2019–2020
FORTY-SECOND EDITION

Texas School Directory

A State Guide to K-12 Districts, Dioceses, and Schools...

Powered by the Industry's Best Data

- **NEW...8 Additional Administrator Titles!**
- Charter Management Organization Index
- Facebook and Twitter Indicators
- Email Address Availability Highlighted
- Detailed School and District Listings
- Names and Job Titles of Key Personnel
- New Schools and Personnel Index

9781951295424

T0417955

MDR
A Dun & Bradstreet Division

Copyright 2019 Market Data Retrieval | 6 Armstrong Road, Shelton, CT 06484

Copyright 2019 Market Data Retrieval, a D&B Company. All Rights Reserved. No information furnished hereby may be reproduced or transmitted in any form or by any means, electronic or mechanical, including photocopying and recording, or by any information storage or retrieval system, except as may be expressly permitted by MDR, 6 Armstrong Road, Shelton, CT 06484.

The information in this directory is licensed with the express understanding and agreement that the information will be solely for internal use and will not be used for the creation and/or updating of databases, electronic or otherwise, that are sold or provided to any third party without the express written permission of MDR.

51-Volume National Set   ISBN# 978-1-951295-51-6

Individual Bound State Editions

	ISSN#	ISBN#		ISSN#	ISBN#
Alabama	1077-7393	978-1-947802-68-1	Montana	1077-7652	978-1-951295-25-7
Alaska	1077-7407	978-1-951295-00-4	Nebraska	1077-7660	978-1-951295-26-4
Arizona	1077-7415	978-1-951295-01-1	Nevada	1077-7679	978-1-951295-27-1
Arkansas	1077-7423	978-1-951295-02-8	New Hampshire	1077-7687	978-1-951295-28-8
California	1077-7431	978-1-951295-03-5	New Jersey	1077-7695	978-1-951295-29-5
Colorado	1077-744X	978-1-951295-04-2	New Mexico	1077-7709	978-1-951295-30-1
Connecticut	1077-7458	978-1-951295-05-9	New York	1077-7717	978-1-951295-31-8
Delaware	1077-7466	978-1-951295-06-6	North Carolina	1077-7725	978-1-951295-32-5
District of Columbia	1077-7474	978-1-951295-07-3	North Dakota	1077-7733	978-1-951295-33-2
Florida	1077-7482	978-1-951295-08-0	Ohio	1077-7741	978-1-951295-34-9
Georgia	1077-7490	978-1-951295-09-7	Oklahoma	1077-775X	978-1-951295-35-6
Hawaii	1077-7504	978-1-951295-10-3	Oregon	1077-7768	978-1-951295-36-3
Idaho	1077-7512	978-1-951295-11-0	Pennsylvania	1077-7776	978-1-951295-37-0
Illinois	1077-7520	978-1-951295-12-7	Rhode Island	1077-7784	978-1-951295-38-7
Indiana	1077-7539	978-1-951295-13-4	South Carolina	1077-7792	978-1-951295-39-4
Iowa	1077-7547	978-1-951295-14-1	South Dakota	1077-7806	978-1-951295-40-0
Kansas	1077-7555	978-1-951295-15-8	Tennessee	1077-7814	978-1-951295-41-7
Kentucky	1077-7563	978-1-951295-16-5	Texas	1077-7822	978-1-951295-42-4
Louisiana	1077-7571	978-1-951295-17-2	Utah	1077-7830	978-1-951295-43-1
Maine	1077-758X	978-1-951295-18-9	Vermont	1077-7849	978-1-951295-44-8
Maryland	1077-7598	978-1-951295-19-6	Virginia	1077-7857	978-1-951295-45-5
Massachusetts	1077-7601	978-1-951295-20-2	Washington	1077-7865	978-1-951295-46-2
Michigan	1077-761X	978-1-951295-21-9	West Virginia	1077-7873	978-1-951295-47-9
Minnesota	1077-7628	978-1-951295-22-6	Wisconsin	1077-7881	978-1-951295-48-6
Mississippi	1077-7636	978-1-951295-23-3	Wyoming	1077-789X	978-1-951295-49-3
Missouri	1077-7644	978-1-951295-24-0	Sales Manager's Guide	2150-2021	978-1-951295-50-9

If you have any questions or comments concerning this directory, please write to MDR, 6 Armstrong Road, Shelton, CT 06484, or call us toll-free at 800-333-8802 or collect at 203-926-4800.

MDR's School Directory

TABLE OF CONTENTS

Sample Directory Listings iv
- A complete listing of codes, definitions and data elements used throughout this directory.

Directory Statistics (Yellow Section)

State Statistics A1
- An overview of state statistics showing the distribution of districts, schools and personnel by key indicators.

County Statistics B1
- A county-by-county census of districts and schools and their enrollments.

District Buying Power Index C1
- A complete listing of counties and districts ranked by the amount of money they spend on instructional materials.

New Public Schools and Key Personnel Index (Cream Section) NEW1
- A summary of new public schools that have opened for the current school year, plus Superintendents and Principals who are new to their institution.

District and School Listings (White Section) 1
- Complete information provided for each district and school in the state, organized alphabetically by county.
- Listings within each county are in the following order: County Centers and Schools, Public School Districts and Schools, Catholic Diocesan Offices and/or Schools, Other Private Schools and Regional Centers.

Directory Indices

District Index (Ivory Section) Q1
- A complete listing of districts in alphabetical order for each district type: Public School Districts, Catholic Dioceses, County Centers and Regional Centers.
- Includes number of schools, enrollment, county location and page number.

County Index (Tan Section) R1
- A complete alphabetical listing by county of Public School Districts, Catholic Dioceses, County Centers and Regional Centers.

Supervisory Union Index (Gold Section) S1
- Included for the states of Maine, Massachusetts, New Hampshire and Vermont, where several local school districts are administered by the same administrative personnel located at a Supervisory Union office. The index lists each Supervisory Union followed by their local school districts.

District Personnel Index (Gray Section) T1
- A complete listing, in last name sequence, of all district personnel.

Principal Index (Green Section) U1
- A complete listing, in last name sequence, of all school principals.

District and School Telephone Index (Blue Section) V1
- A complete listing of all districts and schools in the state with their telephone and PID numbers.

District URL Index (Salmon Section) W1
- A listing of districts that have URL addresses.

Charter Management Organization (CMO) Index (Orchid Section) CMO1
- An alphabetical listing, by state-CMO sequence, of Charter Management Organizations.
- Includes CMO number, PID, full address and phone number.

Directory Code Reference Guide located on the bottom of each page.

Sample Directory Listings

MDR's School Directories are your complete reference source, providing comprehensive data on public school districts and schools, Catholic and other independent schools, and regional and county centers in all 50 states and the District of Columbia. Every public school district and school entry in MDR's School Directories is updated each year through telephone interviews conducted with school district personnel. These interviews take place from July to September, capturing the most current school year data available. In addition, information obtained from state, district and school directories is used to verify information contained in MDR's School Directories.

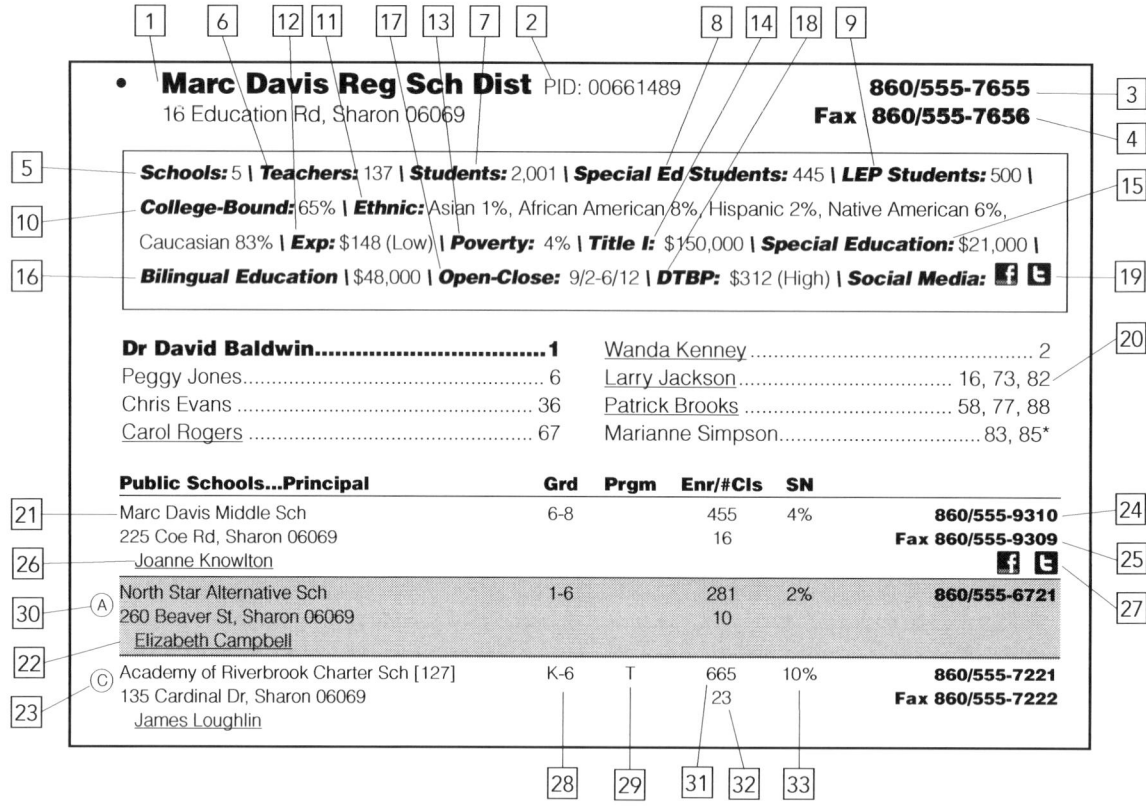

Each directory listing is uniformly organized to reflect the following data as applicable.

Definitions of Codes and Data:

DISTRICT DATA

1 District Name and Address
The physical location address for the superintendent's office is listed. MDR also maintains the mailing address, if different, for each district office. For this alternative mailing address, contact MDR directly at 800-333-8802.

2 District PID Number
Personal Identification Number of the district. Helps identify specific institutions when speaking to an MDR Representative or searching in Education MarketView.

3 Telephone Number
The telephone number of the district's central administration office.

4 Fax Number
The fax number of the district's central administration office. Please use the fax numbers in the directory appropriately.

The FCC prohibits the use of a telephone facsimile machine to send unsolicited advertisements. If you need further clarification of the laws that exist, you can contact the FCC directly at 888-225-5322, or you can visit their website at http://www.fcc.gov.

5 Number of Schools
The number of schools reporting directly to the district. In the case of decentralized large districts (such as Chicago Public Schools), the number of schools reflects those reporting directly to the central school district in addition to those administered directly by each of the subdistrict offices.

6 Number of Teachers
The number of full-time equivalent teachers throughout the district as reported by the U.S. Department of Education.

7 District Enrollment
The projected number of students enrolled in the district for fall 2019.

8 Special Ed Students
The number of students having a written Individualized Education Plan (IEP) indicating their participation in a Special Education Program.

9 LEP Students
The number of Limited-English Proficient students being served in appropriate programs of language assistance (i.e., English as a second language, high-intensity language training, bilingual education).

10 College-Bound Students
The percentage of the district's 12th grade enrollment planning to attend two- or four-year colleges.

11 Student Ethnic Percentages
The student enrollment percentage by ethnic group: Asian, African American, Hispanic, Native American and Caucasian. This information is reported annually by the U.S. Department of Education. Due to rounding, the percentages may not add up to 100%.

12 District Expenditure
The district's expenditure per student for instructional materials. In addition to the actual dollar amount, a level of expenditure is provided as follows:
   High = $300+
   Med = $200-299
   Low = Under $200

13 Poverty Level
This census data reflects the percentage of school-age children in the district from families below the poverty line. Poverty levels are as follows:
   Low = 0-5%
   Med-Low = 6-15%
   Med-High = 16-29%
   High = 30%+

14 Title I
The district's Title I dollar allocation is for the 2018 fiscal year. Funding levels are as follows:
   Highest = $2.5 Million+
   High = $500,000-2.49 Million
   Medium = $150,000-499,999
   Low = Under $150,000

15 Special Education
The sum of federal and state dollars earmarked for special education programs in the district.

16 Bilingual Education
The sum of federal and state dollars earmarked for English Language Acquisition programs in the district.

17 District Opening/Closing Dates
The month and day of the official opening and closing dates of the school district.

18 District Tech Budget Per Pupil
The district's total IT technology budget dollars per pupil. DTBP levels are as follows:
   High = $100+
   Med = $80-99
   Low = $1-79

19 Social Media
The use of Facebook and/or Twitter for information communication, messaging and other content.

20 District-Level Administrators and Job Title Codes
The names of administrative staff with district-wide responsibilities are listed, followed by numeric codes representing their specific areas of responsibility. A full list of job title codes and their descriptions can be found on the bottom of the directory pages.

The names are listed, from left to right, in numeric job title sequence to facilitate identification of individuals responsible for specific administrative areas. In cases where an individual has multiple responsibilities, the job title with the lowest code number is used for sequencing.

An asterisk (*) denotes district administrators who maintain offices at one of the schools in the district rather than at the district office.

Superintendents who are new to the district are printed in **bold** type. Also see our index of new personnel on page NEW1.

An underscore of a district-level administrator indicates an email address at that institution in our database and in Education MarketView.

SCHOOL DATA

21 School Name and Address
The physical location address of the school is listed. MDR also maintains the mailing address, if different, for every school. For this alternative address, contact MDR directly at 800-333-8802.

22 New Schools
The listings of public schools opening for the first time during this school year are shaded for easy identification. Also see our index of new public schools on page NEW1.

23 Charter Management Organization (CMO)
Indicates the CMO number from the CMO Index to which this school reports.

24 Telephone Number
The telephone number of the school's central administration office. Note that in some cases a school district may require that all calls to schools must first go through a central switchboard to be routed to individual schools. In these cases, the central switchboard number is given for all schools affected.

25 Fax Number
The fax number of the school's administration office. Please use the fax numbers in the directory appropriately.

> The FCC prohibits the use of a telephone facsimile machine to send unsolicited advertisements. If you need further clarification of the laws that exist, you can contact the FCC directly at 888-225-5322, or you can visit their website at http://www.fcc.gov.

26 Principal Name
The name of the school principal. When a school has both an elementary and secondary principal, both names are given. The elementary principal is listed first, with the secondary principal listed below.

Principals who are new to their public school are printed in **bold** type. Also see our index of new personnel on page NEW1.

All principals printed with an underscore have an email address at that institution in our database and in Education MarketView.

27 Social Media
The use of Facebook and/or Twitter for information communication, messaging and other content.

28 School Grade Span/Voc, Special, Adult Schools
The lowest and highest grades taught in the school. Schools with dedicated programs in the areas of vocational, special and adult education are designated as Voc, Spec and Adult, respectively.

29 School Program Codes
In addition to the grades taught within the school, schools that have special curriculum programs are indicated with these codes following the school grade span.

- A = Alternative Program: Identifies traditional schools that also provide a special setting/curriculum for students who do not function well in traditional classroom settings.
- G = Adult Classes: Identifies schools that offer adult education classes.
- M = Magnet Program: Identifies traditional schools that also offer an enriched curricula in a special subject area to qualified students.
- T = Title I Schoolwide: Identifies public schools that have a Title I Schoolwide program, allowing greater spending flexibility.
- V = Career & Technical Education Programs: Identifies schools that offer Career & Technical Education programs.

30 Other School Types
Schools that are unique in the curriculum they offer or in the way they operate are indicated to the left of the school name.

- (A) = Alternative School: Identifies schools that provide instruction exclusively for students who do not function well in traditional classroom settings.
- (C) = Charter School: Public schools that have certain freedoms from state and local regulations and policies, having more administrative independence.
- (M) = Magnet School: Identifies schools where all students are offered enriched curricula. Students qualify for admission by competitive exams.
- (Y) = Year-Round School: Schools that operate 12 months a year.

31 Student Enrollment
The projected number of students enrolled for fall 2019.

32 Number of Classrooms
The number of classrooms within a school. The number of classrooms prints below student enrollment when known.

33 Student Need
Percentage of students eligible for the free and reduced-price lunch program at the school.

Texas

A Dun & Bradstreet Division

Texas School Directory

STATE STATISTICS

STATE STATISTICS

DISTRICT PERSONNEL BY JOB FUNCTION

Job Code	Job Description	Total	Under 2,500	Enrollment 2,500-9,000	10,000+
1	SUPERINTENDENT	1,059	732	177	110
2	BUS/FINANCE/PURCHASING	1,204	705	241	217
3	BUILDINGS AND GROUNDS	855	496	203	148
4	FOOD SERVICE	808	515	179	108
5	TRANSPORTATION	723	442	181	99
6	ATHLETIC	819	543	168	107
7	HEALTH SERVICES	425	242	94	82
8	CURRIC/INSTRUCT K-12	786	450	184	130
9	CURRIC/INSTRUCT ELEM	186	85	49	52
10	CURRIC/INSTRUCT SEC	148	56	47	45
11	FEDERAL PROGRAM	956	681	157	98
12	TITLE I	155	114	17	22
13	TITLE V	42	24	10	8
15	ASST SUPERINTENDENT	809	123	260	384
16	INSTRUCTIONAL MEDIA SERVICES	550	366	98	75
17	CHIEF OPERATIONS OFFICER	42	8	10	24
18	CHIEF ACADEMIC OFFICER	51	5	15	31
19	CHIEF FINANCIAL OFFICER	209	56	71	72
20	ART K-12	91	2	15	73
21	ART ELEM	0	0	0	0
22	ART SEC	3	1	2	0
23	MUSIC K-12	95	9	23	63
24	MUSIC ELEM	1	0	0	1
25	MUSIC SEC	1	0	0	1
26	BUSINESS EDUCATION	8	3	3	2
27	CAREER & TECH ED	261	90	69	95
28	TECHNOLOGY EDUCATION	33	10	14	9
29	FAMILY/CONSUMER SCIENCE	10	7	2	1
30	ADULT EDUCATION	52	8	18	21
31	CAREER/SCH-TO-WORK K-12	254	131	44	74
32	CAREER/SCH-TO-WORK ELEM	2	2	0	0
33	CAREER/SCH-TO-WORK SEC	10	8	1	1
34	EARLY CHILDHOOD ED	167	64	45	52
35	HEALTH/PHYS EDUCATION	125	39	41	45
36	GUIDANCE SERVICES K-12	320	186	50	80
37	GUIDANCE SERVICES ELEM	71	59	8	4
38	GUIDANCE SERVICES SEC	91	79	11	1
39	SOCIAL STUDIES K-12	58	2	15	40
40	SOCIAL STUDIES ELEM	10	0	5	5
41	SOCIAL STUDIES SEC	14	1	4	9
42	SCIENCE K-12	55	4	17	33
43	SCIENCE ELEM	20	0	7	13
44	SCIENCE SEC	24	0	7	17
45	MATH K-12	56	4	22	29
46	MATH ELEM	33	0	12	21
47	MATH SEC	35	0	16	19
48	ENGLISH/LANG ARTS K-12	41	5	16	18
49	ENGLISH/LANG ARTS ELEM	27	0	10	17
50	ENGLISH/LANG ARTS SEC	22	1	5	16
51	READING K-12	29	11	7	9
52	READING ELEM	19	8	6	5
53	READING SEC	5	0	2	3
54	REMEDIAL READING K-12	42	21	13	8
55	REMEDIAL READING ELEM	6	4	1	1
56	REMEDIAL READING SEC	0	0	0	0
57	BILINGUAL/ELL	659	402	141	109
58	SPECIAL EDUCATION K-12	817	479	190	128
59	SPECIAL EDUCATION ELEM	45	39	2	4
60	SPECIAL EDUCATION SEC	23	20	1	2
61	FOREIGN/WORLD LANG K-12	29	4	3	22
62	FOREIGN/WORLD LANG ELEM	0	0	0	0
63	FOREIGN/WORLD LANG SEC	3	2	0	1
64	RELIGIOUS EDUCATION K-12	1	0	0	0
65	RELIGIOUS EDUCATION ELEM	0	0	0	0
66	RELIGIOUS EDUCATION SEC	0	0	0	0
67	SCHOOL BOARD PRESIDENT	1,026	732	177	110
68	TEACHER PERSONNEL	419	107	148	148
69	ACADEMIC ASSESSMENT	610	373	129	104
70	RESEARCH/DEVELOPMENT	62	1	13	43
71	PUBLIC INFORMATION	254	26	102	117
72	SUMMER SCHOOL	21	2	11	8
73	INSTRUCTIONAL TECH	1,026	677	194	128
74	INSERVICE TRAINING	170	60	38	64
75	MARKETING/DISTRIBUTIVE	21	6	9	6
76	INFO SYSTEMS	372	144	107	105
77	PSYCHOLOGICAL ASSESSMENT	107	34	25	42
78	AFFIRMATIVE ACTION	39	3	24	11
79	STUDENT PERSONNEL	229	59	67	100
80	DRIVER ED/SAFETY	11	3	6	1
81	GIFTED/TALENTED	141	20	49	71
82	VIDEO SERVICES	100	73	17	10
83	SUBSTANCE ABUSE PREVENTION	502	388	71	42
84	ERATE	205	151	36	18
85	AIDS EDUCATION	205	144	32	26
88	ALTERNATIVE/AT RISK	416	282	86	46
89	MULTI-CULTURAL CURRICULUM	10	1	3	6
90	SOCIAL WORK	40	9	14	17
91	SAFETY/SECURITY	327	116	117	91
92	MAGNET SCHOOL	20	9	2	9
93	PARENTAL INVOLVEMENT	83	25	24	34
95	TECH PREP PROGRAM	38	6	16	16
97	CHIEF INFORMATION OFFICER	23	3	4	16
98	CHIEF TECHNOLOGY OFFICER	67	12	19	34
270	CHARACTER EDUCATION	153	125	14	14
271	MIGRANT EDUCATION	335	216	72	45
273	TEACHER MENTOR	173	100	43	30
274	BEFORE/AFTER SCH	100	48	30	22
275	RESPONSE TO INTERVENTION	150	75	34	39
277	REMEDIAL MATH K-12	16	2	9	5
280	LITERACY COACH	51	19	13	19
285	STEM	122	63	39	20
286	DIGITAL LEARNING	299	181	67	45
288	COMMON CORE STANDARDS	247	178	47	22
294	ACCOUNTABILITY	254	89	80	82
295	NETWORK SYSTEM	575	329	158	84
296	TITLE II PROGRAMS	283	182	71	30
297	WEBMASTER	131	48	42	40
298	GRANT WRITER/PTNRSHIPS	278	152	66	54
750	CHIEF INNOVATION OFFICER	7	0	1	6
751	CHIEF OF STAFF	25	0	2	23
752	SOCIAL EMOTIONAL LEARNING	30	20	3	7

DISTRICTS BY EXPENDITURE AND ENROLLMENT

Expenditure	Total	Under 2500	2500-9999	10,000+
Low (Under $200)	28	9	8	11
Medium ($200 - 299)	157	78	37	42
High ($300+)	836	648	133	55
TOTAL DISTRICTS	1,021	735	178	108

SCHOOLS BY LEVEL AND TYPE

School Level	Total	Public	Private	Catholic
Elementary	5,412	4,905	315	192
Middle/Junior	1,490	1,483	4	3
Senior	1,678	1,599	45	34
K-12 (Combined)	969	620	330	19
Adult/Special/Voc Ed	113	80	32	1
TOTAL SCHOOLS	9,662	8,687	726	249

School Year 2019-2020   800-333-8802

Texas School Directory

COUNTY STATISTICS

COUNTY		DISTRICTS	SCHOOLS	ELEM ENROLL[1]	MIDDLE/JHS ENROLL[2]	SENIOR ENROLL[3]	TOTAL ENROLL[4]	% OF STATE	K-5[5]	K-6	SCHOOLS BY GRADE SPAN K-8	5-8[6]	7-9[7]	7-12[8]	K-12[9]	OTHER[10]
ANDERSON	PUBLIC	7	21	4,796	1,242	2,430	8,510		7	2	1	2	2	5	2	0
	NONPUBLIC	0	1	128	0	0	128		0	0	1	0	2	0	0	0
	TOTAL	7	22	4,924	1,242	2,430	8,638	0.2	7	2	2	2	2	5	2	0
ANDREWS	PUBLIC	1	6	2,043	924	1,099	4,200		3	0	0	1	0	2	0	0
	NONPUBLIC	0	0	0	0	0	0		0	0	0	0	0	0	0	0
	TOTAL	1	6	2,043	924	1,099	4,200	0.1	3	0	0	1	0	2	0	0
ANGELINA	PUBLIC	6	35	8,302	3,534	4,528	16,550		20	1	0	4	1	7	2	0
	NONPUBLIC	0	2	250	0	0	250		1	0	1	0	0	0	0	0
	TOTAL	6	37	8,552	3,534	4,528	16,800	0.3	21	1	1	4	1	7	2	0
ARANSAS	PUBLIC	1	4	933	612	781	2,800		2	0	0	1	0	1	0	0
	NONPUBLIC	0	2	182	0	0	182		2	0	0	0	0	0	0	0
	TOTAL	1	6	1,115	612	781	2,982	0.1	4	0	0	1	0	1	0	0
ARCHER	PUBLIC	3	8	895	349	665	1,886		2	1	0	2	0	3	0	0
	NONPUBLIC	0	0	0	0	0	0		0	0	0	0	0	0	0	0
	TOTAL	3	8	895	349	665	1,886		2	1	0	2	0	3	0	0
ARMSTRONG	PUBLIC	1	1	236	0	94	330		0	0	0	0	0	0	1	0
	NONPUBLIC	0	0	0	0	0	0		0	0	0	0	0	0	0	0
	TOTAL	1	1	236	0	94	330		0	0	0	0	0	0	1	0
ATASCOSA	PUBLIC	5	19	4,436	2,283	2,294	8,980		8	0	0	5	0	5	1	0
	NONPUBLIC	0	1	65	0	0	65		1	0	0	0	0	0	0	0
	TOTAL	5	20	4,501	2,283	2,294	9,045	0.2	9	0	0	5	0	5	1	0
AUSTIN	PUBLIC	3	14	2,774	1,317	1,809	5,800		6	0	0	3	0	3	2	0
	NONPUBLIC	0	1	150	0	60	210		0	0	0	0	0	0	1	0
	TOTAL	3	15	2,924	1,317	1,869	6,010	0.1	6	0	0	3	0	3	3	0
BAILEY	PUBLIC	1	4	742	322	362	1,450		2	0	0	1	0	1	0	0
	NONPUBLIC	0	0	0	0	0	0		0	0	0	0	0	0	0	0
	TOTAL	1	4	742	322	362	1,450		2	0	0	1	0	1	0	0
BANDERA	PUBLIC	2	6	1,267	587	748	2,593		3	0	0	1	0	1	1	0
	NONPUBLIC	0	0	0	0	0	0		0	0	0	0	0	0	0	0
	TOTAL	2	6	1,267	587	748	2,593	0.1	3	0	0	1	0	1	1	0
BASTROP	PUBLIC	4	27	9,230	2,957	5,164	17,870		11	2	0	2	2	8	2	0
	NONPUBLIC	0	1	59	0	24	83		0	0	0	0	0	0	1	0
	TOTAL	4	28	9,289	2,957	5,188	17,953	0.3	11	2	0	2	2	8	3	0

[1] **Elem Enroll** is the school by school total of enrollments in K-4, K-5, K-6, K-8 schools, elementary and middle/JHS students in K-12 schools and students in special ed schools. Public enrollments include public and county-operated schools.

[2] **Middle/JHS Enroll** is the school by school total of enrollments in 5-8 and 7-9 public schools. Public enrollments include public and county-operated schools. Private middle/JHS enrollments are included in Senior Enroll.

[3] **Senior Enroll** is the school by school total of enrollments in 7-12 and 9-12 schools, the secondary students in K-12 schools and students in vocational ed schools. Public enrollments include public and county-operated schools. For private schools, Senior Enroll includes middle/JHS enrollment plus senior enrollment.

[4] **Public Total Enroll** columns are not the sum of school building enrollments. They are projected district-wide Fall enrollments provided to MDR by each school district office, plus county-operated school enrollments.

[5] K-5 includes pre-kindergarten, kindergarten, K-3, K-4, K-5 schools.
[6] 5-8 includes schools with low grades of 4, 5, 6 and high grades of 7, 8, 9 (e.g., 4-8, 5-8, 6-8, 6-9).
[7] 7-9 includes schools with low grades of 7, 8 and high grades of 7, 8, 9 (e.g., 7-7, 7-8, 7-9, 8-9).
[8] 7-12 includes 7-12, 8-12, 9-12, 10-12, etc.
[9] K-12 includes schools with both elementary and secondary grades.
[10] **Other** includes special ed, vocational ed and adult schools.
Public State Totals for all columns can exceed the sum of the counties because state totals include state-operated schools and their enrollments

School Year 2019-2020   800-333-8802   TX—B1

COUNTY STATISTICS — Market Data Retrieval

COUNTY		DISTRICTS	SCHOOLS	ELEM ENROLL[1]	MIDDLE/JHS ENROLL[2]	SENIOR ENROLL[3]	TOTAL ENROLL[4]	% OF STATE	K-5[5]	K-6	K-8	5-8[6]	7-9[7]	7-12[8]	K-12[9]	OTHER[10]
BAYLOR	PUBLIC	1	3	241	176	162	575		1	0	0	1	0	0	0	0
	NONPUBLIC	0	0	0	0	0	0		0	0	0	0	0	0	0	0
	TOTAL	1	3	241	176	162	575		1	0	0	1	0	0	0	0
BEE	PUBLIC	4	12	2,603	1,077	1,446	5,021		5	0	1	2	1	2	1	0
	NONPUBLIC	0	2	171	0	0	171		0	2	0	0	0	0	0	0
	TOTAL	4	14	2,774	1,077	1,446	5,192	0.1	5	2	1	2	1	2	1	0
BELL	PUBLIC	9	106	37,830	15,010	20,197	73,209		60	0	0	24	0	17	4	1
	NONPUBLIC	0	8	1,139	0	397	1,536		1	1	2	0	0	2	2	0
	TOTAL	9	114	38,969	15,010	20,594	74,745	1.4	61	1	2	24	0	19	6	1
BEXAR	PUBLIC	17	457	162,109	67,868	98,531	320,545		267	6	10	72	4	69	20	9
	NONPUBLIC	0	67	14,983	0	5,761	20,744		6	2	29	0	0	6	22	2
	TOTAL	17	524	177,092	67,868	104,292	341,289	6.3	273	8	39	72	4	75	42	11
BLANCO	PUBLIC	2	6	655	477	558	1,684		2	0	0	2	0	2	0	0
	NONPUBLIC	0	0	0	0	0	0		0	0	0	0	0	0	0	0
	TOTAL	2	6	655	477	558	1,684		2	0	0	2	0	2	0	0
BORDEN	PUBLIC	1	1	159	0	71	230		0	0	0	0	0	0	1	0
	NONPUBLIC	0	0	0	0	0	0		0	0	0	0	0	0	0	0
	TOTAL	1	1	159	0	71	230		0	0	0	0	0	0	1	0
BOSQUE	PUBLIC	8	14	1,725	406	811	2,937		3	0	0	1	0	1	9	0
	NONPUBLIC	0	0	0	0	0	0		0	0	0	0	0	0	0	0
	TOTAL	8	14	1,725	406	811	2,937	0.1	3	0	0	1	0	1	9	0
BOWIE	PUBLIC	13	43	9,387	4,339	5,290	18,218		19	2	3	7	1	9	2	0
	NONPUBLIC	0	2	178	0	0	178		0	1	1	0	0	0	0	0
	TOTAL	13	45	9,565	4,339	5,290	18,396	0.3	19	3	4	7	1	9	2	0
BRAZORIA	PUBLIC	8	91	36,952	13,759	20,949	73,029		46	10	1	10	7	14	2	1
	NONPUBLIC	0	11	2,043	0	355	2,398		3	0	2	0	0	0	6	0
	TOTAL	8	102	38,995	13,759	21,304	75,427	1.4	49	10	3	10	7	14	8	1
BRAZOS	PUBLIC	3	44	17,886	4,916	8,605	30,759		24	5	0	0	5	7	2	1
	NONPUBLIC	0	7	1,306	0	509	1,815		0	1	0	0	0	0	6	0
	TOTAL	3	51	19,192	4,916	9,114	32,574	0.6	24	6	0	0	5	7	8	1
BREWSTER	PUBLIC	4	7	580	331	374	1,173		1	0	2	1	0	2	1	0
	NONPUBLIC	0	1	32	0	13	45		0	0	0	0	0	0	1	0
	TOTAL	4	8	612	331	387	1,218		1	0	2	1	0	2	2	0
BRISCOE	PUBLIC	1	1	139	0	56	195		0	0	0	0	0	0	1	0
	NONPUBLIC	0	0	0	0	0	0		0	0	0	0	0	0	0	0
	TOTAL	1	1	139	0	56	195		0	0	0	0	0	0	1	0

[1] **Elem Enroll** is the school by school total of enrollments in K-4, K-5, K-6, K-8 schools, elementary and middle/JHS students in K-12 schools and students in special ed schools. Public enrollments include public and county-operated schools.

[2] **Middle/JHS Enroll** is the school by school total of enrollments in 5-8 and 7-9 public schools. Public enrollments include public and county-operated schools. Private middle/JHS enrollments are included in Senior Enroll.

[3] **Senior Enroll** is the school by school total of enrollments in 7-12 and 9-12 schools, the secondary students in K-12 schools and students in vocational ed schools. Public enrollments include public and county-operated schools. For private schools, Senior Enroll includes middle/JHS enrollment plus senior enrollment.

[4] **Public Total Enroll** columns are not the sum of school building enrollments. They are projected district-wide Fall enrollments provided to MDR by each school district office, plus county-operated school enrollments.

[5] **K-5** includes pre-kindergarten, kindergarten, K-3, K-4, K-5 schools.
[6] **5-8** includes schools with low grades of 4, 5, 6 and high grades of 7, 8, 9 (e.g., 4-8, 5-8, 6-8, 6-9).
[7] **7-9** includes schools with low grades of 7, 8 and high grades of 7, 8, 9 (e.g., 7-7, 7-8, 7-9, 8-9).
[8] **7-12** includes 7-12, 8-12, 9-12, 10-12, etc.
[9] **K-12** includes schools with both elementary and secondary grades.
[10] **Other** includes special ed, vocational ed and adult schools.

*Public State Totals for all columns can exceed the sum of the counties because state totals include state-operated schools and their enrollments

Texas School Directory

COUNTY STATISTICS

COUNTY		DISTRICTS	SCHOOLS	ELEM ENROLL[1]	MIDDLE/JHS ENROLL[2]	SENIOR ENROLL[3]	TOTAL ENROLL[4]	% OF STATE	\\multicolumn{8}{c}{SCHOOLS BY GRADE SPAN}
									K-5[5]	K-6	K-8	5-8[6]	7-9[7]	7-12[8]	K-12[9]	OTHER[10]
BROOKS	PUBLIC	1	4	844	340	405	1,589		2	0	0	0	0	1	0	0
	NONPUBLIC	0	0	0	0	0	0		0	0	0	0	0	0	0	0
	TOTAL	1	4	844	340	405	1,589		2	0	0	0	0	1	0	0
BROWN	PUBLIC	7	21	3,444	1,139	1,968	6,564		7	2	0	3	1	6	2	0
	NONPUBLIC	0	1	82	0	33	115		0	0	0	0	0	0	1	0
	TOTAL	7	22	3,526	1,139	2,001	6,679	0.1	7	2	0	3	1	6	3	0
BURLESON	PUBLIC	3	9	1,404	605	815	2,940		3	0	0	2	0	2	2	0
	NONPUBLIC	0	0	0	0	0	0		0	0	0	0	0	0	0	0
	TOTAL	3	9	1,404	605	815	2,940	0.1	3	0	0	2	0	2	2	0
BURNET	PUBLIC	2	13	3,557	1,713	2,163	7,340		7	0	0	2	0	4	0	0
	NONPUBLIC	0	2	591	0	85	676		0	0	1	0	0	0	1	0
	TOTAL	2	15	4,148	1,713	2,248	8,016	0.2	7	0	1	2	0	4	1	0
CALDWELL	PUBLIC	3	14	3,669	1,726	2,060	8,010		8	0	0	2	0	3	1	0
	NONPUBLIC	0	0	0	0	0	0		0	0	0	0	0	0	0	0
	TOTAL	3	14	3,669	1,726	2,060	8,010	0.2	8	0	0	2	0	3	1	0
CALHOUN	PUBLIC	1	7	2,007	735	1,165	3,985		3	0	1	1	0	2	0	0
	NONPUBLIC	0	1	90	0	0	90		0	0	1	0	0	0	0	0
	TOTAL	1	8	2,097	735	1,165	4,075	0.1	3	0	2	1	0	2	0	0
CALLAHAN	PUBLIC	4	12	1,286	460	762	2,492		3	2	0	2	1	4	0	0
	NONPUBLIC	0	0	0	0	0	0		0	0	0	0	0	0	0	0
	TOTAL	4	12	1,286	460	762	2,492	0.1	3	2	0	2	1	4	0	0
CAMERON	PUBLIC	10	146	44,908	21,494	31,774	97,281		79	3	0	25	4	30	5	0
	NONPUBLIC	0	15	2,977	0	1,255	4,232		0	3	6	1	0	3	2	0
	TOTAL	10	161	47,885	21,494	33,029	101,513	1.9	79	6	6	26	4	33	7	0
CAMP	PUBLIC	1	5	1,324	373	647	2,344		2	1	0	0	1	1	0	0
	NONPUBLIC	0	0	0	0	0	0		0	0	0	0	0	0	0	0
	TOTAL	1	5	1,324	373	647	2,344		2	1	0	0	1	1	0	0
CARSON	PUBLIC	3	6	677	167	410	1,310		1	1	0	1	0	2	1	0
	NONPUBLIC	0	0	0	0	0	0		0	0	0	0	0	0	0	0
	TOTAL	3	6	677	167	410	1,310		1	1	0	1	0	2	1	0
CASS	PUBLIC	7	18	2,631	1,238	1,597	5,528		5	0	0	4	0	4	5	0
	NONPUBLIC	0	0	0	0	0	0		0	0	0	0	0	0	0	0
	TOTAL	7	18	2,631	1,238	1,597	5,528	0.1	5	0	0	4	0	4	5	0
CASTRO	PUBLIC	3	7	854	455	519	1,695		2	0	0	1	0	2	2	0
	NONPUBLIC	0	0	0	0	0	0		0	0	0	0	0	0	0	0
	TOTAL	3	7	854	455	519	1,695		2	0	0	1	0	2	2	0

[1] **Elem Enroll** is the school by school total of enrollments in K-4, K-5, K-6, K-8 schools, elementary and middle/JHS students in K-12 schools and students in special ed schools. Public enrollments include public and county-operated schools.

[2] **Middle/JHS Enroll** is the school by school total of enrollments in 5-8 and 7-9 public schools. Public enrollments include public and county-operated schools. Private middle/JHS enrollments are included in Senior Enroll.

[3] **Senior Enroll** is the school by school total of enrollments in 7-12 and 9-12 schools, the secondary students in K-12 schools and students in vocational ed schools. Public enrollments include public and county-operated schools. For private schools, Senior Enroll includes middle/JHS enrollment plus senior enrollment.

[4] **Public Total Enroll** columns are not the sum of school building enrollments. They are projected district-wide Fall enrollments provided to MDR by each school district office, plus county-operated school enrollments.

[5] **K-5** includes pre-kindergarten, kindergarten, K-3, K-4, K-5 schools.

[6] **5-8** includes schools with low grades of 4, 5, 6 and high grades of 7, 8, 9 (e.g., 4-8, 5-8, 6-8, 6-9).

[7] **7-9** includes schools with low grades of 7, 8 and high grades of 7, 8, 9 (e.g., 7-7, 7-8, 7-9, 8-9).

[8] **7-12** includes 7-12, 8-12, 9-12, 10-12, etc.

[9] **K-12** includes schools with both elementary and secondary grades.

[10] **Other** includes special ed, vocational ed and adult schools.

*****Public State Totals** for all columns can exceed the sum of the counties because state totals include state-operated schools and their enrollments

School Year 2019-2020   800-333-8802   TX—B3

COUNTY STATISTICS — Market Data Retrieval

COUNTY		DISTRICTS	SCHOOLS	ELEM ENROLL[1]	MIDDLE/JHS ENROLL[2]	SENIOR ENROLL[3]	TOTAL ENROLL[4]	% OF STATE	K-5[5]	K-6	K-8	5-8[6]	7-9[7]	7-12[8]	K-12[9]	OTHER[10]
CHAMBERS	PUBLIC	3	15	4,135	1,886	2,368	8,050		7	0	0	4	0	3	1	0
	NONPUBLIC	0	0	0	0	0	0		0	0	0	0	0	0	0	0
	TOTAL	3	15	4,135	1,886	2,368	8,050	0.2	7	0	0	4	0	3	1	0
CHEROKEE	PUBLIC	5	19	4,856	1,359	2,394	8,612		8	2	0	2	1	4	2	0
	NONPUBLIC	0	1	69	0	31	100		0	0	0	0	0	0	1	0
	TOTAL	5	20	4,925	1,359	2,425	8,712	0.2	8	2	0	2	1	4	3	0
CHILDRESS	PUBLIC	1	4	556	246	312	1,100		1	0	0	1	0	1	1	0
	NONPUBLIC	0	0	0	0	0	0		0	0	0	0	0	0	0	0
	TOTAL	1	4	556	246	312	1,100		1	0	0	1	0	1	1	0
CLAY	PUBLIC	4	7	944	226	581	1,657		1	1	0	1	0	2	2	0
	NONPUBLIC	0	0	0	0	0	0		0	0	0	0	0	0	0	0
	TOTAL	4	7	944	226	581	1,657		1	1	0	1	0	2	2	0
COCHRAN	PUBLIC	2	6	360	158	218	725		2	0	0	1	0	2	1	0
	NONPUBLIC	0	0	0	0	0	0		0	0	0	0	0	0	0	0
	TOTAL	2	6	360	158	218	725		2	0	0	1	0	2	1	0
COKE	PUBLIC	2	3	338	0	214	535		0	1	0	0	0	1	1	0
	NONPUBLIC	0	0	0	0	0	0		0	0	0	0	0	0	0	0
	TOTAL	2	3	338	0	214	535		0	1	0	0	0	1	1	0
COLEMAN	PUBLIC	3	6	649	248	401	1,293		1	1	0	1	0	2	1	0
	NONPUBLIC	0	0	0	0	0	0		0	0	0	0	0	0	0	0
	TOTAL	3	6	649	248	401	1,293		1	1	0	1	0	2	1	0
COLLIN	PUBLIC	14	276	105,838	47,626	62,144	210,165		155	24	0	44	9	39	2	3
	NONPUBLIC	0	33	8,002	0	3,009	11,011		7	3	6	0	0	1	16	0
	TOTAL	14	309	113,840	47,626	65,153	221,176	4.1	162	27	6	44	9	40	18	3
COLLINGSWORTH	PUBLIC	1	3	324	112	152	580		1	0	0	1	0	1	0	0
	NONPUBLIC	0	0	0	0	0	0		0	0	0	0	0	0	0	0
	TOTAL	1	3	324	112	152	580	0.1	1	0	0	1	0	1	0	0
COLORADO	PUBLIC	3	14	1,659	754	1,167	3,480		6	0	0	3	0	5	0	0
	NONPUBLIC	0	2	265	0	0	265		0	0	2	0	0	0	0	0
	TOTAL	3	16	1,924	754	1,167	3,745		6	0	2	3	0	5	0	0
COMAL	PUBLIC	2	46	15,263	9,409	9,262	33,020		28	0	0	9	0	8	1	0
	NONPUBLIC	0	7	1,082	0	318	1,400		1	0	2	0	0	1	3	0
	TOTAL	2	53	16,345	9,409	9,580	34,420	0.6	29	0	2	9	0	9	4	0
COMANCHE	PUBLIC	4	9	1,299	465	592	2,342		3	0	0	2	0	2	2	0
	NONPUBLIC	0	0	0	0	0	0		0	0	0	0	0	0	0	0
	TOTAL	4	9	1,299	465	592	2,342		3	0	0	2	0	2	2	0

[1] **Elem Enroll** is the school by school total of enrollments in K-4, K-5, K-6, K-8 schools, elementary and middle/JHS students in K-12 schools and students in special ed schools. Public enrollments include public and county-operated schools.
[2] **Middle/JHS Enroll** is the school by school total of enrollments in 5-8 and 7-9 public schools. Public enrollments include public and county-operated schools. Private middle/JHS enrollments are included in Senior Enroll.
[3] **Senior Enroll** is the school by school total of enrollments in 7-12 and 9-12 schools, the secondary students in K-12 schools and students in vocational ed schools. Public enrollments include public and county-operated schools. For private schools, Senior Enroll includes middle/JHS enrollment plus senior enrollment.
[4] **Public Total Enroll** columns are not the sum of school building enrollments. They are projected district-wide Fall enrollments provided to MDR by each school district office, plus county-operated school enrollments.
[5] **K-5** includes pre-kindergarten, kindergarten, K-3, K-4, K-5 schools.
[6] **5-8** includes schools with low grades of 4, 5, 6 and high grades of 7, 8, 9 (e.g., 4-8, 5-8, 6-8, 6-9).
[7] **7-9** includes schools with low grades of 7, 8 and high grades of 7, 8, 9 (e.g., 7-7, 7-8, 7-9, 8-9).
[8] **7-12** includes 7-12, 8-12, 9-12, 10-12, etc.
[9] **K-12** includes schools with both elementary and secondary grades.
[10] **Other** includes special ed, vocational and adult schools.

*****Public State Totals** for all columns can exceed the sum of the counties because state totals include state-operated schools and their enrollments

Texas School Directory — COUNTY STATISTICS

COUNTY		DISTRICTS	SCHOOLS	ELEM ENROLL[1]	MIDDLE/JHS ENROLL[2]	SENIOR ENROLL[3]	TOTAL ENROLL[4]	% OF STATE	K-5[5]	K-6	K-8	5-8[6]	7-9[7]	7-12[8]	K-12[9]	OTHER[10]
CONCHO	PUBLIC	2	3	386	50	135	455		1	0	0	0	0	0	2	0
	NONPUBLIC	0	0	0	0	0	0		0	0	0	0	0	0	0	0
	TOTAL	2	3	386	50	135	455		1	0	0	0	0	0	2	0
COOKE	PUBLIC	8	16	3,951	724	2,038	6,668		3	3	2	0	1	4	3	0
	NONPUBLIC	0	2	368	0	81	449		0	0	1	0	0	0	1	0
	TOTAL	8	18	4,319	724	2,119	7,117	0.1	3	3	3	0	1	4	4	0
CORYELL	PUBLIC	5	19	6,168	2,183	3,350	11,728		9	1	0	2	1	3	3	0
	NONPUBLIC	0	0	0	0	0	0		0	0	0	0	0	0	0	0
	TOTAL	5	19	6,168	2,183	3,350	11,728	0.2	9	1	0	2	1	3	3	0
COTTLE	PUBLIC	1	1	150	0	60	210		0	0	0	0	0	0	1	0
	NONPUBLIC	0	0	0	0	0	0		0	0	0	0	0	0	0	0
	TOTAL	1	1	150	0	60	210		0	0	0	0	0	0	1	0
CRANE	PUBLIC	1	3	571	261	324	1,155		1	0	0	1	0	1	0	0
	NONPUBLIC	0	0	0	0	0	0		0	0	0	0	0	0	0	0
	TOTAL	1	3	571	261	324	1,155		1	0	0	1	0	1	0	0
CROCKETT	PUBLIC	1	3	388	178	192	758		1	0	0	1	0	1	0	0
	NONPUBLIC	0	0	0	0	0	0		0	0	0	0	0	0	0	0
	TOTAL	1	3	388	178	192	758		1	0	0	1	0	1	0	0
CROSBY	PUBLIC	3	8	589	200	360	1,125		2	1	0	1	0	3	1	0
	NONPUBLIC	0	0	0	0	0	0		0	0	0	0	0	0	0	0
	TOTAL	3	8	589	200	360	1,125		2	1	0	1	0	3	1	0
CULBERSON	PUBLIC	1	1	286	0	114	400		0	0	0	0	0	0	1	0
	NONPUBLIC	0	0	0	0	0	0		0	0	0	0	0	0	0	0
	TOTAL	1	1	286	0	114	400		0	0	0	0	0	0	1	0
DALLAM	PUBLIC	2	5	981	392	564	1,885		2	0	0	1	0	1	1	0
	NONPUBLIC	0	3	252	0	0	252		0	2	1	0	0	0	0	0
	TOTAL	2	8	1,233	392	564	2,137		2	2	1	1	0	1	1	0
DALLAS	PUBLIC	16	639	243,504	86,339	128,963	462,419		323	70	22	82	17	94	25	6
	NONPUBLIC	0	121	26,869	0	10,089	36,958		13	14	35	0	0	10	40	9
	TOTAL	16	760	270,373	86,339	139,052	499,377	9.2	336	84	57	82	17	104	65	15
DAWSON	PUBLIC	4	8	1,432	409	703	2,439		2	0	0	1	0	2	3	0
	NONPUBLIC	0	0	0	0	0	0		0	0	0	0	0	0	0	0
	TOTAL	4	8	1,432	409	703	2,439		2	0	0	1	0	2	3	0
DE WITT	PUBLIC	6	15	2,200	937	1,389	4,417		6	0	2	3	0	3	1	0
	NONPUBLIC	0	1	73	0	0	73		0	1	0	0	0	0	0	0
	TOTAL	6	16	2,273	937	1,389	4,490	0.1	6	1	2	3	0	3	1	0

[1] **Elem Enroll** is the school by school total of enrollments in K-4, K-5, K-6, K-8 schools, elementary and middle/JHS students in K-12 schools and students in special ed schools. Public enrollments include public and county-operated schools.

[2] **Middle/JHS Enroll** is the school by school total of enrollments in 5-8 and 7-9 public schools. Public enrollments include public and county-operated schools. Private middle/JHS enrollments are included in Senior Enroll.

[3] **Senior Enroll** is the school by school total of enrollments in 7-12 and 9-12 schools, the secondary students in K-12 schools and students in vocational ed schools. Public enrollments include public and county-operated schools. For private schools, Senior Enroll includes middle/JHS enrollment plus senior enrollment.

[4] **Public Total Enroll** columns are not the sum of school building enrollments. They are projected district-wide Fall enrollments provided to MDR by each school district office, plus county-operated school enrollments.

[5] **K-5** includes pre-kindergarten, kindergarten, K-3, K-4, K-5 schools.

[6] **5-8** includes schools with low grades of 4, 5, 6 and high grades of 7, 8, 9 (e.g., 4-8, 5-8, 6-8, 6-9).

[7] **7-9** includes schools with low grades of 7, 8 and high grades of 7, 8, 9 (e.g., 7-7, 7-8, 7-9, 8-9).

[8] **7-12** includes 7-12, 8-12, 9-12, 10-12, etc.

[9] **K-12** includes schools with both elementary and secondary grades.

[10] **Other** includes special ed, vocational ed and adult schools.

*Public **State Totals** for all columns can exceed the sum of the counties because state totals include state-operated schools and their enrollments

School Year 2019-2020 800-333-8802

COUNTY STATISTICS — Market Data Retrieval

COUNTY		DISTRICTS	SCHOOLS	ELEM ENROLL[1]	MIDDLE/JHS ENROLL[2]	SENIOR ENROLL[3]	TOTAL ENROLL[4]	% OF STATE	K-5[5]	K-6	K-8	5-8[6]	7-9[7]	7-12[8]	K-12[9]	OTHER[10]
DEAF SMITH	PUBLIC	2	12	2,583	906	1,135	4,225		7	1	0	1	1	2	0	0
	NONPUBLIC	0	2	179	0	0	179		0	2	0	1	0	0	0	0
	TOTAL	2	14	2,762	906	1,135	4,404	0.1	7	3	0	1	1	2	0	0
DELTA	PUBLIC	2	4	482	220	294	900		2	0	0	0	0	0	2	0
	NONPUBLIC	0	0	0	0	0	0		0	0	0	0	0	0	0	0
	TOTAL	2	4	482	220	294	900		2	0	0	0	0	0	2	0
DENTON	PUBLIC	11	184	62,298	28,874	37,521	129,337		106	3	1	33	3	30	4	4
	NONPUBLIC	0	15	4,143	0	1,448	5,591		3	0	3	0	0	0	9	0
	TOTAL	11	199	66,441	28,874	38,969	134,928	2.5	109	3	4	33	3	30	13	4
DICKENS	PUBLIC	2	2	258	0	103	361		0	0	0	0	0	0	2	0
	NONPUBLIC	0	0	0	0	0	0		0	0	0	0	0	0	0	0
	TOTAL	2	2	258	0	103	361		0	0	0	0	0	0	2	0
DIMMIT	PUBLIC	1	4	1,252	333	612	2,200		1	1	0	1	0	1	0	0
	NONPUBLIC	0	0	0	0	0	0		0	0	0	0	0	0	0	0
	TOTAL	1	4	1,252	333	612	2,200		1	1	0	1	0	1	0	0
DONLEY	PUBLIC	2	4	325	108	160	720		1	1	0	1	0	1	0	0
	NONPUBLIC	0	0	0	0	0	0		0	0	0	0	0	0	0	0
	TOTAL	2	4	325	108	160	720	0.1	1	1	0	1	0	1	0	0
DUVAL	PUBLIC	4	9	1,360	519	758	2,637		2	2	0	2	0	3	0	0
	NONPUBLIC	0	0	0	0	0	0		0	0	0	0	0	0	0	0
	TOTAL	4	9	1,360	519	758	2,637	0.1	2	2	0	2	0	3	0	0
EASTLAND	PUBLIC	5	13	1,452	536	869	2,777		3	1	0	3	0	5	1	0
	NONPUBLIC	0	0	0	0	0	0		0	0	0	0	0	0	0	0
	TOTAL	5	13	1,452	536	869	2,777	0.1	3	1	0	3	0	5	1	0
ECTOR	PUBLIC	1	42	16,742	7,011	8,302	31,500		30	0	0	6	0	5	1	0
	NONPUBLIC	0	4	680	0	21	701		0	0	3	0	0	1	0	0
	TOTAL	1	46	17,422	7,011	8,323	32,201	0.6	30	0	3	6	0	6	1	0
EDWARDS	PUBLIC	2	3	375	0	313	560		0	1	0	0	0	1	1	0
	NONPUBLIC	0	0	0	0	0	0		0	0	0	0	0	0	0	0
	TOTAL	2	3	375	0	313	560		0	1	0	0	0	1	1	0
EL PASO	PUBLIC	9	242	86,849	32,601	54,447	168,071		112	25	8	40	6	44	4	3
	NONPUBLIC	0	33	5,405	0	2,147	7,552		5	2	12	0	0	3	10	1
	TOTAL	9	275	92,254	32,601	56,594	175,623	3.2	117	27	20	40	6	47	14	4
ELLIS	PUBLIC	10	62	17,522	8,423	10,775	36,701		32	4	1	8	2	11	4	0
	NONPUBLIC	0	4	627	0	163	790		0	0	2	0	0	0	2	0
	TOTAL	10	66	18,149	8,423	10,938	37,491	0.7	32	4	3	8	2	11	6	0

[1] **Elem Enroll** is the school by school total of enrollments in K-4, K-5, K-6, K-8 schools, elementary and middle/JHS students in K-12 schools and students in special ed schools. Public enrollments include public and county-operated schools.
[2] **Middle/JHS Enroll** is the school by school total of enrollments in 5-8 and 7-9 public schools. Public enrollments include public and county-operated schools. Private middle/JHS enrollments are included in Senior Enroll.
[3] **Senior Enroll** is the school by school total of enrollments in 7-12 and 9-12 schools, the secondary students in K-12 schools and students in vocational ed schools. Public enrollments include public and county-operated schools. For private schools, Senior Enroll includes middle/JHS enrollment plus senior enrollment.
[4] **Public Total Enroll** columns are not the sum of school building enrollments. They are projected district-wide Fall enrollments provided to MDR by each school district office, plus county-operated school enrollments.
[5] **K-5** includes pre-kindergarten, kindergarten, K-3, K-4, K-5 schools.
[6] **5-8** includes schools with low grades of 4, 5, 6 and high grades of 7, 8, 9 (e.g., 4-8, 5-8, 6-8, 6-9).
[7] **7-9** includes schools with low grades of 7, 8 and high grades of 7, 8, 9 (e.g., 7-7, 7-8, 7-9, 8-9).
[8] **7-12** includes 7-12, 8-12, 9-12, 10-12, etc.
[9] **K-12** includes schools with both elementary and secondary grades.
[10] **Other** includes special ed, vocational and adult schools.

Public State Totals for all columns can exceed the sum of the counties because state totals include state-operated schools and their enrollments

Texas School Directory — COUNTY STATISTICS

COUNTY		DISTRICTS	SCHOOLS	ELEM ENROLL[1]	MIDDLE/JHS ENROLL[2]	SENIOR ENROLL[3]	TOTAL ENROLL[4]	% OF STATE	K-5[5]	K-6	K-8	5-8[6]	7-9[7]	7-12[8]	K-12[9]	OTHER[10]
ERATH	PUBLIC	7	15	3,613	523	1,842	5,943		4	2	2	0	1	3	3	0
	NONPUBLIC	0	1	57	0	0	57		0	1	0	0	0	0	0	0
	TOTAL	7	16	3,670	523	1,842	6,000	0.1	4	3	2	0	1	3	3	0
FALLS	PUBLIC	4	8	1,310	343	557	2,325		1	1	1	1	1	2	1	0
	NONPUBLIC	0	0	0	0	0	0		0	0	0	0	0	0	0	0
	TOTAL	4	8	1,310	343	557	2,325	0.1	1	1	1	1	1	2	1	0
FANNIN	PUBLIC	8	20	3,043	802	1,595	5,323		6	2	0	3	1	5	3	0
	NONPUBLIC	0	0	0	0	0	0		0	0	0	0	0	0	0	0
	TOTAL	8	20	3,043	802	1,595	5,323	0.1	6	2	0	3	1	5	3	0
FAYETTE	PUBLIC	5	12	2,396	599	1,211	4,228		2	3	0	0	1	2	3	0
	NONPUBLIC	0	2	311	0	0	311		0	1	1	0	0	0	0	1
	TOTAL	5	14	2,707	599	1,211	4,539	0.1	2	4	1	0	1	2	3	1
FISHER	PUBLIC	2	4	346	51	151	560		1	0	0	0	0	1	1	0
	NONPUBLIC	0	0	0	0	0	0		0	0	0	0	0	0	0	0
	TOTAL	2	4	346	51	151	560		1	0	0	0	0	1	1	0
FLOYD	PUBLIC	2	5	677	103	344	1,160		1	1	0	1	0	2	0	0
	NONPUBLIC	0	0	0	0	0	0		0	0	0	0	0	0	0	0
	TOTAL	2	5	677	103	344	1,160		1	1	0	1	0	2	0	0
FOARD	PUBLIC	1	2	119	0	98	200		0	0	1	0	0	1	0	0
	NONPUBLIC	0	0	0	0	0	0		0	0	0	0	0	0	0	0
	TOTAL	1	2	119	0	98	200		0	0	1	0	0	1	0	0
FORT BEND	PUBLIC	5	206	95,002	41,867	58,739	202,427		122	7	0	31	7	31	6	2
	NONPUBLIC	0	20	3,504	0	1,314	4,818		5	1	6	1	0	1	6	0
	TOTAL	5	226	98,506	41,867	60,053	207,245	3.8	127	8	6	32	7	32	12	2
FRANKLIN	PUBLIC	1	3	633	523	469	1,620		1	0	0	1	0	1	0	0
	NONPUBLIC	0	0	0	0	0	0		0	0	0	0	0	0	0	0
	TOTAL	1	3	633	523	469	1,620		1	0	0	1	0	1	0	0
FREESTONE	PUBLIC	4	13	1,860	764	1,118	3,657		5	0	1	3	0	4	0	0
	NONPUBLIC	0	0	0	0	0	0		0	0	0	0	0	0	0	0
	TOTAL	4	13	1,860	764	1,118	3,657	0.1	5	0	1	3	0	4	0	0
FRIO	PUBLIC	2	8	1,599	703	1,067	3,100		3	0	0	2	0	3	0	0
	NONPUBLIC	0	1	25	0	10	35		0	0	0	0	0	0	1	0
	TOTAL	2	9	1,624	703	1,077	3,135	0.1	3	0	0	2	0	3	1	0
GAINES	PUBLIC	3	10	1,851	836	988	3,702		4	0	0	2	0	2	2	0
	NONPUBLIC	0	0	0	0	0	0		0	0	0	0	0	0	0	0
	TOTAL	3	10	1,851	836	988	3,702	0.1	4	0	0	2	0	2	2	0

[1] **Elem Enroll** is the school by school total of enrollments in K-4, K-5, K-6, K-8 schools, elementary and middle/JHS students in K-12 schools and students in special ed schools. Public enrollments include public and county-operated schools.

[2] **Middle/JHS Enroll** is the school by school total of enrollments in 5-8 and 7-9 public schools. Public enrollments include public and county-operated schools. Private middle/JHS enrollments are included in Senior Enroll.

[3] **Senior Enroll** is the school by school total of enrollments in 7-12 and 9-12 schools, the secondary students in K-12 schools and students in vocational ed schools. Public enrollments include public and county-operated schools. For private schools, Senior Enroll includes middle/JHS enrollment plus senior enrollment.

[4] **Public Total Enroll** columns are not the sum of school building enrollments. They are projected district-wide Fall enrollments provided to MDR by each school district office, plus county-operated school enrollments.

[5] **K-5** includes pre-Kindergarten, kindergarten, K-3, K-4, K-5 schools.

[6] **5-8** includes schools with low grades of 4, 5, 6 and high grades of 7, 8, 9 (e.g., 4-8, 5-8, 6-8, 6-9).

[7] **7-9** includes schools with low grades of 7, 8 and high grades of 7, 8, 9 (e.g., 7-7, 7-8, 7-9, 8-9).

[8] **7-12** includes 7-12, 8-12, 9-12, 10-12, etc.

[9] **K-12** includes schools with both elementary and secondary grades.

[10] **Other** includes special ed, vocational ed and adult schools.

*****Public State Totals** for all columns can exceed the sum of the counties because state totals include state-operated schools and their enrollments.

School Year 2019-2020 — 800-333-8802 — TX–B7

COUNTY STATISTICS

Market Data Retrieval

COUNTY		DISTRICTS	SCHOOLS	ELEM ENROLL[1]	MIDDLE/JHS ENROLL[2]	SENIOR ENROLL[3]	TOTAL ENROLL[4]	% OF STATE	K-5[5]	K-6	K-8	5-8[6]	7-9[7]	7-12[8]	K-12[9]	OTHER[10]
GALVESTON	PUBLIC	8	100	38,515	17,896	24,489	83,138		54	4	1	18	3	15	4	1
	NONPUBLIC	0	12	1,725	0	387	2,112		1	2	6	0	0	1	2	0
	TOTAL	8	112	40,240	17,896	24,876	85,250	1.6	55	6	7	18	3	16	6	1
GARZA	PUBLIC	2	4	522	163	263	942		1	0	0	1	0	1	1	0
	NONPUBLIC	0	0	0	0	0	0		0	0	0	0	0	0	0	0
	TOTAL	2	4	522	163	263	942		1	0	0	1	0	1	1	0
GILLESPIE	PUBLIC	3	10	1,738	871	1,182	3,525		4	0	1	2	0	3	0	0
	NONPUBLIC	0	3	430	0	80	510		0	0	1	0	0	0	2	0
	TOTAL	3	13	2,168	871	1,262	4,035	0.1	4	0	2	2	0	3	2	0
GLASSCOCK	PUBLIC	1	1	221	0	89	310		0	0	0	0	0	0	0	0
	NONPUBLIC	0	0	0	0	0	0		0	0	0	0	0	0	0	0
	TOTAL	1	1	221	0	89	310		0	0	0	0	0	0	0	0
GOLIAD	PUBLIC	1	3	734	190	417	1,340		0	1	0	0	1	1	0	0
	NONPUBLIC	0	0	0	0	0	0		0	0	0	0	0	0	0	0
	TOTAL	1	3	734	190	417	1,340		0	1	0	0	1	1	0	0
GONZALES	PUBLIC	3	10	2,327	761	1,186	4,295		4	1	0	1	1	2	1	0
	NONPUBLIC	0	1	16	0	7	23		0	0	0	0	0	0	1	0
	TOTAL	3	11	2,343	761	1,193	4,318	0.1	4	1	0	1	1	2	2	0
GRAY	PUBLIC	4	10	2,150	794	1,085	3,950		4	0	0	1	0	2	2	0
	NONPUBLIC	0	1	71	0	0	71		0	1	1	0	0	0	0	0
	TOTAL	4	11	2,221	794	1,085	4,021	0.1	4	1	1	1	0	2	2	0
GRAYSON	PUBLIC	13	54	12,213	4,351	6,761	23,068		25	3	0	9	2	14	1	0
	NONPUBLIC	0	7	722	0	150	872		1	1	1	0	0	0	4	0
	TOTAL	13	61	12,935	4,351	6,911	23,940	0.4	26	4	1	9	2	14	5	0
GREGG	PUBLIC	7	41	12,855	4,855	6,611	24,073		21	1	0	8	1	9	1	0
	NONPUBLIC	0	7	927	0	375	1,302		0	0	1	0	0	0	6	1
	TOTAL	7	48	13,782	4,855	6,986	25,375	0.5	21	1	1	8	1	9	7	1
GRIMES	PUBLIC	4	11	2,383	868	1,322	4,522		4	1	0	1	0	3	2	0
	NONPUBLIC	0	1	1,200	0	0	1,200		1	0	0	0	0	0	0	0
	TOTAL	4	12	3,583	868	1,322	5,722	0.1	5	1	0	1	0	3	2	0
GUADALUPE	PUBLIC	4	38	13,432	4,821	8,164	26,477		19	4	0	3	3	7	2	0
	NONPUBLIC	0	5	949	0	103	1,052		0	0	2	0	0	0	3	0
	TOTAL	4	43	14,381	4,821	8,267	27,529	0.5	19	4	2	3	3	7	5	0
HALE	PUBLIC	5	18	3,765	1,544	1,994	7,307		8	0	0	4	0	4	2	0
	NONPUBLIC	0	1	152	0	61	213		0	0	0	0	0	0	1	0
	TOTAL	5	19	3,917	1,544	2,055	7,520	0.1	8	0	0	4	0	4	3	0

[1] **Elem Enroll** is the school by school total of enrollments in K-4, K-5, K-6, K-8 schools, elementary and middle/JHS students in K-12 schools and students in special ed schools. Public enrollments include public and county-operated schools.

[2] **Middle/JHS Enroll** is the school by school total of enrollments in 5-8 and 7-9 public schools. Public enrollments include public and county-operated schools. Private middle/JHS enrollments are included in Senior Enroll.

[3] **Senior Enroll** is the school by school total of enrollments in 7-12 and 9-12 schools, the secondary students in K-12 schools and students in vocational ed schools. Public enrollments include public and county-operated schools. For private schools, Senior Enroll includes middle/JHS enrollment plus senior enrollment.

[4] **Public Total Enroll** columns are not the sum of school building enrollments. They are projected district-wide Fall enrollments provided to MDR by each school district office, plus county-operated school enrollments.

[5] K-5 includes pre-kindergarten, kindergarten, K-3, K-4, K-5 schools.

[6] 5-8 includes schools with low grades of 4, 5, 6 and high grades of 7, 8, 9 (e.g., 4-8, 5-8, 6-8, 6-9).

[7] 7-9 includes schools with low grades of 7, 8 and high grades of 7, 8, 9 (e.g., 7-7, 7-8, 7-9, 8-9).

[8] 7-12 includes 7-12, 8-12, 9-12, 10-12, etc.

[9] K-12 includes schools with both elementary and secondary grades.

[10] Other includes special ed, vocational ed and adult schools.

***Public State Totals** for all columns can exceed the sum of the counties because state totals include state-operated schools and their enrollments.

Texas School Directory — COUNTY STATISTICS

COUNTY		DISTRICTS	SCHOOLS	ELEM ENROLL[1]	MIDDLE/JHS ENROLL[2]	SENIOR ENROLL[3]	TOTAL ENROLL[4]	% OF STATE	SCHOOLS BY GRADE SPAN							
									K-5[5]	K-6	K-8	5-8[6]	7-9[7]	7-12[8]	K-12[9]	OTHER[10]
HALL	PUBLIC	2	5	412	102	196	707		2	0	0	0	0	1	1	0
	NONPUBLIC	0	0	0	0	0	0		0	0	0	0	0	0	0	0
	TOTAL	2	5	412	102	196	707		2	0	0	0	0	1	1	0
HAMILTON	PUBLIC	2	5	741	296	405	1,450		2	0	0	1	0	1	0	0
	NONPUBLIC	0	0	0	0	0	0		0	0	0	0	0	0	1	0
	TOTAL	2	5	741	296	405	1,450		2	0	0	1	0	1	1	0
HANSFORD	PUBLIC	3	7	692	337	398	1,375		2	0	0	1	0	1	0	0
	NONPUBLIC	0	0	0	0	0	0		0	0	0	0	0	0	1	0
	TOTAL	3	7	692	337	398	1,375		2	0	0	1	0	1	1	0
HARDEMAN	PUBLIC	2	5	364	132	254	773		1	1	0	1	0	2	0	0
	NONPUBLIC	0	0	0	0	0	0		0	0	0	0	0	0	0	0
	TOTAL	2	5	364	132	254	773		1	1	0	1	0	2	0	0
HARDIN	PUBLIC	5	19	5,818	1,951	3,133	10,783		8	2	0	2	2	5	0	0
	NONPUBLIC	0	0	0	0	0	0		0	0	0	0	0	0	0	0
	TOTAL	5	19	5,818	1,951	3,133	10,783	0.2	8	2	0	2	2	5	0	0
HARRIS	PUBLIC	18	888	406,469	149,490	218,712	774,917		530	25	12	130	19	132	30	10
	NONPUBLIC	0	176	37,907	0	13,286	51,193		21	9	66	1	0	19	53	7
	TOTAL	18	1,064	444,376	149,490	231,998	826,110	15.2	551	34	78	131	19	151	83	17
HARRISON	PUBLIC	6	22	6,094	3,137	3,653	13,503		11	0	1	5	0	5	0	0
	NONPUBLIC	0	2	155	0	56	211		0	0	1	0	0	1	0	0
	TOTAL	6	24	6,249	3,137	3,709	13,714	0.3	11	0	2	5	0	6	0	0
HARTLEY	PUBLIC	2	2	300	0	120	420		0	0	0	0	0	0	2	0
	NONPUBLIC	0	0	0	0	0	0		0	0	0	0	0	0	0	0
	TOTAL	2	2	300	0	120	420		0	0	0	0	0	0	2	0
HASKELL	PUBLIC	3	5	453	107	224	798		1	0	0	1	0	1	2	0
	NONPUBLIC	0	0	0	0	0	0		0	0	0	0	0	0	0	0
	TOTAL	3	5	453	107	224	798		1	0	0	1	0	1	2	0
HAYS	PUBLIC	4	47	18,319	8,538	11,836	37,445		27	0	0	11	0	8	1	0
	NONPUBLIC	0	12	978	0	523	1,501		1	3	2	0	0	1	5	0
	TOTAL	4	59	19,297	8,538	12,359	38,946	0.7	28	3	2	11	0	9	6	0
HEMPHILL	PUBLIC	1	4	449	201	280	930		2	0	0	1	0	1	0	0
	NONPUBLIC	0	0	0	0	0	0		0	0	0	0	0	0	0	0
	TOTAL	1	4	449	201	280	930		2	0	0	1	0	1	0	0
HENDERSON	PUBLIC	8	27	5,376	1,869	2,890	10,206		10	2	1	4	1	6	3	0
	NONPUBLIC	0	2	93	0	13	106		0	1	0	0	0	0	1	0
	TOTAL	8	29	5,469	1,869	2,903	10,312	0.2	10	3	1	4	1	6	4	0

[1] **Elem Enroll** is the school by school total of enrollments in K-4, K-5, K-6, K-8 schools, elementary and middle/JHS students in K-12 schools and students in special ed schools. Public enrollments include public and county-operated schools.
[2] **Middle/JHS Enroll** is the school by school total of enrollments in 5-8 and 7-9 public schools. Public enrollments include public and county-operated schools. Private middle/JHS enrollments are included in Senior Enroll.
[3] **Senior Enroll** is the school by school total of enrollments in 7-12 and 9-12 schools, the secondary students in K-12 schools and students in vocational schools. Public enrollments include public and county-operated schools. For private schools, Senior Enroll includes middle/JHS enrollment plus senior enrollment.
[4] **Public Total Enroll** columns are not the sum of school building enrollments. They are projected district-wide Fall enrollments provided to MDR by each school district office, plus county-operated school enrollments.

[5] **K-5** includes pre-kindergarten, kindergarten, K-3, K-4, K-5 schools.
[6] **5-8** includes schools with low grades of 4, 5, 6 and high grades of 7, 8, 9 (e.g., 4-8, 5-8, 6-8, 6-9).
[7] **7-9** includes schools with low grades of 7, 8 and high grades of 7, 8, 9 (e.g., 7-7, 7-8, 7-9, 8-9).
[8] **7-12** includes 7-12, 8-12, 9-12, 10-12, etc.
[9] **K-12** includes schools with both elementary and secondary grades.
[10] **Other** includes special ed, vocational and adult schools.

*** **Public State Totals** for all columns can exceed the sum of the counties because state totals include state-operated schools and their enrollments

COUNTY STATISTICS — Market Data Retrieval

COUNTY		DISTRICTS	SCHOOLS	ELEM ENROLL[1]	MIDDLE/JHS ENROLL[2]	SENIOR ENROLL[3]	TOTAL ENROLL[4]	% OF STATE	K-5[5]	K-6	K-8	5-8[6]	7-9[7]	7-12[8]	K-12[9]	OTHER[10]
HIDALGO	PUBLIC	16	354	112,143	50,150	65,359	240,591		194	8	1	64	3	53	31	0
	NONPUBLIC	0	20	3,177	0	535	3,712		4	2	6	0	0	1	7	0
	TOTAL	16	374	115,320	50,150	65,894	244,303	4.5	198	10	7	64	3	54	38	0
HILL	PUBLIC	12	23	3,813	991	1,800	6,485		6	1	2	2	1	4	7	0
	NONPUBLIC	0	0	0	0	0	0		0	0	0	0	0	0	0	0
	TOTAL	12	23	3,813	991	1,800	6,485	0.1	6	1	2	2	1	4	7	0
HOCKLEY	PUBLIC	6	14	2,636	740	1,399	4,724		5	1	0	2	0	3	3	0
	NONPUBLIC	0	1	48	0	0	48		0	0	1	0	0	0	0	0
	TOTAL	6	15	2,684	740	1,399	4,772	0.1	5	1	1	2	0	3	3	0
HOOD	PUBLIC	3	15	4,278	1,914	2,366	8,418		7	0	0	3	0	3	2	0
	NONPUBLIC	0	2	230	0	97	327		0	0	0	0	0	0	2	0
	TOTAL	3	17	4,508	1,914	2,463	8,745	0.2	7	0	0	3	0	3	4	0
HOPKINS	PUBLIC	7	16	4,042	1,039	1,937	6,862		7	0	0	1	0	1	7	0
	NONPUBLIC	0	1	60	0	0	60		1	0	0	0	0	0	0	0
	TOTAL	7	17	4,102	1,039	1,937	6,922	0.1	8	0	0	1	0	1	7	0
HOUSTON	PUBLIC	5	13	1,719	400	1,032	3,236		3	2	0	2	0	5	1	0
	NONPUBLIC	0	0	0	0	0	0		0	0	0	0	0	0	0	0
	TOTAL	5	13	1,719	400	1,032	3,236	0.1	3	2	0	2	0	5	1	0
HOWARD	PUBLIC	3	14	3,329	980	1,542	5,812		7	1	0	1	1	3	1	0
	NONPUBLIC	0	0	0	0	0	0		0	0	0	0	0	0	0	0
	TOTAL	3	14	3,329	980	1,542	5,812	0.1	7	1	0	1	1	3	1	0
HUDSPETH	PUBLIC	3	5	309	100	156	565		1	0	0	1	0	1	2	0
	NONPUBLIC	0	0	0	0	0	0		0	0	0	0	0	0	0	0
	TOTAL	3	5	309	100	156	565		1	0	0	1	0	1	2	0
HUNT	PUBLIC	10	43	7,943	2,807	4,361	15,410		17	2	0	8	1	10	5	0
	NONPUBLIC	0	3	454	0	106	560		0	0	1	0	0	0	2	0
	TOTAL	10	46	8,397	2,807	4,467	15,970	0.3	17	2	1	8	1	10	7	0
HUTCHINSON	PUBLIC	4	13	2,341	711	1,201	4,304		5	1	0	2	1	3	1	0
	NONPUBLIC	0	0	0	0	0	0		0	0	0	0	0	0	0	0
	TOTAL	4	13	2,341	711	1,201	4,304	0.1	5	1	0	2	1	3	1	0
IRION	PUBLIC	1	2	121	0	132	275		0	1	0	0	0	1	0	0
	NONPUBLIC	0	0	0	0	0	0		0	0	0	0	0	0	0	0
	TOTAL	1	2	121	0	132	275		0	1	0	0	0	1	0	0
JACK	PUBLIC	3	6	898	230	509	1,635		1	1	0	1	0	2	1	0
	NONPUBLIC	0	1	644	0	257	901		0	0	0	0	0	0	1	0
	TOTAL	3	7	1,542	230	766	2,536	0.1	1	1	0	1	0	2	2	0

[1] **Elem Enroll** is the school by school total of enrollments in K-4, K-5, K-6, K-8 schools, elementary and middle/JHS students in K-12 schools and students in special ed schools. Public enrollments include public and county-operated schools.

[2] **Middle/JHS Enroll** is the school by school total of enrollments in 5-8 and 7-9 public schools. Public enrollments include public and county-operated schools. Private middle/JHS enrollments are included in Senior Enroll.

[3] **Senior Enroll** is the school by school total of enrollments in 7-12 and 9-12 schools, the secondary students in K-12 schools and students in vocational ed schools. Public enrollments include public and county-operated schools. For private schools, Senior Enroll includes middle/JHS enrollment plus senior enrollment.

[4] **Public Total Enroll** columns are not the sum of school building enrollments. They are projected district-wide Fall enrollments provided to MDR by each school district office, plus county-operated school enrollments.

[5] **K-5** includes pre-kindergarten, kindergarten, K-3, K-4, K-5 schools.

[6] **5-8** includes schools with low grades of 4, 5, 6 and high grades of 7, 8, 9 (e.g., 4-8, 5-8, 6-8, 6-9).

[7] **7-9** includes schools with low grades of 7, 8 and high grades of 7, 8, 9 (e.g., 7-7, 7-8, 7-9, 8-9).

[8] **7-12** includes 7-12, 8-12, 9-12, 10-12, etc.

[9] **K-12** includes schools with both elementary and secondary grades.

[10] **Other** includes special ed, vocational ed and adult schools.

Public State Totals for all columns can exceed the sum of the counties because state totals include state-operated schools and their enrollments

Texas School Directory — COUNTY STATISTICS

COUNTY		DISTRICTS	SCHOOLS	ELEM ENROLL[1]	MIDDLE/JHS ENROLL[2]	SENIOR ENROLL[3]	TOTAL ENROLL[4]	% OF STATE	K-5[5]	K-6	K-8	5-8[6]	7-9[7]	7-12[8]	K-12[9]	OTHER[10]
JACKSON	PUBLIC	3	11	1,682	788	1,034	3,428		4	0	0	3	0	3	1	0
	NONPUBLIC	0	0	0	0	0	0		0	0	0	0	0	0	0	0
	TOTAL	3	11	1,682	788	1,034	3,428	0.1	4	0	0	3	0	3	1	0
JASPER	PUBLIC	5	13	3,336	1,264	1,798	6,112		4	0	1	3	0	4	1	0
	NONPUBLIC	0	0	0	0	0	0		0	0	0	0	0	0	0	0
	TOTAL	5	13	3,336	1,264	1,798	6,112	0.1	4	0	1	3	0	4	1	0
JEFF DAVIS	PUBLIC	2	3	127	54	80	260		1	0	0	0	0	0	2	0
	NONPUBLIC	0	0	0	0	0	0		0	0	0	0	0	0	0	0
	TOTAL	2	3	127	54	80	260		1	0	0	0	0	0	2	0
JEFFERSON	PUBLIC	6	68	20,567	8,611	10,040	40,375		36	1	0	12	1	10	6	2
	NONPUBLIC	0	9	1,602	0	551	2,153		0	0	5	0	0	1	1	0
	TOTAL	6	77	22,169	8,611	10,591	42,528	0.8	36	1	5	12	1	11	9	2
JIM HOGG	PUBLIC	1	3	577	262	312	1,151		1	0	0	0	0	1	0	0
	NONPUBLIC	0	0	0	0	0	0		0	0	0	0	0	0	0	0
	TOTAL	1	3	577	262	312	1,151		1	0	0	0	0	1	0	0
JIM WELLS	PUBLIC	5	18	4,469	1,294	2,257	7,858		8	4	0	1	1	3	1	0
	NONPUBLIC	0	3	311	0	8	319		0	1	1	0	0	0	1	0
	TOTAL	5	21	4,780	1,294	2,265	8,177	0.2	8	5	1	1	1	3	2	0
JOHNSON	PUBLIC	9	64	17,485	7,812	10,115	36,090		31	2	0	10	3	17	1	0
	NONPUBLIC	0	8	678	0	224	902		0	0	4	0	0	1	3	0
	TOTAL	9	72	18,163	7,812	10,339	36,992	0.7	31	2	4	10	3	18	4	0
JONES	PUBLIC	5	13	1,356	513	813	2,643		3	1	1	3	0	5	0	0
	NONPUBLIC	0	0	0	0	0	0		0	0	0	0	0	0	0	0
	TOTAL	5	13	1,356	513	813	2,643	0.1	3	1	1	3	0	5	0	0
KARNES	PUBLIC	4	11	1,435	417	842	2,495		3	1	0	2	0	4	1	0
	NONPUBLIC	0	0	0	0	0	0		0	0	0	0	0	0	0	0
	TOTAL	4	11	1,435	417	842	2,495	0.1	3	1	0	2	0	4	1	0
KAUFMAN	PUBLIC	7	52	15,738	4,945	8,425	28,513		17	11	0	5	3	10	6	0
	NONPUBLIC	0	2	253	0	77	330		0	1	0	0	0	0	1	0
	TOTAL	7	54	15,991	4,945	8,502	28,843	0.5	17	12	0	5	3	10	7	0
KENDALL	PUBLIC	2	14	4,592	2,420	3,262	10,100		4	3	0	1	2	3	1	0
	NONPUBLIC	0	4	612	0	216	828		0	0	1	0	0	0	3	0
	TOTAL	2	18	5,204	2,420	3,478	10,928	0.2	4	3	1	1	2	3	4	0
KENEDY	PUBLIC	1	1	72	0	0	72		0	1	0	0	0	0	0	0
	NONPUBLIC	0	0	0	0	0	0		0	0	0	0	0	0	0	0
	TOTAL	1	1	72	0	0	72		0	1	0	0	0	0	0	0

[1] **Elem Enroll** is the school by school total of enrollments in K-4, K-5, K-6, K-8 schools, elementary and middle/JHS students in K-12 schools and students in special ed schools. Public enrollments include public and county-operated schools.

[2] **Middle/JHS Enroll** is the school by school total of enrollments in 5-8 and 7-9 public schools. Public enrollments include public and county-operated schools. Private middle/JHS enrollments are included in Senior Enroll.

[3] **Senior Enroll** is the school by school total of enrollments in 7-12 and 9-12 schools, the secondary students in K-12 schools and students in vocational ed schools. Public enrollments include public and county-operated schools. For private schools, Senior Enroll includes middle/JHS enrollment plus senior enrollment.

[4] **Public Total Enroll** columns are not the sum of school building enrollments. They are projected district-wide Fall enrollments provided to MDR by each school district office, plus county-operated school enrollments.

[5] **K-5** includes pre-kindergarten, kindergarten, K-3, K-4, K-5 schools.

[6] **5-8** includes schools with low grades of 4, 5, 6 and high grades of 7, 8, 9 (e.g., 4-8, 5-8, 6-8, 6-9).

[7] **7-9** includes schools with low grades of 7, 8 and high grades of 7, 8, 9 (e.g., 7-7, 7-8, 7-9, 8-9).

[8] **7-12** includes 7-12, 8-12, 9-12, 10-12, etc.

[9] **K-12** includes schools with both elementary and secondary grades.

[10] **Other** includes special ed, vocational and adult schools.

*Public State Totals for all columns can exceed the sum of the counties because state totals include state-operated schools and their enrollments.

School Year 2019-2020 800-333-8802

COUNTY STATISTICS — Market Data Retrieval

COUNTY		DISTRICTS	SCHOOLS	ELEM ENROLL[1]	MIDDLE/JHS ENROLL[2]	SENIOR ENROLL[3]	TOTAL ENROLL[4]	% OF STATE	K-5[5]	K-6	K-8	5-8[6]	7-9[7]	7-12[8]	K-12[9]	OTHER[10]
KENT	PUBLIC	1	1	116	0	47	163		0	0	0	0	0	0	1	0
	NONPUBLIC	0	0	0	0	0	0		0	0	0	0	0	0	0	0
	TOTAL	1	1	116	0	47	163		0	0	0	0	0	0	1	0
KERR	PUBLIC	5	18	3,856	1,130	1,948	6,662		7	2	1	2	1	5	0	0
	NONPUBLIC	0	3	147	0	110	257		0	0	2	0	0	1	1	0
	TOTAL	5	21	4,003	1,130	2,058	6,919	0.1	7	2	3	2	1	6	1	0
KIMBLE	PUBLIC	1	3	306	136	173	615		0	0	0	1	0	1	0	0
	NONPUBLIC	0	0	0	0	0	0		0	0	0	0	0	0	0	0
	TOTAL	1	3	306	136	173	615		0	0	0	1	0	1	0	0
KING	PUBLIC	1	1	74	0	30	104		1	0	0	0	0	0	1	0
	NONPUBLIC	0	0	0	0	0	0		0	0	0	0	0	0	0	0
	TOTAL	1	1	74	0	30	104		1	0	0	0	0	0	1	0
KINNEY	PUBLIC	1	3	282	136	167	569		0	0	0	0	0	0	0	0
	NONPUBLIC	0	0	0	0	0	0		0	0	0	0	0	0	0	0
	TOTAL	1	3	282	136	167	569		0	0	0	0	0	0	0	0
KLEBERG	PUBLIC	4	13	3,250	415	1,574	4,909		4	2	2	0	1	4	0	0
	NONPUBLIC	0	2	25	0	140	165		1	0	0	0	0	1	0	0
	TOTAL	4	15	3,275	415	1,714	5,074	0.1	5	2	2	0	1	5	0	0
KNOX	PUBLIC	3	6	458	72	241	752		1	1	0	1	0	2	1	0
	NONPUBLIC	0	0	0	0	0	0		0	0	0	0	0	0	0	0
	TOTAL	3	6	458	72	241	752		1	1	0	1	0	2	1	0
LA SALLE	PUBLIC	1	4	703	316	361	1,400		2	0	0	1	0	1	0	0
	NONPUBLIC	0	0	0	0	0	0		0	0	0	0	0	0	0	0
	TOTAL	1	4	703	316	361	1,400		2	0	0	1	0	1	0	0
LAMAR	PUBLIC	4	22	4,570	1,580	2,278	8,560		11	1	0	3	1	4	2	0
	NONPUBLIC	0	0	0	0	0	0		0	0	0	0	1	0	0	0
	TOTAL	4	22	4,570	1,580	2,278	8,560	0.2	11	1	0	3	1	4	2	0
LAMB	PUBLIC	5	12	1,763	430	876	2,890		3	0	2	2	0	4	1	0
	NONPUBLIC	0	0	0	0	0	0		0	0	0	0	0	0	0	0
	TOTAL	5	12	1,763	430	876	2,890	0.1	3	0	2	2	0	4	1	0
LAMPASAS	PUBLIC	2	6	1,791	757	1,095	3,695		3	0	0	1	0	1	1	0
	NONPUBLIC	0	0	0	0	0	0		0	0	0	0	0	0	0	0
	TOTAL	2	6	1,791	757	1,095	3,695	0.1	3	0	0	1	0	1	1	0
LAVACA	PUBLIC	6	10	1,270	338	800	2,440		1	2	3	1	0	3	0	0
	NONPUBLIC	0	3	544	0	168	712		0	0	1	0	0	0	2	0
	TOTAL	6	13	1,814	338	968	3,152	0.1	1	2	4	1	0	3	2	0

[1] **Elem Enroll** is the school by school total of enrollments in K-4, K-5, K-6, K-8 schools, elementary and middle/JHS students in K-12 schools and students in special ed schools. Public enrollments include public and county-operated schools.

[2] **Middle/JHS Enroll** is the school by school total of enrollments in 5-8 and 7-9 public schools. Public enrollments include public and county-operated schools. Private middle/JHS enrollments are included in Senior Enroll.

[3] **Senior Enroll** is the school by school total of enrollments in 7-12 and 9-12 schools, the secondary students in K-12 schools and students in vocational ed schools. Public enrollments include public and county-operated schools. For private schools, Senior Enroll includes middle/JHS enrollment plus senior enrollment.

[4] **Public Total Enroll** columns are not the sum of school building enrollments. They are projected district-wide Fall enrollments provided to MDR by each school district office, plus county-operated school enrollments.

[5] **K-5** includes pre-kindergarten, kindergarten, K-3, K-4, K-5 schools.

[6] **5-8** includes schools with low grades of 4, 5, 6 and high grades of 7, 8, 9 (e.g., 4-8, 5-8, 6-8, 6-9).

[7] **7-9** includes schools with low grades of 7, 8 and high grades of 7, 8, 9 (e.g., 7-7, 7-8, 7-9, 8-9).

[8] **7-12** includes 7-12, 8-12, 9-12, 10-12, etc.

[9] **K-12** includes schools with both elementary and secondary grades.

[10] **Other** includes special ed, vocational ed and adult schools.

Public State Totals for all columns can exceed the sum of the counties because state totals include state-operated schools and their enrollments.

School Year 2019-2020

Texas School Directory — COUNTY STATISTICS

COUNTY		DISTRICTS	SCHOOLS	ELEM ENROLL[1]	MIDDLE/JHS ENROLL[2]	SENIOR ENROLL[3]	TOTAL ENROLL[4]	% OF STATE	SCHOOLS BY GRADE SPAN							
									K-5[5]	K-6	K-8	5-8[6]	7-9[7]	7-12[8]	K-12[9]	OTHER[10]
LEE	PUBLIC	3	8	1,485	660	942	3,095		3	0	0	2	0	2	1	0
	NONPUBLIC	0	2	233	0	0	233		0	0	2	0	0	0	0	0
	TOTAL	3	10	1,718	660	942	3,328	0.1	3	0	2	2	0	2	1	0
LEON	PUBLIC	5	14	1,612	523	1,064	3,157		4	2	0	3	0	5	0	0
	NONPUBLIC	0	0	0	0	0	0		0	0	0	0	0	0	0	0
	TOTAL	5	14	1,612	523	1,064	3,157	0.1	4	2	0	3	0	5	0	0
LIBERTY	PUBLIC	7	28	8,722	3,203	4,586	18,196		12	1	1	5	1	8	0	0
	NONPUBLIC	0	0	0	0	0	0		0	0	0	0	0	0	0	0
	TOTAL	7	28	8,722	3,203	4,586	18,196	0.3	12	1	1	5	1	8	0	0
LIMESTONE	PUBLIC	3	11	2,247	730	1,073	3,669		4	1	0	1	1	2	1	1
	NONPUBLIC	0	0	0	0	0	0		0	0	0	0	0	0	0	0
	TOTAL	3	11	2,247	730	1,073	3,669	0.1	4	1	0	1	1	2	1	1
LIPSCOMB	PUBLIC	4	5	485	84	222	783		1	0	0	0	0	0	4	0
	NONPUBLIC	0	0	0	0	0	0		0	0	0	0	0	0	0	0
	TOTAL	4	5	485	84	222	783		1	0	0	0	0	0	4	0
LIVE OAK	PUBLIC	2	6	952	170	656	1,778		1	2	0	0	1	2	0	0
	NONPUBLIC	0	0	0	0	0	0		0	0	0	0	0	0	0	0
	TOTAL	2	6	952	170	656	1,778		1	2	0	0	1	2	0	0
LLANO	PUBLIC	1	4	849	405	539	1,800		2	0	0	1	0	1	0	0
	NONPUBLIC	0	1	54	0	22	76		0	0	0	0	0	0	1	1
	TOTAL	1	5	903	405	561	1,876		2	0	0	1	0	1	1	1
LUBBOCK	PUBLIC	8	87	25,036	11,049	13,254	49,512		51	0	0	19	0	12	4	1
	NONPUBLIC	0	10	1,533	0	722	2,255		1	0	2	0	0	0	7	0
	TOTAL	8	97	26,569	11,049	13,976	51,767	1.0	52	0	2	19	0	12	11	1
LYNN	PUBLIC	4	7	895	194	396	1,562		2	0	0	1	0	1	3	0
	NONPUBLIC	0	0	0	0	0	0		0	0	0	0	0	0	0	0
	TOTAL	4	7	895	194	396	1,562		2	0	0	1	0	1	3	0
MADISON	PUBLIC	2	5	1,407	501	755	2,663		2	0	0	1	0	1	1	0
	NONPUBLIC	0	0	0	0	0	0		0	0	0	0	0	0	0	0
	TOTAL	2	5	1,407	501	755	2,663	0.1	2	0	0	1	0	1	1	0
MARION	PUBLIC	1	4	547	375	350	1,272		2	0	0	1	0	0	0	0
	NONPUBLIC	0	2	29	0	40	69		0	0	1	0	0	1	0	0
	TOTAL	1	6	576	375	390	1,341		2	0	1	1	0	2	0	0
MARTIN	PUBLIC	2	4	699	228	345	1,352		1	0	0	0	0	0	1	0
	NONPUBLIC	0	0	0	0	0	0		0	0	0	1	0	1	0	1
	TOTAL	2	4	699	228	345	1,352		1	0	0	1	0	1	1	1

[1] **Elem Enroll** is the school by school total of enrollments in K-4, K-5, K-6, K-8 schools, elementary and middle/JHS students in K-12 schools and students in special ed schools. Public enrollments include public and county-operated schools.

[2] **Middle/JHS Enroll** is the school by school total of enrollments in 5-8 and 7-9 public schools. Public enrollments include public and county-operated schools. Private middle/JHS enrollments are included in Senior Enroll.

[3] **Senior Enroll** is the school by school total of enrollments in 7-12 and 9-12 schools, the secondary students in K-12 schools and students in vocational ed schools. Public enrollments include public and county-operated schools. For private schools, Senior Enroll includes middle/JHS enrollment plus senior enrollment.

[4] **Public Total Enroll** columns are not the sum of school building enrollments. They are projected district-wide Fall enrollments provided to MDR by each school district office, plus county-operated school enrollments.

[5] K-5 includes pre-kindergarten, kindergarten, K-3, K-4, K-5 schools.

[6] 5-8 includes schools with low grades of 4, 5, 6 and high grades of 7, 8, 9 (e.g., 4-8, 5-8, 6-8, 6-9).

[7] 7-9 includes schools with low grades of 7, 8 and high grades of 7, 8, 9 (e.g., 7-7, 7-8, 7-9, 8-9).

[8] 7-12 includes 7-12, 8-12, 9-12, 10-12, etc.

[9] K-12 includes schools with both elementary and secondary grades.

[10] **Other** includes special ed, vocational ed and adult schools.

*****Public State Totals** for all columns can exceed the sum of the counties because state totals include state-operated schools and their enrollments.

School Year 2019-2020 — 800-333-8802 — TX–B13

COUNTY STATISTICS — Market Data Retrieval

COUNTY		DISTRICTS	SCHOOLS	ELEM ENROLL[1]	MIDDLE/JHS ENROLL[2]	SENIOR ENROLL[3]	TOTAL ENROLL[4]	% OF STATE	K-5[5]	K-6	K-8	5-8[6]	7-9[7]	7-12[8]	K-12[9]	OTHER[10]
MASON	PUBLIC	1	3	294	220	214	675		1	0	0	0	0	1	0	0
	NONPUBLIC	0	0	0	0	0	0		0	0	0	1	0	0	0	0
	TOTAL	1	3	294	220	214	675		1	0	0	1	0	1	0	0
MATAGORDA	PUBLIC	5	18	3,702	1,395	2,015	7,356		8	1	1	3	1	4	0	0
	NONPUBLIC	0	1	110	0	0	110		0	1	0	0	0	0	0	0
	TOTAL	5	19	3,812	1,395	2,015	7,466	0.1	8	2	1	3	1	4	0	0
MAVERICK	PUBLIC	1	23	8,007	2,196	4,378	15,000		4	15	0	0	2	2	0	0
	NONPUBLIC	0	2	280	0	0	280		0	1	1	0	0	0	0	0
	TOTAL	1	25	8,287	2,196	4,378	15,280	0.3	4	16	1	0	2	2	0	0
MCCULLOCH	PUBLIC	3	6	813	245	406	1,410		1	0	0	0	0	1	3	0
	NONPUBLIC	0	0	0	0	0	0		0	0	0	1	0	0	0	0
	TOTAL	3	6	813	245	406	1,410		1	0	0	1	0	1	3	0
MCLENNAN	PUBLIC	18	87	22,838	7,439	12,636	43,275		38	9	1	11	4	18	6	0
	NONPUBLIC	0	9	1,137	0	458	1,595		0	2	3	0	0	2	2	0
	TOTAL	18	96	23,975	7,439	13,094	44,870	0.8	38	11	4	11	4	20	8	0
MCMULLEN	PUBLIC	1	1	205	0	82	287		0	0	0	0	0	0	1	0
	NONPUBLIC	0	0	0	0	0	0		0	0	0	0	0	0	0	0
	TOTAL	1	1	205	0	82	287		0	0	0	0	0	0	1	0
MEDINA	PUBLIC	5	18	5,162	2,354	3,077	10,742		9	0	0	4	0	4	1	0
	NONPUBLIC	0	2	145	0	0	145		2	0	0	0	0	0	0	0
	TOTAL	5	20	5,307	2,354	3,077	10,887	0.2	11	0	0	4	0	4	1	0
MENARD	PUBLIC	1	2	225	0	87	300		0	0	1	0	0	0	0	0
	NONPUBLIC	0	0	0	0	0	0		0	0	0	0	0	1	0	0
	TOTAL	1	2	225	0	87	300		0	0	1	0	0	1	0	0
MIDLAND	PUBLIC	2	43	16,359	4,624	7,368	28,831		2	26	0	3	3	8	0	1
	NONPUBLIC	0	7	2,475	0	715	3,190		0	1	1	0	0	0	4	1
	TOTAL	2	50	18,834	4,624	8,083	32,021	0.6	2	27	1	3	3	8	4	2
MILAM	PUBLIC	6	16	2,382	962	1,371	4,667		6	0	1	4	0	4	1	0
	NONPUBLIC	0	1	97	0	0	97		0	0	1	0	0	0	0	0
	TOTAL	6	17	2,479	962	1,371	4,764	0.1	6	0	2	4	0	4	1	0
MILLS	PUBLIC	3	10	427	137	451	800		1	1	0	1	0	4	3	0
	NONPUBLIC	0	0	0	0	0	0		0	0	0	0	0	0	0	0
	TOTAL	3	10	427	137	451	800		1	1	0	1	0	4	3	0
MITCHELL	PUBLIC	3	6	1,018	0	421	1,372		1	0	1	0	0	2	2	0
	NONPUBLIC	0	0	0	0	0	0		0	0	0	0	0	0	0	0
	TOTAL	3	6	1,018	0	421	1,372		1	0	1	0	0	2	2	0

[1] **Elem Enroll** is the school by school total of enrollments in K-4, K-5, K-6, K-8 schools, elementary and middle/JHS students in K-12 schools and students in special ed schools. Public enrollments include public and county-operated schools.
[2] **Middle/JHS Enroll** is the school by school total of enrollments in 5-8 and 7-9 public schools. Public enrollments include public and county-operated schools. Private middle/JHS enrollments are included in Senior Enroll.
[3] **Senior Enroll** is the school by school total of enrollments in 7-12 and 9-12 schools, the secondary students in K-12 schools and students in vocational schools. Public enrollments include public and county-operated schools. For private schools, Senior Enroll includes middle/JHS enrollment plus senior enrollment.
[4] **Public Total Enroll** columns are not the sum of school building enrollments. They are projected district-wide Fall enrollments provided to MDR by each school district office, plus county-operated school enrollments.

[5] **K-5** includes pre-kindergarten, kindergarten, K-3, K-4, K-5 schools.
[6] **5-8** includes schools with low grades of 4, 5, 6 and high grades of 7, 8, 9 (e.g., 4-8, 5-8, 6-8, 6-9).
[7] **7-9** includes schools with low grades of 7, 8 and high grades of 7, 8, 9 (e.g., 7-7, 7-8, 7-9, 8-9).
[8] **7-12** includes 7-12, 8-12, 9-12, 10-12, etc.
[9] **K-12** includes schools with both elementary and secondary grades.
[10] **Other** includes special ed, vocational and adult schools.

*Public State Totals for all columns can exceed the sum of the counties because state totals include state-operated schools and their enrollments

TX—B14   800-333-8802   School Year 2019-2020

Texas School Directory — COUNTY STATISTICS

COUNTY		DISTRICTS	SCHOOLS	ELEM ENROLL[1]	MIDDLE/JHS ENROLL[2]	SENIOR ENROLL[3]	TOTAL ENROLL[4]	% OF STATE	K-5[5]	K-6	K-8	SCHOOLS BY GRADE SPAN 5-8[6]	7-9[7]	7-12[8]	K-12[9]	OTHER[10]
MONTAGUE	PUBLIC	7	13	1,847	552	1,008	3,403		3	1	1	2	0	3	3	0
	NONPUBLIC	0	0	0	0	0	0		0	0	0	0	0	0	0	0
	TOTAL	7	13	1,847	552	1,008	3,403	0.1	3	1	1	2	0	3	3	0
MONTGOMERY	PUBLIC	6	123	61,675	19,591	32,848	111,664		63	16	0	8	10	24	2	0
	NONPUBLIC	0	19	3,514	0	1,230	4,744		1	2	4	0	0	0	12	0
	TOTAL	6	142	65,189	19,591	34,078	116,408	2.1	64	18	4	8	10	24	14	0
MOORE	PUBLIC	2	12	2,778	822	1,231	4,762		6	1	0	1	1	3	0	0
	NONPUBLIC	0	0	0	0	0	0		0	0	0	0	0	0	0	0
	TOTAL	2	12	2,778	822	1,231	4,762	0.1	6	1	0	1	1	3	0	0
MORRIS	PUBLIC	2	7	984	409	524	1,991		3	0	0	2	0	2	0	0
	NONPUBLIC	0	0	0	0	0	0		0	0	0	0	0	0	0	0
	TOTAL	2	7	984	409	524	1,991		3	0	0	2	0	2	0	0
MOTLEY	PUBLIC	1	1	108	0	43	151		0	0	0	0	0	0	1	0
	NONPUBLIC	0	0	0	0	0	0		0	0	0	0	0	0	0	0
	TOTAL	1	1	108	0	43	151		0	0	0	0	0	0	1	0
NACOGDOCHES	PUBLIC	9	25	5,437	2,145	3,014	10,621		10	0	1	5	0	5	4	0
	NONPUBLIC	0	4	407	0	49	456		1	2	0	0	0	0	1	0
	TOTAL	9	29	5,844	2,145	3,063	11,077	0.2	11	2	1	5	0	5	5	0
NAVARRO	PUBLIC	7	23	4,923	1,769	2,886	10,039		10	1	0	3	1	4	4	0
	NONPUBLIC	0	3	289	0	51	340		0	0	1	0	0	0	2	0
	TOTAL	7	26	5,212	1,769	2,937	10,379	0.2	10	1	1	3	1	4	6	0
NEWTON	PUBLIC	2	5	668	205	396	1,276		1	1	0	1	0	2	0	0
	NONPUBLIC	0	1	14	0	6	20		0	0	0	0	0	0	1	0
	TOTAL	2	6	682	205	402	1,296		1	1	0	1	0	2	1	0
NOLAN	PUBLIC	4	10	1,685	631	792	3,223		5	0	0	1	0	1	3	0
	NONPUBLIC	0	0	0	0	0	0		0	0	0	0	0	0	0	0
	TOTAL	4	10	1,685	631	792	3,223	0.1	5	0	0	1	0	1	3	0
NUECES	PUBLIC	12	102	29,887	12,184	18,563	60,514		54	3	1	18	1	20	3	2
	NONPUBLIC	0	19	2,485	0	1,022	3,507		6	2	4	2	0	2	3	0
	TOTAL	12	121	32,372	12,184	19,585	64,021	1.2	60	5	5	20	1	22	6	2
OCHILTREE	PUBLIC	1	6	1,079	528	617	2,217		3	0	0	1	0	2	0	0
	NONPUBLIC	0	1	42	0	0	42		0	1	0	0	0	0	0	0
	TOTAL	1	7	1,121	528	617	2,259		3	1	0	1	0	2	0	0
OLDHAM	PUBLIC	4	7	444	167	348	934		2	0	0	0	0	1	3	0
	NONPUBLIC	0	0	0	0	0	0		0	0	0	0	0	0	0	0
	TOTAL	4	7	444	167	348	934		2	0	0	1	0	1	3	0

[1] **Elem Enroll** is the school by school total of enrollments in K-4, K-5, K-6, K-8 schools, elementary and middle/JHS students in K-12 schools and students in special ed schools. Public enrollments include public and county-operated schools.

[2] **Middle/JHS Enroll** is the school by school total of enrollments in 5-8 and 7-9 public schools. Public enrollments include public and county-operated schools. Private middle/JHS enrollments are included in Senior Enroll.

[3] **Senior Enroll** is the school by school total of enrollments in 7-12 and 9-12 schools, the secondary students in K-12 schools and students in vocational ed schools. Public enrollments include public and county-operated schools. For private schools, Senior Enroll includes middle/JHS enrollment plus senior enrollment.

[4] **Public Total Enroll** columns are not the sum of school building enrollments. They are projected district-wide Fall enrollments provided to MDR by each school district office, plus county-operated school enrollments.

[5] **K-5** includes pre-kindergarten, kindergarten, K-3, K-4, K-5 schools.
[6] **5-8** includes schools with low grades of 4, 5, 6 and high grades of 7, 8, 9 (e.g., 4-8, 5-8, 6-8, 6-9).
[7] **7-9** includes schools with low grades of 7, 8 and high grades of 7, 8, 9 (e.g., 7-7, 7-8, 7-9, 8-9).
[8] **7-12** includes 7-12, 8-12, 9-12, 10-12, etc.
[9] **K-12** includes schools with both elementary and secondary grades.
[10] **Other** includes special ed, vocational and adult schools.

***Public State Totals** for all columns can exceed the sum of the counties because state totals include state-operated schools and their enrollments.

School Year 2019-2020 — 800-333-8802

COUNTY STATISTICS — Market Data Retrieval

COUNTY		DISTRICTS	SCHOOLS	ELEM ENROLL[1]	MIDDLE/JHS ENROLL[2]	SENIOR ENROLL[3]	TOTAL ENROLL[4]	% OF STATE	K-5[5]	K-6	K-8	5-8[6]	7-9[7]	7-12[8]	K-12[9]	OTHER[10]
ORANGE	PUBLIC	6	26	7,882	3,242	4,390	15,875		12	1	0	5	1	6	1	0
	NONPUBLIC	0	2	432	0	93	525		0	0	1	0	0	0	1	0
	TOTAL	6	28	8,314	3,242	4,483	16,400	0.3	12	1	1	5	1	6	2	0
PALO PINTO	PUBLIC	6	13	2,732	630	1,225	4,494		4	2	0	0	1	2	4	0
	NONPUBLIC	0	1	51	0	21	72		0	0	0	0	0	0	1	0
	TOTAL	6	14	2,783	630	1,246	4,566	0.1	4	2	0	0	1	2	5	0
PANOLA	PUBLIC	3	9	2,150	564	1,137	3,892		3	1	0	0	1	1	3	0
	NONPUBLIC	0	1	64	0	26	90		0	0	0	0	0	0	1	0
	TOTAL	3	10	2,214	564	1,163	3,982	0.1	3	1	0	0	1	1	4	0
PARKER	PUBLIC	8	42	11,955	3,328	6,239	21,770		11	11	1	3	5	11	0	0
	NONPUBLIC	0	6	1,579	0	252	1,831		1	0	1	0	0	0	4	0
	TOTAL	8	48	13,534	3,328	6,491	23,601	0.4	12	11	2	3	5	11	4	0
PARMER	PUBLIC	4	11	1,258	454	636	2,330		4	0	0	3	0	3	0	0
	NONPUBLIC	0	0	0	0	0	0		0	0	0	0	0	0	0	0
	TOTAL	4	11	1,258	454	636	2,330		4	0	0	3	0	3	0	0
PECOS	PUBLIC	3	9	1,651	637	859	3,145		4	0	0	2	0	2	1	0
	NONPUBLIC	0	0	0	0	0	0		0	0	0	0	0	0	0	0
	TOTAL	3	9	1,651	637	859	3,145	0.1	4	0	0	2	0	2	1	0
POLK	PUBLIC	6	16	3,770	1,179	2,074	6,758		6	1	0	2	0	4	3	0
	NONPUBLIC	0	0	0	0	0	0		0	0	0	0	0	0	0	0
	TOTAL	6	16	3,770	1,179	2,074	6,758	0.1	6	1	0	2	0	4	3	0
POTTER	PUBLIC	4	65	19,721	7,123	9,879	37,382		40	4	0	8	4	9	0	0
	NONPUBLIC	0	5	1,003	0	165	1,168		1	1	1	0	0	0	2	0
	TOTAL	4	70	20,724	7,123	10,044	38,550	0.7	41	5	1	8	4	9	2	0
PRESIDIO	PUBLIC	2	5	767	397	526	1,504		1	1	0	0	1	1	1	0
	NONPUBLIC	0	0	0	0	0	0		0	0	0	0	0	0	0	0
	TOTAL	2	5	767	397	526	1,504		1	1	0	0	1	1	1	0
RAINS	PUBLIC	1	4	845	381	479	1,650		2	0	0	1	0	0	0	0
	NONPUBLIC	0	0	0	0	0	0		0	0	0	0	0	0	0	0
	TOTAL	1	4	845	381	479	1,650		2	0	0	1	0	1	0	0
RANDALL	PUBLIC	1	16	6,358	1,532	2,891	10,200		8	3	0	0	2	3	0	0
	NONPUBLIC	0	3	124	0	320	444		1	0	0	0	0	0	2	0
	TOTAL	1	19	6,482	1,532	3,211	10,644	0.2	9	3	0	0	2	3	2	0
REAGAN	PUBLIC	1	3	439	191	229	950		1	0	0	1	0	1	0	0
	NONPUBLIC	0	0	0	0	0	0		0	0	0	0	0	0	0	0
	TOTAL	1	3	439	191	229	950		1	0	0	1	0	1	0	0

[1] **Elem Enroll** is the school by school total of enrollments in K-4, K-5, K-6, K-8 schools, elementary and middle/JHS students in K-12 schools and students in special ed schools. Public enrollments include public and county-operated schools.
[2] **Middle/JHS Enroll** is the school by school total of enrollments in 5-8 and 7-9 public schools. Public enrollments include public and county-operated schools. Private middle/JHS enrollments are included in Senior Enroll.
[3] **Senior Enroll** is the school by school total of enrollments in 7-12 and 9-12 schools, the secondary students in K-12 schools and students in vocational ed schools. Public enrollments include public and county-operated schools. For private schools, Senior Enroll includes middle/JHS enrollment plus senior enrollment.
[4] **Public Total Enroll** columns are not the sum of school building enrollments. They are projected district-wide Fall enrollments provided to MDR by each school district office, plus county-operated school enrollments.
[5] **K-5** includes pre-kindergarten, kindergarten, K-3, K-4, K-5 schools.
[6] **5-8** includes schools with low grades of 4, 5, 6 and high grades of 7, 8, 9 (e.g., 4-8, 5-8, 6-8, 6-9).
[7] **7-9** includes schools with low grades of 7, 8 and high grades of 7, 8, 9 (e.g., 7-7, 7-8, 7-9, 8-9).
[8] **7-12** includes 7-12, 8-12, 9-12, 10-12, etc.
[9] **K-12** includes schools with both elementary and secondary grades.
[10] **Other** includes special ed, vocational and adult schools.

*Public State Totals for all columns can exceed the sum of the counties because state totals include state-operated schools and their enrollments

Texas School Directory — COUNTY STATISTICS

COUNTY		DISTRICTS	SCHOOLS	ELEM ENROLL[1]	MIDDLE/JHS ENROLL[2]	SENIOR ENROLL[3]	TOTAL ENROLL[4]	% OF STATE	SCHOOLS BY GRADE SPAN							
									K-5[5]	K-6	K-8	5-8[6]	7-9[7]	7-12[8]	K-12[9]	OTHER[10]
REAL	PUBLIC	1	1	221	0	88	309		0	0	0	0	0	0	1	0
	NONPUBLIC	0	0	0	0	0	0		0	0	0	0	0	0	0	0
	TOTAL	1	1	221	0	88	309		0	0	0	0	0	0	1	0
RED RIVER	PUBLIC	4	10	1,071	454	624	2,225		4	0	0	2	0	2	2	0
	NONPUBLIC	0	0	0	0	0	0		0	0	0	0	0	0	0	0
	TOTAL	4	10	1,071	454	624	2,225		4	0	0	2	0	2	2	0
REEVES	PUBLIC	2	6	1,538	537	720	2,965		3	0	0	1	0	1	1	0
	NONPUBLIC	0	0	0	0	0	0		0	0	0	0	0	0	0	0
	TOTAL	2	6	1,538	537	720	2,965	0.1	3	0	0	1	0	1	1	0
REFUGIO	PUBLIC	3	7	730	135	425	1,250		1	2	0	0	0	2	1	0
	NONPUBLIC	0	0	0	0	0	0		0	0	0	0	1	0	0	0
	TOTAL	3	7	730	135	425	1,250		1	2	0	0	1	2	1	0
ROBERTS	PUBLIC	1	1	157	0	63	220		0	0	0	0	0	0	1	0
	NONPUBLIC	0	0	0	0	0	0		0	0	0	0	0	0	0	0
	TOTAL	1	1	157	0	63	220		0	0	0	0	0	0	1	0
ROBERTSON	PUBLIC	4	10	1,437	594	756	2,631		2	1	0	2	1	3	1	0
	NONPUBLIC	0	0	0	0	0	0		0	0	0	0	0	0	0	0
	TOTAL	4	10	1,437	594	756	2,631	0.1	2	1	0	2	1	3	1	0
ROCKWALL	PUBLIC	2	29	11,779	3,542	6,725	22,570		4	16	0	0	4	5	0	0
	NONPUBLIC	0	2	444	0	108	552		1	0	0	0	0	0	1	0
	TOTAL	2	31	12,223	3,542	6,833	23,122	0.4	5	16	0	0	4	5	1	0
RUNNELS	PUBLIC	4	8	1,061	337	577	1,988		2	0	0	2	0	2	2	0
	NONPUBLIC	0	0	0	0	0	0		0	0	0	0	0	0	0	0
	TOTAL	4	8	1,061	337	577	1,988		2	0	0	2	0	2	2	0
RUSK	PUBLIC	8	20	4,336	1,483	2,361	7,803		8	0	0	3	0	4	5	0
	NONPUBLIC	0	1	93	0	42	135		0	0	0	0	0	0	1	0
	TOTAL	8	21	4,429	1,483	2,403	7,938	0.2	8	0	0	3	0	4	6	0
SABINE	PUBLIC	2	5	697	411	454	1,500		2	0	0	1	0	1	1	0
	NONPUBLIC	0	0	0	0	0	0		0	0	0	0	0	0	0	0
	TOTAL	2	5	697	411	454	1,500		2	0	0	1	0	1	1	0
SAN AUGUSTINE	PUBLIC	2	4	599	246	327	1,163		2	0	0	0	0	0	2	0
	NONPUBLIC	0	0	0	0	0	0		0	0	0	0	0	0	0	0
	TOTAL	2	4	599	246	327	1,163		2	0	0	0	0	0	2	0
SAN JACINTO	PUBLIC	2	8	1,754	748	1,047	3,525		4	0	0	2	0	2	0	0
	NONPUBLIC	0	0	0	0	0	0		0	0	0	0	0	0	0	0
	TOTAL	2	8	1,754	748	1,047	3,525	0.1	4	0	0	2	0	2	0	0

[1] **Elem Enroll** is the school by school total of enrollments in K-4, K-5, K-6, K-8 schools, elementary and middle/JHS students in K-12 schools and students in special ed schools. Public enrollments include public and county-operated schools.

[2] **Middle/JHS Enroll** is the school by school total of enrollments in 5-8 and 7-9 public schools. Public enrollments include public and county-operated schools. Private middle/JHS enrollments are included in Senior Enroll.

[3] **Senior Enroll** is the school by school total of enrollments in 7-12 and 9-12 schools, the secondary students in K-12 schools and students in vocational ed schools. Public enrollments include public and county-operated schools. For private schools, Senior Enroll includes middle/JHS enrollment plus senior enrollment.

[4] **Public Total Enroll** columns are not the sum of school building enrollments. They are projected district-wide Fall enrollments provided to MDR by each school district office, plus county-operated school enrollments.

[5] **K-5** includes pre-kindergarten, kindergarten, K-3, K-4, K-5 schools.

[6] **5-8** includes schools with low grades of 4, 5, 6 and high grades of 7, 8, 9 (e.g., 4-8, 5-8, 6-8, 6-9).

[7] **7-9** includes schools with low grades of 7, 8 and high grades of 8, 9 (e.g., 7-7, 7-8, 7-9, 8-9).

[8] **7-12** includes 7-12, 8-12, 9-12, 10-12, etc.

[9] **K-12** includes schools with both elementary and secondary grades.

[10] **Other** includes special ed, vocational and adult schools.

*Public State Totals for all columns can exceed the sum of the counties because state totals include state-operated schools and their enrollments

COUNTY STATISTICS
Market Data Retrieval

COUNTY		DISTRICTS	SCHOOLS	ELEM ENROLL[1]	MIDDLE/JHS ENROLL[2]	SENIOR ENROLL[3]	TOTAL ENROLL[4]	% OF STATE	K-5[5]	K-6	K-8	SCHOOLS BY GRADE SPAN 5-8[6]	7-9[7]	7-12[8]	K-12[9]	OTHER[10]
SAN PATRICIO	PUBLIC	7	32	7,059	2,786	4,227	14,146		16	1	0	6	1	8	0	0
	NONPUBLIC	0	0	0	0	0	0		0	0	0	0	0	0	0	0
	TOTAL	**7**	**32**	**7,059**	**2,786**	**4,227**	**14,146**	**0.3**	**16**	**1**	**0**	**6**	**1**	**8**	**0**	**0**
SAN SABA	PUBLIC	3	5	496	216	254	980		1	0	0	1	0	1	2	0
	NONPUBLIC	0	0	0	0	0	0		0	0	0	0	0	0	0	0
	TOTAL	**3**	**5**	**496**	**216**	**254**	**980**		**1**	**0**	**0**	**1**	**0**	**1**	**2**	**0**
SCHLEICHER	PUBLIC	1	3	241	163	151	590		1	0	0	1	0	1	0	0
	NONPUBLIC	0	0	0	0	0	0		0	0	0	0	0	0	0	0
	TOTAL	**1**	**3**	**241**	**163**	**151**	**590**		**1**	**0**	**0**	**1**	**0**	**1**	**0**	**0**
SCURRY	PUBLIC	3	6	1,801	622	883	3,170		2	0	0	1	0	1	2	0
	NONPUBLIC	0	0	0	0	0	0		0	0	0	0	0	0	0	0
	TOTAL	**3**	**6**	**1,801**	**622**	**883**	**3,170**	**0.1**	**2**	**0**	**0**	**1**	**0**	**1**	**2**	**0**
SHACKELFORD	PUBLIC	2	3	370	0	258	620		0	1	0	1	0	1	1	0
	NONPUBLIC	0	0	0	0	0	0		0	0	0	0	0	0	0	0
	TOTAL	**2**	**3**	**370**	**0**	**258**	**620**		**0**	**1**	**0**	**1**	**0**	**1**	**1**	**0**
SHELBY	PUBLIC	6	17	2,927	1,057	1,487	5,330		6	0	1	4	0	4	2	0
	NONPUBLIC	0	1	30	0	12	42		0	0	0	0	0	0	1	0
	TOTAL	**6**	**18**	**2,957**	**1,057**	**1,499**	**5,372**	**0.1**	**6**	**0**	**1**	**4**	**0**	**4**	**3**	**0**
SHERMAN	PUBLIC	2	4	370	183	152	700		2	0	0	1	0	1	0	0
	NONPUBLIC	0	0	0	0	0	0		0	0	0	0	0	0	0	0
	TOTAL	**2**	**4**	**370**	**183**	**152**	**700**		**2**	**0**	**0**	**1**	**0**	**1**	**0**	**0**
SMITH	PUBLIC	9	68	19,228	6,710	10,126	37,344		35	3	0	9	3	11	5	2
	NONPUBLIC	0	14	2,247	0	1,934	4,181		4	0	1	0	0	1	8	0
	TOTAL	**9**	**82**	**21,475**	**6,710**	**12,060**	**41,525**	**0.8**	**39**	**3**	**1**	**9**	**3**	**12**	**13**	**2**
SOMERVELL	PUBLIC	1	4	862	417	527	1,882		2	0	0	1	0	1	0	0
	NONPUBLIC	0	0	0	0	0	0		0	0	0	0	0	0	0	0
	TOTAL	**1**	**4**	**862**	**417**	**527**	**1,882**		**2**	**0**	**0**	**1**	**0**	**1**	**0**	**0**
STARR	PUBLIC	3	29	8,891	4,004	5,063	16,526		16	0	0	6	0	4	3	0
	NONPUBLIC	0	1	141	0	0	141		0	0	1	0	0	0	0	0
	TOTAL	**3**	**30**	**9,032**	**4,004**	**5,063**	**16,667**	**0.3**	**16**	**0**	**1**	**6**	**0**	**4**	**3**	**0**
STEPHENS	PUBLIC	1	5	844	238	419	1,465		2	1	0	0	1	1	0	0
	NONPUBLIC	0	0	0	0	0	0		0	0	0	0	0	0	0	0
	TOTAL	**1**	**5**	**844**	**238**	**419**	**1,465**		**2**	**1**	**0**	**0**	**1**	**1**	**0**	**0**
STERLING	PUBLIC	1	2	141	64	86	320		1	0	0	0	0	0	1	0
	NONPUBLIC	0	0	0	0	0	0		0	0	0	0	0	0	0	0
	TOTAL	**1**	**2**	**141**	**64**	**86**	**320**		**1**	**0**	**0**	**0**	**0**	**0**	**1**	**0**

[1] **Elem Enroll** is the school by school total of enrollments in K-4, K-5, K-6, K-8 schools, elementary and middle/JHS students in K-12 schools and students in special ed schools. Public enrollments include public and county-operated schools.

[2] **Middle/JHS Enroll** is the school by school total of enrollments in 5-8 and 7-9 public schools. Public enrollments include public and county-operated schools. Private middle/JHS enrollments are included in Senior Enroll.

[3] **Senior Enroll** is the school by school total of enrollments in 7-12 and 9-12 schools, the secondary students in K-12 schools and students in vocational ed schools. Public enrollments include public and county-operated schools. For private schools, Senior Enroll includes middle/JHS enrollment plus senior enrollment.

[4] **Public Total Enroll** columns are not the sum of school building enrollments. They are projected district-wide Fall enrollments provided to MDR by each school district office, plus county-operated school enrollments.

[5] **K-5** includes pre-kindergarten, kindergarten, K-3, K-4, K-5 schools.

[6] **5-8** includes schools with low grades of 4, 5, 6 and high grades of 7, 8, 9 (e.g., 4-8, 5-8, 6-8, 6-9).

[7] **7-9** includes schools with low grades of 7, 8 and high grades of 7, 8, 9 (e.g., 7-7, 7-8, 7-9, 8-9).

[8] **7-12** includes 7-12, 8-12, 9-12, 10-12, etc.

[9] **K-12** includes schools with both elementary and secondary grades.

[10] **Other** includes special ed, vocational ed and adult schools.

*****Public State Totals** for all columns can exceed the sum of the counties because state totals include state-operated schools and their enrollments

Texas School Directory — COUNTY STATISTICS

COUNTY		DISTRICTS	SCHOOLS	ELEM ENROLL[1]	MIDDLE/JHS ENROLL[2]	SENIOR ENROLL[3]	TOTAL ENROLL[4]	% OF STATE	K-5[5]	K-6	K-8	5-8[6]	7-9[7]	7-12[8]	K-12[9]	OTHER[10]
STONEWALL	PUBLIC	1	2	104	53	70	240		1	0	0	0	0	0	1	0
	NONPUBLIC	0	0	0	0	0	0		0	0	0	0	0	0	0	0
	TOTAL	1	2	104	53	70	240		1	0	0	0	0	0	1	0
SUTTON	PUBLIC	1	3	387	181	249	760		0	1	0	0	1	1	0	0
	NONPUBLIC	0	0	0	0	0	0		0	0	0	0	0	0	0	0
	TOTAL	1	3	387	181	249	760		0	1	0	0	1	1	0	0
SWISHER	PUBLIC	3	8	841	241	532	1,633		2	2	0	1	0	3	0	0
	NONPUBLIC	0	0	0	0	0	0		0	0	0	0	0	0	0	0
	TOTAL	3	8	841	241	532	1,633		2	2	0	1	0	3	0	0
TARRANT	PUBLIC	16	497	185,787	65,389	104,889	349,355		216	101	2	41	38	76	10	13
	NONPUBLIC	0	79	16,344	0	5,764	22,108		8	9	18	0	0	7	30	7
	TOTAL	16	576	202,131	65,389	110,653	371,463	6.8	224	110	20	41	38	83	40	20
TAYLOR	PUBLIC	5	41	11,965	5,605	6,323	24,180		22	0	0	8	0	7	1	3
	NONPUBLIC	0	5	628	0	86	714		3	0	1	0	0	0	1	0
	TOTAL	5	46	12,593	5,605	6,409	24,894	0.5	25	0	1	8	0	7	2	3
TERRELL	PUBLIC	1	1	93	0	37	130		0	0	0	0	0	0	1	0
	NONPUBLIC	0	0	0	0	0	0		0	0	0	0	0	0	0	0
	TOTAL	1	1	93	0	37	130		0	0	0	0	0	0	1	0
TERRY	PUBLIC	3	7	1,388	358	630	2,327		3	0	0	1	0	1	2	0
	NONPUBLIC	0	0	0	0	0	0		0	0	0	0	0	0	0	0
	TOTAL	3	7	1,388	358	630	2,327		3	0	0	1	0	1	2	0
THROCKMORTON	PUBLIC	2	2	232	0	93	325		0	0	0	0	0	0	2	0
	NONPUBLIC	0	0	0	0	0	0		0	0	0	0	0	0	0	0
	TOTAL	2	2	232	0	93	325		0	0	0	0	0	0	2	0
TITUS	PUBLIC	3	12	4,203	946	1,864	6,990		6	1	1	0	1	2	0	0
	NONPUBLIC	0	1	7	0	3	10		0	0	0	1	0	0	1	0
	TOTAL	3	13	4,210	946	1,867	7,000	0.1	6	1	1	1	1	2	1	0
TOM GREEN	PUBLIC	6	37	8,560	3,930	5,000	17,697		20	1	0	5	0	7	4	0
	NONPUBLIC	0	4	403	0	84	487		0	0	2	0	0	0	2	0
	TOTAL	6	41	8,963	3,930	5,084	18,184	0.3	20	1	2	5	0	7	6	0
TRAVIS	PUBLIC	7	208	76,476	31,639	40,225	147,735		127	9	0	36	0	29	4	3
	NONPUBLIC	0	46	8,124	0	3,870	11,994		6	0	16	2	0	7	11	4
	TOTAL	7	254	84,600	31,639	44,095	159,729	2.9	133	9	16	38	0	36	15	7
TRINITY	PUBLIC	4	9	1,142	468	730	2,377		2	2	0	1	0	3	1	0
	NONPUBLIC	0	0	0	0	0	0		0	0	0	0	0	0	0	0
	TOTAL	4	9	1,142	468	730	2,377		2	2	0	1	0	3	1	0

[1] **Elem Enroll** is the school by school total of enrollments in K-4, K-5, K-6, K-8 schools, elementary and middle/JHS students in K-12 schools and students in special ed schools. Public enrollments include public and county-operated schools.
[2] **Middle/JHS Enroll** is the school by school total of enrollments in 5-8 and 7-9 public schools. Public enrollments include public and county-operated schools. Private middle/JHS enrollments are included in Senior Enroll.
[3] **Senior Enroll** is the school by school total of enrollments in 7-12 and 9-12 schools, the secondary students in K-12 schools and students in vocational ed schools. Public enrollments include public and county-operated schools. For private schools, Senior Enroll includes middle/JHS enrollment plus senior enrollment.
[4] **Public Total Enroll** columns are not the sum of school building enrollments. They are projected district-wide Fall enrollments provided to MDR by each school district office, plus county-operated school enrollments.
[5] **K-5** includes pre-kindergarten, kindergarten, K-3, K-4, K-5 schools.
[6] **5-8** includes schools with low grades of 4, 5, 6 and high grades of 7, 8, 9 (e.g., 4-8, 5-8, 6-8, 6-9).
[7] **7-9** includes schools with low grades of 7, 8 and high grades of 7, 8, 9 (e.g., 7-7, 7-8, 7-9, 8-9).
[8] **7-12** includes 7-12, 8-12, 9-12, 10-12, etc.
[9] **K-12** includes schools with both elementary and secondary grades.
[10] **Other** includes special ed, vocational ed and adult schools.
***Public State Totals** for all columns can exceed the sum of the counties because state totals include state-operated schools and their enrollments.

School Year 2019-2020 — 800-333-8802 — TX—B19

COUNTY STATISTICS — Market Data Retrieval

COUNTY		DISTRICTS	SCHOOLS	ELEM ENROLL[1]	MIDDLE/JHS ENROLL[2]	SENIOR ENROLL[3]	TOTAL ENROLL[4]	% OF STATE	K-5[5]	K-6	K-8	5-8[6]	7-9[7]	7-12[8]	K-12[9]	OTHER[10]
TYLER	PUBLIC	5	14	1,904	737	1,076	3,760		6	1	0	2	0	3	2	0
	NONPUBLIC	0	1	28	0	0	28		1	0	0	0	0	0	0	0
	TOTAL	5	15	1,932	737	1,076	3,788	0.1	7	1	0	2	0	3	2	0
UPSHUR	PUBLIC	7	20	3,879	1,208	2,154	7,318		6	2	0	4	1	6	1	0
	NONPUBLIC	0	0	0	0	0	0		0	0	0	0	0	0	0	0
	TOTAL	7	20	3,879	1,208	2,154	7,318	0.1	6	2	0	4	1	6	1	0
UPTON	PUBLIC	2	5	419	163	251	880		2	0	0	1	0	2	0	0
	NONPUBLIC	0	0	0	0	0	0		0	0	0	0	0	0	0	0
	TOTAL	2	5	419	163	251	880		2	0	0	1	0	2	0	0
UVALDE	PUBLIC	4	11	3,352	714	1,514	5,428		4	2	0	0	1	1	3	0
	NONPUBLIC	0	2	145	0	0	145		1	1	0	0	0	0	0	0
	TOTAL	4	13	3,497	714	1,514	5,573	0.1	5	3	0	0	1	1	3	0
VAL VERDE	PUBLIC	2	13	6,131	1,545	3,023	10,699		8	1	0	0	1	2	0	0
	NONPUBLIC	0	3	613	0	0	613		1	0	0	0	0	0	1	0
	TOTAL	2	16	6,744	1,545	3,023	11,312	0.2	9	1	0	0	1	2	1	0
VAN ZANDT	PUBLIC	7	26	5,117	1,775	2,891	9,880		11	2	0	4	2	6	1	0
	NONPUBLIC	0	1	26	0	11	37		0	0	2	0	0	0	1	0
	TOTAL	7	27	5,143	1,775	2,902	9,917	0.2	11	2	2	4	2	6	2	0
VICTORIA	PUBLIC	3	28	7,286	3,313	4,106	14,920		17	0	0	5	0	4	1	1
	NONPUBLIC	0	8	1,556	0	431	1,987		1	0	4	0	0	1	1	1
	TOTAL	3	36	8,842	3,313	4,537	16,907	0.3	18	0	4	5	0	5	2	2
WALKER	PUBLIC	2	13	4,050	1,124	2,098	7,100		7	1	0	1	1	2	1	0
	NONPUBLIC	0	2	366	0	154	520		0	0	0	0	0	0	2	0
	TOTAL	2	15	4,416	1,124	2,252	7,620	0.1	7	1	0	1	1	2	3	0
WALLER	PUBLIC	3	15	5,703	2,387	2,918	11,700		8	0	0	4	0	3	0	0
	NONPUBLIC	0	0	0	0	0	0		0	0	0	0	0	0	0	0
	TOTAL	3	15	5,703	2,387	2,918	11,700	0.2	8	0	0	4	0	3	0	0
WARD	PUBLIC	2	7	1,468	367	678	2,485		2	1	0	0	1	2	1	0
	NONPUBLIC	0	0	0	0	0	0		0	0	0	0	0	0	0	0
	TOTAL	2	7	1,468	367	678	2,485	0.1	2	1	0	0	1	2	1	0
WASHINGTON	PUBLIC	2	9	2,747	787	1,679	5,455		3	2	0	0	1	3	0	0
	NONPUBLIC	0	4	384	0	0	384		1	1	2	0	0	0	0	0
	TOTAL	2	13	3,131	787	1,679	5,839	0.1	4	3	2	0	1	3	0	0
WEBB	PUBLIC	3	83	33,386	14,599	19,996	69,009		50	0	0	15	0	16	2	0
	NONPUBLIC	0	7	1,859	0	627	2,486		0	1	5	0	0	1	0	0
	TOTAL	3	90	35,245	14,599	20,623	71,495	1.3	50	1	5	15	0	17	2	0

[1] **Elem Enroll** is the school by school total of enrollments in K-4, K-5, K-6, K-8 schools, elementary and middle/JHS students in K-12 schools and students in special ed schools. Public enrollments include public and county-operated schools.

[2] **Middle/JHS Enroll** is the school by school total of enrollments in 5-8 and 7-9 public schools. Public enrollments include public and county-operated schools. Private middle/JHS enrollments are included in Senior Enroll.

[3] **Senior Enroll** is the school by school total of enrollments in 7-12 and 9-12 schools, the secondary students in K-12 schools and students in vocational ed schools. Public enrollments include public and county-operated schools. For private schools, Senior Enroll includes middle/JHS enrollment plus senior enrollment.

[4] **Public Total Enroll** columns are not the sum of school building enrollments. They are projected district-wide Fall enrollments provided to MDR by each school district office, plus county-operated school enrollments.

[5] **K-5** includes pre-kindergarten, kindergarten, K-3, K-4, K-5 schools.

[6] **5-8** includes schools with low grades of 4, 5, 6 and high grades of 7, 8, 9 (e.g., 4-8, 5-8, 6-8, 6-9).

[7] **7-9** includes schools with low grades of 7, 8 and high grades of 7, 8, 9 (e.g., 7-7, 7-8, 7-9, 8-9).

[8] **7-12** includes 7-12, 8-12, 9-12, 10-12, etc.

[9] **K-12** includes schools with both elementary and secondary grades.

[10] **Other** includes special ed, vocational ed and adult schools.

*****Public State Totals** for all columns can exceed the sum of the counties because state totals include state-operated schools and their enrollments.

Texas School Directory — COUNTY STATISTICS

COUNTY		DISTRICTS	SCHOOLS	ELEM ENROLL[1]	MIDDLE/JHS ENROLL[2]	SENIOR ENROLL[3]	TOTAL ENROLL[4]	% OF STATE	K-5[5]	K-6	K-8	5-8[6]	7-9[7]	7-12[8]	K-12[9]	OTHER[10]
WHARTON	PUBLIC	5	19	4,035	1,868	2,505	8,147		7	1	0	4	1	6	0	0
	NONPUBLIC	0	2	401	0	29	430		0	0	1	0	0	0	1	0
	TOTAL	5	21	4,436	1,868	2,534	8,577	0.2	7	1	1	4	1	6	1	0
WHEELER	PUBLIC	4	6	708	100	305	1,146		1	0	0	1	0	1	3	0
	NONPUBLIC	0	0	0	0	0	0		0	0	0	0	0	0	0	0
	TOTAL	4	6	708	100	305	1,146		1	0	0	1	0	1	3	0
WICHITA	PUBLIC	5	43	10,959	4,008	5,701	21,177		24	3	0	5	0	7	3	1
	NONPUBLIC	0	4	511	0	211	722		0	0	0	0	0	0	4	0
	TOTAL	5	47	11,470	4,008	5,912	21,899	0.4	24	3	0	5	0	7	7	1
WILBARGER	PUBLIC	3	8	1,164	471	676	2,040		3	0	0	1	0	1	3	0
	NONPUBLIC	0	0	0	0	0	0		0	0	0	0	0	0	0	0
	TOTAL	3	8	1,164	471	676	2,040		3	0	0	1	0	1	3	0
WILLACY	PUBLIC	4	11	2,256	812	1,258	4,213		3	0	1	2	0	4	1	0
	NONPUBLIC	0	0	0	0	0	0		0	0	0	0	0	0	0	0
	TOTAL	4	11	2,256	812	1,258	4,213	0.1	3	0	1	2	0	4	1	0
WILLIAMSON	PUBLIC	11	149	56,032	27,056	35,850	122,018		87	1	1	29	1	24	5	1
	NONPUBLIC	0	13	2,447	0	796	3,243		0	2	6	0	0	2	3	0
	TOTAL	11	162	58,479	27,056	36,646	125,261	2.3	87	3	7	29	1	26	8	1
WILSON	PUBLIC	4	15	4,214	2,051	2,831	9,003		6	0	0	4	0	4	1	0
	NONPUBLIC	0	2	105	0	5	110		1	0	0	0	0	0	1	0
	TOTAL	4	17	4,319	2,051	2,836	9,113	0.2	7	0	0	4	0	4	2	0
WINKLER	PUBLIC	2	5	898	416	538	1,858		1	1	0	1	0	2	0	0
	NONPUBLIC	0	0	0	0	0	0		0	0	0	0	0	0	0	0
	TOTAL	2	5	898	416	538	1,858		1	1	0	1	0	2	0	0
WISE	PUBLIC	7	26	4,580	1,790	2,905	9,560		11	1	0	5	1	6	2	0
	NONPUBLIC	0	1	286	0	115	401		0	0	0	0	0	0	1	0
	TOTAL	7	27	4,866	1,790	3,020	9,961	0.2	11	1	0	5	1	6	3	0
WOOD	PUBLIC	6	17	3,001	1,446	1,739	6,202		7	0	0	4	0	4	2	0
	NONPUBLIC	0	0	0	0	0	0		0	0	0	0	0	0	0	0
	TOTAL	6	17	3,001	1,446	1,739	6,202	0.1	7	0	0	4	0	4	2	0
YOAKUM	PUBLIC	2	8	1,061	503	605	2,171		3	0	0	2	0	3	0	0
	NONPUBLIC	0	0	0	0	0	0		0	0	0	0	0	0	0	0
	TOTAL	2	8	1,061	503	605	2,171		3	0	0	2	0	3	0	0
YOUNG	PUBLIC	3	9	1,646	696	902	3,270		4	0	0	2	0	2	1	0
	NONPUBLIC	0	0	0	0	0	0		0	0	0	0	0	0	0	0
	TOTAL	3	9	1,646	696	902	3,270	0.1	4	0	0	2	0	2	1	0

[1] **Elem Enroll** is the school by school total of enrollments in K-4, K-5, K-6, K-8 schools, elementary and middle/JHS students in K-12 schools and students in special ed schools. Public enrollments include public and county-operated schools.

[2] **Middle/JHS Enroll** is the school by school total of enrollments in 5-8 and 7-9 public schools. Public enrollments include public and county-operated schools. Private middle/JHS enrollments are included in Senior Enroll.

[3] **Senior Enroll** is the school by school total of enrollments in 7-12 and 9-12 schools, the secondary students in K-12 schools and students in vocational ed schools. Public enrollments include public and county-operated schools. For private schools, Senior Enroll includes middle/JHS enrollment plus senior enrollment.

[4] **Public Total Enroll** columns are not the sum of school building enrollments. They are projected district-wide Fall enrollments provided to MDR by each school district office, plus county-operated school enrollments.

[5] **K-5** includes pre-kindergarten, kindergarten, K-3, K-4, K-5 schools.

[6] **5-8** includes schools with low grades of 4, 5, 6 and high grades of 7, 8, 9 (e.g., 4-8, 5-8, 6-8, 6-9).

[7] **7-9** includes schools with low grades of 7, 8 and high grades of 7, 8 and high grades of 7, 8, 9 (e.g., 7-7, 7-8, 7-9, 8-9).

[8] **7-12** includes 7-12, 8-12, 9-12, 10-12, etc.

[9] **K-12** includes schools with both elementary and secondary grades.

[10] **Other** includes special ed, vocational ed and adult schools.

*****Public State Totals** for all columns can exceed the sum of the counties because state totals include state-operated schools and their enrollments

COUNTY STATISTICS

Market Data Retrieval

COUNTY		DISTRICTS	SCHOOLS	ELEM ENROLL[1]	MIDDLE/JHS ENROLL[2]	SENIOR ENROLL[3]	TOTAL ENROLL[4]	% OF STATE	SCHOOLS BY GRADE SPAN							
									K-5[5]	K-6	K-8	5-8[6]	7-9[7]	7-12[8]	K-12[9]	OTHER[10]
ZAPATA	PUBLIC	1	6	1,826	772	923	3,521		4	0	0	1	0	1	0	0
	NONPUBLIC	0	0	0	0	0	0		0	0	0	0	0	0	0	0
	TOTAL	1	6	1,826	772	923	3,521	0.1	4	0	0	1	0	1	0	0
ZAVALA	PUBLIC	2	7	967	282	729	2,000		2	2	0	0	1	2	0	0
	NONPUBLIC	0	0	0	0	0	0		0	0	0	0	0	0	0	0
	TOTAL	2	7	967	282	729	2,000		2	2	0	0	1	2	0	0
STATE TOTAL	PUBLIC*	1,027	8,687	2,649,076	1,031,866	1,496,615	5,424,742		3,976	560	107	1,199	239	1,461	473	73
	NONPUBLIC	0	975	183,732	0	64,127	247,859		121	84	302	7	0	79	349	33
	TOTAL	1,027	9,662	2,832,808	1,031,866	1,560,742	5,672,601		4,097	644	409	1,206	239	1,540	822	106

[1] **Elem Enroll** is the school by school total of enrollments in K-4, K-5, K-6, K-8 schools, elementary and middle/JHS students in K-12 schools and students in special ed schools. Public enrollments include public and county-operated schools.

[2] **Middle/JHS Enroll** is the school by school total of enrollments in 5-8 and 7-9 public schools. Public enrollments include public and county-operated schools. Private middle/JHS enrollments are included in Senior Enroll.

[3] **Senior Enroll** is the school by school total of enrollments in 7-12 and 9-12 schools, the secondary students in K-12 schools and students in vocational ed schools. Public enrollments include public and county-operated schools. For private schools, Senior Enroll includes middle/JHS enrollment plus senior enrollment.

[4] **Public Total Enroll** columns are not the sum of school building enrollments. They are projected district-wide Fall enrollments provided to MDR by each school district office, plus county-operated school enrollments.

[5] **K-5** includes pre-kindergarten, kindergarten, K-3, K-4, K-5 schools.

[6] **5-8** includes schools with low grades of 4, 5, 6 and high grades of 7, 8, 9 (e.g., 4-8, 5-8, 6-8, 6-9).

[7] **7-9** includes schools with low grades of 7, 8 and high grades of 7, 8, 9 (e.g., 7-7, 7-8, 7-9, 8-9).

[8] **7-12** includes 7-12, 8-12, 9-12, 10-12, etc.

[9] **K-12** includes schools with both elementary and secondary grades.

[10] **Other** includes special ed, vocational and adult schools.

***Public State Totals** for all columns can exceed the sum of the counties because state totals include state-operated schools and their enrollments

Texas School Directory

DISTRICT BUYING POWER INDEX

DISTRICT BUYING POWER INDEX
COUNTIES RANKED BY PERCENTAGE OF STATE SPENDING

COUNTY / DISTRICT	PID	COUNTY % OF STATE	DISTRICT % OF COUNTY	DISTRICT % OF STATE	NUMBER OF SCHOOLS	ENROLL	EXP	POV
HARRIS		11.73						
Houston Ind School Dist	01023770		28.86	3.38	275	206,052	MED	MED-HIGH
Cypress-Fairbanks Ind Sch Dist	01023184		12.92	1.52	91	116,249	MED	MED-LOW
Aldine Ind School Dist	01022697		8.53	1.00	82	69,768	MED	HIGH
Spring Ind School Dist	01027465		6.61	0.77	41	35,391	HIGH	MED-HIGH
Alief Ind School Dist	01022972		6.54	0.77	45	46,241	MED	MED-HIGH
Pasadena Ind School Dist	01026631		6.20	0.73	68	54,000	MED	MED-HIGH
Spring Branch Ind School Dist	01027087		4.83	0.57	47	34,975	MED	MED-HIGH
Klein Ind School Dist	01026289		4.64	0.54	49	53,868	LOW	MED-LOW
Galena Park Ind School Dist	01023419		3.95	0.46	27	24,000	HIGH	MED-HIGH
Goose Creek Cons Ind Sch Dist	01023562		3.73	0.44	28	24,000	HIGH	MED-HIGH
Humble Ind School Dist	01026150		3.01	0.35	46	44,802	LOW	MED-LOW
Tomball Ind School Dist	01027568		2.08	0.24	20	16,289	MED	MED-LOW
Channelview Ind School Dist	01023079		1.83	0.21	13	9,700	HIGH	MED-HIGH
Sheldon Ind School Dist	01027013		1.74	0.20	11	8,500	HIGH	MED-HIGH
Deer Park Ind School Dist	01023316		1.49	0.17	16	13,000	MED	MED-LOW
Crosby Ind School Dist	01023134		1.21	0.14	7	6,300	HIGH	MED-HIGH
La Porte Ind School Dist	01026370		1.06	0.12	12	7,679	MED	MED-LOW
Huffman Ind School Dist	01026112		0.78	0.09	4	3,600	HIGH	MED-LOW
DALLAS		8.78						
Dallas Ind School Dist	01008354		42.19	3.70	230	156,100	HIGH	MED-HIGH
Garland Ind School Dist	01010395		15.55	1.37	72	56,471	HIGH	MED-HIGH
Mesquite Ind School Dist	01011399		7.73	0.68	47	39,900	MED	MED-HIGH
Grand Prairie Ind School Dist	01010814		7.66	0.67	42	29,339	HIGH	MED-HIGH
Irving Ind School Dist	01011105		5.97	0.52	39	33,188	MED	MED-HIGH
Carrollton-Farmers Branch ISD	01008134		4.45	0.39	37	26,000	MED	MED-LOW
Richardson Ind School Dist	01011624		4.00	0.35	57	39,103	LOW	MED-HIGH
DeSoto Ind School Dist	01010242		2.70	0.24	14	9,872	HIGH	MED-HIGH
Duncanville Ind School Dist	01010292		2.59	0.23	19	12,800	MED	MED-HIGH
Cedar Hill Ind School Dist	01008275		2.55	0.22	14	7,866	HIGH	MED-LOW
Coppell Ind School Dist	01008328		1.95	0.17	18	13,500	MED	LOW
Lancaster Ind School Dist	01011337		1.57	0.14	11	7,600	HIGH	MED-HIGH
Highland Park Ind Sch Dist	01011038		0.55	0.05	7	7,000	LOW	LOW
Sunnyvale Ind School Dist	01012018		0.54	0.05	3	1,950	HIGH	MED-LOW
BEXAR		6.37						
San Antonio Ind School Dist	00998366		28.05	1.79	96	49,000	HIGH	HIGH
Northside Ind School Dist	00998017		25.06	1.60	122	105,856	MED	MED-LOW
North East Ind School Dist	00997661		13.80	0.88	74	64,359	MED	MED-LOW
Harlandale Ind School Dist	00997350		5.99	0.38	24	14,500	HIGH	MED-HIGH
Judson Ind School Dist	00997582		5.61	0.36	33	23,000	MED	MED-HIGH
Southwest Ind School Dist	00999578		4.86	0.31	19	13,580	HIGH	MED-HIGH
Edgewood Ind School Dist	00997075		4.65	0.30	21	10,881	HIGH	HIGH
South San Antonio Ind Sch Dist	00999384		2.83	0.18	16	8,800	HIGH	MED-HIGH
East Central Ind School Dist	00996992		2.75	0.18	12	10,146	MED	MED-HIGH
Southside Ind School Dist	00999516		1.84	0.12	9	5,800	HIGH	MED-HIGH
Ft Sam Houston Ind School Dist	01534949		1.07	0.07	2	1,580	HIGH	MED-LOW
Lackland Ind School Dist	01808829		1.04	0.07	2	1,053	HIGH	MED-LOW
Somerset Ind School Dist	00999346		1.02	0.07	7	3,990	MED	HIGH
Alamo Heights Ind School Dist	00996928		0.76	0.05	5	4,900	LOW	MED-LOW
Randolph Field Ind School Dist	01601786		0.66	0.04	3	1,300	HIGH	MED-LOW
TARRANT		6.19						
Ft Worth Ind School Dist	01052525		25.02	1.55	134	86,000	MED	MED-HIGH
Keller Ind School Dist	01053983		17.59	1.09	42	34,512	HIGH	LOW
Arlington Ind School Dist	01051624		13.72	0.85	78	60,000	MED	MED-HIGH
Birdville Ind School Dist	01052032		7.44	0.46	33	23,513	HIGH	MED-LOW
Mansfield Ind School Dist	01054119		7.00	0.43	44	34,309	MED	MED-LOW
Crowley Ind School Dist	01052355		4.49	0.28	25	15,215	HIGH	MED-LOW
Hurst-Euless-Bedford ISD	01053737		4.21	0.26	31	23,000	LOW	MED-LOW
Eagle Mtn-Saginaw Ind Sch Dist	01052408		3.40	0.21	27	21,000	LOW	MED-LOW
Azle Ind School Dist	01051973		3.03	0.19	12	6,000	HIGH	MED-LOW
Grapevine-Colleyville Ind SD	01053672		2.90	0.18	21	14,000	MED	MED-LOW
Everman Ind School Dist	01052460		2.84	0.18	11	6,800	HIGH	MED-HIGH
Castleberry Ind School Dist	01052290		2.29	0.14	7	3,900	HIGH	MED-HIGH
Carroll Independent Sch Dist	01052252		2.08	0.13	11	8,000	MED	LOW
White Settlement Ind Sch Dist	01054183		1.47	0.09	9	6,906	MED	MED-LOW
Lake Worth Ind School Dist	01054078		1.35	0.08	6	3,000	HIGH	MED-HIGH
Kennedale Ind School Dist	01054030		1.18	0.07	6	3,200	HIGH	MED-LOW
HIDALGO		4.92						
La Joya Ind School Dist	01029841		18.37	0.90	41	27,000	HIGH	HIGH
Pharr-San Juan-Alamo Ind SD	01030333		16.07	0.79	42	32,500	HIGH	HIGH
Edinburg Cons Ind School Dist	01029671		14.85	0.73	43	34,500	HIGH	HIGH

School Year 2019-2020   800-333-8802

DISTRICT BUYING POWER INDEX

COUNTIES RANKED BY PERCENTAGE OF STATE SPENDING

COUNTY / DISTRICT	PID	COUNTY % OF STATE	DISTRICT % OF COUNTY	DISTRICT % OF STATES	NUMBER OF SCHOOLS	ENROLL	EXP	POV
McAllen Ind School Dist	01029918		12.83	0.63	31	24,000	HIGH	HIGH
Mission Cons Ind School Dist	01030228		7.65	0.38	23	16,000	HIGH	HIGH
Weslaco Ind School Dist	01030589		7.64	0.38	19	18,000	HIGH	HIGH
Sharyland Ind School Dist	01030527		5.36	0.26	14	10,295	HIGH	MED-HIGH
Donna Ind School Dist	01029554		5.14	0.25	22	14,459	MED	HIGH
Edcouch Elsa Ind School Dist	01029621		4.73	0.23	8	5,450	HIGH	HIGH
Valley View Ind School Dist	01030565		2.34	0.12	8	4,329	HIGH	HIGH
Mercedes Ind School Dist	01030149		2.17	0.11	9	4,781	HIGH	HIGH
Monte Alto Ind School Dist	01030319		1.16	0.06	3	900	HIGH	HIGH
Progreso Ind School Dist	01030503		0.72	0.04	5	1,750	MED	HIGH
Hidalgo Ind School Dist	01029827		0.72	0.04	7	3,300	LOW	HIGH
La Villa Ind School Dist	01029891		0.24	0.01	3	579	HIGH	HIGH
EL PASO		4.13						
El Paso Ind School Dist	01015450		29.29	1.21	89	54,824	HIGH	MED-HIGH
Ysleta Ind School Dist	01016296		27.68	1.14	61	40,691	HIGH	HIGH
Socorro Ind School Dist	01016208		26.03	1.07	50	47,000	HIGH	MED-HIGH
Clint Ind School Dist	01015424		7.97	0.33	14	11,522	HIGH	HIGH
San Elizario Ind School Dist	01016179		3.79	0.16	6	3,560	HIGH	HIGH
Canutillo Ind School Dist	01015383		2.35	0.10	10	6,200	MED	MED-HIGH
Fabens Ind School Dist	01016129		1.17	0.05	5	2,300	HIGH	HIGH
Tornillo Ind School Dist	01016260		1.14	0.05	4	1,135	HIGH	HIGH
Anthony Ind School Dist	01015357		0.59	0.02	3	839	HIGH	MED-HIGH
FORT BEND		3.31						
Katy Ind School Dist	01026227		43.02	1.42	71	83,599	HIGH	MED-LOW
Ft Bend Ind School Dist	01018115		35.08	1.16	79	78,000	MED	MED-LOW
Lamar Cons Ind School Dist	01018232		17.61	0.58	45	34,000	HIGH	MED-LOW
Needville Ind School Dist	01018347		2.17	0.07	4	3,228	HIGH	MED-LOW
Stafford Municipal Sch Dist	02228624		2.12	0.07	7	3,600	HIGH	MED-LOW
COLLIN		3.15						
Frisco Ind School Dist	01006186		24.08	0.76	72	62,386	MED	LOW
Plano Ind School Dist	01006344		21.91	0.69	73	53,952	MED	LOW
McKinney Ind School Dist	01006241		17.58	0.55	31	24,335	HIGH	LOW
Wylie Ind School Dist	01006605		9.65	0.30	20	17,000	HIGH	LOW
Allen Ind School Dist	01005986		7.17	0.23	24	21,404	LOW	LOW
Prosper Ind School Dist	01006552		4.43	0.14	15	7,600	HIGH	LOW
Anna Ind School Dist	01006021		2.87	0.09	6	3,800	HIGH	MED-LOW
Princeton Ind School Dist	01006502		2.60	0.08	8	5,000	HIGH	MED-LOW
Melissa Ind School Dist	01006320		2.08	0.07	4	2,792	HIGH	LOW
Lovejoy Ind School Dist	01006227		2.08	0.07	6	4,424	MED	LOW
Farmersville Ind School Dist	01006148		1.96	0.06	4	1,750	HIGH	MED-LOW
Community Ind School Dist	01006124		1.83	0.06	4	2,262	HIGH	MED-LOW
Celina Ind School Dist	01006083		1.24	0.04	6	2,600	MED	MED-LOW
Blue Ridge Ind School Dist	01006057		0.53	0.02	3	860	HIGH	MED-LOW
CAMERON		2.55						
Brownsville Ind School Dist	01003445		40.46	1.03	54	43,355	HIGH	HIGH
San Benito Cons Ind Sch Dist	01004140		16.81	0.43	18	10,643	HIGH	HIGH
Los Fresnos Cons Ind Sch Dist	01004009		11.69	0.30	16	10,700	HIGH	MED-HIGH
Harlingen Cons Ind School Dist	01003756		11.60	0.30	31	18,600	MED	HIGH
South Texas Ind School Dist	01808984		9.17	0.23	6	4,245	HIGH	
La Feria Ind School Dist	01003940		4.00	0.10	7	3,347	HIGH	HIGH
Point Isabel Ind Sch Dist	01004061		2.42	0.06	4	2,500	HIGH	HIGH
Rio Hondo Ind School Dist	01004102		1.73	0.04	3	1,900	HIGH	HIGH
Santa Rosa Ind School Dist	01004322		1.44	0.04	3	1,300	HIGH	HIGH
Santa Maria Ind School Dist	01004308		0.68	0.02	4	691	HIGH	HIGH
TRAVIS		2.31						
Austin Ind School Dist	01055993		46.37	1.07	121	80,100	MED	MED-HIGH
Pflugerville Ind School Dist	01056935		16.89	0.39	33	26,269	MED	MED-LOW
Del Valle Ind School Dist	01056789		16.29	0.38	15	12,100	HIGH	MED-HIGH
Manor Ind School Dist	01056894		9.98	0.23	16	9,200	HIGH	MED-HIGH
Lake Travis Ind School Dist	02178653		5.61	0.13	10	10,410	MED	LOW
Eanes Ind School Dist	01056844		3.88	0.09	9	8,156	LOW	LOW
Lago Vista Ind School Dist	01056870		0.98	0.02	4	1,500	MED	MED-LOW
DENTON		2.11						
Denton Ind School Dist	01013220		28.39	0.60	42	29,152	HIGH	MED-LOW
Lewisville Ind School Dist	01013402		25.55	0.54	70	52,000	LOW	MED-LOW
Northwest Ind School Dist	01013517		19.78	0.42	30	24,000	HIGH	LOW
Little Elm Ind School Dist	01013490		7.37	0.16	9	7,400	HIGH	MED-LOW
Aubrey Ind School Dist	01013191		4.83	0.10	4	2,000	HIGH	MED-LOW
Lake Dallas Ind School Dist	01013373		3.84	0.08	5	4,000	HIGH	LOW
Argyle Ind School Dist	01013177		2.72	0.06	5	3,000	HIGH	LOW
Krum Ind School Dist	01013347		2.51	0.05	5	2,050	HIGH	MED-LOW

Texas School Directory

DISTRICT BUYING POWER INDEX

COUNTIES RANKED BY PERCENTAGE OF STATE SPENDING

COUNTY / DISTRICT	PID	COUNTY % OF STATE	DISTRICT % OF COUNTY	DISTRICT % OF STATES	NUMBER OF SCHOOLS	ENROLL	EXP	POV
Sanger Ind School Dist	01013646		2.08	0.04	7	2,660	MED	MED-LOW
Pilot Point Ind School Dist	01013581		1.48	0.03	4	1,500	HIGH	MED-LOW
Ponder Ind School Dist	01013610		1.46	0.03	3	1,575	HIGH	MED-LOW
WILLIAMSON		2.05						
Round Rock Ind School Dist	01061083		38.49	0.79	54	50,546	MED	LOW
Leander Ind School Dist	01061007		32.01	0.66	43	41,000	MED	LOW
Georgetown Ind School Dist	01060869		10.12	0.21	17	10,946	HIGH	MED-LOW
Hutto Ind School Dist	01060948		8.24	0.17	9	7,500	HIGH	LOW
Liberty Hill Ind School Dist	01061069		3.37	0.07	6	4,476	HIGH	LOW
Taylor Ind School Dist	01061162		2.85	0.06	7	3,280	HIGH	MED-LOW
Jarrell Ind School Dist	01060974		1.89	0.04	5	1,850	HIGH	MED-LOW
Florence Ind School Dist	01060833		1.36	0.03	3	1,065	HIGH	MED-LOW
Thrall Ind School Dist	01061227		0.90	0.02	3	720	HIGH	MED-LOW
Granger Ind School Dist	01060912		0.61	0.01	1	460	HIGH	MED-LOW
Coupland Ind School Dist	01060819		0.17	0.00	1	175	HIGH	MED-HIGH
BELL		1.86						
Killeen Ind School Dist	00996423		63.15	1.18	53	45,583	HIGH	MED-HIGH
Temple Ind School Dist	00996708		16.03	0.30	15	8,700	HIGH	MED-HIGH
Belton Ind School Dist	00996318		11.90	0.22	17	11,950	HIGH	MED-LOW
Troy Ind School Dist	00996899		2.72	0.05	4	1,600	HIGH	MED-LOW
Salado Ind School Dist	00996679		2.51	0.05	3	1,900	HIGH	MED-LOW
Rogers Ind School Dist	00996643		1.19	0.02	3	875	HIGH	MED-LOW
Academy Ind School Dist	00996253		1.15	0.02	5	1,559	MED	MED-LOW
Holland Ind School Dist	00996394		0.94	0.02	3	692	HIGH	MED-HIGH
Bartlett Ind School Dist	00996289		0.41	0.01	3	350	HIGH	MED-HIGH
MONTGOMERY		1.79						
Conroe Ind School Dist	01042439		49.89	0.89	64	63,000	MED	MED-LOW
New Caney Ind School Dist	01042661		18.13	0.33	19	15,000	HIGH	MED-HIGH
Magnolia Ind School Dist	01042582		11.61	0.21	16	13,100	MED	MED-HIGH
Montgomery Ind School Dist	01042623		7.46	0.13	10	8,864	MED	MED-LOW
Willis Ind School Dist	01042764		7.08	0.13	9	7,500	HIGH	MED-LOW
Splendora Ind School Dist	01042726		5.84	0.10	5	4,200	HIGH	MED-LOW
BRAZORIA		1.47						
Alvin Ind School Dist	01001382		49.58	0.73	29	25,926	HIGH	MED-LOW
Pearland Ind School Dist	01001849		21.05	0.31	23	21,917	MED	MED-LOW
Brazosport Ind School Dist	01001540		13.89	0.20	18	12,345	MED	MED-LOW
Angleton Ind School Dist	01001473		7.13	0.10	9	6,787	MED	MED-LOW
Columbia Brazoria ISD	01001710		4.13	0.06	5	3,135	HIGH	MED-LOW
Sweeny Ind School Dist	01001904		2.38	0.03	3	1,969	MED	MED-HIGH
Danbury Ind School Dist	01001813		1.57	0.02	3	750	HIGH	MED-LOW
Damon Ind School Dist	01001796		0.28	0.00	1	200	HIGH	MED-HIGH
LUBBOCK		1.45						
Lubbock Ind School Dist	01038490		65.25	0.95	48	27,759	HIGH	MED-HIGH
Frenship Ind School Dist	01038402		14.46	0.21	13	9,900	HIGH	MED-LOW
Lubbock-Cooper Ind Sch Dist	01039030		8.44	0.12	9	6,000	HIGH	MED-LOW
Slaton Ind School Dist	01039195		2.57	0.04	4	1,340	HIGH	HIGH
Idalou Ind School Dist	01038452		2.39	0.03	3	1,003	HIGH	MED-LOW
Shallowater Ind School Dist	01039157		2.36	0.03	4	1,600	HIGH	MED-LOW
Roosevelt Ind School Dist	01039119		2.35	0.03	3	1,150	HIGH	MED-HIGH
New Deal Ind School Dist	01039080		2.18	0.03	3	760	HIGH	MED-HIGH
WEBB		1.40						
United Ind School Dist	01059470		67.48	0.94	47	45,000	HIGH	MED-HIGH
Laredo Ind School Dist	01059183		31.15	0.43	33	23,737	HIGH	HIGH
Webb Cons Ind School Dist	01059145		1.37	0.02	3	272	HIGH	HIGH
NUECES		1.32						
Corpus Christi Ind Sch Dist	01044176		63.83	0.84	58	38,094	HIGH	MED-HIGH
Tuloso-Midway Ind School Dist	01045015		7.48	0.10	5	4,000	HIGH	MED-HIGH
Flour Bluff Ind School Dist	01044815		6.49	0.09	7	5,750	MED	MED-LOW
Calallen Ind School Dist	01044114		5.70	0.08	6	4,000	HIGH	MED-LOW
Robstown Ind School Dist	01044906		4.66	0.06	7	2,000	HIGH	HIGH
West Oso Ind School Dist	01045065		4.46	0.06	4	2,104	HIGH	MED-HIGH
Bishop Cons Ind School Dist	01044059		2.57	0.03	5	1,472	HIGH	MED-HIGH
Banquete Ind School Dist	01044011		1.99	0.03	3	954	HIGH	MED-HIGH
Agua Dulce Ind School Dist	01043988		0.95	0.01	2	370	HIGH	MED-HIGH
London Ind School Dist	01044865		0.81	0.01	1	900	LOW	MED-LOW
Driscoll Ind School Dist	01044798		0.72	0.01	1	320	HIGH	MED-HIGH
Port Aransas Ind School Dist	01044889		0.36	0.00	3	550	LOW	MED-LOW
GALVESTON		1.23						
Clear Creek Ind School Dist	01018816		44.41	0.55	45	44,099	MED	MED-LOW

School Year 2019-2020

DISTRICT BUYING POWER INDEX

COUNTIES RANKED BY PERCENTAGE OF STATE SPENDING

COUNTY / DISTRICT	PID	COUNTY % OF STATE	DISTRICT % OF COUNTY	DISTRICT % OF STATES	NUMBER OF SCHOOLS	ENROLL	EXP	POV
Dickinson Ind School Dist	01018969		17.54	0.22	14	10,400	HIGH	MED-HIGH
Texas City Ind School Dist	01019470		13.14	0.16	14	9,000	MED	MED-HIGH
Galveston Ind School Dist	01019078		8.25	0.10	12	7,000	MED	MED-HIGH
Friendswood Ind Sch Dist	01019028		6.25	0.08	6	6,000	MED	LOW
Santa Fe Ind School Dist	01019432		6.14	0.08	4	4,794	MED	MED-LOW
Hitchcock Ind School Dist	01019274		3.89	0.05	4	1,700	HIGH	MED-HIGH
High Island Ind Sch Dist	01019250		0.39	0.00	1	145	HIGH	MED-HIGH
JEFFERSON		1.01						
Beaumont Ind School Dist	01034092		46.49	0.47	28	18,697	HIGH	HIGH
Port Arthur Ind School Dist	01033749		27.13	0.27	16	9,000	HIGH	HIGH
Nederland Ind School Dist	01033660		14.77	0.15	8	5,214	HIGH	MED-LOW
Port Neches-Groves Ind SD	01033957		6.52	0.07	10	5,150	MED	MED-LOW
Hamshire Fannett Ind Sch Dist	01033610		3.68	0.04	4	1,900	HIGH	MED-LOW
Sabine Pass Ind School Dist	01034066		1.40	0.01	1	372	HIGH	MED-HIGH
ELLIS		0.92						
Midlothian Ind School Dist	01015137		26.78	0.25	11	9,500	HIGH	LOW
Waxahachie Ind School Dist	01015292		24.18	0.22	16	9,481	HIGH	MED-LOW
Ennis Ind School Dist	01014963		15.00	0.14	11	5,800	HIGH	MED-HIGH
Red Oak Ind School Dist	01015242		13.79	0.13	8	6,000	HIGH	MED-LOW
Ferris Ind School Dist	01015034		8.45	0.08	5	2,400	HIGH	MED-HIGH
Palmer Ind School Dist	01015216		4.10	0.04	3	1,250	HIGH	MED-LOW
Maypearl Ind School Dist	01015101		2.74	0.03	4	1,040	HIGH	LOW
Italy Ind School Dist	01015072		2.10	0.02	2	600	HIGH	MED-LOW
Avalon Ind School Dist	01014937		1.73	0.02	1	350	HIGH	MED-LOW
Milford Ind School Dist	01015187		1.13	0.01	1	280	HIGH	MED-LOW
MCLENNAN		0.89						
Waco Ind School Dist	01040132		35.13	0.31	24	15,050	HIGH	MED-HIGH
Midway Ind School Dist	01039937		13.65	0.12	10	8,411	MED	MED-LOW
La Vega Ind School Dist	01039779		8.74	0.08	5	3,099	HIGH	MED-HIGH
China Spring Ind School Dist	01039614		8.14	0.07	5	2,748	HIGH	MED-LOW
Connally Ind School Dist	01039640		6.86	0.06	6	2,300	HIGH	MED-HIGH
Lorena Ind School Dist	01039822		4.46	0.04	4	1,725	HIGH	MED-LOW
Robinson Ind School Dist	01040039		3.62	0.03	5	2,200	MED	MED-LOW
McGregor Ind School Dist	01039896		3.00	0.03	4	1,550	HIGH	MED-HIGH
Axtell Ind School Dist	01039535		2.91	0.03	2	740	HIGH	MED-HIGH
Bosqueville Ind School Dist	01039561		2.50	0.02	3	705	HIGH	MED-LOW
Moody Ind School Dist	01039975		2.30	0.02	3	690	HIGH	MED-HIGH
Bruceville-Eddy Ind Sch Dist	01039585		2.13	0.02	4	641	HIGH	MED-LOW
Riesel Ind School Dist	01040003		1.75	0.02	2	620	HIGH	MED-LOW
Crawford Ind School Dist	01039705		1.59	0.01	2	530	HIGH	MED-LOW
West Ind School Dist	01040481		1.32	0.01	4	1,350	LOW	MED-LOW
Mart Ind School Dist	01039858		0.82	0.01	2	500	MED	MED-HIGH
Gholson Ind School Dist	01039731		0.78	0.01	1	255	HIGH	MED-HIGH
Hallsburg Ind School Dist	01039755		0.30	0.00	1	161	MED	MED-LOW
KAUFMAN		0.79						
Kaufman Ind School Dist	01035606		23.52	0.19	7	3,500	HIGH	MED-HIGH
Forney Ind School Dist	01035565		19.11	0.15	14	9,681	MED	MED-LOW
Terrell Ind School Dist	01035759		19.06	0.15	9	4,711	HIGH	MED-HIGH
Crandall Ind School Dist	01035539		17.07	0.13	7	4,500	HIGH	MED-LOW
Mabank Ind School Dist	01035682		12.39	0.10	8	3,500	HIGH	MED-HIGH
Kemp Ind School Dist	01035656		5.06	0.04	4	1,586	HIGH	MED-HIGH
Scurry Rosser Ind School Dist	01035723		3.78	0.03	3	1,035	HIGH	MED-HIGH
POTTER		0.78						
Amarillo Ind School Dist	01047128		90.28	0.71	55	33,754	HIGH	MED-HIGH
Bushland Ind School Dist	01047568		3.98	0.03	3	1,500	HIGH	MED-LOW
River Road Ind School Dist	01047609		3.73	0.03	4	1,278	HIGH	MED-HIGH
Highland Park Ind School Dist	01047582		2.01	0.02	3	850	MED	MED-HIGH
HAYS		0.74						
Hays Cons Ind School Dist	01029059		50.42	0.37	25	20,445	HIGH	MED-LOW
San Marcos Cons Ind Sch Dist	01029114		24.31	0.18	11	8,200	HIGH	MED-LOW
Dripping Springs Ind Sch Dist	01029011		19.73	0.15	7	6,400	HIGH	LOW
Wimberley Ind School Dist	02903408		5.54	0.04	4	2,400	MED	MED-LOW
SMITH		0.74						
Tyler Ind School Dist	01050747		45.60	0.34	30	18,600	HIGH	MED-HIGH
Chapel Hill Ind School Dist	01050606		12.50	0.09	5	3,513	HIGH	MED-HIGH
Whitehouse Ind School Dist	01050993		12.07	0.09	8	4,800	HIGH	MED-LOW
Lindale Ind School Dist	01050656		10.96	0.08	6	4,200	HIGH	MED-LOW
Bullard Ind School Dist	01050577		7.43	0.06	6	2,500	HIGH	MED-LOW
Troup Ind School Dist	01050709		4.27	0.03	3	1,081	HIGH	MED-HIGH
Winona Ind School Dist	01051038		4.05	0.03	4	1,050	HIGH	HIGH

Texas School Directory

DISTRICT BUYING POWER INDEX

DISTRICT BUYING POWER INDEX
COUNTIES RANKED BY PERCENTAGE OF STATE SPENDING

COUNTY / DISTRICT	PID	COUNTY % OF STATE	DISTRICT % OF COUNTY	DISTRICT % OF STATES	NUMBER OF SCHOOLS	ENROLL	EXP	POV
Arp Ind School Dist	01050541		3.12	0.02	3	900	HIGH	MED-HIGH
BRAZOS		0.70						
Bryan Ind School Dist	01002013		57.53	0.40	24	16,134	HIGH	MED-HIGH
College Station Ind Sch Dist	01001954		40.83	0.29	19	14,000	HIGH	MED-LOW
Mumford Ind School Dist	01048691		1.64	0.01	1	625	HIGH	MED-HIGH
GUADALUPE		0.62						
Seguin Ind School Dist	01021631		49.58	0.31	13	7,127	HIGH	MED-HIGH
Schertz-Cibolo-Univ City ISD	01021552		30.64	0.19	17	15,931	LOW	MED-LOW
Navarro Ind School Dist	01021526		14.02	0.09	4	1,911	HIGH	MED-LOW
Marion Ind School Dist	01021485		5.75	0.04	4	1,508	HIGH	MED-LOW
JOHNSON		0.62						
Burleson Ind School Dist	01034810		22.40	0.14	17	12,742	LOW	MED-LOW
Cleburne Ind School Dist	01034872		17.59	0.11	12	6,749	HIGH	MED-HIGH
Godley Ind School Dist	01034963		13.33	0.08	5	2,027	HIGH	MED-LOW
Joshua Ind School Dist	01035022		11.80	0.07	10	5,626	MED	MED-LOW
Alvarado Ind School Dist	01034767		10.94	0.07	6	3,650	HIGH	MED-LOW
Venus Ind School Dist	01035163		8.92	0.06	4	2,200	HIGH	MED-LOW
Keene Ind School Dist	01035060		6.14	0.04	4	1,070	HIGH	MED-HIGH
Grandview Ind School Dist	01034999		5.65	0.03	3	1,276	HIGH	MED-HIGH
Rio Vista Ind School Dist	01035137		3.22	0.02	3	750	HIGH	MED-HIGH
GRAYSON		0.58						
Denison Ind School Dist	01020297		24.99	0.14	9	4,500	HIGH	MED-HIGH
Sherman Ind School Dist	01020596		24.27	0.14	12	7,300	HIGH	MED-HIGH
Whitesboro Ind School Dist	01020780		7.13	0.04	4	1,600	HIGH	MED-HIGH
Howe Ind School Dist	01020479		6.76	0.04	4	1,100	HIGH	MED-HIGH
Van Alstyne Ind School Dist	01020742		6.36	0.04	4	1,598	HIGH	MED-LOW
Pottsboro Ind School Dist	01020510		5.82	0.03	3	1,450	HIGH	MED-HIGH
S & S Cons Ind School Dist	01020560		4.92	0.03	3	950	HIGH	MED-LOW
Whitewright Ind School Dist	01020821		4.32	0.03	3	850	HIGH	MED-HIGH
Tioga Ind School Dist	01020699		3.88	0.02	1	700	HIGH	MED-LOW
Bells Ind School Dist	01020235		3.12	0.02	3	845	HIGH	MED-LOW
Gunter Ind School Dist	01020443		2.99	0.02	3	970	HIGH	MED-LOW
Collinsville Ind School Dist	01020261		2.86	0.02	2	530	HIGH	MED-LOW
Tom Bean Ind School Dist	01020716		2.58	0.01	3	675	HIGH	MED-LOW
BASTROP		0.51						
Bastrop Ind School Dist	00995833		61.84	0.32	15	11,000	HIGH	MED-HIGH
Elgin Ind School Dist	00995883		27.96	0.14	6	4,700	HIGH	MED-HIGH
Smithville Ind School Dist	00995974		7.96	0.04	5	1,780	HIGH	MED-HIGH
McDade Ind School Dist	00995936		2.24	0.01	1	390	HIGH	HIGH
COMAL		0.50						
Comal Ind School Dist	01006887		63.80	0.32	31	23,800	MED	MED-LOW
New Braunfels Ind School Dist	01006966		36.20	0.18	15	9,220	HIGH	MED-LOW
GREGG		0.50						
Longview Ind School Dist	01020986		32.67	0.16	13	8,700	HIGH	MED-HIGH
Kilgore Ind School Dist	01020900		17.94	0.09	5	4,076	HIGH	MED-HIGH
Pine Tree Ind School Dist	01021148		17.19	0.09	8	4,700	HIGH	MED-HIGH
Spring Hill Ind School Dist	01021253		9.81	0.05	4	1,980	HIGH	MED-LOW
Sabine Ind School Dist	01021215		8.87	0.04	3	1,397	HIGH	MED-LOW
Gladewater Ind School Dist	01020857		7.16	0.04	4	1,700	HIGH	MED-HIGH
White Oak Ind School Dist	01021306		6.36	0.03	4	1,520	HIGH	MED-HIGH
BOWIE		0.45						
Texarkana Ind School Dist	01001215		36.74	0.16	13	7,174	HIGH	HIGH
Liberty-Eylau Ind School Dist	01000948		12.16	0.05	4	2,500	HIGH	MED-HIGH
Pleasant Grove Ind School Dist	01001112		11.08	0.05	4	2,200	HIGH	MED-LOW
Redwater Ind School Dist	01001150		8.04	0.04	4	1,150	HIGH	MED-LOW
New Boston Ind School Dist	01001069		7.81	0.03	4	1,340	HIGH	MED-HIGH
Hooks Ind School Dist	01000857		6.79	0.03	3	942	HIGH	MED-HIGH
De Kalb Ind School Dist	01000819		5.04	0.02	3	900	HIGH	MED-HIGH
Maud Ind School Dist	01001033		4.33	0.02	1	480	HIGH	MED-HIGH
Red Lick Ind School Dist	01001136		4.10	0.02	1	530	HIGH	MED-HIGH
Simms Ind School Dist	01001186		2.60	0.01	3	516	HIGH	MED-HIGH
Malta Ind School Dist	01001019		0.60	0.00	1	241	MED	MED-LOW
Leary Ind School Dist	01000924		0.41	0.00	1	125	MED	MED-HIGH
Hubbard Ind School Dist	01000900		0.28	0.00	1	120	MED	MED-HIGH
PARKER		0.44						
Weatherford Ind School Dist	01046564		36.49	0.16	12	8,000	HIGH	MED-LOW
Springtown Ind School Dist	01046514		20.38	0.09	6	3,470	HIGH	MED-LOW
Aledo Ind School Dist	01046306		19.51	0.09	10	6,000	MED	LOW
Millsap Ind School Dist	01046394		7.03	0.03	3	994	HIGH	MED-LOW

DISTRICT BUYING POWER INDEX

Market Data Retrieval

DISTRICT BUYING POWER INDEX
COUNTIES RANKED BY PERCENTAGE OF STATE SPENDING

COUNTY / DISTRICT	PID	COUNTY % OF STATE	DISTRICT % OF COUNTY	DISTRICT % OF STATES	NUMBER OF SCHOOLS	ENROLL	EXP	POV
Peaster Ind School Dist	01046423		6.90	0.03	3	1,200	HIGH	MED-LOW
Brock Ind School Dist	01046344		6.58	0.03	4	1,376	HIGH	LOW
Poolville Ind School Dist	01046459		2.21	0.01	3	530	HIGH	MED-HIGH
Garner Ind School Dist	01046370		0.90	0.00	1	200	HIGH	MED-LOW
TOM GREEN		0.43						
San Angelo Ind School Dist	01055539		74.94	0.32	25	14,362	HIGH	MED-HIGH
Grape Creek Ind School Dist	01055515		8.64	0.04	3	1,160	HIGH	MED-HIGH
Wall Ind School Dist	01055840		7.16	0.03	4	1,100	HIGH	MED-LOW
Christoval Ind School Dist	01055486		4.75	0.02	2	500	HIGH	MED-LOW
Water Valley Ind School Dist	01055888		3.32	0.01	2	300	HIGH	MED-HIGH
Veribest Ind School Dist	01055826		1.20	0.01	1	275	HIGH	MED-HIGH
ROCKWALL		0.39						
Rockwall Ind School Dist	01048718		73.66	0.29	20	16,270	HIGH	MED-LOW
Royse City Ind School Dist	01048770		26.34	0.10	9	6,300	HIGH	MED-LOW
TAYLOR		0.38						
Abilene Ind School Dist	01054523		75.79	0.28	26	17,000	MED	MED-HIGH
Wylie Ind School Dist	01055008		11.78	0.04	7	4,600	LOW	MED-LOW
Merkel Ind School Dist	01054925		5.66	0.02	3	1,100	HIGH	MED-HIGH
Jim Ned Cons Ind School Dist	01054896		4.90	0.02	4	1,300	MED	MED-LOW
Trent Ind School Dist	01054987		1.88	0.01	1	180	HIGH	MED-HIGH
LIBERTY		0.34						
Cleveland Ind School Dist	01037719		42.24	0.14	6	6,719	HIGH	MED-HIGH
Dayton Ind School Dist	01037771		17.49	0.06	7	5,400	LOW	MED-LOW
Liberty Ind School Dist	01037927		14.18	0.05	4	2,200	HIGH	MED-HIGH
Tarkington Ind School Dist	01037977		10.93	0.04	4	1,800	HIGH	MED-HIGH
Hardin Ind School Dist	01037848		7.66	0.03	3	1,400	MED	MED-HIGH
Hull Daisetta Ind School Dist	01037886		5.90	0.02	3	477	HIGH	MED-LOW
Devers Ind School Dist	01037824		1.60	0.01	1	200	HIGH	MED-HIGH
ECTOR		0.33						
Ector Co Ind School Dist	01014547		100.00	0.33	42	31,500	LOW	MED-HIGH
ORANGE		0.33						
Vidor Ind School Dist	01045754		40.43	0.13	7	5,000	HIGH	MED-HIGH
Little Cypress Mauriceville SD	01045651		20.03	0.07	6	3,100	HIGH	MED-HIGH
Bridge City Ind School Dist	01045601		12.43	0.04	4	2,953	MED	MED-LOW
West Orange-Cove Cons ISD	01045819		12.21	0.04	4	2,487	MED	HIGH
Orangefield Ind School Dist	01045704		12.08	0.04	3	1,785	HIGH	MED-LOW
Deweyville Ind School Dist	01043718		2.82	0.01	2	550	MED	MED-HIGH
SAN PATRICIO		0.33						
Gregory-Portland Ind Sch Dist	01049530		33.14	0.11	7	4,600	HIGH	MED-LOW
Sinton Ind School Dist	01049762		16.32	0.05	4	2,202	HIGH	MED-HIGH
Taft Ind School Dist	01049827		12.15	0.04	3	1,100	HIGH	MED-HIGH
Ingleside Ind School Dist	01049592		11.32	0.04	5	2,235	MED	MED-HIGH
Odem-Edroy Ind School Dist	01049700		9.75	0.03	4	900	HIGH	HIGH
Mathis Ind School Dist	01049645		8.89	0.03	4	1,635	MED	HIGH
Aransas Pass Ind School Dist	01049487		8.42	0.03	5	1,474	HIGH	HIGH
WICHITA		0.33						
Wichita Falls Ind School Dist	01060132		49.48	0.16	28	14,500	MED	MED-HIGH
Burkburnett Ind Sch Dist	01059925		19.57	0.07	6	3,350	HIGH	MED-HIGH
Iowa Park Consolidated Ind SD	01060065		16.47	0.05	4	1,839	HIGH	MED-LOW
City View Ind School Dist	01059999		12.73	0.04	2	1,058	HIGH	MED-HIGH
Electra Ind School Dist	01060015		1.75	0.01	3	430	MED	MED-HIGH
STARR		0.32						
Rio Grande City Ind Sch Dist	01051117		60.66	0.19	18	9,876	MED	HIGH
Roma Ind School Dist	01051222		37.66	0.12	10	6,400	HIGH	HIGH
San Isidro Ind School Dist	01051296		1.68	0.01	1	250	HIGH	HIGH
ANGELINA		0.31						
Lufkin Ind School Dist	00994932		40.10	0.12	15	8,000	MED	MED-HIGH
Diboll Ind School Dist	00994815		16.67	0.05	5	1,890	HIGH	MED-HIGH
Hudson Ind School Dist	00994853		15.23	0.05	5	3,000	MED	MED-HIGH
Huntington Ind School Dist	00994891		13.38	0.04	5	1,750	HIGH	MED-HIGH
Central Ind School Dist	00994774		11.53	0.04	3	1,550	HIGH	MED-HIGH
Zavalla Ind School Dist	00995089		3.08	0.01	2	360	HIGH	MED-HIGH
HUNT		0.29						
Quinlan Ind School Dist	01032575		25.56	0.07	5	2,725	HIGH	MED-HIGH
Greenville Ind School Dist	01032446		21.71	0.06	12	5,400	MED	MED-HIGH
Commerce Independent Sch Dist	01032381		11.66	0.03	4	1,603	HIGH	MED-HIGH
Caddo Mills Ind Sch Dist	01032290		9.68	0.03	5	1,850	MED	MED-LOW
Wolfe City Ind School Dist	01032616		8.34	0.02	3	690	HIGH	MED-HIGH

DISTRICT BUYING POWER INDEX

COUNTIES RANKED BY PERCENTAGE OF STATE SPENDING

COUNTY / DISTRICT	PID	COUNTY % OF STATE	DISTRICT % OF COUNTY	DISTRICT % OF STATES	NUMBER OF SCHOOLS	ENROLL	EXP	POV
Lone Oak Ind School Dist	01032549		6.82	0.02	4	1,050	HIGH	MED-LOW
Celeste Ind School Dist	01032355		5.99	0.02	3	512	HIGH	MED-HIGH
Bland Ind School Dist	01032238		5.18	0.02	3	730	HIGH	MED-HIGH
Boles Ind School Dist	01032264		3.35	0.01	3	540	MED	MED-HIGH
Campbell Ind School Dist	01032329		1.71	0.00	1	310	MED	MED-HIGH
MIDLAND		0.29						
Midland Ind School Dist	01041423		77.29	0.23	39	26,000	LOW	MED-LOW
Greenwood Ind School Dist	01041394		22.71	0.07	4	2,831	HIGH	MED-HIGH
VICTORIA		0.28						
Victoria Ind School Dist	01058440		81.54	0.23	23	13,900	MED	MED-HIGH
Bloomington Ind School Dist	01058311		17.73	0.05	4	900	HIGH	MED-HIGH
Nursery ISD School Dist	01058414		0.73	0.00	1	120	MED	MED-HIGH
HENDERSON		0.27						
Athens Ind School Dist	01029231		34.31	0.09	5	3,118	HIGH	MED-HIGH
Brownsboro Ind School Dist	01029322		27.39	0.07	7	2,800	HIGH	MED-HIGH
Malakoff Ind School Dist	01029449		12.13	0.03	5	1,400	HIGH	MED-HIGH
Cross Roads Ind School Dist	01029360		10.20	0.03	3	545	HIGH	MED-HIGH
Eustace Ind School Dist	01029384		8.82	0.02	4	1,550	MED	MED-HIGH
La Poynor Ind School Dist	01029413		4.59	0.01	1	453	HIGH	MED-HIGH
Trinidad Ind School Dist	01029504		1.66	0.00	1	165	HIGH	MED-HIGH
Murchison Ind Sch Dist	01029487		0.90	0.00	1	175	MED	HIGH
NACOGDOCHES		0.27						
Nacogdoches Ind School Dist	01043275		57.14	0.16	10	6,300	HIGH	HIGH
Garrison Ind School Dist	01043213		8.40	0.02	3	600	HIGH	MED-HIGH
Central Heights Ind Sch Dist	01043079		7.35	0.02	3	1,181	MED	MED-HIGH
Woden Ind School Dist	01043354		5.84	0.02	3	725	HIGH	MED-HIGH
Cushing Ind School Dist	01043134		5.66	0.02	2	551	HIGH	MED-HIGH
Chireno ISD School Dist	01043108		5.39	0.01	1	304	HIGH	HIGH
Martinsville Ind School Dist	01043249		4.97	0.01	1	400	HIGH	HIGH
Douglass Ind School Dist	01043160		3.22	0.01	1	460	HIGH	MED-HIGH
Etoile Ind School Dist	01043196		2.04	0.01	1	100	HIGH	HIGH
WALLER		0.27						
Waller Ind School Dist	01058866		65.37	0.18	8	7,700	HIGH	MED-HIGH
Royal Ind School Dist	01058816		18.49	0.05	4	2,400	HIGH	MED-HIGH
Hempstead Ind School Dist	01058775		16.14	0.04	3	1,600	HIGH	MED-HIGH
HARRISON		0.26						
Marshall Ind School Dist	01028603		41.70	0.11	7	5,345	HIGH	MED-HIGH
Hallsville Ind School Dist	01028483		26.15	0.07	5	5,500	MED	MED-HIGH
Waskom Ind School Dist	01028744		18.36	0.05	3	890	HIGH	MED-HIGH
Elysian Fields Ind School Dist	01028433		6.30	0.02	3	910	HIGH	MED-HIGH
Harleton Ind School Dist	01028536		5.40	0.01	3	734	HIGH	MED-HIGH
Karnack Ind School Dist	01028574		2.08	0.01	1	124	HIGH	HIGH
MAVERICK		0.26						
Eagle Pass Ind School Dist	01041057		100.00	0.26	23	15,000	MED	HIGH
HARDIN		0.23						
Lumberton Ind School Dist	01022544		38.68	0.09	5	4,123	HIGH	MED-LOW
Silsbee Ind School Dist	01022582		23.69	0.06	4	2,800	HIGH	MED-HIGH
Hardin Jefferson Ind Sch Dist	01022439		17.61	0.04	4	2,200	HIGH	MED-LOW
Kountze Ind School Dist	01022491		12.80	0.03	4	1,135	HIGH	MED-HIGH
West Hardin Co Cons Sch Dist	01022659		7.22	0.02	2	525	HIGH	MED-LOW
VAL VERDE		0.23						
San Felipe-Del Rio Cons Ind SD	01057941		97.18	0.22	12	10,472	HIGH	HIGH
Comstock Ind School Dist	01057898		2.82	0.01	1	227	HIGH	HIGH
WHARTON		0.23						
El Campo Ind School Dist	01059602		39.85	0.09	5	3,600	HIGH	MED-HIGH
Wharton Ind School Dist	01059690		33.03	0.08	5	2,097	HIGH	MED-HIGH
East Bernard Ind Sch Dist	01059573		11.57	0.03	3	950	HIGH	MED-HIGH
Boling Ind School Dist	01059535		10.80	0.02	3	1,000	HIGH	MED-HIGH
Louise Ind School Dist	01059664		4.75	0.01	3	500	HIGH	MED-HIGH
LAMAR		0.22						
Paris Ind School Dist	01036698		53.38	0.12	8	3,900	HIGH	HIGH
North Lamar Ind School Dist	01036636		27.25	0.06	7	2,500	HIGH	MED-LOW
Prairiland Ind School Dist	01036789		12.30	0.03	4	1,160	HIGH	MED-LOW
Chisum Ind School Dist	01036600		7.07	0.02	3	1,000	MED	HIGH
VAN ZANDT		0.22						
Van Ind School Dist	01058232		35.75	0.08	5	2,400	HIGH	MED-HIGH
Canton Ind School Dist	01058086		17.45	0.04	4	2,300	MED	MED-LOW

DISTRICT BUYING POWER INDEX

Market Data Retrieval

DISTRICT BUYING POWER INDEX
COUNTIES RANKED BY PERCENTAGE OF STATE SPENDING

COUNTY / DISTRICT	PID	COUNTY % OF STATE	DISTRICT % OF COUNTY	DISTRICT % OF STATES	NUMBER OF SCHOOLS	ENROLL	EXP	POV
Wills Point Ind School Dist	01058270		15.92	0.04	5	2,415	MED	MED-HIGH
Edgewood Ind School Dist	01058115		9.80	0.02	4	975	HIGH	MED-LOW
Grand Saline Ind School Dist	01058165		8.43	0.02	4	1,100	MED	MED-HIGH
Fruitvale Ind School Dist	01058141		6.77	0.02	3	460	HIGH	MED-HIGH
Martin's Mill Ind Sch Dist	01058191		5.87	0.01	1	230	HIGH	MED-HIGH
CORYELL		0.21						
Copperas Cove Ind School Dist	01007556		62.60	0.13	11	8,200	MED	MED-HIGH
Gatesville Ind School Dist	01007661		25.29	0.05	5	2,788	HIGH	MED-HIGH
Evant Ind School Dist	01007635		5.01	0.01	1	235	HIGH	MED-HIGH
Jonesboro Ind School Dist	01007714		4.50	0.01	1	340	HIGH	MED-HIGH
Oglesby Ind School Dist	01007740		2.60	0.01	1	165	HIGH	HIGH
NAVARRO		0.21						
Corsicana Ind School Dist	01043421		51.29	0.11	9	6,000	HIGH	MED-HIGH
Kerens Ind School Dist	01043586		10.75	0.02	3	600	HIGH	HIGH
Rice Ind School Dist	01043641		10.64	0.02	4	895	HIGH	MED-HIGH
Dawson Ind School Dist	01043524		10.00	0.02	1	500	HIGH	MED-HIGH
Mildred Ind School Dist	01043615		7.10	0.01	1	720	HIGH	MED-LOW
Blooming Grove Ind School Dist	01043392		6.15	0.01	3	924	MED	MED-HIGH
Frost Ind School Dist	01043550		4.06	0.01	2	400	HIGH	MED-HIGH
ANDERSON		0.20						
Palestine Ind School Dist	00994528		46.70	0.09	6	3,450	HIGH	MED-HIGH
Westwood Ind School Dist	00994669		19.85	0.04	4	1,600	HIGH	MED-LOW
Elkhart Ind School Dist	00994437		11.14	0.02	4	1,250	HIGH	MED-LOW
Frankston Ind School Dist	00994463		11.06	0.02	3	825	HIGH	MED-HIGH
Cayuga Ind School Dist	00994401		4.73	0.01	1	570	MED	MED-HIGH
Slocum ISD School Dist	00994633		3.32	0.01	1	415	MED	MED-HIGH
Neches Ind School Dist	00994499		3.20	0.01	2	400	MED	MED-HIGH
CHEROKEE		0.20						
Jacksonville Ind School Dist	01005235		53.73	0.11	8	5,091	HIGH	MED-HIGH
Rusk Ind School Dist	01005364		23.02	0.05	5	2,015	HIGH	MED-HIGH
Alto Ind School Dist	01005209		9.91	0.02	3	671	HIGH	HIGH
New Summerfield Ind Sch Dist	01005340		7.46	0.01	1	550	HIGH	MED-HIGH
Wells Ind School Dist	01005405		5.89	0.01	2	285	HIGH	MED-HIGH
WALKER		0.20						
Huntsville Ind School Dist	01058672		92.54	0.18	9	6,100	HIGH	MED-HIGH
New Waverly Ind School Dist	01058737		7.46	0.01	4	1,000	MED	MED-HIGH
CHAMBERS		0.19						
Barbers Hill Ind School Dist	01005118		48.63	0.09	8	5,214	MED	MED-LOW
East Chambers Ind School Dist	01005156		32.23	0.06	4	1,500	HIGH	MED-LOW
Anahuac Ind School Dist	01005077		19.14	0.04	3	1,336	HIGH	MED-HIGH
HILL		0.19						
Hillsboro Ind School Dist	01030852		28.55	0.05	5	2,000	HIGH	MED-HIGH
Whitney Ind School Dist	01031052		18.75	0.04	4	1,425	HIGH	MED-HIGH
Itasca Ind School Dist	01030955		13.85	0.03	3	660	HIGH	MED-HIGH
Aquilla Ind School Dist	01030735		8.56	0.02	1	325	HIGH	MED-LOW
Abbott Ind School Dist	01030709		6.81	0.01	1	242	HIGH	MED-LOW
Covington ISD School Dist	01030826		6.00	0.01	1	293	HIGH	MED-LOW
Blum Ind School Dist	01030761		4.21	0.01	1	370	HIGH	MED-LOW
Hubbard Ind School Dist	01030917		4.10	0.01	2	400	HIGH	MED-HIGH
Penelope ISD School Dist	01031026		2.96	0.01	1	210	HIGH	MED-LOW
Mt Calm Ind School Dist	01031002		2.90	0.01	2	210	HIGH	HIGH
Bynum Ind School Dist	01030797		1.90	0.00	1	185	HIGH	MED-HIGH
Malone Independent School Dist	01030981		1.39	0.00	1	165	MED	MED-LOW
HOPKINS		0.19						
Sulphur Springs Ind Sch Dist	01031624		58.07	0.11	9	4,400	HIGH	MED-HIGH
Como Pickton Cons Ind SD	01031466		12.45	0.02	1	753	HIGH	MED-HIGH
North Hopkins Ind School Dist	01031545		11.85	0.02	1	525	HIGH	MED-HIGH
Miller Grove Ind School Dist	01031521		6.65	0.01	1	329	HIGH	MED-LOW
Cumby Ind School Dist	01031492		4.20	0.01	2	400	HIGH	MED-LOW
Saltillo Ind School Dist	01031571		4.13	0.01	1	240	HIGH	MED-LOW
Sulphur Bluff Ind School Dist	01031595		2.65	0.01	1	215	HIGH	MED-LOW
WISE		0.19						
Decatur Ind School Dist	01061655		42.12	0.08	5	3,390	HIGH	MED-LOW
Bridgeport Ind School Dist	01061588		25.05	0.05	5	2,062	HIGH	MED-HIGH
Boyd Ind School Dist	01061552		11.69	0.02	4	1,317	MED	MED-LOW
Alvord Ind School Dist	01061526		7.12	0.01	3	709	HIGH	MED-LOW
Paradise Ind School Dist	01061722		7.02	0.01	4	1,200	LOW	MED-LOW
Chico Ind School Dist	01061629		5.28	0.01	3	600	MED	MED-HIGH
Slidell Ind School Dist	01061758		1.72	0.00	2	282	MED	MED-LOW

Texas School Directory

DISTRICT BUYING POWER INDEX

DISTRICT BUYING POWER INDEX
COUNTIES RANKED BY PERCENTAGE OF STATE SPENDING

COUNTY / DISTRICT	PID	COUNTY % OF STATE	DISTRICT % OF COUNTY	DISTRICT % OF STATES	NUMBER OF SCHOOLS	ENROLL	EXP	POV
COOKE		0.18						
Gainesville Ind School Dist	01007348		47.49	0.09	6	3,100	HIGH	MED-HIGH
Callisburg Ind School Dist	01007271		19.96	0.04	2	1,100	HIGH	MED-HIGH
Valley View ISD-Cooke Co	01007506		13.29	0.02	1	815	HIGH	MED-HIGH
Lindsay Ind School Dist	01007427		6.81	0.01	2	510	HIGH	MED-LOW
Era Ind School Dist	01007312		5.30	0.01	1	500	HIGH	MED-LOW
Muenster Ind School Dist	01007453		5.27	0.01	2	500	HIGH	LOW
Walnut Bend Ind School Dist	01007532		0.98	0.00	1	75	HIGH	MED-HIGH
Sivells Bend Ind School Dist	01007489		0.89	0.00	1	68	HIGH	MED-LOW
HOOD		0.18						
Granbury Ind School Dist	01031375		85.29	0.15	11	7,218	HIGH	MED-HIGH
Tolar Ind School Dist	01031430		8.77	0.02	3	780	HIGH	MED-LOW
Lipan Ind School Dist	01031416		5.94	0.01	1	420	HIGH	MED-HIGH
MATAGORDA		0.18						
Bay City Ind School Dist	01040819		52.95	0.10	5	3,700	HIGH	MED-HIGH
Van Vleck Ind School Dist	01041019		19.98	0.04	4	1,050	HIGH	MED-HIGH
Tidehaven Ind School Dist	01040962		15.59	0.03	4	980	HIGH	MED-HIGH
Palacios Ind School Dist	01040912		10.92	0.02	4	1,506	MED	MED-HIGH
Matagorda Ind School Dist	01040895		0.56	0.00	1	120	LOW	MED-HIGH
RUSK		0.18						
Henderson Ind School Dist	01048976		39.37	0.07	6	3,040	HIGH	MED-HIGH
Tatum Ind School Dist	01049188		17.09	0.03	4	1,622	HIGH	MED-HIGH
West Rusk Co Cons Ind Sch Dist	01049217		13.96	0.03	4	1,150	HIGH	MED-HIGH
Carlisle Ind School Dist	01048940		10.71	0.02	1	650	HIGH	MED-HIGH
Overton Ind School Dist	01049152		7.77	0.01	2	500	HIGH	MED-HIGH
Mt Enterprise Ind School Dist	01049126		5.20	0.01	1	400	HIGH	MED-HIGH
Laneville Ind School Dist	01049061		3.02	0.01	1	182	HIGH	MED-HIGH
Leveretts Chapel Ind Sch Dist	01049097		2.88	0.01	1	259	HIGH	MED-LOW
TITUS		0.18						
Mt Pleasant Ind School Dist	01055369		63.15	0.12	8	5,300	HIGH	MED-HIGH
Chapel Hill Ind School Dist	01055307		28.74	0.05	3	1,050	HIGH	MED-HIGH
Harts Bluff Ind School Dist	01055345		8.11	0.01	1	640	HIGH	MED-HIGH
UPSHUR		0.18						
Gilmer Ind School Dist	01057408		27.35	0.05	4	2,437	HIGH	MED-HIGH
New Diana Ind School Dist	01057484		14.96	0.03	3	1,071	HIGH	MED-HIGH
Union Grove Ind School Dist	01057551		14.46	0.03	2	750	HIGH	MED-LOW
Big Sandy Ind School Dist	01057379		13.76	0.03	3	650	HIGH	MED-HIGH
Harmony Ind School Dist	01057458		12.31	0.02	4	1,060	HIGH	MED-LOW
Ore City Ind School Dist	01057525		10.26	0.02	3	950	HIGH	MED-HIGH
Union Hill Ind School Dist	01057587		6.90	0.01	1	400	HIGH	MED-HIGH
BROWN		0.17						
Brownwood Ind School Dist	01002489		59.48	0.10	7	3,595	HIGH	MED-HIGH
Bangs Ind School Dist	01002398		15.09	0.03	3	875	HIGH	MED-HIGH
Early Ind School Dist	01002556		12.60	0.02	4	1,200	MED	MED-HIGH
Zephyr Ind School Dist	01002611		4.32	0.01	1	217	HIGH	MED-HIGH
Blanket Ind School Dist	01002427		4.21	0.01	1	187	HIGH	MED-LOW
May Ind School Dist	01002582		3.00	0.00	2	290	MED	MED-HIGH
Brookesmith Ind School Dist	01002453		1.30	0.00	3	200	LOW	MED-LOW
CALDWELL		0.17						
Lockhart Ind School Dist	01003031		75.77	0.13	9	6,350	HIGH	MED-HIGH
Luling Ind School Dist	01003093		21.67	0.04	4	1,450	HIGH	MED-HIGH
Prairie Lea Ind School Dist	01003122		2.56	0.00	1	210	HIGH	MED-LOW
ERATH		0.17						
Stephenville Ind School Dist	01017135		67.59	0.12	6	3,650	HIGH	MED-LOW
Dublin Ind School Dist	01017018		15.28	0.03	3	1,200	HIGH	MED-HIGH
Bluff Dale Ind Sch Dist	01016997		5.65	0.01	1	243	HIGH	MED-LOW
Lingleville Ind School Dist	01017082		3.49	0.01	1	275	HIGH	MED-HIGH
Three Way Ind School Dist	01017185		3.08	0.01	2	190	HIGH	MED-LOW
Huckabay Ind School Dist	01017056		2.87	0.00	1	260	HIGH	MED-LOW
Morgan Mill Ind School Dist	01017111		2.04	0.00	1	125	HIGH	MED-LOW
FANNIN		0.17						
Bonham Ind School Dist	01017367		36.42	0.06	5	1,890	HIGH	MED-HIGH
Leonard Ind School Dist	01017501		18.88	0.03	4	820	HIGH	MED-LOW
Sam Rayburn Ind School Dist	01017549		12.71	0.02	1	500	HIGH	MED-LOW
Honey Grove Ind School Dist	01017472		11.85	0.02	3	605	HIGH	MED-HIGH
Trenton Ind School Dist	01017604		6.62	0.01	3	568	HIGH	MED-LOW
Dodd City Ind School Dist	01017422		5.52	0.01	1	370	HIGH	MED-LOW
Savoy Ind School Dist	01017575		4.03	0.01	2	320	HIGH	MED-LOW
Ector Ind School Dist	01017458		3.97	0.01	1	250	HIGH	MED-LOW

School Year 2019-2020   800-333-8802

DISTRICT BUYING POWER INDEX

COUNTIES RANKED BY PERCENTAGE OF STATE SPENDING

COUNTY / DISTRICT	PID	COUNTY % OF STATE	DISTRICT % OF COUNTY	DISTRICT % OF STATES	NUMBER OF SCHOOLS	ENROLL	EXP	POV
MEDINA		0.17						
Medina Valley Ind School Dist	01041277		40.68	0.07	5	5,087	MED	MED-HIGH
Devine Ind School Dist	01041198		20.89	0.04	4	2,000	MED	MED-HIGH
Hondo Ind School Dist	01041239		16.67	0.03	4	2,200	MED	MED-HIGH
Natalia Ind School Dist	01041320		15.76	0.03	4	1,060	HIGH	MED-HIGH
D'Hanis Ind School Dist	01041162		6.00	0.01	1	395	HIGH	MED-HIGH
KENDALL		0.16						
Boerne Ind School Dist	01035814		81.05	0.13	11	9,000	MED	MED-LOW
Comfort Ind School Dist	01035864		18.95	0.03	3	1,100	HIGH	MED-HIGH
POLK		0.16						
Livingston Ind School Dist	01047075		53.15	0.09	7	3,963	HIGH	MED-HIGH
Corrigan-Camden Ind Sch Dist	01046980		17.27	0.03	3	850	HIGH	MED-HIGH
Onalaska Ind School Dist	01809809		15.60	0.03	2	1,000	HIGH	MED-HIGH
Big Sandy Ind School Dist	01046954		8.21	0.01	1	525	HIGH	MED-HIGH
Leggett Ind School Dist	01047051		3.39	0.01	1	185	HIGH	MED-HIGH
Goodrich Ind School Dist	01047025		2.37	0.00	2	235	HIGH	MED-HIGH
RANDALL		0.16						
Canyon Ind School Dist	01047934		100.00	0.16	16	10,200	MED	MED-LOW
WOOD		0.16						
Winnsboro Ind School Dist	01061942		29.94	0.05	3	1,496	HIGH	MED-HIGH
Quitman Ind School Dist	01061904		24.13	0.04	3	1,121	HIGH	MED-HIGH
Mineola Ind School Dist	01061851		19.30	0.03	4	1,630	HIGH	MED-HIGH
Alba-Golden Ind School Dist	01061784		10.88	0.02	2	850	HIGH	MED-HIGH
Hawkins Ind School Dist	01061813		10.66	0.02	3	735	HIGH	MED-HIGH
Yantis Ind School Dist	01061980		5.09	0.01	2	370	HIGH	MED-HIGH
ATASCOSA		0.15						
Pleasanton Ind School Dist	00995431		35.02	0.05	4	3,477	MED	MED-HIGH
Lytle Ind School Dist	00995405		19.77	0.03	4	1,693	MED	MED-HIGH
Poteet Ind School Dist	00995493		19.20	0.03	4	1,735	MED	MED-HIGH
Jourdanton Ind School Dist	00995376		15.47	0.02	4	1,600	MED	MED-HIGH
Charlotte Ind School Dist	00995338		10.55	0.02	3	475	HIGH	MED-HIGH
HALE		0.15						
Plainview Ind School Dist	01021904		61.47	0.09	10	5,450	MED	MED-HIGH
Abernathy Ind School Dist	01021746		14.34	0.02	3	780	HIGH	MED-HIGH
Hale Center Ind School Dist	01021813		9.93	0.01	3	647	HIGH	MED-HIGH
Petersburg Ind School Dist	01021863		9.53	0.01	1	300	HIGH	MED-HIGH
Cotton Center Ind School Dist	01021784		4.72	0.01	1	130	HIGH	HIGH
SHELBY		0.15						
Center Ind School Dist	01050278		49.02	0.08	6	2,600	HIGH	MED-HIGH
Joaquin Ind School Dist	01050357		13.29	0.02	3	650	HIGH	MED-HIGH
Timpson Ind School Dist	01050450		12.75	0.02	3	630	HIGH	HIGH
Tenaha Ind School Dist	01050424		12.22	0.02	1	570	HIGH	HIGH
Shelbyville Ind School Dist	01050395		10.50	0.02	3	790	HIGH	HIGH
Excelsior Ind School Dist	01050321		2.22	0.00	1	90	HIGH	MED-HIGH
UVALDE		0.15						
Uvalde Cons Ind School Dist	01057795		78.32	0.11	7	4,221	HIGH	HIGH
Sabinal Ind School Dist	01057733		11.01	0.02	2	500	HIGH	MED-HIGH
Knippa Ind School Dist	01057692		7.41	0.01	1	475	HIGH	HIGH
Utopia Ind School Dist	01057769		3.26	0.00	1	232	HIGH	MED-HIGH
WILSON		0.15						
La Vernia Ind School Dist	01061318		44.42	0.07	4	3,360	HIGH	MED-LOW
Floresville Ind School Dist	01061265		32.13	0.05	5	4,000	MED	MED-LOW
Stockdale Ind School Dist	01061382		11.97	0.02	3	803	HIGH	MED-HIGH
Poth Ind School Dist	01061344		11.47	0.02	3	840	HIGH	MED-LOW
CASS		0.14						
Atlanta Ind School Dist	01004671		34.09	0.05	5	1,760	HIGH	HIGH
Hughes Springs Ind Sch Dist	01004786		23.42	0.03	3	1,230	HIGH	MED-HIGH
Queen City Ind School Dist	01004920		16.62	0.02	4	1,045	HIGH	MED-HIGH
Linden Kildare Cons Ind SD	01004827		8.97	0.01	3	700	MED	MED-HIGH
McLeod Ind School Dist	01004891		8.08	0.01	1	388	HIGH	HIGH
Bloomburg Ind School Dist	01004750		5.07	0.01	1	270	HIGH	MED-HIGH
Avinger Ind School Dist	01004724		3.75	0.01	1	135	HIGH	MED-HIGH
HOWARD		0.14						
Big Spring Ind School Dist	01031870		65.08	0.09	9	4,000	HIGH	MED-HIGH
Forsan Ind School Dist	01032094		18.39	0.03	2	812	HIGH	MED-LOW
Coahoma Ind School Dist	01032056		16.53	0.02	3	1,000	HIGH	MED-HIGH

Texas School Directory

DISTRICT BUYING POWER INDEX

DISTRICT BUYING POWER INDEX
COUNTIES RANKED BY PERCENTAGE OF STATE SPENDING

COUNTY / DISTRICT	PID	COUNTY % OF STATE	DISTRICT % OF COUNTY	DISTRICT % OF STATES	NUMBER OF SCHOOLS	ENROLL	EXP	POV
JIM WELLS		0.14						
Alice Ind School Dist	01034511		49.18	0.07	9	4,784	MED	HIGH
Orange Grove Ind School Dist	01034688		21.83	0.03	4	1,850	MED	HIGH
Premont Ind School Dist	01034717		19.09	0.03	2	587	HIGH	HIGH
Ben Bolt-Palito Blanco ISD	01034638		7.38	0.01	2	512	MED	MED-HIGH
La Gloria Ind School Dist	01034664		2.53	0.00	1	125	HIGH	HIGH
MILAM		0.14						
Cameron Ind School Dist	01041758		36.09	0.05	4	1,800	HIGH	HIGH
Rockdale Ind School Dist	01041851		27.66	0.04	4	1,530	HIGH	MED-HIGH
Milano Ind School Dist	01041825		15.30	0.02	3	460	HIGH	HIGH
Thorndale Ind School Dist	01041904		13.04	0.02	3	567	HIGH	MED-HIGH
Buckholts Ind School Dist	01041722		5.43	0.01	1	140	HIGH	HIGH
Gause Ind School Dist	01041801		2.48	0.00	1	170	HIGH	HIGH
WILLACY		0.14						
Lyford Cons Ind School Dist	01060651		49.24	0.07	3	1,551	HIGH	HIGH
Raymondville Ind Sch Dist	01060716		36.38	0.05	5	2,000	HIGH	HIGH
Lasara Ind School Dist	01060637		9.08	0.01	2	380	HIGH	HIGH
San Perlita Ind School Dist	01060780		5.31	0.01	1	282	HIGH	HIGH
AUSTIN		0.13						
Bellville Ind School Dist	00995534		42.48	0.05	6	2,200	HIGH	MED-HIGH
Sealy Ind School Dist	00995584		41.29	0.05	4	2,900	HIGH	MED-LOW
Brazos Ind School Dist	00995625		16.23	0.02	4	700	HIGH	MED-LOW
DE WITT		0.13						
Yoakum Ind School Dist	01013804		36.72	0.05	5	1,500	HIGH	MED-HIGH
Cuero Ind School Dist	01013684		33.65	0.04	4	2,000	HIGH	MED-HIGH
Yorktown Ind School Dist	01013866		16.08	0.02	3	550	HIGH	MED-HIGH
Nordheim Ind School Dist	01013751		8.04	0.01	1	150	HIGH	MED-HIGH
Westhoff Ind School Dist	01013787		3.11	0.00	1	85	HIGH	HIGH
Meyersville Ind School Dist	01013737		2.40	0.00	1	132	HIGH	MED-LOW
HOCKLEY		0.13						
Levelland Ind School Dist	01031129		51.49	0.07	6	2,936	HIGH	MED-HIGH
Sundown Ind School Dist	01031301		15.25	0.02	3	585	HIGH	MED-LOW
Smyer Ind School Dist	01031272		11.73	0.02	2	420	HIGH	MED-HIGH
Ropes Ind School Dist	01031234		10.80	0.01	1	430	HIGH	MED-HIGH
Anton ISD School Dist	01031090		6.67	0.01	1	180	HIGH	MED-HIGH
Whitharral Ind School Dist	01031349		4.06	0.01	1	173	HIGH	MED-HIGH
KERR		0.13						
Kerrville Ind School Dist	01036076		60.31	0.08	10	4,800	MED	MED-HIGH
Ingram Ind School Dist	01036052		21.02	0.03	3	1,070	HIGH	MED-HIGH
Center Point Ind School Dist	01035979		16.35	0.02	3	570	HIGH	MED-HIGH
Hunt Ind School Dist	01036038		2.15	0.00	1	200	MED	MED-LOW
Divide Ind School Dist	01036014		0.18	0.00	1	22	MED	MED-HIGH
PALO PINTO		0.13						
Mineral Wells Ind School Dist	01046019		68.57	0.09	6	3,200	HIGH	MED-HIGH
Santo Ind School Dist	01046124		11.07	0.01	2	475	HIGH	MED-HIGH
Graford Ind School Dist	01045986		7.41	0.01	2	340	HIGH	MED-LOW
Strawn Ind School Dist	01046150		6.68	0.01	1	167	HIGH	MED-HIGH
Gordon Ind School Dist	01045950		3.15	0.00	1	200	HIGH	MED-LOW
Palo Pinto Ind Sch Dist 906	01046100		3.12	0.00	1	112	HIGH	MED-HIGH
GONZALES		0.12						
Gonzales Ind School Dist	01019860		70.46	0.08	6	2,875	HIGH	MED-HIGH
Nixon-Smiley Cons Ind Sch Dist	01019937		24.09	0.03	3	1,100	HIGH	MED-HIGH
Waelder Ind School Dist	01020003		5.45	0.01	1	320	HIGH	MED-HIGH
JASPER		0.12						
Jasper Ind School Dist	01033244		38.95	0.05	4	2,390	HIGH	HIGH
Buna Ind School Dist	01033177		20.27	0.02	3	1,480	MED	MED-LOW
Kirbyville Cons Ind Sch Dist	01033282		17.17	0.02	3	1,400	MED	HIGH
Brookeland Ind School Dist	01033141		15.57	0.02	1	392	HIGH	MED-HIGH
Evadale Ind School Dist	01033218		8.05	0.01	2	450	HIGH	MED-HIGH
NOLAN		0.12						
Sweetwater ISD School Dist	01043914		48.50	0.06	5	2,200	HIGH	MED-HIGH
Roscoe Collegiate Ind Sch Dist	01043885		33.07	0.04	3	620	HIGH	MED-HIGH
Blackwell Cons Ind Sch Dist	01043794		13.08	0.02	1	153	HIGH	MED-HIGH
Highland Ind School Dist	01043859		5.35	0.01	1	250	HIGH	MED-HIGH
BEE		0.11						
Beeville Ind School Dist	00996069		68.21	0.08	6	3,200	HIGH	HIGH
Skidmore Tynan Ind SD	00996215		17.43	0.02	3	850	HIGH	MED-HIGH

DISTRICT BUYING POWER INDEX

Market Data Retrieval

DISTRICT BUYING POWER INDEX
COUNTIES RANKED BY PERCENTAGE OF STATE SPENDING

COUNTY / DISTRICT	PID	COUNTY % OF STATE	DISTRICT % OF COUNTY	DISTRICT % OF STATES	NUMBER OF SCHOOLS	ENROLL	EXP	POV
Pettus Ind School Dist	00996174		11.25	0.01	2	421	HIGH	MED-HIGH
Pawnee Ind School Dist	00996148		3.12	0.00	1	550	LOW	MED-HIGH
GAINES		0.11						
Seminole Ind School Dist	01018751		54.47	0.06	6	2,983	HIGH	MED-HIGH
Seagraves Ind School Dist	01018713		33.10	0.03	3	569	HIGH	HIGH
Loop Ind School Dist	01018684		12.44	0.01	1	150	HIGH	MED-HIGH
GRIMES		0.11						
Navasota Ind School Dist	01021409		73.25	0.08	6	3,000	HIGH	MED-HIGH
Anderson-Shiro Cons Ind SD	01021344		13.60	0.02	2	850	MED	MED-LOW
Iola Ind School Dist	01021370		10.52	0.01	2	502	HIGH	MED-HIGH
Richards Ind School Dist	01021459		2.62	0.00	1	170	HIGH	MED-HIGH
KLEBERG		0.11						
Kingsville Ind School Dist	01036258		64.13	0.07	8	3,050	HIGH	HIGH
Santa Gertrudis Ind Sch Dist	01809536		16.90	0.02	2	753	HIGH	HIGH
Riviera Ind School Dist	01036399		10.85	0.01	2	435	HIGH	MED-LOW
Ricardo Ind School Dist	01036375		8.12	0.01	1	671	MED	MED-HIGH
LAMPASAS		0.11						
Lampasas Ind School Dist	01037111		90.77	0.10	5	3,400	HIGH	MED-HIGH
Lometa Ind School Dist	01037161		9.23	0.01	1	295	HIGH	MED-HIGH
WASHINGTON		0.11						
Brenham Ind School Dist	01059042		82.43	0.09	7	5,000	HIGH	MED-HIGH
Burton Ind School Dist	01059107		17.57	0.02	2	455	HIGH	MED-HIGH
BURNET		0.10						
Burnet Cons Ind Sch Dist	01002752		61.81	0.06	6	3,186	HIGH	MED-HIGH
Marble Falls Ind School Dist	01002817		38.19	0.04	7	4,154	LOW	MED-HIGH
DIMMIT		0.10						
Carrizo Spgs Cons Ind SD	01014030		100.00	0.10	4	2,200	HIGH	HIGH
JACKSON		0.10						
Edna Ind School Dist	01032991		49.43	0.05	4	1,500	HIGH	MED-HIGH
Industrial Ind School Dist	01033086		31.23	0.03	4	1,178	HIGH	MED-HIGH
Ganado Ind School Dist	01033050		19.33	0.02	3	750	HIGH	MED-HIGH
MOORE		0.10						
Dumas Ind School Dist	01042817		84.28	0.09	9	4,212	HIGH	MED-HIGH
Sunray Ind School Dist	01042910		15.72	0.02	3	550	HIGH	MED-LOW
PANOLA		0.10						
Carthage Ind School Dist	01046215		68.53	0.07	6	2,692	HIGH	MED-HIGH
Beckville Ind School Dist	01046186		16.70	0.02	2	700	HIGH	MED-HIGH
Gary Ind School Dist	01046277		14.78	0.01	1	500	HIGH	MED-HIGH
SAN JACINTO		0.10						
Shepherd Ind School Dist	01049449		62.83	0.06	4	2,000	HIGH	MED-HIGH
Coldspring-Oakhurst Cons ISD	01049401		37.17	0.04	4	1,525	HIGH	MED-HIGH
ARANSAS		0.09						
Aransas Co Ind School Dist	00995120		100.00	0.09	4	2,800	HIGH	MED-HIGH
COLORADO		0.09						
Rice Cons Ind School Dist	01006784		41.85	0.04	7	1,325	HIGH	MED-HIGH
Columbus Ind School Dist	01006746		41.01	0.04	4	1,494	HIGH	MED-HIGH
Weimar Ind School Dist	01006849		17.13	0.02	3	661	HIGH	MED-HIGH
DEAF SMITH		0.09						
Hereford Ind School Dist	01012989		91.38	0.09	11	4,100	HIGH	MED-HIGH
Walcott Ind School Dist	01013086		8.62	0.01	1	125	HIGH	MED-HIGH
DUVAL		0.09						
Freer Ind School Dist	01809196		47.26	0.04	3	807	HIGH	HIGH
San Diego Ind School Dist	01014274		41.01	0.04	3	1,460	HIGH	HIGH
Benavides Ind School Dist	01014171		10.12	0.01	2	340	HIGH	HIGH
Ramirez Common School Dist	01014250		1.62	0.00	1	30	HIGH	MED-HIGH
FRIO		0.09						
Pearsall Ind School Dist	01018610		50.11	0.04	4	2,100	HIGH	HIGH
Dilley Ind School Dist	01018579		49.89	0.04	4	1,000	HIGH	HIGH
HOUSTON		0.09						
Crockett Ind School Dist	01031715		45.83	0.04	5	1,331	HIGH	HIGH
Latexo Ind School Dist	01031820		19.80	0.02	2	500	HIGH	MED-HIGH
Lovelady Ind School Dist	01031844		18.15	0.02	2	510	HIGH	MED-HIGH
Grapeland Ind School Dist	01031753		8.26	0.01	3	615	MED	MED-HIGH
Kennard Ind Sch Dist	01031791		7.97	0.01	1	280	HIGH	MED-HIGH

TX—C12   800-333-8802   **School Year 2019-2020**

Texas School Directory

DISTRICT BUYING POWER INDEX

DISTRICT BUYING POWER INDEX
COUNTIES RANKED BY PERCENTAGE OF STATE SPENDING

COUNTY / DISTRICT	PID	COUNTY % OF STATE	DISTRICT % OF COUNTY	DISTRICT % OF STATES	NUMBER OF SCHOOLS	ENROLL	EXP	POV
HUTCHINSON		0.09						
Borger Ind School Dist	01032642		65.29	0.06	6	2,800	HIGH	MED-HIGH
Sanford-Fritch Ind School Dist	01032771		17.91	0.02	3	737	HIGH	MED-LOW
Plemons-Stinnett-Phillips CISD	01032836		10.90	0.01	3	675	MED	MED-HIGH
Spring Creek Ind School Dist	01032812		5.90	0.01	1	92	HIGH	MED-LOW
LIMESTONE		0.09						
Groesbeck Ind School Dist	01038048		47.84	0.04	4	1,560	HIGH	MED-HIGH
Mexia Ind School Dist	01038086		40.00	0.04	5	1,800	HIGH	MED-HIGH
Coolidge Ind School Dist	01038012		12.16	0.01	2	309	HIGH	HIGH
TYLER		0.09						
Woodville Ind School Dist	01057331		38.04	0.03	4	1,300	HIGH	HIGH
Warren Ind School Dist	01057288		37.28	0.03	4	1,400	HIGH	MED-HIGH
Colmesneil Ind School Dist	01057226		11.92	0.01	2	475	HIGH	MED-HIGH
Spurger Ind School Dist	01057252		8.09	0.01	2	385	HIGH	MED-HIGH
Chester Ind School Dist	01057197		4.67	0.00	2	200	HIGH	MED-HIGH
BAILEY		0.08						
Muleshoe Ind School Dist	00995699		100.00	0.08	4	1,450	HIGH	MED-HIGH
BOSQUE		0.08						
Valley Mills Ind School Dist	01000754		27.41	0.02	3	630	HIGH	MED-HIGH
Clifton Ind School Dist	01808893		25.38	0.02	3	1,000	HIGH	MED-HIGH
Meridian Ind School Dist	01000699		16.35	0.01	3	480	HIGH	MED-HIGH
Cranfills Gap ISD School Dist	01000601		7.62	0.01	1	125	HIGH	MED-HIGH
Walnut Springs Ind Sch Dist	01000780		7.53	0.01	1	190	HIGH	HIGH
Morgan Ind School Dist	01000728		6.90	0.01	1	142	HIGH	HIGH
Kopperl Ind School Dist	01000663		6.22	0.01	1	225	HIGH	MED-HIGH
Iredell Ind School Dist	01000637		2.58	0.00	1	145	MED	MED-HIGH
CALHOUN		0.08						
Calhoun Co Ind School Dist	01003158		100.00	0.08	7	3,985	HIGH	MED-HIGH
FREESTONE		0.08						
Fairfield Ind School Dist	01018452		48.04	0.04	4	1,817	HIGH	MED-HIGH
Teague Ind School Dist	01018505		27.60	0.02	5	1,160	MED	MED-HIGH
Wortham Ind School Dist	01018543		20.62	0.02	3	500	HIGH	MED-HIGH
Dew Ind School Dist	01018438		3.74	0.00	1	180	HIGH	MED-LOW
JONES		0.08						
Stamford Ind School Dist	01035321		36.03	0.03	3	670	HIGH	MED-HIGH
Anson Ind School Dist	01035199		27.34	0.02	3	700	HIGH	MED-HIGH
Hawley Ind School Dist	01035266		21.16	0.02	3	769	HIGH	MED-HIGH
Hamlin Ind School Dist	01035228		9.50	0.01	2	400	HIGH	HIGH
Lueders-Avoca Ind School Dist	01035292		5.98	0.00	2	104	HIGH	MED-HIGH
KARNES		0.08						
Karnes City Ind School Dist	01035395		42.96	0.04	5	1,085	HIGH	MED-HIGH
Kenedy Ind School Dist	01035450		25.29	0.02	3	800	HIGH	MED-HIGH
Runge Ind School Dist	01035503		17.54	0.01	1	250	HIGH	MED-HIGH
Falls City Ind School Dist	01035369		14.22	0.01	2	360	HIGH	MED-LOW
LAMB		0.08						
Littlefield Ind School Dist	01036911		37.64	0.03	4	1,300	HIGH	MED-HIGH
Olton Ind School Dist	01036973		21.74	0.02	3	600	HIGH	MED-HIGH
Sudan Ind School Dist	01037082		18.49	0.02	2	495	HIGH	MED-HIGH
Springlake-Earth Ind Sch Dist	01037044		14.59	0.01	2	350	HIGH	MED-LOW
Amherst Ind School Dist	01036882		7.54	0.01	1	145	HIGH	MED-HIGH
MONTAGUE		0.08						
Bowie Ind School Dist	01042180		37.25	0.03	4	1,720	MED	MED-HIGH
Nocona Ind School Dist	01042336		32.45	0.03	3	770	HIGH	MED-HIGH
St Jo Ind School Dist	01042403		10.49	0.01	2	283	HIGH	MED-LOW
Forestburg Ind School Dist	01042257		7.13	0.01	1	160	HIGH	MED-HIGH
Gold-Burg Ind School Dist	01042283		6.04	0.00	1	140	HIGH	MED-HIGH
Montague Ind School Dist	01042312		3.80	0.00	1	160	HIGH	MED-HIGH
Prairie Valley Ind School Dist	01042374		2.83	0.00	1	170	MED	MED-HIGH
SCURRY		0.08						
Snyder Ind School Dist	01050101		79.00	0.06	4	2,650	HIGH	MED-HIGH
Ira Ind School Dist	01050072		10.96	0.01	1	270	HIGH	MED-LOW
Hermleigh Ind School Dist	01050046		10.04	0.01	1	250	HIGH	MED-LOW
WARD		0.08						
Monahans-Wickett-Pyote ISD	01058957		89.13	0.07	6	2,300	HIGH	MED-HIGH
Grandfalls-Royalty Ind SD	01058919		10.87	0.01	1	185	HIGH	MED-HIGH

DISTRICT BUYING POWER INDEX

Market Data Retrieval

DISTRICT BUYING POWER INDEX
COUNTIES RANKED BY PERCENTAGE OF STATE SPENDING

COUNTY / DISTRICT	PID	COUNTY % OF STATE	DISTRICT % OF COUNTY	DISTRICT % OF STATES	NUMBER OF SCHOOLS	ENROLL	EXP	POV
BURLESON		0.07						
Caldwell Ind School Dist	01002647		68.90	0.05	5	1,800	HIGH	MED-HIGH
Snook Ind School Dist	01002685		19.10	0.01	1	500	HIGH	MED-HIGH
Somerville Ind School Dist	01002714		12.00	0.01	3	640	MED	HIGH
CALLAHAN		0.07						
Clyde Consolidated Ind SD	01003316		42.97	0.03	4	1,450	HIGH	MED-HIGH
Cross Plains Ind Sch Dist	01003354		26.45	0.02	2	368	HIGH	MED-HIGH
Baird Ind School Dist	01003287		17.01	0.01	3	274	HIGH	MED-HIGH
Eula Ind School Dist	01003380		13.58	0.01	3	400	HIGH	MED-HIGH
FAYETTE		0.07						
La Grange Ind School Dist	01017721		45.27	0.03	4	2,350	MED	MED-LOW
Flatonia Ind School Dist	01017692		20.51	0.01	3	580	HIGH	MED-HIGH
Schulenburg Ind School Dist	01017800		17.57	0.01	2	750	MED	MED-HIGH
Fayetteville Ind School Dist	01017666		11.40	0.01	1	265	HIGH	MED-LOW
Round Top-Carmine Ind Sch Dist	01017771		5.26	0.00	2	283	MED	MED-LOW
GILLESPIE		0.07						
Fredericksburg Ind School Dist	01019688		82.87	0.06	6	2,900	HIGH	MED-HIGH
Harper Ind School Dist	01019731		15.44	0.01	3	600	HIGH	MED-LOW
Doss Consolidated Common SD	01019664		1.69	0.00	1	25	HIGH	MED-LOW
JACK		0.07						
Jacksboro Ind Sch Dist	01032927		75.58	0.05	3	1,050	HIGH	MED-HIGH
Perrin-Whitt Cons Ind Sch Dist	01032965		14.14	0.01	2	330	HIGH	MED-LOW
Bryson Ind School Dist	01032898		10.28	0.01	1	255	HIGH	HIGH
LEE		0.07						
Giddings Ind School Dist	01037458		63.07	0.04	4	1,905	HIGH	MED-HIGH
Lexington Ind School Dist	01037496		28.94	0.02	3	1,030	HIGH	MED-LOW
Dime Box Ind School Dist	01037422		7.99	0.01	1	160	HIGH	MED-LOW
LEON		0.07						
Buffalo Ind School Dist	01037551		29.52	0.02	4	970	HIGH	MED-HIGH
Centerville Ind School Dist	01037587		23.81	0.02	2	700	HIGH	MED-HIGH
Leon Ind School Dist	01037628		22.57	0.02	3	715	HIGH	MED-HIGH
Normangee Ind School Dist	01037654		15.60	0.01	3	572	HIGH	MED-HIGH
Oakwood Ind School Dist	01037680		8.49	0.01	2	200	HIGH	MED-HIGH
OCHILTREE		0.07						
Perryton Ind School Dist	01045455		100.00	0.07	6	2,217	HIGH	MED-HIGH
PECOS		0.07						
Ft Stockton Ind School Dist	01046837		72.19	0.05	5	2,479	HIGH	MED-HIGH
Iraan-Sheffield Ind Sch Dist	01046904		17.95	0.01	3	422	HIGH	MED-HIGH
Buena Vista Ind School Dist	01046801		9.86	0.01	1	244	HIGH	HIGH
SWISHER		0.07						
Tulia Ind School Dist	01051571		74.71	0.05	4	1,099	HIGH	MED-HIGH
Kress Ind School Dist	01051545		14.34	0.01	2	280	HIGH	MED-HIGH
Happy Ind School Dist	01051519		10.95	0.01	2	254	HIGH	MED-HIGH
TERRY		0.07						
Brownfield Ind Sch Dist	01055084		71.70	0.05	5	1,700	HIGH	MED-HIGH
Wellman Union Ind School Dist	01055199		16.44	0.01	1	347	HIGH	MED-HIGH
Meadow Ind School Dist	01055149		11.86	0.01	1	280	HIGH	HIGH
WINKLER		0.07						
Kermit Ind School Dist	01061423		76.70	0.06	3	1,418	HIGH	MED-HIGH
Wink Loving Ind School Dist	01061485		23.30	0.02	2	440	HIGH	MED-HIGH
YOUNG		0.07						
Graham Ind School Dist	01062104		65.33	0.05	5	2,390	HIGH	MED-HIGH
Olney Ind School Dist	01062192		23.07	0.02	3	700	HIGH	MED-HIGH
Newcastle Ind School Dist	01062166		11.60	0.01	1	180	HIGH	HIGH
ARCHER		0.06						
Holliday Ind School Dist	00995211		44.11	0.02	3	1,007	HIGH	MED-LOW
Archer City Ind School Dist	00995182		34.37	0.02	2	474	HIGH	MED-HIGH
Windthorst Ind School Dist	00995273		21.52	0.01	3	405	HIGH	MED-LOW
CASTRO		0.06						
Dimmitt Ind School Dist	01004968		73.33	0.04	4	1,225	HIGH	MED-HIGH
Hart Ind School Dist	01005015		14.49	0.01	2	230	HIGH	HIGH
Nazareth Ind School Dist	01005041		12.19	0.01	1	240	HIGH	MED-LOW
CLAY		0.06						
Henrietta Ind School Dist	01005546		66.16	0.04	3	940	HIGH	MED-HIGH
Petrolia Cons Ind School Dist	01005601		22.37	0.01	2	440	HIGH	MED-HIGH

DISTRICT BUYING POWER INDEX

COUNTIES RANKED BY PERCENTAGE OF STATE SPENDING

COUNTY / DISTRICT	PID	COUNTY % OF STATE	DISTRICT % OF COUNTY	DISTRICT % OF STATES	NUMBER OF SCHOOLS	ENROLL	EXP	POV
Midway Ind School Dist	01005584		7.10	0.00	1	137	HIGH	MED-LOW
Bellevue Ind School Dist	01005481		4.37	0.00	1	140	HIGH	MED-LOW
COMANCHE		0.06						
Comanche Ind School Dist	01007051		49.96	0.03	4	1,325	HIGH	MED-HIGH
De Leon Ind School Dist	01007099		24.44	0.01	3	716	HIGH	MED-HIGH
Sidney Ind School Dist	01007154		15.94	0.01	1	140	HIGH	MED-HIGH
Gustine Ind School Dist	01007128		9.66	0.01	1	161	HIGH	MED-HIGH
DALLAM		0.06						
Dalhart Ind School Dist	01008067		79.35	0.05	4	1,700	HIGH	MED-LOW
Texline Ind School Dist	01008108		20.65	0.01	1	185	HIGH	MED-LOW
DAWSON		0.06						
Lamesa Ind School Dist	01012862		65.19	0.04	5	1,800	HIGH	MED-HIGH
Sands Consolidated ISD	01012941		16.12	0.01	1	254	HIGH	MED-HIGH
Klondike Ind School Dist	01012824		13.74	0.01	1	275	HIGH	MED-HIGH
Dawson Ind School Dist	01012795		4.95	0.00	1	110	HIGH	MED-HIGH
EASTLAND		0.06						
Eastland Ind School Dist	01014406		35.15	0.02	3	1,130	HIGH	MED-HIGH
Cisco Independent Sch Dist	01014353		26.27	0.02	4	850	HIGH	MED-HIGH
Ranger Ind School Dist	01014470		15.67	0.01	1	350	HIGH	MED-HIGH
Gorman Ind School Dist	01014444		12.99	0.01	3	300	HIGH	MED-HIGH
Rising Star Ind Sch Dist	01014511		9.92	0.01	2	147	HIGH	MED-HIGH
FALLS		0.06						
Marlin Ind School Dist	01017238		49.89	0.03	3	1,000	HIGH	HIGH
Rosebud-Lott Ind School Dist	01017276		24.14	0.01	3	630	HIGH	MED-HIGH
Chilton Ind School Dist	01017202		20.30	0.01	1	540	HIGH	MED-HIGH
Westphalia Ind School Dist	01017329		5.66	0.00	1	155	HIGH	MED-LOW
GRAY		0.06						
Pampa Ind School Dist	01020132		77.99	0.05	7	3,500	LOW	MED-HIGH
McLean Ind School Dist	01020106		12.50	0.01	1	240	HIGH	MED-HIGH
Lefors Ind School Dist	01020077		7.49	0.00	1	160	HIGH	HIGH
Grandview-Hopkins Ind Sch Dist	01020053		2.02	0.00	1	50	HIGH	MED-LOW
LAVACA		0.06						
Hallettsville Ind Sch Dist	01037288		55.59	0.03	3	1,130	HIGH	MED-HIGH
Shiner Ind School Dist	01037355		22.45	0.01	2	660	HIGH	MED-LOW
Moulton Ind School Dist	01037329		12.55	0.01	2	300	HIGH	MED-HIGH
Sweet Home Ind School Dist	01037381		4.68	0.00	1	150	MED	MED-LOW
Ezzell Ind School Dist	01037264		2.64	0.00	1	85	MED	MED-LOW
Vysehrad Ind School Dist	01037408		2.09	0.00	1	115	LOW	MED-LOW
MADISON		0.06						
Madisonville Cons ISD	01040596		85.46	0.05	4	2,358	HIGH	MED-HIGH
North Zulch Ind School Dist	01040637		14.54	0.01	1	305	HIGH	MED-LOW
MARTIN		0.06						
Stanton Ind School Dist	01040754		80.90	0.05	3	1,092	HIGH	MED-HIGH
Grady Ind School Dist	01040730		19.10	0.01	1	260	HIGH	MED-HIGH
MCCULLOCH		0.06						
Brady Ind School Dist	01039420		71.88	0.04	4	1,120	HIGH	MED-HIGH
Rochelle Ind School Dist	01039509		19.27	0.01	1	200	HIGH	MED-HIGH
Lohn Ind School Dist	01039482		8.85	0.01	1	90	HIGH	HIGH
RED RIVER		0.06						
Clarksville Ind School Dist	01048110		30.25	0.02	2	585	HIGH	MED-HIGH
Detroit Ind School Dist	01048172		28.82	0.02	3	540	HIGH	MED-HIGH
Rivercrest Ind School Dist	01048213		28.00	0.02	3	735	HIGH	MED-HIGH
Avery Ind School Dist	01048081		12.93	0.01	2	365	HIGH	MED-HIGH
REEVES		0.06						
Pecos-Barstow-Toyah Ind SD	01048304		84.88	0.05	5	2,800	HIGH	MED-HIGH
Balmorhea Ind School Dist	01048251		15.12	0.01	1	165	HIGH	MED-LOW
ROBERTSON		0.06						
Franklin Ind School Dist	01048615		39.62	0.02	3	1,100	HIGH	MED-HIGH
Hearne Ind School Dist	01048641		33.40	0.02	3	860	HIGH	MED-HIGH
Bremond Ind School Dist	01048550		22.13	0.01	3	507	HIGH	MED-HIGH
Calvert Ind School Dist	01048586		4.86	0.00	1	164	MED	HIGH
RUNNELS		0.06						
Winters Ind School Dist	01048914		44.05	0.03	3	544	HIGH	MED-HIGH
Ballinger Ind School Dist	01048809		25.73	0.02	3	911	HIGH	MED-HIGH
Miles Ind School Dist	01048847		18.11	0.01	1	440	HIGH	MED-LOW
Olfen Ind School Dist	01048873		12.11	0.01	1	93	HIGH	MED-HIGH

DISTRICT BUYING POWER INDEX

Market Data Retrieval

DISTRICT BUYING POWER INDEX
COUNTIES RANKED BY PERCENTAGE OF STATE SPENDING

COUNTY / DISTRICT	PID	COUNTY % OF STATE	DISTRICT % OF COUNTY	DISTRICT % OF STATES	NUMBER OF SCHOOLS	ENROLL	EXP	POV
SABINE		0.06						
Hemphill Ind School Dist	01049267		75.53	0.05	3	900	HIGH	MED-HIGH
West Sabine Ind Sch Dist	01049293		24.47	0.02	2	600	HIGH	MED-HIGH
ZAPATA		0.06						
Zapata Co Ind School Dist	01062245		100.00	0.06	6	3,521	MED	HIGH
ANDREWS		0.05						
Andrews Ind School Dist	00994700		100.00	0.05	6	4,200	MED	MED-HIGH
BANDERA		0.05						
Bandera Ind School Dist	00995778		79.71	0.04	4	2,283	MED	MED-HIGH
Medina Ind School Dist	00995807		20.29	0.01	2	310	HIGH	MED-HIGH
BREWSTER		0.05						
Alpine Ind School Dist	01002192		79.71	0.04	3	1,000	HIGH	MED-HIGH
Marathon Ind School Dist	01002233		10.49	0.00	1	55	HIGH	MED-LOW
Terlingua Common School Dist	01002283		6.96	0.00	2	105	HIGH	MED-HIGH
San Vicente Ind School Dist	01002269		2.84	0.00	1	13	HIGH	MED-LOW
CAMP		0.05						
Pittsburg Ind School Dist	01004504		100.00	0.05	5	2,344	HIGH	HIGH
CARSON		0.05						
Panhandle Ind School Dist	01004592		52.06	0.02	3	700	HIGH	MED-LOW
Groom Ind School Dist	01004554		29.43	0.01	1	160	HIGH	MED-HIGH
White Deer Ind School Dist	01004633		18.51	0.01	2	450	HIGH	LOW
LYNN		0.05						
Tahoka Ind School Dist	01039341		41.24	0.02	3	680	HIGH	MED-HIGH
New Home Ind School Dist	01039274		26.65	0.01	1	447	HIGH	MED-HIGH
O'Donnell Ind School Dist	01039315		20.43	0.01	2	306	HIGH	MED-HIGH
Wilson Ind School Dist	01039391		11.68	0.01	1	129	HIGH	HIGH
MITCHELL		0.05						
Colorado Ind School Dist	01042063		52.28	0.03	4	940	HIGH	MED-HIGH
Westbrook Ind School Dist	01042154		36.11	0.02	1	272	HIGH	HIGH
Loraine Ind School Dist	01042128		11.62	0.01	1	160	HIGH	MED-HIGH
NEWTON		0.05						
Newton Ind School Dist	01043744		82.60	0.04	3	1,026	HIGH	MED-HIGH
Burkeville Ind School Dist	01043677		17.40	0.01	2	250	HIGH	HIGH
OLDHAM		0.05						
Vega Ind School Dist	01045558		32.78	0.02	2	380	HIGH	MED-LOW
Boys Ranch Ind School Dist	01484461		31.61	0.02	3	254	HIGH	MED-LOW
Wildorado Ind Sch Dist	01045584		20.96	0.01	1	180	HIGH	MED-HIGH
Adrian Ind School Dist	01045522		14.64	0.01	1	120	HIGH	MED-LOW
PARMER		0.05						
Friona Ind School Dist	01046734		34.38	0.02	4	1,117	MED	MED-HIGH
Bovina Ind School Dist	01046655		30.74	0.02	3	490	HIGH	MED-HIGH
Farwell Ind School Dist	01046693		28.48	0.01	3	522	HIGH	MED-HIGH
Lazbuddie Ind School Dist	01046772		6.40	0.00	1	201	MED	MED-LOW
PRESIDIO		0.05						
Presidio Ind School Dist	01047867		79.84	0.04	3	1,162	HIGH	HIGH
Marfa Ind School Dist	01047829		20.16	0.01	2	342	HIGH	HIGH
SOMERVELL		0.05						
Glen Rose Ind School Dist	01051088		100.00	0.05	4	1,882	HIGH	MED-LOW
TRINITY		0.05						
Trinity Ind School Dist	01057147		47.80	0.03	3	1,280	HIGH	HIGH
Groveton Ind School Dist	01057109		37.53	0.02	2	750	HIGH	HIGH
Apple Springs Ind School Dist	01057044		9.59	0.01	2	220	HIGH	HIGH
Centerville Ind School Dist	01057070		5.08	0.00	2	127	HIGH	MED-HIGH
WILBARGER		0.05						
Vernon Ind School Dist	01060560		75.16	0.04	6	1,700	HIGH	MED-HIGH
Northside Ind School Dist	01060534		17.43	0.01	1	230	HIGH	MED-HIGH
Harrold Ind School Dist	01060508		7.40	0.00	1	110	HIGH	MED-LOW
YOAKUM		0.05						
Denver City Ind School Dist	01062013		64.92	0.03	5	1,741	HIGH	MED-HIGH
Plains Ind School Dist	01062063		35.08	0.02	3	430	HIGH	MED-HIGH
BROOKS		0.04						
Brooks Co Ind School Dist	01002336		100.00	0.04	4	1,589	HIGH	HIGH

Texas School Directory

DISTRICT BUYING POWER INDEX

DISTRICT BUYING POWER INDEX
COUNTIES RANKED BY PERCENTAGE OF STATE SPENDING

COUNTY / DISTRICT	PID	COUNTY % OF STATE	DISTRICT % OF COUNTY	DISTRICT % OF STATES	NUMBER OF SCHOOLS	ENROLL	EXP	POV
COLEMAN		0.04						
Coleman Ind School Dist	01005819		63.30	0.02	3	885	HIGH	HIGH
Santa Anna Ind School Dist	01005924		28.62	0.01	2	259	HIGH	HIGH
Panther Creek Cons Ind SD	01005950		8.08	0.00	1	149	MED	HIGH
CROSBY		0.04						
Ralls Ind School Dist	01007984		36.10	0.01	4	500	HIGH	MED-HIGH
Crosbyton Cons Ind Sch Dist	01007908		35.46	0.01	2	375	HIGH	HIGH
Lorenzo Ind School Dist	01007958		28.44	0.01	2	250	HIGH	HIGH
DELTA		0.04						
Cooper Ind School Dist	01013103		89.34	0.03	2	750	HIGH	MED-HIGH
Fannindel Ind School Dist	01013141		10.66	0.00	2	150	HIGH	MED-HIGH
FLOYD		0.04						
Floydada Ind School Dist	01017977		71.57	0.03	2	730	HIGH	MED-HIGH
Lockney Independent Sch Dist	01018024		28.43	0.01	3	430	HIGH	HIGH
GOLIAD		0.04						
Goliad Ind School Dist	01019810		100.00	0.04	3	1,340	HIGH	MED-HIGH
HAMILTON		0.04						
Hamilton Ind School Dist	01022166		65.87	0.03	3	850	HIGH	MED-HIGH
Hico Ind School Dist	01022192		34.13	0.02	2	600	HIGH	MED-HIGH
LIVE OAK		0.04						
Three Rivers Ind School Dist	01038309		59.59	0.02	2	678	HIGH	MED-HIGH
George West Ind School Dist	01038256		40.41	0.02	4	1,100	MED	MED-HIGH
LLANO		0.04						
Llano Ind School Dist	01038347		100.00	0.04	4	1,800	HIGH	MED-HIGH
MARION		0.04						
Jefferson Ind School Dist	01040687		100.00	0.04	4	1,272	HIGH	HIGH
MILLS		0.04						
Goldthwaite Consolidated ISD	01041942		75.94	0.03	3	595	HIGH	MED-HIGH
Mullin Ind School Dist	01041978		16.01	0.01	6	94	HIGH	MED-HIGH
Priddy Ind School Dist	01042001		8.05	0.00	1	111	HIGH	MED-HIGH
MORRIS		0.04						
Pewitt Cons Ind School Dist	01043005		52.45	0.02	3	891	HIGH	MED-HIGH
Daingerfield-Lone Star Ind SD	01042946		47.55	0.02	4	1,100	HIGH	HIGH
REAGAN		0.04						
Reagan Co Ind School Dist	01048017		100.00	0.04	3	950	HIGH	MED-HIGH
SAN AUGUSTINE		0.04						
San Augustine Ind School Dist	01049360		64.91	0.02	2	763	HIGH	HIGH
Broaddus Ind School Dist	01049334		35.09	0.01	2	400	HIGH	HIGH
UPTON		0.04						
Rankin Ind School Dist	01057654		69.98	0.02	2	320	HIGH	MED-LOW
McCamey Ind School Dist	01057616		30.02	0.01	3	560	HIGH	MED-HIGH
ZAVALA		0.04						
Crystal City Ind School Dist	01062295		70.47	0.03	5	1,500	MED	HIGH
La Pryor Ind School Dist	01062374		29.53	0.01	2	500	HIGH	HIGH
BLANCO		0.03						
Blanco Ind School Dist	01000481		59.64	0.02	3	1,025	HIGH	MED-HIGH
Johnson City Ind School Dist	01000510		40.36	0.01	3	659	HIGH	MED-LOW
CHILDRESS		0.03						
Childress Ind School Dist	01005431		100.00	0.03	4	1,100	HIGH	MED-HIGH
CRANE		0.03						
Crane Ind School Dist	01007817		100.00	0.03	3	1,155	HIGH	MED-LOW
FRANKLIN		0.03						
Mt Vernon Ind School Dist	01018385		100.00	0.03	3	1,620	HIGH	MED-HIGH
GARZA		0.03						
Post Ind School Dist	01019597		89.16	0.03	3	810	HIGH	MED-HIGH
Southland Ind School Dist	01019638		10.84	0.00	1	132	HIGH	MED-HIGH
HANSFORD		0.03						
Spearman Ind School Dist	01022312		63.31	0.02	3	860	HIGH	MED-HIGH
Gruver Ind School Dist	01022257		26.58	0.01	3	400	HIGH	MED-LOW
Pringle-Morse Cons ISD	01022295		10.11	0.00	1	115	HIGH	MED-LOW

DISTRICT BUYING POWER INDEX

Market Data Retrieval

DISTRICT BUYING POWER INDEX
COUNTIES RANKED BY PERCENTAGE OF STATE SPENDING

COUNTY / DISTRICT	PID	COUNTY % OF STATE	DISTRICT % OF COUNTY	DISTRICT % OF STATES	NUMBER OF SCHOOLS	ENROLL	EXP	POV
HUDSPETH		0.03						
Ft Hancock Ind School Dist	01032173		53.39	0.02	3	410	HIGH	MED-HIGH
Sierra Blanca Ind School Dist	01032202		24.91	0.01	1	90	HIGH	MED-HIGH
Dell City Ind School Dist	01032147		21.71	0.01	1	65	HIGH	MED-HIGH
JIM HOGG		0.03						
Jim Hogg Co Ind School Dist	01034470		100.00	0.03	3	1,151	HIGH	HIGH
KIMBLE		0.03						
Junction Ind School Dist	01036155		100.00	0.03	3	615	HIGH	HIGH
KNOX		0.03						
Munday Consolidated Ind SD	01036533		53.04	0.02	2	375	HIGH	HIGH
Benjamin Ind School Dist	01036442		24.39	0.01	1	107	HIGH	MED-HIGH
Knox City-O'Brien Cons Ind SD	01036507		22.56	0.01	3	270	HIGH	MED-HIGH
LA SALLE		0.03						
Cotulla Ind School Dist	01037197		100.00	0.03	4	1,400	HIGH	HIGH
LIPSCOMB		0.03						
Booker Ind School Dist	01038139		51.22	0.02	2	398	HIGH	MED-LOW
Follett Ind School Dist	01038191		20.45	0.01	1	140	HIGH	MED-HIGH
Higgins Ind School Dist	01038220		15.17	0.00	1	125	HIGH	HIGH
Darrouzett Ind School Dist	01038165		13.16	0.00	1	120	HIGH	MED-HIGH
MASON		0.03						
Mason Ind School Dist	01040780		100.00	0.03	3	675	HIGH	MED-HIGH
RAINS		0.03						
Rains Ind School Dist	01047893		100.00	0.03	4	1,650	HIGH	MED-HIGH
REFUGIO		0.03						
Woodsboro Ind School Dist	01048495		48.07	0.01	2	420	HIGH	MED-HIGH
Refugio Ind School Dist	01048457		40.47	0.01	3	690	MED	MED-HIGH
Austwell Tivoli Ind SD	01048419		11.46	0.00	2	140	HIGH	HIGH
SAN SABA		0.03						
San Saba Ind School Dist	01049944		70.03	0.02	3	750	HIGH	MED-HIGH
Richland Springs Ind Sch Dist	01049918		21.11	0.01	1	120	HIGH	MED-LOW
Cherokee Ind School Dist	01049889		8.85	0.00	1	110	HIGH	MED-LOW
STEPHENS		0.03						
Breckenridge Ind School Dist	01051325		100.00	0.03	5	1,465	HIGH	MED-HIGH
SUTTON		0.03						
Sonora Ind School Dist	01051478		100.00	0.03	3	760	HIGH	MED-HIGH
WHEELER		0.03						
Wheeler Ind School Dist	01059896		35.84	0.01	1	487	HIGH	MED-HIGH
Shamrock Ind School Dist	01059858		31.93	0.01	3	426	HIGH	MED-HIGH
Kelton Ind School Dist	01059808		16.58	0.01	1	95	HIGH	MED-LOW
Ft Elliott Cons Ind Sch Dist	01059779		15.65	0.00	1	138	HIGH	MED-LOW
BAYLOR		0.02						
Seymour Ind School Dist	00996021		100.00	0.02	3	575	HIGH	MED-HIGH
BORDEN		0.02						
Borden Co Ind School Dist	01000546		100.00	0.02	1	230	HIGH	MED-HIGH
COCHRAN		0.02						
Whiteface Con Ind School Dist	01005728		53.93	0.01	2	325	HIGH	HIGH
Morton Ind School Dist	01005675		46.07	0.01	4	400	HIGH	HIGH
CONCHO		0.02						
Paint Rock Ind School Dist	01007245		60.91	0.01	1	240	HIGH	HIGH
Eden Cons Ind School Dist	01007180		39.09	0.01	2	215	HIGH	MED-HIGH
CULBERSON		0.02						
Culberson Co Allamoore Ind SD	01008029		100.00	0.02	1	400	HIGH	HIGH
DONLEY		0.02						
Clarendon Cons Ind Sch Dist	01014119		69.66	0.01	3	600	HIGH	HIGH
Hedley Ind School Dist	01014145		30.34	0.01	1	120	HIGH	MED-HIGH
EDWARDS		0.02						
Rocksprings Ind School Dist	01014901		57.45	0.01	1	290	HIGH	HIGH
Nueces Canyon Cons Ind SD	01014872		42.55	0.01	2	270	HIGH	HIGH
FISHER		0.02						
Roby Cons Ind School Dist	01017886		61.51	0.01	2	310	HIGH	MED-HIGH
Rotan Ind School Dist	01017915		38.49	0.01	2	250	HIGH	MED-HIGH

Texas School Directory

DISTRICT BUYING POWER INDEX

DISTRICT BUYING POWER INDEX
COUNTIES RANKED BY PERCENTAGE OF STATE SPENDING

COUNTY / DISTRICT	PID	COUNTY % OF STATE	DISTRICT % OF COUNTY	DISTRICT % OF STATES	NUMBER OF SCHOOLS	ENROLL	EXP	POV
GLASSCOCK		0.02						
Glasscock Co Ind School Dist	01019781		100.00	0.02	1	310	HIGH	MED-LOW
HALL		0.02						
Memphis Ind School Dist	01022087		75.71	0.02	4	500	HIGH	HIGH
Turkey-Quitaque Cons Ind SD	01022130		24.29	0.01	1	207	HIGH	HIGH
HARDEMAN		0.02						
Quanah Ind School Dist	01022398		76.41	0.02	3	525	HIGH	MED-HIGH
Chillicothe ISD School Dist	01022350		23.59	0.01	2	248	HIGH	HIGH
HASKELL		0.02						
Haskell Cons Ind School Dist	01028873		69.00	0.02	3	566	HIGH	MED-HIGH
Paint Creek Ind School Dist	01028914		22.19	0.01	1	102	HIGH	MED-HIGH
Rule Ind School Dist	01028964		8.82	0.00	1	130	MED	HIGH
KINNEY		0.02						
Brackett Ind School Dist	01036222		100.00	0.02	3	569	HIGH	MED-HIGH
SCHLEICHER		0.02						
Schleicher Co Ind Sch Dist	01049982		100.00	0.02	3	590	HIGH	MED-HIGH
SHACKELFORD		0.02						
Albany Ind School Dist	01050216		89.75	0.02	2	500	HIGH	MED-HIGH
Moran Ind School Dist	01050242		10.25	0.00	1	120	HIGH	HIGH
SHERMAN		0.02						
Stratford Ind School Dist	01050486		89.23	0.02	3	585	HIGH	MED-HIGH
Texhoma Ind School Dist	01050527		10.77	0.00	1	115	MED	MED-LOW
STERLING		0.02						
Sterling City Ind School Dist	01051387		100.00	0.02	2	320	HIGH	MED-HIGH
THROCKMORTON		0.02						
Woodson Ind School Dist	01055254		57.75	0.01	1	150	HIGH	MED-HIGH
Throckmorton Ind School Dist	01055228		42.25	0.01	1	175	HIGH	MED-HIGH
ARMSTRONG		0.01						
Claude Ind School Dist	00995302		100.00	0.01	1	330	HIGH	MED-LOW
BRISCOE		0.01						
Silverton Ind School Dist	01002300		100.00	0.01	1	195	HIGH	MED-HIGH
COKE		0.01						
Robert Lee Ind School Dist	01005780		58.53	0.01	1	290	HIGH	MED-HIGH
Bronte Ind School Dist	01005754		41.47	0.01	2	245	HIGH	MED-HIGH
COLLINGSWORTH		0.01						
Wellington Ind School Dist	01006708		100.00	0.01	3	580	HIGH	MED-HIGH
COTTLE		0.01						
Paducah Ind School Dist	01007776		100.00	0.01	1	210	HIGH	HIGH
CROCKETT		0.01						
Crockett Co Cons Common SD	01007855		100.00	0.01	3	758	HIGH	MED-HIGH
DICKENS		0.01						
Spur Ind School Dist	01013969		66.37	0.01	1	250	HIGH	MED-HIGH
Patton Springs Ind School Dist	01013933		33.63	0.00	1	111	HIGH	HIGH
FOARD		0.01						
Crowell Ind School Dist	01018086		100.00	0.01	2	200	HIGH	MED-HIGH
HARTLEY		0.01						
Hartley Ind School Dist	01028823		69.99	0.01	1	239	HIGH	MED-LOW
Channing Ind School Dist	01028794		30.01	0.00	1	181	HIGH	MED-LOW
HEMPHILL		0.01						
Canadian Ind School Dist	01029205		100.00	0.01	4	930	LOW	MED-LOW
IRION		0.01						
Irion Co Ind School Dist	01032862		100.00	0.01	2	275	HIGH	MED-LOW
JEFF DAVIS		0.01						
Fort Davis Ind School Dist	01033323		63.78	0.01	2	230	HIGH	MED-HIGH
Valentine Ind School Dist	01033359		36.22	0.00	1	30	HIGH	MED-HIGH
KENEDY		0.01						
Kenedy Co Wide Common Sch Dist	01035905		100.00	0.01	1	72	HIGH	MED-LOW
KING		0.01						
Guthrie Common School Dist	01036193		100.00	0.01	1	104	HIGH	MED-HIGH

DISTRICT BUYING POWER INDEX

Market Data Retrieval

DISTRICT BUYING POWER INDEX
COUNTIES RANKED BY PERCENTAGE OF STATE SPENDING

COUNTY / DISTRICT	PID	COUNTY % OF STATE	DISTRICT % OF COUNTY	DISTRICT % OF STATES	NUMBER OF SCHOOLS	ENROLL	EXP	POV
MCMULLEN		0.01						
McMullen Co Ind Sch Dist	01040560		100.00	0.01	1	287	HIGH	MED-LOW
MENARD		0.01						
Menard Ind School Dist	01041368		100.00	0.01	2	300	HIGH	HIGH
REAL		0.01						
Leakey Ind School Dist	01048055		100.00	0.01	1	309	HIGH	HIGH
ROBERTS		0.01						
Miami Ind School Dist	01048536		100.00	0.01	1	220	HIGH	MED-LOW
KENT		0.00						
Jayton-Girard Ind School Dist	01035931		100.00	0.00	1	163	HIGH	MED-HIGH
MOTLEY		0.00						
Motley Co Ind School Dist	01043043		100.00	0.00	1	151	HIGH	MED-HIGH
STONEWALL		0.00						
Aspermont Ind School Dist	01051416		100.00	0.00	2	240	HIGH	MED-HIGH
TERRELL		0.00						
Terrell Co Ind School Dist	01055046		100.00	0.00	1	130	HIGH	MED-HIGH

TX—C20   800-333-8802   School Year 2019-2020

Texas School Directory

NEW PUBLIC SCHOOLS AND KEY PERSONNEL

NEW SCHOOLS/NEW PRINCIPALS

SCHOOL	PRINCIPAL	GRADES	ENROLLMENT	COUNTY	PAGE
Charter Oak Elem Sch	Conner, Jennifer	K-5	400	Bell	26
Marshall Law & Med Svc Mag HS	Bray, Margaret	9-12	175	Bexar	38
Ywla Primary	McLerran, Delia	PK-1	159	Bexar	41
Anna Education Center	Medrano, Gabriel	6-6	401	Collin	77
Lowe Elem Sch	Coburn, Jeff	PK-5	450	Collin	84
Canyon Ranch Elem Sch	Minton, Ashley	K-5	700	Dallas	98
Lance Thompson Elem Sch	Howell, Amy	PK-5	500	Denton	125
Union Park Elem Sch	Salas, Lorena	PK-5	450	Denton	121
Cactus Trails Elem Sch	Thomas, Leslie	PK-5	401	El Paso	136
Joe M Adams Junior High Sch	Brodt, Elisabeth	6-8	135	Fort Bend	152
Olga Leonard Elem Sch	Vaughan, Stephanie	PK-5	670	Fort Bend	152
Florence Campbell Sch	Tite, Erin	PK-5	700	Galveston	159
Rose M Avalos P-Tech Sch	Delpilar, Diana	9-12	126	Harris	180
Spring Leadership Acad Mid Sch	Banks, Kevin	5-7	401	Harris	203
Springwoods Village Mid Sch	Culley, Kimberly	6-8	401	Harris	203
Idea Clg Prep-Achieve	Kim, Jaeil	5-7	250	Hidalgo	218
Young Women's Leadership Acad	Seybert, Jennifer	6-7	100	Midland	286
Suchma Elementary	Vandermark, Tara, Dr	PK-6	897	Montgomery	292
Arlington College & Career HS	Bholan, Ben, Dr	9-12	500	Tarrant	343
June W Davis Elem Sch	Hunt, Kevin	PK-5	550	Tarrant	348
Marine Creek Middle Sch	Knowles, Danny	6-8	1,000	Tarrant	349
Bee Cave Middle Sch	Prehn, Amanda	6-8	401	Travis	370
I Go Elem Sch	Wilson, Jack	PK-5	401	Williamson	396
Larkspur Elem Sch	Montanio, Tracie	K-5	440	Williamson	397

NEW PRINCIPALS

SCHOOL	PRINCIPAL	GRADES	ENROLLMENT	COUNTY	PAGE
Elkhart Middle Sch	Huff, Rebecca	6-8	277	Anderson	15
Frankston Middle Sch	Rodriguez, Edgar	6-8	219	Anderson	15
Andrews Alternative Sch	Johnson, Carlton	9-12	43	Andrews	16
Andrews High Sch	Carranco, John	9-12	1,056	Andrews	16
Andrews Middle Sch	Lowder, David	6-8	924	Andrews	16
Anderson Elem Sch	Fain, Amy	3-5	288	Angelina	18
Central Elem Sch	Wright, Amanda	PK-4	658	Angelina	17
Slack Elem Sch	Clifton, Yaneth	3-5	521	Angelina	18
Zavalla Elem Sch	Peyton, Angela	PK-5	178	Angelina	18
Zavalla High Sch	Cross, Patricia	6-12	190	Angelina	18
Rockport-Fulton High Sch	Mieth, Rhonda	9-12	781	Aransas	19
Archer City High Sch	Stafford, Amanda	7-12	219	Archer	19
Windthorst Junior High Sch	Longcrier, Roy	6-8	92	Archer	20
Charlotte High Sch	Brock, Brianne	9-12	150	Atascosa	20
Charlotte Middle Sch	Brock, Brianne	5-8	151	Atascosa	20
Jourdanton High Sch	Parsons, Virginia	9-12	429	Atascosa	20
Lytle Junior High Sch	Stewart, Elizabeth	6-8	394	Atascosa	21
Poteet Junior High Sch	Poth, Julie	6-8	381	Atascosa	21
Prairie Harbor Alternative Sch	Glover, Michael	5-12	50	Austin	22
Bandera Middle Sch	Sizemore, Patrick	6-8	518	Bandera	23
Bastrop High Sch	Gosselink, John	9-12	1,404	Bastrop	23
Lost Pines Elem Sch	Trost, Stacy	PK-4	632	Bastrop	24
Neidig Elem Sch	Borowicz, Sarah	PK-5	660	Bastrop	24
Red Rock Elem Sch	Hubley, Kelly	PK-4	641	Bastrop	24
Seymour High Sch	Arredondo, Adam	9-12	162	Baylor	25
Pettus Secondary Sch	DeLeon, Ricardo	6-12	234	Bee	25
Academy Elem Sch	Chaney, Andrea	PK-2	386	Bell	26
Academy High Sch	Remschel, Alex	9-12	453	Bell	26
Harker Heights High Sch	Soldevila, Jorge	9-12	2,550	Bell	28
Holland Elem Sch	Kinard, Lori	PK-5	311	Bell	27
Holland High Sch	Edwards, Robby	9-12	214	Bell	27
Liberty Hill Middle Sch	Brown, Latricia	6-8	847	Bell	28
Meridith-Dunbar EC Academy	Murphy, Nikki	PK-PK	514	Bell	29
Montague Village Elem Sch	Cue, Natalie	PK-5	605	Bell	28
Nolan Middle Sch	York, Ashley	6-8	757	Bell	28
Palo Alto Middle Sch	Hill, Kernisha	6-8	652	Bell	28
Reeces Creek Elem Sch	Watson, Sara	PK-5	900	Bell	28
STEM Academy-Killeen	Wolf, Chad	6-12	14	Bell	28
Thomas Arnold Elem Sch	Mullins, Julie	PK-5	887	Bell	29
Thornton Elem Sch	Moore, Michelle	K-5	734	Bell	29
West Ward Elem Sch	Thornhill, Tammy	PK-5	504	Bell	28
Western Hills Elem Sch	Vestal, Tiffany	PK-5	224	Bell	29
Willow Springs Elem Sch	Locke, Connie	PK-5	937	Bell	28

School Year 2019-2020 **800-333-8802**

NEW PUBLIC SCHOOLS AND KEY PERSONNEL

Market Data Retrieval

School	Contact	Grades	Enrollment	County	
Alamo Heights High Sch	Garinger, Debbie	9-12	1,578	Bexar	30
Alan B Shepard Middle Sch	Zavala, Frank	6-8	556	Bexar	42
Antonio Margil Academy	Galinzoga, Sandra	PK-5	557	Bexar	39
Bella Cameron Elem Sch	Lewis, Brandy	PK-5	454	Bexar	40
Bob Lewis Elem Sch	Merrell, Kendra	PK-5	698	Bexar	36
Bradley Middle Sch	Cerroni, Brenda	6-8	1,288	Bexar	34
Briscoe Academy	Emerson, Jennifer	PK-5	492	Bexar	40
Bush Middle Sch	Guthrie, Stuart	6-8	1,201	Bexar	34
Cable Elem Sch	Pinon, Debra	PK-5	679	Bexar	36
Carl Wanke Elem Sch	Sanchez, Claudia	PK-5	803	Bexar	36
Carroll Bell Elem Sch	Christenson, Gina, Dr	PK-5	469	Bexar	32
Carroll Early Chldhd Center	Barraza, Alejandra, Dr	PK-PK	306	Bexar	40
Cast STEM High Sch	Gardner, Aja, Dr	9-12	401	Bexar	43
Coronado Village Elem Sch	Guerrero, Liza	PK-5	283	Bexar	33
De Zavala Elem Sch	Finch, Donna	PK-5	600	Bexar	40
Democracy Prep Stewart [227]	Silva, Vivian	PK-5	448	Bexar	40
Dolores Linton Elem Sch	Ortega, Marty	PK-5	546	Bexar	37
Dr Harmon W Kelley Elem Sch	Peterson, Tiffany	PK-6	301	Bexar	42
Edgewood Fine Arts Academy	Pina, Daniel	9-12	200	Bexar	31
F R Scobee Elem Sch	Dudney, Jocelyn	PK-5	575	Bexar	37
Ferdinand Herff Academy	Allen, Kelly	PK-5	477	Bexar	40
Fields Elem Sch	Hammond, P Jennifer	PK-5	862	Bexar	37
Francis R Scobee Middle Sch	Cruz, Jorge	6-8	855	Bexar	43
Frank M Tejeda Academy	Balleza, Geraldine	6-12	185	Bexar	32
Frank Tejeda Middle Sch	Reyes, Martha	6-8	1,155	Bexar	35
Harmony Hills Elem Sch	Rochkus, Alan	PK-5	597	Bexar	35
Henry Metzger Middle Sch	Valree, Tracey	6-8	1,008	Bexar	33
Herbert Boldt Elem Sch	Siller, Ms	K-5	636	Bexar	37
Hillcrest Elem Sch	Lopez, Santa	PK-5	538	Bexar	40
Huppertz Elem Sch	Rios-Garcia, Linda	PK-5	400	Bexar	40
Inez Foster Academy	Diaz, Johnny	PK-5	604	Bexar	40
James Masters Elem Sch	Baker, Latanya	PK-5	279	Bexar	33
James Russell Lowell Mid Sch	Hernandez, Yvonne	6-8	407	Bexar	40
Jhw Inspire Acad-Williams Hse	Knox, Lois	3-12	34	Bexar	31
Jimmy Elrod Elem Sch	Flores, Mrs	PK-5	457	Bexar	37
Johnson High Sch	Comalander, Gary	9-12	3,086	Bexar	35
Kindred Elem Sch	Boysen, Eric	PK-5	409	Bexar	42
Kirby Middle Sch	Arredondo, Elizabeth	6-8	775	Bexar	33
Knox Early Chldhd Center	Kwiatkowski, Perla	PK-PK	256	Bexar	40
L B Johnson Elem Sch	Gearhart, Ellie	PK-5	515	Bexar	32
Las Lomas Elem Sch	Massey, Harold	PK-5	486	Bexar	35
Legacy of Educl Excellence HS	Crowe, David	9-12	2,642	Bexar	35
Loma Park Elem Sch	Gonzales, Roger	PK-5	696	Bexar	32
Medio Creek Elem Sch	Garza, Amy	PK-5	597	Bexar	43
Neil Armstrong Elem Sch	De La Pena, Phillip	PK-5	396	Bexar	42
Nimitz Middle Sch	Cooper, Jennifer	6-8	1,285	Bexar	35
Northern Hills Elem Sch	Wulfsberg, Marisa	PK-5	679	Bexar	35
Northside Alt Middle Sch South	Persyn, Anthony	6-8	125	Bexar	38
Northside Alt Middle Sch-North	Persyn, Anthony	6-8	120	Bexar	38
Oak Grove Elem Sch	Bloom, Taleen	PK-5	375	Bexar	35
Oak Hills Terrace Elem Sch	Robinson, Angela	PK-5	649	Bexar	38
Oak Meadow Elem Sch	Campos, Lisa	PK-5	449	Bexar	35
Patricia J Blattman Elem Sch	Macias, Raymond	PK-5	550	Bexar	38
Pershing Elem Sch	Handford, Thamesia	PK-5	424	Bexar	41
Rayburn Elem Sch	Santos, Juanita	PK-5	441	Bexar	33
Redland Oaks Elem Sch	Barr, Randy	PK-5	425	Bexar	35
Rhodes Middle Sch	Flores, Rick	6-8	685	Bexar	41
Roosevelt Elem Sch	Ortiz, Patricia, Dr	PK-5	497	Bexar	32
Roosevelt High Sch	Norwood, Bryan	9-12	2,819	Bexar	35
Roy Cisneros Elem Sch	Herrera, Jennifer, Dr	PK-5	502	Bexar	32
Savannah Heights Interm Sch	Falletich, Maru	5-6	642	Bexar	42
Serna Elem Sch	Lomas, Jennifer	PK-5	479	Bexar	35
Sidney Lanier High Sch	Ortiz, Moises	9-12	1,693	Bexar	41
Somerset Elem Sch	Padilla, Tracy	1-4	694	Bexar	42
Stafford Elem Sch	Salazar, Wendy	PK-5	493	Bexar	32
Stone Oak Elem Sch	Karrer, Ann	PK-5	855	Bexar	35
Thousand Oaks Elem Sch	Salazar, Holly	PK-5	743	Bexar	36
Tradition Elem Sch	Kopeck, Karen	PK-5	900	Bexar	31
West Campus High Sch	Hernandez, Lee, Dr	9-9	401	Bexar	43
Wetmore Elem Sch	Leach, Catherine	PK-5	681	Bexar	36
Winston Churchill High Sch	Bloomer, Todd	9-12	2,932	Bexar	36
Zamora Middle Sch	Mauldin, Daniel	6-8	776	Bexar	43
Blanco Middle Sch	Kinney, Brad	6-8	269	Blanco	46
Lyndon B Johnson High Sch	Maedgen, Russell	9-12	240	Blanco	46
Lyndon B Johnson Middle Sch	Norton, Michael	5-8	208	Blanco	46
Borden County Sch	Gordon, Britt	K-12	230	Borden	46

Texas School Directory

NEW PUBLIC SCHOOLS AND KEY PERSONNEL

School	Contact	Grades	Enrollment	County	Page
Kopperl Sch	Underwood, Jay	PK-12	225	Bosque	47
De Kalb Elem Sch	Hodgson, Melinda	PK-4	331	Bowie	48
Eschool Prep Virtual Sch	Power, Nanette	5-11	1,000	Bowie	50
James Bowie High Sch	Hudgeons, Lisa	9-12	165	Bowie	50
Oakview Primary Sch	Reid, Melissa	PK-2	379	Bowie	49
Pleasant Grove High Sch	Marshall, Todd	9-12	671	Bowie	49
Redwater High Sch	Cook, Brad	9-12	341	Bowie	49
Assets Academy	Johanson, Brandy	9-12	156	Brazoria	51
Berry Miller Junior High Sch	Barcelona, Tony	7-8	906	Brazoria	53
Challenger Elem Sch	Morris, Becky	PK-4	683	Brazoria	53
Damon Sch	Hayward, David	PK-8	200	Brazoria	53
Danbury High Sch	Pounds, Crystal	9-12	231	Brazoria	53
G W Harby Junior High Sch	Lawson, Elizabeth	6-8	756	Brazoria	51
Manvel High Sch	Flowers, Aneiqua	9-12	1,826	Brazoria	51
O M Roberts Elem Sch	Nabors, Jennifer	PK-4	519	Brazoria	52
Pomona Elem Sch	Kwan, Victoria	PK-5	402	Brazoria	51
Creek View Elem Sch	Roraback, Annette	PK-4	595	Brazos	55
Fannin Elem Sch	Caperton, Desiree, Dr	PK-4	460	Brazos	55
Johnson Elem Sch	Thomman, Amy	PK-4	404	Brazos	55
Mary Catherine Harris Sch	Kaspar, Karen	9-12	228	Brazos	55
River Bend Elem Sch	Jones, Robyn	PK-4	450	Brazos	56
Southwood Valley Elem Sch	DeLuna, Alison	PK-4	638	Brazos	56
Spring Creek Elem Sch	Casper-Teague, Laura	PK-4	640	Brazos	56
Sul Ross Elem Sch	Bay, Amy	PK-4	507	Brazos	55
Alpine High Sch	Gonzales, Justin	9-12	314	Brewster	56
Bangs High Sch	Patrick, Scott	9-12	327	Brown	58
Coggin Intermediate Sch	Spruell, Sandra	4-6	700	Brown	58
Early High Sch	Ozuna, Judy	9-12	370	Brown	59
East Elem Sch	Wright, Dee	PK-3	320	Brown	58
Genesis Academy	Hughes, Mercathia	6-8	35	Brown	58
May High Sch	Heupel, Nicholas	7-12	152	Brown	59
Caldwell Middle Sch	Savage, Shaunna	6-8	413	Burleson	59
Snook Sch	Everett, Christi	PK-12	500	Burleson	59
Snook Sch	Frauenberger, Rick	PK-12	500	Burleson	59
Somerville Intermediate Sch	Pinkerton, Joshua	5-7	192	Burleson	60
Bertram Elem Sch	Harris, Alicia	PK-5	376	Burnet	60
Burnet Middle Sch	LeJeune, Jeremy	6-8	762	Burnet	60
Highland Lakes Elem Sch	Talamantes, Leslie	PK-5	603	Burnet	60
R J Richey Elem Sch	Steiner, Bobbie	3-5	559	Burnet	60
Prairie Lea Sch	Guillory, Monica	PK-12	210	Caldwell	61
Seadrift Sch	Bermea, Lynda	PK-8	294	Calhoun	62
Cross Plains Elem Sch	Barron, Jeanette	PK-6	204	Callahan	62
Cross Plains High Sch	Jones, Wesley	7-12	164	Callahan	62
Eula High Sch	Damron, Wayland	9-12	106	Callahan	63
Angela Leal Elem Sch	Ramirez, Rudy	PK-5	426	Cameron	67
Burns Elem Sch	Rodriguez-Bohn, Leticia	PK-5	802	Cameron	63
College Career & Tech Acad	Gomez, Jeri	9-12	31	Cameron	66
Cromack Elem Sch	Hernandez, L	PK-5	594	Cameron	63
Dr C M Cash Elem Sch	Araiza, Marleen	PK-5	608	Cameron	67
Elma Barrera Elem Sch	Camarillo, Gregorio	PK-5	531	Cameron	67
Frank Roberts Elem Sch	Diaz, Rolando	PK-5	340	Cameron	67
Gutierriez Middle Sch	Mike Reyes, Gutierrez	6-8	841	Cameron	65
Harlingen High Sch	Bauer, Vivian	9-12	1,827	Cameron	65
Judge Oscar De La Fuente ES	Flores, Olivia	PK-5	398	Cameron	67
Laureles Elem Sch	Larrasquitu, Claudia	PK-5	636	Cameron	66
Liberty Middle Sch	Garza, Annice	6-8	788	Cameron	66
Los Fresnos Elem Sch	Grimaldo, Veronica	PK-5	603	Cameron	66
Memorial Middle Sch	Snavely, William	6-8	806	Cameron	65
Rancho Verde Elem Sch	Chavez, Mary	PK-5	663	Cameron	66
Rio Hondo Middle Sch	Moreno, Ramiro	5-8	405	Cameron	66
Rodriguez Elem Sch	Arellano, Adriana	PK-5	731	Cameron	65
Sam Houston Elem Sch	Cazares, Hector	PK-4	514	Cameron	65
Santa Maria High Sch	Vela, Jose	9-12	201	Cameron	67
STEM2 Preparatory Academy	Brandenburg, Sonya	6-8	250	Cameron	65
Panhandle Elem Sch	Mitchell, Allison	PK-5	341	Carson	69
Bloomburg Sch	Barron, Amy	PK-12	270	Cass	70
Daep Center	Boyce, Pamela	K-12	20	Cass	69
McLeod Sch	Whittemore, Shana	K-12	388	Cass	70
McLeod Sch	Lance, Jennifer	K-12	388	Cass	70
McLeod Sch	Lambeth, Erin	K-12	388	Cass	70
Queen City High Sch	Holmes, Steve	9-12	314	Cass	71
Richardson Elem Sch	Flores, Marittsa	PK-4	560	Castro	71
Barbers Hill Middle Sch South	Wagner, Dennis	6-8	695	Chambers	72
East Chambers Elem Sch	Dale, Becky	3-5	300	Chambers	72
East Chambers High Sch	Duoto, Tom	9-12	435	Chambers	72
Jacksonville High Sch	Peacock, Ben	9-12	1,311	Cherokee	73

NEW PUBLIC SCHOOLS AND KEY PERSONNEL

School	Contact	Grades	Enrollment	County	
Rusk High Sch	Snow, Ronny	9-12	601	Cherokee	73
Rusk Intermediate Sch	Evans, Jan	4-5	310	Cherokee	73
Petrolia Elem Sch	Travis, Barnes	PK-6	282	Clay	74
Bronte High Sch	Phillips, John	7-12	131	Coke	75
Coleman Junior High Sch	King, Thomas	5-8	248	Coleman	76
Santa Anna High Sch	Sturgeon, James	7-12	116	Coleman	76
Bennett & Alma Griffin Mid Sch	Hill, Tommy	6-8	867	Collin	78
Benton A Staley Middle Sch	Robinson, Anita	6-8	662	Collin	78
Billy Vandeventer Middle Sch	Taylor, Stephanie	6-8	1,084	Collin	79
Boon Elem Sch	Cypert, Lauren	PK-6	702	Collin	76
Calvin Bledsoe Elem Sch	Klingenberg, Sherry	K-5	683	Collin	79
Carylene McClendon Elem Sch	Salinas, Gilberto	PK-5	605	Collin	78
Community High Sch	Westfall, Michael	9-12	622	Collin	78
Comstock Elem Sch	Dalton, Amanda	K-5	732	Collin	79
Farmersville Jr High Sch	Warren, Dave	6-8	418	Collin	78
Frisco High Sch	Barrentine, Daniel	9-12	1,525	Collin	79
Frisco ISD Early Childhood Sch	Birdwell, Bethany	PK-PK	760	Collin	79
Furr Elem Sch	Zukowski, Cindy	K-5	760	Collin	84
Gene M Reed Elem Sch	Streitmatter, Ardath	PK-6	583	Collin	77
George Anderson Elem Sch	Koder, Chris	PK-6	521	Collin	77
Harrington Elem Sch	Jamar, Jacye	PK-5	411	Collin	82
Harry McKillop Elem Sch	Womack, Krissy	PK-5	834	Collin	81
Hays Middle Sch	Jones, Nicholas	6-8	800	Collin	84
Heritage High Sch	Gray, Katey, Dr	9-12	2,188	Collin	79
JW & Ruth Christie Elem Sch	Brewer, Paige	K-5	534	Collin	79
Lamar & Norma Hunt Middle Sch	Clark, Chris	6-8	811	Collin	79
Lizzie Nell C McClure Elem Sch	Hafner, Maria	K-5	645	Collin	81
Mitchell Elem Sch	Liner, Lariza	PK-5	798	Collin	83
Naomi Press Elem Sch	Constantinescu, Rachel	K-5	584	Collin	81
Olson Elem Sch	Miller, Susanne	PK-6	651	Collin	77
Plano Head Start Center	Lohmiller, Denise, Dr	PK-PK	146	Collin	83
Plano ISD Academy High Sch	Ojeda, Lynn	9-12	447	Collin	83
Reba Cobb Carroll Elem Sch	Waldrip, John	K-5	528	Collin	80
Robert Cobb Middle Sch	Lakey, Jamie	6-8	949	Collin	80
Robinson Middle Sch	Roberston, Kennitra	6-8	1,011	Collin	83
Rogers Middle Sch	Jetton, Jason	6-8	1,420	Collin	84
Roy Lee Walker Elem Sch	Raleeh, Melanie	K-5	567	Collin	81
Sam & Ann Roach Middle Sch	McDonald, Natasha	6-8	855	Collin	80
Schell Elem Sch	Farris, Bob	K-5	673	Collin	83
Stuber Elem Sch	Hinson, Jennifer, Dr	K-5	780	Collin	84
Student Opportunity Center	Theodore, Kecia	9-12	150	Collin	80
Tibbals Elem Sch	Fletcher, Jamie	PK-4	686	Collin	85
Wally Watkins Elem Sch	Wiseman, Jennifer	PK-4	562	Collin	85
Williams High Sch	Endsley, Matthew	9-10	1,107	Collin	83
Wellington Junior High Sch	Beck, Edward	6-8	112	Collingsworth	86
Columbus Alternative Sch	Koehl, Michael	7-12	60	Colorado	86
Rice Junior High Sch	Leist, Brian	6-8	251	Colorado	87
Clear Spring Elem Sch	Hardin, Janelle	PK-5	759	Comal	88
Comal Academy	Lehmberg, Lori	11-12	51	Comal	88
County Line Elem Sch	Danielle, Taylor	PK-5	368	Comal	88
Indian Springs Elem Sch	Stults, Mary	PK-5	810	Comal	88
Klein Road Elem Sch	Lopez, Marisela	PK-5	483	Comal	88
Lamar Elem Sch	Russell, Christopher	PK-5	371	Comal	88
Seele Elem Sch	Callahan, Deanna	PK-5	408	Comal	89
Veramendi Elem Sch	Droddy, Leah	PK-5	743	Comal	89
Comanche High Sch	Lewis, Steven	9-12	323	Comanche	89
Gustine Sch	Eudy, Kenny	PK-12	161	Comanche	90
Callisburg Elem Sch	Herring, Lisa	PK-5	565	Cooke	90
Callisburg Middle High Sch	Werts, Bronwyn	6-12	590	Cooke	90
Callisburg Middle High Sch	Hooper, Jason	6-12	590	Cooke	90
Gainesville Jr High Sch	Beal, Krista	7-8	471	Cooke	91
Valley View Sch	Newton, Jesse	PK-12	815	Cooke	91
Copperas Cove High Sch	Shuck, Jimmy, Dr	9-12	2,214	Coryell	92
Gatesville Elem Sch	Webb, Keegan	1-3	619	Coryell	93
Gatesville Intermediate Sch	Register, Bridget	4-6	594	Coryell	93
Crane High Sch	Cross, Stephen	9-12	324	Crane	93
Crane Middle Sch	Heredia, Arick	6-8	261	Crane	93
Ralls Elem Sch	Feaster, Amy	PK-5	280	Crosby	94
Van Horn Schools	Gonzalez, Charles	PK-12	400	Culberson	95
A C New Middle Sch	Jackson, Regina	6-8	980	Dallas	110
Ann Richards Steam Academy	Shaw, Natasha	6-8	1,324	Dallas	98
Anne Frank Elem Sch	Ford, Beverly	PK-5	1,145	Dallas	98
Arch H McCulloch Interm Sch	Moran, Clifton	5-6	1,133	Dallas	108
Arlington Park ECC	Molinares, Mary	PK-PK	150	Dallas	99
Austin Middle Sch	Barrett, Channa, Dr	6-8	992	Dallas	109
Back Elem Sch	Ramos, Amanda	PK-5	450	Dallas	105

Texas School Directory

NEW PUBLIC SCHOOLS AND KEY PERSONNEL

School	Contact	Grades	Enrollment	District	Page
Beaver Tech Ctr-Math & Science	Devantier, Vicki	PK-5	573	Dallas	105
Ben Tisinger Elem Sch	Relf, Amanda	PK-5	824	Dallas	110
Berkner High Sch	Cage, Kristy	9-12	2,642	Dallas	112
Billy Earl Dade Middle Sch	Stewart, Rockell	6-8	894	Dallas	99
Bradfield Elem Sch	Bados, Cecilia	PK-5	498	Dallas	105
Bray Elem Sch	Barnes, Eric	PK-5	272	Dallas	97
Bussey Middle Sch	Oliphant, Jeremiah	6-8	944	Dallas	105
C J & Anne Hyman Elem Sch	Ross, Derrick	PK-4	668	Dallas	104
Cedar Crest Elem Sch	Jawaid, Constance	PK-5	410	Dallas	99
Cedar Hill Collegiate High Sch	Stevens, Deidrea	9-12	403	Dallas	97
Cedar Hill High Sch	Miller, Jason	10-12	1,707	Dallas	97
Celestino Mauricio Soto ES	Barrayam, Norma	PK-5	588	Dallas	99
Cesar Chavez Learning Center	Wilson, Sheryl	PK-5	470	Dallas	99
Charles M Blalack Middle Sch	Davis, Keith	6-8	969	Dallas	96
Cisneros Pre-K Sch	Kiser, Andy	PK-PK	566	Dallas	105
Colin Powell Elem Sch	Sterling, Marchelle	PK-5	534	Dallas	107
Coppell High Sch	Springer, Laura	10-12	3,000	Dallas	98
Coppell Middle School East	Glover, Steve	6-8	972	Dallas	98
Coyle Middle Sch	Washington, Kenneth	6-8	1,033	Dallas	105
Crockett Middle Sch	Johnson, Bianca	6-8	909	Dallas	109
Dallas Environmental Sci Acad	Rider, Aris	6-8	443	Dallas	99
Dan D Rogers Elem Sch	Limon, Marissa	PK-5	503	Dallas	99
Daniels Academy of Science and	Maynard-Walter, Marva	PK-5	439	Dallas	107
Dr Linda Henrie Elem Sch	Lovato, Lisa	PK-6	961	Dallas	111
Duncanville High Sch	McDonald, Michael	9-12	4,268	Dallas	104
Duncanville HS Collegiate Acad	Thomas, Pamela	9-12	210	Dallas	104
E S McKenzie Elem Sch	Langston, Emmalee	K-6	538	Dallas	111
East Middle Sch	Hannible, Deidre	6-8	596	Dallas	104
Ebby Halliday Elem Sch	Ward, Amy	PK-5	638	Dallas	99
Ed Vanston Middle Sch	Smith, Melissa	7-8	805	Dallas	111
Esperanza Medrano Elementary	Mondragon, Mario	PK-5	398	Dallas	100
Fairmeadows Elem Sch	Villarreal, Sugey	PK-4	482	Dallas	105
Farmers Branch Elem Sch	Brown, Shanah	PK-5	550	Dallas	97
Frank D Moates Elem Sch	Lunkin, Tarsha	PK-5	768	Dallas	104
Franklin D Roosevelt High Sch	Tyson, Troy	9-12	712	Dallas	100
Franklin Monroe Gilbert ES	Ruiz, Claudia	K-5	715	Dallas	109
Frederick Douglass Elem Sch	Allen, Tenisha	PK-5	481	Dallas	100
Galloway Elem Sch	Sarpy, April	PK-6	732	Dallas	111
Geneva Heights Elem Sch	Ruiz, Michael	PK-5	348	Dallas	100
Gilbreath-Reed Career Tech Ctr	Bruman, Coleman	Voc	500	Dallas	106
Grand Prairie Early Clg HS	Boyle, Laigha	9-12	150	Dallas	107
Grand Prairie High Sch	Boyle, Laigha	9-12	2,806	Dallas	107
Hastings Elem Sch	Simpson, Wendy	PK-4	591	Dallas	105
Hector P Garcia Middle Sch	Lee, David	6-8	764	Dallas	100
Herbert Marcus Elem Sch	Romero, Jonatan	PK-5	780	Dallas	100
Hickman Elem Sch	Beltran, Karla	PK-5	499	Dallas	106
High Pointe Elem Sch	Whittaker, Shay	PK-5	486	Dallas	97
Highland Meadows Elem Sch	Bahena, Jo'Anna	PK-5	760	Dallas	100
Highland Park Middle Sch	Gilbert, Jeremy	7-8	1,106	Dallas	108
Hudson Middle Sch	Hope, Amber	6-8	1,232	Dallas	106
I N Range Elem Sch	Locke, Kelly	K-6	763	Dallas	111
Int'l Ldrshp TX-Keller Saginaw	Layne, Valerie	9-12	550	Dallas	109
Int'l Ldrshp TX-Wml-Orem HS	Mott, Stephanie	9-9	100	Dallas	109
Jack E Singley Academy	Kibodeaux, Melanie	9-12	1,733	Dallas	109
Janie Stark Elem Sch	Putman, Jennifer	PK-5	745	Dallas	97
Jerry Junkins Elem Sch	Spurlock, Oscar	PK-5	676	Dallas	100
Jess Harben Elem Sch	Newman, Sharon	PK-6	391	Dallas	112
John F Peeler Elem Sch	Carballo, Janie	PK-5	323	Dallas	101
John L Patton Academic Center	Brooks, Marlon	9-12	210	Dallas	101
John Q Adams Elem Sch	Totsuka, Maria	PK-5	749	Dallas	101
Juan Seguin Elem Sch	Rodriguez, Amanda	PK-5	487	Dallas	107
Katherine Johnson Tech Mag Sch	Batiste, Angela	K-5	810	Dallas	104
Kimberlin Acad for Excellence	Sullivan, Tammy	PK-5	485	Dallas	106
L F Blanton Elem Sch	Badillo, Patricia	PK-5	419	Dallas	97
L G Pinkston High Sch	Brooks, Marlon	9-12	906	Dallas	101
Lake Ridge Elem Sch	McCullum, Marquita	PK-5	328	Dallas	97
Lee A McShan Jr Elem Sch	Medaris, Joseph	PK-5	641	Dallas	101
Liberty Grove Elem Sch	Bottoms, Debra	PK-5	499	Dallas	106
Mark Twain Elem Sch	Traylor, Pertricee	PK-5	299	Dallas	101
Martin Luther King Jr Lrng Ctr	Sneed, Romikianta	PK-5	439	Dallas	101
Maya Angelou High Sch	Bratton, Billy	6-12	24	Dallas	101
Memorial Pathway Academy	Perales, Ida	6-12	249	Dallas	106
Mesquite Academy Aec of Choice	Joseph, Abram	9-12	167	Dallas	111
Mesquite High Sch	Sarpy, Gerald	9-12	2,904	Dallas	111
Montclair Elem Sch	Massey, Karla	PK-5	551	Dallas	106
Mt Auburn Elem Sch	Swanson, Brittany	PK-4	710	Dallas	102

School Year 2019-2020

NEW PUBLIC SCHOOLS AND KEY PERSONNEL — Market Data Retrieval

School	Contact	Grades	Enrollment	County	Code
N W Harllee Early Chldhd Ctr	Shields, Amber	PK-2	206	Dallas	102
Naaman Forest High Sch	Ellis, Keith, Dr	9-12	2,150	Dallas	106
Nimitz High Sch	Miranda, Francisco	9-12	2,480	Dallas	110
Nita Pearson Elem Sch	Wilson, Cherelle	PK-5	677	Dallas	106
O'Banion Middle Sch	Gilmore, Earl	6-8	1,110	Dallas	106
Obadiah Knight Elem Sch	Rojo, Blanca	PK-5	511	Dallas	102
Otis Brown Elem Sch	Bloomfield, Maria	K-5	816	Dallas	110
Pathfinder Achievement Center	Ajibola, Lacey	Spec	46	Dallas	106
Ronald E McNair Elem Sch	Bell, Demetria	PK-5	602	Dallas	102
Rosemont Primary Sch	Barker, Marco	PK-2	540	Dallas	102
Rowlett Elem Sch	Bain, Kim	PK-5	549	Dallas	106
Rowlett High Sch	Blakey, Carmen	9-12	2,577	Dallas	106
Skyline High Sch	Simmons, Dwain	9-12	4,535	Dallas	102
Smith Elem Sch	Stephens, Celee	PK-4	355	Dallas	105
Spring Creek Elem Sch	McCutcheon, Teresa	PK-5	613	Dallas	106
Summit Education Center	Brown, Mekasha	K-12	140	Dallas	105
Sunnyvale High Sch	Nickel, Brian	9-12	528	Dallas	113
Tom C Gooch Elem Sch	Johnson, Kay	PK-5	428	Dallas	103
Tom W Field Elem Sch	Deboskie, Selena	PK-5	263	Dallas	103
Townsell Elem Sch	Brooks, Amber	K-5	795	Dallas	110
Townview Mag HS-Bus & Mngmnt	Rivera, Israel	9-12	491	Dallas	103
Village Fair-Elem Daep	Bratton, Billy	K-6	4	Dallas	103
Vivian Field Middle Sch	Hunter, Chad	6-8	1,006	Dallas	97
Walnut Hill Elem Sch	Potter, Phillip	PK-5	358	Dallas	103
Waterford Oaks Elem Sch	Phillips, Bill	PK-5	565	Dallas	97
Watson Tech Center Math & Sci	Leday, Adrian	PK-5	583	Dallas	107
Weaver Elem Sch	Thomason, Jennifer	PK-5	583	Dallas	107
Webb Middle Sch	Wilson, Nikketta, Dr	6-8	1,137	Dallas	107
West Middle Sch	Hawthorne, Shana	6-8	673	Dallas	104
Whitt Fine Arts Academy	Wyatt, April	PK-5	649	Dallas	108
Yale Elem Sch	Greer, Carrie	PK-6	427	Dallas	113
Young Womens Leadership Acad	Burns, Janna	6-12	895	Dallas	108
Zan Wesley Holmes Jr Mid Sch	Carter, Tangela	6-8	952	Dallas	104
Klondike Sch	Therwhanger, Danielle	PK-12	275	Dawson	117
Tierra Blanca Early Child Cent	Bice, Brenda	PK-PK	340	Deaf Smith	119
Cooper Jr Sr High Sch	Roan, Richard	6-12	427	Delta	120
Alice Moore Elementary	Henderson, Lindsay	PK-5	582	Denton	121
Arbor Creek Middle Sch	Obenhaus, Amy	6-8	910	Denton	122
Argyle West Elem Sch	Funderburg, Renee	PK-5	401	Denton	120
Brent Elem Sch	Kuster, Karie	PK-5	691	Denton	124
Career Center East	Moreno, Adrian	Voc	450	Denton	122
Clear Creek Intermediate Sch	Herrell, Sally	3-5	386	Denton	126
Dale Jackson Career Center	Gilbreath, Justin	Voc	500	Denton	123
Downing Middle Sch	Martin, Curt	6-8	546	Denton	123
Flower Mound Elem Sch	Van Scoyoc, Christy	PK-5	475	Denton	123
Flower Mound High Sch	Russell, Chad	10-12	2,619	Denton	123
Fred Moore High Sch	San Miguel, Jacqueline	9-12	49	Denton	121
Griffin Middle Sch	Garrison, Heather	6-8	805	Denton	123
Hodge Elem Sch	Hare, Andrea	PK-5	584	Denton	121
Lakeland Elem Sch	Asbun, Vanesa	PK-5	844	Denton	123
Lakeview Middle Sch	Deister, Beri	6-8	707	Denton	123
Lamar Middle Sch	Casal, Kristy	6-8	718	Denton	123
Lewisville HS-Killough	Tyler, Kyndra	9-10	1,125	Denton	123
Lizzie Curtis Elem Sch	Pierce, Carrie	PK-5	507	Denton	125
Monaco Elem Sch	Pitt, Barbara	PK-5	551	Denton	120
O A Peterson Elem Sch	Grimes, Danielle	PK-5	769	Denton	125
Oak Point Elem Sch	Werth, Kori	PK-5	722	Denton	124
Pecan Creek Elem Sch	Bomar, Amanda	PK-5	703	Denton	121
Peters Colony Elem Sch	Chirinos, Rebecca	PK-5	662	Denton	124
Purnell Support Center	LaRocque, Shawnda	Spec	100	Denton	124
Rockbrook Elem Sch	Guy, Patrick	PK-5	757	Denton	124
Sanger Middle Sch	Cain, Jim	7-8	405	Denton	126
Stewart's Creek Elem Sch	Smith, Andrea	PK-5	370	Denton	124
Thomas O Hicks Elem Sch	Bevill-Nelson, Misty	PK-5	596	Denton	124
Tomas Rivera Elem Sch	White, Marvyn	PK-5	604	Denton	121
Bernarda Jaime Jr High Sch	Vela, Nita	6-8	333	Duval	128
Collins-Parr Elem Sch	Perez, Monica	PK-5	748	Duval	128
Ramirez Elem Sch	Gonzalez, Yliana	PK-6	30	Duval	128
Gorman High Sch	Kunkel, Kelly	9-12	83	Eastland	129
Gorman Middle Sch	Kunkel, Kelly	6-8	72	Eastland	129
Maxfield Elem Sch	Sandoval, Fernando	PK-5	151	Eastland	129
Siebert Elem Sch	Chesser, Brandon	PK-5	563	Eastland	129
Bowie Middle Sch	Ellington, Brian	6-8	1,223	Ector	130
Dowling Elem Sch	Regalado, Kristabel	K-5	516	Ector	130
Dr Lee Buice Elem Sch	Rickman, Jessica	K-5	649	Ector	130
Ector Clg Prep Success Acad	Quintela, Charles	6-8	1,568	Ector	130

Texas School Directory

NEW PUBLIC SCHOOLS AND KEY PERSONNEL

School	Principal	Grades	Enrollment	County	Page
Ector Co Youth Alt Center	Portillo, Adam	6-12	104	Ector	130
George W Bush New Tech Odessa	Ramirez, Gerardo	9-12	333	Ector	130
Gonzales Elem Sch	Moad, Angie	K-5	416	Ector	130
Lauro Cavazos Elem Sch	Montelongo, Amanda	K-5	764	Ector	130
Noel Elem Sch	Chavez, Jennie	3-5	534	Ector	130
Odessa Career Tch Early Clg HS	Miller, Karl	9-9	174	Ector	130
Travis Magnet Elem Sch	Voss, Linda	K-5	333	Ector	130
Wilson & Young Middle Sch	Garza, Anthony	6-8	961	Ector	130
Nueces Canyon Elem Sch	Moore, Shawna	PK-6	168	Edwards	131
Rocksprings Sch	McCraw, Brian	PK-12	290	Edwards	131
About Face Alternative ES	Martinez, Bertha	K-5	44	El Paso	133
Aoy Elem Sch	Haynes, Sylvia	PK-5	477	El Paso	133
Armendariz Middle Sch	Ontiveros, Cynthia, Dr	6-8	541	El Paso	134
Brown Middle Sch	Favela, Corina	6-8	963	El Paso	134
Burges High Sch	Smith, Christopher	9-12	1,553	El Paso	134
Campestre Elem Sch	Avila, Jennifer	PK-5	587	El Paso	136
Canutillo Middle Sch	Medina, Daniel	6-8	585	El Paso	132
Carroll T Welch Elem Sch	Vasquez, Alma	PK-5	902	El Paso	132
Cesar Chavez Academy	Nava, Lionel	7-12	72	El Paso	137
Cielo Vista Elem Sch	Rodriguez, Bertha	PK-5	402	El Paso	133
Clardy Elem Sch	Booker, Mark	PK-5	489	El Paso	133
College Career Technology Acad	Rojas, Fred	9-12	352	El Paso	134
Crosby Elem Sch	Barraza, Alonzo	PK-5	542	El Paso	133
Desert View Middle Sch	Salgado, Javier	7-8	350	El Paso	137
Douglass Elem Sch	Guerra, Maria	PK-5	343	El Paso	133
Fabens High Sch	Prado, Anthony	9-12	761	El Paso	135
Fabens Middle Sch	Torres, Nancy	6-8	499	El Paso	135
Franklin High Sch	Mena, Shawn	9-12	2,806	El Paso	134
Gonzalo & Sofia Garcia ES	Heimer, Teresa	PK-5	504	El Paso	132
Guillen Middle Sch	Lyons, Monica	6-8	777	El Paso	134
Henderson Middle Sch	Yturralde, Jason	6-8	731	El Paso	135
Hueco Elem Sch	Garcia, Daisy	PK-5	546	El Paso	136
Jefferson High Sch	Gallegos, Armando, Dr	9-12	1,056	El Paso	134
Johnson Elem Sch	Gustafson, Peggy	PK-5	472	El Paso	133
Lebarron Park Elem Sch	Balderrama, Maritza	K-5	640	El Paso	138
Lujan-Chavez Elem Sch	Eksaengsri, Jina	PK-5	1,126	El Paso	136
Mesa Vista Elem Sch	Sierra, Norma	PK-6	442	El Paso	138
Morehead Middle Sch	Gustafson, Peggy	6-8	640	El Paso	135
Moye Elem Sch	Medina, Jessie	PK-5	518	El Paso	133
North Star Elem Sch	Lahrman, Stephanie	PK-6	478	El Paso	138
O'Shea Keleher Elem Sch	Lujan-Garcia, Laura	PK-5	893	El Paso	136
Parkland Middle Sch	Reyna, Angela	6-8	1,282	El Paso	138
Parkland Pre-K Center	Lopez, Rita	PK-PK	347	El Paso	138
Paul Moreno Elem Sch	Pancoast, Robert	PK-5	488	El Paso	134
Pebble Hills Elem Sch	Youngs, Irene	PK-5	768	El Paso	138
Ramona Elem Sch	Ahumada, Irene	PK-6	293	El Paso	138
Riverside Middle Sch	Valtierra, Jacob	7-8	525	El Paso	138
Scotsdale Elem Sch	Guzman, Juan	PK-6	850	El Paso	138
Silva Health Magnet High Sch	Gallegos, Armando, Dr	9-12	721	El Paso	134
Terrace Hills Middle Sch	Ewing, Leticia	6-8	488	El Paso	135
Tierra Del Sol Elem Sch	Romero, Michelle	PK-6	718	El Paso	138
Young Women's Steam Prep Acad	Ontiveros, Cynthia, Dr	6-7	401	El Paso	134
Ysleta Pre-K Center	Karns, Heather	PK-PK	691	El Paso	138
Avalon Sch	Hernandez, Tony	PK-12	350	Ellis	140
Avalon Sch	Tennery, Jody	PK-12	350	Ellis	140
Baxter Elem Sch	Timm, Ryan	PK-5	613	Ellis	141
Ferris High Sch	Gilbert, Andru	9-12	758	Ellis	140
Ferris Junior High Sch	Lowery, C	7-8	586	Ellis	140
Italy Jr Sr High Sch	Lawson, Jason	6-12	281	Ellis	141
Maypearl Middle Sch	Garrison, Matthew	5-8	217	Ellis	141
Russell Schupmann Elem Sch	Jackson, Ashley	PK-5	411	Ellis	142
Shackelford Elem Sch	East, Rusty	PK-5	602	Ellis	142
Turner Prekindergarten Academy	Foster, Stefani	PK-PK	188	Ellis	142
Waxahachie High Sch	Harris, Tonya	9-12	2,204	Ellis	142
Central Elem Sch	Tucker, Esther	PK-K	413	Erath	144
Dublin Elem Sch	Mitchell, Kalley	PK-3	416	Erath	143
Dublin Intermediate Sch	Schneider, Chesta	4-6	289	Erath	143
Huckabay Sch	Corzine, Wes	K-12	260	Erath	143
Chilton Sch	Darden, Leon	PK-12	540	Falls	144
Rosebud-Lott High Sch	Barton, Jerrod	9-12	203	Falls	145
Bonham High Sch	Scown, Panchi	9-12	489	Fannin	145
Dodd City Sch	Maupin, Bruce	PK-12	370	Fannin	145
Honey Grove Elem Sch	Sherwood, Mitzi	PK-5	275	Fannin	146
Leonard High Sch	Plake, Cody	9-12	291	Fannin	146
Sam Rayburn Sch	Symanik, Julie	PK-12	500	Fannin	146
Savoy Elem Sch	Henderson, Danny	PK-6	190	Fannin	146

NEW PUBLIC SCHOOLS AND KEY PERSONNEL

Market Data Retrieval

School	Contact	Grades	Enrollment	County	Code
Lockney Elem Sch	Michaleson, Micheal	PK-5	216	Floyd	149
Crowell Elem Sch	Flinn, Christie	PK-8	119	Foard	149
Arizona Fleming Elem Sch	Dudley, Porsha	PK-5	659	Fort Bend	149
Austin Parkway Elem Sch	Macklin, Audrey	PK-5	715	Fort Bend	149
Barrington Place Elem Sch	Riha, Ruth	PK-5	621	Fort Bend	149
Beckendorff Junior High Sch	Moussavi, Paul	6-8	1,739	Fort Bend	151
Bentley Elem Sch	Nehls, Jill	PK-5	654	Fort Bend	153
Brazos Bend Elem Sch	Viado, Stephanie	PK-5	705	Fort Bend	150
Briargate Elem Sch	Garrett, Latoya, Dr	PK-5	428	Fort Bend	150
Briscoe Junior High Sch	Zebold, Jennifer	7-8	891	Fort Bend	153
Cornerstone Elem Sch	Murphy, Margaret	PK-5	1,131	Fort Bend	150
Culver Elem Sch	Thomas, Carla	K-5	615	Fort Bend	153
Dulles High Sch	King-Knowles, Melissa	9-12	2,485	Fort Bend	150
First Colony Middle Sch	Muceus, Courtney	6-8	1,275	Fort Bend	150
George Ranch High Sch	Patterson, Heather	9-12	2,641	Fort Bend	154
Heritage Rose Elem Sch	Garza, Gabriella	PK-5	932	Fort Bend	150
Huggins Elem Sch	Cunningham, Bethany	PK-5	679	Fort Bend	154
Jane Wessendorff Middle Sch	Callis, Lorana	6-6	404	Fort Bend	154
Lantern Lane Elem Sch	Williams, Lavanta	PK-5	446	Fort Bend	150
Madden Elem Sch	Durham, Kristi	PK-5	961	Fort Bend	150
Martha Raines High Sch	Linares, Diego, Dr	10-12	190	Fort Bend	152
Oyster Creek Elem Sch	Olson, Deanna	PK-5	848	Fort Bend	151
Pecan Grove Elem Sch	Hill, Trenae, Dr	PK-5	695	Fort Bend	151
Polly Ryon Middle Sch	Croft, Kevin	6-6	679	Fort Bend	154
Quest Academy	Allen, Carlotta	10-11	20	Fort Bend	155
Reading Junior High Sch	Sanzo, Sonya, Dr	6-8	1,200	Fort Bend	154
Ridgegate Elem Sch	Rivas, Marta	PK-5	552	Fort Bend	151
Ridgemont Elem Sch	Diaz, Framy	2-5	764	Fort Bend	151
Roberts Middle Sch	Harvey, Janice	6-6	415	Fort Bend	154
Sartartia Middle Sch	Oglesby, Cholly	6-8	1,295	Fort Bend	151
Scanlan Oaks Elem Sch	Craig, Lori	PK-5	1,017	Fort Bend	151
Settlers Way Elem Sch	Emery, Danny	PK-5	640	Fort Bend	151
Sienna Crossing Elem Sch	Rosier, Rachel	PK-5	1,080	Fort Bend	151
Stafford Alt Ed Campus	Jenkins, Carlotta	6-12	25	Fort Bend	155
Stafford Elem Sch	Hynes, Twyla	2-4	799	Fort Bend	155
Stafford Middle Sch	Gayle, Ginny	7-8	527	Fort Bend	155
Stafford Primary Sch	Hynes, Twyla	PK-1	690	Fort Bend	155
Sugar Mill Elem Sch	Geis, Jaimie	PK-5	588	Fort Bend	151
T H McDonald Junior High Sch	Caruso, Carrie	6-8	928	Fort Bend	153
Terry High Sch	Nava, Juan	9-12	2,084	Fort Bend	154
Townewest Elem Sch	Briceno, Felipa	PK-5	707	Fort Bend	151
Ursula Stephens Elem Sch	Schwartz, Michael	PK-5	692	Fort Bend	153
Wertheimer Middle Sch	Kitto, Sharyn	6-6	428	Fort Bend	154
West Memorial Elem Sch	Marron, Rebecca	PK-5	822	Fort Bend	153
William B Travis High Sch	LaBerge, Sarah	9-12	2,618	Fort Bend	151
Mt Vernon Middle Sch	Payne, James	5-8	523	Franklin	156
Teague Elem Sch	Adams, Crystal	PK-3	355	Freestone	156
Teague High Sch	Ezell, Tracie	9-12	410	Freestone	156
Dilley High Sch	Solis, Roger	9-12	300	Frio	157
Pearsall Intermediate Sch	Cantu, Gilbert	3-5	512	Frio	157
Seagraves Junior High Sch	Humphries, Jame	6-8	144	Gaines	157
Dunbar Middle Sch	Brown, Temeka	5-6	674	Galveston	159
North Pointe Elem Sch	Kattner, Diana	PK-5	747	Galveston	159
Santa Fe High Sch	Harris, Rachel	9-12	1,443	Galveston	161
Texas City High Sch	Keown, Holly	9-12	1,893	Galveston	161
Zue S Bales Intermediate Sch	Patton, J T	3-5	300	Galveston	160
Southland Sch	Johnson, Gregg	K-12	132	Garza	162
Gillespie County High Sch	Kirchner, Dalen	10-12	25	Gillespie	163
Stonewall Elem Sch	Chalberg, Amie	K-5	90	Gillespie	163
Nixon-Smiley High Sch	Weaver, Jim	9-12	300	Gonzales	164
Austin Elem Sch	Floyd, Kristal	K-5	396	Gray	165
Lamar Elem Sch	McClendon, Troy	PK-5	606	Gray	165
Pampa Junior High Sch	Winborne, Jamie	6-8	794	Gray	165
Travis Elem Sch	May, Byron	K-5	406	Gray	165
Bells High Sch	Rolen, Clay	9-12	261	Grayson	165
Collinsville Elem Sch	Shackelford, Catherine	PK-6	302	Grayson	166
Crutchfield Elem Sch	Roelke, Leda	K-4	430	Grayson	167
Howe High Sch	Kempson, Phil	9-12	341	Grayson	166
Howe Intermediate Sch	Witten, Tammy	3-5	300	Grayson	166
Jefferson Elem Sch	Jung, Nancy	K-4	227	Grayson	167
Pottsboro Middle Sch	Springer, Gerald	5-8	457	Grayson	167
S & S Elem Sch	Reynolds, Shanna	PK-5	441	Grayson	167
Summit Hill Elem Sch	Doty, Clarissa	PK-2	200	Grayson	166
Terrell Elem Sch	Neidert, Amy	PK-4	314	Grayson	166
Everhart Mgnt Acad/Cltrl Study	James, Cassandria	1-5	742	Gregg	169
Excel High Sch	Wadley, Cleotis	9-12	55	Gregg	170

TX-NEW8 800-333-8802 School Year 2019-2020

Texas School Directory

NEW PUBLIC SCHOOLS AND KEY PERSONNEL

School	Principal	Grades	Enrollment	County	Page
Forest Park Middle Sch	Andrews, Wilbert, Dr	6-8	478	Gregg	170
Judson Steam Academy	Pandant, Melanie	6-8	498	Gregg	170
Brule Elem Sch	Leggett, Vanikin	4-5	384	Grimes	172
High Point Elem Sch	Bathke, John	PK-5	433	Grimes	172
Iola Elem Sch	Sajewski, Kristin	PK-6	289	Grimes	172
John C Webb Elem Sch	Nichols, Emily	PK-3	750	Grimes	172
Richards Independent Sch	Portwood, John	PK-12	170	Grimes	172
A L Steele Enhanced Lrng Ctr	Newman, Lisa	9-12	82	Guadalupe	173
George Vogel Elem Sch	Flack, Laura	K-5	409	Guadalupe	174
Green Valley Elem Sch	Denman, Amy	PK-4	742	Guadalupe	173
Jim Barnes Middle Sch	Bittings, Nikki	6-8	863	Guadalupe	174
Lizzie Burgess Alt Sch	Freeman, Erma	2-12	40	Guadalupe	174
Navarro Elem Sch	Wilson, Laurel	PK-3	535	Guadalupe	173
Abernathy Elem Sch	Chambers, Jenci	PK-5	354	Hale	174
Akin Elem Sch	Hutton, Jeff	PK-4	281	Hale	175
Edgemere Elem Sch	Richburg, Leslie	PK-5	471	Hale	175
Thunderbird Elem Sch	Dunn, Karla	PK-5	484	Hale	175
Quanah High Sch	Bibler, Amy	9-12	155	Hardeman	177
Travis Middle Sch	Turner, Virginia	6-8	132	Hardeman	177
Lumberton High Sch	White, John	9-12	1,126	Hardin	178
Lumberton Middle Sch	Edgerton, Travis	7-8	624	Hardin	178
Silsbee High Sch	Schwartz, Scott	9-12	784	Hardin	178
West Hardin High Sch	Smith, Michael	7-12	239	Hardin	179
Academy of Choice	Purdy, Angel	6-12	187	Harris	200
Adella Young Elem Sch	McClellen, Amy	PK-4	606	Harris	198
Anderson Elem Sch	Everett, Deshonta, Dr	PK-5	758	Harris	193
Andy Dekaney High Sch	Reynolds, Alonzo	9-12	2,363	Harris	202
Atascocita Springs Elem Sch	Cheryl, Fennell	PK-5	985	Harris	195
B F Adam Elem Sch	Thomas, Stephanie	PK-5	843	Harris	184
Bammel Middle Sch	Hyder, H, Dr	6-8	941	Harris	202
Baylor Clg of Medicine Acad	Edwards, Tanya	6-8	728	Harris	192
Bear Branch Elem Sch	Palmer, Kakie	PK-5	605	Harris	195
Bernshausen Elem Sch	Farmer, Carrie	PK-5	905	Harris	197
Berry Elem Sch	Steuernagel, Philip	PK-5	799	Harris	190
Bill Worsham Elem Sch	Doria, Sandra	1-5	868	Harris	181
Blackshear Elem Sch	White, Meagan	PK-5	1,042	Harris	197
Blanche K Bruce Elem Sch	Nickerson, Shawn	PK-5	495	Harris	188
Browning Elem Sch	Campos, Evangeline	PK-5	489	Harris	191
Cage Charter Elem Sch	Patenotte, Lisa, Dr	PK-5	520	Harris	189
Chavez High Sch	Landa, Luis	9-12	2,882	Harris	189
Clemente Martinez Elem Sch	Lopez, Alejandro	PK-5	412	Harris	191
Community Services Sch	Williams, Cicely	PK-12	154	Harris	191
Cook Middle Sch	Drayton, Martin	6-8	1,584	Harris	184
Cornelius Elem Sch	Gomez, Zaira	PK-5	867	Harris	192
Cornerstone Academy	Purdy, Angel	6-8	373	Harris	201
Crosby High Sch	Bromley, Dustin	9-12	1,745	Harris	183
Crosby Kindergarten Center	Davis, Kriste	PK-K	651	Harris	183
De Chaumes Elem Sch	Silerio, Enedith	PK-5	841	Harris	190
Deepwater Junior High Sch	Ramos, Rosa	6-8	657	Harris	186
Deer Park High Sch-N Campus	Davis, Scott	9-9	1,073	Harris	186
DeWalt Alternative Sch	Pohl, Candace	6-12	67	Harris	198
Dogan Elem Sch	Tovar, Margarita	PK-5	607	Harris	188
Dueitt Middle Sch	Rodgers, Stacy	6-8	1,162	Harris	202
Durham Elem Sch	Flores, Carrie	PK-5	571	Harris	191
Duryea Elem Sch	Williams, Tomicka	PK-5	950	Harris	184
Elmore Elem Sch	Fugit, Faith	K-5	588	Harris	190
Energized for Excellence ES	Chavez-Pinto, Claudia	K-5	522	Harris	193
Energized for STEM Academy HS	Clark, Shavon	9-12	200	Harris	193
Energized for STEM Academy MS	Perez, Ranier	6-8	333	Harris	193
Fleming Middle Sch	Ayen Metoyer, Nicole	6-8	486	Harris	190
Floyd Hoffman Middle Sch	Morrison-Adams, Jeana	6-8	783	Harris	181
Fondren Middle Sch	Narcisse, Tiffany	6-8	1,013	Harris	193
Francone Elem Sch	Martin, Melissa	PK-5	979	Harris	184
Franklin Elem Sch	Moran, Tammie	PK-5	431	Harris	189
Frazier Elem Sch	Pagano, Michael	PK-5	702	Harris	184
George W Carver Elem Sch	Mancini, Angela	PK-5	736	Harris	187
Grace Raymond Academy	Maddox, Tannessa	1-5	960	Harris	180
Gregory-Lincoln Education Ctr	Wilson, Angel	PK-8	740	Harris	188
Griggs EC-PK-K Sch	Moton, Gladys	PK-K	865	Harris	181
Hamilton Elem Sch	Papaioannou, Sage	PK-5	1,083	Harris	185
HCC Life Skills	Punch, Shawna	12-12	61	Harris	194
Heights High Sch	Ford, Cynthia	9-12	2,377	Harris	191
Helms Elem Sch	Perejon, Lola	PK-5	473	Harris	191
Heritage Elem Sch	Russell, Trenn	PK-5	667	Harris	202
High School Ahead Acad MS	Austin, Ericka	6-8	205	Harris	188
High School for Law & Justice	Garcia, Stacy	9-12	469	Harris	189

NEW PUBLIC SCHOOLS AND KEY PERSONNEL

School	Contact	Grades	Enrollment	County	Code
Highland Heights Elem Sch	Flowers, John	PK-5	517	Harris	188
Hogg Middle Sch	Roque, Tiffany	6-8	984	Harris	191
Holland Middle Sch	Resendiz, Pablo	6-8	673	Harris	189
Hollibrook Elem Sch	Taylor, Anabel	PK-5	763	Harris	201
Horne Elem Sch	Bennett, Tracey	PK-5	955	Harris	185
Hoyland Elem Sch	Cole, Elisa	PK-5	797	Harris	202
Humble Elem Sch	Hernandez, Veronica	PK-5	587	Harris	196
Inspired for Excellence Acad W	Gilmore, Letha	5-8	227	Harris	194
J Henderson Elem Sch	Guerra, Maria	PK-5	783	Harris	189
J Ruth Smith Academy	Carter, Ida	1-5	574	Harris	179
James R Reynolds Elem Sch	Marshall, Renesiaha	PK-5	467	Harris	192
Jersey Village High Sch	Wiley, Maggie	9-12	3,521	Harris	185
Joan Postma Elem Sch	Bell, Terry	PK-5	862	Harris	185
Juan N Seguin Elem Sch	Garcia-Olivo, Mayte	PK-5	544	Harris	193
Judson Robinson Elem Sch	Aguilar, Ana	PK-5	521	Harris	190
Kelso Elem Sch	Walker, Shanda	PK-5	448	Harris	193
Kirk Elem Sch	Bell, Breyanna	PK-5	952	Harris	185
Klein Alternative Ed Center	Marr, Brian	K-12	100	Harris	197
Krahn Elem Sch	Kompelien, Leslie	PK-5	746	Harris	197
L L Pugh Elem Sch	Ortiz, Jorge	PK-5	390	Harris	189
Labay Middle Sch	Bellamy, Catherine	6-8	1,279	Harris	185
Lanier Middle Sch	Wheat, Dave	6-8	1,464	Harris	194
Lewis Elem Sch	Rodriguez, Jorge	1-5	791	Harris	190
Lion Lane Sch	Gabriel, Michele	PK-PK	304	Harris	201
Mabel B Wesley Elem Sch	Cotter, Thomas	PK-5	344	Harris	189
Madison High Sch	Brown, Carlotta	9-12	1,736	Harris	189
Mandarin Immersion Magnet Sch	Ying, Chung	PK-8	748	Harris	194
Margaret Long Wisdom High Sch	Wagner, Michelle	9-12	2,023	Harris	194
Marshall Elem Sch	Price, Lauren	PK-5	944	Harris	191
Marshall Middle Sch	Miller, Queinnise	6-8	794	Harris	192
McReynolds Middle Sch	Giron, Jasmine	6-8	595	Harris	191
Meadow Wood Elem Sch	Barry, Lynne	PK-5	505	Harris	201
Memorial Drive Elem Sch	Jeremiassen, Kathleen	PK-5	447	Harris	201
Meyerland Perf-Visual Arts MS	Sarabia, Auden	6-8	1,574	Harris	194
Middle College at HCC Fraga	Santos, Jose	9-12	128	Harris	190
Middle College at HCC Gulfton	Gibson, Holly	9-12	162	Harris	190
Milton Cooper Elem Sch	Garcia, Mayra	PK-5	791	Harris	202
Miraibeau B Lamar Elem Sch	Rosas Gonzalez, Maria	PK-5	699	Harris	188
Mittelstadt Elem Sch	Shumake, Julie	PK-5	865	Harris	197
Navarro Mid Sch	Vaughn, Kelly	6-8	682	Harris	190
Nimitz 9th Grade Sch	Adams, Aisley	9-9	702	Harris	180
Nitsch Elem Sch	Ward, Frank	K-5	777	Harris	197
Northbrook High Sch	Adami, Randolph	9-12	2,517	Harris	201
Northline Elem Sch	Sandoval, Mario	PK-5	560	Harris	191
Northpointe Intermediate Sch	McReynolds, Darrell	5-6	709	Harris	203
Oakcrest Intermediate Sch	Flores, George	5-6	631	Harris	203
Oates Elem Sch	Melchor, Melissa	PK-5	386	Harris	190
Ortiz Middle Sch	Martinez, Marlen	6-8	1,067	Harris	190
Osborne Elem Sch	Parnell, Jacqueline	PK-5	407	Harris	191
Panda Path Sch	Ruiz, Amanda	PK-PK	203	Harris	201
Parker Elem Sch	Mitchell, Chavis	PK-5	883	Harris	194
Pasadena High Sch	Gomez, Laura	9-12	2,711	Harris	199
Patrick Henry Middle Sch	Davila, Jason	6-8	829	Harris	189
Peck Elem Sch	Bell, Myra	PK-5	528	Harris	193
Post Elem Sch	Stockton, Karen	PK-5	1,146	Harris	185
Project Chrysalis Middle Sch	Rodriguez, Lisa, Dr	6-8	279	Harris	190
Quest Early College High Sch	Scott, Nachelle	9-12	430	Harris	196
R C Conley Elem Sch	Hodge, Lashawn	1-5	789	Harris	180
R P Harris Elem Sch	Avie, Erica	PK-5	569	Harris	190
Ray Daily Elem Sch	Tiet, Cindy	PK-5	768	Harris	194
Riverwood Middle Sch	Roser, Matthew	6-8	1,051	Harris	196
Rosehill Elem Sch	Vasquez, Gloria	PK-4	484	Harris	203
Ross Elem Sch	West, Treasure	PK-5	372	Harris	191
Ruby Thompson Elem Sch	Brame, Erica	PK-5	413	Harris	193
Rucker Elem Sch	Puente, Eileen	PK-5	428	Harris	190
School at St George Place	McClish, Sean	PK-5	793	Harris	194
Sheridan Elem Sch	McIntyre, Rene	PK-5	1,156	Harris	185
Sherman Elem Sch	Rosenbalm, Racquel	PK-5	570	Harris	191
Sherwood Elem Sch	Salas, Sarah	PK-5	456	Harris	201
Smith Elem Sch	Daugherty, Melinda	PK-5	862	Harris	192
South Houston Intermediate Sch	Swenson, Jessica	7-8	725	Harris	200
Spring Branch Acad Institute	Kassir, Patricia	K-9	45	Harris	201
Spring Branch Middle Sch	Spencer, Stefanie	6-8	1,112	Harris	201
Spring Woods Middle Sch	Delariva, Cristian	6-8	876	Harris	201
Stevens Elem Sch	Trent, Erin	PK-5	648	Harris	189
Strack Intermediate Sch	Ovalle, Jason	6-8	1,369	Harris	197

Texas School Directory

NEW PUBLIC SCHOOLS AND KEY PERSONNEL

School	Principal	Grades	Enrollment	County	Page
Sutton Elem Sch	Akala, Beatrice	PK-5	1,121	Harris	194
Sylvan Rodriguez Elem Sch	Deanda, Luz	PK-5	958	Harris	194
T H Rogers Sch	Mike, Tiffany	K-12	979	Harris	194
Thornwood Elem Sch	Lullo, Vicki	PK-5	431	Harris	201
Tice Elem Sch	Gouard, Toshia	PK-5	690	Harris	187
Tomball High Sch	Scott, Chris	9-12	1,931	Harris	203
Tomball Intermediate Sch	Davis, Samora	5-6	753	Harris	203
Tomball Memorial High Sch	Metz, Mike	9-12	2,247	Harris	203
Treasure Forest Elem Sch	Williams, Jerona	PK-5	570	Harris	201
Truitt Middle Sch	Garcia, Yvette	6-8	1,366	Harris	185
W T Hall Education Center	Strahan, Marcie	9-12	239	Harris	180
Walter Matthys Elem Sch	Vargas, Becky	PK-4	664	Harris	200
West University Elem Sch	Disch, Scott	K-5	1,273	Harris	195
Westside High Sch	Stewart, Marguerite	9-12	2,897	Harris	195
Whidby Elem Sch	Lam, Mimi	PK-5	590	Harris	193
Whispering Pines Elem Sch	Anaya, Wendy	PK-5	686	Harris	196
Wilchester Elem Sch	Goodman, Anna	PK-5	793	Harris	201
Woodcreek Middle Sch	Moye, Alan	6-8	1,736	Harris	196
Woodland Acres Middle Sch	Escalante, Manuel	6-8	534	Harris	187
Woodland Hills Elem Sch	Barker, Cindy	PK-5	565	Harris	196
Young Elem Sch	Mitchell, Shanica	PK-5	301	Harris	193
Zwink Elem Sch	Vaglienty, Stacey	PK-5	1,086	Harris	198
Harleton High Sch	Newman, Crystal	9-12	223	Harrison	208
Harleton Junior High Sch	Wright, Randall	6-8	184	Harrison	208
Marshall Junior High Sch	Adams Pegues, Nakeisha	6-8	1,271	Harrison	209
William B Travis Elem Sch	Johnson, Tamekia	K-5	678	Harrison	209
Paint Creek Sch	Wallace, Ken	PK-12	102	Haskell	210
Rule Sch	Frazier, Kenneth	PK-12	130	Haskell	210
Bonham Pre-Kindergarten Sch	Gonzalez, Jennifer	PK-PK	433	Hays	211
Camino Real Elem Sch	Soliz, Elva	PK-5	799	Hays	211
Carpenter Hill Elem Sch	Bordeau, Ginger	PK-5	678	Hays	211
De Zavala Elem Sch	Sanchezvillanu, Elena	K-5	602	Hays	212
Dripping Springs High Sch	Gamez, Angela	9-12	1,869	Hays	210
Johnson High Sch	Miksch, Brett	9-12	1,091	Hays	211
Lehman High Sch	Zuniga, Karen	9-12	2,566	Hays	211
Rooster Springs Elem Sch	Novickas, Steve	PK-5	793	Hays	210
San Marcos High Sch	Presley, Denisha	9-12	2,334	Hays	212
Science Hall Elem Sch	Ramos, Iric	PK-5	754	Hays	211
Walnut Springs Elem Sch	Gardner, Melinda	PK-5	719	Hays	211
Canadian Elem Sch	Risley, Reagan	PK-2	233	Hemphill	213
Brownsboro High Sch	Cooper, Brent	9-12	764	Henderson	213
Brownsboro Intermediate Sch	Beasley, Billy	4-6	334	Henderson	213
Eustace Primary Sch	Gray, Julie	PK-2	416	Henderson	214
South Athens Elem Sch	Mason, Nicole	PK-5	483	Henderson	213
Aida Escobar Elem Sch	Espinoza, Catarina	PK-5	810	Hidalgo	223
Alamo Middle Sch	Esparza, Cristina	6-8	615	Hidalgo	223
Carlos Truan Jr High Sch	Aguilar, Alfredo	6-8	1,074	Hidalgo	216
Carmen Anaya Elem Sch	Cantu, Bertha	PK-5	400	Hidalgo	223
Disciplinary Alt Ed Program	Perez, Jose	6-12	60	Hidalgo	225
Dr Javier Saenz Middle Sch	Salinas, Carlota	6-8	816	Hidalgo	219
Edcouch Elsa High Sch	Tijerina, Janie	9-12	1,394	Hidalgo	216
Francisco Barrientes Mid Sch	Rivera, David	6-8	1,308	Hidalgo	216
Hidalgo Academy	De Hoyos, Brenda	9-12	34	Hidalgo	217
Idea Academy-Achieve	Johnson, Shandra	PK-3	250	Hidalgo	217
Idea Clg Prep-Harvey Najim	Hall, Theresa	6-7	500	Hidalgo	218
Idea Clg Prep-Montopolis	Rubio, Cristopher	6-12	116	Hidalgo	219
James Bonham Elem Sch	Infante, Leticia	PK-5	294	Hidalgo	221
Juan N Seguin Elem Sch	Cerda, Sandra	PK-5	629	Hidalgo	220
Juarez-Lincoln High Sch	Estrada, Ricardo	9-12	2,528	Hidalgo	220
La Villa Early Clg High Sch	Layton, Antonio	9-12	162	Hidalgo	220
Lamar Academy	Nino, Jeanette	9-12	124	Hidalgo	221
Lloyd M Bentsen Elem Sch	Mendoza, Hilda	PK-5	617	Hidalgo	220
Memorial Middle Sch	Martinez, Belen	6-8	758	Hidalgo	220
Mercedes Early College HS	Venecia, Jeanne	9-12	400	Hidalgo	221
N L Trevino Elem Sch	Alonzo, Brenda	PK-5	597	Hidalgo	217
Pfc Mario Ybarra Elem Sch	Hernandez, Linda	PK-5	554	Hidalgo	225
Progreso Elem Sch	Garcia, Marivel	3-5	380	Hidalgo	224
Psja Elvis J Ballew Echs	Cuellar, Darcia	9-12	358	Hidalgo	223
Psja Memorial HS	Vela, Rowdy, Dr	9-12	1,843	Hidalgo	224
Psja T Jefferson Echs	Maldonado, Virna	9-12	775	Hidalgo	224
Robert E Lee Elem Sch	Navarro, Alonda	PK-5	411	Hidalgo	217
Rosendo Benavides Elem Sch	Benavidez, Romeo, Dr	PK-5	400	Hidalgo	220
Sam Rayburn Elem Sch	Partida, Clarissa	PK-5	474	Hidalgo	221
Santos Livas Elem Sch	Hernandez, Rodrigo	PK-5	640	Hidalgo	224
Sgt Leonel Trevino Elem Sch	Carriaga, Benito	PK-5	520	Hidalgo	224
Truman Price Elem Sch	Cervantes, Olga	PK-5	507	Hidalgo	215

NEW PUBLIC SCHOOLS AND KEY PERSONNEL

Market Data Retrieval

School	Contact	Grades	Enrollment	County	Code
Weslaco East High Sch	Gamboa, David	9-12	2,047	Hidalgo	225
Covington Sch	Blalock, Joel	PK-12	293	Hill	227
Hillsboro Intermediate Sch	Jones, Wendy	3-6	478	Hill	227
Malone Elem Sch	Johnson, Lakeshia	PK-8	165	Hill	228
Penelope Sch	Timmons, David	PK-12	210	Hill	228
Whitney Middle Sch	Booth, Paul	6-8	339	Hill	228
Anton Sch	Betencourt, Deeanne	PK-12	180	Hockley	229
Anton Sch	Cox, David	PK-12	180	Hockley	229
Levelland Middle Sch	Clanton, Brad	6-8	607	Hockley	229
Whitharral Sch	McCollister, Alex	PK-12	173	Hockley	230
Acton Elem Sch	Willmeth, Karla	PK-5	870	Hood	230
Granbury Middle Sch	Clark, Tammy	6-8	775	Hood	230
Lipan Sch	Phillips, Jennifer	PK-12	420	Hood	230
Cumby Elem Sch	Wicks, Douglas	PK-5	185	Hopkins	231
Sulphur Bluff Sch	Daniel, Amy	PK-12	215	Hopkins	232
Crockett Junior High Sch	Gomez, Juan	6-8	281	Houston	232
Lovelady Jr Sr High Sch	Martinez, Jo	7-12	230	Houston	233
Forsan Jr Sr High Sch	Carter, Hanna	6-12	396	Howard	234
Kentwood Early Childhood Ctr	Chesworth, Jennifer	PK-PK	104	Howard	233
Moss Elem Sch	Wommack, Carman	K-2	487	Howard	233
Washington Elem Sch	Jeffrey, Kaitlin	K-5	400	Howard	234
Butler Intermediate Sch	Walker, Lindsay	3-5	559	Hunt	237
Ford High Sch	Wallen, Jason	9-12	821	Hunt	237
Kathryn Griffis Elem Sch	Brutonr, Jennifer	PK-5	457	Hunt	235
Travis Elem Sch	Vincent, Dawes	K-6	349	Hunt	236
Wolfe City Elem Sch	White, Ginger	PK-5	323	Hunt	237
Wolfe City High Sch	Gardner, Rose	9-12	204	Hunt	237
West Texas Elem Sch	Lamb, Shawna	PK-5	333	Hutchinson	238
Bryson Sch	Kirby, Gary	PK-12	255	Jack	238
Jacksboro High Sch	Sanders, Starla	9-12	284	Jack	239
Ganado Elem Sch	Stephenson, Jennifer	PK-5	369	Jackson	239
Industrial Elem Sch East	Baughman, Lisa	PK-5	314	Jackson	240
Industrial Elem Sch West	Sides, Barbara	K-5	219	Jackson	240
Industrial Junior High Sch	Schaefer, Kim	6-8	294	Jackson	240
Buna Elem Sch	Hebert, Karen	PK-5	762	Jasper	240
Buna High Sch	Brewster, Mike	9-12	413	Jasper	240
Central Middle Sch	Gomez, Natalie	5-8	746	Jefferson	243
Hamshire Fannett Interm Sch	Gilmore, Marla	4-6	450	Jefferson	242
Langham Elem Sch	Latiolais, Toby	PK-4	462	Jefferson	243
Marshall Middle Sch	Breaux, Paul	6-8	849	Jefferson	242
Pathways Alt Learning Center	Colvin, Charles	6-12	56	Jefferson	242
Regina-Howell Elem Sch	Screen, Kimberly	PK-5	812	Jefferson	242
Thomas Jefferson Middle Sch	Oliva, Melissa, Dr	6-8	925	Jefferson	243
Ben Bolt-Palito Blanco ES	Hamill, Gloria	PK-6	287	Jim Wells	245
Ben Bolt-Palito Blanco HS	Barrera, Gus	7-12	250	Jim Wells	245
Dubose Intermediate Sch	Orta, Lorie	5-6	457	Jim Wells	245
Orange Grove Elem & Inter Sch	Bridges, Jeanne	2-5	559	Jim Wells	245
Premont Collegiate High Sch	Garcia, Claudette	6-12	283	Jim Wells	246
Salazar Elem Sch	Vidaurri, Maria	PK-4	255	Jim Wells	245
A G Elder Elem Sch	Brakel, Debra	PK-5	527	Johnson	248
Burleson Collegiate High Sch	Wieland, Amanda	9-12	76	Johnson	246
Centennial High Sch	Holder, Ikie	9-12	1,738	Johnson	247
Cleburne High Sch	Renner, Ben	9-12	1,750	Johnson	247
Crossroads High Sch	Canonico, Marcus	9-12	83	Johnson	247
Frazier Elem Sch	Lyday, Tricia	PK-5	596	Johnson	247
Godley High Sch	Flood, Kurtis	9-12	537	Johnson	247
Godley Intermediate Sch	Block, Melissa	2-6	481	Johnson	247
Irving Elem Sch	Jackson, Sherqueena	PK-5	495	Johnson	247
Jack Taylor Elem Sch	Ketchum, Ana	PK-5	516	Johnson	247
Judy Hajek Elem Sch	Basham, Cretia	PK-5	639	Johnson	247
Links Academy	Sveum, Michelle	9-12	40	Johnson	247
Phoenix Alt Campus 817	Smith, Loyd	1-12	250	Johnson	247
Rio Vista High Sch	Mims, Charles	9-12	239	Johnson	248
Steam Academy at Stribling	Hinkle, Rebekah	K-5	420	Johnson	247
Venus High Sch	Woodworth, Karen	9-12	590	Johnson	249
Hamlin Elem Sch	Jones, C	PK-6	241	Jones	249
Lueders-Avoca High Sch	Cummings, Robert	9-12	36	Jones	250
Stamford High Sch	Seelke, Chase	9-12	184	Jones	250
Kenedy High Sch	Del Bosque, Deborah	9-12	214	Karnes	251
Gilbert Willie Sr Elem Sch	Navaja, Brenda	K-5	664	Kaufman	253
Herman Furlough Jr Middle Sch	Navaja, Brenda	6-8	588	Kaufman	253
Mabank High Sch	Haugh, Brett	9-12	1,035	Kaufman	253
Terrell High Sch	Thompson, Jay	9-12	1,190	Kaufman	253
W H Burnett Early Chldhd Ctr	Nichols, Melissa	PK-PK	568	Kaufman	253
Boerne Middle School South	Watson, Angela, Dr	7-8	1,286	Kendall	254
Comfort Middle Sch	Colvin, Michael	6-8	253	Kendall	254

School	Contact	Grades	Enrollment	County	Page
Curington Elem Sch	Myers, Matt	PK-5	589	Kendall	254
Fred H Tally Elem Sch	Robertson, Gena	K-5	522	Kerr	256
Guthrie Sch	Hill, Lynn	PK-12	104	King	257
Academy High Sch	Sandoval, Juan	9-12	360	Kleberg	258
Gillett Intermediate Sch	Garnez, Belinda	5-6	428	Kleberg	257
H M King High Sch	Daniel, Mahogany	9-12	966	Kleberg	257
Harvey Elem Sch	Barton, Abigayle	PK-4	425	Kleberg	257
N M Harrel Elem Sch	Trevino, John	PK-4	329	Kleberg	257
Perez Elem Sch	Villarreal, Albert	PK-4	475	Kleberg	257
Ricardo Elem Middle Sch	Braswell, Marci, Dr	PK-8	671	Kleberg	258
Ricardo Elem Middle Sch	Vilches, Gina	PK-8	671	Kleberg	258
Amherst Sch	Gonzales, Jose	PK-12	145	Lamb	260
Littlefield High Sch	Read, Mike	9-12	374	Lamb	261
Springlake-Earth Elem Mid Sch	Johnson, Jimmi	PK-8	380	Lamb	261
Hanna Springs Elem Sch	Duhon, Lindsay	PK-5	632	Lampasas	261
Normangee Senior High Sch	Mark, Ruffin	9-12	203	Leon	264
Stephen F Austin Elem Sch	Wortham, Atiya	K-5	895	Liberty	265
Enge-Washington Interm Sch	Westhoff, Beth	3-6	586	Limestone	267
Groesbeck High Sch	Bomar, Bonnie, Dr	9-12	484	Limestone	267
H O Whitehurst Elem Sch	Carter, Kimberly	PK-5	600	Limestone	267
Mexia High Sch	White, Robert	9-12	506	Limestone	267
Follett Sch	Robertson, Megan	PK-12	140	Lipscomb	268
George West Elem Sch	De La Rosa, Omar	4-6	238	Live Oak	268
George West Primary Sch	Cortez, Christina	PK-3	349	Live Oak	268
Three Rivers Elem Sch	Miller, Cindy	PK-6	365	Live Oak	268
Alderson Elem Sch	Coleman, Drue	PK-5	569	Lubbock	270
Bennett Elem Sch	Bessire, Chera	PK-5	667	Lubbock	269
Central Elem Sch	Cox, Colter	PK-5	600	Lubbock	271
Coronado High Sch	Stephen, Julia	9-12	2,134	Lubbock	270
Evans Middle Sch	Newman, Justin	6-8	900	Lubbock	270
Frenship High Sch	Hernandez, Gregory	9-12	2,697	Lubbock	269
Heritage Middle Sch	Campbell, Chelsey	6-8	701	Lubbock	269
Legacy Elem Sch	Kidd, Carole	PK-3	484	Lubbock	269
Maedgen Elem Sch	Mendez, Ofelia	PK-5	350	Lubbock	270
Overton Elem Sch	Archer, Ann	PK-5	330	Lubbock	270
Parsons Elem Sch	Avey, Yvonne	PK-5	475	Lubbock	270
Ramirez Charter Sch	Serenil, Melissa	PK-5	506	Lubbock	270
Reese Education Center	Spear, Stephanie	6-12	75	Lubbock	269
Roy Roberts Elem Sch	Briseno, Anissa	PK-5	706	Lubbock	270
Shallowater Intermediate Sch	Southard, Michelle	2-4	386	Lubbock	272
Willow Bend Elem Sch	Fisher, Vivian	PK-5	580	Lubbock	269
New Home Sch	Baum, Kelly	PK-12	447	Lynn	273
Tahoka Elem Sch	Scott, Donald	PK-5	336	Lynn	273
Wilson Sch	Portillo, Jp	PK-12	129	Lynn	273
Jefferson Junior High Sch	Phy, Tim	5-8	375	Marion	274
Stanton Middle Sch	Ruiz, Jennifer	6-8	228	Martin	274
Mason Elem Sch	Holbrook, Ryan	PK-4	294	Mason	275
Mason High Sch	Burns, Kade	9-12	214	Mason	275
Mason Junior High Sch	Holbrook, Ryan	5-8	220	Mason	275
Matagorda Sch	Phillips, Susan	PK-8	120	Matagorda	275
Matagorda Sch	Thurmon, Kyle	PK-8	120	Matagorda	275
O H Herman Middle Sch	Hood, Brandon	6-8	249	Matagorda	276
Van Vleck High Sch	Townsend, Chris	9-12	328	Matagorda	276
Axtell High Sch	Beseda, Sunny	6-12	162	McLennan	278
Carver Middle Sch	Perry, Phillip	6-8	477	McLennan	282
Connally Early Childhood Ctr	Gerik, Misty	PK-K	319	McLennan	279
Crestview Elem Sch	Craytor, Samantha	PK-5	608	McLennan	282
Hillcrest Prof Dev Sch	Lundquist, Jennifer	PK-5	430	McLennan	282
La Vega High Sch	Gibson, Sandra	9-12	865	McLennan	280
Riesel High Sch	Wilson, Krystal	7-12	342	McLennan	281
Robinson High Sch	Dietzman, Kati	9-12	701	McLennan	281
Speegleville Elem Sch	Bronstad, Mandi	PK-4	295	McLennan	281
Tennyson Middle Sch	Rambo, Matt	6-8	930	McLennan	282
West Elem Sch	Kazda, Carrie	PK-5	541	McLennan	282
West High Sch	Snook, Don	9-12	425	McLennan	282
West Middle Sch	Klander, Charles	6-8	326	McLennan	282
Woodway Elem Sch	Olson, Beth	PK-4	581	McLennan	281
Medina Valley High Sch	Lange, Tanner	9-12	1,429	Medina	284
Medina Valley Lacoste ES	Vera, Elizabeth	PK-5	746	Medina	284
Medina Valley Middle Sch	Solis, Lesli	6-8	1,209	Medina	284
Menard Elem Middle Sch	Bannowsky, Amy	PK-8	225	Menard	285
Menard High Sch	Kruse, Cheryl	9-12	87	Menard	285
Alamo Junior High Sch	Hidalgo, Paul	7-8	732	Midland	285
Bonham Elem Sch	Teran, Tricia	PK-6	631	Midland	285
Emerson Elem Sch	Reeves, Christin	PK-6	496	Midland	285
Gen Tommy Franks Elem Sch	Jones, Andra	PK-6	398	Midland	286

NEW PUBLIC SCHOOLS AND KEY PERSONNEL

Market Data Retrieval

School	Contact	Grades	Enrollment	County	Code
Goddard Junior High Sch	Copeland, Brandy	7-8	1,212	Midland	286
Greathouse Elem Sch	Sanchez, Tonya	PK-6	779	Midland	286
Greenwood Elem Sch	Goodrum, Leslie	PK-2	600	Midland	285
Greenwood Interm Sch	Hopkins, Crysten	3-5	522	Midland	285
James R Brooks Middle Sch	Brown-Griffin, Kristi	6-8	846	Midland	285
Long Elem Sch	Rimer, Terri	PK-6	518	Midland	286
Pease Communication/Tech Acad	Moya, Gabriel	K-6	621	Midland	286
Sam Houston Elem Sch	Ramos, Stephanie	PK-6	464	Midland	286
Washington STEM Academy	Newton, Ann	K-6	464	Midland	286
Ben Milam Elem Sch	Jordan, Tracey	PK-2	546	Milam	287
Milano High Sch	Steinbecker, Catrina	9-12	174	Milam	287
Thorndale Middle Sch	Frei, Scott	6-8	140	Milam	288
Mullin Middle High Sch	Feist, Chayden	7-12	55	Mills	288
Colorado High Sch	Russell, Rebecca	9-12	284	Mitchell	289
Loraine Sch	Anders, Dustin	PK-12	160	Mitchell	289
Bowie High Sch	Menchaca, Sergio	9-12	498	Montague	290
Gold-Burg Sch	Flinchum, Thomas	PK-12	140	Montague	290
Bear Branch Elem Sch	Gassaway, Jim	K-4	637	Montgomery	292
Bear Branch Junior High Sch	Petty, Ben	7-8	977	Montgomery	293
Brookwood Forest Elem Sch	Gutierrez, Ericka	PK-5	500	Montgomery	293
Bush Elem Sch	Lambert, Jarod, Dr	PK-4	732	Montgomery	291
Dolly F Vogel Intermediate Sch	Haymark, Christa	5-6	1,104	Montgomery	291
Giesinger Elem Sch	Ralston, Melissa	PK-4	702	Montgomery	291
Kings Manor Elem Sch	Paine, Stacey	PK-5	737	Montgomery	293
Lake Creek High Sch	Eaton, Phil	9-12	331	Montgomery	293
Lamar Elem Sch	Belcher, Kristen	PK-4	741	Montgomery	292
Lincoln Elem Sch	Dyer, Courtney	PK-5	495	Montgomery	293
Magnolia High Sch	Quinn, Greg	9-12	1,961	Montgomery	293
New Caney Elem Sch	Andjelic, Jennifer	PK-5	617	Montgomery	294
New Caney High Sch	Holton, Eric	9-12	1,946	Montgomery	294
New Caney Middle Sch	Ray, Holly	6-8	795	Montgomery	294
Oak Ridge High Sch	Papadimitriou, Michael, Dr	10-12	2,839	Montgomery	292
Oak Ridge HS 9th Grade Campus	Bujnoch, Melanie	9-9	1,179	Montgomery	292
Robert Brabham Middle Sch	Ray, Richard	6-8	889	Montgomery	294
Sorters Mill Elem Sch	Tomhave, Kindy	PK-5	854	Montgomery	294
Tom R Ellisor Elem Sch	Boyd, Kristin	PK-5	752	Montgomery	293
Willie E Williams Elem Sch	Dominguez, Claudia	PK-5	719	Montgomery	293
Morningside Elem Sch	Pingelton, Erin	PK-4	397	Moore	295
Daingerfield High Sch	Stewart, Tommy	9-12	282	Morris	296
Pewitt High Sch	Wylie, Jay	9-12	242	Morris	296
Pewitt Junior High Sch	Giles, Tom	6-8	200	Morris	296
South Elem Sch	Reeder, Angie	3-5	228	Morris	296
Garrison Senior High Sch	Barnett, Clark	9-12	201	Nacogdoches	298
Nettie Marshall Elem Sch	Rodriguez, Joseph	K-5	369	Nacogdoches	298
Woden High Sch	Stroud, Jesse	9-12	209	Nacogdoches	298
Corsciana Middle Sch	Johnson, Janice	7-8	830	Navarro	299
Fannin Elem Sch	Horne, Dallas	K-4	470	Navarro	299
Navarro Co Alt Educ Ctr	Richardson, Melinda	K-12	70	Navarro	300
Rice Intermediate Middle Sch	Metcalfe, Monnie	5-8	435	Navarro	300
Sam Houston Elem Sch	Corrington, Molly	K-4	323	Navarro	299
Highland Sch	Acevedo, David	PK-12	250	Nolan	301
Roscoe Collegiate High Sch	Althof, Gregory	6-12	257	Nolan	301
Roscoe Collegiate Mont ECC	Althof, Crystal	PK-K	160	Nolan	301
Calallen Charter High Sch	Marquez-Neth, Yvonne	11-12	80	Nueces	302
Calallen Middle Sch	Saenz, Rey	6-8	973	Nueces	302
Club Estates Elem Sch	Bircher, Kay	PK-5	405	Nueces	303
Early Childhood Dev Center	Loving, Kellye	PK-6	187	Nueces	303
Hicks Elem Sch	Garza, Alicia	PK-5	704	Nueces	303
Miller HS-Metro Sch of Design	Wilson, Bruce	7-12	1,345	Nueces	304
Olsen Elem Sch	Garcie, Kelye	PK-5	259	Nueces	305
Perryton High Sch	Finch, Danny	9-12	577	Ochiltree	307
Adrian Sch	Brooks, Dawn	PK-12	120	Oldham	307
Mimi Farley Elem Sch	Martinez, Joanna	PK-5	36	Oldham	307
Bridge City Intermediate Sch	Motomura, Julie	3-5	725	Orange	308
Bridge City Middle Sch	Hoffman, Amanda	6-8	637	Orange	308
Deweyville Jr Sr High Sch	East, Brian	6-12	312	Orange	308
Orangefield Junior High Sch	Wrinkle, Rea	6-8	560	Orange	309
West Orange-Stark High Sch	Holifield, Rolanda	9-12	579	Orange	309
Graford Jr Sr High Sch	Womack, Clifton	6-12	152	Palo Pinto	310
Mineral Wells High Sch	Funk, Doug, Dr	9-12	855	Palo Pinto	310
Gary Sch	Davis, Brittney	PK-12	500	Panola	311
Crockett Elem Sch	Moore, Marilisa	PK-6	524	Parker	314
Goshen Creek Elem Sch	Jones, Kelly	PK-4	602	Parker	313
Joe Tison Middle Sch	Bradley, Jeffrey	7-8	597	Parker	314
McAnally Intermediate Sch	Hearn, Dennis	5-6	834	Parker	312
Peaster Middle Sch	Carlisle, Scott	6-8	178	Parker	313

Texas School Directory

NEW PUBLIC SCHOOLS AND KEY PERSONNEL

School	Contact	Grades	Enrollment	County	Code
Poolville High Sch	Shifflett, Jennifer	9-12	163	Parker	313
Poolville Junior High Sch	Dunnam, Jamie	6-8	94	Parker	313
Reno Elem Sch	Showers, Jenna	PK-4	381	Parker	313
Shirley Hall Middle Sch	Wynne, Stephanie	7-8	633	Parker	314
Weatherford 9th Grade Center	Pool, Lynn	9-9	618	Parker	314
Weatherford High Sch	Kidd, Brannon	10-12	1,700	Parker	314
Lazbuddie Sch	Bailey, Bryan	PK-12	201	Parmer	315
Buena Vista Sch	Alcala, Adelina	PK-12	244	Pecos	315
Ft Stockton High Sch	Alvarado, Roy	9-12	672	Pecos	315
Iraan Elem Sch	Frazier, Amy	PK-5	236	Pecos	316
Iraan High Sch	Andrews, Blake	9-12	117	Pecos	316
Big Sandy Sch	Tillery, Shelby	PK-12	525	Polk	316
Big Sandy Sch	Houston, Diane	PK-12	525	Polk	316
Goodrich Middle High Sch	Isaacs, Calobe	6-12	106	Polk	316
Onalaska Jr Sr High Sch	Thornton, Robyn	7-12	438	Polk	317
Timber Creek Elem Sch	Murphy, Sheri	PK-3	445	Polk	317
Emerson Elem Sch	Bales, Amanda	PK-5	538	Potter	318
Hamlet Elem Sch	Favela, Victor	PK-5	329	Potter	318
Highland Park High Sch	Shettel, Dixie	9-12	223	Potter	319
Humphrey's Highland Elem Sch	Prickett, Erin	PK-5	572	Potter	318
Lawndale Elem Sch	Toliver, Jana	PK-5	388	Potter	318
Lorenzo De Zavala Middle Sch	Manchee, Mike	5-8	420	Potter	318
Paramount Terrace Elem Sch	Greenhouse, Lisa	PK-5	362	Potter	318
Puckett Elem Sch	Hess, Cheri	PK-5	404	Potter	318
South Georgia Elem Sch	Newman, Heather	PK-5	405	Potter	318
Stephen F Austin Middle Sch	Self, Brandy	6-8	826	Potter	318
Whittier Elem Sch	Rangel, Linda	PK-5	529	Potter	318
William B Travis 6th GR Campus	Newman, Casey	6-6	346	Potter	318
Windsor Elem Sch	Woodington, Allison	PK-5	494	Potter	318
Presidio High Sch	Tibayan, Dr	10-12	440	Presidio	320
Rains Intermediate Sch	Vance, J	3-5	377	Rains	320
Hillside Elem Sch	Brown, Brittany	K-4	420	Randall	321
Reagan Co High Sch	Valeriano, Rene	9-12	229	Reagan	321
Reagan Co Middle Sch	Brown, Clifton	6-8	191	Reagan	321
Leakey Sch	Goebel, Vicki	PK-12	309	Real	322
Austin Elem Sch	McGraw, Leeann	1-3	682	Reeves	323
Austwell Tivoli Jr Sr High Sch	Cortez, John	6-12	55	Refugio	323
Woodsboro Jr Sr High Sch	Piwetz, Tisha	7-12	192	Refugio	324
Hearne High Sch	Mott, Caroline	9-12	220	Robertson	325
Winters Elem Sch	Garcia, Edward	PK-5	248	Runnels	327
West Rusk Junior High Sch	Keith, Brian	6-8	235	Rusk	328
San Augustine Mid High Sch	Perkins, Hugh	6-12	359	San Augustine	329
Faulk Early Childhood Center	Mansfield, Jason	PK-1	281	San Patricio	330
Mathis High Sch	Riojas, Jesse, Dr	9-12	411	San Patricio	331
Odem High Sch	Bowers, Calvin	9-12	288	San Patricio	331
Odem Intermediate Sch	Tapia, Erica	3-5	201	San Patricio	331
Odem Junior High Sch	Vela, Joe	6-8	224	San Patricio	331
Stephen F Austin Elem Sch	Brinkman, Brenda	PK-5	481	San Patricio	331
Taft High Sch	Lohse, Matthew	9-12	318	San Patricio	332
Wildcat Learning Alt Center	Haynes, Terra	9-12	50	San Patricio	331
Richland Springs Sch	Wyatt, Rhonda	K-12	120	San Saba	332
San Saba Elem Sch	Deckard, Denise	PK-4	337	San Saba	332
Nancy Smith Elem Sch	Gallagher, John	PK-6	284	Shackelford	334
Center Intermediate Sch	Masterson, Lee	4-5	388	Shelby	334
Arp High Sch	Hurst, Bryan	9-12	266	Smith	336
Bell Elem Sch	Taylor, Sheri	PK-5	454	Smith	338
Chapel Hill Middle Sch	Strode, Matt	6-8	799	Smith	337
Hollaway Sixth Grade Sch	Pineda, Stacy	6-6	389	Smith	339
James S Hogg Middle Sch	Taylor, Sheri	6-8	341	Smith	338
Lindale High Sch	Chilek, Jeremy	9-12	1,156	Smith	337
Owens Elem Sch	Sherman, Rachel	PK-5	584	Smith	338
Peete Elem Sch	Chapa, Cassandra	PK-5	294	Smith	338
Troup Middle Sch	Cooksey, Stephen	6-8	247	Smith	337
Winona Elem Sch	Caldwell, Jason	PK-3	387	Smith	339
Wise Elem Fine Arts Magnet Sch	Reagan, Cyndy	PK-5	510	Smith	337
General Ricardo Sanchez ES	Garcia, Teresa	PK-5	729	Starr	340
Grulla Elem Sch	Gonzalez, Epigmenio	PK-5	547	Starr	340
La Union Elem Sch	Trevino, Lorena	PK-5	372	Starr	340
Roma High Sch	Saldivar, Ildefonso	9-12	1,781	Starr	341
San Isidro Sch	Garcia, Anna	PK-12	250	Starr	341
North Elem Sch	Freeman, Prairie	2-3	206	Stephens	341
Sterling Elem Sch	Keele, Jami	PK-5	141	Sterling	342
Aspermont High Sch	Van Meter, Trent	6-12	123	Stonewall	342
Kress Elem Sch	Langston, Robert	PK-6	155	Swisher	343
Tulia High Sch	Perez, Perla	9-12	317	Swisher	343
Amos Elem Sch	Tufts, Carin	PK-6	431	Tarrant	343

School Year 2019-2020   800-333-8802

NEW PUBLIC SCHOOLS AND KEY PERSONNEL

Market Data Retrieval

School	Contact	Grades	Enrollment	County	Code
Anderson Elem Sch	Peragine, Angela	PK-6	657	Tarrant	343
Ashworth Elem Sch	Maddoux, Stacey	PK-6	466	Tarrant	343
Azle Hornet Academy	Boone, Dianne	9-12	80	Tarrant	345
Bear Creek Intermediate Sch	Riebkes, Brenda	5-6	991	Tarrant	354
Bell Manor Elem Sch	McCarty, Keri	PK-6	740	Tarrant	354
Birdville Elem Sch of Fine Art	Pope, Tammy	PK-5	426	Tarrant	346
Boulevard Heights Sch	Guthrie, Terry, Dr	Spec	50	Tarrant	350
Bryson Elem Sch	Gillard, Jennifer	PK-5	489	Tarrant	348
Butler Elem Sch	Bohannon, Jennifer	PK-6	627	Tarrant	344
Carroll Peak Elem Sch	Sanjacinto, Kalyn	PK-5	626	Tarrant	350
Charles E Nash Elem Sch	Galindo, Mrs	PK-5	276	Tarrant	350
Chisholm Ridge Elem Sch	Green, Krystle	PK-5	664	Tarrant	348
Corey Acad Fine Arts	Zaravar, Nidia	PK-6	580	Tarrant	344
Cross Timbers Elem Sch	Wynns, Shelly	PK-4	539	Tarrant	345
Crouch Elem Sch	Stephens, Jaime	PK-6	651	Tarrant	344
D McRae Elem Sch	Angel, Aura	PK-5	615	Tarrant	350
Daggett Montessori Elem Sch	Eugenio, Victorius	K-8	508	Tarrant	350
Dallas Park Elem Sch	DelGado, Veronica	PK-4	741	Tarrant	348
David L Walker Interm Sch	Randall, Melanie	5-6	603	Tarrant	348
Deer Creek Elem Sch	Roe, Anna	PK-4	514	Tarrant	348
Elkins Elem Sch	Cowden, Randiann	K-5	651	Tarrant	348
Erma Nash Elem Sch	McAdams, Kia	PK-4	580	Tarrant	356
Fine Arts Academy	Cooper, Kerry	K-6	302	Tarrant	357
Foster Village Elem Sch	Gamble, Sherri	PK-5	495	Tarrant	346
Goodman Elem Sch	Savala, Stephanie	PK-6	561	Tarrant	344
Grapevine Elem Sch	Hale, Nancy	PK-5	526	Tarrant	353
Greenfield Elem Sch	Ramsey, Kelly	PK-5	709	Tarrant	348
Gunn Junior High Sch	Varnell, Matt, Dr	7-8	442	Tarrant	344
Hafley Development Center	De Hoyos, Stacey	PK-PK	296	Tarrant	348
Harlean Beal Elem Sch	Courtade, Jodie	PK-5	448	Tarrant	350
Hazel Harvey Peace Elem Sch	Avery, Anthony	PK-5	571	Tarrant	351
Heritage Elem Sch	West-Dukes, Edwina	K-4	529	Tarrant	355
Hurst Junior High Sch	Smith, Michael	7-9	1,099	Tarrant	354
I M Terrell Elem Sch	Brown, Baldwin	PK-5	244	Tarrant	351
Iuniversity Prep Virtual Acad	Rogers, Klinetta	4-12	427	Tarrant	353
J P Elder Middle Sch	Trimble, David, Dr	6-8	1,290	Tarrant	351
James A Arthur Interm Sch	Blackstone, Caroline	5-6	503	Tarrant	355
Jean McClung Middle Sch	McWilliams, Marron	6-8	741	Tarrant	351
Keller Middle Sch	Burruel, Amanda	7-8	987	Tarrant	355
Kennedale Alternative Ed Prog	Bryson, Carol	1-12	100	Tarrant	356
Kennedale Junior High Sch	Rhines, Reggie	7-8	491	Tarrant	356
Kenneth Davis Elem Sch	Goad, Lacye	PK-4	492	Tarrant	357
Lake Worth High Sch	Stults, Bobby	9-12	868	Tarrant	356
Leonard Middle Sch	Williams, Cathy	6-8	772	Tarrant	351
Liberty Elem Sch	Koehler, Lisa	PK-4	491	Tarrant	345
Liberty Elem Sch	Dickinson, Michael	PK-4	640	Tarrant	357
Luella Merrett Elem Sch	Merrett, Luella	PK-5	631	Tarrant	351
Mansfield High Sch	Dowd, Trent	9-12	2,468	Tarrant	357
Martha Reid Elem Sch	McGuinness, Catherine	PK-4	633	Tarrant	357
Mary Louise Phillips Elem Sch	Hill, Laura	PK-5	489	Tarrant	351
Mary Moore Elem Sch	Prange, Nathan	K-6	672	Tarrant	344
Meadowbrook Middle Sch	Gentry, Mr	6-8	850	Tarrant	351
Metro Opportunity Sch	Bohanon, Aundra	9-12	30	Tarrant	351
Morningside Elem Sch	Cuarenta, Vanessa	PK-5	620	Tarrant	351
N A Howry Intermediate Sch	Mynyk, Ted	5-6	483	Tarrant	356
Nichols Junior High Sch	Claiborne, Catherine	7-8	788	Tarrant	344
North Riverside Elem Sch	Boyd, Allison	K-4	433	Tarrant	355
O H Stowe Elem Sch	Nathan, Frymark	PK-5	662	Tarrant	346
Richard J Wilson Elem Sch	Ayala, Irma	PK-5	588	Tarrant	351
Richland High Sch	McCanlies, Mark	9-12	2,158	Tarrant	346
Richland Middle Sch	Fadely, Jody	6-8	662	Tarrant	346
S S Dillow Elem Sch	Flagler, Duvaughn	PK-5	568	Tarrant	352
Sam Houston High Sch	Villarreal, Juan	9-12	3,627	Tarrant	345
Seminary Hills Park Elem Sch	Ferrales, Lorena	PK-5	380	Tarrant	352
Silver Lake Elem Sch	Whiteside, Nicole	PK-5	601	Tarrant	353
South Davis Elem Sch	Wall, Debra	PK-6	676	Tarrant	345
TCC South-Fwisd Collegiate HS	Collins, Quanda	9-10	75	Tarrant	352
Timberline Elem Sch	Hilcher, Liz	PK-5	704	Tarrant	353
Van Zandt-Guinn Elem Sch	Fuentes, Debora	PK-5	595	Tarrant	352
Vista Ridge Middle Sch	Arsenault, Tracy	5-7	251	Tarrant	355
Watauga Middle Sch	Houston, Shannon	6-8	711	Tarrant	346
Wayside Middle Sch	Fahey, Raymond	6-8	880	Tarrant	349
Wimbish World Language Academy	Hardy, Delisse	PK-6	527	Tarrant	345
Young Junior High Sch	Humbles, Stacie	7-8	850	Tarrant	345
Atems High Sch	Howle, Jeffrey	9-12	357	Taylor	360
Byron Craig Middle Sch	Gonzales, Guadalupe	6-8	962	Taylor	360

Texas School Directory

NEW PUBLIC SCHOOLS AND KEY PERSONNEL

School	Principal	Grades	Enrollment	County	Page
Cooper High Sch	Williamson, Lyndsey	9-12	1,787	Taylor	360
Johnston Elem Sch	Brokovich, Jeffrey	K-5	484	Taylor	360
Merkel Elem Sch	Kotara, Daniel	PK-5	570	Taylor	361
Merkel High Sch	Stevens, James	9-12	314	Taylor	361
Taylor Elem Sch	Thornburg, Keri	PK-5	643	Taylor	360
Trent Sch	Oakley, Vanessa	PK-12	180	Taylor	361
Ward Elem Sch	Ripple, Dawn	PK-5	565	Taylor	360
Wylie East Elem Sch	McMillan, Kim	PK-4	940	Taylor	361
Wylie East Junior High Sch	Goodenough, Rob	5-8	678	Taylor	361
Wylie High Sch	Smith, Tim	9-12	1,164	Taylor	361
Wylie Intermediate Sch	Boone, Phil	3-4	692	Taylor	361
Wylie West Junior High Sch	Amonett, Aaron	5-8	686	Taylor	361
Colonial Heights Elem Sch	Brisendine, Susan	K-1	253	Terry	362
Oak Grove Elem Sch	Hathaway, Vicki	2-5	518	Terry	362
Throckmorton Sch	Riley, Rhonda	PK-12	175	Throckmorton	363
Mt Pleasant High Sch	Bailey, Craig	9-12	1,505	Titus	364
P E Wallace Middle Sch	Rider, Nathan	5-6	750	Titus	364
Alta Loma Elem Sch	Herndon, Lauri	PK-5	335	Tom Green	364
Carver Learning Center	Becerra, Claudia	K-12	47	Tom Green	365
Glenmore Elem Sch	Gould, Teri	PK-5	474	Tom Green	365
Lincoln Middle Sch	Gandar, Joe	6-8	862	Tom Green	365
Wall Elem Sch	Granzin, Kelly	PK-5	515	Tom Green	365
Water Valley Elem Sch	Blanton, Deeanna	PK-6	211	Tom Green	365
A N McCallum High Sch	Hosack, Brandi	9-12	1,761	Travis	368
Alternative Learning Center	Jones, Chris	6-12	101	Travis	368
Andrews Elem Sch	Vallejo, Diana	PK-6	504	Travis	367
Clifton Career Dev Sch	Dishner, Tony	Voc	200	Travis	368
Cook Elem Sch	Sanchez, Priscilla	PK-5	453	Travis	367
Cowan Elem Sch	Brunner, Travis	PK-5	841	Travis	366
Delco Primary Sch	Castillo, Miguel	PK-2	697	Travis	371
Dessau Middle Sch	Torres-Solis, Valerie	6-8	860	Travis	372
Doss Elem Sch	Steenport, Nathan	PK-5	835	Travis	367
Frank & Sue McBee Elem Sch	Celorio-Reyes, Yvette	PK-5	395	Travis	367
Guerrero Thompson Elem Sch	Garcia, Briana	PK-5	633	Travis	367
Harris Elem Sch	Dwiggins, Ana Maria	PK-5	650	Travis	367
Highland Park Elem Sch	Ruiz, Lizbeth	PK-5	641	Travis	372
Hill Elem Sch	Drummond, Jack	PK-5	954	Travis	368
Houston Elem Sch	Diaz-Camarillo, Elia	PK-5	642	Travis	366
Joslin Elem Sch	Chang, Chaolin	PK-5	282	Travis	366
Lake Travis Middle Sch	Wolff, Lester	6-8	1,420	Travis	370
Lamar Middle Sch	Mondik, Mayra	6-8	1,130	Travis	369
Linder Elem Sch	Rodriguez, Melissa	1-5	306	Travis	367
Lyndon B Johnson High Sch	Wright, Traci Lynn	9-12	799	Travis	368
Manor Elem Early Learning Ctr	Aguirre, Nicole	PK-PK	295	Travis	371
Manor High Sch	Bailey, Jon	9-10	900	Travis	371
Manor Senior High Sch	Matthews, John	11-12	900	Travis	371
Murchison Middle Sch	Newton, Beth	6-8	1,392	Travis	369
Navarro Early College High Sch	Covin, Steven	9-12	1,586	Travis	368
Newton Collins Elem Sch	Wallace, Suzi	PK-5	600	Travis	369
Northeast Early Clg High Sch	Longoria, Alisia	9-12	1,252	Travis	368
Northwest Elem Sch	Tidwell, Tere	PK-5	530	Travis	372
Oak Springs Elem Sch	Woods, Monica	PK-5	322	Travis	368
Ojeda Middle Sch	Torrez, Alex	6-8	906	Travis	369
Paredes Middle Sch	Torres-Solis, Valerie	6-8	892	Travis	369
Pease Elem Sch	Foss, Stacy	PK-6	233	Travis	368
Pecan Springs Elem Sch	Williams, Andrea	PK-5	454	Travis	368
Pickle Elem Sch	Davalos, Lauro	PK-5	544	Travis	368
Ridgetop Elem Sch	Schultz, Kara	PK-5	371	Travis	368
Small Middle Sch	Nelson, Matthew	6-8	1,231	Travis	369
Spring Hill Elem Sch	Longoria, Camille	PK-5	597	Travis	372
Sunset Valley Elem Sch	Marquez, Marizza	PK-5	543	Travis	367
Timothy Baranoff Elem Sch	Cantu, Beth	PK-5	1,014	Travis	367
Travis Early College High Sch	Harrington, Christina	9-12	1,233	Travis	369
Webb Primary Sch	Lopez, Yolanda	PK-5	258	Travis	368
Williams Elem Sch	Villanueva, Natalie	PK-5	466	Travis	367
Chester Elem Sch	Loughner, Katie	PK-5	110	Tyler	374
Fred Elem Sch	Hicks, Katy	PK-5	211	Tyler	375
Spurger Elem Sch	Drake, Jason	PK-5	204	Tyler	375
Wheat Elem Sch	Greaff, Gina	PK-2	382	Tyler	375
Woodville Middle Sch	Hollingsworth, Elton	6-8	321	Tyler	375
Gilmer Intermediate Sch	Treadway, Gina	5-6	389	Upshur	376
Comstock Sch	Parker, Laura	K-12	227	Val Verde	379
San Felipe Memorial Middle Sch	Zuniga-Barrera, Celia	6-6	771	Val Verde	379
Earnest O Woods Interm Sch	Brown, David	2-4	534	Van Zandt	381
Edgewood Intermediate Sch	Orsborn, Shannon	3-5	213	Van Zandt	380
Grand Saline Middle Sch	Hand, Leland	6-8	221	Van Zandt	380

School Year 2019-2020   800-333-8802

NEW PUBLIC SCHOOLS AND KEY PERSONNEL

Market Data Retrieval

School	Contact	Grades	Enrollment	County	Code
Van High Sch	Hutchins, Jeffery	9-12	807	Van Zandt	381
Van Junior High Sch	Peterson, Jeremy	7-8	352	Van Zandt	381
Bloomington Elem Sch	Frisch, Carl	2-5	264	Victoria	381
Bloomington Middle Sch	Torres, Lou	6-8	195	Victoria	381
Crain Elem Sch	Harper, Renee	PK-5	381	Victoria	382
Dudley Magnet Sch	Carroll, Steven	PK-5	473	Victoria	382
Placedo Elem Sch	Torres, Lou	PK-1	164	Victoria	382
Shields Elem Sch	Gabrysch, Kelly	PK-5	466	Victoria	382
Hempstead High Sch	Mullens, Eric	9-12	415	Waller	384
Herman Jones Elem Sch	Kinney, Ashley	PK-5	636	Waller	384
It Holleman Elem Sch	Abke, Ashley	PK-5	706	Waller	384
Royal Early Childhood Center	Green, Aronda	PK-K	341	Waller	384
Royal Elem Sch	Green, Aronda	1-5	932	Waller	384
Royal Junior High Sch	Vargas, Orlando	6-8	495	Waller	384
Waller Junior High Sch	Carrejo, Tanya	6-8	740	Waller	385
Grandfalls Royalty Sch	Starkweather, Brett	PK-12	185	Ward	385
Burton High Sch	Wamble, Matthew	7-12	208	Washington	386
Bruni High Sch	Garza, H	9-12	78	Webb	388
Clark Middle Sch	Arredondo, Pamela	6-8	731	Webb	387
Finley Elem Sch	Chapa, Kristina	PK-5	474	Webb	387
Francisco Farias Elem Sch	Garza, San Juana	PK-5	655	Webb	386
Hector Garcia Early Clg HS	Iznaola, Jose	9-12	438	Webb	386
United Middle Sch	Arizola, Rosana	6-8	1,126	Webb	388
East Bernard Jr High Sch	Janczak, Jay	5-8	290	Wharton	389
El Campo Middle Sch	Figirova, Gary	6-8	863	Wharton	389
Iago Junior High Sch	Floyd, Gerald	6-8	278	Wharton	389
Newgulf Elem Sch	Kucera, Inez	PK-5	490	Wharton	389
Wharton High Sch	Barron, Jerrell	9-12	586	Wharton	390
Wharton Junior High Sch	Oduwole, Olatunji	7-8	304	Wharton	390
Shamrock Elem Sch	Glass, Andy	PK-5	193	Wheeler	391
Wheeler Sch	Bailey, Mike	PK-12	487	Wheeler	391
Booker T Washington ES	Davis, Mark	PK-5	286	Wichita	392
City View Elem Sch	Davis, Ronda	PK-6	605	Wichita	391
City View Jr Sr High Sch	Boswell, Scott	7-12	453	Wichita	391
Electra Jr Senior High Sch	Russell, Jim	7-12	156	Wichita	391
Farris Early Childhood Center	Willis, Letitia	PK-PK	211	Wichita	392
North West Head Start Center	Willis, Letitia	PK-PK	51	Wichita	392
Rosewood Head Start Center	Willis, Letitia	PK-PK	101	Wichita	392
Lasara Elem Sch	Quintanilla, Israel	PK-8	298	Willacy	394
Raymondville High Sch	Garcia, Frank	9-12	529	Willacy	394
Anderson Mill Elem Sch	Molina, Amanda	PK-5	523	Williamson	398
Bill Burden Elem Sch	Lambert, Tanya	PK-4	652	Williamson	398
Blackland Prairie Elem Sch	Hildebrand, Sue	PK-5	804	Williamson	398
Deer Creek Elem Sch	Calkins, Matthew	PK-5	687	Williamson	397
Eastview High Sch	Easter, Latoya	9-12	1,573	Williamson	395
Four Points Middle Sch	Crawford, Steve	6-8	773	Williamson	397
Georgetown Alt Program	Kelly, Spiller	6-12	23	Williamson	395
Howard Norman Elem Sch	Abrams, Carrie	PK-5	660	Williamson	396
Joe Lee Johnson Elem Sch	Scott, Marc	PK-5	729	Williamson	399
Laurel Mountain Elem Sch	Marvel, Doriane	PK-5	758	Williamson	399
Main Street Imtermediate Sch	Cobb, Marcelina	4-5	427	Williamson	399
Nadine Johnson Elem Sch	Almquist, Lindsie	PK-5	424	Williamson	396
Neysa Callison Elem Sch	Oates, Penny	PK-5	805	Williamson	399
Old Town Elem Sch	Schock, Jessica	PK-5	749	Williamson	399
Pat Cooper Elem Sch	Ptomey, Tish	PK-5	553	Williamson	395
Pfc Robert Hernandez Mid Sch	Ephlin, Patricia, Dr	6-8	752	Williamson	399
Ray Elem Sch	Campbell, Alexis	PK-5	675	Williamson	396
Ronald Reagan Elem Sch	Haug, Eric	PK-5	863	Williamson	397
Spicewood Elem Sch	Allen, Teyan	K-5	807	Williamson	399
Taylor Middle Sch	Ellison, Chelsey	6-8	710	Williamson	400
Taylor Opportunity Center	Maddox, Andrew	6-12	50	Williamson	400
Vic Robertson Elem Sch	Borel, Kyle	PK-5	431	Williamson	399
Wells Branch Elem Sch	Gordon, Eliza	PK-5	479	Williamson	399
Westside Elem Sch	Lillard, Amanda	PK-5	574	Williamson	397
La Vernia Junior High Sch	Carter, Andrea	6-8	720	Wilson	401
La Vernia Primary Sch	Keck, Shelley	PK-2	808	Wilson	401
Poth Elem Sch	Brysch, Karla	PK-5	411	Wilson	401
Poth High Sch	Deaver, Todd	9-12	244	Wilson	401
Poth Junior High Sch	Kroll, Laura	6-8	180	Wilson	401
Stockdale Elem Sch	Lucas, Brigit	PK-5	389	Wilson	401
Kermit Junior High Sch	Miller, Laura	5-8	416	Winkler	402
Bridgeport Middle Sch	Valkenaar, Steven	6-8	446	Wise	403
Slidell Secondary Sch	Stevens, Theresa	5-12	153	Wise	403
Hawkins High Sch	Henninger, Elisa	9-12	222	Wood	404
Dr Tomas Rivera Elem Sch	Guerrero, Andi	PK-1	200	Zavala	407
La Pryor High Sch	Lambert, Rachel	7-12	204	Zavala	407

Texas School Directory

NEW PUBLIC SCHOOLS AND KEY PERSONNEL

Lorenzo De Zavala Elem Sch	Hoffman, Veronica	2-4	200	Zavala	407

NEW SUPERINTENDENTS

DISTRICT	SUPERINTENDENT	GRADES	ENROLLMENT	COUNTY	PAGE
Poteet Ind School Dist	Mills, Cheryl	PK-12	1,735	Atascosa	21
Pettus Ind School Dist	Hornann, Mike	PK-12	421	Bee	25
Academy Ind School Dist	Harlan, Billy	K-12	1,559	Bell	26
Bartlett Ind School Dist	Clevenger, Theodore	K-12	350	Bell	26
Belton Ind School Dist	Battershell, Robin, Dr	PK-12	11,950	Bell	26
Holland Ind School Dist	Downing, Shane	PK-12	692	Bell	27
Harlandale Ind School Dist	Gallegos, Samantha	PK-12	14,500	Bexar	32
North East Ind School Dist	Maika, Sean, Dr	PK-12	64,359	Bexar	34
Pleasant Grove Ind School Dist	Pirtele, Chad	PK-12	2,200	Bowie	49
Alvin Ind School Dist	Nelson, Carol	PK-12	25,926	Brazoria	50
Calhoun Co Ind School Dist	Nichols, Larry	PK-12	3,985	Calhoun	61
Cross Plains Ind Sch Dist	Cosby, Dade	PK-12	368	Callahan	62
Brownsville Ind School Dist	Gutierrez, Rene, Dr	PK-12	43,355	Cameron	63
Pittsburg Ind School Dist	Waldrep, Terry	PK-12	2,344	Camp	68
Wells Ind School Dist	Moore, James	PK-12	285	Cherokee	73
Whiteface Con Ind School Dist	Wheeler, Nate	PK-12	325	Cochran	75
Blue Ridge Ind School Dist	Kimball, Matt	PK-12	860	Collin	77
Lovejoy Ind School Dist	Goddard, Michael, Dr	PK-12	4,424	Collin	80
Sidney Ind School Dist	Rucker, James	PK-12	140	Comanche	90
Cedar Hill Ind School Dist	Hudson, Gerald, Dr	K-12	7,866	Dallas	97
Grand Prairie Ind School Dist	Ellis, Linda	PK-12	29,339	Dallas	107
Dawson Ind School Dist	Steets, Layne	K-12	110	Dawson	116
Yorktown Ind School Dist	Kuenstler, Katherine	PK-12	550	De Witt	118
Sanger Ind School Dist	Hunter, Tommy, Dr	PK-12	2,660	Denton	126
Carrizo Spgs Cons Ind SD	Gonzales, Alberto, Dr	PK-12	2,200	Dimmit	127
Hedley Ind School Dist	Baines, Garrett	PK-12	120	Donley	127
Benavides Ind School Dist	Chapa, Marisa, Dr	PK-12	340	Duval	128
Ramirez Common School Dist	Gonzalez, Yliana	PK-6	30	Duval	128
San Diego Ind School Dist	Pena, Rodrigo, Dr	PK-12	1,460	Duval	128
Cisco Independent Sch Dist	Steel, Ryan, Dr	PK-12	850	Eastland	128
Rising Star Ind Sch Dist	Atkins, Mary Jane	PK-12	147	Eastland	129
Ector Co Ind School Dist	Muri, Scott, Dr	PK-12	31,500	Ector	129
Anthony Ind School Dist	Troncoso, Oscar	PK-12	839	El Paso	131
Avalon Ind School Dist	Marshall, Khristopher	PK-12	350	Ellis	140
Red Oak Ind School Dist	Dixon, Ann, Dr	PK-12	6,000	Ellis	142
Waxahachie Ind School Dist	Cain, Bonny	PK-12	9,481	Ellis	142
Marlin Ind School Dist	Godfrey, Remy	PK-12	1,000	Falls	144
Roby Cons Ind School Dist	Cook, Keith	PK-12	310	Fisher	148
Mt Vernon Ind School Dist	McCullough, Jason	PK-12	1,620	Franklin	155
Loop Ind School Dist	Blackman, Heath	PK-12	150	Gaines	157
Seminole Ind School Dist	Lynch, Kyle	PK-12	2,983	Gaines	158
Dickinson Ind School Dist	Voelkel, Carla	PK-12	10,400	Galveston	159
Hitchcock Ind School Dist	Edwards, Travis	PK-12	1,700	Galveston	161
Gonzales Ind School Dist	Schumacker, John	PK-12	2,875	Gonzales	164
Grandview-Hopkins Ind Sch Dist	Hargis, Kent	K-6	50	Gray	164
Bells Ind School Dist	Meek, Tricia	PK-12	845	Grayson	165
Kilgore Ind School Dist	Baker, Andrew, Dr	PK-12	4,076	Gregg	169
Cotton Center Ind School Dist	Bobo, Ryan	PK-12	130	Hale	174
Petersburg Ind School Dist	Bibb, Brian, Dr	PK-12	300	Hale	175
Quanah Ind School Dist	Baird, Jerry	PK-12	525	Hardeman	177
Hardin Jefferson Ind Sch Dist	McEachern, Brad	PK-12	2,200	Hardin	177
Klein Ind School Dist	McGowan, Jenny, Dr	PK-12	53,868	Harris	196
Spring Branch Ind School Dist	Blaine, Jennifer	PK-12	34,975	Harris	200
Brownsboro Ind School Dist	Hampton, Keri, Dr	PK-12	2,800	Henderson	213
Malakoff Ind School Dist	Layton, Done	PK-12	1,400	Henderson	214
Edcouch Elsa Ind School Dist	Riberou, Richard, Dr	PK-12	5,450	Hidalgo	215
Edinburg Cons Ind School Dist	Garza, Gilbert	PK-12	34,500	Hidalgo	216
La Joya Ind School Dist	Saenz, Gisela, Dr	PK-12	27,000	Hidalgo	219
Mercedes Ind School Dist	Mendiola, Carolyn	PK-12	4,781	Hidalgo	221
Monte Alto Ind School Dist	Cobarrubias, Rosie, Dr	PK-12	900	Hidalgo	222
Progreso Ind School Dist	Coronado, Sergio	PK-12	1,750	Hidalgo	224
Hubbard Ind School Dist	Norman, Tim	PK-12	400	Hill	227
Lipan Ind School Dist	Overton, Jodi	PK-12	420	Hood	230
Irion Co Ind School Dist	Clausen, Donny	K-12	275	Irion	238
Buna Ind School Dist	Lee, Donny, Dr	PK-12	1,480	Jasper	240
Jasper Ind School Dist	Hyden, Steve, Dr	PK-12	2,390	Jasper	240
Kirbyville Cons Ind Sch Dist	Sayers, Georgia	PK-12	1,400	Jasper	241
Hawley Ind School Dist	McBrayer, Cassidy, Dr	K-12	769	Jones	250
Lueders-Avoca Ind School Dist	Spikes, Bob	PK-12	104	Jones	250
Crandall Ind School Dist	Eldredge, Wendy, Dr	PK-12	4,500	Kaufman	251

NEW PUBLIC SCHOOLS AND KEY PERSONNEL

District	Contact	Grade	Enrollment	County	Code
North Lamar Ind School Dist	Stewart, Kelli	PK-12	2,500	Lamar	259
Shiner Ind School Dist	Remschel, Alex	PK-12	660	Lavaca	262
Normangee Ind School Dist	Ruffin, Mark	PK-12	572	Leon	264
Oakwood Ind School Dist	Holden, Russell	PK-12	200	Leon	264
Hull Daisetta Ind School Dist	Bartram, Timothy	K-12	477	Liberty	266
Darrouzett Ind School Dist	Parish, Deidre	PK-12	120	Lipscomb	267
George West Ind School Dist	Rosebrock, James, Dr	PK-12	1,100	Live Oak	268
Three Rivers Ind School Dist	Dragon, Les	PK-12	678	Live Oak	268
Tahoka Ind School Dist	Van Hoose, Dick	PK-12	680	Lynn	273
McGregor Ind School Dist	Lenamon, James	PK-12	1,550	McLennan	280
Riesel Ind School Dist	Cope, Brandon	PK-12	620	McLennan	281
Waco Ind School Dist	Kincannon, Susan	PK-12	15,050	McLennan	281
Cameron Ind School Dist	Sprinkles, Kevin	PK-12	1,800	Milam	287
Bowie Ind School Dist	Enlow, Blake	PK-12	1,720	Montague	289
Pewitt Cons Ind School Dist	Forsyth, Skip	PK-12	891	Morris	296
Chireno ISD School Dist	Kelly, Arnie	PK-12	304	Nacogdoches	297
Douglass Ind School Dist	Keeling, Justin	K-12	460	Nacogdoches	297
Garrison Ind School Dist	Spivey, Reid	PK-12	600	Nacogdoches	297
Agua Dulce Ind School Dist	Lopez, Nora	PK-12	370	Nueces	302
Flour Bluff Ind School Dist	Freeman, David, Dr	PK-12	5,750	Nueces	304
Gordon Ind School Dist	Wilkins, Dewanye	PK-12	200	Palo Pinto	310
Poolville Ind School Dist	Kirby, Jeff	PK-12	530	Parker	313
Onalaska Ind School Dist	Roberts, Anthony	PK-12	1,000	Polk	317
Amarillo Ind School Dist	Loomis, Doug	PK-12	33,754	Potter	317
Rains Ind School Dist	Johnson, Jennifer	PK-12	1,650	Rains	320
Detroit Ind School Dist	Thompson, Kathy	PK-12	540	Red River	322
Austwell Tivoli Ind SD	Vela, Dolores	K-12	140	Refugio	323
Henderson Ind School Dist	Lamb, Thurston, Dr	PK-12	3,040	Rusk	327
West Sabine Ind Sch Dist	Stephenson, Jane	PK-12	600	Sabine	329
Broaddus Ind School Dist	Hollway, Lucas	PK-12	400	San Augustine	329
Hermleigh Ind School Dist	Petty, Cathy	PK-12	250	Scurry	333
Albany Ind School Dist	Scott, Jonathan	PK-12	500	Shackelford	334
Joaquin Ind School Dist	Fuller, Ryan	PK-12	650	Shelby	335
Rio Grande City Ind Sch Dist	Garza, Velma	PK-12	9,876	Starr	340
Aspermont Ind School Dist	Morris, Zack	PK-12	240	Stonewall	342
Jim Ned Cons Ind School Dist	Teal, Glen, Dr	PK-12	1,300	Taylor	361
Wellman Union Ind School Dist	Foote, David	PK-12	347	Terry	362
Del Valle Ind School Dist	Villerot, Annette	PK-12	12,100	Travis	369
Warren Ind School Dist	Boyette, Tammy, Dr	PK-12	1,400	Tyler	375
Woodville Ind School Dist	Meysembourg, Lisa	PK-12	1,300	Tyler	375
Canton Ind School Dist	Dunlap, Jim	PK-12	2,300	Van Zandt	380
Edgewood Ind School Dist	Hernandez, Eduardo, Dr	PK-12	975	Van Zandt	380
Bloomington Ind School Dist	Anglin, Mark	PK-12	900	Victoria	381
Kelton Ind School Dist	Taylor, Carl	PK-12	95	Wheeler	390
Electra Ind School Dist	West, Ted	PK-12	430	Wichita	391
Leander Ind School Dist	Gearing, Bruce, Dr	PK-12	41,000	Williamson	396
Boyd Ind School Dist	Vann, Leslie	PK-12	1,317	Wise	402
Chico Ind School Dist	Higgins, William	PK-12	600	Wise	403
Newcastle Ind School Dist	Cardwell, Evan	PK-12	180	Young	406
Crystal City Ind School Dist	Chruchillo, Edward	PK-12	1,500	Zavala	407

Texas School Directory

TEXAS

- **Texas Dept of Education** PID: 00994396   512/463-9734
  1701 N Congress Ave, Austin 78701   Fax 512/463-9838

Schools: 599

Mike Morath 1	Alejandro DelGado 2,15
Leo Lopez 2,19	Shirley Beaulieu 2
Barney Fudge 7,80,85,91	Shelly Ramos 8
David Marx 11	Cory Green 12,298
A Crabill 15,70,298	Martin Winchester 15,68
Megan Aghazadian 15	Kelsey Kling 20
Ryan Merrit 27	Jacquie Porter 34
Irene Pickhardt 42	James Slack 45
Karin Miller 48,51	Susie Coultress 57
Lawrence Allen 67	Gene Acuna 71
Ryan Franklin 74	Marian Schutte 76
Melody Parrish 76	Monica Brewer 81
Kerry Ballast 286	

STATE-OPERATED SCHOOLS

State Schs..Principal	Grd	Prgm	Enr/#Cls	SN	
© A Plus Academy Elementary [272] 10327 Rylie Rd, Dallas 75217 Michelle Thrash	PK-6		610		972/557-5578 Fax 972/557-4128
© A Plus Academy Secondary [272] 445 S Masters Dr, Dallas 75217 Norman Lee	7-12		554		469/677-1000
© A Plus Up-Museum Campus 5555 Hermann Dr, Houston 77004 Thomas McWhorter	6-8	T	67	43%	713/955-7543
© A Plus Up-University Campus 3353 Elgin St, Houston 77004 Rachel Clarke	6-8	T	155	59%	713/955-7583
© A W Brown Leadership Academy 5701 Red Bird Center Dr, Dallas 75237 Chastity Armstead \ Shenikwa Cager	PK-8	T	1,800 32	68%	972/709-4700 Fax 214/339-2273
© Abundant Life Christian Sch 5130 Casey St, La Marque 77568 Cynthia Hallam	PK-12		422		409/935-8773
© Academy of Accelerated Lrng 6025 Chimney Rock Rd, Houston 77081 Janelle Glover	PK-5	T	715 30	98%	713/773-4766 Fax 713/666-2532
© Academy of Dallas-Oak Park [187] 1030 Oak Park Dr, Dallas 75232 Ross Williams	PK-1	T	476 11	99%	214/371-9600 Fax 214/371-1053
© Accel Inter Academy-Lancaster 901 E Belt Line Rd, Lancaster 75146 Lashawn Hoskins	PK-5		250		972/227-2105
© Accelerated Intermediate Acad 12825 Summit Ridge Dr, Houston 77085 Lashawn Hoskins	PK-6		259 15		713/728-9330 Fax 713/283-6190
© Alief Montessori Cmty Sch 12013 6th St, Houston 77072 Delia Presillas	PK-6	T	272 9	39%	281/530-9406 Fax 281/530-2233
© Amarillo Collegiate Academy 6000 S Georgia St, Amarillo 79118 Michael Griffin	K-12		481		806/352-0171 Fax 866/397-5456
© Amarillo Collegiate Academy [297] 6000 S Georgia St, Amarillo 79118 Michael Griffin	PK-12		451	26%	806/352-0171 Fax 806/367-5449
© Ambassadors Preparatory Acad 5001 Avenue U, Galveston 77551 Dr Pat Williams	PK-8	T	308 18	84%	409/762-1115 Fax 409/762-1114
© Amigos Por Vida Charter Sch 5503 El Camino Del Rey St, Houston 77081 Freddy DelGado	PK-8	T	513 15	97%	713/349-9945 Fax 713/349-0671
© Aristoi Classical Academy 5618 11th St, Katy 77493 Terrence Boling \ Matthew Watson	K-12	AT	593	17%	281/391-5003 Fax 281/391-5010
© Arlington Classics Acad-Bowen 5200 S Bowen Rd, Arlington 76017 Teri Rodgers	3-5		525		817/303-1553 Fax 817/549-0246
© Arlington Classics Academy 2800 W Arkansas Ln, Arlington 76016 Melissa Fambrough	K-8		530 25	18%	817/274-2008 Fax 817/274-8768
© Arrow-Champions Academy [273] 2113 Cypress Landing Dr, Houston 77090 Sonja Williams	K-6	T	130	60%	832/446-6762 Fax 832/446-6790
© Arrow-Harvest Preparatory Acad [273] 17770 Imperial Valley Dr, Houston 77060 Michael Blackshire	K-6	T	171	95%	281/872-5201
© Arrow-Las Americas Lrng Ctr 5901 Glenmont Dr Apt 17, Houston 77081 Lillian Martinez	K-7		125		832/582-7327 Fax 832/582-7325
© Arrow-Liberation Academy [273] 401 Present St, Missouri City 77489 Audrey Sanders	K-5	T	166	61%	281/969-7766 Fax 281/969-7762
© Arrow-Save Our Streets Ctr [273] 1700 Groesbeck St, Bryan 77803 Becky Tucker	K-5	T	110	96%	979/703-1810 Fax 979/703-1834
© Austin Achieve Public Sch 5908 Manor Rd, Austin 78723 Reece Hartle \ MacKee Mason	5-12	T	527	89%	512/522-4190 Fax 512/727-0376
© Austin Classical Academy [297] 1504 E 51st St, Austin 78723 Miriam Trollo	K-8		159		512/371-8933 Fax 866/433-9225
© Austin Discovery Academy 8509 FM 969 Ste 200, Austin 78724 Leigh Moss	K-8		524	12%	512/674-0700 Fax 512/674-3133
Aw Brown-Fla Early Childhood 6901 S Westmoreland Rd, Dallas 75237 Chavala Arnold	PK-5		1,240	85%	214/330-8686
© Baker-Ripley Promise Cmty CS 6500 Rookin St Bldg A, Houston 77074 Roel Saldivar	K-6		400		713/273-3731 Fax 713/273-3797
© Basis San Antonio Prim-Med Ctr [011] 8519 Floyd Curl Dr, San Antonio 78240 Jen Neal	K-5		750		210/319-5525 Fax 210/877-9214
© Basis San Antonio Primary N [011] 318 E Ramsey Rd, San Antonio 78216 America Palmer	5-10		600		210/775-4125 Fax 210/855-4888
© Basis San Antonio Shavano [011] 4114 Lockhill Selma Rd, San Antonio 78230 David King	6-12		1,050		210/874-9250 Fax 210/579-6030
© Beatrice Mayes Institute CS 5807 Calhoun Rd, Houston 77021 Beatrice Mayes	K-8	T	445 32	75%	713/747-5629 Fax 281/809-7842
© Beaumont Classical Academy [297] 10255 Eastex Fwy Ste 100, Beaumont 77708 Myrna Ramirez	K-5		157	37%	409/434-4549
© Beta Academy 9701 Almeda Genoa Rd, Houston 77075 Kendra Hampton	K-10	T	585	63%	832/331-2460
© Bexar County Academy [187] 1485 Hillcrest Dr, San Antonio 78228 Edison Marcos	PK-8	T	374 27	99%	210/432-8600 Fax 210/432-8667
ⒶBig Springs-Brune Charter Sch © 10664 N US Highway 83, Leakey 78873 Dr Carmen Boatright	K-12	T	129 7	91%	830/232-7101 Fax 830/232-4279
© Big Springs-Cailloux CS 3522 Junction Hwy 27, Ingram 78025 Dr Maria De'LaCruz	1-12	A	71		830/367-6100 Fax 830/367-6108
© Bob Hope Elem Sch 4301 32nd St, Port Arthur 77642 Virginia Roberts	PK-2		310		409/983-3244
ⒶBob Hope Middle High Sch © 2849 9th Ave, Port Arthur 77642 Bobby Lopez	6-12	T	666	91%	409/983-3244 Fax 409/983-6408

Market Data Retrieval

School	Grades	Type	Enroll	%	Phone
ⓐ Brazos River Charter Sch ⓒ 1964 FM 199, Nemo 76070 Bengie Laning	9-12	T	125 13	56%	254/898-9226 Fax 254/898-2297
ⓒ Brazos Sch Inquiry-Bryan [276] 410 Bethel Ln, Bryan 77802 Chris Osgood	PK-8	T	165 6	84%	979/774-5032 Fax 979/774-5037
ⓒ Brazos Sch Inquiry-Tidwell [276] 1055 W Tidwell Rd, Houston 77091 John Bean	PK-6	T	165	96%	713/681-1960 Fax 713/681-1979
ⓒ Brooks Acad-Science Engineerng [130] 214 E Ashby Pl, San Antonio 78212 Bonnie Salas	K-12	T	1,532 28	69%	210/388-0288 Fax 210/388-0293 f t
ⓒ Brooks Collegiate Academy 4802 Vance Jackson Rd, San Antonio 78230 Lisa Schutz	K-12	T	928	69%	
ⓒ Brooks Estrella Academy 3803 Lyster Rd, San Antonio 78235 Bonnie Salas	K-6		275		210/257-5175 Fax 210/257-8147
ⓒ Brooks Int'l Studies Academy 134 E Lambert St, San Antonio 78204 Patricia Lazono-Landry	K-7	T	162	83%	210/998-4452 Fax 210/998-4454
ⓒ Brooks Lonestar Academy 4802 Vance Jackson Rd, San Antonio 78230 Barry Lemaitre	K-6		95		210/998-4452 Fax 210/998-4454
ⓒ Brooks Oaks Academy 6070 Babcock Rd, San Antonio 78240 Talisa Wilson	PK-5		175		210/627-6013 Fax 210/627-6016
ⓒ Calvin Nelms Charter Sch [275] 20625 Clay Rd, Katy 77449 Mike Dean	6-12	AV	190	39%	281/398-8031 Fax 281/398-8032
ⓒ Carrollton Classical Academy [297] 2400 N Josey Ln, Carrollton 75006 Stephanie Scott	K-8		356 13	32%	972/245-2900 Fax 972/245-2999
ⓒ Cedar Park Charter Academy [295] 201 Buttercup Creek Blvd, Cedar Park 78613 Sylvia Sharp	PK-12		226		512/331-2980 Fax 512/628-6700
ⓒ Cedars International Academy 8416 N Interstate 35, Austin 78753 Heather Rauls	PK-7	T	385 8	76%	512/419-1551 Fax 512/419-1581 t
ⓒ Cedars Intl Next Generation HS 6700 Middle Fiskville Rd, Austin 78752 Steven Zipkes	8-12		116	48%	512/956-4406
ⓒ Cesar E Chavez Academy [294] 4613 S Padre Island Dr, Corp Christi 78411 Sandra Valencia	9-12	T	84	80%	361/561-5651 Fax 361/561-5654 t
ⓒ Chaparral Star Academy 14046 Summit Dr, Austin 78728 Marsha Hagin	K-12		381 19		512/989-2672 Fax 512/251-9799
ⓒ Chapel Hill Academy CS 4640 Sycamore School Rd, Fort Worth 76133 Victoria Sendejo	PK-5	T	510	59%	817/289-0242 Fax 817/289-3657 f t
ⓒ Clay Classical Academy [297] 3303 Potters House Way, Dallas 75236 Jacqueline Mercury-Owens	K-8		275	99%	214/467-4143 Fax 214/467-4066
ⓒ Compass Academy Charter Sch 5530 Billy Hext Rd, Odessa 79765 Valerie Minyen \ Jason Inman	K-10		1,126	17%	432/272-1836 Fax 432/272-1835
ⓒ Compass Rose Academy 8005 Outer Circle Rd, San Antonio 78235 Paul Morrissey	6-12		90		210/540-9265
ⓒ Comquest Academy 207 Peach St, Tomball 77375 Tanis Stanfield	7-12	AT	50 7	67%	281/516-0611 Fax 281/516-9807 t
ⓒ Coppell Classical Academy [297] 140 S Heartz Rd, Coppell 75019 Christopher Sisk	K-8		465	19%	972/393-3077
ⓒ Corinth Classical Academy [297] 3600 Meadowview Dr, Corinth 76210 Christina Wallace \ Allison Leonard	K-10		713		940/497-0059 Fax 866/231-9437
ⓒ Corpus Christi College Prep HS [294] 3501 S Padre Island Dr, Corp Christi 78415 Ashley Trevino	9-12	T	68 10	59%	361/225-4240 Fax 361/541-5967
ⓒ Corpus Christi Montessori Sch 822 Ayers St, Corp Christi 78404 Cerise Weeks	1-8		145	18%	361/852-0707
ⓒ Cove Charter Academy [295] 2205 FM 3046, Copperas Cove 76522 Michael Anderson	PK-12	T	296	46%	254/238-8231 Fax 254/247-3931
ⓒ Crockett Classical Academy [297] 1303 E Houston Ave, Crockett 75835 Frances Spivey	K-6	T	145	50%	936/546-0487 Fax 936/546-0034
ⓒ Crosstimbers Academy 242 Harmony Rd, Weatherford 76087 Dr Kendra Nelson	9-12		150	55%	817/594-6220 Fax 817/594-6227
ⓒ Cumberland Academy 1340 Shiloh Rd, Tyler 75703 Michelle Dean \ Mike Richardson \ Tim Schodowski	K-12		230 28		903/581-2890 Fax 903/581-1476 t
ⓒ Da Vinci School Science & Arts 785 Southwestern Dr, El Paso 79912 Vanessa Ruiz	5-12	T	534	44%	915/584-4024 Fax 915/581-9840
ⓒ Denton Classical Academy [297] 4420 Country Club Rd, Denton 76210 Susan Thomas	K-5		165	25%	940/565-8333
ⓐ Depelchin-Richmond Charter Sch ⓒ 710 S 7th St, Richmond 77469 Dorothy Goodman	K-8	T	20	75%	713/558-3980 Fax 713/558-3985
ⓒ Dr M L Garza-Gonzalez Chtr Sch [283] 4129 Greenwood Dr, Corp Christi 78416 Ricardo Godoy	PK-12	AGT	150	97%	361/881-9988 Fax 361/881-9994 f t
ⓒ Draw Acad Early Learning Ctr 7914 Westglen Dr, Houston 77063 Fernando Donatti	PK-PK	T	138	91%	713/706-3729 Fax 713/706-3711
ⓒ Draw Academy 3920 Stoney Brook Dr, Houston 77063 Patricia Beistegui	K-8	T	360 12	94%	713/706-3729 Fax 713/706-3711
ⓒ E Kolitz Hebrew Language Acad 12500 NW Military Hwy, San Antonio 78231 Kathryn Davis	K-8		319	13%	210/302-6900 Fax 210/302-6913
ⓒ East Austin Clg Prep-SW Key 6002 Jain Ln, Austin 78721 Ricardo Garza	PK-5	T	196 13	97%	512/287-5000
ⓒ East Austin College Prep-MLK 5800 W Martin L King Jr Blvd, Austin 78721 Erica Gonzalez	7-10		556	86%	512/287-5050
ⓒ East Ft Worth Montessori Acad 501 Oakland Blvd, Fort Worth 76103 Shello Tabb	PK-5	T	298 8	78%	817/496-3003 Fax 817/496-3004
ⓒ East Grand Preparatory Academy 6211 E Grand Ave, Dallas 75223 Sonia Webb	PK-9	T	800 16	94%	214/824-4747 Fax 214/824-4447
ⓒ East TX Charter Sch-Chadwick 2402 Alpine Rd, Longview 75601 Terry Lapic	9-12	A	140 13		903/753-9400 Fax 903/753-0285
ⓒ Ecia-Rowlett 8200 Schrade Rd, Rowlett 75088 Donna Townsend	PK-8	T	170	41%	972/412-8080 Fax 214/628-9124
ⓒ Ecia-Royse City 201 N Erby Campbell Blvd, Royse City 75189	K-6		117		972/636-2600 Fax 214/628-9124
ⓒ Ecia-Sunnyvale 302 N Town East Blvd, Sunnyvale 75182 Tonya Harris	PK-8	T	295	47%	214/628-9152 Fax 214/628-9124

1 Superintendent	8 Curric/Instruct K-12	19 Chief Financial Officer	29 Family/Consumer Science	39 Social Studies K-12	49 English/Lang Arts Elem	59 Special Education Elem	69 Academic Assessment
2 Bus/Finance/Purchasing	9 Curric/Instruct Elem	20 Art K-12	30 Adult Education	40 Social Studies Elem	50 English/Lang Arts Sec	60 Special Education Sec	70 Research/Development
3 Buildings And Grounds	10 Curric/Instruct Sec	21 Art Elem	31 Career/Sch-to-Work K-12	41 Social Studies Sec	51 Reading K-12	61 Foreign/World Lang K-12	71 Public Information
4 Food Service	11 Federal Program	22 Art Sec	32 Career/Sch-to-Work Elem	42 Science K-12	52 Reading Elem	62 Foreign/World Lang Elem	72 Summer School
5 Transportation	12 Title I	23 Music K-12	33 Career/Sch-to-Work Sec	43 Science Elem	53 Reading Sec	63 Foreign/World Lang Sec	73 Instructional Tech
6 Athletic	13 Title V	24 Music Elem	34 Early Childhood Ed	44 Science Sec	54 Remedial Reading K-12	64 Religious Education K-12	74 Inservice Training
7 Health Services	15 Asst Superintendent	25 Music Sec	35 Health/Phys Education	45 Math K-12	55 Remedial Reading Elem	65 Religious Education Elem	75 Marketing/Distributive
	16 Instructional Media Svcs	26 Business Education	36 Guidance Services K-12	46 Math Elem	56 Remedial Reading Sec	66 Religious Education Sec	76 Info Systems
	17 Chief Operations Officer	27 Career & Tech Ed	37 Guidance Services Elem	47 Math Sec	57 Bilingual/ELL	67 School Board President	77 Psychological Assess
	18 Chief Academic Officer	28 Technology Education	38 Guidance Services Sec	48 English/Lang Arts K-12	58 Special Education K-12	68 Teacher Personnel	78 Affirmative Action

Texas School Directory

School	Grades	Prog	Enroll	%	Phone
ⓒ Edinburg Classical Academy [297] 2110 S McColl Rd, Edinburg 78539 Elizabeth Alaniz	K-8	T	158	63%	956/720-4361
ⓒ Ehrhart Sch 3380 Fannin St Ste A, Beaumont 77701 Corina Long	PK-8	T	387	82%	409/839-8200 Fax 409/839-8242
ⓒ El Paso Academy East 11000 Argal Ct, El Paso 79935	9-12	T	261 15	67%	915/590-8589 Fax 915/590-8618
ⓒ El Paso Academy West 201 W Redd Rd, El Paso 79932 Beatriz Zavala	9-12	V	192 13		915/845-7997 Fax 915/845-7522 ⓣ
ⓒ El Paso Leadership Academy 1918 Texas Ave, El Paso 79901 Andrew Benitez	6-8	T	192	80%	915/298-3900 Fax 915/400-7971
ⓒ Elite College Prep Acad-Bowie 7310 Bowie St, Houston 77012 Tiffany Wright	PK-12		1,600		832/649-2700 Fax 713/649-8268
ⓒ Enhanced Horizons 149 Camp Scenic Rd, Ingram 78025 Kelly Bluemel	K-12	A	90		830/367-4330 Fax 830/367-2814
ⓒ Etoile Acad Charter Sch 6648 Hornwood Dr, Houston 77074 Kayleigh Colombero	5-5		65		713/201-5714
Evins Regional Juvenile Ctr 3801 E Monte Cristo Rd, Edinburg 78542 Steve Van Nest	9-12	GV	140 15		956/289-5500 Fax 956/381-1425
ⓒ Evolution Academy-Beaumont [279] 3920 W Cardinal Dr, Beaumont 77705 Dr Veronica Durden	9-12		145		409/239-5553 Fax 409/347-7135
ⓒ Evolution Academy-Houston [279] 2414 Spring Cypress Rd, Spring 77388 Julia Askew	9-12		300		281/907-6440 Fax 281/907-6442
ⓒ Evolution Academy-Richardson [279] ⓒ 1101 S Sherman St, Richardson 75081 Tina Shaw	9-12	TV	349 20	65%	972/907-3755 Fax 972/907-3765
ⓐ Excel Academy Charter Sch ⓒ 6500 Chimney Rock Rd, Houston 77081 Henry Gonzales	9-12	T	32	83%	713/222-4577 Fax 713/437-4121
ⓐ Excel Center-Fort Worth ⓒ 1220 W Presidio St, Fort Worth 76102 Carolynn Epperson	K-12		40		817/335-6429 Fax 817/335-7927
ⓒ Excellence In Leadership Acad 915 W Interstate Highway 2, Mission 78572 Ana Mendoza	PK-8	T	230	94%	956/424-9504 Fax 956/585-4673
ⓒ Faith Family Acad-Waxahachie [280] 701 Ovilla Rd, Waxahachie 75167 Monica Kramer	PK-8	T	300 25	94%	972/937-3704 Fax 469/383-3075 ⓕⓣ
ⓒ Faith Family Academy-Oak Cliff [280] 300 W Kiest Blvd, Dallas 75224 Tien Nguyen \ Tara Carter	PK-12	TV	2,150 95	87%	214/375-7682 Fax 214/375-7681 ⓕⓣ
ⓒ Fallbrook Academy [297] 12512 Walters Rd Ste 100, Houston 77014 Dr Dawn Doucet	K-8		203		281/880-1360
ⓒ Foundation School for Autism [297] 2235 Thousand Oaks Dr Ste 130, San Antonio 78232 Rheatha Miller	Spec	T	39	40%	210/402-0253
ⓒ Founders Classical Acad Flower [297] 500 Parker Sq, Flower Mound 75028 Briton Smith	K-8		515	6%	972/899-2521
ⓒ Founders Classical Acad Frisco [297] 10710 Frisco St, Frisco 75033 Melanie Sharpless	K-8		597		972/532-0952
ⓒ Founders Classical Acad Leandr [297] 1303 Leander Dr, Leander 78641 Dr Kathleen O'Toole	K-12		629	3%	512/259-0103 Fax 512/532-6503
ⓒ Founders Classical Acad Lwsvll [297] 1010 Bellaire Blvd, Lewisville 75067 Jason Caros	K-12		917	13%	469/464-3415
ⓒ Founders Classical Acad Mesq [297] 790 Windbell Cir, Mesquite 75149 Linea Dowler \ Daniel Carter	K-11	T	633	86%	469/453-0977
ⓒ Founders Classical Acad Schrtz [297] 8453 E 1518 N, Schertz 78154 James Farmer	K-9		532	32%	210/510-2618 Fax 866/422-4225
ⓒ Frank L Madla Accel Coll Acad [291] 4018 S Presa St, San Antonio 78223 Monica Villarreal	K-8	T	486 30	89%	210/533-3655 Fax 210/533-5077 ⓣ
ⓒ Frank L Madla Early College HS [291] 1400 W Villaret Blvd, San Antonio 78224 Jeff Flores	9-12	T	188	71%	210/486-3686
ⓒ Ft Worth Academy of Fine Arts [306] 3901 S Hulen St, Fort Worth 76109 Jennifer Jackson	3-12		580 40	10%	817/924-1482 Fax 817/926-9932
ⓐ Gainesville State Sch 1379 FM 678, Gainesville 76240 Andre Jenerson	8-12	GV	197 25		940/665-0701 Fax 940/665-9416
ⓒ Garland Classical Academy [297] 3024 Anita Dr, Garland 75041 Dr Alicia Luna	K-8	T	236	82%	972/840-1100 Fax 972/840-1105
ⓒ Gateway Charter Academy 1015 E Wheatland Rd, Dallas 75241 Raymond Edwards	6-12	T	296	31%	214/375-1921 Fax 214/375-2730
ⓒ Gateway Charter Elem Academy 6103 University Hills Blvd, Dallas 75241 Raymond Edwards	PK-5	T	457 18	69%	214/375-2039 Fax 214/375-1842
ⓒ Gateway College Prep Sch [292] 3360 County Road, Georgetown 78626 Kristin Hunt \ Laurie Mattson \ Shawn Lance	K-12		1,256	9%	512/868-4947 Fax 512/868-4946
ⓒ Gateway Tech High Sch [292] 2951 Williams Dr Bldg 2, Georgetown 78628 Jolene Bruce	9-12		74 15	10%	512/868-5299 Fax 512/869-3030
ⓒ George Gervin Academy 6944 S Sunbelt Dr, San Antonio 78218 Keith Thomas \ Tyrone Darden \ Dr Kimberley Conaway	PK-12	ATV	1,209 27	94%	210/568-8800 Fax 210/568-8897 ⓕ
ⓒ George I Sanchez Charter HS 6001 Gulf Fwy, Houston 77023 Giselle Easton	7-12	G	500 45		713/926-1112 Fax 713/926-8129
ⓒ Georgetown Behavioral Hlth CS 3101 S Austin Ave, Georgetown 78626 C Cunningham	6-12		15		254/644-9111
ⓒ Georgetown Charter Academy [295] 302 Serenada Dr, Georgetown 78628 Josiah Perkins	PK-8	T	75	45%	512/863-9236 Fax 512/863-9290
Giddings State Sch 2261 James Turman Rd, Giddings 78942 Dennis Smith	9-12	V	220 24		979/542-4500 Fax 979/542-3886
ⓒ Golden Rule CS-DeSoto [281] 135 W Wintergreen Rd, Desoto 75115 Diana Lara	PK-6	T	213	97%	469/248-4463 Fax 469/248-4471
ⓒ Golden Rule CS-Grand Prairie [281] 1729 Avenue B, Grand Prairie 75051 Cesar Hernandez	PK-3		89		214/988-3257 Fax 214/988-3261
ⓒ Golden Rule CS-Illinois [281] 2602 W Illinois Ave, Dallas 75233 Debra Durling \ Barberina Turner \ Alirio Carruyo	PK-12	T	720 20	92%	214/333-9330 Fax 214/333-9325 ⓣ
ⓒ Golden Rule CS-Pleasant Grove [281] 10747 Bruton Rd, Dallas 75217 Tramaine Reynolds	PK-4		272		469/341-5780 Fax 469/341-5779
ⓒ Golden Rule CS-Sunnyside [281] 622 Sunnyside Ave, Dallas 75211 Jimmy Wright	PK-4		187		214/393-6911

79 Student Personnel	91 Safety/Security	275 Response To Intervention	298 Grant Writer/Ptnrships	**School Programs**		**Social Media**
80 Driver Ed/Safety	92 Magnet School	277 Remedial Math K-12	750 Chief Innovation Officer	A = Alternative Program		
81 Gifted/Talented	93 Parental Involvement	280 Literacy Coach	751 Chief of Staff	G = Adult Classes		ⓕ = Facebook
82 Video Services	95 Tech Prep Program	285 STEM	752 Social Emotional Learning	M = Magnet Program		
83 Substance Abuse Prev	97 Chief Infomation Officer	286 Digital Learning		T = Title I Schoolwide		ⓣ = Twitter
84 Erate	98 Chief Technology Officer	288 Common Core Standards	**Other School Types**	V = Career & Tech Ed Programs		
85 AIDS Education	270 Character Education	294 Accountability	ⓐ = Alternative School			
88 Alternative/At Risk	271 Migrant Education	295 Network System	ⓒ = Charter School	New Schools are shaded		
89 Multi-Cultural Curriculum	273 Teacher Mentor	296 Title II Programs	ⓜ = Magnet School	New Superintendents and Principals are bold		
90 Social Work	274 Before/After Sch	297 Webmaster	ⓨ = Year-Round School	Personnel with email addresses are underscored		

TX-3

Market Data Retrieval

School	Grades		Enroll	%	Phone
© Golden Rule CS-Wilmer [281] 520 N I-45, Wilmer 75172 Cesar Hernandez	PK-K		20		972/525-6204
© Goodwater Mont Charter Sch 710 Stadium Dr, Georgetown 78626	PK-8		350		512/966-5484
© Great Hearts Forest Heights [282] Prue Rd, San Antonio 78240 Jason Doughty	K-5		401		210/892-3665
© Great Hearts Irving [282] 3350 Story Rd W, Irving 75038 Tami Perkins \ Philip Althage	K-10		872	9%	469/759-3030
© Great Hearts Monte Vista-North [282] 319 E Mulberry Ave, San Antonio 78212 William Rutherford	6-12		475	18%	210/888-9485
© Great Hearts Monte Vista-South [282] 211 Belknap Pl, San Antonio 78212 Mandi Cannon	K-5		432	13%	210/888-9485
© Great Hearts Northern Oaks [282] 17223 Jones Maltsberger Rd, San Antonio 78247 Trinette Keffer \ Samuel Heisman	K-10		1,171	9%	210/888-9483 Fax 210/888-9484
© Great Hearts Western Hills [282] 8702 Ingram Rd, San Antonio 78245 Robby Kuhlman	K-6		592		210/888-9488
Ⓐ Gwa Sierra Vista Charter HS [303] © 4620 S Lucy Ave, Laredo 78046 Gerardo Arambula	9-12	T	140	91%	956/723-0345 Fax 956/712-1112
Ⓐ Gwa Townlake CHS [303] © 1230 Townlake Dr, Laredo 78041 Olga Trevino	9-12	GT	181 15	93%	956/722-0747 Fax 956/722-0767
© Harbach-Ripley Charter Sch 6225 Northdale St, Houston 77087 Dawnyell Brown	PK-5		114		713/669-5202 Fax 713/640-7152
© Harmony Sch Achievement-Houstn [284] 16205 Kieth Harrow Blvd, Houston 77084 Melissa Knight	K-5	T	641	52%	281/855-2500 Fax 281/858-2505
© Harmony Sch Adv-Houston [284] 3171 N Sam Houston Pkwy W, Houston 77038 Fatih Oner	9-12	T	622	53%	281/741-8899 Fax 281/741-8006
© Harmony Sch Bus-Dallas [284] 8080 W Pres G Bush Hwy, Dallas 75252 Serif Mercan	6-12	T	400	42%	214/321-0100 Fax 214/919-4352
© Harmony Sch DSC-Houston [284] 6270 Barker Cypress Rd, Houston 77084 Ednan Karanci	6-12	T	730	56%	281/861-5105 Fax 281/656-8525
© Harmony Sch Endeavor-Austin [284] 13415 Ranch Road 620 N, Austin 78717 Waylon Stengler	PK-12		530	26%	512/284-9880 Fax 512/284-9632
© Harmony Sch Endeavor-Houston [284] 5668 W Little York Rd, Houston 77091 Kamil Yilmaz	K-8	T	557	80%	281/999-8400 Fax 281/999-8404
© Harmony Sch Enrichment-Houston [284] 3207 N Sam Houston Pkwy W, Houston 77038 Brent Bardo	K-5		650		281/999-0606
© Harmony Sch Exc-Austin [284] 2100 E Saint Elmo Rd, Austin 78744 Agil Sharifov	6-12	T	540	78%	512/693-0000 Fax 512/693-0008
© Harmony Sch Exc-El Paso [284] 9435 Betel Dr, El Paso 79907 Michelle Melendez	K-6	T	700	71%	915/307-4772 Fax 915/307-3689
© Harmony Sch Exc-Houston [284] 7340 Gessner Rd, Houston 77040 Mugire Ayci	K-8		877	35%	713/983-8668 Fax 713/983-8667
© Harmony Sch Exc-Laredo [284] 4401 San Francisco Ave Bldg B, Laredo 78041 Mustafa Ayik	9-12		357		956/791-0007
© Harmony Sch Exc-San Antonio [284] 2015 SW Loop 410, San Antonio 78227 Bambi Teaff	PK-5	T	530	63%	210/645-7166 Fax 210/645-7178
© Harmony Sch Exc-Sugar Land [284] 1428 Eldridge Rd, Sugar Land 77478 Sefik Ekmen	6-8		570		832/532-0728 Fax 832/532-0738
© Harmony Sch Exploration-Houstn [284] 9305 W Sam Houston Pkwy S, Houston 77099 Nora Morales	K-5	T	637	82%	832/831-7406 Fax 832/831-7408
© Harmony Sch Fine Arts & Tech [284] 9115 Kirby Dr, Houston 77054 Atila Akyurek	K-8	T	696	67%	832/433-7001 Fax 832/433-7083
© Harmony Sch Ingenuity-Houston [284] 10555 Stella Link Rd, Houston 77025 Jasmeen Kohli	6-12	T	600	73%	713/664-1020 Fax 713/664-1025
© Harmony Sch Innov-Austin [284] 2124 E Saint Elmo Rd A, Austin 78744 Tiffany Molina	PK-5	T	432	75%	512/300-0895 Fax 512/330-4225
© Harmony Sch Innov-Brownsville [284] 3451 Dana Ave, Brownsville 78526 Mustafa Altindag	6-12		482		956/544-1348 Fax 956/544-1349
© Harmony Sch Innov-Carrolltn [284] 1024 W Rosemeade Pkwy Bldg 1, Carrollton 75007 Clinton Barnes	K-5		570		469/892-5556 Fax 469/892-5667
© Harmony Sch Innov-El Paso [284] 5210 Fairbanks Dr, El Paso 79924 Riza Gurlek	K-12	T	1,090 22	69%	915/757-2929 Fax 915/757-2202
© Harmony Sch Innov-Euless [284] 701 S Industrial Blvd Ste 105, Euless 76040 Crystal McAnalley	K-6	T	724	52%	817/554-2800
© Harmony Sch Innov-Ft Worth [284] 8100 S Hulen St, Fort Worth 76123 Mehmet Basoglu	6-12	T	868	43%	817/386-5505 Fax 817/977-1727
© Harmony Sch Innov-Garland [284] 2250 Firewheel Pkwy, Garland 75040 Dan Bell	7-12		520		469/814-0059 Fax 469/814-0579
© Harmony Sch Innov-Houston [284] 9421 W Sam Houston Pkwy S, Houston 77099 Ali Yilmaz	6-8	T	507	77%	713/541-3030 Fax 713/541-3032
© Harmony Sch Innov-Laredo [284] 4608 Daugherty Ave, Laredo 78041 Geraldine Salas	K-5	T	648	73%	956/568-9495
© Harmony Sch Innov-San Antonio [284] 8125 Glen Mont, San Antonio 78239 Mert Aykanat	PK-8	T	525	75%	210/265-1715 Fax 210/265-5364
© Harmony Sch Innov-Sugar Land [284] 13522 W Airport Blvd, Sugar Land 77498 Hakan Simsek	9-12	T	692	44%	281/302-6445 Fax 281/302-6745
© Harmony Sch Innov-Waco [284] 1110 S Valley Mills Dr, Waco 76711 Orhan Avci	6-12	T	480	72%	254/235-0321 Fax 254/235-1373
© Harmony Sch Nature & Athletics [284] 8120 W Camp Wisdom Rd, Dallas 75249 Ilker Fidan	6-12	T	540	48%	972/296-1000 Fax 972/296-2125
© Harmony Sch Sci-Austin [284] 11800 Stonehollow Dr Ste 100, Austin 78758 Mehmet Subas	K-5	T	519	48%	512/821-1700 Fax 512/821-1702
© Harmony Sch Sci-Houston [284] 5435 S Braeswood Blvd, Houston 77096 Oguzkaan Torun	K-8	T	335	87%	713/729-4400 Fax 713/729-6600
© Harmony Sch Tech-Houston [284] 3203 N Sam Houston Pkwy W, Houston 77038 Celil Kucukbasol	6-8		660		281/444-1555 Fax 281/444-1015
© Harmony Sci Acad-Austin [284] 930 E Rundberg Ln, Austin 78753 Kyle Borel	PK-8	T	310 11	92%	512/835-7900 Fax 512/835-7901

1 Superintendent	8 Curric/Instruct K-12	19 Chief Financial Officer	29 Family/Consumer Science	39 Social Studies K-12	49 English/Lang Arts Elem	59 Special Education Elem	69 Academic Assessment
2 Bus/Finance/Purchasing	9 Curric/Instruct Elem	20 Art K-12	30 Adult Education	40 Social Studies Elem	50 English/Lang Arts Sec	60 Special Education Sec	70 Research/Development
3 Buildings And Grounds	10 Curric/Instruct Sec	21 Art Elem	31 Career/Sch-to-Work K-12	41 Social Studies Sec	51 Reading K-12	61 Foreign/World Lang K-12	71 Public Information
4 Food Service	11 Federal Program	22 Art Sec	32 Career/Sch-to-Work Elem	42 Science K-12	52 Reading Elem	62 Foreign/World Lang Elem	72 Summer School
5 Transportation	12 Title I	23 Music K-12	33 Career/Sch-to-Work Sec	43 Science Elem	53 Reading Sec	63 Foreign/World Lang Sec	73 Instructional Tech
6 Athletic	13 Title V	24 Music Elem	34 Early Childhood Ed	44 Science Sec	54 Remedial Reading K-12	64 Religious Education K-12	74 Inservice Training
7 Health Services	15 Asst Superintendent	25 Music Sec	35 Health/Phys Education	45 Math K-12	55 Remedial Reading Elem	65 Religious Education Elem	75 Marketing/Distributive
	16 Instructional Media Svcs	26 Business Education	36 Guidance Services K-12	46 Math Elem	56 Remedial Reading Sec	66 Religious Education Sec	76 Info Systems
	17 Chief Operations Officer	27 Career & Tech Ed	37 Guidance Services Elem	47 Math Sec	57 Bilingual/ELL	67 School Board President	77 Psychological Assess
	18 Chief Academic Officer	28 Technology Education	38 Guidance Services Sec	48 English/Lang Arts K-12	58 Special Education K-12	68 Teacher Personnel	78 Affirmative Action

Texas School Directory

School	Grades	Prog	Enroll	%	Phone
© Harmony Sci Acad-Beaumont [284] 4055 Calder Ave, Beaumont 77706 <u>Klediol Murati</u>	K-12	T	551	44%	409/838-4000 Fax 409/838-4009
© Harmony Sci Acad-Brownsville [284] 1124 Central Blvd, Brownsville 78520 <u>Layla Trevino</u>	PK-8	T	490	86%	956/574-9555 Fax 956/574-9558
© Harmony Sci Acad-Bryan [284] 2031 S Texas Ave, Bryan 77802 <u>Laura Mattingly</u>	PK-8	T	370 32	78%	979/779-2100 Fax 979/779-2110
© Harmony Sci Acad-Carrollton [284] 1024 W Rosemeade Pkwy Bldg 2, Carrollton 75007 <u>Huseyin Sari</u>	6-12	T	518	48%	972/394-9560 Fax 469/892-5667
© Harmony Sci Acad-Cedar Park [284] 12200 Anderson Mill Rd, Austin 78726 <u>Ilker Yilmaz</u>	PK-5		448		512/494-5151 Fax 512/494-5177
© Harmony Sci Acad-El Paso [284] 9405 Betel Dr, El Paso 79907 <u>Mucahit Turel</u>	K-12	T	800	72%	915/859-4620 Fax 915/859-4630
© Harmony Sci Acad-Euless [284] 701 S Industrial Blvd Ste 115, Euless 76040 <u>Sevde Aslan</u>	7-12		685		817/354-3000
© Harmony Sci Acad-Ft Worth [284] 5651 Westcreek Dr, Fort Worth 76133 <u>Serena Jackson</u>	K-5		700		817/263-0700 Fax 817/263-0705
© Harmony Sci Acad-Garland [284] 2302 Firewheel Pkwy, Garland 75040 <u>Jennifer Kolb</u>	PK-6		650		972/212-4777 Fax 972/212-4778
© Harmony Sci Acad-Grand Prairie [284] 1102 NW 7th St, Grand Prairie 75050 <u>Angela Knapp</u>	PK-8		500		972/642-9911 Fax 972/642-9922
© Harmony Sci Acad-Houston [284] 9431 W Sam Houston Pkwy S, Houston 77099 <u>Serdar Haytiyev</u>	9-12		632	68%	713/492-0214 Fax 713/383-2839
© Harmony Sci Acad-Katy [284] 22400 Grand Corner Dr, Katy 77494 <u>Meredith Marchante</u>	K-5	T	663	44%	832/437-3926 Fax 832/437-3927
© Harmony Sci Acad-Laredo [284] 4401 San Francisco Ave, Laredo 78041 <u>Abdullah Tatir</u>	6-8	T	741	71%	956/712-1177 Fax 956/712-1188
© Harmony Sci Acad-Lubbock [284] 1516 53rd St, Lubbock 79412 <u>Selcuk Bakir</u>	PK-8	T	387	77%	806/747-1000 Fax 806/747-1005
© Harmony Sci Acad-Odessa [284] 2755 N Grandview Ave, Odessa 79762 <u>Cetin Demir</u>	K-8	T	488	62%	432/363-6000 Fax 432/363-6001
© Harmony Sci Acad-Pflugerville [284] 1421 W Wells Branch Pkwy #200, Pflugerville 78660 <u>Engin Dogan</u>	6-12	T	894	54%	512/251-5000 Fax 512/251-5001
© Harmony Sci Acad-Plano [284] 550 Talbert Dr, Plano 75093 <u>Gregory Coleman</u>	PK-5		304		972/596-0041
© Harmony Sci Acad-San Antonio [284] 8505 Lakeside Pkwy, San Antonio 78245 <u>Klediol Murati</u>	6-12	T	772 40	65%	210/674-7788 Fax 210/674-7766
© Harmony Sci Acad-Sugar Land [284] 13415 W Bellfort Ave, Sugar Land 77478 <u>Afreen Merchant</u>	K-5	T	695	54%	281/265-2525 Fax 281/265-2565
© Harmony Sci Acad-Waco [284] 1900 N Valley Mills Dr, Waco 76710 <u>Lindy Ermoian</u>	PK-6		770		254/751-7878 Fax 254/751-7877
© Harmony Science Acad-Cypress 7047 Greenhouse Rd, Cypress 77433	K-5		401		281/444-1555
© Harmony Science Acad-Dallas [284] 11945 Forestgate Dr, Dallas 75243 <u>Omer Toycu</u>	K-12		1,225		469/730-2477 Fax 469/341-9138
Ⓐ Harris Co Juvenile Justice CS © 1200 Congress St, Houston 77002 <u>Oliver Burbridge</u>	5-12	GV	602		713/222-4100 Fax 713/222-4388
Ⓐ Harris Cty Leadership Academy 9120 Katy Hockley Rd, Katy 77493 <u>Kaoenya Warren</u>	6-12	T	96 8	97%	713/222-4629 Fax 713/222-4630
Ⓐ Helping Hand Charter Sch © 3804 Avenue B, Austin 78751 <u>Holly Engleman</u>	K-6		25		512/751-4534
© Heritage Academy Del Rio 709B Kings Way, Del Rio 78840 <u>Judy Galindo</u>	4-12	T	350	69%	830/774-6230
© Heritage Academy San Antonio 8750 Fourwinds Dr, Windcrest 78239 <u>Eric Davis</u>	PK-8	T	290	83%	210/354-7753 Fax 210/547-9459
© Hfa-Alameda Sch-Art & Design 318 W Houston St, San Antonio 78205 <u>Jeremiah Montez</u>	9-12	T	150	49%	210/226-4031 Fax 210/802-3025
© High Point Academy 1256 N Jim Wright Fwy, Fort Worth 76108 <u>Craig Shreckengast</u>	K-12		457	27%	817/600-6401
© Hill Country Yth Rch-Najim Sch 3522 Junction Hwy 27, Ingram 78025 <u>Kelly Bluemel</u>	K-12		104		830/367-6100 Fax 830/367-2611
© Horizon Montessori Academy I [301] 320 N Main St, McAllen 78501 <u>Miguel Castillo</u>	PK-8		590 19		956/631-0234 Fax 956/668-1404
© Horizon Montessori II [301] 1222 W Sugarcane Dr, Weslaco 78599 <u>Janis De Luna</u>	PK-8	T	305	80%	956/969-0044 Fax 956/969-0065
© Horizon Montessori III [301] 2802 S 77 Sunshine Strip, Harlingen 78550 <u>Annette Salazar</u>	PK-8	T	341	62%	956/423-8200 Fax 956/423-8207
© Houston Gateway Acad-Evergreen 3400 Evergreen Dr, Houston 77087 <u>Yuridia Garcia</u>	PK-8	T	500	96%	713/649-2706 Fax 713/649-8165
© Houston Gateway Academy-Coral 1020 Coral St, Houston 77012 <u>John Smith</u>	PK-12	T	819 29	91%	713/923-5060 Fax 713/923-9070
© Houston Gateway Elite Clg Prep 7310 Bowie St, Houston 77012 <u>Tiffany Wright</u>	PK-5	T	745	90%	832/649-2700 Fax 713/649-8268
© Houston Heights High Sch 1125 Lawrence St, Houston 77008 <u>Erica McCready</u>	9-12	T	204 15	86%	713/868-9797 Fax 713/868-9750 f t
© Howard Burnham Elem Sch 7310 Bishop Flores Dr, El Paso 79912 <u>Mrs Heras-Salas</u>	K-5	GT	380	38%	915/584-9499 Fax 915/585-8814
© Humble Classical Academy [297] 901 Wilson Rd Bldg B, Humble 77338 <u>Alyson Kelly</u>	K-7	T	304	77%	281/913-5107 Fax 866/655-1476
© Hunstville Classical Academy [297] 2407 Sam Houston Ave Ste B, Huntsville 77340 <u>Sherry Sheppard</u>	K-8		321		936/291-0203 Fax 936/293-8096
Ⓐ Huston Academy © 680 Peach Orchard Rd, Stephenville 76401 <u>Carol Taylor</u>	9-12	TV	75 7	77%	254/965-8883 Fax 254/965-8654
© Imagine Intl Academy-N Texas [029] 2860 Virginia Pkwy, McKinney 75071 <u>Holly Baker</u> \ <u>Elisha Upton</u>	K-12		1,020	6%	214/491-1500 Fax 214/491-1504
© Inspired Vision Elem Sch [272] 8421 Bohannon Dr, Dallas 75217 <u>Sherqueena Myles</u>	PK-4	T	742 12	92%	214/391-7964 Fax 214/391-7954
© Inspired Vision Secondary Sch [272] 8501 Bruton Rd, Dallas 75217 <u>Tara Addison</u>	7-12	T	580 25	84%	972/285-5758 Fax 972/285-0061

79 Student Personnel	91 Safety/Security	275 Response To Intervention	298 Grant Writer/Ptnrships	**School Programs**	**Social Media**
30 Driver Ed/Safety	92 Magnet School	277 Remedial Math K-12	750 Chief Innovation Officer	**A** = Alternative Program	
31 Gifted/Talented	93 Parental Involvement	280 Literacy Coach	751 Chief of Staff	**G** = Adult Classes	f = Facebook
32 Video Services	95 Tech Prep Program	285 STEM	752 Social Emotional Learning	**M** = Magnet Program	
33 Substance Abuse Prev	97 Chief Information Officer	286 Digital Learning		**T** = Title I Schoolwide	t = Twitter
34 Erate	98 Chief Technology Officer	288 Common Core Standards	**Other School Types**	**V** = Career & Tech Ed Programs	
35 AIDS Education	270 Character Education	294 Accountability	Ⓐ = Alternative School		
38 Alternative/At Risk	271 Migrant Education	295 Network System	© = Charter School	New Schools are shaded	
39 Multi-Cultural Curriculum	273 Teacher Mentor	296 Title II Programs	Ⓜ = Magnet School	New Superintendents and Principals are bold	
30 Social Work	274 Before/After Sch	297 Webmaster	Ⓨ = Year-Round School	Personnel with email addresses are underscored	**TX—5**

School	Grades		Enrollment		Phone
© Ischool High Lewisville [297] 1800 Lakeway Dr Ste 100, Lewisville 75057 Gary Wilhelmi	9-12		76	13%	972/317-2470
© Ischool High the Woodlands [297] 3232 College Park Dr Ste 212, The Woodlands 77384 Guamma Goff	9-12		266	16%	936/231-8594
© Ischool High University Park [297] 20515 State Highway 249, Houston 77070 Stacy Bare	9-12		313	14%	281/251-5770
© Ischool High-Hickory Creek [297] 800 Point Vista Dr Ste 518, Hickory Creek 75065 Amie Giacumakis	K-12		71	7%	940/321-1144
© Ischool Virtual Academy HS [297] 1301 Waters Ridge Dr, Lewisville 75057 Tammany Olson	9-12		1,501		888/729-0622
© Jasper Classical Academy [297] 1501B S Wheeler St, Jasper 75951 Patricia Oliver	K-7	T	113	53%	409/489-9222 Fax 409/489-9272
© Jean Massieu Acad for the Deaf 823 N Center St, Arlington 76011 Monica Fox	Spec		196 13		817/460-0396 Fax 817/460-9867
© Jubilee Academic Center 4434 Roland Rd, San Antonio 78222 Cheryl Stewart	PK-8	V	620 30		210/333-6227 Fax 210/337-2357
© Jubilee Brownsville [285] 4955 Pablo Kisel Blvd, Brownsville 78526 Carlos Moreno	PK-12		1,100		956/509-2690 Fax 956/509-2326
© Jubilee Destiny [285] 2601 Bothwell Rd, Harlingen 78552 Tanya Perez	PK-7		100		956/708-2040
© Jubilee Harlingen [285] 4501 W Expressway 83, Harlingen 78552 Dr Cindy Sadler	PK-7	T	125	66%	956/708-2030 Fax 956/364-2453
© Jubilee Highland Hills [285] 1515 Goliad Rd, San Antonio 78223 Trina Cardenas	PK-8		503		210/634-7590
© Jubilee Highland Park [285] 901 E Drexel Ave, San Antonio 78210 James Montano	PK-8	T	299	73%	210/801-8030 Fax 210/532-3810
© Jubilee Kingsville [285] 201 N 19th St, Kingsville 78363	PK-8		250		361/516-0840 Fax 361/516-0874
© Jubilee Lake View Univ Prep [285] 325 Castroville Rd, San Antonio 78207 Nadine Pabst	PK-12		450		210/963-3900
© Jubilee Leadership Academy [285] 4150 Jaime J Zapata Ave, Brownsville 78521 Yolanda Cantu	PK-5		218		956/641-4250 Fax 956/641-4255
© Jubilee Livingway [285] 350 Ruben Torres Sr Blvd, Brownsville 78520 Cecilia Septimo	K-5		351		956/708-2020 Fax 956/554-9701
© Jubilee San Antonio [285] 4427 Chandler, San Antonio 78222 Hector Gomez	K-12		300		210/278-3880 Fax 210/278-3929
© Jubilee Wells Branch [285] 15201 Burnet Rd, Austin 78728 Cynthia Sneed	K-9		800	29%	512/872-8440 Fax 512/341-0816
© Jubilee-Wells Academies 3711 Shoreline Dr, Austin 78728 Cynthia Sneed	PK-9		500		512/872-8440
© Katherine Anne Porter Sch 515 FM 2325, Wimberley 78676 Dr Erin Flynn	9-12	ATV	157 15	46%	512/847-6867 Fax 512/847-0737
© Kauffman Leadership Academy 1108 N Anglin St, Cleburne 76031 Dr Theresa Kauffman	5-12		120	13%	682/459-2800 Fax 817/740-7521
© Ki Charter Academy 120 Bert Brown St, San Marcos 78666 Paul Camden	1-12	T	174	98%	512/618-0787
© Kingsland Sch [292] 136 Real St, Kingsland 78639 Meloni Puishes	K-8		225	35%	325/388-0020
© KIPP 3D Academy [288] 500 Tidwell Rd, Houston 77022 Kelsey Lyman	5-8	T	440	88%	832/230-0566 Fax 713/692-1631
© KIPP Acad West MS [288] 8500 Highway 6 S, Houston 77083 Steven Khadam-Hir	5-8	T	324	86%	832/230-0573
© KIPP Academy MS [288] 10711 Kipp Way Dr, Houston 77099 Andrew Rubin	5-8		420 20		832/328-1051 Fax 281/498-4201
© KIPP Aspire Academy [289] 239 Stark, San Antonio 78204 Jaime Jaen	5-8	T	485	88%	210/735-7300 Fax 210/735-7305
© KIPP Austin Acad Arts Letters [286] 8509 FM 969 Ste 619, Austin 78724 Jamie Holley	5-8		455		512/501-3640 Fax 512/501-3641
© KIPP Austin Beacon Prep [286] 5107 S Interstate 35 Ste 8, Austin 78744 Kristi Michaels	5-8		465		512/651-1918 Fax 866/924-2872
© KIPP Austin Brave HS [286] 5107 S Interstate 35 Ste A, Austin 78744 Stephanie Burns	9-11	T	500	87%	512/651-2225 Fax 866/857-6541
© KIPP Austin College Prep [286] 8004 Cameron Rd, Austin 78754 Katie Carpenter	5-8	T	441	92%	512/501-4969 Fax 512/637-6899
© KIPP Austin Collegiate [286] 8004 Cameron Rd, Austin 78754 James Pasto	9-12		713		512/501-3586 Fax 512/501-3587
© KIPP Austin Comunidad [286] 8004 Cameron Rd, Austin 78754 Kelly Doyle	K-4		600		512/501-3911 Fax 512/870-9224
© KIPP Austin Connections ES [286] 8509 FM 969 Ste 629, Austin 78724 Elizabeth Reiter	K-4	T	600	88%	512/651-5537 Fax 512/870-9537
© KIPP Austin Leadership ES [286] 8509 FM 969 Ste 628, Austin 78724 Nicole Seltman	K-4		560		512/651-2168 Fax 866/461-8086
© KIPP Austin Obras [286] 5107 S Interstate 35 Ste A, Austin 78744 Briana Anderson	K-4		596	85%	512/651-2069 Fax 866/700-5197
© KIPP Austin Vista Middle Sch [286] 8509 FM 969 Ste 627, Austin 78724 Breanne Diaz	5-8	T	430	92%	512/651-1921 Fax 512/501-3641
© KIPP Camino Academy [289] 4343 W Commerce St, San Antonio 78237 Delisa Morales	5-8	T	492	89%	210/829-4200 Fax 210/829-4207
© KIPP Climb Academy [288] 8805 Ferndale, Houston 77017 Autumn Figueroa	PK-3		500	83%	832/230-0578
© KIPP Connect Houston High Sch [288] 6700 Bellaire Blvd, Houston 77074 Geoffrey Roy	9-9		160		281/879-3023
© KIPP Connect Houston MS [288] 6700 Bellaire Blvd, Houston 77074 Pegah Taylor	5-8		433	93%	281/879-3023 Fax 713/774-0387
© KIPP Connect Houston Primary [288] 6700 Bellaire Blvd, Houston 77074 Adam Kutac	PK-4	T	843	93%	281/879-3023
© KIPP Courage College Prep [288] 2200 Ridgecrest Dr, Houston 77055 Eric Schmidt	5-8		397		713/251-3800

1 Superintendent	8 Curric/Instruct K-12	19 Chief Financial Officer	29 Family/Consumer Science	39 Social Studies K-12	49 English/Lang Arts Elem	59 Special Education Elem	69 Academic Assessment
2 Bus/Finance/Purchasing	9 Curric/Instruct Elem	20 Art K-12	30 Adult Education	40 Social Studies Elem	50 English/Lang Arts Sec	60 Special Education Sec	70 Research/Development
3 Buildings And Grounds	10 Curric/Instruct Sec	21 Art Elem	31 Career/Sch-to-Work K-12	41 Social Studies Sec	51 Reading K-12	61 Foreign/World Lang K-12	71 Public Information
4 Food Service	11 Federal Program	22 Art Sec	32 Career/Sch-to-Work Elem	42 Science K-12	52 Reading Elem	62 Foreign/World Lang Elem	72 Summer School
5 Transportation	12 Title I	23 Music K-12	33 Career/Sch-to-Work Sec	43 Science Elem	53 Reading Sec	63 Foreign/World Lang Sec	73 Instructional Tech
6 Athletic	13 Title V	24 Music Elem	34 Early Childhood Ed	44 Science Sec	54 Remedial Reading K-12	64 Religious Education K-12	74 Inservice Training
7 Health Services	14 Instructional Media Svcs	25 Music Sec	35 Health/Phys Education	45 Math K-12	55 Remedial Reading Elem	65 Religious Education Elem	75 Marketing/Distributive
	15 Asst Superintendent	26 Business Education	36 Guidance Services K-12	46 Math Elem	56 Remedial Reading Sec	66 Religious Education Sec	76 Info Systems
	16 Instructional Media Svcs	27 Career & Tech Ed	37 Guidance Services Elem	47 Math Sec	57 Bilingual/ELL	67 School Board President	77 Psychological Assess
	17 Chief Operations Officer	28 Technology Education	38 Guidance Services Sec	48 English/Lang Arts K-12	58 Special Education K-12	68 Teacher Personnel	78 Affirmative Action
	18 Chief Academic Officer						

Texas School Directory

School	Grades	Type	Enroll	%	Phone
ⓒ KIPP Destiny Elem Sch [287] 3663 W Camp Wisdom Rd, Dallas 75237 Tori Lee	K-4	T	400	85%	972/323-4220 Fax 972/708-8598
ⓒ KIPP Destiny Middle Sch [287] 3663 W Camp Wisdom Rd, Dallas 75237 Cynite Cooke	5-8	T	120	89%	972/323-4225
ⓒ KIPP Dream Prep [288] 500 Tidwell Rd, Houston 77022 Haley Simonton	PK-4	T	864	93%	832/230-0566
ⓒ KIPP Esperanza Dual Lang Acad [289] 239 Stark, San Antonio 78204 Dorene Benavidez	K-4	T	648	81%	210/888-6601 Fax 210/888-6602
ⓒ KIPP Explore Academy [288] 5402 Lawndale St, Houston 77023 Amy Stabile	PK-4	T	860	95%	832/230-0547 Fax 832/230-0178
ⓒ KIPP Generations Collegiate HS [288] 500 Tidwell Rd, Houston 77022 Amanda Ybarsabal	9-12	T	600	89%	832/230-0566 Fax 832/201-9988
ⓒ KIPP Houston High Sch [288] 10711 Kipp Way Dr, Houston 77099 Mohamad Maarouf	9-12	T	715	92%	832/328-1082 Fax 832/838-4293
ⓒ KIPP Intrepid Prep Sch [288] 5402 Lawndale St, Houston 77023 Arlene Taluyo	5-8	T	382	93%	281/879-3100 Fax 713/924-5046
ⓒ KIPP Legacy Prep Sch [288] 9606 Mesa Dr, Houston 77078 Monique Payton	PK-4	T	964	95%	832/230-0567 Fax 713/491-7311
ⓒ KIPP Liberation College Prep [288] 5400 Martin Luther King Blvd, Houston 77021 Tai Ingram	5-8	T	426	91%	832/230-0564 Fax 713/748-0471
ⓒ KIPP Nexus MS [288] 4211 Watonga Blvd, Houston 77092 Lisa McClinton	5-5		107		832/230-0553
ⓒ KIPP Nexus Primary-Houston [288] 4211 Watonga Blvd, Houston 77092 Lindsay Hatcher	PK-2		90		832/230-0553
ⓒ KIPP Northeast College Prep [288] 9680 Mesa Dr, Houston 77078 John Burnett	9-12	T	538	89%	832/230-0567
ⓒ KIPP Peace Elem Sch [288] 5400 Martin Luther King Blvd, Houston 77021 Precious Parks	PK-4	T	718	90%	832/230-0564 Fax 713/440-0667
ⓒ KIPP Pleasant Grove Mid Sch [287] 2200 N Saint Augustine Dr, Dallas 75227 Delshon Henry	5-5		355		972/323-4235
ⓒ KIPP Pleasant Grove Primary [287] 2200 N Saint Augustine Dr, Dallas 75227 Dexter Chaney	K-3		355	96%	972/323-4230
ⓒ KIPP Poder Academy [289] 128 S Audubon Dr, San Antonio 78212 Nicole Winsett	5-8		460	85%	210/888-6513 Fax 210/888-6515
ⓒ KIPP Polaris Academy for Boys [288] 9636 Mesa Dr, Houston 77078 Jamaal Henry	5-8		328	90%	832/230-0567 Fax 713/633-4783
ⓒ KIPP Prime College Prep [288] 8805 Ferndale, Houston 77017 Rob Gill	5-8		319	90%	832/230-0578
ⓒ KIPP Sharp Prep [288] 8430 Westglen Dr, Houston 77063 Michelle Bennett	PK-4	T	898	88%	281/879-3000 Fax 281/879-3001
ⓒ KIPP Sharpstown College Prep [288] 8440 Westpark Dr, Houston 77063 Rebecca Easterby	5-8	T	426	95%	281/879-3005 Fax 281/915-0074
ⓒ KIPP Shine Prep [288] 10711 Kipp Way Dr, Houston 77099 Deborah Shifrine	PK-4	T	861	93%	832/328-1051 Fax 832/230-0579
ⓒ KIPP Somos Collegiate High Sch [289] 735 Fredericksburg Rd, San Antonio 78201 Jeremy Gray	9-9		160		
ⓒ KIPP Spirit College Prep [288] 11000 Scott St, Houston 77047 Tiffany Prados	5-8		441		832/230-0562 Fax 713/731-1644
ⓒ KIPP Sunnyside High Sch [288] 11000 Scott St, Houston 77047 Dr Rian Wright	9-12	T	550	82%	832/230-0562 Fax 832/201-8695
ⓒ KIPP Truth Academy [287] 1545 S Ewing Ave, Dallas 75216 Ellen Prueitt	5-8	T	477	93%	972/323-4215 Fax 214/375-2990
ⓒ KIPP Truth Elem Sch [287] 1545 S Ewing Ave, Dallas 75216 Katie Jubert	K-3	T	120	96%	972/323-4240
ⓒ KIPP UN Mundo Dual Lang Acad [289] 4343 W Commerce St, San Antonio 78237 Lorraine Bernal	K-4	T	636	87%	210/824-1905 Fax 210/485-1393
ⓒ KIPP Unity Primary [288] 8500 Highway 6 S, Houston 77083 Kaleena Rosenbauer	PK-4		501	86%	832/230-0572 Fax 281/933-8169
ⓒ KIPP University Prep High Sch [289] 239 Stark, San Antonio 78204 Tina De Valk	9-12	T	850	86%	210/290-8720 Fax 210/290-9427
ⓒ KIPP Voyage Academy for Girls [288] 9616 Mesa Dr, Houston 77078 Kristen Pappas	5-8		324	91%	832/230-0567 Fax 713/491-7311
ⓒ KIPP Zenith Academy [288] 11000 Scott St, Houston 77047 Cassandra Cotman	PK-4	T	861	89%	832/230-0562 Fax 713/731-0386
ⓒ La Academia De Estrellas CS 4680 W Kiest Blvd, Dallas 75236 Ivelisse Centeno \ Kemlyn Stephens	PK-8	T	1,088 18	92%	214/946-8908
ⓒ La Fe Preparatory Sch 616 E Father Rahm Ave, El Paso 79901 Nelllie Morales	PK-7		243	96%	915/533-4690 Fax 915/533-4175
ⓒ Lawson Academy 5052 Scott St, Houston 77004 Dr Marthea Raney	6-8		260	57%	713/225-1551 Fax 713/225-1561
ⓒ Leadership Academy 6720 Oak Hill Blvd, Tyler 75703 Louise Dyer	K-7		127		903/561-1002 Fax 903/303-2069
ⓒ Leadership Prep Sch 8500 Teel Pkwy, Frisco 75034 Michelle Creamer	K-4		500	3%	972/294-6921 Fax 972/294-3416
ⓒ Legacy Prep Charter Acad-Plano 601 Accent Dr, Plano 75075 Nicole May	K-12	T	355	39%	469/998-0213 Fax 469/287-8579
ⓒ Legacy Prep Chtr Acad-Mesquite 2727 Military Pkwy, Mesquite 75149 Vivian Rivera \ Javier Chaparro	K-12	T	1,200	73%	469/287-8610 Fax 469/461-0793
ⓒ Legacy Sch of Sport Sciences 2727 Spring Creek Dr, Spring 77373 Ralph Butler	6-11		393		713/396-0837
ⓒ Life High School-Waxahachie [290] 170 Butcher Rd, Waxahachie 75165 Kim Riepe	9-12	T	931	38%	469/708-4444 Fax 469/708-4445
ⓒ Life Middle School Waxahachie [290] 3295 N Highway 77, Waxahachie 75165 Fred Stanmore	7-8	T	530	47%	972/937-0715 Fax 972/937-0503
ⓒ Life School Cedar Hill [290] 129 W Wintergreen Rd, Cedar Hill 75104 Candace Johnson	K-6	T	634	52%	972/293-2825 Fax 972/291-2877
ⓒ Life School Lancaster [290] 950 S Interstate 35 E, Lancaster 75146 Deborah Garton	K-6	T	598	61%	972/274-7950 Fax 972/274-7991

79 Student Personnel	91 Safety/Security	275 Response To Intervention	298 Grant Writer/Ptnrships
80 Driver Ed/Safety	92 Magnet School	277 Remedial Math K-12	750 Chief Innovation Officer
81 Gifted/Talented	93 Parental Involvement	280 Literacy Coach	751 Chief of Staff
82 Video Services	95 Tech Prep Program	285 STEM	752 Social Emotional Learning
83 Substance Abuse Prev	97 Chief Information Officer	286 Digital Learning	
84 Erate	98 Chief Technology Officer	288 Common Core Standards	**Other School Types**
85 AIDS Education	270 Character Education	294 Accountability	Ⓐ = Alternative School
88 Alternative/At Risk	271 Migrant Education	295 Network System	Ⓒ = Charter School
89 Multi-Cultural Curriculum	273 Teacher Mentor	296 Title II Programs	Ⓜ = Magnet School
90 Social Work	274 Before/After Sch	297 Webmaster	Ⓨ = Year-Round School

School Programs
A = Alternative Program
G = Adult Classes
M = Magnet Program
T = Title I Schoolwide
V = Career & Tech Ed Programs

Social Media
 = Facebook
 = Twitter

New Schools are shaded
New Superintendents and Principals are bold
Personnel with email addresses are underscored

School	Grades		Enroll	%	Phone
ⓒ Life School Mountain Creek [290] 5525 W Illinois Ave, Dallas 75211 Eva Mease	K-5	T	444	67%	214/623-0012 Fax 214/613-3166
ⓒ Life School Oak Cliff [290] 4400 S R L Thornton Fwy, Dallas 75224 Anita Sanders \ Anne Beckman	K-12	T	1,545	77%	214/376-8200 Fax 214/371-0297
ⓒ Life School Red Oak [290] 777 S I-35 E, Red Oak 75154 Joy Shepherd	K-6	T	1,030	38%	469/552-9200 Fax 972/617-5765
ⓒ Lighthouse Charter Sch 2718 Frontier Dr, San Antonio 78227 Blanca Gonzales	PK-1	T	85 15	89%	210/674-4100 Fax 210/674-4108
ⓒ Lighthouse Chtr Sch-B Campus 8138 Westshire Dr, San Antonio 78227 Blanca Gonzalez	PK-8	T	220	86%	210/257-6746 Fax 210/254-9284
ⓒ Lone Star Language Academy 5301 Democracy Dr, Plano 75024 Judy Johnston	K-5		162		972/244-7220
Lubbock Adult Learning Center 1601 24th St, Lubbock 79411 Larry Morgan	Adult	V	24 6		806/281-5750 Fax 806/281-5758
ⓒ Lumin E Dallas Community Sch 924 Wayne St, Dallas 75223 Sylvie Fitzgerald	PK-3		102 4		214/824-8950 Fax 214/827-7683
ⓒ Lumin Lindsley Park Cmty Sch 722 Tenison Memorial Dr, Dallas 75223 Rebekah Hardie	PK-3	T	313	64%	214/321-9155 Fax 214/321-0702
ⓒ Magnolia Montessori for All 5100 Pecan Brook Dr, Austin 78724 Madison Schmakel	PK-6	T	479	39%	512/522-2429
ⓒ Mainland Prep Classical Acad [297] 319 Newman Rd, La Marque 77568 Diane Merchant	PK-8	T	492 40	88%	409/934-9100 Fax 409/934-9130
ⓒ Manara Acad Leadership Acad 8001 Jetstar Dr Ste 100, Irving 75063 Denise Woodward	7-11		149	54%	972/304-1155 Fax 972/304-1150
ⓒ Manara Acad-Arlington STEM 6101 S Collins St, Arlington 76018 Luis Valdez	K-8		243		972/304-1155 Fax 972/304-1150
ⓒ Manara Acad-Irving Elem Sch 8201 Tristar Dr, Irving 75063 Dr Monica Hall	PK-6	T	422	37%	972/304-1155 Fax 972/304-1150
ⓐ McLennan Co State Juvenile Sch 116 W Burleson Rd, Mart 76664 Carol Jo Mize	6-12		200 19		254/297-8200 Fax 254/297-8392
ⓐ Meadowland CS Stepping Stones ⓒ 3103 West Ave, San Antonio 78213 James Chavis	1-5		4		830/331-4094
ⓒ Meadowland CS-Oaks Acad 121 Old San Antonio Rd, Boerne 78006 Jerry Zapata	Spec	T	85	87%	830/331-4094 Fax 830/331-4096
ⓒ Meridian World Charter Sch 2555 N Interstate 35, Round Rock 78664 Shannon Haulotte \ Melina Berduo \ Charles Ryder	K-12	T	1,594	8%	512/660-5230 Fax 512/660-5231
ⓒ Meyer High Sch [277] 1020 Elm St Bldg 500, Waco 76704 Tyler Ellis	9-12	T	160	55%	254/754-2288 Fax 254/754-8002
ⓒ Meyerpark Charter Sch 13663 Main St, Houston 77035 Julia Wright	PK-6	T	230	94%	713/729-9712 Fax 713/729-9720
ⓒ Midland Academy Charter Sch 500 N Baird St, Midland 79701 Janet Wallace	PK-9	T	500 36	41%	432/686-0003 Fax 432/686-0845
ⓒ Munday Charter Sch 4800 Manor Rd, Austin 78723 N Whetstone	6-12	A	27		512/791-2270 Fax 512/232-9177
ⓒ Mva Brownsville CHS [303] 944 E Los Ebanos Blvd, Brownsville 78520 Yolanda Chamberlain	9-12		130		956/372-1433
ⓐ Mva McAllen CHS [303] ⓒ 200 N 17th St, McAllen 78501 Jennifer McLelland	9-12		124 8		956/618-2303 Fax 956/618-2323
ⓒ Mva Mercedes CHS [303] 103 E 2nd St, Mercedes 78570 Miscellene Pemelton	9-12		130		956/565-5417 Fax 956/514-2586
ⓒ Nci CS Without Walls 6565 Rookin St, Houston 77074 Cimberli Darrough	PK-PK	T	184	100%	713/779-4856
New Horizons Ranch Sch 850 FM Road Hwy 574W, Goldthwaite 76844 Shelley Williams	K-12	T	70 12	95%	325/938-5513 Fax 325/938-5512
ⓒ Newman Int'l Acad-Arlington 1111 Gibbins Rd, Arlington 76011 Wendy Dansby \ Dr Donna Hart	PK-12	T	870	45%	682/207-5175
ⓒ Newman Int'l Acad-Cedar Hill 1114 W FM 1382, Cedar Hill 75104 Carinia Hornbuckle	K-12		600	39%	972/293-5460
ⓒ Newman Int'l Acad-Ft Worth 6801 Meadowbrook Dr, Fort Worth 76112 Dale Duncan	K-4	T	166	80%	817/655-2255
ⓒ Newman Int'l Acad-Grace 308 W Park Row Dr, Arlington 76010 Shauna Moore	K-6	T	220	60%	682/220-9210
ⓒ Newman Int'l Acad-Mansfield 1201 N State Highway 360, Mansfield 76063 Keith Shull	K-8		273	31%	682/400-4010
ⓒ Nolan Creek Sch [292] 505 E Avenue C, Belton 76513 Ken Wiseman	K-6		84		254/939-4491
ⓒ North Texas Collegiate Acad-E [300] 1851 Oak Grove Pkwy, Little Elm 75068 Susan Taraba	K-8	T	140	72%	972/292-3562 Fax 972/292-3563
ⓒ North Texas Collegiate Acad-N [300] 4601 N Interstate 35, Denton 76207 Amanda Jordan	K-8	T	113	74%	940/383-1972 Fax 940/383-7655
ⓒ North Texas Collegiate Acad-S [300] 968 Raldon St, Lewisville 75067 Donica Hill	PK-8		177 10		972/221-3564 Fax 972/221-3576
ⓒ Nova Academy Cedar Hill 820 E Wintergreen Rd Bldg B, Cedar Hill 75104 Janice Foster	PK-6		62		972/291-1900 Fax 972/293-8049
ⓒ Nova Academy Prichard 2800 Prichard Ln, Dallas 75227 Lashun Jasper	PK-8	T	481	82%	972/808-7470 Fax 972/808-7471
ⓒ Nova Academy Scyene 6459 Scyene Rd, Dallas 75227 Nichole Ward	PK-3	T	192	95%	214/381-3088 Fax 214/381-3499
ⓒ Nova Academy-Prichard 2800 Prichard Ln, Dallas 75227 Lashun Jasper	PK-8	T	500 19	90%	972/808-7470 Fax 972/808-7471
ⓒ Nyos Charter Sch-Lamar Campus 12301 N Lamar Blvd, Austin 78753 Will Jaramillo	4-12	T	641	28%	512/583-6967 Fax 512/583-6973
ⓒ Nyos Charter School-M M Campus 1605 Kramer Ln, Austin 78758 Terry Berkenhoff \ Curtis Wilson	K-12	T	355 5	39%	512/275-1593 Fax 512/287-5258
ⓒ Odyssey Academy 2412 61st St, Galveston 77551 Jennifer Goodman	PK-12	T	1,000 29	40%	409/750-9289 Fax 409/740-3735
ⓒ Olive Tree Montessori Academy 8601 Randol Mill Rd, Fort Worth 76120 Sadia Haq	PK-5	T	79	67%	817/460-5000

1 Superintendent	8 Curric/Instruct K-12	19 Chief Financial Officer	29 Family/Consumer Science	39 Social Studies K-12	49 English/Lang Arts Elem	59 Special Education Elem	69 Academic Assessment
2 Bus/Finance/Purchasing	9 Curric/Instruct Elem	20 Art K-12	30 Adult Education	40 Social Studies Elem	50 English/Lang Arts Sec	60 Special Education Sec	70 Research/Development
3 Buildings And Grounds	10 Curric/Instruct Sec	21 Art Elem	31 Career/Sch-to-Work K-12	41 Social Studies Sec	51 Reading K-12	61 Foreign/World Lang K-12	71 Public Information
4 Food Service	11 Federal Program	22 Art Sec	32 Career/Sch-to-Work Elem	42 Science K-12	52 Reading Elem	62 Foreign/World Lang Elem	72 Summer School
5 Transportation	12 Title I	23 Music K-12	33 Career/Sch-to-Work Sec	43 Science Elem	53 Reading Sec	63 Foreign/World Lang Sec	73 Instructional Tech
6 Athletic	13 Title V	24 Music Elem	34 Early Childhood Ed	44 Science Sec	54 Remedial Reading K-12	64 Religious Education K-12	74 Inservice Training
7 Health Services	15 Asst Superintendent	25 Music Sec	35 Health/Phys Education	45 Math K-12	55 Remedial Reading Elem	65 Religious Education Elem	75 Marketing/Distributive
	16 Instructional Media Svcs	26 Business Education	36 Guidance Services K-12	46 Math Elem	56 Remedial Reading Sec	66 Religious Education Sec	76 Info Systems
	17 Chief Operations Officer	27 Career & Tech Ed	37 Guidance Services Elem	47 Math Sec	57 Bilingual/ELL	67 School Board President	77 Psychological Assess
	18 Chief Academic Officer	28 Technology Education	38 Guidance Services Sec	48 English/Lang Arts K-12	58 Special Education K-12	68 Teacher Personnel	78 Affirmative Action

Texas School Directory

School	Grades	Programs	Enroll	%	Phone
Ⓐ Panola Charter HS [293] ⓒ 1110 FM 10, Carthage 75633 Keith Koonce	8-12	V	27 2	33%	903/693-6355 Fax 903/693-6391
Panola Early College High Sch [293] 1109 W Panola St, Carthage 75633 Robert Bruce	8-12		38	34%	903/693-6355 Fax 903/693-6391
ⓒ Pasadena Classical Academy [297] 6109 Fairmont Pkwy, Pasadena 77505 Lillian Pope	K-6		161	70%	281/372-8999
Ⓐ Pathways 3H Campus ⓒ 110 Youth Ranch Rd, Mountain Home 78058 Sally Arnold	4-12		27		512/560-8132
Ⓐ PCA Dr Sarah Strinden Elem Sch 602 S Raguet St, Lufkin 75904 Dr Jennifer Shaw	K-5	T	401	49%	936/634-5515
Ⓐ PCA Dr Terry Robbins Mid Sch 602 S Raguet St, Lufkin 75904 Jason Perry	6-8	T	245	43%	936/634-5515
ⓒ Pdn Academy-Vista Del Sol 1599 George Dieter Dr, El Paso 79936 Luis Liano	9-12	T	130	88%	915/298-3637 Fax 915/298-3644
ⓒ Pdna Vista Del Sol Mesa CHS [303] 711 N Mesa St, El Paso 79902 Jaime Sanchez	9-12	T	105 15	97%	915/532-7216 Fax 915/356-2205
ⓒ Pegasus Sch Liberal Arts & Sci 601 N Akard St Ste 203, Dallas 75201 Kristen Clements	K-12		653 20		214/740-9991 Fax 214/740-9799
ⓒ Permian Basin Classical Acad [297] 4320 W Illinois Ave Ste A, Midland 79703 Sharla Butler	K-8		266		432/217-6122
ⓒ Pineywoods Community Academy 602 S Raguet St, Lufkin 75904 Jennifer Shaw \ Jason Perry	PK-12	T	1,005 30	39%	936/634-5515 Fax 936/634-5518
ⓒ Por Vida Academy Charter HS [294] 1135 Mission Rd, San Antonio 78210 Loren Franckowiak	9-12	AGTV	119 11	92%	210/775-1132 Fax 210/533-5612 t
ⓒ Positive Solutions Charter Sch 1325 N Flores St Ste 100, San Antonio 78212 Ruby Torres	9-12	AGT	150 11	93%	210/299-1025 Fax 210/299-1052
Ⓐ Premier HS-Abilene [297] ⓒ 3161 S 23rd St Ste 4, Abilene 79605 Sue Pond	9-12	T	136 6	71%	325/698-8111 Fax 325/695-5620
Ⓐ Premier HS-Amarillo [297] ⓒ 3242 Hobbs Rd Ste F, Amarillo 79109 Rebekah Pinson	9-12		217	59%	806/367-5447
Ⓐ Premier HS-American Youthworks [297] ⓒ 1901 E Ben White Blvd, Austin 78741 Cynthia Jones	9-12		73 7		512/744-1954 Fax 866/368-9413
Ⓐ Premier HS-Arlington [297] ⓒ 551 Ryan Plaza Dr, Arlington 76011 Devon Turner	9-12		149	49%	682/350-8865
Ⓐ Premier HS-Brenham Miracle Frm [297] 10632 FM 2621, Brenham 77833 Caty Paben	7-12		14		979/836-0901 Fax 979/277-0939
Ⓐ Premier HS-Brownsville [297] ⓒ 955 Paredes Line Rd, Brownsville 78521 Maria Alvarado	9-12	T	138 10	85%	956/550-0084 Fax 866/677-8626
ⓒ Premier HS-Brownwood Early [297] 819 Early Blvd, Early 76802 Tim Garcia	7-12		40		325/643-3735 Fax 866/363-4987
ⓒ Premier HS-Career Tech Ed Ctr [297] 4701 S Sugar Rd, Edinburg 78539 Julianna Lopez	7-12	T	145	98%	956/386-1793 Fax 877/622-9224
ⓒ Premier HS-Comanche [297] 1008 S Austin St, Comanche 76442 Eutimio Garcia	7-12		26		325/356-9673 Fax 866/892-8875
Ⓐ Premier HS-Dayton [297] ⓒ 1709 County Road 611, Dayton 77535 Suzanne Thomas	9-12		71		936/257-8017
Ⓐ Premier HS-Del Rio [297] ⓒ 1701 Kings Way, Del Rio 78840 Carol Mireles	9-12	TV	104 3	82%	830/703-1631 Fax 830/298-2122
Ⓐ Premier HS-El Paso East [297] 8720 Gateway Blvd E Ste E, El Paso 79907 Osvaldo Morales	9-12		114		915/633-1598 Fax 877/693-5206
ⓒ Premier HS-El Paso West [297] 1035 Belvidere St Ste 116, El Paso 79912 Laura Dominguez	9-12	A	114		915/581-4300
Ⓐ Premier HS-Fort Worth [297] ⓒ 6411 Camp Bowie Blvd Ste B, Fort Worth 76116 Danny Perez	9-12	T	140 8	83%	817/731-2028 Fax 866/728-0824
Ⓐ Premier HS-Granbury [297] ⓒ 919 E US Highway 377 Ste 1, Granbury 76048 Marsha Grissom	9-12		139	23%	817/573-0435 Fax 866/895-9616
Ⓐ Premier HS-Huntsville [297] ⓒ 2407 Sam Houston Ave Ste C, Huntsville 77340 Kevin Nichols	9-12	T	53	50%	936/439-5204
Ⓐ Premier HS-Irving South [297] ⓒ 1081 W Shady Grove Rd, Irving 75060 Dennis Bingham	9-12	T	115	96%	972/254-1016
Ⓐ Premier HS-Laredo [297] ⓒ 2201 Chihuahua St, Laredo 78043 Veronica Khan	9-12	T	96 5	98%	956/723-7788 Fax 956/284-0175
ⓒ Premier HS-Lewisville [297] 1800 Lakeway Dr Ste 100, Lewisville 75057 Gary Wilhelmi	9-12		34	33%	972/521-1592 Fax 866/262-8996
Ⓐ Premier HS-Lubbock [297] ⓒ 2002 W Loop 289 Ste 121, Lubbock 79407 Rodrick Saldana	9-12	T	139 5	58%	806/763-1518 Fax 806/763-9310
Ⓐ Premier HS-Midland [297] ⓒ 4320 W Illinois Ave Ste A, Midland 79703 Jarret Hostas	9-12		129 8		432/682-0384 Fax 432/682-0897
ⓒ Premier HS-Mission [297] 1203 St Claire Blvd, Mission 78572 Laura Thatcher	9-12	T	134	98%	956/424-9290 Fax 866/859-0140
Ⓐ Premier HS-N Austin [297] ⓒ 13801 Burnet Rd Ste 100, Austin 78727 Wayne Williams	9-12		89		512/614-4537
Ⓐ Premier HS-New Braunfels [297] ⓒ 1928 S Seguin Ave Ste 100A, New Braunfels 78130 Richard Ramirez	9-12	T	95	46%	830/609-6606
Ⓐ Premier HS-North Houston [297] ⓒ 12512 Walters Rd, Houston 77014 Kevin Nichols	9-12		100		281/537-7272
ⓒ Premier HS-Palmview [297] 406 W Veterans Blvd, Palmview 78572 Selma Fernat	9-12	T	119 7	97%	956/584-8458
ⓒ Premier HS-Pflugerville [297] 616 FM 685 Ste 204B, Pflugerville 78660 Paulita Zuniga	9-12		115		512/969-5100
Ⓐ Premier HS-Pharr [297] ⓒ 200 E Interstate 2 Ste E, Pharr 78577 Rosario Zamora	9-12	T	96 7	88%	956/781-8800 Fax 877/512-1175
Ⓐ Premier HS-S Austin [297] ⓒ 1701 W Ben White Blvd Ste 100A, Austin 78704 Elizabeth Camarena	9-12	T	210 5	56%	512/444-8442 Fax 866/673-0058
Ⓐ Premier HS-San Angelo [297] ⓒ 4102 Sunset Dr, San Angelo 76904 Bree Sherwood	9-12		97		325/823-7758
Ⓐ Premier HS-San Antonio East [297] ⓒ 8220 Windsor Cross, San Antonio 78239 Dr Luis Gonzalez	9-12		127		210/650-0944 Fax 866/836-6493

79 Student Personnel	91 Safety/Security	275 Response To Intervention	298 Grant Writer/Ptnrships	**School Programs**
30 Driver Ed/Safety	92 Magnet School	277 Remedial Math K-12	750 Chief Innovation Officer	A = Alternative Program
31 Gifted/Talented	93 Parental Involvement	280 Literacy Coach	751 Chief of Staff	G = Adult Classes
32 Video Services	95 Tech Prep Program	285 STEM	752 Social Emotional Learning	M = Magnet Program
33 Substance Abuse Prev	97 Chief Infomation Officer	286 Digital Learning		T = Title I Schoolwide
34 Erate	98 Chief Technology Officer	288 Common Core Standards	**Other School Types**	V = Career & Tech Ed Programs
35 AIDS Education	270 Character Education	294 Accountability	Ⓐ = Alternative Program	
38 Alternative/At Risk	271 Migrant Education	295 Network System	ⓒ = Charter School	**Social Media**
39 Multi-Cultural Curriculum	273 Teacher Mentor	296 Title II Programs	Ⓜ = Magnet School	ⓕ = Facebook
30 Social Work	274 Before/After Sch	297 Webmaster	Ⓨ = Year-Round School	t = Twitter

New Schools are shaded
New Superintendents and Principals are bold
Personnel with email addresses are underscored

TX—9

Market Data Retrieval

School	Grades	Type	Enroll	%	Phone
ⓒ Premier HS-San Antonio West [297] 6218 NW Loop 410, San Antonio 78238 Manuela Allen	9-12	T	145	78%	830/587-4730 Fax 866/864-2743
Ⓐ Premier HS-San Juan [297] ⓒ 1202 E Business Highway 83, San Juan 78589 Alma Prado	9-12		110		956/961-4721
Ⓐ Premier HS-Texarkana [297] ⓒ 3448 Summerhill Rd, Texarkana 75503 Heather McNeill	9-12		74		430/200-4385
Ⓐ Premier HS-Tyler [297] ⓒ 1106 N Glenwood Blvd, Tyler 75702 Joshua Groth	9-12		85 8	88%	903/592-5222 Fax 866/365-0336
Ⓐ Premier HS-Waco [297] ⓒ 4720 N 19th St, Waco 76708 Lisa Linton	9-12		150 4	69%	254/752-0441 Fax 254/752-0445
Ⓐ Pro-Vision Academy ⓒ 4590 Wilmington St, Houston 77051 Kimberly Carroll	3-12	T	400 6	89%	713/748-0030 Fax 713/748-0037
ⓒ Promise Cmty Sch-New Nghbr [274] 6500 Rookin St, Houston 77074 Roel Saldivar	PK-6		36		713/273-3731 Fax 713/273-3797
ⓒ Promise Community Sch Ripley [274] 4410 Navigation Blvd, Houston 77011 Jennifer Galvan	PK-8	T	470 11	94%	713/315-6429 Fax 713/547-8201
ⓒ Ptaa-Greenville Mid High Sch 300 Aerobic Ln, Greenville 75402 Jennifer Cayce	6-12		83		903/454-7153
ⓒ Ptaa-Mesquite Mid High Sch 3200 Oates Dr, Mesquite 75150 Jennifer Cayce	6-11		320		972/375-9672 Fax 469/301-2135
ⓒ Quinn Middle Sch [277] 1020 Elm St Bldg 100, Waco 76704 Tyler Ellis	5-8	T	262 10	69%	254/754-8000 Fax 254/754-8009
ⓒ Ranch Academy 3120 Vzcr 2318, Canton 75103 Bruce Blair	6-12	AT	102 6	42%	903/479-3601 Fax 903/479-1161
ⓒ Ranch Academy-Tyler 3120 Von Van Dt Cr 2318, Canton 75103 Melissa Parduce	K-12		50		903/479-3601 Fax 903/939-8045
ⓒ Rapoport Acad-E Campus ES [277] 2000 J J Flewellen Rd, Waco 76704 Jennifer Whitlark	PK-1		399 15		254/799-4191
ⓒ Rapoport Acad-N Campus ES [277] 2200 MacArthur Dr, Waco 76708 Michelene Bess	2-4		205		254/313-1313
ⓒ Raul Yzaguirre Sch for Success 2255 N Coria St, Brownsville 78520 Maria Knosel	K-8	T	380	99%	956/574-7100 Fax 956/542-2667
ⓒ Raul Yzaguirre Sch for Success [296] 2950 Broadway St, Houston 77017 Mario Sandoval	K-12	T	916 14	94%	713/640-3700 Fax 713/641-1853
ⓒ Reve Preparatory Charter Sch 4315 W Fuqua St, Houston 77045 Traci Thibodeaux	K-5		401		832/982-2083
ⓒ Rhodes School-Lee 11821 East Fwy Ste 400, Houston 77029 William Davis	PK-8		130		281/458-4334 Fax 281/458-7595
ⓒ Richard Milburn Acad-Amarillo [298] 4106 SW 51st Ave, Amarillo 79109 Rebecca Gerhardt	9-12	T	159 15	76%	806/463-2284 Fax 806/463-2331
Ⓐ Richard Milburn Acad-CC [298] ⓒ 5333 Everhart Rd Bldg C, Corp Christi 78411 Elizabeth Hanna	9-12	TV	277 18	72%	361/225-4424 Fax 361/225-4945
Ⓐ Richard Milburn Acad-Ft Worth [298] ⓒ 6785 Camp Bowie Blvd Ste 200, Fort Worth 76116 Susan Richey	9-12	T	194 12	75%	817/731-7627 Fax 817/731-7628
Ⓐ Richard Milburn Acad-Houston [298] ⓒ 713 E Airtex Dr Bldg B, Houston 77073 Greg Nix	9-12	T	182 16	87%	281/209-3505 Fax 281/209-9475
Ⓐ Richard Milburn Acad-Killeen [298] ⓒ 802 N 8th St, Killeen 76541 Lucette Bredt	9-12		255 12		254/634-4444 Fax 254/526-0461
Ⓐ Richard Milburn Acad-Lubbock [298] ⓒ 2333 50th St, Lubbock 79412 Brenda Ewerz	9-12	T	180 9	89%	806/740-0811 Fax 806/740-0804
Ⓐ Richard Milburn Acad-Midland [298] ⓒ 503 E I20 Frontage #110, Midland 79703 Debra Theesfield	9-12	T	181 10	66%	432/203-9829 Fax 432/803-5393
Ⓐ Richard Milburn Acad-Odessa [298] ⓒ 2419 N County Rd W Ste 100, Odessa 79763 Mary Jansen	9-12	T	444 6	53%	432/614-1859 Fax 432/614-1913
Ⓐ Richard Milburn Acad-Pasadena [298] ⓒ 171 Pasadena Town Square Mall, Pasadena 77506 Sandra Nix	9-12		197	96%	832/730-4570
ⓒ Richardson Classical Academy [297] 2101 E Renner Rd, Richardson 75082 Ashley Cooper	K-7	T	99	35%	972/479-9584
ⓒ Richland Collegiate High Sch 12800 Abrams Rd, Dallas 75243 Craig Hinkle	11-12		610	19%	972/761-6888 Fax 972/761-6890
ⓒ Ripley House Middle Sch 4410 Navigation Blvd, Houston 77011 Rachael Purdom	6-8	T	172	95%	713/315-6429 Fax 713/315-6404
ⓒ Rise Academy 207 N Martin Luther King Blvd, Lubbock 79403 Richard Baumgartner	PK-8	T	269 20	88%	806/744-0438 Fax 832/201-7088
ⓒ Rspa Northeast-Humble 600 Charles St, Humble 77338 William Davis	K-8		100		281/319-9300
ⓒ Rspa Northshore 13334 Wallisville Rd, Houston 77049 Tonya McBride	PK-6		100		281/459-9797
ⓒ Rspa Northwest-Living Word 6601 Antoine Dr, Houston 77091 Charles Russell	K-5		108		832/562-2822
ⓒ Rspa-Channelview 1215 Pecan St, Channelview 77530 Ashley Miller	PK-5		115		281/864-7015
ⓒ Rspa-E Northshore 12818 Tidwell Rd, Houston 77044 Joesette Simeon	PK-5	T	534	76%	281/459-9797
ⓒ Rspa-NE Humble 600 Charles St, Humble 77338 William Davis	PK-8		495		281/319-9300
ⓒ Ruth Jones McClendon Mid Sch 3460 Northeast Pkwy, San Antonio 78218 Keith Thomas	6-8		110		210/568-8800
ⓒ Sch of Sci & Tech Advancement [299] 10550 Westoffice Dr, Houston 77042 Haci Dilli	K-8	T	316	74%	713/266-2522 Fax 713/266-2494
ⓒ Sch of Sci & Tech Excellence [299] 330 N Sam Houston Pkwy E, Houston 77060 Hasan Kendirci	PK-7		370		832/672-6671 Fax 832/202-0700
ⓒ Sch of Sci & Tech Main [299] 1450 NE Loop 410, San Antonio 78209 Ahmed Mamedov	6-12	T	484	47%	210/804-0222 Fax 210/822-3422
ⓒ Sch of Sci & Tech Northwest 12042 Culebra Rd, San Antonio 78253	K-5		104		210/530-8366
ⓒ Sch of Sci & Tech-Alamo [299] 12200 Crownpoint, San Antonio 78233 Elizabeth James	K-8	T	452	49%	210/657-6400

1 Superintendent	8 Curric/Instruct K-12	19 Chief Financial Officer	29 Family/Consumer Science	39 Social Studies K-12	49 English/Lang Arts Elem	59 Special Education Elem	69 Academic Assessment
2 Bus/Finance/Purchasing	9 Curric/Instruct Elem	20 Art K-12	30 Adult Education	40 Social Studies Elem	50 English/Lang Arts Sec	60 Special Education Sec	70 Research/Development
3 Buildings And Grounds	10 Curric/Instruct Sec	21 Art Elem	31 Career/Sch-to-Work K-12	41 Social Studies Sec	51 Reading K-12	61 Foreign/World Lang K-12	71 Public Information
4 Food Service	11 Federal Program	22 Art Sec	32 Career/Sch-to-Work Elem	42 Science K-12	52 Reading Elem	62 Foreign/World Lang Elem	72 Summer School
5 Transportation	12 Title I	23 Music K-12	33 Career/Sch-to-Work Sec	43 Science Elem	53 Reading Sec	63 Foreign/World Lang Sec	73 Instructional Tech
6 Athletic	13 Title V	24 Music Elem	34 Early Childhood Ed	44 Science Sec	54 Remedial Reading K-12	64 Religious Education K-12	74 Inservice Training
7 Health Services	15 Asst Superintendent	25 Music Sec	35 Health/Phys Education	45 Math K-12	55 Remedial Reading Elem	65 Religious Education Elem	75 Marketing/Distributive
	16 Instructional Media Svcs	26 Business Education	36 Guidance Services K-12	46 Math Elem	56 Remedial Reading Sec	66 Religious Education Sec	76 Info Systems
	17 Chief Operations Officer	27 Career & Tech Ed	37 Guidance Services Elem	47 Math Sec	57 Bilingual/ELL	67 School Board President	77 Psychological Assess
	18 Chief Academic Officer	28 Technology Education	38 Guidance Services Sec	48 English/Lang Arts K-12	58 Special Education K-12	68 Teacher Personnel	78 Affirmative Action

Texas School Directory

School	Grades	Prog	Enroll	%	Phone
ⓒ Sch of Sci & Tech-Corpus Crsti [299] 4737 Saratoga Blvd, Corp Christi 78413 Ekrem Demirci	K-12	T	900	56%	361/851-2450 Fax 361/851-2475
ⓒ Sch of Sci & Tech-Discovery [299] 5707 Bandera Rd, Leon Valley 78238 Jessica Romero	PK-8	T	483	55%	210/543-1111 Fax 210/543-1112
ⓒ Sch of Sci & Tech-Houston [299] 16200 Tx 249, Houston 77086 Alpaslan Uzgoren	PK-8	T	474	55%	346/270-2101 Fax 346/270-2187
ⓒ Sch of Sci & Tech-Sugarland 10007 Clodine Rd, Richmond 77407	K-5		118		210/530-8366
ⓒ Seashore Learning Center 15801 S Padre Island Dr Ste A, Corp Christi 78418 Genger Holt	K-4		273 14	1%	361/949-1222 Fax 361/949-6762
ⓒ Seashore Middle Academy 15437 S Padre Island Dr, Corp Christi 78418 Barbara Beeler	5-8		215 11		361/654-1134 Fax 361/654-1139
ⓒ Ser-Ninos Charter Middle Sch 5610 Gulfton St, Houston 77081 Charmaine Constantine	6-8		220		713/592-6055
ⓒ Ser-Ninos Charter Sch 5815 Alder Dr, Houston 77081 Esther Villela	PK-8	G	589 35		713/667-6145 Fax 713/667-0645
ⓒ Ser-Ninos Charter School II 5919 Dashwood Dr, Houston 77081 Sheronda Oliphant	PK-5		305		713/432-9400 Fax 713/432-0624
ⓐ Seton Home Charter Education ⓒ 1115 Mission Rd, San Antonio 78210 S Arnold	9-12		25		512/560-8132
ⓒ Shekinah Radiance Acad-Garland 10715 Garland Rd Ste 100, Dallas 75218 Trina Garnes	K-7		91		214/320-2500
ⓐ Shoreline Academy ⓒ 1220 Gregory St, Taft 78390 Elizabeth Phillips	7-12	GT	51 4	95%	361/528-3356 Fax 361/528-3249
ⓒ Shsu CS-Brighton Academy 10801 Falconwing Dr, The Woodlands 77381 Renee O'Neal	K-5		110		281/465-4111
ⓒ Shsu CS-Cypress Trails 22801 Aldine Westfield Rd, Spring 77373 Kendra O'Neal	K-2		260		936/294-3229
ⓒ Shsu CS-Greengate Academy 18490 Kuykendahl Rd, Spring 77379 Katie Statlander	K-2		109		281/288-0880
ⓒ Shsu CS-Little Geniuses Acad 150 Isaacks Rd, Humble 77338 Tanassa Joseph	K-1		99		832/995-5916 Fax 832/218-3758
ⓒ South Plains CHS [303] 4008 Avenue R, Lubbock 79412 Jennifer McLelland	9-12	T	200 16	90%	806/744-0330 Fax 806/744-1341
ⓐ Southwest Prep New Directions [302] ⓒ 1258 Austin Hwy Bldg 1, San Antonio 78209 Carolyn Martinez	6-12	T	141	68%	210/829-8017 Fax 210/829-8514
ⓒ Southwest Prep Sch NE [302] 1258 Austin Hwy, San Antonio 78209 Carolyn Martinez	PK-12	TV	225 8	81%	210/829-8017 Fax 210/829-8514
ⓒ Southwest Prep Sch NW [302] 6535 Culebra Rd, San Antonio 78238 Sheryl Wills-Pacheco	6-12	T	295	71%	210/432-2634 Fax 210/521-2602
ⓒ Southwest Prep Sch SE [302] 735 S WW White Rd, San Antonio 78220 Javier Garcia	PK-12	T	213	90%	210/333-1403 Fax 210/333-3024
ⓒ Southwest Prep-Seguin [302] 2400 E Walnut St, Seguin 78155 Sherry Head	PK-8		210		830/549-5930 Fax 830/433-4534
ⓒ Southwest Preparatory-NW ES 4151 Culebra Rd, San Antonio 78228 Cheryl Wills-Pacheco	PK-5	T	86	91%	210/819-7860 Fax 210/438-8523
ⓒ Southwest Sch-Bissonnet [278] 8440 Bissonnet St, Houston 77074 Pamela Sailors	PK-5	T	445	97%	713/988-5839 Fax 713/270-0076
ⓐ Southwest Sch-Discovery MS [278] ⓒ 6400 Westpark Dr Ste 200, Houston 77057 Deborah Silber	6-8	T	319 25	84%	713/954-9528 Fax 713/785-1014
ⓒ Southwest Sch-Empowerment HS [278] 6400 Westpark Dr Ste 200, Houston 77057 Bianca Clark	9-12	T	356	70%	713/954-9528
ⓒ Southwest Sch-Mangum [278] 4515 Mangum Rd, Houston 77092 Ruben Gomez	PK-5	T	357	93%	713/688-0505 Fax 713/688-3386
ⓒ Southwest Schools-Phoenix [278] 6400 Westpark Dr, Houston 77057 Tonya Woods	K-12		264		346/571-6060 Fax 346/571-6061
ⓒ St Anthony Sch 3732 Myrtle St, Dallas 75215 Mr Ray	K-8		204 13		214/421-3645 Fax 214/421-7416
ⓒ St Mary's Academy Charter Sch 410 N Tyler St, Beeville 78102 Hirma Elizondo	K-6	T	442 15	80%	361/358-5601 Fax 361/358-5704 ⓣ
Staggs Acad Intl STEM Studies 5201 University Blvd, Laredo 78041 Dr Patricia Uribe	11-12		100		956/326-2861 Fax 956/326-2429
ⓒ STEM Academy-Lewisville [297] 650 Bennett Ln, Lewisville 75057 Alan Wimberley	6-12		384		972/829-4492
ⓒ STEM Academy-Lewisville 650 Bennett Ln, Lewisville 75057 Carolyn Anderson	6-12		500	17%	972/316-6700 Fax 972/316-6705
ⓒ Step Charter School II 11250 S Wilcrest Dr, Houston 77099 William Clark	K-6	T	300	68%	281/988-7797 Fax 281/988-7736
ⓒ Stephen F Austin Univ CS 2428 Raguet St, Nacogdoches 75965 Lysa Hagan	K-5		255 6	9%	936/468-5899 Fax 936/468-7015
ⓒ Tekoa Academy-Orange [304] 1408 W Park Ave, Orange 77630 Princess Chretien	PK-8		160		409/886-9864 Fax 409/886-0961
ⓒ Tekoa Academy-Port Arthur [304] 327 Thomas Blvd, Port Arthur 77640 Paula Richardson	PK-12		420 14		409/982-5400 Fax 409/982-9711
ⓒ Temple Charter Academy [295] 7177 Airport Rd, Temple 76502 Jason Osburn	PK-12	T	357 8	53%	254/778-8682 Fax 254/853-4144
ⓒ Texans Can Acad Carrltn-Farmrs [305] 2720 Hollandale Ln, Dallas 75234 Dr Amparo Hakemack	9-12	T	462 20	84%	972/243-2178 Fax 972/243-2669
ⓐ Texans Can Acad Dallas Oak Clf [305] ⓒ 325 W 12th St, Dallas 75208 Cynthia Miles	9-12	GT	689 31	97%	214/943-2244 Fax 214/943-8899
ⓒ Texans Can Acad Dallas Pl Grv [305] 1227 N Masters Dr, Dallas 75217 Mene Khepera	9-12	T	577	95%	972/225-1194 Fax 972/225-1164
ⓐ Texans Can Acad Dallas Ross AV [305] ⓒ 4621 Ross Ave, Dallas 75204 Rufus Johnson	9-12	GT	551 30	90%	214/824-4226 Fax 214/234-8617
ⓒ Texans Can Acad Fw Lancaster [305] 1316 E Lancaster Ave, Fort Worth 76102 Philip Tucker	9-12		364 15		817/735-1515 Fax 817/735-1465
ⓒ Texans Can Acad Fw Westcreek [305] 6620 Westcreek Dr, Fort Worth 76133 Ku-Masi Lewis	9-12	AGT	500 14	84%	817/531-3223 Fax 817/292-3432

79 Student Personnel	91 Safety/Security	275 Response To Intervention	296 Grant Writer/Ptnrships
80 Driver Ed/Safety	92 Magnet School	277 Remedial Math K-12	750 Chief Innovation Officer
81 Gifted/Talented	93 Parental Involvement	280 Literacy Coach	751 Chief of Staff
82 Video Services	95 Tech Prep Program	285 STEM	752 Social Emotional Learning
83 Substance Abuse Prev	97 Chief Infomation Officer	286 Digital Learning	
84 Erate	98 Chief Technology Officer	288 Common Core Standards	**Other School Types**
85 AIDS Education	270 Accountability	294 Accountability	ⓐ = Alternative School
88 Alternative/At Risk	271 Migrant Education	295 Network System	ⓒ = Charter School
89 Multi-Cultural Curriculum	273 Teacher Mentor	296 Title II Programs	ⓜ = Magnet School
90 Social Work	274 Before/After Sch	297 Webmaster	ⓨ = Year-Round School

School Programs
A = Alternative Program
G = Adult Classes
M = Magnet Program
T = Title I Schoolwide
V = Career & Tech Ed Programs

Social Media
☐ = Facebook
ⓣ = Twitter

New Schools are shaded
New Superintendents and Principals are bold
Personnel with email addresses are underscored

TX—11

Market Data Retrieval

School	Grades	Type	Enroll	%	Phone
Ⓐ Texans Can Acad Garland [305] © 2256 Arapaho Rd, Garland 75044 Daniel Johnson	9-12	T	265	67%	972/441-7202
© Texans Can Acad Houston Hobby [305] 9020 Gulf Fwy, Houston 77017 Yardley Williams	9-12	T	412	84%	832/379-4226 Fax 713/944-6736
© Texans Can Acad Houston North [305] 3401 Hardy St, Houston 77009 Leon Gilmore	9-12	AG	450 28		713/659-4226 Fax 713/651-1493
© Texans Can Acad Houston SW [305] 9745 Bissonnet St, Houston 77036 Justin Reyes	9-12	T	378	74%	281/918-4316 Fax 713/271-0257
© Texans Can Acad San Antonio [305] 1807 Centennial Blvd, San Antonio 78211 Debra Cruz	9-12		400 16		210/923-1226 Fax 210/928-3366
Ⓐ Texans Can Academy Austin [305] © 2406 Rosewood Ave, Austin 78702 William Arevalo	9-12		485 13		512/477-4226 Fax 512/477-4223
© Texans Can Academy-Grant East [305] 2901 Morgan Dr, Dallas 75241 Rodney Milliner	9-12	T	341	99%	972/228-4226
Texas Academy Math & Science 1167 Union Circle Rm 320, Denton 76201 Glenisson DeOliveira	11-12		350		940/565-3606 Fax 940/369-8696
© Texas Early College High Sch [293] 3714 E End Blvd S, Marshall 75672 Bob Garcia	8-12		82	45%	903/935-4109 Fax 903/935-4067
Texas Empowerment Academy 6414 N Hampton Dr, Austin 78723 David Nowlin	3-11	T	214	64%	512/928-0118 Fax 512/928-0128
© Texas Empowerment Academy 3613 Bluestein Dr, Austin 78721 Neisha Nunn	K-2	T	100 10	70%	512/494-1076 Fax 512/494-1009
© Texas Leadership CS-Abilene 1840 N 8th St, Abilene 79603 Carmen Crane	PK-12	T	429	56%	325/480-3500 Fax 325/672-2631
© Texas Leadership CS-Arlington 2001 Brown Blvd, Arlington 76006 Brooke Morrison	K-10	T	510	62%	817/385-9338 Fax 817/861-1242
© Texas Leadership CS-Midland 3300 Thomas Ave, Midland 79703 Charlie Gann	K-10	T	438	43%	432/242-7117 Fax 432/262-0994
© Texas Prep School-San Marcos 400 Uhland Rd, San Marcos 78666 Brandy Strait	K-6	T	150 4	65%	512/805-3000 Fax 512/805-7739 🅕🅣
© Texas Preparatory Sch-Austin 7540 Ed Bluestein Blvd, Austin 78723 Daphne McDole	PK-6	T	120	87%	512/928-3000
Texas Sch Blind & Visually Imp 1100 W 45th St, Austin 78756 Miles Fain	Spec	T	150	76%	512/454-8631 Fax 512/206-9450
Texas School for the Deaf 1102 S Congress Ave, Austin 78704 Barbara Hussey \ Karlin Hummel	Spec	TV	524	71%	512/462-5353 Fax 512/462-5313
© Texas School of the Arts [306] 6025 Village Pkwy, Edgecliff Vlg 76134 Joe Morrow	K-6		334 14	10%	817/732-8372 Fax 817/732-8373
Ⓐ Texas Serenity Academy © 8787 N Houston Rosslyn Rd, Houston 77088 Michelle Foreman	K-8	T	295	90%	281/820-9540 Fax 281/820-6204
© Texas Serenity Academy-Gano 4637 Gano St, Houston 77009 Michelle Foreman	K-5		140		713/699-3443 Fax 713/699-3929
© Texas Virtual Acad Hallsville 1955 Lakeway Dr Ste 250B, Lewisville 75057 Daphne Troxell \ Shelby Newman	K-12	T	6,477	48%	866/360-0161
© The Goodwill Excel Center 1015 Norwood Park Blvd, Austin 78753 Charles Moody	9-12	G	337	46%	512/531-5500 Fax 512/339-5299
© The Lawson Academy 5052 Scott St, Houston 77004 Dr Marthea Raney	6-8		230 6		713/225-1551
© The Varnett School-SW [310] 5025 S Willow Dr, Houston 77035 Toni Fisher	PK-6	T	600	95%	713/723-4699 Fax 713/723-5853
© The Woodlands Classical Acad [297] 6565 Research Forest Dr, The Woodlands 77381 Roxana Butler	K-8		377	23%	936/242-1541
Ⓐ Thomas Buzbee Vocational Sch © 143 Forest Svc Rd 233, New Waverly 77358 Will Gollihar	9-12	TV	104 15	97%	936/344-7238 Fax 936/344-6396
© TLC Academy 5687 Melrose Ave, San Angelo 76901 Kevin Reed \ Johnny Burleson	K-12	T	1,700	43%	325/653-3200 Fax 325/942-6795 🅕
© Treetops International Sch 12500 S Pipeline Rd, Euless 76040 Lou Blancher	PK-12	V	381 23	16%	817/283-1771 Fax 817/684-0892
© Trinity Basin Prep-10th Street 831 W 10th St Ste B, Dallas 75208 Candee Martinez	PK-4		590		214/296-9302 Fax 214/296-9306
© Trinity Basin Prep-Ewing 808 N Ewing Ave, Dallas 75203 Kyla Jaramillo	PK-3	T	511	89%	214/942-8846 Fax 214/710-2127
© Trinity Basin Prep-Ft Worth 101 E Pafford St, Fort Worth 76110 Jodi Rebarchek	PK-8		950		817/840-7501 Fax 817/840-7502
© Trinity Basin Prep-Jefferson 855 E 8th St, Dallas 75203 Jennifer Masten	5-8		750		214/941-4881 Fax 214/941-4866
© Trinity Charter Sch-Amarillo [307] 4655 S FM 1258, Amarillo 79118 Jennifer Chappell	7-12		10		512/706-7566
© Trinity Charter Sch-Big Sandy [307] 1085 Private Road 34814, Big Sandy 75755 Nicki Cornejo	1-12		30		903/565-6801 Fax 903/636-9010
© Trinity Charter Sch-Bokenkamp [307] 5517 S Alameda St, Corp Christi 78412 Hilda Vega	K-8	T	150	98%	361/994-1214
© Trinity Charter Sch-New Hope [307] 1000 N McColl Rd, McAllen 78501 Hilga Vega	3-10	T	58	95%	361/563-7979
© Trinity Charter Sch-New Life [307] 650 Scarbourough, Canyon Lake 78133 Joshua Machicek	4-12	T	58 10	93%	830/964-4390 Fax 830/964-4376
© Trinity Charter School-Krause [307] 25752 Kingsland Blvd, Katy 77494 Sandra Flores	6-12	T	57	95%	281/392-7505 Fax 281/392-7560
© Trinity Charter School-Pegasus [307] 896 Robin Ranch Rd, Lockhart 78644 Keely Reynolds	3-12	T	146	98%	512/432-1655 Fax 512/432-1653
© Trinity Charter School-Spring [307] 2929 FM 2920 Rd, Spring 77388 Sandra Flores	8-11		20		512/706-7566
© Trinity Environment Academy 3837 Simpson Stuart Rd, Dallas 75241 Michael Hooten	K-6	T	200	91%	972/920-6558
Ⓐ Triumph Public CHS [303] © 1785 W Business Hwy 77, San Benito 78586 Nancy Ramirez	9-12		146		956/276-9930 Fax 956/276-9943
© Trivium Academy 2205 E Hebron Pkwy, Carrollton 75010 Marsha Cawthon	K-8		150	6%	469/855-5531

1 Superintendent
2 Bus/Finance/Purchasing
3 Buildings And Grounds
4 Food Service
5 Transportation
6 Athletic
7 Health Services
8 Curric/Instruct K-12
9 Curric/Instruct Elem
10 Curric/Instruct Sec
11 Federal Program
12 Title I
13 Title V
15 Asst Superintendent
16 Instructional Media Svcs
17 Chief Operations Officer
18 Chief Academic Officer
19 Chief Financial Officer
20 Art K-12
21 Art Elem
22 Art Sec
23 Music K-12
24 Music Elem
25 Music Sec
26 Business Education
27 Career & Tech Ed
28 Technology Education
29 Family/Consumer Science
30 Adult Education
31 Career/Sch-to-Work K-12
32 Career/Sch-to-Work Elem
33 Career/Sch-to-Work Sec
34 Early Childhood Ed
35 Health/Phys Education
36 Guidance Services K-12
37 Guidance Services Elem
38 Guidance Services Sec
39 Social Studies K-12
40 Social Studies Elem
41 Social Studies Sec
42 Science K-12
43 Science Elem
44 Science Sec
45 Math K-12
46 Math Elem
47 Math Sec
48 English/Lang Arts K-12
49 English/Lang Arts Elem
50 English/Lang Arts Sec
51 Reading K-12
52 Reading Elem
53 Reading Sec
54 Remedial Reading K-12
55 Remedial Reading Elem
56 Remedial Reading Sec
57 Bilingual/ELL
58 Special Education K-12
59 Special Education Elem
60 Special Education Sec
61 Foreign/World Lang K-12
62 Foreign/World Lang Elem
63 Foreign/World Lang Sec
64 Religious Education K-12
65 Religious Education Elem
66 Religious Education Sec
67 School Board President
68 Teacher Personnel
69 Academic Assessment
70 Research/Development
71 Public Information
72 Summer School
73 Instructional Tech
74 Inservice Training
75 Marketing/Distributive
76 Info Systems
77 Psychological Assess
78 Affirmative Action

Texas School Directory

School	Grades	Type	Enroll	%	Phone
© Two Dimensions Prep Academy [308] 12121 Veterans Memorial Dr, Houston 77067 Deateria Akan	PK-5	T	220 14	95%	281/227-4700 Fax 832/232-0032
© Two Dimensions Prep-Vickery [308] 12330 Vickery St, Houston 77039 Shirley Harris	PK-5	T	228	94%	281/227-4700 Fax 281/987-7306
© Two Dimensions-Corsicana [308] 901 E 10th Ave, Corsicana 75110 Shirley Harris	PK-1	T	50	96%	281/227-4700
© TX Can Acad Dallas Ross Ave 4621 Ross Ave, Dallas 75204 Rufus Johnson	PK-12	A	393		214/824-4226 Fax 214/234-8617
© Tyler Classical Academy [297] 3405 E Grande Blvd, Tyler 75707 Paula Biddle	K-10		441		903/504-5690
© Ume Prep Acad-Dallas 3838 Spur 408, Dallas 75236 Joni Holder \ James Tweedy	K-12	T	444	24%	214/445-6243 Fax 972/709-7951
© Ume Prep Acad-Duncanville 415 N Cedar Ridge Dr, Duncanville 75116 Shannon Horton	K-6	T	220	47%	972/296-0084
© Univ of Houston Charter Sch 3855 Holman St, Houston 77204 Patricia Paquin	K-5		127 6	33%	713/743-9111
© Universal Academy-Coppell 1001 E Sandy Lake Rd, Coppell 75019 Dr Dana Job	K-12		750		972/393-5834 Fax 972/393-5657
© Universal Academy-Irving 2616 N MacArthur Blvd, Irving 75062 Sheraton Duffey	PK-12	T	777	81%	972/255-1800 Fax 972/255-6122
ⓐ University High Sch © 2007 University Ave, Austin 78705 Holly Engleman	9-12		22		512/382-0072
© University of Texas Elem CS 2200 E 6th St, Austin 78702 Dr Nicole Whetstone	PK-5	T	295	58%	512/495-3300 Fax 512/495-9631 f t
© Uplift Gradus Preparatory [309] 121 Seahawk Dr, Desoto 75115 Sharon Duplantier	PK-5	T	486	84%	214/451-5551
© Uplift Grand Preparatory [309] 300 E Church St, Grand Prairie 75050 Sarah Chambers \ Allen Anderson	PK-10		288		972/854-0600
© Uplift Hampton Prep Chtr Sch [309] 8915 S Hampton Rd, Dallas 75232 Kecia Clark \ Andrea Anderson \ Brady Cooper	K-12		435		972/421-1982 Fax 972/421-1986 f
© Uplift Heights Prep Prim Sch [309] 2202 Calypso St, Dallas 75212 Kristin Algier	PK-5	T	991	92%	214/873-9700
© Uplift Heights Prep Sch Sec [309] 2650 Canada Dr, Dallas 75212 Elizabeth Kastiel	6-12		1,500		214/442-7094
© Uplift Infinity Prep Sch [309] 1401 S MacArthur Blvd, Irving 75060 Sarah Hobson \ Arlene Barochin \ Mark Forman	PK-12		387		469/621-9200 Fax 469/621-9191
© Uplift Luna Prep Primary [309] 2020 N Lamar St, Dallas 75202 Alieshia Baisy-Dyer	PK-5	T	478	82%	214/442-7882
© Uplift Luna Prep Secondary [309] 2625 Elm St, Dallas 75226 Kristina Nitahara \ Candice Dagnino	6-12	T	250	79%	214/445-3300 f
© Uplift Meridian Preparatory [309] 1801 S Beach St, Fort Worth 76105 Marissa Wells	PK-5	T	345	85%	817/288-1700
© Uplift Mighty Preparatory Acad [309] 3700 Mighty Mite Dr, Fort Worth 76105 April Sandolph \ Anson Jackson	K-12	T	566	84%	817/288-3800
© Uplift North Hills Prep Sch [309] 606 E Royal Ln, Irving 75039 Nicole Wallin \ George Rutzen \ Heather Pereira	K-12		1,600 12	20%	972/501-0645 Fax 972/501-9439
© Uplift Peak Prep Sch [309] 4600 Bryan St, Dallas 75204 Leetha Harper \ Jamila Thomas \ Samina Noorani	PK-12		423		214/276-0879 Fax 214/276-5207
© Uplift Pinnacle Prep Primary [309] 2510 S Vernon Ave, Dallas 75224 Katie Leinenkugel	K-5	T	583	84%	214/442-6100 Fax 214/442-6181
© Uplift Summit Int'l Prep CS [309] 1305 N Center St, Arlington 76011 Amanda Dudley \ Aleia Mims \ Tracy Odom	K-12		1,000		817/287-5121 Fax 817/287-0532
© Uplift Triumph Preparatory [309] 9411 Hargrove Dr, Dallas 75220 Christine Denison	PK-5	T	542	91%	972/590-5100 Fax 972/590-5199
© Uplift White Rock Hills Prep [309] 7370 Valley Glen Dr, Dallas 75228 Christine Lipschitz	PK-4		400		469/914-7500 Fax 469/914-7561
© Uplift Williams Prep Chtr Sch [309] 1750 Viceroy Dr, Dallas 75235 Marygrace Insorio	K-12		445		214/276-0352 Fax 214/637-6393
© Uplift Wisdom Prep Primary Sch [309] 301 W Camp Wisdom Rd, Dallas 75232 Karen Salerno	K-1		401		972/330-7291
© Uplift Wisdom Prep Sec Sch [309] 301 W Camp Wisdom Rd, Dallas 75232 Jacob Stainbrook	6-8		401		972/330-7291
© UT Univ CS-Laurel Ridge 17720 Corporate Woods Dr, San Antonio 78259 Sally Arnold	K-12	A	40	24%	210/491-9400 Fax 210/491-3550
ⓐ UT Univ CS-Memorial Hermann © 3043 Gessner Rd, Houston 77080 Dorothy Goodman	7-12		25		713/939-7272 Fax 713/329-7485
© UT Univ CS-Methodist Children 1111 Herring Ave, Waco 76708 Michelle Arocha	6-12	AT	200	98%	512/471-4864
© UT Univ CS-Settlement Home 1600 Payton Gin Rd, Austin 78758 Holly Engleman	6-12	AT	39	91%	512/836-2150 Fax 512/836-2159
© Utpb STEM Academy 4901 E University Blvd, Odessa 79762 Monica Elizondo \ Cody Griffen	K-10		740	17%	432/552-2580
© Valor South Austin 220 Foremost Dr, Austin 78745 Steve Gordon	K-9		450		512/646-4170
© Vanguard Academy-Beethoven 2215 S Veterans Blvd, Edinburg 78539 Blanca Salinas \ Angelica Martinez	PK-8	T	629	78%	956/318-0211 Fax 956/318-0220
© Vanguard Academy-Mozart 155 E Business 83, Alamo 78516 Federico Gonzalez	PK-5		400		956/702-2548 Fax 956/702-2731
© Vanguard Academy-Picasso 901 S Athol St, Pharr 78577 Jeanette Lerma	PK-5	T	588	82%	956/702-0134 Fax 956/702-0166
© Vanguard Academy-Rembrandt 1200 E Kelly Ave, Pharr 78577 Maria Farias	PK-12	T	1,409	82%	956/781-1701 Fax 956/781-8055
© Varnett School Southeast [310] 12707 Cullen Blvd, Houston 77047 Jessika Hearne	PK-8		52		713/726-7654
© Varnett School-East [310] 804A Maxey Rd, Houston 77013 Gail Voltz	PK-6		344		713/637-6574 Fax 713/637-8319
© Varnett School-NE [310] 8305 Mesa Dr, Houston 77028 Toni Fisher	PK-7	T	501	75%	713/631-4396 Fax 713/491-3597

79 Student Personnel	91 Safety/Security	275 Response To Intervention	298 Grant Writer/Ptnrships
30 Driver Ed/Safety	92 Magnet School	277 Remedial Math K-12	750 Chief Innovation Officer
31 Gifted/Talented	93 Parental Involvement	280 Literacy Coach	751 Chief of Staff
32 Video Services	95 Tech Prep Program	285 STEM	752 Social Emotional Learning
33 Substance Abuse Prev	97 Chief Information Officer	286 Digital Learning	
34 Erate	98 Chief Technology Officer	288 Common Core Standards	**Other School Types**
35 AIDS Education	270 Character Education	294 Accountability	ⓐ = Alternative School
38 Alternative/At Risk	271 Migrant Education	295 Network System	© = Charter School
39 Multi-Cultural Curriculum	273 Teacher Mentor	296 Title II Programs	Ⓜ = Magnet School
40 Social Work	274 Before/After Sch	297 Webmaster	Ⓨ = Year-Round School

School Programs
A = Alternative Program
G = Adult Classes
M = Magnet Program
T = Title I Schoolwide
V = Career & Tech Ed Programs

Social Media
f = Facebook
t = Twitter

New Schools are shaded
New Superintendents and Principals are bold
Personnel with email addresses are underscored

TX—13

Anderson County

Market Data Retrieval

© Village Technical Sch 402 W Danieldale Rd, Duncanville 75137 Brandi Olmstead \ Schretta Mays	PK-12	T	920	34%	469/454-4441 Fax 409/454-4442
© Vista Del Futuro Charter Sch 1671 Bob Hope Dr, El Paso 79936 Fernando Gallardo	K-7	T	450	40%	915/855-8143 Fax 915/855-8179
Waco Center for Youth-Spec Ed 3501 N 19th St, Waco 76708 Charles Freeto	Spec	T	65 11	96%	254/756-2171 Fax 254/745-5398
© Waco Charter Sch 615 N 25th St, Waco 76707 Nancy Cross	PK-5	T	215 15	99%	254/754-8169 Fax 254/754-7389
© Walipp Tsu Prep Academy 5760 Cullen Blvd, Houston 77021 Marthea Raney	6-8		190		713/741-3600 Fax 713/741-3603
© Wayside Altamira Academy 10704 Bradshaw Rd, Austin 78747	PK-5	T	396	63%	512/220-9105
© Wayside Eden Park Academy 6215 Manchaca Rd, Austin 78745 Lisa Drummond	PK-5	T	426 14	35%	512/358-1800
© Wayside Real Learning Academy 6405 S Interstate 35, Austin 78744 Kierstin Howard	PK-5	T	678	64%	512/438-7325
© Wayside Sci-Tech Preparatory 6405 S Interstate 35, Austin 78744 Brian Clason \ Bardo Montelongo	6-12	T	580	49%	512/220-9120
© Westlake Academy 2600 J T Ottinger Rd, Westlake 76262 Stacy Stoyanoff \ Rod Harding	K-12		853 30		817/490-5757 Fax 817/490-5758
© Willis Classical Academy [297] 202 S Thomason St, Willis 77378 Russell Shafer	K-8		174	43%	936/890-0100
© Winfree Academy-Dallas [311] 2550 Beckleymeade Ave Ste 170, Dallas 75237 Brad Landis	9-12		128	79%	469/930-5199 Fax 469/930-5206
© Winfree Academy-Grand Prairie [311] 2985 S State Hwy 360 Ste 160, Grand Prairie 75052 Corrine Johnson	9-12		329	69%	214/204-2030 Fax 817/329-6307
Ⓐ Winfree Academy-Irving [311] © 3110 Skyway Cir S, Irving 75038 Ridwan Williams	9-12		199 6	70%	972/251-2010 Fax 972/251-4301
Ⓐ Winfree Academy-Lewisville [311] © 341 Bennett Ln, Lewisville 75057 David Stubblefield	9-12		141 4	55%	214/222-2200 Fax 214/222-0201
© Winfree Academy-N Rchlnd Hills [311] 6311 Boulevard 26, Richland Hls 76180 Tiranus Edwards	9-12		262	48%	817/590-2240 Fax 817/590-8724
Ⓐ Winfree Academy-Richardson [311] © 1661 Gateway Blvd, Richardson 75080 Madge Ennis	9-12		240	58%	972/234-9855 Fax 972/234-9975
© YES Prep Brays Oaks [312] 9000 W Bellfort Way, Houston 77031 Stephanie Gounder	6-12	T	965	90%	713/967-8400 Fax 713/778-0917
© YES Prep East End [312] 8329 Lawndale St, Houston 77012 Aaron Simmons	6-12	T	930 8	82%	713/967-7800 Fax 713/589-2502
© YES Prep Fifth Ward [312] 1305 Benson St, Houston 77020 Barb Campbell	6-12	T	950	90%	713/924-0600 Fax 713/670-0032
© YES Prep Gulfton [312] 6565 De Moss Dr, Houston 77074 Oscar Romano	6-12	T	1,087	99%	713/967-9805 Fax 713/744-1808
© YES Prep Hoffman [312] 6101 W Little York Rd, Houston 77091 Chase Sander	6-8		402		713/924-5400 Fax 866/618-3781
© YES Prep North Centrl [312] 13703 Aldine Westfield Rd, Houston 77039 Michelle Laflure	6-12	T	965	83%	281/227-2044 Fax 281/227-2090
© YES Prep North Forest [312] 6602 Winfield Rd, Houston 77050 James Mosley	6-12	T	1,005	84%	713/967-8600 Fax 281/442-4466
© YES Prep Northbrook MS [312] 3030 Rosefield Dr, Houston 77080 Eric Newcomer	6-8		435		713/251-4200 Fax 713/251-4209
© YES Prep Northline [312] 5815 Airline Dr, Houston 77076 Brittany McGruder	6-7		300		713/842-5400
© YES Prep Northside [312] 5215 Jensen Dr, Houston 77026 Maureen Israel	6-12	T	945	91%	713/924-0400
© YES Prep Southeast [312] 353 Crenshaw Rd, Houston 77034 Eileen Galligan	6-12	T	1,009 25	78%	713/910-2510 Fax 713/910-2350
© YES Prep Southside [312] 5515 South Loop E, Houston 77033 Ashleigh Fritz	6-9	T	760	89%	713/924-5500
© YES Prep Southwest [312] 4411 Anderson Rd, Houston 77053 Eric Espinoza	6-12	T	925	82%	713/413-0001 Fax 713/413-0003
© YES Prep West [312] 10535 Harwin Dr, Houston 77036 Reem Semaan	6-12	T	895	89%	713/967-8200 Fax 713/541-8518
© YES Prep White Oak [312] 5620 W Tidwell Rd, Houston 77091 Jennifer Greene	6-11	T	655	86%	713/924-5300 Fax 713/956-4874

ANDERSON COUNTY

ANDERSON PUBLIC SCHOOLS

• **Cayuga Ind School Dist** PID: 00994401   903/928-2102
17750 N US Highway 287, Tenn Colony 75861   Fax 903/928-2646

Schools: 1 \ *Teachers:* 52 \ *Students:* 570 \ *Special Ed Students:* 86 \ *LEP Students:* 3 \ *College-Bound:* 43% \ *Ethnic:* Asian 1%, African American 4%, Hispanic 4%, Caucasian 91% \ *Exp:* $275 (Med) \ *Poverty:* 22% \ *Title I:* $148,348 \ *Special Education:* $73,000 \ *Open-Close:* 08/19 - 05/21 \ *DTBP:* $350 (High)

Dr Rick Webb 1,11,288   Kellie Gatewood 2
Leslie Glad 4   Roy Feagins 5
Cody Mohan .... 6*   Tim West 67
Jackie Willingham .... 73,295*   Nancy Griffey 83,85*

Public Schs..Principal	Grd	Prgm	Enr/#Cls	SN	
Cayuga Sch 17750 N US Highway 287, Tenn Colony 75861 Tracie Campbell \ Sherrie McInnis \ Russell Holden	PK-12	V	570 58	31%	903/928-2102

1	Superintendent	8	Curric/Instruct K-12	19	Chief Financial Officer	29	Family/Consumer Science
2	Bus/Finance/Purchasing	9	Curric/Instruct Elem	20	Art K-12	30	Adult Education
3	Buildings And Grounds	10	Curric/Instruct Sec	21	Art Elem	31	Career/Sch-to-Work K-12
4	Food Service	11	Federal Program	22	Art Sec	32	Career/Sch-to-Work Elem
5	Transportation	12	Title I	23	Music K-12	33	Career/Sch-to-Work Sec
6	Athletic	13	Title V	24	Music Elem	34	Early Childhood Ed
7	Health Services	14	Instructional Media Svcs	25	Music Sec	35	Health/Phys Education
		15	Asst Superintendent	26	Business Education	36	Guidance Services K-12
		16	Instructional Media Svcs	27	Career & Tech Ed	37	Guidance Services Elem
		17	Chief Operations Officer	28	Technology Education	38	Guidance Services Sec
		18	Chief Academic Officer				

39	Social Studies K-12	49	English/Lang Arts Elem	59	Special Education Elem	69	Academic Assessment
40	Social Studies Elem	50	English/Lang Arts Sec	60	Special Education Sec	70	Research/Development
41	Social Studies Sec	51	Reading K-12	61	Foreign/World Lang K-12	71	Public Information
42	Science K-12	52	Reading Elem	62	Foreign/World Lang Elem	72	Summer School
43	Science Elem	53	Reading Sec	63	Foreign/World Lang Sec	73	Instructional Tech
44	Science Sec	54	Remedial Reading K-12	64	Religious Education K-12	74	Inservice Training
45	Math K-12	55	Remedial Reading Elem	65	Religious Education Elem	75	Marketing/Distributive
46	Math Elem	56	Remedial Reading Sec	66	Religious Education Sec	76	Info Systems
47	Math Sec	57	Bilingual/ELL	67	School Board President	77	Psychological Assess
48	English/Lang Arts K-12	58	Special Education K-12	68	Teacher Personnel	78	Affirmative Action

Texas School Directory — Anderson County

Elkhart Ind School Dist PID: 00994437
301 E Parker St, Elkhart 75839
903/764-2952
Fax 903/764-2466

Schools: 4 \ **Teachers:** 103 \ **Students:** 1,250 \ **Special Ed Students:** 141 \ **LEP Students:** 16 \ **Ethnic:** Asian 1%, African American 5%, Hispanic 11%, Caucasian 82% \ **Exp:** $303 (High) \ **Poverty:** 15% \ **Title I:** $234,170 \ **Special Education:** $111,000 \ **Open-Close:** 08/14 - 05/29 \ **DTBP:** $350 (High)

Dr Lamont Smith 1	Alana Bacon 2
Ricky Parker 3	Marcus Wilkins 4
Shawn Mattern 5	Jason Fiacco 6
Stephanie Link 7*	Michelle Clark 16,82
Melody Holloway 38*	David Dominguez 57*
Kevin Bush 67	Rj Defreece 73,76,295

Public Schs..Principal	Grd	Prgm	Enr/#Cls	SN	
Elkhart Elem Sch 301 E Parker St, Elkhart 75839 Tana Herring	PK-2	T	337 30	63%	903/764-2979 Fax 903/764-8286
Elkhart High Sch 301 E Parker St, Elkhart 75839 Jason Ives	9-12	TV	383 30	46%	903/764-5161 Fax 903/764-2414
Elkhart Intermediate Sch 301 E Parker St, Elkhart 75839 Greg Herring	3-5	T	237	54%	903/764-8535 Fax 903/764-8287
Elkhart Middle Sch 301 E Parker St, Elkhart 75839 Rebecca Huff	6-8	T	277 25	50%	903/764-2459 Fax 903/764-8288

Frankston Ind School Dist PID: 00994463
100 W Perry St, Frankston 75763
903/876-2556
Fax 903/876-4558

Schools: 3 \ **Teachers:** 59 \ **Students:** 825 \ **Special Ed Students:** 75 \ **LEP Students:** 18 \ **College-Bound:** 62% \ **Ethnic:** Asian 1%, African American 9%, Hispanic 10%, Native American: 1%, Caucasian 79% \ **Exp:** $425 (High) \ **Poverty:** 23% \ **Title I:** $217,159 \ **Special Education:** $88,000 \ **Open-Close:** 08/14 - 05/20 \ **DTBP:** $333 (High) \ f t

John Allen 1	Randi Westbrook 2,19
Kurt Norfleet 3,5	Tina Owen 4
Paul Gould 6*	Amy Porter 7*
Nicci Cook 8,11,15,57,273,296	Bob Whitehurst 67
Edgar Rodriguez 69,88,285*	Ed Prater 73,286,295,298*
Becky Hancock 297	

Public Schs..Principal	Grd	Prgm	Enr/#Cls	SN	
Frankston Elem Sch 100 W Perry St, Frankston 75763 Melanie Blackwell	PK-5	T	405 30	59%	903/876-2214
Frankston High Sch 100 W Perry St, Frankston 75763 Edgar Rodriguez	9-12	TV	249 23	45%	903/876-3219 f t
Frankston Middle Sch 100 W Perry St, Frankston 75763 Edgar Rodriguez	6-8	TV	219 18	51%	903/876-2215 f t

Neches Ind School Dist PID: 00994499
Highway 79 County Rd 346, Neches 75779
903/584-3311
Fax 903/584-3686

Schools: 2 \ **Teachers:** 35 \ **Students:** 400 \ **Special Ed Students:** 38 \ **LEP Students:** 6 \ **College-Bound:** 60% \ **Ethnic:** Asian 1%, African American 7%, Hispanic 13%, Caucasian 79% \ **Exp:** $298 (Med) \ **Poverty:** 20% \ **Title I:** $66,390 \ **Special Education:** $64,000 \ **Open-Close:** 08/19 - 05/22 \ **DTBP:** $359 (High)

Randy Snider 1	Tina Bolton 2
Lynwood Cook 3,85	Kristi Braaton 7*
Sha-Ree Hudson 8,12,69,83,88*	Kimberlyn Snider 11*
Carol Harris 57*	Debbie Gazaway 58
Van Brown 67	Rick Seymour 73,286
Tammy Burnett 288*	

Public Schs..Principal	Grd	Prgm	Enr/#Cls	SN	
Neches Elem Jr High Sch 3055 FM 2574, Neches 75779 Kimberlyn Snider	PK-8		275 18		903/584-3401 Fax 903/584-3278
Neches High Sch 1509 Acr 346, Neches 75779 Trent Cook	9-12	TV	125 14	44%	903/584-3311

Palestine Ind School Dist PID: 00994528
1007 E Park Ave, Palestine 75801
903/731-8000
Fax 877/766-4983

Schools: 6 \ **Teachers:** 264 \ **Students:** 3,450 \ **Special Ed Students:** 305 \ **LEP Students:** 525 \ **College-Bound:** 52% \ **Ethnic:** Asian 1%, African American 29%, Hispanic 41%, Caucasian 29% \ **Exp:** $475 (High) \ **Poverty:** 27% \ **Title I:** $1,233,675 \ **Special Education:** $636,000 \ **Open-Close:** 08/15 - 05/22 \ f

Jason Marshall 1	David Atkeisson 2,19
Jacob Wheeler 3,5	Mimi Spreen 4
Breck Quarles 5	Lance Angel 6
Tobin Mac 7,83,85	Sharon Reed 8,69
Chris Keiser 15	Suzanne Eiben 15,68
Tammy Jones 15,48,51,54,57,88,271	Diane Harding 16*
Rhonda Perrington 22	Chris Kiser 31*
Sarah Johnson 36*	Dee Dietz 58
Brandon Sheeley 67	Mark Schrader 73,76,286*
Sheila Bradley 91	

Public Schs..Principal	Grd	Prgm	Enr/#Cls	SN	
Northside Primary Sch 2509 N State Highway 155, Palestine 75803 Barbara Dutton	K-1	T	504 18	74%	903/731-8020 Fax 877/655-0742
Palestine High Sch 1600 S Loop 256, Palestine 75801 Stephen Cooksey	9-12	ATV	966 60	64%	903/731-8005
Palestine Jr High Sch 233 Ben Milam Dr, Palestine 75801 Joseph Mason	7-8	T	504 60	74%	903/731-8008 Fax 877/655-0731
Southside Elem Sch 201 E Gillespie St, Palestine 75801 Grace Mancilla	2-3	T	488 31	79%	903/731-8023 Fax 877/655-0734
Story Intermediate Sch 5300 N Loop 256, Palestine 75801 Jamie Clark	4-6	T	761 65	81%	903/731-8015 Fax 877/655-0732
Washington Early Childhood Ctr 1020 W Hamlett St, Palestine 75803 Sheila Bradley	PK-PK	T	192	95%	903/731-8030 Fax 877/645-9497

79	Student Personnel	91	Safety/Security	275	Response To Intervention	298	Grant Writer/Ptnrships
80	Driver Ed/Safety	92	Magnet School	277	Remedial Math K-12	750	Chief Innovation Officer
81	Gifted/Talented	93	Parental Involvement	280	Literacy Coach	751	Chief of Staff
82	Video Services	95	Tech Prep Program	285	STEM	752	Social Emotional Learning
83	Substance Abuse Prev	97	Chief Infomation Officer	286	Digital Learning		
84	Erate	98	Chief Technology Officer	288	Common Core Standards		
85	AIDS Education	270	Character Education	294	Accountability		
88	Alternative/At Risk	271	Migrant Education	295	Network System		
89	Multi-Cultural Curriculum	273	Teacher Mentor	296	Title II Programs		
90	Social Work	274	Before/After Sch	297	Webmaster		

School Programs
A = Alternative Program
G = Adult Classes
M = Magnet Program
T = Title I Schoolwide
V = Career & Tech Ed Programs

Other School Types
Ⓐ = Alternative School
Ⓒ = Charter School
Ⓜ = Magnet School
Ⓨ = Year-Round School

Social Media
f = Facebook
t = Twitter

New Schools are shaded
New Superintendents and Principals are bold
Personnel with email addresses are underscored

Andrews County

Market Data Retrieval

- **Slocum ISD School Dist** PID: 00994633 903/478-3624
  5765 E State Highway 294, Elkhart 75839 Fax 903/478-3030

Schools: 1 \ *Teachers:* 39 \ *Students:* 415 \ *Special Ed Students:* 52 \
LEP Students: 4 \ *College-Bound:* 75% \ *Exp:* $263 (Med) \ *Poverty:* 21%
\ *Title I:* $83,183 \ *Special Education:* $66,000 \ *Open-Close:* 08/14 - 05/28
\ *DTBP:* $346 (High) \ f

Cliff Lasiter 1
Todd Flecter 3
Lacey Sloane 37
Daniel Bailey 67
Dana Morgan 2,12
Joel Parker 16,73,298*
Kim Tutt 38,83,85,88,270,275

Public Schs..Principal	Grd	Prgm	Enr/#Cls	SN	
Slocum Sch 5765 E State Highway 294, Elkhart 75839 Mark Leuschner \ Errin Deer	PK-12	V	415 38		903/478-3624 f

- **Westwood Ind School Dist** PID: 00994669 903/729-1776
  4524 W Oak St, Palestine 75801 Fax 903/729-3696

Schools: 4 \ *Teachers:* 123 \ *Students:* 1,600 \ *Special Ed Students:* 169
\ *LEP Students:* 84 \ *College-Bound:* 50% \ *Ethnic:* Asian 1%,
African American 18%, Hispanic 26%, Native American: 1%, Caucasian
54% \ *Exp:* $427 (High) \ *Poverty:* 14% \ *Title I:* $392,597 \
Special Education: $180,000 \ *Open-Close:* 08/21 - 05/22 \ *DTBP:* $350
(High) \ f

Wade Stanford 1
Josh Shultz 3,91
Richard Bishop 6*
Christine Bedre 8
Kenneth Lively 27*
Amy Little 54*
Dr Don Rice 67
Michelle Brooks 76
Kyle Penn 2,288
Phil Nedbalek 5
Kim Gilbreath 7,85*
Tiffany Carwell 11,57,69,83,285,294,298
Rosa Perez 34*
Jennifer Sturm 58
Edwin Schuessler 73,286,295*

Public Schs..Principal	Grd	Prgm	Enr/#Cls	SN	
Westwood Elem Sch 2305 Salt Works Rd, Palestine 75803 Shinnitta Foreman	3-6	T	460 35	66%	903/729-1771 Fax 903/723-0169 f
Westwood High Sch 1820 Panther Blvd, Palestine 75803 Steven Nettles	9-12	ATV	425 39	60%	903/729-1773 Fax 903/723-8695 f
Westwood Junior High Sch 1801 Panther Blvd, Palestine 75803 Sonya Brown	7-8	ATV	242 25	65%	903/723-0423 Fax 903/723-6765 f
Westwood Primary Sch 1701 W Point Tap Rd, Palestine 75803 Rosa Perez	PK-2	T	434 23	68%	903/729-1774 Fax 903/729-8839

ANDERSON PRIVATE SCHOOLS

Private Schs..Principal	Grd	Prgm	Enr/#Cls	SN	
Christian Heritage Academy 1500 Crockett Rd, Palestine 75801 Tammy Patton	K-8		128		903/723-4685

ANDREWS COUNTY

ANDREWS PUBLIC SCHOOLS

- **Andrews Ind School Dist** PID: 00994700 432/523-3640
  405 NW 3rd St, Andrews 79714 Fax 432/523-3343

Schools: 6 \ *Teachers:* 258 \ *Students:* 4,200 \ *Special Ed Students:* 291
\ *LEP Students:* 405 \ *College-Bound:* 51% \ *Ethnic:* African American
1%, Hispanic 68%, Native American: 1%, Caucasian 30% \ *Exp:* $243
(Med) \ *Poverty:* 16% \ *Title I:* $726,297 \ *Special Education:* $873,000 \
Open-Close: 08/15 - 05/22 \ *DTBP:* $147 (High)

Dr Bobby Azam 1
Daniel Webb 3,15,91
Donnie Lloyd 5
Becky Nelson 7
Kevin Vaughan 8,30,58,88,273
Belma Avena 11,69
Kari Walinder 67
Frank Lopez 297*
Bill Butler 2
Pam Yocham 4
Ralph Mason 6
Dennis Haynie 16,73,95*
Diana Villa 68

Public Schs..Principal	Grd	Prgm	Enr/#Cls	SN	
Ⓐ Andrews Alternative Sch 600 Blk NW 3rd St, Andrews 79714 Carlton Johnson	9-12	GT	43 3	38%	432/524-1946
Andrews High Sch 1400 NW Avenue K, Andrews 79714 John Carranco	9-12	GTV	1,056 70	34%	432/524-1910 Fax 432/523-6807
Andrews Middle Sch 600 NW 3rd St, Andrews 79714 David Lowder	6-8	TV	924 45	42%	432/524-1940 Fax 432/524-1904
Clearfork Elem Sch 300 NE Avenue K, Andrews 79714 Suzanne Mata	PK-1	T	785 22	51%	432/524-1930 Fax 432/524-1903
Devonian Elem Sch 1214 NW 11th Avenue, Andrews 79714 Arturo Roman	2-3	T	610 15	44%	432/524-1950 Fax 432/524-1905
Underwood Elem Sch 308 SW 5th St, Andrews 79714 Terry Justice	4-5	T	648 15	45%	432/524-1960 Fax 432/524-1906

ANGELINA COUNTY

ANGELINA PUBLIC SCHOOLS

- **Central Ind School Dist** PID: 00994774 936/853-2216
  7622 N US Highway 69, Pollok 75969 Fax 936/853-2215

Schools: 3 \ *Teachers:* 116 \ *Students:* 1,550 \ *Special Ed Students:* 167
\ *LEP Students:* 54 \ *College-Bound:* 75% \ *Ethnic:* African American
6%, Hispanic 21%, Native American: 1%, Caucasian 72% \ *Exp:* $389
(High) \ *Poverty:* 19% \ *Title I:* $366,663 \ *Special Education:* $294,000 \
Open-Close: 08/19 - 05/20 \ *DTBP:* $39 (Low) \ f t

1	Superintendent	8	Curric/Instruct K-12	19	Chief Financial Officer	29	Family/Consumer Science	39	Social Studies K-12	49 English/Lang Arts Elem	59 Special Education Elem	69 Academic Assessment
2	Bus/Finance/Purchasing	9	Curric/Instruct Elem	20	Art K-12	30	Adult Education	40	Social Studies Elem	50 English/Lang Arts Sec	60 Special Education Sec	70 Research/Development
3	Buildings And Grounds	10	Curric/Instruct Sec	21	Art Elem	31	Career/Sch-to-Work K-12	41	Social Studies Sec	51 Reading K-12	61 Foreign/World Lang K-12	71 Public Information
4	Food Service	11	Federal Program	22	Art Sec	32	Career/Sch-to-Work Elem	42	Science K-12	52 Reading Elem	62 Foreign/World Lang Elem	72 Summer School
5	Transportation	12	Title I	23	Music K-12	33	Career/Sch-to-Work Sec	43	Science Elem	53 Reading Sec	63 Foreign/World Lang Sec	73 Instructional Tech
6	Athletic	13	Title V	24	Music Elem	34	Early Childhood Ed	44	Science Sec	54 Remedial Reading K-12	64 Religious Education K-12	74 Inservice Training
7	Health Services	15	Asst Superintendent	25	Music Sec	35	Health/Phys Education	45	Math K-12	55 Remedial Reading Elem	65 Religious Education Elem	75 Marketing/Distributive
		16	Instructional Media Svcs	26	Business Education	36	Guidance Services K-12	46	Math Elem	56 Remedial Reading Sec	66 Religious Education Sec	76 Info Systems
		17	Chief Operations Officer	27	Career & Tech Ed	37	Guidance Services Elem	47	Math Sec	57 Bilingual/ELL	67 School Board President	77 Psychological Assess
		18	Chief Academic Officer	28	Technology Education	38	Guidance Services Sec	48	English/Lang Arts K-12	58 Special Education K-12	68 Teacher Personnel	78 Affirmative Action

Texas School Directory
Angelina County

Kasey Gargg 2
Heather Brink 4
Justin Risner 8,11,31,57,69,296,298*
Christi Rowe 37*
Rochelle Metts 58*
Robbie Thompson 73
Kyle Ivey 286*
Joe Collmorgen 3
Mark Caldwell 5
Donna Cook 16,82*
Shannon Matthews 37*
Brant Lee 67
Cliff Trevathan 83,91
Shalana Hyde 7*
Emily Meisel 16*
Leslie March 58
Joan Ragland 73*
Teresa Matthews 90*
Robert Inman 295
Lisa Jeffrey 8
Laura Mikeal 34*
Matt Lowe 67
Josh Smith 76,295
Michael Paul Daniel 91
Mark Condron 297

Public Schs..Principal	Grd	Prgm	Enr/#Cls	SN	
Central Elem Sch 7622 N US Highway 69, Pollok 75969 **Amanda Wright**	PK-4	T	658 27	63%	936/853-9390 Fax 936/853-9319
Central High Sch 7622 N US Highway 69, Pollok 75969 Ronald Musgrove	9-12	T	435 29	47%	936/853-2167 Fax 936/853-2208
Central Junior High Sch 7622 N US Highway 69, Pollok 75969 Ty Cauthen	5-8	T	423 25	58%	936/853-2115 Fax 936/853-2348

Public Schs..Principal	Grd	Prgm	Enr/#Cls	SN	
Hudson High Sch Highway 94 W, Lufkin 75904 John Courtney	9-12	TV	824 50	47%	936/875-9232 Fax 936/875-9307
Hudson Middle Sch Highway 94 W, Lufkin 75904 Richard Crenshaw	6-8	T	659 35	49%	936/875-9295 Fax 936/875-9317
Ⓐ Stubblefield Learning Center Ⓨ 502 College Dr, Lufkin 75904 Sally Darmstadter	9-12	GMT	12 6	71%	936/634-1100 Fax 936/634-1102
W F Peavy Primary Sch 6920 State Highway 94, Lufkin 75904 Laura Mikeal	PK-2	T	718 24	61%	936/875-9344 Fax 936/875-9378
W H Bonner Elem Sch 536 FM 3258, Lufkin 75904 Scott Mackey	3-5	T	679 28	54%	936/875-9212 Fax 936/875-9314

• **Diboll Ind School Dist** PID: 00994815 936/829-4718
215 N Temple Dr, Diboll 75941 Fax 936/829-5558

Schools: 5 \ **Teachers:** 140 \ **Students:** 1,890 \ **Special Ed Students:** 217 \ **LEP Students:** 297 \ **College-Bound:** 64% \ **Ethnic:** African American 12%, Hispanic 55%, Caucasian 33% \ **Exp:** $451 (High) \ **Poverty:** 28% \ **Title I:** $646,729 \ **Special Education:** $380,000 \ **Open-Close:** 08/26 - 06/02 \ **DTBP:** $200 (High)

• **Huntington Ind School Dist** PID: 00994891 936/876-4287
908 N Main St, Huntington 75949 Fax 936/876-3212

Schools: 5 \ **Teachers:** 124 \ **Students:** 1,750 \ **Special Ed Students:** 147 \ **LEP Students:** 14 \ **Ethnic:** African American 2%, Hispanic 7%, Native American: 1%, Caucasian 90% \ **Exp:** $398 (High) \ **Poverty:** 22% \ **Title I:** $475,767 \ **Special Education:** $441,000 \ **Open-Close:** 08/15 - 05/21 \ **DTBP:** $356 (High) \ [f]

Vicky Thomas 1
Eric Crager 3
Brandon Sanford 5
Ashlei Clowers 8
Julie Smith 16*
Carol Mettlen 38*
Jay Wyatt 67
Gerald Craig 73,286
Katherina Crager 2
Kerri Sanford 4
Blake Morrison 6*
Daniel Lopez 15
Laura Hobbs 16
Shana Powers 58
Mary Hendry 69
Mavis Trout 294
David Flowers 1
Jon Crane 3
Samantha McElroy 4
Shawn Jones 6*
Shane Stover 10*
Sherri Flynt 38,69*
Tracy Neal 67
Mike Jinkins 91
Glenn Frank 2
Shawn Ricks 3
Todd Ricks 5
Dr Dianne Holbrook ... 8,11,57,69,88,280,285,298
Robert Williams 27*
Molly Stringer 58
Jeffery Baird 73,295

Public Schs..Principal	Grd	Prgm	Enr/#Cls	SN	
Diboll High Sch 1000 Lumberjack Dr, Diboll 75941 John Clements	9-12	TV	490 40	75%	936/829-5626 Fax 936/829-5708
Diboll Junior High Sch 403 Dennis St, Diboll 75941 Mark Kettering	7-8	AT	268 38	70%	936/829-5225 Fax 936/829-5848
Diboll Primary Sch 113 N Hendrix Ave, Diboll 75941 Diana Moore	PK-PK	T	195 30	80%	936/829-4671 Fax 936/829-4977
H G Temple Elem Sch 1303 Lumberjack Dr, Diboll 75941 Nikki Miller	K-3	T	509 38	69%	936/829-6950 Fax 936/829-6960
H G Temple Intermediate Sch 1301 Lumberjack Dr, Diboll 75941 Nikki Miller	4-6	T	430	56%	936/829-6900 Fax 936/829-6910

Public Schs..Principal	Grd	Prgm	Enr/#Cls	SN	
Huntington Elem Sch 408 E Linn St, Huntington 75949 Geoff Gregory	PK-3	T	518 25	63%	936/876-5194 Fax 936/422-4450
Huntington High Sch 908 Gibson St, Huntington 75949 Shane Stover	9-12	TV	511 30	44%	936/876-4150 Fax 936/876-3057
Huntington Intermediate Sch 950 Gibson St, Huntington 75949 Sandy Flowers	4-5	T	271 15	58%	936/876-3432 Fax 936/422-4419
Huntington Middle Sch 906 N Main St, Huntington 75949 Mrs Bosley	6-8	T	398 30	50%	936/876-4722 Fax 936/876-4009
Ⓐ Pride Sch 906 N Main St, Huntington 75949 Lawton Trekell	9-12	TV	21 3	69%	936/876-4287 Fax 936/876-4352

• **Hudson Ind School Dist** PID: 00994853 936/875-3351
6735 Ted Trout Dr, Lufkin 75904 Fax 936/875-9209

Schools: 5 \ **Teachers:** 190 \ **Students:** 3,000 \ **Special Ed Students:** 215 \ **LEP Students:** 178 \ **College-Bound:** 65% \ **Ethnic:** Asian 1%, African American 7%, Hispanic 25%, Native American: 1%, Caucasian 67% \ **Exp:** $269 (Med) \ **Poverty:** 19% \ **Title I:** $569,488 \ **Special Education:** $608,000 \ **Open-Close:** 08/19 - 05/21 \ **DTBP:** $328 (High)

Donny Webb 1,11,57,83
Billy Russell 3
Keith Jennings 5
Barrett Lankford 2,19
Karen Hutto 4
Glen Kimble 6

79 Student Personnel	91 Safety/Security	275 Response To Intervention	298 Grant Writer/Ptnrships
80 Driver Ed/Safety	92 Magnet School	277 Remedial Math K-12	750 Chief Innovation Officer
81 Gifted/Talented	93 Parental Involvement	280 Literacy Coach	751 Chief of Staff
82 Video Services	95 Tech Prep Program	285 STEM	752 Social Emotional Learning
83 Substance Abuse Prev	97 Chief Information Officer	286 Digital Learning	
84 Erate	98 Chief Technology Officer	288 Common Core Standards	**Other School Types**
85 AIDS Education	270 Accountability	294 Accountability	Ⓐ = Alternative School
88 Alternative/At Risk	271 Migrant Education	295 Network System	Ⓒ = Charter School
89 Multi-Cultural Curriculum	273 Teacher Mentor	296 Title II Programs	Ⓜ = Magnet School
90 Social Work	274 Before/After Sch	297 Webmaster	Ⓨ = Year-Round School

School Programs
A = Alternative Program
G = Adult Classes
M = Magnet Program
T = Title I Schoolwide
V = Career & Tech Ed Programs

Social Media
[f] = Facebook
[t] = Twitter

New Schools are shaded
New Superintendents and Principals are bold
Personnel with email addresses are underscored

TX—17

Angelina County

Market Data Retrieval

- **Lufkin Ind School Dist** PID: 00994932 936/634-6696
  101 N Cotton Sq, Lufkin 75904 Fax 936/634-8864

  Schools: 15 \ **Teachers:** 594 \ **Students:** 8,000 \ **Special Ed Students:** 854 \ **LEP Students:** 1,375 \ **College-Bound:** 57% \ **Ethnic:** Asian 2%, African American 30%, Hispanic 42%, Caucasian 27% \ **Exp:** $250 (Med) \ **Poverty:** 26% \ **Title I:** $2,839,637 \ **Special Education:** $1,486,000 \ **Open-Close:** 08/14 - 05/21 \ **DTBP:** $139 (High)

Lynn Torres 1	Charlotte Bynum 2
Tim Hobbs 2	Johnnie Ross 3,91
Amanda Calk 4	Wayne Grissom 5
Todd Quick 6	Barbara Lazarine 9,15,74
Dr Anthony Sorola 13,15,78	Stephen Rhoades 27,31,75*
Vada Hughes 42	Gabe Keese 45
Sylvia Eubanks 57,271	Kim Kassaw 58
Scott Skelton 67	Sheila Adams 71
Brad Stewart 73,295,297*	Kelly Foley 76
Dierdre Harrison 77	Allison Hillis 81
Kurt Stephens 88,294*	Tonja Akridge 90,93
Suzi Jungman 285	Stacey McCarty 286
Jason Carr 295	Josh Williams 295

Public Schs..Principal	Grd	Prgm	Enr/#Cls	SN	
Ⓐ Ace Alternative Sch 1121 Winston 8 Ranch Rd, Lufkin 75904 Scott Walters	K-12		100 12		936/630-4152 Fax 936/632-7209
Anderson Elem Sch 381 Champions Dr, Lufkin 75901 Amy Fain	3-5	T	288 24	80%	936/632-5527 Fax 936/632-5487
Brandon Elem Sch 1612 Sayers St, Lufkin 75904 Mark Keith	3-5	T	439 30	67%	936/632-5513 Fax 936/632-5617
Brookhollow Elem Sch 1009 Live Oak Ln, Lufkin 75904 April Sebesta	3-5	T	298 35	84%	936/639-3100 Fax 936/634-8543
Burley Primary Sch 502 Joyce Ln, Lufkin 75901 Betsy Mijares	K-2	T	440	89%	936/639-3100 Fax 936/633-6222
Coston Elem Sch 707 Trenton St, Lufkin 75901 Kathy Jost	3-5	T	259 22	95%	936/639-3118 Fax 936/639-3289
Dunbar Primary Sch 1807 Martin Luther King, Lufkin 75904 Dorinda Wade	K-2	T	377 17	66%	936/630-4500 Fax 936/630-4511
Garrett Primary Sch 229 Leach St, Lufkin 75904 Cherree Hall	PK-K	T	400 18	99%	936/634-8418 Fax 936/634-8406
Hackney Primary Sch 708 Lubbock St, Lufkin 75901 Kelly Ford-Prout	PK-PK	T	240 13	97%	936/634-3324 Fax 936/634-0463
Herty Primary Sch 2804 Paul Ave, Lufkin 75901 Jill Riggs	PK-2	T	275 24	94%	936/639-2241 Fax 936/633-6516
Kurth Primary Sch 521 York Dr, Lufkin 75901 Karen Vinson	PK-2	T	294 21	82%	936/639-3279 Fax 936/639-3415
Lufkin High Sch 309 S Medford Dr, Lufkin 75901 Brandon Boyd	9-12	TV	2,126 100	67%	936/632-7721 Fax 936/632-8132
Lufkin Middle Sch 900 E Denman Ave, Lufkin 75901 Danny Whisenant	6-8	T	1,705	75%	936/630-4444 Fax 936/632-6664
Slack Elem Sch 1305 Fuller Springs Dr, Lufkin 75901 Yaneth Clifton	3-5	T	521 26	80%	936/639-2279 Fax 936/699-2297

Trout Primary Sch 1014 Allendale Dr, Lufkin 75904 Cindy Nerren	PK-2	T	315 22	87%	936/639-3274 Fax 936/639-3873

- **Zavalla Ind School Dist** PID: 00995089 936/897-2271
  431 E Main St, Zavalla 75980 Fax 936/897-2674

  Schools: 2 \ **Teachers:** 36 \ **Students:** 360 \ **Special Ed Students:** 55 \ **LEP Students:** 3 \ **Ethnic:** African American 1%, Hispanic 3%, Native American: 2%, Caucasian 95% \ **Exp:** $428 (High) \ **Poverty:** 24% \ **Title I:** $149,595 \ **Special Education:** $113,000 \ **Open-Close:** 08/15 - 05/22 \ **DTBP:** $335 (High)

Ricky Oliver 1	Alice Boulware 2
Kathy Caton 8	Kelli Collins 8,36*
Caryn Calhoun 11,58,69*	James Barge 67
James Maglothin 73	

Public Schs..Principal	Grd	Prgm	Enr/#Cls	SN	
Zavalla Elem Sch Highway 63 E, Zavalla 75980 Angela Peyton	PK-5	T	178 12	65%	936/897-2611 Fax 936/897-3586
Zavalla High Sch Highway 63 E, Zavalla 75980 Patricia Cross	6-12	TV	190 24	58%	936/897-2301 Fax 936/897-3101

ANGELINA CATHOLIC SCHOOLS

- **Diocese of Tyler Ed Office** PID: 03014660
  Listing includes only schools located in this county. See District Index for location of Diocesan Offices.

Catholic Schs..Principal	Grd	Prgm	Enr/#Cls	SN	
St Patrick Catholic Sch 2116 Lowery St, Lufkin 75901 G Maisonet	PK-8		50 12		936/634-6719 Fax 936/639-2776

ANGELINA PRIVATE SCHOOLS

Private Schs..Principal	Grd	Prgm	Enr/#Cls	SN	
St Cyprian's Episcopal Sch 1115 S John Redditt Dr, Lufkin 75904 Dr Sherry Durham	PK-5		200 21		936/632-1720 Fax 936/632-3852

1 Superintendent	8 Curric/Instruct K-12	19 Chief Financial Officer	29 Family/Consumer Science	39 Social Studies K-12	49 English/Lang Arts Elem	59 Special Education Elem	69 Academic Assessment
2 Bus/Finance/Purchasing	9 Curric/Instruct Elem	20 Art K-12	30 Adult Education	40 Social Studies Elem	50 English/Lang Arts Sec	60 Special Education Sec	70 Research/Development
3 Buildings And Grounds	10 Curric/Instruct Sec	21 Art Elem	31 Career/Sch-to-Work K-12	41 Social Studies Sec	51 Reading K-12	61 Foreign/World Lang K-12	71 Public Information
4 Food Service	11 Federal Program	22 Art Sec	32 Career/Sch-to-Work Elem	42 Science K-12	52 Reading Elem	62 Foreign/World Lang Elem	72 Summer School
5 Transportation	12 Title V	23 Music K-12	33 Career/Sch-to-Work Sec	43 Science Elem	53 Reading Sec	63 Foreign/World Lang Sec	73 Instructional Tech
6 Athletic	13 Title V	24 Music Elem	34 Early Childhood Ed	44 Science Sec	54 Remedial Reading K-12	64 Religious Education K-12	74 Inservice Training
7 Health Services	15 Asst Superintendent	25 Music Sec	35 Health/Phys Education	45 Math K-12	55 Remedial Reading Elem	65 Religious Education Elem	75 Marketing/Distributive
	16 Instructional Media Svcs	26 Business Education	36 Guidance Services K-12	46 Math Elem	56 Remedial Reading Sec	66 Religious Education Sec	76 Info Systems
	17 Chief Operations Officer	27 Career & Tech Ed	37 Guidance Services Elem	47 Math Sec	57 Bilingual/ELL	67 School Board President	77 Psychological Assess
	18 Chief Academic Officer	28 Technology Education	38 Guidance Services Sec	48 English/Lang Arts K-12	58 Special Education K-12	68 Teacher Personnel	78 Affirmative Action

Texas School Directory

ARANSAS COUNTY

ARANSAS PUBLIC SCHOOLS

• **Aransas Co Ind School Dist** PID: 00995120 361/790-2212
619 N Live Oak St, Rockport 78382 Fax 361/790-2299

Schools: 4 \ **Teachers:** 244 \ **Students:** 2,800 \ **Special Ed Students:** 345 \ **LEP Students:** 137 \ **College-Bound:** 45% \ **Ethnic:** Asian 2%, African American 2%, Hispanic 43%, Caucasian 53% \ **Exp:** $597 (High) \ **Poverty:** 27% \ **Title I:** $1,110,505 \ **Special Education:** $748,000 \ **Open-Close:** 08/14 - 05/22 \ **DTBP:** $183 (High)

Joseph Patek ...1	Gerald Goodwin ...2		
Kathy Henderson ...2,19	Norman Spears ...3,16,73		
Ross Schonhoeft ...4	Robert Douglas ...5		
Jay Seibert ...6	Tonia Ramaker ...7*		
Rose Tran ...8,11,30,68,74,78,79*	Denise Poland ...9		
Tom Jaggard ...10	Molly Adams ...12*		
John Owen ...31*	Jessica Robbins ...57,69		
Alicia Luttman ...58,270	Jack Wright ...67		
Bridget Johnson ...68	Kimberly Lawing ...73		
Sammy Zapata ...91	Chris Garis ...295		

Public Schs..Principal	Grd	Prgm	Enr/#Cls	SN	
Fulton 4-5 Learning Center 314 N 6th St, Fulton 78358 Rose Tran	4-5	T	374 22	57%	361/790-2240 Fax 361/790-2274
Live Oak Learning Center 31 Griffith Dr, Rockport 78382 Robin Rice	1-3	AT	559 60	63%	361/790-2260 Fax 361/790-2207
Rockport-Fulton High Sch 1801 Omohundro St, Rockport 78382 **Rhonda Mieth**	9-12	AGTV	781 80	45%	361/790-2220 Fax 361/790-2206
Rockport-Fulton Middle Sch 1701 Colorado St, Rockport 78382 Michael Hannum	6-8	ATV	612 60	56%	361/790-2230 Fax 361/790-2030

ARANSAS CATHOLIC SCHOOLS

• **Diocese Corpus Christi Ed Off** PID: 01045170
Listing includes only schools located in this county. See District Index for location of Diocesan Offices.

Catholic Schs..Principal	Grd	Prgm	Enr/#Cls	SN	
Sacred Heart Sch 213 S Church St, Rockport 78382 Katherine Barnes	1-5		162 8		361/463-8963

ARANSAS PRIVATE SCHOOLS

Private Schs..Principal	Grd	Prgm	Enr/#Cls	SN	
Coastal Oaks Christian Sch 2002 FM 3036, Rockport 78382 Mary Barlow	K-5		20 3		361/790-9597 Fax 361/729-4481

ARCHER COUNTY

ARCHER PUBLIC SCHOOLS

• **Archer City Ind School Dist** PID: 00995182 940/574-4536
600 S Ash Street, Archer City 76351 Fax 940/574-4051

Schools: 2 \ **Teachers:** 45 \ **Students:** 474 \ **Special Ed Students:** 59 \ **LEP Students:** 3 \ **College-Bound:** 82% \ **Ethnic:** Hispanic 11%, Native American: 1%, Caucasian 88% \ **Exp:** $681 (High) \ **Poverty:** 20% \ **Title I:** $112,073 \ **Open-Close:** 08/15 - 05/22 \

Cd Knobloch ...1,11	Bridget Wylie ...2
Shad Shanna ...6	Amanda Stafford ...8,33,85,288,296
Tiarra Truette ...12,34*	Nan Harlow ...16,82*
Jill Dunkel ...67	Leslie Graham ...69,83,88*
Bethann Oswald ...73,286,298*	Beth Anne Oswald ...84

Public Schs..Principal	Grd	Prgm	Enr/#Cls	SN	
Archer City Elem Sch 600 S Ash, Archer City 76351 Amy Huseman	PK-6	T	255 18	52%	940/574-4506 Fax 940/574-2675
Archer City High Sch 600 S Ash St, Archer City 76351 **Amanda Stafford**	7-12		219 35	27%	940/574-4713 Fax 940/574-2636

• **Holliday Ind School Dist** PID: 00995211 940/586-1281
751 College St, Holliday 76366 Fax 940/586-1492

Schools: 3 \ **Teachers:** 71 \ **Students:** 1,007 \ **Special Ed Students:** 81 \ **LEP Students:** 3 \ **College-Bound:** 4% \ **Ethnic:** Hispanic 8%, Native American: 1%, Caucasian 90% \ **Exp:** $411 (High) \ **Poverty:** 9% \ **Title I:** $63,682 \ **Open-Close:** 08/19 - 05/29 \ **DTBP:** $383 (High) \

Kevin Dyes ...1,11	Dustin Scobee ...2
Cindy Mayfield ...3	Laura Wheatherread ...4
Frank Johnson ...6*	Amber Morrison ...7*
Aniece Anderson ...36,83,88,93,271*	Krystal Southard ...59
Barry Hardin ...67	Kim Booher ...69,79
Karie Miller ...73,84,286	Denise Lawson ...76*

Public Schs..Principal	Grd	Prgm	Enr/#Cls	SN	
Holliday Elem Sch 751 College St, Holliday 76366 Tara Kirkland	PK-5	AT	443 23	29%	940/586-1986 Fax 940/586-0538
Holliday High Sch 751 College St, Holliday 76366 Bruce Patterson	9-12	AV	307 26	19%	940/586-1624 Fax 940/586-9501
Holliday Middle Sch 751 College St, Holliday 76366 Kelly Carver	6-8	ATV	257 14	20%	940/586-1314 Fax 940/583-4480

Armstrong County

Market Data Retrieval

- **Windthorst Ind School Dist** PID: 00995273   940/423-6688
  100 St Marys Street, Windthorst 76389   Fax 940/423-6505

Schools: 3 \ **Teachers:** 35 \ **Students:** 405 \ **Special Ed Students:** 35 \ **LEP Students:** 22 \ **College-Bound:** 52% \ **Ethnic:** African American 1%, Hispanic 30%, Native American: 1%, Caucasian 69% \ **Exp:** $472 (High) \ **Poverty:** 8% \ **Title I:** $25,286 \ **Open-Close:** 07/19 - 05/20 \ **DTBP:** $355 (High)

Lonnie Hise 1,11
Chris Tackett 6
Ann Armendarez 12,57,275*
Chad Steinberger 67
Rob Leopold 73,295*
Juhree Vaughn 2
Lonnie Hise 8,31*
Neal Mellon 58
Darla Tackett 69,270,271*

Public Schs..Principal	Grd	Prgm	Enr/#Cls	SN	
Windthorst Elem Sch 100 St Marys Street, Windthorst 76389 **Ann Armendarez**	PK-5	T	197 30	44%	940/423-6679
Windthorst High Sch 100 St Marys Street, Windthorst 76389 **Roy Longcrier**	9-12	TV	139 15	36%	940/423-6680
Windthorst Junior High Sch 100 St Marys, Windthorst 76389 **Roy Longcrier**	6-8	T	92	45%	940/423-6605

ARMSTRONG COUNTY

ARMSTRONG PUBLIC SCHOOLS

- **Claude Ind School Dist** PID: 00995302   806/226-7331
  500 5th St, Claude 79019   Fax 806/226-2244

Schools: 1 \ **Teachers:** 35 \ **Students:** 330 \ **Special Ed Students:** 40 \ **LEP Students:** 6 \ **College-Bound:** 80% \ **Exp:** $853 (High) \ **Poverty:** 13% \ **Title I:** $45,311 \ **Open-Close:** 08/15 - 05/22 \ **DTBP:** $341 (High) \

Brock Cartwright 1,11
Mike Hook 3,5
John Moffett 6,83,88,273,275,294
Tony Holland 58*
M-Lynn Miller 73,76,286
Angela Taylor 2,11
Annett Stanghellini 4
Amy Taylor 57,77,81,280,296,752*
Amy Lovell 67
Amy Taylor 752

Public Schs..Principal	Grd	Prgm	Enr/#Cls		
Claude Sch 500 5th St, Claude 79019 **Kendra Sherrill** \ Robert Cantu	PK-12	V	330 40		806/226-7331 Fax 806/226-3822

ATASCOSA COUNTY

ATASCOSA PUBLIC SCHOOLS

- **Charlotte Ind School Dist** PID: 00995338   830/277-1431
  102 E Hindes Ave, Charlotte 78011   Fax 830/277-1551

Schools: 3 \ **Teachers:** 45 \ **Students:** 475 \ **Special Ed Students:** 62 \ **LEP Students:** 30 \ **College-Bound:** 50% \ **Ethnic:** Hispanic 92%, Caucasian 8% \ **Exp:** $518 (High) \ **Poverty:** 23% \ **Title I:** $195,603 \ **Open-Close:** 08/19 - 05/28 \ **DTBP:** $325 (High) \

Mario Sotelo 1,83
Martin Chavarria 3,5
Becky Ramos 67
Nora Gaitan 2,11
Natasha Pesqueda 16,82*
Jennifer Swan 76,84

Public Schs..Principal	Grd	Prgm	Enr/#Cls	SN	
Charlotte Elem Sch 168 Watson Avenue, Charlotte 78011 Laura Mikolajczyk	PK-4	T	193 18	76%	830/277-1710 Fax 830/277-1675
Charlotte High Sch 70 Trojan Drive, Charlotte 78011 **Brianne Brock**	9-12	TV	150 26	73%	830/277-1432 Fax 830/277-1605
Charlotte Middle Sch 95 Rose Boulevard, Charlotte 78011 **Brianne Brock**	5-8	T	151 8	75%	830/277-1646 Fax 830/277-1534

- **Jourdanton Ind School Dist** PID: 00995376   830/769-3548
  200 Zanderson Ave, Jourdanton 78026   Fax 830/770-0015

Schools: 4 \ **Teachers:** 121 \ **Students:** 1,600 \ **Special Ed Students:** 133 \ **LEP Students:** 32 \ **College-Bound:** 41% \ **Ethnic:** African American 1%, Hispanic 59%, Caucasian 39% \ **Exp:** $234 (Med) \ **Poverty:** 17% \ **Title I:** $250,709 \ **Open-Close:** 08/15 - 05/28 \ **DTBP:** $553 (High) \

Teresa McCallister 1,73,83
Jacob Reyna 3
Braden Boehme 5
Sarah Guiturrez 7
Christie Kinsler 29
Bertha Curara 57
Sherry Rankin 271*
Angie Balaszi 2
Effron Trevino 4
Darrel Andrus 6*
Pepperjo Barley 11
Marie Fanno 36,69,88*
Barbra Peeler 67
Anna Kindrich 274*

Public Schs..Principal	Grd	Prgm	Enr/#Cls	SN	
Jourdanton Elem Sch 200 Zanderson Ave, Jourdanton 78026 Laurie Daughtrey	PK-5	T	816 40	58%	830/769-2121 Fax 830/769-2208
Jourdanton High Sch 200 Zanderson Ave, Jourdanton 78026 **Virginia Parsons**	9-12	TV	429 26	49%	830/769-2350 Fax 830/769-3065
Jourdanton Junior High Sch 200 Zanderson Ave, Jourdanton 78026 Casandra McGill	6-8	TV	362 23	54%	830/769-2234 Fax 830/769-2998
@ Larry Brown Sch 1508 Campbell Ave, Jourdanton 78026 Jeff Thornton	6-12		8 2		830/769-2925 Fax 830/769-2617

1	Superintendent	8	Curric/Instruct K-12	19	Chief Financial Officer	29	Family/Consumer Science	39	Social Studies K-12	49	English/Lang Arts Elem	59	Special Education Elem	69	Academic Assessment
2	Bus/Finance/Purchasing	9	Curric/Instruct Elem	20	Art K-12	30	Adult Education	40	Social Studies Elem	50	English/Lang Arts Sec	60	Special Education Sec	70	Research/Development
3	Buildings And Grounds	10	Curric/Instruct Sec	21	Art Elem	31	Career/Sch-to-Work K-12	41	Social Studies Sec	51	Reading K-12	61	Foreign/World Lang K-12	71	Public Information
4	Food Service	11	Federal Program	22	Art Sec	32	Career/Sch-to-Work Elem	42	Science K-12	52	Reading Elem	62	Foreign/World Lang Elem	72	Summer School
5	Transportation	12	Title I	23	Music K-12	33	Career/Sch-to-Work Sec	43	Science Elem	53	Reading Sec	63	Foreign/World Lang Sec	73	Instructional Tech
6	Athletic	13	Title V	24	Music Elem	34	Early Childhood Ed	44	Science Sec	54	Remedial Reading K-12	64	Religious Education K-12	74	Inservice Training
7	Health Services	15	Asst Superintendent	25	Music Sec	35	Health/Phys Education	45	Math K-12	55	Remedial Reading Elem	65	Religious Education Elem	75	Marketing/Distributive
		16	Instructional Media Svcs	26	Business Education	36	Guidance Services K-12	46	Math Elem	56	Remedial Reading Sec	66	Religious Education Sec	76	Info Systems
		17	Chief Operations Officer	27	Career & Tech Ed	37	Guidance Services Elem	47	Math Sec	57	Bilingual/ELL	67	School Board President	77	Psychological Assess
		18	Chief Academic Officer	28	Technology Education	38	Guidance Services Sec	48	English/Lang Arts K-12	58	Special Education K-12	68	Teacher Personnel	78	Affirmative Action

Texas School Directory — Austin County

- **Lytle Ind School Dist** PID: 00995405   830/709-5100
  15437 Cottage St, Lytle 78052   Fax 830/709-5104

Schools: 4 \ *Teachers:* 115 \ *Students:* 1,693 \ *Special Ed Students:* 122 \ *LEP Students:* 151 \ *College-Bound:* 45% \ *Ethnic:* African American 1%, Hispanic 81%, Caucasian 18% \ *Exp:* $283 (Med) \ *Poverty:* 22% \ *Title I:* $420,358 \ *Special Education:* $303,000 \ *Open-Close:* 08/23 - 05/25 \ *DTBP:* $311 (High)

Michelle Smith	1	Kathy Duran	2
William Cross	3,5	Deborah Constanzo	5
Laurie Wilson	6	Harry Piles	8,15,275,286,288
Laura Uribe-Center	11,68,296,298	Richard Tollett	16,73,76,82,84
Cassie Hoffman	36,270,273*	Robbie Pierce	58
Leanne Mask	67	Lorianne Magura	71
Sandra Jopling	83		

Public Schs..Principal	Grd	Prgm	Enr/#Cls	SN	
ⓨ Lytle Elem Sch 11550 Laredo St, Lytle 78052 Wendy Conover	2-5	MT	501 24	71%	830/709-5130 Fax 830/709-5119
Lytle High Sch 18975 W FM 2790 S, Lytle 78052 Loretta Zavala	9-12	ATV	449 35	69%	830/709-5105 Fax 830/709-5139 f
ⓨ Lytle Junior High Sch 18975 W FM 2790 S, Lytle 78052 Elizabeth Stewart	6-8	AMTV	394 20	72%	830/709-5115 Fax 830/709-3106
ⓨ Lytle Primary Sch 19126 Prairie St, Lytle 78052 Jammie Fewell	PK-1	MT	348 24	74%	830/709-5140 Fax 830/709-5142

- **Pleasanton Ind School Dist** PID: 00995431   830/569-1200
  831 Stadium Dr, Pleasanton 78064   Fax 830/569-2171

Schools: 4 \ *Teachers:* 234 \ *Students:* 3,477 \ *Special Ed Students:* 293 \ *LEP Students:* 107 \ *College-Bound:* 60% \ *Ethnic:* Hispanic 71%, Caucasian 28% \ *Exp:* $244 (Med) \ *Poverty:* 23% \ *Title I:* $1,175,501 \ *Open-Close:* 08/26 - 05/28 \ *DTBP:* $181 (High)

Dr Matthew Mann	1	Scott Stephen	2,19
Yvonne Little	3,91,295	Christophe Milini	4
David Zertuche	5	Tab Dumont	6
Jennifer Tracy	7*	Renee Cadena	8,31,54,69,275,277,285
Lindsy Pawelk	11,58	Beth Moos	16,82*
Lorene Tullos	27,35,36,83	Keri Cooper	57,288,296
Frank Tudyk	67	Cheryl Barron	68,79
Jody Lemere	73,95,297	Mary Zinda	81*
Sarah Callihan-Lewis	294	Mike Maxwell	295

Public Schs..Principal	Grd	Prgm	Enr/#Cls	SN	
Pleasanton Elem Sch 616 N Main St, Pleasanton 78064 Erica Bernal	2-5	T	992 30	59%	830/569-1340 Fax 830/569-3096 f
Pleasanton High Sch 832 Stadium Dr, Pleasanton 78064 Twila Guajardo	9-12	TV	749 70	47%	830/569-1250 Fax 830/569-4747
Pleasanton Junior High Sch 1140 Jolly St, Pleasanton 78064 Jennifer Garcia	6-8	TV	992 40	56%	830/569-1280 Fax 830/569-1290
Pleasanton Primary Sch 1209 Downey, Pleasanton 78064 Kari Vickers	PK-1	T	744 43	65%	830/569-1325 Fax 830/569-5208

- **Poteet Ind School Dist** PID: 00995493   830/742-3567
  1100 School Dr, Poteet 78065   Fax 830/742-3332

Schools: 4 \ *Teachers:* 118 \ *Students:* 1,735 \ *Special Ed Students:* 147 \ *LEP Students:* 81 \ *College-Bound:* 47% \ *Ethnic:* African American 1%, Hispanic 87%, Caucasian 13% \ *Exp:* $268 (Med) \ *Poverty:* 23% \ *Title I:* $537,037 \ *Open-Close:* 08/26 - 05/29 \ *DTBP:* $553 (High)

Cheryl Mills	1,57	Amanda Garcia	2,3*
Fernando Mendez	4	Paula Lopez	5
Ruth Martinez	7,83,85*	Greta Warner	11
Tonya Abbott	16,82	Carol Wharton	37*
Bernie Bato	58	Jo Marie Cervantez	67
Julie Post	69	Mary Ortiz	90,93
Adam Gonzales	295	Craig Smith	297

Public Schs..Principal	Grd	Prgm	Enr/#Cls	SN	
Poteet Elem Sch 1100 School Dr, Poteet 78065 Donisha Miller	PK-3	T	585 45	82%	830/742-3503 Fax 830/742-8487
Poteet High Sch 1020 Farm Rd 1470, Poteet 78065 Tony Dominguez	9-12	AGTV	512	70%	830/742-3521 Fax 830/742-8497
Poteet Intermediate Campus 838 School Dr, Poteet 78065 Christina Gillespie	4-5	T	257 27	81%	830/742-3697 Fax 830/742-3194
Poteet Junior High Sch 1020 Sn 1470, Poteet 78065 Julie Poth	6-8	TV	381 33	73%	830/742-3571 Fax 830/742-8495 f

ATASCOSA CATHOLIC SCHOOLS

- **Archdiocese San Antonio Ed Off** PID: 00999724
  Listing includes only schools located in this county. See District Index for location of Diocesan Offices.

Catholic Schs..Principal	Grd	Prgm	Enr/#Cls	SN	
Our Lady of Grace Academy 626 Market St, Pleasanton 78064 Jeanette Geyer	PK-5		65		830/569-8073

AUSTIN COUNTY

AUSTIN PUBLIC SCHOOLS

- **Bellville Ind School Dist** PID: 00995534   979/865-3133
  518 S Mathews St, Bellville 77418   Fax 979/865-8591

Schools: 6 \ *Teachers:* 161 \ *Students:* 2,200 \ *Special Ed Students:* 212 \ *LEP Students:* 183 \ *Ethnic:* Asian 1%, African American 10%, Hispanic 31%, Caucasian 59% \ *Exp:* $424 (High) \ *Poverty:* 16% \ *Title I:* $561,233 \ *Special Education:* $413,000 \ *Open-Close:* 08/26 - 05/27 \ *DTBP:* $573 (High) \ t

Mike Coker	1	Dennis Jurek	2,19
JD Higginbotham	3	Cindy Coker	4
Cody Cox	5	Grady Rowe	6*

---

79 Student Personnel	91 Safety/Security	275 Response To Intervention	298 Grant Writer/Ptnrships	School Programs	Social Media
80 Driver Ed/Safety	92 Magnet School	277 Remedial Math K-12	750 Chief Innovation Officer	A = Alternative Program	f = Facebook
81 Gifted/Talented	93 Parental Involvement	280 Literacy Coach	751 Chief of Staff	G = Adult Classes	t = Twitter
82 Video Services	95 Tech Prep Program	285 STEM	752 Social Emotional Learning	M = Magnet Program	
84 Substance Abuse Prev	97 Chief Information Officer	286 Digital Learning		T = Title I Schoolwide	
84 Erate	98 Chief Technology Officer	288 Common Core Standards	Other School Types	V = Career & Tech Ed Programs	
85 AIDS Education	270 Character Education	294 Accountability	Ⓐ = Alternative School		
88 Alternative/At Risk	271 Migrant Education	295 Network System	Ⓒ = Charter School	New Schools are shaded	
89 Multi-Cultural Curriculum	273 Teacher Mentor	296 Title II Programs	Ⓜ = Magnet School	New Superintendents and Principals are bold	
90 Social Work	274 Before/After Sch	297 Webmaster	Ⓨ = Year-Round School	Personnel with email addresses are underscored	

TX—21

Bailey County

Market Data Retrieval

Suzanne Grawunder 7*
Audrau Winkelmann 16*
Grant Lischka 67

Michael Coopersmith 8,11,36,57,69,83,88*
Evelin Sifford 34,37,58
Brian Reid 73,286,295*

John Anderson 4
Shane Mobley 6*
Mary Gajewski 11,88,296
Christopher Summers 15,294
Sarah MaGee 34,58
Ryan Reichardt 67
Shannon Culpepper 91

Randall Krichnak 5
Emily Eschenburg 10,57,271*
Shawn Hiatt 11*
Marie Landry 16,82*
Susan Stritz 37*
Amy Dyer 73,76,295*

Public Schs..Principal	Grd	Prgm	Enr/#Cls	SN
Bellville High Sch 850 Schumann Rd, Bellville 77418 Casey Hollomon	9-12	T	711 40	40% 979/865-3681 Fax 979/865-7080
Bellville Junior High Sch 1305 S Tesch St, Bellville 77418 Daniel Symm	6-8	T	512 47	49% 979/865-5966 Fax 979/865-7060
O'Bryant Intermediate Sch 414 S Tesch St, Bellville 77418 Natalie Jones	4-5	T	287 24	51% 979/865-3671 Fax 979/865-7049
O'Bryant Primary Sch 413 S Tesch St, Bellville 77418 Natalie Jones	PK-3	T	601 26	56% 979/865-5907 Fax 979/865-7039
ⓐ Spicer Alternative Ed Center 518 S Mathews St, Bellville 77418 Sean McEnerney	6-12		44 8	979/865-7095 Fax 979/865-7094
West End Elem Sch 7453 Ernst Pkwy, Industry 78944 Tony Hancock	K-5	T	150 16	36% 979/357-2595 Fax 979/357-4799

Public Schs..Principal	Grd	Prgm	Enr/#Cls	SN
Maggie B Selman Elem Sch 1741 Highway 90 W, Sealy 77474 Mary Gajewski	PK-5	T	953 43	63% 979/885-6659
Sealy Elem Sch 723 FM 2187 Rd, Sealy 77474 Mary Gajewski	PK-5	T	443 25	62% 979/885-3852 Fax 979/885-0162
Sealy High Sch 2372 Championship Dr, Sealy 77474 Megan Oliver	9-12	AGTV	851	51% 979/885-3515 Fax 979/987-3398
Sealy Junior High Sch 939 Tiger Ln, Sealy 77474 Barry Wolf	6-8	T	585 40	55% 979/885-3292 Fax 979/877-0743

AUSTIN PRIVATE SCHOOLS

Private Schs..Principal	Grd	Prgm	Enr/#Cls	SN
Faith Academy 12177 Highway 36, Bellville 77418 Zena Lyth	PK-12		210	979/865-1811 Fax 979/865-2454

BAILEY COUNTY

BAILEY PUBLIC SCHOOLS

• **Muleshoe Ind School Dist** PID: 00995699 806/272-7400
514 W Avenue G, Muleshoe 79347 Fax 806/272-4120

Schools: 4 \ *Teachers:* 116 \ *Students:* 1,450 \ *Special Ed Students:* 183 \ *LEP Students:* 255 \ *College-Bound:* 52% \ *Ethnic:* Asian 1%, Hispanic 85%, Caucasian 14% \ *Exp:* $943 (High) \ *Poverty:* 24% \ *Title I:* $473,313 \ *Special Education:* $310,000 \ *Open-Close:* 08/20 - 05/21 \ *DTBP:* $342 (High) \

Dr R Richards 1,57,83,288
Sam Whalin 3
Lee Walker 6*
Christi Richards 11
Darla Myatt 34,58
Susan Hinojsa 73,286

Lisa Whalin 2
Fiosncio Cortez 5
Jennifer Burrus 9*
Dani Heathington 15
Curtis Preston 67

Public Schs..Principal	Grd	Prgm	Enr/#Cls	SN
Mary DeShazo Elem Sch 514 W Avenue G, Muleshoe 79347 Jennifer Burrus	3-5	T	334 21	84% 806/272-7364 Fax 806/272-7370
Muleshoe High Sch 800 W 3rd St, Muleshoe 79347 Cindy Bessire	9-12	ATV	362 38	70% 806/272-7302 Fax 806/272-7574
Neal Dillman Elem Sch 510 W 18th St, Muleshoe 79347 Letti Tovar	PK-2	T	408 27	88% 806/272-7383 Fax 806/272-7388

• **Brazos Ind School Dist** PID: 00995625 979/478-6551
227 Educator Ln, Wallis 77485 Fax 979/478-2300

Schools: 4 \ *Teachers:* 64 \ *Students:* 700 \ *Special Ed Students:* 83 \ *LEP Students:* 99 \ *College-Bound:* 52% \ *Ethnic:* Asian 1%, African American 10%, Hispanic 51%, Caucasian 39% \ *Exp:* $486 (High) \ *Poverty:* 12% \ *Title I:* $127,612 \ *Special Education:* $192,000 \ *Open-Close:* 08/21 - 05/28 \ *DTBP:* $345 (High)

Brian Thompson 1
Georgina Matula 4
Kim Fisher 7*
Jill Hutchin 16
Nanette Kubena 31,69,83,85*
Kim Somer 58*
Eric Stuessel 73,295*

Courtney Marek 2
Ned Berrier 6*
Teresa Ressler 8,11,57,74,271,294*
Jill Hutchin 16*
Kim Somer 58
Matt Demny 67

Public Schs..Principal	Grd	Prgm	Enr/#Cls	SN
Brazos Elem Sch 9814 Kibler St, Orchard 77464 Shelly Grubert-Dotson	PK-5	T	340 24	67% 979/478-6610 Fax 979/478-2146
Brazos High Sch 16621 Hwy 36 S, Wallis 77485 Eric Cormier	9-12	TV	222 35	56% 979/478-6832 Fax 979/478-6022
Brazos Middle Sch 702 Educators Ln, Wallis 77485 Clay Hudgins	6-8	T	195 16	52% 979/478-6814 Fax 979/478-2574
ⓐ Prairie Harbor Alternative Sch 7146 Highway 60, Wallis 77485 **Michael Glover**	5-12		50	94% 979/478-6020

• **Sealy Ind School Dist** PID: 00995584 979/885-3516
939 Tiger Ln, Sealy 77474 Fax 979/885-6457

Schools: 4 \ *Teachers:* 198 \ *Students:* 2,900 \ *Special Ed Students:* 251 \ *LEP Students:* 360 \ *College-Bound:* 50% \ *Ethnic:* Asian 1%, African American 10%, Hispanic 50%, Caucasian 39% \ *Exp:* $306 (High) \ *Poverty:* 14% \ *Title I:* $565,593 \ *Special Education:* $907,000 \ *Open-Close:* 08/15 - 05/21 \ *DTBP:* $181 (High)

Sheryl Moore 1
Tracey Dorenkamp 2

Lisa Svoboda 2,11,19
Mike Zapaliac 3

1 Superintendent	8 Curric/Instruct K-12	19 Chief Financial Officer	29 Family/Consumer Science	39 Social Studies K-12	49 English/Lang Arts Elem	59 Special Education Elem	69 Academic Assessment
2 Bus/Finance/Purchasing	9 Curric/Instruct Elem	20 Art K-12	30 Adult Education	40 Social Studies Elem	50 English/Lang Arts Sec	60 Special Education Sec	70 Research/Development
3 Buildings And Grounds	10 Curric/Instruct Sec	21 Art Elem	31 Career/Sch-to-Work K-12	41 Social Studies Sec	51 Reading K-12	61 Foreign/World Lang K-12	71 Public Information
4 Food Service	11 Federal Program	22 Art Sec	32 Career/Sch-to-Work Elem	42 Science K-12	52 Reading Elem	62 Foreign/World Lang Elem	72 Summer School
5 Transportation	12 Title I	23 Music K-12	33 Career/Sch-to-Work Sec	43 Science Elem	53 Reading Sec	63 Foreign/World Lang Sec	73 Instructional Tech
6 Athletic	13 Title V	24 Music Elem	34 Early Childhood Ed	44 Science Sec	54 Remedial Reading K-12	64 Religious Education K-12	74 Inservice Training
7 Health Services	15 Asst Superintendent	25 Music Sec	35 Health/Phys Education	45 Math K-12	55 Remedial Reading Elem	65 Religious Education Elem	75 Marketing/Distributive
	16 Instructional Media Svcs	26 Business Education	36 Guidance Services K-12	46 Math Elem	56 Remedial Reading Sec	66 Religious Education Sec	76 Info Systems
	17 Chief Operations Officer	27 Career & Tech Ed	37 Guidance Services Elem	47 Math Sec	57 Bilingual/ELL	67 School Board President	77 Psychological Assess
	18 Chief Academic Officer	28 Technology Education	38 Guidance Services Sec	48 English/Lang Arts K-12	58 Special Education K-12	68 Teacher Personnel	78 Affirmative Action

Texas School Directory

Bastrop County

Watson Junior High Sch 6-8 T 322 82% 806/272-7349
500 W Ave F, Muleshoe 79347   33   Fax 806/272-4983
Melvin Nusser

BANDERA COUNTY

BANDERA PUBLIC SCHOOLS

• **Bandera Ind School Dist** PID: 00995778   830/796-3313
815 Pecan St, Bandera 78003   Fax 830/796-6282

Schools: 4 \ *Teachers:* 144 \ *Students:* 2,283 \ *Special Ed Students:* 250 \ *LEP Students:* 80 \ *College-Bound:* 92% \ *Ethnic:* Asian 1%, African American 1%, Hispanic 33%, Caucasian 65% \ *Exp:* $281 (Med) \ *Poverty:* 20% \ *Title I:* $567,718 \ *Special Education:* $391,000 \ *Open-Close:* 08/19 - 05/22 \ *DTBP:* $237 (High) \ [f]

Jerry Hollingsworth 1	Scott Tipton 2
Ed Barnes 3	Brian Cleary 4
Bryan Crelia 4	Kay Miller 5
Jeff Hamilton 6*	Gary Bitzi 8,36,48,51,74,285
Tracy Thayer 11,31,91,296,298	David Brown 16,73,82,84,295,297
Bonnie Hale 36,69,83,88	Patricia Galm 58
Dr Barbara Skipper 67	

Public Schs..Principal	Grd	Prgm	Enr/#Cls	SN		
Alkek Elem Sch 1798 State Highway 173 S, Bandera 78003 Chip Jackson	PK-5	T	591 33		62%	830/796-6223 Fax 830/796-6232
Bandera High Sch 474 Old San Antonio Hwy, Bandera 78003 Sergio Menchaca	9-12	TV	656 50		45%	830/796-6254 Fax 830/796-6251
Bandera Middle Sch 1005 Cherry St, Bandera 78003 **Patrick Sizemore**	6-8	T	518 48		52%	830/460-3899 Fax 830/460-6945 [f]
Hill Country Elem Sch 6346 FM 1283, Pipe Creek 78063 Laura Klein	PK-5	T	518 47		57%	830/535-6151 Fax 830/535-5111 [f][t]

• **Medina Ind School Dist** PID: 00995807   830/589-2855
1 Bobcat Lane, Medina 78055   Fax 830/589-7150

Schools: 2 \ *Teachers:* 33 \ *Students:* 310 \ *Special Ed Students:* 30 \ *LEP Students:* 7 \ *College-Bound:* 95% \ *Ethnic:* African American 4%, Hispanic 24%, Caucasian 73% \ *Exp:* $513 (High) \ *Poverty:* 18% \ *Title I:* $200,405 \ *Special Education:* $77,000 \ *Open-Close:* 08/26 - 05/22 \ *DTBP:* $379 (High)

Kevin Newsom 1,73	Teresa Blair 2,11,76,298
Lindsay Kuntz 8,16,57,83,288	Janet Murff 11,58
Melinda Wheat 16*	Dana Staump 36
Andy Lautzenheifer 67	

Public Schs..Principal	Grd	Prgm	Enr/#Cls	SN		
Medina Elem Sch 1 Bobcat Lane, Medina 78055 Janel Murff	PK-5		158 12			830/589-2731
Medina Secondary Sch One Bobcat Ln, Medina 78055 Sarah McCrae	6-12	TV	161 20		62%	830/589-2851

BASTROP COUNTY

BASTROP PUBLIC SCHOOLS

• **Bastrop Ind School Dist** PID: 00995833   512/321-2292
906 Farm St, Bastrop 78602   Fax 512/321-1371

Schools: 15 \ *Teachers:* 706 \ *Students:* 11,000 \ *Special Ed Students:* 1,112 \ *LEP Students:* 2,436 \ *College-Bound:* 41% \ *Ethnic:* African American 5%, Hispanic 67%, Caucasian 28% \ *Exp:* $502 (High) \ *Poverty:* 17% \ *Title I:* $2,129,435 \ *Special Education:* $1,846,000 \ *Open-Close:* 08/14 - 05/27 \ *DTBP:* $148 (High) \ [f][t]

Barry Edwards 1	Sandra Callahan 2,19
Scot Bunch 3,91	Andy Sexton 6,13
Luis Portillo 20,23	Kerri Walker 39*
Augustina Lozano 57	Jackie Rodgers 58
Shelly Pietsch 59	James Allen 67
Pene Liefer 68	Dr Kristi Lee 71,298
Randy Sharp 73,84	Les Hudson 79
Noemi Guerra 271	Kayla Russell 274
Emily Bain 286	Heather Christie 294

Public Schs..Principal	Grd	Prgm	Enr/#Cls	SN		
Bastrop High Sch 1614 Chambers St, Bastrop 78602 **John Gosselink**	9-12	T	1,404		48%	512/772-7200 Fax 512/772-7920 [f][t]
Bastrop Intermediate Sch 509 Old Austin Hwy, Bastrop 78602 Daniel Brown	5-6	T	778 40		60%	512/772-7450 Fax 512/321-4348
Bastrop Middle Sch 725 Old Austin Hwy, Bastrop 78602 Krystal Gabriel	7-8	T	771 55		58%	512/772-7400 Fax 512/321-1557
Bluebonnet Elem Sch 416 FM 1209, Bastrop 78602 Alison Hall	PK-4	T	771 34		71%	512/772-7680 Fax 512/308-1306 [f][t]
Cedar Creek Elem Sch 5582 FM 535, Cedar Creek 78612 Dr Delores Godinez	PK-4	T	810 30		78%	512/772-7600 Fax 512/321-6905 [f][t]
Cedar Creek High Sch 793 Union Chapel Rd, Cedar Creek 78612 Bridgette Cornelius	9-12	T	1,569		61%	512/772-7300 Fax 512/772-7930
Cedar Creek Intermediate Sch 151 Voss Pkwy, Cedar Creek 78612 Jennifer Hranitzky	5-6	T	958		71%	512/772-7475 Fax 512/321-3484
Cedar Creek Middle Sch 125 Voss Pkwy, Cedar Creek 78612 Jim Hallamek	7-8	T	841 60		67%	512/772-7425 Fax 512/332-2631
Colorado River Collegiate Acad 1602 Hill St, Bastrop 78602 Martin Conrardy	9-10	T	161		57%	512/772-7230 Fax 512/321-3212
Emile Elem Sch 601 Martin Luther King Dr, Bastrop 78602 Windy Burnett	PK-4	T	777 49		51%	512/772-7620 Fax 512/321-3564
Ⓐ Gateway Daep Sch 1155 Lovers Ln, Bastrop 78602 Patricia Alford	6-12	T	60 9		75%	512/772-7820 Fax 512/332-0498
Geneisis High Sch 1602 Hill St, Bastrop 78602 Martin Conrardy	9-12	T	98		68%	512/772-7230 Fax 512/321-3212 [f][t]

						School Programs	Social Media
9 Student Personnel	91 Safety/Security	275 Response To Intervention	298 Grant Writer/Ptnrships			A = Alternative Program	
0 Driver Ed/Safety	92 Magnet School	277 Remedial Math K-12	750 Chief Innovation Officer			G = Adult Classes	[f] = Facebook
1 Gifted/Talented	93 Parental Involvement	280 Literacy Coach	751 Chief of Staff			M = Magnet Program	
2 Video Services	95 Tech Prep Program	285 STEM	752 Social Emotional Learning			T = Title I Schoolwide	[t] = Twitter
3 Substance Abuse Prev	97 Chief Information Officer	286 Digital Learning				V = Career & Tech Ed Programs	
4 Erate	98 Chief Technology Officer	288 Common Core Standards	**Other School Types**				
5 AIDS Education	270 Character Education	294 Accountability	Ⓐ = Alternative School				
8 Alternative/At Risk	271 Migrant Education	295 Network System	Ⓒ = Charter School			New Schools are shaded	
9 Multi-Cultural Curriculum	273 Teacher Mentor	296 Title II Programs	Ⓜ = Magnet School			New Superintendents and Principals are bold	
0 Social Work	274 Before/After Sch	297 Webmaster	Ⓨ = Year-Round School			Personnel with email addresses are underscored	

TX—23

Baylor County
Market Data Retrieval

Lost Pines Elem Sch 151 Tiger Woods Dr, Bastrop 78602 **Stacy Trost**	PK-4	T	632	84%	512/772-7700 Fax 512/321-2385
Mina Elem Sch 1203 Hill St, Bastrop 78602 Reba King	PK-4	T	613 45	49%	512/772-7640 Fax 512/321-4354
Red Rock Elem Sch 2401 FM 20, Red Rock 78662 Kelly Hubley	PK-4	T	641 30	80%	512/772-7660 Fax 512/332-0126

● **Elgin Ind School Dist** PID: 00995883 512/281-3434
1002 N Avenue C, Elgin 78621 Fax 512/281-9836

Schools: 6 \ *Teachers:* 286 \ *Students:* 4,700 \ *Special Ed Students:* 411 \ *LEP Students:* 957 \ *Ethnic:* African American 13%, Hispanic 65%, Caucasian 22% \ *Exp:* $555 (High) \ *Poverty:* 18% \ *Title I:* $979,674 \ *Special Education:* $804,000 \ *Open-Close:* 08/19 - 05/28 \ *DTBP:* $189 (High)

Dr Jodi Duron 1	Debra George 2,19
Alejandro Guerra 3	Elizabeth Guajardo 4
Larry Moseley 5	Jens Anderson 6
Roberto Vasquez 7,91	Shannon Luis 8,15,54,61,280
Leshell Reeves 9	Michelle Ruthven 10
Debra Mahone 11	Dr Peter Perez 11,15,57,83
Al Rodriguez 15,68,71,78	Armando Martinez 23*
Brian Page 28,73,84,98	Stephanie Oyler 31*
Teresa Hill 36	Norma Saavedra 57
Bonita Homer 58	Lashun Gaines 58
Byron Mitchell 67	Cynthia Pawelek 294
Kathy Moore 298	

Public Schs..Principal	Grd	Prgm	Enr/#Cls	SN	
Booker T Washington Elem Sch 510 M L K Dr, Elgin 78621 Amanda Phillips	PK-5	T	622 32	79%	512/281-3411 Fax 512/281-9749
Elgin Elem School North 1005 W 2nd St, Elgin 78621 Sarah Juarez-Farias	PK-5	T	806	82%	512/281-3457 Fax 512/281-9772
Elgin High Sch 14000 County Line Rd, Elgin 78621 Rick Reyes	9-12	ATV	1,248 80	66%	512/281-3438 Fax 512/281-9804
Elgin Middle Sch 1351 N Avenue C, Elgin 78621 Riza Cooper	6-8	T	935 46	74%	512/281-3382 Fax 512/281-9781
Neidig Elem Sch 13700 County Line Rd, Elgin 78621 **Sarah Borowicz**	PK-5	T	660 35	72%	512/281-9702 Fax 512/281-9703
Phoenix High Sch 902 W 2nd St, Elgin 78621 Cheryl Williams	9-12	T	48 2	59%	512/281-9774 Fax 512/281-9862

● **McDade Ind School Dist** PID: 00995936 512/273-2522
156 Marlin St, Mc Dade 78650 Fax 512/273-2101

Schools: 1 \ *Teachers:* 27 \ *Students:* 390 \ *Special Ed Students:* 35 \ *LEP Students:* 48 \ *College-Bound:* 71% \ *Ethnic:* African American 1%, Hispanic 53%, Caucasian 46% \ *Exp:* $589 (High) \ *Poverty:* 38% \ *Title I:* $170,760 \ *Special Education:* $33,000 \ *Open-Close:* 08/19 - 05/22 \ *DTBP:* $356 (High)

Barbara Marchbanks 1,11,288	Jana Muery 2
Terry Johnson 3,5*	Annette King 4*
Frances Williams 8*	Cliff Spurlin 16,73,295,297*
Mark Dube 67	Grant Hennig 76

Public Schs..Principal	Grd	Prgm	Enr/#Cls	SN	
McDade Sch 156 Marlin St, Mc Dade 78650 Frances Williams	PK-10	T	390 10	68%	512/273-2522

● **Smithville Ind School Dist** PID: 00995974 512/237-2487
901 NE 6th St, Smithville 78957 Fax 512/237-2775

Schools: 5 \ *Teachers:* 149 \ *Students:* 1,780 \ *Special Ed Students:* 153 \ *LEP Students:* 111 \ *College-Bound:* 43% \ *Ethnic:* Asian 1%, African American 8%, Hispanic 32%, Caucasian 58% \ *Exp:* $388 (High) \ *Poverty:* 16% \ *Title I:* $359,146 \ *Special Education:* $211,000 \ *Open-Close:* 08/26 - 05/29 \ *DTBP:* $550 (High)

Cheryl Burns 1	Jeanann McCarthy 2,19
Zachary Harris 3,5	Candance Biehle 4
Cyril Adkins 6*	Weinheimer Sophie 7
David Edwards 11*	Kim Hemphill 16*
Shari Bang 58	Grant Gutierrez 67
Ana Murray 71,97	

Public Schs..Principal	Grd	Prgm	Enr/#Cls	SN	
Brown Primary Sch 403 4th Ave, Smithville 78957 Stephanie Foster	PK-2	T	433 38	71%	512/237-2519 Fax 512/237-5635
Smithville Elem Sch 800 Bishop St, Smithville 78957 Tammie Hewitt	3-5	T	404 23	64%	512/237-2406 Fax 512/237-5614
Smithville High Sch 285 Highway 95, Smithville 78957 Paul Smith	9-12	TV	541 48	52%	512/237-2451 Fax 512/237-5643
Smithville Junior High Sch 801 Wilkes St, Smithville 78957 Bethany Logan	6-8	T	410 22	65%	512/237-2407 Fax 512/237-5624
ⓐ Tiger Academy 301 Royston St, Smithville 78957 David Edwards	9-12		30		512/237-5142

BASTROP PRIVATE SCHOOLS

Private Schs..Principal	Grd	Prgm	Enr/#Cls	SN	
Rosanky Christian Academy 2160 FM 535, Rosanky 78953 Sarah Voigt	PK-12		83		512/360-3109 Fax 512/360-4088

BAYLOR COUNTY

BAYLOR PUBLIC SCHOOLS

● **Seymour Ind School Dist** PID: 00996021 940/889-3525
409 W Idaho St, Seymour 76380 Fax 940/889-5340

Schools: 3 \ *Teachers:* 54 \ *Students:* 575 \ *Special Ed Students:* 68 \ *LEP Students:* 5 \ *College-Bound:* 47% \ *Ethnic:* Asian 1%, African American 2%, Hispanic 21%, Caucasian 75% \ *Exp:* $584 (High) \ *Poverty:* 26% \ *Title I:* $201,359 \ *Open-Close:* 08/20 - 05/21 \ *DTBP:* $373 (High)

---

1 Superintendent	8 Curric/Instruct K-12	19 Chief Financial Officer	29 Family/Consumer Science	39 Social Studies K-12	49 English/Lang Arts Elem	59 Special Education Elem	69 Academic Assessment
2 Bus/Finance/Purchasing	9 Curric/Instruct Elem	20 Art K-12	30 Adult Education	40 Social Studies Elem	50 English/Lang Arts Sec	60 Special Education Sec	70 Research/Development
3 Buildings And Grounds	10 Curric/Instruct Sec	21 Art Elem	31 Career/Sch-to-Work K-12	41 Social Studies Sec	51 Reading K-12	61 Foreign/World Lang K-12	71 Public Information
4 Food Service	11 Federal Program	22 Art Sec	32 Career/Sch-to-Work Elem	42 Science K-12	52 Reading Elem	62 Foreign/World Lang Elem	72 Summer School
5 Transportation	12 Title I	23 Music K-12	33 Career/Sch-to-Work Sec	43 Science Elem	53 Reading Sec	63 Foreign/World Lang Sec	73 Instructional Tech
6 Athletic	13 Title V	24 Music Elem	34 Early Childhood Ed	44 Science Sec	54 Remedial Reading K-12	64 Religious Education K-12	74 Inservice Training
7 Health Services	15 Asst Superintendent	25 Music Sec	35 Health/Phys Education	45 Math K-12	55 Remedial Reading Elem	65 Religious Education Elem	75 Marketing/Distributive
	16 Instructional Media Svcs	26 Business Education	36 Guidance Services K-12	46 Math Elem	56 Remedial Reading Sec	66 Religious Education Sec	76 Info Systems
	17 Chief Operations Officer	27 Career & Tech Ed	37 Guidance Services Elem	47 Math Sec	57 Bilingual/ELL	67 School Board President	77 Psychological Assess
	18 Chief Academic Officer	28 Technology Education	38 Guidance Services Sec	48 English/Lang Arts K-12	58 Special Education K-12	68 Teacher Personnel	78 Affirmative Action

Texas School Directory — Bee County

John Anderson 1	Cindy Davis 2,8,11,83,88,296,298
Phil Holub 3,5	Hugh Farmer 6*
Sunday McAdams 16,82*	Jimmie Carter 27*
Shawn Stout 29*	Edward Wolsch 31,36,69,77*
Carra Carter 34*	Donna Carver 57,271*
Mona Wardlaw 58*	Whitney Martischnig 60*
Bryan Baldwin 67	Courtney Woodward 73,76
Brian Bibb 286,288*	

Public Schs..Principal	Grd	Prgm	Enr/#Cls	SN	
Seymour Elem Sch 300 E Idaho St, Seymour 76380 Kenda Gilbreath	PK-4	AT	241 40	63%	940/889-2533 Fax 940/889-8890
Seymour High Sch 500 Stadium Dr, Seymour 76380 **Adam Arredondo**	9-12	ATV	162 24	46%	940/889-2947 Fax 940/889-1045
Seymour Middle Sch 500 Stadium Dr, Seymour 76380 Donny Hearn	5-8	AT	176 17	57%	940/889-4548 Fax 940/889-4962

BEE COUNTY

BEE PUBLIC SCHOOLS

● **Beeville Ind School Dist** PID: 00996069   361/358-7111
201 N Saint Marys St, Beeville 78102   Fax 361/362-6046

Schools: 6 \ **Teachers:** 227 \ **Students:** 3,200 \ **Special Ed Students:** 350 \ **LEP Students:** 83 \ **College-Bound:** 41% \ **Ethnic:** African American 3%, Hispanic 84%, Caucasian 13% \ **Exp:** $313 (High) \ **Poverty:** 32% \ **Title I:** $1,802,751 \ **Special Education:** $772,000 \ **Open-Close:** 08/19 - 05/22 \ **DTBP:** $137 (High)

Dr Marc Puig 1	Eve Cisneros 2
Victor Ramos 3,27*	Art Provencio 4
Ernest Delbosque 5	Chris Soza 6
Martina Verell 11	Erasmo Rodriguez 15,91
Jay Viertel 27,36*	Rosario Zambrano 57,58
Leticia Munoz 67	Joni Barber 70,294
Lawrence Garcia 73,84	Art Gamez 91

Public Schs..Principal	Grd	Prgm	Enr/#Cls	SN	
A C Jones High Sch 1902 N Adams St, Beeville 78102 Ann Ewing	9-12	TV	1,033	63%	361/362-6000 Fax 361/362-6048
Fadden-McKeown-Chambliss ES 100 T J Pfeil Ln, Beeville 78102 Anita Taylor	1-5	T	580 27	87%	361/362-6050 Fax 361/362-6054
Hampton-Moreno-Dugat ECC 2000 S Musset, Beeville 78102 Annette Sanchez	PK-K	T	402 17	87%	361/362-6040 Fax 361/362-6049
Ⓜ Joe Barnhart Magnet Academy 301 N Minnesota St, Beeville 78102 Jaime Rodriguez	7-8		78		361/358-6262
Moreno Middle Sch Sch 301 N Minnesota St, Beeville 78102 Jaime Rodriguez	6-8	T	687 56	77%	361/358-6262 Fax 361/362-6094
R A Hall Elem Sch 1100 W Huntington St, Beeville 78102 Belinda Aguirre	1-5	T	530 19	87%	361/362-6060 Fax 361/362-6059

● **Pawnee Ind School Dist** PID: 00996148   361/456-7256
6229 FM 798, Pawnee 78145   Fax 361/456-7388

Schools: 1 \ **Teachers:** 22 \ **Students:** 550 \ **Special Ed Students:** 16 \ **LEP Students:** 3 \ **Ethnic:** African American 3%, Hispanic 78%, Caucasian 18% \ **Exp:** $190 (Low) \ **Poverty:** 18% \ **Title I:** $16,129 \ **Open-Close:** 08/12 - 05/20 \ 🅕 🅣

Michelle Hartmann 1,11,84,288	Braden Lyssy 2,3
Monica Flores 4	Brooke Mills 7
Kendra Wuest 8,12,83,88,294*	Pete Dobson 67
Billy Polasek 73*	Mandy Becker 275,752

Public Schs..Principal	Grd	Prgm	Enr/#Cls	SN	
Pawnee Sch 6229 FM 798, Pawnee 78145 Kendra Wuest	PK-8	T	550 17	84%	361/456-7256

● **Pettus Ind School Dist** PID: 00996174   361/375-2296
500 N May St, Pettus 78146   Fax 361/375-2830

Schools: 2 \ **Teachers:** 39 \ **Students:** 421 \ **Special Ed Students:** 40 \ **LEP Students:** 3 \ **College-Bound:** 60% \ **Ethnic:** African American 1%, Hispanic 66%, Native American: 1%, Caucasian 32% \ **Exp:** $481 (High) \ **Poverty:** 25% \ **Title I:** $228,310 \ **Special Education:** $45,000 \ **Open-Close:** 08/15 - 05/27 \ **DTBP:** $48 (Low)

Mike Homann 1,11	Clark Mansker 2
Larry Bailey 3	Mario Monjaras 4*
Micheal Enriquez 6	Steve Sugerek 16,73*
Charla Burns 38,69,83*	Karla Cypert 57*
Jaime Rodriguez 67	

Public Schs..Principal	Grd	Prgm	Enr/#Cls	SN	
Pettus Elem Sch 500 N B Street, Pettus 78146 Karla Cypert	PK-5	T	195 14	72%	361/375-2296 Fax 361/375-2930
Pettus Secondary Sch 500 N May St, Pettus 78146 Ricardo DeLeon	6-12	GTV	234 22	70%	361/375-2296 Fax 361/375-2565

● **Skidmore Tynan Ind SD** PID: 00996215   361/287-3426
224 W Main St, Skidmore 78389   Fax 361/287-3442

Schools: 3 \ **Teachers:** 61 \ **Students:** 850 \ **Special Ed Students:** 86 \ **LEP Students:** 11 \ **College-Bound:** 70% \ **Ethnic:** Asian 1%, African American 1%, Hispanic 68%, Native American: 1%, Caucasian 30% \ **Exp:** $382 (High) \ **Poverty:** 19% \ **Title I:** $135,512 \ **Open-Close:** 08/21 - 05/25 \ **DTBP:** $318 (High) \ 🅕

Dustin Burton 1	Robin Moore 2
Jennifer Franklin 4	Rose Reyna 5
John Livas 6	Amanda Michael ....
Robin Thomas 8,11,69,83,88,288*	Dana Scott 12,296*
Debbie Lopez 16*	Sherri Brown 36,88*
Sherri Nelson 58*	James Bennett 67
Luz Gonzales 73*	Judy Garza 270*

Public Schs..Principal	Grd	Prgm	Enr/#Cls	SN	
Skidmore Tynan Elem Sch 325 Bodcat Trial, Skidmore 78389 Corina Garcia	PK-5	T	346 20	59%	361/287-3425 Fax 361/287-3319
Skidmore Tynan High Sch 213 N Walton, Skidmore 78389 Dana Scott	9-12	TV	279 18	49%	361/287-3426 Fax 361/287-0146

---

*9	Student Personnel	91	Safety/Security	275	Response To Intervention	298	Grant Writer/Ptnrships	
*0	Driver Ed/Safety	92	Magnet School	277	Remedial Math K-12	750	Chief Innovation Officer	
*1	Gifted/Talented	93	Parental Involvement	280	Literacy Coach	751	Chief of Staff	
*2	Video Services	95	Tech Prep Program	285	STEM	752	Social Emotional Learning	
*3	Substance Abuse Prev	97	Chief Information Officer	286	Digital Learning			
*4	Erate	98	Chief Technology Officer	288	Common Core Standards			
*5	AIDS Education	270	Character Education	294	Accountability			
*6	Alternative/At Risk	271	Migrant Education	295	Network System			
*9	Multi-Cultural Curriculum	273	Teacher Mentor	296	Title II Programs			
*0	Social Work	274	Before/After Sch	297	Webmaster			

School Programs
A = Alternative Program
G = Adult Classes
M = Magnet Program
T = Title I Schoolwide
V = Career & Tech Ed Programs

Other School Types
Ⓐ = Alternative School
Ⓒ = Charter School
Ⓜ = Magnet School
Ⓨ = Year-Round School

Social Media
🅕 = Facebook
🅣 = Twitter

New Schools are shaded
New Superintendents and Principals are bold
Personnel with email addresses are underscored

TX—25

Bell County
Market Data Retrieval

Skidmore Tynan Jr High Sch — 6-8 — AT — 212 — 63% — 361/287-3426
201 N 8th St, Skidmore 78389 — 13 — Fax 361/287-0714
Stella Resio

BEE PRIVATE SCHOOLS

Private Schs..Principal	Grd	Prgm	Enr/#Cls	SN	
First Baptist Church Sch 600 N Saint Marys St, Beeville 78102 Dr Susan Warner	PK-6		71 10		361/358-4161 Fax 361/358-4163
St Philip's Episcopal Sch 105 N Adams St, Beeville 78102 Carol Reagan	PK-6		100 18		361/358-6242 Fax 361/358-8232

BELL COUNTY

BELL PUBLIC SCHOOLS

• **Academy Ind School Dist** PID: 00996253 — 254/982-4304
704 E Main St, LTL RVR Acad 76554 — Fax 254/982-0023

Schools: 5 \ *Teachers:* 102 \ *Students:* 1,559 \ *Special Ed Students:* 114 \ *LEP Students:* 72 \ *College-Bound:* 95% \ *Ethnic:* Asian 1%, African American 6%, Hispanic 23%, Native American: 1%, Caucasian 70% \ *Exp:* $227 (Med) \ *Poverty:* 10% \ *Title I:* $117,999 \ *Open-Close:* 08/21 - 05/29 \ *DTBP:* $350 (High) \

Billy Harlan 1
Alex Remchel 3,11,15,83,88,271,274*
Heather Thies 4*
Carlinda Rex 9
Jana Warren 37*
Calvin Eshbaugh 67
Jarrod Newman 73,295
Stephen Ash 85*
Sherry Moore 2
Oscar Martinez 3
Mike Nichols 6*
Callie Poncik 10,74,273*
Nancy Riley 58
Amanda Liebman 69
Connie Bleer 76
Terry Timberlake 295

Public Schs..Principal	Grd	Prgm	Enr/#Cls	SN	
Academy Elem Sch 311 N Bumblebee Dr, LTL RVR Acad 76554 **Andrea Chaney**	PK-2	T	386 20	48%	254/982-4621 Fax 254/982-4584
Academy High Sch 602 E Main St, LTL RVR Acad 76554 **Alex Remschel**	9-12	TV	453 21	27%	254/982-4201 Fax 254/982-4420
Academy Intermediate Sch 107 S Pondalily, LTL RVR Acad 76554 Dana Coleman	3-5	T	376	40%	254/982-0150
Academy Middle Sch 501 E Main St, LTL RVR Acad 76554 Glenell Bankhead	6-8	T	344 25	35%	254/982-4620 Fax 254/982-4776
ⓐ Bell County Alternative Sch 706 E Rio Poco, LTL RVR Acad 76554 Terry Day	6-12		30 3		254/982-3505 Fax 254/982-3506

• **Bartlett Ind School Dist** PID: 00996289 — 254/527-4247
404 N Robinson Street, Bartlett 76511 — Fax 254/527-3340

Schools: 3 \ *Teachers:* 35 \ *Students:* 350 \ *Special Ed Students:* 36 \ *LEP Students:* 34 \ *Ethnic:* African American 10%, Hispanic 63%, Caucasian 27% \ *Exp:* $331 (High) \ *Poverty:* 16% \ *Title I:* $96,993 \ *Open-Close:* 08/19 - 05/22 \ *DTBP:* $360 (High) \

Theodore Clevenger 1
Shirley Hall 2
Angie Peace 8,36,69,88*
Rebecca Beam 12*
Nelson Hall 67
Monica Crouch 2
Elizabeth Maddox 4
Laurie Webb 8,11,36,88
Monica Hauk 16,73,295

Public Schs..Principal	Grd	Prgm	Enr/#Cls	SN	
Bartlett Elem Sch 404 N Robinson Street, Bartlett 76511 Angie Peace	PK-5		203 14		254/527-3353 Fax 254/527-3441
Bartlett High Sch 404 N Robinson Street, Bartlett 76511 Angie Peace	9-12	V	103 20		254/527-3351 Fax 254/527-3515
Bartlett Middle Sch 404 N Robinson St, Bartlett 76511 Angie Peace	6-8	T	75	83%	254/527-4247

• **Belton Ind School Dist** PID: 00996318 — 254/215-2000
400 N Wall St, Belton 76513 — Fax 254/215-2001

Schools: 17 \ *Teachers:* 702 \ *Students:* 11,950 \ *Special Ed Students:* 1,257 \ *LEP Students:* 738 \ *College-Bound:* 65% \ *Ethnic:* Asian 2%, African American 7%, Hispanic 34%, Native American: 1%, Caucasian 56% \ *Exp:* $332 (High) \ *Poverty:* 12% \ *Title I:* $1,405,203 \ *Special Education:* $1,646,000 \ *Open-Close:* 08/19 - 05/27 \ *DTBP:* $181 (High) \

Dr Robin Battershell 1
Kerri Pridemore 2
Rick Martinez 3
Andrew Forrester 5
Charlotte Smith 7*
8,15,88,270,275,286,296,298
Celia Ray 11
Dr Robert Muller 15
Stephanie Ferguson 26,31,75*
Beverly Stephens 36*
Jennifer Ramirez 58
Dawn Schiller 69,70
Rachel Starnes 76
Doug Taylor 91
Dr Rachelle Warren 752
Jennifer Land 2,19
Tammy Shannon 2
Rob Pasichnyk 4
Sanvel Skidmore 6
Dr Deanna Lovesmith ....
Mike Morgan 15,79
Todd Shiller 15,68,78,273
Sue Banfield 34*
Lauren Brisbin 57,280
Sue Jordan 67
Dr Charlotte Trejo 74,273
Barbara Epperson 81
Vickie Dean 294

Public Schs..Principal	Grd	Prgm	Enr/#Cls	SN	
ⓐ Aep Center 302 N Blair St, Belton 76513 Ted Smith	6-12	V	50 2		254/215-2571 Fax 254/215-2551
Belton Early Childhood Sch 501 E 4th Ave, Belton 76513 Sue Banfield	PK-PK	T	427	79%	254/215-3700 Fax 254/215-3701
Belton High Sch 600 Lake Rd, Belton 76513 Jill Ross	9-12	TV	2,843	43%	254/215-2200 Fax 254/215-2201
Charter Oak Elem Sch **8402 Poison Oak Rd, Temple 76502** **Jennifer Conner**	**K-5**		**400**		**254/215-4000**
Chisholm Trail Elem Sch 1082 S Wheat Rd, Belton 76513 Elizabeth McMurtry	K-5	T	765	68%	254/316-5100 Fax 254/316-5101

1 Superintendent	8 Curric/Instruct K-12	19 Chief Financial Officer	29 Family/Consumer Science	39 Social Studies K-12	49 English/Lang Arts Elem	59 Special Education Elem	69 Academic Assessment
2 Bus/Finance/Purchasing	9 Curric/Instruct Elem	20 Art K-12	30 Adult Education	40 Social Studies Elem	50 English/Lang Arts Sec	60 Special Education Sec	70 Research/Development
3 Buildings And Grounds	10 Curric/Instruct Sec	21 Art Elem	31 Career/Sch-to-Work K-12	41 Social Studies Sec	51 Reading K-12	61 Foreign/World Lang K-12	71 Public Information
4 Food Service	11 Federal Program	22 Art Sec	32 Career/Sch-to-Work Elem	42 Science K-12	52 Reading Elem	62 Foreign/World Lang Elem	72 Summer School
5 Transportation	12 Title I	23 Music K-12	33 Career/Sch-to-Work Sec	43 Science Elem	53 Reading Sec	63 Foreign/World Lang Sec	73 Instructional Tech
6 Athletic	14 Title V	24 Music Elem	34 Early Childhood Ed	44 Science Sec	54 Remedial Reading K-12	64 Religious Education K-12	74 Inservice Training
7 Health Services	15 Asst Superintendent	25 Music Sec	35 Health/Phys Education	45 Math K-12	55 Remedial Reading Elem	65 Religious Education Elem	75 Marketing/Distributive
	16 Instructional Media Svcs	26 Business Education	36 Guidance Services K-12	46 Math Elem	56 Remedial Reading Sec	66 Religious Education Sec	76 Info Systems
	17 Chief Operations Officer	27 Career & Tech Ed	37 Guidance Services Elem	47 Math Sec	57 Bilingual/ELL	67 School Board President	77 Psychological Assess
	18 Chief Academic Officer	28 Technology Education	38 Guidance Services Sec	48 English/Lang Arts K-12	58 Special Education K-12	68 Teacher Personnel	78 Affirmative Action

Texas School Directory

Bell County

High Point Elem Sch 1635 Starlight Dr, Temple 76502 Amy Armstrong	K-5	T	716	38%	254/316-5000 Fax 254/316-5001
Joe M Pirtle Elem Sch 714 S Pea Ridge Rd, Temple 76502 Rebecca Vaughn	K-5		762 39	31%	254/215-3400 Fax 254/215-3401
Lake Belton Middle Sch 8818 Tarver Dr, Temple 76502 Kris Hobson	6-8	T	840 65	47%	254/215-2900 Fax 254/780-3493 f t
Lakewood Elem Sch 11200 FM 2305, Belton 76513 Judy Schiller	K-5	T	678 35	28%	254/215-3100 Fax 254/215-3101
Leon Heights Elem Sch 1501 N Main St, Belton 76513 Marcie Beck	K-5	T	280 14	45%	254/215-3200 Fax 254/215-3201 f t
Miller Heights Elem Sch 1110 Fairway Dr, Belton 76513 Jennifer Conner	K-5	T	327 22	74%	254/215-3300 Fax 254/215-3301
New Tech High Sch at Waskow 320 N Blair St, Belton 76513 Benjamin Smith	9-12		527 5	24%	254/215-2500 Fax 254/215-2501
North Belton Middle Sch 7907 Prairie View Rd, Temple 76502 Joe Brown	6-8		959 30	33%	254/316-5200
South Belton Middle Sch 805 Sage Brush, Belton 76513 Kevin Taylor	6-8	T	837	57%	254/215-3000
Southwest Elem Sch 611 Saunders St, Belton 76513 Stacy Cox	K-5	T	381 26	79%	254/215-3500 Fax 254/215-3501
Sparta Elem Sch 1800 Sparta Rd, Belton 76513 Julee Manley	K-5		600 22	33%	254/215-3600 Fax 254/215-3601
Tarver Elem Sch 7949 Stonehollow Dr, Temple 76502 Michelle Tish	K-5	T	587 37	42%	254/215-3800 Fax 254/215-3801 f t

● Holland Ind School Dist PID: 00996394
105 Rose Ln, Holland 76534

254/657-0175
Fax 254/657-0172

Schools: 3 \ **Teachers:** 57 \ **Students:** 692 \ **Special Ed Students:** 53 \ **LEP Students:** 14 \ **College-Bound:** 55% \ **Ethnic:** African American 3%, Hispanic 29%, Caucasian 68% \ **Exp:** $438 (High) \ **Poverty:** 17% \ **Title I:** $117,262 \ **Open-Close:** 08/21 - 05/22 \ **DTBP:** $347 (High)

Shane Downing 1,57
Larry Coufal 3
Brad Talbert 6
Melany Cearley 8,36,79,88,270*
Terri Crum 16*
Jill Marwitz 67
Keith Cabaniss 295*
Tracy Wolf 2,84
Connie Knaus 4
Cynthia Phaestka 7
Robbie Edwards 10,11,57,83,275,285
Nancy Riley 58
Sherry Kallus 274*

Public Schs..Principal	Grd	Prgm	Enr/#Cls	SN	
Holland Elem Sch 503 Crockett St, Holland 76534 **Lori Kinard**	PK-5	T	311 20	59%	254/657-2525 Fax 254/657-2845
Holland High Sch 502 Crockett St, Holland 76534 Robby Edwards	9-12	AV	214 19	40%	254/657-2523 Fax 254/657-2250
Holland Middle Sch 302 Hackberry Rd, Holland 76534 Leah Smith	6-8	ATV	143 11	46%	254/657-2224 Fax 254/657-2872

● Killeen Ind School Dist PID: 00996423
200 N Ws Young Dr, Killeen 76543

254/336-0000
Fax 254/336-0010

Schools: 53 \ **Teachers:** 2,860 \ **Students:** 45,583 \ **Special Ed Students:** 4,957 \ **LEP Students:** 3,906 \ **College-Bound:** 75% \ **Ethnic:** Asian 3%, African American 38%, Hispanic 33%, Native American: 1%, Caucasian 26% \ **Exp:** $440 (High) \ **Poverty:** 18% \ **Title I:** $11,781,062 \ **Special Education:** $6,063,000 \ **Bilingual Education:** $104,000 \ **Open-Close:** 08/26 - 05/28 \ **DTBP:** $199 (High)

Dr John Craft 1
Megan Bradley 2,19
Edward Thomas 5
Vhonda Gilmore 7
Dagmar Harris 10
Dr Eric Penrod 15
Shannon Lumar 36
Dr Jacqueline Pilkey 58
Corbett Lawler 67
Teresa Daugherty 69,294
Cindy Oppermann 76
John Dye 91*
Holly Landez 286
George Ybarra 2
Lori Alejandro 4
Randall Hugg 6
Sharon Davis 8,11,15
David Manley 15
Dr Karen Herrera 20,23
Liodolee Garcia 57,271
Dr Janice Peronto 58
Jo-Lynette Crayton 68,74,273
Taina Maya 71
Sandra Forsythe 79
Cynthia Hodges 285

Public Schs..Principal	Grd	Prgm	Enr/#Cls	SN	
Alice W Douse Elem Sch 700 Rebecca Lynn Ln, Killeen 76542 Stephanie Ford	PK-5		866		254/336-7480 Fax 254/336-7490
Audie Murphy Middle Sch 53393 Sun Dance Dr, Fort Hood 76544 Mike Quinn	6-8	T	800	51%	254/336-6530 Fax 254/200-6579
Bellaire Elem Sch 108 W Jasper Dr, Killeen 76542 Lavonda Loney	PK-5	T	551 37	88%	254/336-1410 Fax 254/336-1437
Brookhaven Elem Sch 3221 Hilliard Ave, Killeen 76543 Iris Felder	PK-5	T	654 38	82%	254/336-1440 Fax 254/336-1463
Cedar Valley Elem Sch 4801 Chantz Dr, Killeen 76542 Connie Morris	PK-5	T	705 43	55%	254/336-1480 Fax 254/336-1496 f
Clarke Elem Sch 51612 Comanche Ave, Fort Hood 76544 Laura Dart	PK-3	T	592 50	63%	254/336-1510 Fax 254/336-1528
Clear Creek Elem Sch 4800 Washington St, Fort Hood 76544 Maryann Ramos	PK-5	T	721 40	72%	254/336-1550 Fax 254/336-1567
Clifton Park Elem Sch 2200 Trimmier Rd, Killeen 76541 Catherine Snyder	PK-5	T	559 29	78%	254/336-1580 Fax 254/336-1598
Early College High Sch 51000 Tank Destroyer Blvd, Fort Hood 76544 Kathleen Burke	9-12		840		254/336-0260 Fax 254/336-0271
Eastern Hills Middle Sch 300 Indian Trl, Harker HTS 76548 Jeremy Key	6-8	T	753 50	56%	254/336-1100 Fax 254/336-1115
Ellison High Sch 909 E Elms Rd, Killeen 76542 David Dominguez	9-12	TV	2,585 98	40%	254/336-0600 Fax 254/336-0606
Fowler Elem Sch 4910 Katy Creek Ln, Killeen 76549 Joyce Lauer	PK-5	T	1,141 40	54%	254/336-1760 Fax 254/336-1789
Ⓐ Gateway High Sch 4100 Zephyr Rd, Killeen 76543 Christopher Halpayne	9-12	V	84 12	66%	254/336-1700 Fax 254/501-1711
Ⓐ Gateway Middle Sch 1307 Gowen Dr, Killeen 76543 Christopher Halpayne	6-8		40 9		254/336-1690 Fax 254/501-1698

9 Student Personnel	91 Safety/Security	275 Response To Intervention	298 Grant Writer/Ptnrships	**School Programs**	**Social Media**
0 Driver Ed/Safety	92 Magnet School	277 Remedial Math K-12	750 Chief Innovation Officer	A = Alternative Program	
1 Gifted/Talented	93 Parental Involvement	280 Literacy Coach	751 Chief of Staff	G = Adult Classes	f = Facebook
2 Video Services	95 Tech Prep Program	285 STEM	752 Social Emotional Learning	M = Magnet Program	
3 Substance Abuse Prev	97 Chief Infomation Officer	286 Digital Learning		T = Title I Schoolwide	t = Twitter
4 Erate	98 Chief Technology Officer	288 Common Core Standards	**Other School Types**	V = Career & Tech Ed Programs	
5 AIDS Education	270 Character Education	294 Accountability	Ⓐ = Alternative School		
8 Alternative/At Risk	271 Migrant Education	295 Network System	Ⓒ = Charter School	New Schools are shaded	
9 Multi-Cultural Curriculum	273 Teacher Mentor	296 Title II Programs	Ⓜ = Magnet School	New Superintendents and Principals are bold	
0 Social Work	274 Before/After Sch	297 Webmaster	Ⓨ = Year-Round School	Personnel with email addresses are underscored	

TX—27

Bell County

School	Grades	Type	Students	%	Phone
Harker Heights Elem Sch 726 S Ann Blvd, Harker HTS 76548 Carolyn Dugger	PK-5	T	725 38	85%	254/336-2050 Fax 254/336-2073
Harker Heights High Sch 1001 E FM 2410 Rd, Harker HTS 76548 **Jorge Soldevila**	9-12	V	2,550	28%	254/336-0800 Fax 254/336-0829
Hay Branch Elem Sch 6101 Westcliff Rd, Killeen 76543 Cassandra Spearman	PK-5	T	680 45	76%	254/336-2080 Fax 254/336-2097
Haynes Elem Sch 3309 Canadian River Loop, Killeen 76549 Angela Donovan	PK-5	T	1,053	47%	254/336-6750 Fax 254/336-2798
Iduma Elem Sch 4400 Foster Ln, Killeen 76549 Katy Bohannon	PK-5	T	913	60%	254/336-2590 Fax 254/336-2598
Ira Cross Jr Elem Sch 1910 Herndon Dr, Killeen 76543 Tomas Sias	PK-5	T	714	84%	254/336-2550 Fax 254/336-2560
Killeen High Sch 500 N 38th St, Killeen 76543 Kara Trevino	9-12	TV	2,362	54%	254/336-7208 Fax 254/336-0413
Killeen ISD Career Center 1320 Stagecoach Rd, Killeen 76542 **Russell Porterfield**		Voc	1,434 12		254/336-3800 Fax 254/519-7737
Liberty Hill Middle Sch 4500 Kit Carson Trl, Killeen 76542 **Latricia Brown**	6-8	T	847 45	43%	254/336-1370 Fax 254/336-1403
Live Oak Ridge Middle Sch 2600 Robinett Rd, Killeen 76549 Wanda Stidom	6-8	T	640	55%	254/336-2490 Fax 254/336-2498
Manor Middle Sch 1700 S W S Young Dr, Killeen 76543 Rhea Bell	6-8	TV	645	62%	254/336-1310 Fax 254/336-1317
Maude Moore Wood Elem Sch 6410 Morganite Ln, Killeen 76542 Norma Baker	PK-5	T	600 31	81%	254/336-1650
Maxdale Elem Sch 2600 Westwood Dr, Killeen 76549 Bobbie Evans	PK-5	T	750 44	40%	254/336-2460 Fax 254/336-2469
Meadows Elem Sch 423 27th St, Fort Hood 76544 Peter Hartley	PK-5		850 40	31%	254/336-1870 Fax 254/336-1893
Montague Village Elem Sch 84001 Clements Dr, Fort Hood 76544 **Natalie Cue**	PK-5	T	605 36	65%	254/336-2230 Fax 254/336-2238
Mountain View Elem Sch 500 Mountain Lion Rd, Harker HTS 76548 Randy Podhaski	PK-5		945 53	34%	254/336-1900 Fax 254/336-1919
Nolan Middle Sch 505 E Jasper Dr, Killeen 76541 **Ashley York**	6-8	TV	757 45	76%	254/336-1150 Fax 254/336-1162
Nolanville Elem Sch 901 Old Nolanville Rd, Nolanville 76559 Wendy Haider	PK-5	I	653 40	50%	254/336-2180 Fax 254/336-2202
Oveta Culp Hobby Elem Sch 53210 Lost Moccasin, Fort Hood 76544 Jennifer Warren	PK-5	AT	553 42	63%	254/336-6500 Fax 254/336-6505
Palo Alto Middle Sch 2301 W Elms Rd, Killeen 76549 **Kernisha Hill**	6-8	T	652 46	66%	254/336-1200 Fax 254/336-1217
Ⓐ Pathways Academic Campus 1322 Stagecoach Rd, Killeen 76542 Dr Bobbie Reeders	9-12		400 12	44%	254/336-7250 Fax 254/336-7298
Patterson Middle Sch 8383 Trimmier Rd, Killeen 76542 Latisha Williams	6-8	T	1,002 51	44%	254/336-7100 Fax 254/336-7136
Peebles Elem Sch 1800 N W S Young Dr, Killeen 76543 Carol Correa	PK-5	T	827 34	80%	254/336-2120 Fax 254/336-2131
Pershing Park Elem Sch 1500 W Central Texas Expy, Killeen 76549 Linda Butler	PK-5	T	609 50	76%	254/336-1790 Fax 254/336-1804
Rancier Middle Sch 3301 Hilliard Ave, Killeen 76543 Alan Gawryszewski	6-8	TV	657 51	65%	254/336-1250 Fax 254/336-1254
Reeces Creek Elem Sch 400 W Stan Schlueter Loop, Killeen 76542 **Sara Watson**	PK-5	T	900 44	71%	254/336-2150 Fax 254/336-2165
Richard E Cavazos Elem Sch 1200 N 10th St, Nolanville 76559 Joe Gullekson	PK-5		657	63%	254/336-7000 Fax 254/336-7030
Robert M Shoemaker High Sch 3302 S Clear Creek Rd, Killeen 76549 Micah Wells	9-12	T	2,199 60	51%	254/336-0900 Fax 254/336-2416
Roy J Smith Middle Sch 6000 Brushy Creek Dr, Killeen 76549 Chad Wolf	6-8		1,211		254/336-1050 Fax 254/336-1056
Saegert Elem Sch 5600 Schorn Dr, Killeen 76542 Eli Lopez	PK-5	AT	909	46%	254/336-6660 Fax 254/336-6684
Skipcha Elem Sch 515 Prospector Trl, Harker HTS 76548 Jane Apodaca	PK-5		1,171	23%	254/336-6690 Fax 254/336-6711
STEM Academy-Killeen 6000 Bushy Creek Dr, Killeen 76549 **Chad Wolf**	6-12		14		254/336-7836
Sugar Loaf Elem Sch 1517 Barbara Ln, Killeen 76549 Violet Simmons	PK-5	T	447 34	72%	254/336-1940 Fax 254/336-1945
Timber Ridge Elem Sch 5402 White Rock Dr, Killeen 76542 Tanya Dockery	PK-5	T	1,114	39%	254/336-6630 Fax 254/336-6653
Trimmier Elem Sch 4400 Success Dr, Killeen 76542 Penny Batts	PK-5	T	819 35	73%	254/336-2270 Fax 254/336-2284
Union Grove Middle Sch 101 E Iowa Dr, Harker HTS 76548 Paula Lawrason	6-8		922	24%	254/336-6580 Fax 254/336-6593
Venable Village Elem Sch 60160 Venable Dr, Fort Hood 76544 Vickie Wasson	PK-5	T	591 50	52%	254/336-1980 Fax 254/336-2015
West Ward Elem Sch 709 W Dean Ave, Killeen 76541 **Tammy Thornhill**	PK-5	T	504 32	81%	254/336-1830 Fax 254/336-1861
Willow Springs Elem Sch 2501 W Stan Schlueter Loop, Killeen 76549 Connie Locke	PK-5	T	937 52	72%	254/336-2020 Fax 254/336-2047

• **Rogers Ind School Dist** PID: 00996643   254/642-3802
1 Eagle Dr, Rogers 76569   Fax 254/642-3851

Schools: 3 \ **Teachers:** 64 \ **Students:** 875 \ **Special Ed Students:** 61 \ **LEP Students:** 28 \ **College-Bound:** 50% \ **Ethnic:** Asian 1%, African American 2%, Hispanic 30%, Caucasian 67% \ **Exp:** $413 (High) \ **Poverty:** 11% \ **Title I:** $101,124 \ **Special Education:** $166,000 \ **Open-Close:** 08/21 - 05/28 \ **DTBP:** $341 (High)

Joe Criag 1,83
Jason Beard 3,5
Charles Roten 6
Becky Ralston 8,69,294
Garrett Layne 12,34,277*
Tracie Malovets 2
Christy Stone 4
Carol Morris 7
Tammy Tucker 11,296,298
Nicolette Wiesman 36,85,88,275,288

1 Superintendent	8 Curric/Instruct K-12	19 Chief Financial Officer	29 Family/Consumer Science	39 Social Studies K-12	49 English/Lang Arts Elem	59 Special Education Elem	69 Academic Assessment
2 Bus/Finance/Purchasing	9 Curric/Instruct Elem	20 Art K-12	30 Adult Education	40 Social Studies Elem	50 English/Lang Arts Sec	60 Special Education Sec	70 Research/Development
3 Buildings And Grounds	10 Curric/Instruct Sec	21 Art Elem	31 Career/Sch-to-Work K-12	41 Social Studies Sec	51 Reading K-12	61 Foreign/World Lang K-12	71 Public Information
4 Food Service	11 Federal Program	22 Art Sec	32 Career/Sch-to-Work Elem	42 Science K-12	52 Reading Elem	62 Foreign/World Lang Elem	72 Summer School
5 Transportation	12 Title I	23 Music K-12	33 Career/Sch-to-Work Sec	43 Science Elem	53 Reading Sec	63 Foreign/World Lang Sec	73 Instructional Tech
6 Athletic	13 Title V	24 Music Elem	34 Early Childhood Ed	44 Science Sec	54 Remedial Reading K-12	64 Religious Education K-12	74 Inservice Training
7 Health Services	15 Asst Superintendent	25 Music Sec	35 Health/Phys Education	45 Math K-12	55 Remedial Reading Elem	65 Religious Education Elem	75 Marketing/Distributive
	16 Instructional Media Svcs	26 Business Education	36 Guidance Services K-12	46 Math Elem	56 Remedial Reading Sec	66 Religious Education Sec	76 Info Systems
	17 Chief Operations Officer	27 Career & Tech Ed	37 Guidance Services Elem	47 Math Sec	57 Bilingual/ELL	67 School Board President	77 Psychological Assess
	18 Chief Academic Officer	28 Technology Education	38 Guidance Services Sec	48 English/Lang Arts K-12	58 Special Education K-12	68 Teacher Personnel	78 Affirmative Action

Texas School Directory — Bell County

Kimberly Marek .....57* Karen Morgan 67
Carol Whitley .....68,91* Glen Kinard 73,295*
Cheyenne Doskocil 297

Public Schs..Principal	Grd	Prgm	Enr/#Cls	SN	
Rogers Elem Sch 802 Cemetery Rd, Rogers 76569 Garrett Layne	PK-5	T	390 22	50%	254/642-3250 Fax 254/642-3145
Rogers High Sch 1 Eagle Dr, Rogers 76569 Lee Moses	9-12	V	289 22	39%	254/642-3224 Fax 254/642-3037
Rogers Middle Sch 1 Eagle Dr, Rogers 76569 Lucinda Smith	6-8	TV	215 12	44%	254/642-3011 Fax 254/642-0033

● **Salado Ind School Dist** PID: 00996679 254/947-6900
601 N Main St, Salado 76571 Fax 254/947-5605

Schools: 3 \ **Teachers:** 115 \ **Students:** 1,900 \ **Special Ed Students:** 100 \ **LEP Students:** 97 \ **College-Bound:** 64% \ **Ethnic:** Asian 1%, African American 1%, Hispanic 24%, Caucasian 74% \ **Exp:** $417 (High) \ **Poverty:** 10% \ **Title I:** $142,348 \ **Open-Close:** 08/21 - 05/27 \ **DTBP:** $342 (High)

Michael Novotny .....1 Brandy Stanford 2,11
Danny Agee .....3,5 Mike Brooks 3,4,5,17
Brenda Hodges .....4* Paul Baird 6
Ashley Faglie .....7* Burt Smith 8,15,36,68,69,91,298
Bobette Bell .....16 Kendra Copeland 57*
Nancy Rielly .....58 Kim Bird 67
Earl Bragg 73

Public Schs..Principal	Grd	Prgm	Enr/#Cls	SN	
Salado High Sch 1880 Williams Rd, Salado 76571 Beth Aycock	9-12	AV	563 45	21%	254/947-6985 Fax 254/947-6984
Salado Junior High Sch 620 Thomas Arnold Rd, Salado 76571 Ted Smith	6-8		413	22%	254/947-6935 Fax 254/947-6934
Thomas Arnold Elem Sch 510 Thomas Arnold Rd, Salado 76571 Julie Mullins	PK-5	T	887 14	32%	254/947-6925 Fax 254/947-6924

● **Temple Ind School Dist** PID: 00996708 254/215-8473
401 Santa Fe Way, Temple 76501 Fax 254/215-6783

Schools: 15 \ **Teachers:** 596 \ **Students:** 8,700 \ **Special Ed Students:** 882 \ **LEP Students:** 847 \ **College-Bound:** 50% \ **Ethnic:** Asian 2%, African American 28%, Hispanic 45%, Caucasian 25% \ **Exp:** $587 (High) \ **Poverty:** 28% \ **Title I:** $3,947,483 \ **Special Education:** $1,872,000 \ **Open-Close:** 08/21 - 05/28 \ **DTBP:** $160 (High) \ f

Dr Bobby Ott .....1 Kallen Vaden 2,19
Kent Boyd .....2,15 Kenneth Wolf 3
Ian Vestal .....4 Patrick Cain 5
Scott Stewart .....6* Kim Glawe 7
Renota Rogers .....8* Beth Giniewicz 9*
Lisa Adams .....10,15 Dr Karen Morgan 11,294,296
Eric Haugeberg .....13,15,79 Joe Palmer 15,68
Catrina Lotspeich .....20,23 Denise Ayres 31
Dr Nichole Riley .....36,83,275* Consuelo Sisneros 57
Consuelo Sisneros .....57 Jennie Mathesen 58
Dan Posey .....67 Amy Hayes 68
David McCauley .....68 Tiffany Vestal 69,294
Christine Parks .....71,97 Marc Sivak 73,84
Carl Pleasant .....88* Gil Hollie 274*
Craig Wilson 286

Public Schs..Principal	Grd	Prgm	Enr/#Cls	SN	
Bonham Middle Sch 4600 Midway Dr, Temple 76502 Sandra Atmar	6-8	TV	576 40	66%	254/215-6600 Fax 254/215-6634
Cater Elem Sch 4111 Lark Trl, Temple 76502 Adrian Lopez	K-5	T	334 17	76%	254/215-7444 Fax 254/215-7479
ⓐ Fred W Edwards Academy 1414 W Barton Ave, Temple 76504 Phillip Perry	9-12	GT	128	50%	254/215-6944 Fax 254/215-6946 f
Hector P Garcia Elem Sch 2525 Lavendusky Dr, Temple 76501 Sandra Reyes	K-5	T	426 35	89%	254/215-6100 Fax 254/215-6122
Jefferson Elem Sch 2616 N 3rd St, Temple 76501 Pamela Demny	K-5	T	578 26	83%	254/215-5500 Fax 254/215-5545
Kennedy-Powell Elem Sch 3707 W Nugent Ave, Temple 76504 Kelly Madden	K-5	T	499 25	67%	254/215-6000 Fax 254/215-6032
Lamar Middle Sch 2120 N 1st St, Temple 76501 Billy Madden	6-8	TV	610 42	82%	254/215-6444 Fax 254/215-6483
Meridith-Dunbar EC Academy 1717 E Avenue J, Temple 76501 Nikki Murphy	PK-PK	T	514 16	92%	254/215-6700 Fax 254/215-6728
Raye-Allen Elem Sch 5015 S 5th St, Temple 76502 Frances Smetana	K-5	T	469 27	81%	254/215-5800 Fax 254/215-5843
Scott Elem Sch 2301 W Avenue P, Temple 76504 Chrystal Thomas	K-5	T	483 18	78%	254/215-6222 Fax 254/215-6251
Temple High Sch 415 N 31st St, Temple 76504 Dr Jason Mayo	9-12	TV	2,145	59%	254/215-7000 Fax 254/899-6926
Thornton Elem Sch 2825 Cottonwood Ln, Temple 76502 Michelle Moore	K-5	T	734 20	67%	254/215-5700 Fax 254/215-5746
Travis Science Academy 1551 S 25th St, Temple 76504 Tiffany Weiss	6-8	TV	691 41	74%	254/215-6300 Fax 254/215-6352
Western Hills Elem Sch 600 Arapaho Dr, Temple 76504 Tiffany Vestal	PK-5	T	224 29	80%	254/215-5600 Fax 254/215-5624
ⓐ Wheatley Alt Ed Center 515 E Avenue D, Temple 76501 Carl Pleasant	1-12	G	39 6	78%	254/215-5655 Fax 254/215-5673

● **Troy Ind School Dist** PID: 00996899 254/938-2595
1 Trojan Rd, Troy 76579 Fax 254/938-7323

Schools: 4 \ **Teachers:** 101 \ **Students:** 1,600 \ **Special Ed Students:** 174 \ **LEP Students:** 40 \ **Ethnic:** African American 1%, Hispanic 27%, Caucasian 71% \ **Exp:** $549 (High) \ **Poverty:** 13% \ **Title I:** $191,092 \ **Special Education:** $10,000 \ **Open-Close:** 08/26 - 05/28 \ **DTBP:** $350 (High) \ t

Neil Jeter .....1 Cindy Holloway 2
Brad McMurtry .....3,68,79,288 Lisa Mays 4
Leah Glenn .....5 Ronnie Porter 6*
Penny Braeuer .....7,85 Dr Darrell Becker 8,11,32,58,69,273
Trista Falcon .....16,82* Mindy Howard 27,33,273*
Dawn Robinson .....34,37* Mollie Huber 38
Pam Bulls .....67 Clay Osburn 73,295
Dwayne Frei 83,88*

Code	Description	Code	Description	Code	Description	School Programs	Social Media
79	Student Personnel	91	Safety/Security	275	Response To Intervention	298 Grant Writer/Ptnrships	
80	Driver Ed/Safety	92	Magnet School	277	Remedial Math K-12	750 Chief Innovation Officer	A = Alternative Program
81	Gifted/Talented	93	Parental Involvement	280	Literacy Coach	751 Chief of Staff	G = Adult Classes	= Facebook
82	Video Services	95	Tech Prep Program	285	STEM	752 Social Emotional Learning	M = Magnet Program	
83	Substance Abuse Prev	97	Chief Information Officer	286	Digital Learning		T = Title I Schoolwide	= Twitter
84	Erate	98	Chief Technology Officer	288	Common Core Standards	Other School Types	V = Career & Tech Ed Programs	
85	AIDS Education	270	Character Education	294	Accountability	Ⓐ = Alternative School		
86	Alternative/At Risk	271	Migrant Education	295	Network System	Ⓒ = Charter School	New Schools are shaded	
89	Multi-Cultural Curriculum	273	Teacher Mentor	296	Title II Programs	Ⓜ = Magnet School	New Superintendents and Principals are bold	
90	Social Work	274	Before/After Sch	297	Webmaster	Ⓨ = Year-Round School	Personnel with email addresses are underscored	

TX—29

Bexar County

Public Schs..Principal	Grd	Prgm	Enr/#Cls	SN	
Edna Bigham Mays Elem Sch 725 W Main St, Troy 76579 Kelli Frisch	PK-1	T	277 15	56%	254/938-0304 Fax 254/938-0233
Raymond Mays Middle Sch 915 W Main St, Troy 76579 Michelle Jolliff	6-8	TV	354 40	48%	254/938-2543 Fax 254/938-2880
Troy Elem Sch 808 E Austin St, Troy 76579 Andrea Durbin	2-5	T	475 47	50%	254/938-2503 Fax 254/938-2080
Troy High Sch 205 N Waco Rd, Troy 76579 Randy Hicks	9-12	V	428 32	41%	254/938-2561 Fax 254/938-2328

BELL CATHOLIC SCHOOLS

- **Diocese of Austin Ed Office** PID: 01420568
  Listing includes only schools located in this county. See District Index for location of Diocesan Offices.

Catholic Schs..Principal	Grd	Prgm	Enr/#Cls	SN	
Holy Trinity Catholic High Sch 6608 W Adams Ave, Temple 76502 Blake Evans	9-12		90 13		254/771-0787 Fax 254/771-2285
St Joseph Catholic Sch 2901 E Rancier Ave, Killeen 76543 Dirk Steffens	PK-6		80 8		254/634-7272 Fax 254/634-1224
St Mary's Catholic Sch 1019 S 7th St, Temple 76504 Theresa Wyles	PK-8		300 22		254/778-8141 Fax 254/778-1396

BELL PRIVATE SCHOOLS

Private Schs..Principal	Grd	Prgm	Enr/#Cls	SN	
American Preparatory Institute 6200 W Central Expy, Killeen 76549 Colvin Davis	9-12		100		254/526-1321 Fax 254/526-1481
Central Texas Christian Sch 4141 W FM 93, Temple 76502 Brenda Russel	PK-12		500 20		254/939-5700 Fax 254/939-5733
Education Connection 1020 Trimmier Rd, Killeen 76541 Nikki Luther	K-5		190		254/526-9299 Fax 254/526-0631
Killeen Adventist Jr Academy 3412 Lake Rd, Killeen 76543 Annemarie Jacobs	PK-8		52 7		254/699-9466 Fax 254/699-0519
Memorial Christian Academy 4001 Trimmier Rd, Killeen 76542 Barbra Carpenter	PK-12		224 25		254/526-5403 Fax 254/634-2030

BEXAR COUNTY

BEXAR PUBLIC SCHOOLS

- **Alamo Heights Ind School Dist** PID: 00996928   210/824-2483
  7101 Broadway St, San Antonio 78209   Fax 210/822-2221

Schools: 5 \ **Teachers:** 345 \ **Students:** 4,900 \ **Special Ed Students:** 369 \ **LEP Students:** 239 \ **College-Bound:** 95% \ **Ethnic:** Asian 4%, African American 2%, Hispanic 42%, Caucasian 52% \ **Exp:** $168 (Low) \ **Poverty:** 7% \ **Title I:** $403,213 \ **Special Education:** $926,000 \ **Open-Close:** 08/19 - 05/21 \ **DTBP:** $156 (High) \ 🇫 🇹

Dr Dana Bashara 1		Mike Hagar 2,15	
Louis Cardenas 3		Richard Mallard 4	
Leah Roudebush 5		Norm Collins 6	
Catherine Widder 7*		Dr Jimmie Walker 8,81	
Frank Alfaro 10,12,15,57,88		Susan Peery 34,72*	
Kris Holliday 58,77,78,90		Lisa Krenger 67	
Frank Stange 68,71		Kristen Ascencao 69	
Jamie Locklin 73,295		Lisa Lucas 83*	
Melissa Arredondo 84		Kevin Lam 295	
Rosalinda Montero 297			

Public Schs..Principal	Grd	Prgm	Enr/#Cls	SN	
Alamo Heights High Sch 6900 Broadway St, San Antonio 78209 Debbie Garinger	9-12	AV	1,578 80	17%	210/820-8850 Fax 210/832-5777
Alamo Heights Jr High Sch 7607 N New Braunfels Ave, San Antonio 78209 Laura Ancira	6-8		1,100 100	20%	210/824-3231 Fax 210/832-5825 🇫 🇹
Cambridge Elem Sch 1001 Townsend Ave, San Antonio 78209 Jana Needham	1-5		822 75	24%	210/822-3611 Fax 210/832-5840 🇫 🇹
Howard Early Childhood Center 7800 Broadway St, San Antonio 78209 Susan Peery	PK-K		391 32	28%	210/832-5900 Fax 210/832-5898 🇫 🇹
Woodridge Elem Sch 100 Woodridge Dr, San Antonio 78209 Gerrie Spellmann	1-5		916 45	21%	210/826-8021 Fax 210/832-5871 🇫 🇹

- **Braination Schools** PID: 11701354   210/638-5000
  10325 Bandera Rd, San Antonio 78250   Fax 210/638-5075

Schools: 8 \ **Students:** 1,200 \ **Ethnic:** Asian 2%, African American 12%, Hispanic 51%, Caucasian 35% \ **Open-Close:** 08/20 - 06/05

Bruce Rockstroh 1		Ymelda Y'Herrera 2,19	
Jennifer Rower 3,5,17,68		Mandy Alandzes 4	
Brenda Murphy 8,18		Orlando De Los Santos 11,298	
Charles Winkler 36,76,84,295		Alethia Phillips 58	
Laura Dominguez 58		Olin Tunnell 67	
Carol Taly 68		Phil Castillo 73	
Renee Mancias 76*		Ronny Almanza 295	

Public Schs..Principal	Grd	Prgm	Enr/#Cls	SN	
© Anne Frank Inspire Academy 11216 Bandera Rd, San Antonio 78250 Nino Etienne	K-12	V	303	20%	210/638-5900 Fax 210/638-5975

1	Superintendent	8	Curric/Instruct K-12	19	Chief Financial Officer	29	Family/Consumer Science	39	Social Studies K-12	49	English/Lang Arts Elem	59	Special Education Elem	69	Academic Assessment
2	Bus/Finance/Purchasing	9	Curric/Instruct Elem	20	Art K-12	30	Adult Education	40	Social Studies Elem	50	English/Lang Arts Sec	60	Special Education Sec	70	Research/Development
3	Buildings And Grounds	10	Curric/Instruct Sec	21	Art Elem	31	Career/Sch-to-Work K-12	41	Social Studies Sec	51	Reading K-12	61	Foreign/World Lang K-12	71	Public Information
4	Food Service	11	Federal Program	22	Art Sec	32	Career/Sch-to-Work Elem	42	Science K-12	52	Reading Elem	62	Foreign/World Lang Elem	72	Summer School
5	Transportation	12	Title I	23	Music K-12	33	Career/Sch-to-Work Sec	43	Science Elem	53	Reading Sec	63	Foreign/World Lang Sec	73	Instructional Tech
6	Athletic	13	Title V	24	Music Elem	34	Early Childhood Ed	44	Science Sec	54	Remedial Reading K-12	64	Religious Education K-12	74	Inservice Training
7	Health Services	15	Asst Superintendent	25	Music Sec	35	Health/Phys Education	45	Math K-12	55	Remedial Reading Elem	65	Religious Education Elem	75	Marketing/Distributive
		16	Instructional Media Svcs	26	Business Education	36	Guidance Services K-12	46	Math Elem	56	Remedial Reading Sec	66	Religious Education Sec	76	Info Systems
		17	Chief Operations Officer	27	Career & Tech Ed	37	Guidance Services Elem	47	Math Sec	57	Bilingual/ELL	67	School Board President	77	Psychological Assess
		18	Chief Academic Officer	28	Technology Education	38	Guidance Services Sec	48	English/Lang Arts K-12	58	Special Education K-12	68	Teacher Personnel	78	Affirmative Action

Texas School Directory — Bexar County

School	Grd	Prgm	Enr/#Cls	SN	Phone
ⓒ Jhw Inspire Acad-Afton Oaks 620 E Afton Oaks Blvd, San Antonio 78232 Asa Cuellar	5-12	T	138	98%	210/638-5500 Fax 210/638-5575
Ⓐ Jhw Inspire Acad-Legacy Ranch ⓒ 13326 N US Highway 183, Gonzales 78629 Patricia Smith	K-6	T	40	88%	210/638-5300
ⓒ Jhw Inspire Acad-Meridell 12550 W State Highway 29, Liberty Hill 78642 Gwyn Rollins	K-12	T	101	97%	512/528-2100 Fax 512/528-2193
ⓒ Jhw Inspire Acad-Rockdale 696 N FM 487, Rockdale 76567 Tamra Vance	6-12	T	61	95%	210/638-5700 Fax 210/638-5775
ⓒ Jhw Inspire Acad-Williams Hse 107 W Railway, Lometa 76853 Lois Knox	3-12	A	34		210/638-5800 Fax 512/515-5875
Ⓐ Jhw Inspire Academy-Bell Co ⓒ 4800 E Rancier Ave, Killeen 76543 Stephanie House	4-12		37		254/618-4280
ⓒ Jhw Inspire Academy-Hays Co 2250 Clovis R Barker Rd, San Marcos 78666 Kayla Heyward	6-12		64 7		210/638-5400 Fax 210/638-5475

● **East Central Ind School Dist** PID: 00996992 210/648-7861
6634 New Sulphur Springs Rd, San Antonio 78263 Fax 210/648-0931

Schools: 12 \ **Teachers:** 608 \ **Students:** 10,146 \
Special Ed Students: 1,063 \ **LEP Students:** 978 \ **College-Bound:** 41%
\ **Ethnic:** African American 9%, Hispanic 76%, Caucasian 15% \ **Exp:** $287
(Med) \ **Poverty:** 18% \ **Title I:** $2,418,844 \ **Special Education:** $1,801,000 \
Open-Close: 08/19 - 05/28 \ **DTBP:** $148 (High)

Roland Toscano 1		Judy Burns 2,19	
Matt Morgan 2		Stephen Priour 3	
Nancy Britton 4		Donald Jurek 5	
Suzette Arriola 6*		Jaelynn Hart 7*	
Jennifer Kasper 8*		Shannon Fuller 8	
Taffi Hertz 8,15		Meredith Rokas 11,31,296	
Dr Alma Rosa Martinez 57		Nina Puth 58	
Steve Bryant 67		Yvette Sanders 68	
Jonathan Hulbert 69		Ashley Chohlis 71,79	
Dirk Dykstra 73		John Hernandez 79	
George Dranowsky 91			

Public Schs..Principal	Grd	Prgm	Enr/#Cls	SN	Phone
Ⓐ Bexar Co Learning Center 3621 Farm Rd, San Antonio 78223 Patricia White	6-12		90 15	91%	210/335-1745 Fax 210/335-1746
East Central Development Ctr 12271 Donop Rd, San Antonio 78223 Damon Trainer	PK-PK	T	164 19	89%	210/633-3020 Fax 210/633-0323
East Central Heritage Mid Sch 8004 New Sulphur Springs Rd, San Antonio 78263 Mary Gomez	6-8	TV	1,172 70	62%	210/648-4546 Fax 210/648-3501
East Central High Sch 7173 FM 1628, San Antonio 78263 Shane McKay	9-12	TV	3,132	58%	210/649-2951 Fax 210/649-2184
Harmony Elem Sch 10625 Green Lake St, San Antonio 78223 Stephanie Orsak	PK-3	T	520 26	74%	210/633-0231 Fax 210/633-2176
Highland Forest Elem Sch 3736 SE Military Dr, San Antonio 78223 Irma Goana	PK-3	T	457 32	72%	210/333-7385 Fax 210/333-4069
Legacy Middle Sch 5903 SE Loop 410, San Antonio 78222 Nicole Lewis	6-8	T	1,264	74%	210/648-3118 Fax 210/648-1068
Oak Crest Elem Sch 7806 New Sulphur Springs Rd, San Antonio 78263 Joette Barnes	K-5	T	769 45	66%	210/648-9484 Fax 210/648-6967
Pecan Valley Elem Sch 3966 E Southcross Blvd, San Antonio 78222 Kristin Wurzbach	PK-3	T	520 27	77%	210/333-1230 Fax 210/359-1352
Salado Intermediate Sch 3602 S WW White Rd, San Antonio 78222 Teresa Triana	4-5	T	761 56	75%	210/648-3310 Fax 210/359-1245
Sinclair Elem Sch 6126 Sinclair Rd, San Antonio 78222 Stacey Johnston	PK-3	T	656 32	71%	210/648-4620 Fax 210/648-0422
Tradition Elem Sch 12885 FM 1346, Saint Hedwig 78152 Karen Kopeck	PK-5		900 37		210/649-2021 Fax 210/649-1226

● **Edgewood Ind School Dist** PID: 00997075 210/444-4500
5358 W Commerce St, San Antonio 78237 Fax 210/444-4525

Schools: 21 \ **Teachers:** 689 \ **Students:** 10,881 \
Special Ed Students: 1,070 \ **LEP Students:** 1,846 \ **College-Bound:** 70%
\ **Ethnic:** African American 1%, Hispanic 98%, Caucasian 1% \ **Exp:** $447
(High) \ **Poverty:** 39% \ **Title I:** $8,054,199 \ **Special Education:** $2,263,000
\ **Open-Close:** 08/19 - 05/22 \ **DTBP:** $201 (High)

Dr Eduardo Hernandez 1		Betty Galindo 2	
Myrna Martinez 2,15,19		Elsa Rosas 3	
Ernesto Cantu 3		Roxanne Ruiz 4	
Will Thornton 5		Robert Gomez 6,35	
Jennifer Milla 7		Stefanie Chatelain 7	
Phillip Chavez 8,15,18		Theresa Salinas 8	
Becky Goodwin 11		Olga Moucoulis 15,751	
Dr Emma Dromgoole 20,23		Chriselda Bazaldua 27,31,285	
Dr Mary Miller-Baker 34*		Rosemary Hernandez 34	
Linda Vargas-Lew 36,78,90		Doris Perez 57,61	
Emily Sauceda 58		Roy Soto 67	
Travis McKelvain 68		Robert Miller 69,70	
Keyhla Calderon-Lugo 71		Juan Vazquez-Cruz 73	
Kimberly Gonzalez 73		Judith Torres 74	
Angelica Garza 76		Angelica Lozano 79	
Dr Bertha Ortiz 81		Valerie Galan 88	
Jesse Quiroga 91		Ron Foster 286	
Sylvia Morales 294*			

Public Schs..Principal	Grd	Prgm	Enr/#Cls	SN	Phone
Alonso S Perales Elem Sch 1507 Ceralvo St, San Antonio 78237 Teresa Silva	PK-5	T	474 28	94%	210/444-8350 Fax 210/444-8373
Brentwood Middle Sch 1626 Thompson Pl, San Antonio 78226 Eva Reyna	6-8	TV	666 40	87%	210/444-7675 Fax 210/444-7698
Burleson Early Chldhd Center 4415 Monterey St, San Antonio 78237 Sheila Ballagh	PK-PK	T	242	96%	210/444-7725 Fax 210/444-7748
Cardenas Center 3300 Ruiz St, San Antonio 78228 Claudia Barrios	PK-PK	T	365	99%	210/444-7826
E T Wrenn Middle Sch 627 S Acme Rd, San Antonio 78237 Nicole Gomez	6-8	TV	646 35	94%	210/444-8475 Fax 210/444-8498
Edgewood Fine Arts Academy 402 Lance St, San Antonio 78237 **Daniel Pina**	9-12		200		210/444-7925 Fax 210/444-7973
Ⓐ Emma Frey Discip Alt Ed Pgrm 900 S San Eduardo Ave, San Antonio 78237 **Daniel Pina**	6-12	V	25 10		210/444-8230 Fax 210/444-8233

9	Student Personnel	91	Safety/Security	275	Response To Intervention	298 Grant Writer/Ptnrships
0	Driver Ed/Safety	92	Magnet School	277	Remedial Math K-12	750 Chief Innovation Officer
1	Gifted/Talented	93	Parental Involvement	280	Literacy Coach	751 Chief of Staff
2	Video Services	95	Tech Prep Program	285	STEM	752 Social Emotional Learning
3	Substance Abuse Prev	97	Chief Information Officer	286	Digital Learning	
4	Erate	98	Chief Technology Officer	288	Common Core Standards	**Other School Types**
5	AIDS Education	270	Character Education	294	Accountability	Ⓐ = Alternative School
8	Alternative/At Risk	271	Migrant Education	295	Network System	ⓒ = Charter School
9	Multi-Cultural Curriculum	273	Teacher Mentor	296	Title II Programs	Ⓜ = Magnet School
0	Social Work	274	Before/After Sch	297	Webmaster	Ⓨ = Year-Round School

School Programs
A = Alternative Program
G = Adult Classes
M = Magnet Program
T = Title I Schoolwide
V = Career & Tech Ed Programs

Social Media
f = Facebook
t = Twitter

New Schools are shaded
New Superintendents and Principals are bold
Personnel with email addresses are underscored

Bexar County

School	Grd	Prgm	Enr/#Cls	SN	Phone
Gardendale Elem Sch 1731 Dahlgreen Ave, San Antonio 78237 Kristin Willmann	PK-5	T	486 45	84%	210/444-8150 Fax 210/444-8173
Gus Garcia Middle Sch 3306 Ruiz St, San Antonio 78228 Christopher Bland	6-8	TV	740 50	85%	210/444-8075 Fax 210/444-8098
H B Gonzalez Elem Sch 2803 Castroville Rd, San Antonio 78237 Tania Moran	PK-5	T	423 29	91%	210/444-7800 Fax 210/444-7823
John F Kennedy High Sch 1922 S General McMullen Dr, San Antonio 78226 Graciela Martinez	9-12	GTV	1,198	84%	210/444-8040 Fax 210/444-8020
L B Johnson Elem Sch 6515 W Commerce St, San Antonio 78227 Ellie Gearhart	PK-5	T	515 29	88%	210/444-8175 Fax 210/444-8198
Las Palmas Elem Sch 115 Las Palmas Dr, San Antonio 78237 Monica Munoz	PK-5	T	455	99%	210/444-8050 Fax 210/444-8073
Loma Park Elem Sch 400 Aurora Ave, San Antonio 78228 Roger Gonzales	PK-5	T	696 39	95%	210/444-8250 Fax 210/444-8273
Memorial High Sch 1227 Memorial St, San Antonio 78228 Pamela Reece	9-12	GTV	1,320 70	86%	210/444-8300 Fax 210/444-8336
Roosevelt Elem Sch 3823 Fortuna Ct, San Antonio 78237 Dr Patricia Ortiz	PK-5	T	497	97%	210/444-8375 Fax 210/444-7798
Roy Cisneros Elem Sch 3011 Ruiz St, San Antonio 78228 Dr Jennifer Herrera	PK-5	T	502 26	96%	210/444-7850 Fax 210/444-7873
Stafford Early Childhd Ctr 611 SW 36th St, San Antonio 78237 Lilly Benavidez	PK-PK	T	406	99%	210/444-7900 Fax 210/444-7923
Stafford Elem Sch 415 SW 36th St, San Antonio 78237 Wendy Salazar	PK-5	T	493 29	97%	210/444-8400 Fax 210/444-8423
Toltech T-STEM Academy 1018 NW 34th St, San Antonio 78228 Dr Rose Narvaez	9-12		320		210/444-8425 Fax 210/444-8448
Winston Elem Sch 2525 S General McMullen Dr, San Antonio 78226 Claudia Sanchez	PK-5	T	433 26	94%	210/444-8450 Fax 210/444-8473

● **Ft Sam Houston Ind School Dist** PID: 01534949   210/368-8701
4005 Winans Rd, San Antonio 78234   Fax 210/368-8741

Schools: 2 \ **Teachers:** 130 \ **Students:** 1,580 \ **Special Ed Students:** 180 \ **LEP Students:** 38 \ **College-Bound:** 63% \ **Ethnic:** Asian 3%, African American 20%, Hispanic 36%, Native American 1%, Caucasian 41% \ **Exp:** $702 (High) \ **Poverty:** 9% \ **Title I:** $130,648 \ **Open-Close:** 08/19 - 05/21 \ **DTBP:** $206 (High) \

Dr Gary Bates 1
Richard Allen 3
Jesse Sandoval 5
Jayne Hatton 8,11,16,57,83,88,285,296
Hans Palmer 34,58
Debbie Kramme 68
Julie Novak 2,11
Roxanne Ruiz 4
Christina Guerreo 6*
Roland Rios 16,73,295*
Lisa Brown 67

Public Schs..Principal	Grd	Prgm	Enr/#Cls	SN	Phone
Ft Sam Houston Elem Sch 4351 Nursery Rd, San Antonio 78234 Dr Joseph Cerna	PK-5		885 40	32%	210/368-8800 Fax 210/368-8801
Robert G Cole Jr/Sr High Sch 4001 Winans Rd, San Antonio 78234 Isabell Clayton	6-12		727	23%	210/368-8730 Fax 210/368-8731

● **Harlandale Ind School Dist** PID: 00997350   210/989-4300
102 Genevieve Dr, San Antonio 78214   Fax 210/989-4481

Schools: 24 \ **Teachers:** 1,012 \ **Students:** 14,500 \ **Special Ed Students:** 1,344 \ **LEP Students:** 2,342 \ **College-Bound:** 51% \ **Ethnic:** Hispanic 98%, Caucasian 2% \ **Exp:** $418 (High) \ **Poverty:** 28% \ **Title I:** $5,294,194 \ **Special Education:** $3,105,000 \ **Open-Close:** 08/26 - 06/04 \ **DTBP:** $201 (High)

Samantha Gallegos 1
Richard Hernandez 2,15
Marcos Rodriguez 4
Isaac Martinez 6,35*
Rosemary Cooremans 9
Nadine Wolfe 11,30,85,271,296,298
Tracy Anderson 27,31
Matthew Simonds 42
Kari Espinoza 48,51,54,61,280
Della Taylor 58
Dr Melinda Salinas 68
Michael Littlefield 73
James Klein 79
Mike Ramirez 91
Ben Mora 2
Gerry Soto 3
Christopher Ramirez 5*
Deborah Hernandez 7
Melissa Casey 10
Connie Montalvo 16
Rubina Pantoja 39
Nora Lugo 45
Rosa Torres 57
Juan Mancha 67
Albert Rosales 71
Myrna Martinez 76,295
Anthony Khosravi 81*
Ruth Zambrano 93

Public Schs..Principal	Grd	Prgm	Enr/#Cls	SN	Phone
Armando Leal Jr Middle Sch 743 W Southcross Blvd, San Antonio 78211 Ricardo Salmon	6-8	T	822 60	94%	210/989-2400 Fax 210/977-1459
Bellaire Elem Sch 142 E Amber St, San Antonio 78221 Elizabeth Lozano	PK-5	T	648 36	92%	210/989-2850 Fax 210/989-2887
Carroll Bell Elem Sch 519 W Harding Blvd, San Antonio 78221 Dr Gina Christenson	PK-5	T	469 47	89%	210/989-2900 Fax 210/989-2936
Collier Elem Sch 834 W Southcross Blvd, San Antonio 78211 Patricia Garcia	PK-5	T	511 26	98%	210/989-2950 Fax 210/989-2986
Columbia Heights Elem Sch 1610 Fitch St, San Antonio 78211 Santos Flores	PK-5	T	435 25	90%	210/989-3000 Fax 210/989-3029
E H Gilbert Elem Sch 931 E Southcross Blvd, San Antonio 78214 Herlinda Longoria	PK-5	T	558 31	94%	210/989-3050 Fax 210/989-3297
Fenley PK Center 934 Flanders Ave, San Antonio 78211 Elaine Jimenez	PK-PK		164		210/921-7000 Fax 210/977-1481
Ⓐ Frank M Tejeda Academy 12121 SE Loop 410, San Antonio 78221 Geraldine Balleza	6-12	GT	185 22	91%	210/989-4900 Fax 210/989-4937
Gillette Elem Sch 625 Gillette Blvd, San Antonio 78221 Lorena Jasso	PK-5	T	616 34	92%	210/989-3100 Fax 210/989-3136
H W Schulze Elem Sch 9131 Yett Ave Bldg 1, San Antonio 78221 Victoria Trevino	PK-5	GT	737 31	86%	210/989-3250 Fax 210/989-3271
Ⓐ Harlandale Alternative Center 4050 Apollo, San Antonio 78214 Andrew Dominguez	6-12	GV	88 16		210/989-5200 Fax 210/989-5236
Harlandale High Sch 114 E Gerald Ave, San Antonio 78214 Fred Anthony	9-12	TV	1,842 100	88%	210/989-1000 Fax 210/989-1082
Harlandale Middle Sch 300 W Huff Ave, San Antonio 78214 Ricardo Marroquin	6-8	T	831	91%	210/989-2000 Fax 210/989-2062
Jewel C Wietzel Center 9131 Yett Ave Bldg B, San Antonio 78221 Jennifer Bernal-Tamaren	Spec	T	15 5		210/989-3280 Fax 210/989-3296

1	Superintendent	8	Curric/Instruct K-12	19	Chief Financial Officer	29	Family/Consumer Science
2	Bus/Finance/Purchasing	9	Curric/Instruct Elem	20	Art K-12	30	Adult Education
3	Buildings And Grounds	10	Curric/Instruct Sec	21	Art Elem	31	Career/Sch-to-Work K-12
4	Food Service	11	Federal Program	22	Art Sec	32	Career/Sch-to-Work Elem
5	Transportation	12	Title I	23	Music K-12	33	Career/Sch-to-Work Sec
6	Athletic	13	Title V	24	Music Elem	34	Early Childhood Ed
7	Health Services	14	Instructional Media Svcs	25	Music Sec	35	Health/Phys Education
		15	Asst Superintendent	26	Business Education	36	Guidance Services K-12
		16	Instructional Media Svcs	27	Career & Tech Ed	37	Guidance Services Elem
		17	Chief Operations Officer	28	Technology Education	38	Guidance Services Sec
		18	Chief Academic Officer				

39	Social Studies K-12	49	English/Lang Arts Elem	59	Special Education Elem	69	Academic Assessment
40	Social Studies Elem	50	English/Lang Arts Sec	60	Special Education Sec	70	Research/Development
41	Social Studies Sec	51	Reading K-12	61	Foreign/World Lang K-12	71	Public Information
42	Science K-12	52	Reading Elem	62	Foreign/World Lang Elem	72	Summer School
43	Science Elem	53	Reading Sec	63	Foreign/World Lang Sec	73	Instructional Tech
44	Science Sec	54	Remedial Reading K-12	64	Religious Education K-12	74	Inservice Training
45	Math K-12	55	Remedial Reading Elem	65	Religious Education Elem	75	Marketing/Distributive
46	Math Elem	56	Remedial Reading Sec	66	Religious Education Sec	76	Info Systems
47	Math Sec	57	Bilingual/ELL	67	School Board President	77	Psychological Assess
48	English/Lang Arts K-12	58	Special Education K-12	68	Teacher Personnel	78	Affirmative Action

Texas School Directory — Bexar County

Public Schs..Principal	Grd	Prgm	Enr/#Cls	SN	
Kingsborough Middle Sch 422 E Ashley Rd, San Antonio 78221 Sylvia Tovar	6-8	T	651 55	87%	210/989-2200 Fax 210/989-2240
McCollum High Sch 500 W Formosa Blvd, San Antonio 78221 Jacob Garcia	9-12	TV	1,553	84%	210/989-1500 Fax 210/989-1580
Morrill Elem Sch 5200 S Flores St, San Antonio 78214 Tina Mireles	PK-5	T	445 39	91%	210/989-3150 Fax 210/989-3186
Rayburn Elem Sch 635 Rayburn Dr, San Antonio 78221 Juanita Santos	PK-5	T	441 25	90%	210/989-3200 Fax 210/977-1541
STEM Early College High Sch 4040 Apollo, San Antonio 78214 Michael Littlefield	9-12		359		210/989-3500 Fax 210/989-3528
Stonewall Flanders Elem Sch 804 Stonewall St, San Antonio 78211 Dr Traci Smith	PK-5	T	727 36	91%	210/989-3300 Fax 210/989-3336
Terrell Wells Middle Sch 422 W Hutchins Pl, San Antonio 78221 Jessie Gipprich	6-8	T	747 53	87%	210/989-2600 Fax 210/989-2640
Verda Mae Adams Elem Sch 135 E Southcross Blvd, San Antonio 78214 Leticia Rodriguez	PK-5	T	723 60	93%	210/989-2800 Fax 210/989-2828
Vestal Elem Sch 1102 Cantrell Dr, San Antonio 78221 Marianela Sanchez	K-5	T	463 44	95%	210/989-3350 Fax 210/989-3386
Wright Elem Sch 115 E Huff Ave, San Antonio 78214 Griselda Raley	PK-5	T	518 25	97%	210/989-3400 Fax 210/989-3444

● Judson Ind School Dist PID: 00997582
8012 Shin Oak Dr, Live Oak 78233
210/945-5100
Fax 210/945-6922

Schools: 33 \ **Teachers:** 1,372 \ **Students:** 23,000 \
Special Ed Students: 2,393 \ **LEP Students:** 1,950 \ **College-Bound:** 45% \
Ethnic: Asian 2%, African American 23%, Hispanic 59%, Caucasian 16% \ **Exp:** $258 (Med) \ **Poverty:** 17% \ **Title I:** $6,514,257 \
Special Education: $3,678,000 \ **Bilingual Education:** $29,000 \
Open-Close: 08/13 - 05/28 \ **DTBP:** $199 (High) \ 🅕 🅣

```
Dr Janette Ball ..................... 1           William Adkin ................. 2,19
Milton Fields .................. 3,15,91         Ruben Moreno .................... 3
Terry Yaklin ........................ 3          Janet Daniel .................... 4
Kenneth Johnson ..................... 5          Mike Miller ..................... 6
Jodi Burton ..................... 11,298         Becky Robinson ................. 15
Cecilia Davis ...................... 15          Nereida Cantu .................. 15
Marsha Bellinger ................... 16          Monica Garcia .................. 36
Luz Ramirez ..................... 57,271         Dr Teresa Arocha-Gill ...... 58,275
Rene Pafchall ...................... 67          Steve Linscomb ................. 71
Jesse Cortinas .................. 73,98          Janlen Waclawczyk .............. 76
Michael Davis ..................... 295
```

Public Schs..Principal	Grd	Prgm	Enr/#Cls	SN	
Candlewood Elem Sch 3635 Candleglenn, San Antonio 78244 Andrea Johnson	PK-5	GT	561 50	83%	210/662-1060 Fax 210/662-9327
Converse Elem Sch 6720 FM 1516 N, Converse 78109 Cynthia Davis	PK-5	T	459 29	65%	210/945-1210 Fax 210/945-6944 🅕🅣
Copperfield Elem Sch 7595 E Loop 1604 N, Converse 78109 Sherri Wrather	PK-5	T	612	54%	210/619-0460 Fax 210/619-0469
Coronado Village Elem Sch 213 Amistad Blvd, Universal Cty 78148 Liza Guerrero	PK-5	T	283 29	58%	210/945-5110 Fax 210/945-6948
Crestview Elem Sch 7710 Narrow Pass St, Live Oak 78233 Linda Cruz	PK-5	T	619 44	62%	210/945-5111 Fax 210/945-6953 🅕🅣
Ed Franz Elem Sch 12301 Welcome Dr, Live Oak 78233 Kelle Lofton	PK-5	GT	458 24	70%	210/655-6241 Fax 210/945-6946 🅕🅣
Elolf Elem Sch 6335 Beech Trail Dr, Converse 78109 Scott Wilson	PK-5	T	568 39	68%	210/661-1130 Fax 210/945-6959
Escondido Elem Sch 5000 Texas Palm Dr, Converse 78109 Mary Tyson	PK-5		342		210/662-2250
Henry Metzger Middle Sch 7475 Binz Engleman Rd, San Antonio 78244 Tracey Valree	6-8	T	1,008	71%	210/662-2210 Fax 210/945-6967
James Masters Elem Sch 2650 Woodlake Pkwy, Converse 78109 Latanya Baker	PK-5	T	279	59%	210/945-1150 Fax 210/945-6963
Joseph Hopkins Elem Sch 2440 Ackerman Rd, San Antonio 78219 Terry Combs	PK-5	T	775 44	82%	210/661-1120 Fax 210/945-6945 🅕🅣
Jstem Academy 9695 Schaefer Rd, Converse 78109 Dawn Worley	6-8		375		210/945-1159
Judson Early College Academy 8230 Palisades Dr, Universal Cty 78148 Josephine Juarez	9-12		374		210/619-0200 Fax 210/945-6981
Judson High Sch 9142 FM 78, Converse 78109 Jesus Hernandez	9-12	TV	2,789 100	52%	210/945-1100 Fax 210/945-6976
Ⓐ Judson Learning Academy 6909 N Loop 1604 E Ste 2010, San Antonio 78247 Latanya Baker	9-12	V	91 1	38%	210/651-4080 Fax 210/945-6980 🅕🅣
Judson Middle Sch 9695 Schaefer Rd, Converse 78109 Liza Guerrero	6-8	T	865	61%	210/357-0801 Fax 210/945-6969
Ⓐ Judson Secondary Alt Sch 102 School St, Converse 78109 Ricci Bethely-Day	6-12	T	76 11	61%	210/619-0330 Fax 210/619-0359
Karen Wagner High Sch 3000 N Foster Rd, San Antonio 78244 Mary Duhart-Toppen	9-12	TV	2,203	71%	210/662-5000 Fax 210/945-6979
Kirby Middle Sch 5441 Seguin Rd, San Antonio 78219 Elizabeth Arredondo	6-8	TV	775 80	84%	210/661-1140 Fax 210/945-6964
Kitty Hawk Middle Sch 840 Old Cimarron Trl, Universal Cty 78148 Beverly Broom	6-8	TV	1,405 96	49%	210/945-1220 Fax 210/945-6965
Mary Hartman Elem Sch 7203 Woodlake Pkwy, San Antonio 78218 Monica Rodriguez	PK-5	T	692 47	70%	210/564-1520 Fax 210/619-0320
Miller's Point Elem Sch 7027 Misty Ridge Dr, Converse 78109 Barbara Smejkal	PK-5	T	572 48	70%	210/945-5114 Fax 210/945-6957
Olympia Elem Sch 8439 Athenian, Universal Cty 78148 Karli Sitton	PK-5		440 31	39%	210/945-5113 Fax 210/945-6955
Park Village Elem Sch 5855 Midcrown Dr, San Antonio 78218 Sharon Balderas	PK-5	T	545 44	90%	210/637-4890 Fax 210/945-6952
Ricardo Salinas Elem Sch 10560 Old Cimarron Trl, Universal Cty 78148 Martin Silverman	PK-5	T	680 36	51%	210/659-5045 Fax 210/945-6962
Rolling Meadows Elem Sch 17222 FM 2252, San Antonio 78266 Michelle La Rue	PK-5		912	36%	210/945-5700 Fax 210/945-6989

---

79 Student Personnel	91 Safety/Security	275 Response To Intervention	298 Grant Writer/Ptnrships	**School Programs**	**Social Media**	
80 Driver Ed/Safety	92 Magnet School	277 Remedial Math K-12	750 Chief Innovation Officer	A = Alternative Program		
81 Gifted/Talented	93 Parental Involvement	280 Literacy Coach	751 Chief of Staff	G = Adult Classes	🅕 = Facebook	
82 Video Services	95 Tech Prep Program	285 STEM	752 Social Emotional Learning	M = Magnet Program		
83 Substance Abuse Prev	97 Chief Information Officer	286 Digital Learning		T = Title I Schoolwide	🅣 = Twitter	
84 Erate	98 Chief Technology Officer	288 Common Core Standards	**Other School Types**	V = Career & Tech Ed Programs		
85 AIDS Education	270 Character Education	294 Accountability	Ⓐ = Alternative School			
86 Alternative/At Risk	271 Migrant Education	295 Network System	Ⓒ = Charter School	New Schools are shaded		
87 Multi-Cultural Curriculum	273 Teacher Mentor	296 Title II Programs	Ⓜ = Magnet School	New Superintendents and Principals are bold		
88 Social Work	274 Before/After Sch	297 Webmaster	Ⓨ = Year-Round School	Personnel with email addresses are underscored		

TX—33

Bexar County

Market Data Retrieval

Spring Meadows Elem Sch 7135 Elm Trail Dr, San Antonio 78244 Destiny Barrera	PK-5	T	621 37	76%	210/662-1050 Fax 210/945-6956
ⓐ Thompson Learning Center 8555 E Loop 1604 N, Converse 78109 Joe Gonzalez	9-12		10		210/945-5053 Fax 210/945-7525
Veterans Memorial High Sch 7618 E Evans Rd, San Antonio 78266 Gregory Brauer	9-12		1,386	50%	210/619-0222 Fax 210/619-0223
William Paschall Elem Sch 6351 Lakeview Dr, San Antonio 78244 Tricia Davila	PK-5	T	526	80%	210/662-2240 Fax 210/945-6961
Woodlake Elem Sch 5501 Lakebend East Dr, San Antonio 78244 Kristin Saunders	PK-5	T	499 34	70%	210/662-2220 Fax 210/945-6954
Woodlake Hills Middle Sch 6625 Woodlake Pkwy, San Antonio 78244 Daniel Brooks	6-8	TV	826 85	76%	210/661-1110 Fax 210/945-6966
Wortham Oaks Elem Sch 5710 Carriage Cpe, San Antonio 78261 Yvonne Munoz	PK-5		241		210/945-5750

● **Lackland Ind School Dist** PID: 01808829   210/357-5000
2460 Kenly Ave Bldg 8265, San Antonio 78236   Fax 210/357-5050

Schools: 2 \ *Teachers:* 83 \ *Students:* 1,053 \ *Special Ed Students:* 129 \ *LEP Students:* 11 \ *College-Bound:* 45% \ *Ethnic:* Asian 1%, African American 21%, Hispanic 26%, Caucasian 52% \ *Exp:* $1,048 (High) \ *Poverty:* 12% \ *Title I:* $87,796 \ *Open-Close:* 08/19 - 05/22 \ *DTBP:* $333 (High)

Dr Bernie Roper 1
Alfredo Concha 3,4,5,73,76,91,295
Edward Rodriguez 4
Jarvis Sims 5
Brian Miller 67
Ben Pease 76
Rebecca Estrada 2,13,19
Steven Rodriguez 3
Maricella Reyna 4
Dr Tonya Hyde 8,11,57,83,88,288
Linda Gottman 69*
Dr Kyle Jones 84

Public Schs..Principal	Grd	Prgm	Enr/#Cls	SN	
Lackland Elem Sch 2460 Kenly Ave Bldg 8265, San Antonio 78236 Teresa Leija	PK-5	T	655 55	34%	210/357-5053 Fax 210/357-5060
Stacey Jr Sr High Sch 2460 Kenly Ave Bldg 8265, San Antonio 78236 Hunter Shelby	6-12		398 31	30%	210/357-5100 Fax 210/357-5109

● **North East Ind School Dist** PID: 00997661   210/407-0000
8961 Tesoro Dr, San Antonio 78217   Fax 210/804-7017

Schools: 74 \ *Teachers:* 4,309 \ *Students:* 64,359 \ *Special Ed Students:* 6,547 \ *LEP Students:* 7,385 \ *College-Bound:* 83% \ *Ethnic:* Asian 4%, African American 8%, Hispanic 61%, Caucasian 28% \ *Exp:* $215 (Med) \ *Poverty:* 14% \ *Title I:* $17,189,960 \ *Special Education:* $11,459,000 \ *Open-Close:* 08/19 - 05/28 \ *DTBP:* $191 (High) \ ▣

Dr Sean Maika 1
Dan Villarreal 2,15,19
Dr Barry Lanford 3
Sharon Glosson 4
Karen Funk 6
Susan Diaz 8
Dr Donna Newman 15
Jim Baldoni 16,73
Rudy Jimenez 30,274
Julia Schneider 34
Millie Reynolds 41
Brian Moy 2
David Bohannon 2
Ron Clary 3,15
Jack Deforrest 5
Maria Perez 7,35*
Eric Wicker 11
Jason Gatell 16
Julie Shore 20,23
Tami Shaw 31
Natalie Hierholzer 36*
Thomas Campsey 42

Rebecca Ortiz 46
Maria Schwab 49
Shannon Grona 67
Chyla Whitton 68
Joel Trevino 68
Laura Witte 69
Marcos Zorola 76
Jorge Ramirez 80
Oteka Gibson 83
Wallace McCampbell 91
Doretta Walker 295
Rosanna Ruiz 47
Gerard Cortez 58,77
Brian Hurley 68
Gina Elliott 68
Mildred Andrews 68
Aubrey Chancellor 71
Dr Brent Brument 79,88,90,270
Roxanne Brown 81
Mark Contreras 91
Roberto Lozano 285*
Victor Garcia 298

Public Schs..Principal	Grd	Prgm	Enr/#Cls	SN	
ⓐ Academy of Creative Education 3736 Perrin Ctl Bldg 2, San Antonio 78217 Patrick Valdez	11-12	V	150 10	35%	210/407-0740 Fax 210/657-8976
Bradley Middle Sch 14819 Heimer Rd, San Antonio 78232 Brenda Cerroni	6-8	V	1,288 65	34%	210/356-2600 Fax 210/491-8314
ⓐ Bssp & Nets 8438 Ahern Dr, San Antonio 78216 Christine Condren	9-12	GV	100		210/356-7520
Bulverde Creek Elem Sch 3839 Canyon Pkwy, San Antonio 78259 Michelle McCoy	PK-5		1,101	26%	210/407-1000 Fax 210/491-8333
Bush Middle Sch 1500 Evans Rd, San Antonio 78258 Stuart Guthrie	6-8		1,201 100	16%	210/356-2900 Fax 210/491-8471
Camelot Elem Sch 5311 Merlin Dr, San Antonio 78218 Wilma Payne	PK-5	T	614 30	91%	210/407-1400 Fax 210/564-1782 ▣
Canyon Ridge Elem Sch 20522 Stone Oak Pkwy, San Antonio 78258 Laura Huggins	PK-5		636	15%	210/407-1600 Fax 210/482-2293 ▣ ▣
Career & Tech Education Center 3736 Perrin Central Bldg 4, San Antonio 78217 Justin Missildine	Voc		150		210/407-0743 Fax 210/637-4992
ⓜ Castle Hills Elem Sch ⓨ 200 Lemonwood Dr, San Antonio 78213 Betsy Asheim	PK-5	M	479 30	39%	210/407-1800 Fax 210/407-1809
Cibolo Green Elem Sch 24315 Bulverde Grn, San Antonio 78261 Adam Schwab	PK-5		957	17%	210/407-1200 Fax 830/435-3540
Clear Spring Elem Sch 4311 Clear Spring Dr, San Antonio 78217 Carlos Hoffman	PK-5	T	406 25	86%	210/407-2000 Fax 210/407-2009
Coker Elem Sch 302 Heimer Rd, San Antonio 78232 Elizabeth Fischer	PK-5	T	837 40	47%	210/407-2200 Fax 210/407-2209 ▣
Colonial Hills Elem Sch 2627 Kerrybrook Ct, San Antonio 78230 Jenae Mai	PK-5	T	744 40	86%	210/407-2400 Fax 210/442-0730
ⓜ Data Design & Technology Acad 5110 Walzem Rd, San Antonio 78218 Christina Mank-Allen	9-12		200		210/356-2237 Fax 210/650-1285
ⓨ David Tex Hill Middle Sch 21314 Bowerde Rd, San Antonio 78259 Charles Reininger	6-8	MV	1,139	19%	210/356-8000 Fax 210/444-2380
Dellview Elem Sch 7235 Dewhurst Rd, San Antonio 78213 Kelli Nungesser	PK-5	T	397 40	80%	210/407-2600 Fax 210/442-0781
Dr Bernard Harris Middle Sch 5300 Knollcreek, San Antonio 78247 Jeremi Niehoff	6-8	T	1,087	45%	210/356-4100 Fax 210/657-8892 ▣
Driscoll Middle Sch 17150 Jones Maltsberger Rd, San Antonio 78247 John Hill	6-8	TV	791 91	50%	210/356-3200 Fax 210/491-6467 ▣

1	Superintendent	8	Curric/Instruct K-12	19	Chief Financial Officer	29	Family/Consumer Science	39	Social Studies K-12	49	English/Lang Arts Elem	59	Special Education Elem	69	Academic Assessment
2	Bus/Finance/Purchasing	9	Curric/Instruct Elem	20	Art K-12	30	Adult Education	40	Social Studies Elem	50	English/Lang Arts Sec	60	Special Education Sec	70	Research/Development
3	Buildings And Grounds	10	Curric/Instruct Sec	21	Art Elem	31	Career/Sch-to-Work K-12	41	Social Studies Sec	51	Reading K-12	61	Foreign/World Lang K-12	71	Public Information
4	Food Service	11	Federal Program	22	Art Sec	32	Career/Sch-to-Work Elem	42	Science K-12	52	Reading Elem	62	Foreign/World Lang Elem	72	Summer School
5	Transportation	12	Title I	23	Music K-12	33	Career/Sch-to-Work Sec	43	Science Elem	53	Reading Sec	63	Foreign/World Lang Sec	73	Instructional Tech
6	Athletic	13	Title V	24	Music Elem	34	Early Childhood Ed	44	Science Sec	54	Remedial Reading K-12	64	Religious Education K-12	74	Inservice Training
7	Health Services	15	Asst Superintendent	25	Music Sec	35	Health/Phys Education	45	Math K-12	55	Remedial Reading Elem	65	Religious Education Elem	75	Marketing/Distributive
		16	Instructional Media Svcs	26	Business Education	36	Guidance Services K-12	46	Math Elem	56	Remedial Reading Sec	66	Religious Education Sec	76	Info Systems
		17	Chief Operations Officer	27	Career & Tech Ed	37	Guidance Services Elem	47	Math Sec	57	Bilingual/ELL	67	School Board President	77	Psychological Assess
		18	Chief Academic Officer	28	Technology Education	38	Guidance Services Sec	48	English/Lang Arts K-12	58	Special Education K-12	68	Teacher Personnel	78	Affirmative Action

TX—34

Texas School Directory — Bexar County

School	Grades	Programs	Enrollment	%	Phone
East Terrell Hills Elem Sch 4415 Bloomdale, San Antonio 78218 Ross McGlothlin	PK-5	T	626 33	87%	210/407-2800 Fax 210/564-1604 [f]
Edward H White Middle Sch 7800 Midcrown Dr, San Antonio 78218 Bethany Lorge	6-8	TV	1,072 65	73%	210/356-5900 Fax 210/650-1443
Eisenhower Middle Sch 8231 Blanco Rd, San Antonio 78216 John Smith	6-8	TV	1,040	56%	210/356-3500 Fax 210/442-0537
El Dorado Elem Sch 12634 El Sendero St, San Antonio 78233 Glenn Forde	PK-5	T	719 30	75%	210/407-3000 Fax 210/407-3009
Encino Park Elem Sch 2550 Encino Rio, San Antonio 78259 James Miller	PK-5	G	638 54	14%	210/407-3200 Fax 210/497-6238
Fox Run Elem Sch 6111 Fox Creek St, San Antonio 78247 Kimberly Orihuela	PK-5	T	699	58%	210/407-3400 Fax 210/564-1732
Frank Tejeda Middle Sch 2909 E Evans Rd, San Antonio 78259 **Martha Reyes**	6-8		1,155 65	19%	210/356-5600 Fax 210/482-2277
Garner Middle Sch 4302 Harry Wurzbach Rd, San Antonio 78209 John Bojescul	6-8	TV	965 40	71%	210/356-3800 Fax 210/805-5138
Hardy Oak Elem Sch 22900 Hardy Oak Blvd, San Antonio 78258 Lola Folkes	PK-5		707 60	8%	210/407-3600 Fax 210/481-4004
Harmony Hills Elem Sch 10727 Memory Ln, San Antonio 78216 Alan Rochkus	PK-5	T	597 40	66%	210/407-3800 Fax 210/407-3809
Hidden Forest Elem Sch 802 Silver Spruce St, San Antonio 78232 Cody Miller	PK-5		564 29	15%	210/407-4000 Fax 210/407-4009
Huebner Elem Sch 16311 Huebner Rd, San Antonio 78248 Carol Pierce	PK-5		703 48	25%	210/407-4200 Fax 210/408-5529 [t]
ⓜ International Sch of Americas 1400 Jackson Keller Rd, San Antonio 78213 Steven Magadance	9-12		488 18	23%	210/356-0900 Fax 210/442-0409
Jackson Middle Sch 4538 Vance Jackson Rd, San Antonio 78230 Erin Deason	6-8	TV	808 70	70%	210/356-4400 Fax 210/442-0580
Jackson-Keller Elem Sch 1601 Jackson Keller Rd, San Antonio 78213 Anna Nicolai	PK-5	T	783 32	89%	210/407-4400 Fax 210/442-0706
Johnson High Sch 23203 Bulverde Rd, San Antonio 78259 **Gary Comalander**	9-12		3,086	16%	210/356-0400 Fax 210/356-0430
Jose M Lopez Middle Sch 23103 Hardy Oak Blvd, San Antonio 78258 Eric Wernli	6-8	V	1,232	8%	210/356-5000 Fax 210/481-4072
Krueger Middle Sch 438 Lanark Dr, San Antonio 78218 Cynthia Rubio	6-8	TV	906	75%	210/356-4700 Fax 210/650-1124
Larkspur Elem Sch 1802 Larkspur Dr, San Antonio 78213 Edward Balderas	PK-5		813		210/407-4600 Fax 210/407-4609
Las Lomas Elem Sch 20303 Hardy Oak Blvd, San Antonio 78258 **Harold Massey**	PK-5		486	18%	210/356-7000 Fax 210/481-4012
Legacy of Educl Excellence HS 1400 Jackson Keller Rd, San Antonio 78213 David Crowe	9-12	AGTV	2,642	65%	210/356-0800 Fax 210/442-0325
Longs Creek Elem Sch 15806 Oconnor Rd, San Antonio 78247 Amy Copes	PK-5		638 46	30%	210/407-4800 Fax 210/657-8754 [t]
MacArthur High Sch 2923 MacArthur Vw, San Antonio 78217 Peter Martinez	9-12	GTV	2,391 100	45%	210/356-7600 Fax 210/650-1195
Madison High Sch 5005 Stahl Rd, San Antonio 78247 Steven Zimmerman	9-12	TV	3,287 100	46%	210/356-1400 Fax 210/637-4435
Montgomery Elem Sch 7047 Montgomery, San Antonio 78239 John Merrill	PK-5	T	504	91%	210/407-5000 Fax 210/564-1758
ⓐ NE Alternative Center 103 W Rampart Dr, San Antonio 78216 Brian Kennedy \ Bryan Norwood	6-12	G	93 27		210/356-7400 Fax 210/442-0623
ⓐ NE Transition Sch 8438 Ahern Dr, San Antonio 78216 Christine Condren	9-12		170		210/356-7520 Fax 210/637-4956
Nimitz Middle Sch 5426 Blanco Rd, San Antonio 78216 Jennifer Cooper	6-8	TV	1,285 48	75%	210/356-5300 Fax 210/442-0489
Northern Hills Elem Sch 13901 Higgins Rd, San Antonio 78217 Marisa Wulfsberg	PK-5	T	679 57	66%	210/407-5200 Fax 210/650-1482
Northwood Elem Sch 519 Pike Rd, San Antonio 78209 Catherine Harper	PK-5	T	416 26	41%	210/407-5400 Fax 210/805-5157 [t]
Oak Grove Elem Sch 3250 Nacogdoches Rd, San Antonio 78217 **Taleen Bloom**	PK-5		375 34	82%	210/407-5600 Fax 210/407-5609 [t]
Oak Meadow Elem Sch 2800 Hunters Green St, San Antonio 78231 Lisa Campos	PK-5		449 36	33%	210/407-5800 Fax 210/407-5809
Olmos Elem Sch 1103 Allena Dr, San Antonio 78213 Gaila Booth	PK-5	T	623 46	88%	210/407-6000 Fax 210/407-6009
Redland Oaks Elem Sch 16650 Redland Rd, San Antonio 78247 **Randy Barr**	PK-5		425 29	33%	210/407-6200 Fax 210/491-8383
Regency Place Elem Sch 10222 Broadway St, San Antonio 78217 Estelia Wallace	PK-5	T	532 28	79%	210/407-6400 Fax 210/407-6409
Ridgeview Elem Sch 8223 McCullough Ave, San Antonio 78216 Veronica Garza	PK-5	T	610 40	85%	210/407-6600 Fax 210/407-6609
Roan Forest Elem Sch 22710 Roan Park, San Antonio 78259 Christopher Specia	PK-5		766	29%	210/407-6800 Fax 210/481-4053
Ronald Reagan High Sch 19000 Ronald Reagan, San Antonio 78258 Brenda Shelton	9-12		3,517	12%	210/356-1800 Fax 210/482-2222
Roosevelt High Sch 5110 Walzem Rd, Windcrest 78218 **Bryan Norwood**	9-12	GTV	2,819	66%	210/356-2200 Fax 210/650-1291
Royal Ridge Elem Sch 5933 Royal Rdg, San Antonio 78239 Jana Carter	PK-5		611	55%	210/407-7000 Fax 210/564-1620
Serna Elem Sch 2569 NE Loop 410, San Antonio 78217 Jennifer Lomas	PK-5	T	479 25	86%	210/407-7200 Fax 210/407-7209
Stahl Elem Sch 5222 Stahl Rd, San Antonio 78247 Emma Yates	PK-5	T	815 44	58%	210/407-7400 Fax 210/564-1682
Steubing Ranch Elem Sch 5100 Knollcreek, San Antonio 78247 Mario Guillen	PK-5	T	972	49%	210/407-7600 Fax 210/650-1248
Stone Oak Elem Sch 21045 Crescent Oaks, San Antonio 78258 **Ann Karrer**	PK-5		855 40	16%	210/407-7800 Fax 210/497-6204

79 Student Personnel
80 Driver Ed/Safety
81 Gifted/Talented
82 Video Services
85 Substance Abuse Prev
84 Erate
85 AIDS Education
88 Alternative/At Risk
89 Multi-Cultural Curriculum
90 Social Work

91 Safety/Security
92 Magnet School
93 Parental Involvement
95 Tech Prep Program
97 Chief Information Officer
98 Chief Technology Officer
270 Character Education
271 Migrant Education
273 Teacher Mentor
274 Before/After Sch

275 Response To Intervention
277 Remedial Math K-12
280 Literacy Coach
285 STEM
286 Digital Learning
288 Common Core Standards
294 Accountability
295 Network System
296 Title II Programs
297 Webmaster

298 Grant Writer/Ptnrships
750 Chief Innovation Officer
751 Chief of Staff
752 Social Emotional Learning

Other School Types
Ⓐ = Alternative Program
Ⓒ = Charter School
Ⓜ = Magnet School
Ⓨ = Year-Round School

School Programs
A = Alternative Program
G = Adult Classes
M = Magnet Program
T = Title I Schoolwide
V = Career & Tech Ed Programs

New Schools are shaded
New Superintendents and Principals are bold
Personnel with email addresses are underscored

Social Media
[f] = Facebook
[t] = Twitter

Bexar County

Thousand Oaks Elem Sch 16080 Henderson Pass, San Antonio 78232 **Holly Salazar**	PK-5	T	743 45	42%	210/407-8000 Fax 210/491-8358
Tuscany Heights Elem Sch 25001 Wilderness Oak, San Antonio 78260 Tara Bailey	PK-5		785	13%	210/407-8200 Fax 830/438-6330
Vineyard Ranch Elem Sch 16818 Huebner Rd, San Antonio 78258 Diadra Williams	PK-5		796	11%	210/356-7200 Fax 210/408-5515
Walzem Elem Sch 4618 Walzem Rd, San Antonio 78218 John Hinds	PK-5	T	656 40	88%	210/407-8400 Fax 210/564-1630
West Avenue Elem Sch 3915 West Ave, San Antonio 78213 Victor Saldana	PK-5		356 26	92%	210/407-8600 Fax 210/442-0756
Wetmore Elem Sch 3250 Thousand Oaks Dr, San Antonio 78247 **Catherine Leach**	PK-5		681 41	45%	210/407-8800 Fax 210/481-4037
Wilderness Oak Elem Sch 21019 Wilderness Oak, San Antonio 78258 Elias Harrington	PK-5		614	13%	210/407-9200 Fax 210/491-8371
Wilshire Elem Sch 6523 Cascade Pl, San Antonio 78218 Stacy Deming-Garcia	PK-5	T	339 24	83%	210/407-9400 Fax 210/805-5181
Windcrest Elem Sch 465 Faircrest Dr, San Antonio 78239 Todd Voges	PK-5	T	571 25	69%	210/407-9600 Fax 210/407-9401
Winston Churchill High Sch 12049 Blanco Rd, San Antonio 78216 **Todd Bloomer**	9-12	GV	2,932 100	34%	210/356-0000 Fax 210/442-0879
Wood Middle Sch 14800 Judson Rd, San Antonio 78233 Marcus Alvarez	6-8	TV	974 60	65%	210/356-6200 Fax 210/650-1309
Woodstone Elem Sch 5602 Fountainwood St, San Antonio 78233 Kelli Halliburton	PK-5	T	600 49	61%	210/407-9800 Fax 210/564-1708

- **Northside Ind School Dist** PID: 00998017   210/397-8500
  5900 Evers Rd, San Antonio 78238   Fax 210/706-8772

> **Schools:** 122 \ **Teachers:** 6,903 \ **Students:** 105,856 \
> **Special Ed Students:** 12,238 \ **LEP Students:** 8,536 \ **College-Bound:** 85%
> \ **Ethnic:** Asian 3%, African American 7%, Hispanic 70%, Caucasian
> 20% \ **Exp:** $248 (Med) \ **Poverty:** 15% \ **Title I:** $25,954,287 \
> **Special Education:** $18,178,000 \ **Bilingual Education:** $203,000 \
> **Open-Close:** 08/26 - 06/04 \ **DTBP:** $181 (High)

Dr Brian Woods	1	David Rastellini	2,15
Wesley Scott	2,15	Leroy San Miguel	3,15
Thomas Wherry	4	Rafael Salazar	5
Stan Laing	6	Jennifer Krueger	7
Shirley Schreiber	7*	Dr Janis Jordan	8,15
Deonna Dean	9	Ginger Fleming	9
Patti Sanchez	9	Anthony Jarrett	10
Melissa Turner	11*	Carolyn Rozelle	12
Don Schmidt	15,79	Henry Acosta	15
Levinia Lara	15	Lori Jones	15,73
Patricia Denham-Hill	15,68	Ray Galindo	15
Stephen Daniel	15	Doug Shudde	16,73
James Miculka	20,23	Lydia Martinez	30,93
Deborah Ruel Schafer	31,34	Dr Kimberly Ridgley	36
Victor Raga	57	Krista Garcia	58
Dr Carol Harle	67	Dr Brenda Ward	69,294
Carla Adermann	69	Barry Perez	71
Diana Ely	74	Melissa Oshman	76
Dr Coleman Heckman	77	Dr Vicky Sullivan	79
Courtney Mayer	81	Kim Stewart	81
Charlie Carnes	91	Sharon Sanchez	298*

Public Schs..Principal	Grd	Prgm	Enr/#Cls	SN	
Adams Hill Elem Sch 9627 Adams Hill Dr, San Antonio 78245 Annette Robinson	PK-5	T	515 32	84%	210/397-1400 Fax 210/678-2937
Allen Elem Sch 101 Dumont Dr, San Antonio 78227 Erika Zagala	PK-5	T	584 30	93%	210/397-0800 Fax 210/678-2946
Anson Jones Middle Sch 1256 Pinn Rd, San Antonio 78227 Michella Wheat	6-8	ATV	1,064 62	89%	210/397-2100 Fax 210/678-2113
Aue Elem Sch 24750 Baywater Stage, San Antonio 78255 Ursula Silberschlag	PK-5		686 52	8%	210/397-6750 Fax 210/698-4422
Bennie Cole Elem Sch 13185 Tillman Rdg, San Antonio 78253 Tod Kuenning	PK-5		799	27%	210/398-2100 Fax 210/678-2127
Bob Beard Elem Sch 8725 Sonoma Pkwy, Helotes 78023 Blanca Hemann	PK-5		713 31	8%	210/397-6600 Fax 210/695-3849
Bob Lewis Elem Sch 1000 Seascape, San Antonio 78251 **Kendra Merrell**	PK-5		698 44	41%	210/397-2650 Fax 210/257-3004
Bobbye Behlau Elem Sch 2355 Camp Light Way, San Antonio 78245 Jody Fries	PK-5	T	1,105	40%	210/398-1000 Fax 210/678-2107
Bonnie Ellison Elem Sch 7132 Oak Dr, San Antonio 78256 Julie Meneses	PK-5		578	21%	210/398-1850 Fax 210/687-1093
Brandeis High Sch 13011 Kyle Seale Pkwy, San Antonio 78249 Dr Geri Berger	9-12	GV	2,702	22%	210/397-8200 Fax 210/561-2000
Braun Station Elem Sch 8631 Tezel Rd, San Antonio 78254 Jack Funkhouser	PK-5		554 38	36%	210/397-1550 Fax 210/706-7463
ⓜ Business Careers High Sch 6500 Ingram Rd, San Antonio 78238 Randolph Neuenfeldt	9-12	V	700 15		210/397-7070 Fax 210/706-7076
Cable Elem Sch 1706 Pinn Rd, San Antonio 78227 **Debra Pinon**	PK-5	T	679 30	96%	210/397-2850 Fax 210/678-2878
Carl Wanke Elem Sch 10419 Old Prue Rd, San Antonio 78249 **Claudia Sanchez**	PK-5		803	39%	210/397-6700 Fax 210/257-4340
Carlos Coon Elem Sch 3110 Timber View Dr, San Antonio 78251 Mark Garcia	PK-5	T	758 35	74%	210/397-7250 Fax 210/706-7288
Carnahan Elem Sch 6839 Babcock Rd, San Antonio 78249 Andi Sosa	PK-5	T	586	59%	210/397-5850 Fax 210/516-2050
Christian Evers Elem Sch 1715 Richland Hills Dr, San Antonio 78251 Talia Hernandez	PK-5	T	844 47	46%	210/397-2550 Fax 210/706-7564
Clarence Galm Elem Sch 1454 Saxonhill Dr, San Antonio 78253 Michelle Alongi	PK-5	T	614 47	47%	210/397-1150 Fax 210/678-2863
Colby Glass Elem Sch 519 Clearview Dr, San Antonio 78228 Jennifer Bock	PK-5	T	604 27	83%	210/397-1950 Fax 210/431-5817
Colonies North Elem Sch 9915 Northampton Dr, San Antonio 78230 Norma Farrell	PK-5	T	751 32	67%	210/397-1700 Fax 210/561-5240
ⓜ Communications Arts High Sch 11600 Culebra Rd, San Antonio 78253 Lisa Baker	9-12		525 15		210/397-6043 Fax 210/688-6092
Construction Careers Academy 9411 W Military Dr, San Antonio 78251 Phillip Edge	Voc		520		210/397-4294

1	Superintendent	8	Curric/Instruct K-12	19	Chief Financial Officer	29	Family/Consumer Science	39	Social Studies K-12
2	Bus/Finance/Purchasing	9	Curric/Instruct Elem	20	Art K-12	30	Adult Education	40	Social Studies Elem
3	Buildings And Grounds	10	Curric/Instruct Sec	21	Art Elem	31	Career/Sch-to-Work K-12	41	Social Studies Sec
4	Food Service	11	Federal Program	22	Art Sec	32	Career/Sch-to-Work Elem	42	Science K-12
5	Transportation	12	Title I	23	Music K-12	33	Career/Sch-to-Work Sec	43	Science Elem
6	Athletic	13	Title V	24	Music Elem	34	Early Childhood Ed	44	Science Sec
7	Health Services	15	Asst Superintendent	25	Music Sec	35	Health/Phys Education	45	Math K-12
		16	Instructional Media Svcs	26	Business Education	36	Guidance Services K-12	46	Math Elem
		17	Chief Operations Officer	27	Career & Tech Ed	37	Guidance Services Elem	47	Math Sec
		18	Chief Academic Officer	28	Technology Education	38	Guidance Services Sec	48	English/Lang Arts K-12

49	English/Lang Arts Elem	59	Special Education Elem	69	Academic Assessment
50	English/Lang Arts Sec	60	Special Education Sec	70	Research/Development
51	Reading K-12	61	Foreign/World Lang K-12	71	Public Information
52	Reading Elem	62	Foreign/World Lang Elem	72	Summer School
53	Reading Sec	63	Foreign/World Lang Sec	73	Instructional Tech
54	Remedial Reading K-12	64	Religious Education K-12	74	Inservice Training
55	Remedial Reading Elem	65	Religious Education Elem	75	Marketing/Distributive
56	Remedial Reading Sec	66	Religious Education Sec	76	Info Systems
57	Bilingual/ELL	67	School Board President	77	Psychological Assess
58	Special Education K-12	68	Teacher Personnel	78	Affirmative Action

Market Data Retrieval

Texas School Directory

Bexar County

School	Grades	Prog	Enroll	%	Phone
Dean H Krueger Elem Sch 9900 Wildhorse Pkwy, San Antonio 78254 Laneil Belko	PK-5		758 48	29%	210/397-3850 Fax 210/257-1130
Dolores Linton Elem Sch 2103 Oakhill Rd, San Antonio 78238 **Marty Ortega**	PK-5	T	546 28	85%	210/397-0750 Fax 210/706-7186
Dolph Briscoe Middle Sch 4265 Lone Star Pkwy, San Antonio 78253 Christina Rather	6-8		1,222	20%	210/398-1100 Fax 210/674-0220
Dr Joe Bernal Middle Sch 14045 Bella Vista Pl, San Antonio 78253 Glenda Munson	6-8		896	30%	210/398-1900 Fax 210/679-8216
Dr Joe Ward Elem Sch 8400 Cavern Hl, San Antonio 78254 Sunday Nelson	PK-5	T	860 48	53%	210/397-6800 Fax 210/257-1195
Dr Martha Mead Elem Sch 3803 Midhorizon Dr, San Antonio 78229 Annette Lopez	PK-5	T	735	86%	210/397-1750 Fax 210/366-0770
Dr Pat Henderson Elem Sch 14605 Kallison Bnd, San Antonio 78254 Thomas Mackey	PK-5		535	32%	210/398-1050 Fax 210/256-0985
Dr Winn Murnin Elem Sch 9019 Dugas Dr, San Antonio 78251 Amber Freeman	PK-5	T	883 40	58%	210/397-4550 Fax 210/257-4335
E M Pease Middle Sch 201 Hunt Ln, San Antonio 78245 Katherine Lyssy	6-8	TV	1,099 75	72%	210/397-2950 Fax 210/678-2974
Earl Rudder Middle Sch 6558 Horn Blvd, San Antonio 78240 Dr Mary Jewell	6-8	AT	970 65	66%	210/397-5000 Fax 210/561-5022
Ed Rawlinson Middle Sch 14100 Vance Jackson Rd, San Antonio 78249 Sherry Mireles	6-8	V	1,294 75	30%	210/397-4900 Fax 210/697-4055
Edmund Cody Elem Sch 10403 Dugas Dr, San Antonio 78245 Kittiya Johnson	PK-5	T	628 45	72%	210/397-1650 Fax 210/678-2797
F R Scobee Elem Sch 11223 Cedar Park, San Antonio 78249 **Jocelyn Dudney**	PK-5	T	575 32	46%	210/397-0700 Fax 210/561-5076
Fields Elem Sch 9570 FM 1560 N, San Antonio 78254 **P Jennifer Hammond**	PK-5		862	44%	210/398-2150 Fax 210/688-0347
Folks Middle Sch 9855 Swayback Rnch, San Antonio 78254 Shawn McKenzie	6-8		1,212	25%	210/398-1600 Fax 210/257-3060
Forester Elem Sch 10726 Rousseau St, San Antonio 78245 Kelly Mantle	PK-5	T	940	51%	210/397-0200 Fax 210/257-1030
Frances M Rhodes Elem Sch 5714 N Knoll, San Antonio 78240 Vicki Kilpatrick	PK-5	T	590 35	61%	210/397-4000 Fax 210/697-4020
Glenoaks Elem Sch 5103 Newcome Dr, San Antonio 78229 Maria Meza	PK-5	T	628 42	73%	210/397-2300 Fax 210/617-5452
Gregorio Esparza Elem Sch 5700 Hemphill Dr, San Antonio 78228 Gabriela Garcia	PK-5	T	656 35	78%	210/397-1850 Fax 210/431-5843
Gregory Luna Middle Sch 200 Grosenbacher Rd N, San Antonio 78253 Lisa Richard	6-8	T	1,358	42%	210/397-5300 Fax 210/645-5246
Harlan High Sch 14350 Culebra Rd, San Antonio 78253 Robert Harris	9-12	V	1,458		210/398-2200 Fax 210/688-0494
Health Careers High Sch 4646 Hamilton Wolfe Rd, San Antonio 78229 Linda Burk	Voc	A	843 40	25%	210/397-5400 Fax 210/617-5423
Hector Garcia Middle Sch 14900 Kyle Seale Pkwy, San Antonio 78255 Tracy Wernli	6-8		1,474	12%	210/397-8400 Fax 210/695-3830
Helotes Elem Sch 13878 Riggs Rd, Helotes 78023 Rhonda Johnson	PK-5		406 26	14%	210/397-3800 Fax 210/695-3827
Henry Brauchle Elem Sch 8555 Bowens Crossing St, San Antonio 78250 Adriana Mata-Tausch	PK-5	T	635 40	64%	210/397-1500 Fax 210/706-7448
Henry Steubing Elem Sch 11655 Braefield, San Antonio 78249 Dr Mary Usrey	PK-5		526 50	30%	210/397-4390 Fax 210/706-4374
Herbert Boldt Elem Sch 310 Hollimon Pkwy, San Antonio 78253 **Ms Siller**	K-5		636	23%	210/398-2000 Fax 210/398-2048
Hoffmann Elem Sch 12118 Volunteer Pkwy, San Antonio 78253 Carrie Squyres	PK-5		1,013	18%	210/397-8350 Fax 210/645-3305
Ⓐ Irene L Chavez Excel Academy 11937 W Interstate 10, San Antonio 78230 Darren Calvert	11-12		93 8	57%	210/397-8120 Fax 210/706-8953
J B Passmore Elem Sch 570 Pinn Rd, San Antonio 78227 Veronica Arteaga	PK-5	T	560 30	90%	210/397-0500 Fax 210/678-2808
Jack C Jordan Middle Sch 1725 Richland Hills Dr, San Antonio 78251 Anabel Romero	6-8	TV	1,289 80	53%	210/397-6150 Fax 210/523-4876
James Carson Elem Sch 8151 Old Tezel Rd, San Antonio 78250 Lori Shaw	PK-5		586 32	37%	210/397-1100 Fax 210/257-1103
Jim G Martin Elem Sch 730 Canterbury, San Antonio 78228 Juan Perez	PK-5	T	719	90%	210/398-1400 Fax 210/431-5810
Jimmy Elrod Elem Sch 8885 Heath Circle Dr, San Antonio 78250 **Mrs Flores**	PK-5	T	457 32	46%	210/397-1800 Fax 210/706-7493
John B Connally Middle Sch 8661 Silent Sunrise, San Antonio 78250 Jaime Liendo	6-8	TV	953 40	45%	210/397-1000 Fax 210/257-1004
John C Holmgreen Center 8580 Ewing Halsell Dr, San Antonio 78229 Melissa Benavidez	Spec	AV	130 20		210/397-6100 Fax 210/617-5476
John Glenn Elem Sch 2385 Horal St, San Antonio 78227 Michelle Fine	PK-5	T	570 55	87%	210/397-2250 Fax 210/678-2891
John Jay High Sch 7611 Marbach Rd, San Antonio 78227 Jay Sumpter	9-12	ATV	3,015	72%	210/397-2700 Fax 210/645-3310
Ⓜ John Jay Sci & Engineer Acad 7611 Marbach Rd, San Antonio 78227 Gretchen Bley	9-12		732 5		210/397-2773 Fax 210/678-2145
John Marshall High Sch 8000 Lobo Ln, San Antonio 78240 Susan Cleveland	9-12	ATV	2,616	43%	210/397-7100 Fax 210/706-7175
John Paul Stevens High Sch 600 N Ellison Dr, San Antonio 78251 Harold Maldonado	9-12	TV	2,913	53%	210/397-6450 Fax 210/257-4304
Judge Andy Mireles Elem Sch 12260 Rockwall Ml, San Antonio 78253 Laura Hernandez	PK-5		945	20%	210/398-1500 Fax 210/257-3044
Kallison Elem Sch 8610 Ranch Vw E, San Antonio 78254 Billy Navin	PK-5		605		210/398-2350 Fax 210/688-9034
Kay Franklin Elem Sch 9180 Silver Spot, San Antonio 78254 Brenda Gallardo	PK-5		814	34%	210/398-1700 Fax 210/257-3013

79 Student Personnel
80 Driver Ed/Safety
81 Gifted/Talented
82 Video Services
83 Substance Abuse Prev
84 Erate
85 AIDS Education
88 Alternative/At Risk
89 Multi-Cultural Curriculum
90 Social Work

91 Safety/Security
92 Magnet School
93 Parental Involvement
95 Tech Prep Program
97 Chief Information Officer
98 Chief Technology Officer
270 Character Education
271 Migrant Education
273 Teacher Mentor
274 Before/After Sch

275 Response To Intervention
277 Remedial Math K-12
280 Literacy Coach
285 STEM
286 Digital Learning
288 Common Core Standards
294 Accountability
295 Network System
296 Title II Programs
297 Webmaster

298 Grant Writer/Ptnrships
750 Chief Innovation Officer
751 Chief of Staff
752 Social Emotional Learning

Other School Types
Ⓐ = Alternative School
Ⓒ = Charter School
Ⓜ = Magnet School
Ⓨ = Year-Round School

School Programs
A = Alternative Program
G = Adult Classes
M = Magnet Program
T = Title I Schoolwide
V = Career & Tech Ed Programs

New Schools are shaded
New Superintendents and Principals are bold
Personnel with email addresses are underscored

Social Media
◻ = Facebook
◻ = Twitter

TX—37

Bexar County

School	Grades		Enroll	%	Phone
Kuentz Elem Sch 12303 Leslie Rd, Helotes 78023 Lori Gallegos	PK-5		726	15%	210/397-8050 Fax 210/695-4810
Leon Springs Elem Sch 23881 W Interstate 10, San Antonio 78257 Gracie Espinoza	PK-5		509 27	14%	210/397-4400 Fax 210/698-4407
Leon Valley Elem Sch 7111 Huebner Rd, San Antonio 78240 Rebecca Barron-Flores	PK-5	T	600 45	73%	210/397-4650 Fax 210/706-7391
Lieck Elem Sch 12600 Reid Ranch Rd, San Antonio 78245 Rachel DelGado	PK-5		760	34%	210/398-1450 Fax 210/678-2108
Lloyd M Knowlton Elem Sch 9500 Timber Path, San Antonio 78250 Dr Maricela Alarcon	PK-5	T	671 40	81%	210/397-2600 Fax 210/706-7534
Locke Hill Elem Sch 5050 De Zavala Rd, San Antonio 78249 Danielle Frei	PK-5	T	641 45	46%	210/397-1600 Fax 210/561-5062
Los Reyes Elem Sch 10785 Triana Pkwy, Helotes 78023 Erika Pruneda	PK-5		586	19%	210/398-1200 Fax 210/695-5394
Marshall Law & Med Svc Mag HS 8000 Lobo Ln, San Antonio 78240 **Margaret Bray**	9-12		175		210/397-7199
Mary Hull Elem Sch 7320 Remuda Dr, San Antonio 78227 Patricia Noriega	PK-5	T	548 27	92%	210/397-0950 Fax 210/678-2917
Mary Lou Fisher Elem Sch 3430 Barrel Pass, San Antonio 78245 Rhapsody Quintero	PK-5	T	780	67%	210/397-4450 Fax 210/645-3911
McAndrew Elem Sch 26615 Toutant Beauregard Rd, Boerne 78006 De'Ann Upright	PK-5		331	3%	210/398-1750 Fax 210/398-1799
McDermott Elem Sch 5111 Usaa Blvd, San Antonio 78240 Belinda Trevinio	PK-5	T	676 47	64%	210/397-5100 Fax 210/561-5118
Meadow Village Elem Sch 1406 Meadow Way Dr, San Antonio 78227 Jennifer Escamilla	PK-5	T	532 30	88%	210/397-0650 Fax 210/678-2846
Michael Elem Sch 3155 Quiet Plain Dr, San Antonio 78245 Melissa Lopez-Brouse	PK-5	T	751 50	72%	210/397-3900 Fax 210/645-3905
Monroe S May Jr Elem Sch 15707 Chase Hill Blvd, San Antonio 78256 Geri Benitez	PK-5		573 70	37%	210/397-2000 Fax 210/561-2024
Mora Elem Sch 1520 American Lotus, San Antonio 78245 Jill Holmes	K-5		485		210/398-2400 Fax 210/678-2739
Murray E Boone Elem Sch 6614 Spring Time St, San Antonio 78249 Manuela Haberer	PK-5	T	602 31	64%	210/397-1450 Fax 210/561-5143
Nellie M Reddix Center 4711 Sid Katz Dr, San Antonio 78229 Robin Fields	Spec		233 4	45%	210/397-2401 Fax 210/615-2411
Nichols Elem Sch 9560 Braun Rd, San Antonio 78254 Jeff Davenport	PK-5	T	470 32	37%	210/397-4050 Fax 210/767-5951
ⓐ Northside Alt Middle Sch South 11937 W Interstate 10, San Antonio 78230 Anthony Persyn	6-8		125 10	90%	210/397-2070 Fax 210/561-2074
ⓐ Northside Alt Middle Sch-North 11937 W Interstate 10, San Antonio 78230 Anthony Persyn	6-8		120 6	73%	210/397-2070 Fax 210/561-2074
ⓐ Northside Alternative High Sch 144 Hunt Ln, San Antonio 78245 Dr Darrell Rice	9-12	V	180 24	76%	210/397-7080 Fax 210/706-7086
Northwest Crossing Elem Sch 10255 Dover Rdg, San Antonio 78250 Priscilla Siano	PK-5	T	539 30	59%	210/397-0600 Fax 210/706-7546
Oak Hills Terrace Elem Sch 5710 Cary Grant Dr, San Antonio 78240 **Angela Robinson**	PK-5	T	649 28	70%	210/397-0550 Fax 210/706-7348
Oliver Wendell Holmes High Sch 6500 Ingram Rd, San Antonio 78238 Ada Bohlken	9-12	TV	2,840	77%	210/397-7000 Fax 210/706-7030
Pat Neff Middle Sch 5227 Evers Rd, San Antonio 78238 Yvonne Correa	6-8	TV	1,176 45	78%	210/397-4100 Fax 210/523-4566
Patricia J Blattman Elem Sch 3300 N Loop 1604 W, San Antonio 78231 **Raymond Macias**	PK-5		550 35	6%	210/397-4600 Fax 210/408-6219
Paul W Ott Elem Sch 100 Grosenbacher Rd N, San Antonio 78253 Madeline Bueno	PK-5	T	713	40%	210/397-5550 Fax 210/645-5235
Powell Elem Sch 6003 Thunder Dr, San Antonio 78238 Priscilla Paul	PK-5	T	502 30	69%	210/397-0450 Fax 210/706-7361
R K Driggers Elem Sch 6901 Shadow Mist, San Antonio 78238 Paul Brusewitz	PK-5	T	574 31	73%	210/397-5900 Fax 210/257-4993
Raba Elem Sch 9740 Raba Dr, San Antonio 78251 Francesca Neal	PK-5	T	774 50	42%	210/397-1350 Fax 210/257-1335
Ralph Langley Elem Sch 14185 Bella Vista Pl, San Antonio 78253 Aydee Ruiz-Ufland	PK-5		462	40%	210/397-0150 Fax 210/645-3325
Raul B Fernandez Elem Sch 6845 Ridgebrook St, San Antonio 78250 Chaisleigh Southworth	PK-5	T	607 57	57%	210/397-1900 Fax 210/706-7376
Sam Rayburn Middle Sch 1400 Cedarhurst Dr, San Antonio 78227 Dr Scott McKenzie	6-8	TV	929 60	80%	210/397-2150 Fax 210/678-2181
Sandra Day O'Connor High Sch 12221 Leslie Rd, Helotes 78023 Jackie Horras	9-12	GV	3,327	21%	210/397-4800 Fax 210/695-4804
Scarborough Elem Sch 12280 Silver Pointe, San Antonio 78254 Mrs Cotton	PK-5		908	34%	210/397-8000 Fax 210/257-1019
Shirley J Howsman Elem Sch 11431 Vance Jackson Rd, San Antonio 78230 Thomas Buente	PK-5	T	712 36	73%	210/397-2350 Fax 210/561-5047
Stevenson Middle Sch 8403 Tezel Rd, San Antonio 78254 Julie Schweers	6-8	TV	1,315 75	39%	210/397-7300 Fax 210/706-7336
Stinson Middle Sch 13200 Skyhawk Dr, San Antonio 78249 Lou Medina	6-8	ATV	1,179 60	42%	210/397-3600 Fax 210/561-3609
Sul Ross Middle Sch 3630 Callaghan Rd, San Antonio 78228 Faustino Ortega	6-8	TV	1,165 83	84%	210/397-6350 Fax 210/431-6383
Thomas Hatchett Elem Sch 10700 Ingram Rd, San Antonio 78245 Adam Bock	PK-5	T	782 40	63%	210/397-6850 Fax 210/645-5222
Timberwilde Elem Sch 8838 Timberwilde St, San Antonio 78250 Wendy Tiemann	PK-5	T	651 42	63%	210/397-0400 Fax 210/706-7478
Tom C Clark High Sch 5150 De Zavala Rd, San Antonio 78249 Dr Jerry Woods	9-12	AV	2,744	31%	210/397-5150 Fax 210/561-5250
Vale Middle Sch 2120 N Ellison Dr, San Antonio 78251 Dana Gilbert-Perry	6-8	T	1,330	49%	210/397-5700 Fax 210/257-1000

1 Superintendent	8 Curric/Instruct K-12	19 Chief Financial Officer	29 Family/Consumer Science	39 Social Studies K-12	49 English/Lang Arts Elem	59 Special Education Elem	69 Academic Assessment
2 Bus/Finance/Purchasing	9 Curric/Instruct Elem	20 Art K-12	30 Adult Education	40 Social Studies Elem	50 English/Lang Arts Sec	60 Special Education Sec	70 Research/Development
3 Buildings And Grounds	10 Curric/Instruct Sec	21 Art Elem	31 Career/Sch-to-Work K-12	41 Social Studies Sec	51 Reading K-12	61 Foreign/World Lang K-12	71 Public Information
4 Food Service	11 Federal Program	22 Art Sec	32 Career/Sch-to-Work Elem	42 Science K-12	52 Reading Elem	62 Foreign/World Lang Elem	72 Summer School
5 Transportation	12 Title I	23 Music K-12	33 Career/Sch-to-Work Sec	43 Science Elem	53 Reading Sec	63 Foreign/World Lang Sec	73 Instructional Tech
6 Athletic	13 Title V	24 Music Elem	34 Early Childhood Ed	44 Science Sec	54 Remedial Reading K-12	64 Religious Education K-12	74 Inservice Training
7 Health Services	15 Asst Superintendent	25 Music Sec	35 Health/Phys Education	45 Math K-12	55 Remedial Reading Elem	65 Religious Education Elem	75 Marketing/Distributive
	16 Instructional Media Svcs	26 Business Education	36 Guidance Services K-12	46 Math Elem	56 Remedial Reading Sec	66 Religious Education Sec	76 Info Systems
	17 Chief Operations Officer	27 Career & Tech Ed	37 Guidance Services Elem	47 Math Sec	57 Bilingual/ELL	67 School Board President	77 Psychological Assess
	18 Chief Academic Officer	28 Technology Education	38 Guidance Services Sec	48 English/Lang Arts K-12	58 Special Education K-12	68 Teacher Personnel	78 Affirmative Action

Texas School Directory — Bexar County

School	Grd	Prgm	Enr/#Cls	SN	Phone
Valley Hi Elem Sch 8503 Ray Ellison Blvd, San Antonio 78227 Andrew Morris	PK-5	T	409 20	78%	210/397-0350 Fax 210/678-2928
Villarreal Elem Sch 2902 White Tail Dr, San Antonio 78228 Roxanne Gutierrez	PK-5	T	713 35	86%	210/397-5800 Fax 210/431-5809
Virginia Myers Elem Sch 3031 Village Pkwy, San Antonio 78251 Tesilia Garza	PK-5	T	680 36	65%	210/397-6650 Fax 210/706-6674
W Z Burke Elem Sch 10111 Terra Oak, San Antonio 78250 Misty Knapp	PK-5	T	490 45	79%	210/397-1300 Fax 210/257-1305
Wallace Jefferson Middle Sch 10900 Shaenfield Rd, San Antonio 78254 Kevin Kearns	6-8		1,509	39%	210/397-3700 Fax 210/257-4988
Warren High Sch 9411 W Military Dr, San Antonio 78251 Valerie Sisk	9-12	TV	3,084	42%	210/397-4200 Fax 210/257-4246
Westwood Terrace Elem Sch 2315 Hackamore Ln, San Antonio 78227 Tom Knapp	PK-5	T	554 25	92%	210/397-0300 Fax 210/678-2786
William Hobby Middle Sch 11843 Vance Jackson Rd, San Antonio 78230 Lawrence Carranco	6-8	TV	1,026 60	51%	210/397-6300 Fax 210/690-6332
William Howard Taft High Sch 11600 Culebra Rd, San Antonio 78253 Martha Fernandez	9-12	AV	2,620	37%	210/397-6000 Fax 210/688-6072
William J Brennan High Sch 2400 Cottonwood Way, San Antonio 78253 John Trimble	9-12		2,649	31%	210/398-1250
William J Thornton Elem Sch 6450 Pembroke Rd, San Antonio 78240 Justin Bledsoe	PK-5	T	607 50	43%	210/397-3950 Fax 210/561-5128
Zachry Middle Sch 9410 Timber Path, San Antonio 78250 Susan Allain	6-8	ATV	948 80	71%	210/397-7400 Fax 210/706-7432

● **Randolph Field Ind School Dist** PID: 01601786   210/357-2300
Bldg 1225 Randolph AFB, Universal Cty 78148   Fax 210/357-2469

Schools: 3 \ **Teachers:** 101 \ **Students:** 1,300 \ **Special Ed Students:** 107 \ **LEP Students:** 10 \ **College-Bound:** 69% \ **Ethnic:** Asian 4%, African American 20%, Hispanic 25%, Caucasian 51% \ **Exp:** $482 (High) \ **Poverty:** 9% \ **Title I:** $45,100 \ **Open-Close:** 08/22 - 05/22 \ **DTBP:** $563 (High) \

Lance Johnson 1
Hossiny Moharam 3
Brandon Casey 5
Susie Wacker 7
Linda Heier 11
Christina Petofi-Casal 58*
Linda Mills 68
Sarah Sanders 81
Lorrie Remick 2,19,71
Cynthia Moczygemba 4
Pete Wesp 6*
Susan Bendele 8,11,69,273,275,277,298
Jennifer Martin 16*
Patrick Luna 67
Brian Grenier 73,98,295

Public Schs..Principal	Grd	Prgm	Enr/#Cls	SN	Phone
Randolph Elem Sch Bldg 146 Harmon -Randolph AFB, Universal Cty 78148 Allana Hemenway	PK-5		654 30	9%	210/357-2345 Fax 210/357-2346
Randolph High Sch Bldg 1225 Randolph AFB, Universal Cty 78148 Mark Malone	9-12		462 40	6%	210/357-2400 Fax 210/357-2475
Randolph Middle Sch Bldg 1225 Randolph AFB, Universal Cty 78148 Merrie Fox	6-8		334 40	9%	210/357-2430 Fax 210/357-2431

● **San Antonio Ind School Dist** PID: 00998366   210/554-2200
141 Lavaca St, San Antonio 78210   Fax 210/299-5580

Schools: 96 \ **Teachers:** 3,226 \ **Students:** 49,000 \
Special Ed Students: 5,341 \ **LEP Students:** 8,841 \ **College-Bound:** 54% \
Ethnic: African American 6%, Hispanic 91%, Caucasian 2% \ **Exp:** $553 (High)
\ **Poverty:** 32% \ **Title I:** $32,376,736 \ **Special Education:** $10,585,000 \
Bilingual Education: $211,000 \ **Open-Close:** 08/12 - 05/27 \ **DTBP:** $197 (High)

Pedro Martinez 1
Kamal Elhabr 3,15
Willie Burroughs 3,17
Ansilee Trevino 4
Kristy Sharpe 4
Nathan Graf 5
Todd Howey 6
Barbara Rodriguez 11
Dr Courtney Gober 15
Dr Joanelda DeLeon 15
Dr Matthew Weber 15
Patti Salzmann 15
Tiffany Grant 15,751
Becky Landa 16,74
Isabel Romero 23
Darlene Volz 30
Raul Salazar 35
Patrick Pyle 39
Stacey Knudson 45
Esmeralda Alday 57
Monica Valderrama 57
Beth Jones 58,77
Patti Radle 67
Liza Rosenthal 69,294
Mohammed Chounhury 70,750
Dr Kenneth Thompson 73,76,97,98
Ashleigh Dennis 81
Estella Garza 90
Dawn Kulpa 275
John Strelchun 298
Larry Garza 2,19
Michael Sanchez 3
Allisan Ramos 4
Jenny Arredondo 4
Samantha Regalado 4
Brian Clancy 6
Gloria Davis 7
Angelica Romero 15
Daniel Girard 15
Dr Judith Solis 15
Olivia Hernandez 15,57,271
Dr Pauline Dow 15
Toni Thompson 15,68,79
James Orozco 20
Johnny Vahalik 27,31
Aleida Perez 34
Victoria Bustos 36
Angela Paskell 42
Laura Gamez 48
Galadriel Friese 57
Myrna Rasmussen 57
Martha Vasquez 61
Jamie Brown 69
Theresa Urrabazo 69,70,294
Leslie Price 71
Lus Zoch 74
Michael Jordan 88
Elsa Pennell 93
Carol Bielke 286

Public Schs..Principal	Grd	Prgm	Enr/#Cls	SN	Phone
Advanced Learning Academy 621 W Euclid Ave, San Antonio 78212 Emily Bieser	PK-3		100		210/738-9760 Fax 210/228-3003
Advanced Learning Academy 637 N Main Ave, San Antonio 78205 Kathy Bieser	4-12		200		210/738-9763 Fax 210/228-3003
Agnes Cotton Academy 1616 Blanco Rd, San Antonio 78212 Rawan Hammoudeh	PK-3	T	437 29	94%	210/738-9780 Fax 210/228-3033
Antonio Margil Academy 1000 Perez St, San Antonio 78207 Sandra Galinzoga	PK-5	T	557 23	95%	210/738-9805 Fax 210/228-3054
Arnold Elem Sch 467 Freiling, San Antonio 78213 Belinda Hernandez	PK-5	T	593 22	92%	210/438-6530 Fax 210/228-3023
Artemisia Bowden Academy 515 Willow, San Antonio 78202 Anita O'Neal	PK-5	T	512 25	97%	210/738-9770 Fax 210/228-3028
© Barkley-Ruiz Academy 1111 S Navidad St, San Antonio 78207 Jacqueline Lanford	PK-5	T	491 28	93%	210/978-7940 Fax 210/228-3025
Baskin Elem Sch 630 Crestview Dr, San Antonio 78201 Valarie Garcia	PK-5	T	523 28	87%	210/438-6535 Fax 210/228-3075
Beacon Hill Academy 1411 W Ashby Pl, San Antonio 78201 Laryn Nelson	PK-5	T	500	93%	210/738-9765 Fax 210/228-3026

79	Student Personnel	91	Safety/Security	275	Response To Intervention	298	Grant Writer/Ptnrships
80	Driver Ed/Safety	92	Magnet School	277	Remedial Math K-12	750	Chief Innovation Officer
81	Gifted/Talented	93	Parental Involvement	280	Literacy Coach	751	Chief of Staff
82	Video Services	95	Tech Prep Program	285	STEM	752	Social Emotional Learning
83	Substance Abuse Prev	97	Chief Infomation Officer	286	Digital Learning		
84	Erate	98	Chief Technology Officer	288	Common Core Standards		Other School Types
85	AIDS Education	270	Character Education	294	Accountability	Ⓐ	= Alternative School
86	Alternative/At Risk	271	Migrant Education	295	Network System	Ⓒ	= Charter School
89	Multi-Cultural Curriculum	273	Teacher Mentor	296	Title II Programs	Ⓜ	= Magnet School
90	Social Work	274	Before/After Sch	297	Webmaster	Ⓨ	= Year-Round School

School Programs
A = Alternative Program
G = Adult Classes
M = Magnet Program
T = Title I Schoolwide
V = Career & Tech Ed Programs

Social Media
⧉ = Facebook
Ⓔ = Twitter

New Schools are shaded
New Superintendents and Principals are bold
Personnel with email addresses are underscored

TX—39

Bexar County — Market Data Retrieval

School	Grades	Type	Enroll	%	Phone
Bella Cameron Elem Sch 3635 Belgium Ln, San Antonio 78219 **Brandy Lewis**	PK-5	T	454 22	95%	210/978-7960 Fax 210/228-3078
© Bonham Academy 925 S Saint Marys St, San Antonio 78205 David Nungaray	PK-8	T	582 25	60%	210/228-3300 Fax 210/228-3027
Brackenridge High Sch 400 Eagleland Dr, San Antonio 78210 Maria Cordova	9-12	TV	1,717 110	90%	210/228-1200 Fax 210/228-3000
Ⓐ Brewer Academy © 906 Merida St, San Antonio 78207 Angie Griffin	6-12	V	31 12		210/438-6825
© Briscoe Academy 2015 S Flores St, San Antonio 78204 **Jennifer Emerson**	PK-5	T	492 50	91%	210/228-3305 Fax 210/228-3077
Burbank High Sch 1002 Edwards, San Antonio 78204 Miguel Elizondo	9-12	TV	1,253 85	88%	210/228-1210 Fax 210/228-3001
Carroll Early Chldhd Center 463 Holmgreen Rd, San Antonio 78220 **Dr Alejandra Barraza**	PK-PK	T	306	99%	210/978-7965 Fax 210/228-3079
Carvajal Early Chldhd Center 225 Arizona, San Antonio 78207 Sonya Cardenas	PK-PK	T	390 25	99%	210/978-7970 Fax 210/228-3031
© Cast Med 2601 Louis Bauer Dr, San Antonio 78235 Dr Eddie Rodriguez	Voc		118		210/228-3380
© Cast Tech High Sch 637 N Main Ave, San Antonio 78205 Melissa Alcala	9-11		147		210/554-2700 Fax 210/228-4601
Charles Clyde Ball Academy 343 Koehler Ct, San Antonio 78223 Gregory Rivers	PK-5	T	531 22	99%	210/438-6845 Fax 210/228-3008
Collins Garden Elem Sch 167 Harriman Pl, San Antonio 78204 Cynthia Delagarza	PK-5	T	509 30	94%	210/228-3310 Fax 210/228-3032
Connell Middle Sch 400 Hot Wells Blvd, San Antonio 78223 Mr Rivers	6-8	V	620 45		210/438-6835 Fax 210/534-6589
Ⓐ Cooper Academy at Navarro 623 S Pecos La Trinidad, San Antonio 78207 Robert Loveland	8-12	G	105 43		210/438-6810 Fax 210/228-3009
David Crockett Academy 2215 Morales St, San Antonio 78207 Anna Garcia	PK-7	T	681 44	97%	210/738-9785 Fax 210/228-3034
Davis Middle Sch 4702 E Houston St, San Antonio 78220 Sharene Dixon	6-8	TV	718 65	99%	210/978-7920 Fax 210/228-3010
De Zavala Elem Sch 2311 San Luis St, San Antonio 78207 **Donna Finch**	PK-5	T	600 40	98%	210/978-7975 Fax 210/228-3035
© Democracy Prep Stewart [227] 1950 Rigsby Ave, San Antonio 78210 **Vivian Silva**	PK-5	T	448 35	96%	210/438-6875 Fax 210/228-3065
Edison High Sch 701 Santa Monica St, San Antonio 78212 Cynthia Carielo	9-12	TV	1,611 75	82%	210/738-9720 Fax 210/228-3002
Eloise Japhet Academy 314 Astor St, San Antonio 78210 Natasha Gould	PK-5	T	508 25	93%	210/228-3345 Fax 210/228-3048
Estrada Achievement Center 1112 S Zarzamora St, San Antonio 78207 Gary Pollock	7-12		107 16		210/438-6820 Fax 210/228-3088
Ferdinand Herff Academy 996 S Hackberry, San Antonio 78210 **Kelly Allen**	PK-5	T	477 26	97%	210/228-3330 Fax 210/228-3042
Fox Technical High Sch 637 N Main Ave, San Antonio 78205 Jennifer Benavides	9-12	GTV	384	77%	210/738-9730 Fax 210/228-3003
Franklin Elem Sch 1915 W Olmos Dr, San Antonio 78201 Hugo Saucedo	PK-5	T	473 28	91%	210/738-9790 Fax 210/228-3039
Frederick Douglass Academy 318 Martin Luther King Dr, San Antonio 78203 Dr Stephanie Ratliff	PK-7	T	360 20	94%	210/228-3315 Fax 210/228-3080
© Gates Elem Sch 510 Morningview Dr, San Antonio 78220 Sonya Mora	PK-5	T	230 100	98%	210/978-7980 Fax 210/228-3081
Graebner Elem Sch 530 Hoover Ave, San Antonio 78225 Noemi Saldivar	PK-5	T	793 41	94%	210/228-3320 Fax 210/228-3040
© Harris Academy 325 Pruitt Ave, San Antonio 78204 Carol Velazquez	6-8	TV	738 48	91%	210/228-1220 Fax 210/228-3011
© Hawthorne Academy 115 W Josephine St, San Antonio 78212 Guadalupe Rodriguez	PK-8	T	821 45	77%	210/738-9795 Fax 210/228-3082
Highland Hills Elem Sch 734 Glamis Ave, San Antonio 78223 Deborah Esparza	PK-5	T	663 42	93%	210/438-6860 Fax 210/228-3043
© Highland Park Elem Sch 635 Rigsby Ave, San Antonio 78210 Rose Engelbrecht	PK-5	T	540 36	95%	210/228-3335 Fax 210/228-3044
Highlands High Sch 3118 Elgin Ave, San Antonio 78210 Julio Garcia	9-12	TV	1,661 80	91%	210/438-6800 Fax 210/228-3004
Hillcrest Elem Sch 211 W Malone Ave, San Antonio 78214 **Santa Lopez**	PK-5	T	538 27	95%	210/228-3340 Fax 210/228-3045
Hirsch Elem Sch 4826 Seabreeze Dr, San Antonio 78220 Mary Rodriguez	PK-5	T	813 21	95%	210/978-7985 Fax 210/228-3046
Huppertz Elem Sch 247 Bangor Dr, San Antonio 78228 **Linda Rios-Garcia**	PK-5	T	400 26	92%	210/438-6580 Fax 210/228-3047
Inez Foster Academy 6718 Pecan Valley Dr, San Antonio 78223 **Johnny Diaz**	PK-5	T	604 35	95%	210/438-6855 Fax 210/228-3038
Ira C Ogden Academy 2215 Leal St, San Antonio 78207 Ixchell Gonzalez	PK-7	T	645 30	98%	210/978-9815 Fax 210/228-3058
© Irving Dual Language Academy 1300 Delgado St, San Antonio 78207 Olivia Almanza-Pena	PK-2		250		210/738-9740 Fax 210/228-3012
Irving Middle Sch 1300 Delgado St, San Antonio 78207 Olivia Almanza	8-8	TV	100 46	95%	210/738-9740 Fax 210/228-3012
J T Brackenridge Elem Sch 1214 Guadalupe St, San Antonio 78207 Marco Morales	PK-5	T	652 44	99%	210/978-7950 Fax 210/228-3030
Ⓐ James F Cooper Acad-Navarro 623 S Pecos La Trinidad, San Antonio 78207 Robert Loveland	9-12	T	318	88%	210/438-6810 Fax 210/228-3009
James Russell Lowell Mid Sch 919 Thompson Pl, San Antonio 78226 **Yvonne Hernandez**	6-8	TV	407 33	95%	210/228-1225 Fax 210/228-3014
Kelly Elem Sch 1026 Thompson Pl, San Antonio 78226 Claudia Ramos-Coto	PK-5	T	283 15	96%	210/228-3350 Fax 210/228-3049
Knox Early Chldhd Center 302 Tipton Ave, San Antonio 78204 **Perla Kwiatkowski**	PK-PK	T	256 17	99%	210/228-3365 Fax 210/228-3051

1 Superintendent	8 Curric/Instruct K-12	19 Chief Financial Officer	29 Family/Consumer Science	39 Social Studies K-12	49 English/Lang Arts Elem	59 Special Education Elem	69 Academic Assessment
2 Bus/Finance/Purchasing	9 Curric/Instruct Elem	20 Art K-12	30 Adult Education	40 Social Studies Elem	50 English/Lang Arts Sec	60 Special Education Sec	70 Research/Development
3 Buildings And Grounds	10 Curric/Instruct Sec	21 Art Elem	31 Career/Sch-to-Work K-12	41 Social Studies Sec	51 Reading K-12	61 Foreign/World Lang K-12	71 Public Information
4 Food Service	11 Federal Program	22 Art Sec	32 Career/Sch-to-Work Elem	42 Science K-12	52 Reading Elem	62 Foreign/World Lang Elem	72 Summer School
5 Transportation	12 Title I	23 Music K-12	33 Career/Sch-to-Work Sec	43 Science Elem	53 Reading Sec	63 Foreign/World Lang Sec	73 Instructional Tech
6 Athletic	13 Title V	24 Music Elem	34 Early Childhood Ed	44 Science Sec	54 Remedial Reading K-12	64 Religious Education K-12	74 Inservice Training
7 Health Services	15 Asst Superintendent	25 Music Sec	35 Health/Phys Education	45 Math K-12	55 Remedial Reading Elem	65 Religious Education Elem	75 Marketing/Distributive
	16 Instructional Media Svcs	26 Business Education	36 Guidance Services K-12	46 Math Elem	56 Remedial Reading Sec	66 Religious Education Sec	76 Info Systems
	17 Chief Operations Officer	27 Career & Tech Ed	37 Guidance Services Elem	47 Math Sec	57 Bilingual/ELL	67 School Board President	77 Psychological Assess
	18 Chief Academic Officer	28 Technology Education	38 Guidance Services Sec	48 English/Lang Arts K-12	58 Special Education K-12	68 Teacher Personnel	78 Affirmative Action

Texas School Directory — Bexar County

School	Grades	Type	Enroll	Staff	%	Phone / Fax
Lamar Elem Sch 201 Parland Pl, San Antonio 78209 Brian Sparks	PK-5	T	226	20	84%	210/738-9800 Fax 210/228-3052
Laura Steele Montessori Acad 722 Haggin St, San Antonio 78210 Laura Christenberry	PK-2		105			210/438-6870 Fax 210/228-3076
Longfellow Middle Sch 1130 E Sunshine Dr, San Antonio 78228 Nancy Rodriguez	6-8	TV	854	30	91%	210/438-6520 Fax 210/228-3013
Madison Elem Sch 2900 W Woodlawn Ave, San Antonio 78228 Lianna Cano	PK-5	T	582	34	92%	210/438-6545 Fax 210/228-3053
Marin B Fenwick Academy 1930 Waverly Ave, San Antonio 78228 Dr Tambrey Ozuna	PK-5	T	462	31	96%	210/438-6540 Fax 210/228-3036
Ⓜ Martin Luther King Academy 3501 Martin Luther King Dr, San Antonio 78220 Natasha Pinnix	PK-8	TV	365	31	93%	210/978-7935 Fax 210/228-3083
Maverick Elem Sch 107 Raleigh Pl, San Antonio 78201 Leila Garza	PK-5	T	571	31	87%	210/438-6550 Fax 210/228-3055
Miller Elem Sch 207 Lincolnshire Dr, San Antonio 78220 Christine Weiland	PK-5	T	262	20	95%	210/978-7995 Fax 210/228-3085
Mission Academy 9210 S Presa St, San Antonio 78223 Noemi Davila	PK-8	T	584		88%	210/438-6880 Fax 210/228-3195
Muriel Vance Forbes Academy 2630 Sally Gay Dr, San Antonio 78223 Erica Lopez	PK-5	T	386	22	96%	210/438-6850 Fax 210/228-3037
Neal Elem Sch 3407 Capitol Ave, San Antonio 78201 Valerie Henry	PK-5	T	547	40	94%	210/738-9810 Fax 210/228-3056
Nelson Early Chldhd Ed Ctr 1014 Waverly Ave, San Antonio 78201 Marisa Mendez	PK-PK		206			210/438-6555 Fax 210/228-3057
New Tech San Antonio High Sch 4635 E Houston St, San Antonio 78220 Ashlan Barrientes	9-12	V	250			210/978-7900
Ollie Perry Storm Elem Sch 435 Brady Blvd, San Antonio 78207 Jacquelyn Navar	PK-5	T	440	45	98%	210/978-8005 Fax 210/228-3066
Page Middle Sch 401 Berkshire, San Antonio 78210 Stephanie Mihleder	6-8	TV	396	35	92%	210/228-1230 Fax 210/228-3015
Pershing Elem Sch 600 Sandmeyer St, San Antonio 78208 **Thamesia Handford**	PK-5	T	424	25	98%	210/738-9820 Fax 210/228-3059
Poe Middle Sch 814 Aransas Ave, San Antonio 78210 Christine Perez	6-8	TV	502	36	96%	210/228-1235 Fax 210/228-3016
Ⓜ Rhodes Middle Sch 3000 Tampico St, San Antonio 78207 **Rick Flores**	6-8	TV	685	40	95%	210/978-7925 Fax 210/228-3017
Riverside Park Academy 202 School St, San Antonio 78210 Cassie McClung	PK-7	T	363	25	97%	210/228-3355 Fax 210/228-3087
Robert B Green Academy 122 W Whittier St, San Antonio 78210 Jeanette Vasquez	PK-5	T	188	17	88%	210/228-3325 Fax 210/228-3041
Rodriguez Elem Sch 3626 W Cesar E Chavez Blvd, San Antonio 78207 Beth Brady	PK-5	T	346	27	95%	210/978-8000 Fax 210/228-3060
Rogers Middle Sch 314 Galway St, San Antonio 78223 Julie May	6-8	T	494	35	94%	210/438-6840 Fax 210/228-3018
Sam Houston High Sch 4635 E Houston St, San Antonio 78220 Mateen Diop	9-12	TV	1,132	100	91%	210/978-7900 Fax 210/228-3005
Sarah King Elem Sch 1001 Ceralvo St, San Antonio 78207 Gloria Martinez	PK-5	T	686	27	97%	210/978-7990 Fax 210/228-3050
Schenck Elem Sch 101 Kate Schenck Ave, San Antonio 78223 Mary Del Toro	PK-5	T	575	48	88%	210/438-6865 Fax 210/228-3062
Sidney Lanier High Sch 1514 W Cesar E Chavez Blvd, San Antonio 78207 Moises Ortiz	9-12	TV	1,693		88%	210/978-7910 Fax 210/228-3007
Smith Elem Sch 823 S Gevers St, San Antonio 78203 Vanessa Fox-Norton	PK-5	T	387	38	96%	210/228-3360 Fax 210/228-3063
St Philip's Early Clg HS 1801 Martin Luther King Dr, San Antonio 78203 Dr Derrick Thomas	9-9	T	146		87%	210/486-2406 Fax 210/228-3094
Tafolla Middle Sch 1303 W Cesar E Chavez Blvd, San Antonio 78207 Jeffrey Price	6-8	TV	694	56	94%	210/978-7930 Fax 210/228-3019
Thomas Jefferson High Sch 723 Donaldson Ave, San Antonio 78201 Ralf Halderman	9-12	ATV	1,740		86%	210/438-6570 Fax 210/228-3006
Ⓒ Travis Early College High Sch 1915 N Main Ave, San Antonio 78212 Adrianna Arredondo	9-12	T	389		68%	210/738-9830 Fax 210/228-3067
Twain MS & Dual Language Acad 2411 San Pedro Ave, San Antonio 78212 David Garcia	PK-8	TV	560	60	94%	210/738-9745 Fax 210/228-3020
Tynan Early Childhood Ctr 925 Gulf, San Antonio 78202 Gregorio Velazquez	PK-PK	T	244	14	99%	210/738-9835 Fax 210/228-3068
Washington Elem Sch 1823 Nolan, San Antonio 78202 Phyllis Foley-Davis	PK-5	T	459	25	99%	210/738-9840 Fax 210/228-3069
Wheatley Middle Sch 415 Gabriel, San Antonio 78202 Sandra Galinzoga	6-8	TV	378	40	98%	210/738-9750 Fax 210/227-9972
Ⓒ Whittier Middle Sch 2101 Edison Dr, San Antonio 78201 Irene Talamantes	6-8	TV	825		92%	210/738-9755 Fax 210/228-3022
Will Rogers Academy 620 McIlvaine, San Antonio 78212 Robby Wilson	PK-5	T	689	35	92%	210/738-9825 Fax 210/228-3061
Wilson Elem Sch 1421 Clower, San Antonio 78201 Jennifer Zavala	PK-5	T	460	27	88%	210/738-9845 Fax 210/228-3071
Woodlawn Academy 1717 W Magnolia Ave, San Antonio 78201 Karen Rose	PK-7	T	615	34	86%	210/438-6560 Fax 210/228-3072
Woodlawn Hills Elem Sch 110 W Quill Dr, San Antonio 78228 Martha Silva	PK-5	T	497	28	93%	210/438-6565 Fax 210/228-3073
Ⓒ Young Men's Leadership Academy 415 Gabriel, San Antonio 78202 Derrick Brown	4-6	T	162		70%	210/354-9652 Fax 210/228-3070
Ⓒ Young Women's Leadership Acad 2123 W Huisache Ave, San Antonio 78201 Delia McLerran	6-12	T	464		53%	210/438-6525 Fax 210/228-3194
Ywla Primary 401 Berkshire Ave, San Antonio 78210 **Delia McLerran**	PK-1		159			210/554-2710

Code	Description	Code	Description	Code	Description
79	Student Personnel	91	Safety/Security	275	Response To Intervention
80	Driver Ed/Safety	92	Magnet School	277	Remedial Math K-12
81	Gifted/Talented	93	Parental Involvement	280	Literacy Coach
82	Video Services	95	Tech Prep Program	285	STEM
83	Substance Abuse Prev	97	Chief Infomation Officer	286	Digital Learning
84	Erate	98	Chief Technology Officer	288	Common Core Standards
85	AIDS Education	270	Character Education	294	Accountability
88	Alternative/At Risk	271	Migrant Education	295	Network System
89	Multi-Cultural Curriculum	273	Teacher Mentor	296	Title II Programs
90	Social Work	274	Before/After Sch	297	Webmaster

298	Grant Writer/Ptnrships
750	Chief Innovation Officer
751	Chief of Staff
752	Social Emotional Learning

Other School Types
- Ⓐ = Alternative School
- Ⓒ = Charter School
- Ⓜ = Magnet School
- Ⓨ = Year-Round School

School Programs
- A = Alternative Program
- G = Adult Classes
- M = Magnet Program
- T = Title I Schoolwide
- V = Career & Tech Ed Programs

Social Media
- ▮ = Facebook
- ▮ = Twitter

New Schools are shaded
New Superintendents and Principals are bold
Personnel with email addresses are underscored

Bexar County

Market Data Retrieval

- **School of Excellence In Ed** PID: 11828823   210/431-9881
  1826 Basse Rd, San Antonio 78213   Fax 210/432-8467

Schools: 4 \ *Teachers:* 61 \ *Students:* 600 \ *Special Ed Students:* 51 \
LEP Students: 137 \ *College-Bound:* 75% \ *Ethnic:* African American 30%, Hispanic 68%, Caucasian 2% \ *Open-Close:* 08/19 - 05/29

Sheilda Madkins 1	Karl Knox 2,11
Sam Reyes 4	Teresa Johnson 11,298
Penelope Borkert 58	Patrick Britton 67
Stephen Trevino 73	Valerie Walker 285

Public Schs..Principal	Grd	Prgm	Enr/#Cls	SN	
© Dr David C Walker Elem Sch 6500 N Interstate 35, San Antonio 78218 Andrea Hall	PK-6	T	164	94%	210/654-4411 Fax 210/590-0376
© Dr Harmon W Kelley Elem Sch 802 Oblate Dr, San Antonio 78216 **Tiffany Peterson**	PK-6	T	301	97%	210/431-9881 Fax 210/253-2198
© Dr Paul Saenz Junior High Sch 1826 Basse Rd, San Antonio 78213 Valarie Walker	7-8	T	73	86%	210/431-9881 Fax 210/582-2547
© Milton B Lee Acad of Sci & Eng 1826 Basse Rd, San Antonio 78213 Valarie Walker	9-12	T	129	87%	210/431-9881 Fax 210/582-2547

- **Somerset Ind School Dist** PID: 00999346   866/852-9858
  7791 6th St, Somerset 78069   Fax 210/750-8470

Schools: 7 \ *Teachers:* 267 \ *Students:* 3,990 \ *Special Ed Students:* 380 \ *LEP Students:* 566 \ *College-Bound:* 40% \ *Ethnic:* African American 1%, Hispanic 88%, Caucasian 11% \ *Exp:* $240 (Med) \ *Poverty:* 31% \ *Title I:* $1,600,806 \ *Special Education:* $925,000 \ *Open-Close:* 08/26 - 05/28 \ *DTBP:* $146 (High)

Saul Hinojosa 1,11	Michael Caralez 2,19
Robert Villafranca 3,15,79	Janet Welch 4*
Laura Vasquez 5	Johan Dinkelmann 6*
Yvette Trevino 7	Kriesti Bunch 8,18,74
Sheila Collazo 8,15,57,271	Diana Barrera 9,88
Shannon Boyd 10	Liliaana Perez 28,95*
Dr Alicia Villarreal 48,51	Dr Ramiro Nava 58
Don Green 67	Gloria Wynkoop 68
Beverley Lee 69,294	Maury Vasquez 71*
Rick Valdez 91	John Kennedy 295

Public Schs..Principal	Grd	Prgm	Enr/#Cls	SN	
Barrera Veterans Elem Sch 4135 Smith Rd, Von Ormy 78073 Geneva Salinas	PK-4	T	630	83%	866/465-8808 Fax 866/465-8818
Early College Leadership Acad 7790 E 3rd St, Somerset 78069 Melissa Holguin	9-10	T	76	66%	855/999-4634
Savannah Heights Interm Sch 5040 Smith Rd, Von Ormy 78073 **Maru Falletich**	5-6	T	642	83%	866/852-9863 Fax 888/488-4341
Somerset Early Chldhd Ctr 19930 Touchstone Rd, Somerset 78069 Sara Gonzales	PK-K	T	365 22	85%	866/852-9865 Fax 866/667-2599
Somerset Elem Sch 7840 6th St, Somerset 78069 **Tracy Padilla**	1-4	T	694 50	83%	866/852-9864 Fax 866/667-2602
Somerset High Sch 7650 S Loop 1604 W, Somerset 78069 Ricky Flores	9-12	ATV	1,078 35	70%	866/852-9861 Fax 866/667-2608
Somerset Junior High Sch 4370 W Loop 1604, Von Ormy 78073 Elida Guerra	7-8	ATV	642 50	75%	866/852-9862 Fax 866/448-2738

- **South San Antonio Ind Sch Dist** PID: 00999384   210/977-7000
  5622 Ray Ellison Blvd, San Antonio 78242   Fax 210/977-7022

Schools: 16 \ *Teachers:* 615 \ *Students:* 8,800 \ *Special Ed Students:* 780 \ *LEP Students:* 1,446 \ *Ethnic:* African American 1%, Hispanic 97%, Caucasian 1% \ *Exp:* $314 (High) \ *Poverty:* 27% \ *Title I:* $3,948,921 \ *Special Education:* $2,408,000 \ *Open-Close:* 08/19 - 05/28 \ *DTBP:* $196 (High)

Alexandro Flores 1	Bettinae Kaiser 2,19
Chad Doucet 2	Ruperto Becerra 3
Scott Stephens 4	Jesse Berlanga 5
Robert Zamora 6	Diane Olivo 7
Delores Sendejo 8,18	Lorraine DeLeon 8,288
David Abundis 11,296	David Cloud 16,73
Bobbie Shannon 27	Rosanna Mercado 34
Arla Chapa 57,271	Julie Silva 58
Connie Prado 67	Sheri Seaman 68
Denise Orosco 70,76	Jennifer Sunga-Collier 71*
Cynthia Bills 73,81,285	Scott Laleman 73,98,295,297
Eugene Tovar 91	

Public Schs..Principal	Grd	Prgm	Enr/#Cls	SN	
Alan B Shepard Middle Sch 5558 Ray Ellison Blvd, San Antonio 78242 **Frank Zavala**	6-8	TV	556 60	83%	210/623-1875 Fax 210/623-1894
Dwight Middle Sch 2454 W Southcross Blvd, San Antonio 78211 Yvonne Hernandez	6-8	T	647 40	97%	210/977-7300 Fax 210/977-7316
Five Palms Elem Sch 7138 Five Palms Dr, San Antonio 78242 Greg Martinez	PK-5	T	471 23	90%	210/645-3850 Fax 210/645-3853
Frank Madla Elem Sch 6100 Royalgate Dr, San Antonio 78242 Joann Buchanan	PK-5	T	533 34	94%	210/645-3800 Fax 210/645-3807
Health Science Academy 8638 Larkia St, San Antonio 78224 Dyanne Martinez-Munoz		Voc	50		210/977-7278 Fax 210/977-7285
Hutchins Elem Sch 1919 W Hutchins Pl, San Antonio 78224 Elizabeth Martinez	PK-5	T	546 30	96%	210/977-7200 Fax 210/977-7211
Kindred Elem Sch 7811 Kindred St, San Antonio 78224 **Eric Boysen**	PK-5	T	409 27	92%	210/977-7575 Fax 210/977-7586
Miguel Carrillo Jr Elem Sch 500 Price Ave, San Antonio 78211 Raul Hinojosa	PK-5	T	471 26	97%	210/977-7550 Fax 210/977-7558
Neil Armstrong Elem Sch 7111 Apple Valley Dr, San Antonio 78242 **Phillip De La Pena**	PK-5	T	396 32	95%	210/623-8787 Fax 210/623-8792
Palo Alto Elem Sch 1725 Palo Alto Rd, San Antonio 78211 Judith Benavidez	PK-5	T	495 32	94%	210/977-7125 Fax 210/977-7132
Price Elem Sch 245 Price Ave, San Antonio 78211 Florinda Castillo	PK-5	T	543 24	92%	210/977-7225 Fax 210/977-7236
Roy P Benavidez Elem Sch 8340 Interstate 35 S, San Antonio 78224 Evelia Montemayor	PK-5	T	654 32	91%	210/977-7175 Fax 210/977-7184
South San Antonio Career Ctr 2615 Navajo St, San Antonio 78224 Charles Ervin		Voc	G	300 17	210/977-7350 Fax 210/977-7356

1	Superintendent	8	Curric/Instruct K-12	19	Chief Financial Officer	29	Family/Consumer Science
2	Bus/Finance/Purchasing	9	Curric/Instruct Elem	20	Art K-12	30	Adult Education
3	Buildings and Grounds	10	Curric/Instruct Sec	21	Art Elem	31	Career/Sch-to-Work K-12
4	Food Service	11	Federal Program	22	Art Sec	32	Career/Sch-to-Work Elem
5	Transportation	12	Title I	23	Music K-12	33	Career/Sch-to-Work Sec
6	Athletic	13	Title V	24	Music Elem	34	Early Childhood Ed
7	Health Services	15	Asst Superintendent	25	Music Sec	35	Health/Phys Education
		16	Instructional Media Svcs	26	Business Education	36	Guidance Services K-12
		17	Chief Operations Officer	27	Career & Tech Ed	37	Guidance Services Elem
		18	Chief Academic Officer	28	Technology Education	38	Guidance Services Sec

39	Social Studies K-12	49	English/Lang Arts Elem	59	Special Education Elem	69	Academic Assessment
40	Social Studies Elem	50	English/Lang Arts Sec	60	Special Education Sec	70	Research/Development
41	Social Studies Sec	51	Reading K-12	61	Foreign/World Lang K-12	71	Public Information
42	Science K-12	52	Reading Elem	62	Foreign/World Lang Elem	72	Summer School
43	Science Elem	53	Reading Sec	63	Foreign/World Lang Sec	73	Instructional Tech
44	Science Sec	54	Remedial Reading K-12	64	Religious Education K-12	74	Inservice Training
45	Math K-12	55	Remedial Reading Elem	65	Religious Education Elem	75	Marketing/Distributive
46	Math Elem	56	Remedial Reading Sec	66	Religious Education Sec	76	Info Systems
47	Math Sec	57	Bilingual/ELL	67	School Board President	77	Psychological Assess
48	English/Lang Arts K-12	58	Special Education K-12	68	Teacher Personnel	78	Affirmative Action

TX—42

Texas School Directory — Bexar County

School	Grd	Prgm	Enr/#Cls	SN	Phone
South San Antonio High Sch 7535 Barlite Blvd, San Antonio 78224 Lee Hernandez	9-12	GTV	2,606 90	90%	210/977-7400 Fax 210/977-7430
West Campus High Sch 5622 Ray Ellison Blvd, San Antonio 78242 Dr Lee Hernandez	9-9		401		
Zamora Middle Sch 8638 Larkia St, San Antonio 78224 Daniel Mauldin	6-8	TV	776 45	77%	210/977-7278 Fax 210/977-7285 [f][t]

● **Southside Ind School Dist** PID: 00999516 210/882-1600
1460 Martinez Losoya Rd, San Antonio 78221 Fax 210/626-0101

Schools: 9 \ **Teachers:** 390 \ **Students:** 5,800 \ **Special Ed Students:** 643 \ **LEP Students:** 922 \ **College-Bound:** 44% \ **Ethnic:** African American 2%, Hispanic 91%, Caucasian 7% \ **Exp:** $353 (High) \ **Poverty:** 27% \ **Title I:** $2,109,526 \ **Special Education:** $905,000 \ **Open-Close:** 08/13 - 05/22 \ **DTBP:** $158 (High) \ [t]

Mark Eads 1		Dr Fred Hayes 2,15		
Julian Monreal 3*		Juana Ramirez 4		
Robert Huffstickler 5		Richard Lock 6*		
Dr Genese Bell 8,15,74		Melonie Hammons 8		
Adriana Bermea 57		Christopher Douglas 58		
Delores Sendejo 67		Cliff Herring 73		
David Zaragoza 91		Christine Rodriguez 297		

Public Schs..Principal	Grd	Prgm	Enr/#Cls	SN	
Col Menchaca ECC 16180 S US Highway 281, San Antonio 78221 Rebecca Herrera	PK-K		350		210/882-1600
Freedom Elem Sch 3845 S Loop 1604 E, San Antonio 78264 Thomasina Montana	1-5	T	645	84%	210/882-1603 Fax 210/626-9866
Heritage Elem Sch 3223 S Loop 1604 E, San Antonio 78264 Elise Puente	1-5	T	573 32	86%	210/882-1607 Fax 210/626-9788
Julien C Gallardo Elem Sch 1300 Del Lago Pkwy, San Antonio 78221 Karen Feldman	1-5	T	645 35	83%	210/882-1609 Fax 210/626-2161
Julius L Matthey Middle Sch 20350 Redforest Ln, San Antonio 78264 Miguel Martell	7-8	T	803 80	81%	210/882-1601 Fax 210/626-0113 [t]
Losoya Intermediate Sch 1610 Martinez Losoya Rd, San Antonio 78221 Joel Gaines	6-6	T	878 34	87%	210/882-1602 Fax 210/626-0116
Southside Alternative Sch 3223 S Loop 1604 E Ste 4, San Antonio 78264 Carveth Hall	1-12	T	6 9	85%	210/882-1604 Fax 210/626-0473
Southside High Sch 19190 US Highway 281 S, San Antonio 78221 Henry Yzaguirre	9-12	T	1,575 80	74%	210/882-1606 Fax 210/626-0119
William Pearce Elem Sch 19190 US Highway 281 S, San Antonio 78221 Brenda Gonzales	1-5	T	529 29	82%	210/882-1605 Fax 210/626-0117

● **Southwest Ind School Dist** PID: 00999578 210/622-4300
11914 Dragon Ln, San Antonio 78252 Fax 210/622-4301

Schools: 19 \ **Teachers:** 896 \ **Students:** 13,580 \ **Special Ed Students:** 1,542 \ **LEP Students:** 2,136 \ **College-Bound:** 45% \ **Ethnic:** African American 3%, Hispanic 92%, Caucasian 5% \ **Exp:** $378 (High) \ **Poverty:** 25% \ **Title I:** $4,631,749 \ **Special Education:** $2,653,000 \ **Open-Close:** 08/26 - 06/04 \ **DTBP:** $186 (High) \ [f][t]

Dr Lloyd Verstuyft 1	Brandon Crisp 2,15	
Thomas Krueger 3	Winston Gatlin 4	
Emanuel Tamyo 5	Peter Wagner 6	
Valarie Maldonado 7,85	Dalia Garcia 8	
Velia Terrazas 9	Francis Gerber 11	
Homero Rodriguez 15	Marisela Rodriguez 16	
Victoria Gaeta 30	Louis Gonzalez 36	
Robert Robinson 58	Michael Frazier 67	
Lisa Boltie 69,294	Janice Hernandez 71	
Jeff Powell 73,84,295	Marie Phelps 79*	

Public Schs..Principal	Grd	Prgm	Enr/#Cls	SN	
Big Country Elem Sch 2250 Pue Rd, San Antonio 78245 Wendy Quillin	PK-5	T	665 45	78%	210/645-7560 Fax 210/645-7561
Bob Hope Elem Sch 3022 Reforma Dr, San Antonio 78211 Brian Pennartz	PK-5	T	410 23	89%	210/927-8180 Fax 210/927-8181
Cast STEM High Sch 4495 SW Verano Pkwy Bldg 100, Von Ormy 78073 Dr Aja Gardner	9-12		401		210/622-4810
Christa McAuliffe Middle Sch 9390 SW Loop 410, San Antonio 78242 Roxie Freeman	6-8	GT	811	92%	210/623-6260 Fax 210/623-6261
Ⓐ Crossroads Alternative Center 11914 Dragon Ln Bldg 203, San Antonio 78252 Odilia Martinez	6-12	V	20		210/622-4670 Fax 210/622-4671
Elm Creek Elem Sch 11535 Pearsall Rd, Atascosa 78002 J Luis Rojas	PK-5	T	690 40	76%	210/622-4430 Fax 210/622-4431
Francis R Scobee Middle Sch 10675 Marbach Rd, San Antonio 78245 Jorge Cruz	6-8	T	855 55	71%	210/645-7500 Fax 210/645-7501
Hidden Cove Elem Sch 5102 Trading Post Dr, San Antonio 78242 Tracy Myers	PK-5	T	565 40	97%	210/623-6220 Fax 210/623-6219
Indian Creek Elem Sch 5830 Old Pearsall Rd, San Antonio 78242 Patricia Chavez	PK-5	T	554 53	96%	210/623-6520 Fax 210/623-6521
Kriewald Road Elem Sch 10355 Kriewald Rd, San Antonio 78245 Rosie Hidalgo	PK-5	T	613 33	73%	210/645-7550 Fax 210/645-7551
Medio Creek Elem Sch 8911 Excellence Dr, San Antonio 78252 Amy Garza	PK-5	T	597	91%	210/622-4950 Fax 210/622-4951
Resnik Middle Sch 4495 SW Verano Pkwy Bldg 100, Von Ormy 78073 Odilia Martinez	6-8	T	837	83%	210/623-6589 Fax 210/623-2700
Ronald E McNair Middle Sch 11553 Pearsall Rd, Atascosa 78002 Anitra Crisp	6-8	T	729 50	73%	210/622-4480 Fax 210/622-4481
Sky Harbor Elem Sch 5902 Fishers Bend St, San Antonio 78242 Sylvia Acuna	PK-5	T	651 45	93%	210/623-6580 Fax 210/623-6584
Southwest Elem Sch 11914 Dragon Ln Bldg 100, San Antonio 78252 Judy Foster	PK-5	T	641 30	74%	210/622-4420 Fax 210/622-4421
Southwest High Sch 11960 Dragon Ln, San Antonio 78252 Aracelie Bunsen	9-12	GTV	2,375 125	76%	210/622-4500 Fax 210/622-4501
Southwest Legacy High Sch 4495 SW Verano Pkwy Bldg 100, Von Ormy 78073 Anita Chavarria	9-12	GV	1,497		210/623-6539 Fax 210/623-2716
Spicewood Park Elem Sch 11303 Tilson Dr, San Antonio 78224 Krista Nail	PK-5	T	637	95%	210/622-4999 Fax 210/622-4131
Sun Valley Elem Sch 6803 SW Loop 410, San Antonio 78227 Veronica Cuenca-Wilson	PK-5	T	620 42	75%	210/645-7570 Fax 210/645-7571

79 Student Personnel	91 Safety/Security	275 Response To Intervention	298 Grant Writer/Ptnrships	**School Programs**
80 Driver Ed/Safety	92 Magnet School	277 Remedial Math K-12	750 Chief Innovation Officer	A = Alternative Program
81 Gifted/Talented	93 Parental Involvement	280 Literacy Coach	751 Chief of Staff	G = Adult Classes
82 Video Services	95 Tech Prep Program	285 STEM	752 Social Emotional Learning	M = Magnet Program
83 Substance Abuse Prev	97 Chief Information Officer	286 Digital Learning		T = Title I Schoolwide
84 Erate	98 Chief Technology Officer	288 Common Core Standards	**Other School Types**	V = Career & Tech Ed Programs
85 AIDS Education	270 Character Education	294 Accountability	Ⓐ = Alternative School	
86 Alternative/At Risk	271 Migrant Education	295 Network System	Ⓒ = Charter School	**Social Media**
89 Multi-Cultural Curriculum	273 Teacher Mentor	296 Title II Programs	Ⓜ = Magnet School	[f] = Facebook
90 Social Work	274 Before/After Sch	297 Webmaster	Ⓨ = Year-Round School	[t] = Twitter

New Schools are shaded
New Superintendents and Principals are bold
Personnel with email addresses are underscored

Bexar County

BEXAR CATHOLIC SCHOOLS

- **Archdiocese San Antonio Ed Off** PID: 00999724   210/734-2620
  2718 W Woodlawn Ave, San Antonio 78228   Fax 210/734-0231

Schools: 39 \ *Students:* 13,062

Listing includes only schools located in this county. See District Index for location of Diocesan Offices.

Marti West 1   Veronica Ball 36,79

Catholic Schs..Principal	Grd	Prgm	Enr/#Cls	SN
Antonian College Prep High Sch 6425 West Ave, San Antonio 78213 Tim Petersen	9-12		702 25	210/344-9265 Fax 210/344-9267
Blessed Sacrament Catholic Sch 600 Oblate Dr, San Antonio 78216 Michael Fierro	PK-8		200 17	210/824-3381 Fax 210/826-6146
Central Catholic High Sch 1403 N Saint Marys St, San Antonio 78215 Stephen Walswick	9-12	G	530 54	210/225-6794 Fax 210/227-9353
Holy Cross of San Antonio Sch 426 N San Felipe Ave, San Antonio 78228 Dr Rene Escobedo	6-12		482 35	210/433-9395 Fax 210/433-1666
Holy Name Catholic Sch 3814 Nash Blvd, San Antonio 78223 Jennifer Tiller	PK-8		200 14	210/333-7356 Fax 210/333-7642
Holy Spirit Catholic Sch 770 W Ramsey Rd, San Antonio 78216 Margaret Webb	PK-8		500 30	210/349-1169 Fax 210/349-1247
Incarnate Word High Sch 727 E Hildebrand Ave, San Antonio 78212 Anna Downey	9-12		620 40	210/829-3100 Fax 210/829-3120
Little Flower Sch 905 Kentucky Ave, San Antonio 78201 Jackie Castro	PK-8		300 14	210/732-9207 Fax 210/732-3214
Mt Sacred Heart Sch 619 Mount Sacred Heart Rd, San Antonio 78216 Sharon Longoria	PK-8		380 28	210/342-6711 Fax 210/342-4032
Providence Catholic Sch 1215 N Saint Marys St, San Antonio 78215 Alicia Garcia	6-12		350	210/224-6651 Fax 210/224-6214
St Anthony Catholic Elem Sch 205 W Huisache Ave, San Antonio 78212 Patricia Ramirez	PK-8		428 26	210/732-8801 Fax 210/732-5968
St Anthony Catholic High Sch 3200 McCullough Ave, San Antonio 78212 Dr Kristina Vidaurri	9-12		400 29	210/832-5600 Fax 210/832-5615
St Gerard Catholic High Sch 521 S New Braunfels Ave, San Antonio 78203 Judith Priest	6-12		125 14	210/533-8061 Fax 210/761-8548
St Gregory the Great Cath Sch 700 Dewhurst Rd, San Antonio 78213 Daniel Martinez	PK-8	G	480 28	210/342-0281 Fax 210/308-7177
St James the Apostle Sch 907 W Theo Ave, San Antonio 78225 Sr Debbie Walker	PK-8		300 25	210/924-1201 Fax 210/924-0201
St John Berchman's Sch 1147 Cupples Rd, San Antonio 78226 Nora Garcia	PK-8		270 18	210/433-0411 Fax 210/433-2335
St John Bosco Sch 5630 W Commerce St, San Antonio 78237 Roxanne LeBlanc	PK-8		400 20	210/432-8011 Fax 866/214-8083
St Jose Sanchez Del Rio Sch 21140 Gathering Oak, San Antonio 78260 Michelle Mendez	PK-8		245 16	210/497-0323 Fax 210/497-5192
St Luke Catholic Sch 4603 Manitou, San Antonio 78228 Mary Cover	PK-8		500 30	210/434-2011 Fax 210/432-2419
St Margaret Mary Sch 1202 Fair Ave, San Antonio 78223 Jackie Castro	PK-8		198 11	210/534-6137 Fax 210/534-2225
St Mary Magdalen Sch 1700 Clower, San Antonio 78201 William Daily	PK-8		310 11	210/735-1381 Fax 210/735-2406
St Matthew Catholic Sch 10703 Wurzbach Rd, San Antonio 78230 Geneva Salinas	PK-8		715 29	210/696-7433 Fax 210/696-7624
St Monica Sch 515 North St, Converse 78109 Abigal Sozar	PK-8		240 22	210/658-6701 Fax 210/658-6945
St Paul Catholic Sch 307 John Adams Dr, San Antonio 78228 Lisa Barrera	PK-8		305 24	210/732-2741 Fax 210/732-7702
St Peter Prince of Apostles 112 Marcia Pl, San Antonio 78209 Gabriel Duarte	PK-8		156 23	210/824-3171 Fax 210/822-4504
St Pius X Catholic Sch 7734 Robin Rest Dr, San Antonio 78209 Jenny Kerr	PK-8		240 9	210/824-6431 Fax 210/824-7454
St Thomas More Catholic Sch 4427 Moana Dr, San Antonio 78218 Kimberly Gutierrez	PK-8		150 10	210/655-2882 Fax 210/655-9603

BEXAR PRIVATE SCHOOLS

Private Schs..Principal	Grd	Prgm	Enr/#Cls	SN
Atonement Academy 15415 Red Robin Rd, San Antonio 78255 James Growdon	PK-12		500	210/695-2240 Fax 210/695-9679
Buckner Fanning Christian Sch 975 Mission Spgs, San Antonio 78258 Sharon Newman	PK-8		220 16	210/402-6905 Fax 210/495-0688
Calvary Chapel Christian Acad 2935 Pat Booker Rd Unit 118, Universal Cty 78148 Will Shank	K-12		130	210/658-8337 Fax 210/658-1708
Cedar Creek Sch 3427 Northeast Pkwy, San Antonio 78218 Julie Brandt	3-12		36	210/822-3792
Child Montessori Sch 2829 Hunters Green St, San Antonio 78231 Jean Carol Stein	PK-5		85 4	210/493-6550
Christian School-Castle Hills 2216 NW Military Hwy, San Antonio 78213 Lisa Jacobs \ Dr Jim Bazar	PK-12		600 75	210/878-1000
Concordia Lutheran Sch 16801 Huebner Rd, San Antonio 78258 Sally McBee	PK-8		435 25	210/479-1477 Fax 210/479-9416
Cornerstone Christian Sch 17702 NW Military Hwy, San Antonio 78257 Peter Barnes \ Robin Davenport	PK-12		1,000	210/979-6161
Eisenhauer Rd Baptist DC PS 3950 Eisenhauer Rd, San Antonio 78218 Lydia Canales	PK-K		60 11	210/655-6831 Fax 210/655-0980
First Baptist Acad-Univ City 1401 Pat Booker Rd, Universal Cty 78148 Bob Payton	PK-12		380 26	210/658-5331 Fax 210/658-7024

1 Superintendent	8 Curric/Instruct K-12	19 Chief Financial Officer	29 Family/Consumer Science	39 Social Studies K-12	49 English/Lang Arts Elem	59 Special Education Elem	69 Academic Assessment
2 Bus/Finance/Purchasing	9 Curric/Instruct Elem	20 Art K-12	30 Adult Education	40 Social Studies Elem	50 English/Lang Arts Sec	60 Special Education Sec	70 Research/Development
3 Buildings And Grounds	10 Curric/Instruct Sec	21 Art Elem	31 Career/Sch-to-Work K-12	41 Social Studies Sec	51 Reading K-12	61 Foreign/World Lang K-12	71 Public Information
4 Food Service	11 Federal Program	22 Art Sec	32 Career/Sch-to-Work Elem	42 Science K-12	52 Reading Elem	62 Foreign/World Lang Elem	72 Summer School
5 Transportation	12 Title I	23 Music K-12	33 Career/Sch-to-Work Sec	43 Science Elem	53 Reading Sec	63 Foreign/World Lang Sec	73 Instructional Tech
6 Athletic	13 Title V	24 Music Elem	34 Early Childhood Ed	44 Science Sec	54 Remedial Reading K-12	64 Religious Education K-12	74 Inservice Training
7 Health Services	15 Asst Superintendent	25 Music Sec	35 Health/Phys Education	45 Math K-12	55 Remedial Reading Elem	65 Religious Education Elem	75 Marketing/Distributive
	16 Instructional Media Svcs	26 Business Education	36 Guidance Services K-12	46 Math Elem	56 Remedial Reading Sec	66 Religious Education Sec	76 Info Systems
	17 Chief Operations Officer	27 Career & Tech Ed	37 Guidance Services Elem	47 Math Sec	57 Bilingual/ELL	67 School Board President	77 Psychological Assess
	18 Chief Academic Officer	28 Technology Education	38 Guidance Services Sec	48 English/Lang Arts K-12	58 Special Education K-12	68 Teacher Personnel	78 Affirmative Action

Texas School Directory — Blanco County

School	Grades		Enr/#Cls	Phone
Gateway Christian Sch 6623 Five Palms Dr, San Antonio 78242 Roger Gaines	K-12		78 5	210/674-5703 Fax 210/674-6811
Healy-Murphy Center 618 Live Oak St, San Antonio 78202 Janie Whitely	9-12	V	123 13	210/223-2944 Fax 210/224-1033
Keystone Sch 119 E Craig Pl, San Antonio 78212 Jeanette Vilagi \ Bill Spedding	PK-12		405	210/735-4022 Fax 210/732-4905
Leafspring School-Sonterra 322 E Sonterra Blvd, San Antonio 78258 Erin Cuny	PK-K		120	210/495-5222 Fax 210/495-5851
Legacy Christian Academy 2255 Horal St, San Antonio 78227 Pedro Garza \ Angie Stewart	PK-12		207 20	210/674-0490
Leon Valley Christian Academy 7990 Grissom Rd, San Antonio 78251 John DuPree	PK-5		73 6	210/684-5662 Fax 210/520-9898
Lutheran High Sch 18104 Babcock Rd, San Antonio 78255 Patrick Maynard	9-12		100	210/694-4962 Fax 210/694-9150
Montessori Sch International 8222 Wurzbach Rd Ste B, San Antonio 78229 Marie Paul	PK-K		50 4	210/614-1665 Fax 210/692-1994
Montessori Sch of San Antonio 17722 Rogers Ranch Pkwy, San Antonio 78258 Chuck Raymer	PK-8		277 12	210/492-3553 Fax 210/492-3484
New Life Christian Academy 6622 W US Highway 90, San Antonio 78227 Anthony Jackson	PK-12		70	210/679-6001 Fax 210/679-6080
Palm Heights Baptist Sch 1106 W Malone Ave, San Antonio 78225 Bertha Rodriguez	PK-8		30 7	210/923-8600 Fax 210/921-2173
River City Christian Sch 5810 Blanco Rd, San Antonio 78216 Erica McCormick \ Larry Romine	K-12		97	210/384-0297 Fax 210/384-0446
Royal Point Academy 9965 Kriewald Rd, San Antonio 78245 Veronica Pena	PK-6		58 5	210/674-5310
Saint Mary's Hall 9401 Starcrest Dr, San Antonio 78217 Khristi Bates \ Sam Hamilton \ Brent Spicer	PK-12		993 30	210/483-9100 Fax 210/483-9299
Salem Sayers Baptist Academy 5212 FM 1628, Adkins 78101 Jason Taylor	PK-12		127	210/649-1178 Fax 210/649-2920
San Antonio Academy-Texas 117 E French Pl, San Antonio 78212 Clint Dubose	PK-8		344 40	210/733-7331 Fax 210/734-0711
San Antonio Christian Mid Sch 19202 Redland Rd, San Antonio 78259 Matt Erbaugh \ Catherine Sheats \ Jared Roan	PK-12		1,000 15	210/248-1635 Fax 210/348-6030
San Antonio Christian Sch 19202 Redland Rd, San Antonio 78259 Matt Erbaugh \ Catherine Sheats \ Jared Roan	PK-12		800	210/340-1864 Fax 210/342-0146
Scenic Hills Christian Academy 11223 Bandera Rd, San Antonio 78250 Jon Dickerson	PK-12		66 4	210/523-2312 Fax 210/684-8155
Shepherd of the Hills Luth Sch 6914 Wurzbach Rd, San Antonio 78240 Sue Gary	PK-8		372 22	210/614-3741
St George Episcopal Sch 6900 West Ave, San Antonio 78213 Rob Devlin	PK-8		500 27	210/342-4263 Fax 210/342-4681
St Luke's Episcopal Sch 15 Saint Lukes Ln, San Antonio 78209 Tom McLaughlin	PK-8		341 23	210/826-0664 Fax 210/826-8520
St Thomas Episcopal Sch 1416 N Loop 1604 E, San Antonio 78232 Allison Newman	PK-5		225 22	210/494-3509 Fax 210/494-0678
Sunnybrook Christian Academy 1620 Pinn Rd, San Antonio 78227 James Hatch	PK-12		111 14	210/674-8000 Fax 210/673-4603
Sunshine Cottage Sch-Deaf Chld 603 E Hildebrand Ave, San Antonio 78212 Jeff Bryan	Spec		120 14	210/824-0579 Fax 210/826-0436
Texas Military Institute 20955 W Tejas Trl, San Antonio 78257 Victoria Banks \ Dr Matthew Blake	6-12		400 45	210/698-7171 Fax 210/698-0903
Town East Christian Sch 5866 US Highway 87 E, San Antonio 78222 J D King	K-12		100 12	210/648-2601 Fax 210/648-1460
Trinity Christian Academy 5401 N Loop 1604 E, San Antonio 78247 Sharon Ausbury	K-8		95 25	210/653-2800 Fax 210/653-0303
Village Parkway Chrn Sch 3002 Village Pkwy, San Antonio 78251 John Turner	PK-6		90 7	210/680-8187 Fax 210/509-3502
Winston School San Antonio 8565 Ewing Halsell Dr, San Antonio 78229 Steven Yocham \ Louise Pastorino	Spec		200 28	210/615-6544 Fax 210/615-6627

BEXAR REGIONAL CENTERS

• **Region 20 Ed Service Center** PID: 00999645   210/370-5200
1314 Hines, San Antonio 78208   Fax 210/370-5750

Dr Jeff Goldhorn 1
Paul Neuhoff 2
Dr Carolyn Castillo 8,15,57
Sherry Marsh 58
Jeff Stone 2,15,73,76
Michael Peterson 3
Kim Vinton 30
Paul Patillo 73,76,98

BLANCO COUNTY

BLANCO PUBLIC SCHOOLS

• **Blanco Ind School Dist** PID: 01000481   830/833-4414
814 11th St, Blanco 78606   Fax 830/833-2019

Schools: 3 \ **Teachers:** 90 \ **Students:** 1,025 \ **Special Ed Students:** 94 \ **LEP Students:** 64 \ **College-Bound:** 61% \ **Ethnic:** African American 1%, Hispanic 40%, Caucasian 59% \ **Exp:** $312 (High) \ **Poverty:** 16% \ **Title I:** $207,444 \ **Special Education:** $325,000 \ **Open-Close:** 08/21 - 05/28 \ **DTBP:** $341 (High)

Clay Rosenbaum 1
Tony Petri 3
Robin Johnson 7*
Dina Johnson 8,11,57,88,271,288,294*
Kathryn Rutherford 58
Collin Gaskamp 73*
Mathew Streger 2,4
William Tesch 6*
Deeanna McLendon 8,31,36,69,83*
Elizabeth Hoff 16,82*
Kirt Felps 67
James Caudell 295

Public Schs..Principal	Grd	Prgm	Enr/#Cls	SN
Blanco Elem Sch 814 11th St, Blanco 78606 Jowie Walker	PK-5	T	444 24	55% 830/833-4338 Fax 830/833-4389

---

79 Student Personnel	91 Safety/Security	275 Response To Intervention	298 Grant Writer/Ptnrships	**School Programs**	**Social Media**
30 Driver Ed/Safety	92 Magnet School	277 Remedial Math K-12	750 Chief Innovation Officer	A = Alternative Program	
31 Gifted/Talented	93 Parental Involvement	280 Literacy Coach	751 Chief of Staff	G = Adult Classes	= Facebook
32 Video Services	95 Tech Prep Program	285 STEM	752 Social Emotional Learning	M = Magnet Program	
33 Substance Abuse Prev	97 Chief Infomation Officer	286 Digital Learning		T = Title I Schoolwide	= Twitter
34 Erate	98 Chief Technology Officer	288 Common Core Standards	**Other School Types**	V = Career & Tech Ed Programs	
35 AIDS Education	270 Character Education	294 Accountability	Ⓐ = Alternative School		
38 Alternative/At Risk	271 Migrant Education	295 Network System	Ⓒ = Charter School	New Schools are shaded	
39 Multi-Cultural Curriculum	273 Teacher Mentor	296 Title II Programs	Ⓜ = Magnet School	New Superintendents and Principals are bold	
90 Social Work	274 Before/After Sch	297 Webmaster	Ⓨ = Year-Round School	Personnel with email addresses are underscored	

TX—45

Borden County   **Market Data Retrieval**

Blanco High Sch	9-12	TV	318	43%	830/833-4337
1215 4th St, Blanco 78606			35		Fax 830/833-5028
Keitha St Clair					
Blanco Middle Sch	6-8	T	269	44%	830/833-5570
1500 Rocky Rd, Blanco 78606			15		Fax 830/833-2507
Brad Kinney					

- **Johnson City Ind School Dist** PID: 01000510   830/868-7410
  303 N Lbj Dr, Johnson City 78636   Fax 830/868-7375

Schools: 3 \ *Teachers:* 60 \ *Students:* 659 \ *Special Ed Students:* 68 \ *LEP Students:* 44 \ *College-Bound:* 68% \ *Ethnic:* Asian 1%, Hispanic 29%, Native American: 1%, Caucasian 70% \ *Exp:* $330 (High) \ *Poverty:* 10% \ *Title I:* $95,648 \ *Special Education:* $216,000 \ *Open-Close:* 08/21 - 05/28 \ *DTBP:* $346 (High)

Richard Kolek	1	Erin Fasel	2,11,15
Vance Marks	3,91	Chelsey Kerr	4
David Sine	6	Amanda Haley	8,57,270,273,288,296*
Regina Allen	16*	Cenny Pulate	58,69
Shelly Wenmohs	67	Kevin Jacks	73*

Public Schs..Principal	Grd	Prgm	Enr/#Cls	SN	
Lyndon B Johnson Elem Sch	PK-4	T	211	44%	830/868-4028
401 E Pecan Dr, Johnson City 78636			14		
Amanda Haley					
Lyndon B Johnson High Sch	9-12	V	240	25%	830/868-4025
505 N Nugent, Johnson City 78636			25		Fax 830/868-9244
Russell Maedgen					
Lyndon B Johnson Middle Sch	5-8		208	32%	830/868-9025
303 N Lbj Dr, Johnson City 78636			16		
Michael Norton					

BORDEN COUNTY

BORDEN PUBLIC SCHOOLS

- **Borden Co Ind School Dist** PID: 01000546   806/756-4313
  240 W Kincaid Ave, Gail 79738   Fax 806/756-4310

Schools: 1 \ *Teachers:* 20 \ *Students:* 230 \ *Special Ed Students:* 17 \ *LEP Students:* 3 \ *College-Bound:* 100% \ *Ethnic:* African American 1%, Hispanic 19%, Caucasian 80% \ *Exp:* $1,105 (High) \ *Poverty:* 17% \ *Title I:* $21,033 \ *Open-Close:* 08/27 - 05/25

Billy Collins	1	Amy Rinehart	2
Bart McMeans	8,11,57,69,88,294,296*	Becky Nix	58,275*
Dennis Poole	67	Ricardo Martinez	295*

Public Schs..Principal	Grd	Prgm	Enr/#Cls	SN	
Borden County Sch	K-12	TV	230	24%	806/756-4313
240 W Kincaid Ave, Gail 79738			14		
Britt Gordon					

BOSQUE COUNTY

BOSQUE PUBLIC SCHOOLS

- **Clifton Ind School Dist** PID: 01808893   254/675-2827
  1102 Key Ave, Clifton 76634   Fax 254/675-4351

Schools: 3 \ *Teachers:* 80 \ *Students:* 1,000 \ *Special Ed Students:* 107 \ *LEP Students:* 74 \ *Ethnic:* Asian 1%, African American 2%, Hispanic 35%, Native American: 1%, Caucasian 61% \ *Exp:* $341 (High) \ *Poverty:* 23% \ *Title I:* $295,408 \ *Special Education:* $196,000 \ *Open-Close:* 08/19 - 05/22 \ *DTBP:* $343 (High) \

Andy Ball	1	Lisa Prescher	2
Joe Adcock	3,5	Jennifer Green	4
Chuck Caniford	6*	Melissa Bosley	8
Viki Villarreal	57*	Karen Schasteen	58
Alex Montes	67	Mary Maddux	68*
Barbi Ernst	73*		

Public Schs..Principal	Grd	Prgm	Enr/#Cls	SN	
Clifton Elem School PK-5	PK-5	T	500	65%	254/675-1875
1000 Key Ave, Clifton 76634			12		Fax 254/675-1257
Ronda Kroll					
Clifton High Sch	9-12	ATV	293	38%	254/675-1845
1101 N Avenue Q, Clifton 76634			28		Fax 254/675-8002
Jimmy Jackson					
Clifton Middle Sch	6-8	AT	214	48%	254/675-1855
1102 Key Ave, Clifton 76634			25		Fax 254/675-2005
Andy Ball					

- **Cranfills Gap ISD School Dist** PID: 01000601   254/597-2505
  505 S 2nd St, Cranfills Gap 76637   Fax 254/597-0001

Schools: 1 \ *Teachers:* 15 \ *Students:* 125 \ *Special Ed Students:* 17 \ *LEP Students:* 9 \ *College-Bound:* 100% \ *Ethnic:* African American 2%, Hispanic 31%, Caucasian 68% \ *Exp:* $748 (High) \ *Poverty:* 21% \ *Title I:* $32,568 \ *Open-Close:* 08/26 - 05/22 \ *DTBP:* $336 (High) \

Monti Parchman	1,11,73,83	Sara Doyle	2
Adam Carroll	6*	Shana Campbell	8,69*
Kenney Wiese	67		

Public Schs..Principal	Grd	Prgm	Enr/#Cls	SN	
Cranfills Gap Sch	PK-12	ATV	125	71%	254/597-2505
505 S 2nd St, Cranfills Gap 76637			11		
Shana Campbell					

- **Iredell Ind School Dist** PID: 01000637   254/364-2411
  501 E McClain St, Iredell 76649   Fax 254/364-2206

Schools: 1 \ *Teachers:* 15 \ *Students:* 145 \ *Special Ed Students:* 19 \ *LEP Students:* 3 \ *College-Bound:* 100% \ *Ethnic:* Hispanic 27%, Caucasian 73% \ *Exp:* $248 (Med) \ *Poverty:* 25% \ *Title I:* $45,771 \ *Open-Close:* 08/26 - 05/29 \ *DTBP:* $363 (High)

Patrick Murphy	1,11,73,83,288	Deborah Burns	2*
Luis Guereca	6*	Jeanne Wallace	58*
Patrick Proffitt	67	Connie White	69,275*
William Kammerer	273*		

1	Superintendent	8	Curric/Instruct K-12	19	Chief Financial Officer	29	Family/Consumer Science	39	Social Studies K-12	49	English/Lang Arts Elem	59	Special Education Elem	69	Academic Assessment
2	Bus/Finance/Purchasing	9	Curric/Instruct Elem	20	Art K-12	30	Adult Education	40	Social Studies Elem	50	English/Lang Arts Sec	60	Special Education Sec	70	Research/Development
3	Buildings And Grounds	10	Curric/Instruct Sec	21	Art Elem	31	Career/Sch-to-Work K-12	41	Social Studies Sec	51	Reading K-12	61	Foreign/World Lang K-12	71	Public Information
4	Food Service	11	Federal Program	22	Art Sec	32	Career/Sch-to-Work Elem	42	Science K-12	52	Reading Elem	62	Foreign/World Lang Elem	72	Summer School
5	Transportation	12	Title I	23	Music K-12	33	Career/Sch-to-Work Sec	43	Science Elem	53	Reading Sec	63	Foreign/World Lang Sec	73	Instructional Tech
6	Athletic	13	Title V	24	Music Elem	34	Early Childhood Ed	44	Science Sec	54	Remedial Reading K-12	64	Religious Education K-12	74	Inservice Training
7	Health Services	15	Asst Superintendent	25	Music Sec	35	Health/Phys Education	45	Math K-12	55	Remedial Reading Elem	65	Religious Education Elem	75	Marketing/Distributive
		16	Instructional Media Svcs	26	Business Education	36	Guidance Services K-12	46	Math Elem	56	Remedial Reading Sec	66	Religious Education Sec	76	Info Systems
		17	Chief Operations Officer	27	Career & Tech Ed	37	Guidance Services Elem	47	Math Sec	57	Bilingual/ELL	67	School Board President	77	Psychological Assess
		18	Chief Academic Officer	28	Technology Education	38	Guidance Services Sec	48	English/Lang Arts K-12	58	Special Education K-12	68	Teacher Personnel	78	Affirmative Action

Texas School Directory

Bowie County

Public Schs..Principal	Grd	Prgm	Enr/#Cls	SN	
Iredell Sch 501 E McClain St, Iredell 76649 Patrick Murphy	PK-12	T	145 10	59%	254/364-2411

Kopperl Ind School Dist PID: 01000663
175 County Road 1240, Kopperl 76652
254/889-3502
Fax 254/889-3545

Schools: 1 \ **Teachers:** 19 \ **Students:** 225 \ **Special Ed Students:** 24 \ **LEP Students:** 3 \ **College-Bound:** 75% \ **Ethnic:** Hispanic 14%, Caucasian 86% \ **Exp:** $363 (High) \ **Poverty:** 27% \ **Title I:** $84,459 \ **Open-Close:** 08/21 - 05/22 \ **DTBP:** $329 (High)

Katrina Adcock 1,73	Yuvonne Wood 2*
John Wood 6	Katrina Adcock 8,11*
Roy Henry 31,36,83*	Paula Allen 58*
Harold Wellborn 67	Robin Flores 76

Public Schs..Principal	Grd	Prgm	Enr/#Cls	SN	
Kopperl Sch 175 County Road 1240, Kopperl 76652 Jay Underwood	PK-12	T	225 50	73%	254/889-3502

Meridian Ind School Dist PID: 01000699
204 2nd St, Meridian 76665
254/435-2081
Fax 254/435-2025

Schools: 3 \ **Teachers:** 51 \ **Students:** 480 \ **Special Ed Students:** 59 \ **LEP Students:** 27 \ **College-Bound:** 75% \ **Ethnic:** African American 4%, Hispanic 36%, Caucasian 60% \ **Exp:** $467 (High) \ **Poverty:** 16% \ **Title I:** $151,385 \ **Open-Close:** 08/26 - 05/28 \ **DTBP:** $231 (High) \ F T

Kim Edwards 1,11,84	Jami Edwards 2
Russell Crawford 3,5	Debbie Sanchez 4*
Stony Coffman 6*	Amy Dirkse 7*
Kim Edwards 12*	Donna Tarmon 32,37*
Dianne Luna 58*	Payton Wallace 67
Karen Robinson 69,83,85,88,273,274*	Tom Woody 73,76,295

Public Schs..Principal	Grd	Prgm	Enr/#Cls	SN	
Ⓐ Meridian Alternative Sch 607 F St, Meridian 76665 Paul Booth	K-12		12 2		254/435-6047
Meridian Elem Sch 550 Yellow Jacket Dr, Meridian 76665 Jaime Leinhauser	PK-5	T	227 20	72%	254/435-2731 Fax 254/435-6099
Meridian Middle High Sch 500 Yellow Jacket Dr, Meridian 76665 Paul Booth	6-12	TV	247 18	57%	254/435-2723 Fax 254/435-2199

Morgan Ind School Dist PID: 01000728
1306 Charles St, Morgan 76671
254/635-2311
Fax 254/635-2129

Schools: 1 \ **Teachers:** 12 \ **Students:** 142 \ **Special Ed Students:** 19 \ **LEP Students:** 7 \ **College-Bound:** 50% \ **Ethnic:** African American 2%, Hispanic 61%, Native American: 2%, Caucasian 35% \ **Exp:** $703 (High) \ **Poverty:** 32% \ **Title I:** $69,418 \ **Open-Close:** 08/26 - 05/29 \ **DTBP:** $414 (High)

John Bryant 1,11,73,83	Janie Pinnell 2*
Edward Avieles 6*	David Pinnell 67

Public Schs..Principal	Grd	Prgm	Enr/#Cls	SN	
Morgan Sch 1306 Charles St, Morgan 76671 Juan Ramirez	PK-12	TV	142 18	90%	254/635-2311

Valley Mills Ind School Dist PID: 01000754
1 Eagle Way, Valley Mills 76689
254/932-5210
Fax 254/932-6601

Schools: 3 \ **Teachers:** 50 \ **Students:** 630 \ **Special Ed Students:** 79 \ **LEP Students:** 41 \ **College-Bound:** 40% \ **Ethnic:** African American 3%, Hispanic 29%, Caucasian 68% \ **Exp:** $569 (High) \ **Poverty:** 18% \ **Title I:** $132,895 \ **Open-Close:** 08/21 - 05/08 \ **DTBP:** $347 (High)

Mike Kelly 1,11	Brenda Byrom 2,68
Cody Gibson 3,91	Lisa Danke 4*
Shelley Sonntag 5*	Sam Moody 6*
Sherri Fisk 7*	Dianna Richardson 16,73,295*
Courtney Hammond 57,83,88*	Mike Jones 67

Public Schs..Principal	Grd	Prgm	Enr/#Cls	SN	
Ⓨ Bosque Co Educational Center 201 Second St, Meridian 76665 John Bullion	K-12	AGMV	88 5		254/435-6098 Fax 254/435-6438
Ⓨ Valley Mills Elem Sch 254/932-5526 102 West Ave C, Valley Mills 76689 Chris Dowdy	PK-5	AGMTV	346 20	62%	Fax 254/932-5861
Ⓨ Valley Millsjr Sr High Sch 254/932-5251 1 Eagle Way, Valley Mills 76689 Jason Sansom	6-12	AGMTV	200 25	51%	

Walnut Springs Ind Sch Dist PID: 01000780
184 Avenue A, Walnut Spgs 76690
254/797-2133
Fax 254/797-2191

Schools: 1 \ **Teachers:** 20 \ **Students:** 190 \ **Special Ed Students:** 23 \ **LEP Students:** 27 \ **College-Bound:** 75% \ **Ethnic:** Hispanic 58%, Caucasian 42% \ **Exp:** $576 (High) \ **Poverty:** 39% \ **Title I:** $127,401 \ **Open-Close:** 08/26 - 05/21 \ **DTBP:** $392 (High)

Pat Garrett 1,11,84	Karen Prescher 2
Tim Trotter 6*	Christy Halbert 8,12,57,88,288*
Sandra Uloth 16*	Jonathan Harbour 58*
Clint Pullin 67	

Public Schs..Principal	Grd	Prgm	Enr/#Cls	SN	
Walnut Springs Sch 184 Avenue A, Walnut Spgs 76690 Christy Halbert	PK-12	ATV	190 23	85%	254/797-2133

BOWIE COUNTY

BOWIE PUBLIC SCHOOLS

De Kalb Ind School Dist PID: 01000819
101 Maple St, De Kalb 75559
903/667-2566
Fax 903/667-3791

Schools: 3 \ **Teachers:** 72 \ **Students:** 900 \ **Special Ed Students:** 87 \ **LEP Students:** 41 \ **College-Bound:** 51% \ **Ethnic:** African American 18%, Hispanic 12%, Native American: 1%, Caucasian 68% \ **Exp:** $449 (High) \ **Poverty:** 19% \ **Title I:** $233,896 \ **Open-Close:** 08/15 - 05/22 \ **DTBP:** $329 (High)

John Booth 1	Matteson Jennifer 2

Legend:

9 Student Personnel	91 Safety/Security	275 Response To Intervention	298 Grant Writer/Ptnrships	**School Programs**	**Social Media**	
10 Driver Ed/Safety	92 Magnet School	277 Remedial Math K-12	750 Chief Innovation Officer	A = Alternative Program		
1 Gifted/Talented	93 Parental Involvement	280 Literacy Coach	751 Chief of Staff	G = Adult Classes	F = Facebook	
2 Video Services	95 Tech Prep Program	285 STEM	752 Social Emotional Learning	M = Magnet Program		
3 Substance Abuse Prev	97 Chief Information Officer	286 Digital Learning		T = Title I Schoolwide	T = Twitter	
4 Erate	98 Chief Technology Officer	288 Common Core Standards	**Other School Types**	V = Career & Tech Ed Programs		
5 AIDS Education	270 Character Education	294 Accountability	Ⓐ = Alternative School			
6 Alternative/At Risk	271 Migrant Education	295 Network System	Ⓒ = Charter School	New Schools are shaded		
9 Multi-Cultural Curriculum	273 Teacher Mentor	296 Title II Programs	Ⓜ = Magnet School	New Superintendents and Principals are bold		
0 Social Work	274 Before/After Sch	297 Webmaster	Ⓨ = Year-Round School	Personnel with email addresses are underscored		

TX—47

Bowie County — Market Data Retrieval

Cortney White 3,5
Emily Lee 11,69
Michael White 23
Blake Hodges 67
Nielan Hensley 91*
Eddy May 6
Randall Brown 16,73,295*
Michele Fannin 52,55,57,59*
Melissa Motes 73
Margie Pate 298

Public Schs..Principal	Grd	Prgm	Enr/#Cls	SN	
De Kalb Elem Sch 101 Maple St, De Kalb 75559 Melinda Hodgson	PK-4	T	331 28	69%	903/667-2328 Fax 903/667-5151
De Kalb High Sch 101 Maple St, De Kalb 75559 Clayton Little	9-12	TV	230 35	58%	903/667-2422 Fax 903/667-4086
De Kalb Middle Sch 101 Maple St, De Kalb 75559 Cody Burgin	5-8	T	270 30	57%	903/667-2834 Fax 903/667-5509

- **Hooks Ind School Dist** PID: 01000857   903/547-6077
  100 E 5th St, Hooks 75561   Fax 903/547-2943

Schools: 3 \ **Teachers:** 75 \ **Students:** 942 \ **Special Ed Students:** 103 \ **LEP Students:** 24 \ **Ethnic:** African American 15%, Hispanic 10%, Caucasian 74% \ **Exp:** $533 (High) \ **Poverty:** 20% \ **Title I:** $221,227 \ **Open-Close:** 08/15 - 05/29 \ **DTBP:** $574 (High) \

Shane Krueger 1
Chris Crawford 3,5
Tracy Cook 8,11,30,34,36,57,288,296
Keith Minter 73,76,295
Judy Cochrane 2
Chris Birdwell 6*
Scot Duncan 67
Beverly Shannon 88*

Public Schs..Principal	Grd	Prgm	Enr/#Cls	SN	
Hooks Elem Sch 401 Precinct Rd, Hooks 75561 Kenny Turner	PK-4	T	329 30	64%	903/547-2291 Fax 903/547-3172
Hooks High Sch 401 E Avenue A, Hooks 75561 Danny Garrett	9-12	TV	352 40	49%	903/547-2215 Fax 903/547-6514
Hooks Junior High Sch 3921 FM 560, Hooks 75561 Craig Mahar	5-8	T	261 22	60%	903/547-2568 Fax 903/547-2595

- **Hubbard Ind School Dist** PID: 01000900   903/667-2645
  3347 US Highway 259 S, De Kalb 75559   Fax 903/667-5835

Schools: 1 \ **Teachers:** 9 \ **Students:** 120 \ **Special Ed Students:** 11 \ **LEP Students:** 7 \ **Ethnic:** Hispanic 23%, Native American: 1%, Caucasian 76% \ **Exp:** $222 (Med) \ **Poverty:** 16% \ **Title I:** $24,324 \ **Open-Close:** 08/15 - 05/22 \ **DTBP:** $350 (High)

Traci Drake 1,11,83
Traci Drake 12*
Johnny Pate 57*
Mechelle McMichael 73,76,270
Cayla Brown 752
Auttumn Owens 2
Becky Buttrum 16*
Brian Tripplett 67
Shellye McDaniel 271*

Public Schs..Principal	Grd	Prgm	Enr/#Cls	SN	
Hubbard Elem Sch 3347 US Highway 259 S, De Kalb 75559 Traci Drake	PK-8	T	120 12	76%	903/667-2645

- **Leary Ind School Dist** PID: 01000924   903/838-8960
  9500 W New Boston Rd, Texarkana 75501   Fax 903/838-6036

Schools: 1 \ **Teachers:** 11 \ **Students:** 125 \ **Special Ed Students:** 16 \ **Ethnic:** African American 5%, Hispanic 6%, Caucasian 90% \ **Exp:** $293 (Med) \ **Poverty:** 18% \ **Title I:** $45,391 \ **Open-Close:** 08/15 - 05/29 \ **DTBP:** $510 (High)

Jennifer Dear 1,11,57
Kim Fernandez 59*
Ken Autrey 67
Auttum Owens 2,288
Tamera Jones 59*
Heath Shelton 73,286*

Public Schs..Principal	Grd	Prgm	Enr/#Cls	SN	
Leary Elem Sch 9500 W New Boston Rd, Texarkana 75501	PK-8	AT	125 15	80%	903/838-8960

- **Liberty-Eylau Ind School Dist** PID: 01000948   903/832-1535
  2901 Leopard Dr, Texarkana 75501   Fax 903/838-9444

Schools: 4 \ **Teachers:** 196 \ **Students:** 2,500 \ **Special Ed Students:** 320 \ **LEP Students:** 35 \ **College-Bound:** 33% \ **Ethnic:** African American 55%, Hispanic 6%, Caucasian 39% \ **Exp:** $359 (High) \ **Poverty:** 25% \ **Title I:** $798,149 \ **Open-Close:** 08/12 - 05/22 \ **DTBP:** $158 (High) \

Ronnie Thompson 1
Jeff Wright 3,15
Malisa Mathews 4*
Klint King 6
Ceretha Levingston 11,15,80,298
Jason Brown 16,73
Linda Block 27
Angela Featherson 58
Matthew Fry 71
Bart Zeal 91
Susie Byrd 2
Wayne Harmon 3
Joyce Wade 5
Ronda Jameson 8
Brandy Burnett 12,68
Madeline Cooper 26*
Jean Ford 57,271*
Chad Turner 67
Diane Niemyer 88
Joseph Lavender 295

Public Schs..Principal	Grd	Prgm	Enr/#Cls	SN	
Liberty-Eylau Early Chldhd Ctr 3105 Norris Cooley Dr, Texarkana 75501 Amy Norwood	PK-K	T	417 14	92%	903/831-5352 Fax 903/831-5354
Liberty-Eylau Elem Sch 5492 US Highway 59 S, Texarkana 75501 Dr Brandon Thirston	1-4	T	662 42	84%	903/831-5390 Fax 903/831-5393
Liberty-Eylau High Sch 2905 Leopard Dr, Texarkana 75501 Kendrick Smith	9-12	GTV	689 68	63%	903/832-1530 Fax 903/831-6113
Liberty-Eylau Middle Sch 5555 Leopard Dr, Texarkana 75501 Jakeb Goff	5-8	TV	738 45	71%	903/838-5555 Fax 903/832-6700

- **Malta Ind School Dist** PID: 01001019   903/667-2950
  6178 W US Highway 82, New Boston 75570   Fax 903/667-0546

Schools: 1 \ **Teachers:** 13 \ **Students:** 241 \ **Special Ed Students:** 9 \ **LEP Students:** 4 \ **Ethnic:** Asian 1%, African American 1%, Hispanic 6%, Native American: 3%, Caucasian 88% \ **Exp:** $238 (Med) \ **Poverty:** 11% \ **Title I:** $12,774 \ **Open-Close:** 08/12 - 05/22 \ **DTBP:** $303 (High)

Stacy Starrett 1,11
Shana Rivas 59*
David Lee 6,9,57,69,74,270*
Doug Russell 67

Public Schs..Principal	Grd	Prgm	Enr/#Cls	SN	
Malta Elem Sch 6178 W US Highway 82, New Boston 75570 David Lee	PK-6	T	241 13	52%	903/667-2950 Fax 903/667-2984

1	Superintendent	8	Curric/Instruct K-12	19	Chief Financial Officer	29	Family/Consumer Science	39	Social Studies K-12	49	English/Lang Arts Elem	59	Special Education Elem	69	Academic Assessment
2	Bus/Finance/Purchasing	9	Curric/Instruct Elem	20	Art K-12	30	Adult Education	40	Social Studies Elem	50	English/Lang Arts Sec	60	Special Education Sec	70	Research/Development
3	Buildings And Grounds	10	Curric/Instruct Sec	21	Art Elem	31	Career/Sch-to-Work K-12	41	Social Studies Sec	51	Reading K-12	61	Foreign/World Lang K-12	71	Public Information
4	Food Service	11	Federal Program	22	Art Sec	32	Career/Sch-to-Work Elem	42	Science K-12	52	Reading Elem	62	Foreign/World Lang Elem	72	Summer School
5	Transportation	12	Title I	23	Music K-12	33	Career/Sch-to-Work Sec	43	Science Elem	53	Reading Sec	63	Foreign/World Lang Sec	73	Instructional Tech
6	Athletic	13	Title V	24	Music Elem	34	Early Childhood Ed	44	Science Sec	54	Remedial Reading K-12	64	Religious Education K-12	74	Inservice Training
7	Health Services	15	Asst Superintendent	25	Music Sec	35	Health/Phys Education	45	Math K-12	55	Remedial Reading Elem	65	Religious Education Elem	75	Marketing/Distributive
		16	Instructional Media Svcs	26	Business Education	36	Guidance Services K-12	46	Math Elem	56	Remedial Reading Sec	66	Religious Education Sec	76	Info Systems
		17	Chief Operations Officer	27	Career & Tech Ed	37	Guidance Services Elem	47	Math Sec	57	Bilingual/ELL	67	School Board President	77	Psychological Assess
		18	Chief Academic Officer	28	Technology Education	38	Guidance Services Sec	48	English/Lang Arts K-12	58	Special Education K-12	68	Teacher Personnel	78	Affirmative Action

Texas School Directory

Bowie County

Maud Ind School Dist PID: 01001033
389 Houston St, Maud 75567
903/585-2219
Fax 903/585-5451

Schools: 1 \ **Teachers:** 39 \ **Students:** 480 \ **Special Ed Students:** 54 \ **College-Bound:** 29% \ **Ethnic:** African American 9%, Hispanic 4%, Native American: 1%, Caucasian 86% \ **Exp:** $662 (High) \ **Poverty:** 18% \ **Title I:** $111,891 \ **Open-Close:** 08/12 - 05/21 \ **DTBP:** $365 (High)

Chris Bradshaw 1	Tommy Van Deaver 2
Debbie Johnson 4*	Josh Turner 6*
Amanda Sanders ... 8,11,57,271,288,296,298*	Mark Forsyth 16,73,76,84,286,295*
Angela Featherson 58	Melford Pierce 67
Ella Duren 69	Kayla Harrell 83,85,88,270*

Public Schs..Principal	Grd	Prgm	Enr/#Cls	SN	
Maud Sch 389 Houston St, Maud 75567 Erica Fouche \ Joel Windham	PK-12	TV	480 50	55%	903/585-2219

New Boston Ind School Dist PID: 01001069
201 Rice St, New Boston 75570
903/628-2521
Fax 903/628-8990

Schools: 4 \ **Teachers:** 123 \ **Students:** 1,340 \ **Special Ed Students:** 178 \ **LEP Students:** 21 \ **College-Bound:** 39% \ **Ethnic:** Asian 1%, African American 25%, Hispanic 8%, Caucasian 66% \ **Exp:** $431 (High) \ **Poverty:** 21% \ **Title I:** $380,333 \ **Open-Close:** 08/12 - 05/22 \ **DTBP:** $363 (High) \ f

Brian Bobbitt 1	Jackie Barnwell 2,12
Clinton Crawford 3*	Jimmie Thomas 5*
Justin Waltz 6	Patty Greene 8,11,57,69,273,298
Justin Dragoescu 16,73,295	Tonya Briggs 27*
Kimberly Fernandez 58,83	Paula Turner 67
Melissa Farris 75*	Tim Williams 84

Public Schs..Principal	Grd	Prgm	Enr/#Cls	SN	
Crestview Elem Sch 604 N McCoy Blvd, New Boston 75570 Melissa Reid	3-5	T	271 28	75%	903/628-6521 Fax 903/628-4205
New Boston High Sch 1 W Lion Dr, New Boston 75570 Neil Koenig	9-12	ATV	404 45	44%	903/628-6551 Fax 903/628-3695
New Boston Middle Sch 1215 N State Highway 8, New Boston 75570 Lindsay Skinner	6-8	T	286 40	62%	903/628-6588 Fax 903/628-5132
Oakview Primary Sch 530 Hospital Dr, New Boston 75570 Melissa Reid	PK-2	T	379	80%	903/628-8900 Fax 903/628-8910

Pleasant Grove Ind School Dist PID: 01001112
8500 N Kings Hwy, Texarkana 75503
903/831-4086
Fax 903/831-4435

Schools: 4 \ **Teachers:** 159 \ **Students:** 2,200 \ **Special Ed Students:** 204 \ **LEP Students:** 48 \ **College-Bound:** 44% \ **Ethnic:** Asian 3%, African American 16%, Hispanic 9%, Caucasian 71% \ **Exp:** $385 (High) \ **Poverty:** 10% \ **Title I:** $221,014 \ **Special Education:** $330,000 \ **Open-Close:** 08/12 - 05/21 \ **DTBP:** $213 (High)

Chad Pirtele 1	Derick Sibley 2,11
Steve Shatto 3	Bill Harp 4,68,83
Gary Stauty 4	Terry Spivey 5,91
Josh Gibson 6*	Lakeisha Girley 7*
Julie McClurg 8,11,58,85,285,296*	Patricia Long 26
Regan Summers 37*	Louanne Smith 38*
Dr Tina Antley 57,63,271	Fred Meisenheimer 67
Jim McClurg 73,297	Shelby DeMuth 75,298*
Kathy Lanier 76	Wanda Wortham 294
Brad Gildon 295	

Public Schs..Principal	Grd	Prgm	Enr/#Cls	SN	
Pleasant Grove Elem Sch 6500 Pleasant Grove Rd, Texarkana 75503 Chad Blain	PK-2	T	505 37	54%	903/838-0528 Fax 903/831-3799
Pleasant Grove High Sch 5406 McKnight Rd, Texarkana 75503 Todd Marshall	9-12	V	671 45	17%	903/832-8005 Fax 903/832-5381
Pleasant Grove Interm Sch 8480 N Kings Hwy, Texarkana 75503 Pam Bradford	3-5		479 30	36%	903/832-0001 Fax 903/832-0147
Pleasant Grove Middle Sch 5605 Cooks Ln, Texarkana 75503 Linda Erie	6-8		473 40	25%	903/831-4295 Fax 903/831-5501

Red Lick Ind School Dist PID: 01001136
3511 N FM 2148, Texarkana 75503
903/838-8230
Fax 903/831-6134

Schools: 1 \ **Teachers:** 35 \ **Students:** 530 \ **Special Ed Students:** 28 \ **Ethnic:** Hispanic 5%, Caucasian 95% \ **Exp:** $594 (High) \ **Poverty:** 17% \ **Title I:** $96,217 \ **Open-Close:** 08/14 - 05/28

Brandon Bynard 1	Lacey McMillon 2*
Neil Kiser 6*	Debbie Cooper 9,11,57,69,74,88*
Crystal Roach 12	Matt Windham 16,73*
Melissa Whitecotton 59*	David Price 67
Jessica Raney 83,85*	

Public Schs..Principal	Grd	Prgm	Enr/#Cls	SN	
Red Lick Sch 3511 N FM 2148, Texarkana 75503 Debbie Cooper	K-8		530 20	13%	903/838-8230

Redwater Ind School Dist PID: 01001150
202 Red River Rd N, Redwater 75573
903/671-3481
Fax 903/671-2019

Schools: 4 \ **Teachers:** 104 \ **Students:** 1,150 \ **Special Ed Students:** 112 \ **LEP Students:** 10 \ **College-Bound:** 65% \ **Ethnic:** Asian 1%, African American 3%, Hispanic 3%, Caucasian 93% \ **Exp:** $538 (High) \ **Poverty:** 10% \ **Title I:** $120,205 \ **Special Education:** $241,000 \ **Open-Close:** 08/19 - 05/28 \ **DTBP:** $333 (High) \ t

Kelly Burns 1	Tess Baker 2
Connie Mears 5	Thomas Graf 6
Laura Magnum 7	Leeann Corbin 8,11,57,69,83,273,288,296
Lori Baffern 16,286	Wendy May 31,36,93,270,271,274
Wendy May 31,36,93,270,271,274*	Anne White 58*
Kenney Cecil 67	Karen Zink 73*
Karen Arnett 79*	Kaye Derrick 88*

Public Schs..Principal	Grd	Prgm	Enr/#Cls	SN	
Redwater Elem Sch 206 Red River Rd N, Redwater 75573 Kasey Coggin	PK-3	T	351 21	49%	903/671-3425 Fax 903/671-3196
Redwater High Sch 120 Red River Rd N, Redwater 75573 Brad Cook	9-12	TV	341 23	27%	903/671-3421 Fax 903/671-3259
Redwater Junior High Sch 204 Red River Rd N, Redwater 75573 Kim Cody	7-8	T	167 19	36%	903/671-3227
Redwater Middle Sch 108 Ware St, Redwater 75573 Audrey Shumate	4-6	T	247 16	38%	903/671-3412 Fax 903/671-2444

---

79 Student Personnel	91 Safety/Security	275 Response To Intervention	298 Grant Writer/Ptnrships	**School Programs**	**Social Media**		
80 Driver Ed/Safety	92 Magnet School	277 Remedial Math K-12	750 Chief Innovation Officer	A = Alternative Program			
81 Gifted/Talented	93 Parental Involvement	280 Literacy Coach	751 Chief of Staff	G = Adult Classes	f = Facebook		
82 Video Services	95 Tech Prep Program	285 STEM	752 Social Emotional Learning	M = Magnet Program			
83 Substance Abuse Prev	97 Chief Infomation Officer	286 Digital Learning		T = Title I Schoolwide	t = Twitter		
84 Erate	98 Chief Technology Officer	288 Common Core Standards	**Other School Types**	V = Career & Tech Ed Programs			
85 AIDS Education	270 Character Education	294 Accountability	Ⓐ = Alternative School				
86 Alternative/At Risk	271 Migrant Education	295 Network System	Ⓒ = Charter School	New Schools are shaded			
89 Multi-Cultural Curriculum	273 Teacher Mentor	296 Title II Programs	Ⓜ = Magnet School	New Superintendents and Principals are bold			
90 Social Work	274 Before/After Sch	297 Webmaster	Ⓨ = Year-Round School	Personnel with email addresses are underscored			

TX—49

Brazoria County — Market Data Retrieval

- **Simms Ind School Dist** PID: 01001186   903/543-2219
  47 James Bowie Ln, Simms 75574   Fax 903/543-2512

Schools: 3 \ **Teachers:** 46 \ **Students:** 516 \ **Special Ed Students:** 78 \ **College-Bound:** 47% \ **Ethnic:** Hispanic 4%, Native American: 1%, Caucasian 95% \ **Exp:** $384 (High) \ **Poverty:** 22% \ **Title I:** $242,412 \ **Open-Close:** 08/19 - 05/22 \ **DTBP:** $396 (High)

Andy Johnson 8,298
Brandy Ceynowa 752

Public Schs..Principal	Grd	Prgm	Enr/#Cls	SN	
James Bowie Elem Sch 47 James Bowie Ln, Simms 75574 Justin Tyndell	PK-5	T	230 26	55%	903/543-2245
James Bowie High Sch 47 James Bowie Ln, Simms 75574 Lisa Hudgeons	9-12	TV	165 25	46%	903/543-2275
James Bowie Middle Sch 47 James Bowie Ln, Simms 75574 Christopher McClure	6-8	T	119	52%	903/543-2275

- **Texarkana Ind School Dist** PID: 01001215   903/794-3651
  4241 Summerhill Rd, Texarkana 75503   Fax 903/792-2632

Schools: 13 \ **Teachers:** 523 \ **Students:** 7,174 \ **Special Ed Students:** 641 \ **LEP Students:** 418 \ **Ethnic:** Asian 1%, African American 46%, Hispanic 15%, Native American: 1%, Caucasian 37% \ **Exp:** $379 (High) \ **Poverty:** 31% \ **Title I:** $2,781,733 \ **Special Education:** $1,204,000 \ **Open-Close:** 08/14 - 05/21 \ **DTBP:** $158 (High) \

Paul Norton 1
David Defoy 2
Christie Lammers 4
Barry Norton 6
Suzie Inman 7*
Holly Tucker 8,18
Shawn Davis 11,58,85,274,275
George Moore 15,88
Dr Sandra Austin 16,286*
Dean Ransdell 30
Lori Bailey 40,49
Jennifer Sells 44,47
Becky Graham 58
Tina Veal-Gooch 71
Kim Icenhower 73
Amanda Manca 76
Tony Dollarhide 83,91
Jennell Ingram 273
Cathy Klopper 285
Anita Clay 2
Myron Stringer 3
Kaye Oliver 5
Suzie Inman 7
Christy Tidwell 8,74
Jamie Friday 8
Autumn Thomas 15
Joann Rice 15,79,93
Rusty Ogburn 27,76,92,295
Kim Lee 40,49
Amy Frierson 43,46
April Davis 58
Amy Nix 68
Jennifer Beck 73
Debra Shelby 74
Monica Harrison 81
Stacy Courson 90*
Georgette Duke 274*
Felita Gilmore 286

Public Schs..Principal	Grd	Prgm	Enr/#Cls	SN	
Dunbar Early Education Center 2315 W 10th St, Texarkana 75501 Lakesha Taylor	PK-PK	AT	306 20	98%	903/794-8112 Fax 903/794-5841
Eschool Prep Virtual Sch 4241 Summerhill Rd, Texarkana 75503 **Nanette Power**	5-11		1,000		903/794-3651
Highland Park Elem Sch 401 W 25th St, Texarkana 75503 Jennifer Cross	PK-5	T	368 17	95%	903/794-8001 Fax 903/793-1702
Jones Early Literacy Center 2600 W 15th St, Texarkana 75501 Melodie White	K-2	T	402 30	99%	903/793-4871 Fax 903/793-7596
Morriss Elem Sch 4826 University Park, Texarkana 75503 Brandy Debenport	K-5		407	22%	903/791-2262 Fax 903/798-6875
Nash Elem Sch 100 E Burton St, Nash 75569 Patti O'Bannon	PK-5	AT	691 27	78%	903/838-4321 Fax 903/831-7158
ⓐ Options Academic High Sch 3201 Lincoln Ave, Texarkana 75503 Amy Doss	9-12	T	64 3	65%	903/793-5632 Fax 903/798-2131
Spring Lake Park Elem Sch 4324 Ghio Fish Blvd, Texarkana 75503 Anne Slade	PK-5	T	374 14	85%	903/794-7525 Fax 903/255-3270
Texas High Sch 4001 Summerhill Rd, Texarkana 75503 Carla DuPree	9-12	TV	1,808 100	51%	903/794-3891 Fax 903/792-8971
Texas Middle Sch 2100 College Dr, Texarkana 75503 Tim Lambert	6-8	T	1,454 90	63%	903/793-5631 Fax 903/792-2935
Waggoner Creek Elem Sch 6335 Gibson Ln, Texarkana 75503 Angie Griffin	K-5		293	50%	903/255-3301 Fax 903/223-7945
Wake Village Elem Sch 400 Wildcat Dr, Wake Village 75501 Mindy Gennings	PK-5	AT	639 38	80%	903/838-4261 Fax 903/255-3272
Westlawn Elem Sch 410 Westlawn Dr, Texarkana 75501 Taryn Givan	3-5	T	347 27	96%	903/223-4252 Fax 903/223-4262

BOWIE PRIVATE SCHOOLS

Private Schs..Principal	Grd	Prgm	Enr/#Cls	SN	
Bethel SDA Sch 489 S Kings Hwy, Texarkana 75501 Galsmine Ellis	K-8		13 2		903/838-4215 Fax 903/832-6216
St James Day Sch 5501 N State Line Ave, Texarkana 75503 Cheryl Brown	PK-6		165 10		903/793-5554 Fax 903/793-1775

BRAZORIA COUNTY

BRAZORIA PUBLIC SCHOOLS

- **Alvin Ind School Dist** PID: 01001382   281/388-1130
  301 E House St, Alvin 77511   Fax 281/388-2719

Schools: 29 \ **Teachers:** 1,535 \ **Students:** 25,926 \ **Special Ed Students:** 2,322 \ **LEP Students:** 3,658 \ **Ethnic:** Asian 10%, African American 18%, Hispanic 43%, Caucasian 29% \ **Exp:** $494 (High) \ **Poverty:** 13% \ **Title I:** $3,076,354 \ **Special Education:** $3,317,000 \ **Open-Close:** 08/15 - 05/22 \ **DTBP:** $181 (High) \

Carol Nelson 1
Dr Daniel Combs 2,15,19,71
David Bolton 3
Jeff Dungen 5
Dr Loree Bruton 7,11,15,36,58
Dr Kathy Windsor 8,68,79*
Allen Roberts 15
Lisa Savage 20,23
Charlotte Liptack 39,48
Erica Price 42
Paula Camacho 57,89,271
Cheryl Ryan 2
Mickie Dietrich 2
Jennifer Basich 4
Mike Bass 6
Jennifer Valdez 8,15,37,270
Kathy Windsor 11
Don Rabalais 16,73,76,98
Christina Rice-Wiltz 27,31,95
Virginia Lively 39*
Diane Peltier 45*
Carl Hauberd 67

1	Superintendent	8	Curric/Instruct K-12	19	Chief Financial Officer	29	Family/Consumer Science	39	Social Studies K-12	49	English/Lang Arts Elem	59	Special Education Elem	69	Academic Assessment
2	Bus/Finance/Purchasing	9	Curric/Instruct Elem	20	Art K-12	30	Adult Education	40	Social Studies Elem	50	English/Lang Arts Sec	60	Special Education Sec	70	Research/Development
3	Buildings And Grounds	10	Curric/Instruct Sec	21	Art Elem	31	Career/Sch-to-Work K-12	41	Social Studies Sec	51	Reading K-12	61	Foreign/World Lang K-12	71	Public Information
4	Food Service	11	Federal Program	22	Art Sec	32	Career/Sch-to-Work Elem	42	Science K-12	52	Reading Elem	62	Foreign/World Lang Elem	72	Summer School
5	Transportation	12	Title I	23	Music K-12	33	Career/Sch-to-Work Sec	43	Science Elem	53	Reading Sec	63	Foreign/World Lang Sec	73	Instructional Tech
6	Athletic	13	Title V	24	Music Elem	34	Early Childhood Ed	44	Science Sec	54	Remedial Reading K-12	64	Religious Education K-12	74	Inservice Training
7	Health Services	15	Asst Superintendent	25	Music Sec	35	Health/Phys Education	45	Math K-12	55	Remedial Reading Elem	65	Religious Education Elem	75	Marketing/Distributive
		16	Instructional Media Svcs	26	Business Education	36	Guidance Services K-12	46	Math Elem	56	Remedial Reading Sec	66	Religious Education Sec	76	Info Systems
		17	Chief Operations Officer	27	Career & Tech Ed	37	Guidance Services Elem	47	Math Sec	57	Bilingual/ELL	67	School Board President	77	Psychological Assess
		18	Chief Academic Officer	28	Technology Education	38	Guidance Services Sec	48	English/Lang Arts K-12	58	Special Education K-12	68	Teacher Personnel	78	Affirmative Action

Texas School Directory

Brazoria County

Kim Alvarez 68
Brent Shaw 69,294
Mike Putnal 91
Melba Morales 68
John Wilds 84,295

Public Schs..Principal	Grd	Prgm	Enr/#Cls	SN	
Alvin Elem Sch 1910 Rosharon Rd, Alvin 77511 Tracy Olvera	3-5	T	523 36	62%	281/585-2511 Fax 281/331-2217
Alvin High Sch 802 S Johnson St, Alvin 77511 Juan Briseno	9-12	ATV	2,766	50%	281/245-3000 Fax 281/331-3053
Alvin ISD Career & Tech Ed Ctr 7381 Lewis Ln, Manvel 77578 Dr Kathy Windsor		Voc	250		281/245-2160
Alvin Junior High Sch 2300 W South St, Alvin 77511 Leroy Castro	6-8	AT	847 60	59%	281/245-2770 Fax 281/331-5926
Alvin Primary Sch 2200 W Parkway Dr, Alvin 77511 Karla Klyng	PK-2	T	588 37	67%	281/585-2531 Fax 281/331-9888
Ⓐ Assets Academy 605 W House St, Alvin 77511 **Brandy Johanson**	9-12	T	156 4	56%	281/331-1690 Fax 281/331-1667
Bill Hasse Elem Sch 1200 House St, Alvin 77511 Diana Baker	PK-5	T	766 26	68%	281/585-3397 Fax 281/331-1190
Don Jeter Elem Sch 2455 County Road 58, Manvel 77578 Tina McCorkle	PK-5	T	826	71%	281/245-3055 Fax 281/489-4630
Ⓨ Dr James Red Duke Elem Sch 11330 Magnolia Pkwy, Manvel 77578 Fulvia Shaw	PK-5	M	533	22%	281/245-3400 Fax 281/489-1760
E C Mason Elem Sch 7400 Lewis Ln, Manvel 77578 Dixie Jones	PK-5	T	690 35	52%	281/245-2832 Fax 281/245-3777
Fairview Junior High Sch 2600 County Road 190, Alvin 77511 Gregory Bingham	6-8	T	723	63%	281/245-3100 Fax 281/245-3213
G W Harby Junior High Sch 1500 Heights Rd, Alvin 77511 **Elizabeth Lawson**	6-8	T	756	65%	281/585-6626 Fax 281/388-2247
Glenn York Elem Sch 2720 Kingsley Dr, Pearland 77584 Lisa Hicks	PK-5		871	20%	281/245-2100 Fax 713/340-1797
Hood-Case Elem Sch 1450 Heights Rd, Alvin 77511 Donna Reynolds	PK-5	T	672 40	73%	281/585-5786 Fax 281/388-0692
Laura Ingalls Wilder Elem Sch 2225 Kingsley Dr, Pearland 77584 Stacie Vanloenen	PK-5		841 42	20%	281/245-3090 Fax 713/340-0694
Manvel High Sch 19601 Highway 6, Manvel 77578 **Aneiqua Flowers**	9-12	TV	1,826	46%	281/245-2232 Fax 281/245-2268
Manvel Junior High Sch 7302 McCoy Rd, Manvel 77578 Robert Ford	6-8		1,132		281/245-3700 Fax 281/692-9078
Mark Twain Elem Sch 345 Kendall Crest Dr, Alvin 77511 Brenda Vincent	PK-5	T	775 43	78%	281/585-5318 Fax 281/331-2584
Mary Burks Marek Elem Sch 1947 Kirby St, Pearland 77584 Roman Nieto	PK-5		764	24%	281/245-3232 Fax 281/436-3796
Melba Passmore Elem Sch 600 Kost Rd, Alvin 77511 Rosemary Reed	PK-5	T	684 55	64%	281/585-6696 Fax 281/331-6697
Meridiana Elem Sch 9815 Meridiana Pkwy, Iowa Colony 77583 Julie Weiss	PK-5	T	708	48%	281/245-3636 Fax 281/245-3665
Nolan Ryan Junior High Sch 11500 Shadow Creek Pkwy, Pearland 77584 Ashley Marquez	6-8		1,099	21%	281/245-3210 Fax 281/245-3221
Pomona Elem Sch 4480 Kirby Dr, Manvel 77578 **Victoria Kwan**	PK-5		402		281/245-3670 Fax 281/245-2412
Robert L Stevenson Primary Sch 4715 Mustang Rd, Alvin 77511 Kim Graham	PK-2	T	595 33	71%	281/585-3349 Fax 281/245-2904
Rodeo Palms Junior High Sch 101 Palm Desert Dr, Manvel 77578 Aeniqua Flowers	6-8	T	969 30	53%	281/245-2078 Fax 281/489-8169
Savannah Lakes Elem Sch 5151 Savannah Pkwy, Rosharon 77583 Charles Bagley	PK-5	T	844	51%	281/245-3214 Fax 281/245-3161
Shadow Creek High Sch 11850 Broadway St, Pearland 77584 Kelly Hestand	9-12		2,180	33%	281/245-3800 Fax 281/245-3901
Shirley Dill Brothers Elem Sch 2910 Half Moon Bay Dr, Pearland 77584 Krystal Hawks	PK-5		770		281/388-1130
Walt Disney Elem Sch 5000 Mustang Rd, Alvin 77511 Dale Tribble	3-5	T	542 30	65%	281/585-6234 Fax 281/585-6503

● **Angleton Ind School Dist** PID: 01001473   979/864-8000
1900 N Downing Rd, Angleton 77515   Fax 979/864-8070

Schools: 9 \ *Teachers:* 413 \ *Students:* 6,787 \ *Special Ed Students:* 648 \ *LEP Students:* 711 \ *College-Bound:* 56% \ *Ethnic:* African American 11%, Hispanic 49%, Native American: 2%, Caucasian 38% \ *Exp:* $268 (Med) \ *Poverty:* 14% \ *Title I:* $1,191,291 \ *Special Education:* $1,201,000 \ *Open-Close:* 08/19 - 05/22 \ *DTBP:* $176 (High) \

Phil Edwards 1
Kirk Crim 3
Tracy Turner 4
Jason Brittain 6*
Vicki Harmon 9
Roy Gardner 16,27,31,88*
Michelle Lebleu 58,77
Cindy Pullen 68
Jeff Stout 73
James Gayle 91*
Allison Hemphill 298
Connie Cox 2
Amy Anderson 4
Angel Kersten 5
Mark Comneck 8,15
Lisa Davis 10
Marbella Hooper 57,81*
Regina Bieri 67
Hanna Chalmers 71
Kalean Bowie 79
Brian Heironimus 295

Public Schs..Principal	Grd	Prgm	Enr/#Cls	SN	
Angleton High Sch 1 Campus Dr, Angleton 77515 Anthony Smedley	9-12	TV	1,995 200	54%	979/864-8001 Fax 979/848-9865
Angleton Junior High Sch 1201 E Henderson Rd, Angleton 77515 Alice Clayton	6-8	TV	1,464 50	63%	979/864-8002 Fax 979/864-8675
Ⓐ Cats Academy-Student Alt Ctr 300 S Walker St, Angleton 77515 Colleen Tribble	5-12	V	6 3		979/864-8003 Fax 979/864-8736
Central Elem Sch 429 E Locust St, Angleton 77515 Maria MacEdo	PK-5	T	640 34	76%	979/864-8004 Fax 979/864-8704
Frontier Elem Sch 5200 Airline Rd, Angleton 77515 Stephanie Ramirez	K-5	T	425 18	59%	979/864-8005 Fax 979/864-8715

79	Student Personnel	91	Safety/Security	275	Response To Intervention	298	Grant Writer/Ptnrships	School Programs	Social Media
80	Driver Ed/Safety	92	Magnet School	277	Remedial Math K-12	750	Chief Innovation Officer	A = Alternative Program	
81	Gifted/Talented	93	Parental Involvement	280	Literacy Coach	751	Chief of Staff	G = Adult Classes	= Facebook
82	Video Services	95	Tech Prep Program	285	STEM	752	Social Emotional Learning	M = Magnet Program	
83	Substance Abuse Prev	97	Chief Infomation Officer	286	Digital Learning			T = Title I Schoolwide	= Twitter
84	Erate	98	Chief Technology Officer	288	Common Core Standards	Other School Types		V = Career & Tech Ed Programs	
85	AIDS Education	270	Character Education	294	Accountability	Ⓐ = Alternative School			
88	Alternative/At Risk	271	Migrant Education	295	Network System	Ⓒ = Charter School		New Schools are shaded	
89	Multi-Cultural Curriculum	273	Teacher Mentor	296	Title II Programs	Ⓜ = Magnet School		New Superintendents and Principals are bold	
90	Social Work	274	Before/After Sch	297	Webmaster	Ⓨ = Year-Round School		Personnel with email addresses are underscored	

TX—51

Brazoria County — Market Data Retrieval

Northside Elem Sch 1000 Ridgecrest St, Angleton 77515 Laurie Gonzalez	PK-5		444 30		979/864-8006 Fax 979/864-8696
Rancho Isabella Elem Sch 100 Corral Loop, Angleton 77515 Christopher Kocurek	PK-5	T	359 20	53%	979/864-8007 Fax 979/864-8725
Southside Elem Sch 1200 Park Ln, Angleton 77515 Jerri McNeill	PK-5	T	388 27	73%	979/864-8008 Fax 979/864-8730
Westside Elem Sch 1001 W Mulberry St, Angleton 77515 Robin Braun	PK-5	T	1,083 30	72%	979/848-8990 Fax 979/864-8686

● **Brazosport Ind School Dist** PID: 01001540   979/730-7000
301 W Brazoswood Dr, Clute 77531   Fax 979/266-2409

Schools: 18 \ *Teachers:* 802 \ *Students:* 12,345 \ *Special Ed Students:* 926
\ *LEP Students:* 1,328 \ *College-Bound:* 83% \ *Ethnic:* Asian 2%,
African American 8%, Hispanic 54%, Native American: 1%, Caucasian
36% \ *Exp:* $273 (Med) \ *Poverty:* 15% \ *Title I:* $2,798,743 \
Special Education: $2,651,000 \ *Open-Close:* 08/14 - 05/21 \ *DTBP:* $188
(High) \ f t

Danny Massey	1	Kaley Crisp	2	
Rebecca Kelley	2,19	Monty Burger	3,17,73,98	
Zeke Whintjen	3	Rachel Arthur	4	
John Craig	5	Dean DeAtley	6*	
Molly James	7,85	Clara Sale-Davis	8,18,288	
John Murtell	9	Ryan Cole	11,34,271	
Brent Jaco	15,751	Jay Whitehead	15,68,74,79,273	
Brian Cole	16,95,286	David Mendoza	28,73,76,295	
Jessie Jennings	31	Alan Weddell	35	
Allison Jasso	36	Angela McCabe	39	
Sandra Consillo	45	Kristen Piper	48,51,54	
Alta Gace-DelGado	57,89,93*	Lorin Furlow	58,77,90,296	
Mason Howard	67	Mari Lou Dodhany	69,73	
Ron Redden	69,294	Kristi Susen	71,97*	
Robin Pelton	79,83,270,275	Dedee Wilson	81,92	
Kristen Demland	286	Lindsey Blackstock	286	
Amber Casey	297			

Public Schs..Principal	Grd	Prgm	Enr/#Cls	SN	
A P Beutel Elem Sch 300 Ligustrum St, Lake Jackson 77566 Laura Morris	PK-4	T	620 50	35%	979/730-7165 Fax 979/292-2821 f t
Bess Brannen Elem Sch 802 That Way St, Lake Jackson 77566 Julie Evans	PK-4	T	579 28	32%	979/730-7170 Fax 979/292-2834 f t
Brazosport High Sch 1800 W 2nd St, Freeport 77541 Richard Yoes	9-12	GTV	1,023 70	64%	979/730-7260 Fax 979/730-7366 f t
Brazoswood High Sch 302 W Brazoswood Dr, Clute 77531 Rita Pintavalle	9-12	V	2,406	33%	979/730-7300 Fax 979/266-2447 f
Clute Intermediate Sch 421 E Main St, Clute 77531 Chris Loftin	5-8	T	905 120	66%	979/730-7230 Fax 979/730-7363
Elisabeth Ney Elem Sch 308 Winding Way St, Lake Jackson 77566 Vicky Parr	PK-4	T	454 50	50%	979/730-7190 Fax 979/292-2829 f t
Freeport Elem Sch 1200 W 11th St, Freeport 77541 Maria Espinoza	PK-1	T	648 20	88%	979/730-7175 Fax 979/233-9671 f t
Freeport Intermediate Sch 1815 W 4th St, Freeport 77541 Ian White	7-8	T	464 40	74%	979/730-7240 Fax 979/237-6329 f t
Gladys Polk Elem Sch 600 Audubon, Richwood 77531 Tara Fulton	PK-4	T	520 25	52%	979/730-7200 Fax 979/730-7350 f t
Grady B Rasco Middle Sch 92 Lake Rd, Lake Jackson 77566 Jennifer Gonzalez	5-6	T	822 40	41%	979/730-7225 Fax 979/292-2817 f t
Lake Jackson Intermediate Sch 100 Oyster Creek Dr, Lake Jackson 77566 Susan Wood	7-8		895 50	33%	979/730-7250 Fax 979/292-2804
ⓐ Lighthouse Learning Center 1035 Dixie Dr, Clute 77531 Dr A'Lesia Land	1-12	T	58 20	65%	979/730-7340 Fax 979/730-7369 f t
Madge Griffith Elem Sch 101 Lexington Ave, Clute 77531 Karen Matt	PK-4		535 28		979/730-7180 Fax 979/266-2469
O M Roberts Elem Sch 110 Cedar St, Lake Jackson 77566 Jennifer Nabors	PK-4	T	519 25	53%	979/730-7205 Fax 979/292-2825
R O'Hara Lanier Middle Sch 522 N Avenue B, Freeport 77541 Bridgette Percle	5-6	T	441 32	82%	979/730-7220 Fax 979/237-6348 f t
Stephen F Austin STEM Academy 7351 Stephen F Austin Rd, Freeport 77541 Brian Brooks	PK-6	T	303 19	63%	979/730-7160 Fax 979/237-6341 f t
T W Ogg Elem Sch 208 N Lazy Ln, Clute 77531 Kristine Traylor	PK-4	T	494 32	79%	979/730-7195 Fax 979/266-2488 f t
Velasco Elem Sch 401 N Gulf Blvd, Freeport 77541 Margaret Meadows	2-4	T	638 40	82%	979/730-7210 Fax 979/237-6318

● **Columbia Brazoria ISD** PID: 01001710   979/345-5147
520 S 16th St, West Columbia 77486   Fax 979/345-4890

Schools: 5 \ *Teachers:* 207 \ *Students:* 3,135 \ *Special Ed Students:* 259
\ *LEP Students:* 168 \ *College-Bound:* 53% \ *Ethnic:* African American
11%, Hispanic 29%, Caucasian 59% \ *Exp:* $322 (High) \ *Poverty:* 11% \
Title I: $498,405 \ *Special Education:* $692,000 \ *Open-Close:* 08/20 -
05/22 \ *DTBP:* $177 (High)

Steven Galloway	1	Jason Tracy	2	
Justen Williams	3	Scott Williams	3	
Ann Edwards	4	Debbie Jones	5	
Herman Ornelas	5	Brant Mascheck	6	
Patti Heidel	8,54,69,275,280	Lynn Grell-Boethel	11,36,57,77,83,88,296	
Chris Miller	15	Greg Fields	16,73,295	
Jennifer Kelly	58*	Jonathan Champagne	67	
Cyndy Pullen	273	Aaron Murphy	295	

Public Schs..Principal	Grd	Prgm	Enr/#Cls	SN	
Barrow Elem Sch 112 Gaines St, Brazoria 77422 Tara Belote	PK-6	T	574 35	63%	979/991-1740 Fax 979/798-6784
Columbia High Sch 521 S 16th St, West Columbia 77486 Robert Mowles	9-12	ATV	898 55	47%	979/799-1720 Fax 979/345-6785
West Brazos Junior High Sch 111 Roustabout Dr, Brazoria 77422 Alfred Black	7-8	AT	488 30	54%	979/991-1730 Fax 979/798-8000
West Columbia Elem Sch 711 S Gray Ave, West Columbia 77486 Roxana Bolton	PK-6	T	824 30	52%	979/799-1760 Fax 979/345-3170
Wild Peach Elem Sch 3311 County Road 353, Brazoria 77422 Mary McCarthy	PK-6	T	351 18	67%	979/991-1750 Fax 979/798-9198

---

1 Superintendent	8 Curric/Instruct K-12	19 Chief Financial Officer	29 Family/Consumer Science	39 Social Studies K-12	49 English/Lang Arts Elem	59 Special Education Elem	69 Academic Assessment
2 Bus/Finance/Purchasing	9 Curric/Instruct Elem	20 Art K-12	30 Adult Education	40 Social Studies Elem	50 English/Lang Arts Sec	60 Special Education Sec	70 Research/Development
3 Buildings And Grounds	10 Curric/Instruct Sec	21 Art Elem	31 Career/Sch-to-Work K-12	41 Social Studies Sec	51 Reading K-12	61 Foreign/World Lang K-12	71 Public Information
4 Food Service	11 Federal Program	22 Art Sec	32 Career/Sch-to-Work Elem	42 Science K-12	52 Reading Elem	62 Foreign/World Lang Elem	72 Summer School
5 Transportation	12 Title I	23 Music K-12	33 Career/Sch-to-Work Sec	43 Science Elem	53 Reading Sec	63 Foreign/World Lang Sec	73 Instructional Tech
6 Athletic	13 Title V	24 Music Elem	34 Early Childhood Ed	44 Science Sec	54 Remedial Reading K-12	64 Religious Education K-12	74 Inservice Training
7 Health Services	15 Asst Superintendent	25 Music Sec	35 Health/Phys Education	45 Math K-12	55 Remedial Reading Elem	65 Religious Education Elem	75 Marketing/Distributive
	16 Instructional Media Svcs	26 Business Education	36 Guidance Services K-12	46 Math Elem	56 Remedial Reading Sec	66 Religious Education Sec	76 Info Systems
	17 Chief Operations Officer	27 Career & Tech Ed	37 Guidance Services Elem	47 Math Sec	57 Bilingual/ELL	67 School Board President	77 Psychological Assess
	18 Chief Academic Officer	28 Technology Education	38 Guidance Services Sec	48 English/Lang Arts K-12	58 Special Education K-12	68 Teacher Personnel	78 Affirmative Action

Texas School Directory

Brazoria County

Damon Ind School Dist PID: 01001796
1211 Mulcahy St, Damon 77430
979/742-3457
Fax 979/742-3275

Schools: 1 \ **Teachers:** 16 \ **Students:** 200 \ **Special Ed Students:** 29 \ **LEP Students:** 31 \ **Ethnic:** African American 2%, Hispanic 56%, Caucasian 43% \ **Exp:** $326 (High) \ **Poverty:** 27% \ **Title I:** $101,790 \ **Open-Close:** 08/26 - 05/29 \ **DTBP:** $340 (High)

David Hayward 1	Bubba Schneider 67	
Shelly Schneider 286*		

Public Schs..Principal	Grd	Prgm	Enr/#Cls	SN	
Damon Sch 1211 Mulcahy Street, Damon 77430 **David Hayward**	PK-8	T	200 12	98%	979/742-3457

Danbury Ind School Dist PID: 01001813
5611 Panther Dr, Danbury 77534
979/922-1218
Fax 979/922-8246

Schools: 3 \ **Teachers:** 54 \ **Students:** 750 \ **Special Ed Students:** 58 \ **LEP Students:** 30 \ **College-Bound:** 67% \ **Ethnic:** Asian 1%, Hispanic 21%, Native American: 1%, Caucasian 77% \ **Exp:** $503 (High) \ **Poverty:** 8% \ **Title I:** $73,047 \ **Open-Close:** 08/15 - 05/21 \ **DTBP:** $73 (Low)

Greg Anderson 1	Cynthia Wendell 2
Disa Schulze 3,4,5,91	Sherry Phillips 11,15,57
Ace Filipp 16*	Debra Murphey 37
Lilly Guu 38*	Daryl Peltier 67
Stacey Matheson 73,76,295*	Sherry Phillips 273*

Public Schs..Principal	Grd	Prgm	Enr/#Cls	SN	
Danbury Elem Sch 2222 Ave F, Danbury 77534 Jennifer Williams	PK-5	AT	343 20	32%	979/922-8787 Fax 979/922-1589
Danbury High Sch 5611 Panther Dr, Danbury 77534 **Crystal Pounds**	9-12	AV	231 15	14%	979/922-1226 Fax 979/922-1051
Danbury Middle Sch 5611 Panther Dr, Danbury 77534 Crystal Pounds	6-8	A	189 11	24%	979/922-1226 Fax 979/922-1051

Pearland Ind School Dist PID: 01001849
1928 N Main St, Pearland 77581
281/485-3203
Fax 281/412-1560

Schools: 23 \ **Teachers:** 1,343 \ **Students:** 21,917 \ **Special Ed Students:** 1,902 \ **LEP Students:** 1,588 \ **Ethnic:** Asian 11%, African American 16%, Hispanic 34%, Caucasian 39% \ **Exp:** $233 (Med) \ **Poverty:** 6% \ **Title I:** $1,652,731 \ **Special Education:** $2,730,000 \ **Open-Close:** 08/15 - 05/21 \ **DTBP:** $182 (High) \ 📘 📧

Dr John Kelly 1	Jorgannie Carter 2,19,76
Don Tellis 3,91	Dorothy Simpson 4
Raul Cruz 5	Ben Pardo 6
Noel Gray 8,54,74,277	Dr Nyla Watson 8,15,77,273
Thomas Bell 8,20*	Dr Brenda Waters 9,15
Sonia Serrano 10,15	Cary Partin 15
Dr David Moody 15,68,79	Nanette Weimer 15
Kim Hocott 16,71	Dr Toby Nix 27,31,95
Greg Bartay 28,295	Chenda Moore 36,83,88,275
Dr Susana Fuenmayor 57	Lisa Nixon 58
Charles Gooden 67	Ellen Akers 69
Victor Bushfield 297*	Donna Tate 298*

Public Schs..Principal	Grd	Prgm	Enr/#Cls	SN	
Alexander Middle Sch 3001 Old Alvin Rd, Pearland 77581 Brad Hayes	5-6		806	26%	832/736-6700 Fax 281/485-1115
Barbara Cockrell Elem Sch 3500 McHard Rd, Pearland 77581 Kathy Behrendsen	PK-4	T	767	31%	832/736-6600 Fax 281/412-7763
Berry Miller Junior High Sch 3301 Manvel Rd, Pearland 77584 **Tony Barcelona**	7-8		906	15%	281/997-3900 Fax 281/997-7893
C J Harris Elem Sch 2314 Schleider Dr, Pearland 77581 Brenda Keimig	PK-4		637 33	40%	281/485-4024 Fax 281/412-1559
Challenger Elem Sch 9434 Hughes Ranch Rd, Pearland 77584 **Becky Morris**	PK-4		683 35	26%	281/485-7912 Fax 281/412-1105
E A Lawhon Elem Sch 5810 Brookside Rd, Pearland 77581 Jennifer Walker	PK-4	T	818 40	54%	281/412-1445 Fax 281/412-1448
Glenda Dawson High Sch 2050 Cullen Pkwy, Pearland 77581 Kelly Holt	9-12	V	2,518	19%	281/412-8800 Fax 281/727-1660
H C Carleston Elem Sch 3010 Harkey Rd, Pearland 77584 Amy Beverly	PK-4	T	814 48	51%	281/412-1412 Fax 281/412-1415
Leon Sablatura Middle Sch 2201 N Galveston Ave, Pearland 77581 Verna Tipton	5-6	T	830 65	37%	281/412-1500 Fax 281/412-1504
Magnolia Elem Sch 5350 Magnolia Pkwy, Pearland 77584 Sharon Gifford	PK-4		867 22	39%	281/727-1750 Fax 281/692-1437
Massey Ranch Elem Sch 3900 Manvel Rd, Pearland 77584 Melanie Grote	PK-4		681	28%	281/727-1700 Fax 281/692-0300
Ⓐ Pace Center 2314 Old Alvin Rd, Pearland 77581 Kimberly Darden	9-12	T	82 14	52%	281/412-1599 Fax 281/412-1580
Pearland High Sch 3775 S Main St, Pearland 77581 John Palombo	9-12	AGV	3,053 189	29%	281/997-7445 Fax 281/412-1113
Pearland Jr High School East 2315 Old Alvin Rd, Pearland 77581 Charles Allen	7-8	A	782 60	25%	281/485-2481 Fax 281/412-1203
Pearland Jr High School South 4719 Bailey Rd, Pearland 77584 Jason Frerking	7-8	T	890 50	42%	281/727-1500 Fax 281/727-1580
Pearland Jr High School West 2337 N Galveston Ave, Pearland 77581 Dana Miles	7-8	AT	816 60	36%	281/412-1222 Fax 281/412-1228
Robert Turner Colege-Career HS 4717 Bailey Rd, Pearland 77584 Kai Bouchard	9-12	V	1,200	28%	281/727-1600 Fax 281/727-1616
Rogers Middle Sch 3121 Manvel Rd, Pearland 77584 Lakesha Vaughn	5-6		814 35	14%	832/736-6400 Fax 281/736-6444
Rustic Oak Elem Sch 1302 Rustic Ln, Pearland 77581 Beth West	PK-4		706 38	22%	281/482-5400 Fax 281/996-3658
Sam Jamison Middle Sch 2506 Woody Rd, Pearland 77581 Sharon Bradley	5-6	T	814 60	39%	281/412-1440 Fax 281/412-1461
Shadycrest Elem Sch 2405 Shadybend Dr, Pearland 77581 Michelle Kiefer	PK-4		683 42	17%	281/412-1404 Fax 281/412-1401
Silvercrest Elem Sch 3003 Southwyck Pkwy, Pearland 77584 Lori Campbell	PK-4		727 40	6%	832/736-6000 Fax 713/436-2209

---

79 Student Personnel	91 Safety/Security	275 Response To Intervention	298 Grant Writer/Ptnrships
80 Driver Ed/Safety	92 Magnet School	277 Remedial Math K-12	750 Chief Innovation Officer
81 Gifted/Talented	93 Parental Involvement	280 Literacy Coach	751 Chief of Staff
82 Video Services	95 Tech Prep Program	285 STEM	752 Social Emotional Learning
83 Substance Abuse Prev	97 Chief Infomation Officer	286 Digital Learning	
84 Erate	98 Chief Technology Officer	288 Common Core Standards	**Other School Types**
85 AIDS Education	270 Character Education	294 Accountability	Ⓐ = Alternative School
88 Alternative/At Risk	271 Migrant Education	295 Network System	Ⓒ = Charter School
89 Multi-Cultural Curriculum	273 Teacher Mentor	296 Title II Programs	Ⓜ = Magnet School
90 Social Work	274 Before/After Sch	297 Webmaster	Ⓨ = Year-Round School

School Programs
A = Alternative Program
G = Adult Classes
M = Magnet Program
T = Title I Schoolwide
V = Career & Tech Ed Programs

Social Media
📘 = Facebook
📧 = Twitter

New Schools are shaded
New Superintendents and Principals are bold
Personnel with email addresses are underscored

TX—53

Brazos County

Market Data Retrieval

Silverlake Elem Sch — PK-4 — 730 — 11% — 713/436-8000
2550 County Road 90, Pearland 77584 — 45 — Fax 713/436-8008
Shayla McGrew

- **Sweeny Ind School Dist** PID: 01001904 — 979/491-8000
1310 N Elm St, Sweeny 77480 — Fax 979/491-8030

Schools: 3 \ *Teachers:* 136 \ *Students:* 1,969 \ *Special Ed Students:* 159 \ *LEP Students:* 52 \ *College-Bound:* 57% \ *Ethnic:* African American 13%, Hispanic 25%, Caucasian 61% \ *Exp:* $296 (Med) \ *Poverty:* 16% \ *Title I:* $462,818 \ *Special Education:* $363,000 \ *Open-Close:* 08/15 - 05/28 \ *DTBP:* $553 (High)

Dr Tory Hill 1	Amy Carter 2,19
Jackie Hornback 2	Stewart Crouc 3
Kathy Wolford 4	Diane McNeill 5
Brett Miksch 6*	Darin Presto 8,294
Amy Pope 11,15,69,83,88,275,294,296	Kelly Bertsch 16,73,84,295
Mark Manley 27	Renee Mitchell 36*
Michael Heinroth 37*	Laura Genella 52*
Betty Bartness 58	Rhonda Alexander 58
Sandra Vandaveer 58	Earl Mathis 67
Gerald Nixon 68	Dedra Phillips 76
Les Kluttz 79	Michael Saul 79
LaBonne Casey 81,298	Jesse Cisneros 91
John Ideus 91*	Stacey Branch 295

Public Schs..Principal	Grd	Prgm	Enr/#Cls	SN		
Sweeny Elem Sch 709 Sycamore St, Sweeny 77480 Michael Heinroth	PK-5	T	938 71	57%	979/491-8300 Fax 979/491-8373	
Sweeny High Sch 600 Ashley Wilson Road, Sweeny 77480 William Mader	9-12	ATV	593 50	39%	979/491-8100 Fax 979/491-8171	
Sweeny Junior High Sch 800 N Elm St, Sweeny 77480 David Smothers	6-8	T	431 40	50%	979/491-8200 Fax 979/491-8274	

BRAZORIA CATHOLIC SCHOOLS

- **Archdiocese Galveston-Houston** PID: 01027855
Listing includes only schools located in this county. See District Index for location of Diocesan Offices.

Catholic Schs..Principal	Grd	Prgm	Enr/#Cls	SN	
Our Lady Queen of Peace Sch 1600 Highway 2004, Richwood 77531 Marianne Mechura	PK-8		285 17		979/265-3909 Fax 979/265-9780
St Helen Sch 2213 Old Alvin Rd, Pearland 77581 Phyliss Coleman	K-8		237 10		281/485-2845 Fax 281/485-7607

BRAZORIA PRIVATE SCHOOLS

Private Schs..Principal	Grd	Prgm	Enr/#Cls	SN	
Angleton Christian Sch 976 Anchor Road, Angleton 77515 Terri Jones \ Steve Davis	PK-12		330 13		979/864-3842
Brazosport Christian Sch 200B Willow Dr, Lake Jackson 77566 Todd Landers	PK-12		220 25		979/297-0722 Fax 979/297-8455
Eagle Heights Christian Acad 3005 Pearland Pkwy, Pearland 77581 Lana Stahl	PK-12		330		281/485-6330 Fax 281/485-8682
First Christian Academy 2411 S Grand Blvd, Pearland 77581 Diane DuVall	PK-12		125		281/760-4201
Heritage Christian Academy 12006 Shadow Creek Pkwy, Pearland 77584 Kara Marsh	PK-5		290		713/436-8422 Fax 713/436-5350
Living Stones Christian Sch 1407 Victory Ln, Alvin 77511 Jessica Sanders	PK-12		150 16		281/331-0086 Fax 281/331-6747
Shiloh Sch 3926 Bahler Ave, Manvel 77578 Brenda Gardner-Valdes	1-12		75		281/489-1290 Fax 281/489-0167
Silverline Montessori Sch 2080 Reflection Bay Dr, Pearland 77584 Teresa Conn	PK-5		300		713/436-5070 Fax 713/436-5076
Sweeny Christian Sch 904 Texas Ave, Sweeny 77480 Lynette McKinney	PK-5		56 7		979/548-6001 Fax 979/548-0210

BRAZOS COUNTY

BRAZOS PUBLIC SCHOOLS

- **Bryan Ind School Dist** PID: 01002013 — 979/209-1000
801 S Ennis St, Bryan 77803 — Fax 979/209-1004

Schools: 24 \ *Teachers:* 1,108 \ *Students:* 16,134 \ *Special Ed Students:* 1,477 \ *LEP Students:* 3,641 \ *College-Bound:* 52% \ *Ethnic:* African American 19%, Hispanic 57%, Caucasian 24% \ *Exp:* $413 (High) \ *Poverty:* 23% \ *Title I:* $6,205,602 \ *Special Education:* $2,913,000 \ *Open-Close:* 08/20 - 05/22 \ *DTBP:* $195 (High)

Dr Christie Whitbeck 1	James Brau 2
Kevin Beesaw 2,15,275	Ronnie O'Neal 2,275
Stefanie Brumfield 2	Norris McDaniel 3
Paul Buckner 3	Steve Peterson 3
Sundy Fryrear 4	Claudell Lipscomb 5
Simeon Gates 5	Warren Lanphier 5
Lance Angel 6	Barbara Ybarra 8,15,294
Christina Richardson 8,81	Dr Leslie Holtkamp 8
Jolyn Bricker 9	Debbie Richards 10,42
Ginger Carrabine 15,751	Denise Kersten 16
Lamanda Jatzlau 16	Rachel Whitely 16
Robin Cox 16	Patrick Corbett 20,23
David Reynolds 27,31	Kevin Ross 27
Larry White 27	Rachel Curlin 34,298
Schronda McKnight 34	Janice Williamson 35
Donna Willett 36,77	Dr Wanda Baker 57,271
Dr Catherine George 58	Kate Patterson 58
Lora Ouren 58	Mark McCall 67
Carol Cune 68	Crystal Goodman 68
Dr Jill Morris 69,70,76	Hugo Ibarra 71
Matthew LeBlanc 71	Jana Wenzel 73
Julea Johnson 73	Kelli Norgaard 74
Jennifer Lemons 76,79	Robert Hayes 76
Dr Shantina Dixon 77	Juana Garcia 271
Charlie Zapalac 295	Chris Cannon 295

1 Superintendent	8 Curric/Instruct K-12	19 Chief Financial Officer	29 Family/Consumer Science	39 Social Studies K-12	49 English/Lang Arts Elem	59 Special Education Elem	69 Academic Assessment
2 Bus/Finance/Purchasing	9 Curric/Instruct Elem	20 Art K-12	30 Adult Education	40 Social Studies Elem	50 English/Lang Arts Sec	60 Special Education Sec	70 Research/Development
3 Buildings And Grounds	10 Curric/Instruct Sec	21 Art Elem	31 Career/Sch-to-Work K-12	41 Social Studies Sec	51 Reading K-12	61 Foreign/World Lang K-12	71 Public Information
4 Food Service	11 Federal Program	22 Art Sec	32 Career/Sch-to-Work Elem	42 Science K-12	52 Reading Elem	62 Foreign/World Lang Elem	72 Summer School
5 Transportation	12 Title I	23 Music K-12	33 Career/Sch-to-Work Sec	43 Science Elem	53 Reading Sec	63 Foreign/World Lang Sec	73 Instructional Tech
6 Athletic	13 Title V	24 Music Elem	34 Early Childhood Ed	44 Science Sec	54 Remedial Reading K-12	64 Religious Education K-12	74 Inservice Training
7 Health Services	15 Asst Superintendent	25 Music Sec	35 Health/Phys Education	45 Math K-12	55 Remedial Reading Elem	65 Religious Education Elem	75 Marketing/Distributive
	16 Instructional Media Svcs	26 Business Education	36 Guidance Services K-12	46 Math Elem	56 Remedial Reading Sec	66 Religious Education Sec	76 Info Systems
	17 Chief Operations Officer	27 Career & Tech Ed	37 Guidance Services Elem	47 Math Sec	57 Bilingual/ELL	67 School Board President	77 Psychological Assess
	18 Chief Academic Officer	28 Technology Education	38 Guidance Services Sec	48 English/Lang Arts K-12	58 Special Education K-12	68 Teacher Personnel	78 Affirmative Action

Texas School Directory — Brazos County

Public Schs..Principal	Grd	Prgm	Enr/#Cls	SN	
Alton O Bowen Elem Sch 3870 Copperfield Dr, Bryan 77802 Bridget Cooper	PK-4	T	395 26	51%	979/209-1300 Fax 979/209-1306
Arthur L Davila Middle Sch 2751 N Earl Rudder Fwy, Bryan 77803 Shannon McGehee	7-8	T	1,049	80%	979/209-7150 Fax 979/209-7151
Bonham Elem Sch 3100 Wilkes St, Bryan 77803 Gloria Rhodes	PK-4	T	641 41	75%	979/209-1200 Fax 979/209-1218
Bryan Adult Learning Center 1700 Palasota Dr, Bryan 77803 Becky Collet	Adult		210 6		979/703-7740 Fax 979/209-7041
Bryan Collegiate High Sch 1901 E Villa Maria Rd, Bryan 77802 Tommy Roberts	9-12	T	466	68%	979/209-2790 Fax 979/209-2704
Crockett Elem Sch 401 Elm Ave, Bryan 77801 Debi Ehrhardt	PK-4	T	449 32	92%	979/209-2960 Fax 979/209-2965
ⓐ Disciplinary Alt Ed Program 1901 E Villa Maria Rd, Bryan 77802 Michael Watts	6-12		150	89%	979/209-2752 Fax 979/209-2754
Fannin Elem Sch 1200 Baker Ave, Bryan 77803 **Dr Desiree Caperton**	PK-4	T	460 27	94%	979/209-3800 Fax 979/209-3826
Henderson Elem Sch 801 Matous Dr, Bryan 77802 Danielle Legg	PK-4	T	580 23	80%	979/209-1560 Fax 979/209-1566
James E Rudder High Sch 3251 Austins Colony Pkwy, Bryan 77808 Mario Bye	9-12	TV	1,649	72%	979/209-7900 Fax 979/209-7901
Johnson Elem Sch 3800 Oak Hill Dr, Bryan 77802 **Amy Thomman**	PK-4	T	404 30	44%	979/209-1460 Fax 979/209-1462
Jones Elem Sch 1400 Pecan St, Bryan 77803 Linda Montoya	PK-4	T	582 21	97%	979/209-3900 Fax 979/209-3912
Kemp-Carver Elem Sch 750 Bruin Trce, Bryan 77803 Alison Boggan	PK-4	T	658 26	95%	979/209-3700 Fax 979/209-3764
Long Intermediate Sch 1106 N Harvey Mitchell Pkwy, Bryan 77803 Cody Satterfield	5-6	V	1,213 65		979/209-6500 Fax 979/209-6566
Mary Branch Elem Sch 2040 W Villa Maria Rd, Bryan 77807 Karen Kaspar	PK-4	T	483 29	76%	979/209-2900 Fax 979/209-2910
ⓐ Mary Catherine Harris Sch 1307 Memorial Dr, Bryan 77802 **Karen Kaspar**	9-12	T	228 6	79%	979/209-2812 Fax 979/209-2813
Mitchell Elem Sch 2500 Austins Colony Pkwy, Bryan 77808 Donna Wallace	PK-4	T	380 26	56%	979/209-1400 Fax 979/209-1420
Navarro Elem Sch 4619 Northwood Dr, Bryan 77803 Sara Rueda	PK-4	T	449 40	89%	979/209-1260 Fax 979/209-1270
Neal Elem Sch 801 W Martin Luther King Jr St, Bryan 77803 Juanita Collins	PK-4	T	426 30	97%	979/209-3860 Fax 979/209-3863
Rayburn Intermediate Sch 1048 N Earl Rudder Fwy, Bryan 77802 Justin Smith	5-6	V	1,186 78		979/209-6600 Fax 979/209-6611
Sam Houston Elem Sch 4501 Canterbury Dr, Bryan 77802 Mandy Wells	PK-4	T	398 21	36%	979/209-1360 Fax 979/209-1364
Stephen F Austin Middle Sch 801 S Ennis St, Bryan 77803 Rachel Layton	7-8	TV	1,189 85	69%	979/209-6700 Fax 979/209-6741
Sul Ross Elem Sch 3300 Parkway Ter, Bryan 77802 **Amy Bay**	PK-4	T	507 18	62%	979/209-1500 Fax 979/209-1513
Travis Bryan High Sch 3450 Campus Dr, Bryan 77802 Lane Buban	9-12	TV	2,309 250	64%	979/209-2400 Fax 979/209-2402

● **College Station Ind Sch Dist** PID: 01001954   979/764-5400
  1812 Welsh Ave, College Sta 77840   Fax 979/764-5492

> **Schools:** 19 \ **Teachers:** 895 \ **Students:** 14,000 \
> **Special Ed Students:** 1,116 \ **LEP Students:** 1,004 \ **College-Bound:** 64%
> \ **Ethnic:** Asian 8%, African American 14%, Hispanic 24%, Caucasian
> 54% \ **Exp:** $361 (High) \ **Poverty:** 12% \ **Title I:** $1,882,826 \
> **Special Education:** $1,806,000 \ **Open-Close:** 08/15 - 05/28 \ **DTBP:** $188
> (High) \

Dr Clark Ealy 1	Carmella Shaffer 2
Mike Martindale 2,15,19	Thad Lasater 2
John Hadley 3	Bridget Goodlett 4
Hector Silva 5	Dr Penny Tramel 8,18
Molley Perry 15,77,751	Chrissy Hester 16,36,79
Karen Ferguson 27,31	Chad Gardner 30,274
Susan Heath 34	Marla Ramirez 57*
Lindsey Fuentes 58,77	Jeff Harris 67
Nkrumah Dixon 68	Stormy Hickman 68
Becky Burghardt 69	Chuck Glenewinkel 71
David Hutchison 73*	Jeff Mann 74*
Jackie Janacek 76	Justin Grimes 83,88*
Brad Recek 295	Keith Slaughter 295

Public Schs..Principal	Grd	Prgm	Enr/#Cls	SN	
A & M Consolidated High Sch 1801 Harvey Mitchell Pkwy S, College Sta 77840 Gwendolyn Elder	9-12	V	1,713	38%	979/764-5500 Fax 979/693-0212
A & M Consolidated Middle Sch 105 Holik St, College Sta 77840 N Omar Espitia	7-8	T	911 50	47%	979/764-5575 Fax 979/764-5577
College Hills Elem Sch 1101 Williams St, College Sta 77840 Josh Hatfield	PK-4	T	734 30	56%	979/764-5565 Fax 979/764-5497
College Station High Sch 4002 Victoria Ave, College Sta 77845 Tiffany Parkerson	9-12	V	1,996		979/694-5800 Fax 979/694-5865
College Station Middle Sch 900 Rock Prairie Rd, College Sta 77845 Oliver Hadnot	7-8		1,067 48	23%	979/764-5545 Fax 979/764-5557
College View High Sch 1300 George Bush Dr, College Sta 77840 Justin Grimes	9-12	AV	65 4	41%	979/764-5540 Fax 979/764-5564
Creek View Elem Sch 1001 Eagle Ave, College Sta 77845 **Annette Roraback**	PK-4		595	35%	979/694-5890 Fax 979/694-5893
Cypress Grove Intermediate Sch 900 Graham Rd, College Sta 77845 Holly Scott	5-6		661 40	28%	979/694-5600 Fax 979/694-5604
Forest Ridge Elem Sch 1950 Greens Prairie Rd W, College Sta 77845 Teresa Katt	PK-4		667	23%	979/694-5801 Fax 979/694-5805
Greens Prairie Elem Sch 4315 Greens Prairie Trl, College Sta 77845 Donna Bairrington	PK-4		768	22%	979/694-5870 Fax 979/694-3871
Oakwood Intermediate Sch 106 Holik St, College Sta 77840 Josh Symank	5-6	T	747 33	45%	979/764-5530 Fax 979/764-5533

---

79 Student Personnel	91 Safety/Security	275 Response To Intervention	298 Grant Writer/Ptnrships	**School Programs**	**Social Media**		
80 Driver Ed/Safety	92 Magnet School	277 Remedial Math K-12	750 Chief Innovation Officer	A = Alternative Program			
81 Gifted/Talented	93 Parental Involvement	280 Literacy Coach	751 Chief of Staff	G = Adult Classes	= Facebook		
82 Video Services	95 Tech Prep Program	285 STEM	752 Social Emotional Learning	M = Magnet Program			
83 Substance Abuse Prev	97 Chief Information Officer	286 Digital Learning		T = Title I Schoolwide	= Twitter		
84 Erate	98 Chief Technology Officer	288 Common Core Standards	**Other School Types**	V = Career & Tech Ed Programs			
85 AIDS Education	270 Character Education	294 Accountability	ⓐ = Alternative School				
86 Alternative/At Risk	271 Migrant Education	295 Network System	ⓒ = Charter School	New Schools are shaded			
89 Multi-Cultural Curriculum	273 Teacher Mentor	296 Title II Programs	Ⓜ = Magnet School	New Superintendents and Principals are bold			
90 Social Work	274 Before/After Sch	297 Webmaster	Ⓨ = Year-Round School	Personnel with email addresses are underscored			

TX—55

Brewster County

Market Data Retrieval

Pebble Creek Elem Sch 200 Parkview Dr, College Sta 77845 Blaire Grande	PK-4		418 31	11% 979/764-5595 Fax 979/764-5478
Pecan Trail Interm Sch 4319 Greens Prairie Trl, College Sta 77845 Kelli Deegear	5-6		611	979/694-5874 Fax 979/694-5869
River Bend Elem Sch 4070 Holleman Dr S, College Sta 77845 Robyn Jones	PK-4		450	979/694-5841
Rock Prairie Elem Sch 3400 Welsh Ave, College Sta 77845 Jeff Durand	PK-4		633 36	38% 979/764-5570 Fax 979/764-5486
South Knoll Elem Sch 1220 Boswell St, College Sta 77840 Laura Richter	PK-4	T	667 31	55% 979/764-5580 Fax 979/764-5485
Southwood Valley Elem Sch 2700 Brothers Blvd, College Sta 77845 Alison DeLuna	PK-4	T	638 35	57% 979/764-5590 Fax 979/764-5488
Spring Creek Elem Sch 2450 Brewster Dr, College Sta 77845 Laura Casper-Teague	PK-4		640	26% 979/694-5838
Wellborn Middle Sch 15510 Royder Rd, College Sta 77845 Julia Mishler	7-8		700	979/694-5880 Fax 979/694-5881

- **Mumford Ind School Dist** PID: 01048691   979/279-3678
  9755 FM 50, Mumford 77807   Fax 979/279-5044

Schools: 1 \ *Teachers:* 38 \ *Students:* 625 \ *Special Ed Students:* 50 \ *LEP Students:* 58 \ *College-Bound:* 75% \ *Exp:* $487 (High) \ *Poverty:* 25% \ *Open-Close:* 08/19 - 05/21 \ *DTBP:* $334 (High)

Blayne Davis 1,11
Barbara Brannon 3,4,5,69,71,74,271*
Melissa McDonough 8,31,36,58,85*
Anthony Scamardo 67
Luanne Lockhart 2
Michael Scarborough 6*
Ann Swaner 16*
Flavio Saucedo 73*

Public Schs..Principal	Grd	Prgm	Enr/#Cls	SN
Mumford Sch 9755 FM 50, Mumford 77867 Blayne Davis	PK-12	V	625 50	979/279-3678

BRAZOS CATHOLIC SCHOOLS

- **Diocese of Austin Ed Office** PID: 01420568
  Listing includes only schools located in this county. See District Index for location of Diocesan Offices.

Catholic Schs..Principal	Grd	Prgm	Enr/#Cls	SN
St Joseph Catholic Sch 600 S Coulter Dr, Bryan 77803 Jim Rike	PK-12		441 31	979/822-6641 Fax 979/779-2810

BRAZOS PRIVATE SCHOOLS

Private Schs..Principal	Grd	Prgm	Enr/#Cls	SN
Aggieland Country Mont Sch 1500 Quail Run, College Sta 77845 Lynn Adams	PK-6		75 3	979/696-1674

Allen Academy 3201 Boonville Rd, Bryan 77802 Matt Rush	PK-12		310 30	979/776-0731 Fax 979/774-7769
Brazos Christian Sch 3000 W Villa Maria Rd, Bryan 77807 Jess McMaster	PK-12		430 32	979/823-1000 Fax 979/823-1774
Cornerstone Christian Academy 3200 Cavitt Ave, Bryan 77801 Rebecca Curry	K-12		93 6	979/694-8200 Fax 979/703-6263
Kor Education Sch 6110 Elmo Weedon Rd, College Sta 77845 Gena Richter	K-12		401	979/777-1213
St Michaels Episcopal Sch 2500 S College Ave, Bryan 77801 Jenny Morris	PK-12		65 23	979/822-2715 Fax 979/823-4971

BREWSTER COUNTY

BREWSTER PUBLIC SCHOOLS

- **Alpine Ind School Dist** PID: 01002192   432/837-7700
  704 W Sul Ross Ave, Alpine 79830   Fax 432/837-7740

Schools: 3 \ *Teachers:* 91 \ *Students:* 1,000 \ *Special Ed Students:* 86 \ *LEP Students:* 94 \ *College-Bound:* 67% \ *Ethnic:* Asian 1%, African American 1%, Hispanic 64%, Caucasian 34% \ *Exp:* $548 (High) \ *Poverty:* 20% \ *Title I:* $247,226 \ *Special Education:* $131,000 \ *Open-Close:* 08/21 - 05/26 \ *DTBP:* $351 (High)

Rebecca McCutchen 1
Chayo Gonzales 3,5
Jonathan Fellows 6*
Verl Obryant 34*
Eddie Netera 67
Tucker Durham 2
Liz Rayburn 4*
Nancy Roll 11,286,296,298
Mesinda Llanez 58
Darin Nance 73,295

Public Schs..Principal	Grd	Prgm	Enr/#Cls	SN
Alpine Elem Sch 200 W Avenue A, Alpine 79830 Judith Pardo	PK-4	T	449 38	57% 432/837-7730 Fax 432/837-7744
Alpine High Sch 300 E Hendryx Ave, Alpine 79830 Justin Gonzales	9-12	ATV	314 32	41% 432/837-7710 Fax 432/837-9813
Alpine Middle Sch 801 Middle School Dr, Alpine 79830 Justin Gonzales	5-8	T	331 30	47% 432/837-7720 Fax 432/837-9814

- **Marathon Ind School Dist** PID: 01002233   432/386-4431
  109 N 5th St, Marathon 79842   Fax 432/386-4395

Schools: 1 \ *Teachers:* 10 \ *Students:* 55 \ *Special Ed Students:* 4 \ *College-Bound:* 50% \ *Ethnic:* Hispanic 66%, Native American: 1%, Caucasian 33% \ *Exp:* $1,251 (High) \ *Poverty:* 10% \ *Open-Close:* 08/19 - 05/29 \ *DTBP:* $331 (High)

Guadalupe Singh 1,11
Monica Pinedo 57,83,271*
Judy Briones 67
Victoria Sanchez 2
Travis Jarrell 58*
Kelly Springfield 69,93,271*

---

1 Superintendent	8 Curric/Instruct K-12	19 Chief Financial Officer	29 Family/Consumer Science	39 Social Studies K-12	49 English/Lang Arts Elem	59 Special Education Elem	69 Academic Assessment
2 Bus/Finance/Purchasing	9 Curric/Instruct Elem	20 Art K-12	30 Adult Education	40 Social Studies Elem	50 English/Lang Arts Sec	60 Special Education Sec	70 Research/Development
3 Buildings And Grounds	10 Curric/Instruct Sec	21 Art Elem	31 Career/Sch-to-Work K-12	41 Social Studies Sec	51 Reading K-12	61 Foreign/World Lang K-12	71 Public Information
4 Food Service	11 Federal Program	22 Art Sec	32 Career/Sch-to-Work Elem	42 Science K-12	52 Reading Elem	62 Foreign/World Lang Elem	72 Summer School
5 Transportation	12 Title I	23 Music K-12	33 Career/Sch-to-Work Sec	43 Science Elem	53 Reading Sec	63 Foreign/World Lang Sec	73 Instructional Tech
6 Athletic	13 Title V	24 Music Elem	34 Early Childhood Ed	44 Science Sec	54 Remedial Reading K-12	64 Religious Education	74 Inservice Training
7 Health Services	15 Asst Superintendent	25 Music Sec	35 Health/Phys Education	45 Math K-12	55 Remedial Reading Elem	65 Religious Education Elem	75 Marketing/Distributive
	16 Instructional Media Svcs	26 Business Education	36 Guidance Services K-12	46 Math Elem	56 Remedial Reading Sec	66 Religious Education Sec	76 Info Systems
	17 Chief Operations Officer	27 Career & Tech Ed	37 Guidance Services Elem	47 Math Sec	57 Bilingual/ELL	67 School Board President	77 Psychological Assess
	18 Chief Academic Officer	28 Technology Education	38 Guidance Services Sec	48 English/Lang Arts K-12	58 Special Education K-12	68 Teacher Personnel	78 Affirmative Action

Texas School Directory | Brooks County

Public Schs..Principal	Grd	Prgm	Enr/#Cls	SN	
Marathon Sch 109 N 5th St, Marathon 79842 Danny Armstrong	PK-12	TV	55 20	87%	432/386-4431

• **San Vicente Ind School Dist** PID: 01002269   432/477-2220
195 Escuela Vista Dr, Bg BND NTL Pk 79834   Fax 432/477-2221

Schools: 1 \ *Teachers:* 5 \ *Students:* 13 \ *Special Ed Students:* 3 \
Ethnic: Hispanic 33%, Caucasian 67% \ *Exp:* $1,781 (High) \ *Poverty:* 12% \
Open-Close: 09/03 - 06/03 \ *DTBP:* $389 (High)

Eric Stoddard 1,11   Rocky Noahrip 2,73
Pamela Priddy ....57*   Mary Gibson 67
Jennifer Pena ....83,85,270*   Jeani Stoddard 285*

Public Schs..Principal	Grd	Prgm	Enr/#Cls	SN	
San Vicente Elem Sch 195 Escuela Vista Dr, Bg BND NTL Pk 79834 Eric Stoddard	PK-8		13 5	32%	432/477-2220

• **Terlingua Common School Dist** PID: 01002283   432/371-2281
550 Roadrunner Cir, Terlingua 79852   Fax 432/371-2245

Schools: 2 \ *Teachers:* 11 \ *Students:* 105 \ *Special Ed Students:* 13
\ *LEP Students:* 41 \ *College-Bound:* 95% \ *Ethnic:* Hispanic 79%,
Native American: 1%, Caucasian 20% \ *Exp:* $425 (High) \ *Poverty:* 28% \
Title I: $102,925 \ *Open-Close:* 08/20 - 06/01 \ *DTBP:* $396 (High)

Reagan Reed 1   Jeanette Hall 2,12
Reagan Reed ....6*   Bobbie Jones 11,83
Jennifer Pena ....36*   Christin Orren 57*
Scott Watkins 67   Ted Arbogast 73,84,285,295

Public Schs..Principal	Grd	Prgm	Enr/#Cls	SN	
Big Bend High Sch 550 Roadrunner Cir, Terlingua 79852 Reagan Reed	9-12	T	44 7	77%	432/371-2281
Terlingua Elem Sch 550 Roadrunner Cir, Terlingua 79852 Reagan Reed	K-8		79 15		432/371-2281

BREWSTER PRIVATE SCHOOLS

Private Schs..Principal	Grd	Prgm	Enr/#Cls	SN	
Alpine Christian Sch 203 N 4th St, Alpine 79830 Caroline Luna	PK-12		45		432/837-5757 Fax 432/837-9057

BRISCOE COUNTY

BRISCOE PUBLIC SCHOOLS

• **Silverton Ind School Dist** PID: 01002300   806/823-2476
700 S Loretta St, Silverton 79257   Fax 806/823-2276

Schools: 1 \ *Teachers:* 20 \ *Students:* 195 \ *Special Ed Students:* 16
\ *LEP Students:* 8 \ *College-Bound:* 100% \ *Ethnic:* African American
1%, Hispanic 39%, Caucasian 60% \ *Exp:* $542 (High) \ *Poverty:* 19% \
Title I: $32,701 \ *Open-Close:* 08/14 - 05/21 \ *DTBP:* $350 (High)

Michelle Francis 1,11   Michael Hayes 2
Mike Juarez ....3,5*   Mary Patino 4
Clyde Parham ....6*   Michelle Francis 8,11,31,68,69,74,88*
Colleen Reed ....27,73,286,295*   Molly Forman 67
Vicki Perry 271

Public Schs..Principal	Grd	Prgm	Enr/#Cls	SN	
Silverton Sch 700 S Loretta St, Silverton 79257 Michael Hayes	PK-12	TV	195 35	54%	806/823-2476 Fax 806/832-2276

BROOKS COUNTY

BROOKS PUBLIC SCHOOLS

• **Brooks Co Ind School Dist** PID: 01002336   361/325-5681
200 E Allen St, Falfurrias 78355   Fax 361/325-1913

Schools: 4 \ *Teachers:* 104 \ *Students:* 1,589 \ *Special Ed Students:* 139
\ *LEP Students:* 43 \ *College-Bound:* 45% \ *Ethnic:* Hispanic 98%,
Caucasian 1% \ *Exp:* $444 (High) \ *Poverty:* 54% \ *Title I:* $1,326,932 \
Open-Close: 08/22 - 06/01 \ *DTBP:* $356 (High)

Dr Maria Casas 1   Alissa Sanchez 2
Romeo Ozuna 3,5   Rosie Perez 4
Harold McGehee ....6,35*   Guadalupe De Luna 7*
Rick Ruiz 8   Maria Anzualda 11,30,88,271
Jose Salinas 27,73,84,295   Patricia Mendez 34,57,58,69
Servando Guerra 67

Public Schs..Principal	Grd	Prgm	Enr/#Cls	SN	
Falfurrias Elem Sch 100 E Allen St, Falfurrias 78355 Ruiz Enrique	2-5	T	461 25	86%	361/325-8040 Fax 361/325-2220
Falfurrias High Sch 100 Jersey Blvd, Falfurrias 78355 Richard Wright	9-12	ATV	405 28	61%	361/325-8091 Fax 361/325-9284
Falfurrias Junior High Sch 600 S Center St, Falfurrias 78355 Dr Cynthia Perez	6-8	ATV	340 33	82%	361/325-8071 Fax 361/325-8156
Lasater Elem Sch 200 W Bennett, Falfurrias 78355 Louella Garcia	PK-1	T	383 17	92%	361/325-8060 Fax 361/325-2673

---

79 Student Personnel	91 Safety/Security	275 Response To Intervention	298 Grant Writer/Ptnrships	**School Programs**	**Social Media**
80 Driver Ed/Safety	92 Magnet School	277 Remedial Math K-12	750 Chief Innovation Officer	A = Alternative Program	
81 Gifted/Talented	93 Parental Involvement	280 Literacy Coach	751 Chief of Staff	G = Adult Classes	▯ = Facebook
82 Video Services	95 Tech Prep Program	285 STEM	752 Social Emotional Learning	M = Magnet Program	
83 Substance Abuse Prev	97 Chief Infomation Officer	286 Digital Learning		T = Title I Schoolwide	▯ = Twitter
84 Erate	98 Chief Technology Officer	288 Common Core Standards	**Other School Types**	V = Career & Tech Ed Programs	
85 AIDS Education	270 Character Education	294 Accountability	Ⓐ = Alternative School		
88 Alternative/At Risk	271 Migrant Education	295 Network System	Ⓒ = Charter School	New Schools are shaded	
89 Multi-Cultural Curriculum	273 Teacher Mentor	296 Title II Programs	Ⓜ = Magnet School	New Superintendents and Principals are bold	**TX—57**
90 Social Work	274 Before/After Sch	297 Webmaster	Ⓨ = Year-Round School	Personnel with email addresses are underscored	

Brown County

BROWN COUNTY

BROWN PUBLIC SCHOOLS

• **Bangs Ind School Dist** PID: 01002398 325/752-6612
200 E Hall St, Bangs 76823 Fax 325/752-6253

Schools: 3 \ *Teachers:* 81 \ *Students:* 875 \ *Special Ed Students:* 92 \ *LEP Students:* 10 \ *College-Bound:* 60% \ *Ethnic:* African American 2%, Hispanic 26%, Caucasian 72% \ *Exp:* $434 (High) \ *Poverty:* 17% \ *Title I:* $211,382 \ *Open-Close:* 08/19 - 05/22 \ *DTBP:* $367 (High) \ f

Tony Truelove 1	Teresa Roberts 2
Randy Sharp 3	Milla McCown 4
Mandy Johnson 5	Kyle Maxfield 6
Trumon Westfall 11,84	Linda Ratliff 12,57*
Shalee Moore 58	Eric Lykins 67
Bridgette Bowen 73,76	Kristi Davis 83*
Bridgette Bowen 295*	

Public Schs..Principal	Grd	Prgm	Enr/#Cls	SN	
Bangs High Sch 305 N Third St, Bangs 76823 Scott Patrick	9-12	ATV	327 27	48%	325/752-6822 Fax 325/752-7028
Bangs Middle Sch 400 N 3rd St, Bangs 76823 Damon Wilson	5-8	T	291 11	47%	325/752-6088 Fax 325/752-6367
J B Stephens Elem Sch 2001 N 6th St, Bangs 76823 Candace Wilson	PK-4	T	341 30	54%	325/752-7236 Fax 325/752-6974

• **Blanket Ind School Dist** PID: 01002427 325/748-5311
901 Avenue H, Blanket 76432 Fax 325/748-3391

Schools: 1 \ *Teachers:* 20 \ *Students:* 187 \ *Special Ed Students:* 29 \ *LEP Students:* 4 \ *College-Bound:* 58% \ *Ethnic:* Asian 1%, African American 1%, Hispanic 33%, Native American: 2%, Caucasian 64% \ *Exp:* $621 (High) \ *Poverty:* 14% \ *Title I:* $49,485 \ *Open-Close:* 08/26 - 06/01 \ *DTBP:* $358 (High)

David Whisenhunt 1,11	Trisha Amos 2
Tyler Tabor 6	Larry Smith 16,73
Chris Furry 67	Deb Jones 69,83,85,88

Public Schs..Principal	Grd	Prgm	Enr/#Cls	SN	
Blanket Sch 901 Avenue H, Blanket 76432 Chris Morrow	PK-12	T	187 26	58%	325/748-3341 Fax 325/748-2110

• **Brookesmith Ind School Dist** PID: 01002453 325/643-3023
13400 FM 586 S, Brookesmith 76827 Fax 325/643-3378

Schools: 3 \ *Teachers:* 16 \ *Students:* 200 \ *Special Ed Students:* 7 \ *College-Bound:* 50% \ *Ethnic:* Hispanic 20%, Caucasian 80% \ *Exp:* $144 (Low) \ *Poverty:* 13% \ *Title I:* $20,362 \ *Open-Close:* 09/03 - 05/28 \ *DTBP:* $64 (Low)

Steve Mickelson 1	Rena Allgood 2,11*
Scott Edmonson 6,35	Sandra Lehman 8,69
Jennifer Barrow 16	Terry Been 67

Public Schs..Principal	Grd	Prgm	Enr/#Cls	SN	
Brookesmith Elem Sch 13400 FM 586 S, Brookesmith 76827 Sandra Lehman	PK-5		70 21		325/643-3023
Brookesmith High Sch 13400 FM 586 S, Brookesmith 76827 Danny Copeland	9-12	T	43 25	49%	325/643-3023 Fax 325/645-3378
Genesis Academy 13400 FM 568 S, Brookesmith 76827 Mercathia Hughes	6-8		35		713/955-4414

• **Brownwood Ind School Dist** PID: 01002489 325/643-5644
2707 4th St, Brownwood 76801 Fax 325/643-5640

Schools: 7 \ *Teachers:* 258 \ *Students:* 3,595 \ *Special Ed Students:* 352 \ *LEP Students:* 100 \ *College-Bound:* 47% \ *Ethnic:* Asian 1%, African American 5%, Hispanic 42%, Caucasian 51% \ *Exp:* $454 (High) \ *Poverty:* 22% \ *Title I:* $1,134,227 \ *Special Education:* $770,000 \ *Open-Close:* 08/21 - 05/28 \ *DTBP:* $157 (High) \ t

Joe Young 1	Katie Burke 2
Bobby August 3	Justin Felts 3
Samuel Burnett 6	Helen Lacy 7*
Liesa Land 8,83,275,298	Heidi Gardner 11,31,57,88,285,296
Hector Martinez 15	Emily Wilson 16*
Landry Blackstock 58	Michael Cloy 67
Mark Stanley 73,286,295	Jimmy Fisher 295

Public Schs..Principal	Grd	Prgm	Enr/#Cls	SN	
Ⓐ Brownwood Accelerated High Sch 2707 4th St, Brownwood 76801 David McUllough	9-12	T	10 6	71%	325/646-1652 Fax 325/646-2477
Brownwood High Sch 2100 Slayden St, Brownwood 76801 Mitchell Moore	9-12	T	951 100	59%	325/646-9549 Fax 325/643-1965
Brownwood Middle Sch 1600 Calvert Rd, Brownwood 76801 Richard Sweaney	7-8	TV	544 35	62%	325/646-9545 Fax 325/646-3785
Coggin Intermediate Sch 800 Rogan St, Brownwood 76801 Sandra Spruell	4-6	T	700 35	63%	325/646-0462 Fax 325/646-9317
East Elem Sch 2700 Vincent St, Brownwood 76801 Dee Wright	PK-3	T	320 14	71%	325/646-2937 Fax 325/646-5900
Northwest Elem Sch 311 Bluffview Dr, Brownwood 76801 Christine Young	PK-3	T	609 39	84%	325/646-0707 Fax 325/646-2449
Woodland Heights Elem Sch 3900 4th St, Brownwood 76801 Jenny Swanzy	PK-3	T	430 25	50%	325/646-8633 Fax 325/641-0109

• **Early Ind School Dist** PID: 01002556 325/646-7934
101 Turtle Creek, Early 76802 Fax 325/646-9238

Schools: 4 \ *Teachers:* 105 \ *Students:* 1,200 \ *Special Ed Students:* 105 \ *LEP Students:* 11 \ *College-Bound:* 95% \ *Ethnic:* Asian 1%, African American 2%, Hispanic 22%, Caucasian 75% \ *Exp:* $292 (Med) \ *Poverty:* 21% \ *Title I:* $270,923 \ *Open-Close:* 08/26 - 05/28 \ *DTBP:* $424 (High)

Wes Beck 1	Becky Seale 2
Stewart Dickerson 3,5	Blake Sandford 6*
Reca Godfrey 8,11,36,57,83	Chalet Moore 58
Shawn Russell 67	Rick Lancaster 73
Terri Brinson 79	

1	Superintendent	8	Curric/Instruct K-12	19	Chief Financial Officer	29	Family/Consumer Science	39	Social Studies K-12	49	English/Lang Arts Elem	59	Special Education Elem	69	Academic Assessment
2	Bus/Finance/Purchasing	9	Curric/Instruct Elem	20	Art K-12	30	Adult Education	40	Social Studies Elem	50	English/Lang Arts Sec	60	Special Education Sec	70	Research/Development
3	Buildings And Grounds	10	Curric/Instruct Sec	21	Art Elem	31	Career/Sch-to-Work K-12	41	Social Studies Sec	51	Reading K-12	61	Foreign/World Lang K-12	71	Public Information
4	Food Service	11	Federal Program	22	Art Sec	32	Career/Sch-to-Work Elem	42	Science K-12	52	Reading Elem	62	Foreign/World Lang Elem	72	Summer School
5	Transportation	12	Title I	23	Music K-12	33	Career/Sch-to-Work Sec	43	Science Elem	53	Reading Sec	63	Foreign/World Lang Sec	73	Instructional Tech
6	Athletic	13	Title V	24	Music Elem	34	Early Childhood Ed	44	Science Sec	54	Remedial Reading K-12	64	Religious Education K-12	74	Inservice Training
7	Health Services	15	Asst Superintendent	25	Music Sec	35	Health/Phys Education	45	Math K-12	55	Remedial Reading Elem	65	Religious Education Elem	75	Marketing/Distributive
		16	Instructional Media Svcs	26	Business Education	36	Guidance Services K-12	46	Math Elem	56	Remedial Reading Sec	66	Religious Education Sec	76	Info Systems
		17	Chief Operations Officer	27	Career & Tech Ed	37	Guidance Services Elem	47	Math Sec	57	Bilingual/ELL	67	School Board President	77	Psychological Assess
		18	Chief Academic Officer	28	Technology Education	38	Guidance Services Sec	48	English/Lang Arts K-12	58	Special Education K-12	68	Teacher Personnel	78	Affirmative Action

Texas School Directory — Burleson County

Public Schs..Principal	Grd	Prgm	Enr/#Cls	SN	
Early Elem Sch 201 Sudderth Dr, Early 76802 Sharon Watson	3-5	T	276 15	53%	325/646-5511 Fax 325/646-5469
Early High Sch 115 Sudderth Dr, Early 76802 Judy Ozuna	9-12	V	370 35	41%	325/643-4593 Fax 325/646-4061
Early Middle Sch 700 Sunrise St, Early 76802 Robert Weyman	6-8	T	269 30	51%	325/643-5665 Fax 325/646-9972
Early Primary Sch 965 Early Blvd, Early 76802 Teresa Cooley	PK-2	AT	274 18	55%	325/643-9622 Fax 325/646-5336

● **May Ind School Dist** PID: 01002582 254/259-2091
3400 E County Road 411, May 76857 Fax 254/259-3514

Schools: 2 \ *Teachers:* 26 \ *Students:* 290 \ *Special Ed Students:* 27 \ *LEP Students:* 12 \ *Ethnic:* African American 2%, Hispanic 21%, Caucasian 77% \ *Exp:* $278 (Med) \ *Poverty:* 19% \ *Title I:* $68,795 \ *Open-Close:* 08/21 - 05/22 \ *DTBP:* $350 (High)

Steve Howard 1,83
Natalie Steele 11
Allison Williams 57,280,285*
Mike Martin 73,76,296*
Tony Norvil 5
Cynthia Wade 16
Jeff Phillips 67

Public Schs..Principal	Grd	Prgm	Enr/#Cls	SN	
May Elem Sch 3400 E County Road 411, May 76857 Nick Heupel	PK-6	T	135 16	68%	254/259-3711 Fax 254/259-2135
May High Sch 3400 E County Road 411, May 76857 Nicholas Heupel	7-12	TV	152 15	60%	254/259-2131 Fax 254/259-2706

● **Zephyr Ind School Dist** PID: 01002611 325/739-5331
11625 County Road 281, Zephyr 76890 Fax 325/739-2126

Schools: 1 \ *Teachers:* 20 \ *Students:* 217 \ *Special Ed Students:* 17 \ *College-Bound:* 70% \ *Ethnic:* Hispanic 13%, Caucasian 87% \ *Exp:* $549 (High) \ *Poverty:* 16% \ *Title I:* $48,121 \ *Open-Close:* 08/14 - 05/22 \ *DTBP:* $386 (High)

Stanton Marwitz 1,83
Ronda King 4
Elizabeth Croutch 12,275*
John Rockefeller 67
Judy Painter 2
Kelsa Blair 11*
Sutton Spieckerman 58*
Wade Lowry 73

Public Schs..Principal	Grd	Prgm	Enr/#Cls	SN	
Zephyr Sch 11625 County Road 281, Zephyr 76890 Kelsa Blair	PK-12	T	217 7	65%	325/739-5331

BROWN PRIVATE SCHOOLS

Private Schs..Principal	Grd	Prgm	Enr/#Cls	SN	
Victory Life Academy 901 C C Woodson Rd, Brownwood 76802 Yesy Sandoval	PK-12		115 14		325/641-2223

BURLESON COUNTY

BURLESON PUBLIC SCHOOLS

● **Caldwell Ind School Dist** PID: 01002647 979/567-2400
203 N Gray St, Caldwell 77836 Fax 979/567-9876

Schools: 5 \ *Teachers:* 130 \ *Students:* 1,800 \ *Special Ed Students:* 130 \ *LEP Students:* 179 \ *College-Bound:* 55% \ *Ethnic:* Asian 1%, African American 11%, Hispanic 37%, Caucasian 50% \ *Exp:* $434 (High) \ *Poverty:* 23% \ *Title I:* $510,323 \ *Open-Close:* 08/22 - 05/28 \ *DTBP:* $541 (High)

Andrew Peters 1,11
Brady Beavers 3
Sally Iselt 5
Dr Alex Salazar 8,15,18,57,88
Kim McManus 69
Deanie Gold 83,85*
Heather Escalante 2
Keith Fortson 4
Matt Langley 6*
Trip Warren 67
Keith Johnson 73,76
Susan Groce 280

Public Schs..Principal	Grd	Prgm	Enr/#Cls	SN	
Ⓐ Burleson Co Alt Sch 203 N Gray St, Caldwell 77836 John Meckel	6-12		27 1		979/567-2670 Fax 979/567-7476
Caldwell Elem Sch 675 Country Rd 300, Caldwell 77836 Erin Supak	PK-2	T	448 27	68%	979/567-2404 Fax 979/567-9422
Caldwell High Sch 550 County Road 307, Caldwell 77836 Vicki Ochs	9-12	T	526 60	48%	979/567-2401 Fax 979/567-6735
Caldwell Intermediate Sch 765 County Road 300, Caldwell 77836 Kimberly Pagach	3-5	T	417 24	62%	979/567-2403 Fax 979/567-7131
Caldwell Middle Sch 200 N Gray St, Caldwell 77836 Shaunna Savage	6-8	T	413 37	57%	979/567-2402 Fax 979/567-7433

● **Snook Ind School Dist** PID: 01002685 979/272-8307
10110 FM2155, Snook 77878 Fax 979/272-5041

Schools: 1 \ *Teachers:* 50 \ *Students:* 500 \ *Special Ed Students:* 51 \ *LEP Students:* 24 \ *College-Bound:* 55% \ *Ethnic:* African American 31%, Hispanic 25%, Caucasian 44% \ *Exp:* $433 (High) \ *Poverty:* 18% \ *Title I:* $114,998 \ *Open-Close:* 08/26 - 05/21 \ *DTBP:* $330 (High)

Brenda Krchnak 1
John Cooper 3
Emily Vacha 7,35
Kristine Brisco 67
Brandon McCord 73,76,286
Darrell Saint Clair 2,13,296,298
Laura Sebesta 5,288*
Jeff Meff 8
Theresa Schoppe 68
Teresa Allen 83,90*

Public Schs..Principal	Grd	Prgm	Enr/#Cls	SN	
Snook Sch 10110 FM 2155, Snook 77878 Christi Everett \ Rick Frauenberger	PK-12	T	500 38	66%	979/272-8307

---

79 Student Personnel | 91 Safety/Security | 275 Response To Intervention | 298 Grant Writer/Ptnrships | School Programs | Social Media
80 Driver Ed/Safety | 92 Magnet School | 277 Remedial Math K-12 | 750 Chief Innovation Officer | A = Alternative Program | = Facebook
81 Gifted/Talented | 93 Parental Involvement | 280 Literacy Coach | 751 Chief of Staff | G = Adult Classes |
82 Video Services | 95 Tech Prep Program | 285 STEM | 752 Social Emotional Learning | M = Magnet Program | = Twitter
83 Substance Abuse Prev | 97 Chief Infomation Officer | 288 Digital Learning | | T = Title I Schoolwide |
84 Erate | 98 Chief Technology Officer | 288 Common Core Standards | Other School Types | V = Career & Tech Ed Programs |
85 AIDS Education | 270 Character Education | 294 Accountability | Ⓐ = Alternative School | |
88 Alternative/At Risk | 271 Migrant Education | 295 Network System | Ⓒ = Charter School | New Schools are shaded |
89 Multi-Cultural Curriculum | 273 Teacher Mentor | 296 Title II Programs | Ⓜ = Magnet School | New Superintendents and Principals are bold |
90 Social Work | 274 Before/After Sch | 297 Webmaster | Ⓨ = Year-Round School | Personnel with email addresses are underscored |

Burnet County

- **Somerville Ind School Dist** PID: 01002714   979/596-2153
  625 8th St, Somerville 77879   Fax 979/596-1778

  Schools: 3 \ **Teachers:** 51 \ **Students:** 640 \ **Special Ed Students:** 54 \ **LEP Students:** 34 \ **College-Bound:** 40% \ **Ethnic:** African American 25%, Hispanic 32%, Caucasian 42% \ **Exp:** $272 (Med) \ **Poverty:** 32% \ **Title I:** $243,129 \ **Open-Close:** 08/28 - 05/27 \ **DTBP:** $343 (High)

  Karla Sparks 1,11,83   Amanda Flencher 2
  Bryan Crook 67

Public Schs..Principal	Grd	Prgm	Enr/#Cls	SN	
Somerville Elem Sch 700 8th St, Somerville 77879 Stephanie Longoria	PK-4	T	182 14	83%	979/596-1502
Somerville High Sch 570 8th St, Somerville 77879 Jennifer Wood	8-12	ATV	146 30	70%	979/596-1534 Fax 979/596-3649
Somerville Intermediate Sch 700 8th St, Somerville 77879 Joshua Pinkerton	5-7		192		979/596-7502

BURNET COUNTY

BURNET PUBLIC SCHOOLS

- **Burnet Cons Ind Sch Dist** PID: 01002752   512/756-2124
  208 E Brier Ln, Burnet 78611   Fax 512/756-7498

  Schools: 6 \ **Teachers:** 206 \ **Students:** 3,186 \ **Special Ed Students:** 360 \ **LEP Students:** 218 \ **College-Bound:** 50% \ **Ethnic:** Asian 1%, African American 1%, Hispanic 31%, Caucasian 67% \ **Exp:** $318 (High) \ **Poverty:** 16% \ **Title I:** $658,907 \ **Special Education:** $658,000 \ **Open-Close:** 08/19 - 05/22 \ **DTBP:** $155 (High)

  Keith McBurnett 1   Clay Goehring 2
  Charlie Goble 3   Pamela Holcomb 4*
  Josh Albro 5   Kurt Jones 6*
  Amy Murray .... 7*   R J Gates 9,11,16,27,57,83,296,298
  Dr Kelly McCord 10   Jennifer Simpson 58
  Andy Field 67   Michele Gilmore 68
  Adam Hermes .... 73*   Rchard Torrez 295

Public Schs..Principal	Grd	Prgm	Enr/#Cls	SN	
Bertram Elem Sch 315 Main St, Bertram 78605 Alicia Harris	PK-5	T	376 21	68%	512/355-2111 Fax 512/355-2261
Burnet High Sch 1000 the Green Mile Rd, Burnet 78611 Casey Burkhart	9-12	TV	899	47%	512/756-6193 Fax 512/756-4553
Burnet Middle Sch 1401 N Main St, Burnet 78611 Jeremy LeJeune	6-8	T	762 25	56%	512/756-6182 Fax 512/756-7955
ⓐ Quest High Sch 702 N Wood St, Burnet 78611 Douglas Marvin	9-12	T	24 9	47%	512/756-6747 Fax 512/756-6289
R J Richey Elem Sch 500 E Graves St, Burnet 78611 Bobbie Steiner	3-5	T	559 18	60%	512/756-2609 Fax 512/756-2624

Shady Grove Elem Sch 111 Shady Grove Rd, Burnet 78611 Tasha Briseno	PK-2	T	581 24	62%	512/756-2126 Fax 512/756-6993

- **Marble Falls Ind School Dist** PID: 01002817   830/693-4357
  1800 Colt Cir, Marble Falls 78654   Fax 830/693-5685

  Schools: 7 \ **Teachers:** 315 \ **Students:** 4,154 \ **Special Ed Students:** 484 \ **LEP Students:** 587 \ **College-Bound:** 48% \ **Ethnic:** Asian 1%, African American 2%, Hispanic 47%, Caucasian 50% \ **Exp:** $145 (Low) \ **Poverty:** 17% \ **Title I:** $837,725 \ **Special Education:** $741,000 \ **Open-Close:** 08/21 - 05/28 \ 🆃

  Dr Chris Allen 1   Jeff Gasaway 2,15
  Melissa Lafferty 2   Jeff Rowland 3
  Mike Phillips 3   Mary Davidson 4
  Gina Solorzano 5   Leslie Baty 9
  Heather Metzgar 10   Soor-El Puga 57
  Dr Shanna Fancher 58   Kevin Naumann 67
  Betsy Russell 68   Melissa Fields 69,294
  Nathan Fink 73,295   Ashley Bernard 285
  Pam Parkman 298

Public Schs..Principal	Grd	Prgm	Enr/#Cls	SN	
Colt Elem Sch 2200 Manzano Mile, Marble Falls 78654 Erika O'Connor	PK-5	T	627 29	67%	830/693-3474 Fax 830/693-7092
ⓐ Falls Career High Sch 1800 Colt Cir, Marble Falls 78654 Yarda Leflet	9-12	T	49 5	73%	830/798-3621 Fax 830/798-3636
Highland Lakes Elem Sch 8200 W FM 1431, Granite SHLS 78654 Leslie Talamantes	PK-5	T	603 31	82%	830/798-3650 Fax 830/598-9349
Marble Falls Elem Sch 901 Avenue U, Marble Falls 78654 Michael Haley	PK-5	T	592 27	66%	830/693-2385 Fax 830/693-5421
Marble Falls High Sch 2101 Mustang Dr, Marble Falls 78654 Damon Adams	9-12	ATV	1,191 75	58%	830/693-4375 Fax 830/693-6079
Marble Falls Middle Sch 1511 Pony Dr, Marble Falls 78654 Roger Barr	6-8	TV	951 63	62%	830/693-4439 Fax 830/693-7788
Spicewood Elem Sch 1005 Spur 191, Spicewood 78669 Susan Cox	PK-5	T	219 19	48%	830/798-3675 Fax 830/798-3676 🆃

BURNET PRIVATE SCHOOLS

Private Schs..Principal	Grd	Prgm	Enr/#Cls	SN	
Faith Academy of Marble Falls 3151 E FM 1431, Marble Falls 78654 Joe Rispoli	K-12		275 11		830/798-1333 Fax 830/798-1332
First Baptist Christian Sch 901 La Ventana, Marble Falls 78654 Dr Sandra Phelps	PK-8		401		830/693-3930

1 Superintendent	8 Curric/Instruct K-12	19 Chief Financial Officer	29 Family/Consumer Science	39 Social Studies K-12
2 Bus/Finance/Purchasing	9 Curric/Instruct Elem	20 Art K-12	30 Adult Education	40 Social Studies Elem
3 Buildings And Grounds	10 Curric/Instruct Sec	21 Art Elem	31 Career/Sch-to-Work K-12	41 Social Studies Sec
4 Food Service	11 Federal Program	22 Art Sec	32 Career/Sch-to-Work Elem	42 Science K-12
5 Transportation	12 Title I	23 Music K-12	33 Career/Sch-to-Work Sec	43 Science Elem
6 Athletic	13 Title V	24 Music Elem	34 Early Childhood Ed	44 Science Sec
7 Health Services	15 Asst Superintendent	25 Music Sec	35 Health/Phys Education	45 Math K-12
	16 Instructional Media Svcs	26 Business Education	36 Guidance Services K-12	46 Math Elem
	17 Chief Operations Officer	27 Career & Tech Ed	37 Guidance Services Elem	47 Math Sec
	18 Chief Academic Officer	28 Technology Education	38 Guidance Services Sec	48 English/Lang Arts K-12

49 English/Lang Arts Elem	59 Special Education Elem	69 Academic Assessment
50 English/Lang Arts Sec	60 Special Education Sec	70 Research/Development
51 Reading K-12	61 Foreign/World Lang K-12	71 Public Information
52 Reading Elem	62 Foreign/World Lang Elem	72 Summer School
53 Reading Sec	63 Foreign/World Lang Sec	73 Instructional Tech
54 Remedial Reading K-12	64 Religious Education K-12	74 Inservice Training
55 Remedial Reading Elem	65 Religious Education Elem	75 Marketing/Distributive
56 Remedial Reading Sec	66 Religious Education Sec	76 Info Systems
57 Bilingual/ELL	67 School Board President	77 Psychological Assess
58 Special Education K-12	68 Teacher Personnel	78 Affirmative Action

Texas School Directory

Calhoun County

CALDWELL COUNTY

CALDWELL PUBLIC SCHOOLS

● **Lockhart Ind School Dist** PID: 01003031 512/398-0000
419 Bois Darc St, Lockhart 78644 Fax 512/398-0031

Schools: 9 \ *Teachers:* 348 \ *Students:* 6,350 \ *Special Ed Students:* 646 \ *LEP Students:* 1,039 \ *College-Bound:* 80% \ *Ethnic:* African American 3%, Hispanic 75%, Caucasian 21% \ *Exp:* $371 (High) \ *Poverty:* 18% \ *Title I:* $1,090,086 \ *Special Education:* $1,495,000 \ *Open-Close:* 08/14 - 05/22 \ *DTBP:* $169 (High)

Mark Estrades	1	Tanya Homann		2
Tina Knudsen	2,19	Lee Raspberry		3*
James Akuna	4	Salanon Torres		5
Todd Moebes	6	Shelly Webber		7
Stephanie Camarillo	8,15	Faith Pope		9
Barry Bacom	10,83	Kim Brents		11,91,270
Adam Galvan	15,73,76,271	Christina Vazques		57,271
Melissa Corona	58,81	Steve Johnson		67
Karla Tate	274	Paul Hodge		295*

Public Schs..Principal	Grd	Prgm	Enr/#Cls	SN	
Alma Brewer Strawn Elem Sch 9000 FM 1854, Dale 78616 Analeasa Holmes	PK-5	T	503	85%	512/398-0630 Fax 512/398-0631
Bluebonnet Elem Sch 211 Mockingbird Ln, Lockhart 78644 Belinda Vasquez	K-5	T	579	73%	512/398-0900 Fax 512/398-0901
Clear Fork Elem Sch 1102 Clearfork St, Lockhart 78644 Rebecca Leonard	1-5	T	489 38	58%	512/398-0450 Fax 512/398-0536
George W Carver Early Ed Ctr 371 Carver St, Lockhart 78644 Karen Nixon	PK-K	T	228 24	87%	512/398-0060 Fax 512/398-0110
Lockhart High Sch 906 Center St, Lockhart 78644 Luciano Castro	9-12	ATV	1,567 59	56%	512/398-0300 Fax 512/398-0302
Lockhart Junior High Sch 500 City Line Rd, Lockhart 78644 Lori Davis	6-8	ATV	1,393 40	68%	512/398-0770 Fax 512/398-0772
ⒶLockhart Pride High Sch 500 Pecos St, Lockhart 78644 Barry Bacom	9-12	T	47 4	73%	512/398-0130 Fax 512/398-0132
Navarro Elem Sch 715 S Medina St, Lockhart 78644 Deanna Juarez	1-5	T	457 20	65%	512/398-0690 Fax 512/398-0692
Plum Creek Elem Sch 710 Flores St, Lockhart 78644 Janey Griebel	1-5	T	550 59	83%	512/398-0570 Fax 512/398-0572

● **Luling Ind School Dist** PID: 01003093 830/875-3191
212 E Bowie St, Luling 78648 Fax 830/875-3193

Schools: 4 \ *Teachers:* 92 \ *Students:* 1,450 \ *Special Ed Students:* 122 \ *LEP Students:* 179 \ *College-Bound:* 40% \ *Ethnic:* African American 5%, Hispanic 68%, Caucasian 27% \ *Exp:* $430 (High) \ *Poverty:* 27% \ *Title I:* $535,515 \ *Open-Close:* 08/26 - 05/28 \ *DTBP:* $604 (High)

Erin Warren	1,11	Menell Martin		2,19
Bryan Tucker	3	Bill Hathaway		4
Diana Dietz	5	Stacey Martin		6*
Haley Almaguer	7	Dr Donna Weikert		9
Errin Jennings	10	Kimberley Hardy		16,82*
Kathleen Murray	37*	Laurinda Webb		57,58*
Jeff Ferry	67	Susan Guzman		68
Rutty DeCou	73,76*	Susan Maxey		83,85,271*
Alicia Cruz	271			

Public Schs..Principal	Grd	Prgm	Enr/#Cls	SN	
Gilbert Gerdes Jr High Sch 214 E Bowie St, Luling 78648 Kelly Meshell	6-8	T	333 20	72%	830/875-2121 Fax 830/875-5482
Leonard Shanklin Elem Sch 122 E Houston St, Luling 78648 Deborah Ewald	2-5	T	440 18	74%	830/875-2515 Fax 830/875-6708
Luling High Sch 218 E Travis St, Luling 78648 Joseph Alvarez	9-12	AGTV	386 35	62%	830/875-2458 Fax 830/875-2751
Luling Primary Sch 118 W Bowie St, Luling 78648 Hank Weikert	PK-1	T	273 12	80%	830/875-2223 Fax 830/875-6712

● **Prairie Lea Ind School Dist** PID: 01003122 512/488-2328
6910 San Marcus Hwy, Prairie Lea 78661 Fax 512/488-9006

Schools: 1 \ *Teachers:* 17 \ *Students:* 210 \ *Special Ed Students:* 16 \ *LEP Students:* 11 \ *College-Bound:* 75% \ *Ethnic:* African American 8%, Hispanic 49%, Caucasian 43% \ *Exp:* $365 (High) \ *Poverty:* 12% \ *Title I:* $36,132 \ *Open-Close:* 08/26 - 05/29 \ *DTBP:* $373 (High)

Larry Markert	1,11	Charlie Simpson		3
Debbie Hardaway	4*	Teresa Acklin		6*
Shelley Hardaway	27*	Kay Markert		57*
Kimberly Durick	58	Margarito Zapata		67
John Ray	73*			

Public Schs..Principal	Grd	Prgm	Enr/#Cls	SN	
Prairie Lea Sch 6910 San Marcus Hwy 80, Prairie Lea 78661 Monica Guillory	PK-12	TV	210 16	76%	512/488-2328 Fax 512/488-2425

CALHOUN COUNTY

CALHOUN PUBLIC SCHOOLS

● **Calhoun Co Ind School Dist** PID: 01003158 361/552-9728
525 N Commerce St, Port Lavaca 77979 Fax 361/551-2649

Schools: 7 \ *Teachers:* 262 \ *Students:* 3,985 \ *Special Ed Students:* 354 \ *LEP Students:* 411 \ *College-Bound:* 39% \ *Ethnic:* Asian 5%, African American 2%, Hispanic 64%, Caucasian 28% \ *Exp:* $330 (High) \ *Poverty:* 22% \ *Title I:* $1,053,147 \ *Special Education:* $648,000 \ *Open-Close:* 08/15 - 05/28 \ *DTBP:* $183 (High)

Larry Nichols	1	Robin Martinez		2,15
Joe Hernandez	3,5,91	Nicole Nguyen		4
Richard Whitaker	6*	Shari Dierlam		7*
Maggie Hernadez	8	Kelly Taylor		13,57,69,74,83,271*
Dana Dworaczyk	27	Gina Bethany		58,275

TX—61

Callahan County

Market Data Retrieval

Dr Bill Harvey 67
Marcus Martinez 73,286,295
Lela Tyson 69
Dwana Finster 88*

Public Schs..Principal	Grd	Prgm	Enr/#Cls	SN	
Calhoun High Sch 201 Sandcrab Blvd, Port Lavaca 77979 Nicole Amason	9-12	TV	1,138	53%	361/552-3775 Fax 361/551-2620
Harrison-Jefferson-Madison ES 605 N Commerce St, Port Lavaca 77979 Tiffany O'Donnell	PK-5	T	723 40	70%	361/552-5253 Fax 361/551-2628
ⓐ Hope High Sch 900 N Virginia St, Port Lavaca 77979 Dwana Finster	9-12	V	27 6	74%	361/552-7084 Fax 361/551-2677
Jackson-Roosevelt Elem Sch 1512 Jackson St, Port Lavaca 77979 Sherry Phillips	PK-5	T	900 50	67%	361/552-3317 Fax 361/551-2699
Port Oconnor Elem Sch 508 Monroe Street, Port O Connor 77982 Kelly Wehmeyer	PK-5	T	90 10	59%	361/983-2341 Fax 361/551-2605
Seadrift Sch 1801 W Broadway, Seadrift 77983 Lynda Bermea	PK-8	T	294 28	59%	361/785-3511 Fax 361/785-5720
Travis Middle Sch 705 N Nueces St, Port Lavaca 77979 Michael Torres	6-8	TV	735 50	62%	361/552-3784 Fax 361/551-2692

CALHOUN CATHOLIC SCHOOLS

- **Diocese of Victoria Ed Office** PID: 02181727
  Listing includes only schools located in this county. See District Index for location of Diocesan Offices.

Catholic Schs..Principal	Grd	Prgm	Enr/#Cls	SN	
Our Lady of the Gulf Cath Sch 301 S San Antonio St, Port Lavaca 77979 Theresa Dent	PK-8		90 9		361/552-6140 Fax 361/552-4300 f

CALLAHAN COUNTY

CALLAHAN PUBLIC SCHOOLS

- **Baird Ind School Dist** PID: 01003287
  600 W 7th St, Baird 79504
  325/854-1400
  Fax 325/854-2058

Schools: 3 \ **Teachers:** 35 \ **Students:** 274 \ **Special Ed Students:** 40 \ **LEP Students:** 3 \ **College-Bound:** 57% \ **Ethnic:** African American 1%, Hispanic 19%, Caucasian 80% \ **Exp:** $668 (High) \ **Poverty:** 25% \ **Title I:** $117,527 \ **Open-Close:** 08/26 - 05/21 \ **DTBP:** $343 (High)

Jarod Bellar 1,11,57
Kevin Davis 3,5
Joel Baker 6
Cynthia Bessent 8,12,271*
Lori Higgins 67
Cindy Clark 2
Tiffany Voights-Pettit 4
Marilu Hall 7
Jennifer Bellar 31,36,69,83,270,294*
Glendell Barr 73,295*

Public Schs..Principal	Grd	Prgm	Enr/#Cls	SN	
Baird Elem Sch 400 W 7th St, Baird 79504 Cynthia Bessent	PK-5	T	156 14	68%	325/854-1400 Fax 325/854-2808
Baird High Sch 600 W 7th St, Baird 79504 Torrey Price	9-12	TV	88 20	61%	325/854-1400 Fax 325/854-2808
Baird Middle Sch 400 W 7th St, Baird 79504 Cynthia Bessent	6-8	T	61	69%	325/854-1400 Fax 325/854-2808

- **Clyde Consolidated Ind SD** PID: 01003316
  526 Shalimar Dr, Clyde 79510
  325/893-4222
  Fax 325/893-4024

Schools: 4 \ **Teachers:** 117 \ **Students:** 1,450 \ **Special Ed Students:** 152 \ **LEP Students:** 5 \ **Ethnic:** African American 1%, Hispanic 14%, Caucasian 84% \ **Exp:** $359 (High) \ **Poverty:** 22% \ **Title I:** $384,347 \ **Open-Close:** 08/22 - 05/22 \ **DTBP:** $340 (High) \ t

Kenny Berry 1
Melanie Brown 4
Lois Burlson 7*
Teresa Howard 16*
Greg Welch 67
Mike Neal 286*
Terry Phillips 2
Scott Campbell 6
Paula Kinslow 8,11,58,69,271,273,298
Carrie Conner 36,83,85,88*
Paul McGuire 73,295*

Public Schs..Principal	Grd	Prgm	Enr/#Cls	SN	
Clyde Elem Sch 318 Forrest Rd, Clyde 79510 Kim Jones	PK-2	T	358 26	58%	325/893-4788 Fax 325/893-5642
Clyde High Sch 500 N Hays Rd, Clyde 79510 Gregg Wilson	9-12	AV	404 42	40%	325/893-2161 Fax 325/893-2993
Clyde Intermediate Sch 505 N Hays Rd, Clyde 79510 Jill Morphis	3-5	T	331 25	57%	325/893-2815 Fax 325/893-3067
Clyde Junior High Sch 211 S 3rd St W, Clyde 79510 Jared Duncum	6-8	T	341 17	54%	325/893-5788 Fax 325/893-2134 f t

- **Cross Plains Ind Sch Dist** PID: 01003354
  700 N Main St, Cross Plains 76443
  254/725-6121
  Fax 254/725-6559

Schools: 2 \ **Teachers:** 34 \ **Students:** 368 \ **Special Ed Students:** 39 \ **LEP Students:** 5 \ **College-Bound:** 80% \ **Ethnic:** Asian 1%, Hispanic 12%, Native American: 1%, Caucasian 87% \ **Exp:** $862 (High) \ **Poverty:** 21% \ **Title I:** $99,123 \ **Open-Close:** 08/27 - 05/21 \ **DTBP:** $342 (High)

Dade Cosby 1
Clarence Tennison 3
Mike Perez 5
Stacy Jones 8,69,83,88,275,294*
Roy Richey 67
Linda Birdwell 2,298
Barbara Barnette 4
Daniel Purvis 6*
Leslie Lawrence 11*
Dave Crosby 73,286,295

Public Schs..Principal	Grd	Prgm	Enr/#Cls	SN	
Cross Plains Elem Sch 800 N Main St, Cross Plains 76443 Jeanette Barron	PK-6	T	204 18	64%	254/725-6123
Cross Plains High Sch 700 N Main St, Cross Plains 76443 Wesley Jones	7-12	TV	164 15	59%	254/725-6121

1 Superintendent	8 Curric/Instruct K-12	19 Chief Financial Officer	29 Family/Consumer Science	39 Social Studies K-12	49 English/Lang Arts Elem	59 Special Education Elem	69 Academic Assessment
2 Bus/Finance/Purchasing	9 Curric/Instruct Elem	20 Art K-12	30 Adult Education	40 Social Studies Elem	50 English/Lang Arts Sec	60 Special Education Sec	70 Research/Development
3 Buildings And Grounds	10 Curric/Instruct Sec	21 Art Elem	31 Career/Sch-to-Work K-12	41 Social Studies Sec	51 Reading K-12	61 Foreign/World Lang Elem	71 Public Information
4 Food Service	11 Federal Program	22 Art Sec	32 Career/Sch-to-Work Elem	42 Science K-12	52 Reading Elem	62 Foreign/World Lang Elem	72 Summer School
5 Transportation	12 Title I	23 Music K-12	33 Career/Sch-to-Work Sec	43 Science Elem	53 Reading Sec	63 Foreign/World Lang Sec	73 Instructional Tech
6 Athletic	13 Title V	24 Music Elem	34 Early Childhood Ed	44 Science Sec	54 Remedial Reading K-12	64 Religious Education K-12	74 Inservice Training
7 Health Services	15 Asst Superintendent	25 Music Sec	35 Health/Phys Education	45 Math K-12	55 Remedial Reading Elem	65 Religious Education Elem	75 Marketing/Distributive
	16 Instructional Media Svcs	26 Business Education	36 Guidance Services K-12	46 Math Elem	56 Remedial Reading Sec	66 Religious Education Sec	76 Info Systems
TX-62	17 Chief Operations Officer	27 Career & Tech Ed	37 Guidance Services Elem	47 Math Sec	57 Bilingual/ELL	67 School Board President	77 Psychological Assess
	18 Chief Academic Officer	28 Technology Education	38 Guidance Services Sec	48 English/Lang Arts K-12	58 Special Education K-12	68 Teacher Personnel	78 Affirmative Action

Texas School Directory

Cameron County

Eula Ind School Dist PID: 01003380
6040 FM 603, Clyde 79510
325/529-3186
Fax 325/529-4461

Schools: 3 \ **Teachers:** 38 \ **Students:** 400 \ **Special Ed Students:** 45 \ **LEP Students:** 3 \ **College-Bound:** 70% \ **Ethnic:** Asian 1%, African American 1%, Hispanic 14%, Native American: 1%, Caucasian 84% \ **Exp:** $393 (High) \ **Poverty:** 18% \ **Title I:** $134,053 \ **Open-Close:** 08/26 - 05/22 \ **DTBP:** $180 (High)

Name	Ref
Tim Kelley	1
Susan Faircloth	2
Sue Pounds	4*
Joye Fuller	7*
Katie Fostel	9,11,69,93,273*
Bill Dean	67
Joshua Fostel	2,6,296*
Glen Smith	3,91
Debra Frazier	5
David Turner	8,16,73,82,83,286*
Lori Oglesby	31*
Kortni Collins	270*

Public Schs..Principal	Grd	Prgm	Enr/#Cls	SN	
Eula Elem Sch 6040 FM 603, Clyde 79510 Cody Williams	PK-6	T	237	58%	325/529-3212 Fax 325/529-2001
Eula High Sch 6040 FM 603, Clyde 79510 Wayland Damron	9-12	TV	106 20	45%	325/529-3605 Fax 325/529-5534
Eula Middle Sch 6040 FM 603, Clyde 79510 Wayland Damron	7-8	T	58 6	57%	325/529-3605 Fax 325/529-5534

CAMERON COUNTY

CAMERON PUBLIC SCHOOLS

Brownsville Ind School Dist PID: 01003445
1900 Price Rd, Brownsville 78521
956/548-8000
Fax 956/574-6497

Schools: 54 \ **Teachers:** 3,026 \ **Students:** 43,355 \ **Special Ed Students:** 5,106 \ **LEP Students:** 14,078 \ **College-Bound:** 95% \ **Ethnic:** Hispanic 98%, Caucasian 1% \ **Exp:** $358 (High) \ **Poverty:** 38% \ **Title I:** $27,913,818 \ **Special Education:** $8,357,000 \ **Bilingual Education:** $102,000 \ **Open-Close:** 08/14 - 05/27 \ **DTBP:** $195 (High)

Name	Ref
Dr Rene Gutierrez	1
Cesar Lopez	3
Eliud Ornelas	5
Rosa Pones	7
Dolores Emerson	9
Mary Lou Esparza	11
Alma Cardenas-Rubio	15
Jimmy Hayes	15*
Dr Timothy Cuff	15
Kathleen Jimenez	20,23
Dr Debbie Alford	30
Fred Tamez	35
Carlos Olvera	57
Minerva Pena	67
Alfonso Guitierrez	71
Luis Martinez	82
Rosalva Larrasquitu	93
Estela Barrientes	271
Dr Gregorio Garcia	298
Mary Garza	2,19
Laura Zelda Villarreal	4
Gilbert Leal	6
Dr Dora Sauceda	8,15
Dr Norma Ibarra-Cantu	10
Mary Tolman	12
Carmelita Rodriguez	15,68
Sandra Lopez	15*
Rosie Ara	16
Dr Juan Chavez	27,31*
Merrill Hammons	31,83
Sara Garza	36
Adriana Lippa	58
Pam Van Ravensway	69,70
Cynthia Castro	74
Oscar Garcia	91
Robby Fisher	95
Joshua Claudio	297

Public Schs..Principal	Grd	Prgm	Enr/#Cls	SN	
Ben L Brite Elem Sch 450 S Browne Ave, Brownsville 78521 Nicole Clint	PK-5	T	613	95%	956/698-3000 Fax 956/831-5146
Benavides Elem Sch 3101 McAllen Rd, Brownsville 78520 Sherry Stout	PK-5	T	761 58	93%	956/350-3250 Fax 956/350-3273
Besteiro Middle Sch 6280 Southmost Rd, Brownsville 78521 Teresa Nunez	6-8	GTV	705	99%	956/544-3900 Fax 956/544-3946
Breeden Elem Sch 3955 Dana Ave, Brownsville 78526 Mandy DelGado	PK-5	T	696	92%	956/554-4730 Fax 956/547-4305
Ⓐ Brownsville Academic Center 3308 Robindale Rd, Brownsville 78526 Hector Hernandez	6-12		152 16		956/504-6305 Fax 956/831-9726
Brownsville Early Clg HS 343 Ringgold Rd, Brownsville 78520 Aimee Garza	9-12	T	412	91%	956/698-1476 Fax 956/574-5600
Ⓐ Brownsville Lrng Acad High Sch 1800 Cummings Pl, Brownsville 78520 Teresita De Saro	6-12		350		956/548-8630 Fax 956/831-8267
Bruce Aiken Elem Sch 6290 Southmost Rd, Brownsville 78521 Dora Fasci-Marquez	PK-5	T	739 33	96%	956/986-5200 Fax 956/986-5208
Burns Elem Sch 1974 E Alton Gloor Blvd, Brownsville 78526 **Leticia Rodriguez-Bohn**	PK-5	T	802 66	98%	956/548-8490 Fax 956/548-8489
Canales Elem Sch 1811 International Blvd, Brownsville 78521 Edward Ude	PK-5	T	811 65	98%	956/548-8900 Fax 956/548-8912
Champion Elem Sch 4750 Bowie Rd, Brownsville 78521 Ricardo Torres	PK-5	T	823 36	98%	956/832-6200 Fax 956/832-6225
Cromack Elem Sch 3200 E 30th St, Brownsville 78521 L Hernandez	PK-5	T	594 60	98%	956/548-8820 Fax 956/548-8824
Del Castillo Elem Sch 105 Morningside Rd, Brownsville 78521 Petra Torres	PK-5	T	351 45	98%	956/982-2600 Fax 956/982-2622
Egly Elem Sch 445 Land O Lakes Dr, Brownsville 78521 Pedro Vidal	PK-5	T	784 40	96%	956/548-8850 Fax 956/982-3074
El Jardin Elem Sch 6911 Boca Chica Blvd, Brownsville 78521 Maria Flores	PK-5	T	551 60	99%	956/831-6000 Fax 956/831-6002
Faulk Middle Sch 2000 Roosevelt St, Brownsville 78521 Benita Villarreal	6-8	T	1,142 60	99%	956/548-8500 Fax 956/548-8507
Filemon B Vela Middle Sch 4905 Paredes Line Rd, Brownsville 78526 Joel Wood	6-8	TV	797 60	93%	956/548-7770 Fax 956/548-7780
Gallegos Elem Sch 2700 Avenida Rancho Viejo, Brownsville 78521 Theresa Villafuerte	PK-5	T	570 48	99%	956/547-4230 Fax 956/547-4232
Garden Park Elem Sch 855 Military Rd, Brownsville 78520 Victor Caballero	PK-5	T	595 60	99%	956/982-2630 Fax 956/982-2644
Garza Elem Sch 200 Esperanza Rd, Brownsville 78521 Maria Lara	PK-5	T	425 60	95%	956/982-2660 Fax 956/982-2682
Ⓜ Gladys Porter Early Clg HS 3500 International Blvd, Brownsville 78521 Maria Solis	9-12	GTV	2,000	100%	956/548-7800 Fax 956/548-7988
Gonzalez Elem Sch 4350 Jaime J Zapata Ave, Brownsville 78521 Billy Cobos	PK-5	T	845 65	94%	956/831-6030 Fax 956/831-6035

Code	Description	Code	Description	Code	Description
79	Student Personnel	91	Safety/Security	275	Response To Intervention
80	Driver Ed/Safety	92	Magnet School	277	Remedial Math K-12
81	Gifted/Talented	93	Parental Involvement	280	Literacy Coach
82	Video Services	95	Tech Prep Program	285	STEM
83	Substance Abuse Prev	97	Chief Infomation Officer	286	Digital Learning
84	Erate	98	Chief Technology Officer	288	Common Core Standards
85	AIDS Education	270	Character Education	294	Accountability
86	Alternative/At Risk	271	Migrant Education	295	Network System
87	Multi-Cultural Curriculum	273	Teacher Mentor	296	Title II Programs
88	Social Work	274	Before/After Sch	297	Webmaster

298	Grant Writer/Ptnrships	
750	Chief Innovation Officer	
751	Chief of Staff	
752	Social Emotional Learning	

School Programs
A = Alternative Program
G = Adult Classes
M = Magnet Program
T = Title I Schoolwide
V = Career & Tech Ed Programs

Other School Types
Ⓐ = Alternative School
Ⓒ = Charter School
Ⓜ = Magnet School
Ⓨ = Year-Round School

Social Media
 = Facebook
 = Twitter

New Schools are shaded
New Superintendents and Principals are bold
Personnel with email addresses are underscored

TX-63

Cameron County

Market Data Retrieval

School	Grd	Prgm	Enr/#Cls		SN	Phone
ⓜ Homer Hanna Early Clg HS 2615 E Price Rd, Brownsville 78521 Blanca Lambarri	9-12	GTV	2,663		92%	956/548-7600 Fax 956/548-7603
Hudson Elem Sch 2980 Ruben Torres Sr Blvd, Brownsville 78526 Rachel Ayala	PK-5	T	804	35	92%	956/574-6400 Fax 956/574-6403
ⓜ James Pace Early Clg HS 314 W Los Ebanos Blvd, Brownsville 78520 Rose Longoria	9-12	GTV	2,057	100	100%	956/548-7700 Fax 956/548-7710
Josephine Castaneda Elem Sch 3201 Lima St, Brownsville 78521 Griselda Camargo	PK-5	T	631	17	98%	956/548-8800 Fax 956/548-8811
Julia Garcia Middle Sch 5701 Ruben Torres Sr Blvd, Brownsville 78526 Luis Segura	6-8	T	1,112		97%	956/832-6300 Fax 956/832-6304
Keller Elem Sch 2540 W Alton Gloor Blvd, Brownsville 78520 Javier Garza	PK-5	T	589		95%	956/547-4400 Fax 956/554-7150
Ⓐ Lincoln Park Sch 7 Orange St, Brownsville 78521 Dawn Hall	6-12	V	107	17	97%	956/548-7880 Fax 956/982-3090
ⓜ Lopez Early College High Sch 3205 S Dakota Ave, Brownsville 78521 Dahlia Aguilar	9-12	GTV	2,051	104	99%	956/982-7400 Fax 956/982-7499
Lucio Middle Sch 300 N Vermillion Ave, Brownsville 78521 Chester Arizmendi	6-8	T	892	55	97%	956/831-4550 Fax 956/838-2298
Manzano Middle Sch 2580 W Alton Gloor Blvd, Brownsville 78520 Marisol Trevino	6-8	T	938		95%	956/548-9800 Fax 956/548-6772
Mary & Frank Yturria Elem Sch 2955 W Tandy Rd, Brownsville 78520 Sandra Cortez	PK-5	T	590	46	85%	956/350-3200 Fax 956/350-3207
Morningside Elem Sch 1025 Morningside Rd, Brownsville 78521 Jose Martinez	PK-5	T	660	60	97%	956/982-2760 Fax 956/982-2787
Oliveira Middle Sch 444 Land O Lakes Dr, Brownsville 78521 Cindy Castro	6-8	T	1,098	120	94%	956/548-8530 Fax 956/544-3968
Ortiz Elem Sch 2500 W Alton Gloor Blvd, Brownsville 78520 Patricia Garza	PK-5	T	655	21	98%	956/698-1100 Fax 956/546-6611
Palm Grove Elem Sch 7942 Southmost Rd, Brownsville 78521 Patricia Chacon	PK-6	T	440	35	97%	956/982-3850 Fax 956/986-5070
Paredes Elem Sch 3700 Heritage Trl, Brownsville 78526 Melissa Werbiski	PK-5	T	882		87%	956/574-5582 Fax 956/574-5584
Pena Elem Sch 4975 Salida De Luna, Brownsville 78526 Yolanda Turbeville	PK-5	T	604		97%	956/547-7100 Fax 956/838-6545
Perez Elem Sch 2514 Shidler Dr, Brownsville 78521 Michael Moreno	PK-5	T	470	35	98%	956/982-2800 Fax 956/982-2806
Perkins Middle Sch 4750 Austin Rd, Brownsville 78521 Beatriz Hernandez	6-8	T	694	75	99%	956/831-8770 Fax 956/831-8789
Pullam Elem Sch 3200 Madrid Ave, Brownsville 78520 Celia De Los Santos	PK-5	T	726		86%	956/547-3700 Fax 956/350-2880
Putegnat Elem Sch 730 E 8th St, Brownsville 78520 Aidee Vasquez	PK-5	T	458	35	99%	956/548-8930 Fax 956/548-8947
R L Martin Elem Sch 1701 Stanford Ave, Brownsville 78520 Gilda Jo Pena	PK-5	T	473	45	94%	956/982-2730 Fax 956/982-3032
Russell Elem Sch 800 Lakeside Blvd, Brownsville 78520 Oscar Cantu	PK-5	T	666	40	100%	956/548-8960 Fax 956/548-8889
Sharp Elem Sch 1439 Palm Blvd, Brownsville 78520 Irma Segura	PK-5	T	498	36	92%	956/982-2930 Fax 956/982-2948
ⓜ Simon Rivera Early Clg HS 6955 Ruben Torres Sr Blvd, Brownsville 78526 Norma Canales	9-12	TV	2,338		99%	956/831-8700 Fax 956/831-8705
Skinner Elem Sch 411 W Saint Charles St, Brownsville 78520 Mary Rodriguez	PK-5	T	474	50	92%	956/982-2830 Fax 956/982-2849
Southmost Elem Sch 5245 Southmost Rd, Brownsville 78521 Anabela Almanza	PK-5	T	396	40	99%	956/548-8870 Fax 956/548-8875
Stell Middle Sch 1105 E Los Ebanos Blvd, Brownsville 78520 Obed Leal	6-8	T	1,041		98%	956/698-0363 Fax 956/548-8666
Stillman Middle Sch 2977 W Tandy Rd, Brownsville 78520 Eduardo Martinez	6-8	T	1,077	85	87%	956/698-1000 Fax 956/350-3231
Vermillion Elem Sch 6895 Ruben Torres Sr Blvd, Brownsville 78526 Socorro Houghtaling	PK-5	T	825	66	99%	956/831-6060 Fax 956/831-1093
Veterans Memorial Early Clg HS 4550 US Highway 281, Brownsville 78520 Norma Gallegos	9-12		1,948		91%	956/574-5600 Fax 956/542-1341
Villa Nueva Elem Sch 7455 Old Military Rd, Brownsville 78520 Melissa Gutierrez	PK-5	T	508	26	94%	956/542-3957 Fax 956/544-0720

● **Harlingen Cons Ind School Dist** PID: 01003756   956/430-9500
407 N 77 Sunshine Strip, Harlingen 78550   Fax 956/430-9514

Schools: 31 \ *Teachers:* 1,272 \ *Students:* 18,600 \
Special Ed Students: 1,791 \ *LEP Students:* 2,478 \ *College-Bound:* 59%
\ *Ethnic:* Hispanic 93%, Caucasian 6% \ *Exp:* $262 (Med) \ *Poverty:* 35% \
Title I: $8,900,352 \ *Special Education:* $3,206,000 \ *Open-Close:* 08/12 -
05/22 \ *DTBP:* $192 (High) \ ⓕ

Art Cavazos 1		Julio Cavazos 2,15,19	
Kimberly Anderson 2		Oscar Tapia 3,4,5,15	
Judy Baker 4,7		Luciano Rubio 5	
Robert Davies 6		Dr Alicia Noyola 8,18	
Loranda Romero 9,15		Lori Romero 9	
Joseph Villareal 10		Thelma Reynolds 11	
Debbie Scogin 15,68		Ronnie Rios 23*	
Luis Solorio 35		Sandra Tovar 36	
Norma Garcia 57		Daniel Garcia 58*	
Alejandra Lara 59*		Dr Nolan Perez 67	
Melissa Nieto 68		Cynthia Castillo 69	
Shane Strubhart 71		Jessica Hruska 73	
Maria Kortan 74		Olga Garcia 76	
Myliss Parker 81		Dr Jose Cavazos 88,93	
Jennifer Maldonado 286		Dalia Garcia 294	
Jessica Martinez 297*			

Public Schs..Principal	Grd	Prgm	Enr/#Cls		SN	
Austin Elem Sch 700 E Austin Ave, Harlingen 78550 Magda Gonzales	PK-5	T	384	32	86%	956/427-3060 Fax 956/427-3063
Ben Milam Elem Sch 1215 S Rangerville Rd, Harlingen 78552 Brenda McKinney	PK-5	T	430	28	92%	956/427-3150 Fax 956/427-3153
Bonham Elem Sch 2400 E Jefferson Ave, Harlingen 78550 Herminia Ramirez	PK-5	T	743	44	85%	956/427-3070 Fax 956/427-3073

TX—64

1	Superintendent	8	Curric/Instruct K-12	19	Chief Financial Officer	29	Family/Consumer Science	39	Social Studies K-12	49	English/Lang Arts Elem	59	Special Education Elem	69	Academic Assessment
2	Bus/Finance/Purchasing	9	Curric/Instruct Elem	20	Art K-12	30	Adult Education	40	Social Studies Elem	50	English/Lang Arts Sec	60	Special Education Sec	70	Research/Development
3	Buildings And Grounds	10	Curric/Instruct Sec	21	Art Elem	31	Career/Sch-to-Work K-12	41	Social Studies Sec	51	Reading K-12	61	Foreign/World Lang K-12	71	Public Information
4	Food Service	11	Federal Program	22	Art Sec	32	Career/Sch-to-Work Elem	42	Science K-12	52	Reading Elem	62	Foreign/World Lang Elem	72	Summer School
5	Transportation	12	Title I	23	Music K-12	33	Career/Sch-to-Work Sec	43	Science Elem	53	Reading Sec	63	Foreign/World Lang Sec	73	Instructional Tech
6	Athletic	13	Title V	24	Music Elem	34	Early Childhood Ed	44	Science Sec	54	Remedial Reading K-12	64	Religious Education K-12	74	Inservice Training
7	Health Services	15	Asst Superintendent	25	Music Sec	35	Health/Phys Education	45	Math K-12	55	Remedial Reading Elem	65	Religious Education Elem	75	Marketing/Distributive
		16	Instructional Media Svcs	26	Business Education	36	Guidance Services K-12	46	Math Elem	56	Remedial Reading Sec	66	Religious Education Sec	76	Info Systems
		17	Chief Operations Officer	27	Career & Tech Ed	37	Guidance Services Elem	47	Math Sec	57	Bilingual/ELL	67	School Board President	77	Psychological Assess
		18	Chief Academic Officer	28	Technology Education	38	Guidance Services Sec	48	English/Lang Arts K-12	58	Special Education K-12	68	Teacher Personnel	78	Affirmative Action

Texas School Directory — Cameron County

School	Grd	Prgm	Enr/#Cls	SN	Phone
Bowie Elem Sch 309 W Lincoln Ave, Harlingen 78550 Jaymie Galan	PK-5	T	339 21	92%	956/427-3080 Fax 956/427-3083
Coakley Middle Sch 1402 S 6th St, Harlingen 78550 Pedro Sanchez	6-8	TV	737 60	79%	956/427-3000 Fax 956/427-3006
Crockett Elem Sch 1406 W Jefferson Ave, Harlingen 78550 Juan Manuel Garcia	PK-5	T	358 23	94%	956/427-3090 Fax 956/427-3093
Dishman Elem Sch 309 Madeley St, Combes 78535 Irma Davis	PK-5	T	338 24	93%	956/427-3100 Fax 956/427-3103
Dr Abraham P Cano Fresh Acad 1701 W Lozano St, Harlingen 78550 Vivian Bauer	9-9	T	1,139	74%	956/430-4900 Fax 956/427-3772
Ⓒ Early College High Sch 2510 Pecan St Bldg R, Harlingen 78550 Dr Pamela Flores	9-12	T	336 13	62%	956/430-9690 Fax 956/430-9693
Gutierriez Middle Sch 3205 Wilson Rd, Harlingen 78552 **Gutierrez Mike Reyes**	6-8	T	841 50	81%	956/430-4400 Fax 956/430-4480
Harlingen High Sch 1201 Marshall St, Harlingen 78550 **Vivian Bauer**	9-12	TV	1,827	78%	956/427-3600 Fax 956/427-3792
Harlingen High School South 1701 Dixieland Rd, Harlingen 78550 Fernando Reyes	9-12	ATV	1,549 60	69%	956/427-3800 Fax 956/427-3995
Harlingen Sch of Health 2302 N 21st St, Harlingen 78550 Tina Garza	8-12	T	414	57%	956/430-4078 Fax 956/427-3763
Houston Elem Sch 301 E Taft Ave, Harlingen 78550 Virgina Armstrong	PK-5	T	462	85%	956/427-3110 Fax 956/427-3114
Jane Long Elem Sch 2601 N 7th St, Harlingen 78550 Bobbie Hushen	PK-5	T	653 42	72%	956/427-3140 Fax 956/427-3144
Jefferson Elem Sch 601 S J St, Harlingen 78550 Alejandra Lara	PK-5	T	356 26	96%	956/427-3120 Fax 956/427-3127
Ⓐ Keys Academy Ⓨ 2809 N 7th St, Harlingen 78550 Isidoro Nieto	8-12	GMT	204 12	72%	956/427-3220 Fax 956/427-3223
Lamar Elem Sch 1100 McLarry Rd, Harlingen 78550 Alma Atkinson	PK-5	T	626 30	83%	956/427-3130 Fax 956/427-3133
Lee H Means Elem Sch 1201 E Loop 499, Harlingen 78550 Mindy Sanchez	PK-5	T	639	71%	956/427-3377 Fax 956/427-3376
Memorial Middle Sch 1901 Rio Hondo Rd, Harlingen 78550 **William Snavely**	6-8	TV	806 35	79%	956/427-3020 Fax 956/427-3024
Moises Vela Middle Sch 801 S Palm Blvd, Harlingen 78552 Tony Gonzales	6-8	TV	857 35	65%	956/427-3479 Fax 956/427-3549
Ⓐ New Pathways Center 208 S F St, Harlingen 78550 Venee Harrell	1-5		15 2		956/427-3250 Fax 956/427-3254
Rodriguez Elem Sch 8402 Wilson Rd, Harlingen 78552 **Adriana Arellano**	PK-5	T	731 43	80%	956/430-4060 Fax 956/430-4065
Ⓐ Secondary Alternative Center 1310 Sam Houston Dr, Harlingen 78550 Dan Araiza	6-12		59 6	89%	956/427-3210 Fax 956/430-4487
STEM2 Preparatory Academy 1920 E Washington Ave, Harlingen 78550 Sonya Brandenburg	6-8		250		956/368-6100 Fax 956/430-4447
Stuart Place Elem Sch 6701 W Business 83, Harlingen 78552 William Snavely	PK-5	T	755 34	56%	956/427-3160 Fax 956/427-3159
Travis Elem Sch 600 E Polk St, Harlingen 78550 Beulah Rangel	PK-5	T	347 24	87%	956/427-3170 Fax 956/427-3173
Treasure Hills Elem Sch 2525 Haine Dr, Harlingen 78550 Roland Ingram	PK-5	T	909 38	68%	956/427-3180 Fax 956/427-3187
Vernon Middle Sch 125 S 13th St, Harlingen 78550 Arely Tamez	6-8	TV	662 54	87%	956/427-3040 Fax 956/427-3046
Wilson Elem Sch 16495 Primera Rd, Harlingen 78552 Michele Todd	PK-5	T	500 40	81%	956/427-3190 Fax 956/427-3197
Zavala Elem Sch 1111 N B St, Harlingen 78550 Tanya Garza	PK-5	T	406 26	97%	956/427-3200 Fax 956/427-3203

● **La Feria Ind School Dist** PID: 01003940   956/797-8300
   505 N Villarreal St, La Feria 78559   Fax 956/797-3737

Schools: 7 \ **Teachers:** 240 \ **Students:** 3,347 \ **Special Ed Students:** 318 \ **LEP Students:** 499 \ **Ethnic:** Hispanic 97%, Caucasian 3% \ **Exp:** $485 (High) \ **Poverty:** 31% \ **Title I:** $1,731,904 \ **Open-Close:** 08/27 - 05/22 \ **DTBP:** $176 (High)

Cathy Hernandez ....1 Antonio Aguilar 2,19
Darrell Guerra ....3,5 Cynthia Casas 4
Oscar Salinas ....6,35* Cynthia Torres 8,15
Dr Isaac Roderiguez ....8 Dr Miriam Guerra 11,27,285
Veronica Torres ....28,73,295 Haydee Rodriguez 36*
Annette Pena ....57 Lilian Ramos 58
Juan Bronis ....67 Cynthia Guajardo 93,271

Public Schs..Principal	Grd	Prgm	Enr/#Cls	SN	Phone
C E Vail Elem Sch 209 W Jessamine Ave, La Feria 78559 Rosie Garza	PK-4	T	489 42	92%	956/797-8460 Fax 956/797-3429
David Sanchez Elem Sch 1601 S Main St, La Feria 78559 Umberto Flores	PK-4	T	409	80%	956/797-8550 Fax 956/797-8530
Ⓐ La Feria Academy 505 N Villarreal St, La Feria 78559 Carlos Verduzco	9-12	T	33	95%	956/797-8360 Fax 956/797-1583
La Feria High Sch 901 N Canal St, La Feria 78559 Cynthia Chairez	9-12	AGTV	963 100	80%	956/797-8370 Fax 956/797-9374
Noemi Dominguez Elem Sch 600 Pancho Maples Dr, La Feria 78559 Yvette Cantu	5-6	T	495 60	85%	956/797-8430 Fax 956/797-2600
Sam Houston Elem Sch 500 Beddoes Rd, La Feria 78559 **Hector Cazares**	PK-4	T	514 21	82%	956/797-8490 Fax 956/797-5169
W B Green Junior High Sch 501 N Canal St, La Feria 78559 Michael Torres	7-8	T	504 45	85%	956/797-8400 Fax 956/797-2157

● **Los Fresnos Cons Ind Sch Dist** PID: 01004009   956/254-5000
   600 N Mesquite St, Los Fresnos 78566   Fax 956/233-4031

Schools: 16 \ **Teachers:** 670 \ **Students:** 10,700 \ **Special Ed Students:** 931 \ **LEP Students:** 2,195 \ **Ethnic:** Hispanic 97%, Caucasian 3% \ **Exp:** $464 (High) \ **Poverty:** 27% \ **Title I:** $3,985,835 \ **Special Education:** $1,523,000 \ **Open-Close:** 08/14 - 05/28 \ **DTBP:** $188 (High)

---

79 Student Personnel	91 Safety/Security	275 Response To Intervention	298 Grant Writer/Ptnrships	**School Programs**	**Social Media**		
30 Driver Ed/Safety	92 Magnet School	277 Remedial Math K-12	750 Chief Innovation Officer	A = Alternative Program			
31 Gifted/Talented	93 Parental Involvement	280 Literacy Coach	751 Chief of Staff	G = Adult Classes	▯ = Facebook		
32 Video Services	95 Tech Prep Program	285 STEM	752 Social Emotional Learning	M = Magnet Program			
33 Substance Abuse Prev	97 Chief Infomation Officer	286 Digital Learning		T = Title I Schoolwide	▯ = Twitter		
34 Erate	98 Chief Technology Officer	288 Common Core Standards	**Other School Types**	V = Career & Tech Ed Programs			
35 AIDS Education	270 Character Education	294 Accountability	Ⓐ = Alternative School				
38 Alternative/At Risk	271 Migrant Education	295 Network System	Ⓒ = Charter School	New Schools are shaded			
39 Multi-Cultural Curriculum	273 Teacher Mentor	296 Title II Programs	Ⓜ = Magnet School	New Superintendents and Principals are bold			
30 Social Work	274 Before/After Sch	297 Webmaster	Ⓨ = Year-Round School	Personnel with email addresses are underscored			

Cameron County

Market Data Retrieval

Gonzalo Salazar 1	David Young 2
Jose Leal 3	Rey Ovalle 4
Suzanne Ramirez 5	Patrick Brown 6*
Denise Davis 7	Sara Tudon 8
Tammy Chambers 8	Valarie Londrie 9,16,27,31,57,69,277,298
Jimmy McDonough 10,16,27,31,57,58,69,298	Noe Guillen 11,271,294,296
Sandra Ruiz 36,69,83,88	Jesus Amaya 67
Ben Estrada 70	Billy Simpson 73,84,295
Joe Vasquez 91	

Public Schs..Principal	Grd	Prgm	Enr/#Cls	SN	
ⓐ AMI Kids Rio Grande Valley 27615 Buena Vista Blvd, Los Fresnos 78566 Javier Ibarra	9-12	V	15 6		956/233-5795 Fax 956/233-3124
ⓐ College Career & Tech Acad 32614 State Highway 100, Los Fresnos 78566 Jeri Gomez	9-12		31		956/254-5296 Fax 956/233-6328
Dora Romero Elem Sch 9705 Cajaun Blvd, Brownsville 78521 Veronica Grimaldo	PK-5	T	539	81%	956/254-5210 Fax 956/350-2645
Las Yescas Elem Sch 24313 FM 803, San Benito 78586 Lynn Martinez	PK-5	T	439 30	90%	956/233-6955 Fax 956/748-2540
Laureles Elem Sch 31393 FM 2893, Los Fresnos 78566 Claudia Larrasquitu	PK-5	T	636 35	85%	956/254-5141 Fax 956/233-3690
Liberty Middle Sch 31579 FM 2893, San Benito 78586 Annice Garza	6-8	T	788	87%	956/233-3900 Fax 956/233-1074
Lopez-Riggins Elem Sch 613 N Mesquite St, Los Fresnos 78566 Oscar De La Rosa	PK-5	T	571 36	82%	956/233-6916 Fax 956/233-3696
Los Cuates Middle Sch 32477 Highway 100, Los Fresnos 78566 Antonio Padilla	6-8	T	797 48	75%	956/254-5182 Fax 956/233-1487
Los Fresnos 9th & 10th GR Sch 33790 Farm Rd 803, San Benito 78586 Jennifer Stumbaugh	9-10		1,657		956/254-5250 Fax 956/399-2047
Los Fresnos Elem Sch 32602 State Highway 100, Los Fresnos 78566 Veronica Grimaldo	PK-5	T	603 37	77%	956/233-6900 Fax 956/233-6235
Los Fresnos High Sch 907 N Arroyo Blvd, Los Fresnos 78566 Justin Stumbaugh	10-12	ATV	1,669 150	78%	956/254-5300 Fax 956/233-3510
Olmito Elem Sch 2500 Arroyo Blvd, Brownsville 78526 Linda Rodriguez	PK-5	T	638	71%	956/233-3950 Fax 956/350-8835
Palmer-Laakso Elem Sch 30515 FM 1847, San Benito 78586 Celia Ontiveros	PK-5	T	564	76%	956/254-5121 Fax 956/233-3659
Rancho Verde Elem Sch 101 Rancho Alegre, Brownsville 78526 Mary Chavez	PK-5	T	663	62%	956/254-5230 Fax 956/350-8843
Resaca Middle Sch 22422 FM 1575, Los Fresnos 78566 Elizabeth Swantner	6-8	T	812 53	64%	956/254-5159 Fax 956/233-6210
Villareal Elem Sch 7700 E Lakeside Blvd, Olmito 78575 Pablo Leal	PK-5	T	387 34	78%	956/233-3975 Fax 956/350-2087

• **Point Isabel Ind Sch Dist** PID: 01004061 956/943-0000
101 Port Rd, Port Isabel 78578 Fax 956/943-0014

Schools: 4 \ **Teachers:** 151 \ **Students:** 2,500 \ **Special Ed Students:** 228 \ **LEP Students:** 849 \ **Ethnic:** Hispanic 92%, Caucasian 7% \ **Exp:** $423 (High) \ **Poverty:** 37% \ **Title I:** $1,395,844 \ **Special Education:** $437,000 \ **Open-Close:** 08/27 - 05/25 \ **DTBP:** $553 (High)

Theresa Alarcon 1	Henry Levrier 2,3,11,27,30,83,296
Audrey Pena-Rodriguez 4	Ernie Mata 5
Jason Strunk 6	Ana Holland 8,16,57,69,72,85,273,274
Kirstie Ramirez 11,270,271	D J Canales 16,73,297
Lindsey Zimmerman 38*	Juan Lopez 58
Jennifer Pinkerton 67	Debbie Hernandez 69

Public Schs..Principal	Grd	Prgm	Enr/#Cls	SN	
Derry Elem Sch 1702 2nd St, Port Isabel 78578 Maribel Valdez	PK-5	T	638 31	89%	956/943-0070 Fax 956/943-0074
Garriga Elem Sch 400 W Adam St, Port Isabel 78578 Reina Salinas	PK-5	T	590 40	89%	956/943-0080 Fax 956/943-0640
Port Isabel High Sch 18000 Highway 100, Port Isabel 78578 William Roach	9-12	ATV	697 45	83%	956/943-0030 Fax 956/943-0648
Port Isabel Junior High Sch 17001 Highway 100, Port Isabel 78578 Nancy Gonzalez	6-8	T	501 35	88%	956/943-0060 Fax 956/943-0055

• **Rio Hondo Ind School Dist** PID: 01004102 956/748-1000
215 W Colorado St, Rio Hondo 78583 Fax 956/748-1038

Schools: 3 \ **Teachers:** 146 \ **Students:** 1,900 \ **Special Ed Students:** 179 \ **LEP Students:** 225 \ **Ethnic:** Hispanic 96%, Caucasian 4% \ **Exp:** $377 (High) \ **Poverty:** 30% \ **Title I:** $1,013,478 \ **Open-Close:** 08/26 - 05/29 \ **DTBP:** $158 (High)

Ismael Garcia 1	Ron De La Garza 2,84
Racao Madrigal 4	Rocky James 6*
Veronica Puente 11,57,58,69	Saul Rodriguez 16,73,295,297
Claudia Villalobos 67	Paul Arce 297

Public Schs..Principal	Grd	Prgm	Enr/#Cls	SN	
Rio Hondo Elem Sch 700 N Reynolds St, Rio Hondo 78583 Ricardo Ortiz	PK-4	T	810 40	84%	956/748-1050 Fax 956/748-1073
Rio Hondo High Sch 22547 State Highway 345, Rio Hondo 78583 Asael Ruvalcaba	9-12	ATV	685 40	85%	956/748-1200 Fax 956/748-1204
Rio Hondo Middle Sch 501 N Reynolds St, Rio Hondo 78583 Ramiro Moreno	5-8	T	405 35	89%	956/748-1150 Fax 956/748-1168

• **San Benito Cons Ind Sch Dist** PID: 01004140 956/361-6100
240 N Crockett St, San Benito 78586 Fax 956/361-6115

Schools: 18 \ **Teachers:** 680 \ **Students:** 10,643 \ **Special Ed Students:** 906 \ **LEP Students:** 2,253 \ **College-Bound:** 55% \ **Ethnic:** Hispanic 99%, Caucasian 1% \ **Exp:** $649 (High) \ **Poverty:** 40% \ **Title I:** $6,600,762 \ **Special Education:** $1,727,000 \ **Open-Close:** 08/14 - 05/28 \ **DTBP:** $187 (High)

Dr Nate Carman 1	Eddie Bacavazos 2
Hilda Rendon 2,15	David Garcia 3
Jana Landrum 4	Erica Flores 5
Dan Gomez 6	Janette Rodriguez 7

1	Superintendent	8	Curric/Instruct K-12	19	Chief Financial Officer	29	Family/Consumer Science	39	Social Studies K-12	49	English/Lang Arts Elem	59	Special Education Elem	69	Academic Assessment
2	Bus/Finance/Purchasing	9	Curric/Instruct Elem	20	Art K-12	30	Adult Education	40	Social Studies Elem	50	English/Lang Arts Sec	60	Special Education Sec	70	Research/Development
3	Buildings And Grounds	10	Curric/Instruct Sec	21	Art Elem	31	Career/Sch-to-Work K-12	41	Social Studies Sec	51	Reading K-12	61	Foreign/World Lang K-12	71	Public Information
4	Food Service	11	Federal Program	22	Art Sec	32	Career/Sch-to-Work Elem	42	Science K-12	52	Reading Elem	62	Foreign/World Lang Elem	72	Summer School
5	Transportation	12	Title I	23	Music K-12	33	Career/Sch-to-Work Sec	43	Science Elem	53	Reading Sec	63	Foreign/World Lang Sec	73	Instructional Tech
6	Athletic	13	Title V	24	Music Elem	34	Early Childhood Ed	44	Science Sec	54	Remedial Reading K-12	64	Religious Education K-12	74	Inservice Training
7	Health Services	14	Asst Superintendent	25	Music Sec	35	Health/Phys Education	45	Math K-12	55	Remedial Reading Elem	65	Religious Education Elem	75	Marketing/Distributive
		15	Instructional Media Svcs	26	Business Education	36	Guidance Services K-12	46	Math Elem	56	Remedial Reading Sec	66	Religious Education Sec	76	Info Systems
		16	Chief Operations Officer	27	Career & Tech Ed	37	Guidance Services Elem	47	Math Sec	57	Bilingual/ELL	67	School Board President	77	Psychological Assess
		18	Chief Academic Officer	28	Technology Education	38	Guidance Services Sec	48	English/Lang Arts K-12	58	Special Education K-12	68	Teacher Personnel	78	Affirmative Action

Texas School Directory — Cameron County

Name	Page
Hector Madrigal	8,15
Connie Cruz	12,271
Leonila Pena	16,76,286
Dr Patricia Quesada	57
Michael Vargas	67
Isabelle Gonzalez	71
Ray Saldana	79*
Luis Gonzales	93
Libby Flores	9
Andrea Cruz	15,68
Rolando Guerra	27
Ernesto Manriquez	58
Gina Ortiz	69,70,294
Stephanie Ramirez	74*
Juan Sosa	91
Terry Padilla	274

Public Schs..Principal	Grd	Prgm	Enr/#Cls	SN	
Angela Leal Elem Sch 33356 FM 732, San Benito 78586 **Rudy Ramirez**	PK-5	T	426	91%	956/276-5055
Berta Cabaza Middle Sch 2901 Shafer Rd, San Benito 78586 Saul Ibarra	6-8	T	851 75	77%	956/361-6600 Fax 956/361-6608
Dr C M Cash Elem Sch 400 Ponciana St, San Benito 78586 **Marleen Araiza**	PK-5	T	608 40	87%	956/361-6700 Fax 956/361-6708
Dr Raul Garza Jr Elem Sch 845 8th St, San Benito 78586 Elsa Lambert	PK-5	T	396 35	82%	956/361-6900 Fax 956/361-6908
Ed Downs Elem Sch 1302 N Dick Dowling St, San Benito 78586 Manuela Lopez	PK-5	T	436 32	62%	956/361-6720 Fax 956/361-6728
Frank Roberts Elem Sch 451 Biddle St, San Benito 78586 Rolando Diaz	PK-5	T	340 20	94%	956/361-6740 Fax 956/361-6748
Fred Booth Elem Sch 705 Zaragosa St, San Benito 78586 Nedia Espinoza	PK-5	T	503 39	86%	956/361-6860 Fax 956/361-6868
Ⓐ Gateway to Graduation Academy 600 N Austin St, San Benito 78586 Alfredo Perez	9-12	T	82	90%	956/361-6446 Fax 956/361-0000
Judge Oscar De La Fuente ES 2700 S Sam Houston St, San Benito 78586 Olivia Flores	PK-5	T	398 30	85%	956/361-6820 Fax 956/361-6828
La Encantada Elem Sch 35001 FM 1577, San Benito 78586 Gracie Martinez	PK-5	T	418 25	92%	956/361-6760 Fax 956/361-6768
La Paloma Elem Sch 35076 Padilla St, San Benito 78586 Ema Gonzalez	PK-5	T	423 30	87%	956/361-6780 Fax 956/361-6788
Miller Jordan Middle Sch 700 N McCullough St, San Benito 78586 Jo Fernandez	6-8	T	825 60	88%	956/361-6650 Fax 956/361-6658
Ⓐ Positive Redirection Center 450 S Dick Dowling St, San Benito 78586 Scott Hausler	6-12	T	25 6		956/361-6275 Fax 956/361-6278
Rangerville Elem Sch 17558 Landrum Park Rd, San Benito 78586 Nora Martinez	PK-5	T	347 18	81%	956/361-6840 Fax 956/361-6848
Riverside Middle Sch 35428 Padilla St, San Benito 78586 Eliza Gomez	6-8	AT	612 40	91%	956/361-6940 Fax 956/361-6948
San Benito High Sch 450 S Williams Rd, San Benito 78586 Maria Solis	10-12	ATV	2,172 50	81%	956/361-6500 Fax 956/361-6473
Sullivan Elem Sch 900 Elizabeth St, San Benito 78586 Diana Atkinson	PK-5	T	419 24	80%	956/361-6880 Fax 956/361-6888
Veterans Memorial Academy 2115 N Williams Rd, San Benito 78586 Gilbert Galvan	9-9	T	766	85%	956/276-6000 Fax 956/276-6008

● **Santa Maria Ind School Dist** PID: 01004308   956/565-6308
11119 Military Road, Santa Maria 78592   Fax 956/565-0598

Schools: 4 \ **Teachers:** 55 \ **Students:** 691 \ **Special Ed Students:** 45 \ **LEP Students:** 242 \ **College-Bound:** 55% \ **Ethnic:** Hispanic 99%, Caucasian 1% \ **Exp:** $385 (High) \ **Poverty:** 37% \ **Title I:** $382,773 \ **Open-Close:** 08/06 - 06/05

Name	Page	Name	Page
Martin Cuellar	1	Enrique Cuellar	2
Adolfo Hinojosa	67	Daniel Kaffka	91

Public Schs..Principal	Grd	Prgm	Enr/#Cls	SN	
Santa Maria High Sch 11224 Military Rd, Santa Maria 78592 Jose Vela	9-12	AGTV	201	97%	956/565-9144 Fax 956/514-1968
Santa Maria Junior High Sch 11142 Military Rd, Santa Maria 78592 Jose Vela	7-8		105		956/565-5348
Santa Maria Middle Sch 11100 Military Rd, Santa Maria 78592 Rogelio Campa	5-6	AT	96 17	96%	956/565-6309 Fax 956/565-6720
Tony Gonzalez Elem Sch 11100 Military Rd, Santa Maria 78592 Mark Aguero	PK-4	T	297 15	99%	956/565-5348 Fax 956/565-2698

● **Santa Rosa Ind School Dist** PID: 01004322   956/636-9800
232 E Jesus T Avila, Santa Rosa 78593   Fax 956/636-1439

Schools: 3 \ **Teachers:** 83 \ **Students:** 1,300 \ **Special Ed Students:** 106 \ **LEP Students:** 149 \ **College-Bound:** 48% \ **Ethnic:** Hispanic 99%, Caucasian 1% \ **Exp:** $554 (High) \ **Poverty:** 35% \ **Title I:** $700,863 \ **Open-Close:** 08/19 - 05/28 \ **DTBP:** $484 (High)

Name	Page	Name	Page
Dr Angela Gonzalez	1	David Robledo	2,4,19
Ren Rergel	3,5	Catherine Diaz	4
Juan Cipriano	6*	Malesa Salera	8,58
Heriberto Villarreal	11,73	Santos Castareda	67
Nephalit Gonzalez	76	Alberto Trevino	274

Public Schs..Principal	Grd	Prgm	Enr/#Cls	SN	
Elma Barrera Elem Sch Hwy 107, Santa Rosa 78593 **Gregorio Camarillo**	PK-5	T	531 33	92%	956/636-9870 Fax 956/362-2747
Jo Nelson Middle Sch 102 S Main, Santa Rosa 78593 Jacinto Sauceda	6-8	ATV	247 17	84%	956/636-9850 Fax 956/636-1519
Santa Rosa High Sch 102 Jesus R Cruz St, Santa Rosa 78593 Jaime Garcia	9-12	ATV	350 40	81%	956/636-9830 Fax 956/636-1496

● **South Texas Ind School Dist** PID: 01808984   956/565-2454
100 Med High Dr, Mercedes 78570   Fax 956/565-9129

Schools: 6 \ **Teachers:** 296 \ **Students:** 4,245 \ **Special Ed Students:** 88 \ **LEP Students:** 100 \ **Ethnic:** Asian 9%, African American 1%, Hispanic 84%, Caucasian 6% \ **Exp:** $927 (High) \ **Special Education:** $541,000 \ **Open-Close:** 08/19 - 05/29 \ **DTBP:** $181 (High)

Name	Page	Name	Page
Marco Antonio Lara	1	Marla Knaub	2,15
Juan Villarreal	3,5,91	Jeff Hembree	11,57,73,76,285,286,295,296
Ann Vickman	16*	Josie Garcia	58*
Doug Buchanan	67	Amanda Odom	71
Maricela Hinojosa	83,88*	Candace Guillen	93*

Codes:
79 Student Personnel | 91 Safety/Security | 275 Response To Intervention | 298 Grant Writer/Ptnrships
80 Driver Ed/Safety | 92 Magnet School | 277 Remedial Math K-12 | 750 Chief Innovation Officer
81 Gifted/Talented | 93 Parental Involvement | 280 Literacy Coach | 751 Chief of Staff
82 Video Services | 95 Tech Prep Program | 285 STEM | 752 Social Emotional Learning
83 Substance Abuse Prev | 97 Chief Infomation Officer | 286 Digital Learning
84 Erate | 98 Chief Technology Officer | 288 Common Core Standards
85 AIDS Education | 270 Character Education | 294 Accountability
88 Alternative/At Risk | 271 Migrant Education | 295 Network System
89 Multi-Cultural Curriculum | 273 Teacher Mentor | 296 Title II Programs
90 Social Work | 274 Before/After Sch | 297 Webmaster

School Programs: A = Alternative Program | G = Adult Classes | M = Magnet Program | T = Title I Schoolwide | V = Career & Tech Ed Programs

Other School Types: Ⓐ = Alternative Program | Ⓒ = Charter School | Ⓜ = Magnet School | Ⓨ = Year-Round School

Social Media: = Facebook | = Twitter

New Schools are shaded
New Superintendents and Principals are bold
Personnel with email addresses are underscored

Camp County

Market Data Retrieval

Public Schs..Principal	Grd	Prgm	Enr/#Cls	SN		
Rising Scholars Acad of S TX 151 Helen Moore Rd, San Benito 78586 Carrie Sauceda	7-8	T	497	44%	956/399-4358 Fax 956/399-3570	
ⓜ S Texas Bus Ed & Tech Acad 510 S Sugar Rd, Edinburg 78539 Efrain Garza	9-12	TV	623 50	61%	956/383-1684 Fax 956/383-8544	
ⓜ Science Acad of South Texas 900 Med High Dr, Mercedes 78570 Irma Castillo	9-12	ATV	801 48	37%	956/565-4620 Fax 956/565-9112	
South Texas Acad Med Professns 10650 N Expressway 77 77/83, Olmito 78575 Harry Goette	9-12	TV	848 25	74%	956/214-6100 Fax 956/399-3570	
ⓜ South Texas HS for Health Prof 700 Med High Dr, Mercedes 78570 Barbara Heater	9-12	TV	861 54	57%	956/565-2237 Fax 956/574-3017	
ⓜ South Texas Prep Academy 724 S Sugar Rd, Edinburg 78539 Ana Castro	7-8	TV	615	40%	956/381-5522 Fax 956/381-1177	

CAMERON CATHOLIC SCHOOLS

- **Diocese of Brownsville Ed Off** PID: 01004372
  Listing includes only schools located in this county. See District Index for location of Diocesan Offices.

Catholic Schs..Principal	Grd	Prgm	Enr/#Cls	SN	
Guadalupe Regional Middle Sch 1214 Lincoln St, Brownsville 78521 Lupita Alvarado	6-8		73 7		956/504-5568 Fax 956/504-9393
Incarnate Word Academy 244 Resaca Blvd, Brownsville 78520 Michael Camarrillo	PK-8		356 19		956/546-4486 Fax 956/504-3960
St Anthony Sch 1015 E Harrison Ave, Harlingen 78550 Kathy Stapleton	PK-8		270 12		956/423-2486 Fax 956/412-0084
St Joseph Academy 101 Saint Joseph Dr, Brownsville 78520 Melissa Valadez	7-12		784 43		956/542-3581 Fax 956/542-4748
St Luke Catholic Sch 2850 E Price Rd, Brownsville 78521 Anne Marie Serrato	PK-8		120 18		956/544-7982 Fax 956/544-4874
St Mary's Sch 1300 E Los Ebanos Blvd, Brownsville 78520 Ana Gomez	PK-6		500 25		956/546-1805 Fax 956/546-0787

CAMERON PRIVATE SCHOOLS

Private Schs..Principal	Grd	Prgm	Enr/#Cls	SN	
Calvary Christian Sch 1815 N 7th St, Harlingen 78550 Karen Zeissel	PK-8		450 25		956/425-1882 Fax 956/412-0324
Episcopal Day Sch 34 N Coria St, Brownsville 78520 Brian Clyne	PK-6		305 20		956/542-5231 Fax 956/504-9486
Faith Christian Academy 1944 E Alton Gloor Blvd, Brownsville 78526 Desi Najera	PK-8		140		956/546-7726
First Baptist Sch 1600 Boca Chica Blvd, Brownsville 78520 Deborah Batsell	PK-12		300 20		956/542-4854 Fax 956/542-6188

Kenmont Montessori Sch 2734 N Coria St, Brownsville 78520 Dr Sonia Saenz	PK-8		350 10		956/542-0500 Fax 956/542-0591
Laguna Madre Christian Academy 30640 Holly Bch, Laguna Vista 78578 Robin Stepan	PK-10		32 4		956/943-4446
Marine Military Academy 320 Iwo Jima Blvd, Harlingen 78550 Dr John Butler	8-12		250 35		956/423-6006 Fax 956/421-9273
St Alban's Episcopal Day Sch 1417 E Austin Ave, Harlingen 78550 Mary Kathryn Duffy	PK-6		245 21		956/428-2326 Fax 956/428-8457
Valley Christian High Sch 1190 MacKintosh Dr, Brownsville 78521 Elizabeth Rivera	9-12		57 5		956/542-5222 Fax 956/544-0038

CAMP COUNTY

CAMP PUBLIC SCHOOLS

- **Pittsburg Ind School Dist** PID: 01004504 903/856-3628
  402 Broach St, Pittsburg 75686 Fax 903/856-0269

Schools: 5 \ *Teachers:* 209 \ *Students:* 2,344 \ *Special Ed Students:* 239 \ *LEP Students:* 413 \ *Ethnic:* Asian 1%, African American 18%, Hispanic 40%, Caucasian 40% \ *Exp:* $359 (High) \ *Poverty:* 30% \ *Title I:* $999,167 \ *Special Education:* $595,000 \ *Open-Close:* 08/19 - 05/22 \ *DTBP:* $345 (High)

Terry Waldrep 1		Julie Wetzel 2	
Joe Marsh 3,5		Chris Hackett 4	
Kenneth Shelton 5		Brad Baca 6	
Laura Smith 7*		Beth Anne Dunavant 8,11,69,88,273,288,294,298	
Neil Morrison 16,73,76,295,297		Kelly Hobbs 34,58	
Jean Carrell 57,271*		Alan Brison 67	
Sherri Seale 68		Diane Stratton 88,91*	

Public Schs..Principal	Grd	Prgm	Enr/#Cls	SN	
Pittsburg Elem Sch 110 Fulton St, Pittsburg 75686 Terri Brown	2-4	AT	555 32	81%	903/856-6472 Fax 903/855-3370
Pittsburg High Sch 300 N Texas St, Pittsburg 75686 Jonathan Hill	9-12	ATV	647 60	70%	903/856-3646 Fax 903/855-3325
Pittsburg Intermediate Sch 209 Lafayette St, Pittsburg 75686 Sarah Richmond	5-6	AT	343 28	74%	903/856-3395 Fax 903/855-3398
Pittsburg Junior High Sch 313 Broach St, Pittsburg 75686 Kristane Moore	7-8	AT	373 34	77%	903/856-6432 Fax 903/855-3357
Pittsburg Primary Sch 405 Broach St, Pittsburg 75686 Jyl Wood	PK-1	AT	426 30	81%	903/856-6482 Fax 903/855-3385

1 Superintendent	8 Curric/Instruct K-12	19 Chief Financial Officer	29 Family/Consumer Science	39 Social Studies K-12	49 English/Lang Arts Elem	59 Special Education Elem	69 Academic Assessment
2 Bus/Finance/Purchasing	9 Curric/Instruct Elem	20 Art K-12	30 Adult Education	40 Social Studies Elem	50 English/Lang Arts Sec	60 Special Education Sec	70 Research/Development
3 Buildings And Grounds	10 Curric/Instruct Sec	21 Art Elem	31 Career/Sch-to-Work K-12	41 Social Studies Sec	51 Reading K-12	61 Foreign/World Lang K-12	71 Public Information
4 Food Service	11 Federal Program	22 Art Sec	32 Career/Sch-to-Work Elem	42 Science K-12	52 Reading Elem	62 Foreign/World Lang Elem	72 Summer School
5 Transportation	12 Title I	23 Music K-12	33 Career/Sch-to-Work Sec	43 Science Elem	53 Reading Sec	63 Foreign/World Lang Sec	73 Instructional Tech
6 Athletic	13 Title V	24 Music Elem	34 Early Childhood Ed	44 Science Sec	54 Remedial Reading K-12	64 Religious Education K-12	74 Inservice Training
7 Health Services	14 Asst Superintendent	25 Music Sec	35 Health/Phys Education	45 Math K-12	55 Remedial Reading Elem	65 Religious Education Elem	75 Marketing/Distributive
	15 Instructional Media Svcs	26 Business Education	36 Guidance Services K-12	46 Math Elem	56 Remedial Reading Sec	66 Religious Education Sec	76 Info Systems
	16 Chief Operations Officer	27 Career & Tech Ed	37 Guidance Services Elem	47 Math Sec	57 Bilingual/ELL	67 School Board President	77 Psychological Assess
	18 Chief Academic Officer	28 Technology Education	38 Guidance Services Sec	48 English/Lang Arts K-12	58 Special Education K-12	68 Teacher Personnel	78 Affirmative Action

Texas School Directory — Cass County

CAMP REGIONAL CENTERS

- **Region 8 Ed Service Center** PID: 01055450   903/575-2600
  4845 US Highway 271 N, Pittsburg 75686   Fax 903/575-2611

Dr David Fitts	1	Michele Leach	2,3,19
Niki Jones	7,271	Debra Crooms	8
Richele Langley	8,11,15	Leonard Beles	11,57,88
Brent Baker	16,73	Dr Jason McCullough	31
Janis McClure	58	Heather McGregor	74,294
Wayne Snyder	76		

CARSON COUNTY

CARSON PUBLIC SCHOOLS

- **Groom Ind School Dist** PID: 01004554   806/248-7474
  304 W 3rd Street, Groom 79039   Fax 806/248-7949

Schools: 1 \ *Teachers:* 20 \ *Students:* 160 \ *Special Ed Students:* 18 \ *LEP Students:* 3 \ *College-Bound:* 100% \ *Ethnic:* African American 2%, Hispanic 14%, Caucasian 84% \ *Exp:* $1,472 (High) \ *Poverty:* 19% \ *Title I:* $21,437 \ *Open-Close:* 08/12 - 05/21 \ *DTBP:* $69 (Low)

Jay Lamb	1,11,84	Tammy Case	2
Kenneth Payton	3	Irma Thias	4
Stephen Vanderpool	8,57,69,275*	Tony Dodson	16,295*
Aimee Fields	58*	Ron Kuehler	67

Public Schs..Principal	Grd	Prgm	Enr/#Cls	SN
Groom Sch 304 W 3rd Street, Groom 79039 Stephen Vanderpool	PK-12	T	160 23	30% 806/248-7474

- **Panhandle Ind School Dist** PID: 01004592   806/537-3568
  1001 Elsie St, Panhandle 79068   Fax 806/537-4055

Schools: 3 \ *Teachers:* 60 \ *Students:* 700 \ *Special Ed Students:* 70 \ *LEP Students:* 4 \ *Ethnic:* African American 1%, Hispanic 11%, Native American: 1%, Caucasian 87% \ *Exp:* $567 (High) \ *Poverty:* 11% \ *Title I:* $73,984 \ *Open-Close:* 08/19 - 05/22 \ *DTBP:* $350 (High) \ 📘 🐦

Blair Brown	1,11	Jamie Moore	2
Joe Bonner	3	Candy Greening	4
Robert Hammer	5	Dane Ashley	6
Taylor Norville	9,74*	Maria Walker	57*
Patricia Heck	58*	Patti Brown	58
Bubba Smith	67	John Strother	69,83,88,270*
Rusty Howes	73,295		

Public Schs..Principal	Grd	Prgm	Enr/#Cls	SN
Panhandle Elem Sch 106 W 9th St, Panhandle 79068 **Allison Mitchell**	PK-5	T	341 27	31% 806/537-3579 Fax 806/537-4230
Panhandle High Sch 106 W 11th St, Panhandle 79068 Brent Kirkland	9-12	AV	217 23	15% 806/537-3851 Fax 806/537-3476
Panhandle Junior High Sch 1001 Elsie Ave, Panhandle 79068 Gary Cates	6-8		167 20	20% 806/537-3541 Fax 806/537-5725

- **White Deer Ind School Dist** PID: 01004633   806/883-2311
  601 Omohundro Street, White Deer 79097   Fax 806/883-2321

Schools: 2 \ *Teachers:* 32 \ *Students:* 450 \ *Special Ed Students:* 39 \ *LEP Students:* 3 \ *College-Bound:* 59% \ *Ethnic:* Hispanic 16%, Caucasian 83% \ *Exp:* $396 (High) \ *Poverty:* 5% \ *Title I:* $19,888 \ *Open-Close:* 08/15 - 05/22 \ *DTBP:* $374 (High) \ 📘 🐦

Dane Richardson	1,11,83	Shane Grange	67
Linda Allen	69,88*	Rosalea McAnally	73*

Public Schs..Principal	Grd	Prgm	Enr/#Cls	SN
White Deer Elem Sch 604 Main Street, White Deer 79097 Rob Groves	PK-6	T	222 25	53% 806/883-2311 Fax 806/883-5008
White Deer Jr Sr High Sch 604 S Doucette Street, White Deer 79097 Darla Forney	7-12	TV	147 18	40% 806/883-2311 Fax 806/883-5029

CASS COUNTY

CASS PUBLIC SCHOOLS

- **Atlanta Ind School Dist** PID: 01004671   903/796-4194
  106 W Main St, Atlanta 75551   Fax 903/796-3487

Schools: 5 \ *Teachers:* 125 \ *Students:* 1,760 \ *Special Ed Students:* 194 \ *LEP Students:* 29 \ *College-Bound:* 50% \ *Ethnic:* Asian 1%, African American 35%, Hispanic 8%, Caucasian 56% \ *Exp:* $469 (High) \ *Poverty:* 36% \ *Title I:* $922,136 \ *Special Education:* $70,000 \ *Open-Close:* 08/15 - 05/21 \ *DTBP:* $348 (High) \ 📘

Sidney Harrist	1	Marilyn Cobb	2,15
Dave Wilcox	3,4,5,10,11,15	Donna Wilkins	4
Matt McClure	6,35,85*	Diane Whatley	9
Dave Wilcox	12	Gloria Herring	16*
Christina Kelley	34,58	Charlotte Stanner	67
Holly Triamrose	68	Brandon Prince	73,286,297*

Public Schs..Principal	Grd	Prgm	Enr/#Cls	SN
Atlanta Elem Sch 902 Abc Ln, Atlanta 75551 Dena McCord	2-4	T	335 35	72% 903/796-7164 Fax 903/799-1018
Atlanta High Sch 705 Rabbit Blvd, Atlanta 75551 Nancy Rinehart	9-12	TV	480 38	54% 903/796-4411 Fax 903/799-1033
Atlanta Middle Sch 600 High School Ln, Atlanta 75551 Colby Boyce	5-8	T	487 35	64% 903/796-7928 Fax 903/796-7290
Atlanta Primary Sch 505 Rabbit Blvd, Atlanta 75551 Donna Rice	PK-1	T	386 30	83% 903/796-8115 Fax 903/799-1014
Ⓐ Daep Center 309 N Buckner St, Atlanta 75551 Pamela Boyce	K-12		20 3	903/799-1044 Fax 903/796-2520

---

79 Student Personnel	91 Safety/Security	275 Response To Intervention	298 Grant Writer/Ptnrships	**School Programs**	**Social Media**
80 Driver Ed/Safety	92 Magnet School	277 Remedial Math K-12	750 Chief Innovation Officer	A = Alternative Program	
81 Gifted/Talented	93 Parental Involvement	280 Literacy Coach	751 Chief of Staff	G = Adult Classes	📘 = Facebook
82 Video Services	95 Tech Prep Program	285 STEM	752 Social Emotional Learning	M = Magnet Program	
83 Substance Abuse Prev	97 Chief Infomation Officer	286 Digital Learning		T = Title I Schoolwide	🐦 = Twitter
84 Erate	98 Chief Technology Officer	288 Common Core Standards	**Other School Types**	V = Career & Tech Ed Programs	
85 AIDS Education	270 Character Education	294 Accountability	Ⓐ = Alternative School		
88 Alternative/At Risk	271 Migrant Education	295 Network System	Ⓒ = Charter School	New Schools are shaded	
89 Multi-Cultural Curriculum	273 Teacher Mentor	296 Title II Programs	Ⓜ = Magnet School	New Superintendents and Principals are bold	
90 Social Work	274 Before/After Sch	297 Webmaster	Ⓨ = Year-Round School	Personnel with email addresses are underscored	

TX—69

Cass County

Market Data Retrieval

- **Avinger Ind School Dist** PID: 01004724 903/562-1355
  245 Conner, Avinger 75630 Fax 903/562-1271

Schools: 1 \ *Teachers:* 17 \ *Students:* 135 \ *Special Ed Students:* 16 \ *LEP Students:* 3 \ *College-Bound:* 50% \ *Ethnic:* Asian 1%, African American 15%, Hispanic 8%, Native American: 1%, Caucasian 75% \ *Exp:* $691 (High) \ *Poverty:* 18% \ *Title I:* $51,992 \ *Open-Close:* 08/19 - 05/22

Jacquelyn Smith 1,11
Doug Jacobs 67
Pam Miller 2
April Grogan 73*

Public Schs..Principal	Grd	Prgm	Enr/#Cls	SN	
Avinger Sch 245 Conner, Avinger 75630 Terry Giddens	PK-12	TV	135 22	80%	903/562-1355

- **Bloomburg Ind School Dist** PID: 01004750 903/728-5216
  307 W Cypress St, Bloomburg 75556 Fax 903/728-5399

Schools: 1 \ *Teachers:* 25 \ *Students:* 270 \ *Special Ed Students:* 24 \ *LEP Students:* 4 \ *College-Bound:* 100% \ *Ethnic:* Asian 2%, African American 3%, Hispanic 2%, Native American: 3%, Caucasian 90% \ *Exp:* $425 (High) \ *Poverty:* 24% \ *Title I:* $67,743 \ *Open-Close:* 08/14 - 05/20 \ *DTBP:* $371 (High)

Brian Stroman 1,11
Mike Carter 3*
Jennifer Camley 7*
Kacie Reneau 58*
Stephen Belk 73*
Shannon Peacock 83*
Kim Ratcliff 2
Chad Sheffield 6
Natalie Imnan 17,69,273
Thresha Jones 67
Cindy Shofner 79

Public Schs..Principal	Grd	Prgm	Enr/#Cls	SN	
Bloomburg Sch 307 W Cypress St, Bloomburg 75556 Amy Barron \ Silvia Stroman	PK-12	ATV	270 28	52%	903/728-5216

- **Hughes Springs Ind Sch Dist** PID: 01004786 903/639-3800
  871 Taylor St, Hughes Spgs 75656 Fax 903/639-2624

Schools: 3 \ *Teachers:* 100 \ *Students:* 1,230 \ *Special Ed Students:* 104 \ *LEP Students:* 36 \ *College-Bound:* 64% \ *Ethnic:* African American 12%, Hispanic 11%, Caucasian 76% \ *Exp:* $428 (High) \ *Poverty:* 27% \ *Title I:* $311,321 \ *Open-Close:* 08/15 - 05/21 \ *DTBP:* $338 (High) \ [f]

Sarah Dildine 1,57
David Hinerman 3,5,91
Chris Edwards 6
Thersa Jennings ... 8,11,16,58,88,288,296,298
Van Hall 67
Doug Stewart 73,76,286*
Jaylyn Setser 2,11
Elizabeth Martinez 4
Brandi Pittman 7*
Vanessa Murphy 37*
Mary Trevino 68

Public Schs..Principal	Grd	Prgm	Enr/#Cls	SN	
Hughes Springs Elem Sch 809 Russell, Hughes Spgs 75656 Scott Hanes	PK-5	T	619 24	64%	903/639-3881 Fax 903/639-3930
Hughes Springs High Sch 701 Russell, Hughes Spgs 75656 Brian Nation	9-12	TV	351	46%	903/639-3841 Fax 903/639-3928
Hughes Springs Jr High Sch 609 Russell, Hughes Spgs 75656 Rusty Duke	6-8	T	279 18	54%	903/639-3812 Fax 903/639-3929

- **Linden Kildare Cons Ind SD** PID: 01004827 903/756-7071
  205 Kildare Rd, Linden 75563 Fax 903/756-7242

Schools: 3 \ *Teachers:* 69 \ *Students:* 700 \ *Special Ed Students:* 87 \ *LEP Students:* 24 \ *College-Bound:* 57% \ *Ethnic:* Asian 1%, African American 20%, Hispanic 9%, Caucasian 71% \ *Exp:* $299 (Med) \ *Poverty:* 29% \ *Title I:* $330,840 \ *Special Education:* $126,000 \ *Open-Close:* 08/15 - 05/21 \ *DTBP:* $31 (Low)

Keri Winters 1,83
Derek Simmons 6*
Ginny Leuba 58
Tyson Knopp 73*
Tony McDuffy 91
Kenneth Hooten 2
Keith Owen 11,88,288,298*
Kay Stephens 67
Shannon Crenshaw 76

Public Schs..Principal	Grd	Prgm	Enr/#Cls	SN	
Linden Elem Sch 205 Kildare Rd, Linden 75563 Carolyn Oliver	PK-5	AT	334 45	61%	903/756-5471 Fax 903/756-5022
Linden Kildare High Sch 2913 Farm Rd 125 S, Linden 75563 Shekita Martin	9-12	ATV	217 35	64%	903/756-5314 Fax 903/756-8512
Mae Luster Stephen Jr High Sch Highway 59 S, Linden 75563 Rebecca Owen	6-8	AT	146 25	67%	903/756-5381 Fax 903/756-8832

- **McLeod Ind School Dist** PID: 01004891 903/796-7181
  19395 Farm Rd 125, Mc Leod 75565 Fax 903/796-8443

Schools: 1 \ *Teachers:* 34 \ *Students:* 388 \ *Special Ed Students:* 37 \ *College-Bound:* 35% \ *Exp:* $491 (High) \ *Poverty:* 36% \ *Title I:* $85,847 \ *Open-Close:* 08/16 - 05/22 \ *DTBP:* $334 (High)

Cathy May 1
Steven Lambeth 6
Shana Whittemore 11,57,271,296*
Kathleen O'Kelley 36*
Don Blackwell 67
Brandie Parker 2
Jennifer Lance 8*
Justin Huckabee 16,73,286,295*
Twyla Davis 52,55*

Public Schs..Principal	Grd	Prgm	Enr/#Cls	SN	
McLeod Sch 19395 FM 125 E, Bivins 75555 Erin Lambeth \ Shana Whittemore \ Jennifer Lance	K-12	V	388 50		903/796-7181

- **Queen City Ind School Dist** PID: 01004920 903/796-8256
  1015 Houston St, Queen City 75572 Fax 903/796-0248

Schools: 4 \ *Teachers:* 82 \ *Students:* 1,045 \ *Special Ed Students:* 99 \ *LEP Students:* 3 \ *College-Bound:* 27% \ *Ethnic:* African American 15%, Hispanic 3%, Native American: 1%, Caucasian 80% \ *Exp:* $371 (High) \ *Poverty:* 25% \ *Title I:* $269,230 \ *Special Education:* $231,000 \ *Open-Close:* 08/19 - 05/22 \ *DTBP:* $350 (High) \ [f]

Charlotte Williams 1
Pam Upchurch 3,5
Eric Droddy 6*
Kendra Bates 38,83*
Angie Parker 68
Yolanda Hawkins 2
Shannon Coats 4
Shannon Henderson 8,11,36,69,72,73,285*
Jonathan Stanmore 67
Heather Bolt 77

Public Schs..Principal	Grd	Prgm	Enr/#Cls	SN	
ⓐ Dawson-Hillmon Alt Ed Center 605 Walker Ln, Queen City 75572 Kippie Hartcraft	5-12	G	20 3		903/796-0774 Fax 903/799-5419
J K Hileman Elem Sch 1013 Houston St, Queen City 75572 David Estes	PK-4	T	399 23	62%	903/796-6304 Fax 903/799-5275

1	Superintendent	8	Curric/Instruct K-12	19	Chief Financial Officer	29	Family/Consumer Science	39	Social Studies K-12	49	English/Lang Arts Elem	59	Special Education Elem	69	Academic Assessment
2	Bus/Finance/Purchasing	9	Curric/Instruct Elem	20	Art K-12	30	Adult Education	40	Social Studies Elem	50	English/Lang Arts Sec	60	Special Education Sec	70	Research/Development
3	Buildings And Grounds	10	Curric/Instruct Sec	21	Art Elem	31	Career/Sch-to-Work K-12	41	Social Studies Sec	51	Reading K-12	61	Foreign/World Lang K-12	71	Public Information
4	Food Service	11	Federal Program	22	Art Sec	32	Career/Sch-to-Work Elem	42	Science K-12	52	Reading Elem	62	Foreign/World Lang Elem	72	Summer School
5	Transportation	12	Title I	23	Music K-12	33	Career/Sch-to-Work Sec	43	Science Elem	53	Reading Sec	63	Foreign/World Lang Sec	73	Instructional Tech
6	Athletic	13	Title V	24	Music Elem	34	Early Childhood Ed	44	Science Sec	54	Remedial Reading K-12	64	Religious Education K-12	74	Inservice Training
7	Health Services	15	Asst Superintendent	25	Music Sec	35	Health/Phys Education	45	Math K-12	55	Remedial Reading Elem	65	Religious Education Elem	75	Marketing/Distributive
		16	Instructional Media Svcs	26	Business Education	36	Guidance Services K-12	46	Math Elem	56	Remedial Reading Sec	66	Religious Education Sec	76	Info Systems
		17	Chief Operations Officer	27	Career & Tech Ed	37	Guidance Services Elem	47	Math Sec	57	Bilingual/ELL	67	School Board President	77	Psychological Assess
		18	Chief Academic Officer	28	Technology Education	38	Guidance Services Sec	48	English/Lang Arts K-12	58	Special Education K-12	68	Teacher Personnel	78	Affirmative Action

Texas School Directory

Chambers County

Morris Upchurch Middle Sch	5-8	T	326	55%	903/796-6412
500 5th St, Queen City 75572			30		Fax 903/796-0834
Steve Holmes					
Queen City High Sch	9-12	GTV	314	51%	903/796-8259
905 Houston St, Queen City 75572			25		Fax 903/796-8258
Steve Holmes					

CASTRO COUNTY

CASTRO PUBLIC SCHOOLS

• **Dimmitt Ind School Dist** PID: 01004968   806/647-3101
608 W Halsell St, Dimmitt 79027   Fax 806/647-5433

Schools: 4 \ *Teachers:* 104 \ *Students:* 1,225 \ *Special Ed Students:* 93 \ *LEP Students:* 219 \ *College-Bound:* 45% \ *Ethnic:* Asian 1%, African American 1%, Hispanic 87%, Caucasian 11% \ *Exp:* $586 (High) \ *Poverty:* 22% \ *Title I:* $304,143 \ *Open-Close:* 08/21 - 05/20 \ *DTBP:* $350 (High)

Bryan Davis 1	Becky Standlee 2	
Larry Leivas 2,3	Vanessa Escarcega 4*	
Richard Rickert 5	Aaron Manous 6	
Stacy Boozer 11,296	Vanesa McClure 16	
Patrice Hill 34,58	Greg Odom 67	
Sue Summers 69*	Karen Newman 73,295*	
Tammy McLain 286		

Public Schs..Principal	Grd	Prgm	Enr/#Cls	SN	
Ⓐ Dimmitt Alternative Center	9-12		10		806/647-5186
210 W Jones St, Dimmitt 79027			1		Fax 806/647-0701
Max Newman					
Dimmitt High Sch	9-12	TV	317	78%	806/647-3105
1405 Western Cir, Dimmitt 79027			35		Fax 806/647-5795
Christine Arnold					
Dimmitt Middle Sch	5-8	TV	355	85%	806/647-3108
1505 Western Cir, Dimmitt 79027			34		Fax 806/647-2996
Tiffany Seaton					
Richardson Elem Sch	PK-4	T	560	85%	806/647-4131
708 W Stinson St, Dimmitt 79027			30		Fax 806/647-4438
Marritssa Flores					

• **Hart Ind School Dist** PID: 01005015   806/938-2143
710 2nd Street, Hart 79043   Fax 806/938-2610

Schools: 2 \ *Teachers:* 26 \ *Students:* 230 \ *Special Ed Students:* 13 \ *LEP Students:* 19 \ *College-Bound:* 50% \ *Ethnic:* African American 1%, Hispanic 94%, Caucasian 6% \ *Exp:* $446 (High) \ *Poverty:* 34% \ *Title I:* $146,776 \ *Open-Close:* 08/21 - 05/22 \ *DTBP:* $265 (High) \ 📘 🐦

Eliazar Castillo 3,5*	Gloria Diaz 4*
Christa Chambers 8	Christa Lara 11,296
Retta Knox 13,35,83,85,88*	Daisy Hernandez 36
Mark Castillo 57	Senaida De La Fuente 58
Ramona Neudorf 73	

Public Schs..Principal	Grd	Prgm	Enr/#Cls	SN	
Hart Elem Sch	PK-5	T	123	88%	806/938-2142
710 2nd Street, Hart 79043			13		Fax 806/938-2188
Krista Lara					📘 🐦
Hart Junior Senior High Sch	6-12	AGV	233		806/938-2141
710 2nd Street, Hart 79043			26		Fax 806/938-2199
Ramona Neudorf					

• **Nazareth Ind School Dist** PID: 01005041   806/945-2231
101 S 1st Avenue, Nazareth 79063   Fax 806/945-2431

Schools: 1 \ *Teachers:* 22 \ *Students:* 240 \ *Special Ed Students:* 13 \ *LEP Students:* 3 \ *College-Bound:* 87% \ *Ethnic:* African American 1%, Hispanic 10%, Native American: 2%, Caucasian 87% \ *Exp:* $480 (High) \ *Poverty:* 10% \ *Title I:* $21,659 \ *Open-Close:* 08/21 - 05/22 \ *DTBP:* $157 (High) \ 📘

Glen Waldo 1,11,84,288	K'Lynn Gerber 2
Ralph Albracht 3,5	Robert O'Connor 8,57*
Nikki Wethington 12	Dana Stanfield 26*
Austin Heck 27*	Mitchell Brockman 67
Cory Hoelting 73,295	

Public Schs..Principal	Grd	Prgm	Enr/#Cls	SN	
Nazareth Sch	PK-12	TV	240	16%	806/945-2231
101 S 1st Avenue, Nazareth 79063			20		
Shad Reed					

CHAMBERS COUNTY

CHAMBERS PUBLIC SCHOOLS

• **Anahuac Ind School Dist** PID: 01005077   409/267-3600
804 Michael Ricks Dr, Anahuac 77514   Fax 409/267-3855

Schools: 3 \ *Teachers:* 95 \ *Students:* 1,336 \ *Special Ed Students:* 119 \ *LEP Students:* 94 \ *Ethnic:* Asian 2%, African American 13%, Hispanic 31%, Native American: 1%, Caucasian 53% \ *Exp:* $455 (High) \ *Poverty:* 16% \ *Title I:* $265,168 \ *Open-Close:* 08/15 - 05/21 \ *DTBP:* $1,182 (High)

Dennis Wagner 1	Rosie Womack 2,5,84
Jim Felice 3	Stacey Medders 3
Marty Murr 6*	Patti Nauman 8
Deanna Humphrey 11,36,57,58,69,83,88*	Kenny Dean 16,73,295*
Kristi Henry 38,79*	Leslie Todd 38*
Lane Bertrand 67	

Public Schs..Principal	Grd	Prgm	Enr/#Cls	SN	
Anahuac Elem Sch	PK-5	T	649	59%	409/267-3600
905 S Ross Sterling Rd, Anahuac 77514			60		Fax 409/267-6119
Mitzi Higginbotham					
Anahuac High Sch	9-12	TV	385	45%	409/267-3600
201 S Kansas St, Anahuac 77514			40		Fax 409/267-5192
Eric Humphrey					
Anahuac Middle Sch	6-8	T	302	54%	409/267-2042
706 Michael Ricks Dr, Anahuac 77514			25		Fax 409/267-3643
Tammy Duhon					

---

79 Student Personnel	91 Safety/Security	275 Response To Intervention	298 Grant Writer/Ptnrships	**School Programs**	**Social Media**	
80 Driver Ed/Safety	92 Magnet School	277 Remedial Math K-12	750 Chief Innovation Officer	A = Alternative Program		
81 Gifted/Talented	93 Parental Involvement	280 Literacy Coach	751 Chief of Staff	G = Adult Classes	📘 = Facebook	
82 Video Services	95 Tech Prep Program	285 STEM	752 Social Emotional Learning	M = Magnet Program		
83 Substance Abuse Prev	97 Chief Information Officer	286 Digital Learning		T = Title I Schoolwide	🐦 = Twitter	
84 Erate	98 Chief Technology Officer	288 Common Core Standards	**Other School Types**	V = Career & Tech Ed Programs		
85 AIDS Education	270 Accountability	294 Accountability	Ⓐ = Alternative School			
88 Alternative/At Risk	271 Migrant Education	295 Network System	Ⓒ = Charter School	New Schools are shaded		
89 Multi-Cultural Curriculum	273 Teacher Mentor	296 Title II Programs	Ⓜ = Magnet School	New Superintendents and Principals are bold		
90 Social Work	274 Before/After Sch	297 Webmaster	Ⓨ = Year-Round School	Personnel with email addresses are underscored		TX–71

Cherokee County

Market Data Retrieval

- **Barbers Hill Ind School Dist** PID: 01005118   281/576-2221
  9600 Eagle Dr, Mont Belvieu 77580   Fax 281/576-5879

Schools: 8 \ *Teachers:* 363 \ *Students:* 5,214 \ *Special Ed Students:* 373 \ *LEP Students:* 141 \ *College-Bound:* 80% \ *Ethnic:* Asian 1%, African American 3%, Hispanic 23%, Caucasian 72% \ *Exp:* $296 (Med) \ *Poverty:* 8% \ *Title I:* $304,363 \ *Special Education:* $699,000 \ *Open-Close:* 08/14 - 05/21 \ *DTBP:* $164 (High)

Dr Greg Poole 1	Becky McManus 2,15
Becky Johnson 3	Stan Frazier 3,5,15,91
Rhonda Cole 4	Susan LeBlanc 4*
Tom Westerberg 6,35*	Colleen Goundrey 7
Sandra Duree 8,15,275,280,286	Linda Gerhart 11,57,271,298*
Barbara Ponder 15,68	Kristen Davis 16,73,76,82,295
Sue Garcia 34,58,77	Stormy Thibodeaux 45
Vicky Moye 48	Lori May 58
Marilyn Ropp 58	Kristen Brown 59
Becky Tice 67	Natasha Holden 69,294
Carla Rabalais 71	Stacy Pennington 73
Denise King 285*	Sebastian Lopez 295
Tim LeBlanc 295	

Public Schs..Principal	Grd	Prgm	Enr/#Cls	SN	
Barbers Hill Elem Sch North PO Box 1108, Mont Belvieu 77580 Stephanie Martin	2-5	T	794	22%	281/567-2221
Barbers Hill Elem Sch South 9600 Eagle Dr, Mont Belvieu 77580 Melissa Barrington	2-5	T	893	16%	281/576-3421 Fax 281/576-3420
Barbers Hill High Sch 9696 Eagle Dr, Mont Belvieu 77580 Rick Kana	9-12	V	1,548 60	11%	281/576-3400 Fax 281/576-3356
Barbers Hill Kindergarten Ctr 9600 Eagle Dr, Mont Belvieu 77580 Lisa Watkins	PK-K	T	470	22%	281/576-3407 Fax 281/576-3412
Barbers Hill Middle Sch North 9600 Eagle Dr, Mont Belvieu 77580 Lance Murphy	6-8		589 34	19%	281/576-2221 Fax 281/576-3353
Barbers Hill Middle Sch South 9600 Eagle Dr, Mont Belvieu 77580 Dennis Wagner	6-8		695 50	16%	281/576-2221 Fax 281/576-3350
Barbers Hill Primary Sch 9600 Eagle Dr, Mont Belvieu 77580 Mandy Malone	1-1	T	387 27	18%	281/576-2221 Fax 281/576-3415
ⓐ Epic Daep Alt Sch 9600 Eagle Dr, Mont Belvieu 77580 Daniel Andrews	6-12		35		281/576-2221 Fax 281/576-3422

- **East Chambers Ind School Dist** PID: 01005156   409/296-6100
  216 Champions Loop, Winnie 77665   Fax 409/296-3528

Schools: 4 \ *Teachers:* 101 \ *Students:* 1,500 \ *Special Ed Students:* 136 \ *LEP Students:* 307 \ *Ethnic:* Asian 1%, African American 7%, Hispanic 44%, Caucasian 47% \ *Exp:* $693 (High) \ *Poverty:* 9% \ *Title I:* $134,092 \ *Special Education:* $250,000 \ *Open-Close:* 08/26 - 05/28 \ *DTBP:* $575 (High)

Scott Campbell 1	Gena Huddleston 2
Darren Smith 3,5,91	Dawn Nelson 4
Russ Sutherland 6*	Katie Sparks 7*
Renee Brawner 8*	Cindy Bull 11,57,58,77,83,88,271,296
Mitchell Long 16,73,288	Maria Garcia 57*
Gary Hoffpauir 67	Nicole Touchet 68
Tammie Gilsillian 69,270	

Public Schs..Principal	Grd	Prgm	Enr/#Cls	SN	
East Chambers Elem Sch 2045 State Highway 124, Winnie 77665 Becky Dale	3-5	T	300	64%	409/296-6100 Fax 409/962-3259
East Chambers High Sch 234 E Buccaneer Dr, Winnie 77665 Tom Duoto	9-12	GV	435 32	45%	409/296-4184 Fax 409/296-9596
East Chambers Jr High Sch 1931 State Highway 124, Winnie 77665 Lou Ann Rainey	6-8		300 20	56%	409/296-4183 Fax 409/296-2724
East Chambers Primary Sch 316 E Fear Rd, Winnie 77665 Andrea Smith	PK-2	T	642 30	63%	409/296-2980 Fax 409/296-3259

CHEROKEE COUNTY

CHEROKEE PUBLIC SCHOOLS

- **Alto Ind School Dist** PID: 01005209   936/858-7101
  244 County Road 2429, Alto 75925   Fax 936/858-2101

Schools: 3 \ *Teachers:* 57 \ *Students:* 671 \ *Special Ed Students:* 73 \ *LEP Students:* 100 \ *College-Bound:* 58% \ *Ethnic:* African American 26%, Hispanic 34%, Caucasian 40% \ *Exp:* $491 (High) \ *Poverty:* 30% \ *Title I:* $273,626 \ *Special Education:* $19,000 \ *Open-Close:* 08/19 - 05/22 \ *DTBP:* $350 (High)

Kelly West 1	Kelly Robertson 2
Kim Bradshaw 3	Donnita Lucas 4
Kerry Birdwell 11	Courtney Marshall 31,83,88*
Janette Moore 57*	Noreen Freeman 58
Jeff Duplichain 67	Adam Knight 73
Paula Low 271	

Public Schs..Principal	Grd	Prgm	Enr/#Cls	SN	
Alto Elem Sch 236 County Road 2429, Alto 75925 Candis Mabry	PK-4	T	278 20	67%	936/587-7174 Fax 936/858-4382
Alto High Sch 248 County Road 2429, Alto 75925 Shanequa Redd-Dorsey	9-12	TV	201 30	63%	936/858-7110 Fax 936/858-4387
Alto Middle Sch 240 County Road 2429, Alto 75925 Brandi Tiner	5-8	T	192 16	73%	936/858-7140 Fax 936/858-4579

- **Jacksonville Ind School Dist** PID: 01005235   903/586-6511
  800 College Ave, Jacksonville 75766   Fax 903/586-3133

Schools: 8 \ *Teachers:* 339 \ *Students:* 5,091 \ *Special Ed Students:* 428 \ *LEP Students:* 1,219 \ *College-Bound:* 54% \ *Ethnic:* Asian 1%, African American 17%, Hispanic 52%, Native American: 1%, Caucasian 30% \ *Exp:* $357 (High) \ *Poverty:* 24% \ *Title I:* $1,616,308 \ *Special Education:* $1,022,000 \ *Open-Close:* 08/28 - 05/28 \ *DTBP:* $157 (High)

Dr Chad Kelly 1	Lindy Finley 2
Troy Parker 2	Tommy Wade 3,91
Clay Carter 4	Mark Turney 5
Wayne Coleman 6*	Nicole Fontenot 7*
Lisa Dailey 8,11,16,83,273,294,298	Lisa Cox 8,72,79,275*

1 Superintendent	8 Curric/Instruct K-12	19 Chief Financial Officer	29 Family/Consumer Science	39 Social Studies K-12	49 English/Lang Arts Elem	59 Special Education Elem	69 Academic Assessment
2 Bus/Finance/Purchasing	9 Curric/Instruct Elem	20 Art K-12	30 Adult Education	40 Social Studies Elem	50 English/Lang Arts Sec	60 Special Education Sec	70 Research/Development
3 Buildings And Grounds	10 Curric/Instruct Sec	21 Art Elem	31 Career/Sch-to-Work K-12	41 Social Studies Sec	51 Reading K-12	61 Foreign/World Lang K-12	71 Public Information
4 Food Service	11 Federal Program	22 Art Sec	32 Career/Sch-to-Work Elem	42 Science K-12	52 Reading Elem	62 Foreign/World Lang Elem	72 Summer School
5 Transportation	12 Title I	23 Music K-12	33 Career/Sch-to-Work Sec	43 Science Elem	53 Reading Sec	63 Foreign/World Lang Sec	73 Instructional Tech
6 Athletic	13 Title V	24 Music Elem	34 Early Childhood Ed	44 Science Sec	54 Remedial Reading K-12	64 Religious Education K-12	74 Inservice Training
7 Health Services	15 Asst Superintendent	25 Music Sec	35 Health/Phys Education	45 Math K-12	55 Remedial Reading Elem	65 Religious Education Elem	75 Marketing/Distributive
	16 Instructional Media Svcs	26 Business Education	36 Guidance Services K-12	46 Math Elem	56 Remedial Reading Sec	66 Religious Education Sec	76 Info Systems
	17 Chief Operations Officer	27 Career & Tech Ed	37 Guidance Services Elem	47 Math Sec	57 Bilingual/ELL	67 School Board President	77 Psychological Assess
	18 Chief Academic Officer	28 Technology Education	38 Guidance Services Sec	48 English/Lang Arts K-12	58 Special Education K-12	68 Teacher Personnel	78 Affirmative Action

Texas School Directory — Cherokee County

Hedda Alexander	16,73,76,84,98,295		Amber Penn		57,89,271
Sara Gill	58		Jeff Horton		67
Brad Stewart	68		Kala Moore		68
Grace Traylor	71		Lynne Bullock		73
Marvin Acker	91*		Buddy Attaway		295

Public Schs..Principal	Grd	Prgm	Enr/#Cls	SN	
ⒶCompass Center 436 SW Loop 456, Jacksonville 75766 Timothy Rucker	PK-12	T	3 7		903/589-3926 Fax 903/586-7158
East Side Elem Sch 711 Fort Worth St, Jacksonville 75766 Jodi Alderete	PK-4	T	573 35	67%	903/586-5146 Fax 903/589-4977
Fred Douglass Elem Sch 1501 E Pine St, Jacksonville 75766 Rachel Sherman	PK-4	T	633 40	83%	903/586-6519 Fax 903/589-4341
Jacksonville High Sch 1210 Corinth Rd, Jacksonville 75766 Ben Peacock	9-12	TV	1,311	71%	903/586-3661 Fax 903/586-8229
Jacksonville Middle Sch 1541 E Pine St, Jacksonville 75766 Patsy Whitaker	7-8	T	688 51	74%	903/586-3686 Fax 903/586-8071
Joe Wright Elem Sch 1055 N Pineda St, Jacksonville 75766 Cindy Slovacek	PK-4	T	516 27	89%	903/586-5286 Fax 903/589-8108
Nichols Intermediate Sch 818 SW Loop 456, Jacksonville 75766 Holly Searcy	5-6	T	803 45	82%	903/541-0213 Fax 903/541-0199
West Side Elem Sch 1105 College Ave, Jacksonville 75766 Alicia Tennison	PK-4	T	465 26	92%	903/586-5165 Fax 903/586-6196

● **New Summerfield Ind Sch Dist** PID: 01005340   903/726-3306
13307 Hwy 110 S, New Summerfld 75780   Fax 903/726-3405

Schools: 1 \ **Teachers:** 47 \ **Students:** 550 \ **Special Ed Students:** 28 \ **LEP Students:** 195 \ **College-Bound:** 59% \ **Ethnic:** Asian 1%, African American 3%, Hispanic 84%, Caucasian 13% \ **Exp:** $455 (High) \ **Poverty:** 18% \ **Title I:** $133,631 \ **Open-Close:** 08/15 - 05/20 \ **DTBP:** $350 (High) \ 🇹

Dr Brian Nichols	1		Lanita Parker-Felder	2
Eric Boyett	3,5*		Dawn Sutlive	4
Kent Willis	6*		Dr Craig Wilcox	8,11,57*
Troy Jenkins	16,73,297*		Michael Davis	67
Ashley Faucett	69,83,270*			

Public Schs..Principal	Grd	Prgm	Enr/#Cls	SN	
New Summerfield Sch 13307 Hwy 110 S, New Summerfld 75780 Angela Tucker \ Joe Brannen \ Joshua Faucett	PK-12	TV	550 38	88%	903/726-3306 Fax 903/726-3421

● **Rusk Ind School Dist** PID: 01005364   903/683-5592
203 E 7th St, Rusk 75785   Fax 903/683-2104

Schools: 5 \ **Teachers:** 156 \ **Students:** 2,015 \ **Special Ed Students:** 255 \ **LEP Students:** 103 \ **Ethnic:** African American 14%, Hispanic 17%, Caucasian 69% \ **Exp:** $362 (High) \ **Poverty:** 18% \ **Title I:** $448,176 \ **Open-Close:** 08/19 - 05/21 \ **DTBP:** $343 (High) \ 🇹

Grey Barton	1		Stacie Young	2,15,294
Greg Dover	3		John Hood	4,11,288*
Joseph Eckel	5		Jowell Hancock	6,35
Teara Newman	7		Betty Collins	8,27,57,74,88,271,296,298
Deborah Welch	9*		Gary Cruseturner	16,28,73,76,295,297
Tammy Hancock	34*		Lisa Cockrum	38*

Theresa Gates	45,69,83,91,275		Donna Tugwell	58,77
Britt Patterson	67		Scott Blackmon	84

Public Schs..Principal	Grd	Prgm	Enr/#Cls	SN	
Rusk Elem Sch 300 N Henderson St, Rusk 75785 Deborah Welch	2-3	T	313 30	72%	903/683-6106 Fax 903/683-6299
Rusk High Sch 495 Eagle Dr, Rusk 75785 Ronny Snow	9-12	ATV	601 35	52%	903/683-5401 Fax 903/683-6090
Rusk Intermediate Sch 1143 Loop 343 W, Rusk 75785 Jan Evans	4-5	T	310	67%	903/683-1726 Fax 903/683-5167
Rusk Junior High Sch 1345 S Main St, Rusk 75785 Jon Burkhalter	6-8	ATV	479 35	60%	903/683-2502 Fax 903/683-4363
Rusk Primary Sch 440 Collins St, Rusk 75785 Tammy Hancock	PK-1	T	407 24	79%	903/683-6106 Fax 903/683-6299

● **Wells Ind School Dist** PID: 01005405   936/867-4466
160 Rusk Ave, Wells 75976   Fax 936/867-4497

Schools: 2 \ **Teachers:** 27 \ **Students:** 285 \ **Special Ed Students:** 34 \ **LEP Students:** 17 \ **College-Bound:** 67% \ **Ethnic:** African American 7%, Hispanic 14%, Caucasian 79% \ **Exp:** $684 (High) \ **Poverty:** 27% \ **Title I:** $133,527 \ **Open-Close:** 08/15 - 05/20 \ **DTBP:** $138 (High)

James Moore	1		Jana Oquinn	2
Mike Petty	3,5		Camille Pinkston	4
Leslie Brown	8,11,69,294*		Kathy Ford	31,34,36,57,83,85,88,270
Joy Weber	58*		Wayne Montes	67
Slade Johnson	73,295,296*		Jill Gaston	275*

Public Schs..Principal	Grd	Prgm	Enr/#Cls	SN	
Wells Elem Sch Highway 69, Wells 75976 Bryan Caughlin	PK-6	T	163 15	70%	936/867-4400 Fax 936/867-4466
Wells High Sch Highway 69, Wells 75976 Jill Gaston	7-12	TV	123 10	56%	936/867-4400

CHEROKEE PRIVATE SCHOOLS

Private Schs..Principal	Grd	Prgm	Enr/#Cls	SN	
Christ the Redeemer Sch 247 S Barron St, Rusk 75785 Debra McCormick	K-12		100		903/683-1404 Fax 903/683-1341

79	Student Personnel	91	Safety/Security	275	Response To Intervention	298	Grant Writer/Ptnrships	**School Programs**
80	Driver Ed/Safety	92	Magnet School	277	Remedial Math K-12	750	Chief Innovation Officer	A = Alternative Program
81	Gifted/Talented	93	Parental Involvement	280	Literacy Coach	751	Chief of Staff	G = Adult Classes
82	Video Services	95	Tech Prep Program	285	STEM	752	Social Emotional Learning	M = Magnet Program
83	Substance Abuse Prev	97	Chief Information Officer	286	Digital Learning			T = Title I Schoolwide
84	Erate	98	Chief Technology Officer	288	Common Core Standards	**Other School Types**		V = Career & Tech Ed Programs
85	AIDS Education	270	Character Education	294	Accountability	Ⓐ = Alternative School		
88	Alternative/At Risk	271	Migrant Education	295	Network System	Ⓒ = Charter School		New Schools are shaded
89	Multi-Cultural Curriculum	273	Teacher Mentor	296	Title II Programs	Ⓜ = Magnet School		New Superintendents and Principals are bold
90	Social Work	274	Before/After Sch	297	Webmaster	Ⓨ = Year-Round School		Personnel with email addresses are underscored

Social Media
f = Facebook
🇹 = Twitter

TX–73

Childress County

CHILDRESS COUNTY

CHILDRESS PUBLIC SCHOOLS

• **Childress Ind School Dist** PID: 01005431 940/937-2501
308 3rd St NW, Childress 79201 Fax 940/937-2938

Schools: 4 \ *Teachers:* 95 \ *Students:* 1,100 \ *Special Ed Students:* 107 \ *LEP Students:* 36 \ *College-Bound:* 50% \ *Ethnic:* Asian 1%, African American 4%, Hispanic 41%, Native American: 1%, Caucasian 53% \ *Exp:* $473 (High) \ *Poverty:* 23% \ *Title I:* $306,802 \ *Open-Close:* 08/16 - 05/21 \ *DTBP:* $377 (High) \

Rick Teran 1,83	Karen Leonard 2
Joel Camacho 3	Tracee Herbstritt 4
Jayson Read 5	Jason Sims 6
Sarah Mills 8,11,58	Janet Word 9*
Faith Self 16*	Roy Novak 27*
Sherry Davis 36*	Alicia Jurado 57*
Mark Keys 67	John Galligan 73,295*

Public Schs..Principal	Grd	Prgm	Enr/#Cls	SN	
Childress Elem Sch 300 3rd St SE, Childress 79201 Janet Word	PK-5	T	556 34	55%	940/937-6313 Fax 940/937-2165
Childress High Sch 800 Avenue J NW, Childress 79201 Paige Steed	9-12	TV	312	47%	940/937-6131 Fax 940/937-2039
Childress Junior High Sch 700 Commerce St, Childress 79201 Marsha Meacham	6-8	T	246 22	45%	940/937-3641 Fax 940/937-8427
ⓐ Gateway Academy 600 Avenue F NW, Childress 79201 Janet Word \ Marsha Meacham	3-12		20 2		940/937-3099

CLAY COUNTY

CLAY PUBLIC SCHOOLS

• **Bellevue Ind School Dist** PID: 01005481 940/928-2104
500 7th Street, Bellevue 76228 Fax 940/928-2583

Schools: 1 \ *Teachers:* 18 \ *Students:* 140 \ *Special Ed Students:* 16 \ *College-Bound:* 75% \ *Ethnic:* African American 1%, Hispanic 8%, Native American: 1%, Caucasian 91% \ *Exp:* $350 (High) \ *Poverty:* 14% \ *Title I:* $22,026 \ *Open-Close:* 08/15 - 05/15 \

Michael Qualls 1,11	Colby Broussard 6*
Cason Bennet 58*	Mark Hanson 67
Johney Chandler 69,88*	Sunny Mitchel 295*

Public Schs..Principal	Grd	Prgm	Enr/#Cls	SN	
Bellevue Sch 500 7th Street, Bellevue 76228 Cason Bennet	PK-12	TV	140 17	58%	940/928-2104

• **Henrietta Ind School Dist** PID: 01005546 940/720-7900
1801 E Crafton St, Henrietta 76365 Fax 940/538-7505

Schools: 3 \ *Teachers:* 79 \ *Students:* 940 \ *Special Ed Students:* 112 \ *LEP Students:* 3 \ *College-Bound:* 59% \ *Ethnic:* Hispanic 7%, Native American: 2%, Caucasian 90% \ *Exp:* $697 (High) \ *Poverty:* 16% \ *Title I:* $154,441 \ *Open-Close:* 08/15 - 05/21 \ *DTBP:* $533 (High)

Jeffrey McClure 1	Joy Campbell 2
Brittanie Brown 4	Larry Gisler 5
Byron West 6*	Jeanette Holding 7*
Scot Clayton 8,11,15,288,296	Mandy Story 16*
Cheryl Holbert 31,69,83,85*	Dr Terell White 58
Betty Ellsworth 67	Derek Leach 73,76
Brandi Watson 88,270	

Public Schs..Principal	Grd	Prgm	Enr/#Cls	SN	
Henrietta Elem Sch 1600 E Crafton St, Henrietta 76365 Kendra Bennett	PK-5	T	464 24	48%	940/720-7910 Fax 940/538-7515
Henrietta High Sch 1700 E Crafton St, Henrietta 76365 Michael Smiley	9-12	V	268 20	32%	940/720-7930 Fax 940/538-7535
Henrietta Junior High Sch 308 E Gilbert St, Henrietta 76365 Terry McCutchen	6-8	T	226 20	41%	940/720-7920 Fax 940/538-7525

• **Midway Ind School Dist** PID: 01005584 940/476-2215
12142 State Highway 148 S, Henrietta 76365 Fax 940/476-2226

Schools: 1 \ *Teachers:* 17 \ *Students:* 137 \ *Special Ed Students:* 13 \ *College-Bound:* 75% \ *Ethnic:* Hispanic 5%, Caucasian 95% \ *Exp:* $523 (High) \ *Poverty:* 14% \ *Title I:* $18,017 \ *Open-Close:* 08/27 - 05/25

Randel Beaver 1	Jennifer Van Pelt 2
Cami Franke 4*	Alan Umholtz 11
Glenda Terry 16*	Treva Byrne 58*
Derek Leach 67	Louis Clayton 73,286*

Public Schs..Principal	Grd	Prgm	Enr/#Cls	SN	
Midway Sch 12142 State Highway 148 S, Henrietta 76365 Cherry Johnston	PK-12	TV	137 13	50%	940/476-2215

• **Petrolia Cons Ind School Dist** PID: 01005601 940/524-3555
701 S Prairie Avenue, Petrolia 76377 Fax 940/524-3370

Schools: 2 \ *Teachers:* 43 \ *Students:* 440 \ *Special Ed Students:* 51 \ *LEP Students:* 4 \ *College-Bound:* 62% \ *Ethnic:* Hispanic 12%, Native American: 1%, Caucasian 86% \ *Exp:* $437 (High) \ *Poverty:* 16% \ *Title I:* $84,786 \ *Open-Close:* 08/14 - 05/21 \ *DTBP:* $362 (High)

David Hedges 1	Theresa Harrison 2,84
David Sizemore 3	Skyla Barger 4*
Eli Rivers 5	Mitch McLamore 6
Dustin Barger 67	Clint Perkins 69,83,88*

Public Schs..Principal	Grd	Prgm	Enr/#Cls	SN	
Petrolia Elem Sch 701 S Prairie Ave, Petrolia 76377 Barnes Travis	PK-6	T	282 15	64%	940/524-3433 Fax 940/524-3302
Petrolia Jr Sr High Sch 8307 FM810, Petrolia 76377 Clint Perkins	7-12	V	234 17	38%	940/524-3264 Fax 940/524-3215

Texas School Directory

COCHRAN COUNTY

COCHRAN PUBLIC SCHOOLS

- **Morton Ind School Dist** PID: 01005675 806/266-5505
  500 Champion Dr, Morton 79346   Fax 806/266-5449

Schools: 4 \ *Teachers:* 43 \ *Students:* 400 \ *Special Ed Students:* 37 \ *LEP Students:* 72 \ *College-Bound:* 80% \ *Ethnic:* African American 7%, Hispanic 80%, Caucasian 13% \ *Exp:* $350 (High) \ *Poverty:* 36% \ *Title I:* $219,146 \ *Open-Close:* 08/19 - 05/22 \ *DTBP:* $350 (High)

Karen Saunders	1	Tera Cruz	2
Jacob Cruz	5	Shean Abston	6*
Holly Boggs	9,11,57,88*	Rina Ramos	9*
Rod Cottrell	16,73,76,295	Russell Hill	16*
Ann Hill	58	Glen Lyon	67
Regina Ingle	271*	Becky Cottrell	274*

Public Schs..Principal	Grd	Prgm	Enr/#Cls	SN	
Morton Elem Sch 500 Champion Dr, Morton 79346 Kellye Kuehler	PK-5		195 18		806/266-5505 Fax 806/266-5123
Morton High Sch 500 Champion Dr, Morton 79346 Regina Ingle	9-12	V	98 15		806/266-5505 Fax 806/266-5780
Morton Junior High Sch 500 Champion Dr, Morton 79346 Smith Glen	6-8		87 12		806/266-5505 Fax 806/266-5739
Ⓐ Pep High Sch Highway 303, Pep 79353 Natasha Newman	9-12	GV	25 10	81%	806/933-4499 Fax 806/933-4699

- **Whiteface Con Ind School Dist** PID: 01005728 806/287-1154
  401 Antelope Blvd, Whiteface 79379   Fax 806/287-1131

Schools: 2 \ *Teachers:* 38 \ *Students:* 325 \ *Special Ed Students:* 32 \ *LEP Students:* 12 \ *College-Bound:* 70% \ *Ethnic:* African American 1%, Hispanic 53%, Caucasian 45% \ *Exp:* $527 (High) \ *Poverty:* 31% \ *Title I:* $73,189 \ *Open-Close:* 08/23 - 05/25 \ *DTBP:* $362 (High)

Nate Wheeler	1	Tammie Bentley	2
Tom Rohmfeld	3,5	Linda Stockman	4
Scott Lucas	9,93,274*	Dr Cassidy McBrayer	11
Carrie Casarez	16*	Bev Byrne	31*
Beverly Byrne	36,69,83,85,88,270	Audra Davis	57,271*
Michael McBrayer	58*	Teresa Desautell	60*
Corey Ayers	67	Joel Dietz	73
Christopher Mendez	280*		

Public Schs..Principal	Grd	Prgm	Enr/#Cls	SN	
Whiteface Elem Sch 2nd St & Arthur St, Whiteface 79379 Scott Lucas	PK-5	T	165 15	58%	806/287-1285
Whiteface High Sch 3 2nd St, Whiteface 79379 Christopher Mendez	6-12	T	166 20	56%	806/287-1104

Coke County

COKE PUBLIC SCHOOLS

- **Bronte Ind School Dist** PID: 01005754 325/473-2511
  210 S Jefferson St, Bronte 76933   Fax 325/473-2313

Schools: 2 \ *Teachers:* 25 \ *Students:* 245 \ *Special Ed Students:* 24 \ *LEP Students:* 4 \ *College-Bound:* 75% \ *Ethnic:* Hispanic 35%, Caucasian 65% \ *Exp:* $384 (High) \ *Poverty:* 17% \ *Title I:* $62,773 \ *Open-Close:* 08/22 - 05/22 \ *DTBP:* $372 (High)

Tim Siler	1,11	Jenney Baker	2
Danielle Queen	4	Natasha Sullivan	5
Rocky Rawls	6*	John Phillips	9,11,52,55
Rebecca Siler	11*	George Tomes	23*
Daisy Sanchez	36,69,83,85,88,270,273*	Jerita Taylor	42*
Paula Connally	58,280	Shane Kelton	67

Public Schs..Principal	Grd	Prgm	Enr/#Cls	SN	
Bronte Elem Sch 210 S Jefferson St, Bronte 76933 Donna Poehls	PK-6		131 10		325/473-2251
Bronte High Sch 210 S Jefferson St, Bronte 76933 **John Phillips**	7-12	ATV	131 16	47%	325/473-2521 Fax 325/473-2022

- **Robert Lee Ind School Dist** PID: 01005780 325/453-4555
  1323 W Hamilton St, Robert Lee 76945   Fax 325/453-2326

Schools: 1 \ *Teachers:* 26 \ *Students:* 290 \ *Special Ed Students:* 40 \ *LEP Students:* 5 \ *College-Bound:* 50% \ *Ethnic:* Asian 1%, Hispanic 36%, Native American: 1%, Caucasian 62% \ *Exp:* $483 (High) \ *Poverty:* 22% \ *Title I:* $64,881 \ *Open-Close:* 08/19 - 05/21 \ *DTBP:* $350 (High)

Aaron Hood	1,11,288	Robin Allen	2
Mariann Hill	12,57*	Sandy Sawyer	16,73,76,286*
Wes Washam	67		

Public Schs..Principal	Grd	Prgm	Enr/#Cls	SN	
Robert Lee Sch 1323 W Hamilton St, Robert Lee 76945 David Odell	PK-12	ATV	290 36	58%	325/453-4555

---

79 Student Personnel	91 Safety/Security	275 Response To Intervention	298 Grant Writer/Ptnrships	**School Programs**	**Social Media**		
30 Driver Ed/Safety	92 Magnet School	277 Remedial Math K-12	750 Chief Innovation Officer	A = Alternative Program			
31 Gifted/Talented	93 Parental Involvement	280 Literacy Coach	751 Chief of Staff	G = Adult Classes	▉ = Facebook		
32 Video Services	95 Tech Prep Program	285 STEM	752 Social Emotional Learning	M = Magnet Program			
33 Substance Abuse Prev	97 Chief Information Officer	286 Digital Learning		T = Title I Schoolwide	▉ = Twitter		
34 Erate	98 Chief Technology Officer	288 Common Core Standards	**Other School Types**	V = Career & Tech Ed Programs			
35 AIDS Education	270 Character Education	294 Accountability	Ⓐ = Alternative School				
38 Alternative/At Risk	271 Migrant Education	295 Network System	Ⓒ = Charter School	New Schools are shaded			
39 Multi-Cultural Curriculum	273 Teacher Mentor	296 Title II Programs	Ⓜ = Magnet School	New Superintendents and Principals are bold			
90 Social Work	274 Before/After Sch	297 Webmaster	Ⓨ = Year-Round School	Personnel with email addresses are underscored			

TX-75

Coleman County

COLEMAN COUNTY

COLEMAN PUBLIC SCHOOLS

- **Coleman Ind School Dist** PID: 01005819 325/625-3575
  300 W Pecan St, Coleman 76834 Fax 325/625-4751

  Schools: 3 \ *Teachers:* 80 \ *Students:* 885 \ *Special Ed Students:* 101 \ *LEP Students:* 16 \ *College-Bound:* 59% \ *Ethnic:* Asian 1%, African American 2%, Hispanic 28%, Caucasian 69% \ *Exp:* $443 (High) \ *Poverty:* 34% \ *Title I:* $457,324 \ *Open-Close:* 08/21 - 05/21 \ *DTBP:* $392 (High)

  Brandon McDowell 1
  Weldon Thompson 3
  Chris Burton 5
  Joy Thompson 8,12,34,57,296*
  Anthony Beggs 27*
  Angelita Stephenson 58*
  Jeanne Ailshie 69*
  Amy Flippin 83,85,270,273*
  Karen Huff 2
  Marsha Ray 4
  John Elder 6*
  Ed Pryor 11
  Alissa Hohmann 36*
  Mark Martinez 67
  Paul Martin 73,76,295,297*

Public Schs..Principal	Grd	Prgm	Enr/#Cls	SN	
Coleman Elem Sch 303 15th St, Coleman 76834 Joy Thompson	PK-4	T	395 30	65%	325/625-3546 Fax 325/625-4064
Coleman High Sch 201 15th St, Coleman 76834 Diana Dobbins	9-12	TV	242 30	44%	325/625-2156 Fax 325/625-4557
Coleman Junior High Sch 301 15th St, Coleman 76834 Thomas King	5-8	T	248 20	55%	325/625-3593 Fax 325/625-3358

- **Panther Creek Cons Ind SD** PID: 01005950 325/357-4449
  Farm Road 503, Voss 76888 Fax 325/357-4470

  Schools: 1 \ *Teachers:* 19 \ *Students:* 149 \ *Special Ed Students:* 16 \ *College-Bound:* 85% \ *Ethnic:* Asian 1%, African American 2%, Hispanic 23%, Caucasian 74% \ *Exp:* $287 (Med) \ *Poverty:* 37% \ *Title I:* $111,455 \ *Open-Close:* 08/15 - 05/19 \ *DTBP:* $382 (High) \

  Dwin Nanny 1,11,83
  Jay Dalton 67
  Jan Romina 2,19
  Mark Romine 73*

Public Schs..Principal	Grd	Prgm	Enr/#Cls	SN	
Panther Creek Sch Farm Road 503, Voss 76888 Dwin Nanny	PK-12	TV	149 34	75%	325/357-4449

- **Santa Anna Ind School Dist** PID: 01005924 325/348-3136
  701 Bowie St, Santa Anna 76878 Fax 325/348-3141

  Schools: 2 \ *Teachers:* 24 \ *Students:* 259 \ *Special Ed Students:* 24 \ *College-Bound:* 75% \ *Ethnic:* African American 3%, Hispanic 28%, Native American: 1%, Caucasian 67% \ *Exp:* $672 (High) \ *Poverty:* 42% \ *Title I:* $205,044 \ *Open-Close:* 08/15 - 05/22 \ *DTBP:* $344 (High) \

  David Robinett 1
  LaVelle Walters 4*
  Laurie Hunter 8,12,79,88,274,275*
  Katrina Guerrero 2,11*
  Austin Simpson 6*
  Nathan Hindman 27
  Kristi Herrod 36,57,69,83,271,285*
  Larry Bostick 73
  Janice Fellers 67

Public Schs..Principal	Grd	Prgm	Enr/#Cls	SN	
Santa Anna Elem Sch 506 Jefferson St, Santa Anna 76878 Aletha Patterson	PK-6	T	148 10	74%	325/348-3138 Fax 325/348-3142
Santa Anna High Sch 701 Bowie St, Santa Anna 76878 James Sturgeon	7-12	TV	116 14	69%	325/348-3137 Fax 325/348-3149

COLLIN COUNTY

COLLIN PUBLIC SCHOOLS

- **Allen Ind School Dist** PID: 01005986 972/727-0511
  612 E Bethany Dr, Allen 75002 Fax 972/727-0500

  Schools: 24 \ *Teachers:* 1,316 \ *Students:* 21,404 \ *Special Ed Students:* 2,272 \ *LEP Students:* 1,151 \ *College-Bound:* 75% \ *Ethnic:* Asian 19%, African American 13%, Hispanic 14%, Native American: 1%, Caucasian 54% \ *Exp:* $179 (Low) \ *Poverty:* 3% \ *Title I:* $497,023 \ *Special Education:* $2,772,000 \ *Open-Close:* 08/14 - 05/22 \ *DTBP:* $181 (High) \

  Scott Niven 1
  Debbie Nye 2
  Brandon Boyter 3
  Steve Hanner 3
  Kyle Pursifull 5
  Jennifer Wilhelm 8,15,294
  Abigal Hobart 11,57
  Robin Bullock 15
  Renee Hernandez 16
  Jeff Turner 20,23
  Montie Parker 58
  Lisa Hodges 68
  Tim Carroll 71,97
  Patrick Tanner 76,295
  Jennifer Atencio 83*
  Regina Taylor 298
  Amber Lasseygne 2
  Greg Cartwright 2,19
  Daniel Pitcock 3,5,15,91,295
  Jackie Anderson 4
  Steve Williams 6
  Larry Labue 8,74
  Dr Maroba Zoeller 11
  Shelia Smith 15,68
  Victoria Selznick 16*
  Becky Hunt 27,31*
  John Montgomery 67
  Sheryl Stewart 69,294
  Bonnie Suttle 76
  Barbara Hinton 81
  Ernie Rodriguez 91

Public Schs..Principal	Grd	Prgm	Enr/#Cls	SN	
Allen High Sch 300 Rivercrest Blvd, Allen 75002 Dr Jason Johnston	9-12	V	4,885 175	13%	972/727-0400 Fax 972/727-0515
Alton Boyd Elem Sch 800 S Jupiter Rd, Allen 75002 Judith Coffman	PK-6	T	660 35	64%	972/727-0560 Fax 972/727-0566
Alvis C Story Elem Sch 1550 Edelweiss Dr, Allen 75002 Amanda Tabor	PK-6		525 45	18%	972/727-0570 Fax 972/727-0573
Beverly Cheatham Elem Sch 1501 Hopewell Dr, Allen 75013 Stephanie Logan	PK-6		565	1%	972/396-3016 Fax 972/396-3035
Boon Elem Sch 1050 Comanche Dr, Allen 75013 Lauren Cypert	PK-6		702	7%	972/747-3331 Fax 972/747-3335
Chandler Elem Sch 1000 Water Oak Dr, Allen 75002 Cindy Blair	PK-6		678	12%	469/467-1400 Fax 469/467-1410

1	Superintendent	8	Curric/Instruct K-12	19	Chief Financial Officer	29	Family/Consumer Science	39	Social Studies K-12	49	English/Lang Arts Elem	59	Special Education Elem	69	Academic Assessment
2	Bus/Finance/Purchasing	9	Curric/Instruct Elem	20	Art K-12	30	Adult Education	40	Social Studies Elem	50	English/Lang Arts Sec	60	Special Education Sec	70	Research/Development
3	Buildings And Grounds	10	Curric/Instruct Sec	21	Art Elem	31	Career/Sch-to-Work K-12	41	Social Studies Sec	51	Reading K-12	61	Foreign/World Lang K-12	71	Public Information
4	Food Service	11	Federal Program	22	Art Sec	32	Career/Sch-to-Work Elem	42	Science K-12	52	Reading Elem	62	Foreign/World Lang Elem	72	Summer School
5	Transportation	12	Title I	23	Music K-12	33	Career/Sch-to-Work Sec	43	Science Elem	53	Reading Sec	63	Foreign/World Lang Sec	73	Instructional Tech
6	Athletic	13	Title V	24	Music Elem	34	Early Childhood Ed	44	Science Sec	54	Remedial Reading K-12	64	Religious Education K-12	74	Inservice Training
7	Health Services	14	Asst Superintendent	25	Music Sec	35	Health/Phys Education	45	Math K-12	55	Remedial Reading Elem	65	Religious Education Elem	75	Marketing/Distributive
		15	Instructional Media Svcs	26	Business Education	36	Guidance Services K-12	46	Math Elem	56	Remedial Reading Sec	66	Religious Education Sec	76	Info Systems
		16	Chief Operations Officer	27	Career & Tech Ed	37	Guidance Services Elem	47	Math Sec	57	Bilingual/ELL	67	School Board President	77	Psychological Assess
		17	Chief Academic Officer	28	Technology Education	38	Guidance Services Sec	48	English/Lang Arts K-12	58	Special Education K-12	68	Teacher Personnel	78	Affirmative Action

Texas School Directory — Collin County

D L Rountree Elem Sch 800 E Main St, Allen 75002 Lara Utecht	PK-6	T	580 35	55%	972/727-0550 Fax 972/727-0555
ⓐ Dillard Spec Achievement Ctr 610 E Bethany Dr, Allen 75002 Eric Pacheco	K-12		100 4		972/727-7163 Fax 972/727-7162
Ereckson Middle Sch 450 Tatum Dr, Allen 75013 Leslie Norris	7-8	V	1,219	13%	972/747-3308 Fax 972/747-3311
Flossie Floyd Green Elem Sch 1315 Comanche Dr, Allen 75013 Stacia Butler	PK-6		596 30	9%	972/727-0370 Fax 972/727-0373
Frances Norton Elem Sch 1120 Newport Dr, Allen 75013 Julie DeLeon	PK-6		513 40	6%	972/396-6918 Fax 972/396-6923
Gene M Reed Elem Sch 1200 Rivercrest Blvd, Allen 75002 **Ardath Streitmatter**	PK-6		583 35	31%	972/727-0580 Fax 972/727-0588
George Anderson Elem Sch 305 N Alder Dr, Allen 75002 **Chris Koder**	PK-6		521 40	13%	972/396-6924 Fax 972/396-6929
James & Margie Marion ES 1595 Stablerun Dr, Allen 75002 Brooke Cherry	PK-6		729 38	9%	214/495-6784 Fax 214/495-6787
James D Kerr Elem Sch 1325 Glendover Dr, Allen 75013 **Ardath Streitmatter**	PK-6		658 41	4%	214/495-6765 Fax 214/495-6771
Lois Lindsey Elem Sch 5730 Wilford Dr, McKinney 75070 Melissa Pursifull	PK-6		669	10%	972/908-4000 Fax 469/319-6999
Lowery Freshman Center 368 N Greenville Ave, Allen 75002 Jill Stafford	9-9	V	1,776	14%	972/396-6975 Fax 972/396-6981
Luther & Anna Bolin Elem Sch 5705 Cheyenne Dr, Parker 75002 Reena Varughese	PK-6		541 39	12%	214/495-6750 Fax 214/495-6756
Mary Evans Elem Sch 1225 Walnut Springs Dr, Allen 75013 Pam Hale	PK-6		698	3%	972/747-3373 Fax 972/747-3376
Max Vaughan Elem Sch 820 Cottonwood Dr, Allen 75002 Tonya Jasenof	PK-6		709 30	17%	972/727-0470 Fax 972/727-0579
Olson Elem Sch 1751 E Exchange Pkwy, Allen 75002 **Susanne Miller**	PK-6		651	11%	972/562-1800 Fax 972/562-1835 f
Pete Ford Middle Sch 630 Park Place Dr, Allen 75002 Matthew Russell	7-8	V	874 70	23%	972/727-0590 Fax 972/727-0596 f t
Preston Elem Sch 2455 Hilliard Dr, Allen 75013 Johnna Walker	K-6		531		972/908-8780
Walter & Lois Curtis Mid Sch 1530 Rivercrest Blvd, Allen 75002 Sonya Pitcock	7-8	V	1,296 58	12%	972/727-0340 Fax 972/727-0345

● **Anna Ind School Dist** PID: 01006021   972/924-1000
501 S Sherley Ave, Anna 75409   Fax 972/924-1001

Schools: 6 \ **Teachers:** 208 \ **Students:** 3,800 \ **Special Ed Students:** 351 \ **LEP Students:** 366 \ **Ethnic:** Asian 1%, African American 10%, Hispanic 33%, Native American: 1%, Caucasian 55% \ **Exp:** $429 (High) \ **Poverty:** 7% \ **Title I:** $230,190 \ **Special Education:** $383,000 \ **Open-Close:** 08/14 - 05/21 \ **DTBP:** $350 (High)

Michael Comeaux 1		Dr Thomas Oneal 2,15,19		
Kenneth Lindsey 3		Mitchell Burney 4		
Jason Heath 6		Sue Akins 8,15		
Paula McMillion 11,57		Brad Duncan 15		
Jay Underwood 15,68,79		Greta Adams 16		
Jennifer Kelly 33		Dr Wendy Stanley 58		
Shelly Conway 67		Denisa Stewart 68		
Mindi Vandagriff 73,286		Patti Matthews 76		
Vince Sharp 77,83		Cane Sweet 88		
Jeff Jones 91		Theodore Mackey 285		

Public Schs..Principal	Grd	Prgm	Enr/#Cls	SN
Anna Education Center 601 S Sherley Ave, Anna 75409 **Gabriel Medrano**	6-6		401	972/924-1340
Anna High Sch 1107 W Rosamond Pkwy, Anna 75409 Shelley Anderson	9-12	V	924 20	36% 972/924-1100 Fax 972/924-1101
Anna Middle Sch 1201 N Powell Pkwy, Anna 75409 Tressi Brown	7-8	T	783 35	39% 972/924-1200 Fax 972/924-1201
Harlow Elem Sch 2412 Leonard Ave, Anna 75409 Karen Reddell	K-5		509	972/924-1320 Fax 972/924-9145
Joe K Bryant Elem Sch 2725 Bryant Farm Rd, Anna 75409 Cinda Owen	K-5	T	658 29	39% 972/924-1300 Fax 972/924-1301
Sue E Rattan Elem Sch 1221 S Ferguson Pkwy, Anna 75409 Todd Frazier	K-5	T	583 42	50% 972/924-1400 Fax 972/924-1401

● **Blue Ridge Ind School Dist** PID: 01006057   972/752-5554
318 School St, Blue Ridge 75424   Fax 972/752-9084

Schools: 3 \ **Teachers:** 54 \ **Students:** 860 \ **Special Ed Students:** 78 \ **LEP Students:** 55 \ **College-Bound:** 66% \ **Ethnic:** Hispanic 24%, Caucasian 76% \ **Exp:** $337 (High) \ **Poverty:** 11% \ **Title I:** $76,793 \ **Open-Close:** 08/15 - 05/28 \ **DTBP:** $350 (High)

Matt Kimball 1		Amanda Ray 2		
Terri Rodriquez 4		Mark Chester 6		
Helen Thompson 7*		Matthew Todd 8,11,69,74,88,294,298*		
Mike McCreary 67		Melissaa Stieney 73		

Public Schs..Principal	Grd	Prgm	Enr/#Cls	SN
Blue Ridge Elem Sch 425 N Church St, Blue Ridge 75424 Greg Smyder	PK-5	T	392 15	53% 972/752-5554 Fax 972/752-9950 f
Blue Ridge High Sch 11020 County Road 504, Blue Ridge 75424 Chris Miller	9-12	TV	233 50	40% 972/752-5554 Fax 972/752-5361
Blue Ridge Middle Sch 710 Tiger Pride Cir, Blue Ridge 75424 Phillip Lentz	6-8	T	200 10	55% 972/752-4243 Fax 972/752-5363 f t

● **Celina Ind School Dist** PID: 01006083   469/742-9100
205 S Colorado St, Celina 75009   Fax 972/382-3607

Schools: 6 \ **Teachers:** 161 \ **Students:** 2,600 \ **Special Ed Students:** 205 \ **LEP Students:** 127 \ **College-Bound:** 50% \ **Ethnic:** Asian 1%, African American 3%, Hispanic 25%, Native American: 1%, Caucasian 70% \ **Exp:** $265 (Med) \ **Poverty:** 6% \ **Title I:** $168,466 \ **Open-Close:** 08/14 - 05/21 \ **DTBP:** $320 (High)

Rick Demasters 1,84		Sarahbeth McCarter 2
William Hemby 3,15*		Ofelia Almendarez 4
Jerry Moore 5		Bill Elliot 6
Missy Tuinstra 7,83,85*		Lori Sitzes 8,11,15

79 Student Personnel	91 Safety/Security	275 Response To Intervention	298 Grant Writer/Ptnrships	**School Programs**
80 Driver Ed/Safety	92 Magnet School	277 Remedial Math K-12	750 Chief Innovation Officer	A = Alternative Program
81 Gifted/Talented	93 Parental Involvement	280 Literacy Coach	751 Chief of Staff	G = Adult Classes
82 Video Services	95 Tech Prep Program	285 STEM	752 Social Emotional Learning	M = Magnet Program
83 Substance Abuse Prev	97 Chief Infomation Officer	286 Digital Learning		T = Title I Schoolwide
84 Erate	98 Chief Technology Officer	288 Common Core Standards	**Other School Types**	V = Career & Tech Ed Programs
85 AIDS Education	270 Accountability	294 Accountability	Ⓐ = Alternative School	
88 Alternative/At Risk	271 Migrant Education	295 Network System	Ⓒ = Charter School	**Social Media**
89 Multi-Cultural Curriculum	273 Teacher Mentor	296 Title II Programs	Ⓜ = Magnet School	f = Facebook
90 Social Work	274 Before/After Sch	297 Webmaster	Ⓨ = Year-Round School	t = Twitter

New Schools are shaded
New Superintendents and Principals are bold
Personnel with email addresses are underscored

TX—77

Collin County
Market Data Retrieval

Starlynn Wells 9,88,294
Vanessa Jaramillo 57
Marilyn Chamberlin 73*

John Matthews 15,68
Kelly Juergens 67
Bobby Manson 91

Public Schs..Principal	Grd	Prgm	Enr/#Cls	SN	
Celina 6th Grade Center 706 E Pecan St, Celina 75009 Kimber Kincaid	6-6	V	200		469/742-9105 Fax 972/382-8543
Celina Elem Sch 550 S Utah St, Celina 75009 Starla Martin	1-5	T	596 24	27%	469/742-9103 Fax 972/382-3789
Celina High Sch 3455 N Preston Rd, Celina 75009 David Wilson	9-12	V	792 20	21%	469/742-9102 Fax 972/382-4830
Celina Junior High Sch 710 E Pecan St, Celina 75009 Russell McDaniel	7-8		426 17	24%	469/742-9101 Fax 972/382-4258
Celina Primary Sch 507 E Malone St, Celina 75009 Nancy Alvarez	PK-K		223	24%	469/742-9104 Fax 972/382-4792
O'Dell Elem Sch 750 Punk Carter Pkwy, Celina 75009 Stacy Ceci	1-5		402		469/742-9106 Fax 214/851-3667

- **Community Ind School Dist** PID: 01006124 972/843-8400
  611 N FM 1138, Nevada 75173   Fax 972/843-8401

Schools: 4 \ *Teachers:* 138 \ *Students:* 2,262 \
Special Ed Students: 193 \ *LEP Students:* 334 \ *College-Bound:* 44% \
Ethnic: Asian 1%, African American 5%, Hispanic 35%, Native American: 1%, Caucasian 58% \ *Exp:* $423 (High) \ *Poverty:* 7% \ *Title I:* $202,945 \
Special Education: $296,000 \ *Open-Close:* 08/15 - 05/27 \ *DTBP:* $354 (High) \

Roosevelt Nivins 1
James Percival 3,5
Jeremy Turner 6
Christi Farish 8,12,18,69,270,271,296
Neil Cardwell 16,73,76,286,295
Michael Shepard 67
Sabreana Marsh 71

Bryan Moore 2,19,288
Cindy Lewis 4
Kathy Coleman 7,85*
Natosha Scott 11,58
Margarita Solis 57
Alphonso Bates 68,79

Public Schs..Principal	Grd	Prgm	Enr/#Cls	SN	
Carylene McClendon Elem Sch 601 N FM 1138, Nevada 75173 **Gilberto Salinas**	PK-5	T	605 32	54%	972/843-6800 Fax 972/843-6801
Community High Sch 620 N FM 1138, Nevada 75173 **Michael Westfall**	9-12	TV	622 45	42%	972/843-6500 Fax 972/843-6501
Edge Middle Sch 615 N FM 1138, Nevada 75173 David Girardi	6-8	T	503 40	46%	972/843-6670 Fax 972/843-6671
Nesmith Elem Sch 801 President Blvd, Lavon 75166 Julie Meek	PK-5		532 17	29%	972/843-6100 Fax 972/843-6101

- **Farmersville Ind School Dist** PID: 01006148 972/782-6601
  501A State Highway 78 N, Farmersville 75442 Fax 972/784-7293

Schools: 4 \ *Teachers:* 109 \ *Students:* 1,750 \ *Special Ed Students:* 175 \
LEP Students: 155 \ *Ethnic:* Asian 1%, African American 3%, Hispanic 36%, Native American: 1%, Caucasian 60% \ *Exp:* $625 (High) \ *Poverty:* 8% \
Title I: $167,158 \ *Special Education:* $260,000 \ *Open-Close:* 08/14 - 05/21 \ *DTBP:* $559 (High)

Jeff Adams 1
Amber Pennell 2,19,271

Ernie Phelps 3,5
Brandon Hankins 6
Garry Jameson 8,15,288,294,296,298
Wiley Sullivan 27,73,295,297*
Tony Gray 67
Brian Alford 91

Tammy Pyle 4
Aimee Howard 7*
Trish Carnagey 11,57,280
Josh Martin 58,69,77,88
Tina Murray 76

Public Schs..Principal	Grd	Prgm	Enr/#Cls	SN	
Farmersville High Sch 499 State Highway 78 N, Farmersville 75442 Wayne Callaway	9-12	ATV	508 40	40%	972/782-7757 Fax 972/782-7245
Farmersville Intermediate Sch 807 N Main St, Farmersville 75442 Tad Myers	2-5	T	477	58%	972/782-8108 Fax 972/782-7527
Farmersville Jr High Sch 501 State Highway 78 N, Farmersville 75442 **Dave Warren**	6-8	AT	418 20	51%	972/782-6202 Fax 972/782-7029
Tatum Elem Sch 405 N Washington St, Farmersville 75442 Ginger Ketcher	PK-1	T	236 25	64%	972/782-7251 Fax 972/782-8109

- **Frisco Ind School Dist** PID: 01006186 469/633-6000
  5515 Ohio Dr, Frisco 75035   Fax 469/633-6050

Schools: 72 \ *Teachers:* 3,814 \ *Students:* 62,386 \
Special Ed Students: 4,989 \ *LEP Students:* 2,788 \ *College-Bound:* 50% \ *Ethnic:* Asian 25%, African American 11%, Hispanic 14%, Native American: 1%, Caucasian 50% \ *Exp:* $223 (Med) \ *Poverty:* 2% \ *Title I:* $715,767 \
Special Education: $4,122,000 \ *Open-Close:* 08/15 - 05/28 \ *DTBP:* $172 (High)

Dr Mike Waldrip 1
Scott Warstler 2
Blake Vaughn 3
Doug Zambiasi 3,17
Doug Becker 5
Kathy Tolbert 7
Mary Webb 9
Gary Nye 11,69,273,294
Stacy Cameron 16
Preston Hazzard 20
Dr Stephanie Cook 36
Christine Davis 58
Tracy Cartas 58
Dr Pamela Linton 68,78
Jamie Driskill 71
Sherri Wakeland 74*
Jennifer Adams 81*
Denise Debaugh 274
John Curran 295

Kimberly Smith 2,19
Todd Fouche 2,15
Cecil Cypert 3
Lisa Jenkins 4
David Kuykendall 6
Phil Evans 8
Angela Romney 10,81
Kenny Chandler 15,79
Dr Wes Cunningham 18
Dianna Manuel 27,31*
Merideth Choate 57
Garrett Jackson 58
Chad Rudy 67
Amanda McCune 71,97
Melissa Fouche 73,76,98,295
Dana Reid 81
Kevin Haller 91
Cheryl McDonald 286

Public Schs..Principal	Grd	Prgm	Enr/#Cls	SN	
Adelle R Clark Middle Sch 4600 Colby Dr, Frisco 75035 Lanina Duffey	6-8		791 45	16%	469/633-4600 Fax 469/633-4650
Anderson Elem Sch 2800 Oakland Hills Dr, Plano 75025 Laura Del Hierro	K-5		646 40	11%	469/633-2300 Fax 469/633-2350
Bennett & Alma Griffin Mid Sch 3703 Eldorado Pkwy, Frisco 75033 **Tommy Hill**	6-8		867	2%	469/633-4900 Fax 469/633-4950
Benton A Staley Middle Sch 6927 Stadium Ln, Frisco 75033 **Anita Robinson**	6-8		662	37%	469/633-4500 Fax 469/633-4550
Bessie Gunstream Elem Sch 7600 Rockyridge Dr, Frisco 75035 David Smolka	PK-5		651	12%	469/633-3100 Fax 469/633-3150

1 Superintendent	8 Curric/Instruct K-12	19 Chief Financial Officer	29 Family/Consumer Science	39 Social Studies K-12	49 English/Lang Arts Elem	59 Special Education Elem	69 Academic Assessment
2 Bus/Finance/Purchasing	9 Curric/Instruct Elem	20 Art K-12	30 Adult Education	40 Social Studies Elem	50 English/Lang Arts Sec	60 Special Education Sec	70 Research/Development
3 Buildings And Grounds	10 Curric/Instruct Sec	21 Art Elem	31 Career/Sch-to-Work K-12	41 Social Studies Sec	51 Reading K-12	61 Foreign/World Lang K-12	71 Public Information
4 Food Service	11 Federal Program	22 Art Sec	32 Career/Sch-to-Work Elem	42 Science K-12	52 Reading Elem	62 Foreign/World Lang Elem	72 Summer School
5 Transportation	12 Title I	23 Music K-12	33 Career/Sch-to-Work Sec	43 Science Elem	53 Reading Sec	63 Foreign/World Lang Sec	73 Instructional Tech
6 Athletic	13 Title V	24 Music Elem	34 Early Childhood Ed	44 Science Sec	54 Remedial Reading K-12	64 Religious Education K-12	74 Inservice Training
7 Health Services	15 Asst Superintendent	25 Music Sec	35 Health/Phys Education	45 Math K-12	55 Remedial Reading Elem	65 Religious Education Elem	75 Marketing/Distributive
	16 Instructional Media Svcs	26 Business Education	36 Guidance Services K-12	46 Math Elem	56 Remedial Reading Sec	66 Religious Education Sec	76 Info Systems
	17 Chief Operations Officer	27 Career & Tech Ed	37 Guidance Services Elem	47 Math Sec	57 Bilingual/ELL	67 School Board President	77 Psychological Assess
	18 Chief Academic Officer	28 Technology Education	38 Guidance Services Sec	48 English/Lang Arts K-12	58 Special Education K-12	68 Teacher Personnel	78 Affirmative Action

TX–78

Texas School Directory — Collin County

School	Grades	Prog	Enroll	%	Phone
Billy Vandeventer Middle Sch 6075 Independence Pkwy, Frisco 75035 Stephanie Taylor	6-8		1,084	5%	469/633-4350 Fax 469/633-4360
Cal & Walt Wester Middle Sch 12293 Shepherds Hill Ln, Frisco 75035 Richard Manuel	6-8		1,010	11%	469/633-4800 Fax 469/633-4850
Calvin Bledsoe Elem Sch 1900 Timber Ridge Dr, Frisco 75036 Sherry Klingenberg	K-5		683	2%	469/633-3600 Fax 469/633-3610
Career & Tech Education Center 9889 Wade Blvd, Frisco 75035 Monica Manuel	Voc		400		469/633-6780 Fax 469/633-6790
Centennial High Sch 6901 Coit Rd, Frisco 75035 Alicia Maphies	9-12	G	2,022	10%	469/633-5600 Fax 469/633-5650
Claude Curtsinger Elem Sch 12450 Jereme Trl, Frisco 75035 Angela Borgarello	K-5		757 37	5%	469/633-2100 Fax 469/633-2150
Comstock Elem Sch 7152 Silverado Trl, McKinney 75070 Amanda Dalton	K-5		732	8%	469/633-3900 Fax 469/633-3910
Dr Erwin & Elizabeth Pink ES 3650 Overhill Dr, Frisco 75033 Danielle Record	K-5		481	1%	469/633-3500 Fax 469/633-3510
Dr JM Ogle Elem Sch 4200 Big Fork Trl, McKinney 75070 Phyllis Pope	K-5	T	685	10%	469/633-3525 Fax 469/633-3535
Edris Childres Elliot Elem Sch 3721 Hudson Xing, McKinney 75070 Natalie Miller	K-5	T	605	27%	469/633-3750 Fax 469/633-3760
Frisco High Sch 6401 Parkwood Blvd, Frisco 75034 Daniel Barrentine	9-12	V	1,525 55	19%	469/633-5500 Fax 469/633-5550
Frisco ISD Early Childhood Sch 10330 Red Cedar Dr, Frisco 75035 Bethany Birdwell	PK-PK		760	27%	469/633-3825 Fax 469/633-3835
George & Deborah Purefoy ES 11880 Teel Pkwy, Frisco 75033 Kena Robertson	K-5		585	4%	469/633-3875 Fax 469/633-3885
Gerald Sonntag Elem Sch 2001 Reagan Dr, McKinney 75072 Shannon Acosta	K-5	T	591	16%	469/633-3850 Fax 469/633-3860
Heritage High Sch 14040 Eldorado Pkwy, Frisco 75035 Dr Katey Gray	9-12		2,188	14%	469/633-5900 Fax 469/633-5950
I S Rogers Elem Sch 10500 Rogers Rd, Frisco 75033 Jenny McGowan	K-5	T	518 34	20%	469/633-2000 Fax 469/633-2050
Ida Lee Bright Elem Sch 7600 Woodstream Dr, Frisco 75034 Serita Dodson	K-5	T	383	49%	469/633-2700 Fax 469/633-2750
Independence High Sch 10555 Independence Pkwy, Frisco 75035 Alan Waligura	9-12		1,958	13%	469/633-5400 Fax 469/633-5450
Isabel Pierce Sem Elem Sch 12721 Honeygrove Dr, Frisco 75035 Jose Mira	K-5		828	8%	469/633-3575 Fax 469/633-3585
Isbell Elem Sch 6000 Maltby Dr, Frisco 75035 Kandra Wooten	K-5		704 40	3%	469/633-3400 Fax 469/633-3450
Izetta Sparks Elem Sch 8200 Otis Dr, Frisco 75036 Amy Baker	PK-5		725 18	4%	469/633-3000 Fax 469/633-3050
James R Newman Elem Sch 12333 Briar Ridge Rd, Frisco 75033 Rachael Gilbert	K-5		813	4%	469/633-3975 Fax 469/633-3985
Janice Stanley Scott Elem Sch 10550 Millbend Dr, McKinney 75072 T Leanne Crane	K-5		728	10%	469/633-4000 Fax 469/633-4010
Justin Wakeland High Sch 10700 Legacy Dr, Frisco 75033 Donna Edge	9-12	AV	2,195	6%	469/633-5700 Fax 469/633-5750
JW & Ruth Christie Elem Sch 10300 Huntington Rd, Frisco 75035 Paige Brewer	K-5	T	534 35	55%	469/633-2400 Fax 469/633-2450
Lamar & Norma Hunt Middle Sch 4900 Legendary Dr, Frisco 75034 Chris Clark	6-8		811	14%	469/633-5200 Fax 469/633-5210
Lawler Middle Sch 12921 Rolater Rd, Frisco 75035 Travis Zambiasi	6-8		600		469/633-4150 Fax 469/633-4160
Lebanon Trail High Sch 5151 Ohio Dr, Frisco 75035 Jacob Duce	9-12		946	9%	469/633-6600 Fax 469/633-6657
Libby Cash Maus Middle Sch 12175 Coit Rd, Frisco 75035 Chakosha Powell	6-8		987	11%	469/633-5250 Fax 469/633-5260
Liberty High Sch 15250 Rolater Rd, Frisco 75035 Ashley Rainwater	9-12		1,983	8%	469/633-5800 Fax 469/633-5850 🅵 🆃
Liscano Elem Sch 11222 Mammoth Cave, Frisco 75035 Michele Lott	K-5		600		469/633-2275 Fax 469/633-2285
Lone Star High Sch 2606 Panther Creek Pkwy, Frisco 75033 Karen Kraft	9-12		2,131	13%	469/633-5300 Fax 469/633-5350
Lucile Rogers Ashley Elem Sch 15601 Christopher Ln, Frisco 75035 Kimberly Frankson	K-5		658 44	3%	469/633-3700 Fax 469/633-3710
Mary M Boals Elem Sch 2035 Jaguar Dr, Frisco 75033 Christina Beran	K-5		689	9%	469/633-3300 Fax 469/633-3350
McSpedden Elem Sch 14140 Countrybrook Dr, Frisco 75035 Kranti Singh	K-5		714	1%	469/633-4025 Fax 469/633-4035
Memorial High Sch 12300 Frisco St, Frisco 75033 Jennifer Redden	9-11	V	600		469/633-7300 Fax 469/633-7350
Miller Elem Sch 300 Cypress Hill Dr, Little Elm 75068 Ashley Miller	K-5		631	12%	469/633-2075 Fax 469/633-2085
Mooneyham Elem Sch 2301 Eden Dr, McKinney 75072 Ingrid Dodd	K-5		826	7%	469/633-3650 Fax 469/633-3660
Nelson Middle Sch 10100 Independence Pkwy, Frisco 75035 Mitzi Garner	6-8		767	6%	469/633-4100 Fax 469/633-4110
Nichols Elem Sch 7411 Nichols Trl, Frisco 75036 Zachary Wiley	K-5		551	1%	469/633-3950 Fax 469/633-3960
Noel A Smith Elem Sch 9800 Sean Dr, Frisco 75035 Catherine Young	K-5		630 37	9%	469/633-2200 Fax 469/633-2250
Norris Elem Sch 10101 Shepton Ln, Frisco 75035 Loryn Tobey	K-5		817	3%	469/633-4075 Fax 469/633-4085
Otis Spears Elem Sch 8500 Wade Blvd, Frisco 75034 Becca Bustillo	K-5	T	734 40	14%	469/633-2900 Fax 469/633-2950
Pat & Katherine Fowler Mid Sch 3801 McDermott Rd, Plano 75025 Donnie Wiseman	6-8	V	1,141	5%	469/633-5050 Fax 469/633-5060

79 Student Personnel	91 Safety/Security	275 Response To Intervention	298 Grant Writer/Ptnrships
80 Driver Ed/Safety	92 Magnet School	277 Remedial Math K-12	750 Chief Innovation Officer
81 Gifted/Talented	93 Parental Involvement	280 Literacy Coach	751 Chief of Staff
82 Video Services	95 Tech Prep Program	285 STEM	752 Social Emotional Learning
83 Substance Abuse Prev	97 Chief Infomation Officer	286 Digital Learning	
84 Erate	98 Chief Technology Officer	288 Common Core Standards	**Other School Types**
85 AIDS Education	270 Character Education	294 Accountability	Ⓐ = Alternative School
88 Alternative/At Risk	271 Migrant Education	295 Network System	Ⓒ = Charter School
89 Multi-Cultural Curriculum	273 Teacher Mentor	296 Title II Programs	Ⓜ = Magnet School
90 Social Work	274 Before/After Sch	297 Webmaster	Ⓨ = Year-Round School

School Programs
A = Alternative Program
G = Adult Classes
M = Magnet Program
T = Title I Schoolwide
V = Career & Tech Ed Programs

Social Media
🅵 = Facebook
🆃 = Twitter

New Schools are shaded
New Superintendents and Principals are bold
Personnel with email addresses are underscored

TX—79

Collin County

Market Data Retrieval

School	Grd	Prgm	Enr/#Cls	SN	Phone	Fax
Pearson Middle Sch 2323 Stonebrook Pkwy, Frisco 75036 Jamie Wisneski	6-8		770	2%	469/633-4450	Fax 469/633-4460
Pete & Gracie Hosp Elem Sch 5050 Lone Star Ranch Pkwy, Frisco 75036 Aaron Else	K-5		743	4%	469/633-4050	Fax 469/633-4060
Phillips Elem Sch 2285 Little River Rd, Frisco 75033 Dana Solomon	K-5		673	6%	469/633-3925	Fax 469/633-3935
Pioneer Heritage Middle Sch 1649 High Shoals Dr, Frisco 75036 Rocky Agan	6-8		877	3%	469/633-4700	Fax 469/633-4750
Polly Tadlock Elem Sch 12515 Godfrey Dr, Frisco 75035 Kellie Rapp	K-5	T	636	12%	469/633-3775	Fax 469/633-3785
Portia Ross Taylor Elem Sch 9865 Gillespie Dr, Plano 75025 Christy Garza	K-5	T	706	14%	469/633-3625	Fax 469/633-3635
Reba Cobb Carroll Elem Sch 4380 Throne Hall Dr, Frisco 75033 John Waldrip	K-5		528	5%	469/633-3725	Fax 469/633-3735
Rick Reedy High Sch 3003 Stonebrook Pkwy, Frisco 75034 Karen Lecocq	9-10		1,335	4%	469/633-6400	Fax 469/633-6450
Riddle Elem Sch 8201 Robinson Rd, Plano 75024 Heather Cox	K-5		772 42	6%	469/633-3200	Fax 469/633-3250
Robert Cobb Middle Sch 9400 Teel Pkwy, Frisco 75033 Jamie Lakey	6-8		949	8%	469/633-4300	Fax 469/633-4310
Robertson Elem Sch 2501 Woodlake Pkwy, Little Elm 75068 Kyla Prusak	K-5		741	8%	469/633-3675	Fax 469/633-3685
Ruth Borchardt Elem Sch 4300 Waskom Dr, Plano 75024 Jodi Davis	PK-5		754	5%	469/633-2800	Fax 469/633-2850
Sam & Ann Roach Middle Sch 12499 Independence Pkwy, Frisco 75035 Natasha McDonald	6-8		855	15%	469/633-5000	Fax 469/633-5010
Scoggins Middle Sch 7070 Stacy Rd, McKinney 75070 Barbara Warner	6-8		1,001	16%	469/633-5150	Fax 469/633-5160
Shawnee Trail Elem Sch 10701 Preston Vineyard Dr, Frisco 75035 Pamela Schaeffer	K-5	T	596 33	14%	469/633-2500	Fax 469/633-2550
ⓐ Student Opportunity Center 6928 Maple St, Frisco 75033 Kecia Theodore	9-12		150 20		469/633-6700	Fax 469/633-6710
Sue Wilson Stafford Middle Sch 2288 Little River Rd, Frisco 75035 Robin Scott	6-8		871	13%	469/633-5100	Fax 469/633-5110 ⓣ
Talley Elem Sch 5900 Colt Rd, Frisco 75035 Jamie Peden	K-5		600		469/633-2175	Fax 469/633-2185
Trent Middle Sch 13131 Coleto Creek Dr, Frisco 75033 Shawn Perry	6-8		887	7%	469/633-4400	Fax 469/633-4410
Vaughn Elem Sch 3535 Guinn Gate Dr, Frisco 75034 Susie Graham	K-5		572	1%	469/633-2575	Fax 469/633-2585
Weldon Corbell Elem Sch 11095 Monarch Dr, Frisco 75033 Brenda Youngblood	K-5		722	16%	469/633-3550	Fax 469/633-3560
William & Abbie Allen Elem Sch 5800 Legacy Dr, Frisco 75034 Chastity Johnson	K-5		630	8%	469/633-3800	Fax 469/633-3810
Wilma Fisher Elem Sch 2500 Old Orchard Rd, Frisco 75033 Nancy Fatheree	K-5		584	3%	469/633-2600	Fax 469/633-2650

● **Lovejoy Ind School Dist** PID: 01006227   469/742-8000
259 Country Club Rd, Allen 75002   Fax 469/742-8001

> **Schools:** 6 \ **Teachers:** 293 \ **Students:** 4,424 \ **Special Ed Students:** 295 \ **LEP Students:** 52 \ **College-Bound:** 96% \ **Ethnic:** Asian 7%, African American 2%, Hispanic 8%, Native American: 1%, Caucasian 82% \ **Exp:** $272 (Med) \ **Poverty:** 3% \ **Title I:** $98,235 \ **Special Education:** $342,000 \ **Open-Close:** 08/19 - 05/29 \ **DTBP:** $181 (High)

Dr Michael Goddard	1	Dee Dee White	2
Shay Adams	2,19	Tina Tomson	2
David Dillon	3,5	Dr Dennis Womack	3,5,15,91
Juliana Elandary	4	Matt McCarty	4
Sunny Cleveland	4	Jim Bob Puckett	6
Sancy Fuller	7,57,58	Dennis Muizers	8,15,69
Mary Mullen	8	Mitci Allen	11,73
Kristin Dawson	16*	Brice McCasland	20
Mary Ruggeri	37*	Cindy Bronson	43
Diana Saylack	46	Kelly Cowan	47*
Megan Frankenberg	52	Chad Collins	67
Stacey Dillon	71	Michael Voth	73
Brie Smith	81	Ajck Vestal	98
Stephanie Kranz	273	Lisa Leirer	274*
Taylor Denison	274	Trevor Davis	295

Public Schs..Principal	Grd	Prgm	Enr/#Cls	SN	Phone	Fax
Hart Elem Sch 450 Country Club Rd, Lucas 75002 Lacey Moser	PK-4	T	465 35	4%	469/742-8200	Fax 469/742-8201
Lovejoy Elem Sch 256 Country Club Rd, Allen 75002 Wendy Craft	PK-4		419 31	3%	469/742-8100	Fax 469/742-8101
Lovejoy High Sch 2350 E States Pkwy, Lucas 75002 Chris Mayfield	9-12		1,484	2%	469/742-8700	Fax 469/742-8701
Puster Elem Sch 856 Stoddard Rd, Fairview 75069 Holly Haynes	PK-4		414	1%	469/742-8300	Fax 469/742-8301
Sloan Creek Intermediate Sch 440 Country Club Rd, Fairview 75069 Ray Winkler	5-6		661	3%	469/742-8400	Fax 469/742-8401
Willow Springs Middle Sch 1101 W Lucas Rd, Allen 75002 Kent Messer	7-8		779	2%	469/742-8500	Fax 469/742-8501

● **McKinney Ind School Dist** PID: 01006241   469/302-4000
1 Duvall St, McKinney 75069   Fax 469/302-4071

> **Schools:** 31 \ **Teachers:** 1,670 \ **Students:** 24,335 \ **Special Ed Students:** 2,689 \ **LEP Students:** 2,519 \ **College-Bound:** 56% \ **Ethnic:** Asian 4%, African American 14%, Hispanic 30%, Native American: 1%, Caucasian 52% \ **Exp:** $368 (High) \ **Poverty:** 5% \ **Title I:** $1,929,245 \ **Special Education:** $3,690,000 \ **Open-Close:** 08/15 - 05/27 \ **DTBP:** $198 (High) \ ⓕ ⓣ

Dr Rick McDaniel	1	Beverly Biering	2
Jason Bird	2,19	Corey Gililland	3
Erica Wright	3	Greg Suttle	3
Justin Price	3	James Shoemake	4
Robert Montgomery	5,91	Shawn Pratt	6
Julie Blankenship	7	Suzanne Woodard	9,15
Melinda DeFelice	10,15	Tamira Griffin	15,68,270,273
Lara Lindsey	16,73	Dan White	20,23
Todd Young	31*	Dr Pamela Parmley	34,274

1 Superintendent	8 Curric/Instruct K-12	19 Chief Financial Officer	29 Family/Consumer Science	39 Social Studies K-12	49 English/Lang Arts Elem	59 Special Education Elem	69 Academic Assessment
2 Bus/Finance/Purchasing	9 Curric/Instruct Elem	20 Art K-12	30 Adult Education	40 Social Studies Elem	50 English/Lang Arts Sec	60 Special Education Sec	70 Research/Development
3 Buildings And Grounds	10 Curric/Instruct Sec	21 Art Elem	31 Career/Sch-to-Work K-12	41 Social Studies Sec	51 Reading K-12	61 Foreign/World Lang K-12	71 Public Information
4 Food Service	11 Federal Program	22 Art Sec	32 Career/Sch-to-Work Elem	42 Science K-12	52 Reading Elem	62 Foreign/World Lang Elem	72 Summer School
5 Transportation	12 Title I	23 Music K-12	33 Career/Sch-to-Work Sec	43 Science Elem	53 Reading Sec	63 Foreign/World Lang Sec	73 Instructional Tech
6 Athletic	13 Title V	24 Music Elem	34 Early Childhood Ed	44 Science Sec	54 Remedial Reading K-12	64 Religious Education K-12	74 Inservice Training
7 Health Services	15 Asst Superintendent	25 Music Sec	35 Health/Phys Education	45 Math K-12	55 Remedial Reading Elem	65 Religious Education Elem	75 Marketing/Distributive
	16 Instructional Media Svcs	26 Business Education	36 Guidance Services K-12	46 Math Elem	56 Remedial Reading Sec	66 Religious Education Sec	76 Info Systems
	17 Chief Operations Officer	27 Career & Tech Ed	37 Guidance Services Elem	47 Math Sec	57 Bilingual/ELL	67 School Board President	77 Psychological Assess
	18 Chief Academic Officer	28 Technology Education	38 Guidance Services Sec	48 English/Lang Arts K-12	58 Special Education K-12	68 Teacher Personnel	78 Affirmative Action

Texas School Directory — Collin County

Karin Kelmm 35	Jennifer Akins 36	
Lisa Witt 41	Kendra Henke 44	
Misty Young 46	Judy Vega 49	
Andrea Coachman 50	Zabi Gonzalez 57	
Adrienne Morris 58,69,77	Sally Riche 58	
Curtis Rippee 67	Chad Teague 68	
Cody Cunningham 71	David Spann 71,73,84,97	
Greg Grimes 76	Jeff Gilliam 76	
Luke Hurst 81	Geoff Sanderson 294	
Shun Ying 295		

Public Schs..Principal	Grd	Prgm	Enr/#Cls	SN	
Albert & Iola Davis Malvern ES 1100 Eldorado Pkwy, McKinney 75069 Rhonda Gilliam	K-5	T	522 34	72%	469/302-5300 Fax 469/302-5301
Arthur McNeil Elem Sch 3650 S Hardin Blvd, McKinney 75070 Tracy Meador	K-5		419 40	28%	469/302-5200 Fax 469/302-5201
Bennett Elem Sch 7760 Coronado Dr, McKinney 75072 Amy Holderman	K-5		515	6%	469/302-5400 Fax 469/302-5401
C T Eddins Elem Sch 311 Peregrine Dr, McKinney 75072 Sharon Havard	K-5		384 35	6%	469/302-6600 Fax 469/302-6601
Earl & Lottie Wolford Elem Sch 6951 Berkshire Rd, McKinney 75072 Francine Gratt	K-5		476 30	11%	469/302-4700 Fax 469/302-4701
Earl Slaughter Elem Sch 2706 Wolford St, McKinney 75071 Nick DeFelice	K-5	T	589 27	53%	469/302-6100 Fax 469/302-6101
Evans Middle Sch 6998 Eldorado Pkwy, McKinney 75070 Darla Jackson	6-8	V	1,120	22%	469/302-7100 Fax 469/302-7101
Fanny Finch Elem Sch 1205 S Tennessee St, McKinney 75069 Erika Echegaray	K-5	GT	388 75	87%	469/302-5600 Fax 469/302-5601
Gibson Caldwell Elem Sch 601 W Louisiana St, McKinney 75069 Kelly Flowers	K-5	T	530 42	68%	469/302-5500 Fax 469/302-5501
Glen Oaks Elem Sch 6100 Glen Oaks Dr, McKinney 75072 Molly Hovan	K-5		477 35	4%	469/302-6400 Fax 469/302-6401
Herman Lawson Early Chldhd Ctr 500 Dowell St, McKinney 75071 Susie Towber	PK-PK	T	590	76%	469/302-2400 Fax 469/302-2401
J B Wilmeth Elem Sch 901 La Cima Dr, McKinney 75071 Kristin Ellis	K-5		671	4%	469/302-7400 Fax 469/302-7401
J W Webb Elem Sch 810 E Louisiana St, McKinney 75069 Kyle Luthi	K-5	GT	394 35	75%	469/302-6000 Fax 469/302-6001
Jack Cockrill Middle Sch 1351 N Hardin Blvd, McKinney 75071 Dr Amber Epperson	6-8		1,322	19%	469/302-7900 Fax 469/302-7901
Jack Faubion Middle Sch 2000 Rollins St, McKinney 75069 Jimmy Bowser	6-8	V	1,291	36%	469/302-6900 Fax 469/302-6901
Jesse McGowen Elem Sch 4300 Columbus Dr, McKinney 75070 Kimberly Luyster	K-5		669	22%	469/302-7500 Fax 469/302-7501
Lizzie Nell C McClure Elem Sch 1753 N Ridge Rd, McKinney 75071 Maria Hafner	K-5		645	10%	469/302-9400 Fax 469/302-9401
McKinney Boyd High Sch 600 N Lake Forest Dr, McKinney 75071 Jennifer Peirson	9-12	AV	2,824	16%	469/302-3400 Fax 469/302-3401
Ⓐ McKinney Daep Learning Center 2100 W White Ave, McKinney 75069 Cynthia Morton	K-12	G	75 6		469/302-7800 Fax 469/302-7801
McKinney High Sch 1400 Wilson Creek Pkwy, McKinney 75069 Alan Arbabi	9-12	GV	2,958	30%	469/302-5700 Fax 469/302-5701
McKinney North High Sch 2550 Wilmeth Rd, McKinney 75071 Jae Gaskill	9-12	V	2,117 90	28%	469/302-4300 Fax 469/302-4301
Minshew Elem Sch 300 Joplin Dr, McKinney 75071 Inetra Nelson	K-5		673	19%	469/302-7300 Fax 469/302-7301
Naomi Press Elem Sch 4101 Shawnee Rd, McKinney 75071 Rachel Constantinescu	K-5	T	584 30	43%	469/302-7600 Fax 469/302-7601
Nell Burks Elem Sch 1801 Hill St, McKinney 75069 Alvin Conley	K-5	T	460 30	80%	469/302-6200 Fax 469/302-6203
Reuben Johnson Elem Sch 3400 Ash Ln, McKinney 75070 Michelle Baumman	K-5		502 38	15%	469/302-6500 Fax 469/302-6501
Roy Lee Walker Elem Sch 4000 Cockrill Dr, McKinney 75072 Melanie Raleeh	K-5		567 35	5%	469/302-4600 Fax 469/302-4601
Ruth Dowell Middle Sch 301 S Ridge Rd, McKinney 75072 Holly Rogers	6-8	GV	1,192 100	22%	469/302-6700 Fax 469/302-6701
Scott Johnson Middle Sch 3400 Community Ave, McKinney 75071 Mitchell Curry	6-8	TV	918 80	48%	469/302-4900 Fax 469/302-4901
Serenity High Sch 2100 W White Ave, McKinney 75069 Stephen Issa	9-12		12 4		469/302-7830 Fax 469/302-7831
Valley Creek Elem Sch 2800 Valley Creek Trl, McKinney 75072 Megan Richards	K-5		551 36	13%	469/302-4800 Fax 469/302-4801
Vega Elem Sch 2511 Cattleman Dr, McKinney 75071 Mike Forsyth	K-5	T	521 34	59%	469/302-5100 Fax 469/302-5101

● **Melissa Ind School Dist** PID: 01006320 — 972/837-2411
1904 Cooper St, Melissa 75454 — Fax 972/837-4233

Schools: 4 \ *Teachers:* 169 \ *Students:* 2,792 \ *Special Ed Students:* 245 \ *LEP Students:* 74 \ *Ethnic:* Asian 1%, African American 7%, Hispanic 19%, Native American: 1%, Caucasian 71% \ *Exp:* $389 (High) \ *Poverty:* 3% \ *Title I:* $35,142 \ *Special Education:* $257,000 \ *Open-Close:* 08/27 - 05/28 \ *DTBP:* $360 (High) \

Keith Murphy 1	Lance Rainey 2	
Kenny Deel 3,4,91	Mike Price 4*	
Weston Bartlett 5	Sharon Carroll 8,11,36,69,294	
Dr Robert Rich 11,68,271,296	Leanne Bush 57	
Adrienne Morris 58,77	Jennifer Clark 58	
George James 67	Kim Boedeker 69	

Public Schs..Principal	Grd	Prgm	Enr/#Cls	SN	
Harry McKillop Elem Sch 3509 Liberty Way, Melissa 75454 **Krissy Womack**	PK-5	T	834 16	19%	972/837-2632 Fax 469/729-7737
Melissa High Sch 3030 Milrany Ln, Melissa 75454 Kenneth Wooten	9-12		827 28	11%	972/837-4216 Fax 972/729-7751
Melissa Middle Sch 3150 Cardinal Dr, Melissa 75454 Marcus Eckert	6-8		672	16%	972/837-4355 Fax 972/729-1150

*9 Student Personnel	91 Safety/Security	275 Response To Intervention	298 Grant Writer/Ptnrships	**School Programs**	**Social Media**
30 Driver Ed/Safety	92 Magnet School	277 Remedial Math K-12	750 Chief Innovation Officer	A = Alternative Program	
31 Gifted/Talented	93 Parental Involvement	280 Literacy Coach	751 Chief of Staff	G = Adult Classes	= Facebook
32 Video Services	95 Tech Prep Program	285 STEM	752 Social Emotional Learning	M = Magnet Program	
33 Substance Abuse Prev	97 Chief Information Officer	286 Digital Learning		T = Title I Schoolwide	= Twitter
34 Erate	98 Chief Technology Officer	288 Common Core Standards	**Other School Types**	V = Career & Tech Ed Programs	
35 AIDS Education	270 Character Education	294 Accountability	Ⓐ = Alternative School		
38 Alternative/At Risk	271 Migrant Education	295 Network System	Ⓒ = Charter School	New Schools are shaded	
39 Multi-Cultural Curriculum	273 Teacher Mentor	296 Title II Programs	Ⓜ = Magnet School	New Superintendents and Principals are bold	
30 Social Work	274 Before/After Sch	297 Webmaster	Ⓨ = Year-Round School	Personnel with email addresses are underscored	

TX—81

Collin County

Market Data Retrieval

North Creek Elem Sch	PK-5	T	459	17%	972/837-4530
4401 Cypress Dr, Melissa 75454					Fax 469/729-7739
Michele Austin					

• **Plano Ind School Dist** PID: 01006344 — 469/752-8100
2700 W 15th St, Plano 75075 — Fax 469/752-8096

> **Schools:** 73 \ **Teachers:** 3,905 \ **Students:** 53,952 \
> **Special Ed Students:** 5,811 \ **LEP Students:** 6,797 \ **College-Bound:** 65%
> \ **Ethnic:** Asian 24%, African American 13%, Hispanic 25%, Caucasian 38% \ **Exp:** $209 (Med) \ **Poverty:** 5% \ **Title I:** $5,122,464 \
> **Special Education:** $8,404,000 \ **Open-Close:** 08/12 - 05/22 \ **DTBP:** $187 (High) \

Sara Bonser 1	John Orr 2		
Randy McDowell 2,19	Juan Ramos 3		
Dr Theresa Williams 3,17	Ashley Hipp 4		
Dr Kary Cooper 4,5,6,15,68,91	Mark Skinner 5		
Gerald Brence 6	Megan Schuler 7		
Amy Bates 8	Dr Katrina Hasley 8,15,27,34,57,58		
Laurie Taylor 9	Ashley Halms 10		
Betsy Gust 11	Dr Beth Brockman 15,68		
Dan Armstrong 15,16,73,76,295	Elaine Cogburn 15		
Karla Oliver 15,71,298	Susan Modisette 15,36,93		
Marylynn Skinner 16	Kathy Kuddes 20,23		
Karen Buechman 27	Molly Pipak 35		
Jana Hancock 36	Mary Swinton 42		
Karen Shepherd 44	Susan Dyer 49		
Deborah Brannon 50	Roxanne Burchfiel 53,54		
Talle Gomez 57*	Janna Crow 58		
Paula Lons 58	Stephany Sipes 61		
Tammy Richards 67	Dr Dash Weerasinghe 69,70,294		
Matt Frey 73	Rhonda Davis 81		
Gary Carter 83*	Joseph Parks 91		
Robin Garcia 274			

Public Schs..Principal	Grd	Prgm	Enr/#Cls	SN		
Aldridge Elem Sch	K-5		615	18%	469/752-0000	
720 Pleasant Valley Ln, Richardson 75080			45		Fax 469/752-0001	
Antreshawn Buhl						
Armstrong Middle Sch	6-8	T	708	72%	469/752-4600	
3805 Timberline Dr, Plano 75074			35		Fax 469/752-4601	
Melissa Blank						
Barksdale Elem Sch	K-5		659	15%	469/752-0100	
2424 Midway Rd, Plano 75093					Fax 469/752-0101	
Jennifer Caplinger						
Barron Elem Sch	K-5	T	394	86%	469/752-0200	
3300 P Ave, Plano 75074			28		Fax 469/752-0201	
Tricia Lancaster						
Beaty Early Childhood Sch	PK-PK		453	20%	469/752-4200	
1717 Nevada Dr, Plano 75093					Fax 469/752-4201	
Kristen Fislar						
Bethany Elem Sch	K-5		384	9%	469/752-0300	
2418 Micarta Dr, Plano 75025					Fax 469/752-0301	
Bryan Bird						
Bettye Haun Elem Sch	K-5		636	9%	469/752-1600	
4500 Quincy Ln, Plano 75024					Fax 469/752-1601	
Jayne Smith						
Bowman Middle Sch	6-8	T	994	62%	469/752-4800	
2501 Jupiter Rd, Plano 75074			100		Fax 469/752-4801	
Brooks Baca						
Brinker Elem Sch	K-5		656	15%	469/752-0500	
3800 Clark Pkwy, Plano 75093			30		Fax 469/752-0501	
Barbara Lange						
C M Rice Middle Sch	6-8		1,080	6%	469/752-6000	
8500 Gifford Dr, Plano 75025					Fax 469/752-6001	
Christopher Glasscock						
Carlisle Elem Sch	K-5		547	20%	469/752-0600	
6525 Old Orchard Dr, Plano 75023			40		Fax 469/752-0601	
Linda Patrick						
Carpenter Middle Sch	6-8	T	671	56%	469/752-5000	
3905 Rainier Rd, Plano 75023					Fax 469/752-5001	
Courtney Washington						
Centennial Elem Sch	K-5		552	8%	469/752-0700	
2609 Ventura Dr, Plano 75093					Fax 469/752-0701	
Sara Stewart						
Christie Elem Sch	PK-5	T	737	57%	469/752-0800	
3801 Rainier Rd, Plano 75023			40		Fax 469/752-0801	
Sean Flynn						
Clark High Sch	9-10	GV	1,453	29%	469/752-7200	
523 W Spring Creek Pkwy, Plano 75023			70		Fax 469/752-7201	
Pamela Clark						
Daffron Elem Sch	K-5	T	587	31%	469/752-0900	
3900 Preston Meadow Dr, Plano 75093					Fax 469/752-0901	
Stefanie Ramos						
David McCall Elem Sch	K-5	T	558	33%	469/752-4500	
6601 Cloverhaven Way, Plano 75074					Fax 469/752-4501	
Stacy Kimbriel						
Davis Elem Sch	K-5		435	39%	469/752-1000	
2701 Parkhaven Dr, Plano 75075			30		Fax 469/752-1001	
Karma Cunningham						
Dennis Miller Elem Sch	K-5		400	11%	469/752-2700	
5651 Coventry Dr, Richardson 75082			38		Fax 469/752-2701	
Jennifer Bero						
Dooley Elem Sch	K-5	T	367	39%	469/752-1100	
2425 San Gabriel Dr, Plano 75074			24		Fax 469/752-1101	
Tramy Tran						
Dr Allan & Carolyn Bird Ed Ctr	Spec	A	80		469/752-2200	
1300 19th St, Plano 75074					Fax 469/752-2201	
Jana Sandall						
Forman Elem Sch	PK-5	T	594	81%	469/752-1200	
3600 Timberline Dr, Plano 75074			40		Fax 469/752-1201	
Carmen Casamayor-Ryan						
Frankford Middle Sch	6-8	T	1,056	38%	469/752-5200	
7706 Osage Plaza Pkwy, Dallas 75252			50		Fax 469/752-5201	
Melanie Schulte						
Gulledge Elem Sch	K-5		662	13%	469/752-1300	
6801 Preston Meadow Dr, Plano 75024					Fax 469/752-1301	
Deni Bleggi						
Haggard Middle Sch	6-8		818	19%	469/752-5400	
2832 Parkhaven Dr, Plano 75075					Fax 469/752-5401	
Shauna Koehne						
Harrington Elem Sch	PK-5		411	24%	469/752-1500	
1540 Baffin Bay Dr, Plano 75075			23		Fax 469/752-1501	
Jacye Jamar						
Hedgcoxe Elem Sch	K-5		429	13%	469/752-1700	
7701 Prescott Dr, Plano 75025					Fax 469/752-1701	
Kristi Graham						
Hendrick Middle Sch	6-8		723	26%	469/752-5600	
7400 Red River Dr, Plano 75025			70		Fax 469/752-5601	
Lisa Long						
Henry Dye Boggess Elem Sch	K-5		566	10%	469/752-4000	
225 Glen Ridge Dr, Murphy 75094					Fax 469/752-4001	
Shurandia Holden						
Hightower Elem Sch	K-5		566	16%	469/752-1800	
2601 Decator Dr, Plano 75093			35		Fax 469/752-1801	
Mariea Sprott						
Huffman Elem Sch	PK-5	T	469	65%	469/752-1900	
5510 Channel Isle Dr, Plano 75093			30		Fax 469/752-1901	
Jamey Allen						
Hughston Elem Sch	K-5		372	16%	469/752-2000	
2601 Cross Bend Rd, Plano 75023					Fax 469/752-2001	
Carrie D'Argo						

1	Superintendent	8	Curric/Instruct K-12	19	Chief Financial Officer	29	Family/Consumer Science	39	Social Studies K-12
2	Bus/Finance/Purchasing	9	Curric/Instruct Elem	20	Art K-12	30	Adult Education	40	Social Studies Elem
3	Buildings And Grounds	10	Curric/Instruct Sec	21	Art Elem	31	Career/Sch-to-Work K-12	41	Social Studies Sec
4	Food Service	11	Federal Program	22	Art Sec	32	Career/Sch-to-Work Elem	42	Science K-12
5	Transportation	12	Title I	23	Music K-12	33	Career/Sch-to-Work Sec	43	Science Elem
6	Athletic	13	Title V	24	Music Elem	34	Early Childhood Ed	44	Science Sec
7	Health Services	15	Asst Superintendent	25	Music Sec	35	Health/Phys Education	45	Math K-12
		16	Instructional Media Svcs	26	Business Education	36	Guidance Services K-12	46	Math Elem
		17	Chief Operations Officer	27	Career & Tech Ed	37	Guidance Services Elem	47	Math Sec
		18	Chief Academic Officer	28	Technology Education	38	Guidance Services Sec	48	English/Lang Arts K-12
49	English/Lang Arts Elem	59	Special Education Elem	69	Academic Assessment				
50	English/Lang Arts Sec	60	Special Education Sec	70	Research/Development				
51	Reading K-12	61	Foreign/World Lang K-12	71	Public Information				
52	Reading Elem	62	Foreign/World Lang Elem	72	Summer School				
53	Reading Sec	63	Foreign/World Lang Sec	73	Instructional Tech				
54	Remedial Reading K-12	64	Religious Education K-12	74	Inservice Training				
55	Remedial Reading Elem	65	Religious Education Elem	75	Marketing/Distributive				
56	Remedial Reading Sec	66	Religious Education Sec	76	Info Systems				
57	Bilingual/ELL	67	School Board President	77	Psychological Assess				
58	Special Education K-12	68	Teacher Personnel	78	Affirmative Action				

TX—82

Texas School Directory — Collin County

School	Grades	Prog	Enroll	%	Phone
Isaacs Early Childhood Sch 3400 E Parker Rd, Plano 75074 Jane Oestreich	PK-PK		426	17%	469/752-3480 Fax 469/752-3481
Jackson Elem Sch 1101 Jackson Dr, Plano 75075 Andrea Cockrell	PK-5	T	550 40	65%	469/752-2100 Fax 469/752-2101
Jasper High Sch 6800 Archgate Dr, Plano 75024 Matthew Endsley	9-10	GV	1,436	8%	469/752-7400 Fax 469/752-7401
ⒶLarry D Guinn Spec Pgrms Ctr 2221 Legacy Dr, Plano 75023 Sonja Pegram	9-12		194		469/752-6900 Fax 469/752-6901
Loreta Hickey Elem Sch 4100 Coldwater Creek Ln, Plano 75074 Dina Rowe	K-5	T	545	33%	469/752-4100 Fax 469/752-4101
Martha Hunt Elem Sch 415 Oriole Dr, Murphy 75094 Arron Moeller	K-5		702	5%	469/752-4400 Fax 469/752-4401
Mathews Elem Sch 7500 Marchman Way, Plano 75025 Ryan Steele	K-5		475 43	6%	469/752-2300 Fax 469/752-2301
McMillen High Sch 750 N Murphy Rd, Plano 75094 Brian Lyons	9-10		1,213	31%	469/752-8600 Fax 469/752-8601
Meadows Elem Sch 2800 18th St, Plano 75074 Katherine Foster	K-5	T	483 34	84%	469/752-2400 Fax 469/752-2401
Memorial Elem Sch 2200 Laurel Ln, Plano 75074 Mary Hardin	PK-5	T	510 27	82%	469/752-2500 Fax 469/752-2501
Mendenhall Elem Sch 1330 19th St, Plano 75074 Jana Prince	PK-5	T	593 49	87%	469/752-2600 Fax 469/752-2601
Mitchell Elem Sch 4223 Briargrove Ln, Dallas 75287 **Lariza Liner**	PK-5	T	798 50	44%	469/752-2800 Fax 469/752-2801
Murphy Middle Sch 620 N Murphy Rd, Murphy 75094 Matt Conrad	6-8		1,261	9%	469/752-7000 Fax 469/752-7001
Otto Middle Sch 504 N Star Rd, Plano 75074 Antoine Spencer	6-8	TV	1,063	29%	469/752-8500 Fax 469/752-8501
Pearson Early Childhood Sch 4000 Eagle Pass, Plano 75023 Jennifer Haugh	PK-PK		332 18	20%	469/752-4300 Fax 469/752-4301
Plano East Senior High Sch 3000 Los Rios Blvd, Plano 75074 King George	9-12	V	3,033	28%	469/752-9000 Fax 469/752-9001
Plano Head Start Center 1600 Rigsbee Dr, Plano 75074 **Dr Denise Lohmiller**	PK-PK	T	146	98%	469/752-7160 Fax 469/752-7161
Plano ISD Academy High Sch 1701 Alma Dr, Plano 75075 **Lynn Ojeda**	9-12		447	10%	972/905-8100 Fax 972/905-8101
Plano Senior High Sch 2200 Independence Pkwy, Plano 75075 Sarah Watkins	11-12	GV	2,714	23%	469/752-9300 Fax 469/752-9301
Plano West Senior High Sch 5601 W Parker Rd, Plano 75093 Janis Williams	11-12		2,765	14%	469/752-9600 Fax 469/752-9601
Rasor Elem Sch 945 Hedgcoxe Rd, Plano 75025 Leigh Earnhart	K-5	T	446 30	48%	469/752-2900 Fax 469/752-2901
Renner Middle Sch 5701 W Parker Rd, Plano 75093 Jill Engelking	6-8		1,251 55	21%	469/752-5800 Fax 469/752-5801
Robinson Middle Sch 6701 Preston Meadow Dr, Plano 75024 **Kennitra Roberston**	6-8		1,011	16%	469/752-6200 Fax 469/752-6201
Rose Haggar Elem Sch 17820 Campbell Rd, Dallas 75252 Katie Brittain	PK-5	T	594 34	34%	469/752-1400 Fax 469/752-1401
Saigling Elem Sch 3600 Matterhorn Dr, Plano 75075 Chris Dunkle	K-5		412	14%	469/752-3000 Fax 469/752-3001
Schell Elem Sch 5301 E Renner Rd, Richardson 75082 **Bob Farris**	K-5		673	19%	469/752-6600 Fax 469/752-6601
Schimelpfenig Middle Sch 2400 Maumelle Dr, Plano 75023 Dr Brant Perry	6-8		859 90	14%	469/752-6400 Fax 469/752-6401
Shepard Elem Sch 1000 Wilson Dr, Plano 75075 Kristin Bishop	K-5		474 30	15%	469/752-3100 Fax 469/752-3101
Shepton High Sch 5505 W Plano Pkwy, Plano 75093 Jeffrey Banner	9-10	V	1,459 85	27%	469/752-7600 Fax 469/752-7601
Sigler Elem Sch 1400 Janwood Dr, Plano 75075 Matthew Arend	PK-5	T	443 31	72%	469/752-3200 Fax 469/752-3201
Skaggs Elem Sch 3201 Russell Creek Dr, Plano 75025 Karen Lee	K-5		417	6%	469/752-3300 Fax 469/752-3301
Stinson Elem Sch 4201 Greenfield Dr, Richardson 75082 Michele Taylor	K-5		647 40	8%	469/752-3400 Fax 469/752-3401
Thomas Elem Sch 1800 Montana Trl, Plano 75023 Zack Pruett	PK-5	T	663	64%	469/752-3500 Fax 469/752-3501
Thomas Wesley Andrews Elem Sch 2520 Scenic Dr, Plano 75025 Joy Lovell	K-5		591	5%	469/752-3900 Fax 469/752-3901
Vines High Sch 1401 Highedge Dr, Plano 75075 Julie-Anne Dean	9-10	V	1,033 70	29%	469/752-7800 Fax 469/752-7801
Weatherford Elem Sch 2941 Mollimar Dr, Plano 75075 Ben Benavides	PK-5	T	487 30	60%	469/752-3600 Fax 469/752-3601
Wells Elem Sch 3427 Mission Ridge Rd, Plano 75023 Sara Meyer	K-5		535 27	14%	469/752-3700 Fax 469/752-3701
William Beverly Elem Sch 715 Duchess Dr, Allen 75013 Cindy Savant	K-5		485 23	13%	469/752-0400 Fax 469/752-0401
Williams High Sch 1717 17th St, Plano 75074 **Matthew Endsley**	9-10	TV	1,107 50	43%	469/752-8300 Fax 469/752-8301
Wilson Middle Sch 1001 Custer Rd, Plano 75075 Mark Letterer	6-8	T	830	38%	469/752-6700 Fax 469/752-6701
Wyatt Elem Sch 8900 Coit Rd, Plano 75025 Cynthia Hentges	K-5		477 34	5%	469/752-3800 Fax 469/752-3801

79 Student Personnel	91 Safety/Security	275 Response To Intervention	298 Grant Writer/Ptnrships	School Programs	Social Media
80 Driver Ed/Safety	92 Magnet School	277 Remedial Math K-12	750 Chief Innovation Officer	A = Alternative Program	
81 Gifted/Talented	93 Parental Involvement	280 Literacy Coach	751 Chief of Staff	G = Adult Classes	= Facebook
82 Video Services	95 Tech Prep Program	285 STEM	752 Social Emotional Learning	M = Magnet Program	
83 Substance Abuse Prev	97 Chief Information Officer	286 Digital Learning		T = Title I Schoolwide	= Twitter
84 Erate	98 Chief Technology Officer	288 Common Core Standards	Other School Types	V = Career & Tech Ed Programs	
85 AIDS Education	270 Character Education	294 Accountability	Ⓐ = Alternative School		
88 Alternative/At Risk	271 Migrant Education	295 Network System	Ⓒ = Charter School	New Schools are shaded	
89 Multi-Cultural Curriculum	273 Teacher Mentor	296 Title II Programs	Ⓜ = Magnet School	New Superintendents and Principals are bold	
90 Social Work	274 Before/After Sch	297 Webmaster	Ⓨ = Year-Round School	Personnel with email addresses are underscored	

TX—83

Collin County
Market Data Retrieval

- **Princeton Ind School Dist** PID: 01006502   469/952-5400
  321 Panther Pkwy, Princeton 75407   Fax 972/736-3505

Schools: 8 \ **Teachers:** 265 \ **Students:** 5,000 \ **Special Ed Students:** 492 \ **LEP Students:** 676 \ **Ethnic:** Asian 1%, African American 7%, Hispanic 48%, Caucasian 44% \ **Exp:** $316 (High) \ **Poverty:** 11% \ **Title I:** $566,743 \ **Special Education:** $634,000 \ **Open-Close:** 08/15 - 05/28 \ **DTBP:** $176 (High)

Name	Code
Philip Anthony	1
Jim Staley	3
Ric Wayman	5
Dacia Jondron	7
Rene Mullins	9
Liz Goen	34,58,88*
Joyce Swift	69
David Vincent	73
Jona Boitmann	2,3,15,298
Kelly Alvis	4
Stacey Dillard	6*
Dr Jackie Hendricks	8,11,15,36,57,83,271,288
Donald McIntyre	10,15,286*
Carol Bodwell	67
Jeanann Collins	71

Public Schs..Principal	Grd	Prgm	Enr/#Cls	SN	Phone
Clark Middle Sch 301 Panther Pkwy, Princeton 75407 Casey Gunnels	6-8	AT	620 40	57%	469/952-5404 Fax 972/736-5903
Godwin Elem Sch 1019 N 6th St, Princeton 75407 Marlena Brown	PK-5	AT	553	66%	469/952-5402 Fax 972/736-3533
Harper Elem Sch 8080 County Road 398, Princeton 75407 Nichole Powell	PK-5	AT	521	69%	469/952-5400 Fax 972/736-2621
Lacy Elem Sch 224 E College St, Princeton 75407 Thomas Osburn	PK-5	AT	545 37	70%	469/952-5401 Fax 972/736-6795
Lowe Elem Sch 540 Beauchamp Blvd, Princeton 75407 Jeff Coburn	PK-5		450		469/952-5400
Princeton High Sch 1000 E Princeton Dr, Princeton 75407 James Lovelady	9-12	ATV	1,174 39	53%	469/952-5405 Fax 972/736-5902
Smith Elem Sch 2101 Forest Meadow Dr, Princeton 75407 Rachel Nicks	PK-5	T	626	41%	469/952-5411 Fax 469/952-5421
Southard Middle Sch 455 Monte Carlo Blvd, Princeton 75407 Richard Boring	6-8	AT	600 20	58%	469/952-5403 Fax 972/736-6162

- **Prosper Ind School Dist** PID: 01006552   469/219-2000
  605 E 7th St, Prosper 75078   Fax 972/346-9247

Schools: 15 \ **Teachers:** 648 \ **Students:** 7,600 \ **Special Ed Students:** 730 \ **LEP Students:** 288 \ **College-Bound:** 57% \ **Ethnic:** Asian 5%, African American 8%, Hispanic 14%, Caucasian 73% \ **Exp:** $305 (High) \ **Poverty:** 2% \ **Title I:** $66,728 \ **Special Education:** $961,000 \ **Open-Close:** 08/14 - 05/22 \ **DTBP:** $147 (High) \ 🇫 🇹

Name	Code	Name	Code
Dr Drew Watkins	1	Annette Folmar	2,19
Rusty Craig	2	Danny Roberts	3
Cassandra Williams	4	Eileen Johnson	4
Leslie Beach	4	Anna Hamrick	5,91
Valerie Little	6*	Dr Karen Kidd	8
Lauri Slicker	12*	Greg Bradley	15
Melissa Gassman	57	Blair Hickey	58
Jim Bridges	67	Chrystal Hankey	71
Brett Hankey	73	Fernando De Velasco	73,98,286,295
Scott Cox	76	Todd Shirley	79
Theresa Biggs	81	Alexis Webb	288

Public Schs..Principal	Grd	Prgm	Enr/#Cls	SN	Phone
Boyer Elem Sch 1616 Montgomery, Prosper 75078 Alissa Andrews	K-5		705		469/219-2240 Fax 972/346-9625
Cockrell Elem Sch 1075 Escalante Trl, Prosper 75078 Glenda Dophied	PK-5		993	2%	469/219-2130 Fax 972/346-2456
Folsom Elem Sch 800 Sommerville Dr, Prosper 75078 Stephanie Cockrell	PK-5		808 30	2%	469/219-2110 Fax 972/346-9245
Furr Elem Sch 551 S Bluestem Dr, McKinney 75072 Cindy Zukowski	K-5		760		469/219-2280
Hays Middle Sch 14441 Hillcrest Rd, Frisco 75035 Nicholas Jones	6-8		800		469/219-2260
Hughes Elem Sch 1551 Prestwick Holw, McKinney 75071 Kimberly Newman	PK-5		977		469/219-2230 Fax 972/346-9620
John A Baker Elem Sch 3125 Bluewood Dr, McKinney 75071 Danielle Wallace	PK-5	T	760	8%	469/219-2120 Fax 972/529-1142 🇫 🇹
Judy Rucker Elem Sch 402 S Craig Rd, Prosper 75078 Shelly Spears	PK-5	T	839	10%	469/219-2100 Fax 972/346-9249
Light Farms Elem Sch 1100 Cypress Creek Way, Celina 75009 Haley Stelly	PK-5		978	2%	469/219-2140 Fax 972/346-9630
Prosper High Sch 301 Eagle Dr, Prosper 75078 John Burdett	9-12	AV	2,974	6%	469/219-2180 Fax 972/346-9246
Reynolds Middle Sch 700 N Coleman St, Prosper 75078 Justin Goldsmith	6-8		1,409	5%	469/219-2165 Fax 972/346-2455
Rogers Middle Sch 1001 S Coit Rd, Prosper 75078 Jason Jetton	6-8		1,420	7%	469/219-2150 Fax 972/346-9248
Spradley Elem Sch 11411 Leona St, Frisco 75035 Machelle Scogin	K-5		810		469/219-2250 Fax 972/346-9635
Stuber Elem Sch 721 Village Park Lane, Prosper 75078 Dr Jennifer Hinson	K-5		780		469/219-2290
Windsong Ranch Elem Sch 800 Copper Canyon Dr, Prosper 75078 Kardel Miller	PK-5		974	9%	469/219-2220 Fax 972/346-9615

- **Wylie Ind School Dist** PID: 01006605   972/429-3000
  951 S Ballard Ave, Wylie 75098   Fax 972/442-5368

Schools: 20 \ **Teachers:** 969 \ **Students:** 17,000 \ **Special Ed Students:** 1,455 \ **LEP Students:** 1,393 \ **College-Bound:** 98% \ **Ethnic:** Asian 10%, African American 15%, Hispanic 22%, Native American: 1%, Caucasian 53% \ **Exp:** $321 (High) \ **Poverty:** 5% \ **Title I:** $824,317 \ **Special Education:** $1,697,000 \ **Bilingual Education:** $16,000 \ **Open-Close:** 08/15 - 05/21 \ **DTBP:** $183 (High) \ 🇫

Name	Code	Name	Code
Dr David Vinson	1	Gina Smilie	2
Lynn Lyon	2	Michele Trongaard	2,15
Jennifer DuPlessis	3	Dawn Lin	4
Kyle Craighead	6	Amy Hillin	7*
Joei Shermer	9,54	Dr Stephen Davis	10
Jessica Branch	11*	Jill Vasquez	11,57,271*
Dr Kim Spicer	15	Scott Winn	15,79
D'Anne Mosby	16*	Glenn Lambert	20*
Jason Hudson	27	Ian Halperin	30,71
Sara Roland	34,58,77	Amanda Martin	36

Code	Description	Code	Description	Code	Description	Code	Description	Code	Description	Code	Description	Code	Description
1	Superintendent	8	Curric/Instruct K-12	19	Chief Financial Officer	29	Family/Consumer Science	39	Social Studies K-12	49	English/Lang Arts K-12	59	Special Education Elem	69	Academic Assessment
2	Bus/Finance/Purchasing	9	Curric/Instruct Elem	20	Art K-12	30	Adult Education	40	Social Studies Elem	50	English/Lang Arts Sec	60	Special Education Sec	70	Research/Development
3	Buildings And Grounds	10	Curric/Instruct Sec	21	Art Elem	31	Career/Sch-to-Work K-12	41	Social Studies Sec	51	Reading K-12	61	Foreign/World Lang K-12	71	Public Information
4	Food Service	11	Federal Program	22	Art Sec	32	Career/Sch-to-Work Elem	42	Science K-12	52	Reading Elem	62	Foreign/World Lang Elem	72	Summer School
5	Transportation	12	Title I	23	Music K-12	33	Career/Sch-to-Work Sec	43	Science Elem	53	Reading Sec	63	Foreign/World Lang Sec	73	Instructional Tech
6	Athletic	13	Title V	24	Music Elem	34	Early Childhood Ed	44	Science Sec	54	Remedial Reading K-12	64	Religious Education K-12	74	Inservice Training
7	Health Services	14	Instructional Media Svcs	25	Music Sec	35	Health/Phys Education	45	Math K-12	55	Remedial Reading Elem	65	Religious Education Elem	75	Marketing/Distributive
		15	Asst Superintendent	26	Business Education	36	Guidance Services K-12	46	Math Elem	56	Remedial Reading Sec	66	Religious Education Sec	76	Info Systems
		16	Chief Operations Officer	27	Career & Tech Ed	37	Guidance Services Elem	47	Math Sec	57	Bilingual/ELL	67	School Board President	77	Psychological Assess
		18	Chief Academic Officer	28	Technology Education	38	Guidance Services Sec	48	English/Lang Arts K-12	58	Special Education K-12	68	Teacher Personnel	78	Affirmative Action

Texas School Directory — Collin County

Mitch Herzog 67
Chris Lamb 71,84,97
James Matthews 76
Belinda Feverbacher 275
Dr Judy Bolen 69,294
Lee Hadaway 74*
Heather Buckley 81*
Doug Bellamy 297

Public Schs..Principal	Grd	Prgm	Enr/#Cls	SN
A B Harrison Intermediate Sch 1001 S Ballard Ave, Wylie 75098 Christa Smyder	5-6		701 36	24% 972/429-3300 Fax 972/442-3971
Achieve Academy 300 Pirate Dr, Wylie 75098 Dana Roberts	Spec	AT	100 9	36% 972/429-2390 Fax 972/941-9720
Bill F Davis Intermediate Sch 950 Park Blvd, Wylie 75098 Cody Summers	5-6		799	25% 972/429-3325 Fax 972/429-9729
Cheri L Cox Elem Sch 7009 Woodbridge Pkwy, Sachse 75048 Krista Wilson	PK-4		668 42	22% 972/429-2500 Fax 972/429-4435
Dodd Elem Sch 1500 Park Blvd, Wylie 75098 Magan Porter	PK-4		563 31	23% 972/429-3440 Fax 972/442-9856
Don Whitt Elem Sch 7520 Woodcreek Way, Sachse 75048 Amber Teamann	PK-4		654	10% 972/429-2560 Fax 972/941-8564
Dr AL Draper Intermediate Sch 103 Hensley Ln, Wylie 75098 Beth Craighead	5-6		1,007	28% 972/429-3350 Fax 972/442-9317
George W Bush Elem Sch 2000 Eagle Aerie Ln, Wylie 75098 Dr Maricella Helm	K-4	T	555	47% 972/429-2600 Fax 469/661-9428
Grady Burnett Jr Senior HS 516 Hilltop Ln, Wylie 75098 Ryan Bickley	7-8	V	772	30% 972/429-3200 Fax 972/442-1447
Hartman Elem Sch 510 S Birmingham St, Wylie 75098 Shawnell Bradshaw	PK-4	GT	577 27	53% 972/429-3480 Fax 972/442-7072
McMillan Junior High Sch 1050 Park Blvd, Wylie 75098 Jon Peters	7-8	V	846 46	27% 972/492-3225 Fax 972/941-6372
P M Akin Elem Sch 1100 Springwood Ln, Wylie 75098 Valerie Mann	PK-4	T	421 31	29% 972/429-3400 Fax 972/442-5744
R V Groves Elem Sch 1100 McCreary Rd, Wylie 75098 Vanessa Hudgins	PK-4	GT	555	36% 972/429-3460 Fax 972/429-7906
Raymond Cooper Junior High Sch 101 Hensley Ln, Wylie 75098 Shawn Miller	7-8		891	23% 972/429-3250 Fax 972/941-9175
Rita Smith Elem Sch 2221 FM 1378, Wylie 75098 Kellye Morton	PK-4		500	16% 972/429-2540 Fax 972/442-5493
T F Birmingham Elem Sch 700 W Brown St, Wylie 75098 Tiffany Doolan	PK-4	T	508 58	37% 972/429-3420 Fax 972/442-1215
Tibbals Elem Sch 621 Waters Edge Way, Murphy 75094 Jamie Fletcher	PK-4		686	9% 972/429-2520 Fax 972/442-2260
Wally Watkins Elem Sch 1301 Elm Dr, Wylie 75098 Jennifer Wiseman	PK-4		562	16% 972/429-2580 Fax 972/429-9345
Wylie East High Sch 3000 E Stone Rd, Wylie 75098 Mike Williams	9-12	V	1,846	28% 972/429-3150 Fax 972/442-2874
Wylie High Sch 2550 W FM 544, Wylie 75098 Virdie Montgomery	9-12	V	2,428	21% 972/429-3100 Fax 972/442-1879

COLLIN CATHOLIC SCHOOLS

- **Diocese of Dallas Ed Office** PID: 01012367
  Listing includes only schools located in this county. See District Index for location of Diocesan Offices.

Catholic Schs..Principal	Grd	Prgm	Enr/#Cls	SN
All Saints Catholic Sch 7777 Osage Plaza Pkwy, Dallas 75252 Shana Druffner	PK-8		300 24	214/217-3300 Fax 214/217-3339
John Paul II High Sch 900 Coit Rd, Plano 75075 Marlene Hammerle	9-12		785	972/867-0005 Fax 972/867-7555
Prince of Peace Catholic Sch 5100 W Plano Pkwy, Plano 75093 Meghan Jones	PK-8		825 27	972/380-5505 Fax 972/380-2570
St Mark Catholic Sch 1201 Alma Dr, Plano 75075 Patricia Opon	K-8		644	972/578-0610 Fax 972/423-3299
St Martin De Porres Cath Sch 4000 W University Dr, Prosper 75078 Susan Flanagan	PK-3		100	469/362-2400 Fax 972/370-2400

- **Diocese of Fort Worth Ed Off** PID: 01054339
  Listing includes only schools located in this county. See District Index for location of Diocesan Offices.

COLLIN PRIVATE SCHOOLS

Private Schs..Principal	Grd	Prgm	Enr/#Cls	SN
Bethany Christian Sch 3300 W Parker Rd, Plano 75075 Dr Marvin Effa	PK-12		103 10	972/596-5811 Fax 972/596-5814
Choices Leadership Academy 18106 Marsh Ln, Dallas 75287 Karen Harkey	K-5		100	972/662-0665 Fax 972/307-3440
Coram Deo Academy-Collin Cnty 9645 Independence Pkwy, Plano 75025 Stephanie Garland \ Toby Oaks	PK-12		400	469/854-1300 Fax 972/692-5140
Cornerstone Christian Academy 808 S College St Ste 101, McKinney 75069 Sandy Hanson	PK-12		360	972/562-8200
Dallas International Sch 17811 Waterview Pkwy, Dallas 75252 Bertrand Ferret	6-12		180	469/250-0001 Fax 214/570-4900
Einstein School Plano 4011 W Plano Pkwy, Plano 75093 Willetta Edinburgh \ Armando Castellanos	K-12		401	972/564-8040
Faith Lutheran Sch 1701 E Park Blvd, Plano 75074 Stephen Kieser	PK-12		130 20	972/423-7448 Fax 972/423-9618
Fusion Academy-Plano 2400 Dallas Pkwy Ste 180Q, Plano 75093 Troy Byrne	6-12		401	972/403-9018
Good Tree Academy 3600 K Ave, Plano 75074 Uzma Khan	PK-12		401	972/836-6322 Fax 972/502-9432
Great Lakes Academy 6000 Custer Rd Ste 7, Plano 75023 Jason Campbell	K-12		60 20	972/517-7498 Fax 972/517-0133

---

79 Student Personnel	91 Safety/Security	275 Response To Intervention	298 Grant Writer/Ptnrships	**School Programs**	**Social Media**
30 Driver Ed/Safety	92 Magnet School	277 Remedial Math K-12	750 Chief Innovation Officer	A = Alternative Program	= Facebook
31 Gifted/Talented	93 Parental Involvement	280 Literacy Coach	751 Chief of Staff	G = Adult Classes	
32 Video Services	95 Tech Prep Program	285 STEM	752 Social Emotional Learning	M = Magnet Program	= Twitter
33 Substance Abuse Prev	97 Chief Infomation Officer	286 Digital Learning		T = Title I Schoolwide	
34 Erate	98 Chief Technology Officer	288 Common Core Standards	**Other School Types**	V = Career & Tech Ed Programs	
35 AIDS Education	270 Character Education	294 Accountability	A = Alternative School		
38 Alternative/At Risk	271 Migrant Education	295 Network System	C = Charter School	New Schools are shaded	
39 Multi-Cultural Curriculum	273 Teacher Mentor	296 Title II Programs	M = Magnet School	New Superintendents and Principals are bold	
90 Social Work	274 Before/After Sch	297 Webmaster	Y = Year-Round School	Personnel with email addresses are underscored	

Collingsworth County

School	Grades	Enr	Phone
Guidepost Montessori-Stonebria 10247 Warren Pkwy, Frisco 75035 Baljeet Jawanda	PK-6	401	214/387-8202
Legacy Christian Academy 5000 Academy Dr, Frisco 75034 Tiffany McCollum \ Glenn Dibley \ Kevin Mosley	PK-12	650	469/633-1330 Fax 469/633-1348
Levine Academy 18011 Hillcrest Rd, Dallas 75252 Liz Lawlor	PK-8	520 80	972/248-3032 Fax 972/248-0695
Lucas Christian Academy 505 W Lucas Rd, Lucas 75002 Ann DeSantis \ Robin Dembicki	K-12	435	972/429-4362 Fax 972/429-5141
McKinney Christian Academy 3601 Bois D Arc Rd, McKinney 75071 Chris Hydock \ David Etheredge \ Laura Smith	PK-12	470	214/544-2658 Fax 972/542-5056
Mona Montessori McKinney 513 N Central Expy, McKinney 75070 Tina Kasturi	PK-K	55 4	972/542-5825 Fax 972/542-7273
Montessori Sch of North Dallas 18303 Davenport Rd, Dallas 75252 Reena Khandtur	PK-3	200 9	972/985-8844
Montessori School at Starcreek 915 Ridgeview Dr, Allen 75013 Monica Cook	PK-6	150	972/727-2800
New Hope Christian Academy 1501 H Ave, Plano 75074 Deedee Mims	PK-4	50	972/656-9951
New Star Sch 7700 San Jacinto Pl Ste 300, Plano 75024 Holly Hao	K-7	200	972/897-9217
Pebblecreek Montessori Sch 8104 Coit Rd, Plano 75025 Pinky Kohli	PK-6	50	972/908-3797 Fax 972/908-3790
Prestonwood Christian Academy 6801 W Park Blvd, Plano 75093 Paige DeLeon \ Bill Wendl \ Wendy Morris	PK-12	1,500 75	972/820-5300 Fax 972/820-5068
Spring Creek Academy 6000 Custer Rd Bldg 5, Plano 75023 Walter Ritchie	1-12	150	972/517-6730
St Philip's Academy-Frisco 6400 Stonebrook Pkwy, Frisco 75034 Beverly Woodson	K-3	40	214/929-7787 Fax 214/387-9531
Torah Day School of Dallas 6921 Frankford Rd, Dallas 75252 Chana Ruderman	PK-8	500	972/964-0090
West Plano Montessori Sch 3425 Ashington Ln, Plano 75023 Adhirai Basaaran	PK-3	120 6	972/618-8844 Fax 972/398-1798
Willow Bend Academy-Plano 2220 Coit Rd Ste 500, Plano 75075 Dr Peter Berner	5-12	100	972/599-7882 Fax 972/672-7858
Wylie Preparatory Academy 4110 Skyview Ct, Wylie 75098 Sara Killian \ Elizabeth Caperton	K-12	230	972/442-1388 Fax 972/429-3568

COLLINGSWORTH COUNTY

COLLINGSWORTH PUBLIC SCHOOLS

- **Wellington Ind School Dist** PID: 01006708   806/447-3102
  609 15th St, Wellington 79095   Fax 806/447-5124

Schools: 3 \ **Teachers:** 54 \ **Students:** 580 \ **Special Ed Students:** 50 \ **LEP Students:** 50 \ **College-Bound:** 60% \ **Ethnic:** African American 3%, Hispanic 53%, Caucasian 44% \ **Exp:** $361 (High) \ **Poverty:** 24% \ **Title I:** $188,070 \ **Open-Close:** 08/19 - 05/20 \ **DTBP:** $402 (High)

Kurt Ashmore 1,11
Toby Silva 3
Reggie Sauder 5
Asheley Long 7
Vicki Decker 16,82*
Lynn Bartlett 67
John Scott 73,295*
Diane Souder 2
Debbie Hungteres 4
Greg Proffitt 6
Diedra Kane 8
Linda Castillo 57,270,271
Renessa Klink 69,83,88*

Public Schs..Principal	Grd	Prgm	Enr/#Cls	SN
Wellington Elem Sch 606 16th St, Wellington 79095 Deidre Kane	PK-5	T	324 25	62% 806/447-3112 Fax 806/447-5097
Wellington High Sch 811 15th St, Wellington 79095 Jermaine Cantu	9-12	TV	152 20	57% 806/447-3172 Fax 806/447-9012
Wellington Junior High Sch 1504 Amarillo St, Wellington 79095 **Edward Beck**	6-8	T	112 20	70% 806/447-3152 Fax 806/447-5089

COLORADO COUNTY

COLORADO PUBLIC SCHOOLS

- **Columbus Ind School Dist** PID: 01006746   979/732-5704
  105 Cardinal Ln, Columbus 78934   Fax 979/732-5960

Schools: 4 \ **Teachers:** 126 \ **Students:** 1,494 \ **Special Ed Students:** 197 \ **LEP Students:** 164 \ **Ethnic:** African American 12%, Hispanic 45%, Caucasian 42% \ **Exp:** $426 (High) \ **Poverty:** 20% \ **Title I:** $396,798 \ **Special Education:** $338,000 \ **Open-Close:** 08/14 - 05/21 \ **DTBP:** $350 (High)

Dr Brian Morris 1
Kenny Koehl 3
Chris Everett 5
Jim Connor 8
Sarah Wanjura 58
Lance Portwood 73,295
Scott Leopold 2
Cheryl Woytek 4
Matt Schobel 6
Amber Berger 11,296
Rick Restivo 67

Public Schs..Principal	Grd	Prgm	Enr/#Cls	SN
Ⓐ Columbus Alternative Sch 1421 Austin St, Columbus 78934 **Michael Koehl**	7-12		60	979/732-2963

---

1 Superintendent	8 Curric/Instruct K-12	19 Chief Financial Officer	29 Family/Consumer Science	39 Social Studies K-12	49 English/Lang Arts Elem	59 Special Education Elem	69 Academic Assessment
2 Bus/Finance/Purchasing	9 Curric/Instruct Elem	20 Art K-12	30 Adult Education	40 Social Studies Elem	50 English/Lang Arts Sec	60 Special Education Sec	70 Research/Development
3 Buildings And Grounds	10 Curric/Instruct Sec	21 Art Elem	31 Career/Sch-to-Work K-12	41 Social Studies Sec	51 Reading K-12	61 Foreign/World Lang K-12	71 Public Information
4 Food Service	11 Federal Program	22 Art Sec	32 Career/Sch-to-Work Elem	42 Science K-12	52 Reading Elem	62 Foreign/World Lang Elem	72 Summer School
5 Transportation	12 Title I	23 Music K-12	33 Career/Sch-to-Work Sec	43 Science Elem	53 Reading Sec	63 Foreign/World Lang Sec	73 Instructional Tech
6 Athletic	13 Title V	24 Music Elem	34 Early Childhood Ed	44 Science Sec	54 Remedial Reading K-12	64 Religious Education K-12	74 Inservice Training
7 Health Services	15 Asst Superintendent	25 Music Sec	35 Health/Phys Education	45 Math K-12	55 Remedial Reading Elem	65 Religious Education Elem	75 Marketing/Distributive
	16 Instructional Media Svcs	26 Business Education	36 Guidance Services K-12	46 Math Elem	56 Remedial Reading Sec	66 Religious Education Sec	76 Info Systems
	17 Chief Operations Officer	27 Career & Tech Ed	37 Guidance Services Elem	47 Math Sec	57 Bilingual/ELL	67 School Board President	77 Psychological Assess
	18 Chief Academic Officer	28 Technology Education	38 Guidance Services Sec	48 English/Lang Arts K-12	58 Special Education K-12	68 Teacher Personnel	78 Affirmative Action

Texas School Directory Comal County

Public Schs..Principal	Grd	Prgm	Enr/#Cls	SN	
Columbus Elem Sch 1324 Bowie St, Columbus 78934 Shana Neisner	PK-5	T	694	69%	979/732-2078 Fax 979/732-8627
Columbus High Sch 103 Cardinal Ln, Columbus 78934 Robert Russell	9-12	ATV	470 40	46%	979/732-5746 Fax 979/732-8862
Columbus Junior High Sch 702 Rampart St, Columbus 78934 Gary Leopold	6-8	AT	330 30	65%	979/732-2891 Fax 979/732-9081

- **Rice Cons Ind School Dist** PID: 01006784   979/234-3531
  1094 Raider Dr, Altair 77412   Fax 979/234-3409

Schools: 7 \ *Teachers:* 103 \ *Students:* 1,325 \ *Special Ed Students:* 145 \ *LEP Students:* 112 \ *College-Bound:* 62% \ *Ethnic:* Asian 1%, African American 19%, Hispanic 58%, Caucasian 22% \ *Exp:* $490 (High) \ *Poverty:* 25% \ *Title I:* $409,896 \ *Open-Close:* 08/21 - 05/27 \ *DTBP:* $349 (High)

Bill Hefner	1,11		Melody Grigar	2,8,11,83,88,288,296,298
Douglas Behlen	3		Rachel Barten	4
Jared Sloan	6		Debbie Ugarte	7*
Connie Gertson	16*		Jacqueline Kovar	31*
Vicki Nelson	57		Amy Bosse	58
John Carey	67		Debra Cummings	69*
Ralph Gertson	73,295		Eric Grogan	271*

Public Schs..Principal	Grd	Prgm	Enr/#Cls	SN	
Eagle Lake Intermediate Sch 701 Tate Ave, Eagle Lake 77434 Gene Glover	3-5	T	203 17	86%	979/234-3531 Fax 979/234-5027
Eagle Lake Primary Sch 600 J D Hutchins Dr, Eagle Lake 77434 Kimberly Etheridge	PK-2	T	294	86%	979/234-3531 Fax 979/234-6337
Garwood Elem Sch Highway 71 S, Garwood 77442 Leroy Stavinoha	PK-5	T	110 6	53%	979/758-3531 Fax 979/758-3751
Ⓐ Rice Challenge Academy 600 FM 3013 W, Eagle Lake 77434 Dan Garza	9-12		63	96%	979/234-3531
Rice High Sch 1095 Raider Dr, Altair 77412 Eric Grogan	9-12	TV	366 30	63%	979/234-3531 Fax 979/234-5901
Rice Junior High Sch 1095 Raider Dr, Altair 77412 Brian Leist	6-8	T	251 19	80%	979/234-3531 Fax 979/234-5901
Sheridan Elem Sch Farm Road 2437, Sheridan 77475 Janet Lumpkins	PK-5	T	63 8	74%	979/234-3531 Fax 979/234-6322

- **Weimar Ind School Dist** PID: 01006849   979/725-9504
  506 W Main St, Weimar 78962   Fax 979/725-8737

Schools: 3 \ *Teachers:* 55 \ *Students:* 661 \ *Special Ed Students:* 58 \ *LEP Students:* 108 \ *College-Bound:* 50% \ *Ethnic:* African American 13%, Hispanic 43%, Caucasian 44% \ *Exp:* $393 (High) \ *Poverty:* 16% \ *Title I:* $123,998 \ *Special Education:* $178,000 \ *Open-Close:* 08/19 - 05/21 \ *DTBP:* $367 (High)

Jonathan Wunderlich	1		Angela Luksovsky	2
Stephen Jurek	3		Theresa Rerich	4*
Ryan McIver	6*		Codi Guenther	11*
Eleazar Moreno	16,76,295		Lisa Marak	57*
Amanda Turlington	58*		Ken Kram	67

Public Schs..Principal	Grd	Prgm	Enr/#Cls	SN	
Weimar Elem Sch 515 W Main St, Weimar 78962 Kristy Janecka	PK-4	T	295 16	60%	979/725-6009 Fax 979/725-9527
Weimar High Sch 506 W Main St, Weimar 78962 Stacy Heger	9-12	V	208 18	31%	979/725-9504 Fax 979/725-9765
Weimar Junior High Sch 101 N West St, Weimar 78962 Stacy Heger	5-8	T	173 8	49%	979/725-9515 Fax 979/725-8383

COLORADO CATHOLIC SCHOOLS

- **Diocese of Victoria Ed Office** PID: 02181727
  Listing includes only schools located in this county. See District Index for location of Diocesan Offices.

Catholic Schs..Principal	Grd	Prgm	Enr/#Cls	SN	
St Anthony Sch 635 Bonham St, Columbus 78934 John O'Leary	PK-8		185 14		979/732-5505 Fax 979/732-9758
St Michael Sch 103 E North St, Weimar 78962 Carolanne McAfee	PK-8		80 12		979/725-8461 Fax 979/725-8344

COMAL COUNTY

COMAL PUBLIC SCHOOLS

- **Comal Ind School Dist** PID: 01006887   830/221-2000
  1404 Interstate Hwy 35 N, New Braunfels 78130   Fax 830/221-2001

Schools: 31 \ *Teachers:* 1,337 \ *Students:* 23,800 \ *Special Ed Students:* 2,289 \ *LEP Students:* 1,224 \ *College-Bound:* 51% \ *Ethnic:* Asian 1%, African American 2%, Hispanic 40%, Caucasian 56% \ *Exp:* $228 (Med) \ *Poverty:* 10% \ *Title I:* $2,590,576 \ *Special Education:* $3,073,000 \ *Open-Close:* 08/27 - 05/28 \ *DTBP:* $180 (High) 📘 🅃

Andrew Kim	1		Catherine Janda	2
David Anderson	2,19		Mike McCuller	3
Jessica Fischer	5		Liana Gombert	6*
Michael Smith	7,35*		Kerry Gain	8,15
Carla Schumann	20,23		Becky Walker	27,31,95
Taylor Keller	42		Janice Rose	58,79
Michele Martella	58		Jason York	67
Mandy Epley	68		Courtney Witherell	69,294
Steve Stanford	71		Jarrett Cochran	73,76,295,297
Hannah Schramm	74		Daniel Mendez	75
Jennifer Johnson	79,275		Tiffany Newkirk	83,90
Sarah Permentor	271			

Public Schs..Principal	Grd	Prgm	Enr/#Cls	SN	
Arlon Seay Elem Sch 20911 State Highway 46 W, Spring Branch 78070 Carla Carter	PK-5		378 20	19%	830/885-8700 Fax 830/885-8701

79	Student Personnel	91	Safety/Security	275	Response To Intervention	298	Grant Writer/Ptnrships
80	Driver Ed/Safety	92	Magnet School	277	Remedial Math K-12	750	Chief Innovation Officer
81	Gifted/Talented	93	Parental Involvement	280	Literacy Coach	751	Chief of Staff
82	Video Services	95	Tech Prep Program	285	STEM	752	Social Emotional Learning
83	Substance Abuse Prev	97	Chief Information Officer	286	Digital Learning		
84	Erate	98	Chief Technology Officer	288	Common Core Standards		
85	AIDS Education	270	Character Education	294	Accountability		
86	Alternative/At Risk	271	Migrant Education	295	Network System		
89	Multi-Cultural Curriculum	273	Teacher Mentor	296	Title II Programs		
90	Social Work	274	Before/After Sch	297	Webmaster		

School Programs
A = Alternative Program
G = Adult Classes
M = Magnet Program
T = Title I Schoolwide
V = Career & Tech Ed Programs

Other School Types
Ⓐ = Alternative School
Ⓒ = Charter School
Ⓜ = Magnet School
Ⓨ = Year-Round School

Social Media
📘 = Facebook
🅃 = Twitter

New Schools are shaded
New Superintendents and Principals are bold
Personnel with email addresses are underscored

TX-87

Comal County

Market Data Retrieval

School	Grd	Prgm	Enr/#Cls	SN	Phone
Bill Brown Elem Sch 20410 State Highway 46 W, Spring Branch 78070 Jillian Jurica	PK-5		678	25%	830/885-1400 Fax 830/885-1401
Canyon High Sch 1510 N Interstate 35 1H, New Braunfels 78130 Casey Whittle	9-12	AGV	2,637 75	30%	830/221-2400 Fax 830/221-2401
Canyon Lake High Sch 8555 Rm 32, Fischer 78623 Kristy Castilleja	9-12	A	1,023	35%	830/885-1700 Fax 830/221-1701
Canyon Middle Sch 2014 FM 1101, New Braunfels 78130 Matthew DeLoach	6-8	TV	1,187 57	39%	830/221-2300 Fax 830/221-2301
Church Hill Middle Sch 1275 N Business Ih 35, New Braunfels 78130 Jaime Calderon	6-8		1,053 38	28%	830/221-2800 Fax 830/221-2801
Clear Spring Elem Sch 550 Avery Pkwy, New Braunfels 78130 Janelle Hardin	PK-5	T	759	49%	830/837-7300 Fax 830/837-7301
Ⓐ Comal Academy 1413 N Business Ih 35, New Braunfels 78130 Lori Lehmberg	11-12		51	29%	830/221-2950
Ⓐ Comal Discipline Center 1413 N Business Ih 35, New Braunfels 78130 Lori Lehmberg	K-12		60	57%	830/221-2950 Fax 830/221-2951
Danville Middle Sch 370 Hubertus Rd, New Braunfels 78132 Julie Cronkhite	6-8		1,000		830/837-7400
Freiheit Elem Sch 2002 FM 1101, New Braunfels 78130 Shelly Crofford	K-5	T	551 23	54%	830/221-2700 Fax 830/221-2701
Garden Ridge Elem Sch 9401 Municipal Pkwy, Garden Ridge 78266 Jennifer Schultz	PK-5		790 22	15%	830/885-1794 Fax 830/837-7001
Goodwin Frazier Elem Sch 1441 N Business Ih 35, New Braunfels 78130 Carolyn Gump	PK-5	T	578 22	60%	830/221-2200 Fax 830/221-2201
Hoffmann Lane Elem Sch 4600 FM 306, New Braunfels 78132 Leslie Durst	PK-5		774 33	4%	830/221-2500 Fax 830/221-2501
Indian Springs Elem Sch 25751 Wilderness Oak, San Antonio 78261 Mary Stults	PK-5		810	5%	830/609-6298 Fax 830/885-9301
Johnson Ranch Elem Sch 30501 Johnson Way, Bulverde 78163 Suzanne Seabolt	PK-5		404	15%	830/885-8600 Fax 830/885-8601
Kinder Ranch Elem Sch 2035 Kinder Pkwy, San Antonio 78260 Nicole DuVall	PK-5		616	31%	830/609-6702 Fax 830/885-8901
M H Specht Elem Sch 25815 Overlook Pkwy, San Antonio 78260 Jackie Sundt	PK-5		753 35	18%	830/885-1500 Fax 830/885-1501
Ⓐ Memorial Early Clg HS 1419 N Business Ih 35, New Braunfels 78130 Meredith Pappas	9-12		324 6	22%	830/885-1798 Fax 830/221-2901
Morningside Elem Sch 3855 Morningside Dr, New Braunfels 78132 Ashley Fredo	PK-5	T	725	70%	830/837-7100 Fax 830/837-7101
Mountain Valley Elem Sch 310 Cannan Rd, Canyon Lake 78133 Jennifer Smith	PK-5		430		830/885-9500 Fax 830/885-9501
Mountain Valley Middle Sch 1165 Sattler Rd, Canyon Lake 78132 Dustin Davisson	6-8	T	748	44%	830/885-1300 Fax 830/855-1301
Oak Creek Elem Sch 3060 Goodwin Ln, New Braunfels 78130 Stacy Wilkie	PK-5		535	36%	830/837-7200 Fax 830/837-7201
Pieper Ranch Middle Sch 1106 Kinder Pkwy, San Antonio 78260 Scott Hammond	6-8		1,000		830/885-9600
Rahe Bulverde Elem Sch 1715 E Ammann Rd, Bulverde 78163 Amy Malone	PK-5		402 10	18%	830/885-1600 Fax 830/885-1601
Rebecca Creek Elem Sch 125 Quest Ave, Spring Branch 78070 Wendy Moore	PK-5	T	542	41%	830/885-1800 Fax 830/885-1801
Smithson Valley High Sch 14001 State Highway 46 W, Spring Branch 78070 Michael Wahl	9-12	AGV	2,759 100	13%	830/885-1000 Fax 830/885-1001
Smithson Valley Middle Sch 6101 FM 311, Spring Branch 78070 Michael Keranen	6-8	V	1,194 30	12%	830/885-1200 Fax 830/885-1201
Spring Branch Middle Sch 21053 State Highway 46 W, Spring Branch 78070 Chris Smith	6-8	V	1,138 30	20%	830/885-8800 Fax 830/885-8801
Startzville Elem Sch 42111 FM 3159, Canyon Lake 78133 Melinda Shinn	PK-5	T	449 30	59%	830/885-8000 Fax 830/885-8001
Timberwood Park Elem Sch 26715 S Glenrose Rd, San Antonio 78260 Kim Lyssy	PK-5		670 38	10%	830/609-6705 Fax 830/885-8501

● **New Braunfels Ind School Dist** PID: 01006966 830/643-5700
430 W Mill St, New Braunfels 78130 Fax 830/643-5701

> **Schools:** 15 \ **Teachers:** 513 \ **Students:** 9,220 \ **Special Ed Students:** 697 \ **LEP Students:** 658 \ **College-Bound:** 48% \ **Ethnic:** Asian 1%, African American 2%, Hispanic 47%, Caucasian 50% \ **Exp:** $353 (High) \ **Poverty:** 13% \ **Title I:** $1,617,842 \ **Special Education:** $1,492,000 \ **Bilingual Education:** $36,000 \ **Open-Close:** 08/26 - 05/28 \ **DTBP:** $176 (High)

Randy Moczygemba 1		Rosanne Stockhorst 2	
Steve Brown 2		Daryl Stoker 3	
Catherine Vanderbrook 4		Brian Gibson 5,91	
Jim Streety 6		Karen Schwind 7	
Victoria Pursch 8,15,34,69,294		Ron Rychel 11	
Matthew Jones 16,73,295		Rachel Behnke 27	
Kimberly Brann 57		Martha Moke 58	
Sherry Harrison 67		Kathy Kenney 68	
Dena Schroeder 69		Rebecca Villarreal 71	
Lori Gruwell 74		Francie Novander 76	
Clay Gillentine 79		Blake Haygood 81	

Public Schs..Principal	Grd	Prgm	Enr/#Cls	SN	Phone
Carl Schurz Elem Sch 633 W Coll St, New Braunfels 78130 Duane Trujillo	PK-5	T	407 24	44%	830/627-6680 Fax 830/627-6681
County Line Elem Sch 1200 W County Line Rd, New Braunfels 78130 Taylor Danielle	PK-5		368 28	33%	830/627-6610 Fax 830/627-6611
Klein Road Elem Sch 2620 Klein Way, New Braunfels 78130 Marisela Lopez	PK-5	T	483	50%	830/221-1700 Fax 830/221-1701
Lamar Elem Sch 240 N Central Ave, New Braunfels 78130 Christopher Russell	PK-5		371 24	24%	830/627-6890 Fax 830/629-2660
Lone Star Early Childhood Ctr 2343 W San Antonio St, New Braunfels 78130 Heather Salas	PK-PK		300		830/627-6820 Fax 830/627-6821
Memorial Elem Sch 1911 S Walnut Ave, New Braunfels 78130 Nicole Haecker	PK-5	T	367 21	51%	830/627-6470 Fax 830/627-6471

1	Superintendent	8	Curric/Instruct K-12	19	Chief Financial Officer	29	Family/Consumer Science
2	Bus/Finance/Purchasing	9	Curric/Instruct Elem	20	Art K-12	30	Adult Education
3	Buildings And Grounds	10	Curric/Instruct Sec	21	Art Elem	31	Career/Sch-to-Work K-12
4	Food Service	11	Federal Program	22	Art Sec	32	Career/Sch-to-Work Elem
5	Transportation	12	Title I	23	Music K-12	33	Career/Sch-to-Work Sec
6	Athletic	13	Title V	24	Music Elem	34	Early Childhood Ed
7	Health Services	14		25	Music Sec	35	Health/Phys Education
		15	Asst Superintendent	26	Business Education	36	Guidance Services K-12
		16	Instructional Media Svcs	27	Career & Tech Ed	37	Guidance Services Elem
		17	Chief Operations Officer	28	Technology Education	38	Guidance Services Sec
		18	Chief Academic Officer				
39	Social Studies K-12	49	English/Lang Arts Elem	59	Special Education Elem	69	Academic Assessment
40	Social Studies Elem	50	English/Lang Arts Sec	60	Special Education Sec	70	Research/Development
41	Social Studies Sec	51	Reading K-12	61	Foreign/World Lang K-12	71	Public Information
42	Science K-12	52	Reading Elem	62	Foreign/World Lang Elem	72	Summer School
43	Science Elem	53	Reading Sec	63	Foreign/World Lang Sec	73	Instructional Tech
44	Science Sec	54	Remedial Reading K-12	64	Religious Education K-12	74	Inservice Training
45	Math K-12	55	Remedial Reading Elem	65	Religious Education Elem	75	Marketing/Distributive
46	Math Elem	56	Remedial Reading Sec	66	Religious Education Sec	76	Info Systems
47	Math Sec	57	Bilingual/ELL	67	School Board President	77	Psychological Assess
48	English/Lang Arts K-12	58	Special Education K-12	68	Teacher Personnel	78	Affirmative Action

Texas School Directory — Comanche County

School	Grades	Prgm	Enr/#Cls	SN	Phone
New Braunfels High Sch 2551 Loop 337, New Braunfels 78130 Kara Bock	9-12	GV	1,813 110	26%	830/627-6000 Fax 830/627-6001
New Braunfels HS 9th GR Ctr 659 S Guenther Ave, New Braunfels 78130 Jeffrey Lightsey	9-9	A	655	29%	830/629-8600 Fax 830/629-8601
New Braunfels Middle Sch 4150 Klein Meadows, New Braunfels 78130 Greg Hughes	6-9	V	1,151 65	35%	830/627-6270 Fax 830/627-6271
Oak Run Middle Sch 415 Oak Run Pt, New Braunfels 78132 Shana Behling	6-8		938 25	31%	830/627-6400 Fax 830/627-6401
Ⓐ School of Choice 659 S Guenther Ave, New Braunfels 78130 Jerry Clark	9-12	T	150 5	38%	830/629-8650 Fax 830/629-8651
Seele Elem Sch 540 Howard St, New Braunfels 78130 **Deanna Callahan**	PK-5	T	408 18	42%	830/627-6750 Fax 830/627-6751
Veramendi Elem Sch 2290 Oak Run Pkwy, New Braunfels 78132 **Leah Droddy**	PK-5		743		830/608-5900 Fax 830/608-5901
Voss Farms Elem Sch 2510 Pahmeyer Rd, New Braunfels 78130 Deborah Cary	PK-5		592		830/608-5800 Fax 830/608-5801
Walnut Springs Elem Sch 1900 S Walnut Ave, New Braunfels 78130 David Lewis	PK-5	T	380 22	32%	830/627-6540 Fax 830/627-6541

COMAL CATHOLIC SCHOOLS

● **Archdiocese San Antonio Ed Off** PID: 00999724
Listing includes only schools located in this county. See District Index for location of Diocesan Offices.

Catholic Schs..Principal	Grd	Prgm	Enr/#Cls	SN	Phone
SS Peter & Paul Sch 198 W Bridge St, New Braunfels 78130 Janet Buras	PK-8		377 20		830/625-4531 Fax 830/606-6916
St John Paul II High Sch 6720 FM 482, New Braunfels 78132 Andrew Iliff	9-12		200		830/643-0802 Fax 830/643-0806

COMAL PRIVATE SCHOOLS

Private Schs..Principal	Grd	Prgm	Enr/#Cls	SN	Phone
Bracken Christian Sch 670 Old Boerne Rd, Bulverde 78163 Frank Riley \ Sheila Kerby	PK-12		250 40		830/438-3211 Fax 830/980-2327 [f] [t]
Cross Lutheran Sch 2171 E Common St, New Braunfels 78130 Corey Brandenburger	PK-8		165 13		830/625-3969 Fax 830/625-5019
Gloria Deo Academy 1100 Bulverde Rd Ste 2, Bulverde 78163 Joe Fesler	K-10		120		830/708-5463
Living Rock Academy 2500 Bulverde Rd, Bulverde 78163 Whitney Chandler	PK-12		88		830/387-2929 Fax 210/787-4091
New Braunfels Chrn Aca-Lower 995 Mission Hills Dr, New Braunfels 78130 Darren West	PK-5		200 15		830/629-6222 Fax 830/629-8049

COMANCHE COUNTY

COMANCHE PUBLIC SCHOOLS

● **Comanche Ind School Dist** PID: 01007051 325/356-2727
200 E Highland Ave, Comanche 76442 Fax 325/356-2312

Schools: 4 \ *Teachers:* 123 \ *Students:* 1,325 \ *Special Ed Students:* 138 \ *LEP Students:* 165 \ *College-Bound:* 68% \ *Ethnic:* Asian 1%, Hispanic 50%, Caucasian 48% \ *Exp:* $361 (High) \ *Poverty:* 23% \ *Title I:* $338,464 \ *Open-Close:* 08/16 - 05/25 \ *DTBP:* $379 (High)

Gary Speegle	1	Kathy Herring	2
Howard Gifford	3	Amy Brooks	4
Chad Brown	5	Jimmy Eaton	5
Lupe Moreno	5	Stephen Hermesmeyer	6*
Mona Clifton	7*	Della Hicks	10,36,69,77,83,85*
Gwinn Smith	37*	Curtis Stahnke	54*
Becky Jones	58	Jason Pate	67
Linda McGinnis	73*	Roxann Gray	76
Scott Carlisle	91*		

Public Schs..Principal	Grd	Prgm	Enr/#Cls	SN	Phone
Comanche Early Childhood Ctr 200 E Highland Ave, Comanche 76442 Scott Carlisle	PK-PK	T	68	96%	325/356-2440 Fax 325/356-1454
Comanche Elem Sch 308 FM 3381, Comanche 76442 Curtis Stahnke	PK-5	T	659 25	67%	325/356-2727 Fax 325/356-3990
Comanche High Sch Highway 16 N, Comanche 76442 **Steven Lewis**	9-12	T	323 50	58%	325/356-2581 Fax 325/356-2658
H R Jefferies Junior High Sch 1 Valley Forge St, Comanche 76442 Joseph Simmons	6-8	T	277 25	66%	325/356-5220 Fax 325/356-1949

● **De Leon Ind School Dist** PID: 01007099 254/893-8210
425 S Texas St, De Leon 76444 Fax 254/893-8214

Schools: 3 \ *Teachers:* 58 \ *Students:* 716 \ *Special Ed Students:* 74 \ *LEP Students:* 30 \ *Ethnic:* Hispanic 32%, Caucasian 67% \ *Exp:* $321 (High) \ *Poverty:* 19% \ *Title I:* $173,962 \ *Special Education:* $5,000 \ *Open-Close:* 08/21 - 05/28 \ *DTBP:* $335 (High)

Dana Marable	1	Nicky Wilkerson	3,5*
Samantha Jones	4*	Andy Dickson	6
Liesa Nowlin	10*	Kaye Quinn	12,31,36,69,85,88,270,296
Michell Simpson	16*	Roxanna Tibo	54*
Deanna Downs	57*	Craig Hopper	58
Josh Mahan	67	David White	73,84

Public Schs..Principal	Grd	Prgm	Enr/#Cls	SN	Phone
De Leon Elem Sch 133 E Pecan Ave, De Leon 76444 Lori Womack	PK-5	T	357 17	66%	254/893-8220 Fax 254/893-8224
De Leon High Sch 200 W Manchaca Ave, De Leon 76444 Liesa Nowlin	9-12	ATV	183 20	49%	254/938-8240 Fax 254/934-4985
Perkins Middle Sch 600 N Johnson St, De Leon 76444 Joshua Sepeda	6-8	T	188 16	54%	254/893-8230 Fax 254/893-8234

---

79 Student Personnel	91 Safety/Security	275 Response To Intervention	298 Grant Writer/Ptnrships	**School Programs**	**Social Media**
80 Driver Ed/Safety	92 Magnet School	277 Remedial Math K-12	750 Chief Innovation Officer	A = Alternative Program	
81 Gifted/Talented	93 Parental Involvement	280 Literacy Coach	751 Chief of Staff	G = Adult Classes	[f] = Facebook
82 Video Services	95 Tech Prep Program	285 STEM	752 Social Emotional Learning	M = Magnet Program	
83 Substance Abuse Prev	97 Chief Information Officer	286 Digital Learning		T = Title I Schoolwide	[t] = Twitter
84 Erate	98 Chief Technology Officer	288 Common Core Standards	**Other School Types**	V = Career & Tech Ed Programs	
85 AIDS Education	270 Character Education	294 Accountability	Ⓐ = Alternative School		
88 Alternative/At Risk	271 Migrant Education	295 Network System	Ⓒ = Charter School	New Schools are shaded	
89 Multi-Cultural Curriculum	273 Teacher Mentor	296 Title II Programs	Ⓜ = Magnet School	New Superintendents and Principals are bold	
90 Social Work	274 Before/After Sch	297 Webmaster	Ⓨ = Year-Round School	Personnel with email addresses are underscored	

Concho County

- **Gustine Ind School Dist** PID: 01007128 325/667-7981
  503 W Main St, Gustine 76455 Fax 325/667-0203

Schools: 1 \ *Teachers:* 21 \ *Students:* 161 \ *Special Ed Students:* 21 \ *LEP Students:* 50 \ *College-Bound:* 70% \ *Ethnic:* Hispanic 66%, Caucasian 34% \ *Exp:* $656 (High) \ *Poverty:* 26% \ *Title I:* $78,628 \ *Open-Close:* 08/12 - 05/22

Patti Blue	1,11,73	Brandy Ruedas ... 57*
Steve Ruedas	67	

Public Schs..Principal	Grd	Prgm	Enr/#Cls	SN	
Gustine Sch 503 W Main St, Gustine 76455 Kenny Eudy	PK-12	TV	161 20	83%	325/667-7303

- **Sidney Ind School Dist** PID: 01007154 254/842-5500
  4100 FM 1689, Sidney 76474 Fax 254/842-5139

Schools: 1 \ *Teachers:* 17 \ *Students:* 140 \ *Special Ed Students:* 19 \ *College-Bound:* 80% \ *Ethnic:* Hispanic 25%, Native American: 1%, Caucasian 74% \ *Exp:* $1,194 (High) \ *Poverty:* 20% \ *Title I:* $23,738 \ *Open-Close:* 08/14 - 05/29 \ *DTBP:* $408 (High)

James Rucker	1,11,73,83	Anita Wright ... 2
Betty Stanley	4*	Sigrid Huddleston ... 8,58,88*
Doug Caffey	67	Deanna Drummond ... 73,98,298*

Public Schs..Principal	Grd	Prgm	Enr/#Cls	SN	
ⓥ Sidney Sch 4100 FM 1689, Sidney 76474 James Rucker	PK-12	MTV	140 10	60%	254/842-5500 Fax 254/842-5731

CONCHO COUNTY

CONCHO PUBLIC SCHOOLS

- **Eden Cons Ind School Dist** PID: 01007180 325/869-4121
  113 W Bryan St, Eden 76837 Fax 325/869-5210

Schools: 2 \ *Teachers:* 20 \ *Students:* 215 \ *Special Ed Students:* 36 \ *LEP Students:* 10 \ *College-Bound:* 70% \ *Exp:* $601 (High) \ *Poverty:* 19% \ *Title I:* $71,609 \ *Open-Close:* 08/21 - 05/21 \ *DTBP:* $378 (High)

Misty Gandy	1	Margo Rucker ... 2
Chris Castillo	3	Dawn Torres ... 4
Jonie Whiteley	16*	Tiffany Estrada ... 31
Geneva Garza	36,57,69,83,270*	Amanda Rurup ... 58
Shan Click	67	Kelli Dillard ... 286*

Public Schs..Principal	Grd	Prgm	Enr/#Cls		
Eden Elem Sch 101 W Bryan, Eden 76837 Deanna Beachum	K-5		215 13		325/869-4121 Fax 325/869-5672
Eden High Sch 180 W Bryan, Eden 76837 Misty Gandy	6-12	V	116 15		325/869-4121 Fax 325/869-5023

- **Paint Rock Ind School Dist** PID: 01007245 325/732-4314
  698 S Sims St, Paint Rock 76866 Fax 325/732-4384

Schools: 1 \ *Teachers:* 25 \ *Students:* 240 \ *Special Ed Students:* 28 \ *LEP Students:* 9 \ *College-Bound:* 70% \ *Ethnic:* Asian 1%, Hispanic 48%, Caucasian 50% \ *Exp:* $917 (High) \ *Poverty:* 45% \ *Title I:* $65,298 \ *Open-Close:* 08/21 - 05/29 \ *DTBP:* $328 (High)

Ron Cline	1,11	Tracy Grimes ... 2*
Allison Tonne	16*	Anthony Brown ... 67
Russell Hoelscher	73*	

Public Schs..Principal	Grd	Prgm	Enr/#Cls	SN	
Paint Rock Sch 698 Sims St, Paint Rock 76866 Allison Tonne	PK-12	T	240 20	77%	325/732-4314

COOKE COUNTY

COOKE PUBLIC SCHOOLS

- **Callisburg Ind School Dist** PID: 01007271 940/665-0540
  148 Dozier St, Gainesville 76240 Fax 940/668-2706

Schools: 2 \ *Teachers:* 84 \ *Students:* 1,100 \ *Special Ed Students:* 105 \ *LEP Students:* 23 \ *College-Bound:* 38% \ *Ethnic:* African American 1%, Hispanic 12%, Native American: 1%, Caucasian 86% \ *Exp:* $530 (High) \ *Poverty:* 16% \ *Title I:* $200,215 \ *Open-Close:* 08/20 - 05/21 \ *DTBP:* $463 (High)

Donald Metzler	1,11	Janie Lewis ... 2,12
Gene May	3,5	Gary Jack ... 6*
Lisa Griffin	31,36*	Vicki Reasor ... 58
Dusty Weaver	67	Steve Goodall ... 76,295

Public Schs..Principal	Grd	Prgm	Enr/#Cls	SN	
Callisburg Elem Sch 648 FM 3164, Gainesville 76240 Lisa Herring	PK-5	T	565 45	48%	940/612-4196 Fax 940/612-4804
Callisburg Middle High Sch 308 Dozier St, Gainesville 76240 Bronwyn Werts \ Jason Hooper	6-12	ATV	590 45	33%	940/665-0961 Fax 940/665-2849

- **Era Ind School Dist** PID: 01007312 940/665-5961
  108 Hargrove St, Era 76238 Fax 940/665-5311

Schools: 1 \ *Teachers:* 40 \ *Students:* 500 \ *Special Ed Students:* 34 \ *LEP Students:* 6 \ *College-Bound:* 80% \ *Ethnic:* Asian 1%, Hispanic 12%, Native American: 1%, Caucasian 86% \ *Exp:* $339 (High) \ *Poverty:* 14% \ *Title I:* $49,379 \ *Open-Close:* 08/15 - 05/22 \ *DTBP:* $352 (High)

Jeremy Thompson	1	Suzette Henderson ... 2,11
Jeremy Diets	5*	Donald New ... 6
Samantha Gumes	7*	Todd Jones ... 8*
Lisa Jones	12,57	Michael Parkhill ... 16,73,295*
John Erwin	31,36,69,83,85*	Vickie Beckham ... 58*
Jeffrey Stevens	67	Leann Spears ... 81*

---

1 Superintendent	8 Curric/Instruct K-12	19 Chief Financial Officer	29 Family/Consumer Science	39 Social Studies K-12	49 English/Lang Arts Elem	59 Special Education Elem	69 Academic Assessment
2 Bus/Finance/Purchasing	9 Curric/Instruct Elem	20 Art K-12	30 Adult Education	40 Social Studies Elem	50 English/Lang Arts Sec	60 Special Education Sec	70 Research/Development
3 Buildings And Grounds	10 Curric/Instruct Sec	21 Art Elem	31 Career/Sch-to-Work K-12	41 Social Studies Sec	51 Reading K-12	61 Foreign/World Lang K-12	71 Public Information
4 Food Service	11 Federal Program	22 Art Sec	32 Career/Sch-to-Work Elem	42 Science K-12	52 Reading Elem	62 Foreign/World Lang Elem	72 Summer School
5 Transportation	12 Title I	23 Music K-12	33 Career/Sch-to-Work Sec	43 Science Elem	53 Reading Sec	63 Foreign/World Lang Sec	73 Instructional Tech
6 Athletic	13 Title V	24 Music Elem	34 Early Childhood Ed	44 Science Sec	54 Remedial Reading K-12	64 Religious Education K-12	74 Inservice Training
7 Health Services	15 Asst Superintendent	25 Music Sec	35 Health/Phys Education	45 Math K-12	55 Remedial Reading Elem	65 Religious Education Elem	75 Marketing/Distributive
	16 Instructional Media Svcs	26 Business Education	36 Guidance Services K-12	46 Math Elem	56 Remedial Reading Sec	66 Religious Education Sec	76 Info Systems
	17 Chief Operations Officer	27 Career & Tech Ed	37 Guidance Services Elem	47 Math Sec	57 Bilingual/ELL	67 School Board President	77 Psychological Assess
	18 Chief Academic Officer	28 Technology Education	38 Guidance Services Sec	48 English/Lang Arts K-12	58 Special Education K-12	68 Teacher Personnel	78 Affirmative Action

Texas School Directory — Cooke County

Public Schs..Principal	Grd	Prgm	Enr/#Cls	SN	
Era Sch 108 Hargrove St, Era 76238 Todd Jones \ Courtney Stevens	PK-12	ATV	500 40	38%	940/665-5961

● **Gainesville Ind School Dist** PID: 01007348   940/665-4362
800 S Morris St, Gainesville 76240   Fax 940/668-0354

Schools: 6 \ *Teachers:* 204 \ *Students:* 3,100 \ *Special Ed Students:* 239 \ *LEP Students:* 618 \ *College-Bound:* 61% \ *Ethnic:* Asian 1%, African American 7%, Hispanic 61%, Native American: 1%, Caucasian 31% \ *Exp:* $511 (High) \ *Poverty:* 23% \ *Title I:* $956,503 \ *Special Education:* $599,000 \ *Open-Close:* 08/14 - 05/28 \ *DTBP:* $203 (High)

Dr Desmontes Stewart 1		Alyce Greer 2,19	
Joe Warren 3		Corey Ray 4	
William Rice 5		James Polk 6	
Lisa Lawson 7,85		Lacrsasha Stille 8,15	
David Glancy 10*		Paula Moore 11,57,68,83,88,271,298	
Reagan Lynch 11		Russ Rutherford 20,23	
Brittanie Polk 58		Corey Hardin 67	
Leslie Crutsinger 71		Jennifer Coleman 73,76,98	

Public Schs..Principal	Grd	Prgm	Enr/#Cls	SN	
Gainesville High Sch 2201 S Interstate 35, Gainesville 76240 Melissa Hutchison	9-12	T	846 40	71%	940/665-5528 Fax 940/612-2795
Gainesville Jr High Sch 1201 S Lindsay St, Gainesville 76240 Krista Beal	7-8	T	471 55	81%	940/665-4062 Fax 940/665-1432
Margaret Galubenski Achiev Ctr 1000 N Radio Hill Rd, Gainesville 76240 Todd Kitchens	7-12		16 3		940/665-0277 Fax 940/665-0154
Robert E Lee Intermediate Sch 2100 N Grand Ave, Gainesville 76240 Nina Coody	5-6	T	447 24	82%	940/668-6662 Fax 940/668-0353
Thomas A Edison Elem Sch 1 Edison Dr, Gainesville 76240 Pablo De Santiago	PK-1	T	614 40	82%	940/665-6091 Fax 940/665-5728
W E Chalmers Elem Sch 600 S Radio Hill Rd, Gainesville 76240 Brittenie Polk	2-4	T	702 43	84%	940/665-4147 Fax 940/665-9290

● **Lindsay Ind School Dist** PID: 01007427   940/668-8923
495 6th St, Lindsay 76250   Fax 940/668-2662

Schools: 2 \ *Teachers:* 36 \ *Students:* 510 \ *Special Ed Students:* 25 \ *College-Bound:* 100% \ *Ethnic:* Asian 2%, Hispanic 3%, Native American: 1%, Caucasian 93% \ *Exp:* $421 (High) \ *Poverty:* 6% \ *Title I:* $27,159 \ *Open-Close:* 08/14 - 05/21

Trevor Rogers 1,11		Diane Zimmerer 2	
Jeff Smiley 6*		Pat Autry 8,11,31,58,273*	
Ben Hawkins 67		James Moats 73	
Todd Armstrong 84			

Public Schs..Principal	Grd	Prgm	Enr/#Cls	SN	
Lindsay Elem Sch 495 W 6th St, Lindsay 76250 Pat Autry	PK-6		259 33	12%	940/668-8923
Lindsay High Sch 631 Knight Dr, Lindsay 76250 Steven Cope	7-12	V	237 20	11%	940/668-8474 Fax 940/665-1637

● **Muenster Ind School Dist** PID: 01007453   940/759-2281
113 E 7th St, Muenster 76252   Fax 940/759-5200

Schools: 2 \ *Teachers:* 42 \ *Students:* 500 \ *Special Ed Students:* 83 \ *LEP Students:* 3 \ *College-Bound:* 76% \ *Ethnic:* Asian 1%, Hispanic 5%, Caucasian 94% \ *Exp:* $318 (High) \ *Poverty:* 5% \ *Title I:* $34,431 \ *Open-Close:* 08/14 - 05/21 \ *DTBP:* $363 (High) \ f

Steven Self 1		Carol Klement 2	
James Koelzer 3		Susie Fleitman 5	
Brady Carney 6		Lou Heers 9,11,271*	
Vickie Eldridge 16*		Kristi Schneider 36,69,83,88,270*	
Vikki Reasor 58		Darren Bindel 67	
Jeffrey Presnall 73*			

Public Schs..Principal	Grd	Prgm	Enr/#Cls	SN	
Muenster Elem Sch 912 N Walnut St, Muenster 76252 Lou Heers	PK-6	T	282 20	16%	940/759-2282 Fax 940/759-5201
Muenster High Sch 135 E 7th Street, Muenster 76252 John York	7-12	ATV	226 27	11%	940/759-2281 Fax 940/759-4614

● **Sivells Bend Ind School Dist** PID: 01007489   940/665-6411
1053 County Road 403, Gainesville 76240   Fax 940/665-2527

Schools: 1 \ *Teachers:* 8 \ *Students:* 68 \ *Special Ed Students:* 13 \ *Ethnic:* African American 3%, Hispanic 19%, Native American: 8%, Caucasian 71% \ *Exp:* $395 (High) \ *Poverty:* 11% \ *Title I:* $1,024 \ *Open-Close:* 08/27 - 06/01 \ *DTBP:* $401 (High)

Lisa Slaughter 1,11,83,288		Angela Beaudin 2*	
Randy Jenkins 3,5*		Rod Tipps 6,16,59,73*	
Cheryl Downey 11*		Coleen Gunter 57*	
Harry Harrell 67			

Public Schs..Principal	Grd	Prgm	Enr/#Cls	SN	
Sivells Bend Sch 1053 County Road 403, Gainesville 76240 Lisa Slaughter	PK-8	T	68 7	78%	940/665-6411

● **Valley View ISD-Cooke Co** PID: 01007506   940/726-3659
106 Newton St, Valley View 76272   Fax 940/726-3614

Schools: 1 \ *Teachers:* 56 \ *Students:* 815 \ *Special Ed Students:* 87 \ *LEP Students:* 74 \ *College-Bound:* 80% \ *Ethnic:* Asian 1%, Hispanic 25%, Caucasian 73% \ *Exp:* $504 (High) \ *Poverty:* 16% \ *Title I:* $98,815 \ *Open-Close:* 08/22 - 05/28 \ *DTBP:* $349 (High)

Willaim Stokes 1		Lori Huber 2	
Kristy Holt 4		Alan Kassen 6*	
Monica Parkhill 8,11,296		Vikki Reasor 58	
Ray Sappinting 67		Mike Wilson 73*	

Public Schs..Principal	Grd	Prgm	Enr/#Cls	SN	
Valley View Sch 106 Newton St, Valley View 76272 Jesse Newton \ Susan Smith	PK-12	T	815 25	37%	940/726-3659

---

79 Student Personnel	91 Safety/Security	275 Response To Intervention	298 Grant Writer/Ptnrships	School Programs	Social Media
30 Driver Ed/Safety	92 Magnet School	277 Remedial Math K-12	750 Chief Innovation Officer	A = Alternative Program	f = Facebook
31 Gifted/Talented	93 Parental Involvement	280 Literacy Coach	751 Chief of Staff	G = Adult Classes	t = Twitter
32 Video Services	95 Tech Prep Program	285 STEM	752 Social Emotional Learning	M = Magnet Program	
83 Substance Abuse Prev	97 Chief Information Officer	286 Digital Learning		T = Title I Schoolwide	
34 Erate	98 Chief Technology Officer	288 Common Core Standards	Other School Types	V = Career & Tech Ed Programs	
35 AIDS Education	270 Accountability	294 Accountability	Ⓐ = Alternative Program		
68 Alternative/At Risk	271 Migrant Education	295 Network System	Ⓒ = Charter School	New Schools are shaded	
39 Multi-Cultural Curriculum	273 Teacher Mentor	296 Title II Programs	Ⓜ = Magnet School	New Superintendents and Principals are bold	
90 Social Work	274 Before/After Sch	297 Webmaster	Ⓨ = Year-Round School	Personnel with email addresses are underscored	

TX—91

Coryell County
Market Data Retrieval

- **Walnut Bend Ind School Dist** PID: 01007532   940/665-5990
  47 County Road 198, Gainesville 76240   Fax 940/665-9660

  Schools: 1 \ **Teachers:** 6 \ **Students:** 75 \ **Special Ed Students:** 7 \
  Ethnic: Hispanic 25%, Caucasian 75% \ **Exp:** $396 (High) \ **Poverty:** 16% \
  Open-Close: 08/20 - 05/21 \ **DTBP:** $360 (High)

  Troy Humphrey 1,11,73,83   Barbara Smith 16*
  Randy Clark 67   Gabby Probst 273*

Public Schs..Principal	Grd	Prgm	Enr/#Cls	SN	
Walnut Bend Elem Sch 47 County Road 198, Gainesville 76240 Troy Humphrey	PK-8		75 6	64%	940/665-5990

COOKE CATHOLIC SCHOOLS

- **Diocese of Fort Worth Ed Off** PID: 01054339
  Listing includes only schools located in this county. See District Index for location of Diocesan Offices.

Catholic Schs..Principal	Grd	Prgm	Enr/#Cls	SN	
Sacred Heart Sch 153 E 6th St, Muenster 76252 Beth Bartush	PK-12		284 22		940/759-2511 Fax 940/759-4422
St Mary's Catholic Sch 931 N Weaver St, Gainesville 76240 Karen Lee	PK-8		165 11		940/665-5395 Fax 940/665-9538

CORYELL COUNTY

CORYELL PUBLIC SCHOOLS

- **Copperas Cove Ind School Dist** PID: 01007556   254/547-1227
  408 S Main St, Copperas Cove 76522   Fax 254/547-1542

  Schools: 11 \ **Teachers:** 538 \ **Students:** 8,200 \ **Special Ed Students:** 817
  \ **LEP Students:** 281 \ **College-Bound:** 55% \ **Ethnic:** Asian 2%,
  African American 20%, Hispanic 29%, Native American: 1%, Caucasian
  49% \ **Exp:** $264 (Med) \ **Poverty:** 19% \ **Title I:** $1,361,047 \
  Special Education: $1,916,000 \ **Open-Close:** 08/20 - 06/04 \ **DTBP:** $187
  (High) \ 🅵 🅴

  Deidra Hall 2   June Crawford 2,11,19
  Gary Elliott 3,5,91   Melissa Bryan 4
  Lisa Edgar 8,12,74,275   Dr Patricia Remissong 8,15,288
  Rick Kirkpatrick 15,91   Henry Blair 16,76,295
  Leah Miller 31,38   Rhonda Burnell 58
  Joan Manning 67   Kayleen Love 68*
  Wendy Sledd 71,298   Dr Earl Parcell 73,286
  Kim Alverez 294

Public Schs..Principal	Grd	Prgm	Enr/#Cls	SN	
Clements-Parsons Elem Sch 1115 Northern Dancer Dr, Copperas Cove 76522 Leah Miller	K-5	T	828 60	56%	254/547-2235 Fax 254/547-0845
Copperas Cove High Sch 400 S 25th St, Copperas Cove 76522 Dr Jimmy Shuck	9-12	T	2,214	43%	254/547-2534 Fax 254/547-9870
Copperas Cove Jr High Sch 702 Sunny Ave, Copperas Cove 76522 Amanda Crawley	6-8	T	827 50	58%	254/547-6959 Fax 254/518-2620
Crossroads High Sch 306 E Avenue E, Copperas Cove 76522 James Irick	9-12	T	66 13	59%	254/547-9164 Fax 254/547-4039
Fairview-Miss Jewel Elem Sch 710 S 5th St, Copperas Cove 76522 Larea Gamble	K-5	T	479 46	80%	254/547-4212 Fax 254/547-6378
Hettie Halstead Elem Sch 910 N Main St, Copperas Cove 76522 Brian Jost	K-5	T	325 27	72%	254/547-3440 Fax 254/547-6896
House Creek Elementray Sch 351 Lutheran Church Rd, Copperas Cove 76522 Todd Williams	K-5	T	693	39%	254/518-3000 Fax 254/518-7400
J L Williams-Lovett Ledger ES 909 Courtney Ln, Copperas Cove 76522 Marla Sullivan	K-5	T	765 25	60%	254/542-1001 Fax 254/542-2794
Mae Stevens Early Learng Acad 302 Manning Dr, Copperas Cove 76522 Mary Derrick	PK-PK	T	591 19	71%	254/547-8289 Fax 254/547-8325
Martin Walker Elem Sch 100 FM 3046, Copperas Cove 76522 Earl Parcell	K-5	T	490 29	57%	254/547-2283 Fax 254/547-5984
S C Lee Junior High Sch 1205 Courtney Ln, Copperas Cove 76522 Melanie Schratwieser	6-8	T	895 34	53%	254/542-7877 Fax 254/542-8103

- **Evant Ind School Dist** PID: 01007635   254/471-3160
  339 Memory Lane, Evant 76525   Fax 254/471-5629

  Schools: 1 \ **Teachers:** 15 \ **Students:** 235 \ **Special Ed Students:** 22
  \ **LEP Students:** 11 \ **College-Bound:** 100% \ **Exp:** $714 (High) \
  Poverty: 23% \ **Title I:** $64,338 \ **Open-Close:** 08/19 - 05/28 \ **DTBP:** $331
  (High) \ 🅵 🅴

  Ken Wimberly 1   Danny Hemphill 2*
  Shane Belanger 3   Lupe Hernandez 4
  Mike Lancaster 5   Philip Martin 6
  Donna Watson 7   Jennifer Ingram 8,13,74,288,294,298*
  Stacey Lowery . 11,57,81,88,271,275,280,296*   Randy Newby 16,73,76,285,295
  Whitie Decker .... 27,31*   Shawn Harrison 35
  Lora Slaughter .... 36,69,79,83,270,286*   Stacey Parrish 58,77*
  Sheila Williams 67   Danny Hemphill 68,84,91

Public Schs..Principal	Grd	Prgm	Enr/#Cls	SN	
Evant Sch 339 Memory Ln, Evant 76525 Jennifer Ingram	PK-12	V	235 25		254/471-5536

- **Gatesville Ind School Dist** PID: 01007661   254/865-7251
  311 S Lovers Ln, Gatesville 76528   Fax 254/865-2279

  Schools: 5 \ **Teachers:** 198 \ **Students:** 2,788 \ **Special Ed Students:** 338
  \ **LEP Students:** 103 \ **College-Bound:** 47% \ **Ethnic:** Asian 1%, African
  American 3%, Hispanic 23%, Native American: 1%, Caucasian 73% \
  Exp: $314 (High) \ **Poverty:** 19% \ **Title I:** $559,651 \ **Open-Close:** 08/19 -
  05/22 \ **DTBP:** $178 (High) \ 🅵 🅴

  Dr Barrett Pollard 1   Darrell Frazier 2,19
  Toby Williams 3   Gail Shelton 4*
  Marty Williams 5   Kyle Cooper 6
  Shane Webb 10   Marsha Worthington ... 11,31,36,69,273,275,288

1	Superintendent	8	Curric/Instruct K-12	19	Chief Financial Officer	29	Family/Consumer Science	39	Social Studies K-12	49	English/Lang Arts Elem	59	Special Education Elem	69	Academic Assessment
2	Bus/Finance/Purchasing	9	Curric/Instruct Elem	20	Art K-12	30	Adult Education	40	Social Studies Elem	50	English/Lang Arts Sec	60	Special Education Sec	70	Research/Development
3	Buildings And Grounds	10	Curric/Instruct Sec	21	Art Elem	31	Career/Sch-to-Work K-12	41	Social Studies Sec	51	Reading K-12	61	Foreign/World Lang K-12	71	Public Information
4	Food Service	11	Federal Program	22	Art Sec	32	Career/Sch-to-Work Elem	42	Science K-12	52	Reading Elem	62	Foreign/World Lang Elem	72	Summer School
5	Transportation	12	Title I	23	Music K-12	33	Career/Sch-to-Work Sec	43	Science Elem	53	Reading Sec	63	Foreign/World Lang Sec	73	Instructional Tech
6	Athletic	13	Title V	24	Music Elem	34	Early Childhood Ed	44	Science Sec	54	Remedial Reading K-12	64	Religious Education K-12	74	Inservice Training
7	Health Services	14	Instructional Media Svcs	25	Music Sec	35	Health/Phys Education	45	Math K-12	55	Remedial Reading Elem	65	Religious Education Elem	75	Marketing/Distributive
		15	Asst Superintendent	26	Business Education	36	Guidance Services K-12	46	Math Elem	56	Remedial Reading Sec	66	Religious Education Sec	76	Info Systems
		16	Chief Operations Officer	27	Career & Tech Ed	37	Guidance Services Elem	47	Math Sec	57	Bilingual/ELL	67	School Board President	77	Psychological Assess
		18	Chief Academic Officer	28	Technology Education	38	Guidance Services Sec	48	English/Lang Arts K-12	58	Special Education K-12	68	Teacher Personnel	78	Affirmative Action

Texas School Directory — Crane County

Mary Leib .... 67 Shelly Harper 73

Public Schs..Principal	Grd	Prgm	Enr/#Cls	SN	
Gatesville Elem Sch 2537 E Main St, Gatesville 76528 **Keegan Webb**	1-3	T	619 22	56%	254/865-7262 Fax 254/248-0077
Gatesville High Sch 205 S Lovers Ln, Gatesville 76528 Yancey Sanderson	9-12	AGTV	859 50	44%	254/865-8281 Fax 254/865-2293
Gatesville Intermediate Sch 311 Hornet Way, Gatesville 76528 Bridget Register	4-6	T	594 30	51%	254/865-2526 Fax 254/865-2932
Gatesville Junior High Sch 307 S Lovers Ln, Gatesville 76528 Cindy Venable	7-8	AT	461 36	51%	254/865-8271 Fax 254/865-2252
Gatesville Primary Sch 308 Hornet Way, Gatesville 76528 Bridget Register	PK-K	T	255 23	67%	254/865-7264 Fax 254/865-2160

● **Jonesboro Ind School Dist** PID: 01007714   254/463-2111
14909 E State Hwy 36, Jonesboro 76538   Fax 254/463-2275

Schools: 1 \ *Teachers:* 21 \ *Students:* 340 \ *Special Ed Students:* 31 \ *LEP Students:* 3 \ *College-Bound:* 25% \ *Ethnic:* Hispanic 15%, Caucasian 85% \ *Exp:* $484 (High) \ *Poverty:* 17% \ *Title I:* $36,748 \ *Open-Close:* 08/26 - 05/22 \ *DTBP:* $303 (High)

Matt Dossey 1,11,73,83   Stacey Lilljedahl 2*
Keith Necessary .... 3*   Kendra Gustin 8,12,286*
Cynthia Cate .... 59*   Chris Simon 60
Keith Taylor 67

Public Schs..Principal	Grd	Prgm	Enr/#Cls	SN	
Jonesboro Sch 14909 E State Hwy 36, Jonesboro 76538 Kendra Gustin	PK-12	TV	340 30	57%	254/463-2111

● **Oglesby Ind School Dist** PID: 01007740   254/456-2271
125 College Ave, Oglesby 76561   Fax 254/456-2522

Schools: 1 \ *Teachers:* 19 \ *Students:* 165 \ *Special Ed Students:* 12 \ *LEP Students:* 9 \ *College-Bound:* 58% \ *Ethnic:* Hispanic 28%, Caucasian 72% \ *Exp:* $502 (High) \ *Poverty:* 32% \ *Title I:* $95,857 \ *Open-Close:* 08/20 - 05/22 \ *DTBP:* $361 (High)

David Maass 1   Kalinda Westbrook 2*
Boone Brinkley 3,5   Ryan Kyle 6
David Maass .... 8,11,16,69,73,286*   Misti Sanders 12
Amanda Fisher 58   Rebbeca Schultz 67
Sheila Hoehn 76

Public Schs..Principal	Grd	Prgm	Enr/#Cls	SN	
Oglesby Sch 125 College Ave, Oglesby 76561 Misti Sanders	PK-12	TV	165 20	69%	254/456-2271 Fax 254/456-2916

COTTLE COUNTY

COTTLE PUBLIC SCHOOLS

● **Paducah Ind School Dist** PID: 01007776   806/492-3524
810 Goodwin St, Paducah 79248   Fax 806/492-2432

Schools: 1 \ *Teachers:* 23 \ *Students:* 210 \ *Special Ed Students:* 26 \ *LEP Students:* 3 \ *College-Bound:* 90% \ *Ethnic:* African American 9%, Hispanic 44%, Native American: 1%, Caucasian 47% \ *Exp:* $663 (High) \ *Poverty:* 34% \ *Title I:* $117,456 \ *Open-Close:* 08/19 - 05/26 \ *DTBP:* $294 (High)

Gary Waltman 1   Irene Blount 2
Marty Smith 3   Elisa Love 4
John York .... 6*   Leslie Hutchinson 8*
Denise Ford 11,294,296   Brad Blount 67

Public Schs..Principal	Grd	Prgm	Enr/#Cls	SN	
Paducah Sch 810 Goodwin Street, Paducah 79248 Will Flemons	PK-12	TV	210 50	71%	806/492-2009 Fax 806/492-2193

CRANE COUNTY

CRANE PUBLIC SCHOOLS

● **Crane Ind School Dist** PID: 01007817   432/558-1022
511 W 8th St, Crane 79731   Fax 432/558-1025

Schools: 3 \ *Teachers:* 97 \ *Students:* 1,155 \ *Special Ed Students:* 92 \ *LEP Students:* 173 \ *College-Bound:* 51% \ *Ethnic:* African American 2%, Hispanic 78%, Caucasian 20% \ *Exp:* $459 (High) \ *Poverty:* 15% \ *Title I:* $180,715 \ *Special Education:* $257,000 \ *Open-Close:* 08/19 - 05/21 \ *DTBP:* $350 (High)

Jan Hunt 1   Leigh McCain 2*
Monty King 3,5   Mendy McCarty 4
Maria Hernandez 7   Nicole Jeffery 12,57,88,271
Shelly Garcia 58   Alan Swinford 67
Thomas Valenzuela 73,295

Public Schs..Principal	Grd	Prgm	Enr/#Cls	SN	
Crane Elem Sch 300 W 7th St, Crane 79731 Pamela Hailey	PK-5	T	571 24	58%	432/558-1050 Fax 432/558-1077
Crane High Sch 509 W 8th St, Crane 79731 **Stephen Cross**	9-12		324 30	41%	432/558-1030 Fax 432/558-1056
Crane Middle Sch 302 W 10th St, Crane 79731 **Arick Heredia**	6-8	T	261 20	52%	432/558-1040 Fax 432/558-1046

9 Student Personnel	91 Safety/Security	275 Response To Intervention	298 Grant Writer/Ptnrships	**School Programs**	**Social Media**		
0 Driver Ed/Safety	92 Magnet School	277 Remedial Math K-12	750 Chief Innovation Officer	A = Alternative Program			
1 Gifted/Talented	93 Parental Involvement	280 Literacy Coach	751 Chief of Staff	G = Adult Classes	▉ = Facebook		
3 Video Services	95 Tech Prep Program	285 STEM	752 Social Emotional Learning	M = Magnet Program			
4 Substance Abuse Prev	97 Chief Infomation Officer	286 Digital Learning		T = Title I Schoolwide	▉ = Twitter		
4 Erate	98 Chief Technology Officer	288 Common Core Standards	**Other School Types**	V = Career & Tech Ed Programs			
5 AIDS Education	270 Character Education	294 Accountability	Ⓐ = Alternative School				
8 Alternative/At Risk	271 Migrant Education	295 Network System	Ⓒ = Charter School	New Schools are shaded			
9 Multi-Cultural Curriculum	273 Teacher Mentor	296 Title II Programs	Ⓜ = Magnet School	New Superintendents and Principals are bold			
0 Social Work	274 Before/After Sch	297 Webmaster	Ⓨ = Year-Round School	Personnel with email addresses are underscored			

Crockett County

Market Data Retrieval

CROCKETT COUNTY

CROCKETT PUBLIC SCHOOLS

• **Crockett Co Cons Common SD** PID: 01007855   325/392-5501
797 Avenue D, Ozona 76943   Fax 325/392-5177

Schools: 3 \ **Teachers:** 66 \ **Students:** 758 \ **Special Ed Students:** 60 \ **LEP Students:** 101 \ **College-Bound:** 40% \ **Ethnic:** African American 1%, Hispanic 76%, Native American: 1%, Caucasian 23% \ **Exp:** $323 (High) \ **Poverty:** 25% \ **Title I:** $264,198 \ **Open-Close:** 08/21 - 05/25 \ **DTBP:** $359 (High) \ t

Raul Chavarria 1
Chuy Martinez 3
Anna Martinez 5
Karen Huffman 7,85*
Janina Savala 11,57,288,296,298
Keith Harmsen 73,295
Jason Davis 286*
Lisa Harmsen 2
Ludy Vargus 4
Kyle Freeman 6
Tonya Poindexter 8,69*
Dwight Childress 67
Mari Sanchez 76

Public Schs..Principal	Grd	Prgm	Enr/#Cls	SN	
Ozona Elem Sch 1701 Avenue E, Ozona 76943 Erica Cruz	PK-5	T	388 19	62%	325/392-5501 Fax 325/392-2327
Ozona High Sch 605 Ave E, Ozona 76943 Tamara McWilliams	9-12	ATV	192 30	49%	325/392-5501 Fax 325/392-3125 t
Ozona Middle Sch 502 Avenue G, Ozona 76943 Cash Jennings	6-8	T	178 25	65%	325/392-5501 Fax 325/392-2910

CROSBY COUNTY

CROSBY PUBLIC SCHOOLS

• **Crosbyton Cons Ind Sch Dist** PID: 01007908   806/675-7331
204 S Harrison St, Crosbyton 79322   Fax 806/675-2409

Schools: 2 \ **Teachers:** 37 \ **Students:** 375 \ **Special Ed Students:** 37 \ **LEP Students:** 5 \ **College-Bound:** 90% \ **Ethnic:** African American 4%, Hispanic 68%, Caucasian 28% \ **Exp:** $617 (High) \ **Poverty:** 43% \ **Title I:** $280,631 \ **Open-Close:** 08/19 - 05/21 \ **DTBP:** $348 (High)

Shawn Mason 1
Gary Hamersley 3,5
Colby Huseman 6*
Stacy Mason 11,69,77*
Meredith Caffey 58
Julie Harrington 73,295
Gary Hardin 2
Susan Guerrero 4
Ashley Luna 7,83
Alva Rodriguez 57,271*
Clifford Trull 67

Public Schs..Principal	Grd	Prgm	Enr/#Cls	SN	
Crosbyton Elem Sch 204 S Harrison St, Crosbyton 79322 Sharon West	PK-5	T	165 25	80%	806/675-7331
Crosbyton High Sch 204 S Harrison St, Crosbyton 79322 Hector Dominguez	6-12	TV	195	66%	806/675-7331

• **Lorenzo Ind School Dist** PID: 01007958   806/634-5591
1003 4th Street, Lorenzo 79343   Fax 806/634-5928

Schools: 2 \ **Teachers:** 37 \ **Students:** 250 \ **Special Ed Students:** 41 \ **LEP Students:** 23 \ **College-Bound:** 74% \ **Ethnic:** African American 3%, Hispanic 83%, Caucasian 14% \ **Exp:** $687 (High) \ **Poverty:** 36% \ **Title I:** $166,315 \ **Open-Close:** 08/26 - 05/22 \ **DTBP:** $354 (High)

Kayla Morrisson 1,11
Omar Villegas 3
Amanda Hare 9,274
April Burguss 16,82
Gladice Salinas 57
Brad Aycock 67
Joe Simpson 2
Dee Ware 5
Jessica Crabb 10,273*
Angela Moreno 31,54,69,83*
Kristopher Lamm 58
Danny Thomas 73*

Public Schs..Principal	Grd	Prgm	Enr/#Cls	SN	
Lorenzo Elem Sch 1003 4th Street, Lorenzo 79343 Jessica Crabb	PK-6	T	144 20	80%	806/634-5593 Fax 806/634-8419
Lorenzo Jr Sr High Sch 1003 4th Street, Lorenzo 79343 Jessica Crabb	7-12	T	115 20	72%	806/634-5592 Fax 806/634-5788

• **Ralls Ind School Dist** PID: 01007984   806/253-2509
1082 4th St, Ralls 79357   Fax 806/253-2508

Schools: 4 \ **Teachers:** 53 \ **Students:** 500 \ **Special Ed Students:** 61 \ **LEP Students:** 6 \ **College-Bound:** 59% \ **Ethnic:** African American 1%, Hispanic 76%, Caucasian 24% \ **Exp:** $426 (High) \ **Poverty:** 27% \ **Title I:** $193,424 \ **Open-Close:** 08/15 - 05/20 \ **DTBP:** $332 (High) \ f

Chris Wade 1
Xavier Rangel 6
Macy Cavazos 8,11,57,58,83,288,296,298
Miguel Salizar 10*
Charla Mills 59*
Aunie Sellers 67
Mindy Bolm 77*
Bobby Casias 5
Lori Peredia 7,35,85*
Brenda Prather 10
Juan Calderon 16,73,286,295*
John Burgess 60*
Jill Calderon 68
Angelica Marquez 271

Public Schs..Principal	Grd	Prgm	Enr/#Cls	SN	
Ralls Elem Sch 1401 16th St, Ralls 79357 **Amy Feaster**	PK-5	T	280 18	82%	806/253-2546 Fax 806/253-3112
Ralls High Sch 1106 10th St, Ralls 79357 Miguel Salizar	9-12	AT	129 20	78%	806/253-2571 Fax 806/253-2609
Ralls Middle Sch 1107 10th St, Ralls 79357 Brenda Prather	6-8	T	116 12	86%	806/253-2549 Fax 806/253-4031
ⓐ Recovery Education Campus 1107 Kent St, Ralls 79357 Marshal Herron	9-12	T	5		806/253-2549 Fax 806/253-4031

1	Superintendent	8	Curric/Instruct K-12	19	Chief Financial Officer	29	Family/Consumer Science	39	Social Studies K-12	49	English/Lang Arts Elem	59	Special Education Elem	69	Academic Assessment
2	Bus/Finance/Purchasing	9	Curric/Instruct Elem	20	Art K-12	30	Adult Education	40	Social Studies Elem	50	English/Lang Arts Sec	60	Special Education Sec	70	Research/Development
3	Buildings And Grounds	10	Curric/Instruct Sec	21	Art Elem	31	Career/Sch-to-Work K-12	41	Social Studies Sec	51	Reading K-12	61	Foreign/World Lang K-12	71	Public Information
4	Food Service	11	Federal Program	22	Art Sec	32	Career/Sch-to-Work Elem	42	Science K-12	52	Reading Elem	62	Foreign/World Lang Elem	72	Summer School
5	Transportation	12	Title I	23	Music K-12	33	Career/Sch-to-Work Sec	43	Science Elem	53	Reading Sec	63	Foreign/World Lang Sec	73	Instructional Tech
6	Athletic	13	Title V	24	Music Elem	34	Early Childhood Ed	44	Science Sec	54	Remedial Reading K-12	64	Religious Education K-12	74	Inservice Training
7	Health Services	15	Asst Superintendent	25	Music Sec	35	Health/Phys Education	45	Math K-12	55	Remedial Reading Elem	65	Religious Education Elem	75	Marketing/Distributive
		16	Instructional Media Svcs	26	Business Education	36	Guidance Services K-12	46	Math Elem	56	Remedial Reading Sec	66	Religious Education Sec	76	Info Systems
		17	Chief Operations Officer	27	Career & Tech Ed	37	Guidance Services Elem	47	Math Sec	57	Bilingual/ELL	67	School Board President	77	Psychological Assess
		18	Chief Academic Officer	28	Technology Education	38	Guidance Services Sec	48	English/Lang Arts K-12	58	Special Education K-12	68	Teacher Personnel	78	Affirmative Action

Texas School Directory — Dallas County

CULBERSON COUNTY

CULBERSON PUBLIC SCHOOLS

• **Culberson Co Allamoore Ind SD** PID: 01008029 — 432/283-2245
400 W 7th St, Van Horn 79855 — Fax 432/283-9062

Schools: 1 \ *Teachers:* 36 \ *Students:* 400 \ *Special Ed Students:* 26 \
LEP Students: 30 \ *College-Bound:* 39% \ *Ethnic:* Asian 1%, Hispanic 90%, Caucasian 9% \ *Exp:* $834 (High) \ *Poverty:* 33% \ *Title I:* $187,357 \
Open-Close: 08/26 - 05/28 \ *DTBP:* $372 (High) \ F T

Kenneth Baugh	1	Marcial Gonzalez	3
Marie Borrego	4	Cornelio Garibay	5
Letty Hernandez	67		

Public Schs..Principal	Grd	Prgm	Enr/#Cls	SN	
Van Horn Schools 400 West 7th St, Van Horn 79855 **Charles Gonzalez**	PK-12	T V	400	68%	432/283-2245 F T

DALLAM COUNTY

DALLAM PUBLIC SCHOOLS

• **Dalhart Ind School Dist** PID: 01008067 — 806/244-7810
701 E 10th St, Dalhart 79022 — Fax 806/244-7822

Schools: 4 \ *Teachers:* 131 \ *Students:* 1,700 \ *Special Ed Students:* 149 \ *LEP Students:* 209 \ *College-Bound:* 50% \ *Ethnic:* Asian 1%, African American 1%, Hispanic 58%, Caucasian 40% \ *Exp:* $500 (High) \ *Poverty:* 13% \ *Title I:* $272,151 \ *Special Education:* $330,000 \
Open-Close: 08/14 - 05/22 \ *DTBP:* $339 (High)

Dr Joe Alcorta	1,11	Brian Walter	2,19
Joe Garcia	3	Ernest Fernandez	4
Frank Subeldoa	5*	Joey Read	6*
Sarah Nutter	8	Misty Bornemeier	16,82
Shannon Wilson	16,82	Christy Dovel	38*
David Rivera	58,275	Robert Ledbetter	67
Brad Powell	73,76,84,295	Kurtis Abla	88
Rachael Rivera	271		

Public Schs..Principal	Grd	Prgm	Enr/#Cls	SN	
Dalhart Elem Sch 1401 Tennessee Ave, Dalhart 79022 Claudia Montoya	PK-3	T	607 34	68%	806/244-7350 Fax 806/244-7352
Dalhart High Sch 2100 Spirit Trl, Dalhart 79022 Scot Wright	9-12	T	511 35	39%	806/244-7300 Fax 806/244-7307
Dalhart Intermediate Sch 801 Oak Ave, Dalhart 79022 Misty Heiskell	4-5	T	242 12	66%	806/244-7380 Fax 806/244-7387 F
Dalhart Junior High Sch 1802 E 16th St, Dalhart 79022 Shannon Marshall	6-8	T	392 32	55%	806/244-7825 Fax 806/244-7835

• **Texline Ind School Dist** PID: 01008108 — 806/362-4667
302 E Pine Street, Texline 79087 — Fax 806/362-4538

Schools: 1 \ *Teachers:* 20 \ *Students:* 185 \ *Special Ed Students:* 12 \
LEP Students: 23 \ *College-Bound:* 85% \ *Ethnic:* African American 2%, Hispanic 52%, Native American: 1%, Caucasian 45% \ *Exp:* $1,237 (High) \
Poverty: 11% \ *Title I:* $33,055 \ *Open-Close:* 08/14 - 05/22 \ *DTBP:* $340 (High)

Terrell Jones	1	Debbie Carter	2,84
Stryker Green	5*	Roff Perschbacher	8,12,69,288*
Misty Luther	16,57,82	Misty Luther	16,82*
Becky Claycomb	31,90*	Megan Moore	31,90
Rayanne McGee	31,58*	Jody Bezner	67
Karen Fernandez	271		

Public Schs..Principal	Grd	Prgm	Enr/#Cls	SN	
Texline Sch 302 E Pine Street, Texline 79087 Ross Perschbacher	PK-12	T V	185 16	58%	806/362-4284 Fax 806/362-4938

DALLAM CATHOLIC SCHOOLS

• **Diocese of Amarillo Ed Office** PID: 01047659
Listing includes only schools located in this county. See District Index for location of Diocesan Offices.

Catholic Schs..Principal	Grd	Prgm	Enr/#Cls	SN	
St Anthony's Elem Sch 410 E 13th St, Dalhart 79022 Shay Batenhorst	K-6		113 7		806/244-4811 Fax 806/244-8062 F T

DALLAM PRIVATE SCHOOLS

Private Schs..Principal	Grd	Prgm	Enr/#Cls	SN	
Dalhart Christian Academy 1000 E 16th St, Dalhart 79022 Debbie Dunham	PK-6		98 10		806/244-6482 Fax 806/244-3542
Stateline Christian Sch 220 Hershey Lane, Texline 79087 Errol Smith	1-8		41 5		806/362-4320

DALLAS COUNTY

DALLAS COUNTY SCHOOLS

• **Dallas Co Schools** PID: 02090673 — 214/944-4545
5151 Samuell Blvd, Dallas 75228 — Fax 214/944-4564

Gary Lindsey	1	Paul King	2
Timothy Jones	3	Leigh Giddens	5
Leatha Mullins	15,71	Deanne Hullender	16,70

Codes:
79 Student Personnel | 91 Safety/Security | 275 Response To Intervention | 298 Grant Writer/Ptnrships
80 Driver Ed/Safety | 92 Magnet School | 277 Remedial Math K-12 | 750 Chief Innovation Officer
81 Gifted/Talented | 93 Parental Involvement | 280 Literacy Coach | 751 Chief of Staff
82 Video Services | 95 Tech Prep Program | 285 STEM | 752 Social Emotional Learning
83 Substance Abuse Prev | 97 Chief Infomation Officer | 286 Digital Learning
84 Erate | 98 Chief Technology Officer | 288 Common Core Standards
85 AIDS Education | 270 Character Education | 294 Accountability
88 Alternative/At Risk | 271 Migrant Education | 295 Network System
89 Multi-Cultural Curriculum | 273 Teacher Mentor | 296 Title II Programs
90 Social Work | 274 Before/After Sch | 297 Webmaster

School Programs: A = Alternative Program | G = Adult Classes | M = Magnet Program | T = Title I Schoolwide | V = Career & Tech Ed Programs

Other School Types: A = Alternative School | C = Charter School | M = Magnet School | Y = Year-Round School

Social Media: F = Facebook | T = Twitter

New Schools are shaded
New Superintendents and Principals are bold
Personnel with email addresses are underscored

TX—95

Dallas County

Gloria Levario 67
Michael Rogger 73

Jerry Martinez 68
Scott Peters 74,77,91

County Schs..Principal	Grd	Prgm	Enr/#Cls	SN	
Ⓐ Dallas Co Jj Aae-Letot Ctr © 10505 Denton Dr, Dallas 75220 Marilena Zuppardo	6-12	T	50	89%	214/956-2036 Fax 214/956-2010
Ⓐ Dallas Co Jj Aae-SAU © 414 S R L Thornton Fwy, Dallas 75203 Jacqueline Bluitt	6-12	T	50	93%	214/860-4370 Fax 214/860-4490
Ⓐ Dallas Co Jj CS-Drc Campus © 1673 Terre Colony Ct, Dallas 75212 Daniel Guillary	6-12	T	110	92%	214/637-6136 Fax 214/637-6779
© Dallas Co Jj CS-Main Camp 1673 Terre Colony Ct, Dallas 75212 Sheterric Malone	5-12	T	175		214/637-6136 Fax 214/637-6130
Ⓐ Dallas Co Jj CS-Medlock © 1508 E Langdon Rd Ste A, Dallas 75241 Aubrey Hooper	6-12		150 8		972/225-9735 Fax 972/225-9763
Ⓐ Dallas Co Jj CS-Youth Village © 1508 E Langdon Rd, Dallas 75241 Aubrey Hooper	5-12		72		972/225-9735 Fax 972/225-9737

DALLAS PUBLIC SCHOOLS

• **Advantage Academy Admin Office**   PID: 11824891   214/276-5800
618 W Wheatland Rd, Duncanville 75116   Fax 214/276-5890

Schools: 4 \ **Teachers:** 99 \ **Students:** 1,650 \ **Special Ed Students:** 95 \
LEP Students: 390 \ **Ethnic:** Asian 1%, African American 22%, Hispanic 63%,
Caucasian 14% \ **Open-Close:** 08/29 - 06/01

Angela McDonald 1
Kevin McDonald 3,5,17
Stella Sisneros 4
Stephanie DeLuna 57
Marie Cox 68
Marco Salazar 73,76,286,295
Denise Clevenger 280

Wilma Mallory-Sneed 2,11,19,298
Manuel Ruiz 3
Aimee Cooper 8
Lisa Lanham 58,88,752
Sherri Busalacchi 71
Tammy Bailey 79

Public Schs..Principal	Grd	Prgm	Enr/#Cls	SN	
© Advantage Acad-Grand Prairie E 300 W Pioneer Pkwy, Grand Prairie 75051 Roy Watts	8-12	V	150		214/276-5800 Fax 972/237-7927
© Advantage Acad-Grand Prairie W 955 Freetown Rd, Grand Prairie 75051 Beverly Compton	PK-8	T	750	75%	214/276-5800 Fax 972/602-2212
© Advantage Acad-N Duncanville 4009 Joseph Hardin Dr, Dallas 75236 Donita White	PK-8	AV	500		214/276-5800 Fax 214/467-2510
© Advantage Academy-Waxahachie 701 W 287 Bypass, Waxahachie 75165 Aimee Barnes	PK-8		335 20		972/937-9851 Fax 972/937-9876

• **Carrollton-Farmers Branch ISD**   PID: 01008134   972/968-6100
1445 N Perry Rd, Carrollton 75006   Fax 972/968-6217

Schools: 37 \ **Teachers:** 1,674 \ **Students:** 26,000 \
Special Ed Students: 2,752 \ **LEP Students:** 6,702 \ **College-Bound:** 55%
\ **Ethnic:** Asian 11%, African American 17%, Hispanic 58%, Caucasian
14% \ **Exp:** $260 (Med) \ **Poverty:** 12% \ **Title I:** $5,067,780 \
Special Education: $4,553,000 \ **Open-Close:** 08/19 - 05/28 \ **DTBP:** $191
(High) \

Dr John Chapman 1
Vicki Pippin 2
Pat Hester 3,17,274
David Hanna 5
Sandra Lieck 7
Dr Pat Franklin 9,93
Michelle Bailey 10,15,79
Kimberly Guinn 12,69,294
Scott Monroe 16,73,76,295
Jo Gillen 27,31,36,69,77,83,88,270
Michael Ramirez 35
Susan Shipp 42,280,285
Tonya Garvey 47
Randi Wells 58
Asheley Brown 68,84
Kathryn Schaeffer 69,81
Trudy Kelly 71
Shelly Gammon 297

Scott Rodrick 2,19
Malcolm Mulroney 3,17
Rachelle Sherrin 4
Renee Putter 6,35
Georgeann Warnock 8,15,74,286
Tracy Smith 9,15,275
Tonya Tillman 11,15
Dr Derrell Coleman 15,751
Brett Farr 20,23
Susan Kelly 34,54
Pier Larsen 39
Karen Spaulding 46,277
Olivia Perez 57,61,89,271
Nancy Cline 67
Jason Liewehr 68
Pam Pena 71
Mario De La Rosa 91

Public Schs..Principal	Grd	Prgm	Enr/#Cls	SN	
Annie Rainwater Elem Sch 1408 E Frankford Rd, Carrollton 75007 Charlotte Thomas	K-5	T	331 25	56%	972/968-2800 Fax 972/968-2810
Barbara Bush Middle Sch 515 Cowboys Pkwy, Irving 75063 Matt Warnock	6-8	T	689 60	55%	972/968-3700 Fax 972/968-3710
Ⓐ Bea Salazar Sch 2416 Keller Springs Rd, Carrollton 75006 Melissa Wesley	K-12	T	150 12	78%	972/968-5900 Fax 972/968-5910
Bernice Chatman Freeman ES 8757 Valley Ranch Pkwy W, Irving 75063 Robyn Campbell	PK-5	T	630	34%	972/968-1700 Fax 972/968-1710
Carrollton Elem Sch 1805 Pearl St, Carrollton 75006 Monica Koen	PK-5	T	591 25	91%	972/968-1200 Fax 972/968-1210
Central Elem Sch 1600 S Perry Rd, Carrollton 75006 Luz Soto-Dimas	PK-5	T	581 21	90%	972/968-1300 Fax 972/968-1310
Charles M Blalack Middle Sch 1706 E Peters Colony Rd, Carrollton 75007 Keith Davis	6-8	T	969 85	53%	972/968-3500 Fax 972/968-3510
Charlie C McKamy Elem Sch 3443 Briargrove Ln, Dallas 75287 Matthew Pruitt	PK-5	T	474 29	71%	972/968-2400 Fax 972/968-2410
Country Place Elem Sch 2115 Raintree Dr, Carrollton 75006 Kimberly Chow-Jackson	PK-5	T	412 20	43%	972/968-1400 Fax 972/968-1410
Creekview High Sch 3201 Old Denton Rd, Carrollton 75007 Joe Lapuma	9-12	T	1,926	48%	972/968-4800 Fax 972/968-4810
Dale B Davis Elem Sch 3205 Dorchester Dr, Carrollton 75007 Lisa Williams	K-5	T	535 26	84%	972/968-1500 Fax 972/968-1510
Dan F Long Middle Sch 2525 Frankford Rd, Dallas 75287 Charde Dockery	6-8	TV	623 70	77%	972/968-4100 Fax 972/968-4110
Dave Blair Elem Sch 14055 Heartside Pl, Farmers BRNCH 75234 Jose Ramos	K-5	T	554 47	87%	972/968-1000 Fax 972/968-1010
DeWitt Perry Middle Sch 1709 E Belt Line Rd, Carrollton 75006 Adam Toy	6-8	TV	1,030 60	78%	972/968-4400 Fax 972/968-4410
E L Kent Elem Sch 1800 W Rosemeade Pkwy, Carrollton 75007 Debbie Williams	K-5	T	377 22	38%	972/968-2000 Fax 972/968-2010
Early College High Sch 3939 Valley View Ln Bldg P, Dallas 75244 Timothy Isaly	9-12	TV	330 9	82%	972/968-6200 Fax 972/968-6270

1 Superintendent	8 Curric/Instruct K-12	19 Chief Financial Officer	29 Family/Consumer Science	39 Social Studies K-12	49 English/Lang Arts Elem	59 Special Education Elem	69 Academic Assessment
2 Bus/Finance/Purchasing	9 Curric/Instruct Elem	20 Art K-12	30 Adult Education	40 Social Studies Elem	50 English/Lang Arts Sec	60 Special Education Sec	70 Research/Development
3 Buildings And Grounds	10 Curric/Instruct Sec	21 Art Elem	31 Career/Sch-to-Work K-12	41 Social Studies Sec	51 Reading K-12	61 Foreign/World Lang K-12	71 Public Information
4 Food Service	11 Federal Program	22 Art Sec	32 Career/Sch-to-Work Elem	42 Science K-12	52 Reading Elem	62 Foreign/World Lang Elem	72 Summer School
5 Transportation	12 Title I	23 Music K-12	33 Career/Sch-to-Work Sec	43 Science Elem	53 Reading Sec	63 Foreign/World Lang Sec	73 Instructional Tech
6 Athletic	13 Title V	24 Music Elem	34 Early Childhood Ed	44 Science Sec	54 Remedial Reading K-12	64 Religious Education K-12	74 Inservice Training
7 Health Services	15 Asst Superintendent	25 Music Sec	35 Health/Phys Education	45 Math K-12	55 Remedial Reading Elem	65 Religious Education Elem	75 Marketing/Distributive
	16 Instructional Media Svcs	26 Business Education	36 Guidance Services K-12	46 Math Elem	56 Remedial Reading Sec	66 Religious Education Sec	76 Info Systems
	17 Chief Operations Officer	27 Career & Tech Ed	37 Guidance Services Elem	47 Math Sec	57 Bilingual/ELL	67 School Board President	77 Psychological Assess
	18 Chief Academic Officer	28 Technology Education	38 Guidance Services Sec	48 English/Lang Arts K-12	58 Special Education K-12	68 Teacher Personnel	78 Affirmative Action

Texas School Directory — Dallas County

School	Grd	Prgm	Enr/#Cls		Phone
Farmers Branch Elem Sch 13521 Tom Field Rd, Farmers BRNCH 75234 Shanah Brown	PK-5	T	550 60	86%	972/968-1600 Fax 972/968-1610
Furneaux Elem Sch 3210 Furneaux Ln, Carrollton 75007 Lori Parker	K-5	T	296 18	59%	972/968-1800 Fax 972/968-1810
Janie Stark Elem Sch 12400 Josey Ln, Farmers BRNCH 75234 **Jennifer Putman**	PK-5	T	745 31	51%	972/968-3300 Fax 972/968-3310
June R Thompson Elem Sch 2915 Scott Mill Rd, Carrollton 75007 Robert Atchison	PK-5	T	541 24	68%	972/968-3400 Fax 972/968-3410
Kathryn S McWhorter Elem Sch 3678 Timberglen Rd, Dallas 75287 Eddie Reed	PK-5	T	589 30	88%	972/968-2600 Fax 972/968-2610
L F Blanton Elem Sch 2525 Scott Mill Rd, Carrollton 75006 **Patricia Badillo**	PK-5	T	419 28	81%	972/968-1100 Fax 972/968-1110
La Villita Elem Sch 1601 Camino Lago, Irving 75039 Dreama Mayfield	K-5		755	20%	972/968-6900 Fax 972/968-6910
Las Colinas Elem Sch 2200 Kinwest Pkwy, Irving 75063 Ahveance Jones	PK-5	T	549 30	22%	972/968-2200 Fax 972/968-2210
Ⓐ Mary Grimes Education Center 1745 Hutton Dr, Carrollton 75006 Jose Ramos	11-12	TV	53 15	51%	972/968-5600 Fax 972/968-5610
McCoy Elem Sch 2425 McCoy Rd, Carrollton 75006 Dawn Rink	K-5	T	441 23	36%	972/968-2300 Fax 972/968-2310
Newman Smith High Sch 2335 N Josey Ln, Carrollton 75006 Michael Arreola	9-12	TV	1,955	64%	972/968-5200 Fax 972/968-5210
R E Good Elem Sch 1012 Study Ln, Carrollton 75006 Shahnaj Ahmad	PK-5	T	527 27	82%	972/968-1900 Fax 972/968-1910
R L Turner High Sch 1600 S Josey Ln, Carrollton 75006 **Jennifer Hall**	9-12	TV	2,048 175	68%	972/968-5400 Fax 972/968-5410
Ranchview High Sch 8401 Valley Ranch Pkwy E, Irving 75063 Sherie Skruch	9-12	TV	878	48%	972/968-5000 Fax 972/968-5010
Riverchase Elem Sch 272 S MacArthur Blvd, Coppell 75019 Pamela Henderson	PK-5	T	358 22	44%	972/968-2900 Fax 972/968-2910
Rosemeade Elem Sch 3550 Kimberly Dr, Carrollton 75007 Laura Gutierrez	PK-5	T	445 19	45%	972/968-3000 Fax 972/968-3010
Sheffield Primary Elem Sch 18111 Kelly Blvd, Dallas 75287 Amy Miller	K-5	T	755 24	84%	972/968-3100 Fax 972/968-3110
Strickland Elem Sch 330 Fyke Rd, Farmers BRNCH 75234 Dianna Madrid-Lacy	K-5	T	600 22	83%	972/968-2500 Fax 972/968-2510
Ted Polk Middle Sch 2001 Kelly Blvd, Carrollton 75006 Kelly O'Sullivan	6-8	TV	1,061 30	71%	972/968-4600 Fax 972/968-4610
Tom Landry Elem Sch 265 Red River Trl, Irving 75063 Stephanie Lopez	PK-5	TV	335 25	70%	972/968-2100 Fax 972/968-2110
Vivian Field Middle Sch 13551 Dennis Ln, Farmers BRNCH 75234 **Chad Hunter**	6-8	TV	1,006	81%	972/968-3900 Fax 972/968-3910

• **Cedar Hill Ind School Dist** PID: 01008275   972/291-1581
285 Uptown Blvd Ste 300, Cedar Hill 75104   Fax 972/291-5231

Schools: 14 \ *Teachers:* 482 \ *Students:* 7,866 \ *Special Ed Students:* 658 \ *LEP Students:* 536 \ *College-Bound:* 55% \ *Ethnic:* Asian 1%, African American 69%, Hispanic 24%, Caucasian 5% \ *Exp:* $471 (High) \ *Poverty:* 14% \ *Title I:* $1,901,331 \ *Special Education:* $1,097,000 \ *Open-Close:* 08/14 - 05/22 \ *DTBP:* $204 (High) \ 🅵 🆃

Dr Gerald Hudson 1	Sherra McGane 2
Josh Skains 3	Jimmy Blades 5
Gina Farmer 6	Pamela Reese-Taylor 7*
Dr Charlotte Ford 8	Dr Darryl Henson 15
Kellie Spencer 15	Tellunce Graham 15,79
Violet Dean 15,68,74,78	Gilberto Prado 19
Tysha Lowe 27,31	Tracey Willyard 28,73,95
Lakimberly Wilson 46	Nicole Rose 47
Patrice Woodson 49	Holly Cunningham 58
Jennifer Lonsford 58	Cheryl Wesley 67
Bryan Ward 69	Jamie Brown 71
Neil Bolton 76,295	Chris Santos 91
Jimmy Hogg 91	Danyell Wells 93
Tierney Tinnin 97	

Public Schs..Principal	Grd	Prgm	Enr/#Cls		SN
Besse Coleman Middle Sch 1208 E Pleasant Run Rd, Cedar Hill 75104 Norman Jones	6-8	T	778	72%	972/293-4505 Fax 469/272-9445
Bray Elem Sch 218 N Broad St, Cedar Hill 75104 Eric Barnes	PK-5	T	272 14	71%	972/291-4231 Fax 972/291-6098
Cedar Hill 9th Grade Center 1515 W Belt Line Rd, Cedar Hill 75104 Zandra Webb	9-9	T	575	69%	469/272-2050 Fax 469/272-3443
Cedar Hill Collegiate High Sch 1533 High Pointe Ln, Cedar Hill 75104 **Deidrea Stevens**	9-12	T	403	45%	469/272-2021 Fax 469/272-3445
Cedar Hill High Sch 1 Longhorn Blvd, Cedar Hill 75104 **Jason Miller**	10-12	GTV	1,707	63%	469/272-2000 Fax 972/293-7125
Collegiate Academy Middle Sch 1533 High Pointe Ln, Cedar Hill 75104 Heath Koenig	6-8		302 40		469/272-2021 Fax 972/291-0646
Collegiate Prep Academy 975 Pickard Dr, Cedar Hill 75104 Shay Whittaker	PK-5	T	484	44%	972/293-4502 Fax 972/291-5213
Ⓐ Discipline Alt Education Pgrm 1515 W Belt Line Rd, Cedar Hill 75104 Patrick Nash	K-12		50 8		972/293-4504 Fax 972/291-7160
High Pointe Elem Sch 1351 High Pointe Ln, Cedar Hill 75104 Shay Whittaker	PK-5	T	486 26	79%	972/291-7874 Fax 972/291-5695
Highlands Elem Sch 131 Sims Dr, Cedar Hill 75104 Damian Patton	PK-5	T	654 40	78%	972/291-0496 Fax 972/291-5764
Lake Ridge Elem Sch 1020 Lake Ridge Pkwy, Cedar Hill 75104 **Marquita McCullum**	PK-5	T	328	72%	972/293-4501 Fax 972/291-5210
Plummer Elem Sch 1203 S Clark Rd, Cedar Hill 75104 Rickyl Wesson	PK-5	T	597 25	81%	972/291-4058 Fax 972/291-4980
W S Permenter Middle Sch 431 W Parkerville Rd, Cedar Hill 75104 Tonya Haddox	6-8	TV	820	76%	972/291-5270 Fax 972/291-5296
Waterford Oaks Elem Sch 401 N Waterford Oaks Dr, Cedar Hill 75104 **Bill Phillips**	PK-5	T	565 26	73%	972/291-5290 Fax 972/293-2381

---

79 Student Personnel	91 Safety/Security	275 Response To Intervention	298 Grant Writer/Ptnrships	**School Programs**	**Social Media**
80 Driver Ed/Safety	92 Magnet School	277 Remedial Math K-12	750 Chief Innovation Officer	A = Alternative Program	
81 Gifted/Talented	93 Parental Involvement	280 Literacy Coach	751 Chief of Staff	G = Adult Classes	🅵 = Facebook
82 Video Services	95 Tech Prep Program	285 STEM	752 Social Emotional Learning	M = Magnet Program	
83 Substance Abuse Prev	97 Chief Information Officer	286 Digital Learning		T = Title I Schoolwide	🆃 = Twitter
84 Erate	98 Chief Technology Officer	288 Common Core Standards	**Other School Types**	V = Career & Tech Ed Programs	
85 AIDS Education	270 Character Education	294 Accountability	Ⓐ = Alternative School		
88 Alternative/At Risk	271 Migrant Education	295 Network System	Ⓒ = Charter School	New Schools are shaded	
89 Multi-Cultural Curriculum	273 Teacher Mentor	296 Title II Programs	Ⓜ = Magnet School	New Superintendents and Principals are bold	
90 Social Work	274 Before/After Sch	297 Webmaster	Ⓨ = Year-Round School	Personnel with email addresses are underscored	

Dallas County — Market Data Retrieval

- **Coppell Ind School Dist** PID: 01008328 214/496-6000
  200 S Denton Tap Rd, Coppell 75019 Fax 214/496-6036

Schools: 18 \ *Teachers:* 750 \ *Students:* 13,500 \ *Special Ed Students:* 688 \ *LEP Students:* 1,223 \ *College-Bound:* 61% \ *Ethnic:* Asian 45%, African American 4%, Hispanic 14%, Caucasian 36% \ *Exp:* $237 (Med) \ *Poverty:* 4% \ *Title I:* $308,154 \ *Special Education:* $1,360,000 \ *Open-Close:* 08/14 - 05/21 \ *DTBP:* $173 (High) \

Name	#	Name	#
Brad Hunt	1	Diana Sircar	2,19
Justin Hill	2	Genaro Lopez	3,5,91
Jean Mosley	4	Kit Pehl	6*
Dr Angie Applegate	8,15,69	Laurie O'Neill	11,298
Kristen Streeter	15,68,79	Sid Grant	15
Evan Whitfield	42	Mary Kemper	45
Patricia Cheatham	57	Stephanie Flores	58
Thom Hulme	67	Kelly Mires	68
Amanda Simpson	71,97	Tamerah Ringo	71
Nancy Garvey	73,286	Steven McGilvary	73,98
Brooke Sims	74*	Angela Brown	75
Carol Freese	76	Janice Duffney	76
Kathy Creek	76	Todd Sissom	76
Deana Dynis	81	Debbie Gauntt	275
Anita Delaisla	280		

Public Schs..Principal	Grd	Prgm	Enr/#Cls	SN	Phone
Barbara S Austin Elem Sch 161 S Moore Rd, Coppell 75019 Lorie Squalls	PK-5	T	716 28	12%	214/496-7300 Fax 214/496-7306
Canyon Ranch Elem Sch 1205 Santa Fe Tr, Irving 75063 Ashley Minton	K-5		700		214/496-7200
Coppell High Sch 185 W Parkway Blvd, Coppell 75019 Laura Springer	10-12	V	3,000 110	10%	214/496-6100 Fax 214/496-6166
Coppell HS 9th Grade 1301 Wrangler Cir, Coppell 75019 Cody Koontz	9-9		925		214/496-3800
Coppell Middle School East 400 Mockingbird Ln, Coppell 75019 Steve Glover	6-8	V	972 60	8%	214/496-6600 Fax 214/496-6603
Coppell Middle School North 120 Natches Trce, Coppell 75019 Greg Axelson	6-8	V	949 60	9%	214/496-7100 Fax 214/496-7103
Coppell Middle School West 2701 Ranch Trail, Coppell 75019 Emily Froese	6-8	TV	1,206 55	11%	214/496-8600 Fax 214/496-8606
Cottonwood Creek Elem Sch 615 Minyard Dr, Coppell 75019 Dr Andra Penny	PK-5		499 26	3%	214/496-8300 Fax 214/496-8306
Denton Creek Elem Sch 250 Natches Trce, Coppell 75019 Shannon Edwards	PK-5	T	464 23	13%	214/496-8100 Fax 214/496-8106
Lakeside Elem Sch 1100 Village Pkwy, Coppell 75019 Gema Hall	PK-5		528 20	1%	214/496-7600 Fax 214/496-7606
Mockingbird Elem Sch 300 Mockingbird Ln, Coppell 75019 Laura Flynn	PK-5		515 25	8%	214/496-8200 Fax 214/496-8206
New Tech High Sch-Coppell 113 Samuel Blvd, Coppell 75019 Steffany Batik	9-12		317	9%	214/496-5900 Fax 214/496-5906
Richard J Lee Elem Sch Olympus Blvd & Ranch Tr, Irving 75063 Chantel Kastorunis	PK-5		824	7%	214/496-7900 Fax 214/496-7906
Town Center Elem Sch 185 N Heartz Rd, Coppell 75019 Jennifer Martin	PK-5	T	582 23	11%	214/496-7800 Fax 214/496-7806
Valley Ranch Elem Sch 9800 Rodeo Dr, Irving 75063 Cynthia Arterbery	PK-5		627 20	4%	214/496-8500 Fax 214/496-8506
Victory Place at Coppell 550 N Denton Tap Rd, Coppell 75019 Jeff Minn	6-12		50 2		214/496-8032 Fax 214/496-8027
W H Wilson Elem Sch 200 S Coppell Rd, Coppell 75019 Cooper Hilton	PK-5	T	476	28%	214/496-7500 Fax 214/496-7506
W W Pinkerton Elem Sch 260 Southwestern Blvd, Coppell 75019 Kristi Mikkelsen	PK-5		420 18	3%	214/496-6800 Fax 214/496-6806

- **Dallas Ind School Dist** PID: 01008354 972/925-3700
  9400 N Central Expy, Dallas 75231 Fax 972/925-3701

Schools: 230 \ *Teachers:* 10,508 \ *Students:* 156,100 \ *Special Ed Students:* 11,846 \ *LEP Students:* 63,835 \ *College-Bound:* 78% \ *Ethnic:* Asian 1%, African American 22%, Hispanic 71%, Caucasian 5% \ *Exp:* $390 (High) \ *Poverty:* 27% \ *Title I:* $92,211,397 \ *Special Education:* $23,695,000 \ *Open-Close:* 08/19 - 05/27 \ *DTBP:* $194 (High) \

Name	#	Name	#
Dr Michael Hinojosa	1	Coy Frazier	3
Scott Layne	3,17	Michael Rosenberger	4
Cassandra Behr	5	Troy Mathieu	6
Jennifer Finley	7	Ivonne Durant	8,18
Vicente Reyes	8,15	Sequetta Marks	11
Dr Cecilia Oakeley	15,69,70,294	Israel Cordero	15
Sherry Christian	15,88	Gay Patrick	16
Dwayne Thompson	19	Tim Linley	20,23
Richard Grimsley	27,31	Alan Cohen	34
Barbara Johnson	35	Dr Sylvia Lopez	36
Shalon Bond	39	Jenny Christian	42
Stej Sanchez	45	Arlena Gaynor	48,51
Cloris Rangel	57	Tanya Browne	58
Amy Anderton	61	Justin Henry	67
Dr Diedrae Bell-Hunter	68	Billy Snow	70,750
Dr Cynthia Wilson	71,97*	Toni Cordova	71
Crystal Rentz	72	Jack Kelanic	73,98*
Roland Antoine	73,76,295	Angie Gaylord	74
George Mallick	76	Dr Connie Rodriguez	77,90
Erik Nickerson	79	Craig Miller	91
Nancy Rubio	92	Charissa Govan	275
Michelle Brown	280	Oswaldo Alvarenga	285
Jacquelyn Cumby	286	Brian Reed	297
Pamela Lear	751		

Public Schs..Principal	Grd	Prgm	Enr/#Cls	SN	Phone
Adelfa Botello Callejo ES 7817 Military Pkwy, Dallas 75227 Sandra Fernandez	PK-5	T	663	96%	972/892-5700 Fax 972/892-5701
Adelle Turner Elem Sch 5505 S Polk St, Dallas 75232 Michael Nickson	PK-5	T	292 24	85%	972/794-6300 Fax 972/794-6301
Alex Sanger Elem Sch 8410 San Leandro Dr, Dallas 75218 Hector Martinez	PK-8	T	652 27	83%	972/749-7600 Fax 972/749-7601
Alex W Spence Middle Sch & Tag 4001 Capitol Ave, Dallas 75204 Shanna Jones	6-8	TV	735 60	89%	972/925-2300 Fax 972/925-2301
Ann Richards Steam Academy 3831 N Prairie Creek Rd, Dallas 75227 Natasha Shaw	6-8	TV	1,324	91%	972/892-5400 Fax 972/892-5401
Anne Frank Elem Sch 5201 Celestial Rd, Dallas 75254 Beverly Ford	PK-5	T	1,145 55	79%	972/502-5900 Fax 972/502-5901

#	Key	#	Key	#	Key	#	Key	#	Key	#	Key	#	Key
1	Superintendent	8	Curric/Instruct K-12	19	Chief Financial Officer	29	Family/Consumer Science	39	Social Studies K-12	49	English/Lang Arts Elem	59	Special Education Elem	69	Academic Assessment
2	Bus/Finance/Purchasing	9	Curric/Instruct Elem	20	Art K-12	30	Adult Education	40	Social Studies Elem	50	English/Lang Arts Sec	60	Special Education Sec	70	Research/Development
3	Buildings And Grounds	10	Curric/Instruct Sec	21	Art Elem	31	Career/Sch-to-Work K-12	41	Social Studies Sec	51	Reading K-12	61	Foreign/World Lang K-12	71	Public Information
4	Food Service	11	Federal Program	22	Art Sec	32	Career/Sch-to-Work Elem	42	Science K-12	52	Reading Elem	62	Foreign/World Lang Elem	72	Summer School
5	Transportation	12	Title I	23	Music K-12	33	Career/Sch-to-Work Sec	43	Science Elem	53	Reading Sec	63	Foreign/World Lang Sec	73	Instructional Tech
6	Athletic	13	Title V	24	Music Elem	34	Early Childhood Ed	44	Science Sec	54	Remedial Reading K-12	64	Religious Education K-12	74	Inservice Training
7	Health Services	15	Asst Superintendent	25	Music Sec	35	Health/Phys Education	45	Math K-12	55	Remedial Reading Elem	65	Religious Education Elem	75	Marketing/Distributive
		16	Instructional Media Svcs	26	Business Education	36	Guidance Services K-12	46	Math Elem	56	Remedial Reading Sec	66	Religious Education Sec	76	Info Systems
		17	Chief Operations Officer	27	Career & Tech Ed	37	Guidance Services Elem	47	Math Sec	57	Bilingual/ELL	67	School Board President	77	Psychological Assess
		18	Chief Academic Officer	28	Technology Education	38	Guidance Services Sec	48	English/Lang Arts K-12	58	Special Education K-12	68	Teacher Personnel	78	Affirmative Action

Texas School Directory — Dallas County

School	Grades	Prog	Enroll/Staff	%	Phone/Fax
Annie Webb Blanton Elem Sch 8915 Greenmound Ave, Dallas 75227 Alicia Iwasko	PK-5	T	669 40	92%	972/794-1700 Fax 972/794-1701
Anson Jones Elem Sch 3901 Meredith Ave, Dallas 75211 Guillermo Cortez	PK-5	T	603 55	96%	972/794-4700 Fax 972/794-4701
Arcadia Park Elem Sch 1300 N Justin Ave, Dallas 75211 Kelly Ohara-Sanchez	PK-5	T	652 30	96%	972/502-5300 Fax 972/502-5301
Arlington Park ECC 5606 Wayside Dr, Dallas 75235 **Mary Molinares**	PK-PK		150		972/749-5500
Arthur Kramer Elem Sch 7131 Midbury Dr, Dallas 75230 Kate Walker	PK-5	T	615 25	68%	972/794-8300 Fax 972/794-8301
Arturo Salazar Elem Sch 1120 S Ravinia Dr, Dallas 75211 Nicole Bixby	PK-5	T	614	95%	972/502-1800 Fax 972/502-1801
Ascher Silberstein Elem Sch 5940 Hollis Ave, Dallas 75227 Richard Heffernan	PK-5	T	738 40	95%	972/794-1900 Fax 972/794-1901
B H Macon Elem Sch 650 Holcomb Rd, Dallas 75217 Antonio Verduzco	PK-5	T	528 32	94%	972/794-1500 Fax 972/794-1501
Ⓜ B T Washington Perform Arts HS 2501 Flora St, Dallas 75201 Scott Rudes	9-12	V	1,002 45	24%	972/925-1200 Fax 972/925-1201
Ⓜ Barack Obama Male Ldrshp Acad 3030 Stag Rd, Dallas 75241 David Welch	6-12		247		972/749-2100 Fax 972/749-2101 f t
Barbara Jordan Elem Sch 1111 W Kiest Blvd, Dallas 75224 Lucy Hopkins	PK-5	T	613 50	98%	972/925-8100 Fax 972/925-8101
Bayles Elem Sch 2444 Telegraph Ave, Dallas 75228 Gloria Kennedy	PK-5	T	545 55	98%	972/749-8900 Fax 972/749-8901
Ben Milam Elem Sch 4200 McKinney Ave, Dallas 75205 Anna Galvan	PK-5	T	293	88%	972/749-5600 Fax 972/749-5601
Benjamin Franklin Middle Sch 6920 Meadow Rd, Dallas 75230 Roger Ceballos	6-8	T	1,035 60	80%	972/502-7100 Fax 972/502-7101
Billy Earl Dade Middle Sch 2727 Al Lipscomb Way, Dallas 75215 **Rockell Stewart**	6-8	T	894 28	100%	972/749-3800 Fax 972/749-3801
Birdie Alexander Elem Sch 1830 Goldwood Dr, Dallas 75232 Valarie Kendrick	PK-5	T	373 20	78%	972/749-3100 Fax 972/749-3101
Boude Storey Middle Sch 3000 Maryland Ave, Dallas 75216 Jacqueline Rivers	6-8	TV	589 63	99%	972/925-8700 Fax 972/925-8701
Bryan Adams High Sch 2101 Millmar Dr, Dallas 75228 Ryan Bott	9-12	TV	2,029	89%	972/502-4900 Fax 972/502-4901
C A Tatum Elem Sch 3002 N Saint Augustine Dr, Dallas 75227 Enrique Rodriguez	K-5	T	514	98%	972/502-2000 Fax 972/502-2001
C F Carr Elem Sch 1952 Bayside St, Dallas 75212 Carlotta Hooks	PK-5	T	559 27	92%	972/794-4300 Fax 972/794-4301
Casa View Elem Sch 2100 N Farola Dr, Dallas 75228 Thania Garibay	PK-5	T	715	90%	972/749-7700 Fax 972/749-7701
Cedar Crest Elem Sch 2020 Mouser Ln, Dallas 75203 **Constance Jawaid**	PK-5	T	410 37	91%	972/925-7400 Fax 972/925-7401 f t
Celestino Mauricio Soto ES 4510 W Jefferson Blvd, Dallas 75211 **Norma Barrayam**	PK-5	T	588	94%	972/502-5100 Fax 972/502-5101
Central Elem Sch 902 Shady Ln, Seagoville 75159 Julie Singleton	PK-5	T	587 28	88%	972/749-6800 Fax 972/749-6801
Cesar Chavez Learning Center 1710 N Carroll Ave, Dallas 75204 **Sheryl Wilson**	PK-5	T	470 60	96%	972/925-1000 Fax 972/925-1001
Chapel Hill Preparatory Sch 12701 Templeton Trl, Dallas 75234 Fabian Hypolite	PK-5	T	512 40	93%	972/794-2400 Fax 972/794-2401
Charles A Gill Elem Sch 10910 Ferguson Rd, Dallas 75228 Shawki Freelon	PK-5	T	892 65	90%	972/749-8400 Fax 972/749-8401
Charles Rice Learning Center 2425 Pine St, Dallas 75215 Jennifer Atkins	PK-5	T	511	95%	972/749-1100 Fax 972/749-1101
City Lab High Sch 912 S Ervay St, Dallas 75201 Lynn Smith	9-9		80		972/749-2700
Clara Oliver Elem Sch 4010 Idaho Ave, Dallas 75216 Cheryl Freeman	PK-5	T	311 15	90%	972/749-3400 Fax 972/749-3401
Clinton P Russell Elem Sch 3031 S Beckley Ave, Dallas 75224 Gerald Bennett	PK-5	T	732 17	93%	972/925-8300 Fax 972/925-8301
D A Hulcy Steam Middle Sch 9339 S Polk St, Dallas 75232 Jonica Lockwood	6-8	T	532	85%	214/932-7400
Ⓜ Dallas Environmental Sci Acad 3531 N Westmoreland Rd, Dallas 75212 **Aris Rider**	6-8	TV	443 6	88%	972/794-3950 Fax 972/794-3951
Dan D Rogers Elem Sch 5314 Abrams Rd, Dallas 75214 **Marissa Limon**	PK-5	T	503 50	78%	972/794-8800 Fax 972/794-8801
Daniel Webster Elem Sch 3815 S Franklin St, Dallas 75233 Clement Alexander	PK-5	T	530 40	94%	972/794-6100 Fax 972/794-6101
David G Burnet Elem Sch 3200 Kinkaid Dr, Dallas 75220 Sonia Loskot	PK-5	T	702 55	99%	972/794-3000 Fax 972/794-3001
David W Carter High Sch 1819 W Wheatland Rd, Dallas 75232 Jonathan Smith	9-12	TV	1,135 79	73%	214/932-5700 Fax 214/932-5701
Ⓐ Dr Wright Lassiter Erly Clg HS 801 Main St, Dallas 75202 Michael St Ama	9-12	T	226	83%	214/860-2356 Fax 214/860-2359
E B Comstock Middle Sch 7044 Hodde St, Dallas 75217 Leslie Swann	6-8	TV	846 100	99%	972/794-1300 Fax 972/794-1301
E D Walker Middle Sch 12532 Nuestra Dr, Dallas 75230 Holly Wallace	6-8	T	761	84%	972/502-6100 Fax 972/502-6101
Ebby Halliday Elem Sch 10210 Teagarden Rd, Dallas 75217 **Amy Ward**	PK-5	T	638	96%	972/925-1800 Fax 972/925-1811
Edna Rowe Elem Sch 4918 Hovenkamp Dr, Dallas 75227 Sharon Alexander	PK-5	T	501 45	91%	972/749-8800 Fax 972/749-8801
Eduardo Mata Elem Sch 7420 La Vista Dr, Dallas 75214 Tomeka Williams	PK-3	GT	492 25	56%	972/749-7500 Fax 972/749-7501
Edward H Cary Middle Sch 3978 Killion Dr, Dallas 75229 Naomi Salas	6-8	GTV	598 83	97%	972/502-7600 Fax 972/502-7601

79 Student Personnel
80 Driver Ed/Safety
81 Gifted/Talented
82 Video Services
83 Substance Abuse Prev
84 Erate
85 AIDS Education
88 Alternative/At Risk
89 Multi-Cultural Curriculum
90 Social Work

91 Safety/Security
92 Magnet School
93 Parental Involvement
95 Tech Prep Program
97 Chief Information Officer
98 Chief Technology Officer
270 Character Education
271 Migrant Education
273 Teacher Mentor
274 Before/After Sch

275 Response To Intervention
277 Remedial Math K-12
280 Literacy Coach
285 STEM
286 Digital Learning
288 Common Core Standards
294 Accountability
295 Network System
296 Title II Programs
297 Webmaster

298 Grant Writer/Ptnrships
750 Chief Innovation Officer
751 Chief of Staff
752 Social Emotional Learning

Other School Types
Ⓐ = Alternative School
Ⓒ = Charter School
Ⓜ = Magnet School
Ⓨ = Year-Round School

School Programs
A = Alternative Program
G = Adult Classes
M = Magnet Program
T = Title I Schoolwide
V = Career & Tech Ed Programs

New Schools are shaded
New Superintendents and Principals are bold
Personnel with email addresses are underscored

Social Media
f = Facebook
t = Twitter

TX—99

Dallas County — Market Data Retrieval

School	Grades	Media	Enroll	%	Phone
Edward Titche Elem Sch 9560 Highfield Dr, Dallas 75227 Damien Stovall	PK-5	T	688 70	84%	972/794-2100 Fax 972/794-2101
Edwin J Kiest Elem Sch 2611 Healey Dr, Dallas 75228 Gerardo Hernandez	PK-5	T	737 39	95%	972/502-5600 Fax 972/502-5601
Eladio Martinez Learning Ctr 4500 Bernal Dr, Dallas 75212 Josefina Murillo	PK-5	T	562 51	95%	972/794-6900 Fax 972/794-6901
Elisha M Pease Elem Sch 2914 Cummings St, Dallas 75216 Sharri Zachary	PK-5	T	482 22	92%	214/932-3800 Fax 214/932-3801
Emmett J Conrad High Sch 7502 Fair Oaks Ave, Dallas 75231 Temesghen Asmerom	9-12	TV	1,307	90%	972/502-2300 Fax 972/502-2301
Esperanza Medrano Elementary 2221 Lucas Dr, Dallas 75219 Mario Mondragon	PK-5	T	398 40	92%	972/794-3300 Fax 972/794-3301
Everette Lee Degolyer Elem Sch 3453 Flair Dr, Dallas 75229 Tara Mays	PK-5	T	365 24	64%	972/794-2800 Fax 972/794-2801
F P Caillet Elem Sch 3033 Merrell Rd, Dallas 75229 Oscar Nandayapa	PK-5	T	677 32	93%	972/794-3200 Fax 972/794-3201
Felix Botello Elem Sch 225 S Marsalis Ave, Dallas 75203 Maria Puentemejia	PK-5	T	559	96%	972/502-4600 Fax 972/502-4601
Francisco Medrano Middle Sch 9815 Brockbank Dr, Dallas 75220 Theresa Sigurdson	6-8	T	962	91%	972/925-1300 Fax 972/925-1301
Frank Guzick Elem Sch 5000 Berridge Ln, Dallas 75227 Adreana Davis	PK-5	T	658	96%	972/502-3900 Fax 972/502-3901
ⓜ Franklin D Roosevelt High Sch 525 Bonnie View Rd, Dallas 75203 Troy Tyson	9-12	GTV	712	94%	972/925-6800 Fax 972/925-6801
Frederick Douglass Elem Sch 226 N Jim Miller Rd, Dallas 75217 Tenisha Allen	PK-5	T	481 20	91%	972/794-1400 Fax 972/794-1401
© Gabe P Allen Charter Sch ⓥ 5220 Nomas St, Dallas 75212 Sheila Ortiz Espinell	PK-5	GMT	471 30	97%	972/794-5100 Fax 972/794-5101
Geneva Heights Elem Sch 2911 Delmar Ave, Dallas 75206 Michael Ruiz	PK-5	T	348 24	71%	972/749-7400 Fax 972/749-7401
ⓜ George B Dealey Mont Intl Acad 6501 Royal Ln, Dallas 75230 Beth Wing	PK-8	T	181 35	33%	972/794-8400 Fax 972/794-8401
George H W Bush Elem Sch 3939 Spring Valley Rd, Addison 75001 Carol Crowling	PK-5	T	670	74%	972/925-1700 Fax 972/925-1701
George Peabody Elem Sch 3101 Raydell Pl, Dallas 75211 Sherri Rogers-Hall	PK-5	T	535 40	88%	972/794-5200 Fax 972/794-5201
George W Truett Elem Sch 1811 Gross Rd, Dallas 75228 Terre Evans	PK-5	T	1,193 70	94%	972/749-8000 Fax 972/749-8001
Gilbert Cuellar Jr Elem Sch 337 Pleasant Vista Dr, Dallas 75217 Lonnie Russell	PK-5	T	722 45	97%	972/749-6400 Fax 972/749-6401
H Grady Spruce High Sch 9733 Old Seagoville Rd, Dallas 75217 Danielle Petters	9-12	TV	1,794 120	88%	972/892-5500 Fax 972/892-5501
H I Holland ES-Lisbon 4203 S Lancaster Rd, Dallas 75216 Shanieka McDonald	PK-5	T	412 30	91%	972/749-1900 Fax 972/749-1901
Harold Lang Middle Sch 1678 Chenault St, Dallas 75228 Kimberly Robinson	6-8	T	907	89%	972/925-2400 Fax 972/925-2401
Harrell Budd Elem Sch 2121 S Marsalis Ave, Dallas 75216 Anita Barnes	PK-5	T	488 40	70%	972/502-8400 Fax 972/502-8401
Harry C Withers Elem Sch 3959 Northaven Rd, Dallas 75229 Wendy Miller	PK-5	T	420 27	55%	972/794-5000 Fax 972/794-5001
Harry Stone Montessori Academy 4747 Veterans Dr, Dallas 75216 Niki Jones	PK-8	T	339 28	59%	972/794-3400 Fax 972/794-3401
Hector P Garcia Middle Sch 700 E 8th St, Dallas 75203 David Lee	6-8	T	764	94%	972/502-5500 Fax 972/502-5501
Henry Gonzales Elem Sch 6610 Lake June Rd, Dallas 75217 Reymundo Guajardo	PK-5	T	657	95%	972/502-3300 Fax 972/502-3301
Henry W Longfellow Academy 5314 Boaz St, Dallas 75209 Lorena Hernandez	6-8	TV	421 32	87%	972/749-5400 Fax 972/749-5401
Herbert Marcus Elem Sch 2911 Northaven Rd, Dallas 75229 Jonatan Romero	PK-5	GT	780 45	99%	972/794-2900 Fax 972/794-2901
Highland Meadows Elem Sch 8939 Whitewing Ln, Dallas 75238 Jo'Anna Bahena	PK-5	T	760	97%	972/502-5200 Fax 972/502-5201
Hillcrest High Sch 9924 Hillcrest Rd, Dallas 75230 Joseph Sotelo	9-12	TV	1,126 80	79%	972/502-6800 Fax 972/502-6801
Ignacio Zaragoza Elem Sch 4550 Worth St, Dallas 75246 Linda Olivarez	PK-5	GT	327	96%	972/749-8600 Fax 972/749-8601
Ignite Middle Sch 2211 Caddo St, Dallas 75204 Dr Michael Gayles	6-8		160		972/794-7770
Innovation Design Entrep Acad 4800 Ross Ave, Dallas 75204 Nakimia Hicks	9-9	T	207	77%	972/794-6800
J L Long Middle Sch 6116 Reiger Ave, Dallas 75214 Chandra Hooper Barnett	6-8	TV	1,480 73	69%	972/502-4700 Fax 972/502-4701
J N Ervin Elem Sch 3722 Black Oak Dr, Dallas 75241 James Wallace	PK-5	T	603 50	97%	972/749-3700 Fax 972/749-3701
ⓜ J P Starks Mst Vanguard 3033 Tips Blvd, Dallas 75216 Evelyn Howard	PK-5	T	312 28	99%	972/502-8800 Fax 972/502-8801
Jack Lowe Sr Elem Sch 7000 Holly Hill Dr, Dallas 75231 Sandra Barrios	PK-5	T	619	83%	972/502-1700 Fax 972/502-1701
James Bowie Elem Sch 330 N Marsalis Ave, Dallas 75203 Caroline Wilson	PK-5	T	523 70	97%	972/925-6600 Fax 972/925-6601
James Madison High Sch 3000 Martin L King Blvd, Dallas 75215 Marian Willard	9-12	GTV	470 50	97%	972/925-2800 Fax 972/925-2801
James S Hogg Elem Sch 1144 N Madison Ave, Dallas 75208 Jairo Casco	PK-5	T	279 55	93%	972/502-8600 Fax 972/502-8601
Jerry Junkins Elem Sch 2808 Running Duke Dr, Carrollton 75006 Oscar Spurlock	PK-5	T	676	74%	972/502-2400 Fax 972/502-2401
Jill Stone-Vickery Meadow ES 6606 Ridgecrest Rd, Dallas 75231 Rosalinda Pratt	PK-5	T	347 25	99%	972/502-7900 Fax 972/502-7901

---

1 Superintendent	8 Curric/Instruct K-12	19 Chief Financial Officer	29 Family/Consumer Science	39 Social Studies K-12	49 English/Lang Arts Elem	59 Special Education Elem	69 Academic Assessment
2 Bus/Finance/Purchasing	9 Curric/Instruct Elem	20 Art K-12	30 Adult Education	40 Social Studies Elem	50 English/Lang Arts Sec	60 Special Education Sec	70 Research/Development
3 Buildings And Grounds	10 Curric/Instruct Sec	21 Art Elem	31 Career/Sch-to-Work K-12	41 Social Studies Sec	51 Reading K-12	61 Foreign/World Lang K-12	71 Public Information
4 Food Service	11 Federal Program	22 Art Sec	32 Career/Sch-to-Work Elem	42 Science K-12	52 Reading Elem	62 Foreign/World Lang Elem	72 Summer School
5 Transportation	12 Title I	23 Music K-12	33 Career/Sch-to-Work Sec	43 Science Elem	53 Reading Sec	63 Foreign/World Lang Sec	73 Instructional Tech
6 Athletic	13 Title V	24 Music Elem	34 Early Childhood Ed	44 Science Sec	54 Remedial Reading K-12	64 Religious Education K-12	74 Inservice Training
7 Health Services	15 Asst Superintendent	25 Music Sec	35 Health/Phys Education	45 Math K-12	55 Remedial Reading Elem	65 Religious Education Elem	75 Marketing/Distributive
	16 Instructional Media Svcs	26 Business Education	36 Guidance Services K-12	46 Math Elem	56 Remedial Reading Sec	66 Religious Education Sec	76 Info Systems
	17 Chief Operations Officer	27 Career & Tech Ed	37 Guidance Services Elem	47 Math Sec	57 Bilingual/ELL	67 School Board President	77 Psychological Assess
	18 Chief Academic Officer	28 Technology Education	38 Guidance Services Sec	48 English/Lang Arts K-12	58 Special Education K-12	68 Teacher Personnel	78 Affirmative Action

Texas School Directory — Dallas County

School	Grades	Programs	Enrollment	%	Phone/Fax
Jimmie Tyler Brashear Elem Sch 2959 S Hampton Rd, Dallas 75224 Sonja Barnes	PK-5	T	651	81%	972/502-2600 Fax 972/502-2601
John F Peeler Elem Sch 810 S Llewellyn Ave, Dallas 75208 **Janie Carballo**	PK-5	T	323 28	96%	972/502-8300 Fax 972/502-8301
John H Reagan Elem Sch 201 N Adams Ave, Dallas 75208 Ruth Roman	PK-5	T	359 36	92%	972/502-8200 Fax 972/502-8201
John Ireland Elem Sch 1515 N Jim Miller Rd, Dallas 75217 Stephanie Amaya	PK-5	T	527 40	98%	972/749-4900 Fax 972/749-4901
John J Pershing Elem Sch 5715 Meaders Ln, Dallas 75229 Margarita Hernandez	PK-5	T	517 36	85%	972/794-8600 Fax 972/794-8601
Ⓐ John L Patton Academic Center 3313 S Beckley Ave, Dallas 75224 **Marlon Brooks**	9-12	T	210	93%	214/932-5160 Fax 214/932-5149
John Neely Bryan Elem Sch 2001 Deer Path Dr, Dallas 75216 Tonya Anderson	PK-5	T	414 30	89%	972/502-8500 Fax 972/502-8501
John Q Adams Elem Sch 8239 Lake June Rd, Dallas 75217 **Maria Totsuka**	PK-5	T	749 50	98%	972/794-1200 Fax 972/794-1201
John W Carpenter Elem Sch 2121 Tosca Ln, Dallas 75224 Verna Farmer	PK-5	T	380 45	94%	972/794-6000 Fax 972/794-6001
John W Runyon Elem Sch 10750 Cradlerock Dr, Dallas 75217 Sherry Williams	PK-5	T	609 45	96%	972/749-6100 Fax 972/749-6101
Jose May Elem Sch 9818 Brockbank Dr, Dallas 75220 Isreal Rivera	PK-5	T	684	96%	972/749-4800 Fax 972/749-4801
Joseph J Rhoads Learning Ctr 4401 S 2nd Ave, Dallas 75210 Chaundra Macklin	PK-5	T	729 40	96%	972/749-1000 Fax 972/749-1001
Ⓜ Judge Barefoot Sanders Law Mag 1201 E 8th St, Dallas 75203 Garet Feimster	9-12	TV	403	80%	972/925-5950 Fax 972/925-6010
Julian T Saldivar Elem Sch 9510 Brockbank Dr, Dallas 75220 Edgar Jaramillo	PK-5	T	724 60	95%	972/794-2000 Fax 972/794-2001
Julius Dorsey Elem Sch 133 N Saint Augustine Dr, Dallas 75217 Rubinna Sanchez	PK-5	T	508 45	91%	972/749-6300 Fax 972/749-6301
Ⓜ Justin F Kimball High Sch 3606 S Westmoreland Rd, Dallas 75233 Llewellyn Smith	9-12	GTV	1,454	78%	972/502-2100 Fax 972/502-2101
Ⓜ K B Polk Elem Sch 6911 Victoria Ave, Dallas 75209 Kourtnei Billups	PK-5	T	348 40	85%	972/794-8900 Fax 972/794-8901
Kathlyn Joy Gilliam Academy 1700 E Camp Wisdom Rd, Dallas 75241 Gayle Smith	9-12	T	346	84%	972/925-1400 Fax 972/925-1401
Kennedy-Curry Middle Sch 6605 Sebring Dr, Dallas 75241 Patrice Ruffin-Brown	6-8	T	743 28	83%	972/925-1600 Fax 214/932-7901
Kleberg Elem Sch 1450 Edd Rd, Dallas 75253 Amy Zbylut	PK-5	T	735 46	90%	972/749-6500 Fax 972/749-6501
Ⓜ L G Pinkston High Sch 2200 Dennison St, Dallas 75212 **Marlon Brooks**	9-12	TV	906 70	92%	972/502-2700 Fax 972/502-2701
L L Hotchkiss Elem Sch 6929 Town North Dr, Dallas 75231 Rocio Bernal	PK-5	T	754 52	99%	972/749-7000 Fax 972/749-7001
L O Donald Elem Sch 1218 Phinney Ave, Dallas 75211 Kathryn Carter	PK-5	T	411 31	92%	972/794-5300 Fax 972/794-5301
L V Stockard Middle Sch 2300 S Ravinia Dr, Dallas 75211 Heather Holland	6-8	TV	1,156 60	96%	972/794-5700 Fax 972/794-5701
Lakewood Elem Sch 3000 Hillbrook St, Dallas 75214 Kate Wilke	K-5		924 41	10%	972/749-7300 Fax 972/749-7301
Larry G Smith Elem Sch 5299 Gus Thomasson Rd, Mesquite 75150 Lora Morris	PK-5	T	776	92%	972/502-4800 Fax 972/502-4801
Lee A McShan Jr Elem Sch 8307 Meadow Rd, Dallas 75231 **Joseph Medaris**	PK-5	T	641	98%	972/502-3800 Fax 972/502-3801
Leila P Cowart Elem Sch 1515 S Ravinia Dr, Dallas 75211 Lucia Salinas	PK-5	T	578 55	95%	972/794-5500 Fax 972/794-5501
Lenore Kirk Hall Elem Sch 2120 Keats Dr, Dallas 75211 Olga Romero	PK-5	T	504 38	93%	972/794-5400 Fax 972/794-5401
Leonides G Cigarroa Elem Sch 9990 Webb Chapel Rd, Dallas 75220 Douglas Burak	PK-5	T	562	98%	972/502-2900 Fax 972/502-2901
Leslie A Stemmons Elem Sch 2727 Knoxville St, Dallas 75211 Efrain Tovar	PK-5	T	746 40	94%	972/794-4900 Fax 972/794-4901
Lida Hooe Elem Sch 2419 Gladstone Dr, Dallas 75211 Fernando Rodriguez	PK-5	T	418 53	90%	972/794-6700 Fax 972/794-6701
Ⓜ Lincoln Humanities/Comm HS 2826 Elsie Faye Heggins St, Dallas 75215 Johnna Weaver	9-12	TV	630	93%	972/925-7600 Fax 972/925-7601
Lorenzo De Zavala Elem Sch 3214 N Winnetka Ave, Dallas 75212 Melissa Gonzalez	PK-5	T	409 26	97%	972/892-6400 Fax 972/892-6401
Louise Wolff Kahn Elem Sch 610 N Franklin St, Dallas 75211 Monica Marquez	PK-5	T	555 41	80%	972/502-1400 Fax 972/502-1401
Maple Lawn Elem Sch 3120 Inwood Rd, Dallas 75235 Oscar Aponte	PK-5	T	447 42	98%	972/925-2500 Fax 972/925-2501
Margaret B Henderson Elem Sch 2200 S Edgefield Ave, Dallas 75224 Ida Escobedo	PK-5	T	487 50	92%	972/749-2900 Fax 972/749-2901
Maria Moreno Elem Sch 2115 S Hampton Rd, Dallas 75224 Tammie Brooks	PK-5	T	445 60	92%	972/502-3100 Fax 972/502-3101
Mark Twain Elem Sch 724 Green Cove Ln, Dallas 75232 Pertricee Traylor	PK-5	T	299 40	91%	972/749-3000 Fax 972/749-3001
Martha Turner Reilly Elem Sch 11230 Lippitt Ave, Dallas 75218 Marion Jackson	PK-5	T	581 75	85%	972/749-7800 Fax 972/749-7801
Martin Luther King Jr Lrng Ctr 1817 Warren Ave, Dallas 75215 **Romikianta Sneed**	PK-5	T	439 36	99%	972/502-8100 Fax 972/502-8101
Martin Weiss Elem Sch 8601 Willoughby Blvd, Dallas 75232 Lakisha Merritt	PK-5	T	523 35	96%	972/749-4000 Fax 972/749-4001
Mary McLeod Bethune Elem Sch 1665 Duncanville Rd, Dallas 75211 Teresa Hernandez	PK-5	T	742 90	91%	972/502-1300 Fax 972/502-1301
Ⓐ Maya Angelou High Sch 3313 S Beckley Ave, Dallas 75204 Billy Bratton	6-12	TV	24 13	82%	972/925-7000 Fax 972/925-2201

Code	Description		Code	Description		Code	Description		Code	Description
9	Student Personnel		91	Safety/Security		275	Response To Intervention		298	Grant Writer/Ptnrships
0	Driver Ed/Safety		92	Magnet School		277	Remedial Math K-12		750	Chief Innovation Officer
1	Gifted/Talented		93	Parental Involvement		280	Literacy Coach		751	Chief of Staff
2	Video Services		95	Tech Prep Program		285	STEM		752	Social Emotional Learning
3	Substance Abuse Prev		97	Chief Information Officer		286	Digital Learning			
4	Erate		98	Chief Technology Officer		288	Common Core Standards			Other School Types
5	AIDS Education		270	Character Education		294	Accountability		Ⓐ	= Alternative School
8	Alternative/At Risk		271	Migrant Education		295	Network System		Ⓒ	= Charter School
9	Multi-Cultural Curriculum		273	Teacher Mentor		296	Title II Programs		Ⓜ	= Magnet School
0	Social Work		274	Before/After Sch		297	Webmaster		Ⓨ	= Year-Round School

School Programs
A = Alternative Program
G = Adult Classes
M = Magnet Program
T = Title I Schoolwide
V = Career & Tech Ed Programs

Social Media
▌f▐ = Facebook
▌t▐ = Twitter

New Schools are shaded
New Superintendents and Principals are bold
Personnel with email addresses are underscored

TX—101

Dallas County | Market Data Retrieval

School	Grades		Enrollment	%	Phone
Mockingbird Elem Sch 5828 E Mockingbird Ln, Dallas 75206 Melanie Mans	K-5		651 40	24%	972/749-7200 Fax 972/749-7201
Moises E Molina High Sch 2355 Duncanville Rd, Dallas 75211 Terry-Ann Rodriguez	9-12	T	2,221 83	94%	972/502-1000 Fax 972/502-1001
Montessori Acad Hernandez ES 5555 Maple Ave, Dallas 75235 Lisa Vega	PK-3	T	322 40	84%	972/925-2700 Fax 972/925-2701
Mt Auburn Elem Sch 6012 E Grand Ave, Dallas 75223 Brittany Swanson	PK-4	T	710 39	86%	972/749-8500 Fax 972/749-8501
Multiple Careers Magnet Center 4528 Rusk Ave, Dallas 75204 Lynn Smith	Spec	AV	115 5		972/925-2200 Fax 972/925-2201
N W Harllee Early Chldhd Ctr 1216 E 8th St, Dallas 75203 Amber Shields	PK-2	T	206	93%	972/925-6500 Fax 972/925-6501
Nancy J Cochran Elem Sch 6000 Keeneland Pkwy, Dallas 75211 Jamila Steen	PK-5	T	529 20	97%	972/794-4600 Fax 972/794-4601
Nancy Moseley Elem Sch 10400 Rylie Rd, Dallas 75217 Carmen Derrick	PK-5	T	772 40	94%	972/749-6700 Fax 972/749-6701
Nathan Adams Elem Sch 12600 Welch Rd, Dallas 75244 Adrian Luna	PK-5	T	506 31	90%	972/794-2600 Fax 972/794-2601
Nathaniel Hawthorne Elem Sch 7800 Umphress Rd, Dallas 75217 Ana Fernandez	PK-5	T	482 57	97%	972/749-4700 Fax 972/749-4701
New Tech HS at BF Darrell 4730 S Lancaster Rd, Dallas 75216 Jameile Choice	9-12	TV	363 70	92%	214/932-7600 Fax 214/932-7601
North Dallas High Sch 3120 N Haskell Ave, Dallas 75204 Katherine Wanserski-Eska	9-12	TV	1,054 100	94%	972/925-1500 Fax 972/925-1501
Obadiah Knight Elem Sch 2615 Anson Rd, Dallas 75235 Blanca Rojo	PK-5	GT	511 42	94%	972/749-5300 Fax 972/749-5301
Oliver W Holmes Academy 2001 E Kiest Blvd, Dallas 75216 Sharron Jackson	6-8	TV	806	94%	972/925-8500 Fax 972/925-8501
Oran M Roberts Elem Sch 4919 E Grand Ave, Dallas 75223 Kimberly Seymore	PK-5	T	588 25	98%	972/749-8700 Fax 972/749-8701
Paul L Dunbar Learning Center 4200 Metropolitan Ave, Dallas 75210 Alpher Garrett-Jones	PK-5	T	570	98%	972/794-6600 Fax 972/794-6601
Personalized Lrng Prep Houston 2827 Throckmorton St, Dallas 75219 Raymie Venable	PK-5	T	204 30	87%	972/749-5800 Fax 972/749-5801
Piedmont Global Academy 7625 Hume Dr, Dallas 75227 Letrice Portley	6-8	TV	1,006 90	98%	972/749-4100 Fax 972/749-4101
Pleasant Grove Elem Sch 1614 N Saint Augustine Dr, Dallas 75217 Anabel Ruiz	PK-5	T	555 50	98%	972/892-5000 Fax 972/892-5001
Preston Hollow Elem Sch 6423 Walnut Hill Ln, Dallas 75230 Vincent Garcia	PK-5	T	500 22	83%	972/794-8500 Fax 972/794-8501
Ⓜ R M Sorrells Sch-Ed & Soc Srvs 1201 E 8th St Ste 111, Dallas 75203 Shelia Brown	9-12	TV	331 9	79%	972/925-5940 Fax 972/925-6004
Ⓜ Rangel Women's Leadership Sch 1718 Robert B Cullum Blvd, Dallas 75210 Beverly Lusk	6-12		269		972/749-5200 Fax 972/502-5201
Raul Quintanilla Middle Sch 2700 Remond Dr, Dallas 75211 Salem Hussain	6-8	T	1,054 70	95%	972/502-3200 Fax 972/502-3201
Reinhardt Elem Sch 10122 Losa Dr, Dallas 75218 Phoebe Montgomery	PK-5	T	565 36	92%	972/749-7900 Fax 972/749-7901
Richard Lagow Elem Sch 637 Edgeworth Dr, Dallas 75217 Jospeh Luedecke	PK-5	T	509 35	96%	972/749-6600 Fax 972/749-6601
Robert L Thornton Elem Sch 6011 Old Ox Rd, Dallas 75241 Christofor Stephens	PK-5	T	372 38	85%	972/794-8000 Fax 972/794-8001
Robert T Hill Middle Sch 505 Easton Rd, Dallas 75218 Candice Ruiz	6-8	TV	894 50	93%	972/502-5700 Fax 972/502-5701
Roger Q Mills Elem Sch 1515 Lynn Haven Ave, Dallas 75216 Marissa Saenz	PK-5	T	322 30	91%	972/925-7500 Fax 972/925-7501
Ronald E McNair Elem Sch 3150 Bainbridge Ave, Dallas 75237 Demetria Bell	PK-5	T	602 38	95%	972/794-6200 Fax 972/794-6201
Rosemont Elem & Prep Lang MS 719 N Montclair Ave, Dallas 75208 Marco Barker	3-8	T	671 40	86%	972/749-5000 Fax 972/749-5001
Rosemont Primary Sch 1919 Stevens Forest Dr, Dallas 75208 Marco Barker	PK-2		540 32		972/502-3850 Fax 972/502-3851
Rufus C Burleson Elem Sch 6300 Elam Rd, Dallas 75217 Lajoyce Johnson	PK-5	T	684 45	99%	972/749-4500 Fax 972/749-4501
S S Conner Elem Sch 3037 Green Meadow Dr, Dallas 75228 Kiashan King-Corbett	PK-5	T	631 38	87%	972/749-8200 Fax 972/749-8201
Sam Tasby Middle Sch 7001 Fair Oaks Ave, Dallas 75231 Audrey Delacruz	6-8	T	969	96%	972/502-1900 Fax 972/502-1901
San Jacinto Elem Sch 7900 Hume Dr, Dallas 75227 Celia Sanchez	PK-5	T	482 50	98%	972/749-4200 Fax 972/749-4201
Sarah Zumwalt Middle Sch 2245 E Ledbetter Dr, Dallas 75216 Troy Tyson	6-8	TV	417 50	97%	972/749-3600 Fax 972/749-3601
Ⓜ Sch Health Prof-Townview Ctr 1201 E 8th St, Dallas 75203 Lasandra Sanders	9-12	TV	546 30	87%	972/925-5930 Fax 972/925-6007
Ⓐ School Cmty Guidance Center 3313 S Beckley Ave, Dallas 75224 Marlon Brooks	K-12	T	125 17	75%	972/925-7000 Fax 214/371-2860
Seagoville Elem Sch 304 N Kaufman St, Seagoville 75159 Katrina Gibson	PK-5	T	701 45	86%	972/892-7900 Fax 972/892-7901
Ⓜ Seagoville High Sch 15920 Seagoville Rd, Dallas 75253 Angela West	9-12	ATV	1,452 60	92%	972/892-5900 Fax 972/892-5901
Seagoville Middle Sch 950 N Woody Rd, Dallas 75253 Jesus Martinez	6-8	TV	1,363 50	90%	972/892-7100 Fax 972/892-7146
Seagoville North Elem Sch 1906 Seagoville Rd, Seagoville 75159 Rocio Gardea	PK-5	T	775	78%	972/892-5300
Sidney Lanier Expressive Arts 1400 Walmsley Ave, Dallas 75208 Alyssa Peraza	PK-5	T	567 60	90%	972/794-4400 Fax 972/794-4401
Ⓜ Skyline High Sch 7777 Forney Rd, Dallas 75227 Dwain Simmons	9-12	TV	4,535	88%	972/502-3400 Fax 972/502-3401

1 Superintendent	8 Curric/Instruct K-12	19 Chief Financial Officer	29 Family/Consumer Science	39 Social Studies K-12	49 English/Lang Arts Elem	59 Special Education Elem	69 Academic Assessment
2 Bus/Finance/Purchasing	9 Curric/Instruct Elem	20 Art K-12	30 Adult Education	40 Social Studies Elem	50 English/Lang Arts Sec	60 Special Education Sec	70 Research/Development
3 Buildings And Grounds	10 Curric/Instruct Sec	21 Art Elem	31 Career/Sch-to-Work K-12	41 Social Studies Sec	51 Reading K-12	61 Foreign/World Lang K-12	71 Public Information
4 Food Service	11 Federal Program	22 Art Sec	32 Career/Sch-to-Work Elem	42 Science K-12	52 Reading Elem	62 Foreign/World Lang Elem	72 Summer School
5 Transportation	12 Title I	23 Music K-12	33 Career/Sch-to-Work Sec	43 Science Elem	53 Reading Sec	63 Foreign/World Lang Sec	73 Instructional Tech
6 Athletic	13 Title V	24 Music Elem	34 Early Childhood Ed	44 Science Sec	54 Remedial Reading K-12	64 Religious Education K-12	74 Inservice Training
7 Health Services	15 Asst Superintendent	25 Music Sec	35 Health/Phys Education	45 Math K-12	55 Remedial Reading Elem	65 Religious Education Elem	75 Marketing/Distributive
	16 Instructional Media Svcs	26 Business Education	36 Guidance Services K-12	46 Math Elem	56 Remedial Reading Sec	66 Religious Education Sec	76 Info Systems
	17 Chief Operations Officer	27 Career & Tech Ed	37 Guidance Services Elem	47 Math Sec	57 Bilingual/ELL	67 School Board President	77 Psychological Assess
	18 Chief Academic Officer	28 Technology Education	38 Guidance Services Sec	48 English/Lang Arts K-12	58 Special Education K-12	68 Teacher Personnel	78 Affirmative Action

Texas School Directory — Dallas County

School	Grades	Type	Enroll	%	Phone
Solar Prep Sch for Girls-Bonhm 2617 N Henderson Ave, Dallas 75206 Nancy Bernardino	K-2	T	194	51%	972/749-4300
Solar Preparatory for Boys 1802 Moser Ave, Dallas 75206 Adriana Gonzalez	PK-2		160		972/794-7100
South Oak Cliff High Sch 4949 Village Fair Dr, Dallas 75224 Dr Willie Johnson	9-12	V	1,204		214/932-7000 Fax 214/932-7001
Stephen C Foster Elem Sch 3700 Clover Ln, Dallas 75220 Irma Delaguardia	PK-5	T	725 54	90%	972/794-8100 Fax 972/794-8101
Stevens Park Elem Sch 2615 W Colorado Blvd, Dallas 75211 Roberto Gonzalez	PK-5	T	657 50	93%	972/794-4200 Fax 972/794-4201
Sudie Williams Elem Sch 4518 Pomona Rd, Dallas 75209 Michael Jackson	PK-5	T	215 19	91%	972/794-8700 Fax 972/794-8701
Sunset High Sch 2120 W Jefferson Blvd, Dallas 75208 Claudia Vega	9-12	TV	1,983	96%	972/502-1500 Fax 972/502-1501
T G Terry Elem Sch 6661 Greenspan Ave, Dallas 75232 Alicia Bradley	PK-5	T	423 45	93%	972/749-3200 Fax 972/749-3201
T W Browne Middle Sch 3333 Sprague Dr, Dallas 75233 Lakisha Thomas	6-8	TV	541 75	91%	972/502-2500 Fax 972/502-2501
Thelma E Page-Richardson ES 7203 Bruton Rd, Dallas 75217 Courtney Loy	PK-5	T	701	96%	972/892-8100
Thomas C Marsh Prep Academy 3838 Crown Shore Dr, Dallas 75244 Martha Bujanda	6-8	TV	917 60	90%	972/502-6600 Fax 972/502-6601
Thomas J Rusk Middle Sch 2929 Inwood Rd, Dallas 75235 Juan Cordoba	6-8	TV	647 42	92%	972/925-2000 Fax 972/925-2001
Thomas Jefferson High Sch 4001 Walnut Hill Ln, Dallas 75229 Sandi Massey	9-12	TV	1,703 60	82%	972/502-7300 Fax 972/502-7301
Thomas L Marsalis Elem Sch 5640 S Marsalis Ave, Dallas 75241 Kimberly Richardson	PK-5	T	545 37	89%	972/749-3500 Fax 972/749-3501
Thomas Tolbert Elem Sch 4000 Blue Ridge Blvd, Dallas 75233 Lakeisha Smith	PK-5	T	536 50	83%	972/794-5900 Fax 972/794-5901
Tom C Gooch Elem Sch 4030 Calculus Dr, Dallas 75244 **Kay Johnson**	PK-5	T	428 19	90%	972/794-2500 Fax 972/794-2501
Tom W Field Elem Sch 2151 Royal Ln, Dallas 75229 Selena Deboskie	PK-5	T	263 37	96%	972/794-2700 Fax 972/794-2701
Ⓜ Townview Mag HS-Bus & Mngmnt 1201 E 8th St Ste 241, Dallas 75203 **Israel Rivera**	9-12	TV	491 15	82%	972/925-5920 Fax 972/925-6001
Ⓜ Townview Mag HS-Sci & Eng 1201 E 8th St, Dallas 75203 Andrew Palacios	9-12	TV	428	67%	972/925-5960 Fax 972/925-6016
Ⓜ Townview Mag HS-Talent & Gift 1201 E 8th St Ste 302, Dallas 75203 Benjamin Mackey	9-12		276 16	37%	972/925-5970 Fax 972/925-6018
Trinidad Garza Early College 4849 W Illinois Ave W53A, Dallas 75211 Macario Hernandez		T	432	87%	214/860-3680 Fax 214/860-3689
Umphrey Lee Elem Sch 7808 Racine Dr, Dallas 75232 Stephanie McCloud	PK-5	T	579 32	92%	972/749-3900 Fax 972/749-3901
Urban Park Elem Sch 6901 Military Pkwy, Dallas 75227 Lisa Falcon	PK-5	T	627 52	96%	972/794-1100 Fax 972/794-1101
Victor H Hexter Elem Sch 9720 Waterview Rd, Dallas 75218 Dr Jennifer Jackson	PK-5	T	560 28	62%	972/502-5800 Fax 972/502-5801
Ⓐ Village Fair-Elem Daep 3313 S Beckley Ave, Dallas 75224 **Billy Bratton**	K-6	T	4 10	67%	972/925-7000 Fax 214/932-5161
Ⓐ Village Fair-Lacey Middle Sch 3313 S Beckley Ave, Dallas 75224 Marlon Brooks	6-8	T	94 10	69%	972/925-7000 Fax 972/925-7061
W A Blair Elem Sch 7720 Gayglen Dr, Dallas 75217 Umoja Turner	PK-5	T	669 35	87%	972/794-1600 Fax 972/794-1601
Ⓨ W B Travis Vanguard & Academy 3001 McKinney Ave, Dallas 75204 Tom Brandt	4-8		297 32	28%	972/794-7500 Fax 972/794-7501
W E Greiner Explor Arts Acad 501 S Edgefield Ave, Dallas 75208 Yvonne Rojas	6-8	TV	1,721	84%	972/925-7100 Fax 972/925-7101
W H Adamson High Sch 309 E 9th St, Dallas 75203 Diana Nunez	9-12	TV	1,480 60	93%	972/749-1400 Fax 972/749-1401
W H Atwell Middle Sch 1303 Reynoldston Ln, Dallas 75232 Shondula Whitfield	6-8	TV	819	74%	972/794-6400 Fax 972/794-6401
W H Gaston Middle Sch 9565 Mercer Dr, Dallas 75228 Janeen Whitmore	6-8	TV	979 62	97%	972/502-5400 Fax 972/502-5401
W T White High Sch 4505 Ridgeside Dr, Dallas 75244 Elena Luna-Bates	9-12	TV	2,230	80%	972/502-6200 Fax 972/502-6201
W W Bushman Elem Sch 4200 Bonnie View Rd, Dallas 75216 Yolanda Knight	PK-5	T	488 30	98%	972/749-1800 Fax 972/749-1801
W W Samuell High Sch 8928 Palisade Dr, Dallas 75217 Jennifer Tecklenburg	9-12	TV	1,945 108	98%	972/892-5100 Fax 972/892-5101
Walnut Hill Elem Sch 10115 Midway Rd, Dallas 75229 **Phillip Potter**	PK-5	T	358 25	83%	972/502-7800 Fax 972/502-7801
Whitney M Young Jr Elem Sch 4601 Veterans Dr, Dallas 75216 Shabranda Mathis	PK-5	T	531 35	97%	972/749-2000 Fax 972/749-2001
William Anderson Elem Sch 620 N Saint Augustine Dr, Dallas 75217 Silvia Garcia	PK-5	T	680 45	97%	972/749-6200 Fax 972/749-6201
William B Miller Elem Sch 3111 Bonnie View Rd, Dallas 75216 Nikki Hudson	PK-5	T	360 22	92%	972/502-8700 Fax 972/502-8701
William Lipscomb Elem Sch 5801 Worth St, Dallas 75214 Michael Sandoval	PK-5	T	511 27	89%	972/794-7300 Fax 972/794-7301
Wilmer Early Chldhd Center 211 Walnut St, Wilmer 75172 Dr Sharonda Pruitt	PK-PK		73		469/660-7296 Fax 214/932-7531
Wilmer-Hutchins Elem Sch 7475 J J Lemmon Rd, Dallas 75241 Michael Gipson	PK-5	T	919	82%	972/925-2600 Fax 972/925-2601
Wilmer-Hutchins High Sch 5520 Langdon Rd, Dallas 75241 Jasen Campbell	9-12	T	857	85%	972/925-2900 Fax 972/925-2901
Winnetka Elem Sch 1151 S Edgefield Ave, Dallas 75208 Lourdes Garduno	PK-5	T	820 54	94%	972/749-5100 Fax 972/749-5101

Code		Code		Code		Code	
79	Student Personnel	91	Safety/Security	275	Response To Intervention	298	Grant Writer/Ptnrships
80	Driver Ed/Safety	92	Magnet School	277	Remedial Math K-12	750	Chief Innovation Officer
81	Gifted/Talented	93	Parental Involvement	280	Literacy Coach	751	Chief of Staff
82	Video Services	95	Tech Prep Program	285	STEM	752	Social Emotional Learning
83	Substance Abuse Prev	97	Chief Information Officer	286	Digital Learning		
84	Erate	98	Chief Technology Officer	288	Common Core Standards		
85	AIDS Education	270	Character Education	294	Accountability		
88	Alternative/At Risk	271	Migrant Education	295	Network System		
89	Multi-Cultural Curriculum	273	Teacher Mentor	296	Title II Programs		
90	Social Work	274	Before/After Sch	297	Webmaster		

School Programs
A = Alternative Program
G = Adult Classes
M = Magnet Program
T = Title I Schoolwide
V = Career & Tech Ed Programs

Other School Types
Ⓐ = Alternative School
Ⓒ = Charter School
Ⓜ = Magnet School
Ⓨ = Year-Round School

Social Media
[f] = Facebook
[t] = Twitter

New Schools are shaded
New Superintendents and Principals are bold
Personnel with email addresses are underscored

TX—103

Dallas County — Market Data Retrieval

Woodrow Wilson High Sch 100 S Glasgow Dr, Dallas 75214 Michael Moran	9-12	TV	1,865 80	59%	972/502-4400 Fax 972/502-4401
Young Mens Ldrshp Acad-Flornce 1625 N Masters Dr, Dallas 75217 Dr Christopher Barksdale	6-8	TV	952 100	99%	972/749-6000 Fax 972/749-6001
Young Women Steam Acad-Blch Sp 710 Cheyenne Rd, Balch Springs 75180 Gabrelle Dickson	6-8	TV	1,227	95%	972/892-5800 Fax 972/892-5801
Zan Wesley Holmes Jr Mid Sch 2939 Saint Rita Dr, Dallas 75233 Tangela Carter	6-8	T	952	90%	214/932-7800 Fax 214/932-7801

● **DeSoto Ind School Dist** PID: 01010242   972/223-6666
200 E Belt Line Rd, Desoto 75115   Fax 972/274-8968

Schools: 14 \ *Teachers:* 646 \ *Students:* 9,872 \ *Special Ed Students:* 870
\ *LEP Students:* 633 \ *Ethnic:* African American 78%, Hispanic 19%,
Caucasian 2% \ *Exp:* $410 (High) \ *Poverty:* 18% \ *Title I:* $2,877,362 \
Special Education: $2,037,000 \ *Open-Close:* 08/19 - 05/28 \ *DTBP:* $182
(High) \ [f]

Dandre Weaver 1
David Scott 2
Don Lester 3
Rhonda Dalfonso 7
Dr Gabrielle Lemonier 15
Mia Stroy 15,68
Nicholas Johnson 27,285
Carl Sherman 67
Kathy Ferrell 69,294
Darrell Baty 73
Bobby LaBorde 2,15
William Wooten 2
Larry Davis 6,35
Dr Michelle Howard-Schwind 8,15
Levatta Levels 15,79
Roberto Torres 16,73,76,286,295
Dr Akweta Hickman 58,77
Dr Darryl Cob 68,78
Tiffanie Blackman Jones 71
Buddy Watson 295,297

Public Schs..Principal	Grd	Prgm	Enr/#Cls	SN	
Amber Terrace Discovery ECC 224 Amber Ln, Desoto 75115 Keishla Coleman	PK-PK	T	394 38	91%	972/223-8757 Fax 972/274-8247 [f]
Cockrell Hill Elem Sch 425 S Cockrell Hill Rd, Desoto 75115 Angela Robinson	PK-5	T	665 25	72%	972/230-1692 Fax 972/274-8081
Ⓐ DeSoto Alt Sch 204 E Belt Line Rd, Desoto 75115 Homer Webb	K-12	T	121 11	52%	972/223-2242 Fax 972/230-1735
DeSoto High Sch 600 Eagle Dr, Desoto 75115 Shon Joseph	9-12	T	3,253 127	64%	972/230-0726 Fax 972/274-8115
East Middle Sch 601 E Belt Line Rd, Desoto 75115 Deidre Hannible	6-8	T	596 48	77%	972/223-0690 Fax 972/274-8156
Frank D Moates Elem Sch 1500 Heritage Blvd, Glenn Heights 75154 Tarsha Lunkin	PK-5	T	768 50	83%	972/230-2881 Fax 972/274-8073
Ⓜ Katherine Johnson Tech Mag Sch 1200 Academy Way, Desoto 75115 Angela Batiste	K-5		810		972/274-8026
McCowan Middle Sch 1500 Majestic Meadows Dr, Glenn Heights 75154 Kelli McWashington	6-8	T	994	73%	972/274-8090 Fax 972/274-8099
Meadows Elem Sch 1016 the Meadows Pkwy, Desoto 75115 Shana Hawthorne	PK-5	T	450 38	77%	972/224-0960 Fax 972/228-7908
Northside Elem Sch 525 Ray Ave, Desoto 75115 Lori Mathis	PK-5	T	426 24	85%	972/224-6709 Fax 972/228-7925 [f]
Ruby Young Elem Sch 707 N Young Blvd, Desoto 75115 Shanta Duren	PK-5	T	572 24	70%	972/223-6505 Fax 972/274-8221 [f]

West Middle Sch 800 N Westmoreland Rd, Desoto 75115 Shana Hawthorne	6-8	T	673 40	69%	972/230-1820 Fax 972/274-8058
Ⓐ Wings 210 E Belt Line Rd, Desoto 75115 Reginald Lewis	9-12		97	37%	972/274-8219
Woodridge Elem Sch 1001 Woodridge Dr, Desoto 75115 Deidre Hannible	PK-5	T	696 23	76%	972/223-3800 Fax 972/274-8204

● **Duncanville Ind School Dist** PID: 01010292   972/708-2000
710 S Cedar Ridge Dr, Duncanville 75137   Fax 972/708-2020

Schools: 19 \ *Teachers:* 827 \ *Students:* 12,800 \
Special Ed Students: 1,081 \ *LEP Students:* 2,230 \ *College-Bound:* 55%
\ *Ethnic:* Asian 1%, African American 41%, Hispanic 53%, Native American:
1%, Caucasian 4% \ *Exp:* $295 (Med) \ *Poverty:* 19% \ *Title I:* $3,967,848 \
Special Education: $2,224,000 \ *Open-Close:* 08/19 - 05/28 \ *DTBP:* $186
(High) \ [f][t]

Dr Marc Smith 1
Dr Ed Bigbee 2,19
Donna Thomas 4
Dwight Weaver 6,35
Cathy Sewell 8,18
Maria Zimora 11
Kathleen Brown 15,68
Leslie Shimomura 16
Shalontae Payne 27,31*
MacKenzie Casall 36,58,77
Devin Hanes 47
Carla Fahey 67
Tiara Richard 71
Sherri Smith 74
Julie Hargrove 79
Nneka Bernard 81*
Chavela Hampton 91
Christi Courson 2
Joe Peterka 3
Brad Hamrick 5
Eva Navarro 7,85*
Dr Samuel Nix 8,69,270,286,288
Joe Copeland 15,79
Melissa Kates 15,751
Shawntee Cowan 16,73,82,95,98,295
Erika Reyas 34,296
Ashley Logan 41
Rosey Sandoval 57
Alexis McClendon 68
Shannon Bennett 72
Melinda Turner 76
Dr Norbert Whitaker 79,93,271
Tijuana Hudson 88*

Public Schs..Principal	Grd	Prgm	Enr/#Cls	SN	
Acton Elem Sch 7095 W Wheatland Rd, Dallas 75249 Kyalla Bowens	PK-4	T	541 22	84%	972/708-2400 Fax 972/708-2424 [f][t]
Alexander Elem Sch 510 Softwood Dr, Duncanville 75137 Erin Frye	PK-4	T	440 50	79%	972/708-2500 Fax 972/708-2525
Brandenburg Intermediate Sch 1903 Blueridge Dr, Duncanville 75137 Tamra Thompson	5-6	T	543 43	78%	972/708-3100 Fax 972/708-3131 [f][t]
Byrd Middle Sch 1040 W Wheatland Rd, Duncanville 75116 Kendria Davis-Martin	7-8	T	690 45	74%	972/708-3400 Fax 972/708-3434
C J & Anne Hyman Elem Sch 8441 Fox Creek Trl, Dallas 75249 Derrick Ross	PK-4	T	668 25	67%	972/708-6700 Fax 972/708-6767
Central Elem Sch 302 E Freeman St, Duncanville 75116 Sherri Smith	PK-4	T	475 25	82%	972/708-2600 Fax 972/708-2626 [f][t]
Daniel Intermediate Sch 1007 Springwood Ln, Duncanville 75137 Kim Edmondson	5-6	T	719 28	76%	972/708-3200 Fax 972/708-3232
Duncanville High Sch 900 W Camp Wisdom Rd, Duncanville 75116 Michael McDonald	9-12	TV	4,268	69%	972/708-3700 Fax 972/708-3737
Duncanville HS Collegiate Acad 900 W Camp Wisdom Rd, Duncanville 75116 Pamela Thomas	9-12		210		972/708-3885

---

1 Superintendent	8 Curric/Instruct K-12	19 Chief Financial Officer	29 Family/Consumer Science	39 Social Studies K-12	49 English/Lang Arts Elem	59 Special Education Elem	69 Academic Assessment
2 Bus/Finance/Purchasing	9 Curric/Instruct Elem	20 Art K-12	30 Adult Education	40 Social Studies Elem	50 English/Lang Arts Sec	60 Special Education Sec	70 Research/Development
3 Buildings And Grounds	10 Curric/Instruct Sec	21 Art Elem	31 Career/Sch-to-Work K-12	41 Social Studies Sec	51 Reading K-12	61 Foreign/World Lang K-12	71 Public Information
4 Food Service	11 Federal Program	22 Art Sec	32 Career/Sch-to-Work Elem	42 Science K-12	52 Reading Elem	62 Foreign/World Lang Elem	72 Summer School
5 Transportation	12 Title I	23 Music K-12	33 Career/Sch-to-Work Sec	43 Science Elem	53 Reading Sec	63 Foreign/World Lang Sec	73 Instructional Tech
6 Athletic	13 Title V	24 Music Elem	34 Early Childhood Ed	44 Science Sec	54 Remedial Reading K-12	64 Religious Education K-12	74 Inservice Training
7 Health Services	15 Asst Superintendent	25 Music Sec	35 Health/Phys Education	45 Math K-12	55 Remedial Reading Elem	65 Religious Education Elem	75 Marketing/Distributive
	16 Instructional Media Svcs	26 Business Education	36 Guidance Services K-12	46 Math Elem	56 Remedial Reading Sec	66 Religious Education Sec	76 Info Systems
	17 Chief Operations Officer	27 Career & Tech Ed	37 Guidance Services Elem	47 Math Sec	57 Bilingual/ELL	67 School Board President	77 Psychological Assess
	18 Chief Academic Officer	28 Technology Education	38 Guidance Services Sec	48 English/Lang Arts K-12	58 Special Education K-12	68 Teacher Personnel	78 Affirmative Action

Texas School Directory — Dallas County

School	Grd	Prgm	Enr/#Cls	SN	Phone
Fairmeadows Elem Sch 101 E Fairmeadows Dr, Duncanville 75116 Sugey Villarreal	PK-4	T	482 26	87%	972/708-2700 Fax 972/708-2727
G W Kennemer Middle Sch 7101 W Wheatland Rd, Dallas 75249 Monica Smith	7-8	T	723 60	78%	972/708-3600 Fax 972/708-3636
Hardin Intermediate Sch 426 E Freeman St, Duncanville 75116 Melanie Lewis	5-6	T	674 30	86%	972/708-3300 Fax 972/708-3333
Hastings Elem Sch 602 W Center St, Duncanville 75116 Wendy Simpson	PK-4	T	591 28	84%	972/708-2800 Fax 972/708-2828
James Bilhartz Jr Elem Sch 6700 Wandt Dr, Dallas 75236 Valerie Nelms-Harris	PK-4	T	588	79%	972/708-6600 Fax 972/708-6666
Ⓐ Mary E Smithey Pace High Sch 502 E Freeman St, Duncanville 75116 Tijuana Hudson	9-12	T	106 10	58%	972/708-2470 Fax 972/708-2474
Merrifield Elem Sch 102 E Vinyard Rd, Duncanville 75137 Tanji Towels	PK-4	T	494 35	87%	972/708-2900 Fax 972/708-2929
Reed Middle Sch 530 E Freeman St, Duncanville 75116 Bryan Byrd	7-8	T	618 60	79%	972/708-3500 Fax 972/708-3535
Smith Elem Sch 1010 Big Stone Gap Rd, Duncanville 75137 Celee Stephens	PK-4	T	355 23	75%	972/708-3000 Fax 972/708-3030
Ⓐ Summit Education Center 900 S Cedar Ridge Dr, Duncanville 75137 Mekasha Brown	K-12		140 6	76%	972/708-2570 Fax 972/708-2585

● Garland Ind School Dist PID: 01010395
501 S Jupiter Rd, Garland 75042

972/494-8201 Fax 972/485-4936

Schools: 72 \ **Teachers:** 3,648 \ **Students:** 56,471 \
Special Ed Students: 4,696 \ **LEP Students:** 14,516 \ **College-Bound:** 52% \
Ethnic: Asian 9%, African American 18%, Hispanic 51%, Native American: 2%, Caucasian 20% \ **Exp:** $395 (High) \ **Poverty:** 17% \ **Title I:** $16,413,729 \
Special Education: $9,602,000 \ **Bilingual Education:** $20,000 \
Open-Close: 08/12 - 05/21 \ **DTBP:** $190 (High) \ 🅃

Dr Ricardo Lopez 1	Brent Ringo 2,19		
Mark Booker 2*	Dr Rene Barajas 2,15		
Joel Falcon 3	Bradford Trudeau 4		
Holly Frias 4	Brian Abbett 5		
Cliff Odenwald 6	Renee Kotsopoulos 7,85*		
Criselda Valdez 9	Dr Rhonda Davis 11,34,92,288,296		
Ashley Westbrook 12	Dr Doug Brubaker 15		
Dr Gradyne Brown 15,68	Dr Wendy Eldredge 15,71,79		
Dr Jovan Wells 18,298	George Jones 20,23		
Dr Phillip Gilbreath 27,31	Stan Maige 28,295		
Sandra Thompson 29	Louise Gartrell 35		
Debbie Lee 36	Tiffany Gilmore 36		
John Hatch 39	Traci Vickery 46		
Kevin Massey 47	Kelley Steinley 49		
Myra Crump 49,93	Mary Shelton 50		
Deb Tietjen 57	Pascuala Sifre 57		
Zaida Saldivar 57	Bebetta Hemphill 58,79		
Dr Debi Buchanan 58	Veronica Joyner 61		
Johnny Beach 67	Atticus Wisener 68		
Dr Linda Chance 68,751	Rodney McHenry 68		
Courtney Clearfield 69,70,294	Dr Kimberly Caddell 69,70,294		
Dr Pam Neblett 69,70,294	Dr Mida Milligan 71		
Tiffany Veno 71	Cathy Barck 73		
Donna Eurex 73	Dr Jasna Aliefendic 73		
Jason Hickman 73	Pam Holcomb 73		
Nelson Orta 74	Cheryl Jacobs 75		
Keli Daughtry 76	Cheryl Beard 81		
Keith Chapman 91	Pat Lamb 91		

Carra King 275

Public Schs..Principal	Grd	Prgm	Enr/#Cls	SN	Phone
Abbett Elem Sch 730 W Muirfield Rd, Garland 75044 Kelly Williams	PK-5	T	749 30	39%	972/675-3000 Fax 972/675-3005
Ⓜ Austin Academy for Excellence 1125 Beverly Dr, Garland 75040 John Fishpaw	6-8	TV	947 48	44%	972/926-2620 Fax 972/926-2628
Back Elem Sch 7300 Bluebonnet Dr, Rowlett 75089 Amanda Ramos	PK-5	T	450 30	68%	972/475-1884 Fax 972/412-5245
Ⓜ Beaver Tech Ctr-Math & Science 3232 March Ln, Garland 75042 Vicki Devantier	PK-5	T	573 30	55%	972/494-8301 Fax 972/494-8702
Bradfield Elem Sch 3817 Bucknell Dr, Garland 75042 Cecilia Bados	PK-5	T	498 22	84%	972/494-8303 Fax 972/494-8729
Bullock Elem Sch 3909 Edgewood Dr, Garland 75042 Brian Trichell	PK-5	T	615 30	87%	972/494-8308 Fax 972/494-8704
Bussey Middle Sch 1204 Travis St, Garland 75040 Jeremiah Oliphant	6-8	GT	944 50	88%	972/494-8391 Fax 972/494-8971
Caldwell Elem Sch 3400 Saturn Rd, Garland 75041 Raelyn Scroggin	PK-5	T	479 20	87%	972/926-2500 Fax 972/926-2505
Centerville Elem Sch 600 Keen Dr, Garland 75041 Amie Pennington	PK-5	T	302 16	89%	972/926-2510 Fax 972/926-2515
Cisneros Pre-K Sch 2826 S 5th St, Garland 75041 Andy Kiser	PK-PK	T	566	84%	972/271-7160 Fax 972/271-7165
Ⓜ Classical Center at Vial Sch 126 Creekview Dr, Garland 75043 Beatris Martinez	PK-5	T	553 31	52%	972/240-3710 Fax 972/240-3711
Ⓜ Classical Center-Brandenburg 626 Nickens Rd, Garland 75043 Elise Mosty	6-8	T	1,110 50	56%	972/926-2630 Fax 972/926-2633
Club Hill Elem Sch 1330 Colonel Dr, Garland 75043 Kerstin Allen	PK-5	T	528 35	75%	972/926-2520 Fax 972/926-2526
Cooper Elem Sch 1200 Kingsbridge Dr, Garland 75040 Bobbie Carter	PK-5	T	581 28	74%	972/675-3010 Fax 972/675-3015
Coyle Middle Sch 4500 Skyline Dr, Rowlett 75088 Kenneth Washington	6-8	TV	1,033 60	55%	972/475-3711 Fax 972/412-7222
Daugherty Elem Sch 500 W Miller Rd, Garland 75041 Bonnie Barrett	PK-5	T	782 18	90%	972/926-2530 Fax 972/926-2535
Davis Elem Sch 1621 McCallum Dr, Garland 75042 Patricia Tatum	PK-5	T	589 23	84%	972/494-8205 Fax 972/494-8707
Ethridge Elem Sch 2301 Sam Houston Dr, Garland 75044 Lucy Vincent	PK-5	T	749	79%	972/675-3020 Fax 972/675-3025
Freeman Elem Sch 1220 W Walnut St, Garland 75040 Kelly Garcia	PK-5	T	306 30	81%	972/494-8371 Fax 972/494-8835
Garland High Sch 310 S Garland Ave, Garland 75040 Holly Hines	9-12	TV	2,495	63%	972/494-8492 Fax 972/494-8415
George Washington Carver ES 2200 Wynn Joyce Rd, Garland 75043 Wendy Williams	PK-5	T	728	74%	972/487-4415 Fax 972/240-8042

---

9 Student Personnel	91 Safety/Security	275 Response To Intervention	298 Grant Writer/Ptnrships	**School Programs**	**Social Media**
10 Driver Ed/Safety	92 Magnet School	277 Remedial Math K-12	750 Chief Innovation Officer	A = Alternative Program	
1 Gifted/Talented	93 Parental Involvement	280 Literacy Coach	751 Chief of Staff	G = Adult Classes	🅵 = Facebook
2 Video Services	95 Tech Prep Program	285 STEM	752 Social Emotional Learning	M = Magnet Program	
3 Substance Abuse Prev	97 Chief Infomation Officer	286 Digital Learning		T = Title I Schoolwide	🅃 = Twitter
4 Erate	98 Chief Technology Officer	288 Common Core Standards	**Other School Types**	V = Career & Tech Ed Programs	
5 AIDS Education	270 Character Education	294 Accountability	Ⓐ = Alternative School		
6 Alternative/At Risk	271 Migrant Education	295 Network System	Ⓒ = Charter School	New Schools are shaded	
9 Multi-Cultural Curriculum	273 Teacher Mentor	296 Title II Programs	Ⓜ = Magnet School	New Superintendents and Principals are bold	
10 Social Work	274 Before/After Sch	297 Webmaster	Ⓨ = Year-Round School	Personnel with email addresses are underscored	

TX—105

Dallas County

School	Grades		Enroll	%	Phone
Giddens Steadham Elem Sch 6200 Danridge Rd, Rowlett 75089 Jade Hobbs	PK-5	T	524 25	47%	972/463-5887 Fax 972/463-7147
Gilbreath-Reed Career Tech Ctr 4885 N George Bush Hwy, Garland 75040 Coleman Bruman	Voc		500		972/487-4588 Fax 972/487-4589
ⓐ Gisd Alternative Ed Center 2015 S Country Club Rd, Garland 75041 Darrin Hemphill	K-12		69 24	64%	972/926-2691 Fax 972/926-2692
Glen Couch Elem Sch 4349 Waterhouse Blvd, Garland 75043 Armenia Smith	PK-5	T	620	65%	972/240-1801 Fax 972/240-9276
Golden Meadows Elem Sch 1726 Travis St, Garland 75042 Jacqueline Rhymes	PK-5	T	561 35	84%	972/494-8373 Fax 972/494-8709
Handley Elem Sch 3725 Broadway Blvd, Garland 75043 Cheryl Alexander	PK-5	T	477 24	84%	972/926-2540 Fax 972/926-2545
Heather Glen Elem Sch 5119 Heather Glen Dr, Garland 75043 Melissa True	PK-5	T	506 45	84%	972/270-2881 Fax 972/681-0078 ⓣ
Herfurth Elem Sch 7500 Miller Rd, Rowlett 75088 Jessica Hicks	PK-5	T	374 36	54%	972/475-7994 Fax 972/475-7391
Hickman Elem Sch 3114 Pinewood Dr, Garland 75044 Karla Beltran	PK-5	T	499	78%	972/675-3150 Fax 972/675-3155
ⓜ Hillside Acad for Excellence 2014 Dairy Rd, Garland 75041 Sonya Palmer	PK-5	T	423 25	55%	972/926-2550 Fax 972/926-2555 ⓣ
Hudson Middle Sch 4405 Hudson Park, Sachse 75048 Amber Hope	6-8	T	1,232 50	38%	972/675-3070 Fax 972/675-3077
ⓜ Jackson Tech Ctr Math Science 1310 Bobbie Ln, Garland 75042 David Dunphy	6-8	TV	1,327 50	63%	972/494-8362 Fax 972/494-8802
John W Armstrong Elem Sch 4750 Ben Davis Rd, Sachse 75048 Brandy Schneider	PK-5	T	844 50	30%	972/414-7480 Fax 972/414-7488
Keeley Elem Sch 8700 Liberty Grove Rd, Rowlett 75089 Sheri Taylor	PK-5		668 45	25%	972/412-2140 Fax 972/412-7061
ⓜ Kimberlin Acad for Excellence 1520 Cumberland Dr, Garland 75040 Tammy Sullivan	PK-5	T	485 35	36%	972/926-2560 Fax 972/926-2565
Lakeview Centennial High Sch 3505 Hayman Dr, Garland 75043 Maresa Bailey	9-12	TV	2,289	61%	972/240-3740 Fax 972/240-3750 ⓣ
Liberty Grove Elem Sch 10201 Liberty Grove Rd, Rowlett 75089 Debra Bottoms	PK-5	T	499 60	50%	972/487-4416 Fax 214/227-5348
Luna Elem Sch 1050 Lochness Ln, Garland 75044 Deborah Wilkerson	PK-5		305 40	34%	972/675-3040 Fax 972/675-3045
Lyles Middle Sch 4655 S Country Club Rd, Garland 75043 Michael Bland	6-8	TV	863 76	79%	972/240-3720 Fax 972/240-3723
Memorial Pathway Academy 2825 S 1st St, Garland 75041 Ida Perales	6-12	V	249 20		972/926-2650 Fax 972/926-2651
Montclair Elem Sch 5200 Marketplace Dr, Garland 75043 Karla Massey	PK-5		551 31	81%	972/279-4041 Fax 972/681-0565
Naaman Forest High Sch 4843 Naaman Forest Blvd, Garland 75040 Dr Keith Ellis	9-12	TV	2,150 112	57%	972/675-3091 Fax 972/675-3100
Nita Pearson Elem Sch 5201 Nita Pearson Dr, Rowlett 75088 Cherelle Wilson	PK-5	T	677 65	60%	972/463-7568 Fax 972/463-7623
Norma Dorsey Elem Sch 6200 Dexham Rd, Rowlett 75089 Leslie Russell	PK-5	T	630 50	45%	972/463-5595 Fax 972/463-1805
North Garland High Sch 2109 W Buckingham Rd, Garland 75042 Glenda Williams	9-12	TV	2,686	66%	972/675-3120 Fax 972/675-3145
Northlake Elem Sch 1626 Bosque Dr, Garland 75040 Dr Kathryn Metzinger	PK-5	T	570 33	79%	972/494-8359 Fax 972/494-8717
O'Banion Middle Sch 700 Birchwood Dr, Garland 75043 Earl Gilmore	6-8	TV	1,110 35	84%	972/279-6103 Fax 972/613-9532
Park Crest Elem Sch 2232 Parkcrest Dr, Garland 75041 Andrea Kleckner	PK-5	T	350 30	84%	972/926-2571 Fax 972/926-2575
Parsons Pre-K Sch 2202 Richoak Dr, Garland 75044 Disa McEwen	PK-PK	T	520	77%	972/675-8065 Fax 972/675-8061
Pathfinder Achievement Center 221 S 9th St, Garland 75040 Lacey Ajibola	Spec		46 6	80%	972/494-8520 Fax 972/494-8629
Routh Roach Elem Sch 1811 Mayfield Ave, Garland 75041 Aurora Trichell	PK-5	T	463 25	76%	972/926-2580 Fax 972/926-2585
Rowlett Elem Sch 3315 Carla Dr, Rowlett 75088 Kim Bain	PK-5	T	549 36	57%	972/475-3380 Fax 972/412-4484
Rowlett High Sch 4700 President George Bush Hwy, Rowlett 75088 Carmen Blakey	9-12	TV	2,577	41%	972/463-1712 Fax 972/412-2951
Sachse High Sch 3901 Miles Rd, Sachse 75048 Shae Creel	9-12	TV	2,765	39%	972/414-7450 Fax 972/414-7458
Sam Houston Middle Sch 2232 Sussex Dr, Garland 75041 Donald Hernandez	6-8	T	1,005 48	87%	972/926-2640 Fax 972/926-2647
Schrade Middle Sch 6201 Danridge Rd, Rowlett 75089 Tobi Schmidt	6-8	T	1,034 50	45%	972/463-8790 Fax 972/463-8793
Sellers Middle Sch 1009 Mars Dr, Garland 75040 Dr Vikki Mahagan	6-8	TV	835 60	83%	972/494-8337 Fax 972/494-8607
Sewell Elem Sch 4400 Hudson Park, Sachse 75048 Kimberly Marsh	PK-5	T	610 32	44%	972/675-3050 Fax 972/675-3053
Shorehaven Elem Sch 600 Shorehaven Dr, Garland 75040 Krista McClure	PK-5	T	404 24	86%	972/494-8346 Fax 972/494-8720
Shugart Elem Sch 4726 Rosehill Rd, Garland 75043 Salina Allen	PK-5	T	580 47	79%	972/240-3700 Fax 972/240-3701
South Garland High Sch 600 Colonel Dr, Garland 75043 Steven Ewing	9-12	TV	2,168 101	79%	972/926-2700 Fax 972/926-2727
Southgate Elem Sch 1115 Mayfield Ave, Garland 75041 Jennifer Fowler	PK-5	T	486 31	86%	972/926-2590 Fax 972/926-2595
Spring Creek Elem Sch 1510 Spring Creek Dr, Garland 75040 Teresa McCutcheon	PK-5	T	613 40	68%	972/675-3060 Fax 972/675-3065
Stephens Elem Sch 3700 Cheyenne Dr, Rowlett 75088 Jeffrey Waller	PK-5	T	655 44	67%	972/463-5790 Fax 972/463-5794

---

1 Superintendent	8 Curric/Instruct K-12	19 Chief Financial Officer	29 Family/Consumer Science	39 Social Studies K-12	49 English/Lang Arts Elem	59 Special Education Elem	69 Academic Assessment
2 Bus/Finance/Purchasing	9 Curric/Instruct Elem	20 Art K-12	30 Adult Education	40 Social Studies Elem	50 English/Lang Arts Sec	60 Special Education Sec	70 Research/Development
3 Buildings And Grounds	10 Curric/Instruct Sec	21 Art Elem	31 Career/Sch-to-Work K-12	41 Social Studies Sec	51 Reading K-12	61 Foreign/World Lang K-12	71 Public Information
4 Food Service	11 Federal Program	22 Art Sec	32 Career/Sch-to-Work Elem	42 Science K-12	52 Reading Elem	62 Foreign/World Lang Elem	72 Summer School
5 Transportation	12 Title I	23 Music K-12	33 Career/Sch-to-Work Sec	43 Science Elem	53 Reading Sec	63 Foreign/World Lang Sec	73 Instructional Tech
6 Athletic	13 Title V	24 Music Elem	34 Early Childhood Ed	44 Science Sec	54 Remedial Reading K-12	64 Religious Education K-12	74 Inservice Training
7 Health Services	15 Asst Superintendent	25 Music Sec	35 Health/Phys Education	45 Math K-12	55 Remedial Reading Elem	65 Religious Education Elem	75 Marketing/Distributive
	16 Instructional Media Svcs	26 Business Education	36 Guidance Services K-12	46 Math Elem	56 Remedial Reading Sec	66 Religious Education Sec	76 Info Systems
	17 Chief Operations Officer	27 Career & Tech Ed	37 Guidance Services Elem	47 Math Sec	57 Bilingual/ELL	67 School Board President	77 Psychological Assess
	18 Chief Academic Officer	28 Technology Education	38 Guidance Services Sec	48 English/Lang Arts K-12	58 Special Education K-12	68 Teacher Personnel	78 Affirmative Action

Texas School Directory — Dallas County

Public Schs..Principal	Grd	Prgm	Enr/#Cls	SN		
Toler Elem Sch 3520 Guthrie Rd, Garland 75043 Kerresha Strickland	PK-5	T	608 35	75%	972/226-3922 Fax 972/226-0262	
Vernal Lister Elem Sch 3131 Mars Dr, Garland 75040 Aishley Cohns	PK-5	T	469	64%	972/675-3030 Fax 972/675-3036	
ⓂWalnut Glen Academy Excellence 3101 Edgewood Dr, Garland 75042 Lisa Alexander	PK-5	T	418 30	56%	972/494-8330 Fax 972/494-8725	
ⓂWatson Tech Center Math & Sci 2601 Dairy Rd, Garland 75041 Adrian Leday	PK-5	T	583 20	54%	972/926-2600 Fax 972/926-2606	
Weaver Elem Sch 805 Pleasant Valley Rd, Garland 75040 Jennifer Thomason	PK-5	T	583 30	78%	972/494-8311 Fax 972/494-8721	
Webb Middle Sch 1610 Spring Creek Dr, Garland 75040 Dr Nikketta Wilson	6-8	TV	1,137 55	68%	972/675-3080 Fax 972/675-3089	
Williams Elem Sch 1821 Oldgate Ln, Garland 75042 Chucky Viernes	PK-5	T	300 20	81%	972/926-2610 Fax 972/926-2615	

● **Grand Prairie Ind School Dist** PID: 01010814 972/264-6141
2602 S Beltline Rd, Grand Prairie 75052 Fax 972/237-5440

Schools: 42 \ *Teachers:* 1,963 \ *Students:* 29,339 \
Special Ed Students: 2,500 \ *LEP Students:* 8,020 \ *College-Bound:* 54% \
Ethnic: Asian 3%, African American 18%, Hispanic 66%, Caucasian 12% \ *Exp:* $379 (High) \ *Poverty:* 18% \ *Title I:* $7,600,375 \
Special Education: $5,066,000 \ *Open-Close:* 08/19 - 05/21 \ *DTBP:* $45 (Low) \ f t

Linda Ellis 1,288	Nancy Bridges 2,15		
Robb Welch 2,15	Vicki Bridges 3,15		
Dominik Peterson 4	Dana Acock 5*		
Gary Bartel 6	Pat Shull 7,85		
Dr Nuggett Cunningham 8,15,69	Patricia Lewis 11,15		
Calvin Harrison 15,79,91	Elna Davis 15		
Gabriel Trujillo 15	Susanna Ramirez 15,34,93		
Traci Davis 15	Dr Vern Alexander 15,72,294		
Tara Cahill 16,286	Troy Mathieu 17		
Winston Minix 27,31	Magda Grape 57		
Dr Dorothea Gordon 58	Burke Hall 67		
Melissa Steger 69	Sam Buchmeyer 71		
Chris Malone 73,76,295	Chris Gasaway 98		
Kasie Roden 285			

Public Schs..Principal	Grd	Prgm	Enr/#Cls	SN		
Austin Elem Science Acad 815 NW 7th St, Grand Prairie 75050 Tanya Gilliam	PK-5	T	502 27	90%	972/343-4600 Fax 972/343-4699	
Bonham Early Ed Sch 1301 E Coral Way, Grand Prairie 75051 Rachel Mendoza	PK-PK	T	334 15	82%	972/262-4255 Fax 972/522-3199	
Bowie Fine Arts Academy 425 Alice Dr, Grand Prairie 75051 Ana Holland	PK-5	T	495 32	90%	972/262-7348 Fax 972/264-6219	
Bush Global Ldrshp Acad 511 E Springdale Ln, Grand Prairie 75052 Dina Jammer	PK-5	T	490 27	84%	972/237-1628 Fax 972/237-1059	
Colin Powell Elem Sch 5009 S Carrier Pkwy, Grand Prairie 75052 **Marchelle Sterling**	PK-5	T	534 25	37%	972/642-3961 Fax 972/642-4049	
Crockett Early Education Sch 1340 Skyline Rd, Grand Prairie 75051 Magdalena Garcia	PK-PK	T	597	94%	972/262-5353 Fax 972/343-6299	
ⒶCrosswinds Accelerated HS 1100 N Carrier Pkwy, Grand Prairie 75050 Dr Suzy Meyer	9-12	T	378 40	78%	972/522-2950 Fax 972/522-2999	
Daniels Academy of Science and 801 SW 19th St, Grand Prairie 75051 **Marva Maynard-Walter**	PK 5	T	439 34	92%	972/264-7803 Fax 972/343-4599	
Data at Adams MS 833 W Tarrant Rd, Grand Prairie 75050 Darwert Johnson	6-8	T	796 60	89%	972/262-1934 Fax 972/522-3099	
Dezavala Envir Sci Acad 3410 Kirby Creek Dr, Grand Prairie 75052 Mary Smith	PK-5	T	862 26	80%	972/642-0448 Fax 972/264-9495	
Dickinson Elem Sch 1902 Palmer Trl, Grand Prairie 75052 Whitney Carlisle	PK-5	T	405 26	73%	972/641-1664 Fax 972/641-8601	
Dubiski Career High Sch 2990 S State Highway 161, Grand Prairie 75052 Larry Jones	9-12	TV	1,735	70%	972/343-7800 Fax 972/343-7899 f t	
Eisenhower Elem Sch 2102 N Carrier Pkwy, Grand Prairie 75050 Dr Shelley Handcock	PK-5	T	809 24	79%	972/262-3717 Fax 972/264-9473 f t	
Fannin Middle Sch 301 NE 28th St, Grand Prairie 75050 Roberto Lopez	6-8	T	506 24	93%	972/262-8668 Fax 972/343-4799	
Florence Hill Elem Sch 4213 S Robinson Rd, Grand Prairie 75052 Catherine Bridges	PK-5	T	594 27	60%	972/264-0802 Fax 972/264-9475	
Garcia Elem Sch 2444 Graham St, Grand Prairie 75050 Martin Zamarripa	PK-5	T	577 41	91%	972/237-0001 Fax 972/237-9660	
Garner Fine Arts Academy 145 W Polo Rd, Grand Prairie 75052 Alisha Crumley	PK-5		1,001 40	44%	972/262-5000 Fax 972/522-3399	
©Grand Prairie Collegiate Inst 1502 College St, Grand Prairie 75050 Darnisha Carreathers	6-12	T	290	58%	972/343-3120 Fax 972/343-3159	
Grand Prairie Early Clg HS 101 Gopher Blvd, Grand Prairie 75050 Laigha Boyle	9-12		150		972/809-5711 Fax 972/809-5775	
Grand Prairie Fine Arts Acad 102 Gopher Blvd, Grand Prairie 75050 Maria Schell	6-12	T	832	41%	972/237-5603 Fax 972/343-6399	
Grand Prairie High Sch 101 High School Dr, Grand Prairie 75050 Laigha Boyle	9-12	TV	2,806 85	85%	972/809-5711 Fax 972/809-5775	
Harry S Truman Middle Sch 1501 Coffeyville Trl, Grand Prairie 75052 Letycia Fowler	6-8	T	593	72%	972/641-7676 Fax 972/522-3999	
Hobbs Williams Elem Sch 1635 SE 14th St, Grand Prairie 75051 Ami Potts	PK-5	T	633 34	85%	972/522-2700 Fax 972/522-2799 f t	
Jackson Middle Sch 3504 Corn Valley Rd, Grand Prairie 75052 Robert Wallace	6-8	T	988 45	79%	972/264-2704 Fax 972/343-7599 f t	
ⒶJohnson Daep 650 Stonewall Dr, Grand Prairie 75052 Kerry Rapier	6-12		73 18	87%	972/262-7244 Fax 972/264-9479 f t	
Juan Seguin Elem Sch 1450 SE 4th St, Grand Prairie 75050 **Amanda Rodriguez**	PK-5	T	487 45	87%	972/522-7100 Fax 972/522-7199	
Lee Elem Sch 401 E Grand Prairie Rd, Grand Prairie 75051 Bianca Green	PK-5	TV	560 89	92%	972/262-6785 Fax 972/343-6099	
Marshall Leadership Academy 1160 W Warrior Trl, Grand Prairie 75052 Gordon Carlisle	PK-5	T	678 31	73%	972/522-7200 Fax 972/522-7299 f t	

89 Student Personnel	91 Safety/Security	275 Response To Intervention	298 Grant Writer/Ptnrships	**School Programs**	**Social Media**
90 Driver Ed/Safety	92 Magnet School	277 Remedial Math K-12	750 Chief Innovation Officer	A = Alternative Program	
91 Gifted/Talented	93 Parental Involvement	280 Literacy Coach	751 Chief of Staff	G = Adult Classes	f = Facebook
92 Video Services	95 Tech Prep Program	285 STEM	752 Social Emotional Learning	M = Magnet Program	
93 Substance Abuse Prev	97 Chief Information Officer	286 Digital Learning		T = Title I Schoolwide	t = Twitter
94 Erate	98 Chief Technology Officer	288 Common Core Standards	**Other School Types**	V = Career & Tech Ed Programs	
95 AIDS Education	270 Character Education	294 Accountability	Ⓐ = Alternative Program		
96 Alternative/At Risk	271 Migrant Education	295 Network System	Ⓒ = Charter School	New Schools are shaded	
97 Multi-Cultural Curriculum	273 Teacher Mentor	296 Title II Programs	Ⓜ = Magnet School	New Superintendents and Principals are bold	
98 Social Work	274 Before/After Sch	297 Webmaster	Ⓨ = Year-Round School	Personnel with email addresses are underscored	

TX–107

Dallas County — Market Data Retrieval

School	Grd	Prgm	Enr/#Cls	SN	Phone
Mike Moseley Elem Sch 1851 W Camp Wisdom Rd, Grand Prairie 75052 Tuyet Huynh	PK-5	T	622	64%	972/522-2800 Fax 972/522-2899
Ochoa/Milam Steam Academy 2030 Proctor Dr, Grand Prairie 75051 Dinnah Escanilla	PK-5	T	794 40	88%	972/262-7131 Fax 972/264-9492
Ronald Reagan Middle Sch 4616 Bardin Rd, Grand Prairie 75052 Wendy Mathis	6-8	T	896	48%	972/522-7300 Fax 972/522-7399
Sallye Moore Clg&Career Prep 3150 Waterwood Dr, Grand Prairie 75052 Nichole Holland	PK-8	T	428 29	69%	972/660-2261 Fax 972/343-4899
Sam Rayburn Steam Acad 2800 Reforma Dr, Grand Prairie 75052 Jennifer Oliver	PK-5	T	566 22	85%	972/264-8900 Fax 972/522-3899
© School for the Highly Gifted 2990 S Highway 161, Grand Prairie 75052 Holly Mohler	1-5		106	35%	972/343-7864
South Grand Prairie 9th GR Ctr 305 W Warrior Trl, Grand Prairie 75052 Donnie Bartlett	9-9		889		972/264-1769 Fax 972/343-7698
South Grand Prairie Echs 305 W Warrior Trl, Grand Prairie 75052 Dr Joanna Slaton	9-12		200		972/343-7640 Fax 972/623-9051
South Grand Prairie High Sch 301 W Warrior Trl, Grand Prairie 75052 Donna Grant	10-12	T	2,368 103	63%	972/343-1500 Fax 972/642-7902
Travis World Language Academy 525 NE 15th St, Grand Prairie 75050 Veronica Kunschik	K-7	T	740	92%	972/262-2990 Fax 972/343-6198
© Uplift Lee Prep Sch [309] 401 E Grand Prairie Rd, Grand Prairie 75051 Dani Erbert	K-5	T	184	84%	972/262-6785
Whitt Fine Arts Academy 3320 S Edelweiss Dr, Grand Prairie 75052 April Wyatt	PK-5	T	649 37	77%	972/264-5024 Fax 972/343-4999
Young Mens Leadership Academy 2205 SE 4th St, Grand Prairie 75051 Joseph Melms	6-8	T	745	88%	972/264-8651 Fax 972/522-3699
Young Womens Leadership Acad 1204 E Marshall Dr, Grand Prairie 75051 Janna Burns	6-12	T	895	85%	972/343-7400 Fax 972/343-7499

• **Highland Park Ind Sch Dist** PID: 01011038   214/780-3000
7015 Westchester Dr, Dallas 75205   Fax 214/780-3099

Schools: 7 \ **Teachers:** 469 \ **Students:** 7,000 \ **Special Ed Students:** 578 \ **LEP Students:** 56 \ **College-Bound:** 92% \ **Ethnic:** Asian 6%, African American 1%, Hispanic 5%, Caucasian 88% \ **Exp:** $113 (Low) \ **Poverty:** 3% \ **Title I:** $171,264 \ **Special Education:** $960,000 \ **Open-Close:** 08/22 - 05/29 \ **DTBP:** $173 (High)

Dr Tom Trigg 1
Mary Witcher 2
Shane Bryan 3
Johnny Ringo 6
Lisa Wilson 8,15,34,45,57,81,90
Lydia Walden 36,77,83,88
Jim Hitzelberger 67
Dr Stephanie Brown 69
Lisa Ham 73
Mark Rowden 91
Chase Park 2
Mike White 2,5,11,15,70
Lynn Prichard 4
Micki Hinojosa 6
Jon Dahlander 15,71,751
Laurie Gagne 58
Brenda West 68
Charlie Jackson 73,76,98
Kim Brooks 81
Mark Hunter 295

Public Schs..Principal	Grd	Prgm	Enr/#Cls	SN	
Arch H McCulloch Interm Sch 3555 Granada Ave, Dallas 75205 Clifton Moran	5-6		1,133 50		214/780-3500 Fax 214/780-3599
Highland Park High Sch 4220 Emerson Ave, Dallas 75205 Walter Kelly	9-12		2,180		214/780-3700 Fax 214/780-3799
Highland Park Middle Sch 3555 Granada Ave, Dallas 75205 Jeremy Gilbert	7-8		1,106 75		214/780-3600 Fax 214/780-3699
John S Armstrong Elem Sch 3600 Cornell Ave, Dallas 75205 Betsy Cummins	PK-4		531 26		214/780-3100 Fax 214/780-3199
John S Bradfield Elem Sch 4300 Southern Ave, Dallas 75205 Regina Dumar	PK-4		692 31		214/780-3200 Fax 214/780-3299
Robert S Hyer Elem Sch 8385 Durham St, Dallas 75225 Debbie Burt	PK-4		697 35		214/780-3300 Fax 214/780-3399
University Park Elem Sch 3505 Amherst Ave, Dallas 75225 Candace Judd	PK-4		652 30		214/780-3400 Fax 214/780-3402

• **Int'l Leadership of Texas Dist** PID: 12261400   972/479-9078
1820 N Glenville Dr, Richardson 75081   Fax 972/479-9129

Schools: 19 \ **Teachers:** 675 \ **Students:** 19,473 \ **Special Ed Students:** 442 \ **LEP Students:** 2,397 \ **Ethnic:** Asian 6%, African American 24%, Hispanic 56%, Caucasian 15% \ **Open-Close:** 08/15 - 05/21

Eddie Conger 1
Frank Crabill 3
Laura Carrasco 8,18
Anthony Palagonia 15
Rodney Cooksy 15
Claudia Neira 68
Jim Croswell 71
Angela Marcellus 79
Ronald Keuhler 2,19
Rodney Minor 5
Krystal Lovato 12
Dr Matilda Orozco 15
James Williams 67
Jason Sturgeon 69
Joyce Wheeler 73,98
Aaron Thorson 751

Public Schs..Principal	Grd	Prgm	Enr/#Cls	SN	
© Int'l Ldrship TX-Lancaster 1900 W Pleasant Run Rd, Lancaster 75146 Senta Wilson	K-8		1,261		469/862-4237
© Int'l Ldrshp TX-Arlington ES 4950 S Bowen Rd, Arlington 76017 Dionel Waters	K-8	T	935	61%	817/496-0400
© Int'l Ldrshp TX-Arlngtn GR PR 2851 Ragland Rd, Grand Prairie 75052 Quentyn Seamster	9-10	T	215	58%	682/808-5960 Fax 817/635-3118
© Int'l Ldrshp TX-College Sta 3610 Longmire Dr, College Sta 77845 Dr Heather McMahan	K-8		950		979/704-6027 Fax 979/704-5332
© Int'l Ldrshp TX-East Ft Worth 5901 Boca Raton Blvd, Fort Worth 76112 Nikia Smith	K-8		1,166		817/395-1766 Fax 817/446-4270
© Int'l Ldrshp TX-Garland 3301 N Shiloh Rd, Garland 75044 Jade Esquivel	K-8		941		972/414-8000 Fax 972/495-2405
© Int'l Ldrshp TX-Garland HS 4413 N Shiloh Rd, Garland 75044 Karen Marx	9-12	T	621	52%	972/414-3414 Fax 469/635-2689
© Int'l Ldrshp TX-Grand Prairie 3501 S Great Southwest Pkwy, Grand Prairie 75052 Valerie Layne	K-8	T	1,406	71%	469/348-7960
© Int'l Ldrshp TX-Katy 24406 Franz Rd, Katy 77493 Dr Sheri Hawthorn	K-8	T	1,314	49%	281/394-9417 Fax 346/387-7044
© Int'l Ldrshp TX-Katy Westpark 20055 Beechnut St, Richmond 77407 Mark Hemphill	9-12		221		832/222-9470 Fax 832/222-9112

1 Superintendent	8 Curric/Instruct K-12	19 Chief Financial Officer	29 Family/Consumer Science	39 Social Studies K-12	49 English/Lang Arts Elem	59 Special Education Elem	69 Academic Assessment
2 Bus/Finance/Purchasing	9 Curric/Instruct Elem	20 Art K-12	30 Adult Education	40 Social Studies Elem	50 English/Lang Arts Sec	60 Special Education Sec	70 Research/Development
3 Buildings And Grounds	10 Curric/Instruct Sec	21 Art Elem	31 Career/Sch-to-Work K-12	41 Social Studies Sec	51 Reading K-12	61 Foreign/World Lang K-12	71 Public Information
4 Food Service	11 Federal Program	22 Art Sec	32 Career/Sch-to-Work Elem	42 Science K-12	52 Reading Elem	62 Foreign/World Lang Elem	72 Summer School
5 Transportation	12 Title I	23 Music K-12	33 Career/Sch-to-Work Sec	43 Science Elem	53 Reading Sec	63 Foreign/World Lang Sec	73 Instructional Tech
6 Athletic	13 Title V	24 Music Elem	34 Early Childhood Ed	44 Science Sec	54 Remedial Reading K-12	64 Religious Education K-12	74 Inservice Training
7 Health Services	14 Asst Superintendent	25 Music Sec	35 Health/Phys Education	45 Math K-12	55 Remedial Reading Elem	65 Religious Education Elem	75 Marketing/Distributive
	15 Instructional Media Svcs	26 Business Education	36 Guidance Services K-12	46 Math Elem	56 Remedial Reading Sec	66 Religious Education Sec	76 Info Systems
	16 Chief Operations Officer	27 Career & Tech Ed	37 Guidance Services Elem	47 Math Sec	57 Bilingual/ELL	67 School Board President	77 Psychological Assess
	18 Chief Academic Officer	28 Technology Education	38 Guidance Services Sec	48 English/Lang Arts K-12	58 Special Education K-12	68 Teacher Personnel	78 Affirmative Action

Texas School Directory — Dallas County

School	Grd	Prgm	Enr/#Cls	SN	Phone
Int'l Ldrshp TX-Keller 2301 Heritage Trace Pkwy, Fort Worth 76177 Armando Rendon	K-8		457	23%	817/665-0646 Fax 817/232-8220
Int'l Ldrshp TX-Keller Saginaw 10537 US Highway 287, Fort Worth 76131 Valerie Layne	9-12		550		682/250-3701
Int'l Ldrshp TX-Lanc-DeSoto HS 901 N Polk St, Desoto 75115 Marco DeLeon	9-9		44		469/786-2850 Fax 972/231-7995
Int'l Ldrshp TX-N RichInd Hill 4131 Rufe Snow Dr, N RichInd Hls 76180 Gerard Doyle	K-8	T	1,351	52%	817/576-9031
Int'l Ldrshp TX-Orem 5445 E Orem Dr, Houston 77048 Joshua Brown	K-8		1,170		713/987-9435
Int'l Ldrshp TX-Saginaw 500 N Old Decatur Rd, Fort Worth 76179 Nanette Coleman	K-8		1,251		682/250-3600
Int'l Ldrshp TX-Westpark 15300 Bellaire Blvd, Houston 77083 Charlie Butler	K-8		1,342		346/203-4126
Int'l Ldrshp TX-Windmill Lakes 9898 Windmill Lakes Blvd, Houston 77075 Mayra Arreola	K-8		1,252		832/667-0453
Int'l Ldrshp TX-Wml-Orem HS 9901 Windmill Lakes Blvd, Houston 77075 Stephanie Mott	9-9		100		832/649-6817 Fax 832/271-7410

● Irving Ind School Dist PID: 01011105
2621 W Airport Fwy, Irving 75062
972/600-5000 Fax 972/215-5003

Schools: 39 \ **Teachers:** 2,283 \ **Students:** 33,188 \ **Special Ed Students:** 2,574 \ **LEP Students:** 12,325 \ **College-Bound:** 60% \ **Ethnic:** Asian 3%, African American 13%, Hispanic 73%, Native American: 2%, Caucasian 9% \ **Exp:** $246 (Med) \ **Poverty:** 21% \ **Title I:** $10,835,435 \ **Special Education:** $6,750,000 \ **Open-Close:** 08/19 - 05/28 \ **DTBP:** $193 (High) \ f t

Magda Hernandez 1
Jim Scrivner 3
Olga Rosenberger 4
Clint Roddy 6
Julie Miller 8
Patricia Alvarado 16
Shawn Blessing 27,31
Dr Sandi Cravens 35,85
Eric Haggard 39
A Jenkins 67
Katie Gilliland 68
Dr Whitcomb Johnstone 70
Bonnie Russell 76
Terry Zettle 91
Vivian Schmitz 271

Gary Micinski 2,19
Thomas Crpiran 3
Don Sturdivant 5,91
Karyn Beauchamp 7
Fernando Natividad 11
Jeff King 20,23
Delia Watley 30
Dr Tracey Brown 36
Rita Ruiz 48
Jorge Acosta 68
Jackie Gorena 69
Alvin McQuarters 73,98,295
Holley Nasky 81*
Denise Courchesne 93
Samantha Echebelem 275

Public Schs..Principal	Grd	Prgm	Enr/#Cls	SN	Phone
Austin Middle Sch 825 E Union Bower Rd, Irving 75061 **Dr Channa Barrett**	6-8	TV	992 60	87%	972/600-3100 Fax 972/600-3105
Ⓐ Barbara Cardwell Career Prep 101 E Union Bower Rd, Irving 75061 Lesley Kelley	6-12	TV	354 60	68%	972/600-6140 Fax 972/273-6188 t
Barton Elem Sch 2931 Conflans Rd, Irving 75061 Manuel Espino	K-5	T	751 43	84%	972/600-4100 Fax 972/600-4110 t
Bowie Middle Sch 600 E 6th St, Irving 75060 Natasha Stewart	6-8	TV	970 70	83%	972/600-3000 Fax 972/600-3044
Brandenburg Elem Sch 2800 Hillcrest Dr, Irving 75062 Netassha Rendon	PK-5	T	850 46	77%	972/600-7100 Fax 972/258-7199
Britain Elem Sch 631 Edmondson Dr, Irving 75060 Adriana Rico	PK-5	T	662 60	88%	972/600-3800 Fax 972/600-3899 f t
Clifton Early Childhood Sch 3950 Pleasant Run Rd, Irving 75038 Leigh Ann McNeese	PK-PK	T	643 17	88%	972/600-4200 Fax 972/261-2849
Crockett Middle Sch 2431 Hancock St, Irving 75061 Bianca Johnson	6-8	TV	909 87	84%	972/600-4700 Fax 972/313-4770 f t
Elliott Elem Sch 1900 S Story Rd, Irving 75060 Sheila Peragine	K-5	T	647 50	78%	972/600-4300 Fax 972/600-4316
Farine Elem Sch 615 Metker St, Irving 75062 Joe Estrada	K-5	T	756 46	67%	972/600-7900 Fax 972/261-2799 t
Franklin Monroe Gilbert ES 1501 E Pioneer Dr, Irving 75061 Claudia Ruiz	K-5	T	715 48	87%	972/600-0400 Fax 972/721-8480
Hanes Elem Sch 2730 Cheyenne St, Irving 75062 Ed Henderson	K-5	T	641 36	81%	972/600-3600 Fax 972/261-2950
Houston Middle Sch 3033 Country Club Dr W, Irving 75038 Jeffrey Dorman	6-8	T	872	80%	972/600-7500 Fax 972/261-2399
Irving High Sch 900 N O Connor Rd, Irving 75061 Ahna Gomez	9-12	GTV	2,571 110	75%	972/600-6300 Fax 972/273-8319
Irving Reg Day Sch Pgrm-Deaf 631 Edmondson Dr, Irving 75060 Sherry Clifton	Spec		50		972/600-3800 Fax 972/554-3899
J O Davis Elem Sch 310 Davis Dr, Irving 75061 Angela Long	K-5	T	867 61	79%	972/600-4900 Fax 972/600-4949
J O Schulze Elem Sch 1200 S Irving Heights Dr, Irving 75060 Robin Bayer	K-5	T	669 40	88%	972/600-3500 Fax 972/600-3599 f
Jack E Singley Academy 4601 N MacArthur Blvd, Irving 75038 **Melanie Kibodeaux**	9-12	T	1,733	72%	972/600-5300 Fax 972/600-5301
John Haley Elem Sch 1100 Schulze Dr, Irving 75060 Lindsey Sanders	K-5	T	693 45	90%	972/600-6600 Fax 972/273-6608
John R Good Elem Sch 1200 E Union Bower Rd, Irving 75061 Alberto Zavala	K-5	T	745 56	89%	972/600-3300 Fax 972/721-3379
Johnston Elem Sch 2801 Rutgers Dr, Irving 75062 Stephen Pollard	K-5	T	829 50	83%	972/600-7700 Fax 972/600-7799
Kinkeade Early Childhood Sch 2333 Cameron Pl, Irving 75060 Jennifer McKee	PK-PK	T	565 22	82%	972/600-6500 Fax 972/600-6549
Lady Bird Johnson Middle Sch 3601 W Pioneer Dr, Irving 75061 James Clark	6-8	T	1,014	78%	972/600-0500 Fax 972/986-6830
Lamar Middle Sch 219 Crandall Rd, Irving 75060 Eric Ogle	6-8	T	839 100	78%	972/600-4400 Fax 972/600-4499
Lee Elem Sch 1600 Carlisle St, Irving 75062 Angel Rico	K-5	T	668 50	77%	972/600-7800 Fax 972/261-2629 f t
Lively Elem Sch 1800 Plymouth Dr W, Irving 75061 Fernando Vadillo	K-5	T	810	78%	972/600-6700 Fax 972/273-6710

9	Student Personnel	91	Safety/Security	275	Response To Intervention	298	Grant Writer/Ptnrships
0	Driver Ed/Safety	92	Magnet School	277	Remedial Math K-12	750	Chief Innovation Officer
1	Gifted/Talented	93	Parental Involvement	280	Literacy Coach	751	Chief of Staff
2	Video Services	95	Tech Prep Program	285	STEM	752	Social Emotional Learning
3	Substance Abuse Prev	97	Chief Information Officer	286	Digital Learning		
4	Erate	98	Chief Technology Officer	288	Common Core Standards		
5	AIDS Education	270	Character Education	294	Accountability		
8	Alternative/At Risk	271	Migrant Education	295	Network System		
9	Multi-Cultural Curriculum	273	Teacher Mentor	296	Title II Programs		
0	Social Work	274	Before/After Sch	297	Webmaster		

School Programs
A = Alternative Program
G = Adult Classes
M = Magnet Program
T = Title I Schoolwide
V = Career & Tech Ed Programs

Other School Types
Ⓐ = Alternative School
Ⓒ = Charter School
Ⓜ = Magnet School
Ⓨ = Year-Round School

Social Media
f = Facebook
t = Twitter

New Schools are shaded
New Superintendents and Principals are bold
Personnel with email addresses are underscored

TX—109

Dallas County — Market Data Retrieval

School	Grd	Prgm	Enr	/#Cls	SN	Phone
Lorenzo De Zavala Middle Sch 707 W Pioneer Dr, Irving 75061 Anika Horgan	6-8	TV	861		82%	972/600-6000 Fax 972/273-8924
MacArthur High Sch 3700 N MacArthur Blvd, Irving 75062 Deeadra Brown	9-12	GTV	2,793	120	61%	972/600-7200 Fax 972/261-2299
Nimitz High Sch 100 W Oakdale Rd, Irving 75060 Francisco Miranda	9-12	TV	2,480	70	72%	972/600-5700 Fax 972/273-8610
Otis Brown Elem Sch 2501 10th St, Irving 75060 Maria Bloomfield	K-5	T	816	60	85%	972/600-4000 Fax 972/600-4099
Paul Keyes Elem Sch 1501 N Britain Rd, Irving 75061 Blanca De La Sierra	K-5	T	698	52	90%	972/600-3400 Fax 972/600-3405
Pierce Early Childhood Sch 901 N Britain Rd, Irving 75061 Jennifer Dickson	PK-PK	T	492	22	89%	972/600-3700 Fax 972/554-3749
Stipes Elem Sch 3100 Cross Timbers Dr, Irving 75060 Kelly Giddens	K-5	T	695		72%	972/600-4500 Fax 972/600-4598
Ⓐ Student Reassignment Ctr 1600 E Shady Grove Rd, Irving 75060 Scott Sralla	6-12		150	12		972/600-3900 Fax 972/721-3205
Thomas Haley Elem Sch 3601 Cheyenne St, Irving 75062 Henry Taylor	K-5	T	851	40	74%	972/600-7000 Fax 972/261-2599
Townley Elem Sch 1030 W Vilbig St, Irving 75060 Liz Munoz	K-5	T	727	50	73%	972/600-6800 Fax 972/600-6877
Townsell Elem Sch 3700 Pleasant Run Rd, Irving 75038 Amber Brooks	K-5	T	795		80%	972/600-5500 Fax 972/255-6008
Travis Middle Sch 1600 Finley Rd, Irving 75062 Denise Anderson	6-8	TV	994	45	65%	972/600-0100 Fax 972/261-2450
Wheeler Transitional Dev Ctr 1600 E Shady Grove Rd, Irving 75060 Nancy Atkinson	Spec		26	12		972/600-3750 Fax 972/554-3769

- **Lancaster Ind School Dist** PID: 01011337
422 S Centre Ave, Lancaster 75146
972/218-1400
Fax 972/218-1401

Schools: 11 \ **Teachers:** 426 \ **Students:** 7,600 \ **Special Ed Students:** 614 \ **LEP Students:** 547 \ **College-Bound:** 65% \ **Ethnic:** African American 77%, Hispanic 20%, Native American: 1%, Caucasian 2% \ **Exp:** $318 (High) \ **Poverty:** 22% \ **Title I:** $2,432,746 \ **Special Education:** $1,131,000 \ **Open-Close:** 08/19 - 05/28 \ **DTBP:** $19 (Low) \

Elijah Granger 1
Shonna Pumphrey 2,19
Dr John Price 3,17
Dawn Rice 5
Karleen Watson 7*
Pamela Brown 15,57,68,79,81
Garry Williams 20*
Crystal Cromer 58
Ellen Clark 67
Kelli Watson 73
Clifford Wherley 91
Sonya Butler 98,295
Lachele Washington 275
Dana Mosley 2
James Thomas 3
Upenda Sibley 4
Beverly Humphrey 6,71
Shemeka Williams 8,15
Tonia Howard 18,74
Sheila Benskin 27,31
Susan Keen 58
Connie Isabel 69
Pamela Carroll 78*
Dr Kanesha Waites 93
Lisa Bacon 274*
Dr Lamont Smith 294

Public Schs..Principal	Grd	Prgm	Enr/#Cls	SN	
Beltline Elem Sch 1355 W Belt Line Rd, Lancaster 75146 Wendy Hawthrone	PK-5	T	630 29	89%	972/218-1608 Fax 972/218-1620
Elsie Robertson Middle Sch 822 W Pleasant Run Rd, Lancaster 75146 Willisa House	7-8	TV	1,007 51	85%	972/218-1660 Fax 972/218-3080
GW Carver 6th GR STEM Lrng Ctr 1005 Westridge Ave, Lancaster 75146 Jamilla Thomas	6-6	T	532	91%	972/218-1577 Fax 972/218-1589
Houston Elem Sch 2929 Marquis Ln, Lancaster 75134 Tatanisha Stevenson	PK-5	T	703 18	89%	972/218-1512 Fax 972/218-1524
Ⓐ J D Hall Learning Center 602 E 2nd St, Lancaster 75146 Antoinette Mathews	1-12	V	60 5		972/218-1441 Fax 972/218-1442
Lancaster High Sch 200 E Wintergreen Rd, Lancaster 75134 Eleanor Webb	9-12	GTV	2,133	78%	972/218-1800 Fax 972/218-5797
Lancaster STEM Early Clg HS 200 E Wintergreen Rd, Lancaster 75134 Anthony Thornhill	9-12		401		972/218-1800
Pleasant Run Elem Sch 427 W Pleasant Run Rd, Lancaster 75146 Marlon Waites	PK-5	T	683 21	94%	972/218-1538 Fax 972/218-1550
Rolling Hills Elem Sch 450 Rolling Hills Pl, Lancaster 75146 Cherish Pipkins	PK-5	T	509 24	91%	972/218-1525 Fax 972/218-1537
Rosa Parks-Millbrook Sch 630 Millbrook Dr, Lancaster 75146 Yvonne Thornton	PK-5	T	496 27	89%	972/218-1564 Fax 972/218-3420
West Main Elem Sch 531 W Main St, Lancaster 75146 Gail Wright	PK-5	T	676 15	90%	972/218-1551 Fax 972/218-1563

- **Mesquite Ind School Dist** PID: 01011399
3819 Towne Crossing Blvd, Mesquite 75150
972/288-6411
Fax 972/882-7787

Schools: 47 \ **Teachers:** 2,610 \ **Students:** 39,900 \ **Special Ed Students:** 4,043 \ **LEP Students:** 9,221 \ **College-Bound:** 52% \ **Ethnic:** Asian 2%, African American 25%, Hispanic 57%, Native American: 1%, Caucasian 15% \ **Exp:** $276 (Med) \ **Poverty:** 20% \ **Title I:** $11,959,051 \ **Special Education:** $7,037,000 \ **Open-Close:** 08/19 - 05/28 \ **DTBP:** $184 (High) \

Dr David Vroonland 1
Scott Owens 3
Beth Dittman 7,85
Jennifer Hulme 12
Dr Karyn Cummings 15*
Mary Woodard 16
Kristi Krajca 27,31
Elaine Whitlock 67
Laura Jobe 71,297
Cara Jackson 73,286
Kristi Mullenix 77
Dr Shelley Garrett 91
Kathryn Bohling 2,3,15
Bette Mogg 4
Dr Treva Franklin 8,11,15,34,83,88,93,296
Beth Nicholas 15,57,58,69,72,275
Mary Randall 15,68,74
Steve Andre 20,23
Kim Johnson 58
Donna McAda 69,288
Karen Lloyd 72,275
Lane King 76
Russell Weeks 81
Debbie Tanton 273

Public Schs..Principal	Grd	Prgm	Enr/#Cls	SN	
A C New Middle Sch 3700 S Belt Line Rd, Mesquite 75181 Regina Jackson	6-8	TV	980 40	90%	972/882-5600 Fax 972/882-5620
Achziger Elem Sch 3300 Ridge Ranch Rd, Mesquite 75181 Kristi Gregory	PK-5	T	971	76%	972/290-4180 Fax 972/882-4190
B J Smith Elem Sch 2300 Mesquite Valley Rd, Mesquite 75149 Charelene Goss	PK-5	T	494 35	60%	972/882-7080 Fax 972/882-7090
Ben Tisinger Elem Sch 1701 Hillcrest St, Mesquite 75149 Amanda Relf	PK-5	T	824 33	88%	972/882-5120 Fax 972/882-5130

1	Superintendent	8	Curric/Instruct K-12	19	Chief Financial Officer	29	Family/Consumer Science	39	Social Studies K-12	49 English/Lang Arts Elem	59 Special Education Elem	69 Academic Assessment
2	Bus/Finance/Purchasing	9	Curric/Instruct Elem	20	Art K-12	30	Adult Education	40	Social Studies Elem	50 English/Lang Arts Sec	60 Special Education Sec	70 Research/Development
3	Buildings And Grounds	10	Curric/Instruct Sec	21	Art Elem	31	Career/Sch-to-Work K-12	41	Social Studies Sec	51 Reading K-12	61 Foreign/World Lang K-12	71 Public Information
4	Food Service	11	Federal Program	22	Art Sec	32	Career/Sch-to-Work Elem	42	Science K-12	52 Reading Elem	62 Foreign/World Lang Elem	72 Summer School
5	Transportation	12	Title I	23	Music K-12	33	Career/Sch-to-Work Sec	43	Science Elem	53 Reading Sec	63 Foreign/World Lang Sec	73 Instructional Tech
6	Athletic	13	Title V	24	Music Elem	34	Early Childhood Ed	44	Science Sec	54 Remedial Reading K-12	64 Religious Education K-12	74 Inservice Training
7	Health Services	15	Asst Superintendent	25	Music Sec	35	Health/Phys Education	45	Math K-12	55 Remedial Reading Elem	65 Religious Education Elem	75 Marketing/Distributive
		16	Instructional Media Svcs	26	Business Education	36	Guidance Services K-12	46	Math Elem	56 Remedial Reading Sec	66 Religious Education Sec	76 Info Systems
		17	Chief Operations Officer	27	Career & Tech Ed	37	Guidance Services Elem	47	Math Sec	57 Bilingual/ELL	67 School Board President	77 Psychological Assess
		18	Chief Academic Officer	28	Technology Education	38	Guidance Services Sec	48	English/Lang Arts Elem	58 Special Education K-12	68 Teacher Personnel	78 Affirmative Action

Texas School Directory — Dallas County

School	Grades	Prog	Enroll	%	Phone
Bonnie Gentry Elem Sch 1901 Twin Oaks Dr, Mesquite 75181 Rashunda Price	PK-6	T	916 35	69%	972/290-4140 Fax 972/290-4150
C W Beasley Elem Sch 919 Green Canyon Dr, Mesquite 75150 Kelly McCollom	PK-6	T	467 30	55%	972/882-5160 Fax 972/882-5161
Charles Tosch Elem Sch 2424 Larchmont Dr, Mesquite 75150 Amy Childress	PK-6	T	872 40	87%	972/882-5000 Fax 972/882-5010
Dr J C Cannaday Elem Sch 2701 Chisolm Trl, Mesquite 75150 Lauren Chism	K-6	T	564 27	73%	972/882-5060 Fax 972/882-5070
Dr James P Terry Middle Sch 2351 Edwards Church Rd, Mesquite 75181 Kelley Prewitt	6-8	T	896 40	57%	972/882-5650 Fax 972/882-5660
Dr Joey Pirrung Elem Sch 1500 Creek Valley Rd, Mesquite 75181 Susan Brison	PK-5	T	434 30	61%	972/882-7170 Fax 972/882-7189
Dr John D Horn High Sch 3300 E Cartwright Rd, Mesquite 75181 Patrick Perkins	9-12	TV	2,386 60	53%	972/882-5200 Fax 972/882-5292
Dr Linda Henrie Elem Sch 253 W Lawson Rd, Dallas 75253 Lisa Lovato	PK-6	T	961	92%	972/290-4200 Fax 972/290-4210
Dr Ralph H Poteet High Sch 3300 Poteet Dr, Mesquite 75150 Taylor Morris	9-12	TV	1,848 53	52%	972/882-5300 Fax 972/882-5355
E S McKenzie Elem Sch 3535 Stephens Green Dr, Mesquite 75150 **Emmalee Langston**	K-6	T	538 30	82%	972/882-5140 Fax 972/882-5151
Ed Vanston Middle Sch 3230 Karla Dr, Mesquite 75150 **Melissa Smith**	7-8	TV	805 30	84%	972/882-5801 Fax 972/882-5848
Elsie Shands Elem Sch 4836 Shands Dr, Mesquite 75150 Brandi Lewis	K-6	T	825 34	83%	972/290-4020 Fax 972/290-4030
Florence Black Elem Sch 328 Newsome Rd, Mesquite 75149 Darla Franklin	PK-6	T	639 30	76%	972/882-7240 Fax 972/882-7250
Frank B Agnew Middle Sch 729 Wilkinson Dr, Mesquite 75149 Kelly Long	7-8	TV	831	76%	972/882-5750 Fax 972/882-5760
Fred McWhorter Elem Sch 1700 Hickory Tree Rd, Mesquite 75149 Tammi Froning	PK-6	T	870 35	91%	972/882-7020 Fax 972/882-7030
G R Porter Elem Sch 517 Via Avenida, Mesquite 75150 Becky Rasco	PK-6	T	605 20	68%	972/290-4000 Fax 972/290-4004
Galloway Elem Sch 200 Clary Dr, Mesquite 75149 **April Sarpy**	PK-6	T	732	81%	972/882-5101 Fax 972/882-5110
Georgia Kimball Elem Sch 4010 Coryell Way, Mesquite 75150 Stacy Sheffield	K-6	T	242 19	59%	972/290-4120 Fax 972/290-4130
Hodges Elem Sch 14401 Spring Oak Dr, Balch Springs 75180 Kim Broadway	PK-6	T	767 35	89%	972/290-4040 Fax 972/290-4046
I N Range Elem Sch 4060 Emerald Dr, Mesquite 75150 **Kelly Locke**	K-6	T	763 28	88%	972/882-5180 Fax 972/882-5190
J C Austin Elem Sch 3020 Poteet Dr, Mesquite 75150 Jonathan Royle	PK-6	T	471 22	65%	972/882-7220 Fax 972/882-7225
J C Rugel Elem Sch 2701 Sybil Dr, Mesquite 75149 Amanda Martin	K-6	T	458 21	75%	972/882-7260 Fax 972/882-7270
J H Florence Elem Sch 4600 Ashwood Dr, Mesquite 75150 Ladonna Gulley	PK-5	T	654 35	84%	972/290-4080 Fax 972/290-4088
Jay Thompson Elem Sch 2525 Helen Ln, Mesquite 75181 Bridget Mitchell	PK-5	T	565 38	59%	972/882-7190 Fax 972/882-7197
Joe Lawrence Elem Sch 3811 Richman Dr, Mesquite 75150 Cathy Swann	PK-6	T	440 23	73%	972/882-7000 Fax 972/882-7010
John Hanby Elem Sch 480 Gross Rd, Mesquite 75149 Jessica Eaton	PK-5	T	929 50	90%	972/882-5040 Fax 972/882-5050
Judge Frank Berry Middle Sch 2675 Bear Dr, Mesquite 75181 Angela Wiggins	6-8	TV	904 55	71%	972/882-5850 Fax 972/882-5888
Mary Moss Elem Sch 1208 New Market Rd, Mesquite 75149 Michael Pierotti	K-6	T	434 33	72%	972/882-7130 Fax 972/882-7146
Ⓐ Mesquite Academy Aec of Choice 2704 Motley Dr, Mesquite 75150 **Abram Joseph**	9-12	GT	167 15	53%	972/882-7570 Fax 972/882-7169
Mesquite High Sch 300 E Davis St, Mesquite 75149 **Gerald Sarpy**	9-12	GTV	2,904 100	71%	972/882-7800 Fax 972/882-7876
North Mesquite High Sch 18201 Lyndon B Johnson Fwy, Mesquite 75150 Douglas Barber	9-12	TV	2,808 115	72%	972/882-7900 Fax 972/882-7908
R S Kimbrough Middle Sch 3900 N Galloway Ave, Mesquite 75150 Chris Brott	7-8	T	825 50	63%	972/882-5900 Fax 972/882-5942
Ruby Shaw Elem Sch 707 Purple Sage Trl, Mesquite 75149 Jennifer Dumaine	PK-6	T	884 34	73%	972/882-7060 Fax 972/882-7070
S M Seabourn Elem Sch 2300 Sandy Ln, Mesquite 75149 Jewel Kern	PK-6	T	724 35	91%	972/882-7040 Fax 972/882-7050
Sam Rutherford Elem Sch 1607 Sierra Dr, Mesquite 75149 Holly Grubbs	PK-5	T	474 35	71%	972/290-4060 Fax 972/290-4068
Sue Ann Mackey Elem Sch 14900 N Spring Ridge Cir, Balch Springs 75180 Artha Noe	K-5	T	805 40	84%	972/290-4160 Fax 972/290-4179
T H McDonald Middle Sch 2930 N Town East Blvd, Mesquite 75150 Debra Bassinger	7-8	TV	1,002 30	81%	972/882-5700 Fax 972/882-5710
Vernon Price Elem Sch 630 Stroud Ln, Garland 75043 Tomika Johnson	PK-6	T	451 24	79%	972/290-4100 Fax 972/290-4110
W O Gray Elem Sch 3500 Pioneer Rd, Balch Springs 75180 Jennifer LaPlante	PK-6	T	634 42	87%	972/882-7280 Fax 972/882-7288
Walter E Floyd Elem Sch 3025 Hickory Tree Rd, Balch Springs 75180 Kelsey Bowles	PK-6	T	798 31	94%	972/882-7100 Fax 972/882-7110
Walter Wilkinson Middle Sch 2100 Crest Park Dr, Mesquite 75149 Molly Purl	6-8	TV	974 53	89%	972/882-5950 Fax 972/882-5988
West Mesquite High Sch 2500 Memorial Blvd, Mesquite 75149 Alesia Austin	9-12	TV	2,077 87	78%	972/882-7600 Fax 972/882-7611
Ⓨ Zack Motley Elem Sch 3719 Moon Dr, Mesquite 75150 Dr Shawna Delamar	PK-6	MT	455 17	84%	972/882-5080 Fax 972/882-5090

9 Student Personnel
10 Driver Ed/Safety
11 Gifted/Talented
12 Video Services
13 Substance Abuse Prev
14 Erate
15 AIDS Education
18 Alternative/At Risk
19 Multi-Cultural Curriculum
20 Social Work
91 Safety/Security
92 Magnet School
93 Parental Involvement
95 Tech Prep Program
97 Chief Infomation Officer
98 Chief Technology Officer
270 Character Education
271 Migrant Education
273 Teacher Mentor
274 Before/After Sch
275 Response To Intervention
277 Remedial Math K-12
280 Literacy Coach
285 STEM
286 Digital Learning
288 Common Core Standards
294 Accountability
295 Network System
296 Title II Programs
297 Webmaster
298 Grant Writer/Ptnrships
750 Chief Innovation Officer
751 Chief of Staff
752 Social Emotional Learning

Other School Types
Ⓐ = Alternative School
Ⓒ = Charter School
Ⓜ = Magnet School
Ⓨ = Year-Round School

School Programs
A = Alternative Program
G = Adult Classes
M = Magnet Program
T = Title I Schoolwide
V = Career & Tech Ed Programs

Social Media
= Facebook
= Twitter

New Schools are shaded
New Superintendents and Principals are bold
Personnel with email addresses are underscored

Dallas County   Market Data Retrieval

- **Richardson Ind School Dist** PID: 01011624   469/593-0000
  400 S Greenville Ave, Richardson 75081   Fax 469/593-0302

> **Schools:** 57 \ **Teachers:** 2,584 \ **Students:** 39,103 \
> **Special Ed Students:** 4,322 \ **LEP Students:** 9,248 \ **College-Bound:** 63%
> \ **Ethnic:** Asian 7%, African American 22%, Hispanic 40%, Caucasian 31% \ **Exp:** $147 (Low) \ **Poverty:** 18% \ **Title I:** $10,194,830 \
> **Special Education:** $6,370,000 \ **Open-Close:** 08/15 - 05/22 \ **DTBP:** $187 (High) \

Name	#	Name	#
Dr Jeannie Stone	1	David Pate	2,19
Melody Greig	2	Sandra Hayes	3,15
Rose Ann Martin	4	Larry Hudson	5
Kevin Pitts	6	Sharon Simpson	7
Brenda Payne	9,15	Kim Fuller	11,298
Dr Christopher Goodson	15,68	Dr Kristin Byno	15
Tabitha Branum	15	Julie Briggs	16*
Jeff Bradford	20	Masud Shamsid-Deen	31,73
Kellie Sellers	35	Milissa Pfeiffer	39
Lakeisha Mitchell	44	Doug Plany	47
Carol Johnson	49*	Emma Selig	57
Cindy Lawrence	58	Kim Malcolm	61
Justin Bono	67	Mary Welch	68
Nancy Kinzie	68	Sandra Moore	68,273
Terry Harris	68	Kathy Milton	69
Chris Moore	71	Mary Worthington	71
Melissa Heller	74	Norma Comer	76,295
Craig Raley	79	Dr Matthew Gibbons	79,83
Monica Simonds	81	Monica Simonds	81*
La'Evening Woodard	91	Michael Freeman	92
Kyndra Johnson	285	Elvia Noriega	294
Andy McCormick	297		

Public Schs..Principal	Grd	Prgm	Enr/#Cls	SN	Phone/Fax
Aikin Elem Sch 12300 Pleasant Valley Dr, Dallas 75243 Roxanne Cheek	PK-6	T	724	86%	469/593-1820 Fax 469/593-1763
Apollo Junior High Sch 1600 Apollo Rd, Richardson 75081 Yolanda Gaither	7-8	T	650 150	52%	469/593-7900 Fax 469/593-7911
ⓜ Arapaho Classical Magnet Sch 1300 Cypress Dr, Richardson 75080 Kristin Strickland	PK-6		582 24	27%	469/593-6400 Fax 469/593-6448
Audelia Creek Elem Sch 12600 Audelia Rd, Dallas 75243 Martha Staufert	PK-6	T	661	80%	469/593-2900 Fax 469/593-1763
Berkner High Sch 1600 E Spring Valley Rd, Richardson 75081 **Kristy Cage**	9-12	TV	2,642 130	52%	469/593-7000 Fax 469/593-7211
Berkner STEM Academy 1600 E Spring Valley Rd, Richardson 75081 Elizabeth Swaner	9-12		99		469/593-7021 Fax 469/593-7211
Big Springs Elem Sch 3301 W Campbell Rd, Garland 75044 Denise May	PK-6		324 29	39%	469/593-8100 Fax 469/593-8114
Bowie Elem Sch 7643 La Manga Dr, Dallas 75248 Staci Low	PK-6		626 40	11%	469/593-6000 Fax 469/593-6066
Brentfield Elem Sch 6767 Brentfield Dr, Dallas 75248 Jason Myatt	PK-6		789 28	5%	469/593-5740 Fax 469/593-5723
Canyon Creek Elem Sch 2100 Copper Ridge Dr, Richardson 75080 Carol Mixon	PK-6		296 20	13%	469/593-6500 Fax 469/593-8114
Carolyn G Bukhair Elem Sch 13900 Esperanza Rd, Dallas 75240 Roxxy Griffin	1-6	T	672	94%	469/593-4900 Fax 469/593-4901
ⓐ Christa McAuliffe Learning Ctr 900 S Greenville Ave, Richardson 75081 Carmen Steward	1-12		62 6	71%	469/593-5800 Fax 469/593-5805
Dartmouth Elem Sch 417 Dartmouth Ln, Richardson 75081 Stacey Marx	PK-6		404 22	30%	469/593-8400 Fax 469/593-8408
Dobie Primary Sch 14040 Rolling Hills Ln, Dallas 75240 Kristyn Hart	PK-K	T	480 35	82%	469/593-4100 Fax 469/593-4011
Dover Elem Sch 700 Dover Dr, Richardson 75080 Brona Hudson	PK-6	T	600 25	83%	469/593-4200 Fax 469/593-4201
Forest Ln Acad of Arts & Comm 9663 Forest Ln, Dallas 75243 Lariza Liner	PK-6	T	732	86%	469/593-1850 Fax 469/593-1919
Forest Meadow Jr High Sch 9373 Whitehurst Dr, Dallas 75243 Kerri Jones	7-8	T	784	67%	469/593-1500 Fax 469/593-1461
Forestridge Elem Sch 10330 Bunchberry Dr, Dallas 75243 Misty Wilson	PK-6	T	676 47	70%	469/593-8500 Fax 469/593-8502
Greenwood Hills Elem Sch 1313 W Shore Dr, Richardson 75080 Misti Lehman	PK-6	T	438 25	75%	469/593-6100 Fax 469/593-6111
ⓜ Hamilton Park Pacesetter Magnt 8301 Towns St, Dallas 75243 Michael Thomas	PK-6	T	658 54	54%	469/593-3900 Fax 469/593-3950
Jess Harben Elem Sch 600 S Glenville Dr, Richardson 75081 **Sharon Newman**	PK-6	T	391 30	55%	469/593-8800 Fax 469/593-8801
Lake Highlands Elem Sch 9501 Ferndale Rd, Dallas 75238 Emily Gruninger	PK-6		756 41	36%	469/593-2100 Fax 469/593-2088
Lake Highlands High Sch 9449 Church Rd, Dallas 75238 Joshua Delich	9-12	TV	2,762 50	54%	469/593-1000 Fax 469/593-1030
Lake Highlands Jr High Sch 10301 Walnut Hill Ln, Dallas 75238 Carrie Breedlove	7-8	T	808	51%	469/593-1600 Fax 469/593-1606
Liberty Junior High Sch 10330 Lawler Rd, Dallas 75243 Cecilia Galvan	7-8	T	616 50	72%	469/593-7888 Fax 469/593-7764
Mark Twain Elem Sch 1200 Larkspur Dr, Richardson 75081 Catherine Kelly	PK-6	T	594 18	81%	469/593-4800 Fax 469/593-4799
ⓜ Math Science & Tech Magnet Sch 450 Abrams Rd, Richardson 75081 Helena Lopez	PK-6	T	616 26	48%	469/593-7300 Fax 469/593-7301
ⓐ Memorial Park Academy 410 S Greenville Ave, Richardson 75081 Bill Gallo	9-12		20		469/593-0450 469/593-0451
Merriman Park Elem Sch 7101 Winedale Dr, Dallas 75231 Susan Burt	PK-6	T	575 25	41%	469/593-2800 Fax 469/593-2741
Mohawk Elem Sch 1500 Mimosa Dr, Richardson 75080 Megan Cox	PK-6		455 17	5%	469/593-6600 Fax 469/593-6610
Moss Haven Elem Sch 9202 Moss Farm Ln, Dallas 75243 Philip Henderson	PK-6		491 25	14%	469/593-2200 Fax 469/593-2158
Northlake Elem Sch 10059 Ravensway Dr, Dallas 75238 Mary Kellagher	PK-6		595 45	83%	469/593-2300 Fax 469/593-2309
Northrich Elem Sch 1301 Custer Rd, Richardson 75080 Lashon Easter	PK-6	T	432 26	60%	469/593-6200 Fax 469/593-6201

1 Superintendent	8 Curric/Instruct K-12	19 Chief Financial Officer	29 Family/Consumer Science	39 Social Studies K-12	49 English/Lang Arts Elem	59 Special Education Elem	69 Academic Assessment
2 Bus/Finance/Purchasing	9 Curric/Instruct Elem	20 Art K-12	30 Adult Education	40 Social Studies Elem	50 English/Lang Arts Sec	60 Special Education Sec	70 Research/Development
3 Buildings And Grounds	10 Curric/Instruct Sec	21 Art Elem	31 Career/Sch-to-Work K-12	41 Social Studies Sec	51 Reading K-12	61 Foreign/World Lang K-12	71 Public Information
4 Food Service	11 Federal Program	22 Art Sec	32 Career/Sch-to-Work Elem	42 Science K-12	52 Reading Elem	62 Foreign/World Lang Elem	72 Summer School
5 Transportation	12 Title I	23 Music K-12	33 Career/Sch-to-Work Sec	43 Science Elem	53 Reading Sec	63 Foreign/World Lang Sec	73 Instructional Tech
6 Athletic	13 Title V	24 Music Elem	34 Early Childhood Ed	44 Science Sec	54 Remedial Reading K-12	64 Religious Education K-12	74 Inservice Training
7 Health Services	15 Asst Superintendent	25 Music Sec	35 Health/Phys Education	45 Math K-12	55 Remedial Reading Elem	65 Religious Education Elem	75 Marketing/Distributive
	16 Instructional Media Svcs	26 Business Education	36 Guidance Services K-12	46 Math Elem	56 Remedial Reading Sec	66 Religious Education Sec	76 Info Systems
	17 Chief Operations Officer	27 Career & Tech Ed	37 Guidance Services Elem	47 Math Sec	57 Bilingual/ELL	67 School Board President	77 Psychological Assess
	18 Chief Academic Officer	28 Technology Education	38 Guidance Services Sec	48 English/Lang Arts K-12	58 Special Education K-12	68 Teacher Personnel	78 Affirmative Action

Texas School Directory — Dallas County

School	Grades	Prgm	Enr/#Cls	SN	Phone
Northwood Hills Elem Sch 14532 Meandering Way, Dallas 75254 Ishii Tavarez	PK-6	T	440 20	62%	469/593-4300 Fax 469/593-4301
O Henry Elem Sch 4100 Tyree Dr, Garland 75042 Jennifer Wills	PK-6	T	453 24	74%	469/593-8200 Fax 469/593-4201
Parkhill Junior High Sch 16500 Shadybank Dr, Dallas 75248 Farrah Smock	7-8		636 40	43%	469/593-5600 Fax 469/593-5500
Pearce High Sch 1600 N Coit Rd, Richardson 75080 Mike Evans	9-12	V	2,383 65	33%	469/593-5000 Fax 469/593-5169
Prairie Creek Elem Sch 2120 E Prairie Creek Dr, Richardson 75080 Kyle Stuard	PK-6		335 18	5%	469/593-6300 Fax 469/593-6308
Prestonwood Elem Sch 6525 La Cosa Dr, Dallas 75248 Pam Aitken	PK-6	T	455 16	44%	469/593-6700 Fax 469/593-6712
Richardson Heights Elem Sch 101 N Floyd Rd, Richardson 75080 Jenny Lanier	PK-6	T	494 26	65%	469/593-4400 Fax 469/593-4401
Richardson High Sch 1250 W Belt Line Rd, Richardson 75080 Christopher Choat	9-12	TV	2,770 110	47%	469/593-3000 Fax 469/593-3010
Richardson North Jr High Sch 1820 N Floyd Rd, Richardson 75080 Joshua Eason	7-8		632 50	43%	469/593-5300
Richardson Terrace Elem Sch 300 N Dorothy Dr, Richardson 75081 Michele Zupa	PK-6	T	527 35	64%	469/593-8700 Fax 469/593-8781
Richardson West Arts & Tech 1309 Holly Dr, Richardson 75080 Kimberly Kindred	7-8	T	711 40	53%	469/593-3700 Fax 469/593-3666
Richland Elem Sch 550 Park Bend Dr, Richardson 75081 Lauren Bolack	PK-6	T	651 26	61%	469/593-4650 Fax 469/593-4654
Risd Academy 13630 Coit Rd, Dallas 75240 Rebeca Carrero	PK-6	T	825 48	95%	469/593-3300 Fax 469/593-3307
Skyview Elem Sch 9229 Meadowknoll Dr, Dallas 75243 Katrina Collins	PK-6	T	769 32	80%	469/593-2400 Fax 469/593-4401
Spring Creek Elem Sch 7667 Roundrock Rd, Dallas 75248 Sharon Erickson	PK-6	T	331 20	16%	469/593-4500 Fax 469/593-4501
Spring Valley Elem Sch 13535 Spring Grove Ave, Dallas 75240 Lanette Stinnett	PK-6	T	416 37	84%	469/593-4600 Fax 469/593-4609
Springridge Elem Sch 1801 E Spring Valley Rd, Richardson 75081 Katie Barrett	PK-6	T	345 21	64%	469/593-8600 Fax 469/593-8603
Stults Road Elem Sch 8700 Stults Rd, Dallas 75243 Jennifer Balch	PK-6	T	738 25	75%	469/593-2500 Fax 469/593-2521
Thurgood Marshall Elem Sch 9666 W Ferris Branch Blvd, Dallas 75243 Charmaine Curtis	PK-6	T	639	83%	469/593-6800 Fax 469/593-6801
Wallace Elem Sch 9921 Kirkhaven Dr, Dallas 75238 Frank Patranella	PK-6	T	809	63%	469/593-2600 Fax 469/593-2610
Warren Center 2625 Anita Dr, Garland 75041 Amy Spawn	Spec		30		972/926-2671
Westwood JHS Math Sci Ldrshp 7630 Arapaho Rd, Dallas 75248 Jennie Bates	7-8	T	675 60	50%	469/593-3600 Fax 469/593-3508
White Rock Elem Sch 9229 Chiswell Rd, Dallas 75238 Lee Walker	PK-6		925 24	12%	469/593-2700 Fax 469/593-2706
Yale Elem Sch 1900 E Collins Blvd, Richardson 75081 Carrie Greer	PK-6		427 27	36%	469/593-8300 Fax 469/593-8362

● **Sunnyvale Ind School Dist** PID: 01012018   972/226-5974
417 E Tripp Rd, Sunnyvale 75182   Fax 972/226-6882

Schools: 3 \ *Teachers:* 113 \ *Students:* 1,950 \ *Special Ed Students:* 158 \ *LEP Students:* 49 \ *Ethnic:* Asian 23%, African American 11%, Hispanic 12%, Caucasian 54% \ *Exp:* $431 (High) \ *Poverty:* 6% \ *Title I:* $89,073 \ *Special Education:* $171,000 \ *Open-Close:* 08/21 - 05/29 \ *DTBP:* $350 (High)

Doug Williams	1	Margret Davis	2
Keith Adams	3	Karl Williams	5
John Settle	6*	Christi Morgan	8,15,298
Erica Lawless	11,58	Michael Fennig	57*
Brad Cravens	67	Glenda McMahan	69,88,270*
Buck Baskins	73	Buck Baskin	76,84
Amy Tutle	294		

Public Schs..Principal	Grd	Prgm	Enr/#Cls	SN	Phone
Sunnyvale Elem Sch 416 Hounsel Ln, Sunnyvale 75182 Brittany Dlabaj	PK-4	T	707	16%	972/226-7601 Fax 972/226-4812
Sunnyvale High Sch 222 N Collins Rd, Sunnyvale 75182 Brian Nickel	9-12	T	528	12%	972/203-4600 Fax 972/226-2834
Sunnyvale Middle Sch 216 N Collins Rd, Sunnyvale 75182 Brandon Tunnell	5-8	T	578 45	16%	972/226-2922 Fax 972/226-0982

DALLAS CATHOLIC SCHOOLS

● **Diocese of Dallas Ed Office** PID: 01012367   214/528-2360
3725 Blackburn St, Dallas 75219   Fax 214/522-1753

Schools: 35 \ *Students:* 14,713

Listing includes only schools located in this county. See District Index for location of Diocesan Offices.

Dr Matthew Vereecke	1	Nan Sayers	2
Joyce Schreitmueller	11,30	Sr Dawn Achs	15,68
Dr Veronica Alonzo	15	Carol Mayo	73

Catholic Schs..Principal	Grd	Prgm	Enr/#Cls	SN	Phone
Bishop Dunne Catholic Sch 3900 Rugged Dr, Dallas 75224 Mary Marchiony	6-12		624 40		214/339-6561 Fax 214/339-1438
Bishop Lynch High Sch 9750 Ferguson Rd, Dallas 75228 Chad Riley	9-12		1,097 50		214/324-3607 Fax 214/324-3600
Christ the King Sch 4100 Colgate Ave, Dallas 75225 Lisa Bosco	K-8		430 18		214/365-1234 Fax 214/365-1236
Cistercian Preparatory Sch 3660 Cistercian Rd, Irving 75039 Paul McCormick	5-12		355 22		469/499-5400 Fax 469/499-5440

---

9 Student Personnel	91 Safety/Security	275 Response To Intervention	298 Grant Writer/Ptnrships	**School Programs**	**Social Media**
0 Driver Ed/Safety	92 Magnet School	277 Remedial Math K-12	750 Chief Innovation Officer	A = Alternative Program	
1 Gifted/Talented	93 Parental Involvement	280 Literacy Coach	751 Chief of Staff	G = Adult Classes	❋ = Facebook
2 Video Services	95 Tech Prep Program	285 STEM	752 Social Emotional Learning	M = Magnet Program	
3 Substance Abuse Prev	97 Chief Infomation Officer	286 Digital Learning		T = Title I Schoolwide	❋ = Twitter
4 Erate	98 Chief Technology Officer	288 Common Core Standards	**Other School Types**	V = Career & Tech Ed Programs	
5 AIDS Education	270 Character Education	294 Accountability	Ⓐ = Alternative School		
8 Alternative/At Risk	271 Migrant Education	295 Network System	Ⓒ = Charter School	New Schools are shaded	
9 Multi-Cultural Curriculum	273 Teacher Mentor	296 Title II Programs	Ⓜ = Magnet School	New Superintendents and Principals are bold	
0 Social Work	274 Before/After Sch	297 Webmaster	Ⓨ = Year-Round School	Personnel with email addresses are underscored	

Dallas County

School	Grd	Enr/#Cls	Phone
Good Shepherd Catholic Sch 214 S Garland Ave, Garland 75040 Gail Bassett	PK-8	227 20	972/272-6533 Fax 972/272-0512
Highlands Sch 1451 E Northgate Dr, Irving 75062 Michael Pennell	PK-12	448 32	972/554-1980 Fax 972/721-1691
Holy Family Catholic Academy 2323 Cheyenne St, Irving 75062 Kathy Carruth	PK-8	257 11	972/255-0205 Fax 972/252-0448
Holy Trinity Catholic Sch 3815 Oak Lawn Ave, Dallas 75219 Marian Davis	PK-8	150 11	214/526-5113 Fax 214/526-4524
Immaculate Conception Sch 400 NE 17th St, Grand Prairie 75050 Linda Santos	PK-8	135 22	972/264-8777 Fax 972/264-7742
Jesuit College Prep Sch 12345 Inwood Rd, Dallas 75244 Tom Garrison	9-12	1,090 47	972/387-8700 Fax 972/661-9349
Mary Immaculate Sch 14032 Dennis Ln, Farmers BRNCH 75234 Linda Coffin	K-8	491 21	972/243-7105 Fax 972/241-7678
Mt Saint Michael Catholic Sch 4500 W Davis St, Dallas 75211 Renee Ozier	PK-8	127 16	214/337-0244 Fax 214/339-1702
Notre Dame Sch 2018 Allen St, Dallas 75204 Theresa Francis	Spec	150 12	214/720-3911 Fax 214/720-3913
Our Lady of Perpetual Help Sch 7625 Cortland Ave, Dallas 75235 Maria Searle	K-8	198 11	214/351-3396 Fax 214/351-9889
Santa Clara Catholic Academy 321 Calumet Ave, Dallas 75211 Stephanie Matous	PK-8	235 14	214/333-9423 Fax 214/333-2556
St Bernard of Clairvaux Sch 1420 Old Gate Ln, Dallas 75218 Michael Davies	PK-8	200 10	214/321-2897 Fax 214/321-4060
St Cecilia Sch 635 Mary Cliff Rd, Dallas 75208 Lisa Hernandez	PK-8	215 11	214/948-8628 Fax 214/948-4956
St Elizabeth of Hungary Sch 4019 S Hampton Rd, Dallas 75224 Rachel Dzurilla	PK-8	250 24	214/331-5139 Fax 214/467-4346
St Joseph Catholic Sch 600 S Jupiter Rd, Richardson 75081 Fran Thompson	K-8	300 22	972/234-4679 Fax 972/692-4594
St Mary of Carmel Sch 1716 Singleton Blvd, Dallas 75212 Kaitlyn Aguilar	PK-8	160 10	214/748-2934 Fax 214/760-9052
St Monica Catholic Sch 4140 Walnut Hill Ln, Dallas 75229 Phillip Riley	PK-8	866 48	214/351-5688 Fax 214/352-2608
St Patrick Sch 9635 Ferndale Rd, Dallas 75238 Julie Hendry	PK-8	555 24	214/348-8070 Fax 214/503-7230
St Paul the Apostle Sch 720 S Floyd Rd, Richardson 75080 Michael Davies	PK-8	300 26	972/235-3263 Fax 972/690-1542
St Philip & St Augustine Acad 8151 Military Pkwy, Dallas 75227 Dianne Brungardt	PK-8	350 12	214/381-4973 Fax 214/381-0466
St Pius X Sch 3030 Gus Thomasson Rd, Dallas 75228 Tana Scott	PK-8	371 18	972/279-2339 Fax 972/613-2059
St Rita Catholic Sch 12525 Inwood Rd, Dallas 75244 Carol Walsh	K-8 G	658 50	972/239-3203 Fax 972/934-0657
St Thomas Aquinas Sch 3741 Abrams Rd, Dallas 75214 Lauren Roberts \ Jennifer Watts	PK-8	895 44	214/826-0566 Fax 214/826-0251
Ursuline Academy 4900 Walnut Hill Ln, Dallas 75229 Andrea Shurley	9-12	820 60	469/232-1800 Fax 469/232-1836

DALLAS PRIVATE SCHOOLS

Private Schs..Principal	Grd	Prgm	Enr/#Cls	SN
Akiba Academy of Dallas 12324 Merit Dr, Dallas 75251 Danielle Rothenberg	PK-8		356	214/295-3400 Fax 214/295-3405
Alcuin Montessori Sch 6144 Churchill Way, Dallas 75230 Paige Whitney \ Verna Salta \ Margaret Davis	PK-12		535 25	972/239-1745 Fax 972/934-8727
Alexander Sch 409 International Pkwy, Richardson 75081 Andrew Cody	8-12		40 20	972/690-9210 Fax 972/690-9284
Ashleys Private Sch 310 W Belt Line Rd, Cedar Hill 75104 Michelle Emmert	PK-5		125	972/291-1313
Autism Treatment Center 10503 Metric Dr, Dallas 75243 Carolyn Garver	Spec		22	972/644-2076 Fax 972/644-5650
Balch Springs Chrn Academy 11524 Seagoville Rd, Balch Springs 75180 Renia Peters	K-12		100 17	972/286-8511 Fax 972/286-1379
Bending Oaks High Sch 11884 Greenville Ave Ste 120, Dallas 75243 Beth Rule	8-12	A	50 10	972/669-0000 Fax 972/232-2290
Berean Christian Academy 1000 E 6th St, Irving 75060 Leon Adkins	K-6		34 4	972/438-1440 Fax 972/554-6807
Berne Acad Private Sch 1311 Johns Ave, Lancaster 75134 Theresa Smith	PK-12		38 8	972/218-7373 Fax 972/218-7372
Brighter Horizons Academy 3145 Medical Plaza Dr, Garland 75044 Dr Iram Shaikh-Jilani	PK-12		800 45	972/675-2062 Fax 972/675-2063
Calvary Lutheran Sch 9807 Church Rd, Dallas 75238 Jim Henrickson	PK-8		85 5	214/343-7457 Fax 214/348-1424
Calvary Temple Christian Acad 3150 South Outline Road, Mesquite 75181 Betty Vickery	PK-12		60 4	972/286-4935 Fax 972/557-0045
Cambridge School of Dallas 3877 Walnut Hill Ln, Dallas 75229 B Paul Wolfe	6-12		100 12	214/357-2995 Fax 214/357-8008
Canterbury Episcopal Sch 1708 N Westmoreland Rd, Desoto 75115 Misty Stern	K-12		200 37	972/572-7200 Fax 972/572-2470
Cathedral of Life Chrn Sch 12908 Seagoville Rd, Balch Springs 75180 David Gibbs	K-12		28 4	972/286-4845 Fax 972/287-4357
Coram Deo Academy-Dallas 6464 Et Lovers Ln, Dallas 75214 Beverly Mullin	PK-8		100	972/385-6410
Covenant Sch 7300 Valley View Ln, Dallas 75240 Charles Evans	K-12		512	214/358-5818 Fax 214/358-5809
Cristo Rey Dallas College Prep 1064 N Saint Augustine Dr, Dallas 75217 Christine Roman	9-11		378	469/844-7956

1 Superintendent	8 Curric/Instruct K-12	19 Chief Financial Officer	29 Family/Consumer Science	39 Social Studies K-12	49 English/Lang Arts Elem	59 Special Education Elem	69 Academic Assessment
2 Bus/Finance/Purchasing	9 Curric/Instruct Elem	20 Art K-12	30 Adult Education	40 Social Studies Elem	50 English/Lang Arts Sec	60 Special Education Sec	70 Research/Development
3 Buildings And Grounds	10 Curric/Instruct Sec	21 Art Elem	31 Career/Sch-to-Work K-12	41 Social Studies Sec	51 Reading K-12	61 Foreign/World Lang K-12	71 Public Information
4 Food Service	11 Federal Program	22 Art Sec	32 Career/Sch-to-Work Elem	42 Science K-12	52 Reading Elem	62 Foreign/World Lang Elem	72 Summer School
5 Transportation	12 Title I	23 Music K-12	33 Career/Sch-to-Work Sec	43 Science Elem	53 Reading Sec	63 Foreign/World Lang Sec	73 Instructional Tech
6 Athletic	13 Title V	24 Music Elem	34 Early Childhood Ed	44 Science Sec	54 Remedial Reading K-12	64 Religious Education K-12	74 Inservice Training
7 Health Services	15 Asst Superintendent	25 Music Sec	35 Health/Phys Education	45 Math K-12	55 Remedial Reading Elem	65 Religious Education Elem	75 Marketing/Distributive
	16 Instructional Media Svcs	26 Business Education	36 Guidance Services K-12	46 Math Elem	56 Remedial Reading Sec	66 Religious Education Sec	76 Info Systems
	17 Chief Operations Officer	27 Career & Tech Ed	37 Guidance Services Elem	47 Math Sec	57 Bilingual/ELL	67 School Board President	77 Psychological Assess
	18 Chief Academic Officer	28 Technology Education	38 Guidance Services Sec	48 English/Lang Arts K-12	58 Special Education K-12	68 Teacher Personnel	78 Affirmative Action

Texas School Directory — Dallas County

School	Grades	Enrollment/Staff	Phone/Fax
Cross of Christ Lutheran Sch 512 N Cockrell Hill Rd, Desoto 75115 Lila Fusssell	PK-K	85 6	972/223-9586
Crossroads Academy 820 E Wintergreen Rd, Cedar Hill 75104 Cindy Lowe	1-12	100	972/293-9093 Fax 972/293-9376
Dallas Academy 950 Tiffany Way, Dallas 75218 Elizabeth Murski	1-12	200 32	214/324-1481 Fax 214/327-8537
Dallas Christian Academy 4025 N Central Expy, Dallas 75204 Maeli Dang	PK-12	140 12	214/528-6327 Fax 214/528-6450
Dallas Christian Sch 1515 Republic Pkwy, Mesquite 75150 Courtney Pine \ Jennifer Webb \ Kristi England	PK-12	866 40	972/270-5495 Fax 972/270-7581
Dallas International Sch 6039 Churchill Way, Dallas 75230 Catherine Levy	PK-12	600	972/991-6379 Fax 972/991-6608
DeSoto Pvt Sch & Day Care Ctr 301 E Belt Line Rd, Desoto 75115 Kenneth Larson	PK-6	400 40	972/223-6450 Fax 972/230-0629
Episcopal Sch Dallas-Mid Upper 4100 Merrell Rd, Dallas 75229 Chelle Wabrek \ Henry Heil	5-12	651	214/358-4368 Fax 214/357-1232
Episcopal Sch of Dallas-Lower 4344 Colgate Ave, Dallas 75225 Chelle Wabrek	PK-4	432 32	214/353-5818 Fax 214/353-5861
Fairhill Sch 16150 Preston Rd, Dallas 75248 Caroline Stamos	Spec	220 23	972/233-1026 Fax 972/233-8205
Family Christian Academy 10715 Garland Rd, Dallas 75218 Richard Mitchell	K-6	61	214/324-4399 Fax 214/324-5549
Faustina Academy 1621 W Grauwyler Rd, Irving 75061 Christina Mehaffey	PK-12	80	972/254-6726
Fellowship Christian Academy 1821 W Camp Wisdom Rd, Dallas 75232 Karen Gosby	PK-8	502	214/672-9200 Fax 214/672-9201
Firewheel Christian Academy 5500 Lavon Dr, Garland 75040 Stephanie Fuchs	PK-9	180 10	972/495-0851 Fax 972/495-3927
First Baptist Academy 7894 Samuell Blvd, Dallas 75228 Julia Shoemaker \ Julie Weyand	PK-12	366 25	972/453-1321
Fusion Academy-Dallas 8128 Park Ln Ste 123, Dallas 75231 Christina Tipton	6-12	401	214/363-4615
Gardner Preparatory Sch 100 N Houston School Rd, Lancaster 75146 Lazonda Gardner	PK-1	50	972/275-1539
Garland Christian Academy 1522 Lavon Dr, Garland 75040 Stephanie Davis	PK-12	320 20	972/487-0043 Fax 972/276-4079
Glen Oaks Sch 12105 Plano Rd, Dallas 75243 Donna Sharber	PK-K	100 11	972/231-3135 Fax 972/644-6373
Good Shepherd Episcopal Sch 11110 Midway Rd, Dallas 75229 Casey Martin \ Lori Rolke	PK-8	530 40	214/357-1610 Fax 214/357-4105
Grace Academy of Dallas 11306A Inwood Rd, Dallas 75229 Jim Clarke	PK-6	220 17	214/696-5648 Fax 214/696-8713
Grace Fellowship Christian Sch 3052 N Belt Line Rd, Sunnyvale 75182 Edris Carr	K-12	62	972/226-4499 Fax 972/226-0242
Greenhill Sch 4141 Spring Valley Rd, Addison 75001 Michael Simpson \ Susan Palmer \ Trevor Worcester	PK-12	1,250	972/628-5400 Fax 972/404-8217
Highland PK Presbyterian Sch 3821 University Blvd, Dallas 75205 Sarah Good	PK-5	280 21	214/525-6500 Fax 214/525-6501
Highlander Sch 9120 Plano Rd, Dallas 75238 Jill Reed	PK-6	150 14	214/348-3220 Fax 214/341-0401
Hockaday Sch 11600 Welch Rd, Dallas 75229 Randal Rhodus \ Linda Kramer \ Lisa Culbertson	PK-12	1,087 180	214/363-6311 Fax 214/360-6527
Iant Quranic Academy 840 Abrams Rd, Richardson 75081 Mathew Moes	K-12	201	972/231-5698 Fax 972/231-6707
Iboc Christian Academy 7710 S Westmoreland Rd, Dallas 75237 Sherrye Vaden	1-3	75 10	972/572-4262 Fax 972/709-3888
Islamic School of Irving 2555 Esters Rd, Irving 75062 Sadia Haq	PK-12	475	972/812-2220 Fax 972/257-8640
Kessler Sch 1215 Turner Ave, Dallas 75208 Vanessa Ullmann	PK-6	140	214/942-2220 Fax 214/942-1223
Kiest Park Christian Academy 2719 S Hampton Rd, Dallas 75224 Armida Ortega	PK-K	69 6	214/331-1536 Fax 214/330-0469
Lake Cities Montessori Sch 1935 E Centerville Rd, Garland 75041 Masi Adibi	PK-2	105	214/440-4930
Lakehill Preparatory Sch 2720 Hillside Dr, Dallas 75214 John Trout \ Kaye Hauschild \ Bob Yttredahl	K-12	400 200	214/826-2931 Fax 214/826-4623
Lutheran High Sch 8494 Stults Rd, Dallas 75243 Bradley Krause \ Todd Nitz	7-12	200 32	214/349-8912 Fax 214/340-3095
Meadow Oaks Academy 1412 S Belt Line Rd, Mesquite 75149 Nancy Albright	PK-5	135	972/285-6895 Fax 972/285-7647
Merit Academy 2825 Valley View Ln Ste 100, Dallas 75234 Darian Fowler	Spec	20	214/736-8375 Fax 214/377-4942
Merrywood Sch 807 S Cockrell Hill Rd, Duncanville 75137 Peggy Ogden	PK-6	200 17	972/298-0130 Fax 972/298-0277
Mesorah High School for Girls 12712 Park Central Dr Ste B190, Dallas 75251 Avraham Kosowsky	9-12	45	214/420-1990 Fax 214/420-1993
Momentous Sch 106 E 10th St, Dallas 75203 Sandy Nobles	PK-5	248 18	214/915-1890
New Life Christian Academy 2626 Gus Thomasson Rd, Dallas 75228 David Galvan	PK-12	35	214/327-6522
Newfound Academy 2155 Marsh Ln, Carrollton 75006 Dr Marsha Guernsey	Spec	20	214/390-1749
North Dallas Adventist Academy 2800 Custer Pkwy, Richardson 75080 Rosy Arizaga \ Becky Clark \ Melonie Wolfe	PK-12	150 15	972/234-6322 Fax 972/234-6325
Oak Crest Private Sch 1200 E Jackson Rd Bldg 2, Carrollton 75006 Hildegard Jessup	PK-8	55	214/483-5400
Oak Hill Academy 9407 Midway Rd, Dallas 75220 Brit Smart \ Anne Acton \ Joya Jacob	PK-12	140 12	214/353-8804 Fax 214/353-8839

---

89 Student Personnel	91 Safety/Security	275 Response To Intervention	298 Grant Writer/Ptnrships
90 Driver Ed/Safety	92 Magnet School	277 Remedial Math K-12	750 Chief Innovation Officer
1 Gifted/Talented	93 Parental Involvement	280 Literacy Coach	751 Chief of Staff
2 Video Services	95 Tech Prep Program	285 STEM	752 Social Emotional Learning
3 Substance Abuse Prev	97 Chief Infomation Officer	286 Digital Learning	
4 Erate	98 Chief Technology Officer	288 Common Core Standards	Other School Types
5 AIDS Education	270 Character Education	294 Accountability	Ⓐ = Alternative School
8 Alternative/At Risk	271 Migrant Education	295 Network System	Ⓒ = Charter School
9 Multi-Cultural Curriculum	273 Teacher Mentor	296 Title II Programs	Ⓜ = Magnet School
0 Social Work	274 Before/After Sch	297 Webmaster	Ⓨ = Year-Round School

School Programs
A = Alternative Program
G = Adult Classes
M = Magnet Program
T = Title I Schoolwide
V = Career & Tech Ed Programs

Social Media
= Facebook
= Twitter

New Schools are shaded
New Superintendents and Principals are bold
Personnel with email addresses are underscored

Dawson County

Market Data Retrieval

Our Redeemer Lutheran Sch 7611 Park Ln, Dallas 75225 Corey Moss	PK-6	140 14	214/368-1371 Fax 214/368-1473
Parish Episcopal Sch 4101 Sigma Rd, Dallas 75244 Jay Riven	PK-12	1,100	972/239-8011 Fax 972/991-1237
Parkside Baptist Academy 1729 Gross Rd, Mesquite 75149 Don Crutcher	K-12	70	972/613-7833
Preston Hollow Presby Sch 9800 Preston Rd, Dallas 75230 Patty McNally	K-6	120 13	214/368-3886 Fax 214/368-2255
Providence Christian Sch 5002 W Lovers Ln, Dallas 75209 Carol Chester \ Tag Green	K-8	450	214/302-2800 Fax 214/357-6251
Qalam Collegiate Academy 1111 Digital Dr # 101, Richardson 75081 Elora Bashir	5-10	19	972/437-2526 Fax 972/437-2524
Radiant STEM Academy 2001 W Walnut Hill Ln, Irving 75038 Nuzhat Hye	PK-7	275	214/245-5125
Redeemer Montessori Sch 2700 Warren Cir, Irving 75062 Shannon Flowers	PK-6	130 6	972/257-3517 Fax 972/258-9882
Rise School of Dallas 600 Preston Rd, Dallas 75205 Kari Zerbe	Spec	56 5	214/373-7473 Fax 214/373-6545
Scofield Christian Sch 7730 Abrams Rd, Dallas 75231 Dr Traci Tucker	PK-6	100 10	214/349-6843 Fax 214/342-2061
Shelton Sch 15720 Hillcrest Rd, Dallas 75248 Christine Davis \ Mellany Barnett \ Jenny Cheatham	Spec	850	972/774-1772
Southwest Adventist Jr Academy 1600 Bonnie View Rd, Dallas 75203 Kymberly Mayes	PK-8	31 3	214/948-1666 Fax 214/948-1125
St John's Episcopal Sch 848 Harter Rd, Dallas 75218 Jayme Johnson \ Pam Jordan	PK-8	500 35	214/328-9131 Fax 214/320-0205
St Mark's School of Texas 10600 Preston Rd, Dallas 75230 Sherri Darver \ Dean Clayman \ Colin Igoe	1-12	855	214/346-8000 Fax 214/346-8002
St Philip's Episcopal Sch 1600 Pennsylvania Ave, Dallas 75215 Kellee Murrell	PK-6 G	255 20	214/421-5221 Fax 214/428-5371
Stonegate Christian Academy 1705 Esters Rd, Irving 75061 Matt Maples	K-12	151 21	972/790-0070
The Humanist Academy 2925 Skyway Cir N V, Irving 75038 Vijay Shah	K-5	16	972/646-1085
The Westwood School-Upper 14240 Midway Rd, Dallas 75244 Heather Lourcey	9-12	60	972/239-8598 Fax 972/239-1028
Trinity Christian Academy 17001 Addison Rd, Addison 75001 Anne Badger \ Scott Berthel \ Kyle Morrill	PK-12	1,500	972/931-8325 Fax 972/931-8923
Trinity Christian Sch 1231 E Pleasant Run Rd, Cedar Hill 75104 James Swearingin \ Debbie Durling	PK-12	501 40	972/291-2505 Fax 972/291-4739
Tyler Street Christian Academy 915 W 9th St, Dallas 75208 Kelly Betts	PK-12	150 22	214/941-9717 Fax 214/941-0324
Vanguard Preparatory Sch 4240 Sigma Rd, Dallas 75244 Becky Hodnett	Spec	100	972/404-1616 Fax 972/404-1641
Wesley Prep Sch 9200 Inwood Rd, Dallas 75220 Carol Johnson	PK-6	315	214/706-9568 Fax 214/346-3462
West Dallas Community Sch 2300 Canada Dr, Dallas 75212 Stan Newton	PK-8	246 25	214/634-1927 Fax 214/688-1928
Westwood Montessori/IB Sch 14340 Proton Rd, Dallas 75244 Heather Lourcey	PK-12	250	972/239-8598 Fax 972/239-1028
White Rock Montessori Sch 1601 Oates Dr, Dallas 75228 Connie Laufersky	PK-8	175 7	214/324-5580 Fax 214/324-5671
White Rock North Sch 9727 White Rock Trl, Dallas 75238 Amy Adams	PK-6	325 15	214/348-7410 Fax 214/348-3109
Winston Sch 5707 Royal Ln, Dallas 75229 Rebbie Evans	Spec	196 36	214/691-6950 Fax 214/691-1509
Xavier Preparatory Sch 7022 Woodwick Dr, Dallas 75232 Lazonda Gardner	PK-3	35	214/372-4524
Yavneh Academy-Dallas 12324 Merit Dr, Dallas 75251 Donna Hutchinson	9-12	130 13	214/295-3500 Fax 214/295-3505
Zion Lutheran Sch 6121 E Lovers Ln, Dallas 75214 Jeff Thorman	PK-8	294 10	214/363-1630 Fax 214/361-2049

DALLAS REGIONAL CENTERS

• **Region 10 Ed Service Center** PID: 01012032   972/348-1700
400 E Spring Valley Rd, Richardson 75081   Fax 972/231-3642

Gordon Taylor 1,11	Sue Hayes 2,19
Mark Keahey 4	Dr Dana West 8
Alison Fears 11	Jana Burns 15
Dr Holly Bishop 16	Angela Neal 34
Cathryn King 58	Stephen Quisenberry 68
Grant Rampy 71	Brent Goerner 73,98
Craig Gray 286	Denise Barker 297

DAWSON COUNTY

DAWSON PUBLIC SCHOOLS

• **Dawson Ind School Dist** PID: 01012795   806/489-7461
Highway 137, Welch 79377   Fax 806/489-7463

Schools: 1 \ *Teachers:* 17 \ *Students:* 110 \ *Special Ed Students:* 9
\ *LEP Students:* 9 \ *College-Bound:* 100% \ *Ethnic:* Hispanic 55%,
Native American: 1%, Caucasian 44% \ *Exp:* $385 (High) \ *Poverty:* 17% \
Title I: $17,672 \ *Open-Close:* 08/21 - 05/27 \ *DTBP:* $362 (High)

Layne Steets 1,11,73	Mike Hendricks 3,4,5*
Jonathan Patrick 6*	Robbie Phipps 7*
Melanie Hayes 36,69,88*	Dana Mahan 58*
Kalith Brown 67	Ruby Castro 271

---

1 Superintendent	8 Curric/Instruct K-12	19 Chief Financial Officer	29 Family/Consumer Science	39 Social Studies K-12	49 English/Lang Arts Elem	59 Special Education Elem	69 Academic Assessment
2 Bus/Finance/Purchasing	9 Curric/Instruct Elem	20 Art K-12	30 Adult Education	40 Social Studies Elem	50 English/Lang Arts Sec	60 Special Education Sec	70 Research/Development
3 Buildings And Grounds	10 Curric/Instruct Sec	21 Art Elem	31 Career/Sch-to-Work K-12	41 Social Studies Sec	51 Reading K-12	61 Foreign/World Lang K-12	71 Public Information
4 Food Service	11 Federal Program	22 Art Sec	32 Career/Sch-to-Work Elem	42 Science K-12	52 Reading Elem	62 Foreign/World Lang Elem	72 Summer School
5 Transportation	12 Title I	23 Music K-12	33 Career/Sch-to-Work Sec	43 Science Elem	53 Reading Sec	63 Foreign/World Lang Sec	73 Instructional Tech
6 Athletic	13 Title V	24 Music Elem	34 Early Childhood Ed	44 Science Sec	54 Remedial Reading K-12	64 Religious Education K-12	74 Inservice Training
7 Health Services	15 Asst Superintendent	25 Music Sec	35 Health/Phys Education	45 Math K-12	55 Remedial Reading Elem	65 Religious Education Elem	75 Marketing/Distributive
	16 Instructional Media Svcs	26 Business Education	36 Guidance Services K-12	46 Math Elem	56 Remedial Reading Sec	66 Religious Education Sec	76 Info Systems
	17 Chief Operations Officer	27 Career & Tech Ed	37 Guidance Services Elem	47 Math Sec	57 Bilingual/ELL	67 School Board President	77 Psychological Assess
	18 Chief Academic Officer	28 Technology Education	38 Guidance Services Sec	48 English/Lang Arts K-12	58 Special Education K-12	68 Teacher Personnel	78 Affirmative Action

Texas School Directory — De Witt County

Public Schs..Principal	Grd	Prgm	Enr/#Cls	SN	
Dawson Sch Highway 137, Welch 79377 Jeffrey Fleenor	PK-12	TV	110 13	57%	806/489-7461 Fax 806/489-7546

● **Klondike Ind School Dist** PID: 01012824   806/462-7334
2911 County Road H, Lamesa 79331   Fax 806/462-7333

Schools: 1 \ **Teachers:** 21 \ **Students:** 275 \ **Special Ed Students:** 10 \ **LEP Students:** 12 \ **College-Bound:** 90% \ **Ethnic:** Asian 1%, African American 1%, Hispanic 34%, Caucasian 64% \ **Exp:** $565 (High) \ **Poverty:** 23% \ **Title I:** $48,888 \ **Open-Close:** 08/15 - 05/15 \ **DTBP:** $255 (High)

Steve McLaren 1,11		Dalton Degraffenreid 2,6	
Dalton Degraffenreid 2*		Evaristo Acevedo 3*	
Dolores Cobos 4		Dolores Cobos 4*	
Terry Morris 5*		Danielle Therwanger 8,83,288	
Julie Dossey 36,69,88,270,271*		Hailey White 58*	
Clay Thixton 67		Randy Leonard 73,295*	

Public Schs..Principal	Grd	Prgm	Enr/#Cls	SN	
Klondike Sch 2911 County Road H, Lamesa 79331 Danielle Therwhanger	PK-12	TV	275 15	35%	806/462-7332

● **Lamesa Ind School Dist** PID: 01012862   806/872-5461
212 N Houston Ave, Lamesa 79331   Fax 806/872-6220

Schools: 5 \ **Teachers:** 133 \ **Students:** 1,800 \ **Special Ed Students:** 179 \ **LEP Students:** 99 \ **College-Bound:** 77% \ **Ethnic:** Asian 1%, African American 4%, Hispanic 81%, Caucasian 14% \ **Exp:** $366 (High) \ **Poverty:** 28% \ **Title I:** $822,708 \ **Open-Close:** 08/14 - 05/20 \ **DTBP:** $372 (High)

Jim Knight 1	Liz Poage 2,294
Sammy Sanchez 3,5,91	Gary Pope 4
Gregg Moreland 6*	Steve Ruiz 7*
Doug Morris 8,11,57,83,286,288,296,298	Keith Emfinger 16,73,286,295*
Stacy Stewart 34,58,77*	Amy Baker 36*
Paige Kennon 37	Kelli Merritt 67
Chris Riggins 68*	Velinda Dimas 68
David Ritchie 88	

Public Schs..Principal	Grd	Prgm	Enr/#Cls	SN	
Lamesa High Sch 600 N 14th St, Lamesa 79331 Jerry Jerabek	9-12	ATV	491 50	80%	806/872-8385 Fax 806/872-6008
Lamesa Middle Sch N Bryan St & S 1st St, Lamesa 79331 Serapio Arguijo	6-8	TV	409 37	89%	806/872-8301 Fax 806/872-2949
Lamesa Success Academy 212 N Houston Ave, Lamesa 79331 David Ritchey	9-12	T	29	90%	806/872-5410
North Elem Sch 601 N 14th St, Lamesa 79331 Jennifer Stewart	3-5	T	439 27	89%	806/872-5428 Fax 806/872-8324
South Elem Sch 2000 S 8th St, Lamesa 79331 Shelley Mann	PK-2	T	537 29	83%	806/872-5401 Fax 806/872-9161

● **Sands Consolidated ISD** PID: 01012941   432/353-4888
101 1st St, Ackerly 79713   Fax 432/353-4650

Schools: 1 \ **Teachers:** 19 \ **Students:** 254 \ **Special Ed Students:** 16 \ **LEP Students:** 23 \ **College-Bound:** 80% \ **Ethnic:** Asian 1%, Hispanic 40%, Native American: 1%, Caucasian 57% \ **Exp:** $666 (High) \ **Poverty:** 18% \ **Title I:** $35,097 \ **Open-Close:** 08/15 - 05/15 \ **DTBP:** $326 (High)

Wayne Henderson 1	Amy Grumbles 2
Chris Spivey 3*	Jana Spivey 4*
Fred Brown 5	Lenny Morrow 8,12*
Tommy Stags 67	Tana Howard 69,83,270*
Scott Ragle 73*	Debi Barraza 271*

Public Schs..Principal	Grd	Prgm	Enr/#Cls	SN	
Sands Sch 101 1st St, Ackerly 79713 Lenny Morrow	PK-12	TV	254 25	51%	432/353-4744

DE WITT COUNTY

DE WITT PUBLIC SCHOOLS

● **Cuero Ind School Dist** PID: 01013684   361/275-1900
960 E Broadway St, Cuero 77954   Fax 361/275-8957

Schools: 4 \ **Teachers:** 148 \ **Students:** 2,000 \ **Special Ed Students:** 224 \ **LEP Students:** 76 \ **College-Bound:** 75% \ **Ethnic:** African American 13%, Hispanic 46%, Caucasian 40% \ **Exp:** $360 (High) \ **Poverty:** 27% \ **Title I:** $570,911 \ **Special Education:** $422,000 \ **Open-Close:** 08/14 - 05/22 \ **DTBP:** $341 (High) \ f t

Dr Micah Dyer 1	Mark Iacoponelli 2,15
Dwayne Noack 3,91	Sandra Hernandez 4
Bo Daniel 5	Travis Reeve 6
Wanda Hays 7	Dr Pamela Long Botham 8,11,57,88,285,288,298
Jennifer Hudgeons 16	Paula Brown 16,73,76,286,295
Stacey Porter 27*	Brittany Braden 36*
Megan Castillo 36*	Cynthia Bammert 38*
Karen Linscomb 58,77	Courtney Moore 67
Dave Truman 84,295	Ruby Rodriguez 93
Connie Phillips 294	

Public Schs..Principal	Grd	Prgm	Enr/#Cls	SN	
Cuero High Sch 920 E Broadway St, Cuero 77954 Paul Fleener	9-12	ATV	682 40	49%	361/275-1900 Fax 361/275-2430
Cuero Junior High Sch 608 Jr High Dr, Cuero 77954 Kim Fleener	6-8	ATV	473 32	61%	361/275-1900 Fax 361/275-6912
Hunt Elem Sch 550 Industrial Blvd, Cuero 77954 Bridgette Cerny	2-5	AT	515 21	71%	361/275-1900 Fax 361/275-3474
John C French Elem Sch 611 E Prairie St, Cuero 77954 Jennifer Bauer	PK-1	AT	326 22	75%	361/275-1900 Fax 361/275-2698

De Witt County

Market Data Retrieval

- **Meyersville Ind School Dist** PID: 01013737 361/277-5817
  1897 Meyersville Rd, Meyersville 77974 Fax 361/275-5034

  Schools: 1 \ **Teachers:** 12 \ **Students:** 132 \ **Special Ed Students:** 7 \
  Ethnic: African American 1%, Hispanic 16%, Caucasian 83% \ **Exp:** $424
  (High) \ **Poverty:** 14% \ **Title I:** $37,489 \ **Open-Close:** 08/14 - 05/21 \
  DTBP: $397 (High)

  Kelly Dunn ....1,11 Gay Davis 16,57,73,295*
  Johnny Jank 67

Public Schs..Principal	Grd	Prgm	Enr/#Cls	SN	
Meyersville Elem Sch 1897 Meyersville Rd, Meyersville 77974 Kelly Dunn	PK-8	T	132 13	32%	361/275-3639

- **Nordheim Ind School Dist** PID: 01013751 361/938-5211
  500 Broadway, Nordheim 78141 Fax 361/938-5266

  Schools: 1 \ **Teachers:** 17 \ **Students:** 150 \ **Special Ed Students:** 11
  \ **College-Bound:** 50% \ **Ethnic:** African American 3%, Hispanic 43%,
  Caucasian 54% \ **Exp:** $1,086 (High) \ **Poverty:** 21% \ **Title I:** $30,902 \
  Open-Close: 08/28 - 06/01 \ **DTBP:** $326 (High)

  John Kevin Wilson ....1 Kimberly Saunders 2,84
  Carlton Williams ....6* Pamela Remmers 67
  Ron Squires 73

Public Schs..Principal	Grd	Prgm	Enr/#Cls	SN	
Nordheim Sch 500 Broadway, Nordheim 78141 Lisa Karnei	PK-12	TV	150 14	38%	361/938-5211

- **Westhoff Ind School Dist** PID: 01013787 830/236-5519
  244 Lynch Ave, Westhoff 77994 Fax 830/236-5583

  Schools: 1 \ **Teachers:** 7 \ **Students:** 85 \ **Special Ed Students:** 4
  \ **LEP Students:** 4 \ **Ethnic:** African American 8%, Hispanic 56%,
  Caucasian 36% \ **Exp:** $823 (High) \ **Poverty:** 33% \ **Title I:** $35,707 \
  Open-Close: 08/14 - 05/20 \ **DTBP:** $293 (High)

  David Kennedy ....1,11,73,83,84 Maryhelen Robles 2
  Paddy Burwell 67

Public Schs..Principal	Grd	Prgm	Enr/#Cls	SN	
Westhoff Elem Sch 244 Lynch Ave, Westhoff 77994 David Kennedy	PK-8	T	85 8	67%	830/236-5519

- **Yoakum Ind School Dist** PID: 01013804 361/293-3162
  315 E Gonzales St, Yoakum 77995 Fax 361/293-6678

  Schools: 5 \ **Teachers:** 154 \ **Students:** 1,500 \ **Special Ed Students:** 222
  \ **LEP Students:** 246 \ **College-Bound:** 50% \ **Ethnic:** African American
  9%, Hispanic 65%, Caucasian 26% \ **Exp:** $497 (High) \ **Poverty:** 23% \
  Title I: $503,765 \ **Open-Close:** 08/14 - 05/21 \ **DTBP:** $342 (High)

  Tom Kelley ....1 Chris Kvinta 2,15,71,91,271
  Eric Thiry ....3 Velma Gomez 4*
  Dwight Watson ....5 Bo Robinson 6
  Amanda Murphree ....7,85 Chad Rothbauer 8,11,57,58,69,77,83,88
  Jason Fling ....16,73,76,84,295,298 Kim Kvinta 37*
  Courtney Zinke ....38* Glen Kusak 67
  Lynette Pate 68,79

Public Schs..Principal	Grd	Prgm	Enr/#Cls	SN	
Yoakum High Sch 104 Poth St, Yoakum 77995 Chris Wegener	9-12	TV	499 65	60%	361/293-3442 Fax 361/293-2145
Yoakum Intermediate Sch 208 Aubrey St, Yoakum 77995 Gabe Adamek	3-5	T	353 20	79%	361/293-3001 Fax 361/293-6562
Yoakum Junior High Sch 103 McKinnon St, Yoakum 77995 Patrick Frank	6-8	TV	353 25	79%	361/293-3111 Fax 361/293-5787
Yoakum Primary Annex Sch 412 Simpson St, Yoakum 77995 Pat Brewer	PK-K		190 9		361/293-3312 Fax 361/293-6937
Yoakum Primary Sch 800 W Grand Ave, Yoakum 77995 Darrin Stansberry	1-2	T	233 13	82%	361/293-2011 Fax 361/293-2688

- **Yorktown Ind School Dist** PID: 01013866 361/564-2252
  331 W Main St, Yorktown 78164 Fax 361/564-2254

  Schools: 3 \ **Teachers:** 43 \ **Students:** 550 \ **Special Ed Students:** 60
  \ **LEP Students:** 9 \ **College-Bound:** 45% \ **Ethnic:** African American
  2%, Hispanic 54%, Caucasian 44% \ **Exp:** $637 (High) \ **Poverty:** 25% \
  Title I: $182,306 \ **Open-Close:** 08/14 - 05/21 \ **DTBP:** $323 (High)

  Katherine Kuenstler ....1 Wendy Peroni 2,11,30,271
  Jason Chapa ....3 Diana Trevino 4
  Mary Romans ....7,85* Dina Menn 37*
  Tracy Heafley ....38 Jeremy Bailey 52,59
  Ciara Ibraheim ....54 Nelda Sertuche 67
  Erin Merts ....68 Blake Bryant 73

Public Schs..Principal	Grd	Prgm	Enr/#Cls	SN	
Yorktown Elem Sch 416 W 4th St, Yorktown 78164 Pamela Edwards-Flores	PK-5	T	259 18	69%	361/564-2252 Fax 361/564-2270
Yorktown High Sch 417 W 4th St, Yorktown 78164 Ashley Chandler	9-12	T	165 30	58%	361/564-2252 Fax 361/564-2274
Yorktown Junior High Sch 418 W 4th St, Yorktown 78164 Ashley Chandler	6-8	T	111 20	67%	361/564-2252 Fax 361/564-2289

DE WITT CATHOLIC SCHOOLS

- **Diocese of Victoria Ed Office** PID: 02181727
  Listing includes only schools located in this county. See District Index for
  location of Diocesan Offices.

Catholic Schs..Principal	Grd	Prgm	Enr/#Cls	SN	
St Michael Sch 208 N McLeod St, Cuero 77954 Jennifer Saenz	PK-6		73 9		361/274-3554 Fax 361/275-3135

1 Superintendent	8 Curric/Instruct K-12	19 Chief Financial Officer	29 Family/Consumer Science	39 Social Studies K-12	49 English/Lang Arts Elem	59 Special Education Elem	69 Academic Assessment
2 Bus/Finance/Purchasing	9 Curric/Instruct Elem	20 Art K-12	30 Adult Education	40 Social Studies Elem	50 English/Lang Arts Sec	60 Special Education Sec	70 Research/Development
3 Buildings And Grounds	10 Curric/Instruct Sec	21 Art Elem	31 Career/Sch-to-Work K-12	41 Social Studies Sec	51 Reading K-12	61 Foreign/World Lang K-12	71 Public Information
4 Food Service	11 Federal Program	22 Art Sec	32 Career/Sch-to-Work Elem	42 Science K-12	52 Reading Elem	62 Foreign/World Lang Elem	72 Summer School
5 Transportation	12 Title I	23 Music K-12	33 Career/Sch-to-Work Sec	43 Science Elem	53 Reading Sec	63 Foreign/World Lang Sec	73 Instructional Tech
6 Athletic	13 Title V	24 Music Elem	34 Early Childhood Ed	44 Science Sec	54 Remedial Reading K-12	64 Religious Education K-12	74 Inservice Training
7 Health Services	15 Asst Superintendent	25 Music Sec	35 Health/Phys Education	45 Math K-12	55 Remedial Reading Elem	65 Religious Education Elem	75 Marketing/Distributive
	16 Instructional Media Svcs	26 Business Education	36 Guidance Services K-12	46 Math Elem	56 Remedial Reading Sec	66 Religious Education Sec	76 Info Systems
	17 Chief Operations Officer	27 Career & Tech Ed	37 Guidance Services Elem	47 Math Sec	57 Bilingual/ELL	67 School Board President	77 Psychological Assess
	18 Chief Academic Officer	28 Technology Education	38 Guidance Services Sec	48 English/Lang Arts K-12	58 Special Education K-12	68 Teacher Personnel	78 Affirmative Action

Texas School Directory

DEAF SMITH COUNTY

DEAF SMITH PUBLIC SCHOOLS

• **Hereford Ind School Dist** PID: 01012989 806/363-7600
601 N 25 Mile Ave, Hereford 79045 Fax 806/363-7699

Schools: 11 \ **Teachers:** 307 \ **Students:** 4,100 \ **Special Ed Students:** 300 \ **LEP Students:** 671 \ **Ethnic:** African American 1%, Hispanic 88%, Caucasian 11% \ **Exp:** $344 (High) \ **Poverty:** 25% \ **Title I:** $1,339,688 \ **Special Education:** $810,000 \ **Open-Close:** 08/14 - 05/22 \ **DTBP:** $157 (High) \ [f]

Sheri Blankenship 1
Rusty Ingram 2,19
Joel Evertt 3
Ruth Evenson 5
Don Delozier 6,35*
Mark Stokes 8,18,45,69
Yolanda Gavina 11,83,271,274
Ruth Vessels 57
Christie Volmer 68
Edward Ingram 2
Joe Mendez 3,16,17,73,84,286,295
Vlada Buck 4
Brenda Kitten 6,35*
Joy Kilian 7,58,72
Adianna Wolf 11,296
Michelle Delozier 28,30,31*
Clay McNeely 67

Public Schs..Principal	Grd	Prgm	Enr/#Cls	SN	
Aikman Elem Sch 900 Avenue K, Hereford 79045 Sandra Maldonado	K-5	T	428 22	86%	806/363-7640
Bluebonnet Elem Sch 221 16th St, Hereford 79045 Andrea Brown	K-5	T	323 18	88%	806/363-7650 Fax 806/363-7657
Hcal 241 Avenue H, Hereford 79045 Tony Barker	9-12	T	44	82%	806/363-7720
Hereford High Sch 200 Avenue F, Hereford 79045 Richard Sauceda	9-12	GTV	1,091 50	76%	806/363-7620 Fax 806/363-7688
Hereford Junior High Sch 704 La Plata St, Hereford 79045 Cuca Salinas	6-7	TV	600 60	83%	806/363-7630 Fax 806/363-7697
Hereford Preparatory Academy 704 La Plata St Ste B, Hereford 79045 Linda Gonzalez	8-8	T	306	81%	806/363-7740 Fax 806/363-7637 [f]
Northwest Elem Sch 400 Moreman St, Hereford 79045 Nancy Neusch	K-5	T	467 21	77%	806/363-7660 Fax 806/363-7662 [f]
Stanton Learning Center 711 E Park Ave, Hereford 79045 **Brenda Bice**	PK-PK	A	320 5		806/363-7610 Fax 806/363-7715
Tierra Blanca Early Child Cent 7615 Columbia Dr, Hereford 79045 **Brenda Bice**	PK-PK		340		806/363-7680
Tierra Blanca Elem Sch 615 Columbia Dr, Hereford 79045 Ortencia Mendez	K-5	T	357 22	86%	806/363-7680 Fax 806/363-7668 [f]
West Central Elem Sch 120 Campbell St, Hereford 79045 Ortencia Mendez	K-5	T	223	88%	806/363-7690

Delta County

• **Walcott Ind School Dist** PID: 01013086 806/289-5222
4275 Highway 214, Hereford 79045 Fax 806/289-5224

Schools: 1 \ **Teachers:** 9 \ **Students:** 125 \ **Special Ed Students:** 13 \ **LEP Students:** 13 \ **Ethnic:** Asian 1%, Hispanic 75%, Caucasian 24% \ **Exp:** $1,067 (High) \ **Poverty:** 16% \ **Open-Close:** 08/28 - 05/25 \ **DTBP:** $192 (High)

Dr Bill McLaughlin 1,11,288
Cindy Hernandez 4
Natalie Sims 16,73*
Tammy Northcutt 59*
Tonya Gruhlkey 271*
Leslynn Arfsten 2
Darla Bryant 12,296*
Vickie Matthews 57*
Lucy McGowan 67

Public Schs..Principal	Grd	Prgm	Enr/#Cls	SN	
Walcott Elem Sch 4275 Highway 214, Hereford 79045 Darla Bryant	PK-6	T	125 8	64%	806/289-5222

DEAF SMITH CATHOLIC SCHOOLS

• **Diocese of Amarillo Ed Office** PID: 01047659
Listing includes only schools located in this county. See District Index for location of Diocesan Offices.

Catholic Schs..Principal	Grd	Prgm	Enr/#Cls	SN	
St Anthony's Elem Sch 120 W Park Ave, Hereford 79045 Ana Copeland	PK-6		109 8		806/364-1952 Fax 806/364-7179

DEAF SMITH PRIVATE SCHOOLS

Private Schs..Principal	Grd	Prgm	Enr/#Cls	SN	
Nazarene Christian Academy 1410 La Plata St, Hereford 79045 Shannon Victor	K-6		70 8		806/364-1697 Fax 806/364-7973

DELTA COUNTY

DELTA PUBLIC SCHOOLS

• **Cooper Ind School Dist** PID: 01013103 903/395-2111
350 W McKinney Ave, Cooper 75432 Fax 903/395-2117

Schools: 2 \ **Teachers:** 64 \ **Students:** 750 \ **Special Ed Students:** 74 \ **LEP Students:** 16 \ **College-Bound:** 49% \ **Ethnic:** Asian 1%, African American 12%, Hispanic 13%, Native American: 1%, Caucasian 72% \ **Exp:** $639 (High) \ **Poverty:** 26% \ **Title I:** $276,818 \ **Open-Close:** 08/15 - 05/21 \ **DTBP:** $348 (High) \ [f] [t]

Denicia Hohenberger 1,11,57
Denice Vaugh 3*
Rod Casterona 6*
Richard Roan 12*
Thomas Darden 67
Rachael Arthur 2,296,298
Lafreceia Robinson 4
Lou Ann Murray 7,85*
Elizabeth Joslien 38,69,83,288
Rachel Darden 68

Denton County

Market Data Retrieval

Charles Rutledge 73,76,295
Jean Howard 271*
Rachel Arthur 296*

Charles Rutledge 76*
Amber Norris 286*

Public Schs..Principal	Grd	Prgm	Enr/#Cls	SN	
Cooper Elem Sch 1401 SW 8th St, Cooper 75432 Julie Silman	PK-5	T	395 24	74%	903/395-2111 Fax 903/395-2019
Cooper Jr Sr High Sch 823 FM 1528, Cooper 75432 **Richard Roan**	6-12	AV	427 40		903/395-2111 Fax 903/395-2382

• **Fannindel Ind School Dist** PID: 01013141   903/367-7251
601 W Main St, Ladonia 75449   Fax 903/367-7252

Schools: 2 \ *Teachers:* 17 \ *Students:* 150 \ *Special Ed Students:* 22 \ *LEP Students:* 5 \ *College-Bound:* 80% \ *Ethnic:* Asian 4%, African American 36%, Hispanic 8%, Native American: 1%, Caucasian 52% \ *Exp:* $360 (High) \ *Poverty:* 21% \ *Title I:* $71,492 \ *Open-Close:* 08/16 - 05/22 \ *DTBP:* $335 (High)

Brad Lane 1,11,73,83
Larry Braley 5
Don Childress 16*

Discha Threlkelb 2
Jamie Babineaux 8,88*
Gwen Beeler 67

Public Schs..Principal	Grd	Prgm	Enr/#Cls	SN	
Fannindel Elem Sch 409 W Main St, Pecan Gap 75469 Drew Thomas	PK-5	T	87 8	89%	903/359-6314 Fax 903/359-6315
Fannindel High Sch 601 W Main St, Ladonia 75449 Jamie Babineaux	6-12	TV	87 12	87%	903/367-7251

DENTON COUNTY

DENTON PUBLIC SCHOOLS

• **Argyle Ind School Dist** PID: 01013177   940/464-7241
800 Eagle Dr, Argyle 76226   Fax 940/464-7297

Schools: 5 \ *Teachers:* 166 \ *Students:* 3,000 \ *Special Ed Students:* 218 \ *LEP Students:* 55 \ *College-Bound:* 90% \ *Ethnic:* Asian 2%, African American 1%, Hispanic 11%, Caucasian 85% \ *Exp:* $352 (High) \ *Poverty:* 3% \ *Title I:* $48,339 \ *Open-Close:* 08/19 - 05/22 \ *DTBP:* $326 (High)

Dr Telena Wright 1
Thomas Ledford 3*
Albert Rutledge 5
Deana Steeber 8,11,15,298
Sam Slaton 67

Elizabeth Stewart 2,19
Amy Bresnahan 4
Todd Rogers 6*
Greg Royar 16,295

Public Schs..Principal	Grd	Prgm	Enr/#Cls	SN	
Argyle High Sch 191 S Highway 377, Argyle 76226 John King	9-12		854 25	6%	940/262-7777 Fax 940/262-7783
Argyle Intermediate Sch 800 Eagle Dr, Argyle 76226 Renee Funderburg	4-5		400	8%	940/464-5100 Fax 940/464-7245
Argyle Middle Sch 6601 Canyon Falls Rd, Argyle 76226 Scott Gibson	6-8		679 32	7%	940/246-2126 Fax 940/262-4039
Argyle West Elem Sch 1741 Old Justin Rd, Argyle 76226 Renee Funderburg	PK-5		401		940/464-7241
Hilltop Elem Sch 1050 Harrison Ln, Argyle 76226 Mandi Murphy	PK-3		783 40	12%	940/464-0564 Fax 940/464-4017

• **Aubrey Ind School Dist** PID: 01013191   940/668-0060
415 Tisdell Ln, Aubrey 76227   Fax 940/365-2627

Schools: 4 \ *Teachers:* 144 \ *Students:* 2,000 \ *Special Ed Students:* 189 \ *LEP Students:* 88 \ *College-Bound:* 60% \ *Ethnic:* Asian 1%, African American 7%, Hispanic 17%, Native American: 1%, Caucasian 74% \ *Exp:* $680 (High) \ *Poverty:* 6% \ *Title I:* $139,539 \ *Open-Close:* 08/14 - 05/21 \ *DTBP:* $315 (High)

Dr David Belding 1,11
Eric Hough 2,19
Lendsey Gibbs 3
Shonna Hart 5
Elizabeth Swaim 7*
Dr Shannon Saylor 15,68,79
Monica Molinar 57,271*
Chris Millican 73,295

Betty Henderson 2,68
Eric Huff 3,17
Sherri Clement 4
Keith Ivy 6
Joanie Rouk 8
Terry McNabb 15
Jim Milacek 67
Sandra Ungerwood 83,85

Public Schs..Principal	Grd	Prgm	Enr/#Cls	SN	
Aubrey High Sch 510 Spring Hill Rd, Aubrey 76227 Matthew Gore	9-12		684 30	24%	940/668-3900 Fax 940/668-3903
Aubrey Middle Sch 815 W Sherman Dr, Aubrey 76227 Karen Wright	6-8		772 12	24%	940/668-0200 Fax 940/668-0228
Brockett Elem Sch 900 Chestnut St, Aubrey 76227 Kari Abrams	K-5	T	488 30	35%	940/668-0036 Fax 940/668-0037
Monaco Elem Sch 9350 Cape Cod Blvd, Aubrey 76227 Barbara Pitt	PK-5	T	551 15	33%	940/668-0000 Fax 940/668-0001

• **Denton Ind School Dist** PID: 01013220   940/369-0000
1307 N Locust St, Denton 76201   Fax 940/369-4982

Schools: 42 \ *Teachers:* 2,068 \ *Students:* 29,152 \ *Special Ed Students:* 3,022 \ *LEP Students:* 3,906 \ *College-Bound:* 59% \ *Ethnic:* Asian 3%, African American 15%, Hispanic 30%, Native American: 1%, Caucasian 51% \ *Exp:* $361 (High) \ *Poverty:* 8% \ *Title I:* $3,348,828 \ *Special Education:* $4,691,000 \ *Open-Close:* 08/13 - 05/21 \ *DTBP:* $186 (High)

Dr Jamie Wilson 1
Julie Simpson 2
Jim Watson 5
Kathy Malmberg 7*
Dr Dan Ford 10
Dr Rich Valenta 15,751
Donna Kearley 16
Carla Ruge 27,31,75,95*
Teresa Luna-Taylor 57,271
Mia Price 67
Julie Zwattr 71,97
Ernie Stripling 73,76,98

Debbie Monschke 2
Chris Bomberger 4
Joey Florence 6
Mary Helen Martin 9
Chris Shade 11,296,298
Robert Stewart 15,68,74
Jackie Demontmollin 20,23
Amy Lawrence 36
Debbie Roybal 58
Lori Hart 69
Dwight Goodwin 73
Lori Mabry 81*

1 Superintendent	8 Curric/Instruct K-12	19 Chief Financial Officer	29 Family/Consumer Science	39 Social Studies K-12	49 English/Lang Arts Elem	59 Special Education Elem	69 Academic Assessment
2 Bus/Finance/Purchasing	9 Curric/Instruct Elem	20 Art K-12	30 Adult Education	40 Social Studies Elem	50 English/Lang Arts Sec	60 Special Education Sec	70 Research/Development
3 Buildings And Grounds	10 Curric/Instruct Sec	21 Art Elem	31 Career/Sch-to-Work K-12	41 Social Studies Sec	51 Reading K-12	61 Foreign/World Lang K-12	71 Public Information
4 Food Service	11 Federal Program	22 Art Sec	32 Career/Sch-to-Work Elem	42 Science K-12	52 Reading Elem	62 Foreign/World Lang Elem	72 Summer School
5 Transportation	12 Title I	23 Music K-12	33 Career/Sch-to-Work Sec	43 Science Elem	53 Reading Sec	63 Foreign/World Lang Sec	73 Instructional Tech
6 Athletic	13 Title V	24 Music Elem	34 Early Childhood Ed	44 Science Sec	54 Remedial Reading K-12	64 Religious Education K-12	74 Inservice Training
7 Health Services	15 Asst Superintendent	25 Music Sec	35 Health/Phys Education	45 Math K-12	55 Remedial Reading Elem	65 Religious Education Elem	75 Marketing/Distributive
	16 Instructional Media Svcs	26 Business Education	36 Guidance Services K-12	46 Math Elem	56 Remedial Reading Sec	66 Religious Education Sec	76 Info Systems
	17 Chief Operations Officer	27 Career & Tech Ed	37 Guidance Services Elem	47 Math Sec	57 Bilingual/ELL	67 School Board President	77 Psychological Assess
	18 Chief Academic Officer	28 Technology Education	38 Guidance Services Sec	48 English/Lang Arts K-12	58 Special Education K-12	68 Teacher Personnel	78 Affirmative Action

Texas School Directory — Denton County

Public Schs..Principal	Grd	Prgm	Enr/#Cls	SN	
Adkins Elem Sch 1701 Monahan Dr, Lantana 76226 Erin Vennell	PK-5		383	8%	940/369-1300 Fax 940/584-0857
Alice Moore Elementary 800 Mack Dr, Denton 76209 **Lindsay Henderson**	PK-5	T	582 35	74%	940/369-3500 Fax 940/369-4918
Bettye Myers Middle Sch 131 N Garza Rd, Shady Shores 76208 Trey Peden	6-8	T	773	62%	940/369-1500 Fax 940/498-0050
Billy Ryan High Sch 5101 E McKinney St, Denton 76208 Vernon Reeves	9-12	AGTV	2,048	52%	940/369-3000 Fax 940/369-4960
Blanton Elem Sch 9501 Stacee Ln, Argyle 76226 Linda Bozeman	PK-5		489	3%	940/369-0700 Fax 940/241-1423
Borman Elem Sch 1201 Parvin St, Denton 76205 Emily McLarty	PK-5	T	469 40	78%	940/369-2500 Fax 940/369-4903
Braswell High Sch 26750 E University Ave, Aubrey 76227 Lesli Guajardo	9-12		1,756	31%	972/347-7700 Fax 972/347-6259
Calhoun Middle Sch 709 W Congress St, Denton 76201 Paul Martinez	6-8	GTV	729 70	69%	940/369-2400 Fax 940/369-4939
Catherine Bell Elem Sch 601 Villa Paloma Blvd, Little Elm 75068 Lauren Shapiro	K-5		801	25%	972/347-7200 Fax 972/347-9990
Cross Oaks Elem Sch 600 Liberty Rd, Crossroads 76227 Matthew Preston	PK-5	T	724	44%	972/347-7100 Fax 940/440-9770
Denton High Sch 1007 Fulton St, Denton 76201 Joel Hays	9-12	AGTV	2,030 70	43%	940/369-2000 Fax 940/369-4953
Eugenia P Rayzor Elem Sch 377 Rayzor Rd, Argyle 76226 Mary Dunlevy	PK-5		395	2%	940/369-4100 Fax 940/455-2658
Evers Park Elem Sch 3300 Evers Pkwy, Denton 76207 Linda Cavazos-Tucker	PK-5	T	574 44	72%	940/369-2600 Fax 940/369-4906
Ⓐ Fred Moore High Sch 815 Cross Timber St, Denton 76205 **Jacqueline San Miguel**	9-12	V	49 7	46%	940/369-4000 Fax 940/369-4957
Ginnings Elem Sch 2525 Yellowstone Pl, Denton 76209 Cornelius Anderson	PK-5	T	569 35	78%	940/369-2700 Fax 940/369-4909
Gonzalez Pre-K Center 1212 Long Rd, Denton 76207 Felicia Sprayberry	PK-PK	T	337	85%	940/369-4360 Fax 940/382-4285
Harpool Middle Sch 9601 Stacee Ln, Argyle 76226 Jeff Smith	6-8		990	12%	940/369-1700 Fax 940/241-1342
Hodge Elem Sch 3900 Grant Pkwy, Denton 76208 **Andrea Hare**	PK-5	T	584 35	81%	940/369-2800 Fax 940/369-4912
Ⓐ Joe Dale Sparks Campus 210 S Woodrow Ln, Denton 76205 Anthony Sims	4-12		54	16%	940/349-2468 Fax 940/369-4993
John H Guyer High Sch 7501 Teasley Ln, Denton 76210 Dr Shaun Perry	9-12		2,524	19%	940/369-1000 Fax 940/369-4965
L A Nelson Elem Sch 3909 Teasley Ln, Denton 76210 Erika Timmons	PK-5		633	28%	940/369-1400 Fax 940/383-3534
LaGrone Advanced Tech Complex 1504 Long Rd, Denton 76207 Marcus Bourland	Voc		850 20		940/369-4850 Fax 940/380-0243
Ⓐ Lester Davis Sch 1125 Davis St, Denton 76209 Ronnie Watkins	K-12	T	56 9	71%	940/369-4050 Fax 940/369-4966
McMath Middle Sch 1900 Jason Dr, Denton 76205 Dr Buddy Dunworth	6-8	T	781 60	44%	940/369-3300 Fax 940/369-4946
McNair Elem Sch 1212 Hickory Creek Rd, Denton 76210 Lacey Hailey	PK-5	T	533 45	35%	940/369-3600 Fax 940/369-4921
Mildred M Hawk Elem Sch 2300 Oakmont Dr, Corinth 76210 Robin Brownell	PK-5		671 36	10%	940/369-1800 Fax 940/321-1872
Navo Middle Sch 1701 Navo Rd, Aubrey 76227 Beth Kelly	6-8	V	937	30%	972/347-7500 Fax 940/304-3404
Newton Rayzor Elem Sch 1400 Malone St, Denton 76201 Cecilia Holt	PK-5	T	624 25	55%	940/369-3700 Fax 940/369-4924
Paloma Creek Elem Sch 1600 Navo Rd, Aubrey 76227 Natalie Mead	PK-5		659 30	30%	972/347-7300 Fax 972/346-9501
Pecan Creek Elem Sch 4400 Lakeview Blvd, Denton 76208 **Amanda Bomar**	PK-5		703	38%	940/369-4400 Fax 940/369-4904
Providence Elem Sch 1000 FM 2931, Aubrey 76227 Jairia Diggs	PK-5		415	26%	940/369-1900 Fax 940/365-2985
Rodriguez Middle Sch 8650 Martop Rd, Aubrey 76227 Renee Koontz	6-8		661		972/347-7050 Fax 972/987-4920
Ronnie Crownover Middle Sch 1901 Creekside Dr, Corinth 76210 Charlene Parham	6-8		927	23%	940/369-4700 Fax 940/321-0502
Sam Houston Elem Sch 3100 Teasley Ln, Denton 76205 Teresa Andress	PK-5		584 35	31%	940/369-2900 Fax 940/369-4915
Savannah Elem Sch 1101 Cotton Exchange Dr, Aubrey 76227 Michael McWilliams	PK-5		719	22%	972/347-7400 Fax 972/346-3352
Stephens Elem Sch 133 N Garza Rd, Shady Shores 76208 Chris Rangel	PK-5	T	447	50%	940/369-0800 Fax 940/321-1318
Strickland Middle Sch 324 E Windsor Dr, Denton 76209 Kathleen Carmona	6-8	GT	881	61%	940/369-4200 Fax 940/369-4950
Tomas Rivera Elem Sch 701 Newton St, Denton 76205 **Marvyn White**	PK-5	T	604 80	86%	940/369-3800 Fax 940/369-4927
Union Park Elem Sch 7401 Fieldwood Way, Aubrey 76227 **Lorena Salas**	PK-5		450		940/369-0900
Wayne Stuart Ryan Elem Sch 201 W Ryan Rd, Denton 76210 Nicole Poole	PK-5	T	672	57%	940/369-4600 Fax 940/369-4936
Windle Sch for Young Children 901 Audra Ln, Denton 76209 Angela Hellman	PK-PK	T	390 23	89%	940/369-3900 Fax 940/369-4930
Woodrow Wilson Elem Sch 1306 E Windsor Dr, Denton 76209 Caleb Leath	PK-5	T	598 35	42%	940/369-4500 Fax 940/369-4933

TX—121

Denton County

Market Data Retrieval

- **Krum Ind School Dist** PID: 01013347 940/482-6000
  1200 Bobcat Blvd, Krum 76249 Fax 940/482-3929

Schools: 5 \ **Teachers:** 158 \ **Students:** 2,050 \ **Special Ed Students:** 230 \ **LEP Students:** 161 \ **Ethnic:** African American 2%, Hispanic 27%, Caucasian 69% \ **Exp:** $415 (High) \ **Poverty:** 7% \ **Title I:** $146,795 \ **Open-Close:** 08/14 - 05/21 \ **DTBP:** $347 (High) \

Cody Carroll	1	Bryan Moore	2
Bobby Carey	3,5	Ashley Doyal	4
Bobby Clark	6*	Nancy Shipley	11,15
Cheryl Eager	16	Tracy Reynolds	37*
Michelle Vanzant	38*	Patricia Jameson	58,88
Eric Borchardt	67	Mark Sprague	73
Marilin Reeves	274*		

Public Schs..Principal	Grd	Prgm	Enr/#Cls	SN	
Blanche Dodd Elem Sch 915 E McCart St, Krum 76249 Patricia Bolz	2-5	T	314 25	37%	940/482-2603 Fax 940/482-3368
Hattie Dyer Elem Sch 304 N 3rd St, Krum 76249 Lindsey Boone	2-5	T	305 20	37%	940/482-2604 Fax 940/482-8203
Krum Early Education Center 1513 Sequoia Dr, Krum 76249 Tammy Morris	PK-1	T	349	45%	940/482-2605 Fax 940/482-6232
Krum High Sch 700A Bobcat Blvd, Krum 76249 Michelle Pieniazek	9-12	V	652 16	28%	940/482-2601 Fax 940/482-2997
Krum Middle Sch 805 E McCart St, Krum 76249 Robert Butler	6-8		503 30	37%	940/482-2602 Fax 940/482-6299

- **Lake Dallas Ind School Dist** PID: 01013373 940/497-4039
  104 Swisher Rd, Lake Dallas 75065 Fax 940/497-3737

Schools: 5 \ **Teachers:** 278 \ **Students:** 4,000 \ **Special Ed Students:** 450 \ **LEP Students:** 335 \ **College-Bound:** 65% \ **Ethnic:** Asian 3%, African American 8%, Hispanic 30%, Native American: 1%, Caucasian 58% \ **Exp:** $340 (High) \ **Poverty:** 5% \ **Title I:** $307,890 \ **Special Education:** $939,000 \ **Open-Close:** 08/15 - 05/22 \ **DTBP:** $175 (High)

Dr Gayle Stinson	1	Anne Haehn	2
Wes Eversole	2,15,19	David Talbert	3
Wendy Konz	3,5	Stephanie Reese	4
Raymond Hagel	5,91	Sharon Mitchell	5
Scott Head	6*	Diane Ramirez	7*
Brenda McOllum	9,57,274	Dr Marci Malcom	15
Sharon Simon	16,82*	Dr Mark Ruggles	58
Lance Stacy	67	Karla Landrum	68
Stephanie Payne	69	Melaynee Broadstreet	71
Mike Dabney	73,286,297	Robin Ballard	73
Vicki Haimlen	77	Mike Cromis	88
Gerry Hamilton	295		

Public Schs..Principal	Grd	Prgm	Enr/#Cls	SN	
Corinth Elem Sch 3501 Cliff Oaks Dr, Corinth 76210 Randall Caldwell	PK-5	T	590 47	37%	940/497-4010 Fax 940/497-8479
Lake Dallas Elem Sch 401 Main St, Lake Dallas 75065 Jennifer Perry	PK-5	T	664 16	59%	940/497-2222 Fax 940/497-2807
Lake Dallas High Sch 3016 Parkridge Dr, Corinth 76210 Dr Kristi Strickland	9-12	AV	1,260 60	32%	940/497-4031 Fax 940/497-1524
Lake Dallas Middle Sch 325 E Hundley Dr, Lake Dallas 75065 Randall Caldwell	6-8	T	907 120	41%	940/497-4037 Fax 940/497-4028
Shady Shores Elem Sch 300 Dobbs Rd, Shady Shores 76208 Jennifer Bryant	PK-5	T	543	36%	940/497-4035 Fax 940/497-4036

- **Lewisville Ind School Dist** PID: 01013402 469/713-5200
  1565 W Main St, Lewisville 75067 Fax 972/350-9500

Schools: 70 \ **Teachers:** 3,815 \ **Students:** 52,000 \ **Special Ed Students:** 5,610 \ **LEP Students:** 7,444 \ **College-Bound:** 71% \ **Ethnic:** Asian 14%, African American 11%, Hispanic 30%, Caucasian 44% \ **Exp:** $169 (Low) \ **Poverty:** 6% \ **Title I:** $5,037,818 \ **Special Education:** $8,383,000 \ **Open-Close:** 08/13 - 05/21 \ **DTBP:** $191 (High) \

Dr Kevin Rogers	1	Michael Ball	2,19
Shawn Barr	3	Mike Herman	4
Dr Joseph Coburn	6,7,72,91	Tim Ford	6
Melanie Vincelette	7	Dr Lori Rapp	8,15
Courtney Hart	11	Dr Buddy Bonner	15,68
Robin Stout	16	Bill Watson	20,23
Heidi Veal	34	Robin Fry	35
Monya Crow	36	Kelly Glos	41
Renee Marts	43	Jennifer Beimer	44
Lindsey Ferguson	46	Kobey Stringer	49
Eric Simpson	50	Jorge Castillo	57
Alex Alexander	58	Dr Kathy Talbert	58
Katherine Sells	67	Dr Sarah Fitzhugh	69,294
Amanda Brim	71	Bryon Kolbeck	73,76,98,295
Dana Sons	73	Shawna Miller	74
David Koonce	76	Rebecca Clark	79
Deborah Roby	81	Sharon Nobis	81
Matthew Garrett	91	Michael Jacobsen	286
Nick Rooney	297		

Public Schs..Principal	Grd	Prgm	Enr/#Cls	SN	
Arbor Creek Middle Sch 2109 Arbor Creek Dr, Carrollton 75010 Amy Obenhaus	6-8		910 50	19%	469/713-5971 Fax 972/350-9163
Bluebonnet Elem Sch 2000 Spinks Rd, Flower Mound 75028 Lana Fisher	PK-5		510 17	5%	469/713-5195 Fax 972/350-9005
Briarhill Middle Sch 2100 Briarhill Blvd, Lewisville 75077 Chris Mattingly	6-8		865 80	4%	469/713-5975 Fax 972/350-9167
Bridlewood Elem Sch 4901 Remington Park Dr, Flower Mound 75028 Robin Block	PK-5		402 20	2%	469/713-5193 Fax 972/350-9007
Camey Elem Sch 4949 Arbor Glen Rd, The Colony 75056 Angela Cortez	PK-5	T	596 30	48%	469/713-5951 Fax 972/350-9015
Career Center East 2553 Parker Rd, Lewisville 75056 Adrian Moreno	Voc		450		469/713-5211 Fax 214/626-1640
Castle Hills Elem Sch 1025 Holy Grail Dr, Lewisville 75056 Donna Taylor	PK-5		641 35	2%	469/713-5952 Fax 972/350-9018
Central Elem Sch 400 High School Dr, Lewisville 75057 Lea Devers	PK-5	T	908 70	91%	469/713-5976 Fax 972/350-9019
Coyote Ridge Elem Sch 4520 Maumee Dr, Carrollton 75010 Padgett Cervantes	PK-5		688	28%	469/713-5994 Fax 972/350-9026
Creek Valley Middle Sch 4109 Creek Valley Blvd, Carrollton 75010 Steffanie Webb	6-8		695	27%	469/713-5184 Fax 972/350-9172

1	Superintendent	8	Curric/Instruct K-12	19	Chief Financial Officer	29	Family/Consumer Science	39	Social Studies K-12	49	English/Lang Arts Elem	59	Special Education Elem	69	Academic Assessment
2	Bus/Finance/Purchasing	9	Curric/Instruct Elem	20	Art K-12	30	Adult Education	40	English/Lang Arts Sec	50	Special Education Sec	70	Research/Development
3	Buildings And Grounds	10	Curric/Instruct Sec	21	Art Elem	31	Career/Sch-to-Work K-12	41	Social Studies Sec	51	Reading K-12	61	Foreign/World Lang K-12	71	Public Information
4	Food Service	11	Federal Program	22	Art Sec	32	Career/Sch-to-Work Elem	42	Science K-12	52	Reading Elem	62	Foreign/World Lang Elem	72	Summer School
5	Transportation	12	Title I	23	Music K-12	33	Career/Sch-to-Work Sec	43	Science Elem	53	Reading Sec	63	Foreign/World Lang Sec	73	Instructional Tech
6	Athletic	13	Title V	24	Music Elem	34	Early Childhood Ed	44	Science Sec	54	Remedial Reading K-12	64	Religious Education K-12	74	Inservice Training
7	Health Services	15	Asst Superintendent	25	Music Sec	35	Health/Phys Education	45	Math K-12	55	Remedial Reading Elem	65	Religious Education Elem	75	Marketing/Distributive
		16	Instructional Media Svcs	26	Business Education	36	Guidance Services K-12	46	Math Elem	56	Remedial Reading Sec	66	Religious Education Sec	76	Info Systems
		17	Chief Operations Officer	27	Career & Tech Ed	37	Guidance Services Elem	47	Math Sec	57	Bilingual/ELL	67	School Board President	77	Psychological Assess
		18	Chief Academic Officer	28	Technology Education	38	Guidance Services Sec	48	English/Lang Arts K-12	58	Special Education K-12	68	Teacher Personnel	78	Affirmative Action

Texas School Directory — Denton County

School	Grades	Prog	Enroll	%	Phone
Creekside Elem Sch 901 Valley View Dr, Lewisville 75067 Rodney McGinnis	PK-5	T	475 50	62%	469/713-5953 Fax 972/350-9027
Dale Jackson Career Center 1597 S Edmonds Ln, Lewisville 75067 **Justin Gilbreath**	Voc		500 14		469/713-5186 Fax 972/350-9342
Degan Elem Sch 1680 College Pkwy, Lewisville 75077 Vanessa Stuart	PK-5	T	628 40	59%	469/713-5967 Fax 972/350-9028
Delay Middle Sch 2103 Savage Ln, Lewisville 75057 Jim Baker	6-8	TV	967 78	86%	469/713-5191 Fax 972/350-9174
Downing Middle Sch 5555 Bridlewood Blvd, Flower Mound 75028 Curt Martin	6-8		546 55	4%	469/713-5962 Fax 972/350-9176
Durham Middle Sch 2075 S Edmonds Ln, Lewisville 75067 Gary Holt	6-8	T	871	58%	469/713-5963 Fax 972/350-9182
Ethridge Elem Sch 6001 Ethridge Dr, The Colony 75056 Tasia Thompson	PK-5		496 35	24%	469/713-5954 Fax 972/350-9036
Flower Mound 9th Grade Center 3411A Peters Colony Rd, Flower Mound 75022 Jeffrey Brown	9-9	A	870	4%	469/713-5999
Flower Mound Elem Sch 4101 Churchill Dr, Flower Mound 75028 **Christy Van Scoyoc**	PK-5		475 35	8%	469/713-5955 Fax 972/350-9046
Flower Mound High Sch 3411 Peters Colony Rd, Flower Mound 75022 **Chad Russell**	10-12	V	2,619 150	4%	469/713-5192 Fax 972/350-9237
Forest Vista Elem Sch 900 Forest Vista Dr, Flower Mound 75028 Dr Patrick Schott	PK-5		492 40	11%	469/713-5194 Fax 972/350-9047
Forestwood Middle Sch 2810 Morriss Rd, Flower Mound 75028 David Tickner	6-8	V	914 60	8%	469/713-5972 Fax 972/350-9184
Garden Ridge Elem Sch 2220 S Garden Ridge Blvd, Flower Mound 75028 Kelly Roden	PK-5		381 28	9%	469/713-5956 Fax 972/350-9052
Griffin Middle Sch 5105 N Colony Blvd, The Colony 75056 **Heather Garrison**	6-8	GTV	805 30	46%	469/713-5973 Fax 972/350-9187
Hebron 9th Grade Campus 4211 Plano Pkwy, Carrollton 75010 Amanda Werneke	9-9		985	22%	469/713-5996 Fax 214/626-1630
Hebron High Sch 4207 Plano Pkwy, Carrollton 75010 Scot Finch	10-12	V	1,648	17%	469/713-5183 Fax 972/350-9255
Hebron Valley Elem Sch 4108 Creek Valley Blvd, Carrollton 75010 Tina Krol	PK-5		565 40	18%	469/713-5182 Fax 972/350-9068
Hedrick Middle Sch 1526 Bellaire Blvd, Lewisville 75067 Barbara Hamric	6-8	TV	668 55	64%	469/713-5188 Fax 972/350-9196
Heritage Elem Sch 100 Barnett Dr, Lewisville 75077 Toby Maxson	K-5		500 22	4%	469/713-5985 Fax 972/350-9072
Highland Village Elem Sch 301 Brazos Blvd, Lewisville 75077 Leslye Mitchell	PK-5		335 24	16%	469/713-5957 Fax 972/350-9079
Homestead Elem Sch 1830 E Branch Hollow Dr, Carrollton 75007 Sean Perry	PK-5		553 30	16%	469/713-5181 Fax 972/350-9083
Huffines Middle Sch 1440 N Valley Pkwy, Lewisville 75077 Estella Rupard	6-8	T	827 50	53%	469/713-5990 Fax 972/350-9199
Independence Elem Sch 2511 Windhaven Pkwy, Lewisville 75056 Theodora Winslow	PK-5	T	874	48%	469/713-5212 Fax 972/350-9479
Indian Creek Elem Sch 2050 Arbor Creek Dr, Carrollton 75010 Amy Teddy	PK-5		536 43	34%	469/713-5180 Fax 972/350-9085
Jackson Early Childhood Center 1651 S Valley Pkwy, Lewisville 75067 Dulia Longoria	PK-PK	T	694 19	79%	469/713-5986 Fax 972/350-9103
Lakeland Elem Sch 800 Fox Ave, Lewisville 75067 **Vanesa Asbun**	PK-5	T	844 33	86%	469/713-5992 Fax 972/350-9092
Lakeview Middle Sch 4300 Keys Dr, The Colony 75056 **Beri Deister**	6-8	TV	707 75	42%	469/713-5974 Fax 972/350-9202
Lamar Middle Sch 4000 Timber Creek Rd, Flower Mound 75028 **Kristy Casal**	6-8	V	718 75	14%	469/713-5966 Fax 972/350-9204
Lewisville Elem Sch 285 W Country Ridge Rd, Lewisville 75067 Lakshmi Natividad	PK-5	T	776	82%	469/713-5995 Fax 214/626-1620
Lewisville High Sch 1098 W Main St, Lewisville 75067 Jeffrey Kajs	11-12	ATV	1,921	55%	469/713-5190 Fax 972/350-9291
Lewisville HS-B Harmon Campus 1250 W Round Grove Rd, Lewisville 75067 Anthony Fontana	9-10		1,256		469/713-5201 Fax 214/626-1680
Lewisville HS-Killough 1301 Summit Ave, Lewisville 75077 **Kyndra Tyler**	9-10	V	1,125 70		469/713-5987 Fax 972/350-9304
Ⓐ Lewisville Learning Center 1601 S Edmonds Ln, Lewisville 75067 Angie Deaton	1-12	T	228 21	45%	469/713-5185 Fax 972/350-9350
Liberty Elem Sch 4600 Quail Run, Flower Mound 75022 Timothy Greenwell	PK-5		520 40	1%	469/713-5958 Fax 972/350-9098
Lisd STEM Academy at Donaldson 2400 Forest Vista Dr, Flower Mound 75028 Michelle Wooten	PK-5		476 35	9%	469/713-5198 Fax 972/350-9033
Marcus 9th Grade Center 5707A Morriss Rd, Flower Mound 75028 Chantell Upshaw	9-9	A	824	8%	469/713-5998
Marcus High Sch 5707 Morriss Rd, Flower Mound 75028 Will Skelton	10-12	GV	2,421 135	6%	469/713-5196 Fax 972/350-9313
McAuliffe Elem Sch 2300 Briarhill Blvd, Lewisville 75077 Jennifer Mattingly	PK-5		541 50	6%	469/713-5959 Fax 972/350-9116
McKamy Middle Sch 2401 Old Settlers Rd, Flower Mound 75022 Kelly Knight	6-8	V	941	2%	469/713-5991 Fax 972/350-9477
Michael G Killian Middle Sch 2561 Parker Rd, Lewisville 75056 Deanne Angonia	6-8		947	26%	469/713-5977 Fax 469/350-9200
Mill St Elem Sch 601 S Mill St, Lewisville 75057 Susan Heintzman	PK-5	T	246 24	63%	469/713-5965 Fax 972/350-9024
Morningside Elem Sch 6350 Paige Rd, The Colony 75056 Rita Bacque	PK-5		383 46	19%	469/713-5970 Fax 972/350-9117
Old Settlers Elem Sch 2525 Old Settlers Rd, Flower Mound 75022 Kelly Hayunga	PK-5	T	569 40	3%	469/713-5993 Fax 972/350-9126
Owen Elem Sch 5640 Squires Dr, The Colony 75056 Jennifer Spitzer	PK-5	T	388 26	49%	469/713-5950 Fax 972/350-9000

Legend:

- 89 Student Personnel
- 90 Driver Ed/Safety
- 91 Safety/Security
- 92 Magnet School
- 93 Parental Involvement
- 94 Gifted/Talented
- 95 Tech Prep Program
- 96 Video Services
- 97 Chief Information Officer
- 98 Chief Technology Officer
- 3 Substance Abuse Prev
- 4 Erate
- 5 AIDS Education
- 6 Alternative/At Risk
- 7 Multi-Cultural Curriculum
- 9 Social Work
- 270 Character Education
- 271 Migrant Education
- 273 Teacher Mentor
- 274 Before/After Sch
- 275 Response To Intervention
- 277 Remedial Math K-12
- 280 Literacy Coach
- 285 STEM
- 286 Digital Learning
- 288 Common Core Standards
- 294 Accountability
- 295 Network System
- 296 Title II Programs
- 297 Webmaster
- 298 Grant Writer/Ptnrships
- 750 Chief Innovation Officer
- 751 Chief of Staff
- 752 Social Emotional Learning

Other School Types
- Ⓐ = Alternative School
- Ⓒ = Charter School
- Ⓜ = Magnet School
- Ⓨ = Year-Round School

School Programs
- A = Alternative Program
- G = Adult Classes
- M = Magnet Program
- T = Title I Schoolwide
- V = Career & Tech Ed Programs

Social Media
- = Facebook
- = Twitter

New Schools are shaded
New Superintendents and Principals are bold
Personnel with email addresses are underscored

Denton County — Market Data Retrieval

School	Grd	Prgm	Enr/#Cls	SN	Phone/Fax
Parkway Elem Sch 2100 S Valley Pkwy, Lewisville 75067 Valerie Parsons	PK-5	T	518 50	58%	469/713-5979 Fax 972/350-9132
Peters Colony Elem Sch 5101 Nash Dr, The Colony 75056 Rebecca Chirinos	PK-5	T	662 34	66%	469/713-5179 Fax 972/350-9133
Polser Elem Sch 1520 Polser Rd, Carrollton 75010 Lisa Phelps	PK-5	T	393 25	49%	469/713-5978 Fax 972/350-9134
Prairie Trail Elem Sch 5555 Timber Creek Rd, Flower Mound 75028 Wendi Vaughn	PK-5		690 30	13%	469/713-5980 Fax 972/350-9135
Purnell Support Center 136 W Purnell Rd, Lewisville 75057 Shawnda LaRocque	Spec		100		469/713-5199 Fax 972/350-9393
Rockbrook Elem Sch 2751 Rockbrook Dr, Lewisville 75067 Patrick Guy	PK-5	T	757	56%	469/713-5968 Fax 972/350-9139
Shadow Ridge Middle Sch 2050 Aberdeen Dr, Flower Mound 75028 Gary Gibson	6-8		721	5%	469/713-5984 Fax 972/350-9215
Southridge Elem Sch 495 W Corporate Dr, Lewisville 75067 Wyvona Ulman	PK-5	T	627	69%	469/713-5187 Fax 972/350-9140
Stewart's Creek Elem Sch 4431 Augusta St, The Colony 75056 Andrea Smith	PK-5	T	370 20	57%	469/713-5960 Fax 972/350-9145
The Colony High Sch 4301 Blair Oaks Dr, The Colony 75056 Tim Baxter	9-12	GTV	2,052 147	37%	469/713-5178 Fax 972/350-9336
Thomas O Hicks Elem Sch 3651 Compass Dr, Frisco 75034 Misty Bevill-Nelson	PK-5		596 38	7%	469/713-5981 Fax 972/350-9075
Timber Creek Elem Sch 1900 Timber Creek Rd, Flower Mound 75028 Amy Acosta	PK-5		498	26%	469/713-5961 Fax 972/350-9146
Valley Ridge Elem Sch 1604 N Garden Ridge Blvd, Lewisville 75077 Rachel Garrett	PK-5		471 35	32%	469/713-5982 Fax 972/350-9155
Vickery Elem Sch 3301 Wager Rd, Flower Mound 75028 Adam Gray	PK-5	T	490	57%	469/713-5969 Fax 972/350-9157
Virtual Learning Academy 5707 Morriss Rd, Flower Mound 75028 Dr Christopher Bigenho	9-12		300		972/350-1870
Wellington Elem Sch 3900 Kenwood Dr, Flower Mound 75022 Tami Braun	PK-5		912 30	3%	469/713-5989 Fax 972/350-9160

• Little Elm Ind School Dist PID: 01013490
300 Lobo Ln, Little Elm 75068
972/947-9340
Fax 972/294-1107

Schools: 9 \ **Teachers:** 453 \ **Students:** 7,400 \ **Special Ed Students:** 591 \ **LEP Students:** 1,255 \ **College-Bound:** 58% \ **Ethnic:** Asian 3%, African American 16%, Hispanic 41%, Caucasian 40% \ **Exp:** $350 (High) \ **Poverty:** 7% \ **Title I:** $603,578 \ **Special Education:** $994,000 \ **Open-Close:** 08/14 - 05/20 \ **DTBP:** $181 (High) \

Daniel Gallagher 1	Anna Chavez 2
Grant Anderson 2,15,19	Danny Cogdell 3
Joel Moses 3	Carolyn Tarver 4
Sandra Howell 6	Toni Nelson 7*
Dr Ashley Glover 8	Dr Cyndy Mika 11,15,70,294
Ross Roberts 15,79	Jeff Wiseman 16,73,286
Dr Tony Tipton 27,31	Cortney Clover 58
Melissa Myers 67	Cleota Epps 68
Cecelia Jones 71	Patricia Robbins 71

Public Schs..Principal	Grd	Prgm	Enr/#Cls	SN	Phone/Fax
Brent Elem Sch 500 Witt Rd, Little Elm 75068 Karie Kuster	PK-5	T	691 13	46%	972/947-9451 Fax 972/947-9330
Cesar Chavez Elem Sch 2600 Hart Rd, Little Elm 75068 Elizabeth Miller	PK-5	T	713	38%	972/947-9452 Fax 972/294-0172
Colin Powell 6th Grade Center 520 Lobo Ln, Little Elm 75068 Elizabeth Miller	6-6		421		972/947-9446
Hackberry Elem Sch 7200 Snug Harbor Cir, Frisco 75036 Stephen Richardson	PK-5	T	627	52%	972/947-9453 Fax 972/947-9327
Lakeside Middle Sch 400 Lobo Ln, Little Elm 75068 Kelley Carr	7-8	AT	850 45	51%	972/947-9445 Fax 972/292-3009
Lakeview Elem Sch 1800 Waterside Dr, Little Elm 75068 John Wofford	PK-5		587	32%	972/947-9454 Fax 972/947-9328
Little Elm High Sch 1900 Walker Ln, Little Elm 75068 Renee Pentecost	9-12	GT	2,090 30	42%	972/947-9443 Fax 972/947-9334
Oak Point Elem Sch 401 Shahan Prairie Rd, Oak Point 75068 Kori Werth	PK-5	T	722	59%	972/947-9455 Fax 972/947-9329
Prestwick STEM Academy 3101 Stonefield, The Colony 75056 Christine Gibson	PK-8	V	758	15%	972/947-9450

• Northwest Ind School Dist PID: 01013517
2001 Texan Dr, Justin 76247
817/215-0000
Fax 817/215-0170

Schools: 30 \ **Teachers:** 1,444 \ **Students:** 24,000 \ **Special Ed Students:** 1,956 \ **LEP Students:** 1,002 \ **College-Bound:** 83% \ **Ethnic:** Asian 4%, African American 8%, Hispanic 21%, Native American: 1%, Caucasian 67% \ **Exp:** $330 (High) \ **Poverty:** 5% \ **Title I:** $993,719 \ **Special Education:** $2,148,000 \ **Open-Close:** 08/20 - 05/22 \ **DTBP:** $164 (High) \

Dr Ryder Warren 1	Brian Carter 2,15,19
Cara Carter 2,16,19,73,76,95,286*	Tim McClure 3,5,15
Joel Johnson 6,35	Dr Mary Seltzer 9
Dr Logan Faris 10	Carri Eddy 12,36,57,83,271,274
Dr Kim Caley 15,68	Dr Rob Thornell 15
Dr Kevin Lacefield 20,27	Cylynn Braswell 27,31,285
Terry Ward 44	Melanie Griffin 47
Dr Sunni Johnson 49,52,55	Brittany Bragg 50
Micah Glerkey 58	Judy Copp 67
Dr Melissa DeSimone 69	Emily Conklin 71
Dr Stephanie Espinosa 74,273,296	Jamie Farber 77,79
Mike Conklin 91	Adam Feind 295

Public Schs..Principal	Grd	Prgm	Enr/#Cls	SN	Phone/Fax
Byron Nelson High Sch 2775 Bobcat Blvd, Trophy Club 76262 Ron Myers	9-12		2,508	12%	817/698-5600 Fax 817/698-5670
Carl E Schluter Elem Sch 1220 Mesa Crest Dr, Haslet 76052 Amy Howell	PK-5		720	11%	817/698-3900 Fax 817/698-3970
Chisholm Trail Middle Sch 583 FM 3433, Rhome 76078 Matrice Raven	6-8	TV	1,067 45	26%	817/215-0600 Fax 817/215-0648

---

1 Superintendent	8 Curric/Instruct K-12	19 Chief Financial Officer	29 Family/Consumer Science	39 Social Studies K-12	49 English/Lang Arts Elem	59 Special Education Elem	69 Academic Assessment
2 Bus/Finance/Purchasing	9 Curric/Instruct Elem	20 Art K-12	30 Adult Education	40 Social Studies Elem	50 English/Lang Arts Sec	60 Special Education Sec	70 Research/Development
3 Buildings And Grounds	10 Curric/Instruct Sec	21 Art Elem	31 Career/Sch-to-Work K-12	41 Social Studies Sec	51 Reading K-12	61 Foreign/World Lang K-12	71 Public Information
4 Food Service	11 Federal Program	22 Art Sec	32 Career/Sch-to-Work Elem	42 Science K-12	52 Reading Elem	62 Foreign/World Lang Elem	72 Summer School
5 Transportation	12 Title I	23 Music K-12	33 Career/Sch-to-Work Sec	43 Science Elem	53 Reading Sec	63 Foreign/World Lang Sec	73 Instructional Tech
6 Athletic	13 Title V	24 Music Elem	34 Early Childhood Ed	44 Science Sec	54 Remedial Reading K-12	64 Religious Education K-12	74 Inservice Training
7 Health Services	15 Asst Superintendent	25 Music Sec	35 Health/Phys Education	45 Math K-12	55 Remedial Reading Elem	65 Religious Education Elem	75 Marketing/Distributive
	16 Instructional Media Svcs	26 Business Education	36 Guidance Services K-12	46 Math Elem	56 Remedial Reading Sec	66 Religious Education Sec	76 Info Systems
	17 Chief Operations Officer	27 Career & Tech Ed	37 Guidance Services Elem	47 Math Sec	57 Bilingual/ELL	67 School Board President	77 Psychological Assess
	18 Chief Academic Officer	28 Technology Education	38 Guidance Services Sec	48 English/Lang Arts K-12	58 Special Education K-12	68 Teacher Personnel	78 Affirmative Action

Texas School Directory — Denton County

School	Grd	Prgm	Enr/#Cls	SN	Phone
Clara Love Elem Sch 16301 Elementary Dr, Justin 76247 Lisa Crosslin	PK-5	T	614	33%	817/698-6600 Fax 817/698-6670
Denton Creek Sch 3505 Haynes Rd, Roanoke 76262 Dr Monty Brown	9-12		35 5		817/215-0920 Fax 817/490-0329
Gene Pike Middle Sch 2200 Texan Dr, Justin 76247 Christopher Jones	6-8	TV	933 50	29%	817/215-0400 Fax 817/215-0425
Haslet Elem Sch 501 Schoolhouse Rd, Haslet 76052 Melissa Webber	PK-5		708 39	9%	817/215-0850 Fax 817/215-0870
J C Thompson Elem Sch 440 E Wishbone Ln, Haslet 76052 Leigh Romer	PK-5		691	20%	817/698-3800 Fax 817/698-3870
J Lyndal Hughes Elem Sch 13824 Lost Spurs Rd, Roanoke 76262 Jessica McDonald	PK-5		632	24%	817/698-1900 Fax 817/698-1915
James Steele Accelerated HS 606 N Walnut St, Roanoke 76262 Robin Ellis	9-12		144	23%	817/698-5800 Fax 817/698-5840
John M Tidwell Middle Sch 3937 Haslet Roanoke Rd, Roanoke 76262 Dr Rhett King	6-8	V	1,212	17%	817/698-5900 Fax 817/698-5870
Justin Elem Sch 425 Boss Range Rd, Justin 76247 Dr Lisa Ransleben	PK-5	T	572 21	27%	817/215-0800 Fax 817/215-0840
Kay Granger Elem Sch 12771 Saratoga Springs Cir, Keller 76244 Michelle McAdams	PK-5		928	7%	817/698-1100 Fax 817/698-1170
Lakeview Elem Sch 100 Village Trl, Trophy Club 76262 Mary Seltzer	PK-5		623 15	3%	817/215-0750 Fax 817/215-0770
Lance Thompson Elem Sch 821 Hawks Way, Argyle 76226 Amy Howell	PK-5		500		817/698-1800 Fax 817/698-1813
Lizzie Curtis Elem Sch 9640 Belle Prairie Trl, Fort Worth 76177 Carrie Pierce	PK-5		507		817/541-8901 Fax 817/541-8999
Medlin Middle Sch 601 Parkview Dr, Trophy Club 76262 Paige Cantrell	6-8	V	1,117 22	9%	817/215-0500 Fax 817/215-0548
Northwest High Sch 2301 Texan Dr, Justin 76247 Carrie Jackson	9-12	V	1,756 114	23%	817/215-0200 Fax 817/215-0251
Northwest Special Program Ctr 1800 Highway 114, Justin 76247 Susan Moore	6-12		85 5		817/215-0900 Fax 817/215-0120
O A Peterson Elem Sch 2000 Winter Hawk Dr, Fort Worth 76177 Danielle Grimes	PK-5		769	24%	817/698-5000 Fax 817/698-5070
Prairie View Elem Sch 609 FM 3433, Rhome 76078 Yolanda Wallace	PK-5	T	447 20	49%	817/215-0550 Fax 817/215-0598
Roanoke Elem Sch 1401 Lancelot Dr, Roanoke 76262 Kristi King	PK-5		754 18	18%	817/215-0650 Fax 817/215-0670
Samuel Beck Elem Sch 401 Parkview Dr, Trophy Club 76262 Sandy Conklin	PK-5		838 22	5%	817/215-0450 Fax 817/215-0498
Sendera Ranch Elem Sch 1216 Diamond Back Ln, Haslet 76052 John Booles	PK-5		565	12%	817/698-3500 Fax 817/698-3515
Seven Hills Elem Sch 654 FM 3433, Newark 76071 Kim Blackburn	PK-5		572 34		817/215-0700 Fax 817/215-0740
Sonny & Allegra Nance ES 701 Tierra Vista Way, Fort Worth 76131 Penny Bowles	PK-5		572	18%	817/698-1950 Fax 817/698-1960
Truett Wilson Middle Sch 14250 Sendera Ranch Blvd, Haslet 76052 Natalie Arnold	6-8		1,050	14%	817/698-7900 Fax 817/698-7970
V R Eaton High Sch 1350 Eagle Dr, Fort Worth 76111 Michael Blankenship	9-10		1,603	16%	817/698-7300 Fax 817/698-7370
W R Hatfield Elem Sch 2051 Texan Dr, Justin 76247 James Mahler	PK-5	T	505 21	33%	817/215-0350 Fax 817/215-0369
Wayne A Cox Elem Sch 1100 Litsey Rd, Roanoke 76262 Kimberly Becan	PK-5		620	7%	817/698-7200 Fax 817/698-7270

● **Pilot Point Ind School Dist** PID: 01013581   940/686-8700
829 S Harrison St, Pilot Point 76258   Fax 940/686-8705

Schools: 4 \ *Teachers:* 111 \ *Students:* 1,500 \ *Special Ed Students:* 110 \ *LEP Students:* 301 \ *Ethnic:* Asian 1%, African American 2%, Hispanic 47%, Native American: 1%, Caucasian 49% \ *Exp:* $371 (High) \ *Poverty:* 11% \ *Title I:* $194,792 \ *Open-Close:* 08/19 - 05/21 \ *DTBP:* $616 (High)

Dan Gist 1   Barbara Ettredge 2,19
Harold Colson 3,15   Cassie Davidson 4
Pam Varnum 5   Danny David 6
James Ramsey 6   Tammy Morgan 8,69,74,273,275
Trina Brown 11,296   Blake Hesteande 27*
Denise Stovola 57   Renee Polk 67
Valerie Wall 73,295

Public Schs..Principal	Grd	Prgm	Enr/#Cls	SN	Phone
Pilot Point Elem Sch 829 S Jefferson St, Pilot Point 76258 Rae Strittmatter	PK-2	T	342 28	61%	940/686-8710 Fax 940/686-8715
Pilot Point High Sch 1300 N Washington St, Pilot Point 76258 Todd Southard	9-12	TV	423 33	45%	940/686-8740 Fax 940/686-8745
Pilot Point Intermediate Sch 501 Carroll St, Pilot Point 76258 Darla Wooten	3-6	T	409 25	61%	940/686-8720 Fax 940/686-8725
Pilot Point Middle Sch 828 S Harrison St, Pilot Point 76258 Robyn Leslie	7-8	T	227 27	48%	940/686-8730 Fax 940/686-8735

● **Ponder Ind School Dist** PID: 01013610   940/479-8200
400 W Bailey St, Ponder 76259   Fax 940/479-8209

Schools: 3 \ *Teachers:* 94 \ *Students:* 1,575 \ *Special Ed Students:* 100 \ *LEP Students:* 93 \ *Ethnic:* African American 2%, Hispanic 24%, Native American: 1%, Caucasian 74% \ *Exp:* $362 (High) \ *Poverty:* 8% \ *Title I:* $112,380 \ *Open-Close:* 08/14 - 05/21 \ *DTBP:* $316 (High)

Bruce Yeager 1   Kent Josselet 2,15,286
Patrick McLarty 3,5   Jeannie Delange 4*
Bill Savaell 6   Tara Allred 8
Elizabeth Wilbanks ....11,34,57,59,274*   Rhonda Brockett 16,82*
Bart Stover ....27*   Richard Hooper 31,73,297
Anne Ivy ....38,88*   Vangee Deussen 67
Chuck Woodall 295

Public Schs..Principal	Grd	Prgm	Enr/#Cls	SN	Phone
Ponder Elem Sch 401 W Bailey St, Ponder 76259 Janell Wilbanks	PK-5	T	655 31	45%	940/479-8230 Fax 940/479-8239

				School Programs	Social Media
9 Student Personnel	91 Safety/Security	275 Response To Intervention	298 Grant Writer/Ptnrships	A = Alternative Program	
0 Driver Ed/Safety	92 Magnet School	277 Remedial Math K-12	750 Chief Innovation Officer	G = Adult Classes	ⓕ = Facebook
1 Gifted/Talented	93 Parental Involvement	280 Literacy Coach	751 Chief of Staff	M = Magnet Program	
3 Video Services	95 Tech Prep Program	285 STEM	752 Social Emotional Learning	T = Title I Schoolwide	ⓣ = Twitter
3 Substance Abuse Prev	97 Chief Infomation Officer	286 Digital Learning		V = Career & Tech Ed Programs	
4 Erate	98 Chief Technology Officer	288 Common Core Standards	Other School Types		
5 AIDS Education	270 Character Education	294 Accountability	Ⓐ = Alternative School		
3 Alternative/At Risk	271 Migrant Education	295 Network System	Ⓒ = Charter School	New Schools are shaded	
9 Multi-Cultural Curriculum	273 Teacher Mentor	296 Title II Programs	Ⓜ = Magnet School	New Superintendents and Principals are bold	
Social Work	274 Before/After Sch	297 Webmaster	Ⓨ = Year-Round School	Personnel with email addresses are underscored	

TX-125

Dickens County

Market Data Retrieval

Ponder High Sch 300 W Bailey St, Ponder 76259 Dr Matthew Birdwell	9-12	AV	418 30	31%	940/479-8210 Fax 940/479-8219
Ponder Junior High Sch 501 Shaffner St, Ponder 76259 Shawn Simmons	6-8	TV	341 22	41%	940/479-8220 Fax 940/479-8229

● **Sanger Ind School Dist** PID: 01013646 940/458-7438
601 Elm St, Sanger 76266 Fax 940/458-5140

Schools: 7 \ *Teachers:* 186 \ *Students:* 2,660 \ *Special Ed Students:* 280 \ *LEP Students:* 192 \ *College-Bound:* 48% \ *Ethnic:* Asian 1%, African American 3%, Hispanic 27%, Native American: 1%, Caucasian 68% \ *Exp:* $276 (Med) \ *Poverty:* 8% \ *Title I:* $294,182 \ *Open-Close:* 08/13 - 05/22 \ *DTBP:* $183 (High) \

Dr Tommy Hunter 1   Susan Kwast 2
Dena Scheffler 3   Paige Hachmeister 4
Terry Gleaton 5   Charles Galbreath 6*
Leann Loyless ....8,270 Jennifer Mulkey 11,57,296
Kim Phillips ....58,84 Ken Scribner 67
Natalie Key 68   Leon Elsbecker 73,295
Tammy Austin 73

Public Schs..Principal	Grd	Prgm	Enr/#Cls	SN	
Butterfield Elem Sch 291 Indian Ln, Sanger 76266 Larry Beam	PK-5	T	550 56	44%	940/458-4377 Fax 940/458-5591
Chisholm Trail Elem Sch 812 Keaton Rd N, Sanger 76266 Alice Ford	K-2	T	321 27	53%	940/458-5297 Fax 940/458-2537
Clear Creek Intermediate Sch 1901 S Stemmons St, Sanger 76266 Sally Herrell	3-5	T	386 24	49%	940/458-7476 Fax 940/458-2539
Ⓐ Linda Tutt High Sch 404 Hughes St, Sanger 76266 Ivy Foss	9-12	T	30 3	50%	940/458-5701 Fax 940/458-5759
Sanger 6th Grade Sch 508 N 7th St, Sanger 76266 Larry Shuman	6-6	T	215 10	42%	940/458-3699 Fax 940/458-3795
Sanger High Sch 100 Indian Ln, Sanger 76266 Jennifer Flaa	9-12	T	819 40	36%	940/458-7497 Fax 940/458-4637
Sanger Middle Sch 105 Berry St, Sanger 76266 Jim Cain	7-8	GT	405 30	41%	940/458-7916 Fax 940/458-5111

DENTON CATHOLIC SCHOOLS

● **Diocese of Fort Worth Ed Off** PID: 01054339
Listing includes only schools located in this county. See District Index for location of Diocesan Offices.

Catholic Schs..Principal	Grd	Prgm	Enr/#Cls	SN	
Immaculate Conception Catholic 2301 N Bonnie Brae St, Denton 76207 Elaine Schad	PK-8		260 15		940/381-1155 Fax 940/381-1837

DENTON PRIVATE SCHOOLS

Private Schs..Principal	Grd	Prgm	Enr/#Cls	SN	
Blossom Valley Academy 1252 College Pkwy, Lewisville 75077 Edith Lam	PK-PK		90 6		972/436-3613
Christian Academy of America 175 Double Oaks Dr, Double Oak 75077 Jonathan Pulaski	K-12		800		972/539-1458 Fax 972/539-9434
Coram Deo Academy 4900 Wichita Trl, Flower Mound 75022 Polly Dwyer	K-12		600		682/237-0232 Fax 972/692-5140
Denton Calvary Academy 1910 E University Dr, Denton 76209 Stacey Baxter	K-12		350		940/320-1944 Fax 940/591-9311
Explorations Preparatory Sch 1501 Flower Mound Rd, Flower Mound 75028 Carolyn Hart	PK-8		120		972/539-0601
Knowledge Seeker Christian Sch 1471 W Corporate Dr, Lewisville 75067 Sandra Goodrich	K-8		6 2		972/353-3981
Lakeland Christian Academy 397 S Stemmons Fwy, Lewisville 75067 Tena Mitchell \ Jesse Erhart	PK-12		500		972/219-3939 Fax 972/219-9601
Liberty Baptist Sch 602 Manco Rd, Lewisville 75067 Doyle Moseley	K-12		55 3		972/436-3493 Fax 972/436-6063
Liberty Christian Sch 1301 S Highway 377, Argyle 76226 Joe Belyeu \ Norman Parker \ Heather Lytle	PK-12		1,300		940/294-2000 Fax 940/294-2035
Montessori Episcopal Sch 602 N Old Orchard Ln, Lewisville 75077 Tracey Reinhart	PK-K		70 10		972/221-3533
Prince of Peace Christian Sch 4004 Midway Rd, Carrollton 75007 Todd Baringer \ Betsy Graham \ Dr Jeromy Lowe	PK-12		1,000 50		972/447-0532 Fax 972/267-4202
Selwyn College Prep Sch 2270 Copper Canyon Rd, Argyle 76226 Melissa Sayler \ Lisa Biles \ Mary Kosednar	PK-12		150 20		940/382-6771 Fax 940/400-2593
Temple Christian Academy 2501 Northshore Blvd, Flower Mound 75028 Todd Hickman	PK-12		170 30		972/874-8700 Fax 972/539-4649
Wellspring Christian Acad 1919 N Elm St, Denton 76201	PK-5		120		940/591-9900 Fax 940/387-1518

DICKENS COUNTY

DICKENS PUBLIC SCHOOLS

● **Patton Springs Ind School Dist** PID: 01013933 806/689-2220
1261 East FM 193, Afton 79220 Fax 806/689-2253

Schools: 1 \ *Teachers:* 11 \ *Students:* 111 \ *Special Ed Students:* 17 \ *College-Bound:* 100% \ *Ethnic:* Hispanic 39%, Caucasian 61% \ *Exp:* $807 (High) \ *Poverty:* 47% \ *Title I:* $34,873 \ *Open-Close:* 08/19 - 05/22 \ *DTBP:* $350 (High)

Bryan White 1,11,57   Becky Hodges 2

---

1 Superintendent	8 Curric/Instruct K-12	19 Chief Financial Officer	29 Family/Consumer Science	39 Social Studies K-12	49 English/Lang Arts Elem	59 Special Education Elem	69 Academic Assessment
2 Bus/Finance/Purchasing	9 Curric/Instruct Elem	20 Art K-12	30 Adult Education	40 Social Studies Elem	50 English/Lang Arts Sec	60 Special Education Sec	70 Research/Development
3 Buildings And Grounds	10 Curric/Instruct Sec	21 Art Elem	31 Career/Sch-to-Work K-12	41 Social Studies Sec	51 Reading K-12	61 Foreign/World Lang K-12	71 Public Information
4 Food Service	11 Federal Program	22 Art Sec	32 Career/Sch-to-Work Elem	42 Science K-12	52 Reading Elem	62 Foreign/World Lang Elem	72 Summer School
5 Transportation	12 Title I	23 Music K-12	33 Career/Sch-to-Work Sec	43 Science Elem	53 Reading Sec	63 Foreign/World Lang Sec	73 Instructional Tech
6 Athletic	13 Title V	24 Music Elem	34 Early Childhood Ed	44 Science Sec	54 Remedial Reading K-12	64 Religious Education K-12	74 Inservice Training
7 Health Services	15 Asst Superintendent	25 Music Sec	35 Health/Phys Education	45 Math K-12	55 Remedial Reading Elem	65 Religious Education Elem	75 Marketing/Distributive
	16 Instructional Media Svcs	26 Business Education	36 Guidance Services K-12	46 Math Elem	56 Remedial Reading Sec	66 Religious Education Sec	76 Info Systems
	17 Chief Operations Officer	27 Career & Tech Ed	37 Guidance Services Elem	47 Math Sec	57 Bilingual/ELL	67 School Board President	77 Psychological Assess
	18 Chief Academic Officer	28 Technology Education	38 Guidance Services Sec	48 English/Lang Arts K-12	58 Special Education K-12	68 Teacher Personnel	78 Affirmative Action

Texas School Directory

Donley County

Bruce Porter	3*	Bryan White			12,288*
Gary Bridge	67	James Stephens			73*

Public Schs..Principal	Grd	Prgm	Enr/#Cls	SN	
Patton Springs Sch 1261 East FM 193, Afton 79220 Sandra Ramirez	PK-12	V	111 18	83%	806/689-2220 Fax 806/689-2470

• **Spur Ind School Dist** PID: 01013969   806/271-3272
800 Williams Ave, Spur 79370   Fax 806/271-4575

Schools: 1 \ *Teachers:* 29 \ *Students:* 250 \ *Special Ed Students:* 39 \ *LEP Students:* 3 \ *College-Bound:* 95% \ *Ethnic:* African American 3%, Hispanic 43%, Caucasian 54% \ *Exp:* $586 (High) \ *Poverty:* 22% \ *Title I:* $71,739 \ *Open-Close:* 08/19 - 05/21 \

Craig Hamilton	1	Jodi Gonzalez		2,11
Chris Barron	3,5*	Michael Norman		6,12*
Josh Watson	16,73	Josh Watson		16,73*
Chad Smith	27*	Dana Conrad		58*
Barry Ferguson	67	Marcella Bilberry		83,85*

Public Schs..Principal	Grd	Prgm	Enr/#Cls	SN	
Spur Sch 800 Williams Ave, Spur 79370 Jose Molina \ Michael Norman	PK-12	TV	250 25	57%	806/271-3385

DIMMIT COUNTY

DIMMIT PUBLIC SCHOOLS

• **Carrizo Spgs Cons Ind SD** PID: 01014030   830/876-3503
300 N 7th St, Carrizo Spgs 78834   Fax 830/876-9317

Schools: 4 \ *Teachers:* 142 \ *Students:* 2,200 \ *Special Ed Students:* 150 \ *LEP Students:* 146 \ *College-Bound:* 75% \ *Ethnic:* Hispanic 94%, Caucasian 5% \ *Exp:* $729 (High) \ *Poverty:* 39% \ *Title I:* $1,321,301 \ *Special Education:* $542,000 \ *Open-Close:* 08/26 - 05/29 \ *DTBP:* $326 (High)

Dr Alberto Gonzales	1	Jesse Muniz		2
Alejandro Orosco	3,5	Erica Vega		4
Richard Ebshire	6	Maria Areal		8,288
Sandra Uriegas	11,57	Michael Uriegas		33,68,78,79,91
Jayda Rodriguez	38	Roxanne Miranda		38*
Gilbert Morales	58	Dr Ninfa Cadena		67
Marco Mendez	73,76,84,295	Eddie Cortez		91

Public Schs..Principal	Grd	Prgm	Enr/#Cls	SN	
Carrizo Springs Elem Sch 605 N 9th St, Carrizo Spgs 78834 Elisa Martinez	PK-3	T	732 20	75%	830/876-3513 Fax 830/876-4138
Carrizo Springs High Sch 335 Farm Rd 1917, Carrizo Spgs 78834 Michelle Gonzalez	9-12	AGTV	612 52	70%	830/876-9393 Fax 830/876-9553
Carrizo Springs Interm Sch 452 Highway 85, Carrizo Spgs 78834 Mario Ruiz	4-6	T	520 15	84%	830/876-3561 Fax 830/876-5132
Carrizo Springs Jr High Sch 286 Farm Rd 1556, Carrizo Spgs 78834 Maria Villarreal	6-8	T	333 45	76%	830/876-2496 Fax 830/876-2497

DONLEY COUNTY

DONLEY PUBLIC SCHOOLS

• **Clarendon Cons Ind Sch Dist** PID: 01014119   806/874-2062
416 S Allen Street, Clarendon 79226   Fax 806/874-2579

Schools: 3 \ *Teachers:* 47 \ *Students:* 600 \ *Special Ed Students:* 41 \ *LEP Students:* 3 \ *College-Bound:* 76% \ *Ethnic:* African American 10%, Hispanic 11%, Caucasian 79% \ *Exp:* $522 (High) \ *Poverty:* 32% \ *Title I:* $185,858 \ *Special Education:* $57,000 \ *Open-Close:* 08/15 - 05/21 \ *DTBP:* $354 (High) \

Mike Norrell	1	Kristen Brown		2
Terry Ralston	3	Pat Ritchie		4*
Chad Hommel	5	Clinit Coonkin		6
Travis Victory	8	Jenay Ashbrooke		11,88
Mike Word	11,93*	Melondy Lusk		58
Wayne Hardin	67	Butch Noble		71,73,97,98,295*

Public Schs..Principal	Grd	Prgm	Enr/#Cls	SN	
Clarendon Elem Sch 922 W 5th St, Clarendon 79226 Mike Word	PK-5	T	239 20	58%	806/874-3855 Fax 806/874-2082
Clarendon High Sch 420 S Allen St, Clarendon 79226 Larry Jeffers	9-12	TV	126 16	47%	806/874-2181 Fax 806/874-3428
Clarendon Junior High Sch 922 W 5th St, Clarendon 79226 Travis Victory	6-8	T	108 9	58%	806/874-3232 Fax 806/874-9748

• **Hedley Ind School Dist** PID: 01014145   806/856-5323
301 Jones St, Hedley 79237   Fax 806/856-5372

Schools: 1 \ *Teachers:* 14 \ *Students:* 120 \ *Special Ed Students:* 8 \ *LEP Students:* 3 \ *College-Bound:* 90% \ *Ethnic:* African American 2%, Hispanic 21%, Native American: 1%, Caucasian 77% \ *Exp:* $1,045 (High) \ *Poverty:* 21% \ *Title I:* $24,960 \ *Open-Close:* 08/15 - 05/21 \ *DTBP:* $392 (High)

Garrett Baines	1,11,73	Tresa Alston		2
Garrett Baines	8*	Christi Willey		58
Dana Bell	67	Jennie Owens		73,295*

Public Schs..Principal	Grd	Prgm	Enr/#Cls	SN	
Hedley Sch 301 Jones St, Hedley 79237 Garrett Baines	PK-12	TV	120 19	78%	806/856-5323

Student Personnel	91 Safety/Security	275 Response To Intervention	298 Grant Writer/Ptnrships	**School Programs**	**Social Media**
Driver Ed/Safety	92 Magnet School	277 Remedial Math K-12	750 Chief Innovation Officer	A = Alternative Program	
Gifted/Talented	93 Parental Involvement	280 Literacy Coach	751 Chief of Staff	G = Adult Classes	= Facebook
Video Services	95 Tech Prep Program	285 STEM	752 Social Emotional Learning	M = Magnet Program	
Substance Abuse Prev	97 Chief Infomation Officer	286 Digital Learning		T = Title I Schoolwide	= Twitter
Erate	98 Chief Technology Officer	288 Common Core Standards	**Other School Types**	V = Career & Tech Ed Programs	
AIDS Education	270 Accountability	294 Accountability	Ⓐ = Alternative School		
Alternative/At Risk	271 Migrant Education	295 Network System	Ⓒ = Charter School	New Schools are shaded	
Multi-Cultural Curriculum	273 Teacher Mentor	296 Title II Programs	Ⓜ = Magnet School	New Superintendents and Principals are bold	
Social Work	274 Before/After Sch	297 Webmaster	Ⓨ = Year-Round School	Personnel with email addresses are underscored	

Duval County

DUVAL COUNTY

DUVAL PUBLIC SCHOOLS

- **Benavides Ind School Dist** PID: 01014171 361/256-3000
  106 W School St, Benavides 78341 Fax 361/256-3002

Schools: 2 \ *Teachers:* 29 \ *Students:* 340 \ *Special Ed Students:* 40 \ *LEP Students:* 15 \ *College-Bound:* 50% \ *Ethnic:* Hispanic 99%, Caucasian 1% \ *Exp:* $447 (High) \ *Poverty:* 33% \ *Title I:* $181,712 \ *Open-Close:* 08/23 - 06/01 \ *DTBP:* $350 (High) \

Dr Marisa Chapa .... 1 Christina Perez 2,5
Odette Panales .... 4 Gilbert Perez 6
Leticia Cervantes .... 36,69,83,288* Jesse Abitua 67
Greg Perez 73,84,285,286

Public Schs..Principal	Grd	Prgm	Enr/#Cls	SN	
Benavides Elem Sch 106 W School St, Benavides 78341 Sandra Perez	PK-6	MTV	175 14	89%	361/256-3030 Fax 361/256-3032
Benavides Secondary Sch 1025 Eagle Dr, Benavides 78341 Raynaldo Perez	7-12	TV	165 18	70%	361/256-3040 Fax 361/256-3043

- **Freer Ind School Dist** PID: 01809196 361/394-6025
  905 S Norton St, Freer 78357 Fax 361/394-5055

Schools: 3 \ *Teachers:* 60 \ *Students:* 807 \ *Special Ed Students:* 108 \ *LEP Students:* 33 \ *College-Bound:* 97% \ *Ethnic:* Hispanic 92%, Caucasian 8% \ *Exp:* $879 (High) \ *Poverty:* 30% \ *Title I:* $259,088 \ *Open-Close:* 08/26 - 05/28 \ *DTBP:* $380 (High)

Conrad Cantu .... 1 Guadalupe Cude 2,11,57,69,271,296
Carolyn Stanfield .... 4 Linda Worsham 5
Gerardo Carpentier .... 6* Maria Cantu 7*
Dr Frances Perez .... 8,15,752 Dina McQuagge 33,38*
Susan Gallagos .... 58 Steve McQuagge 67
Karl Garcia 73,84,295

Public Schs..Principal	Grd	Prgm	Enr/#Cls	SN	
Freer High Sch 905 S Norton St, Freer 78357 Linda Hinojosa	9-12	ATV	214 30	76%	361/394-6717 Fax 361/394-5046
Freer Junior High Sch 615 S Norton St, Freer 78357 Rosalva Campos	6-8	T	186 22	68%	361/394-7102 Fax 361/394-5016
Norman Thomas Elem Sch 1404 S Norton St, Freer 78357 Ramon Garza	PK-5	T	407 21	73%	361/394-6800 Fax 361/394-5014

- **Ramirez Common School Dist** PID: 01014250 361/539-4343
  10492 School St, Realitos 78376 Fax 361/539-4482

Schools: 1 \ *Teachers:* 4 \ *Students:* 30 \ *Special Ed Students:* 3 \ *LEP Students:* 14 \ *Ethnic:* Hispanic 100% \ *Exp:* $735 (High) \ *Poverty:* 25% \ *Title I:* $19,638 \ *Open-Close:* 08/26 - 05/29 \ *DTBP:* $245 (High)

Yliana Gonzalez .... 1 Dalia Bozah 2
George Chavera 67

Public Schs..Principal	Grd	Prgm	Enr/#Cls	SN	
Ramirez Elem Sch 10492 School St, Realitos 78376 Yliana Gonzalez	PK-6	T	30 5	89%	361/539-4343

- **San Diego Ind School Dist** PID: 01014274 361/279-3382
  609 W Labbe St, San Diego 78384 Fax 361/279-1830

Schools: 3 \ *Teachers:* 94 \ *Students:* 1,460 \ *Special Ed Students:* 117 \ *LEP Students:* 25 \ *College-Bound:* 51% \ *Ethnic:* Hispanic 98%, Caucasian 1% \ *Exp:* $421 (High) \ *Poverty:* 44% \ *Title I:* $840,112 \ *Open-Close:* 08/15 - 05/22 \ *DTBP:* $346 (High)

Dr Rodrigo Pena .... 1 Angelina Smith-Wick 2
Gracie Pizzini .... 8,11,15,79 Rosalinda Flores 16*
Rosie Solis .... 58 Librada Vela 67
Oscar Ruiz 73,76*

Public Schs..Principal	Grd	Prgm	Enr/#Cls	SN	
Bernarda Jaime Jr High Sch 609 W Labbe St, San Diego 78384 Nita Vela	6-8	AT	333 38	77%	361/279-3382 Fax 361/279-7160
Collins-Parr Elem Sch 600 S Reforma St, San Diego 78384 Monica Perez	PK-5	AT	748 28	82%	361/279-3382 Fax 361/279-1827
San Diego High Sch 235 S Highway 359, San Diego 78384 Claudette Garcia	9-12	ATV	379 37	75%	361/279-1840 Fax 361/279-5098

EASTLAND COUNTY

EASTLAND PUBLIC SCHOOLS

- **Cisco Independent Sch Dist** PID: 01014353 254/442-3056
  1503 Liggett St, Cisco 76437 Fax 254/442-1412

Schools: 4 \ *Teachers:* 84 \ *Students:* 850 \ *Special Ed Students:* 95 \ *LEP Students:* 8 \ *College-Bound:* 71% \ *Ethnic:* Asian 1%, African American 1%, Hispanic 18%, Native American: 1%, Caucasian 80% \ *Exp:* $312 (High) \ *Poverty:* 29% \ *Title I:* $323,543 \ *Open-Close:* 08/19 - 05/29 \ *DTBP:* $386 (High) \

Dr Ryan Steel .... 1,11 Terri Hanlon 2
Derrick White .... 3,5* Lori Boyd 4*
Brent West .... 6* Pam Duncan 7*
Charlotte Weiser .... 16,73* Julie Patterson 58,74,92*
Cindy Tubb .... 68 Kathy Conring 69*
Charlotte Weiser 84

Public Schs..Principal	Grd	Prgm	Enr/#Cls	SN	
Cisco Elem Sch 503 W 11th St, Cisco 76437 Sharon Wilcoxen	PK-5	T	403 26	59%	254/442-1219 Fax 254/442-4836
Cisco High Sch 1300 Pershing St, Cisco 76437 Craig Kent	9-12	TV	244 45	46%	254/442-3051 Fax 254/442-2516

---

1 Superintendent	8 Curric/Instruct K-12	19 Chief Financial Officer	29 Family/Consumer Science	39 Social Studies K-12	49 English/Lang Arts Elem	59 Special Education Elem	69 Academic Assessment
2 Bus/Finance/Purchasing	9 Curric/Instruct Elem	20 Art K-12	30 Adult Education	40 Social Studies Elem	50 English/Lang Arts Sec	60 Special Education Sec	70 Research/Development
3 Buildings And Grounds	10 Curric/Instruct Sec	21 Art Elem	31 Career/Sch-to-Work K-12	41 Social Studies Sec	51 Reading K-12	61 Foreign/World Lang K-12	71 Public Information
4 Food Service	11 Federal Program	22 Art Sec	32 Career/Sch-to-Work Elem	42 Science K-12	52 Reading Elem	62 Foreign/World Lang Elem	72 Summer School
5 Transportation	12 Title I	23 Music K-12	33 Career/Sch-to-Work Sec	43 Science Elem	53 Reading Sec	63 Foreign/World Lang Sec	73 Instructional Tech
6 Athletic	13 Title V	24 Music Elem	34 Early Childhood Ed	44 Science Sec	54 Remedial Reading K-12	64 Religious Education K-12	74 Inservice Training
7 Health Services	15 Asst Superintendent	25 Music Sec	35 Health/Phys Education	45 Math K-12	55 Remedial Reading Elem	65 Religious Education Elem	75 Marketing/Distributive
	16 Instructional Media Svcs	26 Business Education	36 Guidance Services K-12	46 Math Elem	56 Remedial Reading Sec	66 Religious Education Sec	76 Info Systems
	17 Chief Operations Officer	27 Career & Tech Ed	37 Guidance Services Elem	47 Math Sec	57 Bilingual/ELL	67 School Board President	77 Psychological Assess
	18 Chief Academic Officer	28 Technology Education	38 Guidance Services Sec	48 English/Lang Arts K-12	58 Special Education K-12	68 Teacher Personnel	78 Affirmative Action

Texas School Directory

Ector County

Cisco Junior High Sch	6-8	TV	204	59%	254/442-3004
1200 Pershing St, Cisco 76437			12		Fax 254/442-1832
Tooter Draper					
Cisco Learning Center	9-12	AV	12	75%	254/442-4852
804 Avenue H, Cisco 76437			2		Fax 254/442-1917
Julie Patterson					

● **Eastland Ind School Dist** PID: 01014406   254/631-5120
900 W Plummer St, Eastland 76448   Fax 254/631-5126

> **Schools:** 3 \ **Teachers:** 90 \ **Students:** 1,130 \ **Special Ed Students:** 109 \ **LEP Students:** 66 \ **College-Bound:** 85% \ **Ethnic:** Asian 1%, African American 2%, Hispanic 28%, Caucasian 69% \ **Exp:** $311 (High) \ **Poverty:** 27% \ **Title I:** $375,728 \ **Special Education:** $5,000 \ **Open-Close:** 08/14 - 05/28 \ **DTBP:** $344 (High) \ f t

Jason Cochran 1,83		Mary Jones 2	
Cala Willis 4		Brian Schafer 5	
James Morton 6*		Brandon Chesser 12	
Jeremy Williams 15		Laurah Williams 27*	
David Hullman 67			

Public Schs..Principal	Grd	Prgm	Enr/#Cls	SN	
Eastland High Sch	9-12	ATV	361	40%	254/631-5000
900 W Plummer St Ste 101, Eastland 76448			40		Fax 254/631-5025
Adam Bramlett					
Eastland Middle Sch	6-8	T	260	58%	254/631-5040
900 W Plummer St, Eastland 76448			32		Fax 254/631-5049
Jason Henry					
Siebert Elem Sch	PK-5	T	563	66%	254/631-5080
100 Little Maverick Trl, Eastland 76448			32		Fax 254/631-5085
Brandon Chesser					

● **Gorman Ind School Dist** PID: 01014444   254/734-3171
114 W Lexington Street, Gorman 76454   Fax 254/734-3393

> **Schools:** 3 \ **Teachers:** 30 \ **Students:** 300 \ **Special Ed Students:** 45 \ **LEP Students:** 19 \ **College-Bound:** 80% \ **Ethnic:** African American 1%, Hispanic 41%, Caucasian 58% \ **Exp:** $444 (High) \ **Poverty:** 18% \ **Title I:** $64,454 \ **Open-Close:** 08/19 - 05/28 \ **DTBP:** $350 (High)

Mike Winter 1,11		Randy Lewis 3,5	
Lissa Young 4		Shellie Little 7	
Patricia Hampton 36,83,88*		Debra Sanchez 57,271*	
Vicki Brown 58*		Eldin Straw 67	
Dianne Snider 68		Denise Carlton 73	

Public Schs..Principal	Grd	Prgm	Enr/#Cls	SN	
Gorman High Sch	9-12	TV	83	57%	254/734-3171
114 W Lexington Street, Gorman 76454			13		Fax 254/734-3425
Kelly Kunkel					f t
Gorman Middle Sch	6-8	T	72	77%	254/734-3171
114 W Lexington St, Gorman 76454					Fax 254/734-4729
Kelly Kunkel					f t
Maxfield Elem Sch	PK-5	T	151	75%	254/734-3171
114 W Lexington Street, Gorman 76454			13		Fax 254/734-3445
Fernando Sandoval					f t

● **Ranger Ind School Dist** PID: 01014470   254/647-1187
1842 E Loop 254, Ranger 76470   Fax 254/647-5215

> **Schools:** 1 \ **Teachers:** 41 \ **Students:** 350 \ **Special Ed Students:** 56 \ **LEP Students:** 5 \ **College-Bound:** 50% \ **Ethnic:** African American 1%, Hispanic 24%, Native American: 1%, Caucasian 74% \ **Exp:** $478 (High) \ **Poverty:** 28% \ **Title I:** $178,916 \ **Open-Close:** 08/26 - 05/29 \ **DTBP:** $350 (High)

Mike Thompson 1,73		Joy Felan 2	
Bobby Campbell 6,35*		Michelle Arnold 11*	
June Guess 16*		Nanette Edwards 27,31*	
Trey Felan 36,69,85,270		Karen Clifton 67	

Public Schs..Principal	Grd	Prgm	Enr/#Cls	SN	
Ranger Sch	PK-12	TV	350	64%	254/647-3216
1842 E Loop 254, Ranger 76470			30		Fax 254/647-1895
Jessie Ellerbe					

● **Rising Star Ind Sch Dist** PID: 01014511   254/643-1981
907 N Main St, Rising Star 76471   Fax 254/643-1922

> **Schools:** 2 \ **Teachers:** 16 \ **Students:** 147 \ **Special Ed Students:** 7 \ **LEP Students:** 8 \ **Ethnic:** Hispanic 16%, Caucasian 84% \ **Exp:** $675 (High) \ **Poverty:** 24% \ **Title I:** $82,353 \ **Open-Close:** 08/19 - 05/21 \ **DTBP:** $353 (High) \ f t

Mary Jane Atkins 1		Teresa Lawrence 2	
Tracey Rutledge 4		Ennis Erickson 6	
Creig Hopper 58		Howard Lawrence 67	

Public Schs..Principal	Grd	Prgm	Enr/#Cls	SN	
Rising Star Elem Sch	PK-6	T	85	75%	254/643-2431
113 W Newton St, Rising Star 76471			10		Fax 254/643-1002
Barbara Long					
Rising Star High Sch	7-12	TV	69	67%	254/643-3521
905 N Main St, Rising Star 76471			11		Fax 254/643-5408
Randy Jones					

ECTOR COUNTY

ECTOR PUBLIC SCHOOLS

● **Ector Co Ind School Dist** PID: 01014547   432/456-0000
802 N Sam Houston Ave, Odessa 79761

> **Schools:** 42 \ **Teachers:** 2,021 \ **Students:** 31,500 \ **Special Ed Students:** 2,506 \ **LEP Students:** 4,932 \ **College-Bound:** 55% \ **Ethnic:** Asian 1%, African American 4%, Hispanic 76%, Caucasian 19% \ **Exp:** $152 (Low) \ **Poverty:** 17% \ **Title I:** $7,984,739 \ **Special Education:** $5,870,000 \ **Open-Close:** 08/19 - 05/21 \ **DTBP:** $180 (High)

Dr Scott Muri 1		Albert Valencia 2	
Gary Weatherford 3		Brandon Reyes 4	
Roger Cleere 5		Bruce McCreary 6	
Dr Lilian Nonaz 8,15		Lisa Wills 8	
Julia Willett Weekly 11		Kellie Wilks 16,73,82,98,295	
Aaron Holley 20,23		Carla Byrne 27,31	
Nancy Vanley 36*		Lisa Marroquin 39	

TX—129

Ector County

Ashley Bryant 42
Betsabe Salcido 57
Dr Donna Smith 67
Annette Macias 69,294
Mike Adkins 71
Debbie Bynum 74
Omega Loera 81
Lisa Duncan 45
Dr Tracy Canter 58,77
Dr Gregory Nelson 68,78
Elsa Lazcano 69
Toby Lefevers 73
Heather Potts 76
Jaime Miller 280

Public Schs..Principal	Grd	Prgm	Enr/#Cls	SN	
ⓜ Austin Montessori Elem Sch 901 N Lee Ave, Odessa 79761 Tania Hagood	PK-5	T	449 30	45%	432/456-1029 Fax 432/456-1028
Barbara Jordan Elem Sch 9400 Rainbow Dr, Odessa 79765 Scott Houston	K-5	T	807 55	47%	432/456-1299 Fax 432/456-1298
ⓜ Blackshear Magnet Elem Sch 501 S Dixie Blvd, Odessa 79761 Ms Rivera	K-5	T	692 30	76%	432/456-1279 Fax 432/456-1278 f t
Blanton Elem Sch 4101 Lynbrook Ave, Odessa 79762 Stacey Molyneaux	PK-5	T	425 25	48%	432/456-1259 Fax 432/456-1258
Bonham Middle Sch 2201 E 21st St, Odessa 79761 James Ramage	6-8	TV	899	53%	432/456-0429 Fax 432/456-0428 f t
Bowie Middle Sch 500 W 21st St, Odessa 79761 Brian Ellington	6-8	TV	1,223 65	58%	432/456-0439 Fax 432/456-0438 f t
Burleson Elem Sch 3900 Golder Ave, Odessa 79764 Tristan Specter	K-5	T	428 35	75%	432/456-1039 Fax 432/456-1038
Burnet Elem Sch 3511 Maple Ave, Odessa 79762 Marissa King	K-5		580 35		432/456-1049 Fax 432/456-1048
ⓜ Cameron Dual Lang Magnet Sch 2401 W 8th St, Odessa 79763 Jacob Bargas	PK-5	T	528 36	66%	432/456-1059 Fax 432/456-1058 f t
Carver Early Education Center 600 College Ave, Odessa 79761 Sherry Palmer	PK-PK	T	562 15	83%	432/456-1069 Fax 432/456-1068 t
Crockett Middle Sch 2301 Conover Ave, Odessa 79763 Maribel Aranda	6-8	TV	1,218 52	63%	432/456-0449 Fax 432/456-0448
Dowling Elem Sch 1510 E 17th St, Odessa 79761 Kristabel Regalado	K-5	T	516 40	78%	432/456-1079 Fax 432/456-1078
Dr Lee Buice Elem Sch 1800 E 87th St, Odessa 79765 Jessica Rickman	K-5		649	42%	432/456-1339
ⓜ Ector Clg Prep Success Acad 809 W Clements St, Odessa 79763 Charles Quintela	6-8	TV	1,568 87	66%	432/456-0479 Fax 432/456-0478
ⓐ Ector Co Youth Alt Center 1299 E Yukon Rd, Odessa 79762 Adam Portillo	6-12	V	104 15	18%	432/456-0049 Fax 432/456-5768 f
Edward K Downing Elem Sch 1480 N Knox Ave, Odessa 79763 Marcos Lopez	K-5	T	732	74%	432/456-1319
Falcon Early College High Sch 4901 E University Blvd, Odessa 79762 Lindsey Lumpkin	9-9		140	29%	432/456-6429 f t
ⓨ Gale Pond Alamo Elem Sch 801 E 23rd St, Odessa 79761 Regina Lee	PK-5	MT	418 25	59%	432/456-1019 Fax 432/456-1018
George Buddy West Elem Sch 2225 W Sycamore Dr, Odessa 79763 Gisela Davila	K-5	T	657	73%	432/456-1329
George W Bush New Tech Odessa 300 E 29th St, Odessa 79762 Gerardo Ramirez	9-12		333 60	36%	432/456-6989 Fax 432/456-6988
Goliad Elem Sch 501 E 52nd St, Odessa 79762 Cristabel Gonzales	K-5	T	478 32	76%	432/456-1109 Fax 432/456-1108 f t
Gonzales Elem Sch 2700 Disney St, Odessa 79761 Angie Moad	K-5	T	416 35	50%	432/456-1119 Fax 432/456-1118 f t
ⓜ Hays Magnet Academy 1101 E Monahans St, Odessa 79761 Julie Marshall	PK-5		409 30	44%	432/456-1129 Fax 432/456-1128
ⓜ Ireland Elem Sch 4301 Dawn Ave, Odessa 79762 Katy Ochoa	K-5	T	499 38	49%	432/456-1149 Fax 432/456-1148
Lamar Early Education Center 501 Lettie Lee, Odessa 79761 Maryjane Hutchins	PK-PK	T	652 23	96%	432/456-1159 Fax 432/456-1158
Lauro Cavazos Elem Sch 9301 W 16th St, Odessa 79763 Amanda Montelongo	K-5	T	764 36	68%	432/456-1309 Fax 432/456-1308
Lyndon B Johnson Elem Sch 6401 Amber Dr, Odessa 79762 Alisha Holguin	K-5	T	722 60	48%	432/456-1289 Fax 432/456-1288
ⓜ Milam Magnet Elem Sch 640 College Ave, Odessa 79761 Natalie Fitzgerald	PK-5		517 40		432/456-1169 Fax 432/456-1168 f t
Murry Fly Elem Sch 11688 W Westview Dr, Odessa 79764 Sammy Martinez	PK-5	T	814 38	72%	432/456-1269 Fax 432/456-1268
Nimitz Middle Sch 4900 Maple Ave, Odessa 79762 Teresa Willison	6-8	V	1,097 60	32%	432/456-0469 Fax 432/456-0468 f t
ⓜ Noel Elem Sch 2200 Newcomb Dr, Odessa 79764 Jennie Chavez	3-5	T	534 30	68%	432/456-1249 Fax 432/456-1248
Odessa Career Tch Early Clg HS 201 W University Blvd, Odessa 79764 Karl Miller	9-9	T	174	45%	432/456-6409
Odessa High Sch 1301 Dotsy Ave, Odessa 79763 Mauricio Marquez	9-12	V	3,807 100	46%	432/456-0029 Fax 432/456-5264
Pease Elem Sch 1800 W 22nd St, Odessa 79763 Autumn Sloan	K-5	T	602 50	66%	432/456-1179 Fax 432/456-1178
Permian High Sch 1800 E 42nd St, Odessa 79762 Robert Gex	9-12	V	3,789	35%	432/456-0039 Fax 432/456-0038
ⓜ Reagan Magnet Elem Sch 2321 E 21st St, Odessa 79761 Wayne Squiers	K-5		574 33	18%	432/456-1189 Fax 432/456-1188 f t
Ross Elem Sch 4600 N Everglade Ave, Odessa 79762 Rebecca Phillips	K-5	T	391 32	62%	432/456-1199 Fax 432/456-1198
Sam Houston Elem Sch 300 E 37th St, Odessa 79762 Crystal Marquez	K-5	T	511 30	72%	432/456-1139 Fax 432/456-1138
San Jacinto Elem Sch 1000 W 19th St, Odessa 79763 Erin Bueno	K-5	T	472 34	69%	432/456-1219 Fax 432/456-1218
ⓜ Travis Magnet Elem Sch 1400 S Lee Ave, Odessa 79761 Linda Voss	K-5	T	333 23	77%	432/456-1229 Fax 432/456-1228
Wilson & Young Middle Sch 601 E 38th St, Odessa 79762 Anthony Garza	6-8	TV	961 55	43%	432/456-0459 Fax 432/456-0458

1	Superintendent	8	Curric/Instruct K-12	19	Chief Financial Officer	29	Family/Consumer Science	39	Social Studies K-12	49	English/Lang Arts Elem	59	Special Education Elem	69	Academic Assessment
2	Bus/Finance/Purchasing	9	Curric/Instruct Elem	20	Art K-12	30	Adult Education	40	Social Studies Elem	50	English/Lang Arts Sec	60	Special Education Sec	70	Research/Development
3	Buildings And Grounds	10	Curric/Instruct Sec	21	Art Elem	31	Career/Sch-to-Work K-12	41	Social Studies Sec	51	Reading K-12	61	Foreign/World Lang K-12	71	Public Information
4	Food Service	11	Federal Program	22	Art Sec	32	Career/Sch-to-Work Elem	42	Science K-12	52	Reading Elem	62	Foreign/World Lang Elem	72	Summer School
5	Transportation	12	Title I	23	Music K-12	33	Career/Sch-to-Work Sec	43	Science Elem	53	Reading Sec	63	Foreign/World Lang Sec	73	Instructional Tech
6	Athletic	13	Title V	24	Music Elem	34	Early Childhood Ed	44	Science Sec	54	Remedial Reading K-12	64	Religious Education K-12	74	Inservice Training
7	Health Services	15	Asst Superintendent	25	Music Sec	35	Health/Phys Education	45	Math K-12	55	Remedial Reading Elem	65	Religious Education Elem	75	Marketing/Distributive
		16	Instructional Media Svcs	26	Business Education	36	Guidance Services K-12	46	Math Elem	56	Remedial Reading Sec	66	Religious Education Sec	76	Info Systems
		17	Chief Operations Officer	27	Career & Tech Ed	37	Guidance Services Elem	47	Math Sec	57	Bilingual/ELL	67	School Board President	77	Psychological Assess
		18	Chief Academic Officer	28	Technology Education	38	Guidance Services Sec	48	English/Lang Arts K-12	58	Special Education K-12	68	Teacher Personnel	78	Affirmative Action

Texas School Directory

El Paso County

Zavala Magnet Elem Sch	K-5	T	611	74%	432/456-1239
1201 Clifford St, Odessa 79763			38		Fax 432/456-1238
Tanya Galindo					

ECTOR CATHOLIC SCHOOLS

Diocese of San Angelo Ed Off PID: 01055929
Listing includes only schools located in this county. See District Index for location of Diocesan Offices.

Catholic Schs..Principal	Grd	Prgm	Enr/#Cls SN	
St Mary's Central Catholic Sch	PK-8		310	432/337-6052
1703 Adams Ave, Odessa 79761			13	Fax 432/332-2942
Benjamin Villarreal				

ECTOR PRIVATE SCHOOLS

Private Schs..Principal	Grd	Prgm	Enr/#Cls SN	
Holy Cross Catholic HS	9-12		21	432/713-0143
7601 North Grandview, Odessa 79765				
Carolyn Gonzalez				
Odessa Christian Sch	PK-8		150	432/362-6311
2000 Doran Dr, Odessa 79761			12	Fax 432/550-7086
Nancy Campbell				
St John's Episcopal Sch	PK-8		220	432/337-6431
401 W County Rd N, Odessa 79763			13	Fax 432/335-0815
Emily McDoniel				

EDWARDS COUNTY

EDWARDS PUBLIC SCHOOLS

Nueces Canyon Cons Ind SD PID: 01014872   830/234-3514
200 Taylor Street, Barksdale 78828   Fax 830/234-3435

Schools: 2 \ **Teachers:** 30 \ **Students:** 270 \ **Special Ed Students:** 22 \
LEP Students: 3 \ **College-Bound:** 100% \ **Ethnic:** African American 2%, Hispanic 42%, Native American: 1%, Caucasian 55% \ **Exp:** $555 (High) \
Poverty: 36% \ **Title I:** $137,252 \ **Open-Close:** 08/19 - 05/21

Kristi Powers 1		Billye Smith 2	
Wilma Reading 4*		Steven Smith 5	
Leslie Caillet 7*		Shawna Moore 8,11,36,59,69,88,296*	
Brett Vurner 16,73,298		Richard Kramer 27*	
Christi Collins 58,83*		Toby Kramer 59*	
Danny Irwin 67		Tina Taylor 286*	

Public Schs..Principal	Grd	Prgm	Enr/#Cls SN	
Nueces Canyon Elem Sch	PK-6	T	168	77% 830/597-3218
Highway 337, Camp Wood 78833			12	Fax 830/597-6197
Shawna Moore				
Nueces Canyon Jr Sr High Sch	7-12	TV	230	55% 830/234-3524
200 Taylor Street, Barksdale 78828			16	
Shawna Moore				

Rocksprings Ind School Dist PID: 01014901   830/683-4137
201 N Highway 377, Rocksprings 78880   Fax 830/683-4141

Schools: 1 \ **Teachers:** 29 \ **Students:** 290 \ **Special Ed Students:** 35 \ **LEP Students:** 13 \ **College-Bound:** 50% \ **Ethnic:** Hispanic 83%, Caucasian 17% \ **Exp:** $659 (High) \ **Poverty:** 37% \ **Title I:** $154,418 \
Open-Close: 08/21 - 05/28 \ **DTBP:** $443 (High)

Daron Worrell 1,11		Patty Flores 2	
Manuel Ramos 6*		Brian McCraw 8,12,57,69,88,270*	
Leann Holt 58		Brady Hyde 67	
Mario Gonzales 73*			

Public Schs..Principal	Grd	Prgm	Enr/#Cls SN	
Rocksprings Sch	PK-12	TV	290	73% 830/683-2140
201 N Highway 377, Rocksprings 78880			20	Fax 830/683-8141
Brian McCraw				

EL PASO COUNTY

EL PASO PUBLIC SCHOOLS

Anthony Ind School Dist PID: 01015357   915/886-6500
840 6th St, Anthony 79821   Fax 915/886-2420

Schools: 3 \ **Teachers:** 55 \ **Students:** 839 \ **Special Ed Students:** 92 \
LEP Students: 196 \ **Ethnic:** Hispanic 97%, Caucasian 3% \ **Exp:** $482 (High) \ **Poverty:** 25% \ **Title I:** $235,220 \ **Special Education:** $124,000 \
Open-Close: 08/12 - 05/22 \ **DTBP:** $354 (High)

Oscar Troncoso 1		Jissel Reyes 2	
Jesus Carrasco 4		Jaime Reyes 5	
Raymond Carroll 6,296		Shandra Westen 11,57,58,271	
Karen Paterson 16*		Angel Cuellar 67	
Alex Ramirez 295			

Public Schs..Principal	Grd	Prgm	Enr/#Cls SN	
Anthony Elem Sch	PK-5	T	399	99% 915/886-6510
610 6th St, Anthony 79821			36	Fax 915/886-3205
Oralia Moseley				
Anthony High Sch	9-12	AGTV	239	99% 915/886-6550
825 Wildcat Dr, Anthony 79821			18	Fax 915/886-3876
Fernando Garnica				
Anthony Middle Sch	6-8	T	201	99% 915/886-6530
813 6th St, Anthony 79821				Fax 915/886-3875
Fernando Garnica				

Canutillo Ind School Dist PID: 01015383   915/877-7400
7965 Artcraft Rd, El Paso 79932   Fax 915/877-7525

Schools: 10 \ **Teachers:** 390 \ **Students:** 6,200 \ **Special Ed Students:** 564 \ **LEP Students:** 1,640 \ **College-Bound:** 54% \ **Ethnic:** African American 1%, Hispanic 95%, Caucasian 4% \ **Exp:** $268 (Med) \ **Poverty:** 25% \
Title I: $1,770,147 \ **Special Education:** $895,000 \ **Open-Close:** 08/12 - 05/22 \ **DTBP:** $193 (High) \ 🅕 🅣

Dr Pedro Galaviz 1		Martha Piekarski 2,19	
Bruno Vasquez 3,5		Marco Macias 4	
Scott Brooks 6*		Dr Monica Reyes 7,30,34,36,85,88,93	
Debra Kerney 8*		Marnie Rocha 15	

El Paso County

Tracy Andrews 27*
Stacey Parker 39
Nidia Avila 45*
Natalie Spalloni 48
Carey Chambers 58
Martha Carrasco 68
Liza Rodriguez 71
Carlos Carrillo 91*
Albert Vega 286

Sandra Carrillo 34
Marlena Zimmerman 42
Yirah Valverde 45
Maria Silva 57,271
Sergio Coronado 67
April Galaviz 69,70,294
Lucero Hernandez 88
Marisela Ramos 271

Public Schs..Principal	Grd	Prgm	Enr/#Cls	SN	
Bill Childress Elem Sch 7700 Cap Carter Rd, Vinton 79821 Reyna Salcedo	PK-5	T	400 60	86%	915/877-7700 Fax 915/877-7709
Canutillo Elem Sch 651 Canutillo Ave, Canutillo 79835 Julie Melendez	PK-5	T	569 40	86%	915/877-7600 Fax 915/877-7609
Canutillo High Sch 6675 S Desert Blvd, El Paso 79932 Teresa Clapsaddle	9-12	TV	1,531 90	74%	915/877-7800 Fax 915/877-7807
Canutillo Middle Sch 7311 Bosque Rd, Canutillo 79835 Daniel Medina	6-8	T	585 60	65%	915/877-7900 Fax 915/877-7919
Deanna Davenport Elem Sch 8401 Remington Rd, Canutillo 79835 Marta Strobach	PK-5	T	388 23	91%	915/886-6400 Fax 915/886-6407
Gonzalo & Sofia Garcia ES 6550 Westside Dr, El Paso 79932 **Teresa Heimer**	PK-5	T	504	60%	915/877-1200 Fax 915/877-1219
Jose Alderete Middle Sch 801 Talbot Ave, Canutillo 79835 Dr Oscar Rico	6-8	T	713	75%	915/877-6600 Fax 915/877-6619
Jose Damian Elem Sch 6300 Strahan Rd, El Paso 79932 Jesus Barba	PK-5	T	506 40	61%	915/877-6800 Fax 915/877-6819
Northwest Early College HS 6701 S Desert Blvd, El Paso 79932 Tracy Speaker	9-12	T	356	56%	915/877-1700 Fax 915/877-7033
Silvestre & Reyes Elem Sch 7440 Northern Pass, El Paso 79911 Dr Debra Kerney	PK-5	T	667	44%	915/877-1300 Fax 915/877-2319

• **Clint Ind School Dist** PID: 01015424   915/926-4000
14521 Horizon Blvd, El Paso 79928   Fax 915/926-4009

Schools: 14 \ *Teachers:* 678 \ *Students:* 11,522 \ *Special Ed Students:* 853 \ *LEP Students:* 3,646 \ *College-Bound:* 55% \ *Ethnic:* Hispanic 96%, Caucasian 4% \ *Exp:* $471 (High) \ *Poverty:* 32% \ *Title I:* $4,802,905 \ *Special Education:* $1,776,000 \ *Open-Close:* 07/29 - 06/04 \ *DTBP:* $161 (High) \

Dr Juan Martinez 1
Sandra Odenburg 3
Jonathan Powell 5*
Mike Mackeben 6
Jim Littlejohn 10,15
Manuel Ayala 15,69,294
Jose Ramirez 39
Sandra Martinez 48
Josephine Angerstein 58
Rene Chavez 68
Manuel Verduzco 73,98
Sally Upchurch 91

Donna Cline 2,19
Paul Harrington 4
Mike Mackeben 6
Jennifer Parker 9
Melissa Williams 11
Veronica Booth 27
William Swanson 44
Victor Hernandez 57
Arlene Parada 67
Laura Cade 71
Noe Cantu 73

Public Schs..Principal	Grd	Prgm	Enr/#Cls	SN	
Carroll T Welch Elem Sch 14510 McMahon Ave, El Paso 79928 Alma Vasquez	PK-5	AT	902 45	92%	915/926-4400 Fax 915/852-7230
Clint Early College Academy 13100 Alameda Ave, Clint 79836 Edmond Martinez	9-9	T	342	80%	915/926-8100 Fax 915/851-3459
Clint High Sch 13890 Alameda Ave, Clint 79836 Garrett Ritchey	9-12	AGTV	667 60	79%	915/926-8300 Fax 915/851-5375
Clint Junior High Sch 12625 Alameda Ave, Clint 79836 Noemi Hernandez	6-8	AGT	561 15	83%	915/926-8000 Fax 915/851-3895
Desert Hills Elem Sch 300 N Kenazo Ave, El Paso 79928 Adriana Cantu	PK-5	AT	1,073 45	74%	915/926-4500 Fax 915/852-3570
East Montana Middle Sch 3490 Ascencion St, El Paso 79938 Juanita Guerra	6-8	AT	694 68	84%	915/926-5200 Fax 915/855-0821
Frank Macias Elem Sch 14400 Golden Eagle Dr, Horizon City 79928 Liz Olga	PK-5	AT	1,075 43	84%	915/926-4600 Fax 915/852-7547
Horizon High Sch 14651 Horizon Blvd, El Paso 79928 Elena Acosta	10-12	AT	1,555	79%	915/926-4200 Fax 915/852-0357
Horizon Middle Sch 400 N Kenazo Ave, El Paso 79928 Veronica Candelaria	6-7	AT	687	80%	915/926-4700 Fax 915/852-9274
Montana Vista Elem Sch 3550 Mark Jason Dr, El Paso 79938 Cain Castillo	PK-5	AT	668 40	94%	915/926-5307 Fax 915/857-0631
Mountain View High Sch 14964 Greg Dr, El Paso 79938 Roberto Trejo	9-12	AGTV	812 85	83%	915/926-5000 Fax 915/855-2503
Red Sands Elem Sch 4250 Oshea St, El Paso 79938 Carlos Villalobos	PK-5	AT	759	92%	915/926-5400 Fax 915/855-8294
Ricardo Estrada Middle Sch 851 Darrington Rd, El Paso 79928 Lorraine Vidales	6-8	AT	705	89%	915/926-4800 Fax 915/852-2455
William D Surratt Elem Sch 12675 Alameda Ave, Clint 79836 Melissa Williams	PK-5	AT	1,022 40	88%	915/926-8200 Fax 915/851-3489

• **El Paso Ind School Dist** PID: 01015450   915/230-2000
6531 Boeing Dr, El Paso 79925

Schools: 89 \ *Teachers:* 3,977 \ *Students:* 54,824 \ *Special Ed Students:* 6,262 \ *LEP Students:* 15,295 \ *College-Bound:* 76% \ *Ethnic:* Asian 1%, African American 4%, Hispanic 85%, Caucasian 10% \ *Exp:* $330 (High) \ *Poverty:* 27% \ *Title I:* $26,643,172 \ *Special Education:* $11,730,000 \ *Bilingual Education:* $95,000 \ *Open-Close:* 08/12 - 05/22 \ *DTBP:* $191 (High)

Juan Cabrera 1,288
Ernesto Ortiz 3
Maria Kennedy 6
Dr Tamekia Brown 8,18
Angela Henderson 15
Dr Carla Gonzales 15
Vincent Sheffield 15,68,78
John Adams 35
Norma Calderon 57
Bob Geske 67
Debra Betts 69
Alicia Ramos 71,76,97,295
Edgar Garcia 91

Carmen Candelaria 2,15
Laura Duran 4
Alana Bejarano 7,85
Cecilia Rojero 12*
Dr Blanca Garcia 15
Jose Lopez 15,751*
Eric Winkelman 27,31
Manuel Castruita 36,88
Vanessa Maurizzio 59
Brenda Booth 69
Jeffrey Clay 69,70,294
Melissa Martinez 71
Johnny Quintana 295

Texas School Directory — El Paso County

Public Schs..Principal	Grd	Prgm	Enr/#Cls	SN	
About Face Alternative ES 1440 E Cliff Dr, El Paso 79902 Bertha Martinez	K-5	T	44		915/236-3150
Delta Academy 6400 Delta Dr, El Paso 79905 Christian James	5-12	T	80 12	65%	915/774-0447 Fax 915/881-1245
Raymond Telles/Lafarelle MS 2851 Grant Ave Bldg A, El Paso 79930 Lorenzo Munoz	6-12	T	45 40	77%	915/236-7800 Fax 915/532-0540
San Jacinto Adult Learning Ctr 1216 Olive Ave, El Paso 79901 Arturo Gonzalez	Adult		500 18		915/230-3200 Fax 915/544-7163
YW Steam Research & Prep Acad 2231 Arizona Ave, El Paso 79930 Cynthia Ontiveros	6-12		182		915/236-4830

El Paso ISD-Elementary PID: 11982247   915/230-2485
6531 Boeing Dr, El Paso 79925

Blanca Garcia 15

Public Schs..Principal	Grd	Prgm	Enr/#Cls	SN	
Aoy Elem Sch 901 S Campbell St, El Paso 79901 Sylvia Haynes	PK-5	T	477 60	98%	915/236-0175 Fax 915/313-0163
Barron Elem Sch 11155 Whitey Ford St, El Paso 79934 Lidia Anguiano	PK-5	T	453	69%	915/236-5075 Fax 915/822-1460
Beall Elem Sch 320 S Piedras St, El Paso 79905 Maria Guerra	PK-5	GT	363 33	98%	915/236-8075 Fax 915/533-7044
Bliss Elem Sch 4401 Sheridan Rd, El Paso 79906 Narichica Handy	PK-5	T	519	64%	915/236-5150 Fax 915/566-2806
Bonham Elem Sch 7024 Cielo Vista Dr, El Paso 79925 Sandra Sanchez	PK-5	T	250 30	87%	915/236-8150 Fax 915/778-0525
Bradley Elem Sch 10700 Rushing Rd, El Paso 79924 Kathleen Ese	PK-5	T	395 24	73%	915/236-5225 Fax 915/821-0628
Cielo Vista Elem Sch 9000 Basil Ct, El Paso 79925 Bertha Rodriguez	PK-5	T	402 20	45%	915/236-8375 Fax 915/599-2965
Clardy Elem Sch 5508 Delta Dr, El Paso 79905 Mark Booker	PK-5	T	489 46	92%	915/236-8450 Fax 915/778-1580
Clendenin Elem Sch 2701 Harrison Ave, El Paso 79930 Martha Martinez	PK-5	T	453 30	90%	915/236-5300 Fax 915/566-4459
Coldwell Elem Sch 4101 Altura Ave, El Paso 79903 Jose Gijon	PK-5	T	467 65	87%	915/236-8525 Fax 915/566-4634
Collins Elem Sch 4860 Tropicana Ave, El Paso 79924 Leticia Ewing	PK-5	T	485 35	88%	915/236-5375 Fax 915/759-7315
Cooley Elem Sch 107 N Collingsworth St, El Paso 79905 Elizabeth Prangner	PK-5	T	528 54	94%	915/236-8600 Fax 915/775-1272
Crockett Elem Sch 3200 Wheeling Ave, El Paso 79930 Elco Ramos	PK-5	T	519 60	92%	915/236-8675 Fax 915/566-4950
Crosby Elem Sch 5411 Wren Ave, El Paso 79924 Alonzo Barraza	PK-5	T	542 60	90%	915/236-5450 Fax 915/759-7409
Douglass Elem Sch 101 S Eucalyptus St, El Paso 79905 Maria Guerra	PK-5	GT	343 33	98%	915/236-8750 Fax 915/533-3716
Dowell Elem Sch 5249 Bastille Ave, El Paso 79924 Yeni Ontiveros	PK-5	T	371 35	87%	915/236-5525 Fax 915/759-7713
Dr Nixon Elem Sch 11141 Loma Roja Dr, El Paso 79934 Christine Miles	PK-5	T	675 50	50%	915/236-5900 Fax 915/821-6582
Fannin Elem Sch 5425 Salem Dr, El Paso 79924 Peggy Gustafson	PK-5	T	511 53	86%	915/236-5600 Fax 915/821-0680
General Colin Powell Elem Sch 4750 Ellerthorpe Ave, El Paso 79904 Wilfred Veilleux	PK-5	T	574	81%	915/774-7775 Fax 915/564-5086
Green Elem Sch 5430 Buckley Dr, El Paso 79912 Charlotte Quintana	PK-5	T	399 45	65%	915/236-3000 Fax 915/833-8794
Hart Elem Sch 1110 S Park St, El Paso 79901 Angelica Negrete	PK-5	T	517 40	97%	915/236-8825 Fax 915/533-3726
Hawkins Elem Sch 5816 Stephenson Ave, El Paso 79905 Adriana Ruiz	PK-5	T	298 32	98%	915/236-8900 Fax 915/775-2699
Herrera Elem Sch 350 Coates Dr, El Paso 79932 Diana Provencio	PK-5	T	561	72%	915/774-7700 Fax 915/581-2377
Hillside Elem Sch 4500 Clifton Ave, El Paso 79903 Cynthia Anderson	PK-5	T	508 42	91%	915/236-0100 Fax 915/566-5210
Hughey Elem Sch 6201 Hughey Cir, El Paso 79925 Lilia Aguilera	PK-5	T	576 40	70%	915/236-0250 Fax 915/779-6911
Johnson Elem Sch 499 Cabaret Dr, El Paso 79912 Peggy Gustafson	PK-5	T	472 80	95%	915/236-3925 Fax 915/581-0917
Lamar Elem Sch 1440 E Cliff Dr, El Paso 79902 Bertha Martinez	PK-5	T	419 35	91%	915/236-3150 Fax 915/534-0083
Lee Elem Sch 7710 Pandora St, El Paso 79904 Terry Montes	PK-5	T	534 60	94%	915/236-5675 Fax 915/759-8115
Logan Elem Sch 3200 Ellerthorpe Ave, El Paso 79904 Nancy Hanson	PK-5	T	432 36	76%	915/236-5750 Fax 915/236-5752
Lundy Elem Sch 6201 High Ridge Dr, El Paso 79912 Lourdes Lugo	PK-5		725	12%	915/230-5075 Fax 915/584-1972
MacArthur Elem-Interm Sch 8101 Whitus Dr, El Paso 79925 Rose Martinez	PK-8	T	826 57	65%	915/236-0625 Fax 915/779-2281
Mesita Elem Sch 3307 N Stanton St, El Paso 79902 Laila Ferris	PK-5	T	1,127 35	52%	915/236-6850 Fax 915/532-2068
Milam Elem Sch 5000 Luke St, El Paso 79908 Wanda Johnson	PK-5	T	789 21	40%	915/236-0325 Fax 915/562-6448
Mitzi Bond Elem Sch 250 Lindbergh Ave, El Paso 79932 Rachel Villalobos	PK-5	T	620 49	46%	915/236-2925 Fax 915/581-1220
Moye Elem Sch 4825 Alps Dr, El Paso 79904 Jessie Medina	PK-5	T	518 35	94%	915/774-4000 Fax 915/751-7810
Newman Elem Sch 10275 Alcan St, El Paso 79924 Pauletta Howard	PK-5	T	460 45	87%	915/236-5825 Fax 915/759-8306

- Student Personnel
- Driver Ed/Safety
- Gifted/Talented
- Video Services
- Substance Abuse Prev
- Erate
- AIDS Education
- Alternative/At Risk
- Multi-Cultural Curriculum
- Social Work

91 Safety/Security
92 Magnet School
93 Parental Involvement
95 Tech Prep Education
97 Chief Information Officer
98 Chief Technology Officer
270 Character Education
271 Migrant Education
273 Teacher Mentor
274 Before/After Sch

275 Response To Intervention
277 Remedial Math K-12
280 Literacy Coach
285 STEM
286 Digital Learning
288 Common Core Standards
294 Accountability
295 Network System
296 Title II Programs
297 Webmaster

298 Grant Writer/Ptnrships
750 Chief Innovation Officer
751 Chief of Staff
752 Social Emotional Learning

School Programs
A = Alternative Program
G = Adult Classes
M = Magnet Program
T = Title I Schoolwide
V = Career & Tech Ed Programs

Other School Types
Ⓐ = Alternative School
Ⓒ = Charter School
Ⓜ = Magnet School
Ⓨ = Year-Round School

Social Media
 = Facebook
 = Twitter

New Schools are shaded
New Superintendents and Principals are bold
Personnel with email addresses are underscored

TX—133

El Paso County | Market Data Retrieval

School	Grd	Prgm	Enr/#Cls	SN	Phone
Olga Kohlberg Elem Sch 1445 Nardo Goodman Dr, El Paso 79912 Michelle Pringle	PK-5	T	606 50	43%	915/236-2850 Fax 915/833-4628
Park Elem Sch 3601 Edgar Park Ave, El Paso 79904 Carmen Dwyer	PK-5	T	509 37	86%	915/236-5975 Fax 915/759-8315
Paul Moreno Elem Sch 2300 San Diego Ave, El Paso 79930 Robert Pancoast	PK-5	T	488 30	91%	915/236-0400 Fax 915/566-5163
Polk Elem Sch 940 Belvidere St, El Paso 79912 Sandra Spivey	PK-5		649 45	36%	915/236-2775 Fax 915/236-2849
Putnam Elem Sch 6508 Fiesta Dr, El Paso 79912 Cynthia Sanchez	PK-5	T	415 36	85%	915/236-3225 Fax 915/585-2304
Rivera Elem Sch 6445 Escondido Dr, El Paso 79912 Cindy Contreras	PK-5	T	353 35	82%	915/236-3700 Fax 915/585-2337
Roberts Elem Sch 341 Thorn Ave, El Paso 79932 Rafael Guardado	PK-5	T	431 35	99%	915/236-3775 Fax 915/585-2729
Rosa Guerrero Elem Sch 7530 Lakehurst Rd, El Paso 79912 Jill Crossley	PK-5	T	553 53	76%	915/236-3075 Fax 915/581-4418
Rusk Elem Sch 3601 N Copia St, El Paso 79930 Monica Brinkley	PK-5	T	303 40	94%	915/236-0475 Fax 915/565-1666
Stanton Elem Sch 5414 Hondo Pass Dr, El Paso 79924 Dr Sarah Chavez-Gibson	PK-5	T	446 45	92%	915/236-6125 Fax 915/759-9415
Tippin Elem Sch 6541 Bear Ridge Dr, El Paso 79912 Gina Nunez	PK-5		563	18%	915/230-5150 Fax 915/833-2140
Tom Lea Elem Sch 4851 Marcus Uribe Dr, El Paso 79934 Michelle Casillas	PK-5	T	872	39%	915/230-5450 Fax 915/821-3665
Travis Elem Sch 500 N Stevens St, El Paso 79930 Armando Llanos	PK-5	T	318 37	95%	915/236-6200 Fax 915/565-2013
Western Hills Elem Sch 530 Thunderbird Dr, El Paso 79912 Cristina Benavides	PK-5	T	476 32	55%	915/774-4060 Fax 915/875-0183
Whitaker Elem Sch 4700 Rutherford Dr, El Paso 79924 Antoinette Carpenter	PK-5	T	443 35	75%	915/236-6275 Fax 915/751-9436
Zach White Elem Sch 4256 Roxbury Dr, El Paso 79922 Jocelyn Scott	PK-5	T	474 50	48%	915/236-2700 Fax 915/585-3619
Zavala Elem Sch 51 N Hammett St, El Paso 79905 Alma Brockhoff	PK-5	T	226 27	96%	915/236-0550 Fax 915/542-1760

● **El Paso ISD-High Schools** PID: 11982259 915/236-2500
800 E Schuster Ave, El Paso 79902

Dr Carla Gonzales 15   Mary Ann Clark 92*

Public Schs..Principal	Grd	Prgm	Enr/#Cls	SN	Phone
Andress High Sch 5400 Sun Valley Dr, El Paso 79924 Joseph Manago	9-12	TV	1,560 100	61%	915/236-4000 Fax 915/757-6443
Austin High Sch 3500 Memphis Ave, El Paso 79930 Cynthia Ponce	9-12	TV	1,381 100	82%	915/236-4200 Fax 915/566-7360
Bowie High Sch 801 S San Marcial St, El Paso 79905 Francisco Ordaz	9-12	TV	1,386 60	82%	915/236-7000 Fax 915/532-1918
Burges High Sch 7800 Edgemere Blvd, El Paso 79925 Christopher Smith	9-12	TV	1,553 100	66%	915/236-7200 Fax 915/771-6914
Center for Career & Tech Ed 1170 N Walnut St, El Paso 79930 Matthew Farley	Voc	G	850 38		915/236-7900 Fax 915/544-5976
Chapin High Sch 7000 Dyer St, El Paso 79904 Robert Marsh	9-12	AT	1,853	60%	915/236-4400 Fax 915/565-9716
ⓐ College Career Technology Acad 2851 Grant Ave, El Paso 79930 Fred Rojas	9-12	GTV	352 12	60%	915/236-7700 Fax 915/585-4789
Coronado High Sch 100 Champions Pl, El Paso 79912 Marc Escareno	9-12	TV	2,813	41%	915/236-2000 Fax 915/587-6458
El Paso High Sch 800 E Schuster Ave, El Paso 79902 Mark Paz	9-12	T	1,436 70	65%	915/236-2500 Fax 915/532-2008
Franklin High Sch 900 N Resler Dr, El Paso 79912 Shawn Mena	9-12	TV	2,806	37%	915/236-2200 Fax 915/587-4094
Franklin HS 9th Grade Center 825 E Redd Rd, El Paso 79912 Rose Ann Martinez	9-9		800		915/236-2400 Fax 915/587-5059
Irvin High Sch 9465 Roanoke Dr, El Paso 79924 Mary Anna Giba	9-12	GTV	1,400 130	90%	915/236-4600 Fax 915/757-6450
Jefferson High Sch 4700 Alameda Ave, El Paso 79905 Dr Armando Gallegos	9-12	TV	1,056 150	94%	915/236-7400 Fax 915/532-2033
Ⓜ Silva Health Magnet High Sch 121 Val Verde St, El Paso 79905 Dr Armando Gallegos	9-12	T	721 41	45%	915/236-7600 Fax 915/533-3695
Transmountain Early College HS 9570 Gateway Blvd N, El Paso 79924 Barbara Brinkley-Lopez	9-12	T	454	56%	915/236-5000 Fax 915/751-2011
Young Women's Steam Prep Acad 2231 Arizona Ave, El Paso 79930 Dr Cynthia Ontiveros	6-7		401		915/236-4830

● **El Paso ISD-Middle Schools** PID: 11982261 915/230-2213
6531 Boeing Dr, El Paso 79925

Angela Henderson 15

Public Schs..Principal	Grd	Prgm	Enr/#Cls	SN	Phone
Armendariz Middle Sch 2231 Arizona Ave, El Paso 79930 Dr Cynthia Ontiveros	6-8	T	541 52	89%	915/236-4800 Fax 915/577-0848
Bassett Middle Sch 4400 Elm St, El Paso 79930 Michael Mendoza	6-8	GTV	681 78	89%	915/236-6350 Fax 915/565-1562
Brown Middle Sch 7820 Helen of Troy Dr, El Paso 79912 Corina Favela	6-8	T	963	54%	915/774-4080 Fax 915/581-6424
Canyon Hills Middle Sch 8930 Eclipse St, El Paso 79904 Carlos Gomez	6-8	T	792 61	83%	915/236-6450 Fax 915/757-8067
Dr Hornedo Middle Sch 6101 High Ridge Dr, El Paso 79912 Micaela Varela	6-8	V	1,304	20%	915/236-3300 Fax 915/581-7371
Guillen Middle Sch 900 S Cotton St, El Paso 79901 Monica Lyons	6-8	T	777 75	95%	915/236-4900 Fax 915/532-1143
H E Charles Middle Sch 4909 Trojan Dr, El Paso 79924 David Zamora	6-8	T	648	80%	915/236-6550 Fax 915/821-0505

1	Superintendent	8	Curric/Instruct K-12	19	Chief Financial Officer	29	Family/Consumer Science
2	Bus/Finance/Purchasing	9	Curric/Instruct Elem	20	Art K-12	30	Adult Education
3	Buildings And Grounds	10	Curric/Instruct Sec	21	Art Elem	31	Career/Sch-to-Work K-12
4	Food Service	11	Federal Program	22	Art Sec	32	Career/Sch-to-Work Elem
5	Transportation	12	Title I	23	Music K-12	33	Career/Sch-to-Work Sec
6	Athletic	13	Title V	24	Music Elem	34	Early Childhood Ed
7	Health Services	14		25	Music Sec	35	Health/Phys Education
		15	Asst Superintendent	26	Business Education	36	Guidance Services K-12
		16	Instructional Media Svcs	27	Career & Tech Ed	37	Guidance Services Elem
		17	Chief Operations Officer	28	Technology Education	38	Guidance Services Sec
		18	Chief Academic Officer				

39	Social Studies K-12	49	English/Lang Arts Elem	59	Special Education Elem	69	Academic Assessment
40	Social Studies Elem	50	English/Lang Arts Sec	60	Special Education Sec	70	Research/Development
41	Social Studies Sec	51	Reading K-12	61	Foreign/World Lang K-12	71	Public Information
42	Science K-12	52	Reading Elem	62	Foreign/World Lang Elem	72	Summer School
43	Science Elem	53	Reading Sec	63	Foreign/World Lang Sec	73	Instructional Tech
44	Science Sec	54	Remedial Reading K-12	64	Religious Education K-12	74	Inservice Training
45	Math K-12	55	Remedial Reading Elem	65	Religious Education Elem	75	Marketing/Distributive
46	Math Elem	56	Remedial Reading Sec	66	Religious Education Sec	76	Info Systems
47	Math Sec	57	Bilingual/ELL	67	School Board President	77	Psychological Assess
48	English/Lang Arts K-12	58	Special Education K-12	68	Teacher Personnel	78	Affirmative Action

TX—134

Texas School Directory

El Paso County

School	Grd	Prgm	Enr/#Cls	SN	Phone
Henderson Middle Sch 301 Lisbon St, El Paso 79905 **Jason Yturralde**	6-8	TV	731 100	95%	915/236-0700 Fax 915/772-3425
Lincoln Middle Sch 500 Mulberry Ave, El Paso 79932 **Haidi Appel**	6-8	T	809 64	62%	915/236-3400 Fax 915/581-1371
Magoffin Middle Sch 4931 Hercules Ave, El Paso 79904 **Yvonne Portillo**	6-8	T	744	92%	915/774-4040 Fax 915/757-7675
Morehead Middle Sch 5625 Confetti Dr, El Paso 79912 **Peggy Gustafson**	6-8	T	640 90	79%	915/236-3500 Fax 915/587-5355
Nolan Richardson Middle Sch 11350 Loma Franklin Dr, El Paso 79934 **Ragen Chappell**	6-8	TV	701 50	54%	915/236-6650 Fax 915/822-8812
Ross Middle Sch 6101 Hughey Cir, El Paso 79925 **Jason Yturralde**	6-8	T	862 100	71%	915/236-0800 Fax 915/771-6792
Terrace Hills Middle Sch 4835 Blossom Ave, El Paso 79924 **Leticia Ewing**	6-8	T	488	90%	915/236-6750 Fax 915/759-0615
Wiggs Middle Sch 1300 Circle Dr, El Paso 79902 **Timothy Luther**	6-8	T	957 50	72%	915/236-3600 Fax 915/533-2902

● Fabens Ind School Dist   PID: 01016129
821 NE G Ave, Fabens 79838   915/765-2600   Fax 915/764-3115

Schools: 5 \ **Teachers:** 173 \ **Students:** 2,300 \ **Special Ed Students:** 267 \ **LEP Students:** 963 \ **Ethnic:** Hispanic 99%, Caucasian 1% \ **Exp:** $353 (High) \ **Poverty:** 42% \ **Title I:** $1,736,057 \ **Open-Close:** 08/12 - 05/21 \ **DTBP:** $507 (High)

Dr Veronica Vijil ....1 Yvonne Coupland 2,4
Javier Garay ....3,5* Liz Ramirez 7*
Corina Reese ....15 Manuela Gutierrez 16*
Tamika Young ....31* Jorge Saenz 58*
Orlando Flores ....67 Mario Dominguez 73,91*
Anne Esparza ....79 Pedro Gonzalez 83*

Public Schs..Principal	Grd	Prgm	Enr/#Cls	SN	Phone
Cotton Vly Early College HS 600 NE 4th St, Fabens 79838 Dr Sam Hogue	9-12		250		915/765-2609 Fax 915/764-4358
Fabens Elem Sch 1200 Mike Maros St, Fabens 79838 **Richard Lopez**	PK-3	T	670 47	92%	915/765-2650 Fax 915/765-2655
Fabens High Sch 601 NE G Ave, Fabens 79838 **Anthony Prado**	9-12	ATV	761 60	100%	915/765-2620 Fax 915/765-2568
Fabens Middle Sch 800 Walker St, Fabens 79838 **Nancy Torres**	6-8	T	499 39	90%	915/765-2630 Fax 915/764-7263
O'Donnell Intermediate Sch 301 NE Camp St, Fabens 79838 **Corina Ruiz**	4-5	T	357 45	99%	915/765-2640 Fax 915/764-3339

● San Elizario Ind School Dist   PID: 01016179
1050 Chicken Ranch Rd, San Elizario 79849   915/872-3900   Fax 915/872-3901

Schools: 6 \ **Teachers:** 246 \ **Students:** 3,560 \ **Special Ed Students:** 342 \ **LEP Students:** 1,760 \ **College-Bound:** 85% \ **Ethnic:** Hispanic 99%, \ **Exp:** $670 (High) \ **Poverty:** 39% \ **Title I:** $2,170,517 \ **Special Education:** $692,000 \ **Open-Close:** 08/26 - 06/05 \ **DTBP:** $178 (High)

Dr Jeannie Meza-Chavez ....1 Norberto Rivas 2,19
Jesus Martinez ....3,5 Raul Jacques 4
Christine Jakssch ....6 Robert Gallegos 7,35,83,91
Rogelio Segovia ......8,11,15,70,72,274 Bea Apeldace 12,271
Beatriz Apodaca ....12 Michael Rodriguez 27,36,69*
Georgina Diaz ....39,48,81 Lisa Renegar 39,48,69,81,88,275,294
Debbie Cortez ....42,45,277 Amanda Sanchez 58
Sandra Licon ....67 Blanca Cruz 68
Alice Ramos ....73,76,297* Corina Lugo 93*
Perla Magallon ....95 Horacio Hernandez 295
Vicente Rodriguez 295

Public Schs..Principal	Grd	Prgm	Enr/#Cls	SN	Phone
Alarcon Elem Sch 12501 Socorro Road, San Elizario 79849 **Julissa Esquivel**	1-6	T	628 37	97%	915/872-3930 Fax 915/872-3931
Ann M Garcia-Enriquez Mid Sch 12280 Socorro Rd, San Elizario 79849 **April Marioni**	7-8	T	554 38	98%	915/872-3960 Fax 915/872-3961
Borrego Elem Sch 13300 Chicken Ranch Rd, San Elizario 79849 **Norma Cassillas**	1-6	T	479 28	94%	915/872-3910 Fax 915/872-3911
Josefa L Sambrano Elem Sch 200 Herring Rd, San Elizario 79849 **Teresa Wilks**	1-6	T	537 27	97%	915/872-3950 Fax 915/872-3951
Lorenzo G Loya Primary Sch 13705 Socorro Road, San Elizario 79849 **George Augustain**	PK-K	T	566 32	96%	915/872-3940 Fax 915/872-3941
San Elizario High Sch 13981 Socorro Rd, San Elizario 79849 **Maribel Guillen**	9-12	TV	1,035 80	95%	915/872-3970 Fax 915/872-3971

● Socorro Ind School Dist   PID: 01016208
12440 Rojas Dr, El Paso 79928   915/937-0000   Fax 915/937-0194

Schools: 50 \ **Teachers:** 2,590 \ **Students:** 47,000 \ **Special Ed Students:** 4,073 \ **LEP Students:** 9,001 \ **College-Bound:** 89% \ **Ethnic:** Asian 1%, African American 2%, Hispanic 93%, Caucasian 4% \ **Exp:** $385 (High) \ **Poverty:** 23% \ **Title I:** $14,554,729 \ **Special Education:** $6,156,000 \ **Open-Close:** 07/29 - 05/28 \ **DTBP:** $164 (High)

Dr Jose Espinoza ....1 Samuel Garcia 2
Tony Reza ....2,19 David Carrasco 3
Gabriel Crespo ....3 Tom Eyeington 3,15,17
Shelly Chenausky ....4 Rito Meza 5
Jimmy Calderon ....6 Rebecca Madrid 7
Jessica Macias ....8 Lucia Borrego 8,18
Alisa Zapata-Farmer ....9,15 Carmen Crosse 10,15,288
Adam Starke ....11 Lorena Cartagena 12
Marivel Macias ....15,68,78 Marcy Sparks 16
Armando Martinez ....20,23 George Thomas 27,31
Anthony Fraga ....30 Liza Marquez 34
Tammi Mackeben ....36 Michelle Trujillo 40
Kimberly Baxter ....41 Danielle Navariz 43
Frank McDonald ....43 Fabiola Jordan 45
Veronica Reyes ....57 Richard Ortega 58,275
Cynthia Najera ....67 Rudy Campoya 68
Kelly McBain ....70 Daniel Escobar 71
Hector Reyna ....73,76,98,295,297 Lupe Luhan 79
Dr Magdalena Aguilar ....88* Jose Castorena 91
Corina Goytia ....271 Ann Darnell 298

Public Schs..Principal	Grd	Prgm	Enr/#Cls	SN	Phone
ⓨ Americas High Sch 12101 Pellicano Dr, El Paso 79936 **Patricia Cuevas**	9-12	MT	2,507	59%	915/937-2800 Fax 915/855-6898

---

89 Student Personnel
90 Driver Ed/Safety
91 Gifted/Talented
92 Video Services
93 Substance Abuse Prev
94 Erate
95 AIDS Education
96 Alternative/At Risk
97 Multi-Cultural Curriculum
98 Social Work

91 Safety/Security
92 Magnet School
93 Parental Involvement
95 Tech Prep Program
97 Chief Infomation Officer
98 Chief Technology Officer
270 Character Education
271 Migrant Education
273 Teacher Mentor
274 Before/After Sch

275 Response To Intervention
277 Remedial Math K-12
280 Literacy Coach
285 STEM
286 Digital Learning
288 Common Core Standards
294 Accountability
295 Network System
296 Title II Programs
297 Webmaster

298 Grant Writer/Ptnrships
750 Chief Innovation Officer
751 Chief of Staff
752 Social Emotional Learning

School Programs
A = Alternative Program
G = Adult Classes
M = Magnet Program
T = Title I Schoolwide
V = Career & Tech Ed Programs

Other School Types
Ⓐ = Alternative School
Ⓒ = Charter School
Ⓜ = Magnet School
Ⓨ = Year-Round School

Social Media
◧ = Facebook
◧ = Twitter

New Schools are shaded
New Superintendents and Principals are bold
Personnel with email addresses are underscored

El Paso County

School	Grades		Enroll	%	Phone
ⓥ Benito Martinez Elem Sch 2640 Robert Wynn St, El Paso 79936 Greg Hatch	K-5	MT	588 60	79%	915/937-8001 Fax 915/937-8090
ⓥ Bill Sybert Sch 11530 Edgemere Blvd, El Paso 79936 Gabriela Elliott	PK-8	MT	1,049	77%	915/937-4400 Fax 915/851-7777
Cactus Trails Elem Sch 14701 Ralph Seitsinger Dr, El Paso 79938 **Leslie Thomas**	PK-5		401		915/938-2600
ⓥ Campestre Elem Sch 11399 Socorro Rd, El Paso 79927 **Jennifer Avila**	PK-5	MT	587 49	91%	915/937-7300 Fax 915/851-1715
ⓥ Capt Walter E Clarke Mid Sch 1515 Bob Hope Dr, El Paso 79936 Ivan Ramirez	6-8	MT	938 75	79%	915/937-5600 Fax 915/857-3765
ⓥ Chester Jordan Elem Sch 13995 Jason Crandall Dr, El Paso 79938 Maribel Pidone	PK-5	T	1,097	67%	915/937-8801 Fax 915/937-8889
ⓥ Col John O Ensor Middle Sch 13600 Ryderwood Dr, El Paso 79928 Lisa Estrada	6-8	MT	1,078 43	60%	915/937-6000 Fax 915/851-7590
ⓥ Desert Wind Elem Sch 1100 Colina De Paz, El Paso 79928 Leticia Terrazas	PK-8	MT	899	98%	915/937-7800 Fax 915/851-7840
ⓥ Dr Sue Shook Elem Sch 13777 Paseo Del Este Dr, El Paso 79928 Cristina Chavira	PK-5	T	863	61%	915/937-7100 Fax 915/937-7197
ⓥ Eastlake High Sch 13000 Emerald Pass Ave, El Paso 79928 Gilbert Martinez	9-12	T	2,164	67%	915/937-3600 Fax 915/937-3799
ⓥ El Dorado High Sch 12401 Edgemere Blvd, El Paso 79938 Vanessa Betancourt	9-12	MT	2,010	62%	915/937-3200 Fax 915/937-3290
ⓥ Elfida P Chavez Elem Sch 11720 Pebble Hills Blvd, El Paso 79936 Rosemary Yates	PK-5	MT	792 42	79%	915/937-8300 Fax 915/856-9993
ⓥ Ernesto Serna Elem Sch 11471 Alameda Ave, El Paso 79927 Alejandro Olvera	PK-8	MT	792 42	91%	915/937-4800 Fax 915/851-7580
ⓥ Escontrias Early Childhood Ctr 10400 Alameda Ave, El Paso 79927 Jesse Aguirre	PK-1	MT	387 17	94%	915/937-4200 Fax 915/937-4212
ⓥ Escontrias Elem Sch 205 Buford Rd, El Paso 79927 Jesse Aguirre	2-5	MT	564 40	90%	915/937-4100 Fax 915/937-9212
ⓥ H D Hilley Elem Sch 693 N Rio Vista Rd, El Paso 79927 Fernando Miranda	PK-5	MT	622 40	92%	915/937-8400 Fax 915/937-8490
ⓥ Helen Ball Elem Sch 1950 Firehouse Dr, El Paso 79936 Ana Soto	K-5	MT	760 41	73%	915/937-8201 Fax 915/856-1478
ⓥ Horizon Heights Sch 13601 Ryderwood Dr, El Paso 79928 Jenifer Hansen	PK-5	MT	941 40	63%	915/937-7400 Fax 915/937-7497
ⓥ Hueco Elem Sch 300 Old Hueco Tanks Rd, El Paso 79927 **Daisy Garcia**	PK-5	MT	546 35	92%	915/937-7600 Fax 915/860-1125
ⓥ Hurshel Antwine Elem Sch 3830 Rich Beem, El Paso 79938 Michelle Romero	PK-5	MT	1,088	70%	915/937-6400 Fax 915/851-7830
ⓥ James P Butler Elem Sch 14251 Ralph Seitsinger Dr, El Paso 79938 Rosa Avedician	PK-5	T	1,005	57%	915/937-8901 Fax 915/937-8996
ⓥ Jane A Hambric Sch 3535 Nolan Richardson Dr, El Paso 79936 Joanne Anguiano	PK-8	MT	1,169 75	83%	915/937-4600 Fax 915/851-7560
ⓥ John Drugan Elem Sch 12451 Pellicano Dr, El Paso 79928 Adalberto Garcia	PK-8	MT	1,150	52%	915/937-6800 Fax 915/937-6815
ⓐ Keys Academy ⓥ 12380 Pine Springs Dr, El Paso 79928 Dr Magdalena Aguilar	6-12	MTV	51	73%	915/937-4000 Fax 915/937-4006
ⓐ Keys Elem Academy 205 Buford Rd, El Paso 79927 Jesse Aguirre	1-5		3		915/937-4104 Fax 915/937-9212
ⓥ Loma Verde Elem Sch 12150 Ted Houghton, El Paso 79936 Leslie Chavez	PK-5	MT	682	57%	915/937-8600 Fax 915/851-7780
ⓥ Lujan-Chavez Elem Sch 2200 Sun Country Dr, El Paso 79938 **Jina Eksaengsri**	PK-5	MT	1,126 30	63%	915/937-8700 Fax 915/937-8790
Mission Early College High Sch 10700 Gateway Blvd E, El Paso 79927 Benjamin Ortega	9-12	T	468	72%	915/937-1200 Fax 915/860-2935
Mission Ridge Elem Sch 150 Nonap Rd, El Paso 79928 Jesus Mendez	PK-5	T	820	91%	915/938-2000 Fax 915/852-8559
ⓥ Montwood High Sch 12000 Montwood Dr, El Paso 79936 Carlos Guerra	9-12	MTV	2,656 110	57%	915/937-2400 Fax 915/937-2422
ⓥ Montwood Middle Sch 11710 Pebble Hills Blvd, El Paso 79936 Sylvia Esparza	6-8	MT	710 200	73%	915/937-5800 Fax 915/856-9909
Myrtle Cooper Elem Sch 1515 Rebecca Ann Dr, El Paso 79936 Alicia Miranda	PK-6	T	720 48	82%	915/937-7700 Fax 915/855-7645
ⓥ O'Shea Keleher Elem Sch 1800 Leroy Bonse Dr, El Paso 79936 **Laura Lujan-Garcia**	PK-5	MT	893 44	79%	915/937-7200 Fax 915/921-1506
ⓐ Options High Sch 12380 Pine Springs Dr, El Paso 79928 Dr Magdalena Aguilar	9-12	T	117	92%	915/937-1300 Fax 915/859-2603
ⓥ Paso Del Norte Sch 12300 Tierra Este Rd, El Paso 79938 Nathan Ballard	K-5	MT	1,173	67%	915/937-6200 Fax 915/851-7800
Pebble Hill High Sch 14400 Pebble Hills Blvd, El Paso 79938 Melissa Parham	9-12	T	2,467	60%	915/937-9400 Fax 915/937-9498
Purple Heart Elem Sch 14400 G R Campuzano Dr, El Paso 79938 Deana White	PK-5	T	915	74%	915/938-2200
ⓥ Robert R Rojas Elem Sch 500 Bauman Rd, El Paso 79927 Jacqueline Salas	PK-5	MT	531 35	94%	915/937-8500 Fax 915/937-8590
ⓥ Salvador H Sanchez Middle Sch 321 N Rio Vista Rd, El Paso 79927 Iris Jimenez	6-8	MTV	660 25	90%	915/937-5200 Fax 915/859-6636
Sgt Jose Carrasco Elem Sch 14900 Tierra Mirage De, El Paso 79938 Jesse Sepulveda	PK-5		700		915/938-2400 Fax 915/938-2490
ⓥ Sgt Roberto Ituarte Elem Sch 12860 Tierra Sonora, El Paso 79938 Lynnette Vidales	K-5	MT	913	64%	915/937-7000 Fax 915/937-7095
ⓥ Sierra Vista Elem Sch 1501 Bob Hope Dr, El Paso 79936 Christine De La Cruz	PK-5	MT	698 55	76%	915/937-8100 Fax 915/849-1263
ⓥ Socorro High Sch 10150 Alameda Ave, El Paso 79927 Federico Tovar	9-12	GMTV	2,456	78%	915/937-2000 Fax 915/937-2394
ⓥ Socorro Middle Sch 321 Bovee Rd, El Paso 79927 Mauro Guerrero	6-8	MT	631 50	95%	915/937-5001 Fax 915/859-6955

1 Superintendent	8 Curric/Instruct K-12	19 Chief Financial Officer
2 Bus/Finance/Purchasing	9 Curric/Instruct Elem	20 Art K-12
3 Buildings And Grounds	10 Curric/Instruct Sec	21 Art Elem
4 Food Service	11 Federal Program	22 Art Sec
5 Transportation	12 Title I	23 Music K-12
6 Athletic	13 Title V	24 Music Elem
7 Health Services	14 Asst Superintendent	25 Music Sec
	15 Instructional Media Svcs	26 Business Education
	16	
	17 Chief Operations Officer	27 Career & Tech Ed
	18 Chief Academic Officer	28 Technology Education

29 Family/Consumer Science	39 Social Studies K-12	49 English/Lang Arts Elem	59 Special Education Elem
30 Adult Education	40 Social Studies Elem	50 English/Lang Arts Sec	60 Special Education Sec
31 Career/Sch-to-Work K-12	41 Social Studies Sec	51 Reading K-12	61 Foreign/World Lang K-12
32 Career/Sch-to-Work Elem	42 Science K-12	52 Reading Elem	62 Foreign/World Lang Elem
33 Career/Sch-to-Work Sec	43 Science Elem	53 Reading Sec	63 Foreign/World Lang Sec
34 Early Childhood Ed	44 Science Sec	54 Remedial Reading K-12	64 Religious Education K-12
35 Health/Phys Education	45 Math K-12	55 Remedial Reading Elem	65 Religious Education Elem
36 Guidance Services K-12	46 Math Elem	56 Remedial Reading Sec	66 Religious Education Sec
37 Guidance Services Elem	47 Math Sec	57 Bilingual/ELL	67 School Board President
38 Guidance Services Sec	48 English/Lang Arts K-12	58 Special Education K-12	68 Teacher Personnel
69 Academic Assessment			
70 Research/Development			
71 Public Information			
72 Summer School			
73 Instructional Tech			
74 Inservice Training			
75 Marketing/Distributive			
76 Info Systems			
77 Psychological Assess			
78 Affirmative Action			

Texas School Directory — El Paso County

School	Grd	Prgm	Enr/#Cls	SN	Phone
Spc Rafael Hernando Middle Sch 3451 Rich Beem, El Paso 79938 Valerie Hairston	6-8	T	1,001	70%	915/937-9800 Fax 915/937-9898
Ssg Manuel R Puentes Mid Sch 3216 Tim Foster, El Paso 79938 Monica Castro	6-8	T	990	59%	915/937-9200 Fax 915/856-7855
Ⓨ Sun Ridge Middle Sch 2210 Sun Country Dr, El Paso 79938 Ignacio Estorga	6-8	MT	932 57	59%	915/937-6600 Fax 915/851-7730
Ⓐ Vista Del Sol Sch Ⓨ 11851 Vista Del Sol Dr, El Paso 79936 Cynthia Velasquez	PK-5	MT	546 47	88%	915/937-7500 Fax 915/937-7598
Ⓐ William D Slider Middle Sch 11700 School Ln, El Paso 79936 Manuel Rios	6-8	MT	800 75	69%	915/857-5804

● **Tornillo Ind School Dist** PID: 01016260   915/765-3000
19200 Cobb St, Tornillo 79853   Fax 915/765-3099

Schools: 4 \ **Teachers:** 83 \ **Students:** 1,135 \ **Special Ed Students:** 65 \ **LEP Students:** 546 \ **College-Bound:** 45% \ **Ethnic:** Hispanic 100%, \ **Exp:** $612 (High) \ **Poverty:** 37% \ **Title I:** $592,517 \ **Special Education:** $205,000 \ **Open-Close:** 08/12 - 05/28 \ **DTBP:** $521 (High) \ 🅕 🅣

Rosy Vega-Barrio 1
Rosiosos Salinas 4
Silvia Rodriguez 4*
Rodrigo Portillo 9
Gerogina Miramontes 58
Carlos Garcia 73,76*
Davette Solice 2
Silvia Ramirez 4*
Cody Burris 6*
Lizatte Caroll 57
Marlene Bullard 67
Carmen Beasley 271

Public Schs..Principal	Grd	Prgm	Enr/#Cls	SN	Phone
Tornillo Elem Sch 19200 Gaby Rd, Tornillo 79853 Thomas Cervantes	PK-3	T	268 21	97%	915/765-3100 Fax 915/765-3199
Tornillo High Sch 430 D Oil Mill Rd, Tornillo 79853 Laura Roa	9-12	AGTV	348 20	96%	915/765-3550 Fax 915/765-3599 🅕 🅣
Tornillo Intermediate Sch 410 A Oil Mill Rd, Tornillo 79853 Nadia De La Rosa	4-6	T	256	94%	915/765-3350 Fax 915/765-3399
Tornillo Junior High Sch 300 Oil Mill Rd, Tornillo 79853 Marco Tristan	7-8	T	263 22	93%	915/765-3400 Fax 915/765-3499 🅕

● **Ysleta Ind School Dist** PID: 01016296   915/434-0000
9600 Sims Dr, El Paso 79925   Fax 915/435-9561

Schools: 61 \ **Teachers:** 2,713 \ **Students:** 40,691 \ **Special Ed Students:** 5,058 \ **LEP Students:** 9,733 \ **College-Bound:** 58% \ **Ethnic:** African American 2%, Hispanic 94%, Caucasian 4% \ **Exp:** $454 (High) \ **Poverty:** 33% \ **Title I:** $18,572,673 \ **Special Education:** $7,704,000 \ **Open-Close:** 08/26 - 06/05 \ **DTBP:** $193 (High)

Dr Xavier De La Torre 1
Lynly Leeper 2,17,19
Pedro Solis 4
Mike Williams 6,35
Brenda Chacon 9,15
Connie Fattorini-Vasq 11
Scott Thoreson 20,23
Elizabeth Moya 30*
Michelle Kehrwald 42,45
Ana Esqueda 57
Reymundo Sanchez 58
Bobbi Russell-Garcia 68
Christine Gerlach 2
Mary Haynie 2
Mario Rodriguez 5*
Sylvia Belmontes 7,85
Roberto Basurto 10,15
Dr Catherine Kennedy 15
Fernando Marquez 27,31*
Victor Perez 36,57
Rita Tellez 45
Dr Diana Otero 58
Cruz Ochoa 67
Craig Lahrman 68
Jiovana Gutierrez 68
Gloria Chavez 73,76,98
Cynthia Corrales 93*
Doug Chamlee 295
Sheila Elias 298
Patricia Ayala 71,97
Dr Ron Livermore 74
Raul Medellin 294
Lorena Olmos 297

Public Schs..Principal	Grd	Prgm	Enr/#Cls	SN	Phone
Ⓜ Alicia R Chacon Int'l Lang Sch Ⓨ 221 S Prado Rd, El Paso 79907 Ruben Cadena	PK-8	MT	777 35	67%	915/434-9200 Fax 915/859-2131
Ascarate Elem Sch 7090 Alameda Ave, El Paso 79915 Claudia Ureno Olivaz	PK-6	T	403 27	92%	915/434-7400 Fax 915/772-8051
Bel Air High Sch 731 N Yarbrough Dr, El Paso 79915 Charles Garcia	9-12	GTV	1,936	78%	915/434-2000 Fax 915/593-6110
Bel Air Middle Sch 7909 Ranchland Dr, El Paso 79915 Dana DeRouen	7-8	T	767	90%	915/434-2200 Fax 915/591-9439
Camino Real Middle Sch 9393 Alameda Ave, El Paso 79907 Ida Perales	6-8	TV	576 50	93%	915/434-8300 Fax 915/858-3743
Capistrano Elem Sch 240 Mecca Dr, El Paso 79907 Christopher Puga	K-5	T	450 34	94%	915/434-8600 Fax 915/860-2750
Cedar Grove Elem Sch 218 Barker Rd, El Paso 79915 Dolores Acosta	PK-6	T	511 35	97%	915/434-7600 Fax 915/772-8092
Ⓐ Cesar Chavez Academy 7814 Alameda Ave, El Paso 79915 **Lionel Nava**	7-12	TV	72 15	92%	915/434-9600 Fax 915/779-2068
Constance Hulbert Elem Sch 7755 Franklin Dr, El Paso 79915 James McIntyre	PK-6	T	394	94%	915/434-6900 Fax 915/772-8166
Del Norte Heights Elem Sch 1800 Winslow Rd, El Paso 79915 Claudia Poblano	PK-6	T	332 31	87%	915/434-2400 Fax 915/591-8862
Del Valle Elem Sch 9251 Escobar Dr, El Paso 79907 Sandra Perez	PK-5	T	449	90%	915/434-9300 Fax 915/434-9306
Del Valle High Sch 950 Bordeaux Dr, El Paso 79907 Antonio Acuna	9-12	GT	2,012 96	78%	915/434-3000 Fax 915/858-1427
Del Valle Middle Sch 8674 N Loop Dr, El Paso 79907 Ida Perales	6-8	TV	738 50	86%	915/434-3300 Fax 915/858-3615
Desert View Middle Sch 1641 Billie Marie Dr, El Paso 79936 Javier Salgado	7-8	T	350 41	72%	915/434-5300 Fax 915/591-9327
Desertaire Elem Sch 6301 Tiger Eye Dr, El Paso 79924 Beth Harbison	K-5	T	1,007 47	76%	915/434-6400 Fax 915/821-0634
Dolphin Terrace Elem Sch 9790 Pickerel Dr, El Paso 79924 Lorraine Martinez	K-5	T	746 37	84%	915/434-6500 Fax 915/757-8073
East Point Elem Sch 2400 Zanzibar Rd, El Paso 79925 Dana Boyd	PK-6	T	877 48	69%	915/434-4500 Fax 915/591-8958
Eastwood Heights Elem Sch 10530 Janway Dr, El Paso 79925 Raul Mendoza	PK-6	T	735 30	68%	915/434-4600 Fax 915/591-8960
Eastwood High Sch 2430 McRae Blvd, El Paso 79925 James Boatright	9-12	GT	1,619 100	57%	915/434-4000 Fax 915/594-8014
Eastwood Knolls Elem Sch 10000 Buckwood Ave, El Paso 79925 Robert Martinez	PK-8	T	868 60	50%	915/434-4400 Fax 915/592-0339

El Paso County

School	Grades		Enroll	%	Phone
Eastwood Middle Sch 2612 Chaswood St, El Paso 79935 Sarah Venegas	7-8	T	1,035 53	69%	915/434-4300 Fax 915/591-9426
Edgemere Elem Sch 10300 Edgemere Blvd, El Paso 79925 Jose Perez	PK-6	T	723	75%	915/434-4700 Fax 915/590-8335
Glen Cove Elem Sch 10955 Sam Snead Dr, El Paso 79936 Margarita Mendoza	PK-5	T	854 56	79%	915/434-5500 Fax 915/591-9024
Ⓜ Hacienda Heights Elem Sch 7530 Acapulco Ave, El Paso 79915 Maria Aguilar	K-6	T	480 45	86%	915/434-2500 Fax 915/591-9044
Indian Ridge Middle Sch 11201 Pebble Hills Blvd, El Paso 79936 Pauline Muele	6-8	T	622 52	78%	915/434-5400 Fax 915/591-9447
J M Hanks High Sch 2001 N Lee Trevino Dr, El Paso 79936 Enrique Herrera	9-12	AGTV	1,733 115	69%	915/434-5000 Fax 915/598-4621
Lancaster Elem Sch 9230 Elgin Dr, El Paso 79907 Veronica Frias	PK-5	T	502	86%	915/434-3400 Fax 915/860-2315
Lebarron Park Elem Sch 920 Burgundy Dr, El Paso 79907 **Maritza Balderrama**	K-5	T	640 65	90%	915/434-3500 Fax 915/860-2817
Loma Terrace Elem Sch 8200 Ryland Ct, El Paso 79907 Alejandro Armendariz	PK-6	T	600 46	87%	915/434-2600 Fax 915/591-9111
Marian Manor Elem Sch 8300 Forrest Haven Ct, El Paso 79907 Natalie Alvarez	PK-5	T	324 33	89%	915/434-3600 Fax 915/591-9131
Mesa Vista Elem Sch 8032 Alamo Ave, El Paso 79907 **Norma Sierra**	PK-6	T	442 35	87%	915/434-2700 Fax 915/591-9171
Mission Valley Elem Sch 8674 N Loop Dr, El Paso 79907 Veronica Alvidrez	K-6	T	498 42	97%	915/434-3700 Fax 915/860-0049
North Loop Elem Sch 412 Emerson St, El Paso 79915 Denise Jones	PK-6	T	417 26	96%	915/434-2800 Fax 915/591-9202
North Star Elem Sch 5950 Sean Haggerty Dr, El Paso 79924 **Stephanie Lahrman**	PK-6	T	478	72%	915/434-6700 Fax 915/822-9386
Parkland Elem Sch 6330 Deer Ave, El Paso 79924 Roxanne Merfa	PK-5	T	1,037 30	75%	915/434-6600 Fax 915/757-9458
Parkland High Sch 5932 Quail Ave, El Paso 79924 Penelope Bankston	9-12	GT	1,515 56	75%	915/434-6000 Fax 915/755-2382
Parkland Middle Sch 6045 Nova Way, El Paso 79924 **Angela Reyna**	6-8	TV	1,282 38	80%	915/434-6300 Fax 915/757-6608
Parkland Pre-K Center 10080 Chick A Dee St, El Paso 79924 **Rita Lopez**	PK-PK		347		915/435-7800 Fax 915/435-7896
Pasodale Elem Sch 8253 McElroy Ave, El Paso 79907 David Medina	PK-5	T	691 57	86%	915/434-8500 Fax 915/858-1269
Pebble Hills Elem Sch 11145 Edgemere Blvd, El Paso 79936 **Irene Youngs**	PK-5	T	768 48	76%	915/434-5600 Fax 915/591-9222
Ⓐ Plato Academy 8441 Alameda Ave, El Paso 79907 Gloria Spencer	11-12	TV	100 9	72%	915/434-9000 Fax 915/590-6815
Presa Elem Sch 128 Presa Pl, El Paso 79907 Wendy Banegas	PK-5	T	364 28	90%	915/434-8700 Fax 915/860-2810
Ramona Elem Sch 351 Nichols Rd, El Paso 79915 Irene Ahumada	PK-6	T	293 40	81%	915/434-7700 Fax 915/772-8153
Rio Bravo Middle Sch 525 Greggerson Dr, El Paso 79907 Sandra Calzada	6-8	T	478 20	81%	915/434-8400 Fax 915/872-0269
Riverside High Sch 301 Midway Dr, El Paso 79915 Daniel Gurany	9-12	TV	1,120	87%	915/434-7000 Fax 915/779-6983
Riverside Middle Sch 7615 Mimosa Ave, El Paso 79915 **Jacob Valtierra**	7-8	T	525 40	89%	915/434-7300 Fax 915/772-7549
Robbin E L Washington Elem Sch 3505 N Lee Trevino Dr, El Paso 79936 Mauricio Cano	PK-6	T	551 30	77%	915/434-5900 Fax 915/590-6535
Sageland Elem Sch 7901 Santa Monica Ct, El Paso 79915 Rachael Blair	PK-6	T	537 27	80%	915/434-2900 Fax 915/591-9228
Scotsdale Elem Sch 2901 McRae Blvd, El Paso 79925 Juan Guzman	PK-6	T	850 42	72%	915/434-4800 Fax 915/591-9270
South Loop Elem Sch 520 Southside Rd, El Paso 79907 Norma Myers	PK-5	T	289 27	86%	915/434-8800 Fax 915/860-9075
Ⓐ Tejas School of Choice Ⓨ 7500 Alpha Ave, El Paso 79915 Lucy Lozano-Lerma	9-12	MT	69 14	94%	915/434-9900 Fax 915/772-8366
Thomas Manor Elem Sch 7900 Jersey St, El Paso 79915 Sandra Stresow	PK-6	T	563 40	95%	915/434-7500 Fax 915/858-0873
Tierra Del Sol Elem Sch 1832 Tommy Aaron Dr, El Paso 79936 **Michelle Romero**	PK-6	T	718 39	68%	915/434-5800 Fax 915/591-9271
Valle Verde Early College HS 919 Hunter Dr, El Paso 79915 Paul Covey	9-12	T	389 11	68%	915/434-1500 Fax 915/594-7112
Vista Hills Elem Sch 10801 La Subida Dr, El Paso 79935 Laura Calderon	PK-6	T	653 50	75%	915/434-5700 Fax 915/591-9305
Young Women's Leadership Acad 7615 Yuma Dr, El Paso 79915 Malinda Villalobos	6-7	T	231	51%	915/434-1300 Fax 915/434-1399
Ysleta Community Learning Ctr 121 Padres Dr, El Paso 79907 Louis Martinez	Adult		250 20		915/434-9400 Fax 915/858-6307
Ysleta Elem Sch 8624 Dorbandt Cir, El Paso 79907 Norma Osuna	PK-5	T	511 40	92%	915/434-8900 Fax 915/859-9311
Ysleta High Sch 8600 Alameda Ave, El Paso 79907 Silvia Rendon	9-12	AGTV	1,371	89%	915/434-8000 Fax 915/858-3299
Ysleta Middle Sch 8691 Independence Dr, El Paso 79907 David Gonzalez	6-8	TV	597 43	98%	915/434-8200 Fax 915/858-0261
Ⓨ Ysleta Pre-K Center 7940 Craddock Ave, El Paso 79915 **Heather Karns**	PK-PK	MT	691 26	88%	915/434-9500 Fax 915/591-9325

1 Superintendent	8 Curric/Instruct K-12	19 Chief Financial Officer	29 Family/Consumer Science	39 Social Studies K-12	49 English/Lang Arts Elem	59 Special Education Elem	69 Academic Assessment
2 Bus/Finance/Purchasing	9 Curric/Instruct Elem	20 Art K-12	30 Adult Education	40 Social Studies Elem	50 English/Lang Arts Sec	60 Special Education Sec	70 Research/Development
3 Buildings And Grounds	10 Curric/Instruct Sec	21 Art Elem	31 Career/Sch-to-Work K-12	41 Social Studies Sec	51 Reading K-12	61 Foreign/World Lang K-12	71 Public Information
4 Food Service	11 Federal Program	22 Art Sec	32 Career/Sch-to-Work Elem	42 Science K-12	52 Reading Elem	62 Foreign/World Lang Elem	72 Summer School
5 Transportation	12 Title I	23 Music K-12	33 Career/Sch-to-Work Sec	43 Science Elem	53 Reading Sec	63 Foreign/World Lang Sec	73 Instructional Tech
6 Athletic	13 Title V	24 Music Elem	34 Early Childhood Ed	44 Science Sec	54 Remedial Reading K-12	64 Religious Education K-12	74 Inservice Training
7 Health Services	14 Asst Superintendent	25 Music Sec	35 Health/Phys Education	45 Math K-12	55 Remedial Reading Elem	65 Religious Education Elem	75 Marketing/Distributive
	15 Instructional Media Svcs	26 Business Education	36 Guidance Services K-12	46 Math Elem	56 Remedial Reading Sec	66 Religious Education Sec	76 Info Systems
	16 Chief Operations Officer	27 Career & Tech Ed	37 Guidance Services Elem	47 Math Sec	57 Bilingual/ELL	67 School Board President	77 Psychological Assess
	17 Chief Academic Officer	28 Technology Education	38 Guidance Services Sec	48 English/Lang Arts K-12	58 Special Education K-12	68 Teacher Personnel	78 Affirmative Action

Texas School Directory — El Paso County

EL PASO CATHOLIC SCHOOLS

- **Diocese of El Paso Ed Office** PID: 01016703 915/872-8426
  499 Saint Matthews St, El Paso 79907 Fax 915/872-8464

Schools: 11 \ *Students:* 2,700

Listing includes only schools located in this county. See District Index for location of Diocesan Offices.

Steve Sanchez 1,11,73

Catholic Schs..Principal	Grd	Prgm	Enr/#Cls	SN	
Cathedral High Sch 1309 N Stanton St, El Paso 79902 Adolfo Sanchez	9-12		400 36		915/532-3238 Fax 915/533-8248 [f]
Father Yermo Elem Sch 237 Tobin Pl, El Paso 79905 Sr Yamila Trejo	PK-12		300 11		915/533-4693 Fax 915/532-2827
Father Yermo High Sch 250 Washington St, El Paso 79905 Sister Yamila Prejo	9-12		190 25		915/533-3185
Loretto Acad Elem Sch 4625 Clifton Ave, El Paso 79903 Jane German	PK-5		220 13		915/566-8400 Fax 915/564-0563 [f][t]
Loretto Acad-Middle High Sch 1300 Hardaway St, El Paso 79903 Homero Silva	6-12		477 40		915/566-8400 Fax 915/564-0563
Most Holy Trinity Sch 10000 Pheasant Rd, El Paso 79924 Jim Horan	PK-8		103 12		915/751-2566 Fax 915/751-2596 [f]
St Joseph Sch 1300 Lamar St, El Paso 79903 Marcella Hernandez	PK-8		511 23		915/566-1661 Fax 915/566-1664
St Matthews Catholic Sch 400 W Sunset Rd, El Paso 79922 Veronica De La Cruz	PK-8		300		915/581-8801 Fax 915/581-8816
St Patrick Cathedral Sch 1111 N Stanton St, El Paso 79902 Elizabeth Carreon	PK-8		200 15		915/532-4142 Fax 915/532-8297 [f]
St Pius X Sch 1007 Geronimo Dr, El Paso 79905 Ana Silva	PK-8		486 16		915/772-6598 Fax 915/225-0010
St Raphael Catholic Sch 2310 Woodside Dr, El Paso 79925 Graciela Fernandez	PK-8		400 28		915/598-2241 Fax 915/598-3002 [f]

EL PASO PRIVATE SCHOOLS

Private Schs..Principal	Grd	Prgm	Enr/#Cls	SN	
Bridges Sch 4320 N Stanton St, El Paso 79902 Irma Keys	Spec		46 13		915/532-6647 Fax 915/532-8767
Community of Faith Chrn Sch 4539 Emory Rd, El Paso 79922 Blanca Mixer	PK-8		53		915/584-2561 Fax 915/584-3529
El Paso Adventist Jr Academy 3510 George Dieter Dr, El Paso 79936 Juanita Camacho	PK-9		43 5		915/855-7312 Fax 915/855-0092
El Paso Country Day Sch 220 E Cliff Dr, El Paso 79902 Dr Laura Alpern	PK-8		50 6		915/533-4492 Fax 915/533-9626 [t]
El Paso Jewish Academy 805 Cherry Hill Ln Frnt, El Paso 79912 Kara Jones	1-8		50 8		915/833-0808 Fax 915/833-0819
El Paso NE Children's Ed Ctr 6301 Alabama St, El Paso 79904 Mari Jo Hodges	PK-5		100 10		915/751-9487
Escuela Montessori-Del Valle 212 W Sunset Rd, El Paso 79922 Vanessa Miranda	PK-6		100		915/584-9215 Fax 915/587-6067 [f]
Faith Christian Academy 8960 Escobar Dr, El Paso 79907 Shannon Nyeman	PK-12		550		915/594-3305 Fax 915/593-5474
Immanuel Christian Sch 1201 Hawkins Blvd, El Paso 79925 Linda Johnson	PK-12		550		915/778-6160 Fax 915/772-8207
Jesus Chapel Sch 10200 Album Ave, El Paso 79925 Alba Wilcox	PK-12		180 14		915/593-1153 Fax 915/593-1113
La Paz Language Academy 1035 Belvidere St Ste 200, El Paso 79912 Ely Ferreyra	K-12		200		915/584-5100
Lydia Patterson Institute 517 S Florence St, El Paso 79901 Ernesto Morales	7-12		450 23		915/533-8286 Fax 915/533-5236
Maran-Ata Christian Academy 8800 Cristo Viene Dr, El Paso 79907 Lizbeth Cabrera	K-12		60 8		915/592-1909 Fax 915/592-0303
New World Montessori Sch 3510 N Yarbrough Dr, El Paso 79925 Francisco Portillo	PK-6		150 6		915/593-8091 Fax 915/593-8268
North Loop Christian Academy 8617 N Loop Dr, El Paso 79907 Valerie DeVine	K-12		97 7		915/859-8090 Fax 915/859-3290
Northeast Christian Academy 9901 McCombs St, El Paso 79924 Lillian Ainsworth	PK-12		65 20		915/755-1155 Fax 915/755-8264
Palm Tree Academy 143 Paragon Ln, El Paso 79912 Laura Kassim	PK-5		41		915/229-2190
Radford Sch 2001 Radford St, El Paso 79903 John Doran	PK-12		175 24		915/565-2700 Fax 915/565-2730
St Clement's Parish Sch 600 Montana Ave, El Paso 79902 Priscilla Pelking	PK-8		380 50		915/533-4248 Fax 915/544-1778
St Mark's Sch 5005 Love Rd, El Paso 79922 Linda Smith	PK-8		300 30		915/581-2032 Fax 915/581-4701
Wee Wisdom Kindergarten 1712 Weston Brent Ln, El Paso 79935 Claudia Labrado	PK-1		75 5		915/592-6036
Western Hills Academy 524 Thunderbird Dr, El Paso 79912 Patricia Aguirre	PK-5		250 17		915/584-6642 Fax 915/833-2965

EL PASO REGIONAL CENTERS

- **Region 19 Ed Service Center** PID: 01016246 915/780-5052
  6611 Boeing Dr, El Paso 79925 Fax 915/780-6537

Dr Armando Aguirre .... 1 Royce Cleveland 2
Sonia Eubank .... 2,15 Monica Gonzalez 16,73
Angie Haro .... 27,73 Amy Avina 57
Juan Alderete 58

Ellis County

ELLIS COUNTY

ELLIS PUBLIC SCHOOLS

• **Avalon Ind School Dist** PID: 01014937 972/627-3251
Highway 104 FM 55, Avalon 76623 Fax 972/627-3220

Schools: 1 \ *Teachers:* 28 \ *Students:* 350 \ *Special Ed Students:* 51 \ *LEP Students:* 8 \ *College-Bound:* 100% \ *Ethnic:* African American 2%, Hispanic 32%, Caucasian 67% \ *Exp:* $661 (High) \ *Poverty:* 13% \ *Title I:* $23,780 \ *Open-Close:* 08/15 - 05/26 \ *DTBP:* $92 (Med) \

Khristopher Marshall 1,288
Tony Hernandez 3*
Jody Tennery 9,34*
Dwayne Betik 16,73,295*
Todd Bruner 67
Alice Compton 2
Malcom Cole 6*
Neva Delbosque 11,57,88,273,275,296*
Sandra Berniking 58*

Public Schs..Principal	Grd	Prgm	Enr/#Cls	SN	
Avalon Sch Highway 104 FM 55, Avalon 76623 Jody Tennery \ Tony Hernandez	PK-12	AGT	350 14	53%	972/627-3251

• **Ennis Ind School Dist** PID: 01014963 972/872-7000
303 W Knox St, Ennis 75119 Fax 972/875-8667

Schools: 11 \ *Teachers:* 392 \ *Students:* 5,800 \ *Special Ed Students:* 608 \ *LEP Students:* 695 \ *Ethnic:* African American 13%, Hispanic 57%, Caucasian 29% \ *Exp:* $381 (High) \ *Poverty:* 19% \ *Title I:* $1,402,752 \ *Special Education:* $832,000 \ *Open-Close:* 08/15 - 05/28 \ *DTBP:* $214 (High) \

Lloyd Treadwell 1
Lisa Fincher 2,19,296,298
David Gutierrez 4
David Kilpatrick 6
Dr Lacey Padgett 8
Jennifer Nelson 11,34,58
Scott Short 16,28,73,76,82,286
Mandi Chapman 58
Bill Honza 71
John Steele 295
Laurie Walker 2,11
Jason Gilstrap 3,15,68
Ryan McCabe 5,285*
Kathy Cikanek 8,15,69
Twilla Rex 8,57,69,288
James Sanders 15,68
Cliff Mathes 58
Bramlet Beard 67
Jeremy Scruggs 83,91*

Public Schs..Principal	Grd	Prgm	Enr/#Cls	SN	
ⓐ Alamo Education Center 501 N Gaines St, Ennis 75119 Howard Hughes	6-12	G	115		972/872-7332 Fax 972/875-3834
David S Crockett ECC 1701 W Lampasas St, Ennis 75119 Dee-Dee Gryder	PK-K	T	417	78%	972/872-7131 Fax 972/872-9829
Dorie Miller Interm Sch 2200 W Lampasas St, Ennis 75119 Lindsey Wood	4-6	T	644 23	70%	972/872-3775 Fax 972/872-9370
Ennis High Sch 2301 Ensign Rd, Ennis 75119 Wade Bishop	9-12	TV	1,670 65	62%	972/872-3500 Fax 972/875-6337
Ennis Junior High Sch 3101 Ensign Rd, Ennis 75119 Sheila Thomas-Boone	7-8	ATV	859 55	67%	972/872-3850 Fax 972/875-9044
G W Carver Early Childhood Ctr 600 E Martin Luther King Dr, Ennis 75119 Susan Jones	PK-K	T	334	78%	972/872-3730 Fax 972/875-5038
Jack Lummus Interm Sch 501 N Clay St, Ennis 75119 Rodney McNeill	4-6	T	666	72%	972/872-7060 Fax 972/875-8030
James Bowie Elem Sch 501 Jeter Dr, Ennis 75119 John Peterson	1-3	T	361 36	67%	972/872-7234 Fax 972/875-3407
Sam Houston Elem Sch 1701 S Hall St, Ennis 75119 Lori Redning	1-3	T	288 25	81%	972/872-7285 Fax 972/875-4816
Stephen F Austin Elem Sch 1500 Austin Dr, Ennis 75119 Bobby White	1-3	T	281 18	68%	972/872-7190 Fax 972/875-7216
Wm B Travis Elem Sch 200 N Shawnee St, Ennis 75119 Philip Black	1-3	T	288 15	71%	972/872-7455 Fax 972/875-4205

• **Ferris Ind School Dist** PID: 01015034 972/544-3858
301 E 5th St, Ferris 75125 Fax 972/544-2784

Schools: 5 \ *Teachers:* 187 \ *Students:* 2,400 \ *Special Ed Students:* 259 \ *LEP Students:* 560 \ *College-Bound:* 60% \ *Ethnic:* African American 7%, Hispanic 70%, Caucasian 22% \ *Exp:* $507 (High) \ *Poverty:* 14% \ *Title I:* $362,171 \ *Open-Close:* 08/21 - 05/28 \ *DTBP:* $353 (High) \

James Hartman 1
Dondi Markgraf 3
Brandon Layne 6,35
Kendra Gajdica 9
Dr Melinda Domain 12,15,27,88,296,298
Rebecca Strick 16,82
Robert Scott 67
William Wooten 2
Gay Clark 4*
Jane Dvorak 8,85
Thomas Knight 11,54,57,68,69,74,83,294
Brett Browne 16,73,84,295
Kevin Dixon 58
Joshua Newman 91

Public Schs..Principal	Grd	Prgm	Enr/#Cls	SN	
Ferris High Sch 1025 E 8th St, Ferris 75125 Andru Gilbert	9-12	TV	758 42	79%	972/544-3737 Fax 972/544-3820
Ferris Intermediate Sch 601 W FM Rd 664, Ferris 75125 Lance Keating	4-6	T	374 48	82%	972/544-8662 Fax 972/544-3085
Ferris Junior High Sch 1002 E 8th St, Ferris 75125 C Lowery	7-8	T	586 18	83%	972/544-2279 Fax 972/544-2281
Hazel Ingram Elem Sch 600 S Central St, Ferris 75125 Victoria Griffith	PK-K	GT	405 23	88%	972/544-3212 Fax 972/544-3405
Lucy Mae McDonald Elem Sch 500 FM 983, Ferris 75125 Christopher Hawkins	1-3	T	531 40	84%	972/544-3405 Fax 972/544-2116

• **Italy Ind School Dist** PID: 01015072 972/483-1815
300 College, Italy 76651 Fax 972/483-6152

Schools: 2 \ *Teachers:* 55 \ *Students:* 600 \ *Special Ed Students:* 77 \ *LEP Students:* 48 \ *College-Bound:* 49% \ *Ethnic:* African American 16%, Hispanic 33%, Caucasian 50% \ *Exp:* $535 (High) \ *Poverty:* 10% \ *Title I:* $71,721 \ *Open-Close:* 08/20 - 05/20 \ *DTBP:* $350 (High) \

Dr Michelle Schwind 1
Michael Chambers 3,5
Deedee Hamilton 7*
Cassie Joffre 16*
Angela Green 37*
Allen Richards 67
Natasha Blackburn 2,11,298
Charles Tindol 6*
Lee Joffre 8*
John Woody 31*
Cheryl Allen 57*
Erica Miller 69,88,271*

---

1 Superintendent	8 Curric/Instruct K-12	19 Chief Financial Officer	29 Family/Consumer Science	39 Social Studies K-12	49 English/Lang Arts Elem	59 Special Education Elem	69 Academic Assessment
2 Bus/Finance/Purchasing	9 Curric/Instruct Elem	20 Art K-12	30 Adult Education	40 Social Studies Elem	50 English/Lang Arts Sec	60 Special Education Sec	70 Research/Development
3 Buildings And Grounds	10 Curric/Instruct Sec	21 Art Elem	31 Career/Sch-to-Work K-12	41 Social Studies Sec	51 Reading K-12	61 Foreign/World Lang K-12	71 Public Information
4 Food Service	11 Federal Program	22 Art Sec	32 Career/Sch-to-Work Elem	42 Science K-12	52 Reading Elem	62 Foreign/World Lang Elem	72 Summer School
5 Transportation	12 Title I	23 Music K-12	33 Career/Sch-to-Work Sec	43 Science Elem	53 Reading Sec	63 Foreign/World Lang Sec	73 Instructional Tech
6 Athletic	13 Title V	24 Music Elem	34 Early Childhood Ed	44 Science Sec	54 Remedial Reading K-12	64 Religious Education K-12	74 Inservice Training
7 Health Services	15 Asst Superintendent	25 Music Sec	35 Health/Phys Education	45 Math K-12	55 Remedial Reading Elem	65 Religious Education Elem	75 Marketing/Distributive
	16 Instructional Media Svcs	26 Business Education	36 Guidance Services K-12	46 Math Elem	56 Remedial Reading Sec	66 Religious Education Sec	76 Info Systems
	17 Chief Operations Officer	27 Career & Tech Ed	37 Guidance Services Elem	47 Math Sec	57 Bilingual/ELL	67 School Board President	77 Psychological Assess
	18 Chief Academic Officer	28 Technology Education	38 Guidance Services Sec	48 English/Lang Arts K-12	58 Special Education K-12	68 Teacher Personnel	78 Affirmative Action

Texas School Directory — Ellis County

Oscar McCawley 73,285*

Public Schs..Principal	Grd	Prgm	Enr/#Cls	SN	
Italy Jr Sr High Sch 300 College, Italy 76651 **Jason Lawson**	6-12	T	281 40	53%	972/483-7411 Fax 972/483-1500 [f]
Stafford Elem Sch 301 Harris St, Italy 76651 Lakesha Bass	PK-5	T	304 23	66%	972/483-6342 Fax 972/483-6892

● **Maypearl Ind School Dist** PID: 01015101   972/435-2116
309 Main St, Maypearl 76064   Fax 972/435-1001

Schools: 4 \ **Teachers:** 72 \ **Students:** 1,040 \ **Special Ed Students:** 90 \ **LEP Students:** 44 \ **College-Bound:** 75% \ **Ethnic:** Asian 1%, African American 1%, Hispanic 18%, Caucasian 80% \ **Exp:** $404 (High) \ **Poverty:** 5% \ **Title I:** $64,676 \ **Special Education:** $362,000 \ **Open-Close:** 08/15 - 05/22 \ **DTBP:** $350 (High) \ [f]

Ritchie Bowling 1
Dale Cheek 3,5
Robin Leal 4*
Lisa Hyles 8
Debra Griffin 36,83,85,270*
Tricia Ikard 58
Charles Frame 67
Leighanne McAlister 2
Robert Garcia 3,5,91
Jason Wallen 6,83,270
Barbara Pinson 16*
Barbara Truby 58
Lynne Pipes 59*
Carole Upchurch 73,295

Public Schs..Principal	Grd	Prgm	Enr/#Cls	SN	
Lorene S Kirkpatrick Elem Sch 1024 W 4th, Maypearl 76064 Cristin Votaw	PK-5	AT	378 20	43%	972/435-1010 Fax 972/435-1011
Maypearl High Sch 600 Philips St Hwy 157, Maypearl 76064 Eric Janszen	9-12	AV	374 36	35%	972/435-1020 Fax 972/435-1021
Maypearl Intermediate Sch 400 Panther Ln, Maypearl 76064 Jessica Lee	5-6	T	174	47%	972/435-1099 Fax 972/435-1098
Maypearl Middle Sch 1025 4th St, Maypearl 76064 **Matthew Garrison**	5-8	AT	217 12	33%	972/435-1015 Fax 972/435-1016

● **Midlothian Ind School Dist** PID: 01015137   469/856-5000
100 Walter Stephenson Rd, Midlothian 76065

Schools: 11 \ **Teachers:** 533 \ **Students:** 9,500 \ **Special Ed Students:** 818 \ **LEP Students:** 295 \ **College-Bound:** 64% \ **Ethnic:** Asian 1%, African American 6%, Hispanic 23%, Caucasian 70% \ **Exp:** $463 (High) \ **Poverty:** 5% \ **Title I:** $423,299 \ **Special Education:** $1,056,000 \ **Open-Close:** 08/20 - 05/29 \ **DTBP:** $177 (High) \ [f] [t]

Dr Lane Ledbetter 1
Rola Fadel 3
Deanna Cannon 5
Becki Krsnak 9*
Lisa Knight 11,57,271,296,298
Karen Fitzgerald 15,71,76,750
Melissa Wolfe 58
Natalie Dennington 69,294*
Tim Hicks 91*
Jim Norris 2,15
Peter Pajack 4
John Crawford 6
Nikki Nix 10
Judy Walling 15
Kay Lynn Day 15,79
Matt Sanders 67
Leslie Garakani 73,98
Gregg Burcham 295

Public Schs..Principal	Grd	Prgm	Enr/#Cls	SN	
Baxter Elem Sch 1050 Park Place Blvd, Midlothian 76065 **Ryan Timm**	PK-5		613 36	34%	469/856-6100 [f]
Dolores W McClatchey Elem Sch 6631 Shiloh Rd, Midlothian 76065 Stacy Germany	K-5		626		469/856-6600
Frank Seale Middle Sch 700 George Hopper Rd, Midlothian 76065 Kristopher Vernon	6-8	V	1,164 63	22%	972/775-6145 Fax 972/775-1502
J A Vitovsky Elem Sch 333 Church St, Midlothian 76065 Hollye Walker	PK-5	T	638 30	53%	469/856-6400 [f]
J R Irvin Elem Sch 600 5th St, Midlothian 76065 Joshua Roberts	K-5	T	339 21	36%	469/856-6000
LaRue Miller Elem Sch 2800 Sudith Ln, Midlothian 76065 Shannon West	PK-5		702	15%	469/856-6500
Longbranch Elem Sch 6631 FM 1387, Midlothian 76065 Karena Blackwell	PK-5		582 38	14%	469/856-6200
Midlothian Heritage High Sch 4000 FM 1387, Midlothian 76065 Krista Tipton	9-12		966	10%	469/856-5400
Midlothian High Sch 923 S 9th St, Midlothian 76065 Gary Gates	9-12	AV	1,830 50	20%	469/856-5100
Mountain Peak Elem Sch 5201 FM 663, Midlothian 76065 Shannon Thompson	PK-5		724 32	15%	469/856-6300 [f][t]
Walnut Grove Middle Sch 990 N Walnut Grove Rd, Midlothian 76065 Brian Blackwell	6-8		1,104	20%	469/856-5700

● **Milford Ind School Dist** PID: 01015187   972/493-2911
205 3rd St, Milford 76670   Fax 972/493-4600

Schools: 1 \ **Teachers:** 25 \ **Students:** 280 \ **Special Ed Students:** 28 \ **LEP Students:** 22 \ **College-Bound:** 50% \ **Ethnic:** African American 26%, Hispanic 32%, Caucasian 42% \ **Exp:** $633 (High) \ **Poverty:** 13% \ **Title I:** $40,426 \ **Open-Close:** 08/12 - 05/21 \ **DTBP:** $30 (Low)

Vernon Orndorff 1
Lauren Gray 2,271
Charlene Buzan 4*
Alton Chambers 8,36,69,88*
Mark Jackson 13*
Kimberly Cook 67
April Gilley 2
Mark Garza 3
Ronny Crompton 6*
Joann Dahl 11,296
Flossie Gowin 57*
Kirk Price 73,286,295*

Public Schs..Principal	Grd	Prgm	Enr/#Cls	SN	
Milford Sch 205 3rd St, Milford 76670 Vernon Orndorff	PK-12	TV	280 24	76%	972/493-2921

● **Palmer Ind School Dist** PID: 01015216   972/449-3389
303 Bulldog Way, Palmer 75152   Fax 972/845-2112

Schools: 3 \ **Teachers:** 86 \ **Students:** 1,250 \ **Special Ed Students:** 153 \ **LEP Students:** 94 \ **College-Bound:** 65% \ **Ethnic:** African American 1%, Hispanic 43%, Caucasian 55% \ **Exp:** $516 (High) \ **Poverty:** 11% \ **Title I:** $156,930 \ **Special Education:** $233,000 \ **Open-Close:** 08/19 - 05/21 \ **DTBP:** $157 (High) \ [f]

Kevin Noack 1
Clifford Hurd 5
Joanette Roybal 7
Regina Cottongame 11,58,69,296,298
Leann Jones 31*
Kirk DeCordova 57*
Roxanne Ncelhaney 79
Karla Cochrane 2
Dawn Waddle 6
Brian Fry 8,74,285,286,288
Allison Kemp 29*
Cassie Windham 35*
Christen Vick 67

---

9 Student Personnel
10 Driver Ed/Safety
11 Gifted/Talented
12 Video Services
13 Substance Abuse Prev
14 Erate
15 AIDS Education
18 Alternative/At Risk
19 Multi-Cultural Curriculum
20 Social Work

91 Safety/Security
92 Magnet School
93 Parental Involvement
95 Tech Prep Program
97 Chief Infomation Officer
98 Chief Technology Officer
270 Character Education
271 Migrant Education
273 Teacher Mentor
274 Before/After Sch

275 Response To Intervention
277 Remedial Math K-12
280 Literacy Coach
285 STEM
286 Digital Learning
288 Common Core Standards
294 Accountability
295 Network System
296 Title II Programs
297 Webmaster

298 Grant Writer/Ptnrships
750 Chief Innovation Officer
751 Chief of Staff
752 Social Emotional Learning

Other School Types
Ⓐ = Alternative School
Ⓒ = Charter School
Ⓜ = Magnet School
Ⓨ = Year-Round School

School Programs
A = Alternative Program
G = Adult Classes
M = Magnet Program
T = Title I Schoolwide
V = Career & Tech Ed Programs

Social Media
[f] = Facebook
[t] = Twitter

New Schools are shaded
New Superintendents and Principals are bold
Personnel with email addresses are underscored

Ellis County — Market Data Retrieval

Public Schs..Principal	Grd	Prgm	Enr/#Cls	SN	
Palmer Elem Sch 113 W FM 813, Palmer 75152 Alison Spurgeon	PK-4	T	510 19	53%	972/449-3132 Fax 972/845-2019
Palmer High Sch 422 W Jefferson St, Palmer 75152 Brian Warner	9-12	TV	314 30	45%	972/449-3487 Fax 972/845-3517
Palmer Middle Sch 112 Farm Road 813 W, Palmer 75152 Kristin Middlebrooks	4-8	TV	391 30	56%	972/449-3319 Fax 972/845-3380

• **Red Oak Ind School Dist** PID: 01015242 972/617-2941
109 W Red Oak Rd, Red Oak 75154 Fax 972/617-4333

Schools: 8 \ **Teachers:** 356 \ **Students:** 6,000 \ **Special Ed Students:** 622 \ **LEP Students:** 536 \ **College-Bound:** 71% \ **Ethnic:** Asian 1%, African American 22%, Hispanic 35%, Native American: 1%, Caucasian 41% \ **Exp:** $357 (High) \ **Poverty:** 9% \ **Title I:** $549,727 \ **Special Education:** $1,000,000 \ **Open-Close:** 08/19 - 05/22 \ **DTBP:** $181 (High) \

Dr Ann Dixon 1
Brent Stanford 3,5
Victoria Ybarra 4
Chris Anderson 6,35
Garry Gorman 8
Patrick Torres 8,15,54,277
Stephanie Heimbuch 8
Nancy Toney 11,296,298
Robert Myers 20,23
Rachel Kistner 58
Catrina Reeves 68
Karen Prachyl 76
Shondra Jones 273*
Diane Case 297
Dr Bill Johnston 2,19
Kevin Freels 3,15
Tammy Pickett 5
Sue Brown 7
Lindsay Cadenhead 8
Rebecca Waller 8
Scott Rodgers 10
Michelle Ailara 15,68,79
Lisa Menton 27
John Anderson 67
Mike Bahr 73,76,295
Kevin Denney 83,91
Tia Wilson 274

Public Schs..Principal	Grd	Prgm	Enr/#Cls	SN	
Donald T Shields Elem Sch 223 W Ovilla Rd, Glenn Heights 75154 Shondra Jones	K-4	T	545 32	44%	972/617-4799 Fax 972/617-0495
Eastridge Elem Sch 725 E Ovilla Rd, Red Oak 75154 Michelle Owen	PK-5	T	451 19	51%	972/617-2266 Fax 972/617-4759
H A Wooden Elem Sch 200 Louise Ritter Blvd, Red Oak 75154 Rebecca Vega	PK-4	T	540 25	49%	972/617-2977 Fax 972/617-4760
Ischolars Magnet Academy 109 W Red Oak Rd, Red Oak 75154 Tim Day	3-9		41		972/617-4747
Red Oak Elem Sch 200 Valley Ridge Dr, Red Oak 75154 Megan Corns	PK-4	T	600 28	52%	972/617-3523 Fax 972/576-3423
Red Oak High Sch 220 S State Highway 342, Red Oak 75154 Miller Beaird	9-12	T	1,835 60	38%	972/617-3535 Fax 972/617-4796
Red Oak Middle Sch 154 Louise Ritter Blvd, Red Oak 75154 Howard Gatewood	6-8	T	1,378 40	47%	972/617-0066 Fax 972/617-4786
Russell Schupmann Elem Sch 401 E Ovilla Rd, Glenn Heights 75154 Ashley Jackson	PK-5	T	411 50	58%	972/617-2685 Fax 972/576-5784

• **Waxahachie Ind School Dist** PID: 01015292 972/923-4631
411 N Gibson St, Waxahachie 75165 Fax 972/923-4759

Schools: 16 \ **Teachers:** 592 \ **Students:** 9,481 \ **Special Ed Students:** 999 \ **LEP Students:** 635 \ **Ethnic:** Asian 1%, African American 12%, Hispanic 35%, Native American: 1%, Caucasian 52% \ **Exp:** $435 (High) \ **Poverty:** 11% \ **Title I:** $1,168,116 \ **Special Education:** $1,442,000 \ **Open-Close:** 08/05 - 05/28 \ **DTBP:** $171 (High) \

Bonny Cain 1
Jacob Perry 3
Tiffany Rivera 5
Melissa Bousquet 7*
Julie Hastings 11,298
Lee Auvenshine 15,68
Melissa Cobb 30
Dana James 40
Melissa Abadie 43,285
Stace Johnson 46
Tricia Peyrot 49,52,55
Dusty Autrey 67
Debbie Needham 73
Jeff Robinson 76
Ashley Cieri 286
Ryan Kahlden 2,15
Kam Bridgers 4
Greg Reed 6
Lisa Mott 8
Letty Bernal 12,13,296
Dustin Binnicker 27
Ginger Robinson 36,69,294
Andrea Kline 41
Theresa Smithey 44
Alison Frary 47
Audrey Thomas 58
Jenny Bridges 71
Allison Mendelsohn 76
Mike Morgan 79
Eli Saenz 295

Public Schs..Principal	Grd	Prgm	Enr/#Cls	SN	
Coleman Junior High Sch 1000 N Dallas Hwy, Waxahachie 75165 Brad Andrews	6-8		900		972/923-4790 Fax 972/923-4621
Dunaway Elem Sch 600 S Highway 77, Waxahachie 75165 Emily Camarena	K-5	T	565 30	69%	972/923-4646 Fax 972/923-4752
Eddie Finley Jr High Sch 2401 Brown St, Waxahachie 75165 Derek Zandt	6-8	GTV	650 56	58%	972/923-4680 Fax 972/923-4687
Margaret L Felty Elem Sch 231 Park Place Blvd, Waxahachie 75165 Caroline Kazda	PK-5		651	25%	972/923-4616 Fax 972/923-9394
Marvin Elem Sch 110 Brown St, Waxahachie 75165 Christy Bailey	K-5	T	384 31	71%	972/923-4670 Fax 972/923-4677
Northside Elem Sch 801 Brown St, Waxahachie 75165 Jennifer Burns	PK-5	T	457 26	51%	972/923-4610 Fax 972/923-4750
Oliver E Clift Elem Sch 650 Parks School House Rd, Waxahachie 75165 Christi Kubin	K-5	T	375	71%	972/923-4720 Fax 972/937-5367
Robbie E Howard Jr High Sch 265 Broadhead Rd, Waxahachie 75165 Ryan Cavazos	6-8	T	1,005	42%	972/923-4771 Fax 972/923-3817
Shackelford Elem Sch 1001 Butcher Rd, Waxahachie 75165 Rusty East	PK-5		602 40	29%	972/923-4666 Fax 972/923-4753
Turner Prekindergarten Academy 614 N Getzendaner St, Waxahachie 75165 Stefani Foster	PK-PK		188		972/923-4690 Fax 972/923-4699
Waxahachie Challenge Academy 1000 N Highway 77, Waxahachie 75165 Dr Al Benskin	9-12	A	15		972/923-4695 Fax 972/923-4717
ⓐ Waxahachie Global High Sch 275 Indian Dr, Waxahachie 75165 Ken Lynch	9-12		370 3	26%	972/923-4761 Fax 972/923-4738
Waxahachie High Sch 3001 US Hwy 287 Bypass, Waxahachie 75167 Tonya Harris	9-12	TV	2,204 75	43%	972/923-4600 Fax 972/923-4617
ⓐ Waxahachie HS of Choice 1000 N Highway 77, Waxahachie 75165 Ryan Cavazos	9-12	T	32	60%	972/923-4758 Fax 972/923-4717

---

1 Superintendent	8 Curric/Instruct K-12	19 Chief Financial Officer	29 Family/Consumer Science	39 Social Studies K-12	49 English/Lang Arts Elem	59 Special Education Elem	69 Academic Assessment
2 Bus/Finance/Purchasing	9 Curric/Instruct Elem	20 Art K-12	30 Adult Education	40 Social Studies Elem	50 English/Lang Arts Sec	60 Special Education Sec	70 Research/Development
3 Buildings And Grounds	10 Curric/Instruct Sec	21 Art Elem	31 Career/Sch-to-Work K-12	41 Social Studies Sec	51 Reading K-12	61 Foreign/World Lang K-12	71 Public Information
4 Food Service	11 Federal Program	22 Art Sec	32 Career/Sch-to-Work Elem	42 Science K-12	52 Reading Elem	62 Foreign/World Lang Elem	72 Summer School
5 Transportation	12 Title I	23 Music K-12	33 Career/Sch-to-Work Sec	43 Science Elem	53 Reading Sec	63 Foreign/World Lang Sec	73 Instructional Tech
6 Athletic	13 Title V	24 Music Elem	34 Early Childhood Ed	44 Science Sec	54 Remedial Reading K-12	64 Religious Education K-12	74 Inservice Training
7 Health Services	15 Asst Superintendent	25 Music Sec	35 Health/Phys Education	45 Math K-12	55 Remedial Reading Elem	65 Religious Education Elem	75 Marketing/Distributive
	16 Instructional Media Svcs	26 Business Education	36 Guidance Services K-12	46 Math Elem	56 Remedial Reading Sec	66 Religious Education Sec	76 Info Systems
	17 Chief Operations Officer	27 Career & Tech Ed	37 Guidance Services Elem	47 Math Sec	57 Bilingual/ELL	67 School Board President	77 Psychological Assess
	18 Chief Academic Officer	28 Technology Education	38 Guidance Services Sec	48 English/Lang Arts K-12	58 Special Education K-12	68 Teacher Personnel	78 Affirmative Action

Texas School Directory

Erath County

Wedgeworth Elem Sch	K-5	T	682	61%	972/923-4640
405 Solon Rd, Waxahachie 75165			33		Fax 972/923-4751
Lynda Solis					
Wilemon Steam Academy	K-5		401		972/923-4780
600 W 2nd St, Waxahachie 75165					
Kate Authier					

ELLIS CATHOLIC SCHOOLS

• **Diocese of Dallas Ed Office** PID: 01012367
Listing includes only schools located in this county. See District Index for location of Diocesan Offices.

Catholic Schs..Principal	Grd	Prgm	Enr/#Cls SN	
St Joseph Catholic Sch	PK-8		130	972/937-0956
506 E Marvin Ave, Waxahachie 75165			15	Fax 972/937-1742
Autumn Helland				

ELLIS PRIVATE SCHOOLS

Private Schs..Principal	Grd	Prgm	Enr/#Cls SN	
First Christian Day Sch	PK-8		100	972/937-1952
1109 Brown St, Waxahachie 75165			17	Fax 972/937-1997
Debbie Aday				
Ovilla Christian Sch	PK-12		400	972/617-1177
3251 Ovilla Rd, Red Oak 75154			38	Fax 469/218-0135
Lezlie Rozier \ Steven Johnston				f t
Waxahachie Preparatory Academy	K-12		160	972/937-0440
1000 Butcher Rd, Waxahachie 75165				
Scott Marks				

ERATH COUNTY

ERATH PUBLIC SCHOOLS

• **Bluff Dale Ind Sch Dist** PID: 01016997   254/728-3277
710 W Church St, Bluff Dale 76433   Fax 254/728-3298

Schools: 1 \ **Teachers:** 14 \ **Students:** 243 \ **Special Ed Students:** 7 \ **Ethnic:** Hispanic 8%, Native American: 1%, Caucasian 91% \ **Exp:** $855 (High) \ **Poverty:** 13% \ **Title I:** $18,158 \ **Open-Close:** 08/27 - 06/01

John Taylor 1,11,83,288		Christine Murphy 2*	
Dean Edwards 11,83,288		James Barton 67	
Nancy Lachowicz 69*		Lisa Logan 73,286*	

Public Schs..Principal	Grd	Prgm	Enr/#Cls SN	
Bluff Dale Elem Sch	PK-12	T	243	37% 254/728-3277
710 W Church St, Bluff Dale 76433			10	
John Taylor				

• **Dublin Ind School Dist** PID: 01017018   254/445-3341
420 Post Oak St, Dublin 76446   Fax 254/445-3345

Schools: 3 \ **Teachers:** 97 \ **Students:** 1,200 \ **Special Ed Students:** 78 \ **LEP Students:** 205 \ **College-Bound:** 75% \ **Ethnic:** African American 1%, Hispanic 63%, Caucasian 35% \ **Exp:** $366 (High) \ **Poverty:** 29% \ **Title I:** $587,097 \ **Open-Close:** 08/21 - 05/28 \ f t

Rodney Schnider 1	Ginny Moiser 2	
Clyde Shubert 3,5	Nocona Estes 4*	
Nancy Johnson 7*	Mellissa Summers 8,11,31,57,273,286,288,296	
Peggy Gruell 16*	Samantha Abila 58	
Jeff Weaver 67	Kassi Eads 68,78	
Paige Johnson 69*	Craig Parks 73,84	

Public Schs..Principal	Grd	Prgm	Enr/#Cls SN	
Dublin Elem Sch	PK-3	T	416	80% 254/445-2577
701 Thomas St, Dublin 76446			27	Fax 254/445-2750
Kalley Mitchell				
Dublin High Sch	7-12	GTV	488	72% 254/445-0362
2233 E State Highway 6, Dublin 76446			24	Fax 254/445-1706
Norma Briseno \ Chesta Schneider				f
Dublin Intermediate Sch	4-6	T	289	77% 254/445-2618
609 N Thomas, Dublin 76446			15	Fax 254/445-3383
Chesta Schneider				

• **Huckabay Ind School Dist** PID: 01017056   254/968-5274
200 County Road 421, Stephenville 76401   Fax 254/965-3740

Schools: 1 \ **Teachers:** 21 \ **Students:** 260 \ **Special Ed Students:** 7 \ **LEP Students:** 4 \ **College-Bound:** 70% \ **Ethnic:** Hispanic 17%, Native American: 2%, Caucasian 80% \ **Exp:** $345 (High) \ **Poverty:** 13% \ **Title I:** $31,361 \ **Open-Close:** 08/26 - 05/28 \ **DTBP:** $359 (High)

Troy Roberts 1,83,84	Tammy Shipman 2
Kayla Walls 6*	Shane Stegall 67

Public Schs..Principal	Grd	Prgm	Enr/#Cls SN	
Huckabay Sch	K-12	TV	260	31% 254/968-8476
200 County Road 421, Stephenville 76401			24	Fax 254/965-3140
Wes Corzine				

• **Lingleville Ind School Dist** PID: 01017082   254/968-2596
21261 N FM 219, Lingleville 76461   Fax 254/965-5821

Schools: 1 \ **Teachers:** 23 \ **Students:** 275 \ **Special Ed Students:** 14 \ **LEP Students:** 50 \ **College-Bound:** 65% \ **Ethnic:** Hispanic 48%, Caucasian 52% \ **Exp:** $362 (High) \ **Poverty:** 21% \ **Title I:** $86,357 \ **Open-Close:** 08/26 - 05/28 \ **DTBP:** $367 (High)

Curtis Haley 1,11	Paula Hidditts 2
Oscar Rodriguez 3*	Scott Wells 8,57,88,274,286,288*
Barbara Vaden 16,82*	Melissa Helms 27,31*
Jenny Winter 36,83*	Karen Keith 58*
Larry Griffin 67	Rhonda Bays 73,76*

Public Schs..Principal	Grd	Prgm	Enr/#Cls SN	
Lingleville Sch	PK-12	TV	275	49% 254/968-2596
21261 N FM 219, Lingleville 76461			25	
Scott Wells				

---

9 Student Personnel	91 Safety/Security	275 Response To Intervention	298 Grant Writer/Ptnrships	**School Programs**	**Social Media**	
0 Driver Ed/Safety	92 Magnet School	277 Remedial Math K-12	750 Chief Innovation Officer	A = Alternative Program		
1 Gifted/Talented	93 Parental Involvement	280 Literacy Coach	751 Chief of Staff	G = Adult Classes	f = Facebook	
2 Video Services	95 Tech Prep Program	285 STEM	752 Social Emotional Learning	M = Magnet Program		
3 Substance Abuse Prev	97 Chief Infomation Officer	286 Digital Learning		T = Title I Schoolwide	t = Twitter	
4 Erate	98 Chief Technology Officer	288 Common Core Standards	**Other School Types**	V = Career & Tech Ed Programs		
5 AIDS Education	270 Accountability	294 Accountability	Ⓐ = Alternative School			
3 Alternative/At Risk	271 Migrant Education	295 Network System	Ⓒ = Charter School	New Schools are shaded		
9 Multi-Cultural Curriculum	273 Teacher Mentor	296 Title II Programs	Ⓜ = Magnet School	New Superintendents and Principals are bold		
9 Social Work	274 Before/After Sch	297 Webmaster	Ⓨ = Year-Round School	Personnel with email addresses are underscored		**TX—143**

Falls County

Market Data Retrieval

- **Morgan Mill Ind School Dist** PID: 01017111   254/968-4921
  Highway 281, Morgan Mill 76465   Fax 254/968-4814

Schools: 1 \ **Teachers:** 11 \ **Students:** 125 \ **Special Ed Students:** 7 \ **LEP Students:** 3 \ **Ethnic:** Hispanic 15%, Caucasian 85% \ **Exp:** $469 (High) \ **Poverty:** 8% \ **Title I:** $14,222 \ **Open-Close:** 08/23 - 05/25 \ **DTBP:** $318 (High)

Wendy Sanders 1   Dr Shannon Buchanan 67
Maggie Burton 270,271

Public Schs..Principal	Grd	Prgm	Enr/#Cls	SN	
Morgan Mill Elem Sch Highway 281, Morgan Mill 76465 Barrett Hutchison	PK-8	T	125 9	30%	254/968-4921

- **Stephenville Ind School Dist** PID: 01017135   254/968-7990
  2655 W Overhill Dr, Stephenville 76401   Fax 254/968-5942

Schools: 6 \ **Teachers:** 247 \ **Students:** 3,650 \ **Special Ed Students:** 261 \ **LEP Students:** 359 \ **College-Bound:** 66% \ **Ethnic:** Asian 1%, African American 1%, Hispanic 33%, Native American: 1%, Caucasian 64% \ **Exp:** $529 (High) \ **Poverty:** 14% \ **Title I:** $658,391 \ **Special Education:** $642,000 \ **Open-Close:** 08/21 - 05/28 \ **DTBP:** $158 (High) \ E

Matt Underwood 1   Deborah Hummel 2
Keith Starnes 3,91   Zachery Robinson 3
Cheryl Dowell 4   David Woods 5
Gloria Quiroz 5   Jennifer Ryan 8,57,288
Shelby Womack .... 27,73*   Stephanie Atchley 58*
Dr Ann Calahan 67   Kathy Haynes 68*
Renee Goodwin 69,294   Luke Reagor 73*
Julie Griffin 76   Audrey Warren 80

Public Schs..Principal	Grd	Prgm	Enr/#Cls	SN	
Central Elem Sch 780 W Washington St, Stephenville 76401 **Esther Tucker**	PK-K	T	413 25	61%	254/965-3716 Fax 254/965-5319 E
Chamberlin Elem Sch 1601 W Frey St, Stephenville 76401 Jennifer Salyards	1-2	T	515 28	51%	254/968-2311 Fax 254/968-5399
Gilbert Intermediate Sch 950 N Dale Ave, Stephenville 76401 Victor Sauceda	5-6	T	594 40	50%	254/968-4664 Fax 254/968-8696
Henderson Junior High Sch 2798 W Frey St, Stephenville 76401 Brad Burleson	7-8	T	523 50	42%	254/968-6967 Fax 254/965-7018
Hook Elem Sch 1067 W Jones St, Stephenville 76401 Daresa Rhine	3-4	T	546 24	49%	254/968-3213 Fax 254/968-6758
Stephenville High Sch 2650 W Overhill Dr, Stephenville 76401 Stephanie Traweek	9-12	GV	1,079 54	36%	254/968-4141 Fax 254/968-4897

- **Three Way Ind School Dist** PID: 01017185   254/965-6496
  247 County Road 207, Stephenville 76401   Fax 254/965-3357

Schools: 2 \ **Teachers:** 9 \ **Students:** 190 \ **Special Ed Students:** 3 \ **LEP Students:** 18 \ **Ethnic:** Hispanic 56%, Caucasian 44% \ **Exp:** $734 (High) \ **Poverty:** 11% \ **Title I:** $15,313 \ **Open-Close:** 08/19 - 05/25 \ **DTBP:** $362 (High)

Paul Ryan 1,11,84   Jennifer Bailey 2
Troy Sparks 5   Allison Wright 59*

Tracie Hankins 67   Carlos Ortiz 73

Public Schs..Principal	Grd	Prgm	Enr/#Cls	SN	
Three Way Elem Sch 247 County Road 207, Stephenville 76401 Kayla Sparks	PK-8	T	165 9	83%	254/965-6496
Threeway High Sch 247 County Road 207, Stephenville 76401 Randall Ryan	9-10		47		254/965-9496

ERATH PRIVATE SCHOOLS

Private Schs..Principal	Grd	Prgm	Enr/#Cls	SN	
Stephenville Christian Sch 1120 County Road 351, Stephenville 76401 Greg Judy	PK-6		57 5		254/965-4821

FALLS COUNTY

FALLS PUBLIC SCHOOLS

- **Chilton Ind School Dist** PID: 01017202   254/546-1200
  905 Durango Ave, Chilton 76632   Fax 254/546-1201

Schools: 1 \ **Teachers:** 42 \ **Students:** 540 \ **Special Ed Students:** 61 \ **LEP Students:** 77 \ **College-Bound:** 60% \ **Ethnic:** African American 15%, Hispanic 62%, Caucasian 23% \ **Exp:** $384 (High) \ **Poverty:** 28% \ **Title I:** $157,416 \ **Open-Close:** 08/26 - 05/21 \ **DTBP:** $342 (High)

Brandon Hubbard 1,11   Lahoma Taylor 2
Willis Childers 3   Chris Jones 6*
Leslie Harris .... 8,12,69,88*   Keimesha Alexander 58*
Rodney Hall 67   Ronnie Lawson 73*

Public Schs..Principal	Grd	Prgm	Enr/#Cls	SN	
Chilton Sch 905 Durango Ave, Chilton 76632 Gladys Graves \ **Leon Darden**	PK-12	TV	540 54	86%	254/546-1200

- **Marlin Ind School Dist** PID: 01017238   254/883-3585
  130 Coleman St, Marlin 76661   Fax 254/883-6612

Schools: 3 \ **Teachers:** 77 \ **Students:** 1,000 \ **Special Ed Students:** 96 \ **LEP Students:** 111 \ **College-Bound:** 75% \ **Ethnic:** African American 62%, Hispanic 31%, Caucasian 6% \ **Exp:** $478 (High) \ **Poverty:** 38% \ **Title I:** $692,688 \ **Special Education:** $261,000 \ **Open-Close:** 08/20 - 05/29 \ **DTBP:** $335 (High)

Remy Godfrey 1   Pat Lewis 2,19
Vince Margoitta .... 3,5*   Barbara Brown 4
Marshall Higgins 5   Remy Hodge 8
Dr Michael Seabolt 11   Adam LeJeune 16,288
Nancy Laster .... 16*   Edward Rogers 36*
Billy Johnson 67   Rockney Terry 73*

Texas School Directory — Fannin County

Public Schs..Principal	Grd	Prgm	Enr/#Cls	SN	
Marlin Elem Sch 602 Donnaho St, Marlin 76661 Kimberly McKnight	PK-5	A	419 33		254/883-3232 Fax 254/883-5237
Marlin High Sch 1400 Capps St, Marlin 76661 Pamela Thomas	9-12	ATV	200 22	98%	254/883-2394 Fax 254/883-3470
Marlin Middle Sch 678 Success Dr, Marlin 76661 Patti Ward	6-8	A	240 17		254/883-9241 Fax 254/883-6491

● **Rosebud-Lott Ind School Dist** PID: 01017276   254/583-4510
1789 US Highway 77, Lott 76656   Fax 254/583-4469

Schools: 3 \ *Teachers:* 57 \ *Students:* 630 \ *Special Ed Students:* 85 \ *LEP Students:* 21 \ *Ethnic:* African American 15%, Hispanic 35%, Caucasian 49% \ *Exp:* $363 (High) \ *Poverty:* 24% \ *Title I:* $256,480 \ *Open-Close:* 08/19 - 05/20 \ *DTBP:* $273 (High)

Dr Steve Brownlee 1   Valerie Gausemeier 2*
Robby Sims 3   Steffanie Stone 4
Tony Stone 5   Brad Ballard 6*
Natalie Parcus 11,288   Julie Bennett 67
Larry Dutcher 73   Randall Jennings 73

Public Schs..Principal	Grd	Prgm	Enr/#Cls	SN	
Rosebud-Lott Elem Sch 1813 US Highway 77, Lott 76656 Alushka Driska	PK-6	T	350 9	79%	254/583-7965 Fax 254/583-2642
Rosebud-Lott High Sch 1789 US Highway 77, Lott 76656 **Jerrod Barton**	9-12	T	203	49%	254/583-7967 Fax 254/583-1130
Rosebud-Lott Middle Sch 1789 US Highway 77, Lott 76656 Phil Johanson	7-8	ATV	103 45	66%	254/583-7962 Fax 254/583-2904

● **Westphalia Ind School Dist** PID: 01017329   254/584-4988
124 County Road 3000, Lott 76656   Fax 254/584-2963

Schools: 1 \ *Teachers:* 19 \ *Students:* 155 \ *Special Ed Students:* 17 \ *Ethnic:* African American 1%, Hispanic 16%, Caucasian 84% \ *Exp:* $348 (High) \ *Poverty:* 12% \ *Title I:* $629 \ *Open-Close:* 08/15 - 05/21 \ *DTBP:* $352 (High)

Robert Hudson 1,11   Shelley Thornton 2
Robert Hudson ....6,69,83,270*   Kimberly Nejtek 57,59*
Michelle Weaver 67   Michael Johnson 73,76,295*

Public Schs..Principal	Grd	Prgm	Enr/#Cls	SN	
Westphalia Sch 124 County Road 3000, Lott 76656 Robert Hudson	K-8		155 12	24%	254/584-4988

FANNIN COUNTY

FANNIN PUBLIC SCHOOLS

● **Bonham Ind School Dist** PID: 01017367   903/583-5526
1005 Chestnut St, Bonham 75418   Fax 903/583-8463

Schools: 5 \ *Teachers:* 137 \ *Students:* 1,890 \ *Special Ed Students:* 252 \ *LEP Students:* 198 \ *College-Bound:* 44% \ *Ethnic:* Asian 1%, African American 8%, Hispanic 27%, Native American: 1%, Caucasian 64% \ *Exp:* $544 (High) \ *Poverty:* 18% \ *Title I:* $468,711 \ *Open-Close:* 08/21 - 05/28 \ *DTBP:* $356 (High) \ f t

Alicia Lang 2   Bill Wakefield 3,91
Claude Lewis 3   Phyllis Kinnaird 4
Concan Humphrey 5   Ryan Crock 6*
Lori Flowers ....7*   Faith Anne Cheeck 8,11,288
Angie Richardson 13,58   Kelly Trompler 15,68,74,79,273
April Peterson ....16*   Rory Hilliard 34
Suzanne Kennedy ....34*   Chance Roberts 67

Public Schs..Principal	Grd	Prgm	Enr/#Cls	SN	
Bailey Inglish Erly Chldhd Ctr 201 E 10th St, Bonham 75418 Rory Hillard	PK-PK	T	205 8	92%	903/583-8141 Fax 903/583-0025
Bonham High Sch 1002 War Path St, Bonham 75418 Panchi Scown	9-12	ATV	489 60	57%	903/583-5567 Fax 903/583-5560
Finley-Oates Elem Sch 1901 Albert Broadfoot St, Bonham 75418 Mary Lou Fox	K-3	T	549 31	79%	903/640-4090 Fax 903/640-8140
I W Evans Intermediate Sch 1300 N Main St, Bonham 75418 Karli Fowler	4-6	T	400 21	72%	903/583-2914 Fax 903/640-1056 f
L H Rather Junior High Sch 1201 N Main St, Bonham 75418 Traci Daniel	7-8	TV	252 25	67%	903/583-7474 Fax 903/583-3713 f t

● **Dodd City Ind School Dist** PID: 01017422   903/583-7585
602 N Main St, Dodd City 75438   Fax 903/583-9545

Schools: 1 \ *Teachers:* 33 \ *Students:* 370 \ *Special Ed Students:* 32 \ *LEP Students:* 10 \ *College-Bound:* 75% \ *Ethnic:* Asian 1%, Hispanic 8%, Caucasian 91% \ *Exp:* $413 (High) \ *Poverty:* 10% \ *Title I:* $29,623 \ *Open-Close:* 08/19 - 05/21 \ *DTBP:* $346 (High)

Dr Jon Hill 1,83   Lesia Bridges 2,8,11,16,58,74,294,298*
Alex Stevenson ....6*   Alisha Hale 7
Angie Freeman ....13,31,36,69,77,88* Juliana Wild 57*
Thomas Lackey 67   Joanna Collida 274*

Public Schs..Principal	Grd	Prgm	Enr/#Cls	SN	
Dodd City Sch 602 N Main St, Dodd City 75438 **Bruce Maupin** \ Joanna Collida	PK-12	TV	370 23	42%	903/583-7585

---

79 Student Personnel 91 Safety/Security 275 Response To Intervention 298 Grant Writer/Ptnrships
80 Driver Ed/Safety 92 Magnet School 277 Remedial Math K-12 750 Chief Innovation Officer
81 Gifted/Talented 93 Parental Involvement 280 Literacy Coach 751 Chief of Staff
82 Video Services 95 Tech Prep Program 285 STEM 752 Social Emotional Learning
83 Substance Abuse Prev 97 Chief Information Officer 286 Digital Learning
84 Erate 98 Chief Technology Officer 288 Common Core Standards **Other School Types**
85 AIDS Education 270 Character Education 294 Accountability Ⓐ = Alternative School
88 Alternative/At Risk 271 Migrant Education 295 Network System Ⓒ = Charter School
89 Multi-Cultural Curriculum 273 Teacher Mentor 296 Title II Programs Ⓜ = Magnet School
90 Social Work 274 Before/After Sch 297 Webmaster Ⓨ = Year-Round School

School Programs
A = Alternative Program
G = Adult Classes
M = Magnet Program
T = Title I Schoolwide
V = Career & Tech Ed Programs

Social Media
f = Facebook
t = Twitter

New Schools are shaded
New Superintendents and Principals are bold
Personnel with email addresses are underscored

Fannin County

Ector Ind School Dist PID: 01017458
301 S Main St, Ector 75439
903/961-2355
Fax 903/961-2110

> **Schools:** 1 \ **Teachers:** 24 \ **Students:** 250 \ **Special Ed Students:** 34 \ **LEP Students:** 3 \ **College-Bound:** 85% \ **Ethnic:** Asian 3%, African American 2%, Hispanic 13%, Caucasian 83% \ **Exp:** $487 (High) \ **Poverty:** 14% \ **Title I:** $51,385 \ **Open-Close:** 08/19 - 05/22 \ **DTBP:** $325 (High)

Gary Bohannon 1
Joe Detiller 3*
Terry Johnson 6*
Betty Day 58*
Jeff Glaser 295*
Deborah Williams 2
Roger Morris 5,275*
Dawn Bohannon 16,73*
John Harris 67

Public Schs..Principal	Grd	Prgm	Enr/#Cls	SN	
Ector Sch 301 S Main St, Ector 75439 Jennifer Morris \ Bradford Evans	K-12	T	250 20	38%	903/961-2355

Honey Grove Ind School Dist PID: 01017472
1206 17th St, Honey Grove 75446
903/378-2264
Fax 903/900-4935

> **Schools:** 3 \ **Teachers:** 46 \ **Students:** 605 \ **Special Ed Students:** 71 \ **LEP Students:** 44 \ **College-Bound:** 46% \ **Ethnic:** African American 10%, Hispanic 21%, Native American: 1%, Caucasian 68% \ **Exp:** $535 (High) \ **Poverty:** 20% \ **Title I:** $146,975 \ **Open-Close:** 08/14 - 05/22 \ **DTBP:** $350 (High)

Todd Morrison 1,11
J Caraway 3*
Glenn Schulte 6
Cathrine Sherwood 8,12*
Zeb Tindel 31
Sandra Rubio 57*
Josh Russell 67
Lori Lane 2
Margo Oats 4*
Joy Stroud 7*
Joshua Edmondson 16,73*
Lyn Scott 36,69,77,752
Angie Richardson 58
Michael Goss 298

Public Schs..Principal	Grd	Prgm	Enr/#Cls	SN	
Honey Grove Elem Sch 1206 17th St, Honey Grove 75446 Mitzi Sherwood	PK-5	T	275 25	69%	903/378-2264 Fax 903/900-4725
Honey Grove High Sch 1208 17th St, Honey Grove 75446 Tammy Mariani	9-12	TV	197 23	55%	903/378-2264 Fax 903/900-4725
Honey Grove Middle Sch 1204 17th St, Honey Grove 75446 Lee Frost	6-8	T	148 11	54%	903/378-2264 Fax 903/900-4725

Leonard Ind School Dist PID: 01017501
1 Tiger Aly, Leonard 75452
903/587-2318
Fax 903/587-2845

> **Schools:** 4 \ **Teachers:** 60 \ **Students:** 820 \ **Special Ed Students:** 82 \ **LEP Students:** 30 \ **College-Bound:** 56% \ **Ethnic:** African American 3%, Hispanic 19%, Native American: 2%, Caucasian 76% \ **Exp:** $574 (High) \ **Poverty:** 13% \ **Title I:** $110,793 \ **Open-Close:** 08/19 - 05/22 \ **DTBP:** $341 (High)

Brad Maxwell 1
Dwain Campbell 3,5
Shane Fletcher 6*
Jeff Johnson 11,84,296
John Davis 27
Billy Watson 67
Tracy Howell 271*
Janna Layman 2,298
Sherry Cooper 4*
Nancy Zachary 7*
Pam McCarley 16*
Kacie Littrell 31,36,58,69,83,88*
Kim Wheeler 73,295*

Public Schs..Principal	Grd	Prgm	Enr/#Cls	SN	
Leonard Elem Sch 300 E Mulberry St, Leonard 75452 Regina Blain	PK-3	T	279 17	65%	903/587-2316 Fax 903/587-2392
Leonard High Sch 1000 2N Poplar St, Leonard 75452 Cody Plake	9-12	TV	291 30	46%	903/587-3556 Fax 903/587-8011
Leonard Intermediate Sch 600 E Hackberry, Leonard 75452 Sarah Day	4-5	T	138 7	62%	903/587-8303 Fax 903/587-4414
Leonard Junior High Sch 500 E Hackberry St, Leonard 75452 Tammy Hutchings	6-8	T	212 16	55%	903/587-2315 Fax 903/587-2228

Sam Rayburn Ind School Dist PID: 01017549
9363 E FM 273, Ivanhoe 75447
903/664-2255
Fax 903/664-2406

> **Schools:** 1 \ **Teachers:** 44 \ **Students:** 500 \ **Special Ed Students:** 55 \ **LEP Students:** 12 \ **College-Bound:** 45% \ **Ethnic:** African American 2%, Hispanic 9%, Caucasian 89% \ **Exp:** $654 (High) \ **Poverty:** 15% \ **Title I:** $91,973 \ **Open-Close:** 08/19 - 05/21 \ **DTBP:** $366 (High)

Cole McClendon 1
Kyle Baker 3*
Wendy Keeton 10,60,69,73,286,295*
Stephanie Klein 37*
Lynn Gibbs 67
Patty Foreman 2,12
Jim Shaw 8,11,58,271,273,275*
Kim Hopkins 16*
Jennifer Voan 38*

Public Schs..Principal	Grd	Prgm	Enr/#Cls	SN	
Sam Rayburn Sch 9363 E FM 273, Ivanhoe 75447 Julie Symanik	PK-12	TV	500 30	39%	903/664-2165

Savoy Ind School Dist PID: 01017575
302 W Hayes St, Savoy 75479
903/965-5262
Fax 903/965-7282

> **Schools:** 2 \ **Teachers:** 27 \ **Students:** 320 \ **Special Ed Students:** 26 \ **College-Bound:** 70% \ **Ethnic:** Asian 1%, African American 1%, Hispanic 5%, Native American: 1%, Caucasian 92% \ **Exp:** $356 (High) \ **Poverty:** 9% \ **Title I:** $29,032 \ **Open-Close:** 08/21 - 05/27 \ **DTBP:** $305 (High)

Brian Neal 1
Joe Baca 3,5*
Clay Wilson 6*
Stephanie Sweet 58*
Rapee Sriritarat 73,295*
Denise Pugh 2
Georgina Green 4*
Michael Smith 10*
Terry Lewis 67
Leslie Sanders 85*

Public Schs..Principal	Grd	Prgm	Enr/#Cls	SN	
Savoy Elem Sch 302 W Hayes St, Savoy 75479 Danny Henderson	PK-6	T	190 11	48%	903/965-7738 Fax 903/965-4389
Savoy High Sch 605 E Hayes St, Savoy 75479 Michael Smith	7-12	TV	127	37%	903/965-4024 Fax 903/965-5608

Trenton Ind School Dist PID: 01017604
702 S Ballentine St, Trenton 75490
903/989-2245
Fax 903/989-2767

> **Schools:** 3 \ **Teachers:** 42 \ **Students:** 568 \ **Special Ed Students:** 51 \ **LEP Students:** 15 \ **College-Bound:** 51% \ **Ethnic:** African American 2%, Hispanic 17%, Native American: 2%, Caucasian 79% \ **Exp:** $326 (High) \ **Poverty:** 13% \ **Title I:** $99,127 \ **Open-Close:** 08/20 - 05/25 \ **DTBP:** $367 (High) \

Rick Foreman 1
Kimberly Anderson 2

1	Superintendent	8	Curric/Instruct K-12	19	Chief Financial Officer	29	Family/Consumer Science	39	Social Studies K-12	49	English/Lang Arts Elem	59	Special Education Elem	69	Academic Assessment
2	Bus/Finance/Purchasing	9	Curric/Instruct Elem	20	Art K-12	30	Adult Education	40	Social Studies Elem	50	English/Lang Arts Sec	60	Special Education Sec	70	Research/Development
3	Buildings And Grounds	10	Curric/Instruct Sec	21	Art Elem	31	Career/Sch-to-Work K-12	41	Social Studies Sec	51	Reading K-12	61	Foreign/World Lang K-12	71	Public Information
4	Food Service	11	Federal Program	22	Art Sec	32	Career/Sch-to-Work Elem	42	Science K-12	52	Reading Elem	62	Foreign/World Lang Elem	72	Summer School
5	Transportation	12	Title I	23	Music K-12	33	Career/Sch-to-Work Sec	43	Science Elem	53	Reading Sec	63	Foreign/World Lang Sec	73	Instructional Tech
6	Athletic	13	Title V	24	Music Elem	34	Early Childhood Ed	44	Science Sec	54	Remedial Reading K-12	64	Religious Education K-12	74	Inservice Training
7	Health Services	15	Asst Superintendent	25	Music Sec	35	Health/Phys Education	45	Math K-12	55	Remedial Reading Elem	65	Religious Education Elem	75	Marketing/Distributive
		16	Instructional Media Svcs	26	Business Education	36	Guidance Services K-12	46	Math Elem	56	Remedial Reading Sec	66	Religious Education Sec	76	Info Systems
		17	Chief Operations Officer	27	Career & Tech Ed	37	Guidance Services Elem	47	Math Sec	57	Bilingual/ELL	67	School Board President	77	Psychological Assess
		18	Chief Academic Officer	28	Technology Education	38	Guidance Services Sec	48	English/Lang Arts K-12	58	Special Education K-12	68	Teacher Personnel	78	Affirmative Action

Texas School Directory   Fayette County

Sonya McTee 4	Mike Jones 6*
Kevin Cannon 11,69,296*	Amy Shaw 31,83,85,88,273*
Jarret Tucker 57,271*	Henry Baker 67
Todd Gruhn 73*	Jamie Doan 270

Public Schs..Principal	Grd	Prgm	Enr/#Cls	SN	
Trenton Elem Sch 105 Witherspoon St, Trenton 75490 Mandi Alexander	PK-4	T	213 15	49%	903/989-2244 Fax 903/989-2415
Trenton High Sch 2289 Farm Market 815, Trenton 75490 Jeremy Strickland	9-12	AV	165 15	37%	903/989-2242 Fax 903/989-5173
Trenton Middle Sch 500 Ballentine St, Trenton 75490 Trent Hamilton	5-8	A	190	40%	903/989-2243 Fax 903/989-2668

FAYETTE COUNTY

FAYETTE PUBLIC SCHOOLS

- **Fayetteville Ind School Dist** PID: 01017666   979/378-4242
  618 N Rusk St, Fayetteville 78940   Fax 979/378-4246

Schools: 1 \ *Teachers:* 20 \ *Students:* 265 \ *Special Ed Students:* 19 \ *LEP Students:* 11 \ *College-Bound:* 75% \ *Ethnic:* African American 1%, Hispanic 15%, Caucasian 83% \ *Exp:* $495 (High) \ *Poverty:* 15% \ *Title I:* $33,265 \ *Open-Close:* 08/19 - 05/20 \ *DTBP:* $37 (Low)

Jeff Harvey 1,11,83,288	Michelle Bertsch 2
Clint Jaeger 6*	Brynn Lopez 8,36,270,273
Ray Brothers 16,31,73,295	Lisa Dyer 57*
Vincent Orsak 67	

Public Schs..Principal	Grd	Prgm	Enr/#Cls	SN	
Fayetteville Sch 618 N Rusk St, Fayetteville 78940 Brynn Lopez	PK-12	V	265 22	28%	979/378-4242

- **Flatonia Ind School Dist** PID: 01017692   361/865-2941
  400 E 4th St, Flatonia 78941   Fax 361/865-2940

Schools: 3 \ *Teachers:* 56 \ *Students:* 580 \ *Special Ed Students:* 53 \ *LEP Students:* 43 \ *College-Bound:* 40% \ *Ethnic:* Asian 1%, African American 4%, Hispanic 56%, Caucasian 39% \ *Exp:* $380 (High) \ *Poverty:* 20% \ *Title I:* $140,906 \ *Open-Close:* 08/19 - 05/21 \ *DTBP:* $427 (High)

Dr Andy Reddock 1	Rodney Stryk 2*
Rodney Stryk 2,3,5	Chris Freytag 6*
Ashley Grahmann 8*	Robin Branecky 11*
Deanne Holloway 16,73*	Delia Moeller 16,73*
Tim Rowell 67	Marianna Herrera 271*

Public Schs..Principal	Grd	Prgm	Enr/#Cls	SN	
Flatonia Elem Sch 400 E 4th St, Flatonia 78941 Laura Kutac	PK-5	T	250 20	61%	361/865-2941 Fax 361/865-2945
Flatonia High Sch 400 E 4th St, Flatonia 78941 Tandy Betak	6-12	ATV	297 20	60%	361/865-2941 Fax 361/865-2944
Whispering Hills Achieve Ctr 4110 FM 609, Flatonia 78941 Robin Branecky	Spec		13	81%	361/865-3083

- **La Grange Ind School Dist** PID: 01017721   979/968-7000
  560 N Monroe St, La Grange 78945   Fax 979/968-8155

Schools: 4 \ *Teachers:* 142 \ *Students:* 2,350 \ *Special Ed Students:* 167 \ *LEP Students:* 246 \ *College-Bound:* 56% \ *Ethnic:* Asian 1%, African American 10%, Hispanic 40%, Caucasian 49% \ *Exp:* $274 (Med) \ *Poverty:* 13% \ *Title I:* $300,183 \ *Special Education:* $205,000 \ *Open-Close:* 08/15 - 05/28 \ *DTBP:* $268 (High) \ 🛈

Bill Wagner 1	Neal Miller 3,4,5*
Matt Kates 6	Kari Willrich 7
Shelly Landreth 8*	Nicole Ramirez 11
Stacy Eilers 15	Kim Miori 57*
Kathryn Wyman 58	Gary Drab 67
Michael Mach 73*	Heather Smith 81

Public Schs..Principal	Grd	Prgm	Enr/#Cls	SN	
Hermes Elem Sch 631 E Milam St, La Grange 78945 Stacy Eilers	PK-6	T	1,006 31	57%	979/968-4100 Fax 979/968-6327
La Grange High Sch 820 S Vail St, La Grange 78945 John Pineda	9-12	TV	629 40	40%	979/968-4800 Fax 979/968-6744
La Grange Intermediate Sch 192 S Vail St, La Grange 78945 Ray Morrow	4-6		418 21		979/968-4700 Fax 979/968-5694
La Grange Middle Sch 820 S Vail St, La Grange 78945 Sarah Otto	7-8	T	302 23	49%	979/968-4747 Fax 979/968-6012

- **Round Top-Carmine Ind Sch Dist** PID: 01017771   979/278-3252
  378 Centennial St, Carmine 78932   Fax 979/278-3063

Schools: 2 \ *Teachers:* 25 \ *Students:* 283 \ *Special Ed Students:* 29 \ *LEP Students:* 18 \ *College-Bound:* 92% \ *Ethnic:* African American 6%, Hispanic 20%, Native American: 1%, Caucasian 73% \ *Exp:* $221 (Med) \ *Poverty:* 11% \ *Title I:* $24,349 \ *Open-Close:* 08/20 - 05/20 \ *DTBP:* $337 (High)

Brandon Schovajsa 1,11,83	Gwen Stork 2
Rachelle Kuecker 6,10,88*	Kathryn Schoen 9*
Andrea White 57,271	Calvin Krause 67

Public Schs..Principal	Grd	Prgm	Enr/#Cls	SN	
Round Top Carmine Elem Sch 608 N Washington St, Round Top 78954 Kathryn Schoen	PK-6		156 14	40%	979/249-3200 Fax 979/249-4084
Round Top Carmine High Sch 378 Centennial St, Carmine 78932 John Bathke	7-12		110 20	31%	979/278-3252

- **Schulenburg Ind School Dist** PID: 01017800   979/743-3448
  521 Shorthorn Dr, Schulenburg 78956   Fax 979/743-4721

Schools: 2 \ *Teachers:* 64 \ *Students:* 750 \ *Special Ed Students:* 98 \ *LEP Students:* 54 \ *Ethnic:* Asian 1%, African American 12%, Hispanic 42%, Caucasian 44% \ *Exp:* $259 (Med) \ *Poverty:* 18% \ *Title I:* $175,589 \ *Open-Close:* 08/21 - 05/21 \ *DTBP:* $343 (High)

Lisa Meysembourg 1,11	Lynne Machac 2
Brandon Brown 6*	Brad Lux 27*

79 Student Personnel	91 Safety/Security	275 Response To Intervention	298 Grant Writer/Ptnrships	**School Programs**	**Social Media**
80 Driver Ed/Safety	92 Magnet School	277 Remedial Math K-12	750 Chief Innovation Officer	A = Alternative Program	
81 Gifted/Talented	93 Parental Involvement	280 Literacy Coach	751 Chief of Staff	G = Adult Classes	🅕 = Facebook
82 Video Services	95 Tech Prep Program	285 STEM	752 Social Emotional Learning	M = Magnet Program	
83 Substance Abuse Prev	97 Chief Information Officer	286 Digital Learning		T = Title I Schoolwide	🅣 = Twitter
84 Erate	98 Chief Technology Officer	288 Common Core Standards	**Other School Types**	V = Career & Tech Ed Programs	
85 AIDS Education	270 Character Education	294 Accountability	Ⓐ = Alternative School		
86 Alternative/At Risk	271 Migrant Education	295 Network System	Ⓒ = Charter School	New Schools are shaded	
89 Multi-Cultural Curriculum	273 Teacher Mentor	296 Title II Programs	Ⓜ = Magnet School	New Superintendents and Principals are bold	
90 Social Work	274 Before/After Sch	297 Webmaster	Ⓨ = Year-Round School	Personnel with email addresses are underscored	

TX–147

Fisher County Market Data Retrieval

Misti Tucker 31,36	Sheila Brossman 57*			
Deanna Moore 58	Craig Schultz 67			
Charles Henke 69*	Nick Sanchez 73,295			
Cindy Kalina 85*	Kristi McBride 286			

Public Schs..Principal	Grd	Prgm	Enr/#Cls	SN	
Schulenburg Elem Sch 300 Bucek St, Schulenburg 78956 Brooke De La Garza	PK-5	AT	364 25	69%	979/743-4221 Fax 979/743-4864
Schulenburg High Sch 503 College St, Schulenburg 78956 Callene Zapalac \ Charles Henke	6-12	ATV	396 25	48%	979/743-3605 Fax 979/743-2428

FAYETTE CATHOLIC SCHOOLS

- **Diocese of Austin Ed Office** PID: 01420568
  Listing includes only schools located in this county. See District Index for location of Diocesan Offices.

Catholic Schs..Principal	Grd	Prgm	Enr/#Cls	SN	
Sacred Heart Catholic Sch 545 E Pearl St, La Grange 78945 Ladonna Voelkel	PK-6		151 20		979/968-3223 Fax 979/968-3215
St Rose of Lima Sch 405 Black St, Schulenburg 78956 Roseanne Gallia	PK-8		160 10		979/743-3080 Fax 979/743-4228

- **Diocese of Victoria Ed Office** PID: 02181727
  Listing includes only schools located in this county. See District Index for location of Diocesan Offices.

FISHER COUNTY

FISHER PUBLIC SCHOOLS

- **Roby Cons Ind School Dist** PID: 01017886   325/776-2222
  141 S College St, Roby 79543   Fax 325/267-2622

Schools: 2 \ *Teachers:* 27 \ *Students:* 310 \ *Special Ed Students:* 23 \ *LEP Students:* 12 \ *College-Bound:* 97% \ *Ethnic:* Asian 1%, African American 1%, Hispanic 34%, Caucasian 63% \ *Exp:* $534 (High) \ *Poverty:* 20% \ *Title I:* $57,855 \ *Open-Close:* 08/22 - 05/25 \ *DTBP:* $420 (High)

Keith Cook 1,11	Kandra Lakey 2		
Christi Adkinson 4	Eli Sepeda 5		
Angel Pantoja 6	Jason Carter 8,69,73,285,296,298*		
Tempie West 16*	Lisa Stuart 52*		
Linda De La Santos 57,271	Terry Orr 58*		
Jeff Posey 67	Chrystal Loomis 83,85,88,270,273		

Public Schs..Principal	Grd	Prgm	Enr/#Cls	SN	
Roby Elem Sch 141 S College St, Roby 79543 Misty McWilliams	PK-8	T	220 17	53%	325/776-2222
Roby High Sch 141 S College St, Roby 79543 Jason Carter	9-12		82	43%	325/776-2223

- **Rotan Ind School Dist** PID: 01017915   325/735-2332
  102 N McKinley Ave, Rotan 79546   Fax 325/735-2686

Schools: 2 \ *Teachers:* 27 \ *Students:* 250 \ *Special Ed Students:* 19 \ *LEP Students:* 5 \ *College-Bound:* 90% \ *Ethnic:* African American 3%, Hispanic 54%, Caucasian 43% \ *Exp:* $402 (High) \ *Poverty:* 21% \ *Title I:* $74,627 \ *Special Education:* $6,000 \ *Open-Close:* 08/20 - 05/25 \ *DTBP:* $350 (High) \

Shelby Grooban 2	Guy Nelson 67
Bruce Martin 84	

Public Schs..Principal	Grd	Prgm	Enr/#Cls	SN	
Rotan Elem Sch 102 N McKinley Ave, Rotan 79546 Jody Helms	PK-5	T	126 15	63%	325/735-3182
Rotan High Sch 102 N McKinley Ave, Rotan 79546 Bradley Hayhurst	6-12	TV	120 19	54%	325/735-3041

FLOYD COUNTY

FLOYD PUBLIC SCHOOLS

- **Floydada Ind School Dist** PID: 01017977   806/983-3498
  226 W California St, Floydada 79235   Fax 806/983-5739

Schools: 2 \ *Teachers:* 70 \ *Students:* 730 \ *Special Ed Students:* 77 \ *LEP Students:* 67 \ *College-Bound:* 70% \ *Ethnic:* African American 5%, Hispanic 79%, Caucasian 16% \ *Exp:* $565 (High) \ *Poverty:* 29% \ *Title I:* $335,027 \ *Special Education:* $192,000 \ *Open-Close:* 08/19 - 05/21 \ *DTBP:* $335 (High)

Dr Gilbert Trevino 1	Alicia Bice 2
Todd Bandy 6*	Monica Smith 8
Rex Holcombe 11,57,73,81,84,271,295,296	Alejandra Ramirez 27,75*
Jim Hobbs 34,58	Jennifer Gonzalez 37*
Kristie Rehkopf 38,69*	Lyle Miller 67
Kelly Pachiano 71	

Public Schs..Principal	Grd	Prgm	Enr/#Cls	SN	
A B Duncan Elem Sch 1011 S 8th St, Floydada 79235 Carlos Munoz	PK-6	T	461 14	81%	806/983-5332 Fax 806/983-4950
Floydada High Sch 1 Whirlwind Aly, Floydada 79235 Wayne Morren	7-12	TV	205 32	69%	806/983-2340 Fax 806/983-5843

Texas School Directory — Fort Bend County

- **Lockney Independent Sch Dist** PID: 01018024   806/652-2104
  601 W Poplar St, Lockney 79241   Fax 806/652-4920

Schools: 3 \ *Teachers:* 47 \ *Students:* 430 \ *Special Ed Students:* 45 \ *LEP Students:* 24 \ *College-Bound:* 95% \ *Ethnic:* African American 2%, Hispanic 81%, Caucasian 18% \ *Exp:* $362 (High) \ *Poverty:* 31% \ *Title I:* $196,225 \ *Open-Close:* 08/21 - 05/22

Jim Baum	1	Kenton Hooten	3,5
Calixta Sustaita	4	Stacy Ward	6
Connie Barnett	7*	Carol Lane	8,69,74
Naiomo Jones	11	Vance Lemons	27
Judy Race	57*	Mike Lass	67
Chris Pritchard	73,295	Mindy Petty	83,85*
Shana Hallmark	88,294*	Jeffrey Hallmark	270*
Robin Sherman	280*	Sandra Cummings	286*

Public Schs..Principal	Grd	Prgm	Enr/#Cls	SN	
Lockney Elem Sch 310 SW 8th St, Lockney 79241 **Micheal Michaleson**	PK-5	T	216 16	81%	806/652-3321 Fax 806/652-2956
Lockney High Sch 410 SW 4th St, Lockney 79241 Todd Hallmark	9-12	TV	139 25	61%	806/652-3325 Fax 806/652-4945
Lockney Junior High Sch 406 W Willow St, Lockney 79241 Monte Setliff	6-8	T	103 12	78%	806/652-2236

FOARD COUNTY

FOARD PUBLIC SCHOOLS

- **Crowell Ind School Dist** PID: 01018086   940/684-1403
  400 E Logan Street, Crowell 79227   Fax 940/684-1616

Schools: 2 \ *Teachers:* 20 \ *Students:* 200 \ *Special Ed Students:* 37 \ *LEP Students:* 3 \ *College-Bound:* 94% \ *Ethnic:* Asian 1%, African American 2%, Hispanic 39%, Caucasian 58% \ *Exp:* $620 (High) \ *Poverty:* 28% \ *Title I:* $76,725 \ *Open-Close:* 08/21 - 05/22 \ *DTBP:* $328 (High)

Pam Norwood	1	Sherlene Williams	2,12,73,76,295,298
Ricky Norwood	3	Nora Urquizo	4*
Chuck Chatfield	5	Tom McVey	6*
Megan Clifton	16*	Amber Garvin	48*
Herlinda Delapena	57*	Stephanie Bearden	58*
Joe Haynie	67		

Public Schs..Principal	Grd	Prgm	Enr/#Cls	SN	
Crowell Elem Sch 400 E Logan St, Crowell 79227 **Christie Flinn**	PK-8		119 15		940/684-1878
Crowell High Sch 400 E Logan Street, Crowell 79227 Nathan Hayes	9-12	TV	98 15	73%	940/684-1331 Fax 940/684-1978

FORT BEND COUNTY

FORT BEND PUBLIC SCHOOLS

- **Ft Bend Ind School Dist** PID: 01018115   281/634-1000
  16431 Lexington Blvd, Sugar Land 77479   Fax 281/634-1700

Schools: 79 \ *Teachers:* 4,468 \ *Students:* 78,000 \ *Special Ed Students:* 5,086 \ *LEP Students:* 11,140 \ *College-Bound:* 75% \ *Ethnic:* Asian 26%, African American 29%, Hispanic 27%, Caucasian 18% \ *Exp:* $255 (Med) \ *Poverty:* 10% \ *Title I:* $14,740,958 \ *Special Education:* $11,907,000 \ *Open-Close:* 08/14 - 05/28 \ *DTBP:* $191 (High)

Dr Charles Dupre	1	Brenda Essberg	2
Steven Bassett	2,19	David Moore	3
Oscar Perez	3,17	Gail Stotler	4
Gustavo Rodriguez	5	Micheal Bradsfield	5
Rodney Chnat	6	Diana Barton	7
Diana Sayavedra	8,18,31,69,79	Kristi Durham	9*
Susan Voradakis	10	Deadra Holloway	11
Dr Anthony Indelicato	15,70,751	Elizabeth Martin	15*
Joe Rodriguez	15	Dr Xochitl Rodriguez	15,79
Suzanne Lyons	16	James Drew	20
Meredith Watassek	27*	Marybelle Perez	34*
Steven Shiels	36,79,90,270,271	Kelly Fox	38*
Angela Tran	57	Dr Deena Hill	58
Jason Burdine	67	Gwyn Touchet	68
Kermit Spears	68	Thomas Negri	69
Kim Davis	70	Long Pham	71,76,97
Veronica Sopher	71	Mitzi Patin	73
Crystal Wilson	81	Michael Ewing	88
David Rider	91	Pamela Shaw	93
Cathy Collins	274*	Stephanie Williams	280,285,296
Lynette Meyer	286	Audra Ude	294
Amanda Salazar	298		

Public Schs..Principal	Grd	Prgm	Enr/#Cls	SN	
Anne Sullivan Elem Sch 17828 Winding Waters Ln, Sugar Land 77479 Donna Whisonant	PK-5		1,254	3%	281/327-2860 Fax 281/327-2861
Arizona Fleming Elem Sch 14850 Bissonnet St, Houston 77083 Porsha Dudley	PK-5	T	659	67%	281/634-4600 Fax 281/634-4615
Armstrong Elem Sch 3440 Independence Blvd, Missouri City 77459 Nancy Sanchez	PK-5	T	587	85%	281/634-9410 Fax 281/327-9409
Austin Parkway Elem Sch 4400 Austin Pkwy, Sugar Land 77479 **Audrey Macklin**	PK-5		715 29	15%	281/634-4001 Fax 281/634-4014
Barbara Jordan Elem Sch 17800 W Oaks Village Dr, Richmond 77407 Kandy Bond	PK-5	T	559	47%	281/634-2800 Fax 281/634-2801
Barrington Place Elem Sch 2100 Squire Dobbins Dr, Sugar Land 77478 **Ruth Riha**	PK-5		621 38	34%	281/634-4040 Fax 281/634-4057
Billy Baines Middle Sch 9000 Sienna Ranch Rd, Missouri City 77459 Jennifer Roberts	6-8	V	1,812	23%	281/634-6870 Fax 281/634-6880
Blue Ridge Elem Sch 6241 McHard Rd, Houston 77053 Dr Toron Wooldridge	PK-5	T	495 43	85%	281/634-4520 Fax 281/634-4533

79 Student Personnel	91 Safety/Security	275 Response To Intervention	298 Grant Writer/Ptnrships	School Programs	Social Media
80 Driver Ed/Safety	92 Magnet School	277 Remedial Math K-12	750 Chief Innovation Officer	A = Alternative Program	
81 Gifted/Talented	93 Parental Involvement	280 Literacy Coach	751 Chief of Staff	G = Adult Classes	= Facebook
82 Video Services	95 Tech Prep Program	285 STEM	752 Social Emotional Learning	M = Magnet Program	
83 Substance Abuse Prev	97 Chief Information Officer	286 Digital Learning		T = Title I Schoolwide	= Twitter
84 Erate	98 Chief Technology Officer	288 Common Core Standards	Other School Types	V = Career & Tech Ed Programs	
85 AIDS Education	270 Character Education	294 Accountability	Ⓐ = Alternative School		
86 Alternative/At Risk	271 Migrant Education	295 Network System	Ⓒ = Charter School	New Schools are shaded	
87 Multi-Cultural Curriculum	273 Teacher Mentor	296 Title II Programs	Ⓜ = Magnet School	New Superintendents and Principals are bold	
88 Social Work	274 Before/After Sch	297 Webmaster	Ⓨ = Year-Round School	Personnel with email addresses are underscored	

TX—149

Fort Bend County

School	Grades		Enroll	%	Phone
Brazos Bend Elem Sch 621 Cunningham Creek Blvd, Sugar Land 77479 **Stephanie Viado**	PK-5		705 47	19%	281/634-5180 Fax 281/634-5200
Briargate Elem Sch 15817 Blueridge Rd, Missouri City 77489 **Dr Latoya Garrett**	PK-5	T	428 36	90%	281/634-4560 Fax 281/634-4576
Clements High Sch 4200 Elkins Rd, Sugar Land 77479 David Yaffie	9-12	V	2,551 110	8%	281/634-2150 Fax 281/634-2168
Colony Bend Elem Sch 2720 Planters St, Sugar Land 77479 Elizabeth Williams	PK-5		512 25	19%	281/634-4080 Fax 281/634-4092
Colony Meadows Elem Sch 4510 Sweetwater Blvd, Sugar Land 77479 Melissa Bolding	PK-5		752	8%	281/634-4120 Fax 281/634-4136
Commonwealth Elem Sch 4909 Commonwealth Blvd, Sugar Land 77479 Latecha Bogle	PK-5		939 39	1%	281/634-5120 Fax 281/634-5140
Cornerstone Elem Sch 1800 Chatham Ave, Sugar Land 77479 **Margaret Murphy**	PK-5		1,131 33	3%	281/634-6400 Fax 281/327-6400
David Crockett Middle Sch 19001 Beechnut St, Richmond 77407 Dr Tonya Curtis	6-8	T	1,004	54%	281/634-6380 Fax 281/327-6380
Donald Leonetti Elem Sch 1757 Waters Lake Blvd, Missouri City 77459 Joy Schwinger	PK-5		443		281/327-3190 Fax 281/327-3191
Dulles Elem Sch 630 Dulles Ave, Sugar Land 77478 Kyella Griffin	PK-5	T	726 27	41%	281/634-5830 Fax 281/634-5843
Dulles High Sch 550 Dulles Ave, Sugar Land 77478 **Melissa King-Knowles**	9-12	V	2,485 110	26%	281/634-5600 Fax 281/634-5682
Dulles Middle Sch 500 Dulles Ave, Sugar Land 77478 Dee Knox	6-8	V	1,513 80	33%	281/634-5750 Fax 281/634-5781
E A Jones Elem Sch 302 Martin Ln, Missouri City 77489 Carlo Leiva	PK-5	T	661 30	84%	281/634-4960 Fax 281/634-4974
Edgar Glover Elem Sch 1510 Columbia Blue Dr, Missouri City 77489 Nikki Roberts	PK-5	T	479 42	76%	281/634-4920 Fax 281/634-4934
Elkins High Sch 7007 Knights Ct, Missouri City 77459 Deidra Lyons-Lewis	9-12	V	2,307	25%	281/634-2600 Fax 281/634-2674
Ⓐ Ferndell Henry Center for Lrng 7447 FM 521 Rd, Rosharon 77583 Trevor Lemon	6-12	T	200	59%	281/327-6000 Fax 281/327-6001
First Colony Middle Sch 3225 Austin Pkwy, Sugar Land 77479 **Courtney Muceus**	6-8	V	1,275 85	16%	281/634-3240 Fax 281/634-3267
Fort Settlement Middle Sch 5440 Elkins Rd, Sugar Land 77479 Michael Hejducek	6-8		1,429 70	4%	281/634-6440 Fax 281/634-6456
George Bush High Sch 6707 FM 1464 Rd, Richmond 77407 Felicia James	9-12	TV	2,422	57%	281/634-6060 Fax 281/634-6066
Heritage Rose Elem Sch 636 Glendale Lakes Dr, Rosharon 77583 **Gabriella Garza**	PK-5	T	932	72%	281/327-5400 Fax 281/327-5401
Highlands Elem Sch 2022 Colonist Park Dr, Sugar Land 77478 Angela Dow	PK-5		635 48	24%	281/634-4160 Fax 281/634-4176
Ⓜ Hightower High Sch 3333 Hurricane Ln, Missouri City 77459 John Montelongo	9-12	TV	2,042 75	50%	281/634-5240 Fax 281/634-5333
Hodges Bend Middle Sch 16510 Bissonnet St, Houston 77083 Rachel Cortez	6-8	TV	1,031 70	70%	281/634-3000 Fax 281/634-3028
Hunters Glen Elem Sch 695 Independence Blvd, Missouri City 77489 Crystal Gardner	PK-5	T	413 50	77%	281/634-4640 Fax 281/634-4656
I H Kempner High Sch 14777 Voss Rd, Sugar Land 77498 Lori Oliver	9-12	V	2,257 120	41%	281/634-2300 Fax 281/634-2378
James Bowie Middle Sch 700 Plantation Dr, Richmond 77406 Brian Shillingburg	6-8		1,283	23%	281/327-6200 Fax 281/327-6201
James Neill Elem Sch 3830 Harvest Corner Dr, Richmond 77406 Lori Hoeffken	PK-5		671		281/327-3760 Fax 281/327-3761
James Patterson Elem Sch 18702 Beechnut St, Richmond 77407 Kari Bruhn	PK-5		598		281/327-4260 Fax 281/327-4261
Juan Seguin Elem Sch 7817 Grand Mission Blvd, Richmond 77407 Fidel Wells	PK-5		567	38%	281/634-9850 Fax 281/327-7029
Lake Olympia Middle Sch 3100 Lake Olympia Pkwy, Missouri City 77459 Janis Nott	6-8	TV	1,233	56%	281/634-3520 Fax 281/634-3549
Lakeview Elem Sch 314 Lakeview Dr, Sugar Land 77498 Alena McClanahan	PK-5		484 44	40%	281/634-4200 Fax 281/634-4214
Lantern Lane Elem Sch 3323 Mission Valley Dr, Missouri City 77459 **Lavanta Williams**	PK-5	T	446 35	72%	281/634-4680 Fax 281/634-4694
Lexington Creek Elem Sch 2335 Dulles Ave, Missouri City 77459 Christina Hopkins	PK-5		551 45	24%	281/634-5000 Fax 281/634-5014
Lula Belle Goodman Elem Sch 1100 W Sycamore St, Fresno 77545 Dr Felicia Bolden	PK-5	T	606 40	66%	281/634-5985 Fax 281/634-6000
Macario Garcia Middle Sch 18550 Old Richmond Rd, Sugar Land 77498 Dr Cory Collins	6-8	V	1,156 85	34%	281/634-3160 Fax 281/634-3166
Madden Elem Sch 17727 Abermore Ln, Richmond 77407 **Kristi Durham**	PK-5		961	13%	281/327-2740 Fax 281/327-2742
Mary Austin Holley Elem Sch 16655 Bissonnet St, Houston 77083 Laureen Sanford	PK-5	T	591 46	66%	281/634-3850 Fax 281/634-3856
McAuliffe Middle Sch 16650 S Post Oak Rd, Houston 77053 Andre Roberson	6-8	TV	969 85	84%	281/634-3360 Fax 281/634-3393
Meadows Elem Sch 12037 Pender Ln, Meadows Place 77477 Courtney Dickey	PK-5	T	437 20	45%	281/634-4720 Fax 281/634-4734
Mission Bend Elem Sch 16200 Beechnut St, Houston 77083 Jill Gumbs	PK-5	T	611 46	75%	281/634-4240 Fax 281/634-4250
Mission Glen Elem Sch 16053 Mission Glen Dr, Houston 77083 Dr Yvette Blake	PK-5	T	470 30	65%	281/634-4280 Fax 281/634-4296
Mission West Elem Sch 7325 Clodine Reddick Rd, Houston 77083 Rhonda Mason	PK-5		629 40	76%	281/634-4320 Fax 281/634-4334
Missouri City Middle Sch 202 Martin Ln, Missouri City 77489 Tasha Hamilton	6-8	TV	998 72	78%	281/634-3440 Fax 281/634-3473
Oakland Elem Sch 4455 Waterside Estates Dr D, Richmond 77406 Nancy Hummel	PK-5		791	18%	281/634-3730 Fax 281/634-3738

1	Superintendent	8	Curric/Instruct K-12	19	Chief Financial Officer	29	Family/Consumer Science	39	Social Studies K-12	49	English/Lang Arts Elem	59	Special Education Elem	69	Academic Assessment
2	Bus/Finance/Purchasing	9	Curric/Instruct Elem	20	Art K-12	30	Adult Education	40	Social Studies Elem	50	English/Lang Arts Sec	60	Special Education Sec	70	Research/Development
3	Buildings And Grounds	10	Curric/Instruct Sec	21	Art Elem	31	Career/Sch-to-Work K-12	41	Social Studies Sec	51	Reading K-12	61	Foreign/World Lang K-12	71	Public Information
4	Food Service	11	Federal Program	22	Art Sec	32	Career/Sch-to-Work Elem	42	Science K-12	52	Reading Elem	62	Foreign/World Lang Elem	72	Summer School
5	Transportation	12	Title I	23	Music K-12	33	Career/Sch-to-Work Sec	43	Science Elem	53	Reading Sec	63	Foreign/World Lang Sec	73	Instructional Tech
6	Athletic	13	Title V	24	Music Elem	34	Early Childhood Ed	44	Science Sec	54	Remedial Reading K-12	64	Religious Education K-12	74	Inservice Training
7	Health Services	15	Asst Superintendent	25	Music Sec	35	Health/Phys Education	45	Math K-12	55	Remedial Reading Elem	65	Religious Education Elem	75	Marketing/Distributive
		16	Instructional Media Svcs	26	Business Education	36	Guidance Services K-12	46	Math Elem	56	Remedial Reading Sec	66	Religious Education Sec	76	Info Systems
		17	Chief Operations Officer	27	Career & Tech Ed	37	Guidance Services Elem	47	Math Sec	57	Bilingual/ELL	67	School Board President	77	Psychological Assess
		18	Chief Academic Officer	28	Technology Education	38	Guidance Services Sec	48	English/Lang Arts K-12	58	Special Education K-12	68	Teacher Personnel	78	Affirmative Action

Texas School Directory — Fort Bend County

School	Grd	Prgm	Enr/#Cls	SN	Phone
Oyster Creek Elem Sch 16425 Mellow Oaks Ln, Sugar Land 77498 Deanna Olson	PK-5		848 42	35%	281/634-5910 Fax 281/634-5925 t
Palmer Elem Sch 4208 Crow Valley Dr, Missouri City 77459 Kellie Clay	PK-5		582 40	35%	281/634-4760 Fax 281/634-4773
Pecan Grove Elem Sch 3330 Old South Dr, Richmond 77406 Dr Trenae Hill	PK-5		695 50	20%	281/634-4800 Fax 281/634-4814
Ⓐ Progressive High Sch 1555 Independence Blvd, Missouri City 77489 Lisa Jones	10-12		150 6		281/634-2900 Fax 281/634-2913
Quail Valley Elem Sch 3500 Quail Village Dr, Missouri City 77459 Carla Patton	PK-5	T	480 22	39%	281/634-5040 Fax 281/634-5054
Quail Valley Middle Sch 3019 FM 1092 Rd, Missouri City 77459 Jeffrey Post	6-8	V	1,179 55	30%	281/634-3600 Fax 281/634-3632
Ridge Point High Sch 500 Waters Lake Blvd, Missouri City 77459 Leonard Brogan	9-12	V	2,712	18%	281/327-5200 Fax 281/327-5201
Ridgegate Elem Sch 6015 W Ridgecreek Dr, Houston 77053 Marta Rivas	PK-5	T	552 55	88%	281/634-4840 Fax 281/634-4855
Ridgemont Elem Sch 4910 Raven Ridge Dr, Houston 77053 Framy Diaz	2-5	T	764 43	76%	281/634-4880 Fax 281/634-4896
Rita Drabek Elem Sch 11325 Lake Woodbridge Dr, Sugar Land 77498 Wendy Nunez	PK-5		842	28%	281/634-6570 Fax 281/634-6572
Ronald Thornton Middle Sch 1909 Waters Lake Blvd, Missouri City 77459 Jeanna Sniffin	6-8		1,100		281/327-3870 Fax 281/327-3871
Rosa Parks Elem Sch 19101 Chimney Rock Rd, Fresno 77545 Alfred Holland	PK-5	T	667	67%	281/634-6390 Fax 281/327-6390
Sartartia Middle Sch 8125 Homeward Way, Sugar Land 77479 Cholly Oglesby	6-8		1,295 50	9%	281/634-6310 Fax 281/634-6373
Scanlan Oaks Elem Sch 9000 Camp Sienna Trl, Missouri City 77459 Lori Craig	PK-5		1,017 44	4%	281/634-3950 Fax 281/634-3915
Schiff Elem Sch 7400 Discovery Ln, Missouri City 77459 Lucretia Deflora	PK-5		847	9%	281/634-9450 Fax 281/327-9449 t
Settlers Way Elem Sch 3015 Settlers Way Blvd, Sugar Land 77479 Danny Emery	PK-5		640 26	19%	281/634-4360 Fax 281/634-4376 t
Sienna Crossing Elem Sch 10011 Steep Bank Trce, Missouri City 77459 Rachel Rosier	PK-5		1,080 40	7%	281/634-3680 Fax 281/634-3799
Stephen F Austin High Sch 3434 Pheasant Creek Dr, Sugar Land 77498 Dr Rizvan Quadri	9-12	V	2,276	25%	281/634-2000 Fax 281/634-2074
Sugar Land Middle Sch 321 7th St, Sugar Land 77498 Keith Fickel	6-8	TV	1,243 88	45%	281/634-3080 Fax 281/327-6599
Sugar Mill Elem Sch 13707 Jess Pirtle Blvd, Sugar Land 77498 Jaimie Geis	PK-5		588 32	30%	281/634-4440 Fax 281/634-4459 t
Technical Education Center 540 Dulles Ave, Sugar Land 77478 Kennith Kendziora	Voc		500 10		281/634-5671 Fax 281/634-5700
Thurgood Marshall High Sch 1220 Buffalo Run, Missouri City 77489 Dr Ogechi Uwaga-Sanders	9-12	TV	1,243	65%	281/634-6630 Fax 281/634-6650
Townewest Elem Sch 13927 Old Richmond Rd, Sugar Land 77498 Felipa Briceno	PK-5	T	707 37	74%	281/634-4480 Fax 281/634-4494
Walker Station Elem Sch 6200 Homeward Way, Sugar Land 77479 Kate Kargbo	PK-5		781 59	5%	281/634-4400 Fax 281/634-4413
Walter Moses Burton Elem Sch 1625 Hunter Green Ln, Fresno 77545 Lakisha Anthony	PK-5	T	396 50	60%	281/634-5080 Fax 281/634-5094
William B Travis High Sch 11111 Harlem Rd, Richmond 77406 Sarah LaBerge	9-12	V	2,618	26%	281/634-7000 Fax 281/634-7010
Willowridge High Sch 16301 Chimney Rock Rd, Houston 77053 Terence Hayden	9-12	TV	1,315 105	74%	281/634-2450 Fax 281/634-2513

● **Katy Ind School Dist** PID: 01026227   281/396-6000
6301 S Stadium Ln, Katy 77494   Fax 281/644-1849

Schools: 71 \ *Teachers:* 4,996 \ *Students:* 83,599 \
Special Ed Students: 7,128 \ *LEP Students:* 11,534 \ *College-Bound:* 75%
\ *Ethnic:* Asian 15%, African American 11%, Hispanic 36%, Caucasian
38% \ *Exp:* $308 (High) \ *Poverty:* 9% \ *Title I:* $9,030,091 \
Special Education: $11,340,000 \ *Bilingual Education:* $54,000 \
Open-Close: 08/14 - 05/15 \ *DTBP:* $179 (High) \ f t

Dr Ken Gregorski	1	Chris Smith	2,19
Gloria Truskowski	2	Lee Crews	3,17
Donna Pittenger	4	Dr Bill Wood	5*
Debbie Decker	6	Therese Highnote	7
Dr Christine Caskey	8,18	Dr Kim Lawson	9
Dr Cazilda Steele	10*	Nakia Coy	11
Dr Andrea Grooms	15,71,93	Bonnie Holland	15
Brian Schuss	15,68	Dr Freda Creech	15
Rhonda Ward	15,74,77,79,83*	Dr Steve Robertson	15
Jay Sonnenburg	16	Michael Ouellette	20,23
Sarah Martin	27,51*	Howard Grimet	35
Christy Maeker	36,77	Linda Shepard	57
Dr Brian Malechuk	58	Courtney Doyle	67
Dr Allison Matney	69,70,294	Lisa Kassman	70
Claudia Deschamps	71	Dr John Alawneh	71,76,97,286
Darlene Rankin	73	Laurie Mitchell	75
Alene Lindley	81	Peggy Caruso	91
Terri Walker	275		

Public Schs..Principal	Grd	Prgm	Enr/#Cls	SN	Phone
Amy Campbell Elem Sch 3701 Cross Creek Bnd, Fulshear 77441 Jaime Shipley	PK-5		800		281/234-4500 Fax 281/644-1890
Bear Creek Elem Sch 4815 Hickory Downs Dr, Houston 77084 Alma Zertuche	PK-5	T	629 36	71%	281/237-5600 Fax 281/644-1500
Beckendorff Junior High Sch 8200 S Fry Rd, Katy 77494 Paul Moussavi	6-8		1,739	6%	281/237-8800 Fax 281/644-1635
Bonnie Holland Elem Sch 23720 Seven Meadows Pkwy, Katy 77494 Linnea Griffith	PK-5		1,097	9%	281/234-0500 Fax 281/644-1695
Cardiff Junior High Sch 3900 Dayflower Dr, Katy 77449 Bryan Rounds	6-8	T	886	66%	281/234-0600 Fax 281/644-1855
Catherine Bethke Elem Sch 4535 E Ventana Pkwy, Katy 77493 Carrie Lowery	PK-5		935	34%	281/234-4200
Cimarron Elem Sch 1100 S Peek Rd, Katy 77450 Youshawna Hunt	PK-5		655 41	38%	281/237-6900 Fax 281/644-1505

---

79 Student Personnel	91 Safety/Security	275 Response To Intervention	298 Grant Writer/Ptnrships	**School Programs**	**Social Media**	
80 Driver Ed/Safety	92 Magnet School	277 Remedial Math K-12	750 Chief Innovation Officer	A = Alternative Program		
81 Gifted/Talented	93 Parental Involvement	280 Literacy Coach	751 Chief of Staff	G = Adult Classes	f = Facebook	
82 Video Services	95 Tech Prep Program	285 STEM	752 Social Emotional Learning	M = Magnet Program		
83 Substance Abuse Prev	97 Chief Information Officer	286 Digital Learning		T = Title I Schoolwide	t = Twitter	
84 Erate	98 Chief Technology Officer	288 Common Core Standards	**Other School Types**	V = Career & Tech Ed Programs		
85 AIDS Education	270 Character Education	294 Accountability	Ⓐ = Alternative School			
86 Alternative/At Risk	271 Migrant Education	295 Network System	Ⓒ = Charter School	New Schools are shaded		
89 Multi-Cultural Curriculum	273 Teacher Mentor	296 Title II Programs	Ⓜ = Magnet School	New Superintendents and Principals are bold		
90 Social Work	274 Before/After Sch	297 Webmaster	Ⓨ = Year-Round School	Personnel with email addresses are underscored		

Fort Bend County

School	Grades		Enroll	%	Phone
Cinco Ranch High Sch 23440 Cinco Ranch Blvd, Katy 77494 James Cross	9-12	V	3,144 100	13%	281/237-7000 Fax 281/644-1734
Cinco Ranch Junior High Sch 23420 Cinco Ranch Blvd, Katy 77494 Elizabeth Nicklas	6-8		1,259	17%	281/237-7300 Fax 281/644-1640
Diane Winborn Elem Sch 22555 Prince George St, Katy 77449 Kasey Lowry	PK-5	T	699 75	45%	281/237-6650 Fax 281/644-1510
Edna Mae Fielder Elem Sch 2100 Greenway Village Dr, Katy 77449 Ramona Cardin	PK-5		1,132 55	22%	281/237-6450 Fax 281/664-1515
Franz Elem Sch 2751 N Westgreen Blvd, Katy 77449 Yvette Sylvan	PK-5	T	1,036	65%	281/237-8600 Fax 281/644-1520
Fred and Patti Shafer ES 5150 Ranch Point Dr, Katy 77494 Melissa Salyer	K-5		1,196	6%	281/234-1900 Fax 281/644-1880
Garland McMeans Junior HS 21000 Westheimer Pkwy, Katy 77450 Steve Guzzetta	6-8	V	1,108	14%	281/237-8000 Fax 281/644-1660
Hazel S Pattison Elem Sch 19910 Stonelodge Dr, Katy 77450 Debbie Barker	PK-5		1,015 42	9%	281/237-5450 Fax 281/644-1575
James E Randolph Elem Sch 5303 Flewellen Oaks Ln, Fulshear 77441 Michelle Gaskamp	PK-5		1,272	3%	281/234-3800 Fax 281/644-1930
James E Taylor High Sch 20700 Kingsland Blvd, Katy 77450 Christopher Morgan	9-12	V	2,940 100	20%	281/237-3100 Fax 281/644-1760
James Williams Elem Sch 3900 S Peek Rd, Katy 77450 Angel Bateman	PK-5		695	7%	281/237-7200 Fax 281/644-1545
Jean & Betty Schmalz Elem Sch 18605 Green Land Way, Houston 77084 Charlotte Gilder	PK-5	GT	1,184	59%	281/237-4500 Fax 281/644-1615
Jeanette Hayes Elem Sch 21203 Park Timbers Ln, Katy 77450 Heather Mulcahy	PK-5		682 42	20%	281/237-3200 Fax 281/644-1541
Jo Ella Exley Elem Sch 21800 Westheimer Pkwy, Katy 77450 Juli Noeldner	PK-5		982	20%	281/237-8400 Fax 281/644-1535
Joe M Adams Junior High Sch 4141 Cross Creek Bend Ln, Fulshear 77441 Elisabeth Brodt	6-8		135		281/234-3400
Katy Elem Sch 5726 George Bush Dr, Katy 77493 Beth Grimet	PK-5		665 48	19%	281/237-6550 Fax 281/644-1550
Katy High Sch 6331 Highway Blvd, Katy 77494 Richard Hull	9-12	V	3,401 175	28%	281/237-6700 Fax 281/644-1700
Katy Junior High Sch 5350 Franz Rd, Katy 77493 Dr Jacob LeBlanc	6-8	TV	1,039 68	42%	281/237-6800 Fax 281/644-1645
Keiko Davidson Elem Sch 26906 Pine Mill Rnch, Katy 77494 Jessie Miller	PK-5		1,163	6%	281/234-2500 Fax 281/644-1925
Loraine T Golbow Elem Sch 3535 Lakes of Bridgewater Dr, Katy 77449 Ann Lalime	PK-5	T	783 54	56%	281/237-5350 Fax 281/644-1525
Ⓐ Martha Raines High Sch 1732 Katyland Dr, Katy 77493 Dr Diego Linares	10-12	T	190	46%	281/237-1500 Fax 281/644-1781
Maurice Wolfe Elem Sch 502 Addicks Howell Rd, Houston 77079 Anna Hinojosa	PK-5	T	348 24	55%	281/237-2250 Fax 281/644-1620
Mayde Creek Elem Sch 2698 Greenhouse Rd, Houston 77084 Felicia Sheedy	PK-5	T	840 60	65%	281/237-3950 Fax 281/644-1555
Mayde Creek High Sch 19202 Groeschke Rd, Houston 77084 Ronnie Edwards	9-12	TV	2,705 200	58%	281/237-3000 Fax 281/644-1718
Mayde Creek Junior High Sch 2700 Greenhouse Rd, Houston 77084 Dr David Paz	6-8	TV	1,076 60	64%	281/237-3900 Fax 281/644-1650
Maydell Jenks Elem Sch 27602 Westridge Creek Ln, Katy 77494 Troy Kemp	PK-5		1,542	9%	281/234-4100
Memorial Parkway Elem Sch 21603 Park Tree Ln, Katy 77450 Doreen Martinez	PK-5	T	823 32	51%	281/237-5850 Fax 281/644-1560
Memorial Parkway Jr High Sch 21203 Highland Knolls Dr, Katy 77450 Emily Craig	6-8	V	799 80	29%	281/237-5800 Fax 281/644-1665
Michael L Griffin Elem Sch 7800 S Fry Rd, Katy 77494 Jackie Keithan	PK-5		1,030	6%	281/237-8700 Fax 281/644-1850
Miller Career & Tech Center 1734 Katyland Dr, Katy 77493 Russell Faldyn	Voc		275 25		281/237-6300 Fax 281/644-1775
Morton Ranch Elem Sch 2502 N Mason Rd, Katy 77449 Deborah Hubble	PK-5	T	950	57%	281/234-0300 Fax 281/644-1685
Morton Ranch High Sch 21000 Franz Rd, Katy 77449 Julie Hinson	9-12	T	3,081	58%	281/237-7800 Fax 281/644-1746
Morton Ranch Jr High Sch 2498 N Mason Rd, Katy 77449 Dr Sanee Bell	6-8	T	1,215	64%	281/237-7400 Fax 281/644-1670
Nottingham Country Elem Sch 20500 Kingsland Blvd, Katy 77450 Tracy Stroud	PK-5		790	22%	281/237-5500 Fax 281/644-1566
Obra D Tompkins High Sch 4400 Falcon Landing Blvd, Katy 77494 Mark Grisdale	9-12		3,375	6%	281/234-1000 Fax 281/644-1910
Odessa Kilpatrick Elem Sch 26100 Cinco Ranch Blvd, Katy 77494 Malynn Rodriguez	PK-5		1,194	5%	281/237-7600 Fax 281/664-1570
Olga Leonard Elem Sch 2602 Winchester Ranch Trail, Katy 77493 Stephanie Vaughan	PK-5		670		281/234-4600
Ⓐ Opportunity Awareness Center 1732 Katyland Dr, Katy 77493 Diego Linares	6-12		72 12	57%	281/237-6350 Fax 281/644-1780
Patricia Paetow High Sch 23111 Stockdick Rd, Katy 77493 Mindy Dickerson	9-12		725		281/234-4900
Polly Ann McRoberts Elem Sch 3535 Fry Rd, Katy 77449 Rahsan Smith	PK-5	T	719 55	62%	281/237-2000 Fax 281/644-1580
Ray & Jamie Wolman Elem Sch 28727 N Firethorne Rd, Katy 77494 Kelly Ricks	PK-5		915	5%	281/234-1700 Fax 281/644-1875
Rhoads Elem Sch 19711 Clay Rd, Katy 77449 Amanda Weaver	PK-5	T	1,040	68%	281/237-8500 Fax 281/644-1590
Robert & Felice Bryant ES 29801 Kingsland Blvd, Katy 77494 Dr William Rhodes	PK-5		580		281/234-4300 Fax 281/644-1965
Robert E King Elem Sch 1901 Charlton House Ln, Katy 77493 Tammi Wilhelm	PK-5	T	981	48%	281/237-6850 Fax 281/644-1595

---

1 Superintendent	8 Curric/Instruct K-12	19 Chief Financial Officer	29 Family/Consumer Science	39 Social Studies K-12	49 English/Lang Arts Elem	59 Special Education Elem	69 Academic Assessment
2 Bus/Finance/Purchasing	9 Curric/Instruct Elem	20 Art K-12	30 Adult Education	40 Social Studies Elem	50 English/Lang Arts Sec	60 Special Education Sec	70 Research/Development
3 Buildings And Grounds	10 Curric/Instruct Sec	21 Art Elem	31 Career/Sch-to-Work K-12	41 Social Studies Sec	51 Reading K-12	61 Foreign/World Lang K-12	71 Public Information
4 Food Service	11 Federal Program	22 Art Sec	32 Career/Sch-to-Work Elem	42 Science K-12	52 Reading Elem	62 Foreign/World Lang Elem	72 Summer School
5 Transportation	12 Title I	23 Music K-12	33 Career/Sch-to-Work Sec	43 Science Elem	53 Reading Sec	63 Foreign/World Lang Sec	73 Instructional Tech
6 Athletic	13 Title V	24 Music Elem	34 Early Childhood Ed	44 Science Sec	54 Remedial Reading K-12	64 Religious Education K-12	74 Inservice Training
7 Health Services	15 Asst Superintendent	25 Music Sec	35 Health/Phys Education	45 Math K-12	55 Remedial Reading Elem	65 Religious Education Elem	75 Marketing/Distributive
	16 Instructional Media Svcs	26 Business Education	36 Guidance Services K-12	46 Math Elem	56 Remedial Reading Sec	66 Religious Education Sec	76 Info Systems
	17 Chief Operations Officer	27 Career & Tech Ed	37 Guidance Services Elem	47 Math Sec	57 Bilingual/ELL	67 School Board President	77 Psychological Assess
	18 Chief Academic Officer	28 Technology Education	38 Guidance Services Sec	48 English/Lang Arts K-12	58 Special Education K-12	68 Teacher Personnel	78 Affirmative Action

Texas School Directory — Fort Bend County

School	Grd	Prgm	Enr/#Cls	SN	Phone
Robert R Shaw Ctr for Steam 1730 Katyland Dr, Katy 77493 Steve Adams	6-12		401		281/396-7670
Roberta Rylander Elem Sch 24831 Westheimer Pkwy, Katy 77494 Cheryl Glasser	PK-5		1,125	16%	281/237-8300 Fax 281/644-1600
Rodger & Ellen Beck Jr HS 5200 S Fry Rd, Katy 77450 Carra Daniels	6-8	V	957 57	11%	281/237-3300 Fax 281/644-1630
Roosevelt Alexander Elem Sch 6161 S Fry Rd, Katy 77494 Charmaine Hobin	PK-5		993 35	5%	281/237-7100 Fax 281/644-1585
Seven Lakes High Sch 9251 S Fry Rd, Katy 77494 Kerri Finnesand	9-12	V	3,526	7%	281/237-2800 Fax 281/644-1785
Seven Lakes Junior High Sch 6026 Katy Gaston Rd, Katy 77494 Kristin Harper	6-8		1,924	6%	281/234-2100 Fax 281/644-1885
ⓐ Simon Youth Academy 5000 Katy Mills Cir, Katy 77494 Heather Devires	9-12		51		281/396-6050 Fax 281/644-3800
Stan C Stanley Elem Sch 26633 Cinco Terrace Dr, Katy 77494 Rebecca Wingfield	PK-5		1,039	3%	281/234-1400 Fax 281/644-1865
Stockdick Jr High Sch 4777 Peek Rd, Katy 77449 Mark McCord	6-8		715		281/234-2700 Fax 281/644-1970
Sue Creech Elem Sch 5905 S Mason Rd, Katy 77450 Euberta Lucas	PK-5		888 53	21%	281/237-8850 Fax 281/644-1605
Sundown Elem Sch 20100 Saums Rd, Katy 77449 Martha Pulido	PK-5	GT	822 50	76%	281/237-5400 Fax 281/644-1610
T H McDonald Junior High Sch 3635 Lakes of Bridgewater Dr, Katy 77449 **Carrie Caruso**	6-8	TV	928	60%	281/237-5300 Fax 281/644-1655
Tays Junior High Sch 26721 Hawks Prairie Blvd, Katy 77494 Dr Kris Mitzner	7-8		1,377	6%	281/234-2400 Fax 281/644-1945
Tom Wilson Elem Sch 5200 Falcon Landing Blvd, Katy 77494 Rhonda Henderson	PK-5		1,056	6%	281/234-1600 Fax 281/644-1870
Ursula Stephens Elem Sch 2715 Fry Rd, Katy 77449 **Michael Schwartz**	PK-5	T	692	70%	281/234-0200 Fax 281/644-1680
West Memorial Elem Sch 22605 Provincial Blvd, Katy 77450 **Rebecca Marron**	PK-5	T	822 40	45%	281/237-6600 Fax 281/644-1625
West Memorial Jr High Sch 22311 Provincial Blvd, Katy 77450 **Gina Cobb**	6-8	TV	800 60	46%	281/237-6400 Fax 281/644-1675
Woodcreek Elem Sch 1155 Woodcreek Bend Ln, Katy 77494 Ronnie Mosher	PK-5		1,200 45	9%	281/234-0100 Fax 281/644-1690
Woodcreek Junior High Sch 1801 Woodcreek Bend Ln, Katy 77494 Melinda Stone	6-8		1,477	8%	281/234-0800 Fax 281/644-1860
Zelma Hutsell Elem Sch 5360 Franz Rd, Katy 77493 Margie Blount	PK-5	GT	763 60	69%	281/237-6500 Fax 281/644-1530

⦁ Lamar Cons Ind School Dist   PID: 01018232
3911 Avenue I, Rosenberg 77471   832/223-0000   Fax 832/223-0002

Schools: 45 \ **Teachers:** 1,879 \ **Students:** 34,000 \
Special Ed Students: 2,576 \ **LEP Students:** 3,814 \ **College-Bound:** 89% \
Ethnic: Asian 7%, African American 20%, Hispanic 45%, Caucasian 28% \ **Exp:** $307 (High) \ **Poverty:** 11% \ **Title I:** $4,694,338 \
Special Education: $4,418,000 \ **Open-Close:** 08/26 - 06/04 \ **DTBP:** $189 (High) \

Dr Thomas Randle 1
Michelle Reynolds 2
Mike Jones 5
Jennifer Roberts 7,77,83
Diane Parks 9,79
Mike Rockwood 15,71,751
Joel Garrett 27,31,286
Brian Moore 36,69,70,294
Kay Danziger 67
David Jacobson 73,76
David Eakin 76,95
Trudy Harris 88
Jill Davis 93
Jill Ludwig 2,19
Aaron Morgan 3
Nicole Nelson 6,35
Teresa Mossige 8,18,288
Dr Marva Oneal 11
Ram Estrada 20
Gloria Stewart 30,57
Tiffany Mathis 58
Dr Kathleen Bowen 68
Jamie Vincek 74,273
Valerie Anderson 81
Dallis Warren 91
David Banks 295

Public Schs..Principal	Grd	Prgm	Enr/#Cls	SN	Phone
ⓐ 1621 Place Sch 117 Lane Dr Ste 14, Rosenberg 77471 Randall Donnell	9-12	V	77 3		832/223-0950 Fax 832/223-0951
Adolphus Elem Sch 7910 Winston Ranch Pkwy, Richmond 77406 Stacy Boarman	PK-5		790	13%	832/223-4700 Fax 832/223-4701
ⓐ Alternative Learning Center 1708 Avenue M, Rosenberg 77471 Randal Donnell	K-12	V	80 15	74%	832/223-0900 Fax 832/223-0901
Arredondo Elem Sch 6110 August Green Dr, Richmond 77469 Amber Barbarow	PK-5	T	818	45%	832/223-4800 Fax 832/223-4801
Austin Elem Sch 1630 Pitts Rd, Richmond 77406 Bud Whileyman	PK-5		607 43	23%	832/223-1000 Fax 832/223-1001
Beasley Elem Sch 7511 Avenue J, Beasley 77417 Laura Haugvoll	PK-5	T	396 11	72%	832/223-1100 Fax 832/223-1101
Bentley Elem Sch 9910 FM 359 Rd, Richmond 77406 **Jill Nehls**	PK-5		654	16%	832/223-4900 Fax 832/222-4901
Bowie Elem Sch 2304 Bamore Rd, Rosenberg 77471 Belynda Billings	PK-5	T	608 43	83%	832/223-1200 Fax 832/223-1201
Briscoe Junior High Sch 4300 FM 723 Rd, Richmond 77406 **Jennifer Zebold**	7-8		891	30%	832/223-4000 Fax 832/223-4001
Campbell Elem Sch 1000 Shadow Bend Dr, Sugar Land 77479 Michelle Koerth	PK-5		606 38	5%	832/223-1300 Fax 832/223-1301
Culver Elem Sch 3131 Learning Tree Lane, Rosenberg 77471 **Carla Thomas**	K-5		615		832/223-5600
Dean Leaman Junior High Sch 9320 Charger Way, Fulshear 77441 **Michael Semmler**	7-9		753	15%	832/223-5200 Fax 832/223-5201
Don Carter Elem Sch 7800 A Meyers Rd, Richmond 77469 Henva Medlow	PK-5		606		832/223-5500 Fax 832/223-5501
ⓐ Fort Bend Alternative Sch 3404 Avenue F, Rosenberg 77471 Randall Donnell	6-12		60 3		281/239-3431 Fax 281/341-5293

---

79 Student Personnel	91 Safety/Security	275 Response To Intervention	298 Grant Writer/Ptnrships
40 Driver Ed/Safety	92 Magnet School	277 Remedial Math K-12	750 Chief Innovation Officer
31 Gifted/Talented	93 Parental Involvement	280 Literacy Coach	751 Chief of Staff
32 Video Services	95 Tech Prep Program	285 STEM	752 Social Emotional Learning
33 Substance Abuse Prev	97 Chief Infomation Officer	286 Digital Learning	
44 Erate	98 Chief Technology Officer	288 Common Core Standards	
45 AIDS Education	270 Character Education	294 Accountability	
48 Alternative/At Risk	271 Migrant Education	295 Network System	
49 Multi-Cultural Curriculum	273 Teacher Mentor	296 Title II Programs	
40 Social Work	274 Before/After Sch	297 Webmaster	

School Programs
A = Alternative Program
G = Adult Classes
M = Magnet Program
T = Title I Schoolwide
V = Career & Tech Ed Programs

Other School Types
ⓐ = Alternative School
ⓒ = Charter School
ⓜ = Magnet School
ⓨ = Year-Round School

Social Media
= Facebook
= Twitter

New Schools are shaded
New Superintendents and Principals are bold
Personnel with email addresses are underscored

Fort Bend County — Market Data Retrieval

School	Grades	Prgm	Enr/#Cls	SN	Phone
Frost Elem Sch 3306 Skinner Ln, Richmond 77406 Shannon Hood	PK-5		563 27	12%	832/223-1500 Fax 832/223-1501
Fulshear High Sch 9302 Charger Way, Fulshear 77441 Daniel Ward	9-10		400	16%	832/223-5000 Fax 832/223-5001
George Junior High Sch 4601 Airport Ave, Rosenberg 77471 Stephen Judice	7-8	T	1,066 80	74%	832/223-3600 Fax 832/223-3601
George Ranch High Sch 8181 FM 762 Rd, Richmond 77469 **Heather Patterson**	9-12	V	2,641	21%	832/223-4200 Fax 832/223-4201
Huggins Elem Sch 1 Huggins Dr, Fulshear 77441 **Bethany Cunningham**	PK-5		679 30	16%	832/223-1600 Fax 832/223-1601
Hutchinson Elem Sch 3602 Richmond Pkwy, Richmond 77469 Mark Melendez	PK-5		665	33%	832/223-1700 Fax 832/223-1701
Jackson Elem Sch 301 3rd St, Rosenberg 77471 Deana Gonzalez	PK-5	T	373 30	93%	832/223-1800 Fax 832/223-1801
Jane Long Elem Sch 907 Main St, Richmond 77469 Jill Nehls	PK-5	T	592 35	80%	832/223-1900 Fax 832/223-1901
Jane Wessendorff Middle Sch 5201 Mustang Ave, Rosenberg 77471 **Lorana Callis**	6-6	T	404 32	69%	832/223-3300 Fax 832/223-3301
Joe Hubenak Elem Sch 11344 Rancho Bella Pkwy, Richmond 77406 Diane Parks	PK-5		844	20%	832/223-2900 Fax 832/223-2901
Lamar Consolidated High Sch 4606 Mustang Ave, Rosenberg 77471 Kaye Williams	9-12	TV	1,699 100	56%	832/223-3000 Fax 832/223-3001
Lamar Junior High Sch 4814 Mustang Ave, Rosenberg 77471 Creighton Jaster	7-8	T	848	64%	832/223-3200 Fax 832/223-3201
Lindsey Elem Sch 2431 Joan Collier Trce, Katy 77494 Heather Williams	K-5		700		832/223-5400 Fax 832/223-5401
McNeill Elem Sch 7300 S Mason Rd, Richmond 77407 Toni Scott	PK-5		871	23%	832/223-2800 Fax 832/223-2801
Meyer Elem Sch 1930 J Meyer Rd, Richmond 77469 Lisa McKey	PK-5	T	790 45	66%	832/223-2000 Fax 832/223-2001
Navarro Middle Sch 4700 Avenue N, Rosenberg 77471 Stephanie McElroy	6-6	T	513 35	71%	832/223-3700 Fax 832/223-3701
Polly Ryon Middle Sch 7901 FM 762 Rd, Richmond 77469 **Kevin Croft**	6-6		679	23%	832/223-4500 Fax 832/223-4501
Randolph Foster High Sch 4400 FM 723 Rd, Richmond 77406 Gerard Kipping	9-12	V	2,054 102	24%	832/223-3800 Fax 832/223-3801
Reading Junior High Sch 8101 FM 762 Rd, Richmond 77469 **Dr Sonya Sanzo**	6-8		1,200	24%	832/223-4400 Fax 832/223-4401
Roberts Middle Sch 9230 Charger Way, Fulshear 77441 **Janice Harvey**	6-6		415		832/223-5300
Seguin Early Child Hood Ctr 605 Mabel St, Richmond 77469 Mary Ellen Rocha	PK-PK	T	311 30	62%	832/223-2200 Fax 832/223-2201
Smith Elem Sch 2014 Lamar Dr, Richmond 77469 Carla Thomas	PK-5	T	420 39	77%	832/223-2300 Fax 832/223-2301
Susannah Dickinson Elem Sch 7110 Greatwood Pkwy, Sugar Land 77479 Karen Mumphord	PK-5		544 42	6%	832/223-1400 Fax 832/223-1401
T L Pink Elem Sch 1001 Collins Rd, Richmond 77469 Tiffany Foster	PK-5	T	575 45	88%	832/223-2100 Fax 832/223-2101
Taylor Ray Elem Sch 2611 Avenue N, Rosenberg 77471 Ben Perez	PK-5	T	634 34	87%	832/223-2400 Fax 832/223-2401
Terry High Sch 5500 Avenue N, Rosenberg 77471 **Juan Nava**	9-12	TV	2,084 95	62%	832/223-3400 Fax 832/223-3401
Thomas Elem Sch 6822 Irby Cobb Blvd, Richmond 77469 Vicki Stevenson	PK-5		870	51%	832/223-4600 Fax 832/223-4601
Travis Elem Sch 2700 Avenue K, Rosenberg 77471 Jearine Jordan	PK-5	T	537 34	85%	832/223-2500 Fax 832/223-2501
Wertheimer Middle Sch 4240 FM 723 Rd, Rosenberg 77471 **Sharyn Kitto**	6-6		428	27%	832/223-4100 Fax 832/223-4101
William Velasquez Elem Sch 402 Macek Rd, Richmond 77469 Brian Gibson	PK-5	T	652	52%	832/223-2600 Fax 832/223-2601
Williams Elem Sch 5111 FM 762 Rd, Richmond 77469 Anitra Wilson	PK-5		500	27%	832/223-2700 Fax 832/223-2701

● **Needville Ind School Dist** PID: 01018347   979/793-4158
16227 Highway 36, Needville 77461   Fax 979/793-3823

Schools: 4 \ **Teachers:** 194 \ **Students:** 3,228 \ **Special Ed Students:** 320 \ **LEP Students:** 275 \ **College-Bound:** 68% \ **Ethnic:** African American 3%, Hispanic 46%, Caucasian 50% \ **Exp:** $369 (High) \ **Poverty:** 10% \ **Title I:** $321,220 \ **Open-Close:** 08/26 - 05/22 \ **DTBP:** $155 (High)

Curtis Rhodes 1		Dovie Peschel 2		
Rodney Wieghat 3,5		Michael Giles 6		
Beth Briscoe 8,11,15,69,271		Melissa Rhodes 16*		
Chris Janicek 67		Charles Roehling 68		
Corey Kelly 73		Nick Stockton 295*		

Public Schs..Principal	Grd	Prgm	Enr/#Cls	SN	Phone
Needville Elem Sch 3600 Margaret St, Needville 77461 Stacey Stavinoha	PK-4	T	1,255 40	41%	979/793-4241 Fax 979/793-2299
Needville High Sch 100 Fritzella Rd, Needville 77461 Steve Adamson	9-12	AV	1,044 80	30%	979/793-4158 Fax 979/793-5590
Needville Junior High Sch 16413 Fritzella Road, Needville 77461 Karen Smart	7-8		456 17	36%	979/793-4250 Fax 979/793-4575
Needville Middle Sch 16411 Fritzella Rd, Needville 77461 Marla Sebesta	5-6	T	473 50	41%	979/793-3027 Fax 979/793-7665

● **Stafford Municipal Sch Dist** PID: 02228624   281/261-9200
1625 Staffordshire Rd, Stafford 77477   Fax 281/261-9249

Schools: 7 \ **Teachers:** 210 \ **Students:** 3,600 \ **Special Ed Students:** 285 \ **LEP Students:** 531 \ **College-Bound:** 57% \ **Ethnic:** Asian 6%, African American 43%, Hispanic 46%, Caucasian 4% \ **Exp:** $337 (High) \ **Poverty:** 12% \ **Title I:** $454,931 \ **Special Education:** $579,000 \ **Open-Close:** 08/14 - 05/22 \ **DTBP:** $181 (High)

---

1 Superintendent	20 Art K-12	39 Social Studies K-12	59 Special Education Elem
2 Bus/Finance/Purchasing	21 Art Elem	40 Social Studies Elem	60 Special Education Sec
3 Buildings And Grounds	22 Art Sec	41 Social Studies Sec	61 Foreign/World Lang K-12
4 Food Service	23 Music K-12	42 Science K-12	62 Foreign/World Lang Elem
5 Transportation	24 Music Elem	43 Science Elem	63 Foreign/World Lang Sec
6 Athletic	25 Music Sec	44 Science Sec	64 Religious Education K-12
7 Health Services	26 Business Education	45 Math K-12	65 Religious Education Elem
8 Curric/Instruct K-12	27 Career & Tech Ed	46 Math Elem	66 Religious Education Sec
9 Curric/Instruct Elem	28 Technology Education	47 Math Sec	67 School Board President
10 Curric/Instruct Sec	29 Family/Consumer Science	48 English/Lang Arts K-12	68 Teacher Personnel
11 Federal Program	30 Adult Education	49 English/Lang Arts Elem	69 Academic Assessment
12 Title I	31 Career/Sch-to-Work K-12	50 English/Lang Arts Sec	70 Research/Development
13 Title V	32 Career/Sch-to-Work Elem	51 Reading K-12	71 Public Information
14 Asst Superintendent	33 Career/Sch-to-Work Sec	52 Reading Elem	72 Summer School
15 Instructional Media Svcs	34 Early Childhood Ed	53 Reading Sec	73 Instructional Tech
16 Chief Operations Officer	35 Health/Phys Education	54 Remedial Reading K-12	74 Inservice Training
17 Chief Academic Officer	36 Guidance Services K-12	55 Remedial Reading Elem	75 Marketing/Distributive
18 Chief Financial Officer	37 Guidance Services Elem	56 Remedial Reading Sec	76 Info Systems
19 Chief Financial Officer	38 Guidance Services Sec	57 Bilingual/ELL	77 Psychological Assess
		58 Special Education K-12	78 Affirmative Action

TX—154

Texas School Directory

Franklin County

Dr Robert Bostic 1
Jaci Phenix 3
Greg Jerkins 5
Carlotta Allen 8,273,285
Dr Teresa Sazedj 13,78,296
Steve Perez 16
Jorge Rodgiuez 73,295

Daniel Flores 2
Danny McDonald 4
Ken Savanah 6
Charmaine Garcia 11,58,275
Marva Rasberry .. 16,57,69,74,88,270,288,294
Christopher Caldwell 67
Cherise Roberts 298

Public Schs..Principal	Grd	Prgm	Enr/#Cls	SN	
Ⓐ Quest Academy 1625 Staffordshire Rd, Stafford 77477 **Carlotta Allen**	10-11		20		281/261-9200
Ⓐ Stafford Alt Ed Campus 1625 Staffordshire Rd, Stafford 77477 **Carlotta Jenkins**	6-12		25 2		281/261-9270 Fax 281/208-6118
Stafford Elem Sch 1625 Staffordshire Rd, Stafford 77477 **Twyla Hynes**	2-4	T	799 40	74%	281/261-9229 Fax 281/261-9262
Stafford High Sch 1625 Staffordshire Rd, Stafford 77477 **Raymond Root**	9-12	ATV	1,052 40	59%	281/261-9239 Fax 281/261-9347
Stafford Intermediate Sch 1625 Staffordshire Rd, Stafford 77477 **Desiree James**	5-6	T	539 30	71%	281/208-6100 Fax 281/208-6111
Stafford Middle Sch 1625 Staffordshire Rd, Stafford 77477 **Ginny Gayle**	7-8	T	527 64	68%	281/261-9215 Fax 281/261-9349
Stafford Primary Sch 1625 Staffordshire Rd, Stafford 77477 **Twyla Hynes**	PK-1	T	690 38	76%	281/261-9203 Fax 281/261-9348

FORT BEND CATHOLIC SCHOOLS

• **Archdiocese Galveston-Houston** PID: 01027855
Listing includes only schools located in this county. See District Index for location of Diocesan Offices.

Catholic Schs..Principal	Grd	Prgm	Enr/#Cls	SN	
Holy Rosary Sch 1426 George St, Rosenberg 77471 **Linda Bradford**	PK-8		200 13		281/342-5813 Fax 281/344-1107
St Laurence Catholic Sch 2630 Austin Pkwy, Sugar Land 77479 **Suzanne Barto**	PK-8		680 32		281/980-0500 Fax 281/980-0026
St Theresa Sch 705 St Theresa Blvd, Sugar Land 77498 **Dr Mark Newcomb**	K-5		70		281/494-1156 Fax 281/242-1393

FORT BEND PRIVATE SCHOOLS

Private Schs..Principal	Grd	Prgm	Enr/#Cls	SN	
Bakers Preparatory Sch 504 Murphy Rd Ste H, Stafford 77477 **Dianna Baker**	PK-5		90 7		281/403-2100 Fax 281/403-2101
Calvary Episcopal Sch 1201 Austin St, Richmond 77469 **Malcolm Smith**	PK-12		180 20		281/342-3161 Fax 281/232-9449
Excel Adventist Academy 7950 W Fuqua Dr, Missouri City 77489 **H Phillip Henry**	PK-8		46 5		281/835-0770 Fax 281/835-1275
Focus Academy 130 Industrial Blvd Ste 130, Sugar Land 77478 **Jacquelyn Mulkey**	6-12		15		281/240-0663
Fort Bend Baptist Academy ES 1201 Lakeview Dr, Sugar Land 77478 **Margie Meyer**	PK-5		320 23		281/263-9100 Fax 281/263-9102
Fort Bend Christian Academy MS 1201 Lakeview Dr, Sugar Land 77478 **Ron Bell**	5-8		265 18		281/263-9191 Fax 281/263-9193
Fort Bend Christian Academy-HS 1250 7th St, Sugar Land 77478 **Joshua Gettys**	9-12		350 22		281/263-9175 Fax 281/263-9199
Fusion Academy-Sugarland 13440 University Blvd Ste 260, Sugar Land 77479 **Shayne Horan**	6-12		401		281/207-9506
Global Innovation Sch 2553 Cordes Dr, Sugar Land 77479 **Huda Ahmed**	PK-12	G	170 15		281/980-5800 Fax 281/980-6106
Honor Roll Sch 4111 Sweetwater Blvd, Sugar Land 77479 **Doris Quintero**	PK-8		600 37		281/265-7888 Fax 281/265-7880
Living Water Christian Sch 4808 Airport Ave, Rosenberg 77471 **Gamila Frank**	PK-12		100 13		281/342-6336 Fax 281/342-9951
Logos Preparatory Academy 13303 Southwest Fwy, Sugar Land 77478 **Tammy McIlvoy**	K-12		500		281/565-6467 Fax 713/456-2306
Simonton Christian Academy 9703 FM 1489, Simonton 77476 **Amy Oglesby**	PK-8		45 6		281/346-2303 Fax 281/346-2393 f
Southminster Sch 4200 Cartwright Rd, Missouri City 77459 **Tiera Pennix**	PK-6		250		281/261-8872 Fax 281/499-4430
Towne Creek Sch 3311 Williamsburg Ln, Missouri City 77459 **Judy Feinsteen**	PK-K		200 15		281/499-8030 Fax 281/261-7846
Walden Sch 16103 Lexington Blvd Ste A, Sugar Land 77479 **Mike McGilvray**	PK-2		150		281/980-0022 Fax 281/980-0040
Westlake Lutheran Academy 23300 Bellaire Blvd, Richmond 77406 **Judy Gerber**	PK-8		186		281/341-9910 Fax 281/341-9915

FRANKLIN COUNTY

FRANKLIN PUBLIC SCHOOLS

• **Mt Vernon Ind School Dist** PID: 01018385   903/537-2546
501 Texas Highway 37, Mount Vernon 75457   Fax 903/537-4784

Schools: 3 \ ***Teachers:*** 124 \ ***Students:*** 1,620 \ ***Special Ed Students:*** 155 \ ***LEP Students:*** 149 \ ***Ethnic:*** Asian 1%, African American 5%, Hispanic 27%, Caucasian 66% \ ***Exp:*** $325 (High) \ ***Poverty:*** 20% \ ***Title I:*** $400,070 \ ***Special Education:*** $328,000 \ ***Open-Close:*** 08/19 - 05/21 \ ***DTBP:*** $348 (High) \ f

Jason McCullough 1
Shelley Black 4
Art Briles 6
Diane Ramsay 13,16,286*
Lacey Stephens 36,83,85,88,285*

Pamela Vandeaver 2
Bobby Thompson 5
Chandra White 8,11,15,288
Jason Glover 31*
Craig Watson 58*

9	Student Personnel	91	Safety/Security	275	Response To Intervention	298	Grant Writer/Ptnrships	**School Programs**	**Social Media**
0	Driver Ed/Safety	92	Magnet School	277	Remedial Math K-12	750	Chief Innovation Officer	**A** = Alternative Program	
1	Gifted/Talented	93	Parental Involvement	280	Literacy Coach	751	Chief of Staff	**G** = Adult Classes	f = Facebook
2	Video Services	95	Tech Prep Program	285	STEM	752	Social Emotional Learning	**M** = Magnet Program	
3	Substance Abuse Prev	97	Chief Information Officer	286	Digital Learning			**T** = Title I Schoolwide	t = Twitter
4	Erate	98	Chief Technology Officer	288	Common Core Standards	**Other School Types**		**V** = Career & Tech Ed Programs	
5	AIDS Education	270	Character Education	294	Accountability	Ⓐ = Alternative School			
8	Alternative/At Risk	271	Migrant Education	295	Network System	Ⓒ = Charter School		New Schools are shaded	
9	Multi-Cultural Curriculum	273	Teacher Mentor	296	Title II Programs	Ⓜ = Magnet School		New Superintendents and Principals are bold	
0	Social Work	274	Before/After Sch	297	Webmaster	Ⓨ = Year-Round School		Personnel with email addresses are underscored	

TX−155

Freestone County

Market Data Retrieval

Aaron Sanders	67	Anthony Eilers		73,295
Dara Fisk	77*			

Public Schs..Principal	Grd	Prgm	Enr/#Cls	SN	
Mt Vernon Elem Sch 501 Texas Highway 37, Mount Vernon 75457 Jennifer Driver	PK-4	T	633 30	67%	903/537-2266 Fax 903/537-3815
Mt Vernon High Sch 501 Texas Highway 37, Mount Vernon 75457 Jason Glover	9-12	TV	469 30	51%	903/537-3700 Fax 903/537-2536
Mt Vernon Middle Sch 501 Texas Highway 37, Mount Vernon 75457 James Payne	5-8	TV	523 15	56%	903/537-2267 Fax 903/537-3601

FREESTONE COUNTY

FREESTONE PUBLIC SCHOOLS

- **Dew Ind School Dist** PID: 01018438   903/389-2828
  606 County Road 481, Teague 75860   Fax 903/389-5104

Schools: 1 \ *Teachers:* 17 \ *Students:* 180 \ *Special Ed Students:* 13 \ *LEP Students:* 6 \ *Ethnic:* African American 10%, Hispanic 12%, Caucasian 78% \ *Exp:* $303 (High) \ *Poverty:* 13% \ *Title I:* $23,056 \ *Open-Close:* 08/14 - 05/22 \ *DTBP:* $361 (High) \ 🅕

Darrell Evans	1,11	Nolan Glass	2
Charlotte Winkler	4*	Nicole Sifford	7
Christie Fishbeck	16,73,295,297*	Ginny Blackwell	57,271*
David Fowler	67		

Public Schs..Principal	Grd	Prgm	Enr/#Cls	SN	
Dew Elem Sch 606 County Road 481, Teague 75860 Darrell Evans	PK-8	T	180 7	52%	903/389-2828 🅕 🅣

- **Fairfield Ind School Dist** PID: 01018452   903/389-2532
  615 Post Oak Rd, Fairfield 75840   Fax 903/389-7050

Schools: 4 \ *Teachers:* 142 \ *Students:* 1,817 \ *Special Ed Students:* 114 \ *LEP Students:* 107 \ *Ethnic:* Asian 1%, African American 16%, Hispanic 24%, Caucasian 59% \ *Exp:* $332 (High) \ *Poverty:* 16% \ *Title I:* $357,344 \ *Open-Close:* 08/14 - 05/28 \ *DTBP:* $375 (High)

Jason Adams	1	Sharon Gibson	2
Ron Harris	3	Crystal Thill	4
Carol Cain	5,294	Michael Mertz	5
John Bachtel	6*	Kimberlee Nicholas	7*
Melissa Cox	8,11,57,69,79,280,296,298	Eric Chavers	67
Lisa Tate	68	Arland Thill	73,295
Lindy Neill	83	Billy Barlow	91

Public Schs..Principal	Grd	Prgm	Enr/#Cls	SN	
Fairfield Elem Sch 330 W Main St, Fairfield 75840 Sheila Ransom	PK-2	T	449 40	59%	903/389-2148 Fax 903/389-5314
Fairfield High Sch 631 Post Oak Rd, Fairfield 75840 Von Wade	9-12	TV	537 42	42%	903/389-4177 Fax 903/389-5453
Fairfield Intermediate Sch 605 N Fairway St, Fairfield 75840 Shetonia Scires	3-5	T	433	53%	903/389-7095 Fax 903/389-7101
Fairfield Junior High Sch 701 Post Oak Rd, Fairfield 75840 Bryan Gawryszewski	6-8	T	398 37	55%	903/389-4210 Fax 903/389-5454

- **Teague Ind School Dist** PID: 01018505   254/739-1300
  420 N 10th Ave, Teague 75860   Fax 254/739-5223

Schools: 5 \ *Teachers:* 100 \ *Students:* 1,160 \ *Special Ed Students:* 131 \ *LEP Students:* 69 \ *College-Bound:* 59% \ *Ethnic:* African American 15%, Hispanic 28%, Caucasian 57% \ *Exp:* $277 (Med) \ *Poverty:* 26% \ *Title I:* $385,186 \ *Special Education:* $257,000 \ *Open-Close:* 08/15 - 05/28 \ *DTBP:* $342 (High)

Chris Skinner	1	Emily Evans	2
Debra Lively	4*	Donnie Osborn	6*
Kella Redic	7*	Ray Matthews	15
Lynne Kilman	16*	Christina Fuller	57*
Jeff Gonzales	67	Elizabeth Hernandez	69
Brent Holmes	73,295*	Cathy Schmidt	288,296*

Public Schs..Principal	Grd	Prgm	Enr/#Cls	SN	
Teague Elem Sch 420 N 10th Ave, Teague 75860 Crystal Adams	PK-3	T	355 23	64%	254/739-2611 Fax 254/739-3605
Teague High Sch 420 Highway Loop 225, Teague 75860 Tracie Ezell	9-12	T	410 20	45%	254/739-2532 Fax 254/739-2724
Teague Intermediate Sch 420 Highway Loop 225, Teague 75860 Vickey Little	4-5	T	188 17	59%	254/739-3303 Fax 254/739-3561
Teague Junior High Sch 420 Highway Loop 225, Teague 75860 Drake Paris	6-8	T	262 25	60%	254/739-3011 Fax 254/739-5896
ⓐ Teague Lion Academy 420 N 10th Ave, Teague 75860 Cathy Schmidt	7-12	T	20	82%	254/739-1444

- **Wortham Ind School Dist** PID: 01018543   254/765-3095
  201 S 4th St, Wortham 76693   Fax 254/765-3473

Schools: 3 \ *Teachers:* 43 \ *Students:* 500 \ *Special Ed Students:* 33 \ *LEP Students:* 13 \ *Ethnic:* African American 14%, Hispanic 19%, Caucasian 66% \ *Exp:* $508 (High) \ *Poverty:* 21% \ *Title I:* $98,032 \ *Open-Close:* 08/15 - 05/22 \ *DTBP:* $404 (High)

David Allen	1,11	Sherry Shivers	2
David Hayes	8,271,273*	Jack Rex	16,73*
Deanna Whaley	37,69	Krystal Duke	38
Chad Coker	58*	Jeff Jones	67
Amy Miller	83,85*		

Public Schs..Principal	Grd	Prgm	Enr/#Cls	SN	
Wortham Elem Sch 200 S 5th St, Wortham 76693 Dee Allen	PK-5	T	255 13	62%	254/765-3523 Fax 254/765-3512
Wortham High Sch 109 S 5th St, Wortham 76693 David Hayes	9-12	ATV	151	36%	254/765-3094
Wortham Middle Sch 200 S 5th St, Wortham 76693 David Hayes	6-8	T	104 6	47%	254/765-3523 Fax 254/765-3512

1	Superintendent	8	Curric/Instruct K-12	19	Chief Financial Officer	29	Family/Consumer Science
2	Bus/Finance/Purchasing	9	Curric/Instruct Elem	20	Art K-12	30	Adult Education
3	Buildings And Grounds	10	Curric/Instruct Sec	21	Art Elem	31	Career/Sch-to-Work K-12
4	Food Service	11	Federal Program	22	Art Sec	32	Career/Sch-to-Work Elem
5	Transportation	12	Title I	23	Music K-12	33	Career/Sch-to-Work Sec
6	Athletic	13	Title V	24	Music Elem	34	Early Childhood Ed
7	Health Services	14	Asst Superintendent	25	Music Sec	35	Health/Phys Education
		15	Instructional Media Svcs	26	Business Education	36	Guidance Services K-12
		16	Chief Operations Officer	27	Career & Tech Ed	37	Guidance Services Elem
		18	Chief Academic Officer	28	Technology Education	38	Guidance Services Sec

39	Social Studies K-12	49	English/Lang Arts Elem	59	Special Education Elem	69	Academic Assessment
40	Social Studies Elem	50	English/Lang Arts Sec	60	Special Education Sec	70	Research/Development
41	Social Studies Sec	51	Reading K-12	61	Foreign/World Lang K-12	71	Public Information
42	Science K-12	52	Reading Elem	62	Foreign/World Lang Elem	72	Summer School
43	Science Elem	53	Reading Sec	63	Foreign/World Lang Sec	73	Instructional Tech
44	Science Sec	54	Remedial Reading K-12	64	Religious Education K-12	74	Inservice Training
45	Math K-12	55	Remedial Reading Elem	65	Religious Education Elem	75	Marketing/Distributive
46	Math Elem	56	Remedial Reading Soc	66	Religious Education Sec	76	Info Systems
47	Math Sec	57	Bilingual/ELL	67	School Board President	77	Psychological Assess
48	English/Lang Arts K-12	58	Special Education K-12	68	Teacher Personnel	78	Affirmative Action

TX—156

Texas School Directory

FRIO COUNTY

FRIO PUBLIC SCHOOLS

• **Dilley Ind School Dist** PID: 01018579   830/965-1912
245 W FM 117, Dilley 78017   Fax 830/965-4069

Schools: 4 \ *Teachers:* 78 \ *Students:* 1,000 \ *Special Ed Students:* 101 \ *LEP Students:* 29 \ *College-Bound:* 50% \ *Ethnic:* Asian 1%, Hispanic 89%, Caucasian 10% \ *Exp:* $691 (High) \ *Poverty:* 39% \ *Title I:* $513,682 \ *Open-Close:* 08/14 - 05/21 \ *DTBP:* $349 (High)

Dr Clint McLain 1   Ryan Autry 2
Javier Torres 3   Grace Garza 4
Raul Ramirez 5   Manny Martinez 6
Steve Lozano 11   James Angst 58
Aida Chapa 67   Matthew Agular 73
Inelda Rodriguez ....271*   Melody Carroll 288

Public Schs..Principal	Grd	Prgm	Enr/#Cls	SN	
Dilley Early Clg High Sch 245 W FM 117, Dilley 78017 Jadie Matthew	11-12		100		830/965-1814
Dilley Elem Sch 226 W Curtis St, Dilley 78017 Delma Carrion	PK-5	T	458 40	79%	830/965-1313 Fax 830/965-1178
Dilley High Sch 230 W FM 117, Dilley 78017 Roger Solis	9-12	AGTV	300 25	70%	830/965-1814 Fax 830/965-1276
Mary Harper Middle Sch 208 W Curtis St, Dilley 78017 Jennifer Torres	6-8	T	223 19	70%	830/965-2195 Fax 830/965-2171 f t

• **Pearsall Ind School Dist** PID: 01018610   830/334-8001
318 Berry Ranch Rd, Pearsall 78061   Fax 830/334-8007

Schools: 4 \ *Teachers:* 167 \ *Students:* 2,100 \ *Special Ed Students:* 219 \ *LEP Students:* 122 \ *College-Bound:* 30% \ *Ethnic:* Hispanic 95%, Caucasian 5% \ *Exp:* $311 (High) \ *Poverty:* 31% \ *Title I:* $996,874 \ *Open-Close:* 08/14 - 05/22 \ *DTBP:* $362 (High) \ f t

Dr Norbert Rodriguez 1   Debbie Kloth 2
Andres Cuevas 3   Dan Strakos 3
Shawn Sheets 4   Juan Ventura 5
Edward Bocanegra 6   Sonya Martinez 8,68,69,79
Brandi Feldhouson 11,57,88,271   Jim Angst 58
Tommy Navarro 67   Jesse Hinojosa 73,84,295
Chris Marquez 91

Public Schs..Principal	Grd	Prgm	Enr/#Cls	SN	
Pearsall High Sch 1990 Maverick Dr, Pearsall 78061 Varghese Panachakunnil	9-12	AGTV	667 40	82%	830/334-8011 Fax 830/334-5018
Pearsall Intermediate Sch 415 E Florida St, Pearsall 78061 **Gilbert Cantu**	3-5	T	512 60	85%	830/334-3316 Fax 830/334-5006
Pearsall Junior High Sch 607 E Alabama St, Pearsall 78061 Devon Zamzow	6-8	ATV	480 40	83%	830/334-8021 Fax 830/334-8025
Ted Flores Elem Sch 321 W Pena St, Pearsall 78061 Linda Chavera	PK-2	T	629 38	75%	830/334-4108 Fax 830/334-5047

FRIO PRIVATE SCHOOLS

Private Schs..Principal	Grd	Prgm	Enr/#Cls	SN	
Faith Christian Academy 124 E Leona St, Dilley 78017 Janeen Hartsfield	2-11		35 1		830/965-1324 Fax 830/965-1096

GAINES COUNTY

GAINES PUBLIC SCHOOLS

• **Loop Ind School Dist** PID: 01018684   806/487-6412
1441 Highway 303, Loop 79342   Fax 806/487-6420

Schools: 1 \ *Teachers:* 17 \ *Students:* 150 \ *Special Ed Students:* 9 \ *LEP Students:* 11 \ *College-Bound:* 100% \ *Ethnic:* African American 1%, Hispanic 59%, Caucasian 40% \ *Exp:* $1,404 (High) \ *Poverty:* 18% \ *Title I:* $24,619 \ *Open-Close:* 08/19 - 05/22 \ *DTBP:* $400 (High)

Heath Blackman 1,11,288   **Deanne Bratcher** 2
Rebecca Sescota 4   Vanetta Blackmon 8,69,88*
Charla Scott ....16,27*   Kim McCoral 58*
Norman Crow 67

Public Schs..Principal	Grd	Prgm	Enr/#Cls	SN	
Loop Sch 1441 Highway 303, Loop 79342 Heath Blackmon	PK-12	TV	150 22	58%	806/487-6412 f

• **Seagraves Ind School Dist** PID: 01018713   806/387-2035
1301 16th St, Seagraves 79359   Fax 806/387-2944

Schools: 3 \ *Teachers:* 56 \ *Students:* 569 \ *Special Ed Students:* 32 \ *LEP Students:* 122 \ *Ethnic:* African American 7%, Hispanic 80%, Caucasian 13% \ *Exp:* $965 (High) \ *Poverty:* 34% \ *Title I:* $357,533 \ *Open-Close:* 08/26 - 05/29 \ *DTBP:* $350 (High) \ f

Joshua Goen 1,11,83   Traci Garza 2
Ruben Valles 3,5   Louisa Ayala 4
Jamie Humphries ....6*   Jennifer Floyd 7,85*
Daylan Sellers ....10*   Elaine Daniels 38
Mary Heryford 38   Rose Flores 57*
Tim Carmichael 67   Scott Beck 73*

Public Schs..Principal	Grd	Prgm	Enr/#Cls	SN	
Seagraves Elem Sch 1300 Avenue J, Seagraves 79359 Junior Martinez	PK-5		320 35		806/387-2015 Fax 806/387-3339 f
Seagraves High Sch 1801 Avenue K, Seagraves 79359 Daylan Sellers	9-12	ATV	166 20	73%	806/387-2520 f
Seagraves Junior High Sch 1605 Avenue K, Seagraves 79359 **Jame Humphries**	6-8		144 16		806/387-2646 Fax 806/387-2451 f

---

79 Student Personnel	91 Safety/Security	275 Response To Intervention	298 Grant Writer/Ptnrships	School Programs	Social Media
80 Driver Ed/Safety	92 Magnet School	277 Remedial Math K-12	750 Chief Innovation Officer	A = Alternative Program	
81 Gifted/Talented	93 Parental Involvement	280 Literacy Coach	751 Chief of Staff	G = Adult Classes	f = Facebook
82 Video Services	95 Tech Prep Program	285 STEM	752 Social Emotional Learning	M = Magnet Program	
83 Substance Abuse Prev	97 Chief Infomation Officer	286 Digital Learning		T = Title I Schoolwide	t = Twitter
84 Erate	98 Chief Technology Officer	288 Common Core Standards	Other School Types	V = Career & Tech Ed Programs	
85 AIDS Education	270 Character Education	294 Accountability	A = Alternative School		
88 Alternative/At Risk	271 Migrant Education	295 Network System	C = Charter School	New Schools are shaded	
89 Multi-Cultural Curriculum	273 Teacher Mentor	296 Title II Programs	M = Magnet School	New Superintendents and Principals are bold	
90 Social Work	274 Before/After Sch	297 Webmaster	Y = Year-Round School	Personnel with email addresses are underscored	TX—157

Galveston County

Market Data Retrieval

- **Seminole Ind School Dist** PID: 01018751   432/758-3662
  207 SW 6th St, Seminole 79360   Fax 432/758-9833

Schools: 6 \ **Teachers:** 213 \ **Students:** 2,983 \ **Special Ed Students:** 214 \ **LEP Students:** 382 \ **Ethnic:** Asian 1%, African American 1%, Hispanic 50%, Caucasian 49% \ **Exp:** $340 (High) \ **Poverty:** 19% \ **Title I:** $996,467 \ **Special Education:** $466,000 \ **Open-Close:** 08/15 - 05/22 \ **DTBP:** $379 (High) \ 🅕 🅣

Kyle Lynch 1	Jay Lashaway 2
Bryan Ritchie 3	Cindy Therwhanger 4
Arsenio Ramirez 5	David Williams 6
Cheryl Houston 7,85*	Dr Sylvia Suarez 8,11,15,57,280,288,296
Mary Ortega 30	Cindy Franklin 58
Shane Wimmer 67	Tasha Garcia 69*
Stephanie Stone 73,286,297	Seth Davis 88

Public Schs..Principal	Grd	Prgm	Enr/#Cls	SN	
Seminole Elem Sch 401 SW Avenue B, Seminole 79360 Aine Lopez	4-5	T	430 21	55%	432/758-3615 Fax 432/758-9064
Seminole High Sch 2100 NW Avenue D, Seminole 79360 Reed Chappell	9-12	T	760 80	39%	432/758-5873 Fax 432/758-8146
Seminole Junior High Sch 600 NW Avenue J, Seminole 79360 Randy Hicks	6-8	T	677 50	56%	432/758-9431 Fax 432/758-5795
Seminole Primary Sch 508 SW Avenue D, Seminole 79360 Kathy Moore	2-3	T	443 18	56%	432/758-5841 Fax 432/758-5299
Seminole Success Center 206 SW 3rd St, Seminole 79360 Stephen Davis	6-12	T	34 6	54%	432/758-2772 Fax 432/758-9917
Young Elem Sch 2100 SW Avenue B, Seminole 79360 Sherry Warren	PK-1	T	551 35	65%	432/758-3636 Fax 432/758-2066

GALVESTON COUNTY

GALVESTON PUBLIC SCHOOLS

- **Clear Creek Ind School Dist** PID: 01018816   281/284-0000
  2425 E Main St, League City 77573   Fax 281/284-9901

Schools: 45 \ **Teachers:** 2,466 \ **Students:** 44,099 \ **Special Ed Students:** 4,111 \ **LEP Students:** 3,848 \ **College-Bound:** 80% \ **Ethnic:** Asian 10%, African American 9%, Hispanic 32%, Caucasian 49% \ **Exp:** $221 (Med) \ **Poverty:** 9% \ **Title I:** $4,911,143 \ **Special Education:** $6,029,000 \ **Open-Close:** 08/19 - 05/28 \ **DTBP:** $193 (High)

Dr Greg Smith 1	Paul McLarty 2,3,15
Paul Miller 3	Fred Walker 4
Ezell Brown 5	Debbie Fuchs 6,35
Dr Steven Ebell 8,15,288	Holly Hughes 9,15
Karen Engle 10,15*	Dr Casey Pry 15
Dr Casey O'Pry 15,68,273	Sue Ferrell 16
Greg Goodman 20,23	Dana Morgan 27,31
Christy Lawrence 34*	Natalie Uranga 36
Marny Doepken 39*	Anne Smith 43
Lisa Wooley 44	Rachel Powell 46,277
Lana Zimmer 47	Tacy King 57
Dr Cynthia Short 58,83,90,275	William Eastman 61
Dr Laura DuPont 67	Elaina Polsen 71
Lorrine Pinegar 71	Robert Bayard 73,98,295
Sabina Trevino 76	Pam Moore-Ellis 77
Glenda Holder 81	Brian Palazzi 91
Jessica Vandervoort 297*	

Public Schs..Principal	Grd	Prgm	Enr/#Cls	SN	
Armand Bayou Elem Sch 16000 Hickory Knoll Dr, Houston 77059 Jenny Thomas	PK-5		548 31	35%	281/284-5100 Fax 281/284-5106
Art & Pat Goforth Elem Sch 2610 Webster St, League City 77573 Mark Smith	PK-5		890	19%	281/284-6000 Fax 281/284-6006
Bayside Intermediate Sch 4430 Village Way, League City 77573 James Thomas	6-8		819	19%	281/284-3000 Fax 281/284-3005
Brookside Intermediate Sch 3535 E FM 528 Rd, Friendswood 77546 Lauren Ambeau	6-8	TV	810 88	40%	281/284-3600 Fax 281/284-3605
Brookwood Elem Sch 16850 Middlebrook Dr, Houston 77059 Kathryn Gouger	PK-5		752	33%	281/284-5600 Fax 281/284-5605
C D Landolt Elem Sch 2104 Pilgrims Point Dr, Friendswood 77546 Debra Reno	PK-5	T	865 37	42%	281/284-5200 Fax 281/284-5206
Clear Brook High Sch 4607 FM 2351 Rd, Friendswood 77546 Michele Staley	9-12	V	2,200 120	26%	281/284-2100 Fax 281/284-2105
Clear Creek High Sch 2305 E Main St, League City 77573 James Majewski	9-12	GV	2,354	29%	281/284-1700 Fax 281/284-1705
Clear Creek Intermediate Sch 2451 E Main St, League City 77573 Kimberly Brouillard	6-8	T	805	45%	281/284-2300 Fax 281/284-2306
Clear Falls High Sch 4380 Village Way, League City 77573 Paul House	9-10	V	2,591	16%	281/284-1100 Fax 281/284-1106
Clear Horizons Early Clg HS 13735 Beamer Rd Box 613, Houston 77089 Marshall Ponce	9-12		442	30%	281/929-4657 Fax 281/284-9960
Clear Lake City Elem Sch 1707 Fairwind Rd, Houston 77062 Jepsey Kimble	PK-5	T	589 26	45%	281/284-4200 Fax 281/284-4205
Clear Lake High Sch 2929 Bay Area Blvd, Houston 77058 David Drake	9-12	V	2,332	23%	281/284-1900 Fax 281/286-3249
Clear Lake Intermediate Sch 15545 El Camino Real, Houston 77062 Lonnie Leal	6-8	V	926 70	40%	281/284-3200 Fax 281/284-3205
Ⓐ Clear Path Alt High Sch 1001 Magnolia St, Webster 77598 Jerry Herd	6-12		150	40%	281/284-1600 Fax 281/284-1605
Clear Springs High Sch 501 Palomino St, League City 77573 Michael Houston	9-12		2,721	16%	281/284-1300 Fax 281/284-1305
Ⓐ Clear View High Sch 400 S Walnut St, Webster 77598 Monica Speaks	9-12	T	216 22	35%	281/284-1500 Fax 281/284-1505
Creekside Intermediate Sch 4320 W Main St, League City 77573 Mandy Scott	6-8	V	943 50	21%	281/284-3500 Fax 281/284-3505
Darwin L Gilmore Elem Sch 3552 W League City Pkwy, League City 77573 Suzanne Jones	PK-5		892	14%	281/284-6400 Fax 281/284-6405

1	Superintendent	8	Curric/Instruct K-12	19	Chief Financial Officer	29	Family/Consumer Science	39	Social Studies K-12
2	Bus/Finance/Purchasing	9	Curric/Instruct Elem	20	Art K-12	30	Adult Education	40	Social Studies Elem
3	Buildings And Grounds	10	Curric/Instruct Sec	21	Art Elem	31	Career/Sch-to-Work K-12	41	Social Studies Sec
4	Food Service	11	Federal Program	22	Art Sec	32	Career/Sch-to-Work Elem	42	Science K-12
5	Transportation	12	Title I	23	Music K-12	33	Career/Sch-to-Work Sec	43	Science Elem
6	Athletic	13	Title V	24	Music Elem	34	Early Childhood Ed	44	Science Sec
7	Health Services	15	Asst Superintendent	25	Music Sec	35	Health/Phys Education	45	Math K-12
		16	Instructional Media Svcs	26	Business Education	36	Religious Education K-12	46	Math Elem
		17	Chief Operations Officer	27	Career & Tech Ed	37	Guidance Services Elem	47	Math Sec
		18	Chief Academic Officer	28	Technology Education	38	Guidance Services Sec	48	English/Lang Arts K-12

49	English/Lang Arts Elem	59	Special Education Elem	69	Academic Assessment
50	English/Lang Arts Sec	60	Special Education Sec	70	Research/Development
51	Reading K-12	61	Foreign/World Lang K-12	71	Public Information
52	Reading Elem	62	Foreign/World Lang Elem	72	Summer School
53	Reading Sec	63	Foreign/World Lang Sec	73	Instructional Tech
54	Remedial Reading K-12	64	Religious Education K-12	74	Inservice Training
55	Remedial Reading Elem	65	Religious Education Elem	75	Marketing/Distributive
56	Remedial Reading Sec	66	Religious Education Sec	76	Info Systems
57	Bilingual/ELL	67	School Board President	77	Psychological Assess
58	Special Education K-12	68	Teacher Personnel	78	Affirmative Action

Texas School Directory — Galveston County

School	Grd	Prgm	Enr/#Cls	SN	Phone
Ed White E-STEM Magnet Sch 1708 Les Talley Dr, El Lago 77586 Matthew Paulson	PK-5		608 27	15%	281/284-4300 Fax 281/284-4305
Falcon Pass Elem Sch 2465 Falcon Pass Dr, Houston 77062 Monica Giuffre	PK-5		619	32%	281/284-6200 Fax 281/284-6205
Florence Campbell Sch 6605 W Elem Pkwy, League City 77573 Erin Tite	PK-5		700		281/284-6600 Fax 281/284-6605
G H Whitcomb Elem Sch 900 Reseda Dr, Houston 77062 Diana Kattner	PK-5	T	702 36	58%	281/284-4900 Fax 281/284-4906
G W Robinson Elem Sch 451 Kirby Rd, Seabrook 77586 Yolanda Jones	PK-5		487	20%	281/284-6500 Fax 281/284-6505
Henry Bauerschlag Elem Sch 2051 W League City Pkwy, League City 77573 Kelly Chapman	PK-5		944	11%	281/284-6100 Fax 281/284-6105
I W & Eleanor Hyde Elem Sch 3700 FM 518 Rd E, League City 77573 Suzanne Saunders	PK-5		653 36	23%	281/284-5800 Fax 281/284-5805
James F Bay Elem Sch 1502 Bayport Blvd, Seabrook 77586 Deborah Johnson	PK-5	T	736 42	38%	281/284-4600 Fax 281/284-4606
James H Ross Elem Sch 2401 W Main St, League City 77573 Kelly Sawchak-Mooney	PK-5		623 40	36%	281/284-4500
John F Ward Elem Sch 1440 Bouldercrest Dr, Houston 77062 Elizabeth Pawlowski	K-5		585 36	26%	281/284-5400 Fax 281/284-5405
Lavace Stewart Elem Sch 330 Marina Bay Dr, Kemah 77565 Dr Britani Moses	PK-5	T	874 35	56%	281/284-4700 Fax 281/284-4706
League City Elem Sch 520 E Walker, League City 77573 Xan Wood	PK-5	T	635	69%	281/284-4400 Fax 281/284-4405
League City Intermediate Sch 2588 Webster St, League City 77573 Kimberly Brouillard	6-8	V	1,069 50	15%	281/284-3400 Fax 281/284-3405
Lloyd R Ferguson Elem Sch 1910 S Compass Rose Blvd, League City 77573 Paige Hutchinson	PK-5		762 55	16%	281/284-5500 Fax 281/284-5505
Margaret S McWhirter Elem Sch 300 Pennsylvania St, Webster 77598 Dr Michael Marquez	PK-5	T	882 50	76%	281/284-4800 Fax 281/284-4805
North Pointe Elem Sch 3200 Almond Creek Dr, Houston 77059 Diana Kattner	PK-5		747 45	30%	281/284-5900 Fax 281/284-5905
P H Greene Elem Sch 2903 Friendswood Link Rd, Webster 77598 Lesa Gaffey	PK-5	T	727	44%	281/284-5000 Fax 281/284-5005
Ralph Parr Elem Sch 1315 Highway 3 S, League City 77573 Jane Kelling	PK-5		845	24%	281/284-4100 Fax 281/284-4105
Sandra Mossman Elem Sch 4050 Village Way, League City 77573 Sara Konesheck	PK-5		967	12%	281/284-4000 Fax 281/284-4005
Seabrook Intermediate Sch 2401 N Meyer Ave, Seabrook 77586 Sharon Lopez	6-8		1,019 60	19%	281/284-3100 Fax 281/284-3107
Space Center Intermediate Sch 17400 Saturn Ln, Houston 77058 Ann Thornton	6-8	V	978 75	36%	281/284-3300 Fax 281/284-3305
Victory Lakes Intermediate Sch 2880 W Walker St, League City 77573 Leatrice Sanders	6-8		1,092	18%	281/284-3700 Fax 281/284-3705
Walter Hall Elem Sch 5931 Meadowside St, League City 77573 Stephanie King	PK-5		871 36	12%	281/284-5300 Fax 281/284-5305
Weber Elem Sch 11955 Blackhawk Blvd, Houston 77089 Cheryl Chaney	PK-5	T	932 42	38%	281/284-6300 Fax 281/284-6305
Wedgewood Elem Sch 4000 Friendswood Link Rd, Friendswood 77546 Buffie Johnson	PK-5	T	730	41%	281/284-5700 Fax 281/284-5705
Westbrook Intermediate Sch 302 W El Dorado Blvd, Friendswood 77546 Stephanie Cooper	6-8		1,204	25%	281/284-3800 Fax 281/284-3805

● **Dickinson Ind School Dist** PID: 01018969   281/229-6000
2218 FM 517 Rd E, Dickinson 77539   Fax 281/229-6011

Schools: 14 \ **Teachers:** 738 \ **Students:** 10,400 \
Special Ed Students: 1,125 \ **LEP Students:** 1,178 \ **Ethnic:** Asian 2%, African American 17%, Hispanic 51%, Caucasian 30% \ **Exp:** $325 (High) \ **Poverty:** 18% \ **Title I:** $2,384,722 \ **Special Education:** $1,481,000 \
Open-Close: 08/19 - 05/21 \ **DTBP:** $186 (High) \

Carla Voelkel 1   Ryan Boone 2,3,15
Jimmy Anderson 3   Judy Lee 4
Brian Cmaidalka 5   John Snelson 6*
Robert Cobb 15   Laurie Rodriguez 58,77
David Swartz 67   Kimberly Rich 68,79
Dr Jeff Pack 69,294   Tammy Dowdy 71
Melissa Williams-Scott ....76*   Wendy Chide 88*
Jo Allen 90*

Public Schs..Principal	Grd	Prgm	Enr/#Cls	SN	Phone
Barber Middle Sch 5651 FM 517 Rd E, Dickinson 77539 Lindsey Suarez	5-6	T	645	66%	281/229-6900 Fax 281/229-6901
Bay Colony Elem Sch 101 Bay Colony Elementary Dr, Dickinson 77539 Amy Smith	PK-4	T	741 45	54%	281/229-6200 Fax 281/229-6201
Calder Road Elem Sch 6511 Calder Dr, Dickinson 77539 Sophia Acevedo	PK-4	T	523	49%	281/229-7500 Fax 281/229-7501
Ⓐ Dickinson Alt Lrng Center 2805 Oak Park St, Dickinson 77539 Wendy Chide	9-12	T	64 4	55%	281/229-6300 Fax 281/229-6351
Dickinson High Sch 3800 Baker Dr, Dickinson 77539 Dr Billye Smith	9-12	TV	2,926	55%	281/229-6400 Fax 281/229-6401
Dunbar Middle Sch 2901 23rd St, Dickinson 77539 Temeka Brown	5-6	T	674 26	69%	281/229-6600 Fax 281/229-6601
Elva C Lobit Middle Sch 1251 FM 517 Rd W, Dickinson 77539 Terri Bruce	5-6	T	424	51%	281/229-7700
Hughes Road Elem Sch 11901 Hughes Rd, Dickinson 77539 Kelly Jackson	PK-4	T	613 36	62%	281/229-6700 Fax 281/229-6701
Jake Silbernagel Elem Sch 4201 25th St, Dickinson 77539 Leslie Tracy-Burke	PK-4	T	742 35	75%	281/229-6800 Fax 281/229-6801
Kenneth E Little Elem Sch 622 Oklahoma Ave, Bacliff 77518 Brooke Newell	PK-4	T	711 60	79%	281/229-7000 Fax 281/229-7001
Kranz Junior High Sch 12850 FM 3436 Rd, Dickinson 77539 Kim Kelley	7-8		924		281/309-3600

79	Student Personnel	91	Safety/Security	275	Response To Intervention	298 Grant Writer/Ptnrships
80	Driver Ed/Safety	92	Magnet School	277	Remedial Math K-12	750 Chief Innovation Officer
81	Gifted/Talented	93	Parental Involvement	280	Literacy Coach	751 Chief of Staff
82	Video Services	95	Tech Prep Program	285	STEM	752 Social Emotional Learning
83	Substance Abuse Prev	97	Chief Information Officer	286	Digital Learning	
84	Erate	98	Chief Technology Officer	288	Common Core Standards	**Other School Types**
85	AIDS Education	270	Accountability	294	Accountability	Ⓐ = Alternative School
88	Alternative/At Risk	271	Migrant Education	295	Network System	Ⓒ = Charter School
89	Multi-Cultural Curriculum	273	Teacher Mentor	296	Title II Programs	Ⓜ = Magnet School
90	Social Work	274	Before/After Sch	297	Webmaster	Ⓨ = Year-Round School

School Programs
A = Alternative Program
G = Adult Classes
M = Magnet Program
T = Title I Schoolwide
V = Career & Tech Ed Programs

Social Media
 = Facebook
 = Twitter

New Schools are shaded
New Superintendents and Principals are bold
Personnel with email addresses are underscored

TX−159

Galveston County
Market Data Retrieval

Louis G Lobit Elem Sch 1251 FM 517 Rd W, Dickinson 77539 Stephanie Williams	PK-4	T	547	47%	281/229-7600
R D McAdams Junior High Sch 11415 Hughes Rd, Dickinson 77539 Rachelle Beafneaux	7-8	T	760 55	63%	281/229-7100 Fax 281/229-7101
San Leon Elem Sch 2655 Broadway St, Dickinson 77539 Sherri Blackburn	PK-4	T	705 50	74%	281/229-7400 Fax 281/229-7401

• **Friendswood Ind Sch Dist** PID: 01019028   281/482-1267
302 Laurel Dr, Friendswood 77546   Fax 281/996-2513

Schools: 6 \ **Teachers:** 377 \ **Students:** 6,000 \ **Special Ed Students:** 598
\ **LEP Students:** 138 \ **College-Bound:** 98% \ **Ethnic:** Asian 7%,
African American 2%, Hispanic 15%, Caucasian 75% \ **Exp:** $229 (Med)
\ **Poverty:** 4% \ **Title I:** $181,690 \ **Special Education:** $866,000 \
Open-Close: 08/14 - 05/21 \ **DTBP:** $181 (High) \

Thad Roher 1
David Moynihan 4
Robert Koopman 6*
Diane Myers 15
Tony Hopkins 67
Dana Owen 71,76
Mike Gasiorowski 76
Tonia Meadows 286,295
Amber Petree 2
Dean Lewis 5
Dahria Driskall 13,58
Susan Kirkpatricke 27
Lynn Tunnel 68
Mark Griffon 72*
Erich Kreiter 91
Brian Smith 295

Public Schs..Principal	Grd	Prgm	Enr/#Cls	SN	
C W Cline Elem Sch 505 Briarmeadow Ave, Friendswood 77546 Barry Clifford	PK-2		499 37	5%	281/482-1201 Fax 281/996-2557
Friendswood High Sch 702 Greenbriar Ave, Friendswood 77546 Mark Griffon	9-12		2,111	7%	281/482-3413 Fax 281/996-2523
Friendswood Junior High Sch 1000 Manison Pkwy, Friendswood 77546 Dana Drew	6-8		1,454 65	7%	281/996-6200 Fax 281/996-6262
Westwood-Bales Elem Sch 506 W Edgewood Dr, Friendswood 77546 Kristin Moffitt	PK-2		499 37	16%	281/482-3341 Fax 281/996-2542
Windsong Intermediate Sch 2100 W Parkwood Ave, Friendswood 77546 Nelda Guerra	3-5		300 28	5%	281/482-0111 Fax 281/996-2594
Zue S Bales Intermediate Sch 211 Stadium Ln, Friendswood 77546 J T Patton	3-5		300		281/482-8255 Fax 281/996-2551

• **Galveston Ind School Dist** PID: 01019078   409/766-5100
3904 Avenue T, Galveston 77550   Fax 409/762-8391

Schools: 12 \ **Teachers:** 458 \ **Students:** 7,000 \ **Special Ed Students:** 518
\ **LEP Students:** 1,025 \ **College-Bound:** 71% \ **Ethnic:** Asian 2%,
African American 25%, Hispanic 46%, Caucasian 27% \ **Exp:** $242 (Med)
\ **Poverty:** 22% \ **Title I:** $2,286,254 \ **Special Education:** $1,640,000 \
Bilingual Education: $74,000 \ **Open-Close:** 08/26 - 05/28 \ **DTBP:** $159
(High)

Dr Kelli Moulton 1
Jennifer Douglas 4
Walter Fortune 6,35
Elizabeth Bennett 9*
Mariana Mueller 16,73
Mary Patrick 34,58
Jessica Edwards 58
Dr Matthew Hay 67
Dr Keri Launius 74
Paul Byers 3
John Pruitt 5
Dr Annette Scott 8,11,15
Molly Allmond-Helmer 10*
Eric Paul 27
Desiree Hartnett 57
Jessica Swenson 58*
Dyann Polzin 68,71
John Mathis 76,84,295

Netobia Taylor 76
Leeroy Amador 91

Public Schs..Principal	Grd	Prgm	Enr/#Cls	SN	
Aim College & Career Prep Acad 3014 Sealy St, Galveston 77550 Cheryl Rutledge	6-12	T	80	76%	409/761-6302 Fax 409/770-0918
Ⓜ Austin Middle Sch 1514 N 1/2, Galveston 77550 Matthew Neighbors	5-8	ATV	545 35	48%	409/761-3500 Fax 409/465-5946
Ball High Sch 4115 Avenue O, Galveston 77550 Joseph Pillar	9-12	TV	2,050	60%	409/766-5700 Fax 409/766-5766
Burnet Early Childhood Univ ES 5501 Avenue S, Galveston 77551 Beatriz Rodriguez	PK-4	T	534	92%	409/761-6470
Central Media Arts Academy 3014 Sealy St, Galveston 77550 Monique Lewis	5-8	TV	213 46	87%	409/761-6200 Fax 409/765-2141
Collegiate Academy 7100 Stewart Rd, Galveston 77551 Debra Owens	5-8	T	674	82%	409/761-6100 Fax 409/770-0339
Collegiate Academy at Weis 3014 Sealy St, Galveston 77550 Cheryl Rutledge	5-8	ATV	600 45	86%	409/761-6200
Crenshaw Elem & Mid Sch 416 Highway 87, Crystal Beach 77650 Tracie Camp	PK-8		156		409/761-6350
Greta Oppe Elem Sch 2915 81st St, Galveston 77554 Alice Prets	PK-4	T	662	53%	409/761-6500 Fax 409/744-1905
L A Morgan Elem Sch 1410 37th St, Galveston 77550 Divya Nagpal	PK-4	T	546 28	94%	409/761-6700 Fax 409/763-0122
Parker Elem Sch 6802 Jones Dr, Galveston 77551 Elizabeth Murphy	PK-4	T	578 32	82%	409/761-6600 Fax 409/744-8312
Ⓒ Rosenberg Elem Sch 721 10th St, Galveston 77550 Cathy Van Ness	PK-2	T	207	90%	409/761-6800 Fax 409/765-5674

• **High Island Ind Sch Dist** PID: 01019250   409/286-5317
2113 6th St, High Island 77623   Fax 409/286-5351

Schools: 1 \ **Teachers:** 14 \ **Students:** 145 \ **Special Ed Students:** 14 \
LEP Students: 3 \ **College-Bound:** 50% \ **Exp:** $555 (High) \ **Poverty:** 21%
\ **Title I:** $18,390 \ **Open-Close:** 08/26 - 05/29 \ **DTBP:** $378 (High)

Travis Grubbs 1
Sabrina Bobino 5*
Amanda Jackson 8,11,57,88,273*
Crystal Larson 2
John Jackson 6*
Benny Barrow 67

Public Schs..Principal	Grd	Prgm	Enr/#Cls	SN	
High Island Sch 2113 6th St, High Island 77623 Travis Grubbs	PK-12	T	145 25		409/286-5313 Fax 409/286-2120

• **Hitchcock Ind School Dist** PID: 01019274   409/316-6545
7801 Neville Ave, Hitchcock 77563   Fax 409/986-5141

Schools: 4 \ **Teachers:** 105 \ **Students:** 1,700 \ **Special Ed Students:** 168
\ **LEP Students:** 99 \ **College-Bound:** 55% \ **Ethnic:** African American
44%, Hispanic 31%, Caucasian 25% \ **Exp:** $557 (High) \ **Poverty:** 23% \
Title I: $510,162 \ **Bilingual Education:** $16,000 \ **Open-Close:** 08/15 -
05/22 \ **DTBP:** $520 (High) \

1 Superintendent	8 Curric/Instruct K-12	19 Chief Financial Officer	29 Family/Consumer Science
2 Bus/Finance/Purchasing	9 Curric/Instruct Elem	20 Art K-12	30 Adult Education
3 Buildings And Grounds	10 Curric/Instruct Sec	21 Art Elem	31 Career/Sch-to-Work K-12
4 Food Service	11 Federal Program	22 Art Sec	32 Career/Sch-to-Work Elem
5 Transportation	12 Title I	23 Music K-12	33 Career/Sch-to-Work Sec
6 Athletic	13 Title V	24 Music Elem	34 Early Childhood Ed
7 Health Services	15 Asst Superintendent	25 Music Sec	35 Health/Phys Education
	16 Instructional Media Svcs	26 Business Education	36 Guidance Services K-12
	17 Chief Operations Officer	27 Career & Tech Ed	37 Guidance Services Elem
	18 Chief Academic Officer	28 Technology Education	38 Guidance Services Sec

39 Social Studies K-12	49 English/Lang Arts Elem	59 Special Education Elem	69 Academic Assessment
40 Social Studies Elem	50 English/Lang Arts Sec	60 Special Education Sec	70 Research/Development
41 Social Studies Sec	51 Reading K-12	61 Foreign/World Lang K-12	71 Public Information
42 Science K-12	52 Reading Elem	62 Foreign/World Lang Elem	72 Summer School
43 Science Elem	53 Reading Sec	63 Foreign/World Lang Sec	73 Instructional Tech
44 Science Sec	54 Remedial Reading K-12	64 Religious Education K-12	74 Inservice Training
45 Math K-12	55 Remedial Reading Elem	65 Religious Education Elem	75 Marketing/Distributive
46 Math Elem	56 Remedial Reading Sec	66 Religious Education Sec	76 Info Systems
47 Math Sec	57 Bilingual/ELL	67 School Board President	77 Psychological Assess
48 English/Lang Arts K-12	58 Special Education K-12	68 Teacher Personnel	78 Affirmative Action

TX—160

Texas School Directory
Galveston County

Travis Edwards 1
Christopher Armacost 3,73
Craig Smith 6*
Sarah Roach 12
Chad Allen 67
Patrick Faour 69,294

Jennifer Donovan 2
Bridget Ford 5
Kathy Potts 7*
Evangelina Guerra 58
Linda Leuschen 68

Public Schs..Principal	Grd	Prgm	Enr/#Cls		SN
Crosby Middle Sch 6625 FM 2004 Rd, Hitchcock 77563 Kellie Edmundson	6-8	AT	290 22	78%	409/316-6542 Fax 409/986-9254 t
Hitchcock High Sch 6629 FM 2004 Rd, Hitchcock 77563 Laurie Gilcrease	9-12	ATV	366 30	71%	409/316-6544 Fax 409/986-9339
Hitchcock Primary Sch 5901 FM 2004 Rd, Hitchcock 77563 Angela Mancini	PK-2	T	420	83%	409/316-6467 Fax 409/986-3168 f t
Stewart Elem Sch 7013 Stewart St, Hitchcock 77563 Donette Line	3-5	T	352 29	79%	409/316-6543 Fax 409/986-5563

● **Santa Fe Ind School Dist** PID: 01019432   409/925-3526
4133 Warpath Ave, Santa Fe 77510   Fax 409/925-4002

Schools: 4 \ **Teachers:** 277 \ **Students:** 4,794 \
Special Ed Students: 491 \ **LEP Students:** 133 \ **College-Bound:** 75% \
Ethnic: Asian 1%, African American 1%, Hispanic 20%, Native American: 1%, Caucasian 78% \ **Exp:** $261 (Med) \ **Poverty:** 9% \ **Title I:** $503,246 \
Special Education: $702,000 \ **Open-Close:** 08/19 - 06/04 \ **DTBP:** $181 (High) \ f

Dr Leigh Wall 1
Marianne Junco 2
Cherie Bowers 4
Mark McKinney 5
Dr Jackie Shulman 8,12,34,288
Rick Morril 28,73
Rusty Norman 67
Lois Jones 90
Belinda Slawson 274

Lee Townsend 2,19
Bob Atkins 3
David McMillian 5
Mark Kanipes 6
Dr Jacqueline Shuman 15
Kathy Oliver 58
Patti Hanssard 68,71,79
Walter Braun 91
Sara Ryan 294*

Public Schs..Principal	Grd	Prgm	Enr/#Cls		SN
Dan J Kubacak Elem Sch 4131 Warpath Ave, Santa Fe 77510 Destini Martin	3-5	T	1,094 32	40%	409/925-9600 Fax 409/927-8262
Roy J Wollam Elem Sch 3400 Avenue S, Santa Fe 77510 Michelle Pourchot	PK-2	T	1,191 37	45%	409/925-2770 Fax 409/925-4276
Santa Fe High Sch 16000 Highway 6, Santa Fe 77517 **Rachel Harris**	9-12	AGV	1,443	24%	409/927-3100 Fax 409/925-2773 f
Santa Fe Junior High Sch 4132 Warpath Ave, Santa Fe 77510 Ryan Kopp	6-8	T	1,066	34%	409/925-9300 Fax 409/927-4106

● **Texas City Ind School Dist** PID: 01019470   409/916-0100
1700 9th Ave N, Texas City 77590   Fax 409/942-2655

Schools: 14 \ **Teachers:** 556 \ **Students:** 9,000 \ **Special Ed Students:** 827 \ **LEP Students:** 621 \ **College-Bound:** 94% \ **Ethnic:** African American 34%, Hispanic 38%, Native American: 1%, Caucasian 27% \ **Exp:** $298 (Med) \ **Poverty:** 24% \ **Title I:** $3,448,084 \ **Special Education:** $1,021,000 \ **Open-Close:** 08/28 - 06/04 \ **DTBP:** $198 (High)

Dr Rodney Cavness 1
Jack Haralson 3
John Vandever 4

Margaret Lee 2,15
Marion Godeaux 3
Richard Ressler 5

Anne Anderson 8
Sherri Simmons 10
Marcus Higgs 15,68,78
Donna Peterson 58
Dickey Campbell 67
Melissa Tortorici 71
Tray White 73,76,295,297
Mike Matranga 91

Susan Myers 8,15,16,36,274
Dr Terri Burchfield 12,15,69,79,273,296
Mark Lyon 20,23
Donna Peterson 58*
Christina Hall-Payne 70,298
James Banks 73
Nathan Jackson 79
Lisa Campbell 294

Public Schs..Principal	Grd	Prgm	Enr/#Cls		SN
Blocker Middle Sch 1800 9th Ave N, Texas City 77590 Anthony Furman	7-8	T	905 63	65%	409/916-0700 Fax 409/942-2755
Calvin Vincent ECC 1805 13th Ave N, Texas City 77590 Susan Wilson	PK-PK	T	248	99%	409/916-0512 Fax 409/916-0596
Guajardo Elem Sch 2300 21st St N, Texas City 77590 Debbie Fuller	K-4	T	561 32	59%	409/916-0300 Fax 409/942-2839
Heights Elem Sch 300 N Logan St, Texas City 77590 Erica Allen	PK-4	T	515 30	80%	409/916-0500 Fax 409/942-2450
Industrial Trade Center 1400 9th Ave N, Texas City 77590 Richard Chapa	Voc		200		409/916-0710
Kohfeldt Elem Sch 1705 13th Ave N, Texas City 77590 Matthew Salley	K-4	T	586 27	84%	409/916-0400 Fax 409/916-0496
La Marque Elem Sch 1217 Vauthier St, La Marque 77568 Sharon Williams	2-4	T	574 20	85%	409/908-5056 Fax 409/908-5044
La Marque High Sch 397 Duroux Rd, La Marque 77568 Ricky Nicholson	9-12	TV	665 78	82%	409/938-4261 Fax 409/908-5036
La Marque Middle Sch 1431 Bayou Rd, La Marque 77568 Dr Florence Adkins	5-8	TV	737 75	82%	409/938-4286
La Marque Primary Sch 100 Lake Rd, La Marque 77568 Patti Martin	PK-1	T	457 21	84%	409/935-3020 Fax 409/908-5022
Levi Fry Intermediate Sch 300 25th Ave N, Texas City 77590 Felica Garrett	5-6	T	957	68%	409/916-0600 Fax 409/916-0696
Roosevelt-Wilson Elem Sch 301 16th Ave N, Texas City 77590 Wendy Patterson	K-4	T	685 28	68%	409/916-0200 Fax 409/916-0296
Texas City High Sch 1431 9th Ave N, Texas City 77590 **Holly Keown**	9-12	TV	1,893	58%	409/916-0800
Ⓐ Woodrow Wilson Daep Sch 1508 6th St N, Texas City 77590 Donald Jones	5-12		57 10	76%	409/916-0280 Fax 409/942-2462

GALVESTON CATHOLIC SCHOOLS

● **Archdiocese Galveston-Houston** PID: 01027855
Listing includes only schools located in this county. See District Index for location of Diocesan Offices.

Catholic Schs..Principal	Grd	Prgm	Enr/#Cls		SN
Holy Family Catholic Sch 2601 Avenue N, Galveston 77550 Nadia Canino	PK-8		130 10		409/765-6607 Fax 409/765-5154

79 Student Personnel
80 Driver Ed/Safety
81 Gifted/Talented
82 Video Services
83 Substance Abuse Prev
84 Erate
85 AIDS Education
86 Alternative/At Risk
87 Multi-Cultural Curriculum
88 Social Work

91 Safety/Security
92 Magnet School
93 Parental Involvement
95 Tech Prep Program
97 Chief Infomation Officer
98 Chief Technology Officer
270 Character Education
271 Migrant Education
273 Teacher Mentor
274 Before/After Sch

275 Response To Intervention
277 Remedial Math K-12
280 Literacy Coach
285 STEM
286 Digital Learning
288 Common Core Standards
294 Accountability
295 Network System
296 Title II Programs
297 Webmaster

298 Grant Writer/Ptnrships
750 Chief Innovation Officer
751 Chief of Staff
752 Social Emotional Learning

Other School Types
Ⓐ = Alternative School
Ⓒ = Charter School
Ⓜ = Magnet School
Ⓨ = Year-Round School

School Programs
A = Alternative Program
G = Adult Classes
M = Magnet Program
T = Title I Schoolwide
V = Career & Tech Ed Programs

Social Media
f = Facebook
t = Twitter

New Schools are shaded
New Superintendents and Principals are bold
Personnel with email addresses are underscored

TX-161

Garza County

Private Schs..Principal	Grd	Prgm	Enr/#Cls SN	Phone
O'Connell High Sch 1320 Tremont St, Galveston 77550 Patti Abbot	9-12		128 20	409/765-5534 Fax 409/765-5536
Our Lady of Fatima Sch 1600 9th Ave N, Texas City 77590 Jennifer Lopez	PK-8		80 10	409/945-3326 Fax 409/945-3389
Our Lady of Lourdes Cath Sch 10114 Highway 6, Hitchcock 77563 Dr Emilie Robert	PK-6		70 8	409/925-3224 Fax 409/925-9900
St Mary Catholic Sch 1612 E Walker St, League City 77573 Mrs Halbardier	PK-8		220 30	281/332-4014 Fax 281/332-5148
True Cross Catholic Sch 400 FM 517 Rd E, Dickinson 77539 Yolanda Agrella	PK-8		160 11	281/337-5212 Fax 832/738-1682

GALVESTON PRIVATE SCHOOLS

Private Schs..Principal	Grd	Prgm	Enr/#Cls SN	Phone
Bay Area Christian Sch 4800 W Main St, League City 77573 Linda Mudgett \ Les Rainey \ Melissa Fuqua	K-12		800 40	281/332-4814 Fax 281/554-5495
Galloway Sch 3200 W Bay Area Blvd, Friendswood 77546 Robin Williams	K-5		180 23	281/338-9510 Fax 281/338-9530
Lord of Life Lutheran Sch 4425 FM 2351 Rd, Friendswood 77546 Andy Van Weele	PK-8		52 3	281/482-0481 Fax 281/648-4189
Pine Drive Christian Sch 6601 FM 2004 Rd, Hitchcock 77563 Lynn Deitz	PK-12		45 10	281/534-4881
Satori Elem Sch 2503 Sealy St, Galveston 77550 Claire Wilkins	PK-6		45	409/763-7022
Trinity Episcopal Sch 720 Tremont St, Galveston 77550 Mark Ravelli	PK-8		202 15	409/765-9391 Fax 409/762-7000

GARZA COUNTY

GARZA PUBLIC SCHOOLS

• **Post Ind School Dist** PID: 01019597   806/495-3343
501 S Avenue K, Post 79356   Fax 806/495-2945

Schools: 3 \ *Teachers:* 82 \ *Students:* 810 \ *Special Ed Students:* 102 \ *LEP Students:* 47 \ *Ethnic:* Asian 1%, African American 5%, Hispanic 63%, Native American: 1%, Caucasian 30% \ *Exp:* $576 (High) \ *Poverty:* 23% \ *Title I:* $248,340 \ *Special Education:* $316,000 \ *Open-Close:* 08/15 - 05/21 \ *DTBP:* $344 (High) \

Heath Dickson 1		Gary Graves 3	
Debbie Line 4*		Ollie Abaraham 5	
Michael Pittman 6*		Joanne Travis 7	
Kim Mills-Oller 8,11,15,69,270,273		Lizette Hastey 37*	
Serena Voss 38,83,88*		Tonya Dunn 38*	
Regina Wise 58		Mike Holly 67	
Coty Tidwell 73		Bobby Dean 91	
Randon Torres 295			

Public Schs..Principal	Grd	Prgm	Enr/#Cls SN	Phone
Post Elem Sch 211 W 8th St, Post 79356 Cassandra Petty	PK-5	T	431 32	75% 806/495-3414 Fax 806/495-2381
Post High Sch 307 W 4th St, Post 79356 Shelly Crow	9-12	TV	222 40	60% 806/495-2770 Fax 806/495-2792
Post Middle Sch 405 W 8th St, Post 79356 Robert Wilson	6-8	T	163 24	60% 806/495-2874 Fax 806/495-2426

• **Southland Ind School Dist** PID: 01019638   806/996-5339
190 Eighth St, Southland 79364   Fax 806/496-2745

Schools: 1 \ *Teachers:* 15 \ *Students:* 132 \ *Special Ed Students:* 14 \ *College-Bound:* 65% \ *Ethnic:* African American 2%, Hispanic 60%, Caucasian 39% \ *Exp:* $433 (High) \ *Poverty:* 21% \ *Title I:* $1,831 \ *Open-Close:* 08/21 - 05/22 \ *DTBP:* $543 (High)

Toby Miller 1		Wyanza Basinger 2	
Justin Hyndran 3,5*		Bethany Miller 11,296	
Martha Angerer 58		Joe Basinger 67	
Phillip Maldonado 271*			

Public Schs..Principal	Grd	Prgm	Enr/#Cls SN	Phone
Southland Sch 190 Eighth St, Southland 79364 Gregg Johnson	K-12	TV	132 25	90% 806/996-5339

GILLESPIE COUNTY

GILLESPIE PUBLIC SCHOOLS

• **Doss Consolidated Common SD** PID: 01019664   830/669-2411
11431 Ranch Road 648, Doss 78618   Fax 830/669-2303

Schools: 1 \ *Teachers:* 1 \ *Students:* 25 \ *Ethnic:* Hispanic 17%, Caucasian 83% \ *Exp:* $831 (High) \ *Poverty:* 8% \ *Open-Close:* 08/26 - 05/28 \ *DTBP:* $175 (High)

Mark Stroeher 1   Pam Seippe 11,84,288,296,298,752
Shawn Sattler 67

Public Schs..Principal	Grd	Prgm	Enr/#Cls SN	Phone
Doss Elem Sch 11431 Ranch Road 648, Doss 78618 Mark Stroeher	PK-8		25 4	830/669-2411

• **Fredericksburg Ind School Dist** PID: 01019688   830/997-9551
234 Friendship Ln, Fredericksbrg 78624   Fax 830/997-6164

Schools: 6 \ *Teachers:* 233 \ *Students:* 2,900 \ *Special Ed Students:* 314 \ *LEP Students:* 360 \ *Ethnic:* Hispanic 48%, Caucasian 51% \ *Exp:* $351 (High) \ *Poverty:* 16% \ *Title I:* $665,725 \ *Special Education:* $180,000 \ *Open-Close:* 08/14 - 05/28

Dr Jeff Brasher 1		Deborah Ottmers 2,15	
Brandon Porter 3		Dr Delisa Styles 3,8,16,69,74,277,285,294	
Joyce Fox 4		Evelyn Peese 5	

1 Superintendent	8 Curric/Instruct K-12	19 Chief Financial Officer	29 Family/Consumer Science	39 Social Studies K-12	49 English/Lang Arts Elem	59 Special Education Elem	69 Academic Assessment
2 Bus/Finance/Purchasing	9 Curric/Instruct Elem	20 Art K-12	30 Adult Education	40 Social Studies Elem	50 English/Lang Arts Sec	60 Special Education Sec	70 Research/Development
3 Buildings And Grounds	10 Curric/Instruct Sec	21 Art Elem	31 Career/Sch-to-Work K-12	41 Social Studies Sec	51 Reading K-12	61 Foreign/World Lang K-12	71 Public Information
4 Food Service	11 Federal Program	22 Art Sec	32 Career/Sch-to-Work Elem	42 Science K-12	52 Reading Elem	62 Foreign/World Lang Elem	72 Summer School
5 Transportation	12 Title I	23 Music K-12	33 Career/Sch-to-Work Sec	43 Science Elem	53 Reading Sec	63 Foreign/World Lang Sec	73 Instructional Tech
6 Athletic	13 Title V	24 Music Elem	34 Early Childhood Ed	44 Science Sec	54 Remedial Reading K-12	64 Religious Education K-12	74 Inservice Training
7 Health Services	15 Asst Superintendent	25 Music Sec	35 Health/Phys Education	45 Math K-12	55 Remedial Reading Elem	65 Religious Education Elem	75 Marketing/Distributive
	16 Instructional Media Svcs	26 Business Education	36 Guidance Services K-12	46 Math Elem	56 Remedial Reading Sec	66 Religious Education Sec	76 Info Systems
	17 Chief Operations Officer	27 Career & Tech Ed	37 Guidance Services Elem	47 Math Sec	57 Bilingual/ELL	67 School Board President	77 Psychological Assess
	18 Chief Academic Officer	28 Technology Education	38 Guidance Services Sec	48 English/Lang Arts K-12	58 Special Education K-12	68 Teacher Personnel	78 Affirmative Action

Texas School Directory — Goliad County

Lance Moffett 6*	Judy Mayo 7*	
Donnie Finn 11,15,68,79,91	Patricia Rivera 11,57,81,271,298	
Debbie Lewis 29*	Joan Kramer 30*	
Debra Wilks 34,58,275	Brian Lehne 67	
Carl Oneil 73*	Karen Humphrey-Sauer 88*	

Public Schs..Principal	Grd	Prgm	Enr/#Cls	SN	
Fredericksburg Elem Sch 1608 N Adams St, Fredericksbrg 78624 Monica Ward	1-5	T	1,061 50	57%	830/997-9595 Fax 830/997-7209
Fredericksburg High Sch 1107 S State Highway 16, Fredericksbrg 78624 Joe Gonzalez	9-12	AV	989	36%	830/997-7551 Fax 830/997-8583
Fredericksburg Middle Sch 110 W Travis St, Fredericksbrg 78624 Sheryl Wallace	6-8	T	687	53%	830/997-7657 Fax 830/997-1927
Fredericksburg Primary Sch 1110 S Adams St, Fredericksbrg 78624 Wendy Dietrich	PK-K	T	347 20	74%	830/997-7421 Fax 830/990-0002
Gillespie County High Sch 1110 S Adams St, Fredericksbrg 78624 Dalen Kirchner	10-12		25 2	37%	830/990-4598
Stonewall Elem Sch 220 Peach St, Stonewall 78671 Amie Chalberg	K-5		90 6	30%	830/990-4599 Fax 830/990-4549

• **Harper Ind School Dist** PID: 01019731 830/864-4044
23122 W Highway 290, Harper 78631 Fax 830/864-4748

Schools: 3 \ *Teachers:* 48 \ *Students:* 600 \ *Special Ed Students:* 56 \
LEP Students: 6 \ *Ethnic:* Hispanic 15%, Caucasian 84% \ *Exp:* $320 (High)
\ *Poverty:* 11% \ *Title I:* $68,091 \ *Open-Close:* 08/14 - 05/21 \ *DTBP:* $323 (High)

Chris Stevenson 1	Tina Burnhart 2,68,79	
Dean Eckert 3,5*	Debbie Pascarella 4	
Mark Karchoff 6	Aaron Brooks 8,11,69,74,294,296	
Bonnie Stewart 8,11,69,74,294,296*	Leann Lake 8,31,83	
Jay Harper 9,58*	Toni Marshall 16	
Nancy Cantwell 57,271*	Juanice Grona 67	
Bill Long 73,295		

Public Schs..Principal	Grd	Prgm	Enr/#Cls	SN	
Harper Elem Sch 23122 W Highway 290, Harper 78631 Billy Harper	PK-4	T	215 15	47%	830/864-4044
Harper High Sch 23122 W Highway 290, Harper 78631 Bonnie Stewart	9-12	T	193 20	30%	830/864-4044
Harper Middle Sch 23122 W Hwy 290, Harper 78631 Julie Fiedler	5-8	T	184	38%	830/864-4044

GILLESPIE CATHOLIC SCHOOLS

• **Archdiocese San Antonio Ed Off** PID: 00999724
Listing includes only schools located in this county. See District Index for location of Diocesan Offices.

Catholic Schs..Principal	Grd	Prgm	Enr/#Cls	SN	
St Mary Elem Sch 202 S Orange St, Fredericksbrg 78624 John Mein	PK-8		250 19		830/997-3914 Fax 830/997-2382 [f]

GILLESPIE PRIVATE SCHOOLS

Private Schs..Principal	Grd	Prgm	Enr/#Cls	SN	
Ambleside School of Fredericks 406 Post Oak Rd, Fredericksbrg 78624 Russ York	K-12		60 7		830/990-9059 Fax 877/471-4957
Heritage Sch 310 Smokehouse Rd, Fredericksbrg 78624 Christopher Acton	K-12		200 13		830/997-6597 Fax 830/997-4900

GLASSCOCK COUNTY

GLASSCOCK PUBLIC SCHOOLS

• **Glasscock Co Ind School Dist** PID: 01019781 432/354-2230
240 Bearkat Ln, Garden City 79739 Fax 432/354-2503

Schools: 1 \ *Teachers:* 33 \ *Students:* 310 \ *Special Ed Students:* 19
\ *LEP Students:* 34 \ *College-Bound:* 100% \ *Exp:* $1,050 (High) \
Poverty: 11% \ *Title I:* $28,390 \ *Open-Close:* 08/21 - 05/20 \ *DTBP:* $899 (High)

Scott Bicknell 1,83,288	Kristy Fuchs 2,11,296	
Reeann McKinnon 4*	Jeff Jones 6	
Tiffany Parker 8,31,69,270*	Wayland Pierce 8,12,88,274*	
Holly McDermott 27*	Sasha Goodwin 35,85*	
Laura Dieringer 51,54*	Bea Correa 57*	
Paula Ringo 58*	Sharon McDonald 58*	
Doug Jost 67	David Wood 73,286	

Public Schs..Principal	Grd	Prgm	Enr/#Cls	SN	
Glasscock Co Sch 240 Bearkat Ln, Garden City 79739 Wayland Pierce \ Brian Hastings	PK-12	V	310 30		432/354-2244 Fax 432/354-2611

GOLIAD COUNTY

GOLIAD PUBLIC SCHOOLS

• **Goliad Ind School Dist** PID: 01019810 361/645-3259
161 N Welch St, Goliad 77963 Fax 361/645-3614

Schools: 3 \ *Teachers:* 101 \ *Students:* 1,340 \ *Special Ed Students:* 149
\ *LEP Students:* 23 \ *Ethnic:* African American 5%, Hispanic 49%,
Caucasian 45% \ *Exp:* $527 (High) \ *Poverty:* 23% \ *Title I:* $357,787 \
Open-Close: 08/14 - 05/21 \ *DTBP:* $336 (High)

Dave Plymale 1	Caroly Estes 2	
David Hill 3	Brenda Gohnert 4	
Bobby Nicholson 6*	Chris Ulcak 8,15	
Patricia Huber 9,34*	Debra Bauer 11	
Brandon Huber 67	David Luna 73,295	

Key		
79 Student Personnel	91 Safety/Security	275 Response To Intervention
80 Driver Ed/Safety	92 Magnet School	277 Remedial Math K-12
81 Gifted/Talented	93 Parental Involvement	280 Literacy Coach
82 Video Services	95 Tech Prep Program	285 STEM
83 Substance Abuse Prev	97 Chief Infomation Officer	286 Digital Learning
84 Erate	98 Chief Technology Officer	288 Common Core Standards
85 AIDS Education	270 Character Education	294 Accountability
86 Alternative/At Risk	271 Migrant Education	295 Network System
87 Multi-Cultural Curriculum	273 Teacher Mentor	296 Title II Programs
88 Social Work	274 Before/After Sch	297 Webmaster
298 Grant Writer/Ptnrships		
750 Chief Innovation Officer		
751 Chief of Staff		
752 Social Emotional Learning		

School Programs
A = Alternative Program
G = Adult Classes
M = Magnet Program
T = Title I Schoolwide
V = Career & Tech Ed Programs

Other School Types
Ⓐ = Alternative School
Ⓒ = Charter School
Ⓜ = Magnet School
Ⓨ = Year-Round School

Social Media
[f] = Facebook
[t] = Twitter

New Schools are shaded
New Superintendents and Principals are bold
Personnel with email addresses are underscored

Gonzales County

Market Data Retrieval

Public Schs..Principal	Grd	Prgm	Enr/#Cls	SN	
Goliad Elem Sch 142 W High St, Goliad 77963 Patricia Huber	PK-6	T	734 40	63%	361/645-3206 Fax 361/645-2336
Goliad High Sch 749 Tiger Drive, Goliad 77963 Brandon Enos	9-12	ATV	417 59	44%	361/645-3257 Fax 361/645-8039
Goliad Middle Sch 659 Tiger Dr, Goliad 77963 Mary Tippin	7-8	T	190 23	46%	361/645-3146 Fax 361/645-8040

GONZALES COUNTY

GONZALES PUBLIC SCHOOLS

- **Gonzales Ind School Dist** PID: 01019860   830/672-9551
  1711 N Sarah DeWitt Dr, Gonzales 78629   Fax 830/672-7159

Schools: 6 \ *Teachers:* 180 \ *Students:* 2,875 \ *Special Ed Students:* 296 \ *LEP Students:* 435 \ *Ethnic:* African American 8%, Hispanic 68%, Caucasian 23% \ *Exp:* $499 (High) \ *Poverty:* 25% \ *Title I:* $978,858 \ *Special Education:* $560,000 \ *Open-Close:* 08/19 - 05/27 \ *DTBP:* $154 (High)

John Schumacker 1   Amanda Smith 2,19,81
Gene Kridler 3,5,17   Michael Waldie 6,35
Dr Lydia Bartlett .11,15,57,58,271,294,296,298   Robin Trojcak 11
Jennifer Needham 16,28,73,76,82,297   Glenn Menking 67
Haley Ratliff 68

Public Schs..Principal	Grd	Prgm	Enr/#Cls	SN	
ⓥ East Avenue Primary Sch 1615 Saint Louis St, Gonzales 78629 Damaris Womack	K-2	MT	410 40	70%	830/672-2826 Fax 830/672-6161
Gonzales Elem Sch 1600 Saint Andrew St, Gonzales 78629 Jim Workman	2-4	T	430 35	78%	830/672-1467 Fax 830/672-5758
Gonzales High Sch 1801 N Sarah DeWitt Dr, Gonzales 78629 Michael Garcia	9-12	ATV	795 46	61%	830/672-7535 Fax 830/672-8273
Gonzales Junior High Sch 426 N College St, Gonzales 78629 Roque Thompson	7-8	T	441 34	69%	830/672-8641 Fax 830/672-6446
Gonzales Primary Academy 222 N Saint Joseph St, Gonzales 78629 Dr Renee Fairchild	PK-PK	T	350	81%	830/519-4110 Fax 830/519-4112
North Avenue Interm Sch 1032 N Saint Joseph St, Gonzales 78629 Hector Dominguez	5-6		456 23		830/672-9557 Fax 830/672-4350

- **Nixon-Smiley Cons Ind Sch Dist** PID: 01019937   830/582-1536
  800 N Rancho Rd, Nixon 78140   Fax 830/582-1920

Schools: 3 \ *Teachers:* 83 \ *Students:* 1,100 \ *Special Ed Students:* 122 \ *LEP Students:* 144 \ *College-Bound:* 6% \ *Ethnic:* African American 1%, Hispanic 78%, Caucasian 21% \ *Exp:* $447 (High) \ *Poverty:* 27% \ *Title I:* $407,659 \ *Special Education:* $188,000 \ *Open-Close:* 08/22 - 05/28 \ *DTBP:* $337 (High) \

Cathy Lauer 1,11,83   Jeff VanAuken 2,3,5
Bobby Newman 3   Lora Torres 4
Carlton McKinney ....6*   Jane Dwyer 8,57,69,88,273,286,288,298
Debbie Coleman ....16*   Jacki Tramell 58
Richard Lott 67   Sarah Loer 73*
Brittany Rogers ....274*   Susan Bell 274

Public Schs..Principal	Grd	Prgm	Enr/#Cls	SN	
Nixon-Smiley Elem Sch 500 Anglin Rd, Smiley 78159 Lundy Atkins	PK-4	T	452 25	90%	830/582-1536 Fax 830/587-6558
Nixon-Smiley High Sch 800 N Rancho Rd, Nixon 78140 **Jim Weaver**	9-12	T	300 24	75%	830/582-1536 Fax 830/582-2168
Nixon-Smiley Middle Sch 800 N Rancho Rd, Nixon 78140 Anita Van Auken	5-8	T	320 36	83%	830/582-1536 Fax 830/582-2258

- **Waelder Ind School Dist** PID: 01020003   830/788-7161
  201 US Hwy 90 West, Waelder 78959   Fax 830/788-7429

Schools: 1 \ *Teachers:* 28 \ *Students:* 320 \ *Special Ed Students:* 24 \ *LEP Students:* 71 \ *College-Bound:* 90% \ *Ethnic:* African American 14%, Hispanic 82%, Caucasian 4% \ *Exp:* $337 (High) \ *Poverty:* 27% \ *Title I:* $127,785 \ *Open-Close:* 08/19 - 05/27 \ *DTBP:* $341 (High) \

Jon Orozlo 1,11,73,83   Tiana Landry 2*
Jacob Garcia ....6*   Dora Noyola 67

Public Schs..Principal	Grd	Prgm	Enr/#Cls	SN	
Waelder Sch 109 N Ave C, Waelder 78959 Carveth Hall \ Dr Ron Lilie	PK-12	T	320 10	68%	830/788-7221 Fax 830/788-7323

GONZALES PRIVATE SCHOOLS

Private Schs..Principal	Grd	Prgm	Enr/#Cls	SN	
Emmanuel Christian Sch 1214 Saint Louis St, Gonzales 78629 Carla Holmes	PK-12		23 2		830/519-4086

GRAY COUNTY

GRAY PUBLIC SCHOOLS

- **Grandview-Hopkins Ind Sch Dist** PID: 01020053   806/669-3831
  11676 FM 293, Groom 79039   Fax 806/669-3044

Schools: 1 \ *Teachers:* 5 \ *Students:* 50 \ *Special Ed Students:* 3 \ *Ethnic:* African American 2%, Hispanic 11%, Caucasian 86% \ *Exp:* $398 (High) \ *Poverty:* 15% \ *Open-Close:* 08/21 - 05/21

Kent Hargis 1,11,288   Ryan Davis 67

Public Schs..Principal	Grd	Prgm	Enr/#Cls	SN	
Grandview-Hopkins Elem Sch 11676 FM 293, Groom 79039 John Wilson	PK-6		50 6	39%	806/669-3831

1 Superintendent	8 Curric/Instruct K-12	19 Chief Financial Officer	29 Family/Consumer Science	39 Social Studies K-12	49 English/Lang Arts Elem	59 Special Education Elem	69 Academic Assessment
2 Bus/Finance/Purchasing	9 Curric/Instruct Elem	20 Art K-12	30 Adult Education	40 Social Studies Elem	50 English/Lang Arts Sec	60 Special Education Sec	70 Research/Development
3 Buildings And Grounds	10 Curric/Instruct Sec	21 Art Elem	31 Career/Sch-to-Work K-12	41 Social Studies Sec	51 Reading K-12	61 Foreign/World Lang K-12	71 Public Information
4 Food Service	11 Federal Program	22 Art Sec	32 Career/Sch-to-Work Elem	42 Science K-12	52 Reading Elem	62 Foreign/World Lang Elem	72 Summer School
5 Transportation	12 Title I	23 Music K-12	33 Career/Sch-to-Work Sec	43 Science Elem	53 Reading Sec	63 Foreign/World Lang Sec	73 Instructional Tech
6 Athletic	13 Title V	24 Music Elem	34 Early Childhood Ed	44 Science Sec	54 Remedial Reading K-12	64 Religious Education K-12	74 Inservice Training
7 Health Services	15 Asst Superintendent	25 Music Sec	35 Health/Phys Education	45 Math K-12	55 Remedial Reading Elem	65 Religious Education Elem	75 Marketing/Distributive
	16 Instructional Media Svcs	26 Business Education	36 Guidance Services K-12	46 Math Elem	56 Remedial Reading Sec	66 Religious Education Sec	76 Info Systems
	17 Chief Operations Officer	27 Career & Tech Ed	37 Guidance Services Elem	47 Math Sec	57 Bilingual/ELL	67 School Board President	77 Psychological Assess
	18 Chief Academic Officer	28 Technology Education	38 Guidance Services Sec	48 English/Lang Arts K-12	58 Special Education K-12	68 Teacher Personnel	78 Affirmative Action

Texas School Directory

Grayson County

- **Lefors Ind School Dist** PID: 01020077 806/835-2533
  209 E 5th Street, Lefors 79054 Fax 866/897-9637

Schools: 1 \ *Teachers:* 17 \ *Students:* 160 \ *Special Ed Students:* 15 \ *LEP Students:* 3 \ *College-Bound:* 60% \ *Ethnic:* Asian 1%, African American 1%, Hispanic 16%, Caucasian 83% \ *Exp:* $471 (High) \ *Poverty:* 30% \ *Title I:* $45,673 \ *Open-Close:* 08/19 - 05/21 \ *DTBP:* $295 (High) \ F T

Kelley Porter 1,11	Morgan McBee 2	
Ron Smith 3	Kendra Ray 4	
Johnny Woodard 5	Joe Rally 6*	
Alicia Forsyth 8,11,57*	Lindy Jackson 67	
Tonya Lock 271		

Public Schs..Principal	Grd	Prgm	Enr/#Cls	SN	
Lefors Sch 209 E 5th Street, Lefors 79054 Alicia Forsyth	PK-12	TV	160 30	61%	806/835-2533

- **McLean Ind School Dist** PID: 01020106 806/779-2301
  4th & Rowe Streets, McLean 79057 Fax 806/779-2248

Schools: 1 \ *Teachers:* 21 \ *Students:* 240 \ *Special Ed Students:* 23 \ *LEP Students:* 3 \ *College-Bound:* 75% \ *Ethnic:* Hispanic 18%, Caucasian 82% \ *Exp:* $482 (High) \ *Poverty:* 21% \ *Title I:* $50,719 \ *Open-Close:* 08/15 - 05/22 \ *DTBP:* $162 (High)

Oscar Muniz 1	Amy Calvert 2,71
Rhonda Sparling 4*	Tammy Hanes 7,271*
Shelly Henderson 54,280*	Diana Watson 57*
Sherri Haynes 67	

Public Schs..Principal	Grd	Prgm	Enr/#Cls	SN	
McLean Sch 4th & Rowe Streets, McLean 79057 Raymond Glass	PK-12	TV	240 16	51%	806/779-2301

- **Pampa Ind School Dist** PID: 01020132 806/669-4700
  1233 N Hobart St, Pampa 79065 Fax 806/665-0506

Schools: 7 \ *Teachers:* 259 \ *Students:* 3,500 \ *Special Ed Students:* 404 \ *LEP Students:* 593 \ *Ethnic:* Asian 1%, African American 3%, Hispanic 48%, Caucasian 48% \ *Exp:* $198 (Low) \ *Poverty:* 21% \ *Title I:* $968,672 \ *Open-Close:* 08/20 - 05/21 \ *DTBP:* $154 (High)

Tanya Larkin 1	Anita Russell 2
Bill Hieronymus 5	Stuart Smith 5
Greg Poynor 6	Tamara Gutierrez 7*
Pam Mitchell 8,11,15,30,72	Kelly Vigil 16*
Mark Murray 27,31*	Brittany Stark 38,83,90*
Mark Elms 47*	Tatiana Greer 57,271*
Susan Furgeson 58,81,88	Richard Qualls 67
Nathan Maxwell 68,74,78,273	Molly Brinkley 73
Melody Baker 76	Jana Williamson 93
Dennis Boyd 295	

Public Schs..Principal	Grd	Prgm	Enr/#Cls	SN	
Austin Elem Sch 1900 Duncan St, Pampa 79065 Kristal Floyd	K-5	T	396 21	38%	806/669-4760 Fax 806/669-4731
Lamar Elem Sch 1234 S Nelson St, Pampa 79065 Troy McClendon	PK-5	T	606 30	90%	806/669-4880 Fax 806/669-4735
Pampa High Sch 111 E Harvester Ave, Pampa 79065 Hugh Piatt	9-12	TV	929 130	48%	806/669-4800 Fax 806/669-4826
Pampa Junior High Sch 4000 Bad Cattle Co Rd, Pampa 79065 Jamie Winborne	6-8	T	794 75	59%	806/669-4900 Fax 806/669-4742
Ⓐ Pampa Learning Center 907 N Frost St, Pampa 79065 Carrie Williams	9-12		41 2	62%	806/669-4750 Fax 806/669-4734
Travis Elem Sch 2300 Primrose Ln, Pampa 79065 Byron May	K-5	T	406 20	55%	806/669-4950 Fax 806/669-4737
Wilson Elem Sch 801 E Browning Ave, Pampa 79065 Keana Daughtry	K-5	T	407 19	84%	806/669-4930 Fax 806/669-4736

GRAY PRIVATE SCHOOLS

Private Schs..Principal	Grd	Prgm	Enr/#Cls	SN	
Community Christian Sch 409 N Frost St, Pampa 79065 Marsha Richardson	PK-8		71 8		806/665-3393 Fax 806/665-4105

GRAYSON COUNTY

GRAYSON PUBLIC SCHOOLS

- **Bells Ind School Dist** PID: 01020235 903/965-7721
  1550 Ole Ambrose Rd, Bells 75414 Fax 903/965-7036

Schools: 3 \ *Teachers:* 64 \ *Students:* 845 \ *Special Ed Students:* 72 \ *LEP Students:* 6 \ *College-Bound:* 65% \ *Ethnic:* African American 1%, Hispanic 7%, Native American: 2%, Caucasian 89% \ *Exp:* $365 (High) \ *Poverty:* 12% \ *Title I:* $89,904 \ *Open-Close:* 08/26 - 05/28 \ *DTBP:* $290 (High)

Tricia Meek 1,11	Marilyn Steger 2
Jackie Eller 3	Will Steger 3,5*
Shannon Keating 4	Dale West 6
Scott Ponder 6*	Deborah Williams 7,35,85*
Josh Weger 12	Pamela Pettit 16,82*
Clay Rolen 31,58,77,88,93	E Pettit 67
Ross Chlapecka 73,76,84	

Public Schs..Principal	Grd	Prgm	Enr/#Cls	SN	
Bells Elem Sch 110 Scott Rd, Bells 75414 Yalonda Ivers	PK-5	T	368	48%	903/965-3601 Fax 903/965-0140
Bells High Sch 1500 Ole Ambrose Rd, Bells 75414 **Clay Rolen**	9-12	V	261 30	30%	903/965-3603 Fax 903/965-5205
Pritchard Junior High Sch 1510 Ole Ambrose Rd, Bells 75414 Will Steger	6-8		193 18	30%	903/965-4835 Fax 903/965-7428

---

79 Student Personnel	91 Safety/Security	275 Response To Intervention	298 Grant Writer/Ptnrships	**School Programs**	**Social Media**		
80 Driver Ed/Safety	92 Magnet School	277 Remedial Math K-12	750 Chief Innovation Officer	A = Alternative Program			
81 Gifted/Talented	93 Parental Involvement	280 Literacy Coach	751 Chief of Staff	G = Adult Classes	F = Facebook		
82 Video Services	95 Tech Prep Program	285 STEM	752 Social Emotional Learning	M = Magnet Program			
83 Substance Abuse Prev	97 Chief Information Officer	288 Digital Learning		T = Title I Schoolwide	T = Twitter		
84 Erate	98 Chief Technology Officer	288 Common Core Standards	**Other School Types**	V = Career & Tech Ed Programs			
85 AIDS Education	270 Character Education	294 Accountability	Ⓐ = Alternative School				
88 Alternative/At Risk	271 Migrant Education	295 Network System	Ⓒ = Charter School	New Schools are shaded			
89 Multi-Cultural Curriculum	273 Teacher Mentor	296 Title II Programs	Ⓜ = Magnet School	New Superintendents and Principals are bold			
90 Social Work	274 Before/After Sch	297 Webmaster	Ⓨ = Year-Round School	Personnel with email addresses are underscored			

TX—165

Grayson County

Market Data Retrieval

● **Collinsville Ind School Dist** PID: 01020261   903/429-6272
500 Reeves St, Collinsville 76233   Fax 903/429-6665

Schools: 2 \ **Teachers:** 43 \ **Students:** 530 \ **Special Ed Students:** 32 \
LEP Students: 28 \ **College-Bound:** 85% \ **Ethnic:** African American 1%,
Hispanic 19%, Native American: 1%, Caucasian 79% \ **Exp:** $504 (High) \
Poverty: 13% \ **Title I:** $73,047 \ **Open-Close:** 08/21 - 05/21 \ **DTBP:** $377
(High) \ f

Mark Dykes	1	Galen Ewton		2
Laurie Bishop	4*	Garrett Patterson		6
Dawn Weaver	7,85*	Misty Ward		8,11,296,298
Ken Kemp	16,73,295*	Melissa Baggs		37,69,83*
Catherine Shackelford	58	Justin McDonnell		67

Public Schs..Principal	Grd	Prgm	Enr/#Cls	SN	
Collinsville Elem Sch 500 Reeves St, Collinsville 76233 **Catherine Shackelford**	PK-6	T	302 6	62%	903/429-3077 Fax 903/429-1004
Collinsville High Sch 202 N Broadway St, Collinsville 76233 **David Johnson**	7-12	T	244 24	42%	903/429-6164 Fax 903/429-6493 f

● **Denison Ind School Dist** PID: 01020297   903/462-7000
1201 S Rusk Ave, Denison 75020   Fax 903/462-7002

Schools: 9 \ **Teachers:** 331 \ **Students:** 4,500 \ **Special Ed Students:** 623 \
LEP Students: 238 \ **Ethnic:** Asian 1%, African American 11%, Hispanic 20%,
Native American: 2%, Caucasian 66% \ **Exp:** $534 (High) \ **Poverty:** 21% \
Title I: $1,226,315 \ **Special Education:** $982,000 \ **Open-Close:** 08/15 -
05/22 \ **DTBP:** $155 (High) \ t

Dr Henry Scott	1	Cortney Hunkapillar		2
Randy Reid	2,15,91	David Self		3
Debbie Hosford	4	Randy Taylor		5
Chad Rogers	6*	Heidi Lyons		7*
Shonda Cannon	8,45,51,74,273,298	Amy Neidert		9
Laurie Brand	10	Renee Burroughs		10
Dr David Kirkbride	13,15,68,78,79,83,294,296	Dr Cavin Boettger		31*
Regina Prigge	36,69,271,294	Lori May		58,77
David Hawley	67	Brian Eaves		71*
Dr Dickie Deel	73,295,297			

Public Schs..Principal	Grd	Prgm	Enr/#Cls	SN	
B McDaniel Intemediate Sch 400 S Lillis Ln, Denison 75020 **Alvis Dunlap**	5-6	T	690 52	66%	903/462-7200 Fax 903/462-7328
Denison High Sch 4200 N State Highway 91, Denison 75020 **Dr Cavin Boettger**	9-12	TV	1,312 71	54%	903/462-7125 Fax 903/462-7217
Henry Scott Middle Sch 1901 S Mirick Ave, Denison 75020 **John Parker**	7-8	T	714	60%	903/462-7180 Fax 903/462-7342
Houston Elem Sch 1100 W Morgan St, Denison 75020 **Kyle Uber**	K-4	T	250 17	76%	903/462-7300 Fax 903/462-7419
Hyde Park Elem Sch 1701 S Hyde Park Ave, Denison 75020 **Kerry Kaai**	PK-5	T	470 15	60%	903/462-7350 Fax 903/462-7455
Lamar Elem Sch 1000 S 5th Ave, Denison 75021 **Gena Jackson**	PK-4	T	440 21	75%	903/462-7400 Fax 903/462-7495 t
Mayes Elem Sch 201 Jennie Ln, Denison 75020 **Natalie Hicks**	PK-4	T	500 14	69%	903/462-7500 Fax 903/462-7563

Ⓐ Pathways High Sch   9-12   T   60   53%   903/462-7150
318 W Morgan St, Denison 75020   2   Fax 903/462-7226
Lance San Millan

Terrell Elem Sch   PK-4   T   314   82%   903/462-7550
230 W M L King Jr Blvd, Denison 75020   30   Fax 903/462-7609
Amy Neidert

● **Gunter Ind School Dist** PID: 01020443   903/433-4750
213 N Preston Rd, Gunter 75058   Fax 903/433-1053

Schools: 3 \ **Teachers:** 83 \ **Students:** 970 \ **Special Ed Students:** 53 \
LEP Students: 50 \ **College-Bound:** 62% \ **Ethnic:** African American 1%,
Hispanic 24%, Native American: 1%, Caucasian 74% \ **Exp:** $308 (High) \
Poverty: 8% \ **Title I:** $55,254 \ **Open-Close:** 08/15 - 05/21 \ **DTBP:** $317
(High)

Dr Jill Siler	1	Brittany Floyd		2
Kelley Teems	3,296	Caleb Bell		5
Jacob Fieszel	6*	Dara Arrington		8,11,296
Jacob Waggoner	38,83*	Elsie Wetzel		57,271
Christy Nolen	58	Scott Meyerdirk		67
Heidi Carruthers	68	Shelli Neely		73*
David Kobosky	295*			

Public Schs..Principal	Grd	Prgm	Enr/#Cls	SN	
Gunter Elem Sch 200 Elm St, Gunter 75058 **Dara Arrington**	PK-4	T	369 15	39%	903/433-5315 Fax 903/433-1184
Gunter High Sch 1102 N 8th St, Gunter 75058 **Chris Dodd**	9-12	V	295 30	20%	903/433-1542 Fax 903/433-1492
Gunter Middle Sch 410 Tiger Ln, Gunter 75058 **Kimberly Patterson**	5-8		268 20	25%	903/433-1545 Fax 903/433-9306

● **Howe Ind School Dist** PID: 01020479   903/532-3228
105 W Tutt St, Howe 75459   Fax 903/532-3205

Schools: 4 \ **Teachers:** 84 \ **Students:** 1,100 \ **Special Ed Students:** 99 \
LEP Students: 39 \ **College-Bound:** 64% \ **Ethnic:** African American 1%,
Hispanic 15%, Native American: 1%, Caucasian 83% \ **Exp:** $558 (High) \
Poverty: 16% \ **Title I:** $218,358 \ **Open-Close:** 08/14 - 05/22 \ **DTBP:** $338
(High) \ f

Kevin Wilson	1	Julie Snapp		2
Ricky Brinlee	3,5	Lesia Kirland		4
Bill Jehlings	6*	Darla Williams		8,11,15,58,69*
Melissa Atchison	16	Mary Claire Woodard		31*
K'Lain Ashlock	37*	Pauli Stephens		38
Clint Catching	67	Joe Gandillon		73,76,298*

Public Schs..Principal	Grd	Prgm	Enr/#Cls	SN	
Howe High Sch 200 Ponderosa Rd, Howe 75459 **Phil Kempson**	9-12	ATV	341 25	28%	903/532-3236 Fax 903/532-3237 f
Howe Intermediate Sch 315 Roberts St, Howe 75459 **Tammy Witten**	3-5	AT	300 26	54%	903/532-3320 Fax 903/532-3221
Howe Middle Sch 300 Beatrice St, Howe 75459 **Clayton Wilson**	6-8	AT	250 24	45%	903/532-3286 Fax 903/532-3287
Summit Hill Elem Sch 701 Summit Hill Pkwy, Howe 75459 **Clarissa Doty**	PK-2		200		903/745-4100 Fax 903/745-4101

1	Superintendent	8	Curric/Instruct K-12	19	Chief Financial Officer	29	Family/Consumer Science	39	Social Studies K-12	49	English/Lang Arts Elem	59	Special Education Elem	69	Academic Assessment
2	Bus/Finance/Purchasing	9	Curric/Instruct Elem	20	Art K-12	30	Adult Education	40	Social Studies Elem	50	English/Lang Arts Sec	60	Special Education Sec	70	Research/Development
3	Buildings And Grounds	10	Curric/Instruct Sec	21	Art Elem	31	Career/Sch-to-Work K-12	41	Social Studies Sec	51	Reading K-12	61	Foreign/World Lang K-12	71	Public Information
4	Food Service	11	Federal Program	22	Art Sec	32	Career/Sch-to-Work Elem	42	Science K-12	52	Reading Elem	62	Foreign/World Lang Elem	72	Summer School
5	Transportation	12	Title I	23	Music K-12	33	Career/Sch-to-Work Sec	43	Science Elem	53	Reading Sec	63	Foreign/World Lang Sec	73	Instructional Tech
6	Athletic	13	Title V	24	Music Elem	34	Early Childhood Ed	44	Science Sec	54	Remedial Reading K-12	64	Religious Education K-12	74	Inservice Training
7	Health Services	15	Asst Superintendent	25	Music Sec	35	Health/Phys Education	45	Math K-12	55	Remedial Reading Elem	65	Religious Education Elem	75	Marketing/Distributive
		16	Instructional Media Svcs	26	Business Education	36	Guidance Services K-12	46	Math Elem	56	Remedial Reading Sec	66	Religious Education Sec	76	Info Systems
		17	Chief Operations Officer	27	Career & Tech Ed	37	Guidance Services Elem	47	Math Sec	57	Bilingual/ELL	67	School Board President	77	Psychological Assess
		18	Chief Academic Officer	28	Technology Education	38	Guidance Services Sec	48	English/Lang Arts K-12	58	Special Education K-12	68	Teacher Personnel	78	Affirmative Action

Texas School Directory — Grayson County

• **Pottsboro Ind School Dist** PID: 01020510 903/771-0083
105 Cardinal Lane, Pottsboro 75076 Fax 903/786-9085

Schools: 3 \ **Teachers:** 94 \ **Students:** 1,450 \ **Special Ed Students:** 141 \
LEP Students: 13 \ **College-Bound:** 70% \ **Ethnic:** Asian 1%, Hispanic 7%,
Native American: 3%, Caucasian 89% \ **Exp:** $390 (High) \ **Poverty:** 16% \
Title I: $238,541 \ **Open-Close:** 08/15 - 05/22 \ **DTBP:** $361 (High)

Dr Kevin Matthews 1	Janet Wilson 2*
Paul Wickett 3	Cathy Griffith 4*
Curtis Hendrickson 5	Matt Poe 6
Debbie Ritchie 8,11	Josh Recer 15
Angie Slate 16,82*	Jim Copeland 67
Jason Brown 73,286,295*	

Public Schs..Principal	Grd	Prgm	Enr/#Cls	SN	
Pottsboro Elem Sch 525 Highway 120, Pottsboro 75076 Danielle Curry	PK-4	T	550 23	47%	903/771-2981 Fax 903/786-4903
Pottsboro High Sch 901 E FM 120, Pottsboro 75076 Greg Wright	9-12		429 40	31%	903/771-0085 Fax 903/786-6349
Pottsboro Middle Sch 207 Cardinal Lane, Pottsboro 75076 Gerald Springer	5-8		457 36	34%	903/771-2982 Fax 903/786-4902

• **S & S Cons Ind School Dist** PID: 01020560 903/564-6051
1 Ram Dr, Sadler 76264 Fax 903/564-3492

Schools: 3 \ **Teachers:** 70 \ **Students:** 950 \ **Special Ed Students:** 81 \
LEP Students: 18 \ **Ethnic:** Hispanic 10%, Native American: 2%,
Caucasian 87% \ **Exp:** $516 (High) \ **Poverty:** 15% \ **Title I:** $171,914 \
Open-Close: 08/15 - 05/20 \ **DTBP:** $359 (High)

Roger Reed 1	Stephanie Maher 2
Corgie Fisher 3,5	Deanne Caffey 4
Josh Aleman 6	Lance Johnson 11,83*
Chris Lopez 67	Dustin Wilson 73*

Public Schs..Principal	Grd	Prgm	Enr/#Cls	SN	
S & S Cons High Sch 404 S Main St, Sadler 76264 Mark Youree	9-12	TV	274 20	46%	903/564-3768 Fax 903/564-7308
S & S Cons Middle Sch 200 Ram Ave, Sadler 76264 Greg Pierce	6-8	T	202 15	46%	903/564-7626 Fax 903/564-7857
S & S Elem Sch 4217 Elementary Dr, Southmayd 76268 Shanna Reynolds	PK-5	T	441 27	56%	903/893-0767 Fax 903/891-9338

• **Sherman Ind School Dist** PID: 01020596 903/891-6400
2701 N Loy Lake Rd, Sherman 75090 Fax 903/891-6407

Schools: 12 \ **Teachers:** 542 \ **Students:** 7,300 \ **Special Ed Students:** 866
\ **LEP Students:** 1,431 \ **College-Bound:** 56% \ **Ethnic:** Asian 3%,
African American 14%, Hispanic 41%, Native American: 1%, Caucasian
40% \ **Exp:** $324 (High) \ **Poverty:** 22% \ **Title I:** $2,099,104 \
Special Education: $1,408,000 \ **Bilingual Education:** $69,000 \
Open-Close: 08/14 - 05/21 \ **DTBP:** $157 (High) \ f

Dr David Hicks 1	Mandi Lewis 2
Dr Tyson Bennett 2,15	Scott Conrad 3
Mandy Stephens 4	Brett Counte 5,91
JD Martinez 6	Stacy Phillips 7,36,69,83,275
Susan Whitenack 8,11,88,286,288,296,298	Dr Gayle Smith 9
Blake Hays 10	Dr Tamy Smalskas 15,31
Kimberly Simpson 16,71	Katherine Morris 27*
Stephanie Lippard ...54,57,74,77,271,273,277	Greg Howse 58
Kaye Allen 58,85	Tim Millerick 67
Jill O'Neal 68,79	Mignon Plyler 73,295
Chris Cooper 76	Colin Bell 295
Sean Vanderveer 297	

Public Schs..Principal	Grd	Prgm	Enr/#Cls	SN	
Crutchfield Elem Sch 521 S Dewey Ave, Sherman 75090 Leda Roelke	K-4	T	430 22	82%	903/891-6565 Fax 903/891-6570
Dillingham Intermediate Sch 1701 Gallagher Dr, Sherman 75090 Pamela Voss	5-6	T	1,130 55	68%	903/891-6495 Fax 903/891-6499
Fairview Elem Sch 501 W Taylor St, Sherman 75092 Michelle Eackles	K-4	T	418 60	59%	903/891-6580 Fax 903/891-6585
Fred Douglass Early Chldhd Ctr 505 E College St, Sherman 75090 Deloris Dowell	PK-PK	T	337 13	94%	903/891-6545 Fax 903/891-6549 f
Jefferson Elem Sch 608 N Lee Ave, Sherman 75090 Nancy Jung	K-4	T	227 12	88%	903/891-6610 Fax 903/891-6615
Percy Neblitt Elem Sch 1505 Gallagher Dr, Sherman 75090 Kelli Abohosh	K-4	T	506	75%	903/891-6670 Fax 903/893-0263 f
ⓐ Perrin Alt Learning Center 81 Vandenburg Dr, Denison 75020 Jimmy May	9-12	T	60	71%	903/891-6680 Fax 903/786-4766
Piner Middle Sch 402 W Pecan St, Sherman 75090 Amy Porter	7-8	T	1,036 40	64%	903/891-6470 Fax 903/891-6475
Sherman High Sch 2201 E Lamar St, Sherman 75090 Jennifer Politi	9-12	TV	1,878	55%	903/891-6440 Fax 903/891-6446
Sory Elem Sch 120 Binkley Park Dr, Sherman 75092 Steven Traw	K-4	T	622	61%	903/891-6650 Fax 903/892-6307
Wakefield Elem Sch 400 Sunset Blvd, Sherman 75092 Eartha Linson	K-4	T	349 40	66%	903/891-6595 Fax 903/891-6600
Washington Elem Sch 815 S Travis St, Sherman 75090 Amy Pesina	K-4	T	437 22	92%	903/891-6700 Fax 903/893-0141 f

• **Tioga Ind School Dist** PID: 01020699 940/437-2366
405 N Florence St, Tioga 76271 Fax 940/437-9986

Schools: 1 \ **Teachers:** 45 \ **Students:** 700 \ **Special Ed Students:** 27 \
LEP Students: 24 \ **College-Bound:** 50% \ **Ethnic:** Asian 1%, Hispanic 22%,
Native American: 1%, Caucasian 76% \ **Exp:** $620 (High) \ **Poverty:** 14% \
Title I: $41,795 \ **Open-Close:** 08/15 - 05/21 \ **DTBP:** $410 (High)

Dr Charles Holloway 1	Nancy Whitworth 2
Vickie McNaird 4*	Cody Patton 6*
Diane Mincher 11,88*	Jana Smith 57,271
Paul Rodarmer 67	Elias Khalaf 73*

Public Schs..Principal	Grd	Prgm	Enr/#Cls	SN	
Tioga Sch 405 N Florence St, Tioga 76271 Jana Smith \ Erica Waller	PK-12	T	700 12	38%	940/437-2366 Fax 940/202-2587

79	Student Personnel	91	Safety/Security	275	Response To Intervention	298	Grant Writer/Ptnrships
80	Driver Ed/Safety	92	Magnet School	277	Remedial Math K-12	750	Chief Innovation Officer
81	Gifted/Talented	93	Parental Involvement	280	Literacy Coach	751	Chief of Staff
82	Video Services	95	Tech Prep Program	285	STEM	752	Social Emotional Learning
83	Substance Abuse Prev	97	Chief Information Officer	286	Digital Learning		
84	Erate	98	Chief Technology Officer	288	Common Core Standards		**Other School Types**
85	AIDS Education	270	Accountability	294	Accountability		ⓐ = Alternative School
88	Alternative/At Risk	271	Migrant Education	295	Network System		ⓒ = Charter School
89	Multi-Cultural Curriculum	273	Teacher Mentor	296	Title II Programs		ⓜ = Magnet School
90	Social Work	274	Before/After Sch	297	Webmaster		ⓨ = Year-Round School

School Programs
A = Alternative Program
G = Adult Classes
M = Magnet Program
T = Title I Schoolwide
V = Career & Tech Ed Programs

Social Media
f = Facebook
t = Twitter

New Schools are shaded
New Superintendents and Principals are bold
Personnel with email addresses are underscored

TX-167

Grayson County

Market Data Retrieval

- **Tom Bean Ind School Dist** PID: 01020716 903/546-6076
  100 E Garner St, Tom Bean 75489 Fax 903/546-6104

Schools: 3 \ **Teachers:** 57 \ **Students:** 675 \ **Special Ed Students:** 69 \ **LEP Students:** 7 \ **Ethnic:** African American 1%, Hispanic 6%, Native American: 1%, Caucasian 92% \ **Exp:** $372 (High) \ **Poverty:** 11% \ **Title I:** $101,142 \ **Open-Close:** 08/15 - 05/21 \ **DTBP:** $353 (High)

Kelly Lusk 1	Jennifer Parrish 2
Pam Piper 3	Florence Penrod 4*
Bobbie McAdoo 6	Tiffany Yale 7
John Orozco 8,11,74,79,91,296	John Orozco 10,34*
Cheryl Jones 16,73,82	Marcy Chapman 27*
Chad Ashlock 38	Wanda Johnson 58*
Jesse Farrer 67	Jan Woods-Meals 73
Bobbie Moran 76	

Public Schs..Principal	Grd	Prgm	Enr/#Cls	SN	
Tom Bean Elem Sch 105 Eubanks St, Tom Bean 75489 Patrice Counts	PK-5	T	287 19	52%	903/546-6333 Fax 903/546-6572
Tom Bean High Sch 7719 State Hwy 11, Tom Bean 75489 Sara McCarty	9-12	TV	209 26	37%	903/546-6319
Tom Bean Middle Sch 289 Franklin Rd, Tom Bean 75489 Sara McCarty	6-8	T	171 18	48%	903/546-6161 Fax 903/546-6798

- **Van Alstyne Ind School Dist** PID: 01020742 903/482-8802
  1096 N Waco St, Van Alstyne 75495 Fax 903/482-6086

Schools: 4 \ **Teachers:** 105 \ **Students:** 1,598 \ **Special Ed Students:** 136 \ **LEP Students:** 32 \ **College-Bound:** 60% \ **Ethnic:** Asian 1%, African American 2%, Hispanic 13%, Native American: 1%, Caucasian 84% \ **Exp:** $383 (High) \ **Poverty:** 10% \ **Title I:** $157,332 \ **Open-Close:** 08/15 - 05/21 \ **DTBP:** $338 (High) \

Dr David Brown 1	Reene Maples 2,11
Lannie Barnes 3,5	Denise Richardson 4*
Mikeal Miller 6*	Jamie Martinez 8,12,57
Devin Hill 16*	Sara Williams 37*
Randall Morgan 67	Kenneth Daniel 73

Public Schs..Principal	Grd	Prgm	Enr/#Cls	SN	
Bob & Lola Sandford Elem Sch 300 Williamsburg Way, Van Alstyne 75495 Sherry Stillman	PK-4		308		903/712-1900
John & Nelda Partin Elem Sch 201 Newport Dr, Van Alstyne 75495 Kristina Odom	PK-4	T	308 26	31%	903/482-8805 Fax 903/482-8820
Van Alstyne High Sch 1722 N Waco St, Van Alstyne 75495 Craig Dennis	9-12	V	469 25	24%	903/482-8803 Fax 903/482-8885
Van Alstyne Middle Sch 1314 N Waco St, Van Alstyne 75495 Kelly Moore	5-8		513 40	33%	903/482-8804 Fax 903/482-8890

- **Whitesboro Ind School Dist** PID: 01020780 903/564-4200
  115 4th St, Whitesboro 76273 Fax 903/564-9303

Schools: 4 \ **Teachers:** 110 \ **Students:** 1,600 \ **Special Ed Students:** 157 \ **LEP Students:** 62 \ **Ethnic:** African American 1%, Hispanic 16%, Native American: 2%, Caucasian 81% \ **Exp:** $433 (High) \ **Poverty:** 20% \ **Title I:** $387,106 \ **Open-Close:** 08/22 - 05/22 \ **DTBP:** $547 (High)

Ryan Harper 1	Jamie Brooks 2
Ken Carden 3	Alicia Tracy 4
Alicia Tracy 4*	Mike Pack 5*
Cody Fagan 6*	Jodie Tucker 8
Mattew Davenport 8,15,84	Sharon Bryan 16*
Donna Boiles 36,69,77*	Justin Boren 67
Michael Peterson 73,295*	D M Hampton 91

Public Schs..Principal	Grd	Prgm	Enr/#Cls	SN	
J W Hayes Primary Sch 117 4th St, Whitesboro 76273 Patti Achimon	PK-2	T	409 28	48%	903/564-4281 Fax 903/564-4123
Whitesboro High Sch 1 Bearcat Dr, Whitesboro 76273 Marlene Robinson	9-12	T	457 30	35%	903/564-4114 Fax 903/564-4288
Whitesboro Intermediate Sch 211 N College St, Whitesboro 76273 Gina Henley	3-5	T	373 18	53%	903/564-4180 Fax 903/564-6808
Whitesboro Middle Sch 600 4th St, Whitesboro 76273 Don Keene	6-8	T	343 30	51%	903/564-4236 Fax 903/564-5939

- **Whitewright Ind School Dist** PID: 01020821 903/364-2155
  315 A Highland Dr, Whitewright 75491 Fax 903/364-2839

Schools: 3 \ **Teachers:** 61 \ **Students:** 850 \ **Special Ed Students:** 55 \ **LEP Students:** 25 \ **Ethnic:** Asian 1%, African American 6%, Hispanic 14%, Native American: 1%, Caucasian 79% \ **Exp:** $487 (High) \ **Poverty:** 18% \ **Title I:** $164,608 \ **Open-Close:** 08/19 - 05/21 \ **DTBP:** $105 (High)

Brian Garner 1	Chelsea Menjivar 2
Mario Carpio 3	Sandra Whitt 4
Bobby Worthy 5,8,11,57,74,273,288,294	Ashley Womble 9,93
Lisa Lawson 16,286*	Linda Jester 67
Donna Lucas 73,295	Judy Sims 91
Mike Stephens 91	

Public Schs..Principal	Grd	Prgm	Enr/#Cls	SN	
Whitewright Elem Sch 305 W Highland Dr, Whitewright 75491 Lori Salmond	PK-5	T	378 22	49%	903/364-2155 Fax 903/364-5799
Whitewright High Sch 304 Echols Ln, Whitewright 75491 Steve Morrow	9-12	V	272 21	37%	903/364-2155 Fax 903/364-2579
Whitewright Middle Sch 315 W Highland Dr, Whitewright 75491 Charles Nash	6-8	T	204 17	43%	903/364-2155 Fax 903/364-5263

GRAYSON CATHOLIC SCHOOLS

- **Diocese of Dallas Ed Office** PID: 01012367
  Listing includes only schools located in this county. See District Index for location of Diocesan Offices.

Catholic Schs..Principal	Grd	Prgm	Enr/#Cls	SN	
St Marys Catholic Sch 713 S Travis St, Sherman 75090 Phillip Scheibmeir	PK-8		170 14		903/893-2127 Fax 903/893-3233

1 Superintendent	8 Curric/Instruct K-12	19 Chief Financial Officer	29 Family/Consumer Science	39 Social Studies K-12	49 English/Lang Arts Elem	59 Special Education Elem	69 Academic Assessment
2 Bus/Finance/Purchasing	9 Curric/Instruct Elem	20 Art K-12	30 Adult Education	40 Social Studies Elem	50 English/Lang Arts Sec	60 Special Education Sec	70 Research/Development
3 Buildings And Grounds	10 Curric/Instruct Sec	21 Art Elem	31 Career/Sch-to-Work K-12	41 Social Studies Sec	51 Reading K-12	61 Foreign/World Lang K-12	71 Public Information
4 Food Service	11 Federal Program	22 Art Sec	32 Career/Sch-to-Work Elem	42 Science K-12	52 Reading Elem	62 Foreign/World Lang Elem	72 Summer School
5 Transportation	12 Title I	23 Music K-12	33 Career/Sch-to-Work Sec	43 Science Elem	53 Reading Sec	63 Foreign/World Lang Sec	73 Instructional Tech
6 Athletic	13 Title V	24 Music Elem	34 Early Childhood Ed	44 Science Sec	54 Remedial Reading K-12	64 Religious Education K-12	74 Inservice Training
7 Health Services	15 Asst Superintendent	25 Music Sec	35 Health/Phys Education	45 Math K-12	55 Remedial Reading Elem	65 Religious Education Elem	75 Marketing/Distributive
	16 Instructional Media Svcs	26 Business Education	36 Guidance Services K-12	46 Math Elem	56 Remedial Reading Sec	66 Religious Education Sec	76 Info Systems
	17 Chief Operations Officer	27 Career & Tech Ed	37 Guidance Services Elem	47 Math Sec	57 Bilingual/ELL	67 School Board President	77 Psychological Assess
	18 Chief Academic Officer	28 Technology Education	38 Guidance Services Sec	48 English/Lang Arts K-12	58 Special Education K-12	68 Teacher Personnel	78 Affirmative Action

Texas School Directory

Gregg County

GRAYSON PRIVATE SCHOOLS

Private Schs..Principal	Grd	Prgm	Enr/#Cls	SN	
Grayson Christian Sch 4400 US Highway 82 E, Sherman 75090 Greg Rostyne	PK-12		180 6		903/892-3304 Fax 903/868-2546
Liberty Christian Academy 120 W Mulberry St, Sherman 75090 Katie Gresham	K-12		36		903/328-6037
Montessori Academy-North Texas 906 Cottonwood Dr, Sherman 75090 Angela Majors	PK-6		120		903/893-3500 Fax 972/767-0999
St Luke Sch 427 W Woodard St, Denison 75020 Cheryl Matsumoto	PK-5		60 5		903/465-2653 Fax 903/465-1428
Texoma Christian Sch 3500 W Houston St, Sherman 75092 Linda Yeilding	PK-12		300 30		903/893-7076 Fax 903/891-8486 f
Unity Christian Sch 1901 Woodlawn Blvd, Denison 75020 Harry Shomaker	3-12		6		903/465-1909

GREGG COUNTY

GREGG PUBLIC SCHOOLS

• **Gladewater Ind School Dist** PID: 01020857   903/845-6991
200 Broadway Ave, Gladewater 75647   Fax 903/845-6994

Schools: 4 \ *Teachers:* 142 \ *Students:* 1,700 \ *Special Ed Students:* 209 \ *LEP Students:* 111 \ *Ethnic:* Asian 1%, African American 23%, Hispanic 18%, Caucasian 58% \ *Exp:* $335 (High) \ *Poverty:* 18% \ *Title I:* $488,372 \ *Open-Close:* 08/15 - 05/28 \ *DTBP:* $539 (High) \ t

Sedric Clark 1   Glenda Hickey 2,19,73
Lesa Lynn 2   Darla Allen 3,4
Kim Chatman 3,17   Matt McIntosh 3
John Berry .... 6*   Amanda Langford 8*
Jimmy Lightfoot 15,79   Dr Peggy Oden 58
Jon Keller 67

Public Schs..Principal	Grd	Prgm	Enr/#Cls	SN	
Gladewater High Sch 2201 W Gay Ave, Gladewater 75647 Cathy Bedair	9-12	TV	477 45	65%	903/845-5591 Fax 903/845-3694
Gladewater Middle Sch 414 S Loop 485, Gladewater 75647 Chris Langford	6-8	T	390 40	75%	903/845-2243 Fax 903/844-1738
Gladewater Primary Sch 100 W Gay Ave, Gladewater 75647 Amanda Langford	PK-1	T	370 22	78%	903/845-2254 Fax 903/845-5411
Weldon Elem Sch 314 E Saunders St, Gladewater 75647 Darren Richardson	2-5	T	545 21	70%	903/845-6921 Fax 903/845-6923

• **Kilgore Ind School Dist** PID: 01020900   903/988-3900
301 N Kilgore St, Kilgore 75662   Fax 903/983-3212

Schools: 5 \ *Teachers:* 277 \ *Students:* 4,076 \ *Special Ed Students:* 328 \ *LEP Students:* 682 \ *Ethnic:* Asian 1%, African American 16%, Hispanic 34%, Native American: 1%, Caucasian 49% \ *Exp:* $367 (High) \ *Poverty:* 22% \ *Title I:* $1,033,532 \ *Special Education:* $554,000 \ *Open-Close:* 08/20 - 05/25 \ *DTBP:* $184 (High) \ f t

Dr Andrew Baker 1   Revard Pfeffer 2,19,298
Michael Brown 3,5   Jennie Hammerbacher 4
Mike Wood 6   Zevely Hatcher 8
Richard Nash 11,15   Jerry Stuart 27
Danny Stanley .... 57,69,81*   Gina Akin 58
Reggie Henson 67   Amy Broadus 68
Mark Lane .... 73,82,295,297*   Heather Chism 295

Public Schs..Principal	Grd	Prgm	Enr/#Cls	SN	
Chandler Elem Sch 2500 Chandler St, Kilgore 75662 Cynthia Lindley	2-3	T	609 41	71%	903/988-3904 Fax 903/986-8026 f t
Kilgore High Sch 711 N Longview St, Kilgore 75662 Charles Presley	9-12	TV	1,119 70	52%	903/988-3901 Fax 903/984-0571
Kilgore Intermediate Sch 2300 Whipperwill St, Kilgore 75662 Kim Slayter	4-5	T	631 24	66%	903/988-3903 Fax 903/984-7879
Kilgore Middle Sch 455 Baughman Rd, Kilgore 75662 April Cox	6-8	T	884 46	66%	903/988-3902 Fax 903/984-6225
Kilgore Primary Sch 255 Baughman Rd, Kilgore 75662 Tamara Dean	PK-1	T	833 26	78%	903/988-3905 Fax 903/984-2176

• **Longview Ind School Dist** PID: 01020986   903/381-2200
1301 E Young St, Longview 75602   Fax 903/753-5389

Schools: 13 \ *Teachers:* 581 \ *Students:* 8,700 \ *Special Ed Students:* 669 \ *LEP Students:* 1,557 \ *Ethnic:* Asian 1%, African American 36%, Hispanic 39%, Native American: 1%, Caucasian 22% \ *Exp:* $320 (High) \ *Poverty:* 24% \ *Title I:* $2,875,906 \ *Special Education:* $1,599,000 \ *Open-Close:* 08/19 - 05/27 \ *DTBP:* $158 (High) \ f t

Dr James Wilcox 1   Joey Jones 2,19
Mike Gipson 3   Phyllis Dozier 4
John King .... 6,35*   Dennis Williams 7,15,79,83,88,91,275
Beth Bassett 8,39,42,45,48,51,277,280   Horace Williams 9,15,36,69,77,286,294
Melanie Pondant 10   Sheri Broadwater 11,54,298
Jennifer Smith .... 16,73*   Brian Kasper 31*
Dr Maureen Lewis 58   Virginia Northcutt 67
Dr Jody Clements 68,74,93,296   Loretta Martin 68
Catina Love 69   Matthew Prosser 71
Brian Pitts 73,295   Glen Pierce 76
Latitia Wilson 294

Public Schs..Principal	Grd	Prgm	Enr/#Cls	SN	
Bramlette Elem Sch 111 Tupelo Dr, Longview 75601 Nikita Mumphrey	1-5	T	453 28	84%	903/803-5600 Fax 903/803-5601
East Texas Mont Prep Academy 400 N Eastman Rd, Longview 75601 Dr Jacqueline Burnett	PK-K		1,020		903/803-5000
Ⓜ Everhart Mgnt Acad/Cltrl Study 2919 Tryon Rd, Longview 75605 Cassandria James	1-5	T	742 16	84%	903/803-5400 Fax 903/758-7870

---

79 Student Personnel	91 Safety/Security	275 Response To Intervention	298 Grant Writer/Ptnrships	**School Programs**	**Social Media**
80 Driver Ed/Safety	92 Magnet School	277 Remedial Math K-12	750 Chief Innovation Officer	A = Alternative Program	
81 Gifted/Talented	93 Parental Involvement	280 Literacy Coach	751 Chief of Staff	G = Adult Classes	f = Facebook
82 Video Services	95 Tech Prep Program	285 STEM	752 Social Emotional Learning	M = Magnet Program	
83 Substance Abuse Prev	97 Chief Infomation Officer	286 Digital Learning		T = Title I Schoolwide	t = Twitter
84 Erate	98 Chief Technology Officer	288 Common Core Standards	**Other School Types**	V = Career & Tech Ed Programs	
85 AIDS Education	270 Character Education	294 Accountability	Ⓐ = Alternative School		
88 Alternative/At Risk	271 Migrant Education	295 Network System	Ⓒ = Charter School	New Schools are shaded	
89 Multi-Cultural Curriculum	273 Teacher Mentor	296 Title II Programs	Ⓜ = Magnet School	New Superintendents and Principals are bold	
90 Social Work	274 Before/After Sch	297 Webmaster	Ⓨ = Year-Round School	Personnel with email addresses are underscored	

TX—169

Gregg County

Market Data Retrieval

ⓜ Forest Park Middle Sch	6-8	T	478	88%	903/446-2510
1644 N Eastman Rd, Longview 75601			50		Fax 903/446-2501
Dr Wilbert Andrews					
Foster Middle Sch	6-8	T	736	66%	903/446-2710
1504 S Martin Luther King Blvd, Longview 75602			60		Fax 903/758-2052
Ryan Carroll					
ⓜ Hudson Pep Elem Sch	1-5		602	26%	903/803-5100
1311 Lilly St, Longview 75602			19		Fax 903/803-5101
Sue Wilson					t
Johnston McQueen Elem Sch	PK-5	T	672	60%	903/803-5300
422 FM 2751, Longview 75605			23		Fax 903/663-2135
Dr Jennifer Bailey					t
Judson Steam Academy	6-8	T	498	66%	903/446-2610
5745 Judson Rd, Longview 75605			30		Fax 903/663-2604
Melanie Pandant					t
ⓐ Longview Early Graduation HS	9-12		250		903/381-3921
410 S Green St, Longview 75601			5		Fax 903/381-3925
Kristi Means					
Longview High Sch	9-12	GTV	2,141	59%	903/663-1301
201 E Tomlinson Pwky, Longview 75605					Fax 903/663-7180
James Brewer					
Ned E Williams Elem Sch	1-5	T	402	86%	903/803-5500
5230 Estes Pkwy, Longview 75603					Fax 903/803-5501
Melanie Hamilton					
South Ward Elem Sch	1-5	T	397	95%	903/803-5200
1011 S Mobberly Ave, Longview 75602			30		Fax 903/753-2961
Joaquin Guerrero					
Ware Elem Sch	1-5	T	476	95%	903/803-5700
601 W Garfield Dr, Longview 75602			30		Fax 903/758-7872
Patricia Duck					t

• **Pine Tree Ind School Dist** PID: 01021148 903/295-5000
1701 Pine Tree Rd, Longview 75604 Fax 903/295-5004

Schools: 8 \ **Teachers:** 326 \ **Students:** 4,700 \ **Special Ed Students:** 395 \ **LEP Students:** 597 \ **Ethnic:** Asian 1%, African American 23%, Hispanic 36%, Caucasian 39% \ **Exp:** $312 (High) \ **Poverty:** 24% \ **Title I:** $1,463,754 \ **Special Education:** $755,000 \ **Open-Close:** 08/21 - 05/22 \ **DTBP:** $153 (High) \ f t

Steve Clugston	1	Nikki Benoit	2
Salena Jackson	2	Tony Hollins	3
Michelle Mitchell	4	Jack Irvin	5
Jody Berryhill	6	Dr Eric Cederstrom	8,15
Michele Walker	11,57	Dr Valerie Baxter	15
Tina Luman	16,82*	Dr Lisa Mullins	39,48
Robin White	44,47,285	Kalli VanMeter	58
Frank Richard	67	Melanie Ferguson	68
Debbie Terry	69,288,294	Mary Whitton	71
Amber Hargrove	76	Donna Pruitt	93
Stephen Taft	286,295	Todd Yohn	295

Public Schs..Principal	Grd	Prgm	Enr/#Cls	SN	
Birch Elem Sch	1-4	T	678	65%	903/295-5120
815 Birch St, Longview 75604			37		Fax 903/295-5126
Derrick Conley					
ⓐ Excel High Sch	9-12	G	55	50%	903/295-6753
850 Northwest Dr, Longview 75604					
Cleotis Wadley					
ⓐ Pace Alternative Campus	K-12		25		903/295-5130
1701 Pine Tree Rd, Longview 75604					Fax 903/295-5145
Shalonda Adams					
Parkway Elem Sch	1-4	T	696	66%	903/295-5151
601 Pt Pkwy, Longview 75608			34		Fax 903/295-5155
Melanie Keoun					

Public Schs..Principal	Grd	Prgm	Enr/#Cls	SN	
Pine Tree Junior High Sch	7-8	T	705	58%	903/295-5081
2100 NW Loop 281, Longview 75604			27		Fax 903/295-5082
Vanessa Robinson					
Pine Tree Middle Sch	5-6	T	725	64%	903/295-5160
600 Pt Parkway, Longview 75604			50		Fax 903/295-5162
Mickey White					
Pine Tree Primary Sch	PK-K	T	567	76%	903/295-5095
1808 Silver Falls Rd, Longview 75604			24		Fax 903/295-5098
Cristi Parsons					
Pine Tree Senior High Sch	9-12	GV	1,266	44%	903/295-5031
900 Northwest Dr, Longview 75604			80		Fax 903/295-5029
Cindy Gabehart					

• **Sabine Ind School Dist** PID: 01021215 903/984-8564
5424 FM 1252 W, Gladewater 75647 Fax 903/984-6108

Schools: 3 \ **Teachers:** 107 \ **Students:** 1,397 \ **Special Ed Students:** 123 \ **LEP Students:** 115 \ **College-Bound:** 95% \ **Ethnic:** Asian 1%, African American 6%, Hispanic 19%, Caucasian 73% \ **Exp:** $503 (High) \ **Poverty:** 13% \ **Title I:** $221,502 \ **Open-Close:** 08/19 - 05/21 \ **DTBP:** $553 (High)

Stacey Bryce	1	Kevin Yandell	2
Ken Wilson	3	Sunnie Caldwell	4
Paul Allen	5	Rex Sharp	6
Amanda Madden	7*	Shelley Yates	8,11,83,285,286,288,294,298
Teri Bass	9,34*	Cyndi Bryce	16,82*
Anna Hamilton	22*	Tiffany Braxton	37*
Vicki Thornton	58,77	Tony Raymond	67
Daniel Rich	73*	Randy Cox	73

Public Schs..Principal	Grd	Prgm	Enr/#Cls	SN	
Sabine Elem Sch	PK-5		709		903/984-5320
645 Access Rd, Kilgore 75662			30		Fax 903/984-4101
Teri Bass					
Sabine High Sch	9-12	ATV	423	37%	903/984-8587
5424 FM 1252 W, Gladewater 75647			35		Fax 903/986-1103
Monty Pepper					
Sabine Middle Sch	6-8	T	341	49%	903/984-4767
5424 FM 1252 W, Gladewater 75647			25		Fax 903/984-8823
Stanton Reaves					

• **Spring Hill Ind School Dist** PID: 01021253 903/759-4404
3101 Spring Hill Rd, Longview 75605 Fax 903/297-0141

Schools: 4 \ **Teachers:** 135 \ **Students:** 1,980 \ **Special Ed Students:** 148 \ **LEP Students:** 116 \ **College-Bound:** 70% \ **Ethnic:** Asian 2%, African American 13%, Hispanic 16%, Native American: 1%, Caucasian 68% \ **Exp:** $417 (High) \ **Poverty:** 15% \ **Title I:** $352,916 \ **Special Education:** $10,000 \ **Open-Close:** 08/14 - 05/21 \ **DTBP:** $332 (High)

Dr Wayne Guidry	1	Martin Cobb	2,19
Toby Pleasant	3	Janet Albright	4
Tony White	5	Johnathan Lovier	6
Penny Fleet	8,69,74,294*	Holly Whittington	27,75*
Vicki Thornton	58	Mark White	67
Connie Johnson	69	Stephanie Perez	69
Steve Hardy	73	Roger Askew	91
Amy Doron	270	Kyle Linthicum	295

Public Schs..Principal	Grd	Prgm	Enr/#Cls	SN	
Spring Hill High Sch	9-12	V	525	26%	903/446-3300
3101 Spring Hill Rd, Longview 75605			27		Fax 903/323-7766
Rusty Robinett					

1	Superintendent	8	Curric/Instruct K-12	19	Chief Financial Officer	29	Family/Consumer Science	39	Social Studies K-12	49	English/Lang Arts Elem	59	Special Education Elem	69	Academic Assessment
2	Bus/Finance/Purchasing	9	Curric/Instruct Elem	20	Art K-12	30	Adult Education	40	Social Studies Elem	50	English/Lang Arts Sec	60	Special Education Sec	70	Research/Development
3	Buildings And Grounds	10	Curric/Instruct Sec	21	Art Elem	31	Career/Sch-to-Work K-12	41	Social Studies Sec	51	Reading K-12	61	Foreign/World Lang K-12	71	Public Information
4	Food Service	11	Federal Program	22	Art Sec	32	Career/Sch-to-Work Elem	42	Science K-12	52	Reading Elem	62	Foreign/World Lang Elem	72	Summer School
5	Transportation	12	Title I	23	Music K-12	33	Career/Sch-to-Work Sec	43	Science Elem	53	Reading Sec	63	Foreign/World Lang Sec	73	Instructional Tech
6	Athletic	13	Title V	24	Music Elem	34	Early Childhood Ed	44	Science Sec	54	Remedial Reading K-12	64	Religious Education K-12	74	Inservice Training
7	Health Services	15	Asst Superintendent	25	Music Sec	35	Health/Phys Education	45	Math K-12	55	Remedial Reading Elem	65	Religious Education Elem	75	Marketing/Distributive
		16	Instructional Media Svcs	26	Business Education	36	Guidance Services K-12	46	Math Elem	56	Remedial Reading Sec	66	Religious Education Sec	76	Info Systems
		17	Chief Operations Officer	27	Career & Tech Ed	37	Guidance Services Elem	47	Math Sec	57	Bilingual/ELL	67	School Board President	77	Psychological Assess
		18	Chief Academic Officer	28	Technology Education	38	Guidance Services Sec	48	English/Lang Arts K-12	58	Special Education K-12	68	Teacher Personnel	78	Affirmative Action

Texas School Directory

Grimes County

Spring Hill Intermediate Sch	3-5	T	489	44%	903/323-7701
3101 Spring Hill Rd, Longview 75605			14		Fax 903/323-7762
Dana Robertson					
Spring Hill Junior High Sch	6-8		463	36%	903/323-7718
3101 Spring Hill Rd, Longview 75605			35		Fax 903/323-7765
David Lynch					
Spring Hill Primary Sch	PK-2	T	489	53%	903/323-7848
2700 Spring Hill Rd, Longview 75605			27		Fax 903/323-7847
Deanna Turner					

● **White Oak Ind School Dist** PID: 01021306 903/291-2200
200 S White Oak Rd, White Oak 75693 Fax 903/291-2222

Schools: 4 \ *Teachers:* 111 \ *Students:* 1,520 \ *Special Ed Students:* 130 \ *LEP Students:* 17 \ *College-Bound:* 70% \ *Ethnic:* Asian 1%, African American 3%, Hispanic 9%, Native American: 1%, Caucasian 86% \ *Exp:* $349 (High) \ *Poverty:* 20% \ *Title I:* $352,250 \ *Open-Close:* 08/15 - 05/20 \ *DTBP:* $522 (High) \ t

Michael Gilbert ....1 Tami Demers 2
Kenny Corbell ....3 Laurie Ferguson 4*
Scott Stagner ....5 Kris Iske 6
Susan Willis ....7* Mitzi Neely 8,11,57,83,88,273,294,296
Carol Stewart ....16* Vicki Thorton 34,58
Eric Swanson ....67 Scott Floyd 73,295*
Deanna Boothe 84

Public Schs..Principal	Grd	Prgm	Enr/#Cls	SN	
White Oak High Sch	9-12	V	410	30%	903/291-2004
200 S White Oak Rd, White Oak 75693			46		Fax 903/291-2034
Donna Jennings					
White Oak Intermediate Sch	3-5	T	348	41%	903/291-2101
200 S White Oak Rd, White Oak 75693			16		Fax 903/291-2196
Jennifer Rock					
White Oak Middle Sch	6-8	TV	360	41%	903/291-2055
200 S White Oak Rd, White Oak 75693			27		Fax 903/291-2035
Becky Balboa					
White Oak Primary Sch	PK-2	T	402	45%	903/291-2160
200 S White Oak Rd, White Oak 75693			17		Fax 903/291-2132
Claire Koonce					

GREGG CATHOLIC SCHOOLS

● **Diocese of Tyler Ed Office** PID: 03014660
Listing includes only schools located in this county. See District Index for location of Diocesan Offices.

Catholic Schs..Principal	Grd	Prgm	Enr/#Cls	SN	
St Mary's Catholic Sch	PK-12		200		903/753-1657
405 Hollybrook Dr, Longview 75605			19		Fax 903/758-7347
Dr Darbie Safford					

GREGG PRIVATE SCHOOLS

Private Schs..Principal	Grd	Prgm	Enr/#Cls	SN	
Christian Heritage Sch	K-12		250		903/663-4151
2715 FM 1844, Longview 75605			20		Fax 903/663-4587
Doug Carr					
Crisman Sch	Spec		40		903/758-9741
2455 N Eastman Rd, Longview 75605			7		Fax 903/758-9767
Laura Lea Blanks					

East Texas Christian Sch	PK-12		130		903/757-7891
5621 S FM 2087, Longview 75603			14		Fax 903/619-0349
Chandra Watson					
Longview Christian Academy	K-12		150		903/759-0626
2200 W Loop 281, Longview 75604			15		
Jaime Castillo					
Longview Christian Sch	K-12		250		903/297-3501
1236 Pegues Pl, Longview 75601			15		Fax 903/663-4448
Karen Williams					
Trinity School of Texas	PK-12		282		903/753-0612
215 N Teague St, Longview 75601			45		Fax 903/753-4812
Gary Whitwell					

GREGG REGIONAL CENTERS

● **Region 7 Ed Service Center** PID: 01021291 903/988-6700
1909 N Longview St, Kilgore 75662 Fax 903/988-6708

Elizabeth Abernethy ....1 Carrie Holland 2,15
Katie Chenoweth ....2,68,71 Ronnie Hemann 3,15,68
Elaine Revell ....4 Dr Sheron Darragh 8,74
Diana McBurnett ....11,58 Viki Sparks 11
Dr Beverly Beran ....58 Leesa Green 69,294
Barbara Bruhn ....73,76,286 Henryette Lovely 78

GRIMES COUNTY

GRIMES PUBLIC SCHOOLS

● **Anderson-Shiro Cons Ind SD** PID: 01021344 936/873-4500
458 FM 149 Rd W, Anderson 77830 Fax 936/873-4515

Schools: 2 \ *Teachers:* 67 \ *Students:* 850 \ *Special Ed Students:* 64 \ *LEP Students:* 22 \ *College-Bound:* 48% \ *Ethnic:* African American 8%, Hispanic 14%, Native American: 1%, Caucasian 77% \ *Exp:* $296 (Med) \ *Poverty:* 13% \ *Title I:* $82,864 \ *Special Education:* $20,000 \ *Open-Close:* 08/14 - 05/22 \ *DTBP:* $320 (High) \ f t

Scott Beene ....1 Blake Vezurk 2
Julie Yargo ....4 Brad Hodges 6*
Carolyn Fiaschetti ....11 Christy Nienstedt 38*
Lonnie Owen ....67 Brenda McDonald 73,286*
Melisa Walla 83

Public Schs..Principal	Grd	Prgm	Enr/#Cls	SN	
Anderson-Shiro Elem Sch	PK-5	T	406	46%	936/873-4525
458 FM 149 Rd W, Anderson 77830			14		Fax 936/873-4530
Marcy Pavlock					f
Anderson-Shiro Jr Sr High Sch	6-12	TV	454	36%	936/873-4550
458 FM 149 Rd W, Anderson 77830			35		Fax 936/873-4575
James Thompson					

Guadalupe County

Market Data Retrieval

- **Iola Ind School Dist** PID: 01021370   936/394-2361
  7282 Fort Worth Ave, Iola 77861   Fax 936/394-2132

Schools: 2 \ *Teachers:* 40 \ *Students:* 502 \ *Special Ed Students:* 37 \ *LEP Students:* 3 \ *College-Bound:* 63% \ *Ethnic:* African American 4%, Hispanic 15%, Caucasian 81% \ *Exp:* $393 (High) \ *Poverty:* 21% \ *Title I:* $116,974 \ *Open-Close:* 08/21 - 05/22 \ *DTBP:* $354 (High)

Scott Martindale 1	Sharon Choiniere 2
Tommy Muntean 3*	Nora Wren 4*
Sean Callahan 5	Pete Martinez 6,83,88*
Cindy Braaton 7*	Tammy Brinkman 11,271,273*
Jamie McDougald 16,85*	Mike McManners 27
Lindsay Harris 31,270*	Joan McKown 54*
Gail Swanlund 57*	Doug Richards 58,69*
Renae Rains 59*	Harvey Cannon 60
Jason Gooch 67	Monica Hurst 73,295*

Public Schs..Principal	Grd	Prgm	Enr/#Cls	SN	
Iola Elem Sch 7282 Fort Worth Ave, Iola 77861 **Kristin Sajewski**	PK-6	T	289 20	39%	936/394-2361 Fax 936/394-2051
Iola Junior Senior High Sch 7282 Fort Worth Ave, Iola 77861 **Dwayne Ross**	7-12	T	213 35	35%	936/394-2361 Fax 936/394-4700

- **Navasota Ind School Dist** PID: 01021409   936/825-4200
  705 E Washington Ave, Navasota 77868   Fax 936/825-4297

Schools: 6 \ *Teachers:* 228 \ *Students:* 3,000 \ *Special Ed Students:* 237 \ *LEP Students:* 528 \ *College-Bound:* 95% \ *Ethnic:* African American 22%, Hispanic 51%, Native American: 1%, Caucasian 27% \ *Exp:* $449 (High) \ *Poverty:* 23% \ *Title I:* $935,097 \ *Open-Close:* 08/26 - 05/28 \ *DTBP:* $168 (High) \

Dr Stu Musick 1	Valorie Moore 2
Jeff Neblett 3	Wyvetta Franklin 4
Kacey Dacous 6,35*	Kathleen Busa 7*
Amberly Kolby 8,69	Jeanie Nickle 8,16
Amy Bay-Wetherwax 12*	Ronnie Gonzalez 15
Tracy Brewer 15,68,79	Nancy Bouliane 16*
Francisco Perez 27,73	Beth Klammer 39,48
Julie Horn 42,45	Jenny Boyer 58
Jennifer Ramirez 67	Jeff Dyer 68

Public Schs..Principal	Grd	Prgm	Enr/#Cls	SN	
Brule Elem Sch 203 Brosig Ave, Navasota 77868 **Vanikin Leggett**	4-5	T	384 30	86%	936/825-4275 Fax 936/825-8523
High Point Elem Sch 11937 Highway 105 E, Navasota 77868 **John Bathke**	PK-5	T	433	70%	936/825-1130 Fax 936/894-3195
John C Webb Elem Sch 1605 Neal St, Navasota 77868 **Emily Nichols**	PK-3	T	750 26	84%	936/825-1120 Fax 936/825-2802
Navasota High Sch 9238 Highway 90 S, Navasota 77868 **Derek Bowman**	9-12	T	767 40	68%	936/825-4250 Fax 936/825-4293
Navasota Junior High Sch 9038 Highway 90 S, Navasota 77868 **Melody Hudspeth**	6-8	T	673 50	75%	936/825-4225 Fax 936/825-4260
Ⓐ W B Bizzell Academy 1604 Stacey St, Navasota 77868 **Kristie Jones**	9-12	T	34	68%	936/825-4296

- **Richards Ind School Dist** PID: 01021459   936/851-2364
  9477 Panther Dr, Richards 77873   Fax 936/851-2210

Schools: 1 \ *Teachers:* 19 \ *Students:* 170 \ *Special Ed Students:* 11 \ *LEP Students:* 3 \ *College-Bound:* 60% \ *Ethnic:* African American 9%, Hispanic 3%, Caucasian 88% \ *Exp:* $301 (High) \ *Poverty:* 19% \ *Title I:* $65,591 \ *Open-Close:* 08/26 - 05/29 \ *DTBP:* $327 (High)

William Boyce 1,11,84	Joy Boyce 2
Jeffrey Pote 6*	William Boyce 8,57,73,74,271,295*
Jason Bay 67	

Public Schs..Principal	Grd	Prgm	Enr/#Cls	SN	
Richards Independent Sch 9477 Panther Dr, Richards 77873 **John Portwood**	PK-12	TV	170 16	58%	936/851-2364

GRIMES CATHOLIC SCHOOLS

- **Archdiocese Galveston-Houston** PID: 01027855
  Listing includes only schools located in this county. See District Index for location of Diocesan Offices.

Catholic Schs..Principal	Grd	Prgm	Enr/#Cls	SN	
Sch of Environmental Education FM Rd 1774, Plantersville 77363 **Michael Richmond**	5-5		1,200		936/894-2141

GUADALUPE COUNTY

GUADALUPE PUBLIC SCHOOLS

- **Marion Ind School Dist** PID: 01021485   830/914-2803
  211 W Otto St, Marion 78124   Fax 830/420-3268

Schools: 4 \ *Teachers:* 103 \ *Students:* 1,508 \ *Special Ed Students:* 124 \ *LEP Students:* 48 \ *College-Bound:* 52% \ *Ethnic:* African American 2%, Hispanic 39%, Caucasian 58% \ *Exp:* $403 (High) \ *Poverty:* 12% \ *Title I:* $173,253 \ *Special Education:* $267,000 \ *Open-Close:* 08/19 - 05/22 \ *DTBP:* $350 (High)

Kelly Lindholm 1,83	Bill Orr 2,8
Joe Allen 3	Marie Brooks 4
Ryne Miller 6	Cesily Peeples 8
Daniel Terrazas 11,58*	Courtney Junkin 16,297
Dr Kevin Kunde 67	Jon Lindholm 68

Public Schs..Principal	Grd	Prgm	Enr/#Cls	SN	
Marion High Sch 506 Bulldog Ln, Marion 78124 **Stacia Snyder**	9-12	AV	433 52	39%	830/914-1075 Fax 830/420-3639
Marion Middle Sch 506 S Center St, Marion 78124 **Susan Thetford**	6-8	TV	356 30	45%	830/914-1070 Fax 830/420-3206
Norma Krueger Elem Sch-Karrer 213 W Huebinger St, Marion 78124 **Paul Goetzke**	3-5	T	320	44%	830/914-1065 Fax 830/420-3258

1	Superintendent	8	Curric/Instruct K-12	19	Chief Financial Officer	29	Family/Consumer Science	39	Social Studies K-12	49	English/Lang Arts Elem	59	Special Education Elem	69	Academic Assessment
2	Bus/Finance/Purchasing	9	Curric/Instruct Elem	20	Art K-12	30	Adult Education	40	Social Studies Elem	50	English/Lang Arts Sec	60	Special Education Sec	70	Research/Development
3	Buildings And Grounds	10	Curric/Instruct Sec	21	Art Elem	31	Career/Sch-to-Work K-12	41	Social Studies Sec	51	Reading K-12	61	Foreign/World Lang K-12	71	Public Information
4	Food Service	11	Federal Program	22	Art Sec	32	Career/Sch-to-Work Elem	42	Science K-12	52	Reading Elem	62	Foreign/World Lang Elem	72	Summer School
5	Transportation	12	Title I	23	Music K-12	33	Career/Sch-to-Work Sec	43	Science Elem	53	Reading Sec	63	Foreign/World Lang Sec	73	Instructional Tech
6	Athletic	13	Title V	24	Music Elem	34	Early Childhood Ed	44	Science Sec	54	Remedial Reading K-12	64	Religious Education K-12	74	Inservice Training
7	Health Services	14	Asst Superintendent	25	Music Sec	35	Health/Phys Education	45	Math K-12	55	Remedial Reading Elem	65	Religious Education Elem	75	Marketing/Distributive
		15	Instructional Media Svcs	26	Business Education	36	Guidance Services K-12	46	Math Elem	56	Remedial Reading Sec	66	Religious Education Sec	76	Info Systems
		16	Chief Operations Officer	27	Career & Tech Ed	37	Guidance Services Elem	47	Math Sec	57	Bilingual/ELL	67	School Board President	77	Psychological Assess
		17	Chief Academic Officer	28	Technology Education	38	Guidance Services Sec	48	English/Lang Arts K-12	58	Special Education K-12	68	Teacher Personnel	78	Affirmative Action

Texas School Directory — Guadalupe County

Norma Krueger Elem Sch	PK-2	T	361	51%	830/914-1060
306 S Cunningham St, Marion 78124			43		Fax 830/420-3776
Rachel Robertson					

- **Navarro Ind School Dist** PID: 01021526 — 830/372-1930
  6450 N State Highway 123, Seguin 78155 — Fax 830/372-1853

Schools: 4 \ *Teachers:* 113 \ *Students:* 1,911 \ *Special Ed Students:* 132 \ *LEP Students:* 64 \ *Ethnic:* Asian 1%, African American 2%, Hispanic 45%, Caucasian 53% \ *Exp:* $756 (High) \ *Poverty:* 8% \ *Title I:* $146,094 \ *Special Education:* $339,000 \ *Open-Close:* 08/21 - 05/28 \ *DTBP:* $351 (High) \ f

Dee Carter 1	Jo Ann Speed 2
Martin Mueck 3	Carlett Drabek 4
Kelly Hyde 5	Less Goad 6*
Lacey Gosch 8,11,57,271,273,288,294	Becky Newton 58
Greg Gilcrease 67	Alissa Elley 73,84,286,295,298
Luke Morales 91*	David Hyde 295

Public Schs..Principal	Grd	Prgm	Enr/#Cls SN		
Navarro Elem Sch	PK-3	T	535	45%	830/372-1933
380 Link Rd, Seguin 78155			29		Fax 830/379-3145
Laurel Wilson					
Navarro High Sch	9-12		608	28%	830/372-1931
6350 N State Highway 123, Seguin 78155			33		Fax 830/401-5570
Gary Haass					
Navarro Intermediate Sch	4-6	T	426	39%	830/372-1943
300 Link Rd, Seguin 78155			23		Fax 830/379-3170
Bobbi Supak					
Navarro Junior High Sch	7-8		342	27%	830/401-5550
6450 N State Highway 123, Seguin 78155					Fax 830/379-3135
Luke Morales					f

- **Schertz-Cibolo-Univ City ISD** PID: 01021552 — 210/945-6200
  1060 Elbel Rd, Schertz 78154 — Fax 210/945-6292

Schools: 17 \ *Teachers:* 921 \ *Students:* 15,931 \ *Special Ed Students:* 1,316 \ *LEP Students:* 549 \ *College-Bound:* 46% \ *Ethnic:* Asian 2%, African American 12%, Hispanic 43%, Caucasian 42% \ *Exp:* $199 (Low) \ *Poverty:* 7% \ *Title I:* $1,121,147 \ *Special Education:* $1,791,000 \ *Open-Close:* 08/20 - 05/28 \ *DTBP:* $185 (High) \ f t

Dr Greg Gibson 1	Matt Rivera 2
J D Mosley 3	Maggie Cornejo 4
Francisco Perez 5	Scott Lehnhoff 6,35
Kelly Kovacs 8,69,74	Veronica Goldhorn 9
Dr J Brett Lemley 10	Dr Damon Edwards 15
Wayne Pruski 19	Mike Lipe 20,23
Cassandra Garcia 31,36	Kim Williams 58*
Kimberly Ferguson 58	Robert Westbrook 67
Linda Cannon 68	Windi Hughes 69
Dr Karla Burkholder 73	Karen Blevins 81
Araceli Trejo 294*	

Public Schs..Principal	Grd	Prgm	Enr/#Cls SN		
ⓐ A L Steele Enhanced Lrng Ctr	9-12		82		210/945-6401
204 Wright Ave, Schertz 78154			7		Fax 210/945-6410
Lisa Newman					f t
Barbara C Jordan Interm Sch	5-6		689	22%	210/619-4250
515 Thistle Creek Dr, Cibolo 78108			32		Fax 210/619-4277
Tina Curtis					
Byron P Steele II High Sch	9-12	V	2,391	19%	210/619-4000
1300 FM 1103, Cibolo 78108					Fax 210/619-4057
Jana Cervantes					f t
Cibolo Valley Elem Sch	PK-4		929	27%	210/619-4700
4093 Green Valley Rd, Cibolo 78108					Fax 210/619-4740
Rhonda Jungmichel					
ⓐ Daep	K-12		53		210/945-6413
301 Main St, Schertz 78154					Fax 210/945-6415
Stacy Serna					
Elaine S Schlather Interm Sch	5-6		738	24%	210/619-4300
230 Elaines Schlather Pkwy, Cibolo 78108					Fax 210/619-4340
Yvette Ross					
Green Valley Elem Sch	PK-4		742	29%	210/619-4450
1694 Green Valley Rd, Schertz 78154			33		Fax 210/619-4478
Amy Denman					
J Frank Dobie Jr High Sch	7-8	AV	1,253	22%	210/619-4100
395 W Borgfeld Rd, Cibolo 78108			63		Fax 210/619-4142
Vernon Simmons					f t
John A Sippel Elem Sch	PK-4		746	29%	210/619-4600
420 Fairlawn Ave, Schertz 78154					Fax 210/619-4630
Clarie Bristow					
Laura Ingalls Wilder Inter Sch	5-6	T	826	42%	210/619-4200
806 Savannah Dr, Schertz 78154			38		Fax 210/619-4220
Sarah Dauphinais					
Maxine & Lutrell Watts ES	PK-4		612	33%	210/619-4400
100 Deer Meadow Blvd, Cibolo 78108					Fax 210/619-4419
Deanna Jackson					
Norma J Paschal Elem Sch	PK-4		670	19%	210/619-4500
590 Savannah Dr, Schertz 78154			36		Fax 210/619-4518
Allison Miller					
O G Wiederstein Elem Sch	PK-4		801	35%	210/619-4550
171 W Borgfeld Rd, Cibolo 78108			20		Fax 210/619-4590
Luis Chavez					f t
Ray D Corbett Junior High Sch	7-8	V	1,200	32%	210/619-4150
12000 Ray Corbett Dr, Schertz 78154			45		Fax 210/619-4190
Rashad Ray					
Rose Garden Elem Sch	PK-4	T	536	52%	210/619-4350
10414 E FM 1518 N, Schertz 78154			28		Fax 210/619-4369
Cindy Ward					
Samuel Clemens High Sch	9-12	V	2,657	26%	210/945-6501
1001 Elbel Rd, Schertz 78154			120		Fax 210/945-6590
Melissa Sosa					f t
Schertz Elem Sch	PK-4	T	781	62%	210/619-4650
701 Curtiss St, Schertz 78154			23		Fax 210/619-4690
Geri Pope					

- **Seguin Ind School Dist** PID: 01021631 — 830/401-8600
  1221 E Kingsbury St, Seguin 78155 — Fax 830/379-0392

Schools: 13 \ *Teachers:* 478 \ *Students:* 7,127 \ *Special Ed Students:* 714 \ *LEP Students:* 656 \ *College-Bound:* 37% \ *Ethnic:* African American 5%, Hispanic 71%, Caucasian 24% \ *Exp:* $702 (High) \ *Poverty:* 19% \ *Title I:* $2,032,123 \ *Special Education:* $1,397,000 \ *Open-Close:* 08/22 - 05/28 \ *DTBP:* $184 (High) \ f t

Dr Matthew Gutierrez 1	Anthony Hillberg 2,88,298
James Pizana 3,5,79,91	Robert Gonzales 3
Jacob Galvin 4	Phia Rigney 5
Travis Bush 6*	Jason Schmidt 9,15
Cynthia Borden 11,57,69,77,83,294	Dot Whitmann 15,68
Bill Lewis 16,73,76	Pete Silvius 35
Nilda Vella 42	David Hall 45
Andrea Jaramillo 48	Halcy Dean 58
Haley Martinez 58*	Cinde Thomas-Jimenez 67
Sean Hoffmann 71	Danica Murillo 74
John Hastings 76	Kristen Legore 79,90
Sara Martinez 88	Yvonne Hill 91
Randy Rodgers 286	Jeffrey Lee 295
Leonard Carter 295	

---

79 Student Personnel	91 Safety/Security	275 Response To Intervention	298 Grant Writer/Ptnrships	**School Programs**	**Social Media**		
80 Driver Ed/Safety	92 Magnet School	277 Remedial Math K-12	750 Chief Innovation Officer	A = Alternative Program			
81 Gifted/Talented	93 Parental Involvement	280 Literacy Coach	751 Chief of Staff	G = Adult Classes	f = Facebook		
82 Video Services	95 Tech Prep Program	285 STEM	752 Social Emotional Learning	M = Magnet Program			
83 Substance Abuse Prev	97 Chief Information Officer	286 Digital Learning		T = Title I Schoolwide	t = Twitter		
84 Erate	98 Chief Technology Officer	288 Common Core Standards	**Other School Types**	V = Career & Tech Ed Programs			
85 AIDS Education	270 Accountability	294 Accountability	ⓐ = Alternative School				
86 Alternative/At Risk	271 Migrant Education	295 Network System	ⓒ = Charter School	New Schools are shaded			
89 Multi-Cultural Curriculum	273 Teacher Mentor	296 Title II Programs	ⓜ = Magnet School	New Superintendents and Principals are bold			
90 Social Work	274 Before/After Sch	297 Webmaster	ⓨ = Year-Round School	Personnel with email addresses are underscored			

Hale County

Market Data Retrieval

Public Schs..Principal	Grd	Prgm	Enr/#Cls	SN	
A J Briesemeister Mid Sch 1616 W Court St, Seguin 78155 Amber Gonzales	6-8	T	807 40	69%	830/401-8711 Fax 830/379-0615
Ball Early Childhood Center 812 Shannon Ave, Seguin 78155 Laura Flack	PK-K	T	490 18	94%	830/401-1281 Fax 830/379-5590
F C Weinert Elem Sch 1111 Bruns St, Seguin 78155 Mary Hernandez	K-5	T	513 37	56%	830/401-1241 Fax 830/372-2720
George Vogel Elem Sch 16121 FM 725, Seguin 78155 Laura Flack	K-5	T	409 24	71%	830/401-8745 Fax 830/372-2174
Jefferson Avenue Elem Sch 215 Short Ave, Seguin 78155 Merry White	K-5	T	403 28	86%	830/401-8727 Fax 830/379-0950
Jim Barnes Middle Sch 1539 Joe Carrillo St, Seguin 78155 Nikki Bittings	6-8	T	863	66%	830/401-8756 Fax 830/379-4239
ⓐ Lizzie Burgess Alt Sch 225 N Saunders St, Seguin 78155 Erma Freeman	2-12	T	40 14	71%	830/379-1108 Fax 830/379-0088
McQueeney Elem Sch 8860 FM 725, Mc Queeney 78123 Meredith Stadler	K-5	T	339 28	78%	830/401-8738 Fax 830/557-6981
ⓐ Mercer-Blumberg Learning Ctr 1205 E Kingsbury St, Seguin 78155 Jay Law	9-12	T	150 10	57%	830/401-8690 Fax 830/379-1362
Oralia R Rodriguez Elem Sch 1567 W Kingsbury St, Seguin 78155 Roberto Arriola	K-5	T	544	78%	830/401-8774 Fax 830/386-0001
Robert F Koennecke Elem Sch 1441 Joe Carrillo St, Seguin 78155 Cynthia Moreno	K-5	T	515 40	59%	830/401-8741 Fax 830/372-3317
Seguin High Sch 1315 E Cedar St, Seguin 78155 Hector Esquivel	9-12	TV	1,962	50%	830/401-8000 Fax 830/372-9851
Vincent Patlan Elem Sch 2501 Breustedt St, Seguin 78155 Linda Guzman	K-5	T	445 44	80%	830/401-1221 Fax 830/372-4565

GUADALUPE CATHOLIC SCHOOLS

• **Archdiocese San Antonio Ed Off** PID: 00999724
Listing includes only schools located in this county. See District Index for location of Diocesan Offices.

Catholic Schs..Principal	Grd	Prgm	Enr/#Cls	SN	
Our Lady-Perpetual Help Sch 16075 N Evans Rd, Selma 78154 Francis Burns	PK-8		511 18		210/651-6811 Fax 210/651-5516
St James Catholic Sch 507 S Camp St, Seguin 78155 David Stone	PK-8		180 13		830/379-2878 Fax 830/379-0047

GUADALUPE PRIVATE SCHOOLS

Private Schs..Principal	Grd	Prgm	Enr/#Cls	SN	
Lifegate Christian Sch 395 Lifegate Ln, Seguin 78155 Mark Peters	K-12		174 12		830/372-0850 Fax 830/372-0895

River City Believers Academy 16765 Lookout Rd, Selma 78154 Dr Victor Fordyce	PK-12		147		210/656-2999
Seguin Christian Academy 1456 E Kingsbury St, Seguin 78155 Sarah Olivas	K-10		40 7		830/433-4131

HALE COUNTY

HALE PUBLIC SCHOOLS

• **Abernathy Ind School Dist** PID: 01021746   806/298-2563
505 7th St, Abernathy 79311   Fax 806/298-2400

Schools: 3 \ **Teachers:** 67 \ **Students:** 780 \ **Special Ed Students:** 74 \ **LEP Students:** 13 \ **Ethnic:** African American 1%, Hispanic 57%, Caucasian 42% \ **Exp:** $453 (High) \ **Poverty:** 19% \ **Title I:** $180,441 \ **Open-Close:** 08/21 - 05/21 \ **DTBP:** $359 (High) \

Aaron Waldrip 1
Bobby Grimsley 3,91
Darrell Daily 6
Kara Nick 36
Terry Driscoll 73
Linda Gonzales 271*
Linda Bufe 2
Johnny Pace 5
Shawn Bearden 8
Bil Bubose 67
Ezra Chambers 88,270*

Public Schs..Principal	Grd	Prgm	Enr/#Cls	SN	
Abernathy Elem Sch 505 7th St, Abernathy 79311 Jenci Chambers	PK-5	T	354 34	63%	806/298-4930 Fax 806/298-4995
Abernathy High Sch 505 7th St, Abernathy 79311 Ezra Chambers	9-12	TV	228 25	39%	806/298-2563 Fax 806/298-4653
Abernathy Middle Sch 505 7th St, Abernathy 79311 Kelly Carlisle	6-8	T	183 18	50%	806/298-4921 Fax 806/298-4775

• **Cotton Center Ind School Dist** PID: 01021784   806/879-2160
2345 Farm Rd 179, Cotton Center 79021   Fax 806/879-2175

Schools: 1 \ **Teachers:** 14 \ **Students:** 130 \ **Special Ed Students:** 8 \ **College-Bound:** 75% \ **Ethnic:** Asian 1%, Hispanic 56%, Caucasian 43% \ **Exp:** $975 (High) \ **Poverty:** 30% \ **Title I:** $33,316 \ **Open-Close:** 08/26 - 05/21 \ **DTBP:** $350 (High) \

Ryan Bobo 1
Bruce Welch 3
Sharla Straw 57*
Clint Carthel 67
Alysha Murphy 2
Jamye Moore 27*
Troy Moses 58*
Dan Butler 73,83,88,270*

Public Schs..Principal	Grd	Prgm	Enr/#Cls	SN	
Cotton Center Sch 2345 Farm Rd 179, Cotton Center 79021 Jeff Kirby	PK-12	TV	130 30	87%	806/879-2176

1	Superintendent	8	Curric/Instruct K-12	19	Chief Financial Officer	29	Family/Consumer Science	39	Social Studies K-12	49	English/Lang Arts Elem	59	Special Education Elem	69	Academic Assessment
2	Bus/Finance/Purchasing	9	Curric/Instruct Elem	20	Art K-12	30	Adult Education	40	Social Studies Elem	50	English/Lang Arts Sec	60	Special Education Sec	70	Research/Development
3	Buildings And Grounds	10	Curric/Instruct Sec	21	Art Elem	31	Career/Sch-to-Work K-12	41	Social Studies Sec	51	Reading K-12	61	Foreign/World Lang K-12	71	Public Information
4	Food Service	11	Federal Program	22	Art Sec	32	Career/Sch-to-Work Elem	42	Science K-12	52	Reading Elem	62	Foreign/World Lang Elem	72	Summer School
5	Transportation	12	Title I	23	Music K-12	33	Career/Sch-to-Work Sec	43	Science Elem	53	Reading Sec	63	Foreign/World Lang Sec	73	Instructional Tech
6	Athletic	13	Title V	24	Music Elem	34	Early Childhood Ed	44	Science Sec	54	Remedial Reading K-12	64	Religious Education K-12	74	Inservice Training
7	Health Services	14	Asst Superintendent	25	Music Sec	35	Health/Phys Education	45	Math K-12	55	Remedial Reading Elem	65	Religious Education Elem	75	Marketing/Distributive
		15	Instructional Media Svcs	26	Business Education	36	Guidance Services K-12	46	Math Elem	56	Remedial Reading Sec	66	Religious Education Sec	76	Info Systems
		16	Chief Operations Officer	27	Career & Tech Ed	37	Guidance Services Elem	47	Math Sec	57	Bilingual/ELL	67	School Board President	77	Psychological Assess
		17	Chief Academic Officer	28	Technology Education	38	Guidance Services Sec	48	English/Lang Arts K-12	58	Special Education K-12	68	Teacher Personnel	78	Affirmative Action

TX—174

Texas School Directory — Hall County

Hale Center Ind School Dist PID: 01021813
103 W Cleveland St, Hale Center 79041
806/839-2451
Fax 806/839-2195

Schools: 3 \ **Teachers:** 53 \ **Students:** 647 \ **Special Ed Students:** 44 \ **LEP Students:** 39 \ **College-Bound:** 59% \ **Ethnic:** African American 2%, Hispanic 72%, Native American: 1%, Caucasian 25% \ **Exp:** $394 (High) \ **Poverty:** 22% \ **Title I:** $160,736 \ **Open-Close:** 08/26 - 05/22 \ **DTBP:** $350 (High) \ f t

Steven Pyburn 1
Joe Betancur 5
Monika Berry 11,57,271
Jack Neddham 67
Erica Garcia 4*
Jeff Smith 6
Laurie Johnson 38,83*
Bryan McGan 73

Public Schs..Principal	Grd	Prgm	Enr/#Cls	SN		
Akin Elem Sch 1105 Ave K, Hale Center 79041 **Jeff Hutton**	PK-4	T	281 16	73%	806/839-2121 Fax 806/839-4404	
Carr Middle Sch 410 W 12th St, Hale Center 79041 Alan Berry	5-8	T	156 13	71%	806/839-2141 Fax 806/839-4417	
Hale Center High Sch 411 Owl Dr, Hale Center 79041 Carlon Branson	9-12	ATV	172 24	63%	806/839-2452 Fax 806/839-2059	

Petersburg Ind School Dist PID: 01021863
1411 W 4th St, Petersburg 79250
806/667-3585
Fax 806/667-3463

Schools: 1 \ **Teachers:** 24 \ **Students:** 300 \ **Special Ed Students:** 30 \ **LEP Students:** 36 \ **College-Bound:** 95% \ **Ethnic:** African American 1%, Hispanic 78%, Caucasian 21% \ **Exp:** $843 (High) \ **Poverty:** 24% \ **Title I:** $91,086 \ **Open-Close:** 08/19 - 05/22 \ **DTBP:** $408 (High)

Dr Brian Bibb 1,11,73
Donna Carnigney 8,57,271,274*
Corina Reyes 36*
Chad Byrd 67
Darlenea Robertson 2
Melissa Galoway 10,69,83*
Donna Camigney 58*

Public Schs..Principal	Grd	Prgm	Enr/#Cls	SN	
Petersburg Sch 1411 W 4th St, Petersburg 79250 Donna Carnigney \ Melissa Galoway	PK-12	T	300 14	80%	806/667-3585

Plainview Ind School Dist PID: 01021904
2417 Yonkers St, Plainview 79072
806/296-6392
Fax 806/293-6000

Schools: 10 \ **Teachers:** 366 \ **Students:** 5,450 \ **Special Ed Students:** 516 \ **LEP Students:** 305 \ **College-Bound:** 44% \ **Ethnic:** African American 4%, Hispanic 79%, Caucasian 16% \ **Exp:** $275 (Med) \ **Poverty:** 25% \ **Title I:** $1,782,762 \ **Special Education:** $1,031,000 \ **Open-Close:** 08/15 - 05/26 \ **DTBP:** $155 (High) \ f

Dr H T Sanchez 1
Doris Chapa 2
Victor Hernandez 2
David Lopez 3
Lorrie Coats 5
Robin Straley 8
Edna Garcia 11,57,93,271
Susan Flippin 16
Brandy Merrick 68
Alissa Carter 73
Jeff De La Garza 79
Wayne Jennings 295
Becca Dunlap 2
Luis Trujillo 2
Charles Mooney 3
Manuel Marin 3
Ryan Rhoades 6*
Garrett Katrina 9
Greg Brown 15
Sylvia Delagarza 67
Robin Forbes-Salazar 69,72,294*
Dr Brent Richburg 73,76
Anita Flores 271

Public Schs..Principal	Grd	Prgm	Enr/#Cls	SN	
ⓐ Ash High Sch 908 Ash St, Plainview 79072 Rodney Wallace	9-12	T	83 15	79%	806/293-6010 Fax 806/296-4183
College Hill Elem Sch 707 Canyon St, Plainview 79072 Lori Glenn	PK-5	T	442 18	72%	806/293-6035 Fax 806/296-4102
Coronado Middle Sch 2501 Joliet St, Plainview 79072 Rachel Long	6-8	T	613 36	74%	806/293-6020 Fax 806/296-4177
Edgemere Elem Sch 2600 W 20th St, Plainview 79072 Leslie Richburg	PK-5	T	471 24	78%	806/293-6040 Fax 806/296-4103
Estacado Middle Sch 2200 W 20th St, Plainview 79072 Ritchie Thorton	6-8	T	592 33	78%	806/293-6015 Fax 806/296-4169 f
Highland Elem Sch 1707 W 11th St, Plainview 79072 Becky Buxton	PK-5	T	440 20	82%	806/293-6045 Fax 806/296-4169 f
Hillcrest Elem Sch 315 SW Alpine Dr, Plainview 79072 Yesenia Pardo	PK-5	T	438 21	85%	806/293-6050 Fax 806/296-4106
La Mesa Elem Sch 600 S Ennis St, Plainview 79072 Vickie Young	PK-5	T	548 27	68%	806/293-6055 Fax 806/296-9425
Plainview High Sch 1501 Quincy St, Plainview 79072 Brandt Reagan	9-12	TV	1,388 40	61%	806/293-6005 Fax 806/296-4069
Thunderbird Elem Sch 1200 W 32nd St, Plainview 79072 Karla Dunn	PK-5	T	484 25	91%	806/293-6060 Fax 806/296-4125

HALE PRIVATE SCHOOLS

Private Schs..Principal	Grd	Prgm	Enr/#Cls	SN	
Plainview Christian Academy 310 S Ennis St, Plainview 79072 Jennifer Harrell	PK-12		213 14		806/296-6034 Fax 806/686-0988

HALL COUNTY

HALL PUBLIC SCHOOLS

Memphis Ind School Dist PID: 01022087
1501 High St, Memphis 79245
806/259-5900
Fax 806/259-2515

Schools: 4 \ **Teachers:** 46 \ **Students:** 500 \ **Special Ed Students:** 67 \ **LEP Students:** 52 \ **Ethnic:** African American 8%, Hispanic 58%, Caucasian 33% \ **Exp:** $572 (High) \ **Poverty:** 36% \ **Title I:** $253,144 \ **Special Education:** $42,000 \ **Open-Close:** 08/21 - 05/28 \ **DTBP:** $336 (High) \ f

William Alexander 1
Donnie Bridges 3
Tony Zuniga 5
Kelli Maddox 7*
Brad Woods 37*
Jennifer Lindsey 295*
Brenda Alexander 2
Sherree Foster 4
David Jurado 6*
Trina Hardin 36,57,58,83,88,296*
Timmy Fowler 67

---

79 Student Personnel
80 Driver Ed/Safety
81 Gifted/Talented
82 Video Services
83 Substance Abuse Prev
84 Erate
85 AIDS Education
88 Alternative/At Risk
89 Multi-Cultural Curriculum
90 Social Work

91 Safety/Security
92 Magnet School
93 Parental Involvement
95 Tech Prep Program
97 Chief Information Officer
98 Chief Technology Officer
270 Character Education
271 Migrant Education
273 Teacher Mentor
274 Before/After Sch

275 Response To Intervention
277 Remedial Math K-12
280 Literacy Coach
285 STEM
286 Digital Learning
288 Common Core Standards
294 Accountability
295 Network System
296 Title II Programs
297 Webmaster

298 Grant Writer/Ptnrships
750 Chief Innovation Officer
751 Chief of Staff
752 Social Emotional Learning

Other School Types
ⓐ = Alternative School
ⓒ = Charter School
ⓜ = Magnet School
ⓨ = Year-Round School

School Programs
A = Alternative Program
G = Adult Classes
M = Magnet Program
T = Title I Schoolwide
V = Career & Tech Ed Programs

New Schools are shaded
New Superintendents and Principals are bold
Personnel with email addresses are underscored

Social Media
f = Facebook
t = Twitter

Hamilton County

Market Data Retrieval

Public Schs..Principal	Grd	Prgm	Enr/#Cls	SN		
Austin Elem Sch 519 N 9th St, Memphis 79245 Leighann Hawthorne	3-5	T	112 7	75%	806/259-5930 Fax 806/259-2786
Memphis High Sch 1501 High St, Memphis 79245 Dick Hutcherson	9-12	TV	137 18	67%	806/259-5910 Fax 806/259-3026
Memphis Middle Sch 1120 N 16th St, Memphis 79245 Kennith Hardin	6-8	T	102 10	63%	806/259-5920 Fax 806/259-2051
Travis Elem Sch 710 N 12th St, Memphis 79245 Vicki Davis	PK-2	T	152 15	84%	806/259-5940 Fax 806/259-3119

- **Turkey-Quitaque Cons Ind SD** PID: 01022130 806/455-1411
  11826 Highway 86, Turkey 79261 Fax 806/455-1718

Schools: 1 \ *Teachers:* 23 \ *Students:* 207 \ *Special Ed Students:* 18 \ *LEP Students:* 10 \ *College-Bound:* 95% \ *Ethnic:* African American 4%, Hispanic 31%, Caucasian 64% \ *Exp:* $459 (High) \ *Poverty:* 37% \ *Title I:* $91,461 \ *Open-Close:* 08/22 - 05/25 \ *DTBP:* $276 (High)

Jackie Jenkins ....1,11 Donna Pigg 2
Matt Edwards ....5* Tye Keith 6*
Tina Carson ....16,73* Trica Carson 58*
Lisa Campbell 67

Public Schs..Principal	Grd	Prgm	Enr/#Cls	SN		
Valley Sch 11826 Highway 86, Turkey 79261 Brandon Smith	PK-12	TV	207 26	50%	806/455-1411

HAMILTON COUNTY

HAMILTON PUBLIC SCHOOLS

- **Hamilton Ind School Dist** PID: 01022166 254/386-3149
  400 S College St, Hamilton 76531 Fax 254/386-8885

Schools: 3 \ *Teachers:* 72 \ *Students:* 850 \ *Special Ed Students:* 84 \ *LEP Students:* 32 \ *College-Bound:* 51% \ *Ethnic:* Hispanic 18%, Caucasian 81% \ *Exp:* $573 (High) \ *Poverty:* 21% \ *Title I:* $206,866 \ *Open-Close:* 08/15 - 05/21 \ *DTBP:* $337 (High)

Clay Tarpley ....1 Ken Alexander 2,11,73
Michael Reed ....6* Wendy Cude 7,35,85*
James Sloane ....12* Misti Polster 57*
T Medlock ....67 Lisa Parrish 69*

Public Schs..Principal	Grd	Prgm	Enr/#Cls	SN		
Ann Whitney Elem Sch 400 S College St, Hamilton 76531 James Slone	PK-5	T	436 29	56%	254/386-8166 Fax 254/386-3316
Hamilton High Sch 611 S College St, Hamilton 76531 Gina Poe	9-12	ATV	241 35	41%	254/386-8167 Fax 254/386-4677
Hamilton Junior High Sch 400 S College St, Hamilton 76531 Mona Gloff	6-8	T	173 10	48%	254/386-8168 Fax 254/386-4677

- **Hico Ind School Dist** PID: 01022192 254/796-2182
  901 Cedar St, Hico 76457 Fax 254/796-2446

Schools: 2 \ *Teachers:* 52 \ *Students:* 600 \ *Special Ed Students:* 52 \ *LEP Students:* 38 \ *College-Bound:* 42% \ *Ethnic:* African American 1%, Hispanic 24%, Caucasian 75% \ *Exp:* $426 (High) \ *Poverty:* 25% \ *Title I:* $176,582 \ *Open-Close:* 08/20 - 06/01 \ *DTBP:* $409 (High) \

Jon Hartgraves ....1,11,84 Keith Elrod 2,298
Peggy Waggoner ....4* David Wilkins 5
Rodney Thornton ....6* Lavern Tooley 7,85*
Shelly Stegall ....10,88* Eric Kale 27*
Deborah McGavock ....31,36,69* Dana Broumley 37*
Melissa Jackson ....57* Keith Broumley 67
Sherry Gerber ....73* David Oneill 286*

Public Schs..Principal	Grd	Prgm	Enr/#Cls	SN		
Hico Elem Sch 805 Tiger Rd, Hico 76457 Ben Eubanks	PK-5	T	305 19	59%	254/796-2183 Fax 254/796-4214
Hico Secondary Sch 901 Cedar St, Hico 76457 Shelly Stegall	6-12	TV	287 16	54%	254/796-2184

HANSFORD COUNTY

HANSFORD PUBLIC SCHOOLS

- **Gruver Ind School Dist** PID: 01022257 806/733-2001
  601 Garrett St, Gruver 79040 Fax 806/733-5416

Schools: 3 \ *Teachers:* 42 \ *Students:* 400 \ *Special Ed Students:* 26 \ *LEP Students:* 73 \ *College-Bound:* 80% \ *Ethnic:* Hispanic 50%, Caucasian 50% \ *Exp:* $339 (High) \ *Poverty:* 10% \ *Title I:* $37,612 \ *Open-Close:* 08/21 - 05/22 \ *DTBP:* $178 (High)

Wade Callaway ....1 Karen Fischer 2,11
Terry Felderhoff ....6* Sahala Gaillard 7*
Amber Holland ....9* Kelly Hart 16*
Jill Butler ....57 Melodie Bryant 58
Carolyn Adams ....60* Mike Yanke 67
Raquel Whitehead ....69,88,270* Holly McLean 73

Public Schs..Principal	Grd	Prgm	Enr/#Cls	SN		
Gruver Elem Sch 401 Garrett St, Gruver 79040 Amber Holland	PK-4	T	155 14	50%	806/733-2031 Fax 806/733-5412
Gruver High Sch 601 Garrett St, Gruver 79040 James Bryant	9-12	GTV	131 20	46%	806/733-2477 Fax 806/733-2596
Gruver Junior High Sch 600 Garrett St, Gruver 79040 Lexy Glass	5-8	T	143 13	54%	806/733-2081 Fax 806/733-5523

1	Superintendent	8	Curric/Instruct K-12	19	Chief Financial Officer	29	Family/Consumer Science	39	Social Studies K-12	49	English/Lang Arts Elem	59	Special Education Elem	69	Academic Assessment
2	Bus/Finance/Purchasing	9	Curric/Instruct Elem	20	Art K-12	30	Adult Education	40	Social Studies Elem	50	English/Lang Arts Sec	60	Special Education Sec	70	Research/Development
3	Buildings And Grounds	10	Curric/Instruct Sec	21	Art Elem	31	Career/Sch-to-Work K-12	41	Social Studies Sec	51	Reading K-12	61	Foreign/World Lang K-12	71	Public Information
4	Food Service	11	Federal Program	22	Art Sec	32	Career/Sch-to-Work Elem	42	Science K-12	52	Reading Elem	62	Foreign/World Lang Elem	72	Summer School
5	Transportation	12	Title I	23	Music K-12	33	Career/Sch-to-Work Sec	43	Science Elem	53	Reading Sec	63	Foreign/World Lang Sec	73	Instructional Tech
6	Athletic	13	Title V	24	Music Elem	34	Early Childhood Ed	44	Science Sec	54	Remedial Reading K-12	64	Religious Education K-12	74	Inservice Training
7	Health Services	15	Asst Superintendent	25	Music Sec	35	Health/Phys Education	45	Math K-12	55	Remedial Reading Elem	65	Religious Education Elem	75	Marketing/Distributive
		16	Instructional Media Svcs	26	Business Education	36	Guidance Services K-12	46	Math Elem	56	Remedial Reading Sec	66	Religious Education Sec	76	Info Systems
		17	Chief Operations Officer	27	Career & Tech Ed	37	Guidance Services Elem	47	Math Sec	57	Bilingual/ELL	67	School Board President	77	Psychological Assess
		18	Chief Academic Officer	28	Technology Education	38	Guidance Services Sec	48	English/Lang Arts K-12	58	Special Education K-12	68	Teacher Personnel	78	Affirmative Action

Texas School Directory

Hardin County

- **Pringle-Morse Cons ISD** PID: 01022295 806/733-2507
  100 S 5th St, Morse 79062 Fax 806/733-2351

Schools: 1 \ **Teachers:** 15 \ **Students:** 115 \ **Special Ed Students:** 13 \ **LEP Students:** 18 \ **Ethnic:** Hispanic 45%, Caucasian 55% \ **Exp:** $435 (High) \ **Poverty:** 9% \ **Title I:** $1,195 \ **Open-Close:** 08/14 - 05/19 \ **DTBP:** $398 (High)

Scott Burrow 1,11,73
Jerahiah Martinez 3
Jeff Forrest 6*
Shannon Lane 57*
Shannon Lane 88
Sadie Delacruz 295*
Paige Speck 2,12,84,298
Janice McCloy 4
Monica Schmidt 16*
James Lieb 67
Viann Clark 271

Public Schs..Principal	Grd	Prgm	Enr/#Cls	SN	
Pringle-Morse Sch 100 S 5th St, Morse 79062 Scott Burrow	PK-8	T	115 13	58%	806/733-2507

- **Spearman Ind School Dist** PID: 01022312 806/659-3233
  403 E 11th Ave, Spearman 79081 Fax 806/659-2079

Schools: 3 \ **Teachers:** 81 \ **Students:** 860 \ **Special Ed Students:** 51 \ **LEP Students:** 172 \ **Ethnic:** Asian 1%, Hispanic 70%, Caucasian 30% \ **Exp:** $392 (High) \ **Poverty:** 18% \ **Title I:** $170,639 \ **Open-Close:** 08/19 - 05/15 \ **DTBP:** $353 (High) \

Clay Montgomery 1
Bernice Flores 4*
Aaron Witten 6
Sandi Wheeler 10,88,270
Shane Whiteley 16*
Mary Nine 58
Brianne Eslick 73,95
Brenda Ferguson 2,11
Joe Martinez 5
Sally Swan 7,35,83,85*
Bonnie Morton 16,82
Krista Baird 31,36,69*
Dr Mark Garnett 67

Public Schs..Principal	Grd	Prgm	Enr/#Cls	SN	
Gus Birdwell Elem Sch 511 Townsend St, Spearman 79081 Lizet Olmos	PK-5	T	422 32	63%	806/659-2565 Fax 806/659-2257
Spearman High Sch 403 E 11th Ave, Spearman 79081 Kelly Carrell	9-12	ATV	267 27	55%	806/659-2584 Fax 806/659-3824
Spearman Junior High Sch 313 W 5th Ave, Spearman 79081 Starla Whiteley	6-8	T	194 14	60%	806/659-2563 Fax 806/659-2243

HARDEMAN COUNTY

HARDEMAN PUBLIC SCHOOLS

- **Chillicothe ISD School Dist** PID: 01022350 940/852-5391
  1610 S 6th St, Chillicothe 79225 Fax 940/852-5269

Schools: 2 \ **Teachers:** 21 \ **Students:** 248 \ **Special Ed Students:** 21 \ **LEP Students:** 35 \ **College-Bound:** 60% \ **Ethnic:** African American 1%, Hispanic 45%, Native American: 1%, Caucasian 53% \ **Exp:** $425 (High) \ **Poverty:** 34% \ **Title I:** $87,158 \ **Special Education:** $10,000 \ **Open-Close:** 08/19 - 05/22 \ **DTBP:** $357 (High) \

Todd Wilson 1,11
Donna Prince 36,69,83,85,88
Phyllis Heath 73*
Tammy Daniel 2
Mark Williams 67

Public Schs..Principal	Grd	Prgm	Enr/#Cls	SN	
Chillicothe Elem Sch 400 Ave L, Chillicothe 79225 Brenda Dunlap	PK-6	T	120 7	93%	940/852-5521 Fax 940/852-5012
Chillicothe High Sch 1610 S 6th St, Chillicothe 79225 Tony Martinez	7-12	TV	99 20	87%	940/852-5391 Fax 940/852-5465

- **Quanah Ind School Dist** PID: 01022398 940/663-2281
  801 Elbert St, Quanah 79252 Fax 940/663-2875

Schools: 3 \ **Teachers:** 52 \ **Students:** 525 \ **Special Ed Students:** 58 \ **LEP Students:** 6 \ **College-Bound:** 70% \ **Ethnic:** Asian 1%, African American 3%, Hispanic 33%, Caucasian 63% \ **Exp:** $568 (High) \ **Poverty:** 25% \ **Title I:** $153,236 \ **Open-Close:** 08/21 - 05/22 \ **DTBP:** $355 (High) \

Jerry Baird 1
Armando Leal 3
Matt Garvin 6*
Rusty Brawley 11,58
Amy Bibler 57
Corri Orr 83*
Jana Brandon 2
Lynn Isnhower 4
Tammy Whitten 10,38
John White 16,73,295,297*
Steven Sparkman 67

Public Schs..Principal	Grd	Prgm	Enr/#Cls	SN	
Quanah High Sch 501 W 7th St, Quanah 79252 Amy Bibler	9-12	ATV	155 20	73%	940/663-2791 Fax 940/663-6447
Reagan Elem Sch 205 E 8th St, Quanah 79252 Lillie Cary	PK-5	T	244 23	80%	940/663-2171 Fax 940/663-2209
Travis Middle Sch 600 W 7th St, Quanah 79252 Virginia Turner	6-8	T	132 10	74%	940/663-2226 Fax 940/663-6361

HARDIN COUNTY

HARDIN PUBLIC SCHOOLS

- **Hardin Jefferson Ind Sch Dist** PID: 01022439 409/981-6400
  520 W Herring St, Sour Lake 77659 Fax 409/287-2287

Schools: 4 \ **Teachers:** 153 \ **Students:** 2,200 \ **Special Ed Students:** 185 \ **LEP Students:** 72 \ **College-Bound:** 68% \ **Ethnic:** Asian 1%, African American 10%, Hispanic 9%, Caucasian 80% \ **Exp:** $309 (High) \ **Poverty:** 10% \ **Title I:** $211,606 \ **Special Education:** $132,000 \ **Open-Close:** 08/14 - 05/22 \ **DTBP:** $347 (High) \

Brad McEachern 1
Randy Obannion 3,91
Katie Kibodeaux 5
Druann Mushlian 11,15,57
Deena Van Pelt 58
Paul Geobel 73
Courtney Bagwell 84
Brad Boullion 2,3
Courtney Bulion 4*
Dwayne DeBoise 6
Christian Kemp 28
Michelle Yentzen 67
Lucas Turner 76,295,297

---

79 Student Personnel
80 Driver Ed/Safety
81 Gifted/Talented
82 Video Services
83 Substance Abuse Prev
84 Erate
85 AIDS Education
88 Alternative/At Risk
89 Multi-Cultural Curriculum
90 Social Work
91 Safety/Security
92 Magnet School
93 Parental Involvement
95 Tech Prep Program
97 Chief Infomation Officer
98 Chief Technology Officer
270 Accountability
271 Migrant Education
273 Teacher Mentor
274 Before/After Sch
275 Response To Intervention
277 Remedial Math K-12
280 Literacy Coach
285 STEM
286 Digital Learning
288 Common Core Standards
294 Accountability
295 Network System
296 Title II Programs
297 Webmaster
298 Grant Writer/Ptnrships
750 Chief Innovation Officer
751 Chief of Staff
752 Social Emotional Learning

Other School Types
Ⓐ = Alternative School
Ⓒ = Charter School
Ⓜ = Magnet School
Ⓨ = Year-Round School

School Programs
A = Alternative Program
G = Adult Classes
M = Magnet Program
T = Title I Schoolwide
V = Career & Tech Ed Programs

New Schools are shaded
New Superintendents and Principals are bold
Personnel with email addresses are underscored

Social Media
 = Facebook
 = Twitter

TX—177

Hardin County

Market Data Retrieval

Public Schs..Principal	Grd	Prgm	Enr/#Cls	SN	
China Elem Sch 605 Henderson Ave, China 77613 Dianne Timberlake	PK-5	T	450 20	50%	409/981-6410 Fax 409/752-3623
Hardin-Jefferson High Sch 3155 Highway 326 S, Sour Lake 77659 Patrick Brown	9-12	V	653 40	30%	409/981-6430 Fax 409/287-2558
Henderson Middle Sch 3025 Highway 326 S, Sour Lake 77659 Darrell Westfall	6-8		533 40		409/981-6420 Fax 409/287-1235
Sour Lake Elem Sch 1055 Highway 326, Sour Lake 77659 Danny McFarland	PK-5	T	633 60	42%	409/981-6440 Fax 409/287-3987

● **Kountze Ind School Dist** PID: 01022491 409/246-3352
160 W Vaughn St, Kountze 77625 Fax 409/246-3217

Schools: 4 \ *Teachers:* 91 \ *Students:* 1,135 \ *Special Ed Students:* 109 \ *LEP Students:* 30 \ *College-Bound:* 53% \ *Ethnic:* Asian 1%, African American 12%, Hispanic 6%, Caucasian 81% \ *Exp:* $426 (High) \ *Poverty:* 17% \ *Title I:* $302,984 \ *Open-Close:* 08/26 - 05/28 \ *DTBP:* $15 (Low)

John Ferguson 1
Elizabeth Jordan 4*
Sherry Allen 7*
Teresa Matthews 16*
Spencer Matthews 73,295
Philip Welch 2,19
John French 5
Shane Reyenga 8,11,15,69*
Steve Eppes 67

Public Schs..Principal	Grd	Prgm	Enr/#Cls	SN	
Kountze Elem Sch 565 Park St, Kountze 77625 Thomas Cooley	PK-3	T	365 41	64%	409/246-3877 Fax 409/246-4138
Kountze High Sch 1488 FM 1293 Rd, Kountze 77625 Dr Chet Deaver	9-12	ATV	331 40	35%	409/246-3474 Fax 409/246-8180
Kountze Intermediate Sch 150 Vaughn St, Kountze 77625 Connie Joubert	4-6	T	279	52%	409/246-8230 Fax 409/246-3857
Kountze Middle Sch 1676 FM 1293 Rd, Kountze 77625 James Stevenson	7-8	T	184 20	39%	409/246-3551 Fax 409/246-8907

● **Lumberton Ind School Dist** PID: 01022544 409/923-7580
121 S Main St, Lumberton 77657 Fax 409/755-7848

Schools: 5 \ *Teachers:* 252 \ *Students:* 4,123 \ *Special Ed Students:* 340 \ *LEP Students:* 63 \ *College-Bound:* 58% \ *Ethnic:* Asian 1%, Hispanic 8%, Caucasian 90% \ *Exp:* $374 (High) \ *Poverty:* 10% \ *Title I:* $383,966 \ *Open-Close:* 08/14 - 05/22 \ *DTBP:* $179 (High)

Gerald Chandler 1
Lori Mack 2
Katie Baker 4
Chris Babin 6
Cynthia Lawrence 8
Patty Crouch 11,15,91,285,288,296
Ticia McBride 57
Anna Miller 71
Mike Buffington 80
Gretchen Scoggins 298
Abby Zernial 2
Ricci Pampolina 3
Roy Coleman 5
Amy Morgan 7,85*
Mandy Babin 8
Candace Koran 16,82
James Kersh 67
Mary Johnson 73,286,297*
Daniel Cazares 84,295

Public Schs..Principal	Grd	Prgm	Enr/#Cls	SN	
Early Childhood Sch 1020 S Main St, Lumberton 77657 John Wing	PK-K		386 23	34%	409/923-7695 Fax 409/755-6607
Lumberton High Sch 103 S Lhs Dr, Lumberton 77657 John White	9-12	AV	1,126 98	20%	409/923-7890 Fax 409/755-6576
Lumberton Intermediate Sch 107 S Lhs Dr, Lumberton 77657 Paige Wing	4-6		880 40	29%	409/923-7790 Fax 409/923-7764
Lumberton Middle Sch 123 S Main St, Lumberton 77657 Travis Edgerton	7-8		624 47	25%	409/923-7581 Fax 409/751-0641
Lumberton Primary Sch 128 E Candlestick Dr, Lumberton 77657 Katherine Waldrop	1-3		970 45	33%	409/923-7490 Fax 409/923-7444

● **Silsbee Ind School Dist** PID: 01022582 409/980-7800
415 Highway 327 W, Silsbee 77656 Fax 409/980-7897

Schools: 4 \ *Teachers:* 205 \ *Students:* 2,800 \ *Special Ed Students:* 325 \ *LEP Students:* 34 \ *Ethnic:* African American 18%, Hispanic 8%, Native American: 1%, Caucasian 73% \ *Exp:* $312 (High) \ *Poverty:* 22% \ *Title I:* $862,664 \ *Special Education:* $757,000 \ *Open-Close:* 08/26 - 05/29 \ *DTBP:* $181 (High)

Dr Gregg Weiss 1
Michael Tomas 3
Joseph Reese 5
Michelle Hardy 7*
Judy Honeycutt 27,95*
Tammy McDuff 57,271*
Jamie Parker 69
Dawn Helton 81
Kevin Wharton 88
Danny Young 295
Kirsten Smith 2,15
Michelle Johnson 4
Randy Smith 6*
Sherrie Thornhill 8,11,288,296
Cindy Smith 34,58
Sam Harrell 67
Daniel Elizondo 71
Tyke Cameron 84,295
Ben Hawthorne 91

Public Schs..Principal	Grd	Prgm	Enr/#Cls	SN	
Edwards-Johnson Memorial MS 1140 Highway 327 E, Silsbee 77656 Sunee Stephens	6-8	GTV	610	48%	409/980-7870 Fax 409/980-7884
Laura Reeves Primary Sch 695 Woodrow St, Silsbee 77656 Terry Deaver	PK-K		344 25		409/980-7850 Fax 409/980-7868
Silsbee Elem Sch 770 S 7th St, Silsbee 77656 Terry Deaver	1-5	T	1,190 36	56%	409/980-7856 Fax 409/980-7861
Silsbee High Sch 1575 Highway 96 N, Silsbee 77656 Scott Schwartz	9-12	AGTV	784	46%	409/980-7877 Fax 409/980-7881

● **West Hardin Co Cons Sch Dist** PID: 01022659 936/274-5061
39227 Highway 105, Saratoga 77585 Fax 936/274-4321

Schools: 2 \ *Teachers:* 39 \ *Students:* 525 \ *Special Ed Students:* 50 \ *LEP Students:* 3 \ *College-Bound:* 56% \ *Ethnic:* Hispanic 4%, Native American: 1%, Caucasian 95% \ *Exp:* $464 (High) \ *Poverty:* 6% \ *Title I:* $38,922 \ *Open-Close:* 08/21 - 05/28 \ *DTBP:* $335 (High)

Dr Jim Armstrong 1
Patti Graham 3,5*
Kenny Holfpauir 6*
D'Wanna Rasnick 8,11,69
Gina Strahan 52,55
Shawn Buser 73,273,295*
Penny White 2*
Kathy Lofton 4*
Tammy Adams 7*
Charlene Zwahr 16,82*
Stephanie Battle 57,58

Public Schs..Principal	Grd	Prgm	Enr/#Cls	SN	
West Hardin Elem Sch 39227 Highway 105, Saratoga 77585 Tiffany Merriweather	PK-5	T	321 14	61%	936/274-5061

1 Superintendent	8 Curric/Instruct K-12	19 Chief Financial Officer	29 Family/Consumer Science	39 Social Studies K-12	49 English/Lang Arts Elem	59 Special Education Elem	69 Academic Assessment
2 Bus/Finance/Purchasing	9 Curric/Instruct Elem	20 Art K-12	30 Adult Education	40 Social Studies Elem	50 English/Lang Arts Sec	60 Special Education Sec	70 Research/Development
3 Buildings And Grounds	10 Curric/Instruct Sec	21 Art Elem	31 Career/Sch-to-Work K-12	41 Social Studies Sec	51 Reading K-12	61 Foreign/World Lang K-12	71 Public Information
4 Food Service	11 Federal Program	22 Art Sec	32 Career/Sch-to-Work Elem	42 Science K-12	52 Reading Elem	62 Foreign/World Lang Elem	72 Summer School
5 Transportation	12 Title I	23 Music K-12	33 Career/Sch-to-Work Sec	43 Science Elem	53 Reading Sec	63 Foreign/World Lang Sec	73 Instructional Tech
6 Athletic	13 Title V	24 Music Elem	34 Early Childhood Ed	44 Science Sec	54 Remedial Reading K-12	64 Religious Education K-12	74 Inservice Training
7 Health Services	15 Asst Superintendent	25 Music Sec	35 Health/Phys Education	45 Math K-12	55 Remedial Reading Elem	65 Religious Education Elem	75 Marketing/Distributive
	16 Instructional Media Svcs	26 Business Education	36 Guidance Services K-12	46 Math Elem	56 Remedial Reading Sec	66 Religious Education Sec	76 Info Systems
	17 Chief Operations Officer	27 Career & Tech Ed	37 Guidance Services Elem	47 Math Sec	57 Bilingual/ELL	67 School Board President	77 Psychological Assess
	18 Chief Academic Officer	28 Technology Education	38 Guidance Services Sec	48 English/Lang Arts K-12	58 Special Education K-12	68 Teacher Personnel	78 Affirmative Action

Texas School Directory — Harris County

West Hardin High Sch	7-12	T	239	45%	936/274-5061
39227 Highway 105, Saratoga 77585			20		Fax 936/274-5671
Michael Smith					

HARRIS COUNTY

HARRIS COUNTY SCHOOLS

- **Harris Co Dept of Ed** PID: 02091055 — 713/694-6300
  6300 Irvington Blvd, Houston 77022 — Fax 713/696-0730

James Colbert 1
Rosa Maria Torres 2
Kimberly McLeod 8,15
Eduardo Honold 30
Natasha Truitt 68
Tammy Lanier 71
Ecomet Burley 91
Gayla Rawlinson 298
Jesus Amezcua 2,15
Greg Lookabaugh 3
Jonathan Parker 15
Louis Evans 67
Darlene Breaux 70
Arthur Vu 73
Helen Spencer 295

County Schs..Principal	Grd	Prgm	Enr/#Cls	SN	
Academic Behavior Center-East	Spec		113		713/242-8036
7703 South Loop E, Houston 77012			24		Fax 713/645-5773
Donna Jones					
Academic Behavior Sch-West	Spec		109		713/339-9411
7800 Westglen Dr, Houston 77063			18		Fax 713/978-7662
Dr Victor Keys					
Harris Co Detention Center	3-12	T	184	99%	713/222-4100
1200 Congress St, Houston 77002			16		Fax 713/222-4360
Chris Garcia					
Harris Co Youth Village	6-12	TV	97	97%	281/326-2521
210 J W Mills Dr, Seabrook 77586			12		Fax 713/222-4749
Diane Hubbell					
Highpoint School East	6-12	V	250		713/696-2160
8003 E Sam Houston Pkwy N, Houston 77049			17		Fax 713/696-2161
Marion Cooksey					
Highpoint School North	6-12		250		713/696-2195
11902 Spears Rd, Houston 77067			12		Fax 713/696-2196
David Oquin					

HARRIS PUBLIC SCHOOLS

- **Aldine Ind School Dist** PID: 01022697 — 281/449-1011
  2520 WW Thorne Blvd, Houston 77073 — Fax 281/449-4911

Schools: 82 \ *Teachers:* 4,644 \ *Students:* 69,768 \
Special Ed Students: 5,026 \ *LEP Students:* 21,780 \ *College-Bound:* 75% \
Ethnic: Asian 1%, African American 23%, Hispanic 73%, Caucasian 2% \ *Exp:* $240 (Med) \ *Poverty:* 30% \ *Title I:* $31,501,622 \
Special Education: $12,975,000 \ *Bilingual Education:* $48,000 \
Open-Close: 08/20 - 05/28 \ *DTBP:* $192 (High) \ 🅕 🅣

Dr Latonya Goffney 1
Milo Ortiz 3
Jill Metcalf 5
Maisha Guillory 7
Dr Selena Chapa 15,17
Cynthia Buchanan 16
Refugio Rodriguez 23
Dr Charlotte Davis 36,83,88,275
Dr Tamika Stephens 2,19
Dani Sheffield 4
Dre Thompson 6
Carlos Barron 10
Dr Todd Davis 15,18
Michaelann Kelley 20
Franklin Higgins 27,31
Twiana Collier 36,81
Gwendolyn Lockett 40
Tracy Mansfield 43
Chantay Smith 46
Lisa Edwards 49
Betsy Haisler 57
Steve Mead 67
Denise Simons 69
Mike Keeney 71
Cynthia Bingman 73,76,295
Candice Moore 76,79
Olivia Boatner 92
Deborah Johnson 41
Xandra Earlie 44
Baron Hannsz 47
Charity Bostick 50
Katherine Seals 58
Dawn Rodriguez 69,70,294
Rachel Haller 69
Sheleah Reed 71
Akilah Willery 74
Nikki Reid 91
Deborah McNeely 275

- **Aldine ISD-Elem Sch Team 1** PID: 12107347 — 281/985-6467
  2520 WW Thorne Blvd, Houston 77073

Latonia Amerson 15

Public Schs..Principal	Grd	Prgm	Enr/#Cls	SN	
Ⓜ A B Anderson Academy	1-5	T	516	84%	281/878-0370
7401 Wheatley St, Houston 77088			37		Fax 281/591-8549
Dr E Simpson					
Ⓜ Earl & Hazel Harris Academy	1-5	T	719	93%	281/878-7900
3130 Holder Forest Dr, Houston 77088			45		Fax 281/878-7913
Cicely Bailey					
Gloria B Sammons Elem Sch	1-5	T	782	89%	281/878-0955
2301 Frick Rd, Houston 77038			30		Fax 281/591-8546
Jose Almendarez					
Ⓜ J Ruth Smith Academy	1-5	T	574	98%	713/613-7650
5815 W Little York Rd, Houston 77091			65		Fax 713/613-7653
Ida Carter					
Kujawa Elem Sch	1-5	T	971	84%	281/878-1530
7007 Fallbrook Dr, Houston 77086			35		Fax 281/878-1536
Kimberly Jenkins					
Ⓜ Lola Mae Carter Academy	1-5	T	794	82%	281/878-7760
3111 Fallbrook Dr, Houston 77038			50		Fax 281/878-7767
Lee Wold					
Stehlik Elem Sch	1-5	T	1,009	92%	281/878-0300
400 West Rd, Houston 77038					Fax 281/878-0305
Karen Wilkerson					
Thomas B Gray Elem Sch	1-5	T	837	91%	281/878-0660
700 West Rd, Houston 77038			100		Fax 281/878-0664
Scott Dubberke					
Voyde Caraway Elem Sch	1-5	T	768	89%	281/878-0320
3031 Ellington St, Houston 77088			55		Fax 281/878-0326
Everette Taylor					
William R Carmichael Elem Sch	1-5	T	809	85%	281/878-0345
6902 Silver Star Dr, Houston 77086			40		Fax 281/878-0379
Monica Stogsdill					
Willie B Ermel Elem Sch	1-5	T	698	81%	713/466-5220
7103 Woodsman Trl, Houston 77040			37		Fax 713/856-4256
Martha Escalante					
Wilson Elem Sch	1-5	T	1,038	87%	281/878-0990
3131 Fallbrook Dr, Houston 77038			58		Fax 281/878-0995
Dana Baker					

- **Aldine ISD-Elem Sch Team 2** PID: 12107359 — 281/985-6159
  2520 WW Thorne Blvd, Houston 77073

Dr Faviola Cantu 15

Public Schs..Principal	Grd	Prgm	Enr/#Cls	SN	
Beulah E Johnson Elem Sch	1-5	T	935	89%	281/985-6510
5801 Hamill Rd, Houston 77039			40		Fax 281/985-6494
Pamela Johnson					
Douglas B Bussey Elem Sch	1-5	T	951	93%	281/878-1501
11555 Airline Dr, Houston 77037					Fax 281/878-1506
Kathleen Sandoval					

---

79 Student Personnel	91 Safety/Security	275 Response To Intervention	298 Grant Writer/Ptnrships	**School Programs**	**Social Media**	
80 Driver Ed/Safety	92 Magnet School	277 Remedial Math K-12	750 Chief Innovation Officer	A = Alternative Program		
81 Gifted/Talented	93 Parental Involvement	280 Literacy Coach	751 Chief of Staff	G = Adult Classes	🅕 = Facebook	
82 Video Services	95 Tech Prep Program	285 STEM	752 Social Emotional Learning	M = Magnet Program		
83 Substance Abuse Prev	97 Chief Information Officer	286 Digital Learning		T = Title I Schoolwide	🅣 = Twitter	
84 Erate	98 Chief Technology Officer	288 Common Core Standards	**Other School Types**	V = Career & Tech Ed Programs		
85 AIDS Education	270 Character Education	294 Accountability	Ⓐ = Alternative School			
88 Alternative/At Risk	271 Migrant Education	295 Network System	Ⓒ = Charter School	New Schools are shaded		
89 Multi-Cultural Curriculum	273 Teacher Mentor	296 Title II Programs	Ⓜ = Magnet School	New Superintendents and Principals are bold		
90 Social Work	274 Before/After Sch	297 Webmaster	Ⓨ = Year-Round School	Personnel with email addresses are underscored		

TX–179

Harris County

Public Schs..Principal	Grd	Prgm	Enr/#Cls	SN		
Evelyn S Thompson Elem Sch 220 Casa Grande Dr, Houston 77060 Sandra Doria	1-5	T	792 38	96%	281/878-0333 Fax 281/878-0339	
Gus A Oleson Elem Sch 12345 Vickery St, Houston 77039 Nadia Stafford	1-5	T	966 50	91%	281/985-6530 Fax 281/985-6143	
Hill Elem Sch 2625 W Mount Houston Rd, Houston 77038 Ivan Hepworth	1-5	T	842	87%	281/878-7775 Fax 281/878-7779	
ⓜ Inez Carroll Academy 423 W Gulf Bank Rd, Houston 77037 Jennifer Price	1-5	T	1,025 54	91%	281/878-0340 Fax 281/591-8527	
Kenneth D Black Elem Sch 160 Mill Stream Ln, Houston 77060 Ash Kirk	1-5	T	859 45	92%	281/878-0350 Fax 281/878-0389	
Lawrence A Eckert Elem Sch 1430 Aldine Meadows Rd, Houston 77032 Mark Herndon	1-5	T	803 50	86%	281/985-6380 Fax 281/985-6117	
Mary Walke Stephens Elem Sch 2402 Aldine Mail Route Rd, Houston 77039 Shauna Showers	1-5	T	908 47	88%	281/985-6560 Fax 281/985-6564	
Orange Grove Elem Sch 4514 Mount Houston Rd, Houston 77093 Kelly James	1-5	T	862 42	90%	281/985-6540 Fax 281/985-6544	
ⓜ Ruby M Reed Academy 1616 Lauder Rd, Houston 77039 Jeana Morrison-Adams	1-5	TV	944 65	86%	281/985-6670 Fax 281/985-6679	
Vera Escamilla Elem Sch 5241 Mount Houston Rd, Houston 77093 Susan Rehan	1-5	T	1,092 65	91%	281/985-6390 Fax 281/985-6137	
Weaver Odom Elem Sch 14701 Henry Rd, Houston 77060 Delilah St Julian	1-5	T	749 43	94%	281/878-0390 Fax 281/878-0397	

● **Aldine ISD-Elem Sch Team 3** PID: 12107361   281/985-6956
2520 WW Thorne Blvd, Houston 77073

Latoya Wynne 15

Public Schs..Principal	Grd	Prgm	Enr/#Cls	SN		
Clifford Dunn Elem Sch 2003 WW Thorne Blvd, Houston 77073 Cheryl Davis	1-5	T	840 54	78%	281/233-4320 Fax 281/233-4328	
Cypresswood Elem Sch 6901 Cypresswood Point Ave, Humble 77338 Innetta Carter	1-5	T	863	79%	281/227-3370 Fax 281/446-4039	
Ellen B Lane Sch 2001 Aldine Bender Rd, Houston 77032 Dale Prioleau	Spec	AT	131 34	70%	281/985-6350 Fax 281/985-6358	
ⓜ Grace Raymond Academy 1605 Connorvale Rd, Houston 77039 Tannessa Maddox	1-5	T	960 45	88%	281/985-6550 Fax 281/985-6555	
Greenspoint Elem Sch 18028 Chisholm Trl, Houston 77060 Tami Schuler	1-5	T	700	89%	281/985-7800	
Jones Elem Sch 7903 Forest Point Dr, Humble 77338 Cheryl Fontenot	1-5	T	859	73%	281/446-6168 Fax 281/985-6022	
Marcella Elem Sch 16250 Cotillion Dr, Houston 77060 Demedia Edwards	1-5	T	843	92%	281/878-0860 Fax 281/878-0805	
O V Calvert Elem Sch 1925 Marvell Dr, Houston 77032 Cheryl LaFleur	1-5	T	616 40	91%	281/985-6360 Fax 281/985-6364	
Oticel Parker Elem Sch 19850 E Hardy Rd, Houston 77073 Candace Hardin	1-5	T	1,018 45	83%	281/233-8930 Fax 281/233-8935	
R C Conley Elem Sch 3345 W Greens Rd, Houston 77066 **Lashawn Hodge**	1-5	T	789 30	89%	281/537-5418 Fax 281/895-5005	
Rick Ogden Elem Sch 21919 Rayford Rd, Humble 77338 Margaret Doran	1-5	T	818	74%	281/233-8901 Fax 281/233-8907	
Spence Elem Sch 1300 Gears Rd, Houston 77067 Susana Lomeli-Bazen	1-5	T	593	91%	281/539-4050 Fax 281/539-4054	
Thomas B Francis Elem Sch 14815 Lee Rd, Houston 77032 Dana Stelly	1-5	T	711 43	93%	281/985-6500 Fax 281/985-6504	

● **Aldine ISD-High Sch Team** PID: 12107397   281/985-6427
2520 WW Thorne Blvd, Houston 77073

Todd Lindeman 15

Public Schs..Principal	Grd	Prgm	Enr/#Cls	SN		
Aldine 9th Grade Sch 10650 North Fwy, Houston 77037 Dr Kanisha Wiley	9-9	TV	840 43	92%	281/878-6800 Fax 281/878-6824	
Aldine Senior HS 11101 Airline Dr, Houston 77037 Walter Stewart	9-12	TV	2,463 125	83%	281/448-5231 Fax 281/878-0641	
Blanson Cte High Sch 311 West Rd, Houston 77038 Benjamin Ibarra	9-12	V	401		281/591-4950	
ⓜ Carver High Sch 2100 S Victory Dr, Houston 77088 Anthony Watkins	9-12	TV	901	72%	281/878-0310 Fax 281/591-8579	
Chester W Nimitz High Sch 2005 WW Thorne Blvd, Houston 77073 Dr Crystal Watson	9-12	TV	1,943 120	71%	281/443-7480 Fax 281/233-4331	
Davis 9th Grade Sch 12211 Ella Blvd, Houston 77067 James Metcalf	9-9	T	921	84%	281/873-1800	
Davis Senior High Sch 12525 Ella Blvd, Houston 77067 Thomas Colwell	10-12	T	2,621	82%	281/539-4070 Fax 281/539-4075	
Douglas MacArthur High Sch 4400 Aldine Mail Route Rd, Houston 77039 Heather Peterson	10-12	TV	2,830	85%	281/985-6330 Fax 281/985-6294	
Dwight D Eisenhower High Sch 7922 Antoine Dr, Houston 77088 Todd Lindeman	10-12	TV	1,750 110	76%	281/878-0900 Fax 281/448-2936	
Eisenhower 9th Grade Sch 3550 W Gulf Bank Rd, Houston 77088 Latonia Amerson	9-9	TV	598 60	87%	281/878-7700 Fax 281/878-7736	
MacArthur 9th Grade Sch 12111 Gloger St, Houston 77039 D'Ann DelGado	9-9	T	990 25	88%	281/985-7400 Fax 281/985-7423	
Nimitz 9th Grade Sch 2425 WW Thorne Blvd, Houston 77073 **Aisley Adams**	9-9	T	702 43	81%	281/209-8200 Fax 281/209-8220	
Rose M Avalos P-Tech Sch 2430 Aldine Mail Route Rd, Houston 77039 Diana Delpilar	9-12		126		281/985-2100 Fax 281/985-2119	
Victory Early College HS 4141 Victory Dr, Houston 77088 Dr Phyllis Cormier	9-12	T	408	84%	281/810-5675 Fax 281/810-5698	
W T Hall Education Center 15014 Aldine Westfield Rd, Houston 77032 Marcie Strahan	9-12	AGT	239	83%	281/985-7446 Fax 281/985-7453	

1 Superintendent	8 Curric/Instruct K-12	19 Chief Financial Officer	29 Family/Consumer Science	39 Social Studies K-12	49 English/Lang Arts Elem	59 Special Education Elem	69 Academic Assessment
2 Bus/Finance/Purchasing	9 Curric/Instruct Elem	20 Art K-12	30 Adult Education	40 Social Studies Elem	50 English/Lang Arts Sec	60 Special Education Sec	70 Research/Development
3 Buildings And Grounds	10 Curric/Instruct Sec	21 Art Elem	31 Career/Sch-to-Work K-12	41 Social Studies Sec	51 Reading K-12	61 Foreign/World Lang K-12	71 Public Information
4 Food Service	11 Federal Program	22 Art Sec	32 Career/Sch-to-Work Elem	42 Science K-12	52 Reading Elem	62 Foreign/World Lang Elem	72 Summer School
5 Transportation	12 Title I	23 Music K-12	33 Career/Sch-to-Work Sec	43 Science Elem	53 Reading Sec	63 Foreign/World Lang Sec	73 Instructional Tech
6 Athletic	13 Title V	24 Music Elem	34 Early Childhood Ed	44 Science Sec	54 Remedial Reading K-12	64 Religious Education K-12	74 Inservice Training
7 Health Services	15 Asst Superintendent	25 Music Sec	35 Health/Phys Education	45 Math K-12	55 Remedial Reading Elem	65 Religious Education Elem	75 Marketing/Distributive
	16 Instructional Media Svcs	26 Business Education	36 Guidance Services K-12	46 Math Elem	56 Remedial Reading Sec	66 Religious Education Sec	76 Info Systems
	17 Chief Operations Officer	27 Career & Tech Ed	37 Guidance Services Elem	47 Math Sec	57 Bilingual/ELL	67 School Board President	77 Psychological Assess
	18 Chief Academic Officer	28 Technology Education	38 Guidance Services Sec	48 English/Lang Arts K-12	58 Special Education K-12	68 Teacher Personnel	78 Affirmative Action

Texas School Directory — Harris County

Aldine ISD-Middle Sch Team   PID: 12107385   281/985-6689
2520 WW Thorne Blvd, Houston 77073

Mable Holt 15

Public Schs..Principal	Grd	Prgm	Enr/#Cls	SN	
ⒶAldine Education Center 1702 Aldine Bender Rd, Houston 77032 Gerald Schattle	1-12		384 24		281/985-6685 Fax 281/985-6688
Aldine Middle Sch 14908 Aldine Westfield Rd, Houston 77032 Christi Vanwassenhove	6-8	T	911 70	93%	281/985-6580 Fax 281/985-6480
ⓂCharles R Drew Academy 1910 W Little York Rd, Houston 77091 Earnest Washington	6-8	T	583 30	79%	281/878-0360 Fax 281/447-4694
Floyd Hoffman Middle Sch 6101 W Little York Rd, Houston 77091 Jeana Morrison-Adams	6-8	TV	783 83	81%	713/613-7670 Fax 713/613-7675
Garcia Middle Sch 11000 Rosslyn Rd, Houston 77038 Todd Roede	6-8		1,177		281/878-3730 Fax 281/878-3749
ⓂJewel S Houston Academy 8103 Carver Rd, Houston 77088 Rhonda Shelby	6-8	T	604	85%	281/878-7745 Fax 281/878-7755
Jones Middle Sch 20155 Townsen Blvd, Humble 77338 Marcus Pruitt	6-8		401		281/985-3720 Fax 281/985-3739
Mattie A Teague Middle Sch 21700 Rayford Rd, Humble 77338 Sonya Hicks	6-8	T	1,074 64	78%	281/233-4310 Fax 281/233-4318
Mattie B Hambrick Middle Sch 4600 Aldine Mail Route Rd, Houston 77039 Rebecca Sanford	6-8	T	1,083 80	92%	281/985-6570 Fax 281/442-9036
Mead Middle Sch 3500 Lauder Rd, Houston 77039 Jessica Scott	6-8		401		281/985-3700 Fax 281/985-3719
Plummer Middle Sch 11429 Spears Rd, Houston 77067 Andrea Cain	6-8	T	939	90%	281/539-4000 Fax 281/539-4017
Ray L Shotwell Middle Sch 6515 Trail Valley Way, Houston 77086 Denise Winchester	6-8	T	1,064 61	86%	281/878-0960 Fax 281/591-8564
Thomas J Stovall Middle Sch 11201 Airline Dr, Houston 77037 Elsa Wright	6-8	T	971 74	88%	281/878-0670 Fax 281/448-0636
ⓂThomas S Grantham Academy 13300 Chrisman Rd, Houston 77039 Jessica Scott	6-8	TV	994 80	87%	281/985-6590 Fax 281/985-6595
Vernon & Kathy Lewis Mid Sch 21255 W Hardy Rd, Houston 77073 Cassandra Bell	6-8	T	919	91%	281/209-8257 Fax 281/209-8267

Aldine ISD-Primary Team   PID: 12368280   281/449-1011
2520 WW Thorne Blvd, Houston 77073

Dr Christine Gomez 15

Public Schs..Principal	Grd	Prgm	Enr/#Cls	SN	
Bill Worsham Elem Sch 3007 Hartwick Rd, Houston 77093 Sandra Doria	1-5	T	868 56	92%	281/985-6520 Fax 281/985-6524
Desantia Go EC-PK-K Sch 1420 Aldine Meadows Rd, Houston 77032 Maria Galindo	PK-K	T	711 38	95%	281/985-7500 Fax 281/985-7509
Garcia-Leza EC-PK-K Sch 5311 Mount Houston Rd, Houston 77093 Patricia Willis	PK-K	T	646	96%	281/985-6037 Fax 281/985-6044
Griggs EC-PK-K Sch 801 Regional Park Dr, Houston 77060 Gladys Moton	PK-K		865		281/985-3760 Fax 281/985-3779
Hinojosa EC-PK-K Sch 1620 Lauder Rd, Houston 77039 Denise Meister	PK-K	T	505 36	95%	281/985-4750 Fax 281/985-4754
Jones EC-PK-K Sch 8003 Forest Point Dr, Humble 77338 Gladys Moton	PK-K	T	643	86%	281/446-1576 Fax 281/985-6010
Keeble EC-PK-K Sch 203 W Gulf Bank Rd, Houston 77037 Andrenetta Marshall	PK-K	T	872 50	93%	281/878-6860 Fax 281/878-6869
Kujawa EC-PK-K Sch 7111 Fallbrook Dr, Houston 77086 Andrea Davis	PK-K	T	574	93%	281/878-1514 Fax 281/878-1545
Magrill EC-PK-K Sch 21701 Rayford Rd, Humble 77338 Mark Malo	PK-K	T	702 48	76%	281/233-4300 Fax 281/233-4303
Ralph G Goodman Elem Sch 9325 Deer Trail Dr, Houston 77088 Nereida Ochoa	1-5	T	680 54	87%	281/878-0355 Fax 281/878-0330
ⓂReece EC-PK-K Sch 2223 Esther Dr, Houston 77088 Sharla Rogers	PK-K	T	488 28	91%	281/878-0800 Fax 281/878-0808
ⓂStovall EC-PK-K Sch 3025 Ellington St, Houston 77088 Kimberly Martin	PK-K	T	626 45	86%	281/591-8500 Fax 281/591-8507
Vardeman EC-PK-K Sch 3302 Connorvale Rd, Houston 77039 Orfelinda Todd	PK-K		401		281/985-3740 Fax 281/985-3759
Vines EC-PK-K Sch 7220 Inwood Park Dr, Houston 77088 Linda Reed	PK-K	T	513 26	98%	281/878-7950 Fax 281/878-7959

Alief Ind School Dist   PID: 01022972   281/498-8110
4250 Cook Rd, Houston 77072   Fax 281/988-3037

Schools: 45 \ **Teachers:** 3,377 \ **Students:** 46,241 \
Special Ed Students: 3,370 \ **LEP Students:** 18,211 \ **College-Bound:** 80%
\ **Ethnic:** Asian 12%, African American 29%, Hispanic 53%, Native American:
1%, Caucasian 4% \ **Exp:** $275 (Med) \ **Poverty:** 28% \ **Title I:** $24,115,064
\ **Special Education:** $7,455,000 \ **Bilingual Education:** $126,000 \
Open-Close: 08/14 - 05/21 \ **DTBP:** $189 (High) \ ⓣ

H D Chambers 1		Charles Woods 2,15	
Deanna Wentz 2,15		Jeff Delisle 3	
Heather Hayes-Ramirez 4		Richard Torres 5	
Scott Moehlig 6		Ava Montgomery 8,15	
Kathy Jahn 8		Karla Kessler 11,296,298	
Dr Elizabeth Veloz-Powell 15,68		Charla Hollingsworth 16,280*	
Susan Chiboroski 20,23		Jennifer Baker 27	
Kimberly Crow 27,70,750		Mari Martinez 34*	
Tyra Walker 36		Gretchen Gaskins 39	
Gelyn Roble 43		Dr Karen Jacobs 44,285	
Earl Snyder 46		Anne Hoskin 47	
Michelle Patterson 49		Joann Williams 50	
Patricia Cantu 57,271		Nicole Roberts 58	
Ann Williams 67		Darrell Alexander 68	
Natalie Martinez 69,294		Kimberly Smith 71	
Wally Rakestraw 73,295		Janine Hoke 74	
Al Reaves 76		Jackie Armwood 79	
Dr Tracy Scholz 81		Dan Turner 91	
Tameka Anderson 274		Joni Maniatis 275	
Pamela Lowe 286			

---

79 Student Personnel	91 Safety/Security	275 Response To Intervention	298 Grant Writer/Ptnrships	**School Programs**	**Social Media**
80 Driver Ed/Safety	92 Magnet School	277 Remedial Math K-12	750 Chief Innovation Officer	A = Alternative Program	
81 Gifted/Talented	93 Parental Involvement	280 Literacy Coach	751 Chief of Staff	G = Adult Classes	▫ = Facebook
82 Video Services	95 Tech Prep Program	285 STEM	752 Social Emotional Learning	M = Magnet Program	
83 Substance Abuse Prev	97 Chief Infomation Officer	286 Digital Learning		T = Title I Schoolwide	ⓣ = Twitter
84 Erate	98 Chief Technology Officer	288 Common Core Standards	**Other School Types**	V = Career & Tech Ed Programs	
85 AIDS Education	270 Character Education	294 Accountability	Ⓐ = Alternative School		
88 Alternative/At Risk	271 Migrant Education	295 Network System	Ⓒ = Charter School	New Schools are shaded	
89 Multi-Cultural Curriculum	273 Teacher Mentor	296 Title II Programs	Ⓜ = Magnet School	New Superintendents and Principals are bold	
90 Social Work	274 Before/After Sch	297 Webmaster	Ⓨ = Year-Round School	Personnel with email addresses are underscored	

TX—181

Harris County

Public Schs..Principal	Grd	Prgm	Enr/#Cls	SN	
A J Martin Elem Sch 11718 Hendon Ln, Houston 77072 Dr Ting-Ling Sha	PK-4	T	935 45	86%	281/983-8363 Fax 281/983-7705
Albright Middle Sch 6315 Winkleman Rd, Houston 77083 Lori Wyatt	7-8	TV	1,146 65	76%	281/983-8411 Fax 281/983-8443
Alexander Elem Sch 8500 Brookwulf Dr, Houston 77072 Kathleen Difelice	PK-4	T	805 50	82%	281/983-8300 Fax 281/983-8454
Alief Early College High Sch 2811 Hayes Rd, Houston 77082 Brandi Brotherton	9-12	T	402	82%	281/988-3010 Fax 281/496-4593
Ⓐ Alief Learning Center 4427 Belle Park Dr, Houston 77072 Mindy Robertson	K-12	V	112 10		281/983-8000 Fax 281/983-7701
Alief Middle Sch 4415 Cook Rd, Houston 77072 Sergio Lopez	6-8	TV	966	86%	281/983-8422 Fax 281/983-8053
Alief Taylor High Sch 7555 Howell Sugar Land Rd, Houston 77083 Mary Williams	9-12	T	3,193	77%	281/988-3500 Fax 281/561-7214
Best Elem Sch 10000 Centre Pkwy, Houston 77036 Renee Canales	PK-4	T	854 55	95%	713/988-6445 Fax 713/272-3211
Boone Elem Sch 11400 Bissonnet St, Houston 77099 Angela Chapman	PK-4	T	821 40	86%	281/983-8308 Fax 281/983-8035
Budewig Intermediate Sch 12570 Richmond Ave, Houston 77082 Heather Turner	5-6	T	1,294	84%	281/988-3200 Fax 281/497-7293
Bush Elem Sch 9730 Stroud Dr, Houston 77036 Gloria Harris-Price	PK-4	T	876 51	92%	713/272-3220 Fax 713/272-3230
Chambers Elem Sch 10700 Carvel Ln, Houston 77072 Jannae Jernberg	PK-4	T	734 60	93%	281/983-8313 Fax 281/988-3013
Chancellor Elem Sch 4350 Boone Rd, Houston 77072 Lisa Saarie	PK-5	T	958 56	82%	281/983-8318 Fax 281/983-8033
Collins Elem Sch 9829 Town Park Dr, Houston 77036 Courtney Marshall	PK-5	T	977 100	93%	713/272-3250 Fax 713/272-3260
Ⓐ Crossroads Alt Tech Sch 12360 Bear Ram Rd, Houston 77072 Tremayne Wickliffe	9-12		36	86%	281/988-3266 Fax 281/988-3277
Cummings Elem Sch 10455 S Kirkwood Rd, Houston 77099 Jeanette Byrd	PK-4	T	573 50	82%	281/983-8328 Fax 281/983-8096
Elsik 9th Grade Center 6767 S Dairy Ashford Rd, Houston 77072 Gina Sprang	9-9	V	1,000 75		281/988-3239 Fax 281/988-3319
Elsik High Sch 12601 High Star Dr, Houston 77072 Tina Elzy	9-12	AGTV	4,278	76%	281/988-3150 Fax 281/530-7058
Hastings 9th Grade Center 6750 Cook Rd, Houston 77072 Janie Saxton	9-9	V	1,100		281/988-3139 Fax 281/988-3419
Hastings High Sch 4410 Cook Rd, Houston 77072 Lynette Miller	9-12	TV	3,000 169	80%	281/988-3110 Fax 281/561-5763
Hearne Elem Sch 13939 Rio Bonito Rd, Houston 77083 Johanna Sanchez	PK-4	T	995 42	84%	281/983-8333 Fax 281/988-3020
Heflin Elem Sch 3303 Synott Rd, Houston 77082 Robin Human	PK-4	T	913 36	82%	281/531-1144 Fax 281/988-3014
Hicks Elem Sch 8520 Hemlock Hill Dr, Houston 77083 Mary Kesler	PK-4	T	781 57	80%	281/983-8040 Fax 281/983-8064
Holmquist Elem Sch 15040 Westpark Dr, Houston 77082 Kimberly Toney	PK-4	T	1,127	80%	281/988-3024 Fax 281/556-1050
Holub Middle Sch 9515 S Dairy Ashford Rd, Houston 77099 Pauline Beckley	7-8	TV	925 80	83%	281/983-8433 Fax 281/983-8398
Horn Elem Sch 10734 Bissonnet St, Houston 77099 Alicia Leyva	PK-4	T	999	93%	281/988-3223 Fax 281/530-5262
Kennedy Elem Sch 10200 Huntington Place Dr, Houston 77099 Sara Caldwell	PK-4	T	700 62	85%	281/983-8338 Fax 281/983-8390
Kerr High Sch 8150 Howell Sugar Land Rd, Houston 77083 Vinson Lewis	9-12	T	806 28	63%	281/983-8484 Fax 281/983-8014
Killough Middle Sch 7600 Synott Rd, Houston 77083 Bertran Bilton	7-8	TV	992	84%	281/983-8444 Fax 281/983-8067
Klentzman Intermediate Sch 11100 Stancliff Rd, Houston 77099 Courtney Holman	5-6	T	1,064 54	88%	281/983-8477 Fax 281/983-8373
Landis Elem Sch 10255 Spice Ln, Houston 77072 Kelli Upshaw	PK-4	T	803 50	93%	281/983-8343 Fax 281/983-8072
Liestman Elem Sch 7610 Synott Rd, Houston 77083 Noe Galindo	PK-4	T	823 45	82%	281/983-8348 Fax 281/983-8086
Mahanay Elem Sch 13215 High Star Dr, Houston 77083 Carmilla Nandlal	PK-4	T	651 30	81%	281/983-8355 Fax 281/983-8083
Mata Intermediate Sch 9225 S Dairy Ashford Rd, Houston 77099 Amy Coleman	5-6	T	824 48	88%	281/983-7800 Fax 281/983-7810
Miller Intermediate Sch 15025 Westpark Dr, Houston 77082 Seymour Stewart	5-6	T	942	79%	281/531-3430 Fax 281/531-3446
O'Donnell Middle Sch 14041 Alief Clodine Rd, Houston 77082 Amador Velasquez	7-8	TV	1,320	85%	281/495-6000 Fax 281/568-5029
Olle Middle Sch 9200 Boone Rd, Houston 77099 Nelda Billescas	7-8	TV	1,097 66	90%	281/983-8455 Fax 281/983-8077
Outley Elem Sch 12355 Richmond Ave, Houston 77082 Sharonda Ross-Newby	PK-4	T	1,207 55	66%	281/584-0655 Fax 281/988-3042
Owens Intermediate Sch 6900 Turtlewood Dr, Houston 77072 Lorena Augustus	5-6	T	1,080 70	92%	281/983-8466 Fax 281/983-8098
Petrosky Elem Sch 6703 Winkleman Rd, Houston 77083 Bernadette Bentley	PK-4	T	544 32	72%	281/983-8366 Fax 281/983-7708
Rees Elem Sch 16305 Kensley Dr, Houston 77082 Paul Baez	PK-4	T	604	76%	281/531-1444 Fax 281/531-3429
Smith Elem Sch 11300 Stancliff Rd, Houston 77099 Jennifer Silva	PK-4	T	842	85%	281/983-8380 Fax 281/983-7710
Sneed Elem Sch 9855 Pagewood Ln, Houston 77042 Kristen Creeggan	PK-4	T	1,120	86%	713/789-6979 Fax 713/260-7307
Youens Elem Sch 12141 High Star Dr, Houston 77072 Tangela Hughes-Bestov	PK-5	T	916 50	90%	281/983-8383 Fax 281/983-8055

1	Superintendent	8	Curric/Instruct K-12	19	Chief Financial Officer	29	Family/Consumer Science
2	Bus/Finance/Purchasing	9	Curric/Instruct Elem	20	Art K-12	30	Adult Education
3	Buildings And Grounds	10	Curric/Instruct Sec	21	Art Elem	31	Career/Sch-to-Work K-12
4	Food Service	11	Federal Program	22	Art Sec	32	Career/Sch-to-Work Elem
5	Transportation	12	Title I	23	Music K-12	33	Career/Sch-to-Work Sec
6	Athletic	13	Title V	24	Music Elem	34	Early Childhood Ed
7	Health Services	14	Asst Superintendent	25	Music Sec	35	Health/Phys Education
		15	Instructional Media Svcs	26	Business Education	36	Guidance Services K-12
		16	Chief Operations Officer	27	Career & Tech Ed	37	Guidance Services Elem
		17	Chief Academic Officer	28	Technology Education	38	Guidance Services Sec

39	Social Studies K-12	49	English/Lang Arts Elem	59	Special Education Elem	69	Academic Assessment
40	Social Studies Elem	50	English/Lang Arts Sec	60	Special Education Sec	70	Research/Development
41	Social Studies Sec	51	Reading K-12	61	Foreign/World Lang K-12	71	Public Information
42	Science K-12	52	Reading Elem	62	Foreign/World Lang Elem	72	Summer School
43	Science Elem	53	Reading Sec	63	Foreign/World Lang Sec	73	Instructional Tech
44	Science Sec	54	Remedial Reading K-12	64	Religious Education K-12	74	Inservice Training
45	Math K-12	55	Remedial Reading Elem	65	Religious Education Elem	75	Marketing/Distributive
46	Math Elem	56	Remedial Reading Sec	66	Religious Education Sec	76	Info Systems
47	Math Sec	57	Bilingual/ELL	67	School Board President	77	Psychological Assess
48	English/Lang Arts K-12	58	Special Education K-12	68	Teacher Personnel	78	Affirmative Action

Texas School Directory   Harris County

Youngblood Intermediate Sch 5-6 1,044 281/983-8020
8410 Dairy View Ln, Houston 77072   47   Fax 281/983-8051
Gwendolyn Sandles

Viola Cobb Elem Sch K-5 T 457 79% 281/452-7788
915 Dell Dale St, Channelview 77530   Fax 281/452-7413
Lizette Castelline

• Channelview Ind School Dist PID: 01023079   281/452-8002
828 Sheldon Rd, Channelview 77530   Fax 281/457-9075

• Crosby Ind School Dist PID: 01023134   281/328-9200
706 Runneburg Rd, Crosby 77532   Fax 281/328-9208

Schools: 13 \ **Teachers:** 545 \ **Students:** 9,700 \ **Special Ed Students:** 835 \ **LEP Students:** 2,618 \ **College-Bound:** 53% \ **Ethnic:** Asian 1%, African American 11%, Hispanic 79%, Native American: 1%, Caucasian 8% \ **Exp:** $373 (High) \ **Poverty:** 19% \ **Title I:** $2,329,115 \ **Special Education:** $1,473,000 \ **Open-Close:** 08/15 - 05/22 \ **DTBP:** $181 (High)

Schools: 7 \ **Teachers:** 406 \ **Students:** 6,300 \ **Special Ed Students:** 527 \ **LEP Students:** 696 \ **College-Bound:** 49% \ **Ethnic:** African American 16%, Hispanic 38%, Caucasian 46% \ **Exp:** $393 (High) \ **Poverty:** 18% \ **Title I:** $1,146,202 \ **Special Education:** $962,000 \ **Open-Close:** 08/15 - 05/28 \ **DTBP:** $158 (High) \ f t

Name	Ref
Greg Ollis	1
Michael Lyons	3
Jared Diehl	5
Dr Don Beck	8,15
Pam Latiolais	10
Mike Niemeyer	15
Jennifer Tunink	20,23
Magdalena Garcia	57
Keith Liggett	67
Karen Bryant	69,70
Darrell Cheney	73,84
Ruth Dougherty	76
Marion Barnes	295
Kris Lynn	2,15
David Bienvenu	4
William Jennings	6,7,35,85
Heather Gilpin	9
Patricia Glaeser	11,286,288,294,296,298
Jennifer Carnathan	19
Mia Young	27,31
Gloria Roach	58
Kay Kerr	68,79
Lakeisha LeBlanc	71
Raquel Ochoa	76
Gregg Board	91

Name	Ref
Dr Scott Davis	1
Chuck Murray	3,91
Teresa Evans	4
Jerry Prieto	6
Todd Hicks	10,74,273*
Dr Patricia Kay	15,31,68
Mary Gill	46
Vicki Randolph	49,52,54
Christina Castillo	57
John Swinney	67
Amy Davis	73,295,297
Lisa Jones	2,11,19
Rusty Hollingsworth	3
Renee Davis	5
Sherry Long	9,37
Karen Grey	15,68
Christie Davis	34
Dr Brenda Aleman	47
Tamara Meigh	50
Karla McGee	58
Viviana Killion	71

Public Schs..Principal	Grd	Prgm	Enr/#Cls	SN	
Alice Johnson Jr High Sch 15500 Proctor St, Channelview 77530 Jules Pichon	6-8	T	1,172 68	83%	281/452-8030 Fax 281/452-1022
Anthony Aguirre Junior HS 15726 Wallisville Rd, Houston 77049 Eric Lathan	6-8	T	1,048	80%	281/860-3300 Fax 281/860-3320
B H Hamblen Elem Sch 1019 Dell Dale St, Channelview 77530 Jose Lopez	K-5	T	861 43	77%	281/457-8720 Fax 281/457-8724
Barrett-Lee Early Chldhd Ctr 911 Sheldon Rd, Channelview 77530 Emily Laird	PK-PK	T	489	88%	281/860-3827 Fax 281/860-3810
Channelview High Sch 1100 Sheldon Rd, Channelview 77530 Robert Laird	10-12	TV	1,798	73%	281/452-1450 Fax 281/457-7346
Crenshaw Elem Sch 16204 Wood Dr, Channelview 77530 Audry Lane	K-5	T	616 30	89%	281/457-3080 Fax 281/457-5434
De Zavala Elem Sch 16150 2nd St, Channelview 77530 Ruben Rodriguez	K-5	T	573 30	90%	281/452-6008 Fax 281/452-3562
Ⓐ Endeavor HS-J F Campbell Ctr 915 Sheldon Rd, Channelview 77530 Mark Sims	9-12	T	156 6	79%	281/457-0086 Fax 281/860-3826
H C Schochler Elem Sch 910 Deerpass Dr, Channelview 77530 Ann Marie Garza	K-5	T	514 28	87%	281/452-2880 Fax 281/452-3709
Harvey S Brown Elem Sch 16550 Wallisville Rd, Houston 77049 Troy Michaud	K-5	T	718 47	66%	281/860-1400 Fax 281/860-9916
L W Kolarik 9th Grade Center 1120 Sheldon Rd, Channelview 77530 Steve McCanless	9-9	V	673		713/378-3400 Fax 713/378-3498
McMullan Elem Sch 1290 Dell Dale St, Channelview 77530 Gina Ervin	K-5	T	588 29	88%	281/452-1154 Fax 281/452-1367

Public Schs..Principal	Grd	Prgm	Enr/#Cls	SN	
Barrett Elem Sch 815 FM 1942 Rd, Crosby 77532 Karen Walthall	1-5	T	540 34	61%	281/328-9317 Fax 281/328-9374
Charles R Drew Elem Sch 223 Red Oak Ave, Crosby 77532 Christy Tisdom	1-5	T	500 33	85%	281/328-9306 Fax 281/328-3490
Crosby Elem Sch 14705 FM 2100 Rd, Crosby 77532 Dana Kratky	1-5	T	662	39%	281/328-9360 Fax 281/328-9213
Crosby High Sch 14703 FM 2100 Rd, Crosby 77532 **Dustin Bromley**	9-12	AGTV	1,745 100	42%	281/328-9237 Fax 281/328-0506
Crosby Kindergarten Center 805 Runneburg Rd, Crosby 77532 **Kriste Davis**	PK-K	T	651 27	67%	281/328-9370 Fax 281/328-9379
Crosby Middle Sch 14703 FM 2100 Rd, Crosby 77532 **Dustin Bromley**	6-8	AT	1,375 40	46%	281/328-9264 Fax 281/328-9356
Newport Elem Sch 430 N Diamondhead Blvd, Crosby 77532 Christy Covan	1-5	T	714 60	33%	281/328-9330 Fax 281/328-9378

• Cypress-Fairbanks Ind Sch Dist PID: 01023184   281/897-4000
10300 Jones Rd, Houston 77065   Fax 281/517-2140

Schools: 91 \ **Teachers:** 6,972 \ **Students:** 116,249 \ **Special Ed Students:** 8,988 \ **LEP Students:** 15,367 \ **College-Bound:** 64% \ **Ethnic:** Asian 10%, African American 18%, Hispanic 46%, Native American: 1%, Caucasian 26% \ **Exp:** $217 (Med) \ **Poverty:** 13% \ **Title I:** $25,354,397 \ **Special Education:** $16,667,000 \ **Open-Close:** 08/26 - 05/28 \ **DTBP:** $187 (High) \ f t

Name	Ref
Dr Mark Henry	1
Melissa McAnear	2
Darin Crawford	4
Raymond Zepeda	6,35
Sydne Marshall	7
Diane Garland	8,16
Kathie Sanders	11,298
Carla Brosnahan	15
Christina Cole	15
Connie Morgenroth	2
Roy Sprague	3,15,17
Kayne Smith	5
Loretta Bourn	7
Denise Kubecka	8,15,27
Barbara Levandoski	9,34
Dr Ashley Clayburn	13,15,294
Chairita Franklin	15,68
Dan McIlduff	15,57,58,90,280

79	Student Personnel	91	Safety/Security	275	Response To Intervention	298	Grant Writer/Ptnrships
80	Driver Ed/Safety	92	Magnet School	277	Remedial Math K-12	750	Chief Innovation Officer
81	Gifted/Talented	93	Parental Involvement	280	Literacy Coach	751	Chief of Staff
82	Video Services	95	Tech Prep Program	285	STEM	752	Social Emotional Learning
83	Substance Abuse Prev	97	Chief Infomation Officer	286	Digital Learning		
84	Erate	98	Chief Technology Officer	288	Common Core Standards		
85	AIDS Education	270	Accountability	294	Character Education		
88	Alternative/At Risk	271	Migrant Education	295	Network System		
89	Multi-Cultural Curriculum	273	Teacher Mentor	296	Title II Programs		
90	Social Work	274	Before/After Sch	297	Webmaster		

School Programs
A = Alternative Program
G = Adult Classes
M = Magnet Program
T = Title I Schoolwide
V = Career & Tech Ed Programs

Other School Types
Ⓐ = Alternative School
Ⓒ = Charter School
Ⓜ = Magnet School
Ⓨ = Year-Round School

Social Media
f = Facebook
t = Twitter

New Schools are shaded
New Superintendents and Principals are bold
Personnel with email addresses are underscored

TX—183

Harris County | Market Data Retrieval

Name	Page
Dr Deborah Stewart	15,68
Leslie Francis	15,71
Paula Ross	15,98
Travis Fanning	15
Susan Firth	27,69,81
Franklin Sampson	36*
Linda Sams	45
Lauri Barnes	58
Dr John Ogletree	67
Jennifer Miller	73
Dr Glenda Horner	74,273*
John Crumbley	76
Candy Medlin	79
Eric Mendez	91
Jennifer Ongoco	297
Ify Ogwumike	15,79
Dr Linda Macias	15,294,296
Roy Garcia	15
Mary Running	20,23
Jay Johnson	28
Mary Hestand	37
Maria Trejo	57,271
Jennifer Klaus	61
Dr Tracy McDaniel	69
Rebecca Cook	73,286
Marion Hogan	74
Traci Schluter	77
Kenneth Henry	79
Frankie Jackson	288*

Public Schs..Principal	Grd	Prgm	Enr/#Cls	SN	Phone
A Robison Elem Sch 17100 Robison Woods Rd, Cypress 77429 Kelly Gerletti	PK-5		1,106	26%	281/213-1700 Fax 281/213-1705
Adaptive Behavior Center 12508 Windfern Rd, Houston 77064 Chad Perry	Spec		20 9		281/897-4174 Fax 281/517-2884
Ⓐ Alternative Lrng Ctr-East 12508 Windfern Rd, Houston 77064 Rashad Godbolt	6-12		100 21		281/897-4171 Fax 281/897-4170
Ⓐ Alternative Lrng Ctr-West 19350 Rebel Yell Dr, Katy 77449 Stacie Wicke	6-12		100		281/855-4310 Fax 281/855-4307
Andre Elem Sch 8111 Fry Rd, Cypress 77433 Laura Novacinski	PK-5	T	966	78%	281/463-5500 Fax 281/463-5507
Arnold Middle Sch 11111 Telge Rd, Cypress 77429 Jodi White	6-8	TV	1,406 85	52%	281/897-4700 Fax 281/517-6857
Ault Elem Sch 21010 Maple Village Dr, Cypress 77433 Jeff Lacoke	PK-5		1,045	26%	281/373-2800 Fax 281/373-2823
B F Adam Elem Sch 11303 Honey Grove Ln, Houston 77065 **Stephanie Thomas**	PK-5	T	843	51%	281/897-4485 Fax 281/517-2089
Bane Elem Sch 5804 Premier St, Houston 77040 Carrie Marz	PK-5	T	935	76%	713/460-6140 Fax 713/460-7847
Birkes Elem Sch 8500 Queenston Blvd, Houston 77095 Stacie Everson	K-5		1,154	28%	281/345-3300 Fax 281/345-3305
Black Elem Sch 14155 Grant Rd, Cypress 77429 Melissa LeDoux	PK-5		1,045	32%	281/320-7145 Fax 281/320-7144
Bleyl Middle Sch 10800 Mills Rd, Houston 77070 Stacia Carew	6-8	TV	1,535 90	61%	281/897-4340 Fax 281/897-4353
Bridgeland High Sch 10707 Mason Rd, Cypress 77433 Michael Smith	9-12		1,276		832/349-7600 Fax 832/349-7610
Campbell Middle Sch 11415 Bobcat Rd, Houston 77064 Dr Laura Perry	6-8	TV	1,271 80	71%	281/897-4300 Fax 281/807-8634
Cook Middle Sch 9111 Wheatland Dr, Houston 77064 **Martin Drayton**	6-8	TV	1,584	57%	281/897-4400 Fax 281/517-2657
Copeland Elem Sch 18018 Forest Heights Dr, Houston 77095 Ann Melancon	PK-5		1,011 50	31%	281/856-1400 Fax 281/463-5510
Cy-Fair High Sch 22602 Northwest Fwy, Cypress 77429 Ana Martin	9-12	V	3,526 150	30%	281/897-4600 Fax 281/517-6530
Cypress Creek High Sch 9815 Grant Rd, Houston 77070 Vicki Snokhous	9-12	TV	3,357	45%	281/897-4200 Fax 281/897-4193
Cypress Falls High Sch 9811 Huffmeister Rd, Houston 77095 Becky Denton	9-12	TV	3,499	49%	281/856-1000 Fax 281/856-1445
Cypress Lakes High Sch 5750 Greenhouse Rd, Katy 77449 Sarah Harty	9-12	T	3,523	65%	281/856-3800 Fax 281/856-3808
Cypress Park High Sch 7425 Westgreen Blvd, Cypress 77433 Chris Hecker	9-12	T	551	69%	346/227-6000
Cypress Ranch High Sch 10700 Fry Rd, Cypress 77433 Michael Maness	9-12		3,114	12%	281/373-2300 Fax 281/213-1976
Cypress Ridge High Sch 7900 N Eldridge Pkwy, Houston 77041 Stephanie Meshell	9-12	TV	3,114	66%	281/807-8000 Fax 281/807-8017
Cypress Springs High Sch 7909 Fry Rd, Cypress 77433 Dr Cheryl Henry	9-12	TV	3,027	67%	281/345-3000 Fax 281/345-3010
Cypress Woods High Sch 13550 Woods Spillane Blvd, Cypress 77429 Garold Kinninger	9-12	AV	3,548	18%	281/213-1800 Fax 281/213-1827
Danish Elem Sch 11850 Fallbrook Dr, Houston 77065 Kelly Dalton	PK-5	T	986	70%	281/955-4981 Fax 281/955-4994
David Anthony Middle Sch 10215 Greenhouse Rd, Cypress 77433 Vivian Bennett	6-8	TV	1,471	47%	281/373-5660 Fax 281/373-2560
Dean Middle Sch 14104 Reo St, Houston 77040 Heather Bergman	6-8	TV	1,653	80%	713/460-6153 Fax 713/460-6197
Dorothy Carlton Center 13550 Woods Spillane Blvd, Cypress 77429 Rhonda Turns	Spec		58 15		281/213-1950 Fax 281/213-1951
Duryea Elem Sch 20150 Arbor Creek Dr, Katy 77449 **Tomicka Williams**	PK-5	T	950	75%	281/856-5174 Fax 281/856-5179
Emery Elem Sch 19636 Plantation Myrtle, Katy 77449 Michelle Merricks	PK-5	T	1,060	70%	281/855-9080 Fax 281/855-9380
Emmott Elem Sch 11750 Steeple Way Blvd, Houston 77065 Jessica Hernandez	PK-5	T	875	64%	281/897-4500 Fax 281/897-3888
Farney Elem Sch 14425 Barker Cypress Rd, Cypress 77429 Patricia Reilly	PK-5		1,082 65	25%	281/373-2850 Fax 281/373-2855
Fiest Elem Sch 8425 Pine Falls Dr, Houston 77095 Jeanette Gerault	PK-5		1,131 60	53%	281/463-5838 Fax 281/856-1174
Francone Elem Sch 11250 Perry Rd, Houston 77064 **Melissa Martin**	PK-5		979	82%	281/897-4512 Fax 281/897-4518
Frazier Elem Sch 8300 Little River Rd, Houston 77064 **Michael Pagano**	PK-5	T	702 46	80%	713/896-3475 Fax 713/896-5013
Gleason Elem Sch 9203 Willowbridge Park Blvd, Houston 77064 Christine Melancon	PK-5	T	961	50%	281/517-6800 Fax 281/517-6805
Goodson Middle Sch 17333 Huffmeister Rd, Cypress 77429 Richard Dixon	6-8	V	1,366 50	29%	281/373-2350 Fax 281/373-2355
Hairgrove Elem Sch 7120 N Eldridge Pkwy, Houston 77041 Darynda Klein	PK-5	T	799 54	81%	713/896-5015 Fax 713/896-5020

1 Superintendent	8 Curric/Instruct K-12	19 Chief Financial Officer	29 Family/Consumer Science	39 Social Studies K-12	49 English/Lang Arts Elem	59 Special Education Elem	69 Academic Assessment
2 Bus/Finance/Purchasing	9 Curric/Instruct Elem	20 Art K-12	30 Adult Education	40 Social Studies Elem	50 English/Lang Arts Sec	60 Special Education Sec	70 Research/Development
3 Buildings And Grounds	10 Curric/Instruct Sec	21 Art Elem	31 Career/Sch-to-Work K-12	41 Social Studies Sec	51 Reading K-12	61 Foreign/World Lang K-12	71 Public Information
4 Food Service	11 Federal Program	22 Art Sec	32 Career/Sch-to-Work Elem	42 Science K-12	52 Reading Elem	62 Foreign/World Lang Elem	72 Summer School
5 Transportation	12 Title I	23 Music K-12	33 Career/Sch-to-Work Sec	43 Science Elem	53 Reading Sec	63 Foreign/World Lang Sec	73 Instructional Tech
6 Athletic	13 Title V	24 Music Elem	34 Early Childhood Ed	44 Science Sec	54 Remedial Reading K-12	64 Religious Education K-12	74 Inservice Training
7 Health Services	15 Asst Superintendent	25 Music Sec	35 Health/Phys Education	45 Math K-12	55 Remedial Reading Elem	65 Religious Education Elem	75 Marketing/Distributive
	16 Instructional Media Svcs	26 Business Education	36 Guidance Services K-12	46 Math Elem	56 Remedial Reading Sec	66 Religious Education Sec	76 Info Systems
	17 Chief Operations Officer	27 Career & Tech Ed	37 Guidance Services Elem	47 Math Sec	57 Bilingual/ELL	67 School Board President	77 Psychological Assess
	18 Chief Academic Officer	28 Technology Education	38 Guidance Services Sec	48 English/Lang Arts K-12	58 Special Education K-12	68 Teacher Personnel	78 Affirmative Action

Texas School Directory — Harris County

School	Grades	Prog	Enroll	%	Phone
Hamilton Elem Sch 12050 Old Kluge Rd, Cypress 77429 Sage Papaioannou	PK-5		1,083	9%	281/370-0990 Fax 281/320-7067
Hamilton Middle Sch 12330 Kluge Rd, Cypress 77429 Kim Sempe	6-8		1,396 69	21%	281/320-7000 Fax 281/320-7033
Hemmenway Elem Sch 20400 W Little York Rd, Katy 77449 Dr Renee Silliman	PK-5	T	1,062	75%	281/856-9870
Holbrook Elem Sch 6402 Langfield Rd, Houston 77092 Abelardo Lozano	PK-5	T	1,020	71%	713/460-6165 Fax 713/460-7866
Holmsley Elem Sch 7315 Hudson Oaks Dr, Houston 77095 Ana Diaz	PK-5	T	846	64%	281/463-5885 Fax 281/463-5529
Hoover Elem Sch 6425 Greenhouse Rd, Katy 77449 Michelle Rice	PK-2		802		832/667-7301 Fax 832/667-7310
Hopper Middle Sch 7811 Fry Rd, Cypress 77433 Wendi Witthaus	6-8	T	1,352	78%	281/463-5353 Fax 281/463-5354
Horne Elem Sch 14950 W Little York Rd, Houston 77084 Tracey Bennett	PK-5	T	955 60	74%	281/463-5954 Fax 281/856-1451
Jan Aragon Middle Sch 16823 West Rd, Houston 77095 Maria Mamaux	6-8	V	1,603	34%	281/856-5100 Fax 281/856-5105
Jersey Village High Sch 7600 Solomon St, Jersey Vlg 77040 Maggie Wiley	9-12	TV	3,521	54%	713/896-3400 Fax 713/849-6710
Joan Postma Elem Sch 18425 West Rd, Cypress 77433 Terry Bell	PK-5		862	31%	281/345-3660 Fax 281/345-3545
Jowell Elem Sch 6355 Greenhouse Rd, Katy 77449 Kimberly Criswell	3-5	T	786 37	74%	281/463-5966 Fax 281/345-3628
Kahla Middle Sch 16212 W Little York Rd, Houston 77084 Virgil Maddox	6-8	TV	1,348	73%	281/345-3260 Fax 281/856-5275
Keith Elem Sch 20550 Fairfield Green Blvd, Cypress 77433 Dawn Tryon	K-5		1,019	18%	281/213-1744 Fax 281/213-1749
Kirk Elem Sch 12421 Tanner Rd, Houston 77041 Breyanna Bell	PK-5	T	952 50	70%	713/849-8250 Fax 713/849-8255
Labay Middle Sch 15435 Willow River Dr, Houston 77095 Catherine Bellamy	6-8	TV	1,279	59%	281/463-5800 Fax 281/463-5939
Lamkin Elem Sch 11521 Telge Rd, Cypress 77429 Gale Parker	PK-5	T	922 45	56%	281/897-4775 Fax 281/807-8163
Langham Creek High Sch 17610 FM 529 Rd, Houston 77095 David Hughes	9-12	TV	3,126	47%	281/463-5400 Fax 281/345-3509
Lee Elem Sch 12900 W Little York Rd, Houston 77041 Susan Epperson	PK-5	T	884	67%	713/849-8281 Fax 713/849-8249
Lieder Elem Sch 17003 Kieth Harrow Blvd, Houston 77084 Dr Karen Stockton	PK-5	T	913 43	81%	281/463-5928 Fax 281/463-5531
Lowery Elem Sch 15950 Ridge Park Dr, Houston 77095 April Wright	PK-5	T	941	42%	281/463-5900 Fax 281/463-5516
M Robinson Elem Sch 4321 Westfield Village Dr D, Katy 77449 Rocio Braley	PK-5	T	1,140	77%	281/855-1240 Fax 281/855-0740
Matzke Elem Sch 10002 Mills Rd, Houston 77070 Cathy Jacobs	PK-5	T	1,054 45	56%	281/897-4450 Fax 281/897-4454
McFee Elem Sch 19315 Plantation Cove Ln, Katy 77449 Sharon Whitfield	PK-5	T	1,150	78%	281/463-5380 Fax 281/463-5680
Metcalf Elem Sch 6100 Queenston Blvd, Houston 77084 John Steward	PK-5	T	877 50	81%	281/856-1152 Fax 281/856-1154
Millsap Elem Sch 12424 Huffmeister Rd, Cypress 77429 Joy Dauphin	PK-5	T	823 46	49%	281/897-4470 Fax 281/807-8635
Moore Elem Sch 13734 Lakewood Forest Dr, Houston 77070 Patricia Myers	PK-5		838 42	33%	281/370-4040 Fax 281/320-7978
Owens Elem Sch 7939 Jackrabbit Rd, Houston 77095 Amy Frank	PK-5	T	882	67%	281/463-5915 Fax 281/463-5526
Pope Elem Sch 19019 N Bridgeland Lake Pkwy, Cypress 77433 Elizabeth Bradley	K-5		779	5%	281/373-2340 Fax 281/373-2341
Post Elem Sch 7600 Equador St, Houston 77040 Karen Stockton	PK-5	T	1,146 50	67%	713/896-3488 Fax 713/896-3497
Ramona Bang Elem Sch 8900 Rio Grande Dr, Houston 77064 Erwann Wilson	PK-5	T	1,054 44	62%	281/897-4760 Fax 281/517-2095
Reed Elem Sch 8700 Tami Renee Ln, Houston 77040 Cesar Diaz	PK-5	T	1,053 52	74%	713/896-5035 Fax 713/896-5051
Rennell Elem Sch 19500 Tuckerton Rd, Cypress 77433 Meredith Akers	PK-5		818	15%	281/213-1550
Sadie Woodard Elem Sch 17501 Cypress North Houston Rd, Cypress 77433 Susan Brenz	PK-5		1,089	32%	281/373-2303 Fax 281/373-2304
Salyards Middle Sch 21757 Fairfield Place Dr, Cypress 77433 Liz Wood	6-8		1,601		281/373-2400
Sampson Elem Sch 16002 Coles Crossing Dr, Cypress 77429 Heather Motzny	PK-5		972	2%	281/213-1600 Fax 281/213-1605
Sheridan Elem Sch 19790 Kieth Harrow Blvd, Katy 77449 Rene McIntyre	PK-5	T	1,156 60	64%	281/856-1420 Fax 281/856-1461
Smith Middle Sch 10300 Warner Smith Blvd, Cypress 77433 Rebecca Koop	6-8		1,447	10%	281/213-1010 Fax 281/213-1019
Spillane Middle Sch 13403 Woods Spillane Blvd, Cypress 77429 Jamie Brotemarkle	6-8	V	1,592	16%	281/213-1645 Fax 281/213-1799
Swenke Elem Sch 22400 Fairfield Place Dr, Cypress 77433 Elizabeth Miller	PK-5		1,189	7%	281/213-1200
T S Hancock Elem Sch 13801 Schroeder Rd, Houston 77070 Lissa Archuletta	PK-5	T	831 35	67%	281/897-4523 Fax 281/807-8166
Thornton Middle Sch 19802 Kieth Harrow Blvd, Katy 77449 Reginal Mitchell	6-8	TV	1,653	73%	281/856-1500 Fax 281/856-1548
Tipps Elem Sch 5611 Queenston Blvd, Houston 77084 Kari Hough	PK-5	T	1,028	78%	281/345-3350 Fax 281/345-3355
Truitt Middle Sch 6600 Addicks Satsuma Rd, Houston 77084 Yvette Garcia	6-8	TV	1,366	66%	281/856-1100 Fax 281/856-1104

79 Student Personnel
80 Driver Ed/Safety
81 Gifted/Talented
82 Video Services
83 Substance Abuse Prev
84 Erate
85 AIDS Education
88 Alternative/At Risk
89 Multi-Cultural Curriculum
90 Social Work
91 Safety/Security
92 Magnet School
93 Parental Involvement
95 Tech Prep Program
97 Chief Infomation Officer
98 Chief Technology Officer
270 Character Education
271 Migrant Education
273 Teacher Mentor
274 Before/After Sch
275 Response To Intervention
277 Remedial Math K-12
280 Literacy Coach
285 STEM
286 Digital Learning
288 Common Core Standards
294 Accountability
295 Network System
296 Title II Programs
297 Webmaster
298 Grant Writer/Ptnrships
750 Chief Innovation Officer
751 Chief of Staff
752 Social Emotional Learning

Other School Types
Ⓐ = Alternative School
Ⓒ = Charter School
Ⓜ = Magnet School
Ⓨ = Year-Round School

School Programs
A = Alternative Program
G = Adult Classes
M = Magnet Program
T = Title I Schoolwide
V = Career & Tech Ed Programs

Social Media
= Facebook
= Twitter

New Schools are shaded
New Superintendents and Principals are bold
Personnel with email addresses are underscored

TX-185

Harris County

Market Data Retrieval

Walker Elem Sch — PK-5 — T — 952 — 70% — 281/345-3200 — Fax 281/345-3205
6424 Settlers Village Dr, Katy 77449
Kim Dameron

Warner Elem Sch — K-5 — 1,309 — 9% — 281/213-1650 — Fax 281/213-1651
10400 Warner Smith Blvd, Cypress 77433
Schonda Kidd

Watkins Middle Sch — 6-8 — TV — 1,370 — 70% — 281/463-5850 — Fax 281/856-1583
4800 Cairnvillage St, Houston 77084
Dr Jose Martinez

Wells Elem Sch — K-5 — 426 — 832/349-7400 — Fax 832/349-7410
10607 Mason Rd, Cypress 77433
Cheryl Fisher

Willbern Elem Sch — PK-5 — T — 884 — 65% — 281/897-3820 — Fax 281/517-2162
10811 Goodspring Dr, Houston 77064
Connie Roberson

Wilson Elem Sch — PK-5 — T — 947 / 40 — 58% — 281/463-5941 — Fax 281/463-5944
18015 Kieth Harrow Blvd, Houston 77084
Tamera Felder

Ⓐ Windfern High School of Choice — 11-12 — GV — 250 / 23 — 281/807-8684 — Fax 281/807-8693
12630 Windfern Rd, Houston 77064
Martha Strother

Yeager Elem Sch — PK-5 — T — 1,015 / 60 — 58% — 281/440-4914 — Fax 281/587-7531
13615 Champion Forest Dr, Houston 77069
Laura Barrett

- **Deer Park Ind School Dist** PID: 01023316 — 832/668-7000 — Fax 281/930-4638
  2800 Texas Ave, Deer Park 77536

Schools: 16 \ *Teachers:* 827 \ *Students:* 13,000 \
Special Ed Students: 1,367 \ *LEP Students:* 1,480 \ *College-Bound:* 61%
\ *Ethnic:* Asian 1%, African American 3%, Hispanic 56%, Caucasian 40% \ *Exp:* $223 (Med) \ *Poverty:* 15% \ *Title I:* $2,013,166 \
Special Education: $2,187,000 \ *Open-Close:* 08/21 - 05/28 \ *DTBP:* $185 (High) \

Name	#	Name	#
Victor White	1	John Knowlton	2
Pete Pape	2,15	Stacey McDowell	2
Michelle Keener	4	Jeff Greene	5
Darren Chandler	6	Ronda Kouba	8,15,296
Donna Yost	11	Pam McClean	13,58,77,83
Peaches McCroskey	15,68	Stephen Harrell	15,79,91
Barry Talley	20,23	David Berrier	27,31
Michele Deutschendorf	34,60	Kathryn Andrews	39,81
Denise Haynes	42	Becky Stack	45
Cindy Hart	45	Jessica Reyna	48
Lisa Mayer	48*	Misti Mead	60
Lynn Kirkpatrick	67	Kathy Owings	69,294*
Dr Steven Travis	70	Matt Lucas	71
Kari Murphy	73,286,295	Sue Pike	76
Denise Batchelor	88		

Public Schs..Principal	Grd	Prgm	Enr/#Cls	SN		
Deepwater Elem Sch 309 Glenmore Dr, Pasadena 77503 Angie Cabaniss	3-5	T	811 36	67%	832/668-8300 Fax 713/475-6150	
Deepwater Junior High Sch 501 Glenmore Dr, Pasadena 77503 **Rosa Ramos**	6-8	T	657 60	67%	832/668-7600 Fax 713/475-6138	
Deer Park Elem Sch 2920 Luella Ave, Deer Park 77536 Lisa McLaughlin	K-5		762 35	27%	832/668-8000 Fax 281/930-4930	
Deer Park High Sch-N Campus 402 Ivy Ave, Deer Park 77536 **Scott Davis**	9-9		1,073		832/668-7300 Fax 281/930-4840	
Deer Park High Sch-S Campus 710 W San Augustine St, Deer Park 77536 Steve Corry	10-12	GTV	2,647	38%	832/668-7200 Fax 281/930-4894	
Deer Park Junior High Sch 410 E 9th St, Deer Park 77536 Dr Tiffany Regan	6-8		880	28%	832/668-7500 Fax 281/930-4726	
Ⓐ Deerpark HS Wolters Campus 204 Ivy Ave, Deer Park 77536 Clyde Skarke	9-12		153 18		832/668-7400 Fax 281/930-0525	
Ⓐ Disciplinary Alt Ed Program 601 E 8th St, Deer Park 77536 Roy Adams	6-12		25 2		832/668-7407 Fax 281/930-0064	
Early Childhood Center 401 Glenmore Dr, Pasadena 77503 Jenny Sisco-Martinez	PK-PK	T	411	58%	832/668-8390 Fax 832/668-8395	
Fairmont Elem Sch 4315 Heathfield Dr, Pasadena 77505 Lea Boswell	K-5		828 42	22%	832/668-8500 Fax 281/998-4411	
Fairmont Junior High Sch 4911 Holly Bay Ct, Pasadena 77505 Neil Munro	6-8	T	699 42	33%	832/668-7800 Fax 281/998-4456	
J P Bonnette Jr High Sch 5010 W Pasadena Blvd, Deer Park 77536 John Wegman	6-8	TV	813 55	45%	832/668-7700 Fax 281/930-4756	
J P Dabbs Elem Sch 302 E Lambuth Ln, Deer Park 77536 Mandy Davis	K-5		681 45	48%	832/668-8100 Fax 281/930-4910	
Parkwood Elem Sch 404 Parkwood Dr, Pasadena 77503 Debbie Yampey	K-2	T	645 45	66%	832/668-8200 Fax 713/475-6180	
San Jacinto Elem Sch 1302 E 13th St, Deer Park 77536 Robin Evans	K-5	T	905 31	37%	832/668-7900 Fax 281/930-4950	
W A Carpenter Elem Sch 5002 W Pasadena Blvd, Deer Park 77536 Suzanne Holcomb	K-5	T	853 42	39%	832/668-8400 Fax 281/930-4970	

- **Galena Park Ind School Dist** PID: 01023419 — 832/386-1000 — Fax 832/386-1100
  14705 Woodforest Blvd, Houston 77015

Schools: 27 \ *Teachers:* 1,401 \ *Students:* 24,000 \
Special Ed Students: 1,963 \ *LEP Students:* 6,829 \ *College-Bound:* 55%
\ *Ethnic:* Asian 1%, African American 4%, Hispanic 78%, Caucasian 5% \ *Exp:* $340 (High) \ *Poverty:* 27% \ *Title I:* $8,139,067 \
Special Education: $3,758,000 \ *Open-Close:* 08/21 - 05/28 \ *DTBP:* $185 (High) \

Name	#	Name	#
Dr Angi Williams	1	Sonya George	2,15,19
Emory Ellis	3	Brian Aubin	4
Kenneth Bush	5	Vivian Dancy	6,50
Elizabeth Lalor	8,15	Amy Cole	11,298
Jonathan Moore	15*	Terri Moore	15,71,74
Dr Wanna Giacona	15,68	Sam Harris	20,23
Laura Mann	27,31	Veronica Martinez	57
Wanda Heath-Johnson	67	Dolly Mayeaux	69,294
Michelle Young	73	Kareen Brown	81
Bryan Clements	91	Nicole Johns	275

Public Schs..Principal	Grd	Prgm	Enr/#Cls	SN		
Ⓐ Accelerated Center for Ed 13801 Hollypark Dr, Houston 77015 Julien Guillory	9-12		9 8		832/386-3672 Fax 832/386-3671	
Ⓐ Center for Success 13801 Hollypark Dr, Houston 77015 Sherrhonda Johnson	6-12		70 6		832/386-3637 Fax 832/386-3631	
Cimarron Elem Sch 816 Cimarron St, Houston 77015 Cynthia Galaviz	PK-5	AT	749 63	86%	832/386-3240 Fax 832/386-3241	

1	Superintendent	8	Curric/Instruct K-12	19	Chief Financial Officer	29	Family/Consumer Science	39	Social Studies K-12	49	English/Lang Arts Elem	59	Special Education Elem	69	Academic Assessment
2	Bus/Finance/Purchasing	9	Curric/Instruct Elem	20	Art K-12	30	Adult Education	40	Social Studies Elem	50	English/Lang Arts Sec	60	Special Education Sec	70	Research/Development
3	Buildings And Grounds	10	Curric/Instruct Sec	21	Art Elem	31	Career/Sch-to-Work K-12	41	Social Studies Sec	51	Reading K-12	61	Foreign/World Lang K-12	71	Public Information
4	Food Service	11	Federal Program	22	Art Sec	32	Career/Sch-to-Work Elem	42	Science K-12	52	Reading Elem	62	Foreign/World Lang Elem	72	Summer School
5	Transportation	12	Title I	23	Music K-12	33	Career/Sch-to-Work Sec	43	Science Elem	53	Reading Sec	63	Foreign/World Lang Sec	73	Instructional Tech
6	Athletic	13	Title V	24	Music Elem	34	Early Childhood Ed	44	Science Sec	54	Remedial Reading K-12	64	Religious Education K-12	74	Inservice Training
7	Health Services	15	Asst Superintendent	25	Music Sec	35	Health/Phys Education	45	Math K-12	55	Remedial Reading Elem	65	Religious Education Elem	75	Marketing/Distributive
		16	Instructional Media Svcs	26	Business Education	36	Guidance Services K-12	46	Math Elem	56	Remedial Reading Sec	66	Religious Education Sec	76	Info Systems
		17	Chief Operations Officer	27	Career & Tech Ed	37	Guidance Services Elem	47	Math Sec	57	Bilingual/ELL	67	School Board President	77	Psychological Assess
		18	Chief Academic Officer	28	Technology Education	38	Guidance Services Sec	48	English/Lang Arts K-12	58	Special Education K-12	68	Teacher Personnel	78	Affirmative Action

Texas School Directory — Harris County

School	Grd	Prgm	Enr/#Cls	SN	Phone
Cloverleaf Elem Sch 1035 Frankie St, Houston 77015 Lee Brown	PK-5	T	836 49	91%	832/386-3200 Fax 832/386-3201
Cobb Sixth Grade Campus 6722 Uvalde Rd, Houston 77049 Adrian Hurtado	6-6	T	1,142 60	80%	832/386-2100 Fax 832/386-2101
Dr Shirley J Williamson ES 6720 New Forest Pkwy, Houston 77049 Dr Jonathan Sutton	PK-5	T	688	71%	832/386-4000 Fax 832/386-4025
Galena Park Cte Early Clg HS 5800 Uvalde Rd Bldg N, Houston 77049 Jeff Hutchinson	9-12	V	125		281/459-7198 Fax 281/459-7113
Galena Park Elem Sch 401 N Main St, Galena Park 77547 Jaime Rocha	PK-5	T	603 50	88%	832/386-1670 Fax 832/386-1692
Galena Park High Sch 1000 Keene St, Galena Park 77547 Kimberly Martin	9-12	GTV	2,016 80	78%	832/386-2800 Fax 832/386-2802
Galena Park Middle Sch 400 Keene St, Galena Park 77547 Lee Ramirez	6-8	TV	1,013	86%	832/386-1700 Fax 832/386-1738
Green Valley Elem Sch 13350 Woodforest Blvd, Houston 77015 Grace Devost	PK-5	T	763 55	90%	832/386-4390 Fax 832/386-4391
Jacinto City Elem Sch 10910 Wiggins St, Houston 77029 Becky Gardea	PK-5	T	784 49	86%	832/386-4600 Fax 832/386-4601
James B Havard Elem Sch 15150 Wallisville Rd, Houston 77049 Lisa Hamblen	PK-5	T	690 43	65%	832/386-3710 Fax 832/386-3711
MacArthur Elem Sch 1801 N Main St, Galena Park 77547 Maria Munoz	PK-5	T	768 45	88%	832/386-4630 Fax 832/386-4631
Normandy Crossing Elem Sch 12500 Normandy Crossing Dr, Houston 77015 Irene Benzor	PK-5	T	664 50	78%	832/386-1600 Fax 832/386-1642
North Shore 10th Grade Ctr 353 N Castlegory Rd # 3, Houston 77049 Kenneth Bryant	10-10	V	1,072		832/386-4880 Fax 832/386-4881
North Shore Elem Sch 14310 Duncannon Dr, Houston 77015 Esmeralda Perez	PK-5	T	969 55	89%	832/386-4660 Fax 832/386-4661
North Shore Middle Sch 120 Castlegory Rd, Houston 77015 Dr Christopher Eckford	7-8	TV	1,406	77%	832/386-2600 Fax 832/386-2643
North Shore Ninth Grade Center 13501 Hollypark Dr, Houston 77015 David Pierson	9-9	AV	1,166 50		832/386-3400 Fax 832/386-3401
North Shore Senior High Sch 353 N Castlegory Rd, Houston 77049 Dr Joe Coleman	11-12	TV	2,500	72%	832/386-4100 Fax 832/386-4101
Purple Sage Elem Sch 6500 Purple Sage Rd, Houston 77049 Wendy McGee	PK-5	T	548	84%	832/386-3100 Fax 832/386-3106
Pyburn Elem Sch 12302 Coulson St, Houston 77015 Conrad Rivera	PK-5	T	653 27	86%	832/386-3150 Fax 832/386-3168
Sam Houston Elem Sch 4101 E Sam Houston Pkwy N, Houston 77015 Michelle Cavazos	PK-5	T	837 48	92%	832/386-4430 Fax 832/386-4431
Tice Elem Sch 14120 Wallisville Rd, Houston 77049 Toshia Gouard	PK-5	T	690 50	83%	832/386-4050 Fax 832/386-4053
W C Cunningham Middle Sch 14110 Wallisville Rd, Houston 77049 Shaunte Morris	7-8	TV	988	81%	832/386-4470 Fax 832/386-4471
Woodland Acres Elem Sch 12936 Sarahs Ln, Houston 77015 Sandra Rodriguez	PK-5	T	469 50	79%	832/386-2220 Fax 832/386-2221
Woodland Acres Middle Sch 12947 Myrtle Ln, Houston 77015 **Manuel Escalante**	6-8	TV	534 40	84%	832/386-4700 Fax 832/386-4701

● **Goose Creek Cons Ind Sch Dist** PID: 01023562   281/420-4800
4544 I-10 E, Baytown 77521   Fax 281/420-4854

Schools: 28 \ *Teachers:* 1,482 \ *Students:* 24,000 \
Special Ed Students: 2,420 \ *LEP Students:* 3,281 \ *College-Bound:* 75%
\ *Ethnic:* Asian 2%, African American 16%, Hispanic 63%, Caucasian 20% \ *Exp:* $315 (High) \ *Poverty:* 19% \ *Title I:* $6,048,362 \
Special Education: $4,219,000 \ *Open-Close:* 08/13 - 05/20 \ *DTBP:* $181 (High) \

Randal O'Brien	1	Joseph Villalba	2
Margie Grimes	2,19	Renea Dobbs	2
Herb Mimyard	3	Natalie Edwards	4
Rick Walterscheid	5	Bernard Mulvaney	6
Patricia Pina	7	Becky Robins	8
Dr Melissa Duarte	8,15,296	Ginger McKay	11,298
Anthony Price	15	Eloy Chapa	15,68
Renae Dillon	27,92*	Dr Precious Reimoneng	31,36
Karen Coffey	34,88	Faith Longorio	39
Kevin Wrobleski	42	Pilar Moreno-Recio	57
Janna Crow	58,77	Natalie Hudson	58
Augustine Loredo	67	Ron Wyatt	68
Tyrone Sylvester	68	David Yannotta	69,294
Susan Passmore	71	Matt Flood	73,76,98
Steve Koester	73,286	Christi Leath	74,81,273
Araceli Delacruz	79	Lisa Vaughan	90
Tony Alfaro	91	Jane Paris	271
Cheryl Parker	274	Lindsey Marek	285*
Mima Trujillo	297		

Public Schs..Principal	Grd	Prgm	Enr/#Cls	SN	Phone
Alamo Elem Sch 6100 N Main St, Baytown 77521 Andrea Zepeda	PK-5	T	746 25	69%	281/420-4595 Fax 281/420-4905
Ashbel Smith Elem Sch 403 E James St, Baytown 77520 Katherine Cruz	PK-5	T	784 40	83%	281/420-4615 Fax 281/420-4940
Baytown Junior High Sch 7707 Bayway Dr, Baytown 77520 Brian Aiken	6-8	TV	966 55	75%	281/420-4560 Fax 281/420-4908
Bonnie P Hopper Primary Sch 405 E Houston St, Highlands 77562 Maria Rosas	PK-1	T	527 30	67%	281/420-4685 Fax 281/426-5179
Cedar Bayou Junior High Sch 2610 Elvinta St, Baytown 77520 Michael Curl	6-8	TV	1,052 60	69%	281/420-4570 Fax 281/420-4569
David Crockett Elem Sch 4500 Barkaloo Rd, Baytown 77521 Michelle James	PK-5	T	681 35	63%	281/420-4645 Fax 281/420-4649
Dr Antonio Banuelos Elem Sch 7770 Eastpoint Blvd, Baytown 77521 Renee Meyer	PK-5	T	851	57%	281/420-1230 Fax 281/421-3480
Dr Johnny T Clark Jr Elem Sch 6033 N Highway 146, Baytown 77523 Kemberly Scheidt	PK-5		675		281/420-7450
George H Gentry Jr High Sch 1919 E Archer Rd, Baytown 77521 Kathryn Holland	6-8	TV	1,082 47	49%	281/420-4590 Fax 281/420-4909
George W Carver Elem Sch 600 S Pruett St, Baytown 77520 **Angela Mancini**	PK-5	T	736 50	85%	281/420-4600 Fax 281/420-4983

79 Student Personnel	91 Safety/Security	275 Response To Intervention	298 Grant Writer/Ptnrships	**School Programs**
80 Driver Ed/Safety	92 Magnet School	277 Remedial Math K-12	750 Chief Innovation Officer	A = Alternative Program
81 Gifted/Talented	93 Parental Involvement	280 Literacy Coach	751 Chief of Staff	G = Adult Classes
82 Video Services	95 Tech Prep Program	285 STEM	752 Social Emotional Learning	M = Magnet Program
83 Substance Abuse Prev	97 Chief Infomation Officer	286 Digital Learning		T = Title I Schoolwide
84 Erate	98 Chief Technology Officer	288 Common Core Standards	**Other School Types**	V = Career & Tech Ed Programs
85 AIDS Education	270 Accountability	294 Accountability	Ⓐ = Alternative School	
86 Alternative/At Risk	271 Migrant Education	295 Network System	Ⓒ = Charter School	New Schools are shaded
89 Multi-Cultural Curriculum	273 Teacher Mentor	296 Title II Programs	Ⓜ = Magnet School	New Superintendents and Principals are bold
90 Social Work	274 Before/After Sch	297 Webmaster	Ⓨ = Year-Round School	Personnel with email addresses are underscored

Social Media
 = Facebook
 = Twitter

TX—187

Harris County

Market Data Retrieval

School	Grades	Prgm	Enr/#Cls	SN	Phone
Goose Creek Memorial High Sch 6001 E Wallisville Rd, Baytown 77521 Susan Jackson	9-12	T	2,167	48%	281/421-4400 Fax 281/421-4444
Harlem Elem Sch 3333 I-10, Baytown 77521 Betty Baca	PK-5	T	649 75	84%	281/420-4910 Fax 281/426-5358
Highlands Elem Sch 200 E Wallisville Rd, Highlands 77562 Blanca Capetillo	2-5	T	826 42	67%	281/420-4900 Fax 281/426-5099
Highlands Junior High Sch 1212 E Wallisville Rd, Highlands 77562 Gary Guy	6-8	TV	1,136 33	51%	281/420-4695 Fax 281/426-4301
Horace Mann Junior High Sch 310 S Highway 146, Baytown 77520 Christie Speights	6-8	TV	984	83%	281/420-4585 Fax 281/420-4664
Impact Early College High Sch 1415 Market St, Baytown 77520 Laura Reyes	9-12		385		281/420-4802 Fax 832/556-5781
James Bowie Elem Sch 2200 Clayton Dr, Baytown 77520 Regina Patrick-Sims	PK-5	T	851 37	71%	281/420-4605 Fax 281/420-4609
John M Stuart Career Tech HS 300 W Wye Dr, Baytown 77521 Dr Cap Roder	Voc		450 16		281/420-4550 Fax 281/420-4553
Lorenzo De Zavala Elem Sch 305 Tri City Beach Rd, Baytown 77520 Theresa Keel	PK-5	T	804 46	77%	281/420-4920 Fax 281/420-4342
Miraibeau B Lamar Elem Sch 816 N Pruett St, Baytown 77520 **Maria Rosas Gonzalez**	PK-5	T	699 75	86%	281/420-4625 Fax 281/420-4626
Ⓐ Peter E Hyland Center 1906 Decker Dr, Baytown 77520 Michelle Verdun	9-12	T	150 11	61%	281/420-4555 Fax 281/420-4629
Ⓐ Point Alternative Center 401 Jones Rd, Highlands 77562 Tricia Times	6-12		75	67%	281/420-4630 Fax 281/420-2680
Robert E Lee High Sch 1809 Market St, Baytown 77520 Joseph Farnsworth	9-12	TV	1,548	75%	281/420-4535 Fax 281/420-4548
Ross S Sterling High Sch 300 W Baker Rd, Baytown 77521 Nathan Chaddick	9-12	TV	2,401	53%	281/420-4500 Fax 281/420-4974
San Jacinto Elem Sch 2615 Virginia St, Baytown 77520 Rachel McAdam	PK-5	T	482 35	81%	281/420-4670 Fax 281/420-4599
Stephen F Austin Elem Sch 3022 Massey Tompkins Rd, Baytown 77521 Michelle Duhon	PK-5	T	763 44	55%	281/420-4620 Fax 281/420-4899
Victoria Walker Elem Sch 4711 Seabird St, Baytown 77521 Monica Juarez	PK-5	T	868	41%	281/421-1800 Fax 281/421-3489
William B Travis Elem Sch 100 Robin Rd, Baytown 77520 Adrienne Tessar	PK-5	T	869 44	67%	281/420-4660 Fax 281/420-4986

• Houston Ind School Dist   PID: 01023770
4400 W 18th St, Houston 77092

713/556-6000
Fax 713/556-6323

Schools: 275 \
Teachers: 11,546 \ **Students:** 206,052 \ **Special Ed Students:** 15,455 \ **LEP Students:** 61,671 \ **College-Bound:** 75% \ **Ethnic:** Asian 4%, African American 24%, Hispanic 63%, Caucasian 9% \ **Exp:** $262 (Med) \ **Poverty:** 28% \ **Title I:** $124,530,413 \ **Special Education:** $38,873,000 \ **Bilingual Education:** $223,000 \ **Open-Close:** 08/26 - 05/29 \ **DTBP:** $198 (High) \

Dr Grenita Lathan 1
Eugene Salzar 2
Alishia Jolivette 3
Betti Wiggins 4
Gwen Johnson 7
Margarita Gardea 9
Pamela Evans 11,296
Anna White 15,57
Dr Lachlin Verrett 15,58
Adrian Acosta 16
Cynthia Nemons 36
Dr Hortense Campbell 44
Alyssa Howell 47
Rhonda Skillern-Jones 67
Rebecca Suarez 71,77,97
Lorenzo Moore 77
Malene Golding 280
Angela Brooks 298

Alexis Licata 2,78
Rene Barajas 2,19
Brian Busby 3,17
Andre Walker 6
Cicely Williams 8
Dr Montra Rogers 10
Wanda Thomas 11
Kennith Davis 15,74,273
Silvia Trinh 15,751
Michiel Rozas 34
Donelle Williams 43
Nalsy Perez 46
Marisa Hartling 53
Julia Dimmitt 68
Lenny Schad 73,76,98,295
Paul Cordova 91
Rene Flores 285
Dr Roberta Scott 752

• Houston ISD-Achieve 180   PID: 12310958
400 W 18th St, Houston 77008

713/556-7102

Felicia Adams 15

Public Schs..Principal	Grd	Prgm	Enr/#Cls	SN	Phone
A G Hilliard Elem Sch 8115 E Houston Rd, Houston 77028 Erika Kimble	PK-5		531 30		713/635-3085 Fax 713/635-7905
Ⓜ Attucks Middle Sch 4330 Bellfort St, Houston 77051 Shani Wyllie	6-8	TV	464 50	82%	713/732-3670 Fax 713/732-3677
Ⓜ B T Washington High Sch 4204 Yale St, Houston 77018 Carlos Phillips	9-12	TV	758	73%	713/696-6600 Fax 713/696-6657
Blackshear Elem Sch 2900 Holman St, Houston 77004 Alicia Lewis	PK-5	T	418 35	94%	713/942-1481 Fax 713/942-1486
Blanche K Bruce Elem Sch 510 Jensen Dr, Houston 77020 Shawn Nickerson	PK-5	T	495 30	98%	713/226-4560 Fax 713/226-4562
Cullen Middle Sch 6900 Scott St, Houston 77021 Jacqueline Thompson	6-8	TV	352 52	76%	713/746-8180 Fax 713/746-8181
Deady Middle Sch 2500 Broadway St, Houston 77012 Opal Harrison	6-8	TV	669	98%	713/845-7411 Fax 713/649-5645
Dogan Elem Sch 4202 Liberty Rd, Houston 77026 **Margarita Tovar**	PK-5	T	607 35	86%	713/671-4110 Fax 713/671-4142
Foerster Elem Sch 14200 Fonmeadow Dr, Houston 77035 Latreia Woodard	PK-5	T	723 44	96%	713/726-3604 Fax 713/726-3629
Fondren Elem Sch 12405 Carlsbad St, Houston 77085 Tabitha Dudley	PK-5	T	314 30	90%	713/726-3611 Fax 713/726-3646
Forest Brook Middle Sch 7525 Tidwell Rd, Houston 77016 Tannisha Gentry	6-8	T	828	88%	713/631-7720 Fax 713/636-4114
Gregory-Lincoln Education Ctr 1101 Taft St, Houston 77019 **Angel Wilson**	PK-8	AT	740 30	85%	713/942-1400 Fax 713/942-1406
High School Ahead Acad MS 5320 Yale St, Houston 77091 Ericka Austin	6-8	T	205	98%	713/696-2643 Fax 713/696-2999
© Highland Heights Elem Sch 865 Paul Quinn St, Houston 77091 **John Flowers**	PK-5	T	517 25	87%	713/696-2920 Fax 713/696-2922

TX-188

1 Superintendent	8 Curric/Instruct K-12	19 Chief Financial Officer	29 Family/Consumer Science	39 Social Studies K-12	49 English/Lang Arts Elem	59 Special Education Elem	69 Academic Assessment
2 Bus/Finance/Purchasing	9 Curric/Instruct Elem	20 Art K-12	30 Adult Education	40 Social Studies Elem	50 English/Lang Arts Sec	60 Special Education Sec	70 Research/Development
3 Buildings And Grounds	10 Curric/Instruct Sec	21 Art Elem	31 Career/Sch-to-Work K-12	41 Social Studies Sec	51 Reading K-12	61 Foreign/World Lang K-12	71 Public Information
4 Food Service	11 Federal Program	22 Art Sec	32 Career/Sch-to-Work Elem	42 Science K-12	52 Reading Elem	62 Foreign/World Lang Elem	72 Summer School
5 Transportation	12 Title I	23 Music K-12	33 Career/Sch-to-Work Sec	43 Science Elem	53 Reading Sec	63 Foreign/World Lang Sec	73 Instructional Tech
6 Athletic	13 Title V	24 Music Elem	34 Early Childhood Ed	44 Science Sec	54 Remedial Reading K-12	64 Religious Education K-12	74 Inservice Training
7 Health Services	15 Asst Superintendent	25 Music Sec	35 Health/Phys Education	45 Math K-12	55 Remedial Reading Elem	65 Religious Education Elem	75 Marketing/Distributive
	16 Instructional Media Svcs	26 Business Education	36 Guidance Services K-12	46 Math Elem	56 Remedial Reading Sec	66 Religious Education Sec	76 Info Systems
	17 Chief Operations Officer	27 Career & Tech Ed	37 Guidance Services Elem	47 Math Sec	57 Bilingual/ELL	67 School Board President	77 Psychological Assess
	18 Chief Academic Officer	28 Technology Education	38 Guidance Services Sec	48 English/Lang Arts K-12	58 Special Education K-12	68 Teacher Personnel	78 Affirmative Action

Texas School Directory — Harris County

School	Grd	Prgm	Enr/#Cls	SN	Phone
Holland Middle Sch 1600 Gellhorn Dr, Houston 77029 **Pablo Resendiz**	6-8	T	673	82%	713/671-3860 Fax 713/671-3874
James Butler Bonham Elem Sch 8302 Braes River Dr, Houston 77074 Erica Tran	PK-5	T	945 70	98%	713/778-3480 Fax 713/778-3482
Ⓜ Kashmere High Sch 6900 Wileyvale Rd, Houston 77028 Reginald Bush	9-12	GTV	777	87%	713/636-6400 Fax 713/636-6433
L L Pugh Elem Sch 1147 Kress St, Houston 77020 Jorge Ortiz	PK-5	T	390 18	93%	713/671-3820 Fax 713/671-3825
Lawson Middle Sch 14000 Stancliff St, Houston 77045 Kasey Bailey	6-8	TV	1,210 70	81%	713/434-5600 Fax 713/434-5608
Ⓒ Liberty High Sch 6400 SW Fwy Ste A, Houston 77036 Monico Rivas	9-12		361		713/458-5555 Fax 713/458-5567
Looscan Elem Sch 3800 Robertson St, Houston 77009 Alvaro Montelongo	PK-5	T	326 21	91%	713/696-2760 Fax 713/696-2765
Ⓒ M C Williams Middle Sch 6100 Knox St, Houston 77091 Roshanda Griffin	6-8	TV	496	91%	713/696-2600 Fax 713/696-2604
Ⓒ Mabel B Wesley Elem Sch 800 Dillard St, Houston 77091 **Thomas Cotter**	PK-5	T	344 40	98%	713/696-2860 Fax 713/696-2866
Mading Elem Sch 8511 Crestmont St, Houston 77033 Nicole Haskins	PK-5	T	433 27	95%	713/732-3560 Fax 713/732-3563
Madison High Sch 13719 White Heather Dr, Houston 77045 Carlotta Brown	9-12	TV	1,736 80	75%	713/433-9801 Fax 713/434-5242
Montgomery Elem Sch 4000 Simsbrook Dr, Houston 77045 Dr Faye McNeil	PK-5	T	551 45	95%	713/434-5640 Fax 713/434-5643
North Forest High Sch 10726 Mesa Dr, Houston 77078 Connie Smith	9-12	TV	993	73%	713/636-4300 Fax 713/636-8116
Patrick Henry Middle Sch 10702 E Hardy Rd, Houston 77093 **Jason Davila**	6-8	TV	829 72	98%	713/696-2650 Fax 713/696-2657
Sharpstown High Sch 7504 Bissonnet St, Houston 77074 Daniel De Leon	9-12	TV	1,689	94%	713/771-7215 Fax 713/773-6103
Stevens Elem Sch 1910 La Monte Ln, Houston 77018 Erin Trent	PK-5	T	648 40	94%	713/613-2546 Fax 713/613-2541
Sugar Grove Academy 8405 Bonhomme Rd, Houston 77074 Orlando Reyna	6-8	T	678 40	86%	713/271-0214 Fax 713/771-9342
Ⓒ Texas Connections Academy [181] 10550 Richmond Ave Ste 140, Houston 77042 Catherine Sullivant \ Brita Lindsey	3-12	T	5,680	40%	281/661-8293 Fax 281/754-4813
Wheatley High Sch 4801 Providence St, Houston 77020 Joseph Williams	9-12	TV	873 70	70%	713/671-3900 Fax 713/671-3951
Woodson PK-5 Sch 10720 Southview St, Houston 77047 Stephen Gittens	PK-5	T	643 200	87%	713/732-3600 Fax 713/732-3606
Ⓜ Worthing High Sch 9215 Scott St, Houston 77051 Dr Khalilah Campbell-Rhone	9-12	TV	781 67	74%	713/733-3433 Fax 713/731-5537
Ⓜ Yates High Sch 3703 Sampson St, Houston 77004 Tiffany Guillory	9-12	TV	874 80	62%	713/748-5400 Fax 713/746-8206
Ⓒ Young Scholars Acad Excellence 1809 Louisiana St, Houston 77002 Anella Coleman	PK-8	T	129 15	75%	713/654-1404 Fax 713/654-1401

● **Houston ISD-East Area** PID: 12170253   713/556-8998
4400 W 18th St, Houston 77092

Geovanny Ponce 15

Public Schs..Principal	Grd	Prgm	Enr/#Cls	SN	Phone
Austin High Sch 1700 Dumble St, Houston 77023 Steve Guerrero	9-12	TV	1,685	92%	713/924-1600 Fax 713/923-3157
Bonner Elem Sch 8100 Elrod St, Houston 77017 Klinger Casquete	PK-5	T	790 55	90%	713/943-5740 Fax 713/943-5741
Briscoe Elem Sch 321 Forest Hill Blvd, Houston 77011 Daniel Hernandez	PK-5	T	262 43	82%	713/924-1740 Fax 713/924-1742
Burnet Elem Sch 5403 Canal St, Houston 77011 Ana Cantu	PK-5	T	486 40	96%	713/924-1780 Fax 713/924-1783
Ⓒ Cage Charter Elem Sch 4528 Leeland St, Houston 77023 **Dr Lisa Patenotte**	PK-5	T	520 40	90%	713/924-1700 Fax 713/924-1704
Carrillo Elem Sch 960 S Wayside Dr, Houston 77023 Mary Hallinan	PK-5	T	492 40	86%	713/924-1870 Fax 713/924-1873
Charles H Milby High Sch 1601 Broadway St, Houston 77012 Ruth Ruiz	9-12	GV	1,903		713/928-7401 Fax 713/928-7474
Chavez High Sch 8501 Howard Dr, Houston 77017 Luis Landa	9-12	TV	2,882	81%	713/495-6950 Fax 713/495-6988
Ⓜ Crespo Elem Sch 7500 Office City Dr, Houston 77012 Mayra Ramon	PK-5	T	766 40	93%	713/845-7492 Fax 713/645-4706
Davila Elem Sch 7610 Dahlia St, Houston 77012 Berzayda Ochoa	PK-5	T	403 52	93%	713/924-1851 Fax 713/924-1853
De Zavala Elem Sch 7521 Avenue H, Houston 77012 Victoria Martinez	PK-5	T	542 36	89%	713/924-1888 Fax 713/924-1891
East Early College High Sch 220 N Milby St, Houston 77003 Stephanie Square	9-12	T	476	89%	713/847-4809 Fax 713/847-4813
Ⓒ Eastwood Academy 1315 Dumble St, Houston 77023 Brandi Lira	9-12	T	432 14	83%	713/924-1697 Fax 713/923-3157
Edison Middle Sch 6901 Avenue I, Houston 77011 Karina Lopez	6-8	TV	654 33	95%	713/924-1800 Fax 713/924-1316
Franklin Elem Sch 7101 Canal St, Houston 77011 Tammie Moran	PK-5	T	431 50	96%	713/924-1820 Fax 713/924-1823
Furr High Sch 520 Mercury Dr, Houston 77013 Steven Stapleton	9-12	TV	1,035 55	94%	713/675-1118 Fax 713/671-3612
Gallegos Elem Sch 7415 Harrisburg Blvd, Houston 77011 Dr Alejandro Gonzalez	PK-5	T	357 35	96%	713/924-1830 Fax 713/924-1833
Ⓐ High School for Law & Justice Ⓜ 3505 Coyle St, Houston 77003 **Stacy Garcia**	9-12	T	469 49	75%	713/867-5100 Fax 713/802-4600
J Henderson Elem Sch 1800 Dismuke St, Houston 77023 Maria Guerra	PK-5	T	783 45	86%	713/924-1730 Fax 713/924-1735

---

79 Student Personnel	91 Safety/Security	275 Response To Intervention	298 Grant Writer/Ptnrships	**School Programs**
80 Driver Ed/Safety	92 Magnet School	277 Remedial Math K-12	750 Chief Innovation Officer	A = Alternative Program
81 Gifted/Talented	93 Parental Involvement	280 Literacy Coach	751 Chief of Staff	G = Adult Classes
82 Video Services	95 Tech Prep Program	285 STEM	752 Social Emotional Learning	M = Magnet Program
83 Substance Abuse Prev	97 Chief Infomation Officer	286 Digital Learning		T = Title I Schoolwide
84 Erate	98 Chief Technology Officer	288 Common Core Standards	**Other School Types**	V = Career & Tech Ed Programs
85 AIDS Education	270 Character Education	294 Accountability	Ⓐ = Alternative Program	
88 Alternative/At Risk	271 Migrant Education	295 Network System	Ⓒ = Charter School	**Social Media**
89 Multi-Cultural Curriculum	273 Teacher Mentor	296 Title II Programs	Ⓜ = Magnet School	ⓕ = Facebook
90 Social Work	274 Before/After Sch	297 Webmaster	Ⓨ = Year-Round School	ⓣ = Twitter

New Schools are shaded
New Superintendents and Principals are bold
Personnel with email addresses are underscored

Harris County

School	Grd	Prgm	Enr/#Cls	%	Phone
J R Harris Elem Sch 801 Broadway St, Houston 77012 Judith Garcia	PK-5	T	411 37	90%	713/924-1860 Fax 713/924-1863
Judson Robinson Elem Sch 12425 Wood Forest Dr, Houston 77013 Ana Aguilar	PK-5	T	521	86%	713/450-7107 Fax 713/450-7129
Lantrip Elem Sch 100 Telephone Rd, Houston 77023 Magdalena Strickland	PK-5	T	720 45	81%	713/924-1670 Fax 713/924-1672
Laurenzo ECC 205 N Delmar St, Houston 77011 Maria Lopez-Rogina	PK-K		344 14	96%	713/924-0350 Fax 713/924-0390
Lewis Elem Sch 6745 Tipperary Dr, Houston 77061 Jorge Rodriguez	1-5	T	791 45	77%	713/845-7453 Fax 713/649-5574
ⓐ Middle College at HCC Fraga 301 N Drennan St, Houston 77003 Jose Santos	9-12		128		713/228-3408 Fax 713/228-3418
ⓐ Middle College at HCC Gulfton 5407 Gulfton St Ste 219, Houston 77081 Holly Gibson	9-12		162		713/662-2551 Fax 713/662-2572
ⓐ Mount Carmel Academy ⓒ 7155 Ashburn St, Houston 77061 Maureen Giacchino	9-12	T	340	72%	713/643-2008 Fax 713/645-0078
Navarro Mid Sch 5100 Polk St, Houston 77023 Kelly Vaughn	6-8	TV	682	86%	713/924-1760 Fax 713/924-1768
Oates Elem Sch 10044 Wallisville Rd, Houston 77013 Melissa Melchor	PK-5	T	386 22	93%	713/671-3800 Fax 713/671-3803
Ortiz Middle Sch 6767 Telephone Rd, Houston 77061 Marlen Martinez	6-8	T	1,067	91%	713/845-5650 Fax 713/845-5646
Park Place Elem Sch 8235 Park Place Blvd, Houston 77017 Gerardo Leal	PK-5	T	951 45	94%	713/845-7458 Fax 713/845-7460
Patterson Elem Sch 5302 Allendale Rd, Houston 77017 Juan Gonzalez	PK-5	T	931 55	90%	713/943-5750 Fax 713/943-5755
Pleasantville Elem Sch 1431 Gellhorn Dr, Houston 77029 Gwendolyn Hunter	PK-5	T	266 31	95%	713/671-3840 Fax 713/671-3844
Port Houston Elem Sch 1800 McCarty St, Houston 77029 Victor Garcia	PK-5	T	292 18	98%	713/671-3890 Fax 713/671-3893
Project Chrysalis Middle Sch 4528 Leeland St, Houston 77023 Dr Lisa Rodriguez	6-8	T	279	88%	713/924-1700
R P Harris Elem Sch 1262 Mae Dr, Houston 77015 Erica Avie	PK-5	T	569	88%	713/450-7100 Fax 713/450-7103
Rucker Elem Sch 5201 Vinett Ave, Houston 77017 Eileen Puente	PK-5	T	428 50	90%	713/845-7467 Fax 713/645-0004
Sanchez Elem Sch 2700 Berkley St, Houston 77012 Emeterio Cruz	PK-5	T	581 50	96%	713/845-7472 Fax 713/649-5749
Southmayd Elem Sch 1800 Coral St, Houston 77012 Sandra Cisneros	PK-5	T	581 32	94%	713/924-1720 Fax 713/924-1722
Tijerina Elem Sch 6501 Sherman St, Houston 77011 Alesander Fernandez	PK-5	T	342 45	92%	713/924-1790 Fax 713/924-1792
W I Stevenson Middle Sch 9595 Winkler Dr, Houston 77017 Christyn McCloskey	6-8	T	1,446 80	92%	713/943-5700 Fax 713/943-5711
Whittier Elem Sch 10511 La Crosse St, Houston 77029 Lori Lueptow	PK-5	T	526 38	89%	713/671-3810 Fax 713/671-3812

● **Houston ISD-North Area** PID: 12170239   713/556-8998
4400 W 18th St, Houston 77092

Yolanda Rodriguez 15

Public Schs..Principal	Grd	Prgm	Enr/#Cls	SN	
Atherton Elem Sch 2011 Solo St, Houston 77020 Albert Lemons	PK-6	T	585 28		97% 713/671-4100 Fax 713/671-4104
Barrick Elem Sch 12001 Winfrey Ln, Houston 77076 Yolanda Garrido	PK-5	T	657 38		95% 281/405-2500 Fax 281/405-2502
Berry Elem Sch 2310 Berry Rd, Houston 77093 Philip Steuernagel	PK-5	T	799 27		90% 713/696-2700 Fax 713/696-2701
Burbank Elem Sch 216 Tidwell Rd, Houston 77022 Diego Duran	PK-5	T	912 40		96% 713/696-2690 Fax 713/696-2691
Burbank Middle Sch 315 Berry Rd, Houston 77022 David Knittle	6-8	TV	1,464 85		93% 713/696-2720 Fax 713/696-2723
Burrus Elem Sch 701 E 33rd St, Houston 77022 Jessie Woods	PK-5	T	454 45		95% 713/867-5180 Fax 713/867-5182
Codwell Elem Sch 5225 Tavenor Ln, Houston 77048 Kristy Love	PK-5		410 40		713/732-3580 Fax 713/732-3582
Cook Jr Elem Sch 7115 Lockwood Dr, Houston 77016 Lysette Cooper	PK-5	T	625 10		97% 713/636-6040 Fax 713/636-6088
Coop Elem Sch 10130 Aldine Westfield Rd, Houston 77093 Tudon Martinez	PK-5	T	736 47		98% 713/696-2630 Fax 713/696-2633
De Chaumes Elem Sch 155 Cooper Rd, Houston 77076 Enedith Silerio	PK-5	T	841 36		96% 713/696-2676 Fax 713/696-2680
Durkee Elem Sch 7301 Nordling Rd, Houston 77076 Alicia Puente-Sanchez	PK-5	T	574 58		90% 713/696-2835 Fax 713/696-2837
Eliot Elem Sch 6411 Laredo St, Houston 77020 Zandra Aguilar	PK-5	T	605 44		95% 713/671-3670 Fax 713/671-3676
Elmore Elem Sch 8200 Tate St, Houston 77028 Faith Fugit	K-5	T	588		97% 713/672-7466 Fax 713/671-3565
Farias Early Childhood Center 515 E Rittenhouse St, Houston 77076 Maria Solis	PK-PK	T	434 20		99% 713/691-8730 Fax 713/691-8746
Fleming Middle Sch 4910 Collingsworth St, Houston 77026 Nicole Ayen Metoyer	6-8	TV	486 48		97% 713/671-4170 Fax 713/671-4176
Fonville Middle Sch 725 E Little York Rd, Houston 77076 Irma Sandate	6-8	TV	808 60		90% 713/696-2825 Fax 713/696-2829
Fonwood Early Childhood Center 9709 Mesa Dr, Houston 77078 Christina Jordan	PK-K	T	555		99% 713/633-0781 Fax 713/636-7940
Garcia Elem Sch 9550 Aldine Westfield Rd, Houston 77093 Linda Bellard	PK-5	T	593 45		90% 713/696-2900 Fax 713/696-2904
ⓐ Harper Daep Sch 4425 N Shepherd Dr, Houston 77018 Raymond Glass	6-12	TV	14 35		91% 713/802-4760 Fax 281/986-6475

---

1 Superintendent	8 Curric/Instruct K-12	19 Chief Financial Officer	29 Family/Consumer Science	39 Social Studies K-12	49 English/Lang Arts Elem	59 Special Education Elem	69 Academic Assessment
2 Bus/Finance/Purchasing	9 Curric/Instruct Elem	20 Art K-12	30 Adult Education	40 Social Studies Elem	50 English/Lang Arts Sec	60 Special Education Sec	70 Research/Development
3 Buildings And Grounds	10 Curric/Instruct Sec	21 Art Elem	31 Career/Sch-to-Work K-12	41 Social Studies Sec	51 Reading K-12	61 Foreign/World Lang K-12	71 Public Information
4 Food Service	11 Federal Program	22 Art Sec	32 Career/Sch-to-Work Elem	42 Science K-12	52 Reading Elem	62 Foreign/World Lang Elem	72 Summer School
5 Transportation	12 Title I	23 Music K-12	33 Career/Sch-to-Work Sec	43 Science Elem	53 Reading Sec	63 Foreign/World Lang Sec	73 Instructional Tech
6 Athletic	13 Title V	24 Music Elem	34 Early Childhood Ed	44 Science Sec	54 Remedial Reading K-12	64 Religious Education K-12	74 Inservice Training
7 Health Services	15 Asst Superintendent	25 Music Sec	35 Health/Phys Education	45 Math K-12	55 Remedial Reading Elem	65 Religious Education Elem	75 Marketing/Distributive
	16 Instructional Media Svcs	26 Business Education	36 Guidance Services K-12	46 Math Elem	56 Remedial Reading Sec	66 Religious Education Sec	76 Info Systems
	17 Chief Operations Officer	27 Career & Tech Ed	37 Guidance Services Elem	47 Math Sec	57 Bilingual/ELL	67 School Board President	77 Psychological Assess
	18 Chief Academic Officer	28 Technology Education	38 Guidance Services Sec	48 English/Lang Arts K-12	58 Special Education K-12	68 Teacher Personnel	78 Affirmative Action

Texas School Directory

Harris County

School	Grd	Prgm	Enr	#Cls	SN	Phone
Herrera Elem Sch 525 Bennington St, Houston 77022 Christopher Carnes	PK-5	T	888	40	99%	713/696-2800 Fax 713/696-2804
Janowski Elem Sch 7500 Bauman Rd, Houston 77022 Myrna Bazan	PK-5	T	550	50	95%	713/696-2844 Fax 713/696-2847
Joe E Moreno Elem Sch 620 E Canino Rd, Houston 77037 Adriana Castro	PK-5	T	752		94%	281/405-2150 Fax 281/405-2176
Kashmere Gardens Elem Sch 4901 Lockwood Dr, Houston 77026 Marques Collins	PK-5	T	391	28	89%	713/671-4160 Fax 713/671-4163
Kennedy Elem Sch 400 Victoria Dr, Houston 77022 Haydee Cavazos	PK-5	T	702	25	87%	713/696-2686 Fax 713/696-2689
Ⓜ Key Middle Sch 4000 Kelley St, Houston 77026 Erika Carter	6-8	T	688		75%	713/636-6000 Fax 713/636-6008
Lyons Elem Sch 800 Roxella St, Houston 77076 Olivia Casares	PK-5	T	1,002	35	94%	713/696-2870 Fax 713/696-2877
Marshall Elem Sch 6200 Winfield Rd, Houston 77050 **Lauren Price**	PK-5	T	944	34	95%	281/636-4606 Fax 281/986-6475
McGowen Elem Sch 6820 Homestead Rd, Houston 77028 Jeffrey Whitaker	PK-5	T	452	25	93%	713/636-6979 Fax 713/636-6983
McReynolds Middle Sch 5910 Market St, Houston 77020 Jasmine Giron	6-8	TV	595	40	93%	713/671-3650 Fax 713/671-3657
Ⓜ Mickey Leland College Prep 1700 Gregg St, Houston 77020 Dameion Crook	6-12	T	501		76%	713/226-2668 Fax 713/266-4923
N Q Henderson Elem Sch 701 Solo St, Houston 77020 Alana Holloway	PK-5	T	321	38	99%	713/671-4195 Fax 713/671-4197
Northline Elem Sch 821 Witcher Ln, Houston 77076 **Mario Sandoval**	PK-5	T	560	44	88%	713/696-2890 Fax 713/696-2894
Ⓒ Osborne Elem Sch 800 Ringold St, Houston 77088 **Jacqueline Parnell**	PK-5	T	407	30	85%	281/405-2525 Fax 281/405-2528
Paige Elem Sch 7501 Curry Rd, Houston 77093 Iliana Perez	PK-5	T	462	35	90%	713/696-2855 Fax 713/696-2858
R L Isaacs Elem Sch 3830 Pickfair St, Houston 77026 Lajuana Armstrong	PK-5	T	304	19	94%	713/671-4120 Fax 713/671-4122
Raul C Martinez Elem Sch 7211 Market St, Houston 77020 Keri Ward	PK-5	T	539	44	96%	713/671-3680 Fax 713/671-3684 ⓕ
Ross Elem Sch 2819 Bay St, Houston 77026 **Treasure West**	PK-5	T	372	28	94%	713/226-4550 Fax 713/226-4554
Scarborough Elem Sch 3021 Little York Rd, Houston 77093 Miriam Medina	PK-5		681	44		713/696-2710 Fax 713/696-2712 ⓕ
Scroggins Elem Sch 400 Boyles St, Houston 77020 Dianna Balderas	PK-5	T	523	30	90%	713/671-4130 Fax 713/671-4133
Shadydale Elem Sch 5905 Tidwell Rd, Houston 77016 Kimberly Agnew	PK-5	T	897	36	95%	713/633-5150 Fax 713/636-7925
Shearn Elem Sch 9802 Stella Link Rd, Houston 77025 Mayra Romero	PK-5	T	603	25	95%	713/295-5236 Fax 713/295-5253
Sherman Elem Sch 1909 McKee St, Houston 77009 **Racquel Rosenbalm**	PK-5	T	570	15	96%	713/226-2627 Fax 713/236-8417

● **Houston ISD-Northwest Area** PID: 12179974   713/556-8999
4400 W 18th St, Houston 77092

Cesar Martinez 15

Public Schs..Principal	Grd	Prgm	Enr/#Cls	SN	Phone
Ⓜ Arabic Immersion Magnet Sch 812 W 28th St, Houston 77008 Mahassen Ballouli	PK-3	T	346	57%	713/556-8940 Fax 713/556-8944
Barbara Jordan Career Center 5800 Eastex Fwy, Houston 77026 Ross McAlpine	11-12	TV	141 120	74%	713/636-6900 Fax 713/636-6917
Benbrook Elem Sch 4026 Bolin Rd, Houston 77092 Dana Darden	PK-5	T	588 21	97%	713/613-2502 Fax 713/613-2281
Black Middle Sch 1575 Chantilly Ln, Houston 77018 Rhonda Honore	6-8	T	1,233 70	62%	713/613-2505 Fax 713/613-2533
Browning Elem Sch 607 Northwood St, Houston 77009 **Evangeline Campos**	PK-5	T	489 40	95%	713/867-5140 Fax 713/867-5148
Ⓜ Carnegie-Vanguard High Sch 1501 Taft St, Houston 77019 Ramon Moss	9-12		808 20	32%	713/732-3690 Fax 713/732-3694
Ⓒ Challenge Early Clg High Sch 5601 West Loop S, Houston 77081 Tonya Miller	9-12	T	463	71%	713/664-9712 Fax 713/664-9780
Clemente Martinez Elem Sch 901 Hays St, Houston 77009 Alejandro Lopez	PK-5	T	412 43	97%	713/224-1424 Fax 713/224-1304
Ⓐ Community Services Sch 1102 Telephone Rd, Houston 77023 **Cicely Williams**	PK-12		154	43%	713/967-5285 Fax 713/967-5223
Ⓒ Crockett Charter Elem Sch 2112 Crockett St, Houston 77007 Priscilla Rivas	PK-5	T	582 15	67%	713/802-4780 Fax 713/802-4783
Ⓐ Debakey High Sch-Health Prof Ⓜ 2545 Pressler St, Houston 77030 Agnes Perry	9-12	V	891 50		713/741-2410 Fax 713/746-5211
Ⓜ Durham Elem Sch 4803 Brinkman St, Houston 77018 **Carrie Flores**	PK-5	T	571 23	74%	713/613-2527 Fax 713/613-2515
Field Elem Sch 703 E 17th St, Houston 77008 John Hendrickson	PK-5	T	461 25	87%	713/867-5190 Fax 713/867-5194
Garden Oaks Montessori 901 Sue Barnett Dr, Houston 77018 Lindsey Pollock	PK-8	T	850 30	46%	713/696-2930 Fax 713/696-2932 ⓕ
Ⓜ Hamilton Middle Sch 139 E 20th St, Houston 77008 Robert Johnson	6-8	TV	266 55	85%	713/802-4725 Fax 713/802-4731
Ⓜ Harvard Elem Sch 810 Harvard St, Houston 77007 Laura Alaniz	PK-5		656 27	23%	713/867-5210 Fax 713/867-5215
Heights High Sch 413 E 13th St, Houston 77008 Cynthia Ford	9-12	TV	2,377 90	70%	713/865-4400 Fax 713/867-0876
Helms Elem Sch 503 W 21st St, Houston 77008 **Lola Perejon**	PK-5	T	473 25	75%	713/867-5130 Fax 713/867-5133 ⓕ
Hogg Middle Sch 1100 Merrill St, Houston 77009 **Tiffany Roque**	6-8	TV	984 90	66%	713/802-4700 Fax 713/802-4708 ⓕ ⓣ

79 Student Personnel	91 Safety/Security	275 Response To Intervention	298 Grant Writer/Ptnrships	**School Programs**	**Social Media**	
80 Driver Ed/Safety	92 Magnet School	277 Remedial Math K-12	750 Chief Innovation Officer	A = Alternative Program		
81 Gifted/Talented	93 Parental Involvement	280 Literacy Coach	751 Chief of Staff	G = Adult Classes	ⓕ = Facebook	
82 Video Services	95 Tech Prep Program	285 STEM	752 Social Emotional Learning	M = Magnet Program		
83 Substance Abuse Prev	97 Chief Infomation Officer	286 Digital Learning		T = Title I Schoolwide	ⓣ = Twitter	
84 Erate	98 Chief Technology Officer	288 Common Core Standards	**Other School Types**	V = Career & Tech Ed Programs		
85 AIDS Education	270 Character Education	294 Accountability	Ⓐ = Alternative School			
86 Alternative/At Risk	271 Migrant Education	295 Network System	Ⓒ = Charter School	New Schools are shaded		
89 Multi-Cultural Curriculum	273 Teacher Mentor	296 Title II Programs	Ⓜ = Magnet School	New Superintendents and Principals are bold		TX-191
90 Social Work	274 Before/After Sch	297 Webmaster	Ⓨ = Year-Round School	Personnel with email addresses are underscored		

Harris County

Market Data Retrieval

School	Grd	Prgm	Enr/#Cls	SN	Phone
Houston Academy Int'l Studies 1810 Stuart St, Houston 77004 Melissa Jacobs	9-12	TV	495	68%	713/942-1430 Fax 713/942-1433
Jefferson Elem Sch 5000 Sharman St, Houston 77009 Lilly Rincon	PK-5	T	432 30	88%	713/696-2778 Fax 713/696-2784
Ketelsen Elem Sch 600 Quitman St, Houston 77009 Shelene Livas	PK-5	T	579 12	93%	713/220-5050 Fax 713/220-5074
ⓜ Kinder HS Perform & Visual Art 790 Austin St, Houston 77002 R Scott Allen	9-12		753 60	14%	713/942-1960 Fax 713/942-1968
Love Elem Sch 1120 W 13th St, Houston 77008 Melba Johnson	PK-5	T	377 19	90%	713/867-0840 Fax 713/867-0841
Marshall Middle Sch 1115 Noble St, Houston 77009 **Queinnise Miller**	6-8	GTV	794 70	94%	713/226-2600 Fax 713/226-2605
North Houston Early College HS 8001 Fulton St Bldg C, Houston 77022 Brian Gaston	9-12	T	484	93%	713/696-6168 Fax 713/696-6172
ⓜ Northside High Sch 1101 Quitman St, Houston 77009 Cecilia Gonzales	9-12	TV	1,540 76	96%	713/226-4900 Fax 713/226-4999
ⓜ Oak Forest Elem Sch 1401 W 43rd St, Houston 77018 Andrew Casler	PK-5	T	859 37	27%	713/613-2536 Fax 713/613-2244
ⓜ Rice Sch 7550 Seuss Dr, Houston 77025 Kimberly Hobbs	K-8	T	1,143 65	68%	713/349-1800 Fax 713/349-1828
ⓜ Roosevelt Elem Sch 6700 Fulton St, Houston 77022 Lisa McManus	PK-5	T	645 40	87%	713/696-2820 Fax 713/696-2821
Ruby Sue Clifton Middle Sch 6001 Golden Forest Dr, Houston 77092 Georgina Castilleja	6-8	T	705	85%	713/613-2516 Fax 713/613-2526
Sam Houston Math Sci Tech HS 9400 Irvington Blvd, Houston 77076 Alan Summers	9-12	TV	2,612 170	81%	713/696-0200 Fax 713/696-8984
Scarborough High Sch 4141 Costa Rica Rd, Houston 77092 Roderick Trevino	9-12	TV	752 53	94%	713/613-2200 Fax 713/613-2205
Sinclair Elem Sch 6410 Grovewood Ln, Houston 77008 Lee Mashburn	PK-5	T	577 28	48%	713/867-5161 Fax 713/867-5162
Smith Elem Sch 4802 Chrystell Ln, Houston 77092 **Melinda Daugherty**	PK-5	T	862 45	85%	713/613-2542 Fax 713/613-2578
ⓜ Travis Elem Sch 3311 Beauchamp St, Houston 77009 Thomas Day	PK-5		687 30	23%	713/802-4790 Fax 713/802-4795
Wainwright Elem Sch 5330 Milwee St, Houston 77092 Christina Aguirre	PK-5	T	519 30	93%	713/613-2550 Fax 713/613-2549
Waltrip High Sch 1900 W 34th St, Houston 77018 Michael Niggli	9-12	TV	1,902 97	67%	713/688-1361 Fax 713/957-7743
ⓜ Young Womens College Prep Acad 1906 Cleburne St, Houston 77004 April Williams	6-12	T	477	72%	713/942-1441 Fax 713/942-1448

- **Houston ISD-South Area** PID: 12170241   713/556-4447
  4400 W 18th St, Houston 77092

  Nicole Moore 15

School	Grd	Prgm	Enr/#Cls	SN	Phone
Public Schs..Principal					
Alcott Elem Sch 5859 Bellfort St, Houston 77033 Dimitrie Rainey	PK-5	T	232 30	96%	713/732-3540 Fax 713/732-3542
Almeda Elem Sch 14226 Almeda School Rd, Houston 77047 Gerardo Medina	PK-5	T	839 40	84%	713/434-5620 Fax 713/434-5622
Bastian Elem Sch 5051 Bellfort St, Houston 77033 Everett Hare	PK-5	T	708 25	99%	713/732-5830 Fax 713/732-5837
Baylor Clg Biotech Acad-Rusk 2805 Garrow St, Houston 77003 Jesus Herrera	3-8		484 25		713/226-4543 Fax 713/226-4546
ⓜ Baylor Clg of Medicine Acad 2610 Elgin St, Houston 77004 **Tanya Edwards**	6-8		728		713/942-1932 Fax 713/942-1943
Bellfort Acad Early Chldhd Ctr 7647 Bellfort St, Houston 77061 Darcele Lofton	PK-K	T	399	91%	713/640-0950 Fax 713/640-0957
Billy Reagan K-8 Educ Ctr 4842 Anderson Rd, Houston 77053 Dr Tabitha Davis	PK-8	T	1,004	94%	713/556-9575 Fax 713/556-9576
Brookline Elem Sch 6301 South Loop E, Houston 77087 Rick Nagir	PK-5	T	897 56	94%	713/845-7400 Fax 713/847-4717
Cornelius Elem Sch 7475 Westover St, Houston 77087 Zaira Gomez	PK-5	T	867 58	87%	713/845-7405 Fax 713/845-7448
ⓜ Energy Institute High Sch 3501 Southmore Blvd, Houston 77004 Lori Lambropulos	9-12	T	764	58%	713/802-4620 Fax 713/556-9840
Foster Elem Sch 3919 Ward St, Houston 77021 Traci Lightfoot	PK-5	T	436 21	91%	713/746-8260 Fax 713/746-8263
Frost Elem Sch 5002 Almeda Genoa Rd, Houston 77048 David Terrell	PK-5	T	615 32	97%	713/732-3490 Fax 713/732-3498
Garden Villas Elem Sch 7185 Santa Fe Dr, Houston 77061 Kimberly Thompson	PK-5	T	691 62	78%	713/845-7484 Fax 713/645-0028
Golfcrest Elem Sch 7414 Fairway Dr, Houston 77087 Bertha Espinosa-Garza	PK-5	T	656 42	91%	713/845-7425 Fax 713/645-0034
Gregg Elem Sch 6701 Roxbury Rd, Houston 77087 David Jackson	PK-5	T	553 36	93%	713/845-7432 Fax 713/847-4708
Grissom Elem Sch 4900 Simsbrook Dr, Houston 77045 Meagan Edwards	PK-5	T	527 34	98%	713/434-5660 Fax 713/434-5664
Hartman Middle Sch 7111 Westover St, Houston 77087 Gerrol Johnson	6-8	TV	1,263 85	88%	713/845-7435 Fax 713/643-1627
Hartsfield Elem Sch 5001 Perry St, Houston 77021 Travis Johnson	PK-5	T	407 14	88%	713/746-8280 Fax 713/746-8283
James Deanda Elem Sch 7980 Almeda Genoa Rd, Houston 77075 Lauren Mailhiot	PK-5	T	685	91%	713/556-9550 Fax 713/556-9552
James R Reynolds Elem Sch 9601 Rosehaven Dr, Houston 77051 **Renesiaha Marshall**	PK-5	T	467 50	88%	713/731-5590 Fax 713/731-5598
Jean Hines-Caldwell Elem Sch 5515 W Orem Dr, Houston 77085 Juanette Green	PK-5	T	781 43	93%	713/726-3700 Fax 713/726-3724
Jones Futures Academy 7414 Saint LO Rd, Houston 77033 Nirmol Lim	9-12	TV	390	92%	713/733-1111 Fax 713/732-3450

1 Superintendent	19 Chief Financial Officer	39 Social Studies K-12	59 Special Education Elem	69 Academic Assessment
2 Bus/Finance/Purchasing	20 Art K-12	40 Social Studies Elem	60 Special Education Sec	70 Research/Development
3 Buildings And Grounds	21 Art Elem	41 Social Studies Sec	61 Foreign/World Lang K-12	71 Public Information
4 Food Service	22 Art Sec	42 Science K-12	62 Foreign/World Lang Elem	72 Summer School
5 Transportation	23 Music K-12	43 Science Elem	63 Foreign/World Lang Sec	73 Instructional Tech
6 Athletic	24 Music Elem	44 Science Sec	64 Religious Education K-12	74 Inservice Training
7 Health Services	25 Music Sec	45 Math K-12	65 Religious Education Elem	75 Marketing/Distributive
8 Curric/Instruct K-12	26 Business Education	46 Math Elem	66 Religious Education Sec	76 Info Systems
9 Curric/Instruct Elem	27 Career & Tech Ed	47 Math Sec	67 School Board President	77 Psychological Assess
10 Curric/Instruct Sec	28 Technology Education	48 English/Lang Arts K-12	68 Teacher Personnel	78 Affirmative Action
11 Federal Program	29 Family/Consumer Science	49 English/Lang Arts Elem		
12 Title I	30 Adult Education	50 English/Lang Arts Sec		
13 Title V	31 Career/Sch-to-Work K-12	51 Reading K-12		
14 Instructional Media Svcs	32 Career/Sch-to-Work Elem	52 Reading Elem		
15 Asst Superintendent	33 Career/Sch-to-Work Sec	53 Reading Sec		
16 Chief Operations Officer	34 Early Childhood Ed	54 Remedial Reading K-12		
17 Chief Academic Officer	35 Health/Phys Education	55 Remedial Reading Elem		
18	36 Guidance Services K-12	56 Remedial Reading Sec		
	37 Guidance Services Elem	57 Bilingual/ELL		
	38 Guidance Services Sec	58 Special Education K-12		

TX—192

Texas School Directory — Harris County

School	Grd	Prgm	Enr/#Cls	SN	Phone
Juan N Seguin Elem Sch 5905 Waltrip St, Houston 77087 **Mayte Garcia-Olivo**	PK-5	T	544	89%	713/845-5600 Fax 713/845-5615
Kelso Elem Sch 5800 Southmund St, Houston 77033 **Shanda Walker**	PK-5	T	448 27	95%	713/845-7451 Fax 713/643-3823
King Early Childhood Center 3930 W Fuqua St, Houston 77045 Tremeka Collins	PK-K	T	395	99%	713/797-7900 Fax 713/797-7904
Law Elem Sch 12401 S Coast Dr, Houston 77047 Derrick Estes	PK-5	T	688 40	83%	713/732-3630 Fax 713/732-3633
Ⓜ Lockhart Elem Sch 3200 Rosedale St, Houston 77004 Monica Cooper	PK-5	T	569 23	77%	713/942-1950 Fax 713/942-1953
Mitchell Elem Sch 10900 Gulfdale Dr, Houston 77075 Elizabeth Castillo	PK-5	T	384 42		713/991-8190 Fax 713/991-8193
Peck Elem Sch 5001 Martin Luther King Blvd, Houston 77021 **Myra Bell**	PK-5	T	528 35	87%	713/845-7463 Fax 713/643-3830
Petersen Elem Sch 14404 Waterloo Dr, Houston 77045 Danitra Arredondo	PK-5	T	419 20	95%	713/434-5630 Fax 713/434-5634
Ruby Thompson Elem Sch 6121 Tierwester St, Houston 77021 **Erica Brame**	PK-5	T	413 43	96%	713/746-8250 Fax 713/746-8104
South Early College High Sch 1930 Airport Blvd, Houston 77051 Steve Gourrier	9-12	T	395 14	73%	713/732-3623 Fax 713/732-3425
Ⓜ Sterling Aviation High Sch 11625 Martindale Rd, Houston 77048 Sabrina Cuby	9-12	TV	1,483 67	76%	713/991-0510 Fax 713/991-8111
Thomas Middle Sch 5655 Selinsky Rd, Houston 77048 Vernitra Shivers	6-8	TV	594	93%	713/732-3500 Fax 713/732-3511
Ⓒ Tsu Charter Lab Sch 3100 Cleburne St, Houston 77004 Debbra Collins	PK-2	T	100	89%	713/313-6754 Fax 713/313-6745
W P Hobby Elem Sch 4021 Woodmont Dr, Houston 77045 Isaac Daniels	PK-5	T	830 32	79%	713/434-5650 Fax 713/434-5652
Westbury High Sch 11911 Chimney Rock Rd, Houston 77035 Susan Monaghan	9-12	TV	2,341	78%	713/723-6015 Fax 713/726-2165
Ⓜ Whidby Elem Sch 7625 Springhill St, Houston 77021 **Mimi Lam**	PK-5	T	590 36	85%	713/746-8170 Fax 713/746-8173
Ⓜ Windsor Village Elem Sch 14440 Polo St, Houston 77085 Shantelle Louis	PK-5	T	757 40	91%	713/726-3642 Fax 713/726-3647
Young Elem Sch 3555 Bellfort St, Houston 77051 **Shanica Mitchell**	PK-5	T	301 28	99%	713/732-3590 Fax 713/732-3592

● **Houston ISD-West Area** PID: 12170265   713/556-9123
4400 W 18th St, Houston 77092
James McSwain 15

Public Schs..Principal	Grd	Prgm	Enr/#Cls	SN	Phone
A A Milne Elem Sch 7800 Portal Dr, Houston 77071 Terese Pollard	PK-5	T	559 70	94%	713/778-3420 Fax 713/778-3424
Ⓒ Anderson Elem Sch 5727 Ludington Dr, Houston 77035 **Dr Deshonta Everett**	PK-5	T	758 60	88%	713/726-3600 Fax 713/726-3603
Ashford Elem Sch 1815 Shannon Valley Dr, Houston 77077 Christopher Walker	PK-5	T	651 35	65%	281/368-2120 Fax 281/368-2123
Barbara Bush Elem Sch 13800 Westerloch Dr, Houston 77077 Theresa Rose	PK-5		881 50	14%	281/368-2150 Fax 281/368-2153
Bell Elem Sch 12323 Shaftsbury Dr, Houston 77031 Brishaun Sutton	PK-5	T	706 45	88%	281/983-2800 Fax 281/983-2802
Ⓜ Bellaire High Sch 5100 Maple St, Bellaire 77401 Michael McDonough	9-12	TV	3,307	49%	713/295-3704 Fax 713/295-3763
Benavidez Elem Sch 6262 Gulfton St, Houston 77081 Dorcas Parra-Malek	PK-5	T	1,024 65	99%	713/778-3350 Fax 713/778-3358
Braeburn Elem Sch 7707 Rampart St, Houston 77081 Amanda Rodgers	PK-5	T	638 55	99%	713/295-5210 Fax 713/295-5289
Briargrove Elem Sch 6145 San Felipe St, Houston 77057 Thayer Hutcheson	K-5		881 45	28%	713/917-3600 Fax 713/917-3601
Ⓒ Briarmeadow Charter Sch 3601 Dunvale Rd, Houston 77063 Peter Heinze	PK-8	T	606 20	63%	713/458-5500 Fax 713/458-5506
Condit Elem Sch 7000 S 3rd St, Bellaire 77401 Daniel Greenberg	PK-5		770 32	33%	713/295-5255 Fax 713/668-5738
Cunningham Elem Sch 5100 Gulfton St, Houston 77081 Karen Harris	PK-5	T	696 42	89%	713/295-5223 Fax 713/668-6217
E White Elem Sch 9001 Triola Ln, Houston 77036 Paulette Caston	PK-5	T	759 38	81%	713/778-3490 Fax 713/778-3493
Eleanor Tinsley Elem Sch 11035 Bob White Dr, Houston 77096 Mythesia Johnson	1-5	T	704	97%	713/778-8400 Fax 713/778-8405
Elrod Elem Sch 6230 Dumfries Dr, Houston 77096 Leigh Curry	PK-5	T	763 64	88%	713/778-3330 Fax 713/778-3333
Emerson Elem Sch 9533 Skyline Dr, Houston 77063 Alexander Rodriguez	PK-5	T	920 60	92%	713/917-3630 Fax 713/917-3634
Ⓒ Energized for Excellence ECC 6400 Southwest Fwy, Houston 77074 Jose Cintron	PK-PK	T	667	93%	281/779-4411 Fax 281/779-4414
Ⓒ Energized for Excellence ES 6201 Bissonnet St, Houston 77081 **Claudia Chavez-Pinto**	K-5	T	522 56	93%	713/773-3600 Fax 713/773-3630
Ⓒ Energized for Excellence MS 6107 Bissonnet St, Houston 77081 Arlene Kho	6-8	T	522	66%	713/773-3600 Fax 713/773-3630
Ⓒ Energized for STEM Academy HS 9220 Jutland Rd, Houston 77033 **Shavon Clark**	9-12	T	200	94%	713/641-1630 Fax 713/641-1669
Ⓒ Energized for STEM Academy MS 7055 Beechnut St, Houston 77074 **Ranier Perez**	6-8	T	333		713/773-3600 Fax 713/773-3630
Fondren Middle Sch 6333 S Braeswood Blvd, Houston 77096 **Tiffany Narcisse**	6-8	TV	1,013 66	96%	713/778-3360 Fax 713/778-3362
Gross Elem Sch 12583 S Gessner Rd, Houston 77071 Tracie Hart-Jackson	PK-5	T	632 40	84%	713/778-8450
Halpin Early Chldhd Lrng Ctr 10901 Sandpiper Dr, Houston 77096 Constance Lathan	PK-K	T	432 20	98%	713/778-6720 Fax 713/778-6724

---

79 Student Personnel	91 Safety/Security	275 Response To Intervention	298 Grant Writer/Ptnrships
80 Driver Ed/Safety	92 Magnet School	277 Remedial Math K-12	750 Chief Innovation Officer
81 Gifted/Talented	93 Parental Involvement	280 Literacy Coach	751 Chief of Staff
82 Video Services	95 Tech Prep Program	285 STEM	752 Social Emotional Learning
83 Substance Abuse Prev	97 Chief Infomation Officer	286 Digital Learning	
84 Erate	98 Chief Technology Officer	288 Common Core Standards	**Other School Types**
85 AIDS Education	270 Accountability	294 Accountability	Ⓐ = Alternative School
88 Alternative/At Risk	271 Migrant Education	295 Network System	Ⓒ = Charter School
89 Multi-Cultural Curriculum	273 Teacher Mentor	296 Title II Programs	Ⓜ = Magnet School
90 Social Work	274 Before/After Sch	297 Webmaster	Ⓨ = Year-Round School

School Programs
A = Alternative Program
G = Adult Classes
M = Magnet Program
T = Title I Schoolwide
V = Career & Tech Ed Programs

Social Media
🅕 = Facebook
🅣 = Twitter

New Schools are shaded
New Superintendents and Principals are bold
Personnel with email addresses are underscored

TX–193

Harris County | Market Data Retrieval

School	Grades	Type	Enroll	%	Phone
HCC Life Skills 1301 Alabama St, Houston 77004 **Shawna Punch**	12-12	T	61	79%	713/718-6882 Fax 713/718-6179
Ⓜ Herod Elem Sch 5627 Jason St, Houston 77096 Michelle Turek	PK-5	T	818	45%	713/778-3315 Fax 713/778-3317
Ⓜ Horn Elem Sch 4530 Holly St, Bellaire 77401 Vanessa Flores	PK-5		805 20	14%	713/295-5264 Fax 713/295-5286
© Inspired for Excellence Acad W 12525 Fondren Rd, Houston 77035 **Letha Gilmore**	5-8		227		832/834-5295 Fax 832/834-5687
Ⓜ Jewel Askew Elem Sch 11200 Wood Lodge Dr, Houston 77077 Ebony Cumby	PK-5	T	907 52	68%	281/368-2100 Fax 281/368-2103
Ⓐ Jjaep Sch © 2525 Murworth Dr Ste 100, Houston 77054 Luis Gavito	4-12		12	50%	713/556-7140 Fax 713/556-7282
Ⓜ Kolter Elem Sch 9710 Runny Meade Dr, Houston 77096 Julie Dickinson	PK-5		649 20		713/726-3630 Fax 713/726-3663
Ⓜ Lamar High Sch 3325 Westheimer Rd, Houston 77098 Rita Graves	9-12	TV	3,082 100	47%	713/522-5960 Fax 713/535-3769
© Lanier Middle Sch 2600 Woodhead St, Houston 77098 **Dave Wheat**	6-8	A	1,464 100	26%	713/942-1900 Fax 713/942-1907
Las Americas Newcomer Mid Sch 6501 Bellaire Blvd, Houston 77074 Maria Moreno	4-8	T	198 6	98%	713/773-5300 Fax 713/773-5303
Ⓜ Long Academy 6501 Bellaire Blvd, Houston 77074 Keri Wittpenn	6-12	TV	896	83%	713/778-3380 Fax 713/778-3387
Longfellow Elem Sch 3617 Norris Dr, Houston 77025 Katherine Keafer	PK-5	T	737 30	74%	713/295-5268 Fax 713/295-5257
Louie Welch Middle Sch 11544 S Gessner Rd, Houston 77071 Inge Garibaldi	6-8	TV	727 92	88%	713/778-3300 Fax 713/995-6067
Lovett Elem Sch 8814 S Rice Ave, Houston 77096 Dawn Thompson	K-5		681 29	35%	713/295-5258 Fax 713/295-5291
MacGregor Elem Sch 4801 La Branch St, Houston 77004 Tara Garrett	PK-5		586 55	73%	713/942-1990 Fax 713/942-1993
Ⓜ Mandarin Immersion Magnet Sch 5445 W Alabama St, Houston 77056 **Chung Ying**	PK-8		748	23%	713/295-5276 Fax 713/662-3527
Margaret Long Wisdom High Sch 6529 Beverlyhill St, Houston 77057 **Michelle Wagner**	9-12	T	2,023 150	97%	713/787-1700 Fax 713/787-1723
Ⓜ Mark Twain Elem Sch 7500 Braes Blvd, Houston 77025 Melissa Patin	PK-5		869 34	12%	713/295-5230 Fax 713/295-5283
Mark White Elem Sch 2515 Old Farm Rd, Houston 77063 Lisa Hernandez	PK-5	T	679	66%	713/556-6571 Fax 713/556-7497
Ⓜ McNamara Elem Sch 8714 McAvoy Dr, Houston 77074 Toufic Elachkar	PK-5	T	934 38	92%	713/778-3460 Fax 713/777-1338
Memorial Elem Sch 6401 Arnot St, Houston 77007 Maria Garcia	PK-5	T	340 24	72%	713/867-5150 Fax 713/867-5151
Meyerland Perf-Visual Arts MS 10410 Manhattan Dr, Houston 77096 **Auden Sarabia**	6-8	TV	1,574	68%	713/726-3616 Fax 713/726-3622
Mistral Early Childhood Center 6203 Jessamine St, Houston 77081 Kristina Davis-Troutman	PK-PK	T	355	77%	713/773-6253 Fax 713/773-6257
Neff Early Learning Center 8200 Carvel Ln, Houston 77036 Santrice Jones	PK-1		661	94%	713/778-3470 Fax 713/778-3473
Neff Elem Sch 8301 Neff St, Houston 77036 Amanda Wingard	2-5	T	783	91%	713/556-9566 Fax 713/556-9567
Parker Elem Sch 10626 Atwell Dr, Houston 77096 **Chavis Mitchell**	PK-5	T	883 36	52%	713/726-3634 Fax 713/726-3660
Paul Revere Middle Sch 10502 Briar Forest Dr, Houston 77042 Monijit Katial	6-8	T	1,228 65	86%	713/917-3500 Fax 713/917-3505
Pershing Middle Sch 3838 Blue Bonnet Blvd, Houston 77025 Steven Shetzer	6-8	TV	1,771	44%	713/295-5240 Fax 713/295-5252
Pilgrim Academy 6302 Skyline Dr, Houston 77057 Diana Castillo	PK-8	T	1,135 34	97%	713/458-4672 Fax 713/458-4693
Pin Oak Middle Sch 4601 Glenmont St, Bellaire 77401 Michelle Shoulders	6-8		1,213	29%	713/295-6500 Fax 713/295-6511
Piney Point Elem Sch 8921 Pagewood Ln, Houston 77063 Bobbie Swaby	PK-5	T	1,181 45	95%	713/917-3610 Fax 713/917-3613
Poe Elem Sch 5100 Hazard St, Houston 77098 Jeffrey Amerson	PK-5		863 36	29%	713/535-3780 Fax 713/535-3784
Ray Daily Elem Sch 12909 Briar Forest Dr, Houston 77077 **Cindy Tiet**	PK-5	T	768	57%	281/368-2111 Fax 281/368-7464
Ⓜ River Oaks Elem Sch 2008 Kirby Dr, Houston 77019 Keri Fovargue	K-5		674 20	10%	713/942-1460 Fax 713/942-1463
Roberts Elem Sch 6000 Greenbriar Dr, Houston 77030 Trealla Epps	PK-5		756 29	13%	713/295-5272 Fax 713/295-5282
S C Red Elem Sch 4520 Tonawanda Rd, Houston 77035 Octaviano Trevino	PK-5	T	598 35	55%	713/726-3638 Fax 713/726-3698
School at St George Place 5430 Hidalgo St, Houston 77056 **Sean McClish**	PK-5	T	793 10	46%	713/625-1499 Fax 713/985-7455
Shadowbriar Elem Sch 2650 Shadowbriar Dr, Houston 77077 Mark Samuel	PK-5	T	596 45	69%	281/368-2160 Fax 281/368-2170
Ⓜ Sharpstown International Acad 8330 Triola Ln, Houston 77036 Bryan Bordelon	6-12	TV	1,179 80	93%	713/778-3440 Fax 713/778-3444
Sutton Elem Sch 7402 Albacore Dr, Houston 77074 **Beatrice Akala**	PK-5	T	1,121 70	87%	713/778-3400 Fax 713/778-3407
Sylvan Rodriguez Elem Sch 5858 Chimney Rock Rd, Houston 77081 **Luz Deanda**	PK-5	T	958	98%	713/295-3870 Fax 713/295-3875
Ⓐ T H Rogers Sch 5840 San Felipe St, Houston 77057 **Tiffany Mike**	K-12	V	979 50	29%	713/917-3565 Fax 713/917-3555
Tanglewood Middle Sch 5215 San Felipe St, Houston 77056 Gretchen Kasper-Hoffman	6-8	T	846 45	56%	713/625-1411 Fax 713/625-1415
Valley West Elem Sch 10707 S Gessner Rd, Houston 77071 Brian VanNest	PK-5	T	861 25	90%	713/773-6151 Fax 713/773-6156

1 Superintendent	8 Curric/Instruct K-12	19 Chief Financial Officer	29 Family/Consumer Science	39 Social Studies K-12	49 English/Lang Arts Elem	59 Special Education Elem	69 Academic Assessment
2 Bus/Finance/Purchasing	9 Curric/Instruct Elem	20 Art K-12	30 Adult Education	40 Social Studies Elem	50 English/Lang Arts Sec	60 Special Education Sec	70 Research/Development
3 Buildings And Grounds	10 Curric/Instruct Sec	21 Art Elem	31 Career/Sch-to-Work K-12	41 Social Studies Sec	51 Reading K-12	61 Foreign/World Lang K-12	71 Public Information
4 Food Service	11 Federal Program	22 Art Sec	32 Career/Sch-to-Work Elem	42 Science K-12	52 Reading Elem	62 Foreign/World Lang Elem	72 Summer School
5 Transportation	12 Title I	23 Music K-12	33 Career/Sch-to-Work Sec	43 Science Elem	53 Reading Sec	63 Foreign/World Lang Sec	73 Instructional Tech
6 Athletic	13 Title V	24 Music Elem	34 Early Childhood Ed	44 Science Sec	54 Remedial Reading K-12	64 Religious Education K-12	74 Inservice Training
7 Health Services	15 Asst Superintendent	25 Music Sec	35 Health/Phys Education	45 Math K-12	55 Remedial Reading Elem	65 Religious Education Elem	75 Marketing/Distributive
	16 Instructional Media Svcs	26 Business Education	36 Guidance Services K-12	46 Math Elem	56 Remedial Reading Sec	66 Religious Education Sec	76 Info Systems
	17 Chief Operations Officer	27 Career & Tech Ed	37 Guidance Services Elem	47 Math Sec	57 Bilingual/ELL	67 School Board President	77 Psychological Assess
	18 Chief Academic Officer	28 Technology Education	38 Guidance Services Sec	48 English/Lang Arts K-12	58 Special Education K-12	68 Teacher Personnel	78 Affirmative Action

Texas School Directory — Harris County

School	Grd	Prgm	Enr/#Cls	SN	Phone
Walnut Bend Elem Sch 10620 Briar Forest Dr, Houston 77042 Michele Dahlquist	PK-5	T	761 36	89%	713/917-3540 Fax 713/917-3656
West Briar Middle Sch 13733 Brimhurst Dr, Houston 77077 Gabriel Lopez	6-8	T	1,113	55%	281/368-2140 Fax 281/368-2194
West University Elem Sch 3756 University Blvd, Houston 77005 **Scott Disch**	K-5		1,273 43	1%	713/295-5215 Fax 713/667-8514
Westside High Sch 14201 Briar Forest Dr, Houston 77077 Marguerite Stewart	9-12	TV	2,897	52%	281/920-8000 Fax 281/920-8059
Wharton Dual Language Academy 900 W Gray St, Houston 77019 Jennifer Day	PK-8	T	510 25	49%	713/535-3771 Fax 713/535-3772
Ⓜ Wilson Montessori Elem Sch 2100 Yupon St, Houston 77006 Shameika Salvador	PK-8	GT	600 20	35%	713/942-1470 Fax 713/942-1472
Ⓒ Young Learners Elem Sch [278] 8432 Bissonnet St, Houston 77074 Lillan Conway	PK-PK	T	1,344	100%	713/772-7100 Fax 713/772-7104

● **Huffman Ind School Dist** PID: 01026112 281/324-1871
24302 FM 2100 Rd, Huffman 77336 Fax 281/324-4319

Schools: 4 \ *Teachers:* 221 \ *Students:* 3,600 \ *Special Ed Students:* 286 \ *LEP Students:* 181 \ *College-Bound:* 75% \ *Ethnic:* Asian 1%, African American 2%, Hispanic 21%, Caucasian 76% \ *Exp:* $448 (High) \ *Poverty:* 11% \ *Title I:* $404,621 \ *Special Education:* $545,000 \ *Open-Close:* 08/21 - 05/29 \ *DTBP:* $153 (High)

Dr Benny Soileau 1
Joe Russo 4
Mike McEachern 6
Michelle Davenport 34,57,58,77,88,271
Monica Dorcz 45
Dr Shirley DuPree 68,71
Dena Burngarner 79
Jim Dees 285*

Tim Brittain 2,11,19
Betty Newton 5
Dr Joel Nolte 8,15
Kristin Breaux 39
Matt Dutton 67
David Carpenter 73,84,295
Shannon Jones 91*

Public Schs..Principal	Grd	Prgm	Enr/#Cls	SN	Phone
Falcon Ridge Elem Sch 26503 FM 2100 Rd, Huffman 77336 Amy Turner	K-5		850		281/324-7100 Fax 281/324-2076
Huffman Elem Sch 24403 E Lake Houston Pkwy, Huffman 77336 Melissa Hutchinson	PK-5	T	866 33	39%	281/324-1399 Fax 281/324-1646
Huffman Middle Sch 3407 Huffman Eastgate Rd, Huffman 77336 Adam Skinner	6-8	V	809 35	33%	281/324-2598 Fax 281/324-2710
Willie J Hargrave High Sch 25400 Willy Ln, Huffman 77336 Brandon Perry	9-12	V	1,075 50	29%	281/324-1845 Fax 281/324-3368

● **Humble Ind School Dist** PID: 01026150 281/641-1000
20200 Eastway Village Dr, Humble 77338 Fax 281/641-1050

Schools: 46 \ *Teachers:* 2,679 \ *Students:* 44,802 \ *Special Ed Students:* 3,183 \ *LEP Students:* 3,392 \ *College-Bound:* 60% \ *Ethnic:* Asian 3%, African American 20%, Hispanic 36%, Caucasian 40% \ *Exp:* $145 (Low) \ *Poverty:* 10% \ *Title I:* $4,764,540 \ *Special Education:* $5,603,000 \ *Open-Close:* 08/12 - 05/29 \ *DTBP:* $188 (High) \ f t

Dr Elizabeth Fagen 1
Deborah Connors 2

Billy Beattie 2
Ida Schultz 2

Janice Himpele 2
Shelley Vineyard 2
Shirley Parker 4
Troy Kite 6
Lisa McCorquodale 8
Stephanie Perry 8,275
Rick Gardner 15,68,78,273
Larkin Lesueur 27,31*
Helen Wagner 35*
Matthew Webb 39
Rachel Smith 46*
Myra Herbst 49,51
Dr Lumara Blanco-Lajara 57
Nancy Morrison 67
John Krippel 68
Kelly Gabrisch 68
Jamie Mount 71
Elizabeth King 74
Dr Robert Meaux 76
Dr Charles Ned 81
Dr Warren Roane 294

Robert Seale 2,19
Kenny Kendrick 3
Jerry Burd 5
Dr Ann Johnson 8
Dr Roger Brown 8,15,18,79
Dr Jamie Bryson 11,296
Houston Hayes 20
Ellen Shimer 34
Matt Smith 37
Kathleen Goerner 44
Courtney Peterson 47*
Deborah Perez 50
Thelissa Edwards 58
Jamie Tisdale 68
Kashonda Hurst 68
Christina Trotter 69
Dustin Hardin 73,76
Reggie Boone 76
Nolan Correa 79
Solomon Cook 91
Adrianne Holmes 298

Public Schs..Principal	Grd	Prgm	Enr/#Cls	SN	Phone
Atascocita High Sch 13300 Will Clayton Pkwy, Humble 77346 Bill Daniels	9-12	V	3,625	26%	281/641-7500 Fax 281/641-7517
Atascocita Middle Sch 18810 W Lake Houston Pkwy, Humble 77346 Karl Koehler	6-8	V	1,258 70	27%	281/641-4600 Fax 281/641-4617
Atascocita Springs Elem Sch 13515 Valley Lodge Pkwy, Humble 77346 Fennell Cheryl	PK-5		985	17%	281/641-3600 Fax 281/641-3617
Bear Branch Elem Sch 3500 Garden Lake Dr, Kingwood 77339 Kakie Palmer	PK-5		605 28	8%	281/641-1600 Fax 281/641-1617
Ⓐ Cambridge Sch 18901 Timber Forest Dr, Humble 77346 Tammey Harlan	2-12		100		281/641-7445 Fax 281/641-7399
Career & Technical Ed Center 9155 Will Clayton Pkwy, Humble 77338 Dr Marley Morris	Voc		200 12		281/641-7950 Fax 281/641-7967 t
Ⓐ Community Learning Center 18901 Timber Forest Dr, Humble 77346 Tammy Alexander	1-12	GT	50 52	53%	281/641-7400 Fax 281/641-7417
Creekwood Middle Sch 3603 W Lake Houston Pkwy, Kingwood 77339 Walter Winicki	6-8	V	1,127 60	11%	281/641-4400 Fax 281/641-4417
Deerwood Elem Sch 2920 Forest Garden Dr, Kingwood 77345 MacAire Davies	PK-5		652	11%	281/641-2200 Fax 281/641-2217
Eagle Springs Elem Sch 12500 Will Clayton Pkwy, Humble 77346 April Maldonado	PK-5		768	13%	281/641-3100 Fax 281/641-3117
Elm Grove Elem Sch 2815 Clear Ridge Dr, Kingwood 77339 Donna Fife	PK-5		508 35	36%	281/641-1700 Fax 281/641-1717
Fall Creek Elem Sch 14435 Mesa Dr, Humble 77396 Christy Erb	PK-5		1,014	14%	281/641-3400 Fax 281/641-3417
Foster Elem Sch 1800 Trailwood Village Dr, Kingwood 77339 Diana Zelezinski	PK-5		536 36	35%	281/641-1400 Fax 281/641-1417
Greentree Elem Sch 3502 Brook Shadow Dr, Kingwood 77345 Denise Rodriguez	PK-5		720 35	10%	281/641-1900 Fax 281/641-1917
Groves Elem Sch 11902 Madera Run Pkwy, Humble 77346 Dr Brian Peters	PK-5		705		281/641-5000 Fax 281/641-5017

Code		Code		Code		Code	
79	Student Personnel	91	Safety/Security	275	Response To Intervention	298	Grant Writer/Ptnrships
30	Driver Ed/Safety	92	Magnet School	277	Remedial Math K-12	750	Chief Innovation Officer
31	Gifted/Talented	93	Parental Involvement	280	Literacy Coach	751	Chief of Staff
32	Video Services	95	Tech Prep Program	285	STEM	752	Social Emotional Learning
33	Substance Abuse Prev	97	Chief Information Officer	286	Digital Learning		
34	Erate	98	Chief Technology Officer	288	Common Core Standards		
35	AIDS Education	270	Character Education	294	Accountability		
38	Alternative/At Risk	271	Migrant Education	295	Network System		
39	Multi-Cultural Curriculum	273	Teacher Mentor	296	Title II Programs		
90	Social Work	274	Before/After Sch	297	Webmaster		

School Programs
A = Alternative Program
G = Adult Classes
M = Magnet Program
T = Title I Schoolwide
V = Career & Tech Ed Programs

Other School Types
Ⓐ = Alternative School
Ⓒ = Charter School
Ⓜ = Magnet School
Ⓨ = Year-Round School

Social Media
f = Facebook
t = Twitter

New Schools are shaded
New Superintendents and Principals are bold
Personnel with email addresses are underscored

Harris County

Market Data Retrieval

School	Grd	Prgm	Enr/#Cls	SN	Phone
Hidden Hollow Elem Sch 4104 Appalachian Trl, Kingwood 77345 Janice Wiederhold	PK-5		469 38	12%	281/641-2400 Fax 281/641-2417
Humble Elem Sch 20252 Fieldtree Dr, Humble 77338 Veronica Hernandez	PK-5	T	587 43	71%	281/641-1100 Fax 281/641-1117
Humble High Sch 1700 Wilson Rd, Humble 77338 Donna Ullrich	9-12	TV	2,271	63%	281/641-6300 Fax 281/641-6517
Humble Middle Sch 11207 Will Clayton Pkwy, Humble 77346 Sarahdia Johnson	6-8	TV	1,256	72%	281/641-4000 Fax 281/641-4117
Jack M Fields Sr Elem Sch 2505 S Houston Ave, Humble 77396 Melissa Christensen	PK-5	T	519	80%	281/641-2700 Fax 281/641-2717
Kingwood High Sch 2701 Kingwood Dr, Kingwood 77339 Dr Michael Nasra	9-12	V	2,657	6%	281/641-6900 Fax 281/641-7217
Kingwood Middle Sch 2407 Pine Terrace Dr, Kingwood 77339 Robert Atteberry	6-8	V	1,018 100	27%	281/641-4200 Fax 281/641-4217
Kingwood Park High Sch 4015 Woodland Hills Dr, Kingwood 77339 Lisa Drabing	9-12	V	1,863 50	19%	281/641-6600 Fax 281/641-6617
Lakeland Elem Sch 1500 Montgomery Ln, Humble 77338 Lucy Anderson	PK-5	T	769 47	90%	281/641-1200 Fax 281/641-1220
Lakeshore Elem Sch 13333 Breakwater Path Dr, Houston 77044 Annette Nevermann	PK-5		1,025	14%	281/641-3500 Fax 281/641-3517
Maplebrook Elem Sch 7935 Farmingham Rd, Humble 77346 Tiffany Caseltine	PK-5		686	26%	281/641-2900 Fax 281/641-2917
North Belt Elem Sch 8105 E North Belt, Humble 77396 Christina Morris	PK-5	T	745 28	89%	281/641-1300 Fax 281/641-1317
Oak Forest Elem Sch 6400 Kingwood Glen Dr, Humble 77346 Linda Schmidt	PK-5	T	712 43	43%	281/641-2800 Fax 281/641-2817
Oaks Elem Sch 5858 Upper Lake Dr, Humble 77346 Kerri Smith	PK-5	T	563 36	51%	281/641-1890 Fax 281/641-1817
Park Lakes Elem Sch 4400 Wilson Rd, Humble 77396 Sarah Ballard	PK-5	T	718	63%	281/641-3200 Fax 281/641-3217
Pine Forest Elem Sch 19702 W Lake Houston Pkwy, Humble 77346 Sloane Simmons	PK-5		603 40	23%	281/641-2100 Fax 281/641-2117
Quest Early College High Sch 1700 Wilson Rd Ste 3100, Humble 77338 **Nachelle Scott**	9-12		430	28%	281/641-7300 Fax 281/641-7318
Ridge Creek Elem Sch 15201 Woodland Hills Dr, Humble 77396 Stephanie Davis	PK-5	T	758	64%	281/641-3700 Fax 281/641-3717
River Pines Elem Sch 2400 Cold River Dr, Humble 77396 Sharon Lee	PK-5	T	881	74%	281/641-3300 Fax 281/641-3317
Riverwood Middle Sch 2910 High Valley Dr, Kingwood 77345 **Matthew Roser**	6-8	V	1,051 65	4%	281/641-4800 Fax 281/641-4817
Ross Sterling Middle Sch 1131 Wilson Rd, Humble 77338 Damico Bartley	6-8	TV	867	76%	281/641-6000 Fax 281/641-6017
Shadow Forest Elem Sch 2300 Mills Branch Dr, Kingwood 77345 Lisa Lackey	PK-5		601 30	4%	281/641-2600 Fax 281/641-2617
Summer Creek High Sch 14000 Weckford Blvd, Houston 77044 Brent McDonald	9-12	T	2,230	44%	281/641-5400 Fax 281/641-5417
Summerwood Elem Sch 14000 Summerwood Lakes Dr, Houston 77044 Shannon Lalmansingh	PK-5		767	17%	281/641-3000 Fax 281/641-3017
Timbers Elem Sch 6910 Lonesome Woods Trl, Humble 77346 Alison Pierce	PK-5		699 25	40%	281/641-2000 Fax 281/641-2017
Timberwood Middle Sch 18450 Timber Forest Dr, Humble 77346 Kenneth Buck	6-8		1,585 65	29%	281/641-3800 Fax 281/641-3817
West Lake Middle Sch 11810 Madera Run Pkwy, Humble 77346 Dr Kenneth Hodgkinson	6-8		1,000		281/641-5800 Fax 281/641-5817
Whispering Pines Elem Sch 17321 Woodland Hills Dr, Humble 77346 Wendy Anaya	PK-5	T	686 42	50%	281/641-2500 Fax 281/641-2517
Willow Creek Elem Sch 2002 Willow Terrace Dr, Kingwood 77345 Scott Duncan	PK-5		509 28	1%	281/641-2300 Fax 281/641-2317
Woodcreek Middle Sch 14600 Woodson Park Dr, Houston 77044 Alan Moye	6-8		1,736	29%	281/641-5200 Fax 281/641-5217
Woodland Hills Elem Sch 2222 Tree Ln, Kingwood 77339 Cindy Barker	PK-5		565 30	28%	281/641-1500 Fax 281/641-1517

● **Klein Ind School Dist** PID: 01026289   832/249-4000
7200 Spring Cypress Rd, Klein 77379   Fax 832/249-4015

Schools: 49 \ *Teachers:* 3,382 \ *Students:* 53,868 \
Special Ed Students: 4,429 \ *LEP Students:* 7,057 \ *College-Bound:* 80%
\ *Ethnic:* Asian 9%, African American 15%, Hispanic 42%, Caucasian
34% \ *Exp:* $174 (Low) \ *Poverty:* 13% \ *Title I:* $9,938,587 \
Special Education: $6,983,000 \ *Open-Close:* 08/19 - 05/28 \ *DTBP:* $186
(High) \

Dr Jenny McGowan	1,288	Audrey Ambridge	2
Dan Schaefer	2,19	Jason Gossett	2
Thomas Petrek	2,15	Robert Robertson	3,15
Scott Lazar	3	Doug Massey	4
John Rice	5	Darby Young	6,35
Yvonne Clark	7	Adam Hile	8
Christopher Ruggerio	11	Cheryl Gordy	12
Dr Jan Marek	15	Kelly Schumacher	15,68
Larry Whitehead	15,76	Vicki James	15,79,294
Nicole Shepard	16	Joel Wren	20,23
Debra Broner Westerl	27	Kayla Shaw	36,85
Michelle Thompson	42	Christine Zorn	45
Carrie Farmer	48*	Kathy Vegara	57,89
Dr Kristen Allman	58	George Reitmeier	67
Stacy Kindsfather	69,294	Amanda Salinas	70*
Christine Jackson	71*	Cindy Doyle	71
Chris Cummings	73,84	Kathleen Plott	81
Rick Stockton	83,88	Brian Marr	88*
David Kimberly	91	Dr Joffery Jones	91
Ron Webster	91	Maria Ovalle Lopez	93
Stacy Kindsfather	294*	Denise McLean	297

Public Schs..Principal	Grd	Prgm	Enr/#Cls	SN	Phone
Benfer Elem Sch 18027 Kuykendahl Rd Ste B, Klein 77379 Shannon Strole	PK-5		825 32	42%	832/484-6000 Fax 832/484-7850
Benignus Elem Sch 7225 Alvin A Klein Dr, Klein 77379 Dawn Proctor	PK-5		792	17%	832/484-7750 Fax 832/484-7796

1	Superintendent	8	Curric/Instruct K-12	19	Chief Financial Officer	29	Family/Consumer Science
2	Bus/Finance/Purchasing	9	Curric/Instruct Elem	20	Art K-12	30	Adult Education
3	Buildings And Grounds	10	Curric/Instruct Sec	21	Art Elem	31	Career/Sch-to-Work K-12
4	Food Service	11	Federal Program	22	Art Sec	32	Career/Sch-to-Work Elem
5	Transportation	12	Title I	23	Music K-12	33	Career/Sch-to-Work Sec
6	Athletic	13	Title V	24	Music Elem	34	Early Childhood Ed
7	Health Services	15	Asst Superintendent	25	Music Sec	35	Health/Phys Education
		16	Instructional Media Svcs	26	Business Education	36	Guidance Services K-12
		17	Chief Operations Officer	27	Career & Tech Ed	37	Guidance Services Elem
		18	Chief Academic Officer	28	Technology Education	38	Guidance Services Sec

39	Social Studies K-12	49	English/Lang Arts Elem	59	Special Education Elem	69	Academic Assessment
40	Social Studies Elem	50	English/Lang Arts Sec	60	Special Education Sec	70	Research/Development
41	Social Studies Sec	51	Reading K-12	61	Foreign/World Lang K-12	71	Public Information
42	Science K-12	52	Reading Elem	62	Foreign/World Lang Elem	72	Summer School
43	Science Elem	53	Reading Sec	63	Foreign/World Lang Sec	73	Instructional Tech
44	Science Sec	54	Remedial Reading K-12	64	Religious Education K-12	74	Inservice Training
45	Math K-12	55	Remedial Reading Elem	65	Religious Education Elem	75	Marketing/Distributive
46	Math Elem	56	Remedial Reading Sec	66	Religious Education Sec	76	Info Systems
47	Math Sec	57	Bilingual/ELL	67	School Board President	77	Psychological Assess
48	English/Lang Arts K-12	58	Special Education K-12	68	Teacher Personnel	78	Affirmative Action

Texas School Directory — Harris County

School	Grades	Prog	Enroll	%	Phone
Bernshausen Elem Sch 11116 Mahaffey Rd, Tomball 77375 Carrie Farmer	PK-5	T	905	53%	832/375-8000 Fax 832/375-8050
Blackshear Elem Sch 11211 Lacey Rd, Tomball 77375 Meagan White	PK-5	T	1,042	42%	832/375-7600 Fax 832/375-7725
Brill Elem Sch 9102 Herts Rd, Klein 77379 Sandra Speer	PK-5		758 48	33%	832/484-6150 Fax 832/484-7851
Doerre Intermediate Sch 18218 Theiss Mail Route Rd, Klein 77379 Katherine Land	6-8		1,309 86	14%	832/249-5700 Fax 832/249-4054
Ehrhardt Elem Sch 6603 Rosebrook Ln, Klein 77379 Linda Galicia	PK-5	T	743 40	46%	832/484-6200 Fax 832/484-7853
Eiland Elem Sch 6700 N Klein Circle Dr, Houston 77088 David Menendez	K-5	T	542 40	87%	832/484-6900 Fax 832/484-7854
Epps Island Elem Sch 7403 Smiling Wood Ln, Houston 77086 Maribel Scarbrough	K-5	T	657 52	89%	832/484-5800 Fax 832/484-7856
Frank Elem Sch 9225 Crescent Clover Dr, Klein 77379 Tyra Storie	PK-5		693	5%	832/375-7000 Fax 832/375-7100
French Elem Sch 5802 W Rayford Rd, Spring 77389 Carole Mason	PK-5		675	8%	832/375-8100 Fax 832/375-8175
Ⓨ Grace England ECC 7535 Prairie Oak Dr, Houston 77086 Jaunee Perry	PK-PK	MT	486	74%	832/375-7900 Fax 832/375-7925
Greenwood Forest Elem Sch 12100 Misty Valley Dr, Houston 77066 Alisha Elrod	K-5	T	735 35	60%	832/484-5700 Fax 832/484-7858
Hassler Elem Sch 9325 Lochlea Ridge Dr, Klein 77379 Sarah Brown	PK-5		783	10%	832/484-7100 Fax 832/484-7860
Haude Elem Sch 3111 Louetta Rd, Spring 77388 Rachel Wall	PK-5		729	20%	832/484-5600 Fax 832/484-7862
Hildebrandt Intermediate Sch 22800 Hildebrandt Rd, Spring 77389 Lauren Marti	6-8		1,345 80	30%	832/249-5100 Fax 832/249-4068
Hofius Intermediate Sch 8400 W Rayford Rd, Spring 77389 Christy Goforth	6-8		401		832/375-8800 Fax 832/375-8835
Kaiser Elem Sch 13430 Bammel North Houston Rd, Houston 77066 Betty Zavala	K-5	T	740	88%	832/484-6100 Fax 832/484-7864
Kleb Intermediate Sch 7425 Louetta Rd, Klein 77379 Clay Huggins	6-8		1,356 80	33%	832/249-5500 Fax 832/249-4053
Ⓐ Klein Alternative Ed Center 7302 Kleingreen Ln, Klein 77379 Brian Marr	K-12		100 25	54%	832/249-4801 Fax 832/249-4045
Klein Cain High Sch 10201 Spring Cypress Rd, Houston 77070 Nicole Patin	9-12		1,400		832/375-8400 Fax 832/375-8301
Klein Collins High Sch 20811 Ella Blvd, Spring 77388 Randy Kirk	9-12		3,629 130	28%	832/484-5500 Fax 832/484-7811
Klein Forest High Sch 11400 Misty Valley Dr, Houston 77066 Lance Alexander	9-12	TV	3,708 120	71%	832/484-4500 Fax 832/484-4490
Klein High Sch 16715 Stuebner Airline Rd, Klein 77379 Jessica Haddox	9-12	V	3,683	27%	832/484-4000 Fax 832/484-7821
Klein Intermediate Sch 4710 W Mount Houston Rd, Houston 77088 Charles Woods	6-8	T	1,105	83%	832/249-4900 Fax 832/249-4046
Klein Oak High Sch 22603 Northcrest Dr, Spring 77389 Thomas Hensley	9-12	V	3,938	25%	832/484-5000 Fax 832/484-7831
Klenk Elem Sch 6111 Bourgeois Rd, Houston 77066 Allie Martin	K-5	T	821 35	68%	832/484-6800 Fax 832/484-7866
Kohrville Elem Sch 11600 Woodland Shore Dr, Tomball 77375 Kia Bowie	PK-5	T	669 50	46%	832/484-7200 Fax 832/484-7890
Krahn Elem Sch 9502 Eday Dr, Klein 77379 Leslie Kompelien	PK-5		746	37%	832/484-6500 Fax 832/484-7868
Kreinhop Elem Sch 20820 Ella Blvd, Spring 77388 Lauren Liesberger	PK-5		953	30%	832/484-7400 Fax 832/484-7404
Krimmel Intermediate Sch 7070 FM 2920 Rd, Klein 77379 Prentiss Harper	6-8		1,384	29%	832/375-7200 Fax 832/375-7150
Kuehnle Elem Sch 5510 Winding Ridge Dr, Klein 77379 Julia Funk	PK-5		882 60	18%	832/484-6650 Fax 832/484-7870
Lemm Elem Sch 19034 Joanleigh Dr, Spring 77388 Kathy Brown	PK-5		695		832/484-6300 Fax 832/484-7872
Mahaffey Elem Sch 10255 Mahaffey Rd, Tomball 77375 Holly Mason	K-5		644	41%	832/375-8300 Fax 832/375-8297
McDougle Elem Sch 10410 Kansack Ln, Houston 77086 Kathy Rachal	K-5	T	573	80%	832/484-7550 Fax 832/484-7699
Metzler Elem Sch 8500 W Rayford Rd, Spring 77389 Lakita Combs	PK-5		863	27%	832/484-7900 Fax 832/484-7999
Mittelstadt Elem Sch 7525 Kleingreen Ln, Klein 77379 Julie Shumake	PK-5	T	865 38	47%	832/484-6700 Fax 832/484-7876
Mueller Elem Sch 7074 FM 2920 Rd, Klein 77379 Kathryn Shealy	PK-5		882	29%	832/375-7300 Fax 832/375-7425
Nitsch Elem Sch 4702 W Mount Houston Rd, Houston 77088 Frank Ward	K-5		777	86%	832/484-6400 Fax 832/484-7878
Northampton Elem Sch 6404 Root Rd, Spring 77389 Lisa Campbell	PK-5		567 55	43%	832/484-5550 Fax 832/484-7880
Roth Elem Sch 21623 Castlemont Ln, Spring 77388 Gail McGuire	PK-5		709 40	42%	832/484-6600 Fax 832/484-7882
Schindewolf Intermediate Sch 20903 Ella Blvd, Spring 77388 Curtis Simmons	6-8		1,495	31%	832/249-5900 Fax 832/249-4072
Schultz Elem Sch 7920 Willow Forest Dr, Tomball 77375 Sherri Davenport	PK-5	T	655 70	43%	832/484-7000 Fax 832/484-7884
Strack Intermediate Sch 18027 Kuykendahl Rd Ste S, Klein 77379 Jason Ovalle	6-8		1,369	31%	832/249-5400 Fax 832/249-4051
Theiss Elem Sch 17510 Theiss Mail Route Rd, Klein 77379 Joann Keenan	PK-5		661 32	15%	832/484-5900 Fax 832/484-7886
Ulrich Intermediate Sch 10103 Spring Cypress Rd, Houston 77070 Trevor Woolley	6-8	T	1,283	47%	832/375-7500 Fax 832/375-7599

---

79 Student Personnel	91 Safety/Security	275 Response To Intervention	298 Grant Writer/Ptnrships	**School Programs**	**Social Media**
80 Driver Ed/Safety	92 Magnet School	277 Remedial Math K-12	750 Chief Innovation Officer	A = Alternative Program	
81 Gifted/Talented	93 Parental Involvement	280 Literacy Coach	751 Chief of Staff	G = Adult Classes	= Facebook
82 Video Services	95 Tech Prep Program	285 STEM	752 Social Emotional Learning	M = Magnet Program	
83 Substance Abuse Prev	97 Chief Infomation Officer	286 Digital Learning		T = Title I Schoolwide	= Twitter
84 Erate	98 Chief Technology Officer	288 Common Core Standards	**Other School Types**	V = Career & Tech Ed Programs	
85 AIDS Education	270 Character Education	294 Accountability	Ⓐ = Alternative School		
88 Alternative/At Risk	271 Migrant Education	295 Network System	Ⓒ = Charter School	New Schools are shaded	
89 Multi-Cultural Curriculum	273 Teacher Mentor	296 Title II Programs	Ⓜ = Magnet School	New Superintendents and Principals are bold	
90 Social Work	274 Before/After Sch	297 Webmaster	Ⓨ = Year-Round School	Personnel with email addresses are underscored	

TX—197

Harris County — Market Data Retrieval

ⓐ **Vistas High Sch** 9-12 75 832/484-7650
12550 Bammel North Houston Rd, Houston 77066 Fax 832/484-7697
James Anderson

Wunderlich Intermediate Sch 6-8 T 1,620 72% 832/249-5200
11800 Misty Valley Dr, Houston 77066 85 Fax 832/249-4050
Lesley Aaron

Zwink Elem Sch PK-5 T 1,086 39% 832/375-7800
22200 Frassati Way, Spring 77389 Fax 832/375-7850
Stacey Vaglienty

- **La Porte Ind School Dist** PID: 01026370 281/604-7000
  1002 San Jacinto St, La Porte 77571 Fax 281/604-7010

Schools: 12 \ **Teachers:** 495 \ **Students:** 7,679 \ **Special Ed Students:** 828 \ **LEP Students:** 666 \ **College-Bound:** 60% \ **Ethnic:** Asian 1%, African American 7%, Hispanic 49%, Native American: 1%, Caucasian 43% \ **Exp:** $269 (Med) \ **Poverty:** 11% \ **Title I:** $1,205,794 \ **Special Education:** $1,554,000 \ **Open-Close:** 08/21 - 05/28 \ **DTBP:** $183 (High)

Name	Ref
Lloyd Graham	1
Sheila Cantu	2
Mike Clausen	3,15,17,91
Todd Schoppe	6*
Dr Linda Wadleigh	8,15
Danette Tilley	10
Eddie Hill	16,76,295
Cynthia Andersen	58
Angela Garza-Viator	68
Terri Cook	71
Rhonda Cumbie	2,19
Corey Marlar	3,5,73
Yvonne Bennett	4
Carrie Rife	7
Jewel Whitfield	9
Dr Vonn Murray	11,69,288,294,296,298
Matthew Burke	20,23
Kathy Green	67
Angela Garza-Viator	68,78*

Public Schs..Principal	Grd	Prgm	Enr/#Cls	SN	Phone
Baker 6th Grade Campus 9800 Spencer Hwy, La Porte 77571 Alicia Upchurch	6-6	T	545 50	56%	281/604-6884 Fax 281/604-6885
Bayshore Elem Sch 800 McCabe Rd, La Porte 77571 Donna Spaugh	PK-5	T	583 28	61%	281/604-4600 Fax 281/604-4680
College Park Elem Sch 4315 Luella Ave, Deer Park 77536 Camilla Whitlock	PK-5	T	437 35	65%	281/604-4400 Fax 281/604-4460
ⓐ DeWalt Alternative Sch 401 N 2nd St, La Porte 77571 Candace Pohl	6-12		67 13		281/604-6900 Fax 281/604-6904
Heritage Elem Sch 4301 East Blvd, Deer Park 77536 Grisel Wallace	PK-5	T	520	47%	281/604-2600 Fax 281/604-2605
Jennie Reid Elem Sch 10001 W Fairmont Pkwy, La Porte 77571 Diane Weeden	PK-5	T	461 32	48%	281/604-4500 Fax 281/604-4555
La Porte Elem Sch 725 S Broadway, La Porte 77571 Carol Williams	PK-5	T	555 30	75%	281/604-4700 Fax 281/604-4787
La Porte High Sch 301 E Fairmont Pkwy, La Porte 77571 Carlin Grammer	9-12	GTV	2,162	39%	281/604-7500 Fax 281/604-7516
La Porte Junior High Sch 401 S Broadway St, La Porte 77571 Earnest Brooks	7-8	T	565 55	53%	281/604-6600 Fax 281/604-6605
Leo A Rizzuto Elem Sch 3201 Farrington Blvd, La Porte 77571 Deanna Narciste	PK-5	T	587 32	45%	281/604-6500 Fax 281/604-6555
Lomax Elem Sch 10615 N Avenue L, La Porte 77571 Patricia Herrera	PK-5	T	486 30	41%	281/604-4300 Fax 281/604-4355
Lomax Junior High Sch 9801 N Avenue L, La Porte 77571 Kade Griffin	7-8	T	614	46%	281/604-6700 Fax 281/604-6730

- **Pasadena Ind School Dist** PID: 01026631 713/740-0000
  1515 Cherrybrook Ln, Pasadena 77502 Fax 713/740-4040

Schools: 68 \ **Teachers:** 3,846 \ **Students:** 54,000 \ **Special Ed Students:** 5,374 \ **LEP Students:** 15,699 \ **Ethnic:** Asian 3%, African American 8%, Hispanic 83%, Caucasian 6% \ **Exp:** $213 (Med) \ **Poverty:** 22% \ **Title I:** $19,892,761 \ **Special Education:** $8,728,000 \ **Open-Close:** 08/19 - 05/28 \ **DTBP:** $194 (High) \ 🅵 🅴

Name	Ref
Dr Deeann Powell	1
Carla Merka	2,15,19
Thomas Douglas	3
Robert Stock	5*
Dr Karen Hickman	8,15,288
Erian Comeaux	11
Alyta Harrell	15,70*
Rhonda Parmer	15
Dr Troy McCarley	15,70,71
Tanya Hagar	27*
Rebecca Terry	34
Suzanne Caballero	57,271
Julie Reed	58,294
Cynthia Guerrero	68,273*
Donna Summers	70
Scott Harrell	74
Allen Brown	76
Stewart Russell	91
Bethany Jordan	2
Kevin Fornof	3,15
Mary Harryman	4
Ruperto Jaso	6
Rebecca Benner	8
Gloria Gallegos	11,15,57,271,274,296
Barbara Fuqua	15,294
Dr Steve Fullen	15
Linda Fletcher	20,23
Tom Swan	30*
Pat Sermas	36,69
Debbie Barrett	58
Marshall Kendrick	67
Karen White	69
Arthur Allen	73,98,286
Traci Goodwin	74
Jamie Burt	79
Olivia Daugherty	298

Public Schs..Principal	Grd	Prgm	Enr/#Cls	SN	Phone
Adella Young Elem Sch 4221 Fox Meadow Ln, Pasadena 77504 Amy McClellen	PK-4	T	606 38	89%	713/740-0784 Fax 713/740-4151
Atkinson Elem Sch 9602 Kingspoint Rd, Houston 77075 Lena Ortiz	PK-4	T	480 36	73%	713/740-0520 Fax 713/740-4128
Bailey Elem Sch 2707 Lafferty Rd, Pasadena 77502 Karyn Johnson	PK-4	T	714 58	87%	713/740-0528 Fax 713/740-4129
Beverly Hills Intermediate Sch 11111 Beamer Rd, Houston 77089 Stacy Barber	7-8	T	1,038 41	68%	713/740-0420 Fax 713/740-4051
Bobby Shaw Middle Sch 1201 Houston Ave, Pasadena 77502 Darby Hickman	5-6	T	782	90%	713/740-5268 Fax 713/740-5909
Burnett Elem Sch 11825 Teaneck Dr, Houston 77089 Jae Lee	PK-4	T	484 44	79%	713/740-0536 Fax 713/740-4130
ⓐ Community Sch 1838A E Sam Houston Pkwy S, Pasadena 77503 Tom Swan	11-12		75		713/740-4048
Dr Kirk Lewis Career & Tech HS 1348 Genoa Red Bluff Rd, Houston 77034 Steve Fleming	Voc		500		713/740-5320 Fax 713/740-5910
Elmer Bondy Intermediate Sch 5101 Keith Rd, Pasadena 77505 Roneka Lee	7-8	T	987 55	61%	713/740-0430 Fax 713/740-4152
Felix Morales Elem Sch 305 W Harris Ave, Pasadena 77506 Lisa Haws	PK-4	T	519 36	85%	713/740-0664 Fax 713/740-4104
Fisher Elem Sch 2920 Watters Rd, Pasadena 77502 Norma Valenzuela	PK-5	T	748	83%	713/740-0552 Fax 713/740-4131

#	Code	#	Code	#	Code	#	Code	#	Code	#	Code	#	Code
1	Superintendent	8	Curric/Instruct K-12	19	Chief Financial Officer	29	Family/Consumer Science	39	Social Studies K-12	49	English/Lang Arts Elem	59	Special Education Elem	69	Academic Assessment
2	Bus/Finance/Purchasing	9	Curric/Instruct Elem	20	Art K-12	30	Adult Education	40	Social Studies Elem	50	English/Lang Arts Sec	60	Special Education Sec	70	Research/Development
3	Buildings And Grounds	10	Curric/Instruct Sec	21	Art Elem	31	Career/Sch-to-Work K-12	41	Social Studies Sec	51	Reading K-12	61	Foreign/World Lang K-12	71	Public Information
4	Food Service	11	Federal Program	22	Art Sec	32	Career/Sch-to-Work Elem	42	Science K-12	52	Reading Elem	62	Foreign/World Lang Elem	72	Summer School
5	Transportation	12	Title I	23	Music K-12	33	Career/Sch-to-Work Sec	43	Science Elem	53	Reading Sec	63	Foreign/World Lang Sec	73	Instructional Tech
6	Athletic	13	Title V	24	Music Elem	34	Early Childhood Ed	44	Science Sec	54	Remedial Reading K-12	64	Religious Education K-12	74	Inservice Training
7	Health Services	15	Asst Superintendent	25	Music Sec	35	Health/Phys Education	45	Math K-12	55	Remedial Reading Elem	65	Religious Education Elem	75	Marketing/Distributive
		16	Instructional Media Svcs	26	Business Education	36	Guidance Services K-12	46	Math Elem	56	Remedial Reading Sec	66	Religious Education Sec	76	Info Systems
		17	Chief Operations Officer	27	Career & Tech Ed	37	Guidance Services Elem	47	Math Sec	57	Bilingual/ELL	67	School Board President	77	Psychological Assess
		18	Chief Academic Officer	28	Technology Education	38	Guidance Services Sec	48	English/Lang Arts K-12	58	Special Education K-12	68	Teacher Personnel	78	Affirmative Action

Texas School Directory

Harris County

School	Grades	Prog	Enroll/Staff	%	Phone
Frazier Elem Sch 10503 Hughes Rd, Houston 77089 Wendy Wiseburn	PK-4	T	509 25	76%	713/740-0560 Fax 713/740-4132
Fred Roberts Middle Sch 13402 Conklin Ln, Houston 77034 Jorly Thomas	5-6	T	607	74%	713/740-5390
Freeman Elem Sch 2323 Theta St, Houston 77034 Michael Van Loenen	PK-4	T	507 35	84%	713/740-0568 Fax 713/740-4107
Gardens Elem Sch 1107 Harris Ave, Pasadena 77506 Lindsey Lesniewski	PK-4	T	724 40	89%	713/740-0576 Fax 713/740-4133
Garfield Elem Sch 10301 Hartsook St, Houston 77034 Courtney Merilatt	PK-4	T	721 40	83%	713/740-0584 Fax 713/740-4134
Genoa Elem Sch 12900 Almeda Genoa Rd, Houston 77034 Tiffany Bennett	PK-4	T	728 40	79%	713/740-0592 Fax 713/740-4135
George A Thompson Interm Sch 11309 Sagedowne Ln, Houston 77089 Tanis Griffin	7-8	T	920 69	64%	713/740-0510 Fax 713/740-4083
Golden Acres Elem Sch 5232 Sycamore Ave, Pasadena 77503 Lisa Davis	PK-4	T	462 37	81%	713/740-0600 Fax 713/740-4136
Ⓐ Guidance Center 3010 Bayshore Blvd, Pasadena 77502 Robert Sayavedra	5-12		400 24		713/740-0792 Fax 713/740-4108
Harvey Turner Elem Sch 4333 Lily St, Pasadena 77505 Donna Duke	PK-4	T	633 36	50%	713/740-0768 Fax 713/740-4149
J Frank Dobie High Sch 10220 Blackhawk Blvd, Houston 77089 Franklin Moses	9-12	TV	4,205 125	58%	713/740-0370 Fax 713/740-4158
Jackson Intermediate Sch 1020 E Thomas Ave, Pasadena 77506 Paula Sword	7-8	T	721 69	91%	713/740-0440 Fax 713/740-4109
Jensen Elem Sch 3514 Tulip St, Pasadena 77504 Judy Diaz	PK-5	T	675 31	79%	713/740-0608 Fax 713/740-4137
Jessup Elem Sch 9301 Almeda Genoa Rd, Houston 77075 Ryan Pavone	PK-4	T	680 40	92%	713/740-0616 Fax 713/740-4112
Keller Middle Sch 1711 Magnolia Dr, Pasadena 77503 Daniel Eble	5-6	T	702	88%	713/740-5284 Fax 713/740-5915
Kruse Elem Sch 400 Park Lane, Pasadena 77506 Sandra Buckner	PK-4	T	600 44	94%	713/740-0624 Fax 713/740-4138
L F Smith Elem Sch 2703 Perez Rd, Pasadena 77502 Cathy Danna	PK-5	T	688 42	91%	713/740-0720 Fax 713/740-4113
Laura Bush Elem Sch 9100 Blackhawk Blvd, Houston 77075 Stephanie Miller	PK-4	T	691	61%	713/740-0928 Fax 713/740-4126
Lomax Middle Sch 1519 Genoa Red Bluff Rd, Pasadena 77504 Norma Penny	5-6	T	659	63%	713/740-5230 Fax 713/740-4175
Lorenzo Dezavala Middle Sch 101 E Jackson Ave, Pasadena 77506 Melissa Garza	5-6	T	716 37	90%	713/740-0544 Fax 713/740-4159
Mae Smythe Elem Sch 2424 Burke Rd, Pasadena 77502 Denise Moody	PK-4	T	690 50	85%	713/740-0728 Fax 713/740-4114
Marshall Kendricks Middle Sch 3001 Watters Rd, Pasadena 77504 Melissa Messenger	5-6	T	782	85%	713/740-5380 Fax 713/740-5980
McMasters Elem Sch 1011 Bennett Dr, Pasadena 77503 Andrea Gilger	PK-4	T	466 30	84%	713/740-0640 Fax 713/740-4079
Meador Elem Sch 10701 Seaford Dr, Houston 77089 Beverly Bolton	PK-4	T	604 37	78%	713/740-0648 Fax 713/740-4105
Melillo Middle Sch 9220 Hughes Rd, Houston 77089 Diane Wheeler	5-6	T	704	56%	713/740-5260 Fax 713/740-5908
Milstead Middle Sch 338 Gilpin St, Houston 77034 Scott Pollack	5-6	T	794 38	87%	713/740-5238 Fax 713/740-4176
Morris Middle Sch 10415 Fuqua St, Houston 77089 Allison Lewallen	5-6	T	895	70%	713/740-0672 Fax 713/740-4047
Nelda Sullivan Middle Sch 1112 Queens Rd, Pasadena 77502 Kelly Cook-Costley	5-6	TV	636	89%	713/740-5420
Park View Intermediate Sch 3003 Dabney Dr, Pasadena 77502 Christina Serna	6-8	TV	659 45	82%	713/740-0460 Fax 713/740-4115
Parks Elem Sch 3302 San Augustine Ave, Pasadena 77503 Frances Burley	PK-4	T	483 32	92%	713/740-0680 Fax 713/740-4141
Pasadena High Sch 206 Shaver St, Pasadena 77506 **Laura Gomez**	9-12	GTV	2,711	82%	713/740-0310 Fax 713/740-4085
Pasadena Memorial High Sch 4410 Crenshaw Rd, Pasadena 77504 Jeremy Richardson	9-12	T	3,375 75	62%	713/740-0390 Fax 713/740-4156
Pearl Hall Elem Sch 1504 9th St, South Houston 77587 Allison Tarnez	PK-4	T	751 43	89%	713/740-0688 Fax 713/740-4142
Pomeroy Elem Sch 920 Burke Rd, Pasadena 77506 Stephen Harding	PK-4	T	890 45	90%	713/740-0696 Fax 713/740-4103
Queens Intermediate Sch 1452 Queens St, Houston 77017 Cleveland Lee	6-8	T	646 50	87%	713/740-0470 Fax 713/740-4101
Red Bluff Elem Sch 416 Bearle St, Pasadena 77506 Tammie Hinton	PK-4	T	549 53	89%	713/740-0704 Fax 713/740-4143
Richard Moore Elem Sch 8880 Southbluff Blvd, Houston 77089 Jill Lacamu	PK-4	T	466 30	61%	713/740-0656 Fax 713/740-4140
Richey Elem Sch 610 Richey St, Pasadena 77506 Andrea Zapata	PK-4	T	738 48	88%	713/740-0712 Fax 713/740-4098
Rick Schneider Middle Sch 8420 Easthaven Blvd, Houston 77075 Kristin Still	5-6	T	758 44	85%	713/740-0920 Fax 713/740-4125
Sam Rayburn High Sch 2121 Cherrybrook Ln, Pasadena 77502 Vanessa Reyes	9-12	TV	3,028 140	80%	713/740-0330 Fax 713/740-4157
San Jacinto Intermediate Sch 3600 Red Bluff Rd, Pasadena 77503 Jennifer Phelan	7-8	T	698 75	85%	713/740-0480 Fax 713/740-4153
South Belt Elem Sch 1801 Riverstone Ranch Rd, Houston 77089 Candy Howard	PK-4	T	596	55%	713/740-5276 Fax 713/740-5924
South Houston Elem Sch 900 Main St, South Houston 77587 Edna Zarzosa	PK-4	T	653 36	89%	713/740-0736 Fax 713/740-4144
South Houston High Sch 3820 S Shaver St, South Houston 77587 Andrea Wenke	9-12	TV	2,902	80%	713/740-0350 Fax 713/740-4155

79 Student Personnel	91 Safety/Security	275 Response To Intervention	298 Grant Writer/Ptnrships	**School Programs**	**Social Media**
80 Driver Ed/Safety	92 Magnet School	277 Remedial Math K-12	750 Chief Innovation Officer	A = Alternative Program	
81 Gifted/Talented	93 Parental Involvement	280 Literacy Coach	751 Chief of Staff	G = Adult Classes	📘 = Facebook
82 Video Services	95 Tech Prep Program	285 STEM	752 Social Emotional Learning	M = Magnet Program	
83 Substance Abuse Prev	97 Chief Infomation Officer	286 Digital Learning		T = Title I Schoolwide	🐦 = Twitter
84 Erate	98 Chief Technology Officer	288 Common Core Standards	**Other School Types**	V = Career & Tech Ed Programs	
85 AIDS Accountability	270 Character Education	294 Accountability	Ⓐ = Alternative School		
88 Alternative/At Risk	271 Migrant Education	295 Network System	Ⓒ = Charter School	New Schools are shaded	
89 Multi-Cultural Curriculum	273 Teacher Mentor	296 Title II Programs	Ⓜ = Magnet School	New Superintendents and Principals are bold	
90 Social Work	274 Before/After Sch	297 Webmaster	Ⓨ = Year-Round School	Personnel with email addresses are underscored	

TX—199

Harris County

School	Grd	Prgm	Enr/#Cls	SN	Phone
South Houston Intermediate Sch 900 College Ave, South Houston 77587 Jessica Swenson	7-8	T	725 60	85%	713/740-0490 Fax 713/740-4097
South Shaver Elem Sch 200 West Ave, Pasadena 77502 Erica Lilly	PK-4	T	698 33	92%	713/740-0842 Fax 713/740-4145
Southmore Intermediate Sch 2000 Patricia Ln, Pasadena 77502 John Moody	7-8	T	783 70	87%	713/740-0500 Fax 713/740-4154
Sparks Elem Sch 2503 Southmore Ave, Pasadena 77502 Sherri Means	PK-4	T	460 45	89%	713/740-0744 Fax 713/740-4146
Stuchbery Elem Sch 11210 Hughes Rd, Houston 77089 Jose Hernandez	PK-4	T	700 40	74%	713/740-0752 Fax 713/740-4147
Teague Elem Sch 4200 Crenshaw Rd, Pasadena 77504 Valorie Morris	PK-4	T	697 35	66%	713/740-0760 Fax 713/740-4148
ⓐ Tegeler Career Center 4949 Burke Rd, Pasadena 77504 Jean Cain	6-12	GV	215 10		713/740-0410 Fax 713/740-4077
ⓐ The Summit Sch 1838 E Sam Houston Pkwy S, Pasadena 77503 Robert De Wolfe	6-12	G	156 21	83%	713/740-0290 Fax 713/740-4049
Thomas Hancock Elem Sch 9604 Minnesota St, Houston 77075 Veronica Sandoval	PK-4	T	446	85%	713/740-5430
Vincent W Miller Interm Sch 1002 Fairmont Pkwy, Pasadena 77504 Mikie Escamilla	7-8	T	785 60	84%	713/740-0450 Fax 713/740-4106
Virtual Sch 1832 E Sam Houston Pkwy S, Pasadena 77503 Luci Weaver	9-12		1,000		713/740-0124 Fax 713/740-4026
Walter Matthys Elem Sch 1500 Main St, South Houston 77587 Becky Vargas	PK-4	T	664 55	81%	713/740-0632 Fax 713/740-4139
Williams Elem Sch 1522 Scarborough Ln, Pasadena 77502 Christine Coppedge	PK-5	T	599 40	88%	713/740-0776 Fax 713/740-4150

- **Sheldon Ind School Dist** PID: 01027013   281/727-2000
  11411 C E King Pkwy, Houston 77044   Fax 281/727-2085

Schools: 11 \ **Teachers:** 553 \ **Students:** 8,500 \ **Special Ed Students:** 658 \ **LEP Students:** 2,243 \ **College-Bound:** 54% \ **Ethnic:** African American 21%, Hispanic 71%, Caucasian 6% \ **Exp:** $447 (High) \ **Poverty:** 21% \ **Title I:** $2,110,478 \ **Special Education:** $1,316,000 \ **Open-Close:** 08/26 - 06/03 \ **DTBP:** $173 (High)

King Davis 1	Abraham George 2,19
Cristy Gates 3,17	Monica Tomas 4
Derek Fitzhenry 6,35	Paula Patterson 8,15,18
Juan Duenas 9,288	Dr Keith Brooks 10
Dr Brenda DeArmon 11,298	Demetrius McCall 15
Susan Pansmith 54,58	Quyen Tieu 58
Patricia Archie 67	Kristy Amarantos 68
Derik Moore 71	Becky Zalefnik 73,76,285,286
Marcie Herrera 76	James Webster 79,83

Public Schs..Principal	Grd	Prgm	Enr/#Cls	SN	Phone
C E King High Sch 8540 C E King Pkwy, Houston 77044 Dr Keith Brooks	9-12	T	2,373 55	73%	281/727-3500 Fax 281/459-7346
C E King Middle Sch 8530 C E King Pkwy, Houston 77044 Raffat Saeed	6-8	T	1,043 44	85%	281/727-4300 Fax 281/459-7452
Carroll Elem Sch 10210 C E King Pkwy, Houston 77044 Atina Young	1-5	T	807	81%	281/727-4100 Fax 281/727-4175
Cravens Early Childhood Acad 13210 Tidwell Rd, Houston 77044 Denise Mustin	PK-K	T	579 29	84%	281/727-2100 Fax 281/727-2160
Garrett Elem Sch 12017 Garrett Rd, Houston 77044 Stephanie Chavez	1-5	T	636	84%	281/727-4200 Fax 281/727-4275
L E Monahan Elem Sch 8901 Deep Valley Dr, Houston 77044 Cheri Dixon	1-5	T	601 26	78%	281/454-2900 Fax 281/459-7452
Michael R Null Middle Sch 12117 Garrett Rd, Houston 77044 Leroy Bradley	6-8	T	1,024 32	80%	281/436-2800 Fax 281/436-2875
Royalwood Elem Sch 7715 Royalwood Dr, Houston 77049 Lorena Carrasco	1-5	T	663 27	83%	281/454-2700 Fax 281/454-2775
Sheldon Early Childhood Acad 17010 Beaumont Hwy, Houston 77049 Christopher Dickson	PK-K	T	535	76%	281/456-6800 Fax 281/456-6875
Sheldon Early Clg High Sch 8540 C E King Pkwy, Houston 77044 Robert Hernandez	9-11	A	297		281/727-3500
Sheldon Elem Sch 17203 Hall Shepperd Rd, Houston 77049 Rachelle Ysquierdo	1-5	T	725 40	78%	281/456-6700 Fax 281/456-6775

- **Spring Branch Ind School Dist** PID: 01027087   713/464-1511
  955 Campbell Rd, Houston 77024   Fax 713/251-2215

Schools: 47 \ **Teachers:** 2,246 \ **Students:** 34,975 \ **Special Ed Students:** 2,566 \ **LEP Students:** 11,011 \ **College-Bound:** 62% \ **Ethnic:** Asian 6%, African American 5%, Hispanic 61%, Caucasian 27% \ **Exp:** $269 (Med) \ **Poverty:** 20% \ **Title I:** $10,510,765 \ **Special Education:** $5,636,000 \ **Open-Close:** 08/15 - 05/28 \ **DTBP:** $188 (High) \

Jennifer Blaine 1	Karen Wilson 2,15
Richard Gay 2	Travis Stanford 3,15
Christopher Kamradt 4	Sherri Lawson 5
Paige Hershey 6	Judith Christopherson 7*
Kristin Craft 8,18	Rebecca Brown 8*
Julie Hodson 11,298	Lawana Coffee 12
Bryan Williams 15	Christina Masick 15,71,73,76,97,295
Elliott Witney 15,70	Jennifer Parker 15
Linda Buchman 15,71	Margie Duffey 15
Jessica Lily Hughes 16	David Sablatura 27
Joe Kolenda 27,31*	Michelle Burke 57
Joni Warren 58	Pam Goodson 67
Karen Heeth 68	Dr Keith Haffey 69,294
Mike Thomas 70	

Public Schs..Principal	Grd	Prgm	Enr/#Cls	SN	Phone
ⓐ Academy of Choice 9016 Westview Dr, Houston 77055 Angel Purdy	6-12	V	187 30		713/251-1500 Fax 713/251-1515
Bear Boulevard Pre-School 8860 Westview Dr, Houston 77055 Kimberly Hammer	PK-PK	T	293	90%	713/251-7900 Fax 713/365-4106
Bendwood Sch 12750 Kimberley Ln, Houston 77024 Jana Bassett	Spec	T	100 6	34%	713/251-5200 Fax 713/365-4992
Buffalo Creek Elem Sch 2801 Blalock Rd, Houston 77080 David Rodriguez	PK-5	T	552 35	89%	713/251-5300 Fax 713/392-6605

1	Superintendent	8	Curric/Instruct K-12	19	Chief Financial Officer	29	Family/Consumer Science
2	Bus/Finance/Purchasing	9	Curric/Instruct Elem	20	Art K-12	30	Adult Education
3	Buildings And Grounds	10	Curric/Instruct Sec	21	Art Elem	31	Career/Sch-to-Work K-12
4	Food Service	11	Federal Program	22	Art Sec	32	Career/Sch-to-Work Elem
5	Transportation	12	Title I	23	Music K-12	33	Career/Sch-to-Work Sec
6	Athletic	13	Title V	24	Music Elem	34	Early Childhood Ed
7	Health Services	14	Asst Superintendent	25	Music Sec	35	Health/Phys Education
		15	Instructional Media Svcs	26	Business Education	36	Guidance Services K-12
		16		27	Career & Tech Ed	37	Guidance Services Elem
		17	Chief Operations Officer	28	Technology Education	38	Guidance Services Sec
		18	Chief Academic Officer				

39	Social Studies K-12	49	English/Lang Arts Elem	59	Special Education Elem	69	Academic Assessment
40	Social Studies Elem	50	English/Lang Arts Sec	60	Special Education Sec	70	Research/Development
41	Social Studies Sec	51	Reading K-12	61	Foreign/World Lang K-12	71	Public Information
42	Science K-12	52	Reading Elem	62	Foreign/World Lang Elem	72	Summer School
43	Science Elem	53	Reading Sec	63	Foreign/World Lang Sec	73	Instructional Tech
44	Science Sec	54	Remedial Reading K-12	64	Religious Education K-12	74	Inservice Training
45	Math K-12	55	Remedial Reading Elem	65	Religious Education Elem	75	Marketing/Distributive
46	Math Elem	56	Remedial Reading Sec	66	Religious Education Sec	76	Info Systems
47	Math Sec	57	Bilingual/ELL	67	School Board President	77	Psychological Assess
48	English/Lang Arts K-12	58	Special Education K-12	68	Teacher Personnel	78	Affirmative Action

Texas School Directory — Harris County

School	Grades	Prog	Enroll	%	Phone / Fax
Bunker Hill Elem Sch 11950 Taylorcrest Rd, Houston 77024 Dana Johnson	PK-5		641 35	7%	713/251-5400 Fax 713/365-5059
Cedar Brook Elem Sch 2121 Ojeman Rd, Houston 77080 Alejandra Perez	PK-5	T	795 34	77%	713/251-5500 Fax 713/365-5027
©Cornerstone Academy 9016 C Westview Dr, Houston 77055 Angel Purdy	6-8		373 15	26%	713/251-1600 Fax 713/365-5787
Edgewood Elem Sch 8757 Kempwood Dr, Houston 77080 Jessica Tejada	PK-5	T	641 39	82%	713/251-5600 Fax 713/365-4007
Frostwood Elem Sch 12214 Memorial Dr, Houston 77024 Pamela Pennington	PK-5		707 28	5%	713/251-5700 Fax 713/365-5086
Guthrie Center 10660 Hammerly Blvd, Houston 77043 Joe Kolenda	Voc		181 20		713/251-1300 Fax 713/365-4621
Hollibrook Elem Sch 3602 Hollister St, Houston 77080 Anabel Taylor	PK-5	T	763 30	98%	713/251-5800 Fax 713/329-6440
Housman Elem Sch 6705 Housman St, Houston 77055 Lindy Robertson	PK-5	T	534 36	88%	713/251-5900 Fax 713/613-1706
Hunters Creek Elem Sch 10650 Beinhorn Rd, Houston 77024 Robalyn Snyder	PK-5		673 29	13%	713/251-6000 Fax 713/365-4937
Landrum Middle Sch 2200 Ridgecrest Dr, Houston 77055 Steven Speyrer	6-8	T	670	82%	713/251-3700 Fax 713/365-4040
Lion Lane Sch 2210 Ridgecrest Dr, Houston 77055 Michele Gabriel	PK-PK	T	304 16	95%	713/251-6100 Fax 713/365-4364
Meadow Wood Elem Sch 14230 Memorial Dr, Houston 77079 Lynne Barry	PK-5		505 25	34%	713/251-6200 Fax 281/560-7409
Memorial Drive Elem Sch 11202 Smithdale Rd, Houston 77024 Kathleen Jeremiassen	PK-5		447 23	8%	713/251-6300 Fax 713/365-4967
Memorial High Sch 935 Echo Ln, Houston 77024 Lisa Weir	9-12	V	2,669 120	9%	713/251-2515 Fax 713/365-5138
Memorial Middle Sch 12550 Vindon Dr, Houston 77024 Jane Green	6-8		1,348 75	5%	713/251-3900 Fax 713/365-5411
Northbrook High Sch 1 Raider Cir S, Houston 77080 Randolph Adami	9-12	T	2,517 75	82%	713/251-2800 Fax 713/365-4412
Northbrook Middle Sch 3030 Rosefield Dr, Houston 77080 Sarah Guerrero	6-8	T	879 66	93%	713/251-4100 Fax 713/329-6523
Nottingham Elem Sch 570 Nottingham Oaks Trl, Houston 77079 Roy Moore	PK-5	T	509 26	37%	713/251-6400 Fax 281/560-7469
Panda Path Sch 8575 Pitner Rd, Houston 77080 Amanda Ruiz	PK-PK	T	203 6	97%	713/251-8000 Fax 713/329-6696
Pine Shadows Elem Sch 9900 Neuens Rd, Houston 77080 Christina Winstead	PK-5	T	755 52	80%	713/251-6500 Fax 713/365-4274
Ridgecrest Elem Sch 2015 Ridgecrest Dr, Houston 77055 Michelle Garcia	PK-5	T	760 50	90%	713/251-6600 Fax 713/365-4067
Rummel Creek Elem Sch 625 Brittmoore Rd, Houston 77079 Nancy Harn	PK-5		737 35	3%	713/251-6700 Fax 713/365-5462
Shadow Oaks Elem Sch 1335 Shadowdale Dr, Houston 77043 Julie Baggerly	PK-5	T	665 46	90%	713/251-6800 Fax 713/365-4585
Sherwood Elem Sch 1700 Sherwood Forest St, Houston 77043 Sarah Salas	PK-5	T	456 40	65%	713/251-6900 Fax 713/365-4806
Spring Branch Acad Institute 8390 Westview Dr, Houston 77055 Patricia Kassir	K-9		45		713/251-1901
Spring Branch Elem Sch 1700 Campbell Rd, Houston 77080 Lynn Austin	PK-5	T	566 50	90%	713/251-7000 Fax 713/251-7015
Spring Branch Middle Sch 1000 Piney Point Rd, Houston 77024 Stefanie Spencer	6-8		1,112 75	38%	713/251-4400 Fax 713/365-5515
Spring Forest Middle Sch 14240 Memorial Dr, Houston 77079 Raymorris Barnes	6-8	T	897	49%	713/251-4600 Fax 281/560-7509
Spring Oaks Middle Sch 2150 Shadowdale Dr, Houston 77043 Maria Davalos	6-8	T	712 65	85%	713/251-4800 Fax 713/365-4522
Spring Shadows Elem Sch 9725 Kempwood Dr, Houston 77080 Rachel Martinez	PK-5	T	695 35	86%	713/251-7100 Fax 713/329-6480
Spring Woods High Sch 2045 Gessner Rd, Houston 77080 Jennifer Collier	9-12	TV	2,165	74%	713/251-3100 Fax 713/365-4474
Spring Woods Middle Sch 9810 Neuens Rd, Houston 77080 Cristian Delariva	6-8	T	876 83	87%	713/251-5000 Fax 713/365-4115
Stratford High Sch 14555 Fern Dr, Houston 77079 Chad Crowson	9-12	V	2,148	26%	713/251-3400 Fax 281/560-7578
Terrace Elem Sch 10400 Rothbury St, Houston 77043 April Blanco	PK-5	T	396 31	72%	713/251-7200 Fax 713/329-6406
Thornwood Elem Sch 14400 Fern Dr, Houston 77079 Vicki Lullo	PK-5	T	431 22	77%	713/251-7300 Fax 281/560-7439
Tiger Trail Sch 10406 Tiger Trl, Houston 77043 Vidal Garza	PK-PK	T	305 15	90%	713/251-8100 Fax 713/365-4578
Treasure Forest Elem Sch 7635 Amelia Rd, Houston 77055 Jerona Williams	PK-5	T	570 40	87%	713/251-7400 Fax 713/613-1724
Valley Oaks Elem Sch 8390 Westview Dr, Houston 77055 Kimberly Reynolds	PK-5		670 70	14%	713/251-7500 Fax 713/365-4086
©Westchester Acad Int'l Studies 901 Yorkchester Dr, Houston 77079 Valerie Muniz	6-12	GT	1,031	57%	713/251-1800 Fax 713/365-5686
Westwood Elem Sch 10595 Hammerly Blvd, Houston 77043 Kay Kennard	PK-5	T	589 40	88%	713/251-2100 Fax 713/365-4555
Wilchester Elem Sch 13618 Saint Marys Ln, Houston 77079 Anna Goodman	PK-5	T	793 24	3%	713/251-7700 Fax 713/365-4912
Wildcat Way Sch 12754 Kimberley Ln, Houston 77024 Morella Tapia	PK-PK	T	326 17	46%	713/251-8200 Fax 713/365-4745
Woodview Elem Sch 9749 Cedardale Dr, Houston 77055 Becky Hagan	PK-5	T	620 50	88%	713/251-7800 Fax 713/365-4294

Legend

- 79 Student Personnel
- 80 Driver Ed/Safety
- 81 Gifted/Talented
- 82 Video Services
- 83 Substance Abuse Prev
- 84 Erate
- 85 AIDS Education
- 88 Alternative/At Risk
- 89 Multi-Cultural Curriculum
- 90 Social Work
- 91 Safety/Security
- 92 Magnet School
- 93 Parental Involvement
- 95 Tech Prep Program
- 97 Chief Information Officer
- 98 Chief Technology Officer
- 270 Character Education
- 271 Migrant Education
- 273 Teacher Mentor
- 274 Before/After Sch
- 275 Response To Intervention
- 277 Remedial Math K-12
- 280 Literacy Coach
- 285 STEM
- 286 Digital Learning
- 288 Common Core Standards
- 294 Accountability
- 295 Network System
- 296 Title II Programs
- 297 Webmaster
- 298 Grant Writer/Ptnrships
- 750 Chief Innovation Officer
- 751 Chief of Staff
- 752 Social Emotional Learning

Other School Types
- Ⓐ = Alternative School
- © = Charter School
- Ⓜ = Magnet School
- Ⓨ = Year-Round School

School Programs
- A = Alternative Program
- G = Adult Classes
- M = Magnet Program
- T = Title I Schoolwide
- V = Career & Tech Ed Programs

Social Media
- f = Facebook
- t = Twitter

New Schools are shaded
New Superintendents and Principals are bold
Personnel with email addresses are underscored

Harris County

Market Data Retrieval

● **Spring Ind School Dist** PID: 01027465   281/891-6000
16717 Ella Blvd, Houston 77090   Fax 281/891-6006

Schools: 41 \ **Teachers:** 2,152 \ **Students:** 35,391 \
Special Ed Students: 2,920 \ **LEP Students:** 7,712 \ **College-Bound:** 55%
\ **Ethnic:** Asian 3%, African American 41%, Hispanic 45%, Native American:
2%, Caucasian 8% \ **Exp:** $350 (High) \ **Poverty:** 23% \ **Title I:** $13,546,123 \
Special Education: $3,906,000 \ **Open-Close:** 08/14 - 06/02 \ **DTBP:** $184
(High) \

Dr Rodney Watson 1,288	Ann Westbrooks 2,19
Yvette Washington 2	Fred Sholmire 3
Mark Miranda 3,17	Shelly Copeland 4
Keith Kaup 5	Willie Amendola 6
Jeanne Parker 7	Khechara Bradford 8,280
Kelly Cline 11	Dr Efrain Oliva 15
Dr Jennifer Cobb 15,69,70,294	Julie Hill 15,751
Laquita Carter 15	Michelle Starr 15
Dr Miguel Perez 15	Dr Natasha Watson 15
Pam Faridas 15	Joe Clark 20,23
Cynthia Williams 27,31	Denise Zimmermann 36
Peg Sherwood 58	Rhonda Newhouse 67
Deeone McKeithan 68	Tiffany Dunne-Oldfield 71,93
Jeff Kohrman 73,76,295	Dr Lupita Hinojosa 79
Darryl Simon 91	Kenneth Culbreath 91

Public Schs..Principal	Grd	Prgm	Enr/#Cls	SN		
Anderson Elem Sch 6218 Lynngate Dr, Spring 77373 Kristin Falcon	PK-5	T	608	66%	281/891-8360 Fax 281/891-8361	
Andy Dekaney High Sch 22351 Imperial Valley Dr, Houston 77073 **Alonzo Reynolds**	9-12	ATV	2,363	66%	281/891-7260 Fax 281/891-7261	
B F Clark Primary Sch 12625 River Laurel Dr, Houston 77014 Cynthia Gomez	PK-1	T	725	65%	281/891-8600 Fax 281/880-6396	
Bammel Elem Sch 17309 Red Oak Dr, Houston 77090 Dr Berky Owolabi	PK-5	T	803 40	67%	281/891-8150 Fax 281/587-7167	
Bammel Middle Sch 16711 Ella Blvd, Houston 77090 **Dr H Hyder**	6-8	TV	941	78%	281/891-7900 Fax 281/891-7901	
Beneke Elem Sch 3840 Briarchase Dr, Houston 77014 Latracy Harris	PK-5	T	695	69%	281/891-8450 Fax 281/891-8451	
Carl Wunsche Sr High Sch 900 Wunsche Loop, Spring 77373 Andria Schur	9-12	AGTV	1,199 60	64%	281/891-7650 Fax 281/891-7651	
Carolee Booker Elem Sch 22352 Imperial Valley Dr, Houston 77073 Keisha Womack	PK-5	TV	844	83%	281/891-8750 Fax 281/891-8751	
Chet Burchett Elem Sch 3366 James C Leo Dr, Spring 77373 Yvette Casas	PK-5	T	802	66%	281/891-8630 Fax 281/528-6351	
Clark Intermediate Sch 1825 Rushworth Dr, Houston 77014 Torrance Brooks	2-5	T	768	61%	281/891-8540 Fax 281/891-8541	
Deloras E Thompson Elem Sch 12470 Walters Rd, Houston 77014 De'Monica Amerson	PK-5	T	678	71%	281/891-8480 Fax 281/891-8481	
Donna Lewis Elem Sch 3230 Spears Rd, Houston 77067 Grace Leal	PK-5	T	665	69%	281/891-8720 Fax 281/440-4088	
Dr Edward Roberson Middle Sch 1500 S Ridge Rd, Houston 77090 Tracey Walker-Daniels	6-8	T	921	72%	281/891-7700 Fax 281/891-7701	
Dueitt Middle Sch 1 Eagle Xing, Spring 77373 **Stacy Rodgers**	6-8	T	1,162 67	70%	281/891-7800 Fax 281/528-6611	
Edwin M Wells Middle Sch 4033 Gladeridge Dr, Houston 77068 Dr Robert Long	6-8	T	1,087	81%	281/891-7750 Fax 281/891-7751	
Ginger McNabb Elm Sch 743 E Cypresswood Dr, Spring 77373 Melissa Warford	PK-5	T	731	69%	281/891-8690 Fax 281/528-5980	
Gloria Marshall Elem Sch 24505 Birnamwood Dr, Spring 77373 Debra Broughton	PK-5	T	747	67%	281/491-4900 Fax 281/891-4901	
Helen Major Elm Sch 16855 Sugar Pine Dr, Houston 77090 Shamethia Dillard	PK-5	T	717	60%	281/891-8870 Fax 281/891-8871	
Heritage Elem Sch 12255 T C Jester Blvd, Houston 77067 **Trenn Russell**	PK-5	T	667 45	81%	281/891-8510 Fax 281/891-8511	
Hoyland Elem Sch 2200 Wittershaw Dr, Houston 77090 **Elisa Cole**	PK-5	T	797	70%	281/891-8810 Fax 281/891-8811	
Joan Link Elm Sch 2815 Ridge Hollow Dr, Houston 77067 Justin Jones	PK-5	T	635 40	86%	281/891-8390 Fax 281/891-8391	
John Winship Elem Sch 2175 Spring Creek Dr, Spring 77373 Todd Armelin	PK-5	T	533	51%	281/891-8210 Fax 281/528-9158	
Meyer Elem Sch 16330 Forest Way Dr, Houston 77090 C'Ne Dawkins	PK-5	T	736 50	79%	281/891-8270 Fax 281/895-0807	
Mildred Jenkins Elem Sch 4615 Reynaldo Dr, Spring 77373 Tiffany Weston	PK-5	T	681	78%	281/891-8300 Fax 281/891-8301	
Milton Cooper Elem Sch 18655 Imperial Valley Dr, Houston 77073 **Mayra Garcia**	PK-5	T	791	85%	281/891-8660 Fax 281/209-0035	
Northgate Crossing Elem Sch 23437 Northgate Crossing Blvd, Spring 77373 Kristi Brown	PK-5	T	700	52%	281/891-8780 Fax 281/891-8781	
Pat Reynolds Elem Sch 3975 Gladeridge Dr, Houston 77068 Dr Angeles Perez	PK-5	T	727	74%	281/891-8240 Fax 281/891-8241	
Pearl M Hirsch Elem Sch 2633 Trailing Vine Rd, Spring 77373 John Baker	PK-5	T	711 34	71%	281/891-8330 Fax 281/891-8331	
Ponderosa Elem Sch 17202 Butte Creek Rd, Houston 77090 Shanna Swearingin	PK-5	T	714 36	78%	281/891-8180 Fax 281/891-8181	
Ralph Eickenroht Elem Sch 15252 Grand Point Rd, Houston 77090 Robert Green	PK-5	T	659	78%	281/891-8840 Fax 281/891-8841	
Ricky C Bailey Middle Sch 3377 James C Leo Dr, Spring 77373 Dr George Flores	6-8	T	1,269	70%	281/891-8000 Fax 281/528-8945	
Salyers Elem Sch 25705 W Hardy Rd, Spring 77373 Sharon Carpenter	PK-5	T	723 40	69%	281/891-8570 Fax 281/891-8571	
Smith Elem Sch 26000 Cypresswood Dr, Spring 77373 Shimona Eason	PK-5	T	620 62	63%	281/891-8420 Fax 281/891-8421	
Spring Early College Academy 2700 W W Thorne Dr Ste A104, Houston 77014 Diana Kimberly	9-12	T	417	65%	281/891-6880 Fax 281/891-6881	
Spring High Sch 19428 I-45 N, Spring 77373 Diaka Melendez	9-12	V	3,075		281/891-7000 Fax 281/891-7001	

1	Superintendent	8	Curric/Instruct K-12	19	Chief Financial Officer	29	Family/Consumer Science
2	Bus/Finance/Purchasing	9	Curric/Instruct Elem	20	Art K-12	30	Adult Education
3	Buildings And Grounds	10	Curric/Instruct Sec	21	Art Elem	31	Career/Sch-to-Work K-12
4	Food Service	11	Federal Program	22	Art Sec	32	Career/Sch-to-Work Elem
5	Transportation	12	Title I	23	Music K-12	33	Career/Sch-to-Work Sec
6	Athletic	13	Title V	24	Music Elem	34	Early Childhood Ed
7	Health Services	14	Instructional Media Svcs	25	Music Sec	35	Health/Phys Education
		15	Asst Superintendent	26	Business Education	36	Guidance Services K-12
		16	Instructional Media Svcs	27	Career & Tech Ed	37	Guidance Services Elem
		17	Chief Operations Officer	28	Technology Education	38	Guidance Services Sec
		18	Chief Academic Officer				

39	Social Studies K-12	49	English/Lang Arts Elem	59	Special Education Elem	69	Academic Assessment
40	Social Studies Elem	50	English/Lang Arts Sec	60	Special Education Sec	70	Research/Development
41	Social Studies Sec	51	Reading K-12	61	Foreign/World Lang K-12	71	Public Information
42	Science K-12	52	Reading Elem	62	Foreign/World Lang Elem	72	Summer School
43	Science Elem	53	Reading Sec	63	Foreign/World Lang Sec	73	Instructional Tech
44	Science Sec	54	Remedial Reading K-12	64	Religious Education K-12	74	Inservice Training
45	Math K-12	55	Remedial Reading Elem	65	Religious Education Elem	75	Marketing/Distributive
46	Math Elem	56	Remedial Reading Sec	66	Religious Education Sec	76	Info Systems
47	Math Sec	57	Bilingual/ELL	67	School Board President	77	Psychological Assess
48	English/Lang Arts K-12	58	Special Education K-12	68	Teacher Personnel	78	Affirmative Action

TX—202

Texas School Directory

Harris County

	Grd	Prgm	Enr/#Cls	SN	
Spring Leadership Acad Mid Sch	5-7		401		281/891-8050
14450 T C Jester Blvd, Houston 77014					
Kevin Banks					
Ⓐ Spring Virtual Sch	9-12		930		281/891-6223
22351 Imperial Valley Dr # 96, Houston 77073					Fax 281/891-6176
Dr Rebecca Long					
Springwoods Village Mid Sch	6-8		401		281/891-8100
1120 Crossgate Blvd, Spring 77373					Fax 281/891-8101
Kimberly Culley					
Stelle Claughton Middle Sch	6-8	T	1,264	82%	281/891-7950
3000 Spears Rd, Houston 77067					Fax 281/891-7951
Rodney Louis					
Twin Creeks Middle Sch	6-8	T	1,104 / 59	62%	281/891-7850 / Fax 281/891-7851
27100 Cypresswood Dr, Spring 77373					
Kenisha Williams					
Westfield High Sch	9-12	TV	2,987	63%	281/891-7130
16713 Ella Blvd, Houston 77090					Fax 281/891-7131
David Mason					

● **Tomball Ind School Dist** PID: 01027568   281/357-3100
310 S Cherry St, Tomball 77375   Fax 281/357-3128

Schools: 20 \ **Teachers:** 934 \ **Students:** 16,289 \
Special Ed Students: 1,235 \ **LEP Students:** 1,479 \ **College-Bound:** 64% \ **Ethnic:** Asian 7%, African American 5%, Hispanic 31%, Caucasian 56% \ **Exp:** $285 (Med) \ **Poverty:** 8% \ **Title I:** $1,013,927 \
Special Education: $1,611,000 \ **Open-Close:** 08/20 - 05/28 \ **DTBP:** $188 (High) \ 🅵 🆃

Dr Martha Salazar-Zamora 1   James Ross 2,19
Zachery Boles 2   Juan Trevino 3
Vince Sebo 3,6   Whitney Johnson 4
Beverly Beisert 5   Cathy Pool 7,35,85
Dr Amy Schindewolf 8,18   Valerie Petrzelka 9*
Xochitl Salazar 11   Dr Michael Webb 15
Dr Rick Fernandez 15   J Janda 20,23
Jessica Ozuna 27   James Watson 28,95
Jessica Perez 34   Chris Scott 42,45*
Jennifer Adams 42   David Surdovel 45
Dr Katie Atkins 48   Crystal Romero-Mueller 57,81
Marcy Canady ....57*   Samora Davis 57
Heather Nichols 58,270   Mark Lewandowski 67
Juan Santos 68   Juan Garza 68
Mark White 70,294   Justin Warnasch 71
Nefertari Mundy 74   Mary Beth Barr 280
Christopher Montgomery 295   Cynthia Fowler 295
Thomas Cranshaw 295

Public Schs..Principal	Grd	Prgm	Enr/#Cls	SN	
Canyon Point Elem Sch	PK-4		808	26%	281/357-3122
13002 Northpointe Blvd, Tomball 77377					Fax 281/357-3147
Barbara Coleman					
Creekside Forest Elem Sch	K-6		576	1%	281/357-4526
5949 Creekside Forest Dr, Spring 77389					Fax 281/357-4535
Sherri Trammell					
Creekside Park Jr High Sch	6-8		672	7%	281/357-3282
8711 Creekside Green Dr, The Woodlands 77375					Fax 281/516-9606
Dr Mindy Munoz					
Creekview Elem Sch	K-5		519	8%	281/357-3070
8877 W New Harmony Trl, The Woodlands 77375					Fax 281/357-3071
Niesa Glenewinkel					
Decker Prairie Elem Sch	PK-4	T	650 / 38	41%	281/357-3134 / Fax 281/357-3293 🆃
27427 Decker Prairie Rosehl Rd, Magnolia 77355					
Jo Colson					
Lakewood Elem Sch	PK-4		817	17%	281/357-3260
15614 Gettysburg Dr, Tomball 77377					Fax 281/357-3271 🆃
Deanna Porter					
Northpointe Intermediate Sch	5-6		709	16%	281/357-3020
11855 Northpointe Blvd, Tomball 77377					Fax 281/357-3026
Darrell McReynolds					
Oakcrest Intermediate Sch	5-6		631	18%	281/357-3033
18202 Shaw Rd, Cypress 77429					Fax 281/357-3034
George Flores					
Rosehill Elem Sch	PK-4	T	484 / 20	38%	281/357-3075 / Fax 281/357-3099 🆃
17950 Tomball Waller Rd, Tomball 77377					
Gloria Vasquez					
Timber Creek Elem Sch	PK-6		492	4%	281/357-3060
8455 Creekside Green Dr, The Woodlands 77389					Fax 281/357-3061 🆃
Lauren Thompson					
Ⓐ Tomball Connections Acadamy	5-12		60 / 6		281/357-3281 / Fax 281/357-3291
1302 Keefer Rd Ste A, Tomball 77375					
Bob Thompson					
Tomball Elem Sch	PK-4	T	717 / 35	54%	281/357-3280 / Fax 281/357-3288
1110 Inwood St, Tomball 77375					
Chad Schmidt					
Tomball High Sch	9-12	V	1,931	25%	281/357-3220
30330 Quinn Rd, Tomball 77375					Fax 281/357-3228
Chris Scott					🅵 🆃
Tomball Intermediate Sch	5-6	T	753 / 26	37%	281/357-3150 / Fax 281/357-3148
723 W Main St, Tomball 77375					
Samora Davis					
Tomball Junior High Sch	7-8	TV	740	36%	281/357-3000
30403 Quinn Rd, Tomball 77375					Fax 281/357-3027
Chad Allman					
Tomball Memorial High Sch	9-12		2,247	15%	281/357-3230
19100 Northpointe Ridge Ln, Tomball 77377					Fax 281/357-3240
Mike Metz					
Tomball Star Academy	9-9		104		281/357-3222
30330 Quinn Rd, Tomball 77375					
Kimberle McKinney					
Wildwood Elem Sch	PK-4		928	14%	281/357-3040
13802 Northpointe Blvd, Tomball 77377					Fax 281/357-3041
Samantha Hinson					
Willow Creek Elem Sch	PK-4		798 / 60	20%	281/357-3080 / Fax 281/357-3092
18302 N Eldridge Pkwy, Tomball 77377					
Teresa Sullivan					
Willow Wood Junior High Sch	7-8	V	1,251	16%	281/357-3030
11770 Gregson Rd, Tomball 77377					Fax 281/357-3044
Robert Frost					

HARRIS CATHOLIC SCHOOLS

● **Archdiocese Galveston-Houston** PID: 01027855   713/741-8704
2403 Holcombe Blvd, Houston 77021   Fax 713/741-7379

Schools: 58 \ **Students:** 19,122

Listing includes only schools located in this county. See District Index for location of Diocesan Offices.

Debra Haney 1   Rose Michalec 2
Nancy Macias 4   Laura Rolo 8
Renee Nunez 8,15,69   Angela Johnson 15
Cathy Stephen 15   Kimberly Pursch 15
Lytia Reese 15   Benita Gonzalez 58
Elizabeth Quinn 64   Ernest Forzano 67
Charles Pavlovsky 68   Leslie Barrera 73

Catholic Schs..Principal	Grd	Prgm	Enr/#Cls	SN	
Assumption Catholic Sch	PK-8		257 / 14		281/447-2132 / Fax 281/447-1825
801 Roselane St, Houston 77037					
John Bates					

79 Student Personnel	91 Safety/Security	275 Response To Intervention	298 Grant Writer/Ptnrships	**School Programs**	**Social Media**		
80 Driver Ed/Safety	92 Magnet School	277 Remedial Math K-12	750 Chief Innovation Officer	A = Alternative Program			
81 Gifted/Talented	93 Parental Involvement	280 Literacy Coach	751 Chief of Staff	G = Adult Classes	🅵 = Facebook		
82 Video Services	95 Tech Prep Program	285 STEM	752 Social Emotional Learning	M = Magnet Program			
83 Substance Abuse Prev	97 Chief Infomation Officer	286 Digital Learning		T = Title I Schoolwide	🆃 = Twitter		
84 Erate	98 Chief Technology Officer	288 Common Core Standards	**Other School Types**	V = Career & Tech Ed Programs			
85 AIDS Education	270 Character Education	294 Accountability	Ⓐ = Alternative School				
88 Alternative/At Risk	271 Migrant Education	295 Network System	Ⓒ = Charter School	New Schools are shaded			
89 Multi-Cultural Curriculum	273 Teacher Mentor	296 Title II Programs	Ⓜ = Magnet School	New Superintendents and Principals are bold			
90 Social Work	274 Before/After Sch	297 Webmaster	Ⓨ = Year-Round School	Personnel with email addresses are underscored			

TX—203

Harris County

School	Grades	Enrollment	Phone
Christ the Redeemer Cath Sch 11511 Huffmeister Rd, Houston 77065 Dan Courtney	K-6	250	281/469-8440 Fax 281/984-9669
Corpus Christi Catholic Sch 4005 Cheena Dr, Houston 77025 Mazie McCoy	PK-8	205 10	713/664-3351 Fax 713/664-6095
Duchesne Acad of Sacred Heart 10202 Memorial Dr, Houston 77024 Ginger Montalbano \ Dr Donald Cramp	PK-12	670 65	713/468-8211 Fax 713/465-9809
Frassati Catholic High Sch 22151 Frassati Way, Spring 77389 John Paul	9-12	200	832/616-3217 Fax 281/907-0675
Holy Ghost Catholic Sch 6920 Chimney Rock Rd, Houston 77081 Deborah Crow	PK-8	120 10	713/668-5327 Fax 713/667-4410
Incarnate Word Academy 609 Crawford St, Houston 77002 Mary Aamodt	9-12	273 30	713/227-3637 Fax 713/227-1014
Our Lady of Fatima Sch 1702 9th St, Galena Park 77547 Khanh Pham	PK-6	89 5	713/674-5832 Fax 713/674-3877
Our Lady of Guadalupe Sch 2405 Navigation Blvd, Houston 77003 Irazema Ortiz	PK-8	218 13	713/224-6904 Fax 713/225-2122
Our Lady of Mt Carmel Elem Sch 6703 Whitefriars Dr, Houston 77087 Maribel Mendoza	PK-8	97 20	713/643-0676 Fax 713/649-1835
Queen of Peace Catholic Sch 2320 Oakcliff St, Houston 77023 Jan Krametbauer	PK-8	150 14	713/921-1558 Fax 713/921-0855
Regis Sch of the Sacred Heart 7330 Westview Dr, Houston 77055 Dennis Phillips	PK-8	200 20	713/682-8383 Fax 713/682-8388
Resurrection Catholic Sch 916 Majestic St, Houston 77020 Dora Martinez	PK-8	147 10	713/674-5545 Fax 713/674-2151
Sacred Heart Sch 907 Runneburg Rd, Crosby 77532 Susan Harris	PK-8	204 11	281/328-6561 Fax 281/462-0072
St Agnes Academy 9000 Bellaire Blvd, Houston 77036 Deborah Whalen	9-12	920 30	713/219-5400 Fax 713/219-5499
St Ambrose Sch 4213 Mangum Rd, Houston 77092 Sarah MacDonald	PK-8	281 24	713/686-6990
St Anne Catholic Elem Sch 1111 S Cherry St, Tomball 77375 Joseph Noonan	PK-8	350 20	281/351-0093 Fax 281/357-1905
St Anne Sch 2120 Westheimer Rd, Houston 77098 Dawn Martinez	PK-8	498 30	713/526-3279 Fax 713/526-8025
St Augustine Catholic Sch 5500 Laurel Creek Way, Houston 77017 Denise Rios	PK-8	202 15	713/946-9050 Fax 713/943-3444
St Catherine's Montessori Sch 9821 Timberside Dr, Houston 77025 Susan Tracy	PK-9	235 10	713/665-2195 Fax 713/665-1478
St Cecilia Catholic Sch 11740 Joan of Arc Dr, Houston 77024 Jeff Matthews	PK-8	590 13	713/468-9515 Fax 713/468-4698
St Christopher Catholic Sch 8134 Park Place Blvd, Houston 77017 Claudia Cavazos	PK-8	243 20	713/649-0009 Fax 713/649-1104
St Clare of Assisi Sch 3131 El Dorado Blvd, Houston 77059 Al Varisco	PK-8	222 15	281/286-3395 Fax 281/286-1256
St Edward Catholic Sch 2601 Spring Stuebner Rd, Spring 77389 Erin Makel	PK-8	395 21	281/353-4570 Fax 281/353-8255
St Elizabeth Seton Cath Sch 6646 Addicks Satsuma Rd, Houston 77084 Ignacio Aguilera	PK-8	528 26	281/463-1444 Fax 281/463-8707
St Francis DeSales Sch 8100 Roos Rd, Houston 77036 Diane Wooten	PK-8	470 19	713/774-4447 Fax 713/271-6744
St Francis of Assisi Cath Sch 5100 Dabney St, Houston 77026 Miguel Sanchez	PK-8	50 11	713/674-1966
St Jerome Sch 8825 Kempwood Dr, Houston 77080 Patricia Jackson	PK-8	303 32	713/468-7946 Fax 713/464-0325
St John Paul II Catholic Sch 1400 Parkway Plaza Dr, Houston 77077 Rebecca Bogard	PK-8	712 40	281/496-1500 Fax 281/496-2943
St John XXIII Preparatory HS 1800 W Grand Pkwy N, Katy 77449 Joesph Noonan	9-12	240	281/693-1000 Fax 281/693-1001
St Joseph Sch 1811 Carolina St, Baytown 77520 Deborah Francis	PK-8	115 15	281/422-9749 Fax 281/422-7001
St Martha Catholic Sch 2411 Oak Shores Dr, Kingwood 77339 Jessica Munscher	PK-8	250 21	281/358-5523 Fax 281/358-5526
St Mary Magdalene Sch 530 Ferguson St, Humble 77338 Joshua Raab	PK-8	300 19	281/446-8535 Fax 281/446-8527
St Mary Purification Mont Sch 3002 Rosedale St, Houston 77004 Lois Goudeau	PK-5	120 9	713/522-9276 Fax 713/522-1879
St Michael Catholic Sch 1833 Sage Rd, Houston 77056 Kathleen Cox	PK-8	500 20	713/621-6847 Fax 713/877-8812
St Peter the Apostle Elem Sch 6220 La Salette St, Houston 77021 Toni Marshall	PK-8	40 9	713/747-9484 Fax 713/842-7055
St Pius V Sch 812 Main St, Pasadena 77506 Dr Felicia Nichols	PK-8	250 12	713/472-5172 Fax 713/534-6270
St Pius X High Sch 811 W Donovan St, Houston 77091 Diane Larsen	9-12	695 50	713/692-3581 Fax 713/692-5725
St Rose of Lima Sch 3600 Brinkman St, Houston 77018 Bernadette Drabek	PK-8	346 16	713/691-0104 Fax 713/692-8073
St Theresa Sch 6623 Rodrigo St, Houston 77007 Melissa Ilski	PK-8	275 8	713/864-4536 Fax 713/869-5184
St Thomas High Sch 4500 Memorial Dr, Houston 77007 Aaron Dominguez	9-12	680 80	713/864-6348 Fax 713/864-5750
St Thomas More Sch 5927 Wigton Dr, Houston 77096 Kristen Thome	PK-8	525 25	713/729-3434 Fax 713/721-5644
St Vincent De Paul Sch 6802 Buffalo Speedway, Houston 77025 Carolyn Sears	PK-8	512 22	713/666-2345 Fax 713/663-3562
Strake Jesuit College Prep Sch 8900 Bellaire Blvd, Houston 77036 Ken Lojo	9-12	900 30	713/774-7651 Fax 713/774-6427

---

1 Superintendent
2 Bus/Finance/Purchasing
3 Buildings And Grounds
4 Food Service
5 Transportation
6 Athletic
7 Health Services
8 Curric/Instruct K-12
9 Curric/Instruct Elem
10 Curric/Instruct Sec
11 Federal Program
12 Title I
13 Title V
15 Asst Superintendent
16 Instructional Media Svcs
17 Chief Operations Officer
18 Chief Academic Officer
19 Chief Financial Officer
20 Art K-12
21 Art Elem
22 Art Sec
23 Music K-12
24 Music Elem
25 Music Sec
26 Business Education
27 Career & Tech Ed
28 Technology Education
29 Family/Consumer Science
30 Adult Education
31 Career/Sch-to-Work K-12
32 Career/Sch-to-Work Elem
33 Career/Sch-to-Work Sec
34 Early Childhood Ed
35 Health/Phys Education
36 Guidance Services K-12
37 Guidance Services Elem
38 Guidance Services Sec
39 Social Studies K-12
40 Social Studies Elem
41 Social Studies Sec
42 Science K-12
43 Science Elem
44 Science Sec
45 Math K-12
46 Math Elem
47 Math Sec
48 English/Lang Arts K-12
49 English/Lang Arts Elem
50 English/Lang Arts Sec
51 Reading K-12
52 Reading Elem
53 Reading Sec
54 Remedial Reading K-12
55 Remedial Reading Elem
56 Remedial Reading Sec
57 Bilingual/ELL
58 Special Education K-12
59 Special Education Elem
60 Special Education Sec
61 Foreign/World Lang K-12
62 Foreign/World Lang Elem
63 Foreign/World Lang Sec
64 Religious Education K-12
65 Religious Education Elem
66 Religious Education Sec
67 School Board President
68 Teacher Personnel
69 Academic Assessment
70 Research/Development
71 Public Information
72 Summer School
73 Instructional Tech
74 Inservice Training
75 Marketing/Distributive
76 Info Systems
77 Psychological Assess
78 Affirmative Action

Texas School Directory — Harris County

HARRIS PRIVATE SCHOOLS

Private Schs..Principal	Grd	Prgm	Enr/#Cls	SN
A Plus Unlimited Potential Sch 821 Chelsea Blvd, Houston 77002 Paul Castro	6-8		40	713/658-1881
Abercrombie Academy 17102 Theiss Mail Route Rd, Spring 77379 Kristen Risdal	PK-5		120 10	281/374-1730 Fax 281/257-2207
Abiding Word Lutheran Sch 17123 Red Oak Dr, Houston 77090 Ben Carlovsky	K-8		110 6	281/895-7048 Fax 281/453-2920
Al-Hadi Sch of Accel Lrng 2313 S Voss Rd, Houston 77057 Br Seyed Alireza Abedi	PK-12		250	713/787-5000 Fax 713/513-5315
Alexander Smith Academy 10255 Richmond Ave Ste 100, Houston 77042 Pam Rameau	9-12		63 13	713/266-0920 Fax 713/266-8857
Annunciation Orthodox Sch 3600 Yoakum Blvd, Houston 77006 Sharon Corbett \ Heather Haas	PK-8		710 40	713/470-5630 Fax 713/470-5605
ⓐ Archway Academy 6221 Main St, Houston 77030 Tonya Sanders-Woods	9-12		20	713/328-0780 Fax 713/328-0781
Ascension Episcopal Sch 2525 Seagler Rd, Houston 77042 Nancy Clausey	PK-5		125 16	713/783-0260 Fax 713/787-9162
Avondale House Sch 3737 Omeara Dr, Houston 77025 Becky Ingalls	Spec		60	713/993-9544 Fax 713/993-0751
Awty International Sch 7455 Awty School Ln, Houston 77055 Tim Long \ Tom Beuscher \ Sam Waugh	PK-12		1,600	713/686-4850 Fax 713/686-4956
Banff Sch 13726 Cutten Rd, Houston 77069 Deborah Wasser	PK-12		130 16	281/444-9326 Fax 281/444-3632
Bay Area Montessori House 17222 Mercury Dr, Houston 77058 Tommie Jean Hebert	PK-6		91 4	281/480-7022 Fax 281/461-3597
Baytown Christian Academy 5555 N Main St, Baytown 77521 James Twardowski	PK-12		300 33	281/421-4150 Fax 281/421-4038
Beth Yeshurun Sch 4525 Beechnut St, Houston 77096 Cynthia Kirsch	PK-5		196 30	713/666-1884 Fax 713/666-2924
Branch Sch 1424 Sherwood Forest St, Houston 77043 Emily Smith	PK-8		120	713/465-0288 Fax 713/465-0337
Briarwood Sch 12207 Whittington Dr, Houston 77077 Carole Wills	Spec	V	320 50	281/493-1070 Fax 281/493-1343
British Int'l Sch of Houston 2203 N Westgreen Blvd, Katy 77449 Mark Wilson	PK-12		1,090	713/290-9025 Fax 713/290-9014
Brookhollow Christian Academy 5725 Queenston Blvd, Houston 77084 Markena Kelley	PK-3		401	281/649-6813
Center for Hearing & Speech 3636 W Dallas St, Houston 77019 Renee Davis	PK-1		30 8	713/523-3633 Fax 713/523-8399
Central Christian Academy 2217 Bingle Rd, Houston 77055 Scott Jacobs	PK-12		40 8	713/468-3248 Fax 713/468-7322
Centro Chrn Alpha Omega Acad 5621 North Fwy, Houston 77076 Gerardo Cardenas	PK-12		76	713/697-6726 Fax 713/697-1726
Chinquapin Prep Sch 2615 E Wallisville Rd, Highlands 77562 Dorothy Scrutchin \ Cody Sharma	6-12		150 10	281/426-5551 Fax 281/426-5553
Christian Life Center Academy 806 Russell Palmer Rd, Kingwood 77339 Dr Aaron Miller	K-12		65 14	281/319-4673 Fax 281/446-5501
Concordia Lutheran High Sch 700 E Main St, Tomball 77375 Julie Kangas	9-12		580 24	281/351-2547 Fax 281/255-8806
Connection School of Houston 15815 House Hahl Rd, Cypress 77433 Kathleen Wrobleske	K-12		200	832/544-6031 Fax 855/286-3088
Covenant Academy 11711 Telge Rd, Cypress 77429 Leslie Collins	K-12		214 9	281/373-2233 Fax 281/582-8227
Covenant Preparatory Sch 1711 Hamblen Rd, Humble 77339 Erica Nevenglosky \ Cody Smoot	PK-12		300 20	281/359-1090 Fax 281/359-5560
Cristo Rey Jesuit Clg Prep HS 6700 Mount Carmel St, Houston 77087 Eileen Quinones	9-12		500	281/501-1298 Fax 281/501-3485
Crossroads Sch 5822 Dolores St, Houston 77057 Justin Adams	Spec		70 7	713/977-1221 Fax 713/977-0010
Cunae International Sch 5655 Creekside Forest Dr, Spring 77389 Anji Price	PK-12		120	281/516-3770
Cypress Cmty Christian Sch 11123 Cypress N Houston Rd, Houston 77065 Joy Bezner \ Iva Nell Rhea	K-12		600	281/469-8829 Fax 281/469-6040
Darul Arqam Sch 8830 Galveston Rd, Houston 77034 Zaheer Anwar	PK-6		104 10	713/948-0094 Fax 713/947-6294
Darul Arqam School-North 11815 Adel Rd, Houston 77067 Saboohi Adhami	PK-12		320	281/583-1984 Fax 281/440-8024
Emery Weiner Sch 9825 Stella Link Rd, Houston 77025 Kendall White \ Nathan Barber	6-12		450 50	832/204-5900 Fax 832/204-5910
Epiphany Lutheran Sch 14423 West Rd, Houston 77041 Jon Fraker	PK-8		274	713/896-1316
Episcopal High Sch 4650 Bissonnet St, Bellaire 77401 Kim Randolph	9-12		676	713/512-3400 Fax 713/512-3603
Eternity Christian Sch 1122 West Rd, Houston 77038 Beth Bashinski	PK-8		140	281/999-5107
Faith Christian Academy 3519 Burke Rd, Pasadena 77504 Rachel Mitchell	K-12		70 13	713/943-9978 Fax 713/944-4416
Faith West Academy 2225 Porter Rd, Katy 77493 Mary Strickland	PK-12		600	281/391-5683 Fax 281/391-2606
Family Christian Academy 14718 Woodford Dr, Houston 77015 John Bohacek	PK-12		401	713/455-4483
First Baptist Academy 7450 Memorial Woods Dr, Houston 77024 Dr Mary White \ Kelli Diers	K-8		450	713/290-2500 Fax 713/290-2508
First Baptist Christian Acad 7500 Fairmont Pkwy, Pasadena 77505 Cindy McDonald \ Toni Shuman	PK-12		550 38	281/991-9191 Fax 281/991-7092

---

79 Student Personnel
80 Driver Ed/Safety
81 Gifted/Talented
82 Video Services
83 Substance Abuse Prev
84 Erate
85 AIDS Education
88 Alternative/At Risk
89 Multi-Cultural Curriculum
90 Social Work

91 Safety/Security
92 Magnet School
93 Parental Involvement
95 Tech Prep Program
97 Chief Information Officer
98 Chief Technology Officer
270 Character Education
271 Migrant Education
273 Teacher Mentor
274 Before/After Sch

275 Response To Intervention
277 Remedial Math K-12
280 Literacy Coach
285 STEM
286 Digital Learning
288 Common Core Standards
294 Accountability
295 Network System
296 Title II Programs
297 Webmaster

298 Grant Writer/Ptnrships
750 Chief Innovation Officer
751 Chief of Staff
752 Social Emotional Learning

Other School Types
ⓐ = Alternative Program
ⓒ = Charter School
ⓜ = Magnet School
ⓨ = Year-Round School

School Programs
A = Alternative Program
G = Adult Classes
M = Magnet Program
T = Title I Schoolwide
V = Career & Tech Ed Programs

Social Media
= Facebook
= Twitter

New Schools are shaded
New Superintendents and Principals are bold
Personnel with email addresses are underscored

Harris County — Market Data Retrieval

School	Grades	Enroll	Phone
Founders Christian Sch 24724 Aldine Westfield Rd, Spring 77373 Joe Jones	PK-12	105	281/602-8006
Fusion Acad-Houston Galleria 5065 Westheimer Rd Ste 840, Houston 77056 Elizabeth Beguerie	6-12	50	713/963-9096
Gateway Academy 3721 Dacoma St, Houston 77092 Scott Adams	7-12	36 13	713/659-7900 Fax 713/659-7901
Generation One Academy PO Box 8280, Houston 77288 Tori Dugar	PK-5	45	713/654-8008 Fax 832/767-1619
Grace Christian Academy 14325 Crescent Landing Dr, Houston 77062 Dr Darrell Smith	K-12	354	281/488-4883 Fax 281/480-3287
Grace Sch 10219 Ella Lee Ln, Houston 77042 Leigh Anne Shumate \ Robert Williford	PK-8	440 49	713/782-4421 Fax 713/267-5056
Holy Spirit Episcopal Sch 12535 Perthshire Rd, Houston 77024 Karen Palividas \ Brian Smith	PK-8	250 30	713/468-5138 Fax 713/465-6972
Holy Trinity Episcopal Sch 11810 Lockwood Rd, Houston 77044 Troy Roddy	PK-12	130 11	281/459-4323 Fax 281/459-4302
Houston Christian High Sch 2700 W Sam Houston Pkwy N, Houston 77043 Dr Darren Price	9-12	500 40	713/580-6000 Fax 713/580-6001
Houston Learning Academy 6200 Winfield Rd, Houston 77050 Lesley Boyer	9-12	30 6	281/449-1532 Fax 281/537-2361
Humble Christian Sch 16202 Old Humble Rd, Humble 77396 Ted Howell	PK-12	330 22	281/441-1313 Fax 281/441-1329
Ilm Academy 1209 Conrad Sauer Dr, Houston 77043 Zuhaira Razzack	PK-8	180	713/464-4720
Iman Academy Southeast 10929 Almeda Genoa Rd, Houston 77034 Aliyah Harris \ Ms Nikki	PK-9	140 15	713/910-3626 Fax 713/910-5955
Iman Academy-Southwest 6240 Highway 6 S, Houston 77083 Baha Zaqat \ Abdullah Masias	PK-12	500	281/498-1345 Fax 281/498-5145
Irvin M Shlenker Sch 5600 N Braeswood Blvd Ste A, Houston 77096 Dr Michelle Barton	PK-5	375 30	713/270-6127 Fax 713/270-6114
Joy Sch 1 Chelsea Blvd, Houston 77006 Shara Bumgarner	Spec	150 20	713/523-0660 Fax 713/523-5660
Kardia Christian Academy 10555 Spring Cypress Rd, Houston 77070 Kim Watson	PK-6	57 7	281/378-4040 Fax 281/378-4081
Katy Adventist Christian Sch 1913 East Ave, Katy 77493 Andrea Kiture	PK-8	40	281/392-5603
Kingdom Academy 13334 Wallisville Rd, Houston 77049 Faith Coble	PK-6	53 4	713/450-0021 Fax 713/453-0855
Living Word Christian Academy 6601 Antoine Dr, Houston 77091 Tina Armstrong	PK-PK	55 25	713/686-5538 Fax 713/686-6840
Lutheran High School North 1130 W 34th St, Houston 77018 Dana Gerard	9-12	175 15	713/880-3131 Fax 713/880-5447
Lutheran South Academy 12555 Ryewater Dr, Houston 77089 Debbie Baacke \ Jeremy Brumm \ Steve Garrabrant	PK-12	750 50	281/464-8299 Fax 281/464-6119
Memorial Chrn Academy 1315 S Dairy Ashford Rd Ste F, Houston 77077 Freda Spillman	K-5	75	281/493-3700 Fax 281/493-6233
Memorial Hall High Sch 2501 Central Pkwy Ste A19, Houston 77092 George Aurich	6-12	65 7	713/688-5566 Fax 713/956-9751
Memorial Lutheran Sch 5800 Westheimer Rd, Houston 77057 Darrell Schepmann	PK-8	250 22	713/782-4022 Fax 713/782-1749
Memorial Private High Sch 14333 Fern Dr, Houston 77079 Harry Camp	7-12	44	281/759-2288
Mirus Academy 5561 3rd St, Katy 77493 Laura Hogan	3-12	100	281/392-4477 Fax 832/437-8273
Mission Bend Christian Academy 3710 Highway 6 S, Houston 77082 Wendy Lewis	PK-6	100 7	281/497-4057 Fax 281/497-3395
Monarch Sch 2815 Rosefield Dr, Houston 77080 Patti Pace	Spec	130 14	713/479-0800 Fax 713/464-7499
Montessori School Downtown 4510 Caroline St, Houston 77004 Theresa Devera	PK-5	200	713/520-6801 Fax 713/520-9731
Mountaintop Learning Center 8420 Almeda Genoa Rd, Houston 77075 Latasha Siscer	PK-K	40	713/808-9284 Fax 713/991-4210
New Heights Christian Academy 1700 W 43rd St, Houston 77018 Victoria Grable	K-12	113 8	713/861-9101
Northland Christian Sch 4363 Sylvanfield Dr, Houston 77014 Eric Wietstruck \ Monica Lewis	PK-12	650	281/440-1060 Fax 281/440-7572
Northwood Montessori Sch 14901 Welcome Ln, Houston 77014 Carita Goss	PK-1	79 3	281/444-9433
Oaks Adventist Christian Sch 11735 Grant Rd, Cypress 77429 Brenda Elms	K-12	150 7	713/896-0071
Our Savior Lutheran Sch 5000 W Tidwell Rd, Houston 77091 Lance Gerard	PK-8	250 14	713/290-8277 Fax 713/290-0850
Parish Sch 11001 Hammerly Blvd, Houston 77043 Nancy Bewely	PK-5	140 20	713/467-4696 Fax 713/467-8341
Pilgrim Lutheran Sch 8601 Chimney Rock Rd, Houston 77096 David Topp	PK-8	215 16	713/432-7082 Fax 713/666-6585
Pines Montessori Sch 3535 Cedar Knolls Dr, Kingwood 77339 Patty Sobelman	PK-8	165 12	281/358-8933 Fax 281/358-3162
Post Oak Montessori Sch 4600 Bissonnet St, Bellaire 77401 Jeff Schneider	PK-6	388 17	713/661-6688 Fax 713/661-4959
Presbyterian Sch 5300 Main St, Houston 77004 Christy Heno \ Charles Gramtages	PK-8	531	713/520-0284 Fax 713/620-6391
Providence Classical Sch 1800 Stuebner Airline Rd, Spring 77379 Melissa Martin \ Vinodh Gunasekera	PK-12	200	281/320-0500 Fax 281/379-2039
Rainard School for the Gifted 11059 Timberline Rd, Houston 77043 Erin Chavez	PK-12	65 7	713/647-7246 Fax 713/365-0372
River Oaks Academy 10600 Richmond Ave, Houston 77042 Dr Louie Valdez	K-12	30 6	713/783-7200 Fax 713/783-7286

#	Role	#	Role	#	Role	#	Role	#	Role	#	Role	#	Role
1	Superintendent	8	Curric/Instruct K-12	19	Chief Financial Officer	29	Family/Consumer Science	39	Social Studies K-12	49	English/Lang Arts Elem	59	Special Education Elem	69	Academic Assessment
2	Bus/Finance/Purchasing	9	Curric/Instruct Elem	20	Art K-12	30	Adult Education	40	Social Studies Elem	50	English/Lang Arts Sec	60	Special Education Sec	70	Research/Development
3	Buildings And Grounds	10	Curric/Instruct Sec	21	Art Elem	31	Career/Sch-to-Work K-12	41	Social Studies Sec	51	Reading K-12	61	Foreign/World Lang K-12	71	Public Information
4	Food Service	11	Federal Program	22	Art Sec	32	Career/Sch-to-Work Elem	42	Science K-12	52	Reading Elem	62	Foreign/World Lang Elem	72	Summer School
5	Transportation	12	Title I	23	Music K-12	33	Career/Sch-to-Work Sec	43	Science Elem	53	Reading Sec	63	Foreign/World Lang Sec	73	Instructional Tech
6	Athletic	13	Title V	24	Music Elem	34	Early Childhood Ed	44	Science Sec	54	Remedial Reading K-12	64	Religious Education K-12	74	Inservice Training
7	Health Services	15	Asst Superintendent	25	Music Sec	35	Health/Phys Education	45	Math K-12	55	Remedial Reading Elem	65	Religious Education Elem	75	Marketing/Distributive
		16	Instructional Media Svcs	26	Business Education	36	Guidance Services K-12	46	Math Elem	56	Remedial Reading Sec	66	Religious Education Sec	76	Info Systems
		17	Chief Operations Officer	27	Career & Tech Ed	37	Guidance Services Elem	47	Math Sec	57	Bilingual/ELL	67	School Board President	77	Psychological Assess
		18	Chief Academic Officer	28	Technology Education	38	Guidance Services Sec	48	English/Lang Arts K-12	58	Special Education K 12	68	Teacher Personnel	78	Affirmative Action

Texas School Directory — Harris County

School	Grades	Enrollment/Staff	Phone
River Oaks Baptist Sch 2300 Willowick Rd, Houston 77027 Amy Womack \ Connor Cook	PK-8	848 40	713/623-6938 Fax 713/621-8216
Robert M Beren Academy 11333 Cliffwood Dr, Houston 77035 Dr Dawn McKernan \ Raquel Cedano	PK-12	315 31	713/723-7170 Fax 713/723-8343
Robindell Private Sch 6610 Alder Dr, Houston 77081 Chuck Wall	PK-1	200	713/667-9895 Fax 713/669-9324
Rosehill Christian Sch 19830 FM 2920 Rd, Tomball 77377 Lauren Dyal \ Marshall Priest	PK-12	360 27	281/351-8114 Fax 281/516-3418
Saint Constantine Sch 6000 Dale Carnegie Ln, Houston 77036 Caitlin Gilbert	PK-12	150	832/975-7075
Salem Lutheran Sch 22601 Lutheran Church Rd, Tomball 77377 Amy Boatman	PK-8	377 20	281/351-8223 Fax 281/290-1240 [f]
School for Young Children 810 Sul Ross St, Houston 77006 Sheila McBrinn	Spec	36 6	713/520-8310 Fax 713/520-1109
School of the Woods 1321 Wirt Rd, Houston 77055 Sherry Herron \ Betsy Coe	PK-12	325 13	713/686-8811
Second Baptist Sch 6410 Woodway Dr, Houston 77057 Evette Haberman \ Ellen Barrett \ Jon Konzelman	PK-12	1,100	713/365-2310 Fax 713/365-2355
Sherwood Forest Mont Sch 1331 Sherwood Forest St, Houston 77043 Sara Norton	PK-6	112 4	713/464-5791 Fax 713/464-5810
Southwest Christian Academy 7400 Eldridge Pkwy, Houston 77083 Paula Thurmond	K-12	150	281/561-7400 Fax 281/561-9823
Southwest Cmty Christian Acad 14880 Bellaire Blvd, Houston 77083 Trialica Heard	PK-1	115 18	281/575-9400 Fax 281/575-1449
Spring Baptist Academy 633 E Louetta Rd, Spring 77373 Dr Gloria Hammack	PK-8	209	281/353-5448
St Francis Episcopal Sch 335 Piney Point Rd, Houston 77024 Stephen Lovejoy	PK-10	801	713/458-6100 Fax 713/782-4720
St John Early Childhood Center 15237 Huffmeister Rd, Cypress 77429 Tiffany Bunker	PK-PK	257	281/304-5546
St John's Sch 2401 Claremont Ln, Houston 77019 Thomas McLaughlin \ Margaret Henry \ Hollis Amley	K-12	1,200	713/850-0222 Fax 713/622-2309
St Mark Lutheran Sch 1515 Hillendahl Blvd, Houston 77055 Dalls Lusk	PK-8	324 20	713/468-2623 Fax 713/468-6735
St Mark's Episcopal Sch 3816 Bellaire Blvd, Houston 77025 Bobbye Hicks \ Matthew Burgy	PK-8	420 25	713/667-7030 Fax 713/349-0419 [f]
St Michael's Learning Academy 6220 Westpark Dr Ste 180, Houston 77057 Christine Aboud	9-12	50	713/977-0566 Fax 713/977-0090
St Nicholas Sch 1920 N Braeswood Blvd, Houston 77030 Margot Heard	PK-8	100	713/791-9977 Fax 713/791-9594
St Stephen's Episcopal Sch 1800 Sul Ross St, Houston 77098 Nahla Nasser	PK-8	186 18	713/821-9100 Fax 713/821-9156
St Thomas Apostle Episc Sch 18300 Upper Bay Rd, Houston 77058 C O'Neal	PK-5	120 10	281/333-1340 Fax 281/333-9113
St Thomas' Episcopal Sch 4900 Jackwood St, Houston 77096 Erica Maw \ Ryno Marais \ Dale King	PK-12	630 30	713/666-3111 Fax 713/668-3887 [f]
Step by Step Christian Sch 1119 S Cherry St, Tomball 77375 Pamela Collins	PK-8	250	281/351-2888 Fax 281/516-0253
Tenney Sch 3500 S Gessner Rd Ste 200, Houston 77063 Catherine DeLaRosa	6-12	65	713/783-6990 Fax 713/783-0786
Texas Christian Sch 17810 Kieth Harrow Blvd, Houston 77084 Becky Soliz	PK-12	270 20	281/550-6060
The Bridge Sch 3333 Bering Dr, Houston 77057 Myah Aquil	6-12	250	713/974-2066
The Fay Sch 105 N Post Oak Ln, Houston 77024 Melissa Sherman	PK-5	340	713/681-8300 Fax 713/681-6826
The Kinkaid Sch 201 Kinkaid School Dr, Houston 77024 Krista Babine \ Chelsea Collins \ Peter Behr	PK-12 G	1,300	713/782-1640 Fax 713/782-3543 [f][t]
Torah Day School of Houston 10900 Fondren Rd, Houston 77096 Arlene Lassin	PK-8	130 12	713/777-2000 Fax 713/771-5770 [f]
Torah Girls Academy 10101 Fondren Rd, Houston 77096 Ezra Sarna	9-12	20	713/936-0644
Trafton Academy 4711 McDermed Dr, Houston 77035 Inez Hutchins	PK-8	250	713/723-3732 Fax 713/723-1844
Trinity Lutheran Chldrn's Ctr 1316 Washington Ave, Houston 77002 Darrell Schepmann	PK-8	220 12	713/224-3207
Trinity Lutheran Sch 18926 Klein Church Rd, Spring 77379 Keith Goedecke	PK-8	600 19	281/376-5810 Fax 281/290-4950
Veritas Christian Academy 7000 Ferris St, Bellaire 77401 Alecia Gallegos \ Lina DelGado	PK-8	175	713/773-9605 Fax 713/773-9753
Village Sch 13077 Westella Dr, Houston 77077 Katherine Brewer	PK-12	750 40	281/496-7900 Fax 281/496-7799
Waller Christian Academy 1208 Penick Rd, Waller 77484 Richard Keithley	PK-8	99	936/372-0901 Fax 936/832-2022
Wesley Academy 10570 Westpark Dr, Houston 77042 Heather Williams	PK-8	133 30	713/266-3341 Fax 713/458-4766 [f]
Westbury Christian Sch 10420 Hillcroft St, Houston 77096 Amanda Archer \ Annette Turner \ Nathan Wagner	PK-12	525 40	713/551-8100 Fax 713/551-8116
Western Academy 1511 Butlercrest St, Houston 77080 Jason Hebert	3-8	100	713/461-7000 Fax 832/408-7861
Westview Sch 1900 Kersten Dr, Houston 77043 Dr Carol Harrison \ Russell Avery	Spec	154	713/973-1900 Fax 713/973-1970
Wheeler Ave Christian Academy 3810 Ruth St, Houston 77004 Melanie Singleton	PK-1	40	713/579-2792 Fax 713/579-2790
Woodlands Preparatory Sch 27440 Kuykendahl Rd, Tomball 77375 Erika Velez	K-12	250	281/561-0600 Fax 281/561-1155 [f]
Xavier Educational Academy 10042 Whiteside Ln, Houston 77080 Richard Delacuadra	5-12	140	832/303-9638

---

79 Student Personnel	91 Safety/Security	275 Response To Intervention	298 Grant Writer/Ptnrships	**School Programs**	**Social Media**
80 Driver Ed/Safety	92 Magnet School	277 Remedial Math K-12	750 Chief Innovation Officer	A = Alternative Program	
81 Gifted/Talented	93 Parental Involvement	280 Literacy Coach	751 Chief of Staff	G = Adult Classes	[f] = Facebook
82 Video Services	95 Tech Prep Program	285 STEM	752 Social Emotional Learning	M = Magnet Program	
83 Substance Abuse Prev	97 Chief Infomation Officer	286 Digital Learning		T = Title I Schoolwide	[t] = Twitter
84 Erate	98 Chief Technology Officer	288 Common Core Standards	**Other School Types**	V = Career & Tech Ed Programs	
85 AIDS Education	270 Character Education	294 Accountability	Ⓐ = Alternative School		
88 Alternative/At Risk	271 Migrant Education	295 Network System	Ⓒ = Charter School	New Schools are shaded	
89 Multi-Cultural Curriculum	273 Teacher Mentor	296 Title II Programs	Ⓜ = Magnet School	New Superintendents and Principals are bold	
90 Social Work	274 Before/After Sch	297 Webmaster	Ⓨ = Year-Round School	Personnel with email addresses are underscored	

Harrison County

Market Data Retrieval

Yellowstone Academy	PK-8	309	713/741-8000
3000 Trulley St, Houston 77004		16	Fax 713/741-8006
Deidra Lawson			

Yorkshire Academy	PK-5	160	281/531-6088
14120 Memorial Dr, Houston 77079			
Janet Howard			

HARRIS REGIONAL CENTERS

● **Region 4 Ed Service Center** PID: 01027556 — 713/462-7708
7145 W Tidwell Rd, Houston 77092 — Fax 713/744-6514

Dr Pam Wells 1	Robert Zingelmann 2,3,19
Kelly Ingram 8,15	Dr Robby McGowen 15,79
Dr Jennifer Brock 34,39,48,51,57	Dr Ginger Gates 58
Dr Melody Goffney 68	Kristi Hernandez 71
Pat Shear 73,76	Dr Rene Ruiz 74
Richard Armand 286	Ingrid Lee 294

HARRISON COUNTY

HARRISON PUBLIC SCHOOLS

● **Elysian Fields Ind School Dist** PID: 01028433 — 903/633-2420
2099 FM 451, Elysian Flds 75642 — Fax 903/633-2498

Schools: 3 \ **Teachers:** 78 \ **Students:** 910 \ **Special Ed Students:** 103 \ **LEP Students:** 7 \ **College-Bound:** 70% \ **Ethnic:** Asian 1%, African American 15%, Hispanic 5%, Caucasian 79% \ **Exp:** $302 (High) \ **Poverty:** 21% \ **Title I:** $237,104 \ **Open-Close:** 08/12 - 05/15 \ **DTBP:** $357 (High)

Maynard Chapman 1	Richard Hutsell 2,11
Norman Barr 3	Scott Ford 6
Monica Simmons 8,69	Martha Lovaasen 9*
Katie Woodley 36,83	Emily Dickenson 59,273
Siera Bradshaw 60	Harold Coburn 67
Bill Spencer 73,84	

Public Schs..Principal	Grd	Prgm	Enr/#Cls	SN	
Elysian Fields Elem Sch	PK-5	T	397	58%	903/633-2465
565 FM 451, Elysian Flds 75642			26		Fax 903/633-2187
Martha Lovaasen					
Elysian Fields High Sch	9-12	TV	250	43%	903/633-2455
2400 FM 451, Elysian Flds 75642			40		Fax 903/633-8154
Jackson Parker					
Elysian Fields Middle Sch	6-8	TV	215	51%	903/633-2306
2450 FM 451, Elysian Flds 75642			20		Fax 903/633-2326
Brandon Goswick					

● **Hallsville Ind School Dist** PID: 01028483 — 903/668-5990
311 Willow St, Hallsville 75650

Schools: 5 \ **Teachers:** 365 \ **Students:** 5,500 \ **Special Ed Students:** 394 \ **LEP Students:** 173 \ **College-Bound:** 59% \ **Ethnic:** Asian 1%, African American 7%, Hispanic 15%, Caucasian 77% \ **Exp:** $217 (Med) \ **Poverty:** 16% \ **Title I:** $783,257 \ **Open-Close:** 08/14 - 05/21 \ **DTBP:** $44 (Low)

Jeff Collum 1	Mary Brown 2,19
Ben Avedikian 3	Roy Presley 5
Joe Drennon 6	Amy Whittle 7,11,57,77,83,88,275
Kimberly McGarvey 7,35,85*	Amber Daub 8,31,36,78,79,285
John Martin 15,68,74	Mark Page 16,28,76,82,295,297*
Kathy Gaw 26,27,29,75,95*	Amy Collins 34,58,90
Jay Nelson 67	Lacy Carter 69,83,294
Carol Greer 71,93	Jill Buchanan 76
Anda Juban 81	Kathy Bradford 84
Terrance Turner 91*	

Public Schs..Principal	Grd	Prgm	Enr/#Cls	SN	
East Elem Sch	PK-3	T	777	53%	903/668-5984
420 Galilee Rd, Hallsville 75650					
Melissa Goulden					
Hallsville High Sch	9-12	AGV	1,461	33%	903/668-5990
616 Calyoung Rd, Hallsville 75650			100		
Lindsay Slaten					
Hallsville Intermediate Sch	4-5	T	783	44%	903/668-5989
401 Waldron Ferry Rd, Hallsville 75650			50		
Karen Aikman					
Hallsville Junior High Sch	6-8	AV	1,186	42%	903/668-5986
1 Bobcat Ln, Hallsville 75650			45		
Amy Whittle					
North Elem Sch	K-3	T	736	41%	903/668-5981
200 Billie Martin Pkwy, Hallsville 75650			45		
Danieli Parker					

● **Harleton Ind School Dist** PID: 01028536 — 903/777-8601
17000 State Highway 154, Harleton 75651 — Fax 903/777-2406

Schools: 3 \ **Teachers:** 60 \ **Students:** 734 \ **Special Ed Students:** 85 \ **LEP Students:** 5 \ **College-Bound:** 63% \ **Ethnic:** African American 2%, Hispanic 7%, Native American: 1%, Caucasian 91% \ **Exp:** $312 (High) \ **Poverty:** 16% \ **Title I:** $119,668 \ **Open-Close:** 08/14 - 05/29 \ **DTBP:** $357 (High) \

Sandra Spencer 1	Tina Cox 2
David Clark 3*	Jeff Jones 5
Terry Ward 6*	Shannon Hearron 7*
Angel Johns 8,11,31,69,271,274	Kim Clynch 16
Misty Everhart 34*	Patricia Cunningham 57*
Pat McGill 67	Kevin Jones 73
Tonya Knolton 83,88,273*	Traci Jones 270

Public Schs..Principal	Grd	Prgm	Enr/#Cls	SN	
Harleton Elem Sch	PK-5	T	327	53%	903/777-4092
17240 State Highway 154, Harleton 75651			25		Fax 903/777-2782
Traci Jones					
Harleton High Sch	9-12	AV	223	32%	903/777-2711
17000 State Highway 154, Harleton 75651			12		Fax 903/777-2778
Crystal Newman					
Harleton Junior High Sch	6-8		184	46%	903/777-3010
17240 State Highway 154, Harleton 75651			15		Fax 903/777-3009
Randall Wright					

● **Karnack Ind School Dist** PID: 01028574 — 903/679-3117
655 Fason St, Karnack 75661 — Fax 903/679-4252

Schools: 1 \ **Teachers:** 11 \ **Students:** 124 \ **Special Ed Students:** 9 \ **LEP Students:** 7 \ **Ethnic:** African American 66%, Hispanic 11%, Caucasian 23% \ **Exp:** $596 (High) \ **Poverty:** 32% \ **Title I:** $194,092 \ **Open-Close:** 08/14 - 05/22 \ **DTBP:** $350 (High)

Amy Dickson 1,11	James Gholson 2
Joe Griffin 4	Ray Polk 67
Glen Hicks 73*	

TX—208

1 Superintendent	8 Curric/Instruct K-12	19 Chief Financial Officer	29 Family/Consumer Science	39 Social Studies K-12	49 English/Lang Arts Elem	59 Special Education Elem	69 Academic Assessment
2 Bus/Finance/Purchasing	9 Curric/Instruct Elem	20 Art K-12	30 Adult Education	40 Social Studies Elem	50 English/Lang Arts Sec	60 Special Education Sec	70 Research/Development
3 Buildings And Grounds	10 Curric/Instruct Sec	21 Art Elem	31 Career/Sch-to-Work K-12	41 Social Studies Sec	51 Reading K-12	61 Foreign/World Lang K-12	71 Public Information
4 Food Service	11 Federal Program	22 Art Sec	32 Career/Sch-to-Work Elem	42 Science K-12	52 Reading Elem	62 Foreign/World Lang Elem	72 Summer School
5 Transportation	12 Title I	23 Music K-12	33 Career/Sch-to-Work Sec	43 Science Elem	53 Reading Sec	63 Foreign/World Lang Sec	73 Instructional Tech
6 Athletic	13 Title V	24 Music Elem	34 Early Childhood Ed	44 Science Sec	54 Remedial Reading K-12	64 Religious Education K-12	74 Inservice Training
7 Health Services	15 Asst Superintendent	25 Music Sec	35 Health/Phys Education	45 Math K-12	55 Remedial Reading Elem	65 Religious Education Elem	75 Marketing/Distributive
	16 Instructional Media Svcs	26 Business Education	36 Guidance Services K-12	46 Math Elem	56 Remedial Reading Sec	66 Religious Education Sec	76 Info Systems
	17 Chief Operations Officer	27 Career & Tech Ed	37 Guidance Services Elem	47 Math Sec	57 Bilingual/ELL	67 School Board President	77 Psychological Assess
	18 Chief Academic Officer	28 Technology Education	38 Guidance Services Sec	48 English/Lang Arts K-12	58 Special Education K-12	68 Teacher Personnel	78 Affirmative Action

Texas School Directory — Hartley County

Public Schs..Principal	Grd	Prgm	Enr/#Cls	SN	
George Washington Carver ES 655 Fason St, Karnack 75661 Amy Dickson	PK-8	T	124 13	98%	903/679-3111

• **Marshall Ind School Dist** PID: 01028603   903/927-8700
1305 E Pinecrest Dr, Marshall 75670   Fax 903/935-0203

Schools: 7 \ *Teachers:* 382 \ *Students:* 5,345 \ *Special Ed Students:* 337 \ *LEP Students:* 939 \ *Ethnic:* African American 36%, Hispanic 35%, Native American: 1%, Caucasian 27% \ *Exp:* $331 (High) \ *Poverty:* 25% \ *Title I:* $1,991,297 \ *Special Education:* $1,787,000 \ *Open-Close:* 08/26 - 05/28 \ *DTBP:* $165 (High)

Dr Jerry Gibson 1
Brad Ash 3
Joseph Brinker 5
Jennifer Peters 7
Dr Melinda Jennings 11,296
Sharona Woolen 58
Helen Warwick 67
David Weaver 71
Eddie Mulanax 76
Jessica Warner 2
Cindy Brandon 4
Jake Griedl 6
Anika Perkins 8,27,34,57,81
Beth Rowe 15
Kim Kalina 60
Tiffany Best 68
Ron Lehr 73,84,295
Dayan Durrant 285

Public Schs..Principal	Grd	Prgm	Enr/#Cls	SN	
David Crockett Elem Sch 700 Jasper Dr, Marshall 75672 Angela Fitzpatrick	K-5	T	723 45	79%	903/927-8880 Fax 903/927-8885
Marshall High Sch 1900 Maverick Dr, Marshall 75670 Katina Brown	9-12	TV	1,412	66%	903/927-8800 Fax 903/938-7052
Marshall Junior High Sch 2710 E Travis St, Marshall 75672 Nakeisha Adams Pegues	6-8	V	1,271 65		903/927-8784 Fax 903/927-8837
Price T Young Elem Sch 1501 Sanford St, Marshall 75670 Nakeisha Pegues	K-5		392 25		903/927-8850 Fax 903/927-8858
Sam Houston Elem Sch 2905 E Travis St, Marshall 75672 Jerry Hancock	K-5		477 30		903/927-8860 Fax 903/927-8863
Washington Early Childhood Ctr 1202 Evans St, Marshall 75670 Frances Moore	PK-PK	T	313 16	99%	903/927-8790 Fax 903/927-8794
William B Travis Elem Sch 300 W Carolanne Blvd, Marshall 75670 Tamekia Johnson	K-5	T	678 400	72%	903/927-8780 Fax 903/927-8782

• **Waskom Ind School Dist** PID: 01028744   903/687-3361
365 W School Ave, Waskom 75692   Fax 903/687-3253

Schools: 3 \ *Teachers:* 75 \ *Students:* 890 \ *Special Ed Students:* 75 \ *LEP Students:* 90 \ *College-Bound:* 50% \ *Ethnic:* African American 18%, Hispanic 26%, Caucasian 57% \ *Exp:* $779 (High) \ *Poverty:* 16% \ *Title I:* $145,717 \ *Open-Close:* 08/14 - 05/22 \ *DTBP:* $350 (High)

Jimmy Cox 1
Ray Sudds 3,5,91
Whitney Keeling 6*
Rae Ann Patty 8,69
Debrah Criso 37
Wendy Shelton 57*
Jacob Speight 67
David Dulude 83
Nancy Dillard 2
Joe Griffin 4
Jennifer Swank 7,85*
Jennifer Troqville 11,271,296
Melinda Bowben 38
Staci Green 58
La Vaughn Fields 73,84

Public Schs..Principal	Grd	Prgm	Enr/#Cls	SN	
Waskom Elem Sch 225 School Avenue, Waskom 75692 Shay Thompson	PK-5	T	367 19	66%	903/687-3361
Waskom High Sch 980 School Ave, Waskom 75692 Kassie Watson	9-12	TV	307 22	55%	903/687-3361 Fax 903/687-2897
Waskom Middle Sch 255 School Ave, Waskom 75692 Bonita Cherry	6-8	T	281 16	62%	903/687-3361 Fax 903/687-3224

HARRISON PRIVATE SCHOOLS

Private Schs..Principal	Grd	Prgm	Enr/#Cls	SN	
Heartlight Boarding Sch 7345 E Highway 80, Hallsville 75650 Blake Nelson	7-12		56		903/668-2173 Fax 903/668-3453
Trinity Episcopal Sch 2905 Rosborough Springs Rd, Marshall 75672 Carrie Hammack	PK-8		155 33		903/938-3513 Fax 903/938-8725

HARTLEY COUNTY

HARTLEY PUBLIC SCHOOLS

• **Channing Ind School Dist** PID: 01028794   806/235-3432
900 Greenwood St, Channing 79018   Fax 806/235-2609

Schools: 1 \ *Teachers:* 17 \ *Students:* 181 \ *Special Ed Students:* 23 \ *LEP Students:* 10 \ *Ethnic:* African American 1%, Hispanic 24%, Caucasian 76% \ *Exp:* $330 (High) \ *Poverty:* 15% \ *Title I:* $45,881 \ *Open-Close:* 08/23 - 05/25 \ *DTBP:* $400 (High)

Robert McClain 1,11,57,288
Forrest Hebert 8,74,83*
David Spinhirne 67
Anne Browning 2
Melissa Garcia 58*
Heather White 73,295*

Public Schs..Principal	Grd	Prgm	Enr/#Cls	SN	
Channing Public Sch 900 Greenwood St, Channing 79018 Forrest Hebert	PK-12	TV	181 16	59%	806/235-3719

• **Hartley Ind School Dist** PID: 01028823   806/365-4458
9th & Johnson Street, Hartley 79044   Fax 806/365-4459

Schools: 1 \ *Teachers:* 21 \ *Students:* 239 \ *Special Ed Students:* 10 \ *LEP Students:* 58 \ *College-Bound:* 40% \ *Ethnic:* Hispanic 58%, Caucasian 42% \ *Exp:* $584 (High) \ *Poverty:* 10% \ *Title I:* $21,540 \ *Open-Close:* 08/19 - 05/21 \ *DTBP:* $341 (High) \ F t

Scott Vincent 1
Rebecca Zapata 4
Brandi Parker 16,73
Wade Lenz 67
Anette Melius 2
Dedra Hill 6*
Aaron Castanon 58*
Juana Garcia 271,273*

Haskell County

Public Schs..Principal	Grd	Prgm	Enr/#Cls	SN	
Hartley Sch 9th & Johnson Street, Hartley 79044 Kurtis Koepke	PK-12	ATV	239 14	62%	806/365-4458

HASKELL COUNTY

HASKELL PUBLIC SCHOOLS

- **Haskell Cons Ind School Dist** PID: 01028873   940/864-2602
  605 N Avenue E, Haskell 79521   Fax 940/864-8096

  Schools: 3 \ *Teachers:* 66 \ *Students:* 566 \ *Special Ed Students:* 59 \ *LEP Students:* 12 \ *College-Bound:* 80% \ *Ethnic:* African American 4%, Hispanic 43%, Native American: 2%, Caucasian 51% \ *Exp:* $496 (High) \ *Poverty:* 29% \ *Title I:* $243,269 \ *Open-Close:* 08/16 - 05/21 \ *DTBP:* $322 (High)

Bill Alcorn 1	Brenda Turner 2			
Bart Parhan 3	Edgwyna Flores 4			
Darryl McGhee 5	Brian Hodnett 6*			
Charistie Wheat 7,35,83,85	Michelle Thane 8,11,57,88,273,296,298			
James Foster 9	Jacklyn Wheatley 16,82*			
Tara Hollingsworth 58*	Tyke Meinzer 67			
Belinda Lytle 69,288*	John Rutkowski 73,84,286,295			
Tresa Martinez 271	Patsy Blakley 275*			

Public Schs..Principal	Grd	Prgm	Enr/#Cls	SN	
Haskell Elem Sch 306 S Avenue G, Haskell 79521 James Lisle	PK-5	AT	287 30	76%	940/864-2654 Fax 940/864-2369
Haskell High Sch 600 N Avenue E, Haskell 79521 Jeff York	9-12	ATV	158 30	57%	940/864-8535 Fax 940/864-3977
Haskell Junior High Sch 4th & Main Street, Rochester 79544 Kent Colley	6-8	ATV	107 18	63%	940/864-5981 Fax 940/864-5982

- **Paint Creek Ind School Dist** PID: 01028914   940/864-2471
  4485 FM 600, Haskell 79521   Fax 940/864-8038

  Schools: 1 \ *Teachers:* 18 \ *Students:* 102 \ *Special Ed Students:* 12 \ *College-Bound:* 70% \ *Ethnic:* Hispanic 37%, Caucasian 63% \ *Exp:* $668 (High) \ *Poverty:* 26% \ *Title I:* $18,806 \ *Open-Close:* 08/14 - 05/21 \ *DTBP:* $350 (High)

Cheryl Floyd 1	Stain Terrell 3
Ken Wallace 8*	Molly Blankenship 27*
Valine Bullinger 36,69,83,85,88,270	Samantha Carroll 54,58,271*
Dana Pendegraft 67	Jennifer Prichard 73,295

Public Schs..Principal	Grd	Prgm	Enr/#Cls	SN	
Paint Creek Sch 4485 FM 600, Haskell 79521 **Ken Wallace**	PK-12	TV	102 18	77%	940/864-2471

- **Rule Ind School Dist** PID: 01028964   940/997-2521
  1100 Union Ave, Rule 79547   Fax 940/997-2446

  Schools: 1 \ *Teachers:* 16 \ *Students:* 130 \ *Special Ed Students:* 14 \ *LEP Students:* 6 \ *College-Bound:* 90% \ *Ethnic:* African American 1%, Hispanic 41%, Native American: 1%, Caucasian 57% \ *Exp:* $246 (Med) \ *Poverty:* 35% \ *Title I:* $64,664 \ *Open-Close:* 08/13 - 05/28 \ *DTBP:* $420 (High) \

Brad Jones 1	Sandy Flores 2*
Lisa Saffel 4*	Norma Rios 4*
Ken Frazier 11,83	Leslie Kupatt 31,69,270*
Linda Caddell 57*	Jeffery Murray 67
Jerry Cannon 73*	

Public Schs..Principal	Grd	Prgm	Enr/#Cls	SN	
Rule Sch 1100 Union Ave, Rule 79547 **Kenneth Frazier**	PK-12	TV	130 30	87%	940/997-2521

HAYS COUNTY

HAYS PUBLIC SCHOOLS

- **Dripping Springs Ind Sch Dist** PID: 01029011   512/858-3000
  510 W Mercer St, Dripping Spgs 78620   Fax 512/858-3099

  Schools: 7 \ *Teachers:* 357 \ *Students:* 6,400 \ *Special Ed Students:* 612 \ *LEP Students:* 258 \ *College-Bound:* 65% \ *Ethnic:* Asian 2%, African American 1%, Hispanic 22%, Caucasian 76% \ *Exp:* $380 (High) \ *Poverty:* 5% \ *Title I:* $337,141 \ *Special Education:* $764,000 \ *Open-Close:* 08/20 - 05/29 \ *DTBP:* $151 (High) \

Bruce Gearing 1	Elaine Cogburn 2
Clint Pruett 3	Mike Hruska 3
John Crowley 4	Nanci Freeborg 4
Pam Swanks 5	Galen Zimmerman 6*
Diane Flaim 8,15	Nicole Poenitzsch ....
Kathy Leopold 16,73,76,297	Lucy Hansen 30,31,274
Rhonda Whitman 57,69,74,79,271	Jack Modgling 58,275
Carrie Kroll 67	Tiffany Duncan 68
Dale Whitaker 71	Cindi Wade 84
Kevin Haney 295	

Public Schs..Principal	Grd	Prgm	Enr/#Cls	SN	
Dripping Springs Elem Sch 29400 Ranch Road 12, Dripping Spgs 78620 **Kellie Raymond**	PK-5	T	767	16%	512/858-3700 Fax 512/858-3799
Dripping Springs High Sch 940 W Highway 290, Dripping Spgs 78620 **Angela Gamez**	9-12	AV	1,869	7%	512/858-3100 Fax 512/858-3199
Dripping Springs Middle Sch 111 Tiger Ln, Dripping Spgs 78620 **Jason Certain**	6-8		761 43	10%	512/858-3400 Fax 512/858-3499
Rooster Springs Elem Sch 1001 Belterra Dr, Austin 78737 **Steve Novickas**	PK-5		793	2%	512/465-6200 Fax 512/465-6299
Sycamore Springs Elem Sch 14451 Sawyer Ranch Rd, Austin 78737 **Kristen Ray**	PK-5		798		512/858-3900 Fax 512/858-3999

1 Superintendent	8 Curric/Instruct K-12	19 Chief Financial Officer	29 Family/Consumer Science	39 Social Studies K-12	49 English/Lang Arts Elem	59 Special Education Elem	69 Academic Assessment
2 Bus/Finance/Purchasing	9 Curric/Instruct Elem	20 Art K-12	30 Adult Education	40 Social Studies Elem	50 English/Lang Arts Sec	60 Special Education Sec	70 Research/Development
3 Buildings And Grounds	10 Curric/Instruct Sec	21 Art Elem	31 Career/Sch-to-Work K-12	41 Social Studies Sec	51 Reading K-12	61 Foreign/World Lang K-12	71 Public Information
4 Food Service	11 Federal Program	22 Art Sec	32 Career/Sch-to-Work Elem	42 Science K-12	52 Reading Elem	62 Foreign/World Lang Elem	72 Summer School
5 Transportation	12 Title I	23 Music K-12	33 Career/Sch-to-Work Sec	43 Science Elem	53 Reading Sec	63 Foreign/World Lang Sec	73 Instructional Tech
6 Athletic	13 Title V	24 Music Elem	34 Early Childhood Ed	44 Science Sec	54 Remedial Reading K-12	64 Religious Education K-12	74 Inservice Training
7 Health Services	15 Asst Superintendent	25 Music Sec	35 Health/Phys Education	45 Math K-12	55 Remedial Reading Elem	65 Religious Education Elem	75 Marketing/Distributive
	16 Instructional Media Svcs	26 Business Education	36 Guidance Services K-12	46 Math Elem	56 Remedial Reading Sec	66 Religious Education Sec	76 Info Systems
	17 Chief Operations Officer	27 Career & Tech Ed	37 Guidance Services Elem	47 Math Sec	57 Bilingual/ELL	67 School Board President	77 Psychological Assess
	18 Chief Academic Officer	28 Technology Education	38 Guidance Services Sec	48 English/Lang Arts K 12	58 Special Education K-12	68 Teacher Personnel	78 Affirmative Action

Texas School Directory — Hays County

Public Schs..Principal	Grd	Prgm	Enr/#Cls	SN	
Sycamore Springs Middle Sch 14451 Sawyer Ranch Rd, Austin 78737 Daniel Diehl	6-8		743		512/858-3600 Fax 512/858-3699
Walnut Springs Elem Sch 300 Sportsplex Dr, Dripping Spgs 78620 Melinda Gardner	PK-5	T	719 23	17%	512/858-3800 Fax 512/858-3899

- **Hays Cons Ind School Dist** PID: 01029059   512/268-2141
  21003 Interstate 35, Kyle 78640   Fax 512/268-2147

Schools: 25 \ *Teachers:* 1,198 \ *Students:* 20,445 \
Special Ed Students: 2,027 \ *LEP Students:* 2,831 \ *College-Bound:* 55%
\ *Ethnic:* Asian 1%, African American 3%, Hispanic 65%, Caucasian
31% \ *Exp:* $314 (High) \ *Poverty:* 10% \ *Title I:* $2,440,309 \
Special Education: $2,401,000 \ *Open-Close:* 08/15 - 05/22 \ *DTBP:* $195
(High) \ [f]

Dr Eric Wright 1	Becka Palmer 2
Nicole Turner 2	Randall Rau 2,19
Max Cleaver 3,5,17	Michael Thibodeaux 4
Karrie Walker 7,85	Sandra Dowdy 8,18
Sharah Pharr 11	Tim Savoy 16,71
Suzane Mitchell 27	Charlotte Winkelmann 36
Esperanza Orosco 67	Marivel Sedillo 68
Diane Borreson 73,98,295,297	Yarda Leflet 79
Deborah Brown 275*	Joy Philpott 294*
Alan Duerr 295	

Public Schs..Principal	Grd	Prgm	Enr/#Cls	SN	
Barton Middle Sch 4950 Jack C Hays Trl, Buda 78610 Teri Eubank	6-8		683 60	24%	512/268-1472 Fax 512/268-1610
Blanco Vista Elem Sch 2951 Blanco Vista Blvd, San Marcos 78666 Sean Fox	PK-5	T	815	63%	512/268-8506 Fax 512/393-2082
Buda Elem Sch 300 N San Marcos St, Buda 78610 Timothy Robinson	PK-5		581 20	40%	512/268-8439 Fax 512/295-4014
Camino Real Elem Sch 170 Las Brisas Blvd, Niederwald 78640 Elva Soliz	PK-5	T	799	85%	512/268-8505 Fax 512/398-5599
Carpenter Hill Elem Sch 4410 FM 967, Buda 78610 Ginger Bordeau	PK-5		678	12%	512/268-8509 Fax 512/295-4049
Chapa Middle Sch 3311 Dacy Ln, Kyle 78640 Lisa Walls	6-8	T	806	61%	512/268-8500 Fax 512/295-7824 [f]
Dahlstrom Middle Sch 3600 FM 967, Buda 78610 Dr Michael Watson	6-8		803 60	12%	512/268-8441 Fax 512/295-5346 [t]
Elm Grove Elem Sch 801 S FM 1626, Buda 78610 Kathryn Faulks	K-5		899 42	10%	512/268-8440 Fax 512/295-6809 [f][t]
Hemphill Elem Sch 3995 E FM 150, Kyle 78640 Monica Salas	PK-5	T	828	90%	512/268-4688 Fax 512/268-6208
Ⓐ Impact Center 4125 FM 967, Buda 78610 Sylvia Villejo	6-12		65 5		512/268-8473 Fax 512/295-5006
Jack C Hays High Sch 4800 Jack C Hays Trl, Buda 78610 David Pierce	9-12	AGV	2,905 100	32%	512/268-2911 Fax 512/268-1394
Johnson High Sch 4260 FM 967, Buda 78610 Brett Miksch	9-12		1,091		512/268-2141
Kyle Elem Sch 500 W Blanco St, Kyle 78640 Karen Lucita	PK-5	T	712 60	46%	512/268-3311 Fax 512/268-1417 [t]
Lehman High Sch 1700 Lehman Rd, Kyle 78640 Karen Zuniga	9-12	TV	2,566	55%	512/268-8454 Fax 512/268-5732
Ⓐ Live Oak Academy 4820 Jack C Hays Trl, Buda 78610 Doug Agnew	10-12	T	200 11	38%	512/268-8462 Fax 512/268-4142
McCormick Middle Sch 5700 Dacy Ln, Buda 78610 James Cruz	6-8		742		512/268-8508 Fax 512/295-4696
Negley Elem Sch 5940 McNaughton, Kyle 78640 Melody Crowther	PK-5		769	18%	512/268-8501 Fax 512/268-8582 [f]
Ralph Pfluger Elem Sch 4951 Marsh Ln, Buda 78610 Kathy Noack	PK-5		698	46%	512/268-8510 Fax 512/295-6826 [f]
Red Simon Middle Sch 3839 E FM 150, Kyle 78640 Charli Lennon	6-8	T	757	75%	512/268-8507
Science Hall Elem Sch 1510 Bebee Rd, Kyle 78640 Iric Ramos	PK-5		754	72%	512/268-8502 Fax 512/268-8784 [f][t]
Susie T Fuentes Elem Sch 901 Philomena Dr, Kyle 78640 Regina Butcher	PK-5	T	607	50%	512/268-7827 Fax 512/268-5968
Ⓜ Tobias Elem Sch 1005 E FM 150, Kyle 78640 Alisa DiPalma	PK-5	T	704 27	47%	512/268-8437 Fax 512/268-8447
Tom Green Elem Sch 1301 Old Goforth Rd, Buda 78610 Jennifer Hanna	PK-5	T	757 50	60%	512/268-8438 Fax 512/295-4107
Uhland Elem Sch 2331 High Rd, Uhland 78640 Cynthia Vasquez	PK-5		500		512/268-8503
Wallace Middle Sch 1500 W Center St, Kyle 78640 Sarah Hodges	6-8	T	801 50	52%	512/268-2891 Fax 512/268-1853

- **San Marcos Cons Ind Sch Dist** PID: 01029114   512/393-6700
  501 S Lbj Dr, San Marcos 78666   Fax 512/393-6787

Schools: 11 \ *Teachers:* 550 \ *Students:* 8,200 \ *Special Ed Students:* 895
\ *LEP Students:* 722 \ *College-Bound:* 70% \ *Ethnic:* Asian 1%,
African American 5%, Hispanic 72%, Caucasian 22% \ *Exp:* $361 (High) \
Poverty: 19% \ *Title I:* $2,439,065 \ *Special Education:* $1,594,000 \
Open-Close: 08/26 - 05/29 \ *DTBP:* $181 (High)

Michael Cardona 1	Cindy Casparis 2
Denise Garcia 2	Ulla Durham 2
Jay Wesson 3	Robert Gutierrez 3,91
Mike Boone 4	Doug Wozniak 5
Mark Soto 6	Dyanna Eastwood 7*
Nicole Dray 8,12,36,83,277,294	Laura Lugo 11,69,79,288
Karen Griffith 15	Dr Marcella Vies 15,68
Monica Ruiz Mills 15,68,69	Clarissa Talbert 58
Laura Zunker 58	Tammy Maiorano 58,77
Clementine Cantu 67	Stephanie Munoz 68
Andrew Fernandez 71	Greg Hubanek 73,76,295
Jeremy Connell 295	James Bratton 296*

Public Schs..Principal	Grd	Prgm	Enr/#Cls	SN	
Bonham Pre-Kindergarten Sch 1225 N State Highway 123, San Marcos 78666 Jennifer Gonzalez	PK-PK	T	433	95%	512/393-6031 Fax 512/353-0671

79 Student Personnel	91 Safety/Security	275 Response To Intervention	298 Grant Writer/Ptnrships
80 Driver Ed/Safety	92 Magnet School	277 Remedial Math K-12	750 Chief Innovation Officer
81 Gifted/Talented	93 Parental Involvement	280 Literacy Coach	751 Chief of Staff
82 Video Services	95 Tech Prep Program	285 STEM	752 Social Emotional Learning
83 Substance Abuse Prev	97 Chief Information Officer	286 Digital Learning	
84 Erate	98 Chief Technology Officer	288 Common Core Standards	
85 AIDS Education	270 Accountability	294 Webmaster	
88 Alternative/At Risk	271 Migrant Education	295 Network System	
89 Multi-Cultural Curriculum	273 Teacher Mentor	296 Title II Programs	
90 Social Work	274 Before/After Sch	297 Webmaster	

School Programs
A = Alternative Program
G = Adult Classes
M = Magnet Program
T = Title I Schoolwide
V = Career & Tech Ed Programs

Other School Types
Ⓐ = Alternative School
Ⓒ = Charter School
Ⓜ = Magnet School
Ⓨ = Year-Round School

Social Media
[f] = Facebook
[t] = Twitter

New Schools are shaded
New Superintendents and Principals are bold
Personnel with email addresses are underscored

Hays County — Market Data Retrieval

Bowie Elem Sch 4020 Monterrey Oaks, San Marcos 78666 Pam Thomas	K-5	T	558 35	73%	512/393-6200 Fax 512/393-6210
Crockett Elem Sch 1300 Girard St, San Marcos 78666 Keith Cunningham	K-5	T	624 33	55%	512/393-6400 Fax 512/353-3557
De Zavala Elem Sch 150 E De Zavala Dr, San Marcos 78666 Elena Sanchezvillanu	K-5		602 34		512/393-6250 Fax 512/392-0620
Doris Miller Middle Sch 301 Foxtail Run, San Marcos 78666 Richard DuVall	6-8	TV	782 48	66%	512/393-6660 Fax 512/393-6602
Hernandez Elem Sch 333 Stagecoach Trl, San Marcos 78666 Amber Owens	K-5	T	594 65	71%	512/393-6100 Fax 512/393-6109
Mendez Elem Sch 1805 Peter Garza Dr, San Marcos 78666 Karen McGowan	K-5	T	588	80%	512/393-6060 Fax 512/393-6039
Owen Goodnight Middle Sch 1301 N State Highway 123, San Marcos 78666 Rose Pearson	6-8	TV	1,005 50	74%	512/393-6550 Fax 512/393-6560
ⓐ Phoenix Learning Center 121 E De Zavala Dr, San Marcos 78666 Judy Mitchell	10-12	V	95 5		512/393-6864 Fax 512/393-6871
San Marcos High Sch 2601 Rattler Rd, San Marcos 78666 Denisha Presley	9-12	GTV	2,334 150	63%	512/393-6800 Fax 512/393-6893
Travis Elem Sch 1437 Post Rd, San Marcos 78666 Scott Masini	K-5	T	662 35	79%	512/393-6450 Fax 512/393-6976

- **Wimberley Ind School Dist** PID: 02903408 512/847-2414
  951 FM 2325, Wimberley 78676 Fax 512/847-2142

Schools: 4 \ *Teachers:* 159 \ *Students:* 2,400 \ *Special Ed Students:* 198 \ *LEP Students:* 130 \ *Ethnic:* Asian 1%, Hispanic 25%, Native American: 1%, Caucasian 73% \ *Exp:* $279 (Med) \ *Poverty:* 7% \ *Title I:* $220,209 \ *Special Education:* $462,000 \ *Open-Close:* 08/15 - 05/21

Dwain York 1		Moises Santiago 2,19	
Darrell Rivera 3		Eddie Campbell 3,91	
Mary Tefertiller 4		Owen Baldwin 5	
Doug Warren 6*		Darelle Jordan 7,83,85*	
Dee Howard 8,11,15,286,288,296,298		Jason Grogan 16,73,76,295	
Misty Howard 57		Stephanie Norris 58	
Joe Malone 67		Tracey Ramsey 68	
Jason Valentine 285*			

Public Schs..Principal	Grd	Prgm	Enr/#Cls	SN	
Danforth Junior High Sch 200 Texan Blvd, Wimberley 78676 Greg Howard	6-8	A	627 30	22%	512/847-2181 Fax 512/847-7897
Jacobs Well Elem Sch 3470 FM 2325, Wimberley 78676 Andrea Pope	2-5		678 21	27%	512/847-5558 Fax 512/847-6176
Scudder Primary Sch 400 Green Acres Dr, Wimberley 78676 Dara Richardson	PK-1	T	402 21	33%	512/847-3407 Fax 512/847-2738
Wimberley High Sch 100 Carney Ln, Wimberley 78676 Jason Valentine	9-12	AV	739 40	17%	512/847-5729 Fax 512/847-7269

HAYS CATHOLIC SCHOOLS

- **Diocese of Austin Ed Office** PID: 01420568
  Listing includes only schools located in this county. See District Index for location of Diocesan Offices.

Catholic Schs..Principal	Grd	Prgm	Enr/#Cls	SN	
Santa Cruz Elem Sch 1100 Main St, Buda 78610 Susan Flanagan	PK-3		43		512/312-2137 Fax 512/312-2143

HAYS PRIVATE SCHOOLS

Private Schs..Principal	Grd	Prgm	Enr/#Cls	SN	
Aesa Preparatory Academy 1401 Canonade Rd, Austin 78737 Barbara Garza	5-12		45		512/560-5584 Fax 512/829-4461
Austin Waldorf Sch 8700 South View Rd, Austin 78737 Jonathan Silver	K-12	G	380 18		512/288-5942 Fax 512/301-8997
Dragonfly International Sch 610 W Highway 290, Dripping Spgs 78620 Robin McThompson	PK-6		50 5		512/858-9780
Dripping Springs Christ Acad 800 W Hwy 290 Bldg C Ste 100, Dripping Spgs 78620 Becky Welborn	PK-10		25		512/858-9738
Hill Country Christian Sch 1401 Davis Ln, San Marcos 78666 Joe Lunz	K-12		145 11		512/353-8976 Fax 512/396-3639 f
Masters Sch 1664 Center Point Rd, San Marcos 78666 Tuck Blythe	K-8		131 8		512/392-4322 Fax 512/754-6017
San Marcos Adventist Jr Acad 1523 Old Ranch Road 12, San Marcos 78666 Carrie Suess	PK-10		74 5		512/392-9475 Fax 512/392-2693
San Marcos Baptist Academy 2801 Ranch Road 12, San Marcos 78666 Bob Bryant	7-12		300 36		512/353-2400 Fax 512/753-8031
St Stephen's Episcopal Sch 6000 FM 3237, Wimberley 78676 Will Webber	PK-6		58 12		512/847-9857 Fax 512/847-5275
The King's Academy 203 W Highway 290, Dripping Spgs 78620 Shelby Hubbard	PK-8		50		512/858-4700
Wonderland Sch 302 Country Estates Dr, San Marcos 78666 Jim Fife	PK-6		200 12		512/392-9404 Fax 512/392-9048

#		#		#		#		#		#		#	
1	Superintendent	8	Curric/Instruct K-12	19	Chief Financial Officer	29	Family/Consumer Science	39	Social Studies K-12	49	English/Lang Arts Elem	59	Special Education Elem	69	Academic Assessment
2	Bus/Finance/Purchasing	9	Curric/Instruct Elem	20	Art K-12	30	Adult Education	40	Social Studies Elem	50	English/Lang Arts Sec	60	Special Education Sec	70	Research/Development
3	Buildings And Grounds	10	Curric/Instruct Sec	21	Art Elem	31	Career/Sch-to-Work K-12	41	Social Studies Sec	51	Reading K-12	61	Foreign/World Lang K-12	71	Public Information
4	Food Service	11	Federal Program	22	Art Sec	32	Career/Sch-to-Work Elem	42	Science K-12	52	Reading Elem	62	Foreign/World Lang Elem	72	Summer School
5	Transportation	12	Title I	23	Music K-12	33	Career/Sch-to-Work Sec	43	Science Elem	53	Reading Sec	63	Foreign/World Lang Sec	73	Instructional Tech
6	Athletic	13	Title V	24	Music Elem	34	Early Childhood Ed	44	Science Sec	54	Remedial Reading K-12	64	Religious Education K-12	74	Inservice Training
7	Health Services	15	Asst Superintendent	25	Music Sec	35	Health/Phys Education	45	Math K-12	55	Remedial Reading Elem	65	Religious Education Elem	75	Marketing/Distributive
		16	Instructional Media Svcs	26	Business Education	36	Guidance Services K-12	46	Math Elem	56	Remedial Reading Sec	66	Religious Education Sec	76	Info Systems
		17	Chief Operations Officer	27	Career & Tech Ed	37	Guidance Services Elem	47	Math Sec	57	Bilingual/ELL	67	School Board President	77	Psychological Assess
		18	Chief Academic Officer	28	Technology Education	38	Guidance Services Sec	48	English/Lang Arts K-12	58	Special Education K-12	68	Teacher Personnel	78	Affirmative Action

Texas School Directory

Henderson County

HEMPHILL COUNTY

HEMPHILL PUBLIC SCHOOLS

• **Canadian Ind School Dist** PID: 01029205 806/323-5393
800 Hillside Ave, Canadian 79014 Fax 806/323-8143

Schools: 4 \ **Teachers:** 85 \ **Students:** 930 \ **Special Ed Students:** 54 \ **LEP Students:** 107 \ **College-Bound:** 64% \ **Ethnic:** Asian 1%, Hispanic 47%, Caucasian 52% \ **Exp:** $117 (Low) \ **Poverty:** 14% \ **Title I:** $124,555 \ **Open-Close:** 08/20 - 05/22 \ **DTBP:** $352 (High)

Kyle Lynch	1,11	Cindy Moore	2
Matt Dillon	3	Lydia Nix	4
Shaffer Baxter	5	Bruce Bryant	8*
Lawana Pulliam	8,73	Reagan Oles	9*
Darlene Walker	38*	Larry Smith	67
David Calabrese	73,76,295		

Public Schs..Principal	Grd	Prgm	Enr/#Cls	SN	
Baker Elem Sch 723 Cheyenne Street, Canadian 79014 Jamie Copley	3-5	T	216 9	46%	806/323-5386 Fax 806/323-9916
Canadian Elem Sch 500 Dogwood St, Canadian 79014 Reagan Risley	PK-2	T	233 22	47%	806/323-9331 Fax 806/323-6852
Canadian High Sch 621 S 5th Street, Canadian 79014 Lynn Pulliam	9-12	V	280 26	33%	806/323-5373 Fax 806/323-9345
Canadian Middle Sch 404 S 6th St, Canadian 79014 Bruce Bryant	6-8	T	201 30	40%	806/323-5351 Fax 806/323-8791

HENDERSON COUNTY

HENDERSON PUBLIC SCHOOLS

• **Athens Ind School Dist** PID: 01029231 903/677-6900
104 Hawn St, Athens 75751 Fax 903/677-6908

Schools: 5 \ **Teachers:** 206 \ **Students:** 3,118 \ **Special Ed Students:** 252 \ **LEP Students:** 715 \ **College-Bound:** 95% \ **Ethnic:** Asian 1%, African American 13%, Hispanic 49%, Caucasian 37% \ **Exp:** $500 (High) \ **Poverty:** 22% \ **Title I:** $1,029,231 \ **Special Education:** $614,000 \ **Open-Close:** 08/05 - 05/28 \ **DTBP:** $155 (High)

Blake Stiles	1	Randy Jones	2,19
Barry Choate	3,4,5	Charlie Combs	4
Zac Harrell	6	Dr Cathy Kirkland	8,57,69,78,288
Jami Ivey	10,15	Ginger Morrison	11,68,83,296,298*
Dr Janie Sims	15	Edward Wilbanks	27*
Brooke Brock	58	Alicia Elliott	67
Toni Clay	71	Tony Brooks	73,76,286
Dana Dykes	91		

Public Schs..Principal	Grd	Prgm	Enr/#Cls	SN	
Athens High Sch 708 E College St, Athens 75751 Henry Tracy	9-12	GTV	925 80	68%	903/677-6920 Fax 903/677-6925
Athens Middle Sch 6800 State Highway 19 S, Athens 75751 Jennifer Risinger	6-8	GT	690 45	73%	903/677-3030 Fax 903/677-2111
Bel Air Elem Sch 215 Willowbrook Dr, Athens 75751 Lisa Howell	PK-5	GT	502 29	80%	903/677-6980 Fax 903/677-6986 f
Central Athens Elem Sch 307 Madole St, Athens 75751 Shannon Pursley	PK-5	GT	518 26	84%	903/677-6960 Fax 903/677-6987
South Athens Elem Sch 718 Robbins Rd, Athens 75751 Nicole Mason	PK-5	GT	483 26	83%	903/677-6970 Fax 903/677-3470 f

• **Brownsboro Ind School Dist** PID: 01029322 903/852-3701
14134 State Highway 31 E, Brownsboro 75756 Fax 903/852-3957

Schools: 7 \ **Teachers:** 186 \ **Students:** 2,800 \ **Special Ed Students:** 266 \ **LEP Students:** 124 \ **Ethnic:** African American 8%, Hispanic 16%, Caucasian 76% \ **Exp:** $478 (High) \ **Poverty:** 19% \ **Title I:** $738,825 \ **Special Education:** $504,000 \ **Open-Close:** 08/15 - 05/21 \ **DTBP:** $152 (High) \ f t

Dr Keri Hampton	1	Jonathan Lundmark	2
Jeff Howard	3,5,91*	Brenda Myers	4
Gene Weinkauf	4	Roger Millender	5
Greg Pearson	6,35*	Jerry Feiner	28,73,76,295
Sandra Duke	34,58,77*	Steve Sanders	67
Carol Mayfield	68*	Brent Cooper	83

Public Schs..Principal	Grd	Prgm	Enr/#Cls	SN	
Ⓐ ACES Alternative 14135 State Highway 31 E, Brownsboro 75756 Marion Jones	9-12		14		903/852-8046
Brownsboro Elem Sch 12331 State Highway 31 E, Brownsboro 75756 Robbi McCarter	PK-3	T	461 25	62%	903/852-6461 Fax 903/852-2718
Brownsboro High Sch 13942 State Highway 31 E, Brownsboro 75756 Brent Cooper	9-12	T	764 65	45%	903/852-2321 Fax 903/852-5195
Brownsboro Intermediate Sch 13951 Saylors St, Brownsboro 75756 Billy Beasley	4-6	T	334 18	51%	903/852-7325 Fax 903/852-6745
Brownsboro Junior High Sch 11233 Ingram St, Brownsboro 75756 Brad Robertson	7-8	T	396 30	50%	903/852-6931 Fax 903/852-5238
Chandler Elem Sch 615 N Broad St, Chandler 75758 Ricky Daily	PK-3	T	472 22	59%	903/849-3400 Fax 903/849-3628
Chandler Intermediate Sch 22250 Barron Rd, Chandler 75758 Lisa Brown	4-6	T	293 19	53%	903/849-6436 Fax 903/849-3019

• **Cross Roads Ind School Dist** PID: 01029360 903/489-2001
14434 FM 59, Malakoff 75148 Fax 903/489-1108

Schools: 3 \ **Teachers:** 48 \ **Students:** 545 \ **Special Ed Students:** 59 \ **LEP Students:** 15 \ **College-Bound:** 61% \ **Ethnic:** African American 1%, Hispanic 8%, Caucasian 91% \ **Exp:** $850 (High) \ **Poverty:** 18% \ **Title I:** $124,216 \ **Open-Close:** 08/22 - 05/22 \ **DTBP:** $350 (High)

Richard Tedder	1,11	Ann Hornsby	2*

---

79 Student Personnel	91 Safety/Security	275 Response To Intervention	298 Grant Writer/Ptnrships
80 Driver Ed/Safety	92 Magnet School	277 Remedial Math K-12	750 Chief Innovation Officer
81 Gifted/Talented	93 Parental Involvement	280 Literacy Coach	751 Chief of Staff
82 Video Services	95 Tech Prep Program	285 STEM	752 Social Emotional Learning
83 Substance Abuse Prev	97 Chief Infomation Officer	286 Digital Learning	
84 Erate	98 Chief Technology Officer	288 Common Core Standards	
85 AIDS Education	270 Character Education	294 Accountability	
88 Alternative/At Risk	271 Migrant Education	295 Network System	
89 Multi-Cultural Curriculum	273 Teacher Mentor	296 Title II Programs	
90 Social Work	274 Before/After Sch	297 Webmaster	

School Programs
A = Alternative Program
G = Adult Classes
M = Magnet Program
T = Title I Schoolwide
V = Career & Tech Ed Programs

Other School Types
Ⓐ = Alternative School
Ⓒ = Charter School
Ⓜ = Magnet School
Ⓨ = Year-Round School

Social Media
f = Facebook
t = Twitter

New Schools are shaded
New Superintendents and Principals are bold
Personnel with email addresses are underscored

TX-213

Henderson County

Market Data Retrieval

Daniel Pierce 6*
Kim Mattingly 31,69,85*
Darren Himes 67
Kari Cahill 270,271*
Gary Cahill 16,73*
Pam Taylor 36*
Gina Trammell 68
Dr Tammy Willis 286

Public Schs..Principal	Grd	Prgm	Enr/#Cls	SN	
Cross Roads Elem Sch 14434 FM 59, Malakoff 75148 Kari Cahill	PK-5	T	242 15	68%	903/489-1774 Fax 903/489-1843
Cross Roads High Sch 14434 FM 59, Malakoff 75148 John Miller	9-12	TV	162 18	51%	903/489-1275
Cross Roads Junior High Sch 14434 FM 59, Malakoff 75148 Julie Koepp	6-8	T	141 12	67%	903/489-2667 Fax 903/489-3840

• **Eustace Ind School Dist** PID: 01029384
320 FM 316 S, Eustace 75124
903/425-5151
Fax 903/425-5147

Schools: 4 \ *Teachers:* 122 \ *Students:* 1,550 \ *Special Ed Students:* 224 \ *LEP Students:* 27 \ *College-Bound:* 46% \ *Ethnic:* African American 1%, Hispanic 11%, Caucasian 88% \ *Exp:* $259 (Med) \ *Poverty:* 26% \ *Title I:* $440,174 \ *Special Education:* $354,000 \ *Open-Close:* 08/21 - 05/22 \ *DTBP:* $357 (High) \ 🇫 🇹

Dr Coy Holcombe 1,73
James Beverly 3
Stan Sowers 5,15*
Deanna Haynes 8,12,57
Kathryn Hendrickson 58*
Phyllis Bice 83,85,88*
Rusty Meyners 295
Carol Warren 2
Carolyn Davis 4
Steven Smith 6*
Julie Gray 34*
Ashley McKee 67
Wade Morton 91*

Public Schs..Principal	Grd	Prgm	Enr/#Cls	SN	
Eustace High Sch 318 FM 316 S, Eustace 75124 Christopher Whorton	9-12	ATV	458 45	63%	903/425-5161 Fax 903/425-5227
Eustace Intermediate Sch 205 W Henderson St, Eustace 75124 Robert Reeve	3-5	T	339 28	68%	903/425-5181 Fax 903/425-5294
Eustace Middle Sch 200 FM 316 S, Eustace 75124 Michael Rowland	6-8	T	335 25	63%	903/425-5171 Fax 903/425-5146 🇫 🇹
Eustace Primary Sch 211 W Henderson St, Eustace 75124 Julie Gray	PK-2	T	416 30	79%	903/425-5191 Fax 903/425-5148

• **La Poynor Ind School Dist** PID: 01029413
13155 US Highway 175 E, Larue 75770
903/876-4057
Fax 903/876-4541

Schools: 1 \ *Teachers:* 37 \ *Students:* 453 \ *Special Ed Students:* 38 \ *LEP Students:* 5 \ *College-Bound:* 95% \ *Ethnic:* Asian 1%, African American 14%, Hispanic 5%, Caucasian 80% \ *Exp:* $1,783 (High) \ *Poverty:* 27% \ *Title I:* $163,630 \ *Open-Close:* 08/20 - 05/22 \ *DTBP:* $392 (High)

James Young 1
Ronnie Hambrick 3,5,91*
Dean Nuckolls 6*
Geneva Robinson 31*
Lori Griffith 57*
Krissy Step 73,295*
Kendra Scarborough 2
Cheryl Hill 4*
Pam Penney 7,85*
Melissa Sheffield 36,83,88*
Keith Bristow 67

Public Schs..Principal	Grd	Prgm	Enr/#Cls	SN	
La Poynor Sch 13155 US Highway 175 E, Larue 75770 Marsha Mills \ Crystal Woodard	PK-12	AV	453 24	45%	903/876-4057

• **Malakoff Ind School Dist** PID: 01029449
1308 FM 3062, Malakoff 75148
903/489-1152
Fax 903/489-2566

Schools: 5 \ *Teachers:* 104 \ *Students:* 1,400 \ *Special Ed Students:* 113 \ *LEP Students:* 54 \ *College-Bound:* 41% \ *Ethnic:* Asian 1%, African American 12%, Hispanic 16%, Caucasian 71% \ *Exp:* $423 (High) \ *Poverty:* 29% \ *Title I:* $494,364 \ *Open-Close:* 08/14 - 05/22 \ *DTBP:* $340 (High)

Done Layton 1
Tammy Baker 3,5
Jamie Driskell 6*
Sybil Norris 11,31,57,58,83,271,296,298
Laurie Holcombe 58
Randy Webb 73,95,295
Kim Spencer 2
Jennifer Gonzales 4
Mike Burns 8
Linda McMurtry 16,82*
Rick Vieregge 67
Stacy Hillhouse 91

Public Schs..Principal	Grd	Prgm	Enr/#Cls	SN	
ⓐ Leo Orr Sr Education Center 1209 W Royall Blvd, Malakoff 75148 Danielle Copeland	6-12		10 3		903/489-4132 Fax 903/489-3239
Malakoff Elem Sch 310 N Terry St, Malakoff 75148 Ronnie Snow	PK-5	T	475 45	69%	903/489-0313 Fax 903/489-1536
Malakoff High Sch 15201 FM 3062, Malakoff 75148 Bill Morgan	9-12	GTV	385 50	48%	903/489-1527 Fax 903/489-0971
Malakoff Middle Sch 106 N Cedar St, Malakoff 75148 Quintin Watkins	6-8	T	303 26	61%	903/489-0264 Fax 903/489-1812
Tool Elem Sch 1201 S Tool Dr, Kemp 75143 Christal Calhoun	PK-5	T	224	82%	903/432-2637 Fax 903/432-3666

• **Murchison Ind Sch Dist** PID: 01029487
9661 Bankhead St, Murchison 75778
903/469-3636
Fax 903/469-3887

Schools: 1 \ *Teachers:* 15 \ *Students:* 175 \ *Special Ed Students:* 17 \ *LEP Students:* 7 \ *Ethnic:* Asian 1%, Hispanic 14%, Caucasian 85% \ *Exp:* $245 (Med) \ *Poverty:* 30% \ *Title I:* $58,973 \ *Open-Close:* 08/26 - 05/22 \ *DTBP:* $303 (High)

Kimberly Followwell 1,11,83
Jerid Heathman 6*
Virginia Crow 73,295*
Christy Wherman 2
Lloyd Smith 67

Public Schs..Principal	Grd	Prgm	Enr/#Cls	SN	
Murchison Elem Sch 9661 Bankhead St, Murchison 75778 Susan Miller	PK-8	T	175 10	61%	903/469-3636

• **Trinidad Ind School Dist** PID: 01029504
105 W Eaton St, Trinidad 75163
903/778-2673
Fax 903/778-4120

Schools: 1 \ *Teachers:* 17 \ *Students:* 165 \ *Special Ed Students:* 19 \ *LEP Students:* 4 \ *College-Bound:* 30% \ *Ethnic:* African American 15%, Hispanic 15%, Caucasian 69% \ *Exp:* $433 (High) \ *Poverty:* 28% \ *Title I:* $54,791 \ *Open-Close:* 08/14 - 05/22 \ *DTBP:* $323 (High)

Corey Jenkins 1,11,288
Matthew Mizell 8,274*
Eric Airheart 67
Kristi Boggas 4
Victrina Johnson 57,58

---

1 Superintendent	8 Curric/Instruct K-12	19 Chief Financial Officer	29 Family/Consumer Science	39 Social Studies K-12	49 English/Lang Arts Elem	59 Special Education Elem	69 Academic Assessment
2 Bus/Finance/Purchasing	9 Curric/Instruct Elem	20 Art K-12	30 Adult Education	40 Social Studies Elem	50 English/Lang Arts Sec	60 Special Education Sec	70 Research/Development
3 Buildings And Grounds	10 Curric/Instruct Sec	21 Art Elem	31 Career/Sch-to-Work K-12	41 Social Studies Sec	51 Reading K-12	61 Foreign/World Lang K-12	71 Public Information
4 Food Service	11 Federal Program	22 Art Sec	32 Career/Sch-to-Work Elem	42 Science K-12	52 Reading Elem	62 Foreign/World Lang Elem	72 Summer School
5 Transportation	12 Title I	23 Music K-12	33 Career/Sch-to-Work Sec	43 Science Elem	53 Reading Sec	63 Foreign/World Lang Sec	73 Instructional Tech
6 Athletic	13 Title V	24 Music Elem	34 Early Childhood Ed	44 Science Sec	54 Remedial Reading K-12	64 Religious Education K-12	74 Inservice Training
7 Health Services	15 Asst Superintendent	25 Music Sec	35 Health/Phys Education	45 Math K-12	55 Remedial Reading Elem	65 Religious Education Elem	75 Marketing/Distributive
	16 Instructional Media Svcs	26 Business Education	36 Guidance Services K-12	46 Math Elem	56 Remedial Reading Sec	66 Religious Education Sec	76 Info Systems
	17 Chief Operations Officer	27 Career & Tech Ed	37 Guidance Services Elem	47 Math Sec	57 Bilingual/ELL	67 School Board President	77 Psychological Assess
	18 Chief Academic Officer	28 Technology Education	38 Guidance Services Sec	48 English/Lang Arts K-12	58 Special Education K-12	68 Teacher Personnel	78 Affirmative Action

Texas School Directory

Hidalgo County

Public Schs..Principal	Grd	Prgm	Enr/#Cls	SN	
Trinidad Sch 105 W Eaton St, Trinidad 75163 Matthew Mizell	PK-12	TV	165 30	65%	903/778-2415 Fax 903/778-2663

HENDERSON PRIVATE SCHOOLS

Private Schs..Principal	Grd	Prgm	Enr/#Cls	SN	
Athens Christian Academy 105 S Carroll St, Athens 75751 Brent Williams	K-6		64 14		903/675-5135 Fax 903/675-4708
Open Doors Christian Academy 202 Ranch Rd, Gun Barrel Cy 75156 Debra Turner	K-12		42 9		903/887-3621 Fax 903/713-0220

HIDALGO COUNTY

HIDALGO PUBLIC SCHOOLS

- **Donna Ind School Dist** PID: 01029554   956/464-1600
  116 N 10th St, Donna 78537   Fax 956/464-1752

Schools: 22 \ **Teachers:** 1,058 \
Students: 14,459 \ **Special Ed Students:** 1,197 \ **LEP Students:** 7,016
\ **College-Bound:** 54% \ **Ethnic:** Hispanic 100%, \ **Exp:** $280 (Med) \
Poverty: 51% \ **Title I:** $14,078,136 \ **Special Education:** $2,384,000 \
Open-Close: 08/26 - 05/28 \ **DTBP:** $191 (High) \ f

Dr Hafedn Azaiez 1
Olga Norriega 2
Rebecca Castaneda 11,271
Juanita Rodriguez 15,68,79,273
David Moreno 27,33*
Emily Anderson 43
Diane Villanueva 58,77,275
John Mendoza 88*
Tomas Camez 93
Ludipina Cansino 2,19
Rosa Campos 7,85*
Dr Debra Aceves 13,57,61,81
David Chavez 16,73,76,295*
Stephanie Powelson 39
Rashad Rana 45
Eva Watts 67
Daniel Walden 91

Public Schs..Principal	Grd	Prgm	Enr/#Cls	SN	
Ⓐ 3D Academy 2110 Hester Ave, Donna 78537 Jose Villanueva	9-12	T	142	97%	956/464-1254 Fax 956/464-2375
A P Solis Middle Sch 700 South Ave, Donna 78537 Mary Lou Rodriguez	6-8	T	842	87%	956/464-1650 Fax 956/464-1786
Antonio M Ochoa Elem Sch 424 S 11th St, Donna 78537 Melissa Smith	PK-5	T	439 26	89%	956/464-1900 Fax 956/464-1918
C Stainke Elem Sch 1309 South Ave, Donna 78537 Griselda Alvarez	PK-5	T	557 30	93%	956/464-1940 Fax 956/464-1790
Capt D Salinas II Elem Sch 333 E Business Highway 83, Alamo 78516 Sanjuanito Franco	PK-5	T	589 38	97%	956/783-1332 Fax 956/782-9175
Daniel Singleterry Sr Elem Sch 9113 N Val Verde Rd, Donna 78537 Christopher Park	PK-5	T	536 39	98%	956/464-1845 Fax 956/464-1849
Ⓐ Disciplinary Alt Ed Program 2006 Silver Ave, Donna 78537 John Mendoza	1-12		60 11		956/464-1954 Fax 956/464-1951
Donna High Sch 2301 E Wood Ave, Donna 78537 Nancy Castillo	9-12	GTV	2,045	90%	956/464-1700 Fax 956/464-1629
Donna North High Sch 7250 N Val Verde Rd, Donna 78537 Bernadett Caceres	9-12	ATV	2,162	95%	956/464-4190
Dora M Sauceda Middle Sch 520 N Valley View Rd, Donna 78537 Adela Troncoso	6-8	T	882 100	96%	956/464-1360 Fax 956/464-1349
Eloy Salazar Elem Sch 3207 N Goolie Rd, Donna 78537 Leticia Chavez	PK-5	T	553 37	92%	956/464-1977 Fax 956/464-1983
Guzman Elem Sch 510 S Salinas Blvd, Donna 78537 Emmy Delagarza	PK-5	T	385 25	97%	956/464-1920 Fax 956/464-1926
J S Adame Elem Sch 5001 N Farm Rd 493, Donna 78537 Maria Partida	PK-5	T	657 45	91%	956/461-4010 Fax 956/461-4017
Juan W Caceres Elem Sch 503 S Hutto Rd, Donna 78537 Celia Martinez	PK-5	T	415 29	95%	956/464-1995 Fax 956/464-1743
Le Noir Elem Sch 316 N Main St, Donna 78537 Karen Nieto	PK-5	T	402 35	91%	956/464-1685 Fax 956/464-1877
Magin Rivas Elem Sch 503 S Hutto Rd, Donna 78537 Rosalinda Navarro	PK-5	T	445 33	99%	956/464-1990 Fax 956/464-1869
Maria Alicia P Munoz Sch 1901 E Roosevelt Rd, Donna 78537 Nelda Calderon	PK-5	T	752 45	97%	956/464-1310 Fax 956/464-1316
Patricia S Garza Elem Sch 8801 W Alberta Rd, Donna 78537 Crystal Garza	PK-5	T	602 48	99%	956/464-1886 Fax 956/464-1891
Runn Elem Sch 1701 E Highway 281, Donna 78537 Alicia Sarminto	PK-5	T	311 22	96%	956/464-1864 Fax 956/464-1934
Truman Price Elem Sch 2906 E Roberts Ave, Donna 78537 **Olga Cervantes**	PK-5	T	507 26	93%	956/464-1303 Fax 956/464-1676
Veterans Middle Sch 2711 N Goolie Rd, Donna 78537 Claudia Guerrero	6-8	T	858 35	97%	956/464-1350 Fax 956/464-1356
W A Todd Middle Sch 400 N Salinas Blvd, Donna 78537 Araceli Guerra	6-8	T	732	91%	956/464-1800

- **Edcouch Elsa Ind School Dist** PID: 01029621   956/262-6000
  301 N Yellow Jacket Dr, Edcouch 78538   Fax 956/262-6032

Schools: 8 \ **Teachers:** 325 \ **Students:** 5,450 \ **Special Ed Students:** 400
\ **LEP Students:** 1,362 \ **College-Bound:** 51% \ **Ethnic:** Hispanic 99%, \
Exp: $717 (High) \ **Poverty:** 46% \ **Title I:** $3,982,435 \ **Open-Close:** 08/26 -
05/22 \ **DTBP:** $189 (High)

Dr Richard Riberou 1
Elena Garza 4
Christian Navarro 6,35
Rosalinda DeLeon 9*
Carmen Garcia 11,296
Pete Vallejo 16
Cynthia Brisero 36,85*
Tony Barco 67
Sandra Garza 69
Sylvia Garza 2
Martin Rodregez 5
Denise Frando 9,36*
Nehemias Cantu 10
Frances Rocha 15
Joe Torres 31,73,286
Itza Flores 58
Virginio Gonzalez 68
Melinda Chapa 298

---

79 Student Personnel	91 Safety/Security	275 Response To Intervention	298 Grant Writer/Ptnrships	**School Programs**	**Social Media**
80 Driver Ed/Safety	92 Magnet School	277 Remedial Math K-12	750 Chief Innovation Officer	A = Alternative Program	
81 Gifted/Talented	93 Parental Involvement	280 Literacy Coach	751 Chief of Staff	G = Adult Classes	f = Facebook
82 Video Services	95 Tech Prep Program	285 STEM	752 Social Emotional Learning	M = Magnet Program	
83 Substance Abuse Prev	97 Chief Infomation Officer	286 Digital Learning		T = Title I Schoolwide	t = Twitter
84 Erate	98 Chief Technology Officer	288 Common Core Standards	**Other School Types**	V = Career & Tech Ed Programs	
85 AIDS Education	270 Character Education	294 Accountability	Ⓐ = Alternative School		
88 Alternative/At Risk	271 Migrant Education	295 Network System	Ⓒ = Charter School	New Schools are shaded	
89 Multi-Cultural Curriculum	273 Teacher Mentor	296 Title II Programs	Ⓜ = Magnet School	New Superintendents and Principals are bold	
90 Social Work	274 Before/After Sch	297 Webmaster	Ⓨ = Year-Round School	Personnel with email addresses are underscored	

TX—215

Hidalgo County

Public Schs..Principal	Grd	Prgm	Enr/#Cls	SN	
Carlos Truan Jr High Sch Mile 17 N & Mile 4 W, Edcouch 78538 Alfredo Aguilar	6-8	TV	1,074 44	100%	956/262-5820 Fax 956/262-6079
Early College High Sch PO Box 127, Edcouch 78538 Jaime Garcia	9-9	V	400		956/262-4731
Edcouch Elsa High Sch Mile 17 N & Mile 4W, Edcouch 78538 Janie Tijerina	9-12	ATV	1,394	99%	956/262-6074 Fax 956/262-6060
John F Kennedy Elem Sch 500 W 9th Street, Elsa 78543 Criselda Martinez	K-5	T	477 26	99%	956/262-6027 Fax 956/262-6029
Jorge R Gutierrez ECC 1210 W Santa Rosa Ave, Edcouch 78538 Norma Hernandez	PK-PK	T	420 28	100%	956/262-0040 Fax 956/262-0043
Lyndon Baines Johnson Elem Sch 200 S Fannin Street, Elsa 78543 Aminta Limas	K-5	T	506 25	99%	956/262-2161 Fax 956/626-6012
Ruben Rodriguez Elem Sch 1302 W Santa Rosa Rd, Edcouch 78538 Maricela Olivarez	K-5	T	434 15	99%	956/262-4712 Fax 956/262-6061
Santiago Garcia Elem Sch 101 E Santa Rosa Ave, Edcouch 78538 Jesus Ramos	K-5	T	511 22	99%	956/262-4741 Fax 956/262-6004

- **Edinburg Cons Ind School Dist** PID: 01029671 956/289-2300
  411 N 8th Ave, Edinburg 78541   Fax 956/383-3576

Schools: 43 \ *Teachers:* 2,306 \ *Students:* 34,500 \
Special Ed Students: 2,011 \ *LEP Students:* 10,232 \ *College-Bound:* 61%
\ *Ethnic:* Asian 1%, Hispanic 98%, Caucasian 2% \ *Exp:* $347 (High) \
Poverty: 35% \ *Title I:* $18,800,104 \ *Special Education:* $5,043,000 \
Open-Close: 08/26 - 05/29 \ *DTBP:* $191 (High) \

Gilbert Garza 1
Dr Rebecca Morrison 2,15,72,274,296,298
Jaime Perez 4*
Rogelio Garza 6,35*
Diana Davila 7
Dr Anthony Garza 10*
Melissa Rodriguez 13
Dr Mario Salinas 15
Nelida Villarreal 20,23
Sofia Hinojosa 36,79,83,85,270,275
Mirella Garza 43
Romero Leal 46
Alida Suarez 58,77
Romeo Cantu 71
Ernestina Cano 88*
Sandra Rodriguez 93

Amaro Tijerina 2
Roberto Saenz 3
Alonzo Barbosa 5
Deanna Martinez 7
Dalia Guzman 8,15
Irma Villareal 12
Edwardo Moreno 15,28,73,84,297
Dora Estrada 16,82
Arminda Lozano 27,31
Azel Arredondo 39
Vanessa Arrona 44
Patricio Escamilla 57,271
Xavier Salinas 67
Mara Moats 74,285
Rudy Jemenez 90

Public Schs..Principal	Grd	Prgm	Enr/#Cls	SN	
A Villarreal Elem Sch 4014 N Doolittle Rd, Edinburg 78542 Odilia Villarreal	PK-5	T	644	89%	956/289-2377 Fax 956/381-4782
Alfonso R Ramirez Elem Sch 1700 W Alberta Rd, Edinburg 78539 Clarisa Ramirez	PK-5	T	558	79%	956/289-2425 Fax 956/316-2355
Anne L MaGee Elem Sch 3420 W Rogers Rd, Edinburg 78541 Marla Cavazos	PK-5	T	436	93%	956/289-2306 Fax 956/385-3320
Austin Elem Sch 1023 E Kuhn St, Edinburg 78541 Homero Cano	PK-5	T	387 17	94%	956/289-2331 Fax 956/316-7560
B L Garza Middle Sch 1202 N Monmack Rd, Edinburg 78541 Dale Ramos	6-8	T	1,079 65	82%	956/289-2480 Fax 956/316-3109
Betty Harwell Middle Sch 9207 N Avila Rd, Edinburg 78542 Marisa Garza	6-8	GTV	1,389 76	95%	956/289-2440 Fax 956/316-7303
Brewster Sch 22420 FM 1017, Edinburg 78541 Dora Flores	PK-8	T	378 18	82%	956/289-2334 Fax 956/316-7510
Cano Gonzalez Elem Sch 1701 S Raul Longoria Rd, Edinburg 78542 Nelda Gaytan	PK-5	T	466 31	84%	956/289-2380 Fax 956/316-7457
Canterbury Elem Sch 2821 W Canton Rd, Edinburg 78539 Ricardo Perez	PK-5	T	636 35	49%	956/289-2374 Fax 956/316-7606
Carmen Avila Elem Sch 9205 Carmen Avila Rd, Edinburg 78542 Susana Aguilar	PK-5		617 35		956/289-2307 Fax 956/385-3330
Cavazos Elem Sch 1501 Freddy Gonzales Rd, McAllen 78504 Christine Gordon	PK-5	T	469 28	78%	956/289-2535 Fax 956/384-5147
Crawford Elem Sch 1800 E Davis Rd, Edinburg 78542 Dr David Montemayor	PK-5	T	592	90%	956/289-2410 Fax 956/287-0700
De La Vina Elem Sch 1001 S Jackson Rd, Edinburg 78539 Erika Playle	PK-5	T	531	90%	956/289-2366 Fax 956/316-7782
E B Guerra Elem Sch 10010 Via Fernandez, Edinburg 78541 Lisa Valdez	PK-5	T	589 45	92%	956/289-2530 Fax 956/384-5352
Ⓐ Edinburg Alternative Academy 1301 E Schunior St, Edinburg 78541 Anibal Gorena	6-12		110 12		956/289-2598 Fax 956/316-7391
Edinburg High Sch 2600 E Wisconsin Rd, Edinburg 78542 Yesena Molina	9-12	GTV	2,428	88%	956/289-2400 Fax 956/386-1225
Edinburg North High Sch 3101 N Closner Blvd, Edinburg 78541 Mark Micallef	9-12	TV	2,789	85%	956/289-2500 Fax 956/316-7712
Edinburg South Middle Sch 601 W Freddy Gonzalez Dr, Edinburg 78539 Mary Garza	6-8	TV	1,354 61	67%	956/289-2415 Fax 956/316-8817
Eisenhower Elem Sch 2901 E Mile 17 1/2 Rd, Edinburg 78542 S Faz	PK-5		635 32		956/289-2540 Fax 956/316-7554
Escandon Elem Sch 1100 E Trenton Rd, Edinburg 78542 Ruth Torres	PK-5	T	655 35	85%	956/289-2545 Fax 956/316-7647
Esparza Elem Sch 2510 S Cesar Chavez Rd, Edinburg 78542 Mr Pesina	PK-5	T	437	88%	956/289-2308 Fax 956/385-3310
Flores-Zapata Elem Sch 14000 N Rooth Rd, Edinburg 78542 Victoria Martinez	PK-5	T	532	95%	956/289-2445 Fax 956/383-0957
Francisco Barrientes Mid Sch 1100 E Ebony Ln, Edinburg 78539 **David Rivera**	6-8	T	1,308	86%	956/289-2430 Fax 956/316-7749
Freddy Gonzalez Elem Sch 2401 S Sugar Rd, Edinburg 78539 Naida Torres	PK-5	T	446 29	67%	956/289-2520 Fax 956/316-7420
Hargill Elem Sch 13394 4th St, Hargill 78549 Modesta Segundo	PK-5	T	378 24	95%	956/289-2338 Fax 956/845-6337
Jefferson Elem Sch 904 S 12th Ave, Edinburg 78539 Ana Salinas	PK-5	T	440 26	66%	956/289-2385 Fax 956/316-7427
John F Kennedy Elem Sch 8610 Tex Mex Rd, Edinburg 78542 Gloria Alonzo	PK-5	T	494 36	96%	956/289-2390 Fax 956/384-5131

1	Superintendent	8	Curric/Instruct K-12	19	Chief Financial Officer	29	Family/Consumer Science	39 Social Studies K-12	49 English/Lang Arts Elem	59 Special Education Elem	69 Academic Assessment
2	Bus/Finance/Purchasing	9	Curric/Instruct Elem	20	Art K-12	30	Adult Education	40 Social Studies Elem	50 English/Lang Arts Sec	60 Special Education Sec	70 Research/Development
3	Buildings And Grounds	10	Curric/Instruct Sec	21	Art Elem	31	Career/Sch-to-Work K-12	41 Social Studies Sec	51 Reading K-12	61 Foreign/World Lang K-12	71 Public Information
4	Food Service	11	Federal Program	22	Art Sec	32	Career/Sch-to-Work Elem	42 Science K-12	52 Reading Elem	62 Foreign/World Lang Elem	72 Summer School
5	Transportation	12	Title I	23	Music K-12	33	Career/Sch-to-Work Sec	43 Science Elem	53 Reading Sec	63 Foreign/World Lang Sec	73 Instructional Tech
6	Athletic	13	Title V	24	Music Elem	34	Early Childhood Ed	44 Science Sec	54 Remedial Reading K-12	64 Religious Education K-12	74 Inservice Training
7	Health Services	15	Asst Superintendent	25	Music Sec	35	Health/Phys Education	45 Math K-12	55 Remedial Reading Elem	65 Religious Education Elem	75 Marketing/Distributive
		16	Instructional Media Svcs	26	Business Education	36	Guidance Services K-12	46 Math Elem	56 Remedial Reading Sec	66 Religious Education Sec	76 Info Systems
		17	Chief Operations Officer	27	Career & Tech Ed	37	Guidance Services Elem	47 Math Sec	57 Bilingual/ELL	67 School Board President	77 Psychological Assess
		18	Chief Academic Officer	28	Technology Education	38	Guidance Services Sec	48 English/Lang Arts K 12	58 Special Education K 12	68 Teacher Personnel	78 Affirmative Action

Texas School Directory — Hidalgo County

School	Grd	Prgm	Enr/#Cls	SN	Phone
Johnny Economedes High Sch 1414 N Alamo Rd, Edinburg 78542 Dr Raul D'Lorm	9-12	TV	2,677 200	92%	956/289-2450 Fax 956/385-3050
Lincoln Elem Sch 1319 E Lovett St, Edinburg 78541 Eva Sandoval	PK-5	T	478 25	95%	956/289-2525 Fax 956/384-5208
Longoria Middle Sch 14101 N Rooth Rd, Edinburg 78541 Antonio Ballesteros	6-8		998		956/289-2486 Fax 956/381-6442
Lorenzo De Zavala Elem Sch 3615 W Rogers Rd, Edinburg 78541 Jose Garza	PK-5	T	519	90%	956/289-2350 Fax 956/316-7605
Lyndon B Johnson Elem Sch 1801 E Sprague St, Edinburg 78542 Enrique De La Cruz	PK-5	T	395 25	87%	956/289-2358 Fax 956/316-7630
M D Betts Elem Sch 2720 S Cesar Chavez Rd, Edinburg 78542 Jesus Cantu	PK-5		456 23		956/289-2560 Fax 956/384-5312
MacAria Gorena Elem Sch 1801 E Freddy Gonzalez Dr, Edinburg 78542 Diane Willis	PK-5	T	551	88%	956/289-2460 Fax 956/316-6213
Memorial Middle Sch 3105 N Doolittle Rd, Edinburg 78542 Fernin Gonzalez	6-8	TV	1,239 69	91%	956/289-2470 Fax 956/316-7581
Monte Cristo Elem Sch 4010 N Doolittle Rd, Edinburg 78542 Diana Smith	PK-5	T	732 40	95%	956/289-2362 Fax 956/316-7471
N L Trevino Elem Sch 909 S Mon Mack Rd, Edinburg 78539 Brenda Alonzo	PK-5	T	597 35	52%	956/289-2550 Fax 956/384-5372
Robert E Lee Elem Sch 1215 W Sprague St, Edinburg 78539 Alonda Navarro	PK-5	T	411 30	94%	956/289-2342 Fax 956/316-7596
Robert Vela High Sch 801 E Canton Rd, Edinburg 78539 Sylvia Ledesma	9-12	TV	2,305	67%	956/289-2650 Fax 956/316-7304
San Carlos Elem Sch 505 S 83rd St, Edinburg 78542 Belinda De La Rosa	PK-5	T	500 29	97%	956/289-2370 Fax 956/316-7364
Travis Elem Sch 1200 S 21st Ave, Edinburg 78539 Eliana Flores	PK-5	T	359 21	89%	956/289-2354 Fax 956/316-7637
Truman Elem Sch 701 W Rogers Rd, Edinburg 78541 Leticia Duarte	PK-5	T	631 34	90%	956/289-2555 Fax 956/316-7527
Ⓐ Vision Academy 222 W Kuhn St, Edinburg 78541 Ernestina Cano	12-12	G	130		956/289-2584 Fax 956/287-0812

• **Hidalgo Ind School Dist** PID: 01029827　　956/843-4404
324 Flora Ave, Hidalgo 78557　　Fax 956/843-3343

Schools: 7 \ **Teachers:** 241 \ **Students:** 3,300 \ **Special Ed Students:** 186 \ **LEP Students:** 1,601 \ **Ethnic:** Hispanic 100%, \ **Exp:** $180 (Low) \ **Poverty:** 39% \ **Title I:** $1,535,465 \ **Special Education:** $512,000 \ **Open-Close:** 08/26 - 05/22 \ **DTBP:** $181 (High)

Xavier Salinas .... 1　　Guillermo Ramirez 2,3,91
Nancy Sanchez .... 2,11,19　Rosalinda Galvan 4
Roberto Guerrero .... 5　Monte Stumbaugh 6
Velma Molano .... 7　　Sandra Cavazos 8,58,69
Jennifer Villarreal .... 16　Carmen Pacheco 57,61,271
Lenore Salinas .... 58*　Blanca Lara 67
Eloy Garcia 73,76,84,295

School	Grd	Prgm	Enr/#Cls	SN	Phone
Diaz Junior High Sch 1312 Pirate Dr, Hidalgo 78557 Jorge Guzman	6-8	T	636 60	88%	956/843-4350 Fax 956/843-3198
Dr Alejo Salinas Sch 411 Ebano St, Hidalgo 78557 Jose Esquivel	PK-5	T	408 30	82%	956/843-4250 Fax 956/843-3357
Ⓐ Hidalgo Academy 310 E Esperanza St, Hidalgo 78557 Brenda De Hoyos	9-12	T	34 2	86%	956/843-4390 Fax 956/843-3339
Hidalgo Early College High Sch 910 S Pirate Dr, Hidalgo 78557 Judith Dimas	9-12	T	1,020 75	91%	956/843-4300 Fax 956/843-3322
Hidalgo Elem Sch 601 S 2nd Street, Hidalgo 78557 Rafael Tinoco	PK-5	T	350 30	91%	956/843-4225 Fax 956/843-3158
Hidalgo Park Elem Sch 8700 S Veterans Blvd, Pharr 78577 Gregorio Solano	PK-5	T	366	91%	956/843-4275 Fax 956/781-4631
Kelly Elem Sch 201 E Las Milpas Rd, Pharr 78577 Beatriz Solano	PK-5	T	393 35	94%	956/843-4200 Fax 956/781-5972

• **Idea Public Schools** PID: 11131307　　956/377-8000
2115 W Pike Blvd, Weslaco 78596　Fax 956/447-3796

Schools: 76 \ **Teachers:** 1,279 \ **Students:** 42,748 \
Special Ed Students: 1,406 \ **LEP Students:** 9,222 \ **Ethnic:** Asian 1%,
African American 3%, Hispanic 93%, Caucasian 3% \ **Open-Close:** 08/12 - 05/29 \ **DTBP:** $181 (High) \

Joann Gama .... 1　　Wyatt Truscheit 2,19
Irma Munoz .... 3,4,5,295　　Dolores Gonzalez 8,11,57,69,286
Tricia Lopez .... 58*　　Tom Torkelson 67
Jarney Roberts .... 68　　Sharise Johnson 71
Efren Montenegro 73

School	Grd	Prgm	Enr/#Cls	SN	Phone
Ⓒ Idea Academy-Achieve 1900 Thomas Rd, Haltom City 76117 Shandra Johnson	PK-3		250		817/885-4700
Ⓒ Idea Academy-Alamo 325 State Highway 495, Alamo 78516 Anna Garza	PK-5	T	609	96%	956/588-4005 Fax 956/588-4006
Ⓒ Idea Academy-Bluff Springs 1700 E Slaughter Ln, Austin 78747 Jayne Pocquette	K-4		267	84%	512/822-4200
Ⓒ Idea Academy-Brackenridge 5555 Old Pearsall Rd, San Antonio 78242 Elisha McCardell	PK-2		400		210/239-4300
Ⓒ Idea Academy-Brownsville 4395 Paredes Line Rd, Brownsville 78526 Erica Matamoros	K-5	T	592	84%	956/832-5150 Fax 956/832-5716
Ⓒ Idea Academy-Carver 217 Robinson Pl, San Antonio 78202 Guadalupe Diaz	K-5	T	495	82%	210/223-8885 Fax 210/223-8970
Ⓒ Idea Academy-Donna 401 S 1st St, Donna 78537 Sylvia Verdooran	PK-5		700	94%	956/464-0203 Fax 956/464-8532
Ⓒ Idea Academy-Eastside 2519 Martin Luther King Dr, San Antonio 78203 Myrla Feria	K-5	T	351	93%	210/239-4800
Ⓒ Idea Academy-Edgemere 15101 Edgemere Blvd, El Paso 79938 Rebecca Cobian	PK-2		300		915/444-0200

79 Student Personnel	91 Safety/Security	275 Response To Intervention	298 Grant Writer/Ptnrships	School Programs	Social Media
80 Driver Ed/Safety	92 Magnet School	277 Remedial Math K-12	750 Chief Innovation Officer	A = Alternative Program	= Facebook
81 Gifted/Talented	93 Parental Involvement	280 Literacy Coach	751 Chief of Staff	G = Adult Classes	
82 Video Services	95 Tech Prep Program	285 STEM	752 Social Emotional Learning	M = Magnet Program	= Twitter
83 Substance Abuse Prev	97 Chief Information Officer	286 Digital Learning		T = Title I Schoolwide	
84 Erate	98 Chief Technology Officer	288 Common Core Standards	Other School Types	V = Career & Tech Ed Programs	
85 AIDS Education	270 Character Education	294 Accountability	Ⓐ = Alternative School		
88 Alternative/At Risk	271 Migrant Education	295 Network System	Ⓒ = Charter School	New Schools are shaded	
89 Multi-Cultural Curriculum	273 Teacher Mentor	296 Title II Programs	Ⓜ = Magnet School	New Superintendents and Principals are bold	
90 Social Work	274 Before/After Sch	297 Webmaster	Ⓨ = Year-Round School	Personnel with email addresses are underscored	

Hidalgo County

School	Grades	T	Enroll	%	Phone
© Idea Academy-Edinburg 2553 N Roegiers Rd, Edinburg 78541 Nora Perez	PK-5	T	716	82%	956/287-6100 Fax 956/287-6101
© Idea Academy-Elsa 411 S Fanin Ave, Elsa 78543 Saron Mata	PK-2		300		956/567-4700
© Idea Academy-Ewing Halsell 2523 W Ansley Blvd, San Antonio 78224 Pam Ray	PK-2		374		210/239-4850
© Idea Academy-Frontier 2800 S Dakota Ave, Brownsville 78521 Dora Villegas	K-5	T	712	92%	956/541-2002 Fax 956/544-2004
© Idea Academy-Harvey Najim 926 S WW White Rd, San Antonio 78220 Hope Walker	PK-2		275		210/239-4900
© Idea Academy-Ingram Hills 3115 Majestic Dr, San Antonio 78228 Nancy Bethencourt	PK-2		300		210/529-3700
© Idea Academy-Judson 13427 Judson Rd, San Antonio 78233 Hope Williams	K-4		342	70%	210/529-3600
© Idea Academy-Kyle 640 Philomena Dr, Kyle 78640 Ester Polanco	K-3		372		512/822-4300
© Idea Academy-Mays 1210 Horal Dr, San Antonio 78245 Maria Sepulveda	K-5		349	80%	210/529-3200
© Idea Academy-McAllen 201 N Bentsen Rd, McAllen 78501 Darlene Cavazos	PK-5	T	591	82%	956/429-4100 Fax 956/429-4126
© Idea Academy-Mission 1600 S Schuerbach Rd, Mission 78572 Christina Escamilla	PK-5	T	722	90%	956/583-8315 Fax 956/424-3248
© Idea Academy-Monterrey Park 222 SW 39th St, San Antonio 78237 Martha Short	K-5	T	323	88%	210/239-4200
© Idea Academy-Montopolis 1701 Vargas Rd, Austin 78741 Disha Jain	K-5	T	570	94%	512/646-2800 Fax 512/385-2512
© Idea Academy-North Mission 2706 N Holland Ave, Mission 78574 Adrianna Villarreal	PK-5	T	733	90%	956/424-4300
© Idea Academy-Owassa 1000 E Owassa Rd, Pharr 78577 Cyndi Delafuente	PK-2		300		956/588-4300
© Idea Academy-Pflugerville 1901 E Wells Branch Pkwy, Pflugerville 78660 Mera Dougherty	K-3		300		512/822-4700
© Idea Academy-Pharr 600 E Las Milpas Rd, Pharr 78577 Sonia Aguilar	PK-5	T	876	97%	956/283-1515 Fax 956/783-1557
© Idea Academy-Quest 14001 N Rooth Rd, Edinburg 78541 Rosa Chapa	PK-5		692		956/287-1003 Fax 956/287-2737
© Idea Academy-Rio Grande City 2803 W Monarch Ln, Rio Grande Cy 78582 Fernando Salinas	PK-2		894		956/263-4900
© Idea Academy-Rio Vista 210 N Rio Vista Rd, Socorro 79927 Yanira Aguilar	PK-3		300		915/444-0188
© Idea Academy-Riverview 30 Palm Blvd, Brownsville 78520 Radha Guajardo	PK-5	T	392	96%	956/832-5900
© Idea Academy-Rundberg 9504 N Interstate 35, Austin 78753 Maya Martin	K-10	T	338	91%	512/822-4800
© Idea Academy-San Benito 2151 Russell Ln, San Benito 78586 Christina Villarreal	PK-5	T	688 24	85%	956/399-5252 Fax 956/361-9478
© Idea Academy-San Juan 200 N Nebraska Ave, San Juan 78589 Melissa Finch	PK-5	T	715	90%	956/702-5150 Fax 956/702-4554
© Idea Academy-South Flores 6919 S Flores St, San Antonio 78221 Hailey McCarthy	PK-5	T	486	78%	210/239-4150
© Idea Academy-Tres Lagos 5200 Tres Lagos Blvd, McAllen 78504 Benigna Carcano	PK-3		500		956/375-8550
© Idea Academy-Walzem 6445 Walzem Rd, San Antonio 78239 Ryane Burke	K-5		660	81%	210/239-4600
© Idea Academy-Weslaco 2931 E Sugarcane Dr, Weslaco 78599 Sylvia Mejia	K-5	T	695	88%	956/351-4100 Fax 956/351-4101
© Idea Academy-Weslaco Pike 1000 E Pike Blvd, Weslaco 78596 Silvia Martinez	PK-5	T	352	87%	956/351-4850 Fax 956/351-4851
© Idea Clg Prep-Achieve 1900 Thomas Rd, Haltom City 76117 Jaeil Kim	5-7		250		817/885-4700
© Idea Clg Prep-Alamo 325 E FM 495, Alamo 78516 Mayra Martinez	6-12	T	760	97%	956/588-4005 Fax 956/588-4006
© Idea Clg Prep-Bluff Sprgs 1700 E Slaughter Ln, Austin 78747 Deanna Bruce	6-8		125		512/822-4200
© Idea Clg Prep-Brackenridge 5555 Old Pearsall Rd, San Antonio 78242 Zachary Sting	6-8		118		210/239-4300
© Idea Clg Prep-Brownsville 4395 Paredes Line Rd, Brownsville 78526 Marco Lopez	6-12		358		956/832-5150 Fax 956/832-5716
© Idea Clg Prep-Carver 217 Robinson Pl, San Antonio 78202 Byong Chang Yu	6-12	T	278	86%	210/223-8885
© Idea Clg Prep-Donna 401 S 1st St, Donna 78537 Amanda Canales	6-12	T	757	91%	956/464-0203 Fax 956/464-8532
© Idea Clg Prep-Eastside 2519 Martin Luther King Dr, San Antonio 78203 Deion Brown	6-10		117		210/239-4800
© Idea Clg Prep-Edgemere 15101 Edgemere Blvd, El Paso 79938 Rodrigo Wong	6-7		300		915/444-0200
© Idea Clg Prep-Edinburg 2553 N Roegiers Rd, Edinburg 78541 Ramiro Gomez	6-12	T	477	85%	956/287-6100
© Idea Clg Prep-Elsa 411 S Fanin Ave, Elsa 78543 Antonio Garza	6-7		300		956/567-4700
© Idea Clg Prep-Ewing Halsell 2523 W Ansley Blvd, San Antonio 78224 William Chermak	6-7		119		210/239-4850
© Idea Clg Prep-Frontier 2800 S Dakota Ave, Brownsville 78521 Virginia Callaway	6-12	T	777	90%	956/541-2002 Fax 956/544-2004
© Idea Clg Prep-Harvey Najim 926 S WW White Rd, San Antonio 78220 Theresa Hall	6-7		500		210/239-4900
© Idea Clg Prep-Ingram Hills 3115 Majestic Dr, San Antonio 78228 Jeffrey Rothschild	6-7		300		210/529-3700

#		#		#		#		#		#		#	
1	Superintendent	8	Curric/Instruct K-12	19	Chief Financial Officer	29	Family/Consumer Science	39	Social Studies K-12	49	English/Lang Arts Elem	59	Special Education Elem	69	Academic Assessment
2	Bus/Finance/Purchasing	9	Curric/Instruct Elem	20	Art K-12	30	Adult Education	40	Social Studies Elem	50	English/Lang Arts Sec	60	Special Education Sec	70	Research/Development
3	Buildings And Grounds	10	Curric/Instruct Sec	21	Art Elem	31	Career/Sch-to-Work K-12	41	Social Studies Sec	51	Reading K-12	61	Foreign/World Lang K-12	71	Public Information
4	Food Service	11	Federal Program	22	Art Sec	32	Career/Sch-to-Work Elem	42	Science K-12	52	Reading Elem	62	Foreign/World Lang Elem	72	Summer School
5	Transportation	12	Title I	23	Music K-12	33	Career/Sch-to-Work Sec	43	Science Elem	53	Reading Sec	63	Foreign/World Lang Sec	73	Instructional Tech
6	Athletic	13	Title V	24	Music Elem	34	Early Childhood Ed	44	Science Sec	54	Remedial Reading K-12	64	Religious Education K-12	74	Inservice Training
7	Health Services	14	Asst Superintendent	25	Music Sec	35	Health/Phys Education	45	Math K-12	55	Remedial Reading Elem	65	Religious Education Elem	75	Marketing/Distributive
		15	Instructional Media Svcs	26	Business Education	36	Guidance Services K-12	46	Math Elem	56	Remedial Reading Sec	66	Religious Education Sec	76	Info Systems
		16	Chief Operations Officer	27	Career & Tech Ed	37	Guidance Services Elem	47	Math Sec	57	Bilingual/ELL	67	School Board President	77	Psychological Assess
		17	Chief Academic Officer	28	Technology Education	38	Guidance Services Sec	48	English/Lang Arts K-12	58	Special Education K-12	68	Teacher Personnel	78	Affirmative Action

Texas School Directory — Hidalgo County

School	Grd	Prgm	Enr	%	Phone
ⓒ Idea Clg Prep-Judson 13427 Judson Rd, San Antonio 78233 Joaquin Hernandez	6-8		99		210/529-3600
ⓒ Idea Clg Prep-Kyle 640 Philomena Dr, Kyle 78640 Jorge Chipres	6-7		133		512/822-4300
ⓒ Idea Clg Prep-Mays 1210 Horal Dr, San Antonio 78245 Gerald Boyd	6-8		120	86%	210/529-3200
ⓒ Idea Clg Prep-McAllen 201 N Bentsen Rd, McAllen 78501 Joan Alvarez	6-12	T	363	87%	956/429-4100 Fax 956/429-4126
ⓒ Idea Clg Prep-Mission 1600 S Schuerbach Rd, Mission 78572 Matthew Kyle	6-12	T	801	94%	956/583-8315 Fax 956/424-3248
ⓒ Idea Clg Prep-Monterrey Park 222 SW 39th St, San Antonio 78237 Jonathan Tyrrell	6-10	T	228	89%	210/239-4200
ⓒ Idea Clg Prep-Montopolis 1701 Vargas Rd, Austin 78741 **Cristopher Rubio**	6-12		116		512/646-2800
ⓒ Idea Clg Prep-N Mission 2706 N Holland Ave, McAllen 78502 Dave Wagner	6-10		255		956/424-4300
ⓒ Idea Clg Prep-Owassa 1000 E Owassa Rd, Pharr 78577 Stevie Luera	6-7		300		956/588-4300
ⓒ Idea Clg Prep-Pflugerville 1901 E Wells Branch Pkwy, Pflugerville 78660 Mera Dougherty	6-7		300		512/822-4700
ⓒ Idea Clg Prep-Pharr 600 E Las Milpas Rd, Pharr 78577 Claudia Ash	6-12	T	764	97%	956/283-1515 Fax 956/783-1557
ⓒ Idea Clg Prep-Quest 14001 N Rooth Rd, Edinburg 78541 Jose De Leon	6-12	T	741	84%	956/287-1003 Fax 956/287-2737
ⓒ Idea Clg Prep-Rio Vista 210 N Rio Vista Rd, Socorro 79927 Adrian Hernandez	6-7		300		915/444-0188
ⓒ Idea Clg Prep-Riverview 30 Palm Blvd, Brownsville 78520 Adriana Alvarado	6-9	T	239	92%	956/832-5900
ⓒ Idea Clg Prep-Rundberg 9504 N Interstate 35, Austin 78753 Pike Nichols	6-10	T	253	95%	512/822-4800
ⓒ Idea Clg Prep-San Benito 2151 Russell Ln, San Benito 78586 Janet Crenshaw	6-12	T	787	84%	956/399-5252 Fax 956/361-9478
ⓒ Idea Clg Prep-San Juan 600 E Sioux Rd, San Juan 78589 Lindsey Campbell	6-12	T	739	93%	956/588-4021 Fax 956/702-4554
ⓒ Idea Clg Prep-South Flores 6919 S Flores St, San Antonio 78221 Constantine Polites	6-12		233		210/239-4150
ⓒ Idea Clg Prep-Toros 1000 E Owassa Rd, Pharr 78577 Brad Scott	6-12		123	87%	956/266-3772
ⓒ Idea Clg Prep-Tres Lagos 5200 Tres Lagos Blvd, McAllen 78504 Megan Arenas-Goossen	6-8		123		956/252-9227
ⓒ Idea Clg Prep-Walzem 6445 Walzem Rd, San Antonio 78239 Andrea Lopez	6-10	T	327	84%	210/239-4600
ⓒ Idea Clg Prep-Weslaco 2931 E Sugarcane Dr, Weslaco 78599 Leanna Sarinana	6-12	T	483	89%	956/351-4100
ⓒ Idea Clg Prep-Weslaco Pike 1000 E Pike Blvd, Weslaco 78596 Nate Lowry	6-11	T	119	90%	956/351-4850

● La Joya Ind School Dist PID: 01029841
200 W Expressway 83, La Joya 78560
956/323-2000
Fax 956/323-2010

Schools: 41 \ **Teachers:** 1,984 \ **Students:** 27,000 \ **Special Ed Students:** 2,148 \ **LEP Students:** 14,303 \ **College-Bound:** 60% \ **Ethnic:** Hispanic 100%, \ **Exp:** $561 (High) \ **Poverty:** 48% \ **Title I:** $21,167,319 \ **Special Education:** $4,825,000 \ **Open-Close:** 08/19 - 05/27 \ **DTBP:** $181 (High)

Dr Gisela Saenz 1		Alfredo Vela 2,15	
Joel Trevino 2,15		Sylvia Zapata 2	
Arlando Nacianceno 3		Galina Reyes 4	
Rolando Hernandez 4		Raul Gonzalez 5,271*	
Victor Garza 6		Marissa Morales 7	
Dr Frank Rivera 8,69		Alma Ortega 9	
Dr Ana Oliveira 10		Melinda Flores 10	
Jose Flores 11*		Dr Anysia Trevino 15,68	
Ricardo Villareal 15,79		Jorge Flores 27*	
Myriam Tellez 36		Alejandro Carranza 43	
David Cavazos 44		Rogelio Gomez 44	
Lucy Munoz 46		Alfonso Rodriguez 47	
Claudia Munoz 49		Marta Castillo 49	
Leticia Martinez 50		Veronica Chavez 50	
Irma Zuniga 57		Andrea Garza 58,77	
Rosey Romo 58		Claudia Ochoa 67	
Lilliana Salgado 71		Clem Garza 73,84	
Cynthia Solis 74		Aaron Lara 76,295	
Sandra Ann Villiarreal 81		Bertha Perez 88	
Dr Armando O'Cana 91		Velma Ochoa 93*	
Maria Leal 298			

Public Schs..Principal	Grd	Prgm	Enr/#Cls	SN	
Academy Health Sci Prof-STEM 801 College Dr, La Joya 78560 Leann Herrera	9-12	V	200		956/323-2250 Fax 956/323-2251
Ann Richards Middle Sch 7005 Ann Richards Rd, Mission 78572 Michael Ocana	6-8	T	824 61	97%	956/323-2860 Fax 956/323-2861
Cesar Chavez Middle Sch 78 Showers Rd, Mission 78572 Rolando Rios	6-8	T	832 58	88%	956/323-2800 Fax 956/323-2801
College & Career Center 603 N College Dr, La Joya 78560 Ronny Cabrera	9-12	V	179 12		956/323-2230 Fax 956/323-2231
Corina Pena Elem Sch 4800 Liberty Blvd, Penitas 78576 Raul Luna	PK-5		702 35	94%	956/323-2750 Fax 956/323-2751
Diaz-Villarreal Elem Sch 5543 N La Homa Rd, Mission 78574 Yolanda Meave	PK-5	T	638 40	95%	956/323-2470 Fax 956/323-2471
Domingo Trevino Middle Sch 301 S Inspiration Blvd, Alton 78573 Jose Garcia	6-8	T	821	97%	956/323-2810 Fax 956/323-2811
Dr Americo Paredes Elem Sch 5301 N Bentsen Palm Dr, Mission 78574 Erika Covarrubia	PK-5	T	473 40	96%	956/323-2730 Fax 956/323-2731
Dr Javier Saenz Middle Sch 39200 Mile 7 Rd, Penitas 78576 **Carlota Salinas**	6-8	T	816	98%	956/323-2830 Fax 956/323-2831
Dr Palmira Mendiola Elem Sch 6401 N Abram Rd, Mission 78574 Alicia Gutierrez	PK-5	T	794	97%	956/323-2420 Fax 956/323-2421

79	Student Personnel	91	Safety/Security	275	Response To Intervention	298	Grant Writer/Ptnrships
80	Driver Ed/Safety	92	Magnet School	277	Remedial Math K-12	750	Chief Innovation Officer
81	Gifted/Talented	93	Parental Involvement	280	Literacy Coach	751	Chief of Staff
82	Video Services	95	Tech Prep Program	285	STEM	752	Social Emotional Learning
83	Substance Abuse Prev	97	Chief Infomation Officer	286	Digital Learning		
84	Erate	98	Chief Technology Officer	288	Common Core Standards		
85	AIDS Education	270	Accountability	294	Character Education		
86	Alternative/At Risk	271	Migrant Education	295	Network System		
89	Multi-Cultural Curriculum	273	Teacher Mentor	296	Title II Programs		
90	Social Work	274	Before/After Sch	297	Webmaster		

School Programs
A = Alternative Program
G = Adult Classes
M = Magnet Program
T = Title I Schoolwide
V = Career & Tech Ed Programs

Other School Types
Ⓐ = Alternative School
Ⓒ = Charter School
Ⓜ = Magnet School
Ⓨ = Year-Round School

Social Media
[f] = Facebook
[t] = Twitter

New Schools are shaded
New Superintendents and Principals are bold
Personnel with email addresses are underscored

TX—219

Hidalgo County

School	Grd	Prgm	Enr/#Cls	SN	Phone
E B Reyna Elem Sch 707 E Veterans Blvd, Palmview 78572 Lucina Lara	PK-5	T	501 42	82%	956/323-2390 Fax 956/323-2391
Eligio Kika De La Garza Sch 5441 N La Homa Rd, Mission 78574 Irene Fernandez	PK-5	T	437 50	96%	956/323-2380 Fax 956/323-2381
Elodia R Chapa Elem Sch 5670 N Doffing Rd, Mission 78574 Linda Lopez	PK-5	T	533 42	95%	956/323-2400 Fax 956/323-2401
Emiliano Zapata Elem Sch 9100 N La Homa Rd, Mission 78574 Rosa Gonzalez Vela	PK-5	T	646	97%	956/323-2700 Fax 956/323-2701
Enrique Camarena Elem Sch 2612 N Moorefield Rd, Mission 78574 Mary Garza-Ibarra	PK-5	T	549	79%	956/323-2720 Fax 956/323-2721
Evangelina Garza Elem Sch 8731 N Doffing Rd, Mission 78574 Maria Flores-Guerra	PK-5	T	616	97%	956/323-2350 Fax 956/323-2351
Guillermo Flores Elem Sch 1913 Roque Salinas Rd, Mission 78572 Maria Flores	PK-5	T	499 50	88%	956/323-2760 Fax 956/323-2761
Henry B Gonzalez Elem Sch 3912 N FM 492, Mission 78574 Dianabel Villarreal	PK-5	T	606 57	91%	956/323-2460 Fax 956/323-2461
ⓐ Hope Academy 101 E Expressway 83, La Joya 78560 Lindolfo Zamora	6-12		83	95%	956/323-2900 Fax 956/323-2901
Irene Garcia Middle Sch 933 Paula St, Mission 78574 Santana Galvan	6-8	TV	806	92%	956/323-2840 Fax 956/323-2841
J F Kennedy Elem Sch 1801 Diamond Ave, Penitas 78576 Mrs Guerra	PK-5	T	816 46	76%	956/323-2330 Fax 956/323-2331
Jimmy Carter Early Clg HS 603 N College Dr, La Joya 78560 Claudia Gomez	9-12	T	355	98%	956/323-2200 Fax 956/323-2201
Jose De Escandon Elem Sch 700 N Shuerbach Rd, Mission 78572 Mary Sepulveda	PK-5	T	626 42	87%	956/323-2410 Fax 956/323-2411
Juan D Salinas Middle Sch 6101 N Bentsen Palm Dr, Mission 78574 Nidia Ortiz	6-8	T	832	99%	956/323-2850 Fax 956/323-2851
Juan N Seguin Elem Sch 8500 Western Rd, Mission 78574 Sandra Cerda	PK-5	T	629	97%	956/323-2710 Fax 956/323-2711
Juarez-Lincoln High Sch 7801 W Mile 7 Rd, Mission 78574 Ricardo Estrada	9-12	T	2,528 100	99%	956/323-2890 Fax 956/323-2891
La Joya Early College HS 604 N Coyote Dr, La Joya 78560 Domingo Villarreal	9-12		117		956/323-2930 Fax 956/323-2939
La Joya Senior High Sch 604 N Coyote Dr, La Joya 78560 Antonio Cano	9-12	GTV	2,855	97%	956/323-2870 Fax 956/323-2871
ⓐ La Joya West Academy 215 E Expressway 83, La Joya 78560 Norma Garcia	9-12	G	167 20		956/323-2260 Fax 956/323-2221
Leo J Leo Elem Sch 1625 Roque Salinas Rd, Mission 78572 Maria Jazinski	PK-5	T	502 40	88%	956/323-2370 Fax 956/323-2371
Lloyd M Bentsen Elem Sch 3301 W Mile 3 Rd, Mission 78574 Hilda Mendoza	PK-5	T	617	84%	956/323-2480 Fax 956/323-2481
Lorenzo De Zavala Middle Sch 603 Tabasco Rd, La Joya 78560 Antonio Uresti	6-8	T	702 70	90%	956/323-2770 Fax 956/323-2771
Memorial Middle Sch 2610 N Moorefield Rd, Mission 78574 Belen Martinez	6-8	T	758 80	90%	956/323-2820 Fax 956/323-2821
Narciso Cavazos Elem Sch 4563 N Minnesota Rd, Mission 78574 Marisa Garza	PK-5	T	491 40	95%	956/323-2430 Fax 956/323-2431
Palmview High Sch 3901 N La Homa Rd, Mission 78574 Yvonne Ayala	9-12	T	2,157 85	96%	956/323-2880 Fax 956/323-2881
Patricio Perez Elem Sch 4431 N Minnesota Rd, Mission 78574 Myra Ramos	PK-5	T	591 50	95%	956/323-2450 Fax 956/232-2451
Rosendo Benavides Elem Sch 1885 El Pinto Rd, Sullivan City 78595 Dr Romeo Benavidez	PK-5	T	400 29	94%	956/323-2360 Fax 956/323-2361
ⓜ Salinas STEM Early College Sch 801 College Dr, La Joya 78560 Diana Garcia	9-12	T	422	97%	956/323-2240 Fax 956/323-2241
Sam Fordyce Elem Sch 801 FM 886, Sullivan City 78595 Roxanna Pena	PK-5	T	448 35	94%	956/323-2490 Fax 956/323-2491
Tabasco Elem Sch 223 S Leo Ave, La Joya 78560 Marena Contreras	PK-5	T	734 30	89%	956/323-2440 Fax 956/323-2441
William J Clinton Elem Sch 39202 Mile 7 Rd, Penitas 78576 Martin Munoz	PK-5	T	681 47	97%	956/323-2740 Fax 956/323-2741

• **La Villa Ind School Dist** PID: 01029891   956/262-4755
  500 E 9th Street, La Villa 78562   Fax 956/262-7323

Schools: 3 \ **Teachers:** 42 \ **Students:** 579 \ **Special Ed Students:** 40 \ **LEP Students:** 112 \ **Ethnic:** Hispanic 100%, \ **Exp:** $333 (High) \ **Poverty:** 36% \ **Title I:** $362,718 \ **Open-Close:** 08/28 - 06/01 \ **DTBP:** $539 (High)

Alejos Salazar 1
Marie Garza 4
Daniel Perez 6,69
Dr Jose Cervantes 11
Edward Rivera 57*
Robert Perez 73*
Monica Mata 2
Norma Razo 5
Joy Cortez 7,85*
Stephanie Reece 16,82
Noe Castillo 67
Paul Abundez 274*

Public Schs..Principal	Grd	Prgm	Enr/#Cls	SN	
J B Munoz Elem Sch 810 N Cottonwood St, La Villa 78562 Edward Rivera	PK-5	T	282 15	92%	956/262-9357 Fax 956/262-9452
La Villa Early Clg High Sch 100 W Highway 107, La Villa 78562 Antonio Layton	9-12	TV	162 25	91%	956/262-4715 Fax 956/262-9798
La Villa Middle Sch 500 E 9th St, La Villa 78562 Paul Abundez	6-8	TV	135 15	91%	956/262-4760 Fax 956/262-5243

• **McAllen Ind School Dist** PID: 01029918   956/618-6000
  2000 N 23rd St, McAllen 78501

Schools: 31 \ **Teachers:** 1,615 \ **Students:** 24,000 \ **Special Ed Students:** 2,169 \ **LEP Students:** 6,937 \ **College-Bound:** 69% \ **Ethnic:** Asian 1%, Hispanic 94%, Caucasian 4% \ **Exp:** $443 (High) \ **Poverty:** 36% \ **Title I:** $14,411,349 \ **Special Education:** $5,068,000 \ **Open-Close:** 08/26 - 05/29 \ **DTBP:** $194 (High) \

Dr J Gonzalez 1
Cynthia Richards 2,15,19
Reuben Trevino 3
Ashley Jaime 2
Iris Luna 2
Alexandra Molina 4

---

1 Superintendent	8 Curric/Instruct K-12	19 Chief Financial Officer	29 Family/Consumer Science
2 Bus/Finance/Purchasing	9 Curric/Instruct Elem	20 Art K-12	30 Adult Education
3 Buildings And Grounds	10 Curric/Instruct Sec	21 Art Elem	31 Career/Sch-to-Work K-12
4 Food Service	11 Federal Program	22 Art Sec	32 Career/Sch-to-Work Elem
5 Transportation	12 Title I	23 Music K-12	33 Career/Sch-to-Work Sec
6 Athletic	13 Title V	24 Music Elem	34 Early Childhood Ed
7 Health Services	14 Instructional Media Svcs	25 Music Sec	35 Health/Phys Education
	15 Asst Superintendent	26 Business Education	36 Guidance Services K-12
	16 Chief Operations Officer	27 Career & Tech Ed	37 Guidance Services Elem
	18 Chief Academic Officer	28 Technology Education	38 Guidance Services Sec

39 Social Studies K-12	49 English/Lang Arts Elem	59 Special Education Elem	69 Academic Assessment
40 Social Studies Elem	50 English/Lang Arts Sec	60 Special Education Sec	70 Research/Development
41 Social Studies Sec	51 Reading K-12	61 Foreign/World Lang K-12	71 Public Information
42 Science K-12	52 Reading Elem	62 Foreign/World Lang Elem	72 Summer School
43 Science Elem	53 Reading Sec	63 Foreign/World Lang Sec	73 Instructional Tech
44 Science Sec	54 Remedial Reading K-12	64 Religious Education K-12	74 Inservice Training
45 Math K-12	55 Remedial Reading Elem	65 Religious Education Elem	75 Marketing/Distributive
46 Math Elem	56 Remedial Reading Sec	66 Religious Education Sec	76 Info Systems
47 Math Sec	57 Bilingual/ELL	67 School Board President	77 Psychological Assess
48 English/Lang Arts K-12	58 Special Education K-12	68 Teacher Personnel	78 Affirmative Action

Texas School Directory — Hidalgo County

Name	Page
Paula Gonzalez	6
Sylvia Ibarra	8,15*
Dr Cynthia Bebon	12,271
Jim Egger	20,23
Mario Reyna	35
Wendy Grohler	42
Angie Martinez	57,61
Marco Suarez	67
Norma Zamora-Guerra	71
John Wilde	79
Cris Esquivel	91
Adalia Del Bosque	7,85
Anjanett Garza	11
Jennyann Vega	16,73,82
Lili Silva	27,31
Clarissa Abbott	39
Linda Farias	45
Maribelle Elizondo	58
John Cavazos	68
Judith Escamita	73,76,295
Karen Nitsch	81

Public Schs..Principal	Grd	Prgm	Enr/#Cls	SN	
Achieve Early College High Sch 1601 N 27th St, McAllen 78501 Miguel Carmona	9-12	T	491	74%	956/872-1653 Fax 956/872-1650
Alonzo De Leon Middle Sch 4201 N 29th Ln, McAllen 78504 Philip Grossweiler	6-8	TV	695 65	77%	956/632-8800 Fax 956/632-8805
Andrew Jackson Elem Sch 501 W Harvey St, McAllen 78501 Miguel Herrera	PK-5	T	731 52	89%	956/971-4277 Fax 956/632-5179
Ben Milam Elem Sch 3800 N Main St, McAllen 78501 Christian Quintanilla	PK-5	T	923 43	62%	956/971-4333 Fax 956/972-5649
Blanca E Sanchez Elem Sch 2901 Incarnate Word Ave, McAllen 78504 Cynthia Rodriguez	PK-5	T	480 30	69%	956/971-1100 Fax 956/618-9705
Christa McAuliffe Elem Sch 3000 Daffodil Ave, McAllen 78501 Sandra Pitchford	PK-5	T	538 48	85%	956/971-4400 Fax 956/971-4482
Dorothea Brown Middle Sch 2700 S Ware Rd, McAllen 78503 Alfredo Gutierrez	6-8	TV	727 40	90%	956/632-8700 Fax 956/632-8709
Dr Carlos Castaneda Elem Sch 4100 N 34th St, McAllen 78504 Jessica Rodriguez	PK-5	T	574 45	72%	956/632-8882 Fax 956/632-3627
Dr Pablo Perez Elem Sch 7801 N Main St, McAllen 78504 Albert Irlas	PK-5	T	544	56%	956/971-1125 Fax 956/632-2880
Dr R D Cathey Middle Sch 1800 N Cynthia St, McAllen 78501 Melvin Benford	6-8	TV	1,003 50	52%	956/971-4300 Fax 956/632-2811
Francisca Alvarez Elem Sch 2606 Gumwood Ave, McAllen 78501 Juan Montes	PK-5	T	436 27	92%	956/971-4471 Fax 956/972-5668
Homer J Morris Middle Sch 1400 Trenton Rd, McAllen 78504 Brian McClenny	6-8	TV	959 48	52%	956/618-7300 Fax 956/632-3666
Ⓐ Instruction & Guidance Center 2604 Galveston Ave, McAllen 78501 Fernando Gutierrez	6-12		50 13	90%	956/971-4393 Fax 956/971-4294
James Bonham Elem Sch 2501 Jordan Ave, McAllen 78503 **Leticia Infante**	PK-5	T	294 20	96%	956/971-4440 Fax 956/971-4284 🅵 🆃
James Nikki Rowe High Sch 2101 N Ware Rd, McAllen 78501 Monica Kaufmann	9-12	TV	2,110	67%	956/632-5100 Fax 956/632-8850
Jose De Escandon Elem Sch 2901 Colbath Ave, McAllen 78503 Carlos Mora	PK-5	T	407 24	79%	956/971-4511 Fax 956/971-4508
Juan Seguin Elem Sch 2200 N 29th St, McAllen 78501 Juan Nevarez	PK-5	T	513 45	91%	956/971-4565 Fax 956/971-4589
Ⓐ Lamar Academy 1009 N 10th St, McAllen 78501 Jeanette Nino	9-12	T	124 23	70%	956/632-3222 Fax 956/632-3662
Leonelo H Gonzalez Elem Sch 201 E Martin Ave, McAllen 78504 Christina Hernandez	PK-5		888 39	32%	956/971-4577 Fax 956/971-4575
Lucile M Hendricks Elem Sch 3900 Goldcrest Ave, McAllen 78504 Sandra Salinas	PK-5	T	462 6	75%	956/971-1145 Fax 956/618-9726
McAllen High Sch 2021 La Vista Ave, McAllen 78501 Albert Canales	9-12	GTV	2,296 50	65%	956/632-3100 Fax 956/632-3114
Memorial High Sch 101 E Hackberry Ave, McAllen 78501 Pedro Alvarez	9-12	TV	2,274 115	67%	956/632-5201 Fax 956/632-5226
Michael E Fossum Middle Sch 7800 N Ware Rd, McAllen 78504 Laura Williams	6-8	T	799	54%	956/971-1105 Fax 956/618-9718
Reynaldo G Garza Elem Sch 6300 N 29th St, McAllen 78504 Nancy Valenzuela	PK-5	T	564 46	61%	956/971-4554 Fax 956/971-4235
Sam Houston Elem Sch 3221 Olga Ave, McAllen 78503 Debra Loya-Thomas	PK-5	T	520 32	88%	956/971-4484 Fax 956/971-4295
Sam Rayburn Elem Sch 7000 N Main St, McAllen 78504 **Clarissa Partida**	PK-5	T	474 39	69%	956/971-4363 Fax 956/632-8453
Theodore Roosevelt Elem Sch 4801 S 26th St, McAllen 78503 Gerardo Gonzalez	PK-5	T	538 40	95%	956/971-4424 Fax 956/618-7362
Thigpen-Zavala Elem Sch 2500 Galveston Ave, McAllen 78501 Sonia Casas	PK-5	T	586 26	95%	956/971-4377 Fax 956/972-5660
Victor Fields Elem Sch 500 Dallas Ave, McAllen 78501 Teresa Trdla	PK-5	T	493 21	93%	956/971-4344 Fax 956/971-4351
William B Travis Middle Sch 600 W Houston Ave, McAllen 78501 Efrain Amaya	6-8	TV	541 55	96%	956/971-4242 Fax 956/632-8454
Woodrow Wilson Elem Sch 1200 W Hackberry Ave, McAllen 78501 Kristine Garza	PK-5	T	478 28	92%	956/971-4525 Fax 956/971-4597

● Mercedes Ind School Dist — PID: 01030149
206 W 6th St, Mercedes 78570
956/514-2000
Fax 956/514-2033

Schools: 9 \ *Teachers:* 392 \ *Students:* 4,781 \ *Special Ed Students:* 380 \ *LEP Students:* 1,354 \ *College-Bound:* 80% \ *Ethnic:* Hispanic 99%, Caucasian 1% \ *Exp:* $357 (High) \ *Poverty:* 44% \ *Title I:* $4,039,174 \ *Open-Close:* 08/26 - 06/08 \ *DTBP:* $199 (High)

Name	Page	Name	Page
Carolyn Mendiola	1	Olga Hinds	2,19
Ralph Mendez	2	Rolando Herrera	3
Nancy Garza	4	Adan Vallejo	5
Roger Adame	6*	Lisa Cantu-Reyes	11*
Dr Dana Yates	15	Juanita Mariscal	42
Delia Castillo	58	Oscar Riojas	67
Daniel Runnels	69	Rodolfo Canales	69,88
Roland Handy	73,271	Debbie Lee-Winslow	286

Public Schs..Principal	Grd	Prgm	Enr/#Cls	SN	
John F Kennedy Sch 801 Hidalgo St, Mercedes 78570 Elva Rivera	PK-5	T	481 30	96%	956/514-2300 Fax 956/514-2311
Ⓐ Mercedes Academic Academy 720 S Mile 1 East, Mercedes 78570 Rafael Leal	9-12	T	69	94%	956/825-5076 Fax 956/514-2171
Ⓐ Mercedes Early College HS 837 S Ohio Ave, Mercedes 78570 **Jeanne Venecia**	9-12	TV	400 13	73%	956/825-5180 Fax 956/514-2175

Code	Description	Code	Description	Code	Description	Code	Description
79	Student Personnel	91	Safety/Security	275	Response To Intervention	298	Grant Writer/Ptnrships
60	Driver Ed/Safety	92	Magnet School	277	Remedial Math K-12	750	Chief Innovation Officer
61	Gifted/Talented	93	Parental Involvement	280	Literacy Coach	751	Chief of Staff
62	Video Services	95	Tech Prep Program	285	STEM	752	Social Emotional Learning
63	Substance Abuse Prev	97	Chief Information Officer	286	Digital Learning		
64	Erate	98	Chief Technology Officer	288	Common Core Standards		
85	AIDS Education	270	Character Education	294	Accountability		
68	Alternative/At Risk	271	Migrant Education	295	Network System		
69	Multi-Cultural Curriculum	273	Teacher Mentor	296	Title II Programs		
90	Social Work	274	Before/After Sch	297	Webmaster		

School Programs
A = Alternative Program
G = Adult Classes
M = Magnet Program
T = Title I Schoolwide
V = Career & Tech Ed Programs

Other School Types
Ⓐ = Alternative School
Ⓒ = Charter School
Ⓜ = Magnet School
Ⓨ = Year-Round School

Social Media
🅵 = Facebook
🆃 = Twitter

New Schools are shaded
New Superintendents and Principals are bold
Personnel with email addresses are underscored

Hidalgo County

Market Data Retrieval

Mercedes High Sch 1200 Florida St, Mercedes 78570 Orlando Rodriguez	9-12	TV	1,096 105	90%	956/514-2100 Fax 956/514-2111
Ruben Hinojosa Elem Sch 1551 S Georgia Ave, Mercedes 78570 Michelle Guajardo	PK-5	T	709 44	92%	956/514-2277 Fax 956/514-2292
Sgt Manuel Chacon Middle Sch 801 S Mile 1 E, Mercedes 78570 Orlando Rodriguez	6-8	T	661 38	80%	956/514-2200 Fax 956/514-2212
Sgt William Harrell Middle Sch 2825 N FM 491, Mercedes 78570 Javier Deanda	6-8	T	460	96%	956/825-5140 Fax 956/514-2323
Taylor Elem Sch 900 Missouri St, Mercedes 78570 David Aguirre	PK-5	T	618 35	95%	956/514-2388 Fax 956/514-2377
Travis Elem Sch 1551 S Georgia Ave, Mercedes 78570 Miguel Chacon	PK-5	T	648 33	90%	956/514-2366 Fax 956/514-2373

● **Mission Cons Ind School Dist** PID: 01030228   956/323-5500
1201 Bryce Dr, Mission 78572   Fax 956/323-5523

Schools: 23 \ *Teachers:* 1,006 \ *Students:* 16,000 \
Special Ed Students: 1,154 \ *LEP Students:* 4,838 \ *College-Bound:* 69%
\ *Ethnic:* Hispanic 99%, Caucasian 1% \ *Exp:* $392 (High) \ *Poverty:* 40% \
Title I: $9,195,770 \ *Special Education:* $2,652,000 \ *Open-Close:* 08/19 -
05/28 \ *DTBP:* $193 (High) \

Dr Carol Perez 1
Rumalda Ruiz 2,15
Maria Woodrum 4
Laticia Ibarra 6
Cynthia Wilson 10
Sharon Roberts 15,81
Sergio Pena 27,31
Jamie Shults 42
Jessica Reina-Garza 49
Edgar Ibarra 57
Charlie Garcia 67
Craig Verley 71
Sylvia Cruz 91
Dolores Reyna 298*
Ana Zuniga 2*
Ricardo Rivera 3,15
Carlos Lerma 5
Jessie Trevino 7,79
Kim Risica 11
Jorge Cabazos 16,68,73,76,95,295,297
Faustino Cedillo 39
Adelina Alaniz 45
Diamond Tijerina 50
Tahnee Netro 58
Gerardo Gonzalez 69,77
Eduardo Alaniz 88*
Arminda Ramirez 271

Public Schs..Principal	Grd	Prgm	Enr/#Cls	SN	
Alton Elem Sch 205 N Chicago St, Alton 78573 Araceli Escalona	PK-5	T	461 36	90%	956/323-7600 Fax 956/323-8181
Alton Memorial Junior High Sch 521 S Los Ebanos Blvd, Alton 78573 Silvia Garcia	6-8	TV	923 54	90%	956/323-5000 Fax 956/323-8196
Bryan Elem Sch 1300 Elm Dr, Mission 78572 Linda Sanchez	PK-5	T	741 37	66%	956/323-4800 Fax 956/323-8182
Cantu Elem Sch 920 W Main Ave, Alton 78573 Enrique Alvarez	PK-5	T	430 45	92%	956/323-7400 Fax 956/323-7415
Carl Waitz Elem Sch 843 W Saint Francis Ave, Alton 78573 Rubicela Rodriguez	PK-5	T	576 34	92%	956/323-6600 Fax 956/323-6618
Castro Elem Sch 200 S Mayberry Rd, Mission 78572 Myra Garza	PK-5	T	503 35	92%	956/323-6800 Fax 956/323-6818
Escobar-Rios Elem Sch 3505 N Trosper Rd, Mission 78573 Blanca Lopez	PK-5	T	470	82%	956/323-8400
Hurla M Midkiff Elem Sch 4201 N Mayberry Rd, Palmhurst 78573 Dora Villalobos	PK-5	T	714	72%	956/323-7000 Fax 956/323-7025
Kenneth White Jr High Sch 1101 W Griffin Pkwy, Mission 78572 Brenda Betancourt	6-8	TV	878 180	90%	956/323-3600 Fax 956/323-3631
Leal Elem Sch 318 S Los Ebanos Rd, Mission 78572 Trinidad Pena	PK-5	T	580 42	89%	956/323-4600 Fax 956/326-4615
Marcell Elem Sch 1101 N Holland Ave, Mission 78572 Efrain Zamora	PK-5	T	457 26	86%	956/323-6400 Fax 956/323-6419
Mims Elem Sch 200 E 2 Mile Rd, Mission 78574 Yvonne Zamora	PK-5	T	629 37	60%	956/323-4400 Fax 956/323-4418
Mission Collegiate High Sch 605 S Los Ebanos Rd, Alton 78573 Orlando Farias	9-12		433		956/323-6120
Mission High Sch 1802 Cleo Dawson St, Mission 78572 Edilberto Flores	9-12	TV	2,234	91%	956/323-5700 Fax 956/323-8203
Mission Junior High Sch 415 E 14th St, Mission 78572 Adan Ramirez	6-8	TV	836 53	70%	956/323-3300 Fax 956/323-3338
ⓐ Mission Options Academy 407 E 3rd St, Mission 78572 Dr Mary Aleman	9-12		150		956/323-3960 Fax 956/323-8223
Ollie Ogrady Elem Sch 810 W Griffin Pkwy, Mission 78572 Angelina Garcia	PK-5	T	486 46	89%	956/323-4200 Fax 956/323-4220
Pearson Elem Sch 315 N Holland Ave, Mission 78572 Melissa Davis	PK-5	T	462 35	90%	956/323-4000 Fax 956/323-4015
Rafael Cantu Jr High Sch 5101 N Stewart Rd, Palmhurst 78573 Ana Flores	6-8	T	722	84%	956/323-7800 Fax 956/323-7880
Raquel Cavazos Elem Sch 803 S Los Ebanos Blvd, Mission 78574 Nelly Flores	PK-5	T	535 37	84%	956/323-7200 Fax 956/323-7225
ⓐ Roosevelt Alt Sch 407 E 3rd St, Mission 78572 Eduardo Alaniz	K-12	T	200 7	93%	956/323-3900 Fax 956/323-3925
Salinas Elem Sch 10820 N Conway Ave, Alton 78573 Martina Garcia	PK-5	T	457 50	90%	956/323-6200 Fax 956/323-6219
Veterans Memorial High Sch 700 E Mile 2 Rd, Mission 78574 Fidel Garza	9-12	TV	1,888 55	77%	956/323-3000 Fax 956/323-3280

● **Monte Alto Ind School Dist** PID: 01030319   956/262-1381
25149 1st St, Monte Alto 78538   Fax 956/262-5535

Schools: 3 \ *Teachers:* 78 \ *Students:* 900 \ *Special Ed Students:* 58 \
LEP Students: 313 \ *Ethnic:* Hispanic 99%, Caucasian 1% \ *Exp:* $925
(High) \ *Poverty:* 36% \ *Title I:* $643,246 \ *Open-Close:* 08/26 - 05/28 \
DTBP: $452 (High)

Dr Rosie Cobarrubias 1
Ana Zepeda 8*
Connie Villanueva 67
Ronaldo Robles 2,19
Barbara Cannon 11,57,58,69,73,84,271,294

Public Schs..Principal	Grd	Prgm	Enr/#Cls	SN	
Jose Borrego Middle Sch 25149 1st St, Monte Alto 78538 Perla Benavides	6-8	T	243	96%	956/262-1374 Fax 956/262-1377
Monte Alto Ealry Clg High Sch 9000 Valdez St, Edcouch 78538 Jimmy Padilla	9-12	T	272	90%	956/262-6152 Fax 956/262-1011

1 Superintendent	8 Curric/Instruct K-12	19 Chief Financial Officer	29 Family/Consumer Science	39 Social Studies K-12	49 English/Lang Arts Elem	59 Special Education Elem	69 Academic Assessment
2 Bus/Finance/Purchasing	9 Curric/Instruct Elem	20 Art K-12	30 Adult Education	40 Social Studies Elem	50 English/Lang Arts Sec	60 Special Education Sec	70 Research/Development
3 Buildings And Grounds	10 Curric/Instruct Sec	21 Art Elem	31 Career/Sch-to-Work K-12	41 Social Studies Sec	51 Reading K-12	61 Foreign/World Lang K-12	71 Public Information
4 Food Service	11 Federal Program	22 Art Sec	32 Career/Sch-to-Work Elem	42 Science K-12	52 Reading Elem	62 Foreign/World Lang Elem	72 Summer School
5 Transportation	12 Title I	23 Music K-12	33 Career/Sch-to-Work Sec	43 Science Elem	53 Reading Sec	63 Foreign/World Lang Sec	73 Instructional Tech
6 Athletic	13 Title V	24 Music Elem	34 Early Childhood Ed	44 Science Sec	54 Remedial Reading K-12	64 Religious Education K-12	74 Inservice Training
7 Health Services	14 Asst Superintendent	25 Music Sec	35 Health/Phys Education	45 Math K-12	55 Remedial Reading Elem	65 Religious Education Elem	75 Marketing/Distributive
	15 Instructional Media Svcs	26 Business Education	36 Guidance Services K-12	46 Math Elem	56 Remedial Reading Sec	66 Religious Education Sec	76 Info Systems
	16 Chief Operations Officer	27 Career & Tech Ed	37 Guidance Services Elem	47 Math Sec	57 Bilingual/ELL	67 School Board President	77 Psychological Assess
	17 Chief Academic Officer	28 Technology Education	38 Guidance Services Sec	48 English/Lang Arts K-12	58 Special Education K-12	68 Teacher Personnel	78 Affirmative Action

Texas School Directory — Hidalgo County

Monte Alto Elem Sch — PK-5 — T — 510 — 89% — 956/262-6101
25149 1st St, Monte Alto 78538 — 35 — Fax 956/262-6112
Alma Cerda

• Pharr-San Juan-Alamo Ind SD   PID: 01030333   956/354-2000
601 E Kelly Ave, Pharr 78577   Fax 956/354-3000

Schools: 42 \ *Teachers:* 2,080 \ *Students:* 32,500 \
Special Ed Students: 2,196 \ *LEP Students:* 12,444 \ *College-Bound:* 90%
\ *Ethnic:* Hispanic 99%, Caucasian 1% \ *Exp:* $411 (High) \ *Poverty:* 37% \
Title I: $17,770,199 \ *Special Education:* $5,108,000 \ *Open-Close:* 08/26 -
05/22 \ *DTBP:* $194 (High) \ f t

Dr Daniel King	1	Emily Garza	2
Fernando Lopez	3	Aurora Palacios	4
Orlando Garcia	6	Sulema Solis	7,35,85
Adriana Garcia	8,16,27,31,73,82*	Dr James Curts	10,70,288,298
Dr Nora Contu	10	Rebecca Sanchez	12
Juan Alvarez	15,68*	Rene Campos	15
Arianna Hernandez	16,71	Nora Galvan	16
Janet Robles	19	Jon Taylor	20
Elias Tovar	30	Yvette Mancillas	34
Stephanie Paulson	39	Hilda Gonzalez	48,51*
Olivia Martinez	57,280	Debbie Salinas	58,77
Jesus Zambrano	67	Rebecca Garza	68*
Francis Valacios	69	Jose Garcia	76,295*
Laura Campos	79,294	Orlando Noyola	79*
Jose Palacios	91	Romeo Garza	91
Jose Adrian-Garcia	98	Yolanda Gomez	271*
Angela Salinas	273	Marisela Zepeda	285*
Santiago Zavala	297	Juan Alvarez	751

Public Schs..Principal	Grd	Prgm	Enr/#Cls SN		
Aida Escobar Elem Sch 901 W Kelly Ave, Pharr 78577 **Catarina Espinoza**	PK-5	T	810 35	91% Fax	956/354-2920 956/354-3288
Alamo Middle Sch 1819 W US Highway 83, Alamo 78516 **Cristina Esparza**	6-8	T	615 50	94% Fax	956/354-2550 956/354-3188
Alfred Sorensen Elem Sch 701 E Sam Houston Blvd, San Juan 78589 Maricela Cortez	PK-5	T	686 22	78% Fax	956/354-2910 956/354-3282 f t
Allen & William Arnold ES 615 W Eldora Rd, Pharr 78577 Pedro Trevino	PK-5	T	641 17	80% Fax	956/354-2710 956/354-3238
Arnoldo Cantu Elem Sch 2900 N Raul Longoria Rd, San Juan 78589 Yvette Mancillas	PK-5	T	673 37	85% Fax	956/354-2850 956/354-3244
Audie Murphy Middle Sch 924 Sioux Rd, Alamo 78516 Lizette Longoria	6-8	T	891	92% Fax	956/354-2530 956/354-3224 f t
Augusto Guerra Elem Sch 807 State Highway 495, Alamo 78516 Graciela Gonzales	PK-5	T	665 35	93% Fax	956/354-2810 956/354-3264 f t
Austin Middle Sch 804 S Stewart Rd, San Juan 78589 Larissa Saenz	6-8	T	944 65	81% Fax	956/354-2570 956/354-3194
Berta Palacios Elem Sch 801 E Thomas Rd, Pharr 78577 Michelle Cardoza	PK-5	GT	594 30	96% Fax	956/354-2690 956/354-3242
ⓐ Buell Central High Sch 218 E Juarez Ave, Pharr 78577 Mario Bracamontes	6-12	T	84 21	95% Fax	956/354-2500 956/354-3110
Carmen Anaya Elem Sch 1000 W Dicker Dr, Pharr 78577 **Bertha Cantu**	PK-5	T	400	92%	956/784-8500
Cesar Chavez Elem Sch 401 E Thomas Rd, Pharr 78577 Roel Faz	PK-5	T	480 35	97% Fax	956/354-2720 956/354-3248
ⓐ College Career & Tech Academy ⓨ 1100 E US Highway 83, Pharr 78577 Darcia Cuellar	12-12	MT	173 10	97% Fax	956/784-8515 956/354-3112
Daniel Ramirez Elem Sch 1920 N Hibiscus St, Pharr 78577 Leonel Avila	PK-5	T	555 34	93% Fax	956/354-2880 956/354-3278
Dr William Long Elem Sch 700 N Raiders Dr, Pharr 78577 Concepcion Ipina	PK-5	T	900 35	78% Fax	956/354-2750 956/354-3266
Drs Reed & Mock Elem Sch 400 E Eldora Rd, San Juan 78589 Jose Montelongo	PK-5	T	614 43	82% Fax	956/354-2890 956/354-3280 f t
Edith & Ethel Carman Elem Sch 100 Ridge Rd, San Juan 78589 Adrian Karr	PK-5	T	654 33	67% Fax	956/354-2700 956/354-3246
Farias Elem Sch 1100 W Acacia St, Alamo 78516 Criselda Trevino	PK-5	GT	609 32	91% Fax	956/354-2760 956/354-3254
Garza-Pena Elem Sch 500 E FM 495, San Juan 78589 Judith Canales	PK-5	T	670 35	94% Fax	956/354-2800 956/354-3260
Geraldine Palmer Elem Sch 1200 W Hall Acres Rd, Pharr 78577 Brisa Gonzalez	PK-5	T	673 25	88% Fax	956/354-2860 956/354-3272 f t
Graciela Garcia Elem Sch 1002 W Juan Balli Rd, Pharr 78577 Sandra Garcia	PK-5	T	493 45	94% Fax	956/354-2790 956/354-3258
Henry Ford Elem Sch 1110 E Polk Ave, Pharr 78577 Pricilla Salinas	PK-5	T	779 29	89% Fax	956/354-2770 956/354-3256 f t
Jaime Escalante Middle Schl 6123 S Cage Blvd, Pharr 78577 Raymundo Monrreal	6-8	T	627	97% Fax	956/354-2670 956/354-3200
John Doedyns Elem Sch 1401 N Raul Longoria Rd, San Juan 78589 Maria Guerrero	PK-5	GT	717 33	86% Fax	956/354-2740 956/354-3252 f t
John McKeever Elem Sch 1310 Ridge Rd, Alamo 78516 Irma Gomez	PK-5	T	715	77% Fax	956/354-2680 956/354-3240 f t
Kelly-Pharr Elem Sch 500 E Sam Houston Blvd, Pharr 78577 Lydia Trevino	PK-5	T	759 35	83% Fax	956/354-2870 956/354-3276
Kennedy Middle Sch 600 W Hall Acres Rd, Pharr 78577 Luis Villarreal	6-8	T	669	89% Fax	956/354-2650 956/354-3206
Liberty Middle Sch 1212 S Fir St, Pharr 78577 Alfredo Carrillo	6-8	TV	879 70	85% Fax	956/354-2610 956/354-3218
Lyndon B Johnson Middle Sch 500 E Sioux Rd, Pharr 78577 Linda Soto	6-8	ATV	1,038 77	83% Fax	956/354-2590 956/354-3212 f t
Marcia R Garza Elem Sch 810 El Gato Rd, Alamo 78516 Claudia Gonzalez	PK-5	T	586 21	97% Fax	956/354-2780 956/354-3262
Pharr San Juan Alamo High Sch 805 Ridge Rd, San Juan 78589 Alejandro Elias	9-12	TV	2,114 112	89% Fax	956/354-2300 956/354-3156
Pharr San Juan Alamo North HS 500 E Nolana Loop, Pharr 78577 Liza Diaz	9-12	T	2,197 110	81% Fax	956/354-2360 956/354-3140
ⓐ Psja Elvis J Ballew Echs 1100 US Business 83, Pharr 78577 **Darcia Cuellar**	9-12	T	358 20	98% Fax	956/354-2520 956/354-3116

79 Student Personnel	91 Safety/Security	275 Response To Intervention	298 Grant Writer/Ptnrships	School Programs	Social Media
80 Driver Ed/Safety	92 Magnet School	277 Remedial Math K-12	750 Chief Innovation Officer	A = Alternative Program	
81 Gifted/Talented	93 Parental Involvement	280 Literacy Coach	751 Chief of Staff	G = Adult Classes	f = Facebook
82 Video Services	95 Tech Prep Program	285 STEM	752 Social Emotional Learning	M = Magnet Program	
83 Substance Abuse Prev	97 Chief Information Officer	286 Digital Learning		T = Title I Schoolwide	t = Twitter
84 Erate	98 Chief Technology Officer	288 Common Core Standards	Other School Types	V = Career & Tech Ed Programs	
85 AIDS Education	270 Character Education	294 Accountability	ⓐ = Alternative School		
88 Alternative/At Risk	271 Migrant Education	295 Network System	ⓒ = Charter School	New Schools are shaded	
89 Multi-Cultural Curriculum	273 Teacher Mentor	296 Title II Programs	ⓜ = Magnet School	New Superintendents and Principals are bold	
90 Social Work	274 Before/After Sch	297 Webmaster	ⓨ = Year-Round School	Personnel with email addresses are underscored	

TX—223

Hidalgo County

Market Data Retrieval

Psja Memorial HS 800 S Alamo Rd, Alamo 78516 **Dr Rowdy Vela**	9-12	TV	1,843 100	90%	956/354-2420 Fax 956/354-3124
Ⓐ Psja Sonia Sotomayer HS 1200 E Polk Ave, Pharr 78577 Rosa Rakay	8-12	TV	118 10	97%	956/354-2510 Fax 956/354-3120
Psja Southwest Echs 300 E Javelina Dr, Pharr 78577 Ranulfo Marquez	9-9	T	1,812	96%	956/354-2480 Fax 956/354-3172
Psja T Jefferson Echs 714 E US Highway 83, Pharr 78577 **Virna Maldonado**	9-12	T	775	77%	956/784-8525 Fax 956/354-3100
Raul Longoria Elem Sch 2500 N Cypress St, Pharr 78577 Rosalina Borrego	PK-5	T	702 33	93%	956/354-2820 Fax 956/354-3268
Raul Yzaguirre Middle Sch 605 E FM 495, San Juan 78589 Rebecca Luna	6-8	T	816	86%	956/354-2630 Fax 956/354-3230
Santos Livas Elem Sch 733 N Alamo Rd, Alamo 78516 **Rodrigo Hernandez**	PK-5	T	640 43	89%	956/354-2860 Fax 956/354-3272
Sgt Leonel Trevino Elem Sch 901 E Eldora Rd, San Juan 78589 **Benito Carriaga**	PK-5	T	520 34	92%	956/354-2900 Fax 956/354-3286
Vida N Clover Elem Sch 800 Carroll Ln, San Juan 78589 Guadalupe Garcia	PK-5	T	650 42	90%	956/354-2730 Fax 956/354-3250

● **Progreso Ind School Dist** PID: 01030503   956/565-3002
600 N Business FM 1015, Progreso 78579   Fax 956/565-2128

Schools: 5 \ **Teachers:** 150 \ **Students:** 1,750 \ **Special Ed Students:** 122 \ **LEP Students:** 880 \ **College-Bound:** 50% \ **Ethnic:** Hispanic 100%, \ **Exp:** $280 (Med) \ **Poverty:** 35% \ **Title I:** $1,167,100 \ **Special Education:** $370,000 \ **Open-Close:** 08/26 - 05/28 \ **DTBP:** $515 (High)

Sergio Coronado 1   Wilfredo Mata 2
Armando Cavazos 3,5   Audrey Rocha 4
Margarito Jimenez .... 6*   Maribel Rodriguez 8,58
Salvadore Acosta 11   Zelda Rocha 57,93
Frank Alanis 67

Public Schs..Principal	Grd	Prgm	Enr/#Cls	SN		
Dorothy Thompson Middle Sch 108 Business FM 1015 Rd, Progreso 78579 Yulia Molina	6-8	TV	390	99%	956/565-6539 Fax 956/565-1718
Progreso Early Childhood Sch 1201 Business FM 1015, Progreso 78579 Edith Zuniga	PK-2	T	432	99%	956/565-1168 Fax 956/565-1103
Progreso Early Clg Academy 700 N Business FM 1015, Progreso 78579 Leticia Aquilar	9-12		75		956/565-4142
Progreso Elem Sch 1401 Business FM 1015, Progreso 78579 **Marivel Garcia**	3-5	T	380	99%	956/514-9502 Fax 956/514-9503
Progreso High Sch 700 Business FM 1015, Progreso 78579 Diana Aguilar	9-12	AGTV	560 45	99%	956/565-4142 Fax 956/565-6029

● **Sharyland Ind School Dist** PID: 01030527   956/580-5200
1200 N Shary Rd, Mission 78572   Fax 956/580-2972

Schools: 14 \ **Teachers:** 615 \ **Students:** 10,295 \ **Special Ed Students:** 644 \ **LEP Students:** 2,700 \ **College-Bound:** 74% \ **Ethnic:** Asian 2%, Hispanic 93%, Caucasian 4% \ **Exp:** $439 (High) \ **Poverty:** 22% \ **Title I:** $3,034,602 \ **Special Education:** $1,417,000 \ **Open-Close:** 08/19 - 05/27 \ **DTBP:** $158 (High)

Dr Maria Vidaurri 1   Ismael Gonzalez 2,15
Jamie Ortega 2   Mark Dougherty 3,91
Cynthia Sanchez 4   Enrique Mata 5
Richard Thompson 6   Jake Salcines 8
Pamela Montalvo 8,15   Temoc Paz 9
Dr Esmeralda Munoz 10   Teresa Gonzalez 11,271
Yoelia Nava 27   Elizabeth Gongora 57
Lelia Torres 58   Jose Garcia 67
Deborah Garza 68   Rocio Landin 71
David Culberson 84,295   Sergio Esquivel 297

Public Schs..Principal	Grd	Prgm	Enr/#Cls	SN		
B L Gray Junior High Sch 4400 S Glasscock Rd, Mission 78572 Ericka Carranza	7-8	AT	776 80	56%	956/580-5333 Fax 956/580-5346
Donna Wernecke Elem Sch 4500 Dove McAllen Rd, McAllen 78504 Lela Culberson	PK-6	T	744	64%	956/928-1063 Fax 956/928-0221
Harry Shimotsu Elem Sch 3101 San Mateo St, Mission 78572 Anthony Limon	PK-6		704	34%	956/583-5643 Fax 936/519-1079
Hinojosa Elem Sch 4205 Los Indios Pkwy, Mission 78572 Lou Sarachene	PK-6	T	447	48%	956/584-4990 Fax 956/584-4998
Jessie Jensen Elem Sch Glasscock Rd & 5 Mile Li, Mission 78572 Niranda Flores	PK-6	T	713 40	91%	956/580-5252 Fax 956/580-5266
John H Shary Elem Sch 2300 N Glasscock Rd, Mission 78574 Rebekah Gerlach	PK-6	T	672 51	51%	956/580-5282 Fax 956/580-5294
Lloyd & Dolly Bentsen Elem Sch 2101 S Taylor Rd, McAllen 78503 Cecilia Boyd	PK-6	T	537 35	75%	956/686-0426 Fax 956/668-0430
Olivero Garza Elem Sch 5 Mile Line & Taylor Rd, Mission 78572 Veronica Rodriguez	PK-6	T	640 45	81%	956/580-5353 Fax 956/580-5363
Romulo Martinez Elem Sch 2571 E 4th St, Mission 78572 Nayeli Perez	PK-6	T	622 50	72%	956/584-4900 Fax 956/584-4908
Sharyland Adv Academic Academy 1106 N Shary Rd, Mission 78572 Ivan Karr	9-12	T	298	65%	956/584-6467
Ⓐ Sharyland Alternative Ed Ctr 1501 N Taylor Rd, Mission 78572 Tizoc Silva	K-12		24		956/584-6407 Fax 956/213-8009
Sharyland High Sch 1216 N Shary Rd, Mission 78572 Lori Garza	9-12	ATV	1,510 85	47%	956/580-5300 Fax 956/580-5311
Sharyland North Jr High Sch 5100 W Dove Ave, McAllen 78504 Lorene Bazan	7-8	T	867	63%	956/686-1415 Fax 956/668-0425
Sharyland Pioneer High Sch 10001 N Shary Rd, Mission 78573 James Heath	9-12	T	1,564	60%	956/271-1600

1	Superintendent	8	Curric/Instruct K-12	19	Chief Financial Officer	29	Family/Consumer Science	39	Social Studies K-12
2	Bus/Finance/Purchasing	9	Curric/Instruct Elem	20	Art K-12	30	Adult Education	40	Social Studies Elem
3	Buildings And Grounds	10	Curric/Instruct Sec	21	Art Elem	31	Career/Sch-to-Work K-12	41	Social Studies Sec
4	Food Service	11	Federal Program	22	Art Sec	32	Career/Sch-to-Work Elem	42	Science K-12
5	Transportation	12	Title I	23	Music K-12	33	Career/Sch-to-Work Sec	43	Science Elem
6	Athletic	13	Title V	24	Music Elem	34	Early Childhood Ed	44	Science Sec
7	Health Services	15	Asst Superintendent	25	Music Sec	35	Health/Phys Education	45	Math K-12
		16	Instructional Media Svcs	26	Business Education	36	Guidance Services K-12	46	Math Elem
		17	Chief Operations Officer	27	Career & Tech Ed	37	Guidance Services Elem	47	Math Sec
		18	Chief Academic Officer	28	Technology Education	38	Guidance Services Sec	48	English/Lang Arts K-12

49	English/Lang Arts Elem	59	Special Education Elem	69	Academic Assessment
50	English/Lang Arts Sec	60	Special Education Sec	70	Research/Development
51	Reading K-12	61	Foreign/World Lang K-12	71	Public Information
52	Reading Elem	62	Foreign/World Lang Elem	72	Summer School
53	Reading Sec	63	Foreign/World Lang Sec	73	Instructional Tech
54	Remedial Reading K-12	64	Religious Education K-12	74	Inservice Training
55	Remedial Reading Elem	65	Religious Education Elem	75	Marketing/Distributive
56	Remedial Reading Sec	66	Religious Education Sec	76	Info Systems
57	Bilingual/ELL	67	School Board President	77	Psychological Assess
58	Special Education K-12	68	Teacher Personnel	78	Affirmative Action

Texas School Directory — Hidalgo County

- **Valley View Ind School Dist** PID: 01030565   956/340-1000
  9701 S Jackson Rd, Pharr 78577   Fax 956/843-8688

Schools: 8 \ **Teachers:** 277 \ **Students:** 4,329 \ **Special Ed Students:** 298 \ **LEP Students:** 2,385 \ **College-Bound:** 62% \ **Ethnic:** Hispanic 100%, \ **Exp:** $439 (High) \ **Poverty:** 36% \ **Title I:** $2,316,419 \ **Special Education:** $674,000 \ **Open-Close:** 08/26 - 05/27 \ **DTBP:** $158 (High) \ 📘 🐦

Rolando Ramirez	1	Rolando Moreno	2
Alex DeLeon	3,5	Karla Rodriguez	4
Julio Martinez	6*	Monica Luna	8,15
Camilo Martinez	11,93	Manuel Rodriguez	20,23
Ramiro Balderas	27	Dr Matthew Meyers	57,271
Perla Deangel	58	Jose Rosillo	67
Sergio Coronado	69	Jorge Martinez	73,84
Gustavo Guzman	285*	Victor Pruneda	295

Public Schs..Principal	Grd	Prgm	Enr/#Cls	SN
Valley View 5th Grade Campus 9701 S Jackson Rd, Pharr 78577 Tomas Villagomez	5-5	T	299	88% 956/340-1400 Fax 956/843-3756 📘 🐦
Valley View Early College Sch 3000 E Dicker Rd, Hidalgo 78557 Tammie Garcia	8-9		698	956/340-1200 Fax 956/213-8438 📘 🐦
Valley View Elem Sch 3804 E Anaya St, Hidalgo 78557 Jesus Cerda	PK-4	T	457	956/340-1450 Fax 956/843-8526 📘 🐦
Valley View High Sch 600 N Jackson Rd, Pharr 78577 Jesus Garza	9-12	AGTV	1,222 45	91% 956/340-1500 Fax 956/843-9368 📘 🐦
Valley View Junior High Sch 9601 S Jackson Rd, Pharr 78577 Antonio De La Cerda	6-7	T	665 35	92% 956/340-1300 Fax 956/843-3031
Valley View North Elem Sch 1000 W Anaya Rd, Pharr 78577 Marina Leal	PK-4	T	493 30	94% 956/340-1600 Fax 956/783-1163 📘 🐦
Valley View South Elem Sch 900 S McColl St, Hidalgo 78557 Elizabeth Reyes	PK-4	T	358	90% 956/340-1650 Fax 956/843-7787
Wilbur E Lucas Elem Sch 1300 N McColl St, Hidalgo 78557 Dr Rosemarie Gomez	PK-4	T	408 31	86% 956/340-1700 Fax 956/843-3039

- **Weslaco Ind School Dist** PID: 01030589   956/969-6500
  319 W 4th St, Weslaco 78596   Fax 956/969-2664

Schools: 19 \ **Teachers:** 1,094 \ **Students:** 18,000 \ **Special Ed Students:** 1,459 \ **LEP Students:** 4,748 \ **College-Bound:** 57% \ **Ethnic:** Hispanic 98%, Caucasian 2% \ **Exp:** $329 (High) \ **Poverty:** 38% \ **Title I:** $9,494,095 \ **Special Education:** $2,714,000 \ **Open-Close:** 08/20 - 05/22 \ **DTBP:** $172 (High)

Dr Priscilla Canales	1	Andres Sanchez	2,15
Dora Pena	4	Lupe Garcia	5
Oscar Riojas	6	Janie Pena	8
Susan Peterson	8,15	John Garlic	11
Abel Aguilar	15	Sergio Garcia	15
Elias Trevino	57	Neil Garza	58
Isidoro Nieto	67	Melva Segura	68
Arminda Munoz	71	Carlos Martinez	73,76,295
Scott Amdahl	73,84	Rick Flores	77,294
Norma Brewer	79	Michael De La Rosa	88
Melissa Escalon	91	Erica Garcia	93*
George Lopez	271		

Public Schs..Principal	Grd	Prgm	Enr/#Cls	SN
A N Rico Elem Sch 2202 N Intl Blvd, Weslaco 78596 Jacqueline Padilla	PK-5	T	819 38	88% 956/969-6815 Fax 956/565-4676
Airport Drive Elem Sch 410 N Airport Dr, Weslaco 78596 Ida Cuadra	PK-5	T	568 37	84% 956/969-6770 Fax 956/968-4062
B Garza Middle Sch 1111 W Sugarcane Dr, Weslaco 78599 Johnny Garlic	6-8	T	1,087 47	76% 956/969-6774 Fax 956/447-0484
Central Middle Sch 503 E 6th St, Weslaco 78596 Patricia Munoz	6-8	T	879 70	77% 956/969-6710 Fax 956/969-0779
Cleckler-Heald Elem Sch 1601 W Sugarcane Dr, Weslaco 78599 Monica Vanderveer	PK-5	T	884 50	82% 956/969-6888 Fax 956/968-6808
Cte Early College High Sch 700 S Bridge St, Weslaco 78596 Marco Zamora	9-9	V	189	86% 956/969-6742
Ⓐ Disciplinary Alt Ed Program 104 S Iowa Ave, Weslaco 78596 Jose Perez	6-12		60 4	956/969-6916 Fax 956/969-6782
Dr Armando Cuellar Middle Sch 1201 S Bridge Ave, Weslaco 78596 D Rodriguez	6-8	T	744 56	87% 956/969-6720 Fax 956/973-9797
Dr R E Margo Elem Sch 1701 S Bridge Ave, Weslaco 78596 Rubelina Martinez	PK-5	T	941 83	87% 956/969-6800 Fax 956/969-8868
Justice Raul A Gonzalez ES 3801 N Mile 5 1/2 W, Weslaco 78599 Rosa Garcia	PK-5	T	734 37	93% 956/969-6760 Fax 956/969-9828
Mary Hoge Middle Sch 2302 N Intl Blvd, Weslaco 78596 Pablo Vallejo	6-8	TV	1,048 38	90% 956/969-6730 Fax 956/514-0903
Memorial Elem Sch 1700 S Border Ave, Weslaco 78596 Rhonda Sellman	PK-5	T	917 50	67% 956/969-6780 Fax 956/968-5506
North Bridge Elem Sch 2001 N Bridge Ave, Weslaco 78599 Daniel Budimir	PK-5	T	762 43	956/969-6810 Fax 956/968-1521
Pfc Mario Ybarra Elem Sch 1800 E Mile 10 N, Weslaco 78599 Linda Hernandez	PK-5	T	554 30	96% 956/969-6587 Fax 956/969-6518
Rudy Silva Elem Sch 1001 W Mile 10 N, Weslaco 78599 Sonia Gonzalez	PK-5	T	680 40	78% 956/969-6790 Fax 956/968-6937
Sam Houston Elem Sch 608 N Cantu St, Weslaco 78596 Selma Gutierrez	PK-5	T	738	87% 956/969-6740 Fax 956/973-9404
Ⓐ South Palm Gardens High Sch 3907 Camino Real Viejo, Weslaco 78596 Tina Wells	10-12		93	956/969-6621 Fax 956/565-5994
Weslaco East High Sch 810 S Pleasantview Dr, Weslaco 78596 **David Gamboa**	9-12	T	2,047 110	77% 956/969-6950 Fax 956/968-8693 🐦
Weslaco High Sch 1005 W Pike Blvd, Weslaco 78596 Yvett Morales	9-12	GTV	2,449	72% 956/969-6700 Fax 956/968-8008

---

79 Student Personnel	91 Safety/Security	275 Response To Intervention	298 Grant Writer/Ptnrships	**School Programs**	**Social Media**
80 Driver Ed/Safety	92 Magnet School	277 Remedial Math K-12	750 Chief Innovation Officer	A = Alternative Program	📘 = Facebook
81 Gifted/Talented	93 Parental Involvement	280 Literacy Coach	751 Chief of Staff	G = Adult Classes	
82 Video Services	95 Tech Prep Program	285 STEM	752 Social Emotional Learning	M = Magnet Program	🐦 = Twitter
83 Substance Abuse Prev	97 Chief Infomation Officer	286 Digital Learning		T = Title I Schoolwide	
84 Erate	98 Chief Technology Officer	288 Common Core Standards	**Other School Types**	V = Career & Tech Ed Programs	
85 AIDS Education	270 Accountability	294 Accountability	Ⓐ = Alternative School		
88 Alternative/At Risk	271 Migrant Education	295 Network System	Ⓒ = Charter School	New Schools are shaded	
89 Multi-Cultural Curriculum	273 Teacher Mentor	296 Title II Programs	Ⓜ = Magnet School	New Superintendents and Principals are bold	
90 Social Work	274 Before/After Sch	297 Webmaster	Ⓨ = Year-Round School	Personnel with email addresses are underscored	

Hill County

Market Data Retrieval

HIDALGO CATHOLIC SCHOOLS

- **Diocese of Brownsville Ed Off** PID: 01004372   956/784-5051
  700 Virgen De San Juan Blvd, San Juan 78589   Fax 956/784-5081

Schools: 12 \ *Students:* 2,092

Listing includes only schools located in this county. See District Index for location of Diocesan Offices.

Sr Cynthia Mello 1,11
Sr Maureen Crosby 16
Alberto Zavala 73
Jack Graham 2
Genoveva Trevino 68

Catholic Schs..Principal	Grd	Prgm	Enr/#Cls	SN	
Juan Diego Academy 5208 S FM 494, Mission 78572 Bob Schmidt	9-12		120		956/583-2752 Fax 956/583-3782
Oratory Academy & Athenaeum 1407 W Moore Rd, Pharr 78577 Leo-Francis Daniels	PK-12		440 15		956/781-3056 Fax 956/787-7729
Our Lady of Sorrows Sch 1100 Gumwood Ave, McAllen 78501 Israel Martinez	PK-8		520 22		956/686-3651 Fax 956/686-1996
San Martin De Porres Sch 905 N Texas Blvd, Weslaco 78596 Reyna Ortega	PK-3		79 9		956/973-8642 Fax 956/973-0522
St Joseph Catholic Sch 119 W Fay St, Edinburg 78539 Angelina Karpinski	PK-8		123 14		956/383-3957 Fax 956/318-0681

HIDALGO PRIVATE SCHOOLS

Private Schs..Principal	Grd	Prgm	Enr/#Cls	SN	
Agape Christian Sch 1401 E 24th St, Mission 78574 Moises Gonzales	PK-7		180 9		956/585-9773 Fax 956/585-9775
Covenant Christian Academy 4201 N Ware Rd, McAllen 78504 Maria Bridwell	PK-8		400 25		956/686-7886 Fax 956/686-9470
Faith Christian Academy 4301 N Shary Rd, Palmhurst 78573 Robert Munne	PK-12		140		956/581-1465 Fax 956/581-7786
First Christian Academy 709 S Iowa Ave, Weslaco 78596 Sonja Ortega	K-3		100		956/968-9030 Fax 956/968-9015
Grace Christian Sch 132 N Sugar Rd, Pharr 78577 Robert Logan	PK-12		15 2		956/787-0701 Fax 956/787-5885
Harvest Christian Academy 1000 Las Alamedas, Edinburg 78541 Joe Cruz	PK-12		300		956/383-8967
Immanuel Lutheran Sch 703 W 3rd St, Mercedes 78570 Virginia Guzman	PK-5		12 3		956/565-3208
Mid-Valley Christian Sch 417 S Westgate Dr, Weslaco 78596 Nancy Mullins	PK-12		135 10		956/968-6232 Fax 956/969-3517
South Texas Christian Academy 7001 N Ware Rd, McAllen 78504 Eric Enright	PK-12		317		956/682-1117 Fax 956/682-7398
St John's Episcopal Day Sch 2500 N 10th St, McAllen 78501 Linda McGurk	PK-5		250 21		956/686-0231 Fax 956/686-8779
St Matthew's Episcopal Sch 2620 Crestview Dr, Edinburg 78539 Laurie Cantu	PK-6		135 14		956/383-4202 Fax 956/383-7846
St Paul Lutheran Sch 300 Pecan Blvd, McAllen 78501 Nichole Perez	PK-8		152 10		956/682-2345 Fax 956/682-7148
Taylor Christian Sch 2021 W Jackson Ave, McAllen 78501 Andrea Cooper	PK-8		39 9		956/686-7574 Fax 956/682-4945
The Discovery Sch 1711 W Alberta Rd, Edinburg 78539 Leticia Sanchez	PK-6		155 12		956/381-1117 Fax 956/381-1007
Valley Christian Heritage Sch 932 N Alamo Rd, Alamo 78516 Mary Rydl	PK-12		100 13		956/787-9743 Fax 956/787-1977

HIDALGO REGIONAL CENTERS

- **Region 1 Ed Service Center** PID: 01030553   956/984-6000
  1900 W Schunior St, Edinburg 78541   Fax 956/984-7655

Dr Cornelio Gonzalez 1
Laura Sheneman 16
Todd Larson 58
Connie Lopez 2,15,19
Melissa Lopez 27
Miguel Chuca 73,76,286

HILL COUNTY

HILL PUBLIC SCHOOLS

- **Abbott Ind School Dist** PID: 01030709   254/582-3011
  219 S 1st St, Abbott 76621   Fax 254/582-5430

Schools: 1 \ *Teachers:* 23 \ *Students:* 242 \ *Special Ed Students:* 32 \ *LEP Students:* 3 \ *College-Bound:* 99% \ *Ethnic:* African American 1%, Hispanic 13%, Caucasian 86% \ *Exp:* $750 (High) \ *Poverty:* 11% \ *Title I:* $26,738 \ *Open-Close:* 08/20 - 05/21 \ *DTBP:* $362 (High)

Eric Pustejovsky 1,57
Ed Pustejovsky 3
Ben Pustejovsky 5
Channa Pustejovsky 8,11,58,88,285,288,294*
Jon Coker 57,58,79,280,296*
Deborah Little 298*
Brenda Lenart 2
Carolyn Langford 4*
Terry Crawford 6*
Billy Schulz 16,73,76,286,295*
Bob Pustejovsky 67

Public Schs..Principal	Grd	Prgm	Enr/#Cls	SN	
Abbott Sch 219 S 1st St, Abbott 76621 Jon Coker	PK-12	T	242 25	26%	254/582-3011

1	Superintendent	8	Curric/Instruct K-12	19	Chief Financial Officer	29	Family/Consumer Science	39	Social Studies K-12	49	English/Lang Arts Elem	59	Special Education Elem	69	Academic Assessment
2	Bus/Finance/Purchasing	9	Curric/Instruct Elem	20	Art K-12	30	Adult Education	40	Social Studies Elem	50	English/Lang Arts Sec	60	Special Education Sec	70	Research/Development
3	Buildings And Grounds	10	Curric/Instruct Sec	21	Art Elem	31	Career/Sch-to-Work K-12	41	Social Studies Sec	51	Reading K-12	61	Foreign/World Lang K-12	71	Public Information
4	Food Service	11	Federal Program	22	Art Sec	32	Career/Sch-to-Work Elem	42	Science K-12	52	Reading Elem	62	Foreign/World Lang Elem	72	Summer School
5	Transportation	12	Title I	23	Music K-12	33	Career/Sch-to-Work Sec	43	Science Elem	53	Reading Sec	63	Foreign/World Lang Sec	73	Instructional Tech
6	Athletic	13	Title V	24	Music Elem	34	Early Childhood Ed	44	Science Sec	54	Remedial Reading K-12	64	Religious Education K-12	74	Inservice Training
7	Health Services	15	Asst Superintendent	25	Music Sec	35	Health/Phys Education	45	Math K-12	55	Remedial Reading Elem	65	Religious Education Elem	75	Marketing/Distributive
		16	Instructional Media Svcs	26	Business Education	36	Guidance Services K-12	46	Math Elem	56	Remedial Reading Sec	66	Religious Education Sec	76	Info Systems
		17	Chief Operations Officer	27	Career & Tech Ed	37	Guidance Services Elem	47	Math Sec	57	Bilingual/ELL	67	School Board President	77	Psychological Assess
		18	Chief Academic Officer	28	Technology Education	38	Guidance Services Sec	48	English/Lang Arts K-12	58	Special Education K-12	68	Teacher Personnel	78	Affirmative Action

Texas School Directory — Hill County

- **Aquilla Ind School Dist** PID: 01030735   254/694-3770
  404 N Richards, Aquilla 76622   Fax 254/694-6237

Schools: 1 \ *Teachers:* 24 \ *Students:* 325 \ *Special Ed Students:* 23 \ *LEP Students:* 11 \ *College-Bound:* 50% \ *Ethnic:* African American 2%, Hispanic 16%, Caucasian 82% \ *Exp:* $849 (High) \ *Poverty:* 13% \ *Title I:* $32,702 \ *Open-Close:* 08/21 – 05/29 \ *DTBP:* $353 (High)

Dr David Edison 1,11	Andrew Christian 2,8,88
Shaun Nugent 4*	Josh Ball 6*
Andrew Christian 8,88*	Keith Coffey 12*
Kenneth Langdale 16,73*	Garla Montez 36,57,69
Garla Montez 36,69*	Laura Hendrix 58*
David Snipes 67	Pam Horton 70
Betty Cox 83*	

Public Schs..Principal	Grd	Prgm	Enr/#Cls	SN	
Aquilla Sch 404 N Richards, Aquilla 76622 Keith Coffey \ Shari Page	PK-12	TV	325 19	50%	254/694-3770

- **Blum Ind School Dist** PID: 01030761   254/874-5231
  310 S Avenue F, Blum 76627   Fax 254/874-5233

Schools: 1 \ *Teachers:* 32 \ *Students:* 370 \ *Special Ed Students:* 41 \ *LEP Students:* 5 \ *College-Bound:* 60% \ *Ethnic:* African American 1%, Hispanic 16%, Caucasian 83% \ *Exp:* $381 (High) \ *Poverty:* 12% \ *Title I:* $46,744 \ *Open-Close:* 08/14 – 05/20 \ *DTBP:* $59 (Low) \ [f] [t]

Jeff Sanders 1,11	Dee Bellinger 2*
Kathy Haggerton 4*	Cooper Thornhill 6*
Tracy Bellomy 8*	Liuren McPherson 31,69,83,88*
Chantele Hurt 57*	Julie Laverett 58
Richard McPherson 67	Phillip Williams 73*

Public Schs..Principal	Grd	Prgm	Enr/#Cls	SN	
Blum Sch 310 S Avenue F, Blum 76627 Tracy Bellomy	PK-12	T	370 28	61%	254/874-5231

- **Bynum Ind School Dist** PID: 01030797   254/531-2341
  704 Toliver St, Bynum 76631   Fax 254/531-2342

Schools: 1 \ *Teachers:* 18 \ *Students:* 185 \ *Special Ed Students:* 22 \ *LEP Students:* 6 \ *College-Bound:* 100% \ *Ethnic:* African American 4%, Hispanic 31%, Caucasian 65% \ *Exp:* $339 (High) \ *Poverty:* 17% \ *Title I:* $42,066 \ *Open-Close:* 08/15 – 05/20 \ *DTBP:* $357 (High) \ [f]

Larry Mynarcik 1,11,83	Brandy Faulknor 2
Josh Haws 3,5	Shirley Horrice 4*
Lyndsey Pederson 8,11,58,76,286,288*	Weldon Whalen 27*
Amy Haws 36*	Grif Harris 67
Shelia Beims 79*	

Public Schs..Principal	Grd	Prgm	Enr/#Cls	SN	
Bynum Sch 704 Toliver St, Bynum 76631 Lyndsey Pederson	PK-12	TV	185 25	70%	254/623-4251

- **Covington ISD School Dist** PID: 01030826   254/854-2215
  501 N Main, Covington 76636   Fax 254/854-2272

Schools: 1 \ *Teachers:* 25 \ *Students:* 293 \ *Special Ed Students:* 40 \ *LEP Students:* 4 \ *College-Bound:* 83% \ *Ethnic:* Hispanic 16%, Native American: 1%, Caucasian 83% \ *Exp:* $643 (High) \ *Poverty:* 12% \ *Title I:* $39,248 \ *Open-Close:* 08/21 – 05/22 \ *DTBP:* $354 (High)

Dr Christopher Heskett 1	Pam Frazier 2
Rhonda Kennedy 4*	Charles Steele 6*
Keri Heskett 36,88,270,271*	Andy Lopez 67
Kara Mackey 69,76*	Sonya Lanham 73,295*

Public Schs..Principal	Grd	Prgm	Enr/#Cls	SN	
Covington Sch 501 N Main, Covington 76636 Leslie Edens \ Joel Blalock	PK-12	TV	293 18	43%	254/854-2215

- **Hillsboro Ind School Dist** PID: 01030852   254/582-8585
  121 E Franklin St, Hillsboro 76645   Fax 254/582-4165

Schools: 5 \ *Teachers:* 161 \ *Students:* 2,000 \ *Special Ed Students:* 217 \ *LEP Students:* 266 \ *Ethnic:* Asian 1%, African American 15%, Hispanic 59%, Caucasian 25% \ *Exp:* $467 (High) \ *Poverty:* 25% \ *Title I:* $684,892 \ *Special Education:* $468,000 \ *Open-Close:* 08/20 – 05/29 \ *DTBP:* $340 (High) \ [f]

Vicky Adams 1	Dale Snyder 2
Raymond Nors 3,5	Angela Boyd 8
Stephanie Tucker 11,31,57,58,271	Donald Gordon 16,73,76,295
Dr Christopher Teague 67	Barbara Robinson 68,273

Public Schs..Principal	Grd	Prgm	Enr/#Cls	SN	
Franklin Elem Sch 103 Country Club Rd, Hillsboro 76645 Cathy Patterson	PK-PK	T	178 16	74%	254/582-4130 Fax 254/582-4133
Hillsboro Elem Sch 115 Jane Ln, Hillsboro 76645 Robin Ralston	K-2	T	424 34	74%	254/582-4140 Fax 254/582-4145
Hillsboro High Sch 1600 Abbott Ave, Hillsboro 76645 Keith Hannah	9-12	AGTV	537 45	63%	254/582-4100 Fax 254/582-4108
Hillsboro Intermediate Sch 1000 Old Bynum Rd, Hillsboro 76645 Wendy Jones	3-6	T	478	75%	254/582-4170 Fax 254/582-4175 [f]
Hillsboro Junior High Sch 210 E Walnut St, Hillsboro 76645 Patrick Harvell	7-8	TV	437 25	68%	254/582-4120 Fax 254/582-4122

- **Hubbard Ind School Dist** PID: 01030917   254/576-2564
  Highway 31 W, Hubbard 76648   Fax 254/576-5019

Schools: 2 \ *Teachers:* 33 \ *Students:* 400 \ *Special Ed Students:* 31 \ *LEP Students:* 3 \ *Ethnic:* African American 15%, Hispanic 14%, Native American: 1%, Caucasian 71% \ *Exp:* $344 (High) \ *Poverty:* 19% \ *Title I:* $73,960 \ *Open-Close:* 08/14 – 05/28 \ *DTBP:* $349 (High)

Tim Norman 1,11	Elizabeth Kaluzas 2
Mike Saucke 3	Dianna Walter 4*
Russell Anderson 6	Weldonna Vardeman 8*
Summer Norman 12,31,69,83	Shawn Gilham 67
Kenny Carter 73,295*	

---

79 Student Personnel	91 Safety/Security	275 Response To Intervention	298 Grant Writer/Ptnrships
80 Driver Ed/Safety	92 Magnet School	277 Remedial Math K-12	750 Chief Innovation Officer
81 Gifted/Talented	93 Parental Involvement	280 Literacy Coach	751 Chief of Staff
82 Video Services	95 Tech Prep Program	285 STEM	752 Social Emotional Learning
83 Substance Abuse Prev	97 Chief Infomation Officer	286 Digital Learning	
84 Erate	98 Chief Technology Officer	288 Common Core Standards	Other School Types
85 AIDS Education	270 Character Education	294 Accountability	Ⓐ = Alternative School
88 Alternative/At Risk	271 Migrant Education	295 Network System	Ⓒ = Charter School
89 Multi-Cultural Curriculum	273 Teacher Mentor	296 Title II Programs	Ⓜ = Magnet School
90 Social Work	274 Before/After Sch	297 Webmaster	Ⓨ = Year-Round School

School Programs
A = Alternative Program
G = Adult Classes
M = Magnet Program
T = Title I Schoolwide
V = Career & Tech Ed Programs

Social Media
[f] = Facebook
[t] = Twitter

New Schools are shaded
New Superintendents and Principals are bold
Personnel with email addresses are underscored

TX—227

Hill County

Market Data Retrieval

Public Schs..Principal	Grd	Prgm	Enr/#Cls	SN	
Hubbard Elem Sch 1801 NW 4th St, Hubbard 76648 Donna Vardeman	PK-5	T	197 14	63%	254/576-2359 Fax 254/576-5018
Hubbard High Sch 1801 NW 4th St, Hubbard 76648 Dr Joseph Ferguson	6-12	AGTV	170 15	53%	254/576-2549 Fax 254/576-2477

• Itasca Ind School Dist PID: 01030955
123 N College St, Itasca 76055
254/687-2922
Fax 254/687-2637

Schools: 3 \ **Teachers:** 59 \ **Students:** 660 \ **Special Ed Students:** 69 \ **LEP Students:** 72 \ **College-Bound:** 73% \ **Ethnic:** Asian 1%, African American 8%, Hispanic 46%, Caucasian 45% \ **Exp:** $639 (High) \ **Poverty:** 22% \ **Title I:** $233,624 \ **Open-Close:** 08/22 - 05/22 \ **DTBP:** $440 (High)

Mark Parsons 1
Karen Taber 4
Grace Hennig 36,83*
Brian Basset 67
Richard Wilson 73,295*
Patty Miller 3
Lisa Von Borstel 8,11*
Amy Reyna 57,58,88*
Kristi Sargent 69*

Public Schs..Principal	Grd	Prgm	Enr/#Cls	SN	
Itasca Elem Sch 300 N Files St, Itasca 76055 Holli Merkel	PK-5	T	350 15	72%	254/687-2922
Itasca High Sch 123 N College St, Itasca 76055 Allison Middleton	9-12	ATV	200 18	58%	254/687-2922
Itasca Middle Sch 208 N Files St, Itasca 76055 Kristi Sargent	6-8	TV	142 10	71%	254/687-2922

• Malone Independent School Dist PID: 01030981
202 W Hackberry St, Malone 76660
254/533-2321
Fax 254/533-5660

Schools: 1 \ **Teachers:** 12 \ **Students:** 165 \ **Special Ed Students:** 21 \ **LEP Students:** 24 \ **Ethnic:** African American 6%, Hispanic 52%, Caucasian 42% \ **Exp:** $280 (Med) \ **Poverty:** 11% \ **Title I:** $1,551 \ **Open-Close:** 08/21 - 05/22 \ **DTBP:** $333 (High)

Linda Buffe 1,11,73,84,288
Sharon Campbell 57*
Larry Hancock 67
Leonard Buffe 6,35*
Barbara Christian 58,270,273*
Michael Johnson 76

Public Schs..Principal	Grd	Prgm	Enr/#Cls	SN	
Malone Elem Sch 262 W Hackberry St, Malone 76660 Lakeshia Johnson	PK-8	T	165 10	89%	254/533-2321

• Mt Calm Ind School Dist PID: 01031002
200 N Coates E, Mount Calm 76673
254/993-2611
Fax 254/993-1022

Schools: 2 \ **Teachers:** 18 \ **Students:** 210 \ **Special Ed Students:** 24 \ **LEP Students:** 15 \ **College-Bound:** 70% \ **Ethnic:** African American 6%, Hispanic 24%, Native American: 1%, Caucasian 69% \ **Exp:** $514 (High) \ **Poverty:** 42% \ **Title I:** $105,790 \ **Open-Close:** 08/15 - 05/22 \ **DTBP:** $200 (High)

James Wright 1,11
Rhonda Williams 4*
Kirk Hinkson 6
Kaaron Cornish 58
Kristi Hawkins 2,11
Pam Taylor 5,8,57,275,288
Brittney Coy 16,73,295,297*
Brian Dunlap 67

Public Schs..Principal	Grd	Prgm	Enr/#Cls	SN	
Mt Calm Elem Sch 200 N Coates E, Mount Calm 76673 Pam Taylor	PK-8	T	141 12	78%	254/993-2611
Mt Calm High Sch 100 N Coates E, Mount Calm 76673 Angela Nors	9-12	TV	44	77%	254/993-2611

• Penelope ISD School Dist PID: 01031026
309 Avenue D St, Penelope 76676
254/533-2215
Fax 254/533-2262

Schools: 1 \ **Teachers:** 20 \ **Students:** 210 \ **Special Ed Students:** 39 \ **LEP Students:** 15 \ **Ethnic:** African American 1%, Hispanic 29%, Caucasian 70% \ **Exp:** $399 (High) \ **Poverty:** 12% \ **Title I:** $20,396 \ **Open-Close:** 08/19 - 05/20 \ **DTBP:** $350 (High) \ f t

David Timmons 1
Deborah Westmoreland 4*
Keri Allen 58,69*
Traci Pustejovsky 73*
Samantha Gutierrez 2,11
Amanda Green 57*
David Kucera 67

Public Schs..Principal	Grd	Prgm	Enr/#Cls	SN	
Penelope Sch 309 Avenue D St, Penelope 76676 David Timmons	PK-12	ATV	210 25	73%	254/533-2215

• Whitney Ind School Dist PID: 01031052
305 S San Jacinto St, Whitney 76692
254/694-2254
Fax 254/694-4001

Schools: 4 \ **Teachers:** 109 \ **Students:** 1,425 \ **Special Ed Students:** 180 \ **LEP Students:** 77 \ **Ethnic:** Asian 1%, African American 5%, Hispanic 21%, Caucasian 73% \ **Exp:** $395 (High) \ **Poverty:** 18% \ **Title I:** $335,329 \ **Open-Close:** 08/19 - 05/21 \ **DTBP:** $385 (High) \ f

John McCullough 1
Brian Caperton 3,5,91
Scott Sheffield 5
Jeanne Thompson 7
Angie Rateike 9,36
Melody Haley 11,15,58,271
Bradley Coffelt 27*
Ray Mabry 67
Kim Martin 2
Judy Bailey 4
Mark Byrd 6
Melissa Marbut 8,12,273
Jennifer Penney 10,31,36,69,83,85,88*
Kristy Smith 16,73,297
Maria Herrera 57
Laura Hunt 288,298

Public Schs..Principal	Grd	Prgm	Enr/#Cls	SN	
Whitney Elem Sch 308 S Bosque St, Whitney 76692 Amber Seely	PK-2	T	381 24	68%	254/694-3456 Fax 254/694-2059
Whitney High Sch 1400 N Brazos St, Whitney 76692 Amy Leech	9-12	TV	457 35	55%	254/694-3457 Fax 254/694-4206
Whitney Intermediate Sch 301 S San Jacinto St, Whitney 76692 Russell Gauer	3-5	T	339 18	69%	254/694-7303 Fax 254/694-7029
Whitney Middle Sch 185 Hcr 1240, Whitney 76692 Paul Booth	6-8	T	339 30	58%	254/946-6568 Fax 254/947-7913

1	Superintendent	8	Curric/Instruct K-12	19	Chief Financial Officer	29	Family/Consumer Science	39	Social Studies K-12	49	English/Lang Arts Elem
2	Bus/Finance/Purchasing	9	Curric/Instruct Elem	20	Art K-12	30	Adult Education	40	Social Studies Elem	50	English/Lang Arts Sec
3	Buildings And Grounds	10	Curric/Instruct Sec	21	Art Elem	31	Career/Sch-to-Work K-12	41	Social Studies Sec	51	Reading K-12
4	Food Service	11	Federal Program	22	Art Sec	32	Career/Sch-to-Work Elem	42	Science K-12	52	Reading Elem
5	Transportation	12	Title I	23	Music K-12	33	Career/Sch-to-Work Sec	43	Science Elem	53	Reading Sec
6	Athletic	13	Title V	24	Music Elem	34	Early Childhood Ed	44	Science Sec	54	Remedial Reading K-12
7	Health Services	15	Asst Superintendent	25	Music Sec	35	Health/Phys Education	45	Math K-12	55	Remedial Reading Elem
		16	Instructional Media Svcs	26	Business Education	36	Guidance Services K-12	46	Math Elem	56	Remedial Reading Sec
		17	Chief Operations Officer	27	Career & Tech Ed	37	Guidance Services Elem	47	Math Sec	57	Bilingual/ELL
		18	Chief Academic Officer	28	Technology Education	38	Guidance Services Sec	48	English/Lang Arts K-12	58	Special Education K-12

59	Special Education Elem	69	Academic Assessment
60	Special Education Sec	70	Research/Development
61	Foreign/World Lang K-12	71	Public Information
62	Foreign/World Lang Elem	72	Summer School
63	Foreign/World Lang Sec	73	Instructional Tech
64	Religious Education K-12	74	Inservice Training
65	Religious Education Elem	75	Marketing/Distributive
66	Religious Education Sec	76	Info Systems
67	School Board President	77	Psychological Assess
68	Teacher Personnel	78	Affirmative Action

Texas School Directory

Hockley County

HOCKLEY COUNTY

HOCKLEY PUBLIC SCHOOLS

- **Anton ISD School Dist** PID: 01031090   806/997-2301
  100 Ellwood Boulevard, Anton 79313   Fax 806/997-2062

Schools: 1 \ **Teachers:** 21 \ **Students:** 180 \ **Special Ed Students:** 27 \ **LEP Students:** 10 \ **College-Bound:** 80% \ **Ethnic:** African American 4%, Hispanic 77%, Caucasian 20% \ **Exp:** $637 (High) \ **Poverty:** 24% \ **Title I:** $97,120 \ **Open-Close:** 08/26 - 05/22 \ **DTBP:** $350 (High)

Dwight Rice .... 1 Andrew Alcorta 4*
Deeanne Betencourt .... 8* Brian Reed 67

Public Schs..Principal	Grd	Prgm	Enr/#Cls	SN	
Anton Sch 100 Ellwood Boulevard, Anton 79313 **David Cox** \ Deeanne Betencourt	PK-12	TV	180 25	86%	806/997-5211 Fax 806/997-2312

- **Levelland Ind School Dist** PID: 01031129   806/894-9628
  704 11th St, Levelland 79336   Fax 806/894-2583

Schools: 6 \ **Teachers:** 230 \ **Students:** 2,936 \ **Special Ed Students:** 416 \ **LEP Students:** 210 \ **College-Bound:** 60% \ **Ethnic:** African American 4%, Hispanic 70%, Caucasian 25% \ **Exp:** $387 (High) \ **Poverty:** 23% \ **Title I:** $901,835 \ **Open-Close:** 08/21 - 05/21 \ **DTBP:** $154 (High)

Jeff Northern .... 1 Lance Terrell 2,19
Steve Croyle .... 4 Randi Bullard 5
Andrew Correll .... 6,35 Judy Whisenant 7
Heidi Blair ..... 8,16,36,69,275,285,288,294 Christy Barnett 9
Lyndsay Lucas .... 10* Donna Pugh 11,31,57,88,271,274,296,298
Kathy Hutchinson .... 12,58 Sky Tucker 34*
Tania Moody .... 67 Brady Dalton 73,76,95,286,295,297
Rodney Caddell 91

Public Schs..Principal	Grd	Prgm	Enr/#Cls	SN	
Capitol Elem Sch 401 E Ellis St, Levelland 79336 Joanna Runkles	1-3	T	387 17	71%	806/894-4715 Fax 806/894-2234
Levelland ABC 1412 E Ellis St, Levelland 79336 Sky Tucker	PK-1	T	428 22	76%	806/894-6959 Fax 806/894-5512
Levelland High Sch 1400 Hickory St, Levelland 79336 Robert Phillips	9-12	TV	773 60	65%	806/894-8515 Fax 806/894-6029
Levelland Intermediate Sch 1100 Avenue D, Levelland 79336 Terri White	4-5	T	410 25	70%	806/894-3060 Fax 806/894-8957
Levelland Middle Sch 1402 E Ellis St, Levelland 79336 **Brad Clanton**	6-8	T	607 70	66%	806/894-6355 Fax 806/894-8935
South Elem Sch 1500 Avenue C, Levelland 79336 Shelbi Eugenis	1-3	T	331 18	79%	806/894-6255 Fax 806/894-1283

- **Ropes Ind School Dist** PID: 01031234   806/562-4031
  304 Ranch Rd, Ropesville 79358   Fax 806/562-4059

Schools: 1 \ **Teachers:** 32 \ **Students:** 430 \ **Special Ed Students:** 29 \ **LEP Students:** 4 \ **College-Bound:** 85% \ **Ethnic:** African American 1%, Hispanic 40%, Native American: 1%, Caucasian 59% \ **Exp:** $563 (High) \ **Poverty:** 19% \ **Title I:** $59,084 \ **Open-Close:** 08/20 - 05/20 \ **DTBP:** $342 (High)

Joel Willmon .... 1,11 Delinda DelGado 2
Jimmy Rascon .... 3* Lane Jackson 6*
Wendee Rhoades .... 7* Tim Carter 8,12,273*
Jay Sedberry .... 16,73* Toyia Senter 16*
Melissa Bratcher .... 57* Tami Hayes 58*
Jean McNabb .... 59* Mike Metzig 67
Lindsay Luckie 69,83*

Public Schs..Principal	Grd	Prgm	Enr/#Cls	SN	
Ropes Sch 304 Ranch Rd, Ropesville 79358 Dr Danny McNabb \ Dana Ketchersid	PK-12	AT	430 28	45%	806/562-4031

- **Smyer Ind School Dist** PID: 01031272   806/234-2935
  4th & Lincoln St, Smyer 79367   Fax 806/234-2411

Schools: 2 \ **Teachers:** 39 \ **Students:** 420 \ **Special Ed Students:** 56 \ **LEP Students:** 14 \ **Ethnic:** African American 2%, Hispanic 50%, Caucasian 48% \ **Exp:** $611 (High) \ **Poverty:** 24% \ **Title I:** $106,797 \ **Open-Close:** 08/21 - 05/21 \ **DTBP:** $340 (High)

Dane Kerns .... 1,83 Donna Robertson 2
Leo Martinez .... 3,5* Mike Schaap 6*
Tony Igo .... 9,11,57,271* Bill Black 10,16,69,74*
Juan Cavazos .... 67 Belinda Maye 73,295*
Shelly Bruster 88,270,296

Public Schs..Principal	Grd	Prgm	Enr/#Cls	SN	
Smyer Elem Sch 4th & Lincoln St, Smyer 79367 Tony Igo	PK-6	T	215 21	68%	806/234-2935
Smyer Jr Sr High Sch 4th & Lincoln St, Smyer 79367 Bill Black	7-12	TV	216	60%	806/234-2935

- **Sundown Ind School Dist** PID: 01031301   806/229-3021
  701 School Ave, Sundown 79372   Fax 806/229-2004

Schools: 3 \ **Teachers:** 64 \ **Students:** 585 \ **Special Ed Students:** 46 \ **LEP Students:** 18 \ **College-Bound:** 82% \ **Ethnic:** African American 1%, Hispanic 58%, Caucasian 41% \ **Exp:** $547 (High) \ **Poverty:** 13% \ **Title I:** $59,160 \ **Open-Close:** 08/19 - 05/21 \ **DTBP:** $333 (High)

Scott Marshall .... 1 Kris Thoms 2,11,298
Tim Redden .... 3,5* Alicia Gonazales 4
Adam Cummings .... 6* Brittany Huerta 7
Jeremy Griffith .... 8,34,57 Mike Glaze 16,73
Randel Ramerez .... 16,82,295* Amanda Davis 37,270*
Delwin Britton .... 67 Ann Majors 69,83,85,88,273*

Public Schs..Principal	Grd	Prgm	Enr/#Cls	SN	
Sundown Elem Sch 701 School Ave, Sundown 79372 Jason Powell	PK-5	T	305 30	41%	806/229-5021
Sundown High Sch 701 School Ave, Sundown 79372 Brent Evans	9-12	AV	187 24	25%	806/229-2511

79 Student Personnel	91 Safety/Security	275 Response To Intervention	298 Grant Writer/Ptnrships	**School Programs**	**Social Media**		
80 Driver Ed/Safety	92 Magnet School	277 Remedial Math K-12	750 Chief Innovation Officer	A = Alternative Program		= Facebook	
81 Gifted/Talented	93 Parental Involvement	280 Literacy Coach	751 Chief of Staff	G = Adult Classes			
82 Video Services	95 Tech Prep Program	285 STEM	752 Social Emotional Learning	M = Magnet Program		= Twitter	
83 Substance Abuse Prev	97 Chief Information Officer	286 Digital Learning		T = Title I Schoolwide			
84 Erate	98 Chief Technology Officer	288 Common Core Standards	**Other School Types**	V = Career & Tech Ed Programs			
85 AIDS Education	270 Character Education	294 Accountability	Ⓐ = Alternative School				
88 Alternative/At Risk	271 Migrant Education	295 Network System	Ⓒ = Charter School	New Schools are shaded			
89 Multi-Cultural Curriculum	273 Teacher Mentor	296 Title II Programs	Ⓜ = Magnet School	New Superintendents and Principals are bold			
90 Social Work	274 Before/After Sch	297 Webmaster	Ⓨ = Year-Round School	Personnel with email addresses are underscored			

TX—229

Hood County

Sundown Middle Sch 6-8 T 133 44% 806/229-4691
7th & School Ave, Sundown 79372   13
Jeremy Griffith

- **Whitharral Ind School Dist** PID: 01031349 806/299-1184
  201 2nd Street, Whitharral 79380 Fax 806/299-1257

Schools: 1 \ *Teachers:* 17 \ *Students:* 173 \ *Special Ed Students:* 13 \ *College-Bound:* 100% \ *Ethnic:* African American 2%, Hispanic 42%, Caucasian 55% \ *Exp:* $494 (High) \ *Poverty:* 18% \ *Title I:* $39,207 \ *Open-Close:* 08/14 - 05/22 \ *DTBP:* $342 (High)

Ed Sharp 1,11,73	Adrianna McCollister 2	
Nick McCollister 8,12,36,69,83,270*	Janay Crenshaw 16*	
Susan Pendergrass 57*	Jamie Driver 58*	
Anthony Albus 67		

Public Schs..Principal	Grd	Prgm	Enr/#Cls SN		
Whitharral Sch	PK-12	TV	173	31%	806/299-1135
201 2nd Street, Whitharral 79380			50		
Alex McCollister					

HOCKLEY PRIVATE SCHOOLS

Private Schs..Principal	Grd	Prgm	Enr/#Cls SN	
Levelland Christian Sch	PK-8		48	806/894-6019
1905 Cactus Dr, Levelland 79336			7	
Kendra Gibson				

HOOD COUNTY

HOOD PUBLIC SCHOOLS

- **Granbury Ind School Dist** PID: 01031375 817/408-4000
  217 N Jones St, Granbury 76048 Fax 817/408-4014

Schools: 11 \ *Teachers:* 449 \ *Students:* 7,218 \ *Special Ed Students:* 758 \ *LEP Students:* 532 \ *College-Bound:* 52% \ *Ethnic:* Asian 1%, African American 1%, Hispanic 24%, Native American: 1%, Caucasian 74% \ *Exp:* $348 (High) \ *Poverty:* 16% \ *Title I:* $1,669,413 \ *Special Education:* $1,123,000 \ *Open-Close:* 08/13 - 05/20 \ *DTBP:* $167 (High) \

Dr Jeremy Glenn 1	Dobie Williams 2
Randy Leach 3,91	Linda Williams 4
Brian Caruthers 5	Dwight Butler 6
Latrisha Suitt 7,27,35,70,75,83,88	Sharon Williams 8,11,36,57,273,296,298
Ron Holmgreen 15	Amy Wood 16,28,73,76
Judy Gentry 27	Becky Strain 39,42,45
Diane Fullerton 58	Nancy Alana 67
Wes Jones 68	Amy Gilbert 69,77*
Jeff Meador 71	Rene Jackson 88
Curtis Starnes 295	

Public Schs..Principal	Grd	Prgm	Enr/#Cls SN		
Acton Elem Sch	PK-5	T	870	39%	817/408-4200
3200 Acton School Rd, Granbury 76049					Fax 817/408-4299
Karla Willmeth					
Acton Middle Sch	6-8		950	36%	817/408-4800
1300 James Rd, Granbury 76049			62		Fax 817/408-4849
Jimmy Dawson					
ⓐ Behavior Transition Center	5-12		50		817/408-4400
301 N Hannaford St, Granbury 76048			2		Fax 817/408-4164
Ginna Marks					
Brawner Intermediate Sch	3-5	T	390	59%	817/408-4950
1520 S Meadows Dr, Granbury 76048			17		Fax 817/408-4999
Jincy Ross					
Emma Roberson Elem Sch	PK-2	T	500	69%	817/408-4500
1500 Misty Meadow Dr, Granbury 76048			35		Fax 817/408-4599
Kellie Lambert					
Granbury High Sch	9-12	ATV	1,968	38%	817/408-4600
2000 W Pearl St, Granbury 76048			110		Fax 817/408-4699
Jeremy Ross					
Granbury Middle Sch	6-8	T	775	59%	817/408-4850
2000 Crossland Rd, Granbury 76048			35		Fax 817/408-4899
Tammy Clark					
Nettie Baccus Elem Sch	PK-5	T	519	74%	817/408-4300
901 Loop 567, Granbury 76048			29		Fax 817/408-4399
Robert Herrera					
Oak Woods Sch	PK-5	T	598	42%	817/408-4750
311 Davis Rd, Granbury 76049			52		Fax 817/408-4799
Donnie Cody					
ⓐ Stars Accelerated High Sch	9-12		37		817/408-4450
301 N Hannaford St, Granbury 76048			5		Fax 817/408-4164
Margaret Rodriquez					
The Steam Academy at Mambrino	PK-5	T	744	58%	817/408-4900
3835 Mambrino Hwy, Granbury 76048			60		Fax 817/408-4949
Stacie Brown					

- **Lipan Ind School Dist** PID: 01031416 254/646-2266
  211 N Kickapoo St, Lipan 76462 Fax 254/646-3499

Schools: 1 \ *Teachers:* 31 \ *Students:* 420 \ *Special Ed Students:* 27 \ *LEP Students:* 15 \ *College-Bound:* 50% \ *Ethnic:* African American 1%, Hispanic 12%, Caucasian 87% \ *Exp:* $448 (High) \ *Poverty:* 19% \ *Title I:* $72,438 \ *Open-Close:* 08/15 - 05/28 \ *DTBP:* $346 (High) \

Jodi Overton 1	Clayton Long 3
Tony Phillips 6,8*	Cindi Fields 57*
John Cooper 67	Susan Taylor 73*
Sandy Howard 271	

Public Schs..Principal	Grd	Prgm	Enr/#Cls SN		
Lipan Sch	PK-12	TV	420	52%	254/646-2266
211 N Kickapoo St, Lipan 76462			30		
Jennifer Phillips					

- **Tolar Ind School Dist** PID: 01031430 254/835-4718
  305 S Oak Ln, Tolar 76476 Fax 254/835-4704

Schools: 3 \ *Teachers:* 61 \ *Students:* 780 \ *Special Ed Students:* 54 \ *LEP Students:* 10 \ *College-Bound:* 75% \ *Ethnic:* Asian 1%, African American 1%, Hispanic 6%, Caucasian 92% \ *Exp:* $327 (High) \ *Poverty:* 14% \ *Title I:* $104,060 \ *Open-Close:* 08/21 - 05/28 \ *DTBP:* $383 (High) \

Travis Stilwell 1	Vicki Carr 2*
Jeremy Mullins 6*	Lindsay Morgan 11,58*
Dalton Nix 67	Laura Walker 73,295*

Public Schs..Principal	Grd	Prgm	Enr/#Cls SN		
Tolar Elem Sch	PK-5		357	31%	254/835-4028
401 E 7th St, Tolar 76476			13		Fax 254/835-4319
Kristen Carey					

1	Superintendent	8	Curric/Instruct K-12	19	Chief Financial Officer	29	Family/Consumer Science	39	Social Studies K-12	49	English/Lang Arts Elem	59	Special Education Elem	69	Academic Assessment
2	Bus/Finance/Purchasing	9	Curric/Instruct Elem	20	Art K-12	30	Adult Education	40	Social Studies Elem	50	English/Lang Arts Sec	60	Special Education Sec	70	Research/Development
3	Buildings And Grounds	10	Curric/Instruct Sec	21	Art Elem	31	Career/Sch-to-Work K-12	41	Social Studies Sec	51	Reading K-12	61	Foreign/World Lang K-12	71	Public Information
4	Food Service	11	Federal Program	22	Art Sec	32	Career/Sch-to-Work Elem	42	Science K-12	52	Reading Elem	62	Foreign/World Lang Elem	72	Summer School
5	Transportation	12	Title I	23	Music K-12	33	Career/Sch-to-Work Sec	43	Science Elem	53	Reading Sec	63	Foreign/World Lang Sec	73	Instructional Tech
6	Athletic	13	Title V	24	Music Elem	34	Early Childhood Ed	44	Science Sec	54	Remedial Reading K-12	64	Religious Education K-12	74	Inservice Training
7	Health Services	15	Asst Superintendent	25	Music Sec	35	Health/Phys Education	45	Math K-12	55	Remedial Reading Elem	65	Religious Education Elem	75	Marketing/Distributive
		16	Instructional Media Svcs	26	Business Education	36	Guidance Services K-12	46	Math Elem	56	Remedial Reading Sec	66	Religious Education Sec	76	Info Systems
		17	Chief Operations Officer	27	Career & Tech Ed	37	Guidance Services Elem	47	Math Sec	57	Bilingual/ELL	67	School Board President	77	Psychological Assess
		18	Chief Academic Officer	28	Technology Education	38	Guidance Services Sec	48	English/Lang Arts K-12	58	Special Education K-12	68	Teacher Personnel	78	Affirmative Action

Texas School Directory

Hopkins County

	Grd	Prgm	Enr/#Cls	SN	
Tolar High Sch	9-12	V	241	22%	254/835-4316
301 Rock Church Hwy, Tolar 76476			26		Fax 254/835-4237
Lindsay Morgan					
Tolar Junior High Sch	6-8	T	189	29%	254/835-5207
401 E 7th St, Tolar 76476					Fax 254/835-5208
Brad Morgan					🅵 🅃

HOOD PRIVATE SCHOOLS

Private Schs..Principal	Grd	Prgm	Enr/#Cls	SN	
Cornerstone Christian Academy	PK-12		160		817/910-8076
5150 N Gate Rd, Granbury 76049			19		Fax 817/573-7604
Marci Martinez					🅵
North Central Texas Academy	K-12		167		254/897-4822
3846 N Highway 144, Granbury 76048			32		Fax 254/897-7650
Jennifer Smith					🅵 🅃

HOPKINS COUNTY

HOPKINS PUBLIC SCHOOLS

● **Como Pickton Cons Ind SD** PID: 01031466   903/488-3671
13017 E Texas Highway 11, Como 75431   Fax 903/488-3133

Schools: 1 \ *Teachers:* 62 \ *Students:* 753 \ *Special Ed Students:* 58 \ *LEP Students:* 182 \ *College-Bound:* 40% \ *Ethnic:* Asian 1%, African American 2%, Hispanic 44%, Native American: 1%, Caucasian 53% \ *Exp:* $527 (High) \ *Poverty:* 18% \ *Title I:* $235,782 \ *Special Education:* $149,000 \ *Open-Close:* 08/19 - 05/22 \ *DTBP:* $350 (High)

Greg Bower 1		Lenise Boseman 2*	
Samara Hernandez 4*		Kelly Baird 8*	
Jenna Andrews 11,58,298		Christy Phillips 38*	
Amy Friddle 57,73,76,271,286,288		D Carr 67	

Public Schs..Principal	Grd	Prgm	Enr/#Cls	SN	
Como Pickton Sch	PK-12	TV	753	72%	903/488-3671
13017 E Texas Highway 11, Como 75431			65		
Linda Rankin \ Cassandra Bland \ Kelly Baird					

● **Cumby Ind School Dist** PID: 01031492   903/994-2260
303 Sayle St, Cumby 75433   Fax 903/994-2399

Schools: 2 \ *Teachers:* 37 \ *Students:* 400 \ *Special Ed Students:* 48 \ *LEP Students:* 12 \ *College-Bound:* 47% \ *Ethnic:* African American 2%, Hispanic 9%, Native American: 1%, Caucasian 88% \ *Exp:* $338 (High) \ *Poverty:* 14% \ *Title I:* $79,910 \ *Open-Close:* 08/15 - 05/22 \ *DTBP:* $373 (High)

Shelly Slaughter 1,11	Brenda Salinas 2
Mike Thorman 3,5*	Tom Dracos 6*
Megan Petty 8,36,69,270	Robert Pena 16,73,295
Jason Hudson 67	

Public Schs..Principal	Grd	Prgm	Enr/#Cls	SN	
Cumby Elem Sch	PK-5	TV	185	62%	903/994-2260
303 Sayle St, Cumby 75433			16		Fax 903/994-2847
Douglas Wicks					
Cumby High Sch	6-12	AT	207	47%	903/994-2260
303 Sayle St, Cumby 75433			24		Fax 903/994-2510
Jennifer Dracos					

● **Miller Grove Ind School Dist** PID: 01031521   903/459-3288
7819 FM 275 S, Cumby 75433   Fax 903/459-3744

Schools: 1 \ *Teachers:* 25 \ *Students:* 329 \ *Special Ed Students:* 24 \ *LEP Students:* 21 \ *College-Bound:* 55% \ *Ethnic:* Hispanic 22%, Caucasian 78% \ *Exp:* $638 (High) \ *Poverty:* 12% \ *Title I:* $34,539 \ *Open-Close:* 08/21 - 05/25 \ *DTBP:* $371 (High)

Steve Johnson 1,11,83	Janet Teer 2
Gary Billingsley 6,10*	Jaime Fox 9,57,69,271*
Brandon McClure 27*	Ronnie Stanley 58
Brandon Darrow 67	Davy Moseley 73*

Public Schs..Principal	Grd	Prgm	Enr/#Cls	SN	
Miller Grove Sch	PK-12	T	329	60%	903/459-3288
7819 FM 275 S, Cumby 75433			24		
Jaime Fox \ Gary Billingsley					

● **North Hopkins Ind School Dist** PID: 01031545   903/945-2192
1994 Farm Road 71 W, Sulphur Spgs 75482   Fax 903/945-2531

Schools: 1 \ *Teachers:* 42 \ *Students:* 525 \ *Special Ed Students:* 39 \ *LEP Students:* 49 \ *College-Bound:* 58% \ *Ethnic:* Asian 1%, Hispanic 26%, Native American: 1%, Caucasian 72% \ *Exp:* $1,424 (High) \ *Poverty:* 19% \ *Title I:* $106,482 \ *Open-Close:* 08/21 - 05/28 \ *DTBP:* $393 (High)

Dr Darin Jolly 1	Jan Vaughn 2
Cindy McPherson 4*	Kenneth Cockrum 5
Carolyn Neal 7*	Robert Stanley 11
Robert McPherson 67	Daniel Caldwell 73*
Cody Wright 275*	

Public Schs..Principal	Grd	Prgm	Enr/#Cls	SN	
North Hopkins Sch	PK-12	ATV	525	56%	903/945-2192
1994 Farm Road 71 W, Sulphur Spgs 75482			28		
Kodi Wright \ Brian Lowe					

● **Saltillo Ind School Dist** PID: 01031571   903/537-2386
150 County Rd 3534, Saltillo 75478   Fax 903/537-2191

Schools: 1 \ *Teachers:* 25 \ *Students:* 240 \ *Special Ed Students:* 23 \ *LEP Students:* 23 \ *College-Bound:* 65% \ *Ethnic:* African American 3%, Hispanic 24%, Caucasian 73% \ *Exp:* $528 (High) \ *Poverty:* 19% \ *Title I:* $60,565 \ *Open-Close:* 08/19 - 05/29 \ *DTBP:* $343 (High)

David Stickels 1,11	Janice Teer 2
Timmy White 3*	Susan Smith 4*
Bill Gilse 6	Reta Eubanks 58*
Mark Sustaire 67	Tim Lane 73,286,288

Public Schs..Principal	Grd	Prgm	Enr/#Cls	SN	
Saltillo Sch	PK-12	ATV	240	68%	903/537-2386
150 County Rd 3534, Saltillo 75478			16		
Tim Lane \ David Stickels					

---

79 Student Personnel	91 Safety/Security	275 Response To Intervention	298 Grant Writer/Ptnrships	**School Programs**	**Social Media**
80 Driver Ed/Safety	92 Magnet School	277 Remedial Math K-12	750 Chief Innovation Officer	A = Alternative Program	🅵 = Facebook
81 Gifted/Talented	93 Parental Involvement	280 Literacy Coach	751 Chief of Staff	G = Adult Classes	
82 Video Services	95 Tech Prep Program	285 STEM	752 Social Emotional Learning	M = Magnet Program	🅃 = Twitter
83 Substance Abuse Prev	97 Chief Information Officer	286 Digital Learning		T = Title I Schoolwide	
84 Erate	98 Chief Technology Officer	288 Common Core Standards	**Other School Types**	V = Career & Tech Ed Programs	
85 AIDS Education	270 Accountability	294 Accountability	Ⓐ = Alternative School		
88 Alternative/At Risk	271 Migrant Education	295 Network System	Ⓒ = Charter School	New Schools are shaded	
89 Multi-Cultural Curriculum	273 Teacher Mentor	296 Title II Programs	Ⓜ = Magnet School	New Superintendents and Principals are bold	
90 Social Work	274 Before/After Sch	297 Webmaster	Ⓨ = Year-Round School	Personnel with email addresses are underscored	

TX—231

Houston County

Market Data Retrieval

• **Sulphur Bluff Ind School Dist** PID: 01031595   903/945-2460
1027 County Road 3550, Sulphur Bluff 75481   Fax 903/945-2459

Schools: 1 \ *Teachers:* 19 \ *Students:* 215 \ *Special Ed Students:* 29 \ *LEP Students:* 7 \ *College-Bound:* 100% \ *Ethnic:* African American 3%, Hispanic 11%, Caucasian 85% \ *Exp:* $384 (High) \ *Poverty:* 14% \ *Title I:* $30,805 \ *Open-Close:* 08/20 - 05/25 \ *DTBP:* $316 (High) \ 🛈

Dustin Carr 1,11
Leah Gore 31,36,294*
Jarret Wilson 73*
Amy Northcutt 8,58,69,83,274,275*
Donnie Powers 67

Public Schs..Principal	Grd	Prgm	Enr/#Cls	SN	
Sulphur Bluff Sch 1027 County Road 3550, Sulphur Bluff 75481 **Amy Daniel**	PK-12	ATV	215 15	54%	903/945-2460

• **Sulphur Springs Ind Sch Dist** PID: 01031624   903/885-2153
631 Connally St, Sulphur Spgs 75482   Fax 903/439-6162

Schools: 9 \ *Teachers:* 347 \ *Students:* 4,400 \ *Special Ed Students:* 422 \ *LEP Students:* 522 \ *College-Bound:* 64% \ *Ethnic:* Asian 1%, African American 12%, Hispanic 28%, Caucasian 59% \ *Exp:* $433 (High) \ *Poverty:* 20% \ *Title I:* $1,135,092 \ *Special Education:* $823,000 \ *Open-Close:* 08/20 - 05/21 \ *DTBP:* $153 (High)

Michael Lamb 1
Dan Froneberger 3*
Greg Owens 6*
Kristin Monk 9,15
Rusty Harden 15,68
Jenny Arledge 26,27,31,75,95*
Susan Johnston 58
Jason Evans 69,294
Ben Scott 295
Sherry McGraw 2
Veronica Arnold 4
Lisa Robinson 8
Josh Williams 11,15,36,79,88,296
Rodney White 16,73,295
Anna Aguilar 57,271
Lisa Toliver 67
John Bimmerle 286*

Public Schs..Principal	Grd	Prgm	Enr/#Cls	SN	
ⓐ Austin Academic Center 808 Davis St S, Sulphur Spgs 75482 Julie Ashmore	1-12		90		903/885-4942 Fax 903/439-6142
Barbara Bush Primary Sch 390 N Hillcrest Dr, Sulphur Spgs 75482 Ashanta Alexander	K-1	T	545 31	70%	903/439-6170 Fax 903/439-6177
Bowie Primary Sch 1400 Mockingbird Ln, Sulphur Spgs 75482 Amanda Fenton	K-3	T	242 19	50%	903/885-3772 Fax 903/885-5754
Douglass ECLC 600 Calvert St, Sulphur Spgs 75482 Angela Edwards	PK-K	T	545 14	62%	903/885-4516 Fax 903/439-1181
Lamar Primary Sch 825 Church St, Sulphur Spgs 75482 Rowena Johnson	K-3	T	155 14	76%	903/885-4550 Fax 903/439-6144
Sulphur Springs Elem Sch 829 Bell St, Sulphur Spgs 75482 Holly Folmar	4-5	T	656 14	64%	903/855-8466 Fax 903/885-5451
Sulphur Springs High Sch 1200 Connally St, Sulphur Spgs 75482 Derek Driver	9-12	TV	1,230 75	49%	903/885-2158 Fax 903/885-6669
Sulphur Springs Middle Sch 835 Wildcat Way, Sulphur Spgs 75482 Jena Williams	6-8	T	950 70	58%	903/885-7741 Fax 903/439-6126
Travis Primary Sch 130 Garrison St, Sulphur Spgs 75482 Michelle Wallace	K-3	T	241 25	74%	903/885-5246 Fax 903/438-2251

HOPKINS PRIVATE SCHOOLS

Private Schs..Principal	Grd	Prgm	Enr/#Cls	SN	
Water Oak Sch 631 Davis St N, Sulphur Spgs 75482 Lesley Williams	K-5		60		903/439-3044

HOUSTON COUNTY

HOUSTON PUBLIC SCHOOLS

• **Crockett Ind School Dist** PID: 01031715   936/544-2125
1400 W Austin St, Crockett 75835   Fax 936/544-5727

Schools: 5 \ *Teachers:* 105 \ *Students:* 1,331 \ *Special Ed Students:* 143 \ *LEP Students:* 219 \ *Ethnic:* African American 51%, Hispanic 27%, Caucasian 22% \ *Exp:* $515 (High) \ *Poverty:* 36% \ *Title I:* $779,118 \ *Special Education:* $362,000 \ *Open-Close:* 08/27 - 06/01 \ *DTBP:* $306 (High)

Terry Myers 1
Brian Fiolek 3
Bruce Baker 5
Margaret Tuggle 36
Charlie Bobbitt 73
Gail Hanson 2,11,296
Louann Turner 4
John Emrich 15
Lela Wheeler 67

Public Schs..Principal	Grd	Prgm	Enr/#Cls	SN	
ⓐ Crockett Aec-Pineywoods 1400 W Austin St, Crockett 75835 Mecheal Abbs	9-12	GT	18 3	77%	936/546-5972 Fax 936/546-0721
Crockett Elem Sch 1400 S Loop 304, Crockett 75835 Robin Stowe	1-5		504 29		936/544-3758 Fax 936/544-2088
Crockett High Sch 1600 SW Loop 304, Crockett 75835 Deborah Revels	9-12	TV	345 34	78%	936/544-2193 Fax 936/546-0104
Crockett Junior High Sch 1500 SW Loop 304, Crockett 75835 Juan Gomez	6-8	T	281 30	87%	936/544-2125 Fax 936/544-4164
Early Childhood Center 1300 Mlk Blvd, Crockett 75835 Dylis Bobbitt	PK-K		183 12		936/544-2125 Fax 936/544-9678

• **Grapeland Ind School Dist** PID: 01031753   936/687-4619
116 W Myrtle Street, Grapeland 75844   Fax 936/687-4624

Schools: 3 \ *Teachers:* 44 \ *Students:* 615 \ *Special Ed Students:* 73 \ *LEP Students:* 8 \ *College-Bound:* 75% \ *Ethnic:* African American 26%, Hispanic 11%, Caucasian 63% \ *Exp:* $243 (Med) \ *Poverty:* 28% \ *Title I:* $222,043 \ *Open-Close:* 08/26 - 05/29 \ *DTBP:* $390 (High) \ 🛈

Don Jackson 1,83
Terry Brown 3
Paul Pick 5
Ginger Arbuckle 8
Rick Frauenberger 10*
Samantha Earp 36,69*
Vicki Dial Branch 58
John Norman 76,295*
Julie Martin 2,11
Shamedria Gilmore 4
Terry Ward 6
Cassie Satterwhite 9,11,34,296*
Gary Graham 27,298*
Amy Howard 57,271
James Martin 67
Teri Frauenberger 79*

1	Superintendent	8	Curric/Instruct K-12	19	Chief Financial Officer	29	Family/Consumer Science	39	Social Studies K-12	49	English/Lang Arts Elem	59	Special Education Elem	69	Academic Assessment
2	Bus/Finance/Purchasing	9	Curric/Instruct Elem	20	Art K-12	30	Adult Education	40	Social Studies Elem	50	English/Lang Arts Sec	60	Special Education Sec	70	Research/Development
3	Buildings And Grounds	10	Curric/Instruct Sec	21	Art Elem	31	Career/Sch-to-Work K-12	41	Social Studies Sec	51	Reading K-12	61	Foreign/World Lang K-12	71	Public Information
4	Food Service	11	Federal Program	22	Art Sec	32	Career/Sch-to-Work Elem	42	Science K-12	52	Reading Elem	62	Foreign/World Lang Elem	72	Summer School
5	Transportation	12	Title I	23	Music K-12	33	Career/Sch-to-Work Sec	43	Science Elem	53	Reading Sec	63	Foreign/World Lang Sec	73	Instructional Tech
6	Athletic	13	Title V	24	Music Elem	34	Early Childhood Ed	44	Science Sec	54	Remedial Reading K-12	64	Religious Education K-12	74	Inservice Training
7	Health Services	15	Asst Superintendent	25	Music Sec	35	Health/Phys Education	45	Math K-12	55	Remedial Reading Elem	65	Religious Education Elem	75	Marketing/Distributive
		16	Instructional Media Svcs	26	Business Education	36	Guidance Services K-12	46	Math Elem	56	Remedial Reading Sec	66	Religious Education Sec	76	Info Systems
		17	Chief Operations Officer	27	Career & Tech Ed	37	Guidance Services Elem	47	Math Sec	57	Bilingual/ELL	67	School Board President	77	Psychological Assess
		18	Chief Academic Officer	28	Technology Education	38	Guidance Services Sec	48	English/Lang Arts K-12	58	Special Education K-12	68	Teacher Personnel	78	Affirmative Action

Texas School Directory — Howard County

Public Schs..Principal	Grd	Prgm	Enr/#Cls	SN
Grapeland Elem Sch 796 N Olive St, Grapeland 75844 Cassie Satterwhite	PK-5	TV	248 17	72% 936/687-2317 Fax 936/687-2341
Grapeland Junior High Sch 116 West Myrtle St, Grapeland 75844 Rick Frauenberger	6-8	TV	119 15	61% 936/687-2351 Fax 936/687-5285
Grapeland Secondary Sch 318 N Olive St, Grapeland 75844 Rick Frauenberger	9-12	AGTV	141 10	58% 936/687-4661 Fax 936/687-9739

- **Kennard Ind Sch Dist** PID: 01031791   936/655-2161
  304 State Highway 7 E, Kennard 75847   Fax 936/655-2327

Schools: 1 \ *Teachers:* 25 \ *Students:* 280 \ *Special Ed Students:* 35 \ *College-Bound:* 100% \ *Ethnic:* African American 15%, Hispanic 8%, Native American: 2%, Caucasian 75% \ *Exp:* $429 (High) \ *Poverty:* 29% \ *Title I:* $128,743 \ *Open-Close:* 08/15 - 05/20 \ *DTBP:* $530 (High)

Melinda Lindsey 1,11,73	Cari Parrish 2		
Corey Carden 6*	Cory Carden 6		
Debbie Pilkington 16,82*	Amy Gladden 31,69*		
Rebecca Parker 67			

Public Schs..Principal	Grd	Prgm	Enr/#Cls	SN
Kennard Sch 304 State Highway 7 E, Kennard 75847 Oscar Encarnacion	PK-12	TV	280 40	60% 936/655-2161

- **Latexo Ind School Dist** PID: 01031820   936/544-5664
  298 FM 2663, Latexo 75849   Fax 936/544-5332

Schools: 2 \ *Teachers:* 47 \ *Students:* 500 \ *Special Ed Students:* 49 \ *LEP Students:* 5 \ *College-Bound:* 50% \ *Ethnic:* Asian 1%, African American 4%, Hispanic 9%, Caucasian 86% \ *Exp:* $611 (High) \ *Poverty:* 23% \ *Title I:* $88,737 \ *Open-Close:* 08/19 - 05/22 \ *DTBP:* $421 (High) \ 📘 🐦

Michael Woodard 1	Jo Lane 2
Tammy Luce 4,84	Logan Taylor 5*
Jessica Cutshall 6*	Krystal Patterson 7*
Lena Kelsey 28,286*	Vicki Dial 58
Kelly Nicol 67	Kimberly Watson 69*
Tracey Catoe 73*	

Public Schs..Principal	Grd	Prgm	Enr/#Cls	SN
Latexo Elem Sch 298 FM 2663, Latexo 75849 Sandy Simpson	PK-6	T	267 22	55% 936/546-5630 Fax 936/546-2220
Latexo High Sch 298 FM 2663, Latexo 75849 Kris Whisenant	7-12	T	218 30	38% 936/544-5638 Fax 936/544-8456

- **Lovelady Ind School Dist** PID: 01031844   936/636-7616
  11839 State Highway 19 S, Lovelady 75851   Fax 936/636-2212

Schools: 2 \ *Teachers:* 46 \ *Students:* 510 \ *Special Ed Students:* 54 \ *LEP Students:* 13 \ *College-Bound:* 80% \ *Ethnic:* Asian 1%, African American 10%, Hispanic 6%, Caucasian 83% \ *Exp:* $496 (High) \ *Poverty:* 16% \ *Title I:* $104,956 \ *Open-Close:* 08/21 - 05/22 \ *DTBP:* $357 (High) \ 📘 🐦

Wendy Tullos 1	Rhonda Stone 2
Cody Robinson 3,5,91	Alisha Mosley 4
Will Kirchhoff 6	Winnie McKnight 7*

Todd Stone 8,11,57,58,270,298*	Alice Ham 16,73,76,295
Leslie Gilchrist 36,280*	Jodi Carney 54
Bruce Monk 67	Cindi Burleson 68
Dakota Ham 295	

Public Schs..Principal	Grd	Prgm	Enr/#Cls	SN
Lovelady Elem Middle Sch 11839 Tx State Highway 19S, Lovelady 75851 Rhonda Lowery	PK-6		317 25	936/636-7832 Fax 936/636-2529
Lovelady Jr Sr High Sch 11839 Tx State Highway 19S, Lovelady 75851 Jo Martinez	7-12	V	230 28	37% 936/636-7636 Fax 936/636-2305

HOWARD COUNTY

HOWARD PUBLIC SCHOOLS

- **Big Spring Ind School Dist** PID: 01031870   432/264-3600
  708 E 11th Pl, Big Spring 79720   Fax 432/264-3646

Schools: 9 \ *Teachers:* 261 \ *Students:* 4,000 \ *Special Ed Students:* 341 \ *LEP Students:* 148 \ *Ethnic:* Asian 1%, African American 6%, Hispanic 68%, Caucasian 26% \ *Exp:* $384 (High) \ *Poverty:* 23% \ *Title I:* $1,279,733 \ *Special Education:* $738,000 \ *Open-Close:* 08/19 - 05/21 \ *DTBP:* $157 (High)

Jay McWilliams 1	Susan Bryan 2
John Sparks 3,5*	Judi Rodriguez 4
Dennis Witt 5	Mike Ritchey 6,51
Raemi Thompson 8,12,15,52	Tyler Shepherd 11,34,57,58,88,271,296,298
George Bancroft 15	Vonnie Anderson 27,294
Fabian Serrano 67	Gina Wells 68
Debbie Park 70	Jamie Scott 73,286,295
Gina Slover 79	Daniel Hoard 295
Brenda Mault 297	

Public Schs..Principal	Grd	Prgm	Enr/#Cls	SN
Ⓐ Anderson Accelerated High Sch 229 Airbase Rd, Big Spring 79720 Heidi Wagner	7-12		15 3	432/264-4115 Fax 432/264-3609
Big Spring High Sch 707 E 11th Pl, Big Spring 79720 Michael Ritchey	9-12	TV	1,065	54% 432/264-3641 Fax 432/264-4133
Big Spring Interm Sch 2000 S Goliad St, Big Spring 79720 Patsy Sanchez	5-6	T	640	70% 432/264-4121
Big Spring Junior High Sch 624 E 6th St, Big Spring 79720 Rebecca Otto	7-8	ATV	606 55	74% 432/264-4135 Fax 432/264-4196
Goliad Elem Sch 1801 Goliad St, Big Spring 79720 Rosie Lain	K-4		397 30	432/264-4111 Fax 432/264-3618
Kentwood Early Childhood Ctr 2500 Merrily Dr, Big Spring 79720 Jennifer Chesworth	PK-PK	T	104	84% 432/264-4130 Fax 432/264-3612
Marcy Elem Sch 2101 Wasson Rd, Big Spring 79720 Dana Pannell	K-5	T	365 25	78% 432/264-4144 Fax 432/264-3627
Moss Elem Sch 3200 Fordham Ave, Big Spring 79720 **Carman Wommack**	K-2	T	487 18	70% 432/264-4148 Fax 432/264-3619

79 Student Personnel	91 Safety/Security	275 Response To Intervention	298 Grant Writer/Ptnrships	School Programs	Social Media
80 Driver Ed/Safety	92 Magnet School	277 Remedial Math K-12	750 Chief Innovation Officer	A = Alternative Program	
81 Gifted/Talented	93 Parental Involvement	280 Literacy Coach	751 Chief of Staff	G = Adult Classes	📘 = Facebook
82 Video Services	95 Tech Prep Program	285 STEM	752 Social Emotional Learning	M = Magnet Program	
83 Substance Abuse Prev	97 Chief Infomation Officer	286 Digital Learning		T = Title I Schoolwide	🐦 = Twitter
84 Erate	98 Chief Technology Officer	288 Common Core Standards	Other School Types	V = Career & Tech Ed Programs	
85 AIDS Education	270 Character Education	294 Accountability	Ⓐ = Alternative School		
88 Alternative/At Risk	271 Migrant Education	295 Network System	Ⓒ = Charter School	New Schools are shaded	
89 Multi-Cultural Curriculum	273 Teacher Mentor	296 Title II Programs	Ⓜ = Magnet School	New Superintendents and Principals are bold	
90 Social Work	274 Before/After Sch	297 Webmaster	Ⓨ = Year-Round School	Personnel with email addresses are underscored	

TX—233

Hudspeth County

Market Data Retrieval

Washington Elem Sch   K-5   T   400   76%   432/264-4126
1201 Birdwell Ln, Big Spring 79720   23   Fax 432/264-3611
Kaitlin Jeffrey

- **Coahoma Ind School Dist** PID: 01032056   432/394-5000
  600 Main St, Coahoma 79511   Fax 432/394-4302

Schools: 3 \ *Teachers:* 70 \ *Students:* 1,000 \ *Special Ed Students:* 83 \ *LEP Students:* 9 \ *College-Bound:* 51% \ *Ethnic:* African American 1%, Hispanic 37%, Caucasian 62% \ *Exp:* $384 (High) \ *Poverty:* 16% \ *Title I:* $125,887 \ *Open-Close:* 08/15 - 05/25 \ *DTBP:* $341 (High)

Brad Cox	1,73	Stephanie Rameriz	4
Chris Joslin	6	Alison Alverez	9,11,16,34,57,271*
John Landin	23*	Carissa Hughes	35,83,85*
Christina Cox	58	Kandy Alaman	67
Megan Parrish	73,76,286,295		

Public Schs..Principal	Grd	Prgm	Enr/#Cls	SN	
Coahoma Elem Sch 400 Ramsey Dr, Coahoma 79511 Alison Alverez	PK-5	T	549 23	40%	432/394-5000 Fax 432/394-4419
Coahoma High Sch 606 N Main St, Coahoma 79511 Christina Cox	9-12	AV	251 35	42%	432/394-5000
Coahoma Junior High Sch 500 High School Dr, Coahoma 79511 Ashley Roberts	6-8	AT	204 14	46%	432/394-5000 Fax 432/394-4052

- **Forsan Ind School Dist** PID: 01032094   432/457-2223
  411 W 6th St, Forsan 79733   Fax 432/457-0008

Schools: 2 \ *Teachers:* 52 \ *Students:* 812 \ *Special Ed Students:* 43 \ *LEP Students:* 5 \ *College-Bound:* 67% \ *Ethnic:* Asian 2%, African American 1%, Hispanic 28%, Native American: 1%, Caucasian 68% \ *Exp:* $548 (High) \ *Poverty:* 14% \ *Title I:* $60,640 \ *Open-Close:* 08/15 - 05/21 \ *DTBP:* $350 (High)

Randy Johnson	1	Jason Mims	2
Phillip Schuppert	3	Roxie Thomas	4*
Jason Phillips	6*	Hanna Carter	8,68,79,273*
Mysti Mims	8,57,69,88,271*	Jeanette Lindsey	11,298*
Lewis Boeker	67	Shaun McVicars	73,286*

Public Schs..Principal	Grd	Prgm	Enr/#Cls	SN	
Forsan Elbow Elem Sch 500 W Main St, Forsan 79733 Hanna Carter	PK-5	AT	387 20	35%	432/457-0091 Fax 432/457-0040
Forsan Jr Sr High Sch 411 W 6th Street, Forsan 79733 Hanna Carter	6-12	V	396 33	28%	432/457-2223

HUDSPETH COUNTY

HUDSPETH PUBLIC SCHOOLS

- **Dell City Ind School Dist** PID: 01032147   915/964-2663
  110 N Main St, Dell City 79837   Fax 915/964-2880

Schools: 1 \ *Teachers:* 9 \ *Students:* 65 \ *Special Ed Students:* 9 \ *LEP Students:* 28 \ *College-Bound:* 100% \ *Ethnic:* Hispanic 69%, Native American: 3%, Caucasian 28% \ *Exp:* $1,876 (High) \ *Poverty:* 27% \ *Title I:* $38,986 \ *Special Education:* $17,000 \ *Open-Close:* 08/27 - 06/01 \ *DTBP:* $416 (High)

Ruben Cervantes	1	Rita Archuleta	2,12
Carlos Contreras	8,11,88,285,288,294*	Bernice Mora	57*
Steve Carpenter	67		

Public Schs..Principal	Grd	Prgm	Enr/#Cls	SN	
Dell City Sch 110 N Main St, Dell City 79837 Carlos Contreras	K-12	TV	65 17	74%	915/964-2663

- **Ft Hancock Ind School Dist** PID: 01032173   915/769-3811
  100 School Drive, Fort Hancock 79839   Fax 915/769-3940

Schools: 3 \ *Teachers:* 36 \ *Students:* 410 \ *Special Ed Students:* 28 \ *LEP Students:* 201 \ *College-Bound:* 65% \ *Ethnic:* Hispanic 97%, Caucasian 3% \ *Exp:* $731 (High) \ *Poverty:* 28% \ *Title I:* $199,807 \ *Special Education:* $79,000 \ *Open-Close:* 08/12 - 05/29 \ *DTBP:* $347 (High)

Jose Franco	1	Victoria Gonzalez	2
Norma Muniz	4	Joegr Apodaca	5
Frank Saldane	6	Rosalia Arzate	7*
Yvonne Samaniego	11,57,298	Joe Rodriguez	67
Tomas Chavez	73		

Public Schs..Principal	Grd	Prgm	Enr/#Cls	SN	
Benito Martinez Elem Sch 460 Knox Ave, Fort Hancock 79839 Yadira Munoz	PK-5	T	200 17	91%	915/769-1602 Fax 915/769-0043
Ft Hancock High Sch 100 School Drive, Fort Hancock 79839 Lorena Molinar	9-12	T	110 20	94%	915/769-1604 Fax 915/769-0044
Ft Hancock Middle Sch 100 School Drive, Fort Hancock 79839 Danny Medina	6-8	T	100	91%	915/769-1603 Fax 915/769-0045

- **Sierra Blanca Ind School Dist** PID: 01032202   915/369-3741
  500 Sierra Blanca Ave, Sierra Blanca 79851   Fax 915/369-2605

Schools: 1 \ *Teachers:* 13 \ *Students:* 90 \ *Special Ed Students:* 8 \ *LEP Students:* 7 \ *College-Bound:* 70% \ *Ethnic:* Asian 2%, African American 2%, Hispanic 68%, Caucasian 29% \ *Exp:* $1,227 (High) \ *Poverty:* 21% \ *Title I:* $33,549 \ *Special Education:* $17,000 \ *Open-Close:* 08/26 - 05/21 \ *DTBP:* $257 (High)

Evelyn Loeffler	1,11,73,83	Ismael Ramirez	6*
Joel Sanchez	67		

1	Superintendent	8	Curric/Instruct K-12	19	Chief Financial Officer	29	Family/Consumer Science	39	Social Studies K-12	49	English/Lang Arts Elem	59	Special Education Elem	69	Academic Assessment
2	Bus/Finance/Purchasing	9	Curric/Instruct Elem	20	Art K-12	30	Adult Education	40	Social Studies Elem	50	English/Lang Arts Sec	60	Special Education Sec	70	Research/Development
3	Buildings And Grounds	10	Curric/Instruct Sec	21	Art Elem	31	Career/Sch-to-Work K-12	41	Social Studies Sec	51	Reading K-12	61	Foreign/World Lang K-12	71	Public Information
4	Food Service	11	Federal Program	22	Art Sec	32	Career/Sch-to-Work Elem	42	Science K-12	52	Reading Elem	62	Foreign/World Lang Elem	72	Summer School
5	Transportation	12	Title I	23	Music K-12	33	Career/Sch-to-Work Sec	43	Science Elem	53	Reading Sec	63	Foreign/World Lang Sec	73	Instructional Tech
6	Athletic	13	Title V	24	Music Elem	34	Early Childhood Ed	44	Science Sec	54	Remedial Reading K-12	64	Religious Education K-12	74	Inservice Training
7	Health Services	15	Asst Superintendent	25	Music Sec	35	Health/Phys Education	45	Math K-12	55	Remedial Reading Elem	65	Religious Education Elem	75	Marketing/Distributive
		16	Instructional Media Svcs	26	Business Education	36	Guidance Services K-12	46	Math Elem	56	Remedial Reading Sec	66	Religious Education Sec	76	Info Systems
		17	Chief Operations Officer	27	Career & Tech Ed	37	Guidance Services Elem	47	Math Sec	57	Bilingual/ELL	67	School Board President	77	Psychological Assess
		18	Chief Academic Officer	28	Technology Education	38	Guidance Services Sec	48	English/Lang Arts K-12	58	Special Education K-12	68	Teacher Personnel	78	Affirmative Action

TX—234

Texas School Directory

Hunt County

Public Schs..Principal	Grd	Prgm	Enr/#Cls	SN	
Sierra Blanca Sch 1111 Farm Rd, Sierra Blanca 79851 Beatriz Zavala	PK-12	TV	90 14	68%	915/369-2781

HUNT COUNTY

HUNT PUBLIC SCHOOLS

• **Bland Ind School Dist** PID: 01032238 903/776-2239
2556 Lake Ave, Merit 75458 Fax 903/776-2240

Schools: 3 \ **Teachers:** 52 \ **Students:** 730 \ **Special Ed Students:** 59 \ **LEP Students:** 89 \ **Ethnic:** African American 1%, Hispanic 39%, Native American: 1%, Caucasian 59% \ **Exp:** $366 (High) \ **Poverty:** 24% \ **Title I:** $226,830 \ **Open-Close:** 08/14 - 05/21 \ **DTBP:** $558 (High)

Rick Tidwell 1,83	Bryan Bymaster 2,15,88		
Jean Riley 3	Shelli Wendland 8*		
Mikayle Goff 11	Susan Douglas 16*		
Jason Hammack 57*	Terry Hurst 67		
Charity Morris 69	Ted Capps 73,286*		

Public Schs..Principal	Grd	Prgm	Enr/#Cls	SN	
Bland Elem Sch 5123 FM 2194, Celeste 75423 Jason Hammack	PK-5	T	337 14	60%	903/527-5480 Fax 903/527-5481
Bland High Sch 6164 FM 2194, Farmersville 75442 Dustin Evans	9-12	TV	206 15	46%	903/776-2161 Fax 903/776-2426
Bland Middle Sch 5123 FM 2194, Celeste 75423 Jason Hammack	6-8	T	140 25	57%	903/527-5490 Fax 903/527-5491

• **Boles Ind School Dist** PID: 01032264 903/883-4464
9777 FM 2101, Quinlan 75474 Fax 903/883-4531

Schools: 3 \ **Teachers:** 47 \ **Students:** 540 \ **Special Ed Students:** 53 \ **LEP Students:** 5 \ **College-Bound:** 59% \ **Ethnic:** Asian 1%, African American 3%, Hispanic 16%, Caucasian 80% \ **Exp:** $298 (Med) \ **Poverty:** 19% \ **Title I:** $99,337 \ **Open-Close:** 08/19 - 05/28 \ **DTBP:** $376 (High)

Dr Graham Sweeney 1,83	Mikayle Moreland 2,11,74,296*
Cindy Mitchell 3,5	Tim Dawson 4*
Jeff Thomason 6*	D'Ann Ralson 7*
Patrece Ozment 36,83*	Linda Pitts 67
David Hartford 73,295*	Shirley Duran 93*

Public Schs..Principal	Grd	Prgm	Enr/#Cls	SN	
Boles Elem Sch 9777 FM 2101, Quinlan 75474 Shirley Duran	PK-4	T	216 12	62%	903/883-2161 Fax 903/883-9094
Boles High Sch 9777 FM 2101, Quinlan 75474 Jill Thomason	9-12	ATV	162 20	43%	903/883-2918 Fax 903/883-5109
Boles Middle Sch 9777 FM 2101, Quinlan 75474 Gordon Jordan	5-8	T	165 12	49%	903/883-4464 Fax 903/883-3097

• **Caddo Mills Ind Sch Dist** PID: 01032290 903/527-6056
100 Fox Ln, Caddo Mills 75135 Fax 903/527-4883

Schools: 5 \ **Teachers:** 125 \ **Students:** 1,850 \ **Special Ed Students:** 153 \ **LEP Students:** 52 \ **Ethnic:** Asian 1%, African American 2%, Hispanic 16%, Native American: 1%, Caucasian 80% \ **Exp:** $269 (Med) \ **Poverty:** 15% \ **Title I:** $252,914 \ **Open-Close:** 08/15 - 05/21 \ f

Luke Allison 1	Becky Pfiel 2
Sam Day 5	Steve Sumrow 6
Julie Wiebersch 8	Kendra Moser 9
Michael Goss 11	Kerri Allen 15
Rueben Terry 67	Pete Rowe 73
Stefanie Duffer 73	

Public Schs..Principal	Grd	Prgm	Enr/#Cls	SN	
Ⓐ Caddo Mills Aep 100 Fox Ln, Caddo Mills 75135 Scott Hudspeth	5-12		30 3		903/527-2075 Fax 903/527-3313
Caddo Mills High Sch 2710 Gilmer St, Caddo Mills 75135 Jana Everett	9-12	V	508 20	29%	903/527-3164 Fax 903/527-4772
Caddo Mills Middle Sch 2700 Gilmer St, Caddo Mills 75135 Anne Payne	6-8		386 32	35%	903/527-3161 Fax 903/527-2379
Kathryn Griffis Elem Sch 3639 FM 1565, Caddo Mills 75135 Jennifer Brutonr	PK-5	T	457	33%	903/527-3525 Fax 903/527-3597
Lee Elem Sch 2702 Gilmer St, Caddo Mills 75135 Vonda Farmer	PK-5	T	385 64	32%	903/527-3162 Fax 903/527-0166

• **Campbell Ind School Dist** PID: 01032329 903/862-3259
480 N Patterson St, Campbell 75422 Fax 903/862-2222

Schools: 1 \ **Teachers:** 35 \ **Students:** 310 \ **Special Ed Students:** 36 \ **LEP Students:** 19 \ **College-Bound:** 50% \ **Exp:** $252 (Med) \ **Poverty:** 23% \ **Title I:** $117,844 \ **Open-Close:** 08/19 - 05/15 \ **DTBP:** $350 (High)

Dr Denise Morgan 1,288	Hubert Bares 2
Justin Nicholson 3	Cynthia Long 4
Gary Shultz 6*	Christy Sweeny 7,35
Karen Moore 16,286*	Sara Fields 58*
Frank Owens 67	Anthony Eilers 73,295*

Public Schs..Principal	Grd	Prgm	Enr/#Cls	SN	
Campbell Sch 409 W North St, Campbell 75422 Jason Crow	PK-12	AV	310 28		903/862-3253 Fax 903/862-3547

• **Celeste Ind School Dist** PID: 01032355 903/568-4825
207 S 5th St, Celeste 75423 Fax 903/568-4495

Schools: 3 \ **Teachers:** 44 \ **Students:** 512 \ **Special Ed Students:** 69 \ **LEP Students:** 9 \ **College-Bound:** 49% \ **Ethnic:** African American 2%, Hispanic 14%, Caucasian 84% \ **Exp:** $592 (High) \ **Poverty:** 17% \ **Title I:** $143,452 \ **Open-Close:** 08/19 - 05/22 \ **DTBP:** $251 (High)

Brad Connelly 1	Tammy Shields 2
Mark Harrison 3,5*	Demetrius Rictor 6*
Jennifer Diles 7,85*	Beth Ray 9,34,271*
James Branam 10*	Alice Dills 12,36,69,83,88,273*
Chris Barnard 67	Chris Johnston 73*

---

79 Student Personnel	91 Safety/Security	275 Response To Intervention	298 Grant Writer/Ptnrships	School Programs	Social Media		
80 Driver Ed/Safety	92 Magnet School	277 Remedial Math K-12	750 Chief Innovation Officer	A = Alternative Program			
81 Gifted/Talented	93 Parental Involvement	280 Literacy Coach	751 Chief of Staff	G = Adult Classes	f = Facebook		
82 Video Services	95 Tech Prep Program	285 STEM	752 Social Emotional Learning	M = Magnet Program			
83 Substance Abuse Prev	97 Chief Infomation Officer	286 Digital Learning		T = Title I Schoolwide	t = Twitter		
84 Erate	98 Chief Technology Officer	288 Common Core Standards	Other School Types	V = Career & Tech Ed Programs			
85 AIDS Education	270 Character Education	294 Accountability	Ⓐ = Alternative School				
88 Alternative/At Risk	271 Migrant Education	295 Network System	Ⓒ = Charter School	New Schools are shaded			
89 Multi-Cultural Curriculum	273 Teacher Mentor	296 Title II Programs	Ⓜ = Magnet School	New Superintendents and Principals are bold			
90 Social Work	274 Before/After Sch	297 Webmaster	Ⓨ = Year-Round School	Personnel with email addresses are underscored			

TX—235

Hunt County

Market Data Retrieval

Public Schs..Principal	Grd	Prgm	Enr/#Cls	SN	
Celeste Elem Sch 605 Cockrell St, Celeste 75423 Beth Ray	PK-5	T	204 14	60%	903/568-4721 Fax 903/568-4651
Celeste High Sch 609 FM 1562, Celeste 75423 James Branam	9-12	ATV	170 16	45%	903/568-4721 Fax 903/568-4115
Celeste Junior High Sch 200 S 5th St, Celeste 75423 Staci Beadles	6-8	T	115 10	54%	903/568-4721 Fax 903/568-4277

- **Commerce Independent Sch Dist** PID: 01032381   903/886-3755
  3315 Washington St, Commerce 75428   Fax 903/886-6025

Schools: 4 \ *Teachers:* 113 \ *Students:* 1,603 \ *Special Ed Students:* 170 \ *LEP Students:* 141 \ *College-Bound:* 75% \ *Ethnic:* Asian 2%, African American 23%, Hispanic 23%, Native American: 1%, Caucasian 51% \ *Exp:* $372 (High) \ *Poverty:* 24% \ *Title I:* $546,477 \ *Open-Close:* 08/13 - 05/22 \ *DTBP:* $561 (High) \

Charles Alderman 1,57
Dennis Yoakum 3,5
Jeff Davidson 6*
Patricia Tremmel 15
Rachel Myers 58
Ludonna Smithers 68,71,297
John Walker 2
Anika Whetstone 4
Mary Hendricks 11,296
Dr Andrea Ellis 27,31
Kathleen Hooten 67
Kathy Myers 85*

Public Schs..Principal	Grd	Prgm	Enr/#Cls	SN	
A C Williams Elem Sch 615 Culver St, Commerce 75428 Lisa Palazzetti	3-5	T	348 19	65%	903/886-3758 Fax 903/468-8030
Commerce Elem Sch 2900 FM 3218, Commerce 75428 Wanda Beane	PK-2	T	385 27	74%	903/886-3757 Fax 903/886-6112
Commerce High Sch 3800 Sregit Dr, Commerce 75428 Steve Drummond	9-12	TV	450 30	56%	903/886-3756 Fax 903/886-6209
Commerce Middle Sch 606 Culver St, Commerce 75428 Shenequa Miller	6-8	T	331 20	61%	903/886-3795 Fax 903/886-6102

- **Greenville Ind School Dist** PID: 01032446   903/457-2500
  4004 Moulton St, Greenville 75401   Fax 903/457-2575

Schools: 12 \ *Teachers:* 382 \ *Students:* 5,400 \ *Special Ed Students:* 579 \ *LEP Students:* 1,033 \ *Ethnic:* Asian 1%, African American 17%, Hispanic 45%, Native American: 1%, Caucasian 37% \ *Exp:* $201 (Med) \ *Poverty:* 27% \ *Title I:* $2,002,451 \ *Special Education:* $880,000 \ *Open-Close:* 08/19 - 05/28 \ *DTBP:* $189 (High)

Dr Demetrus Liggins 1
Greg Anderson 3
Kellie Jones 5
Sharon Boothe 8,15,74
Colleen Netterville 58,68
Rachael Driggers 69,70,294
Laureen Payne 81
Deidra Reeves 2,15,19
Sharee Osten 4
Noelle Bares 7,83,88
Dr Michelle Baird 34
John Kelso 67
Shannon Fulp 73,76,295
David Stone 295

Public Schs..Principal	Grd	Prgm	Enr/#Cls	SN	
Bowie Elem Sch 6005 Stonewall St, Greenville 75402 Lauren Habluetzel	K-5		530 22		903/457-2676 Fax 903/457-0725
Carver Elem Sch 2110 College St, Greenville 75401 Stacie Wilson	K-5	T	484 27	90%	903/457-0777 Fax 903/457-0786
Crockett Elem Sch 1316 Wolfe City Dr, Greenville 75401 Stacey Kluttz	K-5	T	319 19	86%	903/457-2684 Fax 903/457-0722
ⓐ Greenville Alt Center 3923 Henry St, Greenville 75401 Harold Gregory	7-12	T	13 4		903/457-2688 Fax 903/457-2689
Greenville High Sch 3515 Lions Lair Rd, Greenville 75402 Heath Jarvis	9-12	GTV	1,363 45	57%	903/457-2550 Fax 903/455-5158
Greenville Middle Sch 3611 Texas St, Greenville 75401 Dale Mason	7-8	TV	741 60	70%	903/457-2620 Fax 903/457-2628
Greenville Sixth Grade Center 3201 Stanford St, Greenville 75401 Lauren Habluetzel	6-6	T	370 50	72%	903/457-2660 Fax 903/457-2533
Katherine G Johnson STEM Acad 9315 Jack Finney Blvd, Greenville 75402 Stacey Kluttz	K-5		235		903/454-5050 Fax 903/454-5070
L P Waters Early Childhood Ctr 2504 Carver St, Greenville 75401 Sebastian Bozas	PK-PK	T	365 13	86%	903/457-2680 Fax 903/457-0745
Lamar Elem Sch 6321 Jack Finney Blvd, Greenville 75402 Lucretia Newton	K-5	T	651 28	53%	903/457-0765 Fax 903/457-0774
ⓐ New Horizons Learning Center 3923 Henry St, Greenville 75401 Harold Gregory	PK-12	T	66 8	76%	903/457-2688 Fax 903/457-2689
Travis Elem Sch 3201 Stanford St, Greenville 75401 Dawes Vincent	K-6		349 18		903/457-2696 Fax 903/457-2533

- **Lone Oak Ind School Dist** PID: 01032549   903/662-5427
  8162 US Highway 69 S, Lone Oak 75453   Fax 903/662-5290

Schools: 4 \ *Teachers:* 84 \ *Students:* 1,050 \ *Special Ed Students:* 132 \ *LEP Students:* 10 \ *Ethnic:* Asian 1%, African American 3%, Hispanic 9%, Native American: 1%, Caucasian 86% \ *Exp:* $318 (High) \ *Poverty:* 15% \ *Title I:* $196,443 \ *Open-Close:* 08/19 - 05/22 \ *DTBP:* $352 (High)

Lance Campbell 1
Wayne Shepherd 3
James Blunt 5
Jeff Hicks 8
Justin Ramm 67
Isaiah Whitehead 295
Gary Sorrells 2
Brenda Standifer 4
Luke Goode 6*
Mikayle Goss 11,84
Cassie Pinkston 73,76,297

Public Schs..Principal	Grd	Prgm	Enr/#Cls	SN	
ⓐ Lone Oak College St Campus 602 College St, Lone Oak 75453 Jared Smith	6-12		30		903/634-2071
Lone Oak Elem Sch 8080 US Highway 69 S, Lone Oak 75453 Elizabeth Luhn	PK-5	T	453 40	42%	903/662-5151 Fax 903/662-0973
Lone Oak High Sch 8204 Highway 69 S, Lone Oak 75453 Janee Carter	9-12	ATV	356 30	38%	903/662-0980 Fax 903/662-0984
Lone Oak Middle Sch 8160 Highway 69 S, Lone Oak 75453 Shannon Wilhite	6-8	T	237 24	47%	903/662-5121 Fax 903/662-5017

1	Superintendent	8	Curric/Instruct K-12	19	Chief Financial Officer	29	Family/Consumer Science	39	Social Studies K-12	49	English/Lang Arts Elem	59	Special Education Elem	69	Academic Assessment
2	Bus/Finance/Purchasing	9	Curric/Instruct Elem	20	Art K-12	30	Adult Education	40	Social Studies Elem	50	English/Lang Arts Sec	60	Special Education Sec	70	Research/Development
3	Buildings And Grounds	10	Curric/Instruct Sec	21	Art Elem	31	Career/Sch-to-Work K-12	41	Social Studies Sec	51	Reading K-12	61	Foreign/World Lang K-12	71	Public Information
4	Food Service	11	Federal Program	22	Art Sec	32	Career/Sch-to-Work Elem	42	Science K-12	52	Reading Elem	62	Foreign/World Lang Elem	72	Summer School
5	Transportation	12	Title I	23	Music K-12	33	Career/Sch-to-Work Sec	43	Science Elem	53	Reading Sec	63	Foreign/World Lang Sec	73	Instructional Tech
6	Athletic	13	Title V	24	Music Elem	34	Early Childhood Ed	44	Science Sec	54	Remedial Reading K-12	64	Religious Education K-12	74	Inservice Training
7	Health Services	14	Asst Superintendent	25	Music Sec	35	Health/Phys Education	45	Math K-12	55	Remedial Reading Elem	65	Religious Education Elem	75	Marketing/Distributive
		15	Instructional Media Svcs	26	Business Education	36	Guidance Services K-12	46	Math Elem	56	Remedial Reading Sec	66	Religious Education Sec	76	Info Systems
		16	Chief Operations Officer	27	Career & Tech Ed	37	Guidance Services Elem	47	Math Sec	57	Bilingual/ELL	67	School Board President	77	Psychological Assess
		17	Chief Academic Officer	28	Technology Education	38	Guidance Services Sec	48	English/Lang Arts K-12	58	Special Education K-12	68	Teacher Personnel	78	Affirmative Action

Texas School Directory — Hutchinson County

- **Quinlan Ind School Dist** PID: 01032575 — 903/356-1200
  401 E Richmond, Quinlan 75474 — Fax 903/356-1201

Schools: 5 \ **Teachers:** 167 \ **Students:** 2,725 \ **Special Ed Students:** 319 \ **LEP Students:** 241 \ **Ethnic:** African American 1%, Hispanic 25%, Native American: 1%, Caucasian 73% \ **Exp:** $469 (High) \ **Poverty:** 21% \ **Title I:** $802,949 \ **Special Education:** $664,000 \ **Open-Close:** 08/19 - 05/21 \ **DTBP:** $158 (High)

Name	Ref
Jeff Irvin	1
Tommy Underwood	3,5,7,91
Gary Overstreet	5
Alice Lafferty	10
Michael Roberts	16,73,295*
Lori Edwards	57*
Kenny Stone	67
Tiffony Upchurch	71
Anna Baker	76
Steve Walden	91
Billie Miller	2
Brenda Stone	4
Todd Wallace	6*
Kathleen Witte	11,57,74,271,285,294,298
Jenifer Hogan	36*
Sheila Jones	58*
Sherry Reville	68
Kathy Goleman	75
Donna Hopson	85*

Public Schs..Principal	Grd	Prgm	Enr/#Cls	SN	
Butler Intermediate Sch 410 Clardy Dr, Quinlan 75474 **Lindsay Walker**	3-5	T	559 29	68%	903/356-1400 Fax 903/356-1499
C B Thompson Middle Sch 423 Panther Path, Quinlan 75474 **Brian Kinsworthy**	6-8	T	545 38	66%	903/356-1500 Fax 903/356-1599
D C Cannon Elem Sch 315 State Highway 34 S, Quinlan 75474 **Angela House**	PK-2	T	705 30	80%	903/356-1300 Fax 903/356-1399
Ⓐ Discipline Ed Alternative Sch 425 Panther Path, Quinlan 75474 **Gary Pamplin**	6-12		25 4		903/356-1575 Fax 903/356-1598
Ford High Sch 10064 State Highway Spur 264, Quinlan 75474 **Jason Wallen**	9-12	GTV	821 50	55%	903/356-1600 Fax 903/356-1699

- **Wolfe City Ind School Dist** PID: 01032616 — 903/496-2283
  505 W Dallas St, Wolfe City 75496 — Fax 903/496-7905

Schools: 3 \ **Teachers:** 55 \ **Students:** 690 \ **Special Ed Students:** 67 \ **LEP Students:** 25 \ **College-Bound:** 10% \ **Ethnic:** Asian 1%, African American 5%, Hispanic 15%, Caucasian 78% \ **Exp:** $598 (High) \ **Poverty:** 17% \ **Title I:** $116,698 \ **Special Education:** $186,000 \ **Open-Close:** 08/13 - 05/28 \ **DTBP:** $345 (High)

Name	Ref
Anthony Figueroa	1,83
Jessie Strayhorn	3,5
Darren Anderson	6
Sheila Gardner	8,73,286,288
Billy Eldridge	31,69,77*
Ola Owens	67
Donna Gazlick	88
Cindy McIlveene	2
Marcie Duncan	4
Kimberly Johnson	7
Mikayle Goss	11,84,271,296
Sondra Northcutt	57,58
Nancy Sanders	76
Vick Lemieux	295

Public Schs..Principal	Grd	Prgm	Enr/#Cls	SN	
Wolfe City Elem Sch 501 W Dallas St, Wolfe City 75496 **Ginger White**	PK-5		323 17		903/496-7333
Wolfe City High Sch 8353 Highway 34 N, Wolfe City 75496 **Rose Gardner**	9-12	TV	204 22	54%	903/496-2891 Fax 903/496-7124
Wolfe City Middle Sch 505 W Dallas St, Wolfe City 75496 **Melanie Williams**	6-8	T	147 12	60%	903/496-7333 Fax 903/496-2112

HUNT PRIVATE SCHOOLS

Private Schs..Principal	Grd	Prgm	Enr/#Cls	SN	
Frisco Montessori Academy 8890 Meadow Hill Dr, Frisco 75033 Jody Rosen	PK-8		202 12		972/712-7400 Fax 972/712-6441
Grace Covenant Academy 8000 Sanctuary Dr, Frisco 75033 Shannon Behrman	K-12		158		972/836-9422 Fax 972/528-7297 f t
Greenville Christian Sch 8420 Jack Finney Blvd, Greenville 75402 Mark Reisner	PK-12		200 30		903/454-1111 Fax 903/455-8470

HUTCHINSON COUNTY

HUTCHINSON PUBLIC SCHOOLS

- **Borger Ind School Dist** PID: 01032642 — 806/273-6481
  200 E 9th St, Borger 79007 — Fax 806/273-1066

Schools: 6 \ **Teachers:** 198 \ **Students:** 2,800 \ **Special Ed Students:** 291 \ **LEP Students:** 252 \ **Ethnic:** African American 3%, Hispanic 47%, Native American: 1%, Caucasian 48% \ **Exp:** $338 (High) \ **Poverty:** 16% \ **Title I:** $504,203 \ **Special Education:** $500,000 \ **Open-Close:** 08/26 - 05/29 \ **DTBP:** $173 (High)

Name	Ref
Chance Welch	1
Jeri Jett	2
Joy Howard	4
Eric Wilson	6
Rachel Ach	16*
Patti Brown	58,275
Barbie Schroader	69,271,285
Brad Carpenter	91
Fay Hooper	2
Pete Loftis	3
Caleb Hidalgo	5
Amy Blansett	11,15,38,57,273,296,298
Danielle Watson	38*
Leslie Sharp	67
Michael Bos	73,84,295

Public Schs..Principal	Grd	Prgm	Enr/#Cls	SN	
Ⓥ Borger High Sch 600 W 1st St, Borger 79007 **Matt Ammerman**	9-12	AMTV	748 40	43%	806/273-1029 Fax 806/273-1036
Borger Intermediate Sch 1321 S Florida St, Borger 79007 **Brandon Harris**	5-6	T	413	54%	806/273-4342 Fax 806/273-4343
Borger Middle Sch 1321 S Florida St, Borger 79007 Michael Cano	7-8	TV	402	53%	806/273-1037 Fax 806/273-1069
Crockett Elem Sch 400 Kaye St, Borger 79007 Randal Hatfield	3-4	T	379 20	52%	806/273-1054 Fax 806/273-1067
Gateway Elem Sch 401 Tristram St, Borger 79007 Teresa Bodey	1-2	T	356 25	59%	806/273-1044 Fax 806/273-1071
Paul Belton Early Chldhd Ctr 800 N McGee St, Borger 79007 Judy Cooper	PK-K	T	438 16	58%	806/273-1059 Fax 806/273-1070

#	Category	#	Category	#	Category
79	Student Personnel	91	Safety/Security	275	Response To Intervention
80	Driver Ed/Safety	92	Magnet School	277	Remedial Math K-12
81	Gifted/Talented	93	Parental Involvement	280	Literacy Coach
82	Video Services	95	Tech Prep Program	285	STEM
83	Substance Abuse Prev	97	Chief Information Officer	286	Digital Learning
84	Erate	98	Chief Technology Officer	288	Common Core Standards
85	AIDS Education	270	Character Education	294	Accountability
88	Alternative/At Risk	271	Migrant Education	295	Network System
89	Multi-Cultural Curriculum	273	Teacher Mentor	296	Title II Programs
90	Social Work	274	Before/After Sch	297	Webmaster

298	Grant Writer/Ptnrships
750	Chief Innovation Officer
751	Chief of Staff
752	Social Emotional Learning

Other School Types
- Ⓐ = Alternative School
- Ⓒ = Charter School
- Ⓜ = Magnet School
- Ⓨ = Year-Round School

School Programs
- A = Alternative Program
- G = Adult Classes
- M = Magnet Program
- T = Title I Schoolwide
- V = Career & Tech Ed Programs

Social Media
- f = Facebook
- t = Twitter

New Schools are shaded
New Superintendents and Principals are bold
Personnel with email addresses are underscored

Irion County

Market Data Retrieval

- **Plemons-Stinnett-Phillips CISD** PID: 01032836   806/878-2858
  603 S Main St, Stinnett 79083   Fax 806/878-3585

Schools: 3 \ **Teachers:** 74 \ **Students:** 675 \ **Special Ed Students:** 77 \ **LEP Students:** 4 \ **College-Bound:** 50% \ **Ethnic:** Hispanic 22%, Native American: 2%, Caucasian 75% \ **Exp:** $229 (Med) \ **Poverty:** 19% \ **Title I:** $104,870 \ **Special Education:** $144,000 \ **Open-Close:** 08/21 - 05/20 \ **DTBP:** $347 (High)

Bill Wiggins 1	Bettye Stevens 2
Greg Drennan 3,5,91	Pamela Shaw 4
Lori Williams 7,35,83,85*	Jimmy Amaro 8,11,15,69,288
Shawna Lamb 34	Kendra Franklin 36,88*
Tim Hall 67	

Public Schs..Principal	Grd	Prgm	Enr/#Cls	SN	
West Texas Elem Sch 600 Stewart St, Stinnett 79083 Shawna Lamb	PK-5	T	333 26	39%	806/878-2103 Fax 806/878-4213
West Texas High Sch 600 Stewart Street, Stinnett 79083 Kent Torbert	9-12	T	215 24	38%	806/878-2456 Fax 806/878-4242
West Texas Middle Sch 22 Farm Rd, Stinnett 79083 Matthew Tucker	6-8	T	140 18	32%	806/878-2247 Fax 806/878-3434

- **Sanford-Fritch Ind School Dist** PID: 01032771   806/397-0159
  540 Eagle Blvd, Fritch 79036   Fax 806/397-0629

Schools: 3 \ **Teachers:** 68 \ **Students:** 737 \ **Special Ed Students:** 109 \ **College-Bound:** 37% \ **Ethnic:** Hispanic 10%, Native American: 1%, Caucasian 88% \ **Exp:** $352 (High) \ **Poverty:** 8% \ **Title I:** $77,353 \ **Special Education:** $206,000 \ **Open-Close:** 08/15 - 05/21 \ **DTBP:** $399 (High)

Jim McClellan 1,83	Richard Hein 2,11,73
Houston Moos 6*	Edie Allen 8,15
Stacey Boothe 67	Brett Field 73,84

Public Schs..Principal	Grd	Prgm	Enr/#Cls	SN	
Sanford Fritch Elem Sch 201 N Hoyne Ave, Fritch 79036 Edie Allen	PK-5	T	358 34	39%	806/397-0159 Fax 806/397-0627
Sanford Fritch High Sch 538 Eagle Blvd, Fritch 79036 Jason Garrison	9-12	GV	210 28	26%	806/359-0159 Fax 806/359-0625
Sanford Fritch Jr High Sch 536 Eagle Blvd, Fritch 79036 Dixie Watson	6-8	T	169 25	45%	806/397-0159 Fax 806/397-0626

- **Spring Creek Ind School Dist** PID: 01032812   806/273-6791
  9849 FM 2171, Skellytown 79080

Schools: 1 \ **Teachers:** 12 \ **Students:** 92 \ **Special Ed Students:** 3 \ **LEP Students:** 3 \ **Ethnic:** Hispanic 15%, Native American: 3%, Caucasian 82% \ **Exp:** $839 (High) \ **Poverty:** 9% \ **Open-Close:** 08/07 - 05/21

Mandy Poer 1,11,73,83	April Cross 8
Heather Weatherford 57,58*	Bob Kasch 67

Public Schs..Principal	Grd	Prgm	Enr/#Cls	SN	
Spring Creek Sch 9849 FM 2171, Skellytown 79080 Shawna Lamb	K-12		92 7	22%	806/273-6791

IRION COUNTY

IRION PUBLIC SCHOOLS

- **Irion Co Ind School Dist** PID: 01032862   325/835-6111
  302 N 3rd St, Mertzon 76941   Fax 325/835-2017

Schools: 2 \ **Teachers:** 27 \ **Students:** 275 \ **Special Ed Students:** 18 \ **College-Bound:** 100% \ **Ethnic:** African American 2%, Hispanic 36%, Caucasian 62% \ **Exp:** $467 (High) \ **Poverty:** 12% \ **Title I:** $33,516 \ **Open-Close:** 08/15 - 05/22 \ **DTBP:** $334 (High)

Donny Clausen 1	Robert Helms 2
Rick Forges 3	Tony Smith 4
Jacob Conner 6*	Gina Feller 7*
Jessica Parker 9	Shannon Chapman 10,11,296*
Kathy Settle 60*	Vincinte Flores 67
Raymond Flores 73,295*	Leann Rutherford 83,88,270*

Public Schs..Principal	Grd	Prgm	Enr/#Cls	SN	
Irion County High Sch 309 N 3rd St, Mertzon 76941 Shannon Chapman	7-12	ATV	132 15	31%	325/835-2881 Fax 325/835-2298
Irion Elem Sch 302 N 3rd St, Mertzon 76941 Jessica Parker	K-6	T	121 20	32%	325/835-3991 Fax 325/835-2281

JACK COUNTY

JACK PUBLIC SCHOOLS

- **Bryson Ind School Dist** PID: 01032898   940/392-3281
  300 N McCloud St, Bryson 76427   Fax 940/392-2086

Schools: 1 \ **Teachers:** 21 \ **Students:** 255 \ **Special Ed Students:** 25 \ **LEP Students:** 7 \ **College-Bound:** 50% \ **Ethnic:** Hispanic 11%, Native American: 1%, Caucasian 88% \ **Exp:** $443 (High) \ **Poverty:** 30% \ **Title I:** $99,385 \ **Open-Close:** 08/14 - 05/20 \ **DTBP:** $386 (High) \ 🅵 🆃

Greg London 1,11	Tina Register 2
Debbie Hearne 8,12,69*	Ann Decker 16,28*
Britney Hanks 58*	Bob Hauger 67

Public Schs..Principal	Grd	Prgm	Enr/#Cls	SN	
Bryson Sch 300 N McCloud St, Bryson 76427 Gary Kirby	PK-12	TV	255 24	49%	940/392-2601 Fax 940/392-2238

---

1 Superintendent	8 Curric/Instruct K-12	19 Chief Financial Officer	29 Family/Consumer Science	39 Social Studies K-12	49 English/Lang Arts Elem	59 Special Education Elem	69 Academic Assessment
2 Bus/Finance/Purchasing	9 Curric/Instruct Elem	20 Art K-12	30 Adult Education	40 Social Studies Elem	50 English/Lang Arts Sec	60 Special Education Sec	70 Research/Development
3 Buildings And Grounds	10 Curric/Instruct Sec	21 Art Elem	31 Career/Sch-to-Work K-12	41 Social Studies Sec	51 Reading K-12	61 Foreign/World Lang K-12	71 Public Information
4 Food Service	11 Federal Program	22 Art Sec	32 Career/Sch-to-Work Elem	42 Science K-12	52 Reading Elem	62 Foreign/World Lang Elem	72 Summer School
5 Transportation	12 Title I	23 Music K-12	33 Career/Sch-to-Work Sec	43 Science Elem	53 Reading Sec	63 Foreign/World Lang Sec	73 Instructional Tech
6 Athletic	13 Title V	24 Music Elem	34 Early Childhood Ed	44 Science Sec	54 Remedial Reading K-12	64 Religious Education K-12	74 Inservice Training
7 Health Services	15 Asst Superintendent	25 Music Sec	35 Health/Phys Education	45 Math K-12	55 Remedial Reading Elem	65 Religious Education Elem	75 Marketing/Distributive
	16 Instructional Media Svcs	26 Business Education	36 Guidance Services K-12	46 Math Elem	56 Remedial Reading Sec	66 Religious Education Sec	76 Info Systems
	17 Chief Operations Officer	27 Career & Tech Ed	37 Guidance Services Elem	47 Math Sec	57 Bilingual/ELL	67 School Board President	77 Psychological Assess
	18 Chief Academic Officer	28 Technology Education	38 Guidance Services Sec	48 English/Lang Arts K-12	58 Special Education K-12	68 Teacher Personnel	78 Affirmative Action

Texas School Directory

Jackson County

• Jacksboro Ind Sch Dist PID: 01032927
750 W Belknap St, Jacksboro 76458
940/567-7203
Fax 940/567-2214

Schools: 3 \ **Teachers:** 79 \ **Students:** 1,050 \ **Special Ed Students:** 96 \
LEP Students: 141 \ **Ethnic:** Asian 1%, African American 1%, Hispanic 33%,
Native American: 1%, Caucasian 64% \ **Exp:** $817 (High) \ **Poverty:** 20% \
Title I: $227,957 \ **Open-Close:** 08/16 - 05/22 \ **DTBP:** $356 (High) \ f t

Dwain Milam	1	
Craig Adkins	3,4,91	
Brannon Rodgers	6,35*	
Wade Wesley	8,11,57,271,275,288,296,298	
Dori Taylor	36,69,83,85*	
Carl Depew	73,76,286	
Christy Thomas	2,84	
Greg Sanders	5*	
Taylor Martin	7*	
Kevin Thomas	27*	
Brent Hackley	67	

Public Schs..Principal	Grd	Prgm	Enr/#Cls	SN	
Jacksboro Elem Sch 1677 N Main St, Jacksboro 76458 Aaron Hannah	PK-5	T	527 26	66%	940/567-7206 Fax 940/567-2603 f t
Jacksboro High Sch 1400 N Main St, Jacksboro 76458 Starla Sanders	9-12	GTV	284 24	49%	940/567-7204 Fax 940/567-6028
Jacksboro Middle Sch 812 W Belknap St, Jacksboro 76458 Sara Mathis	6-8	TV	230 25	67%	940/567-7205 Fax 940/567-2681

• Perrin-Whitt Cons Ind Sch Dist PID: 01032965
216 N Benson St, Perrin 76486
940/798-3718
Fax 940/798-3071

Schools: 2 \ **Teachers:** 29 \ **Students:** 330 \ **Special Ed Students:** 35
\ **LEP Students:** 15 \ **College-Bound:** 54% \ **Ethnic:** Hispanic 19%,
Caucasian 80% \ **Exp:** $466 (High) \ **Poverty:** 12% \ **Title I:** $48,698 \
Open-Close: 08/15 - 05/21 \ **DTBP:** $333 (High) \ f

Cliff Gilmore	1	
Ben Staggs	6,73*	
Dianna Gilmore	36*	
Fran Self	2	
Loren Sell	10*	
Chris Keeney	67	

Public Schs..Principal	Grd	Prgm	Enr/#Cls	SN	
Perrin-Whitt Elem Sch 216 N Benson St, Perrin 76486 Teresa Mathis	PK-6	T	189 16	56%	940/798-2395
Perrin-Whitt High Sch 216 N Benson St, Perrin 76486 Loren Sell	7-12	TV	152 40	53%	940/798-3718

JACK PRIVATE SCHOOLS

Private Schs..Principal	Grd	Prgm	Enr/#Cls	SN	
Grace Christian Academy-Main 1999 W FM 1885, Perrin 76486 Jody McGiothlin	PK-12		901		682/262-9288 f

JACKSON COUNTY

JACKSON PUBLIC SCHOOLS

• Edna Ind School Dist PID: 01032991
601 N Wells St, Edna 77957
361/782-3573
Fax 361/781-1002

Schools: 4 \ **Teachers:** 121 \ **Students:** 1,500 \ **Special Ed Students:** 143
\ **LEP Students:** 158 \ **College-Bound:** 48% \ **Ethnic:** Asian 2%,
African American 14%, Hispanic 47%, Caucasian 37% \ **Exp:** $512 (High)
\ **Poverty:** 22% \ **Title I:** $405,795 \ **Special Education:** $167,000 \
Open-Close: 08/14 - 05/21 \ **DTBP:** $364 (High)

Robert Oconner	1	
Sonny Strelec	3,5,80,91	
Robert Draper	6	
Brandie Roe	8,57,73,83,285,286,288,296	
Andrew Wallace	16*	
Amber Stansberry	34,58,77	
Patrick Brzozowski	67	
Daniel Harper	2,19	
Zach Norris	4	
Katie Fojtik	7	
Madalyn Maresh	11,298	
Dustin Lambden	16,76,295	
April Cubriel	36	

Public Schs..Principal	Grd	Prgm	Enr/#Cls	SN	
Ⓐ Edna Alternative Sch 112 W Ash St, Edna 77957 Sonya Proper	6-12	T	50	77%	361/782-9051
Edna Elem Sch 400 Apollo Dr, Edna 77957 Katie Kucera	PK-5	AT	780	68%	361/782-2953 Fax 361/781-1028
Edna High Sch 1303 W Gayle St, Edna 77957 Scott Kana	9-12	ATV	455	55%	361/782-5255 Fax 361/781-1014
Edna Junior High Sch 505 W Gayle St, Edna 77957 Brandie Roe	6-8	AT	324 30	62%	361/782-2351 Fax 361/781-1025

• Ganado Ind School Dist PID: 01033050
210 S 6th St, Ganado 77962
361/771-4200
Fax 361/771-2280

Schools: 3 \ **Teachers:** 58 \ **Students:** 750 \ **Special Ed Students:** 69
\ **LEP Students:** 78 \ **College-Bound:** 50% \ **Ethnic:** African American
3%, Hispanic 53%, Caucasian 44% \ **Exp:** $407 (High) \ **Poverty:** 18% \
Title I: $119,328 \ **Open-Close:** 08/21 - 05/22 \ **DTBP:** $343 (High) \ t

Dr John Hardwick	1	
Bert Skoruppa	3	
Tracey Galetti	4*	
Brent Bennett	6	
Virgil Knowlton	11,274*	
Manda Lesak	31,69,271	
Jamie Ramey	58	
David Segers	285*	
Wendy Nixon	2	
Tracey Galetti	4	
Anthony Henslay	5	
Sharon Foltyn	8,288	
Jenny Nelson	16,73,286,295,296*	
Manda Lesak	31,69,271*	
Clay Green	67	

Public Schs..Principal	Grd	Prgm	Enr/#Cls	SN	
Ganado Elem Sch 310 S 5th St, Ganado 77962 Jennifer Stephenson	PK-5	T	369	66%	361/771-4250 Fax 361/771-3403
Ganado High Sch 501 W Devers St, Ganado 77962 David Segers	9-12	ATV	228 35	52%	361/771-4300 Fax 361/771-3479

---

79 Student Personnel	91 Safety/Security	275 Response To Intervention	298 Grant Writer/Ptnrships	**School Programs**	**Social Media**
80 Driver Ed/Safety	92 Magnet School	277 Remedial Math K-12	750 Chief Innovation Officer	A = Alternative Program	f = Facebook
81 Gifted/Talented	93 Parental Involvement	280 Literacy Coach	751 Chief of Staff	G = Adult Classes	t = Twitter
82 Video Services	95 Tech Prep Program	285 STEM	752 Social Emotional Learning	M = Magnet Program	
83 Substance Abuse Prev	97 Chief Information Officer	286 Digital Learning		T = Title I Schoolwide	
84 Erate	98 Chief Technology Officer	288 Common Core Standards	**Other School Types**	V = Career & Tech Ed Programs	
85 AIDS Education	270 Accountability	294 Accountability	Ⓐ = Alternative School		
88 Alternative/At Risk	271 Migrant Education	295 Network System	Ⓒ = Charter School	New Schools are shaded	
89 Multi-Cultural Curriculum	273 Teacher Mentor	296 Title II Programs	Ⓜ = Magnet School	New Superintendents and Principals are bold	
90 Social Work	274 Before/After Sch	297 Webmaster	Ⓨ = Year-Round School	Personnel with email addresses are underscored	

TX—239

Jasper County

Market Data Retrieval

Ganado Junior High Sch — 6-8 — AT — 170 — 55% — 361/771-4309
501 West Devers, Ganado 77962 — Fax 361/771-4310
Joey Rosaloz

- **Industrial Ind School Dist** PID: 01033086 — 361/284-3226
  167 5th St, Vanderbilt 77991 — Fax 361/284-3349

Schools: 4 \ *Teachers:* 93 \ *Students:* 1,178 \ *Special Ed Students:* 107 \ *LEP Students:* 43 \ *College-Bound:* 66% \ *Ethnic:* African American 1%, Hispanic 29%, Caucasian 70% \ *Exp:* $428 (High) \ *Poverty:* 16% \ *Title I:* $174,756 \ *Open-Close:* 08/14 - 05/26 \ *DTBP:* $338 (High) \

Paul Darilek	1	Roxanne Rogers	2
Billy Barr	3	Barbara Thedford	4
James Dixon	6	Kathy Kuchler	7
Missy Klimitchek	8,11,74,270,273,294,296	Kristi Cope	16
Houston Cummings	20,23*	Dale Allen	67
Nathan Sappington	73,84,295		

Public Schs..Principal	Grd	Prgm	Enr/#Cls	SN	
Industrial Elem Sch East 390 Main Street, Vanderbilt 77991 **Lisa Baughman**	PK-5	T	314 17	47%	361/284-3317 Fax 361/284-3377
Industrial Elem Sch West Farm Road 444, Inez 77968 **Barbara Sides**	K-5		219 15	24%	361/782-3325 Fax 361/782-0010
Industrial High Sch 187 5th St, Vanderbilt 77991 **Jim Green**	9-12	AV	351 30	29%	361/284-3216 Fax 361/284-3328
Industrial Junior High Sch Three 5th St, Vanderbilt 77991 **Kim Schaefer**	6-8	T	294 17	32%	361/284-3226 Fax 361/284-3049

JASPER COUNTY

JASPER PUBLIC SCHOOLS

- **Brookeland Ind School Dist** PID: 01033141 — 409/698-2677
  187 Wildcat Walk, Brookeland 75931 — Fax 409/698-2533

Schools: 1 \ *Teachers:* 38 \ *Students:* 392 \ *Special Ed Students:* 55 \ *College-Bound:* 50% \ *Ethnic:* African American 4%, Hispanic 5%, Caucasian 90% \ *Exp:* $775 (High) \ *Poverty:* 26% \ *Title I:* $123,837 \ *Open-Close:* 08/26 - 05/29

Kevin McCugh	1,83	Tammi Haden	2
Donna Cooper	3,5*	Kathryn Thomas	4*
Dawn Moon	7*	Charlotte Odom	8,11,27,57,296,298*
Stacey Gillis	8,31,36,69,92,271*	Carol MacLeod	58*
Brett Holloway	67	Michael Defee	73,295*
Tammy Gilbert	81*	Micheal Defee	84
Deene McCland	294	Maranda Hightower	294*

Public Schs..Principal	Grd	Prgm	Enr/#Cls	SN	
Brookeland Sch Loop 149, Brookeland 75931 **Charlotte Odom**	PK-12	TV	392 42	66%	409/698-2677 Fax 409/698-8974

- **Buna Ind School Dist** PID: 01033177 — 409/994-5101
  1022 Tx State Highway 62, Buna 77612 — Fax 409/994-4808

Schools: 3 \ *Teachers:* 118 \ *Students:* 1,480 \ *Special Ed Students:* 152 \ *LEP Students:* 8 \ *College-Bound:* 55% \ *Ethnic:* African American 5%, Hispanic 3%, Native American: 1%, Caucasian 92% \ *Exp:* $271 (Med) \ *Poverty:* 13% \ *Title I:* $260,942 \ *Open-Close:* 08/21 - 05/22

Dr Donny Lee	1	George Talbert	2,3,17
Joe Menard	3,5	Bradley Morgan	6*
Kelley Peck	8,11,76,271	Jerry Gore	58
Keith Mullins	67	James McCaughey	295

Public Schs..Principal	Grd	Prgm	Enr/#Cls	SN	
Buna Elem Sch 650 County Road 725, Buna 77612 **Karen Hebert**	PK-5	T	762 40	42%	409/994-4840 Fax 409/994-5728
Buna High Sch FM 177 253, Buna 77612 **Mike Brewster**	9-12	GV	413 25	31%	409/994-4811 Fax 409/994-4818
Buna Junior High Sch 420 County Rd 751 A, Buna 77612 **Amber Flowers**	6-8	V	358 40	36%	409/994-4860 Fax 409/994-4810

- **Evadale Ind School Dist** PID: 01033218 — 409/276-1337
  908 Hwy 105, Evadale 77615 — Fax 409/276-1908

Schools: 2 \ *Teachers:* 43 \ *Students:* 450 \ *Special Ed Students:* 51 \ *LEP Students:* 4 \ *Ethnic:* Hispanic 5%, Caucasian 95% \ *Exp:* $339 (High) \ *Poverty:* 19% \ *Title I:* $70,123 \ *Special Education:* $93,000 \ *Open-Close:* 08/15 - 05/29 \ *DTBP:* $363 (High)

Gary Fairchild	1,11	Brandy Black	2
Shannon Adams	3,5,91	Pam Cox	4
Mark Williams	6*	Keisha Christian	7,85*
Ashley Powell	8	Chris Fikes	16,73,76,84,286,295
Christie Sylvester	16*	Piper Ayres	57,58,88
Jim Love	67	Margo Calhoun	68,71
Amy Haden	69	Rusty Minyard	83,288*

Public Schs..Principal	Grd	Prgm	Enr/#Cls	SN	
Evadale Elem Jr High Sch Highway 105 S, Evadale 77615 **Cheryl Jones**	PK-8		330 20		409/276-1337 Fax 409/276-1588
Evadale High Sch Highway 105 S, Evadale 77615 **Rusty Minyard**	9-12	V	155 15	21%	409/276-1337 Fax 409/276-1050

- **Jasper Ind School Dist** PID: 01033244 — 409/384-2401
  128 Park Ln, Jasper 75951 — Fax 409/382-1084

Schools: 4 \ *Teachers:* 178 \ *Students:* 2,390 \ *Special Ed Students:* 274 \ *LEP Students:* 184 \ *Ethnic:* African American 43%, Hispanic 18%, Caucasian 38% \ *Exp:* $321 (High) \ *Poverty:* 30% \ *Title I:* $1,224,789 \ *Special Education:* $494,000 \ *Open-Close:* 08/26 - 05/21 \ *DTBP:* $168 (High) \

Dr Steve Hyden	1	Paula Horton	2,294
Ronnie Bryan	3	Kimberly Dean	4
Donna Adams	5	Darrell Barbay	6*
Stacey Woolems	10,11,69,296	Kim Parker	58,77,88
Mike Durand	67	Denitro Headnot	73,76,295
John Sieboldt	91	Jennifer White	295

---

1 Superintendent	8 Curric/Instruct K-12	19 Chief Financial Officer	29 Family/Consumer Science	39 Social Studies K-12	49 English/Lang Arts Elem	59 Special Education Elem	69 Academic Assessment
2 Bus/Finance/Purchasing	9 Curric/Instruct Elem	20 Art K-12	30 Adult Education	40 Social Studies Elem	50 English/Lang Arts Sec	60 Special Education Sec	70 Research/Development
3 Buildings And Grounds	10 Curric/Instruct Sec	21 Art Elem	31 Career/Sch-to-Work K-12	41 Social Studies Sec	51 Reading K-12	61 Foreign/World Lang K-12	71 Public Information
4 Food Service	11 Federal Program	22 Art Sec	32 Career/Sch-to-Work Elem	42 Science K-12	52 Reading Elem	62 Foreign/World Lang Elem	72 Summer School
5 Transportation	12 Title I	23 Music K-12	33 Career/Sch-to-Work Sec	43 Science Elem	53 Reading Sec	63 Foreign/World Lang Sec	73 Instructional Tech
6 Athletic	13 Title V	24 Music Elem	34 Early Childhood Ed	44 Science Sec	54 Remedial Reading K-12	64 Religious Education K-12	74 Inservice Training
7 Health Services	14 Instructional Media Svcs	25 Music Sec	35 Health/Phys Education	45 Math K-12	55 Remedial Reading Elem	65 Religious Education Elem	75 Marketing/Distributive
	15 Asst Superintendent	26 Business Education	36 Guidance Services K-12	46 Math Elem	56 Remedial Reading Sec	66 Religious Education Sec	76 Info Systems
	16 Instructional Media Svcs	27 Career & Tech Ed	37 Guidance Services Elem	47 Math Sec	57 Bilingual/ELL	67 School Board President	77 Psychological Assess
	17 Chief Operations Officer	28 Technology Education	38 Guidance Services Sec	48 English/Lang Arts K-12	58 Special Education K-12	68 Teacher Personnel	78 Affirmative Action
	18 Chief Academic Officer						

Texas School Directory

Jefferson County

Public Schs..Principal	Grd	Prgm	Enr/#Cls	SN		
Jasper High Sch 400 Bulldog Ave, Jasper 75951 Victor Williams	9-12	TV	720		63%	409/384-3242 Fax 409/382-1310 [f]
Jasper Junior High Sch 211 2nd St, Jasper 75951 David Burt	6-8	T	576 60		73%	409/384-3585 Fax 409/384-4585 [f]
Jean C Few Primary Sch 225 Bulldog Ave, Jasper 75951 Ron Vickers	PK-3	T	826 65		84%	409/489-9808 Fax 409/382-1399 [f]
Parnell Elem Sch 151 Park St, Jasper 75951 William Davis	4-5	T	362 40		74%	409/384-2212 Fax 409/382-1114 [f][t]

- **Kirbyville Cons Ind Sch Dist** PID: 01033282   409/423-2284
  206 E Main St, Kirbyville 75956   Fax 409/423-2367

Schools: 3 \ *Teachers:* 103 \ *Students:* 1,400 \ *Special Ed Students:* 115 \ *LEP Students:* 32 \ *College-Bound:* 37% \ *Ethnic:* African American 9%, Hispanic 8%, Caucasian 82% \ *Exp:* $233 (Med) \ *Poverty:* 33% \ *Title I:* $618,831 \ *Open-Close:* 08/14 - 05/21

Georgia Sayers	1,11	James Dodson	3
Cindy Barlow	4	Craig Jones	6
James Gaspard	16,73,295*	Chad George	67

Public Schs..Principal	Grd	Prgm	Enr/#Cls	SN		
Kirbyville Elem Sch 2100 S Margaret Ave, Kirbyville 75956 Kristi Gore	PK-5	T	776		64%	409/423-8526 Fax 409/423-3753
Kirbyville High Sch 1100 S Margaret Ave, Kirbyville 75956 Holli Farias	9-12	V	398 35			409/423-7500 Fax 409/423-5313
Kirbyville Junior High Sch 2200 S Margaret Ave, Kirbyville 75956 Rod Anderson	6-8	T	330 19		59%	409/420-0692 Fax 409/423-6654

JEFF DAVIS COUNTY

JEFF DAVIS PUBLIC SCHOOLS

- **Fort Davis Ind School Dist** PID: 01033323   432/426-4440
  400 W Webster Ave, Fort Davis 79734   Fax 432/426-3841

Schools: 2 \ *Teachers:* 24 \ *Students:* 230 \ *Special Ed Students:* 25 \ *LEP Students:* 39 \ *College-Bound:* 89% \ *Ethnic:* Hispanic 63%, Caucasian 37% \ *Exp:* $452 (High) \ *Poverty:* 20% \ *Title I:* $47,202 \ *Open-Close:* 08/26 - 05/21 \ *DTBP:* $350 (High)

Graydon Hicks	1	Velvet Hardy	2
Luane Porter	11*	Hortencia Aguilar	13
Katie Nolan	37	David Whitesell	67
Curtis Pittman	73*		

Public Schs..Principal	Grd	Prgm	Enr/#Cls	SN		
Dirks-Anderson Sch Highway 17, Fort Davis 79734 Allison Scott	PK-5		106 8			432/426-4454 Fax 432/426-4456
Fort Davis Jr Sr High Sch 401 W Webster Ave, Fort Davis 79734 Luane Porter	6-12	T	125 17		53%	432/426-4444 Fax 432/426-4449

- **Valentine Ind School Dist** PID: 01033359   432/467-2671
  209 E Kentucky St, Valentine 79854   Fax 432/467-2004

Schools: 1 \ *Teachers:* 11 \ *Students:* 30 \ *Special Ed Students:* 3 \ *LEP Students:* 11 \ *College-Bound:* 100% \ *Ethnic:* Asian 2%, Hispanic 65%, Caucasian 33% \ *Exp:* $1,711 (High) \ *Poverty:* 20% \ *Title I:* $2,424 \ *Open-Close:* 08/22 - 05/28 \ *DTBP:* $394 (High)

Debbie Engle	1,11,57,83	Ernie Villarreal	2
Dawn Houy	8,36,288*	William Miller	67
Brad Bernards	73,286,295*		

Public Schs..Principal	Grd	Prgm	Enr/#Cls	SN		
Valentine Sch 209 E Kentucky St, Valentine 79854 William Cook	PK-12		30 11		72%	432/467-2671 Fax 432/467-2114

JEFFERSON COUNTY

JEFFERSON COUNTY SCHOOLS

County Schs..Principal	Grd	Prgm	Enr/#Cls	SN	
ⓐ Jefferson Co Youth Academy 5030 Highway 69 S, Beaumont 77705 Steve Gatewood	6-12		42 5		409/720-4078 Fax 409/720-4051

JEFFERSON PUBLIC SCHOOLS

- **Beaumont Ind School Dist** PID: 01034092   409/617-5000
  3395 Harrison Ave, Beaumont 77706   Fax 409/617-5184

Schools: 28 \ *Teachers:* 1,185 \ *Students:* 18,697 \ *Special Ed Students:* 1,398 \ *LEP Students:* 1,854 \ *College-Bound:* 55% \ *Ethnic:* Asian 3%, African American 60%, Hispanic 24%, Caucasian 13% \ *Exp:* $403 (High) \ *Poverty:* 30% \ *Title I:* $9,018,444 \ *Special Education:* $3,587,000 \ *Open-Close:* 08/14 - 05/28 \ *DTBP:* $200 (High)

Dr John Frossard	1	Cheryl Hernandez	2,19
Tiffany Eckenrod	4	Gwendolyn Lacy	12,34
Anita Frank	15	Dr Shannon Allen	15
Todd Coleman	15	Rosalind Eyre	16
Ronnie Bryant	20,23*	Dr Donna Prudhomme	27,31*
Rodney Saveat	35	Rachel Guidry	36,83
Monica Reynolds	39,81	Patsy MaGee	42
Sherri Wills	45	Julie Corona	57*
Tammy Diller	58	A Bernard	67
Nakisha Burns	71	Dr Kimber Knight	73
Cindy Saveat	79	Jamie Le Jeune	295
Adam Thibodeaux	297	Jody Slaughter	750

Public Schs..Principal	Grd	Prgm	Enr/#Cls	SN		
Amelia Elem Sch 565 S Major Dr, Beaumont 77707 Dimitrise Haynes	PK-5	T	767 27		79%	409/617-6000 Fax 409/617-6024

---

79 Student Personnel	91 Safety/Security	275 Response To Intervention	298 Grant Writer/Ptnrships	School Programs	Social Media	
80 Driver Ed/Safety	92 Magnet School	277 Remedial Math K-12	750 Chief Innovation Officer	A = Alternative Program		
81 Gifted/Talented	93 Parental Involvement	280 Literacy Coach	751 Chief of Staff	G = Adult Classes	[f] = Facebook	
82 Video Services	95 Tech Prep Program	285 STEM	752 Social Emotional Learning	M = Magnet Program		
83 Substance Abuse Prev	97 Chief Information Officer	286 Digital Learning		T = Title I Schoolwide	[t] = Twitter	
84 Erate	98 Chief Technology Officer	288 Common Core Standards	Other School Types	V = Career & Tech Ed Programs		
85 AIDS Education	270 Accountability	294 Accountability	ⓐ = Alternative School			
88 Alternative/At Risk	271 Migrant Education	295 Network System	ⓒ = Charter School	New Schools are shaded		
89 Multi-Cultural Curriculum	273 Teacher Mentor	296 Title II Programs	ⓜ = Magnet School	New Superintendents and Principals are bold		
90 Social Work	274 Before/After Sch	297 Webmaster	ⓨ = Year-Round School	Personnel with email addresses are underscored		

Jefferson County

School	Grades	Prgm	Enr/#Cls	SN	Phone
Beaumont Early Clg High Sch 3410 Austin St, Beaumont 77706 Melanie Pharis	9-12		127		409/617-6600
ⓜ Beaumont United High Sch 3443 Fannett Rd, Beaumont 77705 Ron Jackson	9-12	GV	1,193		409/617-5400 Fax 409/617-5396
Bingham Head Start Ctr 5265 Kenneth Ave, Beaumont 77705 Carolyn Little	PK-PK	T	510 26	99%	409/617-6200 Fax 409/617-6203
Blanchette Elem Sch 2550 Sarah St, Beaumont 77705 April Johnston	PK-5	T	628 25	95%	409/617-6300 Fax 409/617-6203
Caldwood Elem Sch 102 Berkshire Ln, Beaumont 77707 Julie Corona	PK-5	T	616 33	88%	409/617-6025 Fax 409/617-6048
Charlton-Pollard Elem Sch 1695 Irving St, Beaumont 77701 Charisma Popillion	PK-5	T	489 24	96%	409/617-6075 Fax 409/617-6098
Curtis Elem Sch 6225 N Circuit Dr, Beaumont 77706 Glenetta Henley	PK-5	T	571 25	40%	409/617-6050 Fax 409/617-6073
Dishman Elem Sch 3475 Champions Dr, Beaumont 77707 Mellow Tatmon	PK-5	T	586 30	70%	409/617-6250 Fax 409/617-6274
Dr Mae Jones-Clark Elem Sch 3525 Cleveland St, Beaumont 77703 Yvonne DuPont	PK-5	T	683 18	96%	409/617-6350 Fax 409/617-6346
Fehl-Price Elem Sch 3350 Blanchette St, Beaumont 77701 Stephanie Ling	PK-5	T	681 20	95%	409/617-6400 Fax 409/617-6421
Fletcher Elem Sch 1055 Avenue F, Beaumont 77701 Gloria Guillory	PK-5	T	462 35	96%	409/617-6100 Fax 409/617-6123
Guess Elem Sch 8055 Voth Rd, Beaumont 77708 Debra Oge	PK-5	T	558 45	69%	409/617-6125 Fax 409/617-6148
Homer Drive Elem Sch 8950 Homer Dr, Beaumont 77708 Belinda George	PK-5	T	701 28	91%	409/617-6225 Fax 409/617-6248
Lucas Pre-K Center 1750 E Lucas Dr, Beaumont 77703 Valencia Greenwood	PK-PK	T	309 19	95%	409/617-6450 Fax 409/617-6448
M L King Middle Sch 1400 Avenue A, Beaumont 77701 Dion Varnado	6-8	TV	662 35	91%	409/617-5850 Fax 409/617-5873
Marshall Middle Sch 6455 Gladys Ave, Beaumont 77706 **Paul Breaux**	6-8	TV	849 48	52%	409/617-5900 Fax 409/617-5924
Martin Elem Sch 3500 Pine St, Beaumont 77703 Tamara Long	PK-5	T	627 46	97%	409/617-6425 Fax 409/617-6446
ⓜ Odom Academy 2550 W Virginia St, Beaumont 77705 Lachandra Cobb-Eaglin	6-8	TV	847 50	80%	409/617-5925 Fax 409/617-5949
ⓐ Pathways Alt Learning Center 3410 Austin St, Beaumont 77706 **Charles Colvin**	6-12		56 13	92%	409/617-5206 Fax 409/617-5718
ⓐ Paul A Brown Alternative Ctr 1900 Pope St, Beaumont 77703 Paula Hood	9-12		115 25	87%	409/617-5720 Fax 409/617-5738
Pietzsch-MacArthur Elem Sch 4301 Highland Ave, Beaumont 77705 Audrey Collins	PK-5	T	881 70	95%	409/617-6475 Fax 409/617-6498
Regina-Howell Elem Sch 5850 Regina Ln, Beaumont 77706 **Kimberly Screen**	PK-5	T	812 35	42%	409/617-6190 Fax 409/617-6199
ⓜ Smith Magnet Middle Sch 4415 Concord Rd, Beaumont 77703 Shyulanda Randle-Filer	6-8	TV	534 58	94%	409/617-5825 Fax 409/617-5848
South Park Middle Sch 4500 Highland Ave, Beaumont 77705 Calvin Rice	6-8	TV	472	95%	409/617-5875 Fax 409/617-5898
Taylor Career & Tech Ctr 2330 North St, Beaumont 77702 Michael Shelton	Voc	G	500 30		409/617-5740 Fax 409/617-5759
Vincent Middle Sch 350 Eldridge Dr, Beaumont 77707 Missy Gimble	6-8	TV	603 89	80%	409/617-5950 Fax 409/617-5974
West Brook High Sch 8750 Phelan Blvd, Beaumont 77706 Diana Valdez	9-12	GTV	2,435 135	53%	409/617-5500 Fax 409/617-5582

● **Hamshire Fannett Ind Sch Dist** PID: 01033610 409/243-2133
12702 2nd St, Hamshire 77622 Fax 409/243-3437

Schools: 4 \ *Teachers:* 130 \ *Students:* 1,900 \ *Special Ed Students:* 143 \ *LEP Students:* 76 \ *College-Bound:* 59% \ *Ethnic:* Asian 2%, African American 6%, Hispanic 16%, Caucasian 76% \ *Exp:* $318 (High) \ *Poverty:* 11% \ *Title I:* $189,173 \ *Open-Close:* 08/15 - 05/21 \ *DTBP:* $353 (High)

Dr Dwaine Augustine .... 1 Allison Byrd 2,11,15
Angel Wingate .... 4 Mark Wagner 6,35
Jon Burris .... 8,11,88,271,273,294 Stephen Edwards 15,73*
Erin Laughlin .... 16 Casey Hancock 31*
Mandy Cormier .... 34* Marcy Bellenger 36
Bob Thuman .... 67 Rebecca Marshall 69*
David Parker 76,286,295

Public Schs..Principal	Grd	Prgm	Enr/#Cls	SN	Phone
Hamshire Fannett Elem Sch 23395 Burrell Wingate Rd, Beaumont 77705 Byron Miller	PK-3	T	625 30	36%	409/794-1412 Fax 409/794-1049
Hamshire Fannett High Sch 12552 2nd St, Hamshire 77622 Paul Shipman	9-12	AV	553 38	25%	409/243-2131 Fax 409/243-2518
Hamshire Fannett Interm Sch 11407 Dugat Rd, Beaumont 77705 **Marla Gilmore**	4-6	T	450 34	30%	409/794-1558 Fax 409/794-1787
Hamshire Fannett Middle Sch 11375 Dugat Rd, Beaumont 77705 Shawn Clubb	7-8		303 30	27%	409/794-1502 Fax 409/794-3042

● **Nederland Ind School Dist** PID: 01033660 409/724-2391
220 N 17th St, Nederland 77627 Fax 409/724-4280

Schools: 8 \ *Teachers:* 351 \ *Students:* 5,214 \ *Special Ed Students:* 521 \ *LEP Students:* 377 \ *College-Bound:* 66% \ *Ethnic:* Asian 7%, African American 9%, Hispanic 25%, Native American: 1%, Caucasian 59% \ *Exp:* $466 (High) \ *Poverty:* 13% \ *Title I:* $645,722 \ *Special Education:* $1,208,000 \ *Open-Close:* 08/19 - 05/28 \ *DTBP:* $181 (High) \

Dr Robin Perez .... 1 Melissa Wong 2
Kenny Litvik .... 3,5 Rena Bodden 4
Charles Polk .... 5 Monte Barrow 6,35*
Heather Barrow .... 9,81,89,271 Mike Laird 15,68,91,297
Stuart Kieschnick .... 15,57,88 Deidre Powell 34,36,54,58,77,79
Cindi Bordelon .... 38* Micah Molsey 67
Darrell Evans .... 69* Jeff McKinnon 69
Cindy Laird .... 73,84,95 Andre Rosales 295

---

1 Superintendent	8 Curric/Instruct K-12	19 Chief Financial Officer	29 Family/Consumer Science
2 Bus/Finance/Purchasing	9 Curric/Instruct Elem	20 Art K-12	30 Adult Education
3 Buildings And Grounds	10 Curric/Instruct Sec	21 Art Elem	31 Career/Sch-to-Work K-12
4 Food Service	11 Federal Program	22 Art Sec	32 Career/Sch-to-Work Elem
5 Transportation	12 Title I	23 Music K-12	33 Career/Sch-to-Work Sec
6 Athletic	13 Title V	24 Music Elem	34 Early Childhood Ed
7 Health Services	15 Asst Superintendent	25 Music Sec	35 Health/Phys Education
	16 Instructional Media Svcs	26 Business Education	36 Guidance Services K-12
	17 Chief Operations Officer	27 Career & Tech Ed	37 Guidance Services Elem
	18 Chief Academic Officer	28 Technology Education	38 Guidance Services Sec

39 Social Studies K-12	49 English/Lang Arts Elem	59 Special Education Elem	69 Academic Assessment
40 Social Studies Elem	50 English/Lang Arts Sec	60 Special Education Sec	70 Research/Development
41 Social Studies Sec	51 Reading K-12	61 Foreign/World Lang K-12	71 Public Information
42 Science K-12	52 Reading Elem	62 Foreign/World Lang Elem	72 Summer School
43 Science Elem	53 Reading Sec	63 Foreign/World Lang Sec	73 Instructional Tech
44 Science Sec	54 Remedial Reading K-12	64 Religious Education K-12	74 Inservice Training
45 Math K-12	55 Remedial Reading Elem	65 Religious Education Elem	75 Marketing/Distributive
46 Math Elem	56 Remedial Reading Sec	66 Religious Education Sec	76 Info Systems
47 Math Sec	57 Bilingual/ELL	67 School Board President	77 Psychological Assess
48 English/Lang Arts K-12	58 Special Education K-12	68 Teacher Personnel	78 Affirmative Action

Texas School Directory

Jefferson County

Public Schs..Principal	Grd	Prgm	Enr/#Cls	SN	
C O Wilson Middle Sch 2620 Helena Ave, Nederland 77627 Tina Oliver	5-8	V	852 40	33%	409/727-6224 Fax 409/726-2699
Central Middle Sch 200 17th St, Nederland 77627 **Natalie Gomez**	5-8	T	746	55%	409/727-5765 Fax 409/724-4275
Helena Park Elem Sch 2800 Helena Ave, Nederland 77627 Charlotte Junot	PK-4		632 30	32%	409/722-0462 Fax 409/726-2698 [f]
Highland Park Elem Sch 200 S 6th St, Nederland 77627 Charlee Yeaman	PK-4	T	542 25	42%	409/722-0236 Fax 409/726-2694
Hillcrest Elem Sch 2611 Avenue H, Nederland 77627 Kevin Morrison	PK-4	T	607 35	60%	409/722-3484 Fax 409/726-2690
Langham Elem Sch 800 12th Street, Nederland 77627 **Toby Latiolais**	PK-4	T	462 50	53%	409/722-4324 Fax 409/724-4286
Nederland High Sch 2101 18th St, Nederland 77627 Steven Beagle	9-12	V	1,547 100	33%	409/727-2741 Fax 409/726-2679
Ⓐ Netherland Alt Ed Sch 300 S 12th St, Nederland 77627 Jared Walker	5-12		12 3		409/727-5241 Fax 409/724-4236

• Port Arthur Ind School Dist   PID: 01033749
4801 9th Ave, Port Arthur 77642

409/989-6222
Fax 409/989-6229

Schools: 16 \ *Teachers:* 544 \ *Students:* 9,000 \ *Special Ed Students:* 657 \ *LEP Students:* 2,167 \ *College-Bound:* 51% \ *Ethnic:* Asian 4%, African American 44%, Hispanic 48%, Native American: 2%, Caucasian 3% \ *Exp:* $504 (High) \ *Poverty:* 34% \ *Title I:* $4,857,356 \ *Special Education:* $1,783,000 \ *Open-Close:* 08/14 - 05/26 \ *DTBP:* $169 (High)

Dr Mark Porterie 1	Phyllis Geans 2,15		
Stephanie Barth 2	Erika Sampson 4		
Ester Chapman 5	Andre Boutte 6		
Dr Kim Vine 8	Robin Beaty 8,18,286		
Dr Melvin Getwood 10,11,15,36,288,298	Tuyen Tran 16		
Freda Reynolds 34	Courtney Charles 41		
Rita Leger 43,285*	Melony Puz 44,53		
Catherine Whitehead 46	Mekisha Bazile 47*		
Rhonda Calcoat 52	Dr Tatiana Owens 57,271		
Debra Cartwright 58,83,88	Debra Ambroese 67		
Kathy Londow 68,79	Kathy McEwen 69		
Anthony Jackson 73,76,294,295	Kenneth Daigre 73		
Dr Julie Sherman 77	Dr Lawanda Finney 93,273		
Richard Tatar 295	Raul Picon 297		

Public Schs..Principal	Grd	Prgm	Enr/#Cls	SN	
Abraham Lincoln Middle Sch 1023 Abe Lincoln Ave, Port Arthur 77640 Lasonya Baptiste	6-8	T	614 55	82%	409/984-8700 Fax 409/982-2847
Dequeen Elem Sch 740 Dequeen Blvd, Port Arthur 77640 Jerry Gloston	3-5	T	291 32	92%	409/984-8900 Fax 409/982-1843
Dowling Elem Sch 6301 Pat Ave, Port Arthur 77640 Amy Newcomb-Jordan	PK-5	T	406 21	83%	409/984-4960 Fax 409/736-2406
Lee Elem Sch 3900 10th St, Port Arthur 77642 Reuben Sampson	PK-5	T	784 42	86%	409/984-8300 Fax 409/983-1649
Lucian Adams Elem Sch 5701 9th Ave, Port Arthur 77642 Cheryl Tripplett	PK-5	T	456	89%	409/984-4100 Fax 409/982-5564
Memorial 9th Grade Academy 3505 Sgt Lucien Adams Blvd, Port Arthur 77642 Angel Murphy	9-9	V	593 32		409/984-4900 Fax 409/736-0267
Memorial High Sch 3501 Sgt Lucien Adams Blvd, Port Arthur 77642 Dr Glenn Mitchell	10-12	V	1,538 60		409/984-4000 Fax 409/985-3376
Memorial High School-Cate 3501 Sgt Lucien Adams Blvd, Port Arthur 77642 Raymond Polk	Voc	GT	300 14	79%	409/984-4750 Fax 409/983-2204
Ⓐ Port Arthur Alternative Center 1030 Dunbar Ave, Port Arthur 77640 Luther Thompson	6-12		100 12		409/984-8650 Fax 409/983-1108
Sam Houston Elem Sch 3245 36th St, Port Arthur 77642 Marcia Sharp	PK-5	T	606 57	76%	409/984-4800 Fax 409/984-4858
Thomas Jefferson Middle Sch 2200 Jefferson Dr, Port Arthur 77642 **Dr Melissa Oliva**	6-8	GTV	925 75	80%	409/984-4860 Fax 409/960-6057
Travis Elem Sch 1115 Lakeview Ave, Port Arthur 77642 Israel Taylor	PK-5	T	554 40	93%	409/984-4700 Fax 409/984-4740
Tyrrell Elem Sch 4401 Ferndale Dr, Port Arthur 77642 Dr Lisa Chambers	PK-5	T	895 39	85%	409/984-4660 Fax 409/963-2765
Washington Elem Sch 1300 Freeman Ave, Port Arthur 77640 Erica Seastrunt	PK-2	T	293 17	86%	409/984-8600 Fax 409/984-9631
Wheatley Sch Early Childhood 1100 Jefferson Dr, Port Arthur 77642 Fredia Reynolds	PK-PK	T	422 28	96%	409/984-8750 Fax 409/985-5487
Wilson Early College High Sch 1500 Lakeshore Dr, Port Arthur 77640 Dr Gloria Dotson	9-12		300		409/984-8960 Fax 409/984-8978

• Port Neches-Groves Ind SD   PID: 01033957
620 Avenue C, Port Neches 77651

409/722-4244
Fax 409/724-7864

Schools: 10 \ *Teachers:* 362 \ *Students:* 5,150 \ *Special Ed Students:* 470 \ *LEP Students:* 208 \ *College-Bound:* 61% \ *Ethnic:* Asian 6%, African American 3%, Hispanic 24%, Caucasian 67% \ *Exp:* $217 (Med) \ *Poverty:* 14% \ *Title I:* $705,922 \ *Special Education:* $1,122,000 \ *Open-Close:* 08/20 - 05/21 \ *DTBP:* $182 (High)

Dr Mike Gonzales 1	Sheri Drawhorn 2
Jeff Bergeron 3	Melissa Nunnelly 4
Kyle Segura 5	Dr Brenda Duhon .. 8,15,69,73,74,288,294,298
Roxanne Ferguson 9	Staci Gary 9,57*
Jon Deckert 10,280,285*	Misty Higgins 11,58,88*
Julie Gauthier 15,296	Dr Scott Bartlett 67
Dale Fontenot 71,91,295	

Public Schs..Principal	Grd	Prgm	Enr/#Cls	SN	
Ⓐ Alternative Education Center 1810 Port Neches Ave, Port Neches 77651 Scott Ryan	6-12		20 3		409/722-5924 Fax 409/724-1448
Groves Elem Sch 3901 Cleveland Ave, Groves 77619 Mandie Champagne	4-5	T	450 20	40%	409/962-1531 Fax 409/963-2484
Groves Middle Sch 5201 Wilson St, Groves 77619 James Arnett	6-8	T	571 50	41%	409/962-0225 Fax 409/963-1898
Port Neches Elem Sch 2101 Llano St, Port Neches 77651 Kimberly Carter	4-5	T	402 15	34%	409/722-2262 Fax 409/729-7003
Port Neches Middle Sch 749 Central Dr, Port Neches 77651 Kyle Hooper	6-8	T	591 34	32%	409/722-8115 Fax 409/727-8342

79 Student Personnel	91 Safety/Security	275 Response To Intervention	298 Grant Writer/Ptnrships	School Programs	Social Media
80 Driver Ed/Safety	92 Magnet School	277 Remedial Math K-12	750 Chief Innovation Officer	A = Alternative Program	[f] = Facebook
81 Gifted/Talented	93 Parental Involvement	280 Literacy Coach	751 Chief of Staff	G = Adult Classes	
82 Video Services	95 Tech Prep Program	285 STEM	752 Social Emotional Learning	M = Magnet Program	[t] = Twitter
83 Substance Abuse Prev	97 Chief Infomation Officer	286 Digital Learning		T = Title I Schoolwide	
84 Erate	98 Chief Technology Officer	288 Common Core Standards	Other School Types	V = Career & Tech Ed Programs	
85 AIDS Education	270 Character Education	294 Accountability	Ⓐ = Alternative School		
88 Alternative/At Risk	271 Migrant Education	295 Network System	Ⓒ = Charter School	New Schools are shaded	
89 Multi-Cultural Curriculum	273 Teacher Mentor	296 Title II Programs	Ⓜ = Magnet School	New Superintendents and Principals are bold	
90 Social Work	274 Before/After Sch	297 Webmaster	Ⓨ = Year-Round School	Personnel with email addresses are underscored	

TX—243

Jim Hogg County

Port Neches-Groves High Sch 1401 Merriman St, Port Neches 77651 Scott Ryan	9-12	AV	1,477 60	26%	409/729-7644 Fax 409/727-7217
Ridgewood Elem Sch 2820 Merriman St, Port Neches 77651 Kevin Schexnaider	PK-3		427 20	24%	409/722-7641 Fax 409/721-9721
Taft Elem Sch 2500 Taft Ave, Port Arthur 77642 Staci Gary	PK-3	T	436 20	42%	409/962-2262 Fax 409/963-1923
Van Buren Elem Sch 6400 Van Buren St, Groves 77619 Joe Cegielski	PK-3	T	341 18	36%	409/962-6511 Fax 409/962-2043
Woodcrest Elem Sch 1522 Heisler St, Port Neches 77651 Angela Abel	PK-3	T	339 16	39%	409/724-2309 Fax 409/729-9480

- **Sabine Pass Ind School Dist** PID: 01034066   409/971-2321
  5641 S Gulfway, Sabine Pass 77655   Fax 409/971-2120

> **Schools:** 1 \ **Teachers:** 33 \ **Students:** 372 \ **Special Ed Students:** 9
> \ **LEP Students:** 3 \ **College-Bound:** 95% \ **Ethnic:** Asian 1%, African American 22%, Hispanic 37%, Native American: 1%, Caucasian 39% \
> **Exp:** $628 (High) \ **Poverty:** 18% \ **Title I:** $821 \ **Special Education:** $74,000
> \ **Open-Close:** 08/22 - 05/25 \ **DTBP:** $417 (High)

Kristi Heid 1		Duyen Blanton 2,68	
Tom Butler 3,5		Chelsea Berg 4*	
Jason Thibodeaux 6*		Mark Simmons 16,73*	
Isabel Harvey 36,270*		Lane Plauche 67	

Public Schs..Principal	Grd	Prgm	Enr/#Cls	SN	
Sabine Pass Sch 5641 S Gulfway, Sabine Pass 77655 Troy Gragg \ Andrew Bates	PK-12	ATV	372 25	56%	409/971-2321

JEFFERSON CATHOLIC SCHOOLS

- **Diocese of Beaumont Sch Office** PID: 01034339   409/924-4322
  710 Archie St, Beaumont 77701   Fax 409/838-4511

> **Schools:** 5 \ **Students:** 1,700

Listing includes only schools located in this county. See District Index for location of Diocesan Offices.

Marcia Stevens 1	Sabrina Vrooman 2,19	
Elise Fulton 67	Beverly Escamilla 68	
Karen Gilman 71		

Catholic Schs..Principal	Grd	Prgm	Enr/#Cls	SN	
Msgr Kelly Catholic HS 5950 Kelly Dr, Beaumont 77707 Roger Bemis	9-12		460 45		409/866-2351 Fax 409/866-0917
St Anne Catholic Sch 375 N 11th St, Beaumont 77702 Alison Kiker	PK-8		600 33		409/832-5939 Fax 409/832-4655
St Anthony Cathedral Sch 850 Forsythe St, Beaumont 77701 Felicia Runnels	PK-8		200 17		409/832-3486 Fax 409/838-9051
St Catherine of Siena Sch 3840 Woodrow Dr, Port Arthur 77642 K Renee Tolin	PK-8		183 17		409/962-3011 Fax 409/962-5019

JEFFERSON PRIVATE SCHOOLS

Private Schs..Principal	Grd	Prgm	Enr/#Cls	SN	
All Saints Episcopal Sch 4108 Delaware St, Beaumont 77706 Scootie Clark	PK-8		392 23		409/892-1755 Fax 409/892-0166
Friendship Pre-Sch & Chrn Acad 6750 Highway 105, Beaumont 77708 Casey Zimmerman	PK-12		40		409/898-0489
Legacy Christian Academy 8200 Highway 105, Beaumont 77713 Dr Kevin Wharton \ Jolynne McCraw	K-12		184		409/924-0500 Fax 409/924-0953
Triangle Adventist Chrn Sch 2701 West Parkway, Groves 77619 Renee Leite	PK-8		14 2		409/963-3806
Val Verde Christian Academy 3900 Cleveland Ave, Groves 77619 Nick Dignan	PK-12		80		409/962-8822 Fax 409/962-8464

JEFFERSON REGIONAL CENTERS

- **Region 5 Ed Service Center** PID: 01034298   409/951-1700
  350 Pine St Ste 500, Beaumont 77701   Fax 409/951-1800

Dr Danny Lovett 1	Denise Wallace 2	
Concetta Rollins 4	Maris Peno 7,298	
Monica Mahfouz 8,27,31	Brenda Schofield 11,30	
Dr Byron Terrier 15,16,73	Dr Cindy Fussell 58	
Lynda Hoffpauir 76		

JIM HOGG COUNTY

JIM HOGG PUBLIC SCHOOLS

- **Jim Hogg Co Ind School Dist** PID: 01034470   361/527-3203
  210 W Lucille St, Hebbronville 78361   Fax 361/527-4928

> **Schools:** 3 \ **Teachers:** 83 \ **Students:** 1,151 \ **Special Ed Students:** 89
> \ **LEP Students:** 81 \ **Ethnic:** African American 1%, Hispanic 96%, Caucasian 3% \ **Exp:** $490 (High) \ **Poverty:** 38% \ **Title I:** $627,980 \
> **Special Education:** $230,000 \ **Open-Close:** 08/19 - 05/28 \ **DTBP:** $342 (High)

Dr Susana Garza 1	Jennifer Benavides 4	
Roldan Montalvo 6*	Tiffany Forbes 7*	
Etna Ramirez 67	Raquel Perez 73*	

Public Schs..Principal	Grd	Prgm	Enr/#Cls	SN	
Hebbronville Elem Sch 210 W Lucille St, Hebbronville 78361 Leonor Hernandez	PK-5	T	577 45	83%	361/527-3203 Fax 361/527-2133
Hebbronville High Sch 210 Longhorn Ln, Hebbronville 78361 Joann Valderas	9-12	TV	312 30	81%	361/527-3203 Fax 361/527-3678
Hebbronville Jr High Sch 910 N Wilhelma St, Hebbronville 78361 Anna Canales	6-8	T	262 30	84%	361/527-3203 Fax 361/527-3571

1	Superintendent	8	Curric/Instruct K-12	19	Chief Financial Officer	29	Family/Consumer Science	
2	Bus/Finance/Purchasing	9	Curric/Instruct Elem	20	Art K-12	30	Adult Education	
3	Buildings And Grounds	10	Curric/Instruct Sec	21	Art Elem	31	Career/Sch-to-Work K-12	
4	Food Service	11	Federal Program	22	Art Sec	32	Career/Sch-to-Work Elem	
5	Transportation	12	Title I	23	Music K-12	33	Career/Sch-to-Work Sec	
6	Athletic	13	Title V	24	Music Elem	34	Early Childhood Ed	
7	Health Services	15	Asst Superintendent	25	Music Sec	35	Health/Phys Education	
		16	Instructional Media Svcs	26	Business Education	36	Guidance Services K-12	
		17	Chief Operations Officer	27	Career & Tech Ed	37	Guidance Services Elem	
		18	Chief Academic Officer	28	Technology Education	38	Guidance Services Sec	

39	Social Studies K-12	49	English/Lang Arts Elem	59	Special Education Elem	69	Academic Assessment
40	Social Studies Elem	50	English/Lang Arts Sec	60	Special Education Sec	70	Research/Development
41	Social Studies Sec	51	Reading K-12	61	Foreign/World Lang K-12	71	Public Information
42	Science K-12	52	Reading Elem	62	Foreign/World Lang Elem	72	Summer School
43	Science Elem	53	Reading Sec	63	Foreign/World Lang Sec	73	Instructional Tech
44	Science Sec	54	Remedial Reading K-12	64	Religious Education K-12	74	Inservice Training
45	Math K-12	55	Remedial Reading Elem	65	Religious Education Elem	75	Marketing/Distributive
46	Math Elem	56	Remedial Reading Sec	66	Religious Education Sec	76	Info Systems
47	Math Sec	57	Bilingual/ELL	67	School Board President	77	Psychological Assess
48	English/Lang Arts K-12	58	Special Education K-12	68	Teacher Personnel	78	Affirmative Action

Texas School Directory

Jim Wells County

JIM WELLS COUNTY

JIM WELLS PUBLIC SCHOOLS

- **Alice Ind School Dist** PID: 01034511   361/664-0981
  2 Coyote Trl, Alice 78332   Fax 361/660-2123

Schools: 9 \ **Teachers:** 323 \ **Students:** 4,784 \ **Special Ed Students:** 402 \ **LEP Students:** 163 \ **Ethnic:** African American 1%, Hispanic 94%, Caucasian 5% \ **Exp:** $218 (Med) \ **Poverty:** 38% \ **Title I:** $2,839,473 \ **Special Education:** $950,000 \ **Open-Close:** 08/19 - 05/29 \ **DTBP:** $158 (High)

Dr Carl Scarbrough	1	David Flores	2,19
Willie Ruiz	3,5,17,91	Krystle Flores	4
Daniel Galvan	5	Kyle Atwood	6*
Lisa Lozano	7*	Anna Holmgreen	8,15,69,275
Dr Alma Garcia	11,57,270,296	Yolanda Abrigo	16,73,76,82,286,295*
Arnold Garza	23*	Erika Vasquez	42
Vanessa Snyder	45	Marta Salazar	48,93
Grace Garcia	58	Ben Salinas	67
Elida DeLeon	68,273	Faustina Dominguez	79
Laurie Lerma	81		

Public Schs..Principal	Grd	Prgm	Enr/#Cls	SN	
Alice High Sch 1 Coyote Trl, Alice 78332 **Dr Cidonio Cantu**	9-12	AGTV	1,314 100	70%	361/664-0126 Fax 361/660-2128 **f**
Dubose Intermediate Sch 1000 N Cameron St, Alice 78332 **Lorie Orta**	5-6	T	457 25	69%	361/664-7512 Fax 361/660-2074
Hillcrest Elem Sch 1400 Morningside Dr, Alice 78332 **Elisa Carter**	PK-4	T	315 10	94%	361/660-2095 Fax 361/660-2163 **t**
Memorial Intermediate Sch 900 W 3rd St, Alice 78332 **Cristina Lopez**	5-6	T	392 26	88%	361/660-2080 Fax 361/660-2160
Noonan Elem Sch 701 W 3rd St, Alice 78332 **Monica Garcia**	PK-4	T	378 21	92%	361/664-7591 Fax 361/660-2024
Saenz Elem Sch 400 Palo Blanco St, Alice 78332 **Marina Garza**	PK-4	T	553 22	98%	361/664-4981 Fax 361/660-2167
Salazar Elem Sch 1028 Pierce St, Alice 78332 **Maria Vidaurri**	PK-4	T	255 15	92%	361/664-6263 Fax 361/660-2168
Schallert Elem Sch 1001 Jim Wells Dr, Alice 78332 **Paul Looney**	PK-4	T	498 27	74%	361/664-6361 Fax 361/660-2169
William Adams Middle Sch 901 E 3rd St, Alice 78332 **Dr Judy Holmgreen**	7-8	ATV	731 45	77%	361/660-2055 Fax 361/660-2094

- **Ben Bolt-Palito Blanco ISD** PID: 01034638   361/664-9904
  172 Badger Ln, Ben Bolt 78342   Fax 361/668-0446

Schools: 2 \ **Teachers:** 50 \ **Students:** 512 \ **Special Ed Students:** 47 \ **LEP Students:** 29 \ **College-Bound:** 47% \ **Ethnic:** Asian 1%, African American 1%, Hispanic 93%, Caucasian 6% \ **Exp:** $296 (Med) \ **Poverty:** 19% \ **Title I:** $131,715 \ **Special Education:** $152,000 \ **Open-Close:** 08/26 - 05/29 \ **DTBP:** $350 (High)

Dr Mike Barrera	1	Rosario Benavidez	2
Bobby Galvan	8,11,296,298	Zelda Saenz	67

Public Schs..Principal	Grd	Prgm	Enr/#Cls	SN	
Ben Bolt-Palito Blanco ES 401 Whitney Dr, Ben Bolt 78342 Gloria Hamill	PK-6	AT	287 10	71%	361/664-9568 Fax 361/664-5235
Ben Bolt-Palito Blanco HS 172 Badger Ln, Ben Bolt 78342 Gus Barrera	7-12	ATV	250 18	68%	361/664-9822 Fax 361/664-5481

- **La Gloria Ind School Dist** PID: 01034664   361/325-2330
  182 E County Road 401, Falfurrias 78355   Fax 361/325-2533

Schools: 1 \ **Teachers:** 8 \ **Students:** 125 \ **Special Ed Students:** 5 \ **Ethnic:** African American 1%, Hispanic 97%, Caucasian 3% \ **Exp:** $438 (High) \ **Poverty:** 33% \ **Title I:** $20,244 \ **Open-Close:** 08/19 - 05/29 \ **DTBP:** $366 (High)

David Braswell	1,11,73,83,84,288	Fidencio Madrigal	6*
Melonie Miller	16,57,59,273*	Martha Salazar	67

Public Schs..Principal	Grd	Prgm	Enr/#Cls	SN	
La Gloria Elem Sch 182 E County Road 401, Falfurrias 78355 David Braswell	PK-6	T	125 7	50%	361/325-2330

- **Orange Grove Ind School Dist** PID: 01034688   361/384-2495
  504 S Dibrell St, Orange Grove 78372   Fax 361/384-2148

Schools: 4 \ **Teachers:** 124 \ **Students:** 1,850 \ **Special Ed Students:** 189 \ **LEP Students:** 35 \ **College-Bound:** 51% \ **Ethnic:** Hispanic 59%, Caucasian 40% \ **Exp:** $264 (Med) \ **Poverty:** 32% \ **Title I:** $687,080 \ **Open-Close:** 08/20 - 05/28 \ **DTBP:** $322 (High)

Dr Randy Hoyer	1	Jodi Schroedter	2
Alton Goetzel	3,5	Gina Ochoa	4
Mark Delpercio	6	Ernest Henderson	8,11,57,69,73,74,275,294
Lyn Perez	9*	Lisa Jurecek	16,82*
Sandy Clark	36*	Will Klatt	67
Tracy Klatt	73,295*		

Public Schs..Principal	Grd	Prgm	Enr/#Cls	SN	
Orange Grove Elem & Inter Sch 500 S Eugenia St, Orange Grove 78372 **Jeanne Bridges**	2-5	T	559 18	61%	361/384-9358 Fax 361/384-2118
Orange Grove High Sch 701 S Reynolds, Orange Grove 78372 Gildardo Salazar	9-12	ATV	531 50	50%	361/384-2330 Fax 361/384-0206
Orange Grove Jr High Sch 600 Thiel St, Orange Grove 78372 Kenneth Dykes	6-8	T	442 40	62%	361/384-2323 Fax 361/384-9579
Orange Grove Primary Sch 205 Dahme Ave, Orange Grove 78372 Lyn Perez	PK-1	T	346 20	60%	361/384-2316 Fax 361/384-9171

---

79 Student Personnel	91 Safety/Security	275 Response To Intervention	298 Grant Writer/Ptnrships	**School Programs**	**Social Media**	
60 Driver Ed/Safety	92 Magnet School	277 Remedial Math K-12	750 Chief Innovation Officer	A = Alternative Program		
61 Gifted/Talented	93 Parental Involvement	280 Literacy Coach	751 Chief of Staff	G = Adult Classes	**f** = Facebook	
82 Video Services	95 Tech Prep Program	285 STEM	752 Social Emotional Learning	M = Magnet Program		
83 Substance Abuse Prev	97 Chief Infomation Officer	286 Digital Learning		T = Title I Schoolwide	**t** = Twitter	
84 Erate	98 Chief Technology Officer	288 Common Core Standards	**Other School Types**	V = Career & Tech Ed Programs		
85 AIDS Education	270 Character Education	294 Accountability	Ⓐ = Alternative School			
88 Alternative/At Risk	271 Migrant Education	295 Network System	Ⓒ = Charter School	New Schools are shaded		
89 Multi-Cultural Curriculum	273 Teacher Mentor	296 Title II Programs	Ⓜ = Magnet School	New Superintendents and Principals are bold		
90 Social Work	274 Before/After Sch	297 Webmaster	Ⓨ = Year-Round School	Personnel with email addresses are underscored		

TX—245

Johnson County

Market Data Retrieval

- **Premont Ind School Dist** PID: 01034717   361/348-3915
  439 SW 4th St, Premont 78375   Fax 361/348-2882

Schools: 2 \ **Teachers:** 41 \ **Students:** 587 \ **Special Ed Students:** 45 \ **LEP Students:** 34 \ **College-Bound:** 43% \ **Ethnic:** Asian 1%, Hispanic 98%, Caucasian 1% \ **Exp:** $738 (High) \ **Poverty:** 43% \ **Title I:** $476,166 \ **Special Education:** $111,000 \ **Open-Close:** 08/27 - 06/03 \ **DTBP:** $351 (High)

Stephen Vanmatre 1,11,288	Lili Barrera 2
Annette Jaramillo 4	Dr Marisa Chapa 12,15
Ashley Cantu 58	Richard Waterhouse 67
Donita Powell 73*	

Public Schs..Principal	Grd	Prgm	Enr/#Cls	SN	
Premont Collegiate High Sch 510 S Elaine St, Premont 78375 Claudette Garcia	6-12	ATV	283 25	86%	361/348-3915 Fax 361/348-2914
Premont Early College Academy 608 S Delores St, Premont 78375 Misty Benavides	PK-5	T	304	75%	361/348-3915 Fax 361/348-5010

JIM WELLS CATHOLIC SCHOOLS

- **Diocese Corpus Christi Ed Off** PID: 01045170
  Listing includes only schools located in this county. See District Index for location of Diocesan Offices.

Catholic Schs..Principal	Grd	Prgm	Enr/#Cls	SN	
St Elizabeth Sch 615 E 5th St, Alice 78332 Patricia Garcia	PK-6		166 9		361/664-6271
St Joseph Sch 311 Dewey Ave, Alice 78332 K Barrera	PK-8		128 10		361/664-4642 Fax 361/664-5511

JIM WELLS PRIVATE SCHOOLS

Private Schs..Principal	Grd	Prgm	Enr/#Cls	SN	
Alice Christian Sch 1200 N Stadium Rd, Alice 78332	K-12		25 3		361/668-6636 Fax 361/668-0840

JOHNSON COUNTY

JOHNSON PUBLIC SCHOOLS

- **Alvarado Ind School Dist** PID: 01034767   817/783-6800
  102 Bill Jackson Dr, Alvarado 76009   Fax 817/783-3844

Schools: 6 \ **Teachers:** 217 \ **Students:** 3,650 \ **Special Ed Students:** 286 \ **LEP Students:** 490 \ **College-Bound:** 49% \ **Ethnic:** African American 3%, Hispanic 36%, Native American: 1%, Caucasian 60% \ **Exp:** $303 (High) \ **Poverty:** 15% \ **Title I:** $634,667 \ **Special Education:** $659,000 \ **Open-Close:** 08/19 - 05/22 \ **DTBP:** $190 (High) \

Dr Kenneth Estes 1	Rodney Toon 2
Mark Ratcliff 3,15,91	Randel Ward 3
Jack Aspinall 4	Charles Thompson 5
Dr Lori Nunez 7,11,31,34,83,271,296,298	Maribel Diaz 8,18,57,76,286,288
Julie Holland 16,73,295	Micki McCrory 42
Junior Rayburne 45,277	Arlene Gallagher 58
Tom Head 67	Maryann Wood 68,78
Dandy Earley 69	Tommy Brown 71
Macy Ozuna 295	

Public Schs..Principal	Grd	Prgm	Enr/#Cls	SN	
Alvarado Elem North Sch 1500 N Cummings Dr, Alvarado 76009 Louanne Stevens	PK-3	T	372 23	56%	817/783-6863 Fax 817/783-6871
Alvarado Elem South Sch 1000 E Davis Ave, Alvarado 76009 Karla Moore	PK-3	T	383 25	74%	817/783-6880 Fax 817/783-6889
Alvarado High Sch 1301 S Parkway Dr, Alvarado 76009 Christopher MaGee	9-12	T	1,107 45	53%	817/783-6940 Fax 817/783-6944
Alvarado Intermediate Sch 1401 E Davis, Alvarado 76009 Kim Grant	4-6	T	872 20	67%	817/783-6825 Fax 817/783-6837
Alvarado Junior High Sch 1000 N Cummings Dr, Alvarado 76009 Melodye Brooks	7-8	T	614 32	63%	817/783-6840 Fax 817/783-6844
Lillian Elem Sch 5001 FM 2738, Alvarado 76009 Ricky Lewis	PK-3	T	379 30	75%	817/783-6815 Fax 817/783-6823

- **Burleson Ind School Dist** PID: 01034810   817/245-1000
  1160 SW Wilshire Blvd, Burleson 76028   Fax 817/447-5737

Schools: 17 \ **Teachers:** 760 \ **Students:** 12,742 \ **Special Ed Students:** 1,019 \ **LEP Students:** 555 \ **College-Bound:** 96% \ **Ethnic:** Asian 1%, African American 6%, Hispanic 22%, Native American: 1%, Caucasian 70% \ **Exp:** $193 (Low) \ **Poverty:** 9% \ **Title I:** $1,133,562 \ **Special Education:** $1,668,000 \ **Open-Close:** 08/19 - 05/22 \ **DTBP:** $212 (High) \

Dr Bret Jimerson 1	Brenda Mize 2
Regi Brackin 3	Courtney Peets 7*
April Chiarelli 9,34,57	Leighanne Arthur 10
Charles Osborne 11,69	Marcus Cannonico 27
Lucretia Gartrell 36,58	Seth Hickman 42,45*
Andy Pickens 67	Coby Kirkpatrick 68,79
Katelyn Tyler 71	Stephen Logan 76,295
Dr Leslie Bender Jutzi 298	

Public Schs..Principal	Grd	Prgm	Enr/#Cls	SN	
Acad of Leadershp & Tech-Mound 205 SW Thomas St, Burleson 76028 Marla Bennette	PK-5	T	412 36	55%	817/245-3100 Fax 817/447-5845
Academy at Nola Dunn 201 S Dobson St, Burleson 76028 Lindsey Byrd	PK-5		669 26	11%	817/245-3300 Fax 817/447-0523
Academy of Arts at Branson 820 S Hurst Rd, Burleson 76028 Robert Balentine	PK-5		562 25	35%	817/245-3600 Fax 817/447-5888
Brock Elem Sch 12000 Oak Grove Rd S, Burleson 76028 Kim Kimberling	PK-5	T	702	57%	817/245-3800 Fax 817/293-0488
Burleson Collegiate High Sch 201 S Hurst Rd, Burleson 76028 Amanda Wieland	9-12		76	32%	817/245-1600 Fax 817/245-1606
Burleson High Sch 100 Elk Dr, Burleson 76028 Wayne Leek	9-12	V	1,618	39%	817/245-0000 Fax 817/447-5796

1 Superintendent	8 Curric/Instruct K-12	19 Chief Financial Officer	29 Family/Consumer Science	39 Social Studies K-12	49 English/Lang Arts Elem	59 Special Education Elem	69 Academic Assessment
2 Bus/Finance/Purchasing	9 Curric/Instruct Elem	20 Art K-12	30 Adult Education	40 Social Studies Elem	50 English/Lang Arts Sec	60 Special Education Sec	70 Research/Development
3 Buildings And Grounds	10 Curric/Instruct Sec	21 Art Elem	31 Career/Sch-to-Work K-12	41 Social Studies Sec	51 Reading K-12	61 Foreign/World Lang K-12	71 Public Information
4 Food Service	11 Federal Program	22 Art Sec	32 Career/Sch-to-Work Elem	42 Science K-12	52 Reading Elem	62 Foreign/World Lang Elem	72 Summer School
5 Transportation	12 Title I	23 Music K-12	33 Career/Sch-to-Work Sec	43 Science Elem	53 Reading Sec	63 Foreign/World Lang Sec	73 Instructional Tech
6 Athletic	13 Title V	24 Music Elem	34 Early Childhood Ed	44 Science Sec	54 Remedial Reading K-12	64 Religious Education K-12	74 Inservice Training
7 Health Services	15 Asst Superintendent	25 Music Sec	35 Health/Phys Education	45 Math K-12	55 Remedial Reading Elem	65 Religious Education Elem	75 Marketing/Distributive
	16 Instructional Media Svcs	26 Business Education	36 Guidance Services K-12	46 Math Elem	56 Remedial Reading Sec	66 Religious Education Sec	76 Info Systems
	17 Chief Operations Officer	27 Career & Tech Ed	37 Guidance Services Elem	47 Math Sec	57 Bilingual/ELL	67 School Board President	77 Psychological Assess
	18 Chief Academic Officer	28 Technology Education	38 Guidance Services Sec	48 English/Lang Arts K-12	58 Special Education K-12	68 Teacher Personnel	78 Affirmative Action

Texas School Directory — Johnson County

School	Grd	Prgm	Enr/#Cls	SN	Phone
Centennial High Sch 201 S Hurst Rd, Burleson 76028 **Ikie Holder**	9-12		1,738		817/245-0250 Fax 817/447-2152
Ⓐ Crossroads High Sch 505 Pleasant Manor Ave, Burleson 76028 **Marcus Canonico**	9-12	T	83 7	57%	817/245-0500 Fax 817/447-5889
Frazier Elem Sch 1125 NW Summercrest Blvd, Burleson 76028 **Tricia Lyday**	PK-5	T	596 25	42%	817/245-3000 Fax 817/447-4916
Hughes Middle Sch 316 SW Thomas St, Burleson 76028 **Ben Renner**	6-8	T	1,047 70	42%	817/245-0600 Fax 817/447-5748 [t]
Irene Clinkscale Elem Sch 600 Blayke St, Burleson 76028 **Lauri Allen**	PK-5		654	34%	817/245-3900 Fax 817/295-4651
Jack Taylor Elem Sch 400 NE Alsbury Blvd, Burleson 76028 **Ana Ketchum**	PK-5	T	516 28	72%	817/245-3200 Fax 817/447-5841
Judy Hajek Elem Sch 555 NE McAlister Rd, Burleson 76028 **Cretia Basham**	PK-5		639	32%	817/245-3700 Fax 817/447-4921
Kerr Middle Sch 517 SW Johnson Ave, Burleson 76028 **Kalee McMullen**	6-8	T	1,211 53	42%	817/245-0750 Fax 817/447-5742 [f][t]
Norwood Elem Sch 619 Evelyn Ln, Burleson 76028 **Tracey Besgrove**	PK-5	T	441 20	65%	817/245-3400 Fax 817/447-5831 [t]
Steam Academy at Stribling 1881 E Renfro St, Burleson 76028 **Rebekah Hinkle**	K-5		420 50	26%	817/245-3500 Fax 817/447-5835
Steam Middle Sch 900 SW Hillside Dr, Burleson 76028 **Chris Chappotin**	6-8		596	36%	817/245-1500 Fax 817/245-1515

- **Cleburne Ind School Dist** PID: 01034872 817/202-1100
  505 N Ridgeway Dr Ste 100, Cleburne 76033 Fax 817/202-1460

Schools: 12 \ *Teachers:* 471 \ *Students:* 6,749 \ *Special Ed Students:* 643 \ *LEP Students:* 1,250 \ *College-Bound:* 53% \ *Ethnic:* African American 3%, Hispanic 44%, Native American: 1%, Caucasian 52% \ *Exp:* $301 (High) \ *Poverty:* 17% \ *Title I:* $1,558,199 \ *Special Education:* $1,235,000 \ *Open-Close:* 08/14 - 05/26 \ [f][t]

Dr Kyle Heath 1
Barry Hipp 3
Chad Van Winkle 5
Jeri Larson-Hall 6
Andrea Hensley 9
Sarah Taylor 19
Kirza Matamoros 57
John Finnell 67
Janet Helmcamp 69,81
Lisa Magers 71,93
Timothy Grijalva 73
Jane Flynn 286

Heidi Todd 2
Kim Chance 4
Alice Parker 6
Mark Walker 6
Tammy Bright 12,15,296
Ginger Tanem 45
Cory Borden 58
Kyle Boles 68
Dr Chris Jackson 70
Mike Wallace 73
Katie Cunningham 285
Tracy Shea 286

Public Schs..Principal	Grd	Prgm	Enr/#Cls	SN	Phone
Adams Elem Sch 1492 Island Grove Rd, Cleburne 76031 **Dawn Hitt**	PK-5	T	408 28	71%	817/202-2000 Fax 817/202-1482
Cleburne High Sch 850 North Nolan River Rd, Cleburne 76033 **Ben Renner**	9-12	TV	1,750 70	61%	817/202-1200 Fax 817/202-1470
Coleman Elem Sch 920 W Westhill Dr, Cleburne 76033 **Marla Roth**	PK-5	T	523 30	60%	817/202-2030 Fax 817/202-1484
Cooke Elem Sch 902 Phillips St, Cleburne 76033 **Jacob Walker**	PK-5	T	560 28	82%	817/202-2060 Fax 817/202-1483
Gerard Elem Sch 1212 Hyde Park Blvd, Cleburne 76033 **Tracy White**	PK-5	T	543 20	38%	817/202-2130 Fax 817/202-1485 [f][t]
Irving Elem Sch 345 Hix Rd, Cleburne 76031 **Sherqueena Jackson**	PK-5	T	495 20	84%	817/202-2100 Fax 817/202-1486
Marti Elem Sch 2020 W Kilpatrick St, Cleburne 76033 **Mary Boedeker**	PK-5	T	417 30	64%	817/202-1650 Fax 817/202-1487
Ⓐ Phoenix Alt Campus 817 1005 S Anglin St, Cleburne 76031 **Loyd Smith**	1-12		250 7		817/202-2090 Fax 817/202-1498
Santa Fe Elem Sch 1601 E Henderson St, Cleburne 76031 **Sabina Landeros**	PK-5	T	394	90%	817/202-2300 Fax 817/202-1497
Smith Middle Sch 1710 Country Club Rd, Cleburne 76033 **Amber White**	6-8	TV	818 78	58%	817/202-1500 Fax 817/202-1475
Ⓐ Team Sch 1005 S Anglin St, Cleburne 76031 **Georgann Storm**	9-12	GT	34 14	72%	817/202-2160 Fax 817/202-1489
Wheat Middle Sch 810 N Colonial Dr, Cleburne 76033 **Suzanne Keesee**	6-8	T	730 32	77%	817/202-1300 Fax 817/202-1479

- **Godley Ind School Dist** PID: 01034963 817/389-2536
  313 N Pearson St, Godley 76044 Fax 817/389-2543

Schools: 5 \ *Teachers:* 139 \ *Students:* 2,027 \ *Special Ed Students:* 218 \ *LEP Students:* 188 \ *Ethnic:* African American 1%, Hispanic 26%, Native American: 2%, Caucasian 71% \ *Exp:* $675 (High) \ *Poverty:* 15% \ *Title I:* $287,259 \ *Open-Close:* 08/14 - 05/22 \ *DTBP:* $342 (High)

Dr Rich Dear 1
Bobby Reynolds 3
Lacey Manuel 4
Richard Burciaga 5
Mark Chauveaux 6*
Keri Grimsley 9*
Vicki Kattner 16*
Marty Oliver 28,73,295
Angela Gonzalez 58
David Williams 68,79,91*
Danna Allen 76

Bryan Myres 2,11,296
Mona Westerman 3
Penny Reynolds 4
Curtis Lowery 6*
Dr Airemy Caudle 9
Jason Karnes 15
Joe Walker 20,23
Cheryl Villanueva 31,57,69
Matt McKittrick 67
Kelly Hanna 73*

Public Schs..Principal	Grd	Prgm	Enr/#Cls	SN	Phone
Godley Elem Sch 604 N Pearson St, Godley 76044 **Keri Grimsley**	PK-1	T	694 27	59%	817/389-3838 Fax 817/389-3291
Godley High Sch 9501 N Highway 171, Godley 76044 **Kurtis Flood**	9-12	AGTV	537 22	51%	817/592-4320 Fax 817/592-4294
Godley Intermediate Sch 309 N Pearson St, Godley 76044 **Melissa Block**	2-6	T	481 25	57%	817/389-2382 Fax 817/389-3292 [f]
Godley Middle Sch 9401 N Highway 171, Godley 76044 **Leigh Brown**	7-8	T	315 40	61%	817/389-2121 Fax 817/389-3293
Ⓐ Links Academy 409 Bruce Rd, Godley 76044 **Michelle Sveum**	9-12		40		817/592-4212

Johnson County

Market Data Retrieval

- **Grandview Ind School Dist** PID: 01034999
 701 S 5th St, Grandview 76050
 817/866-4500
 Fax 817/866-3351

> **Schools:** 3 \ **Teachers:** 90 \ **Students:** 1,276 \ **Special Ed Students:** 89 \ **LEP Students:** 49 \ **College-Bound:** 53% \ **Ethnic:** Asian 1%, African American 2%, Hispanic 18%, Native American: 1%, Caucasian 79% \ **Exp:** $477 (High) \ **Poverty:** 16% \ **Title I:** $195,834 \ **Open-Close:** 08/21 - 05/28 \ **DTBP:** $353 (High)

Joe Perrin	1	Margie Fuller	2,19
John King	3	Odell Schronk	5
Ryan Ebner	6	Lisa Davis	7,85*
Kristi Rhone	8,11,76,88,285,288,296,298	Katherine Stewart	16*
Clint Jentsch	37*	Stephanie Davis	38,69,83,270*
Clint Ishmael	67	John Clayton	73,95,295*

Public Schs..Principal	Grd	Prgm	Enr/#Cls	SN		
Grandview Elem Sch 301 Zebra Pkwy, Grandview 76050 Katherine Stewart	PK-5	T	537 26	39%	817/866-4600 Fax 817/866-2452	
Grandview High Sch 1009 Carroll Ln, Grandview 76050 Kirby Basham	9-12	V	369 37	28%	817/866-4520 Fax 817/866-2645	
Grandview Junior High Sch 705 S 5th Street, Grandview 76050 Jeff Hudson	6-8	T	310 22	27%	817/866-4660 Fax 817/866-3912	

- **Joshua Ind School Dist** PID: 01035022
 310 E 18th St, Joshua 76058
 817/426-7500
 Fax 817/641-2738

> **Schools:** 10 \ **Teachers:** 371 \ **Students:** 5,626 \ **Special Ed Students:** 395 \ **LEP Students:** 419 \ **College-Bound:** 54% \ **Ethnic:** African American 1%, Hispanic 27%, Caucasian 71% \ **Exp:** $230 (Med) \ **Poverty:** 12% \ **Title I:** $714,440 \ **Special Education:** $897,000 \ **Open-Close:** 08/15 - 05/21 \ **DTBP:** $151 (High)

Fran Marek	1	Candace Fuchs	2
Rebecca Metzger	2,19	Blake Bowman	3
Kari Frederick	4	Gary Robinson	6
Marcie Walker	7*	Jo Lynn Augsburger	8,294
Julie Hampton	9*	Michelle Snell	10
Rick Edwards	15	Brooklyn Shafer	30*
Faviola Arevalo	57	Elizabeth Rosatelli	58*
Ronnie Galbreath	67	Holly Stambaugh	68
Tammy Riemenschneide	69	Patty Webb	73
Julie Hampton	76	Margaret Johnson	98
Lindsey Elliott	274	Jason Smith	295
Elizabeth Rosatelli	296		

Public Schs..Principal	Grd	Prgm	Enr/#Cls	SN	
A G Elder Elem Sch 513 Henderson St, Joshua 76058 Debra Brakel	PK-5	T	527 36	62%	817/202-2500 Fax 817/641-2951
Caddo Grove Elem Sch 7301 FM 1902, Joshua 76058 Julie Rohleder	PK-5	T	635	81%	817/202-2500 Fax 817/645-6420
H D Staples Elem Sch 505 S Main St, Joshua 76058 Toby Cox	PK-5	T	508 29	66%	817/202-2500 Fax 817/556-0450
Joshua 9th Grade Campus 1035 S Broadway St, Joshua 76058 Kenny Bodine	9-9	T	397	41%	817/202-2500 Fax 817/556-4640
Joshua High Sch 909 S Broadway St, Joshua 76058 Celeste Neal	10-12	V	1,100 93	36%	817/202-2500 Fax 817/556-3403

Ⓐ New Horizons High Sch 603 Plum St, Joshua 76058 Kenneth Bodine	9-12	GTV	38 5	63%	817/202-2500 Fax 817/202-8948
North Joshua Elem Sch 100 Ranchway Dr, Burleson 76028 Tammy Watts	PK-5		566 40	23%	817/426-7500 Fax 817/295-9836
Plum Creek Elem Sch 500 Plum St, Joshua 76058 Shelly Green	PK-5	T	477 30	55%	817/202-2500 Fax 817/202-9133
R C Loflin Middle Sch 6801 FM 1902, Joshua 76058 Damon Patterson	7-8	TV	714 50	49%	817/202-2500 Fax 817/202-9140
Tom & Nita Nichols Middle Sch 2845 FM 731, Burleson 76028 Brian Rosatelli	6-8		565		817/202-2500 Fax 817/202-2649

- **Keene Ind School Dist** PID: 01035060
 3625 E Highway 67 Bldg C, Keene 76059
 817/774-5200
 Fax 817/774-5400

> **Schools:** 4 \ **Teachers:** 84 \ **Students:** 1,070 \ **Special Ed Students:** 84 \ **LEP Students:** 200 \ **Ethnic:** African American 6%, Hispanic 45%, Native American: 1%, Caucasian 48% \ **Exp:** $602 (High) \ **Poverty:** 17% \ **Title I:** $269,966 \ **Open-Close:** 08/15 - 05/21 \ **DTBP:** $546 (High)

Ricky Stephens	1	Sandra Denning	2,8,15,19*
Anthony Denning	3	Ella Smith	4
Jason Hill	6*	Sylvia Mora	7,35,85
Ted Oniel	11,88,271	Dana Stockton	12,31,36,69,83,270
Robert Hinerman	16,82	David Diaz	57,63*
Michele Kurmes	58	Donnie Beeson	67
Ronnie Potts	91		

Public Schs..Principal	Grd	Prgm	Enr/#Cls	SN	
Ⓐ Alternative Learning Center 36245 Highway 67 E, Keene 76059 Ted O'Neil	9-12		60 6		817/774-5370 Fax 817/774-5405
Keene Elem Sch 300 E Highway 67, Keene 76059 Kelly Turnage	PK-5	T	491 16	83%	817/774-5320 Fax 817/774-5404
Keene Junior High Sch 402 E 4th St, Keene 76059 Jamie Ingram	6-8	T	240 15	74%	817/774-5311 Fax 817/774-5402
Keene Wanda R Smith High Sch 404 Charger Dr, Keene 76059 Christopher Taylor	9-12	TV	316 20	66%	817/774-5220 Fax 817/774-5401

- **Rio Vista Ind School Dist** PID: 01035137
 100 E Capps Street, Rio Vista 76093
 817/373-2241
 Fax 817/373-2076

> **Schools:** 3 \ **Teachers:** 62 \ **Students:** 750 \ **Special Ed Students:** 68 \ **LEP Students:** 33 \ **College-Bound:** 55% \ **Ethnic:** African American 1%, Hispanic 16%, Caucasian 83% \ **Exp:** $451 (High) \ **Poverty:** 28% \ **Title I:** $312,768 \ **Open-Close:** 08/15 - 05/22 \ **DTBP:** $350 (High)

Tony Martin	1	Billie Thornton	2
Monie Bigham	3,5	Angela Gonzales	58
Chris Pinyan	67	Charles Lister	73,295
Lisa Collins	81*		

Public Schs..Principal	Grd	Prgm	Enr/#Cls	SN	
Rio Vista Elem Sch 501 S Cleburne Whitney Rd, Rio Vista 76093 Jaylynn Cauthen	PK-5	T	344 35	65%	817/373-2151 Fax 817/373-3042
Rio Vista High Sch 100 Eagle Dr, Rio Vista 76093 Charles Mims	9-12	TV	239 24	45%	817/373-2009 Fax 817/373-3047

1	Superintendent	8	Curric/Instruct K-12	19	Chief Financial Officer	29	Family/Consumer Science	39	Social Studies K-12	49	English/Lang Arts Elem	59	Special Education Elem	69	Academic Assessment
2	Bus/Finance/Purchasing	9	Curric/Instruct Elem	20	Art K-12	30	Adult Education	40	Social Studies Elem	50	English/Lang Arts Sec	60	Special Education Sec	70	Research/Development
3	Buildings And Grounds	10	Curric/Instruct Sec	21	Art Elem	31	Career/Sch-to-Work K-12	41	Social Studies Sec	51	Reading K-12	61	Foreign/World Lang K-12	71	Public Information
4	Food Service	11	Federal Program	22	Art Sec	32	Career/Sch-to-Work Elem	42	Science K-12	52	Reading Elem	62	Foreign/World Lang Elem	72	Summer School
5	Transportation	12	Title I	23	Music K-12	33	Career/Sch-to-Work Sec	43	Science Elem	53	Reading Sec	63	Foreign/World Lang Sec	73	Instructional Tech
6	Athletic	13	Title V	24	Music Elem	34	Early Childhood Ed	44	Science Sec	54	Remedial Reading K-12	64	Religious Education K-12	74	Inservice Training
7	Health Services	15	Asst Superintendent	25	Music Sec	35	Health/Phys Education	45	Math K-12	55	Remedial Reading Elem	65	Religious Education Elem	75	Marketing/Distributive
		16	Instructional Media Svcs	26	Business Education	36	Guidance Services K-12	46	Math Elem	56	Remedial Reading Sec	66	Religious Education Sec	76	Info Systems
		17	Chief Operations Officer	27	Career & Tech Ed	37	Guidance Services Elem	47	Math Sec	57	Bilingual/ELL	67	School Board President	77	Psychological Assess
		18	Chief Academic Officer	28	Technology Education	38	Guidance Services Sec	48	English/Lang Arts K-12	58	Special Education K-12	68	Teacher Personnel	78	Affirmative Action

Texas School Directory

Jones County

Rio Vista Middle Sch	6-8	TV	149	54%	817/373-2241
309 S Cleburne Whitney Rd, Rio Vista 76093			20		Fax 817/373-3046
Brent Batch					

• **Venus Ind School Dist** PID: 01035163 972/366-3448
100 Student Dr, Venus 76084 Fax 972/232-2141

Schools: 4 \ *Teachers:* 135 \ *Students:* 2,200 \ *Special Ed Students:* 146 \ *LEP Students:* 457 \ *College-Bound:* 34% \ *Ethnic:* Asian 1%, African American 3%, Hispanic 55%, Native American: 1%, Caucasian 40% \ *Exp:* $429 (High) \ *Poverty:* 15% \ *Title I:* $344,560 \ *Special Education:* $547,000 \ *Open-Close:* 08/15 - 05/25 \ *DTBP:* $321 (High)

James Hopper 1		Michelle Salazar 2,19,84,288	
Ronnie Lisby 3		Tina McCormick 4	
Kathy Windell 5		Steven Nazworth 8,271*	
Hollis Moore 11,15,83		Katherine Roberts 16	
Gay Roden 57		Michelle Gidst-Barrow 58	
Les Owens 67		Kelly Morris 68	
Warren Hudson 73		Jacob Usery 295	

Public Schs..Principal	Grd	Prgm	Enr/#Cls	SN	
Venus Elem Sch	2-5	T	681	76%	972/366-3748
20 Bulldog Dr, Venus 76084			27		Fax 972/366-8808
Steven Nazworth					
Venus High Sch	9-12	TV	590	68%	972/366-8815
12 Bulldog Dr, Venus 76084			44		Fax 972/366-8919
Karen Woodworth					
Venus Middle Sch	6-8	T	503	71%	972/366-3358
1 Bulldog Dr, Venus 76084			40		Fax 972/366-1740
Kim Buck					
Venus Primary Sch	PK-1	T	420	76%	972/366-3268
102 Student Dr, Venus 76084			24		Fax 972/366-1826
Steven Nazworth					f t

JOHNSON PRIVATE SCHOOLS

Private Schs..Principal	Grd	Prgm	Enr/#Cls	SN	
Boulevard Baptist Chrstn Sch	PK-12		50		817/295-4342
315 N Burleson Blvd, Burleson 76028					Fax 817/295-4364
Jack Dunaway					
Chisholm Trail Academy	9-12	V	148		817/641-6626
401 S Old Betsy Rd, Keene 76059			12		Fax 817/556-2009
Tommy Simons					
Cleburne Christian Academy	PK-8		43		817/641-2857
1410 Glenhaven Dr, Cleburne 76033			10		Fax 817/641-2863
John Turner					
Holy Cross Christian Academy	K-8		200		817/295-7232
1233 Tarver Rd, Burleson 76028					Fax 817/295-6307
Karen Matejka					f t
Joshua Christian Academy	K-12		101		817/295-7377
510 N Broadway St, Joshua 76058			15		Fax 817/484-2415
Brian Archer					
Joshua SDA Multi Grade Sch	PK-8		60		817/556-2109
1912 Conveyor Dr, Joshua 76058			4		Fax 817/556-0029
Carol Schneider					
Keene Adventist Elem Sch	PK-8		200		817/645-9125
302 Pecan St, Keene 76059			13		Fax 817/645-9271
Todd Coulter					
Sycamore Academy	K-12		100		817/645-0895
111 E Oakdale St, Keene 76059					
Lorene Nicolas					

JONES COUNTY

JONES PUBLIC SCHOOLS

• **Anson Ind School Dist** PID: 01035199 325/823-3671
1431 Commercial Ave, Anson 79501 Fax 325/823-4444

Schools: 3 \ *Teachers:* 69 \ *Students:* 700 \ *Special Ed Students:* 84 \ *LEP Students:* 13 \ *Ethnic:* Asian 1%, African American 2%, Hispanic 50%, Caucasian 47% \ *Exp:* $457 (High) \ *Poverty:* 22% \ *Title I:* $179,774 \ *Open-Close:* 08/19 - 05/21 \ *DTBP:* $371 (High)

Jay Baccus 1		Marie Hargrove 2	
Logan Vinson 3,5		Bobbi Lytle 11,57,271,296*	
Stephen Sciterm 27,31*		Sherry Meek 38,83*	
Phyllis Davis 58*		Don Heller 67	
Gary Westbrook 73,98,295*			

Public Schs..Principal	Grd	Prgm	Enr/#Cls	SN	
Anson Elem Sch	PK-5	T	365	70%	325/823-3361
922 Avenue M, Anson 79501			45		Fax 325/823-3127
Amy McIntire					
Anson High Sch	9-12	TV	228	60%	325/823-2404
1509 Commercial Ave, Anson 79501			26		Fax 325/823-2514
Troy Hinds					
Anson Middle Sch	6-8	T	178	61%	325/823-2771
1102 Ave M, Anson 79501			20		Fax 325/823-3667
David Hagler					

• **Hamlin Ind School Dist** PID: 01035228 325/576-2722
250 SW Avenue F, Hamlin 79520 Fax 325/576-2152

Schools: 2 \ *Teachers:* 33 \ *Students:* 400 \ *Special Ed Students:* 48 \ *LEP Students:* 26 \ *College-Bound:* 90% \ *Ethnic:* Asian 1%, African American 3%, Hispanic 44%, Caucasian 53% \ *Exp:* $308 (High) \ *Poverty:* 31% \ *Title I:* $212,910 \ *Open-Close:* 08/15 - 05/22 \ *DTBP:* $350 (High)

Dr Randy Burk 1		Becky Terry 2	
Theresa Gholson 3,5		Russell Lucas 6*	
Laurie Pond 8		Cindy Hastings 31,36,88*	
Michelle Jones 58*		Mason VanCleave 67	
Katrina Bogle 73,76,84,295			

Public Schs..Principal	Grd	Prgm	Enr/#Cls	SN	
Hamlin Elem Sch	PK-6	T	241	77%	325/576-3191
405 NW 5th St, Hamlin 79520			14		Fax 325/576-2358
C Jones					
Hamlin High Sch	7-12	T	156	69%	325/576-3624
450 SW Avenue F, Hamlin 79520			18		Fax 325/576-3926
Matt Pond					

• **Hawley Ind School Dist** PID: 01035266 325/537-2214
210 Ave E, Hawley 79525 Fax 325/537-2265

Schools: 3 \ *Teachers:* 73 \ *Students:* 769 \ *Special Ed Students:* 48 \ *LEP Students:* 3 \ *College-Bound:* 51% \ *Ethnic:* African American 1%, Hispanic 21%, Caucasian 78% \ *Exp:* $370 (High) \ *Poverty:* 19% \ *Title I:* $134,511 \ *Open-Close:* 08/21 - 05/21 \ *DTBP:* $345 (High)

---

79 Student Personnel	91 Safety/Security	275 Response To Intervention	298 Grant Writer/Ptnrships	School Programs	Social Media
80 Driver Ed/Safety	92 Magnet School	277 Remedial Math K-12	750 Chief Innovation Officer	A = Alternative Program	
81 Gifted/Talented	93 Parental Involvement	280 Literacy Coach	751 Chief of Staff	G = Adult Classes	f = Facebook
82 Video Services	95 Tech Prep Program	285 STEM	752 Social Emotional Learning	M = Magnet Program	
83 Substance Abuse Prev	97 Chief Information Officer	286 Digital Learning		T = Title I Schoolwide	t = Twitter
84 Erate	98 Chief Technology Officer	288 Common Core Standards	Other School Types	V = Career & Tech Ed Programs	
85 AIDS Education	270 Accountability	294 Accountability	Ⓐ = Alternative School		
88 Alternative/At Risk	271 Migrant Education	295 Network System	Ⓒ = Charter School	New Schools are shaded	
89 Multi-Cultural Curriculum	273 Teacher Mentor	296 Title II Programs	Ⓜ = Magnet School	New Superintendents and Principals are bold	
90 Social Work	274 Before/After Sch	297 Webmaster	Ⓨ = Year-Round School	Personnel with email addresses are underscored	TX—249

Karnes County

Market Data Retrieval

Dr Cassidy McBrayer 1	Melody Collier 2,8,11,57,58,288*
Terry Thompson 3,5,91*	Wende McAndrew 4*
Mitch Ables 6	Martha Anderson 7
Laurie Florence 9*	Karrie Thompson 16,82*
Kevin Stoker 16,73,286*	Regina Siller 27*
Nikki Grisham 31,285*	Nate Knight 67
Nellie Martin 270,271,273*	

Public Schs..Principal	Grd	Prgm	Enr/#Cls	SN	
Hawley Elem Sch 210 Ave E, Hawley 79525 Laurie Florence	PK-5	T	358 20	60%	325/537-2721 Fax 325/537-9099
Hawley High Sch 800 1st St, Hawley 79525 Nikki Grisham	9-12	TV	209 20	37%	325/537-2722 Fax 325/537-4398
Hawley Middle Sch 800 1st St, Hawley 79525 Charles Hoffman	6-8	T	170 20	58%	325/537-2070 Fax 325/537-4399

- **Lueders-Avoca Ind School Dist** PID: 01035292   325/228-4211
  334 Vandeventer St, Lueders 79533   Fax 325/228-4513

Schools: 2 \ **Teachers:** 17 \ **Students:** 104 \ **Special Ed Students:** 17 \ **LEP Students:** 3 \ **College-Bound:** 50% \ **Ethnic:** African American 4%, Hispanic 24%, Caucasian 72% \ **Exp:** $727 (High) \ **Poverty:** 28% \ **Title I:** $42,582 \ **Open-Close:** 08/14 - 05/22 \ **DTBP:** $350 (High)

Bob Spikes 1	Pete Lopez 67

Public Schs..Principal	Grd	Prgm	Enr/#Cls	SN	
Lueders-Avoca Elem Jr High Sch 334 Vandeventer St, Lueders 79533 Bob Spikes	PK-8	T	70 14	86%	325/228-4211
Lueders-Avoca High Sch 8762 County Road 604, Avoca 79503 Robert Cummings	9-12	T	36 8	67%	325/773-2785 Fax 325/773-3072

- **Stamford Ind School Dist** PID: 01035321   325/773-2705
  507 S Orient St, Stamford 79553   Fax 325/773-5684

Schools: 3 \ **Teachers:** 61 \ **Students:** 670 \ **Special Ed Students:** 57 \ **LEP Students:** 19 \ **Ethnic:** Asian 1%, African American 10%, Hispanic 47%, Native American: 1%, Caucasian 42% \ **Exp:** $692 (High) \ **Poverty:** 27% \ **Title I:** $212,019 \ **Open-Close:** 08/16 - 05/22 \ **DTBP:** $180 (High)

Will Brewer 1	Staci Robertson 2
Joe Garcia 3,91	Ronnie Casey 6*
Jennifer Hinds 8,11,296	Belinda Fernandez 16,82*
Leann Mueller 31*	Cindy Ford 35,85*
Angie Gann 58*	Jennifer Caddell 67
Jennifer White 69,83,88,270*	Michael Burfiend 73*

Public Schs..Principal	Grd	Prgm	Enr/#Cls	SN	
Oliver Elem Sch 400 Oliver Street, Stamford 79553 Kyle Chambers	PK-5	T	322 22	72%	325/307-3765 Fax 325/773-4077
Stamford High Sch 507 S Orient St, Stamford 79553 Chase Seelke	9-12	TV	184 22	57%	325/307-3614 Fax 325/773-4015
Stamford Middle Sch 800 E Reynolds Street, Stamford 79553 Kevin White	6-8	T	165 20	64%	325/455-0978 Fax 325/773-4052

KARNES COUNTY

KARNES PUBLIC SCHOOLS

- **Falls City Ind School Dist** PID: 01035369   830/254-3551
  700 N Nelson St, Falls City 78113   Fax 830/254-3354

Schools: 2 \ **Teachers:** 30 \ **Students:** 360 \ **Special Ed Students:** 22 \ **LEP Students:** 9 \ **College-Bound:** 90% \ **Ethnic:** Hispanic 21%, Caucasian 78% \ **Exp:** $545 (High) \ **Poverty:** 14% \ **Title I:** $50,785 \ **Open-Close:** 08/15 - 05/22

Todd Pawelek 1,11,83	Terri Crawford 2
Britt Hart 6*	Elizabeth De Leon 27,69*
Christy Blocker 57,271*	Christy Blocker 57,58,271
Wayne Lyssy 67	Patricia Startz 73,295,298*

Public Schs..Principal	Grd	Prgm	Enr/#Cls	SN	
Falls City Elem Sch 525 N Nelson St, Falls City 78113 Christy Blocker	PK-6		199 14	18%	830/254-3551
Falls City High Sch 700 N Nelson St, Falls City 78113 Christy Blocker	7-12	V	161 16	15%	830/254-3551

- **Karnes City Ind School Dist** PID: 01035395   830/780-2321
  404 N Highway 123, Karnes City 78118   Fax 830/780-3823

Schools: 5 \ **Teachers:** 84 \ **Students:** 1,085 \ **Special Ed Students:** 116 \ **LEP Students:** 47 \ **Ethnic:** African American 1%, Hispanic 73%, Caucasian 26% \ **Exp:** $552 (High) \ **Poverty:** 23% \ **Title I:** $250,921 \ **Open-Close:** 08/14 - 05/21 \ **DTBP:** $326 (High)

Jeanette Winn 1	Ashley Black 2,68
Juan Carlos 3,91	Sidney Martin 4
Gloria Keller 5	Korey Graham 5
James Wood 6*	Bernadette Bluhm 7*
Jo Ann Gutierrez 8,69,288	Lisa Moczygemba 11,57,88,271
Holly Polasek 16*	Micheal Kroll 27,28*
Lyndall Wiatrek 34	Yolanda Solis 36*
Jayma Wood 58*	Terry Johnson 67
Chelleye Block 73*	Jamie McKee 84
Frances Ehrlich 274	Alicia Wieding 298

Public Schs..Principal	Grd	Prgm	Enr/#Cls	SN	
Karnes City Early Clg HS 400 N Highway 123, Karnes City 78118 Raymond Robinson	9-10		45		830/780-2321
Karnes City High Sch 400 N Highway 123, Karnes City 78118 Anthony Annis	9-12	ATV	351 25	56%	830/780-2321 Fax 830/780-4352
Karnes City Junior High Sch 410 N Highway 123, Karnes City 78118 Theresa Molina	6-8	ATV	257 22	58%	830/780-2321 Fax 830/780-4382
Karnes City Primary Sch 203 E Mayfield St, Karnes City 78118 Jennifer Foster	PK-1	T	222	86%	830/780-2321 Fax 830/780-5376
Roger E Sides Elem Sch 221 N Esplanade St, Karnes City 78118 Jennifer Foster	PK-5	T	400 30	74%	830/780-2321 Fax 830/780-4427

1	Superintendent	8	Curric/Instruct K-12	19	Chief Financial Officer	29	Family/Consumer Science	39	Social Studies K-12
2	Bus/Finance/Purchasing	9	Curric/Instruct Elem	20	Art K-12	30	Adult Education	40	Social Studies Elem
3	Buildings And Grounds	10	Curric/Instruct Sec	21	Art Elem	31	Career/Sch-to-Work K-12	41	Social Studies Sec
4	Food Service	11	Federal Program	22	Art Sec	32	Career/Sch-to-Work Elem	42	Science K-12
5	Transportation	12	Title I	23	Music K-12	33	Career/Sch-to-Work Sec	43	Science Elem
6	Athletic	13	Title V	24	Music Elem	34	Early Childhood Ed	44	Science Sec
7	Health Services	15	Asst Superintendent	25	Music Sec	35	Health/Phys Education	45	Math K-12
		16	Instructional Media Svcs	26	Business Education	36	Guidance Services K-12	46	Math Elem
		17	Chief Operations Officer	27	Career & Tech Ed	37	Guidance Services Elem	47	Math Sec
		18	Chief Academic Officer	28	Technology Education	38	Guidance Services Sec	48	English/Lang Arts K-12

49	English/Lang Arts Elem	59	Special Education Elem	69	Academic Assessment
50	English/Lang Arts Sec	60	Special Education Sec	70	Research/Development
51	Reading K-12	61	Foreign/World Lang K-12	71	Public Information
52	Reading Elem	62	Foreign/World Lang Elem	72	Summer School
53	Reading Sec	63	Foreign/World Lang Sec	73	Instructional Tech
54	Remedial Reading K-12	64	Religious Education K-12	74	Inservice Training
55	Remedial Reading Elem	65	Religious Education Elem	75	Marketing/Distributive
56	Remedial Reading Sec	66	Religious Education Sec	76	Info Systems
57	Bilingual/ELL	67	School Board President	77	Psychological Assess
58	Special Education K-12	68	Teacher Personnel	78	Affirmative Action

Texas School Directory

Kaufman County

● **Kenedy Ind School Dist** PID: 01035450   830/583-4100
401 FM 719, Kenedy 78119   Fax 830/583-9950

Schools: 3 \ *Teachers:* 66 \ *Students:* 800 \ *Special Ed Students:* 111
\ *LEP Students:* 38 \ *College-Bound:* 57% \ *Ethnic:* African American 3%, Hispanic 87%, Caucasian 10% \ *Exp:* $431 (High) \ *Poverty:* 29% \
Title I: $308,091 \ *Open-Close:* 08/12 - 05/21 \ *DTBP:* $367 (High)

Diana Ugarte	1,11	Vanessa Pawelek	2
Jerry Garcia	3,91	Johnnie Lopez	5
Shawn Alveraz	6	Kellie Kolodziej	7*
Dimitrio Garica	67	Melanie Witte	69
Curtis Plant	73,84		

Public Schs..Principal	Grd	Prgm	Enr/#Cls	SN	
Kenedy Elem Sch 401 FM 719, Kenedy 78119 Melanie Witte	PK-5	T	435 23	79%	830/583-4100 Fax 830/583-3973
Kenedy High Sch 401 FM 719, Kenedy 78119 Deborah Del Bosque	9-12	T	214 35	58%	830/583-4100 Fax 830/583-9126
Kenedy Middle Sch 401 FM 719, Kenedy 78119 Richard Cardin	6-8	T	160 22	67%	830/583-4100 Fax 830/583-9519

● **Runge Ind School Dist** PID: 01035503   830/239-4315
600 N Reiffert, Runge 78151   Fax 830/239-4816

Schools: 1 \ *Teachers:* 29 \ *Students:* 250 \ *Special Ed Students:* 31
\ *LEP Students:* 3 \ *College-Bound:* 50% \ *Ethnic:* Hispanic 89%, Caucasian 11% \ *Exp:* $874 (High) \ *Poverty:* 22% \ *Title I:* $105,261 \
Open-Close: 08/27 - 05/29 \ *DTBP:* $26 (Low) \ ⓕ ⓣ

Kyle Spivey	1	Randy Ramirez	2
Pete Ybarra	3	Kyle Blalock	6*
Linda Martin	7	Bake Barron	11
Aiden Everett	28,73,286*	Erica Buehring	36,69,83,88*
Gloria Donaubauer	58*	Robert Molina	67
Aiden Everett	84		

Public Schs..Principal	Grd	Prgm	Enr/#Cls	SN	
Runge Sch 600 N Reiffert, Runge 78151 Brenda DeLaRosa	PK-12	ATV	250 30	73%	830/239-4315

KAUFMAN COUNTY

KAUFMAN PUBLIC SCHOOLS

● **Crandall Ind School Dist** PID: 01035539   972/427-6000
400 W Lewis Street, Crandall 75114   Fax 972/427-6036

Schools: 7 \ *Teachers:* 231 \ *Students:* 4,500 \ *Special Ed Students:* 321
\ *LEP Students:* 305 \ *College-Bound:* 60% \ *Ethnic:* Asian 1%, African American 13%, Hispanic 26%, Caucasian 60% \ *Exp:* $641 (High) \
\ *Poverty:* 9% \ *Title I:* $301,554 \ *Special Education:* $544,000 \
Open-Close: 08/21 - 05/25 \ *DTBP:* $350 (High)

Dr Wendy Eldredge	1	Larry Guerry	2,19
Alan Lovell	3	Earnest Lilly	4
Scott Stewart	5	Joe Cary	6
Dr Anjanette Murry	8,11,15,288	Christy Starrett	15,68
Janice Dowlearn	16,31	Sharlene Gonzalez	57
Deann Baker	58	Rick Harrell	67
Monica Aspegren	69	Erin McCann	71
Scott Phipps	73,76,98,286	Emily Christianson	294

Public Schs..Principal	Grd	Prgm	Enr/#Cls	SN	
Barbara Walker Elem Sch 4060 Abbey Rd, Heartland 75126 Abby Baker	PK-5	T	675	40%	972/427-6030 Fax 972/427-6031
Crandall Compass Academy 400 W Lewis St, Crandall 75114 Jennifer Coward	3-12		65 5		972/427-6100 Fax 972/427-8239
Crandall High Sch 13385 FM 3039, Crandall 75114 Jeannia Dykman	9-12		1,082 30	42%	972/427-6150 Fax 972/427-6130
Crandall Middle Sch 500 W Lewis St, Crandall 75114 Amy McAfee	6-8	T	877 50	47%	972/427-6080 Fax 972/427-6129
Hollis T Dietz Elem Sch 2080 Sunnybrook Dr, Heartland 75126 Melissa Smith	PK-6		500		972/427-6050 Fax 972/427-6052
Nola Kathryn Wilson Elem Sch 300 Meadowcreek Dr, Crandall 75114 Ginger Sikes	PK-5	T	553 30	44%	972/427-6040 Fax 972/472-8111
W A Martin Elem Sch 1160 W Highway 175, Crandall 75114 Dave Christensen	PK-5	T	615 30	65%	972/427-6020 Fax 972/427-6039

● **Forney Ind School Dist** PID: 01035565   972/564-4055
600 S Bois D Arc St, Forney 75126   Fax 972/552-3038

Schools: 14 \ *Teachers:* 590 \ *Students:* 9,681 \ *Special Ed Students:* 825
\ *LEP Students:* 580 \ *College-Bound:* 55% \ *Ethnic:* Asian 2%, African American 14%, Hispanic 27%, Caucasian 56% \ *Exp:* $251 (Med)
\ *Poverty:* 6% \ *Title I:* $530,346 \ *Special Education:* $1,116,000 \
Open-Close: 07/19 - 05/22 \ *DTBP:* $155 (High) \ ⓕ

Dr Justin Terry	1	John Chase	2,19
Christopher Gibbs	3	Tracy Money	4
Mickey Krone	5	Neal Weaver	6
Richard Geer	7,88,270	Judy Webber	8,18,27,30,34,69
Tandi Owen	11,294	Stacy Joseph	16,73
Mario Luna	20,23	Stormy Lemond	28
Carmen Delossantos	57	Laura Merchant	58
Greg Pharris	67	Tommy Riggs	68
Kim Morisak	71,73,97,98	Kristin Zastoupil	71
Deborah Hamessley	76	Melanie Harlan	81
Janet Freeman	91	Sandra Whitley	286
Howard Carlin	295		

Public Schs..Principal	Grd	Prgm	Enr/#Cls	SN	
Blackburn Elem Sch 2401 Concord St, Forney 75126 Courtney Parker	PK-6	T	551 36	31%	972/564-7008 Fax 469/355-0491
Brown Middle Sch 1050 Windmill Farms Blvd, Forney 75126 Dr Pamelia Luttrull	7-8		884 30	28%	972/564-3967 Fax 469/355-1099
Claybon Elem Sch 1011 FM 741, Forney 75126 Kristi Crabtree	PK-6		651 30	21%	972/564-7023 Fax 972/552-3274
Criswell Elem Sch 401 FM 740 N, Forney 75126 Rachel Bonner	PK-6		608 30	27%	972/564-1609 Fax 972/552-3304
Crosby Elem Sch 495 Diamond Creek Dr, Forney 75126 Leslie Rader	PK-6	T	598	22%	972/564-7002 Fax 469/355-0531

79	Student Personnel	91	Safety/Security	275	Response To Intervention	298	Grant Writer/Ptnrships
80	Driver Ed/Safety	92	Magnet School	277	Remedial Math K-12	750	Chief Innovation Officer
81	Gifted/Talented	93	Parental Involvement	280	Literacy Coach	751	Chief of Staff
82	Video Services	95	Tech Prep Program	285	STEM	752	Social Emotional Learning
83	Substance Abuse Prev	97	Chief Infomation Officer	286	Digital Learning		
84	Erate	98	Chief Technology Officer	288	Common Core Standards		
85	AIDS Education	270	Character Education	294	Accountability		
88	Alternative/At Risk	271	Migrant Education	295	Network System		
89	Multi-Cultural Curriculum	273	Teacher Mentor	296	Title II Programs		
90	Social Work	274	Before/After Sch	297	Webmaster		

Other School Types
Ⓐ = Alternative School
Ⓒ = Charter School
Ⓜ = Magnet School
Ⓨ = Year-Round School

School Programs
A = Alternative Program
G = Adult Classes
M = Magnet Program
T = Title I Schoolwide
V = Career & Tech Ed Programs

Social Media
ⓕ = Facebook
ⓣ = Twitter

New Schools are shaded
New Superintendents and Principals are bold
Personnel with email addresses are underscored

TX—251

Kaufman County

Market Data Retrieval

Ⓐ Forney Academic Center 4-12   50   469/762-4350
309 S Bois D Arc St, Forney 75126   5   Fax 469/762-4351
Steve Whiffen

Forney High Sch 9-12 GV 1,453 469/762-4200
1800 College Ave, Forney 75126   Fax 469/762-4201
Dr Jonathan Campbell

Henderson Elem Sch PK-6   678 22% 972/564-7100
12755 FM 1641, Forney 75126   34   Fax 972/552-3335
Laurie Branch

Johnson Elem Sch PK-6   518 20% 972/564-3397
701 S Bois D Arc St, Forney 75126   25   Fax 972/552-3336
Nancy McElroy

Lewis Elem Sch PK-6   535 21% 972/564-7102
1309 Luckenbach Dr, Forney 75126   Fax 469/355-2128
Jenny Harstrom

North Forney High Sch 9-12 1,585 24% 469/762-4210
6170 Falcon Way, Forney 75126   Fax 469/762-4211
Courtney Peck

Rhea Elem Sch PK-6 T 672 27% 469/762-4157
250 Monitor Dr, Forney 75126   Fax 469/355-0191
Barbi Donehoo

Smith Elem Sch PK-6 T 696 34% 469/762-4158
1750 Iron Gate Blvd, Forney 75126   30   Fax 469/355-0154
Jeff Hutcheson

Warren Middle Sch 7-8   767 22% 469/762-4156
811 S Bois D Arc St, Forney 75126   Fax 972/552-1693
Joshua Garcia

● **Kaufman Ind School Dist** PID: 01035606   972/932-2622
1000 S Houston St, Kaufman 75142   Fax 972/932-3325

Schools: 7 \ *Teachers:* 259 \ *Students:* 3,500 \ *Special Ed Students:* 358 \ *LEP Students:* 579 \ *College-Bound:* 67% \ *Ethnic:* Asian 1%, African American 5%, Hispanic 46%, Native American: 1%, Caucasian 47% \ *Exp:* $803 (High) \ *Poverty:* 16% \ *Title I:* $798,929 \ *Special Education:* $692,000 \ *Open-Close:* 08/19 - 05/22 \ *DTBP:* $175 (High)

Dr Lori Blaylock 1   Todd Garrison 2,19
John Hughes 3   Kennan Dealy 4
Patrick Cardoza 5   Jeramy Burleson 6*
Joe Nicks 8,15,286,288   Sherry Kerr 11,57,271
Kell Clopton 15,68,88   Julie Johnson 58
Byron Gregg 67   Bonita Hobden 68
Angela Corder 73,76   Marsha Johnson 294

Public Schs..Principal	Grd	Prgm	Enr/#Cls	SN	
Ⓐ Gary W Campbell High Sch 4814 County Road 151, Kaufman 75142 Gary Campbell	6-12	T	40 8	72%	972/932-8789 Fax 972/932-2278
Helen Edwards Early Chldhd Ctr 1605 Rand Rd, Kaufman 75142 Melanie Bowers	PK-K	T	445	68%	972/932-0800 Fax 972/932-6850
J W Monday Elem Sch 905 S Madison St, Kaufman 75142 Kathy Allen	1-5	T	512 28	69%	972/932-3513 Fax 972/932-2758
Kaufman High Sch 3205 S Houston St, Kaufman 75142 Amy Keith	9-12	TV	1,162 66	53%	972/932-2811 Fax 972/932-1948
Lucille Nash Elem Sch 1002 S Houston St, Kaufman 75142 Alicia Thurston	1-5	T	596 25	70%	972/932-6415 Fax 972/932-4028
O P Norman Junior High Sch 3701 S Houston St, Kaufman 75142 Jeremy Melton	6-8	T	597 50	59%	972/932-2410 Fax 972/932-7771

Phillips Elem Sch 1-5 T 603 70% 972/932-4500
1501 Royal Dr, Kaufman 75142   30   Fax 972/932-7633
Kara Holley

● **Kemp Ind School Dist** PID: 01035656   903/498-1314
905 S Main St, Kemp 75143   Fax 903/498-1315

Schools: 4 \ *Teachers:* 112 \ *Students:* 1,586 \ *Special Ed Students:* 176 \ *LEP Students:* 114 \ *Ethnic:* African American 2%, Hispanic 23%, Caucasian 74% \ *Exp:* $419 (High) \ *Poverty:* 17% \ *Title I:* $381,299 \ *Special Education:* $289,000 \ *Open-Close:* 08/21 - 05/22 \ *DTBP:* $340 (High)

Dr Lisa Gonzales 1   Kim Johnson 2
Scott Ellis 3,5   Larhesa Haley 4*
Jane Dvorak 8,11,286   Tara Bachtel 15
Sheri Machel 16   Toni Miller 27
Mary Ann Gregg 57   Angela Barton 58
Sharron Rakin 67   Tobin Brown 73,297

Public Schs..Principal	Grd	Prgm	Enr/#Cls	SN	
Kemp High Sch 220 State Highway 274, Kemp 75143 Jim Lamb	9-12	ATV	470 25	63%	903/498-9222 Fax 903/498-9275
Kemp Intermediate Sch 101 Old State Highway 40 Rd, Kemp 75143 Kim McDowell	3-5	T	374 26	74%	903/498-1362 Fax 903/498-1379
Kemp Junior High Sch 1000 Tolosa Rd, Kemp 75143 Kyle Hutchings	6-8	AT	347 20	71%	903/498-1343 Fax 903/498-1359
Kemp Primary Sch 601 E 8th St, Kemp 75143 Jennifer Welch	PK-2	T	395 28	83%	903/498-1404 Fax 903/498-2136

● **Mabank Ind School Dist** PID: 01035682   903/880-1300
310 E Market St, Mabank 75147   Fax 903/880-1303

Schools: 8 \ *Teachers:* 234 \ *Students:* 3,500 \ *Special Ed Students:* 366 \ *LEP Students:* 80 \ *College-Bound:* 50% \ *Ethnic:* Asian 1%, African American 2%, Hispanic 16%, Caucasian 80% \ *Exp:* $465 (High) \ *Poverty:* 22% \ *Title I:* $896,682 \ *Special Education:* $893,000 \ *Open-Close:* 08/14 - 05/28 \ *DTBP:* $175 (High)

Lee Joffre 1   Scott Adams 2,15
Steve Templin 3,91   Kim LeGrande 4*
Randy Welch 5   Tracy Carter 6*
Pam Odom 7,35,85   Rebecca Stephens ...8,11,57,69,83,88,294
Brad Koskelin 15,68,71   James Pate 16
Shela Koskelin ....31*   Timbra Yoakem 58
Kenneth Odom 67   Jk Hyde 73,295,297

Public Schs..Principal	Grd	Prgm	Enr/#Cls	SN	
Ⓐ Academy 822 W Mason St, Mabank 75147 Ray Duncan	9-12		58		903/880-1600
Central Elem Sch 19119 E US Highway 175, Mabank 75147 Chelsea Capehart	PK-4	T	627 25	61%	903/880-1380 Fax 903/880-1383
Lakeview Elem Sch 306 Harbor Point Rd, Mabank 75156 Kevin Pate	K-4	T	406 22	62%	903/880-1360 Fax 903/880-1363
Ⓐ Mabank Daep 349 E Market St, Mabank 75147 Edna Duncan	K-12		22 4		903/880-1320 Fax 903/880-1323

1	Superintendent	8	Curric/Instruct K-12	19	Chief Financial Officer	29	Family/Consumer Science	39	Social Studies K-12	49	English/Lang Arts Elem	59	Special Education Elem	69	Academic Assessment
2	Bus/Finance/Purchasing	9	Curric/Instruct Elem	20	Art K-12	30	Adult Education	40	Social Studies Elem	50	English/Lang Arts Sec	60	Special Education Sec	70	Research/Development
3	Buildings And Grounds	10	Curric/Instruct Sec	21	Art Elem	31	Career/Sch-to-Work K-12	41	Social Studies Sec	51	Reading K-12	61	Foreign/World Lang K-12	71	Public Information
4	Food Service	11	Federal Program	22	Art Sec	32	Career/Sch-to-Work Elem	42	Science K-12	52	Reading Elem	62	Foreign/World Lang Elem	72	Summer School
5	Transportation	12	Title I	23	Music K-12	33	Career/Sch-to-Work Sec	43	Science Elem	53	Reading Sec	63	Foreign/World Lang Sec	73	Instructional Tech
6	Athletic	13	Title V	24	Music Elem	34	Early Childhood Ed	44	Science Sec	54	Remedial Reading K-12	64	Religious Education K-12	74	Inservice Training
7	Health Services	15	Asst Superintendent	25	Music Sec	35	Health/Phys Education	45	Math K-12	55	Remedial Reading Elem	65	Religious Education Elem	75	Marketing/Distributive
		16	Instructional Media Svcs	26	Business Education	36	Guidance Services K-12	46	Math Elem	56	Remedial Reading Sec	66	Religious Education Sec	76	Info Systems
		17	Chief Operations Officer	27	Career & Tech Ed	37	Guidance Services Elem	47	Math Sec	57	Bilingual/ELL	67	School Board President	77	Psychological Assess
		18	Chief Academic Officer	28	Technology Education	38	Guidance Services Sec	48	English/Lang Arts K-12	58	Special Education K-12	68	Teacher Personnel	78	Affirmative Action

Texas School Directory

Kendall County

Mabank High Sch	9-12	GTV	1,035	55%	903/880-1600
18786 E US Highway 175, Mabank 75147					Fax 903/880-1603
Brett Haugh					
Mabank Intermediate Sch	5-6	T	564	61%	903/880-1640
513 N 3rd St, Mabank 75147			21		Fax 903/880-1643
Debra DeRosa					
Mabank Junior High Sch	7-8	T	481	59%	903/880-1670
822 W Mason St, Mabank 75147					Fax 903/880-1673
Barbie Conrad					
Southside Elem Sch	PK-4	T	400	75%	903/880-1340
109 Paschall Blvd, Mabank 75147			26		Fax 903/880-1343
Brandi Dyer					

• **Scurry Rosser Ind School Dist** PID: 01035723   972/452-8823
10705 S State Highway 34, Scurry 75158   Fax 972/452-8586

Schools: 3 \ *Teachers:* 77 \ *Students:* 1,035 \ *Special Ed Students:* 113 \ *LEP Students:* 35 \ *College-Bound:* 50% \ *Ethnic:* African American 2%, Hispanic 16%, Native American: 1%, Caucasian 82% \ *Exp:* $483 (High) \ *Poverty:* 16%   \ *Title I:* $224,932 \ *Special Education:* $166,000 \ *Open-Close:* 08/19 - 05/21 \ *DTBP:* $349 (High)

James Sanders 1,11,83	Cindy Wiedemann 2	
Chandra Babovec 4	Jess Cleveland 6	
Rebecca Rowe 7,85*	Gail Crow 8	
Kandy Shirey 9,34*	Chad Collins 15	
David Crawford 27*	Heather Jestis 58	
Joanna Horton 67	Mark Sampson 73*	
Erik Scott 91		

Public Schs..Principal	Grd	Prgm	Enr/#Cls	SN	
Scurry Rosser Elem Sch	PK-3	T	324	51%	972/452-8823
9511 Silver Creek Dr, Scurry 75158			20		Fax 972/452-3434
Kandy Shirey					
Scurry Rosser High Sch	9-12	GV	318	38%	972/452-8823
8321 S State Highway 34, Scurry 75158			25		Fax 972/452-3694
Christian Reed					
Scurry Rosser Middle Sch	4-8	TV	387	46%	972/452-8823
10729 S State Highway 34, Scurry 75158			20		Fax 972/452-8902
Grant Miller					

• **Terrell Ind School Dist** PID: 01035759   972/563-7504
700 N Catherine St, Terrell 75160   Fax 972/563-1406

Schools: 9 \ *Teachers:* 274 \ *Students:* 4,711 \ *Special Ed Students:* 392 \ *LEP Students:* 800 \ *Ethnic:* Asian 1%, African American 24%, Hispanic 49%, Caucasian 27% \ *Exp:* $582 (High) \ *Poverty:* 19% \ *Title I:* $1,271,883 \ *Special Education:* $867,000 \ *Open-Close:* 08/20 - 05/22 \ *DTBP:* $185 (High) \ 🅵

Micheal French 1	Crystal Shirley 2
Diana Tidwell 4	Stan Heisel 5,73,76,295
Buster Leaf 6	Melody Stowe 7*
Julie Fisher 11,69,275,288,296	Dr Jason Gomez 15
Larry Polk 15,298	Peggy Bridges 27,31*
Debi Rogers 58	Dena Risinger 67
Stacey Ellis 68,273	Olivia Rice 71
Shuck Wieland 79	Pam Chamberlain 286

Public Schs..Principal	Grd	Prgm	Enr/#Cls	SN	
Dr Bruce Wood Elem Sch	K-5	T	640	80%	972/563-3750
121 Poetry Rd, Terrell 75160			55		Fax 972/563-4774
Tracy Pritchit					🅵
Gilbert Willie Sr Elem Sch	K-5	T	664	79%	972/563-1443
1400 S Rockwall Ave, Terrell 75160			55		Fax 972/563-4783
Brenda Navaja					
Herman Furlough Jr Middle Sch	6-8	TV	588	74%	972/563-7501
1351 Colquitt Rd, Terrell 75160			50		Fax 972/563-5721
Brenda Navaja					
J W Long Elem Sch	K-5	T	701	82%	972/563-1448
300 Creekside Dr, Terrell 75160			17		Fax 972/563-4780
Melissa Nichols					
Ⓐ Phoenix Center	9-12	T	8	50%	972/563-6319
204 W High St, Terrell 75160			2		Fax 972/563-4786
Renae Jones					
Ⓐ Terrell Alternative Ed Center	K-12		45		972/563-6319
305 W College St, Terrell 75160			4		Fax 972/563-4786
Renee Jones					
Terrell High Sch	9-12	TV	1,190	67%	972/563-7525
701 Town North Dr, Terrell 75160			40		Fax 972/563-6318
Jay Thompson					
Tisd Child & Adolescent Ctr	1-12		23	10%	972/551-8960
1200 E Brin St, Terrell 75160			4		Fax 972/551-8848
Dwight Malone					
W H Burnett Early Chldhd Ctr	PK-PK	T	568	86%	972/563-1452
921 S Rockwall Ave, Terrell 75160			31		Fax 972/563-4782
Melissa Nichols					

KAUFMAN PRIVATE SCHOOLS

Private Schs..Principal	Grd	Prgm	Enr/#Cls	SN	
Kaufman Christian Sch	PK-6		80		972/932-4672
401 N Shannon St, Kaufman 75142			12		Fax 972/962-0531
Christy Butler					
Poetry Community Christian Sch	K-12		250		972/563-7227
18688 FM 986, Terrell 75160					Fax 972/563-0025
Ann Horan					

KENDALL COUNTY

KENDALL PUBLIC SCHOOLS

• **Boerne Ind School Dist** PID: 01035814   830/357-2000
235 Johns Rd, Boerne 78006   Fax 830/357-2009

Schools: 11 \ *Teachers:* 519 \ *Students:* 9,000 \ *Special Ed Students:* 689 \ *LEP Students:* 359 \ *College-Bound:* 59% \ *Ethnic:* Asian 1%, African American 1%, Hispanic 30%, Caucasian 68% \ *Exp:* $270 (Med) \ *Poverty:* 7% \ *Title I:* $741,928 \ *Special Education:* $1,075,000 \ *Open-Close:* 08/14 - 05/21 \ *DTBP:* $198 (High)

Thomas Price 1	Tish Grill 2,15
Mark Stahl 3	Cheryl Rayburg 4
Paul Spencer 5	Stan Leech 6,35
Carole Gish 7*	Jodi Spoor 8,15,36,74,81,88,273*
Bibi Bermudez 11,83,270,271	Ashley Stewart 15
Ken Peach 20	Sandie Ford 27
Bret Bunker 39	Chris Ormiston 42
Linda Gann 45	Jayne Burton 48,51
Daphne Morris 49,52	Francis Garcia 54
Bibiana Stosberg 57	Annie Seiter 58
Carlin Friar 67	Elaine Howard 68,79
Jocelyn Durand 71	Jason Essig 73,286
Shana Dillon 81	Hector Hernandez 91

79	Student Personnel	91	Safety/Security	275	Response To Intervention	298	Grant Writer/Ptnrships
80	Driver Ed/Safety	92	Magnet School	277	Remedial Math K-12	750	Chief Innovation Officer
81	Gifted/Talented	93	Parental Involvement	280	Literacy Coach	751	Chief of Staff
82	Video Services	95	Tech Prep Program	285	STEM	752	Social Emotional Learning
83	Substance Abuse Prev	97	Chief Information Officer	286	Digital Learning		
84	Erate	98	Chief Technology Officer	288	Common Core Standards		Other School Types
85	AIDS Education	270	Accountability	294	Character Education	Ⓐ	= Alternative School
88	Alternative/At Risk	271	Migrant Education	295	Network System	Ⓒ	= Charter School
89	Multi-Cultural Curriculum	273	Teacher Mentor	296	Title II Programs	Ⓜ	= Magnet School
90	Social Work	274	Before/After Sch	297	Webmaster	Ⓨ	= Year-Round School

School Programs
A = Alternative Program
G = Adult Classes
M = Magnet Program
T = Title I Schoolwide
V = Career & Tech Ed Programs

Social Media
🅵 = Facebook
🆃 = Twitter

New Schools are shaded
New Superintendents and Principals are bold
Personnel with email addresses are underscored

TX—253

Kenedy County

Market Data Retrieval

Public Schs..Principal	Grd	Prgm	Enr/#Cls	SN	
Ⓐ Boerne Academy 210 Live Oak St, Boerne 78006 Cory Bell	6-12		20 4		830/572-2600 Fax 830/357-2919
Boerne High Sch 1 Greyhound Ln, Boerne 78006 Ross Sproul	9-12	AV	1,170 72	19%	830/357-2200 Fax 830/357-2208
Boerne Middle School North 240 Johns Rd, Boerne 78006 Thomas Hungate	7-8		881 40	26%	830/357-3100 Fax 830/357-3199
Boerne Middle School South 10 Cascade Caverns Rd, Boerne 78015 Dr Angela Watson	7-8		1,286 50	11%	830/357-3300 Fax 830/357-3399
Champion High Sch 210 Charger Blvd, Boerne 78006 Eddie Ashley	9-12	AV	1,760	8%	830/357-2600 Fax 830/357-2699
Cibolo Creek Elem Sch 300 Herff Ranch Blvd, Boerne 78006 Eleanor Maxwell	PK-6		831	14%	830/357-4400 Fax 830/357-4499
Curington Elem Sch 601 Adler St, Boerne 78006 Matt Myers	PK-5		589 41	32%	830/357-4000 Fax 830/357-4099
Fabra Elem Sch 723 Johns Rd, Boerne 78006 Heberto Hinojosa	PK-6		637 32	33%	830/357-4200 Fax 830/357-4299
Fair Oaks Ranch Elem Sch 29085 Ralph Fair Rd, Fair Oaks 78015 Lauren Walch	K-5		629 60	6%	830/357-4800 Fax 830/357-4899
Kendall Elem Sch 141 Old San Antonio Rd, Boerne 78006 Shanda Wolff	K-6		623 42	23%	830/357-4600 Fax 830/357-4699
Van Raub Elem Sch 8776 Dietz Elkhorn Rd, Boerne 78015 Jamie Robinson	PK-5		768		830/357-4100

- **Comfort Ind School Dist** PID: 01035864   830/995-6400
  327 High St, Comfort 78013   Fax 830/995-2236

Schools: 3 \ *Teachers:* 94 \ *Students:* 1,100 \ *Special Ed Students:* 136 \ *LEP Students:* 118 \ *College-Bound:* 25% \ *Ethnic:* Hispanic 59%, Caucasian 40% \ *Exp:* $460 (High) \ *Poverty:* 18% \ *Title I:* $366,471 \ *Open-Close:* 08/19 - 05/28 \ *DTBP:* $102 (High)

Dr Tanya Monroe 1		Barbara Flores 2,11	
Josh Limmer 3,5,91		Kenny Webb 5	
Brandon Easterly 6		Dayna Gwaltney 7,85*	
Dr Jerry Adam 8,12,57,74,83,288		Jodi Klemstein 16*	
Deanna Brummett 38*		Brad Spenrath 67	
Amanda Rust 68		Susan Lantz 73,82,295*	

Public Schs..Principal	Grd	Prgm	Enr/#Cls	SN	
Comfort Elem Sch 605 3rd Street, Comfort 78013 Donald Love	PK-5	GT	515 30	68%	830/995-6410 Fax 830/995-4153
Comfort High Sch 143 Highway 87 N, Comfort 78013 Darren Williams	9-12	ATV	332 23	46%	830/995-6430 Fax 830/995-2261
Comfort Middle Sch 216 High St, Comfort 78013 Michael Colvin	6-8	AT	253 30	45%	830/995-6420 Fax 830/995-2248

KENDALL PRIVATE SCHOOLS

Private Schs..Principal	Grd	Prgm	Enr/#Cls	SN	
Crestmont Christian Prep Sch 631 S School St, Boerne 78006 Susan Maias	K-12		50		210/254-4534
Geneva School of Boerne 113 Cascade Caverns Rd, Boerne 78015 Jessica Gombert \ Jeff Jones \ Rob Shelton	K-12		581		830/755-6101 Fax 830/755-6102
Hill Country Montessori Sch 50 Stone Wall Dr, Boerne 78006 Joanna Balzer	PK-8		110		830/229-5377 Fax 830/229-5378
Summit Christian Academy 631 S School St, Boerne 78006 Beth Miller	K-11		87		210/254-4534 Fax 210/247-9607

KENEDY COUNTY

KENEDY COUNTY SCHOOLS

- **Kenedy Co Schools** PID: 02091342   361/294-5381
  150 E La Para St, Sarita 78385   Fax 361/294-5718

Kristen Tinsley 1   Felix Serna 67
Becky Hagemen 73

KENEDY PUBLIC SCHOOLS

- **Kenedy Co Wide Common Sch Dist** PID: 01035905   361/294-5381
  150 E La Parra St, Sarita 78385   Fax 361/294-5718

Schools: 1 \ *Teachers:* 11 \ *Students:* 72 \ *Special Ed Students:* 11 \ *LEP Students:* 4 \ *Ethnic:* Asian 1%, African American 4%, Hispanic 85%, Caucasian 9% \ *Exp:* $1,277 (High) \ *Poverty:* 14% \ *Title I:* $16,041 \ *Open-Close:* 08/26 - 05/22 \ *DTBP:* $371 (High)

Johnny Johnson 1   Jerry Rosa 6*
Kristen Tinsley ......11,57,88,271,273,286,288*   Felix Serna 67
Becky Hageman ....73*   Maria McGuire 81*

Public Schs..Principal	Grd	Prgm	Enr/#Cls	SN	
Sarita Elem Sch 150 E La Parra St, Sarita 78385 Kristen Tinsley	PK-6	GT	72 11	68%	361/294-5381

---

1 Superintendent	8 Curric/Instruct K-12	19 Chief Financial Officer	29 Family/Consumer Science	39 Social Studies K-12	49 English/Lang Arts Elem	59 Special Education Elem	69 Academic Assessment
2 Bus/Finance/Purchasing	9 Curric/Instruct Elem	20 Art K-12	30 Adult Education	40 Social Studies Elem	50 English/Lang Arts Sec	60 Special Education Sec	70 Research/Development
3 Buildings And Grounds	10 Curric/Instruct Sec	21 Art Elem	31 Career/Sch-to-Work K-12	41 Social Studies Sec	51 Reading K-12	61 Foreign/World Lang K-12	71 Public Information
4 Food Service	11 Federal Program	22 Art Sec	32 Career/Sch-to-Work Elem	42 Science K-12	52 Reading Elem	62 Foreign/World Lang Elem	72 Summer School
5 Transportation	12 Title I	23 Music K-12	33 Career/Sch-to-Work Sec	43 Science Elem	53 Reading Sec	63 Foreign/World Lang Sec	73 Instructional Tech
6 Athletic	13 Title V	24 Music Elem	34 Early Childhood Ed	44 Science Sec	54 Remedial Reading K-12	64 Religious Education K-12	74 Inservice Training
7 Health Services	15 Asst Superintendent	25 Music Sec	35 Health/Phys Education	45 Math K-12	55 Remedial Reading Elem	65 Religious Education Elem	75 Marketing/Distributive
	16 Instructional Media Svcs	26 Business Education	36 Guidance Services K-12	46 Math Elem	56 Remedial Reading Sec	66 Religious Education Sec	76 Info Systems
	17 Chief Operations Officer	27 Career & Tech Ed	37 Guidance Services Elem	47 Math Sec	57 Bilingual/ELL	67 School Board President	77 Psychological Assess
	18 Chief Academic Officer	28 Technology Education	38 Guidance Services Sec	48 English/Lang Arts K-12	58 Special Education K-12	68 Teacher Personnel	78 Affirmative Action

Texas School Directory   Kerr County

KENT COUNTY

KENT PUBLIC SCHOOLS

- **Jayton-Girard Ind School Dist** PID: 01035931   806/237-2991
  700 Madison Ave, Jayton 79528   Fax 806/237-2670

Schools: 1 \ *Teachers:* 19 \ *Students:* 163 \ *Special Ed Students:* 15 \ *College-Bound:* 100% \ *Ethnic:* African American 1%, Hispanic 27%, Caucasian 72% \ *Exp:* $530 (High) \ *Poverty:* 16% \ *Title I:* $19,449 \ *Open-Close:* 08/15 - 05/21 \ *DTBP:* $378 (High) \ t

Trig Overbo 1   Laci Scogin 2*
Lyle Lackey .... 6,8,11,16,36*   Roger Smetak 11,73,295*
Darla Harrison .... 31,69,83,88*   Justin Gibson 58
Kathy Owen 67

Public Schs..Principal	Grd	Prgm	Enr/#Cls	SN	
Jayton-Girard Sch 700 Madison Ave, Jayton 79528 Jon Lackey	PK-12	TV	163 25	32%	806/237-2991 t

KERR COUNTY

KERR PUBLIC SCHOOLS

- **Center Point Ind School Dist** PID: 01035979   830/634-2171
  215 China St, Center Point 78010   Fax 830/634-2254

Schools: 3 \ *Teachers:* 41 \ *Students:* 570 \ *Special Ed Students:* 59 \ *LEP Students:* 109 \ *Ethnic:* African American 2%, Hispanic 55%, Caucasian 43% \ *Exp:* $592 (High) \ *Poverty:* 18% \ *Title I:* $275,952 \ *Special Education:* $111,000 \ *Open-Close:* 08/20 - 05/22 \ *DTBP:* $342 (High) \ f t

Cody Newcomb 1,83   Kim Bishop 2,11
Sam McLarty ....4,5 Guy Walters 6*
Janet Wolf .... 7,85 Casey Johnson 8,12,16,73,79,286*
Beverly Newcomb .... 31*   Kim Bolin 58*
Michael Butler 67

Public Schs..Principal	Grd	Prgm	Enr/#Cls	SN	
Center Point Elem Sch 215 China St, Center Point 78010 Jennifer George	PK-5	T	279 17	82%	830/634-2257 Fax 830/634-2119 f t
Center Point High Sch 207 China St, Center Point 78010 Keith Mills	9-12	ATV	167 25	67%	830/634-2244 Fax 830/634-7430 t
Center Point Middle Sch 207 China St, Center Point 78010 Keith Mills	6-8	ATV	130 9	75%	830/634-2244 Fax 830/634-7430

- **Divide Ind School Dist** PID: 01036014   830/640-3322
  120 Divide School Rd, Mountain Home 78058   Fax 830/640-3323

Schools: 1 \ *Teachers:* 1 \ *Students:* 22 \ *Special Ed Students:* 3 \ *Ethnic:* Hispanic 18%, Caucasian 82% \ *Exp:* $215 (Med) \ *Poverty:* 17% \ *Open-Close:* 08/27 - 05/29 \ *DTBP:* $320 (High)

William Bacon 1,57,73,83   Dana Beatchge 2
Tim Cowden 67

Public Schs..Principal	Grd	Prgm	Enr/#Cls	SN
Divide Elem Sch 120 Divide School Rd, Mountain Home 78058 William Bacon	PK-6		22 3	830/640-3322

- **Hunt Ind School Dist** PID: 01036038   830/238-4893
  115 School Rd, Hunt 78024   Fax 830/238-4691

Schools: 1 \ *Teachers:* 15 \ *Students:* 200 \ *Special Ed Students:* 14 \ *LEP Students:* 28 \ *Ethnic:* Hispanic 41%, Caucasian 59% \ *Exp:* $233 (Med) \ *Poverty:* 13% \ *Title I:* $66,053 \ *Special Education:* $22,000 \ *Open-Close:* 08/26 - 05/22 \ *DTBP:* $436 (High)

Lucy Harman 1,11,73   Gina Walker 2,4
Marybel Walker 3   Lee Poole 6*
Jane Furbush .... 7,83,85*   Cindy Lambert 11,59,275*
Sally West .... 16 Sarah Nichols 16,297*
Verlene Wallace .... 36,69,88,271*   Linda Pipkin 67
Tammy Brown 273,288*

Public Schs..Principal	Grd	Prgm	Enr/#Cls	SN	
Hunt Sch 115 School Rd, Hunt 78024 Tammy Brown	PK-8	GT	200 15	50%	830/238-4893

- **Ingram Ind School Dist** PID: 01036052   830/367-5517
  510 College St, Ingram 78025   Fax 830/367-4869

Schools: 3 \ *Teachers:* 77 \ *Students:* 1,070 \ *Special Ed Students:* 94 \ *LEP Students:* 128 \ *Ethnic:* Hispanic 47%, Caucasian 52% \ *Exp:* $396 (High) \ *Poverty:* 17% \ *Title I:* $425,466 \ *Special Education:* $247,000 \ *Open-Close:* 08/19 - 05/20 \ *DTBP:* $404 (High)

Dr Robert Templeton 1   Bill Orr 2,19
Trey Whitten 3,5   April Steele 4
Duane Kroeker .... 6*   Catherine Kern 7
Mindy Curran 8,11,16,57,83,288,296,298   Holly Lambert 58
Jack Fairchild .... 67 Juan DeLeon 73,76,84,295
Rodney Robins 91   Shanna Sleeper 294

Public Schs..Principal	Grd	Prgm	Enr/#Cls	SN	
Ingram Elem Sch 125 Brave Run, Ingram 78025 Donna Jenschke	PK-5	AT	556 30	81%	830/367-5751 Fax 830/367-7333
Ingram Middle Sch 700 Highway 39, Ingram 78025 Joe McRorey	6-8	T	243	64%	830/367-4111 Fax 830/367-7335
Ingram Tom Moore High Sch 700 Highway 39, Ingram 78025 Justin Crittenden	9-12	ATV	308 60	58%	830/367-4111 Fax 830/367-7332

---

79 Student Personnel   91 Safety/Security   275 Response To Intervention   298 Grant Writer/Ptnrships   **School Programs**   **Social Media**
80 Driver Ed/Safety   92 Magnet School   277 Remedial Math K-12   750 Chief Innovation Officer   A = Alternative Program
81 Gifted/Talented   93 Parental Involvement   280 Literacy Coach   751 Chief of Staff   G = Adult Classes   f = Facebook
82 Video Services   95 Tech Prep Program   285 STEM   752 Social Emotional Learning   M = Magnet Program
83 Substance Abuse Prev   97 Chief Infomation Officer   286 Digital Learning   T = Title I Schoolwide   t = Twitter
84 Erate   98 Chief Technology Officer   288 Common Core Standards   **Other School Types**   V = Career & Tech Ed Programs
85 AIDS Education   270 Character Education   294 Accountability   Ⓐ = Alternative School
88 Alternative/At Risk   271 Migrant Education   295 Network System   Ⓒ = Charter School   New Schools are shaded
89 Multi-Cultural Curriculum 273 Teacher Mentor   296 Title II Programs   Ⓜ = Magnet School   New Superintendents and Principals are bold   TX—255
90 Social Work   274 Before/After Sch   297 Webmaster   Ⓨ = Year-Round School   Personnel with email addresses are underscored

Kimble County

Market Data Retrieval

- **Kerrville Ind School Dist** PID: 01036076 830/257-2200
  1009 Barnett St, Kerrville 78028 Fax 830/257-2249

Schools: 10 \ **Teachers:** 334 \ **Students:** 4,800 \ **Special Ed Students:** 381 \ **LEP Students:** 307 \ **Ethnic:** Asian 1%, African American 2%, Hispanic 47%, Caucasian 49% \ **Exp:** $251 (Med) \ **Poverty:** 21% \ **Title I:** $1,353,469 \ **Special Education:** $983,000 \ **Open-Close:** 08/19 - 05/29 \ **DTBP:** $154 (High)

Name	Codes
Dr Mark Foust	1
Jarrett Jachade	2,15,16,19,73,76,295*
Scott Anglesee	4
Sue Hendrick	5
Katie Jachade	7,35,85*
Lynn Pluao	11,58,83,88,275,298
Sylvia Flannery	27,31,57,81,271
Dr David Sprouse	67
Jimmy Grmela	69
Laurie Rees	273
Brenda Taylor	2
Carolina Hurtado	3,91
Brad Harvey	5
David Jones	6
Heather Engstrom	8,15,288
Wade Ivy	15,68,78,79
Kendall Young	36*
Charli Stehling	68
Holly Bogt	71
Andrea Dixon	286*

Public Schs..Principal	Grd	Prgm	Enr/#Cls	SN	Phone
B T Wilson 6th Grade Sch 605 Tivy St, Kerrville 78028 Harper Stewart	6-6	T	371 25	56%	830/257-2207 Fax 830/257-1316
Daniels Elem Sch 2002 Singing Wind Dr, Kerrville 78028 Amy Billieter	K-5	T	639 32	67%	830/257-2208 Fax 830/257-1310
Early Childhood Campus 1011 3rd St, Kerrville 78028 Susana Alejandro	PK-PK	T	278 11	94%	830/257-1335 Fax 830/257-7885
Fred H Tally Elem Sch 1840 Goat Creek Pkwy, Kerrville 78028 Gena Robertson	K-5	T	522 24	44%	830/257-2222 Fax 830/257-2288
ⓐ Hill Country High Sch 1200 Sidney Baker St, Kerrville 78028 Steve Schwarz	11-12	TV	43 2	39%	830/257-2232 Fax 830/792-5020
ⓐ Kerrville Discipline Alt Sch 1010 Barnett St, Kerrville 78028 Steve Schwarz	7-12		40 3		830/257-1332 Fax 830/895-1481
Nimitz Elem Sch 100 Valley View Dr, Kerrville 78028 Julie Johnson	K-5	T	472 26	62%	830/257-2209 Fax 830/895-7905
Peterson Middle Sch 1607 Sidney Baker St, Kerrville 78028 Tamela Crawford	7-8	TV	757 54	52%	830/257-2204 Fax 830/257-1300
Starkey Elem Sch 1030 W Main St, Kerrville 78028 Jenna Wentrcek	K-5	T	517 29	57%	830/257-2210 Fax 830/792-3727
Tivy High Sch 3250 Loop 534, Kerrville 78028 Shelby Balser	9-12	TV	1,430 80	42%	830/257-2212 Fax 830/895-0411

KERR CATHOLIC SCHOOLS

- **Archdiocese San Antonio Ed Off** PID: 00999724
  Listing includes only schools located in this county. See District Index for location of Diocesan Offices.

Catholic Schs..Principal	Grd	Prgm	Enr/#Cls	SN	Phone
Notre Dame Sch 907 Main St, Kerrville 78028 Sandi Killo	PK-8		130 17		830/257-6707 Fax 830/792-4370

Our Lady of the Hills Cath HS 235 Peterson Farm Rd, Kerrville 78028 Therese Schwarz	9-12		110 5		830/895-0501 Fax 830/895-3470

KERR PRIVATE SCHOOLS

Private Schs..Principal	Grd	Prgm	Enr/#Cls	SN	Phone
Hill Country Adventist Sch 611 Harper Rd, Kerrville 78028 Brendia Bennett	1-8		17 2		830/257-3903

KIMBLE COUNTY

KIMBLE PUBLIC SCHOOLS

- **Junction Ind School Dist** PID: 01036155 325/446-3510
  1700 College St, Junction 76849 Fax 325/446-4413

Schools: 3 \ **Teachers:** 51 \ **Students:** 615 \ **Special Ed Students:** 73 \ **LEP Students:** 13 \ **College-Bound:** 80% \ **Ethnic:** Asian 1%, Hispanic 39%, Caucasian 60% \ **Exp:** $705 (High) \ **Poverty:** 33% \ **Title I:** $270,511 \ **Open-Close:** 08/15 - 05/28 \ **DTBP:** $389 (High)

Name	Codes
Mike Carter	1
Liz Dechert	4
Renee Schulze	11
Robin Gardner	38,83,85,270*
Lainey Simon	58
Kaycie Sullivan	73,295*
Cheryl Herring	2,84
Mitch McLemore	6*
Jennifer Martinez	16,82*
Renee Braswell	57*
Luke Levien	67

Public Schs..Principal	Grd	Prgm	Enr/#Cls	SN	Phone
Junction Elem Sch 1700 College St, Junction 76849 Jurahee Silvers	PK-5	T	306 24	79%	325/446-2055 Fax 325/446-4569
Junction High Sch 1700 College St, Junction 76849 Dana Davis	9-12	T	173 22	55%	325/446-3326 Fax 325/446-8206
Junction Middle Sch 1700 College St, Junction 76849 Joe Jones	6-8	T	136 20	70%	325/446-2464 Fax 325/446-2255

TX–256

#		#		#		#		#		#		#	
1	Superintendent	8	Curric/Instruct K-12	19	Chief Financial Officer	29	Family/Consumer Science	39	Social Studies K-12	49	English/Lang Arts Elem	59	Special Education Elem	69	Academic Assessment
2	Bus/Finance/Purchasing	9	Curric/Instruct Elem	20	Art K-12	30	Adult Education	40	Social Studies Elem	50	English/Lang Arts Sec	60	Special Education Sec	70	Research/Development
3	Buildings And Grounds	10	Curric/Instruct Sec	21	Art Elem	31	Career/Sch-to-Work K-12	41	Social Studies Sec	51	Reading K-12	61	Foreign/World Lang K-12	71	Public Information
4	Food Service	11	Federal Program	22	Art Sec	32	Career/Sch-to-Work Elem	42	Science K-12	52	Reading Elem	62	Foreign/World Lang Elem	72	Summer School
5	Transportation	12	Title I	23	Music K-12	33	Career/Sch-to-Work Sec	43	Science Elem	53	Reading Sec	63	Foreign/World Lang Sec	73	Instructional Tech
6	Athletic	13	Title V	24	Music Elem	34	Early Childhood Ed	44	Science Sec	54	Remedial Reading K-12	64	Religious Education K-12	74	Inservice Training
7	Health Services	15	Asst Superintendent	25	Music Sec	35	Health/Phys Education	45	Math K-12	55	Remedial Reading Elem	65	Religious Education Elem	75	Marketing/Distributive
		16	Instructional Media Svcs	26	Business Education	36	Guidance Services K-12	46	Math Elem	56	Remedial Reading Sec	66	Religious Education Sec	76	Info Systems
		17	Chief Operations Officer	27	Career & Tech Ed	37	Guidance Services Elem	47	Math Sec	57	Bilingual/ELL	67	School Board President	77	Psychological Assess
		18	Chief Academic Officer	28	Technology Education	38	Guidance Services Sec	48	English/Lang Arts K-12	58	Special Education K-12	68	Teacher Personnel	78	Affirmative Action

Texas School Directory

KING COUNTY

KING PUBLIC SCHOOLS

• **Guthrie Common School Dist** PID: 01036193   806/596-4466
301 Jaguar Ln, Guthrie 79236   Fax 806/596-4519

Schools: 1 \ **Teachers:** 20 \ **Students:** 104 \ **Special Ed Students:** 7 \ **College-Bound:** 92% \ **Ethnic:** Hispanic 10%, Caucasian 90% \ **Exp:** $1,142 (High) \ **Poverty:** 20% \ **Title I:** $14,849 \ **Open-Close:** 08/21 - 05/18 \ **DTBP:** $407 (High) \ f t

Kevin Chisum	1,83	Cynthia Fox	2
James Gilbert	3*	Jodi Tarver	7*
Jodie Reel	8,31*	Lynn Hill	12,69,88,294
McKenzie Chisum	57,271*	Sharrmie Bergvall	58,275*
Travis Adams	67	Trent Van Meter	73,295*

Public Schs..Principal	Grd	Prgm	Enr/#Cls	SN	
Guthrie Sch 301 Jaguar Ln, Guthrie 79236 **Lynn Hill**	PK-12	V	104 16		806/596-4466

KINNEY COUNTY

KINNEY PUBLIC SCHOOLS

• **Brackett Ind School Dist** PID: 01036222   830/563-2491
201 N Ann St, Brackettville 78832   Fax 830/563-9264

Schools: 3 \ **Teachers:** 57 \ **Students:** 569 \ **Special Ed Students:** 61 \ **LEP Students:** 33 \ **College-Bound:** 80% \ **Ethnic:** African American 1%, Hispanic 67%, Caucasian 32% \ **Exp:** $528 (High) \ **Poverty:** 24% \ **Title I:** $166,042 \ **Open-Close:** 08/22 - 05/28 \ **DTBP:** $408 (High)

Guillermo Mancha	1	Marla Madrid	2,11
Fernando Quiraz	3	Honey Bee Meyers	4
Isauro Rivas	5	Gary Griffin	6*
Savannah Molinar	7	Jeannie Moulton	37,69
Dario Gonzalez	57*	Michael Paxon	67
Susan Esparza	68	Michael Munoz	73*
Christine Hutchison	77,88*	Lisa Conoly	81*

Public Schs..Principal	Grd	Prgm	Enr/#Cls	SN	
Brackett High Sch 400 N Ann St, Brackettville 78832 **Christy Price**	9-12	ATV	167 40	47%	830/563-2480 Fax 830/563-3213
Brackett Junior High Sch 400 N Ann St, Brackettville 78832 **Daron Worrell**	6-8	AT	136 8	55%	830/563-2480 Fax 830/563-3213
Jones Elem Sch 400 N Ann St, Brackettville 78832 **Tonya Senne**	PK-5	T	282 15	62%	830/563-2492 Fax 830/563-9355

KLEBERG COUNTY

KLEBERG PUBLIC SCHOOLS

• **Kingsville Ind School Dist** PID: 01036258   361/592-3387
207 N 3rd St, Kingsville 78363   Fax 361/595-7805

Schools: 8 \ **Teachers:** 195 \ **Students:** 3,050 \ **Special Ed Students:** 388 \ **LEP Students:** 106 \ **College-Bound:** 50% \ **Ethnic:** Asian 1%, African American 4%, Hispanic 87%, Caucasian 8% \ **Exp:** $341 (High) \ **Poverty:** 33% \ **Title I:** $2,019,860 \ **Open-Close:** 08/26 - 06/05 \ **DTBP:** $169 (High) \ f t

Elida Bera	1	Peter Pitts	2,68
Michelle Butler	4	Michael Davila	6
Lou Wilson	7,85*	Kamara Adams	8,15
Porfirio Mendez	23*	Joe Martinez	28,73
Brian Coufal	67	Rolando Bazan	295

Public Schs..Principal	Grd	Prgm	Enr/#Cls	SN	
Gillett Intermediate Sch 1007 N 17th St, Kingsville 78363 **Belinda Gamez**	5-6	T	428 40	81%	361/595-8200 Fax 361/595-9008 f t
Ⓐ H M K Care Academy 2210 S Brahma Blvd, Kingsville 78363 Ismael Maldonado	9-12		17	23%	361/595-8600
H M King High Sch 2210 S Brahma Blvd, Kingsville 78363 **Mahogany Daniel**	9-12	TV	966 89	57%	361/595-8600 Fax 361/595-9170
Harvey Elem Sch 1301 E Kenedy Ave, Kingsville 78363 **Abigayle Barton**	PK-4	T	425 26	79%	361/592-4327 Fax 361/595-9130
Kleberg Elem Sch 900 N 6th St, Kingsville 78363 Connie Herrera	PK-4	T	337 23	98%	361/592-2615 Fax 361/595-9145
Memorial Middle Sch 915 S Armstrong Ave, Kingsville 78363 Dr Alys Williams	7-8	T	415 45	71%	361/595-8675 Fax 361/595-4198 f t
N M Harrel Elem Sch 925 W Johnston Ave, Kingsville 78363 John Trevino	PK-4	T	329 13	88%	361/592-9305 Fax 361/516-1313
Perez Elem Sch 1111 E Ailsie Ave, Kingsville 78363 **Albert Villarreal**	PK-4	T	475 22	75%	361/592-8511 Fax 361/516-1468

• **Ricardo Ind School Dist** PID: 01036375   361/593-0703
138 W County Road 2160, Kingsville 78363   Fax 361/592-3101

Schools: 1 \ **Teachers:** 45 \ **Students:** 671 \ **Special Ed Students:** 51 \ **LEP Students:** 20 \ **Ethnic:** Asian 1%, African American 1%, Hispanic 79%, Caucasian 19% \ **Exp:** $219 (Med) \ **Poverty:** 27% \ **Title I:** $290,201 \ **Open-Close:** 08/14 - 05/22 \ **DTBP:** $334 (High) \ t

Dr Vita Canales	1	Andrew Smith	2,11,296*
Alfredo Olivarez	3,16,83	Noemie Garza	4*
Frank Lopez	6	Suzie Howard	7,85*
Dr Marci Braswell	9,57*	Charles Saverline	67
Monika Garza	69,88,270	Tim Etzler	73*

---

79 Student Personnel	91 Safety/Security	275 Response To Intervention	298 Grant Writer/Ptnrships	**School Programs**	**Social Media**
80 Driver Ed/Safety	92 Magnet School	277 Remedial Math K-12	750 Chief Innovation Officer	A = Alternative Program	
81 Gifted/Talented	93 Parental Involvement	280 Literacy Coach	751 Chief of Staff	G = Adult Classes	f = Facebook
82 Video Services	95 Tech Prep Program	285 STEM	752 Social Emotional Learning	M = Magnet Program	
83 Substance Abuse Prev	97 Chief Infomation Officer	286 Digital Learning		T = Title I Schoolwide	t = Twitter
84 Erate	98 Chief Technology Officer	288 Common Core Standards	**Other School Types**	V = Career & Tech Ed Programs	
85 AIDS Education	270 Character Education	294 Accountability	Ⓐ = Alternative School		
88 Alternative/At Risk	271 Migrant Education	295 Network System	Ⓒ = Charter School	New Schools are shaded	
89 Multi-Cultural Curriculum	273 Teacher Mentor	296 Title II Programs	Ⓜ = Magnet School	New Superintendents and Principals are bold	
90 Social Work	274 Before/After Sch	297 Webmaster	Ⓨ = Year-Round School	Personnel with email addresses are underscored	

TX-257

Knox County
Market Data Retrieval

Public Schs..Principal	Grd	Prgm	Enr/#Cls	SN	
Ricardo Elem Middle Sch 138 W County Road 2160, Kingsville 78363 Dr Marci Braswell \ Gina Vilches	PK-8	T	671 45	45%	361/592-6465

- **Riviera Ind School Dist** PID: 01036399   361/296-3101
  203 Seahawk Dr, Riviera 78379   Fax 361/296-3108

> *Schools:* 2 \ *Teachers:* 39 \ *Students:* 435 \ *Special Ed Students:* 21 \ *LEP Students:* 21 \ *College-Bound:* 85% \ *Ethnic:* Asian 1%, Hispanic 74%, Caucasian 25% \ *Exp:* $477 (High) \ *Poverty:* 15% \ *Title I:* $59,934 \ *Special Education:* $64,000 \ *Open-Close:* 08/15 - 05/22 \ *DTBP:* $350 (High)

Karen Unterbrink 1		Jose Betancourt 2,4,5,11,91	
Virginia Pena 2		Toby Yaklin 3	
Nathan Borden 6*		Cathy Borden 11,57,58,271,296	
Brooke Hicky 12,31,69,92		Mable Pippin 16	
Burt Bull 67		Rick Gonzalez 73,84	

Public Schs..Principal	Grd	Prgm	Enr/#Cls	SN	
Kaufer High Sch 203 Seahawk Dr, Riviera 78379 Dawn Schuenemann	7-12	ATV	231 20	68%	361/296-3607 Fax 361/296-3845
Nanny Elem Sch 203 Seahawk Dr, Riviera 78379 Tarrah Dobson	PK-6	T	192 13	70%	361/296-2446 Fax 361/296-3461

- **Santa Gertrudis Ind Sch Dist** PID: 01809536   361/384-5087
  Highway 141 King Ranch, Kingsville 78363   Fax 361/592-7736

> *Schools:* 2 \ *Teachers:* 46 \ *Students:* 753 \ *Special Ed Students:* 27 \ *LEP Students:* 3 \ *College-Bound:* 80% \ *Ethnic:* Asian 2%, African American 2%, Hispanic 75%, Caucasian 21% \ *Exp:* $418 (High) \ *Poverty:* 33% \ *Special Education:* $102,000 \ *Open-Close:* 07/31 - 05/22 \ *DTBP:* $349 (High)

Veronica Alfaro 1	Amanda Ramirez 2
Norma Carrales 4*	Julie Greenwood 7,83,85*
Melly Guerra 11,58,271,275,296	Susan Rutherford 16,69,82,294*
Leonor De Los Santos 31	Jesse Garcia 67
Gerry Lopez 73	Julie Wheeler 91

Public Schs..Principal	Grd	Prgm	Enr/#Cls	SN	
ⓥ Academy High Sch 1055 W Santa Gertrudis, Kingsville 78363 Juan Sandoval	9-12	M	360 18	37%	361/384-5041 Fax 361/592-5335
ⓥ Santa Gertrudis Elem MS 803 Santa Rosa, Kingsville 78364 Mike Jones	PK-8	M	393 10	24%	361/384-5046 Fax 361/592-3128

KLEBERG PRIVATE SCHOOLS

Private Schs..Principal	Grd	Prgm	Enr/#Cls	SN	
Epiphany Montessori Sch 206 N 3rd St, Kingsville 78363 Peggy DeRouen	PK-K		25 10		361/592-2871 Fax 361/592-2105
Presbyterian Pan American Sch 223 N FM 772, Kingsville 78363 Ellie Perez	9-12		140 20		361/592-4307 Fax 361/592-6126

KNOX COUNTY

KNOX PUBLIC SCHOOLS

- **Benjamin Ind School Dist** PID: 01036442   940/459-2231
  300 Hayes St, Benjamin 79505   Fax 940/459-2007

> *Schools:* 1 \ *Teachers:* 12 \ *Students:* 107 \ *Special Ed Students:* 10 \ *LEP Students:* 3 \ *College-Bound:* 75% \ *Ethnic:* Hispanic 37%, Caucasian 63% \ *Exp:* $1,157 (High) \ *Poverty:* 21% \ *Title I:* $20,817 \ *Special Education:* $4,000 \ *Open-Close:* 08/19 - 05/21 \ *DTBP:* $319 (High)

Olivia Gloria 1,11,83,84,288	Stacia Propps 2
Shawn Donham 3*	Gracie Homstead 4
James Jackson 6*	Rebecca Clark 7*
Melissa Everson 57,58,271,286*	Stephen Keeler 67

Public Schs..Principal	Grd	Prgm	Enr/#Cls	SN	
Benjamin Sch 300 Hayes St, Benjamin 79505 Olivia Gloria	PK-12	T	107 10	65%	940/459-2231

- **Knox City-O'Brien Cons Ind SD** PID: 01036507   940/657-3521
  606 E Main St, Knox City 79529   Fax 940/657-3379

> *Schools:* 3 \ *Teachers:* 32 \ *Students:* 270 \ *Special Ed Students:* 40 \ *LEP Students:* 23 \ *College-Bound:* 90% \ *Ethnic:* African American 4%, Hispanic 53%, Native American: 1%, Caucasian 42% \ *Exp:* $423 (High) \ *Poverty:* 23% \ *Title I:* $85,078 \ *Open-Close:* 08/15 - 05/22 \ *DTBP:* $350 (High)

Colin Howeth 1,84	Tammy Gonzales 2,4,11
Terry Butler 3	Caleb Calloway 6
Mandi Perry 7	Marsha Quade 9,57,271*
Glen Hill 10,83,88,275	Christie Howeth 34,69,270*
Jennifer Caddell 58	Joe Albus 67
Sharon Wainscott 68	Stony Krusemark 73,88,286*

Public Schs..Principal	Grd	Prgm	Enr/#Cls	SN	
Knox City Elem Sch 300 N 4th Street, Knox City 79529 Marsha Quade	PK-4	T	125 13	73%	940/657-3147
Knox City High Sch 400 N 4th Street, Knox City 79529 Glen Hill	9-12	AGTV	81 20	66%	940/657-3565
O'Brien Middle Sch 711 9th St, O Brien 79539 Mark Tucker	5-8	T	72 14	74%	940/657-3731

- **Munday Consolidated Ind SD** PID: 01036533   940/422-4241
  811 W D Street, Munday 76371   Fax 940/422-5331

> *Schools:* 2 \ *Teachers:* 41 \ *Students:* 375 \ *Special Ed Students:* 63 \ *LEP Students:* 19 \ *College-Bound:* 85% \ *Ethnic:* Asian 1%, African American 7%, Hispanic 53%, Caucasian 39% \ *Exp:* $717 (High) \ *Poverty:* 36% \ *Title I:* $207,195 \ *Open-Close:* 08/22 - 05/25 \ *DTBP:* $378 (High)

Troy Parton 1,11	Cheryl Berryhill 2,68,79

---

1 Superintendent	8 Curric/Instruct K-12	19 Chief Financial Officer	29 Family/Consumer Science	39 Social Studies K-12	49 English/Lang Arts Elem	59 Special Education Elem	69 Academic Assessment
2 Bus/Finance/Purchasing	9 Curric/Instruct Elem	20 Art K-12	30 Adult Education	40 Social Studies Elem	50 English/Lang Arts Sec	60 Special Education Sec	70 Research/Development
3 Buildings And Grounds	10 Curric/Instruct Sec	21 Art Elem	31 Career/Sch-to-Work K-12	41 Social Studies Sec	51 Reading K-12	61 Foreign/World Lang K-12	71 Public Information
4 Food Service	11 Federal Program	22 Art Sec	32 Career/Sch-to-Work Elem	42 Science K-12	52 Reading Elem	62 Foreign/World Lang Elem	72 Summer School
5 Transportation	12 Title I	23 Music K-12	33 Career/Sch-to-Work Sec	43 Science Elem	53 Reading Sec	63 Foreign/World Lang Sec	73 Instructional Tech
6 Athletic	13 Title V	24 Music Elem	34 Early Childhood Ed	44 Science Sec	54 Remedial Reading K-12	64 Religious Education K-12	74 Inservice Training
7 Health Services	14 Instructional Media Svcs	25 Music Sec	35 Health/Phys Education	45 Math K-12	55 Remedial Reading Elem	65 Religious Education Elem	75 Marketing/Distributive
	15 Asst Superintendent	26 Business Education	36 Guidance Services K-12	46 Math Elem	56 Remedial Reading Sec	66 Religious Education Sec	76 Info Systems
	16 Chief Operations Officer	27 Career & Tech Ed	37 Guidance Services Elem	47 Math Sec	57 Bilingual/ELL	67 School Board President	77 Psychological Assess
	17 Chief Academic Officer	28 Technology Education	38 Guidance Services Sec	48 English/Lang Arts K-12	58 Special Education K-12	68 Teacher Personnel	78 Affirmative Action
	18						

Texas School Directory

Terry Hendricks 3*
Patrick Corcoran 6,35*
Kristi Bufkin 9,12,57,288,296*
Jenni Redwine 34*
Sam Hunter 67
Zann Messer 81*
Bob Bowen 5
Mandi Perry 7*
Christel Shahan 27,36,69,77,88,294*
Jennifer Caddell 58
Kimberly Bowman 73,273,286,295*
Leanne Tidwell 271*

Public Schs..Principal	Grd	Prgm	Enr/#Cls	SN	
Munday Elem Sch 1111 W Main Street, Munday 76371 Kristi Bufkin	PK-6	T	257 19	58%	940/422-4321
Munday High Sch 911 W D Street, Munday 76371 Brent Drury	7-12	T	129 23	52%	940/422-4321

LA SALLE COUNTY

LA SALLE PUBLIC SCHOOLS

• **Cotulla Ind School Dist** PID: 01037197   830/879-3073
  310 N Main St, Cotulla 78014   Fax 830/879-3609

Schools: 4 \ **Teachers:** 110 \ **Students:** 1,400 \ **Special Ed Students:** 151 \ **LEP Students:** 96 \ **College-Bound:** 85% \ **Ethnic:** Asian 1%, Hispanic 93%, Caucasian 6% \ **Exp:** $418 (High) \ **Poverty:** 34% \ **Title I:** $524,162 \ **Open-Close:** 08/19 - 05/28 \ **DTBP:** $350 (High)

Dr Jack Seals 1
Sayna Rodriguez 2,294
David Filda 6
Marlene Maldonado 38*
Deonicio Ramirez 67
Alfredo Vela 2,5
Marcena Martinez 4
Heather Ramirez 11
Alecia Rumfield 58
Daniel Garza 73

Public Schs..Principal	Grd	Prgm	Enr/#Cls	SN	
Cotulla High Sch 1034 Highway Highway 97, Cotulla 78014 Scott Norris	9-12	T	361 36	85%	830/879-2374 Fax 830/879-4302
Encinal Elem Sch 503 Encinal Blvd, Encinal 78019 Louisa Franklin	PK-5	T	125 7	88%	956/948-5324 Fax 956/948-5534
Frank Newman Middle Sch 608 Carrizo St, Cotulla 78014 Dr Brenda Jirasek	6-8	T	316 30	87%	830/879-4376 Fax 830/879-4357
Ramirez-Burks Elem Sch 604 Tilden St, Cotulla 78014 Cynthia Perkins	PK-5	T	578 29	87%	830/879-2511 Fax 830/879-4361

Lamar County

LAMAR COUNTY

LAMAR PUBLIC SCHOOLS

• **Chisum Ind School Dist** PID: 01036600   903/737-2830
  3250 S Church St, Paris 75462   Fax 903/737-2831

Schools: 3 \ **Teachers:** 73 \ **Students:** 1,000 \ **Special Ed Students:** 104 \ **LEP Students:** 41 \ **College-Bound:** 59% \ **Ethnic:** African American 5%, Hispanic 6%, Native American: 2%, Caucasian 87% \ **Exp:** $271 (Med) \ **Poverty:** 37% \ **Title I:** $376,795 \ **Open-Close:** 08/15 - 05/21 \ **DTBP:** $360 (High)

Tommy Chalaire 1,11
Lynn Williams 3,5
Darren Pevey 6
Travis Ball 67
Sherri Gribble 294
Kim Williams 2,11
Wanda Armstrong 4
Dusty Felts 38,88
April North 71,76

Public Schs..Principal	Grd	Prgm	Enr/#Cls	SN	
Chisum Elem Sch 3250 S Church St, Paris 75462 Wendy Ruthart	PK-5	TV	440 38	45%	903/737-2820
Chisum High Sch 3250 S Church St, Paris 75462 Clint Miller	9-12		293		903/737-2800
Chisum Middle Sch 3250 S Church St, Paris 75462 Aaron Bridges	6-8		221		903/737-2806

• **North Lamar Ind School Dist** PID: 01036636   903/737-2000
  3201 Lewis Ln, Paris 75460   Fax 903/669-0129

Schools: 7 \ **Teachers:** 252 \ **Students:** 2,500 \ **Special Ed Students:** 374 \ **LEP Students:** 66 \ **College-Bound:** 67% \ **Ethnic:** Asian 1%, African American 4%, Hispanic 10%, Native American: 2%, Caucasian 83% \ **Exp:** $362 (High) \ **Poverty:** 15% \ **Title I:** $490,574 \ **Open-Close:** 08/15 - 05/22 \ **DTBP:** $160 (High)

Kelli Stewart 1
Tami Miles 2,296
Diana McGregor 4*
Aaron Emeyabbi 6*
Angela Chadwick 8
Wes Brown 27,31,271*
Carla Coleman 71
Jodie Ingram 73
Melissa Darrow 2
Rick Landis 3
Clint Hildreath 5
Justine Wideman 7,35,85*
Debbie Basden 16*
Jeff Martin 67
Glenda Parsons 73,95,295*
Launa Doyal 297*

Public Schs..Principal	Grd	Prgm	Enr/#Cls	SN	
Aaron Parker Elem Sch 98 Cr 4412, Powderly 75473 Kristin Hughes	PK-5	T	234 16	71%	903/732-3066 Fax 903/669-0139
Cecil Everett Elem Sch 3201 Lewis Ln, Paris 75460 Lora Sanders	2-3	T	303	50%	903/737-2061 Fax 903/669-0169
Frank Stone Middle Sch 3201 Lewis Ln, Paris 75460 Kelli Stewart	6-8	T	577 55	48%	903/737-2041 Fax 903/669-0149
Geneva Bailey Intermediate Sch 3201 Lewis Ln, Paris 75460 Angela Compton	4-5	T	333 18	45%	903/737-7971 Fax 903/669-0179

Lamb County

Market Data Retrieval

ⓐ Lamar-Delta Alternative Ctr 3201 Lewis Ln, Paris 75460 Tracie Harris	6-12		30 2	903/669-0188 Fax 903/669-0193
North Lamar High Sch 3201 Lewis Ln, Paris 75460 Clayton Scarborough	9-12	V	800 65	39% 903/737-2011 Fax 903/669-0119
W L Higgins Elem Sch 3201 Lewis Ln, Paris 75460 Lori Malone	PK-1	T	303 22	59% 903/737-2081 Fax 903/669-0189

- **Paris Ind School Dist** PID: 01036698   903/737-7473
  1920 Clarksville St, Paris 75460   Fax 903/737-7484

Schools: 8 \ *Teachers:* 313 \ *Students:* 3,900 \ *Special Ed Students:* 457 \ *LEP Students:* 341 \ *College-Bound:* 66% \ *Ethnic:* Asian 1%, African American 36%, Hispanic 24%, Native American: 1%, Caucasian 38% \ *Exp:* $527 (High) \ *Poverty:* 30% \ *Title I:* $1,606,913 \ *Special Education:* $613,000 \ *Open-Close:* 08/15 - 05/22 \ *DTBP:* $224 (High)

Paul Jones 1		Tish Holleman 2	
Terry Anderson 3		Lori McEntyre 4	
Joseph Justiss 5		Steven Hohenberger 6	
Althea Dixon 8,15,294		Jennifer Ray 9,81	
Caleb Tindel 10,27		Karol Ackley 11	
Gary Preston 15,68,273		Eva Williams 34*	
Yesica Munguia 57		Joi Roberts 58	
Lisa Malone 58		George Fisher 67	
Jeanne Kraft 71		Dale Loughmiller 73	
Jennifer Simmons 73		Kay Grubb 85*	
Brad Ruthart 91		Eddie LaRue 295	

Public Schs..Principal	Grd	Prgm	Enr/#Cls	SN
A M Aikin Elem Sch 3100 Pine Mill Rd, Paris 75460 Kimberly Donnan	K-4	T	922 49	76% 903/737-7443 Fax 903/737-7517
Crockett Intermediate Sch 655 S Collegiate Dr, Paris 75460 Brock Blassingame	5-6	T	588 35	77% 903/737-7450 Fax 903/737-7526
Givens Early Childhood Center 655 Martin Luther King Jr Dr, Paris 75460 Sheila Ensey	PK-PK	T	127 28	89% 903/737-7466 Fax 903/737-7531
Lamar Co Head Start Center 1350 6th St NE, Paris 75460 Eva Williams	PK-PK	T	193	98% 903/737-7469 Fax 903/737-7514
Paris High Sch 2255 S Collegiate Dr, Paris 75460 Chris Vaughn	9-12	TV	875 80	68% 903/737-7400 Fax 903/737-7515
Paris Junior High Sch 2400 Jefferson Rd, Paris 75460 Kristi Callihan	7-8	TV	521 26	69% 903/737-7434 Fax 903/737-7534
Thomas Justiss Elem Sch 401 18th St NW, Paris 75460 Renee Elmore	K-4	T	548 28	92% 903/737-7458 Fax 903/737-7530
ⓐ Travis High School of Choice 3270 Graham St, Paris 75460 Stephen Long	1-12	T	90 13	64% 903/737-7560 Fax 903/737-7574

- **Prairiland Ind School Dist** PID: 01036789   903/652-6476
  466 FM 196 S, Pattonville 75468   Fax 903/652-3738

Schools: 4 \ *Teachers:* 85 \ *Students:* 1,160 \ *Special Ed Students:* 111 \ *LEP Students:* 18 \ *Ethnic:* African American 1%, Hispanic 9%, Native American: 1%, Caucasian 90% \ *Exp:* $391 (High) \ *Poverty:* 14% \ *Title I:* $183,249 \ *Open-Close:* 08/16 - 05/22 \ *DTBP:* $345 (High) \ 🅕 🅣

Jeff Ballard 1			Kay Klein 2,296	
Randell Bridges 3			Lesa Clarkson 4	
Greg Mouser 6			Christal Pilip 7*	
Kent Wright 8,16,73*			Jennifer Clark 11,38,69,83,88,270*	
Stacy Walker 16,82*			Michael Sessums 67	

Public Schs..Principal	Grd	Prgm	Enr/#Cls	SN
Blossom Elem Sch 310 High St, Blossom 75416 Leslie Martin	PK-5	T	434 18	54% 903/982-5230 Fax 903/982-5260
Deport Elem Sch 247 Church St, Deport 75435 Lanny Mathews	PK-5	T	145 15	70% 903/652-3325 Fax 903/652-2212
Prairiland High Sch 466 FM 196 S, Pattonville 75468 Jason Hostetler	9-12	TV	310 18	39% 903/652-5681 Fax 903/652-6400
Prairiland Junior High Sch 466 FM 196 S, Pattonville 75468 Brad Bassano	6-8	TV	261 20	50% 903/652-5681 Fax 903/652-3232

LAMB COUNTY

LAMB PUBLIC SCHOOLS

- **Amherst Ind School Dist** PID: 01036882   806/246-7729
  100 Main St, Amherst 79312   Fax 806/246-3265

Schools: 1 \ *Teachers:* 20 \ *Students:* 145 \ *Special Ed Students:* 20 \ *LEP Students:* 52 \ *College-Bound:* 25% \ *Ethnic:* African American 4%, Hispanic 89%, Caucasian 8% \ *Exp:* $621 (High) \ *Poverty:* 28% \ *Title I:* $72,226 \ *Open-Close:* 08/26 - 05/21

Joel Rodgers 1,11,83,288		Susan Meier 2	
Julie Gonzales 4		Ronnie Schroeder 67	
Ashley Hanlin 69,77*		Michael Nace 84,295*	

Public Schs..Principal	Grd	Prgm	Enr/#Cls	SN
Amherst Sch 100 Main St, Amherst 79312 Jose Gonzales	PK-12	ATV	145 24	87% 806/246-3221 Fax 806/246-3494

- **Littlefield Ind School Dist** PID: 01036911   806/385-3844
  1207 E 14th St, Littlefield 79339   Fax 806/385-6297

Schools: 4 \ *Teachers:* 97 \ *Students:* 1,300 \ *Special Ed Students:* 156 \ *LEP Students:* 75 \ *Ethnic:* African American 7%, Hispanic 73%, Caucasian 20% \ *Exp:* $379 (High) \ *Poverty:* 29% \ *Title I:* $520,499 \ *Open-Close:* 08/19 - 05/22 \ *DTBP:* $350 (High)

Robert Dillard 1		Rick Richards 2,5,8,11,79,88,92,298	
Mark Warsing 3		Brent Green 6	
Jan Richards 12,34,57*		Brett Southard 58	
Lance Broadhurst 67		Tim Gau 73,84,295	

Public Schs..Principal	Grd	Prgm	Enr/#Cls	SN
Littlefield Elem Sch 120 N Westside Ave, Littlefield 79339 Tom Whistler	3-5	T	291 17	80% 806/385-6217 Fax 806/385-4193

1 Superintendent	8 Curric/Instruct K-12	19 Chief Financial Officer	29 Family/Consumer Science	39 Social Studies K-12	49 English/Lang Arts Elem	59 Special Education Elem	69 Academic Assessment
2 Bus/Finance/Purchasing	9 Curric/Instruct Elem	20 Art K-12	30 Adult Education	40 Social Studies Elem	50 English/Lang Arts Sec	60 Special Education Sec	70 Research/Development
3 Buildings And Grounds	10 Curric/Instruct Sec	21 Art Elem	31 Career/Sch-to-Work K-12	41 Social Studies Sec	51 Reading K-12	61 Foreign/World Lang K-12	71 Public Information
4 Food Service	11 Federal Program	22 Art Sec	32 Career/Sch-to-Work Elem	42 Science K-12	52 Reading Elem	62 Foreign/World Lang Elem	72 Summer School
5 Transportation	12 Title I	23 Music K-12	33 Career/Sch-to-Work Sec	43 Science Elem	53 Reading Sec	63 Foreign/World Lang Sec	73 Instructional Tech
6 Athletic	13 Title V	24 Music Elem	34 Early Childhood Ed	44 Science Sec	54 Remedial Reading K-12	64 Religious Education K-12	74 Inservice Training
7 Health Services	15 Asst Superintendent	25 Music Sec	35 Health/Phys Education	45 Math K-12	55 Remedial Reading Elem	65 Religious Education Elem	75 Marketing/Distributive
	16 Instructional Media Svcs	26 Business Education	36 Guidance Services K-12	46 Math Elem	56 Remedial Reading Sec	66 Religious Education Sec	76 Info Systems
	17 Chief Operations Officer	27 Career & Tech Ed	37 Guidance Services Elem	47 Math Sec	57 Bilingual/ELL	67 School Board President	77 Psychological Assess
	18 Chief Academic Officer	28 Technology Education	38 Guidance Services Sec	48 English/Lang Arts K-12	58 Special Education K-12	68 Teacher Personnel	78 Affirmative Action

Texas School Directory

Lampasas County

Littlefield High Sch — 9-12 TV 374 63% 806/385-5683
1100 W Waylon Jennings Blvd, Littlefield 79339 — 25 — Fax 806/385-4191
Mike Read

Littlefield Junior High Sch — 6-8 T 298 78% 806/385-3922
105 N Lake Ave, Littlefield 79339 — 20 — Fax 806/385-4192
Mitch McNeese

Littlefield Primary Sch — PK-2 T 386 85% 806/385-3922
815 W 2nd St, Littlefield 79339 — 25 — Fax 806/385-4194
Jan Richards

• **Olton Ind School Dist** PID: 01036973 — 806/285-2641
701 6th Street, Olton 79064 — Fax 806/285-2724

Schools: 3 \ *Teachers:* 60 \ *Students:* 600 \ *Special Ed Students:* 57 \ *LEP Students:* 91 \ *College-Bound:* 52% \ *Ethnic:* African American 1%, Hispanic 76%, Caucasian 23% \ *Exp:* $480 (High) \ *Poverty:* 25% \ *Title I:* $214,883 \ *Open-Close:* 08/19 - 05/21 \ *DTBP:* $350 (High)

Kevin McCasland 1   Fran Trotter 2
Joe Villanueva 3   Manuel Jimenez 5
Ross Lassiter .... 6*   Cathi Freeman 7,85*
Terri Sandoval .... 11,69,294*   Kelli Smith 16,82*
Tara Ford 34   Shayla Torres 35
Connie Maxwell 67   Angela Martin 83
Blanca Pedroza 271   Stephen Miller 295*

Public Schs..Principal	Grd	Prgm	Enr/#Cls	SN	
Olton High Sch 800 Avenue G, Olton 79064 Gregg Ammons	9-12	TV	195 20	65%	806/285-2691 Fax 806/285-3316
Olton Junior High Sch 800 Avenue G, Olton 79064 Brian Hunt	6-8	TV	132 20	68%	806/285-2681 Fax 806/285-3348
Webb Elem Sch 801 Avenue G, Olton 79064 Mark Silva	PK-5	TV	288 31	76%	806/285-2657 Fax 806/285-2438

• **Springlake-Earth Ind Sch Dist** PID: 01037044 — 806/257-3310
Highway 2901, Earth 79031 — Fax 806/257-3927

Schools: 2 \ *Teachers:* 36 \ *Students:* 350 \ *Special Ed Students:* 55 \ *LEP Students:* 41 \ *College-Bound:* 80% \ *Ethnic:* Asian 1%, African American 5%, Hispanic 64%, Caucasian 30% \ *Exp:* $524 (High) \ *Poverty:* 15% \ *Title I:* $66,011 \ *Open-Close:* 08/14 - 05/22 \ *DTBP:* $372 (High)

Denver Crum 1   Rosie Davis 2*
Israel DeLeon .... 6*   Cindy Furr 10,69,270*
Cathy Bean .... 59*   Mark Parrish 67

Public Schs..Principal	Grd	Prgm	Enr/#Cls	SN	
Springlake-Earth Elem Mid Sch Highway 2901, Earth 79031 Jimmi Johnson	PK-8		380 18		806/257-3310
Springlake-Earth High Sch 472 FM 302, Earth 79031 Cindy Furr	8-12	ATV	112 18	74%	806/257-3819 Fax 806/257-3370

• **Sudan Ind School Dist** PID: 01037082 — 806/227-2431
107 Highway 303, Sudan 79371 — Fax 806/227-2146

Schools: 2 \ *Teachers:* 42 \ *Students:* 495 \ *Special Ed Students:* 41 \ *LEP Students:* 29 \ *College-Bound:* 80% \ *Ethnic:* Hispanic 58%, Caucasian 42% \ *Exp:* $537 (High) \ *Poverty:* 23% \ *Title I:* $99,012 \ *Open-Close:* 08/19 - 05/22 \ *DTBP:* $341 (High)

Scott Harrell 1,11   Tonjua Scisson 2
Mark Scisson .... 3*   Brianna Lashbrook 4
Carroll Legg 5   John Cornelius 6
Wendy Swarb .... 7,85*   Chanda Schovajsa 16,82*
Angela Shultz .... 57*   Daniel Guterrez 58*
Tim Rich 67   Kayela Harrell 69,288*
Jonathan Robertson 73,286,298*

Public Schs..Principal	Grd	Prgm	Enr/#Cls	SN	
Sudan Elem Sch 107 Highway 303, Sudan 79371 Deann Wilson	PK-7	T	314 19	57%	806/227-2431
Sudan High Sch Highway 303, Sudan 79371 Gordon Martin	8-12	T	154 25	47%	806/227-2431 Fax 806/227-2121

LAMPASAS COUNTY

LAMPASAS PUBLIC SCHOOLS

• **Lampasas Ind School Dist** PID: 01037111 — 512/556-6224
207 W 8th St, Lampasas 76550 — Fax 512/556-8711

Schools: 5 \ *Teachers:* 230 \ *Students:* 3,400 \ *Special Ed Students:* 360 \ *LEP Students:* 92 \ *College-Bound:* 47% \ *Ethnic:* Asian 1%, African American 2%, Hispanic 28%, Native American: 1%, Caucasian 68% \ *Exp:* $514 (High) \ *Poverty:* 17% \ *Title I:* $768,555 \ *Special Education:* $747,000 \ *Open-Close:* 08/15 - 05/21 \ *DTBP:* $178 (High)

Dr Chane Rascoe 1   Shane Jones 2,19
David Edgar 3   Calvin Pittman 4
Beverley Spencer 5   Troy Rogers 6*
Kim Kuklies .... 7*   Kevin Bott 8,11,57,83,286,288,296,298
Karen Turner 58   Sam Walker 67
Ron Poage .... 73,295 Whitney Walker 79

Public Schs..Principal	Grd	Prgm	Enr/#Cls	SN	
Hanna Springs Elem Sch 604 E Avenue F, Lampasas 76550 **Lindsay Duhon**	PK-5	T	632 60	63%	512/556-2152 Fax 512/556-0225
Kline Whitis Elem Sch 500 S Willis St, Lampasas 76550 Wes Graham	PK-5	T	429 40	55%	512/556-8291 Fax 512/556-8285
Lampasas High Sch 2716 S Highway 281, Lampasas 76550 Joey McQueen	9-12	ATV	1,011	43%	512/564-2310 Fax 512/564-2406
Lampasas Middle Sch 902 S Broad St, Lampasas 76550 Dana Holcomb	6-8	ATV	757 60	49%	512/556-3101 Fax 512/556-0245
Taylor Creek Elem Sch 2096 Big Divide Rd, Copperas Cove 76522 Renee Cummings	PK-5	T	519	50%	512/564-2585 Fax 512/564-2606

---

79 Student Personnel	91 Safety/Security	275 Response To Intervention	298 Grant Writer/Ptnrships	**School Programs**	**Social Media**
80 Driver Ed/Safety	92 Magnet School	277 Remedial Math K-12	750 Chief Innovation Officer	A = Alternative Program	= Facebook
81 Gifted/Talented	93 Parental Involvement	280 Literacy Coach	751 Chief of Staff	G = Adult Classes	
82 Video Services	95 Tech Prep Program	285 STEM	752 Social Emotional Learning	M = Magnet Program	= Twitter
83 Substance Abuse Prev	97 Chief Information Officer	286 Digital Learning		T = Title I Schoolwide	
84 Erate	98 Chief Technology Officer	288 Common Core Standards	**Other School Types**	V = Career & Tech Ed Programs	
85 AIDS Education	270 Character Education	294 Accountability	Ⓐ = Alternative School		
88 Alternative/At Risk	271 Migrant Education	295 Network System	Ⓒ = Charter School	New Schools are shaded	
89 Multi-Cultural Curriculum	273 Teacher Mentor	296 Title II Programs	Ⓜ = Magnet School	New Superintendents and Principals are bold	
90 Social Work	274 Before/After Sch	297 Webmaster	Ⓨ = Year-Round School	Personnel with email addresses are underscored	

Lavaca County

Market Data Retrieval

- **Lometa Ind School Dist** PID: 01037161   512/752-3384
  100 N 8th St, Lometa 76853   Fax 512/752-3424

Schools: 1 \ **Teachers:** 27 \ **Students:** 295 \ **Special Ed Students:** 36 \ **LEP Students:** 37 \ **College-Bound:** 50% \ **Ethnic:** Asian 1%, Hispanic 53%, Native American: 1%, Caucasian 45% \ **Exp:** $621 (High) \ **Poverty:** 22% \ **Title I:** $216,042 \ **Open-Close:** 08/15 - 05/22 \ **DTBP:** $292 (High)

David Fisher	1,11	Ronda Bridges	2
Tim Williams	3*	B J Burnett	4*
Michael Sibberson	5*	D T Torres	6*
Rob Moore	8,16,31,73,273*	Jamie Smart	51*
Heather Oliver	57,271*	Renee Young	58*
John Hines	67	Elizabeth Dickison	69,83,88*

Public Schs..Principal	Grd	Prgm	Enr/#Cls	SN	
Lometa Sch 100 N 8th St, Lometa 76853 Michael Sibberson	PK-12	MTV	295 20	77%	512/752-3384

LAVACA COUNTY

LAVACA PUBLIC SCHOOLS

- **Ezzell Ind School Dist** PID: 01037264   361/798-4448
  20500 FM 531, Hallettsville 77964   Fax 361/798-9331

Schools: 1 \ **Teachers:** 8 \ **Students:** 85 \ **Special Ed Students:** 7 \ **Ethnic:** African American 2%, Hispanic 4%, Caucasian 94% \ **Exp:** $256 (Med) \ **Poverty:** 12% \ **Title I:** $17,793 \ **Open-Close:** 08/15 - 05/21

| Lisa Berckenhoff | 1 | Jackie Goranson | 2 |
| Henri McCord | 67 | | |

Public Schs..Principal	Grd	Prgm	Enr/#Cls	SN	
Ezzell Elem Sch 20500 FM 531, Hallettsville 77964 Lisa Berckenhoff	PK-8	T	85 9	49%	361/798-4448

- **Hallettsville Ind Sch Dist** PID: 01037288   361/798-2242
  302 N Ridge St, Hallettsville 77964   Fax 361/798-5902

Schools: 3 \ **Teachers:** 80 \ **Students:** 1,130 \ **Special Ed Students:** 111 \ **LEP Students:** 19 \ **College-Bound:** 59% \ **Ethnic:** African American 11%, Hispanic 21%, Caucasian 68% \ **Exp:** $494 (High) \ **Poverty:** 16% \ **Title I:** $207,020 \ **Open-Close:** 08/15 - 05/21 \ **DTBP:** $360 (High) \

Joann Bludau	1	Kristin Marak	2
Johnny Densman	3	Thomas Psencik	6
Mandy Bucek	8*	Renae Phillips	16*
Trina Patek	34*	Michele Etzler	35,83,85
Robert Lundy	67	Farrah Jernegen	73,295*

Public Schs..Principal	Grd	Prgm	Enr/#Cls	SN	
Hallettsville Elem Sch 308 N Ridge St, Hallettsville 77964 Trina Patek	PK-4	T	415 20	50%	361/798-2242 Fax 361/798-4349
Hallettsville High Sch 200 N Ridge St, Hallettsville 77964 Darrin Bickham	9-12	ATV	369 40	33%	361/798-2242 Fax 361/798-9297

| Hallettsville Jr High Sch
410 S Russell St, Hallettsville 77964
Sophie Teltschik | 5-8 | TV | 338
35 | 43% | 361/798-2242
Fax 361/798-3573 |

- **Moulton Ind School Dist** PID: 01037329   361/596-4609
  500 N Pecan St, Moulton 77975   Fax 361/596-7578

Schools: 2 \ **Teachers:** 29 \ **Students:** 300 \ **Special Ed Students:** 31 \ **LEP Students:** 28 \ **College-Bound:** 85% \ **Ethnic:** African American 1%, Hispanic 49%, Native American: 1%, Caucasian 50% \ **Exp:** $447 (High) \ **Poverty:** 20% \ **Title I:** $83,600 \ **Open-Close:** 08/19 - 05/15 \ **DTBP:** $315 (High) \

Todd Grandjean	1,11	Robin Rhoades	2
Rose Bartos	4*	Kevin Fishbeck	6*
Deborah Rother	7*	Laura Kusock	36,69
Ellen Brumfield	57,271*	Daniel Beyer	67

Public Schs..Principal	Grd	Prgm	Enr/#Cls	SN	
Moulton Elem Sch 202 W Bobkat, Moulton 77975 David Hayward	PK-6	T	154 12	62%	361/596-4605 Fax 361/596-4894
Moulton High Sch 502 N Pecan St, Moulton 77975 Jamie Dornak	7-12	TV	126 10	40%	361/596-4691

- **Shiner Ind School Dist** PID: 01037355   361/594-3121
  510 County Road 348, Shiner 77984   Fax 361/594-3925

Schools: 2 \ **Teachers:** 49 \ **Students:** 660 \ **Special Ed Students:** 68 \ **LEP Students:** 13 \ **College-Bound:** 70% \ **Ethnic:** Asian 1%, African American 7%, Hispanic 16%, Caucasian 76% \ **Exp:** $341 (High) \ **Poverty:** 10% \ **Title I:** $84,233 \ **Open-Close:** 08/21 - 05/28 \ **DTBP:** $333 (High)

Alex Remschel	1	Dawn Winkenwerder	2,68
Sherri Vincik	2,11	Melvin Brooks	3
Libby Hornacky	7*	Andrew Schacherl	67
Janette Berkovsky	73,295*		

Public Schs..Principal	Grd	Prgm	Enr/#Cls	SN	
Shiner Elem Sch 510 County Road 348, Shiner 77984 Sue Gottwald	PK-6	T	351 18	29%	361/594-8106 Fax 361/594-3251
Shiner High Sch 510 County Road 348, Shiner 77984 Caleb McCain	7-12	TV	305 17	26%	361/594-3131 Fax 361/594-4295

- **Sweet Home Ind School Dist** PID: 01037381   361/293-3221
  7508 FM 531, Sweet Home 77987   Fax 361/741-2499

Schools: 1 \ **Teachers:** 12 \ **Students:** 150 \ **Special Ed Students:** 9 \ **Ethnic:** Hispanic 17%, Caucasian 83% \ **Exp:** $299 (Med) \ **Poverty:** 6% \ **Title I:** $9,365 \ **Open-Close:** 08/15 - 05/21 \

| Shane Wagner | 1,11,73,83,84 | Ricky Raz | 67 |

Public Schs..Principal	Grd	Prgm	Enr/#Cls	SN	
Sweet Home Elem Sch 7508 FM 531, Sweet Home 77987 Shane Wagner	PK-8	T	150 12	16%	361/293-3221

1 Superintendent	8 Curric/Instruct K-12	19 Chief Financial Officer	29 Family/Consumer Science	39 Social Studies K-12	49 English/Lang Arts Elem	59 Special Education Elem	69 Academic Assessment
2 Bus/Finance/Purchasing	9 Curric/Instruct Elem	20 Art K-12	30 Adult Education	40 Social Studies Elem	50 English/Lang Arts Sec	60 Special Education Sec	70 Research/Development
3 Buildings And Grounds	10 Curric/Instruct Sec	21 Art Elem	31 Career/Sch-to-Work K-12	41 Social Studies Sec	51 Reading K-12	61 Foreign/World Lang K-12	71 Public Information
4 Food Service	11 Federal Program	22 Art Sec	32 Career/Sch-to-Work Elem	42 Science K-12	52 Reading Elem	62 Foreign/World Lang Elem	72 Summer School
5 Transportation	12 Title I	23 Music K-12	33 Career/Sch-to-Work Sec	43 Science Elem	53 Reading Sec	63 Foreign/World Lang Sec	73 Instructional Tech
6 Athletic	13 Title V	24 Music Elem	34 Early Childhood Ed	44 Science Sec	54 Remedial Reading K-12	64 Religious Education K-12	74 Inservice Training
7 Health Services	15 Asst Superintendent	25 Music Sec	35 Health/Phys Education	45 Math K-12	55 Remedial Reading Elem	65 Religious Education Elem	75 Marketing/Distributive
	16 Instructional Media Svcs	26 Business Education	36 Guidance Services K-12	46 Math Elem	56 Remedial Reading Sec	66 Religious Education Sec	76 Info Systems
	17 Chief Operations Officer	27 Career & Tech Ed	37 Guidance Services Elem	47 Math Sec	57 Bilingual/ELL	67 School Board President	77 Psychological Assess
	18 Chief Academic Officer	28 Technology Education	38 Guidance Services Sec	48 English/Lang Arts K-12	58 Special Education K-12	68 Teacher Personnel	78 Affirmative Action

Texas School Directory — Lee County

- **Vysehrad Ind School Dist** PID: 01037408   361/798-4118
  595 County Road 182, Hallettsville 77964   Fax 361/798-3131

Schools: 1 \ **Teachers:** 11 \ **Students:** 115 \ **Special Ed Students:** 9 \ **LEP Students:** 3 \ **Ethnic:** Asian 4%, African American 15%, Hispanic 9%, Caucasian 72% \ **Exp:** $172 (Low) \ **Poverty:** 7% \ **Open-Close:** 08/15 - 05/21 \ facebook twitter

Jason Appelt 1,11,83,84
Alice Janak 67
Leann Migl 59,275*
Claudia Baker 73*

Public Schs..Principal	Grd	Prgm	Enr/#Cls	SN	
Vysehrad Elem Sch 595 County Road 182, Hallettsville 77964 Jason Appelt	PK-8		115 10	47%	361/798-4118

LAVACA CATHOLIC SCHOOLS

- **Diocese of Victoria Ed Office** PID: 02181727
  Listing includes only schools located in this county. See District Index for location of Diocesan Offices.

Catholic Schs..Principal	Grd	Prgm	Enr/#Cls	SN	
Sacred Heart Catholic Sch 313 S Texana St, Hallettsville 77964 Kevin Haas	PK-12		310 14		361/798-4251 Fax 361/798-4970
Shiner Catholic School-St Paul 424 S Saint Ludmila St, Shiner 77984 Neely Yackel	PK-12		277 14		361/594-2313 Fax 361/594-8599
St Joseph Catholic Sch 310 Orth St, Yoakum 77995 Sean Mooney	PK-8		125 12		361/293-9000 Fax 361/293-3004

LEE COUNTY

LEE PUBLIC SCHOOLS

- **Dime Box Ind School Dist** PID: 01037422   979/884-2324
  1079 Stephen F Austin Blvd, Dime Box 77853   Fax 979/884-0106

Schools: 1 \ **Teachers:** 20 \ **Students:** 160 \ **Special Ed Students:** 26 \ **LEP Students:** 19 \ **College-Bound:** 50% \ **Ethnic:** African American 40%, Hispanic 37%, Native American: 1%, Caucasian 22% \ **Exp:** $561 (High) \ **Poverty:** 10% \ **Title I:** $20,269 \ **Open-Close:** 08/13 - 05/29 \ **DTBP:** $350 (High)

Nicholas West 1,11,84
Jay Smith 8*
Charles Fritsche 67
Stephanie Kieschnick 2,4
Zach Zgabay 35

Public Schs..Principal	Grd	Prgm	Enr/#Cls	SN	
Dime Box Sch 1079 Stephen F Austin Blvd, Dime Box 77853 Jay Smith	PK-12	ATV	160 25	76%	979/884-3366

- **Giddings Ind School Dist** PID: 01037458   979/542-2854
  2337 N Main St, Giddings 78942   Fax 979/542-9264

Schools: 4 \ **Teachers:** 147 \ **Students:** 1,905 \ **Special Ed Students:** 208 \ **LEP Students:** 308 \ **Ethnic:** Asian 1%, African American 9%, Hispanic 57%, Caucasian 33% \ **Exp:** $386 (High) \ **Poverty:** 21% \ **Title I:** $455,754 \ **Special Education:** $305,000 \ **Open-Close:** 08/14 - 05/21 \ **DTBP:** $356 (High)

Roger Dees 1
Andy Masek 3,5
Curtis Krause 5
Ashton Booth 58
Todd Walsh 73,295
Angie Bloodworth 2,19
Traci Campbell 4
Shane Holman 8,11,57,58,83,88,294,296
Mark Johnson 67

Public Schs..Principal	Grd	Prgm	Enr/#Cls	SN	
Giddings Elem Sch 1402 E Industry St, Giddings 78942 Alisa Niemeyer	PK-3	T	598 30	79%	979/542-2886 Fax 979/542-1153
Giddings High Sch 2335 N Main St, Giddings 78942 Chad Rood	9-12	ATV	607 55	56%	979/542-3351 Fax 979/542-5312
Giddings Intermediate Sch 2337 N Main St, Giddings 78942 Sarah Borowicz	4-5	T	288 20	76%	979/542-4403 Fax 979/542-4327
Giddings Middle Sch 2335 N Main St, Giddings 78942 Charlotte Penn	6-8	T	412 20	68%	979/542-2057 Fax 979/542-3941

- **Lexington Ind School Dist** PID: 01037496   979/773-2254
  8731 N Highway 77, Lexington 78947   Fax 979/773-4455

Schools: 3 \ **Teachers:** 82 \ **Students:** 1,030 \ **Special Ed Students:** 89 \ **LEP Students:** 14 \ **College-Bound:** 50% \ **Ethnic:** African American 8%, Hispanic 16%, Caucasian 75% \ **Exp:** $330 (High) \ **Poverty:** 11% \ **Title I:** $94,587 \ **Special Education:** $218,000 \ **Open-Close:** 08/14 - 05/21 \ **DTBP:** $354 (High)

Tonya Knowlton 1
Allen Retzlaff 3
James Marburger 5
Dusty Mathews 7*
Debbie Johnson 16,82*
Scott Sanders 67
Rebecca French 273,288,296*
Kathy Dube 2
Kathleen Lamb 4*
Kirk Muhl 6
Rebecca French 8,11,74,271
Nancy Stobaugh 58
Curtis Patschke 73,295,297

Public Schs..Principal	Grd	Prgm	Enr/#Cls	SN	
Lexington Elem Sch 222 5th St, Lexington 78947 Bryan Ladd	PK-5	T	485 30	43%	979/773-2525
Lexington High Sch 8783 N Highway 77, Lexington 78947 Sarah Garrison	9-12	ATV	289	40%	979/773-2255
Lexington Middle Sch 121 3rd St, Lexington 78947 Andre Johnson	6-8	T	248 16	39%	979/773-2254

LEE PRIVATE SCHOOLS

Private Schs..Principal	Grd	Prgm	Enr/#Cls	SN	
Immanuel Lutheran Sch 382 N Grimes St, Giddings 78942 Dale Wolfgram	K-8		140 9		979/542-3319 Fax 979/542-9084

---

79 Student Personnel
80 Driver Ed/Safety
81 Gifted/Talented
82 Video Services
83 Substance Abuse Prev
84 Erate
85 AIDS Education
88 Alternative/At Risk
89 Multi-Cultural Curriculum
90 Social Work
91 Safety/Security
92 Magnet School
93 Parental Involvement
95 Tech Prep Program
97 Chief Infomation Officer
98 Chief Technology Officer
270 Character Education
271 Migrant Education
273 Teacher Mentor
274 Before/After Sch
275 Response To Intervention
277 Remedial Math K-12
280 Literacy Coach
285 STEM
286 Digital Learning
288 Common Core Standards
294 Accountability
295 Network System
296 Title II Programs
297 Webmaster
298 Grant Writer/Ptnrships
750 Chief Innovation Officer
751 Chief of Staff
752 Social Emotional Learning

School Programs
A = Alternative Program
G = Adult Classes
M = Magnet Program
T = Title I Schoolwide
V = Career & Tech Ed Programs

Other School Types
Ⓐ = Alternative School
Ⓒ = Charter School
Ⓜ = Magnet School
Ⓨ = Year-Round School

Social Media
facebook = Facebook
twitter = Twitter

New Schools are shaded
New Superintendents and Principals are bold
Personnel with email addresses are underscored

Leon County

Market Data Retrieval

St Paul Lutheran Sch — K-8 — 93 — 979/366-2218
1578 County Road 211, Giddings 78942 — 9 — Fax 979/366-2200
James House

LEON COUNTY

LEON PUBLIC SCHOOLS

- **Buffalo Ind School Dist** PID: 01037551 — 903/322-3765
  708 Cedar Creek Rd, Buffalo 75831 — Fax 903/322-3091

Schools: 4 \ **Teachers:** 79 \ **Students:** 970 \ **Special Ed Students:** 69 \
LEP Students: 140 \ **Ethnic:** Asian 1%, African American 3%, Hispanic 43%,
Caucasian 54% \ **Exp:** $385 (High) \ **Poverty:** 27% \ **Title I:** $320,451 \
Open-Close: 08/14 - 05/20 \ **DTBP:** $332 (High)

Lacy Freeman 1,83	Courtney Rodell 2,11
Rick Frazee 3	Sarah Corbin 4*
Lee George 5	Brandon Houston 6,35*
Erin Stone 7*	Georgeanna Adams-Molina ..11,73,271,286*
Jeaneen Cobbs 57	Jack Helmcamp 67
Becky Poole 68,71	Melonie Menefee 82*
Corey Hickerson 83*	Melissa Smith 88*
Leslie Morman 274*	

Public Schs..Principal	Grd	Prgm	Enr/#Cls	SN	
Buffalo Elem Sch 1700 E Commerce St, Buffalo 75831 Tina Rayborn	PK-2	GT	258 27	71%	903/322-2473 Fax 903/322-4077
Buffalo High Sch 1724 N Buffalo Ave, Buffalo 75831 Corey Hickerson	9-12	ATV	266 15	57%	903/322-2473 Fax 903/322-5806
Buffalo Lower Junior High Sch 335 Bison Trl, Buffalo 75831 Susan Shelton	3-5	A	210 12		903/322-2473 Fax 903/322-4803
Buffalo Upper Junior High Sch 145 Bison Trl, Buffalo 75831 Greg Kennedy	6-8		210		903/322-2473 Fax 903/322-3862

- **Centerville Ind School Dist** PID: 01037587 — 903/536-7812
  813 S Commerce St, Centerville 75833 — Fax 903/536-3133

Schools: 2 \ **Teachers:** 63 \ **Students:** 700 \ **Special Ed Students:** 53
\ **LEP Students:** 15 \ **College-Bound:** 75% \ **Ethnic:** African American
10%, Hispanic 12%, Caucasian 78% \ **Exp:** $427 (High) \ **Poverty:** 18% \
Title I: $158,225 \ **Open-Close:** 08/14 - 05/22 \ **DTBP:** $322 (High)

Jason Jeitz 1	Carole Dickey 2,4,15,298
Nathan Gilber 3	Gary Bladen 5
Kyle Hardee 6*	Cara Dudley 8,11,285,286
Angela Rodell 16,73*	Dotty Sullivan 57
Sandra Welker 58	Charles Nash 67
Layne Gregson 76,295	Rebecca Hall 83

Public Schs..Principal	Grd	Prgm	Enr/#Cls	SN	
Centerville Elem Sch 346 W Church St, Centerville 75833 Dottie Sullivan	PK-6	T	378 22	50%	903/536-2235 Fax 903/536-3525
Centerville Jr Sr High Sch 813 S Commerce St, Centerville 75833 Claudia Mordecai	7-12	V	309 50	38%	903/536-2625

- **Leon Ind School Dist** PID: 01037628 — 903/626-1400
  12168 US Highway 79, Jewett 75846 — Fax 903/626-1420

Schools: 3 \ **Teachers:** 76 \ **Students:** 715 \ **Special Ed Students:** 62
\ **LEP Students:** 100 \ **College-Bound:** 75% \ **Ethnic:** Asian 3%,
African American 1%, Hispanic 29%, Caucasian 67% \ **Exp:** $366 (High) \
Poverty: 18% \ **Title I:** $190,102 \ **Open-Close:** 08/19 - 05/28 \ **DTBP:** $292
(High)

David Raines 1	Jamie Watson 2,298
Britney Taylor 3,5	Donna Johnson 4*
Jeremy Colvert 6*	Jessica Turner 6
Geoffery Bowdoin 8,11,274,296*	Vicki Gresham 16*
Elise Watson 31,36,69*	Shelly Charlton 54*
Collin Robertson 67	Jerrod Hartioz 73

Public Schs..Principal	Grd	Prgm	Enr/#Cls	SN	
Leon Elem Sch 12168 US Highway 79, Jewett 75846 Gail Middleton	PK-5	T	377 35	58%	903/626-1425 Fax 903/626-1440
Leon High Sch 12168 US Highway 79, Jewett 75846 Jay Winn	9-12	ATV	206 22	44%	903/626-1475 Fax 903/626-1490
Leon Junior High Sch 12168 US Highway 79, Jewett 75846 Johnie Foley	6-8	T	176 21	48%	903/626-1450 Fax 903/626-1455

- **Normangee Ind School Dist** PID: 01037654 — 936/396-3111
  35078 Osr St, Normangee 77871 — Fax 936/396-3112

Schools: 3 \ **Teachers:** 43 \ **Students:** 572 \ **Special Ed Students:** 49 \
LEP Students: 28 \ **Ethnic:** Asian 1%, African American 8%, Hispanic 15%,
Caucasian 76% \ **Exp:** $315 (High) \ **Poverty:** 17% \ **Title I:** $117,272 \
Open-Close: 08/14 - 05/22 \ **DTBP:** $365 (High)

Mark Ruffin 1	Jaimie Bell 2
Joel Tedder 3,5,91*	Tara Green 4*
Keith Fitton 6	Erica Sorters 7*
Tera Phillips 9,57,83,270,271,296*	Cara Phillips 10,31*
Kim Tesch 36,69,88*	Phyllis Rogers 58*
Andres Dela-Garza 67	Jeff Kemmerling 73,82,286

Public Schs..Principal	Grd	Prgm	Enr/#Cls	SN	
Normangee Elem Sch 116 Spur 3, Normangee 77871 Cody Gore	PK-5	T	269 40	56%	936/396-9999 Fax 936/396-2609
Normangee Middle Sch 116 Spur 3, Normangee 77871 Jake George	6-8	TV	137	51%	936/396-3111 Fax 936/396-6879
Normangee Senior High Sch 116 Spur 3, Normangee 77871 **Ruffin Mark**	9-12	TV	203	48%	936/396-6111 Fax 936/396-6879

- **Oakwood Ind School Dist** PID: 01037680 — 903/545-2666
  631 N Holly St, Oakwood 75855 — Fax 903/545-2310

Schools: 2 \ **Teachers:** 16 \ **Students:** 200 \ **Special Ed Students:** 10
\ **LEP Students:** 3 \ **College-Bound:** 80% \ **Ethnic:** Asian 1%, African
American 22%, Hispanic 13%, Caucasian 64% \ **Exp:** $523 (High) \
Poverty: 28% \ **Title I:** $67,469 \ **Open-Close:** 08/21 - 05/25 \ **DTBP:** $350
(High)

Russell Holden 1	Diana Neel 2,11,296
Christopher Kuykendall 6*	Lori Olive 8,69*
Mack Botard 67	Lane Gregson 73
Dr Donny Lee 288	

1	Superintendent	8	Curric/Instruct K-12	19	Chief Financial Officer	29	Family/Consumer Science	39	Social Studies K-12	49	English/Lang Arts Elem	59	Special Education Elem	69	Academic Assessment
2	Bus/Finance/Purchasing	9	Curric/Instruct Elem	20	Art K-12	30	Adult Education	40	Social Studies Elem	50	English/Lang Arts Sec	60	Special Education Sec	70	Research/Development
3	Buildings And Grounds	10	Curric/Instruct Sec	21	Art Elem	31	Career/Sch-to-Work K-12	41	Social Studies Sec	51	Reading K-12	61	Foreign/World Lang K-12	71	Public Information
4	Food Service	11	Federal Program	22	Art Sec	32	Career/Sch-to-Work Elem	42	Science K-12	52	Reading Elem	62	Foreign/World Lang Elem	72	Summer School
5	Transportation	12	Title I	23	Music K-12	33	Career/Sch-to-Work Sec	43	Science Elem	53	Reading Sec	63	Foreign/World Lang Sec	73	Instructional Tech
6	Athletic	13	Title V	24	Music Elem	34	Early Childhood Ed	44	Science Sec	54	Remedial Reading K-12	64	Religious Education K-12	74	Inservice Training
7	Health Services	15	Asst Superintendent	25	Music Sec	35	Health/Phys Education	45	Math K-12	55	Remedial Reading Elem	65	Religious Education Elem	75	Marketing/Distributive
		16	Instructional Media Svcs	26	Business Education	36	Guidance Services K-12	46	Math Elem	56	Remedial Reading Sec	66	Religious Education Sec	76	Info Systems
		17	Chief Operations Officer	27	Career & Tech Ed	37	Guidance Services Elem	47	Math Sec	57	Bilingual/ELL	67	School Board President	77	Psychological Assess
		18	Chief Academic Officer	28	Technology Education	38	Guidance Services Sec	48	English/Lang Arts K-12	58	Special Education K-12	68	Teacher Personnel	78	Affirmative Action

Texas School Directory

Liberty County

Public Schs..Principal	Grd	Prgm	Enr/#Cls	SN	
Oakwood Elem Sch 631 N Holly St, Oakwood 75855 Greg Branch	PK-6	T	120 7	89% Fax	903/545-2106 903/545-1130
Oakwood Jr Sr High Sch 631 N Holly St, Oakwood 75855 Dr Sharon Ragland	7-12	TV	80 17	73% Fax	903/545-2140 903/545-1820

LIBERTY COUNTY

LIBERTY PUBLIC SCHOOLS

- **Cleveland Ind School Dist** PID: 01037719   281/592-8717
  316 E Dallas St, Cleveland 77327   Fax 281/592-8283

Schools: 6 \ **Teachers:** 277 \ **Students:** 6,719 \ **Special Ed Students:** 357 \ **LEP Students:** 1,534 \ **College-Bound:** 45% \ **Ethnic:** Asian 1%, African American 8%, Hispanic 62%, Native American: 1%, Caucasian 29% \ **Exp:** $475 (High) \ **Poverty:** 26% \ **Title I:** $1,495,770 \ **Open-Close:** 08/21 - 05/21 \ **DTBP:** $180 (High) \ f

Chris Trotter 1	Karen Billingsley 2,19	
Gerald Lee 3	Jennifer Leos 4	
Larry Smith 5	Norris Taff 6,35	
Valerie Murphy 7*	Maria Silva 8,11,16,57,69,285,294,296	
Pennee Hall 15	Chris Wood 67	
Dawn O'Connor 69,294	Susan Ard 71	
James Gonzalez 73,295		

Public Schs..Principal	Grd	Prgm	Enr/#Cls	SN	
Cleveland High Sch 1600 E Houston St, Cleveland 77327 Glenn Barnes	9-12	ATV	1,417 80	75% Fax	281/592-8752 281/592-7485
Cleveland Middle Sch 2000 E Houston St, Cleveland 77327 Shelia Stephens	6-8	T	722 45	80% Fax	281/593-1148 281/593-3400
Eastside Elem Sch 1602 Shell Ave, Cleveland 77327 Rebecca Smith	PK-5	T	729 28	86% Fax	281/592-0125 281/592-0277
Ⓐ Frederick A Douglass Lrng Acad 900 Sam Wiley Dr, Cleveland 77327 Mary Giles	9-12	T	33	89% Fax	281/592-7595 281/432-2754
Northside Elem Sch 1522 N Blair Ave, Cleveland 77327 Edward Husk	PK-5	T	892 27	86% Fax	281/592-4628 281/592-9678
Southside Elem Sch 303 E Fort Worth St, Cleveland 77327 Janie Snyder	PK-5	T	1,309 40	85% Fax	281/592-0594 281/592-2185 f

- **Dayton Ind School Dist** PID: 01037771   936/258-2667
  100 Cherry Creek Rd, Dayton 77535   Fax 936/258-5616

Schools: 7 \ **Teachers:** 331 \ **Students:** 5,400 \ **Special Ed Students:** 519 \ **LEP Students:** 935 \ **College-Bound:** 50% \ **Ethnic:** African American 8%, Hispanic 41%, Native American: 1%, Caucasian 49% \ **Exp:** $184 (Low) \ **Poverty:** 15% \ **Title I:** $990,755 \ **Special Education:** $984,000 \ **Open-Close:** 08/15 - 05/22 \ **DTBP:** $178 (High)

Dr Jessica Johnson 1   Melissa Vandeventer 2
Tami Pierce 2,15,19   Steve Bell 3
Marcy Rutland 4   Paci Cantu 5
Kay Stratmann ....7*   Allen Painter 8,12,13,36,79,88,288
Shanna McCracken 8   Michael Dyer 11,80,296
Abigail Cumbie 57   Michaelene Morrison 58*
Thomas Payne 67   Maryellen Conner 68,273
Jenny Gunter ....69,294*   Travis Young 71,83*
Nathan Davis 76,295   Suzanne Chachere 84,286
Hector Herrera 91   Julie Chachere 275

Public Schs..Principal	Grd	Prgm	Enr/#Cls	SN	
Colbert Elem Sch 231 S Colbert, Dayton 77535 Jennifer Narvaez	PK-PK	T	220 5	80% Fax	936/258-2727 936/257-4151
Dayton High Sch 3200 N Cleveland Rd, Dayton 77535 Geoff McCracken	9-12	ATV	1,511 80	55% Fax	936/258-2510 936/257-4047
Dr E R Richter Elem Sch 90 Cherry Creek Rd, Dayton 77535 Kristie Kelley	K-5	T	762 50	58% Fax	936/258-7126 936/257-4179
Ⓐ Fredda Nottingham Alt Educ Ctr 302 S Cleveland St, Dayton 77535 Stacie Lott	9-12		3	40% Fax	936/257-4100 936/257-4110
Kimmie M Brown Elem Sch 151 Brown Rd, Dayton 77535 Jessica Ott	K-5	T	787 22	64% Fax	936/257-2796 936/257-4154
Stephen F Austin Elem Sch 701 W Houston St, Dayton 77535 Atiya Wortham	K-5	T	895 44	68% Fax	936/258-2535 936/257-4138
Woodrow Wilson Jr High Sch 309 Highway 146, Dayton 77535 Matt Barnett	6-8	T	1,210 90	58% Fax	936/258-2309 936/257-4109

- **Devers Ind School Dist** PID: 01037824   936/549-7591
  201 S Chism, Devers 77538   Fax 936/549-7595

Schools: 1 \ **Teachers:** 14 \ **Students:** 200 \ **Special Ed Students:** 14 \ **LEP Students:** 31 \ **Ethnic:** African American 4%, Hispanic 32%, Caucasian 65% \ **Exp:** $513 (High) \ **Poverty:** 16% \ **Title I:** $39,636 \ **Open-Close:** 08/08 - 05/28 \ **DTBP:** $354 (High)

Elizabeth Harris 1,11,57,288   Melissa Jordan 2,295
Deidra Hargrave ....4*   Libby Smith 6
Elizabeth Harris .... 12,57,83*   Missy Horelica 16,69*
Michael Rimarez 67   Penny Gilliland 73

Public Schs..Principal	Grd	Prgm	Enr/#Cls	SN	
Devers Elem Sch 201 S Chism St, Devers 77538 Elizabeth Harris	PK-8	TV	200 20	44% Fax	936/549-7591 936/549-7085

- **Hardin Ind School Dist** PID: 01037848   936/298-2112
  209 County Rd 2003 N, Hardin 77561   Fax 936/298-9161

Schools: 3 \ **Teachers:** 101 \ **Students:** 1,400 \ **Special Ed Students:** 107 \ **LEP Students:** 37 \ **College-Bound:** 60% \ **Ethnic:** African American 3%, Hispanic 14%, Native American: 1%, Caucasian 82% \ **Exp:** $289 (Med) \ **Poverty:** 26% \ **Title I:** $468,634 \ **Special Education:** $50,000 \ **Open-Close:** 08/15 - 05/22 \ **DTBP:** $343 (High)

Gerald Nixson 1   Michelle Lee 2,19
Keith Carpenter 3   Larry Haynes 6*
Cami Jones ....8,11,285,296*   Paula Jackson 34
Cody Parrish 67   Todd English 73,286*

---

79 Student Personnel	91 Safety/Security	275 Response To Intervention	298 Grant Writer/Ptnrships	**School Programs**
80 Driver Ed/Safety	92 Magnet School	277 Remedial Math K-12	750 Chief Innovation Officer	A = Alternative Program
81 Gifted/Talented	93 Parental Involvement	280 Literacy Coach	751 Chief of Staff	G = Adult Classes
82 Video Services	95 Tech Prep Program	285 STEM	752 Social Emotional Learning	M = Magnet Program
83 Substance Abuse Prev	97 Chief Infomation Officer	286 Digital Learning		T = Title I Schoolwide
84 Erate	98 Chief Technology Officer	288 Common Core Standards	**Other School Types**	V = Career & Tech Ed Programs
85 AIDS Education	270 Character Education	294 Accountability	Ⓐ = Alternative School	
88 Alternative/At Risk	271 Migrant Education	295 Network System	Ⓒ = Charter School	New Schools are shaded
89 Multi-Cultural Curriculum	273 Teacher Mentor	296 Title II Programs	Ⓜ = Magnet School	New Superintendents and Principals are bold
90 Social Work	274 Before/After Sch	297 Webmaster	Ⓨ = Year-Round School	Personnel with email addresses are underscored

Social Media
f = Facebook
t = Twitter

Limestone County

Market Data Retrieval

Public Schs..Principal	Grd	Prgm	Enr/#Cls	SN	
Hardin Elem Sch 11285 Highway 146 North, Hardin 77561 Paula Jackson	PK-5	T	749	62%	936/298-2114 Fax 936/298-9153
Hardin High Sch 501 FM 834, Liberty 77575 Dr Bryan Taulton	9-12	ATV	337 25	43%	936/298-2118 Fax 936/298-3612
Hardin Junior High Sch 395 FM 834 E, Hardin 77561 Jennifer Stein	6-8		320		936/298-2054 Fax 936/298-3264

- **Hull Daisetta Ind School Dist** PID: 01037886 936/536-6321
  117 N Main St FM 770, Daisetta 77533 Fax 936/536-6251

Schools: 3 \ *Teachers:* 45 \ *Students:* 477 \ *Special Ed Students:* 48 \ *LEP Students:* 8 \ *College-Bound:* 37% \ *Ethnic:* African American 10%, Hispanic 8%, Caucasian 82% \ *Exp:* $693 (High) \ *Poverty:* 9% \ *Title I:* $62,422 \ *Special Education:* $21,000 \ *Open-Close:* 08/15 - 05/22 \ *DTBP:* $424 (High)

Timothy Bartram 1		Erin Stephens 2	
Brenda Brown 4		Cindy Davie 5	
Stan Hodges 6*		Laura Williamson 7,83,85	
Justin Anderson 10,13		Teresa Camp 11,57,58,69,275*	
Kerry Dillard 31*		Kelley Berry 67	
Justus Cook 73,295*		Rhonda Ritter 286*	

Public Schs..Principal	Grd	Prgm	Enr/#Cls	SN	
Hull Daisetta Elem Sch 7243 FM 834 E, Hull 77564 Kevin Frauenberger	PK-6	T	242	83%	936/536-6321 Fax 936/536-3800
Hull Daisetta High Sch 117 N Main St, Daisetta 77533 Quinn Godwin	9-12	ATV	170 14	66%	936/536-6321 Fax 936/536-3839
Hull Daisetta Junior High Sch 117 N Main St, Daisetta 77533 Quinn Godwin	7-8	AT	65 14	76%	936/536-6321 Fax 936/536-3839

- **Liberty Ind School Dist** PID: 01037927 936/336-7213
  1600 Grand Ave, Liberty 77575 Fax 936/336-2283

Schools: 4 \ *Teachers:* 142 \ *Students:* 2,200 \ *Special Ed Students:* 191 \ *LEP Students:* 320 \ *College-Bound:* 58% \ *Ethnic:* Asian 1%, African American 17%, Hispanic 39%, Caucasian 43% \ *Exp:* $376 (High) \ *Poverty:* 20% \ *Title I:* $558,003 \ *Open-Close:* 08/20 - 05/27 \ *DTBP:* $510 (High)

Cody Abshier 1		Annette Taylor 2	
Ginger Ramer 2,19		Sandy Sizemore 4	
Robert Ward 5*		Chad Taylor 6	
Margaret Gardzina 8,11		Dustin McGee 15	
Susan Baker 16*		Keith Ming 33	
Tonya Freeman 37*		Bruce Bell 67	
Lannise Reidland 68		Yvonne Lawrence 69	
Angela Walker 79			

Public Schs..Principal	Grd	Prgm	Enr/#Cls	SN	
Liberty Elem Sch 1002 Bowie St, Liberty 77575 Stephanie Cox	2-5	T	649 48	66%	936/336-3603 Fax 936/336-6077
Liberty High Sch 2615 Jefferson Dr, Liberty 77575 Benicia Bendele	9-12	GTV	595 65	53%	936/336-6483 Fax 936/336-7914
Liberty Middle Sch 2515 Jefferson Dr, Liberty 77575 Rhonda Smith	6-8	T	445 36	59%	936/336-3582 Fax 936/336-1021
San Jacinto Elem Sch 1629 Grand Ave, Liberty 77575 Tom Connelly	PK-1	T	419 35	75%	936/336-3161 Fax 936/336-5751

- **Tarkington Ind School Dist** PID: 01037977 281/592-8781
  2770 FM 163 Rd, Cleveland 77327 Fax 281/592-3969

Schools: 4 \ *Teachers:* 132 \ *Students:* 1,800 \ *Special Ed Students:* 194 \ *LEP Students:* 40 \ *College-Bound:* 41% \ *Ethnic:* African American 1%, Hispanic 10%, Caucasian 88% \ *Exp:* $334 (High) \ *Poverty:* 23% \ *Title I:* $574,407 \ *Open-Close:* 08/21 - 05/28 \ *DTBP:* $553 (High)

Dr Marc Keith 1		Dennis Shew 2,15	
Ronnie Yancey 3		Karen Blum 4*	
Melanie Owens 5		Mary-Jane Moore ...8,11,57,76,85,88,296,298	
Angie Thomas 34*		Jackie Owens 37*	
Grant Cook 67		Renee Padgett 69	
Crystal Dean 73,286,295*		Pam Williams 73	

Public Schs..Principal	Grd	Prgm	Enr/#Cls	SN	
Tarkington High Sch 2770 FM 163 Rd, Cleveland 77327 Lisa Stephens	9-12	V	520 48	38%	281/592-7739 Fax 281/592-0693
Tarkington Intermediate Sch 2770 FM 163 Rd, Cleveland 77327 Calesta House	4-5	T	297 25	47%	281/592-6134 Fax 281/592-2453
Tarkington Middle Sch 2770 FM 163 Rd, Cleveland 77327 Michael Kelley	6-8	T	441	50%	281/592-7737 Fax 281/592-5241
Tarkington Primary Sch 2770 FM 163 Rd, Cleveland 77327 Angie Thomas	PK-3	T	572 34	52%	281/592-7736 Fax 281/592-2361

LIMESTONE COUNTY

LIMESTONE PUBLIC SCHOOLS

- **Coolidge Ind School Dist** PID: 01038012 254/786-2206
  1002 Kirvan St, Coolidge 76635 Fax 254/786-4835

Schools: 2 \ *Teachers:* 30 \ *Students:* 309 \ *Special Ed Students:* 44 \ *LEP Students:* 54 \ *College-Bound:* 80% \ *Ethnic:* African American 17%, Hispanic 58%, Caucasian 25% \ *Exp:* $589 (High) \ *Poverty:* 36% \ *Title I:* $149,709 \ *Special Education:* $80,000 \ *Open-Close:* 07/25 - 05/22 \ *DTBP:* $347 (High)

Dr Robert Lowry 1		Nancy Kuykendall 2	
Donald Erwin 3,5*		Tonya Barnett 4*	
Christina Smiley 12		Ginger Self 58	
Danny Finley 67		Tennie Sumrall 73,95	

Public Schs..Principal	Grd	Prgm	Enr/#Cls	SN	
Coolidge Elem Sch 1000 Kirvan St, Coolidge 76635 Laci Lowry	PK-5	T	164 14	85%	254/786-2206 Fax 254/786-2130
Coolidge Jr Sr High Sch 1002 Kirvan St, Coolidge 76635 Justin Cox	6-12		145 14		254/786-4612 Fax 254/786-2038

---

1 Superintendent	8 Curric/Instruct K-12	19 Chief Financial Officer	29 Family/Consumer Science	39 Social Studies K-12	49 English/Lang Arts Elem	59 Special Education Elem	69 Academic Assessment
2 Bus/Finance/Purchasing	9 Curric/Instruct Elem	20 Art K-12	30 Adult Education	40 Social Studies Elem	50 English/Lang Arts Sec	60 Special Education Sec	70 Research/Development
3 Buildings And Grounds	10 Curric/Instruct Sec	21 Art Elem	31 Career/Sch-to-Work K-12	41 Social Studies Sec	51 Reading K-12	61 Foreign/World Lang K-12	71 Public Information
4 Food Service	11 Federal Program	22 Art Sec	32 Career/Sch-to-Work Elem	42 Science K-12	52 Reading Elem	62 Foreign/World Lang Elem	72 Summer School
5 Transportation	12 Title I	23 Music K-12	33 Career/Sch-to-Work Sec	43 Science Elem	53 Reading Sec	63 Foreign/World Lang Sec	73 Instructional Tech
6 Athletic	13 Title V	24 Music Elem	34 Early Childhood Ed	44 Science Sec	54 Remedial Reading K-12	64 Religious Education K-12	74 Inservice Training
7 Health Services	15 Asst Superintendent	25 Music Sec	35 Health/Phys Education	45 Math K-12	55 Remedial Reading Elem	65 Religious Education Elem	75 Marketing/Distributive
	16 Instructional Media Svcs	26 Business Education	36 Guidance Services K-12	46 Math Elem	56 Remedial Reading Sec	66 Religious Education Sec	76 Info Systems
	17 Chief Operations Officer	27 Career & Tech Ed	37 Guidance Services Elem	47 Math Sec	57 Bilingual/ELL	67 School Board President	77 Psychological Assess
	18 Chief Academic Officer	28 Technology Education	38 Guidance Services Sec	48 English/Lang Arts K-12	58 Special Education K-12	68 Teacher Personnel	78 Affirmative Action

Texas School Directory

Lipscomb County

- **Groesbeck Ind School Dist** PID: 01038048   254/729-4100
  1202 N Ellis St, Groesbeck 76642   Fax 254/729-5167

Schools: 4 \ *Teachers:* 123 \ *Students:* 1,560 \ *Special Ed Students:* 208 \ *LEP Students:* 81 \ *College-Bound:* 65% \ *Ethnic:* Asian 1%, African American 13%, Hispanic 26%, Caucasian 60% \ *Exp:* $387 (High) \ *Poverty:* 22% \ *Title I:* $412,139 \ *Special Education:* $412,000 \ *Open-Close:* 08/14 - 05/21 \ *DTBP:* $355 (High)

Name	Code
James Cowley	1,73
Jackie Ancelet	3
Jenny Flower	7
Melody Sadler	11,58*
Susan Swick	38*
Don Waller	295
Dayne Duncan	2,4,5,91
Jerry Bomar	6
Dr Diana Freeman	8,11,83,88,288,296,298
Tracy Smith	37
Tom Sutton	67

Public Schs..Principal	Grd	Prgm	Enr/#Cls	SN	
Enge-Washington Interm Sch 803 S Ellis St, Groesbeck 76642 **Beth Westhoff**	3-6	T	586 16	64%	254/729-4103 Fax 254/729-5309
Groesbeck High Sch 1202 N Ellis St, Groesbeck 76642 **Dr Bonnie Bomar**	9-12	T	484 50	57%	254/729-4101 Fax 254/729-5458
Groesbeck Middle Sch 410 Elwood Enge Dr, Groesbeck 76642 Dayne Duncan	7-8	T	265 42	61%	254/729-4102 Fax 254/729-8763
H O Whitehurst Elem Sch 801 S Ellis St, Groesbeck 76642 **Kimberly Carter**	PK-5	T	600 24	65%	254/729-4104 Fax 254/729-2798

- **Mexia Ind School Dist** PID: 01038086   254/562-4000
  616 N Red River St, Mexia 76667   Fax 254/562-5508

Schools: 5 \ *Teachers:* 137 \ *Students:* 1,800 \ *Special Ed Students:* 200 \ *LEP Students:* 290 \ *College-Bound:* 69% \ *Ethnic:* Asian 1%, African American 28%, Hispanic 46%, Caucasian 25% \ *Exp:* $317 (High) \ *Poverty:* 28% \ *Title I:* $738,560 \ *Special Education:* $432,000 \ *Open-Close:* 08/13 - 05/21 \ *DTBP:* $350 (High) \ [f]

Name	Code
Dr Lyle Debus	1
Alvis Minter	3,5
Frank Sandoval	6*
Dr Celia Drews	13,296*
Wendy Dunn	38*
Darcy Tyus	58
Cherilyn Zimmer	73
Tracy Porter	286
William Belees	295
Dr Brian Ziener	2,12
Craig Hempel	4
Dr Celia Drews	8,11,15
Donna Scott	37*
Shelli Killingsworth	57,68
Benji Reed	67
Randal Dobson	83,91*
Anthony Brooks	295

Public Schs..Principal	Grd	Prgm	Enr/#Cls	SN	
A B McBay Elem Sch 1000 N Ross Ave, Mexia 76667 Joe Tyus	PK-2	T	463 38	80%	254/562-4030 Fax 254/562-0074
Mexia High Sch 1120 N Ross Ave, Mexia 76667 **Robert White**	9-12	T	506 55	73%	254/562-4010 Fax 254/562-7072
Mexia Junior High Sch 1 Blackcat Dr, Mexia 76667 **Brian Bartlett**	6-8	T	403 45	84%	254/562-4020 Fax 254/562-5053
Misd Developmental Center 616 N Red River St, Mexia 76667 Galen Remmers	Spec	AT	31	87%	254/562-4023 Fax 254/562-4024
R Q Sims Intermediate Sch 1010 N Ross Ave, Mexia 76667 Kelli Fortner	3-5	T	403 30	84%	254/562-4025 Fax 254/562-4028

LIPSCOMB COUNTY

LIPSCOMB PUBLIC SCHOOLS

- **Booker Ind School Dist** PID: 01038139   806/658-4501
  600 S Main St, Booker 79005   Fax 806/658-4503

Schools: 2 \ *Teachers:* 40 \ *Students:* 398 \ *Special Ed Students:* 40 \ *LEP Students:* 76 \ *College-Bound:* 33% \ *Ethnic:* Hispanic 70%, Caucasian 29% \ *Exp:* $633 (High) \ *Poverty:* 12% \ *Title I:* $50,476 \ *Open-Close:* 08/22 - 05/21 \ *DTBP:* $355 (High)

Name	Code
Dr Brian Holt	1
Griselda Desantiago	4*
Susie Wynn	10,16,69*
Creed Hoover	67
Leah Terrell	73*
Debbie Babitzke	2
Brent Lile	6*
Jenifer Davis	58*
Susy Wynn	69*
Debbie Dempsay	84

Public Schs..Principal	Grd	Prgm	Enr/#Cls	SN	
Bob L Kirksey Elem Sch 600 S Main, Booker 79005 Kelli Cates	PK-5	T	210 20	64%	806/658-4559 Fax 806/658-9279
Booker High Sch 600 S Main St, Booker 79005 Steven Livingston	6-12	TV	196 34	65%	806/658-4521 Fax 806/658-9530

- **Darrouzett Ind School Dist** PID: 01038165   806/624-2221
  102 W Kansas Ave, Darrouzett 79024   Fax 806/624-4361

Schools: 1 \ *Teachers:* 16 \ *Students:* 120 \ *Special Ed Students:* 11 \ *LEP Students:* 3 \ *College-Bound:* 50% \ *Ethnic:* Hispanic 48%, Native American: 1%, Caucasian 51% \ *Exp:* $561 (High) \ *Poverty:* 21% \ *Title I:* $29,036 \ *Open-Close:* 08/20 - 05/22 \ *DTBP:* $280 (High)

Name	Code
Deidre Parish	1,11
Brandi Howell	4
Joyce Coppock	36,275,288*
Randy Miller	67
Tracy Meier	273*
Kim Duke	2
Donavan Ferguson	11
Kelley White	58*
Nieda Schoenhals	73,286,295

Public Schs..Principal	Grd	Prgm	Enr/#Cls	SN	
Darrouzett Sch 102 W Kansas Ave, Darrouzett 79024 Donavan Ferguson	PK-12	TV	120 10	73%	806/624-3001

- **Follett Ind School Dist** PID: 01038191   806/653-2301
  205 E Ivanhoe Ave, Follett 79034   Fax 806/653-2036

Schools: 1 \ *Teachers:* 17 \ *Students:* 140 \ *Special Ed Students:* 10 \ *LEP Students:* 17 \ *College-Bound:* 91% \ *Ethnic:* Asian 1%, Hispanic 29%, Native American: 1%, Caucasian 69% \ *Exp:* $693 (High) \ *Poverty:* 19% \ *Title I:* $28,384 \ *Open-Close:* 08/15 - 05/22 \ *DTBP:* $331 (High)

Name	Code
George Auld	1
Sharon Chadwick	4*
Jamie Copley	11,296
Rusty Stewart	67
Megan Robertson	271*
Trudy Lamb	2
Teresa Robison	8,88,752*
Jr Slater	58
Arlen Barnes	73,76*
Teresa Robison	752

---

79 Student Personnel	91 Safety/Security	275 Response To Intervention	298 Grant Writer/Ptnrships	**School Programs**		**Social Media**
80 Driver Ed/Safety	92 Magnet School	277 Remedial Math K-12	750 Chief Innovation Officer	A = Alternative Program		[f] = Facebook
81 Gifted/Talented	93 Parental Involvement	280 Literacy Coach	751 Chief of Staff	G = Adult Classes		[t] = Twitter
82 Video Services	95 Tech Prep Program	285 STEM	752 Social Emotional Learning	M = Magnet Program		
83 Substance Abuse Prev	97 Chief Infomation Officer	286 Digital Learning		T = Title I Schoolwide		
84 Erate	98 Chief Technology Officer	288 Common Core Standards	**Other School Types**	V = Career & Tech Ed Programs		
85 AIDS Education	270 Accountability	294 Accountability	Ⓐ = Alternative School			
88 Alternative/At Risk	271 Migrant Education	295 Network System	Ⓒ = Charter School	New Schools are shaded		
89 Multi-Cultural Curriculum	273 Teacher Mentor	296 Title II Programs	Ⓜ = Magnet School	New Superintendents and Principals are bold		
90 Social Work	274 Before/After Sch	297 Webmaster	Ⓨ = Year-Round School	Personnel with email addresses are underscored		

Live Oak County

Public Schs..Principal	Grd	Prgm	Enr/#Cls	SN	
Follett Sch 205 E Ivanhoe Ave, Follett 79034 Megan Robertson	PK-12	TV	140 16	51%	806/653-2301

• **Higgins Ind School Dist** PID: 01038220 806/852-2171
406 N Main Street, Higgins 79046 Fax 806/852-3502

Schools: 1 \ **Teachers:** 19 \ **Students:** 125 \ **Special Ed Students:** 21 \ **LEP Students:** 8 \ **College-Bound:** 50% \ **Ethnic:** Asian 1%, African American 1%, Hispanic 22%, Caucasian 76% \ **Exp:** $615 (High) \ **Poverty:** 33% \ **Title I:** $34,327 \ **Open-Close:** 08/12 - 05/22 \ **DTBP:** $277 (High)

Kristy White 1,11,83
James McGinley 3
Javon Hassler 16,73,286*
Jay Barbee 67
Nancy Habekutt 270*
Amy Woods 2
Nic Tarr 6,80*
Jody Wiederstein 58*
Mavonteine Slavin 85

Public Schs..Principal	Grd	Prgm	Enr/#Cls	SN	
Higgins Sch 406 N Main Street, Higgins 79046 Becky Suthers	PK-12		125 15	73%	806/852-2631

LIVE OAK COUNTY

LIVE OAK PUBLIC SCHOOLS

• **George West Ind School Dist** PID: 01038256 361/449-1914
913 Houston St, George West 78022 Fax 361/449-1426

Schools: 4 \ **Teachers:** 81 \ **Students:** 1,100 \ **Special Ed Students:** 93 \ **LEP Students:** 27 \ **College-Bound:** 60% \ **Ethnic:** African American 1%, Hispanic 56%, Caucasian 43% \ **Exp:** $245 (Med) \ **Poverty:** 23% \ **Title I:** $313,158 \ **Special Education:** $104,000 \ **Open-Close:** 08/15 - 05/28 \ **DTBP:** $350 (High) \ 🅕 🅣

Dr James Rosebrock 1
Joe Chappa 3
Sharon Clifton 4
Brent Kornegay 6
Kristy Keach 11,69*
Elda Buenteo 16*
Ethel Murphy 58
Laurl Jones 76
Nita Peck 2
Rena Cuevas 4
Margaret Yarborough 5
Dr Roland Quesada 8,12,57,74,288
Deanna Blackwell 16,73*
Heather Lee 31*
Cheri Moore 67

Public Schs..Principal	Grd	Prgm	Enr/#Cls	SN	
George West Elem Sch 910 Houston St, George West 78022 Omar De La Rosa	4-6	T	238 35	61%	361/449-1914 Fax 361/449-2177
George West High Sch 1013 Houston St, George West 78022 Richard Waterhouse	9-12	ATV	343 35	39%	361/449-1914 Fax 361/449-3128
George West Junior High Sch 900 Houston St, George West 78022 Ashley Lowe	7-8	TV	170 15	59%	361/449-1914 Fax 361/449-3909
George West Primary Sch 405 Travis St, George West 78022 Christina Cortez	PK-3	T	349 20	64%	361/449-1914 Fax 361/449-8921

Market Data Retrieval

• **Three Rivers Ind School Dist** PID: 01038309 361/786-3626
351 S School Rd, Three Rivers 78071 Fax 361/786-2555

Schools: 2 \ **Teachers:** 59 \ **Students:** 678 \ **Special Ed Students:** 60 \ **LEP Students:** 26 \ **College-Bound:** 80% \ **Ethnic:** African American 1%, Hispanic 57%, Caucasian 42% \ **Exp:** $588 (High) \ **Poverty:** 22% \ **Title I:** $166,679 \ **Open-Close:** 08/13 - 05/22 \ **DTBP:** $180 (High)

Les Dragon 1
Whitney Means 4
Audra Huff 11,52,58,286,296
Karl Arnst 67
Stephanie Timms 2
Arturo Lozano 6,85*
Robin Curbello 16*
Daniel Fernandez 73,84

Public Schs..Principal	Grd	Prgm	Enr/#Cls	SN	
Three Rivers Elem Sch 351 S School Rd, Three Rivers 78071 Cindy Miller	PK-6	T	365 24	73%	361/786-3592 Fax 361/786-3594
Three Rivers Jr Sr High Sch 351 S School Rd, Three Rivers 78071 Ross Baker	7-12	ATV	313 20	60%	361/786-3531 Fax 361/786-3533

LLANO COUNTY

LLANO PUBLIC SCHOOLS

• **Llano Ind School Dist** PID: 01038347 325/247-4747
1400 Oatman St, Llano 78643 Fax 325/247-5623

Schools: 4 \ **Teachers:** 133 \ **Students:** 1,800 \ **Special Ed Students:** 207 \ **LEP Students:** 97 \ **College-Bound:** 45% \ **Ethnic:** Asian 1%, African American 1%, Hispanic 25%, Caucasian 73% \ **Exp:** $395 (High) \ **Poverty:** 24% \ **Title I:** $660,637 \ **Special Education:** $511,000 \ **Open-Close:** 08/15 - 05/29 \ **DTBP:** $136 (High)

Mac Edwards 1
Keith Nelson 3
Melissa Pike 5
James Paine 8,11,280,285,286,288,294,298
Jill Dillard 16,82*
Jennifer Watkins 37
Shelly Schuessler 58*
Jim Beasley 73,76,95,295,297
Ryan Turner 270
Jill Minshew 2,19
Amy Grant 4
Matthew Green 6
Kim Stubblefiled 9,11,34,51,54,271
Jenifer Neatherlin 31,83,88*
Courtney Edwards 38
Rick Tisdale 67
Eliabeth Kloepper 85

Public Schs..Principal	Grd	Prgm	Enr/#Cls	SN	
Llano Elem Sch 1600 Oatman St, Llano 78643 Douglas Debord	PK-5	T	374 28	61%	325/247-5718 Fax 325/247-5731
Llano High Sch 2509 S State Highway 16, Llano 78643 Jenifer Neatherlin	9-12	TV	539 45	56%	325/248-2200 Fax 325/247-2122
Llano Junior High Sch 400 E State Highway 71, Llano 78643 Todd Keele	6-8	T	405 50	64%	325/247-4659 Fax 325/247-5821
Packsaddle Elem Sch 150 Pioneer Ln, Kingsland 78639 Ryan Turner	PK-5	T	475 36	84%	325/388-8129 Fax 325/388-7000

---

1 Superintendent	8 Curric/Instruct K-12	19 Chief Financial Officer	29 Family/Consumer Science	39 Social Studies K-12	49 English/Lang Arts Elem	59 Special Education Elem	69 Academic Assessment
2 Bus/Finance/Purchasing	9 Curric/Instruct Elem	20 Art K-12	30 Adult Education	40 Social Studies Elem	50 English/Lang Arts Sec	60 Special Education Sec	70 Research/Development
3 Buildings And Grounds	10 Curric/Instruct Sec	21 Art Elem	31 Career/Sch-to-Work K-12	41 Social Studies Sec	51 Reading K-12	61 Foreign/World Lang K-12	71 Public Information
4 Food Service	11 Federal Program	22 Art Sec	32 Career/Sch-to-Work Elem	42 Science K-12	52 Reading Elem	62 Foreign/World Lang Elem	72 Summer School
5 Transportation	12 Title I	23 Music K-12	33 Career/Sch-to-Work Sec	43 Science Elem	53 Reading Sec	63 Foreign/World Lang Sec	73 Instructional Tech
6 Athletic	13 Title V	24 Music Elem	34 Early Childhood Ed	44 Science Sec	54 Remedial Reading K-12	64 Religious Education K-12	74 Inservice Training
7 Health Services	14 Instructional Media Svcs	25 Music Sec	35 Health/Phys Education	45 Math K-12	55 Remedial Reading Elem	65 Religious Education Elem	75 Marketing/Distributive
	15 Asst Superintendent	26 Business Education	36 Guidance Services K-12	46 Math Elem	56 Remedial Reading Sec	66 Religious Education Sec	76 Info Systems
	16 Instructional Media Svcs	27 Career & Tech Ed	37 Guidance Services Elem	47 Math Sec	57 Bilingual/ELL	67 School Board President	77 Psychological Assess
	17 Chief Operations Officer	28 Technology Education	38 Guidance Services Sec	48 English/Lang Arts K-12	58 Special Education K-12	68 Teacher Personnel	78 Affirmative Action

Texas School Directory

Lubbock County

LLANO PRIVATE SCHOOLS

Private Schs..Principal	Grd	Prgm	Enr/#Cls	SN	
Llano Christian Academy 507 E Green St, Llano 78643 Dr Alice Smith	PK-12		76		325/247-4942

LUBBOCK COUNTY

LUBBOCK PUBLIC SCHOOLS

● **Frenship Ind School Dist** PID: 01038402   806/866-9541
501 7th St, Wolfforth 79382   Fax 806/866-4135

Schools: 13 \ **Teachers:** 622 \ **Students:** 9,900 \ **Special Ed Students:** 796 \ **LEP Students:** 335 \ **College-Bound:** 57% \ **Ethnic:** Asian 3%, African American 4%, Hispanic 42%, Caucasian 50% \ **Exp:** $372 (High) \ **Poverty:** 12% \ **Title I:** $1,301,422 \ **Special Education:** $1,152,000 \ **Open-Close:** 08/19 - 05/22 \ **DTBP:** $137 (High) \ f t

Dr Michelle McCord 1	Farley Reeves 2,15
Tim Williams 2,15	Allen Tanner 3
Derek Cobb 3	Joyce Trevino 4
Michael Brooks 5*	Kenneth Catney 6
Cassandra Slayton 8	Cindy Cobb 8,15,74,273
Melissa Wade 11,85	Amy Baker 27
Regan Lamberson 39*	Julie Rogers 48
Senon Cruz 57	Doug Smith 58
Brad Draper 67	Rhonda Dillard 68,78
Emily Solis 71	Joe Barnett 73,98,297
Laurie Davis 73*	Michelle Traylor 73
Richard Dean 91	Leanne Fisher 288

Public Schs..Principal	Grd	Prgm	Enr/#Cls	SN	
Bennett Elem Sch 101 Donald Preston Dr, Wolfforth 79382 **Chera Bessire**	PK-5	T	667 25	37%	806/866-4443 Fax 806/866-4715
Crestview Elem Sch 6020 81st St, Lubbock 79424 **Stacy Davis**	PK-5		575 29	22%	806/794-3661 Fax 806/798-2373
Frenship High Sch 902 N Dowden Rd, Wolfforth 79382 **Gregory Hernandez**	9-12	V	2,697 115	29%	806/866-4440 Fax 806/866-9370
Frenship Middle Sch 500 Main St, Wolfforth 79382 **Casey Loafman**	6-8		640 40	36%	806/866-4464 Fax 806/866-9137
Heritage Middle Sch 6110 73rd St, Lubbock 79424 **Chelsey Campbell**	6-8		701	32%	806/794-9400 Fax 806/783-8958
Legacy Elem Sch 6424 Kemper Ave, Lubbock 79416 **Carole Kidd**	PK-3	T	484	53%	806/792-3800 Fax 806/792-3801
North Ridge Elem Sch 6302 11th Pl, Lubbock 79416 **Shannon Morrison**	PK-5	T	654 39	47%	806/793-6686 Fax 806/792-3798
Oak Ridge Elem Sch 6514 68th St, Lubbock 79424 **Shane Langen**	PK-5		635	38%	806/794-5200 Fax 806/698-0440
Ⓐ Reese Education Center 9421 W 4th St, Lubbock 79416 **Stephanie Spear**	6-12	T	75 12	56%	806/885-4910 Fax 806/885-2442
Terra Vista Middle Sch 1111 Upland Ave, Lubbock 79416 **Jill Jaquess**	6-8	T	754	51%	806/796-0076 Fax 806/796-1540
Upland Heights Elem Sch 10020 Upland Ave, Lubbock 79424 **Denise Stewart**	PK-5		638	38%	806/698-6611
Westwind Elem Sch 6401 43rd St, Lubbock 79407 **Todd Newberry**	PK-5	T	600 30	64%	806/799-3731
Willow Bend Elem Sch 8816 13 St, Lubbock 79416 **Vivian Fisher**	PK-5	T	580	77%	806/796-0090 Fax 806/796-1517

● **Idalou Ind School Dist** PID: 01038452   806/892-1900
601 Walnut St, Idalou 79329   Fax 806/892-3204

Schools: 3 \ **Teachers:** 78 \ **Students:** 1,003 \ **Special Ed Students:** 85 \ **LEP Students:** 20 \ **College-Bound:** 70% \ **Ethnic:** Hispanic 42%, Caucasian 57% \ **Exp:** $574 (High) \ **Poverty:** 10% \ **Title I:** $88,968 \ **Open-Close:** 08/26 - 05/21 \ **DTBP:** $350 (High)

Jim Waller 1,84	Shelly Kirkendall 2,19
Shelly Tubbs 2,11,71	Darrell Fuller 3
Judy Blackburn 3	Jeff Lofton 6*
Steve Gunter 8,11,274*	Karen Carroll 10,31*
Clay Osburn 16,73	Lori Irwin 57,69,270,271*
Deborah Swanson 58	Johnny Taylor 67

Public Schs..Principal	Grd	Prgm	Enr/#Cls	SN	
Idalou Elem Sch 601 Walnut St, Idalou 79329 **Steve Gunter**	PK-4	T	409 19	43%	806/892-2524 Fax 806/892-2666
Idalou High Sch 601 Walnut St, Idalou 79329 **Karen Carroll**	9-12	TV	292 25	31%	806/892-2123 Fax 806/892-2690
Idalou Middle Sch 403 W 7th St, Idalou 79329 **Josh Damron**	5-8		302 18	32%	806/892-2133 Fax 806/892-2388

● **Lubbock Ind School Dist** PID: 01038490   806/766-1000
1628 19th St, Lubbock 79401   Fax 806/766-1210

Schools: 48 \ **Teachers:** 2,007 \ **Students:** 27,759 \ **Special Ed Students:** 3,041 \ **LEP Students:** 1,164 \ **College-Bound:** 60% \ **Ethnic:** Asian 2%, African American 14%, Hispanic 60%, Caucasian 24% \ **Exp:** $542 (High) \ **Poverty:** 25% \ **Title I:** $11,904,665 \ **Special Education:** $5,809,000 \ **Open-Close:** 08/14 - 05/22 \ **DTBP:** $186 (High) \ t

Kathryn Reno-Rollo 1	Jeff Baum 2,19
Kelley Lewis 2	Nina Waller 2
Bill Craft 3	Lauren Johnson 4*
Mike Meeks 6	Paulett Rozneck 7,83,85*
Misty Rieber 8,15,288	Doyle Volger 9,15
Denise Mattson 11,57,275,296,298	Johnna Weatherbee 12,93
Ricardo Rodriguez 15,68,78,751	Jenny Flores 16*
Andrew Babcock 20,23	Jill Berset 27,31
Bryan Sessom 34	Charlotte Sessom 36*
Joni Rodela 39	Michael Sizemore 42,285
Amador Vasquez 45	Lori Greaves 48,51
Melissa Hernandez 57	Kami Finger 58
Dr Shelly Bratcher 58	Laura Cook 61*
Zack Brady 67	Doug Bawcom 68
Wonderful Loud 68	Pam Leftwich 69,70,294

TX-269

Lubbock County

Jeffrey Klopzman 71
Sherry Mitchell 73,286
Dathan Mullins 76,295
Lynn Akin 79,88
Garrett Luft 81,92,286
Maria Patino 271
Damon Jackson 73,98
Anna Jackson 74*
Dana King 78,90,275
Dr Gail Smith 81
Jody Scifres 91
Sarah Ancell 297*

Public Schs..Principal	Grd	Prgm	Enr/#Cls	SN	
Alderson Elem Sch 219 Walnut Ave, Lubbock 79403 **Drue Coleman**	PK-5	T	569 22	99%	806/219-8000 Fax 806/766-1490
Atkins Middle Sch 5401 Avenue U, Lubbock 79412 Chris Huber	6-8	TV	624 50	82%	806/219-3000 Fax 806/766-2226
Bayless Elem Sch 2115 58th St, Lubbock 79412 Brandi McKinney	PK-5	T	601 38	100%	806/219-5000 Fax 806/766-1651
Bean Elem Sch 3001 Avenue N, Lubbock 79411 Tom Thomas	PK-5	T	553 31	91%	806/219-5100 Fax 806/766-1671
Brown Elem Sch 2315 36th St, Lubbock 79412 Staci Sumners	PK-5	T	365 25	96%	806/219-5300 Fax 806/766-0831
Byron Martin Advanced Tech Ctr 3201 Avenue Q, Lubbock 79411 Charlotte Sessom		Voc	200		806/219-2800
Cavazos Middle Sch 210 N University Ave, Lubbock 79415 Marti Makuta	6-8	TV	581 50	92%	806/219-3200 Fax 806/766-6627
Centennial Elem Sch 1301 N Utica Ave, Lubbock 79416 Davida Burks	PK-5	T	710 31	66%	806/219-7800 Fax 806/766-1982
Coronado High Sch 4910 29th Dr, Lubbock 79410 **Julia Stephen**	9-12	TV	2,134 90	47%	806/219-1100 Fax 806/766-0560
Dunbar College Prep Academy 2010 E 26th St, Lubbock 79404 Gabe Gillespie	6-8	TV	534 50	89%	806/219-3400 Fax 806/766-1320
Dupre Elem Sch 2008 Avenue T, Lubbock 79411 Robin Conkwright	PK-5	T	230 17	92%	806/219-5400 Fax 806/766-1691
Estacado High Sch 1504 East Itasca St, Lubbock 79403 Angelica Wilbanks	9-12	TV	732 53	90%	806/766-1400 Fax 806/766-1952
Evans Middle Sch 4211 58th St, Lubbock 79413 **Justin Newman**	6-8	TV	900	46%	806/219-3600 Fax 806/766-0570
Guadalupe Elem Sch 101 N Avenue P, Lubbock 79401 Alma Cunningtubby	PK-5	T	188 21	93%	806/219-5500 Fax 806/766-1702
Hardwick Elem Sch 1420 Chicago Ave, Lubbock 79416 Kimberly Callison	PK-5	T	400 21	67%	806/219-5600 Fax 806/766-0842
Harwell Elem Sch 4101 Avenue D, Lubbock 79404 Jorge Sanchez	PK-5	T	510 30	91%	806/219-5700 Fax 806/766-1713
Hodges Elem Sch 5001 Avenue P, Lubbock 79412 Dora Jimenez	PK-5	T	383 25	92%	806/219-5800 Fax 806/766-1730
Honey Elem Sch 3615 86th St, Lubbock 79423 Phillip Neeb	PK-5		429 24	32%	806/219-5900 Fax 806/766-0864
Hutchinson Middle Sch 3102 Canton Ave, Lubbock 79410 Heidi Dye	6-8	TV	854 45	39%	806/219-3800 Fax 806/766-0538
Irons Middle Sch 5214 79th St, Lubbock 79424 Philip Riewe	6-8	AV	617 58	40%	806/219-4000 Fax 806/766-2070
Jackson Elem Sch 201 Vernon Ave, Lubbock 79415 Alma Cunningtubby	PK-5	T	209 19	93%	806/219-6000 Fax 806/766-1765
Jayne Ann Miller Elem Sch 6705 Joliet Dr, Lubbock 79413 Kevin Booe	PK-5	T	712 22	39%	806/219-8100 Fax 806/766-0557
Joan Y Ervin Elem Sch 1802 E 28th St, Lubbock 79404 Joshlyn Cotton	PK-5	T	477 30	99%	806/219-8200 Fax 806/766-1875
Lubbock Senior High Sch 2004 19th St, Lubbock 79401 Douglas Young	9-12	TV	1,979	44%	806/219-1600 Fax 806/766-1469
MacKenzie Middle Sch 5402 12th St, Lubbock 79416 John Martinez	6-8	TV	566 45	68%	806/219-4200 Fax 806/766-0510
Maedgen Elem Sch 4401 Nashville Ave, Lubbock 79413 **Ofelia Mendez**	PK-5	T	350 24	85%	806/219-6200 Fax 806/766-0990
Ⓐ Matthews Alt HS/New Directions 417 N Akron Ave, Lubbock 79415 Carolyn Thompson-Conwr	6-12	GV	156 19		806/219-2600 Fax 806/766-1532
McWhorter Elem Sch 2711 1st St, Lubbock 79415 Karla Mann	PK-5	T	590 26	93%	806/219-6100 Fax 806/766-1797
Monterey Senior High Sch 3211 47th St, Lubbock 79413 Les Purkeypile	9-12	ATV	2,120 70	54%	806/219-1900 Fax 806/766-0509
O L Slaton Middle Sch 1602 32nd St, Lubbock 79411 Kris Blodgett	6-8	TV	510 45	90%	806/219-4400 Fax 806/766-1571
Overton Elem Sch 2902 Louisville Ave, Lubbock 79410 **Ann Archer**	PK-5	T	330 21	84%	806/219-6300 Fax 806/766-0895
Parsons Elem Sch 2811 58th St, Lubbock 79413 **Yvonne Avey**	PK-5	T	475 32	81%	806/219-6400 Fax 806/766-0902
Ⓐ Priority Intervention Academy 1324 E 24th St, Lubbock 79404 David Johnson	6-12	V	102 30	75%	806/219-2400 Fax 806/766-1964
Ⓒ Ramirez Charter Sch 702 Avenue T, Lubbock 79401 Melissa Serenil	PK-5	T	506 26	61%	806/219-6500 Fax 806/766-1825
Roscoe Wilson Elem Sch 2807 25th St, Lubbock 79410 Paula January	PK-5		517 26	20%	806/219-7500 Fax 806/766-0525
Roy Roberts Elem Sch 7901 Avenue P, Lubbock 79423 **Anissa Briseno**	PK-5	T	706	64%	806/219-7900 Fax 806/766-6222
Rush Elem Sch 4702 15th St, Lubbock 79416 Mary McGann	PK-5	T	400 29	66%	806/219-6700 Fax 806/766-0929
Smith Elem Sch 8707 Dover Ave, Lubbock 79424 Patsy Latimer	PK-5		656 35	36%	806/219-6800 Fax 806/766-2035
Smylie Wilson Middle Sch 4402 31st St, Lubbock 79410 Kelly Brownfield	6-8	TV	441 20	90%	806/219-4600 Fax 806/766-0814
Stewart Elem Sch 4815 46th St, Lubbock 79414 Jaci Underwood	PK-5	T	400 23	87%	806/219-6900 Fax 806/766-0943
Talkington Sch Young Women 415 N Ivory Ave, Lubbock 79403 Julie Wyatt	6-12	T	472	47%	806/219-2200 Fax 806/766-1738

1	Superintendent	8	Curric/Instruct K-12	19	Chief Financial Officer	29	Family/Consumer Science	39	Social Studies K-12	49 English/Lang Arts Elem	59 Special Education Elem	69 Academic Assessment
2	Bus/Finance/Purchasing	9	Curric/Instruct Elem	20	Art K-12	30	Adult Education	40	Social Studies Elem	50 English/Lang Arts Sec	60 Special Education Sec	70 Research/Development
3	Buildings And Grounds	10	Curric/Instruct Sec	21	Art Elem	31	Career/Sch-to-Work K-12	41	Social Studies Sec	51 Reading K-12	61 Foreign/World Lang K-12	71 Public Information
4	Food Service	11	Federal Program	22	Art Sec	32	Career/Sch-to-Work Elem	42	Science K-12	52 Reading Elem	62 Foreign/World Lang Elem	72 Summer School
5	Transportation	12	Title I	23	Music K-12	33	Career/Sch-to-Work Sec	43	Science Elem	53 Reading Sec	63 Foreign/World Lang Sec	73 Instructional Tech
6	Athletic	13	Title V	24	Music Elem	34	Early Childhood Ed	44	Science Sec	54 Remedial Reading K-12	64 Religious Education K-12	74 Inservice Training
7	Health Services	15	Asst Superintendent	25	Music Sec	35	Health/Phys Education	45	Math K-12	55 Remedial Reading Elem	65 Religious Education Elem	75 Marketing/Distributive
		16	Instructional Media Svcs	26	Business Education	36	Guidance Services K-12	46	Math Elem	56 Remedial Reading Sec	66 Religious Education Sec	76 Info Systems
		17	Chief Operations Officer	27	Career & Tech Ed	37	Guidance Services Elem	47	Math Sec	57 Bilingual/ELL	67 School Board President	77 Psychological Assess
		18	Chief Academic Officer	28	Technology Education	38	Guidance Services Sec	48	English/Lang Arts Sec	58 Special Education K-12	68 Teacher Personnel	78 Affirmative Action

Texas School Directory — Lubbock County

School	Grd	Prgm	Enr/#Cls	SN	Phone
Waters Elem Sch 3006 78th St, Lubbock 79423 Karen Thornton	PK-5	T	622 / 32	62%	806/219-7000 Fax 806/766-6209
Wester Elem Sch 4602 Chicago Ave, Lubbock 79414 Amelia Kimbley	PK-5	T	450 / 19	84%	806/219-7100 Fax 806/766-0962
Wheelock Elem Sch 3008 42nd St, Lubbock 79413 Elizabeth Berridge	PK-5	T	400 / 18	82%	806/219-7200 Fax 806/766-0976
Whiteside Elem Sch 7508 Albany Ave, Lubbock 79424 Brandi Lay	PK-5		562 / 37	43%	806/219-7300 Fax 806/766-2081
Williams Elem Sch 4812 58th St, Lubbock 79414 Denise Neeb	PK-5	T	420 / 22	67%	806/219-7400 Fax 806/766-0989
Wolffarth Elem Sch 3202 Erskine St, Lubbock 79415 Catherine Gillespie	PK-5	T	385 / 17	96%	806/219-7600 Fax 806/766-1893
Wright Elem Sch 1302 Adrian St, Lubbock 79403 Stacy Hurst	PK-5	AT	229 / 6	92%	806/219-7700 Fax 806/766-1906

- **Lubbock-Cooper Ind Sch Dist** PID: 01039030 806/863-7100
  13807 Indiana Ave, Lubbock 79423 Fax 806/863-3130

Schools: 9 \ *Teachers:* 433 \ *Students:* 6,000 \ *Special Ed Students:* 486 \ *LEP Students:* 128 \ *Ethnic:* Asian 2%, African American 2%, Hispanic 35%, Caucasian 61% \ *Exp:* $317 (High) \ *Poverty:* 10% \ *Title I:* $518,822 \ *Special Education:* $884,000 \ *Open-Close:* 08/14 - 05/21 \ *DTBP:* $150 (High)

Keith Bryant 1
John Windham 3
Trevor Edgemon 5
Sandra Beilue 8,294
Betsy Adams Taylor 13,296
Macy Satterwhite 15
Pam Brown 36,69
Tracy Fogerson 58
Britt Spears 68
Jaque Fewin 73
Jay Whitefield 79*
Shay Troutman 280

Ann Ferris 2
Rudy Luna 4*
Katt Winkel 6
Darla Heinrich 11
Danny Davis 15
Deborah Smith 27*
Sandra Jimenez 57,271*
Paul Ehlers 67
Sadie Alderson 71
Donna Hanfeld 76*
Maggie McNab 88*
Jeremy Wagner 285

Public Schs..Principal	Grd	Prgm	Enr/#Cls	SN	Phone
Central Elem Sch 4020 135th St, Lubbock 79423 Colter Cox	PK-5	T	600	32%	806/776-2150 Fax 806/776-2151
East Elem Sch 2727 134th St, Lubbock 79423 Candice Cross	PK-5		360		806/776-2109 Fax 806/776-2110
Laura Bush Middle Sch 3425 118th St, Lubbock 79423 Edna Parr	6-8		872		806/776-0750 Fax 806/776-0751
Lubbock-Cooper High Sch Highway 87 S, Lubbock 79423 Angie Inklebarger	9-12	V	1,519 / 25	27%	806/863-7105 Fax 806/863-7196
Lubbock-Cooper Middle Sch Highway 87 S, Lubbock 79423 Tamara Gunset	6-8	GT	560 / 35	41%	806/863-7104 Fax 806/863-2654
ⓐ New Hope Academy 16302 Loop 493, Lubbock 79423 Phillip Saffel	11-12		50		806/863-7109
North Elem Sch 3202 108th St, Lubbock 79423 Andrea Crawford	PK-5	T	881 / 28	41%	806/776-2700 Fax 806/687-2714
South Elem Sch Highway 87 S, Lubbock 79423 Frances Alonzo	PK-5	T	700 / 56	42%	806/863-7102 Fax 806/863-7120
West Elem Sch 10101 Fulton Ave, Lubbock 79424 Sasha Bennett	PK-5		755	17%	806/776-0700 Fax 806/771-9970

- **New Deal Ind School Dist** PID: 01039080 806/746-5833
  401 S Auburn Ave, New Deal 79350 Fax 806/746-5707

Schools: 3 \ *Teachers:* 57 \ *Students:* 760 \ *Special Ed Students:* 63 \ *LEP Students:* 20 \ *College-Bound:* 54% \ *Ethnic:* African American 2%, Hispanic 50%, Caucasian 48% \ *Exp:* $699 (High) \ *Poverty:* 25% \ *Title I:* $254,686 \ *Open-Close:* 08/19 - 05/21 \ *DTBP:* $342 (High) \ t

Matt Reed 1,11
John Salter 4
Matt Hill 6*
Shelley Carver 8,69
Tricia Williams 38,83,88,270*
Phillip Goodgion 73*

Steve Jerden 2
Derek Copeland 5
Patti Hensley 7,85*
Hannah McCorkle 16*
Sandra Gowens 67

Public Schs..Principal	Grd	Prgm	Enr/#Cls	SN	Phone
New Deal Elem Sch 312 S Monroe Ave, New Deal 79350 Rebecca Cooper	PK-4	T	294 / 18	69%	806/746-5849 Fax 806/746-5142 t
New Deal High Sch 209 S Auburn Ave, New Deal 79350 Matt Reed	9-12	T	213 / 17	50%	806/746-5933 Fax 806/746-5544
New Deal Middle Sch 312 S Monroe Ave, New Deal 79350 Jesus Arenas	5-8	T	244 / 17	61%	806/746-6633 Fax 806/746-5244

- **Roosevelt Ind School Dist** PID: 01039119 806/842-3282
  1406 County Road 3300, Lubbock 79403 Fax 806/842-3266

Schools: 3 \ *Teachers:* 93 \ *Students:* 1,150 \ *Special Ed Students:* 104 \ *LEP Students:* 30 \ *Ethnic:* African American 3%, Hispanic 59%, Native American: 1%, Caucasian 38% \ *Exp:* $518 (High) \ *Poverty:* 24% \ *Title I:* $535,139 \ *Open-Close:* 08/21 - 05/20 \ *DTBP:* $350 (High) \ t

Dallas Grimes 1
Roy Turner 3
Darryl Driver 5
Carla Patchke 7
Stephanie Johnson 37*
James Crawford 73,295*

Kyle Hammock 2
Tony Bruman 4
Jimmy Miller 6
Linda Hernandez 8,11,69,83,273,274,286,296
Jim Warnock 67

Public Schs..Principal	Grd	Prgm	Enr/#Cls	SN	Phone
Roosevelt Elem Sch 1406 County Road 3300, Lubbock 79403 DeLynn Wheeler	PK-5	T	533 / 34	82%	806/842-3284 Fax 806/842-3930
Roosevelt High Sch 1406 County Road 3300, Lubbock 79403 James Ledbetter	9-12	ATV	302 / 50	68%	806/842-3283 Fax 806/842-3931
Roosevelt Junior High Sch 1406 County Road 3300, Lubbock 79403 Tim Crane	6-8	T	258 / 30	77%	806/842-3218 Fax 806/842-3337

79	Student Personnel	91	Safety/Security	275	Response To Intervention	298	Grant Writer/Ptnrships
80	Driver Ed/Safety	92	Magnet School	277	Remedial Math K-12	750	Chief Innovation Officer
81	Gifted/Talented	93	Parental Involvement	280	Literacy Coach	751	Chief of Staff
82	Video Services	95	Tech Prep Program	285	STEM	752	Social Emotional Learning
83	Substance Abuse Prev	97	Chief Information Officer	286	Digital Learning		
84	Erate	98	Chief Technology Officer	288	Common Core Standards		
85	AIDS Education	270	Accountability	294	Alternative School		
88	Alternative/At Risk	271	Migrant Education	295	Network System		
89	Multi-Cultural Curriculum	273	Teacher Mentor	296	Title II Programs		
90	Social Work	274	Before/After Sch	297	Webmaster		

School Programs
A = Alternative Program
G = Adult Classes
M = Magnet Program
T = Title I Schoolwide
V = Career & Tech Ed Programs

Other School Types
ⓐ = Alternative School
ⓒ = Charter School
ⓜ = Magnet School
ⓨ = Year-Round School

Social Media
[f] = Facebook
[t] = Twitter

New Schools are shaded
New Superintendents and Principals are bold
Personnel with email addresses are underscored

Lubbock County

Market Data Retrieval

- **Shallowater Ind School Dist** PID: 01039157   806/832-4531
  1100 Avenue K, Shallowater 79363   Fax 806/832-4350

  Schools: 4 \ *Teachers:* 132 \ *Students:* 1,600 \ *Special Ed Students:* 134 \ *LEP Students:* 39 \ *College-Bound:* 80% \ *Ethnic:* African American 1%, Hispanic 33%, Caucasian 66% \ *Exp:* $346 (High) \ *Poverty:* 13% \ *Title I:* $204,251 \ *Open-Close:* 08/26 - 05/21 \ *DTBP:* $534 (High) \

Dr Kenny Border	1,11	Marcie Romos	2,19
Greg Couch	3	Pat Kerin	4
Brett Holder	5	Mary Hughes	7,12,15,69,275,295*
Tammy Blackburn	8*	J'Rae Tineda	16
Kamber Smith	38*	Tiffany Fisher	57
Barbie Priest	58	Garrett Nelson	67
Stacey Barber	73,84,297		

Public Schs..Principal	Grd	Prgm	Enr/#Cls	SN	
Shallowater Elem Sch 1009 Avenue L, Shallowater 79363 Sherry Oliver	PK-1	T	323 20	48%	806/832-4531 Fax 806/832-4534
Shallowater High Sch 1009 Avenue L, Shallowater 79363 Rob Hollis	9-12	V	443 30	32%	806/832-4531 Fax 806/832-4523
Shallowater Intermediate Sch 1201 Avenue N, Shallowater 79363 **Michelle Southard**	2-4	T	386 15	48%	806/832-4531 Fax 806/832-1884
Shallowater Middle Sch 1009 Avenue L, Shallowater 79363 Aron Strickland	5-8	T	493 18	42%	806/832-4531 Fax 806/832-5543

- **Slaton Ind School Dist** PID: 01039195   806/828-6591
  140 E Panhandle St, Slaton 79364   Fax 806/828-5506

  Schools: 4 \ *Teachers:* 105 \ *Students:* 1,340 \ *Special Ed Students:* 150 \ *LEP Students:* 58 \ *College-Bound:* 26% \ *Ethnic:* African American 5%, Hispanic 69%, Caucasian 26% \ *Exp:* $488 (High) \ *Poverty:* 31% \ *Title I:* $736,058 \ *Open-Close:* 08/21 - 05/20 \ *DTBP:* $572 (High)

Julee Broscoss	1	Art Martin	2
Mike Hernandez	3,5	Paula Garcia	4*
Jeffrey Cassey	6	James Andrus	8,11,15,74,88,275,294*
Felicia Boyd	34*	David Martinez	57*
Denise Kirby	58	Carlos Bentancourt	67
Christian Shute	81*		

Public Schs..Principal	Grd	Prgm	Enr/#Cls	SN	
Cathelene Thomas Elem Sch 615 W Lubbock St, Slaton 79364 Samantha Johnson	1-5	T	462 30	78%	806/828-5805 Fax 806/828-2046
Slaton High Sch 105 N 20th St, Slaton 79364 Shaye Murphy	9-12	TV	356 30	70%	806/828-5833 Fax 806/828-1229
Slaton Junior High Sch 300 W Jean St, Slaton 79364 Kimberly Perry	6-8	T	285 40	78%	806/828-6583 Fax 806/828-2080
Stephen F Austin Primary 740 S 7th St, Slaton 79364 Felicia Boyd	PK-K	T	166 10	73%	806/828-5813 Fax 806/828-2079

LUBBOCK CATHOLIC SCHOOLS

- **Diocese of Lubbock Ed Office** PID: 02204290   806/795-8283
  4620 4th St, Lubbock 79416   Fax 806/792-8109

  Schools: 2 \ *Students:* 360

  Listing includes only schools located in this county. See District Index for location of Diocesan Offices.

Christine Wanjura	1	Christy Duran	2
Claudia Riney	8		

Catholic Schs..Principal	Grd	Prgm	Enr/#Cls	SN	
Christ the King Cathedral Sch 4011 54th St, Lubbock 79413 Gail Ambrose \ Eric Gray	PK-12		300 19		806/795-8283 Fax 806/795-9715
St Joseph Sch 1305 W Division St, Slaton 79364 Karen Hybner	PK-8		57 6		806/828-6761 Fax 806/828-5396

LUBBOCK PRIVATE SCHOOLS

Private Schs..Principal	Grd	Prgm	Enr/#Cls	SN	
All Saints Episcopal Sch 3222 103rd St, Lubbock 79423 Bruce Latta	PK-12		315 27		806/745-7701 Fax 806/748-0454
Kingdom Preparatory Academy PO Box 64028, Lubbock 79464 Jared Squires	PK-12		180 25		806/767-9334 Fax 806/767-9342
Lubbock Christian Sch 2604 Dover Ave, Lubbock 79407 Mark Breaux \ Jerry Lawrence	PK-12		430 28		806/796-8700 Fax 806/791-3569
Lubbock Junior Academy 5302 Elgin Ave, Lubbock 79413 Marybel Orellana	K-8		10		806/793-8614 Fax 806/799-5136
New Life Academy 2102 5th St, Lubbock 79401 Jeff McCreight	K-12	G	104		806/763-0117
Southcrest Christian Sch 3801 S Loop 289, Lubbock 79423 Shonda Mayer \ Susie Driscoll	PK-12		237 7		806/797-7400 Fax 806/797-5100
Trinity Christian Elem Sch 7002 Canton Ave, Lubbock 79413 Jill Roberts	PK-5		350 30		806/791-6581
Trinity Christian Jr Sr HS 6701 University Ave, Lubbock 79413 Tyler Neal	6-12		272 40		806/791-6583

LUBBOCK REGIONAL CENTERS

- **Region 17 Ed Service Center** PID: 01039248   806/792-4000
  1111 W Loop 289, Lubbock 79416   Fax 806/792-1523

Kyle Wargo	1,11	Kerry Wright	2
Wayne Blount	2,3,4,15,76	Syd Sexton	8
Chris Gossett	16,73	Alicia Holligan	36,77
Anna Phillips	58		

---

1 Superintendent	8 Curric/Instruct K-12	19 Chief Financial Officer	29 Family/Consumer Science	39 Social Studies K-12	49 English/Lang Arts Elem	59 Special Education Elem	69 Academic Assessment
2 Bus/Finance/Purchasing	9 Curric/Instruct Elem	20 Art K-12	30 Adult Education	40 Social Studies Elem	50 English/Lang Arts Sec	60 Special Education Sec	70 Research/Development
3 Buildings And Grounds	10 Curric/Instruct Sec	21 Art Elem	31 Career/Sch-to-Work K-12	41 Social Studies Sec	51 Reading K-12	61 Foreign/World Lang K-12	71 Public Information
4 Food Service	11 Federal Program	22 Art Sec	32 Career/Sch-to-Work Elem	42 Science K-12	52 Reading Elem	62 Foreign/World Lang Elem	72 Summer School
5 Transportation	12 Title I	23 Music K-12	33 Career/Sch-to-Work Sec	43 Science Elem	53 Reading Sec	63 Foreign/World Lang Sec	73 Instructional Tech
6 Athletic	13 Title V	24 Music Elem	34 Early Childhood Ed	44 Science Sec	54 Remedial Reading K-12	64 Religious Education K-12	74 Inservice Training
7 Health Services	14 Asst Superintendent	25 Music Sec	35 Health/Phys Education	45 Math K-12	55 Remedial Reading Elem	65 Religious Education Elem	75 Marketing/Distributive
	15 Instructional Media Svcs	26 Business Education	36 Guidance Services K-12	46 Math Elem	56 Remedial Reading Sec	66 Religious Education Sec	76 Info Systems
	16 Chief Operations Officer	27 Career & Tech Ed	37 Guidance Services Elem	47 Math Sec	57 Bilingual/ELL	67 School Board President	77 Psychological Assess
	18 Chief Academic Officer	28 Technology Education	38 Guidance Services Sec	48 English/Lang Arts K 12	58 Special Education K-12	68 Teacher Personnel	78 Affirmative Action

Texas School Directory

LYNN COUNTY

LYNN PUBLIC SCHOOLS

- **New Home Ind School Dist** PID: 01039274 — 806/924-7543
  225 N Main St, New Home 79381 — Fax 806/924-7520

Schools: 1 \ *Teachers:* 36 \ *Students:* 447 \ *Special Ed Students:* 28 \ *LEP Students:* 13 \ *College-Bound:* 70% \ *Ethnic:* Hispanic 28%, Caucasian 71% \ *Exp:* $531 (High) \ *Poverty:* 18% \ *Title I:* $33,820 \ *Open-Close:* 08/19 - 05/22 \ *DTBP:* $345 (High)

Shane Fiedler	1	Monica Maeker	2
Dale Clem	3*	Lisa Alvarado	4*
Ara Sanders	7*	Shane Fiedler	11,286,288*
Lyneil Beck	57*	Kodi Chapman	58*
Travis Smith	67	Shane Moore	73

Public Schs..Principal	Grd	Prgm	Enr/#Cls	SN	
New Home Sch	PK-12	TV	447	25%	806/924-7543
225 N Main St, New Home 79381			20		
Kelly Baum \ Koby Abney					

- **O'Donnell Ind School Dist** PID: 01039315 — 806/428-3241
  400 Small St, Odonnell 79351 — Fax 806/428-3395

Schools: 2 \ *Teachers:* 34 \ *Students:* 306 \ *Special Ed Students:* 26 \ *LEP Students:* 20 \ *College-Bound:* 90% \ *Ethnic:* Hispanic 68%, Caucasian 31% \ *Exp:* $610 (High) \ *Poverty:* 25% \ *Title I:* $94,800 \ *Open-Close:* 08/19 - 05/01 \ *DTBP:* $355 (High)

Dr Cathy Palmer	1,11	Melissa Clark	2
Joseph Luera	3,5	Eva Belossanton	4
Blake Nichols	6*	Tonya Graham	8,42,57,58,69,81*
Mandy Stidham	67	Pam Wilson	73*
Cody White	83,88,298*		

Public Schs..Principal	Grd	Prgm	Enr/#Cls	SN	
O'Donnell Elem Sch	PK-5		148		806/428-3244
300 Small St, Odonnell 79351			14		Fax 806/428-3277
Sharla Edwards					
O'Donnell Jr Sr High Sch	6-12	TV	140	75%	806/428-3247
400 Small St, Odonnell 79351			15		Fax 806/428-3759
Cody White					

- **Tahoka Ind School Dist** PID: 01039341 — 806/561-4105
  2129 Main St, Tahoka 79373 — Fax 806/561-4160

Schools: 3 \ *Teachers:* 56 \ *Students:* 680 \ *Special Ed Students:* 41 \ *LEP Students:* 14 \ *College-Bound:* 80% \ *Ethnic:* African American 3%, Hispanic 65%, Caucasian 32% \ *Exp:* $591 (High) \ *Poverty:* 26% \ *Title I:* $198,824 \ *Open-Close:* 08/22 - 05/25 \ *DTBP:* $376 (High)

Dick Van Hoose	1	Lisa Jones	2,4,12,19
Joey Earrientes	3*	Sam Monsizias	5,91
Stephen Overstreet	6*	Lana Martinez	8,83,88,270,280*
Allan Umholtz	11	Angelica Aguirre	16,73,98,286,295*
Cynthia Jolly	16*	Kaci May	57*
Paige Rivas	58,275*	Clay Taylor	67
Angelica Aguirre	73,98,286		

Madison County

Public Schs..Principal	Grd	Prgm	Enr/#Cls	SN	
Tahoka Elem Sch	PK-5	T	336	67%	806/561-4350
1925 Avenue O, Tahoka 79373			24		Fax 806/561-5334
Donald Scott					
Tahoka High Sch	9-12	T	151	71%	806/561-4538
1925 Avenue P, Tahoka 79373			25		Fax 806/561-6082
Donald Worth					
Tahoka Middle Sch	6-8	T	134	70%	806/561-4539
1925 Avenue P, Tahoka 79373			12		Fax 806/561-6082
Kelly Kieth					

- **Wilson Ind School Dist** PID: 01039391 — 806/628-6261
  1411 Green Ave, Wilson 79381 — Fax 806/628-6441

Schools: 1 \ *Teachers:* 16 \ *Students:* 129 \ *Special Ed Students:* 20 \ *LEP Students:* 13 \ *College-Bound:* 70% \ *Ethnic:* Hispanic 76%, Caucasian 24% \ *Exp:* $806 (High) \ *Poverty:* 36% \ *Title I:* $89,133 \ *Open-Close:* 08/26 - 05/20 \ *DTBP:* $379 (High) \ f t

Jerry Burger	1,83	Rhonda Cox	2
Rhudy Maskew	6*	Keith Church	16*
Juvencio Portillo	31,36,69*	Stefanie Cortez	58*
Doug Boylard	67	Elvira Mendez	271*

Public Schs..Principal	Grd	Prgm	Enr/#Cls	SN	
Wilson Sch	PK-12	TV	129	73%	806/628-6261
1411 Green Ave, Wilson 79381			16		
Jp Portillo					

MADISON COUNTY

MADISON PUBLIC SCHOOLS

- **Madisonville Cons ISD** PID: 01040596 — 936/348-2797
  718 Bacon St, Madisonville 77864 — Fax 936/348-2751

Schools: 4 \ *Teachers:* 165 \ *Students:* 2,358 \ *Special Ed Students:* 170 \ *LEP Students:* 311 \ *Ethnic:* Asian 1%, African American 21%, Hispanic 35%, Caucasian 43% \ *Exp:* $381 (High) \ *Poverty:* 26% \ *Title I:* $753,636 \ *Special Education:* $409,000 \ *Open-Close:* 08/19 - 05/21 \ *DTBP:* $350 (High) \ f t

Keith Smith	1	Scott Singletary	2
Frank Kelly	3,91	Kelley Terry	4
Nelly Vega	4	Rusty Nail	6*
Raelyn Williamson	7,85*	C Keith Smith	11,15,31,36,57,58,88,271
Dr Keith West	15	Joyce Singletary	16*
Shelli Sheppard	27,38,69,75*	Dr Mark Bennett	67
Laney Smith	73		

Public Schs..Principal	Grd	Prgm	Enr/#Cls	SN	
Madisonville Elem Sch	PK-2	T	673	74%	936/348-2261
1000 Raney Ln, Madisonville 77864			36		Fax 936/349-8028
Rhodena Brooks					f t
Madisonville High Sch	9-12	TV	668	61%	936/348-2721
811 S May St A, Madisonville 77864			50		Fax 936/348-5753
Heath Brown					f t
Madisonville Intermediate Sch	3-5	T	516	73%	936/348-2921
926 Raney Ln, Madisonville 77864			40		Fax 936/348-2249
Tawnya Nail					

---

79 Student Personnel	91 Safety/Security	275 Response To Intervention	298 Grant Writer/Ptnrships	**School Programs**	**Social Media**	
80 Driver Ed/Safety	92 Magnet School	277 Remedial Math K-12	750 Chief Innovation Officer	A = Alternative Program		
81 Gifted/Talented	93 Parental Involvement	280 Literacy Coach	751 Chief of Staff	G = Adult Classes	f = Facebook	
82 Video Services	95 Tech Prep Program	285 STEM	752 Social Emotional Learning	M = Magnet Program		
83 Substance Abuse Prev	97 Chief Information Officer	286 Digital Learning		T = Title I Schoolwide	t = Twitter	
84 Erate	98 Chief Technology Officer	288 Common Core Standards	**Other School Types**	V = Career & Tech Ed Programs		
85 AIDS Education	270 Character Education	294 Accountability	Ⓐ = Alternative School			
88 Alternative/At Risk	271 Migrant Education	295 Network System	Ⓒ = Charter School	New Schools are shaded		
89 Multi-Cultural Curriculum	273 Teacher Mentor	296 Title II Programs	Ⓜ = Magnet School	New Superintendents and Principals are bold		
90 Social Work	274 Before/After Sch	297 Webmaster	Ⓨ = Year-Round School	Personnel with email addresses are underscored		

TX—273

Marion County

Madisonville Jr High Sch 6-8 T 501 65% 936/348-3587
724 Raney Ln, Madisonville 77864   30   Fax 936/348-5603
Rhonda Morgan

- **North Zulch Ind School Dist** PID: 01040637   936/241-7100
  11390 5th St, North Zulch 77872   Fax 936/399-2025

Schools: 1 \ *Teachers:* 35 \ *Students:* 305 \ *Special Ed Students:* 27 \
LEP Students: 8 \ *Ethnic:* Asian 2%, African American 1%, Hispanic 15%,
Caucasian 82% \ *Exp:* $433 (High) \ *Poverty:* 15% \ *Title I:* $57,256 \
Open-Close: 08/14 - 05/21 \ *DTBP:* $360 (High)

Alan Andrus	1,11	Dawn Brenner	2*
Brenda Andrews	4*	Jim O'Neal	6,60*
Lea-Ann Andrus	8	Autumn Nauling	16*
Kori Batten	36,752*	Brian Baker	67
Todd Armstrong	73,286,295	Jane Dill	83*

Public Schs..Principal	Grd	Prgm	Enr/#Cls	SN	
North Zulch Sch 11390 5th St, North Zulch 77872 Johan Osth \ Janie Pope	PK-12	TV	305 30	71%	936/241-7100

MARION COUNTY

MARION PUBLIC SCHOOLS

- **Jefferson Ind School Dist** PID: 01040687   903/665-2461
  1600 Martin Luther King Dr, Jefferson 75657   Fax 903/665-7367

Schools: 4 \ *Teachers:* 98 \ *Students:* 1,272 \ *Special Ed Students:* 135
\ *LEP Students:* 15 \ *College-Bound:* 49% \ *Ethnic:* Asian 1%,
African American 37%, Hispanic 6%, Caucasian 56% \ *Exp:* $519 (High)
\ *Poverty:* 35% \ *Title I:* $641,165 \ *Special Education:* $223,000 \
Open-Close: 08/15 - 05/25 \ *DTBP:* $327 (High)

Rob Barnwell	1	Mike Wood	2
Terry Moore	4*	Jack Smith	5
Antwain Jimmerson	6	Debbie Hall	7
Debbie Hall	7*	Lynn Fratangelo	8,31,288
Clinton Coyne	11,34,57,58,61,88,296*	Linda Scott	37*
Jason Bonner	67	Jay Patrick	73,295
Terence Jimerson	88		

Public Schs..Principal	Grd	Prgm	Enr/#Cls	SN	
Jefferson Elem Sch 301 W Harrison St, Jefferson 75657 Lindsey Whitaker	1-4	T	377 20	65%	903/665-2461 Fax 903/665-6401
Jefferson High Sch 1 Bulldog Dr, Jefferson 75657 Michael Walker	9-12	T	350 30	65%	903/665-2461 Fax 903/665-2146
Jefferson Junior High Sch 804 N Alley St, Jefferson 75657 **Tim Phy**	5-8	T	375 57	73%	903/665-2461 Fax 903/665-7149
Jefferson Primary Sch 304 W Broadway St, Jefferson 75657 Lindsey Whitaker	PK-K	T	170	83%	903/665-2461 Fax 903/665-7092

MARION PRIVATE SCHOOLS

Private Schs..Principal	Grd	Prgm	Enr/#Cls	SN	
Cypress Bendadventist ES 2997 FM 728, Jefferson 75657 Peggy Dyke	PK-8		29 3		903/665-7402
Jefferson Christian Academy 3060 FM 728, Jefferson 75657 Lyne Ho	9-12	V	40 7		903/665-3973 Fax 903/665-5987

MARTIN COUNTY

MARTIN PUBLIC SCHOOLS

- **Grady Ind School Dist** PID: 01040730   432/459-2444
  3500 FM 829, Lenorah 79749   Fax 432/459-2729

Schools: 1 \ *Teachers:* 21 \ *Students:* 260 \ *Special Ed Students:* 13
\ *LEP Students:* 9 \ *College-Bound:* 75% \ *Ethnic:* Asian 2%, Hispanic
38%, Caucasian 61% \ *Exp:* $789 (High) \ *Poverty:* 26% \ *Title I:* $56,236 \
Open-Close: 08/14 - 05/20 \ *DTBP:* $333 (High)

Leandro Gonzales	1,83	Bonnie Lucas	2,11,296*
Belen Rodriquez	4*	Sherra Harrell	58*
David Matthews	67		

Public Schs..Principal	Grd	Prgm	Enr/#Cls	SN	
Grady Sch 3500 FM 829, Lenorah 79749 Gary Jones	PK-12	T	260 22	34%	432/459-2445

- **Stanton Ind School Dist** PID: 01040754   432/607-3700
  200 N College St, Stanton 79782   Fax 432/756-2052

Schools: 3 \ *Teachers:* 73 \ *Students:* 1,092 \ *Special Ed Students:* 69
\ *LEP Students:* 60 \ *College-Bound:* 52% \ *Ethnic:* African American
1%, Hispanic 67%, Caucasian 32% \ *Exp:* $832 (High) \ *Poverty:* 17% \
Title I: $193,467 \ *Open-Close:* 08/15 - 05/21 \ *DTBP:* $346 (High)

Dr Merl Brandon	1	Brad Holland	2,19
Pam Shaffer	2	Dennis Simpson	3
George Ramirez	5	Cody Hogan	6
Jan McCown	8,15	Julie Snellgrove	11,271*
Robna Anderson	58	Jermey Louder	67
Jay Baker	73,295		

Public Schs..Principal	Grd	Prgm	Enr/#Cls	SN	
Stanton Elem Sch 911 W Broadway St, Stanton 79782 Leah Mitchell	PK-5	T	513 21	63%	432/756-2285 Fax 432/756-2151
Stanton High Sch 705 Koonce St, Stanton 79782 Matt Turney	9-12	T	271 24	40%	432/756-3326 Fax 432/756-2248
Stanton Middle Sch 200 N Gray St, Stanton 79782 **Jennifer Ruiz**	6-8	T	228 25	51%	432/756-2544 Fax 432/756-2702

1	Superintendent	8	Curric/Instruct K-12	19	Chief Financial Officer	29	Family/Consumer Science	39	Social Studies K-12	49	English/Lang Arts Elem	59	Special Education Elem	69	Academic Assessment
2	Bus/Finance/Purchasing	9	Curric/Instruct Elem	20	Art K-12	30	Adult Education	40	Social Studies Elem	50	English/Lang Arts Sec	60	Special Education Sec	70	Research/Development
3	Buildings And Grounds	10	Curric/Instruct Sec	21	Art Elem	31	Career/Sch-to-Work K-12	41	Social Studies Sec	51	Reading K-12	61	Foreign/World Lang K-12	71	Public Information
4	Food Service	11	Federal Program	22	Art Sec	32	Career/Sch-to-Work Elem	42	Science K-12	52	Reading Elem	62	Foreign/World Lang Elem	72	Summer School
5	Transportation	12	Title I	23	Music K-12	33	Career/Sch-to-Work Sec	43	Science Elem	53	Reading Sec	63	Foreign/World Lang Sec	73	Instructional Tech
6	Athletic	13	Title V	24	Music Elem	34	Early Childhood Ed	44	Science Sec	54	Remedial Reading K-12	64	Religious Education K-12	74	Inservice Training
7	Health Services	14	Asst Superintendent	25	Music Sec	35	Health/Phys Education	45	Math K-12	55	Remedial Reading Elem	65	Religious Education Elem	75	Marketing/Distributive
		15	Instructional Media Svcs	26	Business Education	36	Guidance Services K-12	46	Math Elem	56	Remedial Reading Sec	66	Religious Education Sec	76	Info Systems
		16	Chief Operations Officer	27	Career & Tech Ed	37	Guidance Services Elem	47	Math Sec	57	Bilingual/ELL	67	School Board President	77	Psychological Assess
		17	Chief Academic Officer	28	Technology Education	38	Guidance Services Sec	48	English/Lang Arts K-12	58	Special Education K-12	68	Teacher Personnel	78	Affirmative Action

Texas School Directory

Matagorda County

MASON COUNTY

MASON PUBLIC SCHOOLS

- **Mason Ind School Dist** PID: 01040780   325/347-1144
  200 Ft McKavitt St, Mason 76856   Fax 325/294-4412

Schools: 3 \ **Teachers:** 68 \ **Students:** 675 \ **Special Ed Students:** 55 \ **LEP Students:** 44 \ **College-Bound:** 57% \ **Ethnic:** Asian 1%, Hispanic 36%, Caucasian 63% \ **Exp:** $654 (High) \ **Poverty:** 20% \ **Title I:** $156,038 \ **Special Education:** $155,000 \ **Open-Close:** 08/20 - 05/22 \ **DTBP:** $350 (High)

Teri Price 2	David Davidson 3
Julie Parker 4	Larry Smith 5,88
Michael McLeod 6	Jennifer Moneyhon 7,35*
Holly Whittle 11,57,271,298	Shannon Hofmann 58,752*
Jeff Durst 67	Cathy Felts 68
Julie Armstrong 69*	Merlina Gamel 73
Vondell Jordan 280	Kade Burns 285

Public Schs..Principal	Grd	Prgm	Enr/#Cls	SN	
Mason Elem Sch 807 W College Ave, Mason 76856 **Ryan Holbrook**	PK-4	T	294 23	51%	325/347-1122 Fax 325/347-5461
Mason High Sch 1105 W College Ave, Mason 76856 **Kade Burns**	9-12	TV	214 15	40%	325/347-1122 Fax 325/347-8247
Mason Junior High Sch 807 W College Ave, Mason 76856 **Ryan Holbrook**	5-8	T	220	52%	325/347-1122

MATAGORDA COUNTY

MATAGORDA PUBLIC SCHOOLS

- **Bay City Ind School Dist** PID: 01040819   979/401-1000
  520 7th St, Bay City 77414   Fax 979/245-3175

Schools: 5 \ **Teachers:** 257 \ **Students:** 3,700 \ **Special Ed Students:** 313 \ **LEP Students:** 535 \ **College-Bound:** 53% \ **Ethnic:** Asian 1%, African American 15%, Hispanic 65%, Caucasian 18% \ **Exp:** $449 (High) \ **Poverty:** 27% \ **Title I:** $1,317,970 \ **Open-Close:** 08/26 - 05/28 \ **DTBP:** $172 (High) \ 📘

Marshall Scott 1	Richard Johnson 2,19
Stewart Crouch 3	Mildred Hawkins 4
Lynette Cooper 7*	Lisa Moya 8,18,57,69,88,285,288,294
Lisa Volkmer 11,57,271,273,296	Sonya Sonia 34,58
Robert Klepac 67	Allison Silva 71
Joshua Solis 73,76,98,295	Leroy Cunningham 91*

Public Schs..Principal	Grd	Prgm	Enr/#Cls	SN	
Bay City High Sch 400 7th St, Bay City 77414 **Maria Reyes**	9-12	ATV	979	58%	979/401-1100 Fax 979/245-1220
Bay City Junior High Sch 1507 Sycamore Ave, Bay City 77414 **Dollie Coleman**	6-8	AT	753 46	65%	979/401-1600 Fax 979/245-1419
Cherry Elem Sch 2619 8th St, Bay City 77414 **Merideth Dodd**	PK-5	T	649 20	70%	979/401-1300 Fax 979/245-1702
Holmes Elem Sch 3200 5th St, Bay City 77414 **Kimberly Hickl**	PK-5	T	707 31	81%	979/401-1400 Fax 979/245-1645
Roberts Elem Sch 1212 Whitson St, Bay City 77414 **Rosemarie Cumings**	PK-5	T	483 28	81%	979/401-1500 Fax 979/245-1573

- **Matagorda Ind School Dist** PID: 01040895   979/863-7693
  717 Wightman Street, Matagorda 77457   Fax 979/863-2230

Schools: 1 \ **Teachers:** 12 \ **Students:** 120 \ **Special Ed Students:** 15 \ **LEP Students:** 10 \ **Ethnic:** Hispanic 39%, Caucasian 61% \ **Exp:** $108 (Low) \ **Poverty:** 22% \ **Title I:** $26,609 \ **Special Education:** $1,000 \ **Open-Close:** 08/26 - 05/28 \ **DTBP:** $335 (High)

Susan Phillips 1,11,57,83,288	Tara Simons 2,84,271
Dennis Chambers 3,5*	Jackie Rawlings 4
Ronda Thompson 59*	Ed Derrich 67
Tim Meador 73,295,297	

Public Schs..Principal	Grd	Prgm	Enr/#Cls	SN	
Matagorda Sch 717 Wightman St, Matagorda 77457 **Susan Phillips** \ **Kyle Thurmon**	PK-8	T	120 11	53%	979/863-7693

- **Palacios Ind School Dist** PID: 01040912   361/972-5491
  1209 12th St, Palacios 77465   Fax 361/972-3567

Schools: 4 \ **Teachers:** 104 \ **Students:** 1,506 \ **Special Ed Students:** 146 \ **LEP Students:** 197 \ **Ethnic:** Asian 8%, African American 2%, Hispanic 68%, Caucasian 22% \ **Exp:** $232 (Med) \ **Poverty:** 23% \ **Title I:** $389,996 \ **Open-Close:** 08/14 - 05/22 \ **DTBP:** $350 (High) \ 📘

Dr Missy Glenn 1	Christy Miller 2
Santos Perez 3,5*	Candy Gifford 4
Lisa Harper 7	Dr Julia McMains .. 8,11,16,57,58,271,273,274
Steven Stuhrenberg 67	Dr Brian Williams 68,69,83,294,296,298
Robert Fiorini 73,295*	Becky Aguilera 91

Public Schs..Principal	Grd	Prgm	Enr/#Cls	SN	
Central Elem Sch 1001 5th St, Palacios 77465 **Nancy Flores**	PK-3	T	487 42	69%	361/972-2911 Fax 361/972-5539
East Side Intermediate Sch 901 2nd St, Palacios 77465 **Brian Williams**	4-6	T	329 20	71%	361/972-2544 Fax 361/972-2695
Palacios High Sch 100 Shark Dr, Palacios 77465 **Stephanie Garcia**	9-12	TV	413 65	59%	361/972-2571 Fax 361/972-6287
Palacios Junior High Sch 200 Shark Dr, Palacios 77465 **Buddy Kelley**	7-8	TV	198 20	62%	361/972-2417 Fax 361/972-6372

---

79 Student Personnel	91 Safety/Security	275 Response To Intervention	298 Grant Writer/Ptnrships	**School Programs**	**Social Media**	
80 Driver Ed/Safety	92 Magnet School	277 Remedial Math K-12	750 Chief Innovation Officer	A = Alternative Program		
81 Gifted/Talented	93 Parental Involvement	280 Literacy Coach	751 Chief of Staff	G = Adult Classes	📘 = Facebook	
82 Video Services	95 Tech Prep Program	285 STEM	752 Social Emotional Learning	M = Magnet Program		
83 Substance Abuse Prev	97 Chief Information Officer	286 Digital Learning		T = Title I Schoolwide	🐦 = Twitter	
84 Erate	98 Chief Technology Officer	288 Common Core Standards	**Other School Types**	V = Career & Tech Ed Programs		
85 AIDS Education	270 Character Education	294 Accountability	Ⓐ = Alternative School			
88 Alternative/At Risk	271 Migrant Education	295 Network System	Ⓒ = Charter School	New Schools are shaded		
89 Multi-Cultural Curriculum	273 Teacher Mentor	296 Title II Programs	Ⓜ = Magnet School	New Superintendents and Principals are bold		
90 Social Work	274 Before/After Sch	297 Webmaster	Ⓨ = Year-Round School	Personnel with email addresses are underscored		

TX–275

Maverick County

Market Data Retrieval

- **Tidehaven Ind School Dist** PID: 01040962   979/843-4300
  47 County Road 427, Elmaton 77440   Fax 979/843-4309

  Schools: 4 \ *Teachers:* 65 \ *Students:* 980 \ *Special Ed Students:* 66 \ *LEP Students:* 77 \ *College-Bound:* 64% \ *Ethnic:* African American 3%, Hispanic 54%, Caucasian 43% \ *Exp:* $503 (High) \ *Poverty:* 22% \ *Title I:* $216,925 \ *Special Education:* $4,000 \ *Open-Close:* 08/15 - 05/21 \ *DTBP:* $354 (High) \ f t

Dr Andrew Seigrist	1	Doris Streams	2
Ryan Cobb	3	Karen Black	4
Debra Taska	5,9,11,69,285,296,298	Galvan Migel	5
Mike Galvan	5	David Lucio	6*
Kathy Boyett	8,288*	Tamara Davant	31,36,85
Tamara Davant	31,36,85*	Maria Enoch	57,271*
Stephen Crow	67	Zachary Daugherty	73,295*
Jamie Buis	83,91*	Zachary Daughertyy	295

Public Schs..Principal	Grd	Prgm	Enr/#Cls	SN	
Blessing Elem Sch 231 FM 616, Blessing 77419 Selena Garcia	PK-5	GT	241 15	69%	979/843-4330 Fax 361/588-1150 f t
Markham Elem Sch 299 Ave I North, Markham 77456 Stacie Murry	PK-5	GT	207 16	69%	979/843-4340 Fax 979/843-5018 f t
Tidehaven High Sch Highway 35 & FM 1095, Elmaton 77440 Patrick Talbert	9-12	ATV	295 25	57%	979/843-4310 Fax 361/588-6696 f t
Tidehaven Intermediate Sch 205 FM 1059, Elmaton 77440 Patrick Talbert	6-8	T	195 20	70%	361/843-4320 Fax 361/588-6965 f t

- **Van Vleck Ind School Dist** PID: 01041019   979/323-5000
  142 S Ford St, Van Vleck 77482   Fax 979/245-1214

  Schools: 4 \ *Teachers:* 78 \ *Students:* 1,050 \ *Special Ed Students:* 97 \ *LEP Students:* 17 \ *College-Bound:* 48% \ *Ethnic:* African American 12%, Hispanic 28%, Native American: 1%, Caucasian 59% \ *Exp:* $573 (High) \ *Poverty:* 17% \ *Title I:* $164,256 \ *Special Education:* $109,000 \ *Open-Close:* 08/14 - 05/21 \ t

John O'Brien	1	Gayle Blackmon	2
Louis Ryman	3	Connie Brown	4
Robert Blackmon	6*	Kim Wied	7
Christie Dement	11,27	Amy Matchett	37*
Tony Kucera	67	Randy Keys	73,84

Public Schs..Principal	Grd	Prgm	Enr/#Cls	SN	
E Rudd Intermediate Sch 128 5th St, Van Vleck 77482 Shannon Jedlicka	4-5	T	164 12	56%	979/245-6561 Fax 979/245-3624
O H Herman Middle Sch 719 1st St, Van Vleck 77482 Brandon Hood	6-8	ATV	249 16	48%	979/245-6401 Fax 979/245-8538
Van Vleck Elem Sch 178 S 4th St, Van Vleck 77482 Sarah Roper	PK-3	T	315 17	60%	979/245-8681 Fax 979/323-0479
Van Vleck High Sch 133 S 4th St, Van Vleck 77482 Chris Townsend	9-12	AV	328 20	43%	979/245-4664 Fax 979/244-3485

MATAGORDA CATHOLIC SCHOOLS

- **Diocese of Victoria Ed Office** PID: 02181727
  Listing includes only schools located in this county. See District Index for location of Diocesan Offices.

Catholic Schs..Principal	Grd	Prgm	Enr/#Cls	SN	
Holy Cross Catholic Sch 2001 Katy Ave, Bay City 77414 Angela Kupcho	PK-6		110 9		979/245-5632 Fax 979/245-6120

MAVERICK COUNTY

MAVERICK PUBLIC SCHOOLS

- **Eagle Pass Ind School Dist** PID: 01041057   830/773-5181
  876 Madison St, Eagle Pass 78852   Fax 830/773-7252

  Schools: 23 \ *Teachers:* 898 \ *Students:* 15,000 \ *Special Ed Students:* 1,325 \ *LEP Students:* 4,657 \ *College-Bound:* 58% \ *Ethnic:* Hispanic 97%, Native American: 2%, Caucasian 1% \ *Exp:* $283 (Med) \ *Poverty:* 32% \ *Title I:* $5,786,650 \ *Special Education:* $2,347,000 \ *Open-Close:* 08/26 - 06/03 \ *DTBP:* $166 (High)

Gilberto Gonzalez	1	Ismael Mijares	2,15
Luis Velez	2	Pedro Felan	3,91
Mario Garcia	4*	Humberto Araiza	5
Edward Graf	6,35	David Camarillo	8,294
Samuel Mijares	8,15,81,288	Norma Serna	11,72,271,296,298
Rolando Salinas	15,78,275	Diana Saucedo	16*
Gilbert Sanchez	20,57	Carlos Martinez	23*
Ana Castillon	26,27,28,31	Lana Harper	30,74,83,90,93,273,274
Francis Vilema	39,42*	Rita Carreon	46,277
Rodolfo Musquiz	48,51,54,61,280,298*	Elizabeth Torres	58
Jorge Barrera	67	Jesus Costilla	68,77
Denniella Bryne	71	Jose Munoz	73,82,98,295*
Patrick Salines	73,95	Timito Chares	271
Umberto Duran	297		

Public Schs..Principal	Grd	Prgm	Enr/#Cls	SN	
Armando Cerna Elem Sch 2268 Mondragon Blvd, Eagle Pass 78852 Sandra Lopez	1-6	T	461 13	62%	830/758-7004 Fax 830/773-2731
Benavides Heights Elem Sch 1750 Mesa Dr, Eagle Pass 78852 Olivia Garcia	1-6	T	323 26	83%	830/758-7006 Fax 830/758-0216
C C Winn High Sch 265 Foster Maldonado Blvd, Eagle Pass 78852 Jesus Diaz-Wever	9-12	TV	2,080 58	78%	830/757-0828 Fax 830/757-3268
Eagle Pass High Sch 2020 2nd St, Eagle Pass 78852 John Cox	9-12	TV	2,298 105	72%	830/773-2381 Fax 830/758-1795
Eagle Pass Junior High Sch 1750 N Bibb Ave, Eagle Pass 78852 Mario Escobar	7-8	TV	1,081 50	70%	830/758-7037
Early Childhood Center 636 Kelso Dr, Eagle Pass 78852 Letty Sandoval	PK-K	T	471 25	76%	830/758-7027 Fax 830/757-1153

1 Superintendent	8 Curric/Instruct K-12	19 Chief Financial Officer	29 Family/Consumer Science	39 Social Studies K-12	49 English/Lang Arts Elem	59 Special Education Elem	69 Academic Assessment
2 Bus/Finance/Purchasing	9 Curric/Instruct Elem	20 Art K-12	30 Adult Education	40 Social Studies Elem	50 English/Lang Arts Sec	60 Special Education Sec	70 Research/Development
3 Buildings And Grounds	10 Curric/Instruct Sec	21 Art Elem	31 Career/Sch-to-Work K-12	41 Social Studies Sec	51 Reading K-12	61 Foreign/World Lang K-12	71 Public Information
4 Food Service	11 Federal Program	22 Art Sec	32 Career/Sch-to-Work Elem	42 Science K-12	52 Reading Elem	62 Foreign/World Lang Elem	72 Summer School
5 Transportation	12 Title I	23 Music K-12	33 Career/Sch-to-Work Sec	43 Science Elem	53 Reading Sec	63 Foreign/World Lang Sec	73 Instructional Tech
6 Athletic	13 Title V	24 Music Elem	34 Early Childhood Ed	44 Science Sec	54 Remedial Reading K-12	64 Religious Education K-12	74 Inservice Training
7 Health Services	15 Asst Superintendent	25 Music Sec	35 Health/Phys Education	45 Math K-12	55 Remedial Reading Elem	65 Religious Education Elem	75 Marketing/Distributive
	16 Instructional Media Svcs	26 Business Education	36 Guidance Services K-12	46 Math Elem	56 Remedial Reading Sec	66 Religious Education Sec	76 Info Systems
	17 Chief Operations Officer	27 Career & Tech Ed	37 Guidance Services Elem	47 Math Sec	57 Bilingual/ELL	67 School Board President	77 Psychological Assess
	18 Chief Academic Officer	28 Technology Education	38 Guidance Services Sec	48 English/Lang Arts K-12	58 Special Education K-12	68 Teacher Personnel	78 Affirmative Action

TX—276

Texas School Directory — McCulloch County

School	Grd	Prgm	Enr/#Cls	SN	Phone
Glass Elem Sch 1501 Boehmer Ave, Eagle Pass 78852 Laura Telles	1-6	T	530 28	70%	830/758-7042 Fax 830/773-5989
Graves Elem Sch 720 Kelso Dr, Eagle Pass 78852 Veronica Gonzalez	1-6	T	499 30	74%	830/758-7043 Fax 830/758-0342
Henry B Gonzalez Elem Sch 565 Madison St, Eagle Pass 78852 Juanita Garcia	1-6	T	440 27	83%	830/758-7099 Fax 830/757-3274
Kennedy Elem Sch 1610B Del Rio Blvd, Eagle Pass 78852 Lisa Ruiz	PK-K	T	415 17	70%	830/758-7189 Fax 830/758-7192
Kirchner Elem Sch Crockett St, Quemado 78877 Rosanna Rios	PK-6		100 8		830/758-7045 Fax 830/758-0328
Language Development Center 1681 S Veterans Blvd, Eagle Pass 78852 Rosella Even	PK-K	T	485 23	79%	830/758-7047 Fax 830/757-1528
Liberty Elem Sch 1850 Flowers, Eagle Pass 78852 Rosalinda Barcena	1-6	T	527 35	60%	830/758-7156 Fax 830/757-3237
Memorial Junior High Sch 1800 Lewis St, Eagle Pass 78852 Jose Hernandez	7-8	TV	1,115 70	84%	830/758-7053 Fax 830/773-8900
Perfecto Mancha Elem Sch 3269 Fletcher Rd, Eagle Pass 78852 Sandra Koenig	1-6	T	519	82%	830/758-7216 Fax 830/758-7201
Pete Gallego Elem Sch 565 Madison St, Eagle Pass 78852 Jose Villalobos	1-6	T	405 23	81%	830/758-7130 Fax 830/757-5795
Ray Darr Elem Sch 1420 Eidson Rd, Eagle Pass 78852 Veronica Chacon	1-6	T	485 26	79%	830/758-7060 Fax 830/758-0090
Robert E Lee Elem Sch 300 S Monroe St, Eagle Pass 78852 Blanca Muzquiz	1-6	T	295 30	92%	830/758-7062 Fax 830/773-3471
Rosita Valley Elem Sch 587 Madison St, Eagle Pass 78852 Cynthia Guedea	1-6	T	483 25	85%	830/758-7065 Fax 830/757-2098
Rosita Valley Literacy Academy 811 Rosita Valley Rd, Eagle Pass 78852 Aida Pang-Villa	PK-1	T	361 10	92%	830/758-7067 Fax 830/773-8859
Sam Houston Elem Sch 2789 FM 1021, Eagle Pass 78852 Amalia Riojas	2-6	T	469 26	92%	830/758-7069 Fax 830/757-6639
San Luis Elem Sch 2090 Williams St, Eagle Pass 78852 Sylvia Saucedo	1-6	T	421 30	81%	830/758-7071 Fax 830/773-1632
Seco Mines Elem Sch 1654 S Veterans Blvd, Eagle Pass 78852 Maribel Martinez	1-6	T	318 24	83%	830/758-7073 Fax 830/773-8725

MAVERICK CATHOLIC SCHOOLS

- **Diocese of Laredo Ed Office** PID: 04938095
  Listing includes only schools located in this county. See District Index for location of Diocesan Offices.

Catholic Schs..Principal	Grd	Prgm	Enr/#Cls	SN	Phone
Our Lady of Refuge Sch 577 Washington St, Eagle Pass 78852 Ana Bermea	PK-8		200 13		830/773-3531 Fax 830/773-7310

MAVERICK PRIVATE SCHOOLS

Private Schs..Principal	Grd	Prgm	Enr/#Cls	SN	Phone
Redeemer Episcopal Sch 648 Madison St, Eagle Pass 78852 Jeanette Edwards	PK-6		80 7		830/773-5122 Fax 830/773-3525

MCCULLOCH COUNTY

MCCULLOCH PUBLIC SCHOOLS

- **Brady Ind School Dist** PID: 01039420   325/597-2301
  1003 W 11th St, Brady 76825   Fax 325/597-3984

Schools: 4 \ **Teachers:** 101 \ **Students:** 1,120 \ **Special Ed Students:** 151 \ **LEP Students:** 50 \ **College-Bound:** 61% \ **Ethnic:** Asian 1%, African American 2%, Hispanic 48%, Caucasian 50% \ **Exp:** $621 (High) \ **Poverty:** 26% \ **Title I:** $402,176 \ **Open-Close:** 08/26 - 05/21 \ **DTBP:** $435 (High)

Duane Limbaugh 1,83   Barbara Landry 2
Roy Smith 3   Adriana Flores 4
Mike Hagan 5   Shay Easterwood 6
Kevin White ....11*   Rebbeca Glover 31,38*
Shana Baronet ....37*   Sonia Cain 58
Michael Probst 67   Judy Fincher 73,84

Public Schs..Principal	Grd	Prgm	Enr/#Cls	SN	Phone
Ⓐ Brady Alternative Sch 601 W 11th St, Brady 76825 Hollis Moore	6-12		25 2		325/597-2170 Fax 325/597-7396
Brady Elem Sch 205 W China St, Brady 76825 Angela Bierman	PK-5	T	606 45	69%	325/597-2590 Fax 325/597-0490
Brady High Sch 2301 Highway 190, Brady 76825 Katherine Edwards	9-12	TV	323 35	59%	325/597-2491 Fax 325/597-2147
Brady Middle Sch 2309 Hwy 190, Brady 76825 Shona Moore	6-8	T	245 25	64%	325/597-8110 Fax 325/597-4166

- **Lohn Ind School Dist** PID: 01039482   325/344-5749
  1112 FM 504, Lohn 76852   Fax 325/344-5790

Schools: 1 \ **Teachers:** 15 \ **Students:** 90 \ **Special Ed Students:** 13 \ **College-Bound:** 50% \ **Ethnic:** Hispanic 54%, Caucasian 46% \ **Exp:** $839 (High) \ **Poverty:** 32% \ **Title I:** $888 \ **Open-Close:** 08/26 - 05/22 \ **DTBP:** $344 (High)

Leon Freeman 1,83,84   Christie Snodgrass 11,73*
Robert Swenson 67   Anna Freeman 271*

Public Schs..Principal	Grd	Prgm	Enr/#Cls	SN	Phone
Lohn Sch 1112 FM 504, Lohn 76852 Alett Rosberg	PK-12	ATV	90 16	84%	325/344-5749

---

79 Student Personnel	91 Safety/Security	275 Response To Intervention	298 Grant Writer/Ptnrships	**School Programs**	**Social Media**
80 Driver Ed/Safety	92 Magnet School	277 Remedial Math K-12	750 Chief Innovation Officer	A = Alternative Program	= Facebook
81 Gifted/Talented	93 Parental Involvement	280 Literacy Coach	751 Chief of Staff	G = Adult Classes	
82 Video Services	95 Tech Prep Program	285 STEM	752 Social Emotional Learning	M = Magnet Program	= Twitter
83 Substance Abuse Prev	97 Chief Information Officer	286 Digital Learning		T = Title I Schoolwide	
84 Erate	98 Chief Technology Officer	288 Common Core Standards	**Other School Types**	V = Career & Tech Ed Programs	
85 AIDS Education	270 Accountability	294 Accountability	Ⓐ = Alternative School		
88 Alternative/At Risk	271 Migrant Education	295 Network System	Ⓒ = Charter School	New Schools are shaded	
89 Multi-Cultural Curriculum	273 Teacher Mentor	296 Title II Programs	Ⓜ = Magnet School	New Superintendents and Principals are bold	
90 Social Work	274 Before/After Sch	297 Webmaster	Ⓨ = Year-Round School	Personnel with email addresses are underscored	

McLennan County — Market Data Retrieval

- **Rochelle Ind School Dist** PID: 01039509 325/243-5224
  5902 Lafayette Ave, Rochelle 76872 Fax 325/243-5216

> **Schools:** 1 \ **Teachers:** 22 \ **Students:** 200 \ **Special Ed Students:** 30 \
> **College-Bound:** 30% \ **Ethnic:** Hispanic 22%, Caucasian 78% \ **Exp:** $1,057
> (High) \ **Poverty:** 22% \ **Title I:** $38,295 \ **Open-Close:** 08/15 - 05/15 \
> **DTBP:** $358 (High) \ [f]

Dave Lewis 1,11	Claylene Gossett 2
David Baker 3,5	Anna Wolfe 4
Jeff Corean 6,9,74,288*	Matthew Fields 8*
Tammy Parrish 11,36,69*	Cody Houlbec 27*
Connie Humphreys 58	Mike Wolf 67

Public Schs..Principal	Grd	Prgm	Enr/#Cls	SN	
Rochelle Sch 5902 Lafayette Ave, Rochelle 76872 Matthew Fields	PK-12	TV	200 17	52%	325/243-5224 Fax 325/243-5283 [f]

MCLENNAN COUNTY

MCLENNAN PUBLIC SCHOOLS

- **Axtell Ind School Dist** PID: 01039535 254/863-5301
  308 Ottawa, Axtell 76624 Fax 254/863-5608

> **Schools:** 2 \ **Teachers:** 76 \ **Students:** 740 \ **Special Ed Students:** 122
> \ **LEP Students:** 11 \ **Ethnic:** African American 1%, Hispanic 21%, Native
> American: 1%, Caucasian 78% \ **Exp:** $551 (High) \ **Poverty:** 28% \
> **Title I:** $381,266 \ **Special Education:** $217,000 \ **Open-Close:** 08/21 -
> 05/21 \ **DTBP:** $343 (High) \ [f] [t]

Dr J R Proctor 1	Penny Kocian 2,10,11,35,57,88*
Andy Powell 3	Janice Hornsby 31,73*
Lacey Hollingsworth 58*	Brian Frankum 67
Ashley Hardin 69*	

Public Schs..Principal	Grd	Prgm	Enr/#Cls	SN	
Axtell Elem Sch 1178 Longhorn Pkwy, Axtell 76624 Danette Stranacher	PK-5	T	372 30	56%	254/863-5419 Fax 254/863-5944
Axtell High Sch 308 Ottawa, Axtell 76624 Sunny Beseda	6-12	ATV	162 36	52%	254/863-5301

- **Bosqueville Ind School Dist** PID: 01039561 254/757-3113
  7636 Rock Creek Rd, Waco 76708 Fax 254/752-4909

> **Schools:** 3 \ **Teachers:** 58 \ **Students:** 705 \ **Special Ed Students:** 64
> \ **LEP Students:** 17 \ **College-Bound:** 60% \ **Ethnic:** African American
> 5%, Hispanic 23%, Caucasian 72% \ **Exp:** $519 (High) \ **Poverty:** 14% \
> **Title I:** $65,433 \ **Special Education:** $114,000 \ **Open-Close:** 08/15 - 05/21
> \ **DTBP:** $219 (High)

James Skeeler 1	Catherine Boren 2
Steve Meyer 3*	Mary Mynar 4*
Michael Lamere 5	Clint Zander 6
Eary Penny 7	Kelly Bray 8,11,271,274*
Cliff Heath 10*	Kim Schwarz 16*
Judy Nunn 36,69,83,88,275,285,288,294	Elicia Krunnow 57

Jennifer Riggs 58*	Debbie Wrightwood 67
Rachel Carter 73,286,295*	

Public Schs..Principal	Grd	Prgm	Enr/#Cls	SN	
Bosqueville Elem Sch 1000 Washington Ln, Waco 76708 Kelly Bray	PK-5	T	343 32	42%	254/752-6006 Fax 254/759-7065
Bosqueville Middle Sch 7636 Rock Creek Rd, Waco 76708 Cliff Heath	6-8	T	171	35%	254/759-7077 Fax 254/752-5459 [f]
Bosqueville Secondary Sch 7636 Rock Creek Rd, Waco 76708 Cliff Heath	9-12	TV	197	27%	254/752-8513 Fax 254/752-0326

- **Bruceville-Eddy Ind Sch Dist** PID: 01039585 254/859-5525
  1 Eagle Dr, Eddy 76524 Fax 254/859-4023

> **Schools:** 4 \ **Teachers:** 70 \ **Students:** 641 \ **Special Ed Students:** 72
> \ **LEP Students:** 22 \ **College-Bound:** 49% \ **Ethnic:** African American
> 1%, Hispanic 32%, Native American: 1%, Caucasian 65% \ **Exp:** $432
> (High) \ **Poverty:** 15% \ **Title I:** $143,267 \ **Special Education:** $204,000 \
> **Open-Close:** 08/15 - 05/22 \ **DTBP:** $360 (High)

Richard Kilgore 1	Sheryl Robbins 2,68
Lowell Hill 3	Patricia Novian 4
Mike Hawkins 5*	Kyle Shoppach 6
Lisa Moon 7,85	Joe Woodard 8,288*
Sharon Johnson 9*	Marie Brockett 11,69,294,296,298*
Linda Hargis 16,82*	Stephanie Burkett 31,36,83,88,271*
David Duty 67	Leah Price 73,76,84,286,295

Public Schs..Principal	Grd	Prgm	Enr/#Cls	SN	
Bruceville-Eddy Elem Sch 1 Eagle Dr, Eddy 76524 Sharon Johnson	K-3	AT	167 26	69%	254/859-5525 Fax 254/859-5179
Bruceville-Eddy High Sch 1 Eagle Dr, Eddy 76524 Joe Woodard	9-12	AV	215 25		254/859-5525 Fax 254/859-5001
Bruceville-Eddy Interm Sch 1 Eagle Dr, Eddy 76524 Sharon Johnson	4-6	AT	179 18	64%	254/859-5525 Fax 254/859-5638
Bruceville-Eddy Jr High Sch 1 Eagle Dr, Eddy 76524 Mike Hawkins	7-8	ATV	159 16	60%	254/859-5525 Fax 254/859-3207

- **China Spring Ind School Dist** PID: 01039614 254/836-1115
  12166 Yankie Rd, China Spring 76633 Fax 254/836-0559

> **Schools:** 5 \ **Teachers:** 183 \ **Students:** 2,748 \ **Special Ed Students:** 276
> \ **LEP Students:** 37 \ **Ethnic:** Asian 1%, African American 5%, Hispanic
> 17%, Caucasian 77% \ **Exp:** $437 (High) \ **Poverty:** 9% \ **Title I:** $216,332
> \ **Special Education:** $529,000 \ **Open-Close:** 08/19 - 05/28 \ **DTBP:** $55
> (Low)

Dr Marc Faulkner 1	Brenda Poteet 2
Jim Ditto 3,5	Jill Sanders 4
Mark Bell 6*	Jennifer Crook 8,15,288
Lisa Howard 11,58	Kevin Pitts 15*
Rick Hines 67	Raymond Medina 73,295
Scott Tyner 295	

Public Schs..Principal	Grd	Prgm	Enr/#Cls	SN	
China Spring Elem Sch 200 Bob Johnson Rd, China Spring 76633 Kim Coe	PK-3	T	873 42	29%	254/836-4635 Fax 254/836-4637

1 Superintendent	8 Curric/Instruct K-12	19 Chief Financial Officer	29 Family/Consumer Science	39 Social Studies K-12	49 English/Lang Arts Elem	59 Special Education Elem	69 Academic Assessment
2 Bus/Finance/Purchasing	9 Curric/Instruct Elem	20 Art K-12	30 Adult Education	40 Social Studies Elem	50 English/Lang Arts Sec	60 Special Education Sec	70 Research/Development
3 Buildings And Grounds	10 Curric/Instruct Sec	21 Art Elem	31 Career/Sch-to-Work K-12	41 Social Studies Sec	51 Reading K-12	61 Foreign/World Lang K-12	71 Public Information
4 Food Service	11 Federal Program	22 Art Sec	32 Career/Sch-to-Work Elem	42 Science K-12	52 Reading Elem	62 Foreign/World Lang Elem	72 Summer School
5 Transportation	12 Title I	23 Music K-12	33 Career/Sch-to-Work Sec	43 Science Elem	53 Reading Sec	63 Foreign/World Lang Sec	73 Instructional Tech
6 Athletic	13 Title V	24 Music Elem	34 Early Childhood Ed	44 Science Sec	54 Remedial Reading K-12	64 Religious Education K-12	74 Inservice Training
7 Health Services	15 Asst Superintendent	25 Music Sec	35 Health/Phys Education	45 Math K-12	55 Remedial Reading Elem	65 Religious Education Elem	75 Marketing/Distributive
	16 Instructional Media Svcs	26 Business Education	36 Guidance Services K-12	46 Math Elem	56 Remedial Reading Sec	66 Religious Education Sec	76 Info Systems
	17 Chief Operations Officer	27 Career & Tech Ed	37 Guidance Services Elem	47 Math Sec	57 Bilingual/ELL	67 School Board President	77 Psychological Assess
	18 Chief Academic Officer	28 Technology Education	38 Guidance Services Sec	48 English/Lang Arts K-12	58 Special Education K-12	68 Teacher Personnel	78 Affirmative Action

Texas School Directory — McLennan County

China Spring High Sch 7301 N River Xing, China Spring 76633 Max Rutherford	9-12	V	810 40	18%	254/836-1771 Fax 254/836-1416
China Spring Intermediate Sch 4001 Flat Rock Rd, Waco 76708 Heather Jenkins	4-6		638 19	28%	254/759-1200 Fax 254/759-1208
China Spring Middle Sch 7201 N River Xing, China Spring 76633 Kristen Dutschmann	7-8		427 27	24%	254/836-4611 Fax 254/836-4777
Ⓐ Daep 412 E Cougar Ln, China Spring 76633 Miranda Brown	3-12	T	40		254/836-0676

● **Connally Ind School Dist** PID: 01039640   254/296-6460
200 Cadet Way, Waco 76705   Fax 254/412-5530

Schools: 6 \ *Teachers:* 174 \ *Students:* 2,300 \ *Special Ed Students:* 178 \ *LEP Students:* 192 \ *College-Bound:* 61% \ *Ethnic:* African American 36%, Hispanic 34%, Native American: 1%, Caucasian 29% \ *Exp:* $431 (High) \ *Poverty:* 24% \ *Title I:* $913,566 \ *Special Education:* $592,000 \ *Open-Close:* 08/15 - 05/22 \ *DTBP:* $189 (High)

Wesley Holt 1		James Slater 2,15	
Janes Flater 2,15		Jennifer Moss 2	
Jeremy Richard 3		Amanda Bailey 4	
Terry McHam 5		Shane Anderson 6*	
Pam White 7		Sandra Hancock 8,15	
Thurman Brown 8*		David Wimberly 11	
Laurie Tresl 34,58		Chris Howard 57,69,294	
Greg Davis 67		Larry Cumby 68	
Kevin Tye 73		Ronnie Price 83,91	
Nona King 274			

Public Schs..Principal	Grd	Prgm	Enr/#Cls	SN	
Connally Early Childhood Ctr 100 B B Brown Dr, Waco 76705 **Misty Gerik**	PK-K	T	319	83%	254/750-7160
Connally Early Clg Career Tech 200 Cadet Way, Waco 76705 Herman Pereira	10-12		115		254/296-6700
Connally Elem Sch 300 Cadet Way, Waco 76705 Eric Cantu	3-5	T	360 25	82%	254/750-7100 Fax 254/412-5525
Connally High Sch 901 N Lacy Dr, Waco 76705 Jill Talamantez	9-12	TV	633 50	68%	254/296-6700 Fax 254/412-5549
Connally Junior High Sch 100 Hancock Dr, Elm Mott 76640 Thurman Brown	6-8	TV	507 34	75%	254/296-7700 Fax 254/829-2354
Connally Primary Sch 100 Little Cadet Ln, Elm Mott 76640 Marlo Moore	PK-2	T	600 32	83%	254/296-7600 Fax 254/829-1273

● **Crawford Ind School Dist** PID: 01039705   254/486-2381
200 Pirate Dr, Crawford 76638   Fax 254/486-2198

Schools: 2 \ *Teachers:* 49 \ *Students:* 530 \ *Special Ed Students:* 52 \ *LEP Students:* 3 \ *College-Bound:* 60% \ *Ethnic:* Asian 1%, African American 1%, Hispanic 6%, Caucasian 92% \ *Exp:* $430 (High) \ *Poverty:* 11% \ *Title I:* $62,746 \ *Open-Close:* 08/21 - 05/22 \ *DTBP:* $339 (High) \ 🅕 🅣

Dr Kenneth Hall 1,11		Billy Lynch 2,286	
Robert Erlanson 3		Stephanie Howe 4	
Delbert Kelm 6*		Don Harris 8,73,88*	
Linda Stout 9,57,83,85*		Christine Wilkins 16*	

Joy Allovio 36,69,270	Kevin Harrington 58
Ricky Steinkamp 67	Tami Burch 295*

Public Schs..Principal	Grd	Prgm	Enr/#Cls	SN	
Crawford Elem Sch 100 Leonard Love Dr, Crawford 76638 Linda Stout	PK-6	T	279 18	18%	254/486-9083 Fax 254/486-9085
Crawford High Sch 200 Pirate Dr, Crawford 76638 Monte Pritchett	7-12	T	268 20	21%	254/486-2381

● **Gholson Ind School Dist** PID: 01039731   254/829-1528
137 Hamilton Dr, Waco 76705   Fax 254/829-0054

Schools: 1 \ *Teachers:* 21 \ *Students:* 255 \ *Special Ed Students:* 24 \ *LEP Students:* 8 \ *College-Bound:* 45% \ *Ethnic:* African American 3%, Hispanic 27%, Caucasian 70% \ *Exp:* $451 (High) \ *Poverty:* 21% \ *Title I:* $63,814 \ *Open-Close:* 08/26 - 05/28 \ *DTBP:* $560 (High)

Heather McCartney 1,83,84,288		Carmen Moore 2,13,296	
Carson Moore 3*		Tina McComb 4	
Stephanie Taylor 8,286,752*		Laura Reed 59*	
David Walker 67		Ana Mercado 73	

Public Schs..Principal	Grd	Prgm	Enr/#Cls	SN	
Gholson Sch 137 Hamilton Dr, Waco 76705 Stephanie Taylor	PK-12	T	255 10	80%	254/829-1528

● **Hallsburg Ind School Dist** PID: 01039755   254/875-2331
2313 Hallsburg Rd, Waco 76705   Fax 254/875-2436

Schools: 1 \ *Teachers:* 11 \ *Students:* 161 \ *Special Ed Students:* 13 \ *LEP Students:* 6 \ *Ethnic:* African American 2%, Hispanic 16%, Native American: 1%, Caucasian 81% \ *Exp:* $251 (Med) \ *Poverty:* 13% \ *Title I:* $29,526 \ *Open-Close:* 08/14 - 05/21 \ *DTBP:* $437 (High)

Dr Kent Reynolds 1,11,83,288		Jewell Armstrong 2	
Carol Lewis 4*		Carolyn Scott 6*	
Elzene Barton 57,59*		Norman Huddleston 67	
Elise MaGee 69		Michael Johnson 73,286*	
Gary Parady 752			

Public Schs..Principal	Grd	Prgm	Enr/#Cls	SN	
Hallsburg Elem Sch 2313 Hallsburg Rd, Waco 76705 Kent Reynolds	PK-6	T	161 7	55%	254/875-2331

● **La Vega Ind School Dist** PID: 01039779   254/299-6700
400 E Loop 340, Waco 76705   Fax 254/799-8642

Schools: 5 \ *Teachers:* 201 \ *Students:* 3,099 \ *Special Ed Students:* 217 \ *LEP Students:* 660 \ *Ethnic:* African American 27%, Hispanic 55%, Caucasian 17% \ *Exp:* $416 (High) \ *Poverty:* 29% \ *Title I:* $1,104,162 \ *Special Education:* $659,000 \ *Open-Close:* 08/14 - 05/22 \ *DTBP:* $210 (High) \ 🅕

Dr Sharon Shields 1		Diane Roepke 2	
James Langlotz 3,91		David Thiel 4	
Mandi Livingston 5		Willie Williams 6,35*	
Dr Charla Rudd 8,15		Dr Peggy Johnson 9,11,294,296,298	
Todd Gooden 15,68,74,78,273		Diane Dietiker 16*	
Angela Ward 58		Henry Jennings 67	
Lori Mynarcik 71		Justin Peebles 73,84,295	

---

79 Student Personnel	91 Safety/Security	275 Response To Intervention	298 Grant Writer/Ptnrships	**School Programs**	**Social Media**
80 Driver Ed/Safety	92 Magnet School	277 Remedial Math K-12	750 Chief Innovation Officer	A = Alternative Program	
81 Gifted/Talented	93 Parental Involvement	280 Literacy Coach	751 Chief of Staff	G = Adult Classes	🅕 = Facebook
82 Video Services	95 Tech Prep Program	285 STEM	752 Social Emotional Learning	M = Magnet Program	
83 Substance Abuse Prev	97 Chief Infomation Officer	286 Digital Learning		T = Title I Schoolwide	🅣 = Twitter
84 Erate	98 Chief Technology Officer	288 Common Core Standards	**Other School Types**	V = Career & Tech Ed Programs	
85 AIDS Education	270 Character Education	294 Accountability	Ⓐ = Alternative School		
88 Alternative/At Risk	271 Migrant Education	295 Network System	Ⓒ = Charter School	New Schools are shaded	
89 Multi-Cultural Curriculum	273 Teacher Mentor	296 Title II Programs	Ⓜ = Magnet School	New Superintendents and Principals are bold	
90 Social Work	274 Before/After Sch	297 Webmaster	Ⓨ = Year-Round School	Personnel with email addresses are underscored	

TX—279

McLennan County | Market Data Retrieval

Public Schs..Principal	Grd	Prgm	Enr/#Cls	SN		
La Vega Elem Sch 3100 Wheeler St, Waco 76705 Shaunte Stewart	1-3	AT	687 35	87%	254/299-6755 Fax 254/799-4453	
La Vega High Sch 555 N Loop 340, Waco 76705 **Sandra Gibson**	9-12	ATV	865	83%	254/299-6820 Fax 254/799-0720	f t
La Vega IS-H P Miles Campus 4201 Williams Rd, Bellmead 76705 Kristy Rizo	4-6	T	692 19	96%	254/299-6770 Fax 254/799-9738	
La Vega Junior High Sch 4401 Orchard Ln, Waco 76705 Virginia Ellis	7-8	T	492 45	80%	254/299-6790 Fax 254/799-8943	
La Vega Primary Center 4400 Harrison St, Waco 76705 Lisa Seawright	PK-K	T	363 29	93%	254/299-6730 Fax 254/799-1369	f t

● **Lorena Ind School Dist** PID: 01039822   254/857-3616
308 N Frontage Rd, Lorena 76655   Fax 254/857-4533

> **Schools:** 4 \ **Teachers:** 117 \ **Students:** 1,725 \ **Special Ed Students:** 140
> \ **LEP Students:** 28 \ **College-Bound:** 80% \ **Ethnic:** African American
> 1%, Hispanic 15%, Caucasian 83% \ **Exp:** $373 (High) \ **Poverty:** 8% \
> **Title I:** $136,729 \ **Special Education:** $323,000 \ **Open-Close:** 08/15 - 05/22 \ **DTBP:** $350 (High) \ f t

Dr Joe Kucera 1
Gary Sutherland 3
Elaine George 5
Ray Biles 6
Cheri Borchardt 8,11,31,57,69,275,288
Mary Timmons 67
David Payne 295
Jeff Linnstaedter 2,19
Shirley Oliver 4
Rusty Grimm 5,79,83,91,294
Cindy Fulton 7*
Kourtni Parnell 58
Jennifer Grimm 73,295

Public Schs..Principal	Grd	Prgm	Enr/#Cls	SN	
Lorena Elem Sch 420 N Houston St, Lorena 76655 Liza Cunningham	3-5	T	408 25	30%	254/857-4613 Fax 254/857-9019
Lorena High Sch 1 Leopard Ln, Lorena 76655 Kevin Johnson	9-12	AV	577 40	17%	254/857-4604 Fax 254/857-3883
Lorena Middle Sch 500 Leopard Ln, Lorena 76655 Jennifer Allison	6-8	T	374 33	22%	254/857-4621 Fax 254/857-3419
Lorena Primary Sch 1191 Old Lorena Rd, Lorena 76655 April Jewell	PK-2	T	404	31%	254/857-8909 Fax 254/857-8815

● **Mart Ind School Dist** PID: 01039858   254/876-2523
700 E Navarro Ave, Mart 76664   Fax 254/876-3028

> **Schools:** 2 \ **Teachers:** 47 \ **Students:** 500 \ **Special Ed Students:** 63
> \ **LEP Students:** 23 \ **College-Bound:** 60% \ **Ethnic:** African American
> 27%, Hispanic 18%, Caucasian 55% \ **Exp:** $234 (Med) \ **Poverty:** 16% \
> **Title I:** $190,906 \ **Open-Close:** 08/19 - 05/22 \ **DTBP:** $339 (High) \ f t

Leonard Williams 1
Darrell Wolf 3
Kevin Hoffman 6*
Pete Rowe 67
Rena Graves 2
Paula Abbott 4
John Luedke 16,73,82,297*

Public Schs..Principal	Grd	Prgm	Enr/#Cls	SN	
Mart Elem Sch 1400 E Kensington St, Mart 76664 Amy Stone	PK-6		292 13		254/876-2762 Fax 254/876-2317
Mart High Sch 700 E Navarro Ave, Mart 76664 Betsy Burnett	7-12	ATV	225 20	63%	254/876-2574 Fax 254/876-2576

● **McGregor Ind School Dist** PID: 01039896   254/840-2828
525 Bluebonnet Pkwy, Mc Gregor 76657   Fax 254/840-4077

> **Schools:** 4 \ **Teachers:** 115 \ **Students:** 1,550 \ **Special Ed Students:** 101
> \ **LEP Students:** 156 \ **College-Bound:** 58% \ **Ethnic:** African American
> 6%, Hispanic 52%, Native American: 1%, Caucasian 41% \ **Exp:** $304 (High) \
> **Poverty:** 19% \ **Title I:** $278,355 \ **Open-Close:** 08/14 - 05/27 \ f t

James Lenamon 1
Richard Schwake 3,5
Mike Sheilds 6
Tonya Burgess 9,31*
David Everett 11,15,83
Kevin Harrington 58,275
Lisa Rainey 294
Theresa Kinnear 2
John Carpenter 4
Paul Miller 7,15,91*
Kelly Tharpe 10*
Michelle Lenamon 16
Melissa Seward 73,76,286,295*

Public Schs..Principal	Grd	Prgm	Enr/#Cls	SN	
H G Isbill Junior High Sch 305 S Van Buren St, Mc Gregor 76657 Kelly Tharpe	6-8	T	301 36	72%	254/840-3251 Fax 254/840-3572 f t
McGregor Elem Sch 913 Bluebonnet Pkwy, Mc Gregor 76657 Tonya Burgess	2-5	T	438 27	74%	254/840-3204 Fax 254/840-3540 f t
McGregor High Sch 903 Bluebonnet Pkwy, Mc Gregor 76657 Seth Fortenberry	9-12	ATV	420 29	70%	254/840-2853 Fax 254/840-2489
McGregor Primary Sch 923 Bluebonnet Pkwy, Mc Gregor 76657 Cheri Zacharias	PK-1	T	300	72%	254/840-2973 Fax 254/840-3345 f t

● **Midway Ind School Dist** PID: 01039937   254/761-5600
13885 Woodway Dr, Woodway 76712   Fax 254/761-5789

> **Schools:** 10 \ **Teachers:** 492 \ **Students:** 8,411 \ **Special Ed Students:** 603
> \ **LEP Students:** 247 \ **College-Bound:** 75% \ **Ethnic:** Asian 5%,
> African American 13%, Hispanic 25%, Caucasian 57% \ **Exp:** $249 (Med)
> \ **Poverty:** 8% \ **Title I:** $601,234 \ **Special Education:** $1,283,000 \
> **Open-Close:** 08/20 - 05/28 \ **DTBP:** $147 (High) \ f t

Dr George Kazanas 1
Buddy Freeman 3
Colton Lawrence 4
Brad Shelton 6*
Melissa Sulak 9
Dr Ashley Canuteson 27,31
Jeanette Alexander 41,44*
Lorri Sapp 47
Lisa Cochran 58
Pete Rusek 67
Karen Mayton 69
Susan Fletcher 73,286
Dr Jeanie Johnson 79,91
Ginger Rowe 81
Debbie Perry 273
Wesley Brooks 2,15
Thomas Yourman 3
Brian Fair 5
Dr Aaron Pena 8,15,288
Darrell Umhoefer 20,23
Courtney Jerkins 40,43
Kimberly Johnson 46
Dr Beth Brabham 57,81,271,280
Sharon Blanchard 58,77
Mary-Lou Glaesmann 68,273
Traci Marlin 71
Russell Seiler 76,295
Tammy Smith 79
Brooke Baker 83
Mindy Huime 274

Public Schs..Principal	Grd	Prgm	Enr/#Cls	SN	
Castleman Creek Elem Sch 755 S Hewitt Dr, Hewitt 76643 Amanda Johnson	PK-4	T	620	39%	254/761-5755 Fax 254/761-5759
Hewitt Elem Sch 900 W Panther Way, Hewitt 76643 Christy Watley	PK-4	T	548 30	51%	254/761-5750 Fax 254/666-7540

1	Superintendent	8	Curric/Instruct K-12	19	Chief Financial Officer	29	Family/Consumer Science	39	Social Studies K-12	49	English/Lang Arts Elem	59	Special Education Elem	69	Academic Assessment
2	Bus/Finance/Purchasing	9	Curric/Instruct Elem	20	Art K-12	30	Adult Education	40	Social Studies Elem	50	English/Lang Arts Sec	60	Special Education Sec	70	Research/Development
3	Buildings And Grounds	10	Curric/Instruct Sec	21	Art Elem	31	Career/Sch-to-Work K-12	41	Social Studies Sec	51	Reading K-12	61	Foreign/World Lang K-12	71	Public Information
4	Food Service	11	Federal Program	22	Art Sec	32	Career/Sch-to-Work Elem	42	Science K-12	52	Reading Elem	62	Foreign/World Lang Elem	72	Summer School
5	Transportation	12	Title I	23	Music K-12	33	Career/Sch-to-Work Sec	43	Science Elem	53	Reading Sec	63	Foreign/World Lang Sec	73	Instructional Tech
6	Athletic	13	Title V	24	Music Elem	34	Early Childhood Ed	44	Science Sec	54	Remedial Reading K-12	64	Religious Education K-12	74	Inservice Training
7	Health Services	14	Instructional Media Svcs	25	Music Sec	35	Health/Phys Education	45	Math K-12	55	Remedial Reading Elem	65	Religious Education Elem	75	Marketing/Distributive
		15	Asst Superintendent	26	Business Education	36	Guidance Services K-12	46	Math Elem	56	Remedial Reading Sec	66	Religious Education Sec	76	Info Systems
		16	Chief Operations Officer	27	Career & Tech Ed	37	Guidance Services Elem	47	Math Sec	57	Bilingual/ELL	67	School Board President	77	Psychological Assess
		17	Chief Academic Officer	28	Technology Education	38	Guidance Services Sec	48	English/Lang Arts K-12	58	Special Education K-12	68	Teacher Personnel	78	Affirmative Action

Texas School Directory — McLennan County

School	Grd	Prgm	Enr/#Cls	SN	Phone
Midway High Sch 8200 Mars Dr, Waco 76712 Alison Smith	9-12	AV	2,449 85	25%	254/761-5650 Fax 254/761-5770
Midway Middle Sch 800 N Hewitt Dr, Hewitt 76643 Dr Herb Cox	7-8	AV	1,189 45	29%	254/761-5680 Fax 254/761-5775
River Valley Intermediate Sch 4750 Speegleville Rd, Mc Gregor 76657 Paul Offill	5-6		607		254/761-5699 Fax 254/761-5698
South Bosque Elem Sch 1 Wickson Rd, Waco 76712 Stacey Voigt	PK-4		605 25	15%	254/761-5720 Fax 254/776-2493
Speegleville Elem Sch 101 Maywood Dr, Waco 76712 Mandi Bronstad	PK-4	T	295 25	50%	254/761-5730 Fax 254/761-5733
Spring Valley Elem Sch 610 W Spring Valley Rd, Hewitt 76643 Jay Fischer	PK-4		555 30	30%	254/761-5710 Fax 254/666-4654
Woodgate Intermediate Sch 9400 Chapel Rd, Waco 76712 Aaron Pena	5-6	AT	636 38	38%	254/761-5690 Fax 254/666-0928
Woodway Elem Sch 325 Estates Dr, Waco 76712 Beth Olson	PK-4		581 25	36%	254/761-5740 Fax 254/772-5765

- **Moody Ind School Dist** PID: 01039975   254/853-2172
  12084 S Lone Star Pkwy Unit A, Moody 76557   Fax 254/853-2886

Schools: 3 \ *Teachers:* 59 \ *Students:* 690 \ *Special Ed Students:* 71 \ *LEP Students:* 46 \ *College-Bound:* 80% \ *Ethnic:* African American 7%, Hispanic 31%, Caucasian 62% \ *Exp:* $523 (High) \ *Poverty:* 20% \ *Title I:* $207,745 \ *Open-Close:* 08/20 - 05/22 \ *DTBP:* $332 (High)

Gary Martel 1,11,83   Susan Landua 2
Marty Garcia .... 6*   Belinda Brand 8,12,57,69,286,298
Nancy Molina .... 16,69,73,286*   Staci Evins 67

Public Schs..Principal	Grd	Prgm	Enr/#Cls	SN	
Moody Elem Sch 200 Ave D, Moody 76557 Tina Eaton	K-4	T	229 12	73%	254/853-2155 Fax 254/853-3009
Moody High Sch 11862 S Lone Star Pkwy, Moody 76557 Andrew Miller	9-12	ATV	199 26	60%	254/853-3622 Fax 254/853-3822
Moody Middle Sch 107 Coralee Ln, Moody 76557 Eric Cox	5-8	AT	221 19	70%	254/853-2181 Fax 254/853-9128

- **Riesel Ind School Dist** PID: 01040003   254/896-6411
  600 E Frederick St, Riesel 76682   Fax 254/896-2981

Schools: 2 \ *Teachers:* 48 \ *Students:* 620 \ *Special Ed Students:* 59 \ *LEP Students:* 4 \ *College-Bound:* 60% \ *Ethnic:* African American 3%, Hispanic 21%, Caucasian 75% \ *Exp:* $401 (High) \ *Poverty:* 13% \ *Title I:* $66,337 \ *Open-Close:* 08/21 - 05/28 \ *DTBP:* $350 (High) \ f

Brandon Cope 1   Toni Petrich 2
Jamie Glenn .... 8,11,73,288,296*   Tom McClimtok 67
Rick Ford 286*

Public Schs..Principal	Grd	Prgm	Enr/#Cls	SN	
Dr James D Foster Elem Sch 200 Williams, Riesel 76682 Brittni Summers	PK-6	T	304 23	43%	254/896-2297 Fax 254/896-2319
Riesel High Sch 600 E Frederick St, Riesel 76682 Jody Wood \ **Krystal Wilson**	7-12	ATV	342 30	40%	254/896-3171

- **Robinson Ind School Dist** PID: 01040039   254/662-0194
  500 W Lyndale Ave, Robinson 76706   Fax 254/662-0215

Schools: 5 \ *Teachers:* 177 \ *Students:* 2,200 \ *Special Ed Students:* 213 \ *LEP Students:* 40 \ *Ethnic:* Asian 1%, African American 3%, Hispanic 28%, Caucasian 68% \ *Exp:* $248 (Med) \ *Poverty:* 11% \ *Title I:* $265,830 \ *Special Education:* $483,000 \ *Open-Close:* 08/20 - 05/22 \ *DTBP:* $204 (High) \ f t

Michael Hope 1   Stacey Proctor 2,19
Dennis Ferguson 3   Robyn Lux 4
Tommy Allison .... 6*   Colette Pledger 8,18
Tim VanCleave 11,15   David Wrzesinski 12,58*
Willie Thomas 16   Dawn Griffin 27,31
Danielle Hughes .... 57*   Laura Crawford 67
Bryan Fuqua 73,84   Justin Brink 295

Public Schs..Principal	Grd	Prgm	Enr/#Cls	SN	
Robinson Elem Sch 151 Peplow Dr, Robinson 76706 Shelly Chudej	2-3	T	365 19	38%	254/662-5000 Fax 254/662-3140
Robinson High Sch 700 W Tate St, Robinson 76706 **Kati Dietzman**	9-12	T	701 32	24%	254/662-3840 Fax 254/662-4007
Robinson Intermediate Sch 500 W Lyndale Ave, Robinson 76706 Sara Laughlin	4-5	T	499 16	33%	254/662-6113 Fax 254/662-6183
Robinson Junior High Sch 410 W Lyndale Ave, Robinson 76706 Cynthia McCoy	6-8		371 40	32%	254/662-3843 Fax 254/662-1845
Robinson Primary Sch 541 N Old Robinson Rd, Robinson 76706 Melissa Zacharias	PK-1	T	389 17	44%	254/662-0251 Fax 254/662-3361

- **Waco Ind School Dist** PID: 01040132   254/755-9473
  501 Franklin Ave Ofc, Waco 76701   Fax 254/755-9690

Schools: 24 \ *Teachers:* 995 \ *Students:* 15,050 \ *Special Ed Students:* 1,097 \ *LEP Students:* 2,548 \ *College-Bound:* 53% \ *Ethnic:* African American 29%, Hispanic 62%, Caucasian 9% \ *Exp:* $346 (High) \ *Poverty:* 29% \ *Title I:* $7,282,984 \ *Special Education:* $3,203,000 \ *Open-Close:* 08/20 - 05/28 \ *DTBP:* $200 (High) \ f t

Susan Kincannon 1   Sheryl Davis 2,19
Israel Carrera 3,15   Rolando Gomez 3
Cliff Reece 4   David Gray 5
Johnny Tusa 6   Rhiannon Settles 7
Kim Ellis 8,15   Dr Robin McDurham 10
Dr Robin Wilson 11   Elaine Botello 15
Grace Benson 15,57   Sherry Trotts 15
Yolanda Williams 15   Larry Carpenter 20,23
Donna McKethan 27,31   Tiffany Sommerfeld 36
Robert Glinski 39   Suzanne Hamilton 58*
Angela Tekell 67   Sue Pfleging 68
Kyle DeBeer 71   Darvis Griffin 73,98
Paul Mach 73   Patrick Uptmore 74,273
Cecelia Boswell 81   Scott McClanahan 81
David Williams 91   Pennie Graeber 275
Matt Wolfe 295   Sharla Garcia 298

Public Schs..Principal	Grd	Prgm	Enr/#Cls	SN	
Alta Vista Elem Sch 3637 Alta Vista Dr, Waco 76706 Karmen Logan	PK-5	T	498 24	95%	254/662-3050 Fax 254/662-7353

79	Student Personnel	91	Safety/Security	275	Response To Intervention	298	Grant Writer/Ptnrships
80	Driver Ed/Safety	92	Magnet School	277	Remedial Math K-12	750	Chief Innovation Officer
81	Gifted/Talented	93	Parental Involvement	280	Literacy Coach	751	Chief of Staff
82	Video Services	95	Tech Prep Program	285	STEM	752	Social Emotional Learning
83	Substance Abuse Prev	97	Chief Information Officer	286	Digital Learning		
84	Erate	98	Chief Technology Officer	288	Common Core Standards		
85	AIDS Education	270	Accountability	294	Accountability		
86		271	Migrant Education	295	Network System		
88	Alternative/At Risk	273	Teacher Mentor	296	Title II Programs		
89	Multi-Cultural Curriculum	274	Before/After Sch	297	Webmaster		
90	Social Work						

School Programs
A = Alternative Program
G = Adult Classes
M = Magnet Program
T = Title I Schoolwide
V = Career & Tech Ed Programs

Other School Types
Ⓐ = Alternative School
Ⓒ = Charter School
Ⓜ = Magnet School
Ⓨ = Year-Round School

Social Media
f = Facebook
t = Twitter

New Schools are shaded
New Superintendents and Principals are bold
Personnel with email addresses are underscored

McLennan County

Market Data Retrieval

School	Grade	Prgm	Enr/#Cls	SN	Phone
Bell's Hill Elem Sch 2100 Ross Ave, Waco 76706 Rebekah Mechell	PK-5	T	754 30	97%	254/754-4171 Fax 254/750-3559
Ⓐ Brazos Credit Recovery HS 3005 Edna Ave, Waco 76708 Daphanie Latchison	7-12		250 4		254/754-9422
Brook Ave Elem Sch 720 Brook Ave, Waco 76708 Julie Sapaugh	PK-5	T	372 20	95%	254/750-3562 Fax 254/750-3545 f t
Carver Middle Sch 1601 J J Flewellen Rd, Waco 76704 **Phillip Perry**	6-8	T	477 39	87%	254/757-0787 Fax 254/750-3442 f t
Cedar Ridge Elem Sch 2115 Meridian Ave, Waco 76708 Elizabeth Smith	PK-5	T	567 40	95%	254/756-1241 Fax 254/750-3531
Cesar Chavez Middle Sch 700 S 15th St, Waco 76706 Alonzo McAdoo	6-8	T	847	93%	254/750-3736 Fax 254/750-3739
Crestview Elem Sch 1120 N New Rd, Waco 76710 Samantha Craytor	PK-5	T	608 37	93%	254/776-1704 Fax 254/741-4910
Dean Highland Elem Sch 3300 Maple Ave, Waco 76707 Thia Allen	PK-5	T	739 19	92%	254/752-3751 Fax 254/750-3458
Ⓐ G L Wiley Opportunity Center 1030 E Live Oak St, Waco 76704 Larryl Curtis	6-12		77 11	83%	254/757-3829 Fax 254/750-3772
Ⓜ Hillcrest Prof Dev Sch 4225 Pine Ave, Waco 76710 Jennifer Lundquist	PK-5	T	430 13	70%	254/772-4286 Fax 254/741-4938
Indian Spring Middle Sch 500 N University Parks Dr, Waco 76701 Joseph Alexander	6-8	T	524	94%	254/757-6200 Fax 254/757-6299
J H Hines Elem Sch 301 Garrison St, Waco 76704 Elijah Barefield	PK-5	T	503 35	97%	254/753-1362 Fax 254/750-3799
Kendrick Elem Sch 1801 Kendrick Ln, Waco 76711 Isabel Lozano	PK-5	T	530 21	94%	254/752-3316 Fax 254/750-3472
Ⓜ Lake Air Mont Magnet Sch 4601 Cobbs Dr, Waco 76710 Stephanie Tankersley	PK-8	T	710 25	75%	254/772-1910 Fax 254/741-4945
Ⓐ McLennan Co Challenge Academy 2015 Alexander Ave, Waco 76708 Christopher Rankin	6-12		50 8	84%	254/754-0803 Fax 254/754-6029
Mountainview Elem Sch 5901 Bishop Dr, Waco 76710 Melissa Pritchard	PK-5	T	382 22	75%	254/772-2520 Fax 254/741-4961
Parkdale Elem Sch 6400 Edmond Ave, Waco 76710 Marsha Henry	PK-5	T	620 20	85%	254/772-2170 Fax 254/741-4979
Provident Heights Elem Sch 2415 Bosque Blvd, Waco 76707 Debbie Sims	PK-5	T	386 27	96%	254/750-3930 Fax 254/750-3934
South Waco Elem Sch 2104 Gurley Ln, Waco 76706 Twana Lee	PK-5	T	526 29	94%	254/753-6802 Fax 254/750-3527
Tennyson Middle Sch 6100 Tennyson Dr, Waco 76710 **Matt Rambo**	6-8	T	930 50	76%	254/772-1440 Fax 254/741-4970 f t
University High Sch 3201 S New Rd, Waco 76706 Richard Edison	9-12	TV	1,735	79%	254/756-1843 Fax 254/750-3709
Waco High Sch 2020 N 42nd St, Waco 76710 Ed Love	9-12	TV	1,971	71%	254/776-1150 Fax 254/741-4815
West Ave Elem Sch 1101 N 15th St, Waco 76707 John Weeks	PK-5	T	382 13	98%	254/750-3900 Fax 254/750-3904

• **West Ind School Dist** PID: 01040481   254/981-2050
801 N Reagan St, West 76691

Schools: 4 \ *Teachers:* 93 \ *Students:* 1,350 \ *Special Ed Students:* 104 \ *LEP Students:* 53 \ *College-Bound:* 70% \ *Ethnic:* African American 2%, Hispanic 19%, Caucasian 78% \ *Exp:* $150 (Low) \ *Poverty:* 12% \ *Title I:* $207,330 \ *Special Education:* $389,000 \ *Open-Close:* 08/14 - 05/20 \ *DTBP:* $582 (High) \ f t

David Truitt 1,11,73,83
Kevin Maler 5
Amanda Adams 8
Tory Dobecka 8
Larry Sparks 67
Charles Mikeska 2,3,91
David Woodard 6*
Becky Kersh 8
Carla Sykora 58

Public Schs..Principal	Grd	Prgm	Enr/#Cls	SN	Phone
Ⓐ Brookhaven Sch 5467 Rogers Hill Rd, West 76691 Theresa Soukup	6-12		75		254/981-2240 Fax 254/829-1522
West Elem Sch 209 N Harrison St, West 76691 **Carrie Kazda**	PK-5	T	541 35	43%	254/981-2000 Fax 254/826-3342
West High Sch 1008 Jerry Mashek Dr, West 76691 **Don Snook**	9-12		425	37%	254/981-2050 Fax 254/826-3342
West Middle Sch 1008 Jerry Mashek Dr, West 76691 **Charles Klander**	6-8	T	326 12	40%	254/981-2120 Fax 254/826-3342

MCLENNAN CATHOLIC SCHOOLS

• **Diocese of Austin Ed Office** PID: 01420568
Listing includes only schools located in this county. See District Index for location of Diocesan Offices.

Catholic Schs..Principal	Grd	Prgm	Enr/#Cls	SN	Phone
Reicher Catholic High Sch 2102 N 23rd St, Waco 76708 Mindy Taylor	9-12		135 15		254/752-8349 Fax 254/752-8408
St Louis Catholic Sch 2208 N 23rd St, Waco 76708 Nisa Lagle	PK-8		300 27		254/754-2041 Fax 254/754-2091
St Mary Catholic Sch 507 W Spruce St, West 76691 Ericka Sammon	PK-8		140 11		254/826-5991 Fax 254/826-7047

MCLENNAN PRIVATE SCHOOLS

Private Schs..Principal	Grd	Prgm	Enr/#Cls	SN	Phone
Eagle Christian Academy 6125 Bosque Blvd, Waco 76710 Adrielle Selke	PK-8		115 20		254/772-2122
Live Oak Classical Sch 500 Clay Ave, Waco 76706 Alison Moffatt	PK-12		275		254/714-1007 Fax 254/714-1150

1 Superintendent	8 Curric/Instruct K-12	19 Chief Financial Officer	29 Family/Consumer Science	39 Social Studies K-12	49 English/Lang Arts Elem	59 Special Education Elem	69 Academic Assessment
2 Bus/Finance/Purchasing	9 Curric/Instruct Elem	20 Art K-12	30 Adult Education	40 Social Studies Elem	50 English/Lang Arts Sec	60 Special Education Sec	70 Research/Development
3 Buildings And Grounds	10 Curric/Instruct Sec	21 Art Elem	31 Career/Sch-to-Work K-12	41 Social Studies Sec	51 Reading K-12	61 Foreign/World Lang K-12	71 Public Information
4 Food Service	11 Federal Program	22 Art Sec	32 Career/Sch-to-Work Elem	42 Science K-12	52 Reading Elem	62 Foreign/World Lang Elem	72 Summer School
5 Transportation	12 Title I	23 Music K-12	33 Career/Sch-to-Work Sec	43 Science Elem	53 Reading Sec	63 Foreign/World Lang Sec	73 Instructional Tech
6 Athletic	13 Title V	24 Music Elem	34 Early Childhood Ed	44 Science Sec	54 Remedial Reading K-12	64 Religious Education K-12	74 Inservice Training
7 Health Services	15 Asst Superintendent	25 Music Sec	35 Health/Phys Education	45 Math K-12	55 Remedial Reading Elem	65 Religious Education Elem	75 Marketing/Distributive
	16 Instructional Media Svcs	26 Business Education	36 Guidance Services K-12	46 Math Elem	56 Remedial Reading Sec	66 Religious Education Sec	76 Info Systems
	17 Chief Operations Officer	27 Career & Tech Ed	37 Guidance Services Elem	47 Math Sec	57 Bilingual/ELL	67 School Board President	77 Psychological Assess
	18 Chief Academic Officer	28 Technology Education	38 Guidance Services Sec	48 English/Lang Arts K-12	58 Special Education K-12	68 Teacher Personnel	78 Affirmative Action

Texas School Directory

Parkview Christian Academy	K-12	95	254/753-0159
1100 E Lake Shore Dr, Waco 76708		40	Fax 254/753-0271
Amy Landers			
St Paul's Episcopal Sch	PK-6	70	254/753-0246
517 Columbus Ave, Waco 76701		10	Fax 254/755-7488
M'Lissa Howen			
Vanguard College Prepatory Sch	7-12	215	254/772-8111
2517 Mount Carmel Dr, Waco 76710		29	Fax 254/772-8263
Bill Borg			
Waco Montessori Sch	PK-6	250	254/754-3966
1920 Columbus Ave, Waco 76701			Fax 254/752-2922
Shirley Jansing			

MCLENNAN REGIONAL CENTERS

- **Region 12 Ed Service Center** PID: 01040120 — 254/297-1212
  2101 W Loop 340, Waco 76712 — Fax 254/666-0823

Jerry Maze	1	Terry Marak	2,19
Tammy Becker	8	Linda Roper	12
Dwan Pickens	57	Chris Griffin	58
Larry Robinson	68	Lisa McCray	73
Ed Newman	76	Michelle Butler	77
David McKamie	79	Yolanda Rollins	271

MCMULLEN COUNTY

MCMULLEN PUBLIC SCHOOLS

- **McMullen Co Ind Sch Dist** PID: 01040560 — 361/274-2000
  901 River St, Tilden 78072 — Fax 361/274-3665

Schools: 1 \ *Teachers:* 24 \ *Students:* 287 \ *Special Ed Students:* 13 \ *LEP Students:* 5 \ *College-Bound:* 100% \ *Ethnic:* Asian 2%, Hispanic 37%, Caucasian 60% \ *Exp:* $782 (High) \ *Poverty:* 13% \ *Title I:* $19,118 \ *Open-Close:* 08/14 - 05/21 \ *DTBP:* $299 (High)

Jason Jones	1	Krystal Huschke	2
Larry Garcia	3,5	Tracie Rios	4*
Shannon Taylor	6	Joe Timms	8,31,57,85,273*
Joel Trudeau	11*	Holly Schorch	58,83,88,270*
Walt Franklin	67	Kelly James	69,83,88,270*
Mary Pate	73,76*		

Public Schs..Principal	Grd	Prgm	Enr/#Cls	SN	
McMullen Co Sch	PK-12	V	287	27%	361/274-2000
901 River St, Tilden 78072			20		Fax 361/274-3580
Joe Timms					

Medina County

MEDINA COUNTY

MEDINA PUBLIC SCHOOLS

- **D'Hanis Ind School Dist** PID: 01041162 — 830/363-7216
  6751 County Rd 5216, D Hanis 78850 — Fax 830/363-7390

Schools: 1 \ *Teachers:* 34 \ *Students:* 395 \ *Special Ed Students:* 44 \ *LEP Students:* 3 \ *College-Bound:* 90% \ *Ethnic:* Hispanic 50%, Caucasian 50% \ *Exp:* $451 (High) \ *Poverty:* 21% \ *Title I:* $71,204 \ *Open-Close:* 08/26 - 05/22 \ *DTBP:* $353 (High) \ 📘

Vickie Whorton	2,4	Ray Garza	3*
Todd Craft	6*	Sandra Sexton	16,73*
Annaliza Pieratt	57*	Clay Bell	67

Public Schs..Principal	Grd	Prgm	Enr/#Cls	SN	
D'Hanis Sch	PK-12	T	395	55%	830/363-7216
6751 Cr 5216, D Hanis 78850			30		
Miranda Santos \ Kurt Schumaker					

- **Devine Ind School Dist** PID: 01041198 — 830/851-0795
  605 W Hondo Ave, Devine 78016 — Fax 830/663-6706

Schools: 4 \ *Teachers:* 144 \ *Students:* 2,000 \ *Special Ed Students:* 194 \ *LEP Students:* 68 \ *College-Bound:* 43% \ *Ethnic:* African American 1%, Hispanic 62%, Caucasian 37% \ *Exp:* $298 (Med) \ *Poverty:* 18% \ *Title I:* $412,546 \ *Special Education:* $373,000 \ *Open-Close:* 08/27 - 05/29 \ *DTBP:* $517 (High)

Scott Sostarich	1	Shannon Ramirez	2
Darren Van Fussen	3	David Cardenas	3
Ruben Ramirez	3	Jaime McLaurin	4
Jon Eichman	5	Chad Quisenberry	6*
Daryl Wendel	8,15,68	Lysandra Saldana	9*
Abigail Beadle	11	Roland Cadena	36*
Valerie Dykstra	58	Nancy Pepper	67
Scott Pesato	73*	Dawn Schneider	79

Public Schs..Principal	Grd	Prgm	Enr/#Cls	SN	
Devine High Sch	9-12	AGTV	604	47%	830/851-0895
1225 W Highway 173, Devine 78016			65		Fax 830/663-6792
Derrick Byrd					
Devine Intermediate Sch	3-5	T	440	61%	830/851-0495
900 Atkins Ave, Devine 78016			25		Fax 830/663-6746
Blain Martin					
Devine Middle Sch	6-8	TV	461	55%	830/851-0695
400 Cardinal Dr, Devine 78016			45		Fax 830/663-6769
Kandi Darnell					
John J Ciavarra Elem Sch	PK-2	T	502	68%	830/851-0395
112 Bentson Dr, Devine 78016			29		Fax 830/663-6730
Brenda Gardner					

---

79 Student Personnel	91 Safety/Security	275 Response To Intervention	298 Grant Writer/Ptnrships	**School Programs**
80 Driver Ed/Safety	92 Magnet School	277 Remedial Math K-12	750 Chief Innovation Officer	A = Alternative Program
81 Gifted/Talented	93 Parental Involvement	280 Literacy Coach	751 Chief of Staff	G = Adult Classes
82 Video Services	95 Tech Prep Program	285 STEM	752 Social Emotional Learning	M = Magnet Program
83 Substance Abuse Prev	97 Chief Information Officer	286 Digital Learning		T = Title I Schoolwide
84 Erate	98 Chief Technology Officer	288 Common Core Standards	**Other School Types**	V = Career & Tech Ed Programs
85 AIDS Education	270 Character Education	294 Accountability	Ⓐ = Alternative School	
88 Alternative/At Risk	271 Migrant Education	295 Network System	Ⓒ = Charter School	
89 Multi-Cultural Curriculum	273 Teacher Mentor	296 Title II Programs	Ⓜ = Magnet School	
90 Social Work	274 Before/After Sch	297 Webmaster	Ⓨ = Year-Round School	

Social Media: 📘 = Facebook 🐦 = Twitter

New Schools are shaded
New Superintendents and Principals are bold
Personnel with email addresses are underscored

Medina County

Market Data Retrieval

- **Hondo Ind School Dist** PID: 01041239   830/426-3027
  2604 Avenue E, Hondo 78861   Fax 830/426-7683

  Schools: 4 \ *Teachers:* 154 \ *Students:* 2,200 \ *Special Ed Students:* 186 \ *LEP Students:* 50 \ *Ethnic:* African American 1%, Hispanic 73%, Caucasian 26% \ *Exp:* $238 (Med) \ *Poverty:* 19% \ *Title I:* $485,983 \ *Special Education:* $380,000 \ *Open-Close:* 08/15 - 05/28 \ *DTBP:* $553 (High)

  Dr Alann Truelock 1
  Chuck Beard 3
  Jessie Baez 6*
  Misty Ptasnik 9*
  Stephanie Laughinghouse 11,54,57,83,271,273,275,296
  15,69,74,91
  Kami Neuman 16,82*
  Cynthia Gann 58,77
  Mary Peters 73,286,295*
  Flint Huey 88*

  Patricia Gonzales 2
  Michelle Thacker 4
  Chesney Brown 7*
  Robert Knight 10,31*
  .... Rosemary Mares
  Vanessa Alvarado 30,38*
  Jay Gardenhire 67
  James White 79

Public Schs..Principal	Grd	Prgm	Enr/#Cls	SN	
Hondo High Sch 2603 Avenue H, Hondo 78861 Robert Knight	9-12	ATV	634 50	56%	830/426-3341 Fax 830/426-7691
McDowell Middle Sch 1602 27th St S, Hondo 78861 Scott Backus	6-8	AT	429	59%	830/426-2261 Fax 830/426-7624
Meyer Elem Sch 2502 Avenue Q, Hondo 78861 Misty Ptasnik	PK-2	AT	489 32	71%	830/426-3161 Fax 830/426-7679
Newell E Woolls Interm Sch 2802 Avenue Q, Hondo 78861 Steve Ayers	3-5	AT	450 25	68%	830/426-7666 Fax 830/426-7669

- **Medina Valley Ind School Dist** PID: 01041277   830/931-2243
  8449 FM 471 S, Castroville 78009   Fax 830/931-4050

  Schools: 5 \ *Teachers:* 272 \ *Students:* 5,087 \ *Special Ed Students:* 469 \ *LEP Students:* 219 \ *College-Bound:* 53% \ *Ethnic:* African American 3%, Hispanic 60%, Native American: 1%, Caucasian 35% \ *Exp:* $229 (Med) \ *Poverty:* 19% \ *Title I:* $836,317 \ *Special Education:* $1,642,000 \ *Open-Close:* 08/27 - 06/04 \ *DTBP:* $178 (High)

  Dr Kennith Rohrbach 1
  Paul Holzhaus 2,5,15
  Tommy Ellison 3
  Richard Broome 5
  Chris Soza 6
  Andrea Moreno-Hewitt 8,57,69
  Michael Nesbit 8,15,69
  Leah Graves 45
  Shannon Beasley 67
  Carl Lyles 73,295,297
  Kenneth Englehart 84
  Christine Orozco 93
  Samuel Alaniz 297

  Michael Homann 2,15
  Sylvia Morales 2
  Vicki Beck 4
  Todd Tschirhart 5
  Patricia Mechler 7*
  Arcelia Leon 8,69
  Gabriel Cary 11
  Stephine Keller 58
  Bridget Ayala 69
  Julie Oppelt 81
  Holly Havey 88*
  Nathan Harper 295

Public Schs..Principal	Grd	Prgm	Enr/#Cls	SN	
Castroville Elem Sch 1000 Madrid St, Castroville 78009 Kendall Center	PK-5	T	678 32	58%	830/931-2117 Fax 830/931-3973
Medina Valley High Sch 8365 FM 471 S, Castroville 78009 Tanner Lange	9-12	GTV	1,429	50%	830/931-2243 Fax 830/931-0371
Medina Valley Lacoste ES 16069 Uvalde St, La Coste 78039 Elizabeth Vera	PK-5	T	746 20	64%	830/985-3421 Fax 830/985-3732
Medina Valley Middle Sch 8395 FM 471 S, Castroville 78009 Lesli Solis	6-8	T	1,209 38	52%	830/931-2243 Fax 830/931-3258
Potranco Elem Sch 190 County Road 381 S, San Antonio 78253 Sandy Bermea	PK-5	T	1,025	46%	830/931-2243 Fax 830/931-9575

- **Natalia Ind School Dist** PID: 01041320   830/663-4416
  805 Pearson St, Natalia 78059   Fax 830/663-4186

  Schools: 4 \ *Teachers:* 79 \ *Students:* 1,060 \ *Special Ed Students:* 105 \ *LEP Students:* 65 \ *College-Bound:* 48% \ *Ethnic:* Hispanic 81%, Caucasian 18% \ *Exp:* $409 (High) \ *Poverty:* 20% \ *Title I:* $273,556 \ *Special Education:* $151,000 \ *Open-Close:* 08/26 - 05/29 \ *DTBP:* $350 (High) \ 📧

  Dr Hensley Cone 1
  Paul Michels 2
  Tonya Rodriguez 4
  Ilyan Martinez 6*
  Carmen Maglievaz 9*
  Edgar Camacho 10*
  Eric Smith 67
  Jennett Roberts 73,286,295,297

  Aida Ramos 2
  Philip Riddle 3
  Samuel Bluemel 5
  Lori Robinson 8,271,285
  Dr Andrea Moreno Hewitt 10
  Laticia Buenrostro 11,58,288,296
  Rob Binson 69

Public Schs..Principal	Grd	Prgm	Enr/#Cls	SN	
Early Childhood Center 8th & Pearson Streets, Natalia 78059 Carmen Maglievaz	PK-1		242 17		830/663-9739
Natalia Elem Sch 8th & Pearson Streets, Natalia 78059 Carmen Maglievaz	2-5	T	308 17	77%	830/663-2837 Fax 830/663-9693
Natalia High Sch 8th & Kearny St, Natalia 78059 Dr Andrea Moreno-Hewitt	9-12	ATV	297 36	78%	830/663-4417 Fax 830/663-6410
Natalia Junior High Sch 8th & Pearson Streets, Natalia 78059 Edgar Camacho	6-8	T	255 22	79%	830/663-4027 Fax 830/663-2347

MEDINA CATHOLIC SCHOOLS

- **Archdiocese San Antonio Ed Off** PID: 00999724
  Listing includes only schools located in this county. See District Index for location of Diocesan Offices.

Catholic Schs..Principal	Grd	Prgm	Enr/#Cls	SN	
St Louis Sch 607 Madrid St, Castroville 78009 Dr Jimmy Gouard	PK-3		125 15		830/931-3544 Fax 830/931-9016

MEDINA PRIVATE SCHOOLS

Private Schs..Principal	Grd	Prgm	Enr/#Cls	SN	
DayStar Academy 8406 FM 471 S, Castroville 78009 Jan Carnley	PK-1		20		830/931-0808

1 Superintendent	8 Curric/Instruct K-12	19 Chief Financial Officer	29 Family/Consumer Science	39 Social Studies K-12	49 English/Lang Arts Elem	59 Special Education Elem	69 Academic Assessment
2 Bus/Finance/Purchasing	9 Curric/Instruct Elem	20 Art K-12	30 Adult Education	40 English/Lang Arts Sec	50 English/Lang Arts Sec	60 Special Education Sec	70 Research/Development
3 Buildings And Grounds	10 Curric/Instruct Sec	21 Art Elem	31 Career/Sch-to-Work K-12	41 Social Studies Sec	51 Reading K-12	61 Foreign/World Lang K-12	71 Public Information
4 Food Service	11 Federal Program	22 Art Sec	32 Career/Sch-to-Work Elem	42 Science K-12	52 Reading Elem	62 Foreign/World Lang Elem	72 Summer School
5 Transportation	12 Title I	23 Music K-12	33 Career/Sch-to-Work Sec	43 Science Elem	53 Reading Sec	63 Foreign/World Lang Sec	73 Instructional Tech
6 Athletic	13 Title V	24 Music Elem	34 Early Childhood Ed	44 Science Sec	54 Remedial Reading K-12	64 Religious Education K-12	74 Inservice Training
7 Health Services	14 Instructional Media Svcs	25 Music Sec	35 Health/Phys Education	45 Math K-12	55 Remedial Reading Elem	65 Religious Education Elem	75 Marketing/Distributive
	15 Asst Superintendent	26 Business Education	36 Guidance Services K-12	46 Math Elem	56 Remedial Reading Sec	66 Religious Education Sec	76 Info Systems
	16 Instructional Media Svcs	27 Career & Tech Ed	37 Guidance Services Elem	47 Math Sec	57 Bilingual/ELL	67 School Board President	77 Psychological Assess
	17 Chief Operations Officer	28 Technology Education	38 Guidance Services Sec	48 English/Lang Arts K-12	58 Special Education K 12	68 Teacher Personnel	78 Affirmative Action
	18 Chief Academic Officer						

Texas School Directory

Midland County

MENARD COUNTY

MENARD PUBLIC SCHOOLS

- **Menard Ind School Dist** PID: 01041368   325/396-2404
  221 E San Saba St, Menard 76859   Fax 325/396-2143

Schools: 2 \ **Teachers:** 27 \ **Students:** 300 \ **Special Ed Students:** 31 \ **LEP Students:** 17 \ **College-Bound:** 94% \ **Ethnic:** African American 1%, Hispanic 50%, Caucasian 48% \ **Exp:** $631 (High) \ **Poverty:** 34% \ **Title I:** $145,494 \ **Open-Close:** 08/19 - 05/22 \ **DTBP:** $350 (High)

Amy Bannowsky 1
Beau Tipton 3,5
Felicia Laxson 36,83,88,275*
Arnold Saucedo 67
Holly Bryan 2,68
Johnny Whitson 16,73,295*
Myghan Meadow 58

Public Schs..Principal	Grd	Prgm	Enr/#Cls	SN	
Menard Elem Middle Sch 300 Gay St, Menard 76859 **Amy Bannowsky**	PK-8	T	225 17	78%	325/396-2348 Fax 325/396-2761
Menard High Sch 401 W Travis, Menard 76859 **Cheryl Kruse**	9-12	TV	87 13	63%	325/396-2513 Fax 325/396-2053

MIDLAND COUNTY

MIDLAND PUBLIC SCHOOLS

- **Greenwood Ind School Dist** PID: 01041394   432/683-6461
  2700 FM 1379, Midland 79706   Fax 432/685-7804

Schools: 4 \ **Teachers:** 150 \ **Students:** 2,831 \ **Special Ed Students:** 157 \ **LEP Students:** 166 \ **College-Bound:** 66% \ **Ethnic:** African American 1%, Hispanic 47%, Caucasian 52% \ **Exp:** $414 (High) \ **Poverty:** 17% \ **Title I:** $402,976 \ **Open-Close:** 08/14 - 05/21 \ **DTBP:** $317 (High)

Ariel Elliott 1
Brian Cooper 3*
Rusty Purser 6*
Debra Kiehl 8
Mary Aldarado 57,271*
Justin Brooks 67
Darrell Dodds 2,15
Sandra Smith 4*
Madelaine Gully 7,83,85*
Byron Moreland 11,15
Heidi Delk 59
Debbie Dodds 295*

Public Schs..Principal	Grd	Prgm	Enr/#Cls	SN	
Greenwood Elem Sch 2700 FM 1379, Midland 79706 **Leslie Goodrum**	PK-2	T	600 22	36%	432/685-7821 Fax 432/685-7822
Greenwood High Sch 2700 FM 1379, Midland 79706 **Stacy Jones**	9-12	AV	720 40	26%	432/685-7806 Fax 432/685-7814
Greenwood Interm Sch 2700 FM 1379, Midland 79706 **Crysten Hopkins**	3-5		522		432/685-7819
James R Brooks Middle Sch 2700 FM 1379, Midland 79706 **Kristi Brown-Griffin**	6-8		846 30	36%	432/685-7837 Fax 432/253-6731

- **Midland Ind School Dist** PID: 01041423   432/689-1000
  615 W Missouri Ave, Midland 79701   Fax 432/689-1932

Schools: 39 \ **Teachers:** 1,573 \ **Students:** 26,000 \ **Special Ed Students:** 1,648 \ **LEP Students:** 2,752 \ **College-Bound:** 58% \ **Ethnic:** Asian 2%, African American 8%, Hispanic 63%, Caucasian 27% \ **Exp:** $151 (Low) \ **Poverty:** 14% \ **Title I:** $5,650,017 \ **Special Education:** $3,319,000 \ **Open-Close:** 08/14 - 05/22 \ **DTBP:** $197 (High)

Orlando Riddick 1
James Riggen 3,17,70,91
John Feldt 6
Patrick Jones 8,18
Lisa Neighbors 9
Teresa Moore 11
Kim Evans 27,31*
Ron Moss 36
Rob Pena 42
Linda Hill 47
Leticia Amaya 57
Debbie Oliver 61
Tony DeLaRosa 68
Michael Lloyd 73
Jill Rivera 74
Judy Bridges 81
Josh Tipton 297
Darla Moss 2,19
Willie Tarleton 5
Imo Douglas 7
Diane Lopez 9
Jeff Horner 10
Debbie Shaw 20,23
Della Frye 34
Chris Hightower 39
Wendy DeVault 46
Sylvia Bernal 51
Dawn Miller 58,77
Rick Davis 67
Elaina Ladd 71
Tom Holly 73,76,295,297
Tonia Hale 76
Claudia Alanis 294

Public Schs..Principal	Grd	Prgm	Enr/#Cls	SN	
Abell Junior High Sch 3201 Heritage Blvd, Midland 79707 **Jennifer Seybert**	7-8	TV	1,036 50	42%	432/689-6200 Fax 432/689-6217
Alamo Junior High Sch 3800 W Storey Ave, Midland 79703 **Paul Hidalgo**	7-8	TV	732 50	61%	432/689-1700 Fax 432/689-1712
Bonham Elem Sch 909 Bonham St, Midland 79703 **Tricia Teran**	PK-6	T	631 36	62%	432/240-6000 Fax 432/240-6001
Ⓜ Bowie Fine Arts Academy 805 Elk Ave, Midland 79701 **Melissa Horner**	PK-6		518 24	34%	432/240-6100 Fax 432/689-5121
Bunche Elem Sch 700 S Jackson St, Midland 79701 **Sha Burdsal**	PK-6	T	812	79%	432/240-8600
Burnet Elem Sch 900 Raymond Rd, Midland 79703 **Angela Aron**	PK-6	T	553 29	80%	432/240-6200 Fax 432/689-1783
Bush Elem Sch 5001 Preston Dr, Midland 79707 **Aaron Fong**	PK-6	T	473 23	49%	432/240-6300 Fax 432/689-1879
Carver Center 1300 E Wall St, Midland 79701 **Stephanie Carnett**	Spec		505 20	12%	432/240-6400 Fax 432/689-1426
Dezavala Elem Sch 705 N Lee St, Midland 79701 **Julie Sims**	PK-6	T	588 28	86%	432/240-6600 Fax 432/240-6601
Early College High Sch-Midland 3600 N Garfield St, Midland 79705 **Renee Aldrin**	9-12		299	42%	432/685-4641 Fax 432/685-4669
Emerson Elem Sch 2800 Moss Ave, Midland 79705 **Christin Reeves**	PK-6	T	496 22	44%	432/240-6700 Fax 432/689-6271

79 Student Personnel	91 Safety/Security	275 Response To Intervention	298 Grant Writer/Ptnrships
80 Driver Ed/Safety	92 Magnet School	277 Remedial Math K-12	750 Chief Innovation Officer
81 Gifted/Talented	93 Parental Involvement	280 Literacy Coach	751 Chief of Staff
82 Video Services	95 Tech Prep Program	285 STEM	752 Social Emotional Learning
83 Substance Abuse Prev	97 Chief Information Officer	286 Digital Learning	
84 Erate	98 Chief Technology Officer	288 Common Core Standards	**Other School Types**
85 AIDS Education	270 Character Education	294 Accountability	Ⓐ = Alternative Program
88 Alternative/At Risk	271 Migrant Education	295 Network System	Ⓒ = Charter School
89 Multi-Cultural Curriculum	273 Teacher Mentor	296 Title II Programs	Ⓜ = Magnet School
90 Social Work	274 Before/After Sch	297 Webmaster	Ⓨ = Year-Round School

School Programs
A = Alternative Program
G = Adult Classes
M = Magnet Program
T = Title I Schoolwide
V = Career & Tech Ed Programs

Social Media
= Facebook
= Twitter

New Schools are shaded
New Superintendents and Principals are bold
Personnel with email addresses are underscored

Midland County

School	Grd	Prgm	Enr/#Cls	%	Phone
Fannin Elem Sch 2400 Fannin Ave, Midland 79705 Tara Crockett	PK-6		579 35	35%	432/240-6800 Fax 432/689-1346
Fasken Elem Sch 5806 Val Verde Dr, Midland 79707 Dr Joshua Gamboa	PK-6	T	755	34%	432/240-8400
Gen Tommy Franks Elem Sch 401 E Parker Ave, Midland 79701 Andra Jones	PK-6	T	398 26	86%	432/240-6500 Fax 432/689-1429
Goddard Junior High Sch 2500 Haynes Ave, Midland 79705 Brandy Copeland	7-8	TV	1,212 30	51%	432/689-1300 Fax 432/689-1321
Greathouse Elem Sch 5107 Greathouse Ave, Midland 79707 Tonya Sanchez	PK-6		779 33	31%	432/240-6900 Fax 432/689-6901
Henderson Elem Sch 4800 Graceland Dr, Midland 79703 Ray Portillo	PK-6	T	468 40	53%	432/240-7000 Fax 432/689-1807
Jones Elem Sch 4919 Shadylane Dr, Midland 79703 Lisa Leclear	PK-6	T	373 24	59%	432/240-7200 Fax 432/240-7201
Lamar Elem Sch 3200 Kessler Ave, Midland 79701 Amy Clark	PK-6	T	544 25	78%	432/240-7300 Fax 432/689-1893
Long Elem Sch 4200 Cedar Spring Dr, Midland 79703 Terri Rimer	PK-6	T	518 28	74%	432/240-7400 Fax 432/689-1836
Ⓐ Midland Alternative Program 2101 W Missouri Ave, Midland 79701 Angelina Buck	7-12	T	12	79%	432/240-4700 Fax 432/240-4701
Midland Freshman High Sch 101 E Gist Ave, Midland 79701 Shannon Torres	9-9	AT	842	51%	432/689-1200 Fax 432/689-1209
Midland Senior High Sch 906 W Illinois Ave, Midland 79701 Leslie Sparacello	9-12	AV	2,374 100	31%	432/689-1100 Fax 432/689-1144
Milam Elem Sch 301 E Dormard Ave, Midland 79705 Iliana Bermea	PK-6	T	362 30	81%	432/240-7500 Fax 432/240-7501
Parker Elem Sch 3800 Norwood St, Midland 79707 Tracie Burrow	PK-6		486 20	43%	432/240-7600 Fax 432/240-7601
Ⓜ Pease Communication/Tech Acad 1700 Magnolia Ave, Midland 79705 Gabriel Moya	K-6	T	621 26	61%	432/240-7700 Fax 432/689-1489
Robert E Lee Freshman High Sch 1400 E Oak Ave, Midland 79705 Bobby Stults	9-9	TV	805 52	44%	432/689-1250 Fax 432/689-1253
Robert E Lee Sr High Sch 3500 Neely Ave, Midland 79707 Stan Vanhoozer	9-12	ATV	2,209 100	33%	432/689-1600 Fax 432/689-1647
Rusk Elem Sch 2601 Wedgwood St, Midland 79707 Dora Flores	PK-6	T	415 22	54%	432/240-7800 Fax 432/240-7801
Sam Houston Elem Sch 2000 W Louisiana Ave, Midland 79701 Stephanie Ramos	PK-6	T	464 31	69%	432/240-7100 Fax 432/689-5026
San Jacinto Junior High Sch 1400 N N St, Midland 79701 Deborah Kendricks	6-8	TV	698	53%	432/689-1350 Fax 432/689-1385
Santa Rita Elem Sch 5306 Whitman Dr, Midland 79705 Debra Alba	PK-6	T	600 27	25%	432/240-7900 Fax 432/689-5094
Scharbauer Elem Sch 2115 Hereford Blvd, Midland 79707 Sharla Butler	PK-6	T	766 27	50%	432/240-8000 Fax 432/689-6286
South Elem Sch 200 W Dakota Ave, Midland 79701 Juan Dominguez	PK-6	T	583 26	87%	432/240-8100 Fax 432/689-1539
Travis Elem Sch 900 E Gist Ave, Midland 79701 Terri Matthews	PK-6	T	779 32	84%	432/240-8200 Fax 432/689-5054
Ⓐ Viola M Coleman High Sch 1600 E Golf Course Rd, Midland 79701 David Moore	9-12	T	107 10	49%	432/689-5000 Fax 432/689-5016
Ⓜ Washington STEM Academy 1800 E Wall St, Midland 79701 Ann Newton	K-6		464 23	37%	432/240-8300 Fax 432/689-1593
Yarbrough Elem Sch 6000 Riverfront Dr, Midland 79706 Jill Arthur	PK-6	T	707	43%	432/240-8500 Fax 432/240-8501
Young Women's Leadership Acad 126 Thornridge Dr, Midland 79703 Jennifer Seybert	6-7		100		432/240-8700

MIDLAND CATHOLIC SCHOOLS

- **Diocese of San Angelo Ed Off** PID: 01055929
  1906 W Texas Ave, Midland 79701
  432/684-4563
  Fax 432/687-2468

Schools: 3 \ **Students:** 1,000

Listing includes only schools located in this county. See District Index for location of Diocesan Offices.

Joan Wilmes 1

Catholic Schs..Principal	Grd	Prgm	Enr/#Cls	SN
St Ann's Sch 2000 W Texas Ave, Midland 79701 Joan Wilmes	PK-8	G	363 30	432/684-4563 Fax 432/687-2468 f

MIDLAND PRIVATE SCHOOLS

Private Schs..Principal	Grd	Prgm	Enr/#Cls	SN
Ⓨ Bynum Sch 8404 W County Road 60, Midland 79707 Keri St John	PK-12	M	45	432/520-0075
Hillander Sch 1600 W Wadley Ave, Midland 79705 Buffy Meadore	PK-6		300 20	432/684-8681 Fax 432/684-3863
Hillcrest Sch 2800 N A St, Midland 79705 Betty Starnes	Spec		112 8	432/570-7444 Fax 432/684-9675 f
Midland Christian Sch 2001 Culver Dr, Midland 79705 Judy Wallum \ Jumon Hailey \ Byron Myers	PK-12		1,250	432/694-1661 Fax 432/694-5281
Midland Classical Academy 5711 Whitman Dr, Midland 79705 Kalen Walls	K-12		500	432/694-0995 Fax 432/694-0978
Trinity School of Midland 3500 W Wadley Ave, Midland 79707 Carrie Brown \ Chrystal Myers \ Tim Jones	K-12		620 70	432/697-3281 Fax 432/697-7403

Texas School Directory — Milam County

MIDLAND REGIONAL CENTERS

- **Region 18 Ed Service Center** PID: 01041693 432/563-2380
  2811 La Force Blvd, Midland 79706 Fax 432/567-3290

DeWitt Smith 1	Britt Hayes 2
Nicole Gabriel 7,8,73,74,85	Kirsty Hall 16
Linda Jolly 58	Nancy Dunnam 76

MILAM COUNTY

MILAM PUBLIC SCHOOLS

- **Buckholts Ind School Dist** PID: 01041722 254/593-3011
  203 S 10th St, Buckholts 76518 Fax 254/593-2270

Schools: 1 \ **Teachers:** 15 \ **Students:** 140 \ **Special Ed Students:** 18 \ **LEP Students:** 6 \ **College-Bound:** 85% \ **Ethnic:** Hispanic 54%, Caucasian 46% \ **Exp:** $841 (High) \ **Poverty:** 39% \ **Title I:** $99,760 \ **Open-Close:** 08/19 - 05/22 \ **DTBP:** $338 (High)

Nancy Sandlin 1,11	Sherry Lopez 2,68
Cindy Hernandez 4	James Shelton 6*
Adam Losoya 67	Whilliam Sandlin 73
Kris Shaver 752*	

Public Schs..Principal	Grd	Prgm	Enr/#Cls	SN	
Buckholts Sch 203 S 10th St, Buckholts 76518 Kris Shaver	PK-12	TV	140 25	78%	254/593-2744

- **Cameron Ind School Dist** PID: 01041758 254/697-3512
  304 E 12th St, Cameron 76520 Fax 254/697-2448

Schools: 4 \ **Teachers:** 123 \ **Students:** 1,800 \ **Special Ed Students:** 182 \ **LEP Students:** 141 \ **College-Bound:** 56% \ **Ethnic:** African American 17%, Hispanic 49%, Caucasian 34% \ **Exp:** $437 (High) \ **Poverty:** 39% \ **Title I:** $919,765 \ **Open-Close:** 08/14 - 05/21 \ **DTBP:** $350 (High) \ ▮

Kevin Sprinkles 1	Missi Giesenschlag 2
Abbie Hanke 4	Tommy Brashear 6
Susan Pommerening 8,11,15	Jason Dohnalik 67

Public Schs..Principal	Grd	Prgm	Enr/#Cls	SN	
Ben Milam Elem Sch 1100 E 21st St, Cameron 76520 **Tracey Jordan**	PK-2	T	546 25	80%	254/697-3641 Fax 254/605-0354
C H Yoe High Sch 303 E 12th St, Cameron 76520 Joe Oliver	9-12	ATV	492	66%	254/697-3902 Fax 254/605-0413
Cameron Elem Sch 404 E 22nd St, Cameron 76520 Wendy Mahan	3-5	T	436 23	76%	254/697-2381 Fax 254/605-0356 ▮
Cameron Junior High Sch 404 E 22nd St, Cameron 76520 Wendy Mahan	6-8	ATV	380 27	75%	254/697-2131 Fax 254/605-0379

- **Gause Ind School Dist** PID: 01041801 979/279-5891
  400 College St, Gause 77857 Fax 979/279-5142

Schools: 1 \ **Teachers:** 16 \ **Students:** 170 \ **Special Ed Students:** 17 \ **LEP Students:** 18 \ **Ethnic:** Asian 1%, African American 14%, Hispanic 32%, Caucasian 53% \ **Exp:** $302 (High) \ **Poverty:** 36% \ **Title I:** $77,749 \ **Open-Close:** 08/15 - 05/21 \ **DTBP:** $150 (High)

Brad Jones 1,11,83,288	Diane Lazrine 2
Sondra Sheppard 4	Lynnette Taylor 16,73,295*
Samantha Russell 59,275*	Bill Jones 67

Public Schs..Principal	Grd	Prgm	Enr/#Cls	SN	
Gause Elem Sch 400 College St, Gause 77857 Brad Jones	PK-8	TV	170 17	62%	979/279-5891

- **Milano Ind School Dist** PID: 01041825 512/455-2533
  500 N 5th, Milano 76556 Fax 512/455-9311

Schools: 3 \ **Teachers:** 39 \ **Students:** 460 \ **Special Ed Students:** 34 \ **LEP Students:** 35 \ **College-Bound:** 75% \ **Ethnic:** Asian 1%, African American 6%, Hispanic 27%, Caucasian 66% \ **Exp:** $759 (High) \ **Poverty:** 32% \ **Title I:** $137,056 \ **Open-Close:** 08/21 - 05/28 \ **DTBP:** $368 (High)

Robert Westbrook 1	Stephanie Gage 2,11
Pat Yakesch 3	Dana Gage 4*
Eugene Urbanovsky 5	Wendy King 6*
Courtney Todd 12,57,296	Catrina Steinbecker 36,69,83,85,88
Angie Brashear 58	John Yakesch 67
Kevin Terry 73,295*	

Public Schs..Principal	Grd	Prgm	Enr/#Cls	SN	
Milano Elem Sch 500 N 5th, Milano 76556 Courtney Todd	PK-5	T	175 13	66%	512/455-2062 Fax 512/455-2267
Milano High Sch 600 N 6th St, Milano 76556 **Catrina Steinbecker**	9-12	TV	174 14	44%	512/455-9333 Fax 512/455-9336 ▮ ▮
Milano Junior High Sch 600 N 6th St, Milano 76556 Clint Mc Mahon	6-8	T	104 10	69%	512/455-6701 Fax 512/455-9186

- **Rockdale Ind School Dist** PID: 01041851 512/430-6000
  520 Davilla Street, Rockdale 76567 Fax 512/446-3460

Schools: 4 \ **Teachers:** 116 \ **Students:** 1,530 \ **Special Ed Students:** 140 \ **LEP Students:** 80 \ **College-Bound:** 49% \ **Ethnic:** Asian 1%, African American 11%, Hispanic 49%, Caucasian 39% \ **Exp:** $406 (High) \ **Poverty:** 25% \ **Title I:** $563,652 \ **Open-Close:** 08/15 - 05/28 \ **DTBP:** $350 (High) \ ▮ ▮

Dr Denise Monzingo 1	Genelle Korenek 2
Lance Weidler 3	Sheri Wheeler 4
Robert Hunter 5	Jeff Miller 6
Keari Spence 7*	Pam Kaufmann 8,11,15,58,288,296,298
Rebecca King 16,73,286	Bretina Pesak 27
Kelly Windham 38*	Micki Daniels 57
Troy Zinn 67	Keely Reisner 69,77*
Ken Sweich 73,76,295	Allen Sanders 83

Public Schs..Principal	Grd	Prgm	Enr/#Cls	SN	
Rockdale Elem Sch 625 W Belton Ave, Rockdale 76567 Alesha Eoff	PK-2	T	405 65	78%	512/430-6030 Fax 512/446-5229

---

79 Student Personnel	91 Safety/Security	275 Response To Intervention	298 Grant Writer/Ptnrships	**School Programs**	**Social Media**
80 Driver Ed/Safety	92 Magnet School	277 Remedial Math K-12	750 Chief Innovation Officer	A = Alternative Program	▮ = Facebook
81 Gifted/Talented	93 Parental Involvement	280 Literacy Coach	751 Chief of Staff	G = Adult Classes	▮ = Twitter
82 Video Services	95 Tech Prep Program	285 STEM	752 Social Emotional Learning	M = Magnet Program	
83 Substance Abuse Prev	97 Chief Infomation Officer	286 Digital Learning		T = Title I Schoolwide	
84 Erate	98 Chief Technology Officer	288 Common Core Standards	**Other School Types**	V = Career & Tech Ed Programs	
85 AIDS Education	270 Character Education	294 Accountability	Ⓐ = Alternative School		
88 Alternative/At Risk	271 Migrant Education	295 Network System	Ⓒ = Charter School	New Schools are shaded	
89 Multi-Cultural Curriculum	273 Teacher Mentor	296 Title II Programs	Ⓜ = Magnet School	New Superintendents and Principals are bold	
90 Social Work	274 Before/After Sch	297 Webmaster	Ⓨ = Year-Round School	Personnel with email addresses are underscored	

Mills County — Market Data Retrieval

Rockdale High Sch	9-12	TV	453	58%	512/430-6140
500 Childress Dr, Rockdale 76567			30		Fax 512/446-3512
Tiffany Whitsel					

Rockdale Intermediate Sch	3-5	T	335	69%	512/430-6200
1338 W US Highway 79, Rockdale 76567			21		Fax 512/446-3682
Kathy Pelzel					

Rockdale Junior High Sch	6-8	T	338	70%	512/430-6100
814 Bushdale Rd, Rockdale 76567			28		Fax 512/446-2597
Kelly Blair					

● **Thorndale Ind School Dist** PID: 01041904 — 512/898-2538
300 N Main St, Thorndale 76577 — Fax 512/898-5356

Schools: 3 \ *Teachers:* 51 \ *Students:* 567 \ *Special Ed Students:* 42 \ *LEP Students:* 37 \ *College-Bound:* 51% \ *Ethnic:* African American 1%, Hispanic 27%, Caucasian 71% \ *Exp:* $517 (High) \ *Poverty:* 17% \ *Title I:* $106,852 \ *Open-Close:* 08/14 - 05/22 \ *DTBP:* $375 (High)

Adam Ivy 1,11
Allen Leshber 3
Scott Hawkins 6*
Tricia Cabrera 36,88
Lisa Todd 68
Deby Leschber 73,286,295
Rebecca Peel 2
Bradley Dickerson 6*
Scott Frei 11,83*
David Hall 67
Jennifer Parnum 69*

Public Schs..Principal	Grd	Prgm	Enr/#Cls	SN
Thorndale Elem Sch	PK-5	T	215	57% 512/898-2912
300 N Main St, Thorndale 76577			10	Fax 512/898-5541
Michael Young				
Thorndale High Sch	9-12	TV	212	39% 512/898-2321
300 N Main St, Thorndale 76577			30	Fax 512/898-5090
Lee Hafley				
Thorndale Middle Sch	6-8	TV	140	42% 512/898-2670
300 N Main St, Thorndale 76577			9	Fax 512/898-5505
Scott Frei				

MILAM PRIVATE SCHOOLS

Private Schs..Principal	Grd	Prgm	Enr/#Cls	SN
St Paul Lutheran Sch	PK-8		97	512/898-2711
101 N 3rd St, Thorndale 76577			6	Fax 512/898-5298
David Mueller				

MILAM REGIONAL CENTERS

● **Burleson Milam Spec Serv Co-op** PID: 11551771 — 512/455-7801
400 E Park St, Milano 76556 — Fax 512/455-9681

Angie Brashear 1

MILLS COUNTY

MILLS PUBLIC SCHOOLS

● **Goldthwaite Consolidated ISD** PID: 01041942 — 325/648-3531
1509 Hanna Valley Rd, Goldthwaite 76844 — Fax 325/648-2456

Schools: 3 \ *Teachers:* 58 \ *Students:* 595 \ *Special Ed Students:* 48 \ *LEP Students:* 21 \ *Ethnic:* Asian 1%, Hispanic 27%, Caucasian 72% \ *Exp:* $774 (High) \ *Poverty:* 16% \ *Title I:* $323,629 \ *Open-Close:* 08/21 - 05/21 \ *DTBP:* $338 (High)

Ronny Wright 1,11,83
Ron Griffin 3
Becky Stewart 4*
Keith Virdell 6*
Cheryl Wright 36,69,88,270,271*
Donna Sanders 58
Jenice Benningfield 73,84,298
Glenn Benningfield 2
Becky Stewart 4
Angie Hermesmeyer 6,285*
Leslie Watson 7,85
Rosalinda Martinez 57*
Keri Roberts 67
Annette Watson 286*

Public Schs..Principal	Grd	Prgm	Enr/#Cls	SN
Goldthwaite Elem Sch	PK-5	T	269	54% 325/648-3055
1501 Campbell Street, Goldthwaite 76844			20	Fax 325/648-3528
Arla Wright				
Goldthwaite High Sch	9-12	TV	168	39% 325/648-3081
1509 Hanna Valley Rd, Goldthwaite 76844			20	Fax 325/648-2325
Rusty Hollingsworth				
Goldthwaite Middle Sch	6-8	T	137	46% 325/648-3630
1507 Trent St, Goldthwaite 76844			14	Fax 325/648-3571
Michael Sanderson				

● **Mullin Ind School Dist** PID: 01041978 — 325/985-3374
403 W Bulldog Dr, Mullin 76864 — Fax 325/985-3915

Schools: 6 \ *Teachers:* 40 \ *Students:* 94 \ *Special Ed Students:* 79 \ *LEP Students:* 10 \ *College-Bound:* 70% \ *Ethnic:* African American 20%, Hispanic 32%, Caucasian 48% \ *Exp:* $884 (High) \ *Poverty:* 23% \ *Title I:* $105,485 \ *Special Education:* $21,000 \ *Open-Close:* 08/28 - 06/25 \ *DTBP:* $392 (High)

Kristi Mickelson 1,73
Patricia Eldridge 4*
Justin Hopkins 42*
Marion Ferguson 67
Jesse Griffin 2*
Kristi Mickelson 8,11,83,271,294*
Becky Nelson 57*
Thomas Gravey 273

Public Schs..Principal	Grd	Prgm	Enr/#Cls	SN
Mullin Elem Sch	PK-6	T	53	95% 325/985-3374
403 W Bulldog Dr, Mullin 76864				Fax 325/985-3372
Bryndan Wright				
Mullin Middle High Sch	7-12	ATV	55	93% 325/985-3374
403 W Bulldog Dr, Mullin 76864			24	Fax 325/985-3372
Chayden Feist				
ⓐ Mullin Oaks Sch	9-12	T	91	97% 325/203-5315
800 FM 3254, Brownwood 76801				Fax 325/203-5316
Bryndan Wright				
ⓐ Parkview School-Levelland	K-12		20	806/568-1420
1515 5th St, Levelland 79336				Fax 806/568-1431
Jesse Jalomo				
Parkview School-Lubbock	K-12		17	806/568-1420
2402 Canyon Lake Dr, Lubbock 79415				Fax 806/568-1072
Dr Jesse Jalomo				

---

1 Superintendent	8 Curric/Instruct K-12	19 Chief Financial Officer	29 Family/Consumer Science	39 Social Studies K-12	49 English/Lang Arts Elem	59 Special Education Elem	69 Academic Assessment
2 Bus/Finance/Purchasing	9 Curric/Instruct Elem	20 Art K-12	30 Adult Education	40 Social Studies Elem	50 English/Lang Arts Sec	60 Special Education Sec	70 Research/Development
3 Buildings And Grounds	10 Curric/Instruct Sec	21 Art Elem	31 Career/Sch-to-Work K-12	41 Social Studies Sec	51 Reading K-12	61 Foreign/World Lang K-12	71 Public Information
4 Food Service	11 Federal Program	22 Art Sec	32 Career/Sch-to-Work Elem	42 Science K-12	52 Reading Elem	62 Foreign/World Lang Elem	72 Summer School
5 Transportation	12 Title I	23 Music K-12	33 Career/Sch-to-Work Sec	43 Science Elem	53 Reading Sec	63 Foreign/World Lang Sec	73 Instructional Tech
6 Athletic	13 Title V	24 Music Elem	34 Early Childhood Ed	44 Science Sec	54 Remedial Reading K-12	64 Religious Education K-12	74 Inservice Training
7 Health Services	15 Asst Superintendent	25 Music Sec	35 Health/Phys Education	45 Math K-12	55 Remedial Reading Elem	65 Religious Education Elem	75 Marketing/Distributive
	16 Instructional Media Svcs	26 Business Education	36 Guidance Services K-12	46 Math Elem	56 Remedial Reading Sec	66 Religious Education Sec	76 Info Systems
	17 Chief Operations Officer	27 Career & Tech Ed	37 Guidance Services Elem	47 Math Sec	57 Bilingual/ELL	67 School Board President	77 Psychological Assess
	18 Chief Academic Officer	28 Technology Education	38 Guidance Services Sec	48 English/Lang Arts K-12	58 Special Education K-12	68 Teacher Personnel	78 Affirmative Action

Texas School Directory

Ⓐ Pecan Ridge High Sch 9-12 94 97% 325/372-4091
PO Box 128, Mullin 76864
Sara McDowell

• **Priddy Ind School Dist** PID: 01042001 325/966-3323
1375 Highway 16, Priddy 76870 Fax 325/966-3380

Schools: 1 \ **Teachers:** 16 \ **Students:** 111 \ **Special Ed Students:** 13 \ **College-Bound:** 25% \ **Ethnic:** African American 1%, Hispanic 30%, Caucasian 70% \ **Exp:** $424 (High) \ **Poverty:** 18% \ **Title I:** $16,232 \ **Open-Close:** 08/14 - 05/20 \ **DTBP:** $346 (High) \ 📘

Dr Adrianne Burden 1,11,57,73,83,84
Landon Buffe 27*
Dean Cagle 67
John Smith 286*
Melanie Connally 2
Stephanie Smith 58*
Tani Menchaca 271

Public Schs..Principal	Grd	Prgm	Enr/#Cls	SN		
Priddy Sch 1375 Highway 16, Priddy 76870 Carl Spruell	PK-12	TV	111 13	75%	325/966-3323	

MITCHELL COUNTY

MITCHELL PUBLIC SCHOOLS

• **Colorado Ind School Dist** PID: 01042063 325/728-5312
534 E 11th St, Colorado City 79512 Fax 325/728-1015

Schools: 4 \ **Teachers:** 79 \ **Students:** 940 \ **Special Ed Students:** 96 \ **LEP Students:** 22 \ **College-Bound:** 51% \ **Ethnic:** Asian 1%, African American 10%, Hispanic 49%, Caucasian 39% \ **Exp:** $479 (High) \ **Poverty:** 25% \ **Title I:** $302,704 \ **Open-Close:** 08/15 - 05/20 \ **DTBP:** $341 (High)

Reggy Spencer 1
Becky Sanford 4
Dan Gainey 6*
Denise Farmer 8,12,15,83,88,296
Kaci Griffith 38*
Pam Alvarez 73,295*
Shelia Redwine 2,11
Robert Oliver 5
Kelsee Graham 7,85*
Jody Womack 37*
Sally Neff 67

Public Schs..Principal	Grd	Prgm	Enr/#Cls	SN		
Colorado Elem Sch 1244 E 10th St, Colorado City 79512 Melinda Alexander	PK-2		284 19		325/728-3471 Fax 325/728-1036	
Colorado High Sch 1500 Lone Wolf Blvd, Colorado City 79512 Rebecca Russell	9-12	T	284 30	46%	325/728-3424 Fax 325/728-1068	
Colorado Middle Sch 1244 E 10th St, Colorado City 79512 Robby Russell	3-8		426 20		325/728-2673 Fax 325/728-1051	
Wallace Accelerated High Sch 149 S Highway 208, Colorado City 79512 Steven Reese	9-12	T	13	77%	325/728-2392 Fax 325/728-1025	

Montague County

• **Loraine Ind School Dist** PID: 01042128 325/737-2225
800 S Lightfoot St, Loraine 79532 Fax 325/737-2701

Schools: 1 \ **Teachers:** 17 \ **Students:** 160 \ **Special Ed Students:** 13 \ **LEP Students:** 3 \ **College-Bound:** 50% \ **Ethnic:** African American 6%, Hispanic 53%, Native American: 1%, Caucasian 40% \ **Exp:** $666 (High) \ **Poverty:** 22% \ **Title I:** $95,469 \ **Open-Close:** 08/19 - 05/22 \ **DTBP:** $408 (High)

Dustin Anders 1
Teresa Bruton 4*
Michael Barrientez 31*
Ron Gibson 67
Debbie Finley 2
Jacob Popham 6*
Jana Edmonds 58*
John Rawlings 73,295

Public Schs..Principal	Grd	Prgm	Enr/#Cls	SN		
Loraine Sch 800 S Lightfoot St, Loraine 79532 Dustin Anders	PK-12	TV	160 21	72%	325/737-2225	

• **Westbrook Ind School Dist** PID: 01042154 325/644-2311
102 Bertner St, Westbrook 79565 Fax 325/644-5101

Schools: 1 \ **Teachers:** 26 \ **Students:** 272 \ **Special Ed Students:** 32 \ **College-Bound:** 50% \ **Ethnic:** African American 1%, Hispanic 33%, Native American: 1%, Caucasian 66% \ **Exp:** $1,312 (High) \ **Poverty:** 32% \ **Title I:** $60,147 \ **Open-Close:** 08/15 - 05/22 \ **DTBP:** $374 (High)

Todd Burleson 1
Nick Lopez 3,5*
Jim Hill 6*
Peggy Hill 12,57*
Hayden Walters 58*
Renee Dawson 67
Leslie Moody 2
Jackie Waldrep 4*
Sherry Rowden 8*
Carolyn Redwine 16,82*
Tina Miles 59*
Jackie White 73*

Public Schs..Principal	Grd	Prgm	Enr/#Cls	SN		
Westbrook Sch 102 Bertner St, Westbrook 79565 Sherry Rowden	PK-12	T	272 16	33%	325/644-2311 Fax 325/644-5101	

MONTAGUE COUNTY

MONTAGUE PUBLIC SCHOOLS

• **Bowie Ind School Dist** PID: 01042180 940/872-1151
100 W Wichita St, Bowie 76230 Fax 940/872-5979

Schools: 4 \ **Teachers:** 128 \ **Students:** 1,720 \ **Special Ed Students:** 165 \ **LEP Students:** 93 \ **Ethnic:** African American 1%, Hispanic 18%, Native American: 1%, Caucasian 80% \ **Exp:** $287 (Med) \ **Poverty:** 19% \ **Title I:** $395,990 \ **Open-Close:** 08/22 - 05/22 \ **DTBP:** $369 (High)

Blake Enlow 1
Lauri Crescenzo 5
Brant Farris 16,286,297
Jim Britt 73,84,295
John Meek 3
Christie Walker 8,11,57,58,77,88,288,294
Jacky Betts 67
Brad Costello 88

Public Schs..Principal	Grd	Prgm	Enr/#Cls	SN		
Bowie Elem Sch 405 Lovers Ln, Bowie 76230 Steven Valkenaar	PK-2	T	458 28	67%	940/689-2950 Fax 940/872-3041	

---

79 Student Personnel
80 Driver Ed/Safety
81 Gifted/Talented
82 Video Services
83 Substance Abuse Prev
84 Erate
85 AIDS Education
88 Alternative/At Risk
89 Multi-Cultural Curriculum
90 Social Work

91 Safety/Security
92 Magnet School
93 Parental Involvement
95 Tech Prep Program
97 Chief Information Officer
98 Chief Technology Officer
270 Accountability
271 Migrant Education
273 Teacher Mentor
274 Before/After Sch

275 Response To Intervention
277 Remedial Math K-12
280 Literacy Coach
285 STEM
286 Digital Learning
288 Common Core Standards
294 Character Education
295 Network System
296 Title II Programs
297 Webmaster

298 Grant Writer/Ptnrships
750 Chief Innovation Officer
751 Chief of Staff
752 Social Emotional Learning

Other School Types
Ⓐ = Alternative School
Ⓒ = Charter School
Ⓜ = Magnet School
Ⓨ = Year-Round School

School Programs
A = Alternative Program
G = Adult Classes
M = Magnet Program
T = Title I Schoolwide
V = Career & Tech Ed Programs

New Schools are shaded
New Superintendents and Principals are bold
Personnel with email addresses are underscored

Social Media
📘 = Facebook
🐦 = Twitter

Montague County

Market Data Retrieval

Bowie High Sch 9-12 TV 498 44% 940/689-2840
341 US Highway 287 N Access Rd, Bowie 76230   50   Fax 940/689-2922
Sergio Menchaca

Bowie Intermediate Sch 3-5 T 382 53% 940/689-2895
800 N Mill St, Bowie 76230   40   Fax 940/872-1299
Russell Black

Bowie Junior High Sch 6-8 T 376 52% 940/689-2975
501 E Tarrant St, Bowie 76230   28   Fax 940/872-8921
Jeneanne Fleming

- **Forestburg Ind School Dist** PID: 01042257 940/964-2323
  16346 Highway 455 W, Forestburg 76239 Fax 940/964-2531

> **Schools:** 1 \ **Teachers:** 18 \ **Students:** 160 \ **Special Ed Students:** 19 \
> **College-Bound:** 95% \ **Ethnic:** Hispanic 14%, Caucasian 86% \ **Exp:** $512
> (High) \ **Poverty:** 16% \ **Title I:** $29,667 \ **Open-Close:** 08/15 - 05/22 \
> **DTBP:** $350 (High) \

John Metzler 1   Cori Hayes 6*
Candi Raney ....11*   Karen Wiley 51,54,270*
Julie Sandusky ....58*   Jimmy Raney 67
Rich Lewis 73,286*

Public Schs..Principal	Grd	Prgm	Enr/#Cls	SN	
Forestburg Sch 10346 Highway 455 W, Forestburg 76239 Karen Wiley	PK-12	GTV	160 25	47%	940/964-2323

- **Gold-Burg Ind School Dist** PID: 01042283 940/872-3562
  468 Prater Rd, Bowie 76230 Fax 940/872-5933

> **Schools:** 1 \ **Teachers:** 15 \ **Students:** 140 \ **Special Ed Students:** 11 \
> **LEP Students:** 5 \ **College-Bound:** 82% \ **Ethnic:** Hispanic 11%, Native
> American: 1%, Caucasian 88% \ **Exp:** $748 (High) \ **Poverty:** 22% \
> **Title I:** $33,111 \ **Open-Close:** 08/15 - 05/22

Roger Ellis 1   Carla Karl 3*
Thomas Flinchum ....8,11,36,69,83,88* Charlotte Haley 16,73,286*
David Winingham ......41*   Pam Demoss 58*
Becky Case 67

Public Schs..Principal	Grd	Prgm	Enr/#Cls	SN	
Gold-Burg Sch 468 Prater Rd, Bowie 76230 Thomas Flinchum	PK-12	TV	140 18	58%	940/872-3562

- **Montague Ind School Dist** PID: 01042312 940/894-2811
  8020 Highway 175, Montague 76251 Fax 940/894-6605

> **Schools:** 1 \ **Teachers:** 10 \ **Students:** 160 \ **Special Ed Students:** 13 \
> **Ethnic:** Hispanic 9%, Caucasian 91% \ **Exp:** $320 (High) \ **Poverty:** 29% \
> **Title I:** $33,722 \ **Open-Close:** 08/19 - 05/22 \ **DTBP:** $350 (High)

Carla Hennessey 1,11,83   T Thompson 2
Todd Minor 3,5   Stephanie Love 4
Angela Kleinhans ....16,73*   Taygon Jones 67

Public Schs..Principal	Grd	Prgm	Enr/#Cls	SN	
Montague Elem Sch 8020 Highway 175, Montague 76251 Angela Kleinhans	PK-8	T	160 8	48%	940/894-2811

- **Nocona Ind School Dist** PID: 01042336 940/825-3267
  220 Clay St, Nocona 76255 Fax 940/825-4945

> **Schools:** 3 \ **Teachers:** 73 \ **Students:** 770 \ **Special Ed Students:** 83 \
> **LEP Students:** 89 \ **College-Bound:** 63% \ **Ethnic:** African American 1%,
> Hispanic 32%, Native American: 1%, Caucasian 66% \ **Exp:** $562 (High) \
> **Poverty:** 25% \ **Title I:** $264,177 \ **Open-Close:** 08/15 - 05/28 \ **DTBP:** $358
> (High)

David Waters 1   Paula Peterson 2
John Blim ....3,5*   Walter Waters 4
Bradley Keck ....6*   Sandy Phipps 16,82*
Tracy Pierce ....57,271,275* Guy Hill 67
Deborah Ulibarri ....69,88*   Malissa Swofford 73,76*
Karri Hackley 81*

Public Schs..Principal	Grd	Prgm	Enr/#Cls	SN	
Nocona Elem Sch 300 Montague St, Nocona 76255 Rod Bailey	PK-5	T	360 29	71%	940/825-3151 Fax 940/825-4253
Nocona High Sch 1012 Clay St, Nocona 76255 Stephanie Wright	9-12	TV	244 34	51%	940/825-3264 Fax 940/825-7270
Nocona Middle Sch 220 Clay St, Nocona 76255 Amy Murphey	6-8	T	176 12	59%	940/825-3121 Fax 940/825-6151

- **Prairie Valley Ind School Dist** PID: 01042374 940/825-4425
  12920 FM 103, Nocona 76255 Fax 940/825-4650

> **Schools:** 1 \ **Teachers:** 16 \ **Students:** 170 \ **Special Ed Students:** 13 \
> **College-Bound:** 75% \ **Ethnic:** Hispanic 8%, Caucasian 92% \ **Exp:** $253
> (Med) \ **Poverty:** 17% \ **Title I:** $22,213 \ **Open-Close:** 08/15 - 05/22 \
> **DTBP:** $181 (High)

Tim West 1,84   Brittany Womack 27*
Krysta Woods ....29*   Jesse Kincy 60*
Scott Carpenter 67   Carol Luton 69*
Stacey Ward ....73*   Cathy Harris 79

Public Schs..Principal	Grd	Prgm	Enr/#Cls	SN	
Prairie Valley Sch 12920 FM 103, Nocona 76255 Lisa Sadler	PK-12	T	170 18	57%	940/825-4425

- **St Jo Ind School Dist** PID: 01042403 940/995-2668
  206 W Evans St, Saint Jo 76265 Fax 940/995-2026

> **Schools:** 2 \ **Teachers:** 28 \ **Students:** 283 \ **Special Ed Students:** 35
> \ **LEP Students:** 3 \ **College-Bound:** 60% \ **Ethnic:** Hispanic 13%,
> Native American: 1%, Caucasian 86% \ **Exp:** $500 (High) \ **Poverty:** 9% \
> **Title I:** $41,191 \ **Open-Close:** 08/26 - 05/29 \ **DTBP:** $356 (High) \

Curtis Elridge 1   Cherkoee Brewer 3,5
Kelly Durham ....36,69*   Jerry Bray 60*
Leeton Phillips 67   Julie Kline 73,76,82*
Denise Thurman 83*

Public Schs..Principal	Grd	Prgm	Enr/#Cls	SN	
St Jo Elem Sch 206 W Evans St, Saint Jo 76265 Denise Thurman	PK-6	T	152 11	52%	940/995-2541
St Jo High Sch 206 W Evans St, Saint Jo 76265 Katie Morman	7-12	TV	131 13	50%	940/995-2532 Fax 940/995-2087

#		#		#		#		#		#		#	
1	Superintendent	8	Curric/Instruct K-12	19	Chief Financial Officer	29	Family/Consumer Science	39	Social Studies K-12	49	English/Lang Arts Elem	59	Special Education Elem	69	Academic Assessment
2	Bus/Finance/Purchasing	9	Curric/Instruct Elem	20	Art K-12	30	Adult Education	40	Social Studies Sec	50	English/Lang Arts Sec	60	Special Education Sec	70	Research/Development
3	Buildings And Grounds	10	Curric/Instruct Sec	21	Art Elem	31	Career/Sch-to-Work K-12	41	Social Studies Sec	51	Reading K-12	61	Foreign/World Lang K-12	71	Public Information
4	Food Service	11	Federal Program	22	Art Sec	32	Career/Sch-to-Work Elem	42	Science K-12	52	Reading Elem	62	Foreign/World Lang Elem	72	Summer School
5	Transportation	12	Title I	23	Music K-12	33	Career/Sch-to-Work Sec	43	Science Elem	53	Reading Sec	63	Foreign/World Lang Sec	73	Instructional Tech
6	Athletic	13	Title V	24	Music Elem	34	Early Childhood Ed	44	Science Sec	54	Remedial Reading K-12	64	Religious Education K-12	74	Inservice Training
7	Health Services	15	Asst Superintendent	25	Music Sec	35	Health/Phys Education	45	Math K-12	55	Remedial Reading Elem	65	Religious Education Elem	75	Marketing/Distributive
		16	Instructional Media Svcs	26	Business Education	36	Guidance Services K-12	46	Math Elem	56	Remedial Reading Sec	66	Religious Education Sec	76	Info Systems
		17	Chief Operations Officer	27	Career & Tech Ed	37	Guidance Services Elem	47	Math Sec	57	Bilingual/ELL	67	School Board President	77	Psychological Assess
		18	Chief Academic Officer	28	Technology Education	38	Guidance Services Sec	48	English/Lang Arts K 12	58	Special Education K-12	68	Teacher Personnel	78	Affirmative Action

Texas School Directory

Montgomery County

MONTGOMERY COUNTY

MONTGOMERY PUBLIC SCHOOLS

• **Conroe Ind School Dist** PID: 01042439   936/709-7752
3205 W Davis St, Conroe 77304   Fax 936/709-9701

Schools: 64 \ **Teachers:** 3,628 \ **Students:** 63,000 \
Special Ed Students: 4,839 \ **LEP Students:** 7,700 \ **College-Bound:** 58%
\ **Ethnic:** Asian 4%, African American 7%, Hispanic 37%, Caucasian
50% \ **Exp:** $250 (Med) \ **Poverty:** 9% \ **Title I:** $8,598,048 \
Special Education: $10,658,000 \ **Open-Close:** 08/14 - 05/28 \ **DTBP:** $181
(High)

Dr Curtis Null 1	Darrin Rice 2,19
Rick Reeves 2	Easy Foster 3
Marshall Schroeder 3	Robyn Hughes 4
Sam Davila 5	Danny Long 6
Rodrigo Chaves 7,30,88,93,271	Dr Hedith Sauceda-Upshaw 8,74,273
Dr Pamela Zoda 11,298	Dr Chris Hines 15
Krissy Calhoun 16,73	Dr Robert Horton 20,23
Greg Shipp 27,31	Dr R Matthew Clark 31
Jepilyn Matthis 34,49	Dr Sharon Sterchy 35
Denise Cipolla 36	Richard Woodruff 39
Sheryl Hime 42	Holly Berger 45
Debra McNeely 50,63	Dayren Carlisle 57
Lauren Hickman 58	Teresa Canon 58,77
Datren Williams 67	Dr Kathy Sharples 68
Dr Tamika Taylor 69,294	Teri Ross 76,295
Kim Earthman 79	Chris Reichelt 81
Bill Harness 91	

Public Schs..Principal	Grd	Prgm	Enr/#Cls SN	
Academy Careers Engr Science 27330 Oak Ridge School Rd, Conroe 77385 Dr Michael Papadimitriou	9-9		77	832/482-6700 Fax 832/482-6706
Academy of Science & Tech 3701 College Park Dr, The Woodlands 77384 Dr Susan Caffery	9-12		285 8	936/709-3250 Fax 936/709-3299
ⓜ Academy-Science & Health Prof 3200 W Davis St, Conroe 77304 Terri Benson	9-12		385	936/709-5731 Fax 936/709-5842
Anderson Elem Sch 1414 E Dallas St, Conroe 77301 Laura Acevedo	PK-4	T	646 50	82% 936/709-5300 Fax 936/709-5312
Armstrong Elem Sch 110 Gladstell St, Conroe 77301 Patricia Thacker	PK-4	T	700 25	91% 936/709-3400 Fax 936/709-3415
Austin Elem Sch 14796 Highway 105 E, Conroe 77306 Dr Serena Pierson	PK-4	T	1,014 30	76% 936/709-8400 Fax 936/709-8403
Birnham Woods Elem Sch 31150 Birnham Woods Dr, Spring 77386 Natalie Buckley	PK-4		984	11% 832/663-4200 Fax 832/863-4299
Bozman Intermediate Sch 800 Beach Airport Rd, Conroe 77301 Amber Debeaumont	5-6	T	797	64% 936/709-1800 Fax 936/709-1899
Bradley Elem Sch 4200 Falls Lake Dr, Spring 77386 Dr Christine Butler	PK-4		793	832/482-6800 Fax 832/482-6899
Buckalew Elem Sch 4909 Alden Bridge Dr, The Woodlands 77382 Jill Price	PK-4		632 48	3% 281/465-3400 Fax 281/465-3499
Bush Elem Sch 7420 Crownridge Dr, The Woodlands 77382 **Dr Jarod Lambert**	PK-4		732 55	10% 936/709-1600 Fax 936/709-1699
Caney Creek High Sch 13470 FM 1485 Rd, Conroe 77306 Jeffrey Stichler	9-12	TV	2,042 65	66% 936/709-2000 Fax 936/709-2099
Clark Intermediate Sch 4182 Trench Ln, Spring 77386 Lindsay Ardoin	5-6		801	281/939-0600 Fax 281/939-0699
Colin Powell Elem Sch 7332 Cochrans Crossing Dr, The Woodlands 77381 Lisa Garrison	PK-4		897 45	11% 936/709-1700 Fax 936/709-1799 f t
Collins Intermediate Sch 6020 Shadow Bend Pl, The Woodlands 77381 Shelli LeBlanc	5-6		757 24	9% 281/298-3800 Fax 281/298-3803
Conroe 9th Grade High Sch 400 Sgt Ed Holcomb Blvd N, Conroe 77304 Dennis Gorka	9-9	A	1,000	936/709-4000 Fax 936/709-4099
Conroe High Sch 3200 W Davis St, Conroe 77304 Rotasha Smith	10-12	TV	2,600	58% 936/709-5700 Fax 936/709-5772
Coulson Tough Elem Sch 11660 Cranebrook Dr, Spring 77382 Shawn Creswell	PK-6		889	2% 281/465-5900 Fax 281/465-5959
Creighton Elem Sch 12089 FM 1485 Rd, Conroe 77306 Jennifer Watson	PK-4	T	876 45	81% 936/709-2900 Fax 936/709-2999
Cryar Intermediate Sch 2375 Montgomery Park Blvd, Conroe 77304 Bethany Medford	5-6	T	707	55% 936/709-7300 Fax 936/709-7313
David Elem Sch 5301 Shadow Bend Pl, The Woodlands 77381 Lee Allen	PK-4		707	9% 281/298-4700 Fax 281/298-4703
Deretchin Elem Sch 11000 Merit Oaks Dr, The Woodlands 77382 Alicia Reeves	PK-6		949	4% 832/592-8700 Fax 832/592-8780
Dolly F Vogel Intermediate Sch 27125 Geffert Wright Rd, Spring 77386 **Christa Haymark**	5-6	T	1,104	38% 832/663-4300 Fax 832/663-4399
Ford Elem Sch 25460 Richards Rd, Spring 77386 Paola Gorman	PK-4	T	833	50% 832/592-5700 Fax 832/592-5709
Galatas Elem Sch 9001 Cochrans Crossing Dr, The Woodlands 77381 Denae Wilker	PK-4		639 40	2% 936/709-5000 Fax 936/709-5003
Giesinger Elem Sch 2323 White Oak Blvd, Conroe 77304 **Melissa Ralston**	PK-4		702 44	25% 936/709-2600 Fax 936/709-2699
Glen Loch Elem Sch 27505 Glen Loch Dr, The Woodlands 77381 Cassie Hertzenberg	PK-4		676 40	44% 281/298-4900 Fax 281/298-4903
Grand Oaks High Sch 4800 Riley Fuzzel Rd, Spring 77386 Dr Christopher Povich	9-10		1,300	281/939-0000 Fax 281/939-0099
Grangerland Interm Sch 16283 FM 3083 Rd, Conroe 77302 Karen Jones	5-6	T	1,092 45	77% 936/709-3500 Fax 936/709-3565
Hailey Elem Sch 12051 Sawmill Rd, The Woodlands 77380 Tracy Horne	PK-4		786 34	39% 832/663-4100 Fax 832/663-4199
ⓐ Hauke Academic Alt High Sch 701 N 3rd St, Conroe 77301 John Williams	8-12	TV	142 22	58% 936/709-3420 Fax 936/709-3499
Houser Elem Sch 27370 Oak Ridge School Rd, Conroe 77385 Angela Lozano	PK-4	T	824 50	54% 832/663-4000 Fax 832/663-4076

79 Student Personnel	91 Safety/Security	275 Response To Intervention	298 Grant Writer/Ptnrships	**School Programs**	**Social Media**
80 Driver Ed/Safety	92 Magnet School	277 Remedial Math K-12	750 Chief Innovation Officer	A = Alternative Program	
81 Gifted/Talented	93 Parental Involvement	280 Literacy Coach	751 Chief of Staff	G = Adult Classes	f = Facebook
82 Video Services	95 Tech Prep Program	285 STEM	752 Social Emotional Learning	M = Magnet Program	
83 Substance Abuse Prev	97 Chief Infomation Officer	286 Digital Learning		T = Title I Schoolwide	t = Twitter
84 Erate	98 Chief Technology Officer	288 Common Core Standards	**Other School Types**	V = Career & Tech Ed Programs	
85 AIDS Education	270 Character Education	294 Accountability	ⓐ = Alternative School		
88 Alternative/At Risk	271 Migrant Education	295 Network System	ⓒ = Charter School	New Schools are shaded	
89 Multi-Cultural Curriculum	273 Teacher Mentor	296 Title II Programs	ⓜ = Magnet School	New Superintendents and Principals are bold	
90 Social Work	274 Before/After Sch	297 Webmaster	ⓨ = Year-Round School	Personnel with email addresses are underscored	

TX—291

Montgomery County

Houston Elem Sch — PK-4 — T — 680 / 35 — 90% — 936/709-5100 — Fax 936/709-5103
1000 N Thompson St, Conroe 77301
Viviana Harris

Irons Junior High Sch — 7-8 — V — 1,088 — 31% — 936/709-8500 — Fax 936/709-8599
16780 Needham Rd, Conroe 77385
Jeff Fuller

Jean E Stewart Elem Sch — PK-6 — 729 — 22% — 936/709-4200 — Fax 936/709-4299
680 Fish Creek Thoroughfare, Montgomery 77316
Julie English

Kaufman Elem Sch — PK-4 — 866 — 13% — 832/592-5600 — Fax 832/592-5617
2760 Northridge Forest Dr D, Spring 77386
Tina Oliver

Knox Junior High Sch — 7-8 — V — 1,415 / 80 — 19% — 832/592-8400 — Fax 832/592-8410
12104 Sawmill Rd, The Woodlands 77380
Donny Daw

Lamar Elem Sch — PK-4 — 741 / 36 — 33% — 832/592-5800 — Fax 832/592-5810
1300 Many Pines Rd, The Woodlands 77380
Kristen Belcher

McCullough Junior High Sch — 7-8 — V — 2,208 — 6% — 832/592-5100 — Fax 832/592-5116
3800 S Panther Creek Dr, Spring 77381
Robert McCord

Milam Elem Sch — PK-4 — T — 784 / 43 — 76% — 936/709-5200 — Fax 936/709-5203
16415 FM 3083 Rd, Conroe 77302
Gilberto Lozano

Mitchell Intermediate Sch — 5-6 — 1,242 / 40 — 6% — 832/592-8500 — Fax 832/592-8518
6800 Alden Bridge Dr, The Woodlands 77382
Paula Klapesky

Moorhead Junior High Sch — 7-8 — TV — 1,102 / 60 — 72% — 936/709-2400 — Fax 936/709-2499
13475 FM 1485 Rd, Conroe 77306
Roberto Garcia

Oak Ridge Elem Sch — PK-4 — T — 751 / 24 — 43% — 832/592-5900 — Fax 832/592-5968
19675 Interstate 45 S, Conroe 77385
Tami Eldridge

Oak Ridge High Sch — 10-12 — V — 2,839 / 125 — 24% — 832/592-5300 — Fax 832/592-5544
27330 Oak Ridge School Rd, Conroe 77385
Dr Michael Papadimitriou

Oak Ridge HS 9th Grade Campus — 9-9 — V — 1,179 — 281/465-5000 — Fax 281/465-5099
27310 Oak Ridge School Rd, Conroe 77385
Melanie Bujnoch

Patterson Elem Sch — PK-4 — T — 802 — 72% — 936/709-4300 — Fax 936/709-4399
670 Beach Airport Rd, Conroe 77301
Julie Miller

Peet Junior High Sch — 7-8 — TV — 1,426 — 52% — 936/709-3700 — Fax 936/709-3828
1895 Longmire Rd, Conroe 77304
Christopher Kuempel

Reaves Elem Sch — PK-4 — T — 708 / 38 — 71% — 936/709-5400 — Fax 936/709-5407
1717 N Loop 336 W, Conroe 77304
Nicole Walker

Rice Elem Sch — PK-4 — T — 595 / 26 — 58% — 936/709-2700 — Fax 936/709-2799
904 Gladstell Rd, Conroe 77304
Malinda Stewart

Runyan Elem Sch — PK-4 — T — 606 / 40 — 78% — 936/709-2800 — Fax 936/709-2899
1101 Foster Dr, Conroe 77301
Tracy Voelker

Sally K Ride Elem Sch — PK-4 — 728 — 9% — 281/465-2800 — Fax 281/465-2803
4920 W Panther Creek Dr, The Woodlands 77381
Megan Burnham

San Jacinto Elem Sch — PK-4 — T — 708 / 41 — 78% — 281/465-7700 — Fax 281/465-7799
17601 FM 1314 Rd, Conroe 77302
Jamie Almond

Snyder Elem Sch — PK-4 — 949 — 17% — 832/663-4400 — Fax 832/663-4499
28601 Birnham Woods Dr, Spring 77386
Crystal Poncho

Suchma Elementary — PK-6 — 897 — 936/709-4400 — Fax 936/709-4499
10261 Harpers School Rd, Conroe 77301
Dr Tara Vandermark

Sue Park Broadway Elem Sch — PK-4 — 891 — 11% — 281/465-2900 — Fax 281/465-2903
2855 Spring Trails Bnd, Spring 77386
Shannon Conley

The Woodlands High Sch — 10-12 — V — 3,234 — 3% — 936/709-1200 — Fax 936/709-1299
6101 Research Forest Dr, The Woodlands 77381
Ted Landry

The Woodlands HS-9th GR Campus — 9-9 — V — 1,108 — 832/592-8200 — Fax 832/592-8299
10010 Branch Crossing Dr, The Woodlands 77382
Jill Houser

The Woodlands-College Park HS — 9-12 — 3,101 — 14% — 936/709-3000 — Fax 936/709-3019
3701 College Park Dr, The Woodlands 77384
Dr Mark Murrell

Tom Cox Intermediate Sch — 5-6 — 1,478 — 15% — 281/465-3200 — Fax 281/465-3299
3333 Waterbend Cv, Spring 77386
Deborah Spoon

Travis Intermediate Sch — 5-6 — T — 647 / 30 — 92% — 936/709-7000 — Fax 936/709-7019
1100 N Thompson St, Conroe 77301
Charita Smith

Washington Junior High Sch — 7-8 — TV — 758 / 65 — 85% — 936/709-7400 — Fax 936/709-7492
507 Dr Mlk Pl N, Conroe 77301
Hartwell Brown

Wilkerson Intermediate Sch — 5-6 — 785 / 45 — 37% — 832/592-8900 — Fax 832/592-8910
12312 Sawmill Rd, The Woodlands 77380
Jennifer Daw

Wilkinson Elem Sch — PK-4 — T — 714 — 38% — 936/709-1500 — Fax 936/709-1599
2575 Ed Kharbat Dr, Conroe 77301
Victor Uher

York Junior High Sch — 7-8 — V — 1,379 / 68 — 16% — 832/592-8600 — Fax 832/592-8684
3515 Waterbend Cv, Spring 77386
Brian Lee

• **Magnolia Ind School Dist** PID: 01042582 — 281/356-3571 — Fax 281/252-2235
31141 Nichols Sawmill Rd, Magnolia 77355

Schools: 16 \ *Teachers:* 843 \ *Students:* 13,100 \
Special Ed Students: 1,097 \ *LEP Students:* 1,539 \ *College-Bound:* 70%
\ *Ethnic:* Asian 1%, African American 2%, Hispanic 34%, Native American: 1%, Caucasian 62% \ *Exp:* $270 (Med) \ *Poverty:* 16% \ *Title I:* $2,942,879 \ *Special Education:* $1,766,000 \ *Open-Close:* 08/14 - 05/22 \ *DTBP:* $169 (High) \

Dr Todd Stephens	1	Adam Stearns	2
Erich Morris	2,15	Allen Meeks	3
Kimberly Ohlendorf	4	Joe Dives	5
JD Berna	6	Amy Locker	8,69
Brandon Garza	11,36,275,294	Tammy Haley	13,58
Anita Hebert	15	Dr Jason Bullock	15
Foy Cambell	20,23	Rod Leer	27,31,39
Sherry Galamore	42	Susan Johnson	45
Shay Garland	48	Nancy Rodriguez	57
Kendra Wiggins	58	Gary Blizzard	67
Sam Bell	68	Denise Meyer	71
Rob Stewart	79,91	Mona Johnson	286

Public Schs..Principal	Grd	Prgm	Enr/#Cls	SN		
ⒶAlpha Academy 919 Cloyd Dr, Magnolia 77355 Bryan Cooper	9-12	T	101 10	41%	281/252-2265 Fax 281/252-2268	
ⒶAlternative Education Ctr 919 Cloyd Dr, Magnolia 77355 Fowler Robert	9-12		120		281/252-2275 Fax 281/252-2278	
Bear Branch Elem Sch 8909 FM 1488 Rd, Magnolia 77354 Jim Gassaway	K-4		637 38	19%	281/356-4771 Fax 281/252-2074	
Bear Branch Intermediate Sch 8040 Ken Lake Dr, Magnolia 77354 Tommy Burns	5-6		1,200		281/252-2031 Fax 281/252-2032	

1 Superintendent	8 Curric/Instruct K-12	19 Chief Financial Officer	29 Family/Consumer Science	39 Social Studies K-12	49 English/Lang Arts Elem	59 Special Education Elem	69 Academic Assessment
2 Bus/Finance/Purchasing	9 Curric/Instruct Elem	20 Art K-12	30 Adult Education	40 Social Studies Elem	50 English/Lang Arts Sec	60 Special Education Sec	70 Research/Development
3 Buildings And Grounds	10 Curric/Instruct Sec	21 Art Elem	31 Career/Sch-to-Work K-12	41 Social Studies Sec	51 Reading K-12	61 Foreign/World Lang K-12	71 Public Information
4 Food Service	11 Federal Program	22 Art Sec	32 Career/Sch-to-Work Elem	42 Science K-12	52 Reading Elem	62 Foreign/World Lang Elem	72 Summer School
5 Transportation	12 Title I	23 Music K-12	33 Career/Sch-to-Work Sec	43 Science Elem	53 Reading Sec	63 Foreign/World Lang Sec	73 Instructional Tech
6 Athletic	13 Title V	24 Music Elem	34 Early Childhood Ed	44 Science Sec	54 Remedial Reading K-12	64 Religious Education K-12	74 Inservice Training
7 Health Services	15 Asst Superintendent	25 Music Sec	35 Health/Phys Education	45 Math K-12	55 Remedial Reading Elem	65 Religious Education Elem	75 Marketing/Distributive
	16 Instructional Media Svcs	26 Business Education	36 Guidance Services K-12	46 Math Elem	56 Remedial Reading Sec	66 Religious Education Sec	76 Info Systems
	17 Chief Operations Officer	27 Career & Tech Ed	37 Guidance Services Elem	47 Math Sec	57 Bilingual/ELL	67 School Board President	77 Psychological Assess
	18 Chief Academic Officer	28 Technology Education	38 Guidance Services Soc	48 English/Lang Arts K-12	58 Special Education K-12	68 Teacher Personnel	78 Affirmative Action

Texas School Directory — Montgomery County

School	Grd	Prgm	Enr/#Cls	SN	Phone
Bear Branch Junior High Sch 31310 FM 2978 Rd, Magnolia 77354 **Ben Petty**	7-8	V	977 56	29%	281/356-6088 Fax 281/252-2060
Cedric C Smith Elem Sch 28747 Hardin Store Rd, Magnolia 77354 Dion Rivera	PK-5	T	804 30	62%	281/252-2300 Fax 281/252-2304
J L Lyons Elem Sch 27035 Nichols Sawmill Rd, Magnolia 77355 Erin Vance	PK-5	T	819 50	61%	281/356-8115 Fax 281/252-2170
Magnolia Elem Sch 31900 Nichols Sawmill Rd, Magnolia 77355 Letitia Roman	PK-5	T	844 50	59%	281/356-6434 Fax 281/252-2150
Magnolia High Sch 14350 FM 1488 Rd, Magnolia 77354 **Greg Quinn**	9-12	V	1,961 80	22%	281/356-3572 Fax 281/252-2092
Magnolia Intermediate Sch 110 S Magnolia Blvd, Magnolia 77355 Lisa Bertrand	5-6		1,200 35		281/252-2033 Fax 281/252-2024 f t
Magnolia Junior High Sch 31138 Nichols Sawmill Rd, Magnolia 77355 David Slater	7-8	TV	1,056 45	45%	281/356-1327 Fax 281/252-2125
Magnolia Parkway Elem Sch 11745 FM 1488 Rd, Magnolia 77354 Megan Baker	PK-5		713	38%	281/252-7440 Fax 281/252-7446
Magnolia West High Sch 42202 FM 1774 Rd, Magnolia 77354 Ben King	9-12	V	2,034	41%	281/252-2550 Fax 281/252-2560
Nichols-Saw Mill Elem Sch 28750 Nichols Sawmill Rd, Magnolia 77355 Carrie Quinn	PK-5		626 45	37%	281/252-2133 Fax 281/252-2138
Tom R Ellisor Elem Sch 33040 Egypt Ln, Magnolia 77354 **Kristin Boyd**	PK-5		752	23%	281/252-7400 Fax 281/252-7401
Willie E Williams Elem Sch 18101 FM 1488 Rd, Magnolia 77354 Claudia Dominguez	PK-5	T	719 34	68%	281/356-6866 Fax 281/252-2204

• Montgomery Ind School Dist PID: 01042623
20774 Eva St, Montgomery 77356
936/276-2000 Fax 936/276-2009

Schools: 10 \ **Teachers:** 519 \ **Students:** 8,864 \
Special Ed Students: 547 \ **LEP Students:** 177 \ **College-Bound:** 57% \
Ethnic: Asian 1%, African American 3%, Hispanic 15%, Native American: 1%, Caucasian 80% \ **Exp:** $269 (Med) \ **Poverty:** 8% \ **Title I:** $665,181 \
Special Education: $911,000 \ **Open-Close:** 08/15 - 05/21 \ **DTBP:** $158 (High)

Dr Beau Rees 1	Kristy Conrad 2,19
Arthur Ford 3	Bobby Morris 3,17
Lena Neugebauer 4	Mike Foster 5
Clint Heard 6,35	Sonja Lopez 7,15,68,71,273
Wendy Graves 9,11,15,16,34,57,270,274	Duane McFadden 10,15
Meredith Burg 58,79	Jim Dossey 67
Amy Busby 73	Jerry Krusleski 73,76,286,295
Jada Mullins 79	Marlon Runnels 91

Public Schs..Principal	Grd	Prgm	Enr/#Cls	SN	Phone
Keenan Elem Sch 19180 Keenan Cut Off Rd, Montgomery 77316 Mallory Kirby	PK-5		770 45		936/276-5500 Fax 936/597-5501
Lake Creek High Sch 20639 FM 2854 Rd, Montgomery 77316 **Phil Eaton**	9-12		331		936/276-4000
Lincoln Elem Sch 700 Dr Martin Luther King Dr, Montgomery 77356 Courtney Dyer	PK-5		495		936/276-4700 Fax 936/276-4701
Lone Star Elem Sch 16600 FM 2854 Rd, Montgomery 77316 Dr Catherine Bartlett	PK-5		769	16%	936/276-4500 Fax 936/276-4501
Madeley Ranch Elem Sch 3500 Madeley Ranch Rd, Montgomery 77356 Shelby Smith	PK-5		775	16%	936/276-4600 Fax 936/276-4601
Montgomery Elem Sch 13755 Liberty St, Montgomery 77316 Carrie Fitzpatrick	PK-5		425 30		936/597-6333 Fax 936/276-3601
Montgomery High Sch 22825 Highway 105 W, Montgomery 77356 Brandi Hendrix	9-12	V	1,775	19%	936/276-3000 Fax 936/276-3001
Montgomery Junior High Sch 19000 Stuart Creek Rd, Montgomery 77356 Angela Chapman	6-8		1,151 45	25%	936/276-3300 Fax 936/276-3301 f t
Oak Hills Junior High Sch 19190 Keenan Cut Off Rd, Montgomery 77316 Tim Williams	6-8		1,081 34		936/276-4300 Fax 936/276-4301
Stewart Creek Elem Sch 18990 Stewart Creek Rd, Montgomery 77356 Michele Salter	PK-5	T	780	42%	936/276-3500 Fax 936/276-3501

• New Caney Ind School Dist PID: 01042661
21580 Loop 494, New Caney 77357
281/577-8600 Fax 281/354-2639

Schools: 19 \ **Teachers:** 956 \ **Students:** 15,000 \
Special Ed Students: 1,255 \ **LEP Students:** 3,985 \ **College-Bound:** 36% \ **Ethnic:** Asian 2%, African American 4%, Hispanic 58%, Caucasian 36% \ **Exp:** $450 (High) \ **Poverty:** 17% \ **Title I:** $2,538,905 \
Special Education: $2,004,000 \ **Open-Close:** 08/12 - 05/22 \ **DTBP:** $141 (High) \ f t

Kenn Franklin 1	Brandy Fain 2
Michelle Marable 3	Paul Batchelder 3
Tim Battenfield 3	Debbie Needham 4
Joshua Rice 5	Brent Sipe 6
Christina Nunez 7*	Kristi Shofner 8
Karen Smithson 9	Dr Mark Weatherly 10
Brande Bass 11,83,88,296	Brande Bass 11,83,88,296*
Matt Calvert 15	Mike Milling 15
Patrick Paris 20,23	Warren Stripling 27
Yolanda Rios 57,271	Sarah Chase 58
Chad Turner 67	Steve Freeman 68
Dr Scott Powers 71	Ben Rice 73
Doug Bonsal 74	Dan Casteel 76
Laura Sunosky 78	Scott Castleberry 79
Loree Munro 81	Troy Wooten 91
Jeanie Reed 286	Crosby Doug 295

Public Schs..Principal	Grd	Prgm	Enr/#Cls	SN	Phone
Bens Branch Elem Sch 24160 Briar Berry Ln, Porter 77365 Catherine Olano	PK-5	T	947	52%	281/577-8700 Fax 281/354-4296
Brookwood Forest Elem Sch 25545 Sorters Rd, Porter 77365 **Ericka Gutierrez**	PK-5		500		281/577-8820
Dogwood Elem Sch 600 Dogwood, New Caney 77357 Kerry Hamilton	PK-5		701		281/577-2960
Infinity Early College HS 26751 Sorters Rd, Porter 77365 Patricia Beal	9-10	T	124	63%	281/577-2890
Keefer Crossing Middle Sch 20350 FM 1485 Rd, New Caney 77357 Cesar Condarco	7-8	TV	875 35	72%	281/577-8841 Fax 281/399-9859 f t
Kings Manor Elem Sch 21111 Royal Crossing Dr, Kingwood 77339 Stacey Paine	PK-5		737 41	26%	281/577-2940 Fax 281/359-6391

---

79 Student Personnel	91 Safety/Security	275 Response To Intervention	298 Grant Writer/Ptnrships	**School Programs**	**Social Media**
80 Driver Ed/Safety	92 Magnet School	277 Remedial Math K-12	750 Chief Innovation Officer	A = Alternative Program	
81 Gifted/Talented	93 Parental Involvement	280 Literacy Coach	751 Chief of Staff	G = Adult Classes	f = Facebook
82 Video Services	95 Tech Prep Program	285 STEM	752 Social Emotional Learning	M = Magnet Program	
83 Substance Abuse Prev	97 Chief Infomation Officer	286 Digital Learning		T = Title I Schoolwide	t = Twitter
84 Erate	98 Chief Technology Officer	288 Common Core Standards	**Other School Types**	V = Career & Tech Ed Programs	
85 AIDS Education	270 Accountability	294 Character Education	A = Alternative School		
88 Alternative/At Risk	271 Migrant Education	295 Network System	C = Charter School	New Schools are shaded	
89 Multi-Cultural Curriculum	273 Teacher Mentor	296 Title II Programs	M = Magnet School	New Superintendents and Principals are bold	
90 Social Work	274 Before/After Sch	297 Webmaster	Y = Year-Round School	Personnel with email addresses are underscored	

Montgomery County

Market Data Retrieval

ⓐ Learning Center 20419 FM 1485 Rd, New Caney 77357 Jack Dumesnil	1-12		50 12	71%	281/577-2850 Fax 281/399-4005
New Caney Elem Sch 20501 FM 1485 Rd, New Caney 77357 **Jennifer Andjelic**	PK-5	T	617 48	78%	281/577-8720 Fax 281/399-2174
New Caney High Sch 21650 Loop 494, New Caney 77357 **Eric Holton**	9-12	TV	1,946 100	61%	281/577-2800 Fax 281/354-0186
New Caney Middle Sch 22784 Highway 59, Porter 77365 **Holly Ray**	6-8	T	795	66%	281/577-8860 Fax 281/354-8725
Oakley Elem Sch 22320 Loop 494, New Caney 77357 **Erica Gruber**	PK-5	T	821	77%	281/577-5970
Porter Elem Sch 22256 Ford Rd, Porter 77365 Sheri Bonsal	PK-5	T	651 35	74%	281/577-2920 Fax 281/354-7583
Porter High Sch 22625 Sandy Ln, Porter 77365 Jeremy Harris	9-12	T	1,990	46%	281/577-5900
Robert L Crippen Elem Sch 18690 Cumberland Blvd, Porter 77365 Crystal Mayes	PK-5	T	842 61	71%	281/577-8740 Fax 281/354-6823
Sorters Mill Elem Sch 23300 Sorters Rd, Porter 77365 **Kindy Tomhave**	PK-5	T	854	63%	281/577-8780 Fax 281/354-0164
Tavola Elem Sch 18885 Winding Summit Dr, New Caney 77357 Sheri Lowe	PK-5	T	511 35	78%	281/577-2900 Fax 281/399-9946
Valley Ranch Elem Sch 21700 Valley Ranch Crossing Dr, Porter 77365 Nicole Land	PK-5	T	739	56%	281/577-8760 Fax 281/577-9209
White Oak Middle Sch 24161 Briar Berry Ln, Porter 77365 Everett Simons	6-8	TV	857 60	57%	281/577-8800 Fax 281/354-5186
Woodridge Forest Middle Sch 4540 Woodridge Pkwy, Porter 77365 Bridgett Heine	6-8	TV	842	53%	281/577-8880

● **Splendora Ind School Dist** PID: 01042726 281/689-3128
23419 FM 2090 Rd, Splendora 77372 Fax 281/689-7509

Schools: 5 \ *Teachers:* 251 \ *Students:* 4,200 \ *Special Ed Students:* 332 \ *LEP Students:* 507 \ *College-Bound:* 43% \ *Ethnic:* African American 1%, Hispanic 37%, Caucasian 62% \ *Exp:* $433 (High) \ *Poverty:* 14% \ *Title I:* $663,551 \ *Open-Close:* 08/14 - 05/28 \ *DTBP:* $142 (High)

Dr Jeff Burke	1	Darla Baker	2
Kevin Lynch	2,3,11,15	Rusty Lewis	3
Veronica Castille	3	Nancy Montalbo	4
Darcas Moody	5	Marcus Schulz	6*
Tami Greggerson	8,69,72,81,88,271,285	Richard Kershner	15,273
Rhea Young	16*	Chris Pratt	23*
Adam Lira	27,31*	Loydette Youngblood	36*
Jennifer Stewart	58	Suzanne Soto	67
Brian Kroeger	68	Lisa Foster	71,93,274
Buddy Denman	73,295	Dale Martin	73
Ryan Hamilton	76	Rex Evans	83,91
Lisa Birch	286		

Public Schs..Principal	Grd	Prgm	Enr/#Cls	SN	
Greenleaf Elem Sch 26275 FM 2090 Rd, Splendora 77372 Dr Carolyn King	K-5	T	745 33	80%	281/689-8020 Fax 281/689-3213

Peach Creek Elem Sch 14455 Cox St, Splendora 77372 Duana Brashear	K-5	T	458	57%	281/689-3114 Fax 281/689-7128
Piney Woods Elem Sch 23395 FM 2090 Rd, Splendora 77372 Heath Lucas	PK-5	T	780	54%	281/689-3073 Fax 281/689-7975
Splendora High Sch 23747 FM 2090 Rd, Splendora 77372 Dianna Archer	9-12	TV	1,156 55	51%	281/689-8008 Fax 281/689-8675
Splendora Junior High Sch 23411 FM 2090 Rd, Splendora 77372 Kent Broussard	6-8	TV	877 33	57%	281/689-6343 Fax 281/689-5198

● **Willis Ind School Dist** PID: 01042764 936/856-1200
204 W Rogers St, Willis 77378 Fax 936/856-5182

Schools: 9 \ *Teachers:* 410 \ *Students:* 7,500 \ *Special Ed Students:* 575 \ *LEP Students:* 1,045 \ *College-Bound:* 51% \ *Ethnic:* Asian 1%, African American 8%, Hispanic 37%, Caucasian 54% \ *Exp:* $301 (High) \ *Poverty:* 14% \ *Title I:* $1,430,556 \ *Special Education:* $1,120,000 \ *Open-Close:* 08/14 - 05/22 \ *DTBP:* $177 (High) \

Tim Harkrider	1	Tammy Moore	2,15
Joe Morgan	3	Paul Dusebout	3,4
James Ringo	5	Mike Wall	6
Dr Brian Greeney	8,15	Patricia Musick	9
Robert Whitman	15,68*	Travis Utech	27,31
Sara Goolsby	57,81,275	Debbie Walker	58
Cliff Williams	67	Tracy Jackson	69
Jamie Fails	71	Deborah Menefee	73
Dr Tim Walsh	79	Leslee Zemlicka	91

Public Schs..Principal	Grd	Prgm	Enr/#Cls	SN	
A R Turner Elem Sch 10575 Hwy 75 N, Willis 77378 Kameron Wilder	PK-5	T	722 38	32%	936/856-1289 Fax 936/856-1677
C C Hardy Elem Sch 701 Gerald St, Willis 77378 Eric Burns	PK-5	T	618	83%	936/856-1241 Fax 936/856-1242
Edward B Cannan Elem Sch 7639 County Line Rd, Willis 77378 Tamara Good	PK-5	T	689 40	71%	936/890-8660 Fax 936/890-2616
Lynn Lucas Middle Sch 1304 N Campbell St, Willis 77378 Kim Sprayberry	6-8	TV	815 45	72%	936/856-1274 Fax 936/856-1065
Meador Elem Sch 10020 FM 830 Rd, Willis 77318 Nan Seith	PK-5	T	771	58%	936/890-7550 Fax 936/890-7540
Mel Parmley Elem Sch 600 N Campbell St, Willis 77378 Kelley Moore	PK-5	T	758 25	67%	936/856-1231 Fax 936/856-1239
Robert Brabham Middle Sch 10000 FM 830 Rd, Willis 77318 **Richard Ray**	6-8	T	889	48%	936/856-2312 Fax 936/856-2910
ⓐ Stubblefield Alternative Acad 207 Philpot St, Willis 77378 Tanya Maddin	1-12		22 9		936/856-1302 Fax 936/890-0312
Willis High Sch 10005 Highway 75 N, Willis 77378 Stephanie Hodgins	9-12	TV	1,994 100	52%	936/856-1250 Fax 936/856-3391

---

1 Superintendent	8 Curric/Instruct K-12	19 Chief Financial Officer	29 Family/Consumer Science	39 Social Studies K-12	49 English/Lang Arts Elem	59 Special Education Elem	69 Academic Assessment
2 Bus/Finance/Purchasing	9 Curric/Instruct Elem	20 Art K-12	30 Adult Education	40 Social Studies Elem	50 English/Lang Arts Sec	60 Special Education Sec	70 Research/Development
3 Buildings And Grounds	10 Curric/Instruct Sec	21 Art Elem	31 Career/Sch-to-Work K-12	41 Social Studies Sec	51 Reading K-12	61 Foreign/World Lang K-12	71 Public Information
4 Food Service	11 Federal Program	22 Art Sec	32 Career/Sch-to-Work Elem	42 Science K-12	52 Reading Elem	62 Foreign/World Lang Elem	72 Summer School
5 Transportation	12 Title I	23 Music K-12	33 Career/Sch-to-Work Sec	43 Science Elem	53 Reading Sec	63 Foreign/World Lang Sec	73 Instructional Tech
6 Athletic	13 Title V	24 Music Elem	34 Early Childhood Ed	44 Science Sec	54 Remedial Reading K-12	64 Religious Education K-12	74 Inservice Training
7 Health Services	15 Asst Superintendent	25 Music Sec	35 Health/Phys Education	45 Math K-12	55 Remedial Reading Elem	65 Religious Education Elem	75 Marketing/Distributive
	16 Instructional Media Svcs	26 Business Education	36 Guidance Services K-12	46 Math Elem	56 Remedial Reading Sec	66 Religious Education Sec	76 Info Systems
	17 Chief Operations Officer	27 Career & Tech Ed	37 Guidance Services Elem	47 Math Sec	57 Bilingual/ELL	67 School Board President	77 Psychological Assess
	18 Chief Academic Officer	28 Technology Education	38 Guidance Services Sec	48 English/Lang Arts K-12	58 Special Education K-12	68 Teacher Personnel	78 Affirmative Action

Texas School Directory — Moore County

MONTGOMERY CATHOLIC SCHOOLS

• **Archdiocese Galveston-Houston** PID: 01027855
Listing includes only schools located in this county. See District Index for location of Diocesan Offices.

Catholic Schs..Principal	Grd	Prgm	Enr/#Cls	SN	
Sacred Heart Sch 615 McDade St, Conroe 77301 Deb Brown	PK-8		318 18		936/756-3848 Fax 936/756-4097
St Anthony of Padua Sch 7901 Bay Branch Dr, The Woodlands 77382 Veronica Tucker	PK-8		458 20		281/296-0300 Fax 281/296-7236

MONTGOMERY PRIVATE SCHOOLS

Private Schs..Principal	Grd	Prgm	Enr/#Cls	SN	
Academy at World Champions Ctr 28865 Birnham Dr, Spring 77386 Dr Amelia Robinson	K-12		25		281/292-6284
Adventist Christian Academy 3601 S Loop 336 E, Conroe 77301 Jim Donlon	PK-12		102 6		936/756-5078
Calvary Baptist Sch 3401 N Frazier St, Conroe 77303 Becky Burchett	PK-12		199 13		936/756-0743 Fax 936/756-0764
Central Baptist Academy 37135 FM 1774 Rd, Magnolia 77355 Jason Messer	PK-12		52 6		281/356-2861 Fax 281/259-5120
Christ Community Sch 1488 Wellman Rd, Shenandoah 77384 Sonya Meldahl	PK-6		140 16		936/321-6300 Fax 936/460-3096
Covenant Christian Sch 4503 Interstate 45 N, Conroe 77304 Sara Cummins \ Dathan Petruccio	PK-12	GV	300 30		936/890-8080 Fax 936/890-5343
Esprit International Sch 4890 W Panther Creek Dr, The Woodlands 77381 Rosemary Brumbelow	PK-12		150		281/298-9200 Fax 832/415-0486
Fusion Academy-the Woodlands 1201 Lake Woodlands Dr #4000, The Woodlands 77380 Joseph Thompson	6-12		401		281/419-1436
Glenwood Private Sch 912 W Lewis St, Conroe 77301 Abbey Brawner	PK-2		120 11		936/756-1223
John Cooper Sch 1 John Cooper Dr, The Woodlands 77381 Michael Maher	PK-12		1,000 50		281/367-0900 Fax 281/292-9201
Legacy Preparatory Chrn Acad 9768 Research Forest Dr, Magnolia 77354 Shannon Jones \ Lisa Bontrager	K-12		140		936/337-2000
Lifestyle Christian Sch 3993 Interstate 45 N, Conroe 77304 Clarice Neal	K-12		192 15		936/756-9383 Fax 936/760-3003
Montgomery Christian Academy 12681 FM 149 Rd, Montgomery 77316 Stacy Grant	PK-6		72		936/622-4598
Rubicon Academy 14211 Horseshoe Bnd, The Woodlands 77384 Franci Roberts	PK-8		40 7		936/273-9111
Sojourn Academy 27420 Robinson Rd, Conroe 77385 Becky Staggs	PK-12		160		281/298-5800 Fax 281/292-2818
The Woodlands Methodist Sch 1915 Lake Front Cir, Spring 77380 Tim Patton	K-8		325		281/882-8220
Woodlands Christian Academy 5800 Academy Way, The Woodlands 77384 Peter Laugen \ Patty Bruha	PK-12		550		936/273-2555 Fax 936/271-3115

MOORE COUNTY

MOORE PUBLIC SCHOOLS

• **Dumas Ind School Dist** PID: 01042817
421 W 4th St, Dumas 79029
806/935-6461
Fax 806/935-6275

Schools: 9 \ *Teachers:* 331 \ *Students:* 4,212 \ *Special Ed Students:* 435 \ *LEP Students:* 1,209 \ *Ethnic:* Asian 7%, African American 2%, Hispanic 72%, Caucasian 18% \ *Exp:* $322 (High) \ *Poverty:* 17% \ *Title I:* $844,855 \ *Special Education:* $779,000 \ *Open-Close:* 08/14 - 05/29 \ *DTBP:* $154 (High) \

Monty Hysinger	1
Eddie Crossland	3,5,91
Stan Stroebel	6,35
Lisa Hatley	9
Phillip Guerra	15
Patty Willis	67
Jake Aragon	73,76,95,295
Kim Schnucker	274
Rhonda Artho	286
Daniel West	2,19
Patty Woods	4
Kelly Legg	8,11,88,296
Sally Heaton	10,280
James Bussard	34,58*
Larry Payne	71,83*
Cindy Rhoades	79,294
Frankie Blue	275

Public Schs..Principal	Grd	Prgm	Enr/#Cls	SN	
Cactus Elem Sch 100 South Drive, Cactus 79013 Thomas Funderburg	PK-4	T	357 35	95%	806/966-5102 Fax 806/966-5561
Dumas Intermediate Sch 400 Texas Ave, Dumas 79029 Philip Rhodes	5-6	T	665	70%	806/935-6474 Fax 806/935-6484
Dumas Junior High Sch 700 E 5th St, Dumas 79029 Kurt Baxter	7-8	T	670 50	69%	806/935-4155 Fax 806/934-1434
Ⓐ Dumas Senior High Sch 300 S Klein Ave, Dumas 79029 Brett Beesley	9-12	TV	1,060 60	56%	806/935-4151 Fax 806/934-1433
Green Acres Elem Sch 300 Oak Ave, Dumas 79029 Andrea Cox	PK-4	T	480 27	79%	806/935-4157 Fax 806/934-1444
Hillcrest Elem Sch 514 Pear Ave, Dumas 79029 Stephanie Schilling	PK-4	T	314 23	45%	806/935-5629 Fax 806/934-1439
Morningside Elem Sch 623 Powell Ave, Dumas 79029 **Erin Pingelton**	PK-4	T	397 23	65%	806/935-4153 Fax 806/934-1438
Ⓐ North Plains Opportunity Ctr 1015 N Maddox Ave, Dumas 79029 Carl Clements	9-12	T	35	70%	806/935-8774 Fax 806/935-6376
Sunset Elem Sch 401 W 14th St, Dumas 79029 Caynon Strickland	PK-4	T	333 37	85%	806/935-2127 Fax 806/934-1441

---

79 Student Personnel	91 Safety/Security	275 Response To Intervention	298 Grant Writer/Ptnrships	School Programs	Social Media
80 Driver Ed/Safety	92 Magnet School	277 Remedial Math K-12	750 Chief Innovation Officer	A = Alternative Program	
81 Gifted/Talented	93 Parental Involvement	280 Literacy Coach	751 Chief of Staff	G = Adult Classes	📘 = Facebook
82 Video Services	95 Tech Prep Program	285 STEM	752 Social Emotional Learning	M = Magnet Program	
83 Substance Abuse Prev	97 Chief Infomation Officer	286 Digital Learning		T = Title I Schoolwide	🅃 = Twitter
84 Erate	98 Chief Technology Officer	288 Common Core Standards	Other School Types	V = Career & Tech Ed Programs	
85 AIDS Education	270 Character Education	294 Accountability	Ⓐ = Alternative Program		
88 Alternative/At Risk	271 Migrant Education	295 Network System	Ⓒ = Charter School	New Schools are shaded	
89 Multi-Cultural Curriculum	273 Teacher Mentor	296 Title II Programs	Ⓜ = Magnet School	New Superintendents and Principals are bold	
90 Social Work	274 Before/After Sch	297 Webmaster	Ⓨ = Year-Round School	Personnel with email addresses are underscored	

Morris County

Market Data Retrieval

- **Sunray Ind School Dist** PID: 01042910   806/948-4411
  400 E 7th St, Sunray 79086   Fax 806/948-5274

Schools: 3 \ *Teachers:* 51 \ *Students:* 550 \ *Special Ed Students:* 48 \ *LEP Students:* 94 \ *Ethnic:* Hispanic 55%, Native American: 1%, Caucasian 44% \ *Exp:* $476 (High) \ *Poverty:* 10% \ *Title I:* $54,162 \ *Open-Close:* 08/19 - 05/22 \ *DTBP:* $339 (High) \

Marshall Harrison 1,11,57
Misty Lowman 4*
Marybeth Jones 35,36,69,83*
Mandy Trailor 88,285
Chad Ely 3,5
Matt Stricklen 6,35*
Scott Peeples 67
Mary Jones 275*

Public Schs..Principal	Grd	Prgm	Enr/#Cls	SN	
Sunray Elem Sch 509 Ave Q, Sunray 79086 Cody McDowell	PK-4	T	232 18	64%	806/948-4222 Fax 806/948-4180
Sunray High Sch 900 Ave Q, Sunray 79086 Mandy Traylor	9-12	AV	171 35	35%	806/948-5515 Fax 806/948-5399
Sunray Middle Sch 400 East 7th St, Sunray 79086 Pam Kiesling	5-8	T	152 15	57%	806/948-4444 Fax 806/948-4208

MORRIS COUNTY

MORRIS PUBLIC SCHOOLS

- **Daingerfield-Lone Star Ind SD** PID: 01042946   903/645-2239
  200 Tiger Dr, Daingerfield 75638   Fax 903/645-2137

Schools: 4 \ *Teachers:* 87 \ *Students:* 1,100 \ *Special Ed Students:* 141 \ *LEP Students:* 89 \ *College-Bound:* 64% \ *Ethnic:* Asian 1%, African American 42%, Hispanic 20%, Caucasian 37% \ *Exp:* $309 (High) \ *Poverty:* 31% \ *Title I:* $585,233 \ *Open-Close:* 08/19 - 05/22 \ *DTBP:* $343 (High)

Sandra Quarles 1
Davin Nelson 6*
Daniel Pritchett 11
Vickie Lilley 34,58,275
Ben Rameriz 270
Jamie Bess 4
Martha Campbell 8,11,69,74,79,273,294
Jason Johnson 16,73,295
Neil Roney 67
Ben Rameriz 270*

Public Schs..Principal	Grd	Prgm	Enr/#Cls	SN	
Daingerfield High Sch 202 Tiger Dr, Daingerfield 75638 Tommy Stewart	9-12	ATV	282 45	73%	903/645-3968 Fax 903/645-7662
Daingerfield Jr High Sch 200 Texas St, Daingerfield 75638 Amy Billingslea	6-8	T	209 35	77%	903/645-2261 Fax 903/645-4010
South Elem Sch 1301 Linda Dr, Daingerfield 75638 Angie Reeder	3-5	T	228 12	87%	903/645-3501 Fax 903/645-2295
West Elem Sch 1305 W Watson Blvd, Daingerfield 75638 Lesia Lewis	PK-2	T	307 18	86%	903/645-2901 Fax 903/645-7178

- **Pewitt Cons Ind School Dist** PID: 01043005   903/884-2136
  1330 US Highway 67 W, Omaha 75571   Fax 903/884-2866

Schools: 3 \ *Teachers:* 77 \ *Students:* 891 \ *Special Ed Students:* 109 \ *LEP Students:* 47 \ *College-Bound:* 52% \ *Ethnic:* African American 15%, Hispanic 13%, Caucasian 71% \ *Exp:* $392 (High) \ *Poverty:* 20% \ *Title I:* $266,036 \ *Open-Close:* 08/21 - 05/28 \ *DTBP:* $214 (High)

Skip Forsyth 1
Chris Cobb 3,17*
Christopher Cobb 5*
Holly Tucker 11,288*
Michael Jarvis 67
Sean Rhyne 76
Karla Davlin 2,19
Monica Buford 4
Triston Abron 6
Vickie Lilley 58
Darla Shumate 73,98,295

Public Schs..Principal	Grd	Prgm	Enr/#Cls	SN	
Pewitt Elem Sch 374 County Rd 4108, Omaha 75571 Amy Barron	PK-5	T	449 24	74%	903/884-2404 Fax 903/884-3076
Pewitt High Sch 1216 US Highway 67 W, Omaha 75571 Jay Wylie	9-12	TV	242 29	57%	903/884-2293 Fax 903/884-3111
Pewitt Junior High Sch US Highway 67 West, Omaha 75571 Tom Giles	6-8	T	200 20	67%	903/884-2505 Fax 903/884-3111

MOTLEY COUNTY

MOTLEY PUBLIC SCHOOLS

- **Motley Co Ind School Dist** PID: 01043043   806/347-2676
  1600 Bundy St, Matador 79244   Fax 806/347-2871

Schools: 1 \ *Teachers:* 17 \ *Students:* 151 \ *Special Ed Students:* 18 \ *College-Bound:* 80% \ *Ethnic:* Hispanic 26%, Caucasian 74% \ *Exp:* $453 (High) \ *Poverty:* 29% \ *Title I:* $68,121 \ *Open-Close:* 08/20 - 05/22 \ *DTBP:* $359 (High)

William Cochran 1
Jimmy Erickson 2
Mike Bigham 6*
Licey Rankin 57*
Lewis Drum 67
Shelley Cox 73*
Darlene Thomas 2
Chuck Ream 5*
Becky Decker 11
Tanya Givins 58*
Kathy Gillespie 69*

Public Schs..Principal	Grd	Prgm	Enr/#Cls	SN	
Motley Co Sch 1600 Bundy St, Matador 79244 James Richards	PK-12	TV	151 27	74%	806/347-2676

1	Superintendent	8	Curric/Instruct K-12	19	Chief Financial Officer	29	Family/Consumer Science	39	Social Studies K-12	49	English/Lang Arts Elem	59	Special Education Elem	69	Academic Assessment
2	Bus/Finance/Purchasing	9	Curric/Instruct Elem	20	Art K-12	30	Adult Education	40	Social Studies Elem	50	English/Lang Arts Sec	60	Special Education Sec	70	Research/Development
3	Buildings And Grounds	10	Curric/Instruct Sec	21	Art Elem	31	Career/Sch-to-Work K-12	41	Social Studies Sec	51	Reading K-12	61	Foreign/World Lang K-12	71	Public Information
4	Food Service	11	Federal Program	22	Art Sec	32	Career/Sch-to-Work Elem	42	Science K-12	52	Reading Elem	62	Foreign/World Lang Elem	72	Summer School
5	Transportation	12	Title I	23	Music K-12	33	Career/Sch-to-Work Sec	43	Science Elem	53	Reading Sec	63	Foreign/World Lang Sec	73	Instructional Tech
6	Athletic	13	Title V	24	Music Elem	34	Early Childhood Ed	44	Science Sec	54	Remedial Reading K-12	64	Religious Education K-12	74	Inservice Training
7	Health Services	15	Asst Superintendent	25	Music Sec	35	Health/Phys Education	45	Math K-12	55	Remedial Reading Elem	65	Religious Education Elem	75	Marketing/Distributive
		16	Instructional Media Svcs	26	Business Education	36	Guidance Services K-12	46	Math Elem	56	Remedial Reading Sec	66	Religious Education Sec	76	Info Systems
		17	Chief Operations Officer	27	Career & Tech Ed	37	Guidance Services Elem	47	Math Sec	57	Bilingual/ELL	67	School Board President	77	Psychological Assess
		18	Chief Academic Officer	28	Technology Education	38	Guidance Services Sec	48	English/Lang Arts K-12	58	Special Education K 12	68	Teacher Personnel	78	Affirmative Action

Texas School Directory

Nacogdoches County

NACOGDOCHES COUNTY

NACOGDOCHES PUBLIC SCHOOLS

- **Central Heights Ind Sch Dist** PID: 01043079 936/564-2681
  10317 US Highway 259, Nacogdoches 75965 Fax 936/569-6889

Schools: 3 \ *Teachers:* 82 \ *Students:* 1,181 \ *Special Ed Students:* 76 \ *LEP Students:* 51 \ *College-Bound:* 48% \ *Ethnic:* Asian 1%, African American 4%, Hispanic 17%, Caucasian 77% \ *Exp:* $295 (Med) \ *Poverty:* 26% \ *Title I:* $237,224 \ *Open-Close:* 08/27 - 05/27 \ *DTBP:* $395 (High) \

David Russell	1	Norma Rogers	2
Tanya Bryant	4	Kevin Matheny	5
Kevin Herron	6*	Jana Muckleroy	8,16,57,271,274*
Andy Binford	10*	Martha Labbit	11,76,296,298*
Julie Feasel	13,37*	Allison Thorn	27,31*
Lauren Tyler	38,69,83,85,88	Don Shoemaker	67
Jeffery Hightower	73*	Martha Labbit	84

Public Schs..Principal	Grd	Prgm	Enr/#Cls	SN	
Central Heights Elem Sch	PK-5	T	504	44%	936/552-3424
10317 US Highway 259, Nacogdoches 75965			30		Fax 936/560-2099
Jana Muckleroy					
Central Heights High Sch	9-12		350	32%	936/552-3408
10471 US Highway 259, Nacogdoches 75965			35		Fax 936/560-2016
David Russell					
Central Heights Middle Sch	6-8		279	36%	936/552-3441
1471 Highway 259N, Nacogdoches 75965					Fax 936/560-2016
Andy Binford					

- **Chireno ISD School Dist** PID: 01043108 936/362-2132
  901 Main St, Chireno 75937 Fax 936/362-2490

Schools: 1 \ *Teachers:* 34 \ *Students:* 304 \ *Special Ed Students:* 43 \ *LEP Students:* 31 \ *College-Bound:* 88% \ *Exp:* $621 (High) \ *Poverty:* 36% \ *Title I:* $169,386 \ *Open-Close:* 08/14 - 05/22 \ *DTBP:* $345 (High)

Arnie Kelly	1	Jeanne Holloway	2,11
Kirk Turner	3*	Amber Evans	4*
Brian King	8,273*	Heather Hagle	8,11,79,275,294,296*
Kevin Helmer	16,73,295*	Sam Thomas	27*
Sandy Pinner	36,57,88,271*	Crystal Zienko	58
Michael Sanford	67	Summer Norman	69,83,93*

Public Schs..Principal	Grd	Prgm	Enr/#Cls	SN	
Chireno Sch	PK-12	V	304		936/362-2132
901 Main St, Chireno 75937			23		
Brandy Gray					

- **Cushing Ind School Dist** PID: 01043134 936/326-4890
  1088 W Bearkat Dr, Cushing 75760 Fax 936/326-4115

Schools: 2 \ *Teachers:* 47 \ *Students:* 551 \ *Special Ed Students:* 50 \ *LEP Students:* 25 \ *College-Bound:* 40% \ *Ethnic:* Asian 1%, African American 7%, Hispanic 15%, Native American: 1%, Caucasian 77% \ *Exp:* $461 (High) \ *Poverty:* 28% \ *Title I:* $184,894 \ *Open-Close:* 08/26 - 05/22 \ *DTBP:* $340 (High)

Michael Davis	1	Martha Lee	2
Casey Copelan	3,73	Brenda Marshall	4
Shane Johnson	5,83,91	Shane Smelley	6*
Dee Cruz	7,11,57,69,271,296*	Lynda Langham	67
Tammy Smith	79	Shane Johnson	83,91*

Public Schs..Principal	Grd	Prgm	Enr/#Cls	SN	
Cushing Elem Sch	PK-5	T	271	65%	936/326-4234
1165 Bearcat Dr, Cushing 75760			14		Fax 936/326-4265
Stefani Jackson					
Cushing Jr Sr High Sch	6-12	AGTV	287	56%	936/326-4890
1088 Bearcat Dr, Cushing 75760			20		Fax 936/326-4131
Andy Gresham					

- **Douglass Ind School Dist** PID: 01043160 936/569-9804
  20712 S FM 225, Douglass 75943 Fax 936/569-9446

Schools: 1 \ *Teachers:* 38 \ *Students:* 460 \ *Special Ed Students:* 38 \ *LEP Students:* 23 \ *College-Bound:* 100% \ *Ethnic:* Asian 1%, African American 6%, Hispanic 16%, Native American: 1%, Caucasian 76% \ *Exp:* $305 (High) \ *Poverty:* 25% \ *Title I:* $120,560 \ *Open-Close:* 08/19 - 05/28 \ *DTBP:* $341 (High)

Justin Keeling	1	Casey Watson	2
Brian Gandy	8,57,271,273	Sue Paul	36,69,83,88,270
Craig Matson	58*	Bobby Hobson	67
Ty Porterfield	73,76,286		

Public Schs..Principal	Grd	Prgm	Enr/#Cls	SN	
Douglass Sch	K-12	AV	460	39%	936/569-9804
20712 S FM 225, Douglass 75943			25		
Phil Gersback \ Jason Purke					

- **Etoile Ind School Dist** PID: 01043196 936/465-9404
  16039 FM 226, Etoile 75944 Fax 936/854-2241

Schools: 1 \ *Teachers:* 13 \ *Students:* 100 \ *Special Ed Students:* 20 \ *Ethnic:* Hispanic 4%, Native American: 1%, Caucasian 96% \ *Exp:* $627 (High) \ *Poverty:* 33% \ *Title I:* $108,821 \ *Open-Close:* 08/15 - 05/21 \ *DTBP:* $365 (High) \

Sarah Hottman	1,11,57,288	Rose Pate	2,28
Skipper Eberlan	3,5	Delayne Di Donato	6*
Stephenie Ellisor	7*	Mark Whitehead	59,69*
Gayle Riley	67	Adam Craft	73,286*

Public Schs..Principal	Grd	Prgm	Enr/#Cls	SN	
Etoile Elem Sch	PK-8	T	100	82%	936/465-9404
16039 FM 226, Etoile 75944			12		
Adam Craft					

- **Garrison Ind School Dist** PID: 01043213 936/347-7000
  459 N US Highway 59, Garrison 75946 Fax 936/347-2529

Schools: 3 \ *Teachers:* 67 \ *Students:* 600 \ *Special Ed Students:* 67 \ *LEP Students:* 12 \ *College-Bound:* 55% \ *Ethnic:* Asian 1%, African American 19%, Hispanic 11%, Caucasian 69% \ *Exp:* $524 (High) \ *Poverty:* 25% \ *Title I:* $170,661 \ *Open-Close:* 08/21 - 05/21 \ *DTBP:* $294 (High)

Reid Spivey	1	Patterson Hill	2
Andrew Schmidt	3	Kathy Hammack	4*
Christopher Lee	5	Larry Prince	6*
Amie Adkison	7	Colleen Hill	11*
William Weeks	16,73,84	Eugenia Uribe	36,57,85*
Joya Konderla	37	Leslie McFadden	58*

Nacogdoches County

Market Data Retrieval

Bart Reneau 67
Daphne Dolese 274*

Joel Barton 83*

Public Schs..Principal	Grd	Prgm	Enr/#Cls	SN	
Garrison Elem Sch 459 N US Highway 59, Garrison 75946 Colleen Hill	PK-5	T	360 28	55%	936/347-7010 Fax 936/347-7004
Garrison Middle Sch 459 N US Highway 59, Garrison 75946 Clark Bynum	6-8	T	168 14	40%	936/347-7020 Fax 936/347-7004
Garrison Senior High Sch 459 N US Highway 59, Garrison 75946 Clark Barnett	9-12	T	201 28	39%	936/347-7030 Fax 936/347-7059

- **Martinsville Ind School Dist** PID: 01043249 936/564-3455
  12952 E State Highway 7, Nacogdoches 75961 Fax 936/569-0498

> *Schools:* 1 \ *Teachers:* 35 \ *Students:* 400 \ *Special Ed Students:* 39 \ *LEP Students:* 18 \ *College-Bound:* 52% \ *Ethnic:* African American 4%, Hispanic 15%, Caucasian 81% \ *Exp:* $565 (High) \ *Poverty:* 34% \ *Title I:* $130,189 \ *Open-Close:* 08/26 - 05/22 \ *DTBP:* $320 (High)

Dr David Simmons 1
Zach Crawford 8,57,69,74,92,271*
Mong Waller 11,36,83,85*
Linda Lunsford 68*

Lindsay Lunsford 2
Shelia Cobb 9,12,58,275,296*
Teresa Weaver 67
Chad Huckaby 73,76

Public Schs..Principal	Grd	Prgm	Enr/#Cls	SN	
Martinsville Sch 12952 E State Highway 7, Nacogdoches 75961 Shelia Cobb \ Zach Crawford	PK-12	TV	400 22	49%	936/564-3455

- **Nacogdoches Ind School Dist** PID: 01043275 936/569-5000
  420 S Shawnee St, Nacogdoches 75961 Fax 936/569-5798

> *Schools:* 10 \ *Teachers:* 416 \ *Students:* 6,300 \ *Special Ed Students:* 523 \ *LEP Students:* 1,641 \ *College-Bound:* 58% \ *Ethnic:* Asian 1%, African American 29%, Hispanic 49%, Caucasian 21% \ *Exp:* $400 (High) \ *Poverty:* 37% \ *Title I:* $4,050,601 \ *Special Education:* $1,313,000 \ *Open-Close:* 08/26 - 05/28 \ *DTBP:* $158 (High) \

Alton Frailey 1,83
Ralph LaRue 3
Stacy Lampkin 5
Dr Daya Hill 8,18
Mike Owens 16,73,76,297
Cindy Ivy 36,69
Kayla Hughes 58
Michael Martin 68
Eddie Harwell 90

Lisa Barbarick 2,19
Robin Thacker 4
Darren Allman 6
Dr Jolynn Corley 11,294
Donald Hasley 27*
Evelyn Sauceda 57,271
G W Neal 67
Les Linebarger 71

Public Schs..Principal	Grd	Prgm	Enr/#Cls	SN	
Brooks-Quinn Jones Elem Sch 907 N Sanders St, Nacogdoches 75961 Tom Miller	PK-5	T	763 26	91%	936/569-5040 Fax 936/569-5796
Carpenter Elem Sch 1005 Leroy St, Nacogdoches 75961 Lola Moore	K-5	T	370 24	97%	936/569-5070 Fax 936/569-3165
Fredonia Elem Sch 1326 S Fredonia St, Nacogdoches 75964 Melinda Wiebold	PK-5	T	419 26	90%	936/569-5080 Fax 936/569-3168
ⓐ Malcolm Rector Technical HS 6003 North St, Nacogdoches 75965 James Adams	9-12	T	99 14	83%	936/205-1000
McMichael Middle Sch 4330 SE Stallings Dr, Nacogdoches 75961 Tim Mullican	6-8	T	744	82%	936/552-0519 Fax 936/552-0523
Mike Moses Middle Sch 2801 Park St, Nacogdoches 75961 Stephen Autrey	6-8	T	652 50	80%	936/569-5001 Fax 936/569-5031
Nacogdoches High Sch 4310 Appleby Sand Rd, Nacogdoches 75965 Romulo Crespo	9-12	V	1,648 60	67%	936/564-2466 Fax 936/560-8162
Nettie Marshall Elem Sch 422 W Cox St, Nacogdoches 75964 Joseph Rodriguez	K-5	T	369 16	93%	936/569-5062 Fax 936/569-5038
Raguet Elem Sch 2708 Raguet St, Nacogdoches 75965 Julia Wells	K-5	T	585 26	70%	936/569-5052 Fax 936/569-5060
Thomas J Rusk Elem Sch 411 N Mound St, Nacogdoches 75961 Paula Harshbarger	K-5	T	516 36	91%	936/569-3100 Fax 936/569-5759

- **Woden Ind School Dist** PID: 01043354 936/564-2073
  5263 Farm Rd 226, Nacogdoches 75961 Fax 936/564-1250

> *Schools:* 3 \ *Teachers:* 64 \ *Students:* 725 \ *Special Ed Students:* 52 \ *LEP Students:* 51 \ *College-Bound:* 98% \ *Ethnic:* Asian 1%, African American 1%, Hispanic 22%, Caucasian 76% \ *Exp:* $356 (High) \ *Poverty:* 25% \ *Title I:* $238,751 \ *Special Education:* $106,000 \ *Open-Close:* 08/15 - 05/21 \ *DTBP:* $356 (High)

Brady Taylor 1
Jodee Woodcock 8,11,294,296,298
Brandi Bentley 58
Malinda Holzapfel 73,76*

Walter Peddy 2
Susan Harrison 16*
Perry Grimes 67

Public Schs..Principal	Grd	Prgm	Enr/#Cls	SN	
Woden Elem Sch Farm Road 226, Woden 75978 Jesse Stroud	PK-5	T	359 45	61%	936/564-2386 Fax 936/564-3322
Woden High Sch Farm Road 226, Woden 75978 Jesse Stroud	9-12	TV	209	50%	936/564-7903 Fax 936/462-4962
Woden Junior High Sch 5263 FM 226, Woden 75978 Dr Jerry Meador	6-8	T	179 12	54%	936/564-2481 Fax 936/564-3322

NACOGDOCHES PRIVATE SCHOOLS

Private Schs..Principal	Grd	Prgm	Enr/#Cls	SN	
Christ Episcopal Sch 1430 N Mound St, Nacogdoches 75961 Catherine Oliver	PK-6		114 11		936/564-0621 Fax 936/552-7120
Fredonia Hill Baptist Academy 1711 South St, Nacogdoches 75964 Peggy Fedun	PK-6		130 14		936/564-4472 Fax 936/564-0518
Nacogdoches Christian Academy 211 SE Stallings Dr, Nacogdoches 75964 Donna Baker	PK-K		54		936/462-1021 Fax 936/462-1176
Regents Academy 200 NE Stallings Dr, Nacogdoches 75961 Shannon Henry \ Lance Vermillion	K-12		158		936/559-7343 Fax 936/559-7344

1	Superintendent	8	Curric/Instruct K-12	19	Chief Financial Officer	29	Family/Consumer Science	39	Social Studies K-12	49	English/Lang Arts Elem	59	Special Education Elem	69	Academic Assessment
2	Bus/Finance/Purchasing	9	Curric/Instruct Elem	20	Art K-12	30	Adult Education	40	Social Studies Elem	50	English/Lang Arts Sec	60	Special Education Sec	70	Research/Development
3	Buildings And Grounds	10	Curric/Instruct Sec	21	Art Elem	31	Career/Sch-to-Work K-12	41	Social Studies Sec	51	Reading K-12	61	Foreign/World Lang K-12	71	Public Information
4	Food Service	11	Federal Program	22	Art Sec	32	Career/Sch-to-Work Elem	42	Science K-12	52	Reading Elem	62	Foreign/World Lang Elem	72	Summer School
5	Transportation	12	Title I	23	Music K-12	33	Career/Sch-to-Work Sec	43	Science Elem	53	Reading Sec	63	Foreign/World Lang Sec	73	Instructional Tech
6	Athletic	13	Title V	24	Music Elem	34	Early Childhood Ed	44	Science Sec	54	Remedial Reading K-12	64	Religious Education K-12	74	Inservice Training
7	Health Services	14	Asst Superintendent	25	Music Sec	35	Health/Phys Education	45	Math K-12	55	Remedial Reading Elem	65	Religious Education Elem	75	Marketing/Distributive
		15	Instructional Media Svcs	26	Business Education	36	Guidance Services K-12	46	Math Elem	56	Remedial Reading Sec	66	Religious Education Sec	76	Info Systems
		17	Chief Operations Officer	27	Career & Tech Ed	37	Guidance Services Elem	47	Math Sec	57	Bilingual/ELL	67	School Board President	77	Psychological Assess
		18	Chief Academic Officer	28	Technology Education	38	Guidance Services Sec	48	English/Lang Arts K-12	58	Special Education K-12	68	Teacher Personnel	78	Affirmative Action

Texas School Directory — Navarro County

NAVARRO COUNTY

NAVARRO PUBLIC SCHOOLS

- **Blooming Grove Ind School Dist** PID: 01043392 903/695-2541
  212 W Grady St, Blooming GRV 76626 Fax 903/695-2594

Schools: 3 \ **Teachers:** 65 \ **Students:** 924 \ **Special Ed Students:** 67 \ **LEP Students:** 92 \ **College-Bound:** 66% \ **Ethnic:** African American 3%, Hispanic 31%, Caucasian 66% \ **Exp:** $226 (Med) \ **Poverty:** 19% \ **Title I:** $188,604 \ **Open-Close:** 08/22 - 05/29 \ **DTBP:** $382 (High) \ f

Jack Lee 1	Amy Nicholason 2
Kenneth Hutchison 3,5,7	Sharen Lewis 4*
Ervin Chandler 6	Jessica Lee 8,285,288,298
Tiffany Munoz 11,69*	Lori Kirby 37
Stephanie Chiselbrook 37*	Jon Southard 67
Dennis Williams 73,76,295*	

Public Schs..Principal	Grd	Prgm	Enr/#Cls	SN	
Blooming Grove Elem Sch 601 N Elm St, Blooming GRV 76626 Tiffany Munoz	PK-5	AT	444 24	64%	903/695-2541 Fax 903/695-2009
Blooming Grove High Sch 212 W Grady St, Blooming GRV 76626 John Gillen	9-12	ATV	284 27	46%	903/695-2541
Blooming Grove Junior High Sch 604 Ramsey St, Blooming GRV 76626 Doyle Bell	6-8	AT	219 15	62%	903/695-2541 Fax 903/695-4601

- **Corsicana Ind School Dist** PID: 01043421 903/874-7441
  2200 W 4th Ave, Corsicana 75110 Fax 903/602-8515

Schools: 9 \ **Teachers:** 405 \ **Students:** 6,000 \ **Special Ed Students:** 501 \ **LEP Students:** 1,241 \ **College-Bound:** 67% \ **Ethnic:** Asian 1%, African American 18%, Hispanic 52%, Caucasian 29% \ **Exp:** $300 (High) \ **Poverty:** 22% \ **Title I:** $1,589,472 \ **Special Education:** $918,000 \ **Open-Close:** 08/14 - 05/22 \ **DTBP:** $104 (High) \ f t

Dr Diane Frost 1	Brenda Poteet 2,8,15,296
Richie Cutrer 3,5,83,91*	Shirrell Jessie 4
Shade Boulwave 6*	Carla Whitt 7,85*
Kim Holcomb 8,15,34,39	Elmer Avellaneda 11,58,77
Rhonda Dulworth 31*	Danzel Lee 36,79,294
Debbie Cottar 57,88	Leah Blackard 67
Paula Simpson 69*	Susan Johnson 71,76,93,297
Austin Contreras 73,295	Carla Stanford 288

Public Schs..Principal	Grd	Prgm	Enr/#Cls	SN	
Bowie Elem Sch 1800 Bowie Dr, Corsicana 75110 Hollye Usery	K-4	T	533 35	56%	903/872-6541 Fax 903/872-6298
Carroll Elem Sch 1101 E 13th Ave, Corsicana 75110 Cheryl Murdock	K-4	T	408 36	95%	903/872-3074 Fax 903/641-4153
Collins Intermediate Sch 1500 Dobbins Rd, Corsicana 75110 Scott Doring	5-6		421 40		903/872-3979 Fax 903/874-1423 f t
Corsciana Middle Sch 4101 FM 744, Corsicana 75110 Janice Johnson	7-8		830 45		430/775-6200 Fax 903/874-1423
Corsicana High Sch 3701 W State Highway 22, Corsicana 75110 Shade Boulware	9-12	T	1,658 55	65%	903/874-8211 Fax 903/874-7403 f t
Drane Learning Center 110 S 18th St, Corsicana 75110 Mickey White	PK-PK	T	279	76%	903/874-8281 Fax 903/641-4130
Fannin Elem Sch 3201 N Beaton St, Corsicana 75110 **Dallas Horne**	K-4	T	470 35	85%	903/874-3728 Fax 903/874-0758 f t
Jose Antonio Navarro Elem Sch 601 S 45th St, Corsicana 75110 Tim Betts	K-4	T	504 44	87%	903/874-1011 Fax 903/874-3874 f t
Sam Houston Elem Sch 1213 W 4th Ave, Corsicana 75110 Molly Corrington	K-4	T	323	70%	903/874-6971 Fax 903/641-4114 f t

- **Dawson Ind School Dist** PID: 01043524 254/578-1031
  199 N School Ave, Dawson 76639 Fax 254/578-1721

Schools: 1 \ **Teachers:** 36 \ **Students:** 500 \ **Special Ed Students:** 41 \ **LEP Students:** 21 \ **College-Bound:** 50% \ **Exp:** $716 (High) \ **Poverty:** 29% \ **Title I:** $194,995 \ **Open-Close:** 08/19 - 05/28 \ **DTBP:** $335 (High)

Stacy Henderson 1	Kelly Miller 2
Aaron Hogue 3,5*	Lori James 4*
Ronnie Striplin 6*	Sheryl Bragg 8,13,31,38,69,286,288*
Andrea Farish 9,12,57*	Robert Bray 11,83,88,271*
Lisa Murray 58*	David Mathews 67
Cameron Shaw 73,76,295*	

Public Schs..Principal	Grd	Prgm	Enr/#Cls	SN	
Dawson Sch 199 N School Ave, Dawson 76639 Robert Bray / Andrea Farish	PK-12	AV	500 24		254/578-1031

- **Frost Ind School Dist** PID: 01043550 903/682-2711
  208 N Wyrick St, Frost 76641 Fax 903/682-2107

Schools: 2 \ **Teachers:** 36 \ **Students:** 400 \ **Special Ed Students:** 34 \ **LEP Students:** 54 \ **College-Bound:** 75% \ **Ethnic:** African American 2%, Hispanic 31%, Caucasian 66% \ **Exp:** $342 (High) \ **Poverty:** 20% \ **Title I:** $102,473 \ **Open-Close:** 08/19 - 05/22 \ **DTBP:** $350 (High)

Mickie Jackson 1	Deanna Harrington 2*
Larry Kern 3,5	Aubrey May 4
Randy Fulton 6	Dan Lunsford 10,74*
Terry Barrett 16,73,76,295*	Lisa Bland 51,54*
Kari Richter 58	Jason Curl 67

Public Schs..Principal	Grd	Prgm	Enr/#Cls	SN	
Frost Elem Sch 208 N Wyrick St, Frost 76641 Natalie Rose	PK-5	ATV	209	53%	903/682-2541
Frost High Sch 208 N Wyrick St, Frost 76641 Dan Lunsford	6-12	ATV	204 45	52%	903/682-2541

- **Kerens Ind School Dist** PID: 01043586 903/396-2924
  200 Bobcat Ln, Kerens 75144 Fax 903/396-2334

Schools: 3 \ **Teachers:** 46 \ **Students:** 600 \ **Special Ed Students:** 52 \ **LEP Students:** 23 \ **College-Bound:** 75% \ **Ethnic:** African American 26%, Hispanic 25%, Caucasian 48% \ **Exp:** $619 (High) \ **Poverty:** 30% \ **Title I:** $270,026 \ **Open-Close:** 08/14 - 05/21 \ **DTBP:** $461 (High) \ f

---

79 Student Personnel	91 Safety/Security	275 Response To Intervention	298 Grant Writer/Ptnrships
80 Driver Ed/Safety	92 Magnet School	277 Remedial Math K-12	750 Chief Innovation Officer
81 Gifted/Talented	93 Parental Involvement	280 Literacy Coach	751 Chief of Staff
82 Video Services	95 Tech Prep Program	285 STEM	752 Social Emotional Learning
83 Substance Abuse Prev	97 Chief Infomation Officer	286 Digital Learning	
84 Erate	98 Chief Technology Officer	288 Common Core Standards	
85 AIDS Education	270 Character Education	294 Accountability	
88 Alternative/At Risk	271 Migrant Education	295 Network System	
89 Multi-Cultural Curriculum	273 Teacher Mentor	296 Title II Programs	
90 Social Work	274 Before/After Sch	297 Webmaster	

School Programs
- A = Alternative Program
- G = Adult Classes
- M = Magnet Program
- T = Title I Schoolwide
- V = Career & Tech Ed Programs

Other School Types
- Ⓐ = Alternative School
- Ⓒ = Charter School
- Ⓜ = Magnet School
- Ⓨ = Year-Round School

Social Media
- f = Facebook
- t = Twitter

New Schools are shaded
New Superintendents and Principals are bold
Personnel with email addresses are underscored

TX—299

Newton County
Market Data Retrieval

Martin Brumit 1,11,83
Cliff Davis 3
Terrell Harris 6*
Janice Quinn 16
Robin Williams 38,69
Teresa Jennings 67
Jim Kendall 2
Kayla Duncan 4
Shana Owen 9*
Misty Blue 37,57*
Kayce Bonner 58

Public Schs..Principal	Grd	Prgm	Enr/#Cls	SN	
Kerens Elem Sch 200 Bobcat Ln, Kerens 75144 Shana Owen	PK-4		229 25		903/396-7941
Kerens High Sch 200 Bobcat Ln, Kerens 75144 Greg Priddy	9-12	T	180 21	79%	903/396-2931
Kerens Middle Sch 200 Bobcat Ln, Kerens 75144 Greg Priddy	6-8		198 19		903/396-2570

- **Mildred Ind School Dist** PID: 01043615   903/872-6505
  5475 S US Highway 287, Corsicana 75109   Fax 903/872-1341

Schools: 1 \ *Teachers:* 59 \ *Students:* 720 \ *Special Ed Students:* 47 \ *LEP Students:* 19 \ *Ethnic:* African American 2%, Hispanic 15%, Native American: 1%, Caucasian 82% \ *Exp:* $334 (High) \ *Poverty:* 10% \ *Title I:* $86,047 \ *Open-Close:* 08/07 - 05/21

Shannon Baker 1,11
Tim Gorden 3,5
Tiffany Morgan 36,69,83,85,270*
Beverly McQuary 2
Cody Fagan 6*
Bradley Boyte 67

Public Schs..Principal	Grd	Prgm	Enr/#Cls	SN	
Mildred Sch 5475 S US Highway 287, Corsicana 75109 Janice Schwarz \ Michelle Coker \ Aaron Tidwell	K-12	ATV	720 50	39%	903/872-6505

- **Rice Ind School Dist** PID: 01043641   903/326-4287
  1302 SW McKinney St, Rice 75155   Fax 903/326-4164

Schools: 4 \ *Teachers:* 72 \ *Students:* 895 \ *Special Ed Students:* 56 \ *LEP Students:* 209 \ *Ethnic:* African American 3%, Hispanic 62%, Caucasian 35% \ *Exp:* $414 (High) \ *Poverty:* 23% \ *Title I:* $216,164 \ *Open-Close:* 08/19 - 05/21 \ *DTBP:* $342 (High) ◼

Lynn Jantzen 1
Troy Cox 3,5
Andy Mills 6
Robert Allen 8,83
Justin Bruton 16
Kathleen Evans 57
Robert Gray 91
Julie Obanon 2,11,58,68,88
Lisa Thedford 4
Rachel Tidwell 7*
Kelly Walters 9*
Casey Sellers 31
Shannna Lopez 67
Mary Kirby 295

Public Schs..Principal	Grd	Prgm	Enr/#Cls	SN	
Ⓐ Navarro Co Alt Educ Ctr 705 N Beaton St, Corsicana 75110 Melinda Richardson	K-12		70		903/872-4502
Rice Elem Sch 1500 SW McKinney St, Rice 75155 Kelly Walters	PK-2	T	200 19	77%	903/326-4151 Fax 903/326-4900
Rice High Sch 1400 SW McKinney St, Rice 75155 Robert Allen	9-12	TV	260 20	60%	903/326-4502 Fax 903/326-5042
Rice Intermediate Middle Sch 1402 SW McKinney St, Rice 75155 Monnie Metcalfe	5-8	T	435	70%	903/326-4190 Fax 903/326-4620

NAVARRO CATHOLIC SCHOOLS

- **Diocese of Dallas Ed Office** PID: 01012367
  Listing includes only schools located in this county. See District Index for location of Diocesan Offices.

Catholic Schs..Principal	Grd	Prgm	Enr/#Cls	SN	
James L Collins Catholic Sch 3000 W State Highway 22, Corsicana 75110 Vicky Morrison	PK-8		160 10		903/872-1751 Fax 903/872-1186

NAVARRO PRIVATE SCHOOLS

Private Schs..Principal	Grd	Prgm	Enr/#Cls	SN	
Agape Christian Academy 3116 W State Highway 22, Corsicana 75110 Kathi McMullan	PK-12		120		903/641-0900 Fax 903/641-0905
Park Meadows Academy 3401 Country Club Rd, Corsicana 75110 Paul Davis	PK-12		60		903/872-2391

NEWTON COUNTY

NEWTON PUBLIC SCHOOLS

- **Burkeville Ind School Dist** PID: 01043677   409/565-2201
  231 County Road 2099, Burkeville 75932   Fax 409/565-2012

Schools: 2 \ *Teachers:* 21 \ *Students:* 250 \ *Special Ed Students:* 27 \ *LEP Students:* 3 \ *College-Bound:* 25% \ *Ethnic:* African American 25%, Hispanic 1%, Caucasian 74% \ *Exp:* $480 (High) \ *Poverty:* 31% \ *Title I:* $130,113 \ *Special Education:* $78,000 \ *Open-Close:* 08/13 - 05/15 \ *DTBP:* $402 (High)

Dr Brant Graham 1,11
Donnie Dickerson 3,5*
Phylis Stephens 8,31,57,83,88,275,294
Ronald Graham 67
Pam Dickerson 2,286
Betty Jennings 4*
Donna Graham 58
Trista Wood 73*

Public Schs..Principal	Grd	Prgm	Enr/#Cls	SN	
Burkeville Elem Sch 231 County Road 2099, Burkeville 75932 Kimberly Urie	PK-6	T	144 30	81%	409/565-4284 Fax 409/565-4558
Burkeville Jr Sr High Sch 231 County Road 2099, Burkeville 75932 Kimberly Urie	7-12	T	99 18	60%	409/565-4284 Fax 409/565-4558

---

1 Superintendent	8 Curric/Instruct K-12	19 Chief Financial Officer	29 Family/Consumer Science	39 Social Studies K-12	49 English/Lang Arts Elem	59 Special Education Elem	69 Academic Assessment
2 Bus/Finance/Purchasing	9 Curric/Instruct Elem	20 Art K-12	30 Adult Education	40 Social Studies Elem	50 English/Lang Arts Sec	60 Special Education Sec	70 Research/Development
3 Buildings And Grounds	10 Curric/Instruct Sec	21 Art Elem	31 Career/Sch-to-Work K-12	41 Social Studies Sec	51 Reading K-12	61 Foreign/World Lang K-12	71 Public Information
4 Food Service	11 Federal Program	22 Art Sec	32 Career/Sch-to-Work Elem	42 Science K-12	52 Reading Elem	62 Foreign/World Lang Elem	72 Summer School
5 Transportation	12 Title I	23 Music K-12	33 Career/Sch-to-Work Sec	43 Science Elem	53 Reading Sec	63 Foreign/World Lang Sec	73 Instructional Tech
6 Athletic	13 Title V	24 Music Elem	34 Early Childhood Ed	44 Science Sec	54 Remedial Reading K-12	64 Religious Education K-12	74 Inservice Training
7 Health Services	15 Asst Superintendent	25 Music Sec	35 Health/Phys Education	45 Math K-12	55 Remedial Reading Elem	65 Religious Education Elem	75 Marketing/Distributive
	16 Instructional Media Svcs	26 Business Education	36 Guidance Services K-12	46 Math Elem	56 Remedial Reading Sec	66 Religious Education Sec	76 Info Systems
	17 Chief Operations Officer	27 Career & Tech Ed	37 Guidance Services Elem	47 Math Sec	57 Bilingual/ELL	67 School Board President	77 Psychological Assess
	18 Chief Academic Officer	28 Technology Education	38 Guidance Services Sec	48 English/Lang Arts K-12	58 Special Education K-12	68 Teacher Personnel	78 Affirmative Action

Texas School Directory — Nolan County

- **Newton Ind School Dist** PID: 01043744   409/420-6600
  720 Rusk St, Newton 75966   Fax 409/379-2189

Schools: 3 \ **Teachers:** 89 \ **Students:** 1,026 \ **Special Ed Students:** 123 \ **College-Bound:** 51% \ **Ethnic:** Asian 1%, African American 41%, Hispanic 5%, Caucasian 54% \ **Exp:** $615 (High) \ **Poverty:** 27% \ **Title I:** $454,498 \ **Special Education:** $289,000 \ **Open-Close:** 08/15 - 05/22 \ **DTBP:** $363 (High)

Michelle Barrow	1,11	Malinda Ortolon	2
Kathy Morrow	4	Drew Johnston	6
Debbie Johnston	8,69	Johnny Metz	15
Bill Gobblin	58,88	Donnie Meek	67
Connie Richardson	84		

Public Schs..Principal	Grd	Prgm	Enr/#Cls	SN	
Newton Elem Sch 414 Main St, Newton 75966 Bonetha Christopher	PK-5	T	524 37	70%	409/420-6600 Fax 409/379-2801
Newton High Sch 2812 US Highway 190 E, Newton 75966 Lydia Bean	9-12	TV	297 30	56%	409/420-6600 Fax 409/379-3321
Newton Middle Sch 2814 US Highway 190 E, Newton 75966 Cathy Marshall	6-8	T	205 27	66%	409/420-6600 Fax 409/379-5082

NEWTON PRIVATE SCHOOLS

Private Schs..Principal	Grd	Prgm	Enr/#Cls	SN	
Agape Christian Academy 216 Glover Dr, Newton 75966 Holly Hopson	K-12		20		409/379-4611

NOLAN COUNTY

NOLAN PUBLIC SCHOOLS

- **Blackwell Cons Ind Sch Dist** PID: 01043794   325/282-2311
  610 N Alamo St, Blackwell 79506   Fax 325/282-2027

Schools: 1 \ **Teachers:** 23 \ **Students:** 153 \ **Special Ed Students:** 15 \ **LEP Students:** 3 \ **College-Bound:** 98% \ **Ethnic:** Hispanic 17%, Native American: 1%, Caucasian 82% \ **Exp:** $1,646 (High) \ **Poverty:** 21% \ **Title I:** $42,838 \ **Open-Close:** 08/14 - 05/15 \ **DTBP:** $373 (High)

Abe Gott	1,84	Jill Jones	2*
Ronnie Harris	3,5*	Beverly Williams	4
Clint Lowry	6*	Bryan Shipman	8,11,31,36,58,69,83*
Cassie Olivas	16*	Bryce Barnett	27*
Sherie Smith	57*	Jason Jones	67
Lindsey Colsen	270		

Public Schs..Principal	Grd	Prgm	Enr/#Cls	SN	
Blackwell Sch 610 N Alamo St, Blackwell 79506 Jason Powers \ Bryan Shipman	PK-12	AV	153 30	42%	325/282-2311 Fax 325/282-4384

- **Highland Ind School Dist** PID: 01043859   325/766-3652
  6625 FM 608, Roscoe 79545   Fax 325/766-2281

Schools: 1 \ **Teachers:** 21 \ **Students:** 250 \ **Special Ed Students:** 17 \ **College-Bound:** 98% \ **Ethnic:** Hispanic 20%, Caucasian 80% \ **Exp:** $459 (High) \ **Poverty:** 29% \ **Title I:** $25,466 \ **Open-Close:** 08/20 - 05/25 \ **DTBP:** $342 (High)

Duane Hyde	1,11	Lynn Duniven	2
Bradley Hall	3,5	Kyle Jeffrey	6*
Shahala Hoelscher	36,69*	Leigh Petty	57
Brent Allen	67	Brooke Sanford	73*

Public Schs..Principal	Grd	Prgm	Enr/#Cls	SN	
Highland Sch 6625 FM 608, Roscoe 79545 David Acevedo	PK-12	TV	250 17	38%	325/766-3651

- **Roscoe Collegiate Ind Sch Dist** PID: 01043885   325/766-3629
  1101 W 7th St, Roscoe 79545   Fax 325/766-3138

Schools: 3 \ **Teachers:** 46 \ **Students:** 620 \ **Special Ed Students:** 27 \ **LEP Students:** 43 \ **College-Bound:** 90% \ **Ethnic:** African American 2%, Hispanic 50%, Caucasian 48% \ **Exp:** $1,073 (High) \ **Poverty:** 26% \ **Title I:** $110,615 \ **Open-Close:** 08/08 - 05/15 \ **DTBP:** $365 (High)

Dr Kim Alexander	1	Rita Fried	2
Joe Smith	3,5	Jake Freeman	6*
Gregory Althof	8*	Crystal Althof	11*
Jared Seals	16,73	Marsha Alexander	36,83,88,271,273*
Lindsey Freeman	57	Janie Abrigo	58
Wes Williams	67	Andrew Wilson	285*

Public Schs..Principal	Grd	Prgm	Enr/#Cls	SN	
Roscoe Collegiate High Sch 700 Elm St, Roscoe 79545 Gregory Althof	6-12	TV	257 12	48%	325/766-3327 Fax 325/766-3419
Roscoe Collegiate Mont ECC 1006 Main St, Roscoe 79545 Crystal Althof	PK-K		160		325/766-3323 Fax 325/766-3605
Roscoe Elem Sch 800 Elm St, Roscoe 79545 Crystal Althof	1-5	T	250 10	49%	325/766-3323 Fax 325/766-3605

- **Sweetwater ISD School Dist** PID: 01043914   325/235-8601
  207 Musgrove St, Sweetwater 79556   Fax 325/235-5561

Schools: 5 \ **Teachers:** 158 \ **Students:** 2,200 \ **Special Ed Students:** 293 \ **LEP Students:** 52 \ **Ethnic:** African American 7%, Hispanic 56%, Caucasian 37% \ **Exp:** $473 (High) \ **Poverty:** 27% \ **Title I:** $806,921 \ **Open-Close:** 08/20 - 05/27 \ **DTBP:** $328 (High) \

Dr George McFarland	1	Casey Bills	2
Tim Hampton	3,91	Barbara Woolsey	4*
Angela Duran	5	Ben McGeehee	6,35
Nancy Soles	7,85	Melinda McCarty	11,15,57,61
Rebecca Duncan	27*	Amy Clark	31,38,88*
Kirk Stroman	58	Jeff Allen	67
Tammi Stafford	69	Nick Rutherford	76,84,95,286

Public Schs..Principal	Grd	Prgm	Enr/#Cls	SN	
East Ridge Elem Sch 1700 E 12th St, Sweetwater 79556 Jimmy Bennett	2-3	T	335 15	74%	325/235-5282 Fax 325/235-3740

Nueces County

Market Data Retrieval

Southeast Elem Sch — PK-1 T 322 76% 325/235-9222
1201 Mustang Dr, Sweetwater 79556 — Fax 325/235-0260
Peggy Elliott

Sweetwater High Sch — 9-12 ATV 530 58% 325/235-4371
1205 Ragland St, Sweetwater 79556 — Fax 325/235-4861
Jeff Perez

Sweetwater Intermediate Sch — 4-5 T 330 75% 325/235-3491
705 E 3rd St, Sweetwater 79556 — 17 — Fax 325/235-8016
Mandy Welch

Sweetwater Middle Sch — 6-8 T 521 70% 325/236-6303
305 Lamar St, Sweetwater 79556 — 47 — Fax 325/236-6941
Jeff Withrow

NUECES COUNTY

NUECES PUBLIC SCHOOLS

- **Agua Dulce Ind School Dist** PID: 01043988 — 361/998-2542
1 Longhorn Drive, Agua Dulce 78330 — Fax 361/998-2816

Schools: 2 \ *Teachers:* 29 \ *Students:* 370 \ *Special Ed Students:* 26 \ *LEP Students:* 3 \ *College-Bound:* 44% \ *Ethnic:* African American 1%, Hispanic 80%, Caucasian 19% \ *Exp:* $614 (High) \ *Poverty:* 20% \ *Title I:* $91,743 \ *Special Education:* $25,000 \ *Open-Close:* 08/20 - 06/01 \ *DTBP:* $368 (High)

Nora Lopez 1   James Schumann 2
Rachel Vardeman ....8,11,57,58,69,270*   Noel Estrada 67
Tom Sorrell 73,84

Public Schs..Principal	Grd	Prgm	Enr/#Cls	SN		
Agua Dulce Elem Sch 1 Longhorn Drive, Agua Dulce 78330 Nora Lopez	PK-5	T	150 16		80%	361/998-2335 Fax 361/998-2333
Agua Dulce Secondary Sch 1 Longhorn Drive, Agua Dulce 78330 Dr Christopher Daniels	6-12	T	188 18		65%	361/998-2214 Fax 361/998-2994

- **Banquete Ind School Dist** PID: 01044011 — 361/387-2551
4339 4th St, Banquete 78339 — Fax 361/387-7188

Schools: 3 \ *Teachers:* 70 \ *Students:* 954 \ *Special Ed Students:* 87 \ *LEP Students:* 31 \ *College-Bound:* 100% \ *Ethnic:* African American 1%, Hispanic 82%, Caucasian 17% \ *Exp:* $468 (High) \ *Poverty:* 18% \ *Title I:* $190,552 \ *Open-Close:* 08/14 - 05/29 \ *DTBP:* $385 (High)

Dr Max Thompson 1,11,84   Adrian Pena 2
Yvonne Reagan 2   Leah Civis 4*
Kevin Hermes ....6*   Kerry Thompson 8
Roel Garza ....27*   Denise Blanchard 33,285*
Jennifer Garcia ....58,77*   Tracy Wright 67

Public Schs..Principal	Grd	Prgm	Enr/#Cls	SN		
Banquete Elem Sch 5436 Bulldog Ln, Banquete 78339 Adriana Tagle	PK-5	T	437 34		74%	361/387-4329 Fax 361/767-8105
Banquete High Sch 5519 E Highway 44, Banquete 78339 Denise Blanchard	9-12	TV	268 18		69%	361/387-8588 Fax 361/767-6504

Banquete Junior High Sch — 6-8 T 227 75% 361/387-2551
4339 4th St, Banquete 78339 — 15 — Fax 361/387-7051
Ramiro Pena

- **Bishop Cons Ind School Dist** PID: 01044059 — 361/584-3591
719 E 6th St, Bishop 78343 — Fax 361/584-3147

Schools: 5 \ *Teachers:* 91 \ *Students:* 1,472 \ *Special Ed Students:* 163 \ *LEP Students:* 49 \ *College-Bound:* 64% \ *Ethnic:* African American 1%, Hispanic 85%, Caucasian 14% \ *Exp:* $383 (High) \ *Poverty:* 19% \ *Title I:* $246,835 \ *Special Education:* $261,000 \ *Open-Close:* 08/26 - 05/21 \ *DTBP:* $553 (High)

Christina Gutierrez 1   Manuel Tamez 2
Charles Farek 3,5   Rachel DelGado 4
George Luna ....6*   Dr Eden Hernandez ... 8,11,34,58,69,73,81,83
Dr Andrea Kuyatt ....11,57,296*   Sheri Hayes 16,82,84
Lorena Garcia ....27,75*   Tracy Smith 39,48*
Shirley Barrington 42,45   Marc Morales 67

Public Schs..Principal	Grd	Prgm	Enr/#Cls	SN		
Bishop Elem Sch 200 S Fir Ave, Bishop 78343 Rosie Trevino	3-5	T	256 14		69%	361/584-3571
Bishop High Sch 100 Badger Ln, Bishop 78343 Dr Andrea Kuyatt	9-12	ATV	489 50		54%	361/584-2547 Fax 361/584-3593
Bishop Primary Sch 705 W Main St, Bishop 78343 Emily Salazar	PK-2	T	270 21		76%	361/584-2434 Fax 361/584-7600
Lillion E Luehrs Jr High Sch 717 E 6th St, Bishop 78343 Ray Garza	6-8	AT	350 20		66%	361/584-3576 Fax 361/584-3592
Petronila Elem Sch 2391 County Road 67, Robstown 78380 Rick Gutierrez	PK-5	T	107 7		80%	361/387-2834 Fax 361/584-3880

- **Calallen Ind School Dist** PID: 01044114 — 361/242-5600
4205 Wildcat Dr, Corp Christi 78410 — Fax 361/242-5620

Schools: 6 \ *Teachers:* 280 \ *Students:* 4,000 \ *Special Ed Students:* 408 \ *LEP Students:* 116 \ *College-Bound:* 54% \ *Ethnic:* Asian 1%, African American 2%, Hispanic 60%, Caucasian 37% \ *Exp:* $312 (High) \ *Poverty:* 11% \ *Title I:* $624,059 \ *Special Education:* $808,000 \ *Open-Close:* 08/14 - 05/28 \ *DTBP:* $96 (Med) \ ▣

Dr Arturo Almendarez 1   Kelsey Ramos 2
Randall Curtis 3,91   Leticia Gracia 4
Scott Chapman 5   Phil Danaher 6*
Teresa Shaw ....7,85*   Dr Anita Danaher 8,11,16
Rosanne Meyer 9,57   Blare McLear 10,69
Melana Silva 10   Emily Lorenz 15,68,83
Sony Durrwachter 34,57,58,72,88,271   Jason Floyd 67
Candy Morris 69   Kevin Beatty 73*

Public Schs..Principal	Grd	Prgm	Enr/#Cls	SN		
© Calallen Charter High Sch 2402 Cornett Dr, Corp Christi 78410 Yvonne Marquez-Neth	11-12	TV	80		40%	361/242-6800
Calallen High Sch 4001 Wildcat Dr, Corp Christi 78410 Yvonne Marquez-Neth	9-12	AV	1,256 105		38%	361/242-5626 Fax 361/242-5632
Calallen Middle Sch 4602 Cornett Dr, Corp Christi 78410 Rey Saenz	6-8	T	973 65		47%	361/242-5672 Fax 361/242-0628

1 Superintendent	8 Curric/Instruct K-12	19 Chief Financial Officer	29 Family/Consumer Science	39 Social Studies K-12	49 English/Lang Arts Elem	59 Special Education Elem	69 Academic Assessment
2 Bus/Finance/Purchasing	9 Curric/Instruct Elem	20 Art K-12	30 Adult Education	40 Social Studies Elem	50 English/Lang Arts Sec	60 Special Education Sec	70 Research/Development
3 Buildings And Grounds	10 Curric/Instruct Sec	21 Art Elem	31 Career/Sch-to-Work K-12	41 Social Studies Sec	51 Reading K-12	61 Foreign/World Lang K-12	71 Public Information
4 Food Service	11 Federal Program	22 Art Sec	32 Career/Sch-to-Work Elem	42 Science K-12	52 Reading Elem	62 Foreign/World Lang Elem	72 Summer School
5 Transportation	12 Title I	23 Music K-12	33 Career/Sch-to-Work Sec	43 Science Elem	53 Reading Sec	63 Foreign/World Lang Sec	73 Instructional Tech
6 Athletic	13 Title V	24 Music Elem	34 Early Childhood Ed	44 Science Sec	54 Remedial Reading K-12	64 Religious Education K-12	74 Inservice Training
7 Health Services	15 Asst Superintendent	25 Music Sec	35 Health/Phys Education	45 Math K-12	55 Remedial Reading Elem	65 Religious Education Elem	75 Marketing/Distributive
	16 Instructional Media Svcs	26 Business Education	36 Guidance Services K-12	46 Math Elem	56 Remedial Reading Sec	66 Religious Education Sec	76 Info Systems
	17 Chief Operations Officer	27 Career & Tech Ed	37 Guidance Services Elem	47 Math Sec	57 Bilingual/ELL	67 School Board President	77 Psychological Assess
	18 Chief Academic Officer	28 Technology Education	38 Guidance Services Sec	48 English/Lang Arts K-12	58 Special Education K-12	68 Teacher Personnel	78 Affirmative Action

Texas School Directory — Nueces County

School	Grd	Prgm	Enr/#Cls	SN	Phone
East Elem Sch 3709 Lott Ave, Corp Christi 78410 Kimberly Rodriguez	PK-3	T	593 18	60%	361/242-5938 Fax 361/242-5944
MaGee Elem Sch 4201 Calallen Dr, Corp Christi 78410 Dalia Torres	4-5	T	559 38	49%	361/242-5900 Fax 361/242-5913
Wood River Elem Sch 15118 Dry Creek Dr, Corp Christi 78410 Dr Debbie Litton	PK-3	T	653 28	39%	361/242-7560 Fax 361/387-3114

● **Corpus Christi Ind Sch Dist** PID: 01044176   361/695-7200
801 Leopard St, Corp Christi 78401   Fax 361/886-9209

Schools: 58 \ **Teachers:** 2,299 \ **Students:** 38,094 \
Special Ed Students: 3,365 \ **LEP Students:** 2,173 \ **College-Bound:** 50%
\ **Ethnic:** Asian 2%, African American 4%, Hispanic 80%, Caucasian 14% \ **Exp:** $366 (High) \ **Poverty:** 21% \ **Title I:** $13,295,779 \
Special Education: $6,734,000 \ **Open-Close:** 08/26 - 05/28 \ **DTBP:** $190 (High) \ 🅕 🅣

Dr Roland Hernandez 1	Roxanne Douglas 2
Brett Bostian 3	Jody Houston 4
Kyle Pelichet 5	Brenda Marshall 6
Angie Guerrero 7*	Dr James Rosebrock 8,18
Dr Susan Holt 8,288	Kelli Powell 10
Dr Laura Stout 10,273	Valarie Buhidar 12,40
Jennifer Arismendi 13,58,77	Elizabeth Ortega Ruiz 20
Orlando Salazar 27,36,79,90,285	Iris Estrada 34
Dr Ada Besinaiz 36,83	Ruben Rocha 41
Luci Sosa 43	Wendy DeVoe 44
Cindy Penez 46	Dr Shere Salinas 47
Catherine Susser 67	Debbie Nunez 68
Dr Elda Garcia 69,294	Leanne Libby 71
Irma Ibanez 73	Marilyn Doughty 76,295
Kirby Warnke 91	Angie Ramirez 273
Dr Ralph Silva 273	Cynthia Hernandez 280

Public Schs..Principal	Grd	Prgm	Enr/#Cls	SN	Phone
Berlanga Elem Sch 4120 Carroll Ln, Corp Christi 78411 Aurelia Barrera	PK-5	T	690	78%	361/878-2160 Fax 361/878-2303
Blanche Moore Elem Sch 6121 Durant Dr, Corp Christi 78414 Christine Marroquin	PK-5	T	587 40	79%	361/878-2660 Fax 361/994-3619
C P Yeager Elem Sch 5414 Tripoli Dr, Corp Christi 78411 Tammy Gathright	PK-5	T	323 25	73%	361/878-2920 Fax 361/878-1832
Calk-Wilson Elem Sch 3925 Fort Worth St, Corp Christi 78411 Sheila Thomas	PK-5	T	761 26	70%	361/878-2860 Fax 361/878-1831
Carl O Hamlin Middle Sch 3900 Hamlin Dr, Corp Christi 78411 Prudence Farrell	6-8	ATV	612 45	79%	361/878-4210 Fax 361/878-1839
Claude Cunningham Middle Sch 2901 McArdle Rd, Corp Christi 78416 Irosema Salinas-DeLeon	6-8	TV	510 56	92%	361/878-4720 Fax 361/878-1844
Club Estates Elem Sch 5222 Merganser Dr, Corp Christi 78413 **Kay Bircher**	PK-5	T	405 24	55%	361/878-3780 Fax 361/994-3615
Ⓐ Coles High Sch & Ed Center 924 Winnebago St, Corp Christi 78401 Monica Bayarena	9-12	TV	250 14	89%	361/878-7380 Fax 361/844-0436
Collegiate High Sch 101 Baldwin Blvd - St, Corp Christi 78404 Tracie Rodriguez	9-12		399 13		361/698-2425 Fax 361/698-2427
David Crockett Elem Sch 2625 Belton St, Corp Christi 78416 Dr Olivia Ballesteros	PK-5	T	471 25	89%	361/878-2220 Fax 361/878-2366
Dawson Elem Sch 6821 Sanders Dr, Corp Christi 78413 Roberto Arredondo	PK-5	T	572 34	55%	361/878-0140 Fax 361/878-4805 🅕 🅣
Dorothy Adkins Middle Sch 2402 Ennis Joslin Rd, Corp Christi 78414 Norma Cullum	6-8	T	678	53%	361/878-3800 Fax 361/878-3828
Driscoll Middle Sch 3501 Kenwood Dr, Corp Christi 78408 George Lerma	6-8	TV	779 60	92%	361/878-4660 Fax 361/886-9890
E E & Jovita Mireles Elem Sch 7658 Cimarron Blvd, Corp Christi 78414 Alexis Soulas	PK-5		656 40	31%	361/878-0120 Fax 361/994-6970
Early Childhood Dev Center 6300 Ocean Dr Unit 5834, Corp Christi 78412 Kellye Loving	PK-6	T	187 8	49%	361/825-3366 Fax 361/825-3301
Ella Barnes Elem Sch 2829 Oso Pkwy, Corp Christi 78414 Katherine Gorman	PK-5	T	663 30	47%	361/878-7330 Fax 361/994-0860
Elliot Grant Middle Sch 4350 Aaron Dr, Corp Christi 78413 Carla Villarreal	6-8	T	947 125	48%	361/878-3740 Fax 361/878-1865
Evans Elem Sch 1315 Comanche St, Corp Christi 78401 Amanda Cameron	PK-5	T	411 23	98%	361/878-2240 Fax 361/886-9877
Faye Webb Elem Sch 6953 Boardwalk Ave, Corp Christi 78414 Kristina Kahil	PK-5		761 30	37%	361/878-2740 Fax 361/991-2167
Foy H Moody High Sch 1818 Trojan Dr, Corp Christi 78416 Dr Sandra Clement	9-12	TV	1,614	77%	361/878-7340 Fax 361/857-8253
Fred R Sanders Elem Sch 4102 Republic Dr, Corp Christi 78413 John Prezas	PK-5	T	408 25	78%	361/878-2820 Fax 361/878-1829
Harold Branch Acad Career/Tech 3902 Morgan Ave, Corp Christi 78405 Dr Tracie Rodriguez	Voc	AGT	222	61%	361/878-4780 Fax 361/885-7797
Harold C Kaffie Middle Sch 5922 Brockhampton St, Corp Christi 78414 Jamie Copeland	6-8	V	1,070 40	35%	361/878-3700 Fax 361/994-3604
Hicks Elem Sch 3602 McArdle Rd, Corp Christi 78415 **Alicia Garza**	PK-5	T	704 21	83%	361/878-2200 Fax 361/806-0578
J A Garcia Elem Sch 1945 Gollihar Rd, Corp Christi 78416 Norma DeLeon	PK-5	T	663 23	94%	361/878-2280 Fax 361/878-2367
James W Fannin Elem Sch 2730 Gollihar Rd, Corp Christi 78415 Analisa Farah	PK-5	T	450 40	87%	361/878-2260 Fax 361/878-1820
Kolda Elem Sch 3730 Rodd Field Rd, Corp Christi 78414 Josie Alvarez	PK-5		719	27%	361/878-2980 Fax 361/980-1136
Kostoryz Elem Sch 3602 Panama Dr, Corp Christi 78415 Kelsie Morris	PK-5	T	473 35	93%	361/878-2540 Fax 361/878-2329
Lorenzo De Zavala Spec Emp Sch 3125 Ruth St, Corp Christi 78405 Judith Hinojosa	PK-5	T	646 32	93%	361/878-2720 Fax 361/886-9884
Los Encinos Ses Elem Sch 1826 Frio St, Corp Christi 78417 Christine Sierra	PK-5	T	404 22	84%	361/878-2600 Fax 361/878-1826
Luther Jones Elem Sch 7533 Lipes Blvd, Corp Christi 78413 Lisa Bowers	PK-5		552 30	33%	361/878-0100 Fax 361/994-3616
Martin Middle Sch 3502 Greenwood Dr, Corp Christi 78416 Javier Granados	6-8	TV	609 45	100%	361/878-4690 Fax 361/878-2455

79 Student Personnel	91 Safety/Security	275 Response To Intervention	298 Grant Writer/Ptnrships
80 Driver Ed/Safety	92 Magnet School	277 Remedial Math K-12	750 Chief Innovation Officer
81 Gifted/Talented	93 Parental Involvement	280 Literacy Coach	751 Chief of Staff
82 Video Services	95 Tech Prep Program	285 STEM	752 Social Emotional Learning
83 Substance Abuse Prev	97 Chief Infomation Officer	286 Digital Learning	
84 Erate	98 Chief Technology Officer	288 Common Core Standards	**Other School Types**
85 AIDS Education	270 Character Education	294 Accountability	Ⓐ = Alternative School
88 Alternative/At Risk	271 Migrant Education	295 Network System	Ⓒ = Charter School
89 Multi-Cultural Curriculum	273 Teacher Mentor	296 Title II Programs	Ⓜ = Magnet School
90 Social Work	274 Before/After Sch	297 Webmaster	Ⓨ = Year-Round School

School Programs
A = Alternative Program
G = Adult Classes
M = Magnet Program
T = Title I Schoolwide
V = Career & Tech Ed Programs

Social Media
🅕 = Facebook
🅣 = Twitter

New Schools are shaded
New Superintendents and Principals are bold
Personnel with email addresses are underscored

TX—303

Nueces County — Market Data Retrieval

School	Grd	Prgm	Enr/#Cls	SN	Phone
Marvin P Baker Middle Sch 3445 Pecan St, Corp Christi 78411 John Dobbins	6-8	TV	1,040 40	52%	361/878-4600 Fax 361/878-1834
Mary Carroll High Sch 5301 Weber Rd, Corp Christi 78411 Kelly Manlove	9-12	TV	1,591 140	53%	361/878-5140 Fax 361/878-2403
Mary Grett Sch 4402 Castenon St, Corp Christi 78416 Dr Debra Stanley	Spec	T	82 16	72%	361/878-1738 Fax 361/878-2301
Meadowbrook Elem Sch 901 Meadowbrook Dr, Corp Christi 78412 Dr Latricia Johnson	PK-5	T	433 32	64%	361/878-2620 Fax 361/994-3650
Metro Elem School of Design 1707 Ayers St, Corp Christi 78404 Cori Gilbert	K-6	TV	608 100	69%	361/878-2780 Fax 361/878-1818
Miller HS-Metro Sch of Design 1 Battlin Buc Blvd, Corp Christi 78408 Bruce Wilson	7-12	TV	1,345 85	71%	361/878-5100 Fax 361/883-1928
Montclair Elem Sch 5241 Kentner St, Corp Christi 78412 Roy Barrera	PK-5	T	336 29	41%	361/878-0160 Fax 361/994-6940
Moses Menger Elem Sch 2401 S Alameda St, Corp Christi 78404 Christina Barrera	PK-5	T	344 25	89%	361/878-2640 Fax 361/886-9880
Oak Park Special Emphasis Sch 3801 Leopard St, Corp Christi 78408 Kellye Loving	PK-5	T	663 29	99%	361/878-2120 Fax 361/886-2139
Paul R Haas Middle Sch 6630 McArdle Rd, Corp Christi 78412 Lynda DeLeon	6-8	TV	378 40	79%	361/878-4240 Fax 361/994-3626
Rafael Galvan Elem Sch 3126 Masterson Dr, Corp Christi 78415 Diana Ybarra	PK-5	T	653 37	62%	361/878-2800 Fax 361/878-1821
Richard King High Sch 5225 Gollihar Rd, Corp Christi 78412 Elizabeth Perez	9-12	TV	1,522 80	52%	361/906-3400 Fax 361/994-6918
Sam Houston Elem Sch 363 Norton St, Corp Christi 78415 Zonia Lopez	PK-5	T	463 35	89%	361/878-2520 Fax 361/878-1823
Schanen Estates Elem Sch 5717 Killarmet Dr, Corp Christi 78413 David Crabtree	PK-5	T	410 32	69%	361/878-2940 Fax 361/878-1830
Shaw Spec Emphasis Sch 2920 Soledad St, Corp Christi 78405 Rebecca Casas	PK-5	T	527 39	99%	361/878-2100 Fax 361/878-2109
South Park Middle Sch 2901 McArdle Rd, Corp Christi 78415 Anna Fuentes	6-8	TV	432 33	82%	361/878-4720 Fax 361/878-1844
Ⓐ Student Support Center 4401 Greenwood Dr, Corp Christi 78416 Enrique Vela	1-12	V	102	88%	361/878-2840 Fax 361/878-1437
T G Allen Elem Sch 1414 18th St, Corp Christi 78404 Elodia Gutierrez	PK-5	T	349 28	97%	361/878-2140 Fax 361/886-9874
Tom Browne Middle Sch 4301 Schanen Blvd, Corp Christi 78413 Dr John Trevino	6-8	TV	567 50	59%	361/878-4270 Fax 361/878-1836
Veterans Memorial High Sch 3750 Cimarron Blvd, Corp Christi 78414 Kimberly James	9-12		2,159	29%	361/878-7900 Fax 361/878-7910
W B Ray High Sch 1002 Texan Trl, Corp Christi 78411 Roxanne Cuevas	9-12	TV	2,074	64%	361/878-7300 Fax 361/852-6528
Weldon Gibson Elem Sch 5723 Hampshire Rd, Corp Christi 78408 Julissa Segovia	PK-5		469 25	91%	361/878-2500 Fax 361/289-7406
Weldon Smith Elem Sch 6902 Williams Dr, Corp Christi 78412 Rebecca Raesz	PK-5	T	463 29	79%	361/878-2760 Fax 361/994-3681
William B Travis Elem Sch 3210 Churchill Dr, Corp Christi 78415 Laura Quiroz-Colunga	PK-5	T	484 20	99%	361/878-2700 Fax 361/884-0341
Windsor Park Elem Sch 4525 S Alameda St, Corp Christi 78412 Dr Kimberly Bissell	1-5		589 31	28%	361/878-3770 Fax 361/994-3621
Woodlawn Elem Sch 1110 Woodlawn Dr, Corp Christi 78412 Kathryn Ortiz	PK-5	T	330 24	74%	361/878-2900 Fax 361/994-3622

● **Driscoll Ind School Dist** PID: 01044798 361/387-7349
310 W Dragon St, Driscoll 78351

Schools: 1 \ *Teachers:* 25 \ *Students:* 320 \ *Special Ed Students:* 25 \ *LEP Students:* 5 \ *Exp:* $494 (High) \ *Poverty:* 25% \ *Title I:* $110,960 \ *Special Education:* $55,000 \ *Open-Close:* 07/26 - 05/25 \ *DTBP:* $348 (High)

Dr Cindy Garcia ....1 Annette Vasquez 2,11
Mark Gonzalez ....3* Minerva Zapata 4
Danny Vasquez ....6* Lynn Landenberger 8*
Monica Morin .... 9,37,57,69,88,93,270* Veronica Ramon 67
Patricia Myers 73*

Public Schs..Principal	Grd	Prgm	Enr/#Cls	SN	
Driscoll Sch 310 W Dragon St, Driscoll 78351 Lynn Landenberger	PK-8		320 26		361/387-7349

● **Flour Bluff Ind School Dist** PID: 01044815 361/694-9000
2505 Waldron Rd, Corp Christi 78418 Fax 361/694-9800

Schools: 7 \ *Teachers:* 365 \ *Students:* 5,750 \ *Special Ed Students:* 580 \ *LEP Students:* 164 \ *College-Bound:* 59% \ *Ethnic:* Asian 2%, African American 3%, Hispanic 45%, Caucasian 50% \ *Exp:* $254 (Med) \ *Poverty:* 14% \ *Title I:* $942,299 \ *Special Education:* $955,000 \ *Open-Close:* 08/26 - 05/28 \ *DTBP:* $147 (High) \ 🅵 🅴

Dr David Freeman ....1 Emily Youngblood 2
Clayton Pocius ....3,5 Gina Valdez 4
Christopher Steinbruck ....6 Allison Schaum 8,12,13,15*
Dr Linda Barganski ....11,83,298 Louise Day 15
Victor Lara ....23* Edgar Van Geem 58,77*
Shirley Thornton ....67 Jeanette Revels 68
Kimberly Sneed ....71 Alex Puente 73,76,84,295
Ron Fisher 91

Public Schs..Principal	Grd	Prgm	Enr/#Cls	SN	
Early Childhood Center 2505 Waldron Rd, Corp Christi 78418 Amy Seeds	PK-K	T	497 24	59%	361/694-9036 Fax 361/694-9810 🅵 🅴
Flour Bluff Elem Sch 2505 Waldron Rd, Corp Christi 78418 Dr Nikol Youngberg	3-4	T	794	50%	361/694-9500 Fax 361/694-9805 🅵 🅴
Flour Bluff High Sch 2505 Waldron Rd, Corp Christi 78418 James Crenshaw	9-12	AV	1,885 90	34%	361/694-9100 Fax 361/694-9802
Flour Bluff Interm Sch 2505 Waldron Rd, Corp Christi 78418 Sal Alvarado	5-6	T	824 33	47%	361/694-9400 Fax 361/694-9804
Flour Bluff Junior High Sch 2505 Waldron Rd, Corp Christi 78418 Brodie Wallace	7-8	T	890 25	46%	361/694-9300 Fax 361/694-9803

1 Superintendent	8 Curric/Instruct K-12	19 Chief Financial Officer	29 Family/Consumer Science	39 Social Studies K-12	49 English/Lang Arts Elem	59 Special Education Elem	69 Academic Assessment
2 Bus/Finance/Purchasing	9 Curric/Instruct Elem	20 Art K-12	30 Adult Education	40 Social Studies Elem	50 English/Lang Arts Sec	60 Special Education Sec	70 Research/Development
3 Buildings And Grounds	10 Curric/Instruct Sec	21 Art Elem	31 Career/Sch-to-Work K-12	41 Social Studies Sec	51 Reading K-12	61 Foreign/World Lang K-12	71 Public Information
4 Food Service	11 Federal Program	22 Art Sec	32 Career/Sch-to-Work Elem	42 Science K-12	52 Reading Elem	62 Foreign/World Lang Elem	72 Summer School
5 Transportation	12 Title I	23 Music K-12	33 Career/Sch-to-Work Sec	43 Science Elem	53 Reading Sec	63 Foreign/World Lang Sec	73 Instructional Tech
6 Athletic	13 Title V	24 Music Elem	34 Early Childhood Ed	44 Science Sec	54 Remedial Reading K-12	64 Religious Education K-12	74 Inservice Training
7 Health Services	14 Asst Superintendent	25 Music Sec	35 Health/Phys Education	45 Math K-12	55 Remedial Reading Elem	65 Religious Education Elem	75 Marketing/Distributive
	15 Instructional Media Svcs	26 Business Education	36 Guidance Services K-12	46 Math Elem	56 Remedial Reading Sec	66 Religious Education Sec	76 Info Systems
	16 Chief Operations Officer	27 Career & Tech Ed	37 Guidance Services Elem	47 Math Sec	57 Bilingual/ELL	67 School Board President	77 Psychological Assess
	18 Chief Academic Officer	28 Technology Education	38 Guidance Services Sec	48 English/Lang Arts K-12	58 Special Education K-12	68 Teacher Personnel	78 Affirmative Action

Texas School Directory — Nueces County

School	Grd	Prgm	Enr/#Cls	SN	Phone
Flour Bluff Primary Sch 2505 Waldron Rd, Corp Christi 78418 Shea Hernanadez	1-2	T	780 40	53%	361/694-9400 Fax 361/694-9806
University Preparatory HS 2505 Waldron Rd, Corp Christi 78418 Kim Alamo	9-12		302 8		361/694-9780 Fax 361/694-9814

● **London Ind School Dist** PID: 01044865 361/855-0183
1306 FM 43, Corp Christi 78415 Fax 361/855-0198

Schools: 1 \ *Teachers:* 65 \ *Students:* 900 \ *Special Ed Students:* 57 \ *LEP Students:* 5 \ *Ethnic:* Asian 2%, African American 2%, Hispanic 46%, Native American: 1%, Caucasian 49% \ *Exp:* $197 (Low) \ *Poverty:* 6% \ *Title I:* $32,662 \ *Special Education:* $93,000 \ *Open-Close:* 07/18 - 05/25 \ *DTBP:* $169 (High)

Dr David Freeman 1
Carlos Vargas 3,5
Cassie Freeman 11
Linda Bartlett 16,73*
Holly Salazar 58
Rebecca Hitchcock 74,88*
Vickie George 2,4
Roxanne Bright 4
Jessica Gutierrez 12,271*
Marcella Lockett 57*
Scott Frasier 67
Margo Glover 93*

Public Schs..Principal	Grd	Prgm	Enr/#Cls	SN	Phone
ⓨ London Sch 1306 FM 43, Corp Christi 78415 Jessica Gutierrez \ Amanda Barmore \ Rebecca Hitchcock	PK-12	M	900 23	11%	361/855-0092

● **Port Aransas Ind School Dist** PID: 01044889 361/749-1200
100 S Station St, Port Aransas 78373 Fax 361/749-1215

Schools: 3 \ *Teachers:* 47 \ *Students:* 550 \ *Special Ed Students:* 47 \ *LEP Students:* 4 \ *College-Bound:* 85% \ *Ethnic:* Asian 2%, Hispanic 21%, Caucasian 77% \ *Exp:* $181 (Low) \ *Poverty:* 12% \ *Title I:* $66,992 \ *Special Education:* $124,000 \ *Open-Close:* 08/20 - 05/28 \ *DTBP:* $553 (High)

Sharon McKinney 1,11
Steve Reaves 6*
Meghan Zigmond 16*
Marnie Pate 67
Tom Driver 73*
Carolsue Hipp 2,12
Kelye Garcie 9
Laura Cazalis 58
Danny Welch 69,83,85,93*
Tisha Piwetz 298

Public Schs..Principal	Grd	Prgm	Enr/#Cls	SN	Phone
Brundreet Middle Sch 100 S Station St, Port Aransas 78373 James Garrett	6-8	T	118 14	26%	361/749-1209 Fax 361/749-1218
Olsen Elem Sch 100 S Station St, Port Aransas 78373 **Kelye Garcie**	PK-5	T	259 20	46%	361/749-1212 Fax 361/749-1219
Port Aransas High Sch 100 S Station St, Port Aransas 78373 Jim Potts	9-12	TV	148 25	18%	361/749-1206 Fax 361/749-1226 f t

● **Robstown Ind School Dist** PID: 01044906 361/767-6600
801 N 1st St, Robstown 78380 Fax 361/387-6311

Schools: 7 \ *Teachers:* 190 \ *Students:* 2,000 \ *Special Ed Students:* 299 \ *LEP Students:* 95 \ *College-Bound:* 36% \ *Ethnic:* African American 1%, Hispanic 97%, Caucasian 2% \ *Exp:* $360 (High) \ *Poverty:* 33% \ *Title I:* $1,846,087 \ *Special Education:* $633,000 \ *Open-Close:* 08/12 - 05/20 \ *DTBP:* $200 (High)

Dr Jose Moreno 1
Lee Gonzalez 3
Nina Conway 2,19
Lisa Mendoza 4
Richard Gonzalez 5,27,73,76,84,286
Rosi Moreno 7*
Lornea Ceballos 8
Dr Daniel Ceballos 15
Maricela Pena 30*
Oscar Lopez 67
Delma Salinas 81
Michelle Delapena 93
Arturo Garcia 6
Diana Silvas 8,15,36,68,285,288
Yolanda Reyna 11,57,83*
Charles Cabrera 23*
Pamela Kiawatski 58
Kelsey Picou 71
Eric Gonzalez 88,275

Public Schs..Principal	Grd	Prgm	Enr/#Cls	SN	Phone
Lotspeich Elem Sch 1100 Ruben Chavez Rd, Robstown 78380 Angelita Lopez	K-3		242 24		361/767-6655 Fax 361/387-6019
Robert Driscoll Jr Elem Sch 122 W Avenue H, Robstown 78380 Manuel Lunoff	K-3	T	300 29	91%	361/767-6641 Fax 361/767-6610
Robstown High Sch 609 Highway 44, Robstown 78380 Sylvia Romero	9-12	AGTV	690 50	81%	361/387-5999 Fax 361/767-6629
ⓐ Salazar Crossroads Academy 701 N 1st St, Robstown 78380 Belinda Alaniz	9-12	T	59 9	92%	361/767-6600
San Pedro Elem Sch 800 W Avenue D, Robstown 78380 Laura Cueva	PK-3	T	199 21	89%	361/767-6648 Fax 361/767-2243
Seale Junior High Sch 401 E Avenue G, Robstown 78380 Maribel Trevino	6-8	T	556 43	88%	361/767-6631 Fax 361/767-2272
Solomon P Ortiz Interm Sch 208 E Avenue H, Robstown 78380 Dalia Rodriguez	4-5	T	424 24	87%	361/767-6662 Fax 361/767-2651

● **Tuloso-Midway Ind School Dist** PID: 01045015 361/903-6400
9760 La Branch Dr, Corp Christi 78410 Fax 361/241-5836

Schools: 5 \ *Teachers:* 286 \ *Students:* 4,000 \ *Special Ed Students:* 357 \ *LEP Students:* 220 \ *College-Bound:* 52% \ *Ethnic:* African American 1%, Hispanic 78%, Caucasian 20% \ *Exp:* $431 (High) \ *Poverty:* 20% \ *Title I:* $642,138 \ *Special Education:* $586,000 \ *Open-Close:* 07/16 - 05/28 \ *DTBP:* $144 (High) \ t

Rodney Sumner 1
Patrick Hernandez 3,5
Wade Miller 6
Christopher Casarez 15,91
Paul Mostella 67
David Wiltshire 295
Philip Carroll 2,19,75
Stephanie Gallegos 4
Holly Alderson 8,11,57,92,296
Yolanda Alvaro 58
Anna Elizando 68,78
Robin Murray 298

Public Schs..Principal	Grd	Prgm	Enr/#Cls	SN	Phone
ⓐ Academic Career Center 7601 Leopard St, Corp Christi 78409 Melodie McClarren	9-12	TV	21 7	89%	361/903-6450 Fax 361/289-5642
Tuloso-Midway High Sch 2653 McKinzie Rd, Corp Christi 78410 Ann Bartosh	9-12	ATV	1,179 85	43%	361/903-6700 Fax 361/241-4258
Tuloso-Midway Intermediate Sch 1921 Overland Trl, Corp Christi 78410 David Calk	3-5	T	890 34	61%	361/903-6550 Fax 361/903-6572
Tuloso-Midway Middle Sch 9768 La Branch Dr, Corp Christi 78410 Priscilla Vega	6-8		894 35		361/903-6600 Fax 361/242-9829
Tuloso-Midway Primary Sch 3125 Dear Run Dr, Corp Christi 78410 Alejandra Quintanilla	PK-2	T	894	63%	361/903-6500 Fax 361/241-5617

79 Student Personnel
80 Driver Ed/Safety
81 Gifted/Talented
82 Video Services
83 Substance Abuse Prev
84 Erate
85 AIDS Education
88 Alternative/At Risk
89 Multi-Cultural Curriculum
90 Social Work
91 Safety/Security
92 Magnet School
93 Parental Involvement
95 Tech Prep Program
97 Chief Infomation Officer
98 Chief Technology Officer
270 Character Education
271 Migrant Education
273 Teacher Mentor
274 Before/After Sch
275 Response To Intervention
277 Remedial Math K-12
280 Literacy Coach
285 STEM
286 Digital Learning
288 Common Core Standards
294 Accountability
295 Network System
296 Title II Programs
297 Webmaster
298 Grant Writer/Ptnrships
750 Chief Innovation Officer
751 Chief of Staff
752 Social Emotional Learning

School Programs
A = Alternative Program
G = Adult Classes
M = Magnet Program
T = Title I Schoolwide
V = Career & Tech Ed Programs

Other School Types
ⓐ = Alternative School
ⓒ = Charter School
ⓜ = Magnet School
ⓨ = Year-Round School

Social Media
f = Facebook
t = Twitter

New Schools are shaded
New Superintendents and Principals are bold
Personnel with email addresses are underscored

Nueces County

Market Data Retrieval

• **West Oso Ind School Dist** PID: 01045065   361/806-5900
5050 Rockford Dr, Corp Christi 78416   Fax 361/225-8308

> **Schools:** 4 \ **Teachers:** 143 \ **Students:** 2,104 \ **Special Ed Students:** 225 \ **LEP Students:** 122 \ **College-Bound:** 40% \ **Ethnic:** African American 9%, Hispanic 88%, Caucasian 2% \ **Exp:** $465 (High) \ **Poverty:** 27% \ **Title I:** $675,859 \ **Special Education:** $513,000 \ **Open-Close:** 08/06 - 05/28 \ **DTBP:** $214 (High)

Conrado Garcia 1	David Palacios 2
Denise Hernandez 3,5	Ray Williams 4*
Cheryl Fillmore 6	Christopher Summers 11
R Alvarado 58	Juan Canales 67
Isabel Olivarez 69,294	Lindie Hagdorn 73,297
Kimberly Moore 285	

Public Schs..Principal	Grd	Prgm	Enr/#Cls	SN	
Kennedy Elem Sch 1102 Villarreal Dr, Corp Christi 78416 Marcella Davis	PK-2	T	570 25	84%	361/806-5920 Fax 361/806-5969
West Oso Elem Sch 1526 Cliff Maus Dr, Corp Christi 78416 Fernando Gonzalez	3-5	T	449 40	86%	361/806-5930 Fax 361/225-8956
West Oso High Sch 754 Flato Rd, Corp Christi 78405 Terry Avery	9-12	TV	612 50	82%	361/806-5960 Fax 361/806-5961
West Oso Junior High Sch 5202 Bear Ln, Corp Christi 78405 Margaret Evans	6-8	AT	473 40	84%	361/806-5950 Fax 361/299-3111

NUECES CATHOLIC SCHOOLS

• **Diocese Corpus Christi Ed Off** PID: 01045170   361/882-6191
555 N Carancahua St Ste 750, Corp Christi 78401   Fax 361/693-6798

> **Schools:** 16 \ **Students:** 3,300

Listing includes only schools located in this county. See District Index for location of Diocesan Offices.

Dr Rosemary Henry 1,11	April Esparza 7
Nannette Hatch 15	Monica Maldonado 73

Catholic Schs..Principal	Grd	Prgm	Enr/#Cls	SN	
Bishop Garriga Middle Sch 3114 Saratoga Blvd, Corp Christi 78415 Rene Gonzalez	6-8		86 9		361/851-0853 Fax 361/853-5145
Holy Family Catholic Sch 2526 Soledad St, Corp Christi 78416 Sr Marilyn Springs	PK-5		120 15		361/884-9142 Fax 361/884-1750
Incarnate Word Academy 2910 S Alameda St, Corp Christi 78404 Jose Torres	9-12		245 32		361/883-0857 Fax 361/881-8742
Incarnate Word Elem Sch 450 Chamberlain St, Corp Christi 78404 Pamela Carrillo	PK-5		245 15		361/883-0857 Fax 361/881-9519
Incarnate Word Middle Sch 2917 Austin St, Corp Christi 78404 Adolfo Garza	6-8		199 24		361/883-0857 Fax 361/882-9193
Most Precious Catholic Sch 3502 Saratoga Blvd, Corp Christi 78415 Nelda Bazan	PK-5		204 12		361/852-4800 Fax 361/855-8707
Our Lady of Perpetual Help Sch 5814 Williams Dr, Corp Christi 78412 Raul Ramon	PK-8		206 13		361/991-3305 Fax 361/994-3305
Our Lady of the Rosary Sch 2237 Waldron Rd, Corp Christi 78418 Sr Claudia	PK-K		15		361/939-9847 Fax 361/937-0890
SS Cyril & Methodius Sch 5002 Kostoryz Rd, Corp Christi 78415 Lilly Samaniego	PK-5		140 15		361/853-9392 Fax 361/853-0280
St Anthony Sch 203 Dunne Ave, Robstown 78380 Sr Fe Gamotin	PK-8		350 11		361/387-3814 Fax 361/387-3842
St John Paul II High Sch 3036 Saratoga Blvd, Corp Christi 78415 Jim Brannigan	9-12		314		361/855-5744 Fax 361/855-1343
St Patrick Sch 3340 S Alameda St, Corp Christi 78411 Evelyn Burton	PK-6		316 21		361/852-1211 Fax 361/852-4855
St Pius X Sch 737 Saint Pius Dr, Corp Christi 78412 Delia Rosenbaum	PK-6		190 9		361/992-1343 Fax 361/992-0329

NUECES PRIVATE SCHOOLS

Private Schs..Principal	Grd	Prgm	Enr/#Cls	SN	
Annapolis Christian Academy 3875 S Staples St Ste A, Corp Christi 78411 Travis Lockyer \ Ty Hensley	PK-12		280 40		361/991-6004 Fax 361/232-5629
Arlington Heights Chrn Sch 9550 Leopard St, Corp Christi 78410 Leanne Isom	PK-12		140		361/241-0090 Fax 361/242-9284
Cogin Memorial Elem Sch 6645 Downing St, Corp Christi 78414 Ana Luna	PK-8		23 3		361/991-6968
St James Episcopal Sch 602 S Carancahua St, Corp Christi 78401 Galen Hoffstadt	PK-8		200 24		361/883-0835 Fax 361/883-0837
St Paul Lutheran Sch 801 E Main St, Bishop 78343 Tawnya Denkeler	PK-4		32 4		361/584-2778
Yorktown Christian Academy 5025A Yorktown Blvd, Corp Christi 78413 John Gilbert	PK-12		202		361/985-9960 Fax 361/985-9821

NUECES REGIONAL CENTERS

• **Ed Service Center Region 2** PID: 01045003   361/561-8400
209 N Water St, Corp Christi 78401   Fax 361/883-3442

Rick Alvarado 1,11	Ryan Johnston 2,76
Randy Purdy 8,16,73	Sonia Zyla 58

TX—306

1	Superintendent	8	Curric/Instruct K-12	19	Chief Financial Officer	29	Family/Consumer Science	39	Social Studies K-12	49	English/Lang Arts Elem	59	Special Education Elem	69	Academic Assessment
2	Bus/Finance/Purchasing	9	Curric/Instruct Elem	20	Art K-12	30	Adult Education	40	Social Studies Elem	50	English/Lang Arts Sec	60	Special Education Sec	70	Research/Development
3	Buildings And Grounds	10	Curric/Instruct Sec	21	Art Elem	31	Career/Sch-to-Work K-12	41	Social Studies Sec	51	Reading K-12	61	Foreign/World Lang K-12	71	Public Information
4	Food Service	11	Federal Program	22	Art Sec	32	Career/Sch-to-Work Elem	42	Science K-12	52	Reading Elem	62	Foreign/World Lang Elem	72	Summer School
5	Transportation	12	Title I	23	Music K-12	33	Career/Sch-to-Work Sec	43	Science Elem	53	Reading Sec	63	Foreign/World Lang Sec	73	Instructional Tech
6	Athletic	13	Title V	24	Music Elem	34	Early Childhood Ed	44	Science Sec	54	Remedial Reading K-12	64	Religious Education K-12	74	Inservice Training
7	Health Services	15	Asst Superintendent	25	Music Sec	35	Health/Phys Education	45	Math K-12	55	Remedial Reading Elem	65	Religious Education Elem	75	Marketing/Distributive
		16	Instructional Media Svcs	26	Business Education	36	Guidance Services K-12	46	Math Elem	56	Remedial Reading Sec	66	Religious Education Sec	76	Info Systems
		17	Chief Operations Officer	27	Career & Tech Ed	37	Guidance Services Elem	47	Math Sec	57	Bilingual/ELL	67	School Board President	77	Psychological Assess
		18	Chief Academic Officer	28	Technology Education	38	Guidance Services Sec	48	English/Lang Arts K-12	58	Special Education K-12	68	Teacher Personnel	78	Affirmative Action

Texas School Directory

OCHILTREE COUNTY

OCHILTREE PUBLIC SCHOOLS

- **Perryton Ind School Dist** PID: 01045455   806/435-5478
  821 SW 17th Ave, Perryton 79070   Fax 806/435-4689

Schools: 6 \ *Teachers:* 198 \ *Students:* 2,217 \ *Special Ed Students:* 167 \ *LEP Students:* 625 \ *College-Bound:* 46% \ *Ethnic:* Hispanic 73%, Caucasian 26% \ *Exp:* $475 (High) \ *Poverty:* 17% \ *Title I:* $467,435 \ *Open-Close:* 08/19 - 05/21 \ *DTBP:* $338 (High)

Name	Code	Name	Code
Dr Tim Little	1	Doug Kile	2,19
Allen Kemp	3	Shelli Walker	4
Dustin Klaska	6*	Todd White	8,11,57,88,271,298
Kelly Vernon	11	Cindy Boxwell	16*
Stacy Tanner	29*	Valerie Merkel	36*
Paige Waide	38*	Mary Nine	58
Monty Kinnard	67	Darin Clark	71
Rodney Throgmorton	73,295	Danny Finch	83

Public Schs..Principal	Grd	Prgm	Enr/#Cls	SN	
Edwin F Williams Interm Sch 902 SW 19th Ave, Perryton 79070 Read Cates	4-5	T	347 17	68%	806/435-3436 Fax 806/435-9231
James L Wright Elem Sch 1702 S Grinnell St, Perryton 79070 Tiffany Bietz	1-3	T	496	66%	806/435-2371 Fax 806/434-8844
Perryton High Sch 1200 S Jefferson St, Perryton 79070 Danny Finch	9-12	T	577 40	50%	806/435-3633 Fax 806/435-2602
Perryton Junior High Sch 510 S Eton St, Perryton 79070 Dimitri Garcia	6-8	T	528 30	61%	806/435-3601 Fax 806/435-3624
Perryton Kindergarten 410 S Eton St, Perryton 79070 Dent Felix	PK-K	T	236 22	76%	806/435-2463 Fax 806/435-6093
Top of TX Accelerated Ed Ctr 605 N Main St, Perryton 79070 Ludi Martin	9-12	T	40 6	79%	806/434-0389 Fax 806/434-0402

OCHILTREE PRIVATE SCHOOLS

Private Schs..Principal	Grd	Prgm	Enr/#Cls	SN	
Victory Christian Academy 2322 S Main St, Perryton 79070 Kathy Sparks	PK-6		42 6		806/435-3476 Fax 806/435-9256

Oldham County

OLDHAM COUNTY

OLDHAM PUBLIC SCHOOLS

- **Adrian Ind School Dist** PID: 01045522   806/538-6203
  301 Matador Dr, Adrian 79001   Fax 806/538-6291

Schools: 1 \ *Teachers:* 17 \ *Students:* 120 \ *Special Ed Students:* 16 \ *LEP Students:* 8 \ *Ethnic:* Hispanic 62%, Caucasian 38% \ *Exp:* $1,097 (High) \ *Poverty:* 11% \ *Special Education:* $13,000 \ *Open-Close:* 08/20 - 05/25

Name	Code	Name	Code
Steve Reynolds	1,11	Stephanie Green	2
Debra Jones	7*	Maritsa Flores	8,288*
Morris Blackenship	67	Monty Hale	73,286,295*

Public Schs..Principal	Grd	Prgm	Enr/#Cls	SN	
Adrian Sch 301 Matador Dr, Adrian 79001 Dawn Brooks	PK-12	TV	120 20	63%	806/538-6203

- **Boys Ranch Ind School Dist** PID: 01484461   806/534-2221
  163 River Rd, Boys Ranch 79010   Fax 806/534-2384

Schools: 3 \ *Teachers:* 55 \ *Students:* 254 \ *Special Ed Students:* 47 \ *LEP Students:* 4 \ *College-Bound:* 50% \ *Ethnic:* African American 7%, Hispanic 24%, Caucasian 69% \ *Exp:* $1,093 (High) \ *Poverty:* 10% \ *Title I:* $533,598 \ *Special Education:* $43,000 \ *Open-Close:* 08/27 - 05/25 \ *DTBP:* $335 (High)

Name	Code	Name	Code
Kenneth Brown	1	Meleta Bailey	2
Paul Jones	6,15,275	Kaylia Thomas	8,16
Maggie Taylor	11,15,298	Kelli Boydstun	27,31,36*
Ken Teel	67	Randy Carter	73,295

Public Schs..Principal	Grd	Prgm	Enr/#Cls	SN	
Blakemore Middle Sch 30 Julian Bivins Blvd, Boys Ranch 79010 Brandon Sanders	6-8	AT	65 14	77%	806/534-2361 Fax 806/534-0041
Boys Ranch High Sch 163 River Rd, Boys Ranch 79010 Shawn Read	9-12	ATV	183 40	91%	806/534-0032 Fax 806/534-0033
Mimi Farley Elem Sch 29 Ag Lane, Boys Ranch 79010 Joanna Martinez	PK-5	T	36 12	38%	806/534-2248 Fax 806/534-0111

- **Vega Ind School Dist** PID: 01045558   806/267-2123
  200 Longhorn Dr, Vega 79092   Fax 806/267-2146

Schools: 2 \ *Teachers:* 38 \ *Students:* 380 \ *Special Ed Students:* 21 \ *LEP Students:* 11 \ *College-Bound:* 95% \ *Ethnic:* Asian 1%, Hispanic 19%, Native American: 1%, Caucasian 80% \ *Exp:* $797 (High) \ *Poverty:* 12% \ *Title I:* $31,078 \ *Special Education:* $2,000 \ *Open-Close:* 08/22 - 05/22 \ *DTBP:* $318 (High)

Name	Code	Name	Code
Jody Johnson	1,11	Haylie Lookingbill	2
Jason Porton	6*	Tammie Cook	8,31,36,69,83,270*
Amy Kirkland	16,73*	Mehgan Graves	58*
Tj Barclay	67	Terri Richardson	286*

---

79 Student Personnel	91 Safety/Security	275 Response To Intervention	298 Grant Writer/Ptnrships	**School Programs**	**Social Media**		
80 Driver Ed/Safety	92 Magnet School	277 Remedial Math K-12	750 Chief Innovation Officer	A = Alternative Program			
81 Gifted/Talented	93 Parental Involvement	280 Literacy Coach	751 Chief of Staff	G = Adult Classes	= Facebook		
82 Video Services	95 Tech Prep Program	285 STEM	752 Social Emotional Learning	M = Magnet Program			
83 Substance Abuse Prev	97 Chief Infomation Officer	286 Digital Learning		T = Title I Schoolwide	= Twitter		
84 Erate	98 Chief Technology Officer	288 Common Core Standards	**Other School Types**	V = Career & Tech Ed Programs			
85 AIDS Education	270 Character Education	294 Accountability	Ⓐ = Alternative School				
88 Alternative/At Risk	271 Migrant Education	295 Network System	Ⓒ = Charter School	New Schools are shaded			
89 Multi-Cultural Curriculum	273 Teacher Mentor	296 Title II Programs	Ⓜ = Magnet School	New Superintendents and Principals are bold			
90 Social Work	274 Before/After Sch	297 Webmaster	Ⓨ = Year-Round School	Personnel with email addresses are underscored			

TX-307

Orange County

Public Schs..Principal	Grd	Prgm	Enr/#Cls	SN	
Vega Elem Sch 200 Longhorn Dr, Vega 79092 Johnett Stribling	PK-4	T	172 20	31%	806/267-2126
Vega Jr Sr High Sch 200 Longhorn Dr, Vega 79092 Tracey Bell \ Kassidy Rosas	5-12	TV	203 20	24%	806/267-2126

● **Wildorado Ind Sch Dist** PID: 01045584
1523 S Locust St, Wildorado 79098
806/426-3317
Fax 806/426-3523

Schools: 1 \ **Teachers:** 11 \ **Students:** 180 \ **Special Ed Students:** 11 \ **Ethnic:** African American 2%, Hispanic 17%, Caucasian 81% \ **Exp:** $1,291 (High) \ **Poverty:** 25% \ **Title I:** $21,500 \ **Open-Close:** 08/14 - 05/22 \ **DTBP:** $337 (High)

Troy Duck 1,11,73
Michael Dickerson 3
Sherry Clark 12
Shannon Leavitt 67
Sandy Luster 2,271
Loretta Gouldy 7*
Robin Welch 57*

Public Schs..Principal	Grd	Prgm	Enr/#Cls	SN	
Wildorado Elem Sch 1523 S Locust St, Wildorado 79098 Mike Cheverzer	PK-10	T	180 8	33%	806/426-3317

ORANGE COUNTY

ORANGE PUBLIC SCHOOLS

● **Bridge City Ind School Dist** PID: 01045601
1031 W Round Bunch Rd, Bridge City 77611
409/735-1501
Fax 409/735-1512

Schools: 4 \ **Teachers:** 187 \ **Students:** 2,953 \ **Special Ed Students:** 219 \ **LEP Students:** 117 \ **College-Bound:** 51% \ **Ethnic:** Asian 3%, African American 2%, Hispanic 16%, Caucasian 80% \ **Exp:** $230 (Med) \ **Poverty:** 12% \ **Title I:** $276,268 \ **Special Education:** $859,000 \ **Open-Close:** 08/14 - 05/21 \ **DTBP:** $178 (High) \

Todd Lintzen 1
Maggie Joubert 4
Terra Fountain 8,16,88,288,296
Arron Conner 27*
Johnna Smith 37*
Corrin Gonzales 58
Natasha Ray 73
Shane Preston 295
Melinda James 2
Allen DeShazo 6
Gina Mannino 11,15,271,274,294
Nichole Harris 36*
Jennifer Rumsey 38*
Judy Cole 67
Steve Brinson 83,91

Public Schs..Principal	Grd	Prgm	Enr/#Cls	SN	
Bridge City Elem Sch 1035 W Round Bunch Rd, Bridge City 77611 Melanie Toups	PK-2	T	833 17	43%	409/735-0900 Fax 409/735-0906
Bridge City High Sch 2690 Texas Ave, Bridge City 77611 Tim Woolley	9-12	TV	793 75	28%	409/735-1600 Fax 409/735-1606
Bridge City Intermediate Sch 1029 W Round Bunch Rd, Bridge City 77611 Julie Motomura	3-5	T	725 30	39%	409/792-8800 Fax 409/792-8806
Bridge City Middle Sch 300 Bower Dr, Bridge City 77611 Amanda Hoffman	6-8	T	637 50	32%	409/735-1700 Fax 409/735-1706

● **Deweyville Ind School Dist** PID: 01043718
43200 State Highway 87 S, Orange 77632
409/746-2731
Fax 409/349-9338

Schools: 2 \ **Teachers:** 51 \ **Students:** 550 \ **Special Ed Students:** 70 \ **College-Bound:** 44% \ **Ethnic:** African American 1%, Hispanic 3%, Native American: 1%, Caucasian 95% \ **Exp:** $268 (Med) \ **Poverty:** 19% \ **Title I:** $123,036 \ **Special Education:** $160,000 \ **Open-Close:** 08/26 - 05/29 \ **DTBP:** $358 (High) \

Dr Keith Jones 1,11
Sharlene Hryhorchuk 4
Brandon Prouse 6
Jennifer Parkhurst 12
Carmen Purgahn 58*
Janae Welch 2
Michael Richarb 5
Lisa Brinson 7,85*
Cheryl Inboden 16*
Luke Smith 67

Public Schs..Principal	Grd	Prgm	Enr/#Cls	SN	
Deweyville Elem Sch 43200 State Highway 87 S, Orange 77632 Lajuan Addison	PK-5	T	265 30	70%	409/746-2731 Fax 409/746-7700
Deweyville Jr Sr High Sch 171 State Highway 12 W, Orange 77632 Brian East	6-12	TV	312 25	55%	409/746-2685

● **Little Cypress Mauriceville SD** PID: 01045651
6586 FM 1130, Orange 77632
409/883-2232
Fax 409/883-3509

Schools: 6 \ **Teachers:** 239 \ **Students:** 3,100 \ **Special Ed Students:** 422 \ **LEP Students:** 68 \ **College-Bound:** 62% \ **Ethnic:** Asian 2%, African American 8%, Hispanic 11%, Caucasian 79% \ **Exp:** $335 (High) \ **Poverty:** 16% \ **Title I:** $695,860 \ **Special Education:** $1,442,000 \ **Open-Close:** 08/15 - 05/20 \ **DTBP:** $168 (High)

Dr Pauline Hargrove 1
Phillip Matthews 3,91
Michele Leblew 5
Kelly Meadows 7*
Todd Loupe 10,30,36,69,85,88*
Laurie Gordon 11
Sandy Reynolds 16
Marlene Courmier 67
Greg Perry 2,15
Suzanne MaGee 4
Randall Crouch 6*
Julia Dickerson 9,57,81,271,288*
Beverly Knight 11,58,68,72,270
Roy Mazzagate 16,297
Kristine Brown 35,75*
Kim Allen 73,84

Public Schs..Principal	Grd	Prgm	Enr/#Cls	SN	
Little Cypress Elem Sch 5723 Meeks Dr, Orange 77632 Kayla Casey	PK-3	T	544 35	41%	409/886-2838 Fax 409/886-8172
Little Cypress Interm Sch 2300 Allie Payne Rd, Orange 77632 Michael Ridout	4-5	T	345 18	34%	409/886-4245 Fax 409/886-1828
Little Cypress Jr High Sch 6765 FM 1130, Orange 77632 Jason Yeaman	6-8		453 36	39%	409/883-2317 Fax 409/670-4626
Little Cypress-Mauriceville HS 7327 Highway 87 N, Orange 77632 Ryan Dubose	9-12	AV	1,009 95	28%	409/886-5821 Fax 409/886-5762
Mauriceville Elem Sch 20040 FM 1130, Orange 77632 Carie Broussard	PK-5	T	546 38	44%	409/745-1615 Fax 409/670-4641
Mauriceville Middle Sch 19952 FM 1130, Orange 77632 Kim Cox	6-8		309 25	40%	409/745-3970 Fax 409/670-4636

1	Superintendent	8	Curric/Instruct K-12	19	Chief Financial Officer	29	Family/Consumer Science	39	Social Studies K-12	49	English/Lang Arts Elem	59	Special Education Elem	69	Academic Assessment
2	Bus/Finance/Purchasing	9	Curric/Instruct Elem	20	Art K-12	30	Adult Education	40	Social Studies Elem	50	English/Lang Arts Sec	60	Special Education Sec	70	Research/Development
3	Buildings And Grounds	10	Curric/Instruct Sec	21	Art Elem	31	Career/Sch-to-Work K-12	41	Social Studies Sec	51	Reading K-12	61	Foreign/World Lang K-12	71	Public Information
4	Food Service	11	Federal Program	22	Art Sec	32	Career/Sch-to-Work Elem	42	Science K-12	52	Reading Elem	62	Foreign/World Lang Elem	72	Summer School
5	Transportation	12	Title I	23	Music K-12	33	Career/Sch-to-Work Sec	43	Science Elem	53	Reading Sec	63	Foreign/World Lang Sec	73	Instructional Tech
6	Athletic	13	Title V	24	Music Elem	34	Early Childhood Ed	44	Science Sec	54	Remedial Reading K-12	64	Religious Education K-12	74	Inservice Training
7	Health Services	15	Asst Superintendent	25	Music Sec	35	Health/Phys Education	45	Math K-12	55	Remedial Reading Elem	65	Religious Education Elem	75	Marketing/Distributive
		16	Instructional Media Svcs	26	Business Education	36	Guidance Services K-12	46	Math Elem	56	Remedial Reading Sec	66	Religious Education Sec	76	Info Systems
		17	Chief Operations Officer	27	Career & Tech Ed	37	Guidance Services Elem	47	Math Sec	57	Bilingual/ELL	67	School Board President	77	Psychological Assess
		18	Chief Academic Officer	28	Technology Education	38	Guidance Services Sec	48	English/Lang Arts K-12	58	Special Education K-12	68	Teacher Personnel	78	Affirmative Action

Texas School Directory

Orange County

- **Orangefield Ind School Dist** PID: 01045704   409/735-5337
  9974 FM 105, Orange 77630   Fax 409/735-2080

Schools: 3 \ *Teachers:* 123 \ *Students:* 1,785 \ *Special Ed Students:* 145 \ *LEP Students:* 33 \ *College-Bound:* 65% \ *Ethnic:* Asian 2%, Hispanic 9%, Caucasian 89% \ *Exp:* $373 (High) \ *Poverty:* 13% \ *Title I:* $300,033 \ *Special Education:* $320,000 \ *Open-Close:* 08/14 - 05/21 \ *DTBP:* $6 (Low)

Dr Stephen Patterson 1
Brian Ousley 4
Beena Vanpelt 8
Dr Dayna Smith .. 11,34,57,58,88,271,275,296
Candi Patterson 31,36,69,83,93*
Jennifer Gauthier 73,76,84,295
Shaun McAlpin 2,15,298
Josh Smalley 6
Kim Smalley 8,273,286,288
Sunshine Copeland 16*
Dr Ronald Risinger 67
Matthew Lanier 295

Public Schs..Principal	Grd	Prgm	Enr/#Cls	SN	
Orangefield Elem Sch 10288 FM 105, Orange 77630 Amanda Jenkins	PK-5	TV	728 32	36%	409/735-5346 Fax 409/735-3940
Orangefield High Sch 10058 FM 105, Orange 77630 Zach Quinn	9-12	V	499 45	31%	409/735-3851 Fax 409/697-2301
Orangefield Junior High Sch 7745 Sand Bar Rd, Orange 77630 Rea Wrinkle	6-8		560 50	36%	409/735-6737 Fax 409/792-9605

- **Vidor Ind School Dist** PID: 01045754   409/951-8700
  120 E Bolivar St, Vidor 77662   Fax 409/769-0093

Schools: 7 \ *Teachers:* 341 \ *Students:* 5,000 \ *Special Ed Students:* 610 \ *LEP Students:* 53 \ *Ethnic:* Asian 1%, Hispanic 7%, Caucasian 91% \ *Exp:* $559 (High) \ *Poverty:* 18% \ *Title I:* $987,808 \ *Special Education:* $1,119,000 \ *Open-Close:* 08/19 - 05/29 \ *DTBP:* $177 (High)

Dr Jay Killgo 1,84
Sheila Schoen 2
Mary Ellen Vivreet 4
Jeff Matthews 6,35*
Bunny Adams 9,11,93,286,288,296,298
Jana Cash 16
Penny Singleton 27,31,75*
Heather Watson 39,48
Sally Andrews 71
Barbara Silver 76
Mike Sanchez 91
David Croak 2
Ronnie Davis 3
Jeanne Taylor 5
Deena Bunting 7
Travis Maines 15,68
Kana Philips 23*
Karrie Clark 34,58,77
David Camp 67
Jim Gordon 73
Janet Bradley 76
Laniece Sollock 93

Public Schs..Principal	Grd	Prgm	Enr/#Cls	SN	
Ⓐ Aim Center High Sch 690 Orange St, Vidor 77662 Brandy Antill	9-12	GT	55 6	50%	409/951-8780 Fax 409/769-0443
Oak Forest Elem Sch 2400 Highway 12, Vidor 77662 Carolyn Wedgeworth	PK-4	T	650 39	58%	409/951-8860 Fax 409/769-2678
Pine Forest Elem Sch 4150 N Main St, Vidor 77662 Preston Clark	PK-4	T	606 36	51%	409/951-8800 Fax 409/786-1728
Vidor Elem Sch 400 Old Highway 90 E, Vidor 77662 Jeff Leger	PK-4		629 48		409/951-8830 Fax 409/769-0211
Vidor High Sch 500 Orange St, Vidor 77662 James McDowell	9-12	T	1,277 60	39%	409/951-8900 Fax 409/769-6767
Vidor Junior High Sch 945 N Tram Rd, Vidor 77662 Aaron Herrington	7-8	T	634 50	49%	409/951-8970 Fax 409/769-6754
Vidor Middle Sch 2500 Highway 12, Vidor 77662 Kerri Pierce	5-6	T	701 36	50%	409/951-8880 Fax 409/783-0309

- **West Orange-Cove Cons ISD** PID: 01045819   409/882-5437
  902 W Park Ave, Orange 77630   Fax 409/882-5467

Schools: 4 \ *Teachers:* 164 \ *Students:* 2,487 \ *Special Ed Students:* 254 \ *LEP Students:* 138 \ *Ethnic:* Asian 1%, African American 63%, Hispanic 16%, Caucasian 20% \ *Exp:* $271 (Med) \ *Poverty:* 33% \ *Title I:* $1,283,259 \ *Special Education:* $726,000 \ *Open-Close:* 08/26 - 06/03 \ *DTBP:* $183 (High) \ 📘

Rickie Harris 1
Greg Willis 3
Manuel Vera 5
Ashton Knox 8
Larry Haynes 11
Vickie Brice 34*
Ruth Hancock 67
Alicia Sigee 79
Robin Hathaway 2
Danielle Robinson 4
Cornel Thompson 6*
Dr Nina LeBlanc 8,11,57,58,90,91,273,288
Elvis Rushing 16,73,82*
Heather Knox 58,90,91
Lorraine Shannon 71

Public Schs..Principal	Grd	Prgm	Enr/#Cls	SN	
North Early Learning Center 801 Cordrey St, Orange 77630 Vickie Oceguera	PK-PK	T	269 18	99%	409/882-5434 Fax 409/882-5449
West Orange-Stark Elem Sch 2605 Martin Luther King Jr Dr, Orange 77630 Troy Bethley	K-5	T	1,041 29	74%	409/882-5630 Fax 409/882-5644
West Orange-Stark High Sch 1400 Newton St, Orange 77630 Rolanda Holifield	9-12	ATV	579 40	76%	409/882-5570 Fax 409/882-5573
West Orange-Stark Middle Sch 1402 Green Ave, Orange 77630 Brodrick McGrew	6-8	ATV	515	81%	409/882-5520 Fax 409/882-5545

ORANGE CATHOLIC SCHOOLS

- **Diocese of Beaumont Sch Office** PID: 01034339
  Listing includes only schools located in this county. See District Index for location of Diocesan Offices.

Catholic Schs..Principal	Grd	Prgm	Enr/#Cls	SN	
St Mary Catholic Sch 2600 Bob Hall Rd, Orange 77630 Katie Sanders	PK-8		200 14		409/883-8913 Fax 409/883-0827

ORANGE PRIVATE SCHOOLS

Private Schs..Principal	Grd	Prgm	Enr/#Cls	SN	
Community Christian Sch 3400 M L King Dr, Orange 77632 Macey Jackson	PK-12		325 30		409/883-4531 Fax 409/883-8855

---

79 Student Personnel	91 Safety/Security	275 Response To Intervention	298 Grant Writer/Ptnrships
80 Driver Ed/Safety	92 Magnet School	277 Remedial Math K-12	750 Chief Innovation Officer
81 Gifted/Talented	93 Parental Involvement	280 Literacy Coach	751 Chief of Staff
82 Video Services	95 Tech Prep Program	285 STEM	752 Social Emotional Learning
83 Substance Abuse Prev	97 Chief Information Officer	286 Digital Learning	
84 Erate	98 Chief Technology Officer	288 Common Core Standards	
85 AIDS Education	270 Accountability	294 Character Education	
88 Alternative/At Risk	271 Migrant Education	295 Network System	
89 Multi-Cultural Curriculum	273 Teacher Mentor	296 Title II Programs	
90 Social Work	274 Before/After Sch	297 Webmaster	

School Programs
A = Alternative Program
G = Adult Classes
M = Magnet Program
T = Title I Schoolwide
V = Career & Tech Ed Programs

Other School Types
Ⓐ = Alternative School
Ⓒ = Charter School
Ⓜ = Magnet School
Ⓨ = Year-Round School

Social Media
📘 = Facebook
🐦 = Twitter

New Schools are shaded
New Superintendents and Principals are bold
Personnel with email addresses are underscored

Palo Pinto County

PALO PINTO COUNTY

PALO PINTO PUBLIC SCHOOLS

- **Gordon Ind School Dist** PID: 01045950   254/693-5582
  112-116 Rusk Street, Gordon 76453   Fax 254/693-5503

Schools: 1 \ *Teachers:* 21 \ *Students:* 200 \ *Special Ed Students:* 18 \ *College-Bound:* 60% \ *Ethnic:* Asian 1%, African American 2%, Hispanic 21%, Caucasian 77% \ *Exp:* $387 (High) \ *Poverty:* 15% \ *Title I:* $32,534 \ *Open-Close:* 08/05 - 05/29 \ *DTBP:* $323 (High) \

Dewanye Wilkins	1,83	Jessica Hendrickson	2,19
Patty Hopkins	4	Mike Reed	6*
Holly Campbell	8,11,16,74,275*	Katie Elrod	36*
Michael Rouse	67	Rick Spear	73,295

Public Schs..Principal	Grd	Prgm	Enr/#Cls	SN	
Gordon Sch 112-116 Rusk Street, Gordon 76453 Holly Campbell	PK-12	T	200 20	48%	254/693-5342

- **Graford Ind School Dist** PID: 01045986   940/664-3101
  400 W Division St, Graford 76449   Fax 940/664-2123

Schools: 2 \ *Teachers:* 31 \ *Students:* 340 \ *Special Ed Students:* 26 \ *LEP Students:* 11 \ *Ethnic:* Asian 1%, Hispanic 14%, Native American: 1%, Caucasian 85% \ *Exp:* $448 (High) \ *Poverty:* 15% \ *Title I:* $59,436 \ *Open-Close:* 08/15 - 05/21 \ *DTBP:* $331 (High)

Dennis Holt	1	Michelle Davis	2
David Taylor	3	Rodney Hall	5,83*
Ty Tabor	6*	Lori Henderson	12,79,296
Heather Thompson	57*	Tina Alverado	59
Travis Rogers	67	Chris Thompson	73,295*

Public Schs..Principal	Grd	Prgm	Enr/#Cls	SN	
Graford Elem Sch 400 W Division St, Graford 76449 Clifton Womack	PK-5	T	217 11	57%	940/664-3101 Fax 940/664-2765
Graford Jr Sr High Sch 400 W Division St, Graford 76449 Clifton Womack	6-12	TV	152 20	53%	940/664-3101

- **Mineral Wells Ind School Dist** PID: 01046019   940/325-6404
  906 SW 5th Ave, Mineral Wells 76067   Fax 940/325-6378

Schools: 6 \ *Teachers:* 236 \ *Students:* 3,200 \ *Special Ed Students:* 283 \ *LEP Students:* 275 \ *College-Bound:* 45% \ *Ethnic:* African American 4%, Hispanic 42%, Native American: 1%, Caucasian 54% \ *Exp:* $512 (High) \ *Poverty:* 26% \ *Title I:* $1,238,387 \ *Open-Close:* 08/15 - 05/27 \ *DTBP:* $93 (Med)

Dr John Kuhn	1	Paul Hearn	2,19
James Bradford	3,91	Carrie Martin	4
Brett Barrick	5	Brett Barrick	5*
Gerald Perry	6*	Wanda Voelcker	7,35,85*
Carey Carter	8,16,54,69,74,273,294	Natalie Griffin	11,57,81,271,298
David Tarver	15,68	Deeann Hampton	31*
Parisa Lerma	58,275	Maria Jones	67

Karyn Bullock	71	Janna Lee Martin	73
Justin Lascsak	286	Saugato Ray	295

Public Schs..Principal	Grd	Prgm	Enr/#Cls	SN	
Houston Elem Sch 300 SW 13th St, Mineral Wells 76067 Amy Salazar	2-3	T	487 27	80%	940/325-3427 Fax 940/325-7683
Lamar Elem Sch 2012 SE 12th St, Mineral Wells 76067 Kendra Fowler	PK-1	T	707 45	81%	940/325-5303 Fax 940/328-0152
ⓐ Mineral Wells Academy 3810 Ram Blvd, Mineral Wells 76067 Jeffery Smith	9-12	T	32 3	72%	940/325-3033 Fax 940/325-6044
Mineral Wells High Sch 3801 Ram Blvd, Mineral Wells 76067 Dr Doug Funk	9-12	TV	855 39	58%	940/325-4408 Fax 940/325-7623
Mineral Wells Jr High Sch 1301 SE 14th Ave, Mineral Wells 76067 Shanna Coker	7-8	T	455 44	74%	940/325-0711 Fax 940/328-0450
Travis Elem Sch 1001 SE M L King Jr St, Mineral Wells 76067 David Wells	4-6	T	745	75%	940/325-7801 Fax 940/328-0972

- **Palo Pinto Ind Sch Dist 906** PID: 01046100   940/659-2745
  821 Oak St, Palo Pinto 76484   Fax 940/659-2936

Schools: 1 \ *Teachers:* 11 \ *Students:* 112 \ *Special Ed Students:* 10 \ *LEP Students:* 9 \ *Ethnic:* Hispanic 24%, Caucasian 76% \ *Exp:* $624 (High) \ *Poverty:* 27% \ *Title I:* $44,322 \ *Open-Close:* 08/19 - 05/21 \ *DTBP:* $304 (High) \

Wendell Barker	1,84	Wendell Barker	9,36,57,69,88,271,273*
Eric Cederstrom	11,73,83	Bud Price	67
Danita Ivy	85*		

Public Schs..Principal	Grd	Prgm	Enr/#Cls	SN	
Palo Pinto Elem Sch 821 Oak St, Palo Pinto 76484 Natalie Rogers	PK-6	T	112 8	61%	940/659-2745

- **Santo Ind School Dist** PID: 01046124   940/769-2835
  406 S FM 2201, Santo 76472   Fax 940/769-3116

Schools: 2 \ *Teachers:* 39 \ *Students:* 475 \ *Special Ed Students:* 40 \ *LEP Students:* 16 \ *College-Bound:* 67% \ *Ethnic:* Hispanic 18%, Caucasian 81% \ *Exp:* $541 (High) \ *Poverty:* 29% \ *Title I:* $205,987 \ *Open-Close:* 08/15 - 05/21

Greg Gilbert	1	Cindy Rucker	2,84
Stacy Finley	4	Cathy Longley	12*
Monica Van Remmen	57	Amy Bryan	67

Public Schs..Principal	Grd	Prgm	Enr/#Cls	SN	
Santo Elem Sch Farm Road 2201, Santo 76472 Cathy Longley	PK-5	T	202 15	50%	940/769-3215
Santo Jr Sr High Sch 406 S FM 2201, Santo 76472 Darla Henry	6-12	TV	256 30	42%	940/769-3847 Fax 940/769-2796

1	Superintendent	8	Curric/Instruct K-12	19	Chief Financial Officer	29	Family/Consumer Science	39	Social Studies K-12	49	English/Lang Arts Elem	59	Special Education Elem	69	Academic Assessment
2	Bus/Finance/Purchasing	9	Curric/Instruct Elem	20	Art K-12	30	Adult Education	40	Social Studies Elem	50	English/Lang Arts Sec	60	Special Education Sec	70	Research/Development
3	Buildings And Grounds	10	Curric/Instruct Sec	21	Art Elem	31	Career/Sch-to-Work K-12	41	Social Studies Sec	51	Reading K-12	61	Foreign/World Lang K-12	71	Public Information
4	Food Service	11	Federal Program	22	Art Sec	32	Career/Sch-to-Work Elem	42	Science K-12	52	Reading Elem	62	Foreign/World Lang Elem	72	Summer School
5	Transportation	12	Title I	23	Music K-12	33	Career/Sch-to-Work Sec	43	Science Elem	53	Reading Sec	63	Foreign/World Lang Sec	73	Instructional Tech
6	Athletic	13	Title V	24	Music Elem	34	Early Childhood Ed	44	Science Sec	54	Remedial Reading K-12	64	Religious Education K-12	74	Inservice Training
7	Health Services	14	Asst Superintendent	25	Music Sec	35	Health/Phys Education	45	Math K-12	55	Remedial Reading Elem	65	Religious Education Elem	75	Marketing/Distributive
		15	Instructional Media Svcs	26	Business Education	36	Guidance Services K-12	46	Math Elem	56	Remedial Reading Sec	66	Religious Education Sec	76	Info Systems
		16	Chief Operations Officer	27	Career & Tech Ed	37	Guidance Services Elem	47	Math Sec	57	Bilingual/ELL	67	School Board President	77	Psychological Assess
		17	Chief Academic Officer	28	Technology Education	38	Guidance Services Sec	48	English/Lang Arts K-12	58	Special Education K-12	68	Teacher Personnel	78	Affirmative Action

Texas School Directory — Panola County

- **Strawn Ind School Dist** PID: 01046150   254/672-5313
  224 E Walnut Street, Strawn 76475   Fax 254/672-5662

Schools: 1 \ **Teachers:** 17 \ **Students:** 167 \ **Special Ed Students:** 17 \ **LEP Students:** 22 \ **College-Bound:** 80% \ **Ethnic:** African American 1%, Hispanic 38%, Native American: 1%, Caucasian 60% \ **Exp:** $850 (High) \ **Poverty:** 19% \ **Title I:** $38,324 \ **Open-Close:** 08/26 - 05/29 \ f t

Richard Mitchell 1,11	Kathryn Lynn 2			
Darryl Atkins 3,5	Nancy Montgomery 4			
Dewaine Lee 6	Joyce Gray 57*			
Mindy Hodgkins 67	Shan Nowak 73*			
Jessica Mallory 288*				

Public Schs..Principal	Grd	Prgm	Enr/#Cls	SN	
Strawn Sch 224 E Walnut St, Strawn 76475 Melanie Cormack	PK-12	TV	167 12	57%	254/672-5313

PALO PINTO PRIVATE SCHOOLS

Private Schs..Principal	Grd	Prgm	Enr/#Cls	SN	
Community Christian Sch 2501 Garrett Morris Pkwy, Mineral Wells 76067 William Jefferson	PK-12		72 13		940/328-1333 Fax 940/328-1277

PANOLA COUNTY

PANOLA PUBLIC SCHOOLS

- **Beckville Ind School Dist** PID: 01046186   903/678-3311
  4398 State Highway 149, Beckville 75631   Fax 903/678-2157

Schools: 2 \ **Teachers:** 66 \ **Students:** 700 \ **Special Ed Students:** 53 \ **LEP Students:** 16 \ **College-Bound:** 85% \ **Ethnic:** African American 6%, Hispanic 12%, Caucasian 82% \ **Exp:** $415 (High) \ **Poverty:** 18% \ **Title I:** $107,692 \ **Special Education:** $118,000 \ **Open-Close:** 08/15 - 05/29 \ **DTBP:** $347 (High)

Devin Tate 1	Charmaine Chappell 2
Gay Harris 3,5	Jaime Swanson 4
Cody Ross 6	Dr Georgia King 8,11,58,83,286,296,298*
Veronica Wilkerson 16	Amy English 57*
Casey Travis 67	Trecia Woodall 73*

Public Schs..Principal	Grd	Prgm	Enr/#Cls	SN	
Beckville Jr Sr High Sch 169 N Washington St, Beckville 75631 Loretta Blair \ Phillip Works	6-12	TV	353 25	39%	903/678-3851 Fax 903/678-3827
Beckville Sunset Elem Sch 4378 State Highway 149, Beckville 75631 Jason Bridges	PK-5	T	312 24	33%	903/678-3601 Fax 903/678-2257

- **Carthage Ind School Dist** PID: 01046215   903/693-3806
  1 Bulldog Dr, Carthage 75633   Fax 903/693-2511

Schools: 6 \ **Teachers:** 197 \ **Students:** 2,692 \ **Special Ed Students:** 291 \ **LEP Students:** 242 \ **College-Bound:** 52% \ **Ethnic:** Asian 1%, African American 23%, Hispanic 19%, Caucasian 57% \ **Exp:** $421 (High) \ **Poverty:** 18% \ **Title I:** $584,992 \ **Open-Close:** 08/19 - 05/22 \ **DTBP:** $153 (High)

John Wink 1	Kathy Ballard 2
Bill Black 3	Steve Zurline 3,15
Llyod Williams 4	Renee Reysinger 5
Scott Surratt 6,35*	Bonnie McMillian 7*
Donna Porter ...8,11,57,88,285,288,296,298*	Bonnie Pope 16*
Shannon Royce 38,270	Angie Bishop 58
Dr Ben Donald 67	Jean Thomas 71
Richard Sullivan 73,76,95,295	

Public Schs..Principal	Grd	Prgm	Enr/#Cls	SN	
Baker Koonce Intermediate Sch 320 N Daniels St, Carthage 75633 Clarinda Collins	4-6	T	593 49	59%	903/693-8611 Fax 903/693-5948
Carthage High Sch 1600 West Panola, Carthage 75633 Jason Harris	9-12	T	792 60	46%	903/693-2552 Fax 903/693-9752
Carthage Junior High Sch 616 Holly St, Carthage 75633 Wade Watson	7-8	T	413 35	56%	903/693-2751 Fax 903/694-9582
Carthage Primary Sch 510 N Adams St, Carthage 75633 Kiley Schumacher	PK-1	T	485 33	65%	903/693-2254 Fax 903/693-3287
Libby Elem Sch 419 Davis St, Carthage 75633 Staci Davis	2-3	T	403 22	59%	903/693-8862 Fax 903/693-4696
Ⓐ Pace Academy 320 W College St, Carthage 75633 Mike Baysinger	6-12		30		903/694-7554

- **Gary Ind School Dist** PID: 01046277   903/685-2291
  132 Bobcat Trl, Gary 75643   Fax 903/685-2639

Schools: 1 \ **Teachers:** 40 \ **Students:** 500 \ **Special Ed Students:** 47 \ **LEP Students:** 16 \ **Ethnic:** Hispanic 7%, Caucasian 92% \ **Exp:** $518 (High) \ **Poverty:** 21% \ **Title I:** $83,467 \ **Special Education:** $86,000 \ **Open-Close:** 08/16 - 05/22 \ **DTBP:** $329 (High)

Todd Greer 1	Jason Woodfin 2,3,5,11,88
Mark Brown 6*	Janie Thomas 7*
Dr Richard Ballenger 8,15,58,69*	Tiffany Brown 57*
Stacy Cransord 67	Mark Baisden 73*
Tonja Coleman 81	

Public Schs..Principal	Grd	Prgm	Enr/#Cls	SN	
Gary Sch 132 Bobcat Trl, Gary 75643 **Brittney Davis** \ Michael Powell	PK-12	ATV	500 30	44%	903/685-2291

PANOLA PRIVATE SCHOOLS

Private Schs..Principal	Grd	Prgm	Enr/#Cls	SN	
Northside Christian Academy 108 E Ash St, Carthage 75633 Scott Dragoo	PK-12		90 5		903/693-7700 Fax 903/694-9272

79 Student Personnel	91 Safety/Security	275 Response To Intervention	298 Grant Writer/Ptnrships	**School Programs**	**Social Media**
80 Driver Ed/Safety	92 Magnet School	277 Remedial Math K-12	750 Chief Innovation Officer	A = Alternative Program	
81 Gifted/Talented	93 Parental Involvement	280 Literacy Coach	751 Chief of Staff	G = Adult Classes	f = Facebook
82 Video Services	95 Tech Prep Program	285 STEM	752 Social Emotional Learning	M = Magnet Program	
83 Substance Abuse Prev	97 Chief Infomation Officer	286 Digital Learning		T = Title I Schoolwide	t = Twitter
84 Erate	98 Chief Technology Officer	288 Common Core Standards	**Other School Types**	V = Career & Tech Ed Programs	
85 AIDS Education	270 Character Education	294 Accountability	Ⓐ = Alternative School		
88 Alternative/At Risk	271 Migrant Education	295 Network System	Ⓒ = Charter School	New Schools are shaded	
89 Multi-Cultural Curriculum	273 Teacher Mentor	296 Title II Programs	Ⓜ = Magnet School	New Superintendents and Principals are bold	
90 Social Work	274 Before/After Sch	297 Webmaster	Ⓨ = Year-Round School	Personnel with email addresses are underscored	

Parker County

PARKER COUNTY

PARKER PUBLIC SCHOOLS

• **Aledo Ind School Dist** PID: 01046306 817/441-8327
1008 Bailey Ranch Rd, Aledo 76008 Fax 817/441-4845

Schools: 10 \ *Teachers:* 307 \ *Students:* 6,000 \ *Special Ed Students:* 394 \ *LEP Students:* 134 \ *College-Bound:* 61% \ *Ethnic:* Asian 1%, African American 1%, Hispanic 13%, Caucasian 84% \ *Exp:* $260 (Med) \ *Poverty:* 5% \ *Title I:* $287,131 \ *Special Education:* $675,000 \ *Open-Close:* 08/20 - 05/28 \ *DTBP:* $151 (High) \ f t

Dr Susan Bohn	1	Buffy Hanson	2	
Earl Husfeld	2,19	Randy Campbell	3	
Patty Willhite	4	Ken Burns	5	
Steve Wood	6	Amber Crissey	8	
Lynn McKinney	11,15,296	Julie Baker	16,82*	
Mary Smith	27	Candace Summerhill	57,74,273,294	
Cheryl Wooten	58	Hoyt Harris	67	
Sherry Taylor	68	Rick Herrin	71	
Brooks Moore	73,98,295	Melissa Quisenberry	73	
Scott Kessel	88*			

Public Schs..Principal	Grd	Prgm	Enr/#Cls	SN	
Aledo High Sch 1000 Bailey Ranch Rd, Aledo 76008 Dan Peterson	9-12	V	1,274 55	10%	817/441-8711 Fax 817/441-5136
ⓐ Aledo Learning Center 1016 Bailey Ranch Rd, Aledo 76008 Cheryl Jones	9-12	G	25 5		817/441-5176 Fax 817/441-9488
Aledo Middle Sch 416 S FM 1187, Aledo 76008 Mandy Musselwhite	7-8		882 45	10%	817/441-5198 Fax 817/441-5133
Coder Elem Sch 12 Vernon Rd, Aledo 76008 Amy Sadler	PK-4	T	541 22	26%	817/441-6095 Fax 817/441-5135
Don R Daniel 9th Grade Campus 990 Bailey Ranch Rd, Aledo 76008 Angela Tims	9-9		464	11%	817/441-4504 Fax 817/441-2146
McAnally Intermediate Sch 151 S FM 5, Aledo 76008 Dennis Hearn	5-6		834	12%	817/441-8347 Fax 817/441-5177
McCall Elem Sch 400 Scenic Trl, Willow Park 76087 Julie Choate	PK-4	T	423	22%	817/441-4500 Fax 817/441-4535
Stuard Elem Sch 200 Thunder Head Ln, Aledo 76008 Ron Shelton	PK-4		579 23	4%	817/441-5103 Fax 817/441-5116
Vandagriff Elem Sch 408 S FM 1187, Aledo 76008 Stephanie Covington	PK-4	T	541 20	11%	817/441-8771 Fax 817/441-5150
Walsh Elem Sch 1 Dean Dr, Aledo 76008 Kerry Cooper	PK-5		334		817/207-3355

• **Brock Ind School Dist** PID: 01046344 817/594-7642
410 Eagle Spirit Ln, Brock 76087 Fax 817/599-3246

Schools: 4 \ *Teachers:* 90 \ *Students:* 1,376 \ *Special Ed Students:* 92 \ *LEP Students:* 17 \ *Ethnic:* African American 1%, Hispanic 8%, Native American: 1%, Caucasian 90% \ *Exp:* $357 (High) \ *Poverty:* 5% \ *Title I:* $59,053 \ *Open-Close:* 08/15 - 05/21 \ *DTBP:* $329 (High) \ t

Dr Cade Smith	1	Mike McSwain	2,19
Burt Green	3	Mere Marcus	4*
Jeff Fulmer	5	Chad Massey	6*
Dee Ann Mills	12,298	Charlie King	16,73*
Dr Martin Ivey	67		

Public Schs..Principal	Grd	Prgm	Enr/#Cls	SN	
Brock Elem Sch 3000 FM 1189, Brock 76087 Erin Griffith	PK-2		300 18		817/592-6555 Fax 817/599-5117
Brock High Sch 410 Eagle Spirit Ln, Weatherford 76087 Bobby Atchley	9-12	V	403 20	7%	817/596-7425 Fax 817/594-2509
Brock Intermediate Sch 100 Grindstone Rd, Brock 76087 Ingia Saxton	3-6		447		817/594-8017
Brock Junior High Sch 300 Grindstone Rd, Brock 76087 Andy Hudson	7-8		200 25	9%	817/594-3195 Fax 817/594-3191

• **Garner Ind School Dist** PID: 01046370 940/682-4251
2222 Garner School Rd, Weatherford 76088 Fax 940/682-4141

Schools: 1 \ *Teachers:* 17 \ *Students:* 200 \ *Special Ed Students:* 18 \ *LEP Students:* 12 \ *Ethnic:* Hispanic 23%, Native American: 1%, Caucasian 77% \ *Exp:* $335 (High) \ *Poverty:* 9% \ *Title I:* $28,095 \ *Open-Close:* 08/21 - 05/21 \ *DTBP:* $362 (High) \ f

Rebecca Hallmark	1	Carolyn Jones	2,13
Jay DeRoche	3,5	Vicki McBride	4
Tony Smith	6*	Diane Shawi	7,91*
Jaycy Roach	11,16,69*	Diane Shaw	12,34*
Clay Yougblood	67	Jimmy Autry	73*

Public Schs..Principal	Grd	Prgm	Enr/#Cls	SN	
Garner Elem Sch 2222 Garner School Rd, Weatherford 76088 Diane Shaw	PK-8	T	200 15	57%	940/682-4251

• **Millsap Ind School Dist** PID: 01046394 940/682-4994
201 E Brazos St, Millsap 76066 Fax 940/682-4476

Schools: 3 \ *Teachers:* 79 \ *Students:* 994 \ *Special Ed Students:* 86 \ *LEP Students:* 25 \ *College-Bound:* 43% \ *Ethnic:* Asian 1%, African American 1%, Hispanic 13%, Native American: 1%, Caucasian 85% \ *Exp:* $519 (High) \ *Poverty:* 11% \ *Title I:* $84,766 \ *Open-Close:* 08/19 - 05/22 \ *DTBP:* $347 (High) \ f t

Deann Lee	1,11	Kim Alexander	2
Norman Adkins	3	Tina Stevens	4
Brad Littlefields	5	Stephanie Gast	7*
Edi Martin	15,296	Pam Davis	34*
Dr Dene Herbel	67	John Briese	73
Zach Greer	73*		

Texas School Directory — Parker County

Public Schs..Principal	Grd	Prgm	Enr/#Cls	SN	
Millsap Elem Sch 101 Wilson Bend Rd, Millsap 76066 Cathy Bradshaw	PK-5	T	491 23	44%	940/682-4489
Millsap High Sch 600 Bulldog Dr, Millsap 76066 Tammy Addison	9-12	AV	300 30	42%	940/682-4994 Fax 940/682-4035
Millsap Middle Sch 301 E Brazos St, Millsap 76066 Jeffrey Clark	6-8	TV	203	46%	940/682-4489

● **Peaster Ind School Dist** PID: 01046423   817/341-5000
3602 Harwell Lake Rd, Weatherford 76088   Fax 817/341-5003

Schools: 3 \ **Teachers:** 102 \ **Students:** 1,200 \ **Special Ed Students:** 100 \ **LEP Students:** 33 \ **Ethnic:** African American 1%, Hispanic 13%, Caucasian 85% \ **Exp:** $482 (High) \ **Poverty:** 9% \ **Title I:** $103,815 \ **Open-Close:** 08/21 - 05/21 \ **DTBP:** $353 (High)

Matt Adams 1
Jay Lionberger 3
Michael Rudock 5,8,11,68,69,78,83,298*
Kim Hubbard 12,271*
Kathy Gilbert 58*
Nicole Elliott 73,76,286,295
Sarah Kirk 2
Paula Melton 4
Michelle Madison 9,57,88*
Melinda Cofper 16
Mike Bowling 67
Nick Rudolph 288

Public Schs..Principal	Grd	Prgm	Enr/#Cls	SN	
Peaster Elem Sch 3400 Harwell Lake Rd, Weatherford 76088 Michelle Madison	PK-6	T	471 26	39%	817/341-5000 Fax 817/594-1890
Peaster High Sch 3600 Harwell Lake Rd, Weatherford 76088 Chris Pennington	9-12	AV	335 40	26%	817/341-5000 Fax 817/341-5027
Peaster Middle Sch 8512 FM 920, Weatherford 76088 Scott Carlisle	6-8	T	178 23	37%	817/341-5000 Fax 817/341-5052

● **Poolville Ind School Dist** PID: 01046459   817/594-4452
16025 FM 920, Poolville 76487   Fax 817/594-2651

Schools: 3 \ **Teachers:** 49 \ **Students:** 530 \ **Special Ed Students:** 52 \ **LEP Students:** 43 \ **Ethnic:** Hispanic 19%, Caucasian 81% \ **Exp:** $313 (High) \ **Poverty:** 17% \ **Title I:** $123,196 \ **Open-Close:** 08/14 - 05/22 \ **DTBP:** $333 (High)

Jeff Kirby 1
John Shari 6
Doug Bryant 8,16,73*
Lindsay Back 36,83,270*
Paula Hall 2
Cathy Pennington . 8,11,57,58,69,271,296,298
Kathy Pierce 9,59*
Lynn DuVall 67

Public Schs..Principal	Grd	Prgm	Enr/#Cls	SN	
Poolville Elem Sch 16025 FM 920, Poolville 76487 Kathy Pierce	PK-5	T	261 25	63%	817/599-3308 Fax 817/599-6593
Poolville High Sch 1001 Lone Star Rd, Poolville 76487 Jennifer Shifflett	9-12	T	163 40	51%	817/599-5134 Fax 817/599-5171
Poolville Junior High Sch 16025 FM 920, Poolville 76487 Jamie Dunnam	6-8	T	94 12	51%	817/594-4539 Fax 817/594-0081

● **Springtown Ind School Dist** PID: 01046514   817/220-7243
301 E 5th St, Springtown 76082   Fax 817/523-5766

Schools: 6 \ **Teachers:** 237 \ **Students:** 3,470 \ **Special Ed Students:** 267 \ **LEP Students:** 155 \ **Ethnic:** African American 1%, Hispanic 18%, Native American: 1%, Caucasian 79% \ **Exp:** $432 (High) \ **Poverty:** 13% \ **Title I:** $547,254 \ **Special Education:** $667,000 \ **Open-Close:** 08/19 - 05/22 \ **DTBP:** $163 (High)

Mike Kelley 1
Jerrell Rutherford 3
Micheal Chavez 5,79*
Tiffany Cano 9
Dr Lisa Kirkpatrick 11,31,57,83,88,271,296,298
Stacy Johnson 34,58
Wesley Thomas 69
Sheila Schram 76
Gary Shaw 2,19
Kim Nash 4
Brian Hulett 6*
Michelle Bateman 10
Shane Strickland 15,68,273
Amy Walker 67
Robert McHenry 73,98,286,295

Public Schs..Principal	Grd	Prgm	Enr/#Cls	SN	
Goshen Creek Elem Sch 401 S PO Jo Dr, Springtown 76082 Kelly Jones	PK-4	T	602 14	56%	817/220-0272 Fax 817/220-0471
Reno Elem Sch 172 W Reno Rd, Azle 76020 Jenna Showers	PK-4	T	381 21	71%	817/221-5001 Fax 817/677-1214
Springtown Elem Sch 416 E 3rd St, Springtown 76082 Pearl Russell	PK-4	T	543 35	64%	817/220-2498 Fax 817/523-4094
Springtown High Sch 915 W Highway 199, Springtown 76082 Dr Scott McPherson	9-12	TV	982 64	45%	817/220-3888 Fax 817/523-5290
Springtown Intermediate Sch 300 PO Jo Dr, Springtown 76082 Joe Brown	5-6	T	533 25	53%	817/220-1219 Fax 817/220-0889
Springtown Middle Sch 500 PO Jo Dr, Springtown 76082 Mark Wilson	7-8	T	541 28	50%	817/220-7455 Fax 817/220-0279

● **Weatherford Ind School Dist** PID: 01046564   817/598-2800
1100 Longhorn Dr, Weatherford 76086   Fax 817/598-2951

Schools: 12 \ **Teachers:** 518 \ **Students:** 8,000 \ **Special Ed Students:** 740 \ **LEP Students:** 626 \ **College-Bound:** 58% \ **Ethnic:** Asian 1%, African American 3%, Hispanic 26%, Caucasian 71% \ **Exp:** $339 (High) \ **Poverty:** 12% \ **Title I:** $1,252,895 \ **Special Education:** $1,274,000 \ **Open-Close:** 08/22 - 05/28 \ **DTBP:** $180 (High) \

Dr Jeffrey Hanks 1
Sharon Landrum 2
J P Kechnie 3
Monte Chapman 5,15,68,78
Shaelee Mitchell 7,83*
Racheal Rife 9,69,74,81,752
Janet McNeely 11
Andy Donaghey 23,27
Kady Donaghey 27,31,75*
Jennie Morris 30
Melanie Gonzalez 46
Amy Hall 48
Marie Hernandez 57
Mike Guest 67
Rhiannon Montgomery 73*
Cody Lee 76,286
Grant Priess 88*
Luis Duenez 91
Jennifer Holcomb 274*
Patricia Melendez 2,298
Bob Bridges 3
Alicia Hernandez 4
Richard Scoggin 6
Rachel Rife 8,74,273,285,288*
Marie Hernandez 10,280*
John Tarrant 16,82*
James Buckner 23*
Donnie McGowen 30
Linda Bourland 42
Amy Cribbs 47
Amanda McCown 50
Leslie Ackmann 58,275
Rhiannon Montgomery 73
Rebecca Nelson 74
Lynn Pool 78,79
Bruno Diaz 91
Charlette LaGrone 93
Tracy Montgomery 295

---

79 Student Personnel
80 Driver Ed/Safety
81 Gifted/Talented
82 Video Services
83 Substance Abuse Prev
84 Erate
85 AIDS Education
88 Alternative/At Risk
89 Multi-Cultural Curriculum
90 Social Work

91 Safety/Security
92 Magnet School
93 Parental Involvement
95 Tech Prep Program
97 Chief Information Officer
98 Chief Technology Officer
270 Character Education
271 Migrant Education
273 Teacher Mentor
274 Before/After Sch

275 Response To Intervention
277 Remedial Math K-12
280 Literacy Coach
285 STEM
286 Digital Learning
288 Common Core Standards
294 Accountability
295 Network System
296 Title II Programs
297 Webmaster

298 Grant Writer/Ptnrships
750 Chief Innovation Officer
751 Chief of Staff
752 Social Emotional Learning

School Programs
A = Alternative Program
G = Adult Classes
M = Magnet Program
T = Title I Schoolwide
V = Career & Tech Ed Programs

Other School Types
Ⓐ = Alternative School
Ⓒ = Charter School
Ⓜ = Magnet School
Ⓨ = Year-Round School

Social Media
 = Facebook
 = Twitter

New Schools are shaded
New Superintendents and Principals are bold
Personnel with email addresses are underscored

Parmer County

Market Data Retrieval

Public Schs..Principal	Grd	Prgm	Enr/#Cls	SN	
Austin Elem Sch 1776 Texas Dr, Weatherford 76086 Kelsey Smith	PK-6		658 50	32%	817/598-2848 Fax 817/598-2978
Bill W Wright Elem Sch 1309 Charles St, Weatherford 76086 Tra Hall	PK-6	T	644	57%	817/598-2828 Fax 817/598-2830
Bose Ikard Elem Sch 100 Ikard Ln, Weatherford 76086 Christy Burton	PK-6	T	647 22	65%	817/598-2818 Fax 817/598-2805
Ⓐ Bridge Academy 1007 S Main St, Weatherford 76086 Ben Schoonover	10-12		50		817/598-2847 Fax 817/598-2928
Crockett Elem Sch 1015 Jameson St, Weatherford 76086 **Marilisa Moore**	PK-6	T	524 27	41%	817/598-2811 Fax 817/598-2813
Curtis Elem Sch 501 W Russell St, Weatherford 76086 Lorie Bratcher	PK-6	T	741 34	47%	817/598-2838 Fax 817/598-2840
Joe Tison Middle Sch 102 Meadowview Rd Ste 100, Weatherford 76087 Jeffrey Bradley	7-8	TV	597 65	39%	817/598-2960 Fax 817/598-2963
Juan Seguin Elem Sch 499 E 8th St, Weatherford 76086 Jessica Shugart	PK-6	T	602 34	62%	817/598-2814 Fax 817/598-2826
Mary Martin Elem Sch 719 N Oakridge Dr, Weatherford 76087 Amy Crippen	PK-6		658 28	18%	817/598-2910 Fax 817/598-2912
Shirley Hall Middle Sch 902 Charles St, Weatherford 76086 **Stephanie Wynne**	7-8	TV	633 40	42%	817/598-2822 Fax 817/598-2854
Weatherford 9th Grade Center 1007 S Main St, Weatherford 76086 **Lynn Pool**	9-9	V	618		817/598-2847 Fax 817/598-2928
Weatherford High Sch 2121 Bethel Rd, Weatherford 76087 **Brannon Kidd**	10-12	AV	1,700	34%	817/598-2858 Fax 817/598-2881

PARKER PRIVATE SCHOOLS

Private Schs..Principal	Grd	Prgm	Enr/#Cls	SN	
Aledo Christian Sch 400 Queen St, Aledo 76008 Kay Ross	PK-12		150 9		817/441-7357 Fax 817/441-2713
Grace Christian Academy-Brock 127 Lazy Bend Rd, Brock 76087 Jody McGlothlin	K-8		901		682/262-9288
The Academy 1200 S Main St, Weatherford 76086 Kathy Peck	PK-K		50 5		817/598-0722
Trinity Christian Academy 4954 E I-20 Service Rd S, Willow Park 76087 Dr Steve Newby \ Ken Nobles	PK-12		400 31		817/441-7901 Fax 817/441-7912
Victory Baptist Academy 1311 E Bankhead Dr, Weatherford 76086 Patti Catuto	PK-12		100		817/596-2711 Fax 817/550-6207
Weatherford Christian Sch 111 E Columbia St, Weatherford 76086 Amy Butler \ Karen Mooney	PK-12		230		817/596-7807 Fax 817/596-0529

PARMER COUNTY

PARMER PUBLIC SCHOOLS

• **Bovina Ind School Dist** PID: 01046655   806/251-1336
500 Halsell Street, Bovina 79009   Fax 806/251-1578

Schools: 3 \ *Teachers:* 45 \ *Students:* 490 \ *Special Ed Students:* 32 \ *LEP Students:* 124 \ *College-Bound:* 67% \ *Ethnic:* Hispanic 96%, Caucasian 4% \ *Exp:* $514 (High) \ *Poverty:* 17% \ *Title I:* $114,010 \ *Open-Close:* 08/16 - 05/22 \ *DTBP:* $350 (High)

Denise Anderson	1	Darlene Miller	2
Richard Villarreal	3,5	Rachel Avalos	7,85*
Darla Sealey	8,11	Joanne Belcher	58
George Villarreal	67	Stan Miller	73,84,295
Roseo Monto	88	Lory Saenz	271

Public Schs..Principal	Grd	Prgm	Enr/#Cls	SN	
Bovina Elem Sch 500 Halsell Street, Bovina 79009 Kaylene Davis	PK-5	T	251 24	87%	806/251-1336
Bovina High Sch 500 Halsell St, Bovina 79009 Dan Castillo	9-12	TV	134	85%	806/251-1336
Bovina Middle Sch 500 Halsell St, Bovina 79009 Mark Barnes	6-8	T	106	85%	806/251-1336

• **Farwell Ind School Dist** PID: 01046693   806/481-3371
705 6th St, Farwell 79325   Fax 806/481-9275

Schools: 3 \ *Teachers:* 53 \ *Students:* 522 \ *Special Ed Students:* 56 \ *LEP Students:* 87 \ *College-Bound:* 43% \ *Ethnic:* Hispanic 52%, Caucasian 48% \ *Exp:* $433 (High) \ *Poverty:* 16% \ *Title I:* $80,835 \ *Open-Close:* 08/21 - 05/21 \ *DTBP:* $231 (High)

Colby Waldrop	1	Edy Kalbas	2,11
Tim Kasel	3,5,91	Leticia Olmos	4
Shane Perkins	6*	Michelle Jaime	7,83*
Hayley Christian	36,88,270*	Deirdre Guthals	57*
Jay Be Barrett	67	Karen Schilling	69*
Kathy Curtis	73,76,295*	Yvonne Ortega	93*

Public Schs..Principal	Grd	Prgm	Enr/#Cls	SN	
Farwell Elem Sch 602 Avenue G, Farwell 79325 Tonya O'Neill	PK-5	T	267 17	62%	806/481-9131 Fax 806/481-3255
Farwell High Sch 801 Avenue G, Farwell 79325 Coby Norman	9-12	TV	147 15	53%	806/481-3351 Fax 806/481-3531
Farwell Junior High Sch 701 Avenue G, Farwell 79325 Kristy White	6-8	T	125 12	56%	806/481-9260 Fax 806/481-9258

---

1 Superintendent	8 Curric/Instruct K-12	19 Chief Financial Officer	29 Family/Consumer Science	39 Social Studies K-12	49 English/Lang Arts Elem	59 Special Education Elem	69 Academic Assessment
2 Bus/Finance/Purchasing	9 Curric/Instruct Elem	20 Art K-12	30 Adult Education	40 Social Studies Elem	50 English/Lang Arts Sec	60 Special Education Sec	70 Research/Development
3 Buildings And Grounds	10 Curric/Instruct Sec	21 Art Elem	31 Career/Sch-to-Work K-12	41 Social Studies Sec	51 Reading K-12	61 Foreign/World Lang K-12	71 Public Information
4 Food Service	11 Federal Program	22 Art Sec	32 Career/Sch-to-Work Elem	42 Science K-12	52 Reading Elem	62 Foreign/World Lang Elem	72 Summer School
5 Transportation	12 Title I	23 Music K-12	33 Career/Sch-to-Work Sec	43 Science Elem	53 Reading Sec	63 Foreign/World Lang Sec	73 Instructional Tech
6 Athletic	13 Title V	24 Music Elem	34 Early Childhood Ed	44 Science Sec	54 Remedial Reading K-12	64 Religious Education K-12	74 Inservice Training
7 Health Services	15 Asst Superintendent	25 Music Sec	35 Health/Phys Education	45 Math K-12	55 Remedial Reading Elem	65 Religious Education Elem	75 Marketing/Distributive
	16 Instructional Media Svcs	26 Business Education	36 Guidance Services K-12	46 Math Elem	56 Remedial Reading Sec	66 Religious Education Sec	76 Info Systems
	17 Chief Operations Officer	27 Career & Tech Ed	37 Guidance Services Elem	47 Math Sec	57 Bilingual/ELL	67 School Board President	77 Psychological Assess
	18 Chief Academic Officer	28 Technology Education	38 Guidance Services Sec	48 English/Lang Arts K-12	58 Special Education K-12	68 Teacher Personnel	78 Affirmative Action

Texas School Directory

Pecos County

• Friona Ind School Dist PID: 01046734
909 E 11th St, Friona 79035
806/250-2747
Fax 806/250-3805

Schools: 4 \ **Teachers:** 105 \ **Students:** 1,117 \ **Special Ed Students:** 109 \ **LEP Students:** 281 \ **Ethnic:** African American 1%, Hispanic 89%, Caucasian 11% \ **Exp:** $252 (Med) \ **Poverty:** 19% \ **Title I:** $222,902 \ **Open-Close:** 08/14 - 05/21 \ **DTBP:** $350 (High)

Jimmy Burns	1	Dianna Wright	2*
Daniel Hidalgo	3	Laura Romero	4
Serapio Cabavule	5	Jimmy Arias	6*
Teresa Echavaria	7	Ashley Smith	8
Karen Barnes	11	Amy Cook	16*
Carrie Arias	34,58	Loy McLellan	37,83*
Antonio Rocha	67	Trisha Steelman	73,76,286,295

Public Schs..Principal	Grd	Prgm	Enr/#Cls	SN	
Friona Elem Sch 200 W 8th St, Friona 79035 M'Kell Jeter	2-5	T	327 29	77%	806/250-2240 Fax 806/250-5078
Friona High Sch 810 Chieftain Way, Friona 79035 Erika Montana	9-12	TV	298 50	60%	806/250-3951 Fax 806/250-2188
Friona Junior High Sch 1001 Euclid St, Friona 79035 Jesse Galdean	6-8	T	223 30	79%	806/250-2788 Fax 806/250-8155
Friona Primary Sch 802 Euclid Ave, Friona 79035 Deirdre Osborn	PK-1	T	269 16	72%	806/250-3935 Fax 806/250-3937

• Lazbuddie Ind School Dist PID: 01046772
675 FM 1172, Lazbuddie 79053
806/965-2156
Fax 806/965-2892

Schools: 1 \ **Teachers:** 18 \ **Students:** 201 \ **Special Ed Students:** 18 \ **LEP Students:** 22 \ **College-Bound:** 89% \ **Ethnic:** African American 1%, Hispanic 35%, Native American: 2%, Caucasian 63% \ **Exp:** $261 (Med) \ **Poverty:** 13% \ **Title I:** $23,559 \ **Open-Close:** 08/15 - 05/22 \ **DTBP:** $307 (High)

Steve Wolf	1,73	Carolyn Scott	2
Lyneldon Randolph	3,5*	Lareta Barber	7*
Candice Weaver	67	Ken Hoskins	285*

Public Schs..Principal	Grd	Prgm	Enr/#Cls	SN	
Ⓐ Lazbuddie Sch 675 FM 1172, Lazbuddie 79053 **Bryan Bailey**	PK-12	TV	201 22	67%	806/965-2153

PECOS COUNTY

PECOS PUBLIC SCHOOLS

• Buena Vista Ind School Dist PID: 01046801
404 W State Highway 11, Imperial 79743
432/536-2225
Fax 432/536-2469

Schools: 1 \ **Teachers:** 16 \ **Students:** 244 \ **Special Ed Students:** 10 \ **LEP Students:** 27 \ **College-Bound:** 70% \ **Ethnic:** African American 2%, Hispanic 76%, Native American: 1%, Caucasian 21% \ **Exp:** $498 (High) \ **Poverty:** 31% \ **Title I:** $64,571 \ **Open-Close:** 08/21 - 05/25 \ **DTBP:** $408 (High)

Mark Dominguez	1,11,83	John Benavidez	2,6
Julian Castillo	11,57*	Cruz Gomez	67
David Whaley	73		

Public Schs..Principal	Grd	Prgm	Enr/#Cls	SN	
Buena Vista Sch 404 W State Highway 11, Imperial 79743 **Adelina Alcala**	PK-12	TV	244 21	49%	432/536-2336 f

• Ft Stockton Ind School Dist PID: 01046837
101 W Division St, Fort Stockton 79735
432/336-4000
Fax 432/336-4008

Schools: 5 \ **Teachers:** 161 \ **Students:** 2,479 \ **Special Ed Students:** 155 \ **LEP Students:** 215 \ **College-Bound:** 43% \ **Ethnic:** Asian 1%, African American 1%, Hispanic 87%, Caucasian 12% \ **Exp:** $359 (High) \ **Poverty:** 25% \ **Title I:** $744,894 \ **Special Education:** $576,000 \ **Open-Close:** 08/19 - 05/21 \ **DTBP:** $374 (High) \ f t

Ralph Traynham	1	Maria Gomez	2
Robert Stallard	3*	Paul Casias	4
Cecil Bradshaw	5	Mike Peters	6
Cynthia Milan	7	Robin Derington	8
Gil Madrid	15	Sylvia Ogas	57
Dr Zana Hanson	58	Billy Espino	67
Debra Ezell	73,76	Omar Sanchez	73
Robert Knight	83*	Irene Vargas	271
Amy Porras	274	Chris Terry	295
Gabriel Cyfton	295	Reba Subia	297

Public Schs..Principal	Grd	Prgm	Enr/#Cls	SN	
Alamo Elem Sch 804 S US Highway 385, Fort Stockton 79735 Adrienne Horton	PK-3	T	498 32	73%	432/336-4016 Fax 432/336-4028
Apache Elem Sch 208 W 18th St, Fort Stockton 79735 Betty McCallister	K-3	T	309 14	70%	432/336-4161 Fax 432/336-4167
Ft Stockton High Sch 1200 W 17th St, Fort Stockton 79735 **Roy Alvarado**	9-12	ATV	672 60	53%	432/336-4101 Fax 432/336-4113
Ft Stockton Intermediate Sch 1100 W 2nd St, Fort Stockton 79735 Amanda Urias	4-5	AT	434 21	73%	432/336-4141 Fax 432/336-4147
Ft Stockton Middle Sch 2400 W 5th St, Fort Stockton 79735 **Roy Alvarado**	6-8	AT	566 32	71%	432/336-4131 Fax 432/336-4136

79 Student Personnel	91 Safety/Security	275 Response To Intervention	298 Grant Writer/Ptnrships	**School Programs**	**Social Media**
80 Driver Ed/Safety	92 Magnet School	277 Remedial Math K-12	750 Chief Innovation Officer	A = Alternative Program	f = Facebook
81 Gifted/Talented	93 Parental Involvement	280 Literacy Coach	751 Chief of Staff	G = Adult Classes	
82 Video Services	95 Tech Prep Program	285 STEM	752 Social Emotional Learning	M = Magnet Program	t = Twitter
83 Substance Abuse Prev	97 Chief Infomation Officer	286 Digital Learning		T = Title I Schoolwide	
84 Erate	98 Chief Technology Officer	288 Common Core Standards	**Other School Types**	V = Career & Tech Ed Programs	
85 AIDS Education	270 Character Education	294 Accountability	Ⓐ = Alternative School		
88 Alternative/At Risk	271 Migrant Education	295 Network System	Ⓒ = Charter School	New Schools are shaded	
89 Multi-Cultural Curriculum	273 Teacher Mentor	296 Title II Programs	Ⓜ = Magnet School	New Superintendents and Principals are bold	
90 Social Work	274 Before/After Sch	297 Webmaster	Ⓨ = Year-Round School	Personnel with email addresses are underscored	

TX—315

Polk County

Market Data Retrieval

- **Iraan-Sheffield Ind Sch Dist** PID: 01046904   432/639-2512
  100 S Farr Street, Iraan 79744   Fax 432/639-2501

Schools: 3 \ Teachers: 42 \ Students: 422 \ Special Ed Students: 45 \ LEP Students: 50 \ College-Bound: 80% \ Ethnic: African American 1%, Hispanic 69%, Native American: 1%, Caucasian 30% \ Exp: $438 (High) \ Poverty: 20% \ Title I: $80,104 \ Open-Close: 08/14 - 05/22 \ DTBP: $342 (High)

Mike Meek 1,11
Kurt Hannah 3,73,76,286,295
Matthew Luddeke 6
Stacey Meek 16*
Norma Whaley 58
Melissa Hanna 2
Katrina Kent 4*
Monica Lopez 7,83,85*
Nikki Parker 31,69,79,88,270*
Steve Garlock 67

Public Schs..Principal	Grd	Prgm	Enr/#Cls	SN	
Iraan Elem Sch 100 S Farr Street, Iraan 79744 Amy Frazier	PK-5	T	236 14	50%	432/639-2524 Fax 432/639-2201
Iraan High Sch 100 S Farr Street, Iraan 79744 Blake Andrews	9-12	GV	117 15	44%	432/639-2512 Fax 432/639-2272
Iraan Junior High Sch 100 S Farr Street, Iraan 79744 Amy Frazier	6-8	T	71 10	56%	432/639-2512 Fax 432/639-2381

POLK COUNTY

POLK PUBLIC SCHOOLS

- **Big Sandy Ind School Dist** PID: 01046954   936/563-1000
  9180 FM 1276, Livingston 77351   Fax 936/563-1010

Schools: 1 \ Teachers: 41 \ Students: 525 \ Special Ed Students: 52 \ College-Bound: 45% \ Ethnic: Asian 1%, African American 1%, Hispanic 10%, Native American: 22%, Caucasian 67% \ Exp: $433 (High) \ Poverty: 25% \ Title I: $158,832 \ Open-Close: 08/14 - 05/22 \ DTBP: $397 (High)

Eric Carpenter 1,11
Kimberley Moore 4
Sally Elester 8,31,69,83,88*
Glen Goodwin 67
Linda Kidd 2
Kevin Foster 6*
Jan Slack 58*
Susan Crawford 73,295*

Public Schs..Principal	Grd	Prgm	Enr/#Cls	SN	
Big Sandy Sch 9180 FM 1276, Dallardsville 77332 Shelby Tillery \ Diane Houston \ Stephanie Hendrix	PK-12	ATV	525 50	49%	936/563-1000

- **Corrigan-Camden Ind Sch Dist** PID: 01046980   936/398-4040
  504 S Home St, Corrigan 75939   Fax 936/398-4616

Schools: 3 \ Teachers: 75 \ Students: 850 \ Special Ed Students: 86 \ LEP Students: 122 \ Ethnic: African American 27%, Hispanic 39%, Caucasian 34% \ Exp: $519 (High) \ Poverty: 29% \ Title I: $473,944 \ Open-Close: 08/12 - 05/21 \ DTBP: $300 (High)

Richard Cooper 1
James Kemper 3,5
Seven Armstrong 6*
Cindy Owens 2
Debbie Hueske 4
Paula Martin 8,11,16,57,286,288,296,298

Sage Taylor 38
Sean Burks 67
Tracy Cobb 58
Susan Torrez 73*

Public Schs..Principal	Grd	Prgm	Enr/#Cls	SN	
Corrigan-Camden Elem Sch 1664 US Highway 287 W, Corrigan 75939 Larry Cupit	PK-5	T	429 13	75%	936/398-2501 Fax 936/398-5042
Corrigan-Camden High Sch 504 S Home St, Corrigan 75939 Diana Locke	9-12	T	273 30	75%	936/398-2543 Fax 936/398-2685
Corrigan-Camden Jr High Sch 502 S Mathews St, Corrigan 75939 Robert Elliott	6-8	T	190 20	72%	936/398-2962 Fax 936/398-4608

- **Goodrich Ind School Dist** PID: 01047025   936/365-1100
  234 Katie Simpson Ave, Goodrich 77335   Fax 936/365-3518

Schools: 2 \ Teachers: 21 \ Students: 235 \ Special Ed Students: 16 \ LEP Students: 52 \ College-Bound: 83% \ Ethnic: Asian 1%, African American 16%, Hispanic 46%, Caucasian 38% \ Exp: $358 (High) \ Poverty: 19% \ Title I: $138,614 \ Open-Close: 08/15 - 05/21 \ DTBP: $327 (High)

Bryan Taulton 1,11,83
Climet Hutchins 3,5
Caloby Isaacs 8,288
Walter Risner 295
Gwen Messiner 2
Lester King 6*
Brenda Bennett 67

Public Schs..Principal	Grd	Prgm	Enr/#Cls	SN	
Goodrich Elem Sch 234 Katie Simpson Ave, Goodrich 77335 Dr Kathryn Washington	PK-5	T	129 25	88%	936/365-1100 Fax 936/365-2375
Goodrich Middle High Sch 234 Katie Simpson Ave, Goodrich 77335 Calobe Isaacs	6-12	T	106 15	94%	936/365-1100 Fax 936/365-2371

- **Leggett Ind School Dist** PID: 01047051   936/398-2804
  254 E FM 942, Leggett 77350   Fax 936/398-9109

Schools: 1 \ Teachers: 15 \ Students: 185 \ Special Ed Students: 16 \ LEP Students: 7 \ College-Bound: 85% \ Exp: $1,400 (High) \ Poverty: 22% \ Title I: $86,705 \ Open-Close: 08/26 - 05/28 \ DTBP: $362 (High)

Jana Lowe 1,11,73
Mike Watts 3,5
Amanda Lawson 36,69,88*
Chrystal Tinker 83
Cathy Leloux 2,4,11
Robin Lee 16
Curtis Jefferson 67

Public Schs..Principal	Grd	Prgm	Enr/#Cls	SN	
Leggett Sch 254 E FM 942, Leggett 77350 Jana Lowe	PK-12	GV	185 25		936/398-2412 Fax 936/398-0889

- **Livingston Ind School Dist** PID: 01047075   936/328-2100
  1412 S Houston Ave, Livingston 77351   Fax 936/967-8603

Schools: 7 \ Teachers: 280 \ Students: 3,963 \ Special Ed Students: 417 \ LEP Students: 294 \ College-Bound: 27% \ Ethnic: Asian 1%, African American 10%, Hispanic 24%, Caucasian 65% \ Exp: $356 (High) \ Poverty: 26% \ Title I: $1,477,241 \ Special Education: $676,000 \ Open-Close: 08/14 - 05/29 \ DTBP: $196 (High) \

Dr Brent Hawkins 1
Lisa Pearson 2
Ben Davidson 2,19
Stewart Russell 3,91

1 Superintendent	19 Chief Financial Officer	40 Social Studies Elem	60 Special Education Sec
2 Bus/Finance/Purchasing	20 Art K-12	29 Family/Consumer Science	39 Social Studies K-12	49 English/Lang Arts Elem	59 Special Education Elem	69 Academic Assessment
3 Buildings And Grounds	21 Art Elem	30 Adult Education	50 English/Lang Arts Sec	70 Research/Development
4 Food Service	10 Curric/Instruct Sec	31 Career/Sch-to-Work K-12	41 Social Studies Sec	51 Reading K-12	61 Foreign/World Lang K-12	71 Public Information
5 Transportation	11 Federal Program	22 Art Sec	32 Career/Sch-to-Work Elem	42 Science K-12	52 Reading Elem	62 Foreign/World Lang Elem	72 Summer School
6 Athletic	12 Title I	23 Music K-12	33 Career/Sch-to-Work Sec	43 Science Elem	53 Reading Sec	63 Foreign/World Lang Sec	73 Instructional Tech
7 Health Services	13 Title V	24 Music Elem	34 Early Childhood Ed	44 Science Sec	54 Remedial Reading K-12	64 Religious Education K-12	74 Inservice Training
	15 Asst Superintendent	25 Music Sec	35 Health/Phys Education	45 Math K-12	55 Remedial Reading Elem	65 Religious Education Elem	75 Marketing/Distributive
	16 Instructional Media Svcs	26 Business Education	36 Guidance Services K-12	46 Math Elem	56 Remedial Reading Sec	66 Religious Education Sec	76 Info Systems
	17 Chief Operations Officer	27 Career & Tech Ed	37 Guidance Services Elem	47 Math Sec	57 Bilingual/ELL	67 School Board President	77 Psychological Assess
	18 Chief Academic Officer	28 Technology Education	38 Guidance Services Sec	48 English/Lang Arts K 12	58 Special Education K-12	68 Teacher Personnel	78 Affirmative Action

Texas School Directory — Potter County

Mark Young	4	Donna Soto	5
Finis Vanover	6	Janan Moore	8,18,69,74
Lana Smith	9,11,57,68,79,83,88,751	Jennifer Birdwell	16
Tracey Ludwig	37	Christine Jackson	42,45
Pamela Mitchell	58	Ben Ogletree	67
Ben Wilroy	68	Emily Williamson	73
Lily Hopson	294	Mike Wallace	295

Public Schs..Principal	Grd	Prgm	Enr/#Cls	SN	
Cedar Grove Elem Sch 819 W Church St, Livingston 77351 Erin Barnes	PK-1	T	485	67%	936/328-2240 Fax 936/328-2259
Creekside Elem Sch 1 Lions Ave, Livingston 77351 Elisha Bell	1-5	T	645 27	71%	936/328-2150 Fax 936/328-2149
ⓐ Livingston High Sch Academy 400 FM 350 S, Livingston 77351 Lana Smith	9-12	T	45	78%	936/328-8600
Livingston High Sch 400 FM 350 S, Livingston 77351 Paul Drake	9-12	AGTV	1,054 55	55%	936/967-1600
Livingston Junior High Sch 1801 Highway 59 Loop N, Livingston 77351 Jared Nettles	6-8	TV	944 35	63%	936/328-2120 Fax 936/328-2139
Pine Ridge Elem Sch 1200 Mill Rdg, Livingston 77351 Mary Hill	PK-3	T	458 66	81%	936/328-2160 Fax 936/328-2162
Timber Creek Elem Sch 701 N Willis Ave, Livingston 77351 Sheri Murphy	PK-3	T	445 28	79%	936/328-2180 Fax 936/328-2199

- **Onalaska Ind School Dist** PID: 01809809 936/646-1000
  134 N FM 356, Onalaska 77360 Fax 936/646-2605

Schools: 2 \ **Teachers:** 74 \ **Students:** 1,000 \ **Special Ed Students:** 115 \ **LEP Students:** 12 \ **College-Bound:** 20% \ **Ethnic:** Asian 1%, African American 1%, Hispanic 8%, Caucasian 90% \ **Exp:** $376 (High) \ **Poverty:** 27% \ **Title I:** $465,365 \ **Open-Close:** 08/26 - 05/29 \ **DTBP:** $349 (High) \

Anthony Roberts	1	Angela Foster	2,84
James Ard	3,4	Mike Skaggs	5
Nicholas Tyerman	6*	Robyn Thornton	8,11,16,57,58,69,88*
Ted Wiggins	67	Charles Boyce	73,286

Public Schs..Principal	Grd	Prgm	Enr/#Cls	SN	
Onalaska Elem Sch 391 Old Trinity S, Onalaska 77360 David Murphy	PK-6	T	672 21	75%	936/646-1010 Fax 936/646-1019
Onalaska Jr Sr High Sch 1885 FM 3459, Onalaska 77360 Robyn Thornton	7-12	T	438 41	60%	936/646-1020 Fax 936/646-1022

POTTER COUNTY

POTTER PUBLIC SCHOOLS

- **Amarillo Ind School Dist** PID: 01047128 806/326-1000
  7200 W Interstate 40, Amarillo 79106 Fax 806/354-4303

Schools: 55 \ **Teachers:** 2,259 \ **Students:** 33,754 \ **Special Ed Students:** 3,462 \ **LEP Students:** 4,491 \ **College-Bound:** 50% \ **Ethnic:** Asian 6%, African American 11%, Hispanic 48%, Caucasian 35% \ **Exp:** $345 (High) \ **Poverty:** 20% \ **Title I:** $9,675,065 \ **Special Education:** $5,783,000 \ **Open-Close:** 08/13 - 05/22 \ **DTBP:** $203 (High)

Doug Loomis	1	Gary Elliott	2
Pati Buchenau	2,19	Tim Loan	3
Brad Thiessen	6	Patricia Miranda	7,85
Lisa Morgan	8,18,83,88	Sandy Whitlow	8,18
Debbie Chapman	11,298	Dr Christopher Reidlinger	23
Karyn Pierce	27,31	Jeff Roller	28,73,76,84,98
Tracey Morman	36,270	Devia Cearlock	39
Cayla Cielencki	42	Gay Bonjour	45*
Laura Ramos	54	Shannon Davis	57
Sylvia Hughes	57,271	Camillia Johnston	58
Kelly Guillen	58	Robin Malone	67
Chris Tatum	68	Holly Shelton	71
Keitha Ivey	76	Maria Chrzanowski	81
Denise Blanchard	93	Paul Bourguin	275
John Holman	286	Stefan Bressler	298

Public Schs..Principal	Grd	Prgm	Enr/#Cls	SN	
Alice Landergin Elem Sch 3209 S Taylor St, Amarillo 79110 Ramon Garcia	PK-5	T	330 25	90%	806/326-4650 Fax 806/371-6035
Allen 6th Grade Campus 700 N Lincoln St, Amarillo 79107 Dalea Tatum	6-6	T	216	96%	806/326-3770 Fax 806/371-5829
Amarillo Area Ctr Advance Lrng 1100 N Forest St, Amarillo 79106 Jay Barrett	9-12	V	21 18	16%	806/326-2800 Fax 806/371-6100
Amarillo High Sch 4225 Danbury Dr, Amarillo 79109 David Vincent	9-12	V	2,116 106	18%	806/326-2000 Fax 806/354-5092
Avondale Elem Sch 1500 S Avondale St, Amarillo 79106 Randalyn Huyck	PK-5	T	515 25	77%	806/326-4000 Fax 806/354-4498
Belmar Elem Sch 6342 Adirondack Trl, Amarillo 79106 Nicki Roush	PK-5	T	404 20	45%	806/326-4050 Fax 806/354-5081
Bivins Elem Sch 1500 S Fannin St, Amarillo 79102 Benny Barraza	PK-5	T	537 25	71%	806/326-4100 Fax 806/371-6133
CapRock High Sch 3001 SE 34th Ave, Amarillo 79103 Chad Huseman	9-12	TV	1,956 120	75%	806/326-2200 Fax 806/371-6042
Ⓜ Carver Academy Elem Sch 1905 NW 12th Ave, Amarillo 79107 Melody Fox	2-5	T	327 23	73%	806/326-4150 Fax 806/371-6081
Carver Early Childhood Academy 1800 N Travis St, Amarillo 79107 Mitzi Malcolm	PK-1	T	358 21	49%	806/326-4200 Fax 806/371-6178

79 Student Personnel	91 Safety/Security	275 Response To Intervention	298 Grant Writer/Ptnrships	**School Programs**	**Social Media**	
80 Driver Ed/Safety	92 Magnet School	277 Remedial Math K-12	750 Chief Innovation Officer	A = Alternative Program		
81 Gifted/Talented	93 Parental Involvement	280 Literacy Coach	751 Chief of Staff	G = Adult Classes	= Facebook	
82 Video Services	95 Tech Prep Program	285 STEM	752 Social Emotional Learning	M = Magnet Program		
83 Substance Abuse Prev	97 Chief Infomation Officer	286 Digital Learning		T = Title I Schoolwide	= Twitter	
84 Erate	98 Chief Technology Officer	288 Common Core Standards	**Other School Types**	V = Career & Tech Ed Programs		
85 AIDS Education	270 Accountability	294 Accountability	Ⓐ = Alternative School			
88 Alternative/At Risk	271 Migrant Education	295 Network System	Ⓒ = Charter School	New Schools are shaded		
89 Multi-Cultural Curriculum	273 Teacher Mentor	296 Title II Programs	Ⓜ = Magnet School	New Superintendents and Principals are bold		
90 Social Work	274 Before/After Sch	297 Webmaster	Ⓨ = Year-Round School	Personnel with email addresses are underscored		

TX—317

Potter County

School	Grades	Type	Enrollment	%	Phone
Coronado Elem Sch 3210 Wimberly Rd, Amarillo 79109 Bria Galt	PK-5	T	501 24	64%	806/326-4250 Fax 806/356-4821
David Crockett Middle Sch 4720 Floyd Ave, Amarillo 79106 Lisa Loan	6-8	V	855 60	29%	806/326-3300 Fax 806/356-4873
Eastridge Elem Sch 1314 Evergreen St, Amarillo 79107 Genie Baca	PK-5	T	793 39	96%	806/326-4300 Fax 806/381-7333
Emerson Elem Sch 600 N Cleveland St, Amarillo 79107 **Amanda Bales**	PK-5	T	538 21	97%	806/326-4350 Fax 806/371-6055
Forest Hill Elem Sch 3515 E Amarillo Blvd, Amarillo 79107 Bethany Rose	PK-5	T	592 34	95%	806/326-4400 Fax 806/381-7221
Glenwood Elem Sch 2407 S Houston St, Amarillo 79103 Holly Holder	PK-5	T	450 27	93%	806/326-4450 Fax 806/371-5848
Hamlet Elem Sch 705 Sycamore St, Amarillo 79107 **Victor Favela**	PK-5	T	329 30	95%	806/326-4500 Fax 806/381-7366
Horace Mann Middle Sch 610 N Buchanan St, Amarillo 79107 Tammie Villarreal	7-8	TV	450 40	94%	806/326-3700 Fax 806/371-5617
Humphrey's Highland Elem Sch 3901 SE 15th Ave, Amarillo 79104 **Erin Prickett**	PK-5	T	572 39	93%	806/326-4550 Fax 806/371-5822
James Bonham Middle Sch 5600 SW 49th Ave, Amarillo 79109 Andrea Pfeifer	6-8	V	820	25%	806/326-3100 Fax 806/356-4865
James Bowie 6th Grade Campus 2905 Tee Anchor Blvd, Amarillo 79104 Derek Davis	6-6	T	378	87%	806/326-3270 Fax 806/322-3687
James Bowie Middle Sch 2901 Tee Anchor Blvd, Amarillo 79104 Joann Ramirez	7-8	TV	730 80	84%	806/326-3200 Fax 806/371-5719
James W Fannin Middle Sch 4627 S Rusk St, Amarillo 79110 Nathan Culwell	6-8	TV	678 36	70%	806/326-3500 Fax 806/354-4588
Lamar Elem Sch 3800 S Lipscomb St, Amarillo 79110 Ginny Smith	PK-5	T	337 36	80%	806/326-4600 Fax 806/356-4871
Lawndale Elem Sch 2215 S Bivins St, Amarillo 79103 **Jana Toliver**	PK-5	T	388 30	83%	806/326-4700 Fax 806/371-5687
Lorenzo De Zavala Middle Sch 2801 N Coulter St, Amarillo 79124 **Mike Manchee**	5-8		420 30	25%	806/326-3400 Fax 806/354-4286
Margaret Wills Elem Sch 3500 SW 11th Ave, Amarillo 79106 Chris Altman	PK-5	T	588 22	93%	806/326-5650 Fax 806/371-5842
Mesa Verde Elem Sch 4011 Beaver Dr, Amarillo 79107 Charla Cobb	PK-5	T	521 17	96%	806/326-4800 Fax 806/381-7323
Ⓐ North Heights Alt Sch 607 N Hughes St, Amarillo 79107 Mark Leach	7-12	T	429 15	41%	806/326-2850 Fax 806/371-5715
Oak Dale Elem Sch 2711 S Hill St, Amarillo 79103 Amy Barragan	PK-5	T	420 26	81%	806/326-4850 Fax 806/371-6106
Olsen Park Elem Sch 2409 Anna St, Amarillo 79106 Kris Schellhamer	PK-5	T	442 18	45%	806/326-4900 Fax 806/356-4944
Palo Duro High Sch 1400 N Grant St, Amarillo 79107 Amy Dorris	9-12	TV	2,008 60	86%	806/326-2400 Fax 806/381-7166
Paramount Terrace Elem Sch 3906 Cougar Dr, Amarillo 79109 **Lisa Greenhouse**	PK-5	T	362 17	54%	806/326-4950 Fax 806/354-4623
Pleasant Valley Elem Sch 4413 River Rd, Amarillo 79108 Curtis Crump	PK-5	T	331 19	85%	806/326-5000 Fax 806/381-7372
Puckett Elem Sch 6700 Oakhurst Dr, Amarillo 79109 **Cheri Hess**	PK-5		404 19	22%	806/326-5050 Fax 806/356-4833
Ridgecrest Elem Sch 5306 SW 37th Ave, Amarillo 79109 Lesley McCoy	PK-5	T	464 25	53%	806/326-5100 Fax 806/356-4835
Robert E Lee Elem Sch 119 NE 15th Ave, Amarillo 79107 Margarita Ogden	PK-5	T	347 32	98%	806/326-4750 Fax 806/371-6046
Sam Houston Middle Sch 815 S Independence St, Amarillo 79106 Melody Stephenson	6-8	TV	765 59	83%	806/326-3600 Fax 806/371-5577
San Jacinto Elem Sch 3400 SW 4th Ave, Amarillo 79106 Justin Ruiz	PK-5	T	622 27	97%	806/326-5200 Fax 806/371-5843
Sanborn Elem Sch 700 S Roberts St, Amarillo 79102 Sandra Tudon	PK-5	T	520 27	96%	806/326-5250 Fax 806/371-6171
Sleepy Hollow Elem Sch 3435 Reeder Dr, Amarillo 79121 Amy Krieger	PK-5		557 20	13%	806/326-5300 Fax 806/354-5079
South Georgia Elem Sch 5018 Susan Dr, Amarillo 79110 **Heather Newman**	PK-5	T	405 24	57%	806/326-5350 Fax 806/356-4959
South Lawn Elem Sch 4719 Bowie St, Amarillo 79110 Donna Harris	PK-5	T	448 25	78%	806/326-5400 Fax 806/356-4879
Stephen F Austin Middle Sch 1808 Wimberly Rd, Amarillo 79109 **Brandy Self**	6-8	TV	826 45	60%	806/326-3000 Fax 806/356-4802
Sunrise Elem Sch 5123 SE 14th Ave, Amarillo 79104 Shelley Baloglou	PK-5	T	295 24	91%	806/326-5450 Fax 806/371-5841
Tascosa High Sch 3921 Westlawn St, Amarillo 79102 John Smith	9-12	TV	2,270 110	54%	806/326-2600 Fax 806/354-4702
Tradewind Elem Sch 4300 S Williams St, Amarillo 79118 Kim Bentley	PK-5	T	659	74%	806/326-5500 Fax 806/371-6535
Western Plateau Elem Sch 4927 Shawnee Trl, Amarillo 79109 Lori Berryman	PK-5	T	417 23	49%	806/326-5550 Fax 806/356-4872
Whittier Elem Sch 2004 N Marrs St, Amarillo 79107 **Linda Rangel**	PK-5	T	529 60	94%	806/326-5600 Fax 806/381-7322
Will Rogers Elem Sch 920 N Mirror St, Amarillo 79107 Terri Huseman	PK-5	T	545 38	97%	806/326-5150 Fax 806/371-5718
William B Travis 6th GR Campus 2801 NE 24th Ave, Amarillo 79107 **Casey Newman**	6-6	T	346	93%	806/326-3870 Fax 806/322-3690
William B Travis Middle Sch 2815 Martin Rd, Amarillo 79107 Jennifer Wilkerson	7-8	GTV	687 65	94%	806/326-3800 Fax 806/381-7207
Windsor Elem Sch 6700 Hyde Pkwy, Amarillo 79109 **Allison Woodington**	PK-5		494 25	21%	806/326-5700 Fax 806/356-4999
Wolflin Elem Sch 2026 S Hughes St, Amarillo 79109 Stephanie Chew	PK-5		365 22	60%	806/326-5750 Fax 806/371-6101

1 Superintendent
2 Bus/Finance/Purchasing
3 Buildings And Grounds
4 Food Service
5 Transportation
6 Athletic
7 Health Services
8 Curric/Instruct K-12
9 Curric/Instruct Elem
10 Curric/Instruct Sec
11 Federal Program
12 Title I
13 Title V
14 Music Elem
15 Asst Superintendent
16 Instructional Media Svcs
17 Chief Operations Officer
18 Chief Academic Officer
19 Chief Financial Officer
20 Art K-12
21 Art Elem
22 Art Sec
23 Music K-12
24 Music Elem
25 Music Sec
26 Business Education
27 Career & Tech Ed
28 Technology Education
29 Family/Consumer Science
30 Adult Education
31 Career/Sch-to-Work K-12
32 Career/Sch-to-Work Elem
33 Career/Sch-to-Work Sec
34 Early Childhood Ed
35 Health/Phys Education
36 Guidance Services K-12
37 Guidance Services Elem
38 Guidance Services Sec
39 Social Studies K-12
40 Social Studies Elem
41 Social Studies Sec
42 Science K-12
43 Science Elem
44 Science Sec
45 Math K-12
46 Math Elem
47 Math Sec
48 English/Lang Arts K-12
49 English/Lang Arts Elem
50 English/Lang Arts Sec
51 Reading K-12
52 Reading Elem
53 Reading Sec
54 Remedial Reading K-12
55 Remedial Reading Elem
56 Remedial Reading Sec
57 Bilingual/ELL
58 Special Education K-12
59 Special Education Elem
60 Special Education Sec
61 Foreign/World Lang K-12
62 Foreign/World Lang Elem
63 Foreign/World Lang Sec
64 Religious Education K-12
65 Religious Education Elem
66 Religious Education Sec
67 School Board President
68 Teacher Personnel
69 Academic Assessment
70 Research/Development
71 Public Information
72 Summer School
73 Instructional Tech
74 Inservice Training
75 Marketing/Distributive
76 Info Systems
77 Psychological Assess
78 Affirmative Action

Texas School Directory — Potter County

Woodlands Elem Sch — PK-4 — 416 — 806/326-5800
2501 N Coulter St, Amarillo 79124 — 14 — Fax 806/356-4926
Traci Gabel

• Bushland Ind School Dist PID: 01047568
2400 Wells St, Amarillo 79124
806/359-6683
Fax 806/359-6769

Schools: 3 \ **Teachers:** 121 \ **Students:** 1,500 \ **Special Ed Students:** 175 \ **LEP Students:** 10 \ **Ethnic:** African American 1%, Hispanic 15%, Native American: 1%, Caucasian 84% \ **Exp:** $354 (High) \ **Poverty:** 9% \ **Title I:** $99,269 \ **Special Education:** $205,000 \ **Open-Close:** 08/19 - 05/22 \ **DTBP:** $331 (High)

Chris Wigington	1	Karen Grantham	2*
James Falkner	3,5	Billy Maples	4
Jimmy Thomas	6*	Angie Watson	8,11,15,74,296
Paula Schwertner	16*	Michelle Lancaster	31*
Stephanie Donnell	37,83,85*	Tiffany Fisk	38,83*
Angie Noll	57,271,294	Terri Moss	58*
Holly Jefferys	67	Kristen Diamond	73,286
Randy Tinsley	91	Anthony Montelongo	295,297*
Kristin Lavender	752		

Public Schs..Principal	Grd	Prgm	Enr/#Cls	SN	
Bushland Elem Sch	PK-4	T	526	25%	806/359-5410
2400 Wells St, Amarillo 79124			30		Fax 806/322-1166
Brandi Rankin					
Bushland High Sch	9-12	V	464	11%	806/359-6683
1201 S FM 2381, Amarillo 79124					Fax 806/322-1180
Kristi Culpepper					f t
Bushland Middle Sch	5-8	V	468	19%	806/359-5418
20101 25th St, Bushland 79012					Fax 806/355-2841
Jessica Garrett					

• Highland Park Ind School Dist PID: 01047582
15300 E Amarillo Blvd, Amarillo 79108
806/335-2823
Fax 806/335-3547

Schools: 3 \ **Teachers:** 65 \ **Students:** 850 \ **Special Ed Students:** 104 \ **LEP Students:** 62 \ **College-Bound:** 51% \ **Ethnic:** Asian 9%, African American 3%, Hispanic 38%, Native American: 1%, Caucasian 49% \ **Exp:** $292 (Med) \ **Poverty:** 23% \ **Title I:** $199,644 \ **Special Education:** $161,000 \ **Open-Close:** 08/21 - 05/22 \ **DTBP:** $223 (High)

Jimmy Hannon	1	Lisa Messner	2
Garry Leafloor	3*	Garon Newton	4
Wade Wilson	6	Rala Underwood	38*
Kristi Waters	58*	Tonya Detten	67
Susan Looney	73*	Mark Glick	83,91

Public Schs..Principal	Grd	Prgm	Enr/#Cls	SN	
Highland Park Elem Sch	PK-5	T	453	66%	806/335-1334
15300 E Amarillo Blvd, Amarillo 79108			23		Fax 806/335-3184
Vanette Barnett					f
Highland Park High Sch	9-12	ATV	223	52%	806/335-2821
15300 E Amarillo Blvd, Amarillo 79108			16		Fax 806/335-3215
Dixie Shettel					
Highland Park Middle Sch	6-8	TV	218	65%	806/335-2821
15300 E Amarillo Blvd, Amarillo 79108					Fax 806/335-3215
Neila Malcom					

• River Road Ind School Dist PID: 01047609
9500 N US Highway 287, Amarillo 79108
806/381-7800
Fax 806/381-1357

Schools: 4 \ **Teachers:** 92 \ **Students:** 1,278 \ **Special Ed Students:** 133 \ **LEP Students:** 36 \ **Ethnic:** Asian 1%, African American 2%, Hispanic 25%, Native American: 1%, Caucasian 72% \ **Exp:** $379 (High) \ **Poverty:** 16% \ **Title I:** $244,634 \ **Special Education:** $238,000 \ **Open-Close:** 08/19 - 05/22 \ **DTBP:** $348 (High)

Richard Kelley	1	Andy Nies	2,8,11,74,88,270,294,296
David Perry	3	Kim Terry	4*
Bryan Perryman	5	Bryan Welps	6*
Kim Franks	7*	Robin Wood	34,57,58,69,271*
Amanda Brown	67	Gina Montgomery	73,295*
Gina Montgomery	84,295		

Public Schs..Principal	Grd	Prgm	Enr/#Cls	SN	
River Road High Sch	9-12	T	392	50%	806/383-8867
101 W Mobley St, Amarillo 79108			45		Fax 806/381-7818
Dean Birkes					
River Road Middle Sch	7-8	T	206	58%	806/383-8721
9500 N US Highway 287, Amarillo 79108			12		Fax 806/381-7815
Penny Rosson					f
Rolling Hills Elem Sch	PK-4	T	479	75%	806/383-8621
2800 W Cherry Ave, Amarillo 79108			70		Fax 806/381-7814
Erin Brandstatt					f
Willow Vista Intermediate Sch	5-6	T	201	71%	806/383-8820
7600 Pavillard Dr, Amarillo 79108			10		Fax 806/381-7827
Mike Cheverier					

POTTER CATHOLIC SCHOOLS

• Diocese of Amarillo Ed Office PID: 01047659
4512 NE 24th Ave, Amarillo 79107
806/383-2243
Fax 806/383-8452

Schools: 5 \ **Students:** 850

Listing includes only schools located in this county. See District Index for location of Diocesan Offices.

Christina Wanjura 1   Phil Whitson 2

Catholic Schs..Principal	Grd	Prgm	Enr/#Cls	SN	
St Maryis Cathedral Sch	PK-5		218		806/376-9112
1200 S Washington St, Amarillo 79102			10		Fax 806/376-4314
Linda Aranda					

POTTER PRIVATE SCHOOLS

Private Schs..Principal	Grd	Prgm	Enr/#Cls	SN	
Mosaic Academy	PK-12		100		817/204-0300
1400 College Ave, Amarillo 79104					
Kristen Bray					
San Jacinto Christian Academy	PK-12		475		806/372-2285
501 S Carolina St, Amarillo 79106			50		Fax 806/376-6712
Amy Sternenberg \ Chandra Barnes \ Ed Thomas					f
St Andrew's Episcopal Day Sch	PK-8		300		806/376-9501
1515 S Georgia St, Amarillo 79102					Fax 806/376-8421
Joel Bicknell					
Trinity Lutheran Sch	PK-6		75		806/352-5620
5005 W Interstate 40, Amarillo 79106			8		Fax 806/353-7785
Rick Ryan					f

Code	Description	Code	Description	Code	Description	Code	Description
79	Student Personnel	91	Safety/Security	275	Response To Intervention	298	Grant Writer/Ptnrships
80	Driver Ed/Safety	92	Magnet School	277	Remedial Math K-12	750	Chief Innovation Officer
81	Gifted/Talented	93	Parental Involvement	280	Literacy Coach	751	Chief of Staff
82	Video Services	95	Tech Prep Program	285	STEM	752	Social Emotional Learning
83	Substance Abuse Prev	97	Chief Infomation Officer	286	Digital Learning		
84	Erate	98	Chief Technology Officer	288	Common Core Standards		
85	AIDS Education	270	Character Education	294	Accountability		
88	Alternative/At Risk	271	Migrant Education	295	Network System		
89	Multi-Cultural Curriculum	273	Teacher Mentor	296	Title II Programs		
90	Social Work	274	Before/After Sch	297	Webmaster		

School Programs
A = Alternative Program
G = Adult Classes
M = Magnet Program
T = Title I Schoolwide
V = Career & Tech Ed Programs

Other School Types
Ⓐ = Alternative School
Ⓒ = Charter School
Ⓜ = Magnet School
Ⓨ = Year-Round School

Social Media
f = Facebook
t = Twitter

New Schools are shaded
New Superintendents and Principals are bold
Personnel with email addresses are underscored

Presidio County

PRESIDIO COUNTY

PRESIDIO PUBLIC SCHOOLS

- **Marfa Ind School Dist** PID: 01047829 — 432/729-4252
  400 W Lincoln St, Marfa 79843 — Fax 432/729-4310

Schools: 2 \ **Teachers:** 33 \ **Students:** 342 \ **Special Ed Students:** 35 \ **LEP Students:** 62 \ **College-Bound:** 42% \ **Ethnic:** African American 1%, Hispanic 87%, Caucasian 12% \ **Exp:** $495 (High) \ **Poverty:** 35% \ **Title I:** $165,023 \ **Open-Close:** 08/27 - 05/29 \ **DTBP:** $292 (High)

Oscar Aguero 1   Linda Ojeda 6*
Katie Fowlkes 67

Public Schs..Principal	Grd	Prgm	Enr/#Cls	SN	
Marfa Elem Sch 413 W Columbia St, Marfa 79843 Amy White	PK-5		202 23		432/729-4252 Fax 432/729-3417
Marfa Jr Sr High Sch 300 N Gonzales St, Marfa 79843 John Sherrill	6-12	TV	151 30	74%	432/729-4252 Fax 432/729-4053

- **Presidio Ind School Dist** PID: 01047867 — 432/229-3275
  701 E Market St, Presidio 79845 — Fax 432/229-4228

Schools: 3 \ **Teachers:** 107 \ **Students:** 1,162 \ **Special Ed Students:** 84 \ **LEP Students:** 677 \ **College-Bound:** 50% \ **Ethnic:** Asian 2%, Hispanic 97%, Caucasian 1% \ **Exp:** $520 (High) \ **Poverty:** 35% \ **Title I:** $507,046 \ **Open-Close:** 08/14 - 05/28 \ **DTBP:** $371 (High)

Ray Vasquez 1   Raquel Baeza 2
Ruben Armendariz 3,5   Hezila Ramos 6
Dr Laura Postillo 8,11,57,58,271,298   Samuel Carrasco 30
Yvette Deanda .... 31,36,69,83*   Ethel Barriga 67
Larry Quintna 73   Jaime Sanchez 295

Public Schs..Principal	Grd	Prgm	Enr/#Cls	SN	
Lucy Rede Franco Middle Sch 1515 E Highland St, Presidio 79845 Yvette Deanda	7-9	AT	332 29	94%	432/229-3113 Fax 432/229-4087
Presidio Elem Sch 701 E Market Street, Presidio 79845 Dr Edgar Tibayan \ Ernesto Monte	PK-6	T	565 50	93%	432/229-3200 Fax 432/229-4267
Presidio High Sch 701 Highway 170 E, Presidio 79845 Dr Tibayan	10-12	AT	440 34	94%	432/229-3365 Fax 432/229-4625

RAINS COUNTY

RAINS PUBLIC SCHOOLS

- **Rains Ind School Dist** PID: 01047893 — 903/473-2222
  1759 W US Highway 69, Emory 75440 — Fax 903/473-3053

Schools: 4 \ **Teachers:** 127 \ **Students:** 1,650 \ **Special Ed Students:** 190 \ **LEP Students:** 94 \ **College-Bound:** 54% \ **Ethnic:** African American 2%, Hispanic 17%, Native American: 1%, Caucasian 79% \ **Exp:** $339 (High) \ **Poverty:** 23% \ **Title I:** $479,710 \ **Special Education:** $537,000 \ **Open-Close:** 08/26 - 05/28 \ **DTBP:** $340 (High)

Jennifer Johnson 1,11   Jeff Fisher 2,15
Dereck Rowland 3   Tracy Musgrove 16*
Angie Trull .... 34*   Jennifer Melton 58
Phillip Alexander 67   Lisa Clark 73,295*
Lauri Evans 76

Public Schs..Principal	Grd	Prgm	Enr/#Cls	SN	
Rains Elem Sch 372 FM 3299, Mumford 77867 Angie Trull	PK-2	T	468 28	66%	903/473-2222 Fax 903/473-7259
Rains High Sch 1651 W US Highway 69, Emory 75440 Randell Wellman	9-12	ATV	479 46	51%	903/473-2222 Fax 903/473-5584
Rains Intermediate Sch 409 FM 3299, Emory 75440 J Vance	3-5	T	377 20	58%	903/473-2222 Fax 903/473-5162
Rains Junior High Sch 1755 W US Highway 69, Emory 75440 Gina Hildebrandt	6-8	T	381 30	62%	903/473-2222 Fax 903/473-5162

RANDALL COUNTY

RANDALL PUBLIC SCHOOLS

- **Canyon Ind School Dist** PID: 01047934 — 806/677-2600
  3301 N 23rd St, Canyon 79015 — Fax 806/677-2659

Schools: 16 \ **Teachers:** 612 \ **Students:** 10,200 \ **Special Ed Students:** 1,059 \ **LEP Students:** 165 \ **College-Bound:** 55% \ **Ethnic:** Asian 1%, African American 3%, Hispanic 25%, Native American: 1%, Caucasian 71% \ **Exp:** $265 (Med) \ **Poverty:** 8% \ **Title I:** $885,263 \ **Special Education:** $1,568,000 \ **Open-Close:** 08/14 - 05/22 \ **DTBP:** $181 (High)

Darryl Flusche 1   Bryon McCafferty 2
Heather Wilson 2,15   Jeff Millner 3
Ken Robinson 4   Kirk Self 5,91
Toby Tucker 6   Cameron Rosser 8,273
Yolanda DeLaney 9   Marc Hamil 10,27,31
Robyn Cranmer 11,57,93,270,271   Bridget Johnson 58
Bruce Cobb 67   April McDaniel 71
Chris Norton 73,285,286   Michael Keough 76

1	Superintendent	8	Curric/Instruct K-12	19	Chief Financial Officer	29	Family/Consumer Science	39	Social Studies K-12	49	English/Lang Arts Elem	59	Special Education Elem	69	Academic Assessment
2	Bus/Finance/Purchasing	9	Curric/Instruct Elem	20	Art K-12	30	Adult Education	40	Social Studies Elem	50	English/Lang Arts Sec	60	Special Education Sec	70	Research/Development
3	Buildings And Grounds	10	Curric/Instruct Sec	21	Art Elem	31	Career/Sch-to-Work K-12	41	Social Studies Sec	51	Reading K-12	61	Foreign/World Lang K-12	71	Public Information
4	Food Service	11	Federal Program	22	Art Sec	32	Career/Sch-to-Work Elem	42	Science K-12	52	Reading Elem	62	Foreign/World Lang Elem	72	Summer School
5	Transportation	12	Title I	23	Music K-12	33	Career/Sch-to-Work Sec	43	Science Elem	53	Reading Sec	63	Foreign/World Lang Sec	73	Instructional Tech
6	Athletic	13	Title V	24	Music Elem	34	Early Childhood Ed	44	Science Sec	54	Remedial Reading K-12	64	Religious Education K-12	74	Inservice Training
7	Health Services	15	Asst Superintendent	25	Music Sec	35	Health/Phys Education	45	Math K-12	55	Remedial Reading Elem	65	Religious Education Elem	75	Marketing/Distributive
		16	Instructional Media Svcs	26	Business Education	36	Guidance Services K-12	46	Math Elem	56	Remedial Reading Sec	66	Religious Education Sec	76	Info Systems
		17	Chief Operations Officer	27	Career & Tech Ed	37	Guidance Services Elem	47	Math Sec	57	Bilingual/ELL	67	School Board President	77	Psychological Assess
		18	Chief Academic Officer	28	Technology Education	38	Guidance Services Sec	48	English/Lang Arts K-12	58	Special Education K-12	68	Teacher Personnel	78	Affirmative Action

Texas School Directory — Reagan County

Kenneth Boehs 295

Public Schs..Principal	Grd	Prgm	Enr/#Cls	SN
Arden Road Elem Sch 6801 Learning Tree Ln, Amarillo 79119 John Forbis	PK-4		476 25	24% 806/677-2360 Fax 806/677-2379
Canyon High Sch 1701 23rd St, Canyon 79015 Jennifer Boren	9-12	V	1,128 60	23% 806/677-2740 Fax 806/677-2779
Canyon Intermediate Sch 506 8th St, Canyon 79015 Tricia Cook	5-6	T	637 50	34% 806/677-2800 Fax 806/677-2829
Canyon Junior High Sch 910 9th Ave, Canyon 79015 Kirk Kear	7-8	T	640 33	33% 806/677-2700 Fax 806/677-2739 t
City View Elem Sch 3400 Knoll Dr, Amarillo 79118 Andrew Burgoon	PK-4		533	21% 806/677-2500 Fax 806/677-2519
Crestview Elem Sch 80 Hunsley Rd, Canyon 79015 Amy Meek	PK-4		474 23	19% 806/677-2780 Fax 806/677-2799
Gene Howe Elem Sch 5108 Pico Blvd, Amarillo 79110 Kandi Kempf	PK-4	T	374 26	44% 806/677-2380 Fax 806/677-2399 t
Greenways Intermediate Sch 8100 Pineridge Dr, Amarillo 79119 Toby King	5-6		951 60	32% 806/677-2460 Fax 806/677-2499
Hillside Elem Sch 9600 Perry Ave, Amarillo 79119 **Brittany Brown**	K-4		420	23% 806/677-2520 Fax 806/677-2539
Lakeview Elem Sch 6407 Lair Rd, Amarillo 79118 Krystal Hare	PK-4	T	481 24	66% 806/677-2830 Fax 806/677-2849
Ⓐ Midway Alternative High Sch 1403 23rd St, Canyon 79015 Shawn Neeley	11-12		63	39% 806/677-2455 Fax 806/677-2459
Pinnacle Intermediate Sch 4545 Meadow Ridge Dr, Amarillo 79118 Kimberly Lackey	5-6		575	806/677-2570
Randall High Sch 5800 Attebury Dr, Amarillo 79118 Steven Singleton	9-12	V	1,700 85	23% 806/677-2333 Fax 806/677-2329
Reeves Hinger Elem Sch 1005 21st St, Canyon 79015 Nicole Johnston	PK-4	T	767	39% 806/677-2870 Fax 806/677-2889
Sundown Lane Elem Sch 4715 W Sundown Ln, Amarillo 79118 Noe Renteria	K-4	T	670 12	51% 806/677-2400 Fax 806/677-2419
Westover Park Jr High Sch 7200 Pinnacle Dr, Amarillo 79119 Doug Voran	7-8		892 40	30% 806/677-2420 Fax 806/356-2439

RANDALL CATHOLIC SCHOOLS

• **Diocese of Amarillo Ed Office** PID: 01047659
Listing includes only schools located in this county. See District Index for location of Diocesan Offices.

Catholic Schs..Principal	Grd	Prgm	Enr/#Cls	SN
Holy Cross Catholic Academy 4110 S Bonham St, Amarillo 79110 Angela Seidenberger	6-12		120 13	806/355-9637 Fax 806/353-9520
St Joseph Elem Sch 4118 S Bonham St, Amarillo 79110 David Hernandez	PK-5		124 10	806/359-1604 Fax 806/359-1605

RANDALL PRIVATE SCHOOLS

Private Schs..Principal	Grd	Prgm	Enr/#Cls	SN
Ascension Academy 9301 Ascension Pkwy, Amarillo 79119 William Summerhill	6-12		200 15	806/342-0515 Fax 806/342-0535

RANDALL REGIONAL CENTERS

• **Region 16 Ed Service Center** PID: 01047984
5800 Bell St, Amarillo 79109
806/677-5000
Fax 806/677-5001

Ray Cogburn ....1 Cole Cordell 2
Melissa Shaver ....34 Kelisa Nelson 58,77
Michelle Wilson ....68 Greg Stockstill 73

REAGAN COUNTY

REAGAN PUBLIC SCHOOLS

• **Reagan Co Ind School Dist** PID: 01048017
1111 E 12th St, Big Lake 76932
325/884-3705
Fax 325/884-3021

Schools: 3 \ *Teachers:* 78 \ *Students:* 950 \ *Special Ed Students:* 54 \ *LEP Students:* 94 \ *College-Bound:* 59% \ *Ethnic:* African American 1%, Hispanic 81%, Caucasian 18% \ *Exp:* $690 (High) \ *Poverty:* 18% \ *Title I:* $166,013 \ *Special Education:* $213,000 \ *Open-Close:* 08/21 - 05/28 \ *DTBP:* $690 (High) \ f

Bobby Fryar ....1 Susan Gunnels 2,79
Jamal Rivers ....3,5 April Martinez 4
Blake Weston ....6* Eric Hallmark 11,15,57*
Jed Hruska ....67 Teressa Tekell 69*
Tracey McPhaul ....73,295 Rene Valeriano 83,88

Public Schs..Principal	Grd	Prgm	Enr/#Cls	SN
Reagan Co Elem Sch 501 N Texas Ave, Big Lake 76932 Mandy Traylor	PK-5	T	439 29	62% 325/884-3741 Fax 325/884-2194
Reagan Co High Sch 1111 E 12th St, Big Lake 76932 Rene Valeriano	9-12		229 26	54% 325/884-3714 Fax 325/884-5759
Reagan Co Middle Sch 500 N Pennsylvania Ave, Big Lake 76932 **Clifton Brown**	6-8	T	191 20	65% 325/884-3728 Fax 325/884-2327

---

79 Student Personnel
80 Driver Ed/Safety
81 Gifted/Talented
82 Video Services
83 Substance Abuse Prev
84 Erate
85 AIDS Education
88 Alternative/At Risk
89 Multi-Cultural Curriculum
90 Social Work
91 Safety/Security
92 Magnet School
93 Parental Involvement
95 Tech Prep Program
97 Chief Information Officer
98 Chief Technology Officer
270 Character Education
271 Migrant Education
273 Teacher Mentor
274 Before/After Sch
275 Response To Intervention
277 Remedial Math K-12
280 Literacy Coach
285 STEM
286 Digital Learning
288 Common Core Standards
294 Accountability
295 Network System
296 Title II Programs
297 Webmaster
298 Grant Writer/Ptnrships
750 Chief Innovation Officer
751 Chief of Staff
752 Social Emotional Learning

Other School Types
Ⓐ = Alternative School
Ⓒ = Charter School
Ⓜ = Magnet School
Ⓨ = Year-Round School

School Programs
A = Alternative Program
G = Adult Classes
M = Magnet Program
T = Title I Schoolwide
V = Career & Tech Ed Programs

New Schools are shaded
New Superintendents and Principals are bold
Personnel with email addresses are underscored

Social Media
f = Facebook
t = Twitter

TX-321

Real County

REAL COUNTY

REAL PUBLIC SCHOOLS

- **Leakey Ind School Dist** PID: 01048055
  429 N US Highway 83, Leakey 78873
  830/232-5595
  Fax 830/232-5535

Schools: 1 \ **Teachers:** 23 \ **Students:** 309 \ **Special Ed Students:** 29 \ **LEP Students:** 20 \ **College-Bound:** 60% \ **Ethnic:** Hispanic 39%, Caucasian 61% \ **Exp:** $760 (High) \ **Poverty:** 32% \ **Title I:** $127,433 \ **Open-Close:** 08/26 - 05/21 \ **DTBP:** $389 (High)

Chris Yeschke	1	Kathy Antes	2,297
Jim Couvillion	3	Leann Waligura	4
Carolyn Jones	5	Donnie Dutton	6*
Patrish Sewell	8,36,83,88,275*	Deanna Lanton	9,11,58,69,271,294*
Rick Davis	16,73,295*	Esmarelda Ruiz	57*
Brandi Pichardo	67		

Public Schs..Principal	Grd	Prgm	Enr/#Cls	SN	
Leakey Sch 429 N US Highway 83, Leakey 78873 **Vicki Goebel**	PK-12	TV	309 20	55%	830/232-5595

RED RIVER COUNTY

RED RIVER PUBLIC SCHOOLS

- **Avery Ind School Dist** PID: 01048081
  150 San Antonio St, Avery 75554
  903/684-3460
  Fax 903/684-3294

Schools: 2 \ **Teachers:** 34 \ **Students:** 365 \ **Special Ed Students:** 45 \ **LEP Students:** 7 \ **College-Bound:** 54% \ **Ethnic:** African American 1%, Hispanic 9%, Native American: 3%, Caucasian 86% \ **Exp:** $333 (High) \ **Poverty:** 20% \ **Title I:** $58,282 \ **Open-Close:** 08/23 - 05/29 \ **DTBP:** $333 (High) \

Debbie Drew	1	Kelli House	2
Judy Peeks	4	Bret Harp	6
Jullia Lennon	7*	Jill Maham	11
Karen Downs	11,296*	Jeannie Beaman	16,73,286,295*
Ann Stephenson	59*	Stacie Moore	67

Public Schs..Principal	Grd	Prgm	Enr/#Cls	SN	
Avery Elem Sch 150 San Antonio St, Avery 75554 Karen Downs	PK-5	T	176 9	60%	903/684-3116 Fax 903/684-3093
Avery Secondary Sch 150 San Antonio St, Avery 75554 Jill Mahan	6-12	TV	173 13	50%	903/684-3431 Fax 903/684-3059

- **Clarksville Ind School Dist** PID: 01048110
  1500 W Main St, Clarksville 75426
  903/427-3891
  Fax 903/427-5071

Schools: 2 \ **Teachers:** 41 \ **Students:** 585 \ **Special Ed Students:** 53 \ **LEP Students:** 50 \ **College-Bound:** 40% \ **Ethnic:** African American 55%, Hispanic 28%, Caucasian 16% \ **Exp:** $476 (High) \ **Poverty:** 28% \ **Title I:** $324,850 \ **Special Education:** $172,000 \ **Open-Close:** 08/23 - 05/25 \ **DTBP:** $361 (High)

Kermit Ward	1	Melissa Darrow	2
Pamela Vandeaver	2,3	Sheryl Scott	4
Lonnie Rushing	5	Henry Sharp	11
Mikki Perry	11,58	Robert Beaty	67
Howard Taylor	73*		

Public Schs..Principal	Grd	Prgm	Enr/#Cls	SN	
Cheatham Elem Sch 1500 W Main St, Clarksville 75426 Marianne Whitehouse	PK-5	T	292 35	91%	903/427-3891 Fax 903/427-4118
Clarksville Middle High Sch 202 S Donoho St, Clarksville 75426 James Johnson	6-12		293 20		903/427-3891 Fax 903/427-1344

- **Detroit Ind School Dist** PID: 01048172
  110 E Garner St, Detroit 75436
  903/674-6131
  Fax 903/674-2478

Schools: 3 \ **Teachers:** 48 \ **Students:** 540 \ **Special Ed Students:** 61 \ **LEP Students:** 3 \ **Ethnic:** African American 12%, Hispanic 3%, Caucasian 84% \ **Exp:** $527 (High) \ **Poverty:** 24% \ **Title I:** $103,933 \ **Open-Close:** 08/19 - 05/28 \ **DTBP:** $353 (High)

Kathy Thompson	1	Greg Jones	2,11
Sandra Galley	4,79*	Bobby George	5
Jeff Allensworth	6*	Christie Welch	36*
Cheryl Marquez	57*	Carrie Gray	58
Doug Miller	67	David Williams	73*

Public Schs..Principal	Grd	Prgm	Enr/#Cls	SN	
Detroit Elem Sch 110 E Garner St, Detroit 75436 Henry Sharp	PK-5	T	274 14	70%	903/674-3137 Fax 903/674-2407
Detroit High Sch 110 E Garner St, Detroit 75436 Jonathan Lloyd	9-12	ATV	150 14	45%	903/674-2646 Fax 903/674-2815
Detroit Middle Sch 110 E Garner St, Detroit 75436 Amanda Tidwell	6-8	T	98 15	69%	903/674-2646 Fax 903/674-2815

- **Rivercrest Ind School Dist** PID: 01048213
  4100 US Highway 271 S, Bogata 75417
  903/632-5203
  Fax 903/632-4691

Schools: 3 \ **Teachers:** 60 \ **Students:** 735 \ **Special Ed Students:** 76 \ **LEP Students:** 29 \ **College-Bound:** 77% \ **Ethnic:** African American 5%, Hispanic 14%, Native American: 1%, Caucasian 80% \ **Exp:** $385 (High) \ **Poverty:** 25% \ **Title I:** $181,909 \ **Open-Close:** 08/26 - 05/28 \ **DTBP:** $363 (High) \

Stanley Jessee	1	Tiffany Mabe	2,8,11,288,294,296,298
Lisa Roach	4*	Ricky Moore	5
Lance Connot	6*	Kelly Tietjan	16,82*
Tasha Blagg	36,83,85,88*	Latrishia English	57
Joseph Rose	67	Stephen Reese	73,295

1 Superintendent	8 Curric/Instruct K-12	19 Chief Financial Officer	29 Family/Consumer Science	39 Social Studies K-12	49 English/Lang Arts Elem	59 Special Education Elem	69 Academic Assessment
2 Bus/Finance/Purchasing	9 Curric/Instruct Elem	20 Art K-12	30 Adult Education	40 Social Studies Elem	50 English/Lang Arts Sec	60 Special Education Sec	70 Research/Development
3 Buildings And Grounds	10 Curric/Instruct Sec	21 Art Elem	31 Career/Sch-to-Work K-12	41 Social Studies Sec	51 Reading K-12	61 Foreign/World Lang K-12	71 Public Information
4 Food Service	11 Federal Program	22 Art Sec	32 Career/Sch-to-Work Elem	42 Science K-12	52 Reading Elem	62 Foreign/World Lang Elem	72 Summer School
5 Transportation	12 Title I	23 Music K-12	33 Career/Sch-to-Work Sec	43 Science Elem	53 Reading Sec	63 Foreign/World Lang Sec	73 Instructional Tech
6 Athletic	13 Title V	24 Music Elem	34 Early Childhood Ed	44 Science Sec	54 Remedial Reading K-12	64 Religious Education K-12	74 Inservice Training
7 Health Services	15 Asst Superintendent	25 Music Sec	35 Health/Phys Education	45 Math K-12	55 Remedial Reading Elem	65 Religious Education Elem	75 Marketing/Distributive
	16 Instructional Media Svcs	26 Business Education	36 Guidance Services K-12	46 Math Elem	56 Remedial Reading Sec	66 Religious Education Sec	76 Info Systems
	17 Chief Operations Officer	27 Career & Tech Ed	37 Guidance Services Elem	47 Math Sec	57 Bilingual/ELL	67 School Board President	77 Psychological Assess
	18 Chief Academic Officer	28 Technology Education	38 Guidance Services Sec	48 English/Lang Arts K-12	58 Special Education K-12	68 Teacher Personnel	78 Affirmative Action

Texas School Directory

Refugio County

Public Schs..Principal	Grd	Prgm	Enr/#Cls	SN	
Rivercrest Elem Sch 4220 US Highway 271 S, Bogata 75417 Carrie Gray	PK-5	T	329 25	58%	903/632-5214 Fax 903/632-2424 🇫 🇹
Rivercrest High Sch 4126 US Highway 271 S, Bogata 75417 Ronny Alsup	9-12	ATV	208 20	46%	903/632-5204 Fax 903/632-5231
Rivercrest Junior High Sch 4100 US Highway 271 S, Bogata 75417 Lee Wilson	6-8	AT	156 15	59%	903/632-0878

REEVES COUNTY

REEVES PUBLIC SCHOOLS

- **Balmorhea Ind School Dist** PID: 01048251   432/375-2223
  608 W 1st St, Balmorhea 79718   Fax 432/375-2511

Schools: 1 \ Teachers: 18 \ Students: 165 \ Special Ed Students: 15 \ LEP Students: 11 \ College-Bound: 100% \ Ethnic: Hispanic 93%, Caucasian 7% \ Exp: $849 (High) \ Poverty: 14% \ Title I: $47,943 \ Open-Close: 08/27 - 05/22 \ DTBP: $339 (High)

Douglas Moore 1,11	Rosela Rivera 2
Robert Jones 6*	Jim Workman 8,74,271*
Jim Workman 13,296	Able Garcia 57
Christine Morris 58,286*	Tommy Dominguez 67
Michelle Workman 69*	Richard Galindo 73*

Public Schs..Principal	Grd	Prgm	Enr/#Cls	SN	
Balmorhea Sch 608 W 1st St, Balmorhea 79718 Jim Workman	PK-12	TV	165 36	89%	432/375-2224

- **Pecos-Barstow-Toyah Ind SD** PID: 01048304   432/447-7201
  1302 S Park St, Pecos 79772   Fax 432/447-2690

Schools: 5 \ Teachers: 180 \ Students: 2,800 \ Special Ed Students: 213 \ LEP Students: 257 \ College-Bound: 37% \ Ethnic: Asian 1%, African American 1%, Hispanic 92%, Caucasian 6% \ Exp: $318 (High) \ Poverty: 29% \ Title I: $880,342 \ Special Education: $717,000 \ Open-Close: 08/15 - 05/21 \ DTBP: $350 (High)

Dr Jose Cervantes 1	Eddie Ramerez 2,15
Tim Gilbert 3	Wayne North 3
Joy Peters 4	Lee Serrano 5
Chris Jones 6,35	Simona Acosta 7*
Rosie Salcido 37*	Donna Davis 58
Sam Contreras 67	Cynthia Fields 69
Wendi Russell 271	

Public Schs..Principal	Grd	Prgm	Enr/#Cls	SN	
Austin Elem Sch 1501 W Normandy, Pecos 79772 Leeann McGraw	1-3	T	682 32	63%	432/447-7541 Fax 432/447-4248
Bessie Haynes Elem Sch 800 E 11th St, Pecos 79772 Omar Salgado	4-5	T	460 28	71%	432/447-7497 Fax 432/445-1612
Crockett Middle Sch 1801 S Missouri St, Pecos 79772 Cindy Duke	6-8	T	537 18	73%	432/447-7461 Fax 432/447-4853
Pecos High Sch 1201 S Park St, Pecos 79772 Latanya Sadler	9-12	TV	673 60	52%	432/447-7400 Fax 432/447-9055
Pecos Kindergarten 300 W 10th St, Pecos 79772 Leeann McGraw	PK-K	T	278 17	53%	432/447-7596 Fax 432/445-4203

REFUGIO COUNTY

REFUGIO PUBLIC SCHOOLS

- **Austwell Tivoli Ind SD** PID: 01048419   361/286-3212
  207 Redfish St, Tivoli 77990   Fax 361/286-3637

Schools: 2 \ Teachers: 19 \ Students: 140 \ Special Ed Students: 18 \ College-Bound: 75% \ Ethnic: African American 1%, Hispanic 75%, Caucasian 24% \ Exp: $433 (High) \ Poverty: 47% \ Title I: $99,439 \ Open-Close: 08/27 - 06/01 \ 🇫 🇹

Dolores Vela 1	Becky Carter 4*
Eric Cortez 11,57,88	Melanie Wright 16*
William Lumpkins 36*	Linda Duenez 60*
Carlton Hopper 67	Leslie Sessions 73,295*
Dr Antonio Aguirre 83	Armand Gonzalez 285*

Public Schs..Principal	Grd	Prgm	Enr/#Cls	SN	
Austwell Tivoli Elem Sch 207 Redfish St, Tivoli 77990 Eric Cortez	PK-5	T	80 9	70%	361/286-3222
Austwell Tivoli Jr Sr High Sch 207 Redfish St, Tivoli 77990 John Cortez	6-12	T	55 10	57%	361/286-3212 🇫

- **Refugio Ind School Dist** PID: 01048457   361/526-2325
  212 W Vance St, Refugio 78377   Fax 361/526-2326

Schools: 3 \ Teachers: 66 \ Students: 690 \ Special Ed Students: 75 \ LEP Students: 36 \ Ethnic: African American 11%, Hispanic 66%, Caucasian 23% \ Exp: $293 (Med) \ Poverty: 23% \ Title I: $187,291 \ Open-Close: 08/27 - 05/29 \ DTBP: $365 (High)

Melissa Gonzalez 1	Lisa Herring 2,11,57,69,74,270,294,298
Albert Van Ness 3*	Jason Herring 6*
Emilee Cox 7,85*	Anna Garcia 16,82*
Lori Homeyer 58	Andy Rocha 67
Cliff Smith 73,295	

Public Schs..Principal	Grd	Prgm	Enr/#Cls	SN	
Refugio Elem Sch 601 Crockett St, Refugio 78377 Twyla Thomas	PK-6	T	392 32	71%	361/526-4844 Fax 361/526-1053 🇫 🇹
Refugio High Sch 212 W Vance St, Refugio 78377 Brandon Duncan	9-12	ATV	202 23	57%	361/526-2344 Fax 361/526-1075
Refugio Junior High Sch 212 W Vance St, Refugio 78377 Melissa Gonzales	7-8	T	111	65%	361/526-2434 Fax 361/526-1054

---

79 Student Personnel	91 Safety/Security	275 Response To Intervention	298 Grant Writer/Ptnrships
80 Driver Ed/Safety	92 Magnet School	277 Remedial Math K-12	750 Chief Innovation Officer
81 Gifted/Talented	93 Parental Involvement	280 Literacy Coach	751 Chief of Staff
82 Video Services	95 Tech Prep Program	285 STEM	752 Social Emotional Learning
83 Substance Abuse Prev	97 Chief Information Officer	286 Digital Learning	
84 Erate	98 Chief Technology Officer	288 Common Core Standards	Other School Types
85 AIDS Education	270 Character Education	294 Accountability	Ⓐ = Alternative School
88 Alternative/At Risk	271 Migrant Education	295 Network System	Ⓒ = Charter School
89 Multi-Cultural Curriculum	273 Teacher Mentor	296 Title II Programs	Ⓜ = Magnet School
90 Social Work	274 Before/After Sch	297 Webmaster	Ⓨ = Year-Round School

School Programs
A = Alternative Program
G = Adult Classes
M = Magnet Program
T = Title I Schoolwide
V = Career & Tech Ed Programs

Social Media
🇫 = Facebook
🇹 = Twitter

New Schools are shaded
New Superintendents and Principals are bold
Personnel with email addresses are underscored

TX—323

Roberts County

Market Data Retrieval

- **Woodsboro Ind School Dist** PID: 01048495   361/543-4518
  408 South Kasten, Woodsboro 78393   Fax 361/543-4856

Schools: 2 \ **Teachers:** 42 \ **Students:** 420 \ **Special Ed Students:** 69 \ **College-Bound:** 80% \ **Ethnic:** Asian 1%, African American 3%, Hispanic 51%, Caucasian 45% \ **Exp:** $545 (High) \ **Poverty:** 22% \ **Title I:** $120,110 \ **Open-Close:** 08/19 - 05/28 \ **DTBP:** $387 (High)

Janice Sykora 1,11	Angela Carrasco 2
Mary Alice Ortega 4	Gary Carpenter 6
Carolyn Baker 7*	Chantel Schulz 8,27,31,36,69,83,88,288
Leslie Garza 9,11*	Tom Diles 10,273
Lori Homeyer 58	Robert Thomas 67
Casey Newman 73,91	Christina Grey 73,79,295
Sharon Musich 275	

Public Schs..Principal	Grd	Prgm	Enr/#Cls	SN	
Woodsboro Elem Sch 105 Myrtle St, Woodsboro 78393 Leslie Garza	PK-6	T	258 22	66%	361/543-4518 Fax 361/543-5478
Woodsboro Jr Sr High Sch 508 Kasten Ave, Woodsboro 78393 Tisha Piwetz	7-12	ATV	192 18	44%	361/543-4622 Fax 361/543-5140

ROBERTS COUNTY

ROBERTS PUBLIC SCHOOLS

- **Miami Ind School Dist** PID: 01048536   806/868-3971
  800 Warrior Way, Miami 79059   Fax 806/868-3171

Schools: 1 \ **Teachers:** 23 \ **Students:** 220 \ **Special Ed Students:** 15 \ **College-Bound:** 80% \ **Ethnic:** African American 1%, Hispanic 9%, Native American: 1%, Caucasian 89% \ **Exp:** $646 (High) \ **Poverty:** 6% \ **Title I:** $10,302 \ **Open-Close:** 08/15 - 05/21 \ **DTBP:** $302 (High) \ f t

Donna Hale 1	Liz Poage 2
Ron Carr 3,5	Dann Gonzales 16*
Tara Royal 16,73,295*	Shelly Brooks 57*
Tealer Wilkes 58*	Logan Hudson 67
Karen Alston 275*	

Public Schs..Principal	Grd	Prgm	Enr/#Cls	SN	
Miami Sch 800 Warrior Way, Miami 79059 Mark Driskell	PK-12	TV	220 20	24%	806/868-3971

ROBERTSON COUNTY

ROBERTSON PUBLIC SCHOOLS

- **Bremond Ind School Dist** PID: 01048550   254/746-7145
  601 W Collins St, Bremond 76629   Fax 254/746-7726

Schools: 3 \ **Teachers:** 43 \ **Students:** 507 \ **Special Ed Students:** 41 \ **LEP Students:** 15 \ **College-Bound:** 75% \ **Ethnic:** Asian 1%, African American 12%, Hispanic 17%, Caucasian 69% \ **Exp:** $428 (High) \ **Poverty:** 20% \ **Title I:** $131,415 \ **Open-Close:** 08/23 - 05/25 \ **DTBP:** $350 (High)

Daryl Stuard 1	Victor Boudreaux 3
Margaret Smith 4	John Burnett 5,9,11,57,58,270,271*
Lynn Pruett 7*	Steve English 10,83,88*
Rose Kujawa 16*	Tina Rowe 27*
Randy Yanowski 67	Rosemary Wilganowski 69*
Josh Hymer 73,76*	Bev Swick 286*

Public Schs..Principal	Grd	Prgm	Enr/#Cls	SN	
Bremond Elem Sch 601 W Collins St, Bremond 76629 Shelli McNutt	PK-5	T	257 30	57%	254/746-7145 f t
Bremond High Sch 601 W Collins St, Bremond 76629 Kenneth Groholski	9-12	T	140	44%	254/746-7061
Bremond Middle Sch 601 W Collins St, Bremond 76629 John Burnett	6-8	T	110 11	45%	254/746-5022

- **Calvert Ind School Dist** PID: 01048586   979/364-2824
  310 Hickory St, Calvert 77837   Fax 979/364-2468

Schools: 1 \ **Teachers:** 18 \ **Students:** 164 \ **Special Ed Students:** 17 \ **Ethnic:** African American 77%, Hispanic 10%, Caucasian 13% \ **Exp:** $291 (Med) \ **Poverty:** 43% \ **Title I:** $190,612 \ **Open-Close:** 08/22 - 06/01 \ **DTBP:** $350 (High) \ t

Dr Thyrun Hurst 1	Jan Manning 2
Marcus Wortham 6*	Maxie Morgan 11,84
Bryan Himphill 58	James Whitaker 67
Daniel Arnold 73,83*	

Public Schs..Principal	Grd	Prgm	Enr/#Cls	SN	
Calvert Sch 310 Hickory St, Calvert 77837 Ronnell Trotter	PK-12	GTV	164 9	70%	979/364-2845 Fax 979/364-2043

- **Franklin Ind School Dist** PID: 01048615   979/828-7000
  1216 FM 1644, Franklin 77856   Fax 979/828-1910

Schools: 3 \ **Teachers:** 105 \ **Students:** 1,100 \ **Special Ed Students:** 121 \ **LEP Students:** 30 \ **Ethnic:** Asian 1%, African American 7%, Hispanic 17%, Caucasian 74% \ **Exp:** $310 (High) \ **Poverty:** 19% \ **Title I:** $212,954 \ **Open-Close:** 08/21 - 05/22 \ **DTBP:** $350 (High)

Bret Lowry 1	Michelle Mathews 2
Harold Rowan 3,5	Ashley Charanza 4*
Stacy Ely 8,11,74,294,296*	Joe Squiers 16,28,73,297*

---

1 Superintendent	8 Curric/Instruct K-12	19 Chief Financial Officer	29 Family/Consumer Science	39 Social Studies K-12	49 English/Lang Arts Elem	59 Special Education Elem	69 Academic Assessment
2 Bus/Finance/Purchasing	9 Curric/Instruct Elem	20 Art K-12	30 Adult Education	40 Social Studies Elem	50 English/Lang Arts Sec	60 Special Education Sec	70 Research/Development
3 Buildings And Grounds	10 Curric/Instruct Sec	21 Art Elem	31 Career/Sch-to-Work K-12	41 Social Studies Sec	51 Reading K-12	61 Foreign/World Lang Elem	71 Public Information
4 Food Service	11 Federal Program	22 Art Sec	32 Career/Sch-to-Work Elem	42 Science K-12	52 Reading Elem	62 Foreign/World Lang Sec	72 Summer School
5 Transportation	12 Title I	23 Music K-12	33 Career/Sch-to-Work Sec	43 Science Elem	53 Reading Sec	63 Foreign/World Lang Sec	73 Instructional Tech
6 Athletic	13 Title V	24 Music Elem	34 Early Childhood Ed	44 Science Sec	54 Remedial Reading K-12	64 Religious Education K-12	74 Inservice Training
7 Health Services	15 Asst Superintendent	25 Music Sec	35 Health/Phys Education	45 Math K-12	55 Remedial Reading Elem	65 Religious Education Elem	75 Marketing/Distributive
	16 Instructional Media Svcs	26 Business Education	36 Guidance Services K-12	46 Math Elem	56 Remedial Reading Sec	66 Religious Education Sec	76 Info Systems
	17 Chief Operations Officer	27 Career & Tech Ed	37 Guidance Services Elem	47 Math Sec	57 Bilingual/ELL	67 School Board President	77 Psychological Assess
	18 Chief Academic Officer	28 Technology Education	38 Guidance Services Sec	48 English/Lang Arts K-12	58 Special Education K-12	68 Teacher Personnel	78 Affirmative Action

Texas School Directory — Rockwall County

Deanna May	57
Melissa Medcalf	58
Martha Barnett	69
Leslee Falco	58
Dennis Varvel	67
Becky Permann	295*

Public Schs..Principal	Grd	Prgm	Enr/#Cls	SN	
Franklin High Sch 1252 FM 1644, Franklin 77856 Russell White	9-12	AV	349 50	28%	979/828-7100 Fax 979/828-3364
Franklin Middle Sch 1098 W Decherd St, Franklin 77856 Susan Nelson	5-8	ATV	366 20	38%	979/828-7200 Fax 979/828-7207
Roland Reynolds Elem Sch 317 N Owensville, Franklin 77856 Christie Smitherman	PK-4	T	539 26	42%	979/828-7300 Fax 979/828-5048

● **Hearne Ind School Dist** PID: 01048641   979/279-3200
900 Wheelock St, Hearne 77859   Fax 979/279-3631

Schools: 3 \ **Teachers:** 73 \ **Students:** 860 \ **Special Ed Students:** 130 \ **LEP Students:** 132 \ **College-Bound:** 35% \ **Ethnic:** African American 48%, Hispanic 41%, Caucasian 11% \ **Exp:** $380 (High) \ **Poverty:** 26% \ **Title I:** $486,342 \ **Open-Close:** 08/19 - 05/29 \ **DTBP:** $350 (High) \

Dr Adrian Johnson	1	Erica Duplechain	2
Joe Taylor	3	Rhonda Cloud	4
Ricky Sargent	6	Jeremy Gaston	16,73,82,295*
Leslee Falco	58	Maryjane Rameriz	67
Jay Davis	79		

Public Schs..Principal	Grd	Prgm	Enr/#Cls	SN	
Hearne Elem Sch 1210 Hackberry St, Hearne 77859 Stephanie Heinchon	PK-6	T	524 42	99%	979/279-3341 Fax 979/279-8011
Hearne High Sch 1201 W Brown St, Hearne 77859 Caroline Mott	9-12	ATV	220 25	84%	979/279-2332 Fax 979/279-8006
Hearne Junior High Sch 1201B W Brown St, Hearne 77859 Lucinda McDaniel	7-8	T	118 20	97%	979/279-2449 Fax 979/279-8033

ROCKWALL COUNTY

ROCKWALL PUBLIC SCHOOLS

● **Rockwall Ind School Dist** PID: 01048718   972/771-0605
1050 Williams St, Rockwall 75087   Fax 972/771-2637

Schools: 20 \ **Teachers:** 958 \ **Students:** 16,270 \ **Special Ed Students:** 1,526 \ **LEP Students:** 1,057 \ **College-Bound:** 80% \ **Ethnic:** Asian 3%, African American 8%, Hispanic 22%, Native American: 1%, Caucasian 66% \ **Exp:** $301 (High) \ **Poverty:** 6% \ **Title I:** $1,025,213 \ **Special Education:** $2,255,000 \ **Open-Close:** 08/19 - 05/28 \ **DTBP:** $194 (High) \

Dr John Villarreal	1	David Carter	2,19
Jamie Tomalin	2	Will Salee	3
Kim Pugsley	4	Terry Penn	5
Russ Reeves	6	Adrienne Hergert	7,35*
Dr Amy Ellis	8	Dr Amy Anderson	8,18,273
Dr Mary Johnston	8,18	Sonya Carpenter	11,34,88,298

Luann Hughes	16,73,76,82,295
Alison Belliveau	27
Jennifer Penton	40,280
Katie Braden	43
Megan Humphrey	46
Doug Frank	57
Melissa Melton	58
Joey Byrum	68
Linda Reid	69,77,294
Dr Tom Maglisceau	79*
Missy Wall	90
Chris Kosterman	20,23
Bart Walters	27,31
Dr Matthew Redman	41
Joey Belgard	44
Dr Bianca Coker	47
Patricia Martinez	57
Stephanie Adams	67
Mark Speck	68,74,79
Renae Murphy	71
Jennifer Leal	81*

Public Schs..Principal	Grd	Prgm	Enr/#Cls	SN	
Amanda Rochell Elem Sch 899 Rochell Ct, Rockwall 75032 Kelli Crossland	PK-6	T	557 30	53%	972/771-2112 Fax 972/772-0829
Amy Parks-Heath Elem Sch 330 Laurence Dr, Heath 75032 Megan Smith	PK-6		550 26	6%	972/772-4300 Fax 972/772-2098
Billie Stevenson Elem Sch 636 Stevenson Dr, Rockwall 75087 Mike Pitcher	PK-6		645	12%	469/698-7474
Celia Hays Elem Sch 1880 Tannerson Dr, Rockwall 75087 Tammi Schmitt	PK-6		824 19	8%	469/698-2800 Fax 469/698-2809
Doris Cullins-Lake Pointe ES 5701 Scenic Dr, Rowlett 75088 Dr Mary Pugh	PK-6	T	698 45	39%	972/412-3070 Fax 972/475-7920
Dorothy Smith Pullen Elem Sch 6492 FM 3097, Rockwall 75032 Michael Stuart	PK-6		559 36	15%	972/772-1177 Fax 972/772-2424
Dorris Jones Elem Sch 2051 Trail Gln, Rockwall 75032 Teresa Twedell	PK-6	T	648 44	46%	972/772-1070 Fax 972/772-5789
Grace Hartman Elem Sch 1325 Petaluma Dr, Rockwall 75087 Rebecca Reidling	PK-6		556	9%	972/772-2080 Fax 972/772-5794
Herman E Utley Middle Sch 1201 T L Townsend Dr, Rockwall 75087 Dane Steinberger	7-8		893	26%	972/771-5281 Fax 972/772-1164
Howard Dobbs Elem Sch 901 E Interurban St, Rockwall 75087 Ruth Johnson	PK-6	T	630 33	59%	972/771-5232 Fax 972/772-1145
J W Williams Middle Sch 625 E FM 552, Rockwall 75087 David Blake	7-8		844 56	16%	972/771-8313 Fax 972/772-2033
Linda Lyon Elem Sch 2186 Trophy Dr, Heath 75126 Megan Gist	PK-6		437		214/771-4910
Maurine Cain Middle Sch 6620 FM 3097, Rockwall 75032 Derrice Randle	7-8		941 60	26%	972/772-1170 Fax 972/772-2414
Nebbie Williams Elem Sch 350 Dalton Rd, Rockwall 75087 Lisa Gielow	PK-6		504 22	7%	972/772-0502 Fax 972/772-2046
Ouida Springer Elem Sch 3025 Limestone Hill Ln, Rockwall 75032 Sara Reeves	PK-6	T	657	46%	972/772-7160 Fax 972/772-2464
Rockwall High Sch 901 W Yellowjacket Ln, Rockwall 75087 Kevin Samples	9-12	V	2,598 65	15%	972/771-7339 Fax 972/772-2099
ⓐ **Rockwall Quest Academy** 1050 Williams St, Rockwall 75087 Brian Nickel	7-12	GTV	59 7	34%	972/772-2077 Fax 972/772-1055
Rockwall-Heath High Sch 801 Laurence Dr, Heath 75032 Todd Bradford	9-12		2,401	26%	972/772-2474 Fax 469/698-2608

79 Student Personnel	91 Safety/Security	275 Response To Intervention	298 Grant Writer/Ptnrships	**School Programs**	**Social Media**
80 Driver Ed/Safety	92 Magnet School	277 Remedial Math K-12	750 Chief Innovation Officer	A = Alternative Program	
81 Gifted/Talented	93 Parental Involvement	280 Literacy Coach	751 Chief of Staff	G = Adult Classes	= Facebook
82 Video Services	95 Tech Prep Program	285 STEM	752 Social Emotional Learning	M = Magnet Program	
83 Substance Abuse Prev	97 Chief Infomation Officer	286 Digital Learning		T = Title I Schoolwide	= Twitter
84 Erate	98 Chief Technology Officer	288 Common Core Standards	**Other School Types**	V = Career & Tech Ed Programs	
85 AIDS Education	270 Accountability	294 Accountability	Ⓐ = Alternative School		
88 Alternative/At Risk	271 Migrant Education	295 Network System	Ⓒ = Charter School	New Schools are shaded	
89 Multi-Cultural Curriculum	273 Teacher Mentor	296 Title II Programs	Ⓜ = Magnet School	New Superintendents and Principals are bold	
90 Social Work	274 Before/After Sch	297 Webmaster	Ⓨ = Year-Round School	Personnel with email addresses are underscored	

TX-325

Runnels County

Sharon Shannon Elem Sch — PK-6 — 710 — 25% — 469/698-2900
3130 Fontana Blvd, Rockwall 75032 — Fax 469/698-2909
Steven Pesek

Virginia Reinhardt Elem Sch — PK-6 — 584 — 21% — 972/771-5247
101 S Clark St, Rockwall 75087 — 19 — Fax 972/772-2097
Amanda Payne

- **Royse City Ind School Dist** PID: 01048770 — 972/636-2413
  810 E Old Greenville Rd, Royse City 75189 — Fax 972/635-7037

Schools: 9 \ Teachers: 361 \ Students: 6,300 \
Special Ed Students: 495 \ LEP Students: 542 \ College-Bound: 45% \
Ethnic: Asian 1%, African American 6%, Hispanic 33%, Native American: 1%, Caucasian 59% \ Exp: $309 (High) \ Poverty: 7% \ Title I: $369,918 \
Special Education: $695,000 \ Open-Close: 08/15 - 05/22 \ DTBP: $161 (High)

Kevin Worthy 1	Angel McCrary 2
Byron Bryant 2,19	Jim Lawson 3
Cohnie Harris 4	Tammy Loveless 5
David Petroff 6	Deborah Summers 7*
Julia Robinson 8	Kenny Hudson 11,15,296
Jeff Webb 15,68,273	Zach Snow 27,73,285,286
Linda Taylor 38	Dana Grieb 39,50
Valerie James 46	Kristen Weichel 49
Shannon Hayes 58,79*	Scott Muckensturm 67
Kathy Milton 69,294	Adi Bryant 71,298
Zach Allen 73,98,295	Jere Craighead 88,275*
Lloyd Blaine 91	Mike Medlin 274

Public Schs..Principal	Grd	Prgm	Enr/#Cls	SN	
Anita Scott Elem Sch	PK-4	T	552	41%	972/636-3300
1401 Erby Campbell Blvd, Royse City 75189					Fax 972/635-6503
Teresa Atkins					
ⓐ Browning Learning Center	9-12		12	42%	972/635-5077
810 E Old Greenville Rd, Royse City 75189			4		Fax 972/635-2504
Jere Craighead					
Davis Elem Sch	PK-4	T	553	37%	972/636-9549
1500 FM 1777, Royse City 75189			28		Fax 972/635-2535
Cynthia Pense					
Harry H Herndon Interm Sch	5-6	T	463	38%	469/721-8101
300 Blackland Rd, Fate 75132					Fax 469/874-2186
Shanna Brown					
Miss May Vernon Elem Sch	PK-4	T	633	30%	972/635-5006
100 Miss May Drive, Fate 75132					Fax 972/722-8577
Brittany Lancaster					
Royse City High Sch	9-12	V	1,655	29%	972/636-9991
700 S FM 2642, Royse City 75189			50		Fax 972/635-2906
Sean Walker					
Royse City Middle Sch	7-8		864	35%	972/636-9544
1310 E Highway 66, Royse City 75189			40		Fax 972/635-5093
Angelee Morales					
Ruth Cherry Interm Sch	5-6	T	465	37%	972/636-3301
1400 FM 1777, Royse City 75189			16		Fax 972/635-5008
Richard Pense					
W R Fort Elem Sch	PK-4	T	554	35%	972/636-3304
2801 Epps Rd, Royse City 75189					Fax 469/874-4050
Wendy Prater					

ROCKWALL PRIVATE SCHOOLS

Private Schs..Principal	Grd	Prgm	Enr/#Cls	SN	
Fulton Sch	PK-5		200		972/772-4445
1626 Smirl Dr, Heath 75032					
Marnie Cooper					

Heritage Christian Academy — K-12 — 352 — 972/772-3003
1408 S Goliad St, Rockwall 75087 — 30 — Fax 972/772-3770
Leslie Minter \ Dr Brad Wheeler

RUNNELS COUNTY

RUNNELS PUBLIC SCHOOLS

- **Ballinger Ind School Dist** PID: 01048809 — 325/365-3588
  802 Conda Ave, Ballinger 76821 — Fax 325/365-5920

Schools: 3 \ Teachers: 83 \ Students: 911 \ Special Ed Students: 80 \ LEP Students: 16 \ College-Bound: 85% \ Ethnic: Asian 1%, African American 2%, Hispanic 46%, Caucasian 51% \ Exp: $308 (High) \ Poverty: 24% \ Title I: $297,760 \ Open-Close: 08/19 - 05/20 \ DTBP: $348 (High)

Jeff Butts 1	Liz Garza 2
Tony Harral 3,5	Caroline Toliver 8,11,286,288,296,298
Tessa Knickerbocker 38	Brian Arrott 58*
Manuel Galvan 67	Billy Mobley 73

Public Schs..Principal	Grd	Prgm	Enr/#Cls	SN	
Ballinger Elem Sch	PK-5	T	433	67%	325/365-3527
800 Broad Ave, Ballinger 76821			26		Fax 325/365-2943
Jamie Dudley					
Ballinger High Sch	9-12	ATV	259	45%	325/365-3547
2107 N Broadway St, Ballinger 76821			40		Fax 325/365-5366
Ryan Knickerbocker					
Ballinger Junior High Sch	6-8	T	206	52%	325/365-3537
1006 Conda Ave, Ballinger 76821			20		Fax 325/365-3102
Stacy Tucker					

- **Miles Ind School Dist** PID: 01048847 — 325/468-2861
  1001 Robinson St, Miles 76861 — Fax 325/468-2179

Schools: 1 \ Teachers: 40 \ Students: 440 \ Special Ed Students: 25 \ LEP Students: 24 \ College-Bound: 53% \ Ethnic: Asian 1%, African American 1%, Hispanic 36%, Caucasian 62% \ Exp: $438 (High) \ Poverty: 13% \ Title I: $47,281 \ Open-Close: 08/20 - 05/28 \ DTBP: $350 (High)

Clint Askins 1	Debra Blackwell 2
Bud Hunt 3,5	Charles Boles 6
Curt McNelly 9	Jamie Rouse 10,88*
Joan McCleery 11,45,57,83,270,271,273	Sarah Crouch 12,51*
Leann Mika-Mendez 16*	Paige Ernhart 31*
Karen Brown 36*	Kimberly Niehues 58,69
Mark Sklenarik 67	Janna Rouse 73*

Public Schs..Principal	Grd	Prgm	Enr/#Cls	SN	
Miles Sch	PK-12	V	440	25%	325/468-2861
1001 Robinson St, Miles 76861					
Curt McKneely \ Jamie Rouse					

---

1 Superintendent	8 Curric/Instruct K-12	19 Chief Financial Officer	29 Family/Consumer Science	39 Social Studies K-12	49 English/Lang Arts Elem	59 Special Education Elem	69 Academic Assessment
2 Bus/Finance/Purchasing	9 Curric/Instruct Elem	20 Art K-12	30 Adult Education	40 Social Studies Elem	50 English/Lang Arts Sec	60 Special Education Sec	70 Research/Development
3 Buildings And Grounds	10 Curric/Instruct Sec	21 Art Elem	31 Career/Sch-to-Work K-12	41 Social Studies Sec	51 Reading K-12	61 Foreign/World Lang K-12	71 Public Information
4 Food Service	11 Federal Program	22 Art Sec	32 Career/Sch-to-Work Elem	42 Science K-12	52 Reading Elem	62 Foreign/World Lang Elem	72 Summer School
5 Transportation	12 Title I	23 Music K-12	33 Career/Sch-to-Work Sec	43 Science Elem	53 Reading Sec	63 Foreign/World Lang Sec	73 Instructional Tech
6 Athletic	13 Title V	24 Music Elem	34 Early Childhood Ed	44 Science Sec	54 Remedial Reading K-12	64 Religious Education K-12	74 Inservice Training
7 Health Services	15 Asst Superintendent	25 Music Sec	35 Health/Phys Education	45 Math K-12	55 Remedial Reading Elem	65 Religious Education Elem	75 Marketing/Distributive
	16 Instructional Media Svcs	26 Business Education	36 Guidance Services K-12	46 Math Elem	56 Remedial Reading Sec	66 Religious Education Sec	76 Info Systems
	17 Chief Operations Officer	27 Career & Tech Ed	37 Guidance Services Elem	47 Math Sec	57 Bilingual/ELL	67 School Board President	77 Psychological Assess
	18 Chief Academic Officer	28 Technology Education	38 Guidance Services Sec	48 English/Lang Arts K-12	58 Special Education K-12	68 Teacher Personnel	78 Affirmative Action

Texas School Directory

Rusk County

• **Olfen Ind School Dist** PID: 01048873 325/442-4301
1122 PR 2562, Rowena 76875 Fax 325/442-2133

Schools: 1 \ **Teachers:** 8 \ **Students:** 93 \ **Special Ed Students:** 9 \ **LEP Students:** 4 \ **Ethnic:** African American 4%, Hispanic 58%, Caucasian 38% \ **Exp:** $1,277 (High) \ **Poverty:** 21% \ **Open-Close:** 08/12 - 05/21 \ **DTBP:** $300 (High)

Gabe Zamora 1,11,57	Debbie Fisher 4
Travis Tennison 6*	Jb Fuchs 67
Russell Hoelscher 73,295*	

Public Schs..Principal	Grd	Prgm	Enr/#Cls	SN	
Olfen Sch 1122 Private Rd 2562, Rowena 76875 Lizette Paceley	PK-12		93 8	89%	325/442-4301

• **Winters Ind School Dist** PID: 01048914 325/754-5574
603 N Heights St, Winters 79567 Fax 325/754-5374

Schools: 3 \ **Teachers:** 51 \ **Students:** 544 \ **Special Ed Students:** 55 \ **LEP Students:** 22 \ **Ethnic:** Asian 1%, African American 1%, Hispanic 63%, Caucasian 35% \ **Exp:** $871 (High) \ **Poverty:** 26% \ **Title I:** $205,543 \ **Special Education:** $130,000 \ **Open-Close:** 08/21 - 05/21 \ **DTBP:** $339 (High) \ f

Bruce Davis 1	Rhonda Neal 2,11
Gordon Fenwick 3	June Watson 4
Mark Bridgman 5	Mike Morath 7
Kari Callcoat 9	Brian Arrott 58
Dan Killough 67	Michelle Alexander 68
Josh Clinard 73,295	

Public Schs..Principal	Grd	Prgm	Enr/#Cls	SN	
Winters Elem Sch 702 N Heights St, Winters 79567 Edward Garcia	PK-5	T	248 21	81%	325/754-5577 Fax 325/754-4686
Winters High Sch 205 Jones St, Winters 79567 Randy Gartman	9-12	TV	165 17	59%	325/754-5516 Fax 325/754-5085 t
Winters Junior High Sch 705 Rogers Rd, Winters 79567 Terry Payne	6-8	T	131 11	61%	325/754-5518 Fax 325/754-5085

RUSK COUNTY

RUSK PUBLIC SCHOOLS

• **Carlisle Ind School Dist** PID: 01048940 903/861-3801
8960 FM 13 W, Henderson 75654 Fax 903/861-3932

Schools: 1 \ **Teachers:** 61 \ **Students:** 650 \ **Special Ed Students:** 58 \ **LEP Students:** 170 \ **College-Bound:** 61% \ **Ethnic:** African American 4%, Hispanic 55%, Native American: 1%, Caucasian 40% \ **Exp:** $512 (High) \ **Poverty:** 16% \ **Title I:** $137,548 \ **Open-Close:** 08/14 - 05/21 \ **DTBP:** $527 (High)

Michael Payne 1,11,83	Jill Spearman 2
Andy Hodkinson 3,5*	Margaret Wilson 4*
Rocky Baker 6*	Connie Barton 7*
Jennifer Hale 8,31,69,270*	Andrea Loyola 16*
Lisha Smith 31,36*	Stephanie Rowan 57,274*
Drew Bennett 58*	Kevin Curvo 67
Brian Jennings 73,74,76,295*	

Public Schs..Principal	Grd	Prgm	Enr/#Cls	SN	
Carlisle Sch 8960 FM 13 W, Henderson 75654 Stephanie Rowan \ Sarah Baker	PK-12	T	650 150	82%	903/861-3801 Fax 903/861-0100

• **Henderson Ind School Dist** PID: 01048976 903/655-5000
200 N High St, Henderson 75652 Fax 903/657-9271

Schools: 6 \ **Teachers:** 241 \ **Students:** 3,040 \ **Special Ed Students:** 292 \ **LEP Students:** 407 \ **College-Bound:** 54% \ **Ethnic:** Asian 1%, African American 19%, Hispanic 29%, Native American: 1%, Caucasian 50% \ **Exp:** $349 (High) \ **Poverty:** 19% \ **Title I:** $787,246 \ **Special Education:** $965,000 \ **Open-Close:** 08/15 - 05/20 \ **DTBP:** $193 (High) \ f

Dr Thurston Lamb 1	Christen Byrd 2
Craig Hurt 3,5,91	Tonya Davis 4
Phil Castles 6	Leandrea Cally 7,35,85
Stephanie Boonau 8,11,57,280,285,288,296,298	Mindy Rucker 45
Eileen Jhonson 58	James Holmes 67
Amanda Wallace 68,71	Kevin Bryan 73,84,295
Kim Free 76	Chad Bradley 83*
Clay Freeman 88,286	Gray Young 295

Public Schs..Principal	Grd	Prgm	Enr/#Cls	SN	
Henderson High Sch 1900 State Highway 64 W, Henderson 75652 Terry Everitt	9-12	ATV	953	57%	903/655-5000 Fax 903/655-5500
Henderson Middle Sch 501 Richardson Dr, Henderson 75654 Hardy Dotson	6-8	AT	757 70	62%	903/655-5400 Fax 903/657-6499
Ⓐ Montgomery Achievement Center 308 Smith St, Henderson 75654 Clay Freeman	11-12		25		903/655-5552
Northside Interm Sch 800 N Van Buren St, Henderson 75652 Dea Henry	4-5	T	547 24	65%	903/655-5300 Fax 903/657-5238
Wylie Elem Sch 1735 US Highway 259 S, Henderson 75654 Deidra Sutton	1-3	T	782 14	66%	903/655-5200 Fax 903/657-5299
Wylie Primary Sch 1735 US Highway 259 S, Henderson 75654 Deana Griffith	PK-K	T	400 29	80%	903/655-5100 Fax 903/655-5199

• **Laneville Ind School Dist** PID: 01049061 903/863-5353
7415 FM 1798 W, Laneville 75667 Fax 903/863-5319

Schools: 1 \ **Teachers:** 15 \ **Students:** 182 \ **Special Ed Students:** 16 \ **LEP Students:** 23 \ **College-Bound:** 50% \ **Ethnic:** African American 51%, Hispanic 29%, Caucasian 21% \ **Exp:** $507 (High) \ **Poverty:** 19% \ **Title I:** $61,309 \ **Open-Close:** 08/22 - 05/22 \ **DTBP:** $350 (High) \ f t

Theresa Shelton 1,11	Sandra Upshaw 2
Gay Harper 4	Jose Lee 6
Susie Davis 7,85*	Nathan Templeton 8,34,74,83,88,271,273*
Cynthia Thurmond 16*	Shirley McDaniel 36,58,69,83*
Jean Kelly 50	Robert Loftis 67
Jason Rich 73,295*	Julia Faye Anderson 92,93,270*
Susie Owens 294	

79 Student Personnel	91 Safety/Security	275 Response To Intervention	298 Grant Writer/Ptnrships	School Programs	Social Media	
80 Driver Ed/Safety	92 Magnet School	277 Remedial Math K-12	750 Chief Innovation Officer	A = Alternative Program	f = Facebook	
81 Gifted/Talented	93 Parental Involvement	280 Literacy Coach	751 Chief of Staff	G = Adult Classes		
82 Video Services	95 Tech Prep Program	285 STEM	752 Social Emotional Learning	M = Magnet Program	t = Twitter	
83 Substance Abuse Prev	97 Chief Infomation Officer	286 Digital Learning		T = Title I Schoolwide		
84 Erate	98 Chief Technology Officer	288 Common Core Standards	Other School Types	V = Career & Tech Ed Programs		
85 AIDS Education	270 Accountability	294 Accountability	Ⓐ = Alternative School			
88 Alternative/At Risk	271 Migrant Education	295 Network System	Ⓒ = Charter School	New Schools are shaded		
89 Multi-Cultural Curriculum	273 Teacher Mentor	296 Title II Programs	Ⓜ = Magnet School	New Superintendents and Principals are bold		
90 Social Work	274 Before/After Sch	297 Webmaster	Ⓨ = Year-Round School	Personnel with email addresses are underscored		

Rusk County

Market Data Retrieval

Public Schs..Principal	Grd	Prgm	Enr/#Cls	SN	
Laneville Sch 7415 FM 1798 W, Laneville 75667 Joshua Tremont	PK-12	TV	182 25	94%	903/863-5353 Fax 903/863-2736

● **Leveretts Chapel Ind Sch Dist** PID: 01049097 — 903/834-6675
8956 Highway 42/135 N, Overton 75684 — Fax 903/834-6602

Schools: 1 \ **Teachers:** 28 \ **Students:** 259 \ **Special Ed Students:** 17 \ **LEP Students:** 51 \ **College-Bound:** 90% \ **Exp:** $339 (High) \ **Poverty:** 12% \ **Title I:** $28,522 \ **Open-Close:** 08/19 - 05/22 \ **DTBP:** $330 (High)

Donna Johnson 1
Ben Kain 3*
Georgia Pierce 12*
Stephanie Leplante 57*
Jimmie Waller 67
Teresa Melton 271
Debby Herrin 2,11,298
Rickey Hammontree 6*
Nick Leplante 16,73*
Steffani Greer-Jones 58*
Brenda Smith 83*

Public Schs..Principal	Grd	Prgm	Enr/#Cls	SN	
Leveretts Chapel Sch 8956 Highway 42/135 N, Overton 75684 Matt Everett \ Nikki Saxton	PK-12	AV	259 14		903/834-3181

● **Mt Enterprise Ind School Dist** PID: 01049126 — 903/822-3575
301 NW 3rd St, Mt Enterprise 75681 — Fax 903/822-3633

Schools: 1 \ **Teachers:** 37 \ **Students:** 400 \ **Special Ed Students:** 49 \ **LEP Students:** 16 \ **College-Bound:** 60% \ **Ethnic:** African American 16%, Hispanic 10%, Native American: 1%, Caucasian 72% \ **Exp:** $384 (High) \ **Poverty:** 17% \ **Title I:** $53,509 \ **Open-Close:** 08/19 - 05/22 \ **DTBP:** $380 (High)

Byron Jordan 1,11
Jeremy Jenkins 6
Michelle Lee 16,270*
Kimberly Fryman 57*
Don Rogers 67
Andy Lee 2,68,73,76*
Dr Chance Mays 10*
Tiffanie Jones 36,69,83,88*
Akiko Jones 58
Andy Lee 84

Public Schs..Principal	Grd	Prgm	Enr/#Cls	SN	
Mt Enterprise Sch 301 NW 3rd St, Mt Enterprise 75681 Dr Chance Mays \ Lawren McDermand	PK-12	ATV	400 24	51%	903/822-3545

● **Overton Ind School Dist** PID: 01049152 — 903/834-6145
111 E McKay St, Overton 75684 — Fax 903/834-6755

Schools: 2 \ **Teachers:** 48 \ **Students:** 500 \ **Special Ed Students:** 48 \ **LEP Students:** 3 \ **Ethnic:** African American 14%, Hispanic 9%, Caucasian 76% \ **Exp:** $452 (High) \ **Poverty:** 21% \ **Title I:** $150,291 \ **Open-Close:** 08/20 - 05/22 \ **DTBP:** $318 (High)

Steven Dubose 1
Jerry Thornton 3,5
Wendy Jackosn 8,36,69,85
Irana Hendrick 16
Cindy Smith 58
William Mansfield 73
Matthew Blake 2
Justin Arnold 6*
Nikki Senter 12*
Cindy Bundrick 27*
Shane McCasland 67
Kristi Dubose 275*

Public Schs..Principal	Grd	Prgm	Enr/#Cls	SN	
Overton Elem Sch 501 E Henderson St, Overton 75684 Nichole Fenter	PK-5	T	276 13	68%	903/834-6144 Fax 903/834-3913
Overton Secondary Sch 501 E Henderson St, Overton 75684 Cindy Bundrick	6-12	ATV	249 13	50%	903/834-6143 Fax 903/834-3256

● **Tatum Ind School Dist** PID: 01049188 — 903/947-6482
510 Crystal Farms Rd, Tatum 75691 — Fax 903/947-3295

Schools: 4 \ **Teachers:** 109 \ **Students:** 1,622 \ **Special Ed Students:** 130 \ **LEP Students:** 168 \ **College-Bound:** 52% \ **Ethnic:** African American 24%, Hispanic 28%, Caucasian 48% \ **Exp:** $321 (High) \ **Poverty:** 22% \ **Title I:** $283,059 \ **Open-Close:** 08/14 - 05/21 \ **DTBP:** $331 (High)

Dr J Richardson 1
Bob Garcia 3,5*
Andy Evans 6*
Jennifer Malone 15,69
Wes Boyd 16,73,76,84,295
Cindy Smith 58
Drenon Fite 68
Pat Parks 2
Kathy Goodwin 4*
John Wink 8,11,57,73,83,271,288,296
Cindy Haston 16*
Megan Keifler 38
Matt Crawford 67

Public Schs..Principal	Grd	Prgm	Enr/#Cls	SN	
Tatum Elem Sch 1525 N Hill St, Tatum 75691 Jennifer Malone	3-5	T	356 14	61%	903/947-0352 Fax 903/947-3299
Tatum High Sch 600 Crystal Farms Rd, Tatum 75691 Matthew Quick	9-12	TV	482 45	52%	903/947-6482 Fax 903/765-7816
Tatum Middle Sch 410 N Hill St, Tatum 75691 Kin Bryan	6-8	TV	384 19	57%	903/947-6482 Fax 903/765-7782
Tatum Primary Sch 1200 N Hill St, Tatum 75691 Tamara Fite	PK-2	T	400 20	68%	903/947-6485 Fax 903/765-7376

● **West Rusk Co Cons Ind Sch Dist** PID: 01049217 — 903/392-7850
10705 S Main St, New London 75682 — Fax 903/392-7866

Schools: 4 \ **Teachers:** 79 \ **Students:** 1,150 \ **Special Ed Students:** 97 \ **LEP Students:** 118 \ **College-Bound:** 53% \ **Ethnic:** African American 15%, Hispanic 23%, Native American: 2%, Caucasian 60% \ **Exp:** $395 (High) \ **Poverty:** 20% \ **Title I:** $265,384 \ **Open-Close:** 08/26 - 05/29 \ **DTBP:** $350 (High)

Lawrence Coleman 1
Richard Donnelly 3
Bruce Mason 5
Megan Wriggle 7*
Leah Bobbitt 15
Sandra Smith 67
Vivian Sharp 73
Belinda Walker 2
Steve Alexander 4
Nick Harrison 6
Gwen Gilliam 11,16,69,271,296,298
Judy Chapman 57*
Cody Walker 73,295
Paul Thompson 91

Public Schs..Principal	Grd	Prgm	Enr/#Cls	SN	
West Rusk Elem Sch 10705 S Main St, New London 75682 Carlette Mills	PK-2		239 23		903/895-0179
West Rusk High Sch 10705 S Main, New London 75682 Jake Jackson	9-12	TV	333 40	70%	903/392-7857
West Rusk Intermediate Sch 10705 S Main, New London 75682 Burt Langley	3-5	T	271	78%	903/895-4685
West Rusk Junior High Sch 10705 S Main St, New London 75682 Brian Keith	6-8	T	235 15	74%	903/392-7855

---

1 Superintendent	8 Curric/Instruct K-12	19 Chief Financial Officer	29 Family/Consumer Science	39 Social Studies K-12	49 English/Lang Arts Elem	59 Special Education Elem	69 Academic Assessment
2 Bus/Finance/Purchasing	9 Curric/Instruct Elem	20 Art K-12	30 Adult Education	40 Social Studies Elem	50 English/Lang Arts Sec	60 Special Education Sec	70 Research/Development
3 Buildings And Grounds	10 Curric/Instruct Sec	21 Art Elem	31 Career/Sch-to-Work K-12	41 Social Studies Sec	51 Reading K-12	61 Foreign/World Lang K-12	71 Public Information
4 Food Service	11 Federal Program	22 Art Sec	32 Career/Sch-to-Work Elem	42 Science K-12	52 Reading Elem	62 Foreign/World Lang Elem	72 Summer School
5 Transportation	12 Title I	23 Music K-12	33 Career/Sch-to-Work Sec	43 Science Elem	53 Reading Sec	63 Foreign/World Lang Sec	73 Instructional Tech
6 Athletic	13 Title V	24 Music Elem	34 Early Childhood Ed	44 Science Sec	54 Remedial Reading K-12	64 Religious Education K-12	74 Inservice Training
7 Health Services	15 Asst Superintendent	25 Music Sec	35 Health/Phys Education	45 Math K-12	55 Remedial Reading Elem	65 Religious Education Elem	75 Marketing/Distributive
	16 Instructional Media Svcs	26 Business Education	36 Guidance Services K-12	46 Math Elem	56 Remedial Reading Sec	66 Religious Education Sec	76 Info Systems
	17 Chief Operations Officer	27 Career & Tech Ed	37 Guidance Services Elem	47 Math Sec	57 Bilingual/ELL	67 School Board President	77 Psychological Assess
	18 Chief Academic Officer	28 Technology Education	38 Guidance Services Sec	48 English/Lang Arts K-12	58 Special Education K-12	68 Teacher Personnel	78 Affirmative Action

Texas School Directory

San Augustine County

RUSK PRIVATE SCHOOLS

Private Schs..Principal	Grd	Prgm	Enr/#Cls	SN	
Full Armor Christian Academy	K-12		135		903/655-8489
2324 FM 3135 E, Henderson 75652			12		Fax 903/657-8267
Chris Ford					

SABINE COUNTY

SABINE PUBLIC SCHOOLS

• **Hemphill Ind School Dist** PID: 01049267   409/787-3371
1000 Milam St, Hemphill 75948   Fax 409/787-4005

Schools: 3 \ *Teachers:* 72 \ *Students:* 900 \ *Special Ed Students:* 99 \ *LEP Students:* 14 \ *College-Bound:* 50% \ *Ethnic:* African American 10%, Hispanic 10%, Caucasian 79% \ *Exp:* $878 (High) \ *Poverty:* 29% \ *Title I:* $368,624 \ *Open-Close:* 08/12 - 05/21 \ *DTBP:* $359 (High)

Reese Briggs 1		Sally Butler 2,11,271	
Wayne Alford 3,5*		Margaret White 4	
Gary Vanya 6,35*		Cecily Bridges 7,85*	
Marc Griffin 8,36,74,83,88,274,288*		Susan Smith 9,273*	
Shelly Starr 16*		Jeremy McDaniel 58*	
Lynn Lindsey 67		Monica Butler 69,77*	
Eric Heslip 73,295			

Public Schs..Principal	Grd	Prgm	Enr/#Cls	SN	
Hemphill Elem Sch	PK-4	T	374	70%	409/787-3371
1000 Milam St, Hemphill 75948			30		Fax 409/787-4137
Susan Smith					
Hemphill Middle Sch	5-8	T	264	65%	409/787-3371
1000 Milam St, Hemphill 75948			18		Fax 409/787-2252
Jeremy McDaniel					
Hemphill Senior High Sch	9-12	TV	259	48%	409/787-3371
1000 Milam St, Hemphill 75948			35		Fax 409/787-1259
Marc Griffin					

• **West Sabine Ind Sch Dist** PID: 01049293   409/584-2655
101 Timberland Hwy W, Pineland 75968   Fax 409/584-2139

Schools: 2 \ *Teachers:* 58 \ *Students:* 600 \ *Special Ed Students:* 65 \ *LEP Students:* 7 \ *College-Bound:* 50% \ *Ethnic:* African American 9%, Hispanic 5%, Caucasian 86% \ *Exp:* $384 (High) \ *Poverty:* 25% \ *Title I:* $165,009 \ *Open-Close:* 08/14 - 05/22 \ *DTBP:* $397 (High)

Jane Stephenson 1	Natasha McClelland 2,296
Tammy Rogers 4	Jerred Wallace 6*
Karianna Grant 12,88*	Daniel Havard 16,73,295*
Marie Smith 57*	Cody McBride 67
Patricia Jacks 69,83*	

Public Schs..Principal	Grd	Prgm	Enr/#Cls	SN	
West Sabine Elem Sch	PK-5	T	323	82%	409/584-2205
459 N Temple Rd, Pineland 75968			22		Fax 409/584-3096
Deborah Lane					
West Sabine Jr Sr High Sch	6-12	ATV	342	69%	409/584-2525
109 Timberland Hwy W, Pineland 75968			23		Fax 409/584-2695
Ryan Fuller					

SAN AUGUSTINE COUNTY

SAN AUGUSTINE PUBLIC SCHOOLS

• **Broaddus Ind School Dist** PID: 01049334   936/872-3041
1 Bulldog Plaza, Broaddus 75929   Fax 936/872-3699

Schools: 2 \ *Teachers:* 36 \ *Students:* 400 \ *Special Ed Students:* 48 \ *LEP Students:* 15 \ *College-Bound:* 75% \ *Ethnic:* African American 1%, Hispanic 9%, Caucasian 90% \ *Exp:* $501 (High) \ *Poverty:* 37% \ *Title I:* $216,289 \ *Open-Close:* 08/19 - 05/22 \ *DTBP:* $255 (High)

Lucas Hollway 1,83	Leah Hollway 2,11
Brandon Weatherford 3	Victor Turcios 3
Sheila Williams 4*	Henry Hoya 5
Murray Wall 5	Amanda Sowell 7,85*
Natile Hand 8,11,36,69,88,275,294	Gary Mitchell 16,73,295
Faith Kilmer 57*	Travis Elizalde 67
Leigh Stewart 76	

Public Schs..Principal	Grd	Prgm	Enr/#Cls	SN	
Broaddus Elem Sch	PK-5	T	195	80%	936/872-3315
215 Buchanan St, Broaddus 75929			17		Fax 936/872-3439
Benjamin Holloway					
Broaddus High Sch	6-12	AGTV	214	78%	936/872-3610
16405 Highway 147 S, Broaddus 75929			30		Fax 936/872-9020
Brad Hranicky					

• **San Augustine Ind School Dist** PID: 01049360   936/275-2306
1002 Barrett St, San Augustine 75972   Fax 936/275-9776

Schools: 2 \ *Teachers:* 65 \ *Students:* 763 \ *Special Ed Students:* 85 \ *LEP Students:* 67 \ *Ethnic:* African American 54%, Hispanic 23%, Caucasian 23% \ *Exp:* $497 (High) \ *Poverty:* 30% \ *Title I:* $360,852 \ *Special Education:* $177,000 \ *Open-Close:* 08/14 - 05/22 \ *DTBP:* $341 (High)

Virginia Liepman 1	Patti McLerran 2
Allen Eberlan 3,91	Sharon Taylor 4
Rick Russell 5	Marty Murr 6*
Jason Mixon 8,11,69	Ryan Ham 16,31,73
Anna Short 58	Charles Boyette 67
Veronica Porter 294	

Public Schs..Principal	Grd	Prgm	Enr/#Cls	SN	
San Augustine Elem Sch	PK-5	TV	404	92%	936/275-3424
101 S Milam St, San Augustine 75972					Fax 936/275-9719
Rebecca Whitton					
San Augustine Mid High Sch	6-12	TV	359	77%	936/275-9603
702 N Clark St, San Augustine 75972			20		Fax 936/275-9829
Hugh Perkins					

---

79 Student Personnel	91 Safety/Security	275 Response To Intervention	298 Grant Writer/Ptnrships	**School Programs**	**Social Media**
80 Driver Ed/Safety	92 Magnet School	277 Remedial Math K-12	750 Chief Innovation Officer	A = Alternative Program	
81 Gifted/Talented	93 Parental Involvement	280 Literacy Coach	751 Chief of Staff	G = Adult Classes	= Facebook
82 Video Services	95 Tech Prep Program	285 STEM	752 Social Emotional Learning	M = Magnet Program	
83 Substance Abuse Prev	97 Chief Infomation Officer	286 Digital Learning		T = Title I Schoolwide	= Twitter
84 Erate	98 Chief Technology Officer	288 Common Core Standards	**Other School Types**	V = Career & Tech Ed Programs	
85 AIDS Education	270 Accountability	294 Accountability	Ⓐ = Alternative School		
88 Alternative/At Risk	271 Migrant Education	295 Network System	Ⓒ = Charter School	New Schools are shaded	
89 Multi-Cultural Curriculum	273 Teacher Mentor	296 Title II Programs	Ⓜ = Magnet School	New Superintendents and Principals are bold	
90 Social Work	274 Before/After Sch	297 Webmaster	Ⓨ = Year-Round School	Personnel with email addresses are underscored	

San Jacinto County

SAN JACINTO COUNTY

SAN JACINTO PUBLIC SCHOOLS

- **Coldspring-Oakhurst Cons ISD** PID: 01049401   936/653-1115
  125 FM 1514 Rd, Coldspring 77331   Fax 936/653-2197

Schools: 4 \ *Teachers:* 106 \ *Students:* 1,525 \ *Special Ed Students:* 156 \ *LEP Students:* 10 \ *College-Bound:* 42% \ *Ethnic:* African American 20%, Hispanic 9%, Caucasian 71% \ *Exp:* $408 (High) \ *Poverty:* 27% \ *Title I:* $657,599 \ *Special Education:* $314,000 \ *Open-Close:* 08/26 - 05/29 \ *DTBP:* $394 (High) \

Dr Leland Moore 1
Charles Cotton 3,5
Ken Stanley 6,35
Vikki Curry 8,15,288
Mary Seago 16
Tony Sewell 67
Charles Camden 73,295
Roosevelt Joseph 91
Adam Jenke 2
Dawn Smith 4
Kristi Benastante 7
Jeff Eichman 11
Sheri Wilson 58
Candy Yager 68
Missy Eichman 73,286

Public Schs..Principal	Grd	Prgm	Enr/#Cls	SN
Coldspring Intermediate Sch 1510 Hwy 150, Coldspring 77331 Paula McClendon	3-5	T	358 30	65% 936/653-1152 Fax 936/653-3689
Coldspring-Oakhurst High Sch 14100 State Highway 150 W, Coldspring 77331 Donna Thompson	9-12	ATV	458 58	62% 936/653-1140 Fax 936/653-3687
James Street Elem Sch 125 Jones Ave, Coldspring 77331 Paula McClendon	PK-2	T	371 19	67% 936/653-1187 Fax 936/653-3690
Lincoln Junior High Sch 13605 Sh 156, Coldspring 77331 Frank Brown	6-8	ATV	345 60	64% 936/653-1166 Fax 936/653-3688

- **Shepherd Ind School Dist** PID: 01049449   936/628-3396
  1401 S Byrd Ave, Shepherd 77371   Fax 936/628-3841

Schools: 4 \ *Teachers:* 131 \ *Students:* 2,000 \ *Special Ed Students:* 140 \ *LEP Students:* 272 \ *College-Bound:* 43% \ *Ethnic:* African American 5%, Hispanic 32%, Caucasian 62% \ *Exp:* $524 (High) \ *Poverty:* 25% \ *Title I:* $685,117 \ *Open-Close:* 08/14 - 05/28 \ *DTBP:* $350 (High) \

Rick Hartley 1
Brandon Barrow 3,5
Miles Robison 6*
Holly Oliphant 7*
Rebecca Bany 16*
Susan Bailes 67
Tommy Hues 73,84
Deanna Clavell 2
Randy Milton 4
Holly Oliphant 7
Dr Elizabeth Torres 11,57,88,271,288,298
Shannon Wallace 58
Brenda Cronin 68,74

Public Schs..Principal	Grd	Prgm	Enr/#Cls	SN
Shepherd High Sch 1 Pirate Ln, Shepherd 77371 Daniel Barton	9-12	T	589 55	60% 936/628-3371 Fax 936/628-6986
Shepherd Intermediate Sch 420 S Railroad Ave, Shepherd 77371 Ronnie Seagroves	3-5	T	485 23	77% 936/628-6764 Fax 936/628-6507
Shepherd Middle Sch 1401 S Byrd Ave, Shepherd 77371 Denise Weatherford	6-8	T	403 30	75% 936/628-3377 Fax 936/628-6749
Shepherd Primary Sch 10300 Highway 150, Shepherd 77371 Heather Gore	PK-2	T	540 29	82% 936/628-3302 Fax 936/628-6459

SAN PATRICIO COUNTY

SAN PATRICIO PUBLIC SCHOOLS

- **Aransas Pass Ind School Dist** PID: 01049487   361/758-3466
  2300 McMullen Ln Ste 600, Aransas Pass 78336   Fax 361/758-2962

Schools: 5 \ *Teachers:* 131 \ *Students:* 1,474 \ *Special Ed Students:* 168 \ *LEP Students:* 149 \ *College-Bound:* 45% \ *Ethnic:* African American 2%, Hispanic 65%, Caucasian 32% \ *Exp:* $312 (High) \ *Poverty:* 30% \ *Title I:* $776,405 \ *Special Education:* $506,000 \ *Open-Close:* 08/26 - 05/28 \ *DTBP:* $615 (High)

Mrs Cooke 1
Charlie Ochoa 3,5
Ryan Knostman 6*
Shelly Domingueze 8,16,57,88,271,273,286,288
Susan Coleman 16*
Carla Dees 37*
Victor Galvan 67
Cheryle Stansberry 2
Lanell Jones 4
Sally McCutchan 7*
Mark Kemp 11
Wayne Bennett 31*
Christine Johnson 58
Jason Brou 73

Public Schs..Principal	Grd	Prgm	Enr/#Cls	SN
A C Blunt Middle Sch 2103 Demory Ln, Aransas Pass 78336 Derick King	6-8	T	348 40	74% 361/758-2711 Fax 361/758-4690
Aransas Pass High Sch 450 S Avenue A, Aransas Pass 78336 Wayne Bennett	9-12	ATV	441 34	62% 361/758-3248 Fax 361/758-3251
Charlie Marshall Elem Sch 2300 McMullen Ln, Aransas Pass 78336 Jeremy Saegert	4-5	T	195 18	77% 361/758-3455 Fax 361/758-3046
Faulk Early Childhood Center 430 S 8th St, Aransas Pass 78336 Jason Mansfield	PK-1	T	281 26	80% 361/758-3141 Fax 361/758-5493
Kieberger Elem Sch 748 W Goodnight Ave, Aransas Pass 78336 Jason Mansfield	2-3	T	209 18	75% 361/758-3113 Fax 361/758-3605

- **Gregory-Portland Ind Sch Dist** PID: 01049530   361/777-1091
  608 College St, Portland 78374   Fax 361/777-1093

Schools: 7 \ *Teachers:* 300 \ *Students:* 4,600 \ *Special Ed Students:* 401 \ *LEP Students:* 171 \ *College-Bound:* 60% \ *Ethnic:* Asian 1%, African American 2%, Hispanic 57%, Caucasian 40% \ *Exp:* $393 (High) \ *Poverty:* 14% \ *Title I:* $672,378 \ *Special Education:* $893,000 \ *Open-Close:* 08/12 - 05/21 \ *DTBP:* $181 (High)

Dr Paul Clore 1
Bridget Clark 2,19,91
Jeff Atkinson 4
Rick Rhodes 6*
Sharon Reckaway 10,69,88,270,271,273
Andrew Guerra 16,73,84,295
Barbie Tumlinson 34,58
Alberto Silguero 2
Ernesto Polomo 3
Alton Coleman 5
Velma Soliz-Garcia 8,15,68
Dr Leslie Faught 15
Crystal Matern 16
Geoffrey Rickerhauser 42,45

---

1 Superintendent	8 Curric/Instruct K-12	19 Chief Financial Officer	29 Family/Consumer Science	39 Social Studies K-12	49 English/Lang Arts Elem	59 Special Education Elem	69 Academic Assessment
2 Bus/Finance/Purchasing	9 Curric/Instruct Elem	20 Art K-12	30 Adult Education	40 Social Studies Elem	50 English/Lang Arts Sec	60 Special Education Sec	70 Research/Development
3 Buildings And Grounds	10 Curric/Instruct Sec	21 Art Elem	31 Career/Sch-to-Work K-12	41 Social Studies Sec	51 Reading K-12	61 Foreign/World Lang K-12	71 Public Information
4 Food Service	11 Federal Program	22 Art Sec	32 Career/Sch-to-Work Elem	42 Science K-12	52 Reading Elem	62 Foreign/World Lang Elem	72 Summer School
5 Transportation	12 Title I	23 Music K-12	33 Career/Sch-to-Work Sec	43 Science Elem	53 Reading Sec	63 Foreign/World Lang Sec	73 Instructional Tech
6 Athletic	13 Title V	24 Music Elem	34 Early Childhood Ed	44 Science Sec	54 Remedial Reading K-12	64 Religious Education K-12	74 Inservice Training
7 Health Services	15 Asst Superintendent	25 Music Sec	35 Health/Phys Education	45 Math K-12	55 Remedial Reading Elem	65 Religious Education Elem	75 Marketing/Distributive
	16 Instructional Media Svcs	26 Business Education	36 Guidance Services K-12	46 Math Elem	56 Remedial Reading Sec	66 Religious Education Sec	76 Info Systems
	17 Chief Operations Officer	27 Career & Tech Ed	37 Guidance Services Elem	47 Math Sec	57 Bilingual/ELL	67 School Board President	77 Psychological Assess
	18 Chief Academic Officer	28 Technology Education	38 Guidance Services Sec	48 English/Lang Arts K-12	58 Special Education K-12	68 Teacher Personnel	78 Affirmative Action

Texas School Directory

San Patricio County

Victor Hernandez 67

Public Schs..Principal	Grd	Prgm	Enr/#Cls	SN	
East Cliff Elem Sch 1140 Broadway Blvd, Portland 78374 **Penny Armstrong**	PK-5		541 20	23%	361/777-4255 Fax 361/777-4256
Gregory-Portland High Sch 4601 Wildcat Dr, Portland 78374 **Kyde Eddleman**	9-12	V	1,421 93	32%	361/777-4251 Fax 361/777-4272
Gregory-Portland Mid Sch 4600 Wildcat Dr, Portland 78374 **Gabe Alvarado**	6-8	T	729 50	40%	361/777-4042 Fax 361/643-3187
Stephen F Austin Elem Sch 308 N Gregory Ave, Gregory 78359 **Brenda Brinkman**	PK-5	T	481	64%	361/777-4252 Fax 361/777-4261
T M Clark Elem Sch 2250 Memorial Pkwy, Portland 78374 **Bobby Rister**	PK-5	T	685 35	56%	361/777-4045 Fax 361/777-4046
W C Andrews Elem Sch 4015 Moore Ave, Portland 78374 **Julie Verstuyft**	PK-5	T	495 25	52%	361/777-4048 Fax 361/643-0775
Ⓐ Wildcat Learning Alt Center 1100 Lang Rd, Portland 78374 **Terra Haynes**	9-12		50		361/777-4051

● **Ingleside Ind School Dist** PID: 01049592   361/776-7631
2664 San Angelo Ave, Ingleside 78362   Fax 361/776-0267

Schools: 5 \ *Teachers:* 149 \ *Students:* 2,235 \ *Special Ed Students:* 188 \ *LEP Students:* 157 \ *College-Bound:* 60% \ *Ethnic:* Asian 1%, African American 2%, Hispanic 57%, Native American: 1%, Caucasian 40% \ *Exp:* $276 (Med) \ *Poverty:* 18% \ *Title I:* $445,317 \ *Special Education:* $220,000 \ *Open-Close:* 08/19 - 05/21 \ *DTBP:* $540 (High) \ 🄵 🅃

Troy Mircovich 1
Ross Schonhoeft 4
Karen Mircovich 11,57,69,83
Camille Burger 58
Steven Snyder 71
Danny Glover 79
Ronald Robles 3,5,92
Lynne Porter 8,15
Selena Villaneda 16*
Julio Salinas 67
Delana Lightfoot 73,286

Public Schs..Principal	Grd	Prgm	Enr/#Cls	SN	
Blaschke-Sheldon Elem Sch 2624 Mustang Dr, Ingleside 78362 **Stephanie McNew**	5-6	T	324 20	61%	361/776-3050 Fax 361/776-7912
Gilbert Mircovich Elem Sch 2720 Big Oak Ln, Ingleside 78362 **Heather Cohea**	2-4	T	508 31	62%	361/776-1683 Fax 361/775-0509
Ingleside High Sch 2807 Mustang Dr, Ingleside 78362 **Dawn Whidden**	9-12	ATV	648 54	46%	361/776-2712 Fax 361/776-5200
Ingleside Primary Sch 2100 Achievement Blvd, Ingleside 78362 **Stephanie Dotson**	PK-1	T	411 23	62%	361/776-3060 Fax 361/775-2070
Leon Taylor Junior High Sch 2739 Mustang Dr, Ingleside 78362 **Heather Waugh-Freeze**	7-8	AT	344 27	58%	361/776-2232 Fax 361/776-2192

● **Mathis Ind School Dist** PID: 01049645   361/547-3378
602 E San Patricio Ave, Mathis 78368   Fax 361/547-9474

Schools: 4 \ *Teachers:* 114 \ *Students:* 1,635 \ *Special Ed Students:* 158 \ *LEP Students:* 47 \ *College-Bound:* 31% \ *Ethnic:* African American 1%, Hispanic 90%, Caucasian 8% \ *Exp:* $297 (Med) \ *Poverty:* 39% \ *Title I:* $984,535 \ *Open-Close:* 08/19 - 05/27 \ *DTBP:* $490 (High)

Benny Hernandez 1,11,57,83
David Martinez 3
Rosie Huerta 5
Antonia Vervin 16,73
Christina Alvarado 36,69
Veronica Garza 58
Sylvia Padilla 68
Gail Shepler 2,84
Suanne Martinez 4
Rod Blunt 6*
Ricardo Leal 27*
Lacy Dobbins 48,51
Melinda Barajas 67
Leobardo Cano 88*

Public Schs..Principal	Grd	Prgm	Enr/#Cls	SN	
Mathis Elem Sch 315 S Duval St, Mathis 78368 **Jesse Dolin**	PK-2	T	469 37	84%	361/547-4106 Fax 361/547-4162
Mathis High Sch 1615 E San Patricio Ave, Mathis 78368 **Dr Jesse Riojas**	9-12	AGTV	411 42	72%	361/547-3322 Fax 361/547-4139
Mathis Intermediate Sch 550 E San Patricio Ave, Mathis 78368 **Cynthia Westbrook**	3-5	T	367 24	86%	361/547-2472 Fax 361/547-4119
Mathis Middle Sch 1627 E San Patricio Ave, Mathis 78368 **Randy Tiemann**	6-8	T	388 24	79%	361/547-2381 Fax 361/547-4156

● **Odem-Edroy Ind School Dist** PID: 01049700   361/368-8121
1 Owl Sq, Odem 78370   Fax 361/368-2879

Schools: 4 \ *Teachers:* 70 \ *Students:* 900 \ *Special Ed Students:* 58 \ *LEP Students:* 35 \ *College-Bound:* 90% \ *Ethnic:* Hispanic 86%, Caucasian 13% \ *Exp:* $539 (High) \ *Poverty:* 34% \ *Title I:* $517,237 \ *Special Education:* $154,000 \ *Open-Close:* 08/21 - 05/19 \ *DTBP:* $606 (High)

Yolanda Carr 1
Arnold Maldonado 3*
Armando Huerta 6*
Esmeralda Martinez 34*
Jacob Romero 67
Lisa Perez 83,85*
Tonya Romero 2
Janie Luna 4
Lori Schulze 10,11,285
Jana Kieshhnick 57,58
Joey Avila 73,84,286
Lupita Carrizales 274*

Public Schs..Principal	Grd	Prgm	Enr/#Cls	SN	
Odem Elem Sch 1 Owl Sq, Odem 78370 **Esmeralda Martinez**	PK-2	T	276 31	80%	361/368-8121 Fax 361/368-2317
Odem High Sch 1 Owl Sq Ste A, Odem 78370 **Calvin Bowers**	9-12	ATV	288 31	72%	361/368-8121 Fax 361/368-3781
Odem Intermediate Sch 1 Owl Sq, Odem 78370 **Erica Tapia**	3-5		201		361/368-8121
Odem Junior High Sch 1 Owl Sq, Odem 78370 **Joe Vela**	6-8	T	224 16	80%	361/368-8121 Fax 361/368-2033

---

79 Student Personnel	91 Safety/Security	275 Response To Intervention	298 Grant Writer/Ptnrships	**School Programs**	**Social Media**	
80 Driver Ed/Safety	92 Magnet School	277 Remedial Math K-12	750 Chief Innovation Officer	A = Alternative Program		
81 Gifted/Talented	93 Parental Involvement	280 Literacy Coach	751 Chief of Staff	G = Adult Classes	🄵 = Facebook	
82 Video Services	95 Tech Prep Program	285 STEM	752 Social Emotional Learning	M = Magnet Program		
83 Substance Abuse Prev	97 Chief Information Officer	286 Digital Learning		T = Title I Schoolwide	🅃 = Twitter	
84 Erate	98 Chief Technology Officer	288 Common Core Standards	**Other School Types**	V = Career & Tech Ed Programs		
85 AIDS Education	270 Character Education	294 Accountability	Ⓐ = Alternative School			
88 Alternative/At Risk	271 Migrant Education	295 Network System	Ⓒ = Charter School	New Schools are shaded		
89 Multi-Cultural Curriculum	273 Teacher Mentor	296 Title II Programs	Ⓜ = Magnet School	New Superintendents and Principals are bold		
90 Social Work	274 Before/After Sch	297 Webmaster	Ⓨ = Year-Round School	Personnel with email addresses are underscored		

San Saba County

Market Data Retrieval

- **Sinton Ind School Dist** PID: 01049762   361/364-6800
  322 S Archer St, Sinton 78387   Fax 361/364-6905

Schools: 4 \ **Teachers:** 153 \ **Students:** 2,202 \ **Special Ed Students:** 233 \ **LEP Students:** 15 \ **College-Bound:** 48% \ **Ethnic:** African American 1%, Hispanic 83%, Caucasian 15% \ **Exp:** $405 (High) \ **Poverty:** 25% \ **Title I:** $610,693 \ **Special Education:** $486,000 \ **Open-Close:** 08/14 - 05/21 \ **DTBP:** $558 (High)

Chad Jones 1
Donald Mercier 3
Joseph Buffa 5,73,76,295
Gina Guajardo 11,83,296
Michael Elbert 58
Eileen Troup 71
Heidi Menchaca 271
Melissa Villarreal 2,15
Filke West 4
Lori Soliz 7*
Dana Allen 15,68
Linda Rodriguez 67
Rosie Salinas 73,84
Mary Lankford 285*

Public Schs..Principal	Grd	Prgm	Enr/#Cls	SN	
E Merle Smith Middle Sch 900 S San Patricio St, Sinton 78387 Jennifer Davis	6-8	T	518 26	74%	361/364-6840 Fax 361/364-6856
Sinton Elem Sch 200 S Bowie St, Sinton 78387 Lori Trevino	3-5	T	497 25	77%	361/364-6900 Fax 361/364-6914
Sinton High Sch 400 N Pirate Blvd, Sinton 78387 Daniel Smith	9-12	TV	650 60	63%	361/364-6650 Fax 361/364-6668
Welder Elem Sch 901 Hamilton St, Sinton 78387 Luci Rodriguez	PK-2	T	562 24	73%	361/364-6600 Fax 361/364-6608

- **Taft Ind School Dist** PID: 01049827   361/528-2636
  400 College St, Taft 78390   Fax 361/528-2223

Schools: 3 \ **Teachers:** 80 \ **Students:** 1,100 \ **Special Ed Students:** 115 \ **LEP Students:** 22 \ **College-Bound:** 100% \ **Ethnic:** Hispanic 89%, Caucasian 10% \ **Exp:** $598 (High) \ **Poverty:** 28% \ **Title I:** $409,779 \ **Special Education:** $227,000 \ **Open-Close:** 08/26 - 05/28 \ **DTBP:** $613 (High)

Joe Lopez 1
Ismael Olivares 3
Joe Richard Castellano 6
Ricardo Trevino 12
Freddy Ramos 73
Vangie Lopez 271
Ivonne Banda 2
Margie Longoria 4
Brenda Meyer 8
Ruben Lopez 67
Tony Arsuaga 83,91

Public Schs..Principal	Grd	Prgm	Enr/#Cls	SN	
Taft High Sch 502 Rincon Rd, Taft 78390 **Matthew Lohse**	9-12	GTV	318 26	83%	361/528-2636 Fax 361/528-3918
Taft Junior High Sch 1150 Gregory St, Taft 78390 Christine Acosta	6-8	GTV	235 30	87%	361/528-2636 Fax 361/528-5477
Woodroe Petty Elem Sch 401 Peach St, Taft 78390 Joshua Rombs	PK-5	T	557 17	89%	361/528-2636 Fax 361/528-3570

SAN SABA COUNTY

SAN SABA PUBLIC SCHOOLS

- **Cherokee Ind School Dist** PID: 01049889   325/622-4298
  305 S Indian Ave, Cherokee 76832   Fax 325/622-4430

Schools: 1 \ **Teachers:** 19 \ **Students:** 110 \ **Special Ed Students:** 17 \ **College-Bound:** 75% \ **Ethnic:** Asian 1%, African American 2%, Hispanic 30%, Caucasian 68% \ **Exp:** $438 (High) \ **Poverty:** 15% \ **Title I:** $79,521 \ **Open-Close:** 08/21 - 05/25 \ **DTBP:** $356 (High)

Eldon Franco 1,11,73,83,84
Jennifer Bordner 8,12,58,296*
Denise Woolsey 2
Tommy Morrison 67

Public Schs..Principal	Grd	Prgm	Enr/#Cls	SN	
Cherokee Sch 305 S Indian Ave, Cherokee 76832 Jennifer Bordner	K-12	TV	110 8	52%	325/622-4298

- **Richland Springs Ind Sch Dist** PID: 01049918   325/452-3524
  700 W Coyote Trl, Richland Spgs 76871   Fax 325/452-3230

Schools: 1 \ **Teachers:** 13 \ **Students:** 120 \ **Special Ed Students:** 15 \ **LEP Students:** 3 \ **College-Bound:** 90% \ **Ethnic:** Hispanic 20%, Native American: 1%, Caucasian 79% \ **Exp:** $916 (High) \ **Poverty:** 13% \ **Title I:** $38,950 \ **Open-Close:** 08/16 - 05/22 \ **DTBP:** $438 (High)

Don Fowler 1,11
Shannon Sutherland 4
Rhonda Wyatt 8*
Jason Lewis 67
Linda Morris 2
Rhonda Wyatt 8
Shawn Rogers 58*
Pamela Starr 73*

Public Schs..Principal	Grd	Prgm	Enr/#Cls	SN	
Richland Springs Sch 700 W Coyote Trl, Richland Spgs 76871 **Rhonda Wyatt**	K-12	ATV	120 16	55%	325/452-3427 Fax 325/452-3580

- **San Saba Ind School Dist** PID: 01049944   325/372-3771
  808 W Wallace St, San Saba 76877   Fax 325/372-5977

Schools: 3 \ **Teachers:** 72 \ **Students:** 750 \ **Special Ed Students:** 99 \ **LEP Students:** 115 \ **College-Bound:** 40% \ **Ethnic:** Asian 1%, Hispanic 53%, Caucasian 46% \ **Exp:** $536 (High) \ **Poverty:** 28% \ **Title I:** $236,129 \ **Open-Close:** 08/22 - 05/29 \ **DTBP:** $333 (High) \ 📘

Wayne Kelly 1,83
Kenneth Groomes 3
Alton Tinney 5
Brenda Martinez 8,11,15,57,88,288,296
Kevin Shahan 67
Buck Martin 2
Dianna Wood 4*
Andreas Aguirre 6
Deanne Cromer 16*
Tim Cooper 73,286,295

Public Schs..Principal	Grd	Prgm	Enr/#Cls	SN	
San Saba Elem Sch 808 W Wallace St, San Saba 76877 **Denise Deckard**	PK-4	T	337 20	68%	325/372-3019 Fax 325/372-6187
San Saba High Sch S 8th St, San Saba 76877 Dr Scott Snyder	9-12	T	183 19	41%	325/372-3786 Fax 325/372-3478

1 Superintendent	8 Curric/Instruct K-12	19 Chief Financial Officer	29 Family/Consumer Science	39 Social Studies K-12	49 English/Lang Arts Elem	59 Special Education Elem	69 Academic Assessment
2 Bus/Finance/Purchasing	9 Curric/Instruct Elem	20 Art K-12	30 Adult Education	40 Social Studies Elem	50 English/Lang Arts Sec	60 Special Education Sec	70 Research/Development
3 Buildings And Grounds	10 Curric/Instruct Sec	21 Art Elem	31 Career/Sch-to-Work K-12	41 Social Studies Sec	51 Reading K-12	61 Foreign/World Lang K-12	71 Public Information
4 Food Service	11 Federal Program	22 Art Sec	32 Career/Sch-to-Work Elem	42 Science K-12	52 Reading Elem	62 Foreign/World Lang Elem	72 Summer School
5 Transportation	12 Title I	23 Music K-12	33 Career/Sch-to-Work Sec	43 Science Elem	53 Reading Sec	63 Foreign/World Lang Sec	73 Instructional Tech
6 Athletic	13 Title V	24 Music Elem	34 Early Childhood Ed	44 Science Sec	54 Remedial Reading K-12	64 Religious Education K-12	74 Inservice Training
7 Health Services	15 Asst Superintendent	25 Music Sec	35 Health/Phys Education	45 Math K-12	55 Remedial Reading Elem	65 Religious Education Elem	75 Marketing/Distributive
	16 Instructional Media Svcs	26 Business Education	36 Guidance Services K-12	46 Math Elem	56 Remedial Reading Sec	66 Religious Education Sec	76 Info Systems
	17 Chief Operations Officer	27 Career & Tech Ed	37 Guidance Services Elem	47 Math Sec	57 Bilingual/ELL	67 School Board President	77 Psychological Assess
	18 Chief Academic Officer	28 Technology Education	38 Guidance Services Sec	48 English/Lang Arts K-12	58 Special Education K-12	68 Teacher Personnel	78 Affirmative Action

Texas School Directory

San Saba Middle Sch 5-8 T 216 61% 325/372-3200
10th St, San Saba 76877   22   Fax 325/372-5228
Joshua Ham

SCHLEICHER COUNTY

SCHLEICHER PUBLIC SCHOOLS

- **Schleicher Co Ind Sch Dist** PID: 01049982 325/853-2514
  205 Fields Ave, Eldorado 76936 Fax 325/853-2695

Schools: 3 \ *Teachers:* 57 \ *Students:* 590 \ *Special Ed Students:* 37 \ *LEP Students:* 43 \ *Ethnic:* Hispanic 74%, Caucasian 25% \ *Exp:* $474 (High) \ *Poverty:* 21% \ *Title I:* $155,249 \ *Special Education:* $8,000 \ *Open-Close:* 08/21 - 05/21 \ *DTBP:* $367 (High)

Robert Gibson 1,11
Oscar Martinez 3
Joey Jones 5
Lu Ann Shipman 16*
Sandra Robledo 68
JD Doyle 73,286,295*
Ray Ballew 2
Vikki Cathey 4
Michael Johnson 6
Kriss Griffin 67
Lyndi Oneil 69,85,88,270,288*
Sharon Spinks 285,298

Public Schs..Principal	Grd	Prgm	Enr/#Cls	SN	
Eldorado Elem Sch 205 W Fields Ave, Eldorado 76936 Michael Rudewick	PK-4	T	241 20	69%	325/853-2514 Fax 325/853-2177
Eldorado High Sch 205 W Fields Ave, Eldorado 76936 Perry Graves	9-12	T	151 27	42%	325/853-2514 Fax 325/853-2710
Eldorado Middle Sch 205 W Fields Ave, Eldorado 76936 Ezra Walling	5-8	T	163 25	62%	325/853-2514 Fax 325/853-2895

SCURRY COUNTY

SCURRY PUBLIC SCHOOLS

- **Hermleigh Ind School Dist** PID: 01050046 325/863-2451
  8010 Business 84 H, Hermleigh 79526 Fax 325/863-2713

Schools: 1 \ *Teachers:* 21 \ *Students:* 250 \ *Special Ed Students:* 14 \ *LEP Students:* 12 \ *College-Bound:* 75% \ *Ethnic:* African American 2%, Hispanic 37%, Caucasian 61% \ *Exp:* $502 (High) \ *Poverty:* 13% \ *Title I:* $36,658 \ *Open-Close:* 08/15 - 05/25 \ *DTBP:* $358 (High)

Cathy Petty 1
Alan Culp 3*
Cheyenne Thomas 57,59*
Roy Gill 67
Marci Beard 2
Amber Palmer 8*
Christina Espinoza 60*
Heath Gibson 73

Public Schs..Principal	Grd	Prgm	Enr/#Cls	SN	
Hermleigh Sch 8010 Business 84 H, Hermleigh 79526 Amber Palmer	PK-12	TV	250 16	54%	325/863-2451

- **Ira Ind School Dist** PID: 01050072 325/573-2628
  6190 W FM 1606, Ira 79527 Fax 325/573-0705

Schools: 1 \ *Teachers:* 22 \ *Students:* 270 \ *Special Ed Students:* 20 \ *LEP Students:* 7 \ *College-Bound:* 90% \ *Ethnic:* Hispanic 23%, Caucasian 77% \ *Exp:* $540 (High) \ *Poverty:* 12% \ *Title I:* $13,111 \ *Open-Close:* 08/21 - 05/22 \ *DTBP:* $350 (High)

Brian Patterson 1
Brian Patterson 6*
Bobbie Hale 8,11,57,69,270,271,273*
Dave Hanes 16,73,295*
Dirk Dunn 67
Keeli Hines 2
Kati Patrick 7*
Dale Jones 13*
Leo Sellers 27*
Lacee Cox 88*

Public Schs..Principal	Grd	Prgm	Enr/#Cls	SN	
Ira Sch 6190 W FM 1606, Ira 79527 Dale Jones	K-12	V	270 18	27%	325/573-2628

- **Snyder Ind School Dist** PID: 01050101 325/574-8900
  2901 37th St, Snyder 79549 Fax 325/573-9025

Schools: 4 \ *Teachers:* 194 \ *Students:* 2,650 \ *Special Ed Students:* 263 \ *LEP Students:* 244 \ *Ethnic:* Asian 1%, African American 2%, Hispanic 63%, Native American: 1%, Caucasian 33% \ *Exp:* $369 (High) \ *Poverty:* 24% \ *Title I:* $857,637 \ *Special Education:* $714,000 \ *Open-Close:* 08/15 - 05/21 \ *DTBP:* $158 (High)

Eddie Bland 1
Clay Cade 3
Rachael McClain 8*
Rosie Lopez 57
Ralph Ramon 67
Morgan Preston 2
Wes Wood 6
Kathy Scott 11,79
Cheryl Bricken 58*
Jeff McGinnis 73*

Public Schs..Principal	Grd	Prgm	Enr/#Cls	SN	
Snyder High Sch 3801 Austin Ave, Snyder 79549 Janell Martin	9-12	V	729 45	38%	325/574-8800 Fax 325/573-9500
Snyder Intermediate Sch 3301 El Paso Ave, Snyder 79549 Jerry Russell	4-5	T	384	59%	325/574-8650 Fax 325/574-6024
Snyder Junior High Sch 3300 El Paso St, Snyder 79549 Rebecca Mebane	6-8	TV	622 30	51%	325/574-8700 Fax 325/574-6024
Snyder Primary Sch 3601 El Paso Ave, Snyder 79549 Canita Rhodes	1-3	T	1,051 26	58%	325/574-8600 Fax 325/573-0342

---

79 Student Personnel
80 Driver Ed/Safety
81 Gifted/Talented
82 Video Services
83 Substance Abuse Prev
84 Erate
85 AIDS Education
88 Alternative/At Risk
89 Multi-Cultural Curriculum
90 Social Work
91 Safety/Security
92 Magnet School
93 Parental Involvement
95 Tech Prep Program
97 Chief Information Officer
98 Chief Technology Officer
270 Character Education
271 Migrant Education
273 Teacher Mentor
274 Before/After Sch
275 Response To Intervention
277 Remedial Math K-12
280 Literacy Coach
285 STEM
286 Digital Learning
288 Common Core Standards
294 Accountability
295 Network System
296 Title II Programs
297 Webmaster
298 Grant Writer/Ptnrships
750 Chief Innovation Officer
751 Chief of Staff
752 Social Emotional Learning

Other School Types
Ⓐ = Alternative School
Ⓒ = Charter School
Ⓜ = Magnet School
Ⓨ = Year-Round School

School Programs
A = Alternative Program
G = Adult Classes
M = Magnet Program
T = Title I Schoolwide
V = Career & Tech Ed Programs

Social Media
 = Facebook
 = Twitter

New Schools are shaded
New Superintendents and Principals are bold
Personnel with email addresses are underscored

Shackelford County

Market Data Retrieval

SHACKELFORD COUNTY

SHACKELFORD PUBLIC SCHOOLS

- **Albany Ind School Dist** PID: 01050216   325/762-2823
  501 E S 1st St, Albany 76430   Fax 325/762-3876

  Schools: 2 \ *Teachers:* 44 \ *Students:* 500 \ *Special Ed Students:* 44 \ *LEP Students:* 5 \ *College-Bound:* 99% \ *Ethnic:* African American 2%, Hispanic 17%, Caucasian 81% \ *Exp:* $722 (High) \ *Poverty:* 17% \ *Title I:* $99,071 \ *Open-Close:* 08/15 - 05/20 \ *DTBP:* $350 (High) \ 📧

Jonathan Scott 1	Angelyn Faith 2
Debra Boyett 4*	Ryder Peacock 6*
Edward Morales 10*	Morgan Whitley 15
Jenny Scott 16,38*	Robert Montgomery 67
Dan Key 73*	

Public Schs..Principal	Grd	Prgm	Enr/#Cls	SN	
Albany Jr Sr High Sch 501 E S 1st St, Albany 76430 Edward Morales	7-12	TV	224 50	33%	325/762-3974 Fax 325/762-3850
Nancy Smith Elem Sch 741 Griffin Rd, Albany 76430 **John Gallagher**	PK-6	T	284 27	43%	325/762-3384 Fax 325/762-3070 📧

- **Moran Ind School Dist** PID: 01050242   325/945-3101
  900 Main St, Moran 76464   Fax 325/945-2741

  Schools: 1 \ *Teachers:* 17 \ *Students:* 120 \ *Special Ed Students:* 17 \ *College-Bound:* 50% \ *Ethnic:* Hispanic 8%, Caucasian 92% \ *Exp:* $324 (High) \ *Poverty:* 32% \ *Title I:* $31,237 \ *Open-Close:* 08/26 - 05/29 \ *DTBP:* $327 (High)

Danny Freeman 1,11	Diedre Cauble 2
Charles Russek 3,5*	Tiffany Cambell 4
Lee Lewis 6*	Kim Holland 8,69,288*
Elizabeth Walls 58,83*	Jimmie Roller 67
Anita Wheat 73,295*	Jeannie Tencate 271*

Public Schs..Principal	Grd	Prgm	Enr/#Cls	SN	
Moran Sch 900 Main St, Moran 76464 **Danny Freeman**	PK-12	TV	120 12	81%	325/945-3101

SHELBY COUNTY

SHELBY PUBLIC SCHOOLS

- **Center Ind School Dist** PID: 01050278   936/598-5642
  107 PR 605, Center 75935   Fax 936/598-1515

  Schools: 6 \ *Teachers:* 207 \ *Students:* 2,600 \ *Special Ed Students:* 312 \ *LEP Students:* 716 \ *College-Bound:* 56% \ *Ethnic:* Asian 2%, African American 21%, Hispanic 44%, Caucasian 33% \ *Exp:* $446 (High) \ *Poverty:* 28% \ *Title I:* $854,152 \ *Special Education:* $612,000 \ *Open-Close:* 08/14 - 05/22 \ *DTBP:* $158 (High)

Dr James Hockenberry 1	Betty McDaniel 2,19
Rick Baker 3,5	Tina Byrnes 4
Scott Ponder 6	Jennifer Guillory 11,37,57,271*
Carey Herew 34,58	Sommer Herndon 38,69*
Matthew Mettauer 67	Holly Mikesh 68
Richard Miller 73,76	Jeremy Wallace 88
Teresa Richard 275	

Public Schs..Principal	Grd	Prgm	Enr/#Cls	SN	
Center Elem Sch 621 Rough Rider Dr, Center 75935 Shelly Norvell	1-3	T	568 19	84%	936/598-3625 Fax 936/598-1507
Center High Sch 658 Rough Rider Dr, Center 75935 Matthew Gregory	9-12	ATV	678 70	74%	936/598-6173 Fax 936/598-1527
Center Intermediate Sch 624 Malone Dr, Center 75935 **Lee Masterson**	4-5	T	388 20	81%	936/598-6148 Fax 936/598-1555
Center Middle Sch 302 Kennedy St, Center 75935 Jake Henson	6-8	TV	541 65	78%	936/598-5619 Fax 936/598-1534
Ⓐ Center Roughrider Academy 658 Rough Rider Dr, Center 75935 Jill Gaston	6-12		61		936/598-1540 Fax 936/591-8374
F L Moffett Primary Sch 294 Stadium Dr, Center 75935 Inez Hughes	PK-K	T	434 36	83%	936/598-6266 Fax 936/598-1545

- **Excelsior Ind School Dist** PID: 01050321   936/598-5866
  11270 State Highway 7W, Center 75935   Fax 936/598-2076

  Schools: 1 \ *Teachers:* 11 \ *Students:* 90 \ *Special Ed Students:* 18 \ *LEP Students:* 3 \ *Ethnic:* African American 1%, Hispanic 7%, Caucasian 92% \ *Exp:* $595 (High) \ *Poverty:* 27% \ *Title I:* $41,484 \ *Open-Close:* 08/26 - 05/28 \ *DTBP:* $335 (High)

Wayne Mason 1	Terre Noble 2
Sonya Nutt 6,83*	Judy Andrews 9,11,69
Barbara Scates 16,73,295,297*	Rebecca Adkison 34*
Benny Russell 67	

Public Schs..Principal	Grd	Prgm	Enr/#Cls	SN	
Excelsior Elem Sch 11270 State Highway 7W, Center 75935 Johnny Lewis	PK-8	T	90 10	58%	936/598-5866

1	Superintendent	8	Curric/Instruct K-12	19	Chief Financial Officer	29	Family/Consumer Science	39	Social Studies K-12	49	English/Lang Arts Elem	59	Special Education Elem	69	Academic Assessment
2	Bus/Finance/Purchasing	9	Curric/Instruct Elem	20	Art K-12	30	Adult Education	40	Social Studies Elem	50	English/Lang Arts Sec	60	Special Education Sec	70	Research/Development
3	Buildings And Grounds	10	Curric/Instruct Sec	21	Art Elem	31	Career/Sch-to-Work K-12	41	Social Studies Sec	51	Reading K-12	61	Foreign/World Lang K-12	71	Public Information
4	Food Service	11	Federal Program	22	Art Sec	32	Career/Sch-to-Work Elem	42	Science K-12	52	Reading Elem	62	Foreign/World Lang Elem	72	Summer School
5	Transportation	12	Title I	23	Music K-12	33	Career/Sch-to-Work Sec	43	Science Elem	53	Reading Sec	63	Foreign/World Lang Sec	73	Instructional Tech
6	Athletic	13	Title V	24	Music Elem	34	Early Childhood Ed	44	Science Sec	54	Remedial Reading K-12	64	Religious Education K-12	74	Inservice Training
7	Health Services	15	Asst Superintendent	25	Music Sec	35	Health/Phys Education	45	Math K-12	55	Remedial Reading Elem	65	Religious Education Elem	75	Marketing/Distributive
		16	Instructional Media Svcs	26	Business Education	36	Guidance Services K-12	46	Math Elem	56	Remedial Reading Sec	66	Religious Education Sec	76	Info Systems
		17	Chief Operations Officer	27	Career & Tech Ed	37	Guidance Services Elem	47	Math Sec	57	Bilingual/ELL	67	School Board President	77	Psychological Assess
		18	Chief Academic Officer	28	Technology Education	38	Guidance Services Sec	48	English/Lang Arts K-12	58	Special Education K-12	68	Teacher Personnel	78	Affirmative Action

Texas School Directory
Shelby County

- **Joaquin Ind School Dist** PID: 01050357 936/269-3128
  11109 US Highway 84 E, Joaquin 75954   Fax 936/269-3615

Schools: 3 \ **Teachers:** 56 \ **Students:** 650 \ **Special Ed Students:** 77 \ **LEP Students:** 51 \ **College-Bound:** 56% \ **Ethnic:** African American 6%, Hispanic 16%, Caucasian 78% \ **Exp:** $472 (High) \ **Poverty:** 27% \ **Title I:** $242,456 \ **Special Education:** $157,000 \ **Open-Close:** 08/16 - 05/22 \ **DTBP:** $344 (High)

Ryan Fuller ...1	Joel Bumback ...2,12
Mark Bonner ...3*	Judy Strong ...4*
Rodny Prnka ...5*	Steven McCann ...6*
Sherri Scruggs ...8*	Kathy Carrington ...11,58*
Justin Wilburn ...16,73,76,295	Lisa Barton ...16*
Ashley Rambin ...36,57,271*	Chrisco Bragg ...67
Donna Vergo ...68	

Public Schs..Principal	Grd	Prgm	Enr/#Cls	SN	
Joaquin Elem Sch 120 Southern St, Joaquin 75954 Sherry Scruggs	PK-5	T	346 26	64%	936/269-3128 Fax 936/269-3324
Joaquin High Sch 10901 US Highway 84 E, Joaquin 75954 Rodny Prnka	9-12	TV	201 50	55%	936/269-3128 Fax 936/269-9123
Joaquin Junior High Sch 10901 US Highway 84 E, Joaquin 75954 Terri Gray	6-8	TV	171 15	58%	936/269-3128 Fax 936/269-9123

- **Shelbyville Ind School Dist** PID: 01050395 936/598-2641
  5322 State Highway 87 S, Shelbyville 75973   Fax 936/598-6842

Schools: 3 \ **Teachers:** 66 \ **Students:** 790 \ **Special Ed Students:** 84 \ **LEP Students:** 35 \ **Ethnic:** Asian 1%, African American 21%, Hispanic 13%, Caucasian 65% \ **Exp:** $357 (High) \ **Poverty:** 30% \ **Title I:** $253,987 \ **Special Education:** $164,000 \ **Open-Close:** 08/20 - 05/20 \ **DTBP:** $339 (High)

Dr Ray West ...1	Joyce Dean ...2
Terry Walton ...3*	Brenda Hogue ...4*
Thomas Swearengen ...5,8,83,85,88*	David Bendon ...6
Jeane Taylor ...7*	Jill Baty ...11,15,270,271,274
Catherine Duvon ...13,57,58*	Kaelee Fallin ...27
Patricia Bays ...31*	Sonya Parker ...39*
Etola Jones ...67	Mike Furlow ...69,273*
Scott Gilchrist ...73*	

Public Schs..Principal	Grd	Prgm	Enr/#Cls	SN	
S W Carter Elem Sch 343 Farm Rd 417 W, Shelbyville 75973 Mike Furlow	PK-5		390 25		936/598-7363 Fax 936/598-6843
Shelbyville High Sch 5322 State Highway 87 S, Shelbyville 75973 Mario Osby	9-12	V	228 7		936/598-7323 Fax 936/598-3868
Shelbyville Middle Sch 343 Farm Rd 417 W, Shelbyville 75973 Thomas Swearengen	6-8	TV	177 14	68%	936/598-5146 Fax 936/598-3830

- **Tenaha Ind School Dist** PID: 01050424 936/248-5000
  138 College St, Tenaha 75974   Fax 936/248-3902

Schools: 1 \ **Teachers:** 42 \ **Students:** 570 \ **Special Ed Students:** 74 \ **LEP Students:** 106 \ **College-Bound:** 66% \ **Ethnic:** African American 28%, Hispanic 40%, Caucasian 32% \ **Exp:** $538 (High) \ **Poverty:** 32% \ **Title I:** $206,102 \ **Special Education:** $106,000 \ **Open-Close:** 08/19 - 05/28 \ **DTBP:** $311 (High) \ [f]

Scott Tyner ...1	Emily LeMoine ...2,294*
Joshua Campbell ...3*	Melanie Duncan ...4*
Terry Bowlin ...5,298*	Greg Jenkins ...6*
Stella Baker ...7*	Karen Fallin ...8,13,36,83,88,270*
Martha Boren ...8,11,69*	Linda Jacobs-Worrell ...9*
Ray Jackson ...16,73,295*	Laurie Sisk ...57,271
Judy Monroe ...58*	Aaron Roland ...67
Emily Bowlin ...68	

Public Schs..Principal	Grd	Prgm	Enr/#Cls	SN	
Tenaha Sch 1 Tiger Drive, Tenaha 75974 Linda Jacobs-Worrell	PK-12	TV	570 18	91%	936/248-5000

- **Timpson Ind School Dist** PID: 01050450 936/254-2463
  836 Bear Dr, Timpson 75975   Fax 936/254-3878

Schools: 3 \ **Teachers:** 55 \ **Students:** 630 \ **Special Ed Students:** 85 \ **LEP Students:** 34 \ **College-Bound:** 90% \ **Ethnic:** African American 24%, Hispanic 17%, Caucasian 59% \ **Exp:** $517 (High) \ **Poverty:** 36% \ **Title I:** $386,400 \ **Special Education:** $178,000 \ **Open-Close:** 08/27 - 05/25 \ **DTBP:** $347 (High) \ [f] [t]

Dr Mid Johnson ...1	Janie Raines ...2
Ginger Lee ...4	Fred Wilcox ...5
Kerry Therwhanger ...6	Brittany Kimbro ...7
Dana Evans ...58	George Duke ...67
Dale Flournoy ...73	Kim Graham ...91
Calvin Smith ...285*	

Public Schs..Principal	Grd	Prgm	Enr/#Cls	SN	
Timpson Elem Sch 836 Bear Dr, Timpson 75975 DeWayne Carrington	PK-5	T	304 20	73%	936/254-2462 Fax 936/254-3261
Timpson High Sch 836 Bear Dr, Timpson 75975 Ronald Lindgren	9-12	TV	182 20	57%	936/254-3125 Fax 936/254-3263
Timpson Middle Sch 836 Bear Dr, Timpson 75975 Calvin Smith	6-8	T	142	62%	936/254-2078 Fax 936/254-2355

SHELBY PRIVATE SCHOOLS

Private Schs..Principal	Grd	Prgm	Enr/#Cls	SN	
Central Baptist Christian Sch 909 Cora St, Center 75935 Danny Dodson	PK-12		42 9		936/598-3642 Fax 936/598-9175

79	Student Personnel	91	Safety/Security	275	Response To Intervention	298	Grant Writer/Ptnrships
80	Driver Ed/Safety	92	Magnet School	277	Remedial Math K-12	750	Chief Innovation Officer
81	Gifted/Talented	93	Parental Involvement	280	Literacy Coach	751	Chief of Staff
82	Video Services	95	Tech Prep Program	285	STEM	752	Social Emotional Learning
83	Substance Abuse Prev	97	Chief Information Officer	286	Digital Learning		
84	Erate	98	Chief Technology Officer	288	Common Core Standards		
85	AIDS Accountability	270	Character Education	294	Accountability		
88	Alternative/At Risk	271	Migrant Education	295	Network System		
89	Multi-Cultural Curriculum	273	Teacher Mentor	296	Title II Programs		
90	Social Work	274	Before/After Sch	297	Webmaster		

School Programs
A = Alternative Program
G = Adult Classes
M = Magnet Program
T = Title I Schoolwide
V = Career & Tech Ed Programs

Other School Types
Ⓐ = Alternative School
Ⓒ = Charter School
Ⓜ = Magnet School
Ⓨ = Year-Round School

Social Media
[f] = Facebook
[t] = Twitter

New Schools are shaded
New Superintendents and Principals are bold
Personnel with email addresses are underscored

Sherman County

Market Data Retrieval

SHERMAN COUNTY

SHERMAN PUBLIC SCHOOLS

- **Stratford Ind School Dist** PID: 01050486 806/366-3300
  503 8th St, Stratford 79084 Fax 806/366-3304

Schools: 3 \ *Teachers:* 59 \ *Students:* 585 \ *Special Ed Students:* 48 \ *LEP Students:* 75 \ *College-Bound:* 80% \ *Ethnic:* African American 1%, Hispanic 66%, Caucasian 33% \ *Exp:* $583 (High) \ *Poverty:* 16% \ *Title I:* $97,186 \ *Open-Close:* 08/20 - 05/21 \ *DTBP:* $345 (High)

Mike Dominquez 1,73,83	Lynette Kautz 2,11,84,296			
Frank Castaneda 3	Charlotte Moczygemba 4			
Jeff Kautz 5	Matt Lovrn 6*			
Doug Rawlins 8,15	Ashley Lavake 12			
Mary Rawlins 13	Misti McBryde 36,57,58,69,79,85			
Bryan Clift 67	Beatrice Coreo 271			

Public Schs..Principal	Grd	Prgm	Enr/#Cls	SN	
Mary Allen Elem Sch 501 N Shirley Ave, Stratford 79084 Jennifer Deanda	PK-4	T	255 25	61%	806/366-3340 Fax 806/366-3343
Stratford High Sch 503 8th St, Stratford 79084 Phillip Hanna	9-12	AGTV	152 30	51%	806/366-3330
Stratford Junior High Sch 503 8th St, Stratford 79084 Clint Seward	5-8	T	183 30	60%	806/366-3320 Fax 806/366-3307

- **Texhoma Ind School Dist** PID: 01050527 806/827-7400
  402 W Denver St, Texhoma 73960 Fax 806/827-7657

Schools: 1 \ *Teachers:* 8 \ *Students:* 115 \ *Special Ed Students:* 19 \ *LEP Students:* 68 \ *Ethnic:* Hispanic 52%, Native American: 1%, Caucasian 47% \ *Exp:* $216 (Med) \ *Poverty:* 7% \ *Open-Close:* 08/15 - 05/21 \ *DTBP:* $367 (High)

James Mireles 1	Danielle Harland 2,71
Alejo Ortega 3	Billie Hyde 4*
Kayla Yates 11,73,83,275,286,288,296*	Cody Cartwright 67
Ofelia Porras 271*	Jim Pierce 295

Public Schs..Principal	Grd	Prgm	Enr/#Cls	SN	
Texhoma Elem Sch 402 W Denver St, Texhoma 73960 Kayla Yates	PK-4	T	115 16	67%	806/827-7400

SMITH COUNTY

SMITH PUBLIC SCHOOLS

- **Arp Ind School Dist** PID: 01050541 903/859-8482
  101 Toney Dr, Arp 75750 Fax 903/859-2621

Schools: 3 \ *Teachers:* 76 \ *Students:* 900 \ *Special Ed Students:* 74 \ *LEP Students:* 18 \ *College-Bound:* 52% \ *Ethnic:* Asian 1%, African American 15%, Hispanic 13%, Caucasian 71% \ *Exp:* $426 (High) \ *Poverty:* 19% \ *Title I:* $222,338 \ *Open-Close:* 08/15 - 05/20 \ *DTBP:* $341 (High)

John Arrington 1	Daniella Sanders 2
Randal Wilson 3,5	Kim Wood 4*
Dale Irwin 6*	Shelby Brown 7,85*
Lana Brady 8,11,74,273*	Dr Joy Rousseau 16,73,270,286,295*
Donna Lowery 38*	Lara Parker 38,57,81*
Sanya Burnette 58	Ernest Stroupe 67

Public Schs..Principal	Grd	Prgm	Enr/#Cls	SN	
Arp Elem Sch 16438 Co Rd 294, Arp 75750 Stephanie Schminkey	PK-5	T	443 21	60%	903/859-4650 Fax 903/859-3683
Arp High Sch 101 Toney Dr, Arp 75750 Bryan Hurst	9-12	TV	266 25	51%	903/859-4917 Fax 903/859-1541
Arp Junior High Sch 105 School St, Arp 75750 Bryan Hurst	6-8	T	191 20	60%	903/859-4936 Fax 903/859-3980

- **Bullard Ind School Dist** PID: 01050577 903/894-6639
  1426B S Houston St, Bullard 75757 Fax 903/894-9291

Schools: 6 \ *Teachers:* 190 \ *Students:* 2,500 \ *Special Ed Students:* 287 \ *LEP Students:* 57 \ *Ethnic:* African American 4%, Hispanic 7%, Caucasian 88% \ *Exp:* $366 (High) \ *Poverty:* 14% \ *Title I:* $339,739 \ *Open-Close:* 08/21 - 05/22 \ *DTBP:* $341 (High)

Todd Schneider 1	Gloria West 2
Billy Hawkins 3	Lee Sleeper 3,73*
Stephanie Hayes 4	Dalton Smith 5
Dalton Smith 5*	Scott Callaway 6
Amy Bickersfaff 8	Jan Hill 8,11,88,271
Carol Martin 16*	Lisa Williams 58
Jason Campbell 67	Jodie Albritton 69*
Kory Prince 73	

Public Schs..Principal	Grd	Prgm	Enr/#Cls	SN	
Bullard Early Childhood Center 318 Schoolhouse Rd, Bullard 75757 Amanda Goode	PK-K		249		903/894-6389
Bullard Elem Sch 2008 Panther Crossing, Bullard 75757 Jenny Kasson	3-4	T	385 41	33%	903/894-2930 Fax 903/894-2931
Bullard High Sch 1426 S Houston St, Bullard 75757 Mr Blain	9-12		773 37	28%	903/894-3272 Fax 903/894-3051
Bullard Intermediate Sch 218 Schoolhouse Rd, Bullard 75757 Jodie Albritton	5-6	T	378 13	30%	903/894-6793 Fax 903/894-3982

1 Superintendent	8 Curric/Instruct K-12	19 Chief Financial Officer	29 Family/Consumer Science	39 Social Studies K-12	49 English/Lang Arts Elem	59 Special Education Elem	69 Academic Assessment
2 Bus/Finance/Purchasing	9 Curric/Instruct Elem	20 Art K-12	30 Adult Education	40 Social Studies Elem	50 English/Lang Arts Sec	60 Special Education Sec	70 Research/Development
3 Buildings And Grounds	10 Curric/Instruct Sec	21 Art Elem	31 Career/Sch-to-Work K-12	41 Social Studies Sec	51 Reading K-12	61 Foreign/World Lang K-12	71 Public Information
4 Food Service	11 Federal Program	22 Art Sec	32 Career/Sch-to-Work Elem	42 Science K-12	52 Reading Elem	62 Foreign/World Lang Elem	72 Summer School
5 Transportation	12 Title I	23 Music K-12	33 Career/Sch-to-Work Sec	43 Science Elem	53 Reading Sec	63 Foreign/World Lang Sec	73 Instructional Tech
6 Athletic	13 Title V	24 Music Elem	34 Early Childhood Ed	44 Science Sec	54 Remedial Reading K-12	64 Religious Education K-12	74 Inservice Training
7 Health Services	15 Asst Superintendent	25 Music Sec	35 Health/Phys Education	45 Math K-12	55 Remedial Reading Elem	65 Religious Education Elem	75 Marketing/Distributive
	16 Instructional Media Svcs	26 Business Education	36 Guidance Services K-12	46 Math Elem	56 Remedial Reading Sec	66 Religious Education Sec	76 Info Systems
	17 Chief Operations Officer	27 Career & Tech Ed	37 Guidance Services Elem	47 Math Sec	57 Bilingual/ELL	67 School Board President	77 Psychological Assess
	18 Chief Academic Officer	28 Technology Education	38 Guidance Services Sec	48 English/Lang Arts K-12	58 Special Education K-12	68 Teacher Personnel	78 Affirmative Action

Texas School Directory — Smith County

Bullard Middle Sch	7-8		392	33%	903/894-6533
909 W Main St, Bullard 75757			32		Fax 903/894-7592
Kenley Dover					
Bullard Primary Sch	1-2	T	383	37%	903/894-2890
2016 Panther Crossing, Bullard 75757					Fax 903/894-2893
Kim Murphy					

E J Moss Intermediate Sch	4-6	T	956	44%	903/881-4200
411 Eagle Spirit Dr, Lindale 75771			24		Fax 903/881-4201
Kyle Wright					
Early Childhood Center	PK-K	T	432	63%	903/881-4400
201 Stadium Dr, Lindale 75771			21		Fax 903/881-4401
Kaela Deslatte					
Lindale High Sch	9-12	TV	1,156	37%	903/881-4050
920 E Hubbard St, Lindale 75771			80		Fax 903/882-2813
Jeremy Chilek					
Lindale Junior High Sch	7-8	T	616	44%	903/881-4150
15000 County Rd 463, Lindale 75771			40		Fax 903/882-2842
Jeremy Chilek					
Velma Penny Elem Sch	1-3	T	453	50%	903/881-4250
1000 Mt Silvan Hwy, Lindale 75771			26		Fax 903/881-4251
Monica Moore					

• Chapel Hill Ind School Dist PID: 01050606
11134 County Road 2249, Tyler 75707
903/566-2441 Fax 903/566-8935

Schools: 5 \ *Teachers:* 241 \ *Students:* 3,513 \ *Special Ed Students:* 331 \ *LEP Students:* 690 \ *College-Bound:* 23% \ *Ethnic:* Asian 1%, African American 18%, Hispanic 48%, Caucasian 33% \ *Exp:* $439 (High) \ *Poverty:* 19% \ *Title I:* $867,421 \ *Special Education:* $623,000 \ *Open-Close:* 08/20 - 05/28 \ *DTBP:* $222 (High)

LaMond Dean 1
Sharon Deason 2
Jason Hooker 6*
Lisa Krumm 10*
April Munoz 57
Martin Ibarra 67
Chuck Munoz 73,84,95
Tony Gibbs 295
Lisa Lemon 2
Dean Rodgers 3,4,5,91
Helyn Morris 9*
Joe Hall 34,58,90
Joe Bob 58
Teresa Whitaker 68
Shielda Divine 76

Public Schs..Principal	Grd	Prgm	Enr/#Cls	SN
Chapel Hill High Sch 13172 State Highway 64 E, Tyler 75707 William Houff	9-12	ATV	1,054 90	68% 903/566-2311 Fax 903/565-5155
Chapel Hill Middle Sch 13174 State Highway 64 E, Tyler 75707 Matt Strode	6-8	AT	799 55	76% 903/566-1491 Fax 903/565-5125
Jackson Elem Sch 16406 FM 2767, Tyler 75705 Jill Clay	PK-4	T	411 24	90% 903/566-3411 Fax 903/565-5185
Kissam Elem Sch 12800 State Highway 64 E, Tyler 75707 Charla McClure	PK-5	T	739 30	82% 903/566-8334 Fax 903/565-5195
Ⓜ Wise Elem Fine Arts Magnet Sch 10659 State Highway 64 E, Tyler 75707 Cyndy Reagan	PK-5	T	510 30	71% 903/566-2271 Fax 903/565-5135

• Lindale Ind School Dist PID: 01050656
505 Pierce St, Lindale 75771
903/881-4000 Fax 903/881-4004

Schools: 6 \ *Teachers:* 277 \ *Students:* 4,200 \ *Special Ed Students:* 435 \ *LEP Students:* 150 \ *College-Bound:* 70% \ *Ethnic:* Asian 1%, African American 7%, Hispanic 17%, Native American: 1%, Caucasian 75% \ *Exp:* $337 (High) \ *Poverty:* 15% \ *Title I:* $660,148 \ *Special Education:* $740,000 \ *Open-Close:* 08/19 - 05/29 \ *DTBP:* $181 (High)

Stan Surratt 1
Ed Rhinehart 3
Cindy McClenny 4
Mike Maddox 6,35,83
Jane Silvey 8,74,273
Lori Anderson 11
Brent Berryman 27
Deb Kellas 57*
Mike Combs 67
Randy Anderson 73,84,295
Michelle Tate 2
Jamie Holder 3,15,76
Pete Ridge 5*
Traci Fountain 7*
Summer Carlton 8
Rhonda Walker 16*
David Ramsey 36,69*
Christy Clouse 58
Courtney Sanguinetti 71
Joey King 91

Public Schs..Principal	Grd	Prgm	Enr/#Cls	SN
College Street Elem Sch 106 N College St, Lindale 75771 Ashley Smith	1-3	T	462 23	46% 903/881-4350 Fax 903/881-4351

• Troup Ind School Dist PID: 01050709
201 N Carolina St, Troup 75789
903/842-3067 Fax 903/842-4563

Schools: 3 \ *Teachers:* 81 \ *Students:* 1,081 \ *Special Ed Students:* 74 \ *LEP Students:* 46 \ *College-Bound:* 52% \ *Ethnic:* Asian 1%, African American 13%, Hispanic 13%, Caucasian 73% \ *Exp:* $486 (High) \ *Poverty:* 20% \ *Title I:* $237,232 \ *Special Education:* $5,000 \ *Open-Close:* 08/14 - 05/22 \ *DTBP:* $99 (Med) \

Tammy Jones 1
Teresa Gillespie 4
John Eastman 6*
David Smith 8,11,57,69,83,88,273
Karen Agnew 33*
Judy Daniel 274*
Lisa White 2,68
Preston Lindsey 5
Laurie Larison 7*
Shannon Capps 16,73*
Shane Jasper 67

Public Schs..Principal	Grd	Prgm	Enr/#Cls	SN
Troup Elem Sch 201 E Bryant St, Troup 75789 Amy Ledford	PK-5	T	510 40	60% 903/842-3071 Fax 903/842-3197
Troup High Sch 927 Arp Dr, Troup 75789 Bobby Dyess	9-12	ATV	324 25	47% 903/842-3065 Fax 903/842-5199
Troup Middle Sch 817 Arp Dr, Troup 75789 Stephen Cooksey	6-8	T	247 30	55% 903/842-3081 Fax 903/842-2866

• Tyler Ind School Dist PID: 01050747
1319 Earl Campbell Pkwy, Tyler 75701
903/262-1000 Fax 903/262-1174

Schools: 30 \ *Teachers:* 1,237 \ *Students:* 18,600 \ *Special Ed Students:* 1,240 \ *LEP Students:* 4,050 \ *College-Bound:* 63% \ *Ethnic:* Asian 2%, African American 29%, Hispanic 46%, Caucasian 23% \ *Exp:* $311 (High) \ *Poverty:* 19% \ *Title I:* $6,061,465 \ *Special Education:* $3,258,000 \ *Open-Close:* 08/19 - 05/22 \ *DTBP:* $184 (High) \

Dr Marty Crawford 1
Tim Loper 3
John Bagert 5
Rachel Barber 7
Shauna Hittle 9,37
Vernora Jones 12
Ron Jones 15,68,751
Leslie George 34,58
Susan Gronow 39
Laura Cano 68
John Johnson 79
Danny Brown 83,91
Tosha Bjork 2,19
Victor Olivares 4
Greg Priest 6,85
Dr Christy Hanson 8,15
Stacy Miles 11*
Rawly Sanchez 15
Sandra Newton 20,23
Jennifer Jones 36
Wade Watsmen 67
Johnita Ward 69,294
Nicole Schumer 81
Joseph Jacks 84

79	Student Personnel	91	Safety/Security	275	Response To Intervention	298	Grant Writer/Ptnrships
80	Driver Ed/Safety	92	Magnet School	277	Remedial Math K-12	750	Chief Innovation Officer
81	Gifted/Talented	93	Parental Involvement	280	Literacy Coach	751	Chief of Staff
82	Video Services	95	Tech Prep Program	285	STEM	752	Social Emotional Learning
83	Substance Abuse Prev	97	Chief Information Officer	286	Digital Learning		
84	Erate	98	Chief Technology Officer	288	Common Core Standards		
85	AIDS Education	270	Character Education	294	Accountability		
88	Alternative/At Risk	271	Migrant Education	295	Network System		
89	Multi-Cultural Curriculum	273	Teacher Mentor	296	Title II Programs		
90	Social Work	274	Before/After Sch	297	Webmaster		

School Programs
A = Alternative Program
G = Adult Classes
M = Magnet Program
T = Title I Schoolwide
V = Career & Tech Ed Programs

Other School Types
Ⓐ = Alternative School
Ⓒ = Charter School
Ⓜ = Magnet School
Ⓨ = Year-Round School

Social Media
 = Facebook
 = Twitter

New Schools are shaded
New Superintendents and Principals are bold
Personnel with email addresses are underscored

Smith County

Market Data Retrieval

Public Schs..Principal	Grd	Prgm	Enr/#Cls	SN	
Austin Elem Sch 1105 W Franklin St, Tyler 75702 Brandy Holland	PK-5	T	430 30	77%	903/262-1765 Fax 903/262-1767
Bell Elem Sch 1409 E Hankerson St, Tyler 75701 Sheri Taylor	PK-5	T	454 28	75%	903/262-1820 Fax 903/262-1821
Birdwell Elem Sch 2010 S Talley Ave, Tyler 75701 Bethany Moody	PK-5	T	545 30	82%	903/262-1870 Fax 903/262-1871
Bonner Elem Sch 235 S Saunders Ave, Tyler 75702 Julie Shumake	PK-5	T	381 31	73%	903/262-1920 Fax 903/262-1921
Ⓜ Boulter Middle Sch 2926 Garden Valley Rd, Tyler 75702 Tara Hinton	6-8	TV	886 50	81%	903/262-1390 Fax 903/262-1392
Caldwell Arts Academy 331 S College Ave, Tyler 75702 Bobby Markle	PK-5	T	649 25	66%	903/262-2250 Fax 903/262-2252
ⓨ Clarkston Elem Sch 2915 Williamsburg Dr, Tyler 75701 Gretchen Nabi	PK-5	MT	355 30	68%	903/262-1980 Fax 903/262-1981
Dixie Elem Sch 213 Patton Ln, Tyler 75704 Joanne Saul	PK-5	T	691 35	63%	903/262-2040 Fax 903/262-2041
Douglas Elem Sch 1525 N Carlyle Ave, Tyler 75702 Christy Roach	PK-5	T	562 33	69%	903/262-2100 Fax 903/262-2101
Dr Bryan C Jack Elem Sch 1900 Balsam Gap, Tyler 75703 Brett Shelby	PK-5		776 30	31%	903/262-3260 Fax 903/262-3329
Griffin Elem Sch 2650 N Broadway Ave, Tyler 75702 Eleanore Malone	PK-5	T	666 35	80%	903/262-2310 Fax 903/262-2311
Hubbard Middle Sch 1300 Hubbard Dr, Tyler 75703 Geoffrey Sherman	6-8	TV	534 58	48%	903/262-1560 Fax 903/262-1566
James S Hogg Middle Sch 920 S Broadway Ave, Tyler 75701 Sheri Taylor	6-8	TV	341 47	92%	903/262-1500 Fax 903/262-1501
John Tyler High Sch 1120 N Northwest Loop 323, Tyler 75702 Chanel Howard-Veazy	9-12	TV	2,154	76%	903/262-2850 Fax 903/593-8655
Jones Elem Sch 3450 Chandler Hwy, Tyler 75702 Natasha Crain	PK-5	T	327 14	68%	903/262-2360 Fax 903/262-2362
Ⓜ Moore Mst Magnet Sch 2101 E Devine St, Tyler 75701 Claude Lane	6-8	TV	849 55	61%	903/262-1640 Fax 903/262-1648
Orr Elem Sch 3350 Pine Haven Rd, Tyler 75702 Steve Young	PK-5	T	645 38	71%	903/262-2400 Fax 903/262-2401
Owens Elem Sch 11780 County Road 168, Tyler 75703 Rachel Sherman	PK-5		584 44	36%	903/262-2175 Fax 903/262-2176
Peete Elem Sch 1511 Bellwood Rd, Tyler 75701 Cassandra Chapa	PK-5	T	294 25	71%	903/262-2460 Fax 903/262-2461
ⓐ Plyler Alternative Educ Sch 807 W Glenwood Blvd, Tyler 75701 Vanessa Choice	1-12		153 18		903/262-3070 Fax 903/262-3078
Ramey Elem Sch 2000 N Forest Ave, Tyler 75702 Cassandra Chapa	PK-5	T	459 35	75%	903/262-2505 Fax 903/262-2506
Rice Elem Sch 5215 Old Bullard Rd, Tyler 75703 Shelly Bosley	PK-5	T	626 38	39%	903/262-2555 Fax 903/262-2556
ⓐ Rise Academy 2800 W Shaw St, Tyler 75701 Dexter Floyd	9-12		142 8		903/262-3040 Fax 903/262-3041
Robert E Lee High Sch 411 E Southeast Loop 323, Tyler 75701 Daniel Crawford	9-12	GTV	2,222	45%	903/262-2625 Fax 903/262-2630
ⓨ St Louis Early Childhood Ctr 2800 Walton Rd, Tyler 75701 Gloria Bell	PK-PK	MT	98 18	97%	903/262-1180 Fax 903/262-1351
ⓨ Three Lakes Middle Sch 2445 Three Lakes Pkwy, Tyler 75703 Christopher Blake	6-8	MTV	883 50	52%	903/952-4400 Fax 903/534-2871
Tyler Career & Technology Ctr 3013 Earl Campbell Pkwy, Tyler 75701 Vanessa Holmes		Voc	300		903/262-1024 Fax 903/526-0889
Tyler Early College High Sch 2800 W Shaw St, Tyler 75701 Delsena Frazier	9-12		279		903/262-3040 Fax 903/262-3041
Wayne D Boshears Center 3450 Chandler Hwy, Tyler 75702 Lora King		Spec	80		903/262-1350 Fax 903/262-1351
Woods Elem Sch 3131 Fry Ave, Tyler 75701 Georgeanna Jones	PK-5	T	677 33	52%	903/262-1280 Fax 903/262-1281

- **UT Tyler University Acad Dist** PID: 12317047   903/730-3988
  3900 University Blvd, Tyler 75799   Fax 903/705-4330

Schools: 3 \ *Students:* 700 \ *College-Bound:* 100% \ *Ethnic:* Asian 4%, African American 6%, Hispanic 16%, Native American: 1%, Caucasian 74% \
Open-Close: 08/19 - 05/29

Dr Joann Simmons 1   Christian Chesnut 2
Juan Cabrera 3   J'Ann Sartain 4
Jaclyn Pedersen 8,298   Kathy Parker 8,18
Becky Rutledge 12   Katie Adams 27
Chelsea Nardozza 58   Dr Yanira Oliveras-Ortiz 67
Brian Weaver 69   Dalton Abrams 73

Public Schs..Principal	Grd	Prgm	Enr/#Cls	SN	
ⓒ UT Tyler Univ Acad-Longview 3201 N Eastman Rd, Longview 75605 Rachel Hawkins	2-11		218		903/663-8219
ⓒ UT Tyler Univ Acad-Palestine 1820 W Spring St, Palestine 75803 Dr Becky Rutlage	2-11		201		903/705-4330
ⓒ UT Tyler Univ Acad-Tyler 3900 University Blvd, Tyler 75799 Aimee Dennis	K-12		281	18%	903/705-4330

- **Whitehouse Ind School Dist** PID: 01050993   903/839-5500
  104 Highway 110 N, Whitehouse 75791   Fax 903/839-5515

Schools: 8 \ *Teachers:* 314 \ *Students:* 4,800 \ *Special Ed Students:* 420 \ *LEP Students:* 157 \ *College-Bound:* 59% \ *Ethnic:* Asian 4%, African American 13%, Hispanic 13%, Caucasian 69% \ *Exp:* $316 (High) \ *Poverty:* 14% \ *Title I:* $864,045 \ *Special Education:* $808,000 \
Open-Close: 08/21 - 05/29 \ *DTBP:* $176 (High)

Chris Moran 1   Clint Ray 2,19
Duane Barber .... 4,5,15*   Theresa Wilson 4
Kevin Whitman 5   Betty Lough 8,11,57,74,85,273,274,296
Susanna Campbell 8   Jackie Vigtema 11,58,271
Travis Bass 15   Sonya Johnston 36,69,83
Kathryn Pratt 39   Ann Butler 42,81
Melanie Tidwell 46   Mary Skinner 47

1 Superintendent	8 Curric/Instruct K-12	19 Chief Financial Officer	29 Family/Consumer Science	39 Social Studies K-12
2 Bus/Finance/Purchasing	9 Curric/Instruct Elem	20 Art K-12	30 Adult Education	40 Social Studies Elem
3 Buildings And Grounds	10 Curric/Instruct Sec	21 Art Elem	31 Career/Sch-to-Work K-12	41 Social Studies Sec
4 Food Service	11 Federal Program	22 Art Sec	32 Career/Sch-to-Work Elem	42 Science K-12
5 Transportation	12 Title I	23 Music K-12	33 Career/Sch-to-Work Sec	43 Science Elem
6 Athletic	13 Title V	24 Music Elem	34 Early Childhood Ed	44 Science Sec
7 Health Services	15 Asst Superintendent	25 Music Sec	35 Health/Phys Education	45 Math K-12
	16 Instructional Media Svcs	26 Business Education	36 Guidance Services K-12	46 Math Elem
	17 Chief Operations Officer	27 Career & Tech Ed	37 Guidance Services Elem	47 Math Sec
	18 Chief Academic Officer	28 Technology Education	38 Guidance Services Sec	48 English/Lang Arts K-12

49 English/Lang Arts Elem	59 Special Education Elem	69 Academic Assessment
50 English/Lang Arts Sec	60 Special Education Sec	70 Research/Development
51 Reading K-12	61 Foreign/World Lang K-12	71 Public Information
52 Reading Elem	62 Foreign/World Lang Elem	72 Summer School
53 Reading Sec	63 Foreign/World Lang Sec	73 Instructional Tech
54 Remedial Reading K-12	64 Religious Education K-12	74 Inservice Training
55 Remedial Reading Elem	65 Religious Education Elem	75 Marketing/Distributive
56 Remedial Reading Sec	66 Religious Education Sec	76 Info Systems
57 Bilingual/ELL	67 School Board President	77 Psychological Assess
58 Special Education K-12	68 Teacher Personnel	78 Affirmative Action

Texas School Directory — Smith County

Denise Martin	50,53	Jaculyn Zigtema	58		
Greg Hood	67	Kelley Vannatta	68		
Monet Brown	68	Scott Starkey	73		
Tony Black	73,95,297				

Public Schs..Principal	Grd	Prgm	Enr/#Cls	SN	
Ⓐ Aim Center 110 Wildcat Dr, Whitehouse 75791 Gary Jacobs	K-12		150 8		903/839-5556 Fax 903/839-5384
Gus Winston Cain Elem Sch 801 State Highway 110 S, Whitehouse 75791 Laurie Blain	PK-5	T	644 32	45%	903/839-5600 Fax 903/839-5604
Higgins Elem Sch 306 Bascom Rd, Whitehouse 75791 Forrest Kaiser	PK-5	T	671 37	55%	903/839-5580 Fax 903/839-5584
Hollaway Sixth Grade Sch 701 E Main St, Whitehouse 75791 Stacy Pineda	6-6	T	389 35	42%	903/839-5656 Fax 903/839-1568
Mozelle Brown Elem Sch 104 State Highway 110 N, Whitehouse 75791 Lisa Schwartz	PK-5	T	283 16	39%	903/839-5610 Fax 903/839-5607
Stanton-Smith Elem Sch 500 Zavala Trl, Whitehouse 75791 Sterling Haskell	PK-5	T	595 30	44%	903/839-5730 Fax 903/839-5744
Whitehouse High Sch 901 E Main St, Whitehouse 75791 Josh Garred	9-12	V	1,378 70	32%	903/839-5551 Fax 903/839-5530
Whitehouse Junior High Sch 108 Wildcat Dr, Whitehouse 75791 William Ripley	7-8	T	754 50	41%	903/839-5590 Fax 903/839-5518

● **Winona Ind School Dist** PID: 01051038   903/939-4000
611 Wildcat Dr, Winona 75792   Fax 903/877-9387

Schools: 4 \ **Teachers:** 72 \ **Students:** 1,050 \ **Special Ed Students:** 122 \ **LEP Students:** 98 \ **College-Bound:** 52% \ **Ethnic:** Asian 1%, African American 18%, Hispanic 30%, Caucasian 51% \ **Exp:** $464 (High) \ **Poverty:** 30% \ **Title I:** $414,340 \ **Special Education:** $165,000 \ **Open-Close:** 08/14 - 05/15 \ **DTBP:** $361 (High)

Cody Mize	1	Sheila Bowie	2,298
Ronnie Marsh	3	Terry Gibbs	3
Angela Nick	4	Carla Davis	5
Keylon Kincade	6	Amanda Marsh	8
Heather Carnes	11,271*	Josh Groves	12,296
Angela Adams	13,58	Jamie McNutt	16,82*
Natasha Martinez	57*	Randy Hawkins	67
Kyle Pugh	73,84	Keith Sparkman	88*
Fabian Arteaga	91	Joshua Snook	91*
Wanda Hensley	271*		

Public Schs..Principal	Grd	Prgm	Enr/#Cls	SN	
Winona Elem Sch 605 Wildcat Dr, Winona 75792 Jason Caldwell	PK-3	T	387 25	74%	903/939-4800 Fax 903/877-2457
Winona High Sch 102 Wildcat Dr, Winona 75792 Damenion Miller	9-12	TV	309 40	62%	903/939-4100 Fax 903/939-4199
Winona Intermediate Sch 611 Wildcat Dr, Winona 75792 Jason Caldwell	4-5	T	160	76%	903/939-4800 Fax 903/877-2457
Winona Middle Sch 611 Wildcat Dr, Winona 75792 Mark McDonald	6-8	T	218 13	66%	903/939-4040 Fax 903/877-9150

SMITH CATHOLIC SCHOOLS

● **Diocese of Tyler Ed Office** PID: 03014660   903/534-1077
1015 E Southeast Loop 323, Tyler 75701   Fax 903/534-1370

Schools: 4 \ **Students:** 1,300

Listing includes only schools located in this county. See District Index for location of Diocesan Offices.

Robin Perry 1,11

Catholic Schs..Principal	Grd	Prgm	Enr/#Cls	SN	
Bishop T K Gorman Cath Sch 1405 E Southeast Loop 323, Tyler 75701 Zachary Allen	6-12		405 30		903/561-2424 Fax 903/561-2645
St Gregory Cathedral Sch 500 S College Ave, Tyler 75702 Robin Perry	PK-5		180 17		903/595-4109 Fax 903/592-8626

SMITH PRIVATE SCHOOLS

Private Schs..Principal	Grd	Prgm	Enr/#Cls	SN	
All Saints Episcopal Sch 2695 S Southwest Loop 323, Tyler 75701 Karla Long	PK-12		700 40		903/579-6000 Fax 903/579-6002
Brook Hill Sch 1051 N Houston St, Bullard 75757 Jonathan Kegler \ Kris Shustella \ Michelle Rozell	PK-12		605		903/894-5000 Fax 903/894-6332
Brook Hills Lower Sch 1010 N Rather St, Bullard 75757 Jonathan Kegler	K-5		240		903/894-4164 Fax 903/894-4674
Christian Heritage Sch 961 County Road 1143, Tyler 75704 Barbara Kilkenny	K-12		100 15		903/593-2702 Fax 903/531-2226
East Texas Christian Academy 2448 Roy Rd, Tyler 75707 Curtis Williams	PK-12		215 23		903/561-8642 Fax 903/561-9620
Good Shepherd Sch 2525 Old Jacksonville Rd, Tyler 75701 Mark Hoyt	PK-12		200		903/592-4045 Fax 903/596-7149
Grace Community Jr Sr High Sch 3001 University Blvd, Tyler 75701 Joe Dirksen \ Brian Benscoter	6-12		582 30		903/566-5661 Fax 903/566-5639
Grace Community Sch 3001 University Blvd, Tyler 75701 Jennifer Dozier	PK-5		427 27		903/593-1977 Fax 903/593-2897
Kingdom Life Academy 7330 S Broadway Ave, Tyler 75703 Joel Inge	8-12		401		903/283-3444
Kings Academy Chrn Sch 7330 S Broadway Ave, Tyler 75703 Erin Baggs	K-12		77 13		903/534-9992 Fax 903/526-7929
Promise Academy 504 W 32nd St, Tyler 75702 Sarah Cumming	K-2		36		903/630-7369
Tyler Adventist Sch 2931 S Southeast Loop 323, Tyler 75701 Dorothy Sauder	K-8		13 2		903/595-6706

79 Student Personnel	91 Safety/Security	275 Response To Intervention	298 Grant Writer/Ptnrships	**School Programs**	**Social Media**
80 Driver Ed/Safety	92 Magnet School	277 Remedial Math K-12	750 Chief Innovation Officer	A = Alternative Program	
81 Gifted/Talented	93 Parental Involvement	280 Literacy Coach	751 Chief of Staff	G = Adult Classes	= Facebook
82 Video Services	95 Tech Prep Program	285 STEM	752 Social Emotional Learning	M = Magnet Program	
83 Substance Abuse Prev	97 Chief Infomation Officer	286 Digital Learning		T = Title I Schoolwide	= Twitter
84 Erate	98 Chief Technology Officer	288 Common Core Standards	**Other School Types**	V = Career & Tech Ed Programs	
85 AIDS Education	270 Character Education	294 Accountability	Ⓐ = Alternative School		
88 Alternative/At Risk	271 Migrant Education	295 Network System	Ⓒ = Charter School	New Schools are shaded	
89 Multi-Cultural Curriculum	273 Teacher Mentor	296 Title II Programs	Ⓜ = Magnet School	New Superintendents and Principals are bold	
90 Social Work	274 Before/After Sch	297 Webmaster	Ⓨ = Year-Round School	Personnel with email addresses are underscored	

Somervell County

Market Data Retrieval

SOMERVELL COUNTY

SOMERVELL PUBLIC SCHOOLS

• **Glen Rose Ind School Dist** PID: 01051088   254/898-3900
1102 Stadium Dr, Glen Rose 76043   Fax 254/897-3651

Schools: 4 \ *Teachers:* 134 \ *Students:* 1,882 \ *Special Ed Students:* 108 \ *LEP Students:* 173 \ *College-Bound:* 80% \ *Ethnic:* Asian 1%, African American 1%, Hispanic 31%, Native American: 1%, Caucasian 66% \ *Exp:* $478 (High) \ *Poverty:* 14% \ *Title I:* $249,699 \ *Open-Close:* 08/14 - 05/21 \ *DTBP:* $342 (High)

Wayne Rotan 1	Kayla O'Quinn 2		
Tommy Corcan 3,5,15,68,83,91	Jill Lawson 4		
Cliff Watkins 6	Susan Wright 8,11,58,275,296,298		
Shelly Statler 16*	Kelley Snodgrass 67		
Doug McClure 73,76,295	Patty Flanary 286		

Public Schs..Principal	Grd	Prgm	Enr/#Cls	SN
Glen Rose Elem Sch 601 Stadium Dr, Glen Rose 76043 Debbie Morris	PK-2	T	441 30	58% 254/898-3500 Fax 254/897-3086
Glen Rose High Sch 900 Stadium Dr, Glen Rose 76043 Kelly Shackelford	9-12	AV	527 46	31% 254/898-3800 Fax 254/897-9871
Glen Rose Intermediate Sch 201 Allen Dr, Glen Rose 76043 Lauri Mapes	3-5	T	421 31	42% 254/898-3600 Fax 254/897-9707
Glen Rose Junior High Sch 805 College St, Glen Rose 76043 Vicki Goebel	6-8	TV	417 50	39% 254/898-3700 Fax 254/897-4059

STARR COUNTY

STARR PUBLIC SCHOOLS

• **Rio Grande City Ind Sch Dist** PID: 01051117   956/716-6702
1 S Fort Ringgold St, Rio Grande Cy 78582   Fax 956/487-8506

Schools: 18 \ *Teachers:* 785 \ *Students:* 9,876 \ *Special Ed Students:* 1,051 \ *LEP Students:* 6,881 \ *Ethnic:* Hispanic 98%, Caucasian 2% \ *Exp:* $293 (Med) \ *Poverty:* 34% \ *Title I:* $6,110,570 \ *Special Education:* $1,978,000 \ *Open-Close:* 08/19 - 05/27 \ *DTBP:* $171 (High)

Velma Garza 1	Deanna Robles Mendez 2,19
Epigmenio Gonzaloz 3	Patsy Ramirez 4
Ricardo Solis 5	Rolando Barrera 7*
Eddie Saenz 8,16,73,76,82,84	Olga Smedley 9
Dr Leticia Trevino 10,15,36,69	Virginia Gonzalez 11,296
Adolfo Pena 15	Rogerio Olivarez 23
Adelina Villarreal 27	Norma McKee 34
Jesus Martinez 57	Daniel Garcia 67
Clarissa Ibannez 69,294	Omar Riojas 71

Javier Garcia ....91*   Dr Paul Doyno 298

Public Schs..Principal	Grd	Prgm	Enr/#Cls	SN
ⓜ Academy Academic Enhancemnt-ES 1 S Fort Ringgold St, Rio Grande Cy 78582 Patricia Soto	1-5		415	956/716-6941 Fax 956/716-6797
ⓜ Academy Academic Enhancemnt-MS 144 FM Rd 3167, Rio Grande Cy 78582 Monique Villarreal	6-8		267	956/352-6324 Fax 956/488-6063
Alto Bonito Elem Sch 753 N FM 2360, Rio Grande Cy 78582 Yvette Pena	PK-5	T	570 35	94% 956/487-6295 Fax 956/487-5755
Dr Mario Ramirez Elem Sch 8001 Trophy St, Rio Grande Cy 78582 Daniel Ramirez	PK-5	T	502 23	94% 956/487-4457 Fax 956/487-4415
General Ricardo Sanchez ES 2801 W Eisenhower Rd, Rio Grande Cy 78582 Teresa Garcia	PK-5	T	729 32	79% 956/487-7043 Fax 956/487-7133
Grulla Elem Sch 599 Old Military Rd, Rio Grande Cy 78582 Epigmenio Gonzalez	PK-5	T	547 32	87% 956/487-3306 Fax 956/716-8615
Grulla High Sch 6884 E Highway 83, Rio Grande Cy 78582 Adolfo Pena	9-12		933	956/487-7278 Fax 956/487-4312
Grulla Middle Sch FM 2360, Grulla 78548 Rene Pena	6-8	T	682 56	93% 956/487-5558 Fax 956/487-5633
John & Olive Hinojosa Elem Sch 2448 Embassy St, Rio Grande Cy 78582 Marissa Saldivar	PK-5	T	486 35	90% 956/487-3710 Fax 956/487-4942
La Union Elem Sch 6300 NE Highway 83, Rio Grande Cy 78582 Lorena Trevino	PK-5	T	372 25	74% 956/487-3404 Fax 956/487-4076
North Grammar Elem Sch 1400 N Lopez St, Rio Grande Cy 78582 Nora Rivera	PK-5	T	535 26	87% 956/716-6618 Fax 956/716-8634
Prep for Early College HS 144 FM 3167, Rio Grande Cy 78582 Tina Gorena	9-12		477	71% 956/352-6349 Fax 956/352-6387
Ringgold Elem Sch 1 S Fort Ringgold St, Rio Grande Cy 78582 Idani Salinas	PK-5	T	465 27	73% 956/716-6929 Fax 956/716-6930
Ringgold Middle Sch 1 S Fort Ringgold St, Rio Grande Cy 78582 Lillian Jones	6-8	T	753 120	90% 956/716-6851 Fax 956/716-6807
Rio Grande City High Sch 5726 N FM 755, Rio Grande Cy 78582 Jorge Pena	9-12	T	1,761	66% 956/488-6000 Fax 956/488-6050
Roque Guerra Jr Elem Sch 1600 W Main St, Rio Grande Cy 78582 Laura Barrera	PK-5	T	754 41	99% 956/716-6982 Fax 956/487-1046
Seas Alternative Ed Center 6667 FM 1430, Garciasville 78547 Mariselda Tanguma	1-12		60 6	956/488-0014 Fax 956/487-7311
Veterans Middle Sch 2700 W Eisenhower St, Rio Grande Cy 78582 Enrique Cantu	6-8	T	894	65% 956/488-0252 Fax 956/488-0261

1	Superintendent	8	Curric/Instruct K-12	19	Chief Financial Officer	29	Family/Consumer Science	
2	Bus/Finance/Purchasing	9	Curric/Instruct Elem	20	Art K-12	30	Adult Education	
3	Buildings And Grounds	10	Curric/Instruct Sec	21	Art Elem	31	Career/Sch-to-Work K-12	
4	Food Service	11	Federal Program	22	Art Sec	32	Career/Sch-to-Work Elem	
5	Transportation	12	Title I	23	Music K-12	33	Career/Sch-to-Work Sec	
6	Athletic	13	Title V	24	Music Elem	34	Early Childhood Ed	
7	Health Services	14	Asst Superintendent	25	Music Sec	35	Health/Phys Education	
		15	Instructional Media Svcs	26	Business Education	36	Guidance Services K-12	
		16	Chief Operations Officer	27	Career & Tech Ed	37	Guidance Services Elem	
		18	Chief Academic Officer	28	Technology Education	38	Guidance Services Sec	
39	Social Studies K-12	49	English/Lang Arts Elem	59	Special Education Elem	69	Academic Assessment	
40	Social Studies Elem	50	English/Lang Arts Sec	60	Special Education Sec	70	Research/Development	
41	Social Studies Sec	51	Reading K-12	61	Foreign/World Lang K-12	71	Public Information	
42	Science K-12	52	Reading Elem	62	Foreign/World Lang Elem	72	Summer School	
43	Science Elem	53	Reading Sec	63	Foreign/World Lang Sec	73	Instructional Tech	
44	Science Sec	54	Remedial Reading K-12	64	Religious Education K-12	74	Inservice Training	
45	Math K-12	55	Remedial Reading Elem	65	Religious Education Elem	75	Marketing/Distributive	
46	Math Elem	56	Remedial Reading Sec	66	Religious Education Sec	76	Info Systems	
47	Math Sec	57	Bilingual/ELL	67	School Board President	77	Psychological Assess	
48	English/Lang Arts K-12	58	Special Education K-12	68	Teacher Personnel	78	Affirmative Action	

Texas School Directory
Stephens County

- **Roma Ind School Dist** PID: 01051222 956/849-1377
  608 N Garcia St, Roma 78584 Fax 956/849-3118

Schools: 10 \ **Teachers:** 448 \ **Students:** 6,400 \ **Special Ed Students:** 413 \ **LEP Students:** 4,091 \ **College-Bound:** 70% \ **Ethnic:** Hispanic 100%, \ **Exp:** $308 (High) \ **Poverty:** 44% \ **Title I:** $4,651,810 \ **Special Education:** $1,060,000 \ **Open-Close:** 08/26 - 05/29 \ **DTBP:** $158 (High)

Name	Ref
Carlos Guzman	1
Juan Trevino	4*
Jaime Escobar	6,35*
Yadira Diaz	8,51
Luis Garza	15,68,83,273
Noe Muniz	27,31,83,88*
Hartadelia Barrera	58
Helen Escobar	71
Francisco Rodriguez	286
Alfonso Perez	2
Ricardo Esparza	5
Rosa Nelda Flores	7
Mary Lou Cruz	11,88,270,271,296,298
Leticia Cadena	16,73,84,89,297
Marissa Belmontes	57,81*
Raul Moreno	67
Manuel Garcia	76

Public Schs..Principal	Grd	Prgm	Enr/#Cls	SN	
Delia Gonzalez Garcia ES 4186 W US Highway 83, Rio Grande Cy 78582 Edgar Garza	PK-5	T	545 33	90%	956/849-8450 Fax 956/849-4566
Emma Vera Elem Sch 2015 N Hwy 83, Roma 78584 Yvonne Guerrero	PK-5	T	421 33	87%	956/849-4552 Fax 956/849-1118
Florence J Scott Elem Sch 800 Pfc Angel J Moreno St, Roma 78584 Diana Salinas	PK-5	T	589 30	91%	956/849-1175 Fax 956/849-7274
Rafaela T Barrera Elem Sch 126 N FM 649, Roma 78584 Olga Gonzalez	PK-5	T	474 38	87%	956/486-2475 Fax 956/486-2474
Ramiro Barrera Middle Sch 2 1/2 Miles N FM 649, Roma 78584 Rodrigo Bazan	6-8	GTV	622	90%	956/486-2670 Fax 956/486-2607
Roel & Celia Saenz Elem Sch 310 S Gate Rd, Roma 78584 Odette Garcia	PK-5	T	580	91%	956/849-7230 Fax 956/849-7250
Roma High Sch 2021 N US Highway 83, Roma 78584 **Ildefonso Saldivar**	9-12	TV	1,781 110	85%	956/849-1333 Fax 956/849-2655
Ⓐ Roma Instructional Sch 807 N Raucon St, Roma 78584 Maria Ramirez	6-12		35 5		956/849-2803 Fax 956/849-4421
Roma Middle Sch 2047 N Hwy 83, Roma 78584 Danelo Gonzalez	6-8	TV	771 60	84%	956/849-1434 Fax 956/849-1895
Veterans Memorial Elem Sch 4772 E Highway 83, Roma 78584 Leida Reyez	PK-5	T	688	94%	956/849-1717 Fax 956/849-3854

- **San Isidro Ind School Dist** PID: 01051296 956/481-3100
  5175 FM 1017, San Isidro 78588 Fax 956/481-3597

Schools: 1 \ **Teachers:** 24 \ **Students:** 250 \ **Special Ed Students:** 29 \ **LEP Students:** 40 \ **College-Bound:** 85% \ **Exp:** $376 (High) \ **Poverty:** 34% \ **Title I:** $109,801 \ **Special Education:** $49,000 \ **Open-Close:** 08/26 - 05/29 \ **DTBP:** $367 (High)

Name	Ref
Mario Alvarado	1,73,83,84
Luis Alvardo	3
Jesse Rodriquez	8,11,16,57,273,280,285*
Sara Wexler	58*
Leonel Olivarez	2,4
Rolando Garza	6*
Marisa Garza	36,88*
Velinda Reyes	67

Public Schs..Principal	Grd	Prgm	Enr/#Cls	SN	
San Isidro Sch 5175 FM 1017, San Isidro 78588 Anna Garcia	PK-12	V	250 25		956/481-3100 Fax 956/481-3224

STARR CATHOLIC SCHOOLS

- **Diocese of Brownsville Ed Off** PID: 01004372
  Listing includes only schools located in this county. See District Index for location of Diocesan Offices.

Catholic Schs..Principal	Grd	Prgm	Enr/#Cls	SN	
Immaculate Conception Sch 305 N Britton Ave, Rio Grande Cy 78582 Maria Olivarez	PK-8		141 12		956/487-2558 Fax 956/487-6478

STEPHENS COUNTY

STEPHENS PUBLIC SCHOOLS

- **Breckenridge Ind School Dist** PID: 01051325 254/559-2278
  208 N Miller St, Breckenridge 76424 Fax 254/559-3180

Schools: 5 \ **Teachers:** 114 \ **Students:** 1,465 \ **Special Ed Students:** 146 \ **LEP Students:** 118 \ **College-Bound:** 70% \ **Ethnic:** African American 1%, Hispanic 34%, Native American: 1%, Caucasian 63% \ **Exp:** $330 (High) \ **Poverty:** 27% \ **Title I:** $524,979 \ **Special Education:** $304,000 \ **Open-Close:** 08/15 - 05/21 \ **DTBP:** $349 (High) \ [facebook]

Name	Ref
Tim Seymore	1
Bryan Dieterich	3*
Casey Hubble	6*
Molly Johnson	8,11,69,88,273,296
Dwayne Dove	28,73,297*
Susan Britting	58*
Lou Simmons	2
Mark Nelson	4
Tonya McKenzie	7*
Beth Hand	16*
Marjorie Thompson	57*
Graham Reaugh	67

Public Schs..Principal	Grd	Prgm	Enr/#Cls	SN	
Breckenridge High Sch 500 W Lindsey St, Breckenridge 76424 William Paul	9-12	ATV	419 50	50%	254/559-2231 Fax 254/559-7485
Breckenridge Jr High Sch 502 W Lindsey St, Breckenridge 76424 Mary Perkins	7-8	AT	238 33	63%	254/559-6581 Fax 254/559-1082
East Elem Sch 1310 E Elm St, Breckenridge 76424 Barbara Collinsworth	PK-1	T	281 19	77%	254/559-6531 Fax 254/559-3001
North Elem Sch 300 W 7th St, Breckenridge 76424 Prairie Freeman	2-3	T	206 13	69%	254/559-6511 Fax 254/559-3670
South Elem Sch 1001 W Elliott St, Breckenridge 76424 Kenna Rainey	4-6	T	357 20	68%	254/559-6554 Fax 254/559-2307

Code	Description	Code	Description	Code	Description	Code	Description
79	Student Personnel	91	Safety/Security	275	Response To Intervention	298	Grant Writer/Ptnrships
80	Driver Ed/Safety	92	Magnet School	277	Remedial Math K-12	750	Chief Innovation Officer
81	Gifted/Talented	93	Parental Involvement	280	Literacy Coach	751	Chief of Staff
82	Video Services	95	Tech Prep Program	285	STEM	752	Social Emotional Learning
83	Substance Abuse Prev	97	Chief Information Officer	286	Digital Learning		
84	Erate	98	Chief Technology Officer	288	Common Core Standards		
85	AIDS Education	270	Accountability	294	Accountability		
88	Alternative/At Risk	271	Migrant Education	295	Network System		
89	Multi-Cultural Curriculum	273	Teacher Mentor	296	Title II Programs		
90	Social Work	274	Before/After Sch	297	Webmaster		

School Programs
A = Alternative Program
G = Adult Classes
M = Magnet Program
T = Title I Schoolwide
V = Career & Tech Ed Programs

Other School Types
Ⓐ = Alternative School
Ⓒ = Charter School
Ⓜ = Magnet School
Ⓨ = Year-Round School

Social Media
[f] = Facebook
[t] = Twitter

New Schools are shaded
New Superintendents and Principals are bold
Personnel with email addresses are underscored

Sterling County

STERLING COUNTY

STERLING PUBLIC SCHOOLS

- **Sterling City Ind School Dist** PID: 01051387   325/378-4781
  700 7th St, Sterling City 76951   Fax 325/378-2283

Schools: 2 \ *Teachers:* 25 \ *Students:* 320 \ *Special Ed Students:* 31 \ *LEP Students:* 12 \ *College-Bound:* 60% \ *Ethnic:* Hispanic 44%, Caucasian 56% \ *Exp:* $878 (High) \ *Poverty:* 16% \ *Title I:* $54,649 \ *Open-Close:* 07/23 - 05/22 \ *DTBP:* $304 (High)

Name	Ref	Name	Ref
Bob Rauch	1	Danetta Ferguson	2
Brent Harmon	3	Carol Spindler	4*
Trey Sisco	6	Michelle Guetersloh	11
Stephanie Stafford	36,69,83,85*	Sarah Miller	57,58
Jason Cox	67	Shelli Long	68
Dow Ferguson	73,286	Ty Stevens	285*

Public Schs..Principal	Grd	Prgm	Enr/#Cls	SN	
Sterling Elem Sch 700 7th St, Sterling City 76951 Jami Keele	PK-5	T	141 17	45%	325/378-5821 Fax 325/378-2087
Sterling Middle High Sch 700 7th St, Sterling City 76951 Ty Stevens	6-12	ATV	150	39%	325/378-5821 Fax 325/378-2087

STONEWALL COUNTY

STONEWALL PUBLIC SCHOOLS

- **Aspermont Ind School Dist** PID: 01051416   940/989-3355
  528 E 7th St, Aspermont 79502   Fax 940/989-3353

Schools: 2 \ *Teachers:* 24 \ *Students:* 240 \ *Special Ed Students:* 12 \ *LEP Students:* 7 \ *College-Bound:* 60% \ *Ethnic:* Asian 2%, African American 3%, Hispanic 33%, Caucasian 61% \ *Exp:* $337 (High) \ *Poverty:* 19% \ *Title I:* $47,640 \ *Open-Close:* 08/15 - 05/22 \ *DTBP:* $357 (High)

Name	Ref	Name	Ref
Zack Morris	1	Charla Leonard	2
James Albright	3,91	Tanya Haurdhty	4
Mark Weaver	6	Allison Martin	11
Nicki Edison	11	Teddye Myers	36,69,83,88,270,271,275*
Lacy English	67	Cesioy Hecks	73

Public Schs..Principal	Grd	Prgm	Enr/#Cls	SN	
Aspermont Elem Sch 528 E 7th St, Aspermont 79502 Chuck Chesser	PK-5	T	104 9	60%	940/989-3323 Fax 940/989-2954
Aspermont High Sch 528 E 7th St, Aspermont 79502 Trent Van Meter	6-12		123 15	49%	940/989-2707 Fax 940/989-3486

SUTTON COUNTY

SUTTON PUBLIC SCHOOLS

- **Sonora Ind School Dist** PID: 01051478   325/387-6940
  807 S Concho Ave, Sonora 76950   Fax 325/387-5090

Schools: 3 \ *Teachers:* 84 \ *Students:* 760 \ *Special Ed Students:* 79 \ *LEP Students:* 83 \ *College-Bound:* 64% \ *Ethnic:* Hispanic 71%, Caucasian 28% \ *Exp:* $614 (High) \ *Poverty:* 23% \ *Title I:* $181,459 \ *Special Education:* $223,000 \ *Open-Close:* 08/20 - 05/22 \ *DTBP:* $355 (High)

Name	Ref	Name	Ref
Ross Aschenbeck	1	Greta Ramsdell	2
Josie Torres	4*	Kevin Sherrill	6
Stephanie Taylor	8,11,27,58,88*	Lindsey Geske	16*
Kay Friess	38*	Laura Valeriano	54
Dawn Cahill	67	Karen Evans	73,84,286
Tamie Love	85*		

Public Schs..Principal	Grd	Prgm	Enr/#Cls	SN	
Sonora Elememtary Sch 907 S Concho Ave, Sonora 76950 Michael Kissire	PK-6	T	387 26	68%	325/387-6940 Fax 325/387-9604
Sonora High Sch 1717 Tayloe Ave, Sonora 76950 Sean Leamon	9-12	ATV	249 35	45%	325/387-6940 Fax 325/387-5348
Sonora Middle Sch 408 E 1st St, Sonora 76950 Sean Leamon	7-8	T	181 20	56%	325/387-6940 Fax 325/387-2007

SWISHER COUNTY

SWISHER PUBLIC SCHOOLS

- **Happy Ind School Dist** PID: 01051519   806/558-5331
  500 NW 3rd St, Happy 79042   Fax 806/209-0077

Schools: 2 \ *Teachers:* 27 \ *Students:* 254 \ *Special Ed Students:* 17 \ *LEP Students:* 10 \ *College-Bound:* 80% \ *Ethnic:* African American 2%, Hispanic 19%, Caucasian 80% \ *Exp:* $465 (High) \ *Poverty:* 16% \ *Title I:* $43,924 \ *Open-Close:* 08/21 - 05/20 \ *DTBP:* $372 (High)

Name	Ref	Name	Ref
Ray Keith	1	Shannon Bressler	2,11,296
Ike Lawson	3,5	Diane McPherson	4
Glenda Birkenfeild	7	Julie Dempsey	8,16
Krista Ellison	9,45,48,51,85,274	Sara Reinart	27,30,31*
Staci Wyatt	36	Cindy Givens	58*
Mace Middleton	67	Rowdy Bryan	73,286,295,297

Public Schs..Principal	Grd	Prgm	Enr/#Cls	SN	
Happy Elem Sch 400 NW 3rd St, Happy 79042 Toni Waldo	PK-6	T	145 13	45%	806/558-2561 Fax 806/558-2484

#		#		#		#		#		#		#	
1	Superintendent	8	Curric/Instruct K-12	19	Chief Financial Officer	29	Family/Consumer Science	39	Social Studies K-12	49	English/Lang Arts Elem	59	Special Education Elem	69	Academic Assessment
2	Bus/Finance/Purchasing	9	Curric/Instruct Elem	20	Art K-12	30	Adult Education	40	Social Studies Elem	50	English/Lang Arts Sec	60	Special Education Sec	70	Research/Development
3	Buildings And Grounds	10	Curric/Instruct Sec	21	Art Elem	31	Career/Sch-to-Work K-12	41	Social Studies Sec	51	Reading K-12	61	Foreign/World Lang K-12	71	Public Information
4	Food Service	11	Federal Program	22	Art Sec	32	Career/Sch-to-Work Elem	42	Science K-12	52	Reading Elem	62	Foreign/World Lang Elem	72	Summer School
5	Transportation	12	Title I	23	Music K-12	33	Career/Sch-to-Work Sec	43	Science Elem	53	Reading Sec	63	Foreign/World Lang Sec	73	Instructional Tech
6	Athletic	13	Title V	24	Music Elem	34	Early Childhood Ed	44	Science Sec	54	Remedial Reading K-12	64	Religious Education K-12	74	Inservice Training
7	Health Services	15	Asst Superintendent	25	Music Sec	35	Health/Phys Education	45	Math K-12	55	Remedial Reading Elem	65	Religious Education Elem	75	Marketing/Distributive
		16	Instructional Media Svcs	26	Business Education	36	Guidance Services K-12	46	Math Elem	56	Remedial Reading Sec	66	Religious Education Sec	76	Info Systems
		17	Chief Operations Officer	27	Career & Tech Ed	37	Guidance Services Elem	47	Math Sec	57	Bilingual/ELL	67	School Board President	77	Psychological Assess
		18	Chief Academic Officer	28	Technology Education	38	Guidance Services Sec	48	English/Lang Arts K-12	58	Special Education K-12	68	Teacher Personnel	78	Affirmative Action

Texas School Directory

Tarrant County

Happy Middle High Sch	7-12	ATV	118	31%	806/558-5311
401 NW 3rd St, Happy 79042			16		Fax 806/558-4301
Stacy Barnett					

● **Kress Ind School Dist** PID: 01051545   806/684-2652
200 E 5th St, Kress 79052   Fax 806/684-2687

Schools: 2 \ *Teachers:* 26 \ *Students:* 280 \ *Special Ed Students:* 26 \ *LEP Students:* 22 \ *College-Bound:* 75% \ *Ethnic:* African American 4%, Hispanic 61%, Caucasian 35% \ *Exp:* $636 (High) \ *Poverty:* 24% \ *Title I:* $68,153 \ *Open-Close:* 08/16 - 05/18 \ *DTBP:* $316 (High)

Leah Zeigler 1,11,73,84
Laura Reyes 4*
Shawn Langston 9*
Michelle Goss 16,82*
Gennie Jackson 60*
Melinda Thomas 69,83,270*
Dianna Vuittonet 2
Mickey Bye 5*
Phil Zolman 11,73,286,294,295,298*
Sheri Warren 58*
Tiffany Reed 67

Public Schs..Principal	Grd	Prgm	Enr/#Cls	SN	
Kress Elem Sch	PK-6	T	155	77%	806/684-2326
401 Ripley Ave, Kress 79052			15		Fax 806/684-2778
Robert Langston					
Kress Jr Sr High Sch	7-12	T	97	68%	806/684-2651
500 Ripley St, Kress 79052			20		
Phil Zolman					

● **Tulia Ind School Dist** PID: 01051571   806/995-4591
702 NW 8th St, Tulia 79088   Fax 806/995-3169

Schools: 4 \ *Teachers:* 99 \ *Students:* 1,099 \ *Special Ed Students:* 119 \ *LEP Students:* 68 \ *Ethnic:* African American 10%, Hispanic 62%, Caucasian 28% \ *Exp:* $760 (High) \ *Poverty:* 29% \ *Title I:* $407,296 \ *Open-Close:* 08/14 - 05/21 \ *DTBP:* $338 (High)

Tim Glover 1
Dusty George 3
Tim Gibbons 5
Jaclyn Street 7,85*
Danee Puga 34,58,275
Gary Eastwood 67
Kris Friel 84,295
Daniel Keith 286
Mike Huseman 2
Debbie Earl 4*
Duane Tolliver 6
Brandi DeLong 8,11,57,285,288,298
Dixie Johnson 58
Johnny McCasland 73,76,295
Mary Verver 271

Public Schs..Principal	Grd	Prgm	Enr/#Cls	SN	
Highland Elem Sch	PK-2	T	298	85%	806/995-4141
800 NW 9th St, Tulia 79088			46		Fax 806/995-2265
Pam Miner					
Tulia High Sch	9-12	TV	317	68%	806/995-2759
501 Hornet Pl, Tulia 79088			42		Fax 806/995-4413
Perla Perez					
Tulia Junior High Sch	6-8	T	241	80%	806/995-4842
421 NE 3rd St, Tulia 79088			26		Fax 806/995-4498
Casey McBroom					
W V Swinburn Elem Sch	3-5	T	243	85%	806/995-4309
300 N Dallas Ave, Tulia 79088			15		Fax 806/995-4448
Johnny Lara					

TARRANT COUNTY

TARRANT PUBLIC SCHOOLS

● **Arlington Ind School Dist** PID: 01051624   682/867-4611
1203 W Pioneer Pkwy, Arlington 76013   Fax 817/459-7286

Schools: 78 \ *Teachers:* 4,238 \ *Students:* 60,000 \ *Special Ed Students:* 5,156 \ *LEP Students:* 14,932 \ *College-Bound:* 73% \ *Ethnic:* Asian 6%, African American 25%, Hispanic 47%, Caucasian 21% \ *Exp:* $228 (Med) \ *Poverty:* 18% \ *Title I:* $20,577,378 \ *Special Education:* $9,707,000 \ *Open-Close:* 08/19 - 05/28 \ *DTBP:* $192 (High) \ [f] [t]

Dr Marcelo Cavazos 1
Tammy Craig 2
Kelly Horn 3
Tim Collins 5
Connie Wallace 8
Dr Tamela Horton 8
A Tracie Brown 15
Chad Branum 15,73
Michael Hill 15
Dr Theodore Jarchow 15
Susan Patterson 27
Kandi Hunter 45
Kecia Mays 67
Dr Kevin Barlow 70,294
Barry Fox 76
Patty Bustamante 79
Wendy Carrington 88
Aaron Perales 93
John Atchison 295
Brenda Lohse 298
Cindy Powell 2,19
Tony Drollinger 2
David Lewis 4
Eric White 6
Dr Steven Wurtz 8,18
Julie McGuire 11
Beth Hollinger 15
Dr Christi Buell 15
Scott Kahl 15,68,79
Dr Christopher Anderson 20
Telisa Brown 36
Cassandra Perez 57,61
Dr Peggy Porterfield 69
Elita Driskill 73
Mark Murray 76*
Dr Karen Zeske 81
David Stevens 91
Steve Simpson 286
Frank Sack 297
Luis Valdespino 752

Public Schs..Principal	Grd	Prgm	Enr/#Cls	SN	
Adams Elem Sch	PK-6	T	817	86%	682/867-2130
2220 Sherry St, Arlington 76010					
Lesley Rhodes					
Agriculture Science Center		Voc	700		682/867-9500
2101 Browning Dr, Arlington 76010					Fax 682/867-9505
Ginger Polster					
Amos Elem Sch	PK-6	AT	431	87%	682/867-4700
3100 Daniel Dr, Arlington 76014			30		Fax 817/419-4705
Carin Tufts					
Anderson Elem Sch	PK-6	AT	657	93%	682/867-7750
1101 Timberlake Dr, Arlington 76010					Fax 682/867-7773
Angela Peragine					
Arlington College & Career HS	9-12		500		682/867-9600
4900 W Arkansas Ln, Arlington 76016					
Dr Ben Bholan					
Arlington Collegiate High Sch	9-12		404		817/515-3550
2224 Southeast Pkwy, Arlington 76018					Fax 817/515-3540
Jeff Krieger					
Arlington High Sch	9-12	TV	2,769	53%	682/867-8100
818 W Park Row Dr, Arlington 76013			120		Fax 682/867-8119
Shahveer Dhalla					
Ashworth Elem Sch	PK-6	AT	466	61%	682/867-4800
6700 Silo Rd, Arlington 76002			38		Fax 682/867-4808
Stacey Maddoux					
Atherton Elem Sch	PK-6	AT	615	86%	682/867-4900
2101 Overbrook Dr, Arlington 76014			70		Fax 682/867-4916
Nidia Zaravar					

79 Student Personnel	91 Safety/Security	275 Response To Intervention	298 Grant Writer/Ptnrships	**School Programs**	**Social Media**		
80 Driver Ed/Safety	92 Magnet School	277 Remedial Math K-12	750 Chief Innovation Officer	A = Alternative Program	[f] = Facebook		
81 Gifted/Talented	93 Parental Involvement	280 Literacy Coach	751 Chief of Staff	G = Adult Classes			
82 Video Services	95 Tech Prep Program	285 STEM	752 Social Emotional Learning	M = Magnet Program	[t] = Twitter		
83 Substance Abuse Prev	97 Chief Information Officer	286 Digital Learning		T = Title I Schoolwide			
84 Erate	98 Chief Technology Officer	288 Common Core Standards	**Other School Types**	V = Career & Tech Ed Programs			
85 AIDS Education	270 Accountability	294 Alternative School	Ⓐ = Alternative School				
88 Alternative/At Risk	271 Migrant Education	295 Network System	Ⓒ = Charter School	New Schools are shaded			
89 Multi-Cultural Curriculum	273 Teacher Mentor	296 Title II Programs	Ⓜ = Magnet School	New Superintendents and Principals are bold			
90 Social Work	274 Before/After Sch	297 Webmaster	Ⓨ = Year-Round School	Personnel with email addresses are underscored			

TX—343

Tarrant County — Market Data Retrieval

School	Grades	Codes	Enroll	%	Phone
Bailey Junior High Sch 2411 Winewood Ln, Arlington 76013 Tiffany Benavides	7-8	T	844 40	57%	682/867-0700 Fax 682/867-0708
Barnett Junior High Sch 2101 E Sublett Rd, Arlington 76018 Stephanie Hawthorne	7-8	TV	874 25	65%	682/867-5000 Fax 682/867-5096
Bebensee Elem Sch 5900 Inks Lake Dr, Arlington 76018 Charlotte Carter	PK-6	AT	685 65	73%	682/867-5100 Fax 817/419-5105
Beckham Elem Sch 1700 Southeast Pkwy, Arlington 76018 Susan Mitchell	PK-6	AT	566 25	65%	682/867-6600 Fax 817/375-6605
Berry Elem Sch 1800 Joyce St, Arlington 76010 Tammy Rogers	PK-6	AT	678 37	94%	682/867-0850 Fax 817/801-0905
Blanton Elem Sch 1900 S Collins St, Arlington 76010 Joshua Leonard	PK-6	AT	623 49	92%	682/867-1000 Fax 817/801-0955
Boles Junior High Sch 3900 SW Green Oaks Blvd, Arlington 76017 Dr Angela Smith	7-8	V	672 55	34%	682/867-8000 Fax 682/867-8067
Bryant Elem Sch 2201 Havenwood Dr, Arlington 76018 Randi Smith	PK-6	AT	530	68%	682/867-5200 Fax 817/419-5205
Burgin Elem Sch 401 E Mayfield Rd, Arlington 76014 Christi Wilks	PK-6	AT	590 60	88%	682/867-1300 Fax 817/419-1416
Butler Elem Sch 2121 Margaret Dr, Arlington 76012 **Jennifer Bohannon**	PK-6	A	627 36	22%	682/867-1010 Fax 817/801-1015
Carter Junior High Sch 701 Tharp St, Arlington 76010 Claudia Herrera	7-8	TV	1,149 50	95%	682/867-1700 Fax 682/867-1721
Corey Acad Fine Arts 5200 Kelly Elliott Rd, Arlington 76017 **Nidia Zaravar**	PK-6	AT	580 60	40%	682/867-3900 Fax 682/867-3904
Crouch Elem Sch 2810 Prairie Hill Dr, Grand Prairie 75051 **Jaime Stephens**	PK-6	AT	651	94%	682/867-0200 Fax 972/595-0205
Crow Leadership Academy 1201 Coke Dr, Arlington 76010 Jamie MacDougall	PK-6	AT	376 46	92%	682/867-1850 Fax 817/801-1855
Dan Dipert Career & Tech Ctr 2101 Browning Dr, Arlington 76010 Ginger Polster	Voc		1,000		682/867-9500
Diane Patrick Elem Sch 755 Timber Oaks Ln, Grand Prairie 75051 Ena Meyers	PK-6	MT	832	89%	682/867-0600
Ditto Elem Sch 3001 Quail Ln, Arlington 76016 Karie Kuster	PK-6	A	720 75	26%	682/867-3100 Fax 682/867-3176
Duff Elem Sch 3100 Lynnwood Dr, Arlington 76013 Cynthia Harbison	PK-6	A	622	39%	682/867-2000 Fax 817/801-2005
Dunn Elem Sch 2201 Woodside Dr, Arlington 76013 Mary Helen Burnett	PK-6	AT	561 45	59%	682/867-3200 Fax 817/492-3205
Eddy & Debbie Peach Elem Sch 2020 Baird Farm Rd, Arlington 76006 Dr Stephanie Lee	PK-6	T	909	84%	682/867-6100
Ellis Elem Sch 2601 Shadow Ridge Dr, Arlington 76006 Keith Boyd	PK-6	AT	704 40	79%	682/867-7900 Fax 817/652-7905
Emma Ousley Jr HS 950 Southeast Pkwy, Arlington 76018 Grayson Toperzer	7-8	TV	976 50	68%	682/867-5700 Fax 682/867-5775
Farrell Elem Sch 3410 Paladium Dr, Grand Prairie 75052 Glen Brunk	PK-6	AT	651 50	67%	682/867-0300 Fax 682/867-0370
Fitzgerald Elem Sch 5201 Creek Valley Dr, Arlington 76018 Cindy Brown	PK-6	AT	501 47	80%	682/867-5300 Fax 817/419-5305
Foster Elem Sch 1025 High Point Rd, Arlington 76015 Jacquelyn Burden	PK-6	AT	579 38	84%	682/867-5350 Fax 817/419-5355
Goodman Elem Sch 1400 Rebecca Ln, Arlington 76014 **Stephanie Savala**	PK-6	AT	561 40	92%	682/867-2200 Fax 817/801-2205
Gunn Junior High Sch 3000 S Fielder Rd, Arlington 76015 **Dr Matt Varnell**	7-8	T	442 40	71%	682/867-5400 Fax 817/419-5405
Hale Elem Sch 2400 E Mayfield Rd, Arlington 76014 Natasha Harris	PK-6	AT	567 43	87%	682/867-1530 Fax 817/419-1535
Hill Elem Sch 2020 W Tucker Blvd, Arlington 76013 Kasie Longonia	PK-6	A	528 34	31%	682/867-2300 Fax 682/867-2375
James Bowie High Sch 2101 Highbank Dr, Arlington 76018 Reny Lizardo	9-12	TV	2,716	60%	682/867-4400 Fax 682/867-4406
James Martin High Sch 4501 W Pleasant Ridge Rd, Arlington 76016 Marlene Roddy	9-12	V	3,451 185	27%	682/867-8600 Fax 682/867-8609
Johns Elem Sch 1900 Sherry St, Arlington 76010 Vanessa Colon	PK-6	AT	718 38	93%	682/867-2500 Fax 682/867-2502
Jones Aca of Fine Arts & Dual 2001 Van Buren Dr, Arlington 76011 Katiuska Herrador	PK-6	A	484 40	68%	682/867-3580 Fax 817/801-3505
Juan Seguin High Sch 7001 Silo Rd, Arlington 76002 Ray Borden	9-12	T	1,596	60%	682/867-6700 Fax 817/375-6705
Key Elem Sch 3621 Roosevelt Dr, Arlington 76016 Hallema Jackson	PK-6	AT	483 30	58%	682/867-5500 Fax 817/419-5505
Kooken Educational Center 423 N Center St, Arlington 76011 Dr Connie Spence	PK-PK	T	351 13	85%	682/867-7152 Fax 817/459-7155
Larson Elem Sch 2620 E Avenue K, Grand Prairie 75050 Teri Conely	PK-6	AT	558 50	64%	682/867-0000 Fax 682/867-0079
Little Elem Sch 3721 Little Rd, Arlington 76016 Beth Woodward	PK-6	A	754 43	38%	682/867-3300 Fax 817/492-3305
M B Lamar High Sch 1400 W Lamar Blvd, Arlington 76012 Andy Hagman	9-12	TV	2,841 120	60%	682/867-8300 Fax 682/867-6959
Mary Moore Elem Sch 5500 Park Springs Blvd, Arlington 76017 **Nathan Prange**	K-6	A	672 45	41%	682/867-8900 Fax 817/561-8905
Miller Elem Sch 6401 W Pleasant Ridge Rd, Arlington 76016 Shelly Osten	PK-6	AT	634 48	58%	682/867-8400 Fax 817/561-8405
Morton Elem Sch 2900 Barrington Pl, Arlington 76014 Tashalon McDonald	PK-6	T	572 53	92%	682/867-5600 Fax 682/867-5679
Newcomer Center 600 SE Green Oaks Blvd, Arlington 76018 Greg Meeks	7-12	TV	247 18	93%	682/867-7100 Fax 682/867-7146
Nichols Junior High Sch 2201 Ascension Blvd, Arlington 76006 **Catherine Claiborne**	7-8	T	788 30	80%	682/867-2600 Fax 682/867-2649

#		#		#		#		#		#		#	
1	Superintendent	8	Curric/Instruct K-12	19	Chief Financial Officer	29	Family/Consumer Science	39	Social Studies K-12	49	English/Lang Arts Elem	59	Special Education Elem	69	Academic Assessment
2	Bus/Finance/Purchasing	9	Curric/Instruct Elem	20	Art K-12	30	Adult Education	40	Social Studies Elem	50	English/Lang Arts Sec	60	Special Education Sec	70	Research/Development
3	Buildings And Grounds	10	Curric/Instruct Sec	21	Art Elem	31	Career/Sch-to-Work K-12	41	Social Studies Sec	51	Reading K-12	61	Foreign/World Lang K-12	71	Public Information
4	Food Service	11	Federal Program	22	Art Sec	32	Career/Sch-to-Work Elem	42	Science K-12	52	Reading Elem	62	Foreign/World Lang Elem	72	Summer School
5	Transportation	12	Title I	23	Music K-12	33	Career/Sch-to-Work Sec	43	Science Elem	53	Reading Sec	63	Foreign/World Lang Sec	73	Instructional Tech
6	Athletic	13	Title V	24	Music Elem	34	Early Childhood Ed	44	Science Sec	54	Remedial Reading K-12	64	Religious Education K-12	74	Inservice Training
7	Health Services	15	Asst Superintendent	25	Music Sec	35	Health/Phys Education	45	Math K-12	55	Remedial Reading Elem	65	Religious Education Elem	75	Marketing/Distributive
		16	Instructional Media Svcs	26	Business Education	36	Guidance Services K-12	46	Math Elem	56	Remedial Reading Sec	66	Religious Education Sec	76	Info Systems
		17	Chief Operations Officer	27	Career & Tech Ed	37	Guidance Services Elem	47	Math Sec	57	Bilingual/ELL	67	School Board President	77	Psychological Assess
		18	Chief Academic Officer	28	Technology Education	38	Guidance Services Sec	48	English/Lang Arts K-12	58	Special Education K-12	68	Teacher Personnel	78	Affirmative Action

Texas School Directory — Tarrant County

School	Grd	Prgm	Enr/#Cls	SN	Phone
Pearcy STEM Academy 601 E Harris Rd, Arlington 76002 Codi Van Duzee	PK-6	AT	480 45	62%	682/867-5555 Fax 817/419-5554
Pope Elem Sch 901 Chestnut Dr, Arlington 76012 Celina Kilgore	PK-6	AT	551 27	76%	682/867-2750 Fax 682/867-2795
Rankin Elem Sch 1900 Oleander St, Arlington 76010 Lori Mosley	PK-6	AT	687 32	95%	682/867-2800 Fax 817/801-2805
Remynse Elem Sch 2720 Fall Dr, Grand Prairie 75052 Selina Ozuna	PK-6	AT	515 25	87%	682/867-0500 Fax 972/595-0505
Roark Elem Sch 2401 Roberts Cir, Arlington 76010 Anna Anderson	PK-6	AT	468 44	94%	682/867-2900 Fax 817/801-2905
Sam Houston High Sch 2000 Sam Houston Dr, Arlington 76014 Juan Villarreal	9-12	TV	3,627	87%	682/867-8200 Fax 682/867-6290
Sandy McNutt Elem Sch 3609 S Center St, Arlington 76014 Ginger Cole-Leffel	PK-6	T	680	85%	682/867-9100
Shackelford Junior High Sch 2000 N Fielder Rd, Arlington 76012 Jerod Zahn	7-8	TV	703	67%	682/867-3600 Fax 682/867-3603
Sherrod Elem Sch 2626 Lincoln Dr, Arlington 76006 Dr Michelle Cummings	PK-6	AT	665 48	81%	682/867-3700 Fax 817/801-3705
Short Elem Sch 2000 California Ln, Arlington 76015 Katina Martinez	PK-6	AT	536 32	84%	682/867-5850 Fax 817/419-5855
South Davis Elem Sch 2001 S Davis Dr, Arlington 76013 **Debra Wall**	PK-6	AT	676 34	93%	682/867-3800 Fax 817/801-3805
Speer Elem Sch 811 Fuller St, Arlington 76012 Selina Elizondo	PK-6	AT	738	93%	682/867-4000 Fax 817/801-4005
Starrett Elem Sch 2675 Fairmont Dr, Grand Prairie 75052 Allison Gilmore	PK-6	AT	573 40	72%	682/867-0400 Fax 972/595-0405
Swift Elem Sch 1101 S Fielder Rd, Arlington 76013 Bailey Morris	PK-6	AT	478 33	75%	682/867-4100 Fax 817/801-4105
Thornton Elem Sch 2301 E Park Row Dr, Arlington 76010 Alicia Rodriguez	PK-6	AT	770 65	95%	682/867-4200 Fax 817/801-4205
ⓐ Turning Point Secondary Sch 2209 N Davis Dr, Arlington 76012 Jeanne Muldrew	7-12	V	200 26	71%	682/867-3050 Fax 682/867-3045
Veda Knox Elem Sch 2315 Stonegate St, Arlington 76010 Rose Ravin	PK-6	AT	535	92%	682/867-2051 Fax 817/801-2056
ⓐ Venture High Sch 600 SE Green Oaks Blvd, Arlington 76018 Greg Meeks	9-12	GV	316 30		682/867-6400 Fax 682/867-6441
Webb Elem Sch 1200 N Cooper St, Arlington 76011 Elena Lopez	PK-6	AT	689 50	95%	682/867-4300 Fax 817/801-4305
West Elem Sch 2911 Kingswood Blvd, Grand Prairie 75052 Wendy Britton	PK-6	AT	675 37	54%	682/867-0100 Fax 682/867-0190
Williams Elem Sch 4915 Red Birch Dr, Arlington 76018 Mark Kammlah	PK-6	AT	696 60	76%	682/867-5900 Fax 817/419-5905
Wimbish World Language Academy 1601 Wright St, Arlington 76012 **Delisse Hardy**	PK-6	AT	527 35	84%	682/867-6000 Fax 817/801-6005
Wood Elem Sch 3300 Pimlico Dr, Arlington 76017 David Dillard	PK-6	AT	802 50	42%	682/867-1100 Fax 817/419-1105
Workman Junior High Sch 701 E Arbrook Blvd, Arlington 76014 Jacquelyn McClendon	7-8	TV	1,501	89%	682/867-1200 Fax 682/867-1218
Young Junior High Sch 3200 Woodside Dr, Arlington 76016 **Stacie Humbles**	7-8		850 60	34%	682/867-3400 Fax 817/492-3405 ⓣ

● **Azle Ind School Dist** PID: 01051973 817/444-3235
300 Roe St, Azle 76020 Fax 817/444-6866

Schools: 12 \ *Teachers:* 389 \ *Students:* 6,000 \ *Special Ed Students:* 598 \ *LEP Students:* 253 \ *College-Bound:* 50% \ *Ethnic:* Asian 1%, African American 1%, Hispanic 21%, Native American: 1%, Caucasian 77% \ *Exp:* $520 (High) \ *Poverty:* 14% \ *Title I:* $1,155,323 \ *Special Education:* $1,203,000 \ *Open-Close:* 08/21 - 05/28 \ *DTBP:* $169 (High)

Tanya Anderson	1	Monica Miller 2,11
Almarie Rivera	4	Becky Spurlock 6
Amanda Wimpee	8	Rebecca Trotter 11
Todd Smith	15	Eddie Alford 16,73,297
Suzanne Murr	27	Gwen Gordon 58
Bill Lane	67	Mark Kehoe 68
Jaime Westbrook	90	

Public Schs..Principal	Grd	Prgm	Enr/#Cls	SN	Phone
ⓐ Alt Edu Program Phoenix Campus 1010 Boyd Rd, Azle 76020 Diane Boone	4-12		80 7		817/444-4564 Fax 817/270-0830
Azle Elem Sch 1200 Lakeview Dr, Azle 76020 Gina Lee	5-6	T	593 20	37%	817/444-1312 Fax 817/444-6934
Azle High Sch 1200 Boyd Rd, Azle 76020 Randy Cobb	9-12	TV	1,814	39%	817/444-5555 Fax 817/444-8884
Azle Hornet Academy 1010 Boyd Rd, Azle 76020 **Dianne Boone**	9-12	T	80	49%	817/444-4564
Azle Junior High Sch 201 School St, Azle 76020 Brian Roberts	7-8		536 25	37%	817/444-2564 Fax 817/270-0880
Cross Timbers Elem Sch 831 Jackson Trl, Azle 76020 **Shelly Wynns**	PK-4	T	539 24	60%	817/444-3802 Fax 817/444-0730
Eagle Heights Elem Sch 6505 Lucerne Dr, Fort Worth 76135 Amy Rollman	PK-4	T	448 32	51%	817/237-4161 Fax 817/237-0656
Hoover Elem Sch 484 Sandy Beach Rd, Azle 76020 Joni Bettis	5-6	T	433 18	57%	817/444-7766 Fax 817/270-1425
Liberty Elem Sch 11450 Liberty School Rd, Azle 76020 **Lisa Koehler**	PK-4	T	491 22	68%	817/444-1317 Fax 817/444-1937
Santo J Forte Jr High Sch 479 Sandy Beach Rd, Azle 76020 William Manley	7-8	T	456 47	52%	817/270-1133 Fax 817/270-1157
Silver Creek Elem Sch 10300 S FM 730, Azle 76020 Heidi Nelson	PK-4	T	587 33	34%	817/444-0257 Fax 817/270-2383
Walnut Creek Elem Sch 500 Stribling Dr, Azle 76020 Jessica Hanson	PK-4	T	519 21	43%	817/444-4045 Fax 817/270-2576

79 Student Personnel	91 Safety/Security	275 Response To Intervention	298 Grant Writer/Ptnrships	**School Programs**	**Social Media**
80 Driver Ed/Safety	92 Magnet School	277 Remedial Math K-12	750 Chief Innovation Officer	A = Alternative Program	ⓕ = Facebook
81 Gifted/Talented	93 Parental Involvement	280 Literacy Coach	751 Chief of Staff	G = Adult Classes	ⓣ = Twitter
82 Video Services	95 Tech Prep Program	285 STEM	752 Social Emotional Learning	M = Magnet Program	
83 Substance Abuse Prev	97 Chief Infomation Officer	286 Digital Learning		T = Title I Schoolwide	
84 Erate	98 Chief Technology Officer	288 Common Core Standards	**Other School Types**	V = Career & Tech Ed Programs	
85 AIDS Education	270 Character Education	294 Accountability	ⓐ = Alternative School		
88 Alternative/At Risk	271 Migrant Education	295 Network System	ⓒ = Charter School	New Schools are shaded	
89 Multi-Cultural Curriculum	273 Teacher Mentor	296 Title II Programs	ⓜ = Magnet School	New Superintendents and Principals are bold	
90 Social Work	274 Before/After Sch	297 Webmaster	ⓨ = Year-Round School	Personnel with email addresses are underscored	

Tarrant County

Market Data Retrieval

- **Birdville Ind School Dist** PID: 01052032   817/547-5700
  6125 E Belknap St, Haltom City 76117   Fax 817/547-5530

Schools: 33 \ **Teachers:** 1,566 \ **Students:** 23,513 \
Special Ed Students: 2,182 \ **LEP Students:** 4,187 \ **College-Bound:** 57%
\ **Ethnic:** Asian 5%, African American 9%, Hispanic 43%, Native American: 1%,
Caucasian 42% \ **Exp:** $320 (High) \ **Poverty:** 14% \ **Title I:** $5,004,683 \
Special Education: $4,827,000 \ **Open-Close:** 08/19 - 05/28 \ **DTBP:** $184
(High) \

Name	Code
Dr Darrell Brown	1
Sharay Boynton	2
John Hughes	3
Dave Powers	5
Michelle Province	7*
Dr Elizabeth Clark	8,15
James Smith	9,34*
Adrienne Walker	11,296,298
Skip Baskerville	15,68
Danny Detrick	20,23
Leann Carroll	36,77,83,85,88
Dawna Schweitzer	42
Ralph Kunkel	67
David Holland	69,294*
Dave Lambson	73,76,295,297
Chris Reese	91
Katie Bowman	2
Shelley Freeman	2
Judy Sargent	4
Chris Feris	6
Donna Solley	8*
Clarence Simmons	9
Lorene Ownby	9
Dr Laura Holt	12,58
Kelli Montgomery	16,286
Allison Vinson	27,30,31,73*
Jennifer Miller	39,59
Brenda Mesa	45
Paige Curry	68
Mark Thomas	71
Joseph Showell	79,93

Public Schs..Principal	Grd	Prgm	Enr/#Cls	SN		
Academy at Carrie F Thomas 8200 O Brian Way, N Richlnd Hls 76180 Dr Sabrina Lindsey	PK-5	T	627 27		74%	817/547-3000 Fax 817/581-5490
Alliene Mullendore Elem Sch 4100 Flory St, N Richlnd Hls 76180 William Pope	PK-5	T	359 21		65%	817/547-1900 Fax 817/581-5326
Birdville Elem Sch of Fine Art 3111 Carson St, Haltom City 76117 Tammy Pope	PK-5	T	426 23		84%	817/547-1500 Fax 817/831-5736
Birdville High Sch 9100 Mid Cities Blvd, N Richlnd Hls 76180 Jason Wells	9-12	GV	2,074		35%	817/547-8000 Fax 817/547-8009
Bisd Ctr Tech & Advanced Lrng 7020 Mid Cities Blvd, N Richlnd Hls 76180 Carol Adcocok	Voc		300			817/547-3800 Fax 817/503-8965
David E Smith Elem Sch 3701 Haltom Rd, Haltom City 76117 Jennifer Martin	PK-5	T	459 25		79%	817/547-1600 Fax 817/831-5817
Foster Village Elem Sch 6800 Springdale Ln, N Richlnd Hls 76182 Sherri Gamble	PK-5	T	495 28		53%	817/547-3100 Fax 817/581-5832
Grace E Hardeman Elem Sch 6100 Whispering Ln, Watauga 76148 Katie Moran	PK-5	T	646 36		60%	817/547-2800 Fax 817/581-5496
Green Valley Elem Sch 7900 Smithfield Rd, N Richlnd Hls 76182 Dawn Demas	PK-5		483 26		17%	817/547-3400 Fax 817/581-5477
Haltom High Sch 5501 Haltom Rd, Haltom City 76137 David Hamilton	9-12	TV	2,641 170		68%	817/547-6000 Fax 817/581-5385
Haltom Middle Sch 5000 Hires Ln, Haltom City 76117 Jill Balzer	6-8	TV	928 50		86%	817/547-4000 Fax 817/831-5778
Holiday Heights Elem Sch 5221 Susan Lee Ln, N Richlnd Hls 76180 Lisa Walker	PK-5	T	613 40		59%	817/547-2600 Fax 817/581-5396
Jack C Binion Elem Sch 7400 Glenview Dr, Richland Hls 76180 Hilda Hager	PK-5	T	800 33		77%	817/547-1800 Fax 817/595-5111
John D Spicer Elem Sch 4300 Estes Park Rd, Haltom City 76137 Dr Cheryl Waddell	PK-5	T	595		66%	817/547-3300 Fax 817/581-5497
Major Cheney ES-S Birdville 2600 Solona St, Haltom City 76117 Darrell Brown	PK-5	T	447 21		92%	817/547-2300 Fax 817/831-5798
North Oaks Middle Sch 4800 Jordan Park Dr, Haltom City 76117 Dr Jennifer Klaerner	6-8	TV	571 60		69%	817/547-4600 Fax 817/581-5352
North Richland Middle Sch 4801 Redondo St, N Richlnd Hls 76180 Stephen Ellis	6-8	TV	891 50		61%	817/547-4200 Fax 817/581-5372
North Ridge Elem Sch 7331 Holiday Ln, N Richlnd Hls 76182 Deborah Coulson	PK-5		491 35		29%	817/547-3200 Fax 817/581-5440
North Ridge Middle Sch 7332 Douglas Ln, N Richlnd Hls 76182 John Davis	6-8	V	746 49		34%	817/547-5200 Fax 817/581-5460
O H Stowe Elem Sch 4201 Rita Ln, Haltom City 76117 Frymark Nathan	PK-5	T	662 39		75%	817/547-2400 Fax 817/581-5328
Richland Elem Sch 3250 Scruggs Park Dr, Richland Hls 76118 Kerri Sands	PK-5	T	296 22		77%	817/547-2000 Fax 817/595-5110
Richland High Sch 5201 Holiday Ln, N Richlnd Hls 76180 Mark McCanlies	9-12	TV	2,158 110		38%	817/547-7000 Fax 817/581-5454
Richland Middle Sch 7400 Hovenkamp Ave, Richland Hls 76118 Jody Fadely	6-8	TV	662 40		69%	817/547-4400 Fax 817/595-5139
Ⓐ Shannon High Sch 6010 Walker St, Haltom City 76117 David Williams	9-12	GV	50 15		57%	817/547-5400 Fax 817/831-5847
Smithfield Elem Sch 6724 Smithfield Rd, N Richlnd Hls 76182 Melissa Minix	PK-5	T	449 30		38%	817/547-2100 Fax 817/581-5377
Smithfield Middle Sch 8400 Main St, N Richlnd Hls 76182 Kyle Pekurney	6-8	V	819 50		21%	817/547-5000 Fax 817/581-5480
Snow Heights Elem Sch 4801 Vance Rd, N Richlnd Hls 76180 Susan Nall	PK-5	T	373 15		40%	817/547-2200 Fax 817/581-5323
W A Porter Elem Sch 2750 Prestondale Dr, Hurst 76054 Greg Bicknell	PK-5		524 35		17%	817/547-2900 Fax 817/581-5381
W T Francisco Elem Sch 3701 Layton Ave, Haltom City 76117 Angela Limon	PK-5	T	351 19		78%	817/547-1700 Fax 817/831-5724
Walker Creek Elem Sch 8780 Bridge St, N Richlnd Hls 76180 Marsha Perry	PK-5		615 33		27%	817/547-3500 Fax 817/581-2932
Watauga Elem Sch 5937 Whitley Rd, Watauga 76148 Sara Uppchurch	PK-5	T	811 48		72%	817/547-2700 Fax 817/581-5425
Watauga Middle Sch 6300 Maurie Dr, Watauga 76148 Shannon Houston	6-8	T	711 75		69%	817/547-4800 Fax 817/581-5369
West Birdville Elementary 3001 Layton Ave, Haltom City 76117 Tim Drysdale	PK-5	T	726 50		86%	817/547-2500 Fax 817/831-5795

1	Superintendent	8	Curric/Instruct K-12	19	Chief Financial Officer	29	Family/Consumer Science	39	Social Studies K-12
2	Bus/Finance/Purchasing	9	Curric/Instruct Elem	20	Art K-12	30	Adult Education	40	Social Studies Elem
3	Buildings And Grounds	10	Curric/Instruct Sec	21	Art Elem	31	Career/Sch-to-Work K-12	41	Social Studies Sec
4	Food Service	11	Federal Program	22	Art Sec	32	Career/Sch-to-Work Elem	42	Science K-12
5	Transportation	12	Title I	23	Music K-12	33	Career/Sch-to-Work Sec	43	Science Elem
6	Athletic	13	Title V	24	Music Elem	34	Early Childhood Ed	44	Science Sec
7	Health Services	15	Asst Superintendent	25	Music Sec	35	Health/Phys Education	45	Math K-12
		16	Instructional Media Svcs	26	Business Education	36	Guidance Services K-12	46	Math Elem
		17	Chief Operations Officer	27	Career & Tech Ed	37	Guidance Services Elem	47	Math Sec
		18	Chief Academic Officer	28	Technology Education	38	Guidance Services Sec	48	English/Lang Arts K-12

49	English/Lang Arts Elem	59	Special Education Elem	69	Academic Assessment
50	English/Lang Arts Sec	60	Special Education Sec	70	Research/Development
51	Reading K-12	61	Foreign/World Lang K-12	71	Public Information
52	Reading Elem	62	Foreign/World Lang Elem	72	Summer School
53	Reading Sec	63	Foreign/World Lang Sec	73	Instructional Tech
54	Remedial Reading K-12	64	Religious Education K-12	74	Inservice Training
55	Remedial Reading Elem	65	Religious Education Elem	75	Marketing/Distributive
56	Remedial Reading Sec	66	Religious Education Sec	76	Info Systems
57	Bilingual/ELL	67	School Board President	77	Psychological Assess
58	Special Education K-12	68	Teacher Personnel	78	Affirmative Action

Texas School Directory

Tarrant County

- **Carroll Independent Sch Dist** PID: 01052252 817/949-8222
  2400 N Carroll Ave, Southlake 76092 Fax 817/949-8228

Schools: 11 \ **Teachers:** 555 \ **Students:** 8,000 \ **Special Ed Students:** 551 \ **LEP Students:** 146 \ **College-Bound:** 75% \ **Ethnic:** Asian 15%, African American 2%, Hispanic 9%, Caucasian 73% \ **Exp:** $260 (Med) \ **Poverty:** 3% \ **Title I:** $164,401 \ **Special Education:** $923,000 \ **Open-Close:** 08/19 - 05/28 \ **DTBP:** $184 (High) \

Dr David Faltys	1	Scott Wrehe	2,15
Bob Carabajal	3	Suzanne Teal	3
Susan Wilson	4	Ranjan George	5
Steve Keasler	6	Gina Peddy	8,61,81
Tyisha Nelson	11,27,57,58,88	Julie Thannum	15,71,297
Matt Miller	15,68	Julie Stephens	16,43,46
Jaclyn Hemmila	22,44,47	Melanie Ringman	35,41,50
Angela Hammond	40,49	Sheri Mills	67
Carie Barthelemess	69,294	Randy Stuart	73
Janet McDade	79		

Public Schs..Principal	Grd	Prgm	Enr/#Cls	SN	
Carroll Elem Sch 1705 W Continental Blvd, Southlake 76092 Stacy Wagnon	PK-4		604 33	1%	817/949-4300 Fax 817/949-4343
Carroll High Sch 800 N White Chapel Blvd, Southlake 76092 Pj Giamanco	9-10		1,388	1%	817/949-5600 Fax 817/949-5656
Carroll Middle Sch 1800 Kirkwood Blvd, Southlake 76092 Stephanie Mangels	7-8		733 60	1%	817/949-5400 Fax 817/949-5454
Carroll Senior High Sch 1501 W Southlake Blvd, Southlake 76092 Shawn Duhon	11-12	A	1,352 80	1%	817/949-5800 Fax 817/949-5858
Cleburn Eubanks Interm Sch 500 S Kimball Ave, Southlake 76092 Mary Stockton	5-6		588 27	1%	817/949-5200 Fax 817/949-5252
Don Durham Intermediate Sch 801 Shady Oaks Dr, Southlake 76092 Mike Wyrick	5-6		683 23		817/949-5300 Fax 817/949-5353
George Dawson Middle Sch 400 S Kimball Ave, Southlake 76092 Ryan Wilson	7-8		628 150	1%	817/949-5500 Fax 817/949-5555
Jack D Johnson Elem Sch 1301 N Carroll Ave, Southlake 76092 Rene Moses	K-4		526 30	2%	817/949-4500 Fax 817/949-4545
Old Union Elem Sch 1050 S Carroll Ave, Southlake 76092 Jon Fike	PK-4		473 30	4%	817/949-4600 Fax 817/949-4646
Rockenbaugh Elem Sch 301 Byron Nelson Pkwy, Southlake 76092 Janet Blackwell	PK-4		543 30	1%	817/949-4700 Fax 817/949-4747
Walnut Grove Elem Sch 2520 N White Chapel Blvd, Southlake 76092 Mike Landers	PK-4		701 24	2%	817/949-4400 Fax 817/949-4444

- **Castleberry Ind School Dist** PID: 01052290 817/252-2000
  5228 Ohio Garden Rd, Fort Worth 76114 Fax 817/252-2099

Schools: 7 \ **Teachers:** 244 \ **Students:** 3,900 \ **Special Ed Students:** 311 \ **LEP Students:** 1,447 \ **Ethnic:** African American 1%, Hispanic 80%, Caucasian 19% \ **Exp:** $588 (High) \ **Poverty:** 22% \ **Title I:** $1,195,398 \ **Special Education:** $1,074,000 \ **Open-Close:** 08/19 - 05/22 \ **DTBP:** $181 (High) \

John Ramos	1	Deanne Page	2
Sophia Quiorov	2	Sara Bytren	4
Lenny Lasher	6,7,35	Ken Caserves	8,11,83,88,288,296,298
Micheele Sprambler	9*	Kenneth Casarez	10
Kelli Kelsoe	16*	Abigail Crawford	20,23
Wanda Byther	31*	Denise Fisher	42
Scott Hutching	45,54,277	Stacie Adams	48*
Ruth Martin	57	Lynn Jamison	58
David Holder	67	David Rodriguez	68,273*
Renee Smith-Faulkner	71,73,95,286	Heather Mayfield	76
Jacob Bowser	76	Brian Huff	84,295
Samiel Cervantez	91	Laura Little	294

Public Schs..Principal	Grd	Prgm	Enr/#Cls	SN	
A V Cato Elem Sch 4501 Barbara Rd, Fort Worth 76114 Meredith Strambler	PK-5	T	721 18	78%	817/252-2400 Fax 817/252-2499
Castleberry Elem Sch 1100 Roberts Cut Off Rd, Fort Worth 76114 Michelle Stapp	PK-5	T	753 50	80%	817/252-2300 Fax 817/625-1884
Castleberry High Sch 215 Churchill Rd, Fort Worth 76114 Elizabeth Priddy	9-12	GTV	1,008 70	75%	817/252-2100 Fax 817/252-2575
Irma Marsh Middle Sch 415 Hagg Dr, Fort Worth 76114 Mareka Austin	6-8	TV	881 60	82%	817/252-2200 Fax 817/738-3454
Joy James Elem Sch 5300 Buchanan St, Fort Worth 76114 Leighann Turner	PK-5	T	492 24	87%	817/252-2500 Fax 817/252-2599
Reach High Sch 1101 Merritt St, Fort Worth 76114 Wanda Byther	9-12	AGTV	46 4	86%	817/252-2390 Fax 817/252-2398
Ⓐ Truce Learning Center 1101 Merritt St, Fort Worth 76114 Wanda Byther	6-12	T	25 2	77%	817/252-2490 Fax 817/252-2499

- **Crowley Ind School Dist** PID: 01052355 817/297-5800
  512 Peach St, Crowley 76036 Fax 817/297-5805

Schools: 25 \ **Teachers:** 1,014 \ **Students:** 15,215 \ **Special Ed Students:** 1,440 \ **LEP Students:** 2,114 \ **College-Bound:** 52% \ **Ethnic:** Asian 4%, African American 45%, Hispanic 32%, Native American: 1%, Caucasian 18% \ **Exp:** $303 (High) \ **Poverty:** 14% \ **Title I:** $3,711,131 \ **Special Education:** $2,439,000 \ **Open-Close:** 08/15 - 05/25 \ **DTBP:** $175 (High) \

Dr Michael McFarland	1	Dwayne Jones	2
Stacy Adrian	2,19	Randy Reaves	3
Jason Lowery	5	Charles Lincoln	6
Paige Williams	7*	Maryann Middleton	8
Ted Kretchmar	11,294,296	Billy Johnson	15,79,83,85
Theresa Paschall	36	Maria Anguiano	57
Ruby Batiste	58	June Davis	67
Dr Theresa Kohler	68	Anthony Kirchner	71
Jerald Allen	73,95,98*	Jaretha Jordan	74
Stan Swann	79	Dr John Hamlett	88
Pat Panek	91	Bradley Parker	286
Matt Hoover	297	Crystel Polk	298*
Veronica Kunschik	750	Stefani Allen	752

Public Schs..Principal	Grd	Prgm	Enr/#Cls	SN	
Bess Race Elem Sch 537 S Heights Dr, Crowley 76036 Holly Anderson	PK-4	T	577 33	48%	817/297-5080 Fax 817/297-5084
Bill R Johnson Cte Center 1033 McCart Ave, Crowley 76036 Markeba Warfield	Voc	G	610		817/297-3018 Fax 817/297-1839
Crowley High Sch 1005 W Main St, Crowley 76036 Daryle Moffett	10-12	TV	1,500	50%	817/297-5810 Fax 817/297-5854

79	Student Personnel	91	Safety/Security	275	Response To Intervention	298	Grant Writer/Ptnrships
80	Driver Ed/Safety	92	Magnet School	277	Remedial Math K-12	750	Chief Innovation Officer
81	Gifted/Talented	93	Parental Involvement	280	Literacy Coach	751	Chief of Staff
82	Video Services	95	Tech Prep Program	285	STEM	752	Social Emotional Learning
83	Substance Abuse Prev	97	Chief Infomation Officer	286	Digital Learning		
84	Erate	98	Chief Technology Officer	288	Common Core Standards		
85	AIDS Education	270	Character Education	294	Accountability		
88	Alternative/At Risk	271	Migrant Education	295	Network System		
89	Multi-Cultural Curriculum	273	Teacher Mentor	296	Title II Programs		
90	Social Work	274	Before/After Sch	297	Webmaster		

School Programs
A = Alternative Program
G = Adult Classes
M = Magnet Program
T = Title I Schoolwide
V = Career & Tech Ed Programs

Other School Types
Ⓐ = Alternative School
Ⓒ = Charter School
Ⓜ = Magnet School
Ⓨ = Year-Round School

Social Media
 = Facebook
 = Twitter

New Schools are shaded
New Superintendents and Principals are bold
Personnel with email addresses are underscored

TX—347

Tarrant County

Market Data Retrieval

Crowley HS 9th Grade Campus 9-9 V 540 817/297-5845
1016 FM 1187 W, Crowley 76036 50 Fax 817/297-5847
Christopher White

Ⓐ Crowley Learning Center 3-12 150 817/297-6992
1008 FM 1187 W, Crowley 76036 11 Fax 817/297-4087
Rashad Muhammad

Crowley Middle Sch 7-8 TV 681 66% 817/370-5650
3800 W Risinger Rd, Fort Worth 76123 45 Fax 817/370-5656
Omarian Brown

Dallas Park Elem Sch PK-4 T 741 43% 817/370-5620
8700 Viridian Ln, Fort Worth 76123 37 Fax 817/370-5624
Veronica DelGado

David L Walker Interm Sch 5-6 T 603 74% 817/568-2745
9901 Hemphill St, Fort Worth 76134 Fax 817/568-2209
Melanie Randall

Deer Creek Elem Sch PK-4 T 514 48% 817/297-5880
805 S Crowley Rd, Crowley 76036 30 Fax 817/297-5884
Anna Roe

Ⓐ Global Prep Academy 7-12 75 817/297-3018
1033 McCart Ave, Crowley 76036
Kady Donaghey

H F Stevens Middle Sch 7-8 TV 881 63% 817/297-5840
940 N Crowley Rd, Crowley 76036 35 Fax 817/297-5850
Kimberly Buckhalton

J A Hargrave Elem Sch PK-4 T 559 67% 817/370-5630
9200 Poynter St, Fort Worth 76123 Fax 817/370-5635
Kimberly Sherfield

Jackie Carden Elem Sch PK-4 T 515 67% 817/370-5600
3701 Garden Springs Dr, Fort Worth 76123 32 Fax 817/370-5604
Paula Brooks

June W Davis Elem Sch PK-5 550 817/885-5700
6301 Rockrose Tr, Fort Worth 76123 Fax 817/885-8720
Kevin Hunt

Mary Harris Intermediate Sch 5-6 T 587 70% 817/370-7571
8400 W Cleburne Rd, Fort Worth 76123 Fax 817/294-1594
Clarence Williams

Meadowcreek Elem Sch PK-4 T 558 72% 817/370-5690
2801 Country Creek Ln, Fort Worth 76123 30 Fax 817/370-5694
Tonya Coleman

North Crowley 9th Grade Campus 9-9 V 656 817/297-5896
4630 McPherson Blvd, Fort Worth 76123 Fax 817/297-5878
Camcea Stapinski

North Crowley High Sch 10-12 TV 1,759 48% 817/263-1250
9100 S Hulen St, Fort Worth 76123 100 Fax 817/263-1282
Daryl Porter

Oakmont Elem Sch PK-4 T 632 57% 817/370-5610
6651 Oakmont Trl, Fort Worth 76132 40 Fax 817/370-5615
Kimberly Scoggins

Parkway Elem Sch PK-4 T 656 87% 817/568-5710
1320 W Everman Pkwy, Fort Worth 76134 34 Fax 817/568-5714
Roslyn Bell

S H Crowley Intermediate Sch 5-6 T 531 817/297-5960
10525 McCart Ave, Crowley 76036 Fax 817/297-5964
Deidra Castro

Sidney Poynter Elem Sch PK-4 T 545 62% 817/568-5730
521 Ashdale Dr, Fort Worth 76140 40 Fax 817/568-5734
Shaketa Traylor

Sue Crouch Intermediate Sch 5-6 T 631 53% 817/370-5670
8036 Cedar Lake Ln, Fort Worth 76123 Fax 817/370-5676
Arthurlyn Morgan

Summer Creek Middle Sch 7-8 TV 800 49% 817/297-5090
10236 Summercreek Dr, Crowley 76036 Fax 817/297-5094
Cayla Grossman

Sycamore Elem Sch PK-4 T 627 69% 817/568-5700
1601 Country Manor Rd, Fort Worth 76134 28 Fax 817/568-5704
Rebekah Hunt

• **Eagle Mtn-Saginaw Ind Sch Dist** PID: 01052408 817/232-0880
1200 Old Decatur Rd, Saginaw 76179 Fax 817/847-6124

Schools: 27 \ **Teachers:** 1,213 \ **Students:** 21,000 \
Special Ed Students: 1,725 \ **LEP Students:** 1,643 \ **College-Bound:** 54%
\ **Ethnic:** Asian 4%, African American 11%, Hispanic 39%, Native American:
1%, Caucasian 45% \ **Exp:** $179 (Low) \ **Poverty:** 9% \ **Title I:** $1,941,660 \
Special Education: $2,382,000 \ **Open-Close:** 08/19 - 05/29 \ **DTBP:** $187
(High) \

Dr Jim Chadwell 1
Jim Schiele 2,19
Charles Hamilton 3
Aaron Wylie 4
Cheryl Phalen 7
Stacy Summerhill 8
Shawn Bell 20,23
Dr Dana Barnes 27,30,31*
Dr Heather Hughes 58,77
Dr Deborah Dockens 68,79
Dr Philo Waters 68
Kirk Murdock 73,295
Belinda Newman 76
Ally Surface 298
Jane Valdez 2
Lucia Cieszlak 2
Clete Welch 3,5,17
Brent Barker 6
Dr Linda Parker 8,15,34,74,294
Dr Mary Jones 11,69,88,271,296
Dana Eldredge 27*
Mariella Alvarado 36
Steven Newcom 67
Dr Maria Gamell 68
Megan Overman 71
Karen Miller 74,273
Dr Barry Baker 91

Public Schs..Principal	Grd	Prgm	Enr/#Cls	SN
Bryson Elem Sch 8601 Old Decatur Rd, Fort Worth 76179 **Jennifer Gillard**	PK-5	T	489 35	44% 817/237-8306 Fax 817/238-8991
Chisholm Ridge Elem Sch 8301 Running River Ln, Fort Worth 76131 **Krystle Green**	PK-5	T	664	42% 817/232-0715 Fax 817/306-4391
Chisholm Trail High Sch 3100 NW College Dr, Fort Worth 76179 **Walter Berringer**	9-12	TV	2,078	44% 817/232-7112 Fax 817/306-1327
Comanche Springs Elem Sch 8100 Comanche Springs Dr, Fort Worth 76131 **Melissa Davis**	PK-5		662 26	27% 817/847-8700 Fax 817/847-0941
Creekview Middle Sch 6716 Bob Hanger St, Fort Worth 76179 **Anthe Anagnostis**	6-8	TV	902	43% 817/237-4261 Fax 817/237-2387
Dozier Elem Sch 6201 Redeagle Creek Dr, Fort Worth 76179 Beth Epps	K-5	T	450	51% 817/847-6340 Fax 817/237-8015
Eagle Mountain Elem Sch 9700 Morris Dido Newark Rd, Fort Worth 76179 **Jason Beaty**	PK-5		650 31	17% 817/236-7191 Fax 817/236-1461
Ed Willkie Middle Sch 6129 Texas Shiner Dr, Fort Worth 76179 **Daniel Knowles**	6-8	T	959	42% 817/237-9631 Fax 817/237-9643
Elkins Elem Sch 7259 Elkins School Rd, Fort Worth 76179 **Randiann Cowden**	K-5	T	651 36	53% 817/237-0805 Fax 817/237-0948
Ⓐ Elmer C Watson High Sch 5900 Hereford Dr, Fort Worth 76179 **Melanie Stitt**	9-12	GT	90 25	51% 817/238-7925 Fax 817/237-0753
Greenfield Elem Sch 6020 Ten Mile Bridge Rd, Fort Worth 76135 **Kelly Ramsey**	PK-5	T	709 38	39% 817/237-0357 Fax 817/237-5809
Hafley Development Center 616 W McLeroy Blvd, Fort Worth 76179 **Stacey De Hoyos**	PK-PK	GT	296 18	72% 817/232-2071 Fax 817/232-5126
High Country Elem Sch 1301 High Country Trl, Fort Worth 76131 **Elizabeth Sanders**	PK-5	T	532 35	40% 817/306-8007 Fax 817/306-5852
Highland Middle Sch 1001 E Bailey Boswell Rd, Fort Worth 76131 **David Coker**	6-8	TV	856 50	50% 817/847-5143 Fax 817/847-1922

---

1 Superintendent	8 Curric/Instruct K-12	19 Chief Financial Officer	29 Family/Consumer Science
2 Bus/Finance/Purchasing	9 Curric/Instruct Elem	20 Art K-12	30 Adult Education
3 Buildings And Grounds	10 Curric/Instruct Sec	21 Art Elem	31 Career/Sch-to-Work K-12
4 Food Service	11 Federal Program	22 Art Sec	32 Career/Sch-to-Work Elem
5 Transportation	12 Title I	23 Music K-12	33 Career/Sch-to-Work Sec
6 Athletic	13 Title V	24 Music Elem	34 Early Childhood Ed
7 Health Services	15 Asst Superintendent	25 Music Sec	35 Health/Phys Education
	16 Instructional Media Svcs	26 Business Education	36 Guidance Services K-12
	17 Chief Operations Officer	27 Career & Tech Ed	37 Guidance Services Elem
	18 Chief Academic Officer	28 Technology Education	38 Guidance Services Sec

39 Social Studies K-12	49 English/Lang Arts Elem	59 Special Education Elem	69 Academic Assessment
40 Social Studies Elem	50 English/Lang Arts Sec	60 Special Education Sec	70 Research/Development
41 Social Studies Sec	51 Reading K-12	61 Foreign/World Lang K-12	71 Public Information
42 Science K-12	52 Reading Elem	62 Foreign/World Lang Elem	72 Summer School
43 Science Elem	53 Reading Sec	63 Foreign/World Lang Sec	73 Instructional Tech
44 Science Sec	54 Remedial Reading K-12	64 Religious Education K-12	74 Inservice Training
45 Math K-12	55 Remedial Reading Elem	65 Religious Education Elem	75 Marketing/Distributive
46 Math Elem	56 Remedial Reading Sec	66 Religious Education Sec	76 Info Systems
47 Math Sec	57 Bilingual/ELL	67 School Board President	77 Psychological Assess
48 English/Lang Arts K-12	58 Special Education K-12	68 Teacher Personnel	78 Affirmative Action

Texas School Directory

Tarrant County

Public Schs..Principal	Grd	Prgm	Enr/#Cls	SN	
Hollenstein Career & Tech Ctr 5501 Marine Creek Pkwy, Fort Worth 76179 Dr Dana Barnes	Voc		1,600		817/306-1925 Fax 817/306-1327
L A Gililland Elem Sch 701 Waggoman Rd, Fort Worth 76131 Christina Fehler	PK-5	T	501 39	70%	817/232-0331 Fax 817/232-8822
Lake Pointe Elem Sch 5501 Park Dr, Fort Worth 76179 Audrey Arnold	PK-5		699	24%	817/236-8801 Fax 817/236-8805
Marine Creek Middle Sch 5825 Marine Creek Pkwy, Fort Worth 76179 **Danny Knowles**	6-8		1,000		817/847-2945
Northbrook Elem Sch 2500 Cantrell Sansom Rd, Fort Worth 76131 Gina Mayfield	PK-5	T	597	69%	817/232-0086 Fax 817/232-9861
Parkview Elem Sch 6225 Crystal Lake Dr, Fort Worth 76179 Mindy Miller	PK-5	T	493	45%	817/237-5121 Fax 817/237-5187
Prairie Vista Middle Sch 8000 Comanche Springs Dr, Fort Worth 76131 Dr Anna King	6-8	T	820	49%	817/847-9210 Fax 817/847-4255
Remington Point Elem Sch 6000 Old Decatur Rd, Fort Worth 76179 Chaney Curran	PK-5	T	490 37	48%	817/232-1342 Fax 817/232-2594
Saginaw Elem Sch 301 W McLeroy Blvd, Fort Worth 76179 Amber Beene	PK-5	T	375 50	62%	817/232-0631 Fax 817/232-3357
Saginaw High Sch 800 N Blue Mound Rd, Fort Worth 76131 Karen Pressley	9-12	TV	1,898	42%	817/306-0914 Fax 817/306-1344
W E Boswell High Sch 5805 W Bailey Boswell Rd, Fort Worth 76179 Nika Davis	9-12	GV	1,898 100	29%	817/237-3314 Fax 817/238-8706
Wayside Middle Sch 1300 Old Decatur Rd, Fort Worth 76179 **Raymond Fahey**	6-8	V	880 60	30%	817/232-0541 Fax 817/232-2391
Willow Creek Elem Sch 1100 W McLeroy Blvd, Saginaw 76179 Christal Hollinger	PK-5		598	44%	817/232-2845 Fax 817/847-1859

- **Everman Ind School Dist** PID: 01052460 817/568-3500
  1520 Everman Pkwy, Fort Worth 76140 Fax 817/568-3508

Schools: 11 \ **Teachers:** 342 \ **Students:** 6,800 \ **Special Ed Students:** 452 \ **LEP Students:** 1,586 \ **College-Bound:** 56% \ **Ethnic:** Asian 1%, African American 37%, Hispanic 58%, Caucasian 4% \ **Exp:** $503 (High) \ **Poverty:** 26% \ **Title I:** $2,024,713 \ **Special Education:** $995,000 \ **Open-Close:** 08/15 - 05/28 \ **DTBP:** $171 (High)

Curtis Amos 1		Joee Gainer 2,19	
Glenn Brown 3		Rebecca Noon 4,34	
Felicia Donaldson 5,7,15,36,68,78,80,298		Jason Gillis 5	
Dale Matlock 6*		Kentrell Phillips 8,15,73	
Jennifer Samuel 9,69,288		Colette Kotula 11	
Susan Geye 16,73,286,295*		Susan Alvey 27	
Pam McCoy 34,57		Melissa Sigler 47*	
Diane Walker 58		Ginna Marks 58	
Rickey Burgess 67		Gina Sanderson 68	
Dr Nikita Russell 71		Hubert Pickett 79	
James King 79,91			

Public Schs..Principal	Grd	Prgm	Enr/#Cls	SN	
Baxter Junior High Sch 3038 Shelby Rd, Fort Worth 76140 Kentrel Phillips	7-8	AT	969 30	95%	817/568-3530 Fax 817/568-3594
Dan Powell Intermediate Sch 8875 Oak Grove Rd, Fort Worth 76140 Tanisha Boone	5-5	T	493 36	96%	817/568-3523 Fax 817/568-3533
Davis 9th Grade Center 615 Townley Dr, Everman 76140 Patrick Lamers	9-9	AGV	433		817/568-5280 Fax 817/568-3538
E Ray Elem Sch 7309 Sheridan Rd, Fort Worth 76134 Eva Quinonez	PK-4	T	495 25	93%	817/568-3545 Fax 817/568-3544
Ⓐ Everman Academy High Sch 300 Shelby Rd, Everman 76140 Cherie Pace	9-12	T	67	86%	817/568-3520 Fax 817/568-3516
Everman Joe C Bean High Sch 1000 S Race St, Everman 76140 Jason Miller	9-12	AGT	1,515 125	80%	817/568-5200 Fax 817/568-5219
Hommel Elem Sch 308 W Enon Ave, Everman 76140 Martin DeHoyos	PK-4	T	399 25	98%	817/568-3540 Fax 817/568-3543
J W Bishop Elem Sch 501 Vaughn Ave, Everman 76140 Ollie Clark	PK-4	T	516 37	95%	817/568-3575 Fax 817/568-3572
Ray Johnson 6th Grade Ctr 8901 Oak Grove Rd, Fort Worth 76140 Mary Preston	6-6	T	473	92%	817/615-3670 Fax 817/615-3675
Souder Elem Sch 201 N Forest Hill Dr, Everman 76140 Logan Jones	PK-4	T	529 30	92%	817/568-3580 Fax 817/568-3589
Townley Elem Sch 2200 McPherson Rd, Everman 76140 Tamika Dees	PK-4	T	382	92%	817/568-3560 Fax 817/568-5177

- **Ft Worth Ind School Dist** PID: 01052525 817/871-2000
  100 N University Dr, Fort Worth 76107 Fax 817/814-1935

Schools: 134 \ **Teachers:** 5,689 \ **Students:** 86,000 \ **Special Ed Students:** 7,043 \ **LEP Students:** 24,714 \ **College-Bound:** 57% \ **Ethnic:** Asian 2%, African American 23%, Hispanic 64%, Caucasian 11% \ **Exp:** $294 (Med) \ **Poverty:** 25% \ **Title I:** $38,908,050 \ **Special Education:** $14,267,000 \ **Open-Close:** 08/19 - 05/28 \ **DTBP:** $129 (High) \ 📘 🅣

Dr Kent Scribner 1		Jonathan Bey 2	
Arturo Cavazos 3,15		Glenn Headlee 4	
Bill Ray 5		Todd Vesely 6	
Alice Turner Jackson 7		Charles Carroll 8,18	
Khechara Bradford 8,15		Mirgitt Crespo 11	
Dr Becky Navarre 15,95		Dr Cherie Washington 15	
Dr Maria Sheffield 15,58		Michael Steinert 15,79,83	
Sara Arispe 15,294		Sherry Breed 15,79	
Carter Cook 16		Elsie Schiro 19	
Beverly Fletcher 20		Dick Clardy 23	
Dinah Menger 24		Don Devous 25	
Edward Spears 30		Dr Cassandra Morris-Surles 34	
Georgiann Roberts 35		Kathryn Everest 36	
Joseph Niedziela 39		Dr Herman Jackson 42	
Shannon Hernandez 45		Melvina Robinson 46	
Cherron Ukpaka 52,280		Michelle McCone 53,280	
Suann Claunch 57		Dr Corey Goloms 58	
Elda Rojas 61		Jacinto Ramos 67	
Ken Torres 69		Tracy Marshall 70,298	
Barbara Griffith 71		Dr Karla Lester 73	
Dr Lezley Lewis 74		Dr Carlos Antoline 77	
Danny Sutton 91		Miguel Garcia 274	
Patricia Sutton 275		John Cope 297	
Karen Molinar 751			

79	Student Personnel	91	Safety/Security	275	Response To Intervention	298	Grant Writer/Ptnrships
80	Driver Ed/Safety	92	Magnet School	277	Remedial Math K-12	750	Chief Innovation Officer
81	Gifted/Talented	93	Parental Involvement	280	Literacy Coach	751	Chief of Staff
82	Video Services	95	Tech Prep Program	285	STEM	752	Social Emotional Learning
83	Substance Abuse Prev	97	Chief Infomation Officer	286	Digital Learning		
84	Erate	98	Chief Technology Officer	288	Common Core Standards		
85	AIDS Education	270	Accountability	294	Network School		
88	Alternative/At Risk	271	Migrant Education	295	Network System		
89	Multi-Cultural Curriculum	273	Teacher Mentor	296	Title II Programs		
90	Social Work	274	Before/After Sch	297	Webmaster		

Other School Types
Ⓐ = Alternative School
Ⓒ = Charter School
Ⓜ = Magnet School
Ⓨ = Year-Round School

School Programs
A = Alternative Program
G = Adult Classes
M = Magnet Program
T = Title I Schoolwide
V = Career & Tech Ed Programs

Social Media
📘 = Facebook
🅣 = Twitter

New Schools are shaded
New Superintendents and Principals are bold
Personnel with email addresses are underscored

TX—349

Tarrant County

Market Data Retrieval

Public Schs..Principal	Grd	Prgm	Enr/#Cls	SN	
ⓨ A M Pate Elem Sch 3800 Anglin Dr, Fort Worth 76119 Rochelle Horton	PK-5	MT	522 35	93%	817/815-3800 Fax 817/815-3850
Adult Education Center 5701 Meadowbrook Dr Bldg 1, Fort Worth 76112 Sofia Zamarripa	Adult	V	500 5		817/492-7960 Fax 817/492-7977
ⓨ Alice Carlson Applied Lrng Ctr 3320 W Cantey St, Fort Worth 76109 Janis Harris	PK-5	M	393 17	17%	817/815-5700 Fax 817/815-5750
Alice Contreras Elem Sch 4100 Lubbock Ave, Fort Worth 76115 Amelia Cortes-Rangel	PK-5	T	668	87%	817/814-7800 Fax 817/814-7850
Amon Carter-Riverside High Sch 3301 Yucca Ave, Fort Worth 76111 Greg Ruthart	9-12	TV	1,267	86%	817/814-9000 Fax 817/814-9050
ⓨ Applied Learning Academy 7060 Camp Bowie Blvd, Fort Worth 76116 Alice Buckley	6-8	MT	317 20	55%	817/815-5500 Fax 817/815-5550
Arlington Heights High Sch 4501 West Fwy, Fort Worth 76107 Sarah Weeks	9-12	TV	1,934 75	44%	817/815-1000 Fax 817/815-1050
Atwood McDonald Elem Sch 1850 Barron Ln, Fort Worth 76112 Nkosi Geary-Smith	PK-5	T	494	83%	817/815-4800 Fax 817/815-4850
Benbrook Elem Sch 800 Mercedes St, Fort Worth 76126 Shelly Mayer	PK-5		658 25	38%	817/815-6400 Fax 817/815-6450
Benbrook Middle High Sch 201 Overcrest Dr, Fort Worth 76126 Richard Penland	6-12	T	1,598	43%	817/815-7100 Fax 817/815-7150
Bill J Elliott Elem Sch 2501 Cooks Ln, Fort Worth 76120 Latonya Ordaz	PK-5	T	456 38	83%	817/815-4600 Fax 817/815-4650
Bonnie Brae Elem Sch 3504 Kimbo Rd, Fort Worth 76111 Samantha Gonzalez	PK-5	T	468 22	88%	817/814-3700 Fax 817/814-3750
Boulevard Heights Sch 5100 El Campo Ave, Fort Worth 76107 Dr Terry Guthrie	Spec		50 9	78%	817/814-6400 Fax 817/814-6450
Bruce Shulkey Elem Sch 5533 Whitman Ave, Fort Worth 76133 Vanessa Tritten	PK-5	T	511 28	78%	817/814-8400 Fax 817/814-8450
Burton Hill Elem Sch 519 Burton Hill Rd, Fort Worth 76114 Terrance Bigley	PK-5	T	543 25	52%	817/815-1400 Fax 817/815-1450
Carroll Peak Elem Sch 1201 E Jefferson Ave, Fort Worth 76104 Kalyn Sanjacinto	PK-5	T	626 24	92%	817/814-0700 Fax 817/814-0750
Carter Park Elem Sch 1204 E Broadus Ave, Fort Worth 76115 Howard Robinson	PK-5	T	643 25	95%	817/815-8600 Fax 817/815-8650
Cesar Chavez Elem Sch 3710 Deen Rd, Fort Worth 76106 Monica Ordaz	PK-5	T	547	93%	817/815-0300 Fax 817/815-0350
Charles E Nash Elem Sch 401 Samuels Ave, Fort Worth 76102 Mrs Galindo	PK-5	T	276 12	74%	817/814-9400 Fax 817/814-9450
Christene Moss Elem Sch 4108 Eastland St, Fort Worth 76119 Charla Staten	PK-5	T	418 31	85%	817/815-3600 Fax 817/815-3650
Clifford Davis Elem Sch 4300 Campus Dr, Fort Worth 76119 Pamela Henderson	PK-5	T	789 24	88%	817/815-8700 Fax 817/815-8750
ⓜ Como Montessori Sch 4001 Littlepage St, Fort Worth 76107 Ronnita Carridine	K-8	T	320 19	65%	817/815-7200 Fax 817/815-7250
ⓨ D McRae Elem Sch 3316 Avenue N, Fort Worth 76105 Aura Angel	PK-5	MT	615 32	93%	817/814-0500 Fax 817/814-0550
Daggett Montessori Elem Sch 801 W Jessamine St, Fort Worth 76110 Victorius Eugenio	K-8	T	508	48%	817/814-6300 Fax 817/814-6350
David K Sellars Elem Sch 4200 Dorsey St, Fort Worth 76119 Steven Mattic	PK-5	T	642 28	92%	817/815-9200 Fax 817/815-9250
ⓨ De Zavala Elem Sch 1419 College Ave, Fort Worth 76104 Victorius Eugenio	PK-5	MT	303 30	87%	817/814-5600 Fax 817/814-5650
Diamond Hill Elem Sch 2000 Dewey St, Fort Worth 76106 Maryln Martinez	PK-5	T	676 32	92%	817/814-0400 Fax 817/814-0450
Diamond Hill-Jarvis High Sch 1411 Maydell St, Fort Worth 76106 James Garcia	9-12	TV	936	84%	817/815-0000 Fax 817/815-0050
Dolores Huerta Elem Sch 3309 W Long Ave, Fort Worth 76106 Carla Coscia	PK-5	T	552	95%	817/814-4400 Fax 817/814-4450
E M Daggett Elem Sch 958 Page Ave, Fort Worth 76110 Kendall Miller	PK-5	T	724 35	86%	817/815-5500 Fax 817/815-5550
E M Daggett Middle Sch 1108 Carlock St, Fort Worth 76110 Monica Garrett	6-8	TV	393 35	90%	817/814-5200 Fax 817/814-5250
East Handley Elem Sch 2617 Mims St, Fort Worth 76112 Alleia Hobbs	PK-5	T	427 19	89%	817/815-4400 Fax 817/815-4450
Eastern Hills Elem Sch 5917 Shelton St, Fort Worth 76112 Whitney Scott	PK-5	T	567 30	84%	817/815-4500 Fax 817/815-4550
Eastern Hills High Sch 5701 Shelton St, Fort Worth 76112 Katrina Smith	9-12	GTV	1,150	60%	817/815-4000 Fax 817/815-4050
ⓨ Edward J Briscoe Elem Sch 2751 Yuma Ave, Fort Worth 76104 Octavia Gray	PK-5	MT	464 25	96%	817/814-0300 Fax 817/814-0350
ⓨ Forest Oak Middle Sch 3221 Pecos St, Fort Worth 76119 Seretha Lofton	6-8	MTV	823 50	82%	817/815-8200 Fax 817/815-8250
George Clarke Elem Sch 3300 S Henderson St, Fort Worth 76110 Kimberly Benavides	PK-5	T	476 38	89%	817/814-6100 Fax 817/814-6150
Glen Park Elem Sch 3601 Pecos St, Fort Worth 76119 Ellen Verreault	PK-5	T	646 37	93%	817/815-8800 Fax 817/815-8850
Glencrest 6th Grade Middle Sch 4801 Eastline Dr, Fort Worth 76119 Cassandra McCalister	6-6	T	449 50	89%	817/815-8400 Fax 817/815-8450
Green B Trimble Tech High Sch 1003 W Cannon St, Fort Worth 76104 E Omar Ramos	9-12	TV	1,698 100	69%	817/815-2500 Fax 817/815-2550
Greenbriar Elem Sch 1605 Grady Lee St, Fort Worth 76134 Nicole Montalvo	PK-5	T	647 39	90%	817/814-7400 Fax 817/814-7450
H V Helbing Elem Sch 3524 N Crump St, Fort Worth 76106 Ana Morales	PK-5	TV	467 29	91%	817/815-0500 Fax 817/815-0550
Handley Middle Sch 2801 Patino Rd, Fort Worth 76112 Reginald Terrell	6-8	TV	435 30	67%	817/815-4200 Fax 817/815-4250
Harlean Beal Elem Sch 5615 Forest Hill Dr, Fort Worth 76119 Jodie Courtade	PK-5	T	448 25	72%	817/815-8500 Fax 817/531-7738

---

1 Superintendent	8 Curric/Instruct K-12	19 Chief Financial Officer	29 Family/Consumer Science	39 Social Studies K-12	49 English/Lang Arts Elem	59 Special Education Elem	69 Academic Assessment
2 Bus/Finance/Purchasing	9 Curric/Instruct Elem	20 Art K-12	30 Adult Education	40 Social Studies Elem	50 English/Lang Arts Sec	60 Special Education Sec	70 Research/Development
3 Buildings And Grounds	10 Curric/Instruct Sec	21 Art Elem	31 Career/Sch-to-Work K-12	41 Social Studies Sec	51 Reading K-12	61 Foreign/World Lang K-12	71 Public Information
4 Food Service	11 Federal Program	22 Art Sec	32 Career/Sch-to-Work Elem	42 Science K-12	52 Reading Elem	62 Foreign/World Lang Elem	72 Summer School
5 Transportation	12 Title I	23 Music K-12	33 Career/Sch-to-Work Sec	43 Science Elem	53 Reading Sec	63 Foreign/World Lang Sec	73 Instructional Tech
6 Athletic	13 Title V	24 Music Elem	34 Early Childhood Ed	44 Science Sec	54 Remedial Reading K-12	64 Religious Education K-12	74 Inservice Training
7 Health Services	15 Asst Superintendent	25 Music Sec	35 Health/Phys Education	45 Math K-12	55 Remedial Reading Elem	65 Religious Education Elem	75 Marketing/Distributive
	16 Instructional Media Svcs	26 Business Education	36 Guidance Services K-12	46 Math Elem	56 Remedial Reading Sec	66 Religious Education Sec	76 Info Systems
	17 Chief Operations Officer	27 Career & Tech Ed	37 Guidance Services Elem	47 Math Sec	57 Bilingual/ELL	67 School Board President	77 Psychological Assess
	18 Chief Academic Officer	28 Technology Education	38 Guidance Services Sec	48 English/Lang Arts K-12	58 Special Education K-12	68 Teacher Personnel	78 Affirmative Action

Texas School Directory — Tarrant County

School	Grades	Prog	Enroll/Staff	%	Phone/Fax
Hazel Harvey Peace Elem Sch 7555 Trail Lake Dr, Fort Worth 76133 **Anthony Avery**	PK-5	T	571	76%	817/814-8800 Fax 817/814-8850
ⓨ Hubbard Heights Elem Sch 1333 W Spurgeon St, Fort Worth 76115 Amparo Martinez	PK-5	MT	615 / 35	93%	817/814-7500 Fax 817/814-7550
I M Terrell Elem Sch 1411 I M Terrell Cir S, Fort Worth 76102 **Baldwin Brown**	PK-5	T	244 / 12	98%	817/815-1900 Fax 817/871-1950
ⓨ International Newcomer Academy 7060 Camp Bowie Blvd, Fort Worth 76116 Angelia Ross	6-9	AMT	460 / 44	81%	817/815-5600 Fax 817/815-5650
J Martin Jacquet Middle Sch 2501 Stalcup Rd, Fort Worth 76119 Dr Cheryl Johnson	6-8	TV	736 / 38	80%	817/815-3500 Fax 817/815-3550
J P Elder Middle Sch 709 NW 21st St, Fort Worth 76164 **Dr David Trimble**	6-8	TV	1,290 / 58	88%	817/814-4100 Fax 817/814-4150
J T Stevens Elem Sch 6161 Wrigley Way, Fort Worth 76133 Jessica Johnson	PK-5	T	482 / 25	70%	817/814-8500 Fax 817/814-8550
Jean McClung Middle Sch 3000 Forest Ave, Fort Worth 76112 **Marron McWilliams**	6-8	T	741	85%	817/815-5300 Fax 817/815-5350
ⓨ Jo Kelly Sch 201 N Bailey Ave, Fort Worth 76107 Leslie Riddell	Spec	M	43 / 13	60%	817/815-5900 Fax 817/815-5950
John T White Elem Sch 7300 John T White Rd, Fort Worth 76120 Tamera Dugan	PK-5	T	586	87%	817/814-7900 Fax 817/814-7950
ⓨ Kirkpatrick Middle Sch 3201 Refugio Ave, Fort Worth 76106 Jeffrey Bartolotta	6-8	MT	512	95%	817/814-4200 Fax 817/814-4250
Leadership Acad Como ES 4000 Horne St, Fort Worth 76107 Valencia Rhines	PK-5	T	460	90%	817/815-6500 Fax 817/815-6550
ⓨ Leadership Acad Mitchell Blvd 3601 Mitchell Blvd, Fort Worth 76105 Aileen Quinones	PK-5	MT	391 / 30	90%	817/815-9000 Fax 817/815-9050
Leonard Middle Sch 8900 Chapin Rd, Fort Worth 76116 **Cathy Williams**	6-8	TV	772 / 65	81%	817/815-6200 Fax 817/815-6250
Lily B Clayton Elem Sch 2000 Park Place Ave, Fort Worth 76110 Stephanie Hughes	PK-5	T	560 / 25	34%	817/814-5400 Fax 817/814-5450
Lowery Road Elem Sch 7600 Lowery Rd, Fort Worth 76120 Debra Williamson	PK-5	T	670 / 43	79%	817/815-4700 Fax 817/815-4750
Luella Merrett Elem Sch 7325 Kermit Ave, Fort Worth 76116 **Luella Merrett**	PK-5	T	631	80%	817/815-6600 Fax 817/815-6650
M G Ellis Primary Sch 215 NE 14th St, Fort Worth 76164 Leticia Sparks	PK-K	T	457 / 22	88%	817/814-3800 Fax 817/814-3850
M H Moore Elem Sch 1809 NE 36th St, Fort Worth 76106 Elizabeth Yoder	PK-5	T	564 / 16	93%	817/815-0600 Fax 817/815-0650
Manuel Jara Elem Sch 2100 Lincoln Ave, Fort Worth 76164 Marta Plata	1-5	T	589 / 45	93%	817/814-4500 Fax 817/814-4550
Marine Creek Collegiate HS 4801 Marine Creek Pkwy, Fort Worth 76179 Thomas Fraire	9-12	T	354	72%	817/515-7784 Fax 817/515-7094
Mary Louise Phillips Elem Sch 3020 Bigham Blvd, Fort Worth 76116 **Laura Hill**	PK-5	T	489 / 35	83%	817/815-1600 Fax 817/815-1650
ⓨ Maude I Logan Elem Sch 2300 Dillard St, Fort Worth 76105 Steven Moore	PK-5	MT	445 / 21	89%	817/815-3700 Fax 817/815-3750
Maudrie M Walton Elem Sch 5816 Rickenbacker Pl, Fort Worth 76112 Dr Christina Hanson	PK-5	T	431 / 24	87%	817/815-3300 Fax 817/815-3350
McLean Sixth Grade Sch 3201 South Hills Ave, Fort Worth 76109 Karen Brown	6-6	T	561 / 21	59%	817/814-5700 Fax 817/814-5750
Meadowbrook Elem Sch 4330 Meadowbrook Dr, Fort Worth 76103 Suzelle Birkmire	PK-5	T	645 / 40	93%	817/815-4900 Fax 817/815-4950
Meadowbrook Middle Sch 2001 Ederville Rd S, Fort Worth 76103 **Mr Gentry**	6-8	TV	850 / 40	91%	817/815-4300 Fax 817/815-4350
Ⓐ Metro Opportunity Sch 2720 Cullen St, Fort Worth 76107 Aundra Bohanon	9-12	V	30 / 30	55%	817/814-6700 Fax 817/814-6750
Ⓐ Middle Level Learning Center ⓨ 3813 Valentine St, Fort Worth 76107 Aundra Bohanon	6-8	MV	50 / 11	63%	817/814-6800 Fax 817/814-6850
ⓨ Milton L Kirkpatrick Elem Sch 3229 Lincoln Ave, Fort Worth 76106 Christine Renteria	PK-5	MT	389 / 20	96%	817/814-4600 Fax 817/814-4650
Morningside Elem Sch 2601 Evans Ave, Fort Worth 76104 **Vanessa Cuarenta**	PK-5	T	620 / 60	83%	817/814-0600 Fax 817/814-0650
Morningside Middle Sch 2751 Mississippi Ave, Fort Worth 76104 Justin Edwards	6-8	T	689 / 28	95%	817/815-8300 Fax 817/815-8350
Nathan Howell Elem Sch 1324 Kings Hwy, Haltom City 76117 Monica Granados	PK-5	T	439 / 25	85%	817/814-9300 Fax 817/814-9350
ⓨ North Hi Mount Elem Sch 3801 W 7th St, Fort Worth 76107 Myrna Blanchard	PK-5	MT	404 / 13	52%	817/815-1500 Fax 817/815-1550
North Side High Sch 2211 McKinley Ave, Fort Worth 76164 Antonio Martinez	9-12	TV	1,657 / 87	77%	817/814-4000 Fax 817/814-4050
O D Wyatt High Sch 2400 E Seminary Dr, Fort Worth 76119 Mario Layne	9-12	TV	1,443	95%	817/815-8000 Fax 817/815-8050
Oakhurst Elem Sch 2700 Yucca Ave, Fort Worth 76111 Guadalupe Cortez	PK-5	T	605 / 32	90%	817/814-9500 Fax 817/814-9550
Oaklawn Elem Sch 3220 Hardeman St, Fort Worth 76119 Sonia Anguiano	PK-5	T	586 / 26	86%	817/815-9100 Fax 817/815-9150
Paul Laurence Dunbar High Sch 5700 Ramey Ave, Fort Worth 76112 Oscar Adams	9-12	TV	933	80%	817/815-3000 Fax 817/815-3050
Polytechnic High Sch 1300 Conner Ave, Fort Worth 76105 Nick Torrez	9-12	TV	1,209 / 74	70%	817/814-0000 Fax 817/814-0050
R L Paschal High Sch 3001 Forest Park Blvd, Fort Worth 76110 Troy Langston	9-12	TV	2,522 / 120	52%	817/814-5000 Fax 817/814-5050
Richard J Wilson Elem Sch 900 W Fogg St, Fort Worth 76110 **Irma Ayala**	PK-5	T	588 / 34	95%	817/814-7700 Fax 817/814-7750
Ridglea Hills Elem Sch 6817 Cumberland Rd, Fort Worth 76116 Crenesha Cotton	PK-5	T	786 / 36	33%	817/815-1700 Fax 817/815-1750
ⓨ Riverside Applied Lrng Center 3600 Fossil Dr, Fort Worth 76111 Joann Dickerson	Spec	MT	284	71%	817/815-5800 Fax 817/815-5850

Legend

- 79 Student Personnel
- 80 Driver Ed/Safety
- 81 Gifted/Talented
- 82 Video Services
- 83 Substance Abuse Prev
- 84 Erate
- 85 AIDS Education
- 88 Alternative/At Risk
- 89 Multi-Cultural Curriculum
- 90 Social Work
- 91 Safety/Security
- 92 Magnet School
- 93 Parental Involvement
- 95 Tech Prep Program
- 97 Chief Infomation Officer
- 98 Chief Technology Officer
- 270 Character Education
- 271 Migrant Education
- 273 Teacher Mentor
- 274 Before/After Sch
- 275 Response To Intervention
- 277 Remedial Math K-12
- 280 Literacy Coach
- 285 STEM
- 286 Digital Learning
- 288 Common Core Standards
- 294 Accountability
- 295 Network System
- 296 Title II Programs
- 297 Webmaster
- 298 Grant Writer/Ptnrships
- 750 Chief Innovation Officer
- 751 Chief of Staff
- 752 Social Emotional Learning

School Programs
- A = Alternative Program
- G = Adult Classes
- M = Magnet Program
- T = Title I Schoolwide
- V = Career & Tech Ed Programs

Other School Types
- Ⓐ = Alternative School
- Ⓒ = Charter School
- Ⓜ = Magnet School
- ⓨ = Year-Round School

Social Media
- = Facebook
- = Twitter

New Schools are shaded
New Superintendents and Principals are bold
Personnel with email addresses are underscored

TX-351

Tarrant County

Market Data Retrieval

School	Grades	Media	Enroll	%	Phone
ⓎRiverside Middle Sch 1600 Bolton St, Fort Worth 76111 Victor Alfaro	6-8	MTV	943	87%	817/814-9200 Fax 817/814-9250
Rosemont 6th Grade Center 3908 McCart Ave, Fort Worth 76110 Kathrina Andersen	6-6	I	473 25	92%	817/814-7300 Fax 817/814-7350
Rosemont Elem Sch 1401 W Seminary Dr, Fort Worth 76115 Rodolfo Valdez	PK-5	T	599	94%	817/815-5200 Fax 817/815-5250
Rosemont Middle Sch 1501 W Seminary Dr, Fort Worth 76115 Miguel Del Toro	7-8	GTV	950 36	85%	817/814-7200 Fax 817/814-7250
Rufino Mendoza Elem Sch 1412 Denver Ave, Fort Worth 76164 Jennifer Sanchez	1-5	T	439 23	92%	817/814-4700 Fax 817/814-4750
S S Dillow Elem Sch 4000 Avenue N, Fort Worth 76105 **Duvaughn Flagler**	PK-5	T	568 50	87%	817/814-0400 Fax 817/814-0450
ⓎSagamore Hill Elem Sch 701 S Hughes Ave, Fort Worth 76103 Dirrick Butler	PK-5	MT	700	95%	817/815-5000 Fax 817/815-5050
Sam Rosen Elem Sch 2613 Roosevelt Ave, Fort Worth 76164 Alberto Herrera	PK-5	T	552 26	90%	817/814-4800 Fax 817/814-4850
Seminary Hills Park Elem Sch 5037 Townsend Dr, Fort Worth 76115 **Lorena Ferrales**	PK-5	T	380	96%	817/814-7600 Fax 817/814-7650
South Hi Mount Elem Sch 4101 Birchman Ave, Fort Worth 76107 Melissa Bryan	PK-5	T	539 35	75%	817/815-1800 Fax 817/815-1850
South Hills Elem Sch 3009 Bilglade Rd, Fort Worth 76133 Melissa Russell	PK-5	T	851 46	88%	817/814-5800 Fax 817/814-5850
South Hills High Sch 6101 McCart Ave, Fort Worth 76133 Rodrigo Durbin	9-12	TV	2,152 78	79%	817/814-7000 Fax 817/814-7050
Southwest High Sch 4100 Altamesa Blvd, Fort Worth 76133 John Engel	9-12	GTV	1,310 86	55%	817/814-8000 Fax 817/814-8050
Springdale Elem Sch 3207 Hollis St, Fort Worth 76111 Leann Moreno	PK-5	GT	555 25	88%	817/814-9600 Fax 817/814-9650
ⒶSuccess High Sch 1003 W Cannon St, Fort Worth 76104 Ingrid Williams	9-12	T	269	63%	817/815-2700 Fax 817/815-2750
Sunrise-McMillian Elem Sch 3409 Stalcup Rd, Fort Worth 76119 Latres Cole	PK-5	T	387 35	82%	817/815-3900 Fax 817/815-3950
T A Sims Elem Sch 3500 Crenshaw Ave, Fort Worth 76105 Andrea Harper	PK-5	T	772 50	93%	817/814-0800 Fax 817/814-0850
Tanglewood Elem Sch 3060 Overton Park Dr W, Fort Worth 76109 Connie Smith	PK-5		875 28	5%	817/814-5900 Fax 817/814-5950
TCC South-Fwisd Collegiate HS 5301 Campus Dr, Fort Worth 76119 **Quanda Collins**	9-10		75		817/515-4402 Fax 817/515-4208
ⓂTexas Academy of Biomed Sci 300 Trinity Campus Cir, Fort Worth 76102 Jack Henson	9-12	V	387		817/515-1660 Fax 817/515-2350
Transition Center 5100 El Campo Ave, Fort Worth 76107 Terry Guthrie	Spec		69	23%	817/814-6418 Fax 817/814-6451
ⓎVan Zandt-Guinn Elem Sch 600 S Kentucky Ave, Fort Worth 76104 **Debora Fuentes**	PK-5	MT	595 15	83%	817/815-2000 Fax 817/815-2050
ⓎVersia L Williams Elem Sch 901 Baurline St, Fort Worth 76111 Angela Wright	PK-5	MT	449 22	90%	817/814-9700 Fax 817/814-9750
W A Meacham Middle Sch 3600 Weber St, Fort Worth 76106 Oscar Martinez	6-8	TV	814 55	93%	817/815-0200 Fax 817/815-0250
ⓎW C Stripling Middle Sch 2100 Clover Ln, Fort Worth 76107 Amy Chritian	6-8	AMTV	692 47	67%	817/815-1300 Fax 817/815-1350
ⓎW J Turner Elem Sch 3000 NW 26th St, Fort Worth 76106 Elida Gonzales	PK-5	MT	483 39	87%	817/814-4900 Fax 817/814-4950
W M Green Elem Sch 4612 David Strickland Rd, Fort Worth 76119 Edra Bailey	PK-5	T	803 80	88%	817/815-8900 Fax 817/815-8950
W P McLean Middle Sch 3816 Stadium Dr, Fort Worth 76109 Barbara Ozuna	6-8	TV	1,100 50	51%	817/815-5300
Washington Heights Elem Sch 3124 Clinton Ave, Fort Worth 76106 Maryjane Cantu	PK-5	T	340 18	94%	817/815-0700 Fax 817/815-0750
Waverly Park Elem Sch 3604 Cimmaron Trl, Fort Worth 76116 Roberto Gutierrez	PK-5	T	724 35	60%	817/815-6700 Fax 817/815-6750
Wedgwood 6th Grade Middle Sch 4212 Belden Ave, Fort Worth 76132 Tremanya Thomas	6-6	T	454 40	78%	817/814-8300 Fax 817/814-8350
Wedgwood Middle Sch 3909 Wilkie Way, Fort Worth 76133 Robert Burrell	7-8	TV	956 62	71%	817/814-8200 Fax 817/814-8250
West Handley Elem Sch 2749 Putnam St, Fort Worth 76112 Julie Moynihan	PK-5	T	525 25	89%	817/815-5100 Fax 817/815-5150
Westcliff Elem Sch 4300 Clay Ave, Fort Worth 76109 Sara Gillaspie	PK-5	T	566 22	71%	817/814-6000 Fax 817/814-6050
ⓎWestcreek Elem Sch 3401 Walton Ave, Fort Worth 76133 Julia Cortina	PK-5	MT	643 45	89%	817/814-8600 Fax 817/814-8650
Western Hills Elem Sch 2805 Laredo Dr, Fort Worth 76116 Alexandra Montes	2-5	T	836 42	90%	817/815-6800 Fax 817/815-6850
Western Hills High Sch 3600 Boston Ave, Benbrook 76116 Keri Flores	9-12	TV	918 75	49%	817/815-6000 Fax 817/815-6050
Western Hills Primary Sch 8300 Mojave Trl, Fort Worth 76116 Sonya Kelly	PK-1	T	603	90%	817/815-6900 Fax 817/815-6950
Westpark Elem Sch 10202 Jerry Dunn Pkwy, Fort Worth 76126 Susan Hill	PK-5		730 19		817/815-7000 Fax 817/815-7050
William James Middle Sch 1101 Nashville Ave, Fort Worth 76105 Joycelyn Barnett	6-8	TV	950 68	69%	817/814-0200 Fax 817/814-0250
William Monnig Middle Sch 3136 Bigham Blvd, Fort Worth 76116 Kellye Kirkpatrick	6-8	TV	665 47	70%	817/815-1200 Fax 817/815-1250
ⓎWoodway Elem Sch 6701 Woodway Dr, Fort Worth 76133 Bryan Johnson	PK-5	MT	692 36	79%	817/814-8700 Fax 817/814-8750
World Languages Institute 4921 Benbrook Hwy, Fort Worth 76116 Guadalupe Barreto	6-8	T	221	81%	817/815-2200 Fax 817/815-2250
ⓎWorth Heights Elem Sch 519 E Butler St, Fort Worth 76110 Andrea Lange	PK-5	MT	645 44	91%	817/814-6200 Fax 817/814-6250

#		#		#		#		#		#		#	
1	Superintendent	8	Curric/Instruct K-12	19	Chief Financial Officer	29	Family/Consumer Science	39	Social Studies K-12	49	English/Lang Arts Elem	59	Special Education Elem	69	Academic Assessment
2	Bus/Finance/Purchasing	9	Curric/Instruct Elem	20	Art K-12	30	Adult Education	40	Social Studies Elem	50	English/Lang Arts Sec	60	Special Education Sec	70	Research/Development
3	Buildings And Grounds	10	Curric/Instruct Sec	21	Art Elem	31	Career/Sch-to-Work K-12	41	Social Studies Sec	51	Reading K-12	61	Foreign/World Lang K-12	71	Public Information
4	Food Service	11	Federal Program	22	Art Sec	32	Career/Sch-to-Work Elem	42	Science K-12	52	Reading Elem	62	Foreign/World Lang Elem	72	Summer School
5	Transportation	12	Title I	23	Music K-12	33	Career/Sch-to-Work Sec	43	Science Elem	53	Reading Sec	63	Foreign/World Lang Sec	73	Instructional Tech
6	Athletic	13	Title V	24	Music Elem	34	Early Childhood Ed	44	Science Sec	54	Remedial Reading K-12	64	Religious Education K-12	74	Inservice Training
7	Health Services	14	Asst Superintendent	25	Music Sec	35	Health/Phys Education	45	Math K-12	55	Remedial Reading Elem	65	Religious Education Elem	75	Marketing/Distributive
		15	Instructional Media Svcs	26	Business Education	36	Guidance Services K-12	46	Math Elem	56	Remedial Reading Sec	66	Religious Education Sec	76	Info Systems
		16	Chief Operations Officer	27	Career & Tech Ed	37	Guidance Services Elem	47	Math Sec	57	Bilingual/ELL	67	School Board President	77	Psychological Assess
		17	Chief Academic Officer	28	Technology Education	38	Guidance Services Sec	48	English/Lang Arts K-12	58	Special Education K-12	68	Teacher Personnel	78	Affirmative Action

Texas School Directory — Tarrant County

	Grd	Prgm	Enr/#Cls	SN	
Young Men's Leadership Academy 5100 Willie St, Fort Worth 76105 Rodney White	6-10	T	308	64%	817/815-3400 Fax 817/815-3450
Young Women's Leadership Acad 401 E 8th St, Fort Worth 76102 Tamara Albury	6-12	T	391	62%	817/815-2400 Fax 817/815-2450 [f]

● **Grapevine-Colleyville Ind SD** PID: 01053672   817/251-5200
3051 Ira E Woods Ave, Grapevine 76051   Fax 817/251-5375

Schools: 21 \ *Teachers:* 944 \ *Students:* 14,000 \
Special Ed Students: 1,088 \ *LEP Students:* 1,129 \ *College-Bound:* 90% \ *Ethnic:* Asian 10%, African American 6%, Hispanic 26%, Caucasian 58% \ *Exp:* $222 (Med) \ *Poverty:* 6% \ *Title I:* $1,432,388 \
Special Education: $2,145,000 \ *Open-Close:* 08/19 - 05/28 \ *DTBP:* $188 (High) \ [f] [t]

Dr Robin Ryan 1	Christi Drilling 2	
Daiann Mooney 2,19	Paula Barbaroux 3,17	
Ramon Castanuela 3	Julie Telesca 4	
Manny Rubio 5	Bryan Gerlich 6*	
Amy Howard 7,35	Dr Suzanne Newell 8,11,16,20,27,36	
Dr Brad Schnautz 15	Lindsey Hopkins 30,88	
Rick Bracy 31	Khristie Brown 34	
Emberly Hill 36*	Jodi Cox 57,61	
Dr Joann Wiechmann 58	Lisa Pardo 67	
Gema Padgett 68	Shannon Kovar 69	
Kyle Berger 73,98	Marina Flores 79	
Robin Davis 83*	Alan Smith 91	
Megan Scarbourgh 274	Tony Zahn 285	

Public Schs..Principal	Grd	Prgm	Enr/#Cls	SN	
Bear Creek Elem Sch 401 Bear Creek Dr, Euless 76039 Bryan Calvert	PK-5	T	704 31	30%	817/305-4860 Fax 817/267-3863
Bransford Elem Sch 601 Glade Rd, Colleyville 76034 Jamie Halliburton	PK-5		474 36	9%	817/305-4920 Fax 817/428-1203
Ⓐ Bridges Accel Lrng Ctr 5800 Colleyville Blvd, Colleyville 76034 Lindsey Hopkins	9-12	GV	45 5	32%	817/251-5474 Fax 817/581-4893
Cannon Elem Sch 1300 W College St, Grapevine 76051 Tona Blizzard	PK-5	T	578 26	39%	817/251-5680 Fax 817/421-0982
Collegiate Acad Tarrant Clg 828 W Harwood Rd, Hurst 76054 Bobbe Knutz	9-12	T	325	37%	817/515-6775 Fax 817/515-6766
Colleyville Elem Sch 5911 Pleasant Run Rd, Colleyville 76034 Sheila Shimmick	PK-5		470 25	2%	817/305-4940 Fax 817/498-2062
Colleyville Heritage High Sch 5401 Heritage Ave, Colleyville 76034 Lance Groppel	9-12	V	2,001 120	14%	817/305-4700 Fax 817/358-4765
Colleyville Middle Sch 1100 Bogart Dr, Colleyville 76034 David Arencibia	6-8	V	658 54	4%	817/305-4900 Fax 817/498-9764
Cross Timbers Middle Sch 2301 Pool Rd, Grapevine 76051 Alex Fingers	6-8	TV	851 51	31%	817/251-5320 Fax 817/424-4296
Dove Elem Sch 1932 Dove Rd, Grapevine 76051 Heather Landrum	PK-5	T	494 26	34%	817/251-5700 Fax 817/481-6730
Glenhope Elem Sch 6600 Glenhope Cir N, Colleyville 76034 Wynette Griffin	PK-5		493 22	17%	817/251-5720 Fax 817/329-5618
Grapevine Elem Sch 1801 Hall Johnson Rd, Grapevine 76051 Nancy Hale	PK-5		526 32	10%	817/251-5735 Fax 817/481-6451
Grapevine High Sch 3223 Mustang Dr, Grapevine 76051 David Denning	9-12	GV	1,856 110	18%	817/251-5210 Fax 817/481-5957
Grapevine Middle Sch 301 Pony Pkwy, Grapevine 76051 Laura Koehler	6-8	TV	764 60	37%	817/251-5660 Fax 817/424-1626
Heritage Elem Sch 4500 Heritage Ave, Grapevine 76051 Jill Hemme	PK-5		477 31	6%	817/305-4820 Fax 817/540-2892
Heritage Middle Sch 5300 Heritage Ave, Colleyville 76034 Scott Saettel	6-8	V	849 60	17%	817/305-4790 Fax 817/267-9929
Iuniversity Prep Virtual Acad 3051 Ira E Woods Ave, Grapevine 76051 Klinetta Rogers	4-12		427		855/779-7357 Fax 888/342-4927 [f]
O C Taylor Elem Sch 5300 Pool Rd, Colleyville 76034 Lisa Young	PK-5		490 27	4%	817/305-4870 Fax 817/540-3940
Silver Lake Elem Sch 1301 N Dooley St, Grapevine 76051 Nicole Whiteside	PK-5	T	601 25	50%	817/251-5750 Fax 817/329-4536
Timberline Elem Sch 3220 Timberline Dr, Grapevine 76051 Liz Hilcher	PK-5	T	704 35	78%	817/251-5770 Fax 817/329-5666
Ⓐ Vista Alt Learning Center 5800 Colleyville Blvd, Colleyville 76034 Roger Alzamora	K-12		60 5		817/251-5466 Fax 817/581-9140 [f][t]

● **Hurst-Euless-Bedford ISD** PID: 01053737   817/283-4461
1849 Central Dr, Bedford 76022   Fax 817/354-3311

Schools: 31 \ *Teachers:* 1,360 \ *Students:* 23,000 \
Special Ed Students: 2,049 \ *LEP Students:* 2,985 \ *College-Bound:* 61% \ *Ethnic:* Asian 8%, African American 20%, Hispanic 33%, Caucasian 39% \ *Exp:* $188 (Low) \ *Poverty:* 13% \ *Title I:* $4,264,313 \
Special Education: $3,793,000 \ *Open-Close:* 08/19 - 05/28 \ *DTBP:* $188 (High) \ [f] [t]

Steve Chapman 1	David Garcia 2,15
Josh Minor 3	Mariella Naugher 4
Brian Merchant 5	Mike Fielder 6
Lydia Martin 8,15	Dr Joe Harrington 10,15
Mary Morris 11,298	Cicely Tuttle 15,68
Scott Forester 15,73,295	Kiera Elledge 16,285
Mark Chandler 20,23	Lisa Karr 27,28*
Carla Docken 36,88,270	Marci Deal 39,89
Wade Carrington 42	Garri Adcox 46
Kristen Manning 47	Ladonna Schwobell 49
Terri Smith 50	Rene Riek 58*
Julie Cole 67	Gail Long 69
Deanne Hullender 71	Ann Rodriguez 74
John Sellgren 76	Marianne White 274
David Nielsen 297	

Public Schs..Principal	Grd	Prgm	Enr/#Cls	SN	
Ⓐ Alternative Education Program 1100 Raider Dr, Euless 76040 Dr June Jacoby	6-12	T	175 9	58%	817/354-3398 Fax 817/358-5001
Bedford Heights Elem Sch 1000 Cummings Dr, Bedford 76021 Brad Mengwasser	PK-6		787 36	17%	817/788-3150 Fax 817/788-3112
Bedford Junior High Sch 325 Carolyn Dr, Bedford 76021 Michael Martinak	7-9	V	832 60	34%	817/788-3101 Fax 817/788-3105 [f]

79 Student Personnel	91 Safety/Security	275 Response To Intervention	298 Grant Writer/Ptnrships	**School Programs**
80 Driver Ed/Safety	92 Magnet School	277 Remedial Math K-12	750 Chief Innovation Officer	A = Alternative Program
81 Gifted/Talented	93 Parental Involvement	280 Literacy Coach	751 Chief of Staff	G = Adult Classes
82 Video Services	95 Tech Prep Program	285 STEM	752 Social Emotional Learning	M = Magnet Program
83 Substance Abuse Prev	97 Chief Infomation Officer	286 Digital Learning		T = Title I Schoolwide
84 Erate	98 Chief Technology Officer	288 Common Core Standards	**Other School Types**	V = Career & Tech Ed Programs
85 AIDS Education	270 Accountability	294 Accountability	Ⓐ = Alternative School	
88 Alternative/At Risk	271 Migrant Education	295 Network System	Ⓒ = Charter School	**Social Media**
89 Multi-Cultural Curriculum	273 Teacher Mentor	296 Title II Programs	Ⓜ = Magnet School	[f] = Facebook
90 Social Work	274 Before/After Sch	297 Webmaster	Ⓨ = Year-Round School	[t] = Twitter

New Schools are shaded
New Superintendents and Principals are bold
Personnel with email addresses are underscored

TX—353

Tarrant County

School	Grd	Prgm	Enr/#Cls	SN	Phone
Bell Manor Elem Sch 1300 Winchester Way, Bedford 76022 **Keri McCarty**	PK-6	T	740 35	59%	817/354-3370 Fax 817/354-3374
Bellaire Elem Sch 501 Bellaire Dr, Hurst 76053 Katina Rhodes	PK-6	T	743 32	90%	817/285-3230 Fax 817/285-3203 f
Central Junior High Sch 3191 W Pipeline Rd, Euless 76040 Randy Belcher	7-9	TV	1,097 55	57%	817/354-3350 Fax 817/354-3357
Donna Park Elem Sch 1125 Scott Dr, Hurst 76053 Julie McAvoy	PK-6	T	542 24	64%	817/285-3285 Fax 817/285-3289
Euless Junior High Sch 306 Airport Fwy, Euless 76039 Sonya Stanton	7-9	TV	1,048 44	63%	817/354-3340 Fax 817/354-3345 f
Gene A Buinger Cte Academy 1849 Central Dr Bldg E, Bedford 76022 Lisa Karr	Voc		600 12		817/354-3542 Fax 817/354-3546
Harrison Lane Elem Sch 1000 Harrison Ln, Hurst 76053 Kathleen Harrell	PK-6	T	708 25	74%	817/285-3270 Fax 817/285-3207
Harwood Junior High Sch 3000 Martin Dr, Bedford 76021 Dr Toby Givens	7-9	V	1,000	33%	817/354-3360 Fax 817/354-3365
Hurst Hills Elem Sch 525 Billie Ruth Ln, Hurst 76053 Misty Donaho	PK-6	T	509 38	42%	817/285-3295 Fax 817/285-3208
Hurst Junior High Sch 500 Harmon Rd, Hurst 76053 **Michael Smith**	7-9	TV	1,099	61%	817/285-3220 Fax 817/285-3225 f
Ⓐ Keys Learning Center 1100 Raider Dr, Euless 76040 Jan Joseph	9-12	T	100 15	61%	817/354-3580 Fax 817/354-3586
Lakewood Elem Sch 1600 Donley Dr, Euless 76039 Cameron Ramirez	PK-6	T	645 36	43%	817/354-3375 Fax 817/354-3525 f t
Lawrence D Bell High Sch 1601 Brown Trl, Hurst 76054 Jim Bannister	10-12	TV	2,318	42%	817/282-2551 Fax 817/285-3200
Meadow Creek Elem Sch 3001 Harwood Rd, Bedford 76021 Doreen Mengwasser	PK-6		799 36	22%	817/354-3500 Fax 817/354-3329 f
Midway Park Elem Sch 409 N Ector Dr, Euless 76039 Liesl James	PK-6	T	764 35	72%	817/354-3380 Fax 817/354-3332 f t
North Euless Elem Sch 1101 Denton Dr, Euless 76039 Melissa Meadows	PK-6	T	750 27	66%	817/354-3505 Fax 817/354-3334 f
Oakwood Terrace Elem Sch 700 Ranger St, Euless 76040 Anmarie Garcia	PK-6	T	600 45	80%	817/354-3386 Fax 817/354-3335 f t
River Trails Elem Sch 8850 Elbe Trl, Fort Worth 76118 Tammy Daggs	PK-6		642 41	37%	817/285-3235 Fax 817/285-3238
Shady Brook Elem Sch 2601 Shady Brook Dr, Bedford 76021 Shannon Gauntt	PK-6	T	647 26	50%	817/354-3513 Fax 817/354-3336 f t
Shady Oaks Elem Sch 1400 Cavender Dr, Hurst 76053 Darla Clark	PK-6	T	589 28	62%	817/285-3240 Fax 817/285-3209 f t
South Euless Elem Sch 605 S Main St, Euless 76040 Maureen Sterling	PK-6	T	644 65	62%	817/354-3521 Fax 817/354-3523 f
Spring Garden Elem Sch 2400 Cummings Dr, Bedford 76021 Sarah Williams	PK-6	T	647 40	48%	817/354-3395 Fax 817/354-3337
Stonegate Elem Sch 900 Bedford Rd, Bedford 76022 Talana Bean	PK-6	T	537 26	69%	817/285-3250 Fax 817/285-3210
Transition Center 1849 Central Dr, Bedford 76022 Rene Riek	Spec		44 1		817/354-3537 Fax 817/354-3540
Trinity High Sch 500 N Industrial Blvd, Euless 76039 Mike Harris	10-12	TV	2,529 100	48%	817/571-0271 Fax 817/354-3322
Viridian Elem Sch 4001 Cascade Sky Dr, Arlington 76005 Dr Aungelique Brading	PK-6		774	29%	817/864-0550 Fax 817/354-3280
West Hurst Elem Sch 501 Precinct Line Rd, Hurst 76053 Debra Day	PK-6	T	533 40	65%	817/285-3290 Fax 817/285-3212 f t
Wilshire Elem Sch 420 Wilshire Dr, Euless 76040 Jodie Ramos	PK-6	T	756	53%	817/354-3529 Fax 817/354-3338 f t

• **Keller Ind School Dist** PID: 01053983
350 Keller Pkwy, Keller 76248
817/744-1000
Fax 817/337-3261

Schools: 42 \ **Teachers:** 2,296 \ **Students:** 34,512 \
Special Ed Students: 3,196 \ **LEP Students:** 2,576 \ **Ethnic:** Asian 9%, African American 9%, Hispanic 24%, Native American: 1%, Caucasian 58% \ **Exp:** $504 (High) \ **Poverty:** 5% \ **Title I:** $2,521,897 \
Special Education: $4,871,000 \ **Open-Close:** 08/14 - 05/21 \ **DTBP:** $67 (Low) \ f t

Dr Rick Westfall	1	Kristin Williams	2
Lori Tudor	2	Mark Youngs	2,19
Hudson Huff	3	David Smith	4*
Jim Koons	5	Eric Persyn	6*
Cindy Parsons	7,83,85	Lindsay Anderson	8,15,288
Sara Kopowski	8,275,296	Leigh Cook	11,298
Tommie Johnson	15,68	Kim Blann	20,23
Leslee Shepherd	27*	Dr Robert Wright	27,31,286*
Karin Mahlenkamp	34*	Jennifer Fleming	36
Suzanne McGahey	39	Tracy Hosek	42*
Chrissy Greeling	46	Shannon Bryant	47
Sheree Felan	50*	Dawn Bailey	52
Marie Coker	57	Mary Martin	57
Dr Gena Koster	58	Brandy Crow	61*
Cindy Lotten	67	Jennifer Price	69,294
Shellie Johnson	71	Joe Griffin	73,76,98,295
Vicki Arrington	74	Joseph Copeland	79
Donna Hodge	81*	Marcene Weatherall	83
Kevin Kinley	91		

Public Schs..Principal	Grd	Prgm	Enr/#Cls	SN	Phone
Basswood Elem Sch 3100 Clay Mountain Trl, Fort Worth 76137 Tony Johnson	K-4	T	650	56%	817/744-6500 Fax 817/744-6538
Bear Creek Intermediate Sch 801 Bear Creek Pkwy, Keller 76248 **Brenda Riebkes**	5-6		991 34	5%	817/744-3650 Fax 817/744-3738 f t
Bette Perot Elem Sch 9345 General Worth Dr, Keller 76244 Lisa Young	K-4		639 42	12%	817/744-4600 Fax 817/744-4638
Bluebonnet Elem Sch 7000 Teal Dr, Fort Worth 76137 Rhonda McGee	K-4	T	617 65	39%	817/744-4500 Fax 817/744-4538
CapRock Elem Sch 12301 Grey Twig Dr, Keller 76244 Amy Erb	K-4	T	672	48%	817/744-6400 Fax 817/744-6438
Central High Sch 9450 Ray White Rd, Fort Worth 76244 David Hinson	9-12	G	2,547	22%	817/744-2000 Fax 817/744-2038

1	Superintendent	8	Curric/Instruct K-12	19	Chief Financial Officer	29	Family/Consumer Science
2	Bus/Finance/Purchasing	9	Curric/Instruct Elem	20	Art K-12	30	Adult Education
3	Buildings And Grounds	10	Curric/Instruct Sec	21	Art Elem	31	Career/Sch-to-Work K-12
4	Food Service	11	Federal Program	22	Art Sec	32	Career/Sch-to-Work Elem
5	Transportation	12	Title I	23	Music K-12	33	Career/Sch-to-Work Sec
6	Athletic	13	Title V	24	Music Elem	34	Early Childhood Ed
7	Health Services	14	Instructional Media Svcs	25	Music Sec	35	Health/Phys Education
		15	Asst Superintendent	26	Business Education	36	Guidance Services K-12
		16	Instructional Media Svcs	27	Career & Tech Ed	37	Guidance Services Elem
		17	Chief Operations Officer	28	Technology Education	38	Guidance Services Sec
		18	Chief Academic Officer				

39	Social Studies K-12	49	English/Lang Arts Elem	59	Special Education Elem	69	Academic Assessment
40	Social Studies Elem	50	English/Lang Arts Sec	60	Special Education Sec	70	Research/Development
41	Social Studies Sec	51	Reading K-12	61	Foreign/World Lang K-12	71	Public Information
42	Science K-12	52	Reading Elem	62	Foreign/World Lang Elem	72	Summer School
43	Science Elem	53	Reading Sec	63	Foreign/World Lang Sec	73	Instructional Tech
44	Science Sec	54	Remedial Reading K-12	64	Religious Education K-12	74	Inservice Training
45	Math K-12	55	Remedial Reading Elem	65	Religious Education Elem	75	Marketing/Distributive
46	Math Elem	56	Remedial Reading Sec	66	Religious Education Sec	76	Info Systems
47	Math Sec	57	Bilingual/ELL	67	School Board President	77	Psychological Assess
48	English/Lang Arts K-12	58	Special Education K-12	68	Teacher Personnel	78	Affirmative Action

Texas School Directory — Tarrant County

School	Grd	Prgm	Enr/#Cls	SN	Phone
Chisholm Trail Interm Sch 3901 Summerfields Blvd, Fort Worth 76137 Trish McKeel	5-6	T	886	52%	817/744-3800 Fax 817/744-3838
Eagle Ridge Elem Sch 4600 Alta Vista Rd, Keller 76244 Stacy Blevins	K-4		664 31	13%	817/744-6300 Fax 817/744-6338
Early Learning Ctr North 10310 N Riverside Dr, Fort Worth 76244 David Rische	PK-PK	T	373	45%	817/744-6700
Early Learning Ctr South 3975 Summerfields Blvd, Fort Worth 76137 Christy Johnson	PK-PK		314	64%	817/743-8300
Florence Elem Sch 3095 Johnson Rd, Southlake 76092 Jacqueline Hughes	K-4		484 32	5%	817/744-4700 Fax 817/744-4738
Fossil Hill Middle Sch 3821 Staghorn Cir S, Fort Worth 76137 Jennifer Gonzales	7-8	T	1,030 53	49%	817/744-3050 Fax 817/744-3138
Fossil Ridge High Sch 4101 Thompson Rd, Fort Worth 76244 Dave Hadley	9-12	T	2,318 150	43%	817/744-1700 Fax 817/744-1738
Freedom Elem Sch 5401 Wall Price Keller Rd, Keller 76244 Gary Mantz	K-4		566 33	25%	817/744-4800 Fax 817/744-4838
Friendship Elem Sch 5400 Shiver Rd, Keller 76244 Casey Necessary	K-4	T	549	39%	817/744-6200 Fax 817/744-6238
Heritage Elem Sch 4001 Thompson Rd, Keller 76244 **Edwina West-Dukes**	K-4	GT	529 35	41%	817/744-4900 Fax 817/744-4938
Hidden Lakes Elem Sch 900 Preston Ln, Keller 76248 Melanie Graham	K-4		423 36	2%	817/744-5000 Fax 817/744-5038
Hillwood Middle Sch 8250 Parkwood Hill Blvd, Fort Worth 76137 Kathleen Eckert	7-8		1,165 20	26%	817/744-3350 Fax 817/744-3438
Independence Elem Sch 11773 Bray Birch Ln, Fort Worth 76244 Mark Basham	K-4		552	16%	817/744-6100 Fax 817/744-6138
Indian Springs Middle Sch 305 Bursey Rd, Keller 76248 Sandy Troudt	5-8		1,040 40	13%	817/744-3200 Fax 817/744-3238
Keller Ctr Advanced Learning 201 Bursey Rd, Keller 76248 Leslee Shepherd	9-12	V	4,000		817/743-8000 Fax 817/743-8038
Keller High Sch 601 Pate Orr Rd N, Keller 76248 Lisa Simmons	9-12	GV	2,996	5%	817/744-1400 Fax 817/744-1438
Ⓐ Keller Learning Center 250 College Ave, Keller 76248 Dr Angel Lara	9-12	V	57 7	31%	817/744-4465 Fax 817/741-1269
Keller Middle Sch 300 College Ave, Keller 76248 **Amanda Burruel**	7-8	V	987 40	7%	817/744-2900 Fax 817/744-2938
Keller-Harvel Elem Sch 635 Norma Ln, Keller 76248 Leslie Tewell	K-4		502 34	18%	817/744-5100 Fax 817/744-5138
Liberty Elem Sch 1101 W McDonwell School Rd, Colleyville 76034 Janet Travis	K-4		421 25	5%	817/744-6000 Fax 817/744-6038
Lone Star Elem Sch 4647 Shiver Rd, Fort Worth 76244 Steve Hurst	K-4		813 38	16%	817/744-5200 Fax 817/744-5238
North Riverside Elem Sch 7900 N Riverside Dr, Fort Worth 76137 Allison Boyd	K-4	T	433	56%	817/744-5300 Fax 817/744-5338
Park Glen Elem Sch 5100 Glen Canyon Rd, Fort Worth 76137 Marcia Formby	K-4		579 32	17%	817/744-5400 Fax 817/744-5438
Parkview Elem Sch 6900 Bayberry Dr, Fort Worth 76137 Erin Appling	K-4	GT	528 38	56%	817/744-5500 Fax 817/744-5538
Parkwood Hill Intermediate Sch 8201 Parkwood Hill Blvd, Fort Worth 76137 Brad Taylor	5-6		1,200	30%	817/744-4000 Fax 817/744-4038
Ridgeview Elem Sch 1601 Marshall Ridge Pkwy, Keller 76248 Becky Wilder	K-4		704	12%	817/744-6600 Fax 817/744-6638
Shady Grove Elem Sch 1400 Sarah Brooks Dr, Keller 76248 Anna Renfro	K-4		464 36	5%	817/744-5600 Fax 817/744-5638
Sunset Valley Elem Sch 2032 Canchim St, Fort Worth 76131 Kristen Eriksen	K-4		385	33%	817/743-8200
Timber Creek High Sch 12350 Timberland Blvd, Fort Worth 76244 Michelle Somerhalder	9-12		3,237	19%	817/744-2300 Fax 817/744-2338
Timberview Middle Sch 10300 N Riverside Dr, Fort Worth 76244 Charles Erwin	5-8		1,216	16%	817/744-2600 Fax 817/744-2638
Trinity Meadows Interm Sch 3500 Keller Hicks Rd, Keller 76244 Susan Mackey	5-6		909	28%	817/744-4300 Fax 817/744-4338
Trinity Springs Middle Sch 3550 Keller Hicks Rd, Fort Worth 76244 Justin Barrett	7-8		1,003	24%	817/744-3500 Fax 817/744-3538
Vista Ridge Middle Sch 3201 Thompson Rd, Fort Worth 76177 **Tracy Arsenault**	5-7		251		817/743-8400
Whitley Road Elem Sch 7600 Whitley Rd, Watauga 76148 Rodrigo Cano	K-4	T	430 38	56%	817/744-5800 Fax 817/744-5838
Willis Lane Elem Sch 1620 Willis Ln, Keller 76248 Cheryl Hudson	K-4		517 40	14%	817/744-5700 Fax 817/744-5738
Woodland Springs Elem Sch 12120 Woodland Springs Dr, Keller 76244 Cindy Daniel	K-4		586	15%	817/744-5900 Fax 817/744-5938

● **Kennedale Ind School Dist** PID: 01054030   817/563-8000
120 W Kennedale Pkwy, Kennedale 76060   Fax 817/483-3610

Schools: 6 \ *Teachers:* 206 \ *Students:* 3,200 \ *Special Ed Students:* 269 \ *LEP Students:* 209 \ *Ethnic:* Asian 4%, African American 23%, Hispanic 25%, Caucasian 48% \ *Exp:* $380 (High) \ *Poverty:* 11% \ *Title I:* $444,838 \ *Special Education:* $503,000 \ *Open-Close:* 08/12 - 05/22 \ *DTBP:* $176 (High) \

Chad Gee 1		Jimmy Adams 2	
Eileen Mode 3		Laurie Humiston 4*	
Richard Barrett 6,83		Teresa Vasquez 7*	
Charity Woods 8,58		Jan Cleere 8,69,73*	
Dr Melissa Glenn ..8,11,57,68,88,294,296,298		Dr Julie Vu 15	
Alison Boubel 16*		Stephanie Devlin 36*	
John Hunt 67		Brandy King 68	
Tracy Williams 71		Logan Barrett 91	
Brian Franklin 295			

Public Schs..Principal	Grd	Prgm	Enr/#Cls	SN	
James A Arthur Interm Sch 100 E Mistletoe Dr, Kennedale 76060 **Caroline Blackstone**	5-6	T	503 20	47%	817/563-8300 Fax 817/483-3628

---

79 Student Personnel
80 Driver Ed/Safety
81 Gifted/Talented
82 Video Services
83 Substance Abuse Prev
84 Erate
85 AIDS Education
88 Alternative/At Risk
89 Multi-Cultural Curriculum
90 Social Work
91 Safety/Security
92 Magnet School
93 Parental Involvement
95 Tech Prep Program
97 Chief Infomation Officer
98 Chief Technology Officer
270 Character Education
271 Migrant Education
273 Teacher Mentor
274 Before/After Sch
275 Response To Intervention
277 Remedial Math K-12
280 Literacy Coach
285 STEM
286 Digital Learning
288 Common Core Standards
294 Accountability
295 Network System
296 Title II Programs
297 Webmaster
298 Grant Writer/Ptnrships
750 Chief Innovation Officer
751 Chief of Staff
752 Social Emotional Learning

Other School Types
Ⓐ = Alternative Program
Ⓒ = Charter School
Ⓜ = Magnet School
Ⓨ = Year-Round School

School Programs
A = Alternative Program
G = Adult Classes
M = Magnet Program
T = Title I Schoolwide
V = Career & Tech Ed Programs

Social Media
🅕 = Facebook
🅣 = Twitter

New Schools are shaded
New Superintendents and Principals are bold
Personnel with email addresses are underscored

Tarrant County

Market Data Retrieval

James F DeLaney Elem Sch 180 W Kennedale Pkwy, Kennedale 76060 Kari Pride	PK-4	T	661 25	40%	817/563-8400 Fax 817/483-3653
Ⓐ Kennedale Alternative Ed Prog 100 W Kennedale Pkwy, Kennedale 76060 Carol Bryson	1-12		100 3		817/563-8060 Fax 817/483-3674
Kennedale High Sch 901 Wildcat Way, Kennedale 76060 Michael Cagle	9-12	T	1,021	31%	817/563-8100 Fax 817/563-3718
Kennedale Junior High Sch 930 Corry A Edwards Dr, Kennedale 76060 Reggie Rhines	7-8	T	491	38%	817/563-8200 Fax 817/483-3655
R F Patterson Elem Sch 6621 Kelly Elliott Rd, Arlington 76001 Khourie Jones	K-4	T	451 23	45%	817/563-8600 Fax 817/483-3638

• **Lake Worth Ind School Dist** PID: 01054078   817/306-4200
6805 Telephone Rd, Lake Worth 76135   Fax 817/237-5284

> **Schools:** 6 \ **Teachers:** 238 \ **Students:** 3,000 \ **Special Ed Students:** 312 \
> **LEP Students:** 686 \ **Ethnic:** Asian 1%, African American 15%, Hispanic 59%,
> Native American: 1%, Caucasian 25% \ **Exp:** $417 (High) \ **Poverty:** 20% \
> **Title I:** $823,629 \ **Special Education:** $580,000 \ **Open-Close:** 08/14 -
> 05/28 \ **DTBP:** $316 (High)

Rose Neshyba 1
Tina Robinson 4
Tracy Welch 6
Eric Tingle 8,294
Gwen Steele 10,280
Donna Hutson 67
Karen Reed 69
Cassandra Darst 79

Becky Campbell 2
Carla Dodd 5
Maribell Mandoza 7
Robbin Church 9,57*
Sherry Dickens 11,298
Hali Hunt 68
Sonya Butler 73,76,295
Olivia Mathis 297

Public Schs..Principal	Grd	Prgm	Enr/#Cls	SN
Effie Morris Elem Sch 3801 Merrett Dr, Lake Worth 76135 Eric Moore	PK-4	AT	354 37	81% 817/306-4260 Fax 817/237-3625
Lake Worth High Sch 4210 Boat Club Rd, Lake Worth 76135 Bobby Stults	9-12	ATV	868 50	75% 817/306-4200 Fax 817/237-0697
Lucyle Collins Middle Sch 3651 Santos Dr, Fort Worth 76106 Kathy Harmon	7-8	AT	503 38	81% 817/306-4250 Fax 817/624-7058
Marilyn J Miller Elem Sch 5250 Estrella St, Fort Worth 76106 Brent McClain	PK-4	AT	601 28	91% 817/306-4280 Fax 817/624-9007
Marine Creek Elem Sch 4801 Huffines Blvd, Lake Worth 76135 Carrie Harrison	PK-4	AT	543 16	76% 817/306-4200 Fax 817/238-6726
N A Howry Intermediate Sch 4000 Dakota Trl, Lake Worth 76135 Ted Mynyk	5-6	ATV	483 41	81% 817/306-4200 Fax 817/237-3687

• **Mansfield Ind School Dist** PID: 01054119   817/299-6300
605 E Broad St, Mansfield 76063   Fax 817/473-5465

> **Schools:** 44 \ **Teachers:** 2,176 \ **Students:** 34,309 \
> **Special Ed Students:** 2,922 \ **LEP Students:** 3,192 \ **Ethnic:** Asian 7%,
> African American 30%, Hispanic 27%, Caucasian 36% \ **Exp:** $212 (Med)
> \ **Poverty:** 9% \ **Title I:** $4,216,426 \ **Special Education:** $5,491,000 \
> **Open-Close:** 08/14 - 05/28 \ **DTBP:** $188 (High) \ Ⓣ

Dr Jim Vaszauskas 1
Karen Wiesman 2,15
Dr Paul Cash 3

Ed Harper 2
Jeff Brogden 3,5,15
Scott Shafer 3

Rita Denton 4
Dr Sean Scott 8,15,288,294
Dr Kimberley Cantu 15,68,752
Dr Russell Sanders 20,23*
Holly McCanlies 36,83
Amy Senato 43*
Lesa Shocklee 58
Jennifer Stoecker 68
Dr Kelvin Stroy 79
Jimmy Womack 91
Lynn Phears 295

Phillip O'Neal 6
Donald Williams 15,71
Janice North 16,73
Christie Alfred 27,31,74*
Marie Medina 39,81
Joshua Garcia 57
Karen Marcucci 67
David Wright 79
Terri Franks 81*
Staci Buck 275
Alicia Alford 297

Public Schs..Principal	Grd	Prgm	Enr/#Cls	SN
Alice Ponder Elem Sch 101 Pleasant Ridge Dr, Mansfield 76063 David Thayer	PK-4	T	647 35	63% 817/299-7700 Fax 817/473-5658 Ⓣ
Anna May Daulton Elem Sch 2607 N Grand Peninsula Dr, Grand Prairie 75054 Alycen Phan	PK-4		705 50	13% 817/299-6640 Fax 817/453-6570
Annette Perry Elem Sch 1261 S Main St, Mansfield 76063 Willie Wimbrey	PK-4	T	378	53% 817/804-2800 Fax 817/453-6760
Asa Low Jr Intermediate Sch 1526 N Walnut Creek Dr, Mansfield 76063 Jason Short	5-6		789	35% 817/299-3640 Fax 817/453-6577 Ⓣ
Ben Barber Innovation Academy 1120 W Debbie Ln, Mansfield 76063 Catharine Hudgins	Voc	G	1,200	682/314-1600 Fax 817/453-6840
Brooks Wester Middle Sch 1520 N Walnut Creek Dr, Mansfield 76063 Jennifer Powers	7-8	GV	949	33% 682/314-1800 Fax 817/453-7213 Ⓣ
Carol Holt Elem Sch 7321 Ledbetter Rd, Arlington 76001 Thelma Foster	PK-4	T	438 35	45% 817/299-6460 Fax 817/561-3888
Charlotte Anderson Elem Sch 2122 W Nathan Lowe Rd, Arlington 76017 Sheira Petty	PK-4	T	447 52	63% 817/299-7760 Fax 817/472-3216
Cora Spencer Elem Sch 3140 S Camino Lagos, Grand Prairie 75054 Georgie Swize	PK-4		736	17% 817/299-6680 Fax 817/453-6580
Cross Timbers Intermediate Sch 2934 Russell Rd, Arlington 76001 Gina Rietfors	5-6	T	830 60	63% 817/299-3560 Fax 817/561-3814 Ⓣ
D P Morris Elem Sch 7900 Tin Cup Dr, Arlington 76001 Tara Sublette	PK-4	T	578 55	73% 817/299-7860 Fax 817/473-5362
Danny Jones Middle Sch 4500 E Broad St, Mansfield 76063 Travis Moore	7-8		1,068 60	19% 682/314-4600 Fax 817/453-7380
Della Icenhower Interm Sch 8100 Webb Ferrell Rd, Arlington 76002 Mendy Gregory	5-6		895	50% 817/299-2700 Fax 817/453-6890
Donna Shepard Intermediate Sch 1280 Highway 1187, Mansfield 76063 Matthew Brown	5-6	T	838 60	47% 817/299-5940 Fax 817/453-6812
Early College HS at Timberview 7700 S Watson Rd, Arlington 76002 Erica Bennett	9-9		72	682/314-1391 Fax 817/472-2978
Elizabeth Smith Elem Sch 701 S Holland Rd, Mansfield 76063 Lea Boiles	PK-4		610	21% 817/299-6980 Fax 817/453-7340
Erma Nash Elem Sch 1050 Magnolia St, Mansfield 76063 Kia McAdams	PK-4	T	580 36	72% 817/299-6900 Fax 817/453-7300 Ⓣ
Frontier High Sch 1120 W Debbie Ln, Mansfield 76063 Catherine Hudgins	11-12		171	28% 682/314-1600 Fax 817/453-6840

1	Superintendent	8	Curric/Instruct K-12	19	Chief Financial Officer	29	Family/Consumer Science	39	Social Studies K-12
2	Bus/Finance/Purchasing	9	Curric/Instruct Elem	20	Art K-12	30	Adult Education	40	Social Studies Elem
3	Buildings And Grounds	10	Curric/Instruct Sec	21	Art Elem	31	Career/Sch-to-Work K-12	41	Social Studies Sec
4	Food Service	11	Federal Program	22	Art Sec	32	Career/Sch-to-Work Elem	42	Science K-12
5	Transportation	12	Title I	23	Music K-12	33	Career/Sch-to-Work Sec	43	Science Elem
6	Athletic	13	Title V	24	Music Elem	34	Early Childhood Ed	44	Science Sec
7	Health Services	15	Asst Superintendent	25	Music Sec	35	Health/Phys Education	45	Math K-12
		16	Instructional Media Svcs	26	Business Education	36	Guidance Services K-12	46	Math Elem
		17	Chief Operations Officer	27	Career & Tech Ed	37	Guidance Services Elem	47	Math Sec
		18	Chief Academic Officer	28	Technology Education	38	Guidance Services Sec	48	English/Lang Arts K-12

49	English/Lang Arts Elem	59	Special Education Elem	69	Academic Assessment
50	English/Lang Arts Sec	60	Special Education Sec	70	Research/Development
51	Reading K-12	61	Foreign/World Lang K-12	71	Public Information
52	Reading Elem	62	Foreign/World Lang Elem	72	Summer School
53	Reading Sec	63	Foreign/World Lang Sec	73	Instructional Tech
54	Remedial Reading K-12	64	Religious Education K-12	74	Inservice Training
55	Remedial Reading Elem	65	Religious Education Elem	75	Marketing/Distributive
56	Remedial Reading Sec	66	Religious Education Sec	76	Info Systems
57	Bilingual/ELL	67	School Board President	77	Psychological Assess
58	Special Education K-12	68	Teacher Personnel	78	Affirmative Action

Texas School Directory — Tarrant County

School	Grd	Prgm	Enr/#Cls	SN	Phone
Glenn Harmon Elem Sch 5700 Petra Dr, Arlington 76017 Robyn Rinearson	PK-4	T	629 51	80%	817/299-7780 Fax 817/472-3228
Imogene Gideon Elem Sch 1201 Mansfield Webb Rd, Arlington 76002 Shanee Charles	PK-4	T	462 36	59%	817/299-7800 Fax 817/472-3292
J L Boren Elem Sch 1401 Country Club Dr, Mansfield 76063 Tracy Johnson	PK-4	T	558 30	19%	817/299-7740 Fax 817/473-5727
James L Coble Middle Sch 1200 Ballweg Rd, Arlington 76002 Winston Gipson	7-8	T	942	51%	682/314-4900 Fax 817/453-7331
Janet Brockett Elem Sch 810 Dove Meadows Dr, Arlington 76002 Tamara Liddell	PK-4	T	589 45	48%	817/299-6620 Fax 817/453-6835
Judy K Miller Elem Sch 403 N Holland Rd, Mansfield 76063 Jenny Roberson	PK-4	T	462	17%	817/299-7550 Fax 817/473-5706
Kenneth Davis Elem Sch 900 Eden Rd, Arlington 76001 **Lacye Goad**	PK-4	T	492 39	61%	817/299-7840 Fax 817/472-3267
Linda Jobe Middle Sch 2491 Gertie Barrett Rd, Mansfield 76063 Trent Dowd	7-8	T	933	41%	682/314-4400 Fax 817/561-3899
Louise Cabaniss Elem Sch 6080 Mirabella Blvd, Grand Prairie 75052 Sheryl Suchsland	PK-4	T	582	47%	817/299-6480 Fax 817/472-3030
Mansfield High Sch 3001 E Broad St, Mansfield 76063 **Trent Dowd**	9-12	GV	2,468	21%	682/314-0100 Fax 817/473-5424
Mansfield Lake Ridge High Sch 101 N Day Miar Rd, Mansfield 76063 Brandon Johnson	9-12		2,413	26%	682/314-0400 Fax 817/548-2110
Mansfield Legacy High Sch 1263 N Main St, Mansfield 76063 Dr Shelly Butler	9-12		2,061	38%	682/314-0600 Fax 817/453-7653
Mansfield Summit High Sch 1071 Turner Warnell Rd, Arlington 76001 Todd Taylor	9-12	TV	2,182 120	57%	682/314-0800 Fax 817/473-5732
Mansfield Timberview High Sch 7700 S Watson Rd, Arlington 76002 Derrell Douglas	9-12	T	1,853	48%	682/314-1300 Fax 817/472-2978
Martha Reid Elem Sch 500 Country Club Dr, Arlington 76002 **Catherine McGuinness**	PK-4		633 37	36%	817/299-6960 Fax 817/453-7360
Mary Jo Sheppard Elem Sch 1701 FM 1187, Mansfield 76063 **Darrell LeJeune**	PK-4	T	478	52%	817/299-6600 Fax 817/453-6870
Mary Lillard Intermediate Sch 1301 N Day Miar Rd, Mansfield 76063 Matthew Herzberg	5-6		1,049	16%	817/276-6260 Fax 817/548-2285
Mary Orr Intermediate Sch 2900 E Broad St, Mansfield 76063 Duane Thurston	5-6		830 50	36%	817/299-2600 Fax 817/473-5747
Nancy Neal Elem Sch 280 Nelson Wyatt Rd, Mansfield 76063 Tameka Patton	PK-4		442	30%	817/299-1270 Fax 817/561-3820
Roberta Tipps Elem Sch 3001 N Walnut Creek Dr, Mansfield 76063 Cristina Hernandez	PK-4		613	28%	817/299-6920 Fax 817/453-7320
Rogene Worley Middle Sch 500 Pleasant Ridge Dr, Mansfield 76063 Julia McMains	7-8	V	920 59	37%	682/314-5100 Fax 817/473-5623
T A Howard Middle Sch 7501 Calender Rd, Arlington 76001 Dr Kisha McDonald	7-8	TV	921 80	64%	682/314-1050 Fax 817/561-3840
Tarver-Rendon Elem Sch 6065 Retta Mansfield Rd, Burleson 76028 Jamie Norwood-Miller	PK-4	T	660 27	46%	817/299-7880 Fax 817/453-6599
ⓐ The Phoenix Academy 902 E Broad St, Mansfield 76063 Regenia Crane	7-12	GT	150 35	58%	682/314-1700 Fax 817/473-5477
Thelma Jones Elem Sch 7650 S Watson Rd, Arlington 76002 Dameon Gray	PK-4	T	475	53%	817/299-6940 Fax 817/472-3247
Willie E Brown Elem Sch 1860 Cannon Dr, Mansfield 76063 Kyna Eastlick	PK-4	T	614 29	16%	817/299-5860 Fax 817/473-5392

● **White Settlement Ind Sch Dist** PID: 01054183   817/367-1300
401 S Cherry Ln, Fort Worth 76108   Fax 817/367-1351

Schools: 9 \ *Teachers:* 425 \ *Students:* 6,906 \ *Special Ed Students:* 682 \ *LEP Students:* 740 \ *Ethnic:* Asian 1%, African American 8%, Hispanic 41%, Native American: 1%, Caucasian 50% \ *Exp:* $228 (Med) \ *Poverty:* 13% \ *Title I:* $1,068,657 \ *Special Education:* $1,226,000 \ *Open-Close:* 08/20 - 05/21 \ *DTBP:* $181 (High) \

Frank Molinar	1	David Bitters		2,3,5,15,73,78,85,91
Janette Owens	2	Kathy Huey		4
Todd Peterman	6	Todd Peterman		6*
Candace Summerhill	8	Chris Jenkins		8,11,15,16,58,83,271,295
Lee Duncan	8	Ronda Wright		11
Jennifer Heddins	30,80*	Dr Karen Gonzales		34
Amy Ferguson	57	Michael Pogue		58
Randy Armstrong	67	Tim Duncan		68
Desiree Coyle	71	Carla Nored		73
Honey Lee	88*	Christie Beaty		273

Public Schs..Principal	Grd	Prgm	Enr/#Cls	SN	Phone
Blue Haze Elem Sch 601 Blue Haze Dr, Fort Worth 76108 Emily Estes	PK-4	T	692 27	40%	817/367-2583 Fax 817/367-1381
Brewer High Sch 1025 W Loop 820 N, Fort Worth 76108 Jeff Seeton	9-12	T	1,954 70	47%	817/367-1200 Fax 817/367-1241
Brewer Middle Sch 1000 S Cherry Ln, Fort Worth 76108 Sherri Kottwitz	7-8	T	1,018 55	52%	817/367-1267 Fax 817/367-1268
ⓐ Daep 7911 Gibbs Dr, WHT Settlemt 76108 Jennifer Heddins	9-12	T	53	64%	817/367-1364 Fax 817/367-1366
ⓜ Fine Arts Academy 8301 Downe Dr, Fort Worth 76108 **Kerry Cooper**	K-6		302 15	39%	817/367-5396 Fax 817/367-1396
Liberty Elem Sch 7976 Whitney Dr, Fort Worth 76108 **Michael Dickinson**	PK-4	GT	640 38	78%	817/367-1312 Fax 817/367-1313
North Elem Sch 9850 Legacy Dr, Fort Worth 76108 Connie Bitters	PK-4	T	737 30	61%	817/367-1323 Fax 817/367-1308
Tannahill Intermediate Sch 701 American Flyer Blvd, Fort Worth 76108 Randy Summerhill	5-6	T	995 46	61%	817/367-1370 Fax 817/367-1371
West Elem Sch 8901 White Settlement Rd, Fort Worth 76108 Lisa Edmunds	PK-4	T	515 22	79%	817/367-1334 Fax 817/367-1333

---

79 Student Personnel
80 Driver Ed/Safety
81 Gifted/Talented
82 Video Services
83 Substance Abuse Prev
84 Erate
85 AIDS Education
88 Alternative/At Risk
89 Multi-Cultural Curriculum
90 Social Work
91 Safety/Security
92 Magnet School
93 Parental Involvement
95 Tech Prep Program
97 Chief Infomation Officer
98 Chief Technology Officer
270 Character Education
271 Migrant Education
273 Teacher Mentor
274 Before/After Sch
275 Response To Intervention
277 Remedial Math K-12
280 Literacy Coach
285 STEM
286 Digital Learning
288 Common Core Standards
294 Accountability
295 Network System
296 Title II Programs
297 Webmaster
298 Grant Writer/Ptnrships
750 Chief Innovation Officer
751 Chief of Staff
752 Social Emotional Learning

Other School Types
ⓐ = Alternative School
ⓒ = Charter School
ⓜ = Magnet School
ⓨ = Year-Round School

School Programs
A = Alternative Program
G = Adult Classes
M = Magnet Program
T = Title I Schoolwide
V = Career & Tech Ed Programs

Social Media
= Facebook
= Twitter

New Schools are shaded
New Superintendents and Principals are bold
Personnel with email addresses are underscored

Tarrant County

Market Data Retrieval

TARRANT CATHOLIC SCHOOLS

- **Diocese of Fort Worth Ed Off** PID: 01054339 — 817/560-3300
  800 W Loop 820 S, Fort Worth 76108 — Fax 817/244-8839

Schools: 19 \ *Students:* 5,961

Listing includes only schools located in this county. See District Index for location of Diocesan Offices.

Jennifer Pelletier	1	Donald Wagner	2,19
Nancy Benson	2	Michael Carlson	6
Nancy Eder	7	Erin Vader	8,70
Melissa Button	15		

Catholic Schs..Principal	Grd	Prgm	Enr/#Cls	SN
All Saints Catholic Sch 2006 N Houston St, Fort Worth 76164 Arica Prado	PK-8		155 8	817/624-2670 Fax 817/624-1221
Cassata High Sch 1400 Hemphill St, Fort Worth 76104 Brian Lott	9-12	GV	100 7	817/926-1745 Fax 817/926-3132
Holy Family Catholic Sch 6146 Pershing Ave, Fort Worth 76107 Ann Walters	PK-8		232 16	817/737-4201 Fax 817/738-1542
Holy Trinity Catholic Sch 3750 William D Tate Ave, Grapevine 76051 Jeffrey Heiple	PK-8		300 30	817/421-8000 Fax 817/421-4468
Nolan Catholic High Sch 4501 Bridge St, Fort Worth 76103 Leah Rios	9-12		797 55	817/457-2920 Fax 817/496-9775
Our Lady of Victory Sch 3320 Hemphill St, Fort Worth 76110 Linda Kuntz	PK-8		104 9	817/924-5123 Fax 817/923-9621
St Andrew Catholic Sch 3304 Dryden Rd, Fort Worth 76109 Maria Macias	PK-8		695 30	817/924-8917 Fax 817/921-1490
St Elizabeth Ann Seton Sch 2016 Willis Ln, Keller 76248 Sam Vanderplas	PK-8		482 28	817/431-4845 Fax 817/431-1865
St George Sch 824 Hudgins Ave, Fort Worth 76111 Mary Longoria	PK-8		180 10	817/222-1221 Fax 817/838-0424
St John the Apostle Cath Sch 7421 Glenview Dr, N Richlnd Hls 76180 Amy Felton	PK-8		210 20	817/284-2228 Fax 817/284-1800
St Joseph Catholic Sch 2015 SW Green Oaks Blvd, Arlington 76017 Diane Price	PK-8		464 20	817/419-6800 Fax 817/419-7080
St Maria Goretti Sch 1200 S Davis Dr, Arlington 76013 Laura Behee	PK-8		455 20	817/275-5081 Fax 817/460-0048
St Peter School the Apostle 1201 S Cherry Ln, WHT Settlemt 76108 Lisa Giardino	PK-8		100 10	817/246-2032 Fax 817/246-4900
St Rita Catholic Sch 712 Weiler Blvd, Fort Worth 76112 Mary Burns	PK-8		175 11	817/451-9383 Fax 817/446-4465

TARRANT PRIVATE SCHOOLS

Private Schs..Principal	Grd	Prgm	Enr/#Cls	SN
All Saints Episcopal Sch 9700 Saints Cir, Fort Worth 76108 Dr Thaddeus Bird	PK-12		1,000 50	817/560-5700 Fax 817/560-5716
Azle Christian Sch 1801 S Stewart St, Azle 76020 April Geeslin	PK-12		110	817/444-9964 Fax 817/444-9914
Barbara Gordon Montessori Sch 1513 Hall Johnson Rd, Colleyville 76034 Charlane Baccus	PK-6		160 8	817/354-6670 Fax 817/354-6665
Bethesda Christian Sch 4700 N Beach St, Fort Worth 76137 Freda Chadwick	K-12		400 28	817/281-6446 Fax 817/281-1560
Burton Adventist Academy 4611 Kelly Elliott Rd, Arlington 76017 Darlene White	PK-12		325 21	817/572-0081 Fax 817/561-4237
Calvary Christian Academy 1401 Oakhurst Scenic Dr, Fort Worth 76111 Sue Tidwell	PK-12		400 30	817/332-3351 Fax 817/332-4621
Christian Life Preparatory Sch 5253 Altamesa Blvd, Fort Worth 76123 Zachary Henry	K-12		200	817/293-1500
Clariden Sch 100 Clariden Ranch Rd, Southlake 76092 Sallie Wells	PK-12		87 10	682/237-0400 Fax 682/831-0300
Country Day Sch of Arlington 1105 W Randol Mill Rd, Arlington 76012 Joyce Hunt-French	PK-1		83 20	817/275-0851 Fax 817/275-0263
Covenant Christian Academy 901 Cheek Sparger Rd, Colleyville 76034 Myrandi Ballesteros \ Susan Cook \ Justice Kerr	PK-12		416	817/281-4333 Fax 682/334-0367
Covenant Classical Sch 1701 Wind Star Way, Fort Worth 76108 Eric Cook	K-12		161	817/820-0884 Fax 817/246-5027
Crossroads Christian Academy 3512 Roberts Cut Off Rd, Fort Worth 76114 Chuck Mays	8-12		52 1	817/378-0100 Fax 817/378-8778
Crown of Life Lutheran Sch 6605 Pleasant Run Rd, Colleyville 76034 Laura Cleland	PK-8		160 15	817/251-1881 Fax 817/421-9263
Ekklesia Christian Sch 1200 Bessie St, Fort Worth 76104 Michele Chambers	PK-6		31 3	817/332-1202
Faith Christian Sch 730 E Worth St, Grapevine 76051 Sharon Neely \ Kory Hicks \ Keith Hall	PK-12		800 31	817/442-9144 Fax 817/442-9904
Fellowship Academy 1021 N Bowman Springs Rd, Kennedale 76060 Shannon Stoker	PK-12		320 17	817/483-2400 Fax 817/483-2404
Flint Academy 2111 Roosevelt Dr, Arlington 76013 Dr Paula Flint	PK-12		90 17	817/277-0620 Fax 817/549-0004
Fort Worth Academy 7301 Dutch Branch Rd, Fort Worth 76132 Shannon Elders	K-8		240 24	817/370-1191 Fax 817/294-1323
Fort Worth Christian Sch 6200 Holiday Ln, N Richlnd Hls 76180 Elizabeth Green \ Jill Shelby \ Nick Hinrichsen	PK-12		850 70	817/281-6504 Fax 817/281-7063
Ft Worth Adventist Jr Academy 3040 Sycamore School Rd, Fort Worth 76133 Fred Esquivel	PK-8		85 5	817/370-7177

1 Superintendent	8 Curric/Instruct K-12	19 Chief Financial Officer	29 Family/Consumer Science	39 Social Studies K-12	49 English/Lang Arts Elem	59 Special Education Elem	69 Academic Assessment
2 Bus/Finance/Purchasing	9 Curric/Instruct Elem	20 Art K-12	30 Adult Education	40 Social Studies Elem	50 English/Lang Arts Sec	60 Special Education Sec	70 Research/Development
3 Buildings And Grounds	10 Curric/Instruct Sec	21 Art Elem	31 Career/Sch-to-Work K-12	41 Social Studies Sec	51 Reading K-12	61 Foreign/World Lang K-12	71 Public Information
4 Food Service	11 Federal Program	22 Art Sec	32 Career/Sch-to-Work Elem	42 Science K-12	52 Reading Elem	62 Foreign/World Lang Elem	72 Summer School
5 Transportation	12 Title I	23 Music K-12	33 Career/Sch-to-Work Sec	43 Science Elem	53 Reading Sec	63 Foreign/World Lang Sec	73 Instructional Tech
6 Athletic	13 Title V	24 Music Elem	34 Early Childhood Ed	44 Science Sec	54 Remedial Reading K-12	64 Religious Education Elem	74 Inservice Training
7 Health Services	15 Asst Superintendent	25 Music Sec	35 Health/Phys Education	45 Math K-12	55 Remedial Reading Elem	65 Religious Education Elem	75 Marketing/Distributive
	16 Instructional Media Svcs	26 Business Education	36 Guidance Services K-12	46 Math Elem	56 Remedial Reading Sec	66 Religious Education Sec	76 Info Systems
	17 Chief Operations Officer	27 Career & Tech Ed	37 Guidance Services Elem	47 Math Sec	57 Bilingual/ELL	67 School Board President	77 Psychological Assess
	18 Chief Academic Officer	28 Technology Education	38 Guidance Services Sec	48 English/Lang Arts K-12	58 Special Education K-12	68 Teacher Personnel	78 Affirmative Action

Texas School Directory — Tarrant County

School	Grades	Enrollment/Staff	Phone/Fax
Ft Worth Country Day Sch 4200 Country Day Ln, Fort Worth 76109 Trey Blair \ John Stephens \ Stephen Stackhouse	K-12	1,100 75	817/732-7718 Fax 817/377-3425
Fusion Academy-Southlake 301 State St Ste 200, Southlake 76092 Stephen Schwartz	6-12	401	817/416-0306
Grace Prep Academy PO Box 170958, Arlington 76003 Dr Marc Evans	K-12	450 18	817/557-3399 Fax 817/557-4300
Green Oaks Sch 5508 Chaperito Trl, Arlington 76016 Leigh Weedman	Spec	65	817/496-5100 Fax 817/496-5104
Harvest Christian Academy 7200 Denton Hwy, Watauga 76148 Sheila Bothe	PK-12	600 40	817/485-1660 Fax 817/514-6279
High Point Prep Academy 2400 E Arbrook Blvd, Arlington 76014 Stephen Collins	K-12	157 25	817/394-3100 Fax 817/394-3101
Hill School of Fort Worth 4817 Odessa Ave, Fort Worth 76133 Roxanne Breyer	Spec	175 23	817/923-9482 Fax 817/923-4894 f
Inspire Academy 55 Main St Ste 290, Colleyville 76034 Dana Judd	Spec	30	817/966-4821
Key Sch 3947 E Loop 820 S, Fort Worth 76119 Leslie Vasquez \ Chad Meeks \ Leigh Bryant	Spec G	100 22	817/446-3738 Fax 817/496-3299
Lake Country Christian Sch 7050 Lake Country Dr, Fort Worth 76179 Sarah Deckert \ Josh Williams	PK-12	410 31	817/236-8703 Fax 817/236-1103
Legacy Classical Chrn Academy 12501 Highway 287, Haslet 76052 Belinda Henson	PK-12	85	817/382-2322
Merryhill Sch 711 W Arbrook Blvd, Arlington 76015 Michelle Bechtel	PK-6	300	817/472-9494 Fax 817/468-8348 f
Messiah Luth Classical Academy 1308 Whitley Rd, Keller 76248 Alison Smith	PK-9	155	817/431-5486 Fax 817/898-0365
Metroplex Chapel Academy 601 E Airport Fwy, Euless 76039 Renee Delorge	PK-6	100 7	817/267-1000 Fax 817/267-5000
Montessori Academy-Arlington 3428 W Arkansas Ln, Arlington 76016 Pam Dunbar	PK-6	260 12	817/274-1548 Fax 817/274-6951
Montessori Children's House 3420 Clayton Rd E, Fort Worth 76116 Amy Henderson	PK-8	200 5	817/732-0252 Fax 817/732-6601
Nazarene Christian Academy 2001 E Main St, Crowley 76036 Nancy Shonamon	K-12	385	817/297-7003 Fax 817/297-1509
New Life Academy 601 E Airport Fwy, Euless 76039 Renee Delorge	PK-6	60	817/267-1000
North Park Christian Academy 7025 Mid Cities Blvd, N Richlnd Hls 76182 Jane Edwards	PK-3	40 5	817/498-8456 Fax 817/428-2060
North Texas Leadership Academy 10200 Alta Vista Rd, Keller 76244 Jennifer Pasteur	PK-4	75	817/562-2931 Fax 817/562-2058
Northstar Sch 4620 Park Springs Blvd, Arlington 76017 Lisa Odom	7-12	52	817/478-5852 Fax 817/478-7252
Novus Academy 204 N Dooley St Ste 100, Grapevine 76051 Kathleen Edwards	K-12	70	817/488-4555 Fax 817/488-4533
Pantego Christian Academy 2351 Country Club Dr, Mansfield 76063 Elizabeth Birdwell	PK-5	150 13	817/522-5900 Fax 682/518-0823
Pantego Christian Academy 2201 W Park Row Dr, Arlington 76013 Elizabeth Birdwell \ Michael Beeson	PK-12	797 50	817/460-3315 Fax 817/548-9288 t
Park Row Chrn Academy 915 W Park Row Dr, Arlington 76013 Paula Gibson	PK-6	200 15	817/277-1021 Fax 817/277-1385
Premier Academy 4040 Heritage Trace Pkwy, Keller 76244 Chris Cross	PK-5	250 14	817/745-0034 Fax 817/741-4588
Redeemer Lutheran Sch 4513 Williams Rd, Fort Worth 76116 Page Nickell	PK-5	50 8	817/560-0032
Rivertree Academy 5439 Bonnell Ave, Fort Worth 76107 Emily Williams	PK-5	30	817/420-9310
Saint Peters Classical Sch 7601 Bellaire Dr S, Fort Worth 76132 Jeanette Johnson	K-12	75 13	817/294-0124 Fax 817/288-0180 f
Southwest Christian Sch-Prep 6901 Altamesa Blvd, Fort Worth 76123 Dr Joey Richards \ Coby Bird	7-12	603	817/294-9596
Southwest Christian Sch 6801 Dan Danciger Rd, Fort Worth 76133 Justin Kirk	PK-6	400 25	817/294-0350 Fax 817/294-0752
Spurling Christian Academy 1200 High Point Rd, Arlington 76015 Linda Sands	PK-12	25	817/465-1122 Fax 817/391-1443
St Ignatius College Prep Sch 8109 Shelton Dr, Fort Worth 76120 Victor Nguyen	9-12	200	817/801-4801
St Paul Lutheran Sch 1800 West Fwy, Fort Worth 76102 Scott Browning	PK-8	223 13	817/332-4563 Fax 817/332-2640 f
St Paul's Preparatory Academy 6900 US 287 Hwy, Arlington 76001 Amy Maumus \ Gayla Rockwell	PK-12	290	817/561-3500 Fax 817/561-3408
Starpoint Sch 2825 Stadium Dr, Fort Worth 76109 Marilyn Tolbert	Spec	66 6	817/257-7141 Fax 817/257-7168
Tate Springs Christian Sch 4001 Little Rd, Arlington 76016 Halley Steinhilber	K-6	325	817/478-7091 Fax 817/483-8283
Temple Christian Sch 6824 Randol Mill Rd, Fort Worth 76120 Shelena Schweitzer	K-12	475 26	817/457-0770 Fax 817/457-0777
The Jane Justin Sch 1300 W Lancaster Ave, Fort Worth 76102 Casey Mann	Spec	70	817/390-2831 Fax 817/390-2851
The Oakridge Sch 5900 W Pioneer Pkwy, Arlington 76013 Dr Sarah Schecter \ Britt Robinson	PK-12	850	817/451-4994 Fax 817/457-6681
Trinity Baptist Temple Academy 6045 Wj Boaz Rd, Fort Worth 76179 Br Michael Crain	PK-12	135 13	817/237-4255 Fax 817/237-5233
Trinity Valley Sch 7500 Dutch Branch Rd, Fort Worth 76132 Ian Craig	K-12 V	971 78	817/321-0100 Fax 817/321-0105 f t
Vanguard International Academy 1600 S Center St, Arlington 76010 Ibrahim Abu Abdulrahman	8-11	23	817/274-6444
Walnut Creek Private Sch 1751 N Walnut Creek Dr, Mansfield 76063 Ladonna Morgan	PK-5	150	817/473-4406 Fax 817/453-8755

79 Student Personnel
80 Driver Ed/Safety
81 Gifted/Talented
82 Video Services
83 Substance Abuse Prev
84 Erate
85 AIDS Education
88 Alternative/At Risk
89 Multi-Cultural Curriculum
90 Social Work
91 Safety/Security
92 Magnet School
93 Parental Involvement
95 Tech Prep Program
97 Chief Infomation Officer
98 Chief Technology Officer
270 Accountability
271 Migrant Education
273 Teacher Mentor
274 Before/After Sch
275 Response To Intervention
277 Remedial Math K-12
280 Literacy Coach
285 STEM
286 Digital Learning
288 Common Core Standards
294 Accountability
295 Network System
296 Title II Programs
297 Webmaster
298 Grant Writer/Ptnrships
750 Chief Innovation Officer
751 Chief of Staff
752 Social Emotional Learning

Other School Types
Ⓐ = Alternative School
Ⓒ = Charter School
Ⓜ = Magnet School
Ⓨ = Year-Round School

School Programs
A = Alternative Program
G = Adult Classes
M = Magnet Program
T = Title I Schoolwide
V = Career & Tech Ed Programs

Social Media
f = Facebook
t = Twitter

New Schools are shaded
New Superintendents and Principals are bold
Personnel with email addresses are underscored

Taylor County

Market Data Retrieval

Wedgewood Academy   Spec   61   817/924-9095
4833 Selkirk Dr, Fort Worth 76109
Rachel Wittich

TARRANT REGIONAL CENTERS

- **Region 11 Ed Service Center** PID: 01054171   817/740-3600
  1451 S Cherry Ln, WHT Settlemt 76108   Fax 817/740-7600

  Dr Clyde Steelman 1,11   Brandilyn DePalma 2
  Laura Weir 2   John Petree 15,58,69,73,74
  Rory Peacock 15,295   Tiffany Green 68
  Teela Watson 70   Lori Burton 71
  David Sons 76   Shari King 298

TAYLOR COUNTY

TAYLOR PUBLIC SCHOOLS

- **Abilene Ind School Dist** PID: 01054523   325/677-1444
  241 Pine St, Abilene 79601   Fax 325/794-1324

  Schools: 26 \ *Teachers:* 1,126 \ *Students:* 17,000 \
  Special Ed Students: 1,866 \ *LEP Students:* 793 \ *College-Bound:* 48%
  \ *Ethnic:* Asian 2%, African American 14%, Hispanic 45%, Caucasian
  39% \ *Exp:* $277 (Med) \ *Poverty:* 23% \ *Title I:* $5,758,633 \
  Special Education: $3,440,000 \ *Open-Close:* 08/21 - 05/22 \ *DTBP:* $188
  (High)

  Dr David Young 1   Lisa Metcalf 2
  Melissa Irby 2   Juan Rodriguez 3
  Scott McLean 3,4,5,15   Phil Blue 6,35
  Linda Langston 7   Kimberly Brumley 8
  Alison Sims 9   Gustavo Villanueva 10,15,27,31
  Cheryl Cunningham 11,48,57   Joseph Waldron 15,68
  Jay Lester 20,23   Mignon Lawson 30*
  Jennifer Putnam ....34*   Ross Thomas 39
  Teri Reece 58   Randy Piersall 67
  Jeannette Forehand 69,294   Gregory Fleming 71
  Cary Owens 76,295   Dr Dan Dukes 79
  Charles Caddell 297

Public Schs..Principal	Grd	Prgm	Enr/#Cls	SN	
Abilene High Sch 2800 N 6th St, Abilene 79603 Michael Garcia	9-12	TV	2,137	64%	325/677-1731 Fax 325/794-1387
Adult Education 1929 S 11th St, Abilene 79602 Mignon Lawson	Adult		250 8		325/671-4419 Fax 325/794-1327
Ⓜ Atems High Sch 650 US Highway 80 E, Abilene 79601 Jeffrey Howle	9-12	V	357	48%	325/794-4140
Austin Elem Sch 2341 Greenbriar Dr, Abilene 79605 Alison Camp	PK-5	T	592 25	46%	325/690-3920 Fax 325/794-1350
Bassetti Elem Sch 5749 US Highway 277 S, Abilene 79606 Keri Thornburg	PK-5	T	510 30	73%	325/690-3720 Fax 325/794-1351
Bonham Elem Sch 4250 Potomac Ave, Abilene 79605 Stevanie Jackson	PK-5	T	538 28	73%	325/690-3745 Fax 325/794-1352
Bowie Elem Sch 2034 Jeanette St, Abilene 79602 Tina Jones	PK-5	T	558 32	84%	325/671-4770 Fax 325/794-1353
Byron Craig Middle Sch 702 S Judge Ely Blvd, Abilene 79602 Guadalupe Gonzales	6-8	TV	962	70%	325/794-4100 Fax 325/794-1385
Clack Middle Sch 1610 Corsicana Ave, Abilene 79605 Ernest Bramwell	6-8	TV	845 55	72%	325/692-1961 Fax 325/794-1371
Cooper High Sch 3639 Sayles Blvd, Abilene 79605 Lyndsey Williamson	9-12	TV	1,787	61%	325/691-1000 Fax 325/794-1375
Dyess Elem Sch 402 Delaware Rd, Abilene 79605 Michael Newton	PK-5	T	549	51%	325/690-3795 Fax 325/794-1355
Holland Medical High Sch 2200 Hickory St, Abilene 79601 Lyndsey Williamson	Voc		150		325/794-4120 Fax 325/794-1372
Jackson Elem Sch 2650 S 32nd St, Abilene 79605 Debra Hollingsworth	PK-5	T	541	72%	325/690-3602 Fax 325/794-1357
Jefferson Achievement Ctr 1741 S 14th St, Abilene 79602 Jane Allred	Spec		80 6	79%	325/794-4150 Fax 325/794-1367
Johnston Elem Sch 3602 N 12th St, Abilene 79603 Jeffrey Brokovich	K-5	T	484 25	83%	325/671-4845 Fax 325/794-1358
Lee Elem Sch 1026 N Pioneer Dr, Abilene 79603 Andy Blessing	K-5	T	420 40	87%	325/671-4895 Fax 325/794-1359
Long Early Childhood Center 3600 Sherry Ln, Abilene 79603 Jennifer Putnam	PK-PK	T	346 18	84%	325/671-4594 Fax 325/794-1368
Madison Middle Sch 3145 Barrow St, Abilene 79605 Joshua Newton	6-8	TV	989 40	69%	325/692-5661 Fax 325/794-1313
Mann Middle Sch 2545 Mimosa Dr, Abilene 79603 Kathryn Walker	6-8	TV	890 31	75%	325/672-8493 Fax 325/794-1374
Martinez Elem Sch 1250 Merchant St, Abilene 79603 Mildred Petty	PK-5	T	570 20	94%	325/794-4160
Ortiz Elem Sch 2550 Vogel St, Abilene 79603 Debra Stewart	PK-5	T	604 36	93%	325/671-4945 Fax 325/794-1361
Reagan Elem Sch 5340 Hartford St, Abilene 79605 Leslye Roberts	PK-5	T	411 34	85%	325/690-3627 Fax 325/794-1362
Taylor Elem Sch 916 E North 13th St, Abilene 79601 Keri Thornburg	PK-5	T	643 25	63%	325/671-4970 Fax 325/794-1364
Thomas Elem Sch 1240 Lakeside Dr, Abilene 79602 Cindy Hay	PK-5	T	451 26	77%	325/671-4995 Fax 325/794-1365
Ward Elem Sch 3750 Paint Brush Dr, Abilene 79606 Dawn Ripple	PK-5	T	565 29	51%	325/690-3666 Fax 325/794-1366
Ⓐ Woodson Center for Excellence 342 Cockerell Dr, Abilene 79601 Jaime Tindall	9-12		166 9	84%	325/671-4736 Fax 325/676-1528

1 Superintendent	8 Curric/Instruct K-12	19 Chief Financial Officer	29 Family/Consumer Science	39 Social Studies K-12	49 English/Lang Arts Elem	59 Special Education Elem	69 Academic Assessment
2 Bus/Finance/Purchasing	9 Curric/Instruct Elem	20 Art K-12	30 Adult Education	40 Social Studies Elem	50 English/Lang Arts Sec	60 Special Education Sec	70 Research/Development
3 Buildings And Grounds	10 Curric/Instruct Sec	21 Art Elem	31 Career/Sch-to-Work K-12	41 Social Studies Sec	51 Reading K-12	61 Foreign/World Lang K-12	71 Public Information
4 Food Service	11 Federal Program	22 Art Sec	32 Career/Sch-to-Work Elem	42 Science K-12	52 Reading Elem	62 Foreign/World Lang Elem	72 Summer School
5 Transportation	12 Title I	23 Music K-12	33 Career/Sch-to-Work Sec	43 Science Elem	53 Reading Sec	63 Foreign/World Lang Sec	73 Instructional Tech
6 Athletic	13 Title V	24 Music Elem	34 Early Childhood Ed	44 Science Sec	54 Remedial Reading K-12	64 Religious Education K-12	74 Inservice Training
7 Health Services	15 Asst Superintendent	25 Music Sec	35 Health/Phys Education	45 Math K-12	55 Remedial Reading Elem	65 Religious Education Elem	75 Marketing/Distributive
	16 Instructional Media Svcs	26 Business Education	36 Guidance Services K-12	46 Math Elem	56 Remedial Reading Sec	66 Religious Education Sec	76 Info Systems
	17 Chief Operations Officer	27 Career & Tech Ed	37 Guidance Services Elem	47 Math Sec	57 Bilingual/ELL	67 School Board President	77 Psychological Assess
	18 Chief Academic Officer	28 Technology Education	38 Guidance Services Sec	48 English/Lang Arts K-12	58 Special Education K-12	68 Teacher Personnel	78 Affirmative Action

Texas School Directory

Taylor County

Jim Ned Cons Ind School Dist PID: 01054896
441 Graham Ave, Tuscola 79562
325/554-7500
Fax 325/554-7740

Schools: 4 \ **Teachers:** 93 \ **Students:** 1,300 \ **Special Ed Students:** 103 \ **College-Bound:** 75% \ **Ethnic:** African American 1%, Hispanic 12%, Caucasian 87% \ **Exp:** $251 (Med) \ **Poverty:** 9% \ **Title I:** $108,634 \ **Open-Close:** 08/19 - 05/21 \ **DTBP:** $348 (High)

Dr Glen Teal 1	Hunter Cooley 2,11,19,294
Douglas Taylor 4*	Bobby Easterling 5*
Raenese Byrom 7,85	Cristi Doty 8,288*
Debbie Harris 12	Marja Swart 16,82*
Carla Cooley 38,69,83,88*	Mendi Jeter 58
Matt Higgins 67	Dana Kiner 73,286,295*

Public Schs..Principal	Grd	Prgm	Enr/#Cls	SN	
Buffalo Gap Elem Sch 665 Vine St, Buffalo Gap 79508 Cristi Doty	PK-5		328 12	25%	325/572-3533 Fax 325/572-4824
Jim Ned High Sch 830 Garza Ave, Tuscola 79562 Treva Gambrell	9-12	V	347 30	20%	325/554-7755 Fax 325/554-7733
Jim Ned Middle Sch 830 Garza Ave, Tuscola 79562 Jay Wise	6-8		293 24	21%	325/554-7870 Fax 325/554-7750
Lawn Elem Sch 525 4th Street, Lawn 79530 Debbie Harris	PK-5		251 35		325/583-2256 Fax 325/583-2679

Merkel Ind School Dist PID: 01054925
1512 S 5th, Merkel 79536
325/928-5813
Fax 325/928-3910

Schools: 3 \ **Teachers:** 95 \ **Students:** 1,100 \ **Special Ed Students:** 140 \ **LEP Students:** 19 \ **College-Bound:** 44% \ **Ethnic:** African American 1%, Hispanic 27%, Native American: 1%, Caucasian 71% \ **Exp:** $310 (High) \ **Poverty:** 18% \ **Title I:** $261,845 \ **Open-Close:** 08/19 - 05/22 \ **DTBP:** $486 (High)

Bryan Allen 1	Lane Petty 2
Royce Fowler 3	Robert Whitehead 5
Brian Ramsey 6	Nan Wiley 57,271
Kyle Doan 67	Rachael Byers 69,83,88*

Public Schs..Principal	Grd	Prgm	Enr/#Cls	SN	
Merkel Elem Sch 1602 S 5th, Merkel 79536 **Daniel Kotara**	PK-5	T	570 17	62%	325/928-4795 Fax 325/928-3174
Merkel High Sch 2000 S 7th St, Merkel 79536 **James Stevens**	9-12	ATV	314 40	54%	325/928-4667 Fax 325/928-4684
Merkel Middle Sch 302 Ash, Merkel 79536 Larry Bills	6-8	T	262 27	53%	325/928-5511 Fax 325/928-3138

Trent Ind School Dist PID: 01054987
12821 E I 20, Trent 79561
325/862-6125
Fax 325/862-6448

Schools: 1 \ **Teachers:** 19 \ **Students:** 180 \ **Special Ed Students:** 9 \ **LEP Students:** 3 \ **College-Bound:** 85% \ **Ethnic:** Asian 1%, Hispanic 9%, Caucasian 91% \ **Exp:** $710 (High) \ **Poverty:** 16% \ **Title I:** $23,432 \ **Open-Close:** 08/15 - 05/22 \ **DTBP:** $352 (High)

Guy Birdwell 1,11,83,288	Teresa Bryan 2*
Greg Rains 3*	Patsy Williams 4*
Juan Rios 6*	Patricia West 16*
Marie Alambar 57,58*	J Pickens 67
Tricia Spikes 73,295*	

Public Schs..Principal	Grd	Prgm	Enr/#Cls	SN	
Trent Sch 12821 East I 20, Trent 79561 Vanessa Oakley	PK-12	TV	180 23	49%	325/862-6125

Wylie Ind School Dist PID: 01055008
6251 Buffalo Gap Rd, Abilene 79606
325/692-4353
Fax 325/695-3438

Schools: 7 \ **Teachers:** 265 \ **Students:** 4,600 \ **Special Ed Students:** 276 \ **LEP Students:** 41 \ **College-Bound:** 60% \ **Ethnic:** Asian 2%, African American 4%, Hispanic 19%, Caucasian 75% \ **Exp:** $175 (Low) \ **Poverty:** 7% \ **Title I:** $286,570 \ **Special Education:** $591,000 \ **Open-Close:** 08/21 - 05/21 \ **DTBP:** $153 (High)

Joey Light 1	Carol Smith 2,11,296,298
Craig Bessent 3,5,91	Melanie Brewer 4
Hugh Sandifer 6*	Corrissa Parris 7*
Terry Hagler 8	Jennifer Greenough 16
Lisa Salmon 34,57,69,83,273*	Greggory Ruffin 35*
Brenda Sandifer 36,85,88,271*	Shauni Vaughn 58,271
Steve Keenum 67	Tony Spradlin 73,84
Jackie Powell 76	Kimberly Cheek 81*

Public Schs..Principal	Grd	Prgm	Enr/#Cls	SN	
Wylie East Elem Sch 7401 Maple St, Abilene 79602 **Kim McMillan**	PK-4		940		325/437-2330 Fax 325/437-2379
Wylie East Junior High Sch 1682 Colony Hill Rd, Abilene 79602 Rob Goodenough	5-8		678	18%	325/437-2360 Fax 325/692-5786
Wylie High Sch 4502 Antilley Rd, Abilene 79606 **Tim Smith**	9-12		1,164 65	11%	325/690-1181 Fax 325/690-0320
Wylie Intermediate Sch 3158 Beltway S, Abilene 79606 **Phil Boone**	3-4		692 28	21%	325/692-7961 Fax 325/695-4647
Wylie West Early Childhood Ctr 6249 Buffalo Gap Rd, Abilene 79606 Lisa Salmon	PK-K		495	27%	325/437-2351 Fax 325/695-4645
Wylie West Elem Sch 7650 Hardwick Rd, Abilene 79606 Lisa Bessent	1-2		698 19	20%	325/692-6554 Fax 325/695-4645
Wylie West Junior High Sch 4134 Beltway S, Abilene 79606 **Aaron Amonett**	5-8		686 30	17%	325/695-1910 Fax 325/692-5786

TAYLOR PRIVATE SCHOOLS

Private Schs..Principal	Grd	Prgm	Enr/#Cls	SN	
A Habitat for Learning Daycare 3242 Beltway S, Abilene 79606 Michelle Van Horn	PK-PK		40		325/692-2481 Fax 325/691-0655
Abilene Christian Sch 2550 N Judge Ely Blvd, Abilene 79601 Cindy Johnson \ Van Gravitt	PK-12		300 20		325/672-6200 Fax 325/672-1202
Cornerstone Christian Sch 718 Barrow St, Abilene 79605 Robbye Benningfield	PK-5		45 6		325/676-8232 Fax 325/437-2432
Kenley Sch 1434 Matador St, Abilene 79605 Qi Hang	1-8		69 5		325/698-3220 Fax 325/692-7387

---

79 Student Personnel	91 Safety/Security	275 Response To Intervention	298 Grant Writer/Ptnrships	**School Programs**	**Social Media**
80 Driver Ed/Safety	92 Magnet School	277 Remedial Math K-12	750 Chief Innovation Officer	A = Alternative Program	☐ = Facebook
81 Gifted/Talented	93 Parental Involvement	280 Literacy Coach	751 Chief of Staff	G = Adult Classes	
82 Video Services	95 Tech Prep Program	285 STEM	752 Social Emotional Learning	M = Magnet Program	☐ = Twitter
83 Substance Abuse Prev	97 Chief Infomation Officer	286 Digital Learning		T = Title I Schoolwide	
84 Erate	98 Chief Technology Officer	288 Common Core Standards	**Other School Types**	V = Career & Tech Ed Programs	
85 AIDS Education	270 Accountability	294 Alternative School	Ⓐ = Alternative School		
88 Alternative/At Risk	271 Migrant Education	295 Network System	Ⓒ = Charter School	New Schools are shaded	
89 Multi-Cultural Curriculum	273 Teacher Mentor	296 Title II Programs	Ⓜ = Magnet School	New Superintendents and Principals are bold	
90 Social Work	274 Before/After Sch	297 Webmaster	Ⓨ = Year-Round School	Personnel with email addresses are underscored	

TX—361

Terrell County
Market Data Retrieval

St John's Episcopal Sch   PK-5   260   325/695-8870
1600 Sherman Dr, Abilene 79605   14   Fax 325/698-1532
Rebecca McMillion

TAYLOR REGIONAL CENTERS

- **Region 14 Ed Service Center** PID: 01054975   325/675-8600
  1850 State Highway 351, Abilene 79601   Fax 325/675-8659

Ronnie Kincaid	1	Emily Jeffrey	2
Dr Rose Burks	7,8,27,31,88	Emilia Moreno	11,57
Lisa White	36,58,77	Dr Gene Shelhamer	67
Robb McClellan	73	Misty Bloomingdale	74
Rod Pruitt	83,85	Donna Scherr	275

TERRELL COUNTY

TERRELL PUBLIC SCHOOLS

- **Terrell Co Ind School Dist** PID: 01055046   432/345-2515
  302 2nd St, Sanderson 79848   Fax 432/345-2404

Schools: 1 \ **Teachers:** 16 \ **Students:** 130 \ **Special Ed Students:** 16 \ **LEP Students:** 4 \ **College-Bound:** 50% \ **Ethnic:** Hispanic 65%, Caucasian 35% \ **Exp:** $347 (High) \ **Poverty:** 21% \ **Title I:** $36,663 \ **Open-Close:** 08/15 - 05/22 \ **DTBP:** $428 (High) \

Amanda Mangallan	1	Blain Chriesman	2
Sam Mangallan	3	Violita McDonald	13,83*
Thad Cleveland	67	David Carrasco	73*

Public Schs..Principal	Grd	Prgm	Enr/#Cls	SN
Sanderson Public Sch 302 2nd Street, Sanderson 79848 Amanda Magallan	PK-12	TV	130 20	48% 432/345-2515

TERRY COUNTY

TERRY PUBLIC SCHOOLS

- **Brownfield Ind Sch Dist** PID: 01055084   806/637-2591
  601 E Tahoka Rd, Brownfield 79316   Fax 806/637-9208

Schools: 5 \ **Teachers:** 134 \ **Students:** 1,700 \ **Special Ed Students:** 145 \ **LEP Students:** 140 \ **College-Bound:** 40% \ **Ethnic:** African American 3%, Hispanic 76%, Caucasian 20% \ **Exp:** $445 (High) \ **Poverty:** 27% \ **Title I:** $727,608 \ **Special Education:** $378,000 \ **Open-Close:** 08/14 - 05/22 \ **DTBP:** $340 (High) \

Chris Smith	1	Teresa Montemayor	2,19,68
Brian Paiva	3	Beverly Webb	4
Melissa Oliva	8,15	Sarah Douglas	31*

Geoff Cooper	67	Christina Martinez	73*
Mary Valdonado	271	Lauren Phelps	752

Public Schs..Principal	Grd	Prgm	Enr/#Cls	SN
Bright Beginnings Academic Ctr 1202 Seagraves Rd, Brownfield 79316 Paul Coronado	PK-PK	T	169	95% 806/637-0757 Fax 806/637-0119
Brownfield High Sch 701 Cub Dr, Brownfield 79316 Gionet Cooper	9-12	ATV	451 54	65% 806/637-4523 Fax 806/637-3801
Brownfield Middle Sch 1001 E Broadway St, Brownfield 79316 Artemio Ontiveros	6-8	TV	358 30	76% 806/637-7521 Fax 806/637-2919
Colonial Heights Elem Sch 1100 E Reppto St, Brownfield 79316 Susan Brisendine	K-1	T	253 15	86% 806/637-4282 Fax 806/637-1815
Oak Grove Elem Sch 1000 E Cactus Ln, Brownfield 79316 Vicki Hathaway	2-5	T	518 29	81% 806/637-6455 Fax 806/637-3636

- **Meadow Ind School Dist** PID: 01055149   806/539-2246
  604 4th St, Meadow 79345   Fax 806/539-2529

Schools: 1 \ **Teachers:** 31 \ **Students:** 280 \ **Special Ed Students:** 25 \ **LEP Students:** 15 \ **College-Bound:** 90% \ **Ethnic:** Hispanic 70%, Native American: 1%, Caucasian 29% \ **Exp:** $477 (High) \ **Poverty:** 39% \ **Title I:** $132,408 \ **Open-Close:** 08/15 - 05/21 \ **DTBP:** $327 (High)

Darrian Dover	1	Brandon Hopper	6
Stacey Dover	11,60	Stacy Gamez	34*
Sherryll Barclay	36*	Keith Harrison	67
Blane Britton	73*		

Public Schs..Principal	Grd	Prgm	Enr/#Cls	SN
Meadow Sch 604 4th St, Meadow 79345 Dennis Berger \ Bric Turner	PK-12	T	280 35	73% 806/539-2246

- **Wellman Union Ind School Dist** PID: 01055199   806/637-4910
  505 Terry St, Wellman 79378   Fax 806/637-2585

Schools: 1 \ **Teachers:** 23 \ **Students:** 347 \ **Special Ed Students:** 23 \ **LEP Students:** 35 \ **College-Bound:** 70% \ **Ethnic:** Hispanic 47%, Caucasian 53% \ **Exp:** $595 (High) \ **Poverty:** 29% \ **Title I:** $76,678 \ **Open-Close:** 08/21 - 05/21 \ **DTBP:** $338 (High)

David Foote	1,11	Deborah Lambert	2
Rudy Alvarado	3*	Angie Cavazos	4*
Rudy Alvarado	5	Brian Sepkowipz	6
Bridget Brown	12,271,275*	Megan Becker	36,69,83,85,88*
James Harlan	67	Roger Chase	73,286*

Public Schs..Principal	Grd	Prgm	Enr/#Cls	SN
Wellman-Union Sch 505 Terry St, Wellman 79378 Bridget Brown \ Ben Prowell	PK-12	TV	347 30	66% 806/637-4619

Texas School Directory

THROCKMORTON COUNTY

THROCKMORTON PUBLIC SCHOOLS

- **Throckmorton Ind School Dist** PID: 01055228 940/849-2411
  210 College St, Throckmorton 76483 Fax 940/849-3345

Schools: 1 \ *Teachers:* 16 \ *Students:* 175 \ *Special Ed Students:* 11 \ *College-Bound:* 85% \ *Ethnic:* African American 1%, Hispanic 24%, Caucasian 75% \ *Exp:* $798 (High) \ *Poverty:* 24% \ *Title I:* $50,644 \ *Open-Close:* 08/19 - 05/22 \ *DTBP:* $350 (High) \

Dr Michelle Cline 1		Brittney Woods 2	
Ray Fowler 3,5		Rhonda Riley 8,11,74,275,294	
Amy Anthony 36,69,270		Alexandra Fauntleroy 58	
Kathy Thorp 67		Candi Key 73,84,295	

Public Schs..Principal	Grd	Prgm	Enr/#Cls	SN
Throckmorton Sch 210 College St, Throckmorton 76483 **Rhonda Riley**	PK-12	T	175 10	63% 940/849-9981

- **Woodson Ind School Dist** PID: 01055254 940/345-6521
  207 E Hill St, Woodson 76491 Fax 940/345-6549

Schools: 1 \ *Teachers:* 17 \ *Students:* 150 \ *Special Ed Students:* 18 \ *LEP Students:* 3 \ *College-Bound:* 67% \ *Ethnic:* Hispanic 20%, Caucasian 80% \ *Exp:* $929 (High) \ *Poverty:* 23% \ *Title I:* $18,983 \ *Open-Close:* 08/12 - 05/20 \ *DTBP:* $632 (High) \

Casey Adams 1,11,83,84,288		Melissa Vickers 2,298
Caleb Hagle 3		Rhonda Brockman 4*
Brent Mills 8,57,76		Margaret Mathiews 58,79*
Gary Brockman 67		

Public Schs..Principal	Grd	Prgm	Enr/#Cls	SN
Woodson Sch 207 E Hill St, Woodson 76491 **Brent Mills**	PK-12	TV	150 14	61% 940/345-6521

TITUS COUNTY

TITUS PUBLIC SCHOOLS

- **Chapel Hill Ind School Dist** PID: 01055307 903/572-8096
  1069 County Road 4660, Mt Pleasant 75455 Fax 903/572-1086

Schools: 3 \ *Teachers:* 82 \ *Students:* 1,050 \ *Special Ed Students:* 119 \ *LEP Students:* 167 \ *College-Bound:* 58% \ *Ethnic:* Asian 1%, African American 3%, Hispanic 37%, Caucasian 59% \ *Exp:* $845 (High) \ *Poverty:* 23% \ *Title I:* $204,045 \ *Special Education:* $196,000 \ *Open-Close:* 08/15 - 05/21 \ *DTBP:* $350 (High) \

Marc Levesque 1		Mike Hall 2
Justin Edwards 3,5		Sherry Eargle 4
Lacy Robinson 8,11,57,271,273,298		Stacy Elledge 8,11,57,271,273,298
Stacy Elledge 8,11,57,271,273,298*		Cassie Crane 38
Christina Reid 58		Christina Reid 58*
Mike Edwards 67		Telly Hall 73,286
Jessie Bratton 274*		

Public Schs..Principal	Grd	Prgm	Enr/#Cls	SN
Chapel Hill Elem Sch 1069 County Road 4660, Mt Pleasant 75455 Misty Lake	PK-5	T	447 25	50% 903/572-4586 Fax 903/577-9176
Chapel Hill High Sch 1069 County Road 4660, Mt Pleasant 75455 Marcus Ysasi	9-12	ATV	359	47% 903/572-3925 Fax 903/572-3850
Chapel Hill Junior High Sch 1069 County Road 4660, Mt Pleasant 75455 Matthew Dunn	6-8	TV	232 21	50% 903/572-3925 Fax 903/572-9747

- **Harts Bluff Ind School Dist** PID: 01055345 903/577-1146
  1402 Farm Rd, Mt Pleasant 75455 Fax 903/577-8710

Schools: 1 \ *Teachers:* 40 \ *Students:* 640 \ *Special Ed Students:* 29 \ *LEP Students:* 186 \ *Ethnic:* Asian 1%, African American 1%, Hispanic 49%, Caucasian 50% \ *Exp:* $409 (High) \ *Poverty:* 16% \ *Title I:* $140,635 \ *Open-Close:* 08/21 - 05/21 \ *DTBP:* $357 (High)

Dr Bobby Rice 1,11,83		Craig Craven 2
Ray Flinn 3*		Wayne Phillips 5,73*
Michael Thomasson 8,275*		Tracie Rose 9*
Carole Dickerson 12,16,57,69,88,270,273*		Penny Parker 59*
Dr Bradshaw Colton 67		Sabrina Stobnicki 79,90*
Melissa Rice 271*		Carole Dickerson 296

Public Schs..Principal	Grd	Prgm	Enr/#Cls	SN
Harts Bluff Elem Sch 1402 Farm Rd, Mt Pleasant 75455 Tracie Rose	PK-8	AT	640 32	63% 903/577-1146

- **Mt Pleasant Ind School Dist** PID: 01055369 903/575-2000
  2230 N Edwards Ave, Mt Pleasant 75455 Fax 903/575-2014

Schools: 8 \ *Teachers:* 377 \ *Students:* 5,300 \ *Special Ed Students:* 518 \ *LEP Students:* 1,843 \ *College-Bound:* 62% \ *Ethnic:* Asian 1%, African American 12%, Hispanic 69%, Caucasian 18% \ *Exp:* $377 (High) \ *Poverty:* 23% \ *Title I:* $1,480,737 \ *Open-Close:* 08/21 - 05/21 \ *DTBP:* $158 (High) \

Judd Marshall 1		Stacie Thompson 2,19
Russell Luck 3		Laura Stewart 4*
Ritchie Pinkard 6		Debra Malone 7,15,68
Shirley Peterson 11*		Mike Lide 15
Eva Beles 57*		Marilyn Logan 58
Yvonne Hampton 67		Shelley Derrick 69*
Kelly Cowan 71*		Noe Arzate 73,76,295*
Brian McAdams 79		Gina Landrum 81
Ronnie Humphrey 91		

Public Schs..Principal	Grd	Prgm	Enr/#Cls	SN
Annie Sims Elem Sch 1801 E 1st St, Mt Pleasant 75455 Tonya Murray	K-4	T	553 30	78% 903/575-2062 Fax 903/575-2067
E C Brice Elem Sch 311 Cedar St, Mt Pleasant 75455 Steven Toney	K-4	T	491 26	77% 903/575-2057 Fax 903/575-2061

---

79 Student Personnel	91 Safety/Security	275 Response To Intervention	298 Grant Writer/Ptnrships	**School Programs**	**Social Media**
80 Driver Ed/Safety	92 Magnet School	277 Remedial Math K-12	750 Chief Innovation Officer	A = Alternative Program	= Facebook
81 Gifted/Talented	93 Parental Involvement	280 Literacy Coach	751 Chief of Staff	G = Adult Classes	
82 Video Services	95 Tech Prep Program	285 STEM	752 Social Emotional Learning	M = Magnet Program	= Twitter
83 Substance Abuse Prev	97 Chief Infomation Officer	286 Digital Learning		T = Title I Schoolwide	
84 Erate	98 Chief Technology Officer	288 Common Core Standards	**Other School Types**	V = Career & Tech Ed Programs	
85 AIDS Education	270 Character Education	294 Accountability	Ⓐ = Alternative School		
88 Alternative/At Risk	271 Migrant Education	295 Network System	Ⓒ = Charter School	New Schools are shaded	
89 Multi-Cultural Curriculum	273 Teacher Mentor	296 Title II Programs	Ⓜ = Magnet School	New Superintendents and Principals are bold	
90 Social Work	274 Before/After Sch	297 Webmaster	Ⓨ = Year-Round School	Personnel with email addresses are underscored	

TX—363

Tom Green County

Frances Corprew Elem Sch 909 School St, Mt Pleasant 75455 Amanda Jones	K-4	T	353 24	94%	903/575-2050 Fax 903/575-2052
Mt Pleasant Child Dev Center 1602 W Ferguson Rd, Mt Pleasant 75455 Jamie Cook	PK-PK	T	527 25	89%	903/575-2092 Fax 903/575-2077
Mt Pleasant High Sch 2110 N Edwards Ave, Mt Pleasant 75455 **Craig Bailey**	9-12	TV	1,505 104	73%	903/575-2020 Fax 903/575-2036
Mt Pleasant Junior High Sch 2801 Old Paris Rd, Mt Pleasant 75455 Jeff Turner	7-8	T	714 45	83%	903/575-2110 Fax 903/575-2117
P E Wallace Middle Sch 504 Dunn Ave, Mt Pleasant 75455 **Nathan Rider**	5-6	T	750 49	83%	903/575-2040 Fax 903/575-2047
Vivian Fowler Elem Sch 502 N Otyson St, Mt Pleasant 75455 Cindy Davis	K-4	T	442 24	94%	903/575-2070 Fax 903/575-2075

TITUS PRIVATE SCHOOLS

Private Schs..Principal	Grd	Prgm	Enr/#Cls	SN	
Mt Pleasant Christian Sch 300 S Florey Ave, Mt Pleasant 75455 Tony McNatt	1-12		10 3		903/577-1550

TOM GREEN COUNTY

TOM GREEN PUBLIC SCHOOLS

• **Christoval Ind School Dist** PID: 01055486   325/896-2520
20065 3rd St, Christoval 76935   Fax 325/896-7405

Schools: 2 \ **Teachers:** 44 \ **Students:** 500 \ **Special Ed Students:** 37 \
LEP Students: 3 \ **College-Bound:** 84% \ **Ethnic:** Hispanic 21%, Native American: 1%, Caucasian 78% \ **Exp:** $655 (High) \ **Poverty:** 12% \
Title I: $58,292 \ **Open-Close:** 08/21 - 05/28 \ **DTBP:** $342 (High)

Dr David Walker 1   Sherry Wheeler 2
Dave Goad 3   Isabel Salinas 4
Tracy McDonald 5   Scott Richardson 6*
Tracy Knighton ....9,11,88*   John Choate 10,60,73,288,296*
Staci Jenkins ....10,69*   Jill Novak 59*
Deidre Scherz ....60*   Duff Hallman 67
Cindy Jackson 76   Josh Terrill 295*

Public Schs..Principal	Grd	Prgm	Enr/#Cls	SN	
Christoval Elem Sch 20000 Rudd Rd, Christoval 76935 Tracy Knighton	PK-5	T	217 15	24%	325/896-2446 Fax 325/896-1145
Christoval Jr Sr High Sch 20454 Ranch Rd 2084, Christoval 76935 John Choate	6-12	AV	298 21	20%	325/896-2355 Fax 325/896-2671

• **Grape Creek Ind School Dist** PID: 01055515   325/658-7823
8207 US Highway 87 N, San Angelo 76901   Fax 325/658-8719

Schools: 3 \ **Teachers:** 91 \ **Students:** 1,160 \ **Special Ed Students:** 145 \ **LEP Students:** 53 \ **College-Bound:** 37% \ **Ethnic:** African American 1%, Hispanic 43%, Caucasian 55% \ **Exp:** $473 (High) \ **Poverty:** 19% \
Title I: $362,574 \ **Open-Close:** 08/26 - 05/21 \ **DTBP:** $219 (High)

Angie Smetana 1   Theresa Bird 2
David Augustine 5   Jajean Johnston 7*
Jordan Cox ....11,57,58,285,286,288,296*   Renita Dylan 38*
Dianne James 67   Kimberly Hancock 69,88*
Caleb Rodriguez 73   Dan LaFave 297*
Teri Deweber 298

Public Schs..Principal	Grd	Prgm	Enr/#Cls	SN	
Grape Creek Elem Sch 9633 N Grape Creek Rd, San Angelo 76901 Dana Felts \ Denver Bilyeu	PK-5	T	284 45	63%	325/655-1735 Fax 325/658-2623
Grape Creek High Sch 8834 N Grape Creek Rd, San Angelo 76901 Roger Henderson	9-12	T	300 25	49%	325/653-1852 Fax 325/653-3568
Grape Creek Middle Sch 9633 N Grape Creek Rd, San Angelo 76901 Timothy Jetton	6-8	T	273 35	59%	325/655-1735 Fax 325/657-2997

• **San Angelo Ind School Dist** PID: 01055539   325/947-3700
1621 University Ave, San Angelo 76904   Fax 325/947-3822

Schools: 25 \ **Teachers:** 944 \ **Students:** 14,362 \
Special Ed Students: 1,482 \ **LEP Students:** 664 \ **Ethnic:** Asian 1%, African American 4%, Hispanic 60%, Caucasian 34% \ **Exp:** $370 (High)
\ **Poverty:** 20% \ **Title I:** $4,430,832 \ **Special Education:** $3,219,000 \
Open-Close: 08/21 - 05/29 \ **DTBP:** $167 (High) \

Dr Carl Dethloff 1   Dr Jeff Bright 2,15
David Creek 3   Michelle Helms 4
Brent McCallie 6,35   Melissa Schumpert 7
Dr Jana Rueter 8,15   Shelly Huddleston 8,18
Wesley Underwood 8,18   Stephanie Free 11
Shelly Hullihen 15   Joy Gay 27,31
Dian Underwood 58   Lanny Layman 67
Rebecca Cline .... 69*   Charlyn Doyle 73,76,84,297
Laura Howard 73   Sharon Wermuth 76
Jennifer Crutchfield .... 81*   Monte Althaus 91*

Public Schs..Principal	Grd	Prgm	Enr/#Cls	SN	
Alta Loma Elem Sch 1700 N Garfield St, San Angelo 76901 **Lauri Herndon**	PK-5	T	335 17	81%	325/947-3914 Fax 325/947-3952
Austin Elem Sch 700 N Van Buren St, San Angelo 76901 Brooke Kalnbach	PK-5	T	462 45	79%	325/659-3636 Fax 325/657-4089
Belaire Elem Sch 700 Stephen St, San Angelo 76905 Lindsay Carr	K-5	T	300 20	73%	325/659-3639 Fax 325/657-4093
Bonham Elem Sch 4630 Southland Blvd, San Angelo 76904 Heidi Wierzowiecki	K-5		562 23	24%	325/947-3917 Fax 325/947-3945
Bowie Elem Sch 3700 Forest Trl, San Angelo 76904 Cindy Lee	K-5	T	438 24	56%	325/947-3921 Fax 325/947-3947
Bradford Elem Sch 2302 Bradford St, San Angelo 76903 Berta Carrasco	PK-5		399 20	94%	325/659-3645 Fax 325/659-3692

1	Superintendent	8	Curric/Instruct K-12	19	Chief Financial Officer	29	Family/Consumer Science	
2	Bus/Finance/Purchasing	9	Curric/Instruct Elem	20	Art K-12	30	Adult Education	
3	Buildings And Grounds	10	Curric/Instruct Sec	21	Art Elem	31	Career/Sch-to-Work K-12	
4	Food Service	11	Federal Program	22	Art Sec	32	Career/Sch-to-Work Elem	
5	Transportation	12	Title I	23	Music K-12	33	Career/Sch-to-Work Sec	
6	Athletic	13	Title V	24	Music Elem	34	Early Childhood Ed	
7	Health Services	15	Asst Superintendent	25	Music Sec	35	Health/Phys Education	
		16	Instructional Media Svcs	26	Business Education	36	Guidance Services K-12	
		17	Chief Operations Officer	27	Career & Tech Ed	37	Guidance Services Elem	
		18	Chief Academic Officer	28	Technology Education	38	Guidance Services Sec	

39	Social Studies K-12	49	English/Lang Arts Elem	59	Special Education Elem	69	Academic Assessment	
40	Social Studies Elem	50	English/Lang Arts Sec	60	Special Education Sec	70	Research/Development	
41	Social Studies Sec	51	Reading K-12	61	Foreign/World Lang K-12	71	Public Information	
42	Science K-12	52	Reading Elem	62	Foreign/World Lang Elem	72	Summer School	
43	Science Elem	53	Reading Sec	63	Foreign/World Lang Sec	73	Instructional Tech	
44	Science Sec	54	Remedial Reading K-12	64	Religious Education K-12	74	Inservice Training	
45	Math K-12	55	Remedial Reading Elem	65	Religious Education Elem	75	Marketing/Distributive	
46	Math Elem	56	Remedial Reading Sec	66	Religious Education Sec	76	Info Systems	
47	Math Sec	57	Bilingual/ELL	67	School Board President	77	Psychological Assess	
48	English/Lang Arts K-12	58	Special Education K-12	68	Teacher Personnel	78	Affirmative Action	

Texas School Directory — Tom Green County

School	Grd	Prgm	Enr/#Cls	SN	Phone
Ⓐ Carver Learning Center 301 W 9th St, San Angelo 76903 **Claudia Becerra**	K-12		47 9	85%	325/659-3648 Fax 325/657-4087
Central Freshman Campus 218 N Oakes St, San Angelo 76903 Tim Reid	9-9	TV	765	53%	325/659-3576 Fax 325/659-3583
Central High Sch 655 Caddo St, San Angelo 76901 Bill Waters	10-12	GTV	2,042 120	42%	325/659-3434 Fax 325/659-3413
Crockett Elem Sch 2104 Johnson Ave, San Angelo 76904 Clayton Hubbard	K-5	T	362 30	62%	325/947-3925 Fax 325/947-3951
Fannin Elem Sch 1702 Wilson St, San Angelo 76901 Dave Danner	PK-5	T	363 22	87%	325/947-3930 Fax 325/947-3944
Ⓜ Ft Concho Elem Sch 310 E Washington Dr, San Angelo 76903 Lori Barton	K-5	T	468 23	41%	325/659-3654 Fax 325/657-4083 ⓣ
Glenmore Elem Sch 323 Penrose St, San Angelo 76903 **Teri Gould**	PK-5	T	474 23	55%	325/659-3657 Fax 325/657-4086
Glenn Middle Sch 2201 University Ave, San Angelo 76904 Michael Kalnbach	6-8	TV	1,309 55	52%	325/947-3841 Fax 325/947-3847
Goliad Elem Sch 120 E 39th St, San Angelo 76903 Zachary Ramirez	K-5	T	548 27	78%	325/659-3660 Fax 325/657-4097
Holiman Elem Sch 1900 Ricks Dr, San Angelo 76905 Ginger Luther	K-5	T	408 20	58%	325/659-3663 Fax 325/659-3696
Lake View High Sch 900 E 43rd St, San Angelo 76903 Jason Skelton	9-12	TV	1,051 55	69%	325/659-3500 Fax 325/653-8661
Lamar Elem Sch 3444 School House Dr, San Angelo 76904 Sharon Lane	K-5	T	591 32	45%	325/947-3900 Fax 325/947-3901
Lee Middle Sch 2500 Sherwood Way, San Angelo 76901 Rikke Black	6-8	TV	1,080 53	57%	325/947-3871 Fax 325/947-3890
Lincoln Middle Sch 255 Lake View Heroes Dr, San Angelo 76903 Joe Gandar	6-8	TV	862 58	78%	325/659-3550 Fax 325/659-3559
McGill Elem Sch 201 Millspaugh St, San Angelo 76901 Dr John Rueter	PK-5	T	341 29	69%	325/947-3934 Fax 325/947-3946
Pays Sch 1820 Knickerbocker Rd, San Angelo 76904 Karan Henson	11-12	AV	62		325/947-3912 Fax 325/949-4323
Reagan Elem Sch 1600 Volney St, San Angelo 76903 Brandy Tyner	PK-5	T	333 20	91%	325/659-3666 Fax 325/657-4096
San Jacinto Elem Sch 800 Spaulding St, San Angelo 76903 Kimberly Spurgers	K-5	T	331 26	87%	325/659-3675 Fax 325/657-4092 ⓣ
Ⓜ Santa Rita Elem Sch 615 S Madison St, San Angelo 76901 Kay Scott	K-5	T	389 25	43%	325/659-3672 Fax 325/657-4094 ⓣ

● **Veribest Ind School Dist** PID: 01055826   325/655-2851
10062 Highway 380, Veribest 76886   Fax 325/655-3355

Schools: 1 \ *Teachers:* 24 \ *Students:* 275 \ *Special Ed Students:* 34 \ *LEP Students:* 17 \ *College-Bound:* 75% \ *Exp:* $317 (High) \ *Poverty:* 16% \ *Title I:* $47,300 \ *Open-Close:* 08/21 - 05/22 \ *DTBP:* $345 (High)

Ryder Appleton 1,11,288   Denise Dusek 2

Brenda Neill ....4*   Rick Lancaster 5
Laura Eubank 9   Glen Jones 10
Kelly Hannah 12,69,83,270   Chrys Martin 16
Lee Cauley ....51*   Mark Kellermeier 67
Lahne Burns 73,286*

Public Schs..Principal	Grd	Prgm	Enr/#Cls	SN	
Veribest Sch 10062 FM Highway 380, Veribest 76886 Laura Eubank \ Glen Jones	PK-12	AV	275 30		325/655-2851 Fax 325/655-0551

● **Wall Ind School Dist** PID: 01055840   325/651-7790
8065 Loop 570, Wall 76957

Schools: 4 \ *Teachers:* 114 \ *Students:* 1,100 \ *Special Ed Students:* 64 \ *LEP Students:* 13 \ *College-Bound:* 95% \ *Ethnic:* Hispanic 19%, Caucasian 80% \ *Exp:* $485 (High) \ *Poverty:* 10% \ *Title I:* $102,079 \ *Open-Close:* 08/21 - 05/21 \ *DTBP:* $357 (High)

Russell Dacy 1,11   Charlotte Weishuhn 2
Lanier Duderstadt 3,91   Lisa Glasscock 4*
Jeremy Williams 5,6,8,85,92   Kim Rollwitz 7*
Kelly Granzin 9   Dr Mildred Seimonds 57
Brandy York 58   Christine Wilde 67
Cheryl Marsh 68   Suzette McIntyre 73,295*

Public Schs..Principal	Grd	Prgm	Enr/#Cls	SN	
Ⓐ Fairview Accelerated Sch 2405 Fairview School Rd, San Angelo 76904 Bert Johnson	6-12		42 6		325/651-7656 Fax 325/651-8504
Wall Elem Sch 8065 Loop 570, Wall 76957 **Kelly Granzin**	PK-5	T	515 25	16%	325/651-7790
Wall High Sch 8065 Loop 570, Wall 76957 Ryan Snowden	9-12		354 30	9%	325/651-7521 Fax 325/651-9419
Wall Middle Sch 8065 Loop 570, Wall 76957 Matt Rivers	6-8		260 29	12%	325/651-7648 Fax 325/651-9664

● **Water Valley Ind School Dist** PID: 01055888   325/484-2478
18000 Wildcat Dr, Water Valley 76958   Fax 325/484-3359

Schools: 2 \ *Teachers:* 31 \ *Students:* 300 \ *Special Ed Students:* 45 \ *LEP Students:* 3 \ *College-Bound:* 90% \ *Ethnic:* Asian 1%, African American 1%, Hispanic 22%, Native American: 1%, Caucasian 76% \ *Exp:* $675 (High) \ *Poverty:* 17% \ *Title I:* $65,415 \ *Open-Close:* 08/21 - 05/22 \ *DTBP:* $375 (High)

Fabian Gomez 1,83   Tanis McCoy 2,11
Dant Hughes 3,5   Cheryl Schobajsa 4*
Nathan Hayes 6   Tracy Randolf 7
Deenna Blanton 8,16,31,58,83,271,273,288   Pamela Ashley 36,69,88*
Perri Brown ....57*   Renee Clark 59
Stanley Treadaway 67   James Ditmore 73,297*

Public Schs..Principal	Grd	Prgm	Enr/#Cls	SN	
Water Valley Elem Sch 15575 Adams Ave, Water Valley 76958 **Deeanna Blanton**	PK-6	AT	211 11	56%	325/484-2478 Fax 325/484-2473
Water Valley Jr Sr High Sch 17886 Wildcat Dr, Water Valley 76958 Dane Hoover	7-12	AT	139 20	52%	325/484-2478 Fax 325/484-2462

---

79 Student Personnel   91 Safety/Security   275 Response To Intervention   298 Grant Writer/Ptnrships   **School Programs**   **Social Media**
80 Driver Ed/Safety   92 Magnet School   277 Remedial Math K-12   750 Chief Innovation Officer   A = Alternative Program
81 Gifted/Talented   93 Parental Involvement   280 Literacy Coach   751 Chief of Staff   G = Adult Classes   🅕 = Facebook
82 Video Services   95 Tech Prep Program   285 STEM   752 Social Emotional Learning   M = Magnet Program
83 Substance Abuse Prev   97 Chief Information Officer   288 Digital Learning   T = Title I Schoolwide   ⓣ = Twitter
84 Erate   98 Chief Technology Officer   288 Common Core Standards   **Other School Types**   V = Career & Tech Ed Programs
85 AIDS Education   270 Character Education   294 Accountability   Ⓐ = Alternative School
88 Alternative/At Risk   271 Migrant Education   295 Network System   Ⓒ = Charter School   New Schools are shaded
89 Multi-Cultural Curriculum   273 Teacher Mentor   296 Title II Programs   Ⓜ = Magnet School   New Superintendents and Principals are bold
90 Social Work   274 Before/After Sch   297 Webmaster   Ⓨ = Year-Round School   Personnel with email addresses are underscored

Travis County

Market Data Retrieval

TOM GREEN CATHOLIC SCHOOLS

- **Diocese of San Angelo Ed Off** PID: 01055929
  Listing includes only schools located in this county. See District Index for location of Diocesan Offices.

Catholic Schs..Principal	Grd	Prgm	Enr/#Cls	SN
Angelo Catholic Sch 2315 A and M Ave, San Angelo 76904 Becky Trojcak	PK-8		128 8	325/949-1747 Fax 325/942-1547

TOM GREEN PRIVATE SCHOOLS

Private Schs..Principal	Grd	Prgm	Enr/#Cls	SN
Cornerstone Christian Sch 1502 N Jefferson St, San Angelo 76901 Cynthia Robinson	PK-12		200 16	325/655-3439 Fax 325/658-8998
San Angelo Christian Academy 518 Country Club Rd, San Angelo 76904 Betty Shook	K-12		87 8	325/651-8363 Fax 325/651-1682
Trinity Lutheran Sch 3516 Lutheran Way, San Angelo 76904 Ron Fritsche	PK-8		72 9	325/947-1275 Fax 325/947-1377

TOM GREEN REGIONAL CENTERS

- **Region 15 Ed Service Center** PID: 01055814   325/658-6571
  612 S Irene St, San Angelo 76903   Fax 325/655-4823

Casey Callahan 1,11	Charity Vasquez 2
David Bedford 8	Laura Strube 15
Hector Pineda 34	Jam Page 58
Randon Lance 295	

TRAVIS COUNTY

TRAVIS PUBLIC SCHOOLS

- **Austin Ind School Dist** PID: 01055993   512/414-1700
  4000 S Ih 35 Frontage Rd, Austin 78704   Fax 512/414-1486

Schools: 121 \ **Teachers:** 5,793 \ **Students:** 80,100 \
Special Ed Students: 8,781 \ **LEP Students:** 20,613 \ **College-Bound:** 89%
\ **Ethnic:** Asian 4%, African American 8%, Hispanic 59%, Caucasian
29% \ **Exp:** $214 (Med) \ **Poverty:** 16% \ **Title I:** $26,733,814 \
Special Education: $15,124,000 \ **Bilingual Education:** $133,000 \
Open-Close: 08/20 - 05/28 \ **DTBP:** $192 (High) \

Dr Paul Cruz 1	Nicole Conley-Johnson 2
Louis Zachary 3	Matias Segura 3
Anneliese Tanner 4	Kris Hafezizadeh 5
Leal Anderson 6	Tracy Spinner 7
Dr Lisa Goodnow 8,288	Dr Mary Thomas 11,296,298,752
Jacob Reach 15,751	Elizabeth Polk 16

Alan Lambert 20,23	Tammy Caesar 31
Ami Cortez 34	Michele Rusnak 35
Tracilynn Wright 36,88	Akweta Hickman 58
Erin Barbier 61	Geronimo Rodriguez 67
Dr Fernando Medina 68	Melissa Sabatino 71
Reyne Telles 71	Kevin Schwartz 73,76,295
Dr Andri Lyons 79	Ronda Boyer 81
Ashley Gonzalez 91	Dennis McFall 274
Debra Ready 294	Tim Carrington 295
Camille Lochet 297	

- **Austin ISD Elem School Area 1** PID: 04032316   512/414-1708
  1111 W 6th St, Austin 78703   Fax 512/414-1761

Sandra Creswell 15

Public Schs..Principal	Grd	Prgm	Enr/#Cls	SN
Allison Elem Sch 515 Vargas Rd, Austin 78741 Lupe Molina	PK-5	T	435 30	85% 512/414-2004 Fax 512/385-0905
Barton Hills Elem Sch 2108 Barton Hills Dr, Austin 78704 Kathryn Achtermann	PK-6		455 40	6% 512/414-2013 Fax 512/841-3849
Becker Elem Sch 906 W Milton St, Austin 78704 Valerie Borchers	PK-5	T	437 25	39% 512/414-2019 Fax 512/442-1759
Blazier Elem Sch 8601 Vertex Blvd, Austin 78744 Leti Pena-Wilk	PK-5	T	860 45	70% 512/841-8800 Fax 512/841-8801
Boone Elem Sch 8101 Croftwood Dr, Austin 78749 Alan Stevens	PK-5	T	535 44	40% 512/414-2537 Fax 512/280-3307
Brooke Elem Sch 3100 E 4th St, Austin 78702 Griselda Galindo-Vargas	PK-5	T	246 22	92% 512/414-2043 Fax 512/385-3862
Casey Elem Sch 9400 Texas Oaks Dr, Austin 78748 Lina Villarreal	PK-5	T	616 42	60% 512/841-6900 Fax 512/841-6925
Clayton Elem Sch 7525 La Crosse Ave, Austin 78739 Amy Gonzales	PK-5	T	838 40	1% 512/841-9200 Fax 512/841-9201
Cowan Elem Sch 2817 Kentish Dr, Austin 78748 **Travis Brunner**	PK-5		841 29	29% 512/841-2700 Fax 512/841-2755
Cunningham Elem Sch 2200 Berkeley Ave, Austin 78745 Heather Petruzzini	PK-5	T	394	57% 512/414-2067 Fax 512/441-6006
Dawson Elem Sch 3001 S 1st St, Austin 78704 Tania Jedele	PK-5	T	352 23	80% 512/414-2070 Fax 512/442-5765
Galindo Elem Sch 3800 S 2nd St, Austin 78704 Natascha Barreto-Romero	PK-5	T	586 54	85% 512/414-1756 Fax 512/414-0448
Govalle Elem Sch 3601 Govalle Ave, Austin 78702 Paula Reyes	PK-5	T	408 30	88% 512/414-2078 Fax 512/926-4820
Houston Elem Sch 5409 Ponciana Dr, Austin 78744 Elia Diaz-Camarillo	PK-5	T	642	83% 512/414-2517 Fax 512/448-4869
Joslin Elem Sch 4500 Manchaca Rd, Austin 78745 **Chaolin Chang**	PK-5	T	282	67% 512/414-2094 Fax 512/443-3011
Kiker Elem Sch 5913 La Crosse Ave, Austin 78739 David Crissey	PK-5		1,111	3% 512/414-2584 Fax 512/288-5779
Kocurek Elem Sch 9800 Curlew Dr, Austin 78748 Heather Parmelee	PK-5	T	578 33	62% 512/414-2547 Fax 512/282-7824

TX—366

1 Superintendent	8 Curric/Instruct K-12	19 Chief Financial Officer	29 Family/Consumer Science	39 Social Studies K-12	49 English/Lang Arts Elem	59 Special Education Elem	69 Academic Assessment
2 Bus/Finance/Purchasing	9 Curric/Instruct Elem	20 Art K-12	30 Adult Education	40 Social Studies Elem	50 English/Lang Arts Sec	60 Special Education Sec	70 Research/Development
3 Buildings And Grounds	10 Curric/Instruct Sec	21 Art Elem	31 Career/Sch-to-Work K-12	41 Social Studies Sec	51 Reading K-12	61 Foreign/World Lang K-12	71 Public Information
4 Food Service	11 Federal Program	22 Art Sec	32 Career/Sch-to-Work Elem	42 Science K-12	52 Reading Elem	62 Foreign/World Lang Elem	72 Summer School
5 Transportation	12 Title I	23 Music K-12	33 Career/Sch-to-Work Sec	43 Science Elem	53 Reading Sec	63 Foreign/World Lang Sec	73 Instructional Tech
6 Athletic	13 Title V	24 Music Elem	34 Early Childhood Ed	44 Science Sec	54 Remedial Reading K-12	64 Religious Education	74 Inservice Training
7 Health Services	15 Asst Superintendent	25 Music Sec	35 Health/Phys Education	45 Math K-12	55 Remedial Reading Elem	65 Religious Education Elem	75 Marketing/Distributive
	16 Instructional Media Svcs	26 Business Education	36 Guidance Services K-12	46 Math Elem	56 Remedial Reading Sec	66 Religious Education Sec	76 Info Systems
	17 Chief Operations Officer	27 Career & Tech Ed	37 Guidance Services Elem	47 Math Sec	57 Bilingual/ELL	67 School Board President	77 Psychological Assess
	18 Chief Academic Officer	28 Technology Education	38 Guidance Services Sec	48 English/Lang Arts K-12	58 Special Education K-12	68 Teacher Personnel	78 Affirmative Action

Texas School Directory — Travis County

Public Schs..Principal	Grd	Prgm	Enr/#Cls		SN	
Langford Elem Sch 2206 Blue Meadow Dr, Austin 78744 Dounna Poth	PK-5	T	540 65	94%	512/414-1765 Fax 512/447-4808	
Linder Elem Sch 2800 Metcalfe Rd, Austin 78741 **Melissa Rodriguez**	1-5	T	306 41	93%	512/414-2398 Fax 512/447-3222	
Menchaca Elem Sch 12120 Manchaca Rd, Austin 78748 Eliza Loyola	PK-5		717 38		512/414-2333 Fax 512/282-4043	
Metz Elem Sch 84 Robert T Martinez Jr St, Austin 78702 Martha Castillo	PK-5	T	285 32	82%	512/414-4408 Fax 512/472-3412	
Mills Elem Sch 6201 Davis Ln, Austin 78749 Lalla Beachum	PK-5		854 50	7%	512/841-2400 Fax 512/841-2490	
Oak Hill Elem Sch 6101 Patton Ranch Rd, Austin 78735 Lori Komassa	PK-5	T	868 40	36%	512/414-2336 Fax 512/892-2279	
Odom Elem Sch 1010 Turtle Creek Blvd, Austin 78745 Sondra McWilliams	PK-5		463 38	86%	512/414-2388 Fax 512/443-6170	
Ortega Elem Sch 1135 Garland Ave, Austin 78721 Jen Stephens	PK-5	T	276 18	84%	512/414-4417 Fax 512/929-7906	
Palm Elem Sch 7601 Dixie Dr, Austin 78744 Rhoda Coleman	PK-5	T	449 35	80%	512/414-2545 Fax 512/280-2769	
Patton Elem Sch 6001 Westcreek Dr, Austin 78749 Amanda Brantley	PK-5		984 40	20%	512/414-1780 Fax 512/892-6541	
Perez Elem Sch 7500 S Pleasant Valley Rd, Austin 78744 Kara Santibanez	PK-5		650	82%	512/841-9100 Fax 512/841-9101	
Pleasant Hill Elem Sch 6405 Circle S Rd, Austin 78745 Kristi Cisneros	PK-5	T	465 46	82%	512/414-4453 Fax 512/442-4741	
Rodriguez Elem Sch 4400 Franklin Park Dr, Austin 78744 Monica Mills	PK-5	T	503 53	95%	512/841-7200 Fax 512/841-7205	
Ross Baldwin Elem Sch 12200 Meridian Park Blvd, Austin 78739 Jennifer Murray	PK-5		810	11%	512/841-8900 Fax 512/841-8901	
Sanchez Elem Sch 73 San Marcos St, Austin 78702 Azucena Garcia	PK-5	T	258 25	94%	512/414-4423 Fax 512/472-9493	
St Elmo Elem Sch 600 W Saint Elmo Rd, Austin 78745 Ben McCormack	PK-5	T	297 30	79%	512/414-4477 Fax 512/442-6871	
Sunset Valley Elem Sch 3000 Jones Rd, Austin 78745 **Marizza Marquez**	PK-5	T	543 32	50%	512/414-2392 Fax 512/892-7206	
Timothy Baranoff Elem Sch 12009 Buckingham Gate Rd, Austin 78748 **Beth Cantu**	PK-5	T	1,014 41	12%	512/841-7100 Fax 512/841-7104	
Travis Heights Elem Sch 2010 Alameda Dr, Austin 78704 Michelle Navarro	PK-5	T	518 40	63%	512/414-4495 Fax 512/442-9537 f t	
Uphaus Early Childhood Center 5200 Freidrich Ln, Austin 78744 Claudia Santamaria	PK-K	T	340	83%	512/414-5520 Fax 512/326-1031	
Widen Elem Sch 5605 Nuckols Crossing Rd, Austin 78744 Jennifer Pace	PK-5	T	522 40	86%	512/414-2556 Fax 512/441-8971	
Williams Elem Sch 500 Mairo St, Austin 78748 **Natalie Villanueva**	PK-5	T	466	78%	512/414-2525 Fax 512/292-3041	
Zavala Elem Sch 310 Robert T Martinez Jr St, Austin 78702 Jose Mejia	PK-5	T	373 30	83%	512/414-2318 Fax 512/477-2361	
Zilker Elem Sch 1900 Bluebonnet Ln, Austin 78704 Alicia Hill	PK-5		547 30	20%	512/414-2327 Fax 512/442-3992	

• **Austin ISD Elem School Area 2** PID: 04032304   512/414-0038
1111 W 6th St, Austin 78703   Fax 512/414-9977

Gilbert Hicks 15

Public Schs..Principal	Grd	Prgm	Enr/#Cls		SN	
Andrews Elem Sch 6801 Northeast Dr, Austin 78723 **Diana Vallejo**	PK-6	T	504 40	94%	512/414-1770 Fax 512/926-6635 f t	
Barrington Elem Sch 400 Cooper Dr, Austin 78753 Gilma Sanchez	PK-5	T	620	77%	512/414-2008 Fax 512/836-4077	
Blackshear Elem Sch 1712 E 11th St, Austin 78702 Rick Garner	PK-5	T	378 17	70%	512/414-2021 Fax 512/477-7640	
Blanton Elem Sch 5408 Westminster Dr, Austin 78723 Dora Molina	PK-6	T	516 40	75%	512/414-2026 Fax 512/926-8553	
Brentwood Elem Sch 6700 Arroyo Seco, Austin 78757 Amber LaRoche	PK-5		675 17	22%	512/414-2039 Fax 512/453-8928	
Brown Elem Sch 400 Cooper Dr, Austin 78753 Veronica Sharp	PK-6		272 30		512/414-2047 Fax 512/452-6097	
Bryker Woods Elem Sch 3309 Kerbey Ln, Austin 78703 Kristina Muehling	PK-6		458 21	10%	512/414-2054 Fax 512/459-9047	
Campbell Elem Sch 2613 Rogers Ave, Austin 78722 Keith Moore	PK-5	T	187 35	88%	512/414-2056 Fax 512/841-1246	
Casis Elem Sch 2710 Exposition Blvd, Austin 78703 Samuel Tinnon	PK-5		765 40	3%	512/414-2062 Fax 512/477-1776	
Cook Elem Sch 1511 Cripple Creek Dr, Austin 78758 **Priscilla Sanchez**	PK-5		453 46	94%	512/414-2510 Fax 512/837-5983	
Davis Elem Sch 5214 Duval Rd, Austin 78727 Jennifer Daniels	PK-5		807 35	21%	512/414-2580 Fax 512/346-7384	
Doss Elem Sch 7005 Northledge Dr, Austin 78731 **Nathan Steenport**	PK-5		835 36	15%	512/414-2365 Fax 512/345-0013	
Frank & Sue McBee Elem Sch 1001 W Braker Ln, Austin 78758 **Yvette Celorio-Reyes**	PK-5		395 35	94%	512/841-2500 Fax 512/841-2333	
Graham Elem Sch 11211 Tom Adams Dr, Austin 78753 Ercilia Paredes	PK-5	T	610 55	84%	512/414-2395 Fax 512/835-4562 f t	
Guerrero Thompson Elem Sch 102 E Rundberg Ln, Austin 78753 **Briana Garcia**	PK-5	T	633	82%	512/414-8400 Fax 512/414-8401	
Gullett Elem Sch 6310 Treadwell Blvd, Austin 78757 Tisha Brown	PK-5		569 25	9%	512/414-2082 Fax 512/451-2036	
Harris Elem Sch 1711 Wheless Ln, Austin 78723 **Ana Maria Dwiggins**	PK-5	T	650 44	95%	512/414-2085 Fax 512/929-4640	
Hart Elem Sch 8301 Furness Dr, Austin 78753 Sonia Tosh	PK-5	T	682 37	96%	512/841-2100 Fax 512/841-2190	

---

79 Student Personnel	91 Safety/Security	275 Response To Intervention	298 Grant Writer/Ptnrships	**School Programs**	**Social Media**
80 Driver Ed/Safety	92 Magnet School	277 Remedial Math K-12	750 Chief Innovation Officer	A = Alternative Program	
81 Gifted/Talented	93 Parental Involvement	280 Literacy Coach	751 Chief of Staff	G = Adult Classes	f = Facebook
82 Video Services	95 Tech Prep Program	285 STEM	752 Social Emotional Learning	M = Magnet Program	
83 Substance Abuse Prev	97 Chief Infomation Officer	286 Digital Learning		T = Title I Schoolwide	t = Twitter
84 Erate	98 Chief Technology Officer	288 Common Core Standards	**Other School Types**	V = Career & Tech Ed Programs	
85 AIDS Education	270 Character Education	294 Accountability	Ⓐ = Alternative School		
88 Alternative/At Risk	271 Migrant Education	295 Network System	Ⓒ = Charter School	New Schools are shaded	
89 Multi-Cultural Curriculum	273 Teacher Mentor	296 Title II Programs	Ⓜ = Magnet School	New Superintendents and Principals are bold	
90 Social Work	274 Before/After Sch	297 Webmaster	Ⓨ = Year-Round School	Personnel with email addresses are underscored	

Travis County

Market Data Retrieval

School	Grd	Prgm	Enr/#Cls	SN	Phone
Highland Park Elem Sch 4900 Fairview Dr, Austin 78731 Katie Pena	PK-5		641 26	4%	512/414-2090 Fax 512/414-2626
Hill Elem Sch 8601 Tallwood Dr, Austin 78759 Jack Drummond	PK-5		954 35	8%	512/414-2369 Fax 512/841-8105
Jordan Elem Sch 6711 Johnny Morris Rd, Austin 78724 Adrienne Williams	PK-5	T	769 40	88%	512/414-2578 Fax 512/926-8299
Lee Elem Sch 3308 Hampton Rd, Austin 78705 John Hewlett	PK-6		443 20	15%	512/414-2098 Fax 512/478-4463
Lucy Read Pre-K Sch 2608 Richcreek Rd, Austin 78757 Ami Cortes	PK-PK		304	76%	512/419-9400 Fax 512/414-9401
Maplewood Elem Sch 3808 Maplewood Ave, Austin 78722 Vickie Jacobson	PK-6	G	485 16	40%	512/414-4402 Fax 512/472-8559
Mathews Elem Sch 906 W Lynn St, Austin 78703 Grace Brewster	PK-6	T	437 24	29%	512/414-4406 Fax 512/476-2108
Norman Elem Sch 1203 Springdale Rd, Austin 78721 Wendy Mills	PK-5	T	305 28	93%	512/414-2347 Fax 512/926-6321
Oak Springs Elem Sch 3601 Webberville Rd, Austin 78702 Monica Woods	PK-5	T	322 20	92%	512/414-4413 Fax 512/472-5005
Overton Elem Sch 7201 Colony Loop Dr, Austin 78724 Courtney Colvin	PK-5	T	680	85%	512/841-9300 Fax 512/841-9316
Padron Elem Sch 2011 W Rundberg Ln, Austin 78758 Rafael Soriano	PK-5		759		512/841-9600 Fax 512/719-3135
Pease Elem Sch 1106 Rio Grande St, Austin 78701 Stacy Foss	PK-6		233 14	16%	512/414-4428 Fax 512/477-3009
Pecan Springs Elem Sch 3100 Rogge Ln, Austin 78723 Andrea Williams	PK-5	T	454 47	89%	512/414-4445 Fax 512/926-0001
Pickle Elem Sch 1101 Wheatley Ave, Austin 78752 Lauro Davalos	PK-5	T	544 34	90%	512/841-8400 Fax 512/841-8444
Pillow Elem Sch 3025 Crosscreek Dr, Austin 78757 Yvette Cardenas	PK-5	T	519 35	72%	512/414-2350 Fax 512/467-2513
Reilly Elem Sch 405 Denson Dr, Austin 78752 Corrine Saenz	PK-5	T	238 22	69%	512/414-4464 Fax 512/453-1193
Ridgetop Elem Sch 5005 Caswell Ave, Austin 78751 Kara Schultz	PK-5	T	371 14	34%	512/414-4469 Fax 512/459-9187
Rosedale Sch 2117 W 49th St, Austin 78756 Elizabeth Dickey	Spec		123 13	37%	512/414-3617 Fax 512/458-6754
Sims Elem Sch 1203 Springdale Rd, Austin 78721 Wendy Mills	PK-5	T	250 24	92%	512/414-4488 Fax 512/841-1282
Summitt Elem Sch 12207 Brigadoon Ln, Austin 78727 Kelly Friede	PK-5		844 33	30%	512/414-4484 Fax 512/832-1458
Walnut Creek Elem Sch 401 W Braker Ln, Austin 78753 Dinorah Bores	PK-5	T	657 51	83%	512/414-4499 Fax 512/837-6789
Webb Primary Sch 601 E Saint Johns Ave, Austin 78752 Yolanda Lopez	PK-5	T	258	96%	512/414-8830 Fax 512/414-8834
Winn Elem Sch 3500 Susquehanna Ln, Austin 78723 Anayansi Blessum	PK-5	T	325 40	85%	512/414-2390 Fax 512/926-9211
Wooldridge Elem Sch 1412 Norseman Ter, Austin 78758 Sheri Mull	PK-5	T	532 44	93%	512/414-2353 Fax 512/339-6583
Wooten Elem Sch 1406 Dale Dr, Austin 78757 Angelo San Segundo	PK-5	T	503 45	84%	512/414-2315 Fax 512/459-9227

● **Austin ISD High School Area** PID: 04032328 512/414-4471
1111 W 6th St, Austin 78703 Fax 512/414-1782

Craig Shapiro 15

Public Schs..Principal	Grd	Prgm	Enr/#Cls	SN	Phone
A N McCallum High Sch 5600 Sunshine Dr, Austin 78756 Brandi Hosack	9-12	V	1,761	27%	512/414-2519 Fax 512/453-2599
Akins High Sch 10701 S 1st St, Austin 78748 Kristina Salazar	9-12	T	2,765 120	62%	512/841-9900 Fax 512/841-9903
ⓐ Alternative Learning Center 4900 Gonzales St, Austin 78702 Chris Jones	6-12		101 9	69%	512/414-2554 Fax 512/476-2809
Anderson High Sch 8403 Mesa Dr, Austin 78759 Sammi Harrison	9-12	AV	2,222	23%	512/414-2538 Fax 512/338-1293
Austin High Sch 1715 W Cesar Chavez St, Austin 78703 Amy Taylor	9-12	AV	2,267	28%	512/414-2505 Fax 512/414-7373
Clifton Career Dev Sch 1519 Coronado Hills Dr, Austin 78752 Tony Dishner	Voc		200		512/414-3614 Fax 512/323-2646
Crockett High Sch 5601 Manchaca Rd, Austin 78745 Kori Crawford	9-12	ATV	1,466 100	62%	512/414-2532 Fax 512/447-0489
Eastside Memorial High Sch 1012 Arthur Stiles Rd, Austin 78721 Miguel Garcia	9-12	ATV	491 80	85%	512/414-5810 Fax 512/841-5935
Garza Independence High Sch 1600 Chicon St, Austin 78702 Dr Linda Webb	11-12	GV	162 10	34%	512/414-8600 Fax 512/414-8610
ⓐ Graduation Prep Acad-Navarro ⓒ 1201 Payton Gin Rd, Austin 78758 Kevin Owens	9-12		77	75%	512/414-2896 Fax 512/832-1203
ⓐ Graduation Prep Academy-Travis ⓒ 1211 E Oltorf St, Austin 78704 Eliseo Reyna	9-12		164	83%	512/414-6635 Fax 512/707-0050
International High Sch 1012 Arthur Stiles Rd, Austin 78721 Leticia Vega	9-10		375	96%	512/414-6817 Fax 512/841-5621
James Bowie High Sch 4103 W Slaughter Ln, Austin 78749 Mark Robinson	9-12	AV	2,880	12%	512/414-5247 Fax 512/292-0527
ⓜ Liberal Arts & Science Academy 7309 Lazy Creek Dr, Austin 78724 Stacia Crescenzi	9-12		1,186	7%	512/414-5272 Fax 512/414-6050
Lyndon B Johnson High Sch 7309 Lazy Creek Dr, Austin 78724 Traci Lynn Wright	9-12	ATV	799	78%	512/414-2543 Fax 512/929-3955
Navarro Early College High Sch 1201 Payton Gin Rd, Austin 78758 Steven Covin	9-12	TV	1,586	84%	512/414-2514 Fax 512/832-1203
Northeast Early Clg High Sch 7104 Berkman Dr, Austin 78752 Alisia Longoria	9-12	ATV	1,252	81%	512/414-2523 Fax 512/452-7089

---

1 Superintendent	8 Curric/Instruct K-12	19 Chief Financial Officer	29 Family/Consumer Science	39 Social Studies K-12	49 English/Lang Arts Elem	59 Special Education Elem	69 Academic Assessment
2 Bus/Finance/Purchasing	9 Curric/Instruct Elem	20 Art K-12	30 Adult Education	40 Social Studies Elem	50 English/Lang Arts Sec	60 Special Education Sec	70 Research/Development
3 Buildings And Grounds	10 Curric/Instruct Sec	21 Art Elem	31 Career/Sch-to-Work K-12	41 Social Studies Sec	51 Reading K-12	61 Foreign/World Lang K-12	71 Public Information
4 Food Service	11 Federal Program	22 Art Sec	32 Career/Sch-to-Work Elem	42 Science K-12	52 Reading Elem	62 Foreign/World Lang Elem	72 Summer School
5 Transportation	12 Title I	23 Music K-12	33 Career/Sch-to-Work Sec	43 Science Elem	53 Reading Sec	63 Foreign/World Lang Sec	73 Instructional Tech
6 Athletic	13 Title V	24 Music Elem	34 Early Childhood Ed	44 Science Sec	54 Remedial Reading K-12	64 Religious Education K-12	74 Inservice Training
7 Health Services	15 Asst Superintendent	25 Music Sec	35 Health/Phys Education	45 Math K-12	55 Remedial Reading Elem	65 Religious Education Elem	75 Marketing/Distributive
	16 Instructional Media Svcs	26 Business Education	36 Guidance Services K-12	46 Math Elem	56 Remedial Reading Sec	66 Religious Education Sec	76 Info Systems
	17 Chief Operations Officer	27 Career & Tech Ed	37 Guidance Services Elem	47 Math Sec	57 Bilingual/ELL	67 School Board President	77 Psychological Assess
	18 Chief Academic Officer	28 Technology Education	38 Guidance Services Sec	48 English/Lang Arts K-12	58 Special Education K-12	68 Teacher Personnel	78 Affirmative Action

Texas School Directory — Travis County

Richards Young Women Leaders 2206 Prather Ln, Austin 78704 Kristina Waugh	6-12		827	56%	512/414-3236 Fax 512/441-5208
Travis Early College High Sch 1211 E Oltorf St, Austin 78704 Christina Harrington	9-12	ATV	1,233	77%	512/414-2527 Fax 512/707-0050

• Austin ISD Middle School Area PID: 12033332
1111 W 6th St, Austin 78703
512/414-4481
Fax 512/414-9977

Raul Moreno 15

Public Schs..Principal	Grd	Prgm	Enr/#Cls	SN	
Bailey Middle Sch 4020 Lost Oasis Holw, Austin 78739 John Rocha	6-8	V	1,006 75	30%	512/414-4990 Fax 512/292-0898
Bedichek Middle Sch 6800 Bill Hughes Rd, Austin 78745 Michael Herbin	6-8	GTV	846 60	82%	512/414-3265 Fax 512/444-4382
Burnet Middle Sch 8401 Hathaway Dr, Austin 78757 Marvelia De La Rosa	6-8	TV	967 76	90%	512/414-3225 Fax 512/452-0695
Covington Middle Sch 3700 Convict Hill Rd, Austin 78749 Tai Choice	6-8	TV	660 60	63%	512/414-3276 Fax 512/892-4547
Dobie Middle Sch 1200 E Rundberg Ln, Austin 78753 Jesse De La Huerta	6-8	TV	579	90%	512/414-3270 Fax 512/836-8411 f t
Garcia Young Men's Leadership 7414 Johnny Morris Rd, Austin 78724 Sterlin McGruder	6-8	T	390	94%	512/841-9400 Fax 512/841-9401
Gorzycki Middle Sch 7412 W Slaughter Ln, Austin 78749 Cathryn Mitchell	6-8		1,275	5%	512/841-8600 Fax 512/841-8601 f t
Kealing Middle Sch 1607 Pennsylvania Ave, Austin 78702 Kenisha Coburn	6-8	TV	1,223 30	27%	512/414-3214 Fax 512/478-9133
Lamar Middle Sch 6201 Wynona Ave, Austin 78757 **Mayra Mondik**	6-8	V	1,130 60	25%	512/414-3217 Fax 512/467-6862
Ⓜ Lively Middle Sch 201 E Mary St, Austin 78704 Stacie Holiday	6-8	TV	998 70	62%	512/414-3207 Fax 512/441-3129
Martin Middle Sch 1601 Haskell St, Austin 78702 Monica Conness	6-8	TV	450 55	94%	512/414-3243 Fax 512/320-0125
Means Young Womens Ldrshp Acad 6401 N Hampton Dr, Austin 78723 Christina Almaraz	6-8	V	388		512/414-3234 Fax 512/926-6146
Mendez Middle Sch 5106 Village Square Dr, Austin 78744 Joanna Rowley	6-8	GTV	646	93%	512/414-3284 Fax 512/442-5738
Murchison Middle Sch 3700 N Hills Dr, Austin 78731 **Beth Newton**	6-8		1,392	22%	512/414-3254 Fax 512/343-1710
O Henry Middle Sch 2610 W 10th St, Austin 78703 Marlo Malott	6-8	V	862 980	27%	512/414-3229 Fax 512/477-7428
Paredes Middle Sch 10100 S Mary Moore Searight Dr, Austin 78748 Valerie Torres-Solis	6-8	T	892	73%	512/841-6800 Fax 512/841-7036
Small Middle Sch 4801 Monterey Oaks Blvd, Austin 78749 **Matthew Nelson**	6-8	V	1,231	27%	512/841-6700 Fax 512/841-6703
Webb Middle Sch 601 E Saint Johns Ave, Austin 78752 Raul Sanchez	6-8	TV	664	93%	512/414-3258 Fax 512/452-9683

• Del Valle Ind School Dist PID: 01056789
5301 Ross Rd Ste 103, Del Valle 78617
512/386-3010
Fax 512/386-3015

Schools: 15 \ **Teachers:** 823 \ **Students:** 12,100 \
Special Ed Students: 1,189 \ **LEP Students:** 3,936 \ **Ethnic:** Asian 1%,
African American 9%, Hispanic 85%, Caucasian 6% \ **Exp:** $568 (High) \
Poverty: 22% \ **Title I:** $4,374,094 \ **Special Education:** $2,269,000 \
Open-Close: 08/26 - 06/04 \ **DTBP:** $143 (High) \ t

Annette Villerot 1
David Edgar 2,15
Steven Alves 3,91
Humberto Araiza 5
Ray Prentice 11
Scott Wille 34
Rebecca Miller 42
Gaylen Clevenger 58
Rebecca Birch 67
Gabril Munoz 79
Robert Garcia 294
David Edgas 2,19
Janice Patterson 2
Karen Kovach 4
Tawni Angel 6
Juan Orozco 16
Leticia Hallmark 39
Sonja Howard 48
Jonathan Harris 58,79
Todd Gratehouse 73,76,84,98,295
Rocky Zepeda 88
Jena Gonzales 298

Public Schs..Principal	Grd	Prgm	Enr/#Cls	SN	
Baty Elem Sch 2101 Faro Dr, Austin 78741 Laura Gonzalez	PK-5	T	652	97%	512/386-3450 Fax 512/386-3455
Creedmoor Elem Sch 5604 FM 1327, Creedmoor 78610 Tj Moreno	PK-5	T	640	94%	512/386-3950 Fax 512/386-3955
Dailey Middle Sch 14000 Westall, Austin 78725 Mario Palacios	6-8	T	676	86%	512/386-3600 Fax 512/386-3605
Ⓐ Del Valle Dist Alt Ed Program 4305 McKinney Falls Pkwy, Austin 78744 George Meave	PK-12		150		512/386-3180 Fax 512/386-3179
Del Valle Elem Sch 5400 Ross Rd, Del Valle 78617 Jay Maines	PK-5	T	794	85%	512/386-3350 Fax 512/386-3355
Del Valle High Sch 5201 Ross Rd, Del Valle 78617 Joseph Welch	9-12	T	3,126 70	78%	512/386-3200 Fax 512/386-3205
Del Valle Middle Sch 5500 Ross Rd, Del Valle 78617 Natasha Staten	6-8	T	958	87%	512/386-3400 Fax 512/247-3087
Del Valle Opportunity Center 5301 Ross Rd Ste B, Del Valle 78617 Ray Macias	9-12	T	185 13	90%	512/386-3300 Fax 512/386-3316
Hillcrest Elem Sch 6910 E William Cannon Dr, Austin 78744 Jennifer Eberly	PK-5	T	563 54	96%	512/386-3550 Fax 512/386-3555
Hornsby-Dunlap Elem Sch 13901 FM 969, Austin 78724 Helen Garcia	PK-5	T	569 32	90%	512/386-3650 Fax 512/386-3655
Joseph Gilbert Elem Sch 5412 Gilbert Rd, Austin 78724 Lindsay Gonzales	PK-5	T	631	92%	512/386-3800 Fax 512/386-3805
Newton Collins Elem Sch 7609 Apogee Blvd, Austin 78744 **Suzi Wallace**	PK-5		600		512/386-3900
Ojeda Middle Sch 4900 McKinney Falls Pkwy, Austin 78744 **Alex Torrez**	6-8	T	906	87%	512/386-3500 Fax 512/386-3505
Popham Elem Sch 7014 Elroy Rd, Del Valle 78617 Carrie Abrams	PK-5	T	760 42	89%	512/386-3750 Fax 512/386-3755
Smith Elem Sch 4209 Smith School Rd, Austin 78744 Francisca Maldonado	PK-5	T	735 47	92%	512/386-3850 Fax 512/386-3855

79	Student Personnel	91	Safety/Security	275	Response To Intervention	298 Grant Writer/Ptnrships
80	Driver Ed/Safety	92	Magnet School	277	Remedial Math K-12	750 Chief Innovation Officer
81	Gifted/Talented	93	Parental Involvement	280	Literacy Coach	751 Chief of Staff
82	Video Services	95	Tech Prep Program	285	STEM	752 Social Emotional Learning
83	Substance Abuse Prev	97	Chief Infomation Officer	286	Digital Learning	
84	Erate	98	Chief Technology Officer	288	Common Core Standards	**Other School Types**
85	AIDS Education	270	Character Education	294	Accountability	Ⓐ = Alternative School
88	Alternative/At Risk	271	Migrant Education	295	Network System	Ⓒ = Charter School
89	Multi-Cultural Curriculum	273	Teacher Mentor	296	Title II Programs	Ⓜ = Magnet School
90	Social Work	274	Before/After Sch	297	Webmaster	Ⓨ = Year-Round School

School Programs
A = Alternative Program
G = Adult Classes
M = Magnet Program
T = Title I Schoolwide
V = Career & Tech Ed Programs

Social Media
f = Facebook
t = Twitter

New Schools are shaded
New Superintendents and Principals are bold
Personnel with email addresses are underscored

TX—369

Travis County

Market Data Retrieval

- **Eanes Ind School Dist** PID: 01056844   512/732-9000
  601 Camp Craft Rd, Austin 78746   Fax 512/732-9038

> **Schools:** 9 \ **Teachers:** 598 \ **Students:** 8,156 \ **Special Ed Students:** 689
> \ **LEP Students:** 175 \ **College-Bound:** 98% \ **Ethnic:** Asian 13%, African American 1%, Hispanic 13%, Caucasian 73% \ **Exp:** $186 (Low) \ **Poverty:** 3%
> \ **Title I:** $189,421 \ **Special Education:** $1,649,000 \ **Open-Close:** 08/21 - 05/28 \ **DTBP:** $171 (High) \

Dr Tom Leonard 1	Chris Scott 2
Maria Rockstead 2	Sylvie Pouget 2
Brian Bolek 3	Jeremy Trimble 3,17
Jerri Yznaga 3	Norman Hopkins 3
Steve Stracke 4	Todd Dodge 6
Todd Washburn 8,15,36,275	Carolyn Foote 16*
Kerry Taylor 20,23	Lisa Groover 30,274
Molly May 58	Jennifer Champagne 67
Laura Lee 68	Claudia McWhorter 71
Eric Wright 76	Kimberley Israel 76
Linda Rawlings 79,752	Jerri Lamirand 81,285
Matthew Zemo 88	Matt Greer 91
Beth Keith 275	Preston Jinnette 295
Pamela Van Dyke 297	

Public Schs..Principal	Grd	Prgm	Enr/#Cls	SN	
Barton Creek Elem Sch 1314 Patterson Rd, Austin 78733 Tiffany Phelps	K-5		474 23	1%	512/732-9180 Fax 512/732-9189
Bridge Point Elem Sch 6401 Cedar St, Austin 78746 Heather Meek	K-5		655 37	2%	512/732-9200 Fax 512/732-9209
Cedar Creek Elem Sch 3301 Pinnacle Rd, Austin 78746 Susan Fambrough	K-5		518 18	3%	512/732-9120 Fax 512/732-9129
Eanes Elem Sch 4101 Bee Caves Rd, Austin 78746 Lesley Ryan	PK-5		628 27	2%	512/732-9100 Fax 512/732-9109
Forest Trail Elem Sch 1203 S Capital of Texas Hwy, Austin 78746 Cody Spraberry	K-5		577	1%	512/732-9160 Fax 512/732-9169
Hill Country Middle Sch 1300 Walsh Tarlton Ln, Austin 78746 Kathleen Sullivan	6-8	V	1,072 55	2%	512/732-9220 Fax 512/732-9229
Valley View Elem Sch 1201 S Capital of Texas Hwy, Austin 78746 Jennifer Dusek	K-5		514 35	6%	512/732-9140 Fax 512/732-9149
West Ridge Middle Sch 9201 Scenic Bluff Dr, Austin 78733 Dianne Carter	6-8	V	922 60	3%	512/732-9240 Fax 512/732-9249
Westlake High Sch 4100 Westbank Dr, Austin 78746 Steven Ramsey	9-12	GV	2,541 100	3%	512/732-9280 Fax 512/732-9296

- **Lago Vista Ind School Dist** PID: 01056870   512/267-8300
  8039 Bar K Ranch Rd, Lago Vista 78645   Fax 512/267-8304

> **Schools:** 4 \ **Teachers:** 97 \ **Students:** 1,500 \ **Special Ed Students:** 134
> \ **LEP Students:** 64 \ **College-Bound:** 61% \ **Ethnic:** African American 1%, Hispanic 21%, Caucasian 77% \ **Exp:** $255 (Med) \ **Poverty:** 9% \
> **Title I:** $163,175 \ **Special Education:** $213,000 \ **Open-Close:** 08/14 - 05/21 \ **DTBP:** $363 (High)

Darren Webb 1	Jason Stoner 2,19
Kevin Lovell 3	Mark Beall 3
Stacey Widdecombe 4	Lisa Gordon 5
Craten Phillips 6*	Regina Carmichael 7,83,85*
Dr Suzy Lofton 8,11,15,296	Krystal Colhoff 58,69
David Scott 67	Russell Maynard 73*

Public Schs..Principal	Grd	Prgm	Enr/#Cls	SN	
Lago Vista Elem Sch 20311 Dawn Dr, Lago Vista 78645 Michelle Jackson	PK-3		407 32	33%	512/267-8340 Fax 512/267-8362
Lago Vista High Sch 5185 Lohmans Ford Rd, Lago Vista 78645 Heather Stoner	9-12	AV	447 32	17%	512/267-8300 Fax 512/267-8330
Lago Vista Intermediate Sch 20801 FM 1431, Lago Vista 78645 Stacie Davis	4-5		247	31%	512/267-8300 Fax 512/267-8363
Lago Vista Middle Sch 20801 FM 1431, Lago Vista 78645 Eric Holt	6-8		374 35	23%	512/267-8300 Fax 512/267-8329

- **Lake Travis Ind School Dist** PID: 02178653   512/533-6000
  3322 Ranch Road 620 S, Austin 78738   Fax 512/533-6001

> **Schools:** 10 \ **Teachers:** 581 \ **Students:** 10,410 \ **Special Ed Students:** 756
> \ **LEP Students:** 532 \ **College-Bound:** 68% \ **Ethnic:** Asian 6%, African American 1%, Hispanic 21%, Caucasian 72% \ **Exp:** $226 (Med) \
> **Poverty:** 5% \ **Title I:** $402,696 \ **Special Education:** $1,357,000 \
> **Open-Close:** 08/14 - 05/22 \ **DTBP:** $157 (High) \

Dr Brad Lancaster 1	Angie Marsh 2
Brad Goerke 2	Johnny Hill 2,15
Rufus Myers 2	Tamara Odenthal 2
Richard Harrison 3	Robert Winovitch 3
Wesley Perkins 3	Marcie Kissko 4
Ryan Mikolaycik 4	Tanya Breazeale 4
Dan Lee 5	Rhonda Davis 5
Hank Carter 6	Michael Drinkwater 6
Jennifer Lyon 7	Elizabeth Deterra 8
Liz Sims 9,57	Mary Patin 11,15,286
Evalene Murphy 15,68	Holly Morris-Kuentz 15
Charles Aguillon 20,23	Rachel Behnke 27
Laura Abbott 58,271	Kim Flasch 67
Danielle Hinson 68	Kim Heinen 68
Kathy Burbank 69,73,294	Katie Kauffman 70
Dr Kevin Claypool 70	Marco Alvarado 71
Chris Woehl 73,76,295	Janis Jordan 74
Kathleen Hassenfratz 83,85,270*	Kenneth Debord 88
Dionne Burnett 93,274	

Public Schs..Principal	Grd	Prgm	Enr/#Cls	SN	
Bee Cave Elem Sch 14300 Hamilton Pool Rd, Austin 78738 Kim Kellner	PK-5		750 32	5%	512/533-6250 Fax 512/533-6251
Bee Cave Middle Sch 5400 Vail Divide, Austin 78738 Amanda Prehn	6-8		401		737/931-2400
Hudson Bend Middle Sch 15600 Lariat Trl, Austin 78734 Thomas Payne	6-8		1,170	15%	512/533-6400 Fax 512/533-6401
Lake Pointe Elem Sch 11801 Sonoma Dr, Austin 78738 Kelly Freed	PK-5		739 40	4%	512/533-6500 Fax 512/533-6501
Lake Travis Elem Sch 15303 Kollmeyer Dr, Austin 78734 Angela Frankhouser	PK-5	T	895	47%	512/533-6300 Fax 512/533-6301
Lake Travis High Sch 3324 Ranch Road 620 S, Austin 78738 Gordon Butler	9-12		3,080	9%	512/533-6100 Fax 512/533-6101
Lake Travis Middle Sch 4932 Bee Creek Rd, Spicewood 78669 Lester Wolff	6-8		1,420	5%	512/533-6200 Fax 512/264-2247

1 Superintendent	8 Curric/Instruct K-12	19 Chief Financial Officer	29 Family/Consumer Science	39 Social Studies K-12	49 English/Lang Arts Elem	59 Special Education Elem	69 Academic Assessment
2 Bus/Finance/Purchasing	9 Curric/Instruct Elem	20 Art K-12	30 Adult Education	40 Social Studies Elem	50 English/Lang Arts Sec	60 Special Education Sec	70 Research/Development
3 Buildings And Grounds	10 Curric/Instruct Sec	21 Art Elem	31 Career/Sch-to-Work K-12	41 Social Studies Sec	51 Reading K-12	61 Foreign/World Lang K-12	71 Public Information
4 Food Service	11 Federal Program	22 Art Sec	32 Career/Sch-to-Work Elem	42 Science K-12	52 Reading Elem	62 Foreign/World Lang Elem	72 Summer School
5 Transportation	12 Title I	23 Music K-12	33 Career/Sch-to-Work Sec	43 Science Elem	53 Reading Sec	63 Foreign/World Lang Sec	73 Instructional Tech
6 Athletic	13 Title V	24 Music Elem	34 Early Childhood Ed	44 Science Sec	54 Remedial Reading K-12	64 Religious Education K-12	74 Inservice Training
7 Health Services	15 Asst Superintendent	25 Music Sec	35 Health/Phys Education	45 Math K-12	55 Remedial Reading Elem	65 Religious Education Elem	75 Marketing/Distributive
	16 Instructional Media Svcs	26 Business Education	36 Guidance Services K-12	46 Math Elem	56 Remedial Reading Sec	66 Religious Education Sec	76 Info Systems
	17 Chief Operations Officer	27 Career & Tech Ed	37 Guidance Services Elem	47 Math Sec	57 Bilingual/ELL	67 School Board President	77 Psychological Assess
	18 Chief Academic Officer	28 Technology Education	38 Guidance Services Sec	48 English/Lang Arts K-12	58 Special Education K-12	68 Teacher Personnel	78 Affirmative Action

Texas School Directory — Travis County

Lakeway Elem Sch	PK-5		679	5%	512/533-6350
1701 Lohmans Crossing Rd, Austin 78734				40	Fax 512/533-6351
Sam Hicks					📘 🐦
Serene Hills Elem Sch	PK-5		880	6%	512/533-7400
3301 Serene Hills Ct, Austin 78738					Fax 512/533-7401
Julie Nederveld					
West Cypress Hills Elem Sch	PK-5		797	8%	512/533-7500
6112 Cypress Ranch Blvd, Spicewood 78669					Fax 512/533-7599
Melanie Beninga					📘

● **Manor Ind School Dist** PID: 01056894   512/278-4000
10335 US Highway 290 E, Manor 78653   Fax 512/278-4017

Schools: 16 \ **Teachers:** 554 \ **Students:** 9,200 \ **Special Ed Students:** 743 \ **LEP Students:** 3,032 \ **College-Bound:** 50% \ **Ethnic:** Asian 4%, African American 21%, Hispanic 67%, Caucasian 8% \ **Exp:** $425 (High) \ **Poverty:** 17% \ **Title I:** $1,755,351 \ **Special Education:** $1,275,000 \ **Open-Close:** 08/15 - 05/22 \ **DTBP:** $126 (High) \ 📘 🐦

Dr Royce Avery	1	Carla Stevens	2
Karen Chapoton	2	Melanie Boutwell	2
George Townsend	4	Jackie Fields	5
Jimmie Mitchell	6	Dr Brian Yearwood	8,11,15,69,81,294,298
Mikaela Perkins	8,69,280,294,298*	Creslond Fannin	11
Alfredo Laredo	16,73,98,286	Renferd Joseph	20,23
Jill Ranucci	27	Tamo King	27
Stacy Signaigo	34	Nanette Deaton	36
Courtney Webster	39	Claire Hodgin	43
Tammy Mayberry	44	Lakeyshia Brown	46
Dora Jackson	47	Lisa Kutsch	47,69,285
Lo DeWalt	49	Meredith Roddy	57
Michele McKinley	58	Elmer Fisher	67
Daniel Vera	68	Scott Thomas	71
Beth Chapoton	76	Chris Tawater	76
Rebecca Lott	83	Ryan Marcum	91
Dr Nathan Balasubcamania	294	David Gonzalez	295

Public Schs..Principal	Grd	Prgm	Enr/#Cls	SN	
Blake Manor Elem Sch	PK-5	T	565	86%	512/278-4200
18010 Blake Manor Rd, Manor 78653					Fax 512/278-4209
Maeloisa Morales					📘 🐦
Bluebonnet Trail Elem Sch	PK-5	T	568	67%	512/278-4125
11316 Farmhaven Rd, Austin 78754			23		Fax 512/278-4140
Angel DeLuna					
Decker Elem Sch	PK-5	T	724	97%	512/278-4141
8500 Decker Ln, Austin 78724			44		Fax 512/278-4174
Brandon Powell					
Decker Middle Sch	6-8	T	750	80%	512/278-4630
8104 Decker Ln, Austin 78724					Fax 512/278-4654
Dayna Anthony-Swain					
Lagos Elem Sch	PK-5		391		512/278-4000
11817 Murchison St, Manor 78653					
Malaki Hawkins					
Manor Elem Early Learning Ctr	PK-PK	T	295	83%	512/278-4100
12904 Gregg Manor Rd, Manor 78653			35		Fax 512/278-4104
Nicole Aguirre					
Ⓐ Manor Excel Academy	9-12	T	59	90%	512/278-4075
600 E Parsons St, Manor 78653					Fax 512/278-4859
Jerry Statos					
Manor High Sch	9-10		900		512/278-4800
12700 Gregg Manor Rd, Manor 78653					Fax 512/278-4803
Jon Bailey					
Manor Middle Sch	6-8	T	684	77%	512/278-4600
12900 Gregg Manor Rd, Manor 78653			80		Fax 512/278-4285
Don Wise					🐦
Manor New Tech High Sch	Voc	T	433	58%	512/278-4875
10323 US Highway 290 E, Manor 78653					Fax 512/278-4880
Bobby Garcia					
Manor New Tech Middle Sch	6-8		562		512/278-4663
12116 Joyce Turner Dr, Manor 78653					
Christopher Smith					
Manor Senior High Sch	11-12	GTV	900	72%	512/278-4665
14832 N FM 973 Rd, Manor 78653			53		Fax 512/278-4666
John Matthews					
Oak Meadows Elem Sch	PK-5	T	676	97%	512/278-4175
5600 Decker Ln, Austin 78724					Fax 512/278-4199
Salvador Vega					
Pioneer Crossing Elem Sch	PK-5	T	621	65%	512/278-4250
11300 Samsung Blvd, Austin 78754					Fax 512/278-4259
Eddwina Flowers					📘 🐦
Presidential Meadows Elem Sch	PK-5	T	585	75%	512/278-4225
13252 George Bush St, Manor 78653					Fax 512/278-4231
Lanica Failey					
Shadowglen Elem Sch	PK-5	T	583	67%	512/278-4700
12000 Shadowglen Trce, Manor 78653					Fax 512/278-4701
Niccole Delestre					

● **Pflugerville Ind School Dist** PID: 01056935   512/594-0000
1401 W Pecan St, Pflugerville 78660   Fax 512/594-0011

Schools: 33 \ **Teachers:** 1,737 \ **Students:** 26,269 \ **Special Ed Students:** 2,523 \ **LEP Students:** 4,884 \ **College-Bound:** 57% \ **Ethnic:** Asian 8%, African American 17%, Hispanic 51%, Caucasian 24% \ **Exp:** $264 (Med) \ **Poverty:** 12% \ **Title I:** $4,360,834 \ **Special Education:** $3,631,000 \ **Bilingual Education:** $25,000 \ **Open-Close:** 08/15 - 05/28 \ **DTBP:** $75 (Low) \ 📘 🐦

Dr Douglas Killian	1	Craig Pruett	2
Eduardo Ramos	2,3,17	David Vessling	3
Geoff Holle	4	Todd Raymond	6
Denise Kablaitis	7,91	Brandi Baker	8,15
Christine Fox	11	Dr Troy Galow	15,751
Victor Valdez	16,73,76,295	Manuel Gamez	20,23
Traci Hendrix	27	Gema Henson	57
Cara Schwartz	58	Hutchison Hill	58
Vernagene Mott	67	Willie Watson	68
Tamara Spencer	71	David Greiner	76
Shirley Bachus	81	Karen Shah	294

Public Schs..Principal	Grd	Prgm	Enr/#Cls	SN	
Barron Elem Sch	PK-5	T	689	81%	512/594-4300
14850 Harris Ridge Blvd, Pflugerville 78660					Fax 512/594-4305
Virginia Caudle					📘 🐦
Brookhollow Elem Sch	PK-5	T	471	48%	512/594-5200
1200 N Railroad Ave, Pflugerville 78660			40		Fax 512/594-5205
Lisa Harris					
Caldwell Elem Sch	PK-5	T	655	51%	512/594-6400
1718 Picadilly Dr, Round Rock 78664					Fax 512/594-6405
Colby Self					
Cele Middle Sch	6-8	TV	1,044	40%	512/594-3000
6000 Cele Rd, Pflugerville 78660					
Brian Ernest					
Copperfield Elem Sch	PK-5	T	413	75%	512/594-5800
12135 Thompkins Dr, Austin 78753			55		Fax 512/594-5805
Georgie Arenaz					
Dearing Elem Sch	PK-5	T	574	45%	512/594-4500
4301 Gattis School Rd, Round Rock 78664					Fax 512/594-4505
Christy Chandler					
Delco Primary Sch	PK-2	T	697	83%	512/594-6200
12900 Dessau Rd Ste A, Austin 78754					Fax 512/594-6205
Miguel Castillo					📘 🐦
Dessau Elem Sch	3-5	T	608	80%	512/594-4600
1501 Dessau Ridge Ln, Austin 78754			33		Fax 512/594-4605
Carolyn Parker					

79	Student Personnel	91	Safety/Security	275	Response To Intervention
80	Driver Ed/Safety	92	Magnet School	277	Remedial Math K-12
81	Gifted/Talented	93	Parental Involvement	280	Literacy Coach
82	Video Services	95	Tech Prep Program	285	STEM
83	Substance Abuse Prev	97	Chief Infomation Officer	286	Digital Learning
84	Erate	98	Chief Technology Officer	288	Common Core Standards
85	AIDS Education	270	Character Education	294	Accountability
88	Alternative/At Risk	271	Migrant Education	295	Network System
89	Multi-Cultural Curriculum	273	Teacher Mentor	296	Title II Programs
90	Social Work	274	Before/After Sch	297	Webmaster

298	Grant Writer/Ptnrships		
750	Chief Innovation Officer		
751	Chief of Staff		
752	Social Emotional Learning		

Other School Types
Ⓐ = Alternative School
Ⓒ = Charter School
Ⓜ = Magnet School
Ⓨ = Year-Round School

School Programs
A = Alternative Program
G = Adult Classes
M = Magnet Program
T = Title I Schoolwide
V = Career & Tech Ed Programs

Social Media
📘 = Facebook
🐦 = Twitter

New Schools are shaded
New Superintendents and Principals are bold
Personnel with email addresses are underscored

Travis County

School	Grades	Prgm	Enr/#Cls	FRL	Phone
Dessau Middle Sch 12900 Dessau Rd, Austin 78754 Valerie Torres-Solis	6-8	T	860	76%	512/594-2600 Fax 512/594-2605
Hendrickson High Sch 19201 Colorado Sand Dr, Pflugerville 78660 Daniel Garcia	9-12	V	2,618 135	34%	512/594-1100 Fax 512/594-1105
Highland Park Elem Sch 428 Kingston Lacy Blvd, Pflugerville 78660 Lizbeth Ruiz	PK-5	T	641	40%	512/594-6800 Fax 512/594-6805
John B Connally High Sch 13212 N Lamar Blvd, Austin 78753 Sheila Finley-Reed	9-12	TV	1,857 50	65%	512/594-0800 Fax 512/594-0805
Kelly Lane Middle Sch 18900 Falcon Pointe Blvd, Pflugerville 78660 Dina Schaefer	6-8	V	1,078 90	24%	512/594-2800 Fax 512/594-2805
Murchison Elem Sch 2215 Kelly Ln, Pflugerville 78660 Reese Weirich	PK-5		816	11%	512/594-6000 Fax 512/594-6005
Northwest Elem Sch 14014 Thermal Dr, Austin 78728 Tere Tidwell	PK-5	T	530 32	71%	512/594-4400 Fax 512/594-4405
Pace Sch 1401 W Pecan St B, Pflugerville 78660 Mike Harvey	9-12		112		512/594-1900 Fax 512/594-1905
Park Crest Middle Sch 1500 N Railroad Ave, Pflugerville 78660 Zachary Kleypas	6-8	TV	948 50	38%	512/594-2400 Fax 512/594-2405
Parmer Lane Elem Sch 1806 W Parmer Ln, Austin 78727 Barry Miller	PK-5	T	501 37	64%	512/594-4000 Fax 512/594-4005
Pflugerville Elem Sch 701 Immanuel Rd, Pflugerville 78660 Genia Antoine	PK-5	T	453 29	48%	512/594-3800 Fax 512/594-3805
Pflugerville High Sch 1301 W Pecan St, Pflugerville 78660 Ameka Durham-Hunt	9-12	TV	2,055	43%	512/594-0500 Fax 512/594-0505
Pflugerville Middle Sch 1600 Settlers Valley Dr, Pflugerville 78660 Robert Stell	6-8	TV	1,017 50	51%	512/594-2000 Fax 512/594-2005
Provan Opportunity Center 1401-A W Pecan St, Pflugerville 78660 Philip Clayton	K-12		450 5		512/594-3600 Fax 512/594-3605
Riojas Elem Sch 3400 Crispin Hall Ln, Pflugerville 78660 Christi Siegel	PK-5		668	21%	512/594-4100 Fax 512/594-4105
River Oaks Elem Sch 12401 Scofield Farms Dr, Austin 78758 Aracely Suarez	PK-5	T	561 25	78%	512/594-5000 Fax 512/594-5005
Rowe Lane Elem Sch 3112 Speidel Dr, Pflugerville 78660 Ben O'Connor	PK-5		791 34	12%	512/594-6600 Fax 512/594-6605
Spring Hill Elem Sch 600 S Heatherwilde Blvd, Pflugerville 78660 Camille Longoria	PK-5	T	597 30	66%	512/594-5400 Fax 512/594-5405
Timmerman Elem Sch 412 Swenson Farms Blvd, Pflugerville 78660 Sara Watson	PK-5	T	535 25	44%	512/594-4200 Fax 512/594-4205
Vernagene Mott Elem Sch 20101 Hodde Ln, Pflugerville 78660 Tammy Rebecek	PK-5		706		512/594-4700
Weiss High Sch 5201 Wolf Pack Dr, Pflugerville 78660 Paula Gamble	9-10		807		512/594-1400
Westview Middle Sch 1805 Scofield Ln, Austin 78727 Jorge Franco	6-8	TV	801 54	70%	512/594-2200 Fax 512/594-2205
Wieland Elem Sch 900 Tudor House Rd, Pflugerville 78660 Jared Stevenson	PK-5	T	435 27	66%	512/594-3900 Fax 512/594-3905
Windermere Elem Sch 1100 Picadilly Dr, Pflugerville 78660 Kate Shaum	3-5	T	402 26	46%	512/594-4800 Fax 512/594-4805
Windermere Primary Sch 429 Grand Avenue Pkwy, Pflugerville 78660 Terri Floyd	PK-2	T	398	54%	512/594-5600 Fax 512/594-5605

TRAVIS CATHOLIC SCHOOLS

• **Diocese of Austin Ed Office** PID: 01420568   512/949-2497
6225 E Highway 290, Austin 78723   Fax 512/949-2520

Schools: 21 \ **Students:** 5,000

Listing includes only schools located in this county. See District Index for location of Diocesan Offices.

Misty Poe 1,11   Robert Whitworth 8,15

Catholic Schs..Principal	Grd	Prgm	Enr/#Cls	SN	
Cathedral School of St Mary 910 San Jacinto Blvd, Austin 78701 Robert Legros	PK-8		185 11		512/476-1480 Fax 512/476-9922
San Juan Diego Cath High Sch 2512 S 1st St, Austin 78704 Travis Butler	8-12		180 17		512/804-1935 Fax 512/804-1937
St Austin Catholic Sch 1911 San Antonio St, Austin 78705 Tara Cevallos	PK-8		205 16		512/477-3751 Fax 512/477-3079
St Gabriel's Catholic Sch 2500 Wimberly Ln, Austin 78735 Colleen Lynch \ Daniel McKenna	PK-8		430 23		512/327-7755 Fax 512/327-4334
St Ignatius Martyr Cath Sch 120 W Oltorf St, Austin 78704 Fred Valle	PK-8		250 13		512/442-8547 Fax 512/442-8685
St Louis Catholic Sch 2114 Saint Joseph Blvd, Austin 78757 Cindy Gee	PK-8		230 18		512/454-0384 Fax 512/454-7252
St Michael's Catholic Academy 3000 Barton Creek Blvd, Austin 78735 Dr Dawn Nichols	9-12		400 29		512/328-2323 Fax 512/328-2327
St Theresa's Catholic Sch 4311 Small Dr, Austin 78731 Rachel Eckert	PK-8		400 20		512/451-7105 Fax 512/451-8808

TRAVIS PRIVATE SCHOOLS

Private Schs..Principal	Grd	Prgm	Enr/#Cls	SN	
Academy of Thought & Industry 1701 Toomey Rd, Austin 78704 Michael Strong	9-12		401		512/910-8980
Acton Academy 1404 E Riverside Dr, Austin 78741 Laura Sandefer	5-8		100		512/320-0596
Austin Eco Bilingual Sch-South 8707 Mountain Crest Dr, Austin 78735 Adriana Rodriguez	K-5		125		512/299-5731 Fax 512/432-5317

1	Superintendent	8	Curric/Instruct K-12	19	Chief Financial Officer	29	Family/Consumer Science	39	Social Studies K-12	49	English/Lang Arts Elem	59	Special Education Elem	69	Academic Assessment
2	Bus/Finance/Purchasing	9	Curric/Instruct Elem	20	Art K-12	30	Adult Education	40	Social Studies Elem	50	English/Lang Arts Sec	60	Special Education Sec	70	Research/Development
3	Buildings And Grounds	10	Curric/Instruct Sec	21	Art Elem	31	Career/Sch-to-Work K-12	41	Social Studies Sec	51	Reading K-12	61	Foreign/World Lang K-12	71	Public Information
4	Food Service	11	Federal Program	22	Art Sec	32	Career/Sch-to-Work Elem	42	Science K-12	52	Reading Elem	62	Foreign/World Lang Elem	72	Summer School
5	Transportation	12	Title I	23	Music K-12	33	Career/Sch-to-Work Sec	43	Science Elem	53	Reading Sec	63	Foreign/World Lang Sec	73	Instructional Tech
6	Athletic	13	Title V	24	Music Elem	34	Early Childhood Ed	44	Science Sec	54	Remedial Reading K-12	64	Religious Education K-12	74	Inservice Training
7	Health Services	15	Asst Superintendent	25	Music Sec	35	Health/Phys Education	45	Math K-12	55	Remedial Reading Elem	65	Religious Education Elem	75	Marketing/Distributive
		16	Instructional Media Svcs	26	Business Education	36	Guidance Services K-12	46	Math Elem	56	Remedial Reading Sec	66	Religious Education Sec	76	Info Systems
		17	Chief Operations Officer	27	Career & Tech Ed	37	Guidance Services Elem	47	Math Sec	57	Bilingual/ELL	67	School Board President	77	Psychological Assess
		18	Chief Academic Officer	28	Technology Education	38	Guidance Services Sec	48	English/Lang Arts K-12	58	Special Education K-12	68	Teacher Personnel	78	Affirmative Action

Texas School Directory — Travis County

School	Grades	Enrollment/Staff	Phone/Fax
Austin International Sch 4001 Adelphi Ln, Austin 78727 Emily Hopkins	PK-5	90 7	512/331-7806 Fax 512/219-5201 f t
Austin Jewish Academy 7300 Hart Ln, Austin 78731 Chris Aguero	K-8	130 18	512/735-8350 Fax 512/735-8351 f
Austin Montessori Sch 5006 Sunset Trl, Austin 78745 Grae Baker	PK-9	330 13	512/892-0253 Fax 512/891-9875
Austin Peace Academy 5110 Manor Rd B, Austin 78723 Diana Abdi	PK-12	220 14	512/926-1737 Fax 512/926-9688
Brentwood Christian Sch 11908 N Lamar Blvd, Austin 78753 Mara Ashley \ Leah Smith \ Carol Johnson	PK-12	700 45	512/835-5983 Fax 512/835-2184
Capitol School-Austin 2011 W Koenig Ln, Austin 78756 Jeannette Young	PK-4	55 7	512/467-7006 Fax 512/467-7025
Childrens Sch 2825 Hancock Dr, Austin 78731 Sheryl Wallin	PK-3	165 10	512/453-1126
Fusion Academy-Austin 4701 Bee Caves Rd Ste 101, Austin 78746 Cody Pileski	6-12	80	512/330-0188
Girls' School of Austin 2007 McCall Rd, Austin 78703 Cathleen Eclarinal	K-8	144	512/478-7827 Fax 512/478-5456 f t
Griffin Sch 5001 Evans Ave, Austin 78751 Adam Wilson	9-12	80	512/454-5797 Fax 512/454-5798
Headwaters Sch 6305 Manchaca Rd, Austin 78745 Susie Demarest	PK-5	545	512/443-8843
Headwaters Sch 807 Rio Grande St, Austin 78701 Ted Graf	6-12	500	512/480-8142 Fax 512/480-0277
Hebrew Prep School of Austin 2127 W Palmer Ln, Austin 78727 Rochel Levertov	PK-5	50 6	512/977-0770 Fax 512/499-8202
Hill Country Christian Sch 12124 Ranch Road 620 N, Austin 78750 Jessica Tracy \ Matt Donnowitz	PK-12	565	512/331-7036 Fax 512/257-4190
Huntington-Surrey Sch 4700 Grover Ave, Austin 78756 Catherine Cotman	9-12	70 6	512/502-5400 Fax 512/457-0235
Hyde Park Elem Middle Sch 3901 Speedway, Austin 78751 Kimmarie Suhr \ Dr Adam Creasy	PK-8	430	512/465-8338 Fax 512/371-1433
Hyde Park High Sch 11400 N Mopac Expy, Austin 78759 Dr Chris Coy	9-12	172	512/465-8333 Fax 512/827-2020
Kirby Hall Sch 306 W 29th St, Austin 78705 Helen Roberts	PK-12	100 16	512/474-1770 Fax 512/474-1117 f
Magellan Int'l Sch-Anderson Ln 7938 Great Northern Blvd, Austin 78757 Sagrario Arguelles \ Nicolas Puga	K-8	145	512/782-2327
Odyssey Sch 4407 Red River St, Austin 78751 John Brinson	Spec	65 7	512/472-2262 Fax 512/236-9385 f
Paragon Prep Middle Sch 2001 W Koenig Ln, Austin 78756 David McGrath	5-8	160 8	512/459-5040 Fax 512/459-1875
Rawson Saunders Sch 2614A Exposition Blvd, Austin 78703 Laura Steinbach	1-8	100	512/476-8382 Fax 512/476-1132 f t
Redeemer Lutheran Sch 1500 W Anderson Ln, Austin 78757 Carol Mueller	PK-8	500 28	512/451-6478 Fax 512/610-8809 f
Regents School of Austin 3230 Travis Country Cir, Austin 78735 Dr Dan Peterson	K-12	1,000	512/899-8095 Fax 512/899-8623
Regina Mater 1320B E 51st St, Austin 78723 Jarin Schiavolin	PK-12	25	512/524-1799
Rise School of Austin 4800 Manor Rd Bldg J, Austin 78723 Emily Greer	Spec	40	512/891-1682 Fax 512/494-4096 f t
St Andrew's Episcopal Sch 1112 W 31st St, Austin 78705 Kama Bruce	K-12	675 48	512/452-5779 Fax 512/299-9822 f t
St Francis Sch 300 E Huntland Dr, Austin 78752 Barbara Porter	PK-8	402	512/454-0848
St Stephen's Episcopal Sch 6500 Saint Stephens Dr, Austin 78746 Christopher Gunnin	6-12	650	512/327-1213 Fax 512/327-1311 f t
Stonehill Christian Academy 4301 Kelly Ln, Pflugerville 78660 Chinyere Ukegbu	PK-8	13 4	512/763-2776
Texas Neurorehab Center 1106 W Dittmar Rd, Austin 78745 Dottie Goodman	Spec GV	53 7	512/444-4835 Fax 512/462-6636
Trinity Episcopal Sch 3901 Bee Caves Rd, Austin 78746 Jennifer Morgan \ Shanna Weiss	K-8	458	512/472-9525 Fax 512/472-2337 f t
Veritas Academy 13401 Escarpment Blvd, Austin 78739 Jef Fowler	PK-12	301 15	512/891-1673 Fax 512/891-1693
Waterloo Sch 1511 S Congress Ave, Austin 78704 Craig Doerksen	9-12	15	512/447-7781
William's Community Sch 5209 Duval Rd, Austin 78727 Patsy Harris	Spec	60	512/250-5700

TRAVIS REGIONAL CENTERS

- **Region 13 Ed Service Center** PID: 02101545   512/919-5313
  5701 Springdale Rd, Austin 78723   Fax 512/919-5374

Dr Richard Elsasser 1,11   Jesse Lopez 8,15
Craig Spinn 15   Millie Klein 15

---

79 Student Personnel	91 Safety/Security	275 Response To Intervention	298 Grant Writer/Ptnrships	**School Programs**	**Social Media**	
80 Driver Ed/Safety	92 Magnet School	277 Remedial Math K-12	750 Chief Innovation Officer	A = Alternative Program	f = Facebook	
81 Gifted/Talented	93 Parental Involvement	280 Literacy Coach	751 Chief of Staff	G = Adult Classes		
82 Video Services	95 Tech Prep Program	285 STEM	752 Social Emotional Learning	M = Magnet Program	t = Twitter	
83 Substance Abuse Prev	97 Chief Infomation Officer	286 Digital Learning		T = Title I Schoolwide		
84 Erate	98 Chief Technology Officer	288 Common Core Standards	**Other School Types**	V = Career & Tech Ed Programs		
85 AIDS Education	270 Character Education	294 Accountability	Ⓐ = Alternative School			
88 Alternative/At Risk	271 Migrant Education	295 Network System	Ⓒ = Charter School	New Schools are shaded		
89 Multi-Cultural Curriculum	273 Teacher Mentor	296 Title II Programs	Ⓜ = Magnet School	New Superintendents and Principals are bold		
90 Social Work	274 Before/After Sch	297 Webmaster	Ⓨ = Year-Round School	Personnel with email addresses are underscored		

Trinity County

Market Data Retrieval

TRINITY COUNTY

TRINITY PUBLIC SCHOOLS

- **Apple Springs Ind School Dist** PID: 01057044   936/831-3344
  9120 FM 2501, Apple Springs 75926   Fax 936/831-2824

Schools: 2 \ *Teachers:* 20 \ *Students:* 220 \ *Special Ed Students:* 23 \ *College-Bound:* 67% \ *Ethnic:* African American 4%, Hispanic 7%, Native American: 1%, Caucasian 89% \ *Exp:* $425 (High) \ *Poverty:* 44% \ *Title I:* $141,581 \ *Open-Close:* 08/15 - 05/29

Cody Moree 1	Cody Moree 2,6,19,31,273*
Greg Cambell 3*	Renee Turner 4*
Renee Turner 4	Kevin Plott 8
Loretta Eddins 11,36,58,69,88,270,271*	Amanda Roden 67
Lawanda Vazquez 73,76,98*	

Public Schs..Principal	Grd	Prgm	Enr/#Cls	SN
Apple Springs Elem Sch 9120 Farm Road FM 2501, Apple Springs 75926 Kevin Plotts	PK-6	T	122 10	58% 936/831-2241
Apple Springs High Sch 9120 FM 2501, Apple Springs 75926 Kevin Plotts	7-12	TV	77 14	56% 936/831-2241

- **Centerville Ind School Dist** PID: 01057070   936/642-1597
  10327 N State Highway 94, Groveton 75845   Fax 936/642-2810

Schools: 2 \ *Teachers:* 17 \ *Students:* 127 \ *Special Ed Students:* 9 \ *LEP Students:* 3 \ *College-Bound:* 70% \ *Ethnic:* Hispanic 8%, Caucasian 92% \ *Exp:* $376 (High) \ *Poverty:* 29% \ *Title I:* $44,973 \ *Open-Close:* 08/16 - 05/29 \ *DTBP:* $322 (High)

Mark Brown 1,11	Terry Whittlesey 2
Charles Ashworth 6*	Andja Sailer 8,13,27,36,85,88,271*
Sheila Smith 58	James Due 67
Jennifer Westbrook 73*	

Public Schs..Principal	Grd	Prgm	Enr/#Cls	SN
Centerville Elem Sch 10327 N State Highway 94, Groveton 75845 Andja Sailer	PK-6	T	70 20	60% 936/642-1597 Fax 936/645-2810
Centerville High Sch 10327 N State Highway 94, Groveton 75845 Andja Sailer	7-12	TV	64 14	56% 936/642-1597 Fax 936/645-2810

- **Groveton Ind School Dist** PID: 01057109   936/642-1473
  207 North Main St, Groveton 75845   Fax 936/642-1628

Schools: 2 \ *Teachers:* 64 \ *Students:* 750 \ *Special Ed Students:* 90 \ *LEP Students:* 12 \ *Ethnic:* Asian 1%, African American 6%, Hispanic 14%, Caucasian 79% \ *Exp:* $430 (High) \ *Poverty:* 32% \ *Title I:* $335,862 \ *Open-Close:* 08/12 - 05/29 \ *DTBP:* $345 (High)

Don Hamilton 1,11,57,83	Luther Cockrell 3
Debbie Wilson 4*	John Abshier 5
Richard Steubing 6	Virginia Redden 7,35,85*
Amanda Stubblefield 9,74,91	Bryan Finch 10,88,270
Teresa Anderson 16,82*	Dorothy Kennedy 36,69*

Susan Kitchens 54*	Mark Folds 67
Melody Benton 68	Jack Ledbetter 73,83,295*

Public Schs..Principal	Grd	Prgm	Enr/#Cls	SN
Groveton Elem Sch 421 N Magee St, Groveton 75845 Amanda Stubblefield	PK-5	T	366 24	69% 936/642-1182 Fax 936/642-3254
Groveton Jr Sr High Sch 207 North Main Street, Groveton 75845 Bryan Finch	6-12	ATV	403 30	56% 936/642-1128 Fax 936/642-1616

- **Trinity Ind School Dist** PID: 01057147   936/594-3569
  101 W Jefferson St, Trinity 75862   Fax 936/594-8425

Schools: 3 \ *Teachers:* 91 \ *Students:* 1,280 \ *Special Ed Students:* 105 \ *LEP Students:* 104 \ *College-Bound:* 50% \ *Ethnic:* African American 18%, Hispanic 24%, Caucasian 58% \ *Exp:* $340 (High) \ *Poverty:* 32% \ *Title I:* $521,448 \ *Special Education:* $281,000 \ *Open-Close:* 08/26 - 05/28 \ *DTBP:* $350 (High)

John Kaufman 1	Luann Gallant 2,11,74,84,296
Gill Cambelle 3,4,5,11,288	Patrick Goodman 6
Rachel Kriner 7*	Natalie Barrett 8
Emily Murray 27	David Keithley 58
Kevin Searcy 67	Ashley LaRue 69,83*
Barry Coleman 73,84,295	

Public Schs..Principal	Grd	Prgm	Enr/#Cls	SN
Lansberry Elem Sch 400 S Maple St, Trinity 75862 Kelli Robinson	PK-5	T	584 50	81% 936/594-3567 Fax 936/594-2646
Trinity High Sch 500 E Caroline St, Trinity 75862 Eric Kelley	9-12	GTV	359 20	59% 936/594-3560 Fax 936/594-2162
Trinity Middle Sch 500 E Caroline St, Trinity 75862 Brittaney Cassidy	6-8	T	295 20	76% 936/594-2321 Fax 936/594-3041

TYLER COUNTY

TYLER PUBLIC SCHOOLS

- **Chester Ind School Dist** PID: 01057197   936/969-2211
  273 Yellow Jacket Dr, Chester 75936   Fax 936/969-2080

Schools: 2 \ *Teachers:* 18 \ *Students:* 200 \ *Special Ed Students:* 26 \ *College-Bound:* 66% \ *Ethnic:* African American 5%, Hispanic 5%, Caucasian 90% \ *Exp:* $334 (High) \ *Poverty:* 19% \ *Title I:* $52,565 \ *Open-Close:* 08/15 - 05/29 \ *DTBP:* $331 (High) \ 📘

Cory Hines 1,83	Stephanie Williams 2,84
Marty Thompson 3	Amanda Poundes 4
Betty Whitworth 16*	Shelly Wilkinson 58
Shelly Wilkinson 58*	Ray McKnight 67
Michelle Cowan 73	

Public Schs..Principal	Grd	Prgm	Enr/#Cls	SN
Chester Elem Sch 273 Yellow Jacket Dr, Chester 75936 Katie Loughner	PK-5	T	110 8	61% 936/969-2211 Fax 936/969-3079

---

1 Superintendent	8 Curric/Instruct K-12	19 Chief Financial Officer	29 Family/Consumer Science	39 Social Studies K-12	49 English/Lang Arts Elem	59 Special Education Elem	69 Academic Assessment
2 Bus/Finance/Purchasing	9 Curric/Instruct Elem	20 Art K-12	30 Adult Education	40 Social Studies Elem	50 English/Lang Arts Sec	60 Special Education Sec	70 Research/Development
3 Buildings And Grounds	10 Curric/Instruct Sec	21 Art Elem	31 Career/Sch-to-Work K-12	41 Social Studies Sec	51 Reading K-12	61 Foreign/World Lang K-12	71 Public Information
4 Food Service	11 Federal Program	22 Art Sec	32 Career/Sch-to-Work Elem	42 Science K-12	52 Reading Elem	62 Foreign/World Lang Elem	72 Summer School
5 Transportation	12 Title I	23 Music K-12	33 Career/Sch-to-Work Sec	43 Science Elem	53 Reading Sec	63 Foreign/World Lang Sec	73 Instructional Tech
6 Athletic	13 Title V	24 Music Elem	34 Early Childhood Ed	44 Science Sec	54 Remedial Reading K-12	64 Religious Education K-12	74 Inservice Training
7 Health Services	15 Asst Superintendent	25 Music Sec	35 Health/Phys Education	45 Math K-12	55 Remedial Reading Elem	65 Religious Education Elem	75 Marketing/Distributive
	16 Instructional Media Svcs	26 Business Education	36 Guidance Services K-12	46 Math Elem	56 Remedial Reading Sec	66 Religious Education Sec	76 Info Systems
	17 Chief Operations Officer	27 Career & Tech Ed	37 Guidance Services Elem	47 Math Sec	57 Bilingual/ELL	67 School Board President	77 Psychological Assess
	18 Chief Academic Officer	28 Technology Education	38 Guidance Services Sec	48 English/Lang Arts K-12	58 Special Education K-12	68 Teacher Personnel	78 Affirmative Action

Texas School Directory — Tyler County

Chester High Sch	6-12	TV	96	48%	936/969-2211
273 Yellow Jacket Dr, Chester 75936			12		Fax 936/969-3079
Emily Watson					

● **Colmesneil Ind School Dist** PID: 01057226   409/837-5757
610 W Elder St, Colmesneil 75938   Fax 409/837-9107

Schools: 2 \ **Teachers:** 39 \ **Students:** 475 \ **Special Ed Students:** 56 \ **College-Bound:** 49% \ **Ethnic:** African American 3%, Hispanic 4%, Caucasian 93% \ **Exp:** $370 (High) \ **Poverty:** 19% \ **Title I:** $92,278 \ **Open-Close:** 08/14 - 05/29 \ **DTBP:** $335 (High)

Angela Matterson 1		Wonda Ryan 2	
Dana Setwalker 4*		Ramon Follmar 5	
Ross McMurry 6*		Kathy Gobert 16,73,295*	
Curtis Pittman 67		Walter McAlpin 69,88,271,275*	

Public Schs..Principal	Grd	Prgm	Enr/#Cls	SN	
Colmesneil Elem Sch	PK-6	T	267	65%	409/837-5757
610 W Elder St, Colmesneil 75938			14		Fax 409/837-9119
Yvette Carlton					
Colmesneil High Sch	7-12	GTV	208	55%	409/837-2225
610 W Elder St, Colmesneil 75938			8		Fax 409/837-5759
Walter McAlpin					

● **Spurger Ind School Dist** PID: 01057252   409/429-3464
12212 Highway 92 S, Spurger 77660   Fax 409/429-3770

Schools: 2 \ **Teachers:** 35 \ **Students:** 385 \ **Special Ed Students:** 43 \ **LEP Students:** 5 \ **College-Bound:** 85% \ **Ethnic:** Hispanic 8%, Native American: 1%, Caucasian 91% \ **Exp:** $304 (High) \ **Poverty:** 26% \ **Title I:** $125,050 \ **Open-Close:** 08/15 - 05/22 \ **DTBP:** $430 (High)

Morgan Wright 1	Connie Griffith 2
Doug Jenkins 3,5	Leona Callaway 4*
Arlene Robinson 9,69,83*	Joyce Tippett 16*
Buck Hudson 27*	Randall Rose 57*
Patti Tucker 58*	Carroll Hatton 67
Andrea Wilson 73,295	Stefanie Miller 92,271

Public Schs..Principal	Grd	Prgm	Enr/#Cls	SN	
Spurger Elem Sch	PK-5	T	204	67%	409/429-3464
12212 Highway 92 N, Spurger 77660			16		
Jason Drake					
Spurger High Sch	6-12	T	189	58%	409/429-3464
12212 Highway 92 S, Spurger 77660			20		
Stefanie Miller					

● **Warren Ind School Dist** PID: 01057288   409/547-2241
375 FM 3290, Warren 77664   Fax 409/547-3405

Schools: 4 \ **Teachers:** 89 \ **Students:** 1,400 \ **Special Ed Students:** 96 \ **LEP Students:** 10 \ **College-Bound:** 40% \ **Ethnic:** Asian 1%, African American 1%, Hispanic 6%, Native American: 1%, Caucasian 91% \ **Exp:** $422 (High) \ **Poverty:** 17% \ **Title I:** $191,658 \ **Open-Close:** 08/15 - 05/29 \ **DTBP:** $341 (High)

Dr Tammy Boyette 1	Terry Ling 2
Mark Hardy 3,5	Tammy Heriard 4
Jay Buckner 6*	Mike Paddie 8,11,74,83
Dr Steven Cox 8,11,61,296	Carrie Standley 16*
Rex Currie 27*	Paula Chesser 29*
Bridgette Toelr 58,69	Rocky Burks 67
Cheri Stanley 73,295	

Public Schs..Principal	Grd	Prgm	Enr/#Cls	SN	
Fred Elem Sch	PK-5	T	211	65%	409/429-3240
140-County Road 4650, Fred 77616			15		Fax 409/429-3488
Katy Hicks					
Warren Elem Sch	PK-5	T	436	58%	409/547-2247
307 FM 3290 S, Warren 77664			28		Fax 409/547-0146
Robyn Glosson					
Warren High Sch	9-12	V	361	43%	409/547-2243
395 FM 3290 S, Warren 77664			25		Fax 409/547-0214
James Swinney					
Warren Junior High Sch	6-8	T	294	45%	409/547-2246
395 FM 3290 S, Warren 77664			25		Fax 409/547-2740
Kristina Wiedman					

● **Woodville Ind School Dist** PID: 01057331   409/283-3752
505 N Charlton St, Woodville 75979   Fax 409/283-7962

Schools: 4 \ **Teachers:** 107 \ **Students:** 1,300 \ **Special Ed Students:** 181 \ **LEP Students:** 36 \ **College-Bound:** 75% \ **Ethnic:** Asian 1%, African American 23%, Hispanic 8%, Native American: 3%, Caucasian 66% \ **Exp:** $418 (High) \ **Poverty:** 30% \ **Title I:** $556,304 \ **Open-Close:** 08/15 - 05/29 \ **DTBP:** $337 (High)

Lisa Meysembourg 1,57	Cody Jarrott 2,11,15
Johnny McKee 3	Linda Johnson 4
Ronald Brown 5	Karen Ford 11,288,298
Jennifer Dunsom 58	Jimmy Tucker 67
Jeremy Coker 73,76,84,295	Angela Hollingsworth 83,85*
Jason Hicks 88*	Bernard Collins 91

Public Schs..Principal	Grd	Prgm	Enr/#Cls	SN	
Wheat Elem Sch	PK-2	T	382	73%	409/283-2452
306 Kirby Dr, Woodville 75979			20		Fax 409/331-3409
Gina Greaff					
Woodville High Sch	9-12	ATV	344	56%	409/283-3714
700 Eagle Dr, Woodville 75979			63		Fax 409/331-3427
Terry Young					
Woodville Intermediate Sch	3-5	T	294	71%	409/283-2549
401 N Charlton St, Woodville 75979			21		Fax 409/331-3412
Ashley Weatherford					
Woodville Middle Sch	6-8	TV	321	65%	409/283-3714
500 Eagle Dr, Woodville 75979			25		Fax 409/331-3418
Elton Hollingsworth					

TYLER PRIVATE SCHOOLS

Private Schs..Principal	Grd	Prgm	Enr/#Cls	SN	
St Paul's Episcopal Sch	PK-5		28		409/283-7555
1707 W Bluff St, Woodville 75979			3		
Sharon Brown					

---

79 Student Personnel	91 Safety/Security	275 Response To Intervention	298 Grant Writer/Ptnrships	**School Programs**	**Social Media**
80 Driver Ed/Safety	92 Magnet School	277 Remedial Math K-12	750 Chief Innovation Officer	A = Alternative Program	▯ = Facebook
81 Gifted/Talented	93 Parental Involvement	280 Literacy Coach	751 Chief of Staff	G = Adult Classes	
82 Video Services	95 Tech Prep Program	285 STEM	752 Social Emotional Learning	M = Magnet Program	
83 Substance Abuse Prev	97 Chief Infomation Officer	286 Digital Learning		T = Title I Schoolwide	▯ = Twitter
84 Erate	98 Chief Technology Officer	288 Common Core Standards	**Other School Types**	V = Career & Tech Ed Programs	
85 AIDS Education	270 Accountability	294 Character Education	Ⓐ = Alternative School		
88 Alternative/At Risk	271 Migrant Education	295 Network System	Ⓒ = Charter School	New Schools are shaded	
89 Multi-Cultural Curriculum	273 Teacher Mentor	296 Title II Programs	Ⓜ = Magnet School	New Superintendents and Principals are bold	
90 Social Work	274 Before/After Sch	297 Webmaster	Ⓨ = Year-Round School	Personnel with email addresses are underscored	

Upshur County

UPSHUR COUNTY

UPSHUR PUBLIC SCHOOLS

- **Big Sandy Ind School Dist** PID: 01057379   903/636-5287
  401 N Wildcat Dr, Big Sandy 75755   Fax 903/636-5117

  Schools: 3 \ *Teachers:* 73 \ *Students:* 650 \ *Special Ed Students:* 66 \ *LEP Students:* 13 \ *Ethnic:* African American 11%, Hispanic 10%, Caucasian 78% \ *Exp:* $584 (High) \ *Poverty:* 20% \ *Title I:* $237,856 \ *Special Education:* $266,000 \ *Open-Close:* 08/26 - 05/28 \ *DTBP:* $358 (High)

Jay Ratcliff	1,11	Mary Troboy	2
Joan Ford	4	Michael Crews	5
Larry Minter	6*	Susan Williams	7*
Peggy Oden	58,93	Jamey Childress	67
Moriah Phillips	73,76,84,286,295		

Public Schs..Principal	Grd	Prgm	Enr/#Cls	SN	
Big Sandy Elem Sch 401 N Wildcat Dr, Big Sandy 75755 Donna Varnado	PK-5	T	328 35	70%	903/636-5287 Fax 903/636-5311
Big Sandy High Sch 401 N Wildcat Dr, Big Sandy 75755 Kim Stradley	9-12	TV	219 17	48%	903/636-5287 Fax 903/636-5111
Big Sandy Junior High Sch 401 N Wildcat Dr, Big Sandy 75755 Kimberly Stradley	6-8	T	168 10	66%	903/636-5287 Fax 903/636-5111

- **Gilmer Ind School Dist** PID: 01057408   903/841-7400
  500 S Trinity St, Gilmer 75644   Fax 903/843-5279

  Schools: 4 \ *Teachers:* 178 \ *Students:* 2,437 \ *Special Ed Students:* 199 \ *LEP Students:* 178 \ *College-Bound:* 49% \ *Ethnic:* African American 13%, Hispanic 20%, Native American: 1%, Caucasian 65% \ *Exp:* $340 (High) \ *Poverty:* 22% \ *Title I:* $766,230 \ *Special Education:* $279,000 \ *Open-Close:* 08/27 - 06/01 \ *DTBP:* $510 (High) \

Rick Albritton	1	Beverly Grimes	2
Hoby Holder	3	Jerry Davis	3
Roberta Jones	4	Greg Hanlin	5
Matt Turner	6*	Delinda Wall	8,57,83,271
Dawn Harris	11,15,273	Dr Peggy Oden	58
Mark Skinner	67	Jeff Hamilton	71
Rusty Ivey	73		

Public Schs..Principal	Grd	Prgm	Enr/#Cls	SN	
Bruce Junior High Sch 111 Bruce St, Gilmer 75645 Bill Bradshaw	7-8	T	353 25	64%	903/841-7600 Fax 903/843-6108
Gilmer Elem Sch 1625 US Highway 271 N, Gilmer 75644 Kim Kemp	PK-4	T	1,002 30	74%	903/841-7700 Fax 903/843-4754
Gilmer High Sch 850 Buffalo St, Gilmer 75644 John Bowman	9-12	TV	697 60	58%	903/841-7500 Fax 903/843-2171
Gilmer Intermediate Sch 1623 US Highway 271 N, Gilmer 75644 Gina Treadway	5-6	T	389 16	72%	903/841-7800 Fax 903/797-6346

- **Harmony Ind School Dist** PID: 01057458   903/725-5492
  9788 State Highway 154 W, Big Sandy 75755   Fax 903/725-6737

  Schools: 4 \ *Teachers:* 87 \ *Students:* 1,060 \ *Special Ed Students:* 68 \ *LEP Students:* 54 \ *Ethnic:* African American 1%, Hispanic 15%, Caucasian 84% \ *Exp:* $347 (High) \ *Poverty:* 15% \ *Title I:* $164,865 \ *Open-Close:* 08/19 - 05/29 \ *DTBP:* $352 (High)

Dennis Glenn	1,83	Lena Williamson	2
Mike Powell	3	Terry Ward	4
Bo Bohannan	5	Tim Russell	6*
Carolyn Duke	8,11,69,288,296,298	Tabatha Morris	57*
Dr Peggy Oden	58	Jerry Key	67
Tory Cunningham	73,76		

Public Schs..Principal	Grd	Prgm	Enr/#Cls	SN	
Harmony High Sch 9788 State Highway 154 W, Big Sandy 75755 Michael Alphin	9-12	T	322 24	35%	903/725-7270 Fax 903/725-5485
Harmony Irons-Smith Interm Sch 9788 State Highway 154 W, Big Sandy 75755 Diane Chevalier	4-5	T	174 8	49%	903/725-7270 Fax 903/725-5485
Harmony Junior High Sch 9788 State Highway 154 W, Big Sandy 75755 Lonnie Henry	6-8	T	250 24	53%	903/725-5485 Fax 903/725-7270
James E Poole Elem Sch 9788 State Highway 154 W, Big Sandy 75755 Cara Rendon	PK-3	T	329 23	59%	903/725-7270 Fax 903/725-5485

- **New Diana Ind School Dist** PID: 01057484   903/663-8000
  1373 US Highway 259 S, Diana 75640   Fax 903/241-7393

  Schools: 3 \ *Teachers:* 72 \ *Students:* 1,071 \ *Special Ed Students:* 52 \ *LEP Students:* 22 \ *College-Bound:* 68% \ *Ethnic:* African American 7%, Hispanic 12%, Caucasian 80% \ *Exp:* $427 (High) \ *Poverty:* 20% \ *Title I:* $226,252 \ *Special Education:* $99,000 \ *Open-Close:* 08/19 - 05/22 \ *DTBP:* $333 (High) \

Carl Key	1	Melinda Benson	2,71,97
Bruce Jeffery	3*	Toni Druschke	4*
Scott Farler	8,57,58,69,271,274,288	Jeff Hamilton	67
Sharon Wager	73,295*		

Public Schs..Principal	Grd	Prgm	Enr/#Cls	SN	
New Diana High Sch 11826 State Highway 154 E, Diana 75640 Mark Ferrer	9-12	AV	316 23	30%	903/663-8001 Fax 903/663-2200
New Diana Middle Sch 11854 State Highway 154 E, Diana 75640 John Gross	6-8	T	241 12	40%	903/663-8002 Fax 903/663-1812
Robert F Hunt Elem Sch 11150 State Highway 154 E, Diana 75640 Teresa Beckham	PK-5	T	500 25	42%	903/663-8004 Fax 903/663-7375

- **Ore City Ind School Dist** PID: 01057525   903/968-3300
  100 Rebel Rd N, Ore City 75683   Fax 903/968-3797

  Schools: 3 \ *Teachers:* 72 \ *Students:* 950 \ *Special Ed Students:* 93 \ *LEP Students:* 44 \ *Ethnic:* African American 7%, Hispanic 15%, Native American: 1%, Caucasian 78% \ *Exp:* $332 (High) \ *Poverty:* 27% \ *Title I:* $310,596 \ *Special Education:* $140,000 \ *Open-Close:* 08/19 - 05/21 \ *DTBP:* $343 (High) \

Lynn Heflin	1	Talina McElhany	2
Jim West	3,5	Donna Denton	4

---

1 Superintendent	8 Curric/Instruct K-12	19 Chief Financial Officer	29 Family/Consumer Science	39 Social Studies K-12	49 English/Lang Arts Elem	59 Special Education Elem	69 Academic Assessment
2 Bus/Finance/Purchasing	9 Curric/Instruct Elem	20 Art K-12	30 Adult Education	40 Social Studies Elem	50 English/Lang Arts Sec	60 Special Education Sec	70 Research/Development
3 Buildings And Grounds	10 Curric/Instruct Sec	21 Art Elem	31 Career/Sch-to-Work K-12	41 Social Studies Sec	51 Reading K-12	61 Foreign/World Lang K-12	71 Public Information
4 Food Service	11 Federal Program	22 Art Sec	32 Career/Sch-to-Work Elem	42 Science K-12	52 Reading Elem	62 Foreign/World Lang Elem	72 Summer School
5 Transportation	12 Title I	23 Music K-12	33 Career/Sch-to-Work Sec	43 Science Elem	53 Reading Sec	63 Foreign/World Lang Sec	73 Instructional Tech
6 Athletic	13 Title V	24 Music Elem	34 Early Childhood Ed	44 Science Sec	54 Remedial Reading K-12	64 Religious Education K-12	74 Inservice Training
7 Health Services	15 Asst Superintendent	25 Music Sec	35 Health/Phys Education	45 Math K-12	55 Remedial Reading Elem	65 Religious Education Elem	75 Marketing/Distributive
	16 Instructional Media Svcs	26 Business Education	36 Guidance Services K-12	46 Math Elem	56 Remedial Reading Sec	66 Religious Education Sec	76 Info Systems
	17 Chief Operations Officer	27 Career & Tech Ed	37 Guidance Services Elem	47 Math Sec	57 Bilingual/ELL	67 School Board President	77 Psychological Assess
	18 Chief Academic Officer	28 Technology Education	38 Guidance Services Sec	48 English/Lang Arts K-12	58 Special Education K-12	68 Teacher Personnel	78 Affirmative Action

Texas School Directory

Upton County

Ron Bruhmer 6	Mindy Hamilton 7*
Charae Ford 33*	Elise Peterson 37
Lesa Wright 38,285*	Teddy Ott 58,270
Ms Berryman 67	Shelly Draper 68
Zack Thomas 73	Kim Freeman 88*

Public Schs..Principal	Grd	Prgm	Enr/#Cls	SN	
Ore City Elem Sch 1000 US Highway 259 S, Ore City 75683 Chad Miller	PK-5	TV	466 30	76%	903/968-3300 Fax 903/968-6903
Ore City High Sch 100 Rebel Rd N, Ore City 75683 Nathan Heflin	9-12	T	277 20	66%	903/968-3300 Fax 903/968-8726
Ore City Middle Sch 100 Rebel Rd N, Ore City 75683 Beau Vincent	6-8	T	196 12	71%	903/968-3300 Fax 903/968-4446

- **Union Grove Ind School Dist** PID: 01057551 903/845-5509
  11220 Union Grove Rd, Gladewater 75647 Fax 903/845-6178

Schools: 2 \ *Teachers:* 63 \ *Students:* 750 \ *Special Ed Students:* 39 \ *LEP Students:* 11 \ *College-Bound:* 58% \ *Ethnic:* Hispanic 6%, Native American: 1%, Caucasian 93% \ *Exp:* $585 (High) \ *Poverty:* 15% \ *Title I:* $142,049 \ *Open-Close:* 08/15 - 05/22 \ *DTBP:* $553 (High) \ F t

Kelly Moore 1	Laurice Marshall 2,11
Chris Wayt 3,5	Cynthia Vance 4*
Scotty Lament 6	Jodie Mayhan 7
Lynn Whitaker 11,296*	Inga Davis 16,82*
December Wimberley 57,271*	Tracy Webb 58*
Terri Woodfin 68	Kelly Klein 298

Public Schs..Principal	Grd	Prgm	Enr/#Cls	SN	
Union Grove Elem Sch 11220 Union Grove Rd, Gladewater 75647 Lynn Whitaker	PK-6	T	405 25	49%	903/845-3481 Fax 903/845-6270
Union Grove Jr Sr High Sch 11220 Union Grove Rd, Gladewater 75647 Rachel Evers	7-12	T	209 34	37%	903/845-5506 Fax 903/845-3003 F t

- **Union Hill Ind School Dist** PID: 01057587 903/762-2140
  2197 FM 2088, Gilmer 75644 Fax 903/762-6845

Schools: 1 \ *Teachers:* 35 \ *Students:* 400 \ *Special Ed Students:* 18 \ *LEP Students:* 11 \ *College-Bound:* 85% \ *Ethnic:* African American 9%, Hispanic 15%, Caucasian 76% \ *Exp:* $557 (High) \ *Poverty:* 21% \ *Title I:* $84,417 \ *Open-Close:* 08/14 - 05/21 \ *DTBP:* $1,257 (High)

Dr Troy Batts 1,11	Melissa Helton 2
Don Sinquefield 3,5	Hilda Nelms 4*
Dr John Denson 8*	Dr John Denson 8
Sara Batts 10,88,271*	Michel Lain 16*
James Parker 67	Mark Massingill 73*

Public Schs..Principal	Grd	Prgm	Enr/#Cls	SN	
Union Hill Sch 2197 FM 2088, Gilmer 75644 Sara Batts \ Dr John Denson	PK-12	TV	400 28	59%	903/762-2138 Fax 903/762-6742

UPTON COUNTY

UPTON PUBLIC SCHOOLS

- **McCamey Ind School Dist** PID: 01057616 432/652-3666
  112 E 11th St, Mc Camey 79752 Fax 432/652-4219

Schools: 3 \ *Teachers:* 44 \ *Students:* 560 \ *Special Ed Students:* 44 \ *LEP Students:* 27 \ *Ethnic:* African American 2%, Hispanic 72%, Caucasian 26% \ *Exp:* $317 (High) \ *Poverty:* 25% \ *Title I:* $156,877 \ *Open-Close:* 08/19 - 05/22 \ *DTBP:* $329 (High)

Ronnie Golson 1	Gail Molder 2,11,26
Luis Valenzuela 3	Michelle Falcon 4
Dana McWilliams 5,295,297	Michael Woodard 6
Blanca Smith 10,57*	Michael Valencia 10*
Sara Hill 23	Luann Elliott 31,36,69,83,85,88*
Norma Whalley 58	Charollete Jones 67

Public Schs..Principal	Grd	Prgm	Enr/#Cls	SN	
McCamey High Sch 1201 S Burleson, Mc Camey 79752 Michael Valencia	9-12	TV	143 25	48%	432/652-3666 Fax 432/652-4245
McCamey Middle Sch 200 E 11th St, Mc Camey 79752 Blanca Smith	5-8	T	163 16	59%	432/652-3666 Fax 432/652-4246
McCamey Primary Sch 400 E 11th St, Mc Camey 79752 Michelle Schreiner	PK-4	T	250 20	67%	432/652-3666 Fax 432/652-4247

- **Rankin Ind School Dist** PID: 01057654 432/693-2461
  406 W 12th St, Rankin 79778 Fax 432/693-2353

Schools: 2 \ *Teachers:* 31 \ *Students:* 320 \ *Special Ed Students:* 19 \ *LEP Students:* 11 \ *College-Bound:* 75% \ *Ethnic:* Hispanic 44%, Native American: 1%, Caucasian 55% \ *Exp:* $1,419 (High) \ *Poverty:* 10% \ *Title I:* $25,286 \ *Open-Close:* 08/14 - 05/22 \ *DTBP:* $337 (High)

Samuel Wyatt 1	Dawn Wyatt 2
Tracy Clanton 3,5*	Reyna Rodriguez 4
Garret Avalos 6*	Carla Jackson 7*
Elidia Gallardo 11	Jon Bright 58*
Carrie Templeton 60*	Amanda Evridge 67
Michele Ricker 73,295*	Adrian Gallardo 83,88*

Public Schs..Principal	Grd	Prgm	Enr/#Cls	SN	
James D Gossett Elem Sch 511 W 12th St, Rankin 79778 Brad Riker	PK-5	T	169 14	48%	432/693-2455 Fax 432/693-2552
Rankin High Sch 1201 Upton St, Rankin 79778 Adrian Gallardo	7-12	TV	108 20	55%	432/693-2451 Fax 432/693-2453

---

79 Student Personnel	91 Safety/Security	275 Response To Intervention	298 Grant Writer/Ptnrships
80 Driver Ed/Safety	92 Magnet School	277 Remedial Math K-12	750 Chief Innovation Officer
81 Gifted/Talented	93 Parental Involvement	280 Literacy Coach	751 Chief of Staff
82 Video Services	95 Tech Prep Program	285 STEM	752 Social Emotional Learning
83 Substance Abuse Prev	97 Chief Infomation Officer	286 Digital Learning	
84 Erate	98 Chief Technology Officer	288 Common Core Standards	Other School Types
85 AIDS Education	270 Accountability	294 Accountability	Ⓐ = Alternative School
88 Alternative/At Risk	271 Migrant Education	295 Network System	Ⓒ = Charter School
89 Multi-Cultural Curriculum	273 Teacher Mentor	296 Title II Programs	Ⓜ = Magnet School
90 Social Work	274 Before/After Sch	297 Webmaster	Ⓨ = Year-Round School

School Programs
A = Alternative Program
G = Adult Classes
M = Magnet Program
T = Title I Schoolwide
V = Career & Tech Ed Programs

Social Media
F = Facebook
t = Twitter

New Schools are shaded
New Superintendents and Principals are bold
Personnel with email addresses are underscored

TX–377

Uvalde County

Market Data Retrieval

UVALDE COUNTY

UVALDE PUBLIC SCHOOLS

- **Knippa Ind School Dist** PID: 01057692   830/934-2176
  100 Kessler Ln, Knippa 78870   Fax 830/934-2490

  Schools: 1 \ *Teachers:* 31 \ *Students:* 475 \ *Special Ed Students:* 15 \ *LEP Students:* 13 \ *College-Bound:* 100% \ *Ethnic:* Asian 2%, Hispanic 57%, Caucasian 41% \ *Exp:* $393 (High) \ *Poverty:* 46% \ *Title I:* $139,883 \ *Open-Close:* 08/19 - 05/22 \ *DTBP:* $322 (High) \

  Elda Alejandro 1   Melissa Garza 8,12,298
  Ted Sanderlin 67   Joe Cordova 73*

Public Schs..Principal	Grd	Prgm	Enr/#Cls	SN	
Knippa Sch 100 Kessler Ln, Knippa 78870 Melissa Garza	PK-12	T	475 17	30%	830/934-2176 Fax 830/934-2390

- **Sabinal Ind School Dist** PID: 01057733   830/988-2472
  409 W Cullins St, Sabinal 78881   Fax 830/988-7151

  Schools: 2 \ *Teachers:* 38 \ *Students:* 500 \ *Special Ed Students:* 59 \ *LEP Students:* 25 \ *College-Bound:* 72% \ *Ethnic:* Hispanic 79%, Caucasian 20% \ *Exp:* $520 (High) \ *Poverty:* 22% \ *Title I:* $137,717 \ *Open-Close:* 08/26 - 05/21 \ *DTBP:* $341 (High)

  Richard Grill 1   Michael Neuman 2,8,11,36,69,77,91*
  Andy Lopez .... 3,5*   Shea Gilleland 4
  Jason Keller .... 6*   Cecilia Reyes 7*
  Michael Neuman 15   Monica DeLeon 16*
  Michael Casas .... 23*   Beatriz Valenzuela 38*
  Bob Nunley 67   Howard Karre 73,286,295*
  Steve Alvarado 88   Beth Brady 275*

Public Schs..Principal	Grd	Prgm	Enr/#Cls	SN	
Sabinal Elem Sch 900 W Pickford St, Sabinal 78881 Dr Jimmy Gouard	PK-5	T	191 20	67%	830/988-2436 Fax 830/988-7142
Sabinal High Sch 409 W Cullins St, Sabinal 78881 Steve Alvarado	6-12	TV	108 40	71%	830/988-2475 Fax 830/988-7170

- **Utopia Ind School Dist** PID: 01057769   830/966-1928
  258 School St, Utopia 78884   Fax 830/966-6162

  Schools: 1 \ *Teachers:* 21 \ *Students:* 232 \ *Special Ed Students:* 21 \ *LEP Students:* 14 \ *College-Bound:* 70% \ *Ethnic:* African American 1%, Hispanic 21%, Caucasian 77% \ *Exp:* $330 (High) \ *Poverty:* 24% \ *Title I:* $50,600 \ *Open-Close:* 08/19 - 05/15 \ *DTBP:* $358 (High)

  Jessy Milum 1,288   Kathy Burns 2,12
  Marsha Sheedy .... 4*   Stacey Keeney 6*
  Patti McCaleb .... 7*   Ashely Kay 8,74,271,274*
  Theresa Loman .... 16*   Cammie Morgan 36,69,79,83,88,270*
  Gerry Gebhard .... 57*   Carol Calk 58*
  Steve Darden 67   Joan Saldana 73,76*

Public Schs..Principal	Grd	Prgm	Enr/#Cls	SN	
Utopia Sch 258 School St, Utopia 78884 Bryan Hernandez	PK-12	TV	232 30	43%	830/966-3339

- **Uvalde Cons Ind School Dist** PID: 01057795   830/278-6655
  1000 N Getty St, Uvalde 78801   Fax 830/591-4909

  Schools: 7 \ *Teachers:* 326 \ *Students:* 4,221 \ *Special Ed Students:* 511 \ *LEP Students:* 287 \ *College-Bound:* 90% \ *Ethnic:* Hispanic 90%, Caucasian 10% \ *Exp:* $400 (High) \ *Poverty:* 33% \ *Title I:* $2,359,973 \ *Special Education:* $1,107,000 \ *Open-Close:* 08/19 - 05/22 \ *DTBP:* $158 (High)

  Dr Hal Harrell 1   Jimmy Rutherford 3
  Aurora Barrera 4   Russell Lee 5
  Traci Dillard .... 7*   Michael Rodriguez 8,15,285
  Dr Sandra Zuniga 10   Beth Reavis 11,15,296
  Mario Feron 57   Victor Baron 58
  Javier Flores 67   Anne Marie Espinoza 71
  Cash Keith 73

Public Schs..Principal	Grd	Prgm	Enr/#Cls	SN	
Anthon Elem Sch 224 N Benson Rd, Uvalde 78801 Bryan Perez	1-2	T	678 32	85%	830/591-2988 Fax 830/591-2993
Batesville Elem Sch 496 Garden St, Batesville 78829 Hector Lopez	PK-6	T	118 14	94%	830/376-4221 Fax 830/376-4223
Dalton Early Childhood Center 600 N 4th St, Uvalde 78801 Abraham Contreras	PK-K	T	589 36	81%	830/591-4933 Fax 830/591-4936
Flores Elem Sch 901 N Getty St, Uvalde 78801 Michelle Rodriguez	5-6		603 18		830/591-2976 Fax 830/591-2987
Morales Junior High Sch 615 Studer St, Uvalde 78801 Isidro Escamilla	7-8	TV	668 52	79%	830/591-2980 Fax 830/591-2975
Robb Elem Sch 715 Old Carrizo Rd, Uvalde 78801 Becky Reinhardt	3-4	T	668 27	82%	830/591-4947 Fax 830/591-4937
Uvalde High Sch 1 Coyote Trl, Uvalde 78801 Elizabeth Sandoval	9-12	TV	1,250	71%	830/591-2950 Fax 830/591-2961

UVALDE CATHOLIC SCHOOLS

- **Archdiocese San Antonio Ed Off** PID: 00999724
  Listing includes only schools located in this county. See District Index for location of Diocesan Offices.

Catholic Schs..Principal	Grd	Prgm	Enr/#Cls	SN	
Sacred Heart Sch 401 W Leona St, Uvalde 78801 Janice Estrada	PK-6		80 8		830/278-2661 Fax 830/279-0634

1	Superintendent	8	Curric/Instruct K-12	19	Chief Financial Officer	29	Family/Consumer Science	39	Social Studies K-12	49	English/Lang Arts Elem	59	Special Education Elem	69	Academic Assessment
2	Bus/Finance/Purchasing	9	Curric/Instruct Elem	20	Art K-12	30	Adult Education	40	Social Studies Elem	50	English/Lang Arts Sec	60	Special Education Sec	70	Research/Development
3	Buildings And Grounds	10	Curric/Instruct Sec	21	Art Elem	31	Career/Sch-to-Work K-12	41	Social Studies Sec	51	Reading K-12	61	Foreign/World Lang K-12	71	Public Information
4	Food Service	11	Federal Program	22	Art Sec	32	Career/Sch-to-Work Elem	42	Science K-12	52	Reading Elem	62	Foreign/World Lang Elem	72	Summer School
5	Transportation	12	Title I	23	Music K-12	33	Career/Sch-to-Work Sec	43	Science Elem	53	Reading Sec	63	Foreign/World Lang Sec	73	Instructional Tech
6	Athletic	13	Title V	24	Music Elem	34	Early Childhood Ed	44	Science Sec	54	Remedial Reading K-12	64	Religious Education K-12	74	Inservice Training
7	Health Services	14	Instructional Media Svcs	25	Music Sec	35	Health/Phys Education	45	Math K-12	55	Remedial Reading Elem	65	Religious Education Elem	75	Marketing/Distributive
		15	Asst Superintendent	26	Business Education	36	Guidance Services K-12	46	Math Elem	56	Remedial Reading Sec	66	Religious Education Sec	76	Info Systems
		16	Chief Operations Officer	27	Career & Tech Ed	37	Guidance Services Elem	47	Math Sec	57	Bilingual/ELL	67	School Board President	77	Psychological Assess
		17	Chief Academic Officer	28	Technology Education	38	Guidance Services Sec	48	English/Lang Arts K-12	58	Special Education K-12	68	Teacher Personnel	78	Affirmative Action

Texas School Directory — Val Verde County

UVALDE PRIVATE SCHOOLS

Private Schs..Principal	Grd	Prgm	Enr/#Cls	SN	
St Philip's Episcopal Sch 343 N Getty St, Uvalde 78801 Jean Chisum	PK-3		65 7		830/278-1350 Fax 830/278-2093

VAL VERDE COUNTY

VAL VERDE PUBLIC SCHOOLS

• **Comstock Ind School Dist** PID: 01057898   432/292-4444
101 Sanderson St, Comstock 78837   Fax 432/292-4436

Schools: 1 \ **Teachers:** 20 \ **Students:** 227 \
Special Ed Students: 20 \ **LEP Students:** 5 \ **College-Bound:** 100% \
Ethnic: Asian 1%, African American 1%, Hispanic 45%, Native American: 1%, Caucasian 53% \ **Exp:** $500 (High) \ **Poverty:** 34% \ **Title I:** $37,027 \
Special Education: $28,000 \ **Open-Close:** 08/14 - 05/20 \ **DTBP:** $304 (High) \ f t

Orlie Wolfenbarger 1,11,83	Tina Meza 2	
Queta Vela 4*	Rita Sanchez 4,58,69,73*	
Laura Parker 6,8,69,74,273,274	Valarie Sanchez 12	
Karin Greene 16*	Bill Zuberbueler 67	

Public Schs..Principal	Grd	Prgm	Enr/#Cls	SN	
Comstock Sch 101 Sanderson St, Comstock 78837 Laura Parker	K-12	T	227 18	29%	432/292-4444

• **San Felipe-Del Rio Cons Ind SD** PID: 01057941   830/778-4000
315 Griner St, Del Rio 78840   Fax 830/774-9840

Schools: 12 \ **Teachers:** 637 \ **Students:** 10,472 \ **Special Ed Students:** 901 \ **LEP Students:** 1,738 \ **Ethnic:** African American 1%, Hispanic 93%, Caucasian 5% \ **Exp:** $361 (High) \ **Poverty:** 30% \ **Title I:** $3,786,249 \
Special Education: $1,825,000 \ **Open-Close:** 08/19 - 05/22 \ **DTBP:** $172 (High) \ f t

Carlos Rios 1	Henry Arredondo 2,19
Ric Smith 6	Aida Gomez 8
Waymond Meza 67	Aidee Garcia 68
Leslie Hayenga 73,286	Michelle Gonzalez 280
Gilbert Vazquez 295	

Public Schs..Principal	Grd	Prgm	Enr/#Cls	SN	
Buena Vista Elem Sch 100 Echo Valley Dr, Del Rio 78840 Jennifer Sutton	K-5	T	670 34	50%	830/778-4600 Fax 830/774-9875
Del Rio Freshman Sch 90 Memorial Dr, Del Rio 78840 Patricia Rodriguez	9-9	V	819		830/778-4400 Fax 830/774-9873
Del Rio High Sch 100 Memorial Dr, Del Rio 78840 Jose Perez	10-12	ATV	2,134 100	68%	830/778-4300 Fax 830/774-9320
Del Rio Middle Sch 720 E De La Rosa St, Del Rio 78840 Sergio Jimenez	7-8	TV	1,545	75%	830/778-4500 Fax 830/778-4912
Dr Fermin Calderon Elem Sch Highway 90 E, Del Rio 78840 Jane Villarreal	K-5	T	650 38	89%	830/778-4620 Fax 830/774-9975
Dr Lonnie Green Elem Sch 905 W Cantu Rd, Del Rio 78840 Cheryl Pond	PK-5	T	795 60	74%	830/778-4750 Fax 830/774-9532
Garfield Elem Sch 300 W Martin St, Del Rio 78840 Denise Rubio	K-5	T	717 46	90%	830/778-4700 Fax 830/774-9928
Irene C Cardwell Elem Sch 1009 Avenue J, Del Rio 78840 Rufina Adams	PK-PK	T	531 32	94%	830/778-4650 Fax 830/774-9855
Lamar Elem Sch 301 Waters Ave, Del Rio 78840 Maryvel Flores	K-5	T	575 52	88%	830/778-4730 Fax 830/774-9493
North Heights Elem Sch 2003 N Main St, Del Rio 78840 Maytte Soliz	K-5	T	724 22	79%	830/778-4777 Fax 830/778-4772
Ruben Chavira Elem Sch 2253 S US Hwy 277, Del Rio 78840 Maria Correa	K-5	T	541 40	81%	830/778-4660 Fax 830/778-4921
San Felipe Memorial Middle Sch 1207 W Garza St, Del Rio 78840 Celia Zuniga-Barrera	6-6	T	771 35	79%	830/778-4560 Fax 830/778-4920

VAL VERDE CATHOLIC SCHOOLS

• **Archdiocese San Antonio Ed Off** PID: 00999724
Listing includes only schools located in this county. See District Index for location of Diocesan Offices.

Catholic Schs..Principal	Grd	Prgm	Enr/#Cls	SN	
Sacred Heart Sch 209 E Greenwood St, Del Rio 78840 Aracely Faz	PK-8		266 16		830/775-3274 Fax 830/774-2836

VAL VERDE PRIVATE SCHOOLS

Private Schs..Principal	Grd	Prgm	Enr/#Cls	SN	
Bible Way Christian Academy 409 E Cortinas St, Del Rio 78840 Cynthia McCrea	PK-8		200		830/775-9921 Fax 830/775-2475
St James Episcopal Sch 206 W Greenwood St, Del Rio 78840 Kate Delosontas	PK-5		147 18		830/775-9911 Fax 830/488-6228

---

79 Student Personnel	91 Safety/Security	275 Response To Intervention	298 Grant Writer/Ptnrships
80 Driver Ed/Safety	92 Magnet School	277 Remedial Math K-12	750 Chief Innovation Officer
81 Gifted/Talented	93 Parental Involvement	280 Literacy Coach	751 Chief of Staff
82 Video Services	95 Tech Prep Program	285 STEM	752 Social Emotional Learning
83 Substance Abuse Prev	97 Chief Information Officer	286 Digital Learning	
84 Erate	98 Chief Technology Officer	288 Common Core Standards	**Other School Types**
85 AIDS Education	270 Character Education	294 Accountability	Ⓐ = Alternative School
88 Alternative/At Risk	271 Migrant Education	295 Network System	Ⓒ = Charter School
89 Multi-Cultural Curriculum	273 Teacher Mentor	296 Title II Programs	Ⓜ = Magnet School
90 Social Work	274 Before/After Sch	297 Webmaster	Ⓨ = Year-Round School

School Programs
A = Alternative Program
G = Adult Classes
M = Magnet Program
T = Title I Schoolwide
V = Career & Tech Ed Programs

Social Media
f = Facebook
t = Twitter

New Schools are shaded
New Superintendents and Principals are bold
Personnel with email addresses are underscored

TX—379

Van Zandt County

VAN ZANDT COUNTY

VAN ZANDT PUBLIC SCHOOLS

- **Canton Ind School Dist** PID: 01058086 903/567-4179
  1045 S Buffalo St, Canton 75103 Fax 903/567-2370

Schools: 4 \ *Teachers:* 145 \ *Students:* 2,300 \ *Special Ed Students:* 157 \ *LEP Students:* 68 \ *College-Bound:* 63% \ *Ethnic:* Asian 1%, African American 2%, Hispanic 12%, Native American: 1%, Caucasian 83% \ *Exp:* $297 (Med) \ *Poverty:* 10% \ *Title I:* $199,852 \ *Special Education:* $390,000 \ *Open-Close:* 08/19 - 05/22 \ *DTBP:* $344 (High)

Name	Code	Name	Code
Jim Dunlap	1	Denise Stone	2,84
Thomas Stewart	3	Christy McClelen	4
Dawn Loftin	5	Robert Ivey	6*
Sunday Elerson	7	Brenda Sanford	8,11,69
Kristin Rose	16,82*	Christie Guy	57*
Daphne Thompson	58	Kenith Pruitt	67
Stan Jontra	73,295*	Kari Webster	76,79

Public Schs..Principal	Grd	Prgm	Enr/#Cls	SN	
Canton Elem Sch 1163 S Buffalo St, Canton 75103 Kelly Lamar	PK-2	T	548 30	50%	903/567-6521 Fax 903/567-5373
Canton High Sch 1110 W Highway 243, Canton 75103 Dusty Spencer	9-12		627 60	27%	903/567-6561 Fax 903/567-6562
Canton Intermediate Sch 1190 W Highway 243, Canton 75103 Angela McLeod	3-5	T	519 35	44%	903/567-6418 Fax 903/567-2956
Canton Junior High Sch 1115 S Buffalo St, Canton 75103 Wes Rhoten	6-8	T	490 30	38%	903/567-4329 Fax 903/567-1298

- **Edgewood Ind School Dist** PID: 01058115 903/896-4332
  804 E Pine St, Edgewood 75117 Fax 903/896-4306

Schools: 4 \ *Teachers:* 76 \ *Students:* 975 \ *Special Ed Students:* 109 \ *LEP Students:* 21 \ *College-Bound:* 42% \ *Ethnic:* African American 4%, Hispanic 10%, Caucasian 86% \ *Exp:* $368 (High) \ *Poverty:* 14% \ *Title I:* $143,778 \ *Special Education:* $11,000 \ *Open-Close:* 08/21 - 05/22 \ *DTBP:* $330 (High) \

Name	Code	Name	Code
Dr Eduardo Hernandez	1	Sharon Jones	2
William Thornton	3,5	Jay Jameson	6*
Kathy Harper	7	Kristin Prater	8,69,88*
Kristin Prater	11,83,288	Meggie Erwin	36*
Nikki Tyndell	57*	Emily Sauceda	58
Roy Soto	67	Faye McBride	68
Lori Robert	73*		

Public Schs..Principal	Grd	Prgm	Enr/#Cls	SN	
Edgewood Elem Sch 804 E Pine St, Edgewood 75117 Kristi Jones	PK-2	T	227 11	50%	903/896-4332
Edgewood High Sch 804 E Pine St, Edgewood 75117 Mark Kellogg	9-12	T	276 35	42%	903/896-4856 Fax 903/896-1050
Edgewood Intermediate Sch 804 E Pine St, Edgewood 75117 Shannon Orsborn	3-5	T	213 21	41%	903/896-2134
Edgewood Middle Sch 804 E Pine St, Edgewood 75117 Kassi Mays	6-8	T	272 15	48%	903/896-1530 Fax 903/896-7349

- **Fruitvale Ind School Dist** PID: 01058141 903/896-1191
  244 Vz County Road 1910, Fruitvale 75127 Fax 903/896-1011

Schools: 3 \ *Teachers:* 32 \ *Students:* 460 \ *Special Ed Students:* 36 \ *LEP Students:* 13 \ *College-Bound:* 49% \ *Ethnic:* Asian 1%, African American 1%, Hispanic 10%, Native American: 1%, Caucasian 88% \ *Exp:* $559 (High) \ *Poverty:* 16% \ *Title I:* $63,255 \ *Special Education:* $127,000 \ *Open-Close:* 08/19 - 05/22 \ *DTBP:* $350 (High)

Name	Code	Name	Code
Rebecca Bain	1	Susan McCann	2,19,73,298
Wallie Kroontje	3*	Angela Clark	8,11,89,296*
Terry Furrh	57*	Linda Eddy	58
Heath Yates	67	Amanda Masterson	69,85,88,270*
Zach Masterson	93*	Randy Mills	98,295*
Charles Hartford	285		

Public Schs..Principal	Grd	Prgm	Enr/#Cls	SN	
Fruitvale Junior High Sch 141 Vz County Road 1901, Fruitvale 75127 Charles Harford	6-8	T	90 19	66%	903/896-4363 Fax 903/896-4216
Fruitvale Senior High Sch 141 Vz County Road 1901, Fruitvale 75127 Charles Harford	9-12	GTV	116 15	47%	903/896-4363 Fax 903/896-4216
Hallie Randall Elem Sch 131 Vz County Road 1901, Fruitvale 75127 Zach Masterson	PK-5	T	244 15	75%	903/896-4466 Fax 903/896-4800

- **Grand Saline Ind School Dist** PID: 01058165 903/962-7546
  400 Stadium Dr, Grand Saline 75140 Fax 903/962-7464

Schools: 4 \ *Teachers:* 93 \ *Students:* 1,100 \ *Special Ed Students:* 104 \ *LEP Students:* 111 \ *College-Bound:* 5% \ *Ethnic:* Hispanic 30%, Caucasian 69% \ *Exp:* $287 (Med) \ *Poverty:* 23% \ *Title I:* $390,494 \ *Special Education:* $5,000 \ *Open-Close:* 08/26 - 05/22 \ *DTBP:* $354 (High)

Name	Code	Name	Code
Micha Lewis	1	Laura Griffith	2
Pat Odonnell	3,5,91	Patricia Vaughn	4
Michael Ridge	6*	Debby Morse	8,11,57,73,286,288,296,298
Robin Goff	31,274*	Kim Brewington	58
Jeramiah Carns	67	Lori Hooton	82*

Public Schs..Principal	Grd	Prgm	Enr/#Cls	SN	
Grand Saline Elem Sch 405 Stadium Dr, Grand Saline 75140 Lori Hooton	PK-2	T	319 15	74%	903/962-7526 Fax 903/962-7438
Grand Saline High Sch 500 Stadium Dr, Grand Saline 75140 Ricky LaPrade	9-12	ATV	316 20	51%	903/962-7533 Fax 903/962-7482
Grand Saline Intermediate Sch 200 Stadium Dr, Grand Saline 75140 Tina Core	3-5	T	236 25	67%	903/962-5515 Fax 903/962-3783
Grand Saline Middle Sch 400 Stadium Dr, Grand Saline 75140 Leland Hand	6-8	TV	221 20	60%	903/962-7537 Fax 903/962-7474

Texas School Directory

Victoria County

- **Martin's Mill Ind Sch Dist** PID: 01058191 903/479-3872
  301 FM 1861, Ben Wheeler 75754 Fax 903/479-3711

Schools: 1 \ *Teachers:* 45 \ *Students:* 230 \ *Special Ed Students:* 52 \ *LEP Students:* 40 \ *College-Bound:* 75% \ *Ethnic:* African American 3%, Hispanic 17%, Caucasian 79% \ *Exp:* $966 (High) \ *Poverty:* 27% \ *Title I:* $186,835 \ *Special Education:* $79,000 \ *Open-Close:* 08/21 - 05/28 \ *DTBP:* $357 (High)

James Oliver 1	Michelle Butcher 2*
Gary Gordon 3,5	Tina Morse 4*
Jake Bell 6*	Rachel Martin 8,16,73,82*
Suzette Stringer 8,16,73,286*	Tina Stringer 9,11,88,296,298*
Robin Gandy 36,57,69,83,270*	Casey Swain 58*
Dan Morrow 67	Casey Swain 77
Amber McLemore 85*	

Public Schs..Principal	Grd	Prgm	Enr/#Cls	SN	
Martin's Mill Sch 301 FM 1861, Ben Wheeler 75754 Suzette Stringer	PK-12	ATV	230 35	34%	903/479-3234 Fax 903/479-3486

- **Van Ind School Dist** PID: 01058232 903/963-8713
  549 E Texas St, Van 75790 Fax 903/963-8797

Schools: 5 \ *Teachers:* 149 \ *Students:* 2,400 \ *Special Ed Students:* 248 \ *LEP Students:* 139 \ *Ethnic:* African American 3%, Hispanic 21%, Native American: 1%, Caucasian 76% \ *Exp:* $548 (High) \ *Poverty:* 16% \ *Title I:* $499,653 \ *Special Education:* $386,000 \ *Open-Close:* 08/22 - 05/22 \ *DTBP:* $363 (High) \

Don Dunn 1	Danny Morrow 2,3,19,76
Jared Moffatt 6	Dr Donna Wallace 8,54,69,288,294,296
Richard Pride 11,58	Karla Rainey 27*
Scott Thomas 67	Jason Johnson 73
Thomas Robertson 80	Glenn Hervieux 84
Thomas Robertson 91*	Randy Stancill 295

Public Schs..Principal	Grd	Prgm	Enr/#Cls	SN	
J E Rhodes Elem Sch 250 N Pecan St, Van 75790 Jonnie Smith	PK-1	T	389 40	62%	903/963-8386 Fax 903/963-5586
Van High Sch 985 N Maple, Van 75790 Jeffery Hutchins	9-12	TV	807 50	44%	903/963-8623 Fax 903/963-5591
Van Intermediate Sch 349 E Texas, Van 75790 Marty Moore	2-3	T	353	52%	903/963-8331 Fax 903/963-5582
Van Junior High Sch 630 S Oak St, Van 75790 Jeremy Peterson	7-8	T	352 33	48%	903/963-8321 Fax 903/963-3277
Van Middle Sch 14300 State Hwy 110, Van 75790 Shelby Davidson	4-6	T	523	52%	903/963-1461 Fax 903/963-1472

- **Wills Point Ind School Dist** PID: 01058270 903/873-3161
  338 W North Commerce St, Wills Point 75169 Fax 903/873-2462

Schools: 5 \ *Teachers:* 181 \ *Students:* 2,415 \ *Special Ed Students:* 257 \ *LEP Students:* 175 \ *College-Bound:* 43% \ *Ethnic:* African American 6%, Hispanic 24%, Native American: 1%, Caucasian 68% \ *Exp:* $245 (Med) \ *Poverty:* 20% \ *Title I:* $626,654 \ *Special Education:* $433,000 \ *Open-Close:* 08/14 - 05/22 \ *DTBP:* $158 (High) \

Scott Caloss 1	Cheree Ivy 2
Mike Williams 3	Susan Pace 4
Brian Stokes 5	Greg Cranfill 6*
Tammi Lide 7*	Barbi McMath 8,15,285,286,288,294,298
Kendrea Entrop 11,16,58	Jeff Russell 15
Melanie Mullin 16,73	George Wilcoxson 67
Nancy Morris 73	

Public Schs..Principal	Grd	Prgm	Enr/#Cls	SN	
Earnest O Woods Interm Sch 307 Wingo Way, Wills Point 75169 David Brown	2-4	T	534 30	72%	903/873-5100 Fax 903/873-3134
Wills Point High Sch 1800 W South Commerce St, Wills Point 75169 Jeffrey Russell	9-12	TV	683 50	56%	903/873-5100 Fax 903/873-6008
Wills Point Junior High Sch 200 Tiger Dr, Wills Point 75169 Casey Cochran	7-8	T	350 35	58%	903/873-5100 Fax 903/873-4873
Wills Point Middle Sch 101 School St, Wills Point 75169 Kimberly Calvery	5-6	T	397 26	65%	903/873-5100 Fax 903/873-2465
Wills Point Primary Sch 447 Terrace Dr, Wills Point 75169 Kimberly Cole-White	PK-1	T	451 25	78%	903/873-5100 Fax 903/873-3051

VAN ZANDT PRIVATE SCHOOLS

Private Schs..Principal	Grd	Prgm	Enr/#Cls	SN	
New Frontiers Christian Acad 24385 Interstate 20, Wills Point 75169 Dawn Perez	K-12		37		903/873-2440

VICTORIA COUNTY

VICTORIA PUBLIC SCHOOLS

- **Bloomington Ind School Dist** PID: 01058311 361/333-8016
  2875 FM 616, Bloomington 77951 Fax 361/333-8026

Schools: 4 \ *Teachers:* 64 \ *Students:* 900 \ *Special Ed Students:* 115 \ *LEP Students:* 144 \ *Ethnic:* African American 4%, Hispanic 88%, Caucasian 8% \ *Exp:* $959 (High) \ *Poverty:* 27% \ *Title I:* $332,933 \ *Open-Close:* 08/14 - 05/21 \ *DTBP:* $345 (High)

Mark Anglin 1	Misty Brasfield 2,5,11,15,84
Jeraldo Diaz 3,91	Gary Hatter 4*
Chris Horn 6*	Sylvia Hernandez 8*
Dora Hernandez 58*	Deloris White 67

Public Schs..Principal	Grd	Prgm	Enr/#Cls	SN	
Bloomington Elem Sch 200 N Leonard St, Bloomington 77951 Carl Frisch	2-5	T	264 32	85%	361/333-8003 Fax 361/333-8007
Bloomington Middle Sch 2875 FM 616, Bloomington 77951 Lou Torres	6-8	TV	195 12	88%	361/333-8008 Fax 361/333-8010
Bloomington Senior High Sch 2781 FM 616, Bloomington 77951 Lina Moore	9-12	ATV	244 25	80%	361/333-8011 Fax 361/333-8015

---

79 Student Personnel	91 Safety/Security	275 Response To Intervention	298 Grant Writer/Ptnrships	**School Programs**	**Social Media**
80 Driver Ed/Safety	92 Magnet School	277 Remedial Math K-12	750 Chief Innovation Officer	A = Alternative Program	
81 Gifted/Talented	93 Parental Involvement	280 Literacy Coach	751 Chief of Staff	G = Adult Classes	= Facebook
82 Video Services	95 Tech Prep Program	285 STEM	752 Social Emotional Learning	M = Magnet Program	
83 Substance Abuse Prev	97 Chief Infomation Officer	286 Digital Learning		T = Title I Schoolwide	= Twitter
84 Erate	98 Chief Technology Officer	288 Common Core Standards	**Other School Types**	V = Career & Tech Ed Programs	
85 AIDS Education	270 Character Education	294 Accountability	Ⓐ = Alternative School		
88 Alternative/At Risk	271 Migrant Education	295 Network System	Ⓒ = Charter School	New Schools are shaded	
89 Multi-Cultural Curriculum	273 Teacher Mentor	296 Title II Programs	Ⓜ = Magnet School	New Superintendents and Principals are bold	
90 Social Work	274 Before/After Sch	297 Webmaster	Ⓨ = Year-Round School	Personnel with email addresses are underscored	

TX-381

Victoria County

Market Data Retrieval

Placedo Elem Sch 167 N William St, Placedo 77977 Lou Torres	PK-1	T	164 12	89%	361/333-8000 Fax 361/333-8002

- **Nursery ISD School Dist** PID: 01058414   361/575-6882
  13254 Nursery Dr, Victoria 77904   Fax 361/576-9212

> **Schools:** 1 \ **Teachers:** 11 \ **Students:** 120 \ **Special Ed Students:** 12
> \ **LEP Students:** 4 \ **Ethnic:** African American 5%, Hispanic 44%,
> Caucasian 51% \ **Exp:** $295 (Med) \ **Poverty:** 17% \ **Title I:** $52,926 \
> **Open-Close:** 08/14 - 05/21 \ **DTBP:** $350 (High)

Chris Ulcak 1,11,73,288   Lisa Sauceda 4*
Jennifer Thibodeaux .... 6*   Jennifer Southern 12*
Neal Stevenson 67

Public Schs..Principal	Grd	Prgm	Enr/#Cls	SN	
Nursery Elem Sch 13254 Nursery Drive, Victoria 77904 Chris Ulcak	PK-5	T	120 8	65%	361/575-6882

- **Victoria Ind School Dist** PID: 01058440   361/576-3131
  102 Profit Dr, Victoria 77901   Fax 361/788-9643

> **Schools:** 23 \ **Teachers:** 1,023 \ **Students:** 13,900 \
> **Special Ed Students:** 1,465 \ **LEP Students:** 767 \ **College-Bound:** 60%
> \ **Ethnic:** Asian 1%, African American 7%, Hispanic 66%, Caucasian
> 26% \ **Exp:** $269 (Med) \ **Poverty:** 21% \ **Title I:** $4,283,784 \
> **Special Education:** $3,476,000 \ **Bilingual Education:** $84,000 \
> **Open-Close:** 08/15 - 05/28 \ **DTBP:** $185 (High)

Dr Quintin Shepherd 1   Frances Koch 2,15
John Urbano 3,91   Dana Bigham 4
Angie Sherman 5   Bobby Jackwright 6
Murphey Stuart 7   Dr Susanne Carroll 8,15,74
Tammy Sestak 9,93   Sherri Hathaway 10
Michelle Yates 11   Tammy Nobles 13,79
Dr Gregory Bonewald 15,68   Lisa Blundell 15
Linda Dueser 16,82,286   Jason Levin 20,23
Carol Dippel 34   Kim Motley 36
Teralee Barnett 40   Mica Hernandez 41
Susan Johnson 47   Ashlee Dornak 49
Sarah Bradley 50   Alejandro Mojica 57,89,271
Kelli Cotton .... 58,77*   Tammy Keeling 67
Carla Schaefer 69,294   Shawna Currie 71
Samantha Schulte 73,76,295   Alyese Tate 81
Roberto Gonzalez .... 83*   Melanie Rodriguez 297

Public Schs..Principal	Grd	Prgm	Enr/#Cls	SN	
Aloe Elem Sch 62 Chaparral Rd, Victoria 77905 Kristina Hurley	PK-5	T	492 27	58%	361/788-9509 Fax 361/788-9662
Career & Technology Institute 104 Profit Dr, Victoria 77901 Melissa Correll	Voc		200 9		361/788-9288 Fax 361/788-9656
Chandler Elem Sch 5105 Guy Grant Rd, Victoria 77904 Melanie Steed	PK-5	T	592 27	68%	361/788-9587 Fax 361/788-9590
ⓨ Crain Elem Sch 2706 N Azalea St, Victoria 77901 Renee Harper	PK-5	MT	381 50	86%	361/573-7453 Fax 361/788-9603
DeLeon Elem Sch 1002 Santa Barbara St, Victoria 77904 Selina Reyna	PK-5	T	567 25	47%	361/788-9553 Fax 361/788-9634
ⓜ Dudley Magnet Sch 3307 Callis St, Victoria 77901 Steven Carroll	PK-5	T	473 27	84%	361/788-9517 Fax 361/788-9523
Ella Schorlemmer Elem Sch 2564 Mallette St, Victoria 77904 Elizabeth Chandler	PK-5	T	537	50%	361/788-2860 Fax 361/788-9283
Harold Cade Middle Sch 611 Tropical Dr, Victoria 77904 Jill Lau	6-8	T	865	47%	361/788-2840 Fax 361/788-2886
ⓨ Hopkins Elem Sch 110 Hopkins St, Victoria 77901 Leandra Hill	PK-5	MT	489 30	95%	361/788-9527 Fax 361/788-9635
Howell Middle Sch 2502 Fannin Dr, Victoria 77901 Jo Jones	6-8	T	900 64	57%	361/578-1561 Fax 361/788-9547
Ⓐ Liberty Campus 1110 Sam Houston Dr, Victoria 77901 Sheila Garcia	9-12	T	228 10	63%	361/788-9650 Fax 361/788-9649
Mission Valley Elem Sch 12063 FM 236, Victoria 77905 Eric Amsler	PK-5	T	251 12	44%	361/788-9514 Fax 361/788-9689
ⓨ O'Connor Elem Sch 3402 Bobolink St, Victoria 77901 Vickie Dunseth	PK-5	MT	378 33	85%	361/788-9572 Fax 361/788-9575
Patti Welder Middle Sch 1604 E North St, Victoria 77901 Denise Canchola	6-8	T	609 80	80%	361/575-4553 Fax 361/788-9629
Rowland Elem Sch 2706 Leary Ln, Victoria 77901 Tammy Garza	PK-5	T	471 27	86%	361/788-9549 Fax 361/788-9902
Shields Elem Sch 3400 Bluebonnet St, Victoria 77901 Kelly Gabrysch	PK-5	T	466 42	83%	361/788-9593 Fax 361/788-9691
Smith Elem Sch 2901 Erwin Ave, Victoria 77901 Michelle Graves	PK-5	T	531 35	77%	361/788-9605 Fax 361/788-9688
Stroman Middle Sch 3002 E North St, Victoria 77901 Dawn Maroney	6-8	T	729	85%	361/578-2711 Fax 361/788-9800
Torres Elem Sch 4208 Lone Tree Rd, Victoria 77901 Crystal Rice	PK-5	T	533	84%	361/788-2850 Fax 361/788-9278
Vickers Elem Sch 708 Glascow St, Victoria 77904 Troy White	PK-5	T	577 20	40%	361/788-9579 Fax 361/788-9663
Victoria East High Sch 4103 E Mockingbird Ln, Victoria 77904 Clark Motley	9-12	TV	1,879 100	59%	361/788-2820 Fax 361/788-2826
Ⓐ Victoria Juv Justice Center ⓨ 97 Foster Field Dr, Victoria 77904 Christine Martin	6-12	M	35	93%	361/575-0399
Victoria West High Sch 307 Tropical Dr, Victoria 77904 Debbie Crick	9-12	TV	1,735	51%	361/788-2830 Fax 361/788-2836

VICTORIA CATHOLIC SCHOOLS

- **Diocese of Victoria Ed Office** PID: 02181727   361/573-0828
  1505 E Mesquite Ln, Victoria 77901   Fax 361/573-5725

> **Schools:** 13 \ **Students:** 2,827

Listing includes only schools located in this county. See District Index for location of Diocesan Offices.

Dr John Quary 1   Tony Martinez 2

1	Superintendent	8	Curric/Instruct K-12	19	Chief Financial Officer	29	Family/Consumer Science	39	Social Studies K-12	49	English/Lang Arts Elem	59	Special Education Elem	69	Academic Assessment
2	Bus/Finance/Purchasing	9	Curric/Instruct Elem	20	Art K-12	30	Adult Education	40	Social Studies Elem	50	English/Lang Arts Sec	60	Special Education Sec	70	Research/Development
3	Buildings And Grounds	10	Curric/Instruct Sec	21	Art Elem	31	Career/Sch-to-Work K-12	41	Social Studies Sec	51	Reading K-12	61	Foreign/World Lang K-12	71	Public Information
4	Food Service	11	Federal Program	22	Art Sec	32	Career/Sch-to-Work Elem	42	Science K-12	52	Reading Elem	62	Foreign/World Lang Elem	72	Summer School
5	Transportation	12	Title I	23	Music K-12	33	Career/Sch-to-Work Sec	43	Science Elem	53	Reading Sec	63	Foreign/World Lang Sec	73	Instructional Tech
6	Athletic	13	Title V	24	Music Elem	34	Early Childhood Ed	44	Science Sec	54	Remedial Reading K-12	64	Religious Education K-12	74	Inservice Training
7	Health Services	15	Asst Superintendent	25	Music Sec	35	Health/Phys Education	45	Math K-12	55	Remedial Reading Elem	65	Religious Education Elem	75	Marketing/Distributive
		16	Instructional Media Svcs	26	Business Education	36	Guidance Services K-12	46	Math Elem	56	Remedial Reading Sec	66	Religious Education Sec	76	Info Systems
		17	Chief Operations Officer	27	Career & Tech Ed	37	Guidance Services Elem	47	Math Sec	57	Bilingual/ELL	67	School Board President	77	Psychological Assess
		18	Chief Academic Officer	28	Technology Education	38	Guidance Services Sec	48	English/Lang Arts K-12	58	Special Education K-12	68	Teacher Personnel	78	Affirmative Action

Texas School Directory

Walker County

Catholic Schs..Principal	Grd	Prgm	Enr/#Cls	SN
Nazareth Academy 206 W Convent St, Victoria 77901 Evelyn Korenek	PK-8		356 20	361/573-6651 Fax 361/573-1829
Our Lady of Victory Sch 1311 E Mesquite Ln, Victoria 77901 Justin Matias	PK-8		501 20	361/575-5391 Fax 361/575-3473
St Joseph High Sch 110 E Red River St, Victoria 77901 Gretchen Boyle	9-12		337 30	361/573-2446 Fax 361/573-4221 f

VICTORIA PRIVATE SCHOOLS

Private Schs..Principal	Grd	Prgm	Enr/#Cls	SN
Faith Academy 2002 E Mockingbird Ln, Victoria 77904 Larry Long \ Terry Neinast	PK-12		329 17	361/573-2484 Fax 361/572-4602 f t
Northside Baptist Sch 4100 N Laurent St, Victoria 77901 Jan Chilcoat	PK-5		128 9	361/578-1568
Trinity Episcopal Sch 1504 N Moody St, Victoria 77901 Kristy Nelson	PK-8		220 20	361/573-3220 Fax 361/573-2964
Victoria Christian Sch 3310 N Ben Jordan St, Victoria 77901 Catherine Key	PK-8		98	361/573-5345 Fax 361/578-3367
Vine Sch 2911 N Azalea St, Victoria 77901 Erin Hatley	Spec		18	361/212-8463

VICTORIA REGIONAL CENTERS

- **Region 3 Ed Service Center** PID: 01058438   361/573-0731
  1905 Leary Ln, Victoria 77901   Fax 361/576-4804

Charlotte Baker 1
Laura Ratliff 2,3,15
Linda Ledwig 15,34
Mitzi McAfee 15
Lisa Hernandez 298
Jennifer Sappington 2,19
Carly Shock 4
Marybeth Matula 15,76
Laura Sprinkle 286

WALKER COUNTY

WALKER PUBLIC SCHOOLS

- **Huntsville Ind School Dist** PID: 01058672   936/435-6300
  441 FM 2821 Rd E, Huntsville 77320   Fax 936/435-6648

Schools: 9 \ **Teachers:** 400 \ **Students:** 6,100 \ **Special Ed Students:** 557 \
LEP Students: 823 \ **Ethnic:** Asian 1%, African American 27%, Hispanic 34%,
Caucasian 37% \ **Exp:** $483 (High) \ **Poverty:** 22% \ **Title I:** $1,887,217 \
Special Education: $1,053,000 \ **Open-Close:** 08/15 - 05/21 \ **DTBP:** $159 (High)

Dr Scott Sheppard 1
Paul Brown 2,19
Kevin Stanford 2,15,76
Larry Brown 3
Rodney Merek 3
Charles McGowen 5
Dr Mina Schnitta 10
Marcus Forney 15,36,83,88,270
Marcus Walker 27
Rissie Owens 67
Shannon Duncan 71
Donna Gutierrez 76
Matthew Lahey 286*
Henery Tapia 4
Rodney Southern 6
Linda Marshall 11,296
John Green 23*
Kelley Tieterse 58
Angee Andrus 69,294
Nadine Pharries 73
Sally Dallas 90
Morllo Faulkner 295

Public Schs..Principal	Grd	Prgm	Enr/#Cls	SN
Estella Stewart Elem Sch 3400 Boettcher Dr, Huntsville 77340 Lauren Hodge	K-4	T	507 40	69% 936/435-6700 Fax 936/293-2809
Huntsville Elem Sch 87 M L King Blvd, Huntsville 77320 Christy Cross	K-4	T	577 44	74% 936/293-2888 Fax 936/293-2896
Huntsville High Sch 515 FM 2821 Rd E, Huntsville 77320 William Roberts	9-12	T	1,784 80	51% 936/435-6100 Fax 936/293-2609
Huntsville Intermediate Sch 431 Highway 190 E, Huntsville 77340 Beth Burt	5-6	T	916 60	69% 936/293-2717 Fax 936/293-2712
Mance Park Middle Sch 1010 8th St, Huntsville 77320 Joshua Campbell	7-8	T	895 67	58% 936/435-6400 Fax 936/435-6617
Mary McAshan Gibbs PK Center 1800 19th St, Huntsville 77340 Jessie Anderson	PK-PK	T	354 17	89% 936/435-6550 Fax 936/293-2826
Samuel Houston Elem Sch 1641 7th St, Huntsville 77320 Renee Royal	K-4	T	529 30	66% 936/435-6750 Fax 936/439-1223
Scott Johnson Elem Sch 603 Highway 190 E, Huntsville 77340 Shannon Williams	K-4	T	641 28	70% 936/293-2866 Fax 936/293-2876
Texas Online Preparatory Sch 1955 Lakeway Dr, Lewisville 75057 Blanda Watt \ Elizabeth Nelson \ Rebecca Finka	3-12		2,000	888/263-6497

- **New Waverly Ind School Dist** PID: 01058737   936/344-6751
  355 Front St, New Waverly 77358   Fax 936/344-2438

Schools: 4 \ **Teachers:** 83 \ **Students:** 1,000 \ **Special Ed Students:** 96
\ **LEP Students:** 39 \ **College-Bound:** 10% \ **Ethnic:** African American
19%, Hispanic 14%, Native American: 1%, Caucasian 66% \ **Exp:** $229
(Med) \ **Poverty:** 26% \ **Title I:** $320,031 \ **Special Education:** $207,000 \
Open-Close: 08/26 - 05/19 \ **DTBP:** $350 (High)

Dr Darol Hail 1
James Sanders 3
Roland Oliphant 5
Celeste Roberts 7*
Debbie Choate 36,85,286
Kim Shoulders 58*
Cade Reece 83,88*
Michele Chitwood 2
Jewel Gregory 4
Dean Schaub 6*
Stephanie Brock 8,11,288,298*
Candice Reynolds 37*
Terry Munoz 67

Public Schs..Principal	Grd	Prgm	Enr/#Cls	SN
New Waverly Elem Sch 335 FM 1375 West, New Waverly 77358 Tiffany Wedgeworth	PK-3	T	370 37	57% 936/344-2900 Fax 936/344-2905
New Waverly High Sch 9464 Highway 75 S, New Waverly 77358 Kristopher Drane	9-12	T	314 25	40% 936/344-6451 Fax 936/344-6113
New Waverly Intermediate Sch 215 Clara Rudd Ln, New Waverly 77358 Kathy Lepley	4-5	T	156 8	56% 936/344-6601 Fax 936/344-2331

---

79 Student Personnel	91 Safety/Security	275 Response To Intervention	298 Grant Writer/Ptnrships	**School Programs**	**Social Media**
80 Driver Ed/Safety	92 Magnet School	277 Remedial Math K-12	750 Chief Innovation Officer	A = Alternative Program	
81 Gifted/Talented	93 Parental Involvement	280 Literacy Coach	751 Chief of Staff	G = Adult Classes	f = Facebook
82 Video Services	95 Tech Prep Program	285 STEM	752 Social Emotional Learning	M = Magnet Program	
83 Substance Abuse Prev	97 Chief Infomation Officer	286 Digital Learning		T = Title I Schoolwide	t = Twitter
84 Erate	98 Chief Technology Officer	288 Common Core Standards	**Other School Types**	V = Career & Tech Ed Programs	
85 AIDS Education	270 Character Education	294 Accountability	A = Alternative School		
88 Alternative/At Risk	271 Migrant Education	295 Network System	C = Charter School	New Schools are shaded	
89 Multi-Cultural Curriculum	273 Teacher Mentor	296 Title II Programs	M = Magnet School	New Superintendents and Principals are bold	
90 Social Work	274 Before/After Sch	297 Webmaster	Y = Year-Round School	Personnel with email addresses are underscored	TX—383

Waller County

Market Data Retrieval

New Waverly Junior High Sch 6-8 T 229 47% 936/344-2246
1111 Front St, New Waverly 77358 19 Fax 936/344-8313
Dudley Hawkes

WALKER PRIVATE SCHOOLS

Private Schs..Principal	Grd	Prgm	Enr/#Cls	SN	
Alpha Omega Academy	PK-12		400		936/438-8833
3891 Highway 30 W, Huntsville 77340			40		Fax 936/438-8844
Paul Davidheizar					
Summit Christian Academy	1-12		120		936/295-9601
3122 Montgomery Rd, Huntsville 77340			8		Fax 936/295-9236
Krystal Nunez					

WALKER REGIONAL CENTERS

• **Region 6 Ed Service Center** PID: 01058763 936/435-8400
3332 Montgomery Rd, Huntsville 77340 Fax 936/435-8484

Michael Holland 1   Robert Lindeman 2,19
Dr Brian Zemlicka 15,71   Tally Jo Stout 27,31
Kristine Haymae 30   Dr Catherine George 58
Bonney Monjaras 68   Jayne Tavenner 69
Dr John Conley 73

WALLER COUNTY

WALLER PUBLIC SCHOOLS

• **Hempstead Ind School Dist** PID: 01058775 979/826-3304
1440 13th St, Hempstead 77445 Fax 979/826-5510

Schools: 3 \ *Teachers:* 117 \ *Students:* 1,600 \ *Special Ed Students:* 123 \ *LEP Students:* 356 \ *Ethnic:* African American 29%, Hispanic 57%, Caucasian 13% \ *Exp:* $458 (High) \ *Poverty:* 29% \ *Title I:* $770,345 \ *Special Education:* $216,000 \ *Open-Close:* 08/26 - 05/29 \ *DTBP:* $558 (High)

Dr Angela Gutsch 1,11   Kevin Mathis 2,19
Eddie Brown 5   Bobby Spain 6*
Melissa Skinner 8   Eric Mullens 11,69,88,271,274,296,298
Mandy Dempsey ....16,82* Consuelo Mayorquin 57
Yuki Yamaguchi 57   Courtney Williams 58
Ricky Pearce 67   Mabisha Stubblefield 68,74
Laurie Bettis 71   Alex Miller 73,98,295,297
Aaron Meadow 88

Public Schs..Principal	Grd	Prgm	Enr/#Cls	SN	
Hempstead Elem Sch	PK-5	T	867	76%	979/826-2452
1340 13th St, Hempstead 77445			50		Fax 979/826-5524
Samantha Ray-Mullens					
Hempstead High Sch	9-12	AGTV	415	65%	979/826-3331
801 Donoho Street, Hempstead 77445			50		Fax 979/826-4779
Eric Mullens					
Hempstead Middle Sch	6-8	TV	320	73%	979/826-2530
2532 9th St, Hempstead 77445			48		Fax 979/826-5583
Erika Douglas					

• **Royal Ind School Dist** PID: 01058816 281/934-2248
3714 FM 359, Pattison 77466 Fax 281/934-2846

Schools: 4 \ *Teachers:* 166 \ *Students:* 2,400 \ *Special Ed Students:* 201 \ *LEP Students:* 871 \ *College-Bound:* 57% \ *Ethnic:* African American 16%, Hispanic 74%, Caucasian 10% \ *Exp:* $355 (High) \ *Poverty:* 24% \ *Title I:* $762,488 \ *Special Education:* $387,000 \ *Open-Close:* 08/14 - 05/21 \ *DTBP:* $331 (High)

Stacy Ackley 1   Gladys Hein 2
Sandy Mayberry 2   Derrick Dabney 3,5
Greg Anderson 6   Kendra Strange 8
Susan Cardiff 11,69,294,296,298   Ronnie Melton 27,31*
Tonya Woods Gage 58   Elton Foster 67
Debbie Ulrich 68   Mike Nicholas 73,295
Stephanie Hein 79

Public Schs..Principal	Grd	Prgm	Enr/#Cls	SN	
Royal Early Childhood Center	PK-K	T	341	84%	281/934-3147
2300 Durkin Rd, Brookshire 77423			17		Fax 281/934-4122
Aronda Green					
Royal Elem Sch	1-5	T	932	85%	281/934-3166
2222 Durkin Rd, Brookshire 77423			16		Fax 281/934-3358
Aronda Green					
Royal High Sch	9-12	ATV	642	71%	281/934-2215
34499 Royal Rd, Brookshire 77423			45		Fax 281/934-2866
Tony Runnels					
Royal Junior High Sch	6-8	ATV	495	85%	281/934-2241
2520 Durkin Road, Brookshire 77423			30		Fax 281/934-2329
Orlando Vargas					

• **Waller Ind School Dist** PID: 01058866 936/931-3685
2214 Waller St, Waller 77484 Fax 936/372-5576

Schools: 8 \ *Teachers:* 399 \ *Students:* 7,700 \ *Special Ed Students:* 428 \ *LEP Students:* 1,732 \ *College-Bound:* 53% \ *Ethnic:* Asian 1%, African American 9%, Hispanic 54%, Caucasian 36% \ *Exp:* $450 (High) \ *Poverty:* 16% \ *Title I:* $1,361,047 \ *Special Education:* $910,000 \ *Open-Close:* 08/26 - 05/28 \ *DTBP:* $153 (High)

Kevin Moran 1   Kim Peinly 2
Mike Marcus 2,19   Guy Thomas 3
Molly Warzon 4   Joe Mooneyham 5,91
Jim Phillips ....6*   Kelly Baehren 8,11,18,288,298,752
Sharon Bey 36   Diane Dewease 47
Carrie Lentz 49   Jorge Alvarado 57
Jan Oatess 58   David Kaminski 67
Mike Brooks 68   Donna Suggitt 69
Sarah Marcus 71   Rosa Ojeda 76,97,286

Public Schs..Principal	Grd	Prgm	Enr/#Cls	SN	
Evelyn Turlington Elem Sch	PK-5	T	771	68%	936/372-0100
23400 Hegar Rd, Hockley 77447					Fax 936/372-3868
Kristen Eckerman					
Fields Store Elem Sch	PK-5	T	748	53%	936/931-4050
31670 Giboney Rd, Waller 77484			41		Fax 936/372-4100
Melissa Crosby					
Herman Jones Elem Sch	PK-5		636		936/372-4200
35723 Owens Rd, Prairie View 77446			12		Fax 936/857-5050
Ashley Kinney					
It Holleman Elem Sch	PK-5	T	706	66%	936/372-9196
2200 Brazeal St, Waller 77484			36		Fax 936/372-2468
Ashley Abke					
Roberts Road Elem Sch	PK-5	T	702	72%	936/931-0300
24920 Zube Rd, Hockley 77447			50		Fax 281/373-3164
Amy Carranza					

1 Superintendent	8 Curric/Instruct K-12	19 Chief Financial Officer	29 Family/Consumer Science	39 Social Studies K-12	49 English/Lang Arts Elem	59 Special Education Elem	69 Academic Assessment
2 Bus/Finance/Purchasing	9 Curric/Instruct Elem	20 Art K-12	30 Adult Education	40 Social Studies Elem	50 English/Lang Arts Sec	60 Special Education Sec	70 Research/Development
3 Buildings And Grounds	10 Curric/Instruct Sec	21 Art Elem	31 Career/Sch-to-Work K-12	41 Social Studies Sec	51 Reading K-12	61 Foreign/World Lang K-12	71 Public Information
4 Food Service	11 Federal Program	22 Art Sec	32 Career/Sch-to-Work Elem	42 Science K-12	52 Reading Elem	62 Foreign/World Lang Elem	72 Summer School
5 Transportation	12 Title I	23 Music K-12	33 Career/Sch-to-Work Sec	43 Science Elem	53 Reading Sec	63 Foreign/World Lang Sec	73 Instructional Tech
6 Athletic	13 Title V	24 Music Elem	34 Early Childhood Ed	44 Science Sec	54 Remedial Reading K-12	64 Religious Education K-12	74 Inservice Training
7 Health Services	15 Asst Superintendent	25 Music Sec	35 Health/Phys Education	45 Math K-12	55 Remedial Reading Elem	65 Religious Education Elem	75 Marketing/Distributive
	16 Instructional Media Svcs	26 Business Education	36 Guidance Services K-12	46 Math Elem	56 Remedial Reading Sec	66 Religious Education Sec	76 Info Systems
	17 Chief Operations Officer	27 Career & Tech Ed	37 Guidance Services Elem	47 Math Sec	57 Bilingual/ELL	67 School Board President	77 Psychological Assess
	18 Chief Academic Officer	28 Technology Education	38 Guidance Services Sec	48 English/Lang Arts K-12	58 Special Education K-12	68 Teacher Personnel	78 Affirmative Action

Texas School Directory — Washington County

School	Grd	Prgm	Enr/#Cls	SN	Phone
Schultz Junior High Sch 19010 Stokes Rd, Waller 77484 Hannah Gates	6-8	T	832 52	59%	936/931-9103 Fax 936/372-9302
Waller High Sch 20950 Fields Store Rd, Waller 77484 Stephanie Fletcher	9-12	T	1,861	56%	936/372-3654 Fax 936/372-4114
Waller Junior High Sch 2402 Waller St, Waller 77484 Tanya Carrejo	6-8	T	740 50	68%	936/931-1353 Fax 936/931-4044
Sudderth Elem Sch 701 N Carol Ave, Monahans 79756 Adam Alaniz	4-6	T	543 13	52%	432/943-5101 Fax 432/943-2685
Tatom Elem Sch 1600 S Calvin Ave, Monahans 79756 Jill Steen	1-3	T	571 14	59%	432/943-2769 Fax 432/943-3952
Walker Junior High Sch 800 S Faye Ave, Monahans 79756 Mayna Benavides	7-8	T	367 24	33%	432/943-4622 Fax 432/943-3723

WARD COUNTY

WARD PUBLIC SCHOOLS

• **Grandfalls-Royalty Ind SD** PID: 01058919 432/547-2266
115 Ave C, Grandfalls 79742 Fax 432/547-2960

Schools: 1 \ *Teachers:* 15 \ *Students:* 185 \ *Special Ed Students:* 10 \ *College-Bound:* 40% \ *Ethnic:* African American 1%, Hispanic 75%, Caucasian 24% \ *Exp:* $843 (High) \ *Poverty:* 22% \ *Title I:* $30,249 \ *Open-Close:* 08/19 - 05/22 \ *DTBP:* $359 (High)

Joe Helms 1,11		Lorraine Natividad 2	
Rosa Vasquez 4		Joe Howell 6,8*	
Linda Kuhn 58*		Mark Kuhn 67	
Brett Starkweather 73*		Toy Eaton 83,752	

Public Schs..Principal	Grd	Prgm	Enr/#Cls	SN	Phone
Grandfalls Royalty Sch 115 Ave C, Grandfalls 79742 **Brett Starkweather**	PK-12	T	185 35	81%	432/547-2266

• **Monahans-Wickett-Pyote ISD** PID: 01058957 432/943-6711
606 S Betty Ave, Monahans 79756 Fax 432/943-2307

Schools: 6 \ *Teachers:* 144 \ *Students:* 2,300 \ *Special Ed Students:* 187 \ *LEP Students:* 185 \ *College-Bound:* 50% \ *Ethnic:* Asian 1%, African American 6%, Hispanic 59%, Native American: 1%, Caucasian 34% \ *Exp:* $509 (High) \ *Poverty:* 18% \ *Title I:* $459,776 \ *Special Education:* $375,000 \ *Open-Close:* 08/19 - 05/22 \ *DTBP:* $347 (High)

Kellye Riley 1	Sarah Harris 2
Jeff Jones 3	Tammy Sanchez 4*
Leif Tefertiller 5	Frederek Staugh 6
Ann McCallester 7*	Doug Doege 8,11,57,69,298
Kimberley Thomas 30,38*	Anthony Ayundis 58
Donna Garcia 67	Allen Fox 73,295,297*
Allen Fox 84	

Public Schs..Principal	Grd	Prgm	Enr/#Cls	SN	Phone
Cullender Kindergarten 1100 S Leon Ave, Monahans 79756 Marielena Saenz	PK-K	T	222 14	57%	432/943-5252 Fax 432/943-4768
Ⓐ Monahans Education Center HS 813 S Alice Ave, Monahans 79756 Chad Smith	9-12	T	23 4	44%	432/943-2019 Fax 432/943-2593
Monahans High Sch 809 S Betty Ave, Monahans 79756 Patty Acosta	9-12	TV	602 40	41%	432/943-2519 Fax 432/943-3327

WASHINGTON COUNTY

WASHINGTON PUBLIC SCHOOLS

• **Brenham Ind School Dist** PID: 01059042 979/277-3700
711 E Mansfield St, Brenham 77833 Fax 979/277-3701

Schools: 7 \ *Teachers:* 352 \ *Students:* 5,000 \ *Special Ed Students:* 604 \ *LEP Students:* 544 \ *College-Bound:* 57% \ *Ethnic:* Asian 2%, African American 22%, Hispanic 35%, Caucasian 41% \ *Exp:* $308 (High) \ *Poverty:* 18% \ *Title I:* $1,034,988 \ *Special Education:* $1,107,000 \ *Open-Close:* 08/14 - 05/21 \ *DTBP:* $156 (High)

Dr Walter Jackson 1	Kim Weatherby 2
Kim Horne 2	Phillip Derkowski 3
Sandra Baxter 4	Omian Torres 5
Elliot Allen 6	Dr Jamey Johnson 8,15
Mark Strauss 8,294	Marie Ruiz 11,57,83
Paul Aschenbeck 15	Kim Strauss 16,73,76,295
Eric Rettig 23*	Cody Stelter 27,28*
Leslie Broesche 34,58,275*	Steve Skrla 36
Natalie Lange 67	Christie Olivarez 68
Jessica Johnston 71	Lori Wamble 81
Susan Pritchard 274	

Public Schs..Principal	Grd	Prgm	Enr/#Cls	SN	Phone
Alton Elem Sch 1210 S Market St, Brenham 77833 Michael Ogg	PK-4	T	474 40	82%	979/277-3870 Fax 979/277-3871
Brenham Elem Sch 1000 W Blue Bell Rd, Brenham 77833 Jennifer Vest	PK-4	T	603 41	60%	979/277-3880 Fax 979/277-3881
Brenham High Sch 525 A H Ehrig Dr, Brenham 77833 Joseph Chandler	9-12	V	1,471 200	44%	979/277-3800 Fax 979/277-3801
Brenham Junior High Sch 1200 Carlee Dr, Brenham 77833 **Bryan Bryant**	7-8	T	787 60	51%	979/277-3830 Fax 979/277-3831
Brenham Middle Sch 1600 S Blue Bell Rd, Brenham 77833 Peggy Still	5-6	T	744 30	58%	979/277-3845 Fax 979/277-3846
Krause Elem Sch 2201 E Stone St, Brenham 77833 Courtney Mason	PK-4	T	678 50	62%	979/277-3860 Fax 979/277-3861
Ⓐ Pride Academy 1301 S Market St, Brenham 77833 Allan Colvin	11-12	T	30 5	46%	979/277-3890 Fax 979/277-3891

---

79 Student Personnel	91 Safety/Security	275 Response To Intervention	298 Grant Writer/Ptnrships
80 Driver Ed/Safety	92 Magnet School	277 Remedial Math K-12	750 Chief Innovation Officer
81 Gifted/Talented	93 Parental Involvement	280 Literacy Coach	751 Chief of Staff
82 Video Services	95 Tech Prep Program	285 STEM	752 Social Emotional Learning
83 Substance Abuse Prev	97 Chief Information Officer	286 Digital Learning	
84 Erate	98 Chief Technology Officer	288 Common Core Standards	**Other School Types**
85 AIDS Education	270 Character Education	294 Accountability	Ⓐ = Alternative School
88 Alternative/At Risk	271 Migrant Education	295 Network System	Ⓒ = Charter School
89 Multi-Cultural Curriculum	273 Teacher Mentor	296 Title II Programs	Ⓜ = Magnet School
90 Social Work	274 Before/After Sch	297 Webmaster	Ⓨ = Year-Round School

School Programs
A = Alternative Program
G = Adult Classes
M = Magnet Program
T = Title I Schoolwide
V = Career & Tech Ed Programs

Social Media
 = Facebook
 = Twitter

New Schools are shaded
New Superintendents and Principals are bold
Personnel with email addresses are underscored

Webb County

Market Data Retrieval

- **Burton Ind School Dist** PID: 01059107   979/289-3131
  701 N Railroad St, Burton 77835   Fax 979/289-3076

Schools: 2 \ **Teachers:** 39 \ **Students:** 455 \ **Special Ed Students:** 47 \ **LEP Students:** 26 \ **Ethnic:** African American 15%, Hispanic 22%, Caucasian 62% \ **Exp:** $719 (High) \ **Poverty:** 16% \ **Title I:** $79,020 \ **Open-Close:** 08/21 - 05/22 \ **DTBP:** $344 (High) \ [f]

Name	Ref
Dr Edna Kennedy	1,73,83
Ronnie Hohlt	3
Jason Hodde	6*
Angela Rhodes	31,79,88,270
Demetrius Colvin	67
Caitlyn Blakey	2
Kristie Manley	4
Melinda Fuchs	8,12,69,88,270,288,296*
Kristie Hess	58
Tracie Kramer	68

Public Schs..Principal	Grd	Prgm	Enr/#Cls	SN	
Burton Elem Sch 12504 W Cedar St, Burton 77835 Melinda Fuchs	PK-6	T	248 12	57%	979/289-2175 Fax 979/289-0170
Burton High Sch 917 N Main St, Burton 77835 **Matthew Wamble**	7-12	TV	208 14	50%	979/289-3830 Fax 979/289-4609

WASHINGTON PRIVATE SCHOOLS

Private Schs..Principal	Grd	Prgm	Enr/#Cls	SN	
Citadel Christian Sch 2111 S Blue Bell Rd, Brenham 77833 Shelia Suders	PK-8		28 16		979/830-8480 Fax 979/830-1687
First Baptist Church Sch 302 Pahl St, Brenham 77833 Nancy Jahns	PK-6		275 15		979/836-6411 Fax 979/836-3269
Grace Lutheran Sch 1212 W Jefferson St, Brenham 77833 Thomas Obersat	PK-8		78 10		979/836-2030 Fax 979/836-0510
Johnson Ferguson Academy 1102 E Main St, Brenham 77833 Dr Patricia Larke	K-4		3 1		979/836-4156 Fax 979/836-1361

WEBB COUNTY

WEBB PUBLIC SCHOOLS

- **Laredo Ind School Dist** PID: 01059183   956/273-1000
  1702 Houston St, Laredo 78040   Fax 956/273-1403

Schools: 33 \ **Teachers:** 1,450 \ **Students:** 23,737 \ **Special Ed Students:** 1,887 \ **LEP Students:** 12,316 \ **College-Bound:** 69% \ **Ethnic:** Hispanic 99%, Caucasian 1% \ **Exp:** $300 (High) \ **Poverty:** 46% \ **Title I:** $17,550,535 \ **Special Education:** $5,096,000 \ **Open-Close:** 08/12 - 05/27 \ **DTBP:** $195 (High)

Name	Ref	Name	Ref
Dr Silvia Rios	1	Flor Ayala	2,19
Hector Mejia	2	Roberto Cuellar	4
Esteban Rangel	5	Silvia Barrera	6,35
Dr Gerardo Cruz	8	Myrtala Ramirez	9
Oralia Cortez	11*	Oralia Cortez	11
Roberta Ramirez	15,68	Mely Paez	16
Rogelio Garcia	27,31	Rogelio Garcia	27,31*
Brenda Sepulveda	34,73,76	Itzamara Rendon	34
Rosina Silva	36,88	Cynthia Cruz	57
Raul Gomez	58	Hector Garcia	67
Delma Alaniz-Ramos	69,294	Veronica Castillon	71
Maggie Martinez	79,83	Scott Roberts	298

Public Schs..Principal	Grd	Prgm	Enr/#Cls	SN	
Alma A Pierce Elem Sch 800 E Eistetter St, Laredo 78041 Noralva Johnson	PK-5	T	839 45	90%	956/273-4300 Fax 956/273-4395
Anita T Dovalina Elem Sch 1700 Anna Ave, Laredo 78040 Alma Castillo	PK-5	T	504 40	99%	956/273-3320 Fax 956/273-3395
Antonio Bruni Elem Sch 1508 San Eduardo Ave, Laredo 78040 Miguel Castillo	PK-5	T	618 35	97%	956/273-3000 Fax 956/273-3095
C L Milton Elem Sch 2500 E Ash St, Laredo 78043 Flor Diaz	PK-5	T	881 47	90%	956/273-4200 Fax 956/795-4295
C M MacDonell Elem Sch 1606 Benavides St, Laredo 78040 Cathy DeLeon	PK-5	T	539 30	99%	956/273-4000 Fax 956/273-4095
D D Hachar Elem Sch 3000 Guadalupe St, Laredo 78043 Cynthia Villarreal	PK-5	T	541 28	94%	956/273-3500 Fax 956/273-3595
Don Jose Gallego Elem Sch 520 Clark Blvd, Laredo 78040 Imelda Martinez	PK-5	T	775 33	94%	956/273-3100 Fax 956/273-3195
Ⓜ Dr Dennis Cantu Health Sci Sch 2002 San Bernardo Ave, Laredo 78040 Geraldine Arredondo	9-12	V	305		956/795-3874 Fax 956/795-3875
Dr Joaquin Cigarroa Middle Sch 2600 Palo Blanco St, Laredo 78046 Jose Cerda	6-8	ATV	1,319 88	93%	956/273-6100 Fax 956/273-6195
Dr Leo Cigarroa High Sch 2600 Zacatecas St, Laredo 78046 Laura Flores	9-12	ATV	1,602 100	95%	956/273-6800 Fax 956/795-3814
Francisco Farias Elem Sch 1510 Chicago St, Laredo 78041 **San Juana Garza**	PK-5	T	655 42	95%	956/273-3400 Fax 956/273-3495
Ⓐ Francisco S Lara Academy Ⓜ 2901 E Travis St, Laredo 78043 Armando Molina	6-12	G	70 20	96%	956/273-7900 Fax 956/726-0350
H B Zachry Elem Sch 3200 Chacota St, Laredo 78046 Diana Martinez	PK-5	T	635 35	93%	956/273-4900 Fax 956/273-4995
Ⓜ Hector Garcia Early Clg HS 5241 University Blvd Cowart Hl, Laredo 78041 Jose Iznaola	9-12	T	438	78%	956/273-7700 Fax 956/273-7795
Heights Elem Sch 1208 Market St, Laredo 78040 Adriana Padilla	PK-5	T	553 25	89%	956/273-3600 Fax 956/273-3695
Honore Ligarde Elem Sch 2800 S Canada Ave, Laredo 78046 Elba Contreras	PK-5	T	729 45	92%	956/273-3900 Fax 956/273-3995
J A Kawas Elem Sch 2100 S Milmo Ave, Laredo 78046 Vanessa Ortegon	PK-5	T	578 32	96%	956/273-3700 Fax 956/273-3795
J W Nixon High Sch 2000 E Plum St, Laredo 78043 Cassandra Mendoza	9-12	ATV	2,188 80	84%	956/273-7400 Fax 956/273-7495
J Z Leyendecker Elem Sch 1311 Garden St, Laredo 78040 Maria Oviedo	PK-5	T	509 40	95%	956/273-3800 Fax 956/273-3895
Ⓐ Jose A Valdez High Sch 1619 Victoria St, Laredo 78040 Lizzy Newsome	9-12		100		956/273-8000 Fax 956/273-8095

1	Superintendent	8	Curric/Instruct K-12	19	Chief Financial Officer	29	Family/Consumer Science	39	Social Studies K-12	49	English/Lang Arts Elem	59	Special Education Elem	69	Academic Assessment
2	Bus/Finance/Purchasing	9	Curric/Instruct Elem	20	Art K-12	30	Adult Education	40	Social Studies Elem	50	English/Lang Arts Sec	60	Special Education Sec	70	Research/Development
3	Buildings And Grounds	10	Curric/Instruct Sec	21	Art Elem	31	Career/Sch-to-Work K-12	41	Social Studies Sec	51	Reading K-12	61	Foreign/World Lang K-12	71	Public Information
4	Food Service	11	Federal Program	22	Art Sec	32	Career/Sch-to-Work Elem	42	Science K-12	52	Reading Elem	62	Foreign/World Lang Elem	72	Summer School
5	Transportation	12	Title I	23	Music K-12	33	Career/Sch-to-Work Sec	43	Science Elem	53	Reading Sec	63	Foreign/World Lang Sec	73	Instructional Tech
6	Athletic	13	Title V	24	Music Elem	34	Early Childhood Ed	44	Science Sec	54	Remedial Reading K-12	64	Religious Education K-12	74	Inservice Training
7	Health Services	15	Asst Superintendent	25	Music Sec	35	Health/Phys Education	45	Math K-12	55	Remedial Reading Elem	65	Religious Education Elem	75	Marketing/Distributive
		16	Instructional Media Svcs	26	Business Education	36	Guidance Services K-12	46	Math Elem	56	Remedial Reading Sec	66	Religious Education Sec	76	Info Systems
		17	Chief Operations Officer	27	Career & Tech Ed	37	Guidance Services Elem	47	Math Sec	57	Bilingual/ELL	67	School Board President	77	Psychological Assess
		18	Chief Academic Officer	28	Technology Education	38	Guidance Services Sec	48	English/Lang Arts K-12	58	Special Education K-12	68	Teacher Personnel	78	Affirmative Action

Texas School Directory — Webb County

School	Grd	Prgm	Enr/#Cls	SN	Phone
Joseph C Martin Elem Sch 1600 Monterrey Ave, Laredo 78040 Manuel Escalante	PK-5	T	607 28	99%	956/273-4100 Fax 956/273-4195
Katherine Tarver Elem Sch 3200 Tilden Ave, Laredo 78040 Sara Montemayor	PK-5	T	506 33	93%	956/273-4800 Fax 956/273-4895
L J Christen Middle Sch 2001 Santa Maria Ave, Laredo 78040 Sandra Garcia	6-8	ATV	1,233 100	95%	956/273-6400 Fax 956/273-6495
Leon Daiches Elem Sch 1401 Green St, Laredo 78040 Lisa Soto	PK-5	T	597 34	96%	956/273-3200 Fax 956/273-3295
M B Lamar Middle Sch 1818 N Arkansas Ave, Laredo 78043 Eduardo Lopez	6-8	ATV	1,369 60	100%	956/273-6200 Fax 956/273-6395
M S Ryan Elem Sch 2401 Clark Blvd, Laredo 78043 Elsa Flores	PK-5		898 45		956/273-4400 Fax 956/273-4495
Memorial Middle Sch 2002 Marcella Ave, Laredo 78040 Melissa Valdez	6-8	ATV	763 45	94%	956/273-6600 Fax 956/273-6795
Raymond & Tirza Martin HS 2002 San Bernardo Ave, Laredo 78040 Guillermo Pro	9-12	ATV	2,026 100	93%	956/273-7100 Fax 956/273-7394
Ⓜ Sabas Perez Eng & Tech Sch 2600 Zacatecas St, Laredo 78046 Alfredo Perez	9-12	V	305		956/795-3800 Fax 956/273-9075
Sanchez-Ochoa Elem Sch 211 E Ash St, Laredo 78040 Rosalba Martinez	PK-5	T	719 40	96%	956/273-4500 Fax 956/273-4595
Santa Maria Elem Sch 3817 Santa Maria Ave, Laredo 78041 Jose De Leon	PK-5	T	666 35	97%	956/273-4600 Fax 956/273-4695
Santo Nino Elem Sch 2701 Bismark St, Laredo 78043 Jose Perez	PK-5	T	694 45	91%	956/273-4700 Fax 956/273-4795
Ⓜ Trevino Comm & Fine Art Sch 2102 E Lyon St, Laredo 78043 Dr Martha Villarreal	9-12		687 28		956/273-7800 Fax 956/273-7895

● **United Ind School Dist** PID: 01059470   956/473-6201
201 Lindenwood Dr, Laredo 78045   Fax 956/473-6476

Schools: 47 \ **Teachers:** 2,541 \ **Students:** 45,000 \
Special Ed Students: 3,598 \ **LEP Students:** 15,365 \ **College-Bound:** 51%
\ **Ethnic:** Hispanic 99%, Caucasian 1% \ **Exp:** $333 (High) \ **Poverty:** 29% \
Title I: $18,465,550 \ **Special Education:** $7,305,000 \ **Open-Close:** 08/14 - 05/28 \ **DTBP:** $191 (High)

Roberto Santos 1		Cordelia Flores-Jackson 2	
Laida Benavides 2,15		Enrique Rangel 3,15	
Juan Davila 3		Ray Garner 3,17,91	
Raul Ramirez 4		Joe Aranda 5	
Bobby Cruz 6		Irene Rosales 7,85	
David Gonzalez 8,15		Cynthia Rodriguez 9,288*	
David Canales 10		Dolores Barrera 10*	
Rebecca Morales 11,95,296		David Garcia 15,68	
Eduardo Zuniga 15,79,275		Gloria Rendon 15	
Susan Carlson 16		Javier Vera 20,23	
Angelica Sanchez 27,31*		Melissa Chapa Ramirez 36,83	
Luciel Gonzalez 44		Thelma Elizondo 46	
Cindy Monsivais 47*		Veronica Slaughter 48,52,57	
Susan Ramirez 52		Maria Arambula 57,61	
Cynthia Ramirez 58*		Ramiro Veliz 67	
Rocio Moore 71		Hector Perez 73,76,286	
Judith Garcia 73*		Celia Taboada 74	
Lisa Marie Dunn-Flores 81		Rene Cruz 84,295	
Ofelia Roeminguez 88		Roxann Villagomez 274	

Emma Leza 294   Rolando Juerrero 297
Dr Edith Landeck 298*

Public Schs..Principal	Grd	Prgm	Enr/#Cls	SN	Phone
Alicia Ruiz Elem Sch 1717 Los Presidentes Ave, Laredo 78046 Michelle Cantu	PK-5	T	866 65	80%	956/473-3300 Fax 956/473-3399
Amparo Gutierrez Elem Sch 505 Calle Del Norte, Laredo 78041 Laura Vasquez	PK-5	T	496 51	78%	956/473-4400 Fax 956/473-4499
Antonio Gonzalez Middle Sch 5208 Santa Claudia, Laredo 78043 Clotilde Gamez	6-8	T	1,129	88%	956/473-7000 Fax 956/473-7099
Barbara Fasken Elem Sch 11111 Atlanta Dr, Laredo 78045 Melba Gutierrez	PK-5	T	883	63%	956/473-4700 Fax 956/473-4799
Bonnie Garcia Elem Sch 1453 Concord Hills Blvd, Laredo 78046 Patricia Lanas	PK-5	T	400	85%	956/473-8900 Fax 956/473-8999
Charles Borchers Elem Sch 9551 Backwoods Trl, Laredo 78045 Mucia Flores	PK-5	T	885 35	42%	956/473-7200 Fax 956/473-7299
Clark Elem Sch 500 W Hillside Rd, Laredo 78041 Gabriela Perez	PK-5	T	443 32	90%	956/473-4600 Fax 956/473-4699
Clark Middle Sch 500 W Hillside Rd, Laredo 78041 **Pamela Arredondo**	6-8	T	731 52	80%	956/473-7500 Fax 956/473-7599
Col Santos Benavides Elem Sch 10702 Kirby Dr, Laredo 78045 Adriana Vela	PK-5	T	1,044 60	33%	956/473-4900 Fax 956/473-4999
Dr Henry Cuellar Elem Sch 6431 Casa Del Sol Blvd, Laredo 78043 Andrea Sanchez	PK-5	T	657 34	91%	956/473-2700 Fax 956/473-2799
Dr Malakoff Elem Sch 2810 Havana Dr, Laredo 78045 Anna Martinez	PK-5	T	1,013	49%	956/473-4800 Fax 956/473-4899
Dr S Perez Elem Sch 500 Sierra Vista Blvd, Laredo 78046 Salud Hernandez	PK-5	T	658 48	92%	956/473-3600 Fax 956/473-3699
Finley Elem Sch 2001 Lowry Rd, Laredo 78045 **Kristina Chapa**	PK-5	T	474 35	88%	956/473-4500 Fax 956/473-4599
Freedom Elem Sch 415 Eg Ranch Rd, Laredo 78046 Laura De Los Santos	PK-5		608		956/473-1600 Fax 956/473-1699
George Washington Middle Sch 10306 Riverbank Dr, Laredo 78045 Dorothy Porter	6-8	AT	500 74	78%	956/473-7600 Fax 956/473-7699
J B Alexander 9th Grade HS 4601 Victory Dr, Laredo 78041 Eva Alicia Calcaneo	9-9		900		956/473-1300 Fax 956/473-1399
J B Alexander High Sch 3600 E Del Mar Blvd, Laredo 78041 Ernesto Sandoval	10-12	TV	1,892 125	59%	956/473-5800 Fax 956/473-5999
J B Jones Muller Elem Sch 4430 Muller Blvd, Laredo 78045 Mayra Ramirez	PK-5	T	915 40	76%	956/473-3900 Fax 956/473-3999
J W Arndt Elem Sch 610 Santa Martha Blvd, Laredo 78046 Juanita Zepeda	PK-5	T	794 40	94%	956/473-2800 Fax 956/473-2899
Juarez-Lincoln Elem Sch 1003 Espejo Molina Rd, Laredo 78046 Roberto Ortiz	PK-5	T	685 40	94%	956/473-3000 Fax 956/473-3099
Kazen Elem Sch 9620 Albany Dr, Laredo 78045 Maria Arambula-Ruiz	PK-5	T	494 50	88%	956/473-4200 Fax 956/473-4299

79 Student Personnel	91 Safety/Security	275 Response To Intervention	298 Grant Writer/Ptnrships	**School Programs**	**Social Media**
80 Driver Ed/Safety	92 Magnet School	277 Remedial Math K-12	750 Chief Innovation Officer	A = Alternative Program	
81 Gifted/Talented	93 Parental Involvement	280 Literacy Coach	751 Chief of Staff	G = Adult Classes	= Facebook
82 Video Services	95 Tech Prep Program	285 STEM	752 Social Emotional Learning	M = Magnet Program	
83 Substance Abuse Prev	97 Chief Infomation Officer	286 Digital Learning		T = Title I Schoolwide	= Twitter
84 Erate	98 Chief Technology Officer	288 Common Core Standards	**Other School Types**	V = Career & Tech Ed Programs	
85 AIDS Education	270 Accountability	294 Accountability	Ⓐ = Alternative School		
88 Alternative/At Risk	271 Migrant Education	295 Network System	Ⓒ = Charter School	New Schools are shaded	
89 Multi-Cultural Curriculum	273 Teacher Mentor	296 Title II Programs	Ⓜ = Magnet School	New Superintendents and Principals are bold	
90 Social Work	274 Before/After Sch	297 Webmaster	Ⓨ = Year-Round School	Personnel with email addresses are underscored	

TX—387

Webb County   Market Data Retrieval

School	Grades	Prgm	Enr/#Cls	SN	Phone
Kennedy-Zapata Elem Sch 3809 Espejo Molina Rd, El Cenizo 78046 Thelma Martinez	PK-5	T	408	95%	956/473-4100 Fax 956/473-4199
Killam Elem Sch 5315 Fairfield Dr, Laredo 78043 Agapito Palizo	PK-5	T	695	87%	956/473-2600 Fax 956/473-2699
Lamar Bruni Vergara Middle Sch 5910 Saint Luke, Laredo 78046 Clarissa Flores	6-8	T	984	95%	956/473-6600 Fax 956/473-6699
Los Obispos Middle Sch 4801 S Ejido Ave, Laredo 78046 Jessica Salazar	6-8	TV	943	95%	956/473-7800 Fax 956/473-7899
Lyndon B Johnson High Sch 5626 Cielito Lindo, Laredo 78046 Armando Salazar	9-12	AGTV	2,949	94%	956/473-5100 Fax 956/473-5281
Matias De Llano Jr Elem Sch 1415 Shiloh Dr, Laredo 78045 Diana Korrodi	PK-5	T	300 32	58%	956/473-4000 Fax 956/473-4099
Newman Elem Sch 1300 Alta Vista Dr, Laredo 78041 Leticia Garcia	PK-5	T	649 33	85%	956/473-3800 Fax 956/473-3899
Nye Elem Sch 101 E Del Mar Blvd, Laredo 78041 Cynthia Caballero	PK-5	T	810 53	70%	956/473-3700 Fax 956/473-3799
Paciano Prada Elem Sch 510 Soria Dr, Laredo 78046 Vanessa Saldana	PK-5	T	698 45	92%	956/473-3500 Fax 956/473-3599
Raul Perales Middle Sch 410 Eg Ranch Rd, Laredo 78043 Martha Alvarez	6-8		800		956/473-6800 Fax 956/473-6899
Rodolfo Centeno Elem Sch 2710 La Pita Mangana Rd, Laredo 78046 Amabilia Gonzalez	PK-5	T	884	95%	956/473-8800 Fax 956/473-8899
Roosevelt Elem Sch 3301 Sierra Vista Dr, Laredo 78046 Sylvia Ruiz	PK-5	T	680 47	97%	956/473-3400 Fax 956/473-3499
Salinas Elem Sch 3611 Alfredo Cantu Dr, Laredo 78046 Abraham Rodriguez	PK-5	T	830 35	82%	956/473-3200 Fax 956/473-3299
Salvador Garcia Middle Sch 499 Pena Dr, Laredo 78046 Quetzalcoatl Palapa	6-8	AT	470 40	96%	956/473-5000 Fax 956/473-5099
San Isidro Elem Sch 11021 Bucky Houdman Blvd, Laredo 78045 Dr Myrtha Villareal	PK-5		800		956/473-6700 Fax 956/473-6799
Senator Judith Zaffirini ES 5210 Santa Claudia, Laredo 78043 Claudia Benavides	PK-5	T	556	87%	956/473-2900 Fax 956/473-2999
Trautmann Elem Sch 810 Lindenwood Dr, Laredo 78045 Melissa Shinn	PK-5	T	791 40	45%	956/473-3100 Fax 956/473-3199
Trautmann Middle Sch 8501 Curly Ln, Laredo 78045 Leticia Menchaca	6-8	TV	1,763 50	47%	956/473-7400 Fax 956/473-7499
United High 9th Grade HS 2811 Hillcroft Dr, Laredo 78045 Arlene Trevino	9-9		1,000		956/473-2400 Fax 956/473-2499
United High Sch 2811 United Ave, Laredo 78045 Alberto Aleman	10-12	TV	2,200 100	60%	956/473-5600 Fax 956/473-1980
United Middle Sch 700 E Del Mar Blvd, Laredo 78041 **Rosana Arizola**	6-8	T	1,126	51%	956/473-7300 Fax 956/473-7399
United South High 9th Grade HS 3819 Aguanieve Dr, Laredo 78046 Olga Cantu	9-9		900		956/473-1400 Fax 956/473-1499
United South High Sch 4001 Los Presidentes Ave, Laredo 78046 Adriana Ramirez	10-12	TV	2,300	85%	956/473-5400 Fax 956/473-5599
United South Middle Sch 3707 Los Presidentes Ave, Laredo 78046 Carlos Valdez	6-8	GT	1,319 40	81%	956/473-7700 Fax 956/473-7799
Ⓐ United Step Academy 1600 Espejo Molina Rd, Laredo 78046 Gerardo Rodriguez	6-12	T	150 16	89%	956/473-6500 Fax 956/473-6599
Veterans Memorial Elem Sch 5909 Saint Luke, Laredo 78046 Luz Serna Ramirez	PK-5	T	789	92%	956/473-1200 Fax 956/473-1299

- **Webb Cons Ind School Dist** PID: 01059145   361/747-5415
  619 Avenue F, Bruni 78344   Fax 361/747-5202

Schools: 3 \ *Teachers:* 37 \ *Students:* 272 \ *Special Ed Students:* 33 \ *LEP Students:* 16 \ *College-Bound:* 56% \ *Ethnic:* Hispanic 96%, Caucasian 4% \ *Exp:* $1,168 (High) \ *Poverty:* 44% \ *Title I:* $220,868 \ *Special Education:* $56,000 \ *Open-Close:* 07/24 - 05/25 \ *DTBP:* $350 (High)

Beto Gonzalez 1
Ruben Davila 3
Jay Maldonado 5,12*
Hopie Esperanza 7
Melissa Pena 67
Tenett Black 296
Martha Gonzalez 2,4
Alvaro Carreon 5*
Robbie Silguero 6
Sandra Castillo 8,11,16,57,58,69,275*
Alfonso Gonzalez 73,286*

Public Schs..Principal	Grd	Prgm	Enr/#Cls	SN	Phone
Bruni High Sch 619 Avenue F, Bruni 78344 H Garza	9-12	ATV	78	60%	361/747-5415 Fax 361/747-5301
Bruni Middle Sch 619 Avenue F, Bruni 78344 Josie Castillo	6-8	T	56 10	66%	361/747-5415
Oilton Elem Sch 619 Avenue F, Bruni 78344 Josie Castillo	PK-5	T	138 16	79%	361/586-5415 Fax 361/586-4979

WEBB CATHOLIC SCHOOLS

- **Diocese of Laredo Ed Office** PID: 04938095   956/753-5208
  1201 Corpus Christi St, Laredo 78040   Fax 956/753-5203

Schools: 6 \ *Students:* 2,131 \ *Open-Close:* 08/17 - 05/27

Listing includes only schools located in this county. See District Index for location of Diocesan Offices.

Guadalupe Perez 1
Melinda Sepulveda 68
Lizzy Flores 2
Luis Martinez 76,295

Catholic Schs..Principal	Grd	Prgm	Enr/#Cls	SN	Phone
Blessed Sacrament Sch 1501 N Bartlett Ave, Laredo 78043 Selma Santos	PK-8		250 13		956/722-1222 Fax 956/712-2002
Our Lady of Guadalupe Sch 400 Callaghan St, Laredo 78040 Herlinda Martinez	PK-6		125 9		956/722-3915 Fax 956/727-2840
St Augustine Elem Middle Sch 1300 Galveston St, Laredo 78040 Barbra Zurita	PK-8		300 10		956/724-1176 Fax 956/724-9891

#		#		#		#		#		#	
1	Superintendent	8	Curric/Instruct K-12	19	Chief Financial Officer	29	Family/Consumer Science	39	Social Studies K-12	49	English/Lang Arts Elem	59	Special Education Elem	69	Academic Assessment
2	Bus/Finance/Purchasing	9	Curric/Instruct Elem	20	Art K-12	30	Adult Education	40	Social Studies Elem	50	English/Lang Arts Sec	60	Special Education Sec	70	Research/Development
3	Buildings And Grounds	10	Curric/Instruct Sec	21	Art Elem	31	Career/Sch-to-Work K-12	41	Social Studies Sec	51	Reading K-12	61	Foreign/World Lang K-12	71	Public Information
4	Food Service	11	Federal Program	22	Art Sec	32	Career/Sch-to-Work Elem	42	Science K-12	52	Reading Elem	62	Foreign/World Lang Elem	72	Summer School
5	Transportation	12	Title I	23	Music K-12	33	Career/Sch-to-Work Sec	43	Science Elem	53	Reading Sec	63	Foreign/World Lang Sec	73	Instructional Tech
6	Athletic	13	Title V	24	Music Elem	34	Early Childhood Ed	44	Science Sec	54	Remedial Reading K-12	64	Religious Education K-12	74	Inservice Training
7	Health Services	14	Asst Superintendent	25	Music Sec	35	Health/Phys Education	45	Math K-12	55	Remedial Reading Elem	65	Religious Education Elem	75	Marketing/Distributive
		15	Instructional Media Svcs	26	Business Education	36	Guidance Services K-12	46	Math Elem	56	Remedial Reading Sec	66	Religious Education Sec	76	Info Systems
		16	Chief Operations Officer	27	Career & Tech Ed	37	Guidance Services Elem	47	Math Sec	57	Bilingual/ELL	67	School Board President	77	Psychological Assess
		17	Chief Academic Officer	28	Technology Education	38	Guidance Services Sec	48	English/Lang Arts K-12	58	Special Education K-12	68	Teacher Personnel	78	Affirmative Action

Texas School Directory — Wharton County

St Augustine High Sch	9-12	627	956/724-8131
1300 Galveston St, Laredo 78040		38	Fax 956/724-2770
Olga Gentry			
St Peter's Memorial Sch	PK-8	180	956/723-6302
1519 Houston St, Laredo 78040		11	Fax 956/725-2671
Sr Beth Yoest			

WEBB PRIVATE SCHOOLS

Private Schs..Principal	Grd	Prgm	Enr/#Cls	SN
Mary Help of Christians Sch	K-8		614	956/722-3966
10 E Del Mar Blvd, Laredo 78041			33	Fax 956/722-1413
Sr Vuong DO				
United Day Sch	PK-8		390	956/723-7261
1701 San Isidro Pkwy, Laredo 78045			25	Fax 956/718-4048
Jessica Rivera				

WHARTON COUNTY

WHARTON PUBLIC SCHOOLS

• **Boling Ind School Dist** PID: 01059535 979/657-2770
301 Texas Ave, Boling 77420 Fax 979/657-3265

Schools: 3 \ *Teachers:* 70 \ *Students:* 1,000 \ *Special Ed Students:* 75 \ *LEP Students:* 64 \ *College-Bound:* 67% \ *Ethnic:* Asian 1%, African American 9%, Hispanic 54%, Caucasian 36% \ *Exp:* $373 (High) \ *Poverty:* 16% \ *Title I:* $146,661 \ *Open-Close:* 08/15 - 05/20 \ *DTBP:* $301 (High)

Wade Stidevent 1,83		Cherry Page 2		
Larry Fisher 3,5		Mark Salais 4		
Kevin Urbanek 6		Nicole Folmar 7*		
Inez Kucera 9		Bryan Blanar 11,15,58,84,285,298		
Sarah Wilkins 36*		Linda Taylor 57		
Donald Sciba 67		Terrell Jessen 73*		

Public Schs..Principal	Grd	Prgm	Enr/#Cls	SN
Boling High Sch	9-12	T	328	42% 979/657-2816
407 Atlantic St, Boling 77420			25	Fax 979/657-2026
Keith Jedlicka				
Iago Junior High Sch	6-8	TV	278	55% 979/657-2826
200 Gift St, Boling 77420			20	Fax 979/657-2828
Gerald Floyd				
Newgulf Elem Sch	PK-5	AT	490	55% 979/657-2837
1867 Burning Stone Dr, Boling 77420			30	Fax 979/657-3604
Inez Kucera				

• **East Bernard Ind Sch Dist** PID: 01059573 979/335-7519
723 College St, East Bernard 77435 Fax 979/335-6561

Schools: 3 \ *Teachers:* 79 \ *Students:* 950 \ *Special Ed Students:* 67 \ *LEP Students:* 45 \ *Ethnic:* African American 6%, Hispanic 29%, Caucasian 64% \ *Exp:* $460 (High) \ *Poverty:* 17% \ *Title I:* $169,996 \ *Open-Close:* 08/15 - 05/27 \ *DTBP:* $350 (High) \ 📘 🅣

Courtney Hudgins 1	Becky Kovar 2,11,294,296	
Wade Bosse 6*	Sandra Dusek 7*	
Kimberly Sulak 8,31,83,88,270,271*	Philip Gaudette 9,273*	
Lacey Christ 58	Brian Mica 67	
Jennifer Rieger 69	Jackson Williams 73,84,295	

Public Schs..Principal	Grd	Prgm	Enr/#Cls	SN
East Bernard Elem Sch	PK-4	T	340	46% 979/335-7519
723 College St, East Bernard 77435			17	Fax 979/335-6341
Philip Gaudette				
East Bernard High Sch	9-12	AV	324	26% 979/335-7519
723 College St, East Bernard 77435			35	Fax 979/335-6085
Jeremy Janczak				
East Bernard Jr High Sch	5-8		290	33% 979/335-7519
723 College St, East Bernard 77435			17	Fax 979/335-6415
Jay Janczak				

• **El Campo Ind School Dist** PID: 01059602 979/543-6771
700 W Norris St, El Campo 77437 Fax 979/543-1670

Schools: 5 \ *Teachers:* 236 \ *Students:* 3,600 \ *Special Ed Students:* 339 \ *LEP Students:* 396 \ *Ethnic:* African American 11%, Hispanic 64%, Caucasian 25% \ *Exp:* $420 (High) \ *Poverty:* 27% \ *Title I:* $1,293,968 \ *Open-Close:* 08/14 - 05/25 \ *DTBP:* $159 (High)

Kelly Waters 1	David Bright 2,3,15,17
Greg Anderson 3,17	Jeff Balcar 3,91
Scott Gelardi 4	Chris Burrow 5*
Wayne Condra 6*	Monica Ott 7*
Doloris Trevino 8,15,18,57,271,274	Alicia Stary 11,294,296
Christopher Skinner 16,73,82*	Amy Bosse 58
James Russell 67	Terese Faas 68,79
Tana Martin 69	Thomas Krenek 76,84,286
Donald Oldag 295	

Public Schs..Principal	Grd	Prgm	Enr/#Cls	SN
El Campo High Sch	9-12	ATV	1,114	55% 979/543-6341
600 W Norris St, El Campo 77437			82	Fax 979/543-2528
Demetric Wells				
El Campo Middle Sch	6-8	AT	863	72% 979/543-6362
4010 FM 2765 Rd, El Campo 77437			50	Fax 979/541-5210
Gary Figirova				
Hutchins Elem Sch	2-3	T	563	74% 979/543-5481
1006 Roberts St, El Campo 77437			41	Fax 979/543-2418
Elizabeth Tupa				🅣
Myatt Elem Sch	PK-1	T	653	85% 979/543-7514
501 W Webb St, El Campo 77437			35	Fax 979/543-5188
Mauri Couey				
Northside Elem Sch	4-5	T	549	71% 979/543-5812
2610 Meadow Ln, El Campo 77437			24	Fax 979/578-0682
Rebecca Crowell				

• **Louise Ind School Dist** PID: 01059664 979/648-2982
408 2nd St, Louise 77455 Fax 979/648-2520

Schools: 3 \ *Teachers:* 38 \ *Students:* 500 \ *Special Ed Students:* 20 \ *LEP Students:* 63 \ *College-Bound:* 53% \ *Ethnic:* Asian 1%, African American 5%, Hispanic 56%, Caucasian 38% \ *Exp:* $348 (High) \ *Poverty:* 18% \ *Title I:* $98,520 \ *Open-Close:* 08/27 - 06/01 \ *DTBP:* $345 (High)

Dr Garth Oliver 1	Pam Wagner 2
Mike Briden 3,5,91	Shae Barker 4
Heath Clawson 6*	Kathryn Peterson 8
Traci Harvey 38	Donna Kutac 57*
Linda Alderson 67	Sandra Holik 73,286,295

---

79 Student Personnel	91 Safety/Security	275 Response To Intervention	298 Grant Writer/Ptnrships	**School Programs**	**Social Media**	
80 Driver Ed/Safety	92 Magnet School	277 Remedial Math K-12	750 Chief Innovation Officer	A = Alternative Program	📘 = Facebook	
81 Gifted/Talented	93 Parental Involvement	280 Literacy Coach	751 Chief of Staff	G = Adult Classes		
82 Video Services	95 Tech Prep Program	285 STEM	752 Social Emotional Learning	M = Magnet Program	🅣 = Twitter	
83 Substance Abuse Prev	97 Chief Infomation Officer	286 Digital Learning		T = Title I Schoolwide		
84 Erate	98 Chief Technology Officer	288 Common Core Standards	**Other School Types**	V = Career & Tech Ed Programs		
85 AIDS Education	270 Character Education	294 Accountability	Ⓐ = Alternative School			
88 Alternative/At Risk	271 Migrant Education	295 Network System	Ⓒ = Charter School	New Schools are shaded		
89 Multi-Cultural Curriculum	273 Teacher Mentor	296 Title II Programs	Ⓜ = Magnet School	New Superintendents and Principals are bold		
90 Social Work	274 Before/After Sch	297 Webmaster	Ⓨ = Year-Round School	Personnel with email addresses are underscored		

TX—389

Wheeler County

Market Data Retrieval

Public Schs..Principal	Grd	Prgm	Enr/#Cls	SN	
Louise Elem Sch 408 2nd St, Louise 77455 Pamela Lechler	PK-5	T	233 21	63%	979/648-2262
Louise High Sch 505 Hackberry St, Louise 77455 Donna Kutac	9-12	T	153 16	48%	979/648-2202 Fax 979/648-2142
Louise Junior High Sch 408 2nd St, Louise 77455 Brady Peterson	6-8	T	133	58%	979/648-2262

● **Wharton Ind School Dist** PID: 01059690   979/532-3612
2100 N Fulton St, Wharton 77488   Fax 979/532-6228

Schools: 5 \ *Teachers:* 169 \ *Students:* 2,097 \ *Special Ed Students:* 196 \ *LEP Students:* 223 \ *Ethnic:* Asian 1%, African American 27%, Hispanic 59%, Caucasian 14% \ *Exp:* $598 (High) \ *Poverty:* 22% \ *Title I:* $635,103 \ *Special Education:* $527,000 \ *Open-Close:* 08/15 - 05/28 \ *DTBP:* $360 (High) \

Tina Herrington 1
Emilio Vargas 3,15
Alison Robeledo 4
Diana Garcia 7*
David Calbert 58
Rachel Rust 67
Anna Sanders 82*
Randy Hill 2
Randall Meyer 3,15,68
Tim Finn 6*
Gayle Parenica 8
Kimberly Somer 58,90*
Sheri Ganske 73,297

Public Schs..Principal	Grd	Prgm	Enr/#Cls	SN	
C G Sivells Elem Sch 1605 N Alabama Rd, Wharton 77488 Trisha Terrell	PK-2	T	532 70	91%	979/532-6866 Fax 979/532-6873
ⓐ Wharton Alternative Sch 1010 N Rusk St, Wharton 77488 Kim Harris	7-12	V	60 4		979/532-6262 Fax 979/532-6266
Wharton Elem Sch 2030 E Boling Hwy, Wharton 77488 Jennifer Spears	3-6	T	675 45	86%	979/532-6882 Fax 979/532-6884
Wharton High Sch 1 Tiger Ave, Wharton 77488 **Jerrell Barron**	9-12	TV	586 60	67%	979/532-6800 Fax 979/532-6807
Wharton Junior High Sch 1120 N Rusk St, Wharton 77488 **Olatunji Oduwole**	7-8	GT	304 44	85%	979/532-6840 Fax 979/532-6849

WHARTON CATHOLIC SCHOOLS

● **Diocese of Victoria Ed Office** PID: 02181727
Listing includes only schools located in this county. See District Index for location of Diocesan Offices.

Catholic Schs..Principal	Grd	Prgm	Enr/#Cls	SN	
St Philip Catholic Sch 302 W Church St, El Campo 77437 Gwen Edwards	PK-8		330 12		979/543-2901 Fax 979/578-8835

WHARTON PRIVATE SCHOOLS

Private Schs..Principal	Grd	Prgm	Enr/#Cls	SN	
Faith Christian Academy 5227 FM 1301 Rd, Wharton 77488 Sandra Allen	PK-12		100		979/531-1000

WHEELER COUNTY

WHEELER PUBLIC SCHOOLS

● **Ft Elliott Cons Ind Sch Dist** PID: 01059779   806/375-2454
501 E Wilson Ave, Briscoe 79011   Fax 806/375-2327

Schools: 1 \ *Teachers:* 22 \ *Students:* 138 \ *Special Ed Students:* 19 \ *College-Bound:* 80% \ *Ethnic:* Hispanic 9%, Caucasian 91% \ *Exp:* $586 (High) \ *Poverty:* 9% \ *Title I:* $14,048 \ *Open-Close:* 08/22 - 05/21 \ *DTBP:* $350 (High)

Frank Belcher 1,11,73,83
Brandon Mahler 8,88,273
Susan Hughes 58*
Gwen Gibson 2*
Kevin Meek 27*
Bret Begert 67

Public Schs..Principal	Grd	Prgm	Enr/#Cls	SN	
Ft Elliott Sch 501 E Wilson Road, Briscoe 79011 Brandon Mahler	PK-12	V	138 18	19%	806/375-2454

● **Kelton Ind School Dist** PID: 01059808   806/826-5795
16703 FM 2697, Wheeler 79096   Fax 806/826-5737

Schools: 1 \ *Teachers:* 19 \ *Students:* 95 \ *Special Ed Students:* 8 \ *LEP Students:* 8 \ *College-Bound:* 100% \ *Ethnic:* Asian 1%, Hispanic 37%, Caucasian 62% \ *Exp:* $998 (High) \ *Poverty:* 14% \ *Open-Close:* 08/26 - 05/22

Carl Taylor 1,57,288
Kathleen Reynolds 16*
Bret Buckingham 67
Barbara Harris 7*
Karen Byrum 58*

Public Schs..Principal	Grd	Prgm	Enr/#Cls	SN	
Kelton Sch 16703 FM 2697, Wheeler 79096	PK-12		95 29	62%	806/826-5795

● **Shamrock Ind School Dist** PID: 01059858   806/256-3492
100 S Illinois St, Shamrock 79079   Fax 806/256-3628

Schools: 3 \ *Teachers:* 41 \ *Students:* 426 \ *Special Ed Students:* 41 \ *LEP Students:* 15 \ *College-Bound:* 80% \ *Ethnic:* Asian 1%, African American 8%, Hispanic 31%, Native American: 3%, Caucasian 58% \ *Exp:* $379 (High) \ *Poverty:* 26% \ *Title I:* $134,669 \ *Open-Close:* 08/28 - 05/25 \ *DTBP:* $340 (High)

Kenneth Shields 1
Christi Evans 4*
Amanda Bell 7*
Laramie Jernigan 16,73*
Connie Jones 2
Jody Guy 6*
Kenneth Shields 12,57
Lanna Reeves 34,58

---

1 Superintendent	8 Curric/Instruct K-12	19 Chief Financial Officer	29 Family/Consumer Science	39 Social Studies K-12	49 English/Lang Arts Elem	59 Special Education Elem	69 Academic Assessment
2 Bus/Finance/Purchasing	9 Curric/Instruct Elem	20 Art K-12	30 Adult Education	40 Social Studies Elem	50 English/Lang Arts Sec	60 Special Education Sec	70 Research/Development
3 Buildings And Grounds	10 Curric/Instruct Sec	21 Art Elem	31 Career/Sch-to-Work K-12	41 Social Studies Sec	51 Reading K-12	61 Foreign/World Lang K-12	71 Public Information
4 Food Service	11 Federal Program	22 Art Sec	32 Career/Sch-to-Work Elem	42 Science K-12	52 Reading Elem	62 Foreign/World Lang Elem	72 Summer School
5 Transportation	12 Title I	23 Music K-12	33 Career/Sch-to-Work Sec	43 Science Elem	53 Reading Sec	63 Foreign/World Lang Sec	73 Instructional Tech
6 Athletic	13 Title V	24 Music Elem	34 Early Childhood Ed	44 Science Sec	54 Remedial Reading K-12	64 Religious Education K-12	74 Inservice Training
7 Health Services	15 Asst Superintendent	25 Music Sec	35 Health/Phys Education	45 Math K-12	55 Remedial Reading Elem	65 Religious Education Elem	75 Marketing/Distributive
	16 Instructional Media Svcs	26 Business Education	36 Guidance Services K-12	46 Math Elem	56 Remedial Reading Sec	66 Religious Education Sec	76 Info Systems
	17 Chief Operations Officer	27 Career & Tech Ed	37 Guidance Services Elem	47 Math Sec	57 Bilingual/ELL	67 School Board President	77 Psychological Assess
	18 Chief Academic Officer	28 Technology Education	38 Guidance Services Sec	48 English/Lang Arts K-12	58 Special Education K-12	68 Teacher Personnel	78 Affirmative Action

Texas School Directory — Wichita County

Richard Hall 67   Ed Berngen 69*

Public Schs..Principal	Grd	Prgm	Enr/#Cls	SN	
Shamrock Elem Sch 100 S Illinois St, Shamrock 79079 **Andy Glass**	PK-5	T	193 14	70%	806/256-3227
Shamrock High Sch 100 S Illinois St, Shamrock 79079 Blaze Herring	9-12	TV	100 25	55%	806/256-2241
Shamrock Junior High Sch 100 S Illinois St, Shamrock 79079 Frank Berngen	6-8	T	100 20	67%	806/256-3227

• **Wheeler Ind School Dist** PID: 01059896   806/826-5241
1 Mustang Dr, Wheeler 79096   Fax 806/826-3118

Schools: 1 \ *Teachers:* 42 \ *Students:* 487 \ *Special Ed Students:* 45 \ *LEP Students:* 82 \ *College-Bound:* 72% \ *Ethnic:* Hispanic 61%, Caucasian 39% \ *Exp:* $389 (High) \ *Poverty:* 22% \ *Title I:* $110,945 \ *Open-Close:* 08/21 - 05/22 \ *DTBP:* $424 (High)

Bryan Markham 1,11,83   Stacie Horton 2,19,298
Randi Barr .... 4*   Chris Evans 6*
David Dale .... 8,81,270,273*   Heather Hardcastle 12,296*
Cecil Thomas .... 16,73*   Angie Ware 27*
Stacey Finsterwald .... 57*   Jennifer Houska 58
Dr Leanne Hillhouse 67   Erin Shaw 69*

Public Schs..Principal	Grd	Prgm	Enr/#Cls	SN	
Wheeler Sch 1 Mustang Dr, Wheeler 79096 **Mike Bailey** \ David Dale	PK-12	T	487 40	51%	806/826-5241

WICHITA COUNTY

WICHITA PUBLIC SCHOOLS

• **Burkburnett Ind Sch Dist** PID: 01059925   940/569-3326
100 N Avenue D, Burkburnett 76354   Fax 940/569-4776

Schools: 6 \ *Teachers:* 246 \ *Students:* 3,350 \ *Special Ed Students:* 338 \ *LEP Students:* 44 \ *Ethnic:* Asian 1%, African American 8%, Hispanic 18%, Native American: 1%, Caucasian 73% \ *Exp:* $323 (High) \ *Poverty:* 16% \ *Title I:* $643,531 \ *Special Education:* $796,000 \ *Open-Close:* 08/16 - 05/22 \ *DTBP:* $184 (High) \ ⨍

Tylor Chaplin 1   Laura Richards 2
Scott Simmons 3,91   Debbie Welch 4
Anthony West 5   Danny Nix 6*
Missy Mayfield 8,27,57,69,74,88,286,288   Dr Jim Russell 11,15
Brad Owen 16,73,82,295   Casey Hunter 27,298
Audrey Ash 58,271   Frank Andrajack 67
Elizabeth Nolan .... 81*   Anna Black 83,88*

Public Schs..Principal	Grd	Prgm	Enr/#Cls	SN	
Burkburnett High Sch 109 W Kramer Rd, Burkburnett 76354 Vance Morris	9-12	TV	889 80	44%	940/569-1411 Fax 940/569-9700
Burkburnett Middle Sch 108 S Avenue D, Burkburnett 76354 Michael Baughman	6-8	T	647 80	51%	940/569-3381 Fax 940/569-7116
ⓐ Gateway Alternative Ed Center 200 E 3rd St, Burkburnett 76354 Anna Black	1-12		25 4		940/569-0850 Fax 940/569-3030
I C Evans Elem Sch 1015 S Berry St, Burkburnett 76354 Michelle Wiese	PK-5	T	734 26	54%	940/569-3311 Fax 940/569-2719
John Tower Elem Sch 5200 Hooper Dr, Wichita Falls 76306 Jason Nolan	PK-5	T	495 38	50%	940/855-3221 Fax 940/855-9812
Overton Ray Elem Sch 345 D W Taylor Pathway, Burkburnett 76354 Kendy Johnston	3-5	T	458 53	71%	940/569-5253

• **City View Ind School Dist** PID: 01059999   940/855-4042
1025 City View Dr, Wichita Falls 76306   Fax 940/851-8889

Schools: 2 \ *Teachers:* 82 \ *Students:* 1,058 \ *Special Ed Students:* 113 \ *LEP Students:* 22 \ *College-Bound:* 51% \ *Ethnic:* Asian 1%, African American 9%, Hispanic 31%, Native American: 1%, Caucasian 58% \ *Exp:* $666 (High) \ *Poverty:* 23% \ *Title I:* $227,448 \ *Open-Close:* 08/19 - 05/21 \ *DTBP:* $216 (High)

Tony Bushong 1   Debbie McDaris 2
Dub Ewing 3   Daphne Ramsey 4
Kevin Coffman 5   Rudy Hawkins 6*
Holly Hawkins 8,11   Cindy Leaverton 10,31,83*
Chuck Thompson .... 16*   Holley Hawkins 16,57,69,88,273
Zach Ward 27   Gypsy Karr 67
Ann Park 68   Jeff St Andre 73,84
Lana Wampler 76   Steve Messinger 295

Public Schs..Principal	Grd	Prgm	Enr/#Cls	SN	
City View Elem Sch 1023 City View Dr, Wichita Falls 76306 Ronda Davis	PK-6	T	605 31	69%	940/855-2351 Fax 940/855-7943
City View Jr Sr High Sch 1600 City View Dr, Wichita Falls 76306 Scott Boswell	7-12	ATV	453 32	64%	940/855-7511 Fax 940/851-5027

• **Electra Ind School Dist** PID: 01060015   940/495-3683
400 E Roosevelt Ave, Electra 76360   Fax 940/495-3945

Schools: 3 \ *Teachers:* 43 \ *Students:* 430 \ *Special Ed Students:* 45 \ *LEP Students:* 3 \ *College-Bound:* 47% \ *Ethnic:* Asian 1%, African American 7%, Hispanic 16%, Caucasian 76% \ *Exp:* $233 (Med) \ *Poverty:* 20% \ *Title I:* $129,418 \ *Open-Close:* 08/26 - 05/22 \ *DTBP:* $606 (High)

Ted West 1   Laura Lee Brock 2,8,11,27,31,88,273
Debra Malone 4   Brian Ramsey 6*
Steven Wallace .... 9,54*   Janet Goodwin 11,57,271*
Angela Schlegel 58   Wayne Cranford 67
Renneth Reed .... 73,295*   Scott Hogue 83
Rayann Stevens 275*

Public Schs..Principal	Grd	Prgm	Enr/#Cls	SN	
Electra Elem Sch 621 S Bailey St, Electra 76360 Steven Wallace	PK-6	T	259 24	77%	940/432-3815 Fax 940/495-3627
Electra Jr Senior High Sch 200 Anderson Ave, Electra 76360 Jim Russell	7-12	TV	156 23	58%	940/432-3812 Fax 940/257-2815

---

79 Student Personnel	91 Safety/Security	275 Response To Intervention	298 Grant Writer/Ptnrships	**School Programs**	**Social Media**		
80 Driver Ed/Safety	92 Magnet School	277 Remedial Math K-12	750 Chief Innovation Officer	A = Alternative Program			
81 Gifted/Talented	93 Parental Involvement	280 Literacy Coach	751 Chief of Staff	G = Adult Classes	⨍ = Facebook		
82 Video Services	95 Tech Prep Program	285 STEM	752 Social Emotional Learning	M = Magnet Program			
83 Substance Abuse Prev	97 Chief Infomation Officer	286 Digital Learning		T = Title I Schoolwide	ⓣ = Twitter		
84 Erate	98 Chief Technology Officer	288 Common Core Standards	**Other School Types**	V = Career & Tech Ed Programs			
85 AIDS Education	270 Character Education	294 Accountability	ⓐ = Alternative School				
88 Alternative/At Risk	271 Migrant Education	295 Network System	ⓒ = Charter School	New Schools are shaded			
89 Multi-Cultural Curriculum	273 Teacher Mentor	296 Title II Programs	ⓜ = Magnet School	New Superintendents and Principals are bold			
90 Social Work	274 Before/After Sch	297 Webmaster	ⓨ = Year-Round School	Personnel with email addresses are underscored			

Wichita County

Market Data Retrieval

Ⓐ Texoma Alternative Center 4-12 40 940/592-1410
205 N Colorado St, Iowa Park 76367 4 Fax 940/592-1486
Rosie Flanigan

• **Iowa Park Consolidated Ind SD** PID: 01060065 940/592-4193
328 E Hwy, Iowa Park 76367 Fax 940/592-2136

Schools: 4 \ *Teachers:* 128 \ *Students:* 1,839 \ *Special Ed Students:* 203 \ *LEP Students:* 13 \ *Ethnic:* Asian 1%, African American 1%, Hispanic 11%, Native American: 1%, Caucasian 87% \ *Exp:* $496 (High) \ *Poverty:* 11% \ *Title I:* $209,427 \ *Open-Close:* 08/15 - 05/20 \ *DTBP:* $550 (High) \ f t

Steve Moody 1
Tim Kingcade 3
Ned Miller 5
Jodie Schlaud 8,73,285,286,288
Anjela Schlegel 58
Cindy Bartow 68
Cindy Teichman 79
Sharon Godwin 2,11,19,298
Serena Criswell 4
Aubrey Sims 6*
Brandy Rhoades 36*
Jeff Rhoades 67
Mike Parchman 76

Public Schs..Principal	Grd	Prgm	Enr/#Cls	SN	
Bradford Elem Sch 809 Texowa Rd, Iowa Park 76367 Brandi Swenson	3-5	T	405 26	42%	940/592-5841 Fax 940/592-2059
Iowa Park High Sch 1 Bob Dawson Dr, Iowa Park 76367 Leah Russell	9-12	V	535 50	35%	940/592-2144 Fax 940/592-2583
Kidwell Elem Sch 1200 N 3rd St, Iowa Park 76367 James Kennedy	PK-2	T	482 28	50%	940/592-4322 Fax 940/592-2487
W F George Middle Sch 412 E Cash St, Iowa Park 76367 Darla Biddy	6-8	T	417 40	41%	940/592-2196 Fax 940/592-2801

• **Wichita Falls Ind School Dist** PID: 01060132 940/235-1000
1104 Broad St, Wichita Falls 76301

Schools: 28 \ *Teachers:* 1,032 \ *Students:* 14,500 \ *Special Ed Students:* 1,678 \ *LEP Students:* 928 \ *College-Bound:* 46% \ *Ethnic:* Asian 3%, African American 15%, Hispanic 37%, Native American: 1%, Caucasian 45% \ *Exp:* $249 (Med) \ *Poverty:* 21% \ *Title I:* $4,081,410 \ *Special Education:* $2,602,000 \ *Open-Close:* 08/15 - 05/21 \ *DTBP:* $187 (High) \ f

Michael Kuhrt 1
Denise Brown 2
Christopher Fain 3
Debi Mills 7
Debbie Dippery 10,36
Peter Griffiths 15,286
Kelly Strenski 20,23
Synthia Kirby 27,31,73,95*
Julie Henderson 35,83,85
Greta Benavides 57
Elizabeth Yeager 67
Shannon Kuhrt 69
Frank Murray 73
Ward Roberts 81
Bill Horton 91
Alicia Woodard 2
Tim Sherrod 2,19
Scot Hafley 6
Misti Spear 9
Jackie Wheat 11
Shad McGaha 16,73,76,98,295
Michelle Wood 27,31
Dr Travis Armstrong 34
Sherry Parker 39
Alefia Paris-Toulon 58
Cyndy Kohl 68
Ashley Thomas 71
Dr Linda Muehlberger 79,93
Betsi Morton 88
Jessica Wilkins 297

Public Schs..Principal	Grd	Prgm	Enr/#Cls	SN	
Ⓜ Barwise Middle Sch 3807 Kemp Blvd, Wichita Falls 76308 Peter Braveboy	6-8	TV	1,137 39	67%	940/235-1108 Fax 940/235-1348
Booker T Washington ES 1300 Harding St, Wichita Falls 76301 Mark Davis	PK-5	T	286 15	96%	940/235-1196 Fax 940/235-1197
Brook Village Eec 2222 Brook Ave, Wichita Falls 76301 Letitia Willis	PK-K		251 14		940/235-1132 Fax 940/235-1133
Ⓜ Burgess Elem Sch 3106 Maurine St, Wichita Falls 76306 Jeff Hill	PK-5	T	283 36	96%	940/235-1136 Fax 940/235-1137
Career Education Center 500 E Hatton Rd, Wichita Falls 76302 Synthia Kirby	Voc		150		940/235-4316
Crockett Elem Sch 3015 Avenue I, Wichita Falls 76309 Lee Farris	K-5	T	524 35	61%	940/235-1140 Fax 940/235-1141
Cunningham Elem Sch 4100 Pool St, Wichita Falls 76308 Ashley Davis	PK-5	T	457 28	68%	940/235-1144 Fax 940/235-1145
Ⓐ Denver Alternative Center 1823 5th St, Wichita Falls 76301 Linda Nichols	K-12		150 9		940/235-1101 Fax 940/235-1102
Fain Elem Sch 1562 Norman St, Wichita Falls 76302 Clarisa Richie	PK-5	T	505 27	54%	940/235-1148 Fax 940/235-1149
Farris Early Childhood Center 710 Burkburnett Rd, Wichita Falls 76306 Letitia Willis	PK-PK	T	211 16	99%	940/235-4302 Fax 940/235-4303
Fowler Elem Sch 5100 Ridgecrest Dr, Wichita Falls 76310 Alexandra Martin	PK-5	T	556 28	43%	940/235-1152 Fax 940/235-1153
Franklin Elem Sch 2112 Speedway Ave, Wichita Falls 76308 Angie Betts	PK-5	T	481 36	57%	940/235-1156 Fax 940/235-1157
Haynes Northwest Academy 1705 Katherine Dr, Wichita Falls 76306 Lori Apple	PK-5	T	220 25	77%	940/235-1160 Fax 940/235-1161
Ⓜ Hirschi High Sch 3106 Borton St, Wichita Falls 76306 Doug Albus	9-12	TV	918 80	69%	940/235-1070 Fax 940/235-1300
Jefferson Elem Sch 4628 Mistletoe Dr, Wichita Falls 76310 Erica Adkins	PK-5	T	444 23	56%	940/235-1168 Fax 940/235-1169
Ⓜ Kirby Middle Sch 1715 Loop 11, Wichita Falls 76306 Shannon Cunningham	6-8	TV	631 39	83%	940/235-1113 Fax 940/235-1114
Lamar Elem Sch 2206 Lucas Ave, Wichita Falls 76301 Amanda Garcia	PK-5	T	358 25	93%	940/235-1172 Fax 940/235-1173
Ⓜ McNiel Middle Sch 4712 Barnett Rd, Wichita Falls 76310 Summer Bynum	6-8	TV	1,176 50	47%	940/235-1118 Fax 940/235-1119
Milam Elem Sch 2901 Boren Ave, Wichita Falls 76308 Naomi Alejandro	PK-5	T	504 34	61%	940/235-1176 Fax 940/235-1305 f
North West Head Start Center 2310 Seymour Hwy, Wichita Falls 76301 Letitia Willis	PK-PK	T	51	94%	940/322-1905
Ⓜ Rider High Sch 4611 Cypress Ave, Wichita Falls 76310 Dr Cody Blair	9-12	TV	1,494 90	32%	940/235-1077 Fax 940/235-1301
Rosewood Head Start Center 503 N Rosewood Ave, Wichita Falls 76301 Letitia Willis	PK-PK	T	101 7	97%	940/235-4309 Fax 940/766-4126
Ⓜ Scotland Park Elem Sch 1415 N 5th St, Wichita Falls 76306 Laura Scott	PK-5	T	467 26	95%	940/235-1180 Fax 940/235-1303
Sheppard AFB Elem Sch 301 Anderson Dr, Sheppard Afb 76311 Cindy Waddell	PK-6		317 18	15%	940/235-1184 Fax 940/235-1185

1 Superintendent	8 Curric/Instruct K-12	19 Chief Financial Officer	29 Family/Consumer Science	39 Social Studies K-12	49 English/Lang Arts Elem	59 Special Education Elem	69 Academic Assessment
2 Bus/Finance/Purchasing	9 Curric/Instruct Elem	20 Art K-12	30 Adult Education	40 Social Studies Elem	50 English/Lang Arts Sec	60 Special Education Sec	70 Research/Development
3 Buildings And Grounds	10 Curric/Instruct Sec	21 Art Elem	31 Career/Sch-to-Work K-12	41 Social Studies Sec	51 Reading K-12	61 Foreign/World Lang K-12	71 Public Information
4 Food Service	11 Federal Program	22 Art Sec	32 Career/Sch-to-Work Elem	42 Science K-12	52 Reading Elem	62 Foreign/World Lang Elem	72 Summer School
5 Transportation	12 Title I	23 Music K-12	33 Career/Sch-to-Work Sec	43 Science Elem	53 Reading Sec	63 Foreign/World Lang Sec	73 Instructional Tech
6 Athletic	13 Title V	24 Music Elem	34 Early Childhood Ed	44 Science Sec	54 Remedial Reading K-12	64 Religious Education K-12	74 Inservice Training
7 Health Services	15 Asst Superintendent	25 Music Sec	35 Health/Phys Education	45 Math K-12	55 Remedial Reading Elem	65 Religious Education Elem	75 Marketing/Distributive
	16 Instructional Media Svcs	26 Business Education	36 Guidance Services K-12	46 Math Elem	56 Remedial Reading Sec	66 Religious Education Sec	76 Info Systems
	17 Chief Operations Officer	27 Career & Tech Ed	37 Guidance Services Elem	47 Math Sec	57 Bilingual/ELL	67 School Board President	77 Psychological Assess
	18 Chief Academic Officer	28 Technology Education	38 Guidance Services Sec	48 English/Lang Arts K-12	58 Special Education K-12	68 Teacher Personnel	78 Affirmative Action

Texas School Directory

Wilbarger County

Southern Hills Elem Sch 3920 Armory Rd, Wichita Falls 76302 Jeremy Lopez	PK-5	T	478 29	74%	940/235-1188 Fax 940/235-1304
West Foundation Elem Sch 5220 Lake Wellington Pkwy, Wichita Falls 76310 Kim Smith	PK-5		463 28	32%	940/235-1192 Fax 940/235-1193
Ⓜ Wichita Falls High Sch 2149 Avenue H, Wichita Falls 76309 Christy Nash	9-12	TV	1,248	60%	940/235-1084 Fax 940/235-1310
Zundy Elem Sch 1706 Polk St, Wichita Falls 76309 Stacey Darnall	PK-5	T	547 25	87%	940/235-1123 Fax 940/235-1124

WICHITA CATHOLIC SCHOOLS

• **Diocese of Fort Worth Ed Off** PID: 01054339
Listing includes only schools located in this county. See District Index for location of Diocesan Offices.

Catholic Schs..Principal	Grd	Prgm	Enr/#Cls SN	
Notre Dame Catholic Sch 2821 Lansing Blvd, Wichita Falls 76309 Rachel Gutgsell	PK-12		260 25	940/692-6041 Fax 940/692-2811

WICHITA PRIVATE SCHOOLS

Private Schs..Principal	Grd	Prgm	Enr/#Cls SN	
Bible Baptist Christian Sch 1606 30th St, Wichita Falls 76302 Dj James	PK-12		22 3	940/723-2446 Fax 940/763-0712
Christ Academy 5105 Stone Lake Dr, Wichita Falls 76310 Tim Callaway	PK-12		240 20	940/692-2853 Fax 940/692-2657 🅵
Wichita Christian Sch 1615 Midwestern Pkwy, Wichita Falls 76302 Courtney Cummings \ Julie Foster	K-12		200	940/763-1347 Fax 940/687-0744

WICHITA REGIONAL CENTERS

• **Region 9 Ed Service Center** PID: 01060120   940/322-6928
301 Loop 11, Wichita Falls 76306   Fax 940/767-3836

Wes Pierce 1		Janay Litz 2	
Cindy Moses 8,58,77,275		Darren Francis 15,16,73	
Michael Chapman 27,31,36			

WILBARGER COUNTY

WILBARGER PUBLIC SCHOOLS

• **Harrold Ind School Dist** PID: 01060508   940/886-2213
18106 Stewart St, Harrold 76364   Fax 940/886-2215

Schools: 1 \ *Teachers:* 14 \ *Students:* 110 \ *Special Ed Students:* 11 \ *College-Bound:* 90% \ *Ethnic:* Asian 2%, African American 3%, Hispanic 39%, Native American: 1%, Caucasian 56% \ *Exp:* $589 (High) \ *Poverty:* 14% \ *Open-Close:* 08/22 - 05/21 \ 🅵

David Thweatt 1,11,73		Lynn Dhane 2,16,271*	
Craig Templeton 8,57,69,83,88,273*		Carla Clayton 58*	
Tim Clouse 67			

Public Schs..Principal	Grd	Prgm	Enr/#Cls SN	
Harrold Sch 18106 Stewart St, Harrold 76364 Craig Templeton	PK-12	V	110 17	66% 940/886-2213

• **Northside Ind School Dist** PID: 01060534   940/552-2551
18040 US Highway 283, Vernon 76384   Fax 940/553-4919

Schools: 1 \ *Teachers:* 18 \ *Students:* 230 \ *Special Ed Students:* 13 \ *LEP Students:* 3 \ *College-Bound:* 75% \ *Ethnic:* Asian 1%, African American 3%, Hispanic 27%, Caucasian 68% \ *Exp:* $739 (High) \ *Poverty:* 26% \ *Title I:* $13,645 \ *Open-Close:* 08/15 - 05/22 \ *DTBP:* $341 (High) \ 🅵 🆃

Mark Haught 1		Karen Skinner 2,84	
Debra Vincent 4		Jeremy Reeder 6*	
Kim Bria 7*		Molly Lemon 8,11,73*	
Lori Woods 57*		Dawn Wilkinson 58,88*	
Phoebe Reeves 67		Shari Coody 286*	

Public Schs..Principal	Grd	Prgm	Enr/#Cls SN	
Northside Sch 18040 US Highway 283, Vernon 76384 Molly Lemon	K-12	TV	230 20	33% 940/552-2551 🅵 🆃

• **Vernon Ind School Dist** PID: 01060560   940/553-1900
1713 Wilbarger St Ste 203, Vernon 76384   Fax 940/553-3802

Schools: 6 \ *Teachers:* 163 \ *Students:* 1,700 \ *Special Ed Students:* 243 \ *LEP Students:* 194 \ *Ethnic:* Asian 4%, African American 9%, Hispanic 44%, Native American: 1%, Caucasian 41% \ *Exp:* $301 (High) \ *Poverty:* 21% \ *Title I:* $527,265 \ *Open-Close:* 08/15 - 05/22 \ *DTBP:* $333 (High) \ 🅵 🆃

Jeff Byrd 1		Tammi Wrinkle 2	
Jimmy Anderson 3,5		Tammie Newcomer 4	
Matthew Hoover 6*		Hope Appel 8,11,57,69,288,294,298	
Blaise Boswell 16,73,295		Toni Waldo 58,275,286	
Emory Byars 67		Trisha Dillingham 83,90	

Public Schs..Principal	Grd	Prgm	Enr/#Cls SN	
Central Elem Sch 1300 Paradise St, Vernon 76384 Kacy Hunter	2-3	T	278 20	72% 940/553-1859 Fax 940/553-1138

---

79 Student Personnel	91 Safety/Security	275 Response To Intervention	298 Grant Writer/Ptnrships	**School Programs**		**Social Media**	
80 Driver Ed/Safety	92 Magnet School	277 Remedial Math K-12	750 Chief Innovation Officer	A = Alternative Program		🅵 = Facebook	
81 Gifted/Talented	93 Parental Involvement	280 Literacy Coach	751 Chief of Staff	G = Adult Classes			
82 Video Services	95 Tech Prep Program	285 STEM	752 Social Emotional Learning	M = Magnet Program		🆃 = Twitter	
83 Substance Abuse Prev	97 Chief Infomation Officer	286 Digital Learning		T = Title I Schoolwide			
84 Erate	98 Chief Technology Officer	288 Common Core Standards	**Other School Types**	V = Career & Tech Ed Programs			
85 AIDS Education	270 Accountability	294 Accountability	Ⓐ = Alternative School				
88 Alternative/At Risk	271 Migrant Education	295 Network System	Ⓒ = Charter School	New Schools are shaded			
89 Multi-Cultural Curriculum	273 Teacher Mentor	296 Title II Programs	Ⓜ = Magnet School	New Superintendents and Principals are bold			
90 Social Work	274 Before/After Sch	297 Webmaster	Ⓨ = Year-Round School	Personnel with email addresses are underscored			

Willacy County

McCord Elem Sch 2915 Sand Rd, Vernon 76384 Scott Mills	PK-1	T	338 25	81%	940/553-4381 Fax 940/552-0056
Shive Elem Sch 3130 Bacon St, Vernon 76384 Stefanie Merrell	4-5	T	310 17	71%	940/553-4309 Fax 940/552-5597
Vernon High Sch 2102 Yucca Ln, Vernon 76384 Tommy Cummings	9-12	ATV	574 45	55%	940/553-3377 Fax 940/553-4531
Vernon Middle Sch 2200 Yamparika St, Vernon 76384 Blaise Boswell	6-8	ATV	471 40	66%	940/552-6231 Fax 940/552-0504
Ⓐ Visd Alternative Ed Sch 2211 London St, Vernon 76384 Joe Hennessee	K-12		20 2		940/552-2252 Fax 940/552-6999

WILLACY COUNTY

WILLACY PUBLIC SCHOOLS

• **Lasara Ind School Dist** PID: 01060637 956/642-3271
11932 Jones St, Lasara 78561 Fax 956/642-3751

Schools: 2 \ *Teachers:* 35 \ *Students:* 380 \ *Special Ed Students:* 37 \ *LEP Students:* 55 \ *College-Bound:* 42% \ *Ethnic:* Hispanic 98%, Native American: 1%, Caucasian 1% \ *Exp:* $506 (High) \ *Poverty:* 43% \ *Title I:* $206,239 \ *Open-Close:* 08/26 - 05/28 \ *DTBP:* $350 (High) \ 🅕 🅣

Sara Alvarado 1
Mary Cazares 4*
Roy Vega 6*
Ray Garza 16,73,295
Christina Vargas 58*
Rogelio Cantu 2,68,91
Ted Gutierrez 5*
Cynthia Ramos 8,11,69,74,271,273,285*
Karen McInnis 36,83,88,270,275*
Rolando Velazquez 67

Public Schs..Principal	Grd	Prgm	Enr/#Cls	SN	
Lasara Elem Sch 11932 Jones St, Lasara 78561 **Israel Quintanilla**	PK-8	GTV	298 25	77%	956/642-3271 🅕 🅣
Lasara High Sch 11932 Jones St, Lasara 78561 Israel Quintanilla	9-12	T	112	78%	956/642-3271

• **Lyford Cons Ind School Dist** PID: 01060651 956/347-3900
8204 Simon Gomez Rd, Lyford 78569 Fax 956/347-5588

Schools: 3 \ *Teachers:* 109 \ *Students:* 1,551 \ *Special Ed Students:* 126 \ *LEP Students:* 149 \ *College-Bound:* 55% \ *Ethnic:* Hispanic 97%, Caucasian 2% \ *Exp:* $726 (High) \ *Poverty:* 42% \ *Title I:* $844,567 \ *Open-Close:* 08/26 - 05/29 \ *DTBP:* $359 (High)

Eduardo Infante 1
Gilbert Vela 3,5
Juan Salinas 4
Israel Gonzalez 6
Kristin Brown 8,15,69
Senaida Garza 11,58,76
Allison Bosse-Savage 67
Milissa Pimepel 69*
Gilbert Gonzalez 73
Gil Saldivar 295,297*
Elisa Rosas 2
Joe Guerra 3
Aurelio Manriquez 5
Bibiana Bernal 7
Melissa Pimentel 8
Pilar Trevino 16,82,93
Veronica Sanches 68
Clarisa De La Fuente 71
Jesse Orozco 91

Public Schs..Principal	Grd	Prgm	Enr/#Cls	SN	
Lyford Elem Sch 13094 High School Circle, Lyford 78569 Veronica Lerma	PK-5	T	700 36	83%	956/347-3911 Fax 956/347-3577
Lyford High Sch 8201 High School Circle, Lyford 78569 Michelle DeWitt	9-12	ATV	475 40	83%	956/347-3909 Fax 956/347-5034
Lyford Middle Sch 12820 Glen Lofton Ave, Lyford 78569 Raul Gonzalez	6-8	AT	376 30	77%	956/347-3910 Fax 956/347-2351

• **Raymondville Ind Sch Dist** PID: 01060716 956/689-2471
419 FM 3168, Raymondville 78580 Fax 956/689-8180

Schools: 5 \ *Teachers:* 148 \ *Students:* 2,000 \ *Special Ed Students:* 170 \ *LEP Students:* 150 \ *College-Bound:* 42% \ *Ethnic:* Hispanic 99%, Caucasian 1% \ *Exp:* $411 (High) \ *Poverty:* 43% \ *Title I:* $1,343,043 \ *Open-Close:* 08/26 - 05/29 \ *DTBP:* $350 (High)

Stetson Roane 1
Kayla Arce 2
Norma Cavazos 4
Frank Cantu 6
Ben Clinton 11,15
John Solis 67
David Longoria 2,19
Oscar Gutierrez 3,5
Santos Zuniga 5
Andrea Mungia 8,69
Denise Butler 58
David Flores 73

Public Schs..Principal	Grd	Prgm	Enr/#Cls	SN	
L C Smith Elem Sch 700 N 1st St, Raymondville 78580 Antonio Guerra	PK-5	T	442 32	91%	956/689-8172 Fax 956/689-5871
Myra Green Middle Sch 419 FM 3168, Raymondville 78580 Raul Valdez	6-8	AT	436 50	90%	956/689-8171 Fax 956/689-2302
Pittman Elem Sch 258 E Harris St, Raymondville 78580 Sulema Davila	PK-5	T	615 47	88%	956/689-8173 Fax 956/689-1141
Raymondville High Sch 601 FM 3168, Raymondville 78580 **Frank Garcia**	9-12	ATV	529 60	86%	956/689-8170 Fax 956/689-3640
Ⓐ Raymondville Options Academy 512 E Rodriguez Ave, Raymondville 78580 Frank Garcia	9-12		61		956/689-8185

• **San Perlita Ind School Dist** PID: 01060780 956/248-5563
22987 Trojan Dr, San Perlita 78590 Fax 956/248-5561

Schools: 1 \ *Teachers:* 24 \ *Students:* 282 \ *Special Ed Students:* 33 \ *LEP Students:* 28 \ *College-Bound:* 100% \ *Ethnic:* Hispanic 85%, Caucasian 15% \ *Exp:* $463 (High) \ *Poverty:* 41% \ *Title I:* $131,425 \ *Open-Close:* 08/14 - 05/22 \ *DTBP:* $361 (High) \ 🅕 🅣

Albert Pena 1
Nathaniel Garza 6*
Janie Livas 11,298*
Crystal Rodriguez 69,83*
Debra Rodriguez 2
Adrian Montemayor 8,58*
Melissa Guadiana 67
Armando Torres 73,295*

Public Schs..Principal	Grd	Prgm	Enr/#Cls	SN	
San Perlita Sch 22987 Trojan Dr, San Perlita 78590 Adrian Montemayor \ Laurie Kilborn	PK-12	T	282 30	69%	956/248-5250 Fax 956/248-5103

1 Superintendent	8 Curric/Instruct K-12	19 Chief Financial Officer	29 Family/Consumer Science	39 Social Studies K-12	49 English/Lang Arts Elem	59 Special Education Elem	69 Academic Assessment
2 Bus/Finance/Purchasing	9 Curric/Instruct Elem	20 Art K-12	30 Adult Education	40 Social Studies Elem	50 English/Lang Arts Sec	60 Special Education Sec	70 Research/Development
3 Buildings And Grounds	10 Curric/Instruct Sec	21 Art Elem	31 Career/Sch-to-Work K-12	41 Social Studies Sec	51 Reading K-12	61 Foreign/World Lang K-12	71 Public Information
4 Food Service	11 Federal Program	22 Art Sec	32 Career/Sch-to-Work Elem	42 Science K-12	52 Reading Elem	62 Foreign/World Lang Elem	72 Summer School
5 Transportation	12 Title I	23 Music K-12	33 Career/Sch-to-Work Sec	43 Science Elem	53 Reading Sec	63 Foreign/World Lang Sec	73 Instructional Tech
6 Athletic	13 Title V	24 Music Elem	34 Early Childhood Ed	44 Science Sec	54 Remedial Reading K-12	64 Religious Education	74 Inservice Training
7 Health Services	15 Asst Superintendent	25 Music Sec	35 Health/Phys Education	45 Math K-12	55 Remedial Reading Elem	65 Religious Education Elem	75 Marketing/Distributive
	16 Instructional Media Svcs	26 Business Education	36 Guidance Services K-12	46 Math Elem	56 Remedial Reading Sec	66 Religious Education Sec	76 Info Systems
	17 Chief Operations Officer	27 Career & Tech Ed	37 Guidance Services Elem	47 Math Sec	57 Bilingual/ELL	67 School Board President	77 Psychological Assess
	18 Chief Academic Officer	28 Technology Education	38 Guidance Services Sec	48 English/Lang Arts K-12	58 Special Education K-12	68 Teacher Personnel	78 Affirmative Action

Texas School Directory

Williamson County

WILLIAMSON COUNTY

WILLIAMSON PUBLIC SCHOOLS

- **Coupland Ind School Dist** PID: 01060819   512/856-2422
  620 S Commerce St, Coupland 78615   Fax 512/856-2222

Schools: 1 \ **Teachers:** 12 \ **Students:** 175 \ **Special Ed Students:** 6 \ **LEP Students:** 9 \ **Ethnic:** Asian 1%, African American 4%, Hispanic 31%, Native American: 1%, Caucasian 62% \ **Exp:** $347 (High) \ **Poverty:** 16% \ **Title I:** $39,391 \ **Open-Close:** 08/14 - 05/21 \ **DTBP:** $365 (High)

Tammy Brinkman 1,11,57,83
Cecilia Stuckly 16,82*
Cindy Olson 2,71,274,294,298
Kandice Samuelson 67

Public Schs..Principal	Grd	Prgm	Enr/#Cls	SN	
Coupland Elem Sch 620 S Commerce St, Coupland 78615 Tammy Brinkman	K-8		175 13	36%	512/856-2422

- **Florence Ind School Dist** PID: 01060833   254/793-2850
  306 College Ave, Florence 76527   Fax 254/793-3055

Schools: 3 \ **Teachers:** 81 \ **Students:** 1,065 \ **Special Ed Students:** 94 \ **LEP Students:** 219 \ **Ethnic:** African American 2%, Hispanic 50%, Caucasian 48% \ **Exp:** $441 (High) \ **Poverty:** 9% \ **Title I:** $117,999 \ **Special Education:** $190,000 \ **Open-Close:** 08/15 - 05/28 \ **DTBP:** $353 (High) \

Paul Michaelewicz 1
Dalton West 3
Lisa Ragsdale 5
Lila West 8*
Jenny Strack 16,82*
Ed Navarette 67
Chad Blackman 73,98,295*
Eric Banfield 2,19
Lillian Barnet 4
Drew Bridges 6
Sharon Gibson 11,58,296
Vanessa Freed 57
Amy Branton 68
Judy Stapper 76

Public Schs..Principal	Grd	Prgm	Enr/#Cls	SN	
Florence Elem Sch 304 College Ave, Florence 76527 Dr Kay Bradford	PK-5	T	473 25	71%	254/793-2497 Fax 254/793-3158
Florence High Sch 401 FM 970, Florence 76527 Steve Elder	9-12	ATV	317 30	59%	254/793-2495 Fax 254/793-3784
Florence Middle Sch 12551 S Hwy 195, Florence 76527 Catherine Beckerley	6-8	T	258 19	62%	254/793-2504 Fax 254/793-3054

- **Georgetown Ind School Dist** PID: 01060869   512/943-5000
  507 E University Ave, Georgetown 78626   Fax 512/943-5004

Schools: 17 \ **Teachers:** 787 \ **Students:** 10,946 \ **Special Ed Students:** 1,062 \ **LEP Students:** 1,449 \ **College-Bound:** 59% \ **Ethnic:** Asian 1%, African American 4%, Hispanic 44%, Caucasian 51% \ **Exp:** $301 (High) \ **Poverty:** 7% \ **Title I:** $1,054,558 \ **Special Education:** $1,499,000 \ **Open-Close:** 08/15 - 05/28 \ **DTBP:** $188 (High) \

Dr Fred Brent 1
Pam Sanchez 2,19
David Biesheuvel 3
Jason Dean 6
Melinda Golden 8,15,275
Lisa Napper 15,68
Tony Bonazzi 45
Jessica Neyman 68
Lannon Heflin 70,73,98,750
Donnie Bruton 73
Terri Conrad 273
Kim Garcia 286
Carol Malcik 2
Tonya Blesing 2
Dr Bryan Hallmark 4,15,68,79
David Raniey 7,36
Tiffany Walker 11,57,58,271,285,296
Paige Hoellen 42
Scott Stribling 67
Gabby Nino 69
Melinda Brocher 71
Mary Mitchum 76,79
Carey Thornell 274*
Michael McKenzie 295

Public Schs..Principal	Grd	Prgm	Enr/#Cls	SN	
Annie Purl Elem Sch 1953 Maple St, Georgetown 78626 Denisse Baldwin	PK-5	T	810 37	71%	512/943-5080 Fax 512/943-5089
Carver Elem Sch 4901 Scenic Lake Dr, Georgetown 78626 Nancy Bottlinger	PK-5	T	790 33	50%	512/943-5070 Fax 512/943-5079
Charles Forbes Middle Sch 1911 NE Inner Loop, Georgetown 78626 Justin Del Bosque	6-8	T	675 80	46%	512/943-5150 Fax 512/943-5159
ⒶChip Richarte High Sch 2295 N Austin Ave, Georgetown 78626 Roby Dyer	9-12	GTV	66 8	64%	512/943-5120 Fax 512/943-5121
Dell Pickett Elem Sch 1100 Thousand Oaks Blvd, Georgetown 78628 Natalie Ramback	PK-5	T	286 22	51%	512/943-5050 Fax 512/943-5059
Douglas Benold Middle Sch 3407 Northwest Blvd, Georgetown 78628 Brandon Jayroe	6-8	T	891 40	26%	512/943-5090 Fax 512/943-5099
Eastview High Sch 4490 E University Ave, Georgetown 78626 **Latoya Easter**	9-12	TV	1,573 60	49%	512/943-1800 Fax 512/943-5139
George Wagner Middle Sch 1621 Rockride Ln, Georgetown 78626 Lindsay Harris	6-8		400		512/943-1830 Fax 512/943-1839
ⒶGeorgetown Alt Program 502 County Road 104, Georgetown 78626 **Spiller Kelly**	6-12	T	23 4	35%	512/943-5196 Fax 512/943-5197
Georgetown High Sch 2211 N Austin Ave, Georgetown 78626 Wes Vanicek	9-12	V	1,960	25%	512/943-5100 Fax 512/943-5109
Jack Frost Elem Sch 711 Lakeway Dr, Georgetown 78628 Janet Mormon	PK-5	T	355 28	65%	512/943-5020 Fax 512/943-5028
James Mitchell Elem Sch 1601 Rockride Ln, Georgetown 78626 Meredith Gandy	PK-5	T	726	65%	512/943-1820 Fax 512/943-1829
James Tippit Middle Sch 1601 Leander Rd, Georgetown 78626 Alfonso Longoria	6-8	T	683	55%	512/943-5040 Fax 512/943-5049
Jo Ann Ford Elem Sch 210 Woodlake Dr, Georgetown 78633 Jessica McMullen	PK-5		565	14%	512/943-5180 Fax 512/943-5189
Pat Cooper Elem Sch 1921 NE Inner Loop, Georgetown 78626 **Tish Ptomey**	PK-5	T	553 30	59%	512/943-5060 Fax 512/943-5069
Raye McCoy Elem Sch 401 Bellaire Dr, Georgetown 78628 Jennifer Guidry	PK-5		611 22	19%	512/943-5030 Fax 512/943-5039
Village Elem Sch 400 Village Commons Blvd, Georgetown 78633 Laura Sloan	PK-5	T	555 18	42%	512/943-5140 Fax 512/943-5149

---

79 Student Personnel	91 Safety/Security	275 Response To Intervention	298 Grant Writer/Ptnrships
80 Driver Ed/Safety	92 Magnet School	277 Remedial Math K-12	750 Chief Innovation Officer
81 Gifted/Talented	93 Parental Involvement	280 Literacy Coach	751 Chief of Staff
82 Video Services	95 Tech Prep Program	285 STEM	752 Social Emotional Learning
83 Substance Abuse Prev	97 Chief Infomation Officer	286 Digital Learning	
84 Erate	98 Chief Technology Officer	288 Common Core Standards	**Other School Types**
85 AIDS Education	270 Character Education	294 Accountability	Ⓐ = Alternative School
88 Alternative/At Risk	271 Migrant Education	295 Network System	Ⓒ = Charter School
89 Multi-Cultural Curriculum	273 Teacher Mentor	296 Title II Programs	Ⓜ = Magnet School
90 Social Work	274 Before/After Sch	297 Webmaster	Ⓨ = Year-Round School

School Programs
A = Alternative Program
G = Adult Classes
M = Magnet Program
T = Title I Schoolwide
V = Career & Tech Ed Programs

Social Media
❑ = Facebook
❑ = Twitter

New Schools are shaded
New Superintendents and Principals are bold
Personnel with email addresses are underscored

TX—395

Williamson County

Market Data Retrieval

- **Granger Ind School Dist** PID: 01060912   512/859-2613
  300 N Colorado St, Granger 76530   Fax 512/859-2446

Schools: 1 \ *Teachers:* 36 \ *Students:* 460 \ *Special Ed Students:* 42 \ *LEP Students:* 33 \ *College-Bound:* 62% \ *Ethnic:* African American 3%, Hispanic 45%, Caucasian 52% \ *Exp:* $465 (High) \ *Poverty:* 12% \ *Title I:* $61,203 \ *Open-Close:* 08/26 - 05/28 \ *DTBP:* $341 (High) \

Randy Willis 1	Louise Thornton 2,19
Marlena Sustaita 4	Walt Brock 6*
Erica Moczygemba 7*	Sara Cooper 8*
Amber Thorsen 12,13,36,69,83,296*	Tommy Filla 67
Andrea Dolan 73*	Jimmie Baker 286*

Public Schs..Principal	Grd	Prgm	Enr/#Cls	SN	
Granger Sch 300 N Colorado St, Granger 76530 Mike Abbott	PK-12	TV	460 45	59%	512/859-2173

- **Hutto Ind School Dist** PID: 01060948   512/759-3771
  200 College St, Hutto 78634   Fax 512/759-4797

Schools: 9 \ *Teachers:* 437 \ *Students:* 7,500 \ *Special Ed Students:* 786 \ *LEP Students:* 639 \ *College-Bound:* 55% \ *Ethnic:* Asian 1%, African American 14%, Hispanic 44%, Caucasian 40% \ *Exp:* $373 (High) \ *Poverty:* 5% \ *Title I:* $373,664 \ *Special Education:* $784,000 \ *Open-Close:* 08/20 - 05/28 \ *DTBP:* $135 (High) \

Dr Celina Thomas 1	Glen Graham 2,15
Jeffri Orosco 2	Anna Martin 4
David Uecker 5	Robert Sormani 8,15,68,79,88,288
Elda Torres 57,294,296	Dr Stacy Koerth 58
Connie Gooding 67	Melissa Haney 69
Todd Robison 71	Travis Brown 73,76,295

Public Schs..Principal	Grd	Prgm	Enr/#Cls	SN	
Cottonwood Creek Elem Sch 3160 Limmer Loop, Hutto 78634 Linda Pachicano	PK-5	T	615	44%	512/759-5430 Fax 512/759-5431
Farley Middle Sch 303 County Road 137, Hutto 78634 Mark Willoughby	6-8	T	892 60	40%	512/759-2050 Fax 512/759-2110
Howard Norman Elem Sch 101 Llano River Trl, Hutto 78634 Carrie Abrams	PK-5	T	660	35%	512/759-5480 Fax 512/759-5481
Hutto Elem Sch 100 Mager Ln, Hutto 78634 Gaye Rosser	PK-5	T	458 42	34%	512/759-2094 Fax 512/759-4778
Hutto High Sch 101 Chris Kelley Blvd, Hutto 78634 Roy Christian	9-12	V	1,985 50	41%	512/759-4700 Fax 512/759-4757
Hutto Middle Sch 1005 Exchange Blvd, Hutto 78634 Jason McAuliffe	6-8	T	802 30	44%	512/759-4541 Fax 512/759-4753
Nadine Johnson Elem Sch 480 Carl Stern Dr, Hutto 78634 Lindsie Almquist	PK-5	T	424 40	39%	512/759-5400 Fax 512/759-5401
Ray Elem Sch 225 Swindoll Ln, Hutto 78634 Alexis Campbell	PK-5	T	675	43%	512/759-5450 Fax 512/759-5451
Veterans Hill Elem Sch 555 Limmer Loop, Round Rock 78665 Misty Patureau	PK-5	TV	725	58%	512/759-3030 Fax 512/759-5485

- **Jarrell Ind School Dist** PID: 01060974   512/746-2124
  312 N 5th St, Jarrell 76537   Fax 512/746-2518

Schools: 5 \ *Teachers:* 108 \ *Students:* 1,850 \ *Special Ed Students:* 153 \ *LEP Students:* 192 \ *Ethnic:* Asian 1%, African American 4%, Hispanic 51%, Caucasian 44% \ *Exp:* $415 (High) \ *Poverty:* 8% \ *Title I:* $119,905 \ *Special Education:* $218,000 \ *Open-Close:* 08/15 - 05/28 \ *DTBP:* $350 (High) \

Dr Bill Chapman 1	James Garrett 2
Gretchen Mathys 3	Tim Copeland 3
Maria Manzo 4	Jackie Ivicic 5
Drew Sumner 6	Kathleen Crowe 8,285,298
Shanda Bizel 27	Laura Buckley 37,273*
Melanie Kasper 58,275	Michael Cosimeno 67
Vanessa Ashcraft 73	Krissy Gryseeles 76
Joseph Hubbard 295	

Public Schs..Principal	Grd	Prgm	Enr/#Cls	SN	
I Go Elem Sch 1601 County Rd 314, Jarrell 76537 Jack Wilson	PK-5		401		512/746-4805
Jarrell Elem Sch 1615 County Road 313, Jarrell 76537 Andrea David	PK-3	T	479	62%	512/746-2170 Fax 512/746-2575
Jarrell High Sch 1100 W FM 487, Jarrell 76537 Lindsie Almquist	9-12	TV	462	48%	512/746-2188
Jarrell Intermediate Sch 502 N 5th St, Jarrell 76537 Jack Wilson	4-5	T	250	60%	512/746-4805
Jarrell Middle Sch 101 E Avenue F, Jarrell 76537 Abbe Lester	6-8	TV	362	56%	512/746-4180 Fax 512/746-4280

- **Leander Ind School Dist** PID: 01061007   512/570-0000
  204 W South St, Leander 78641   Fax 512/570-0054

Schools: 43 \ *Teachers:* 2,529 \ *Students:* 41,000 \ *Special Ed Students:* 4,052 \ *LEP Students:* 1,915 \ *College-Bound:* 70% \ *Ethnic:* Asian 7%, African American 4%, Hispanic 25%, Caucasian 63% \ *Exp:* $279 (Med) \ *Poverty:* 4% \ *Title I:* $1,008,405 \ *Special Education:* $4,564,000 \ *Open-Close:* 08/15 - 05/29 \ *DTBP:* $174 (High) \

Dr Bruce Gearing 1	Dana Paulson 2
Gage Loots 2	Lucas Janda 2,19
Jimmy Disler 3,17	Steve Smith 4
Ann Hatton 5	Jody Hormann 6
Matt Smith 8,15,288,751	Matt Bentz 8,18
Chrysta Carlin 10	Kendra Winans 11
Laurie Traynham 12	John Graham 15
Laurelyn Arterbury 15	Laurie Vondersaar 15,73,76,295
Sarah Grissom 15	Jason Johnston 16
Peter Warshaw 20,23	Darla Humes 35,88,91
Steve Clark 36,83,90	Tina Dozier 57
Sandy Khan 58	Maria Vaso 61*
Trish Bode 67	Karie McSpadden 68
Lisa Gibbs 68	Brenda Cruz 69,70,294
Corey Ryan 71,97	Susan Cole 74,273
Brad Mansfield 79	Bryan Miller 79
Dr Tiffany Spicer 81	

Public Schs..Principal	Grd	Prgm	Enr/#Cls	SN	
Bagdad Elem Sch 800 Deercreek Ln, Leander 78641 Christine Hilbun	PK-5	T	592	60%	512/570-5900 Fax 512/570-5905

---

1 Superintendent	8 Curric/Instruct K-12	19 Chief Financial Officer	29 Family/Consumer Science	39 Social Studies K-12	49 English/Lang Arts Elem	59 Special Education Elem	69 Academic Assessment
2 Bus/Finance/Purchasing	9 Curric/Instruct Elem	20 Art K-12	30 Adult Education	40 Social Studies Elem	50 English/Lang Arts Sec	60 Special Education Sec	70 Research/Development
3 Buildings And Grounds	10 Curric/Instruct Sec	21 Art Elem	31 Career/Sch-to-Work K-12	41 Social Studies Sec	51 Reading K-12	61 Foreign/World Lang K-12	71 Public Information
4 Food Service	11 Federal Program	22 Art Sec	32 Career/Sch-to-Work Elem	42 Science K-12	52 Reading Elem	62 Foreign/World Lang Elem	72 Summer School
5 Transportation	12 Title I	23 Music K-12	33 Career/Sch-to-Work Sec	43 Science Elem	53 Reading Sec	63 Foreign/World Lang Sec	73 Instructional Tech
6 Athletic	13 Title V	24 Music Elem	34 Early Childhood Ed	44 Science Sec	54 Remedial Reading K-12	64 Religious Education K-12	74 Inservice Training
7 Health Services	15 Asst Superintendent	25 Music Sec	35 Health/Phys Education	45 Math K-12	55 Remedial Reading Elem	65 Religious Education Elem	75 Marketing/Distributive
	16 Instructional Media Svcs	26 Business Education	36 Guidance Services K-12	46 Math Elem	56 Remedial Reading Sec	66 Religious Education Sec	76 Info Systems
	17 Chief Operations Officer	27 Career & Tech Ed	37 Guidance Services Elem	47 Math Sec	57 Bilingual/ELL	67 School Board President	77 Psychological Assess
	18 Chief Academic Officer	28 Technology Education	38 Guidance Services Sec	48 English/Lang Arts K-12	58 Special Education K-12	68 Teacher Personnel	78 Affirmative Action

Texas School Directory — Williamson County

School	Grades	Prog	Enroll	%	Phone / Fax
Block House Creek Elem Sch 401 Creek Run Dr, Leander 78641 Dr Deana Cady	PK-5		626 41	21%	512/570-7600 Fax 512/570-7605
Camacho Elem Sch 501 Municipal Dr, Leander 78641 Gena Fleming	PK-5	T	781	34%	512/570-7800 Fax 512/570-7805
Canyon Ridge Middle Sch 12601 Country Trl, Austin 78732 Kimberly Waltmon	6-8		1,305 80	2%	512/570-3500 Fax 512/570-3505
Cedar Park High Sch 2150 Cypress Creek Rd, Cedar Park 78613 John Sloan	9-12	V	2,026	10%	512/570-1200 Fax 512/570-1205
Cedar Park Middle Sch 2100 Sunchase Blvd, Cedar Park 78613 Sandra Stewart	6-8		1,357	11%	512/570-3100 Fax 512/570-3105
Cox Elem Sch 1001 Brushy Creek Rd, Cedar Park 78613 Charlie Rodriguez	PK-5		574	16%	512/570-6000 Fax 512/570-6005
Cypress Elem Sch 2900 El Salido Pkwy, Cedar Park 78613 Kristen Alex	PK-5		684 40	10%	512/570-5400 Fax 512/570-5405
Deer Creek Elem Sch 2420 Zeppelin Dr, Cedar Park 78613 **Matthew Calkins**	PK-5		687	6%	512/570-6300 Fax 512/570-6305
Faubion Elem Sch 1209 Cypress Creek Rd, Cedar Park 78613 Bobbie Steiner	PK-5		480 32	27%	512/570-7500 Fax 512/570-7505
Four Points Middle Sch 9700 McNeil Dr, Austin 78750 **Steve Crawford**	6-8		773	13%	512/570-3700 Fax 512/570-3705
Giddens Elem Sch 1500 Timberwood Dr, Cedar Park 78613 Sally Hill	PK-5		533	37%	512/570-5600 Fax 512/570-5605
Glenn High Sch 1320 Collaborative Way, Leander 78641 Arturo Lomeli	9-12	T	1,137	38%	512/570-1400 Fax 512/570-1405
Grandview Hills Elem Sch 12024 Vista Parke Dr, Austin 78726 Kathy Sparksgoecke	PK-5		479	25%	512/570-6800 Fax 512/570-6805
Henry Middle Sch 100 N Vista Ridge Pkwy, Cedar Park 78613 Dr David Ellis	6-8		1,355	21%	512/570-3400 Fax 512/570-3405
Knowles Elem Sch 2101 Cougar Country, Cedar Park 78613 Lara Labbe-Maginel	PK-5	T	641 55	55%	512/570-6200 Fax 512/570-6205
Larkspur Elem Sch 424 Rusk Bluff Ave, Leander 78641 **Tracie Montanio**	K-5		440		512/570-8100
Laura Welch Bush Elem Sch 12600 Country Trails Ln, Austin 78732 Kristine Kline	PK-5		716 38	1%	512/570-6100 Fax 512/570-6105
Leander High Sch 3301 S Bagdad Rd, Leander 78641 Chris Simpson	9-12	AV	2,197	29%	512/570-1000 Fax 512/570-1005
Leander Middle Sch 410 S West Dr, Leander 78641 Mark Koller	6-8	T	1,024	37%	512/570-3200 Fax 512/570-3205
Ⓐ Leo Center 300 S West Dr, Leander 78641 Cathy White	K-12	V	30 9		512/570-2230 Fax 512/570-2234
Mason Elem Sch 1501 N Lakeline Blvd, Cedar Park 78613 Abby Kennell	PK-5		617 47	29%	512/570-5500 Fax 512/570-5505
Monta Jane Akin Elem Sch 3261 Barley Rd, Leander 78641 Beckie Webster	PK-5		761		512/570-8000 Fax 512/570-8005
Naumann Elem Sch 1201 Brighton Bend Ln, Cedar Park 78613 Keith Morgan	PK-5		469 56	21%	512/570-5800 Fax 512/570-5805
Ⓐ New Hope High Sch 401 S West Dr, Leander 78641 Barbara Spelman	9-12	V	43 4	18%	512/570-2200 Fax 512/570-2204
Parkside Elem Sch 301 Garner Park Dr, Georgetown 78628 Lauren Meeks	PK-5		842	2%	512/570-7100 Fax 512/570-7105
Plain Elem Sch 501 S Brook Dr, Leander 78641 Evelyn Crisp	PK-5		838	26%	512/570-6600 Fax 512/570-6605
Pleasant Hill Elem Sch 1800 Horizon Park Blvd, Leander 78641 Heather Robbins	PK-5		646	23%	512/570-6400 Fax 512/570-6405
Reed Elem Sch 1515 Little Elm Trl, Cedar Park 78613 Paige Collier	PK-5		749		512/570-7700 Fax 512/570-7705
River Place Elem Sch 6500 Sitio Del Rio Blvd, Austin 78730 Christina Pasak	PK-5		792	11%	512/570-6900 Fax 512/570-6905
River Ridge Elem Sch 12900 Tierra Grande Trl, Austin 78732 Shelley Roberts	PK-5		715	1%	512/570-7300 Fax 512/570-7305
Ronald Reagan Elem Sch 1700 E Park St, Cedar Park 78613 **Eric Haug**	PK-5		863	8%	512/570-7200 Fax 512/570-7205
Rouse High Sch 1222 Raider Way, Leander 78641 Christine Simpson	9-12	A	1,849	20%	512/570-2000 Fax 512/570-2005
Running Brushy Middle Sch 2303 N Lakeline Blvd, Cedar Park 78613 Jim Rose	6-8		1,246 50	33%	512/570-3300 Fax 512/570-3305
Rutledge Elem Sch 11501 Staked Plains Dr, Austin 78717 Elizabeth Mohler	PK-5		831	8%	512/570-6500 Fax 512/570-6505
Steiner Ranch Elem Sch 4001 N Quinlan Park Rd, Austin 78732 Angela Hodges	PK-5		543 37	10%	512/570-5700 Fax 512/570-5705
Stiles Middle Sch 3250 Barley Rd, Leander 78641 Melody Maples	6-8		1,286	8%	512/570-3800 Fax 512/570-3805
Vandegrift High Sch 9500 McNeil Dr, Austin 78750 Charles Little	9-12		2,579	6%	512/570-2300 Fax 512/570-2305
Vista Ridge High Sch 200 S Vista Ridge Pkwy, Cedar Park 78613 Paul Johnson	9-12		2,326	16%	512/570-1800 Fax 512/570-1805
Westside Elem Sch 300 Ryan Jordan Ln, Cedar Park 78613 **Amanda Lillard**	PK-5		574	6%	512/570-7000 Fax 512/570-7005
Whitestone Elem Sch 2000 Crystal Falls Pkwy, Leander 78641 Niki Prindle	PK-5		774 60	34%	512/570-7400 Fax 512/570-7405
Wiley Middle Sch 1526 Raider Way, Leander 78641 Brandon Evans	6-8		1,023	29%	512/570-3600 Fax 512/570-3605
Winkley Elem Sch 2100 Pow Wow, Leander 78641 Donna Brady	PK-5		684	8%	512/570-6700 Fax 512/570-6705

79 Student Personnel
80 Driver Ed/Safety
81 Gifted/Talented
82 Video Services
83 Substance Abuse Prev
84 Erate
85 AIDS Education
88 Alternative/At Risk
89 Multi-Cultural Curriculum
90 Social Work
91 Safety/Security
92 Magnet School
93 Parental Involvement
95 Tech Prep Program
97 Chief Infomation Officer
98 Chief Technology Officer
270 Character Education
271 Migrant Education
273 Teacher Mentor
274 Before/After Sch
275 Response To Intervention
277 Remedial Math K-12
280 Literacy Coach
285 STEM
286 Digital Learning
288 Common Core Standards
294 Accountability
295 Network System
296 Title II Programs
297 Webmaster
298 Grant Writer/Ptnrships
750 Chief Innovation Officer
751 Chief of Staff
752 Social Emotional Learning

Other School Types
Ⓐ = Alternative School
Ⓒ = Charter School
Ⓜ = Magnet School
Ⓨ = Year-Round School

School Programs
A = Alternative Program
G = Adult Classes
M = Magnet Program
T = Title I Schoolwide
V = Career & Tech Ed Programs

Social Media
= Facebook
= Twitter

New Schools are shaded
New Superintendents and Principals are bold
Personnel with email addresses are underscored

Williamson County
Market Data Retrieval

- **Liberty Hill Ind School Dist** PID: 01061069   512/260-5580
  301 Forrest St, Liberty Hill 78642   Fax 512/260-5581

Schools: 6 \ **Teachers:** 251 \ **Students:** 4,476 \ **Special Ed Students:** 318 \ **LEP Students:** 101 \ **Ethnic:** African American 1%, Hispanic 20%, Caucasian 78% \ **Exp:** $327 (High) \ **Poverty:** 5% \ **Title I:** $173,253 \ **Special Education:** $481,000 \ **Open-Close:** 08/14 - 05/21 \ **DTBP:** $148 (High)

Steven Snell 1
Jennifer Hanna 2,19
Meleia Cox 5
Kelly Keene 7
Summer Neary 11,296
Jay Olivier 16
Kristy Kercheville 31,57*
Lara Chapman 38*
Elyse Tarlton 58,69
Paul Urban 76
Erin Jarrett 2
Mary Sheffield 4
Jeff Walker 6,35,85*
Dr Toni Hicks 8,15,88,294
Brad Mansfield 15
Lauaren Claymon 16,82*
Laura Elder 37
Candy Tijerina 57,271
Clay Cole 67

Public Schs..Principal	Grd	Prgm	Enr/#Cls	SN	
Bill Burden Elem Sch 315 Stonewall Pkwy, Liberty Hill 78642 **Tanya Lambert**	PK-4		652	30%	512/260-4400 Fax 512/260-4410
Liberty Hill Elem Sch 1400 Loop 332, Liberty Hill 78642 **Heather Collison**	PK-4		369 21	35%	512/379-3260 Fax 512/379-3256
Liberty Hill High Sch 16500 W State Highway 29, Liberty Hill 78642 **Jonathan Bever**	9-12		1,121 45	17%	512/260-5500 Fax 512/260-5510
Liberty Hill Intermediate Sch 101 Loop 332, Liberty Hill 78642 **Josh Curtis**	5-6		618 20	26%	512/379-3200 Fax 512/379-3210
Liberty Hill Middle Sch 13125 W State Highway 29, Liberty Hill 78642 **Annette Coe**	7-8		656 35	21%	512/379-3300 Fax 512/379-3310
Rancho Sienna Elem Sch 751 Bonnet Blvd, Georgetown 78628 **Melanie Bowman**	PK-4		605		512/260-4450 Fax 512/260-4460

- **Round Rock Ind School Dist** PID: 01061083   512/464-5000
  1311 Round Rock Ave, Round Rock 78681   Fax 512/464-5090

Schools: 54 \ **Teachers:** 3,379 \ **Students:** 50,546 \ **Special Ed Students:** 4,437 \ **LEP Students:** 4,136 \ **College-Bound:** 64% \ **Ethnic:** Asian 16%, African American 9%, Hispanic 32%, Caucasian 43% \ **Exp:** $272 (Med) \ **Poverty:** 5% \ **Title I:** $3,990,577 \ **Special Education:** $7,941,000 \ **Bilingual Education:** $61,000 \ **Open-Close:** 08/15 - 05/21 \ **DTBP:** $203 (High) \

Dr Steve Flores 1
David Hoedebeck 3
Kelly Grones 4
Dwayne Weirich 6
Darrell Emanuel 8
Dr Amy Grosso 11,298
Margo Vogelpohl 12
Kenneth Adix 19
Sheri Bonds 27,31
Brian Bushart 46
Maria Gonzalez 58*
Annette Vierra 68
Debbie Lewis 69,294
Jenny Lacoste-Caputo 71
Mark Gabehart 76
Michelle Swain 81,92
Kimberly Berry-Corie 275
Rosanna Guerrero 2
Terry Worcester 3,17
Fritz Klabunde 5
Elaine Douville 7,83*
Mandy Estes 8,18
Laura Segers 11
Jeffrey Uselman 16,73,82,286*
Peggy Mica 27
Dr Christina Wiswell 36
Maria Green 57
Charles Chadwell 67
Dr Cathy Malerba 69
Dr Daniel Presley 70
Edie Binns 74
Scott Stansbury 76,84,295,297
Mario De La Rosa 91
Rachelle Finck 752

Public Schs..Principal	Grd	Prgm	Enr/#Cls	SN	
Anderson Mill Elem Sch 10610 Salt Mill Holw, Austin 78750 **Amanda Molina**	PK-5	T	523 20	55%	512/428-3700 Fax 512/428-3790
Blackland Prairie Elem Sch 2005 Via Sonoma Dr, Round Rock 78665 **Sue Hildebrand**	PK-5		804 38	11%	512/424-8600 Fax 512/424-8690
Bluebonnet Elem Sch 1010 Chisholm Valley Dr, Round Rock 78681 **Samuel Soto**	PK-5	T	369 32	81%	512/428-7700 Fax 512/428-7790
Brushy Creek Elem Sch 3800 Stonebridge Dr, Round Rock 78681 **Jennifer Strong**	PK-5		763 40	21%	512/428-3000 Fax 512/428-3080
C D Fulkes Middle Sch 300 W Anderson Ave, Round Rock 78664 **Rebekah Van Ryn**	6-8	TV	713	63%	512/428-3100 Fax 512/428-3240
Cactus Ranch Elem Sch 2901 Goldenoak Cir, Round Rock 78681 **Vicki Crain**	PK-5		979 32	1%	512/424-8000 Fax 512/424-8090
Caldwell Heights Elem Sch 4010 Eagles Nest St, Round Rock 78665 **Michelle Montalvo**	PK-5	T	737 25	46%	512/428-7300 Fax 512/428-7390
Canyon Creek Elem Sch 10210 Ember Glen Dr, Austin 78726 **April Crawford**	PK-5		429 31	2%	512/428-2800 Fax 512/428-2890
Canyon Vista Middle Sch 8455 Spicewood Springs Rd, Austin 78759 **Nicole Hagerty**	6-8	V	1,347	10%	512/464-8100 Fax 512/464-8210
Cedar Ridge High Sch 2801 Gattis School Rd, Round Rock 78664 **Jiae Kim-Batra**	9-12		2,765	26%	512/704-0100 Fax 512/704-0280
Cedar Valley Middle Sch 8139 Racine Trl, Austin 78717 **Zac Oldham**	6-8	V	1,277 45	11%	512/428-2300 Fax 512/428-2420
Chandler Oaks Elem Sch 3800 Stone Oak Dr, Round Rock 78681 **Kelley Hirt**	PK-5		559	8%	512/704-0400 Fax 512/704-0490
Chisholm Trail Middle Sch 500 Oakridge Dr, Round Rock 78681 **Steven Swain**	6-8	V	952 69	35%	512/428-2500 Fax 512/428-2629
Claude Berkman Elem Sch 400 W Anderson Ave, Round Rock 78664 **Kathy Cawthron**	PK-5	T	476 39	83%	512/464-8250 Fax 512/464-8315
Deep Wood Elem Sch 705 Saint Williams Ave, Round Rock 78681 **Reba Mussey**	PK-5		353 22	31%	512/464-4400 Fax 512/464-4494
Deerpark Middle Sch 8849 Anderson Mill Rd, Austin 78729 **Jonathan Smith**	6-8	TV	900	39%	512/464-6600 Fax 512/464-6740
Double File Trail Elem Sch 2400 Chandler Creek Blvd, Round Rock 78665 **Alifia Britton**	PK-5	T	652 34	40%	512/428-7400 Fax 512/428-7490
Early Clg High Sch 4400 College Park, Round Rock 78665 **Veronica Coss**	9-10		250		512/704-1650
England Elem Sch 8801 Pearson Ranch Rd, Austin 78717 **Jana Stowe**	PK-5		1,104	5%	512/704-1200 Fax 512/704-1290
Fern Bluff Elem Sch 17815 Park Valley Dr, Round Rock 78681 **Dr Elizabeth Wilson**	PK-5		619 52	8%	512/428-2100 Fax 512/428-2160
Forest Creek Elem Sch 3505 Forest Creek Dr, Round Rock 78664 **Denise Sharp**	PK-5		832 45	11%	512/464-5350 Fax 512/464-5430
Forest North Elem Sch 13414 Broadmeade Ave, Austin 78729 **Amy Jacobs**	PK-5	T	352	47%	512/464-6750 Fax 512/464-6794

1	Superintendent	8	Curric/Instruct K-12	19	Chief Financial Officer	29	Family/Consumer Science	39 Social Studies K-12 49 English/Lang Arts Elem 59 Special Education Elem 69 Academic Assessment
2	Bus/Finance/Purchasing	9	Curric/Instruct Elem	20	Art K-12	30	Adult Education	40 Social Studies Elem 50 English/Lang Arts Sec 60 Special Education Sec 70 Research/Development
3	Buildings And Grounds	10	Curric/Instruct Sec	21	Art Elem	31	Career/Sch-to-Work K-12	41 Social Studies Sec 51 Reading K-12 61 Foreign/World Lang K-12 71 Public Information
4	Food Service	11	Federal Program	22	Art Sec	32	Career/Sch-to-Work Elem	42 Science K-12 52 Reading Elem 62 Foreign/World Lang Elem 72 Summer School
5	Transportation	12	Title I	23	Music K-12	33	Career/Sch-to-Work Sec	43 Science Elem 53 Reading Sec 63 Foreign/World Lang Sec 73 Instructional Tech
6	Athletic	13	Title V	24	Music Elem	34	Early Childhood Ed	44 Science Sec 54 Remedial Reading K-12 64 Religious Education K-12 74 Inservice Training
7	Health Services	15	Asst Superintendent	25	Music Sec	35	Health/Phys Education	45 Math K-12 55 Remedial Reading Elem 65 Religious Education Elem 75 Marketing/Distributive
		16	Instructional Media Svcs	26	Business Education	36	Guidance Services K-12	46 Math Elem 56 Remedial Reading Sec 66 Religious Education Sec 76 Info Systems
		17	Chief Operations Officer	27	Career & Tech Ed	37	Guidance Services Elem	47 Math Sec 57 Bilingual/ELL 67 School Board President 77 Psychological Assess
		18	Chief Academic Officer	28	Technology Education	38	Guidance Services Sec	48 English/Lang Arts K-12 58 Special Education K-12 68 Teacher Personnel 78 Affirmative Action

TX—398

Texas School Directory — Williamson County

School	Grd	Prgm	Enr/#Cls	SN	Phone
Gattis Elem Sch 2920 Round Rock Ranch Blvd, Round Rock 78665 Jennifer Lucas	PK-5	T	740 45	39%	512/428-2000 Fax 512/428-2065 ⓣ
Goals Learning Center 1311 Round Rock Ave Bldg 800, Round Rock 78681 Dennis Hardesty	Spec		50		512/464-5153 Fax 512/428-7940
Great Oaks Elem Sch 16455 S Great Oaks Dr, Round Rock 78681 Heath Frazer	PK-5		720 50	10%	512/464-6850 Fax 512/464-6930
Hopewell Middle Sch 1535 Gulf Way, Round Rock 78665 Lynda Garinger	6-8	V	1,116	32%	512/464-5200 Fax 512/464-5349
James Garland Walsh Middle Sch 3850 Walsh Ranch Blvd, Round Rock 78681 Brenda Heath-Agnew	6-8		1,461	9%	512/704-0800 Fax 512/704-0940
Joe Lee Johnson Elem Sch 2800 Sauls Dr, Austin 78728 **Marc Scott**	PK-5		729	50%	512/704-1400 Fax 512/704-1490
Jollyville Elem Sch 6720 Corpus Christi Dr, Austin 78729 Scott Morgan	PK-5		466 30	35%	512/428-2200 Fax 512/428-2299
Kathy Caraway Elem Sch 11104 Oak View Dr, Austin 78759 Katrina Bailey	PK-5		825 25	11%	512/464-5500 Fax 512/464-5590
Laurel Mountain Elem Sch 10111 D K Ranch Rd, Austin 78759 **Doriane Marvel**	PK-5		758 38	3%	512/464-4300 Fax 512/464-4390 ⓣ
Linda Herrington Elem Sch 2850 Paloma Lake Blvd, Round Rock 78665 Julie Nelson	PK-5		1,042	22%	512/704-1900 Fax 512/704-1990
Live Oak Elem Sch 8607 Anderson Mill Rd, Austin 78729 Katie Holding	PK-5	T	543 40	36%	512/428-3800 Fax 512/428-3890
McNeil High Sch 5720 McNeil Dr, Austin 78729 Amanda Johnson	9-12	V	2,664 100	21%	512/464-6300 Fax 512/464-6550
Neysa Callison Elem Sch 1750 Thompson Trl, Round Rock 78664 **Penny Oates**	PK-5	T	805	63%	512/704-0700 Fax 512/704-0790
Noel Grisham Middle Sch 10805 School House Ln, Austin 78750 Paige Hadziselimovic	6-8	V	655 45	26%	512/428-2650 Fax 512/428-2790
Old Town Elem Sch 2200 Chaparral Dr, Round Rock 78681 **Jessica Schock**	PK-5		749 36	29%	512/428-7600 Fax 512/428-7690
Patsy Sommer Elem Sch 16200 Avery Ranch Blvd, Austin 78717 Nancy Varljen	PK-5		1,241	2%	512/704-0600 Fax 512/704-0690
Pearson Ranch Middle Sch 8901 Pearson Ranch Rd, Austin 78717 Kim Winters	6-8		668		512/704-1500
Pfc Robert Hernandez Mid Sch 1901 Sunrise Rd, Round Rock 78664 **Dr Patricia Ephlin**	6-8	T	752	54%	512/424-8800 Fax 512/424-8940
Pond Springs Elem Sch 7825 Elkhorn Mountain Trl, Austin 78729 Brooke Elarms	PK-5		643 43	25%	512/464-4200 Fax 512/464-4290
Purple Sage Elem Sch 11801 Tanglebriar Trl, Austin 78750 Sara Nelson	PK-5		446 11	36%	512/428-3500 Fax 512/428-3590
Ridgeview Middle Sch 2000 Via Sonoma Dr, Round Rock 78665 Travis Mutscher	6-8		1,355 60	17%	512/424-8400 Fax 512/424-8540
Round Rock High Sch 201 Deep Wood Dr, Round Rock 78681 Matthew Groff	9-12	GV	3,359	13%	512/464-6000 Fax 512/464-6190
Ⓐ Round Rock Opportunity Center 931 Luther Peterson, Round Rock 78665 Rene Posey	6-12		250 22	48%	512/428-2900 Fax 512/428-2943
Spicewood Elem Sch 11601 Olson Dr, Austin 78750 Teyan Allen	K-5		807 32	6%	512/428-3600 Fax 512/428-3690
Stony Point High Sch 1801 Tiger Trl, Round Rock 78664 Anthony Watson	9-12	TV	2,604	38%	512/428-7000 Fax 512/428-7280
Ⓐ Success High Sch 500 Gattis School Rd, Round Rock 78664 Thomasine Stewart	9-12		313	38%	512/704-1300 Fax 512/704-1390
Teravista Elem Sch 4419 Teravista Club Dr, Round Rock 78665 Michael Wakefield	PK-5		876	13%	512/704-0500 Fax 512/704-0590
Union Hill Elem Sch 1511 Gulf Way, Round Rock 78665 Kimberly Connelly	PK-5	T	735 39	68%	512/424-8700 Fax 512/424-8790
Vic Robertson Elem Sch 1415 Bayland St, Round Rock 78664 Kyle Borel	PK-5	T	431 30	73%	512/428-3300 Fax 512/428-3370
Wells Branch Elem Sch 14650 Merrilltown Rd, Austin 78728 **Eliza Gordon**	PK-5	T	479 39	55%	512/428-3400 Fax 512/428-3490
Westwood High Sch 12400 Mellow Meadow Dr, Austin 78750 Mario Acosta	9-12	GV	2,742 130	12%	512/464-4000 Fax 512/464-4020
Xenia Voigt Elem Sch 1201 Cushing Dr, Round Rock 78664 Cheryl Hester	PK-5	T	539	74%	512/428-7500 Fax 512/428-7590

● **Taylor Ind School Dist** PID: 01061162   512/365-1391
3101 N Main St Ste 104, Taylor 76574   Fax 512/365-3800

Schools: 7 \ **Teachers:** 238 \ **Students:** 3,280 \ **Special Ed Students:** 343 \ **LEP Students:** 380 \ **College-Bound:** 51% \ **Ethnic:** Asian 1%, African American 10%, Hispanic 63%, Caucasian 27% \ **Exp:** $303 (High) \ **Poverty:** 14% \ **Title I:** $623,711 \ **Open-Close:** 08/15 - 05/21 \ **DTBP:** $178 (High)

Keith Brown 1		Lorine David 2	
Johnnie Horn 3		Lori Wilbanks 3	
Edward Kotar 4		Carl Caldwell 5	
Robert Little 6		Dr George Willey 8,18,275	
Jennifer Patschke 11,296,298		Rodney Fausett 15	
Sandra Martinez 57,271		Sandra Martinez 57*	
Robert Stevens 58		Marco Ortiz 67	
Debbie Matthys 69		Tim Crow 71,76	
Andrew Maddox 88*		Robert Borgne 295	

Public Schs..Principal	Grd	Prgm	Enr/#Cls	SN	Phone
Legacy Early College High Sch 516 N Main St, Taylor 76574 Ron Roth	9-12		178		512/352-9596
Main Street Imtermediate Sch 3101 N Main St Ste 105, Taylor 76574 **Marcelina Cobb**	4-5	T	427 32	66%	512/352-3634 Fax 512/365-8533
Naomi Pasemann Elem Sch 2809 North Dr, Taylor 76574 Renee Duckworth	1-3	T	662 33	69%	512/352-1016 Fax 512/365-2280
T H Johnson Elem Sch 3100 Duck Ln, Taylor 76574 Jenni Cork	PK-K	T	373	77%	512/365-7114 Fax 512/365-7112
Taylor High Sch 355 FM 973, Taylor 76574 Andrew Maddox	9-12	AGTV	1,017 80	54%	512/365-6326 Fax 512/365-1351

---

79 Student Personnel
80 Driver Ed/Safety
81 Gifted/Talented
82 Video Services
83 Substance Abuse Prev
84 Erate
85 AIDS Education
88 Alternative/At Risk
89 Multi-Cultural Curriculum
90 Social Work
91 Safety/Security
92 Magnet School
93 Parental Involvement
95 Tech Prep Program
97 Chief Infomation Officer
98 Chief Technology Officer
270 Character Education
271 Migrant Education
273 Teacher Mentor
274 Before/After Sch
275 Response To Intervention
277 Remedial Math K-12
280 Literacy Coach
285 STEM
286 Digital Learning
288 Common Core Standards
294 Accountability
295 Network System
296 Title II Programs
297 Webmaster
298 Grant Writer/Ptnrships
750 Chief Innovation Officer
751 Chief of Staff
752 Social Emotional Learning

Other School Types
Ⓐ = Alternative School
Ⓒ = Charter School
Ⓜ = Magnet School
Ⓨ = Year-Round School

School Programs
A = Alternative Program
G = Adult Classes
M = Magnet Program
T = Title I Schoolwide
V = Career & Tech Ed Programs

Social Media
 = Facebook
ⓣ = Twitter

New Schools are shaded
New Superintendents and Principals are bold
Personnel with email addresses are underscored

Wilson County — Market Data Retrieval

Taylor Middle Sch 304 Carlos G Parker Blvd NW, Taylor 76574 Chelsey Ellison	6-8	AT	710 45	63%	512/352-2815 Fax 512/365-8589
Ⓐ Taylor Opportunity Center 1004 Dellinger St, Taylor 76574 Andrew Maddox	6-12		50		512/365-8089 Fax 512/309-4481

- **Thrall Ind School Dist** PID: 01061227   512/898-0062
  201 S Bounds St, Thrall 76578   Fax 512/898-5349

> *Schools:* 3 \ *Teachers:* 52 \ *Students:* 720 \ *Special Ed Students:* 64 \ *LEP Students:* 15 \ *College-Bound:* 71% \ *Ethnic:* African American 1%, Hispanic 30%, Caucasian 68% \ *Exp:* $459 (High) \ *Poverty:* 8% \ *Title I:* $59,936 \ *Open-Close:* 08/21 - 05/21 \ *DTBP:* $376 (High)

Tom Hooker	1	Shaun Karch	2
Nancy Hollowell	4	Jason Cole	6*
Jolena Pokorny	11,285*	Bryan Holubec	67
Susan Burkhart	73,84		

Public Schs..Principal	Grd	Prgm	Enr/#Cls SN		
Thrall Elem Sch 201 S Bounds St, Thrall 76578 Sherri Maruska	PK-5	T	305 17	33%	512/898-5293 Fax 512/898-2879
Thrall High Sch 201 S Bounds St, Thrall 76578 Travis Dube	9-12	AV	216 12	26%	512/898-5193 Fax 512/898-2132
Thrall Middle Sch 201 S Bounds St, Thrall 76578 Kim Luton	6-8		152 10	30%	512/898-5328 Fax 512/898-2132

WILLIAMSON CATHOLIC SCHOOLS

- **Diocese of Austin Ed Office** PID: 01420568
  Listing includes only schools located in this county. See District Index for location of Diocesan Offices.

Catholic Schs..Principal	Grd	Prgm	Enr/#Cls SN	
Holy Family Catholic Sch 9400 Neenah Ave, Austin 78717 Kelly Laster	PK-8		515	512/246-4455 Fax 512/246-4454
St Dominic Savio Catholic HS 9300 Neenah Ave, Austin 78717 Enrique Garcia	9-12		400	512/388-8846 Fax 512/388-1335
St Helen Catholic Sch 2700 E University Ave, Georgetown 78626 Mary Sims	PK-8		165 8	512/868-0744 Fax 512/869-3244
St Mary's Sch 520 Washburn St, Taylor 76574 Heidi Altman	PK-8		155 10	512/352-2313 Fax 512/365-5313

WILLIAMSON PRIVATE SCHOOLS

Private Schs..Principal	Grd	Prgm	Enr/#Cls SN	
Applegate Adventist Jr Academy 4 Applegate Cir, Round Rock 78665 Ingrid Stanley	PK-8		24	512/388-7870
Challenger School-Avery Rnch 15101 Avery Ranch Blvd, Austin 78717 Molly Bauer	PK-7		116	512/341-8000 Fax 512/331-2951

Community Montessori Sch 500 Pleasant Valley Dr, Georgetown 78626 Becki Hardie	PK-6		148 9		512/863-7920 Fax 512/819-9617
Concordia High Sch 1500 Royston Ln Ste A, Round Rock 78664 Mike Doering	9-12		101 10		512/248-2547 Fax 512/252-3839
Grace Academy 225 Grace Blvd, Georgetown 78633 Dr David Diener	K-12		188 11		512/864-9500 Fax 512/868-5429
Guidepost Montessori-Brush Crk 3017 Polar Ln, Cedar Park 78613	PK-6		401		512/259-3333 Fax 512/259-3331
Round Rock Christian Academy 301 N Lake Creek Dr, Round Rock 78681 Tiffany Jaksch \ Kelly Counts	PK-12		530		512/255-4491
Summit Christian Academy 2121 Cypress Creek Rd, Cedar Park 78613 Shelley Jordan	PK-12		300 20		512/250-1369 Fax 512/257-1851
Zion Lutheran Sch 6101 FM 1105, Georgetown 78626 Thomas Wrege	PK-8		200 12		512/863-5345 Fax 512/869-5659

WILSON COUNTY

WILSON PUBLIC SCHOOLS

- **Floresville Ind School Dist** PID: 01061265   830/393-5300
  1200 5th St, Floresville 78114   Fax 830/393-5399

> *Schools:* 5 \ *Teachers:* 247 \ *Students:* 4,000 \ *Special Ed Students:* 388 \ *LEP Students:* 174 \ *College-Bound:* 45% \ *Ethnic:* African American 1%, Hispanic 65%, Caucasian 33% \ *Exp:* $210 (Med) \ *Poverty:* 13% \ *Title I:* $666,710 \ *Special Education:* $611,000 \ *Open-Close:* 08/19 - 05/28 \ *DTBP:* $184 (High) \

Dr Sherri Bays	1	William Atkins	2,15,91
Darrell Towley	3	Richmon Harris	4
Mary Aaron	5	Andrew Rohrf	6
Donna Lynn	7,85*	Dr Rhonda Wade	8,36
Jacquelyn Miller	15,68,78,79,273	Laura Bittprt	27
Penny Smith	67	James Urbanczyk	73,295,297
Angela Garcia	88,274*	Ben Reed	90*
Melvin Albert	295		

Public Schs..Principal	Grd	Prgm	Enr/#Cls SN		
Ⓐ Floresville Alternative Ctr 335 Alternative Ln, Floresville 78114 Angela Garcia	6-12		85 5		830/393-5368 Fax 830/393-5706
Floresville High Sch 1813 Tiger Ln, Floresville 78114 Michael Schroller	9-12	TV	1,234 60	43%	830/393-5370 Fax 830/393-5719
Floresville Middle Sch 2601 B St, Floresville 78114 Marcia Gonzales	6-8	T	924 80	48%	830/393-5350 Fax 830/393-5359
Floresville North Elem Sch 14905 FM 775, Floresville 78114 Heather Brooks	PK-5	T	903 29	53%	830/393-5310 Fax 830/393-5315
Floresville South Elem Sch 2000 Tiger Ln, Floresville 78114 Leanne Marshall	PK-5	T	927 39	64%	830/393-5325 Fax 830/393-5746

1	Superintendent	8	Curric/Instruct K-12	19	Chief Financial Officer	29	Family/Consumer Science	39	Social Studies K-12	49	English/Lang Arts Elem	59	Special Education Elem	69	Academic Assessment
2	Bus/Finance/Purchasing	9	Curric/Instruct Elem	20	Art K-12	30	Adult Education	40	Social Studies Elem	50	English/Lang Arts Sec	60	Special Education Sec	70	Research/Development
3	Buildings And Grounds	10	Curric/Instruct Sec	21	Art Elem	31	Career/Sch-to-Work K-12	41	Social Studies Sec	51	Reading K-12	61	Foreign/World Lang K-12	71	Public Information
4	Food Service	11	Federal Program	22	Art Sec	32	Career/Sch-to-Work Elem	42	Science K-12	52	Reading Elem	62	Foreign/World Lang Elem	72	Summer School
5	Transportation	12	Title I	23	Music K-12	33	Career/Sch-to-Work Sec	43	Science Elem	53	Reading Sec	63	Foreign/World Lang Sec	73	Instructional Tech
6	Athletic	13	Title V	24	Music Elem	34	Early Childhood Ed	44	Science Sec	54	Remedial Reading K-12	64	Religious Education K-12	74	Inservice Training
7	Health Services	14	Asst Superintendent	25	Music Sec	35	Health/Phys Education	45	Math K-12	55	Remedial Reading Elem	65	Religious Education Elem	75	Marketing/Distributive
		15	Instructional Media Svcs	26	Business Education	36	Guidance Services K-12	46	Math Elem	56	Remedial Reading Sec	66	Religious Education Sec	76	Info Systems
		17	Chief Operations Officer	27	Career & Tech Ed	37	Guidance Services Elem	47	Math Sec	57	Bilingual/ELL	67	School Board President	77	Psychological Assess
		18	Chief Academic Officer	28	Technology Education	38	Guidance Services Sec	48	English/Lang Arts K-12	58	Special Education K-12	68	Teacher Personnel	78	Affirmative Action

Texas School Directory

Winkler County

• **La Vernia Ind School Dist** PID: 01061318 830/779-6600
13600 US Highway 87 W, La Vernia 78121 Fax 830/779-2304

Schools: 4 \ **Teachers:** 208 \ **Students:** 3,360 \ **Special Ed Students:** 311 \ **LEP Students:** 105 \ **College-Bound:** 55% \ **Ethnic:** African American 1%, Hispanic 29%, Caucasian 69% \ **Exp:** $338 (High) \ **Poverty:** 7% \ **Title I:** $222,887 \ **Special Education:** $460,000 \ **Open-Close:** 08/21 - 05/22 \ **DTBP:** $141 (High) \ [f] [t]

Dr Trent Lovette 1	Amy Cowley 2,3,5,15
Adellea Freeman-Wright 4	Chris Taber 6*
Kasey Dickson 7,83,85*	Toni Riester-Wood 8
Brenda Oates 58	Cynthia Burkle 67
Max Flores 68	Dr Jordan Ziemer 71
Angela Turner 73,98,295,297	Joshua Gutierrez 91

Public Schs..Principal	Grd	Prgm	Enr/#Cls	SN	
La Vernia High Sch	9-12	V	1,057	18%	830/779-6630
225 Bluebonnet Rd, La Vernia 78121					Fax 830/779-3218
Kimberley Martin					
La Vernia Intermediate Sch	3-5		776	26%	830/779-6640
369 S FM 1346, La Vernia 78121			38		Fax 830/779-6642
Helen Hubert					
La Vernia Junior High Sch	6-8		720	27%	830/779-6650
195 Bluebonnet Rd, La Vernia 78121			25		Fax 830/779-6651
Andrea Carter					
La Vernia Primary Sch	PK-2		808	28%	830/779-6660
249 S FM 1346, La Vernia 78121			29		Fax 830/779-7031
Shelley Keck					

• **Poth Ind School Dist** PID: 01061344 830/484-3330
510 Titcomb St, Poth 78147 Fax 830/484-2961

Schools: 3 \ **Teachers:** 65 \ **Students:** 840 \ **Special Ed Students:** 79 \ **LEP Students:** 45 \ **College-Bound:** 58% \ **Ethnic:** African American 1%, Hispanic 48%, Caucasian 51% \ **Exp:** $351 (High) \ **Poverty:** 7% \ **Title I:** $53,381 \ **Special Education:** $126,000 \ **Open-Close:** 08/14 - 05/20 \ **DTBP:** $345 (High) \ [f]

Paula Renken 1,11	Jennifer Johnson 2
James Molina 3	Betty Moy 4
Jeffrey Luna 6*	Casse Landrum 7,35*
Karla Brysch 12*	Ronnie Wieding 27*
Nicole Dziuk 31,36,83*	Lori Spencer 58*
Les Miller 67	Susie Martinez 69*
Max Calhoun 73	

Public Schs..Principal	Grd	Prgm	Enr/#Cls	SN	
Poth Elem Sch	PK-5	T	411	44%	830/484-3321
210 Brinkoeter St, Poth 78147			19		Fax 830/484-1271
Karla Brysch					[f]
Poth High Sch	9-12		244	28%	830/484-3322
506 N Dickson St, Poth 78147			22		Fax 830/484-3304
Todd Deaver					
Poth Junior High Sch	6-8		180	38%	830/484-3323
505 N Dickson St, Poth 78147			22		Fax 830/484-3682
Laura Kroll					

• **Stockdale Ind School Dist** PID: 01061382 830/996-3551
503 S 4th St, Stockdale 78160 Fax 830/996-1071

Schools: 3 \ **Teachers:** 74 \ **Students:** 803 \ **Special Ed Students:** 109 \ **LEP Students:** 24 \ **Ethnic:** African American 1%, Hispanic 49%, Caucasian 50% \ **Exp:** $370 (High) \ **Poverty:** 25% \ **Title I:** $283,646 \ **Open-Close:** 08/21 - 05/28 \ **DTBP:** $346 (High)

Daniel Fuller 1	Becky Stewart 2
Samaris Velazquez 4	Roxanne Moczygemba 8,69
Sandra Lynn 10*	Roxanne Moczygemba 11,296
Sharon Dunn 35,88,288*	Venicia Monita 57*
Salvadore Urrabazo 67	Billy Polasek 73
Pam Burrier 76	

Public Schs..Principal	Grd	Prgm	Enr/#Cls	SN	
Stockdale Elem Sch	PK-5	T	389	55%	830/996-1612
503 S 4th St, Stockdale 78160			21		Fax 830/996-3236
Brigit Lucas					
Stockdale High Sch	9-12	TV	247	44%	830/996-3103
503 S 4th St, Stockdale 78160			15		Fax 830/996-9071
Sandra Lynn					
Stockdale Junior High Sch	6-8	T	191	48%	830/996-3153
503 S 4th St, Stockdale 78160			10		Fax 830/996-3055
Sharon Dunn					

WILSON CATHOLIC SCHOOLS

• **Archdiocese San Antonio Ed Off** PID: 00999724
Listing includes only schools located in this county. See District Index for location of Diocesan Offices.

Catholic Schs..Principal	Grd	Prgm	Enr/#Cls	SN	
Sacred Heart Catholic Sch	PK-5		95		830/393-2117
1007 Trail St, Floresville 78114			6		Fax 830/393-6968
Hilary Reile					[f] [t]

WILSON PRIVATE SCHOOLS

Private Schs..Principal	Grd	Prgm	Enr/#Cls	SN	
La Vernia Christian Agape Acad	K-12		15		830/779-6361
10688 US Highway 87 W, La Vernia 78121					Fax 830/779-2402
Bob Middleton					

WINKLER COUNTY

WINKLER PUBLIC SCHOOLS

• **Kermit Ind School Dist** PID: 01061423 432/586-1000
601 S Poplar St, Kermit 79745 Fax 432/586-1016

Schools: 3 \ **Teachers:** 89 \ **Students:** 1,418 \ **Special Ed Students:** 122 \ **LEP Students:** 224 \ **Ethnic:** Asian 1%, African American 2%, Hispanic 78%, Caucasian 19% \ **Exp:** $647 (High) \ **Poverty:** 21% \ **Title I:** $347,728 \ **Open-Close:** 08/26 - 05/29 \ **DTBP:** $352 (High)

Dr Denise Shetter 1	Gayle Fuqua 2
Gabe Espino 3,5,91	Iyana Matthews 4
Charles Ross 6	Remona Sherry 7
William Armstrong 8,83,88,288,294,298	Mark Patrick 16,73,295*
Amanda Urias 31,36,270*	Roxanne Greer 58
Lee Lentz-Edwards 67	Angela Florez 79

---

79 Student Personnel	91 Safety/Security	275 Response To Intervention	298 Grant Writer/Ptnrships	**School Programs**	**Social Media**	
80 Driver Ed/Safety	92 Magnet School	277 Remedial Math K-12	750 Chief Innovation Officer	A = Alternative Program	[f] = Facebook	
81 Gifted/Talented	93 Parental Involvement	280 Literacy Coach	751 Chief of Staff	G = Adult Classes		
82 Video Services	95 Tech Prep Program	285 STEM	752 Social Emotional Learning	M = Magnet Program	[t] = Twitter	
83 Substance Abuse Prev	97 Chief Infomation Officer	286 Digital Learning		T = Title I Schoolwide		
84 Erate	98 Chief Technology Officer	288 Common Core Standards	**Other School Types**	V = Career & Tech Ed Programs		
85 AIDS Education	270 Character Education	294 Accountability	Ⓐ = Alternative School			
88 Alternative/At Risk	271 Migrant Education	295 Network System	Ⓒ = Charter School	New Schools are shaded		
89 Multi-Cultural Curriculum	273 Teacher Mentor	296 Title II Programs	Ⓜ = Magnet School	New Superintendents and Principals are bold		
90 Social Work	274 Before/After Sch	297 Webmaster	Ⓨ = Year-Round School	Personnel with email addresses are underscored		

Wise County

Market Data Retrieval

Public Schs..Principal	Grd	Prgm	Enr/#Cls	SN	
Kermit Elem Sch 201 N East Ave, Kermit 79745 Sonia Gonzales	PK-4	T	636 18	73%	432/586-1020 Fax 432/586-1023
Kermit High Sch 912 E Tommy Thompson St, Kermit 79745 Daniel Sharp	9-12	TV	366 35	64%	432/586-1050 Fax 432/586-1055
Kermit Junior High Sch 1000 Tommy Thompson St, Kermit 79745 Laura Miller	5-8	TV	416 30	73%	432/586-1040 Fax 432/586-1045

• **Wink Loving Ind School Dist** PID: 01061485
200 N Rosey Dodd Ave, Wink 79789
432/527-3880
Fax 432/527-3505

Schools: 2 \ **Teachers:** 40 \ **Students:** 440 \ **Special Ed Students:** 29 \ **LEP Students:** 10 \ **Ethnic:** African American 2%, Hispanic 40%, Native American: 1%, Caucasian 57% \ **Exp:** $642 (High) \ **Poverty:** 21% \ **Title I:** $65,703 \ **Open-Close:** 08/19 - 05/22 \ **DTBP:** $340 (High)

Scotty Carman 1
Greg Rogers 3,5
Brian Gibson 6*
Kittie Gibson 8*
Lance Wineinger 9*
Kimberly Licon 51,271*
Roxanne Greer 58
Peter Lara 61*
Micheal Dawkins 73,76,286,295*
Geanna Coker 2
Mickey Underwood 4
Courtney Woody 7,85*
Priscilla Salgado 8,11,36,69,83,88,93*
Darryl Schwierjohn 23*
Karen Jones 57
Judy White 60*
Brad White 67
Greg Rogers 298*

Public Schs..Principal	Grd	Prgm	Enr/#Cls	SN	
Wink Elem Sch 200 Rosey Dodd St, Wink 79789 Lance Wineinger	PK-6	AT	262 18	36%	432/527-3880
Wink High Sch 200 Rosey Dodd St, Wink 79789 Kittie Gibson	7-12	AGTV	172 28	32%	432/527-3880

WISE COUNTY

WISE PUBLIC SCHOOLS

• **Alvord Ind School Dist** PID: 01061526
100 Mosley Ln, Alvord 76225
940/427-5975
Fax 940/427-2313

Schools: 3 \ **Teachers:** 56 \ **Students:** 709 \ **Special Ed Students:** 69 \ **LEP Students:** 31 \ **Ethnic:** African American 1%, Hispanic 14%, Caucasian 84% \ **Exp:** $310 (High) \ **Poverty:** 9% \ **Title I:** $72,605 \ **Open-Close:** 08/15 - 05/21

Dr Randy Brown 1
Jeremy Russell 5
Asisela Palmer 7,85*
Charles Mann 11,73,295*
Cindy Tackett 2
Peter Hart 6*
Bonnie Foreman 8,69,83,270*
Daniel Ruddick 67

Public Schs..Principal	Grd	Prgm	Enr/#Cls	SN	
Alvord Elem Sch 711 W Stadium Dr, Alvord 76225 Bridget Williams	PK-5	T	325 31	40%	940/427-2881 Fax 940/427-2213
Alvord High Sch 1049 W Bypass 287, Alvord 76225 Aaron Tefertiller	9-12	V	212	23%	940/427-9643 Fax 940/427-9648
Alvord Middle Sch 328 S FM 1655, Alvord 76225 Jessica Bull	6-8		172 11	32%	940/427-5511 Fax 940/427-2461

• **Boyd Ind School Dist** PID: 01061552
600 Knox Ave, Boyd 76023
940/433-2327
Fax 940/433-9569

Schools: 4 \ **Teachers:** 90 \ **Students:** 1,317 \ **Special Ed Students:** 87 \ **LEP Students:** 41 \ **College-Bound:** 53% \ **Ethnic:** African American 1%, Hispanic 16%, Native American: 1%, Caucasian 81% \ **Exp:** $271 (Med) \ **Poverty:** 11% \ **Title I:** $135,212 \ **Open-Close:** 08/15 - 05/21 \ **DTBP:** $349 (High)

Leslie Vann 1
James McDonald 3
Brandon Hopkins 6*
Krystle Duncan 58
Kayla Haynie 73
Linda Ratliff 2
Sharon Nelson 5
Anke Bracey 11,296*
Bill Childress 67

Public Schs..Principal	Grd	Prgm	Enr/#Cls	SN	
Boyd Elem Sch 500 E Morton Ave, Boyd 76023 Anke Bracey	PK-3	T	439 20	61%	940/433-9520 Fax 940/433-9536
Boyd High Sch 700 Knox Ave, Boyd 76023 Susan Foster	9-12	ATV	400 22	40%	940/433-9580 Fax 940/433-9593
Boyd Intermediate Sch 550 Knox Ave, Boyd 76023 Daniel Bourgeois	4-6	T	284 14	45%	940/433-9540
Boyd Middle Sch 550 Knox Ave, Boyd 76023 Daniel Bourgeois	7-8	T	212 20	43%	940/433-9560 Fax 940/433-9568

• **Bridgeport Ind School Dist** PID: 01061588
2107 15th St, Bridgeport 76426
940/683-5124
Fax 940/683-4268

Schools: 5 \ **Teachers:** 161 \ **Students:** 2,062 \ **Special Ed Students:** 198 \ **LEP Students:** 439 \ **College-Bound:** 43% \ **Ethnic:** African American 1%, Hispanic 51%, Native American: 1%, Caucasian 47% \ **Exp:** $376 (High) \ **Poverty:** 19% \ **Title I:** $554,325 \ **Open-Close:** 08/15 - 05/20 \ **DTBP:** $343 (High)

Brandon Peavey 1
Kurt Kronenberger 3,5,15,68
Terry Rye 5*
Dr Adam Hile 8,15,72
Travis Hood 58
Leslie Henson 73
Debi Meng 2
Shelley Laaser 4
Shannon Wilson 6
Patricia Hernandez .. 11,57,69,271,288,296,298
Tom Talley 67
Roger Egle 73,76,286,295*

Public Schs..Principal	Grd	Prgm	Enr/#Cls	SN	
Ⓐ Alternative Learning Center 1101 17th St, Bridgeport 76426 Jennifer Miller	1-12		25 4		940/683-1830 Fax 940/683-3582
Bridgeport Elem Sch 1408 Elementary Dr, Bridgeport 76426 Martha Bock	PK-2	T	484 50	72%	940/683-5955 Fax 940/683-5079
Bridgeport High Sch 1 Maroon Dr, Bridgeport 76426 Jaime Sturdivant	9-12	ATV	651 45	55%	940/683-4064 Fax 940/683-4014
Bridgeport Intermediate Sch 1400 US Highway 380, Bridgeport 76426 Mallory Marr	3-5	T	481 32	66%	940/683-5784 Fax 940/683-4086

---

1 Superintendent	8 Curric/Instruct K-12	19 Chief Financial Officer	29 Family/Consumer Science	39 Social Studies K-12	49 English/Lang Arts Elem	59 Special Education Elem	69 Academic Assessment
2 Bus/Finance/Purchasing	9 Curric/Instruct Elem	20 Art K-12	30 Adult Education	40 Social Studies Elem	50 English/Lang Arts Sec	60 Special Education Sec	70 Research/Development
3 Buildings And Grounds	10 Curric/Instruct Sec	21 Art Elem	31 Career/Sch-to-Work K-12	41 Social Studies Sec	51 Reading K-12	61 Foreign/World Lang K-12	71 Public Information
4 Food Service	11 Federal Program	22 Art Sec	32 Career/Sch-to-Work Elem	42 Science K-12	52 Reading Elem	62 Foreign/World Lang Elem	72 Summer School
5 Transportation	12 Title I	23 Music K-12	33 Career/Sch-to-Work Sec	43 Science Elem	53 Reading Sec	63 Foreign/World Lang Sec	73 Instructional Tech
6 Athletic	13 Title V	24 Music Elem	34 Early Childhood Ed	44 Science Sec	54 Remedial Reading K-12	64 Religious Education K-12	74 Inservice Training
7 Health Services	15 Asst Superintendent	25 Music Sec	35 Health/Phys Education	45 Math K-12	55 Remedial Reading Elem	65 Religious Education Elem	75 Marketing/Distributive
	16 Instructional Media Svcs	26 Business Education	36 Guidance Services K-12	46 Math Elem	56 Remedial Reading Sec	66 Religious Education Sec	76 Info Systems
	17 Chief Operations Officer	27 Career & Tech Ed	37 Guidance Services Elem	47 Math Sec	57 Bilingual/ELL	67 School Board President	77 Psychological Assess
	18 Chief Academic Officer	28 Technology Education	38 Guidance Services Sec	48 English/Lang Arts K-12	58 Special Education K-12	68 Teacher Personnel	78 Affirmative Action

Texas School Directory — Wise County

Bridgeport Middle Sch	6-8	ATV	446	64%	940/683-2273
702 17th St, Bridgeport 76426			36		Fax 940/683-5812
Steven Valkenaar					

• Chico Ind School Dist PID: 01061629   940/644-2228
503 W Sherman St, Chico 76431   Fax 940/644-0055

Schools: 3 \ **Teachers:** 51 \ **Students:** 600 \ **Special Ed Students:** 54 \ **LEP Students:** 50 \ **College-Bound:** 52% \ **Ethnic:** African American 1%, Hispanic 28%, Native American: 1%, Caucasian 71% \ **Exp:** $269 (Med) \ **Poverty:** 16% \ **Title I:** $136,854 \ **Open-Close:** 08/15 - 05/21 \ **DTBP:** $365 (High)

William Higgins	1	Kaylinn Hudson	2
Shelli Lieser	4	Maury Martin	5,11,57,58,88,273,285,294
Randi Miller	6	Brent Hand	8*
Linda Duck	12,280*	Paula Buckner	59*
Tim Raley	67	Breann Cox	73
Karen Decker	275*	Debbie Peyton	295,297

Public Schs..Principal	Grd	Prgm	Enr/#Cls	SN	
Chico Elem Sch	PK-5	AT	307	57%	940/644-2220
1120 Park Rd, Chico 76431			23		Fax 940/644-2847
Karen Decker					
Chico High Sch	9-12	ATV	163	56%	940/644-5783
263 FM 2952, Chico 76431			22		Fax 940/644-1932
Randy Brawner					
Chico Junior High Sch	6-8	AT	138	66%	940/644-5550
1205 W Sherman St, Chico 76431			12		Fax 940/644-5876
Monte Sewell					

• Decatur Ind School Dist PID: 01061655   940/393-7100
307 S Cates St, Decatur 76234   Fax 940/627-3141

Schools: 5 \ **Teachers:** 207 \ **Students:** 3,390 \ **Special Ed Students:** 303 \ **LEP Students:** 411 \ **College-Bound:** 59% \ **Ethnic:** Asian 1%, African American 1%, Hispanic 36%, Caucasian 62% \ **Exp:** $393 (High) \ **Poverty:** 13% \ **Title I:** $406,442 \ **Special Education:** $624,000 \ **Open-Close:** 08/14 - 05/20 \ **DTBP:** $181 (High) \ f

Dr Judi Whitis	1	Cindy Tatum	2,15
Rusty Berg	3	Shelly Lasser	4
Steve White	5	Mike Fuller	6
Dr Shane Conklin	8,31,57,69,70,271,274	Meredith Culpepper	11,68,83,88,298
April Whisenant	58	Cheri Boyd	67
Jennifer Terrell	69	Troy Bagwell	73*
David Jackson	295		

Public Schs..Principal	Grd	Prgm	Enr/#Cls	SN	
Carson Elem Sch	PK-5	T	464	43%	940/393-7500
2100 S Business 287, Decatur 76234			30		Fax 940/627-4792
Craig Weston					
Decatur High Sch	9-12	V	1,054	37%	940/393-7200
750 E Eagle Smt, Decatur 76234			55		Fax 940/626-4520 f
Christopher Mogan					
McCarroll Middle Sch	6-8	TV	485	45%	940/393-7300
1201 W Thompson St, Decatur 76234			25		Fax 940/627-2497 f
Brett Phipps					
Rann Elem Sch	PK-5	T	563	52%	940/393-7600
1300 Deer Park Rd, Decatur 76234			35		Fax 940/627-6198
Roby Nunn					
Young Elem Sch	PK-5	T	520	61%	940/393-7400
379 Buchanan Rd, Decatur 76234					Fax 940/627-0082
Lana Coffman					

• Paradise Ind School Dist PID: 01061722   940/969-2501
338 School House Rd, Paradise 76073   Fax 940/969-5008

Schools: 4 \ **Teachers:** 93 \ **Students:** 1,200 \ **Special Ed Students:** 121 \ **LEP Students:** 34 \ **College-Bound:** 47% \ **Ethnic:** Hispanic 12%, Native American: 1%, Caucasian 87% \ **Exp:** $182 (Low) \ **Poverty:** 13% \ **Title I:** $187,528 \ **Open-Close:** 08/15 - 05/21 \ **DTBP:** $340 (High) \ f

Dr Paul Uttley	1	Summer Mathis	2,19
Greg Fletcher	3	Joe Koch	6
Patti Seckman	8,11,15,74,271,296	Dr Joyce Hardy	15,69
Lana McGehee	16*	Robin Garrett	37*
Cherie Gopffarth	38,83,88	Jennifer Crawford	59*
Homer Mundy	67	Doug Bryant	73,76,286

Public Schs..Principal	Grd	Prgm	Enr/#Cls	SN	
Paradise Elem Sch	PK-3	T	386	31%	940/969-5046
340 Schoolhouse Rd, Paradise 76073			18		Fax 940/969-5043
Robyn Gibson					
Paradise High Sch	9-12	V	349	18%	940/969-5010
338 School House Rd, Paradise 76073			20		Fax 940/969-5009
Mark Mathis					
Paradise Intermediate Sch	4-5		198	31%	940/969-5032
338 School House Rd, Paradise 76073			12		Fax 940/969-5031
Kristin Gage					
Paradise Junior High Sch	6-8	V	260	27%	940/969-5034
338 School House Rd, Paradise 76073					Fax 940/969-5025
Greg Fletcher					

• Slidell Ind School Dist PID: 01061758   940/535-5260
1 Greyhound Ln, Slidell 76267   Fax 940/466-3062

Schools: 2 \ **Teachers:** 25 \ **Students:** 282 \ **Special Ed Students:** 16 \ **LEP Students:** 29 \ **College-Bound:** 30% \ **Ethnic:** Hispanic 29%, Caucasian 71% \ **Exp:** $209 (Med) \ **Poverty:** 12% \ **Title I:** $41,206 \ **Open-Close:** 08/14 - 05/20 \ **DTBP:** $532 (High)

Taylor Williams	1	Irene Wilson	2,12
Robert Oney	3,5,73,76,295*	Casey Pierce	6*
Marty Bratcher-Hair	8,11,15,16,57,58,286*	Marty Bratcher-Hair	15,58
Tim Fletcher	67		

Public Schs..Principal	Grd	Prgm	Enr/#Cls	SN	
Slidell Elem Sch	PK-3		129		940/466-3118
17347 FM 455, Decatur 76234			10		Fax 940/466-3016
Theresa Stevens					
Slidell Secondary Sch	5-12	T	153	54%	940/535-5260
1 Greyhound Ln, Slidell 76267			12		
Theresa Stevens					

WISE PRIVATE SCHOOLS

Private Schs..Principal	Grd	Prgm	Enr/#Cls	SN	
Victory Christian Academy	PK-12		401		940/626-4730
600 W Mulberry St, Decatur 76234					Fax 972/954-3492
Allen Bates					

---

79 Student Personnel	91 Safety/Security	275 Response To Intervention	298 Grant Writer/Ptnrships	**School Programs**	**Social Media**
80 Driver Ed/Safety	92 Magnet School	277 Remedial Math K-12	750 Chief Innovation Officer	A = Alternative Program	f = Facebook
81 Gifted/Talented	93 Parental Involvement	280 Literacy Coach	751 Chief of Staff	G = Adult Classes	t = Twitter
82 Video Services	95 Tech Prep Program	285 STEM	752 Social Emotional Learning	M = Magnet Program	
83 Substance Abuse Prev	97 Chief Infomation Officer	286 Digital Learning		T = Title I Schoolwide	
84 Erate	98 Chief Technology Officer	288 Common Core Standards	**Other School Types**	V = Career & Tech Ed Programs	
85 AIDS Education	270 Accountability	294 Character Education	A = Alternative School		
88 Alternative/At Risk	271 Migrant Education	295 Network System	C = Charter School	New Schools are shaded	
89 Multi-Cultural Curriculum	273 Teacher Mentor	296 Title II Programs	M = Magnet School	New Superintendents and Principals are bold	
90 Social Work	274 Before/After Sch	297 Webmaster	Y = Year-Round School	Personnel with email addresses are underscored	

TX—403

Wood County

WOOD COUNTY

WOOD PUBLIC SCHOOLS

- **Alba-Golden Ind School Dist** PID: 01061784   903/768-2472
  1373 County Road 2377, Alba 75410   Fax 903/768-2130

Schools: 2 \ *Teachers:* 74 \ *Students:* 850 \ *Special Ed Students:* 89 \ *LEP Students:* 16 \ *College-Bound:* 37% \ *Ethnic:* Hispanic 10%, Caucasian 89% \ *Exp:* $327 (High) \ *Poverty:* 19% \ *Title I:* $276,304 \ *Open-Close:* 08/26 - 05/29 \ *DTBP:* $340 (High)

Dwayne Ellis	1	Brenda Kelley	2
Derek Smith	6*	Deitra Bizzell	8*
Michele Glidewell	9*	Jennifer Wigington	11
Michelle Randell	58*	Jason Stovall	67
Dina Allred	69*	Michael Scott	73,98
Starla Bryant	88*		

Public Schs..Principal	Grd	Prgm	Enr/#Cls	SN	
Alba-Golden Elem Sch 1373 County Road 2377, Alba 75410 Kevin Wright	PK-5	T	444 22	55%	903/768-2472 Fax 903/768-2593
Alba-Golden Jr Sr High Sch 1373 County Road 2377, Alba 75410 Brandon Bohannan \ Michael Mize	6-12	T	438 56	50%	903/768-2472 Fax 903/768-2303

- **Hawkins Ind School Dist** PID: 01061813   903/769-2181
  179 Hawk Dr, Hawkins 75765   Fax 903/769-0505

Schools: 3 \ *Teachers:* 63 \ *Students:* 735 \ *Special Ed Students:* 73 \ *LEP Students:* 5 \ *College-Bound:* 75% \ *Ethnic:* African American 12%, Hispanic 5%, Caucasian 83% \ *Exp:* $412 (High) \ *Poverty:* 28% \ *Title I:* $278,500 \ *Open-Close:* 08/14 - 05/22 \ *DTBP:* $378 (High)

Morris Lyon	1,84	Robby Fair	2
Sharyn Loven	2	Lesa Gibson	4*
Troy Love	5	Scott Evans	6,91
Natalie Hlavenka	7*	Dionne Williams	8,11,58,83,88,296,298
Kathy Boyd	16,82*	Robbie White	67
Mike Henderson	73,295*		

Public Schs..Principal	Grd	Prgm	Enr/#Cls	SN	
Hawkins Elem Sch 231 Hawk Dr, Hawkins 75765 Stephanie McConnell	PK-5	T	320 25	60%	903/769-0536 Fax 903/769-0513
Hawkins High Sch 231 Hawk Dr, Hawkins 75765 **Elisa Henninger**	9-12	ATV	222 35	55%	903/769-0571 Fax 903/769-0573
Hawkins Middle Sch 231 Hawk Dr, Hawkins 75765 Gregg Weiss	6-8	T	145 15	54%	903/769-0552 Fax 903/769-0573

- **Mineola Ind School Dist** PID: 01061851   903/569-2448
  1695 W Loop 564, Mineola 75773   Fax 903/569-5155

Schools: 4 \ *Teachers:* 126 \ *Students:* 1,630 \ *Special Ed Students:* 127 \ *LEP Students:* 146 \ *College-Bound:* 55% \ *Ethnic:* Asian 1%, African American 7%, Hispanic 33%, Native American: 1%, Caucasian 57% \ *Exp:* $317 (High) \ *Poverty:* 25% \ *Title I:* $512,649 \ *Open-Close:* 08/15 - 05/22 \ *DTBP:* $353 (High)

Dr Kim Tunnell	1,83,84	William Bjork	2,15
Rick Browning	3	Kim Myers	4
Sherri Harding	5	Luke Blackwell	6*
Jennifer Knipp	8,57,58,69,74,88,271,286	Mark Parkerson	11,27,73,77,295
Carolyn Standford	16	Dr John Abott	67
Melisia Foster	85*		

Public Schs..Principal	Grd	Prgm	Enr/#Cls	SN	
Mineola Elem Sch 900 W Patten St, Mineola 75773 Stacy Morris	3-5	T	372 20	64%	903/569-2466 Fax 903/569-3061
Mineola High Sch 900 W Patten St, Mineola 75773 David Sauer	9-12	TV	466 34	54%	903/569-3000 Fax 903/569-1930
Mineola Middle Sch 1050 W Loop 564, Mineola 75773 Kendall Gould	6-8	GT	362 30	55%	903/569-5338 Fax 903/569-5339
Mineola Primary Sch 1695 W Loop 564, Mineola 75773 Jole Ray	PK-2	GT	414 25	72%	903/569-5488 Fax 903/569-5489

- **Quitman Ind School Dist** PID: 01061904   903/763-5000
  1201 E Goode St, Quitman 75783   Fax 903/763-2710

Schools: 3 \ *Teachers:* 88 \ *Students:* 1,121 \ *Special Ed Students:* 116 \ *LEP Students:* 47 \ *College-Bound:* 48% \ *Ethnic:* African American 2%, Hispanic 17%, Native American: 1%, Caucasian 79% \ *Exp:* $572 (High) \ *Poverty:* 20% \ *Title I:* $292,660 \ *Open-Close:* 08/21 - 05/22 \ *DTBP:* $350 (High)

Rhonda Turner	1	Kayla Mars	2,68
Steve Schoon	3,5,91	Vinny Bass	4
Teresa Bradshaw	5	Bryan Oakes	6
Stacy Vandersthaas	7*	Chris Mason	8,11,57,69,88,285,296,298
June Sims	37*	Dr Jeremy Smith	67
Scott Turner	73,84,295		

Public Schs..Principal	Grd	Prgm	Enr/#Cls	SN	
Quitman Elem Sch 902 E Goode St, Quitman 75783 Mary Nichols	PK-5	T	530 41	58%	903/763-5000 Fax 903/763-4151
Quitman High Sch 1101 E Goode St, Quitman 75783 Dana Hamrick	9-12	TV	294 30	48%	903/763-5000 Fax 903/763-2589
Quitman Junior High Sch 1101 E Goode St, Quitman 75783 Chrystal Ballard	6-8	ATV	297 20	59%	903/763-5000 Fax 903/763-2589

Texas School Directory

Yoakum County

- **Winnsboro Ind School Dist** PID: 01061942   903/342-3737
  207 E Pine St, Winnsboro 75494   Fax 903/342-3380

Schools: 3 \ *Teachers:* 108 \ *Students:* 1,496 \ *Special Ed Students:* 120 \ *LEP Students:* 79 \ *College-Bound:* 80% \ *Ethnic:* Asian 1%, African American 2%, Hispanic 16%, Native American: 1%, Caucasian 81% \ *Exp:* $522 (High) \ *Poverty:* 18% \ *Title I:* $315,341 \ *Special Education:* $210,000 \ *Open-Close:* 08/15 - 05/28 \ *DTBP:* $341 (High)

Susan Morton ...1	Mary Ann Lanier ...2
Roger Spakes ...3,5	Kisha Smith ...4*
William Cummings ...5	Steve Pinnell ...6*
Erika Martin ...7	Torri Miller ...8,11,58,76,286,288,298*
Debbie May ...38,85,88*	Rena Wagner ...57*
Mary Ellen Knight ...58	Chris McElyea ...67
Craig Anderson ...73,84,295	Adriana Weems ...76
Jody Hettich ...91*	David Pinell ...285*

Public Schs..Principal	Grd	Prgm	Enr/#Cls	SN	
Memorial Middle Sch 505 S Chestnut St, Winnsboro 75494 Jeff Akin	5-8	T	454 40	50%	903/342-5711 Fax 903/342-6689
Winnsboro Elem Sch 310 W Coke Rd, Winnsboro 75494 Pam Gambrel	PK-4	T	605 36	64%	903/342-3548 Fax 903/342-6858
Winnsboro High Sch 409 Newsome St, Winnsboro 75494 David Pinell	9-12	T	463 32	40%	903/342-3641 Fax 903/342-3645

- **Yantis Ind School Dist** PID: 01061980   903/383-2463
  105 W Oak St, Yantis 75497   Fax 903/383-7620

Schools: 2 \ *Teachers:* 37 \ *Students:* 370 \ *Special Ed Students:* 24 \ *LEP Students:* 36 \ *College-Bound:* 50% \ *Ethnic:* Hispanic 26%, Caucasian 73% \ *Exp:* $366 (High) \ *Poverty:* 25% \ *Title I:* $124,092 \ *Open-Close:* 08/28 - 06/01 \ *DTBP:* $350 (High)

Tracey Helfferich ...1	Kathleen Young ...2
Mitzi McLane ...4	Staci Gammill ...7*
Tracey Helfferich ...8,11,298*	Steve Hardy ...16,82
Shelia Aaron ...29*	Kenda Armstrong ...57*
Deanna Alexander ...58*	Melissa Stephens ...67
Jon Pollard ...73,84	

Public Schs..Principal	Grd	Prgm	Enr/#Cls	SN	
Imagene Glenn Elem Sch 105 W Oak St, Yantis 75497 Tracey Helfferich	PK-5	T	205 13	58%	903/383-2462 Fax 903/383-2463
Yantis Sch 105 W Oak St, Yantis 75497 Tracey Helfferich \ Buddy Winstead	PK-12	ATV	155 27	51%	903/383-2462 Fax 903/383-2463

YOAKUM COUNTY

YOAKUM PUBLIC SCHOOLS

- **Denver City Ind School Dist** PID: 01062013   806/592-5900
  501 Mustang Dr, Denver City 79323   Fax 806/592-5909

Schools: 5 \ *Teachers:* 132 \ *Students:* 1,741 \ *Special Ed Students:* 99 \ *LEP Students:* 256 \ *College-Bound:* 52% \ *Ethnic:* Asian 1%, African American 1%, Hispanic 82%, Caucasian 17% \ *Exp:* $323 (High) \ *Poverty:* 16% \ *Title I:* $259,138 \ *Open-Close:* 08/20 - 05/21 \ *DTBP:* $133 (High)

Gary Davis ...1	Lachrisa Rains ...2,19
Shannon Bressler ...2	Butch Johnson ...3
Jennifer Jordon ...4	Kelly Adams ...4,8,11,58,83,88,271*
Alonzo Diaz ...5	Steve Taylor ...6*
Vee Ann Carter ...7,85*	Priscilla Summers ...16,82*
Jerry Fortenberry ...27,73	Kristy Kostelich ...27*
Kelli Hilburn ...37*	Brad Woosley ...67
Angie Benningield ...68	Kathy Guetersloh ...77*
Cindy Bessire ...79	

Public Schs..Principal	Grd	Prgm	Enr/#Cls	SN	
Denver City High Sch 601 Mustang Dr, Denver City 79323 Ricky Martinez	9-12	TV	487 45	39%	806/592-5950 Fax 806/592-5959
Dodson Primary Sch 600 N Soland Ave, Denver City 79323 Angela Sutton	PK-2	T	434	70%	806/592-5931
Excalibur Sch 601 Mustang Dr, Denver City 79323 Rick Martinez	9-12		6 1		806/592-5950 Fax 806/592-5959
Kelley Elem Sch 500 N Soland Ave, Denver City 79323 Lori Alexander	3-5	T	402 48	60%	806/592-5920 Fax 806/592-5929
William G Gravitt Jr High Sch 419 Mustang Dr, Denver City 79323 Billy Moore	6-8	TV	366 40	56%	806/592-5940 Fax 806/592-5949

- **Plains Ind School Dist** PID: 01062063   806/456-7401
  811 Cowboy Way, Plains 79355   Fax 806/456-4325

Schools: 3 \ *Teachers:* 38 \ *Students:* 430 \ *Special Ed Students:* 28 \ *LEP Students:* 46 \ *College-Bound:* 93% \ *Ethnic:* Hispanic 68%, Caucasian 32% \ *Exp:* $707 (High) \ *Poverty:* 18% \ *Title I:* $112,741 \ *Open-Close:* 08/21 - 05/22 \ *DTBP:* $331 (High) \ 🇫 🇹

Robert McClean ...1,11,83	Jesenia Suarez ...2
Mary Parra ...4	Mike Taylor ...5
Ron Welch ...6	Kim Gass ...16*
Michelle Frerich ...36*	Gloria Covarrubias ...57,271*
Kyle Martin ...67	Hector Limon ...73,295*
Nate Wheeler ...76	

Public Schs..Principal	Grd	Prgm	Enr/#Cls	SN	
Plains Elem Sch 811 Cowboy Way, Plains 79355 Traci Heflin	PK-5	T	225 17	68%	806/456-7401

79 Student Personnel	91 Safety/Security	275 Response To Intervention	298 Grant Writer/Ptnrships
80 Driver Ed/Safety	92 Magnet School	277 Remedial Math K-12	750 Chief Innovation Officer
81 Gifted/Talented	93 Parental Involvement	280 Literacy Coach	751 Chief of Staff
82 Video Services	95 Tech Prep Program	285 STEM	752 Social Emotional Learning
83 Substance Abuse Prev	97 Chief Information Officer	286 Digital Learning	
84 Erate	98 Chief Technology Officer	288 Common Core Standards	
85 AIDS Education	270 Character Education	294 Accountability	
88 Alternative/At Risk	271 Migrant Education	295 Network System	
89 Multi-Cultural Curriculum	273 Teacher Mentor	296 Title II Programs	
90 Social Work	274 Before/After Sch	297 Webmaster	

School Programs
A = Alternative Program
G = Adult Classes
M = Magnet Program
T = Title I Schoolwide
V = Career & Tech Ed Programs

Other School Types
Ⓐ = Alternative School
Ⓒ = Charter School
Ⓜ = Magnet School
Ⓨ = Year-Round School

Social Media
🇫 = Facebook
🇹 = Twitter

New Schools are shaded
New Superintendents and Principals are bold
Personnel with email addresses are underscored

TX—405

Young County Market Data Retrieval

Plains High Sch 811 Cowboy Way, Plains 79355 Jorge Mendez	9-12	ATV	112 12	58%	806/456-7401
Plains Middle Sch 811 Cowboy Way, Plains 79355 Benjamin Taylor	5-8	TV	137 14	66%	806/456-7401

YOUNG COUNTY

YOUNG PUBLIC SCHOOLS

● **Graham Ind School Dist** PID: 01062104   940/549-0595
400 3rd St, Graham 76450   Fax 940/549-8656

Schools: 5 \ *Teachers:* 171 \ *Students:* 2,390 \ *Special Ed Students:* 236 \ *LEP Students:* 275 \ *Ethnic:* Asian 1%, African American 1%, Hispanic 30%, Native American: 1%, Caucasian 67% \ *Exp:* $312 (High) \ *Poverty:* 22% \ *Title I:* $620,006 \ *Special Education:* $565,000 \ *Open-Close:* 08/14 - 05/22 \ *DTBP:* $317 (High) \ f

Sonny Cruse 1
Jerry Davidson 3,5,91
Kenneth Davidson 6*
Gary Browning 8,288
Robert Loomis 15,38,68,69,296
Jayne Beale 73,286*
Chris Rasile 295
Don Davis 2,15
Jodi Arispie 4*
Stacy Key 7*
Natalie Husen 11,58*
Meredith Lucas 67
Blake Davis 83,91

Public Schs..Principal	Grd	Prgm	Enr/#Cls	SN	
Crestview Elem Sch 1317 Old Jacksboro Rd, Graham 76450 Amanda Townley	1-3	T	534 27	61%	940/549-6023 Fax 940/549-6025
Graham High Sch 1000 Brazos St, Graham 76450 Joe Gordy	9-12	T	675 65	47%	940/549-1504 Fax 940/549-4031
Graham Junior High Sch 1000 2nd St, Graham 76450 Ginger Robbins	6-8	T	538 38	56%	940/549-2002 Fax 940/549-6991
Pioneer Elem Sch 1425 1st St, Graham 76450 Donna Gatlin	PK-K	T	272 13	69%	940/549-2442 Fax 940/549-2460 f t
Woodland Elem Sch 1219 Cliff Dr, Graham 76450 Audra Barrett	4-5	T	368 18	58%	940/549-4090 Fax 940/549-4093

● **Newcastle Ind School Dist** PID: 01062166   940/846-3531
505 Washington Ave, Newcastle 76372   Fax 940/846-3452

Schools: 1 \ *Teachers:* 19 \ *Students:* 180 \ *Special Ed Students:* 19 \ *LEP Students:* 4 \ *College-Bound:* 55% \ *Ethnic:* African American 1%, Hispanic 13%, Caucasian 86% \ *Exp:* $600 (High) \ *Poverty:* 33% \ *Title I:* $117,159 \ *Open-Close:* 08/14 - 05/22 \ *DTBP:* $370 (High)

Evan Cardwell 1,11,83
Elaine Manuel 3,5
Gena Phillips 7
Debbie Wilkinson 58,73,288*
Sherri McMillan 270*
Shirley Rhodes 2,84
Teresa Keene 4
Melanie Lowe 54,57*
Bruce Bailey 67
Christy Eli 286,295*

Public Schs..Principal	Grd	Prgm	Enr/#Cls	SN	
Newcastle Sch 505 Washington Ave, Newcastle 76372 Debbie Wilkinson	PK-12	TV	180 23	66%	940/846-3531

● **Olney Ind School Dist** PID: 01062192   940/564-3519
809 W Hamilton St, Olney 76374   Fax 940/564-5205

Schools: 3 \ *Teachers:* 69 \ *Students:* 700 \ *Special Ed Students:* 95 \ *LEP Students:* 27 \ *College-Bound:* 64% \ *Ethnic:* African American 2%, Hispanic 39%, Caucasian 58% \ *Exp:* $407 (High) \ *Poverty:* 22% \ *Title I:* $190,644 \ *Open-Close:* 08/14 - 05/15 \ *DTBP:* $350 (High) \ f t

Dr Greg Roach 1
Tim Orsak 2
Tony Nichol 16,73
Cristi Little 58
Jenny Walker 68
Debbie Pace 2
Elaine Reno 8,12,288,298
Charlotte Mahler 57*
Jake Bailey 67

Public Schs..Principal	Grd	Prgm	Enr/#Cls	SN	
Olney Elem Sch 801 W Hamilton St, Olney 76374 Gunter Rodriguez	PK-5	T	343 30	71%	940/564-5608 Fax 940/564-3518
Olney High Sch 704 W Grove St, Olney 76374 Matt Caffey	9-12	AT	176 20	53%	940/564-5637 Fax 940/564-5733
Olney Junior High Sch 300 S Avenue H, Olney 76374 Amanda Barrientes	6-8	T	158 14	68%	940/564-3517 Fax 940/564-8824 f t

ZAPATA COUNTY

ZAPATA PUBLIC SCHOOLS

● **Zapata Co Ind School Dist** PID: 01062245   956/765-6546
1302 Glenn St, Zapata 78076   Fax 956/765-8350

Schools: 6 \ *Teachers:* 238 \ *Students:* 3,521 \ *Special Ed Students:* 345 \ *LEP Students:* 941 \ *Ethnic:* Hispanic 99%, Caucasian 1% \ *Exp:* $268 (Med) \ *Poverty:* 43% \ *Title I:* $2,238,236 \ *Special Education:* $577,000 \ *Open-Close:* 08/12 - 05/21 \ *DTBP:* $158 (High)

Carlos Gonzalez 1
Theresa Hein 2
Lesvia Cuellar 4
Claudia Arambula 8
Crisella Gutierrez 8
Suzette Barrera 11,294,298
Rebecca Flores 57
Ricardo Ramirez 67
Anna Martinez 69
Rogelio Gonzalez 79
Patricia Gonzalez 2
Pedro Morales 3,5
Joel Lopez 6
Connie Gray 8,42,93,288*
Hildeliza Villarreal 8
Janie Rodriguez 31,36,81,85,88
Carmen Zavala 58
Rogelia Gonzales 68
Gilbert Flores 73,76,84,286,295
Raymond Moya 91

Public Schs..Principal	Grd	Prgm	Enr/#Cls	SN	
A L Benavides Elem Sch 307 Lincoln Ave, San Ygnacio 78067 Diana Brandon	PK-5	T	90 6	82%	956/765-5611 Fax 956/765-3942
Villarreal Elem Sch 805 Mira Flores Ave, Zapata 78076 Marlen Guerra	PK-5	T	521 35	93%	956/765-4321 Fax 956/765-5124

---

1 Superintendent	8 Curric/Instruct K-12	19 Chief Financial Officer	29 Family/Consumer Science	39 Social Studies K-12	49 English/Lang Arts Elem	59 Special Education Elem	69 Academic Assessment
2 Bus/Finance/Purchasing	9 Curric/Instruct Elem	20 Art K-12	30 Adult Education	40 Social Studies Elem	50 English/Lang Arts Sec	60 Special Education Sec	70 Research/Development
3 Buildings And Grounds	10 Curric/Instruct Sec	21 Art Elem	31 Career/Sch-to-Work K-12	41 Social Studies Sec	51 Reading K-12	61 Foreign/World Lang K-12	71 Public Information
4 Food Service	11 Federal Program	22 Art Sec	32 Career/Sch-to-Work Elem	42 Science K-12	52 Reading Elem	62 Foreign/World Lang Elem	72 Summer School
5 Transportation	12 Title I	23 Music K-12	33 Career/Sch-to-Work Sec	43 Science Elem	53 Reading Sec	63 Foreign/World Lang Sec	73 Instructional Tech
6 Athletic	13 Title V	24 Music Elem	34 Early Childhood Ed	44 Science Sec	54 Remedial Reading K-12	64 Religious Education K-12	74 Inservice Training
7 Health Services	15 Asst Superintendent	25 Music Sec	35 Health/Phys Education	45 Math K-12	55 Remedial Reading Elem	65 Religious Education Elem	75 Marketing/Distributive
	16 Instructional Media Svcs	26 Business Education	36 Guidance Services K-12	46 Math Elem	56 Remedial Reading Sec	66 Religious Education Sec	76 Info Systems
	17 Chief Operations Officer	27 Career & Tech Ed	37 Guidance Services Elem	47 Math Sec	57 Bilingual/ELL	67 School Board President	77 Psychological Assess
	18 Chief Academic Officer	28 Technology Education	38 Guidance Services Sec	48 English/Lang Arts K-12	58 Special Education K-12	68 Teacher Personnel	78 Affirmative Action

Texas School Directory

Zavala County

School	Grade	Prgm	Enr/#Cls	SN	Phone
Zapata High Sch 2009 State Highway 16, Zapata 78076 Jerry Garcia	9-12	TV	923 66	84%	956/765-0280 Fax 956/765-0274
Zapata Middle Sch 702 E 17th Ave, Zapata 78076 Elsa Martinez	6-8	T	772 60	85%	956/765-6542 Fax 956/765-9204
Zapata North Elem Sch 1302 Glenn St, Zapata 78076 Elma Almaraz	PK-5	T	620 28	84%	956/765-6917 Fax 956/765-8512
Zapata South Elem Sch 500 Delmar St, Zapata 78076 Dahlia Garcia	PK-5	T	595 25	74%	956/765-4332 Fax 956/765-3320

ZAVALA COUNTY

ZAVALA PUBLIC SCHOOLS

• **Crystal City Ind School Dist** PID: 01062295   830/374-2367
613 W Zavala St, Crystal City 78839   Fax 830/374-8022

Schools: 5 \ *Teachers:* 143 \ *Students:* 1,500 \ *Special Ed Students:* 196 \ *LEP Students:* 64 \ *Ethnic:* African American 1%, Hispanic 99%, \ *Exp:* $268 (Med) \ *Poverty:* 41% \ *Title I:* $1,203,715 \ *Special Education:* $472,000 \ *Open-Close:* 08/20 - 05/29 \ *DTBP:* $350 (High)

Edward Chruchillo	1	Magdalena Flores	4	
Norbert Salina	4	Irene Melendrez	5	
David Lopez	6*	Marina Pruvino	7,85	
Sandra Alvarado	16*	Erma Martinez	57	
Alma Serndejo	58	Victor Bonilla	67	
Pablo Briseno	69	Jesse Guajardo	73	
Dina Briones	752			

Public Schs..Principal	Grd	Prgm	Enr/#Cls	SN	Phone
Benito Juarez Middle Sch 1000 Javalina Dr, Crystal City 78839 Carmel Diaz	5-6	T	300 20	63%	830/374-8105 Fax 830/374-0043
Crystal City High Sch 1101 N 11th St, Crystal City 78839 Jorge Cerna	9-12	TV	525 30	60%	830/374-2341 Fax 830/374-8012
Dr Tomas Rivera Elem Sch 909 Javelina Dr, Crystal City 78839 **Andi Guerrero**	PK-1		200		830/374-8078 Fax 830/374-8024
Lorenzo De Zavala Elem Sch 901 Javelina Dr, Crystal City 78839 **Veronica Hoffman**	2-4	T	200 25	83%	830/374-8080 Fax 830/374-8092
Sterling H Fly Jr High Sch 715 E Crockett Street, Crystal City 78839 Sarah Garcia	7-8	T	282 25	69%	830/374-2371 Fax 830/374-9124

• **La Pryor Ind School Dist** PID: 01062374   830/365-4000
311 E Highway 57, La Pryor 78872   Fax 830/365-4006

Schools: 2 \ *Teachers:* 44 \ *Students:* 500 \ *Special Ed Students:* 44 \ *LEP Students:* 23 \ *College-Bound:* 51% \ *Ethnic:* Hispanic 94%, Caucasian 6% \ *Exp:* $462 (High) \ *Poverty:* 37% \ *Title I:* $247,600 \ *Special Education:* $93,000 \ *Open-Close:* 08/14 - 05/21 \ *DTBP:* $343 (High) \

Matthew McHazlett	1	Becky Garcia	2	
John Gaitan	3,5,91	Elispo Aguero	6	
Reina Gallegos	11,296	Maryann Perez	57	
Rick Rodriguez	58	Marcel Valdez	67	
Roque Olaslaugua	73	Aimee Mann	88	

Public Schs..Principal	Grd	Prgm	Enr/#Cls	SN	Phone
La Pryor Elem Sch 511 Estes St, La Pryor 78872 Esequiel De La Fuente	PK-6	T	267 15	83%	830/365-4009 Fax 830/365-4021
La Pryor High Sch 315 E Edith St, La Pryor 78872 **Rachel Lambert**	7-12	ATV	204	71%	830/365-4007 Fax 830/365-4026

---

79 Student Personnel	91 Safety/Security	275 Response To Intervention	298 Grant Writer/Ptnrships	**School Programs**	**Social Media**		
80 Driver Ed/Safety	92 Magnet School	277 Remedial Math K-12	750 Chief Innovation Officer	A = Alternative Program			
81 Gifted/Talented	93 Parental Involvement	280 Literacy Coach	751 Chief of Staff	G = Adult Classes	= Facebook		
82 Video Services	95 Tech Prep Program	285 STEM	752 Social Emotional Learning	M = Magnet Program			
83 Substance Abuse Prev	97 Chief Infomation Officer	286 Digital Learning		T = Title I Schoolwide	= Twitter		
84 Erate	98 Chief Technology Officer	288 Common Core Standards	**Other School Types**	V = Career & Tech Ed Programs			
85 AIDS Education	270 Character Education	294 Accountability	Ⓐ = Alternative School				
88 Alternative/At Risk	271 Migrant Education	295 Network System	Ⓒ = Charter School	New Schools are shaded			
89 Multi-Cultural Curriculum	273 Teacher Mentor	296 Title II Programs	Ⓜ = Magnet School	New Superintendents and Principals are bold			
90 Social Work	274 Before/After Sch	297 Webmaster	Ⓨ = Year-Round School	Personnel with email addresses are underscored			

TX—407

Texas School Directory

DISTRICT INDEX

SCHOOL DISTRICT	NO. OF SCHOOLS	ENROLL-MENT	COUNTY	PAGE
PUBLIC SCHOOL DISTRICTS				
Abbott Ind School Dist	1	242	Hill	226
Abernathy Ind School Dist	3	780	Hale	174
Abilene Ind School Dist	26	17,000	Taylor	360
Academy Ind School Dist	5	1,559	Bell	26
Adrian Ind School Dist	1	120	Oldham	307
Advantage Academy Admin Office	4	1,650	Dallas	96
Agua Dulce Ind School Dist	2	370	Nueces	302
Alamo Heights Ind School Dist	5	4,900	Bexar	30
Alba-Golden Ind School Dist	2	850	Wood	404
Albany Ind School Dist	2	500	Shackelford	334
Aldine Ind School Dist	82	69,768	Harris	179
Aldine ISD-Elem Sch Team 1			Harris	179
Aldine ISD-Elem Sch Team 2			Harris	179
Aldine ISD-Elem Sch Team 3			Harris	180
Aldine ISD-High Sch Team			Harris	180
Aldine ISD-Middle Sch Team			Harris	181
Aldine ISD-Primary Team			Harris	181
Aledo Ind School Dist	10	6,000	Parker	312
Alice Ind School Dist	9	4,784	Jim Wells	245
Alief Ind School Dist	45	46,241	Harris	181
Allen Ind School Dist	24	21,404	Collin	76
Alpine Ind School Dist	3	1,000	Brewster	56
Alto Ind School Dist	3	671	Cherokee	72
Alvarado Ind School Dist	6	3,650	Johnson	246
Alvin Ind School Dist	29	25,926	Brazoria	50
Alvord Ind School Dist	3	709	Wise	402
Amarillo Ind School Dist	55	33,754	Potter	317
Amherst Ind School Dist	1	145	Lamb	260
Anahuac Ind School Dist	3	1,336	Chambers	71
Anderson-Shiro Cons Ind SD	2	850	Grimes	171
Andrews Ind School Dist	6	4,200	Andrews	16
Angleton Ind School Dist	9	6,787	Brazoria	51
Anna Ind School Dist	6	3,800	Collin	77
Anson Ind School Dist	3	700	Jones	249
Anthony Ind School Dist	3	839	El Paso	131
Anton ISD School Dist	1	180	Hockley	229
Apple Springs Ind School Dist	2	220	Trinity	374
Aquilla Ind School Dist	1	325	Hill	227
Aransas Co Ind School Dist	4	2,800	Aransas	19
Aransas Pass Ind School Dist	5	1,474	San Patricio	330
Archer City Ind School Dist	2	474	Archer	19
Argyle Ind School Dist	5	3,000	Denton	120
Arlington Ind School Dist	78	60,000	Tarrant	343
Arp Ind School Dist	3	900	Smith	336
Aspermont Ind School Dist	2	240	Stonewall	342
Athens Ind School Dist	5	3,118	Henderson	213
Atlanta Ind School Dist	5	1,760	Cass	69
Aubrey Ind School Dist	4	2,000	Denton	120
Austin Ind School Dist	121	80,100	Travis	366
Austin ISD Elem School Area 1			Travis	366
Austin ISD Elem School Area 2			Travis	367
Austin ISD High School Area			Travis	368
Austin ISD Middle School Area			Travis	369
Austwell Tivoli Ind SD	2	140	Refugio	323
Avalon Ind School Dist	1	350	Ellis	140
Avery Ind School Dist	2	365	Red River	322
Avinger Ind School Dist	1	135	Cass	70
Axtell Ind School Dist	2	740	McLennan	278
Azle Ind School Dist	12	6,000	Tarrant	345
Baird Ind School Dist	3	274	Callahan	62
Ballinger Ind School Dist	3	911	Runnels	326
Balmorhea Ind School Dist	1	165	Reeves	323
Bandera Ind School Dist	4	2,283	Bandera	23
Bangs Ind School Dist	3	875	Brown	58
Banquete Ind School Dist	3	954	Nueces	302
Barbers Hill Ind School Dist	8	5,214	Chambers	72
Bartlett Ind School Dist	3	350	Bell	26
Bastrop Ind School Dist	15	11,000	Bastrop	23
Bay City Ind School Dist	5	3,700	Matagorda	275
Beaumont Ind School Dist	28	18,697	Jefferson	241
Beckville Ind School Dist	2	700	Panola	311
Beeville Ind School Dist	6	3,200	Bee	25
Bellevue Ind School Dist	1	140	Clay	74
Bells Ind School Dist	3	845	Grayson	165
Bellville Ind School Dist	6	2,200	Austin	21
Belton Ind School Dist	17	11,950	Bell	26
Ben Bolt-Palito Blanco ISD	2	512	Jim Wells	245
Benavides Ind School Dist	2	340	Duval	128
Benjamin Ind School Dist	1	107	Knox	258
Big Sandy Ind School Dist	1	525	Polk	316
Big Sandy Ind School Dist	3	650	Upshur	376
Big Spring Ind School Dist	9	4,000	Howard	233
Birdville Ind School Dist	33	23,513	Tarrant	346
Bishop Cons Ind School Dist	5	1,472	Nueces	302
Blackwell Cons Ind Sch Dist	1	153	Nolan	301
Blanco Ind School Dist	3	1,025	Blanco	45
Bland Ind School Dist	3	730	Hunt	235
Blanket Ind School Dist	1	187	Brown	58
Bloomburg Ind School Dist	1	270	Cass	70
Blooming Grove Ind School Dist	3	924	Navarro	299
Bloomington Ind School Dist	4	900	Victoria	381
Blue Ridge Ind School Dist	3	860	Collin	77
Bluff Dale Ind Sch Dist	1	243	Erath	143
Blum Ind School Dist	1	370	Hill	227
Boerne Ind School Dist	11	9,000	Kendall	253
Boles Ind School Dist	3	540	Hunt	235
Boling Ind School Dist	3	1,000	Wharton	389
Bonham Ind School Dist	5	1,890	Fannin	145
Booker Ind School Dist	2	398	Lipscomb	267
Borden Co Ind School Dist	1	230	Borden	46
Borger Ind School Dist	6	2,800	Hutchinson	237
Bosqueville Ind School Dist	3	705	McLennan	278
Bovina Ind School Dist	3	490	Parmer	314
Bowie Ind School Dist	4	1,720	Montague	289
Boyd Ind School Dist	4	1,317	Wise	402
Boys Ranch Ind School Dist	3	254	Oldham	307
Brackett Ind School Dist	3	569	Kinney	257
Brady Ind School Dist	4	1,120	McCulloch	277
Braination Schools	8	1,200	Bexar	30
Brazos Ind School Dist	4	700	Austin	22
Brazosport Ind School Dist	18	12,345	Brazoria	52
Breckenridge Ind School Dist	5	1,465	Stephens	341
Bremond Ind School Dist	3	507	Robertson	324
Brenham Ind School Dist	7	5,000	Washington	385
Bridge City Ind School Dist	4	2,953	Orange	308
Bridgeport Ind School Dist	5	2,062	Wise	402
Broaddus Ind School Dist	2	400	San Augustine	329
Brock Ind School Dist	4	1,376	Parker	312
Bronte Ind School Dist	2	245	Coke	75
Brookeland Ind School Dist	1	392	Jasper	240
Brookesmith Ind School Dist	3	200	Brown	58
Brooks Co Ind School Dist	4	1,589	Brooks	57
Brownfield Ind Sch Dist	5	1,700	Terry	362
Brownsboro Ind School Dist	7	2,800	Henderson	213
Brownsville Ind School Dist	54	43,355	Cameron	63
Brownwood Ind School Dist	7	3,595	Brown	58
Bruceville-Eddy Ind Sch Dist	4	641	McLennan	278
Bryan Ind School Dist	24	16,134	Brazos	54
Bryson Ind School Dist	1	255	Jack	238
Buckholts Ind School Dist	1	140	Milam	287
Buena Vista Ind School Dist	1	244	Pecos	315
Buffalo Ind School Dist	4	970	Leon	264
Bullard Ind School Dist	6	2,500	Smith	336
Buna Ind School Dist	3	1,480	Jasper	240
Burkburnett Ind Sch Dist	6	3,350	Wichita	391
Burkeville Ind School Dist	2	250	Newton	300
Burleson Ind School Dist	17	12,742	Johnson	246
Burnet Cons Ind Sch Dist	6	3,186	Burnet	60
Burton Ind School Dist	2	455	Washington	386
Bushland Ind School Dist	3	1,500	Potter	319
Bynum Ind School Dist	1	185	Hill	227
Caddo Mills Ind Sch Dist	5	1,850	Hunt	235

School Year 2019-2020   800-333-8802   TX-Q1

DISTRICT INDEX

Market Data Retrieval

SCHOOL DISTRICT	NO. OF SCHOOLS	ENROLL-MENT	COUNTY	PAGE
Calallen Ind School Dist	6	4,000	Nueces	302
Caldwell Ind School Dist	5	1,800	Burleson	59
Calhoun Co Ind School Dist	7	3,985	Calhoun	61
Callisburg Ind School Dist	2	1,100	Cooke	90
Calvert Ind School Dist	1	164	Robertson	324
Cameron Ind School Dist	4	1,800	Milam	287
Campbell Ind School Dist	1	310	Hunt	235
Canadian Ind School Dist	4	930	Hemphill	213
Canton Ind School Dist	4	2,300	Van Zandt	380
Canutillo Ind School Dist	10	6,200	El Paso	131
Canyon Ind School Dist	16	10,200	Randall	320
Carlisle Ind School Dist	1	650	Rusk	327
Carrizo Spgs Cons Ind SD	4	2,200	Dimmit	127
Carroll Independent Sch Dist	11	8,000	Tarrant	347
Carrollton-Farmers Branch ISD	37	26,000	Dallas	96
Carthage Ind School Dist	6	2,692	Panola	311
Castleberry Ind School Dist	7	3,900	Tarrant	347
Cayuga Ind School Dist	1	570	Anderson	14
Cedar Hill Ind School Dist	14	7,866	Dallas	97
Celeste Ind School Dist	3	512	Hunt	235
Celina Ind School Dist	6	2,600	Collin	77
Center Ind School Dist	6	2,600	Shelby	334
Center Point Ind School Dist	3	570	Kerr	255
Centerpoint Ind School Dist	2	700	Leon	264
Centerville Ind School Dist	2	127	Trinity	374
Central Heights Ind Sch Dist	3	1,181	Nacogdoches	297
Central Ind School Dist	3	1,550	Angelina	16
Channelview Ind School Dist	13	9,700	Harris	183
Channing Ind School Dist	1	181	Hartley	209
Chapel Hill Ind School Dist	5	3,513	Smith	337
Chapel Hill Ind School Dist	3	1,050	Titus	363
Charlotte Ind School Dist	3	475	Atascosa	20
Cherokee Ind School Dist	1	110	San Saba	332
Chester Ind School Dist	2	200	Tyler	374
Chico Ind School Dist	3	600	Wise	403
Childress Ind School Dist	4	1,100	Childress	74
Chillicothe ISD School Dist	2	248	Hardeman	177
Chilton Ind School Dist	1	540	Falls	144
China Spring Ind School Dist	5	2,748	McLennan	278
Chireno ISD School Dist	1	304	Nacogdoches	297
Chisum Ind School Dist	3	1,000	Lamar	259
Christoval Ind School Dist	2	500	Tom Green	364
Cisco Independent Sch Dist	4	850	Eastland	128
City View Ind School Dist	2	1,058	Wichita	391
Clarendon Cons Ind Sch Dist	3	600	Donley	127
Clarksville Ind School Dist	2	585	Red River	322
Claude Ind School Dist	1	330	Armstrong	20
Clear Creek Ind School Dist	45	44,099	Galveston	158
Cleburne Ind School Dist	12	6,749	Johnson	247
Cleveland Ind School Dist	6	6,719	Liberty	265
Clifton Ind School Dist	3	1,000	Bosque	46
Clint Ind School Dist	14	11,522	El Paso	132
Clyde Consolidated Ind SD	4	1,450	Callahan	62
Coahoma Ind School Dist	3	1,000	Howard	234
Coldspring-Oakhurst Cons ISD	4	1,525	San Jacinto	330
Coleman Ind School Dist	3	885	Coleman	76
College Station Ind Sch Dist	19	14,000	Brazos	55
Collinsville Ind School Dist	2	530	Grayson	166
Colmesneil Ind School Dist	2	475	Tyler	375
Colorado Ind School Dist	4	940	Mitchell	289
Columbia Brazoria ISD	5	3,135	Brazoria	52
Columbus Ind School Dist	4	1,494	Colorado	86
Comal Ind School Dist	31	23,800	Comal	87
Comanche Ind School Dist	4	1,325	Comanche	89
Comfort Ind School Dist	3	1,100	Kendall	254
Commerce Independent Sch Dist	4	1,603	Hunt	236
Community Ind School Dist	4	2,262	Collin	78
Como Pickton Cons Ind SD	1	753	Hopkins	231
Comstock Ind School Dist	1	227	Val Verde	379
Connally Ind School Dist	6	2,300	McLennan	279
Conroe Ind School Dist	64	63,000	Montgomery	291
Coolidge Ind School Dist	2	309	Limestone	266
Cooper Ind School Dist	2	750	Delta	119
Coppell Ind School Dist	18	13,500	Dallas	98
Copperas Cove Ind School Dist	11	8,200	Coryell	92
Corpus Christi Ind Sch Dist	58	38,094	Nueces	303
Corrigan-Camden Ind Sch Dist	3	850	Polk	316
Corsicana Ind School Dist	9	6,000	Navarro	299
Cotton Center Ind School Dist	1	130	Hale	174
Cotulla Ind School Dist	4	1,400	La Salle	259
Coupland Ind School Dist	1	175	Williamson	395
Covington ISD School Dist	1	293	Hill	227
Crandall Ind School Dist	7	4,500	Kaufman	251
Crane Ind School Dist	3	1,155	Crane	93
Cranfills Gap ISD School Dist	1	125	Bosque	46
Crawford Ind School Dist	2	530	McLennan	279
Crockett Co Cons Common SD	3	758	Crockett	94
Crockett Ind School Dist	5	1,331	Houston	232
Crosby Ind School Dist	7	6,300	Harris	183
Crosbyton Cons Ind Sch Dist	2	375	Crosby	94
Cross Plains Ind Sch Dist	2	368	Callahan	62
Cross Roads Ind School Dist	3	545	Henderson	213
Crowell Ind School Dist	2	200	Foard	149
Crowley Ind School Dist	25	15,215	Tarrant	347
Crystal City Ind School Dist	5	1,500	Zavala	407
Cuero Ind School Dist	4	2,000	De Witt	117
Culberson Co Allamoore Ind SD	1	400	Culberson	95
Cumby Ind School Dist	2	400	Hopkins	231
Cushing Ind School Dist	2	551	Nacogdoches	297
Cypress-Fairbanks Ind Sch Dist	91	116,249	Harris	183
D'Hanis Ind School Dist	1	395	Medina	283
Daingerfield-Lone Star Ind SD	4	1,100	Morris	296
Dalhart Ind School Dist	4	1,700	Dallam	95
Dallas Ind School Dist	230	156,100	Dallas	98
Damon Ind School Dist	1	200	Brazoria	53
Danbury Ind School Dist	3	750	Brazoria	53
Darrouzett Ind School Dist	1	120	Lipscomb	267
Dawson Ind School Dist	1	110	Dawson	116
Dawson Ind School Dist	1	500	Navarro	299
Dayton Ind School Dist	7	5,400	Liberty	265
De Kalb Ind School Dist	3	900	Bowie	47
De Leon Ind School Dist	3	716	Comanche	89
Decatur Ind School Dist	5	3,390	Wise	403
Deer Park Ind School Dist	16	13,000	Harris	186
Del Valle Ind School Dist	15	12,100	Travis	369
Dell City Ind School Dist	1	65	Hudspeth	234
Denison Ind School Dist	9	4,500	Grayson	166
Denton Ind School Dist	42	29,152	Denton	120
Denver City Ind School Dist	5	1,741	Yoakum	405
DeSoto Ind School Dist	14	9,872	Dallas	104
Detroit Ind School Dist	3	540	Red River	322
Devers Ind School Dist	1	200	Liberty	265
Devine Ind School Dist	4	2,000	Medina	283
Dew Ind School Dist	1	180	Freestone	156
Deweyville Ind School Dist	2	550	Orange	308
Diboll Ind School Dist	5	1,890	Angelina	17
Dickinson Ind School Dist	14	10,400	Galveston	159
Dilley Ind School Dist	4	1,000	Frio	157
Dime Box Ind School Dist	1	160	Lee	263
Dimmitt Ind School Dist	4	1,225	Castro	71
Divide Ind School Dist	1	22	Kerr	255
Dodd City Ind School Dist	1	370	Fannin	145
Donna Ind School Dist	22	14,459	Hidalgo	215
Doss Consolidated Common SD	1	25	Gillespie	162
Douglass Ind School Dist	1	460	Nacogdoches	297
Dripping Springs Ind Sch Dist	7	6,400	Hays	210
Driscoll Ind School Dist	1	320	Nueces	304
Dublin Ind School Dist	3	1,200	Erath	143
Dumas Ind School Dist	9	4,212	Moore	295
Duncanville Ind School Dist	19	12,800	Dallas	104
Eagle Mtn-Saginaw Ind Sch Dist	27	21,000	Tarrant	348
Eagle Pass Ind School Dist	23	15,000	Maverick	276
Eanes Ind School Dist	9	8,156	Travis	370
Early Ind School Dist	4	1,200	Brown	58

Texas School Directory — DISTRICT INDEX

SCHOOL DISTRICT	NO. OF SCHOOLS	ENROLLMENT	COUNTY	PAGE
East Bernard Ind Sch Dist	3	950	Wharton	389
East Central Ind School Dist	12	10,146	Bexar	31
East Chambers Ind School Dist	4	1,500	Chambers	72
Eastland Ind School Dist	3	1,130	Eastland	129
Ector Co Ind School Dist	42	31,500	Ector	129
Ector Ind School Dist	1	250	Fannin	146
Edcouch Elsa Ind School Dist	8	5,450	Hidalgo	215
Eden Cons Ind School Dist	2	215	Concho	90
Edgewood Ind School Dist	21	10,881	Bexar	31
Edgewood Ind School Dist	4	975	Van Zandt	380
Edinburg Cons Ind School Dist	43	34,500	Hidalgo	216
Edna Ind School Dist	4	1,500	Jackson	239
El Campo Ind School Dist	5	3,600	Wharton	389
El Paso Ind School Dist	89	54,824	El Paso	132
El Paso ISD-Elementary			El Paso	133
El Paso ISD-High Schools			El Paso	134
El Paso ISD-Middle Schools			El Paso	134
Electra Ind School Dist	3	430	Wichita	391
Elgin Ind School Dist	6	4,700	Bastrop	24
Elkhart Ind School Dist	4	1,250	Anderson	15
Elysian Fields Ind School Dist	3	910	Harrison	208
Ennis Ind School Dist	11	5,800	Ellis	140
Era Ind School Dist	1	500	Cooke	90
Etoile Ind School Dist	1	100	Nacogdoches	297
Eula Ind School Dist	3	400	Callahan	63
Eustace Ind School Dist	4	1,550	Henderson	214
Evadale Ind School Dist	2	450	Jasper	240
Evant Ind School Dist	1	235	Coryell	92
Everman Ind School Dist	11	6,800	Tarrant	349
Excelsior Ind School Dist	1	90	Shelby	334
Ezzell Ind School Dist	1	85	Lavaca	262
Fabens Ind School Dist	5	2,300	El Paso	135
Fairfield Ind School Dist	4	1,817	Freestone	156
Falls City Ind School Dist	2	360	Karnes	250
Fannindel Ind School Dist	2	150	Delta	120
Farmersville Ind School Dist	4	1,750	Collin	78
Farwell Ind School Dist	3	522	Parmer	314
Fayetteville Ind School Dist	1	265	Fayette	147
Ferris Ind School Dist	5	2,400	Ellis	140
Flatonia Ind School Dist	3	580	Fayette	147
Florence Ind School Dist	3	1,065	Williamson	395
Floresville Ind School Dist	5	4,000	Wilson	400
Flour Bluff Ind School Dist	7	5,750	Nueces	304
Floydada Ind School Dist	2	730	Floyd	148
Follett Ind School Dist	1	140	Lipscomb	267
Forestburg Ind School Dist	1	160	Montague	290
Forney Ind School Dist	14	9,681	Kaufman	251
Forsan Ind School Dist	2	812	Howard	234
Fort Davis Ind School Dist	2	230	Jeff Davis	241
Franklin Ind School Dist	3	1,100	Robertson	324
Frankston Ind School Dist	3	825	Anderson	15
Fredericksburg Ind School Dist	6	2,900	Gillespie	162
Freer Ind School Dist	3	807	Duval	128
Frenship Ind School Dist	13	9,900	Lubbock	269
Friendswood Ind Sch Dist	6	6,000	Galveston	160
Friona Ind School Dist	4	1,117	Parmer	315
Frisco Ind School Dist	72	62,386	Collin	78
Frost Ind School Dist	2	400	Navarro	299
Fruitvale Ind School Dist	3	460	Van Zandt	380
Ft Bend Ind School Dist	79	78,000	Fort Bend	149
Ft Elliott Cons Ind Sch Dist	1	138	Wheeler	390
Ft Hancock Ind School Dist	3	410	Hudspeth	234
Ft Sam Houston Ind School Dist	2	1,580	Bexar	32
Ft Stockton Ind School Dist	5	2,479	Pecos	315
Ft Worth Ind School Dist	134	86,000	Tarrant	349
Gainesville Ind School Dist	6	3,100	Cooke	91
Galena Park Ind School Dist	27	24,000	Harris	186
Galveston Ind School Dist	12	7,000	Galveston	160
Ganado Ind School Dist	3	750	Jackson	239
Garland Ind School Dist	72	56,471	Dallas	105
Garner Ind School Dist	1	200	Parker	312
Garrison Ind School Dist	3	600	Nacogdoches	297
Gary Ind School Dist	1	500	Panola	311
Gatesville Ind School Dist	5	2,788	Coryell	92
Gause Ind School Dist	1	170	Milam	287
George West Ind School Dist	4	1,100	Live Oak	268
Georgetown Ind School Dist	17	10,946	Williamson	395
Gholson Ind School Dist	1	255	McLennan	279
Giddings Ind School Dist	4	1,905	Lee	263
Gilmer Ind School Dist	4	2,437	Upshur	376
Gladewater Ind School Dist	4	1,700	Gregg	169
Glasscock Co Ind School Dist	1	310	Glasscock	163
Glen Rose Ind School Dist	4	1,882	Somervell	340
Godley Ind School Dist	5	2,027	Johnson	247
Gold-Burg Ind School Dist	1	140	Montague	290
Goldthwaite Consolidated ISD	3	595	Mills	288
Goliad Ind School Dist	3	1,340	Goliad	163
Gonzales Ind School Dist	6	2,875	Gonzales	164
Goodrich Ind School Dist	2	235	Polk	316
Goose Creek Cons Ind Sch Dist	28	24,000	Harris	187
Gordon Ind School Dist	1	200	Palo Pinto	310
Gorman Ind School Dist	3	300	Eastland	129
Grady Ind School Dist	1	260	Martin	274
Graford Ind School Dist	2	340	Palo Pinto	310
Graham Ind School Dist	5	2,390	Young	406
Granbury Ind School Dist	11	7,218	Hood	230
Grand Prairie Ind School Dist	42	29,339	Dallas	107
Grand Saline Ind School Dist	4	1,100	Van Zandt	380
Grandfalls-Royalty Ind SD	1	185	Ward	385
Grandview Ind School Dist	3	1,276	Johnson	248
Grandview-Hopkins Ind Sch Dist	1	50	Gray	164
Granger Ind School Dist	1	460	Williamson	396
Grape Creek Ind School Dist	3	1,160	Tom Green	364
Grapeland Ind School Dist	3	615	Houston	232
Grapevine-Colleyville Ind SD	21	14,000	Tarrant	353
Greenville Ind School Dist	12	5,400	Hunt	236
Greenwood Ind School Dist	4	2,831	Midland	285
Gregory-Portland Ind Sch Dist	7	4,600	San Patricio	330
Groesbeck Ind School Dist	4	1,560	Limestone	267
Groom Ind School Dist	1	160	Carson	69
Groveton Ind School Dist	2	750	Trinity	374
Gruver Ind School Dist	3	400	Hansford	176
Gunter Ind School Dist	3	970	Grayson	166
Gustine Ind School Dist	1	161	Comanche	90
Guthrie Common School Dist	1	104	King	257
Hale Center Ind School Dist	3	647	Hale	175
Hallettsville Ind Sch Dist	3	1,130	Lavaca	262
Hallsburg Ind School Dist	1	161	McLennan	279
Hallsville Ind School Dist	5	5,500	Harrison	208
Hamilton Ind School Dist	3	850	Hamilton	176
Hamlin Ind School Dist	2	400	Jones	249
Hamshire Fannett Ind Sch Dist	4	1,900	Jefferson	242
Happy Ind School Dist	2	254	Swisher	342
Hardin Ind School Dist	3	1,400	Liberty	265
Hardin Jefferson Ind Sch Dist	4	2,200	Hardin	177
Harlandale Ind School Dist	24	14,500	Bexar	32
Harleton Ind School Dist	3	734	Harrison	208
Harlingen Cons Ind School Dist	31	18,600	Cameron	64
Harmony Ind School Dist	4	1,060	Upshur	376
Harper Ind School Dist	3	600	Gillespie	163
Harrold Ind School Dist	1	110	Wilbarger	393
Hart Ind School Dist	2	230	Castro	71
Hartley Ind School Dist	1	239	Hartley	209
Harts Bluff Ind School Dist	1	640	Titus	363
Haskell Cons Ind School Dist	3	566	Haskell	210
Hawkins Ind School Dist	3	735	Wood	404
Hawley Ind School Dist	3	769	Jones	249
Hays Cons Ind School Dist	25	20,445	Hays	211
Hearne Ind School Dist	3	860	Robertson	325
Hedley Ind School Dist	1	120	Donley	127
Hemphill Ind School Dist	3	900	Sabine	329
Hempstead Ind School Dist	3	1,600	Waller	384
Henderson Ind School Dist	6	3,040	Rusk	327
Henrietta Ind School Dist	3	940	Clay	74

School Year 2019-2020 800-333-8802 TX-Q3

DISTRICT INDEX

Market Data Retrieval

SCHOOL DISTRICT	NO. OF SCHOOLS	ENROLL- MENT	COUNTY	PAGE
Hereford Ind School Dist	11	4,100	Deaf Smith	119
Hermleigh Ind School Dist	1	250	Scurry	333
Hico Ind School Dist	2	600	Hamilton	176
Hidalgo Ind School Dist	7	3,300	Hidalgo	217
Higgins Ind School Dist	1	125	Lipscomb	268
High Island Ind Sch Dist	1	145	Galveston	160
Highland Ind School Dist	1	250	Nolan	301
Highland Park Ind Sch Dist	7	7,000	Dallas	108
Highland Park Ind School Dist	3	850	Potter	319
Hillsboro Ind School Dist	5	2,000	Hill	227
Hitchcock Ind School Dist	4	1,700	Galveston	160
Holland Ind School Dist	3	692	Bell	27
Holliday Ind School Dist	3	1,007	Archer	19
Hondo Ind School Dist	4	2,200	Medina	284
Honey Grove Ind School Dist	3	605	Fannin	146
Hooks Ind School Dist	3	942	Bowie	48
Houston Ind School Dist	275	206,052	Harris	188
Houston ISD-Achieve 180			Harris	188
Houston ISD-East Area			Harris	189
Houston ISD-North Area			Harris	190
Houston ISD-Northwest Area			Harris	191
Houston ISD-South Area			Harris	192
Houston ISD-West Area			Harris	193
Howe Ind School Dist	4	1,100	Grayson	166
Hubbard Ind School Dist	1	120	Bowie	48
Hubbard Ind School Dist	2	400	Hill	227
Huckabay Ind School Dist	1	260	Erath	143
Hudson Ind School Dist	5	3,000	Angelina	17
Huffman Ind School Dist	4	3,600	Harris	195
Hughes Springs Ind Sch Dist	3	1,230	Cass	70
Hull Daisetta Ind School Dist	3	477	Liberty	266
Humble Ind School Dist	46	44,802	Harris	195
Hunt Ind School Dist	1	200	Kerr	255
Huntington Ind School Dist	5	1,750	Angelina	17
Huntsville Ind School Dist	9	6,100	Walker	383
Hurst-Euless-Bedford ISD	31	23,000	Tarrant	353
Hutto Ind School Dist	9	7,500	Williamson	396
Idalou Ind School Dist	3	1,003	Lubbock	269
Idea Public Schools	76	42,748	Hidalgo	217
Industrial Ind School Dist	4	1,178	Jackson	240
Ingleside Ind School Dist	5	2,235	San Patricio	331
Ingram Ind School Dist	3	1,070	Kerr	255
Int'l Leadership of Texas Dist	19	19,473	Dallas	108
Iola Ind School Dist	2	502	Grimes	172
Iowa Park Consolidated Ind SD	4	1,839	Wichita	392
Ira Ind School Dist	1	270	Scurry	333
Iraan-Sheffield Ind Sch Dist	3	422	Pecos	316
Iredell Ind School Dist	1	145	Bosque	46
Irion Co Ind School Dist	2	275	Irion	238
Irving Ind School Dist	39	33,188	Dallas	109
Italy Ind School Dist	2	600	Ellis	140
Itasca Ind School Dist	3	660	Hill	228
Jacksboro Ind Sch Dist	3	1,050	Jack	239
Jacksonville Ind School Dist	8	5,091	Cherokee	72
Jarrell Ind School Dist	5	1,850	Williamson	396
Jasper Ind School Dist	4	2,390	Jasper	240
Jayton-Girard Ind School Dist	1	163	Kent	255
Jefferson Ind School Dist	4	1,272	Marion	274
Jim Hogg Co Ind School Dist	3	1,151	Jim Hogg	244
Jim Ned Cons Ind School Dist	4	1,300	Taylor	361
Joaquin Ind School Dist	3	650	Shelby	335
Johnson City Ind School Dist	3	659	Blanco	46
Jonesboro Ind School Dist	1	340	Coryell	93
Joshua Ind School Dist	10	5,626	Johnson	248
Jourdanton Ind School Dist	4	1,600	Atascosa	20
Judson Ind School Dist	33	23,000	Bexar	33
Junction Ind School Dist	3	615	Kimble	256
Karnack Ind School Dist	1	124	Harrison	208
Karnes City Ind School Dist	5	1,085	Karnes	250
Katy Ind School Dist	71	83,599	Fort Bend	151
Kaufman Ind School Dist	7	3,500	Kaufman	252
Keene Ind School Dist	4	1,070	Johnson	248
Keller Ind School Dist	42	34,512	Tarrant	354
Kelton Ind School Dist	1	95	Wheeler	390
Kemp Ind School Dist	4	1,586	Kaufman	252
Kenedy Co Wide Common Sch Dist	1	72	Kenedy	254
Kenedy Ind School Dist	3	800	Karnes	251
Kennard Ind Sch Dist	1	280	Houston	233
Kennedale Ind School Dist	6	3,200	Tarrant	355
Kerens Ind School Dist	3	600	Navarro	299
Kermit Ind School Dist	3	1,418	Winkler	401
Kerrville Ind School Dist	10	4,800	Kerr	256
Kilgore Ind School Dist	5	4,076	Gregg	169
Killeen Ind School Dist	53	45,583	Bell	27
Kingsville Ind School Dist	8	3,050	Kleberg	257
Kirbyville Cons Ind Sch Dist	3	1,400	Jasper	241
Klein Ind School Dist	49	53,868	Harris	196
Klondike Ind School Dist	1	275	Dawson	117
Knippa Ind School Dist	1	475	Uvalde	378
Knox City-O'Brien Cons Ind SD	3	270	Knox	258
Kopperl Ind School Dist	1	225	Bosque	47
Kountze Ind School Dist	4	1,135	Hardin	178
Kress Ind School Dist	2	280	Swisher	343
Krum Ind School Dist	5	2,050	Denton	122
La Feria Ind School Dist	7	3,347	Cameron	65
La Gloria Ind School Dist	1	125	Jim Wells	245
La Grange Ind School Dist	4	2,350	Fayette	147
La Joya Ind School Dist	41	27,000	Hidalgo	219
La Porte Ind School Dist	12	7,679	Harris	198
La Poynor Ind School Dist	1	453	Henderson	214
La Pryor Ind School Dist	2	500	Zavala	407
La Vega Ind School Dist	5	3,099	McLennan	279
La Vernia Ind School Dist	4	3,360	Wilson	401
La Villa Ind School Dist	3	579	Hidalgo	220
Lackland Ind School Dist	2	1,053	Bexar	34
Lago Vista Ind School Dist	4	1,500	Travis	370
Lake Dallas Ind School Dist	5	4,000	Denton	122
Lake Travis Ind School Dist	10	10,410	Travis	370
Lake Worth Ind School Dist	6	3,000	Tarrant	356
Lamar Cons Ind School Dist	45	34,000	Fort Bend	153
Lamesa Ind School Dist	5	1,800	Dawson	117
Lampasas Ind School Dist	5	3,400	Lampasas	261
Lancaster Ind School Dist	11	7,600	Dallas	110
Laneville Ind School Dist	1	182	Rusk	327
Laredo Ind School Dist	33	23,737	Webb	386
Lasara Ind School Dist	2	380	Willacy	394
Latexo Ind School Dist	2	500	Houston	233
Lazbuddie Ind School Dist	1	201	Parmer	315
Leakey Ind School Dist	1	309	Real	322
Leander Ind School Dist	43	41,000	Williamson	396
Leary Ind School Dist	1	125	Bowie	48
Lefors Ind School Dist	1	160	Gray	165
Leggett Ind School Dist	1	185	Polk	316
Leon Ind School Dist	3	715	Leon	264
Leonard Ind School Dist	4	820	Fannin	146
Levelland Ind School Dist	6	2,936	Hockley	229
Leveretts Chapel Ind Sch Dist	1	259	Rusk	328
Lewisville Ind School Dist	70	52,000	Denton	122
Lexington Ind School Dist	3	1,030	Lee	263
Liberty Hill Ind School Dist	6	4,476	Williamson	398
Liberty Ind School Dist	4	2,200	Liberty	266
Liberty-Eylau Ind School Dist	4	2,500	Bowie	48
Lindale Ind School Dist	6	4,200	Smith	337
Linden Kildare Cons Ind SD	3	700	Cass	70
Lindsay Ind School Dist	2	510	Cooke	91
Lingleville Ind School Dist	1	275	Erath	143
Lipan Ind School Dist	1	420	Hood	230
Little Cypress Mauriceville SD	6	3,100	Orange	308
Little Elm Ind School Dist	9	7,400	Denton	124
Littlefield Ind School Dist	4	1,300	Lamb	260
Livingston Ind School Dist	7	3,963	Polk	316
Llano Ind School Dist	4	1,800	Llano	268
Lockhart Ind School Dist	9	6,350	Caldwell	61
Lockney Independent Sch Dist	3	430	Floyd	149

Texas School Directory — DISTRICT INDEX

SCHOOL DISTRICT	NO. OF SCHOOLS	ENROLLMENT	COUNTY	PAGE
Lohn Ind School Dist	1	90	McCulloch	277
Lometa Ind School Dist	1	295	Lampasas	262
London Ind School Dist	1	900	Nueces	305
Lone Oak Ind School Dist	4	1,050	Hunt	236
Longview Ind School Dist	13	8,700	Gregg	169
Loop Ind School Dist	1	150	Gaines	157
Loraine Ind School Dist	1	160	Mitchell	289
Lorena Ind School Dist	4	1,725	McLennan	280
Lorenzo Ind School Dist	2	250	Crosby	94
Los Fresnos Cons Ind Sch Dist	16	10,700	Cameron	65
Louise Ind School Dist	3	500	Wharton	389
Lovejoy Ind School Dist	6	4,424	Collin	80
Lovelady Ind School Dist	2	510	Houston	233
Lubbock Ind School Dist	48	27,759	Lubbock	269
Lubbock-Cooper Ind Sch Dist	9	6,000	Lubbock	271
Lueders-Avoca Ind School Dist	2	104	Jones	250
Lufkin Ind School Dist	15	8,000	Angelina	18
Luling Ind School Dist	4	1,450	Caldwell	61
Lumberton Ind School Dist	5	4,123	Hardin	178
Lyford Cons Ind School Dist	3	1,551	Willacy	394
Lytle Ind School Dist	4	1,693	Atascosa	21
Mabank Ind School Dist	8	3,500	Kaufman	252
Madisonville Cons ISD	4	2,358	Madison	273
Magnolia Ind School Dist	16	13,100	Montgomery	292
Malakoff Ind School Dist	5	1,400	Henderson	214
Malone Independent School Dist	1	165	Hill	228
Malta Ind School Dist	1	241	Bowie	48
Manor Ind School Dist	16	9,200	Travis	371
Mansfield Ind School Dist	44	34,309	Tarrant	356
Marathon Ind School Dist	1	55	Brewster	56
Marble Falls Ind School Dist	7	4,154	Burnet	60
Marfa Ind School Dist	2	342	Presidio	320
Marion Ind School Dist	4	1,508	Guadalupe	172
Marlin Ind School Dist	3	1,000	Falls	144
Marshall Ind School Dist	7	5,345	Harrison	209
Mart Ind School Dist	2	500	McLennan	280
Martin's Mill Ind Sch Dist	1	230	Van Zandt	381
Martinsville Ind School Dist	1	400	Nacogdoches	298
Mason Ind School Dist	3	675	Mason	275
Matagorda Ind School Dist	1	120	Matagorda	275
Mathis Ind School Dist	4	1,635	San Patricio	331
Maud Ind School Dist	1	480	Bowie	49
May Ind School Dist	2	290	Brown	59
Maypearl Ind School Dist	4	1,040	Ellis	141
McAllen Ind School Dist	31	24,000	Hidalgo	220
McCamey Ind School Dist	3	560	Upton	377
McDade Ind School Dist	1	390	Bastrop	24
McGregor Ind School Dist	4	1,550	McLennan	280
McKinney Ind School Dist	31	24,335	Collin	80
McLean Ind School Dist	1	240	Gray	165
McLeod Ind School Dist	1	388	Cass	70
McMullen Co Ind Sch Dist	1	287	McMullen	283
Meadow Ind School Dist	1	280	Terry	362
Medina Ind School Dist	2	310	Bandera	23
Medina Valley Ind School Dist	5	5,087	Medina	284
Melissa Ind School Dist	4	2,792	Collin	81
Memphis Ind School Dist	4	500	Hall	175
Menard Ind School Dist	2	300	Menard	285
Mercedes Ind School Dist	9	4,781	Hidalgo	221
Meridian Ind School Dist	3	480	Bosque	47
Merkel Ind School Dist	3	1,100	Taylor	361
Mesquite Ind School Dist	47	39,900	Dallas	110
Mexia Ind School Dist	5	1,800	Limestone	267
Meyersville Ind School Dist	1	132	De Witt	118
Miami Ind School Dist	1	220	Roberts	324
Midland Ind School Dist	39	26,000	Midland	285
Midlothian Ind School Dist	11	9,500	Ellis	141
Midway Ind School Dist	1	137	Clay	74
Midway Ind School Dist	10	8,411	McLennan	280
Milano Ind School Dist	3	460	Milam	287
Mildred Ind School Dist	1	720	Navarro	300
Miles Ind School Dist	1	440	Runnels	326
Milford Ind School Dist	1	280	Ellis	141
Miller Grove Ind School Dist	1	329	Hopkins	231
Millsap Ind School Dist	3	994	Parker	312
Mineola Ind School Dist	4	1,630	Wood	404
Mineral Wells Ind School Dist	6	3,200	Palo Pinto	310
Mission Cons Ind School Dist	23	16,000	Hidalgo	222
Monahans-Wickett-Pyote ISD	6	2,300	Ward	385
Montague Ind School Dist	1	160	Montague	290
Monte Alto Ind School Dist	3	900	Hidalgo	222
Montgomery Ind School Dist	10	8,864	Montgomery	293
Moody Ind School Dist	3	690	McLennan	281
Moran Ind School Dist	1	120	Shackelford	334
Morgan Ind School Dist	1	142	Bosque	47
Morgan Mill Ind School Dist	1	125	Erath	144
Morton Ind School Dist	4	400	Cochran	75
Motley Co Ind School Dist	1	151	Motley	296
Moulton Ind School Dist	2	300	Lavaca	262
Mt Calm Ind School Dist	2	210	Hill	228
Mt Enterprise Ind School Dist	1	400	Rusk	328
Mt Pleasant Ind School Dist	8	5,300	Titus	363
Mt Vernon Ind School Dist	3	1,620	Franklin	155
Muenster Ind School Dist	2	500	Cooke	91
Muleshoe Ind School Dist	4	1,450	Bailey	22
Mullin Ind School Dist	6	94	Mills	288
Mumford Ind School Dist	1	625	Brazos	56
Munday Consolidated Ind SD	2	375	Knox	258
Murchison Ind Sch Dist	1	175	Henderson	214
Nacogdoches Ind School Dist	10	6,300	Nacogdoches	298
Natalia Ind School Dist	4	1,060	Medina	284
Navarro Ind School Dist	4	1,911	Guadalupe	173
Navasota Ind School Dist	6	3,000	Grimes	172
Nazareth Ind School Dist	1	240	Castro	71
Neches Ind School Dist	2	400	Anderson	15
Nederland Ind School Dist	8	5,214	Jefferson	242
Needville Ind School Dist	4	3,228	Fort Bend	154
New Boston Ind School Dist	4	1,340	Bowie	49
New Braunfels Ind School Dist	15	9,220	Comal	88
New Caney Ind School Dist	19	15,000	Montgomery	293
New Deal Ind School Dist	3	760	Lubbock	271
New Diana Ind School Dist	3	1,071	Upshur	376
New Home Ind School Dist	1	447	Lynn	273
New Summerfield Ind Sch Dist	1	550	Cherokee	73
New Waverly Ind School Dist	4	1,000	Walker	383
Newcastle Ind School Dist	1	180	Young	406
Newton Ind School Dist	3	1,026	Newton	301
Nixon-Smiley Cons Ind Sch Dist	3	1,100	Gonzales	164
Nocona Ind School Dist	3	770	Montague	290
Nordheim Ind School Dist	1	150	De Witt	118
Normangee Ind School Dist	3	572	Leon	264
North East Ind School Dist	74	64,359	Bexar	34
North Hopkins Ind School Dist	1	525	Hopkins	231
North Lamar Ind School Dist	7	2,500	Lamar	259
North Zulch Ind School Dist	1	305	Madison	274
Northside Ind School Dist	122	105,856	Bexar	36
Northside Ind School Dist	1	230	Wilbarger	393
Northwest Ind School Dist	30	24,000	Denton	124
Nueces Canyon Cons Ind SD	2	270	Edwards	131
Nursery ISD School Dist	1	120	Victoria	382
O'Donnell Ind School Dist	2	306	Lynn	273
Oakwood Ind School Dist	2	200	Leon	264
Odem-Edroy Ind School Dist	4	900	San Patricio	331
Oglesby Ind School Dist	1	165	Coryell	93
Olfen Ind School Dist	1	93	Runnels	327
Olney Ind School Dist	3	700	Young	406
Olton Ind School Dist	3	600	Lamb	261
Onalaska Ind School Dist	2	1,000	Polk	317
Orange Grove Ind School Dist	4	1,850	Jim Wells	245
Orangefield Ind School Dist	3	1,785	Orange	309
Ore City Ind School Dist	3	950	Upshur	376
Overton Ind School Dist	2	500	Rusk	328
Paducah Ind School Dist	1	210	Cottle	93
Paint Creek Ind School Dist	1	102	Haskell	210

DISTRICT INDEX

Market Data Retrieval

SCHOOL DISTRICT	NO. OF SCHOOLS	ENROLL-MENT	COUNTY	PAGE
Paint Rock Ind School Dist	1	240	Concho	90
Palacios Ind School Dist	4	1,506	Matagorda	275
Palestine Ind School Dist	6	3,450	Anderson	15
Palmer Ind School Dist	3	1,250	Ellis	141
Palo Pinto Ind Sch Dist 906	1	112	Palo Pinto	310
Pampa Ind School Dist	7	3,500	Gray	165
Panhandle Ind School Dist	3	700	Carson	69
Panther Creek Cons Ind SD	1	149	Coleman	76
Paradise Ind School Dist	4	1,200	Wise	403
Paris Ind School Dist	8	3,900	Lamar	260
Pasadena Ind School Dist	68	54,000	Harris	198
Patton Springs Ind School Dist	1	111	Dickens	126
Pawnee Ind School Dist	1	550	Bee	25
Pearland Ind School Dist	23	21,917	Brazoria	53
Pearsall Ind School Dist	4	2,100	Frio	157
Peaster Ind School Dist	3	1,200	Parker	313
Pecos-Barstow-Toyah Ind SD	5	2,800	Reeves	323
Penelope ISD School Dist	1	210	Hill	228
Perrin-Whitt Cons Ind Sch Dist	2	330	Jack	239
Perryton Ind School Dist	6	2,217	Ochiltree	307
Petersburg Ind School Dist	1	300	Hale	175
Petrolia Cons Ind School Dist	2	440	Clay	74
Pettus Ind School Dist	2	421	Bee	25
Pewitt Cons Ind School Dist	3	891	Morris	296
Pflugerville Ind School Dist	33	26,269	Travis	371
Pharr-San Juan-Alamo Ind SD	42	32,500	Hidalgo	223
Pilot Point Ind School Dist	4	1,500	Denton	125
Pine Tree Ind School Dist	8	4,700	Gregg	170
Pittsburg Ind School Dist	5	2,344	Camp	68
Plains Ind School Dist	3	430	Yoakum	405
Plainview Ind School Dist	10	5,450	Hale	175
Plano Ind School Dist	73	53,952	Collin	82
Pleasant Grove Ind School Dist	4	2,200	Bowie	49
Pleasanton Ind School Dist	4	3,477	Atascosa	21
Plemons-Stinnett-Phillips CISD	3	675	Hutchinson	238
Point Isabel Ind Sch Dist	4	2,500	Cameron	66
Ponder Ind School Dist	3	1,575	Denton	125
Poolville Ind School Dist	3	530	Parker	313
Port Aransas Ind School Dist	3	550	Nueces	305
Port Arthur Ind School Dist	16	9,000	Jefferson	243
Port Neches-Groves Ind SD	10	5,150	Jefferson	243
Post Ind School Dist	3	810	Garza	162
Poteet Ind School Dist	4	1,735	Atascosa	21
Poth Ind School Dist	3	840	Wilson	401
Pottsboro Ind School Dist	3	1,450	Grayson	167
Prairie Lea Ind School Dist	1	210	Caldwell	61
Prairie Valley Ind School Dist	1	170	Montague	290
Prairiland Ind School Dist	4	1,160	Lamar	260
Premont Ind School Dist	2	587	Jim Wells	246
Presidio Ind School Dist	3	1,162	Presidio	320
Priddy Ind School Dist	1	111	Mills	289
Princeton Ind School Dist	8	5,000	Collin	84
Pringle-Morse Cons ISD	1	115	Hansford	177
Progreso Ind School Dist	5	1,750	Hidalgo	224
Prosper Ind School Dist	15	7,600	Collin	84
Quanah Ind School Dist	3	525	Hardeman	177
Queen City Ind School Dist	4	1,045	Cass	70
Quinlan Ind School Dist	5	2,725	Hunt	237
Quitman Ind School Dist	3	1,121	Wood	404
Rains Ind School Dist	4	1,650	Rains	320
Ralls Ind School Dist	4	500	Crosby	94
Ramirez Common School Dist	1	30	Duval	128
Randolph Field Ind School Dist	3	1,300	Bexar	39
Ranger Ind School Dist	1	350	Eastland	129
Rankin Ind School Dist	2	320	Upton	377
Raymondville Ind Sch Dist	5	2,000	Willacy	394
Reagan Co Ind School Dist	3	950	Reagan	321
Red Lick Ind School Dist	1	530	Bowie	49
Red Oak Ind School Dist	8	6,000	Ellis	142
Redwater Ind School Dist	4	1,150	Bowie	49
Refugio Ind School Dist	3	690	Refugio	323
Ricardo Ind School Dist	1	671	Kleberg	257
Rice Cons Ind School Dist	7	1,325	Colorado	87
Rice Ind School Dist	4	895	Navarro	300
Richards Ind School Dist	1	170	Grimes	172
Richardson Ind School Dist	57	39,103	Dallas	112
Richland Springs Ind Sch Dist	1	120	San Saba	332
Riesel Ind School Dist	2	620	McLennan	281
Rio Grande City Ind Sch Dist	18	9,876	Starr	340
Rio Hondo Ind School Dist	3	1,900	Cameron	66
Rio Vista Ind School Dist	3	750	Johnson	248
Rising Star Ind Sch Dist	2	147	Eastland	129
River Road Ind School Dist	4	1,278	Potter	319
Rivercrest Ind School Dist	3	735	Red River	322
Riviera Ind School Dist	2	435	Kleberg	258
Robert Lee Ind School Dist	1	290	Coke	75
Robinson Ind School Dist	5	2,200	McLennan	281
Robstown Ind School Dist	7	2,000	Nueces	305
Roby Cons Ind School Dist	2	310	Fisher	148
Rochelle Ind School Dist	1	200	McCulloch	278
Rockdale Ind School Dist	4	1,530	Milam	287
Rocksprings Ind School Dist	1	290	Edwards	131
Rockwall Ind School Dist	20	16,270	Rockwall	325
Rogers Ind School Dist	3	875	Bell	28
Roma Ind School Dist	10	6,400	Starr	341
Roosevelt Ind School Dist	3	1,150	Lubbock	271
Ropes Ind School Dist	1	430	Hockley	229
Roscoe Collegiate Ind Sch Dist	3	620	Nolan	301
Rosebud-Lott Ind School Dist	3	630	Falls	145
Rotan Ind School Dist	2	250	Fisher	148
Round Rock Ind School Dist	54	50,546	Williamson	398
Round Top-Carmine Ind Sch Dist	2	283	Fayette	147
Royal Ind School Dist	4	2,400	Waller	384
Royse City Ind School Dist	9	6,300	Rockwall	326
Rule Ind School Dist	1	130	Haskell	210
Runge Ind School Dist	1	250	Karnes	251
Rusk Ind School Dist	5	2,015	Cherokee	73
S & S Cons Ind School Dist	3	950	Grayson	167
Sabinal Ind School Dist	2	500	Uvalde	378
Sabine Ind School Dist	3	1,397	Gregg	170
Sabine Pass Ind School Dist	1	372	Jefferson	244
Salado Ind School Dist	3	1,900	Bell	29
Saltillo Ind School Dist	1	240	Hopkins	231
Sam Rayburn Ind School Dist	1	500	Fannin	146
San Angelo Ind School Dist	25	14,362	Tom Green	364
San Antonio Ind School Dist	96	49,000	Bexar	39
San Augustine Ind School Dist	2	763	San Augustine	329
San Benito Cons Ind Sch Dist	18	10,643	Cameron	66
San Diego Ind School Dist	3	1,460	Duval	128
San Elizario Ind School Dist	6	3,560	El Paso	135
San Felipe-Del Rio Cons Ind SD	12	10,472	Val Verde	379
San Isidro Ind School Dist	1	250	Starr	341
San Marcos Cons Ind Sch Dist	11	8,200	Hays	211
San Perlita Ind School Dist	1	282	Willacy	394
San Saba Ind School Dist	3	750	San Saba	332
San Vicente Ind School Dist	1	13	Brewster	57
Sands Consolidated ISD	1	254	Dawson	117
Sanford-Fritch Ind School Dist	3	737	Hutchinson	238
Sanger Ind School Dist	7	2,660	Denton	126
Santa Anna Ind School Dist	2	259	Coleman	76
Santa Fe Ind School Dist	4	4,794	Galveston	161
Santa Gertrudis Ind Sch Dist	2	753	Kleberg	258
Santa Maria Ind School Dist	4	691	Cameron	67
Santa Rosa Ind School Dist	3	1,300	Cameron	67
Santo Ind School Dist	2	475	Palo Pinto	310
Savoy Ind School Dist	2	320	Fannin	146
Schertz-Cibolo-Univ City ISD	17	15,931	Guadalupe	173
Schleicher Co Ind Sch Dist	3	590	Schleicher	333
School of Excellence In Ed	4	600	Bexar	42
Schulenburg Ind School Dist	2	750	Fayette	147
Scurry Rosser Ind School Dist	3	1,035	Kaufman	253
Seagraves Ind School Dist	3	569	Gaines	157
Sealy Ind School Dist	4	2,900	Austin	22
Seguin Ind School Dist	13	7,127	Guadalupe	173

Texas School Directory — DISTRICT INDEX

SCHOOL DISTRICT	NO. OF SCHOOLS	ENROLLMENT	COUNTY	PAGE	SCHOOL DISTRICT	NO. OF SCHOOLS	ENROLLMENT	COUNTY	PAGE
Seminole Ind School Dist	6	2,983	Gaines	158	Terrell Ind School Dist	9	4,711	Kaufman	253
Seymour Ind School Dist	3	575	Baylor	24	Texarkana Ind School Dist	13	7,174	Bowie	50
Shallowater Ind School Dist	4	1,600	Lubbock	272	Texas City Ind School Dist	14	9,000	Galveston	161
Shamrock Ind School Dist	3	426	Wheeler	390	Texhoma Ind School Dist	1	115	Sherman	336
Sharyland Ind School Dist	14	10,295	Hidalgo	224	Texline Ind School Dist	1	185	Dallam	95
Shelbyville Ind School Dist	3	790	Shelby	335	Thorndale Ind School Dist	3	567	Milam	288
Sheldon Ind School Dist	11	8,500	Harris	200	Thrall Ind School Dist	3	720	Williamson	400
Shepherd Ind School Dist	4	2,000	San Jacinto	330	Three Rivers Ind School Dist	2	678	Live Oak	268
Sherman Ind School Dist	12	7,300	Grayson	167	Three Way Ind School Dist	2	190	Erath	144
Shiner Ind School Dist	2	660	Lavaca	262	Throckmorton Ind School Dist	1	175	Throckmorton	363
Sidney Ind School Dist	1	140	Comanche	90	Tidehaven Ind School Dist	4	980	Matagorda	276
Sierra Blanca Ind School Dist	1	90	Hudspeth	234	Timpson Ind School Dist	3	630	Shelby	335
Silsbee Ind School Dist	4	2,800	Hardin	178	Tioga Ind School Dist	1	700	Grayson	167
Silverton Ind School Dist	1	195	Briscoe	57	Tolar Ind School Dist	3	780	Hood	230
Simms Ind School Dist	3	516	Bowie	50	Tom Bean Ind School Dist	3	675	Grayson	168
Sinton Ind School Dist	4	2,202	San Patricio	332	Tomball Ind School Dist	20	16,289	Harris	203
Sivells Bend Ind School Dist	1	68	Cooke	91	Tornillo Ind School Dist	4	1,135	El Paso	137
Skidmore Tynan Ind SD	3	850	Bee	25	Trent Ind School Dist	1	180	Taylor	361
Slaton Ind School Dist	4	1,340	Lubbock	272	Trenton Ind School Dist	3	568	Fannin	146
Slidell Ind School Dist	2	282	Wise	403	Trinidad Ind School Dist	1	165	Henderson	214
Slocum ISD School Dist	1	415	Anderson	16	Trinity Ind School Dist	3	1,280	Trinity	374
Smithville Ind School Dist	5	1,780	Bastrop	24	Troup Ind School Dist	3	1,081	Smith	337
Smyer Ind School Dist	2	420	Hockley	229	Troy Ind School Dist	4	1,600	Bell	29
Snook Ind School Dist	1	500	Burleson	59	Tulia Ind School Dist	4	1,099	Swisher	343
Snyder Ind School Dist	4	2,650	Scurry	333	Tuloso-Midway Ind School Dist	5	4,000	Nueces	305
Socorro Ind School Dist	50	47,000	El Paso	135	Turkey-Quitaque Cons Ind SD	1	207	Hall	176
Somerset Ind School Dist	7	3,990	Bexar	42	Tyler Ind School Dist	30	18,600	Smith	337
Somerville Ind School Dist	3	640	Burleson	60	Union Grove Ind School Dist	2	750	Upshur	377
Sonora Ind School Dist	3	760	Sutton	342	Union Hill Ind School Dist	1	400	Upshur	377
South San Antonio Ind Sch Dist	16	8,800	Bexar	42	United Ind School Dist	47	45,000	Webb	387
South Texas Ind School Dist	6	4,245	Cameron	67	UT Tyler University Acad Dist	3	700	Smith	338
Southland Ind School Dist	1	132	Garza	162	Utopia Ind School Dist	1	232	Uvalde	378
Southside Ind School Dist	9	5,800	Bexar	43	Uvalde Cons Ind School Dist	7	4,221	Uvalde	378
Southwest Ind School Dist	19	13,580	Bexar	43	Valentine Ind School Dist	1	30	Jeff Davis	241
Spearman Ind School Dist	3	860	Hansford	177	Valley Mills Ind School Dist	3	630	Bosque	47
Splendora Ind School Dist	5	4,200	Montgomery	294	Valley View Ind School Dist	8	4,329	Hidalgo	225
Spring Branch Ind School Dist	47	34,975	Harris	200	Valley View ISD-Cooke Co	1	815	Cooke	91
Spring Creek Ind School Dist	1	92	Hutchinson	238	Van Alstyne Ind School Dist	4	1,598	Grayson	168
Spring Hill Ind School Dist	4	1,980	Gregg	170	Van Ind School Dist	5	2,400	Van Zandt	381
Spring Ind School Dist	41	35,391	Harris	202	Van Vleck Ind School Dist	4	1,050	Matagorda	276
Springlake-Earth Ind Sch Dist	2	350	Lamb	261	Vega Ind School Dist	2	380	Oldham	307
Springtown Ind School Dist	6	3,470	Parker	313	Venus Ind School Dist	4	2,200	Johnson	249
Spur Ind School Dist	1	250	Dickens	127	Veribest Ind School Dist	1	275	Tom Green	365
Spurger Ind School Dist	2	385	Tyler	375	Vernon Ind School Dist	6	1,700	Wilbarger	393
St Jo Ind School Dist	2	283	Montague	290	Victoria Ind School Dist	23	13,900	Victoria	382
Stafford Municipal Sch Dist	7	3,600	Fort Bend	154	Vidor Ind School Dist	7	5,000	Orange	309
Stamford Ind School Dist	3	670	Jones	250	Vysehrad Ind School Dist	1	115	Lavaca	263
Stanton Ind School Dist	3	1,092	Martin	274	Waco Ind School Dist	24	15,050	McLennan	281
Stephenville Ind School Dist	6	3,650	Erath	144	Waelder Ind School Dist	1	320	Gonzales	164
Sterling City Ind School Dist	2	320	Sterling	342	Walcott Ind School Dist	1	125	Deaf Smith	119
Stockdale Ind School Dist	3	803	Wilson	401	Wall Ind School Dist	4	1,100	Tom Green	365
Stratford Ind School Dist	3	585	Sherman	336	Waller Ind School Dist	8	7,700	Waller	384
Strawn Ind School Dist	1	167	Palo Pinto	311	Walnut Bend Ind School Dist	1	75	Cooke	92
Sudan Ind School Dist	2	495	Lamb	261	Walnut Springs Ind Sch Dist	1	190	Bosque	47
Sulphur Bluff Ind School Dist	1	215	Hopkins	232	Warren Ind School Dist	4	1,400	Tyler	375
Sulphur Springs Ind Sch Dist	9	4,400	Hopkins	232	Waskom Ind School Dist	3	890	Harrison	209
Sundown Ind School Dist	3	585	Hockley	229	Water Valley Ind School Dist	2	300	Tom Green	365
Sunnyvale Ind School Dist	3	1,950	Dallas	113	Waxahachie Ind School Dist	16	9,481	Ellis	142
Sunray Ind School Dist	3	550	Moore	296	Weatherford Ind School Dist	12	8,000	Parker	313
Sweeny Ind School Dist	3	1,969	Brazoria	54	Webb Cons Ind School Dist	3	272	Webb	388
Sweet Home Ind School Dist	1	150	Lavaca	262	Weimar Ind School Dist	3	661	Colorado	87
Sweetwater ISD School Dist	5	2,200	Nolan	301	Wellington Ind School Dist	3	580	Collingsworth	86
Taft Ind School Dist	3	1,100	San Patricio	332	Wellman Union Ind School Dist	1	347	Terry	362
Tahoka Ind School Dist	3	680	Lynn	273	Wells Ind School Dist	2	285	Cherokee	73
Tarkington Ind School Dist	4	1,800	Liberty	266	Weslaco Ind School Dist	19	18,000	Hidalgo	225
Tatum Ind School Dist	4	1,622	Rusk	328	West Hardin Co Cons Sch Dist	2	525	Hardin	178
Taylor Ind School Dist	7	3,280	Williamson	399	West Ind School Dist	4	1,350	McLennan	282
Teague Ind School Dist	5	1,160	Freestone	156	West Orange-Cove Cons ISD	4	2,487	Orange	309
Temple Ind School Dist	15	8,700	Bell	29	West Oso Ind School Dist	4	2,104	Nueces	306
Tenaha Ind School Dist	1	570	Shelby	335	West Rusk Co Cons Ind Sch Dist	4	1,150	Rusk	328
Terlingua Common School Dist	2	105	Brewster	57	West Sabine Ind Sch Dist	2	600	Sabine	329
Terrell Co Ind School Dist	1	130	Terrell	362	Westbrook Ind School Dist	1	272	Mitchell	289

School Year 2019-2020   800-333-8802

DISTRICT INDEX

SCHOOL DISTRICT	NO. OF SCHOOLS	ENROLL-MENT	COUNTY	PAGE
Westhoff Ind School Dist	1	85	De Witt	118
Westphalia Ind School Dist	1	155	Falls	145
Westwood Ind School Dist	4	1,600	Anderson	16
Wharton Ind School Dist	5	2,097	Wharton	390
Wheeler Ind School Dist	1	487	Wheeler	391
White Deer Ind School Dist	2	450	Carson	69
White Oak Ind School Dist	4	1,520	Gregg	171
White Settlement Ind Sch Dist	9	6,906	Tarrant	357
Whiteface Con Ind School Dist	2	325	Cochran	75
Whitehouse Ind School Dist	8	4,800	Smith	338
Whitesboro Ind School Dist	4	1,600	Grayson	168
Whitewright Ind School Dist	3	850	Grayson	168
Whitharral Ind School Dist	1	173	Hockley	230
Whitney Ind School Dist	4	1,425	Hill	228
Wichita Falls Ind School Dist	28	14,500	Wichita	392
Wildorado Ind Sch Dist	1	180	Oldham	308
Willis Ind School Dist	9	7,500	Montgomery	294
Wills Point Ind School Dist	5	2,415	Van Zandt	381
Wilson Ind School Dist	1	129	Lynn	273
Wimberley Ind School Dist	4	2,400	Hays	212
Windthorst Ind School Dist	3	405	Archer	20
Wink Loving Ind School Dist	2	440	Winkler	402
Winnsboro Ind School Dist	3	1,496	Wood	405
Winona Ind School Dist	4	1,050	Smith	339
Winters Ind School Dist	3	544	Runnels	327
Woden Ind School Dist	3	725	Nacogdoches	298
Wolfe City Ind School Dist	3	690	Hunt	237
Woodsboro Ind School Dist	2	420	Refugio	324
Woodson Ind School Dist	1	150	Throckmorton	363
Woodville Ind School Dist	4	1,300	Tyler	375
Wortham Ind School Dist	3	500	Freestone	156
Wylie Ind School Dist	20	17,000	Collin	84
Wylie Ind School Dist	7	4,600	Taylor	361
Yantis Ind School Dist	2	370	Wood	405
Yoakum Ind School Dist	5	1,500	De Witt	118
Yorktown Ind School Dist	3	550	De Witt	118
Ysleta Ind School Dist	61	40,691	El Paso	137
Zapata Co Ind School Dist	6	3,521	Zapata	406
Zavalla Ind School Dist	2	360	Angelina	18
Zephyr Ind School Dist	1	217	Brown	59

CATHOLIC DIOCESE

SCHOOL DISTRICT	NO. OF SCHOOLS	ENROLL-MENT	COUNTY	PAGE
Archdiocese Galveston-Houston	58	19,122	Harris	203
Archdiocese San Antonio Ed Off	39	13,062	Bexar	44
Diocese Corpus Christi Ed Off	16	3,300	Nueces	306
Diocese of Amarillo Ed Office	5	850	Potter	319
Diocese of Austin Ed Office	21	5,000	Travis	372
Diocese of Beaumont Sch Office	5	1,700	Jefferson	244
Diocese of Brownsville Ed Off	12	2,092	Hidalgo	226
Diocese of Dallas Ed Office	35	14,713	Dallas	113
Diocese of El Paso Ed Office	11	2,700	El Paso	139
Diocese of Fort Worth Ed Off	19	5,961	Tarrant	358
Diocese of Laredo Ed Office	6	2,131	Webb	388
Diocese of Lubbock Ed Office	2	360	Lubbock	272
Diocese of San Angelo Ed Off	3	1,000	Midland	286
Diocese of Tyler Ed Office	4	1,300	Smith	339
Diocese of Victoria Ed Office	13	2,827	Victoria	382

COUNTY CENTERS

SCHOOL DISTRICT	NO. OF SCHOOLS	ENROLL-MENT	COUNTY	PAGE
Dallas Co Schools			Dallas	95
Harris Co Dept of Ed			Harris	179
Kenedy Co Schools			Kenedy	254

Texas School Directory

COUNTY INDEX

COUNTY District/City	NO. OF SCHOOLS	ENROLL-MENT	PAGE
ANDERSON			
Cayuga Ind School Dist/*Tenn Colony*	1	570	14
Elkhart Ind School Dist/*Elkhart*	4	1,250	15
Frankston Ind School Dist/*Frankston*	3	825	15
Neches Ind School Dist/*Neches*	2	400	15
Palestine Ind School Dist/*Palestine*	6	3,450	15
Slocum ISD School Dist/*Elkhart*	1	415	16
Westwood Ind School Dist/*Palestine*	4	1,600	16
ANDREWS			
Andrews Ind School Dist/*Andrews*	6	4,200	16
ANGELINA			
Central Ind School Dist/*Pollok*	3	1,550	16
Diboll Ind School Dist/*Diboll*	5	1,890	17
Hudson Ind School Dist/*Lufkin*	5	3,000	17
Huntington Ind School Dist/*Huntington*	5	1,750	17
Lufkin Ind School Dist/*Lufkin*	15	8,000	18
Zavalla Ind School Dist/*Zavalla*	2	360	18
ARANSAS			
Aransas Co Ind School Dist/*Rockport*	4	2,800	19
ARCHER			
Archer City Ind School Dist/*Archer City*	2	474	19
Holliday Ind School Dist/*Holliday*	3	1,007	19
Windthorst Ind School Dist/*Windthorst*	3	405	20
ARMSTRONG			
Claude Ind School Dist/*Claude*	1	330	20
ATASCOSA			
Charlotte Ind School Dist/*Charlotte*	3	475	20
Jourdanton Ind School Dist/*Jourdanton*	4	1,600	20
Lytle Ind School Dist/*Lytle*	4	1,693	21
Pleasanton Ind School Dist/*Pleasanton*	4	3,477	21
Poteet Ind School Dist/*Poteet*	4	1,735	21
AUSTIN			
Bellville Ind School Dist/*Bellville*	6	2,200	21
Brazos Ind School Dist/*Wallis*	4	700	22
Sealy Ind School Dist/*Sealy*	4	2,900	22
BAILEY			
Muleshoe Ind School Dist/*Muleshoe*	4	1,450	22
BANDERA			
Bandera Ind School Dist/*Bandera*	4	2,283	23
Medina Ind School Dist/*Medina*	2	310	23
BASTROP			
Bastrop Ind School Dist/*Bastrop*	15	11,000	23
Elgin Ind School Dist/*Elgin*	6	4,700	24
McDade Ind School Dist/*Mc Dade*	1	390	24
Smithville Ind School Dist/*Smithville*	5	1,780	24
BAYLOR			
Seymour Ind School Dist/*Seymour*	3	575	24
BEE			
Beeville Ind School Dist/*Beeville*	6	3,200	25
Pawnee Ind School Dist/*Pawnee*	1	550	25
Pettus Ind School Dist/*Pettus*	2	421	25
Skidmore Tynan Ind SD/*Skidmore*	3	850	25
BELL			
Academy Ind School Dist/*LTL RVR Acad*	5	1,559	26
Bartlett Ind School Dist/*Bartlett*	3	350	26
Belton Ind School Dist/*Belton*	17	11,950	26
Holland Ind School Dist/*Holland*	3	692	27
Killeen Ind School Dist/*Killeen*	53	45,583	27
Rogers Ind School Dist/*Rogers*	3	875	28
Salado Ind School Dist/*Salado*	3	1,900	29
Temple Ind School Dist/*Temple*	15	8,700	29
Troy Ind School Dist/*Troy*	4	1,600	29
BEXAR			
Alamo Heights Ind School Dist/*San Antonio*	5	4,900	30
Archdiocese San Antonio Ed Off/*San Antonio*	39	13,062	44
Braination Schools/*San Antonio*	8	1,200	30
East Central Ind School Dist/*San Antonio*	12	10,146	31
Edgewood Ind School Dist/*San Antonio*	21	10,881	31
Ft Sam Houston Ind School Dist/*San Antonio*	2	1,580	32
Harlandale Ind School Dist/*San Antonio*	24	14,500	32
Judson Ind School Dist/*Live Oak*	33	23,000	33
Lackland Ind School Dist/*San Antonio*	2	1,053	34
North East Ind School Dist/*San Antonio*	74	64,359	34
Northside Ind School Dist/*San Antonio*	122	105,856	36
Randolph Field Ind School Dist/*Universal Cty*	3	1,300	39
Region 20 Ed Service Center/*San Antonio*			45
San Antonio Ind School Dist/*San Antonio*	96	49,000	39
School of Excellence In Ed/*San Antonio*	4	600	42
Somerset Ind School Dist/*Somerset*	7	3,990	42
South San Antonio Ind Sch Dist/*San Antonio*	16	8,800	42
Southside Ind School Dist/*San Antonio*	9	5,800	43
Southwest Ind School Dist/*San Antonio*	19	13,580	43
BLANCO			
Blanco Ind School Dist/*Blanco*	3	1,025	45
Johnson City Ind School Dist/*Johnson City*	3	659	46
BORDEN			
Borden Co Ind School Dist/*Gail*	1	230	46
BOSQUE			
Clifton Ind School Dist/*Clifton*	3	1,000	46
Cranfills Gap ISD School Dist/*Cranfills Gap*	1	125	46
Iredell Ind School Dist/*Iredell*	1	145	46
Kopperl Ind School Dist/*Kopperl*	1	225	47
Meridian Ind School Dist/*Meridian*	3	480	47
Morgan Ind School Dist/*Morgan*	1	142	47
Valley Mills Ind School Dist/*Valley Mills*	3	630	47
Walnut Springs Ind Sch Dist/*Walnut Spgs*	1	190	47
BOWIE			
De Kalb Ind School Dist/*De Kalb*	3	900	47
Hooks Ind School Dist/*Hooks*	3	942	48
Hubbard Ind School Dist/*De Kalb*	1	120	48
Leary Ind School Dist/*Texarkana*	1	125	48
Liberty-Eylau Ind School Dist/*Texarkana*	4	2,500	48
Malta Ind School Dist/*New Boston*	1	241	48
Maud Ind School Dist/*Maud*	1	480	49
New Boston Ind School Dist/*New Boston*	4	1,340	49
Pleasant Grove Ind School Dist/*Texarkana*	4	2,200	49
Red Lick Ind School Dist/*Texarkana*	1	530	49
Redwater Ind School Dist/*Redwater*	4	1,150	49
Simms Ind School Dist/*Simms*	3	516	50
Texarkana Ind School Dist/*Texarkana*	13	7,174	50
BRAZORIA			
Alvin Ind School Dist/*Alvin*	29	25,926	50
Angleton Ind School Dist/*Angleton*	9	6,787	51
Brazosport Ind School Dist/*Clute*	18	12,345	52
Columbia Brazoria ISD/*West Columbia*	5	3,135	52
Damon Ind School Dist/*Damon*	1	200	53
Danbury Ind School Dist/*Danbury*	3	750	53
Pearland Ind School Dist/*Pearland*	23	21,917	53
Sweeny Ind School Dist/*Sweeny*	3	1,969	54
BRAZOS			
Bryan Ind School Dist/*Bryan*	24	16,134	54
College Station Ind Sch Dist/*College Sta*	19	14,000	55
Mumford Ind School Dist/*Mumford*	1	625	56
BREWSTER			
Alpine Ind School Dist/*Alpine*	3	1,000	56
Marathon Ind School Dist/*Marathon*	1	55	56
San Vicente Ind School Dist/*Bg BND NTL Pk*	1	13	57
Terlingua Common School Dist/*Terlingua*	2	105	57
BRISCOE			
Silverton Ind School Dist/*Silverton*	1	195	57
BROOKS			
Brooks Co Ind School Dist/*Falfurrias*	4	1,589	57
BROWN			
Bangs Ind School Dist/*Bangs*	3	875	58
Blanket Ind School Dist/*Blanket*	1	187	58
Brookesmith Ind School Dist/*Brookesmith*	3	200	58
Brownwood Ind School Dist/*Brownwood*	7	3,595	58
Early Ind School Dist/*Early*	4	1,200	58
May Ind School Dist/*May*	2	290	59
Zephyr Ind School Dist/*Zephyr*	1	217	59
BURLESON			
Caldwell Ind School Dist/*Caldwell*	5	1,800	59
Snook Ind School Dist/*Snook*	1	500	59
Somerville Ind School Dist/*Somerville*	3	640	60
BURNET			
Burnet Cons Ind Sch Dist/*Burnet*	6	3,186	60
Marble Falls Ind School Dist/*Marble Falls*	7	4,154	60
CALDWELL			
Lockhart Ind School Dist/*Lockhart*	9	6,350	61
Luling Ind School Dist/*Luling*	4	1,450	61

School Year 2019-2020 800-333-8802 TX-R1

COUNTY INDEX

Market Data Retrieval

COUNTY District/City	NO. OF SCHOOLS	ENROLL- MENT	PAGE
Prairie Lea Ind School Dist/*Prairie Lea*	1	210	61
CALHOUN			
Calhoun Co Ind School Dist/*Port Lavaca*	7	3,985	61
CALLAHAN			
Baird Ind School Dist/*Baird*	3	274	62
Clyde Consolidated Ind SD/*Clyde*	4	1,450	62
Cross Plains Ind Sch Dist/*Cross Plains*	2	368	62
Eula Ind School Dist/*Clyde*	3	400	63
CAMERON			
Brownsville Ind School Dist/*Brownsville*	54	43,355	63
Harlingen Cons Ind School Dist/*Harlingen*	31	18,600	64
La Feria Ind School Dist/*La Feria*	7	3,347	65
Los Fresnos Cons Ind Sch Dist/*Los Fresnos*	16	10,700	65
Point Isabel Ind Sch Dist/*Port Isabel*	4	2,500	66
Rio Hondo Ind School Dist/*Rio Hondo*	3	1,900	66
San Benito Cons Ind Sch Dist/*San Benito*	18	10,643	66
Santa Maria Ind School Dist/*Santa Maria*	4	691	67
Santa Rosa Ind School Dist/*Santa Rosa*	3	1,300	67
South Texas Ind School Dist/*Mercedes*	6	4,245	67
CAMP			
Pittsburg Ind School Dist/*Pittsburg*	5	2,344	68
Region 8 Ed Service Center/*Pittsburg*			69
CARSON			
Groom Ind School Dist/*Groom*	1	160	69
Panhandle Ind School Dist/*Panhandle*	3	700	69
White Deer Ind School Dist/*White Deer*	2	450	69
CASS			
Atlanta Ind School Dist/*Atlanta*	5	1,760	69
Avinger Ind School Dist/*Avinger*	1	135	70
Bloomburg Ind School Dist/*Bloomburg*	1	270	70
Hughes Springs Ind Sch Dist/*Hughes Spgs*	3	1,230	70
Linden Kildare Cons Ind SD/*Linden*	3	700	70
McLeod Ind School Dist/*Mc Leod*	1	388	70
Queen City Ind School Dist/*Queen City*	4	1,045	70
CASTRO			
Dimmitt Ind School Dist/*Dimmitt*	4	1,225	71
Hart Ind School Dist/*Hart*	2	230	71
Nazareth Ind School Dist/*Nazareth*	1	240	71
CHAMBERS			
Anahuac Ind School Dist/*Anahuac*	3	1,336	71
Barbers Hill Ind School Dist/*Mont Belvieu*	8	5,214	72
East Chambers Ind School Dist/*Winnie*	4	1,500	72
CHEROKEE			
Alto Ind School Dist/*Alto*	3	671	72
Jacksonville Ind School Dist/*Jacksonville*	8	5,091	72
New Summerfield Ind Sch Dist/*New Summerfld*	1	550	73
Rusk Ind School Dist/*Rusk*	5	2,015	73
Wells Ind School Dist/*Wells*	2	285	73
CHILDRESS			
Childress Ind School Dist/*Childress*	4	1,100	74
CLAY			
Bellevue Ind School Dist/*Bellevue*	1	140	74
Henrietta Ind School Dist/*Henrietta*	3	940	74
Midway Ind School Dist/*Henrietta*	1	137	74
Petrolia Cons Ind School Dist/*Petrolia*	2	440	74
COCHRAN			
Morton Ind School Dist/*Morton*	4	400	75
Whiteface Con Ind School Dist/*Whiteface*	2	325	75
COKE			
Bronte Ind School Dist/*Bronte*	2	245	75
Robert Lee Ind School Dist/*Robert Lee*	1	290	75
COLEMAN			
Coleman Ind School Dist/*Coleman*	3	885	76
Panther Creek Cons Ind SD/*Voss*	1	149	76
Santa Anna Ind School Dist/*Santa Anna*	2	259	76
COLLIN			
Allen Ind School Dist/*Allen*	24	21,404	76
Anna Ind School Dist/*Anna*	6	3,800	77
Blue Ridge Ind School Dist/*Blue Ridge*	3	860	77
Celina Ind School Dist/*Celina*	6	2,600	77
Community Ind School Dist/*Nevada*	4	2,262	78
Farmersville Ind School Dist/*Farmersville*	4	1,750	78
Frisco Ind School Dist/*Frisco*	72	62,386	78
Lovejoy Ind School Dist/*Allen*	6	4,424	80

COUNTY District/City	NO. OF SCHOOLS	ENROLL- MENT	PAGE
McKinney Ind School Dist/*McKinney*	31	24,335	80
Melissa Ind School Dist/*Melissa*	4	2,792	81
Plano Ind School Dist/*Plano*	73	53,952	82
Princeton Ind School Dist/*Princeton*	8	5,000	84
Prosper Ind School Dist/*Prosper*	15	7,600	84
Wylie Ind School Dist/*Wylie*	20	17,000	84
COLLINGSWORTH			
Wellington Ind School Dist/*Wellington*	3	580	86
COLORADO			
Columbus Ind School Dist/*Columbus*	4	1,494	86
Rice Cons Ind School Dist/*Altair*	7	1,325	87
Weimar Ind School Dist/*Weimar*	3	661	87
COMAL			
Comal Ind School Dist/*New Braunfels*	31	23,800	87
New Braunfels Ind School Dist/*New Braunfels*	15	9,220	88
COMANCHE			
Comanche Ind School Dist/*Comanche*	4	1,325	89
De Leon Ind School Dist/*De Leon*	3	716	89
Gustine Ind School Dist/*Gustine*	1	161	90
Sidney Ind School Dist/*Sidney*	1	140	90
CONCHO			
Eden Cons Ind School Dist/*Eden*	2	215	90
Paint Rock Ind School Dist/*Paint Rock*	1	240	90
COOKE			
Callisburg Ind School Dist/*Gainesville*	2	1,100	90
Era Ind School Dist/*Era*	1	500	90
Gainesville Ind School Dist/*Gainesville*	6	3,100	91
Lindsay Ind School Dist/*Lindsay*	2	510	91
Muenster Ind School Dist/*Muenster*	2	500	91
Sivells Bend Ind School Dist/*Gainesville*	1	68	91
Valley View ISD-Cooke Co/*Valley View*	1	815	91
Walnut Bend Ind School Dist/*Gainesville*	1	75	92
CORYELL			
Copperas Cove Ind School Dist/*Copperas Cove*	11	8,200	92
Evant Ind School Dist/*Evant*	1	235	92
Gatesville Ind School Dist/*Gatesville*	5	2,788	92
Jonesboro Ind School Dist/*Jonesboro*	1	340	93
Oglesby Ind School Dist/*Oglesby*	1	165	93
COTTLE			
Paducah Ind School Dist/*Paducah*	1	210	93
CRANE			
Crane Ind School Dist/*Crane*	3	1,155	93
CROCKETT			
Crockett Co Cons Common SD/*Ozona*	3	758	94
CROSBY			
Crosbyton Cons Ind Sch Dist/*Crosbyton*	2	375	94
Lorenzo Ind School Dist/*Lorenzo*	2	250	94
Ralls Ind School Dist/*Ralls*	4	500	94
CULBERSON			
Culberson Co Allamoore Ind SD/*Van Horn*	1	400	95
DALLAM			
Dalhart Ind School Dist/*Dalhart*	4	1,700	95
Texline Ind School Dist/*Texline*	1	185	95
DALLAS			
Advantage Academy Admin Office/*Duncanville*	4	1,650	96
Carrollton-Farmers Branch ISD/*Carrollton*	37	26,000	96
Cedar Hill Ind School Dist/*Cedar Hill*	14	7,866	97
Coppell Ind School Dist/*Coppell*	18	13,500	98
Dallas Co Schools/*Dallas*			95
Dallas Ind School Dist/*Dallas*	230	156,100	98
DeSoto Ind School Dist/*Desoto*	14	9,872	104
Diocese of Dallas Ed Office/*Dallas*	35	14,713	113
Duncanville Ind School Dist/*Duncanville*	19	12,800	104
Garland Ind School Dist/*Garland*	72	56,471	105
Grand Prairie Ind School Dist/*Grand Prairie*	42	29,339	107
Highland Park Ind Sch Dist/*Dallas*	7	7,000	108
Int'l Leadership of Texas Dist/*Richardson*	19	19,473	108
Irving Ind School Dist/*Irving*	39	33,188	109
Lancaster Ind School Dist/*Lancaster*	11	7,600	110
Mesquite Ind School Dist/*Mesquite*	47	39,900	110
Region 10 Ed Service Center/*Richardson*			116
Richardson Ind School Dist/*Richardson*	57	39,103	112
Sunnyvale Ind School Dist/*Sunnyvale*	3	1,950	113
DAWSON			

Texas School Directory

COUNTY INDEX

COUNTY District/City	NO. OF SCHOOLS	ENROLL-MENT	PAGE
Dawson Ind School Dist/*Welch*	1	110	116
Klondike Ind School Dist/*Lamesa*	1	275	117
Lamesa Ind School Dist/*Lamesa*	5	1,800	117
Sands Consolidated ISD/*Ackerly*	1	254	117
DE WITT			
Cuero Ind School Dist/*Cuero*	4	2,000	117
Meyersville Ind School Dist/*Meyersville*	1	132	118
Nordheim Ind School Dist/*Nordheim*	1	150	118
Westhoff Ind School Dist/*Westhoff*	1	85	118
Yoakum Ind School Dist/*Yoakum*	5	1,500	118
Yorktown Ind School Dist/*Yorktown*	3	550	118
DEAF SMITH			
Hereford Ind School Dist/*Hereford*	11	4,100	119
Walcott Ind School Dist/*Hereford*	1	125	119
DELTA			
Cooper Ind School Dist/*Cooper*	2	750	119
Fannindel Ind School Dist/*Ladonia*	2	150	120
DENTON			
Argyle Ind School Dist/*Argyle*	5	3,000	120
Aubrey Ind School Dist/*Aubrey*	4	2,000	120
Denton Ind School Dist/*Denton*	42	29,152	120
Krum Ind School Dist/*Krum*	5	2,050	122
Lake Dallas Ind School Dist/*Lake Dallas*	5	4,000	122
Lewisville Ind School Dist/*Lewisville*	70	52,000	122
Little Elm Ind School Dist/*Little Elm*	9	7,400	124
Northwest Ind School Dist/*Justin*	30	24,000	124
Pilot Point Ind School Dist/*Pilot Point*	4	1,500	125
Ponder Ind School Dist/*Ponder*	3	1,575	125
Sanger Ind School Dist/*Sanger*	7	2,660	126
DICKENS			
Patton Springs Ind School Dist/*Afton*	1	111	126
Spur Ind School Dist/*Spur*	1	250	127
DIMMIT			
Carrizo Spgs Cons Ind SD/*Carrizo Spgs*	4	2,200	127
DONLEY			
Clarendon Cons Ind Sch Dist/*Clarendon*	3	600	127
Hedley Ind School Dist/*Hedley*	1	120	127
DUVAL			
Benavides Ind School Dist/*Benavides*	2	340	128
Freer Ind School Dist/*Freer*	3	807	128
Ramirez Common School Dist/*Realitos*	1	30	128
San Diego Ind School Dist/*San Diego*	3	1,460	128
EASTLAND			
Cisco Independent Sch Dist/*Cisco*	4	850	128
Eastland Ind School Dist/*Eastland*	3	1,130	129
Gorman Ind School Dist/*Gorman*	3	300	129
Ranger Ind School Dist/*Ranger*	1	350	129
Rising Star Ind Sch Dist/*Rising Star*	2	147	129
ECTOR			
Ector Co Ind School Dist/*Odessa*	42	31,500	129
EDWARDS			
Nueces Canyon Cons Ind SD/*Barksdale*	2	270	131
Rocksprings Ind School Dist/*Rocksprings*	1	290	131
EL PASO			
Anthony Ind School Dist/*Anthony*	3	839	131
Canutillo Ind School Dist/*El Paso*	10	6,200	131
Clint Ind School Dist/*El Paso*	14	11,522	132
Diocese of El Paso Ed Office/*El Paso*	11	2,700	139
El Paso Ind School Dist/*El Paso*	89	54,824	132
El Paso ISD-Elementary/*El Paso*			133
El Paso ISD-High Schools/*El Paso*			134
El Paso ISD-Middle Schools/*El Paso*			134
Fabens Ind School Dist/*Fabens*	5	2,300	135
Region 19 Ed Service Center/*El Paso*			139
San Elizario Ind School Dist/*San Elizario*	6	3,560	135
Socorro Ind School Dist/*El Paso*	50	47,000	135
Tornillo Ind School Dist/*Tornillo*	4	1,135	137
Ysleta Ind School Dist/*El Paso*	61	40,691	137
ELLIS			
Avalon Ind School Dist/*Avalon*	1	350	140
Ennis Ind School Dist/*Ennis*	11	5,800	140
Ferris Ind School Dist/*Ferris*	5	2,400	140
Italy Ind School Dist/*Italy*	2	600	140
Maypearl Ind School Dist/*Maypearl*	4	1,040	141
Midlothian Ind School Dist/*Midlothian*	11	9,500	141
Milford Ind School Dist/*Milford*	1	280	141

COUNTY District/City	NO. OF SCHOOLS	ENROLL-MENT	PAGE
Palmer Ind School Dist/*Palmer*	3	1,250	141
Red Oak Ind School Dist/*Red Oak*	8	6,000	142
Waxahachie Ind School Dist/*Waxahachie*	16	9,481	142
ERATH			
Bluff Dale Ind Sch Dist/*Bluff Dale*	1	243	143
Dublin Ind School Dist/*Dublin*	3	1,200	143
Huckabay Ind School Dist/*Stephenville*	1	260	143
Lingleville Ind School Dist/*Lingleville*	1	275	143
Morgan Mill Ind School Dist/*Morgan Mill*	1	125	144
Stephenville Ind School Dist/*Stephenville*	6	3,650	144
Three Way Ind School Dist/*Stephenville*	2	190	144
FALLS			
Chilton Ind School Dist/*Chilton*	1	540	144
Marlin Ind School Dist/*Marlin*	3	1,000	144
Rosebud-Lott Ind School Dist/*Lott*	3	630	145
Westphalia Ind School Dist/*Lott*	1	155	145
FANNIN			
Bonham Ind School Dist/*Bonham*	5	1,890	145
Dodd City Ind School Dist/*Dodd City*	1	370	145
Ector Ind School Dist/*Ector*	1	250	146
Honey Grove Ind School Dist/*Honey Grove*	3	605	146
Leonard Ind School Dist/*Leonard*	4	820	146
Sam Rayburn Ind School Dist/*Ivanhoe*	1	500	146
Savoy Ind School Dist/*Savoy*	2	320	146
Trenton Ind School Dist/*Trenton*	3	568	146
FAYETTE			
Fayetteville Ind School Dist/*Fayetteville*	1	265	147
Flatonia Ind School Dist/*Flatonia*	3	580	147
La Grange Ind School Dist/*La Grange*	4	2,350	147
Round Top-Carmine Ind Sch Dist/*Carmine*	2	283	147
Schulenburg Ind School Dist/*Schulenburg*	2	750	147
FISHER			
Roby Cons Ind School Dist/*Roby*	2	310	148
Rotan Ind School Dist/*Rotan*	2	250	148
FLOYD			
Floydada Ind School Dist/*Floydada*	2	730	148
Lockney Independent Sch Dist/*Lockney*	3	430	149
FOARD			
Crowell Ind School Dist/*Crowell*	2	200	149
FORT BEND			
Ft Bend Ind School Dist/*Sugar Land*	79	78,000	149
Katy Ind School Dist/*Katy*	71	83,599	151
Lamar Cons Ind School Dist/*Rosenberg*	45	34,000	153
Needville Ind School Dist/*Needville*	4	3,228	154
Stafford Municipal Sch Dist/*Stafford*	7	3,600	154
FRANKLIN			
Mt Vernon Ind School Dist/*Mount Vernon*	3	1,620	155
FREESTONE			
Dew Ind School Dist/*Teague*	1	180	156
Fairfield Ind School Dist/*Fairfield*	4	1,817	156
Teague Ind School Dist/*Teague*	5	1,160	156
Wortham Ind School Dist/*Wortham*	3	500	156
FRIO			
Dilley Ind School Dist/*Dilley*	4	1,000	157
Pearsall Ind School Dist/*Pearsall*	4	2,100	157
GAINES			
Loop Ind School Dist/*Loop*	1	150	157
Seagraves Ind School Dist/*Seagraves*	3	569	157
Seminole Ind School Dist/*Seminole*	6	2,983	158
GALVESTON			
Clear Creek Ind School Dist/*League City*	45	44,099	158
Dickinson Ind School Dist/*Dickinson*	14	10,400	159
Friendswood Ind Sch Dist/*Friendswood*	6	6,000	160
Galveston Ind School Dist/*Galveston*	12	7,000	160
High Island Ind Sch Dist/*High Island*	1	145	160
Hitchcock Ind School Dist/*Hitchcock*	4	1,700	160
Santa Fe Ind School Dist/*Santa Fe*	4	4,794	161
Texas City Ind School Dist/*Texas City*	14	9,000	161
GARZA			
Post Ind School Dist/*Post*	3	810	162
Southland Ind School Dist/*Southland*	1	132	162
GILLESPIE			
Doss Consolidated Common SD/*Doss*	1	25	162
Fredericksburg Ind School Dist/*Fredericksbrg*	6	2,900	162

School Year 2019-2020   800-333-8802   TX-R3

COUNTY INDEX

Market Data Retrieval

COUNTY District/City	NO. OF SCHOOLS	ENROLL- MENT	PAGE
Harper Ind School Dist/*Harper*	3	600	163
GLASSCOCK			
Glasscock Co Ind School Dist/*Garden City*	1	310	163
GOLIAD			
Goliad Ind School Dist/*Goliad*	3	1,340	163
GONZALES			
Gonzales Ind School Dist/*Gonzales*	6	2,875	164
Nixon-Smiley Cons Ind Sch Dist/*Nixon*	3	1,100	164
Waelder Ind School Dist/*Waelder*	1	320	164
GRAY			
Grandview-Hopkins Ind Sch Dist/*Groom*	1	50	164
Lefors Ind School Dist/*Lefors*	1	160	165
McLean Ind School Dist/*McLean*	1	240	165
Pampa Ind School Dist/*Pampa*	7	3,500	165
GRAYSON			
Bells Ind School Dist/*Bells*	3	845	165
Collinsville Ind School Dist/*Collinsville*	2	530	166
Denison Ind School Dist/*Denison*	9	4,500	166
Gunter Ind School Dist/*Gunter*	3	970	166
Howe Ind School Dist/*Howe*	4	1,100	166
Pottsboro Ind School Dist/*Pottsboro*	3	1,450	167
S & S Cons Ind School Dist/*Sadler*	3	950	167
Sherman Ind School Dist/*Sherman*	12	7,300	167
Tioga Ind School Dist/*Tioga*	1	700	167
Tom Bean Ind School Dist/*Tom Bean*	3	675	168
Van Alstyne Ind School Dist/*Van Alstyne*	4	1,598	168
Whitesboro Ind School Dist/*Whitesboro*	4	1,600	168
Whitewright Ind School Dist/*Whitewright*	3	850	168
GREGG			
Gladewater Ind School Dist/*Gladewater*	4	1,700	169
Kilgore Ind School Dist/*Kilgore*	5	4,076	169
Longview Ind School Dist/*Longview*	13	8,700	169
Pine Tree Ind School Dist/*Longview*	8	4,700	170
Region 7 Ed Service Center/*Kilgore*			171
Sabine Ind School Dist/*Gladewater*	3	1,397	170
Spring Hill Ind School Dist/*Longview*	4	1,980	170
White Oak Ind School Dist/*White Oak*	4	1,520	171
GRIMES			
Anderson-Shiro Cons Ind SD/*Anderson*	2	850	171
Iola Ind School Dist/*Iola*	2	502	172
Navasota Ind School Dist/*Navasota*	6	3,000	172
Richards Ind School Dist/*Richards*	1	170	172
GUADALUPE			
Marion Ind School Dist/*Marion*	4	1,508	172
Navarro Ind School Dist/*Seguin*	4	1,911	173
Schertz-Cibolo-Univ City ISD/*Schertz*	17	15,931	173
Seguin Ind School Dist/*Seguin*	13	7,127	173
HALE			
Abernathy Ind School Dist/*Abernathy*	3	780	174
Cotton Center Ind School Dist/*Cotton Center*	1	130	174
Hale Center Ind School Dist/*Hale Center*	3	647	175
Petersburg Ind School Dist/*Petersburg*	1	300	175
Plainview Ind School Dist/*Plainview*	10	5,450	175
HALL			
Memphis Ind School Dist/*Memphis*	4	500	175
Turkey-Quitaque Cons Ind SD/*Turkey*	1	207	176
HAMILTON			
Hamilton Ind School Dist/*Hamilton*	3	850	176
Hico Ind School Dist/*Hico*	2	600	176
HANSFORD			
Gruver Ind School Dist/*Gruver*	3	400	176
Pringle-Morse Cons ISD/*Morse*	1	115	177
Spearman Ind School Dist/*Spearman*	3	860	177
HARDEMAN			
Chillicothe ISD School Dist/*Chillicothe*	2	248	177
Quanah Ind School Dist/*Quanah*	3	525	177
HARDIN			
Hardin Jefferson Ind Sch Dist/*Sour Lake*	4	2,200	177
Kountze Ind School Dist/*Kountze*	4	1,135	178
Lumberton Ind School Dist/*Lumberton*	5	4,123	178
Silsbee Ind School Dist/*Silsbee*	4	2,800	178
West Hardin Co Cons Sch Dist/*Saratoga*	2	525	178
HARRIS			
Aldine Ind School Dist/*Houston*	82	69,768	179

COUNTY District/City	NO. OF SCHOOLS	ENROLL- MENT	PAGE
Aldine ISD-Elem Sch Team 1/*Houston*			179
Aldine ISD-Elem Sch Team 2/*Houston*			179
Aldine ISD-Elem Sch Team 3/*Houston*			180
Aldine ISD-High Sch Team/*Houston*			180
Aldine ISD-Middle Sch Team/*Houston*			181
Aldine ISD-Primary Team/*Houston*			181
Alief Ind School Dist/*Houston*	45	46,241	181
Archdiocese Galveston-Houston/*Houston*	58	19,122	203
Channelview Ind School Dist/*Channelview*	13	9,700	183
Crosby Ind School Dist/*Crosby*	7	6,300	183
Cypress-Fairbanks Ind Sch Dist/*Houston*	91	116,249	183
Deer Park Ind School Dist/*Deer Park*	16	13,000	186
Galena Park Ind School Dist/*Houston*	27	24,000	186
Goose Creek Cons Ind Sch Dist/*Baytown*	28	24,000	187
Harris Co Dept of Ed/*Houston*			179
Houston Ind School Dist/*Houston*	275	206,052	188
Houston ISD-Achieve 180/*Houston*			188
Houston ISD-East Area/*Houston*			189
Houston ISD-North Area/*Houston*			190
Houston ISD-Northwest Area/*Houston*			191
Houston ISD-South Area/*Houston*			192
Houston ISD-West Area/*Houston*			193
Huffman Ind School Dist/*Huffman*	4	3,600	195
Humble Ind School Dist/*Humble*	46	44,802	195
Klein Ind School Dist/*Klein*	49	53,868	196
La Porte Ind School Dist/*La Porte*	12	7,679	198
Pasadena Ind School Dist/*Pasadena*	68	54,000	198
Region 4 Ed Service Center/*Houston*			208
Sheldon Ind School Dist/*Houston*	11	8,500	200
Spring Branch Ind School Dist/*Houston*	47	34,975	200
Spring Ind School Dist/*Houston*	41	35,391	202
Tomball Ind School Dist/*Tomball*	20	16,289	203
HARRISON			
Elysian Fields Ind School Dist/*Elysian Flds*	3	910	208
Hallsville Ind School Dist/*Hallsville*	5	5,500	208
Harleton Ind School Dist/*Harleton*	3	734	208
Karnack Ind School Dist/*Karnack*	1	124	208
Marshall Ind School Dist/*Marshall*	7	5,345	209
Waskom Ind School Dist/*Waskom*	3	890	209
HARTLEY			
Channing Ind School Dist/*Channing*	1	181	209
Hartley Ind School Dist/*Hartley*	1	239	209
HASKELL			
Haskell Cons Ind School Dist/*Haskell*	3	566	210
Paint Creek Ind School Dist/*Haskell*	1	102	210
Rule Ind School Dist/*Rule*	1	130	210
HAYS			
Dripping Springs Ind Sch Dist/*Dripping Spgs*	7	6,400	210
Hays Cons Ind School Dist/*Kyle*	25	20,445	211
San Marcos Cons Ind Sch Dist/*San Marcos*	11	8,200	211
Wimberley Ind School Dist/*Wimberley*	4	2,400	212
HEMPHILL			
Canadian Ind School Dist/*Canadian*	4	930	213
HENDERSON			
Athens Ind School Dist/*Athens*	5	3,118	213
Brownsboro Ind School Dist/*Brownsboro*	7	2,800	213
Cross Roads Ind School Dist/*Malakoff*	3	545	213
Eustace Ind School Dist/*Eustace*	4	1,550	214
La Poynor Ind School Dist/*Larue*	1	453	214
Malakoff Ind School Dist/*Malakoff*	5	1,400	214
Murchison Ind Sch Dist/*Murchison*	1	175	214
Trinidad Ind School Dist/*Trinidad*	1	165	214
HIDALGO			
Diocese of Brownsville Ed Off/*San Juan*	12	2,092	226
Donna Ind School Dist/*Donna*	22	14,459	215
Edcouch Elsa Ind School Dist/*Edcouch*	8	5,450	215
Edinburg Cons Ind School Dist/*Edinburg*	43	34,500	216
Hidalgo Ind School Dist/*Hidalgo*	7	3,300	217
Idea Public Schools/*Weslaco*	76	42,748	217
La Joya Ind School Dist/*La Joya*	41	27,000	219
La Villa Ind School Dist/*La Villa*	3	579	220
McAllen Ind School Dist/*McAllen*	31	24,000	220
Mercedes Ind School Dist/*Mercedes*	9	4,781	221
Mission Cons Ind School Dist/*Mission*	23	16,000	222
Monte Alto Ind School Dist/*Monte Alto*	3	900	222
Pharr-San Juan-Alamo Ind SD/*Pharr*	42	32,500	223
Progreso Ind School Dist/*Progreso*	5	1,750	224
Region 1 Ed Service Center/*Edinburg*			226
Sharyland Ind School Dist/*Mission*	14	10,295	224
Valley View Ind School Dist/*Pharr*	8	4,329	225

TX-R4   800-333-8802   School Year 2019-2020

Texas School Directory

COUNTY INDEX

COUNTY / District/City	NO. OF SCHOOLS	ENROLLMENT	PAGE
Weslaco Ind School Dist/Weslaco	19	18,000	225
HILL			
Abbott Ind School Dist/Abbott	1	242	226
Aquilla Ind School Dist/Aquilla	1	325	227
Blum Ind School Dist/Blum	1	370	227
Bynum Ind School Dist/Bynum	1	185	227
Covington ISD School Dist/Covington	1	293	227
Hillsboro Ind School Dist/Hillsboro	5	2,000	227
Hubbard Ind School Dist/Hubbard	2	400	227
Itasca Ind School Dist/Itasca	3	660	228
Malone Independent School Dist/Malone	1	165	228
Mt Calm Ind School Dist/Mount Calm	2	210	228
Penelope ISD School Dist/Penelope	1	210	228
Whitney Ind School Dist/Whitney	4	1,425	228
HOCKLEY			
Anton ISD School Dist/Anton	1	180	229
Levelland Ind School Dist/Levelland	6	2,936	229
Ropes Ind School Dist/Ropesville	1	430	229
Smyer Ind School Dist/Smyer	2	420	229
Sundown Ind School Dist/Sundown	3	585	229
Whitharral Ind School Dist/Whitharral	1	173	230
HOOD			
Granbury Ind School Dist/Granbury	11	7,218	230
Lipan Ind School Dist/Lipan	1	420	230
Tolar Ind School Dist/Tolar	3	780	230
HOPKINS			
Como Pickton Cons Ind SD/Como	1	753	231
Cumby Ind School Dist/Cumby	2	400	231
Miller Grove Ind School Dist/Cumby	1	329	231
North Hopkins Ind School Dist/Sulphur Spgs	1	525	231
Saltillo Ind School Dist/Saltillo	1	240	231
Sulphur Bluff Ind School Dist/Sulphur Bluff	1	215	232
Sulphur Springs Ind Sch Dist/Sulphur Spgs	9	4,400	232
HOUSTON			
Crockett Ind School Dist/Crockett	5	1,331	232
Grapeland Ind School Dist/Grapeland	3	615	232
Kennard Ind Sch Dist/Kennard	1	280	233
Latexo Ind School Dist/Latexo	2	500	233
Lovelady Ind School Dist/Lovelady	2	510	233
HOWARD			
Big Spring Ind School Dist/Big Spring	9	4,000	233
Coahoma Ind School Dist/Coahoma	3	1,000	234
Forsan Ind School Dist/Forsan	2	812	234
HUDSPETH			
Dell City Ind School Dist/Dell City	1	65	234
Ft Hancock Ind School Dist/Fort Hancock	3	410	234
Sierra Blanca Ind School Dist/Sierra Blanca	1	90	234
HUNT			
Bland Ind School Dist/Merit	3	730	235
Boles Ind School Dist/Quinlan	3	540	235
Caddo Mills Ind Sch Dist/Caddo Mills	5	1,850	235
Campbell Ind School Dist/Campbell	1	310	235
Celeste Ind School Dist/Celeste	3	512	235
Commerce Independent Sch Dist/Commerce	4	1,603	236
Greenville Ind School Dist/Greenville	12	5,400	236
Lone Oak Ind School Dist/Lone Oak	4	1,050	236
Quinlan Ind School Dist/Quinlan	5	2,725	237
Wolfe City Ind School Dist/Wolfe City	3	690	237
HUTCHINSON			
Borger Ind School Dist/Borger	6	2,800	237
Plemons-Stinnett-Phillips CISD/Stinnett	3	675	238
Sanford-Fritch Ind School Dist/Fritch	3	737	238
Spring Creek Ind School Dist/Skellytown	1	92	238
IRION			
Irion Co Ind School Dist/Mertzon	2	275	238
JACK			
Bryson Ind School Dist/Bryson	1	255	238
Jacksboro Ind Sch Dist/Jacksboro	3	1,050	239
Perrin-Whitt Cons Ind Sch Dist/Perrin	2	330	239
JACKSON			
Edna Ind School Dist/Edna	4	1,500	239
Ganado Ind School Dist/Ganado	3	750	239
Industrial Ind School Dist/Vanderbilt	4	1,178	240
JASPER			
Brookeland Ind School Dist/Brookeland	1	392	240
Buna Ind School Dist/Buna	3	1,480	240
Evadale Ind School Dist/Evadale	2	450	240
Jasper Ind School Dist/Jasper	4	2,390	240
Kirbyville Cons Ind Sch Dist/Kirbyville	3	1,400	241
JEFF DAVIS			
Fort Davis Ind School Dist/Fort Davis	2	230	241
Valentine Ind School Dist/Valentine	1	30	241
JEFFERSON			
Beaumont Ind School Dist/Beaumont	28	18,697	241
Diocese of Beaumont Sch Office/Beaumont	5	1,700	244
Hamshire Fannett Ind Sch Dist/Hamshire	4	1,900	242
Nederland Ind School Dist/Nederland	8	5,214	242
Port Arthur Ind School Dist/Port Arthur	16	9,000	243
Port Neches-Groves Ind SD/Port Neches	10	5,150	243
Region 5 Ed Service Center/Beaumont			244
Sabine Pass Ind School Dist/Sabine Pass	1	372	244
JIM HOGG			
Jim Hogg Co Ind School Dist/Hebbronville	3	1,151	244
JIM WELLS			
Alice Ind School Dist/Alice	9	4,784	245
Ben Bolt-Palito Blanco ISD/Ben Bolt	2	512	245
La Gloria Ind School Dist/Falfurrias	1	125	245
Orange Grove Ind School Dist/Orange Grove	4	1,850	245
Premont Ind School Dist/Premont	2	587	246
JOHNSON			
Alvarado Ind School Dist/Alvarado	6	3,650	246
Burleson Ind School Dist/Burleson	17	12,742	246
Cleburne Ind School Dist/Cleburne	12	6,749	247
Godley Ind School Dist/Godley	5	2,027	247
Grandview Ind School Dist/Grandview	3	1,276	248
Joshua Ind School Dist/Joshua	10	5,626	248
Keene Ind School Dist/Keene	4	1,070	248
Rio Vista Ind School Dist/Rio Vista	3	750	248
Venus Ind School Dist/Venus	4	2,200	249
JONES			
Anson Ind School Dist/Anson	3	700	249
Hamlin Ind School Dist/Hamlin	2	400	249
Hawley Ind School Dist/Hawley	3	769	249
Lueders-Avoca Ind School Dist/Lueders	2	104	250
Stamford Ind School Dist/Stamford	3	670	250
KARNES			
Falls City Ind School Dist/Falls City	2	360	250
Karnes City Ind School Dist/Karnes City	5	1,085	250
Kenedy Ind School Dist/Kenedy	3	800	251
Runge Ind School Dist/Runge	1	250	251
KAUFMAN			
Crandall Ind School Dist/Crandall	7	4,500	251
Forney Ind School Dist/Forney	14	9,681	251
Kaufman Ind School Dist/Kaufman	7	3,500	252
Kemp Ind School Dist/Kemp	4	1,586	252
Mabank Ind School Dist/Mabank	8	3,500	252
Scurry Rosser Ind School Dist/Scurry	3	1,035	253
Terrell Ind School Dist/Terrell	9	4,711	253
KENDALL			
Boerne Ind School Dist/Boerne	11	9,000	253
Comfort Ind School Dist/Comfort	3	1,100	254
KENEDY			
Kenedy Co Schools/Sarita			254
Kenedy Co Wide Common Sch Dist/Sarita	1	72	254
KENT			
Jayton-Girard Ind School Dist/Jayton	1	163	255
KERR			
Center Point Ind School Dist/Center Point	3	570	255
Divide Ind School Dist/Mountain Home	1	22	255
Hunt Ind School Dist/Hunt	1	200	255
Ingram Ind School Dist/Ingram	3	1,070	255
Kerrville Ind School Dist/Kerrville	10	4,800	256
KIMBLE			
Junction Ind School Dist/Junction	3	615	256
KING			
Guthrie Common School Dist/Guthrie	1	104	257
KINNEY			
Brackett Ind School Dist/Brackettville	3	569	257
KLEBERG			

School Year 2019-2020   800-333-8802

COUNTY INDEX

Market Data Retrieval

COUNTY District/City	NO. OF SCHOOLS	ENROLL- MENT	PAGE
Kingsville Ind School Dist/*Kingsville*	8	3,050	257
Ricardo Ind School Dist/*Kingsville*	1	671	257
Riviera Ind School Dist/*Riviera*	2	435	258
Santa Gertrudis Ind Sch Dist/*Kingsville*	2	753	258
KNOX			
Benjamin Ind School Dist/*Benjamin*	1	107	258
Knox City-O'Brien Cons Ind SD/*Knox City*	3	270	258
Munday Consolidated Ind SD/*Munday*	2	375	258
LA SALLE			
Cotulla Ind School Dist/*Cotulla*	4	1,400	259
LAMAR			
Chisum Ind School Dist/*Paris*	3	1,000	259
North Lamar Ind School Dist/*Paris*	7	2,500	259
Paris Ind School Dist/*Paris*	8	3,900	260
Prairiland Ind School Dist/*Pattonville*	4	1,160	260
LAMB			
Amherst Ind School Dist/*Amherst*	1	145	260
Littlefield Ind School Dist/*Littlefield*	4	1,300	260
Olton Ind School Dist/*Olton*	3	600	261
Springlake-Earth Ind Sch Dist/*Earth*	2	350	261
Sudan Ind School Dist/*Sudan*	2	495	261
LAMPASAS			
Lampasas Ind School Dist/*Lampasas*	5	3,400	261
Lometa Ind School Dist/*Lometa*	1	295	262
LAVACA			
Ezzell Ind School Dist/*Hallettsville*	1	85	262
Hallettsville Ind Sch Dist/*Hallettsville*	3	1,130	262
Moulton Ind School Dist/*Moulton*	2	300	262
Shiner Ind School Dist/*Shiner*	2	660	262
Sweet Home Ind School Dist/*Sweet Home*	1	150	262
Vysehrad Ind School Dist/*Hallettsville*	1	115	263
LEE			
Dime Box Ind School Dist/*Dime Box*	1	160	263
Giddings Ind School Dist/*Giddings*	4	1,905	263
Lexington Ind School Dist/*Lexington*	3	1,030	263
LEON			
Buffalo Ind School Dist/*Buffalo*	4	970	264
Centerville Ind School Dist/*Centerville*	2	700	264
Leon Ind School Dist/*Jewett*	3	715	264
Normangee Ind School Dist/*Normangee*	3	572	264
Oakwood Ind School Dist/*Oakwood*	2	200	264
LIBERTY			
Cleveland Ind School Dist/*Cleveland*	6	6,719	265
Dayton Ind School Dist/*Dayton*	7	5,400	265
Devers Ind School Dist/*Devers*	1	200	265
Hardin Ind School Dist/*Hardin*	3	1,400	265
Hull Daisetta Ind School Dist/*Daisetta*	3	477	266
Liberty Ind School Dist/*Liberty*	4	2,200	266
Tarkington Ind School Dist/*Cleveland*	4	1,800	266
LIMESTONE			
Coolidge Ind School Dist/*Coolidge*	2	309	266
Groesbeck Ind School Dist/*Groesbeck*	4	1,560	267
Mexia Ind School Dist/*Mexia*	5	1,800	267
LIPSCOMB			
Booker Ind School Dist/*Booker*	2	398	267
Darrouzett Ind School Dist/*Darrouzett*	1	120	267
Follett Ind School Dist/*Follett*	1	140	267
Higgins Ind School Dist/*Higgins*	1	125	268
LIVE OAK			
George West Ind School Dist/*George West*	4	1,100	268
Three Rivers Ind School Dist/*Three Rivers*	2	678	268
LLANO			
Llano Ind School Dist/*Llano*	4	1,800	268
LUBBOCK			
Diocese of Lubbock Ed Office/*Lubbock*	2	360	272
Frenship Ind School Dist/*Wolfforth*	13	9,900	269
Idalou Ind School Dist/*Idalou*	3	1,003	269
Lubbock Ind School Dist/*Lubbock*	48	27,759	269
Lubbock-Cooper Ind Sch Dist/*Lubbock*	9	6,000	271
New Deal Ind School Dist/*New Deal*	3	760	271
Region 17 Ed Service Center/*Lubbock*			272
Roosevelt Ind School Dist/*Lubbock*	3	1,150	271
Shallowater Ind School Dist/*Shallowater*	4	1,600	272
Slaton Ind School Dist/*Slaton*	4	1,340	272

COUNTY District/City	NO. OF SCHOOLS	ENROLL- MENT	PAGE
LYNN			
New Home Ind School Dist/*New Home*	1	447	273
O'Donnell Ind School Dist/*Odonnell*	2	306	273
Tahoka Ind School Dist/*Tahoka*	3	680	273
Wilson Ind School Dist/*Wilson*	1	129	273
MADISON			
Madisonville Cons ISD/*Madisonville*	4	2,358	273
North Zulch Ind School Dist/*North Zulch*	1	305	274
MARION			
Jefferson Ind School Dist/*Jefferson*	4	1,272	274
MARTIN			
Grady Ind School Dist/*Lenorah*	1	260	274
Stanton Ind School Dist/*Stanton*	3	1,092	274
MASON			
Mason Ind School Dist/*Mason*	3	675	275
MATAGORDA			
Bay City Ind School Dist/*Bay City*	5	3,700	275
Matagorda Ind School Dist/*Matagorda*	1	120	275
Palacios Ind School Dist/*Palacios*	4	1,506	275
Tidehaven Ind School Dist/*Elmaton*	4	980	276
Van Vleck Ind School Dist/*Van Vleck*	4	1,050	276
MAVERICK			
Eagle Pass Ind School Dist/*Eagle Pass*	23	15,000	276
MCCULLOCH			
Brady Ind School Dist/*Brady*	4	1,120	277
Lohn Ind School Dist/*Lohn*	1	90	277
Rochelle Ind School Dist/*Rochelle*	1	200	278
MCLENNAN			
Axtell Ind School Dist/*Axtell*	2	740	278
Bosqueville Ind School Dist/*Waco*	3	705	278
Bruceville-Eddy Ind Sch Dist/*Eddy*	4	641	278
China Spring Ind School Dist/*China Spring*	5	2,748	278
Connally Ind School Dist/*Waco*	6	2,300	279
Crawford Ind School Dist/*Crawford*	2	530	279
Gholson Ind School Dist/*Waco*	1	255	279
Hallsburg Ind School Dist/*Waco*	1	161	279
La Vega Ind School Dist/*Waco*	5	3,099	279
Lorena Ind School Dist/*Lorena*	4	1,725	280
Mart Ind School Dist/*Mart*	2	500	280
McGregor Ind School Dist/*Mc Gregor*	4	1,550	280
Midway Ind School Dist/*Woodway*	10	8,411	280
Moody Ind School Dist/*Moody*	3	690	281
Region 12 Ed Service Center/*Waco*			283
Riesel Ind School Dist/*Riesel*	2	620	281
Robinson Ind School Dist/*Robinson*	5	2,200	281
Waco Ind School Dist/*Waco*	24	15,050	281
West Ind School Dist/*West*	4	1,350	282
MCMULLEN			
McMullen Co Ind Sch Dist/*Tilden*	1	287	283
MEDINA			
D'Hanis Ind School Dist/*D Hanis*	1	395	283
Devine Ind School Dist/*Devine*	4	2,000	283
Hondo Ind School Dist/*Hondo*	4	2,200	284
Medina Valley Ind School Dist/*Castroville*	5	5,087	284
Natalia Ind School Dist/*Natalia*	4	1,060	284
MENARD			
Menard Ind School Dist/*Menard*	2	300	285
MIDLAND			
Diocese of San Angelo Ed Off/*Midland*	3	1,000	286
Greenwood Ind School Dist/*Midland*	4	2,831	285
Midland Ind School Dist/*Midland*	39	26,000	285
Region 18 Ed Service Center/*Midland*			287
MILAM			
Buckholts Ind School Dist/*Buckholts*	1	140	287
Burleson Milam Spec Serv Co-op/*Milano*			288
Cameron Ind School Dist/*Cameron*	4	1,800	287
Gause Ind School Dist/*Gause*	1	170	287
Milano Ind School Dist/*Milano*	3	460	287
Rockdale Ind School Dist/*Rockdale*	4	1,530	287
Thorndale Ind School Dist/*Thorndale*	3	567	288
MILLS			
Goldthwaite Consolidated ISD/*Goldthwaite*	3	595	288
Mullin Ind School Dist/*Mullin*	6	94	288
Priddy Ind School Dist/*Priddy*	1	111	289

Texas School Directory

COUNTY INDEX

COUNTY District/City	NO. OF SCHOOLS	ENROLL-MENT	PAGE
MITCHELL			
Colorado Ind School Dist/*Colorado City*	4	940	289
Loraine Ind School Dist/*Loraine*	1	160	289
Westbrook Ind School Dist/*Westbrook*	1	272	289
MONTAGUE			
Bowie Ind School Dist/*Bowie*	4	1,720	289
Forestburg Ind School Dist/*Forestburg*	1	160	290
Gold-Burg Ind School Dist/*Bowie*	1	140	290
Montague Ind School Dist/*Montague*	1	160	290
Nocona Ind School Dist/*Nocona*	3	770	290
Prairie Valley Ind School Dist/*Nocona*	1	170	290
St Jo Ind School Dist/*Saint Jo*	2	283	290
MONTGOMERY			
Conroe Ind School Dist/*Conroe*	64	63,000	291
Magnolia Ind School Dist/*Magnolia*	16	13,100	292
Montgomery Ind School Dist/*Montgomery*	10	8,864	293
New Caney Ind School Dist/*New Caney*	19	15,000	293
Splendora Ind School Dist/*Splendora*	5	4,200	294
Willis Ind School Dist/*Willis*	9	7,500	294
MOORE			
Dumas Ind School Dist/*Dumas*	9	4,212	295
Sunray Ind School Dist/*Sunray*	3	550	296
MORRIS			
Daingerfield-Lone Star Ind SD/*Daingerfield*	4	1,100	296
Pewitt Cons Ind School Dist/*Omaha*	3	891	296
MOTLEY			
Motley Co Ind School Dist/*Matador*	1	151	296
NACOGDOCHES			
Central Heights Ind Sch Dist/*Nacogdoches*	3	1,181	297
Chireno ISD School Dist/*Chireno*	1	304	297
Cushing Ind School Dist/*Cushing*	2	551	297
Douglass Ind School Dist/*Douglass*	1	460	297
Etoile Ind School Dist/*Etoile*	1	100	297
Garrison Ind School Dist/*Garrison*	3	600	297
Martinsville Ind School Dist/*Nacogdoches*	1	400	298
Nacogdoches Ind School Dist/*Nacogdoches*	10	6,300	298
Woden Ind School Dist/*Nacogdoches*	3	725	298
NAVARRO			
Blooming Grove Ind School Dist/*Blooming GRV*	3	924	299
Corsicana Ind School Dist/*Corsicana*	9	6,000	299
Dawson Ind School Dist/*Dawson*	1	500	299
Frost Ind School Dist/*Frost*	2	400	299
Kerens Ind School Dist/*Kerens*	3	600	299
Mildred Ind School Dist/*Corsicana*	1	720	300
Rice Ind School Dist/*Rice*	4	895	300
NEWTON			
Burkeville Ind School Dist/*Burkeville*	2	250	300
Newton Ind School Dist/*Newton*	3	1,026	301
NOLAN			
Blackwell Cons Ind Sch Dist/*Blackwell*	1	153	301
Highland Ind School Dist/*Roscoe*	1	250	301
Roscoe Collegiate Ind Sch Dist/*Roscoe*	3	620	301
Sweetwater ISD School Dist/*Sweetwater*	5	2,200	301
NUECES			
Agua Dulce Ind School Dist/*Agua Dulce*	2	370	302
Banquete Ind School Dist/*Banquete*	3	954	302
Bishop Cons Ind School Dist/*Bishop*	5	1,472	302
Calallen Ind School Dist/*Corp Christi*	6	4,000	302
Corpus Christi Ind Sch Dist/*Corp Christi*	58	38,094	303
Diocese Corpus Christi Ed Off/*Corp Christi*	16	3,300	306
Driscoll Ind School Dist/*Driscoll*	1	320	304
Ed Service Center Region 2/*Corp Christi*			306
Flour Bluff Ind School Dist/*Corp Christi*	7	5,750	304
London Ind School Dist/*Corp Christi*	1	900	305
Port Aransas Ind School Dist/*Port Aransas*	3	550	305
Robstown Ind School Dist/*Robstown*	7	2,000	305
Tuloso-Midway Ind School Dist/*Corp Christi*	5	4,000	305
West Oso Ind School Dist/*Corp Christi*	4	2,104	306
OCHILTREE			
Perryton Ind School Dist/*Perryton*	6	2,217	307
OLDHAM			
Adrian Ind School Dist/*Adrian*	1	120	307
Boys Ranch Ind School Dist/*Boys Ranch*	3	254	307
Vega Ind School Dist/*Vega*	2	380	307
Wildorado Ind Sch Dist/*Wildorado*	1	180	308
ORANGE			
Bridge City Ind School Dist/*Bridge City*	4	2,953	308
Deweyville Ind School Dist/*Orange*	2	550	308
Little Cypress Mauriceville SD/*Orange*	6	3,100	308
Orangefield Ind School Dist/*Orange*	3	1,785	309
Vidor Ind School Dist/*Vidor*	7	5,000	309
West Orange-Cove Cons ISD/*Orange*	4	2,487	309
PALO PINTO			
Gordon Ind School Dist/*Gordon*	1	200	310
Graford Ind School Dist/*Graford*	2	340	310
Mineral Wells Ind School Dist/*Mineral Wells*	6	3,200	310
Palo Pinto Ind Sch Dist 906/*Palo Pinto*	1	112	310
Santo Ind School Dist/*Santo*	2	475	310
Strawn Ind School Dist/*Strawn*	1	167	311
PANOLA			
Beckville Ind School Dist/*Beckville*	2	700	311
Carthage Ind School Dist/*Carthage*	6	2,692	311
Gary Ind School Dist/*Gary*	1	500	311
PARKER			
Aledo Ind School Dist/*Aledo*	10	6,000	312
Brock Ind School Dist/*Brock*	4	1,376	312
Garner Ind School Dist/*Weatherford*	1	200	312
Millsap Ind School Dist/*Millsap*	3	994	312
Peaster Ind School Dist/*Weatherford*	3	1,200	313
Poolville Ind School Dist/*Poolville*	3	530	313
Springtown Ind School Dist/*Springtown*	6	3,470	313
Weatherford Ind School Dist/*Weatherford*	12	8,000	313
PARMER			
Bovina Ind School Dist/*Bovina*	3	490	314
Farwell Ind School Dist/*Farwell*	3	522	314
Friona Ind School Dist/*Friona*	4	1,117	315
Lazbuddie Ind School Dist/*Lazbuddie*	1	201	315
PECOS			
Buena Vista Ind School Dist/*Imperial*	1	244	315
Ft Stockton Ind School Dist/*Fort Stockton*	5	2,479	315
Iraan-Sheffield Ind Sch Dist/*Iraan*	3	422	316
POLK			
Big Sandy Ind School Dist/*Livingston*	1	525	316
Corrigan-Camden Ind Sch Dist/*Corrigan*	3	850	316
Goodrich Ind School Dist/*Goodrich*	2	235	316
Leggett Ind School Dist/*Leggett*	1	185	316
Livingston Ind School Dist/*Livingston*	7	3,963	316
Onalaska Ind School Dist/*Onalaska*	2	1,000	317
POTTER			
Amarillo Ind School Dist/*Amarillo*	55	33,754	317
Bushland Ind School Dist/*Amarillo*	3	1,500	319
Diocese of Amarillo Ed Office/*Amarillo*	5	850	319
Highland Park Ind School Dist/*Amarillo*	3	850	319
River Road Ind School Dist/*Amarillo*	4	1,278	319
PRESIDIO			
Marfa Ind School Dist/*Marfa*	2	342	320
Presidio Ind School Dist/*Presidio*	3	1,162	320
RAINS			
Rains Ind School Dist/*Emory*	4	1,650	320
RANDALL			
Canyon Ind School Dist/*Canyon*	16	10,200	320
Region 16 Ed Service Center/*Amarillo*			321
REAGAN			
Reagan Co Ind School Dist/*Big Lake*	3	950	321
REAL			
Leakey Ind School Dist/*Leakey*	1	309	322
RED RIVER			
Avery Ind School Dist/*Avery*	2	365	322
Clarksville Ind School Dist/*Clarksville*	2	585	322
Detroit Ind School Dist/*Detroit*	3	540	322
Rivercrest Ind School Dist/*Bogata*	3	735	322
REEVES			
Balmorhea Ind School Dist/*Balmorhea*	1	165	323
Pecos-Barstow-Toyah Ind SD/*Pecos*	5	2,800	323
REFUGIO			
Austwell Tivoli Ind SD/*Tivoli*	2	140	323
Refugio Ind School Dist/*Refugio*	3	690	323
Woodsboro Ind School Dist/*Woodsboro*	2	420	324
ROBERTS			

School Year 2019-2020 800-333-8802

COUNTY INDEX

Market Data Retrieval

COUNTY District/City	NO. OF SCHOOLS	ENROLL-MENT	PAGE
Miami Ind School Dist/*Miami*	1	220	324
ROBERTSON			
Bremond Ind School Dist/*Bremond*	3	507	324
Calvert Ind School Dist/*Calvert*	1	164	324
Franklin Ind School Dist/*Franklin*	3	1,100	324
Hearne Ind School Dist/*Hearne*	3	860	325
ROCKWALL			
Rockwall Ind School Dist/*Rockwall*	20	16,270	325
Royse City Ind School Dist/*Royse City*	9	6,300	326
RUNNELS			
Ballinger Ind School Dist/*Ballinger*	3	911	326
Miles Ind School Dist/*Miles*	1	440	326
Olfen Ind School Dist/*Rowena*	1	93	327
Winters Ind School Dist/*Winters*	3	544	327
RUSK			
Carlisle Ind School Dist/*Henderson*	1	650	327
Henderson Ind School Dist/*Henderson*	6	3,040	327
Laneville Ind School Dist/*Laneville*	1	182	327
Leveretts Chapel Ind Sch Dist/*Overton*	1	259	328
Mt Enterprise Ind School Dist/*Mt Enterprise*	1	400	328
Overton Ind School Dist/*Overton*	2	500	328
Tatum Ind School Dist/*Tatum*	4	1,622	328
West Rusk Co Cons Ind Sch Dist/*New London*	4	1,150	328
SABINE			
Hemphill Ind School Dist/*Hemphill*	3	900	329
West Sabine Ind Sch Dist/*Pineland*	2	600	329
SAN AUGUSTINE			
Broaddus Ind School Dist/*Broaddus*	2	400	329
San Augustine Ind School Dist/*San Augustine*	2	763	329
SAN JACINTO			
Coldspring-Oakhurst Cons ISD/*Coldspring*	4	1,525	330
Shepherd Ind School Dist/*Shepherd*	4	2,000	330
SAN PATRICIO			
Aransas Pass Ind School Dist/*Aransas Pass*	5	1,474	330
Gregory-Portland Ind Sch Dist/*Portland*	7	4,600	330
Ingleside Ind School Dist/*Ingleside*	5	2,235	331
Mathis Ind School Dist/*Mathis*	4	1,635	331
Odem-Edroy Ind School Dist/*Odem*	4	900	331
Sinton Ind School Dist/*Sinton*	4	2,202	332
Taft Ind School Dist/*Taft*	3	1,100	332
SAN SABA			
Cherokee Ind School Dist/*Cherokee*	1	110	332
Richland Springs Ind Sch Dist/*Richland Spgs*	1	120	332
San Saba Ind School Dist/*San Saba*	3	750	332
SCHLEICHER			
Schleicher Co Ind Sch Dist/*Eldorado*	3	590	333
SCURRY			
Hermleigh Ind School Dist/*Hermleigh*	1	250	333
Ira Ind School Dist/*Ira*	1	270	333
Snyder Ind School Dist/*Snyder*	4	2,650	333
SHACKELFORD			
Albany Ind School Dist/*Albany*	2	500	334
Moran Ind School Dist/*Moran*	1	120	334
SHELBY			
Center Ind School Dist/*Center*	6	2,600	334
Excelsior Ind School Dist/*Center*	1	90	334
Joaquin Ind School Dist/*Joaquin*	3	650	335
Shelbyville Ind School Dist/*Shelbyville*	3	790	335
Tenaha Ind School Dist/*Tenaha*	1	570	335
Timpson Ind School Dist/*Timpson*	3	630	335
SHERMAN			
Stratford Ind School Dist/*Stratford*	3	585	336
Texhoma Ind School Dist/*Texhoma*	1	115	336
SMITH			
Arp Ind School Dist/*Arp*	3	900	336
Bullard Ind School Dist/*Bullard*	6	2,500	336
Chapel Hill Ind School Dist/*Tyler*	5	3,513	337
Diocese of Tyler Ed Office/*Tyler*	4	1,300	339
Lindale Ind School Dist/*Lindale*	6	4,200	337
Troup Ind School Dist/*Troup*	3	1,081	337
Tyler Ind School Dist/*Tyler*	30	18,600	337
UT Tyler University Acad Dist/*Tyler*	3	700	338
Whitehouse Ind School Dist/*Whitehouse*	8	4,800	338
Winona Ind School Dist/*Winona*	4	1,050	339

COUNTY District/City	NO. OF SCHOOLS	ENROLL-MENT	PAGE
SOMERVELL			
Glen Rose Ind School Dist/*Glen Rose*	4	1,882	340
STARR			
Rio Grande City Ind Sch Dist/*Rio Grande Cy*	18	9,876	340
Roma Ind School Dist/*Roma*	10	6,400	341
San Isidro Ind School Dist/*San Isidro*	1	250	341
STEPHENS			
Breckenridge Ind School Dist/*Breckenridge*	5	1,465	341
STERLING			
Sterling City Ind School Dist/*Sterling City*	2	320	342
STONEWALL			
Aspermont Ind School Dist/*Aspermont*	2	240	342
SUTTON			
Sonora Ind School Dist/*Sonora*	3	760	342
SWISHER			
Happy Ind School Dist/*Happy*	2	254	342
Kress Ind School Dist/*Kress*	2	280	343
Tulia Ind School Dist/*Tulia*	4	1,099	343
TARRANT			
Arlington Ind School Dist/*Arlington*	78	60,000	343
Azle Ind School Dist/*Azle*	12	6,000	345
Birdville Ind School Dist/*Haltom City*	33	23,513	346
Carroll Independent Sch Dist/*Southlake*	11	8,000	347
Castleberry Ind School Dist/*Fort Worth*	7	3,900	347
Crowley Ind School Dist/*Crowley*	25	15,215	347
Diocese of Fort Worth Ed Off/*Fort Worth*	19	5,961	358
Eagle Mtn-Saginaw Ind Sch Dist/*Saginaw*	27	21,000	348
Everman Ind School Dist/*Fort Worth*	11	6,800	349
Ft Worth Ind School Dist/*Fort Worth*	134	86,000	349
Grapevine-Colleyville Ind SD/*Grapevine*	21	14,000	353
Hurst-Euless-Bedford ISD/*Bedford*	31	23,000	353
Keller Ind School Dist/*Keller*	42	34,512	354
Kennedale Ind School Dist/*Kennedale*	6	3,200	355
Lake Worth Ind School Dist/*Lake Worth*	6	3,000	356
Mansfield Ind School Dist/*Mansfield*	44	34,309	356
Region 11 Ed Service Center/*WHT Settlemt*			360
White Settlement Ind Sch Dist/*Fort Worth*	9	6,906	357
TAYLOR			
Abilene Ind School Dist/*Abilene*	26	17,000	360
Jim Ned Cons Ind School Dist/*Tuscola*	4	1,300	361
Merkel Ind School Dist/*Merkel*	3	1,100	361
Region 14 Ed Service Center/*Abilene*			362
Trent Ind School Dist/*Trent*	1	180	361
Wylie Ind School Dist/*Abilene*	7	4,600	361
TERRELL			
Terrell Co Ind School Dist/*Sanderson*	1	130	362
TERRY			
Brownfield Ind Sch Dist/*Brownfield*	5	1,700	362
Meadow Ind School Dist/*Meadow*	1	280	362
Wellman Union Ind School Dist/*Wellman*	1	347	362
THROCKMORTON			
Throckmorton Ind School Dist/*Throckmorton*	1	175	363
Woodson Ind School Dist/*Woodson*	1	150	363
TITUS			
Chapel Hill Ind School Dist/*Mt Pleasant*	3	1,050	363
Harts Bluff Ind School Dist/*Mt Pleasant*	1	640	363
Mt Pleasant Ind School Dist/*Mt Pleasant*	8	5,300	363
TOM GREEN			
Christoval Ind School Dist/*Christoval*	2	500	364
Grape Creek Ind School Dist/*San Angelo*	3	1,160	364
Region 15 Ed Service Center/*San Angelo*			366
San Angelo Ind School Dist/*San Angelo*	25	14,362	364
Veribest Ind School Dist/*Veribest*	1	275	365
Wall Ind School Dist/*Wall*	4	1,100	365
Water Valley Ind School Dist/*Water Valley*	2	300	365
TRAVIS			
Austin Ind School Dist/*Austin*	121	80,100	366
Austin ISD Elem School Area 1/*Austin*			366
Austin ISD Elem School Area 2/*Austin*			367
Austin ISD High School Area/*Austin*			368
Austin ISD Middle School Area/*Austin*			369
Del Valle Ind School Dist/*Del Valle*	15	12,100	370
Diocese of Austin Ed Office/*Austin*	21	5,000	372
Eanes Ind School Dist/*Austin*	9	8,156	370
Lago Vista Ind School Dist/*Lago Vista*	4	1,500	370

TX-R8   800-333-8802   **School Year 2019-2020**

Texas School Directory

COUNTY INDEX

COUNTY District/City	NO. OF SCHOOLS	ENROLL- MENT	PAGE
Lake Travis Ind School Dist/*Austin*	10	10,410	370
Manor Ind School Dist/*Manor*	16	9,200	371
Pflugerville Ind School Dist/*Pflugerville*	33	26,269	371
Region 13 Ed Service Center/*Austin*			373
TRINITY			
Apple Springs Ind School Dist/*Apple Springs*	2	220	374
Centerville Ind School Dist/*Groveton*	2	127	374
Groveton Ind School Dist/*Groveton*	2	750	374
Trinity Ind School Dist/*Trinity*	3	1,280	374
TYLER			
Chester Ind School Dist/*Chester*	2	200	374
Colmesneil Ind School Dist/*Colmesneil*	2	475	375
Spurger Ind School Dist/*Spurger*	2	385	375
Warren Ind School Dist/*Warren*	4	1,400	375
Woodville Ind School Dist/*Woodville*	4	1,300	375
UPSHUR			
Big Sandy Ind School Dist/*Big Sandy*	3	650	376
Gilmer Ind School Dist/*Gilmer*	4	2,437	376
Harmony Ind School Dist/*Big Sandy*	4	1,060	376
New Diana Ind School Dist/*Diana*	3	1,071	376
Ore City Ind School Dist/*Ore City*	3	950	376
Union Grove Ind School Dist/*Gladewater*	2	750	377
Union Hill Ind School Dist/*Gilmer*	1	400	377
UPTON			
McCamey Ind School Dist/*Mc Camey*	3	560	377
Rankin Ind School Dist/*Rankin*	2	320	377
UVALDE			
Knippa Ind School Dist/*Knippa*	1	475	378
Sabinal Ind School Dist/*Sabinal*	2	500	378
Utopia Ind School Dist/*Utopia*	1	232	378
Uvalde Cons Ind School Dist/*Uvalde*	7	4,221	378
VAL VERDE			
Comstock Ind School Dist/*Comstock*	1	227	379
San Felipe-Del Rio Cons Ind SD/*Del Rio*	12	10,472	379
VAN ZANDT			
Canton Ind School Dist/*Canton*	4	2,300	380
Edgewood Ind School Dist/*Edgewood*	4	975	380
Fruitvale Ind School Dist/*Fruitvale*	3	460	380
Grand Saline Ind School Dist/*Grand Saline*	4	1,100	380
Martin's Mill Ind Sch Dist/*Ben Wheeler*	1	230	381
Van Ind School Dist/*Van*	5	2,400	381
Wills Point Ind School Dist/*Wills Point*	5	2,415	381
VICTORIA			
Bloomington Ind School Dist/*Bloomington*	4	900	381
Diocese of Victoria Ed Office/*Victoria*	13	2,827	382
Nursery ISD School Dist/*Victoria*	1	120	382
Region 3 Ed Service Center/*Victoria*			383
Victoria Ind School Dist/*Victoria*	23	13,900	382
WALKER			
Huntsville Ind School Dist/*Huntsville*	9	6,100	383
New Waverly Ind School Dist/*New Waverly*	4	1,000	383
Region 6 Ed Service Center/*Huntsville*			384
WALLER			
Hempstead Ind School Dist/*Hempstead*	3	1,600	384
Royal Ind School Dist/*Pattison*	4	2,400	384
Waller Ind School Dist/*Waller*	8	7,700	384
WARD			
Grandfalls-Royalty Ind SD/*Grandfalls*	1	185	385
Monahans-Wickett-Pyote ISD/*Monahans*	6	2,300	385
WASHINGTON			
Brenham Ind School Dist/*Brenham*	7	5,000	385
Burton Ind School Dist/*Burton*	2	455	386
WEBB			
Diocese of Laredo Ed Office/*Laredo*	6	2,131	388
Laredo Ind School Dist/*Laredo*	33	23,737	386
United Ind School Dist/*Laredo*	47	45,000	387
Webb Cons Ind School Dist/*Bruni*	3	272	388
WHARTON			
Boling Ind School Dist/*Boling*	3	1,000	389
East Bernard Ind Sch Dist/*East Bernard*	3	950	389
El Campo Ind School Dist/*El Campo*	5	3,600	389
Louise Ind School Dist/*Louise*	3	500	389
Wharton Ind School Dist/*Wharton*	5	2,097	390
WHEELER			
Ft Elliott Cons Ind Sch Dist/*Briscoe*	1	138	390
Kelton Ind School Dist/*Wheeler*	1	95	390
Shamrock Ind School Dist/*Shamrock*	3	426	390
Wheeler Ind School Dist/*Wheeler*	1	487	391
WICHITA			
Burkburnett Ind Sch Dist/*Burkburnett*	6	3,350	391
City View Ind School Dist/*Wichita Falls*	2	1,058	391
Electra Ind School Dist/*Electra*	3	430	391
Iowa Park Consolidated Ind SD/*Iowa Park*	4	1,839	392
Region 9 Ed Service Center/*Wichita Falls*			393
Wichita Falls Ind School Dist/*Wichita Falls*	28	14,500	392
WILBARGER			
Harrold Ind School Dist/*Harrold*	1	110	393
Northside Ind School Dist/*Vernon*	1	230	393
Vernon Ind School Dist/*Vernon*	6	1,700	393
WILLACY			
Lasara Ind School Dist/*Lasara*	2	380	394
Lyford Cons Ind School Dist/*Lyford*	3	1,551	394
Raymondville Ind Sch Dist/*Raymondville*	5	2,000	394
San Perlita Ind School Dist/*San Perlita*	1	282	394
WILLIAMSON			
Coupland Ind School Dist/*Coupland*	1	175	395
Florence Ind School Dist/*Florence*	3	1,065	395
Georgetown Ind School Dist/*Georgetown*	17	10,946	395
Granger Ind School Dist/*Granger*	1	460	396
Hutto Ind School Dist/*Hutto*	9	7,500	396
Jarrell Ind School Dist/*Jarrell*	5	1,850	396
Leander Ind School Dist/*Leander*	43	41,000	396
Liberty Hill Ind School Dist/*Liberty Hill*	6	4,476	398
Round Rock Ind School Dist/*Round Rock*	54	50,546	398
Taylor Ind School Dist/*Taylor*	7	3,280	399
Thrall Ind School Dist/*Thrall*	3	720	400
WILSON			
Floresville Ind School Dist/*Floresville*	5	4,000	400
La Vernia Ind School Dist/*La Vernia*	4	3,360	401
Poth Ind School Dist/*Poth*	3	840	401
Stockdale Ind School Dist/*Stockdale*	3	803	401
WINKLER			
Kermit Ind School Dist/*Kermit*	3	1,418	401
Wink Loving Ind School Dist/*Wink*	2	440	402
WISE			
Alvord Ind School Dist/*Alvord*	3	709	402
Boyd Ind School Dist/*Boyd*	4	1,317	402
Bridgeport Ind School Dist/*Bridgeport*	5	2,062	402
Chico Ind School Dist/*Chico*	3	600	403
Decatur Ind School Dist/*Decatur*	5	3,390	403
Paradise Ind School Dist/*Paradise*	4	1,200	403
Slidell Ind School Dist/*Slidell*	2	282	403
WOOD			
Alba-Golden Ind School Dist/*Alba*	2	850	404
Hawkins Ind School Dist/*Hawkins*	3	735	404
Mineola Ind School Dist/*Mineola*	4	1,630	404
Quitman Ind School Dist/*Quitman*	3	1,121	404
Winnsboro Ind School Dist/*Winnsboro*	3	1,496	405
Yantis Ind School Dist/*Yantis*	2	370	405
YOAKUM			
Denver City Ind School Dist/*Denver City*	5	1,741	405
Plains Ind School Dist/*Plains*	3	430	405
YOUNG			
Graham Ind School Dist/*Graham*	5	2,390	406
Newcastle Ind School Dist/*Newcastle*	1	180	406
Olney Ind School Dist/*Olney*	3	700	406
ZAPATA			
Zapata Co Ind School Dist/*Zapata*	6	3,521	406
ZAVALA			
Crystal City Ind School Dist/*Crystal City*	5	1,500	407
La Pryor Ind School Dist/*La Pryor*	2	500	407

Texas School Directory

DISTRICT PERSONNEL INDEX

NAME/District	JOB FUNCTIONS	PAGE

A

NAME/District	JOB FUNCTIONS	PAGE
Aaron, Mary/*Floresville Ind School Dist*	5	400
Aaron, Shelia/*Yantis Ind School Dist*	29	405
Abadie, Melissa/*Waxahachie Ind School Dist*	43,285	142
Abaraham, Ollie/*Post Ind School Dist*	5	162
Abbett, Brian/*Garland Ind School Dist*	5	105
Abbott, Clarissa/*McAllen Ind School Dist*	39	221
Abbott, Laura/*Lake Travis Ind School Dist*	58,271	370
Abbott, Paula/*Mart Ind School Dist*	4	280
Abbott, Tonya/*Poteet Ind School Dist*	16,82	21
Abernethy, Elizabeth/*Region 7 Ed Service Center*	1	171
Abila, Samantha/*Dublin Ind School Dist*	58	143
Abitua, Jesse/*Benavides Ind School Dist*	67	128
Abla, Kurtis/*Dalhart Ind School Dist*	88	95
Ables, Mitch/*Hawley Ind School Dist*	6	250
Abott, John, Dr/*Mineola Ind School Dist*	67	404
Abrams, Dalton/*UT Tyler University Acad Dist*	73	338
Abrigo, Janie/*Roscoe Collegiate Ind Sch Dist*	58	301
Abrigo, Yolanda/*Alice Ind School Dist*	16,73,76,82,286,295	245
Abron, Triston/*Pewitt Cons Ind School Dist*	6	296
Abshier, Cody/*Liberty Ind School Dist*	1	266
Abshier, John/*Groveton Ind School Dist*	5	374
Abston, Shean/*Morton Ind School Dist*	6	75
Abundez, Paul/*La Villa Ind School Dist*	274	220
Abundis, David/*South San Antonio Ind Sch Dist*	11,296	42
Acevedo, Evaristo/*Klondike Ind School Dist*	3	117
Aceves, Debra, Dr/*Donna Ind School Dist*	13,57,61,81	215
Ach, Rachel/*Borger Ind School Dist*	16	237
Achs, Dawn, Sr/*Diocese of Dallas Ed Office*	15,68	113
Acker, Marvin/*Jacksonville Ind School Dist*	91	73
Ackley, Karol/*Paris Ind School Dist*	11	260
Ackley, Stacy/*Royal Ind School Dist*	1	384
Acklin, Teresa/*Prairie Lea Ind School Dist*	6	61
Ackmann, Leslie/*Weatherford Ind School Dist*	58,275	313
Acock, Dana/*Grand Prairie Ind School Dist*	5	107
Acosta, Adrian/*Houston Ind School Dist*	16	188
Acosta, Henry/*Northside Ind School Dist*	15	36
Acosta, Jorge/*Irving Ind School Dist*	68	109
Acosta, Salvadore/*Progreso Ind School Dist*	11	224
Acosta, Simona/*Pecos-Barstow-Toyah Ind SD*	7	323
Acuna, Gene/*Texas Dept of Education*	71	1
Adam, Jerry, Dr/*Comfort Ind School Dist*	8,12,57,74,83,288	254
Adame, Roger/*Mercedes Ind School Dist*	6	221
Adams-Molina, Georgeanna/*Buffalo Ind School Dist*	11,73,271,286	264
Adams, Amanda/*West Ind School Dist*	8	282
Adams, Angela/*Winona Ind School Dist*	13,58	339
Adams, Bunny/*Vidor Ind School Dist*	9,11,93,286,288,296,298	309
Adams, Carolyn/*Gruver Ind School Dist*	60	176
Adams, Casey/*Woodson Ind School Dist*	1,11,83,84,288	363
Adams, Donna/*Jasper Ind School Dist*	5	240
Adams, Felicia/*Houston ISD-Achieve 180*	15	188
Adams, Greta/*Anna Ind School Dist*	16	77
Adams, Jason/*Fairfield Ind School Dist*	1	156
Adams, Jeff/*Farmersville Ind School Dist*	1	78
Adams, Jennifer/*Frisco Ind School Dist*	81	78
Adams, Jennifer/*Tomball Ind School Dist*	42	203
Adams, Jimmy/*Kennedale Ind School Dist*	2	355
Adams, John/*El Paso Ind School Dist*	35	132
Adams, Kamara/*Kingsville Ind School Dist*	8,15	257
Adams, Katie/*UT Tyler University Acad Dist*	27	338
Adams, Keith/*Sunnyvale Ind School Dist*	3	113
Adams, Kelly/*Denver City Ind School Dist*	4,8,11,58,83,88,271	405
Adams, Lisa/*Temple Ind School Dist*	10,15	29
Adams, Matt/*Peaster Ind School Dist*	1	313
Adams, Molly/*Aransas Co Ind School Dist*	12	19
Adams, Scott/*Mabank Ind School Dist*	2,15	252
Adams, Shannon/*Evadale Ind School Dist*	3,5,91	240
Adams, Shay/*Lovejoy Ind School Dist*	2,19	80
Adams, Sheila/*Lufkin Ind School Dist*	71	18
Adams, Stacie/*Castleberry Ind School Dist*	48	347
Adams, Stephanie/*Rockwall Ind School Dist*	67	325
Adams, Tammy/*West Hardin Co Cons Sch Dist*	7	178
Adams, Travis/*Guthrie Common School Dist*	67	257
Adams, Vicky/*Hillsboro Ind School Dist*	1	227
Adcock, Joe/*Clifton Ind School Dist*	3,5	46
Adcock, Katrina/*Kopperl Ind School Dist*	1,73	47
Adcock, Katrina/*Kopperl Ind School Dist*	8,11	47
Adcox, Garri/*Hurst-Euless-Bedford ISD*	46	353
Adermann, Carla/*Northside Ind School Dist*	69	36
Adix, Kenneth/*Round Rock Ind School Dist*	19	398
Adkin, William/*Judson Ind School Dist*	2,19	33
Adkins, Craig/*Jacksboro Ind Sch Dist*	3,4,91	239
Adkins, Cyril/*Smithville Ind School Dist*	6	24
Adkins, Mike/*Ector Co Ind School Dist*	71	130
Adkins, Norman/*Millsap Ind School Dist*	3	312
Adkinson, Christi/*Roby Cons Ind School Dist*	4	148
Adkison, Amie/*Garrison Ind School Dist*	7	297
Adkison, Rebecca/*Excelsior Ind School Dist*	34	334
Adrian-Garcia, Jose/*Pharr-San Juan-Alamo Ind SD*	98	223
Adrian, Stacy/*Crowley Ind School Dist*	2,19	347
Agee, Danny/*Salado Ind School Dist*	3,5	29
Aghazadian, Megan/*Texas Dept of Education*	15	1
Agnew, Karen/*Troup Ind School Dist*	33	337
Aguero, Elispo/*La Pryor Ind School Dist*	6	407
Aguero, Oscar/*Marfa Ind School Dist*	1	320
Aguilar, Abel/*Weslaco Ind School Dist*	15	225
Aguilar, Anna/*Sulphur Springs Ind Sch Dist*	57,271	232
Aguilar, Antonio/*La Feria Ind School Dist*	2,19	65
Aguilar, Hortencia/*Fort Davis Ind School Dist*	13	241
Aguilar, Magdalena, Dr/*Socorro Ind School Dist*	88	135
Aguilera, Becky/*Palacios Ind School Dist*	91	275
Aguillon, Charles/*Lake Travis Ind School Dist*	20,23	370
Aguirre, Andreas/*San Saba Ind School Dist*	6	332
Aguirre, Angelica/*Tahoka Ind School Dist*	73,98,286	273
Aguirre, Angelica/*Tahoka Ind School Dist*	16,73,98,286,295	273
Aguirre, Antonio, Dr/*Austwell Tivoli Ind SD*	83	323
Aguirre, Armando, Dr/*Region 19 Ed Service Center*	1	139
Agular, Matthew/*Dilley Ind School Dist*	73	157
Ailara, Michelle/*Red Oak Ind School Dist*	15,68,79	142
Ailshie, Jeanne/*Coleman Ind School Dist*	69	76
Airheart, Eric/*Trinidad Ind School Dist*	67	214
Akers, Ellen/*Pearland Ind School Dist*	69	53
Akin, Gina/*Kilgore Ind School Dist*	58	169
Akin, Lynn/*Lubbock Ind School Dist*	79,88	270
Akins, Jennifer/*McKinney Ind School Dist*	36	81
Akins, Sue/*Anna Ind School Dist*	8,15	77
Akridge, Tonja/*Lufkin Ind School Dist*	90,93	18
Akuna, James/*Lockhart Ind School Dist*	4	61
Alaman, Kandy/*Coahoma Ind School Dist*	67	234
Alambar, Marie/*Trent Ind School Dist*	57,58	361
Alana, Nancy/*Granbury Ind School Dist*	67	230
Alandzes, Mandy/*Braination Schools*	4	30
Alanis, Claudia/*Midland Ind School Dist*	294	285
Alanis, Frank/*Progreso Ind School Dist*	67	224
Alaniz-Ramos, Delma/*Laredo Ind School Dist*	69,294	386
Alaniz, Adelina/*Mission Cons Ind School Dist*	45	222
Alaniz, Eduardo/*Mission Cons Ind School Dist*	88	222
Alaniz, Samuel/*Medina Valley Ind School Dist*	297	284
Alarcon, Theresa/*Point Isabel Ind Sch Dist*	1	66
Alawneh, John, Dr/*Katy Ind School Dist*	71,76,97,286	151
Albert, Melvin/*Floresville Ind School Dist*	295	400
Albracht, Ralph/*Nazareth Ind School Dist*	3,5	71
Albright, James/*Aspermont Ind School Dist*	3,91	342
Albright, Janet/*Spring Hill Ind School Dist*	4	170
Albritton, Jodie/*Bullard Ind School Dist*	69	336
Albritton, Rick/*Gilmer Ind School Dist*	1	376
Albro, Josh/*Burnet Cons Ind Sch Dist*	5	60
Albus, Anthony/*Whitharral Ind School Dist*	67	230
Albus, Joe/*Knox City-O'Brien Cons Ind SD*	67	258
Alcorn, Bill/*Haskell Cons Ind School Dist*	1	210
Alcorta, Andrew/*Anton ISD School Dist*	4	229
Alcorta, Joe, Dr/*Dalhart Ind School Dist*	1,11	95
Aldarado, Mary/*Greenwood Ind School Dist*	57,271	285
Alday, Esmeralda/*San Antonio Ind School Dist*	57	39
Alderete, Juan/*Region 19 Ed Service Center*	58	139
Alderman, Charles/*Commerce Independent Sch Dist*	1,57	236
Alderson, Holly/*Tuloso-Midway Ind School Dist*	8,11,57,92,296	305
Alderson, Linda/*Louise Ind School Dist*	67	389
Alderson, Sadie/*Lubbock-Cooper Ind Sch Dist*	71	271
Alejandro, Elda/*Knippa Ind School Dist*	1	378

School Year 2019-2020   800-333-8802   TX-T1

DISTRICT PERSONNEL INDEX

Market Data Retrieval

NAME/District	JOB FUNCTIONS	PAGE
Alejandro, Lori/*Killeen Ind School Dist*	4	27
Aleman, Brenda, Dr/*Crosby Ind School Dist*	47	183
Aleman, Josh/*S & S Cons Ind School Dist*	6	167
Alexander, Alex/*Lewisville Ind School Dist*	58	122
Alexander, Brenda/*Memphis Ind School Dist*	2	175
Alexander, Darrell/*Alief Ind School Dist*	68	181
Alexander, Deanna/*Yantis Ind School Dist*	58	405
Alexander, Hedda/*Jacksonville Ind School Dist*	16,73,76,84,98,295	73
Alexander, Jeanette/*Midway Ind School Dist*	41,44	280
Alexander, Keimesha/*Chilton Ind School Dist*	58	144
Alexander, Ken/*Hamilton Ind School Dist*	2,11,73	176
Alexander, Kim/*Millsap Ind School Dist*	2	312
Alexander, Kim, Dr/*Roscoe Collegiate Ind Sch Dist*	1	301
Alexander, Marsha/*Roscoe Collegiate Ind Sch Dist*	36,83,88,271,273	301
Alexander, Michelle/*Winters Ind School Dist*	68	327
Alexander, Phillip/*Rains Ind School Dist*	67	320
Alexander, Rhonda/*Sweeny Ind School Dist*	58	54
Alexander, Steve/*West Rusk Co Cons Ind Sch Dist*	4	328
Alexander, Vern, Dr/*Grand Prairie Ind School Dist*	15,72,294	107
Alexander, William/*Memphis Ind School Dist*	1	175
Alfaro, Frank/*Alamo Heights Ind School Dist*	10,12,15,57,88	30
Alfaro, Tony/*Goose Creek Cons Ind Sch Dist*	91	187
Alfaro, Veronica/*Santa Gertrudis Ind School Dist*	1	258
Alford, Alicia/*Mansfield Ind School Dist*	297	356
Alford, Brian/*Farmersville Ind School Dist*	91	78
Alford, Debbie, Dr/*Brownsville Ind School Dist*	30	63
Alford, Eddie/*Azle Ind School Dist*	16,73,297	345
Alford, Wayne/*Hemphill Ind School Dist*	3,5	329
Alfred, Christie/*Mansfield Ind School Dist*	27,31,74	356
Aliefendic, Jasna, Dr/*Garland Ind School Dist*	73	105
Allen, Arthur/*Pasadena Ind School Dist*	73,98,286	198
Allen, Brent/*Highland Ind School Dist*	67	301
Allen, Bryan/*Merkel Ind School Dist*	1	361
Allen, Carlotta/*Stafford Municipal Sch Dist*	8,273,285	155
Allen, Chad/*Hitchcock Ind School Dist*	67	161
Allen, Cheryl/*Italy Ind School Dist*	57	140
Allen, Chris, Dr/*Marble Falls Ind School Dist*	1	60
Allen, Dale/*Industrial Ind School Dist*	67	240
Allen, Dana/*Sinton Ind School Dist*	15,68	332
Allen, Danna/*Godley Ind School Dist*	76	247
Allen, Darla/*Gladewater Ind School Dist*	3,4	169
Allen, David/*Wortham Ind School Dist*	1,11	156
Allen, Edie/*Sanford-Fritch Ind School Dist*	8,15	238
Allen, Elliot/*Brenham Ind School Dist*	6	385
Allen, James/*Bastrop Ind School Dist*	67	23
Allen, Jeff/*Sweetwater ISD School Dist*	67	301
Allen, Jerald/*Crowley Ind School Dist*	73,95,98	347
Allen, Jo/*Dickinson Ind School Dist*	90	159
Allen, Joe/*Marion Ind School Dist*	3	172
Allen, John/*Frankston Ind School Dist*	1	15
Allen, Kaye/*Sherman Ind School Dist*	58,85	167
Allen, Keri/*Penelope ISD School Dist*	58,69	228
Allen, Kerri/*Caddo Mills Ind School Dist*	15	235
Allen, Kim/*Little Cypress Mauriceville SD*	73,84	308
Allen, Lawrence/*Texas Dept of Education*	67	1
Allen, Linda/*White Deer Ind School Dist*	69,88	69
Allen, Mitci/*Lovejoy Ind School Dist*	11,73	80
Allen, Paul/*Sabine Ind School Dist*	5	170
Allen, Paula/*Kopperl Ind School Dist*	58	47
Allen, Regina/*Johnson City Ind School Dist*	16	46
Allen, Richard/*Ft Sam Houston Ind School Dist*	3	32
Allen, Robert/*Rice Ind School Dist*	8,83	300
Allen, Robin/*Robert Lee Ind School Dist*	2	75
Allen, Shannon, Dr/*Beaumont Ind School Dist*	15	241
Allen, Sherry/*Kountze Ind School Dist*	7	178
Allen, Stefani/*Crowley Ind School Dist*	752	347
Allen, Teresa/*Snook Ind School Dist*	83,90	59
Allen, Zach/*Royse City Ind School Dist*	73,98,295	326
Allensworth, Jeff/*Detroit Ind School Dist*	6	322
Allgood, Rena/*Brooksmith Ind School Dist*	2,11	58
Allison, Luke/*Caddo Mills Ind Sch Dist*	1	235
Allison, Tommy/*Robinson Ind School Dist*	6	281
Allman, Darren/*Nacogdoches Ind School Dist*	6	298
Allman, Kristen, Dr/*Klein Ind School Dist*	58	196
Allmond-Helmer, Molly/*Galveston Ind School Dist*	10	160
Allovio, Joy/*Crawford Ind School Dist*	36,69,270	279
Allred, Dina/*Alba-Golden Ind School Dist*	69	404
Allred, Tara/*Ponder Ind School Dist*	8	125
Almaguer, Haley/*Luling Ind School Dist*	7	61
Almanza, Ronny/*Braination Schools*	295	30
Almendarez, Arturo, Dr/*Calallen Ind School Dist*	1	302
Almendarez, Ofelia/*Celina Ind School Dist*	4	77
Alonzo, Veronica, Dr/*Diocese of Dallas Ed Office*	15	113
Alston, Karen/*Miami Ind School Dist*	275	324
Alston, Tresa/*Hedley Ind School Dist*	2	127
Althaus, Monte/*San Angelo Ind School Dist*	91	364
Althof, Crystal/*Roscoe Collegiate Ind Sch Dist*	11	301
Althof, Gregory/*Roscoe Collegiate Ind Sch Dist*	8	301
Alvarado, Christina/*Mathis Ind School Dist*	36,69	331
Alvarado, Jorge/*Waller Ind School Dist*	57	384
Alvarado, Lisa/*New Home Ind School Dist*	4	273
Alvarado, Marco/*Lake Travis Ind School Dist*	71	370
Alvarado, Mariella/*Eagle Mtn-Saginaw Ind Sch Dist*	36	348
Alvarado, Mario/*San Isidro Ind School Dist*	1,73,83,84	341
Alvarado, Patricia/*Irving Ind School Dist*	16	109
Alvarado, R/*West Oso Ind School Dist*	58	306
Alvarado, Rick/*Ed Service Center Region 2*	1,11	306
Alvarado, Rudy/*Wellman Union Ind School Dist*	5	362
Alvarado, Rudy/*Wellman Union Ind School Dist*	3	362
Alvarado, Sandra/*Crystal City Ind School Dist*	16	407
Alvarado, Sara/*Lasara Ind School Dist*	1	394
Alvarado, Steve/*Sabinal Ind School Dist*	88	378
Alvarado, Vanessa/*Hondo Ind School Dist*	30,38	284
Alvardo, Luis/*San Isidro Ind School Dist*	3	341
Alvarenga, Oswaldo/*Dallas Ind School Dist*	285	98
Alvarez, Juan/*Pharr-San Juan-Alamo Ind SD*	751	223
Alvarez, Juan/*Pharr-San Juan-Alamo Ind SD*	15,68	223
Alvarez, Kim/*Alvin Ind School Dist*	68	51
Alvarez, Pam/*Colorado Ind School Dist*	73,295	289
Alvaro, Yolanda/*Tuloso-Midway Ind School Dist*	58	305
Alverado, Tina/*Graford Ind School Dist*	59	310
Alveraz, Shawn/*Kenedy Ind School Dist*	6	251
Alverez, Alison/*Coahoma Ind School Dist*	9,11,16,34,57,271	234
Alverez, Kim/*Copperas Cove Ind School Dist*	294	92
Alves, Steven/*Del Valle Ind School Dist*	3,91	369
Alvey, Susan/*Everman Ind School Dist*	27	349
Alvis, Kelly/*Princeton Ind School Dist*	4	84
Amador, Leeroy/*Galveston Ind School Dist*	91	160
Amarantos, Kristy/*Sheldon Ind School Dist*	68	200
Amaro, Jimmy/*Plemons-Stinnett-Phillips CISD*	8,11,15,69,288	238
Amaya, Jesus/*Los Fresnos Cons Ind Sch Dist*	67	66
Amaya, Leticia/*Midland Ind School Dist*	57	285
Ambridge, Audrey/*Klein Ind School Dist*	2	196
Ambrosee, Debra/*Port Arthur Ind School Dist*	67	243
Amdahl, Scott/*Weslaco Ind School Dist*	73,84	225
Amendola, Willie/*Spring Ind School Dist*	6	202
Amerson, Latonia/*Aldine ISD-Elem Sch Team 1*	15	179
Amezcua, Jesus/*Harris Co Dept of Ed*	2,15	179
Amos, Curtis/*Everman Ind School Dist*	1	349
Amos, Trisha/*Blanket Ind School Dist*	2	58
Ancelet, Jackie/*Groesbeck Ind School Dist*	3	267
Ancell, Sarah/*Lubbock Ind School Dist*	297	270
Anders, Dustin/*Loraine Ind School Dist*	1	289
Andersen, Cynthia/*La Porte Ind School Dist*	58	198

#										
1 Superintendent	16 Instructional Media Svcs	30 Adult Education	44 Science Sec	58 Special Education K-12	72 Summer School	88 Alternative/At Risk	277 Remedial Math K-12
2 Bus/Finance/Purchasing	17 Chief Operations Officer	31 Career/Sch-to-Work K-12	45 Math K-12	59 Special Education Elem	73 Instructional Tech	89 Multi-Cultural Curriculum	280 Literacy Coach
3 Buildings And Grounds	18 Chief Academic Officer	32 Career/Sch-to-Work Elem	46 Math Elem	60 Special Education Sec	74 Inservice Training	90 Social Work	285 STEM
4 Food Service	19 Chief Financial Officer	33 Career/Sch-to-Work Sec	47 Math Sec	61 Foreign/World Lang K-12	75 Marketing/Distributive	91 Safety/Security	286 Digital Learning
5 Transportation	20 Art K-12	34 Early Childhood Ed	48 English/Lang Arts K-12	62 Foreign/World Lang Elem	76 Info Systems	92 Magnet School	288 Common Core Standards
6 Athletic	21 Art Elem	35 Health/Phys Education	49 English/Lang Arts Elem	63 Foreign/World Lang Sec	77 Psychological Assess	93 Parental Involvement	294 Accountability
7 Health Services	22 Art Sec	36 Guidance Services K-12	50 English/Lang Arts Sec	64 Religious Education K-12	78 Affirmative Action	95 Tech Prep Program	295 Network System
8 Curric/Instruct K-12	23 Music K-12	37 Guidance Services Elem	51 Reading K-12	65 Religious Education Elem	79 Student Personnel	97 Chief Information Officer	296 Title II Programs
9 Curric/Instruct Elem	24 Music Elem	38 Guidance Services Sec	52 Reading Elem	66 Religious Education Sec	80 Driver Ed/Safety	98 Chief Technology Officer	297 Webmaster
10 Curric/Instruct Sec	25 Music Sec	39 Social Studies K-12	53 Reading Sec	67 School Board President	81 Gifted/Talented	270 Character Education	298 Grant Writer/Ptnrships
11 Federal Program	26 Business Education	40 Social Studies Elem	54 Remedial Reading K-12	68 Teacher Personnel	82 Video Services	271 Migrant Education	750 Chief Innovation Officer
12 Title I	27 Career & Tech Ed	41 Social Studies Sec	55 Remedial Reading Elem	69 Academic Assessment	83 Substance Abuse Prev	273 Teacher Mentor	751 Chief of Staff
13 Title V	28 Technology Education	42 Science K-12	56 Remedial Reading Sec	70 Research/Development	84 Erate	274 Before/After Sch	752 Social Emotional Learning
15 Asst Superintendent	29 Family/Consumer Science	43 Science Elem	57 Bilingual/ELL	71 Public Information	85 AIDS Education	275 Response To Intervention	

Texas School Directory

DISTRICT PERSONNEL INDEX

NAME/District	JOB FUNCTIONS	PAGE
Anderson, Amy/Angleton Ind School Dist	4	51
Anderson, Amy, Dr/Rockwall Ind School Dist	8,18,273	325
Anderson, Aniece/Holliday Ind School Dist	36,83,88,93,271	19
Anderson, Anne/Texas City Ind School Dist	8	161
Anderson, Chris/Red Oak Ind School Dist	6,35	142
Anderson, Christopher, Dr/Arlington Ind School Dist	20	343
Anderson, Craig/Winnsboro Ind School Dist	73,84,295	405
Anderson, Darren/Wolfe City Ind School Dist	6	237
Anderson, David/Comal Ind School Dist	2,19	87
Anderson, Denise/Bovina Ind School Dist	1	314
Anderson, Emily/Donna Ind School Dist	43	215
Anderson, Grant/Little Elm Ind School Dist	2,15,19	124
Anderson, Greg/Danbury Ind School Dist	1	53
Anderson, Greg/El Campo Ind School Dist	3,17	389
Anderson, Greg/Greenville Ind School Dist	3	236
Anderson, Greg/Royal Ind School Dist	6	384
Anderson, Jackie/Allen Ind School Dist	4	76
Anderson, Jens/Elgin Ind School Dist	6	24
Anderson, Jimmy/Dickinson Ind School Dist	3	159
Anderson, Jimmy/Vernon Ind School Dist	3,5	393
Anderson, John/Red Oak Ind School Dist	67	142
Anderson, John/Sealy Ind School Dist	4	22
Anderson, John/Seymour Ind School Dist	1	25
Anderson, Julia Faye/Laneville Ind School Dist	92,93,270	327
Anderson, Justin/Hull Daisetta Ind School Dist	10,13	266
Anderson, Kimberly/Harlingen Cons Ind School Dist	2	64
Anderson, Kimberly/Trenton Ind School Dist	2	146
Anderson, Leal/Austin Ind School Dist	6	366
Anderson, Lindsay/Keller Ind School Dist	8,15,288	354
Anderson, Lori/Lindale Ind School Dist	11	337
Anderson, Martha/Hawley Ind School Dist	7	250
Anderson, Randy/Lindale Ind School Dist	73,84,295	337
Anderson, Robna/Stanton Ind School Dist	58	274
Anderson, Russell/Hubbard Ind School Dist	6	227
Anderson, Shane/Connally Ind School Dist	6	279
Anderson, Tameka/Alief Ind School Dist	274	181
Anderson, Tanya/Azle Ind School Dist	1	345
Anderson, Teresa/Groveton Ind School Dist	16,82	374
Anderson, Terry/Paris Ind School Dist	3	260
Anderson, Tracy/Harlandale Ind School Dist	27,31	32
Anderson, Valerie/Lamar Cons Ind School Dist	81	153
Anderson, Vonnie/Big Spring Ind School Dist	27,294	233
Anderton, Amy/Dallas Ind School Dist	61	98
Andrajack, Frank/Burkburnett Ind Sch Dist	67	391
Andre, Steve/Mesquite Ind School Dist	20,23	110
Andrews, Brenda/North Zulch Ind School Dist	4	274
Andrews, Jenna/Como Pickton Cons Ind SD	11,58,298	231
Andrews, Judy/Excelsior Ind School Dist	9,11,69	334
Andrews, Kathryn/Deer Park Ind School Dist	39,81	186
Andrews, Mildred/North East Ind School Dist	68	34
Andrews, Sally/Vidor Ind School Dist	71	309
Andrews, Tracy/Canutillo Ind School Dist	27	132
Andrus, Alan/North Zulch Ind School Dist	1,11	274
Andrus, Angee/Huntsville Ind School Dist	69,294	383
Andrus, Darrel/Jourdanton Ind School Dist	6	20
Andrus, James/Slaton Ind School Dist	8,11,15,74,88,275,294	272
Andrus, Lea-Ann/North Zulch Ind School Dist	8	274
Angel, Lance/Bryan Ind School Dist	6	54
Angel, Lance/Palestine Ind School Dist	6	15
Angel, Tawni/Del Valle Ind School Dist	6	369
Angerer, Martha/Southland Ind School Dist	58	162
Angerstein, Josephine/Clint Ind School Dist	58	132
Anglesee, Scott/Kerrville Ind School Dist	4	256
Anglin, Mark/Bloomington Ind School Dist	1	381
Angst, James/Dilley Ind School Dist	58	157
Angst, Jim/Pearsall Ind School Dist	58	157
Anguiano, Maria/Crowley Ind School Dist	57	347
Antes, Kathy/Leakey Ind School Dist	2,297	322
Anthony, Amy/Throckmorton Ind School Dist	36,69,270	363
Anthony, Philip/Princeton Ind School Dist	1	84
Antley, Tina, Dr/Pleasant Grove Ind School Dist	57,63,271	49
Antoine, Roland/Dallas Ind School Dist	73,76,295	98
Antoline, Carlos, Dr/Ft Worth Ind School Dist	77	349
Antonio Lara, Marco/South Texas Ind School Dist	1	67
Anzualda, Maria/Brooks Co Ind School Dist	11,30,88,271	57
Apeldace, Bea/San Elizario Ind School Dist	12,271	135

NAME/District	JOB FUNCTIONS	PAGE
Apodaca, Beatriz/San Elizario Ind School Dist	12	135
Apodaca, Joegr/Ft Hancock Ind School Dist	5	234
Appel, Hope/Vernon Ind School Dist	8,11,57,69,288,294,298	393
Appelt, Jason/Vysehrad Ind School Dist	1,11,83,84	263
Applegate, Angie, Dr/Coppell Ind School Dist	8,15,69	98
Appleton, Ryder/Veribest Ind School Dist	1,11,288	365
Ara, Rosie/Brownsville Ind School Dist	16	63
Aragon, Jake/Dumas Ind School Dist	73,76,95,295	295
Araiza, Humberto/Del Valle Ind School Dist	5	369
Araiza, Humberto/Eagle Pass Ind School Dist	5	276
Arambula, Claudia/Zapata Co Ind School Dist	8	406
Arambula, Maria/United Ind School Dist	57,61	387
Aranda, Joe/United Ind School Dist	5	387
Arbogast, Ted/Terlingua Common School Dist	73,84,285,295	57
Arbuckle, Ginger/Grapeland Ind School Dist	8	232
Arce, Kayla/Raymondville Ind Sch Dist	2	394
Arce, Paul/Rio Hondo Ind School Dist	297	66
Archie, Patricia/Sheldon Ind School Dist	67	200
Archuleta, Rita/Dell City Ind School Dist	2,12	234
Ard, James/Onalaska Ind School Dist	3,4	317
Ard, Susan/Cleveland Ind School Dist	71	265
Areal, Maria/Carrizo Spgs Cons Ind SD	8,288	127
Arevalo, Faviola/Joshua Ind School Dist	57	248
Arfsten, Leslynn/Walcott Ind School Dist	2	119
Arias, Carrie/Friona Ind School Dist	34,58	315
Arias, Jimmy/Friona Ind School Dist	6	315
Arismendi, Jennifer/Corpus Christi Ind Sch Dist	13,58,77	303
Arispe, Sara/Ft Worth Ind School Dist	15,294	349
Arispie, Jodi/Graham Ind School Dist	4	406
Arledge, Jenny/Sulphur Springs Ind Sch Dist	26,27,31,75,95	232
Armacost, Christopher/Hitchcock Ind School Dist	3,73	161
Armand, Richard/Region 4 Ed Service Center	286	208
Armendarez, Ann/Windthorst Ind School Dist	12,57,275	20
Armendariz, Ruben/Presidio Ind School Dist	3,5	320
Armstrong, Dan/Plano Ind School Dist	15,16,73,76,295	82
Armstrong, Jewell/Hallsburg Ind School Dist	2	279
Armstrong, Jim, Dr/West Hardin Co Cons Sch Dist	1	178
Armstrong, Julie/Mason Ind School Dist	69	275
Armstrong, Kenda/Yantis Ind School Dist	57	405
Armstrong, Randy/White Settlement Ind Sch Dist	67	357
Armstrong, Seven/Corrigan-Camden Ind Sch Dist	6	316
Armstrong, Todd/Lindsay Ind School Dist	84	91
Armstrong, Todd/North Zulch Ind School Dist	73,286,295	274
Armstrong, Travis, Dr/Wichita Falls Ind School Dist	34	392
Armstrong, Wanda/Chisum Ind School Dist	4	259
Armstrong, William/Kermit Ind School Dist	8,83,88,288,294,298	401
Armwood, Jackie/Alief Ind School Dist	79	181
Arnett, Karen/Redwater Ind School Dist	79	49
Arnold, Daniel/Calvert Ind School Dist	73,83	324
Arnold, Justin/Overton Ind School Dist	6	328
Arnold, Michelle/Ranger Ind School Dist	11	129
Arnold, Veronica/Sulphur Springs Ind Sch Dist	4	232
Arnst, Karl/Three Rivers Ind School Dist	67	268
Arocha-Gill, Teresa, Dr/Judson Ind School Dist	58,275	33
Arredondo, Azel/Edinburg Cons Ind School Dist	39	216
Arredondo, Henry/San Felipe-Del Rio Cons Ind SD	2,19	379
Arredondo, Jenny/San Antonio Ind School Dist	4	39
Arredondo, Melissa/Alamo Heights Ind School Dist	84	30
Arrington, Dara/Gunter Ind School Dist	8,11,296	166
Arrington, John/Arp Ind School Dist	1	336
Arrington, Vicki/Keller Ind School Dist	74	354
Arriola, Suzette/East Central Ind School Dist	6	31
Arrona, Vanessa/Edinburg Cons Ind School Dist	44	216
Arrott, Brian/Ballinger Ind School Dist	58	326
Arrott, Brian/Winters Ind School Dist	58	327
Arsuaga, Tony/Taft Ind School Dist	83,91	332
Arteaga, Fabian/Winona Ind School Dist	91	339
Arterbury, Laurelyn/Leander Ind School Dist	15	396
Artho, Rhonda/Dumas Ind School Dist	286	295
Arthur, Leighanne/Burleson Ind School Dist	10	246
Arthur, Rachael/Cooper Ind School Dist	2,296,298	119
Arthur, Rachel/Brazosport Ind School Dist	4	52
Arthur, Rachel/Cooper Ind School Dist	296	120
Arzate, Noe/Mt Pleasant Ind School Dist	73,76,295	363
Arzate, Rosalia/Ft Hancock Ind School Dist	7	234
Ascencao, Kristen/Alamo Heights Ind School Dist	69	30

School Year 2019-2020   800-333-8802   TX-T3

DISTRICT PERSONNEL INDEX

Market Data Retrieval

NAME/District	JOB FUNCTIONS	PAGE
Aschenbeck, Paul/*Brenham Ind School Dist*	15	385
Aschenbeck, Ross/*Sonora Ind School Dist*	1	342
Ash, Audrey/*Burkburnett Ind Sch Dist*	58,271	391
Ash, Brad/*Marshall Ind School Dist*	3	209
Ash, Stephen/*Academy Ind School Dist*	85	26
Ashbrooke, Jenay/*Clarendon Cons Ind Sch Dist*	11,88	127
Ashcraft, Vanessa/*Jarrell Ind School Dist*	73	396
Ashley, Dane/*Panhandle Ind School Dist*	6	69
Ashley, Pamela/*Water Valley Ind School Dist*	36,69,88	365
Ashlock, Chad/*Tom Bean Ind School Dist*	38	168
Ashlock, K'Lain/*Howe Ind School Dist*	37	166
Ashmore, Kurt/*Wellington Ind School Dist*	1,11	86
Ashworth, Charles/*Centerville Ind School Dist*	6	374
Askew, Roger/*Spring Hill Ind School Dist*	91	170
Askins, Clint/*Miles Ind School Dist*	1	326
Aspegren, Monica/*Crandall Ind School Dist*	69	251
Aspinall, Jack/*Alvarado Ind School Dist*	4	246
Atchison, John/*Arlington Ind School Dist*	295	343
Atchison, Melissa/*Howe Ind School Dist*	16	166
Atchley, Stephanie/*Stephenville Ind School Dist*	58	144
Atencio, Jennifer/*Allen Ind School Dist*	83	76
Atkeisson, David/*Palestine Ind School Dist*	2,19	15
Atkins, Bob/*Santa Fe Ind School Dist*	3	161
Atkins, Darryl/*Strawn Ind School Dist*	3,5	311
Atkins, Katie, Dr/*Tomball Ind School Dist*	48	203
Atkins, Mary Jane/*Rising Star Ind Sch Dist*	1	129
Atkins, William/*Floresville Ind School Dist*	2,15,91	400
Atkinson, Jeff/*Gregory-Portland Ind Sch Dist*	4	330
Attaway, Buddy/*Jacksonville Ind School Dist*	295	73
Atwood, Kyle/*Alice Ind School Dist*	6	245
Aubin, Brian/*Galena Park Ind School Dist*	4	186
Augsburger, Jo Lynn/*Joshua Ind School Dist*	8,294	248
August, Bobby/*Brownwood Ind School Dist*	3	58
Augustine, David/*Grape Creek Ind School Dist*	5	364
Augustine, Dwaine, Dr/*Hamshire Fannett Ind Sch Dist*	1	242
Auld, George/*Follett Ind School Dist*	1	267
Austin, Sandra, Dr/*Texarkana Ind School Dist*	16,286	50
Austin, Tammy/*Sanger Ind School Dist*	73	126
Autrey, Dusty/*Waxahachie Ind School Dist*	67	142
Autrey, Ken/*Leary Ind School Dist*	67	48
Autry, Jimmy/*Garner Ind School Dist*	73	312
Autry, Pat/*Lindsay Ind School Dist*	8,11,31,58,273	91
Autry, Ryan/*Dilley Ind School Dist*	2	157
Auvenshine, Lee/*Waxahachie Ind School Dist*	15,68	142
Avalos, Garret/*Rankin Ind School Dist*	6	377
Avalos, Rachel/*Bovina Ind School Dist*	7,85	314
Avedikian, Ben/*Hallsville Ind School Dist*	3	208
Avellaneda, Elmer/*Corsicana Ind School Dist*	11,58,77	299
Avena, Belma/*Andrews Ind School Dist*	11,69	16
Avery, Royce, Dr/*Manor Ind School Dist*	1	371
Avieles, Edward/*Morgan Ind School Dist*	6	47
Avila, Joey/*Odem-Edroy Ind School Dist*	73,84,286	331
Avila, Nidia/*Canutillo Ind School Dist*	45	132
Avina, Amy/*Region 19 Ed Service Center*	57	139
Ayala, Bridget/*Medina Valley Ind School Dist*	69	284
Ayala, Flor/*Laredo Ind School Dist*	2,19	386
Ayala, Louisa/*Seagraves Ind School Dist*	4	157
Ayala, Manuel/*Clint Ind School Dist*	15,69,294	132
Ayala, Patricia/*Ysleta Ind School Dist*	71,97	137
Aycock, Brad/*Lorenzo Ind School Dist*	67	94
Ayers, Corey/*Whiteface Con Ind School Dist*	67	75
Ayres, Denise/*Temple Ind School Dist*	31	29
Ayres, Piper/*Evadale Ind School Dist*	57,58,88	240
Ayundis, Anthony/*Monahans-Wickett-Pyote ISD*	58	385
Azaiez, Hafedn, Dr/*Donna Ind School Dist*	1	215
Azam, Bobby, Dr/*Andrews Ind School Dist*	1	16

NAME/District	JOB FUNCTIONS	PAGE
B		
Babcock, Andrew/*Lubbock Ind School Dist*	20,23	269
Babin, Chris/*Lumberton Ind School Dist*	6	178
Babin, Mandy/*Lumberton Ind School Dist*	8	178
Babineaux, Jamie/*Fannindel Ind School Dist*	8,88	120
Babitzke, Debbie/*Booker Ind School Dist*	2	267
Babovec, Chandra/*Scurry Rosser Ind School Dist*	4	253
Baca, Brad/*Pittsburg Ind School Dist*	6	68
Baca, Joe/*Savoy Ind School Dist*	3,5	146
Bacavazos, Eddie/*San Benito Cons Ind Sch Dist*	2	66
Baccus, Jay/*Anson Ind School Dist*	1	249
Bachtel, John/*Fairfield Ind School Dist*	6	156
Bachtel, Tara/*Kemp Ind School Dist*	15	252
Bachus, Shirley/*Pflugerville Ind School Dist*	81	371
Back, Lindsay/*Poolville Ind School Dist*	36,83,270	313
Bacom, Barry/*Lockhart Ind School Dist*	10,83	61
Bacon, Alana/*Elkhart Ind School Dist*	2	15
Bacon, Lisa/*Lancaster Ind School Dist*	274	110
Bacon, William/*Divide Ind School Dist*	1,57,73,83	255
Baehren, Kelly/*Waller Ind School Dist*	8,11,18,288,298,752	384
Baez, Jessie/*Hondo Ind School Dist*	6	284
Baeza, Raquel/*Presidio Ind School Dist*	2	320
Baffern, Lori/*Redwater Ind School Dist*	16,286	49
Bagert, John/*Tyler Ind School Dist*	5	337
Baggs, Melissa/*Collinsville Ind School Dist*	37,69,83	166
Bagwell, Courtney/*Hardin Jefferson Ind Sch Dist*	84	177
Bagwell, Troy/*Decatur Ind School Dist*	73	403
Bahr, Mike/*Red Oak Ind School Dist*	73,76,295	142
Bailes, Susan/*Shepherd Ind School Dist*	67	330
Bailey, Amanda/*Connally Ind School Dist*	4	279
Bailey, Bruce/*Newcastle Ind School Dist*	67	406
Bailey, Daniel/*Slocum ISD School Dist*	67	16
Bailey, Dawn/*Keller Ind School Dist*	52	354
Bailey, Jake/*Olney Ind School Dist*	67	406
Bailey, Jennifer/*Three Way Ind School Dist*	2	144
Bailey, Jeremy/*Yorktown Ind School Dist*	52,59	118
Bailey, Judy/*Whitney Ind School Dist*	4	228
Bailey, Larry/*Pettus Ind School Dist*	3	25
Bailey, Lori/*Texarkana Ind School Dist*	40,49	50
Bailey, Meleta/*Boys Ranch Ind School Dist*	2	307
Bailey, Michelle/*Carrollton-Farmers Branch ISD*	10,15,79	96
Bailey, Tammy/*Advantage Academy Admin Office*	79	96
Bain, Emily/*Bastrop Ind School Dist*	286	23
Bain, Rebecca/*Fruitvale Ind School Dist*	1	380
Baines, Garrett/*Hedley Ind School Dist*	1,11,73	127
Baines, Garrett/*Hedley Ind School Dist*	8	127
Baird, Jeffery/*Huntington Ind School Dist*	73,295	17
Baird, Jerry/*Quanah Ind School Dist*	1	177
Baird, Kelly/*Como Pickton Cons Ind SD*	8	231
Baird, Krista/*Spearman Ind School Dist*	31,36,69	177
Baird, Michelle, Dr/*Greenville Ind School Dist*	34	236
Baird, Paul/*Salado Ind School Dist*	6	29
Baisden, Mark/*Gary Ind School Dist*	73	311
Baker, Amy/*Frenship Ind School Dist*	27	269
Baker, Amy/*Lamesa Ind School Dist*	36	117
Baker, Andrew, Dr/*Kilgore Ind School Dist*	1	169
Baker, Anna/*Quinlan Ind School Dist*	76	237
Baker, Barry, Dr/*Eagle Mtn-Saginaw Ind Sch Dist*	91	348
Baker, Brandi/*Pflugerville Ind School Dist*	8,15	371
Baker, Brent/*Region 8 Ed Service Center*	16,73	69
Baker, Brian/*North Zulch Ind School Dist*	67	274
Baker, Brooke/*Midway Ind School Dist*	83	280
Baker, Bruce/*Crockett Ind School Dist*	5	232
Baker, Carolyn/*Woodsboro Ind School Dist*	7	324
Baker, Charlotte/*Region 3 Ed Service Center*	1	383
Baker, Claudia/*Vysehrad Ind School Dist*	73	263
Baker, Darla/*Splendora Ind School Dist*	2	294

1	Superintendent	16	Instructional Media Svcs	30	Adult Education	44	Science Sec	58	Special Education K-12	72	Summer School
2	Bus/Finance/Purchasing	17	Chief Operations Officer	31	Career/Sch-to-Work K-12	45	Math K-12	59	Special Education Elem	74	Inservice Training
3	Buildings And Grounds	18	Chief Academic Officer	32	Career/Sch-to-Work Elem	46	Math Elem	60	Special Education Sec	75	Marketing/Distributive
4	Food Service	19	Chief Financial Officer	33	Career/Sch-to-Work Sec	47	Math Sec	61	Foreign/World Lang K-12	76	Info Systems
5	Transportation	20	Art K-12	34	Early Childhood Ed	48	English/Lang Arts K-12	62	Foreign/World Lang Elem	77	Psychological Assess
6	Athletic	21	Art Elem	35	Health/Phys Education	49	English/Lang Arts Elem	63	Foreign/World Lang Sec	78	Affirmative Action
7	Health Services	22	Art Sec	36	Guidance Services K-12	50	English/Lang Arts Sec	64	Religious Education K-12	79	Student Personnel
8	Curric/Instruct K-12	23	Music K-12	37	Guidance Services Elem	51	Reading K-12	65	Religious Education Elem	80	Driver Ed/Safety
9	Curric/Instruct Elem	24	Music Elem	38	Guidance Services Sec	52	Reading Elem	66	Religious Education Sec	81	Gifted/Talented
10	Curric/Instruct Sec	25	Music Sec	39	Social Studies K-12	53	Reading Sec	67	School Board President	82	Video Services
11	Federal Program	26	Business Education	40	Social Studies Elem	54	Remedial Reading K-12	68	Teacher Personnel	83	Substance Abuse Prev
12	Title I	27	Career & Tech Ed	41	Social Studies Sec	55	Remedial Reading Elem	69	Academic Assessment	84	Erate
13	Title V	28	Technology Education	42	Science K-12	56	Remedial Reading Sec	70	Research/Development	85	AIDS Education
15	Asst Superintendent	29	Family/Consumer Science	43	Science Elem	57	Bilingual/ELL	71	Public Information		

88	Alternative/At Risk	277	Remedial Math K-12	
89	Multi-Cultural Curriculum	280	Literacy Coach	
90	Social Work	285	STEM	
91	Safety/Security	286	Digital Learning	
92	Magnet School	288	Common Core Standards	
93	Parental Involvement	294	Accountability	
95	Tech Prep Program	295	Network System	
97	Chief Information Officer	296	Title II Programs	
98	Chief Technology Officer	297	Webmaster	
270	Character Education	298	Grant Writer/Ptnrships	
271	Migrant Education	750	Chief Innovation Officer	
273	Teacher Mentor	751	Chief of Staff	
274	Before/After Sch	752	Social Emotional Learning	
275	Response To Intervention			

Texas School Directory

DISTRICT PERSONNEL INDEX

NAME/District	JOB FUNCTIONS	PAGE
Baker, David/*Rochelle Ind School Dist*	3,5	278
Baker, Deann/*Crandall Ind School Dist*	58	251
Baker, Henry/*Trenton Ind School Dist*	67	147
Baker, Jay/*Stanton Ind School Dist*	73,295	274
Baker, Jenney/*Bronte Ind School Dist*	2	75
Baker, Jennifer/*Alief Ind School Dist*	27	181
Baker, Jimmie/*Granger Ind School Dist*	286	396
Baker, Joel/*Baird Ind School Dist*	6	62
Baker, Judy/*Harlingen Cons Ind School Dist*	4,7	64
Baker, Julie/*Aledo Ind School Dist*	16,82	312
Baker, Katie/*Lumberton Ind School Dist*	4	178
Baker, Kyle/*Sam Rayburn Ind School Dist*	3	146
Baker, Melody/*Pampa Ind School Dist*	76	165
Baker, Rick/*Center Ind School Dist*	3,5	334
Baker, Rocky/*Carlisle Ind School Dist*	6	327
Baker, Shannon/*Mildred Ind School Dist*	1,11	300
Baker, Stella/*Tenaha Ind School Dist*	7	335
Baker, Susan/*Liberty Ind School Dist*	16	266
Baker, Tammy/*Malakoff Ind School Dist*	3,5	214
Baker, Tess/*Redwater Ind School Dist*	2	49
Baker, Wanda, Dr/*Bryan Ind School Dist*	57,271	54
Balasubcamania, Nathan, Dr/*Manor Ind School Dist*	294	371
Balaszi, Angie/*Jourdanton Ind School Dist*	2	20
Balcar, Jeff/*El Campo Ind School Dist*	3,91	389
Balderas, Ramiro/*Valley View Ind School Dist*	27	225
Baldoni, Jim/*North East Ind School Dist*	16,73	34
Baldwin, Bryan/*Seymour Ind School Dist*	67	25
Baldwin, Owen/*Wimberley Ind School Dist*	5	212
Ball, Amanda/*Little Elm Ind School Dist*	74	124
Ball, Andy/*Clifton Ind School Dist*	1	46
Ball, Janette, Dr/*Judson Ind School Dist*	1	33
Ball, Josh/*Aquilla Ind School Dist*	6	227
Ball, Michael/*Lewisville Ind School Dist*	2,19	122
Ball, Travis/*Chisum Ind School Dist*	67	259
Ball, Veronica/*Archdiocese San Antonio Ed Off*	36,79	44
Ballard, Brad/*Rosebud-Lott Ind School Dist*	6	145
Ballard, Jeff/*Prairiland Ind School Dist*	1	260
Ballard, Kathy/*Carthage Ind School Dist*	2	311
Ballard, Robin/*Lake Dallas Ind School Dist*	73	122
Ballast, Kerry/*Texas Dept of Education*	286	1
Ballenger, Richard, Dr/*Gary Ind School Dist*	8,15,58,69	311
Ballew, Ray/*Schleicher Co Ind Sch Dist*	2	333
Bammert, Cynthia/*Cuero Ind School Dist*	38	117
Bancroft, George/*Big Spring Ind School Dist*	15	233
Banda, Ivonne/*Taft Ind School Dist*	2	332
Bandy, Todd/*Floydada Ind School Dist*	6	148
Banfield, Eric/*Florence Ind School Dist*	2,19	395
Banfield, Sue/*Belton Ind School Dist*	34	26
Bang, Shari/*Smithville Ind School Dist*	58	24
Banks, David/*Lamar Cons Ind School Dist*	295	153
Banks, James/*Texas City Ind School Dist*	73	161
Bannowsky, Amy/*Menard Ind School Dist*	1	285
Bany, Rebecca/*Shepherd Ind School Dist*	16	330
Barajas, Melinda/*Mathis Ind School Dist*	67	331
Barajas, Rene/*Houston Ind School Dist*	2,19	188
Barajas, Rene, Dr/*Garland Ind School Dist*	2,15	105
Barbarick, Lisa/*Nacogdoches Ind School Dist*	2,19	298
Barbaroux, Paula/*Grapevine-Colleyville Ind SD*	3,17	353
Barbay, Darrell/*Jasper Ind School Dist*	6	240
Barbee, Jay/*Higgins Ind School Dist*	67	268
Barber, Duane/*Whitehouse Ind School Dist*	4,5,15	338
Barber, Joni/*Beeville Ind School Dist*	70,294	25
Barber, Lareta/*Lazbuddie Ind School Dist*	7	315
Barber, Rachel/*Tyler Ind School Dist*	7	337
Barber, Stacey/*Shallowater Ind School Dist*	73,84,297	272
Barbier, Erin/*Austin Ind School Dist*	61	366
Barbosa, Alonzo/*Edinburg Cons Ind School Dist*	5	216
Barck, Cathy/*Garland Ind School Dist*	73	105
Barclay, Sherryll/*Meadow Ind School Dist*	36	362
Barclay, TJ/*Vega Ind School Dist*	67	307
Barco, Tony/*Edcouch Elsa Ind School Dist*	67	215
Bares, Hubert/*Campbell Ind School Dist*	2	235
Bares, Noelle/*Greenville Ind School Dist*	7,83,88	236
Barganski, Linda, Dr/*Flour Bluff Ind School Dist*	11,83,298	304
Barge, James/*Zavalla Ind School Dist*	67	18
Barger, Dustin/*Petrolia Cons Ind School Dist*	67	74
Barger, Skyla/*Petrolia Cons Ind School Dist*	4	74
Barker, Brent/*Eagle Mtn-Saginaw Ind Sch Dist*	6	348
Barker, Denise/*Region 10 Ed Service Center*	297	116
Barker, Shae/*Louise Ind School Dist*	4	389
Barker, Wendell/*Palo Pinto Ind Sch Dist 906*	1,84	310
Barker, Wendell/*Palo Pinto Ind Sch Dist 906*	9,36,57,69,88,271,273	310
Barley, Pepperjo/*Jourdanton Ind School Dist*	11	20
Barlow, Billy/*Fairfield Ind School Dist*	91	156
Barlow, Cindy/*Kirbyville Cons Ind Sch Dist*	4	241
Barlow, Kevin, Dr/*Arlington Ind School Dist*	70,294	343
Barnard, Chris/*Celeste Ind School Dist*	67	235
Barnes, Arlen/*Follett Ind School Dist*	73,76	267
Barnes, Dana, Dr/*Eagle Mtn-Saginaw Ind Sch Dist*	27,30,31	348
Barnes, Ed/*Bandera Ind School Dist*	3	23
Barnes, Karen/*Friona Ind School Dist*	11	315
Barnes, Lannie/*Van Alstyne Ind School Dist*	3,5	168
Barnes, Lauri/*Cypress-Fairbanks Ind Sch Dist*	58	184
Barnes, Marion/*Channelview Ind School Dist*	295	183
Barnet, Lillian/*Florence Ind School Dist*	4	395
Barnett, Bryce/*Blackwell Cons Ind Sch Dist*	27	301
Barnett, Christy/*Levelland Ind School Dist*	9	229
Barnett, Connie/*Lockney Independent Sch Dist*	7	149
Barnett, Joe/*Frenship Ind School Dist*	73,98,297	269
Barnett, Martha/*Franklin Ind School Dist*	69	325
Barnett, Teralee/*Victoria Ind School Dist*	40	382
Barnett, Tonya/*Coolidge Ind School Dist*	4	266
Barnette, Barbara/*Cross Plains Ind Sch Dist*	4	62
Barnwell, Jackie/*New Boston Ind School Dist*	2,12	49
Barnwell, Rob/*Jefferson Ind School Dist*	1	274
Baron, Victor/*Uvalde Cons Ind School Dist*	58	378
Baronet, Shana/*Brady Ind School Dist*	37	277
Barr, Billy/*Industrial Ind School Dist*	3	240
Barr, Glendell/*Baird Ind School Dist*	73,295	62
Barr, Mary Beth/*Tomball Ind School Dist*	280	203
Barr, Norman/*Elysian Fields Ind School Dist*	3	208
Barr, Randi/*Wheeler Ind School Dist*	4	391
Barr, Shawn/*Lewisville Ind School Dist*	3	122
Barraza, Debi/*Sands Consolidated ISD*	271	117
Barrera, Aurora/*Uvalde Cons Ind School Dist*	4	378
Barrera, Diana/*Somerset Ind School Dist*	9,88	42
Barrera, Dolores/*United Ind School Dist*	10	387
Barrera, Hartadelia/*Roma Ind School Dist*	58	341
Barrera, Jorge/*Eagle Pass Ind School Dist*	67	276
Barrera, Leslie/*Archdiocese Galveston-Houston*	73	203
Barrera, Lili/*Premont Ind School Dist*	2	246
Barrera, Mike, Dr/*Ben Bolt-Palito Blanco ISD*	1	245
Barrera, Rolando/*Rio Grande City Ind Sch Dist*	7	340
Barrera, Silvia/*Laredo Ind School Dist*	6,35	386
Barrera, Suzette/*Zapata Co Ind School Dist*	11,294,298	406
Barrett, Debbie/*Pasadena Ind School Dist*	58	198
Barrett, Jay Be/*Farwell Ind School Dist*	67	314
Barrett, Logan/*Kennedale Ind School Dist*	91	355
Barrett, Natalie/*Trinity Ind School Dist*	8	374
Barrett, Richard/*Kennedale Ind School Dist*	6,83	355
Barrett, Terry/*Frost Ind School Dist*	16,73,76,295	299
Barrick, Brett/*Mineral Wells Ind School Dist*	5	310
Barrick, Brett/*Mineral Wells Ind School Dist*	5	310
Barrientes, Estela/*Brownsville Ind School Dist*	271	63
Barrientez, Michael/*Loraine Ind School Dist*	31	289
Barriga, Ethel/*Presidio Ind School Dist*	67	320
Barrington, Shirley/*Bishop Cons Ind School Dist*	42,45	302
Barron, Bake/*Runge Ind School Dist*	11	251
Barron, Carlos/*Aldine Ind School Dist*	10	179
Barron, Cheryl/*Pleasanton Ind School Dist*	68,79	21
Barron, Chris/*Spur Ind School Dist*	3,5	127
Barrow, Benny/*High Island Ind Sch Dist*	67	160
Barrow, Brandon/*Shepherd Ind School Dist*	3,5	330
Barrow, Heather/*Nederland Ind School Dist*	9,81,89,271	242
Barrow, Jennifer/*Brookesmith Ind School Dist*	16	58
Barrow, Michelle/*Newton Ind School Dist*	1,11	301
Barrow, Monte/*Nederland Ind School Dist*	6,35	242
Bartay, Greg/*Pearland Ind School Dist*	28,295	53
Bartel, Gary/*Grand Prairie Ind School Dist*	6	107
Barten, Rachel/*Rice Cons Ind School Dist*	4	87
Barth, Stephanie/*Port Arthur Ind School Dist*	2	243
Barthelemess, Carie/*Carroll Independent Sch Dist*	69,294	347

DISTRICT PERSONNEL INDEX

Market Data Retrieval

NAME/District	JOB FUNCTIONS	PAGE
Bartlett, Linda/London Ind School Dist	16,73	305
Bartlett, Lydia, Dr/Gonzales Ind School Dist	11,15,57,58,271,294,296,298	164
Bartlett, Lynn/Wellington Ind School Dist	67	86
Bartlett, Scott, Dr/Port Neches-Groves Ind SD	67	243
Bartlett, Weston/Melissa Ind School Dist	5	81
Bartness, Betty/Sweeny Ind School Dist	58	54
Barton, Angela/Kemp Ind School Dist	58	252
Barton, Connie/Carlisle Ind School Dist	7	327
Barton, Diana/Ft Bend Ind School Dist	7	149
Barton, Elzene/Hallsburg Ind School Dist	57,59	279
Barton, Grey/Rusk Ind School Dist	1	73
Barton, James/Bluff Dale Ind Sch Dist	67	143
Barton, Joel/Garrison Ind School Dist	83	298
Barton, Lisa/Joaquin Ind School Dist	16	335
Bartos, Rose/Moulton Ind School Dist	4	262
Bartow, Cindy/Iowa Park Consolidated Ind SD	68	392
Bartram, Timothy/Hull Daisetta Ind School Dist	1	266
Basden, Debbie/North Lamar Ind School Dist	16	259
Bashara, Dana, Dr/Alamo Heights Ind School Dist	1	30
Basich, Jennifer/Alvin Ind School Dist	4	50
Basinger, Joe/Southland Ind School Dist	67	162
Basinger, Wyanza/Southland Ind School Dist	2	162
Baskerville, Skip/Birdville Ind School Dist	15,68	346
Baskin, Buck/Sunnyvale Ind School Dist	76,84	113
Baskins, Buck/Sunnyvale Ind School Dist	73	113
Bass, Brande/New Caney Ind School Dist	11,83,88,296	293
Bass, Brande/New Caney Ind School Dist	11,83,88,296	293
Bass, Mike/Alvin Ind School Dist	6	50
Bass, Teri/Sabine Ind School Dist	9,34	170
Bass, Travis/Whitehouse Ind School Dist	15	338
Bass, Vinny/Quitman Ind School Dist	4	404
Basset, Brian/Itasca Ind School Dist	67	228
Bassett, Beth/Longview Ind School Dist	8,39,42,45,48,51,277,280	169
Bassett, Steven/Ft Bend Ind School Dist	2,19	149
Basurto, Ruperto/Ysleta Ind School Dist	10,15	137
Batchelder, Paul/New Caney Ind School Dist	3	293
Batchelor, Denise/Deer Park Ind School Dist	88	186
Bateman, Michelle/Springtown Ind School Dist	10	313
Bates, Alphonso/Community Ind School Dist	68,79	78
Bates, Amy/Plano Ind School Dist	8	82
Bates, Gary, Dr/Ft Sam Houston Ind School Dist	1	32
Bates, Kendra/Queen City Ind School Dist	38,83	70
Batiste, Ruby/Crowley Ind School Dist	58	347
Bato, Bernie/Poteet Ind School Dist	58	21
Batten, Kori/North Zulch Ind School Dist	36,752	274
Battenfield, Tim/New Caney Ind School Dist	3	293
Battershell, Robin, Dr/Belton Ind School Dist	1	26
Battle, Stephanie/West Hardin Co Cons Sch Dist	57,58	178
Batts, Sara/Union Hill Ind School Dist	10,88,271	377
Batts, Troy, Dr/Union Hill Ind School Dist	1,11	377
Baty, Darrell/DeSoto Ind School Dist	73	104
Baty, Jill/Shelbyville Ind School Dist	11,15,270,271,274	335
Baty, Leslie/Marble Falls Ind School Dist	9	60
Bauer, Debra/Goliad Ind School Dist	11	163
Baugh, Kenneth/Culberson Co Allamoore Ind SD	1	95
Baum, Jeff/Lubbock Ind School Dist	2,19	269
Baum, Jim/Lockney Independent Sch Dist	1	149
Bawcom, Doug/Lubbock Ind School Dist	68	269
Baxter, Kimberly/Socorro Ind School Dist	41	135
Baxter, Sandra/Brenham Ind School Dist	4	385
Baxter, Shaffer/Canadian Ind School Dist	5	213
Baxter, Valerie, Dr/Pine Tree Ind School Dist	15	170
Bay-Wetherwax, Amy/Navasota Ind School Dist	12	172
Bay, Jason/Richards Ind School Dist	67	172
Bayard, Robert/Clear Creek Ind School Dist	73,98,295	158
Bays, Patricia/Shelbyville Ind School Dist	31	335
Bays, Rhonda/Lingleville Ind School Dist	73,76	143

NAME/District	JOB FUNCTIONS	PAGE
Bays, Sherri, Dr/Floresville Ind School Dist	1	400
Bazaldua, Chriselda/Edgewood Ind School Dist	27,31,285	31
Bazan, Rolando/Kingsville Ind School Dist	295	257
Bazile, Mekisha/Port Arthur Ind School Dist	47	243
Beach, Johnny/Garland Ind School Dist	67	105
Beach, Leslie/Prosper Ind School Dist	4	84
Beadle, Abigail/Devine Ind School Dist	11	283
Beale, Jayne/Graham Ind School Dist	73,286	406
Beall, Mark/Lago Vista Ind School Dist	3	370
Beam, Rebecca/Bartlett Ind School Dist	12	26
Beaman, Jeannie/Avery Ind School Dist	16,73,286,295	322
Bean, Cathy/Springlake-Earth Ind Sch Dist	59	261
Beard, Bramlet/Ennis Ind School Dist	67	140
Beard, Cheryl/Garland Ind School Dist	81	105
Beard, Chuck/Hondo Ind School Dist	3	284
Beard, Jason/Rogers Ind School Dist	3,5	28
Beard, Marci/Hermleigh Ind School Dist	2	333
Bearden, Shawn/Abernathy Ind School Dist	8	174
Bearden, Stephanie/Crowell Ind School Dist	58	149
Beasley, Carmen/Tornillo Ind School Dist	271	137
Beasley, Jim/Llano Ind School Dist	73,76,95,295,297	268
Beasley, Shannon/Medina Valley Ind School Dist	67	284
Beatchge, Dana/Divide Ind School Dist	2	255
Beattie, Billy/Humble Ind School Dist	2	195
Beatty, Kevin/Calallen Ind School Dist	73	302
Beaty, Christie/White Settlement Ind Sch Dist	273	357
Beaty, Robert/Clarksville Ind School Dist	67	322
Beaty, Robin/Port Arthur Ind School Dist	8,18,286	243
Beauchamp, Karyn/Irving Ind School Dist	7	109
Beaudin, Angela/Sivells Bend Ind School Dist	2	91
Beaulieu, Shirley/Texas Dept of Education	2	1
Beaver, Randel/Midway Ind School Dist	1	74
Beavers, Brady/Caldwell Ind School Dist	3	59
Bebon, Cynthia, Dr/McAllen Ind School Dist	12,271	221
Becerra, Ruperto/South San Antonio Ind Sch Dist	3	42
Beck, Don, Dr/Channelview Ind School Dist	8,15	183
Beck, Jennifer/Texarkana Ind School Dist	73	50
Beck, Lyneil/New Home Ind School Dist	57	273
Beck, Scott/Seagraves Ind School Dist	73	157
Beck, Vicki/Medina Valley Ind School Dist	4	284
Beck, Wes/Early Ind School Dist	1	58
Becker, Darrell, Dr/Troy Ind School Dist	8,11,32,58,69,273	29
Becker, Doug/Frisco Ind School Dist	5	78
Becker, Mandy/Pawnee Ind School Dist	275,752	25
Becker, Megan/Wellman Union Ind School Dist	36,69,83,85,88	362
Becker, Tammy/Region 12 Ed Service Center	8	283
Beckham, Vickie/Era Ind School Dist	58	90
Bedford, David/Region 15 Ed Service Center	8	366
Bedre, Christine/Westwood Ind School Dist	8	16
Beeler, Gwen/Fannindel Ind School Dist	67	120
Been, Terry/Brookesmith Ind School Dist	67	58
Beene, Scott/Anderson-Shiro Cons Ind SD	1	171
Beesaw, Kevin/Bryan Ind School Dist	2,15,275	54
Beeson, Donnie/Keene Ind School Dist	67	248
Begert, Bret/Ft Elliott Cons Ind Sch Dist	67	390
Beggs, Anthony/Coleman Ind School Dist	2	76
Behlen, Douglas/Rice Cons Ind School Dist	3	87
Behnke, Rachel/Lake Travis Ind School Dist	27	370
Behnke, Rachel/New Braunfels Ind School Dist	27	88
Behr, Cassandra/Dallas Ind School Dist	5	98
Beilue, Sandra/Lubbock-Cooper Ind Sch Dist	8,294	271
Beimer, Jennifer/Lewisville Ind School Dist	44	122
Beims, Shelia/Bynum Ind School Dist	79	227
Beisert, Beverly/Tomball Ind School Dist	5	203
Bejarano, Alana/El Paso Ind School Dist	7,85	132
Belanger, Shane/Evant Ind School Dist	3	92
Belcher, Frank/Ft Elliott Cons Ind Sch Dist	1,11,73,83	390

#		#		#		#		#		#	
1	Superintendent	16	Instructional Media Svcs	30	Adult Education	44	Science Sec	58	Special Education K-12	72	Summer School
2	Bus/Finance/Purchasing	17	Chief Operations Officer	31	Career/Sch-to-Work K-12	45	Math K-12	59	Special Education Elem	73	Instructional Tech
3	Buildings And Grounds	18	Chief Academic Officer	32	Career/Sch-to-Work Elem	46	Math Elem	60	Special Education Sec	74	Inservice Training
4	Food Service	19	Chief Financial Officer	33	Career/Sch-to-Work Sec	47	Math Sec	61	Foreign/World Lang K-12	75	Marketing/Distributive
5	Transportation	20	Art K-12	34	Early Childhood Ed	48	English/Lang Arts K-12	62	Foreign/World Lang Elem	76	Info Systems
6	Athletic	21	Art Elem	35	Health/Phys Education	49	English/Lang Arts Elem	63	Foreign/World Lang Sec	77	Psychological Assess
7	Health Services	22	Art Sec	36	Guidance Services K-12	50	English/Lang Arts Sec	64	Religious Education K-12	78	Affirmative Action
8	Curric/Instruct K-12	23	Music K-12	37	Guidance Services Elem	51	Reading K-12	65	Religious Education Elem	79	Student Personnel
9	Curric/Instruct Elem	24	Music Elem	38	Guidance Services Sec	52	Reading Elem	66	Religious Education Sec	80	Driver Ed/Safety
10	Curric/Instruct Sec	25	Music Sec	39	Social Studies K-12	53	Reading Sec	67	School Board President	81	Gifted/Talented
11	Federal Program	26	Business Education	40	Social Studies Elem	54	Remedial Reading K-12	68	Teacher Personnel	82	Video Services
12	Title I	27	Career & Tech Ed	41	Social Studies Sec	55	Remedial Reading Elem	69	Academic Assessment	83	Substance Abuse Prev
13	Title V	28	Technology Education	42	Science K-12	56	Remedial Reading Sec	70	Research/Development	84	Erate
15	Asst Superintendent	29	Family/Consumer Science	43	Science Elem	57	Bilingual/ELL	71	Public Information	85	AIDS Education

#		#	
88	Alternative/At Risk	277	Remedial Math K-12
89	Multi-Cultural Curriculum	280	Literacy Coach
90	Social Work	285	STEM
91	Safety/Security	286	Digital Learning
92	Magnet School	288	Common Core Standards
93	Parental Involvement	294	Accountability
95	Tech Prep Program	295	Network System
97	Chief Information Officer	296	Title II Programs
98	Chief Technology Officer	297	Webmaster
270	Character Education	298	Grant Writer/Ptnrships
271	Migrant Education	750	Chief Innovation Officer
273	Teacher Mentor	751	Chief of Staff
274	Before/After Sch	752	Social Emotional Learning
275	Response To Intervention		

TX-T6

Texas School Directory
DISTRICT PERSONNEL INDEX

NAME/District	JOB FUNCTIONS	PAGE
Belcher, Joanne/*Bovina Ind School Dist*	58	314
Belding, David, Dr/*Aubrey Ind School Dist*	1,11	120
Belees, William/*Mexia Ind School Dist*	295	267
Beles, Eva/*Mt Pleasant Ind School Dist*	57	363
Beles, Leonard/*Region 8 Ed Service Center*	11,57,88	69
Belgard, Joey/*Rockwall Ind School Dist*	44	325
Belk, Stephen/*Bloomburg Ind School Dist*	73	70
Bell-Hunter, Diedrae, Dr/*Dallas Ind School Dist*	68	98
Bell, Amanda/*Shamrock Ind School Dist*	7	390
Bell, Bobette/*Salado Ind School Dist*	16	29
Bell, Bruce/*Liberty Ind School Dist*	67	266
Bell, Caleb/*Gunter Ind School Dist*	5	166
Bell, Clay/*D'Hanis Ind School Dist*	67	283
Bell, Colin/*Sherman Ind School Dist*	295	167
Bell, Dana/*Hedley Ind School Dist*	67	127
Bell, Genese, Dr/*Southside Ind School Dist*	8,15,74	43
Bell, Jaimie/*Normangee Ind School Dist*	2	264
Bell, Jake/*Martin's Mill Ind Sch Dist*	6	381
Bell, Mark/*China Spring Ind School Dist*	6	278
Bell, Sam/*Magnolia Ind School Dist*	68	292
Bell, Shawn/*Eagle Mtn-Saginaw Ind Sch Dist*	20,23	348
Bell, Steve/*Dayton Ind School Dist*	3	265
Bell, Susan/*Nixon-Smiley Cons Ind Sch Dist*	274	164
Bell, Thomas/*Pearland Ind School Dist*	8,20	53
Bellamy, Doug/*Wylie Ind School Dist*	297	85
Bellar, Jarod/*Baird Ind School Dist*	1,11,57	62
Bellar, Jennifer/*Baird Ind School Dist*	31,36,69,83,270,294	62
Bellenger, Marcy/*Hamshire Fannett Ind Sch Dist*	36	242
Bellinger, Dee/*Blum Ind School Dist*	2	227
Bellinger, Marsha/*Judson Ind School Dist*	16	33
Belliveau, Alison/*Rockwall Ind School Dist*	27	325
Bellomy, Tracy/*Blum Ind School Dist*	8	227
Belmontes, Marissa/*Roma Ind School Dist*	57,81	341
Belmontes, Sylvia/*Ysleta Ind School Dist*	7,85	137
Belossanton, Eva/*O'Donnell Ind School Dist*	4	273
Benastante, Kristi/*Coldspring-Oakhurst Cons ISD*	7	330
Benavides, Greta/*Wichita Falls Ind School Dist*	57	392
Benavides, Jennifer/*Jim Hogg Co Ind School Dist*	4	244
Benavides, Laida/*United Ind School Dist*	2,15	387
Benavidez, John/*Buena Vista Ind School Dist*	2,6	315
Benavidez, Rosario/*Ben Bolt-Palito Blanco ISD*	2	245
Bendele, Susan/*Randolph Field Ind School Dist*	8,11,69,273,275,277,298	39
Bender Jutzi, Leslie, Dr/*Burleson Ind School Dist*	298	246
Bendon, David/*Shelbyville Ind School Dist*	6	335
Benner, Rebecca/*Pasadena Ind School Dist*	8	198
Bennet, Cason/*Bellevue Ind School Dist*	58	74
Bennett, Brenda/*Goodrich Ind School Dist*	67	316
Bennett, Brent/*Ganado Ind School Dist*	6	239
Bennett, Drew/*Carlisle Ind School Dist*	58	327
Bennett, Elizabeth/*Galveston Ind School Dist*	9	160
Bennett, James/*Skidmore Tynan Ind SD*	67	25
Bennett, Julie/*Rosebud-Lott Ind School Dist*	67	145
Bennett, Mark, Dr/*Madisonville Cons ISD*	67	273
Bennett, Shannon/*Duncanville Ind School Dist*	72	104
Bennett, Tyson, Dr/*Sherman Ind School Dist*	2,15	167
Bennett, Wayne/*Aransas Pass Ind School Dist*	31	330
Bennett, Yvonne/*La Porte Ind School Dist*	4	198
Benningfield, Glenn/*Goldthwaite Consolidated ISD*	2	288
Benningfield, Jenice/*Goldthwaite Consolidated ISD*	73,84,298	288
Benningield, Angie/*Denver City Ind School Dist*	68	405
Benoit, Nikki/*Pine Tree Ind School Dist*	2	170
Benskin, Sheila/*Lancaster Ind School Dist*	27,31	110
Benson, Grace/*Waco Ind School Dist*	15,57	281
Benson, Melinda/*New Diana Ind School Dist*	2,71,97	376
Benson, Nancy/*Diocese of Fort Worth Ed Off*	2	358
Bentancourt, Carlos/*Slaton Ind School Dist*	67	272
Bentley, Brandi/*Woden Ind School Dist*	58	298
Bentley, Tammie/*Whiteface Con Ind School Dist*	2	75
Benton, Melody/*Groveton Ind School Dist*	68	374
Bentz, Matt/*Leander Ind School Dist*	8,18	396
Bera, Elida/*Kingsville Ind School Dist*	1	257
Beran, Beverly, Dr/*Region 7 Ed Service Center*	58	171
Berckenhoff, Lisa/*Ezzell Ind School Dist*	1	262
Berg, Chelsea/*Sabine Pass Ind School Dist*	4	244
Berg, Rusty/*Decatur Ind School Dist*	3	403
Berger, Amber/*Columbus Ind School Dist*	11,296	86
Berger, Holly/*Conroe Ind School Dist*	45	291
Berger, Kyle/*Grapevine-Colleyville Ind SD*	73,98	353
Bergeron, Jeff/*Port Neches-Groves Ind SD*	3	243
Bergvall, Sharrmie/*Guthrie Common School Dist*	58,275	257
Berkovsky, Janette/*Shiner Ind School Dist*	73,295	262
Berlanga, Jesse/*South San Antonio Ind Sch Dist*	5	42
Bermea, Adriana/*Southside Ind School Dist*	57	43
Bermudez, Bibi/*Boerne Ind School Dist*	11,83,270,271	253
Berna, Jd/*Magnolia Ind School Dist*	6	292
Bernal, Bibiana/*Lyford Cons Ind School Dist*	7	394
Bernal, Letty/*Waxahachie Ind School Dist*	12,13,296	142
Bernal, Sylvia/*Midland Ind School Dist*	51	285
Bernard, A/*Beaumont Ind School Dist*	67	241
Bernard, Ashley/*Marble Falls Ind School Dist*	285	60
Bernard, Nneka/*Duncanville Ind School Dist*	81	104
Bernards, Brad/*Valentine Ind School Dist*	73,286,295	241
Berngen, Ed/*Shamrock Ind School Dist*	69	391
Berniking, Sandra/*Avalon Ind School Dist*	58	140
Berrier, David/*Deer Park Ind School Dist*	27,31	186
Berrier, Ned/*Brazos Ind School Dist*	6	22
Berry-Corie, Kimberly/*Round Rock Ind School Dist*	275	398
Berry, John/*Gladewater Ind School Dist*	6	169
Berry, Kelley/*Hull Daisetta Ind School Dist*	67	266
Berry, Kenny/*Clyde Consolidated Ind SD*	1	62
Berry, Monika/*Hale Center Ind School Dist*	11,57,271	175
Berryhill, Cheryl/*Munday Consolidated Ind SD*	2,68,79	258
Berryhill, Jody/*Pine Tree Ind School Dist*	6	170
Berryman, Brent/*Lindale Ind School Dist*	27	337
Berryman, Ms/*Ore City Ind School Dist*	67	377
Berset, Jill/*Lubbock Ind School Dist*	27,31	269
Bertrand, Lane/*Anahuac Ind School Dist*	67	71
Bertsch, Kelly/*Sweeny Ind School Dist*	16,73,84,295	54
Bertsch, Michelle/*Fayetteville Ind School Dist*	2	147
Besinaiz, Ada, Dr/*Corpus Christi Ind Sch Dist*	36,83	303
Bess, Jamie/*Daingerfield-Lone Star Ind SD*	4	296
Bessent, Craig/*Wylie Ind School Dist*	3,5,91	361
Bessent, Cynthia/*Baird Ind School Dist*	8,12,271	62
Bessire, Cindy/*Denver City Ind School Dist*	79	405
Best, Tiffany/*Marshall Ind School Dist*	68	209
Betancourt, Jose/*Riviera Ind School Dist*	2,4,5,11,91	258
Betancur, Joe/*Hale Center Ind School Dist*	5	175
Betencourt, Deeanne/*Anton ISD School Dist*	8	229
Bethany, Gina/*Calhoun Co Ind School Dist*	58,275	61
Betik, Dwayne/*Avalon Ind School Dist*	16,73,295	140
Bettis, Laurie/*Hempstead Ind School Dist*	71	384
Betts, Debra/*El Paso Ind School Dist*	69	132
Betts, Jacky/*Bowie Ind School Dist*	67	289
Beverly, James/*Eustace Ind School Dist*	3	214
Bey, Jonathan/*Ft Worth Ind School Dist*	2	349
Bey, Sharon/*Waller Ind School Dist*	36	384
Beyer, Daniel/*Moulton Ind School Dist*	67	262
Bezner, Jody/*Texline Ind School Dist*	67	95
Bibb, Brian/*Seymour Ind School Dist*	286,288	25
Bibb, Brian, Dr/*Petersburg Ind School Dist*	1,11,73	175
Bibler, Amy/*Quanah Ind School Dist*	57	177
Bice, Alicia/*Floydada Ind School Dist*	2	148
Bice, Phyllis/*Eustace Ind School Dist*	83,85,88	214
Bickerstaff, Amy/*Bullard Ind School Dist*	8	336
Bicknell, Scott/*Glasscock Co Ind School Dist*	1,83,288	163
Biehle, Candance/*Smithville Ind School Dist*	4	24
Bielke, Carol/*San Antonio Ind School Dist*	286	39
Bienvenu, David/*Channelview Ind School Dist*	4	183
Bieri, Regina/*Angleton Ind School Dist*	67	51
Biering, Beverly/*McKinney Ind School Dist*	2	80
Biesheuvel, David/*Georgetown Ind School Dist*	3	395
Bigbee, Ed, Dr/*Duncanville Ind School Dist*	2,19	104
Biggs, Theresa/*Prosper Ind School Dist*	81	84
Bigham, Dana/*Victoria Ind School Dist*	4	382
Bigham, Mike/*Motley Co Ind School Dist*	6	296
Bigham, Monie/*Rio Vista Ind School Dist*	3,5	248
Bilberry, Marcella/*Spur Ind School Dist*	83,85	127
Biles, Ray/*Lorena Ind School Dist*	6	280
Billingsley, Gary/*Miller Grove Ind School Dist*	6,10	231
Billingsley, Karen/*Cleveland Ind School Dist*	2,19	265
Bills, Casey/*Sweetwater ISD School Dist*	2	301
Bills, Cynthia/*South San Antonio Ind Sch Dist*	73,81,285	42

School Year 2019-2020   800-333-8802

DISTRICT PERSONNEL INDEX

Market Data Retrieval

NAME/District	JOB FUNCTIONS	PAGE
Bimmerle, John/Sulphur Springs Ind Sch Dist	286	232
Bindel, Darren/Muenster Ind School Dist	67	91
Binford, Andy/Central Heights Ind Sch Dist	10	297
Bingman, Cynthia/Aldine Ind School Dist	73,76,295	179
Binnicker, Dustin/Waxahachie Ind School Dist	27	142
Binns, Edie/Round Rock Ind School Dist	74	398
Binson, Rob/Natalia Ind School Dist	69	284
Birch, Lisa/Splendora Ind School Dist	286	294
Birch, Rebecca/Del Valle Ind School Dist	67	369
Bird, Jason/McKinney Ind School Dist	2,19	80
Bird, Kim/Salado Ind School Dist	67	29
Bird, Theresa/Grape Creek Ind School Dist	2	364
Birdwell, Chris/Hooks Ind School Dist	6	48
Birdwell, Guy/Trent Ind School Dist	1,11,83,288	361
Birdwell, Jennifer/Livingston Ind School Dist	16	317
Birdwell, Kerry/Alto Ind School Dist	11	72
Birdwell, Linda/Cross Plains Ind Sch Dist	2,298	62
Birkenfeild, Glenda/Happy Ind School Dist	7	342
Bishop, Angie/Carthage Ind School Dist	58	311
Bishop, Holly, Dr/Region 10 Ed Service Center	16	116
Bishop, Kim/Center Point Ind School Dist	2,11	255
Bishop, Laurie/Collinsville Ind School Dist	4	166
Bishop, Richard/Westwood Ind School Dist	6	16
Bitters, David/White Settlement Ind Sch Dist	2,3,5,15,73,78,85,91	357
Bittprt, Laura/Floresville Ind School Dist	27	400
Bitzi, Gary/Bandera Ind School Dist	8,36,48,51,74,285	23
Bizel, Shanda/Jarrell Ind School Dist	27	396
Bizzell, Deitra/Alba-Golden Ind School Dist	8	404
Bjork, Tosha/Tyler Ind School Dist	2,19	337
Bjork, William/Mineola Ind School Dist	2,15	404
Black, Anna/Burkburnett Ind Sch Dist	83,88	391
Black, Ashley/Karnes City Ind School Dist	2,68	250
Black, Bill/Carthage Ind School Dist	3	311
Black, Bill/Smyer Ind School Dist	10,16,69,74	229
Black, Brandy/Evadale Ind School Dist	2	240
Black, Karen/Tidehaven Ind School Dist	4	276
Black, Shelley/Mt Vernon Ind School Dist	4	155
Black, Tenett/Webb Cons Ind School Dist	296	388
Black, Tony/Whitehouse Ind School Dist	73,95,297	339
Blackard, Leah/Corsicana Ind School Dist	67	299
Blackburn, Judy/Idalou Ind School Dist	3	269
Blackburn, Natasha/Italy Ind School Dist	2,11,298	140
Blackburn, Tammy/Shallowater Ind School Dist	8	272
Blackenship, Morris/Adrian Ind School Dist	67	307
Blackman Jones, Tiffanie/DeSoto Ind School Dist	71	104
Blackman, Chad/Florence Ind School Dist	73,98,295	395
Blackman, Heath/Loop Ind School Dist	1,11,288	157
Blackmon, Gayle/Van Vleck Ind School Dist	2	276
Blackmon, Robert/Van Vleck Ind School Dist	6	276
Blackmon, Scott/Rusk Ind School Dist	84	73
Blackmon, Vanetta/Loop Ind School Dist	8,69,88	157
Blackstock, Landry/Brownwood Ind School Dist	58	58
Blackstock, Lindsey/Brazosport Ind School Dist	286	52
Blackwell, Deanna/George West Ind School Dist	16,73	268
Blackwell, Debra/Miles Ind School Dist	2	326
Blackwell, Don/McLeod Ind School Dist	67	70
Blackwell, Ginny/Dew Ind School Dist	57,271	156
Blackwell, Luke/Mineola Ind School Dist	6	404
Bladen, Gary/Centerville Ind School Dist	5	264
Blades, Jimmy/Cedar Hill Ind School Dist	5	97
Blagg, Tasha/Rivercrest Ind School Dist	36,83,85,88	322
Blaine, Jennifer/Spring Branch Ind School Dist	1	200
Blaine, Lloyd/Royse City Ind School Dist	91	326
Blair, Heidi/Levelland Ind School Dist	8,16,36,69,275,285,288,294	229
Blair, Henry/Copperas Cove Ind School Dist	16,76,295	92
Blair, Kelsa/Zephyr Ind School Dist	11	59
Blair, Teresa/Medina Ind School Dist	2,11,76,298	23
Blake, Matthew/Overton Ind School Dist	2	328
Blakey, Caitlyn/Burton Ind School Dist	2	386
Blakley, Patsy/Haskell Cons Ind School Dist	275	210
Blalock, Kyle/Runge Ind School Dist	6	251
Blanar, Bryan/Boling Ind School Dist	11,15,58,84,285,298	389
Blanchard, Denise/Amarillo Ind School Dist	93	317
Blanchard, Denise/Banquete Ind School Dist	33,285	302
Blanchard, Sharon/Midway Ind School Dist	58,77	280
Blanco-Lajara, Lumara, Dr/Humble Ind School Dist	57	195
Bland, Eddie/Snyder Ind School Dist	1	333
Bland, Lisa/Frost Ind School Dist	51,54	299
Blankenship, Julie/McKinney Ind School Dist	7	80
Blankenship, Molly/Paint Creek Ind School Dist	27	210
Blankenship, Sheri/Hereford Ind School Dist	1	119
Blann, Kim/Keller Ind School Dist	20,23	354
Blansett, Amy/Borger Ind School Dist	11,15,38,57,273,296,298	237
Blanton, Deenna/Water Valley Ind School Dist	8,16,31,58,83,271,273,288	365
Blanton, Duyen/Sabine Pass Ind School Dist	2,68	244
Blaylock, Lori, Dr/Kaufman Ind School Dist	1	252
Bleer, Connie/Academy Ind School Dist	76	26
Blesing, Tonya/Georgetown Ind School Dist	2	395
Blessing, Shawn/Irving Ind School Dist	27,31	109
Blevins, Karen/Schertz-Cibolo-Univ City ISD	81	173
Blim, John/Nocona Ind School Dist	3,5	290
Blizzard, Gary/Magnolia Ind School Dist	67	292
Block, Chelleye/Karnes City Ind School Dist	73	250
Block, Linda/Liberty-Eylau Ind School Dist	27	48
Blocker, Christy/Falls City Ind School Dist	57,271	250
Blocker, Christy/Falls City Ind School Dist	57,58,271	250
Bloodworth, Angie/Giddings Ind School Dist	2,19	263
Bloomingdale, Misty/Region 14 Ed Service Center	74	362
Blount, Brad/Paducah Ind School Dist	67	93
Blount, Irene/Paducah Ind School Dist	2	93
Blount, Wayne/Region 17 Ed Service Center	2,3,4,15,76	272
Bludau, Joann/Hallettsville Ind Sch Dist	1	262
Blue, Frankie/Dumas Ind School Dist	275	295
Blue, Misty/Kerens Ind School Dist	37,57	300
Blue, Patti/Gustine Ind School Dist	1,11,73	90
Blue, Phil/Abilene Ind School Dist	6,35	360
Bluemel, Samuel/Natalia Ind School Dist	5	284
Bluhm, Bernadette/Karnes City Ind School Dist	7	250
Blum, Karen/Tarkington Ind School Dist	4	266
Blundell, Lisa/Victoria Ind School Dist	15	382
Blunt, James/Lone Oak Ind School Dist	5	236
Blunt, Rod/Mathis Ind School Dist	6	331
Board, Gregg/Channelview Ind School Dist	91	183
Boatner, Olivia/Aldine Ind School Dist	92	179
Bob, Joe/Chapel Hill Ind School Dist	58	337
Bobbitt, Brian/New Boston Ind School Dist	1	49
Bobbitt, Charlie/Crockett Ind School Dist	73	232
Bobbitt, Leah/West Rusk Co Cons Ind Sch Dist	15	328
Bobino, Sabrina/High Island Ind Sch Dist	5	160
Bobo, Ryan/Cotton Center Ind School Dist	1	174
Bocanegra, Edward/Pearsall Ind School Dist	6	157
Bodden, Rena/Nederland Ind School Dist	4	242
Bode, Trish/Leander Ind School Dist	67	396
Bodwell, Carol/Princeton Ind School Dist	67	84
Boedeker, Kim/Melissa Ind School Dist	69	81
Boehme, Braden/Jourdanton Ind School Dist	5	20
Boehs, Kenneth/Canyon Ind School Dist	295	321
Boeker, Lewis/Forsan Ind School Dist	67	234
Boettger, Cavin, Dr/Denison Ind School Dist	31	166
Boggas, Kristi/Trinidad Ind School Dist	4	214
Boggs, Holly/Morton Ind School Dist	9,11,57,88	75
Bogle, Katrina/Hamlin Ind School Dist	73,76,84,295	249
Bogt, Holly/Kerrville Ind School Dist	71	256
Bohannan, Bo/Harmony Ind School Dist	5	376

1 Superintendent	16 Instructional Media Svcs	30 Adult Education	44 Science Sec	58 Special Education K-12	72 Summer School	88 Alternative/At Risk	277 Remedial Math K-12
2 Bus/Finance/Purchasing	17 Chief Operations Officer	31 Career/Sch-to-Work K-12	45 Math K-12	59 Special Education Elem	73 Instructional Tech	89 Multi-Cultural Curriculum	280 Literacy Coach
3 Buildings And Grounds	18 Chief Academic Officer	32 Career/Sch-to-Work Elem	46 Math Elem	60 Special Education Sec	74 Inservice Training	90 Social Work	285 STEM
4 Food Service	19 Chief Financial Officer	33 Career/Sch-to-Work Sec	47 Math Sec	61 Foreign/World Lang K-12	75 Marketing/Distributive	91 Safety/Security	286 Digital Learning
5 Transportation	20 Art K-12	34 Early Childhood Ed	48 English/Lang Arts K-12	62 Foreign/World Lang Elem	76 Info Systems	92 Magnet School	288 Common Core Standards
6 Athletic	21 Art Elem	35 Health/Phys Education	49 English/Lang Arts Elem	63 Foreign/World Lang Sec	77 Psychological Assess	93 Parental Involvement	294 Accountability
7 Health Services	22 Art Sec	36 Guidance Services K-12	50 English/Lang Arts Sec	64 Religious Education K-12	78 Affirmative Action	95 Tech Prep Program	295 Network System
8 Curric/Instruct K-12	23 Music K-12	37 Guidance Services Elem	51 Reading K-12	65 Religious Education Elem	79 Student Personnel	97 Chief Information Officer	296 Title II Programs
9 Curric/Instruct Elem	24 Music Elem	38 Guidance Services Sec	52 Reading Elem	66 Religious Education Sec	80 Driver Ed/Safety	98 Chief Technology Officer	297 Webmaster
10 Curric/Instruct Sec	25 Music Sec	39 Social Studies K-12	53 Reading Sec	67 School Board President	81 Gifted/Talented	270 Character Education	298 Grant Writer/Ptnrships
11 Federal Program	26 Business Education	40 Social Studies Elem	54 Remedial Reading K-12	68 Teacher Personnel	82 Video Services	271 Migrant Education	750 Chief Innovation Officer
12 Title I	27 Career & Tech Ed	41 Social Studies Sec	55 Remedial Reading Elem	69 Academic Assessment	83 Substance Abuse Prev	273 Teacher Mentor	751 Chief of Staff
13 Title V	28 Technology Education	42 Science K-12	56 Remedial Reading Sec	70 Research/Development	84 Erate	274 Before/After Sch	752 Social Emotional Learning
15 Asst Superintendent	29 Family/Consumer Science	43 Science Elem	57 Bilingual/ELL	71 Public Information	85 AIDS Education	275 Response To Intervention	

Texas School Directory
DISTRICT PERSONNEL INDEX

NAME/District	JOB FUNCTIONS	PAGE
Bohannon, David/*North East Ind School Dist*	2	34
Bohannon, Dawn/*Ector Ind School Dist*	16,73	146
Bohannon, Gary/*Ector Ind School Dist*	1	146
Bohling, Kathryn/*Mesquite Ind School Dist*	2,3,15	110
Bohn, Susan, Dr/*Aledo Ind School Dist*	1	312
Boiles, Donna/*Whitesboro Ind School Dist*	36,69,77	168
Boitmann, Jona/*Princeton Ind School Dist*	2,3,15,298	84
Bolek, Brian/*Eanes Ind School Dist*	3	370
Bolen, Judy, Dr/*Wylie Ind School Dist*	69,294	85
Boles, Charles/*Miles Ind School Dist*	6	326
Boles, Kyle/*Cleburne Ind School Dist*	68	247
Boles, Zachery/*Tomball Ind School Dist*	2	203
Bolin, Kim/*Center Point Ind School Dist*	58	255
Bolm, Mindy/*Ralls Ind School Dist*	77	94
Bolt, Heather/*Queen City Ind School Dist*	77	70
Boltie, Lisa/*Southwest Ind School Dist*	69,294	43
Bolton, David/*Alvin Ind School Dist*	3	50
Bolton, Neil/*Cedar Hill Ind School Dist*	76,295	97
Bolton, Tina/*Neches Ind School Dist*	2	15
Bomar, Jerry/*Groesbeck Ind School Dist*	6	267
Bomberger, Chris/*Denton Ind School Dist*	4	120
Bonazzi, Tony/*Georgetown Ind School Dist*	45	395
Bond, Shalon/*Dallas Ind School Dist*	39	98
Bonds, Sheri/*Round Rock Ind School Dist*	27,31	398
Bonewald, Gregory, Dr/*Victoria Ind School Dist*	15,68	382
Bonilla, Victor/*Crystal City Ind School Dist*	67	407
Bonjour, Gay/*Amarillo Ind School Dist*	45	317
Bonner, Buddy, Dr/*Lewisville Ind School Dist*	15,68	122
Bonner, Jason/*Jefferson Ind School Dist*	67	274
Bonner, Joe/*Panhandle Ind School Dist*	3	69
Bonner, Kayce/*Kerens Ind School Dist*	58	300
Bonner, Mark/*Joaquin Ind School Dist*	3	335
Bono, Justin/*Richardson Ind School Dist*	67	112
Bonsal, Doug/*New Caney Ind School Dist*	74	293
Bonser, Sara/*Plano Ind School Dist*	1	82
Booher, Kim/*Holliday Ind School Dist*	69,79	19
Booker, Mark/*Garland Ind School Dist*	2	105
Boonau, Stephanie/*Henderson Ind School Dist*	8,11,57,280,285,288,296,298	327
Boone, Mike/*San Marcos Cons Ind Sch Dist*	4	211
Boone, Reggie/*Humble Ind School Dist*	76	195
Boone, Ryan/*Dickinson Ind School Dist*	2,3,15	159
Booth, Ashton/*Giddings Ind School Dist*	58	263
Booth, Brenda/*El Paso Ind School Dist*	69	132
Booth, John/*De Kalb Ind School Dist*	1	47
Booth, Veronica/*Clint Ind School Dist*	27	132
Boothe, Deanna/*White Oak Ind School Dist*	84	171
Boothe, Sharon/*Greenville Ind School Dist*	8,15,74	236
Boothe, Stacey/*Sanford-Fritch Ind School Dist*	67	238
Boozer, Stacy/*Dimmitt Ind School Dist*	11,296	71
Borchardt, Cheri/*Lorena Ind School Dist*	8,11,31,57,69,275,288	280
Borchardt, Eric/*Krum Ind School Dist*	67	122
Bordelon, Cindi/*Nederland Ind School Dist*	38	242
Borden, Cathy/*Riviera Ind School Dist*	11,57,58,271,296	258
Borden, Cory/*Cleburne Ind School Dist*	58	247
Borden, Cynthia/*Seguin Ind School Dist*	11,57,69,77,83,294	173
Borden, Nathan/*Riviera Ind School Dist*	6	258
Border, Kenny, Dr/*Shallowater Ind School Dist*	1,11	272
Bordner, Jennifer/*Cherokee Ind School Dist*	8,12,58,296	332
Boren, Catherine/*Bosqueville Ind School Dist*	2	278
Boren, Justin/*Whitesboro Ind School Dist*	67	168
Boren, Martha/*Tenaha Ind School Dist*	8,11,69	335
Borgne, Robert/*Taylor Ind School Dist*	295	399
Borkert, Penelope/*School of Excellence In Ed*	58	42
Bornemeier, Misty/*Dalhart Ind School Dist*	16,82	95
Borrego, Lucia/*Socorro Ind School Dist*	8,18	135
Borrego, Marie/*Culberson Co Allamoore Ind SD*	4	95
Borreson, Diane/*Hays Cons Ind School Dist*	73,98,295,297	211
Bos, Michael/*Borger Ind School Dist*	73,84,295	237
Boseman, Lenise/*Como Pickton Cons Ind SD*	2	231
Bosley, Melissa/*Clifton Ind School Dist*	8	46
Bosse-Savage, Allison/*Lyford Cons Ind School Dist*	67	394
Bosse, Amy/*El Campo Ind School Dist*	58	389
Bosse, Amy/*Rice Cons Ind School Dist*	58	87
Bosse, Wade/*East Bernard Ind Sch Dist*	6	389
Bostian, Brett/*Corpus Christi Ind Sch Dist*	3	303
Bostic, Robert, Dr/*Stafford Municipal Sch Dist*	1	155

NAME/District	JOB FUNCTIONS	PAGE
Bostick, Charity/*Aldine Ind School Dist*	50	179
Bostick, Larry/*Santa Anna Ind School Dist*	73	76
Boswell, Blaise/*Vernon Ind School Dist*	16,73,295	393
Boswell, Cecelia/*Waco Ind School Dist*	81	281
Botard, Mack/*Oakwood Ind School Dist*	67	264
Botello, Elaine/*Waco Ind School Dist*	15	281
Bott, Kevin/*Lampasas Ind School Dist*	8,11,57,83,286,288,296,298	261
Boubel, Alison/*Kennedale Ind School Dist*	16	355
Boudreaux, Victor/*Bremond Ind School Dist*	3	324
Bouliane, Nancy/*Navasota Ind School Dist*	16	172
Boullion, Brad/*Hardin Jefferson Ind Sch Dist*	2,3	177
Boulware, Alice/*Zavalla Ind School Dist*	2	18
Boulwave, Shade/*Corsicana Ind School Dist*	6	299
Bourguin, Paul/*Amarillo Ind School Dist*	275	317
Bourland, Linda/*Weatherford Ind School Dist*	42	313
Bourn, Loretta/*Cypress-Fairbanks Ind Sch Dist*	7	183
Bousquet, Melissa/*Waxahachie Ind School Dist*	7	142
Boutte, Andre/*Port Arthur Ind School Dist*	6	243
Boutwell, Melanie/*Manor Ind School Dist*	2	371
Bowben, Melinda/*Waskom Ind School Dist*	38	209
Bowdoin, Geoffery/*Leon Ind School Dist*	8,11,274,296	264
Bowen, Bob/*Munday Consolidated Ind SD*	5	259
Bowen, Bridgette/*Bangs Ind School Dist*	295	58
Bowen, Bridgette/*Bangs Ind School Dist*	73,76	58
Bowen, Kathleen, Dr/*Lamar Cons Ind School Dist*	68	153
Bower, Greg/*Como Pickton Cons Ind SD*	1	231
Bowers, Cherie/*Santa Fe Ind School Dist*	4	161
Bowie, Kalean/*Angleton Ind School Dist*	79	51
Bowie, Sheila/*Winona Ind School Dist*	2,298	339
Bowlin, Emily/*Tenaha Ind School Dist*	68	335
Bowlin, Terry/*Tenaha Ind School Dist*	5,298	335
Bowling, Mike/*Peaster Ind School Dist*	67	313
Bowling, Ritchie/*Maypearl Ind School Dist*	1	141
Bowman, Blake/*Joshua Ind School Dist*	3	248
Bowman, Katie/*Birdville Ind School Dist*	2	346
Bowman, Kimberly/*Munday Consolidated Ind SD*	73,273,286,295	259
Bowser, Jacob/*Castleberry Ind School Dist*	76	347
Boxwell, Cindy/*Perryton Ind School Dist*	16	307
Boyce, Charles/*Onalaska Ind School Dist*	73,286	317
Boyce, Joy/*Richards Ind School Dist*	2	172
Boyce, William/*Richards Ind School Dist*	8,57,73,74,271,295	172
Boyce, William/*Richards Ind School Dist*	1,11,84	172
Boyd, Angela/*Hillsboro Ind School Dist*	8	227
Boyd, Cheri/*Decatur Ind School Dist*	67	403
Boyd, Dennis/*Pampa Ind School Dist*	295	165
Boyd, Felicia/*Slaton Ind School Dist*	34	272
Boyd, Kathy/*Hawkins Ind School Dist*	16,82	404
Boyd, Kent/*Temple Ind School Dist*	2,15	29
Boyd, Lori/*Cisco Independent Sch Dist*	4	128
Boyd, Shannon/*Somerset Ind School Dist*	10	42
Boyd, Wes/*Tatum Ind School Dist*	16,73,76,84,295	328
Boydstun, Kelli/*Boys Ranch Ind School Dist*	27,31,36	307
Boyer, Jenny/*Navasota Ind School Dist*	58	172
Boyer, Ronda/*Austin Ind School Dist*	81	366
Boyett, Debra/*Albany Ind School Dist*	4	334
Boyett, Eric/*New Summerfield Ind Sch Dist*	3,5	73
Boyett, Kathy/*Tidehaven Ind School Dist*	8,288	276
Boyette, Charles/*San Augustine Ind School Dist*	67	329
Boyette, Tammy, Dr/*Warren Ind School Dist*	1	375
Boylard, Doug/*Wilson Ind School Dist*	67	273
Boynton, Sharay/*Birdville Ind School Dist*	2	346
Boyte, Bradley/*Mildred Ind School Dist*	67	300
Boyter, Brandon/*Allen Ind School Dist*	3	76
Bozah, Dalia/*Ramirez Common School Dist*	2	128
Braaton, Cindy/*Iola Ind School Dist*	7	172
Braaton, Kristi/*Neches Ind School Dist*	7	15
Brabham, Beth, Dr/*Midway Ind School Dist*	57,81,271,280	280
Bracey, Anke/*Boyd Ind School Dist*	11,296	402
Brackin, Regi/*Burleson Ind School Dist*	3	246
Bracy, Rick/*Grapevine-Colleyville Ind SD*	31	353
Braden, Brittany/*Cuero Ind School Dist*	36	117
Braden, Katie/*Rockwall Ind School Dist*	43	325
Bradford, James/*Mineral Wells Ind School Dist*	3,91	310
Bradford, Jeff/*Richardson Ind School Dist*	20	112
Bradford, Kathy/*Hallsville Ind School Dist*	84	208
Bradford, Khechara/*Ft Worth Ind School Dist*	8,15	349

School Year 2019-2020 800-333-8802 TX-T9

DISTRICT PERSONNEL INDEX

Market Data Retrieval

NAME/District	JOB FUNCTIONS	PAGE
Bradford, Khechara/Spring Ind School Dist	8,280	202
Bradley, Chad/Henderson Ind School Dist	83	327
Bradley, Greg/Prosper Ind School Dist	15	84
Bradley, Janet/Vidor Ind School Dist	76	309
Bradley, Megan/Killeen Ind School Dist	2,19	27
Bradley, Sarah/Victoria Ind School Dist	50	382
Bradley, Sheila/Palestine Ind School Dist	91	15
Bradsfield, Micheal/Ft Bend Ind School Dist	5	149
Bradshaw, Cecil/Ft Stockton Ind School Dist	5	315
Bradshaw, Chris/Maud Ind School Dist	1	49
Bradshaw, Kim/Alto Ind School Dist	3	72
Bradshaw, Siera/Elysian Fields Ind School Dist	60	208
Bradshaw, Teresa/Quitman Ind School Dist	5	404
Brady, Beth/Sabinal Ind School Dist	275	378
Brady, Lana/Arp Ind School Dist	8,11,74,273	336
Brady, Zack/Lubbock Ind School Dist	67	269
Braeuer, Penny/Troy Ind School Dist	7,85	29
Bragg, Brittany/Northwest Ind School Dist	50	124
Bragg, Chrisco/Joaquin Ind School Dist	67	335
Bragg, Earl/Salado Ind School Dist	73	29
Bragg, Sheryl/Dawson Ind School Dist	8,13,31,38,69,286,288	299
Braley, Larry/Fannindel Ind School Dist	5	120
Branam, James/Celeste Ind School Dist	10	235
Branch, Jessica/Wylie Ind School Dist	11	84
Branch, Stacey/Sweeny Ind School Dist	295	54
Brand, Belinda/Moody Ind School Dist	8,12,57,69,286,298	281
Brand, Laurie/Denison Ind School Dist	10	166
Brandon, Cindy/Marshall Ind School Dist	4	209
Brandon, Jana/Quanah Ind School Dist	2	177
Brandon, Merl, Dr/Stanton Ind School Dist	1	274
Branecky, Robin/Flatonia Ind School Dist	11	147
Brann, Kimberly/New Braunfels Ind School Dist	57	88
Brannon, Barbara/Mumford Ind School Dist	3,4,5,69,71,74,271	56
Brannon, Deborah/Plano Ind School Dist	50	82
Branton, Amy/Florence Ind School Dist	68	395
Branum, Chad/Arlington Ind School Dist	15,73	343
Branum, Tabitha/Richardson Ind School Dist	15	112
Brasfield, Misty/Bloomington Ind School Dist	2,5,11,15,84	381
Brashear, Angie/Burleson Milam Spec Serv Co-op	1	288
Brashear, Angie/Milano Ind School Dist	58	287
Brashear, Tommy/Cameron Ind School Dist	6	287
Brasher, Jeff, Dr/Fredericksburg Ind School Dist	1	162
Braswell, Cylynn/Northwest Ind School Dist	27,31,285	124
Braswell, David/La Gloria Ind School Dist	1,11,73,83,84,288	245
Braswell, Marci, Dr/Ricardo Ind School Dist	9,57	257
Braswell, Renee/Junction Ind School Dist	57	256
Bratcher-Hair, Marty/Slidell Ind School Dist	15,58	403
Bratcher-Hair, Marty/Slidell Ind School Dist	8,11,15,16,57,58,286	403
Bratcher, Deanne/Loop Ind School Dist	2	157
Bratcher, Melissa/Ropes Ind School Dist	57	229
Bratcher, Shelly, Dr/Lubbock Ind School Dist	58	269
Bratton, James/San Marcos Cons Ind Sch Dist	296	211
Bratton, Jessie/Chapel Hill Ind School Dist	274	363
Brau, James/Bryan Ind School Dist	2	54
Braun, Walter/Santa Fe Ind School Dist	91	161
Brawley, Rusty/Quanah Ind School Dist	11,58	177
Brawner, Renee/East Chambers Ind School Dist	8	72
Braxton, Tiffany/Sabine Ind School Dist	37	170
Bray, Jerry/St Jo Ind School Dist	60	290
Bray, Kelly/Bosqueville Ind School Dist	8,11,271,274	278
Bray, Robert/Dawson Ind School Dist	11,83,88,271	299
Breaux, Darlene/Harris Co Dept of Ed	70	179
Breaux, Kristin/Huffman Ind School Dist	39	195
Breazeale, Tanya/Lake Travis Ind School Dist	4	370
Breed, Sherry/Ft Worth Ind School Dist	15,79	349
Brence, Gerald/Plano Ind School Dist	6	82
Brenner, Dawn/North Zulch Ind School Dist	2	274
Brent, Fred, Dr/Georgetown Ind School Dist	1	395
Brents, Kim/Lockhart Ind School Dist	11,91,270	61
Bresnahan, Amy/Argyle Ind School Dist	4	120
Bressler, Shannon/Denver City Ind School Dist	2	405
Bressler, Shannon/Happy Ind School Dist	2,11,296	342
Bressler, Stefan/Amarillo Ind School Dist	298	317
Brewer, Cherkoee/St Jo Ind School Dist	3,5	290
Brewer, Melanie/Wylie Ind School Dist	4	361
Brewer, Monica/Texas Dept of Education	81	1
Brewer, Norma/Weslaco Ind School Dist	79	225
Brewer, Tracy/Navasota Ind School Dist	15,68,79	172
Brewer, Will/Stamford Ind School Dist	1	250
Brewington, Kim/Grand Saline Ind School Dist	58	380
Bria, Kim/Northside Ind School Dist	7	393
Brice, Vickie/West Orange-Cove Cons ISD	34	309
Bricken, Cheryl/Snyder Ind School Dist	58	333
Bricker, Jolyn/Bryan Ind School Dist	9	54
Briden, Mike/Louise Ind School Dist	3,5,91	389
Bridge, Gary/Patton Springs Ind School Dist	67	127
Bridgers, Kam/Waxahachie Ind School Dist	4	142
Bridges, Bob/Weatherford Ind School Dist	3	313
Bridges, Cecily/Hemphill Ind School Dist	7,85	329
Bridges, Donnie/Memphis Ind School Dist	3	175
Bridges, Drew/Florence Ind School Dist	6	395
Bridges, Jenny/Waxahachie Ind School Dist	71	142
Bridges, Jim/Prosper Ind School Dist	67	84
Bridges, Judy/Midland Ind School Dist	81	285
Bridges, Lesia/Dodd City Ind School Dist	2,8,11,16,58,74,294,298	145
Bridges, Nancy/Grand Prairie Ind School Dist	2,15	107
Bridges, Peggy/Terrell Ind School Dist	27,31	253
Bridges, Randell/Prairiland Ind School Dist	3	260
Bridges, Ronda/Lometa Ind School Dist	2	262
Bridges, Vicki/Grand Prairie Ind School Dist	3,15	107
Bridgman, Mark/Winters Ind School Dist	5	327
Briese, John/Millsap Ind School Dist	73	312
Briggs, Julie/Richardson Ind School Dist	16	112
Briggs, Reese/Hemphill Ind School Dist	1	329
Briggs, Tonya/New Boston Ind School Dist	27	49
Bright, David/El Campo Ind School Dist	2,3,15,17	389
Bright, Jeff, Dr/San Angelo Ind School Dist	2,15	364
Bright, Jon/Rankin Ind School Dist	58	377
Bright, Roxanne/London Ind School Dist	4	305
Bright, Tammy/Cleburne Ind School Dist	12,15,296	247
Briles, Art/Mt Vernon Ind School Dist	6	155
Brim, Amanda/Lewisville Ind School Dist	71	122
Brink, Heather/Central Ind School Dist	4	17
Brink, Justin/Robinson Ind School Dist	295	281
Brinker, Joseph/Marshall Ind School Dist	5	209
Brinkley, Boone/Oglesby Ind School Dist	3,5	93
Brinkley, Molly/Pampa Ind School Dist	73	165
Brinkman, Tammy/Coupland Ind School Dist	1,11,57,83	395
Brinkman, Tammy/Iola Ind School Dist	11,271,273	172
Brinlee, Ricky/Howe Ind School Dist	3,5	166
Brinson, Lisa/Deweyville Ind School Dist	7,85	308
Brinson, Steve/Bridge City Ind School Dist	83,91	308
Brinson, Terri/Early Ind School Dist	79	58
Briones, Dina/Crystal City Ind School Dist	752	407
Briones, Judy/Marathon Ind School Dist	67	56
Brisbin, Lauren/Belton Ind School Dist	57,280	26
Brisco, Kristine/Snook Ind School Dist	67	59
Briscoe, Beth/Needville Ind School Dist	8,11,15,69,271	154
Briseno, Pablo/Crystal City Ind School Dist	69	407
Brisero, Cynthia/Edcouch Elsa Ind School Dist	36,85	215
Brison, Alan/Pittsburg Ind School Dist	67	68
Bristow, Keith/La Poynor Ind School Dist	67	214
Britt, Jim/Bowie Ind School Dist	73,84,295	289
Brittain, Jason/Angleton Ind School Dist	6	51

1 Superintendent	16 Instructional Media Svcs	30 Adult Education	44 Science Sec	58 Special Education K-12	72 Summer School	88 Alternative/At Risk	277 Remedial Math K-12
2 Bus/Finance/Purchasing	17 Chief Operations Officer	31 Career/Sch-to-Work K-12	45 Math K-12	59 Special Education Elem	73 Instructional Tech	89 Multi-Cultural Curriculum	280 Literacy Coach
3 Buildings And Grounds	18 Chief Academic Officer	32 Career/Sch-to-Work Elem	46 Math Elem	60 Special Education Sec	74 Inservice Training	90 Social Work	285 STEM
4 Food Service	19 Chief Financial Officer	33 Career/Sch-to-Work Sec	47 Math Sec	61 Foreign/World Lang K-12	75 Marketing/Distributive	91 Safety/Security	286 Digital Learning
5 Transportation	20 Art K-12	34 Early Childhood Ed	48 English/Lang Arts K-12	62 Foreign/World Lang Elem	76 Info Systems	92 Magnet School	288 Common Core Standards
6 Athletic	21 Art Elem	35 Health/Phys Education	49 English/Lang Arts Elem	63 Foreign/World Lang Sec	77 Psychological Assess	93 Parental Involvement	294 Accountability
7 Health Services	22 Art Sec	36 Guidance Services K-12	50 English/Lang Arts Sec	64 Religious Education K-12	78 Affirmative Action	95 Tech Prep Program	295 Network System
8 Curric/Instruct K-12	23 Music K-12	37 Guidance Services Elem	51 Reading K-12	65 Religious Education Elem	79 Student Personnel	97 Chief Infomation Officer	296 Title II Programs
9 Curric/Instruct Elem	24 Music Elem	38 Guidance Services Sec	52 Reading Elem	66 Religious Education Sec	80 Driver Ed/Safety	98 Chief Technology Officer	297 Webmaster
10 Curric/Instruct Sec	25 Music Sec	39 Social Studies K-12	53 Reading Sec	67 School Board President	81 Gifted/Talented	270 Character Education	298 Grant Writer/Ptnrships
11 Federal Program	26 Business Education	40 Social Studies Elem	54 Remedial Reading K-12	68 Teacher Personnel	82 Video Services	271 Migrant Education	750 Chief Innovation Officer
12 Title I	27 Career & Tech Ed	41 Social Studies Sec	55 Remedial Reading Elem	69 Academic Assessment	83 Substance Abuse Prev	273 Teacher Mentor	751 Chief of Staff
13 Title V	28 Technology Education	42 Science K-12	56 Remedial Reading Sec	70 Research/Development	84 Erate	274 Before/After Sch	752 Social Emotional Learning
15 Asst Superintendent	29 Family/Consumer Science	43 Science Elem	57 Bilingual/ELL	71 Public Information	85 AIDS Education	275 Response To Intervention	

Texas School Directory

DISTRICT PERSONNEL INDEX

NAME/District	JOB FUNCTIONS	PAGE
Brittain, Tim/*Huffman Ind School Dist*	2,11,19	195
Britting, Susan/*Breckenridge Ind School Dist*	58	341
Britton, Blane/*Meadow Ind School Dist*	73	362
Britton, Delwin/*Sundown Ind School Dist*	67	229
Britton, Nancy/*East Central Ind School Dist*	4	31
Britton, Patrick/*School of Excellence In Ed*	67	42
Broadhurst, Lance/*Littlefield Ind School Dist*	67	260
Broadstreet, Melaynee/*Lake Dallas Ind School Dist*	71	122
Broadus, Amy/*Kilgore Ind School Dist*	68	169
Broadwater, Sheri/*Longview Ind School Dist*	11,54,298	169
Brocher, Melinda/*Georgetown Ind School Dist*	71	395
Brock, Brooke/*Athens Ind School Dist*	58	213
Brock, Jennifer, Dr/*Region 4 Ed Service Center*	34,39,48,51,57	208
Brock, Laura Lee/*Electra Ind School Dist*	2,8,11,27,31,88,273	391
Brock, Stephanie/*New Waverly Ind School Dist*	8,11,288,298	383
Brock, Walt/*Granger Ind School Dist*	6	396
Brockett, Marie/*Bruceville-Eddy Ind Sch Dist*	11,69,294,296,298	278
Brockett, Rhonda/*Ponder Ind School Dist*	16,82	125
Brockman, Beth, Dr/*Plano Ind School Dist*	15,68	82
Brockman, Gary/*Woodson Ind School Dist*	67	363
Brockman, Mitchell/*Nazareth Ind School Dist*	67	71
Brockman, Rhonda/*Woodson Ind School Dist*	4	363
Broesche, Leslie/*Brenham Ind School Dist*	34,58,275	385
Brogden, Jeff/*Mansfield Ind School Dist*	3,5,15	356
Broner Westerl, Debra/*Klein Ind School Dist*	27	196
Bronis, Juan/*La Feria Ind School Dist*	67	65
Bronson, Cindy/*Lovejoy Ind School Dist*	43	80
Brooks, Aaron/*Harper Ind School Dist*	8,11,69,74,294,296	163
Brooks, Amy/*Comanche Ind School Dist*	4	89
Brooks, Angela/*Houston Ind School Dist*	298	188
Brooks, Anthony/*Mexia Ind School Dist*	295	267
Brooks, Jamie/*Whitesboro Ind School Dist*	2	168
Brooks, Justin/*Greenwood Ind School Dist*	67	285
Brooks, Keith, Dr/*Sheldon Ind School Dist*	10	200
Brooks, Kim/*Highland Park Ind Sch Dist*	81	108
Brooks, Marie/*Marion Ind School Dist*	4	172
Brooks, Melvin/*Shiner Ind School Dist*	3	262
Brooks, Michael/*Frenship Ind School Dist*	5	269
Brooks, Michelle/*Westwood Ind School Dist*	76	16
Brooks, Mike/*Salado Ind School Dist*	3,4,5,17	29
Brooks, Mike/*Waller Ind School Dist*	68	384
Brooks, Scott/*Canutillo Ind School Dist*	6	131
Brooks, Shelly/*Miami Ind School Dist*	57	324
Brooks, Tony/*Athens Ind School Dist*	73,76,286	213
Brooks, Wesley/*Midway Ind School Dist*	2,15	280
Broome, Richard/*Medina Valley Ind School Dist*	5	284
Broscoss, Julee/*Slaton Ind School Dist*	1	272
Brosnahan, Carla/*Cypress-Fairbanks Ind Sch Dist*	15	183
Brossman, Sheila/*Schulenburg Ind School Dist*	57	148
Brothers, Ray/*Fayetteville Ind School Dist*	16,31,73,295	147
Brou, Jason/*Aransas Pass Ind School Dist*	73	330
Broumley, Dana/*Hico Ind School Dist*	37	176
Broumley, Keith/*Hico Ind School Dist*	67	176
Broussard, Colby/*Bellevue Ind School Dist*	6	74
Brown, A Tracie/*Arlington Ind School Dist*	15	343
Brown, Allen/*Pasadena Ind School Dist*	76	198
Brown, Amanda/*River Road Ind School Dist*	67	319
Brown, Angela/*Coppell Ind School Dist*	75	98
Brown, Anthony/*Paint Rock Ind School Dist*	67	90
Brown, Asheley/*Carrollton-Farmers Branch ISD*	68,84	96
Brown, Barbara/*Marlin Ind School Dist*	4	144
Brown, Blair/*Panhandle Ind School Dist*	1,11	69
Brown, Brandon/*Schulenburg Ind School Dist*	6	147
Brown, Brenda/*Hull Daisetta Ind School Dist*	4	266
Brown, Bridget/*Wellman Union Ind School Dist*	12,271,275	362
Brown, Brittanie/*Henrietta Ind School Dist*	4	74
Brown, Cayla/*Hubbard Ind School Dist*	752	48
Brown, Chad/*Comanche Ind School Dist*	5	89
Brown, Chesney/*Hondo Ind School Dist*	7	284
Brown, Connie/*Van Vleck Ind School Dist*	4	276
Brown, Danny/*Tyler Ind School Dist*	83,91	337
Brown, Darrell, Dr/*Birdville Ind School Dist*	1	346
Brown, David/*Bandera Ind School Dist*	16,73,82,84,295,297	23
Brown, David, Dr/*Van Alstyne Ind School Dist*	1	168
Brown, Deborah/*Hays Cons Ind School Dist*	275	211
Brown, Denise/*Wichita Falls Ind School Dist*	2	392
Brown, Eddie/*Hempstead Ind School Dist*	5	384
Brown, Ezell/*Clear Creek Ind School Dist*	5	158
Brown, Fred/*Sands Consolidated ISD*	5	117
Brown, Glenn/*Everman Ind School Dist*	3	349
Brown, Gradyne, Dr/*Garland Ind School Dist*	15,68	105
Brown, Greg/*Plainview Ind School Dist*	15	175
Brown, Jamie/*Cedar Hill Ind School Dist*	71	97
Brown, Jamie/*San Antonio Ind School Dist*	69	39
Brown, Jason/*Liberty-Eylau Ind School Dist*	16,73	48
Brown, Jason/*Pottsboro Ind School Dist*	73,286,295	167
Brown, Kalith/*Dawson Ind School Dist*	67	116
Brown, Kareen/*Galena Park Ind School Dist*	81	186
Brown, Karen/*Miles Ind School Dist*	36	326
Brown, Kathleen/*Duncanville Ind School Dist*	15,68	104
Brown, Keith/*Taylor Ind School Dist*	1	399
Brown, Kenneth/*Boys Ranch Ind School Dist*	1	307
Brown, Khristie/*Grapevine-Colleyville Ind SD*	34	353
Brown, Kristen/*Barbers Hill Ind School Dist*	59	72
Brown, Kristen/*Clarendon Cons Ind Sch Dist*	2	127
Brown, Kristin/*Lyford Cons Ind School Dist*	8,15,69	394
Brown, Kristine/*Little Cypress Mauriceville SD*	35,75	308
Brown, Lakeyshia/*Manor Ind School Dist*	46	371
Brown, Larry/*Huntsville Ind School Dist*	3	383
Brown, Leslie/*Wells Ind School Dist*	8,11,69,294	73
Brown, Lisa/*Ft Sam Houston Ind School Dist*	67	32
Brown, Mark/*Centerville Ind School Dist*	1,11	374
Brown, Mark/*Gary Ind School Dist*	6	311
Brown, Mary/*Hallsville Ind School Dist*	2,19	208
Brown, Melanie/*Clyde Consolidated Ind SD*	4	62
Brown, Michael/*Kilgore Ind School Dist*	3,5	169
Brown, Michelle/*Dallas Ind School Dist*	280	98
Brown, Monet/*Whitehouse Ind School Dist*	68	339
Brown, Pam/*Lubbock-Cooper Ind Sch Dist*	36,69	271
Brown, Pamela/*Lancaster Ind School Dist*	15,57,68,79,81	110
Brown, Patrick/*Los Fresnos Cons Ind Sch Dist*	6	66
Brown, Patti/*Borger Ind School Dist*	58,275	237
Brown, Patti/*Panhandle Ind School Dist*	58	69
Brown, Paul/*Huntsville Ind School Dist*	2,19	383
Brown, Paula/*Cuero Ind School Dist*	16,73,76,286,295	117
Brown, Perri/*Water Valley Ind School Dist*	57	365
Brown, Randall/*De Kalb Ind School Dist*	16,73,295	48
Brown, Randy, Dr/*Alvord Ind School Dist*	1	402
Brown, Rebecca/*Spring Branch Ind School Dist*	8	200
Brown, Roger, Dr/*Humble Ind School Dist*	8,15,18,79	195
Brown, Ronald/*Woodville Ind School Dist*	5	375
Brown, Roxanne/*North East Ind School Dist*	81	34
Brown, Shelby/*Arp Ind School Dist*	7,85	336
Brown, Sherri/*Skidmore Tynan Ind SD*	36,88	25
Brown, Stephanie, Dr/*Highland Park Ind Sch Dist*	69	108
Brown, Steve/*New Braunfels Ind School Dist*	2	88
Brown, Sue/*Red Oak Ind School Dist*	7	142
Brown, Tamekia, Dr/*El Paso Ind School Dist*	8,18	132
Brown, Tammy/*Hunt Ind School Dist*	273,288	255
Brown, Telisa/*Arlington Ind School Dist*	36	343
Brown, Terry/*Grapeland Ind School Dist*	3	232
Brown, Thurman/*Connally Ind School Dist*	8	279
Brown, Tiffany/*Gary Ind School Dist*	57	311
Brown, Tobin/*Kemp Ind School Dist*	73,297	252
Brown, Tommy/*Alvarado Ind School Dist*	71	246
Brown, Tracey, Dr/*Irving Ind School Dist*	36	109
Brown, Travis/*Hutto Ind School Dist*	73,76,295	396
Brown, Trina/*Pilot Point Ind School Dist*	11,296	125
Brown, Van/*Neches Ind School Dist*	67	15
Brown, Vicki/*Gorman Ind School Dist*	58	129
Brown, Wes/*North Lamar Ind School Dist*	27,31,271	259
Browne, Brett/*Ferris Ind School Dist*	16,73,84,295	140
Browne, Tanya/*Dallas Ind School Dist*	58	98
Browning, Anne/*Channing Ind School Dist*	2	209
Browning, Gary/*Graham Ind School Dist*	8,288	406
Browning, Rick/*Mineola Ind School Dist*	3	404
Brownlee, Steve, Dr/*Rosebud-Lott Ind School Dist*	1	145
Brubaker, Doug, Dr/*Garland Ind School Dist*	15	105
Bruhmer, Ron/*Ore City Ind School Dist*	6	377
Bruhn, Barbara/*Region 7 Ed Service Center*	73,76,286	171
Bruman, Tony/*Roosevelt Ind School Dist*	4	271
Brument, Brent, Dr/*North East Ind School Dist*	79,88,90,270	34

School Year 2019-2020   800-333-8802   TX-T11

DISTRICT PERSONNEL INDEX

Market Data Retrieval

NAME/District	JOB FUNCTIONS	PAGE
Brumfield, Ellen/Moulton Ind School Dist	57,271	262
Brumfield, Stefanie/Bryan Ind School Dist	2	54
Brumit, Martin/Kerens Ind School Dist	1,11,83	300
Brumley, Kimberly/Abilene Ind School Dist	8	360
Brummett, Deanna/Comfort Ind School Dist	38	254
Bruner, Todd/Avalon Ind School Dist	67	140
Bruster, Shelly/Smyer Ind School Dist	88,270,296	229
Bruton, Donnie/Georgetown Ind School Dist	73	395
Bruton, Justin/Rice Ind School Dist	16	300
Bruton, Loree, Dr/Alvin Ind School Dist	7,11,15,36,58	50
Bruton, Teresa/Loraine Ind School Dist	4	289
Bryan, Amy/Santo Ind School Dist	67	310
Bryan, Holly/Menard Ind School Dist	2,68	285
Bryan, Kevin/Henderson Ind School Dist	73,84,295	327
Bryan, Melissa/Copperas Cove Ind School Dist	4	92
Bryan, Ronnie/Jasper Ind School Dist	3	240
Bryan, Rowdy/Happy Ind School Dist	73,286,295,297	342
Bryan, Shane/Highland Park Ind Sch Dist	3	108
Bryan, Sharon/Whitesboro Ind School Dist	16	168
Bryan, Susan/Big Spring Ind School Dist	2	233
Bryan, Teresa/Trent Ind School Dist	2	361
Bryant, Adi/Royse City Ind School Dist	71,298	326
Bryant, Ashley/Ector Co Ind School Dist	42	130
Bryant, Blake/Yorktown Ind School Dist	73	118
Bryant, Bruce/Canadian Ind School Dist	8	213
Bryant, Byron/Royse City Ind School Dist	2,19	326
Bryant, Darla/Walcott Ind School Dist	12,296	119
Bryant, Doug/Paradise Ind School Dist	73,76,286	403
Bryant, Doug/Poolville Ind School Dist	8,16,73	313
Bryant, John/Morgan Ind School Dist	1,11,73,83	47
Bryant, Karen/Channelview Ind School Dist	69,70	183
Bryant, Keith/Lubbock-Cooper Ind Sch Dist	1	271
Bryant, Melodie/Gruver Ind School Dist	58	176
Bryant, Ronnie/Beaumont Ind School Dist	20,23	241
Bryant, Shannon/Keller Ind School Dist	47	354
Bryant, Starla/Alba-Golden Ind School Dist	88	404
Bryant, Steve/East Central Ind School Dist	67	31
Bryant, Tanya/Central Heights Ind Sch Dist	4	297
Bryce, Cyndi/Sabine Ind School Dist	16,82	170
Bryce, Stacey/Sabine Ind School Dist	1	170
Bryne, Denniella/Eagle Pass Ind School Dist	71	276
Brysch, Karla/Poth Ind School Dist	12	401
Bryson, Jamie, Dr/Humble Ind School Dist	11,296	195
Brzozowski, Patrick/Edna Ind School Dist	67	239
Bubose, Bil/Abernathy Ind School Dist	67	174
Bucek, Mandy/Hallettsville Ind Sch Dist	8	262
Buchanan, Cynthia/Aldine Ind School Dist	16	179
Buchanan, Debi, Dr/Garland Ind School Dist	58	105
Buchanan, Doug/South Texas Ind School Dist	67	67
Buchanan, Jill/Hallsville Ind School Dist	76	208
Buchanan, Shannon, Dr/Morgan Mill Ind School Dist	67	144
Buchenau, Pati/Amarillo Ind School Dist	2,19	317
Buchman, Linda/Spring Branch Ind School Dist	15,71	200
Buchmeyer, Sam/Grand Prairie Ind School Dist	71	107
Buck, Staci/Mansfield Ind School Dist	275	356
Buck, Vlada/Hereford Ind School Dist	4	119
Buckingham, Bret/Kelton Ind School Dist	67	390
Buckley, Heather/Wylie Ind School Dist	81	85
Buckley, Laura/Jarrell Ind School Dist	37,273	396
Buckner, James/Weatherford Ind School Dist	23	313
Buckner, Jay/Warren Ind School Dist	6	375
Buckner, Paul/Bryan Ind School Dist	3	54
Buckner, Paula/Chico Ind School Dist	59	403
Buechman, Karen/Plano Ind School Dist	27	82
Buehring, Erica/Runge Ind School Dist	36,69,83,88	251
Buell, Christi, Dr/Arlington Ind School Dist	15	343
Buenrostro, Laticia/Natalia Ind School Dist	11,58,288,296	284

NAME/District	JOB FUNCTIONS	PAGE
Buenteo, Elda/George West Ind School Dist	16	268
Bufe, Linda/Abernathy Ind School Dist	2	174
Buffa, Joseph/Sinton Ind School Dist	5,73,76,295	332
Buffe, Landon/Priddy Ind School Dist	27	289
Buffe, Leonard/Malone Independent School Dist	6,35	228
Buffe, Linda/Malone Independent School Dist	1,11,73,84,288	228
Buffington, Mike/Lumberton Ind School Dist	80	178
Bufkin, Kristi/Munday Consolidated Ind SD	9,12,57,288,296	259
Buford, Monica/Pewitt Cons Ind School Dist	4	296
Buhidar, Valarie/Corpus Christi Ind Sch Dist	12,40	303
Buis, Jamie/Tidehaven Ind School Dist	83,91	276
Bulion, Courtney/Hardin Jefferson Ind Sch Dist	4	177
Bull, Burt/Riviera Ind School Dist	67	258
Bull, Cindy/East Chambers Ind School Dist	11,57,58,77,83,88,271,296	72
Bullard, Marlene/Tornillo Ind School Dist	67	137
Bullard, Randi/Levelland Ind School Dist	5	229
Bullinger, Valine/Paint Creek Ind School Dist	36,69,83,85,88,270	210
Bullock, Jason, Dr/Magnolia Ind School Dist	15	292
Bullock, Karyn/Mineral Wells Ind School Dist	71	310
Bullock, Lynne/Jacksonville Ind School Dist	73	73
Bullock, Robin/Allen Ind School Dist	15	76
Bulls, Pam/Troy Ind School Dist	67	29
Bumback, Joel/Joaquin Ind School Dist	2,12	335
Bumgarner, Dena/Huffman Ind School Dist	79	195
Bunch, Kriesti/Somerset Ind School Dist	8,18,74	42
Bunch, Scot/Bastrop Ind School Dist	3,91	23
Bundrick, Cindy/Overton Ind School Dist	27	328
Bunker, Bret/Boerne Ind School Dist	39	253
Bunting, Deena/Vidor Ind School Dist	7	309
Burbank, Kathy/Lake Travis Ind School Dist	69,73,294	370
Burch, Tami/Crawford Ind School Dist	295	279
Burcham, Gregg/Midlothian Ind School Dist	295	141
Burchfiel, Roxanne/Plano Ind School Dist	53,54	82
Burchfield, Terri, Dr/Texas City Ind School Dist	12,15,69,79,273,296	161
Burciaga, Richard/Godley Ind School Dist	5	247
Burd, Jerry/Humble Ind School Dist	5	195
Burden, Adrianne, Dr/Priddy Ind School Dist	1,11,57,73,83,84	289
Burdine, Jason/Ft Bend Ind School Dist	67	149
Burfiend, Michael/Stamford Ind School Dist	73	250
Burg, Meredith/Montgomery Ind School Dist	58,79	293
Burger, Camille/Ingleside Ind School Dist	58	331
Burger, Jerry/Wilson Ind School Dist	1,83	273
Burger, Monty/Brazosport Ind School Dist	3,17,73,98	52
Burgess, John/Ralls Ind School Dist	60	94
Burgess, Rickey/Everman Ind School Dist	67	349
Burgess, Tonya/McGregor Ind School Dist	9,31	280
Burghardt, Becky/College Station Ind Sch Dist	69	55
Burguss, April/Lorenzo Ind School Dist	16,82	94
Burk, Randy, Dr/Hamlin Ind School Dist	1	249
Burke, Jeff, Dr/Splendora Ind School Dist	1	294
Burke, Katie/Brownwood Ind School Dist	2	58
Burke, Matthew/La Porte Ind School Dist	20,23	198
Burke, Michelle/Spring Branch Ind School Dist	57	200
Burkett, Stephanie/Bruceville-Eddy Ind Sch Dist	31,36,83,88,271	278
Burkhart, Susan/Thrall Ind School Dist	73,84	400
Burkholder, Karla, Dr/Schertz-Cibolo-Univ City ISD	73	173
Burkle, Cynthia/La Vernia Ind School Dist	67	401
Burks, Rocky/Warren Ind School Dist	67	375
Burks, Rose, Dr/Region 14 Ed Service Center	7,8,27,31,88	362
Burks, Sean/Corrigan-Camden Ind Sch Dist	67	316
Burleson, Cindi/Lovelady Ind School Dist	68	233
Burleson, Jeramy/Kaufman Ind School Dist	6	252
Burleson, Todd/Westbrook Ind School Dist	1	289
Burley, Ecomet/Harris Co Dept of Ed	91	179
Burlson, Lois/Clyde Consolidated Ind SD	7	62
Burnell, Rhonda/Copperas Cove Ind School Dist	58	92
Burnett, B J/Lometa Ind School Dist	4	262

1 Superintendent	16 Instructional Media Svcs	30 Adult Education	44 Science Sec	58 Special Education K-12	72 Summer School	88 Alternative/At Risk	277 Remedial Math K-12
2 Bus/Finance/Purchasing	17 Chief Operations Officer	31 Career/Sch-to-Work K-12	45 Math K-12	59 Special Education Elem	73 Instructional Tech	89 Multi-Cultural Curriculum	280 Literacy Coach
3 Buildings And Grounds	18 Chief Academic Officer	32 Career/Sch-to-Work Elem	46 Math Elem	60 Special Education Sec	74 Inservice Training	90 Social Work	285 STEM
4 Food Service	19 Chief Financial Officer	33 Career/Sch-to-Work Sec	47 Math Sec	61 Foreign/World Lang K-12	75 Marketing/Distributive	91 Safety/Security	286 Digital Learning
5 Transportation	20 Art K-12	34 Early Childhood Ed	48 English/Lang Arts K-12	62 Foreign/World Lang Elem	76 Info Systems	92 Magnet School	288 Common Core Standards
6 Athletic	21 Art Elem	35 Health/Phys Education	49 English/Lang Arts Elem	63 Foreign/World Lang Sec	77 Psychological Assess	93 Parental Involvement	294 Accountability
7 Health Services	22 Art Sec	36 Guidance Services K-12	50 English/Lang Arts Sec	64 Religious Education K-12	78 Affirmative Action	94 Tech Prep Program	295 Network System
8 Curric/Instruct K-12	23 Music K-12	37 Guidance Services Elem	51 Reading K-12	65 Religious Education Elem	79 Student Personnel	97 Chief Information Officer	296 Title II Programs
9 Curric/Instruct Elem	24 Music Elem	38 Guidance Services Sec	52 Reading Elem	66 Religious Education Sec	80 Driver Ed/Safety	98 Chief Technology Officer	297 Webmaster
10 Curric/Instruct Sec	25 Music Sec	39 Social Studies K-12	53 Reading Sec	67 School Board President	81 Gifted/Talented	270 Character Education	298 Grant Writer/Ptnrships
11 Federal Program	26 Business Education	40 Social Studies Elem	54 Remedial Reading K-12	68 Teacher Personnel	82 Video Services	271 Migrant Education	750 Chief Innovation Officer
12 Title I	27 Career & Tech Ed	41 Social Studies Sec	55 Remedial Reading Elem	69 Academic Assessment	83 Substance Abuse Prev	273 Teacher Mentor	751 Chief of Staff
13 Title V	28 Technology Education	42 Science K-12	56 Remedial Reading Sec	70 Research/Development	84 Erate	274 Before/After Sch	752 Social Emotional Learning
15 Asst Superintendent	29 Family/Consumer Science	43 Science Elem	57 Bilingual/ELL	71 Public Information	85 AIDS Education	275 Response To Intervention	

TX-T12

Texas School Directory

DISTRICT PERSONNEL INDEX

NAME/District	JOB FUNCTIONS	PAGE
Burnett, Brandy/*Liberty-Eylau Ind School Dist*	12,68	48
Burnett, Dionne/*Lake Travis Ind School Dist*	93,274	370
Burnett, John/*Bremond Ind School Dist*	5,9,11,57,58,270,271	324
Burnett, Samuel/*Brownwood Ind School Dist*	6	58
Burnett, Tammy/*Neches Ind School Dist*	288	15
Burnette, Sanya/*Arp Ind School Dist*	58	336
Burney, Mitchell/*Anna Ind School Dist*	4	77
Burnhart, Tina/*Harper Ind School Dist*	2,68,79	163
Burns, Charla/*Pettus Ind School Dist*	38,69,83	25
Burns, Cheryl/*Smithville Ind School Dist*	1	24
Burns, Deborah/*Iredell Ind School Dist*	2	46
Burns, Jana/*Region 10 Ed Service Center*	15	116
Burns, Jimmy/*Friona Ind School Dist*	1	315
Burns, Judy/*East Central Ind School Dist*	2,19	31
Burns, Kade/*Mason Ind School Dist*	285	275
Burns, Kathy/*Utopia Ind School Dist*	2,12	378
Burns, Kelly/*Redwater Ind School Dist*	1	49
Burns, Ken/*Aledo Ind School Dist*	5	312
Burns, Lahne/*Veribest Ind School Dist*	73,286	365
Burns, Mike/*Malakoff Ind School Dist*	8	214
Burns, Nakisha/*Beaumont Ind School Dist*	71	241
Burrier, Pam/*Stockdale Ind School Dist*	76	401
Burris, Cody/*Tornillo Ind School Dist*	6	137
Burris, Jon/*Hamshire Fannett Ind Sch Dist*	8,11,88,271,273,294	242
Burroughs, Renee/*Denison Ind School Dist*	10	166
Burroughs, Willie/*San Antonio Ind School Dist*	3,17	39
Burrow, Chris/*El Campo Ind School Dist*	5	389
Burrow, Scott/*Pringle-Morse Cons ISD*	1,11,73	177
Burrus, Jennifer/*Muleshoe Ind School Dist*	9	22
Burt, Jamie/*Pasadena Ind School Dist*	79	198
Burton, Chris/*Coleman Ind School Dist*	5	76
Burton, Dustin/*Skidmore Tynan Ind SD*	1	25
Burton, Jayne/*Boerne Ind School Dist*	48,51	253
Burton, Jodi/*Judson Ind School Dist*	11,298	33
Burton, Lori/*Region 11 Ed Service Center*	71	360
Burton, Maggie/*Morgan Mill Ind School Dist*	270,271	144
Burwell, Paddy/*Westhoff Ind School Dist*	67	118
Busa, Kathleen/*Navasota Ind School Dist*	7	172
Busalacchi, Sherri/*Advantage Academy Admin Office*	71	96
Busby, Amy/*Montgomery Ind School Dist*	73	293
Busby, Brian/*Houston Ind School Dist*	3,17	188
Buser, Shawn/*West Hardin Co Cons Sch Dist*	73,273,295	178
Bush, Kenneth/*Galena Park Ind School Dist*	5	186
Bush, Kevin/*Elkhart Ind School Dist*	67	15
Bush, Leanne/*Melissa Ind School Dist*	57	81
Bush, Travis/*Seguin Ind School Dist*	6	173
Bushart, Brian/*Round Rock Ind School Dist*	46	398
Bushfield, Victor/*Pearland Ind School Dist*	297	53
Bushong, Tony/*City View Ind School Dist*	1	391
Bussard, James/*Dumas Ind School Dist*	34,58	295
Bustamante, Patty/*Arlington Ind School Dist*	79	343
Bustos, Victoria/*San Antonio Ind School Dist*	36	39
Butcher, Michelle/*Martin's Mill Ind Sch Dist*	2	381
Butler, Ann/*Whitehouse Ind School Dist*	42,81	338
Butler, Bill/*Andrews Ind School Dist*	2	16
Butler, Dan/*Cotton Center Ind School Dist*	73,83,88,270	174
Butler, Denise/*Raymondville Ind Sch Dist*	58	394
Butler, Dwight/*Granbury Ind School Dist*	6	230
Butler, Jill/*Gruver Ind School Dist*	57	176
Butler, Michael/*Center Point Ind School Dist*	67	255
Butler, Michelle/*Kingsville Ind School Dist*	4	257
Butler, Michelle/*Region 12 Ed Service Center*	77	283
Butler, Monica/*Hemphill Ind School Dist*	69,77	329
Butler, Sally/*Hemphill Ind School Dist*	2,11,271	329
Butler, Sonya/*Lake Worth Ind School Dist*	73,76,295	356
Butler, Sonya/*Lancaster Ind School Dist*	98,295	110
Butler, Terry/*Knox City-O'Brien Cons Ind SD*	3	258
Butler, Tom/*Sabine Pass Ind School Dist*	3,5	244
Button, Melissa/*Diocese of Fort Worth Ed Off*	15	358
Buttrum, Becky/*Hubbard Ind School Dist*	16	48
Butts, Jeff/*Ballinger Ind School Dist*	1	326
Buzan, Charlene/*Milford Ind School Dist*	4	141
Byars, Emory/*Vernon Ind School Dist*	67	393
Bye, Mickey/*Kress Ind School Dist*	5	343
Byers, Paul/*Galveston Ind School Dist*	3	160
Byers, Rachael/*Merkel Ind School Dist*	69,83,88	361

NAME/District	JOB FUNCTIONS	PAGE
Bymaster, Bryan/*Bland Ind School Dist*	2,15,88	235
Bynard, Brandon/*Red Lick Ind School Dist*	1	49
Byno, Kristin, Dr/*Richardson Ind School Dist*	15	112
Bynum, Charlotte/*Lufkin Ind School Dist*	2	18
Bynum, Debbie/*Ector Co Ind School Dist*	74	130
Byrd, Allison/*Hamshire Fannett Ind Sch Dist*	2,11,15	242
Byrd, Chad/*Petersburg Ind School Dist*	67	175
Byrd, Christen/*Henderson Ind School Dist*	2	327
Byrd, Jeff/*Vernon Ind School Dist*	1	393
Byrd, Mark/*Whitney Ind School Dist*	6	228
Byrd, Susie/*Liberty-Eylau Ind School Dist*	2	48
Byrne, Bev/*Whiteface Con Ind School Dist*	31	75
Byrne, Beverly/*Whiteface Con Ind School Dist*	36,69,83,85,88,270	75
Byrne, Carla/*Ector Co Ind School Dist*	27,31	129
Byrne, Treva/*Midway Ind School Dist*	58	74
Byrnes, Tina/*Center Ind School Dist*	4	334
Byrom, Brenda/*Valley Mills Ind School Dist*	2,68	47
Byrom, Raenese/*Jim Ned Cons Ind School Dist*	7,85	361
Byrum, Joey/*Rockwall Ind School Dist*	68	325
Byrum, Karen/*Kelton Ind School Dist*	58	390
Byther, Wanda/*Castleberry Ind School Dist*	31	347
Bytren, Sara/*Castleberry Ind School Dist*	4	347

C

NAME/District	JOB FUNCTIONS	PAGE
Caballero, Suzanne/*Pasadena Ind School Dist*	57,271	198
Cabaniss, Keith/*Holland Ind School Dist*	295	27
Cabavule, Serapio/*Friona Ind School Dist*	5	315
Cabazos, Jorge/*Mission Cons Ind School Dist*	16,68,73,76,95,295,297	222
Cabrera, Charles/*Robstown Ind School Dist*	23	305
Cabrera, Juan/*El Paso Ind School Dist*	1,288	132
Cabrera, Juan/*UT Tyler University Acad Dist*	3	338
Cabrera, Tricia/*Thorndale Ind School Dist*	36,88	288
Caddell, Charles/*Abilene Ind School Dist*	297	360
Caddell, Jennifer/*Knox City-O'Brien Cons Ind SD*	58	258
Caddell, Jennifer/*Munday Consolidated Ind SD*	58	259
Caddell, Jennifer/*Stamford Ind School Dist*	67	250
Caddell, Kimberly, Dr/*Garland Ind School Dist*	69,70,294	105
Caddell, Linda/*Rule Ind School Dist*	57	210
Caddell, Rodney/*Levelland Ind School Dist*	91	229
Cade, Clay/*Snyder Ind School Dist*	3	333
Cade, Laura/*Clint Ind School Dist*	71	132
Cadena, Leticia/*Roma Ind School Dist*	16,73,84,89,297	341
Cadena, Ninfa, Dr/*Carrizo Spgs Cons Ind SD*	67	127
Cadena, Renee/*Pleasanton Ind School Dist*	8,31,54,69,275,277,285	21
Cadena, Roland/*Devine Ind School Dist*	36	283
Cadenhead, Lindsay/*Red Oak Ind School Dist*	8	142
Caesar, Tammy/*Austin Ind School Dist*	31	366
Caffey, Deanne/*S & S Cons Ind School Dist*	4	167
Caffey, Doug/*Sidney Ind School Dist*	67	90
Caffey, Meredith/*Crosbyton Cons Ind Sch Dist*	58	94
Cagle, Dean/*Priddy Ind School Dist*	67	289
Cahill, Dawn/*Sonora Ind School Dist*	67	342
Cahill, Gary/*Cross Roads Ind School Dist*	16,73	214
Cahill, Kari/*Cross Roads Ind School Dist*	270,271	214
Cahill, Tara/*Grand Prairie Ind School Dist*	16,286	107
Caillet, Leslie/*Nueces Canyon Cons Ind SD*	7	131
Cain, Bonny/*Waxahachie Ind School Dist*	1	142
Cain, Carol/*Fairfield Ind School Dist*	5,294	156
Cain, Patrick/*Temple Ind School Dist*	5	29
Cain, Sonia/*Brady Ind School Dist*	58	277
Calabrese, David/*Canadian Ind School Dist*	73,76,295	213
Calahan, Ann, Dr/*Stephenville Ind School Dist*	67	144
Calbert, David/*Wharton Ind School Dist*	58	390
Calcoat, Rhonda/*Port Arthur Ind School Dist*	52	243
Calderon-Lugo, Keyhla/*Edgewood Ind School Dist*	71	31
Calderon, Jill/*Ralls Ind School Dist*	68	94
Calderon, Jimmy/*Socorro Ind School Dist*	6	135
Calderon, Juan/*Ralls Ind School Dist*	16,73,286,295	94
Calderon, Norma/*El Paso Ind School Dist*	57	132
Caldwell, Carl/*Taylor Ind School Dist*	5	399
Caldwell, Christopher/*Stafford Municipal Sch Dist*	67	155
Caldwell, Daniel/*North Hopkins Ind School Dist*	73	231
Caldwell, Mark/*Central Ind School Dist*	5	17
Caldwell, Sunnie/*Sabine Ind School Dist*	4	170
Caley, Kim, Dr/*Northwest Ind School Dist*	15,68	124
Calhoun, Caryn/*Zavalla Ind School Dist*	11,58,69	18

DISTRICT PERSONNEL INDEX

Market Data Retrieval

NAME/District	JOB FUNCTIONS	PAGE
Calhoun, Krissy/Conroe Ind School Dist	16,73	291
Calhoun, Margo/Evadale Ind School Dist	68,71	240
Calhoun, Max/Poth Ind School Dist	73	401
Calk, Amanda/Lufkin Ind School Dist	4	18
Calk, Carol/Utopia Ind School Dist	58	378
Callahan, Casey/Region 15 Ed Service Center	1,11	366
Callahan, Sandra/Bastrop Ind School Dist	2,19	23
Callahan, Sean/Iola Ind School Dist	5	172
Callaway, Leona/Spurger Ind School Dist	4	375
Callaway, Scott/Bullard Ind School Dist	6	336
Callaway, Wade/Gruver Ind School Dist	1	176
Callcoat, Kari/Winters Ind School Dist	9	327
Callihan-Lewis, Sarah/Pleasanton Ind School Dist	294	21
Calloway, Caleb/Knox City-O'Brien Cons Ind SD	6	258
Cally, Leandrea/Henderson Ind School Dist	7,35,85	327
Caloss, Scott/Wills Point Ind School Dist	1	381
Calvert, Amy/McLean Ind School Dist	2,71	165
Calvert, Matt/New Caney Ind School Dist	15	293
Camacho, Edgar/Natalia Ind School Dist	10	284
Camacho, Joel/Childress Ind School Dist	3	74
Camacho, Paula/Alvin Ind School Dist	57,89,271	50
Camarillo, David/Eagle Pass Ind School Dist	8,294	276
Camarillo, Stephanie/Lockhart Ind School Dist	8,15	61
Cambell, Foy/Magnolia Ind School Dist	20,23	292
Cambell, Greg/Apple Springs Ind School Dist	3	374
Cambell, Tiffany/Moran Ind School Dist	4	334
Cambelle, Gill/Trinity Ind School Dist	3,4,5,11,288	374
Camden, Charles/Coldspring-Oakhurst Cons ISD	73,295	330
Cameron, Stacy/Frisco Ind School Dist	16	78
Cameron, Tyke/Silsbee Ind School Dist	84,295	178
Camez, Tomas/Donna Ind School Dist	93	215
Camigney, Donna/Petersburg Ind School Dist	58	175
Camley, Jennifer/Bloomburg Ind School Dist	7	70
Camp, David/Vidor Ind School Dist	67	309
Camp, Teresa/Hull Daisetta Ind School Dist	11,57,58,69,275	266
Campbell, Becky/Lake Worth Ind School Dist	2	356
Campbell, Bobby/Ranger Ind School Dist	6,35	129
Campbell, Dickey/Texas City Ind School Dist	67	161
Campbell, Dwain/Leonard Ind School Dist	3,5	146
Campbell, Eddie/Wimberley Ind School Dist	3,91	212
Campbell, Holly/Gordon Ind School Dist	8,11,16,74,275	310
Campbell, Hortense, Dr/Houston Ind School Dist	44	188
Campbell, Jason/Bullard Ind School Dist	67	336
Campbell, Joshua/Tenaha Ind School Dist	3	335
Campbell, Joy/Henrietta Ind School Dist	2	74
Campbell, Lance/Lone Oak Ind School Dist	1	236
Campbell, Lisa/Texas City Ind School Dist	294	161
Campbell, Lisa/Turkey-Quitaque Cons Ind SD	67	176
Campbell, Martha/Daingerfield-Lone Star Ind SD	8,11,69,74,79,273,294	296
Campbell, Randy/Aledo Ind School Dist	3	312
Campbell, Scott/Clyde Consolidated Ind SD	6	62
Campbell, Scott/East Chambers Ind School Dist	1	72
Campbell, Shana/Cranfills Gap ISD School Dist	8,69	46
Campbell, Sharon/Malone Independent School Dist	57	228
Campbell, Susanna/Whitehouse Ind School Dist	8	338
Campbell, Traci/Giddings Ind School Dist	4	263
Campos, Laura/Pharr-San Juan-Alamo Ind SD	79,294	223
Campos, Rene/Pharr-San Juan-Alamo Ind SD	15	223
Campos, Rosa/Donna Ind School Dist	7,85	215
Campoya, Rudy/Socorro Ind School Dist	68	135
Campsey, Thomas/North East Ind School Dist	42	34
Canady, Marcy/Tomball Ind School Dist	57	203
Canales, D J/Point Isabel Ind Sch Dist	16,73,297	66
Canales, David/United Ind School Dist	10	387
Canales, Juan/West Oso Ind School Dist	67	306
Canales, Priscilla, Dr/Weslaco Ind School Dist	1	225
Canales, Rodolfo/Mercedes Ind School Dist	69,88	221
Canales, Vita, Dr/Ricardo Ind School Dist	1	257
Candelaria, Carmen/El Paso Ind School Dist	2,15	132
Caniford, Chuck/Clifton Ind School Dist	6	46
Cannon, Barbara/Monte Alto Ind School Dist	11,57,58,69,73,84,271,294	222
Cannon, Chris/Bryan Ind School Dist	295	54
Cannon, Deanna/Midlothian Ind School Dist	5	141
Cannon, Harvey/Bastrop Ind School Dist	60	172
Cannon, Jerry/Rule Ind School Dist	73	210
Cannon, Kevin/Trenton Ind School Dist	11,69,296	147
Cannon, Linda/Schertz-Cibolo-Univ City ISD	68	173
Cannon, Shonda/Denison Ind School Dist	8,45,51,74,273,298	166
Cannonico, Marcus/Burleson Ind School Dist	27	246
Cano, Ernestina/Edinburg Cons Ind School Dist	88	216
Cano, Laura/Tyler Ind School Dist	68	337
Cano, Leobardo/Mathis Ind School Dist	88	331
Cano, Tiffany/Springtown Ind School Dist	9	313
Canon, Teresa/Conroe Ind School Dist	58,77	291
Cansino, Ludipina/Donna Ind School Dist	2,19	215
Canter, Tracy, Dr/Ector Co Ind School Dist	58,77	130
Cantu-Reyes, Lisa/Mercedes Ind School Dist	11	221
Cantu, Ashley/Premont Ind School Dist	58	246
Cantu, Clementine/San Marcos Cons Ind Sch Dist	67	211
Cantu, Conrad/Freer Ind School Dist	1	128
Cantu, Ernesto/Edgewood Ind School Dist	3	31
Cantu, Faviola, Dr/Aldine ISD-Elem Sch Team 2	15	179
Cantu, Frank/Raymondville Ind Sch Dist	6	394
Cantu, Kimberley, Dr/Mansfield Ind School Dist	15,68,752	356
Cantu, Maria/Freer Ind School Dist	7	128
Cantu, Nehemias/Edcouch Elsa Ind School Dist	10	215
Cantu, Nereida/Judson Ind School Dist	15	33
Cantu, Noe/Clint Ind School Dist	73	132
Cantu, Paci/Dayton Ind School Dist	5	265
Cantu, Patricia/Alief Ind School Dist	57,271	181
Cantu, Rogelio/Lasara Ind School Dist	2,68,91	394
Cantu, Romeo/Edinburg Cons Ind School Dist	71	216
Cantu, Sheila/La Porte Ind School Dist	2	198
Cantwell, Nancy/Harper Ind School Dist	57,271	163
Canuteson, Ashley, Dr/Midway Ind School Dist	27,31	280
Caperton, Brian/Whitney Ind School Dist	3,5,91	228
Capps, Shannon/Troup Ind School Dist	16,73	337
Capps, Ted/Bland Ind School Dist	73,286	235
Carabajal, Bob/Carroll Independent Sch Dist	3	347
Caralez, Michael/Somerset Ind School Dist	2,19	42
Caraway, J/Honey Grove Ind School Dist	3	146
Carden, Corey/Kennard Ind Sch Dist	6	233
Carden, Cory/Kennard Ind Sch Dist	6	233
Carden, Ken/Whitesboro Ind School Dist	3	168
Cardenas-Rubio, Alma/Brownsville Ind School Dist	15	63
Cardenas, David/Devine Ind School Dist	3	283
Cardenas, Louis/Alamo Heights Ind School Dist	3	30
Cardiff, Susan/Royal Ind School Dist	11,69,294,296,298	384
Cardona, Michael/San Marcos Cons Ind Sch Dist	1	211
Cardoza, Patrick/Kaufman Ind School Dist	5	252
Cardwell, Evan/Newcastle Ind School Dist	1,11,83	406
Cardwell, Neil/Community Ind School Dist	16,73,76,286,295	78
Carey, Bobby/Krum Ind School Dist	3,5	122
Carey, John/Rice Cons Ind School Dist	67	87
Carlin, Chrysta/Leander Ind School Dist	10	396
Carlin, Howard/Forney Ind School Dist	295	251
Carlisle, Dayren/Conroe Ind School Dist	57	291
Carlisle, Scott/Comanche Ind School Dist	91	89
Carlos, Juan/Karnes City Ind School Dist	3,91	250
Carlson, Michael/Diocese of Fort Worth Ed Off	6	358
Carlson, Susan/United Ind School Dist	16	387
Carlton, Denise/Gorman Ind School Dist	73	129
Carlton, Summer/Lindale Ind School Dist	8	337
Carman, Nate, Dr/San Benito Cons Ind Sch Dist	1	66

---

1 Superintendent	16 Instructional Media Svcs	30 Adult Education	44 Science Sec	58 Special Education K-12	72 Summer School	88 Alternative/At Risk	277 Remedial Math K-12
2 Bus/Finance/Purchasing	17 Chief Operations Officer	31 Career/Sch-to-Work K-12	45 Math K-12	59 Special Education Elem	73 Instructional Tech	89 Multi-Cultural Curriculum	280 Literacy Coach
3 Buildings And Grounds	18 Chief Academic Officer	32 Career/Sch-to-Work Elem	46 Math Elem	60 Special Education Sec	74 Inservice Training	90 Social Work	285 STEM
4 Food Service	19 Chief Financial Officer	33 Career/Sch-to-Work Sec	47 Math Sec	61 Foreign/World Lang K-12	75 Marketing/Distributive	91 Safety/Security	286 Digital Learning
5 Transportation	20 Art K-12	34 Early Childhood Ed	48 English/Lang Arts K-12	62 Foreign/World Lang Elem	76 Info Systems	92 Magnet School	288 Common Core Standards
6 Athletic	21 Art Elem	35 Health/Phys Education	49 English/Lang Arts Elem	63 Foreign/World Lang Sec	77 Psychological Assess	93 Parental Involvement	294 Accountability
7 Health Services	22 Art Sec	36 Guidance Services K-12	50 English/Lang Arts Sec	64 Religious Education K-12	78 Affirmative Action	95 Tech Prep Program	295 Network System
8 Curric/Instruct K-12	23 Music K-12	37 Guidance Services Elem	51 Reading K-12	65 Religious Education Elem	79 Student Personnel	97 Chief Information Officer	296 Title II Programs
9 Curric/Instruct Elem	24 Music Elem	38 Guidance Services Sec	52 Reading Elem	66 Religious Education Sec	80 Driver Ed/Safety	98 Chief Technology Officer	297 Webmaster
10 Curric/Instruct Sec	25 Music Sec	39 Social Studies K-12	53 Reading Sec	67 School Board President	81 Gifted/Talented	270 Character Education	298 Grant Writer/Ptnrships
11 Federal Program	26 Business Education	40 Social Studies Elem	54 Remedial Reading K-12	68 Teacher Personnel	82 Video Services	271 Migrant Education	750 Chief Innovation Officer
12 Title I	27 Career & Tech Ed	41 Social Studies Sec	55 Remedial Reading Elem	69 Academic Assessment	83 Substance Abuse Prev	273 Teacher Mentor	751 Chief of Staff
13 Title V	28 Technology Education	42 Science K-12	56 Remedial Reading Sec	70 Research/Development	84 Erate	274 Before/After Sch	752 Social Emotional Learning
15 Asst Superintendent	29 Family/Consumer Science	43 Science Elem	57 Bilingual/ELL	71 Public Information	85 AIDS Education	275 Response To Intervention	

Texas School Directory
DISTRICT PERSONNEL INDEX

NAME/District	JOB FUNCTIONS	PAGE
Carman, Scotty/Wink Loving Ind School Dist	1	402
Carmichael, Regina/Lago Vista Ind School Dist	7,83,85	370
Carmichael, Tim/Seagraves Ind School Dist	67	157
Carnagey, Trish/Farmersville Ind School Dist	11,57,280	78
Carnathan, Jennifer/Channelview Ind School Dist	19	183
Carnes, Charlie/Northside Ind School Dist	91	36
Carnes, Heather/Winona Ind School Dist	11,271	339
Carney, Brady/Muenster Ind School Dist	6	91
Carney, Jodi/Lovelady Ind School Dist	54	233
Carnigney, Donna/Petersburg Ind School Dist	8,57,271,274	175
Carns, Jeramiah/Grand Saline Ind School Dist	67	380
Caroll, Lizatte/Tornillo Ind School Dist	57	137
Carpenter, Brad/Borger Ind School Dist	91	237
Carpenter, David/Huffman Ind School Dist	73,84,295	195
Carpenter, Eric/Big Sandy Ind School Dist	1,11	316
Carpenter, Gary/Woodsboro Ind School Dist	6	324
Carpenter, John/McGregor Ind School Dist	4	280
Carpenter, Keith/Hardin Ind School Dist	3	265
Carpenter, Larry/Waco Ind School Dist	20,23	281
Carpenter, Scott/Prairie Valley Ind School Dist	67	290
Carpenter, Sonya/Rockwall Ind School Dist	11,34,88,298	325
Carpenter, Steve/Dell City Ind School Dist	67	234
Carpentier, Gerardo/Freer Ind School Dist	6	128
Carpio, Mario/Whitewright Ind School Dist	3	168
Carr, D/Como Pickton Cons Ind SD	67	231
Carr, Dustin/Sulphur Bluff Ind School Dist	1,11	232
Carr, Jason/Lufkin Ind School Dist	295	18
Carr, Ron/Miami Ind School Dist	3,5	324
Carr, Vicki/Tolar Ind School Dist	2	230
Carr, Yolanda/Odem-Edroy Ind School Dist	1	331
Carrabine, Ginger/Bryan Ind School Dist	15,751	54
Carrales, Norma/Santa Gertrudis Ind Sch Dist	4	258
Carranza, Alejandro/La Joya Ind School Dist	43	219
Carrasco, Angela/Woodsboro Ind School Dist	2	324
Carrasco, David/Socorro Ind School Dist	3	135
Carrasco, David/Terrell Co Ind School Dist	73	362
Carrasco, Jesus/Anthony Ind School Dist	4	131
Carrasco, Laura/Int'l Leadership of Texas Dist	8,18	108
Carrasco, Martha/Canutillo Ind School Dist	68	132
Carrasco, Samuel/Presidio Ind School Dist	30	320
Carrell, Jean/Pittsburg Ind School Dist	57,271	68
Carreon, Alvaro/Webb Cons Ind School Dist	5	388
Carreon, Rita/Eagle Pass Ind School Dist	46,277	276
Carrera, Israel/Waco Ind School Dist	3,15	281
Carrillo, Carlos/Canutillo Ind School Dist	91	132
Carrillo, Sandra/Canutillo Ind School Dist	34	132
Carrington, Kathy/Joaquin Ind School Dist	11,58	335
Carrington, Tim/Austin Ind School Dist	295	366
Carrington, Wade/Hurst-Euless-Bedford ISD	42	353
Carrington, Wendy/Arlington Ind School Dist	88	343
Carrizales, Lupita/Odem-Edroy Ind School Dist	274	331
Carroll, Adam/Cranfills Gap ISD School Dist	6	46
Carroll, Charles/Ft Worth Ind School Dist	8,18	349
Carroll, Cody/Krum Ind School Dist	1	122
Carroll, Karen/Idalou Ind School Dist	10,31	269
Carroll, Leann/Birdville Ind School Dist	36,77,83,85,88	346
Carroll, Melody/Dilley Ind School Dist	288	157
Carroll, Pamela/Lancaster Ind School Dist	78	110
Carroll, Philip/Tuloso-Midway Ind School Dist	2,19,75	305
Carroll, Raymond/Anthony Ind School Dist	6,296	131
Carroll, Samantha/Paint Creek Ind School Dist	54,58,271	210
Carroll, Sharon/Melissa Ind School Dist	8,11,36,69,294	81
Carroll, Susanne, Dr/Victoria Ind School Dist	8,15,74	382
Carroll, Tim/Allen Ind School Dist	71,97	76
Carruthers, Heidi/Gunter Ind School Dist	68	166
Carson, Tina/Turkey-Quitaque Cons Ind SD	16,73	176
Carson, Trica/Turkey-Quitaque Cons Ind SD	58	176
Cartagena, Lorena/Socorro Ind School Dist	12	135
Cartas, Tracy/Frisco Ind School Dist	58	78
Carter, Alissa/Plainview Ind School Dist	73	175
Carter, Amy/Sweeny Ind School Dist	2,19	54
Carter, Becky/Austwell Tivoli Ind SD	4	323
Carter, Brian/Northwest Ind School Dist	2,15,19	124
Carter, Cara/Northwest Ind School Dist	2,16,19,73,76,95,286	124
Carter, Carey/Mineral Wells Ind School Dist	8,16,54,69,74,273,294	310
Carter, Carra/Seymour Ind School Dist	34	25

NAME/District	JOB FUNCTIONS	PAGE
Carter, Clay/Jacksonville Ind School Dist	4	72
Carter, David/Rockwall Ind School Dist	2,19	325
Carter, Debbie/Texline Ind School Dist	2,84	95
Carter, Dee/Navarro Ind School Dist	1	173
Carter, Gary/Plano Ind School Dist	83	82
Carter, Hank/Lake Travis Ind School Dist	6	370
Carter, Hanna/Forsan Ind School Dist	8,68,79,273	234
Carter, Jason/Roby Cons Ind School Dist	8,69,73,285,296,298	148
Carter, Jimmie/Seymour Ind School Dist	27	25
Carter, Jorgannie/Pearland Ind School Dist	2,19,76	53
Carter, Kenny/Hubbard Ind School Dist	73,295	227
Carter, Lacy/Hallsville Ind School Dist	69,83,294	208
Carter, Laquita/Spring Ind School Dist	15	202
Carter, Leonard/Seguin Ind School Dist	295	173
Carter, Mike/Bloomburg Ind School Dist	3	70
Carter, Mike/Junction Ind School Dist	1	256
Carter, Rachel/Bosqueville Ind School Dist	73,286,295	278
Carter, Randy/Boys Ranch Ind School Dist	73,295	307
Carter, Tim/Ropes Ind School Dist	8,12,273	229
Carter, Tracy/Mabank Ind School Dist	6	252
Carter, Vee Ann/Denver City Ind School Dist	7,85	405
Carthel, Clint/Cotton Center Ind School Dist	67	174
Cartwright, Brock/Claude Ind School Dist	1,11	20
Cartwright, Cody/Texhoma Ind School Dist	67	336
Cartwright, Debra/Port Arthur Ind School Dist	58,83,88	243
Cartwright, Greg/Allen Ind School Dist	2,19	76
Caruso, Peggy/Katy Ind School Dist	91	151
Caruthers, Brian/Granbury Ind School Dist	5	230
Carver, Donna/Seymour Ind School Dist	57,271	25
Carver, Shelley/New Deal Ind School Dist	8,69	271
Carwell, Tiffany/Westwood Ind School Dist	11,57,69,83,285,294,298	16
Cary, Gabriel/Medina Valley Ind School Dist	11	284
Cary, Joe/Crandall Ind School Dist	6	251
Casall, MacKenzie/Duncanville Ind School Dist	36,58,77	104
Casarez, Carrie/Whiteface Con Ind School Dist	16	75
Casarez, Christopher/Tuloso-Midway Ind School Dist	15,91	305
Casarez, Kenneth/Castleberry Ind School Dist	10	347
Casas, Cynthia/La Feria Ind School Dist	4	65
Casas, Maria, Dr/Brooks Co Ind School Dist	1	57
Casas, Michael/Sabinal Ind School Dist	23	378
Case, Becky/Gold-Burg Ind School Dist	67	290
Case, Diane/Red Oak Ind School Dist	297	142
Case, Tammy/Groom Ind School Dist	2	69
Caserves, Ken/Castleberry Ind School Dist	8,11,83,88,288,296,298	347
Casey, Amber/Brazosport Ind School Dist	297	52
Casey, Brandon/Randolph Field Ind School Dist	5	39
Casey, LaBonne/Sweeny Ind School Dist	81,298	54
Casey, Melissa/Harlandale Ind School Dist	10	32
Casey, Ronnie/Stamford Ind School Dist	6	250
Cash, Jana/Vidor Ind School Dist	16	309
Cash, Paul, Dr/Mansfield Ind School Dist	3	356
Casias, Bobby/Ralls Ind School Dist	5	94
Casias, Paul/Ft Stockton Ind School Dist	4	315
Caskey, Christine, Dr/Katy Ind School Dist	8,18	151
Casparis, Cindy/San Marcos Cons Ind Sch Dist	2	211
Cassey, Jeffrey/Slaton Ind School Dist	6	272
Castaneda, Frank/Stratford Ind School Dist	3	336
Castaneda, Rebecca/Donna Ind School Dist	11,271	215
Castanon, Aaron/Hartley Ind School Dist	58	209
Castanuela, Ramon/Grapevine-Colleyville Ind SD	3	353
Castareda, Santos/Santa Rosa Ind School Dist	67	67
Casteel, Dan/New Caney Ind School Dist	76	293
Castellano, Joe Richard/Taft Ind School Dist	6	332
Casterona, Rod/Cooper Ind School Dist	6	119
Castille, Veronica/Splendora Ind School Dist	3	294
Castillo, Carolyn, Dr/Region 20 Ed Service Center	8,15,57	45
Castillo, Chris/Eden Cons Ind School Dist	3	90
Castillo, Christina/Crosby Ind School Dist	57	183
Castillo, Cynthia/Harlingen Cons Ind School Dist	69	64
Castillo, Delia/Mercedes Ind School Dist	58	221
Castillo, Eliazar/Hart Ind School Dist	3,5	71
Castillo, Jorge/Lewisville Ind School Dist	57	122
Castillo, Julian/Buena Vista Ind School Dist	11,57	315
Castillo, Linda/Wellington Ind School Dist	57,270,271	86
Castillo, Mark/Hart Ind School Dist	57	71
Castillo, Marta/La Joya Ind School Dist	49	219

School Year 2019-2020 · 800-333-8802

DISTRICT PERSONNEL INDEX

Market Data Retrieval

NAME/District	JOB FUNCTIONS	PAGE
Castillo, Megan/*Cuero Ind School Dist*	36	117
Castillo, Noe/*La Villa Ind School Dist*	67	220
Castillo, Phil/*Braination Schools*	73	30
Castillo, Sandra/*Webb Cons Ind School Dist*	8,11,16,57,58,69,275	388
Castillon, Ana/*Eagle Pass Ind School Dist*	26,27,28,31	276
Castillon, Veronica/*Laredo Ind School Dist*	71	386
Castleberry, Scott/*New Caney Ind School Dist*	79	293
Castles, Phil/*Henderson Ind School Dist*	6	327
Castorena, Jose/*Socorro Ind School Dist*	91	135
Castro, Cynthia/*Brownsville Ind School Dist*	74	63
Castro, Ruby/*Dawson Ind School Dist*	271	116
Castruita, Manuel/*El Paso Ind School Dist*	36,88	132
Catching, Clint/*Howe Ind School Dist*	67	166
Cate, Cynthia/*Jonesboro Ind School Dist*	59	93
Cathey, Vikki/*Schleicher Co Ind Sch Dist*	4	333
Catney, Kenneth/*Frenship Ind School Dist*	6	269
Catoe, Tracey/*Latexo Ind School Dist*	73	233
Caton, Kathy/*Zavalla Ind School Dist*	8	18
Cauble, Diedre/*Moran Ind School Dist*	2	334
Caudell, James/*Blanco Ind School Dist*	295	45
Caudle, Airemy, Dr/*Godley Ind School Dist*	9	247
Cauley, Lee/*Veribest Ind School Dist*	51	365
Cavazos, Angie/*Wellman Union Ind School Dist*	4	362
Cavazos, Armando/*Progreso Ind School Dist*	3,5	224
Cavazos, Art/*Harlingen Cons Ind School Dist*	1	64
Cavazos, Arturo/*Ft Worth Ind School Dist*	3,15	349
Cavazos, David/*La Joya Ind School Dist*	44	219
Cavazos, John/*McAllen Ind School Dist*	68	221
Cavazos, Jose, Dr/*Harlingen Cons Ind School Dist*	88,93	64
Cavazos, Juan/*Smyer Ind School Dist*	67	229
Cavazos, Julio/*Harlingen Cons Ind School Dist*	2,15,19	64
Cavazos, Macy/*Ralls Ind School Dist*	8,11,57,58,83,288,296,298	94
Cavazos, Marcelo, Dr/*Arlington Ind School Dist*	1	343
Cavazos, Norma/*Raymondville Ind Sch Dist*	4	394
Cavazos, Sandra/*Hidalgo Ind School Dist*	8,58,69	217
Cavness, Rodney, Dr/*Texas City Ind School Dist*	1	161
Cazalis, Laura/*Port Aransas Ind School Dist*	58	305
Cazares, Daniel/*Lumberton Ind School Dist*	84,295	178
Cazares, Mary/*Lasara Ind School Dist*	4	394
Cearley, Melany/*Holland Ind School Dist*	8,36,79,88,270	27
Cearlock, Devia/*Amarillo Ind School Dist*	39	317
Ceballos, Daniel, Dr/*Robstown Ind School Dist*	15	305
Ceballos, Lornea/*Robstown Ind School Dist*	8	305
Cecil, Kenney/*Redwater Ind School Dist*	67	49
Cederstorm, Eric, Dr/*Pine Tree Ind School Dist*	8,15	170
Cederstrom, Eric, Dr/*Palo Pinto Ind Sch Dist 906*	11,73,83	310
Cedillo, Faustino/*Mission Cons Ind School Dist*	39	222
Cervantes, Jose, Dr/*La Villa Ind School Dist*	11	220
Cervantes, Jose, Dr/*Pecos-Barstow-Toyah Ind SD*	1	323
Cervantes, Leticia/*Benavides Ind School Dist*	36,69,83,288	128
Cervantes, Ruben/*Dell City Ind School Dist*	1	234
Cervantez, Jo Marie/*Poteet Ind School Dist*	67	21
Cervantez, Samiel/*Castleberry Ind School Dist*	91	347
Ceynowa, Brandy/*Simms Ind School Dist*	752	50
Chachere, Julie/*Dayton Ind School Dist*	275	265
Chachere, Suzanne/*Dayton Ind School Dist*	84,286	265
Chacon, Brenda/*Ysleta Ind School Dist*	9,15	137
Chadwell, Charles/*Round Rock Ind School Dist*	67	398
Chadwell, Jim, Dr/*Eagle Mtn-Saginaw Ind Sch Dist*	1	348
Chadwick, Angela/*North Lamar Ind School Dist*	8	259
Chadwick, Sharon/*Follett Ind School Dist*	4	267
Chalaire, Tommy/*Chisum Ind School Dist*	1,11	259
Chalmers, Hanna/*Angleton Ind School Dist*	71	51
Chamberlain, Pam/*Terrell Ind School Dist*	286	253
Chamberlin, Marilyn/*Celina Ind School Dist*	73	78
Chambers, Alton/*Milford Ind School Dist*	8,36,69,88	141
Chambers, Carey/*Canutillo Ind School Dist*	58	132
Chambers, Christa/*Hart Ind School Dist*	8	71
Chambers, Dennis/*Matagorda Ind School Dist*	3,5	275
Chambers, Ezra/*Abernathy Ind School Dist*	88,270	174
Chambers, H D/*Alief Ind School Dist*	1	181
Chambers, Michael/*Italy Ind School Dist*	3,5	140
Chambers, Tammy/*Los Fresnos Cons Ind Sch Dist*	8	66
Chamlee, Doug/*Ysleta Ind School Dist*	295	137
Champagne, Jonathan/*Columbia Brazoria ISD*	67	52
Champange, Jennifer/*Eanes Ind School Dist*	67	370
Chance, Kim/*Cleburne Ind School Dist*	4	247
Chance, Linda, Dr/*Garland Ind School Dist*	68,751	105
Chancellor, Aubrey/*North East Ind School Dist*	71	34
Chandler, Darren/*Deer Park Ind School Dist*	6	186
Chandler, Ervin/*Blooming Grove Ind School Dist*	6	299
Chandler, Gerald/*Lumberton Ind School Dist*	1	178
Chandler, Johney/*Bellevue Ind School Dist*	69,88	74
Chandler, Kenny/*Frisco Ind School Dist*	15,79	78
Chandler, Mark/*Hurst-Euless-Bedford ISD*	20,23	353
Chapa Ramirez, Melissa/*United Ind School Dist*	36,83	387
Chapa, Aida/*Dilley Ind School Dist*	67	157
Chapa, Arla/*South San Antonio Ind Sch Dist*	57,271	42
Chapa, Doris/*Plainview Ind School Dist*	2	175
Chapa, Eloy/*Goose Creek Cons Ind Sch Dist*	15,68	187
Chapa, Jason/*Yorktown Ind School Dist*	3	118
Chapa, Marisa, Dr/*Benavides Ind School Dist*	1	128
Chapa, Marisa, Dr/*Premont Ind School Dist*	12,15	246
Chapa, Melinda/*Edcouch Elsa Ind School Dist*	298	215
Chapa, Selena, Dr/*Aldine Ind School Dist*	15,17	179
Chaplin, Tylor/*Burkburnett Ind Sch Dist*	1	391
Chapman, Bill, Dr/*Jarrell Ind School Dist*	1	396
Chapman, Debbie/*Amarillo Ind School Dist*	11,298	317
Chapman, Ester/*Port Arthur Ind School Dist*	5	243
Chapman, John, Dr/*Carrollton-Farmers Branch ISD*	1	96
Chapman, Judy/*West Rusk Co Cons Ind Sch Dist*	57	328
Chapman, Keith/*Garland Ind School Dist*	91	105
Chapman, Kodi/*New Home Ind School Dist*	58	273
Chapman, Lara/*Liberty Hill Ind School Dist*	38	398
Chapman, Mandi/*Ennis Ind School Dist*	58	140
Chapman, Marcy/*Tom Bean Ind School Dist*	27	168
Chapman, Maynard/*Elysian Fields Ind School Dist*	1	208
Chapman, Michael/*Region 9 Ed Service Center*	27,31,36	393
Chapman, Monte/*Weatherford Ind School Dist*	5,15,68,78	313
Chapman, Scott/*Calallen Ind School Dist*	5	302
Chapman, Shannon/*Irion Co Ind School Dist*	10,11,296	238
Chapman, Steve/*Hurst-Euless-Bedford ISD*	1	353
Chapoton, Beth/*Manor Ind School Dist*	76	371
Chapoton, Karen/*Manor Ind School Dist*	2	371
Chappa, Joe/*George West Ind School Dist*	3	268
Chappell, Charmaine/*Beckville Ind School Dist*	2	311
Charanza, Ashley/*Franklin Ind School Dist*	4	324
Chares, Timito/*Eagle Pass Ind School Dist*	271	276
Charles, Courtney/*Port Arthur Ind School Dist*	41	243
Charlton, Shelly/*Leon Ind School Dist*	54	264
Chase, John/*Forney Ind School Dist*	2,19	251
Chase, Roger/*Wellman Union Ind School Dist*	73,286	362
Chase, Sarah/*New Caney Ind School Dist*	58	293
Chatelain, Stefanie/*Edgewood Ind School Dist*	7	31
Chatfield, Chuck/*Crowell Ind School Dist*	5	149
Chatman, Kim/*Gladewater Ind School Dist*	3,17	169
Chauveaux, Mark/*Godley Ind School Dist*	6	247
Chavarria, Martin/*Charlotte Ind School Dist*	3,5	20
Chavarria, Raul/*Crockett Co Cons Common SD*	1	94
Chavera, George/*Ramirez Common School Dist*	67	128
Chavers, Eric/*Fairfield Ind School Dist*	67	156
Chaves, Rodrigo/*Conroe Ind School Dist*	7,30,88,93,271	291
Chavez, Anna/*Little Elm Ind School Dist*	2	124
Chavez, David/*Donna Ind School Dist*	16,73,76,295	215

1 Superintendent	16 Instructional Media Svcs	30 Adult Education	44 Science Sec	58 Special Education K-12	72 Summer School	88 Alternative/At Risk	277 Remedial Math K-12
2 Bus/Finance/Purchasing	17 Chief Operations Officer	31 Career/Sch-to-Work K-12	45 Math K-12	59 Special Education Elem	73 Instructional Tech	89 Multi-Cultural Curriculum	280 Literacy Coach
3 Buildings And Grounds	18 Chief Academic Officer	32 Career/Sch-to-Work Elem	46 Math Elem	60 Special Education Sec	74 Inservice Training	90 Social Work	285 STEM
4 Food Service	19 Chief Financial Officer	33 Career/Sch-to-Work Sec	47 Math Sec	61 Foreign/World Lang K-12	75 Marketing/Distributive	91 Safety/Security	286 Digital Learning
5 Transportation	20 Art K-12	34 Early Childhood Ed	48 English/Lang Arts K-12	62 Foreign/World Lang Elem	76 Info Systems	92 Magnet School	288 Common Core Standards
6 Athletic	21 Art Elem	35 Health/Phys Education	49 English/Lang Arts Elem	63 Foreign/World Lang Sec	77 Psychological Assess	93 Parental Involvement	294 Accountability
7 Health Services	22 Art Sec	36 Guidance Services K-12	50 English/Lang Arts Sec	64 Religious Education K-12	78 Affirmative Action	95 Tech Prep Program	295 Network System
8 Curric/Instruct K-12	23 Music K-12	37 Guidance Services Elem	51 Reading K-12	65 Religious Education Elem	79 Student Personnel	97 Chief Information Officer	296 Title II Programs
9 Curric/Instruct Elem	24 Music Elem	38 Guidance Services Sec	52 Reading Elem	66 Religious Education Sec	80 Driver Ed/Safety	98 Chief Technology Officer	297 Webmaster
10 Curric/Instruct Sec	25 Music Sec	39 Social Studies K-12	53 Reading Sec	67 School Board President	81 Gifted/Talented	270 Character Education	298 Grant Writer/Ptnrships
11 Federal Program	26 Business Education	40 Social Studies Elem	54 Remedial Reading K-12	68 Teacher Personnel	82 Video Services	271 Migrant Education	750 Chief Innovation Officer
12 Title I	27 Career & Tech Ed	41 Social Studies Sec	55 Remedial Reading Elem	69 Academic Assessment	83 Substance Abuse Prev	273 Teacher Mentor	751 Chief of Staff
13 Title V	28 Technology Education	42 Science K-12	56 Remedial Reading Sec	70 Research/Development	84 Erate	274 Before/After Sch	752 Social Emotional Learning
15 Asst Superintendent	29 Family/Consumer Science	43 Science Elem	57 Bilingual/ELL	71 Public Information	85 AIDS Education	275 Response To Intervention	

Texas School Directory

DISTRICT PERSONNEL INDEX

NAME/District	JOB FUNCTIONS	PAGE
Chavez, Gloria/*Ysleta Ind School Dist*	73,76,98	137
Chavez, Juan, Dr/*Brownsville Ind School Dist*	27,31	63
Chavez, Micheal/*Springtown Ind School Dist*	5,79	313
Chavez, Phillip/*Edgewood Ind School Dist*	8,15,18	31
Chavez, Rene/*Clint Ind School Dist*	68	132
Chavez, Tomas/*Ft Hancock Ind School Dist*	73	234
Chavez, Veronica/*La Joya Ind School Dist*	50	219
Cheatham, Patricia/*Coppell Ind School Dist*	57	98
Cheeck, Faith Anne/*Bonham Ind School Dist*	8,11,288	145
Cheek, Dale/*Maypearl Ind School Dist*	3,5	141
Cheek, Kimberly/*Wylie Ind School Dist*	81	361
Chenausky, Shelly/*Socorro Ind School Dist*	4	135
Cheney, Darrell/*Channelview Ind School Dist*	73,84	183
Chenoweth, Katie/*Region 7 Ed Service Center*	2,68,71	171
Chesnut, Christian/*UT Tyler University Acad Dist*	2	338
Chesser, Brandon/*Eastland Ind School Dist*	12	129
Chesser, Paula/*Warren Ind School Dist*	29	375
Chester, Mark/*Blue Ridge Ind School Dist*	6	77
Chiarelli, April/*Burleson Ind School Dist*	9,34,57	246
Chiboroski, Susan/*Alief Ind School Dist*	20,23	181
Chide, Wendy/*Dickinson Ind School Dist*	88	159
Childers, Willis/*Chilton Ind School Dist*	3	144
Childress, Bill/*Boyd Ind School Dist*	67	402
Childress, Don/*Fannindel Ind School Dist*	16	120
Childress, Dwight/*Crockett Co Cons Common SD*	67	94
Childress, Jamey/*Big Sandy Ind School Dist*	67	376
Chiselbrook, Stephanie/*Blooming Grove Ind School Dist*	37	299
Chism, Heather/*Kilgore Ind School Dist*	295	169
Chisum, Kevin/*Guthrie Common School Dist*	1,83	257
Chisum, McKenzie/*Guthrie Common School Dist*	57,271	257
Chitwood, Michele/*New Waverly Ind School Dist*	2	383
Chlapecka, Ross/*Bells Ind School Dist*	73,76,84	165
Chnat, Rodney/*Ft Bend Ind School Dist*	6	149
Choate, Barry/*Athens Ind School Dist*	3,4,5	213
Choate, Debbie/*New Waverly Ind School Dist*	36,85,286	383
Choate, John/*Christoval Ind School Dist*	10,60,73,288,296	364
Choate, Merideth/*Frisco Ind School Dist*	57	78
Chohlis, Ashley/*East Central Ind School Dist*	71,79	31
Choiniere, Sharon/*Iola Ind School Dist*	2	172
Choundhury, Mohammed/*San Antonio Ind School Dist*	70,750	39
Chriesman, Blain/*Terrell Co Ind School Dist*	2	362
Christ, Lacey/*East Bernard Ind Sch Dist*	58	389
Christian, Andrew/*Aquilla Ind School Dist*	2,8,88	227
Christian, Andrew/*Aquilla Ind School Dist*	8,88	227
Christian, Barbara/*Malone Independent School Dist*	58,270,273	228
Christian, Hayley/*Farwell Ind School Dist*	36,88,270	314
Christian, Jenny/*Dallas Ind School Dist*	42	98
Christian, Keisha/*Evadale Ind School Dist*	7,85	240
Christian, Sherry/*Dallas Ind School Dist*	15,88	98
Christianson, Emily/*Crandall Ind School Dist*	294	251
Christie, Heather/*Bastrop Ind School Dist*	294	23
Christopherson, Judith/*Spring Branch Ind School Dist*	7	200
Chruchillo, Edward/*Crystal City Ind School Dist*	1	407
Chrzanowski, Maria/*Amarillo Ind School Dist*	81	317
Chuca, Miguel/*Region 1 Ed Service Center*	73,76,286	226
Church, Keith/*Wilson Ind School Dist*	16	273
Church, Robbin/*Lake Worth Ind School Dist*	9,57	356
Cielencki, Cayla/*Amarillo Ind School Dist*	42	317
Cieri, Ashley/*Waxahachie Ind School Dist*	286	142
Cieszlak, Lucia/*Eagle Mtn-Saginaw Ind Sch Dist*	2	348
Cikanek, Kathy/*Ennis Ind School Dist*	8,15,69	140
Cipolla, Denise/*Conroe Ind School Dist*	36	291
Cipriano, Juan/*Santa Rosa Ind School Dist*	6	67
Cisneros, Eve/*Beeville Ind School Dist*	2	25
Cisneros, Jesse/*Sweeny Ind School Dist*	91	54
Civis, Leah/*Banquete Ind School Dist*	4	302
Clancy, Brian/*San Antonio Ind School Dist*	6	39
Clanton, Tracy/*Rankin Ind School Dist*	3,5	377
Clardy, Dick/*Ft Worth Ind School Dist*	23	349
Clark, Amy/*Sweetwater ISD School Dist*	31,38,88	301
Clark, Angela/*Fruitvale Ind School Dist*	8,11,89,296	380
Clark, Bobby/*Krum Ind School Dist*	6	122
Clark, Bridget/*Gregory-Portland Ind Sch Dist*	2,19,91	330
Clark, Cindy/*Baird Ind School Dist*	2	62
Clark, Darin/*Perryton Ind School Dist*	71	307
Clark, David/*Harleton Ind School Dist*	3	208

NAME/District	JOB FUNCTIONS	PAGE
Clark, Elizabeth, Dr/*Birdville Ind School Dist*	8,15	346
Clark, Ellen/*Lancaster Ind School Dist*	67	110
Clark, Gay/*Ferris Ind School Dist*	4	140
Clark, Jennifer/*Melissa Ind School Dist*	58	81
Clark, Jennifer/*Prairiland Ind School Dist*	11,38,69,83,88,270	260
Clark, Joe/*Spring Ind School Dist*	20,23	202
Clark, Karrie/*Vidor Ind School Dist*	34,58,77	309
Clark, Lisa/*Rains Ind School Dist*	73,295	320
Clark, Mary Ann/*El Paso ISD-High Schools*	92	134
Clark, Melissa/*O'Donnell Ind School Dist*	2	273
Clark, Michelle/*Elkhart Ind School Dist*	16,82	15
Clark, R Matthew, Dr/*Conroe Ind School Dist*	31	291
Clark, Randy/*Walnut Bend Ind School Dist*	67	92
Clark, Rebecca/*Benjamin Ind School Dist*	7	258
Clark, Rebecca/*Lewisville Ind School Dist*	79	122
Clark, Renee/*Water Valley Ind School Dist*	59	365
Clark, Sandy/*Orange Grove Ind School Dist*	36	245
Clark, Sedric/*Gladewater Ind School Dist*	1	169
Clark, Sherry/*Wildorado Ind Sch Dist*	12	308
Clark, Steve/*Leander Ind School Dist*	36,83,90	396
Clark, Viann/*Pringle-Morse Cons ISD*	271	177
Clark, Yvonne/*Klein Ind School Dist*	7	196
Clarkson, Lesa/*Prairiland Ind School Dist*	4	260
Clary, Ron/*North East Ind School Dist*	3,15	34
Claudio, Joshua/*Brownsville Ind School Dist*	297	63
Claunch, Suann/*Ft Worth Ind School Dist*	57	349
Clausen, Donny/*Irion Co Ind School Dist*	1	238
Clausen, Mike/*La Porte Ind School Dist*	3,15,17,91	198
Clavell, Deanna/*Shepherd Ind School Dist*	2	330
Clawson, Heath/*Louise Ind School Dist*	6	389
Clay, Anita/*Texarkana Ind School Dist*	2	50
Clay, Jeffrey/*El Paso Ind School Dist*	69,70,294	132
Clay, Toni/*Athens Ind School Dist*	71	213
Clayburn, Ashley, Dr/*Cypress-Fairbanks Ind Sch Dist*	13,15,294	183
Claycomb, Becky/*Texline Ind School Dist*	31,90	95
Claymon, Lauaren/*Liberty Hill Ind School Dist*	16,82	398
Claypool, Kevin, Dr/*Lake Travis Ind School Dist*	70	370
Clayton, Carla/*Harrold Ind School Dist*	58	393
Clayton, John/*Grandview Ind School Dist*	73,95,295	248
Clayton, Louis/*Midway Ind School Dist*	73,286	74
Clayton, Scot/*Henrietta Ind School Dist*	8,11,15,288,296	74
Clearfield, Courtney/*Garland Ind School Dist*	69,70,294	105
Cleary, Brian/*Bandera Ind School Dist*	4	23
Cleaver, Max/*Hays Cons Ind School Dist*	3,5,17	211
Cleere, Jan/*Kennedale Ind School Dist*	8,69,73	355
Cleere, Roger/*Ector Co Ind School Dist*	5	129
Clem, Dale/*New Home Ind School Dist*	3	273
Clement, Sherri/*Aubrey Ind School Dist*	4	120
Clements, Bryan/*Galena Park Ind School Dist*	91	186
Clements, Jody, Dr/*Longview Ind School Dist*	68,74,93,296	169
Cleveland, Jess/*Scurry Rosser Ind School Dist*	6	253
Cleveland, Royce/*Region 19 Ed Service Center*	2	139
Cleveland, Sunny/*Lovejoy Ind School Dist*	4	80
Cleveland, Thad/*Terrell Co Ind School Dist*	67	362
Clevenger, Denise/*Advantage Academy Admin Office*	280	96
Clevenger, Gaylen/*Del Valle Ind School Dist*	58	369
Clevenger, Theodore/*Bartlett Ind School Dist*	1	26
Click, Shan/*Eden Cons Ind School Dist*	67	90
Clift, Bryan/*Stratford Ind School Dist*	67	336
Clifton, Karen/*Ranger Ind School Dist*	67	129
Clifton, Megan/*Crowell Ind School Dist*	16	149
Clifton, Mona/*Comanche Ind School Dist*	7	89
Clifton, Sharon/*George West Ind School Dist*	4	268
Clinard, Josh/*Winters Ind School Dist*	73,295	327
Cline, Donna/*Clint Ind School Dist*	2,19	132
Cline, Kelly/*Spring Ind School Dist*	11	202
Cline, Michelle, Dr/*Throckmorton Ind School Dist*	1	363
Cline, Nancy/*Carrollton-Farmers Branch ISD*	67	96
Cline, Rebecca/*San Angelo Ind School Dist*	69	364
Cline, Ron/*Paint Rock Ind School Dist*	1,11	90
Clinton, Ben/*Raymondville Ind Sch Dist*	11,15	394
Clopton, Kell/*Kaufman Ind School Dist*	15,68,88	252
Clore, Paul, Dr/*Gregory-Portland Ind Sch Dist*	1	330
Cloud, David/*South San Antonio Ind Sch Dist*	16,73	42
Cloud, Rhonda/*Hearne Ind School Dist*	4	325
Clouse, Christy/*Lindale Ind School Dist*	58	337

DISTRICT PERSONNEL INDEX

Market Data Retrieval

NAME/District	JOB FUNCTIONS	PAGE
Clouse, Tim/Harrold Ind School Dist	67	393
Clover, Cortney/Little Elm Ind School Dist	58	124
Clowers, Ashlei/Diboll Ind School Dist	8	17
Cloy, Michael/Brownwood Ind School Dist	67	58
Clugston, Steve/Pine Tree Ind School Dist	1	170
Clynch, Kim/Harleton Ind School Dist	16	208
Cmaidalka, Brian/Dickinson Ind School Dist	5	159
Coachman, Andrea/McKinney Ind School Dist	50	81
Coats, Lorrie/Plainview Ind School Dist	5	175
Coats, Shannon/Queen City Ind School Dist	4	70
Cob, Darryl, Dr/DeSoto Ind School Dist	68,78	104
Cobarrubias, Rosie, Dr/Monte Alto Ind School Dist	1	222
Cobb, Bruce/Canyon Ind School Dist	67	320
Cobb, Chris/Pewitt Cons Ind School Dist	3,17	296
Cobb, Christopher/Pewitt Cons Ind School Dist	5	296
Cobb, Cindy/Frenship Ind School Dist	8,15,74,273	269
Cobb, Derek/Frenship Ind School Dist	3	269
Cobb, Jennifer, Dr/Spring Ind School Dist	15,69,70,294	202
Cobb, Marilyn/Atlanta Ind School Dist	2,15	69
Cobb, Martin/Spring Hill Ind School Dist	2,19	170
Cobb, Melissa/Waxahachie Ind School Dist	30	142
Cobb, Robert/Dickinson Ind School Dist	15	159
Cobb, Ryan/Tidehaven Ind School Dist	3	276
Cobb, Shelia/Martinsville Ind School Dist	9,12,58,275,296	298
Cobb, Tracy/Corrigan-Camden Ind Sch Dist	58	316
Cobbs, Jeaneen/Buffalo Ind School Dist	57	264
Cobos, Dolores/Klondike Ind School Dist	4	117
Cobos, Dolores/Klondike Ind School Dist	4	117
Coburn, Billy/Little Elm Ind School Dist	91	124
Coburn, Harold/Elysian Fields Ind School Dist	67	208
Coburn, Joseph, Dr/Lewisville Ind School Dist	6,7,72,91	122
Cochran, Jarrett/Comal Ind School Dist	73,76,295,297	87
Cochran, Jason/Eastland Ind School Dist	1,83	129
Cochran, Lisa/Midway Ind School Dist	58	280
Cochran, William/Motley Co Ind School Dist	1	296
Cochrane, Judy/Hooks Ind School Dist	2	48
Cochrane, Karla/Palmer Ind School Dist	2	141
Cockrell, Luther/Groveton Ind School Dist	3	374
Cockrum, Kenneth/North Hopkins Ind School Dist	5	231
Cockrum, Lisa/Rusk Ind School Dist	38	73
Coffee, Lawanda/Spring Branch Ind School Dist	12	200
Coffelt, Bradley/Whitney Ind School Dist	27	228
Coffey, Karen/Goose Creek Cons Ind Sch Dist	34,88	187
Coffey, Keith/Aquilla Ind School Dist	12	227
Coffman, Kevin/City View Ind School Dist	5	391
Coffman, Stony/Meridian Ind School Dist	6	47
Cofper, Melinda/Peaster Ind School Dist	16	313
Cogburn, Elaine/Dripping Springs Ind Sch Dist	2	210
Cogburn, Elaine/Plano Ind School Dist	15	82
Cogburn, Ray/Region 16 Ed Service Center	1	321
Cogdell, Danny/Little Elm Ind School Dist	3	124
Cohen, Alan/Dallas Ind School Dist	34	98
Coker, Bianca, Dr/Rockwall Ind School Dist	47	325
Coker, Chad/Wortham Ind School Dist	58	156
Coker, Cindy/Bellville Ind School Dist	4	21
Coker, Geanna/Wink Loving Ind School Dist	2	402
Coker, Jeremy/Woodville Ind School Dist	73,76,84,295	375
Coker, Jon/Abbott Ind School Dist	57,58,79,280,296	226
Coker, Marie/Keller Ind School Dist	57	354
Coker, Mike/Bellville Ind School Dist	1	21
Colbert, James/Harris Co Dept of Ed	1	179
Cole, Amy/Galena Park Ind School Dist	11,298	186
Cole, Brian/Brazosport Ind School Dist	16,95,286	52
Cole, Christina/Cypress-Fairbanks Ind Sch Dist	15	183
Cole, Clay/Liberty Hill Ind School Dist	67	398
Cole, Jason/Thrall Ind School Dist	6	400
Cole, Judy/Bridge City Ind School Dist	67	308

NAME/District	JOB FUNCTIONS	PAGE
Cole, Julie/Hurst-Euless-Bedford ISD	67	353
Cole, Malcom/Avalon Ind School Dist	6	140
Cole, Rhonda/Barbers Hill Ind School Dist	4	72
Cole, Ryan/Brazosport Ind School Dist	11,34,271	52
Cole, Susan/Leander Ind School Dist	74,273	396
Coleman, Alton/Gregory-Portland Ind Sch Dist	5	330
Coleman, Barry/Trinity Ind School Dist	73,84,295	374
Coleman, Carla/North Lamar Ind School Dist	71	259
Coleman, Debbie/Nixon-Smiley Cons Ind Sch Dist	16	164
Coleman, Derrell, Dr/Carrollton-Farmers Branch ISD	15,751	96
Coleman, Jennifer/Gainesville Ind School Dist	73,76,98	91
Coleman, Kathy/Community Ind School Dist	7,85	78
Coleman, Lawrence/West Rusk Co Cons Ind Sch Dist	1	328
Coleman, Roy/Lumberton Ind School Dist	5	178
Coleman, Susan/Aransas Pass Ind School Dist	16	330
Coleman, Todd/Beaumont Ind School Dist	15	241
Coleman, Tonja/Gary Ind School Dist	81	311
Coleman, Wayne/Jacksonville Ind School Dist	6	72
Colhoff, Krystal/Lago Vista Ind School Dist	58,69	370
Collazo, Sheila/Somerset Ind School Dist	8,15,57,271	42
Collida, Joanna/Dodd City Ind School Dist	274	145
Collier, Melody/Hawley Ind School Dist	2,8,11,57,58,288	250
Collier, Twiana/Aldine Ind School Dist	36,81	179
Collins, Amy/Hallsville Ind School Dist	34,58,90	208
Collins, Bernard/Woodville Ind School Dist	91	375
Collins, Betty/Rusk Ind School Dist	8,27,57,74,88,271,296,298	73
Collins, Billy/Borden Co Ind School Dist	1	46
Collins, Cathy/Ft Bend Ind School Dist	274	149
Collins, Chad/Lovejoy Ind School Dist	67	80
Collins, Chad/Scurry Rosser Ind School Dist	15	253
Collins, Christi/Nueces Canyon Cons Ind SD	58,83	131
Collins, Jeanann/Princeton Ind School Dist	71	84
Collins, Kelli/Zavalla Ind School Dist	8,36	18
Collins, Kortni/Eula Ind School Dist	270	63
Collins, Lisa/Rio Vista Ind School Dist	81	248
Collins, Norm/Alamo Heights Ind School Dist	6	30
Collins, Tim/Arlington Ind School Dist	5	343
Collmorgen, Joe/Central Ind School Dist	3	17
Collum, Jeff/Hallsville Ind School Dist	1	208
Colsen, Lindsey/Blackwell Cons Ind Sch Dist	270	301
Colson, Harold/Pilot Point Ind School Dist	3,15	125
Colton, Bradshaw, Dr/Harts Bluff Ind School Dist	67	363
Colvert, Jeremy/Leon Ind School Dist	6	264
Colvin, Demetrius/Burton Ind School Dist	67	386
Combs, Charlie/Athens Ind School Dist	4	213
Combs, Daniel, Dr/Alvin Ind School Dist	2,15,19,71	50
Combs, Mike/Lindale Ind School Dist	67	337
Comeaux, Erian/Pasadena Ind School Dist	11	198
Comeaux, Michael/Anna Ind School Dist	1	77
Comer, Norma/Richardson Ind School Dist	76,295	112
Comneck, Mark/Angleton Ind School Dist	8,15	51
Compton, Alice/Avalon Ind School Dist	2	140
Concha, Alfredo/Lackland Ind School Dist	3,4,5,73,76,91,295	34
Condra, Wayne/El Campo Ind School Dist	6	389
Condron, Mark/Hudson Ind School Dist	297	17
Cone, Hensley, Dr/Natalia Ind School Dist	1	284
Conger, Eddie/Int'l Leadership of Texas Dist	1	108
Conklin, Emily/Northwest Ind School Dist	71	124
Conklin, Mike/Northwest Ind School Dist	91	124
Conklin, Shane, Dr/Decatur Ind School Dist	8,31,57,69,70,271,274	403
Conley-Johnson, Nicole/Austin Ind School Dist	2	366
Conley, John, Dr/Region 6 Ed Service Center	73	384
Connally, Melanie/Priddy Ind School Dist	2	289
Connally, Paula/Bronte Ind School Dist	58,280	75
Connell, Jeremy/San Marcos Cons Ind Sch Dist	295	211
Connelly, Brad/Celeste Ind School Dist	1	235
Conner, Arron/Bridge City Ind School Dist	27	308

---

1 Superintendent	16 Instructional Media Svcs	30 Adult Education	44 Science Sec	58 Special Education K-12	72 Summer School	88 Alternative/At Risk	277 Remedial Math K-12
2 Bus/Finance/Purchasing	17 Chief Operations Officer	31 Career/Sch-to-Work K-12	45 Math K-12	59 Special Education Elem	73 Instructional Tech	89 Multi-Cultural Curriculum	280 Literacy Coach
3 Buildings And Grounds	18 Chief Academic Officer	32 Career/Sch-to-Work Elem	46 Math Elem	60 Special Education Sec	74 Inservice Training	90 Social Work	285 STEM
4 Food Service	19 Chief Financial Officer	33 Career/Sch-to-Work Sec	47 Math Sec	61 Foreign/World Lang K-12	75 Marketing/Distributive	91 Safety/Security	286 Digital Learning
5 Transportation	20 Art K-12	34 Early Childhood Ed	48 English/Lang Arts K-12	62 Foreign/World Lang Elem	76 Info Systems	92 Magnet School	288 Common Core Standards
6 Athletic	21 Art Elem	35 Health/Phys Education	49 English/Lang Arts Elem	63 Foreign/World Lang Sec	77 Psychological Assess	93 Parental Involvement	294 Accountability
7 Health Services	22 Art Sec	36 Guidance Services K-12	50 English/Lang Arts Sec	64 Religious Education K-12	78 Affirmative Action	95 Tech Prep Program	295 Network System
8 Curric/Instruct K-12	23 Music K-12	37 Guidance Services Elem	51 Reading K-12	65 Religious Education Elem	79 Student Personnel	97 Chief Information Officer	296 Title II Programs
9 Curric/Instruct Elem	24 Music Elem	38 Guidance Services Sec	52 Reading Elem	66 Religious Education Sec	80 Driver Ed/Safety	98 Chief Technology Officer	297 Webmaster
10 Curric/Instruct Sec	25 Music Sec	39 Social Studies K-12	53 Reading Sec	67 School Board President	81 Gifted/Talented	270 Character Education	298 Grant Writer/Ptnrships
11 Federal Program	26 Business Education	40 Social Studies Elem	54 Remedial Reading K-12	68 Teacher Personnel	82 Video Services	271 Migrant Education	750 Chief Innovation Officer
12 Title I	27 Career & Tech Ed	41 Social Studies Sec	55 Remedial Reading Elem	69 Academic Assessment	83 Substance Abuse Prev	273 Teacher Mentor	751 Chief of Staff
13 Title V	28 Technology Education	42 Science K-12	56 Remedial Reading Sec	70 Research/Development	84 Erate	274 Before/After Sch	752 Social Emotional Learning
15 Asst Superintendent	29 Family/Consumer Science	43 Science Elem	57 Bilingual/ELL	71 Public Information	85 AIDS Education	275 Response To Intervention	

Texas School Directory
DISTRICT PERSONNEL INDEX

NAME/District	JOB FUNCTIONS	PAGE
Conner, Carrie/*Clyde Consolidated Ind SD*	36,83,85,88	62
Conner, Jacob/*Irion Co Ind School Dist*	6	238
Conner, Maryellen/*Dayton Ind School Dist*	68,273	265
Connor, Jim/*Columbus Ind School Dist*	8	86
Connors, Deborah/*Humble Ind School Dist*	2	195
Connot, Lance/*Rivercrest Ind School Dist*	6	322
Conoly, Lisa/*Brackett Ind School Dist*	81	257
Conrad, Dana/*Spur Ind School Dist*	58	127
Conrad, Kristy/*Montgomery Ind School Dist*	2,19	293
Conrad, Scott/*Sherman Ind School Dist*	3	167
Conrad, Terri/*Georgetown Ind School Dist*	273	395
Conring, Kathy/*Cisco Independent Sch Dist*	69	128
Consillo, Sandra/*Brazosport Ind School Dist*	45	52
Constanzo, Deborah/*Lytle Ind School Dist*	5	21
Contreras, Austin/*Corsicana Ind School Dist*	73,295	299
Contreras, Carlos/*Dell City Ind School Dist*	8,11,88,285,288,294	234
Contreras, Mark/*North East Ind School Dist*	91	34
Contreras, Sam/*Pecos-Barstow-Toyah Ind SD*	67	323
Contu, Nora, Dr/*Pharr-San Juan-Alamo Ind SD*	10	223
Conway, Nina/*Robstown Ind School Dist*	2,19	305
Conway, Shelly/*Anna Ind School Dist*	67	77
Coody, Shari/*Northside Ind School Dist*	286	393
Cook, Amy/*Friona Ind School Dist*	16	315
Cook, Carter/*Ft Worth Ind School Dist*	16	349
Cook, Donna/*Central Ind School Dist*	16,82	17
Cook, Grant/*Tarkington Ind School Dist*	67	266
Cook, Justus/*Hull Daisetta Ind School Dist*	73,295	266
Cook, Keith/*Roby Cons Ind School Dist*	1,11	148
Cook, Kimberly/*Milford Ind School Dist*	67	141
Cook, Laura/*Lubbock Ind School Dist*	61	269
Cook, Leigh/*Keller Ind School Dist*	11,298	354
Cook, Lynwood/*Neches Ind School Dist*	3,85	15
Cook, Nicci/*Frankston Ind School Dist*	8,11,15,57,273,296	15
Cook, Rebecca/*Cypress-Fairbanks Ind Sch Dist*	73,286	184
Cook, Solomon/*Humble Ind School Dist*	91	195
Cook, Stephanie, Dr/*Frisco Ind School Dist*	36	78
Cook, Tammie/*Vega Ind School Dist*	8,31,36,69,83,270	307
Cook, Terri/*La Porte Ind School Dist*	71	198
Cook, Tracy/*Hooks Ind School Dist*	8,11,30,34,36,57,288,296	48
Cooke, Mrs/*Aransas Pass Ind School Dist*	1	330
Cooksy, Rodney/*Int'l Leadership of Texas Dist*	15	108
Cooley, Carla/*Jim Ned Cons Ind School Dist*	38,69,83,88	361
Cooley, Hunter/*Jim Ned Cons Ind School Dist*	2,11,19,294	361
Coonkin, Clinit/*Clarendon Cons Ind Sch Dist*	6	127
Cooper, Aimee/*Advantage Academy Admin Office*	8	96
Cooper, Brent/*Brownsboro Ind School Dist*	83	213
Cooper, Brian/*Greenwood Ind School Dist*	3	285
Cooper, Chris/*Sherman Ind School Dist*	76	167
Cooper, Debbie/*Red Lick Ind School Dist*	9,11,57,69,74,88	49
Cooper, Donna/*Brookeland Ind School Dist*	3,5	240
Cooper, Geoff/*Brownfield Ind Sch Dist*	67	362
Cooper, John/*Lipan Ind School Dist*	67	230
Cooper, John/*Snook Ind School Dist*	3	59
Cooper, Kary, Dr/*Plano Ind School Dist*	4,5,6,15,68,91	82
Cooper, Keri/*Pleasanton Ind School Dist*	57,288,296	21
Cooper, Kyle/*Gatesville Ind School Dist*	6	92
Cooper, Lynette/*Bay City Ind School Dist*	7	275
Cooper, Madeline/*Liberty-Eylau Ind School Dist*	26	48
Cooper, Richard/*Corrigan-Camden Ind Sch Dist*	1	316
Cooper, Sara/*Granger Ind School Dist*	8	396
Cooper, Sherry/*Leonard Ind School Dist*	4	146
Cooper, Tim/*San Saba Ind School Dist*	73,286,295	332
Coopersmith, Michael/*Bellville Ind School Dist*	8,11,36,57,69,83,88	22
Cooremans, Rosemary/*Harlandale Ind School Dist*	9	32
Cope, Brandon/*Riesel Ind School Dist*	1	281
Cope, John/*Ft Worth Ind School Dist*	297	349
Cope, Kristi/*Industrial Ind School Dist*	16	240
Copelan, Casey/*Cushing Ind School Dist*	3,73	297
Copeland, Derek/*New Deal Ind School Dist*	5	271
Copeland, Jim/*Pottsboro Ind School Dist*	67	167
Copeland, Joe/*Duncanville Ind School Dist*	15,79	104
Copeland, Joseph/*Keller Ind School Dist*	79	354
Copeland, Kendra/*Salado Ind School Dist*	57	29
Copeland, Shelly/*Spring Ind School Dist*	4	202
Copeland, Sunshine/*Orangefield Ind School Dist*	16	309
Copeland, Tim/*Jarrell Ind School Dist*	3	396

NAME/District	JOB FUNCTIONS	PAGE
Copley, Jamie/*Follett Ind School Dist*	11,296	267
Copp, Judy/*Northwest Ind School Dist*	67	124
Coppock, Joyce/*Darrouzett Ind School Dist*	36,275,288	267
Corbell, Kenny/*White Oak Ind School Dist*	3	171
Corbett, Patrick/*Bryan Ind School Dist*	20,23	54
Corbin, Leeann/*Redwater Ind School Dist*	8,11,57,69,83,273,288,296	49
Corbin, Sarah/*Buffalo Ind School Dist*	4	264
Corcan, Tommy/*Glen Rose Ind School Dist*	3,5,15,68,83,91	340
Corcoran, Patrick/*Munday Consolidated Ind SD*	6,35	259
Cordell, Cole/*Region 16 Ed Service Center*	2	321
Corder, Angela/*Kaufman Ind School Dist*	73,76	252
Cordero, Israel/*Dallas Ind School Dist*	15	98
Cordova, Joe/*Knippa Ind School Dist*	73	378
Cordova, Paul/*Houston Ind School Dist*	91	188
Cordova, Toni/*Dallas Ind School Dist*	71	98
Corean, Jeff/*Rochelle Ind School Dist*	6,9,74,288	278
Coreo, Beatrice/*Stratford Ind School Dist*	271	336
Corley, Jolynn, Dr/*Nacogdoches Ind School Dist*	11,294	298
Cormier, Mandy/*Hamshire Fannett Ind Sch Dist*	34	242
Cornejo, Maggie/*Schertz-Cibolo-Univ City ISD*	4	173
Cornelius, John/*Sudan Ind School Dist*	6	261
Cornish, Kaaron/*Mt Calm Ind School Dist*	58	228
Corona, Julie/*Beaumont Ind School Dist*	57	241
Corona, Melissa/*Lockhart Ind School Dist*	58,81	61
Coronado, Sergio/*Canutillo Ind School Dist*	67	132
Coronado, Sergio/*Progreso Ind School Dist*	1	224
Coronado, Sergio/*Valley View Ind School Dist*	69	225
Corrales, Cynthia/*Ysleta Ind School Dist*	93	137
Correa, Bea/*Glasscock Co Ind School Dist*	57	163
Correa, Nolan/*Humble Ind School Dist*	79	195
Correll, Andrew/*Levelland Ind School Dist*	6,35	229
Cortez, Ami/*Austin Ind School Dist*	34	366
Cortez, Debbie/*San Elizario Ind School Dist*	42,45,277	135
Cortez, Eddie/*Carrizo Spgs Cons Ind SD*	91	127
Cortez, Eric/*Austwell Tivoli Ind SD*	11,57,88	323
Cortez, Fiosncio/*Muleshoe Ind School Dist*	5	22
Cortez, Gerard/*North East Ind School Dist*	58,77	34
Cortez, Joy/*La Villa Ind School Dist*	7,85	220
Cortez, Oralia/*Laredo Ind School Dist*	11	386
Cortez, Oralia/*Laredo Ind School Dist*	11	386
Cortez, Stefanie/*Wilson Ind School Dist*	58	273
Cortinas, Jesse/*Judson Ind School Dist*	73,98	33
Cosby, Dade/*Cross Plains Ind Sch Dist*	1	62
Cosimeno, Michael/*Jarrell Ind School Dist*	67	396
Costello, Brad/*Bowie Ind School Dist*	88	289
Costilla, Jesus/*Eagle Pass Ind School Dist*	68,77	276
Cottar, Debbie/*Corsicana Ind School Dist*	57,88	299
Cotton, Charles/*Coldspring-Oakhurst Cons ISD*	3,5	330
Cotton, Kelli/*Victoria Ind School Dist*	58,77	382
Cottongame, Regina/*Palmer Ind School Dist*	11,58,69,296,298	141
Cottrell, Becky/*Morton Ind School Dist*	274	75
Cottrell, Rod/*Morton Ind School Dist*	16,73,76,295	75
Couch, Greg/*Shallowater Ind School Dist*	3	272
Coufal, Brian/*Kingsville Ind School Dist*	67	257
Coufal, Larry/*Holland Ind School Dist*	3	27
Coultress, Susie/*Texas Dept of Education*	57	1
Counte, Brett/*Sherman Ind School Dist*	5,91	167
Coupland, Yvonne/*Fabens Ind School Dist*	2,4	135
Courchesne, Denise/*Irving Ind School Dist*	93	109
Courmier, Marlene/*Little Cypress Mauriceville SD*	67	308
Courson, Christi/*Duncanville Ind School Dist*	2	104
Courson, Stacy/*Texarkana Ind School Dist*	90	50
Couvillion, Jim/*Leakey Ind School Dist*	3	322
Covarrubias, Gloria/*Plains Ind School Dist*	57,271	405
Cowan, Kelly/*Lovejoy Ind School Dist*	47	80
Cowan, Kelly/*Mt Pleasant Ind School Dist*	71	363
Cowan, Michelle/*Chester Ind School Dist*	73	374
Cowan, Shawntee/*Duncanville Ind School Dist*	16,73,82,95,98,295	104
Cowden, Tim/*Divide Ind School Dist*	67	255
Cowley, Amy/*La Vernia Ind School Dist*	2,3,5,15	401
Cowley, James/*Groesbeck Ind School Dist*	1,73	267
Cox, Betty/*Aquilla Ind School Dist*	83	227
Cox, Brad/*Coahoma Ind School Dist*	1,73	234
Cox, Breann/*Chico Ind School Dist*	73	403
Cox, Christina/*Coahoma Ind School Dist*	58	234
Cox, Cody/*Bellville Ind School Dist*	5	21

School Year 2019-2020   800-333-8802   TX-T19

DISTRICT PERSONNEL INDEX

Market Data Retrieval

NAME/District	JOB FUNCTIONS	PAGE
Cox, Connie/Angleton Ind School Dist	2	51
Cox, Emilee/Refugio Ind School Dist	7,85	323
Cox, Jason/Sterling City Ind School Dist	67	342
Cox, Jimmy/Waskom Ind School Dist	1	209
Cox, Jodi/Grapevine-Colleyville Ind SD	57,61	353
Cox, Jordan/Grape Creek Ind School Dist	11,57,58,285,286,288,296	364
Cox, Lacee/Ira Ind School Dist	88	333
Cox, Lisa/Jacksonville Ind School Dist	8,72,79,275	72
Cox, Marie/Advantage Academy Admin Office	68	96
Cox, Meleia/Liberty Hill Ind School Dist	5	398
Cox, Melissa/Fairfield Ind School Dist	8,11,57,69,79,280,296,298	156
Cox, Pam/Evadale Ind School Dist	4	240
Cox, Randy/Sabine Ind School Dist	73	170
Cox, Rhonda/Wilson Ind School Dist	2	273
Cox, Robin/Bryan Ind School Dist	16	54
Cox, Scott/Prosper Ind School Dist	76	84
Cox, Shelley/Motley Co Ind School Dist	73	296
Cox, Steven, Dr/Warren Ind School Dist	8,11,61,296	375
Cox, Tina/Harleton Ind School Dist	2	208
Cox, Troy/Rice Ind School Dist	3,5	300
Coy, Brittney/Mt Calm Ind School Dist	16,73,295,297	228
Coy, Nakia/Katy Ind School Dist	11	151
Coyle, Desiree/White Settlement Ind Sch Dist	71	357
Coyne, Clinton/Jefferson Ind School Dist	11,34,57,58,61,88,296	274
Crabb, Jessica/Lorenzo Ind School Dist	10,273	94
Crabill, A/Texas Dept of Education	15,70,298	1
Crabill, Frank/Int'l Leadership of Texas Dist	3	108
Craft, Adam/Etoile Ind School Dist	73,286	297
Craft, Bill/Lubbock Ind School Dist	3	269
Craft, John, Dr/Killeen Ind School Dist	1	27
Craft, Kristin/Spring Branch Ind School Dist	8,18	200
Craft, Todd/D'Hanis Ind School Dist	6	283
Crager, Eric/Diboll Ind School Dist	3	17
Crager, Katherina/Diboll Ind School Dist	2	17
Craig, Gerald/Diboll Ind School Dist	73,286	17
Craig, John/Brazosport Ind School Dist	5	52
Craig, Rusty/Prosper Ind School Dist	2	84
Craig, Tammy/Arlington Ind School Dist	2	343
Craighead, Jere/Royse City Ind School Dist	88,275	326
Craighead, Kyle/Wylie Ind School Dist	6	84
Crane, Cassie/Chapel Hill Ind School Dist	38	363
Crane, Jon/Huntington Ind School Dist	3	17
Cranfill, Greg/Wills Point Ind School Dist	6	381
Cranford, Wayne/Electra Ind School Dist	67	391
Cranmer, Robyn/Canyon Ind School Dist	11,57,93,270,271	320
Cranshaw, Thomas/Tomball Ind School Dist	295	203
Cransord, Stacy/Gary Ind School Dist	67	311
Craven, Craig/Harts Bluff Ind School Dist	2	363
Cravens, Brad/Sunnyvale Ind School Dist	67	113
Cravens, Sandi, Dr/Irving Ind School Dist	35,85	109
Crawford, Abigail/Castleberry Ind School Dist	20,23	347
Crawford, Chris/Hooks Ind School Dist	3,5	48
Crawford, Clinton/New Boston Ind School Dist	3	49
Crawford, Darin/Cypress-Fairbanks Ind Sch Dist	4	183
Crawford, David/Scurry Rosser Ind School Dist	27	253
Crawford, James/Roosevelt Ind School Dist	73,295	271
Crawford, Jennifer/Paradise Ind School Dist	59	403
Crawford, John/Midlothian Ind School Dist	6	141
Crawford, June/Copperas Cove Ind School Dist	2,11,19	92
Crawford, Laura/Robinson Ind School Dist	67	281
Crawford, Marty, Dr/Tyler Ind School Dist	1	337
Crawford, Matt/Tatum Ind School Dist	67	328
Crawford, Russell/Meridian Ind School Dist	3,5	47
Crawford, Susan/Big Sandy Ind School Dist	73,295	316
Crawford, Terri/Falls City Ind School Dist	2	250
Crawford, Terry/Abbott Ind School Dist	6	226
Crawford, Zach/Martinsville Ind School Dist	8,57,69,74,92,271	298
Crayton, Jo-Lynette/Killeen Ind School Dist	68,74,273	27
Creech, Freda, Dr/Katy Ind School Dist	15	151
Creek, David/San Angelo Ind School Dist	3	364
Creek, Kathy/Coppell Ind School Dist	76	98
Crelia, Bryan/Bandera Ind School Dist	4	23
Crenshaw, Janay/Whitharral Ind School Dist	16	230
Crenshaw, Shannon/Linden Kildare Cons Ind SD	76	70
Crescenzo, Lauri/Bowie Ind School Dist	5	289
Crespo, Gabriel/Socorro Ind School Dist	3	135
Crespo, Mirgitt/Ft Worth Ind School Dist	11	349
Creswell, Sandra/Austin ISD Elem School Area 1	15	366
Crews, Lee/Katy Ind School Dist	3,17	151
Crews, Michael/Big Sandy Ind School Dist	5	376
Criag, Joe/Rogers Ind School Dist	1,83	28
Cribbs, Amy/Weatherford Ind School Dist	47	313
Crim, Kirk/Angleton Ind School Dist	3	51
Criso, Debrah/Waskom Ind School Dist	37	209
Crisp, Brandon/Southwest Ind School Dist	2,15	43
Crisp, Kaley/Brazosport Ind School Dist	2	52
Crissey, Amber/Aledo Ind School Dist	8	312
Criswell, Serena/Iowa Park Consolidated Ind SD	4	392
Croak, David/Vidor Ind School Dist	2	309
Crock, Ryan/Bonham Ind School Dist	6	145
Cromer, Crystal/Lancaster Ind School Dist	58	110
Cromer, Deanne/San Saba Ind School Dist	16	332
Cromis, Mike/Lake Dallas Ind School Dist	88	122
Crompton, Ronny/Milford Ind School Dist	6	141
Cronin, Brenda/Shepherd Ind School Dist	68,74	330
Crook, Bryan/Somerville Ind School Dist	67	60
Crook, Jennifer/China Spring Ind School Dist	8,15,288	278
Crooms, Debra/Region 8 Ed Service Center	8	69
Crosby, Dave/Cross Plains Ind Sch Dist	73,286,295	62
Crosby, Maureen, Sr/Diocese of Brownsville Ed Off	16	226
Cross, April/Spring Creek Ind School Dist	8	238
Cross, William/Lytle Ind School Dist	3,5	21
Crosse, Carmen/Socorro Ind School Dist	10,15,288	135
Crossland, Eddie/Dumas Ind School Dist	3,5,91	295
Croswell, Jim/Int'l Leadership of Texas Dist	71	108
Crouc, Stewart/Sweeny Ind School Dist	3	54
Crouch, Monica/Bartlett Ind School Dist	2	26
Crouch, Patty/Lumberton Ind School Dist	11,15,91,285,288,296	178
Crouch, Randall/Little Cypress Mauriceville SD	6	308
Crouch, Sarah/Miles Ind School Dist	12,51	326
Crouch, Stewart/Bay City Ind School Dist	3	275
Croutch, Elizabeth/Zephyr Ind School Dist	12,275	59
Crow, Brandy/Keller Ind School Dist	61	354
Crow, Gail/Scurry Rosser Ind School Dist	8	253
Crow, Janna/Goose Creek Cons Ind Sch Dist	58,77	187
Crow, Janna/Plano Ind School Dist	58	82
Crow, Kimberly/Alief Ind School Dist	27,70,750	181
Crow, Monya/Lewisville Ind School Dist	36	122
Crow, Norman/Loop Ind School Dist	67	157
Crow, Stephen/Tidehaven Ind School Dist	67	276
Crow, Tim/Taylor Ind School Dist	71,76	399
Crow, Virginia/Murchison Ind Sch Dist	73,295	214
Crowe, Kathleen/Jarrell Ind School Dist	8,285,298	396
Crowley, John/Dripping Springs Ind Sch Dist	4	210
Croyle, Steve/Levelland Ind School Dist	4	229
Crpiran, Thomas/Irving Ind School Dist	3	109
Crum, Denver/Springlake-Earth Ind Sch Dist	1	261
Crum, Terri/Holland Ind School Dist	16	27
Crumbley, John/Cypress-Fairbanks Ind Sch Dist	76	184
Crump, Myra/Garland Ind School Dist	49,93	105
Cruse, Sonny/Graham Ind School Dist	1	406
Cruseturner, Gary/Rusk Ind School Dist	16,28,73,76,295,297	73
Crutchfield, Jennifer/San Angelo Ind School Dist	81	364
Crutsinger, Leslie/Gainesville Ind School Dist	71	91

---

1 Superintendent
2 Bus/Finance/Purchasing
3 Buildings And Grounds
4 Food Service
5 Transportation
6 Athletic
7 Health Services
8 Curric/Instruct K-12
9 Curric/Instruct Elem
10 Curric/Instruct Sec
11 Federal Program
12 Title I
13 Title V
15 Asst Superintendent
16 Instructional Media Svcs
17 Chief Operations Officer
18 Chief Academic Officer
19 Chief Financial Officer
20 Art K-12
21 Art Elem
22 Art Sec
23 Music K-12
24 Music Elem
25 Music Sec
26 Business Education
27 Career & Tech Ed
28 Technology Education
29 Family/Consumer Science
30 Adult Education
31 Career/Sch-to-Work K-12
32 Career/Sch-to-Work Elem
33 Career/Sch-to-Work Sec
34 Early Childhood Ed
35 Health/Phys Education
36 Guidance Services K-12
37 Guidance Services Elem
38 Guidance Services Sec
39 Social Studies K-12
40 Social Studies Elem
41 Social Studies Sec
42 Science K-12
43 Science Elem
44 Science Sec
45 Math K-12
46 Math Elem
47 Math Sec
48 English/Lang Arts K-12
49 English/Lang Arts Elem
50 English/Lang Arts Sec
51 Reading K-12
52 Reading Elem
53 Reading Sec
54 Remedial Reading K-12
55 Remedial Reading Elem
56 Remedial Reading Sec
57 Bilingual/ELL
58 Special Education K-12
59 Special Education Elem
60 Special Education Sec
61 Foreign/World Lang K-12
62 Foreign/World Lang Elem
63 Foreign/World Lang Sec
64 Religious Education K-12
65 Religious Education Elem
66 Religious Education Sec
67 School Board President
68 Teacher Personnel
69 Academic Assessment
70 Research/Development
71 Public Information
72 Summer School
73 Instructional Tech
74 Inservice Training
75 Marketing/Distributive
76 Info Systems
77 Psychological Assess
78 Affirmative Action
79 Student Personnel
80 Driver Ed/Safety
81 Gifted/Talented
82 Video Services
83 Substance Abuse Prev
84 Erate
85 AIDS Education
88 Alternative/At Risk
89 Multi-Cultural Curriculum
90 Social Work
91 Safety/Security
92 Magnet School
93 Parental Involvement
95 Tech Prep Program
97 Chief Information Officer
98 Chief Technology Officer
270 Character Education
271 Migrant Education
273 Teacher Mentor
274 Before/After Sch
275 Response To Intervention
277 Remedial Math K-12
280 Literacy Coach
285 STEM
286 Digital Learning
288 Common Core Standards
294 Accountability
295 Network System
296 Title II Programs
297 Webmaster
298 Grant Writer/Ptnrships
750 Chief Innovation Officer
751 Chief of Staff
752 Social Emotional Learning

TX-T20

Texas School Directory

DISTRICT PERSONNEL INDEX

NAME/District	JOB FUNCTIONS	PAGE
Cruz, Alicia/*Luling Ind School Dist*	271	61
Cruz, Andrea/*San Benito Cons Ind Sch Dist*	15,68	67
Cruz, Blanca/*San Elizario Ind School Dist*	68	135
Cruz, Bobby/*United Ind School Dist*	6	387
Cruz, Brenda/*Leander Ind School Dist*	69,70,294	396
Cruz, Connie/*San Benito Cons Ind Sch Dist*	12,271	67
Cruz, Cynthia/*Laredo Ind School Dist*	57	386
Cruz, Dee/*Cushing Ind School Dist*	7,11,57,69,271,296	297
Cruz, Gerardo, Dr/*Laredo Ind School Dist*	8	386
Cruz, Jacob/*Morton Ind School Dist*	5	75
Cruz, Mary Lou/*Roma Ind School Dist*	11,88,270,271,296,298	341
Cruz, Paul, Dr/*Austin Ind School Dist*	1	366
Cruz, Raul/*Pearland Ind School Dist*	5	53
Cruz, Rene/*United Ind School Dist*	84,295	387
Cruz, Senon/*Frenship Ind School Dist*	57	269
Cruz, Sylvia/*Mission Cons Ind School Dist*	91	222
Cruz, Tera/*Morton Ind School Dist*	2	75
Cubriel, April/*Edna Ind School Dist*	36	239
Cude, Guadalupe/*Freer Ind School Dist*	2,11,57,69,271,296	128
Cude, Wendy/*Hamilton Ind School Dist*	7,35,85	176
Cuellar, Angel/*Anthony Ind School Dist*	67	131
Cuellar, Enrique/*Santa Maria Ind School Dist*	2	67
Cuellar, Lesvia/*Zapata Co Ind School Dist*	4	406
Cuellar, Martin/*Santa Maria Ind School Dist*	1	67
Cuellar, Roberto/*Laredo Ind School Dist*	4	386
Cuevas, Andres/*Pearsall Ind School Dist*	3	157
Cuevas, Rena/*George West Ind School Dist*	4	268
Cuff, Timothy, Dr/*Brownsville Ind School Dist*	15	63
Culberson, David/*Sharyland Ind School Dist*	84,295	224
Culbreath, Kenneth/*Spring Ind School Dist*	91	202
Culp, Alan/*Hermleigh Ind School Dist*	3	333
Culpepper, Meredith/*Decatur Ind School Dist*	11,68,83,88,298	403
Culpepper, Shannon/*Sealy Ind School Dist*	91	22
Cumbie, Abigail/*Dayton Ind School Dist*	57	265
Cumbie, Rhonda/*La Porte Ind School Dist*	2,19	198
Cumby, Jacquelyn/*Dallas Ind School Dist*	286	98
Cumby, Larry/*Connally Ind School Dist*	68	279
Cummings, Adam/*Sundown Ind School Dist*	6	229
Cummings, Chris/*Klein Ind School Dist*	73,84	196
Cummings, Debra/*Rice Cons Ind School Dist*	69	87
Cummings, Houston/*Industrial Ind School Dist*	20,23	240
Cummings, Karyn, Dr/*Mesquite Ind School Dist*	15	110
Cummings, Sandra/*Lockney Independent Sch Dist*	286	149
Cummings, William/*Winnsboro Ind School Dist*	5	405
Cune, Carol/*Bryan Ind School Dist*	68	54
Cunningham, Cheryl/*Abilene Ind School Dist*	11,48,57	360
Cunningham, Cody/*McKinney Ind School Dist*	71	81
Cunningham, Holly/*Cedar Hill Ind School Dist*	58	97
Cunningham, Katie/*Cleburne Ind School Dist*	285	247
Cunningham, Leroy/*Bay City Ind School Dist*	91	275
Cunningham, Nuggett, Dr/*Grand Prairie Ind School Dist*	8,15,69	107
Cunningham, Patricia/*Harleton Ind School Dist*	57	208
Cunningham, Tory/*Harmony Ind School Dist*	73,76	376
Cunningham, Wes, Dr/*Frisco Ind School Dist*	18	78
Curara, Bertha/*Jourdanton Ind School Dist*	57	20
Curbello, Robin/*Three Rivers Ind School Dist*	16	268
Curl, Jason/*Frost Ind School Dist*	67	299
Curlin, Rachel/*Bryan Ind School Dist*	34,298	54
Curran, John/*Frisco Ind School Dist*	295	78
Curran, Mindy/*Ingram Ind School Dist*	8,11,16,57,83,288,296,298	255
Currie, Rex/*Warren Ind School Dist*	27	375
Currie, Shawna/*Victoria Ind School Dist*	71	382
Curry, Paige/*Birdville Ind School Dist*	68	346
Curry, Vikki/*Coldspring-Oakhurst Cons ISD*	8,15,288	330
Curtis, Kathy/*Farwell Ind School Dist*	73,76,295	314
Curtis, Randall/*Calallen Ind School Dist*	3,91	302
Curts, James, Dr/*Pharr-San Juan-Alamo Ind SD*	10,70,288,298	223
Curvo, Kevin/*Carlisle Ind School Dist*	67	327
Cutrer, Richie/*Corsicana Ind School Dist*	3,5,83,91	299
Cutshall, Jessica/*Latexo Ind School Dist*	6	233
Cyfton, Gabriel/*Ft Stockton Ind School Dist*	295	315
Cypert, Cecil/*Frisco Ind School Dist*	3	78
Cypert, Karla/*Pettus Ind School Dist*	57	25

D

Dabney, Derrick/*Royal Ind School Dist*	3,5	384

NAME/District	JOB FUNCTIONS	PAGE
Dabney, Mike/*Lake Dallas Ind School Dist*	73,286,297	122
Dacous, Kacey/*Navasota Ind School Dist*	6,35	172
Dacy, Russell/*Wall Ind School Dist*	1,11	365
Dahl, Joann/*Milford Ind School Dist*	11,296	141
Dahlander, Jon/*Highland Park Ind Sch Dist*	15,71,751	108
Daigre, Kenneth/*Port Arthur Ind School Dist*	73	243
Dailey, Lisa/*Jacksonville Ind School Dist*	8,11,16,83,273,294,298	72
Daily, Darrell/*Abernathy Ind School Dist*	6	174
Dale, David/*Wheeler Ind School Dist*	8,81,270,273	391
Dalfonso, Rhonda/*DeSoto Ind School Dist*	7	104
Dallas, Sally/*Huntsville Ind School Dist*	90	383
Dalton, Brady/*Levelland Ind School Dist*	73,76,95,286,295,297	229
Dalton, Jay/*Panther Creek Cons Ind SD*	67	76
Danaher, Anita, Dr/*Calallen Ind School Dist*	8,11,16	302
Danaher, Phil/*Calallen Ind School Dist*	6	302
Dancy, Vivian/*Galena Park Ind School Dist*	6,50	186
Daniel, Bo/*Cuero Ind School Dist*	5	117
Daniel, Janet/*Judson Ind School Dist*	4	33
Daniel, Judy/*Troup Ind School Dist*	274	337
Daniel, Kenneth/*Van Alstyne Ind School Dist*	73	168
Daniel, Michael Paul/*Hudson Ind School Dist*	91	17
Daniel, Stephen/*Northside Ind School Dist*	15	36
Daniel, Tammy/*Chillicothe ISD School Dist*	2	177
Daniels, Elaine/*Seagraves Ind School Dist*	38	157
Daniels, Micki/*Rockdale Ind School Dist*	57	287
Danke, Lisa/*Valley Mills Ind School Dist*	4	47
Danziger, Kay/*Lamar Cons Ind School Dist*	67	153
Darden, Rachel/*Cooper Ind School Dist*	68	119
Darden, Steve/*Utopia Ind School Dist*	67	378
Darden, Thomas/*Cooper Ind School Dist*	67	119
Darilek, Paul/*Industrial Ind School Dist*	1	240
Darnell, Ann/*Socorro Ind School Dist*	298	135
Darragh, Sheron, Dr/*Region 7 Ed Service Center*	8,74	171
Darrow, Brandon/*Miller Grove Ind School Dist*	67	231
Darrow, Melissa/*Clarksville Ind School Dist*	2	322
Darrow, Melissa/*North Lamar Ind School Dist*	2	259
Darst, Cassandra/*Lake Worth Ind School Dist*	79	356
Daub, Amber/*Hallsville Ind School Dist*	8,31,36,78,79,285	208
Daugherty, Olivia/*Pasadena Ind School Dist*	298	198
Daugherty, Teresa/*Killeen Ind School Dist*	69,294	27
Daugherty, Zachary/*Tidehaven Ind School Dist*	73,295	276
Daughertyy, Zachary/*Tidehaven Ind School Dist*	295	276
Daughtry, Keli/*Garland Ind School Dist*	76	105
Davant, Tamara/*Tidehaven Ind School Dist*	31,36,85	276
Davant, Tamara/*Tidehaven Ind School Dist*	31,36,85	276
Davenport, Mattew/*Whitesboro Ind School Dist*	8,15,84	168
Davenport, Michelle/*Huffman Ind School Dist*	34,57,58,77,88,271	195
David, Danny/*Pilot Point Ind School Dist*	6	125
David, Lorine/*Taylor Ind School Dist*	2	399
Davidson, Ben/*Livingston Ind School Dist*	2,19	316
Davidson, Cassie/*Pilot Point Ind School Dist*	4	125
Davidson, David/*Mason Ind School Dist*	3	275
Davidson, Jeff/*Commerce Independent Sch Dist*	6	236
Davidson, Jerry/*Graham Ind School Dist*	3,5,91	406
Davidson, Kenneth/*Graham Ind School Dist*	6	406
Davidson, Mary/*Marble Falls Ind School Dist*	4	60
Davie, Cindy/*Hull Daisetta Ind School Dist*	5	266
Davies, Robert/*Harlingen Cons Ind School Dist*	6	64
Davila, Diana/*Edinburg Cons Ind School Dist*	7	216
Davila, Juan/*United Ind School Dist*	3	387
Davila, Michael/*Kingsville Ind School Dist*	6	257
Davila, Ruben/*Webb Cons Ind School Dist*	3	388
Davila, Sam/*Conroe Ind School Dist*	5	291
Davis, Amanda/*Sundown Ind School Dist*	37,270	229
Davis, Amy/*Crosby Ind School Dist*	73,295,297	183
Davis, April/*Texarkana Ind School Dist*	58	50
Davis, Audra/*Whiteface Con Ind School Dist*	57,271	75
Davis, Blake/*Graham Ind School Dist*	83,91	406
Davis, Blayne/*Mumford Ind School Dist*	1,11	56
Davis, Bruce/*Winters Ind School Dist*	1	327
Davis, Bryan/*Dimmitt Ind School Dist*	1	71
Davis, Carla/*Winona Ind School Dist*	5	339
Davis, Carolyn/*Eustace Ind School Dist*	4	214
Davis, Cecilia/*Judson Ind School Dist*	15	33
Davis, Charlotte, Dr/*Aldine Ind School Dist*	36,83,88,275	179
Davis, Christie/*Crosby Ind School Dist*	34	183

DISTRICT PERSONNEL INDEX

Market Data Retrieval

NAME/District	JOB FUNCTIONS	PAGE
Davis, Christine/Frisco Ind School Dist	58	78
Davis, Cindy/Seymour Ind School Dist	2,8,11,83,88,296,298	25
Davis, Cliff/Kerens Ind School Dist	3	300
Davis, Danny/Lubbock-Cooper Ind Sch Dist	15	271
Davis, Denise/Los Fresnos Cons Ind Sch Dist	7	66
Davis, Don/Graham Ind School Dist	2,15	406
Davis, Donna/Pecos-Barstow-Toyah Ind SD	58	323
Davis, Elna/Grand Prairie Ind School Dist	15	107
Davis, Gary/Denver City Ind School Dist	1	405
Davis, Gay/Meyersville Ind School Dist	16,57,73,295	118
Davis, Gloria/San Antonio Ind School Dist	7	39
Davis, Greg/Connally Ind School Dist	67	279
Davis, Inga/Union Grove Ind School Dist	16,82	377
Davis, Jason/Crockett Co Cons Common SD	286	94
Davis, Jay/Hearne Ind School Dist	79	325
Davis, Jenifer/Booker Ind School Dist	58	267
Davis, Jerry/Gilmer Ind School Dist	3	376
Davis, Jill/Lamar Cons Ind School Dist	93	153
Davis, John/Leonard Ind School Dist	27	146
Davis, June/Crowley Ind School Dist	67	347
Davis, Kennith/Houston Ind School Dist	15,74,273	188
Davis, Kevin/Baird Ind School Dist	3,5	62
Davis, Kim/Ft Bend Ind School Dist	70	149
Davis, King/Sheldon Ind School Dist	1	200
Davis, Kristen/Barbers Hill Ind School Dist	16,73,76,82,295	72
Davis, Kristi/Bangs Ind School Dist	83	58
Davis, Larry/DeSoto Ind School Dist	6,35	104
Davis, Laurie/Frenship Ind School Dist	73	269
Davis, Lisa/Angleton Ind School Dist	10	51
Davis, Lisa/Grandview Ind School Dist	7,85	248
Davis, Margret/Sunnyvale Ind School Dist	2	113
Davis, Michael/Cushing Ind School Dist	1	297
Davis, Michael/Judson Ind School Dist	295	33
Davis, Michael/New Summerfield Ind Sch Dist	67	73
Davis, Michelle/Graford Ind School Dist	2	310
Davis, Nathan/Dayton Ind School Dist	76,295	265
Davis, Pam/Millsap Ind School Dist	34	312
Davis, Phyllis/Anson Ind School Dist	58	249
Davis, Renee/Crosby Ind School Dist	5	183
Davis, Rhonda/Lake Travis Ind School Dist	5	370
Davis, Rhonda/Plano Ind School Dist	81	82
Davis, Rhonda, Dr/Garland Ind School Dist	11,34,92,288,296	105
Davis, Rick/Leakey Ind School Dist	16,73,295	322
Davis, Rick/Midland Ind School Dist	67	285
Davis, Robin/Grapevine-Colleyville Ind SD	83	353
Davis, Ronnie/Vidor Ind School Dist	3	309
Davis, Rosie/Springlake-Earth Ind School Dist	2	261
Davis, Ryan/Grandview-Hopkins Ind Sch Dist	67	164
Davis, Samora/Tomball Ind School Dist	57	203
Davis, Scott, Dr/Crosby Ind School Dist	1	183
Davis, Seth/Seminole Ind School Dist	88	158
Davis, Shannon/Amarillo Ind School Dist	57	317
Davis, Sharon/Killeen Ind School Dist	8,11,15	27
Davis, Shawn/Texarkana Ind School Dist	11,58,85,274,275	50
Davis, Sherry/Childress Ind School Dist	36	74
Davis, Sheryl/Waco Ind School Dist	2,19	281
Davis, Stephanie/Grandview Ind School Dist	38,69,83,270	248
Davis, Stephen, Dr/Wylie Ind School Dist	10	84
Davis, Susie/Laneville Ind School Dist	7,85	327
Davis, Todd, Dr/Aldine Ind School Dist	15,18	179
Davis, Tonya/Henderson Ind School Dist	4	327
Davis, Traci/Grand Prairie Ind School Dist	15	107
Davis, Trevor/Lovejoy Ind School Dist	295	80
Davis, Twyla/McLeod Ind School Dist	52,55	70
Davlin, Karla/Pewitt Cons Ind School Dist	2,19	296
Dawkins, Micheal/Wink Loving Ind School Dist	73,76,286,295	402
Dawson, Kristin/Lovejoy Ind School Dist	16	80
Dawson, Renee/Westbrook Ind School Dist	67	289
Dawson, Tim/Boles Ind School Dist	4	235
Day, Betty/Ector Ind School Dist	58	146
Day, Kay Lynn/Midlothian Ind School Dist	15,79	141
Day, Louise/Flour Bluff Ind School Dist	15	304
Day, Sam/Caddo Mills Ind Sch Dist	5	235
De La Fuente, Clarisa/Lyford Cons Ind School Dist	71	394
De La Fuente, Senaida/Hart Ind School Dist	58	71
De La Garza, Jeff/Plainview Ind School Dist	79	175
De La Garza, Ron/Rio Hondo Ind School Dist	2,84	66
De La Rosa, Mario/Carrollton-Farmers Branch ISD	91	96
De La Rosa, Mario/Round Rock Ind School Dist	91	398
De La Rosa, Michael/Weslaco Ind School Dist	88	225
De La Santos, Linda/Roby Cons Ind School Dist	57,271	148
De La Torre, Xavier, Dr/Ysleta Ind School Dist	1	137
De Leon, Elizabeth/Falls City Ind School Dist	27,69	250
De Los Santos, Leonor/Santa Gertrudis Ind Sch Dist	31	258
De Los Santos, Orlando/Braination Schools	11,298	30
De Luna, Guadalupe/Brooks Co Ind School Dist	7	57
De Velasco, Fernando/Prosper Ind School Dist	73,98,286,295	84
Deal, Marci/Hurst-Euless-Bedford ISD	39,89	353
Dealy, Kennan/Kaufman Ind School Dist	4	252
Dean, Bill/Eula Ind School Dist	67	63
Dean, Bobby/Post Ind School Dist	91	162
Dean, Crystal/Tarkington Ind School Dist	73,286,295	266
Dean, Deonna/Northside Ind School Dist	9	36
Dean, Halcy/Seguin Ind School Dist	58	173
Dean, Jason/Georgetown Ind School Dist	6	395
Dean, Joyce/Shelbyville Ind School Dist	2	335
Dean, Kenny/Anahuac Ind School Dist	16,73,295	71
Dean, Kimberly/Jasper Ind School Dist	4	240
Dean, LaMond/Chapel Hill Ind School Dist	1	337
Dean, Richard/Frenship Ind School Dist	91	269
Dean, Vickie/Belton Ind School Dist	294	26
Dean, Violet/Cedar Hill Ind School Dist	15,68,74,78	97
Deanda, Yvette/Presidio Ind School Dist	31,36,69,83	320
Deangel, Perla/Valley View Ind School Dist	58	225
Dear, Jennifer/Leary Ind School Dist	1,11,57	48
Dear, Rich, Dr/Godley Ind School Dist	1	247
DeArmon, Brenda, Dr/Sheldon Ind School Dist	11,298	200
Deason, Sharon/Chapel Hill Ind School Dist	2	337
DeAtley, Dean/Brazosport Ind School Dist	6	52
Deaton, Nanette/Manor Ind School Dist	36	371
Debaugh, Denise/Frisco Ind School Dist	274	78
DeBeer, Kyle/Waco Ind School Dist	71	281
DeBoise, Dwayne/Hardin Jefferson Ind Sch Dist	6	177
Debord, Kenneth/Lake Travis Ind School Dist	88	370
Debus, Lyle, Dr/Mexia Ind School Dist	1	267
Dechert, Liz/Junction Ind School Dist	4	256
Decker, Ann/Bryson Ind School Dist	16,28	238
Decker, Becky/Motley Co Ind School Dist	11	296
Decker, Debbie/Katy Ind School Dist	6	151
Decker, Karen/Chico Ind School Dist	275	403
Decker, Vicki/Wellington Ind School Dist	16,82	86
Decker, Whitie/Evant Ind School Dist	27,31	92
Deckert, Jon/Port Neches-Groves Ind SD	10,280,285	243
DeCordova, Kirk/Palmer Ind School Dist	57	141
DeCou, Rutty/Luling Ind School Dist	73,76	61
Deel, Dickie, Dr/Denison Ind School Dist	73,295,297	166
Deel, Kenny/Melissa Ind School Dist	3,4,91	81
Dees, Carla/Aransas Pass Ind School Dist	37	330
Dees, Jim/Huffman Ind School Dist	285	195
Dees, Roger/Giddings Ind School Dist	1	263
Defee, Michael/Brookeland Ind School Dist	73,295	240
Defee, Micheal/Brookeland Ind School Dist	84	240
DeFelice, Melinda/McKinney Ind School Dist	10,15	80
Deforrest, Jack/North East Ind School Dist	5	34

1	Superintendent	16	Instructional Media Svcs	30	Adult Education	44	Science Sec	58	Special Education K-12
2	Bus/Finance/Purchasing	17	Chief Operations Officer	31	Career/Sch-to-Work K-12	45	Math K-12	59	Special Education Elem
3	Buildings And Grounds	18	Chief Academic Officer	32	Career/Sch-to-Work Elem	46	Math Elem	60	Special Education Sec
4	Food Service	19	Chief Financial Officer	33	Career/Sch-to-Work Sec	47	Math Sec	61	Foreign/World Lang K-12
5	Transportation	20	Art K-12	34	Early Childhood Ed	48	English/Lang Arts K-12	62	Foreign/World Lang Elem
6	Athletic	21	Art Elem	35	Health/Phys Education	49	English/Lang Arts Elem	63	Foreign/World Lang Sec
7	Health Services	22	Art Sec	36	Guidance Services K-12	50	English/Lang Arts Sec	64	Religious Education K-12
8	Curric/Instruct K-12	23	Music K-12	37	Guidance Services Elem	51	Reading K-12	65	Religious Education Elem
9	Curric/Instruct Elem	24	Music Elem	38	Guidance Services Sec	52	Reading Elem	66	Religious Education Sec
10	Curric/Instruct Sec	25	Music Sec	39	Social Studies K-12	53	Reading Sec	67	School Board President
11	Federal Program	26	Business Education	40	Social Studies Elem	54	Remedial Reading K-12	68	Teacher Personnel
12	Title V	27	Career & Tech Ed	41	Social Studies Sec	55	Remedial Reading Elem	69	Academic Assessment
13	Title VI	28	Technology Education	42	Science K-12	56	Remedial Reading Sec	70	Research/Development
15	Asst Superintendent	29	Family/Consumer Science	43	Science Elem	57	Bilingual/ELL	71	Public Information

72	Summer School	88	Alternative/At Risk	277	Remedial Math K-12
73	Instructional Tech	89	Multi-Cultural Curriculum	280	Literacy Coach
74	Inservice Training	90	Social Work	285	STEM
75	Marketing/Distributive	91	Safety/Security	286	Digital Learning
76	Info Systems	92	Magnet School	288	Common Core Standards
77	Psychological Assess	93	Parental Involvement	294	Accountability
78	Affirmative Action	95	Tech Prep Program	295	Network System
79	Student Personnel	97	Chief Information Officer	296	Title II Programs
80	Driver Ed/Safety	98	Chief Technology Officer	297	Webmaster
81	Gifted/Talented	270	Character Education	298	Grant Writer/Ptnrships
82	Video Services	271	Migrant Education	750	Chief Innovation Officer
83	Substance Abuse Prev	273	Teacher Mentor	751	Chief of Staff
84	Erate	274	Before/After Sch	752	Social Emotional Learning
85	AIDS Education	275	Response to Intervention		

TX-T22

Texas School Directory

DISTRICT PERSONNEL INDEX

NAME/District	JOB FUNCTIONS	PAGE
Defoy, David/*Texarkana Ind School Dist*	2	50
Defreece, Rj/*Elkhart Ind School Dist*	73,76,295	15
Degraffenreid, Dalton/*Klondike Ind School Dist*	2,6	117
Degraffenreid, Dalton/*Klondike Ind School Dist*	2	117
Del Bosque, Adalia/*McAllen Ind School Dist*	7,85	221
Dela-Garza, Andres/*Normangee Ind School Dist*	67	264
Delacruz, Araceli/*Goose Creek Cons Ind Sch Dist*	79	187
Delacruz, Sadie/*Pringle-Morse Cons ISD*	295	177
Delagarza, Sylvia/*Plainview Ind School Dist*	67	175
Delaisla, Anita/*Coppell Ind School Dist*	280	98
DeLaney, Yolanda/*Canyon Ind School Dist*	9	320
Delange, Jeannie/*Ponder Ind School Dist*	4	125
Delapena, Herlinda/*Crowell Ind School Dist*	57	149
Delapena, Michelle/*Robstown Ind School Dist*	93	305
DeLaRosa, Tony/*Midland Ind School Dist*	68	285
Delbosque, Ernest/*Beeville Ind School Dist*	5	25
Delbosque, Neva/*Avalon Ind School Dist*	11,57,88,273,275,296	140
DeLeon, Alex/*Valley View Ind School Dist*	3,5	225
DeLeon, Elida/*Alice Ind School Dist*	68,273	245
DeLeon, Israel/*Springlake-Earth Ind Sch Dist*	6	261
DeLeon, Joanelda, Dr/*San Antonio Ind School Dist*	15	39
DeLeon, Juan/*Ingram Ind School Dist*	73,76,84,295	255
DeLeon, Lorraine/*South San Antonio Ind Sch Dist*	8,288	42
DeLeon, Monica/*Sabinal Ind School Dist*	16	378
DeLeon, Rosalinda/*Edcouch Elsa Ind School Dist*	9	215
DelGado, Alejandro/*Texas Dept of Education*	2,15	1
DelGado, Delinda/*Ropes Ind School Dist*	2	229
DelGado, Rachel/*Bishop Cons Ind School Dist*	4	302
Delisle, Jeff/*Alief Ind School Dist*	3	181
Delk, Heidi/*Greenwood Ind School Dist*	59	285
DeLong, Brandi/*Tulia Ind School Dist*	8,11,57,285,288,298	343
Delossantos, Carmen/*Forney Ind School Dist*	57	251
Delozier, Don/*Hereford Ind School Dist*	6,35	119
Delozier, Michelle/*Hereford Ind School Dist*	28,30,31	119
Delpercio, Mark/*Orange Grove Ind School Dist*	6	245
DeLuna, Stephanie/*Advantage Academy Admin Office*	57	96
Demasters, Rick/*Celina Ind School Dist*	1,84	77
Dement, Christie/*Van Vleck Ind School Dist*	11,27	276
Demers, Tami/*White Oak Ind School Dist*	2	171
Demland, Kristen/*Brazosport Ind School Dist*	286	52
Demny, Matt/*Brazos Ind School Dist*	67	22
Demontmollin, Jackie/*Denton Ind School Dist*	20,23	120
Demoss, Pam/*Gold-Burg Ind School Dist*	58	290
Dempsay, Debbie/*Booker Ind School Dist*	84	267
Dempsey, Julie/*Happy Ind School Dist*	8,16	342
Dempsey, Mandy/*Hempstead Ind School Dist*	16,82	384
DeMuth, Shelby/*Pleasant Grove Ind School Dist*	75,298	49
Denham-Hill, Patricia/*Northside Ind School Dist*	15,68	36
Denison, Taylor/*Lovejoy Ind School Dist*	274	80
Denman, Buddy/*Splendora Ind School Dist*	73,295	294
Denney, Kevin/*Red Oak Ind School Dist*	83,91	142
Denning, Anthony/*Keene Ind School Dist*	3	248
Denning, Sandra/*Keene Ind School Dist*	2,8,15,19	248
Dennington, Natalie/*Midlothian Ind School Dist*	69,294	141
Dennis, Ashleigh/*San Antonio Ind School Dist*	81	39
Densman, Johnny/*Hallettsville Ind Sch Dist*	3	262
Denson, John, Dr/*Union Hill Ind School Dist*	8	377
Denson, John, Dr/*Union Hill Ind School Dist*	8	377
Denton, Donna/*Ore City Ind School Dist*	4	376
Denton, Rita/*Mansfield Ind School Dist*	4	356
DePalma, Brandilyn/*Region 11 Ed Service Center*	2	360
Depew, Carl/*Jacksboro Ind Sch Dist*	73,76,286	239
Derington, Robin/*Ft Stockton Ind School Dist*	8	315
Derkowski, Phillip/*Brenham Ind School Dist*	3	385
DeRoche, Jay/*Garner Ind School Dist*	3,5	312
Derrich, Ed/*Matagorda Ind School Dist*	67	275
Derrick, Kaye/*Redwater Ind School Dist*	88	49
Derrick, Shelley/*Mt Pleasant Ind School Dist*	69	363
Desantiago, Griselda/*Booker Ind School Dist*	4	267
Desautell, Teresa/*Whiteface Con Ind School Dist*	60	75
Deschamps, Claudia/*Katy Ind School Dist*	71	151
DeShazo, Allen/*Bridge City Ind School Dist*	6	308
DeSimone, Melissa, Dr/*Northwest Ind School Dist*	69	124
Deterra, Elizabeth/*Lake Travis Ind School Dist*	8	370
Dethloff, Carl, Dr/*San Angelo Ind School Dist*	1	364
Detiller, Joe/*Ector Ind School Dist*	3	146
Detrick, Danny/*Birdville Ind School Dist*	20,23	346
Detten, Tonya/*Highland Park Ind School Dist*	67	319
Deussen, Vangee/*Ponder Ind School Dist*	67	125
Deutschendorf, Michele/*Deer Park Ind School Dist*	34,60	186
DeVault, Wendy/*Midland Ind School Dist*	46	285
Devlin, Stephanie/*Kennedale Ind School Dist*	36	355
DeVoe, Wendy/*Corpus Christi Ind Sch Dist*	44	303
Devous, Don/*Ft Worth Ind School Dist*	25	349
DeWalt, Lo/*Manor Ind School Dist*	49	371
Dewease, Diane/*Waller Ind School Dist*	47	384
Deweber, Teri/*Grape Creek Ind School Dist*	298	364
Dhane, Lynn/*Harrold Ind School Dist*	2,16,271	393
Di Donato, Delayne/*Etoile Ind School Dist*	6	297
Dial Branch, Vicki/*Grapeland Ind School Dist*	58	232
Dial, Vicki/*Latexo Ind School Dist*	58	233
Diamond, Kristen/*Bushland Ind School Dist*	73,286	319
Diaz, Alonzo/*Denver City Ind School Dist*	5	405
Diaz, Bruno/*Weatherford Ind School Dist*	91	313
Diaz, Catherine/*Santa Rosa Ind School Dist*	4	67
Diaz, David/*Keene Ind School Dist*	57,63	248
Diaz, Georgina/*San Elizario Ind School Dist*	39,48,81	135
Diaz, Gloria/*Hart Ind School Dist*	4	71
Diaz, Jeraldo/*Bloomington Ind School Dist*	3,91	381
Diaz, Maribel/*Alvarado Ind School Dist*	8,18,57,76,286,288	246
Diaz, Susan/*North East Ind School Dist*	8	34
Diaz, Yadira/*Roma Ind School Dist*	8,51	341
Dickens, Sherry/*Lake Worth Ind School Dist*	11,298	356
Dickenson, Emily/*Elysian Fields Ind School Dist*	59,273	208
Dickerson, Bradley/*Thorndale Ind School Dist*	6	288
Dickerson, Carole/*Harts Bluff Ind School Dist*	12,16,57,69,88,270,273	363
Dickerson, Carole/*Harts Bluff Ind School Dist*	296	363
Dickerson, Donnie/*Burkeville Ind School Dist*	3,5	300
Dickerson, Julia/*Little Cypress Mauriceville SD*	9,57,81,271,288	308
Dickerson, Michael/*Wildorado Ind Sch Dist*	3	308
Dickerson, Pam/*Burkeville Ind School Dist*	2,286	300
Dickerson, Stewart/*Early Ind School Dist*	3,5	58
Dickey, Carole/*Centerville Ind School Dist*	2,4,15,298	264
Dickison, Elizabeth/*Lometa Ind School Dist*	69,83,88	262
Dickson, Amy/*Karnack Ind School Dist*	1,11	208
Dickson, Andy/*De Leon Ind School Dist*	6	89
Dickson, Heath/*Post Ind School Dist*	1	162
Dickson, Kasey/*La Vernia Ind School Dist*	7,83,85	401
Diehl, Jared/*Channelview Ind School Dist*	5	183
Dieringer, Laura/*Glasscock Co Ind School Dist*	51,54	163
Dierlam, Shari/*Calhoun Co Ind School Dist*	7	61
Dieterich, Bryan/*Breckenridge Ind School Dist*	3	341
Dietiker, Diane/*La Vega Ind School Dist*	16	279
Dietrich, Mickie/*Alvin Ind School Dist*	2	50
Diets, Jeremy/*Era Ind School Dist*	5	90
Dietz, Dee/*Palestine Ind School Dist*	58	15
Dietz, Diana/*Luling Ind School Dist*	5	61
Dietz, Joel/*Whiteface Con Ind School Dist*	73	75
Dildine, Sarah/*Hughes Springs Ind Sch Dist*	1,57	70
Diles, Jennifer/*Celeste Ind School Dist*	7,85	235
Diles, Tom/*Woodsboro Ind School Dist*	10,273	324
Dill, Jane/*North Zulch Ind School Dist*	83	274
Dillard, Jill/*Llano Ind School Dist*	16,82	268
Dillard, Kelli/*Eden Cons Ind School Dist*	286	90
Dillard, Kerry/*Hull Daisetta Ind School Dist*	31	266
Dillard, Nancy/*Waskom Ind School Dist*	2	209
Dillard, Rhonda/*Frenship Ind School Dist*	68,78	269
Dillard, Robert/*Littlefield Ind School Dist*	1	260
Dillard, Stacey/*Princeton Ind School Dist*	6	84
Dillard, Traci/*Uvalde Cons Ind School Dist*	7	378
Diller, Tammy/*Beaumont Ind School Dist*	58	241
Dillingham, Trisha/*Vernon Ind School Dist*	83,90	393
Dillon, David/*Lovejoy Ind School Dist*	3,5	80
Dillon, Matt/*Canadian Ind School Dist*	3	213
Dillon, Renae/*Goose Creek Cons Ind Sch Dist*	27,92	187
Dillon, Shana/*Boerne Ind School Dist*	81	253
Dillon, Stacey/*Lovejoy Ind School Dist*	71	80
Dills, Alice/*Celeste Ind School Dist*	12,36,69,83,88,273	235
Dimas, Velinda/*Lamesa Ind School Dist*	68	117
Dimmitt, Julia/*Houston Ind School Dist*	68	188
Dinkelmann, Johan/*Somerset Ind School Dist*	6	42
Dippel, Carol/*Victoria Ind School Dist*	34	382

DISTRICT PERSONNEL INDEX

Market Data Retrieval

NAME/District	JOB FUNCTIONS	PAGE
Dippery, Debbie/Wichita Falls Ind School Dist	10,36	392
Dirkse, Amy/Meridian Ind School Dist	7	47
Disler, Jimmy/Leander Ind School Dist	3,17	396
Ditmore, James/Water Valley Ind School Dist	73,297	365
Dittman, Beth/Mesquite Ind School Dist	7,85	110
Ditto, Jim/China Spring Ind School Dist	3,5	278
Dives, Joe/Magnolia Ind School Dist	5	292
Divine, Shielda/Chapel Hill Ind School Dist	76	337
Dixon, Althea/Paris Ind School Dist	8,15,294	260
Dixon, Andrea/Kerrville Ind School Dist	286	256
Dixon, Ann, Dr/Red Oak Ind School Dist	1	142
Dixon, James/Industrial Ind School Dist	6	240
Dixon, Kevin/Ferris Ind School Dist	58	140
Dixon, Nkrumah/College Station Ind Sch Dist	68	55
Dixon, Shantina, Dr/Bryan Ind School Dist	77	54
Doan, Jamie/Trenton Ind School Dist	270	147
Doan, Kyle/Merkel Ind School Dist	67	361
Dobbins, Lacy/Mathis Ind School Dist	48,51	331
Dobbs, Renea/Goose Creek Cons Ind Sch Dist	2	187
Dobecka, Tory/West Ind School Dist	8	282
Dobson, Pete/Pawnee Ind School Dist	67	25
Dobson, Randal/Mexia Ind School Dist	83,91	267
Docken, Carla/Hurst-Euless-Bedford ISD	36,88,270	353
Dockens, Deborah, Dr/Eagle Mtn-Saginaw Ind School Dist	68,79	348
Dodd, Carla/Lake Worth Ind School Dist	5	356
Dodds, Darrell/Greenwood Ind School Dist	2,15	285
Dodds, Debbie/Greenwood Ind School Dist	295	285
Dodge, Todd/Eanes Ind School Dist	6	370
Dodhany, Mari Lou/Brazosport Ind School Dist	69,73	52
Dodson, James/Kirbyville Cons Ind Sch Dist	3	241
Dodson, Tony/Groom Ind School Dist	16,295	69
Doege, Doug/Monahans-Wickett-Pyote ISD	8,11,57,69,298	385
Doepken, Marny/Clear Creek Ind School Dist	39	158
Dohnalik, Jason/Cameron Ind School Dist	67	287
Dolan, Andrea/Granger Ind School Dist	73	396
Dolese, Daphne/Garrison Ind School Dist	274	298
Dollarhide, Tony/Texarkana Ind School Dist	83,91	50
Domain, Melinda, Dr/Ferris Ind School Dist	12,15,27,88,296,298	140
Dominguez, David/Elkhart Ind School Dist	57	15
Dominguez, Faustina/Alice Ind School Dist	79	245
Dominguez, Laura/Braination Schools	58	30
Dominguez, Mario/Fabens Ind School Dist	73,91	135
Dominguez, Mark/Buena Vista Ind School Dist	1,11,83	315
Dominguez, Tommy/Balmorhea Ind School Dist	67	323
Dominquez, Mike/Stratford Ind School Dist	1,73,83	336
Dominqueze, Shelly/Aransas Pass Ind School Dist	8,16,57,88,271,273,286,288	330
Donaghey, Andy/Weatherford Ind School Dist	23,27	313
Donaghey, Kady/Weatherford Ind School Dist	27,31,75	313
Donald, Ben, Dr/Carthage Ind School Dist	67	311
Donaldson, Felicia/Everman Ind School Dist	5,7,15,36,68,78,80,298	349
Donaubauer, Gloria/Runge Ind School Dist	58	251
Donham, Shawn/Benjamin Ind School Dist	3	258
Donnell, Stephanie/Bushland Ind School Dist	37,83,85	319
Donnelly, Richard/West Rusk Co Cons Ind School Dist	3	328
Donovan, Jennifer/Hitchcock Ind School Dist	2	161
Dorcz, Monica/Huffman Ind School Dist	45	195
Dorenkamp, Tracey/Sealy Ind School Dist	2	22
Dornak, Ashlee/Victoria Ind School Dist	49	382
Doron, Amy/Spring Hill Ind School Dist	270	170
Doskocil, Cheyenne/Rogers Ind School Dist	297	29
Dossey, Jim/Montgomery Ind School Dist	67	293
Dossey, Julie/Klondike Ind School Dist	36,69,88,270,271	117
Dossey, Matt/Jonesboro Ind School Dist	1,11,73,83	93
Doty, Cristi/Jim Ned Cons Ind School Dist	8,288	361
Doucet, Chad/South San Antonio Ind School Dist	2	42
Doug, Crosby/New Caney Ind School Dist	295	293
Dougherty, Mark/Sharyland Ind School Dist	3,91	224
Dougherty, Ruth/Channelview Ind School Dist	76	183
Doughty, Marilyn/Corpus Christi Ind Sch Dist	76,295	303
Douglas, Christopher/Southside Ind School Dist	58	43
Douglas, Imo/Midland Ind School Dist	7	285
Douglas, Jennifer/Galveston Ind School Dist	4	160
Douglas, Robert/Aransas Co Ind School Dist	5	19
Douglas, Roxanne/Corpus Christi Ind Sch Dist	2	303
Douglas, Sarah/Brownfield Ind Sch Dist	31	362
Douglas, Susan/Bland Ind School Dist	16	235
Douglas, Thomas/Pasadena Ind School Dist	3	198
Douville, Elaine/Round Rock Ind School Dist	7,83	398
Dove, Dwayne/Breckenridge Ind School Dist	28,73,297	341
Dovel, Christy/Dalhart Ind School Dist	38	95
Dover, Darrian/Meadow Ind School Dist	1	362
Dover, Greg/Rusk Ind School Dist	3	73
Dover, Stacey/Meadow Ind School Dist	11,60	362
Dow, Pauline, Dr/San Antonio Ind School Dist	15	39
Dowdy, Sandra/Hays Cons Ind School Dist	8,18	211
Dowdy, Tammy/Dickinson Ind School Dist	71	159
Dowell, Cheryl/Stephenville Ind School Dist	4	144
Dowlearn, Janice/Crandall Ind School Dist	16,31	251
Downey, Cheryl/Sivells Bend Ind School Dist	11	91
Downing, Shane/Holland Ind School Dist	1,57	27
Downs, Deanna/De Leon Ind School Dist	57	89
Downs, Karen/Avery Ind School Dist	11,296	322
Doyal, Ashley/Krum Ind School Dist	4	122
Doyal, Launa/North Lamar Ind School Dist	297	259
Doyle, Charlyn/San Angelo Ind School Dist	73,76,84,297	364
Doyle, Cindy/Klein Ind School Dist	71	196
Doyle, Courtney/Katy Ind School Dist	67	151
Doyle, Jd/Schleicher Co Ind Sch Dist	73,286,295	333
Doyle, Sara/Cranfills Gap ISD School Dist	2	46
Doyno, Paul, Dr/Rio Grande City Ind Sch Dist	298	340
Dozier, Phyllis/Longview Ind School Dist	4	169
Dozier, Tina/Leander Ind School Dist	57	396
Drab, Gary/La Grange Ind School Dist	67	147
Drabek, Carlett/Navarro Ind School Dist	4	173
Dracos, Tom/Cumby Ind School Dist	6	231
Dragoescu, Justin/New Boston Ind School Dist	16,73,295	49
Dragon, Les/Three Rivers Ind School Dist	1	268
Drake, Traci/Hubbard Ind School Dist	12	48
Drake, Traci/Hubbard Ind School Dist	1,11,83	48
Dranowsky, George/East Central Ind School Dist	91	31
Draper, Brad/Frenship Ind School Dist	67	269
Draper, Robert/Edna Ind School Dist	6	239
Draper, Shelly/Ore City Ind School Dist	68	377
Drawhorn, Sheri/Port Neches-Groves Ind SD	2	243
Dray, Nicole/San Marcos Cons Ind Sch Dist	8,12,36,83,277,294	211
Drennan, Greg/Plemons-Stinnett-Phillips CISD	3,5,91	238
Drennon, Joe/Hallsville Ind School Dist	6	208
Drew, Debbie/Avery Ind School Dist	1	322
Drew, James/Ft Bend Ind School Dist	20	149
Drews, Celia, Dr/Mexia Ind School Dist	8,11,15	267
Drews, Celia, Dr/Mexia Ind School Dist	13,296	267
Driggers, Rachael/Greenville Ind School Dist	69,70,294	236
Drilling, Christi/Grapevine-Colleyville Ind SD	2	353
Drinkwater, Michael/Lake Travis Ind School Dist	6	370
Driscoll, Terry/Abernathy Ind School Dist	73	174
Driskall, Dahria/Friendswood Ind Sch Dist	13,58	160
Driskell, Jamie/Malakoff Ind School Dist	6	214
Driskill, Elita/Arlington Ind School Dist	73	343
Driskill, Jamie/Frisco Ind School Dist	71	78
Driver, Darryl/Roosevelt Ind School Dist	5	271
Driver, Jamie/Whitharral Ind School Dist	58	230
Driver, Tom/Port Aransas Ind School Dist	73	305
Droddy, Eric/Queen City Ind School Dist	6	70
Drollinger, Tony/Arlington Ind School Dist	2	343

---

1 Superintendent
2 Bus/Finance/Purchasing
3 Buildings And Grounds
4 Food Service
5 Transportation
6 Athletic
7 Health Services
8 Curric/Instruct K-12
9 Curric/Instruct Elem
10 Curric/Instruct Sec
11 Federal Program
12 Title I
13 Title V
15 Asst Superintendent
16 Instructional Media Svcs
17 Chief Operations Officer
18 Chief Academic Officer
19 Chief Financial Officer
20 Art K-12
21 Art Elem
22 Art Sec
23 Music K-12
24 Music Elem
25 Music Sec
26 Business Education
27 Career & Tech Ed
28 Technology Education
29 Family/Consumer Science
30 Adult Education
31 Career/Sch-to-Work K-12
32 Career/Sch-to-Work Elem
33 Career/Sch-to-Work Sec
34 Early Childhood Ed
35 Health/Phys Education
36 Guidance Services K-12
37 Guidance Services Elem
38 Guidance Services Sec
39 Social Studies K-12
40 Social Studies Elem
41 Social Studies Sec
42 Science K-12
43 Science Elem
44 Science Sec
45 Math K-12
46 Math Elem
47 Math Sec
48 English/Lang Arts K-12
49 English/Lang Arts Elem
50 English/Lang Arts Sec
51 Reading K-12
52 Reading Elem
53 Reading Sec
54 Remedial Reading K-12
55 Remedial Reading Elem
56 Remedial Reading Sec
57 Bilingual/ELL
58 Special Education K-12
59 Special Education Elem
60 Special Education Sec
61 Foreign/World Lang K-12
62 Foreign/World Lang Elem
63 Foreign/World Lang Sec
64 Religious Education K-12
65 Religious Education Elem
66 Religious Education Sec
67 School Board President
68 Teacher Personnel
69 Academic Assessment
70 Research/Development
71 Public Information
72 Summer School
73 Instructional Tech
74 Inservice Training
75 Marketing/Distributive
76 Info Systems
77 Psychological Assess
78 Affirmative Action
79 Student Personnel
80 Driver Ed/Safety
81 Gifted/Talented
82 Video Services
83 Substance Abuse Prev
84 Erate
85 AIDS Education
88 Alternative/At Risk
89 Multi-Cultural Curriculum
90 Social Work
91 Safety/Security
92 Magnet School
93 Parental Involvement
95 Tech Prep Program
97 Chief Information Officer
98 Chief Technology Officer
270 Character Education
271 Migrant Education
273 Teacher Mentor
274 Before/After Sch
275 Response To Intervention
277 Remedial Math K-12
280 Literacy Coach
285 STEM
286 Digital Learning
288 Common Core Standards
294 Accountability
295 Network System
296 Title II Programs
297 Webmaster
298 Grant Writer/Ptnrships
750 Chief Innovation Officer
751 Chief of Staff
752 Social Emotional Learning

Texas School Directory

DISTRICT PERSONNEL INDEX

NAME/District	JOB FUNCTIONS	PAGE
Dromgoole, Emma, Dr/*Edgewood Ind School Dist*	20,23	31
Drum, Lewis/*Motley Co Ind School Dist*	67	296
Drummond, Deanna/*Sidney Ind School Dist*	73,98,298	90
Druschke, Toni/*New Diana Ind School Dist*	4	376
Duarte, Melissa, Dr/*Goose Creek Cons Ind Sch Dist*	8,15,296	187
Dube, Kathy/*Lexington Ind School Dist*	2	263
Dube, Mark/*McDade Ind School Dist*	67	24
Dubose, Kristi/*Overton Ind School Dist*	275	328
Dubose, Steven/*Overton Ind School Dist*	1	328
Duck, Linda/*Chico Ind School Dist*	12,280	403
Duck, Troy/*Wildorado Ind Sch Dist*	1,11,73	308
Duderstadt, Lanier/*Wall Ind School Dist*	3,91	365
Dudley, Cara/*Centerville Ind School Dist*	8,11,285,286	264
Due, James/*Centerville Ind School Dist*	67	374
Duenas, Juan/*Sheldon Ind School Dist*	9,288	200
Duenez, Linda/*Austwell Tivoli Ind SD*	60	323
Duenez, Luis/*Weatherford Ind School Dist*	91	313
Duerr, Alan/*Hays Cons Ind School Dist*	295	211
Dueser, Linda/*Victoria Ind School Dist*	16,82,286	382
Duffer, Stefanie/*Caddo Mills Ind Sch Dist*	73	235
Duffey, Margie/*Spring Branch Ind School Dist*	15	200
Duffney, Janice/*Coppell Ind School Dist*	76	98
Duhon, Brenda, Dr/*Port Neches-Groves Ind SD*	8,15,69,73,74,288,294,298	243
Duke, Carolyn/*Harmony Ind School Dist*	8,11,69,288,296,298	376
Duke, George/*Timpson Ind School Dist*	67	335
Duke, Georgette/*Texarkana Ind School Dist*	274	50
Duke, Kim/*Darrouzett Ind School Dist*	2	267
Duke, Krystal/*Wortham Ind School Dist*	38	156
Duke, Sandra/*Brownsboro Ind School Dist*	34,58,77	213
Dukes, Dan, Dr/*Abilene Ind School Dist*	79	360
Dulude, David/*Waskom Ind School Dist*	83	209
Dulworth, Rhonda/*Corsicana Ind School Dist*	31	299
Dumont, Tab/*Pleasanton Ind School Dist*	6	21
Dunavant, Beth Anne/*Pittsburg Ind School Dist*	8,11,69,88,273,288,294,298	68
Duncan, Brad/*Anna Ind School Dist*	15	77
Duncan, Dayne/*Groesbeck Ind School Dist*	2,4,5,91	267
Duncan, Kayla/*Kerens Ind School Dist*	4	300
Duncan, Krystle/*Boyd Ind School Dist*	58	402
Duncan, Lee/*White Settlement Ind Sch Dist*	8	357
Duncan, Lisa/*Ector Co Ind School Dist*	45	130
Duncan, Marcie/*Wolfe City Ind School Dist*	4	237
Duncan, Melanie/*Tenaha Ind School Dist*	4	335
Duncan, Pam/*Cisco Independent Sch Dist*	7	128
Duncan, Rebecca/*Sweetwater ISD School Dist*	27	301
Duncan, Scot/*Hooks Ind School Dist*	67	48
Duncan, Shannon/*Huntsville Ind School Dist*	71	383
Duncan, Tiffany/*Dripping Springs Ind Sch Dist*	68	210
Duncan, Tim/*White Settlement Ind Sch Dist*	68	357
Dungen, Jeff/*Alvin Ind School Dist*	5	50
Duniven, Lynn/*Highland Ind School Dist*	2	301
Dunkel, Jill/*Archer City Ind School Dist*	67	19
Dunlap, Becca/*Plainview Ind School Dist*	2	175
Dunlap, Brian/*Mt Calm Ind School Dist*	67	228
Dunlap, Jim/*Canton Ind School Dist*	1	380
Dunn-Flores, Lisa Marie/*United Ind School Dist*	81	387
Dunn, Dirk/*Ira Ind School Dist*	67	333
Dunn, Don/*Van Ind School Dist*	1	381
Dunn, Kelly/*Meyersville Ind School Dist*	1,11	118
Dunn, Sharon/*Stockdale Ind School Dist*	35,88,288	401
Dunn, Tonya/*Post Ind School Dist*	38	162
Dunn, Wendy/*Mexia Ind School Dist*	38	267
Dunnam, Nancy/*Region 18 Ed Service Center*	76	287
Dunne-Oldfield, Tiffany/*Spring Ind School Dist*	71,93	202
Dunsom, Jennifer/*Woodville Ind School Dist*	58	375
Duplechain, Erica/*Hearne Ind School Dist*	2	325
DuPlessis, Jennifer/*Wylie Ind School Dist*	3	84
Duplichain, Jeff/*Alto Ind School Dist*	67	72
DuPont, Laura, Dr/*Clear Creek Ind School Dist*	67	158
Dupre, Charles, Dr/*Ft Bend Ind School Dist*	1	149
DuPree, Shirley, Dr/*Huffman Ind School Dist*	68,71	195
Duran, Angela/*Sweetwater ISD School Dist*	5	301
Duran, Christy/*Diocese of Lubbock Ed Office*	2	272
Duran, Kathy/*Lytle Ind School Dist*	2	21
Duran, Laura/*El Paso Ind School Dist*	4	132
Duran, Shirley/*Boles Ind School Dist*	93	235
Duran, Umberto/*Eagle Pass Ind School Dist*	297	276

NAME/District	JOB FUNCTIONS	PAGE
Durand, Jocelyn/*Boerne Ind School Dist*	71	253
Durand, Mike/*Jasper Ind School Dist*	67	240
Durant, Ivonne/*Dallas Ind School Dist*	8,18	98
Duree, Sandra/*Barbers Hill Ind School Dist*	8,15,275,280,286	72
Duren, Ella/*Maud Ind School Dist*	69	49
Durham, Kelly/*St Jo Ind School Dist*	36,69	290
Durham, Kristi/*Ft Bend Ind School Dist*	9	149
Durham, Tucker/*Alpine Ind School Dist*	2	56
Durham, Ulla/*San Marcos Cons Ind Sch Dist*	2	211
Durick, Kimberly/*Prairie Lea Ind School Dist*	58	61
Duron, Jodi, Dr/*Elgin Ind School Dist*	1	24
Durrant, Dayan/*Marshall Ind School Dist*	285	209
Durrwachter, Sony/*Calallen Ind School Dist*	34,57,58,72,88,271	302
Durst, Jeff/*Mason Ind School Dist*	67	275
Dusebout, Paul/*Willis Ind School Dist*	3,4	294
Dusek, Denise/*Veribest Ind School Dist*	2	365
Dusek, Sandra/*East Bernard Ind Sch Dist*	7	389
Dutcher, Larry/*Rosebud-Lott Ind School Dist*	73	145
Dutton, Donnie/*Leakey Ind School Dist*	6	322
Dutton, Matt/*Huffman Ind School Dist*	67	195
Duty, David/*Bruceville-Eddy Ind Sch Dist*	67	278
DuVall, Lynn/*Poolville Ind School Dist*	67	313
Duvon, Catherine/*Shelbyville Ind School Dist*	13,57,58	335
Dvorak, Jane/*Ferris Ind School Dist*	8,85	140
Dvorak, Jane/*Kemp Ind School Dist*	8,11,286	252
Dworaczyk, Dana/*Calhoun Co Ind School Dist*	27	61
Dwyer, Jane/*Nixon-Smiley Cons Ind Sch Dist*	8,57,69,88,273,286,288,298	164
Dye, John/*Killeen Ind School Dist*	91	27
Dyer, Amy/*Sealy Ind School Dist*	73,76,295	22
Dyer, Jeff/*Navasota Ind School Dist*	68	172
Dyer, Lisa/*Fayetteville Ind School Dist*	57	147
Dyer, Micah, Dr/*Cuero Ind School Dist*	1	117
Dyer, Michael/*Dayton Ind School Dist*	11,80,296	265
Dyer, Susan/*Plano Ind School Dist*	49	82
Dyes, Kevin/*Holliday Ind School Dist*	1,11	19
Dykes, Dana/*Athens Ind School Dist*	91	213
Dykes, Mark/*Collinsville Ind School Dist*	1	166
Dykstra, Dirk/*East Central Ind School Dist*	73	31
Dykstra, Valerie/*Devine Ind School Dist*	58	283
Dylan, Renita/*Grape Creek Ind School Dist*	38	364
Dynis, Deana/*Coppell Ind School Dist*	81	98
Dziuk, Nicole/*Poth Ind School Dist*	31,36,83	401

E

NAME/District	JOB FUNCTIONS	PAGE
Eads, Kassi/*Dublin Ind School Dist*	68,78	143
Eads, Mark/*Southside Ind School Dist*	1	43
Eager, Cheryl/*Krum Ind School Dist*	16	122
Eakin, David/*Lamar Cons Ind School Dist*	76,95	153
Ealy, Clark, Dr/*College Station Ind Sch Dist*	1	55
Eargle, Sherry/*Chapel Hill Ind School Dist*	4	363
Earl, Debbie/*Tulia Ind School Dist*	4	343
Earley, Dandy/*Alvarado Ind School Dist*	69	246
Earlie, Xandra/*Aldine Ind School Dist*	44	179
Earp, Samantha/*Grapeland Ind School Dist*	36,69	232
Earrientes, Joey/*Tahoka Ind School Dist*	3	273
Earthman, Kim/*Conroe Ind School Dist*	79	291
Easterling, Bobby/*Jim Ned Cons Ind School Dist*	5	361
Easterly, Brandon/*Comfort Ind School Dist*	6	254
Easterwood, Shay/*Brady Ind School Dist*	6	277
Eastman, John/*Troup Ind School Dist*	6	337
Eastman, William/*Clear Creek Ind School Dist*	61	158
Eastwood, Dyanna/*San Marcos Cons Ind Sch Dist*	7	211
Eastwood, Gary/*Tulia Ind School Dist*	67	343
Eaton, Jimmy/*Comanche Ind School Dist*	5	89
Eaton, Toy/*Grandfalls-Royalty Ind SD*	83,752	385
Eaves, Brian/*Denison Ind School Dist*	71	166
Ebell, Steven, Dr/*Clear Creek Ind School Dist*	8,15,288	158
Eberlan, Allen/*San Augustine Ind School Dist*	3,91	329
Eberlan, Skipper/*Etoile Ind School Dist*	3,5	297
Ebner, Ryan/*Grandview Ind School Dist*	6	248
Ebshire, Richard/*Carrizo Spgs Cons Ind SD*	6	127
Echavaria, Teresa/*Friona Ind School Dist*	7	315
Echebelem, Samantha/*Irving Ind School Dist*	275	109
Eckel, Joseph/*Rusk Ind School Dist*	5	73
Eckenrod, Tiffany/*Beaumont Ind School Dist*	4	241
Eckert, Dean/*Harper Ind School Dist*	3,5	163

School Year 2019-2020   800-333-8802   TX-T25

DISTRICT PERSONNEL INDEX

Market Data Retrieval

NAME/District	JOB FUNCTIONS	PAGE
Eddins, Loretta/Apple Springs Ind School Dist	11,36,58,69,88,270,271	374
Eddy, Carri/Northwest Ind School Dist	12,36,57,83,271,274	124
Eddy, Linda/Fruitvale Ind School Dist	58	380
Eder, Nancy/Diocese of Fort Worth Ed Off	7	358
Edgar, David/Del Valle Ind School Dist	2,15	369
Edgar, David/Lampasas Ind School Dist	3	261
Edgar, Lisa/Copperas Cove Ind School Dist	8,12,74,275	92
Edgas, David/Del Valle Ind School Dist	2,19	369
Edgemon, Trevor/Lubbock-Cooper Ind Sch Dist	5	271
Edison, David, Dr/Aquilla Ind School Dist	1,11	227
Edison, Nicki/Aspermont Ind School Dist	11	342
Edmonds, Jana/Loraine Ind School Dist	58	289
Edmondson, Joshua/Honey Grove Ind School Dist	16,73	146
Edmonson, Scott/Brookesmith Ind School Dist	6,35	58
Edwards, Ann/Columbia Brazoria ISD	4	52
Edwards, Barry/Bastrop Ind School Dist	1	23
Edwards, Chris/Hughes Springs Ind Sch Dist	6	70
Edwards, Courtney/Llano Ind School Dist	38	268
Edwards, Damon, Dr/Schertz-Cibolo-Univ City ISD	15	173
Edwards, David/Smithville Ind School Dist	11	24
Edwards, Dean/Bluff Dale Ind Sch Dist	11,83,288	143
Edwards, Jami/Meridian Ind School Dist	2	47
Edwards, Jessica/Galveston Ind School Dist	58	160
Edwards, Justin/Chapel Hill Ind School Dist	3,5	363
Edwards, Kim/Meridian Ind School Dist	12	47
Edwards, Kim/Meridian Ind School Dist	1,11,84	47
Edwards, Lisa/Aldine Ind School Dist	49	179
Edwards, Lori/Quinlan Ind School Dist	57	237
Edwards, Mac/Llano Ind School Dist	1	268
Edwards, Matt/Turkey-Quitaque Cons Ind SD	5	176
Edwards, Mike/Chapel Hill Ind School Dist	67	363
Edwards, Nanette/Ranger Ind School Dist	27,31	129
Edwards, Natalie/Goose Creek Cons Ind Sch Dist	4	187
Edwards, Phil/Angleton Ind School Dist	1	51
Edwards, Rick/Joshua Ind School Dist	15	248
Edwards, Robbie/Holland Ind School Dist	10,11,57,83,275,285	27
Edwards, Stephen/Hamshire Fannett Ind Sch Dist	15,73	242
Edwards, Thelissa/Humble Ind School Dist	58	195
Edwards, Travis/Hitchcock Ind School Dist	1	161
Egger, Jim/McAllen Ind School Dist	20,23	221
Egle, Roger/Bridgeport Ind School Dist	73,76,286,295	402
Ehlers, Paul/Lubbock-Cooper Ind Sch Dist	67	271
Ehrlich, Frances/Karnes City Ind School Dist	274	250
Eiben, Suzanne/Palestine Ind School Dist	15,68	15
Eichman, Jeff/Coldspring-Oakhurst Cons ISD	11	330
Eichman, Jon/Devine Ind School Dist	5	283
Eichman, Missy/Coldspring-Oakhurst Cons ISD	73,286	330
Eilers, Anthony/Campbell Ind School Dist	73,295	235
Eilers, Anthony/Mt Vernon Ind School Dist	73,295	156
Eilers, Stacy/La Grange Ind School Dist	15	147
Elandary, Juliana/Lovejoy Ind School Dist	4	80
Elbert, Michael/Sinton Ind School Dist	58	332
Elder, John/Coleman Ind School Dist	6	76
Elder, Laura/Liberty Hill Ind School Dist	37	398
Eldredge, Dana/Eagle Mtn-Saginaw Ind Sch Dist	27	348
Eldredge, Wendy, Dr/Crandall Ind School Dist	1	251
Eldredge, Wendy, Dr/Garland Ind School Dist	15,71,79	105
Eldridge, Billy/Wolfe City Ind School Dist	31,69,77	237
Eldridge, Patricia/Mullin Ind School Dist	4	288
Eldridge, Vickie/Muenster Ind School Dist	16	91
Elerson, Sunday/Canton Ind School Dist	7	380
Elester, Sally/Big Sandy Ind School Dist	8,31,69,83,88	316
Elhabr, Kamal/San Antonio Ind School Dist	3,15	39
Eli, Christy/Newcastle Ind School Dist	286,295	406
Elias, Sheila/Ysleta Ind School Dist	298	137
Elizalde, Travis/Broaddus Ind School Dist	67	329
Elizando, Anna/Tuloso-Midway Ind School Dist	68,78	305
Elizondo, Daniel/Silsbee Ind School Dist	71	178
Elizondo, Maribelle/McAllen Ind School Dist	58	221
Elizondo, Thelma/United Ind School Dist	46	387
Elledge, Kiera/Hurst-Euless-Bedford ISD	16,285	353
Elledge, Stacy/Chapel Hill Ind School Dist	8,11,57,271,273,298	363
Elledge, Stacy/Chapel Hill Ind School Dist	8,11,57,271,273,298	363
Eller, Jackie/Bells Ind School Dist	3	165
Elley, Alissa/Navarro Ind School Dist	73,84,286,295,298	173
Elliot, Bill/Celina Ind School Dist	6	77
Elliott, Alicia/Athens Ind School Dist	67	213
Elliott, Ariel/Greenwood Ind School Dist	1	285
Elliott, Gary/Amarillo Ind School Dist	2	317
Elliott, Gary/Copperas Cove Ind School Dist	3,5,91	92
Elliott, Gina/North East Ind School Dist	68	34
Elliott, Lindsey/Joshua Ind School Dist	274	248
Elliott, Luann/McCamey Ind School Dist	31,36,69,83,85,88	377
Elliott, Nicole/Peaster Ind School Dist	73,76,286,295	313
Ellis, Amy, Dr/Rockwall Ind School Dist	8	325
Ellis, Andrea, Dr/Commerce Independent Sch Dist	27,31	236
Ellis, Dwayne/Alba-Golden Ind School Dist	1	404
Ellis, Emory/Galena Park Ind School Dist	3	186
Ellis, Kim/Waco Ind School Dist	8,15	281
Ellis, Linda/Grand Prairie Ind School Dist	1,288	107
Ellis, Roger/Gold-Burg Ind School Dist	1	290
Ellis, Scott/Kemp Ind School Dist	3,5	252
Ellis, Stacey/Terrell Ind School Dist	68,273	253
Ellison, Krista/Happy Ind School Dist	9,45,48,51,85,274	342
Ellison, Tommy/Medina Valley Ind School Dist	3	284
Ellisor, Stephenie/Etoile Ind School Dist	7	297
Ellsworth, Betty/Henrietta Ind School Dist	67	74
Elms, Mark/Pampa Ind School Dist	47	165
Elridge, Curtis/St Jo Ind School Dist	1	290
Elrod, Katie/Gordon Ind School Dist	36	310
Elrod, Keith/Hico Ind School Dist	2,298	176
Elsasser, Richard, Dr/Region 13 Ed Service Center	1,11	373
Elsbecker, Leon/Sanger Ind School Dist	73,295	126
Ely, Chad/Sunray Ind School Dist	3,5	296
Ely, Diana/Northside Ind School Dist	74	36
Ely, Stacy/Franklin Ind School Dist	8,11,74,294,296	324
Emanuel, Darrell/Round Rock Ind School Dist	8	398
Emerson, Dolores/Brownsville Ind School Dist	9	63
Emeyabbi, Aaron/North Lamar Ind School Dist	6	259
Emfinger, Keith/Lamesa Ind School Dist	16,73,286,295	117
Emrich, John/Crockett Ind School Dist	15	232
Engle, Debbie/Valentine Ind School Dist	1,11,57,83	241
Engle, Karen/Clear Creek Ind School Dist	10,15	158
Englehart, Kenneth/Medina Valley Ind School Dist	84	284
English, Amy/Beckville Ind School Dist	57	311
English, Lacy/Aspermont Ind School Dist	67	342
English, Latrishia/Rivercrest Ind School Dist	57	322
English, Steve/Bremond Ind School Dist	10,83,88	324
English, Todd/Hardin Ind School Dist	73,286	265
Engstrom, Heather/Kerrville Ind School Dist	8,15,288	256
Enlow, Blake/Bowie Ind School Dist	1	289
Enoch, Maria/Tidehaven Ind School Dist	57,271	276
Enriquez, Micheal/Pettus Ind School Dist	6	25
Entrop, Kendrea/Wills Point Ind School Dist	11,16,58	381
Epley, Mandy/Comal Ind School Dist	68	87
Epperson, Barbara/Belton Ind School Dist	81	26
Eppes, Steve/Kountze Ind School Dist	67	178
Epps, Cleota/Little Elm Ind School Dist	68	124
Erickson, Ennis/Rising Star Ind Sch Dist	6	129
Erickson, Jimmy/Motley Co Ind School Dist	2	296
Erlanson, Robert/Crawford Ind School Dist	3	279
Ernhart, Paige/Miles Ind School Dist	31	326
Ernst, Barbi/Clifton Ind School Dist	73	46
Erwin, Donald/Coolidge Ind School Dist	3,5	266

#		#		#		#		#		#	
1	Superintendent	16	Instructional Media Svcs	30	Adult Education	44	Science Sec	58	Special Education K-12	72	Summer School
2	Bus/Finance/Purchasing	17	Chief Operations Officer	31	Career/Sch-to-Work K-12	45	Math K-12	59	Special Education Elem	73	Instructional Tech
3	Buildings And Grounds	18	Chief Academic Officer	32	Career/Sch-to-Work Elem	46	Math Elem	60	Special Education Sec	74	Inservice Training
4	Food Service	19	Chief Financial Officer	33	Career/Sch-to-Work Sec	47	Math Sec	61	Foreign/World Lang K-12	75	Marketing/Distributive
5	Transportation	20	Art K-12	34	Early Childhood Ed	48	English/Lang Arts K-12	62	Foreign/World Lang Elem	76	Info Systems
6	Athletic	21	Art Elem	35	Health/Phys Education	49	English/Lang Arts Elem	63	Foreign/World Lang Sec	77	Psychological Assess
7	Health Services	22	Art Sec	36	Guidance Services K-12	50	English/Lang Arts Sec	64	Religious Education K-12	78	Affirmative Action
8	Curric/Instruct K-12	23	Music K-12	37	Guidance Services Elem	51	Reading K-12	65	Religious Education Elem	79	Student Personnel
9	Curric/Instruct Elem	24	Music Elem	38	Guidance Services Sec	52	Reading Elem	66	Religious Education Sec	80	Driver Ed/Safety
10	Curric/Instruct Sec	25	Music Sec	39	Social Studies K-12	53	Reading Sec	67	School Board President	81	Gifted/Talented
11	Federal Program	26	Business Education	40	Social Studies Elem	54	Remedial Reading K-12	68	Teacher Personnel	82	Video Services
12	Title I	27	Career & Tech Ed	41	Social Studies Sec	55	Remedial Reading Elem	69	Academic Assessment	83	Substance Abuse Prev
13	Title V	28	Technology Education	42	Science K-12	56	Remedial Reading Sec	70	Research/Development	84	Erate
15	Asst Superintendent	29	Family/Consumer Science	43	Science Elem	57	Bilingual/ELL	71	Public Information	85	AIDS Education

#		#	
88	Alternative/At Risk	277	Remedial Math K-12
89	Multi-Cultural Curriculum	280	Literacy Coach
90	Social Work	285	STEM
91	Safety/Security	286	Digital Learning
93	Magnet School	288	Common Core Standards
94	Parental Involvement	294	Accountability
95	Tech Prep Program	295	Network System
97	Chief Infomation Officer	296	Title II Programs
98	Chief Technology Officer	297	Webmaster
270	Character Education	298	Grant Writer/Ptnrships
271	Migrant Education	750	Chief Innovation Officer
273	Teacher Mentor	751	Chief of Staff
274	Before/After Sch	752	Social Emotional Learning
275	Response To Intervention		

TX-T26

Texas School Directory

DISTRICT PERSONNEL INDEX

NAME/District	JOB FUNCTIONS	PAGE
Erwin, John/*Era Ind School Dist*	31,36,69,83,85	90
Erwin, Meggie/*Edgewood Ind School Dist*	36	380
Escalante, Heather/*Caldwell Ind School Dist*	2	59
Escalon, Melissa/*Weslaco Ind School Dist*	91	225
Escamilla, Beverly/*Diocese of Beaumont Sch Office*	68	244
Escamilla, Patricio/*Edinburg Cons Ind School Dist*	57,271	216
Escamita, Judith/*McAllen Ind School Dist*	73,76,295	221
Escarcega, Vanessa/*Dimmitt Ind School Dist*	4	71
Eschenburg, Emily/*Sealy Ind School Dist*	10,57,271	22
Escobar, Daniel/*Socorro Ind School Dist*	71	135
Escobar, Helen/*Roma Ind School Dist*	71	341
Escobar, Jaime/*Roma Ind School Dist*	6,35	341
Eshbaugh, Calvin/*Academy Ind School Dist*	67	26
Eslick, Brianne/*Spearman Ind School Dist*	73,95	177
Esparza, Anne/*Fabens Ind School Dist*	79	135
Esparza, April/*Diocese Corpus Christi Ed Off*	7	306
Esparza, Mary Lou/*Brownsville Ind School Dist*	11	63
Esparza, Ricardo/*Roma Ind School Dist*	5	341
Esparza, Susan/*Brackett Ind School Dist*	68	257
Esperanza, Hopie/*Webb Cons Ind School Dist*	7	388
Espino, Billy/*Ft Stockton Ind School Dist*	67	315
Espino, Gabe/*Kermit Ind School Dist*	3,5,91	401
Espinosa, Stephanie, Dr/*Northwest Ind School Dist*	74,273,296	124
Espinoza, Anne Marie/*Uvalde Cons Ind School Dist*	71	378
Espinoza, Christina/*Hermleigh Ind School Dist*	60	333
Espinoza, Jose, Dr/*Socorro Ind School Dist*	1	135
Espinoza, Kari/*Harlandale Ind School Dist*	48,51,54,61,280	32
Esqueda, Ana/*Ysleta Ind School Dist*	57	137
Esquivel, Cris/*McAllen Ind School Dist*	91	221
Esquivel, Sergio/*Sharyland Ind School Dist*	297	224
Essberg, Brenda/*Ft Bend Ind School Dist*	2	149
Essig, Jason/*Boerne Ind School Dist*	73,286	253
Estes, Caroly/*Goliad Ind School Dist*	2	163
Estes, Kenneth, Dr/*Alvarado Ind School Dist*	1	246
Estes, Mandy/*Round Rock Ind School Dist*	8,18	398
Estes, Nocona/*Dublin Ind School Dist*	4	143
Estrada, Ben/*Los Fresnos Cons Ind Sch Dist*	70	66
Estrada, Dora/*Edinburg Cons Ind School Dist*	16,82	216
Estrada, Iris/*Corpus Christi Ind Sch Dist*	34	303
Estrada, Noel/*Agua Dulce Ind School Dist*	67	302
Estrada, Ram/*Lamar Cons Ind School Dist*	20	153
Estrada, Rebecca/*Lackland Ind School Dist*	2,13,19	34
Estrada, Tiffany/*Eden Cons Ind School Dist*	31	90
Estrades, Mark/*Lockhart Ind School Dist*	1	61
Ettredge, Barbara/*Pilot Point Ind School Dist*	2,19	125
Etzler, Michele/*Hallettsville Ind Sch Dist*	35,83,85	262
Etzler, Tim/*Ricardo Ind School Dist*	73	257
Eubank, Laura/*Veribest Ind School Dist*	9	365
Eubank, Sonia/*Region 19 Ed Service Center*	2,15	139
Eubanks, Reta/*Saltillo Ind School Dist*	58	231
Eubanks, Sylvia/*Lufkin Ind School Dist*	57,271	18
Euler, Kendall/*Little Elm Ind School Dist*	76	124
Eurex, Donna/*Garland Ind School Dist*	73	105
Evans, Amber/*Chireno ISD School Dist*	4	297
Evans, Andy/*Tatum Ind School Dist*	6	328
Evans, Chris/*Wheeler Ind School Dist*	6	391
Evans, Christi/*Shamrock Ind School Dist*	4	390
Evans, Dana/*Timpson Ind School Dist*	58	335
Evans, Darrell/*Dew Ind School Dist*	1,11	156
Evans, Darrell/*Nederland Ind School Dist*	69	242
Evans, Emily/*Teague Ind School Dist*	2	156
Evans, Jason/*Sulphur Springs Ind Sch Dist*	69,294	232
Evans, Karen/*Sonora Ind School Dist*	73,84,286	342
Evans, Kathleen/*Rice Ind School Dist*	57	300
Evans, Kim/*Midland Ind School Dist*	27,31	285
Evans, Lauri/*Rains Ind School Dist*	76	320
Evans, Louis/*Harris Co Dept of Ed*	67	179
Evans, Pamela/*Houston Ind School Dist*	11,296	188
Evans, Phil/*Frisco Ind School Dist*	8	78
Evans, Rex/*Splendora Ind School Dist*	83,91	294
Evans, Scott/*Hawkins Ind School Dist*	6,91	404
Evans, Teresa/*Crosby Ind School Dist*	4	183
Evenson, Ruth/*Hereford Ind School Dist*	5	119
Everest, Kathryn/*Ft Worth Ind School Dist*	36	349
Everett, Aiden/*Runge Ind School Dist*	84	251
Everett, Aiden/*Runge Ind School Dist*	28,73,286	251

NAME/District	JOB FUNCTIONS	PAGE
Everett, Chris/*Columbus Ind School Dist*	5	86
Everett, David/*McGregor Ind School Dist*	11,15,83	280
Everhart, Misty/*Harleton Ind School Dist*	34	208
Eversole, Wes/*Lake Dallas Ind School Dist*	2,15,19	122
Everson, Melissa/*Benjamin Ind School Dist*	57,58,271,286	258
Evertt, Joel/*Hereford Ind School Dist*	3	119
Evins, Staci/*Moody Ind School Dist*	67	281
Evridge, Amanda/*Rankin Ind School Dist*	67	377
Ewing, Dub/*City View Ind School Dist*	3	391
Ewing, Michael/*Ft Bend Ind School Dist*	88	149
Ewton, Galen/*Collinsville Ind School Dist*	2	166
Eyeington, Tom/*Socorro Ind School Dist*	3,15,17	135
Eyre, Rosalind/*Beaumont Ind School Dist*	16	241
Ezell, Debra/*Ft Stockton Ind School Dist*	73,76	315

F

NAME/District	JOB FUNCTIONS	PAGE
Faas, Terese/*El Campo Ind School Dist*	68,79	389
Fadel, Rola/*Midlothian Ind School Dist*	3	141
Fagan, Cody/*Mildred Ind School Dist*	6	300
Fagan, Cody/*Whitesboro Ind School Dist*	6	168
Fagen, Elizabeth, Dr/*Humble Ind School Dist*	1	195
Faglie, Ashley/*Salado Ind School Dist*	7	29
Fahey, Carla/*Duncanville Ind School Dist*	67	104
Fails, Jamie/*Willis Ind School Dist*	71	294
Fain, Brandy/*New Caney Ind School Dist*	2	293
Fain, Christopher/*Wichita Falls Ind School Dist*	3	392
Fair, Brian/*Midway Ind School Dist*	5	280
Fair, Robby/*Hawkins Ind School Dist*	2	404
Fairchild, Gary/*Evadale Ind School Dist*	1,11	240
Fairchild, Jack/*Ingram Ind School Dist*	67	255
Faircloth, Susan/*Eula Ind School Dist*	2	63
Faith, Angelyn/*Albany Ind School Dist*	2	334
Falco, Leslee/*Franklin Ind School Dist*	58	325
Falco, Leslee/*Hearne Ind School Dist*	58	325
Falcon, Joel/*Garland Ind School Dist*	3	105
Falcon, Michelle/*McCamey Ind School Dist*	4	377
Falcon, Trista/*Troy Ind School Dist*	16,82	29
Falkner, James/*Bushland Ind School Dist*	3,5	319
Fallin, Kaelee/*Shelbyville Ind School Dist*	27	335
Fallin, Karen/*Tenaha Ind School Dist*	8,13,36,83,88,270	335
Faltys, David, Dr/*Carroll Independent Sch Dist*	1	347
Fancher, Shanna, Dr/*Marble Falls Ind School Dist*	58	60
Fannin, Creslond/*Manor Ind School Dist*	11	371
Fannin, Michele/*De Kalb Ind School Dist*	52,55,57,59	48
Fanning, Travis/*Cypress-Fairbanks Ind Sch Dist*	15	184
Fanno, Marie/*Jourdanton Ind School Dist*	36,69,88	20
Faour, Patrick/*Hitchcock Ind School Dist*	69,294	161
Farber, Jamie/*Northwest Ind School Dist*	77,79	124
Farek, Charles/*Bishop Cons Ind School Dist*	3,5	302
Farias, Linda/*McAllen Ind School Dist*	45	221
Faridas, Pam/*Spring Ind School Dist*	15	202
Faris, Logan, Dr/*Northwest Ind School Dist*	10	124
Farish, Andrea/*Dawson Ind School Dist*	9,12,57	299
Farish, Christi/*Community Ind School Dist*	8,12,18,69,270,271,296	78
Farler, Scott/*New Diana Ind School Dist*	8,57,58,69,271,274,288	376
Farmer, Carrie/*Klein Ind School Dist*	48	196
Farmer, Denise/*Colorado Ind School Dist*	8,12,15,83,88,296	289
Farmer, Gina/*Cedar Hill Ind School Dist*	6	97
Farmer, Hugh/*Seymour Ind School Dist*	6	25
Farr, Brett/*Carrollton-Farmers Branch ISD*	20,23	96
Farrer, Jesse/*Tom Bean Ind School Dist*	67	168
Farris, Brant/*Bowie Ind School Dist*	16,286,297	289
Farris, Melissa/*New Boston Ind School Dist*	75	49
Fasel, Erin/*Johnson City Ind School Dist*	2,11,15	46
Fattorini-Vasq, Connie/*Ysleta Ind School Dist*	11	137
Faucett, Ashley/*New Summerfield Ind Sch Dist*	69,83,270	73
Faught, Leslie, Dr/*Gregory-Portland Ind Sch Dist*	15	330
Faulkner, Marc, Dr/*China Spring Ind School Dist*	1	278
Faulkner, Morllo/*Huntsville Ind School Dist*	295	383
Faulknor, Brandy/*Bynum Ind School Dist*	2	227
Fauntleroy, Alexandra/*Throckmorton Ind School Dist*	58	363
Fausett, Rodney/*Taylor Ind School Dist*	15	399
Feagins, Roy/*Cayuga Ind School Dist*	5	14
Fears, Alison/*Region 10 Ed Service Center*	11	116
Feasel, Julie/*Central Heights Ind Sch Dist*	13,37	297
Featherson, Angela/*Liberty-Eylau Ind School Dist*	58	48

DISTRICT PERSONNEL INDEX

Market Data Retrieval

NAME/District	JOB FUNCTIONS	PAGE
Featherson, Angela/Maud Ind School Dist	58	49
Feind, Adam/Northwest Ind School Dist	295	124
Feiner, Jerry/Brownsboro Ind School Dist	28,73,76,295	213
Felan, Joy/Ranger Ind School Dist	2	129
Felan, Pedro/Eagle Pass Ind School Dist	3,91	276
Felan, Sheree/Keller Ind School Dist	50	354
Felan, Trey/Ranger Ind School Dist	36,69,85,270	129
Felderhoff, Terry/Gruver Ind School Dist	6	176
Feldhouson, Brandi/Pearsall Ind School Dist	11,57,88,271	157
Feldt, John/Midland Ind School Dist	6	285
Felice, Jim/Anahuac Ind School Dist	3	71
Feller, Gina/Irion Co Ind School Dist	7	238
Fellers, Janice/Santa Anna Ind School Dist	67	76
Fellows, Jonathan/Alpine Ind School Dist	6	56
Felps, Kirt/Blanco Ind School Dist	67	45
Felts, Cathy/Mason Ind School Dist	68	275
Felts, Dusty/Chisum Ind School Dist	38,88	259
Felts, Justin/Brownwood Ind School Dist	3	58
Fennig, Michael/Sunnyvale Ind School Dist	57	113
Fenwick, Gordon/Winters Ind School Dist	3	327
Ferguson, Amy/White Settlement Ind Sch Dist	57	357
Ferguson, Barry/Spur Ind School Dist	67	127
Ferguson, Brenda/Spearman Ind School Dist	2,11	177
Ferguson, Danetta/Sterling City Ind School Dist	2	342
Ferguson, Dennis/Robinson Ind School Dist	3	281
Ferguson, Donavan/Darrouzett Ind School Dist	11	267
Ferguson, Dow/Sterling City Ind School Dist	73,286	342
Ferguson, John/Kountze Ind School Dist	1	178
Ferguson, Karen/College Station Ind Sch Dist	27,31	55
Ferguson, Kimberly/Schertz-Cibolo-Univ City ISD	58	173
Ferguson, Laurie/White Oak Ind School Dist	4	171
Ferguson, Lindsey/Lewisville Ind School Dist	46	122
Ferguson, Marion/Mullin Ind School Dist	67	288
Ferguson, Melanie/Pine Tree Ind School Dist	68	170
Ferguson, Roxanne/Port Neches-Groves Ind SD	9	243
Ferguson, Stephanie/Belton Ind School Dist	26,31,75	26
Feris, Chris/Birdville Ind School Dist	6	346
Fernandez, Andrew/San Marcos Cons Ind Sch Dist	71	211
Fernandez, Belinda/Stamford Ind School Dist	16,82	250
Fernandez, Daniel/Three Rivers Ind School Dist	73,84	268
Fernandez, Ernest/Dalhart Ind School Dist	4	95
Fernandez, Karen/Texline Ind School Dist	271	95
Fernandez, Kim/Leary Ind School Dist	59	48
Fernandez, Kimberly/New Boston Ind School Dist	58,83	49
Fernandez, Rick, Dr/Tomball Ind School Dist	15	203
Feron, Mario/Uvalde Cons Ind School Dist	57	378
Ferrell, Kathy/DeSoto Ind School Dist	69,294	104
Ferrell, Sue/Clear Creek Ind School Dist	16	158
Ferris, Ann/Lubbock-Cooper Ind Sch Dist	2	271
Ferry, Jeff/Luling Ind School Dist	67	61
Feverbacher, Belinda/Wylie Ind School Dist	275	85
Fewin, Jaque/Lubbock-Cooper Ind Sch Dist	73	271
Fiacco, Jason/Elkhart Ind School Dist	6	15
Fiaschetti, Carolyn/Anderson-Shiro Cons Ind SD	11	171
Fiedler, Shane/New Home Ind School Dist	11,286,288	273
Fiedler, Shane/New Home Ind School Dist	1	273
Field, Andy/Burnet Cons Ind Sch Dist	67	60
Field, Brett/Sanford-Fritch Ind School Dist	73,84	238
Fielder, Mike/Hurst-Euless-Bedford ISD	6	353
Fields, Aimee/Groom Ind School Dist	58	69
Fields, Cindi/Lipan Ind School Dist	57	230
Fields, Cynthia/Pecos-Barstow-Toyah Ind SD	69	323
Fields, Greg/Columbia Brazoria ISD	16,73,295	52
Fields, Jackie/Manor Ind School Dist	5	371
Fields, La Vaughn/Waskom Ind School Dist	73,84	209
Fields, Matthew/Rochelle Ind School Dist	8	278
Fields, Melissa/Marble Falls Ind School Dist	69,294	60

NAME/District	JOB FUNCTIONS	PAGE
Fields, Milton/Judson Ind School Dist	3,15,91	33
Fields, Sara/Campbell Ind School Dist	58	235
Fieszel, Jacob/Gunter Ind School Dist	6	166
Figueroa, Anthony/Wolfe City Ind School Dist	1,83	237
Fikes, Chris/Evadale Ind School Dist	16,73,76,84,286,295	240
Filda, David/Cotulla Ind School Dist	6	259
Filipp, Ace/Danbury Ind School Dist	16	53
Filla, Tommy/Granger Ind School Dist	67	396
Fillmore, Cheryl/West Oso Ind School Dist	6	306
Finch, Bryan/Groveton Ind School Dist	10,88,270	374
Finch, Danny/Perryton Ind School Dist	83	307
Fincher, Judy/Brady Ind School Dist	73,84	277
Fincher, Lisa/Ennis Ind School Dist	2,19,296,298	140
Finck, Rachelle/Round Rock Ind School Dist	752	398
Finger, Kami/Lubbock Ind School Dist	58	269
Fink, Nathan/Marble Falls Ind School Dist	73,295	60
Finley, Danny/Coolidge Ind School Dist	67	266
Finley, Debbie/Loraine Ind School Dist	2	289
Finley, Jennifer/Dallas Ind School Dist	7	98
Finley, Lindy/Jacksonville Ind School Dist	2	72
Finley, Stacy/Santo Ind School Dist	4	310
Finn, Donnie/Fredericksburg Ind School Dist	11,15,68,79,91	163
Finn, Tim/Wharton Ind School Dist	6	390
Finnell, John/Cleburne Ind School Dist	67	247
Finney, Lawanda, Dr/Port Arthur Ind School Dist	93,273	243
Finster, Dwana/Calhoun Co Ind School Dist	88	62
Finsterwald, Stacey/Wheeler Ind School Dist	57	391
Fiolek, Brian/Crockett Ind School Dist	3	232
Fiorini, Robert/Palacios Ind School Dist	73,295	275
Firth, Susan/Cypress-Fairbanks Ind Sch Dist	27,69,81	184
Fischer, Jessica/Comal Ind School Dist	5	87
Fischer, Karen/Gruver Ind School Dist	2,11	176
Fishbeck, Christie/Dew Ind School Dist	16,73,295,297	156
Fishbeck, Kevin/Moulton Ind School Dist	6	262
Fisher, Amanda/Oglesby Ind School Dist	58	93
Fisher, Corgie/S & S Cons Ind School Dist	3,5	167
Fisher, David/Lometa Ind School Dist	1,11	262
Fisher, Debbie/Olfen Ind School Dist	4	327
Fisher, Denise/Castleberry Ind School Dist	42	347
Fisher, Elmer/Manor Ind School Dist	67	371
Fisher, George/Paris Ind School Dist	67	260
Fisher, Jeff/Rains Ind School Dist	2,15	320
Fisher, Jimmy/Brownwood Ind School Dist	295	58
Fisher, Julie/Terrell Ind School Dist	11,69,275,288,296	253
Fisher, Kim/Brazos Ind School Dist	7	22
Fisher, Larry/Boling Ind School Dist	3,5	389
Fisher, Leanne/Frenship Ind School Dist	288	269
Fisher, Robby/Brownsville Ind School Dist	95	63
Fisher, Ron/Flour Bluff Ind School Dist	91	304
Fisher, Tiffany/Shallowater Ind School Dist	57	272
Fisk, Dara/Mt Vernon Ind School Dist	77	156
Fisk, Sherri/Valley Mills Ind School Dist	7	47
Fisk, Tiffany/Bushland Ind School Dist	38,83	319
Fite, Drenon/Tatum Ind School Dist	68	328
Fitton, Keith/Normangee Ind School Dist	6	264
Fitts, David, Dr/Region 8 Ed Service Center	1	69
Fitzgerald, Karen/Midlothian Ind School Dist	15,71,76,750	141
Fitzhenry, Derek/Sheldon Ind School Dist	6,35	200
Fitzhugh, Sarah, Dr/Lewisville Ind School Dist	69,294	122
Flaim, Diane/Dripping Springs Ind Sch Dist	8,15	210
Flanary, Patty/Glen Rose Ind School Dist	286	340
Flannery, Sylvia/Kerrville Ind School Dist	27,31,57,81,271	256
Flasch, Kim/Lake Travis Ind School Dist	67	370
Flater, Janes/Connally Ind School Dist	2,15	279
Flecter, Todd/Slocum ISD School Dist	3	16
Fleet, Penny/Spring Hill Ind School Dist	8,69,74,294	170
Fleitman, Susie/Muenster Ind School Dist	5	91

1 Superintendent	16 Instructional Media Svcs	30 Adult Education	44 Science Sec	58 Special Education K-12	72 Summer School	88 Alternative/At Risk	277 Remedial Math K-12
2 Bus/Finance/Purchasing	17 Chief Operations Officer	31 Career/Sch-to-Work K-12	45 Math K-12	59 Special Education Elem	73 Instructional Tech	89 Multi-Cultural Curriculum	280 Literacy Coach
3 Buildings And Grounds	18 Chief Academic Officer	32 Career/Sch-to-Work Elem	46 Math Elem	60 Special Education Sec	74 Inservice Training	90 Social Work	285 STEM
4 Food Service	19 Chief Financial Officer	33 Career/Sch-to-Work Sec	47 Math Sec	61 Foreign/World Lang K-12	75 Marketing/Distributive	91 Safety/Security	286 Digital Learning
5 Transportation	20 Art K-12	34 Early Childhood Ed	48 English/Lang Arts K-12	62 Foreign/World Lang Elem	76 Info Systems	92 Magnet School	288 Common Core Standards
6 Athletic	21 Art Elem	35 Health/Phys Education	49 English/Lang Arts Elem	63 Foreign/World Lang Sec	77 Psychological Assess	93 Parental Involvement	294 Accountability
7 Health Services	22 Art Sec	36 Guidance Services K-12	50 English/Lang Arts Sec	64 Religious Education K-12	78 Affirmative Action	95 Tech Prep Program	295 Network System
8 Curric/Instruct K-12	23 Music K-12	37 Guidance Services Elem	51 Reading K-12	65 Religious Education Elem	79 Student Personnel	97 Chief Information Officer	296 Title II Programs
9 Curric/Instruct Elem	24 Music Elem	38 Guidance Services Sec	52 Reading Elem	66 Religious Education Sec	80 Driver Ed/Safety	98 Chief Technology Officer	297 Webmaster
10 Curric/Instruct Sec	25 Music Sec	39 Social Studies K-12	53 Reading Sec	67 School Board President	81 Gifted/Talented	270 Character Education	298 Grant Writer/Ptnrships
11 Federal Program	26 Business Education	40 Social Studies Elem	54 Remedial Reading K-12	68 Teacher Personnel	82 Video Services	271 Migrant Education	750 Chief Innovation Officer
12 Title I	27 Career & Tech Ed	41 Social Studies Sec	55 Remedial Reading Elem	69 Academic Assessment	83 Substance Abuse Prev	273 Teacher Mentor	751 Chief of Staff
13 Title V	28 Technology Education	42 Science K-12	56 Remedial Reading Sec	70 Research/Development	84 Erate	274 Before/After Sch	752 Social Emotional Learning
15 Asst Superintendent	29 Family/Consumer Science	43 Science Elem	57 Bilingual/ELL	71 Public Information	85 AIDS Education	275 Response To Intervention	

Texas School Directory

DISTRICT PERSONNEL INDEX

NAME/District	JOB FUNCTIONS	PAGE
Fleming, Ginger/Northside Ind School Dist	9	36
Fleming, Gregory/Abilene Ind School Dist	71	360
Fleming, Jennifer/Keller Ind School Dist	36	354
Flencher, Amanda/Somerville Ind School Dist	2	60
Fletcher, Beverly/Ft Worth Ind School Dist	20	349
Fletcher, Greg/Paradise Ind School Dist	3	403
Fletcher, Linda/Pasadena Ind School Dist	20,23	198
Fletcher, Shane/Leonard Ind School Dist	6	146
Fletcher, Susan/Midway Ind School Dist	73,286	280
Fletcher, Tim/Slidell Ind School Dist	67	403
Flinchum, Thomas/Gold-Burg Ind School Dist	8,11,36,69,83,88	290
Fling, Jason/Yoakum Ind School Dist	16,73,76,84,295,298	118
Flinn, Ray/Harts Bluff Ind School Dist	3	363
Flippin, Amy/Coleman Ind School Dist	83,85,270,273	76
Flippin, Susan/Plainview Ind School Dist	16	175
Flood, Matt/Goose Creek Cons Ind Sch Dist	73,76,98	187
Florence, Joey/Denton Ind School Dist	6	120
Florence, Laurie/Hawley Ind School Dist	9	250
Flores-Jackson, Cordelia/United Ind School Dist	2	387
Flores, Adriana/Brady Ind School Dist	4	277
Flores, Alexandro/South San Antonio Ind Sch Dist	1	42
Flores, Anita/Plainview Ind School Dist	271	175
Flores, Barbara/Comfort Ind School Dist	2,11	254
Flores, Bernice/Spearman Ind School Dist	4	177
Flores, Daniel/Stafford Municipal Sch Dist	2	155
Flores, David/Alice Ind School Dist	2,19	245
Flores, David/Raymondville Ind Sch Dist	73	394
Flores, Edgwyna/Haskell Cons Ind School Dist	4	210
Flores, Erica/San Benito Cons Ind Sch Dist	5	66
Flores, Gilbert/Zapata Co Ind School Dist	73,76,84,286,295	406
Flores, Itza/Edcouch Elsa Ind School Dist	58	215
Flores, Javier/Uvalde Cons Ind School Dist	67	378
Flores, Jenny/Lubbock Ind School Dist	16	269
Flores, Jorge/La Joya Ind School Dist	27	219
Flores, Jose/La Joya Ind School Dist	11	219
Flores, Krystle/Alice Ind School Dist	4	245
Flores, Libby/San Benito Cons Ind Sch Dist	9	67
Flores, Lizzy/Diocese of Laredo Ed Office	2	388
Flores, Magdalena/Crystal City Ind School Dist	4	407
Flores, Marina/Grapevine-Colleyville Ind SD	79	353
Flores, Maritsa/Adrian Ind School Dist	8,288	307
Flores, Max/La Vernia Ind School Dist	68	401
Flores, Melinda/La Joya Ind School Dist	10	219
Flores, Monica/Pawnee Ind School Dist	4	25
Flores, Orlando/Fabens Ind School Dist	67	135
Flores, Patty/Rocksprings Ind School Dist	2	131
Flores, Raymond/Irion Co Ind School Dist	73,295	238
Flores, Rebecca/Zapata Co Ind School Dist	57	406
Flores, Rene/Houston Ind School Dist	285	188
Flores, Rick/Weslaco Ind School Dist	77,294	225
Flores, Robin/Kopperl Ind School Dist	76	47
Flores, Rosalinda/San Diego Ind School Dist	16	128
Flores, Rose/Seagraves Ind School Dist	57	157
Flores, Sandy/Rule Ind School Dist	2	210
Flores, Stephanie/Coppell Ind School Dist	58	98
Flores, Steve, Dr/Round Rock Ind School Dist	1	398
Flores, Vincinte/Irion Co Ind School Dist	67	238
Florez, Angela/Kermit Ind School Dist	79	401
Flournoy, Dale/Timpson Ind School Dist	73	335
Flower, Jenny/Groesbeck Ind School Dist	7	267
Flowers, David/Huntington Ind School Dist	1	17
Flowers, Lori/Bonham Ind School Dist	7	145
Floyd, Brittany/Gunter Ind School Dist	2	166
Floyd, Cheryl/Paint Creek Ind School Dist	1	210
Floyd, Jason/Calallen Ind School Dist	67	302
Floyd, Jennifer/Seagraves Ind School Dist	7,85	157
Floyd, Scott/White Oak Ind School Dist	73,295	171
Flusche, Darryl/Canyon Ind School Dist	1	320
Flynn, Jane/Cleburne Ind School Dist	286	247
Flynt, Sherri/Huntington Ind School Dist	38,69	17
Fogerson, Tracy/Lubbock-Cooper Ind Sch Dist	58	271
Fojtik, Katie/Edna Ind School Dist	7	239
Folds, Mark/Groveton Ind School Dist	67	374
Foley, Kelly/Lufkin Ind School Dist	76	18
Follmar, Ramon/Colmesneil Ind School Dist	5	375
Followwell, Kimberly/Murchison Ind Sch Dist	1,11,83	214

NAME/District	JOB FUNCTIONS	PAGE
Folmar, Annette/Prosper Ind School Dist	2,19	84
Folmar, Nicole/Boling Ind School Dist	7	389
Foltyn, Sharon/Ganado Ind School Dist	8,288	239
Fontenot, Dale/Port Neches-Groves Ind SD	71,91,295	243
Fontenot, Nicole/Jacksonville Ind School Dist	7	72
Foote, Carolyn/Eanes Ind School Dist	16	370
Foote, David/Wellman Union Ind School Dist	1,11	362
Forbes-Salazar, Robin/Plainview Ind School Dist	69,72,294	175
Forbes, Tiffany/Jim Hogg Co Ind School Dist	7	244
Ford, Arthur/Montgomery Ind School Dist	3	293
Ford, Bridget/Hitchcock Ind School Dist	5	161
Ford, Charae/Ore City Ind School Dist	33	377
Ford, Charlotte, Dr/Cedar Hill Ind School Dist	8	97
Ford, Cindy/Stamford Ind School Dist	35,85	250
Ford, Dan, Dr/Denton Ind School Dist	10	120
Ford, Denise/Paducah Ind School Dist	11,294,296	93
Ford, Jean/Liberty-Eylau Ind School Dist	57,271	48
Ford, Joan/Big Sandy Ind School Dist	4	376
Ford, Karen/Woodville Ind School Dist	11,288,298	375
Ford, Kathy/Wells Ind School Dist	31,34,36,57,83,85,88,270	73
Ford, Rick/Riesel Ind School Dist	286	281
Ford, Sandie/Boerne Ind School Dist	27	253
Ford, Scott/Elysian Fields Ind School Dist	6	208
Ford, Tara/Olton Ind School Dist	34	261
Ford, Tim/Lewisville Ind School Dist	6	122
Forehand, Jeannette/Abilene Ind School Dist	69,294	360
Foreman, Bonnie/Alvord Ind School Dist	8,69,83,270	402
Foreman, Patty/Sam Rayburn Ind School Dist	2,12	146
Foreman, Rick/Trenton Ind School Dist	1	146
Forester, Scott/Hurst-Euless-Bedford ISD	15,73,295	353
Forges, Rick/Irion Co Ind School Dist	3	238
Forman, Molly/Silverton Ind School Dist	67	57
Forney, Marcus/Huntsville Ind School Dist	15,36,83,88,270	383
Fornof, Kevin/Pasadena Ind School Dist	3,15	198
Forrest, Jeff/Pringle-Morse Cons ISD	6	177
Forrester, Andrew/Belton Ind School Dist	5	26
Forsyth, Alicia/Lefors Ind School Dist	8,11,57	165
Forsyth, Mark/Maud Ind School Dist	16,73,76,84,286,295	49
Forsyth, Skip/Pewitt Cons Ind School Dist	1	296
Forsythe, Sandra/Killeen Ind School Dist	79	27
Fortenberry, Jerry/Denver City Ind School Dist	27,73	405
Fortson, Keith/Caldwell Ind School Dist	4	59
Fortune, Walter/Galveston Ind School Dist	6,35	160
Forzano, Ernest/Archdiocese Galveston-Houston	67	203
Fostel, Joshua/Eula Ind School Dist	2,6,296	63
Fostel, Katie/Eula Ind School Dist	9,11,69,93,273	63
Foster, Angela/Onalaska Ind School Dist	2,84	317
Foster, Easy/Conroe Ind School Dist	3	291
Foster, Elton/Royal Ind School Dist	67	384
Foster, James/Haskell Cons Ind School Dist	9	210
Foster, Kevin/Big Sandy Ind School Dist	6	316
Foster, Lisa/Splendora Ind School Dist	71,93,274	294
Foster, Melisia/Mineola Ind School Dist	85	404
Foster, Mike/Montgomery Ind School Dist	5	293
Foster, Ron/Edgewood Ind School Dist	286	31
Foster, Sherree/Memphis Ind School Dist	4	175
Fouche, Melissa/Frisco Ind School Dist	73,76,98,295	78
Fouche, Todd/Frisco Ind School Dist	2,15	78
Fountain, Terra/Bridge City Ind School Dist	8,16,88,288,296	308
Fountain, Traci/Lindale Ind School Dist	7	337
Foust, Mark, Dr/Kerrville Ind School Dist	1	256
Fowler, Cynthia/Tomball Ind School Dist	295	203
Fowler, David/Dew Ind School Dist	67	156
Fowler, Don/Richland Springs Ind Sch Dist	1,11	332
Fowler, Ray/Throckmorton Ind School Dist	3,5	363
Fowler, Royce/Merkel Ind School Dist	3	361
Fowler, Timmy/Memphis Ind School Dist	67	175
Fowlkes, Katie/Marfa Ind School Dist	67	320
Fox, Allen/Monahans-Wickett-Pyote ISD	73,295,297	385
Fox, Allen/Monahans-Wickett-Pyote ISD	84	385
Fox, Barry/Arlington Ind School Dist	76	343
Fox, Christine/Pflugerville Ind School Dist	11	371
Fox, Cynthia/Guthrie Common School Dist	2	257
Fox, Jaime/Miller Grove Ind School Dist	9,57,69,271	231
Fox, Joyce/Fredericksburg Ind School Dist	4	162
Fox, Kelly/Ft Bend Ind School Dist	38	149

School Year 2019-2020   800-333-8802   TX-T29

DISTRICT PERSONNEL INDEX

Market Data Retrieval

NAME/District	JOB FUNCTIONS	PAGE
Fraga, Anthony/Socorro Ind School Dist	30	135
Frailey, Alton/Nacogdoches Ind School Dist	1,83	298
Frame, Charles/Maypearl Ind School Dist	67	141
Francis, Darren/Region 9 Ed Service Center	15,16,73	393
Francis, Leslie/Cypress-Fairbanks Ind Sch Dist	15,71	184
Francis, Michelle/Silverton Ind School Dist	8,11,31,68,69,74,88	57
Francis, Michelle/Silverton Ind School Dist	1,11	57
Franco, Eldon/Cherokee Ind School Dist	1,11,73,83,84	332
Franco, Jose/Ft Hancock Ind School Dist	1	234
Frando, Denise/Edcouch Elsa Ind School Dist	9,36	215
Frank, Anita/Beaumont Ind School Dist	15	241
Frank, Doug/Rockwall Ind School Dist	57	325
Frank, Glenn/Huntington Ind School Dist	2	17
Franke, Cami/Midway Ind School Dist	4	74
Frankenberg, Megan/Lovejoy Ind School Dist	52	80
Franklin, Brian/Kennedale Ind School Dist	295	355
Franklin, Chairita/Cypress-Fairbanks Ind Sch Dist	15,68	183
Franklin, Cindy/Seminole Ind School Dist	58	158
Franklin, Jennifer/Skidmore Tynan Ind SD	4	25
Franklin, Kendra/Plemons-Stinnett-Phillips CISD	36,88	238
Franklin, Kenn/New Caney Ind School Dist	1	293
Franklin, Pat, Dr/Carrollton-Farmers Branch ISD	9,93	96
Franklin, Ryan/Texas Dept of Education	74	1
Franklin, Treva, Dr/Mesquite Ind School Dist	8,11,15,34,83,88,93,296	110
Franklin, Walt/McMullen Co Ind Sch Dist	67	283
Franklin, Wyvetta/Navasota Ind School Dist	4	172
Franks, Kim/River Road Ind School Dist	7	319
Franks, Terri/Mansfield Ind School Dist	81	356
Frankum, Brian/Axtell Ind School Dist	67	278
Frary, Alison/Waxahachie Ind School Dist	47	142
Frasier, Scott/London Ind School Dist	67	305
Fratangelo, Lynn/Jefferson Ind School Dist	8,31,288	274
Frauenberger, Rick/Grapeland Ind School Dist	10	232
Frauenberger, Teri/Grapeland Ind School Dist	79	232
Frazee, Rick/Buffalo Ind School Dist	3	264
Frazier, Coy/Dallas Ind School Dist	3	98
Frazier, Darrell/Gatesville Ind School Dist	2,19	92
Frazier, Debra/Eula Ind School Dist	5	63
Frazier, Ken/Rule Ind School Dist	11,83	210
Frazier, Michael/Southwest Ind School Dist	67	43
Frazier, Pam/Covington ISD School Dist	2	227
Frazier, Stan/Barbers Hill Ind School Dist	3,5,15,91	72
Frederick, Kari/Joshua Ind School Dist	4	248
Free, Kim/Henderson Ind School Dist	76	327
Free, Stephanie/San Angelo Ind School Dist	11	364
Freeborg, Nanci/Dripping Springs Ind Sch Dist	4	210
Freed, Vanessa/Florence Ind School Dist	57	395
Freels, Kevin/Red Oak Ind School Dist	3,15	142
Freeman-Wright, Adellea/La Vernia Ind School Dist	4	401
Freeman, Angie/Dodd City Ind School Dist	13,31,36,69,77,88	145
Freeman, Anna/Lohn Ind School Dist	271	277
Freeman, Buddy/Midway Ind School Dist	3	280
Freeman, Cassie/London Ind School Dist	11	305
Freeman, Cathi/Olton Ind School Dist	7,85	261
Freeman, Clay/Henderson Ind School Dist	88,286	327
Freeman, Danny/Moran Ind School Dist	1,11	334
Freeman, David, Dr/Flour Bluff Ind School Dist	1	304
Freeman, David, Dr/London Ind School Dist	1	305
Freeman, Diana, Dr/Groesbeck Ind School Dist	8,11,83,88,288,296,298	267
Freeman, Jake/Roscoe Collegiate Ind Sch Dist	6	301
Freeman, Janet/Forney Ind School Dist	91	251
Freeman, Kim/Ore City Ind School Dist	88	377
Freeman, Kyle/Crockett Co Cons Common SD	6	94
Freeman, Lacy/Buffalo Ind School Dist	1,83	264
Freeman, Leon/Lohn Ind School Dist	1,83,84	277
Freeman, Lindsey/Roscoe Collegiate Ind Sch Dist	57	301
Freeman, Michael/Richardson Ind School Dist	92	112

NAME/District	JOB FUNCTIONS	PAGE
Freeman, Noreen/Alto Ind School Dist	58	72
Freeman, Shelley/Birdville Ind School Dist	2	346
Freeman, Steve/New Caney Ind School Dist	68	293
Freeman, Tonya/Liberty Ind School Dist	37	266
Freese, Carol/Coppell Ind School Dist	76	98
Frei, Dwayne/Troy Ind School Dist	83,88	29
Frei, Scott/Thorndale Ind School Dist	11,83	288
French, John/Kountze Ind School Dist	5	178
French, Micheal/Terrell Ind School Dist	1	253
French, Rebecca/Lexington Ind School Dist	8,11,74,271	263
French, Rebecca/Lexington Ind School Dist	273,288,296	263
Frerich, Michelle/Plains Ind School Dist	36	405
Frey, Matt/Plano Ind School Dist	73	82
Freytag, Chris/Flatonia Ind School Dist	6	147
Friar, Carlin/Boerne Ind School Dist	67	253
Frias, Holly/Garland Ind School Dist	4	105
Friday, Jamie/Texarkana Ind School Dist	8	50
Friddle, Amy/Como Pickton Cons Ind SD	57,73,76,271,286,288	231
Fried, Rita/Roscoe Collegiate Ind Sch Dist	2	301
Friel, Kris/Tulia Ind School Dist	84,295	343
Frierson, Amy/Texarkana Ind School Dist	43,46	50
Friese, Galadriel/San Antonio Ind School Dist	57	39
Friess, Kay/Sonora Ind School Dist	38	342
Fritsche, Charles/Dime Box Ind School Dist	67	263
Froneberger, Dan/Sulphur Springs Ind Sch Dist	3	232
Frossard, John, Dr/Beaumont Ind School Dist	1	241
Frost, Diane, Dr/Corsicana Ind School Dist	1	299
Fry, Brian/Palmer Ind School Dist	8,74,285,286,288	141
Fry, Matthew/Liberty-Eylau Ind School Dist	71	48
Fry, Robin/Lewisville Ind School Dist	35	122
Fryar, Bobby/Reagan Co Ind School Dist	1	321
Frye, Della/Midland Ind School Dist	34	285
Fryman, Kimberly/Mt Enterprise Ind School Dist	57	328
Fryrear, Sundy/Bryan Ind School Dist	4	54
Fuchs, Candace/Joshua Ind School Dist	2	248
Fuchs, Debbie/Clear Creek Ind School Dist	6,35	158
Fuchs, JB/Olfen Ind School Dist	67	327
Fuchs, Kristy/Glasscock Co Ind School Dist	2,11,296	163
Fuchs, Melinda/Burton Ind School Dist	8,12,69,88,270,288,296	386
Fudge, Barney/Texas Dept of Education	7,80,85,91	1
Fuenmayor, Susana, Dr/Pearland Ind School Dist	57	53
Fuentes, Lindsey/College Station Ind Sch Dist	58,77	55
Fullen, Steve, Dr/Pasadena Ind School Dist	15	198
Fuller, Christina/Teague Ind School Dist	57	156
Fuller, Daniel/Stockdale Ind School Dist	1	401
Fuller, Darrell/Idalou Ind School Dist	3	269
Fuller, Joye/Eula Ind School Dist	7	63
Fuller, Kim/Richardson Ind School Dist	11,298	112
Fuller, Margie/Grandview Ind School Dist	2,19	248
Fuller, Mike/Decatur Ind School Dist	6	403
Fuller, Ryan/Joaquin Ind School Dist	1	335
Fuller, Sancy/Lovejoy Ind School Dist	7,57,58	80
Fuller, Shannon/East Central Ind School Dist	8	31
Fullerton, Diane/Granbury Ind School Dist	58	230
Fulmer, Jeff/Brock Ind School Dist	5	312
Fulp, Shannon/Greenville Ind School Dist	73,76,295	236
Fulton, Cindy/Lorena Ind School Dist	7	280
Fulton, Elise/Diocese of Beaumont Sch Office	67	244
Fulton, Randy/Frost Ind School Dist	2	299
Funk, Karen/North East Ind School Dist	6	34
Fuqua, Barbara/Pasadena Ind School Dist	15,294	198
Fuqua, Bryan/Robinson Ind School Dist	73,84	281
Fuqua, Gayle/Kermit Ind School Dist	2	401
Furbush, Jane/Hunt Ind School Dist	7,83,85	255
Furgeson, Susan/Pampa Ind School Dist	58,81,88	165
Furlow, Lorin/Brazosport Ind School Dist	58,77,90,296	52
Furlow, Mike/Shelbyville Ind School Dist	69,273	335

1 Superintendent	16 Instructional Media Svcs	30 Adult Education	44 Science Sec	58 Special Education K-12	72 Summer School	88 Alternative/At Risk	277 Remedial Math K-12
2 Bus/Finance/Purchasing	17 Chief Operations Officer	31 Career/Sch-to-Work K-12	45 Math K-12	59 Special Education Elem	73 Instructional Tech	89 Multi-Cultural Curriculum	280 Literacy Coach
3 Buildings And Grounds	18 Chief Academic Officer	32 Career/Sch-to-Work Elem	46 Math Elem	60 Special Education Sec	74 Inservice Training	90 Social Work	285 STEM
4 Food Service	19 Chief Financial Officer	33 Career/Sch-to-Work Sec	47 Math Sec	61 Foreign/World Lang K-12	75 Marketing/Distributive	91 Safety/Security	286 Digital Learning
5 Transportation	20 Art K-12	34 Early Childhood Ed	48 English/Lang Arts K-12	62 Foreign/World Lang Elem	76 Info Systems	92 Magnet School	288 Common Core Standards
6 Athletic	21 Art Elem	35 Health/Phys Education	49 English/Lang Arts Elem	63 Foreign/World Lang Sec	77 Psychological Assess	93 Parental Involvement	294 Accountability
7 Health Services	22 Art Sec	36 Guidance Services K-12	50 English/Lang Arts Sec	64 Religious Education K-12	78 Affirmative Action	95 Tech Prep Program	295 Network System
8 Curric/Instruct K-12	23 Music K-12	37 Guidance Services Elem	51 Reading K-12	65 Religious Education Elem	79 Student Personnel	97 Chief Information Officer	296 Title II Programs
9 Curric/Instruct Elem	24 Music Elem	38 Guidance Services Sec	52 Reading Elem	66 Religious Education Sec	80 Driver Ed/Safety	98 Chief Technology Officer	297 Webmaster
10 Curric/Instruct Sec	25 Music Sec	39 Social Studies K-12	53 Reading Sec	67 School Board President	81 Gifted/Talented	270 Character Education	298 Grant Writer/Ptnrships
11 Federal Program	26 Business Education	40 Social Studies Elem	54 Remedial Reading K-12	68 Teacher Personnel	82 Video Services	271 Migrant Education	750 Chief Innovation Officer
12 Title I	27 Career & Tech Ed	41 Social Studies Sec	55 Remedial Reading Elem	69 Academic Assessment	83 Substance Abuse Prev	273 Teacher Mentor	751 Chief of Staff
13 Title V	28 Technology Education	42 Science K-12	56 Remedial Reading Sec	70 Research/Development	84 Erate	274 Before/After Sch	752 Social Emotional Learning
15 Asst Superintendent	29 Family/Consumer Science	43 Science Elem	57 Bilingual/ELL	71 Public Information	85 AIDS Education	275 Response To Intervention	

TX-T30

Texas School Directory — DISTRICT PERSONNEL INDEX

NAME/District	JOB FUNCTIONS	PAGE
Furr, Cindy/*Springlake-Earth Ind Sch Dist*	10,69,270	261
Furrh, Terry/*Fruitvale Ind School Dist*	57	380
Furry, Chris/*Blanket Ind School Dist*	67	58
Fussell, Cindy, Dr/*Region 5 Ed Service Center*	58	244

G

NAME/District	JOB FUNCTIONS	PAGE
Gabehart, Mark/*Round Rock Ind School Dist*	76	398
Gabriel, Nicole/*Region 18 Ed Service Center*	7,8,73,74,85	287
Gabrisch, Kelly/*Humble Ind School Dist*	68	195
Gace-DelGado, Alta/*Brazosport Ind School Dist*	57,89,93	52
Gaeta, Victoria/*Southwest Ind School Dist*	30	43
Gage, Dana/*Milano Ind School Dist*	4	287
Gage, Stephanie/*Milano Ind School Dist*	2,11	287
Gagne, Laurie/*Highland Park Ind Sch Dist*	58	108
Gaillard, Sahala/*Gruver Ind School Dist*	7	176
Gain, Kerry/*Comal Ind School Dist*	8,15	87
Gainer, Joee/*Everman Ind School Dist*	2,19	349
Gaines, Lashun/*Elgin Ind School Dist*	58	24
Gainey, Dan/*Colorado Ind School Dist*	6	289
Gaitan, John/*La Pryor Ind School Dist*	3,5,91	407
Gaitan, Nora/*Charlotte Ind School Dist*	2,11	20
Gajdica, Kendra/*Ferris Ind School Dist*	9	140
Gajewski, Mary/*Sealy Ind School Dist*	11,88,296	22
Galamore, Sherry/*Magnolia Ind School Dist*	42	292
Galan, Valerie/*Edgewood Ind School Dist*	88	31
Galaviz, April/*Canutillo Ind School Dist*	69,70,294	132
Galaviz, Pedro, Dr/*Canutillo Ind School Dist*	1	131
Galbreath, Charles/*Sanger Ind School Dist*	6	126
Galbreath, Ronnie/*Joshua Ind School Dist*	67	248
Galetti, Tracey/*Ganado Ind School Dist*	4	239
Galetti, Tracey/*Ganado Ind School Dist*	4	239
Galindo, Betty/*Edgewood Ind School Dist*	2	31
Galindo, Ray/*Northside Ind School Dist*	15	36
Galindo, Richard/*Balmorhea Ind School Dist*	73	323
Gallagher, Arlene/*Alvarado Ind School Dist*	58	246
Gallagher, Daniel/*Little Elm Ind School Dist*	1	124
Gallagos, Susan/*Freer Ind School Dist*	58	128
Gallant, Luann/*Trinity Ind School Dist*	2,11,74,84,296	374
Gallardo, Adrian/*Rankin Ind School Dist*	83,88	377
Gallardo, Elidia/*Rankin Ind School Dist*	11	377
Gallegos, Gloria/*Pasadena Ind School Dist*	11,15,57,271,274,296	198
Gallegos, Reina/*La Pryor Ind School Dist*	11,296	407
Gallegos, Robert/*San Elizario Ind School Dist*	7,35,83,91	135
Gallegos, Samantha/*Harlandale Ind School Dist*	1	32
Gallegos, Stephanie/*Tuloso-Midway Ind School Dist*	4	305
Galley, Sandra/*Detroit Ind School Dist*	4,79	322
Galligan, John/*Childress Ind School Dist*	73,295	74
Galloway, Steven/*Columbia Brazoria ISD*	1	52
Galm, Patricia/*Bandera Ind School Dist*	58	23
Galow, Troy, Dr/*Pflugerville Ind School Dist*	15,751	371
Galoway, Melissa/*Petersburg Ind School Dist*	10,69,83	175
Galvan, Adam/*Lockhart Ind School Dist*	15,73,76,271	61
Galvan, Bobby/*Ben Bolt-Palito Blanco ISD*	8,11,296,298	245
Galvan, Daniel/*Alice Ind School Dist*	5	245
Galvan, Manuel/*Ballinger Ind School Dist*	67	326
Galvan, Mike/*Tidehaven Ind School Dist*	5	276
Galvan, Nora/*Pharr-San Juan-Alamo Ind SD*	16	223
Galvan, Rosalinda/*Hidalgo Ind School Dist*	4	217
Galvan, Victor/*Aransas Pass Ind School Dist*	67	330
Galvin, Jacob/*Seguin Ind School Dist*	4	173
Gama, Joann/*Idea Public Schools*	1	217
Gamel, Merlina/*Mason Ind School Dist*	73	275
Gamell, Maria, Dr/*Eagle Mtn-Saginaw Ind Sch Dist*	68	348
Gamez, Art/*Beeville Ind School Dist*	91	25
Gamez, Laura/*San Antonio Ind School Dist*	48	39
Gamez, Manuel/*Pflugerville Ind School Dist*	20,23	371
Gamez, Stacy/*Meadow Ind School Dist*	34	362
Gammill, Staci/*Yantis Ind School Dist*	7	405
Gammon, Shelly/*Carrollton-Farmers Branch ISD*	297	96
Gandillon, Joe/*Howe Ind School Dist*	73,76,298	166
Gandy, Brian/*Douglass Ind School Dist*	8,57,271,273	297
Gandy, Misty/*Eden Cons Ind School Dist*	1	90
Gandy, Robin/*Martin's Mill Ind Sch Dist*	36,57,69,83,270	381
Gann, Angie/*Stamford Ind School Dist*	58	250
Gann, Cynthia/*Hondo Ind School Dist*	58,77	284
Gann, Linda/*Boerne Ind School Dist*	45	253

NAME/District	JOB FUNCTIONS	PAGE
Ganske, Sheri/*Wharton Ind School Dist*	73,297	390
Garakani, Leslie/*Midlothian Ind School Dist*	73,98	141
Garay, Javier/*Fabens Ind School Dist*	3,5	135
Garcia, Able/*Balmorhea Ind School Dist*	57	323
Garcia, Adriana/*Pharr-San Juan-Alamo Ind SD*	8,16,27,31,73,82	223
Garcia, Aidee/*San Felipe-Del Rio Cons Ind SD*	68	379
Garcia, Alma, Dr/*Alice Ind School Dist*	11,57,270,296	245
Garcia, Amanda/*Poteet Ind School Dist*	2,3	21
Garcia, Angela/*Floresville Ind School Dist*	88,274	400
Garcia, Anna/*Refugio Ind School Dist*	16,82	323
Garcia, Arturo/*Robstown Ind School Dist*	6	305
Garcia, Becky/*La Pryor Ind School Dist*	2	407
Garcia, Blanca, Dr/*El Paso Ind School Dist*	15	132
Garcia, Blanca, Dr/*El Paso ISD-Elementary*	15	133
Garcia, Bob/*Tatum Ind School Dist*	3,5	328
Garcia, Carlos/*Tornillo Ind School Dist*	73,76	137
Garcia, Carmen/*Edcouch Elsa Ind School Dist*	11,296	215
Garcia, Cassandra/*Schertz-Cibolo-Univ City ISD*	31,36	173
Garcia, Charlie/*Mission Cons Ind School Dist*	67	222
Garcia, Charmaine/*Stafford Municipal Sch Dist*	11,58,275	155
Garcia, Cindy, Dr/*Driscoll Ind School Dist*	1	304
Garcia, Conrado/*West Oso Ind School Dist*	1	306
Garcia, Dalia/*Harlingen Cons Ind School Dist*	294	64
Garcia, Dalia/*Southwest Ind School Dist*	8	43
Garcia, Daniel/*Harlingen Cons Ind School Dist*	58	64
Garcia, Daniel/*Rio Grande City Ind Sch Dist*	67	340
Garcia, Danny/*Ft Worth Ind School Dist*	91	349
Garcia, David/*Hurst-Euless-Bedford ISD*	2,15	353
Garcia, David/*San Benito Cons Ind Sch Dist*	3	66
Garcia, David/*United Ind School Dist*	15,68	387
Garcia, Denise/*San Marcos Cons Ind Sch Dist*	2	211
Garcia, Diana/*Wharton Ind School Dist*	7	390
Garcia, Donna/*Monahans-Wickett-Pyote ISD*	67	385
Garcia, Edgar/*El Paso Ind School Dist*	91	132
Garcia, Edna/*Plainview Ind School Dist*	11,57,93,271	175
Garcia, Elda, Dr/*Corpus Christi Ind Sch Dist*	69,294	303
Garcia, Eloy/*Hidalgo Ind School Dist*	73,76,84,295	217
Garcia, Erica/*Hale Center Ind School Dist*	4	175
Garcia, Erica/*Weslaco Ind School Dist*	93	225
Garcia, Francis/*Boerne Ind School Dist*	54	253
Garcia, Grace/*Alice Ind School Dist*	58	245
Garcia, Gregorio, Dr/*Brownsville Ind School Dist*	298	63
Garcia, Hector/*Laredo Ind School Dist*	67	386
Garcia, Ismael/*Rio Hondo Ind School Dist*	1	66
Garcia, Jacob/*Waelder Ind School Dist*	6	164
Garcia, Javier/*Rio Grande City Ind Sch Dist*	91	340
Garcia, Jennifer/*Banquete Ind School Dist*	58,77	302
Garcia, Jerry/*Kenedy Ind School Dist*	3,91	251
Garcia, Jesse/*Santa Gertrudis Ind Sch Dist*	67	258
Garcia, Joe/*Dalhart Ind School Dist*	3	95
Garcia, Joe/*Stamford Ind School Dist*	3,91	250
Garcia, Jose/*Pharr-San Juan-Alamo Ind SD*	76,295	223
Garcia, Jose/*Sharyland Ind School Dist*	67	224
Garcia, Joshua/*Mansfield Ind School Dist*	57	356
Garcia, Josie/*South Texas Ind School Dist*	58	67
Garcia, Juana/*Bryan Ind School Dist*	271	54
Garcia, Juana/*Hartley Ind School Dist*	271,273	209
Garcia, Judith/*United Ind School Dist*	73	387
Garcia, Karl/*Freer Ind School Dist*	73,84,295	128
Garcia, Kim/*Georgetown Ind School Dist*	286	395
Garcia, Krista/*Northside Ind School Dist*	58	36
Garcia, Larry/*McMullen Co Ind Sch Dist*	3,5	283
Garcia, Lawrence/*Beeville Ind School Dist*	73,84	25
Garcia, Liodolee/*Killeen Ind School Dist*	57,271	27
Garcia, Lorena/*Bishop Cons Ind School Dist*	27,75	302
Garcia, Lupe/*Weslaco Ind School Dist*	5	225
Garcia, Magdalena/*Channelview Ind School Dist*	57	183
Garcia, Manuel/*Roma Ind School Dist*	76	341
Garcia, Maria/*East Chambers Ind School Dist*	57	72
Garcia, Mario/*Eagle Pass Ind School Dist*	4	276
Garcia, Marty/*Moody Ind School Dist*	6	281
Garcia, Melissa/*Channing Ind School Dist*	58	209
Garcia, Miguel/*Ft Worth Ind School Dist*	274	349
Garcia, Monica/*Judson Ind School Dist*	36	33
Garcia, Norma/*Harlingen Cons Ind School Dist*	57	64
Garcia, Olga/*Harlingen Cons Ind School Dist*	76	64

DISTRICT PERSONNEL INDEX

Market Data Retrieval

NAME/District	JOB FUNCTIONS	PAGE
Garcia, Orlando/Pharr-San Juan-Alamo Ind SD	6	223
Garcia, Oscar/Brownsville Ind School Dist	91	63
Garcia, Paula/Slaton Ind School Dist	4	272
Garcia, Robert/Del Valle Ind School Dist	294	369
Garcia, Robert/Maypearl Ind School Dist	3,5,91	141
Garcia, Robin/Plano Ind School Dist	274	82
Garcia, Rogelio/Laredo Ind School Dist	27,31	386
Garcia, Rogelio/Laredo Ind School Dist	27,31	386
Garcia, Roy/Cypress-Fairbanks Ind Sch Dist	15	184
Garcia, Samuel/Socorro Ind School Dist	2	135
Garcia, Sergio/Weslaco Ind School Dist	15	225
Garcia, Sharla/Waco Ind School Dist	298	281
Garcia, Shelly/Crane Ind School Dist	58	93
Garcia, Sue/Barbers Hill Ind School Dist	34,58,77	72
Garcia, Tasha/Seminole Ind School Dist	69	158
Garcia, Victor/North East Ind School Dist	298	34
Garcie, Kelye/Port Aransas Ind School Dist	9	305
Gardea, Margarita/Houston Ind School Dist	9	188
Gardenhire, Jay/Hondo Ind School Dist	67	284
Gardner, Chad/College Station Ind Sch Dist	30,274	55
Gardner, Heidi/Brownwood Ind School Dist	11,31,57,88,285,296	58
Gardner, Rick/Humble Ind School Dist	15,68,78,273	195
Gardner, Robin/Junction Ind School Dist	38,83,85,270	256
Gardner, Roy/Angleton Ind School Dist	16,27,31,88	51
Gardner, Sheila/Wolfe City Ind School Dist	8,73,286,288	237
Gardzina, Margaret/Liberty Ind School Dist	8,11	266
Gargg, Kasey/Central Ind School Dist	2	17
Garibay, Cornelio/Culberson Co Allamoore Ind SD	5	95
Garica, Dimitrio/Kenedy Ind School Dist	67	251
Garis, Chris/Aransas Co Ind School Dist	295	19
Garland, Diane/Cypress-Fairbanks Ind Sch Dist	8,16	183
Garland, Shay/Magnolia Ind School Dist	48	292
Garlic, John/Weslaco Ind School Dist	11	225
Garlock, Steve/Iraan-Sheffield Ind Sch Dist	67	316
Garner, Brian/Whitewright Ind School Dist	1	168
Garner, Ray/United Ind School Dist	3,17,91	387
Garnett, Mark, Dr/Spearman Ind School Dist	67	177
Garrett, James/Jarrell Ind School Dist	2	396
Garrett, Joel/Lamar Cons Ind School Dist	27,31,286	153
Garrett, Matthew/Lewisville Ind School Dist	91	122
Garrett, Pat/Walnut Springs Ind Sch Dist	1,11,84	47
Garrett, Robin/Paradise Ind School Dist	37	403
Garrett, Shelley, Dr/Mesquite Ind School Dist	91	110
Garrison, Todd/Kaufman Ind School Dist	2,19	252
Gartrell, Louise/Garland Ind School Dist	35	105
Gartrell, Lucretia/Burleson Ind School Dist	36,58	246
Garvey, Nancy/Coppell Ind School Dist	73,286	98
Garvey, Tonya/Carrollton-Farmers Branch ISD	47	96
Garvin, Amber/Crowell Ind School Dist	48	149
Garvin, Matt/Quanah Ind School Dist	6	177
Gary, Staci/Port Neches-Groves Ind SD	9,57	243
Garza-Viator, Angela/La Porte Ind School Dist	68	198
Garza-Viator, Angela/La Porte Ind School Dist	68,78	198
Garza, Andrea/La Joya Ind School Dist	58,77	219
Garza, Angelica/Edgewood Ind School Dist	76	31
Garza, Anjanett/McAllen Ind School Dist	11	221
Garza, Anthony, Dr/Edinburg Cons Ind School Dist	10	216
Garza, Arnold/Alice Ind School Dist	23	245
Garza, Brandon/Magnolia Ind School Dist	11,36,275,294	292
Garza, Clem/La Joya Ind School Dist	73,84	219
Garza, Daniel/Cotulla Ind School Dist	73	259
Garza, Deborah/Sharyland Ind School Dist	68	224
Garza, Elena/Edcouch Elsa Ind School Dist	4	215
Garza, Emily/Pharr-San Juan-Alamo Ind SD	2	223
Garza, Estella/San Antonio Ind School Dist	90	39
Garza, Geneva/Eden Cons Ind School Dist	36,57,69,83,270	90
Garza, Gilbert/Edinburg Cons Ind School Dist	1	216

NAME/District	JOB FUNCTIONS	PAGE
Garza, Grace/Dilley Ind School Dist	4	157
Garza, Juan/Tomball Ind School Dist	68	203
Garza, Judy/Skidmore Tynan Ind SD	270	25
Garza, Larry/San Antonio Ind School Dist	2,19	39
Garza, Leslie/Woodsboro Ind School Dist	9,11	324
Garza, Liz/Ballinger Ind School Dist	2	326
Garza, Luis/Roma Ind School Dist	15,68,83,273	341
Garza, Marie/La Villa Ind School Dist	4	220
Garza, Marisa/San Isidro Ind School Dist	36,88	341
Garza, Mark/Milford Ind School Dist	3	141
Garza, Mary/Brownsville Ind School Dist	2,19	63
Garza, Melissa/Knippa Ind School Dist	8,12,298	378
Garza, Mirella/Edinburg Cons Ind School Dist	43	216
Garza, Monika/Ricardo Ind School Dist	69,88,270	257
Garza, Nancy/Mercedes Ind School Dist	4	221
Garza, Nathaniel/San Perlita Ind School Dist	6	394
Garza, Neil/Weslaco Ind School Dist	58	225
Garza, Noemie/Ricardo Ind School Dist	4	257
Garza, Ray/D'Hanis Ind School Dist	3	283
Garza, Ray/Lasara Ind School Dist	16,73,295	394
Garza, Rebecca/Pharr-San Juan-Alamo Ind SD	68	223
Garza, Roel/Banquete Ind School Dist	27	302
Garza, Rogelio/Edinburg Cons Ind School Dist	6,35	216
Garza, Rolando/San Isidro Ind School Dist	6	341
Garza, Romeo/Pharr-San Juan-Alamo Ind SD	91	223
Garza, Sandra/Edcouch Elsa Ind School Dist	69	215
Garza, Sara/Brownsville Ind School Dist	36	63
Garza, Senaida/Lyford Cons Ind School Dist	11,58,76	394
Garza, Susana, Dr/Jim Hogg Co Ind School Dist	1	244
Garza, Sylvia/Edcouch Elsa Ind School Dist	2	215
Garza, Traci/Seagraves Ind School Dist	2	157
Garza, Velma/Rio Grande City Ind Sch Dist	1	340
Garza, Veronica/Mathis Ind School Dist	58	331
Garza, Victor/La Joya Ind School Dist	6	219
Gasaway, Chris/Grand Prairie Ind School Dist	98	107
Gasaway, Jeff/Marble Falls Ind School Dist	2,15	60
Gasiorowski, Mike/Friendswood Ind Sch Dist	76	160
Gaskamp, Collin/Blanco Ind School Dist	73	45
Gaskins, Gretchen/Alief Ind School Dist	39	181
Gaspard, James/Kirbyville Cons Ind Sch Dist	16,73,295	241
Gass, Kim/Plains Ind School Dist	16	405
Gassman, Melissa/Prosper Ind School Dist	57	84
Gast, Stephanie/Millsap Ind School Dist	7	312
Gaston, Jeremy/Hearne Ind School Dist	16,73,82,295	325
Gaston, Jill/Wells Ind School Dist	275	73
Gatell, Jason/North East Ind School Dist	16	34
Gates, Cristy/Sheldon Ind School Dist	3,17	200
Gates, Ginger, Dr/Region 4 Ed Service Center	58	208
Gates, R J/Burnet Cons Ind Sch Dist	9,11,16,27,57,83,296,298	60
Gates, Simeon/Bryan Ind School Dist	5	54
Gates, Theresa/Rusk Ind School Dist	45,69,83,91,275	73
Gatewood, Kellie/Cayuga Ind School Dist	2	14
Gatlin, Winston/Southwest Ind School Dist	4	43
Gau, Tim/Littlefield Ind School Dist	73,84,295	260
Gaudette, Philip/East Bernard Ind Sch Dist	9,273	389
Gauntt, Debbie/Coppell Ind School Dist	275	98
Gausemeier, Valerie/Rosebud-Lott Ind School Dist	2	145
Gauthier, Jennifer/Orangefield Ind School Dist	73,76,84,295	309
Gauthier, Julie/Port Neches-Groves Ind SD	15,296	243
Gavina, Yolanda/Hereford Ind School Dist	11,83,271,274	119
Gaw, Kathy/Hallsville Ind School Dist	26,27,29,75,95	208
Gay, Joy/San Angelo Ind School Dist	27,31	364
Gay, Richard/Spring Branch Ind School Dist	2	200
Gayle, James/Angleton Ind School Dist	91	51
Gaylord, Angie/Dallas Ind School Dist	74	98
Gaynor, Arlena/Dallas Ind School Dist	48,51	98
Gazaway, Debbie/Neches Ind School Dist	58	15

---

1 Superintendent	16 Instructional Media Svcs	30 Adult Education	44 Science Sec	58 Special Education K-12	72 Summer School	88 Alternative/At Risk	277 Remedial Math K-12
2 Bus/Finance/Purchasing	17 Chief Operations Officer	31 Career/Sch-to-Work K-12	45 Math K-12	59 Special Education Elem	73 Instructional Tech	89 Multi-Cultural Curriculum	280 Literacy Coach
3 Buildings And Grounds	18 Chief Academic Officer	32 Career/Sch-to-Work Elem	46 Math Elem	60 Special Education Sec	74 Inservice Training	90 Social Work	285 STEM
4 Food Service	19 Chief Financial Officer	33 Career/Sch-to-Work Sec	47 Math Sec	61 Foreign/World Lang K-12	75 Marketing/Distributive	91 Safety/Security	286 Digital Learning
5 Transportation	20 Art K-12	34 Early Childhood Ed	48 English/Lang Arts K-12	62 Foreign/World Lang Elem	76 Info Systems	92 Magnet School	288 Common Core Standards
6 Athletic	21 Art Elem	35 Health/Phys Education	49 English/Lang Arts Elem	63 Foreign/World Lang Sec	77 Psychological Assess	93 Parental Involvement	294 Accountability
7 Health Services	22 Art Sec	36 Guidance Services K-12	50 English/Lang Arts Sec	64 Religious Education K-12	78 Affirmative Action	95 Tech Prep Program	295 Network System
8 Curric/Instruct K-12	23 Music K-12	37 Guidance Services Elem	51 Reading K-12	65 Religious Education Elem	79 Student Personnel	97 Chief Information Officer	296 Title II Programs
9 Curric/Instruct Elem	24 Music Elem	38 Guidance Services Sec	52 Reading Elem	66 Religious Education Sec	80 Driver Ed/Safety	98 Chief Technology Officer	297 Webmaster
10 Curric/Instruct Sec	25 Music Sec	39 Social Studies K-12	53 Reading Sec	67 School Board President	81 Gifted/Talented	270 Character Education	298 Grant Writer/Ptnrships
11 Federal Program	26 Business Education	40 Social Studies Elem	54 Remedial Reading K-12	68 Teacher Personnel	82 Video Services	271 Migrant Education	750 Chief Innovation Officer
12 Title I	27 Career & Tech Ed	41 Social Studies Sec	55 Remedial Reading Elem	69 Academic Assessment	83 Substance Abuse Prev	273 Teacher Mentor	751 Chief of Staff
13 Title V	28 Technology Education	42 Science K-12	56 Remedial Reading Sec	70 Research/Development	84 Erate	274 Before/After Sch	752 Social Emotional Learning
15 Asst Superintendent	29 Family/Consumer Science	43 Science Elem	57 Bilingual/ELL	71 Public Information	85 AIDS Education	275 Response To Intervention	

Texas School Directory — DISTRICT PERSONNEL INDEX

NAME/District	JOB FUNCTIONS	PAGE
Gazlick, Donna/*Wolfe City Ind School Dist*	88	237
Geans, Phyllis/*Port Arthur Ind School Dist*	2,15	243
Gearing, Bruce/*Dripping Springs Ind Sch Dist*	1	210
Gearing, Bruce, Dr/*Leander Ind School Dist*	1	396
Gebhard, Gerry/*Utopia Ind School Dist*	57	378
Gee, Chad/*Kennedale Ind School Dist*	1	355
Geer, Richard/*Forney Ind School Dist*	7,88,270	251
Gelardi, Scott/*El Campo Ind School Dist*	4	389
Genella, Laura/*Sweeny Ind School Dist*	52	54
Gentry, Judy/*Granbury Ind School Dist*	27	230
Geobel, Paul/*Hardin Jefferson Ind Sch Dist*	73	177
George, Abraham/*Sheldon Ind School Dist*	2,19	200
George, Bobby/*Detroit Ind School Dist*	5	322
George, Catherine, Dr/*Bryan Ind School Dist*	58	54
George, Catherine, Dr/*Region 6 Ed Service Center*	58	384
George, Chad/*Kirbyville Cons Ind Sch Dist*	67	241
George, Debra/*Elgin Ind School Dist*	2,19	24
George, Dusty/*Tulia Ind School Dist*	3	343
George, Elaine/*Lorena Ind School Dist*	5	280
George, Lee/*Buffalo Ind School Dist*	5	264
George, Leslie/*Tyler Ind School Dist*	34,58	337
George, Ranjan/*Carroll Independent Sch Dist*	5	347
George, Sonya/*Galena Park Ind School Dist*	2,15,19	186
George, Vickie/*London Ind School Dist*	2,4	305
Gerber, Francis/*Southwest Ind School Dist*	11	43
Gerber, K'Lynn/*Nazareth Ind School Dist*	2	71
Gerber, Sherry/*Hico Ind School Dist*	73	176
Gerhart, Linda/*Barbers Hill Ind School Dist*	11,57,271,298	72
Gerlach, Christine/*Ysleta Ind School Dist*	2	137
Gerlich, Bryan/*Grapevine-Colleyville Ind SD*	6	353
Gertson, Connie/*Rice Cons Ind School Dist*	16	87
Gertson, Ralph/*Rice Cons Ind School Dist*	73,295	87
Geske, Bob/*El Paso Ind School Dist*	67	132
Geske, Lindsey/*Sonora Ind School Dist*	16	342
Getwood, Melvin, Dr/*Port Arthur Ind School Dist*	10,11,15,36,288,298	243
Geye, Susan/*Everman Ind School Dist*	16,73,286,295	349
Gholson, James/*Karnack Ind School Dist*	2	208
Gholson, Theresa/*Hamlin Ind School Dist*	3,5	249
Giacona, Wanna, Dr/*Galena Park Ind School Dist*	15,68	186
Gibbons, Matthew, Dr/*Richardson Ind School Dist*	79,83	112
Gibbons, Tim/*Tulia Ind School Dist*	5	343
Gibbs, Christopher/*Forney Ind School Dist*	3	251
Gibbs, Lendsey/*Aubrey Ind School Dist*	3	120
Gibbs, Lisa/*Leander Ind School Dist*	68	396
Gibbs, Lynn/*Sam Rayburn Ind School Dist*	67	146
Gibbs, Terry/*Winona Ind School Dist*	3	339
Gibbs, Tony/*Chapel Hill Ind School Dist*	295	337
Gibson, Brian/*New Braunfels Ind School Dist*	5,91	88
Gibson, Brian/*Wink Loving Ind School Dist*	6	402
Gibson, Cody/*Valley Mills Ind School Dist*	3,91	47
Gibson, Greg, Dr/*Schertz-Cibolo-Univ City ISD*	1	173
Gibson, Gwen/*Ft Elliott Cons Ind Sch Dist*	2	390
Gibson, Heath/*Hermleigh Ind School Dist*	73	333
Gibson, Jerry, Dr/*Marshall Ind School Dist*	1	209
Gibson, Josh/*Pleasant Grove Ind School Dist*	6	49
Gibson, Justin/*Jayton-Girard Ind School Dist*	58	255
Gibson, Kittie/*Wink Loving Ind School Dist*	8	402
Gibson, Lesa/*Hawkins Ind School Dist*	4	404
Gibson, Mary/*San Vicente Ind School Dist*	67	57
Gibson, Oteka/*North East Ind School Dist*	83	34
Gibson, Robert/*Schleicher Co Ind Sch Dist*	1,11	333
Gibson, Ron/*Loraine Ind School Dist*	67	289
Gibson, Sharon/*Fairfield Ind School Dist*	2	156
Gibson, Sharon/*Florence Ind School Dist*	11,58,296	395
Giddens, Leigh/*Dallas Co Schools*	5	95
Gidst-Barrow, Michelle/*Venus Ind School Dist*	58	249
Giesenschlag, Missi/*Cameron Ind School Dist*	2	287
Gifford, Candy/*Palacios Ind School Dist*	4	275
Gifford, Howard/*Comanche Ind School Dist*	3	89
Gilber, Nathan/*Centerville Ind School Dist*	3	264
Gilbert, Amy/*Granbury Ind School Dist*	69,77	230
Gilbert, Greg/*Santo Ind School Dist*	1	310
Gilbert, James/*Guthrie Common School Dist*	3	257
Gilbert, Kathy/*Peaster Ind School Dist*	58	313
Gilbert, Michael/*White Oak Ind School Dist*	1	171
Gilbert, Tammy/*Brookeland Ind School Dist*	81	240
Gilbert, Tim/*Pecos-Barstow-Toyah Ind SD*	3	323
Gilbreath, Kim/*Westwood Ind School Dist*	7,85	16
Gilbreath, Phillip, Dr/*Garland Ind School Dist*	27,31	105
Gilchrist, Leslie/*Lovelady Ind School Dist*	36,280	233
Gilchrist, Scott/*Shelbyville Ind School Dist*	73	335
Gilcrease, Greg/*Navarro Ind School Dist*	67	173
Gildon, Brad/*Pleasant Grove Ind School Dist*	295	49
Giles, Michael/*Needville Ind School Dist*	6	154
Gilham, Shawn/*Hubbard Ind School Dist*	67	227
Gililland, Corey/*McKinney Ind School Dist*	3	80
Gill, Mary/*Crosby Ind School Dist*	46	183
Gill, Roy/*Hermleigh Ind School Dist*	67	333
Gill, Sara/*Jacksonville Ind School Dist*	58	73
Gilleland, Shea/*Sabinal Ind School Dist*	4	378
Gillen, Jo/*Carrollton-Farmers Branch ISD*	27,31,36,69,77,83,88,270	96
Gillentine, Clay/*New Braunfels Ind School Dist*	79	88
Gillespie, Kathy/*Motley Co Ind School Dist*	69	296
Gillespie, Teresa/*Troup Ind School Dist*	4	337
Gilley, April/*Milford Ind School Dist*	2	141
Gilliam, Gwen/*West Rusk Co Cons Ind Sch Dist*	11,16,69,271,296,298	328
Gilliam, Jeff/*McKinney Ind School Dist*	76	81
Gilliland, Katie/*Irving Ind School Dist*	68	109
Gilliland, Penny/*Devers Ind School Dist*	73	265
Gillis, Jason/*Everman Ind School Dist*	5	349
Gillis, Stacey/*Brookeland Ind School Dist*	8,31,36,69,92,271	240
Gilman, Karen/*Diocese of Beaumont Sch Office*	71	244
Gilmore, Cliff/*Perrin-Whitt Cons Ind Sch Dist*	1	239
Gilmore, Dianna/*Perrin-Whitt Cons Ind Sch Dist*	36	239
Gilmore, Felita/*Texarkana Ind School Dist*	286	50
Gilmore, Michele/*Burnet Cons Ind Sch Dist*	68	60
Gilmore, Shamedria/*Grapeland Ind School Dist*	4	232
Gilmore, Tiffany/*Garland Ind School Dist*	36	105
Gilmore, Vhonda/*Killeen Ind School Dist*	7	27
Gilpin, Heather/*Channelview Ind School Dist*	9	183
Gilse, Bill/*Saltillo Ind School Dist*	6	231
Gilsillian, Tammie/*East Chambers Ind School Dist*	69,270	72
Gilstrap, Jason/*Ennis Ind School Dist*	3,15,68	140
Giniewicz, Beth/*Temple Ind School Dist*	9	29
Gipson, Mike/*Longview Ind School Dist*	3	169
Girard, Daniel/*San Antonio Ind School Dist*	15	39
Girley, Lakeisha/*Pleasant Grove Ind School Dist*	7	49
Gish, Carole/*Boerne Ind School Dist*	7	253
Gisler, Larry/*Henrietta Ind School Dist*	5	74
Gist, Dan/*Pilot Point Ind School Dist*	1	125
Givens, Cindy/*Happy Ind School Dist*	58	342
Givins, Tanya/*Motley Co Ind School Dist*	58	296
Glad, Leslie/*Cayuga Ind School Dist*	4	14
Gladden, Amy/*Kennard Ind Sch Dist*	31,69	233
Glaeser, Patricia/*Channelview Ind School Dist*	11,286,288,294,296,298	183
Glaesmann, Mary-Lou/*Midway Ind School Dist*	68,273	280
Glancy, David/*Gainesville Ind School Dist*	10	91
Glaser, Jeff/*Ector Ind School Dist*	295	146
Glass, Nolan/*Dew Ind School Dist*	2	156
Glasscock, Lisa/*Wall Ind School Dist*	4	365
Glawe, Kim/*Temple Ind School Dist*	7	29
Glaze, Mike/*Sundown Ind School Dist*	16,73	229
Gleaton, Terry/*Sanger Ind School Dist*	5	126
Glenewinkel, Chuck/*College Station Ind Sch Dist*	71	55
Glenn, Dennis/*Harmony Ind School Dist*	1,83	376
Glenn, Jamie/*Riesel Ind School Dist*	8,11,73,288,296	281
Glenn, Jeremy, Dr/*Granbury Ind School Dist*	1	230
Glenn, Leah/*Troy Ind School Dist*	5	29
Glenn, Melissa, Dr/*Kennedale Ind School Dist*	8,11,57,68,88,294,296,298	355
Glenn, Missy, Dr/*Palacios Ind School Dist*	1	275
Glerkey, Micah/*Northwest Ind School Dist*	58	124
Glick, Mark/*Highland Park Ind School Dist*	83,91	319
Glidewell, Michele/*Alba-Golden Ind School Dist*	9	404
Glinski, Robert/*Waco Ind School Dist*	39	281
Gloria, Olivia/*Benjamin Ind School Dist*	1,11,83,84,288	258
Glos, Kelly/*Lewisville Ind School Dist*	41	122
Glosson, Sharon/*North East Ind School Dist*	4	34
Glover, Ashley, Dr/*Little Elm Ind School Dist*	8	124
Glover, Danny/*Ingleside Ind School Dist*	79	331
Glover, Jason/*Mt Vernon Ind School Dist*	31	155
Glover, Margo/*London Ind School Dist*	93	305
Glover, Rebbeca/*Brady Ind School Dist*	31,38	277

DISTRICT PERSONNEL INDEX

Market Data Retrieval

NAME/District	JOB FUNCTIONS	PAGE
Glover, Tim/Tulia Ind School Dist	1	343
Goad, Dave/Christoval Ind School Dist	3	364
Goad, Less/Navarro Ind School Dist	6	173
Gobblin, Bill/Newton Ind School Dist	58,88	301
Gober, Courtney, Dr/San Antonio Ind School Dist	15	39
Gobert, Kathy/Colmesneil Ind School Dist	16,73,295	375
Goble, Charlie/Burnet Cons Ind Sch Dist	3	60
Goddard, Michael, Dr/Lovejoy Ind School Dist	1	80
Godeaux, Marion/Texas City Ind School Dist	3	161
Godfrey, Reca/Early Ind School Dist	8,11,36,57,83	58
Godfrey, Remy/Marlin Ind School Dist	1	144
Godwin, Sharon/Iowa Park Consolidated Ind SD	2,11,19,298	392
Goehring, Clay/Burnet Cons Ind Sch Dist	2	60
Goen, Joshua/Seagraves Ind School Dist	1,11,83	157
Goen, Liz/Princeton Ind School Dist	34,58,88	84
Goerke, Brad/Lake Travis Ind School Dist	2	370
Goerner, Brent/Region 10 Ed Service Center	73,98	116
Goerner, Kathleen/Humble Ind School Dist	44	195
Goetzel, Alton/Orange Grove Ind School Dist	3,5	245
Goff, Mikayle/Bland Ind School Dist	11	235
Goff, Robin/Grand Saline Ind School Dist	31,274	380
Goffney, Latonya, Dr/Aldine Ind School Dist	1	179
Goffney, Melody, Dr/Region 4 Ed Service Center	68	208
Gohnert, Brenda/Goliad Ind School Dist	4	163
Gold, Deanie/Caldwell Ind School Dist	83,85	59
Golden, Melinda/Georgetown Ind School Dist	8,15,275	395
Goldhorn, Jeff, Dr/Region 20 Ed Service Center	1	45
Goldhorn, Veronica/Schertz-Cibolo-Univ City ISD	9	173
Golding, Malene/Houston Ind School Dist	280	188
Goleman, Kathy/Quinlan Ind School Dist	75	237
Goloms, Corey, Dr/Ft Worth Ind School Dist	58	349
Golson, Ronnie/McCamey Ind School Dist	1	377
Gombert, Liana/Comal Ind School Dist	6	87
Gomez, Aida/San Felipe-Del Rio Cons Ind SD	8	379
Gomez, Christine, Dr/Aldine ISD-Primary Team	15	181
Gomez, Cruz/Buena Vista Ind School Dist	67	315
Gomez, Dan/San Benito Cons Ind Sch Dist	6	66
Gomez, Fabian/Water Valley Ind School Dist	1,83	365
Gomez, Jason, Dr/Terrell Ind School Dist	15	253
Gomez, Maria/Ft Stockton Ind School Dist	2	315
Gomez, Raul/Laredo Ind School Dist	58	386
Gomez, Robert/Edgewood Ind School Dist	6,35	31
Gomez, Rogelio/La Joya Ind School Dist	44	219
Gomez, Rolando/Waco Ind School Dist	3	281
Gomez, Talle/Plano Ind School Dist	57	82
Gomez, Velma/Yoakum Ind School Dist	4	118
Gomez, Yolanda/Pharr-San Juan-Alamo Ind SD	271	223
Gonazales, Alicia/Sundown Ind School Dist	4	229
Gongora, Elizabeth/Sharyland Ind School Dist	57	224
Gonzales, Adam/Poteet Ind School Dist	295	21
Gonzales, Alberto, Dr/Carrizo Spgs Cons Ind SD	1	127
Gonzales, Angela/Rio Vista Ind School Dist	58	248
Gonzales, Carla, Dr/El Paso Ind School Dist	15	132
Gonzales, Carla, Dr/El Paso ISD-High Schools	15	134
Gonzales, Chayo/Alpine Ind School Dist	3,5	56
Gonzales, Corrin/Bridge City Ind School Dist	58	308
Gonzales, Dann/Miami Ind School Dist	16	324
Gonzales, Jeff/Teague Ind School Dist	67	156
Gonzales, Jena/Del Valle Ind School Dist	298	369
Gonzales, Jennifer/Malakoff Ind School Dist	4	214
Gonzales, Julie/Amherst Ind School Dist	4	260
Gonzales, Karen, Dr/White Settlement Ind Sch Dist	34	357
Gonzales, Leandro/Grady Ind School Dist	1,83	274
Gonzales, Linda/Abernathy Ind School Dist	271	174
Gonzales, Lisa, Dr/Kemp Ind School Dist	1	252
Gonzales, Luis/San Benito Cons Ind Sch Dist	93	67
Gonzales, Luz/Skidmore Tynan Ind SD	73	25
Gonzales, Mario/Rocksprings Ind School Dist	73	131
Gonzales, Mike, Dr/Port Neches-Groves Ind SD	1	243
Gonzales, Patricia/Hondo Ind School Dist	2	284
Gonzales, Robert/Seguin Ind School Dist	3	173
Gonzales, Rogelia/Zapata Co Ind School Dist	68	406
Gonzales, Tammy/Knox City-O'Brien Cons Ind SD	2,4,11	258
Gonzalez, Alfonso/Webb Cons Ind School Dist	73,286	388
Gonzalez, Angela/Godley Ind School Dist	58	247
Gonzalez, Angela, Dr/Santa Rosa Ind School Dist	1	67
Gonzalez, Armand/Austwell Tivoli Ind SD	285	323
Gonzalez, Ashley/Austin Ind School Dist	91	366
Gonzalez, Benita/Archdiocese Galveston-Houston	58	203
Gonzalez, Beto/Webb Cons Ind School Dist	1	388
Gonzalez, Carlos/Zapata Co Ind School Dist	1	406
Gonzalez, Cornelio, Dr/Region 1 Ed Service Center	1	226
Gonzalez, Dario/Brackett Ind School Dist	57	257
Gonzalez, David/Manor Ind School Dist	295	371
Gonzalez, David/United Ind School Dist	8,15	387
Gonzalez, Dolores/Idea Public Schools	8,11,57,69,286	217
Gonzalez, Eric/Robstown Ind School Dist	88,275	305
Gonzalez, Gerardo/Mission Cons Ind School Dist	69,77	222
Gonzalez, Gilbert/Lyford Cons Ind School Dist	73	394
Gonzalez, Gilberto/Eagle Pass Ind School Dist	1	276
Gonzalez, Hilda/Pharr-San Juan-Alamo Ind SD	48,51	223
Gonzalez, Isabelle/San Benito Cons Ind Sch Dist	71	67
Gonzalez, Ismael/Sharyland Ind School Dist	2,15	224
Gonzalez, Israel/Lyford Cons Ind School Dist	6	394
Gonzalez, J, Dr/McAllen Ind School Dist	1	220
Gonzalez, James/Cleveland Ind School Dist	73,295	265
Gonzalez, Jennifer/Floydada Ind School Dist	37	148
Gonzalez, Jodi/Spur Ind School Dist	2,11	127
Gonzalez, Kimberly/Edgewood Ind School Dist	73	31
Gonzalez, Lee/Robstown Ind School Dist	3	305
Gonzalez, Louis/Southwest Ind School Dist	36	43
Gonzalez, Luciel/United Ind School Dist	44	387
Gonzalez, Marcial/Culberson Co Allamoore Ind SD	3	95
Gonzalez, Maria/Round Rock Ind School Dist	58	398
Gonzalez, Mark/Driscoll Ind School Dist	3	304
Gonzalez, Martha/Webb Cons Ind School Dist	2,4	388
Gonzalez, Melanie/Weatherford Ind School Dist	46	313
Gonzalez, Melissa/Refugio Ind School Dist	1	323
Gonzalez, Michelle/San Felipe-Del Rio Cons Ind SD	280	379
Gonzalez, Monica/Region 19 Ed Service Center	16,73	139
Gonzalez, Nephalit/Santa Rosa Ind School Dist	76	67
Gonzalez, Patricia/Zapata Co Ind School Dist	2	406
Gonzalez, Paula/McAllen Ind School Dist	6	221
Gonzalez, Pedro/Fabens Ind School Dist	83	135
Gonzalez, Raul/La Joya Ind School Dist	5,271	219
Gonzalez, Richard/Robstown Ind School Dist	5,27,73,76,84,286	305
Gonzalez, Rick/Riviera Ind School Dist	73,84	258
Gonzalez, Roberto/Victoria Ind School Dist	83	382
Gonzalez, Rogelio/Zapata Co Ind School Dist	79	406
Gonzalez, Ronnie/Navasota Ind School Dist	15	172
Gonzalez, Sharlene/Crandall Ind School Dist	57	251
Gonzalez, Teresa/Sharyland Ind School Dist	11,271	224
Gonzalez, Victoria/Ft Hancock Ind School Dist	2	234
Gonzalez, Virginia/Rio Grande City Ind Sch Dist	11,296	340
Gonzalez, Virginio/Edcouch Elsa Ind School Dist	68	215
Gonzalez, Yliana/Ramirez Common School Dist	1	128
Gonzalez, Zabi/McKinney Ind School Dist	57	81
Gonzaloz, Epigmenio/Rio Grande City Ind Sch Dist	3	340
Gooch, Jason/Iola Ind School Dist	67	172
Goodall, Steve/Callisburg Ind School Dist	76,295	90
Goode, Luke/Lone Oak Ind School Dist	6	236
Gooden, Charles/Pearland Ind School Dist	67	53
Gooden, Todd/La Vega Ind School Dist	15,68,74,78,273	279
Goodgion, Phillip/New Deal Ind School Dist	73	271

#	Job Function	#	Job Function	#	Job Function	#	Job Function	#	Job Function	#	Job Function
1	Superintendent	16	Instructional Media Svcs	30	Adult Education	44	Science Sec	58	Special Education K-12	72	Summer School
2	Bus/Finance/Purchasing	17	Chief Operations Officer	31	Career/Sch-to-Work K-12	45	Math K-12	59	Special Education Elem	73	Instructional Tech
3	Buildings And Grounds	18	Chief Academic Officer	32	Career/Sch-to-Work Elem	46	Math Elem	60	Special Education Sec	74	Inservice Training
4	Food Service	19	Chief Financial Officer	33	Career/Sch-to-Work Sec	47	Math Sec	61	Foreign/World Lang K-12	75	Marketing/Distributive
5	Transportation	20	Art K-12	34	Early Childhood Ed	48	English/Lang Arts K-12	62	Foreign/World Lang Elem	76	Info Systems
6	Athletic	21	Art Elem	35	Health/Phys Education	49	English/Lang Arts Elem	63	Foreign/World Lang Sec	77	Psychological Assess
7	Health Services	22	Art Sec	36	Guidance Services K-12	50	English/Lang Arts Sec	64	Religious Education K-12	78	Affirmative Action
8	Curric/Instruct K-12	23	Music K-12	37	Guidance Services Elem	51	Reading K-12	65	Religious Education Elem	79	Student Personnel
9	Curric/Instruct Elem	24	Music Elem	38	Guidance Services Sec	52	Reading Elem	66	Religious Education Sec	80	Driver Ed/Safety
10	Curric/Instruct Sec	25	Music Sec	39	Social Studies K-12	53	Reading Sec	67	School Board President	81	Gifted/Talented
11	Federal Program	26	Business Education	40	Social Studies Elem	54	Remedial Reading K-12	68	Teacher Personnel	82	Video Services
12	Title I	27	Career & Tech Ed	41	Social Studies Sec	55	Remedial Reading Elem	69	Academic Assessment	83	Substance Abuse Prev
13	Title V	28	Technology Education	42	Science K-12	56	Remedial Reading Sec	70	Research/Development	84	Erate
15	Asst Superintendent	29	Family/Consumer Science	43	Science Elem	57	Bilingual/ELL	71	Public Information	85	AIDS Education

#	Job Function	#	Job Function
88	Alternative/At Risk	277	Remedial Math K-12
89	Multi-Cultural Curriculum	280	Literacy Coach
90	Social Work	285	STEM
91	Safety/Security	286	Digital Learning
92	Magnet School	288	Common Core Standards
93	Parental Involvement	294	Accountability
95	Tech Prep Program	295	Network System
97	Chief Information Officer	296	Title II Programs
98	Chief Technology Officer	297	Webmaster
270	Character Education	298	Grant Writer/Ptnrships
271	Migrant Education	750	Chief Innovation Officer
273	Teacher Mentor	751	Chief of Staff
274	Before/After Sch	752	Social Emotional Learning
275	Response To Intervention		

Texas School Directory

DISTRICT PERSONNEL INDEX

NAME/District	JOB FUNCTIONS	PAGE
Gooding, Connie/Hutto Ind School Dist	67	396
Goodlett, Bridget/College Station Ind Sch Dist	4	55
Goodman, Crystal/Bryan Ind School Dist	68	54
Goodman, Greg/Clear Creek Ind School Dist	20,23	158
Goodman, Patrick/Trinity Ind School Dist	6	374
Goodnow, Lisa, Dr/Austin Ind School Dist	8,288	366
Goodson, Christopher, Dr/Richardson Ind School Dist	15,68	112
Goodson, Pam/Spring Branch Ind School Dist	67	200
Goodwin, Becky/Edgewood Ind School Dist	11	31
Goodwin, Dwight/Denton Ind School Dist	73	120
Goodwin, Gerald/Aransas Co Ind School Dist	2	19
Goodwin, Glen/Big Sandy Ind School Dist	67	316
Goodwin, Janet/Electra Ind School Dist	11,57,271	391
Goodwin, Kathy/Tatum Ind School Dist	4	328
Goodwin, Renee/Stephenville Ind School Dist	69,294	144
Goodwin, Sasha/Glasscock Co Ind School Dist	35,85	163
Goodwin, Traci/Pasadena Ind School Dist	74	198
Goolsby, Sara/Willis Ind School Dist	57,81,275	294
Gopffarth, Cherie/Paradise Ind School Dist	38,83,88	403
Goranson, Jackie/Ezzell Ind School Dist	2	262
Gorden, Tim/Mildred Ind School Dist	3,5	300
Gordon, Donald/Hillsboro Ind School Dist	16,73,76,295	227
Gordon, Dorothea, Dr/Grand Prairie Ind School Dist	58	107
Gordon, Gary/Martin's Mill Ind Sch Dist	3,5	381
Gordon, Gwen/Azle Ind School Dist	58	345
Gordon, Jim/Vidor Ind School Dist	73	309
Gordon, Laurie/Little Cypress Mauriceville SD	11	308
Gordon, Lisa/Lago Vista Ind School Dist	5	370
Gordy, Cheryl/Klein Ind School Dist	12	196
Gore, Jerry/Buna Ind School Dist	58	240
Gore, Leah/Sulphur Bluff Ind School Dist	31,36,294	232
Gorena, Jackie/Irving Ind School Dist	69	109
Gorman, Garry/Red Oak Ind School Dist	8	142
Gosch, Lacey/Navarro Ind School Dist	8,11,57,271,273,288,294	173
Goss, Michael/Caddo Mills Ind Sch Dist	11	235
Goss, Michael/Honey Grove Ind School Dist	298	146
Goss, Michelle/Kress Ind School Dist	16,82	343
Goss, Mikayle/Lone Oak Ind School Dist	11,84	236
Goss, Mikayle/Wolfe City Ind School Dist	11,84,271,296	237
Gossett, Chris/Region 17 Ed Service Center	16,73	272
Gossett, Claylene/Rochelle Ind School Dist	2	278
Gossett, Jason/Klein Ind School Dist	2	196
Gott, Abe/Blackwell Cons Ind Sch Dist	1,84	301
Gottman, Linda/Lackland Ind School Dist	69	34
Gould, Paul/Frankston Ind School Dist	6	15
Gouldy, Loretta/Wildorado Ind Sch Dist	7	308
Goundrey, Colleen/Barbers Hill Ind School Dist	7	72
Govan, Charissa/Dallas Ind School Dist	275	98
Gowens, Sandra/New Deal Ind School Dist	67	271
Gowin, Flossie/Milford Ind School Dist	57	141
Goytia, Corina/Socorro Ind School Dist	271	135
Gracia, Leticia/Calallen Ind School Dist	4	302
Graeber, Pennie/Waco Ind School Dist	275	281
Graf, Edward/Eagle Pass Ind School Dist	6,35	276
Graf, Nathan/San Antonio Ind School Dist	5	39
Graf, Thomas/Redwater Ind School Dist	6	49
Graham, Becky/Texarkana Ind School Dist	58	50
Graham, Brant, Dr/Burkeville Ind School Dist	1,11	300
Graham, Donna/Burkeville Ind School Dist	58	300
Graham, Gary/Grapeland Ind School Dist	27,298	232
Graham, Glen/Hutto Ind School Dist	2,15	396
Graham, Jack/Diocese of Brownsville Ed Off	2	226
Graham, John/Leander Ind School Dist	15	396
Graham, Kelsee/Colorado Ind School Dist	7,85	289
Graham, Kim/Timpson Ind School Dist	91	335
Graham, Korey/Karnes City Ind School Dist	5	250
Graham, Leslie/Archer City Ind School Dist	69,83,88	19
Graham, Lloyd/La Porte Ind School Dist	1	198
Graham, Patti/West Hardin Co Cons Sch Dist	3,5	178
Graham, Ronald/Burkeville Ind School Dist	67	300
Graham, Tellunce/Cedar Hill Ind School Dist	15,79	97
Graham, Tonya/O'Donnell Ind School Dist	8,42,57,58,69,81	273
Grahmann, Ashley/Flatonia Ind School Dist	8	147
Grandjean, Todd/Moulton Ind School Dist	1,11	262
Grange, Shane/White Deer Ind School Dist	67	69
Granger, Elijah/Lancaster Ind School Dist	1	110

NAME/District	JOB FUNCTIONS	PAGE
Grant, Amy/Llano Ind School Dist	4	268
Grant, Karianna/West Sabine Ind Sch Dist	12,88	329
Grant, Sid/Coppell Ind School Dist	15	98
Grant, Tiffany/San Antonio Ind School Dist	15,751	39
Grantham, Karen/Bushland Ind School Dist	2	319
Granzin, Kelly/Wall Ind School Dist	9	365
Grape, Magda/Grand Prairie Ind School Dist	57	107
Gratehouse, Todd/Del Valle Ind School Dist	73,76,84,98,295	369
Graves, Gary/Post Ind School Dist	3	162
Graves, Leah/Medina Valley Ind School Dist	45	284
Graves, Mehgan/Vega Ind School Dist	58	307
Graves, Rena/Mart Ind School Dist	2	280
Graves, Wendy/Montgomery Ind School Dist	9,11,15,16,34,57,270,274	293
Gravey, Thomas/Mullin Ind School Dist	273	288
Grawunder, Suzanne/Bellville Ind School Dist	7	22
Gray, Carrie/Detroit Ind School Dist	58	322
Gray, Connie/Zapata Co Ind School Dist	8,42,93,288	406
Gray, Craig/Region 10 Ed Service Center	286	116
Gray, David/Waco Ind School Dist	5	281
Gray, Joyce/Strawn Ind School Dist	57	311
Gray, Julie/Eustace Ind School Dist	34	214
Gray, Lauren/Milford Ind School Dist	2,271	141
Gray, Noel/Pearland Ind School Dist	8,54,74,277	53
Gray, Robert/Rice Ind School Dist	91	300
Gray, Roxann/Comanche Ind School Dist	76	89
Gray, Tony/Farmersville Ind School Dist	67	78
Greaves, Lori/Lubbock Ind School Dist	48,51	269
Greeling, Chrissy/Keller Ind School Dist	46	354
Green, Amanda/Penelope ISD School Dist	57	228
Green, Angela/Italy Ind School Dist	37	140
Green, Brent/Littlefield Ind School Dist	6	260
Green, Burt/Brock Ind School Dist	3	312
Green, Clay/Ganado Ind School Dist	67	239
Green, Cory/Texas Dept of Education	12,298	1
Green, Don/Somerset Ind School Dist	67	42
Green, Georgina/Savoy Ind School Dist	4	146
Green, Jennifer/Clifton Ind School Dist	4	46
Green, John/Huntsville Ind School Dist	23	383
Green, Kathy/La Porte Ind School Dist	67	198
Green, Leesa/Region 7 Ed Service Center	69,294	171
Green, Maria/Round Rock Ind School Dist	57	398
Green, Matthew/Llano Ind School Dist	6	268
Green, Staci/Waskom Ind School Dist	58	209
Green, Stephanie/Adrian Ind School Dist	2	307
Green, Stryker/Texline Ind School Dist	5	95
Green, Tara/Normangee Ind School Dist	4	264
Green, Tiffany/Region 11 Ed Service Center	68	360
Greene, Jeff/Deer Park Ind School Dist	5	186
Greene, Karin/Comstock Ind School Dist	16	379
Greene, Patty/New Boston Ind School Dist	8,11,57,69,273,298	49
Greeney, Brian, Dr/Willis Ind School Dist	8,15	294
Greening, Candy/Panhandle Ind School Dist	4	69
Greenough, Jennifer/Wylie Ind School Dist	16	361
Greenwood, Julie/Santa Gertrudis Ind Sch Dist	7,83,85	258
Greer-Jones, Steffani/Leveretts Chapel Ind Sch Dist	58	328
Greer, Alyce/Gainesville Ind School Dist	2,19	91
Greer, Carol/Hallsville Ind School Dist	71,93	208
Greer, Matt/Eanes Ind School Dist	91	370
Greer, Roxanne/Kermit Ind School Dist	58	401
Greer, Roxanne/Wink Loving Ind School Dist	58	402
Greer, Tatiana/Pampa Ind School Dist	57,271	165
Greer, Todd/Gary Ind School Dist	1	311
Greer, Zach/Millsap Ind School Dist	73	312
Gregg, Byron/Kaufman Ind School Dist	67	252
Gregg, Mary Ann/Kemp Ind School Dist	57	252
Greggerson, Tami/Splendora Ind School Dist	8,69,72,81,88,271,285	294
Gregorski, Ken, Dr/Katy Ind School Dist	1	151
Gregory, Jewel/New Waverly Ind School Dist	4	383
Gregson, Lane/Oakwood Ind School Dist	73	264
Gregson, Layne/Centerville Ind School Dist	76,295	264
Greig, Melody/Richardson Ind School Dist	2	112
Greiner, David/Pflugerville Ind School Dist	76	371
Grell-Boethel, Lynn/Columbia Brazoria ISD	11,36,57,77,83,88,296	52
Grenier, Brian/Randolph Field Ind School Dist	73,98,295	39
Gresham, Vicki/Leon Ind School Dist	16	264
Grey, Christina/Woodsboro Ind School Dist	73,79,295	324

School Year 2019-2020   800-333-8802   TX-T35

DISTRICT PERSONNEL INDEX

Market Data Retrieval

NAME/District	JOB FUNCTIONS	PAGE
Grey, Karen/*Crosby Ind School Dist*	15,68	183
Gribble, Sherri/*Chisum Ind School Dist*	294	259
Grieb, Dana/*Royse City Ind School Dist*	39,50	326
Griedl, Jake/*Marshall Ind School Dist*	6	209
Griffey, Nancy/*Cayuga Ind School Dist*	83,85	14
Griffin, Chris/*Region 12 Ed Service Center*	58	283
Griffin, Darvis/*Waco Ind School Dist*	73,98	281
Griffin, Dawn/*Robinson Ind School Dist*	27,31	281
Griffin, Debra/*Maypearl Ind School Dist*	36,83,85,270	141
Griffin, Gary/*Brackett Ind School Dist*	6	257
Griffin, Jesse/*Mullin Ind School Dist*	2	288
Griffin, Joe/*Karnack Ind School Dist*	4	208
Griffin, Joe/*Keller Ind School Dist*	73,76,98,295	354
Griffin, Joe/*Waskom Ind School Dist*	4	209
Griffin, Julie/*Stephenville Ind School Dist*	76	144
Griffin, Kriss/*Schleicher Co Ind Sch Dist*	67	333
Griffin, Larry/*Lingleville Ind School Dist*	67	143
Griffin, Lisa/*Callisburg Ind School Dist*	31,36	90
Griffin, Marc/*Hemphill Ind School Dist*	8,36,74,83,88,274,288	329
Griffin, Melanie/*Northwest Ind School Dist*	47	124
Griffin, Natalie/*Mineral Wells Ind School Dist*	11,57,81,271,298	310
Griffin, Ron/*Goldthwaite Consolidated ISD*	3	288
Griffin, Tamira/*McKinney Ind School Dist*	15,68,270,273	80
Griffith, Barbara/*Ft Worth Ind School Dist*	71	349
Griffith, Cathy/*Pottsboro Ind School Dist*	4	167
Griffith, Connie/*Spurger Ind School Dist*	2	375
Griffith, Jeremy/*Sundown Ind School Dist*	8,34,57	229
Griffith, Kaci/*Colorado Ind School Dist*	38	289
Griffith, Karen/*San Marcos Cons Ind Sch Dist*	15	211
Griffith, Laura/*Grand Saline Ind School Dist*	2	380
Griffith, Lori/*La Poynor Ind School Dist*	57	214
Griffiths, Peter/*Wichita Falls Ind School Dist*	15,286	392
Griffon, Mark/*Friendswood Ind Sch Dist*	72	160
Grigar, Melody/*Rice Cons Ind School Dist*	2,8,11,83,88,288,296,298	87
Grijalva, Timothy/*Cleburne Ind School Dist*	73	247
Grill, Richard/*Sabinal Ind School Dist*	1	378
Grill, Tish/*Boerne Ind School Dist*	2,15	253
Grimes, Beverly/*Gilmer Ind School Dist*	2	376
Grimes, Dallas/*Roosevelt Ind School Dist*	1	271
Grimes, Greg/*McKinney Ind School Dist*	76	81
Grimes, Justin/*College Station Ind Sch Dist*	83,88	55
Grimes, Margie/*Goose Creek Cons Ind Sch Dist*	2,19	187
Grimes, Perry/*Woden Ind School Dist*	67	298
Grimes, Tracy/*Paint Rock Ind School Dist*	2	90
Grimet, Howard/*Katy Ind School Dist*	35	151
Grimm, Jennifer/*Lorena Ind School Dist*	73,295	280
Grimm, Rusty/*Lorena Ind School Dist*	5,79,83,91,294	280
Grimsley, Bobby/*Abernathy Ind School Dist*	3,91	174
Grimsley, Keri/*Godley Ind School Dist*	9	247
Grimsley, Richard/*Dallas Ind School Dist*	27,31	98
Grisham, Nikki/*Hawley Ind School Dist*	31,285	250
Grissom, Sarah/*Leander Ind School Dist*	15	396
Grissom, Wayne/*Lufkin Ind School Dist*	5	18
Grmela, Jimmy/*Kerrville Ind School Dist*	69	256
Groce, Susan/*Caldwell Ind School Dist*	280	59
Grogan, April/*Avinger Ind School Dist*	73	70
Grogan, Eric/*Rice Cons Ind School Dist*	271	87
Grogan, Jason/*Wimberley Ind School Dist*	16,73,76,295	212
Grohler, Wendy/*McAllen Ind School Dist*	42	221
Grona, Juanice/*Harper Ind School Dist*	67	163
Grona, Shannon/*North East Ind School Dist*	67	34
Grones, Kelly/*Round Rock Ind School Dist*	4	398
Gronow, Susan/*Tyler Ind School Dist*	39	337
Grooban, Shelby/*Rotan Ind School Dist*	2	148
Groomes, Kenneth/*San Saba Ind School Dist*	3	332
Grooms, Andrea, Dr/*Katy Ind School Dist*	15,71,93	151
Groover, Lisa/*Eanes Ind School Dist*	30,274	370
Grosso, Amy, Dr/*Round Rock Ind School Dist*	11,298	398
Groves, Josh/*Winona Ind School Dist*	12,296	339
Grubb, Kay/*Paris Ind School Dist*	85	260
Grubbs, Travis/*High Island Ind Sch Dist*	1	160
Gruell, Peggy/*Dublin Ind School Dist*	16	143
Gruhlkey, Tonya/*Walcott Ind School Dist*	271	119
Gruhn, Todd/*Trenton Ind School Dist*	73	147
Grumbles, Amy/*Sands Consolidated ISD*	2	117
Gruwell, Lori/*New Braunfels Ind School Dist*	74	88
Gryseeles, Krissy/*Jarrell Ind School Dist*	76	396
Guadiana, Melissa/*San Perlita Ind School Dist*	67	394
Guajardo, Cynthia/*La Feria Ind School Dist*	93,271	65
Guajardo, Elizabeth/*Elgin Ind School Dist*	4	24
Guajardo, Gina/*Sinton Ind School Dist*	11,83,296	332
Guajardo, Jesse/*Crystal City Ind School Dist*	73	407
Guenther, Codi/*Weimar Ind School Dist*	11	87
Guereca, Luis/*Iredell Ind School Dist*	6	46
Guerra, Alejandro/*Elgin Ind School Dist*	3	24
Guerra, Andrew/*Gregory-Portland Ind Sch Dist*	16,73,84,295	330
Guerra, Darrell/*La Feria Ind School Dist*	3,5	65
Guerra, Evangelina/*Hitchcock Ind School Dist*	58	161
Guerra, Joe/*Lyford Cons Ind School Dist*	3	394
Guerra, Melly/*Santa Gertrudis Ind Sch Dist*	11,58,271,275,296	258
Guerra, Miriam, Dr/*La Feria Ind School Dist*	11,27,285	65
Guerra, Noemi/*Bastrop Ind School Dist*	271	23
Guerra, Phillip/*Dumas Ind School Dist*	15	295
Guerra, Rolando/*San Benito Cons Ind Sch Dist*	27	67
Guerra, Servando/*Brooks Co Ind School Dist*	67	57
Guerreo, Christina/*Ft Sam Houston Ind School Dist*	6	32
Guerrero, Angie/*Corpus Christi Ind Sch Dist*	7	303
Guerrero, Cynthia/*Pasadena Ind School Dist*	68,273	198
Guerrero, Katrina/*Santa Anna Ind School Dist*	2,11	76
Guerrero, Roberto/*Hidalgo Ind School Dist*	5	217
Guerrero, Rosanna/*Round Rock Ind School Dist*	2	398
Guerrero, Susan/*Crosbyton Cons Ind Sch Dist*	4	94
Guerry, Larry/*Crandall Ind School Dist*	2,19	251
Guess, June/*Ranger Ind School Dist*	16	129
Guest, Mike/*Weatherford Ind School Dist*	67	313
Guetersloh, Kathy/*Denver City Ind School Dist*	77	405
Guetersloh, Michelle/*Sterling City Ind School Dist*	11	342
Guidry, Rachel/*Beaumont Ind School Dist*	36,83	241
Guidry, Wayne, Dr/*Spring Hill Ind School Dist*	1	170
Guillen, Candace/*South Texas Ind School Dist*	93	67
Guillen, Kelly/*Amarillo Ind School Dist*	58	317
Guillen, Noe/*Los Fresnos Cons Ind Sch Dist*	11,271,294,296	66
Guillory, Jennifer/*Center Ind School Dist*	11,37,57,271	334
Guillory, Maisha/*Aldine Ind School Dist*	7	179
Guinn, Kimberly/*Carrollton-Farmers Branch ISD*	12,69,294	96
Guiterrez, Alfonso/*Brownsville Ind School Dist*	71	63
Guiturrez, Sarah/*Jourdanton Ind School Dist*	7	20
Gully, Madelaine/*Greenwood Ind School Dist*	7,83,85	285
Gumes, Samantha/*Era Ind School Dist*	7	90
Gunnels, Susan/*Reagan Co Ind School Dist*	2,79	321
Gunter, Coleen/*Sivells Bend Ind School Dist*	57	91
Gunter, Jenny/*Dayton Ind School Dist*	69,294	265
Gunter, Steve/*Idalou Ind School Dist*	8,11,274	269
Gust, Betsy/*Plano Ind School Dist*	11	82
Gustin, Kendra/*Jonesboro Ind School Dist*	8,12,286	93
Guterrez, Daniel/*Sudan Ind School Dist*	58	261
Guthals, Deirdre/*Farwell Ind School Dist*	57	314
Gutierrez, Christina/*Bishop Cons Ind School Dist*	1	302
Gutierrez, Crisella/*Zapata Co Ind School Dist*	8	406
Gutierrez, David/*Ennis Ind School Dist*	4	140
Gutierrez, Donna/*Huntsville Ind School Dist*	76	383
Gutierrez, Grant/*Smithville Ind School Dist*	67	24
Gutierrez, Jessica/*London Ind School Dist*	12,271	305
Gutierrez, Jiovana/*Ysleta Ind School Dist*	68	137

#		#		#		#		#		#	
1	Superintendent	16	Instructional Media Svcs	30	Adult Education	44	Science Sec	58	Special Education K-12	72	Summer School
2	Bus/Finance/Purchasing	17	Chief Operations Officer	31	Career/Sch-to-Work K-12	45	Math K-12	59	Special Education Elem	73	Instructional Tech
3	Buildings And Grounds	18	Chief Academic Officer	32	Career/Sch-to-Work Elem	46	Math Elem	60	Special Education Sec	74	Inservice Training
4	Food Service	19	Chief Financial Officer	33	Career/Sch-to-Work Sec	47	Math Sec	61	Foreign/World Lang K-12	75	Marketing/Distributive
5	Transportation	20	Art K-12	34	Early Childhood Ed	48	English/Lang Arts K-12	62	Foreign/World Lang Elem	76	Info Systems
6	Athletic	21	Art Elem	35	Health/Phys Education	49	English/Lang Arts Elem	63	Foreign/World Lang Sec	77	Psychological Assess
7	Health Services	22	Art Sec	36	Guidance Services K-12	50	English/Lang Arts Sec	64	Religious Education K-12	78	Affirmative Action
8	Curric/Instruct K-12	23	Music K-12	37	Guidance Services Elem	51	Reading K-12	65	Religious Education Elem	79	Student Personnel
9	Curric/Instruct Elem	24	Music Elem	38	Guidance Services Sec	52	Reading Elem	66	Religious Education Sec	80	Driver Ed/Safety
10	Curric/Instruct Sec	25	Music Sec	39	Social Studies K-12	53	Reading Sec	67	School Board President	81	Gifted/Talented
11	Federal Program	26	Business Education	40	Social Studies Elem	54	Remedial Reading K-12	68	Teacher Personnel	82	Video Services
12	Title I	27	Career & Tech Ed	41	Social Studies Sec	55	Remedial Reading Elem	69	Academic Assessment	83	Substance Abuse Prev
13	Title V	28	Technology Education	42	Science K-12	56	Remedial Reading Sec	70	Research/Development	84	Erate
15	Asst Superintendent	29	Family/Consumer Science	43	Science Elem	57	Bilingual/ELL	71	Public Information	85	AIDS Education

#		#	
88	Alternative/At Risk	277	Remedial Math K-12
89	Multi-Cultural Curriculum	280	Literacy Coach
90	Social Work	285	STEM
91	Safety/Security	286	Digital Learning
92	Magnet School	288	Common Core Standards
93	Parental Involvement	294	Accountability
95	Tech Prep Program	295	Network System
97	Chief Information Officer	296	Title II Programs
98	Chief Technology Officer	297	Webmaster
270	Character Education	298	Grant Writer/Ptnrships
271	Migrant Education	750	Chief Innovation Officer
273	Teacher Mentor	751	Chief of Staff
274	Before/After Sch	752	Social Emotional Learning
275	Response To Intervention		

TX-T36

Texas School Directory

DISTRICT PERSONNEL INDEX

NAME/District	JOB FUNCTIONS	PAGE
Gutierrez, Jo Ann/*Karnes City Ind School Dist*	8,69,288	250
Gutierrez, Joshua/*La Vernia Ind School Dist*	91	401
Gutierrez, Manuela/*Fabens Ind School Dist*	16	135
Gutierrez, Matthew, Dr/*Seguin Ind School Dist*	1	173
Gutierrez, Oscar/*Raymondville Ind Sch Dist*	3,5	394
Gutierrez, Rene, Dr/*Brownsville Ind School Dist*	1	63
Gutierrez, Robert/*San Marcos Cons Ind Sch Dist*	3,91	211
Gutierrez, Samantha/*Penelope ISD School Dist*	2,11	228
Gutierrez, Tamara/*Pampa Ind School Dist*	7	165
Gutierrez, Ted/*Lasara Ind School Dist*	5	394
Gutsch, Angela, Dr/*Hempstead Ind School Dist*	1,11	384
Guu, Lilly/*Danbury Ind School Dist*	38	53
Guy, Christie/*Canton Ind School Dist*	57	380
Guy, Jody/*Shamrock Ind School Dist*	6	390
Guzman, Carlos/*Roma Ind School Dist*	1	341
Guzman, Dalia/*Edinburg Cons Ind School Dist*	8,15	216
Guzman, Gustavo/*Valley View Ind School Dist*	285	225
Guzman, Susan/*Luling Ind School Dist*	68	61
Gwaltney, Dayna/*Comfort Ind School Dist*	7,85	254

H

NAME/District	JOB FUNCTIONS	PAGE
Habekutt, Nancy/*Higgins Ind School Dist*	270	268
Hachmeister, Paige/*Sanger Ind School Dist*	4	126
Hackett, Chris/*Pittsburg Ind School Dist*	4	68
Hackley, Brent/*Jacksboro Ind Sch Dist*	67	239
Hackley, Karri/*Nocona Ind School Dist*	81	290
Hadaway, Lee/*Wylie Ind School Dist*	74	85
Haden, Amy/*Evadale Ind School Dist*	69	240
Haden, Tammi/*Brookeland Ind School Dist*	2	240
Hadley, John/*College Station Ind Sch Dist*	3	55
Haehn, Anne/*Lake Dallas Ind School Dist*	2	122
Hafezizadeh, Kris/*Austin Ind School Dist*	5	366
Haffey, Keith, Dr/*Spring Branch Ind School Dist*	69,294	200
Hafley, Scot/*Wichita Falls Ind School Dist*	6	392
Hagan, Mike/*Brady Ind School Dist*	5	277
Hagar, Mike/*Alamo Heights Ind School Dist*	2,15	30
Hagar, Tanya/*Pasadena Ind School Dist*	27	198
Hagdorn, Lindie/*West Oso Ind School Dist*	73,297	306
Hagel, Raymond/*Lake Dallas Ind School Dist*	5,91	122
Hageman, Becky/*Kenedy Co Wide Common Sch Dist*	73	254
Hagemen, Becky/*Kenedy Co Schools*	73	254
Haggard, Eric/*Irving Ind School Dist*	39	109
Haggerton, Kathy/*Blum Ind School Dist*	4	227
Hagle, Caleb/*Woodson Ind School Dist*	3	363
Hagle, Heather/*Chireno ISD School Dist*	8,11,79,275,294,296	297
Hagler, Terry/*Wylie Ind School Dist*	8	361
Hail, Darol, Dr/*New Waverly Ind School Dist*	1	383
Haimlen, Vicki/*Lake Dallas Ind School Dist*	77	122
Haisler, Betsy/*Aldine Ind School Dist*	57	179
Halbert, Christy/*Walnut Springs Ind Sch Dist*	8,12,57,88,288	47
Hale, Alisha/*Dodd City Ind School Dist*	7	145
Hale, Bobbie/*Ira Ind School Dist*	8,11,57,69,270,271,273	333
Hale, Bonnie/*Bandera Ind School Dist*	36,69,83,88	23
Hale, Donna/*Miami Ind School Dist*	1	324
Hale, Jennifer/*Carlisle Ind School Dist*	8,31,69,270	327
Hale, Monty/*Adrian Ind School Dist*	73,286,295	307
Hale, Tonia/*Midland Ind School Dist*	76	285
Haley, Amanda/*Johnson City Ind School Dist*	8,57,270,273,288,296	46
Haley, Charlotte/*Gold-Burg Ind School Dist*	16,73,286	290
Haley, Curtis/*Lingleville Ind School Dist*	1,11	143
Haley, Larhesa/*Kemp Ind School Dist*	4	252
Haley, Melody/*Whitney Ind School Dist*	11,15,58,271	228
Haley, Tammy/*Magnolia Ind School Dist*	13,58	292
Hall-Payne, Christina/*Texas City Ind School Dist*	70,298	161
Hall, Amy/*Weatherford Ind School Dist*	48	313
Hall, Bradley/*Highland Ind School Dist*	3,5	301
Hall, Burke/*Grand Prairie Ind School Dist*	67	107
Hall, David/*Seguin Ind School Dist*	45	173
Hall, David/*Thorndale Ind School Dist*	67	288
Hall, Debbie/*Jefferson Ind School Dist*	7	274
Hall, Debbie/*Jefferson Ind School Dist*	7	274
Hall, Deidra/*Copperas Cove Ind School Dist*	2	92
Hall, Jeanette/*Terlingua Common School Dist*	2,12	57
Hall, Joe/*Chapel Hill Ind School Dist*	34,58,90	337
Hall, Kenneth, Dr/*Crawford Ind School Dist*	1,11	279
Hall, Kirsty/*Region 18 Ed Service Center*	16	287

NAME/District	JOB FUNCTIONS	PAGE
Hall, Marilu/*Baird Ind School Dist*	7	62
Hall, Mike/*Chapel Hill Ind School Dist*	2	363
Hall, Nelson/*Bartlett Ind School Dist*	67	26
Hall, Paula/*Poolville Ind School Dist*	2	313
Hall, Pennee/*Cleveland Ind School Dist*	15	265
Hall, Rebecca/*Centerville Ind School Dist*	83	264
Hall, Richard/*Shamrock Ind School Dist*	67	391
Hall, Rodney/*Chilton Ind School Dist*	67	144
Hall, Rodney/*Graford Ind School Dist*	5,83	310
Hall, Shirley/*Bartlett Ind School Dist*	2	26
Hall, Telly/*Chapel Hill Ind School Dist*	73,286	363
Hall, Tim/*Plemons-Stinnett-Phillips CISD*	67	238
Hall, Van/*Hughes Springs Ind Sch Dist*	67	70
Haller, Kevin/*Frisco Ind School Dist*	91	78
Haller, Rachel/*Aldine Ind School Dist*	69	179
Hallman, Duff/*Christoval Ind School Dist*	67	364
Hallmark, Bryan, Dr/*Georgetown Ind School Dist*	4,15,68,79	395
Hallmark, Eric/*Reagan Co Ind School Dist*	11,15,57	321
Hallmark, Jeffrey/*Lockney Independent Sch Dist*	270	149
Hallmark, Leticia/*Del Valle Ind School Dist*	39	369
Hallmark, Rebecca/*Garner Ind School Dist*	1	312
Hallmark, Shana/*Lockney Independent Sch Dist*	88,294	149
Halms, Ashley/*Plano Ind School Dist*	10	82
Halperin, Ian/*Wylie Ind School Dist*	30,71	84
Ham, Alice/*Lovelady Ind School Dist*	16,73,76,295	233
Ham, Dakota/*Lovelady Ind School Dist*	295	233
Ham, Lisa/*Highland Park Ind Sch Dist*	73	108
Ham, Ryan/*San Augustine Ind School Dist*	16,31,73	329
Hambrick, Ronnie/*La Poynor Ind School Dist*	3,5,91	214
Hamersley, Gary/*Crosbyton Cons Ind Sch Dist*	3,5	94
Hamessley, Deborah/*Forney Ind School Dist*	76	251
Hamil, Marc/*Canyon Ind School Dist*	10,27,31	320
Hamilton, Anna/*Sabine Ind School Dist*	22	170
Hamilton, Charles/*Eagle Mtn-Saginaw Ind Sch Dist*	3	348
Hamilton, Craig/*Spur Ind School Dist*	1	127
Hamilton, Deedee/*Italy Ind School Dist*	7	140
Hamilton, Don/*Groveton Ind School Dist*	1,11,57,83	374
Hamilton, Gerry/*Lake Dallas Ind School Dist*	295	122
Hamilton, Jeff/*Bandera Ind School Dist*	6	23
Hamilton, Jeff/*Gilmer Ind School Dist*	71	376
Hamilton, Jeff/*New Diana Ind School Dist*	67	376
Hamilton, Mindy/*Ore City Ind School Dist*	7	377
Hamilton, Ryan/*Splendora Ind School Dist*	76	294
Hamilton, Suzanne/*Waco Ind School Dist*	58	281
Hamlett, John, Dr/*Crowley Ind School Dist*	88	347
Hammack, Jason/*Bland Ind School Dist*	57	235
Hammack, Kathy/*Garrison Ind School Dist*	4	297
Hammer, Robert/*Panhandle Ind School Dist*	5	69
Hammerbacher, Jennie/*Kilgore Ind School Dist*	4	169
Hammock, Kyle/*Roosevelt Ind School Dist*	2	271
Hammond, Angela/*Carroll Independent Sch Dist*	40,49	347
Hammond, Courtney/*Valley Mills Ind School Dist*	57,83,88	47
Hammons, Melonie/*Southside Ind School Dist*	8	43
Hammons, Merrill/*Brownsville Ind School Dist*	31,83	63
Hammontree, Rickey/*Leveretts Chapel Ind Sch Dist*	6	328
Hampton, Chavela/*Duncanville Ind School Dist*	91	104
Hampton, D M/*Whitesboro Ind School Dist*	91	168
Hampton, Deeann/*Mineral Wells Ind School Dist*	31	310
Hampton, Julie/*Joshua Ind School Dist*	76	248
Hampton, Julie/*Joshua Ind School Dist*	9	248
Hampton, Keri, Dr/*Brownsboro Ind School Dist*	1	213
Hampton, Latricia/*Gorman Ind School Dist*	36,83,88	129
Hampton, Tim/*Sweetwater ISD School Dist*	3,91	301
Hampton, Yvonne/*Mt Pleasant Ind School Dist*	67	363
Hamrick, Anna/*Prosper Ind School Dist*	5,91	84
Hamrick, Brad/*Duncanville Ind School Dist*	5	104
Hancock, Becky/*Frankston Ind School Dist*	297	15
Hancock, Casey/*Hamshire Fannett Ind Sch Dist*	31	242
Hancock, Jana/*Plano Ind School Dist*	36	82
Hancock, Jowell/*Rusk Ind School Dist*	6,35	73
Hancock, Kimberly/*Grape Creek Ind School Dist*	69,88	364
Hancock, Larry/*Malone Independent School Dist*	67	228
Hancock, Ruth/*West Orange-Cove Cons ISD*	67	309
Hancock, Sandra/*Connally Ind School Dist*	8,15	279
Hancock, Tammy/*Rusk Ind School Dist*	34	73
Hand, Beth/*Breckenridge Ind School Dist*	16	341

DISTRICT PERSONNEL INDEX

Market Data Retrieval

NAME/District	JOB FUNCTIONS	PAGE
Hand, Brent/Chico Ind School Dist	8	403
Hand, Natile/Broaddus Ind School Dist	8,11,36,69,88,275,294	329
Handy, Roland/Mercedes Ind School Dist	73,271	221
Hanes, Dave/Ira Ind School Dist	16,73,295	333
Hanes, Devin/Duncanville Ind School Dist	47	104
Hanes, Tammy/McLean Ind School Dist	7,271	165
Haney, Debra/Archdiocese Galveston-Houston	1	203
Haney, Kevin/Dripping Springs Ind Sch Dist	295	210
Haney, Melissa/Hutto Ind School Dist	69	396
Hanfeld, Donna/Lubbock-Cooper Ind Sch Dist	76	271
Hanke, Abbie/Cameron Ind School Dist	4	287
Hankey, Brett/Prosper Ind School Dist	73	84
Hankey, Chrystal/Prosper Ind School Dist	71	84
Hankins, Brandon/Farmersville Ind School Dist	6	78
Hankins, Tracie/Three Way Ind School Dist	67	144
Hanks, Britney/Bryson Ind School Dist	58	238
Hanks, Jeffrey, Dr/Weatherford Ind School Dist	1	313
Hanlin, Ashley/Amherst Ind School Dist	69,77	260
Hanlin, Greg/Gilmer Ind School Dist	5	376
Hanlon, Terri/Cisco Independent Sch Dist	2	128
Hanna, David/Carrollton-Farmers Branch ISD	5	96
Hanna, Jennifer/Liberty Hill Ind School Dist	2,19	398
Hanna, Kelly/Godley Ind School Dist	73	247
Hanna, Melissa/Iraan-Sheffield Ind Sch Dist	2	316
Hannah, Kelly/Veribest Ind School Dist	12,69,83,270	365
Hannah, Kurt/Iraan-Sheffield Ind School Dist	3,73,76,286,295	316
Hanner, Steve/Allen Ind School Dist	3	76
Hannon, Jimmy/Highland Park Ind School Dist	1	319
Hannsz, Baron/Aldine Ind School Dist	47	179
Hansen, Lucy/Dripping Springs Ind Sch Dist	30,31,274	210
Hanson, Buffy/Aledo Ind School Dist	2	312
Hanson, Christy, Dr/Tyler Ind School Dist	8,15	337
Hanson, Gail/Crockett Ind School Dist	2,11,296	232
Hanson, Mark/Bellevue Ind School Dist	67	74
Hanson, Zana, Dr/Ft Stockton Ind School Dist	58	315
Hanssard, Patti/Santa Fe Ind School Dist	68,71,79	161
Haralson, Jack/Texas City Ind School Dist	3	161
Harbour, Jonathan/Walnut Springs Ind Sch Dist	58	47
Hardaway, Debbie/Prairie Lea Ind School Dist	4	61
Hardaway, Shelley/Prairie Lea Ind School Dist	27	61
Hardcastle, Heather/Wheeler Ind School Dist	12,296	391
Hardee, Kyle/Centerville Ind School Dist	6	264
Harden, Rusty/Sulphur Springs Ind School Dist	15,68	232
Hardin, Ashley/Axtell Ind School Dist	69	278
Hardin, Barry/Holliday Ind School Dist	67	19
Hardin, Corey/Gainesville Ind School Dist	67	91
Hardin, Dustin/Humble Ind School Dist	73,76	195
Hardin, Gary/Crosbyton Cons Ind Sch Dist	2	94
Hardin, Trina/Memphis Ind School Dist	36,57,58,83,88,296	175
Hardin, Wayne/Clarendon Cons Ind Sch Dist	67	127
Harding, Diane/Palestine Ind School Dist	16	15
Harding, Sherri/Mineola Ind School Dist	5	404
Hardwick, John, Dr/Ganado Ind School Dist	1	239
Hardy, Joyce, Dr/Paradise Ind School Dist	15,69	403
Hardy, Kimberley/Luling Ind School Dist	16,82	61
Hardy, Mark/Warren Ind School Dist	3,5	375
Hardy, Michelle/Silsbee Ind School Dist	7	178
Hardy, Steve/Spring Hill Ind School Dist	73	170
Hardy, Steve/Yantis Ind School Dist	16,82	405
Hardy, Velvet/Fort Davis Ind School Dist	2	241
Hare, Amanda/Lorenzo Ind School Dist	9,274	94
Hargis, Kent/Grandview-Hopkins Ind School Dist	1,11,288	164
Hargis, Linda/Bruceville-Eddy Ind Sch Dist	16,82	278
Hargrave, Deidra/Devers Ind School Dist	4	265
Hargrove, Amber/Pine Tree Ind School Dist	76	170
Hargrove, Julie/Duncanville Ind School Dist	79	104
Hargrove, Marie/Anson Ind School Dist	2	249
Hargrove, Pauline, Dr/Little Cypress Mauriceville SD	1	308
Harkrider, Tim/Willis Ind School Dist	1	294
Harlan, Billy/Academy Ind School Dist	1	26
Harlan, James/Wellman Union Ind School Dist	67	362
Harlan, Melanie/Forney Ind School Dist	81	251
Harland, Danielle/Texhoma Ind School Dist	2,71	336
Harle, Carol, Dr/Northside Ind School Dist	67	36
Harlow, Nan/Archer City Ind School Dist	16,82	19
Harman, Lucy/Hunt Ind School Dist	1,11,73	255
Harmon, Brent/Sterling City Ind School Dist	3	342
Harmon, Vicki/Angleton Ind School Dist	9	51
Harmon, Wayne/Liberty-Eylau Ind School Dist	3	48
Harmsen, Keith/Crockett Co Cons Common SD	73,295	94
Harmsen, Lisa/Crockett Co Cons Common SD	2	94
Harness, Bill/Conroe Ind School Dist	91	291
Haro, Angie/Region 19 Ed Service Center	27,73	139
Harp, Bill/Pleasant Grove Ind School Dist	4,68,83	49
Harp, Bret/Avery Ind School Dist	6	322
Harper, Daniel/Edna Ind School Dist	2,19	239
Harper, Ed/Mansfield Ind School Dist	2	356
Harper, Gay/Laneville Ind School Dist	4	327
Harper, Jay/Harper Ind School Dist	9,58	163
Harper, Kathy/Edgewood Ind School Dist	7	380
Harper, Lana/Eagle Pass Ind School Dist	30,74,83,90,93,273,274	276
Harper, Lisa/Palacios Ind School Dist	7	275
Harper, Nathan/Medina Valley Ind School Dist	295	284
Harper, Ryan/Whitesboro Ind School Dist	1	168
Harper, Shelly/Gatesville Ind School Dist	73	93
Harral, Tony/Ballinger Ind School Dist	3,5	326
Harrell, Alyta/Pasadena Ind School Dist	15,70	198
Harrell, Hal, Dr/Uvalde Cons Ind School Dist	1	378
Harrell, Harry/Sivells Bend Ind School Dist	67	91
Harrell, Kayela/Sudan Ind School Dist	69,288	261
Harrell, Kayla/Maud Ind School Dist	83,85,88,270	49
Harrell, Rick/Crandall Ind School Dist	67	251
Harrell, Sam/Silsbee Ind School Dist	67	178
Harrell, Scott/Pasadena Ind School Dist	74	198
Harrell, Scott/Sudan Ind School Dist	1,11	261
Harrell, Sherra/Grady Ind School Dist	58	274
Harrell, Stephen/Deer Park Ind School Dist	15,79,91	186
Harrell, Zac/Athens Ind School Dist	6	213
Harrington, Deanna/Frost Ind School Dist	2	299
Harrington, Joe, Dr/Hurst-Euless-Bedford ISD	10,15	353
Harrington, Julie/Crosbyton Cons Ind Sch Dist	73,295	94
Harrington, Kevin/Crawford Ind School Dist	58	279
Harrington, Kevin/McGregor Ind School Dist	58,275	280
Harrington, Paul/Clint Ind School Dist	4	132
Harris, Barbara/Kelton Ind School Dist	7	390
Harris, Carol/Neches Ind School Dist	57	15
Harris, Cathy/Prairie Valley Ind School Dist	79	290
Harris, Cohnie/Royse City Ind School Dist	4	326
Harris, Dagmar/Killeen Ind School Dist	10	27
Harris, Dawn/Gilmer Ind School Dist	11,15,273	376
Harris, Debbie/Jim Ned Cons Ind School Dist	12	361
Harris, Don/Crawford Ind School Dist	8,73,88	279
Harris, Elizabeth/Devers Ind School Dist	1,11,57,288	265
Harris, Elizabeth/Devers Ind School Dist	12,57,83	265
Harris, Gay/Beckville Ind School Dist	3,5	311
Harris, Grif/Bynum Ind School Dist	67	227
Harris, Hoyt/Aledo Ind School Dist	67	312
Harris, Jeff/College Station Ind Sch Dist	67	55
Harris, John/Ector Ind School Dist	67	146
Harris, Jonathan/Del Valle Ind School Dist	58,79	369
Harris, Leslie/Chilton Ind School Dist	8,12,69,88	144
Harris, Lindsay/Iola Ind School Dist	31,270	172
Harris, Nichole/Bridge City Ind School Dist	36	308
Harris, Richmon/Floresville Ind School Dist	4	400

Job Function Codes:

1 Superintendent
2 Bus/Finance/Purchasing
3 Buildings And Grounds
4 Food Service
5 Transportation
6 Athletic
7 Health Services
8 Curric/Instruct K-12
9 Curric/Instruct Elem
10 Curric/Instruct Sec
11 Federal Program
12 Title I
13 Title V
15 Asst Superintendent
16 Instructional Media Svcs
17 Chief Operations Officer
18 Chief Academic Officer
19 Chief Financial Officer
20 Art K-12
21 Art Elem
22 Art Sec
23 Music K-12
24 Music Elem
25 Music Sec
26 Business Education
27 Career & Tech Ed
28 Technology Education
29 Family/Consumer Science
30 Adult Education
31 Career/Sch-to-Work K-12
32 Career/Sch-to-Work Elem
33 Career/Sch-to-Work Sec
34 Early Childhood Ed
35 Health/Phys Education
36 Guidance Services K-12
37 Guidance Services Elem
38 Guidance Services Sec
39 Social Studies K-12
40 Social Studies Elem
41 Social Studies Sec
42 Science K-12
43 Science Elem
44 Science Sec
45 Math K-12
46 Math Elem
47 Math Sec
48 English/Lang Arts K-12
49 English/Lang Arts Elem
50 English/Lang Arts Sec
51 Reading K-12
52 Reading Elem
53 Reading Sec
54 Remedial Reading K-12
55 Remedial Reading Elem
56 Remedial Reading Sec
57 Bilingual/ELL
58 Special Education K-12
59 Special Education Elem
60 Special Education Sec
61 Foreign/World Lang K-12
62 Foreign/World Lang Elem
63 Foreign/World Lang Sec
64 Religious Education K-12
65 Religious Education Elem
66 Religious Education Sec
67 School Board President
68 Teacher Personnel
70 Research/Development
71 Public Information
72 Summer School
73 Instructional Tech
74 Inservice Training
75 Marketing/Distributive
76 Info Systems
77 Psychological Assess
78 Affirmative Action
79 Student Personnel
80 Driver Ed/Safety
81 Gifted/Talented
82 Video Services
83 Substance Abuse Prev
84 Erate
85 AIDS Education
88 Alternative/At Risk
89 Multi-Cultural Curriculum
90 Social Work
91 Safety/Security
92 Magnet School
93 Parental Involvement
95 Tech Prep Program
97 Chief Information Officer
98 Chief Technology Officer
270 Character Education
271 Migrant Education
273 Teacher Mentor
274 Before/After Sch
275 Response To Intervention
277 Remedial Math K-12
280 Literacy Coach
285 STEM
286 Digital Learning
288 Common Core Standards
294 Accountability
295 Network System
296 Title II Programs
297 Webmaster
298 Grant Writer/Ptnrships
750 Chief Innovation Officer
751 Chief of Staff
752 Social Emotional Learning

Texas School Directory
DISTRICT PERSONNEL INDEX

NAME/District	JOB FUNCTIONS	PAGE
Harris, Rickie/*West Orange-Cove Cons ISD*	1	309
Harris, Ron/*Fairfield Ind School Dist*	3	156
Harris, Ronnie/*Blackwell Cons Ind Sch Dist*	3,5	301
Harris, Sam/*Galena Park Ind School Dist*	20,23	186
Harris, Sarah/*Monahans-Wickett-Pyote ISD*	2	385
Harris, Terrell/*Kerens Ind School Dist*	6	300
Harris, Terry/*Richardson Ind School Dist*	68	112
Harris, Trudy/*Lamar Cons Ind School Dist*	88	153
Harris, Zachary/*Smithville Ind School Dist*	3,5	24
Harrison, Calvin/*Grand Prairie Ind School Dist*	15,79,91	107
Harrison, Darla/*Jayton-Girard Ind School Dist*	31,69,83,88	255
Harrison, Dierdre/*Lufkin Ind School Dist*	77	18
Harrison, Keith/*Meadow Ind School Dist*	67	362
Harrison, Mark/*Celeste Ind School Dist*	3,5	235
Harrison, Marshall/*Sunray Ind School Dist*	1,11,57	296
Harrison, Monica/*Texarkana Ind School Dist*	81	50
Harrison, Nick/*West Rusk Co Cons Ind Sch Dist*	6	328
Harrison, Richard/*Lake Travis Ind School Dist*	3	370
Harrison, Shawn/*Evant Ind School Dist*	35	92
Harrison, Sherry/*New Braunfels Ind School Dist*	67	88
Harrison, Susan/*Woden Ind School Dist*	16	298
Harrison, Theresa/*Petrolia Cons Ind School Dist*	2,84	74
Harrist, Sidney/*Atlanta Ind School Dist*	1	69
Harryman, Mary/*Pasadena Ind School Dist*	4	198
Hart, Britt/*Falls City Ind School Dist*	6	250
Hart, Cindy/*Deer Park Ind School Dist*	45	186
Hart, Courtney/*Lewisville Ind School Dist*	11	122
Hart, Jaelynn/*East Central Ind School Dist*	7	31
Hart, Kelly/*Gruver Ind School Dist*	16	176
Hart, Lori/*Denton Ind School Dist*	69	120
Hart, Peter/*Alvord Ind School Dist*	6	402
Hart, Shonna/*Aubrey Ind School Dist*	5	120
Hartford, Charles/*Fruitvale Ind School Dist*	285	380
Hartford, David/*Boles Ind School Dist*	73,295	235
Hartgraves, Jon/*Hico Ind School Dist*	1,11,84	176
Hartioz, Jerrod/*Leon Ind School Dist*	73	264
Hartley, Rick/*Shepherd Ind School Dist*	1	330
Hartling, Marisa/*Houston Ind School Dist*	53	188
Hartman, James/*Ferris Ind School Dist*	1	140
Hartmann, Michelle/*Pawnee Ind School Dist*	1,11,84,288	25
Hartnett, Desiree/*Galveston Ind School Dist*	57	160
Harvey, Bill, Dr/*Calhoun Co Ind School Dist*	67	62
Harvey, Brad/*Kerrville Ind School Dist*	5	256
Harvey, Isabel/*Sabine Pass Ind School Dist*	36,270	244
Harvey, Jeff/*Fayetteville Ind School Dist*	1,11,83,288	147
Harvey, Traci/*Louise Ind School Dist*	38	389
Harwell, Eddie/*Nacogdoches Ind School Dist*	90	298
Hasley, Donald/*Nacogdoches Ind School Dist*	27	298
Hasley, Katrina, Dr/*Plano Ind School Dist*	8,15,27,34,57,58	82
Hassenfratz, Kathleen/*Lake Travis Ind School Dist*	83,85,270	370
Hassler, Javon/*Higgins Ind School Dist*	16,73,286	268
Hastey, Lizette/*Post Ind School Dist*	37	162
Hastings, Cindy/*Hamlin Ind School Dist*	31,36,88	249
Hastings, John/*Seguin Ind School Dist*	76	173
Hastings, Julie/*Waxahachie Ind School Dist*	11,298	142
Haston, Cindy/*Tatum Ind School Dist*	16	328
Hatch, John/*Garland Ind School Dist*	39	105
Hatch, Nannette/*Diocese Corpus Christi Ed Off*	15	306
Hatcher, Zevely/*Kilgore Ind School Dist*	8	169
Hathaway, Bill/*Luling Ind School Dist*	4	61
Hathaway, Robin/*West Orange-Cove Cons ISD*	2	309
Hathaway, Sherri/*Victoria Ind School Dist*	10	382
Hatley, Lisa/*Dumas Ind School Dist*	9	295
Hatter, Gary/*Bloomington Ind School Dist*	4	381
Hatton, Ann/*Leander Ind School Dist*	5	396
Hatton, Carroll/*Spurger Ind School Dist*	67	375
Hatton, Jayne/*Ft Sam Houston Ind School Dist*	8,11,16,57,83,88,285,296	32
Hauberd, Carl/*Alvin Ind School Dist*	67	50
Haugeberg, Eric/*Temple Ind School Dist*	13,15,79	29
Hauger, Bob/*Bryson Ind School Dist*	67	238
Haught, Mark/*Northside Ind School Dist*	1	393
Hauk, Monica/*Bartlett Ind School Dist*	16,73,295	26
Haurdhty, Tanya/*Aspermont Ind School Dist*	4	342
Havard, Daniel/*West Sabine Ind Sch Dist*	16,73,295	329
Havey, Holly/*Medina Valley Ind School Dist*	88	284
Hawkins, Ben/*Lindsay Ind School Dist*	67	91

NAME/District	JOB FUNCTIONS	PAGE
Hawkins, Billy/*Bullard Ind School Dist*	3	336
Hawkins, Brent, Dr/*Livingston Ind School Dist*	1	316
Hawkins, Holley/*City View Ind School Dist*	16,57,69,88,273	391
Hawkins, Holly/*City View Ind School Dist*	8,11	391
Hawkins, Kristi/*Mt Calm Ind School Dist*	2,11	228
Hawkins, Mike/*Bruceville-Eddy Ind Sch Dist*	5	278
Hawkins, Mildred/*Bay City Ind School Dist*	4	275
Hawkins, Randy/*Winona Ind School Dist*	67	339
Hawkins, Rudy/*City View Ind School Dist*	6	391
Hawkins, Scott/*Thorndale Ind School Dist*	6	288
Hawkins, Yolanda/*Queen City Ind School Dist*	2	70
Hawley, David/*Denison Ind School Dist*	67	166
Haws, Amy/*Bynum Ind School Dist*	36	227
Haws, Josh/*Bynum Ind School Dist*	3,5	227
Hawthorne, Ben/*Silsbee Ind School Dist*	91	178
Hay, Matthew, Dr/*Galveston Ind School Dist*	67	160
Hayenga, Leslie/*San Felipe-Del Rio Cons Ind SD*	73,286	379
Hayes-Ramirez, Heather/*Alief Ind School Dist*	4	181
Hayes, Amy/*Temple Ind School Dist*	68	29
Hayes, Britt/*Region 18 Ed Service Center*	2	287
Hayes, Cori/*Forestburg Ind School Dist*	6	290
Hayes, David/*Wortham Ind School Dist*	8,271,273	156
Hayes, Fred, Dr/*Southside Ind School Dist*	2,15	43
Hayes, Houston/*Humble Ind School Dist*	20	195
Hayes, Jimmy/*Brownsville Ind School Dist*	15	63
Hayes, Melanie/*Dawson Ind School Dist*	36,69,88	116
Hayes, Michael/*Silverton Ind School Dist*	2	57
Hayes, Nathan/*Water Valley Ind School Dist*	6	365
Hayes, Robert/*Bryan Ind School Dist*	76	54
Hayes, Sandra/*Richardson Ind School Dist*	3,15	112
Hayes, Shannon/*Royse City Ind School Dist*	58,79	326
Hayes, Sheri/*Bishop Cons Ind School Dist*	16,82,84	302
Hayes, Stephanie/*Bullard Ind School Dist*	4	336
Hayes, Sue/*Region 10 Ed Service Center*	2,19	116
Hayes, Tami/*Ropes Ind School Dist*	58	229
Haygood, Blake/*New Braunfels Ind School Dist*	81	88
Haymae, Kristine/*Region 6 Ed Service Center*	30	384
Haynes, Deanna/*Eustace Ind School Dist*	8,12,57	214
Haynes, Denise/*Deer Park Ind School Dist*	42	186
Haynes, Kathy/*Stephenville Ind School Dist*	68	144
Haynes, Larry/*Hardin Ind School Dist*	6	265
Haynes, Larry/*West Orange-Cove Cons ISD*	11	309
Haynes, Sherri/*McLean Ind School Dist*	67	165
Haynie, Dennis/*Andrews Ind School Dist*	16,73,95	16
Haynie, Joe/*Crowell Ind School Dist*	67	149
Haynie, Kayla/*Boyd Ind School Dist*	73	402
Haynie, Mary/*Ysleta Ind School Dist*	2	137
Hays, Blake/*Sherman Ind School Dist*	10	167
Hays, Wanda/*Cuero Ind School Dist*	7	117
Hayward, David/*Damon Ind School Dist*	1	53
Hazzard, Preston/*Frisco Ind School Dist*	20	78
Head, Scott/*Lake Dallas Ind School Dist*	6	122
Head, Tom/*Alvarado Ind School Dist*	67	246
Headlee, Glenn/*Ft Worth Ind School Dist*	4	349
Headnot, Denitro/*Jasper Ind School Dist*	73,76,295	240
Heafley, Tracy/*Yorktown Ind School Dist*	38	118
Heard, Clint/*Montgomery Ind School Dist*	6,35	293
Hearn, Paul/*Mineral Wells Ind School Dist*	2,19	310
Hearne, Debbie/*Bryson Ind School Dist*	8,12,69	238
Hearron, Shannon/*Harleton Ind School Dist*	7	208
Heath-Johnson, Wanda/*Galena Park Ind School Dist*	67	186
Heath, Cliff/*Bosqueville Ind School Dist*	10	278
Heath, Jason/*Anna Ind School Dist*	6	77
Heath, Kyle, Dr/*Cleburne Ind School Dist*	1	247
Heath, Phyllis/*Chillicothe ISD School Dist*	73	177
Heath, Susan/*College Station Ind Sch Dist*	34	55
Heathington, Dani/*Muleshoe Ind School Dist*	15	22
Heathman, Jerid/*Murchison Ind Sch Dist*	6	214
Heaton, Sally/*Dumas Ind School Dist*	10,280	295
Hebert, Anita/*Magnolia Ind School Dist*	15	292
Hebert, Forrest/*Channing Ind School Dist*	8,74,83	209
Heck, Austin/*Nazareth Ind School Dist*	27	71
Heck, Patricia/*Panhandle Ind School Dist*	58	69
Heckman, Coleman, Dr/*Northside Ind School Dist*	77	36
Hecks, Cesioy/*Aspermont Ind School Dist*	73	342
Heddins, Jennifer/*White Settlement Ind Sch Dist*	30,80	357

DISTRICT PERSONNEL INDEX

Market Data Retrieval

NAME/District	JOB FUNCTIONS	PAGE
Hedges, David/Petrolia Cons Ind School Dist	1	74
Heers, Lou/Muenster Ind School Dist	9,11,271	91
Heeth, Karen/Spring Branch Ind School Dist	68	200
Heflin, Lannon/Georgetown Ind School Dist	70,73,98,750	395
Heflin, Lynn/Ore City Ind School Dist	1	376
Hefner, Bill/Rice Cons Ind School Dist	1,11	87
Heid, Kristi/Sabine Pass Ind School Dist	1	244
Heidel, Patti/Columbia Brazoria ISD	8,54,69,275,280	52
Heier, Linda/Randolph Field Ind School Dist	11	39
Heimbuch, Stephanie/Red Oak Ind School Dist	8	142
Hein, Gladys/Royal Ind School Dist	2	384
Hein, Richard/Sanford-Fritch Ind School Dist	2,11,73	238
Hein, Stephanie/Royal Ind School Dist	79	384
Hein, Theresa/Zapata Co Ind School Dist	2	406
Heinen, Kim/Lake Travis Ind School Dist	68	370
Heinrich, Darla/Lubbock-Cooper Ind Sch Dist	11	271
Heinroth, Michael/Sweeny Ind School Dist	37	54
Heironimus, Brian/Angleton Ind School Dist	295	51
Heisel, Stan/Terrell Ind School Dist	5,73,76,295	253
Helfferich, Tracey/Yantis Ind School Dist	1	405
Helfferich, Tracey/Yantis Ind School Dist	8,11,298	405
Heller, Don/Anson Ind School Dist	67	249
Heller, Melissa/Richardson Ind School Dist	74	112
Helmcamp, Jack/Buffalo Ind School Dist	67	264
Helmcamp, Janet/Cleburne Ind School Dist	69,81	247
Helmer, Kevin/Chireno ISD School Dist	16,73,295	297
Helms, Joe/Grandfalls-Royalty Ind SD	1,11	385
Helms, Melissa/Lingleville Ind School Dist	27,31	143
Helms, Michelle/San Angelo Ind School Dist	4	364
Helms, Robert/Irion Co Ind School Dist	2	238
Helton, Dawn/Silsbee Ind School Dist	81	178
Helton, Melissa/Union Hill Ind School Dist	2	377
Hemann, Ronnie/Region 7 Ed Service Center	3,15,68	171
Hembree, Jeff/South Texas Ind School Dist	11,57,73,76,285,286,295,296	67
Hemby, William/Celina Ind School Dist	3,15	77
Hemmila, Jaclyn/Carroll Independent Sch Dist	22,44,47	347
Hempel, Craig/Mexia Ind School Dist	4	267
Hemphill, Allison/Angleton Ind School Dist	298	51
Hemphill, Bebetta/Garland Ind School Dist	58,79	105
Hemphill, Danny/Evant Ind School Dist	68,84,91	92
Hemphill, Danny/Evant Ind School Dist	2	92
Hemphill, Kim/Smithville Ind School Dist	16	24
Henderson, Angela/El Paso Ind School Dist	15	132
Henderson, Angela/El Paso ISD-Middle Schools	15	134
Henderson, Betty/Aubrey Ind School Dist	2,68	120
Henderson, Ernest/Orange Grove Ind School Dist	8,11,57,69,73,74,275,294	245
Henderson, Julie/Wichita Falls Ind School Dist	35,83,85	392
Henderson, Kathy/Aransas Co Ind School Dist	2,19	19
Henderson, Lori/Graford Ind School Dist	12,79,296	310
Henderson, Mike/Hawkins Ind School Dist	73,295	404
Henderson, Shannon/Queen City Ind School Dist	8,11,36,69,72,73,285	70
Henderson, Shelly/McLean Ind School Dist	54,280	165
Henderson, Stacy/Dawson Ind School Dist	1	299
Henderson, Suzette/Era Ind School Dist	2,11	90
Henderson, Wayne/Sands Consolidated ISD	1	117
Hendrick, Irana/Overton Ind School Dist	16	328
Hendrick, Sue/Kerrville Ind School Dist	5	256
Hendricks, Jackie, Dr/Princeton Ind School Dist	8,11,15,36,57,83,271,288	84
Hendricks, Mary/Commerce Independent Sch Dist	11,296	236
Hendricks, Mike/Dawson Ind School Dist	3,4,5	116
Hendricks, Terry/Munday Consolidated Ind SD	3	259
Hendrickson, Curtis/Pottsboro Ind School Dist	5	167
Hendrickson, Jessica/Gordon Ind School Dist	2,19	310
Hendrickson, Kathryn/Eustace Ind School Dist	58	214
Hendrix, Laura/Aquilla Ind School Dist	58	227
Hendrix, Traci/Pflugerville Ind School Dist	27	371
Hendry, Mary/Diboll Ind School Dist	69	17

NAME/District	JOB FUNCTIONS	PAGE
Henke, Charles/Schulenburg Ind School Dist	69	148
Henke, Kendra/McKinney Ind School Dist	44	81
Hennessey, Carla/Montague Ind School Dist	1,11,83	290
Hennig, Grace/Itasca Ind School Dist	36,83	228
Hennig, Grant/McDade Ind School Dist	76	24
Henry, Justin/Dallas Ind School Dist	67	98
Henry, Kenneth/Cypress-Fairbanks Ind Sch Dist	79	184
Henry, Kristi/Anahuac Ind School Dist	38,79	71
Henry, Mark, Dr/Cypress-Fairbanks Ind Sch Dist	1	183
Henry, Rosemary, Dr/Diocese Corpus Christi Ed Off	1,11	306
Henry, Roy/Kopperl Ind School Dist	31,36,83	47
Henslay, Anthony/Ganado Ind School Dist	5	239
Hensley, Andrea/Cleburne Ind School Dist	9	247
Hensley, Nielan/De Kalb Ind School Dist	91	48
Hensley, Patti/New Deal Ind School Dist	7,85	271
Hensley, Wanda/Winona Ind School Dist	271	339
Henson, Darryl, Dr/Cedar Hill Ind School Dist	15	97
Henson, Gema/Pflugerville Ind School Dist	57	371
Henson, Leslie/Bridgeport Ind School Dist	73	402
Henson, Reggie/Kilgore Ind School Dist	67	169
Herbel, Dene, Dr/Millsap Ind School Dist	67	312
Herbst, Myra/Humble Ind School Dist	49,51	195
Herbstritt, Tracee/Childress Ind School Dist	4	74
Herew, Carey/Center Ind School Dist	34,58	334
Hergert, Adrienne/Rockwall Ind School Dist	7,35	325
Heriard, Tammy/Warren Ind School Dist	4	375
Herman, Mike/Lewisville Ind School Dist	4	122
Hermes, Adam/Burnet Cons Ind Sch Dist	73	60
Hermes, Kevin/Banquete Ind School Dist	6	302
Hermesmeyer, Angie/Goldthwaite Consolidated ISD	6,285	288
Hermesmeyer, Stephen/Comanche Ind School Dist	6	89
Hernadez, Maggie/Calhoun Co Ind School Dist	8	61
Hernandez, Alicia/Weatherford Ind School Dist	4	313
Hernandez, Arianna/Pharr-San Juan-Alamo Ind SD	16,71	223
Hernandez, Benny/Mathis Ind School Dist	1,11,57,83	331
Hernandez, Cathy/La Feria Ind School Dist	1	65
Hernandez, Cheryl/Beaumont Ind School Dist	2,19	241
Hernandez, Cindy/Buckholts Ind School Dist	4	287
Hernandez, Cindy/Walcott Ind School Dist	4	119
Hernandez, Cynthia/Corpus Christi Ind Sch Dist	280	303
Hernandez, Daisy/Hart Ind School Dist	36	71
Hernandez, Debbie/Point Isabel Ind Sch Dist	69	66
Hernandez, Deborah/Harlandale Ind School Dist	7	32
Hernandez, Denise/West Oso Ind School Dist	3,5	306
Hernandez, Dora/Bloomington Ind School Dist	58	381
Hernandez, Eden, Dr/Bishop Cons Ind School Dist	8,11,34,58,69,73,81,83	302
Hernandez, Eduardo, Dr/Edgewood Ind School Dist	1	31
Hernandez, Eduardo, Dr/Edgewood Ind School Dist	1	380
Hernandez, Elizabeth/Teague Ind School Dist	69	156
Hernandez, Hector/Boerne Ind School Dist	91	253
Hernandez, Horacio/San Elizario Ind School Dist	295	135
Hernandez, Janice/Southwest Ind School Dist	71	43
Hernandez, Joe/Calhoun Co Ind School Dist	3,5,91	61
Hernandez, John/East Central Ind School Dist	79	31
Hernandez, Kristi/Region 4 Ed Service Center	71	208
Hernandez, Letty/Culberson Co Allamoore Ind SD	67	95
Hernandez, Linda/Roosevelt Ind School Dist	8,11,69,83,273,274,286,296	271
Hernandez, Lisa/Region 3 Ed Service Center	298	383
Hernandez, Lucero/Canutillo Ind School Dist	88	132
Hernandez, Lupe/Evant Ind School Dist	4	92
Hernandez, Magda/Irving Ind School Dist	1	109
Hernandez, Maria/Crane Ind School Dist	7	93
Hernandez, Marie/Weatherford Ind School Dist	57	313
Hernandez, Marie/Weatherford Ind School Dist	10,280	313
Hernandez, Melissa/Lubbock Ind School Dist	57	269
Hernandez, Mica/Victoria Ind School Dist	41	382
Hernandez, Mike/Slaton Ind School Dist	3,5	272

1 Superintendent	16 Instructional Media Svcs	30 Adult Education	44 Science Sec	58 Special Education K-12	72 Summer School	88 Alternative/At Risk	277 Remedial Math K-12
2 Bus/Finance/Purchasing	17 Chief Operations Officer	31 Career/Sch-to-Work K-12	45 Math K-12	59 Special Education Elem	73 Instructional Tech	89 Multi-Cultural Curriculum	280 Literacy Coach
3 Buildings And Grounds	18 Chief Academic Officer	32 Career/Sch-to-Work Elem	46 Math Elem	60 Special Education Sec	74 Inservice Training	90 Social Work	285 STEM
4 Food Service	19 Chief Financial Officer	33 Career/Sch-to-Work Sec	47 Math Sec	61 Foreign/World Lang K-12	75 Marketing/Distribute	91 Safety/Security	286 Digital Learning
5 Transportation	20 Art K-12	34 Early Childhood Ed	48 English/Lang Arts K-12	62 Foreign/World Lang Elem	76 Info Systems	92 Magnet School	288 Common Core Standards
6 Athletic	21 Art Elem	35 Health/Phys Education	49 English/Lang Arts Elem	63 Foreign/World Lang Sec	77 Psychological Assess	93 Parental Involvement	294 Accountability
7 Health Services	22 Art Sec	36 Guidance Services K-12	50 English/Lang Arts Sec	64 Religious Education K-12	78 Affirmative Action	95 Tech Prep Program	295 Network System
8 Curric/Instruct K-12	23 Music K-12	37 Guidance Services Elem	51 Reading K-12	65 Religious Education Elem	79 Student Personnel	97 Chief Information Officer	296 Title II Programs
9 Curric/Instruct Elem	24 Music Elem	38 Guidance Services Sec	52 Reading Elem	66 Religious Education Sec	80 Driver Ed/Safety	98 Chief Technology Officer	297 Webmaster
10 Curric/Instruct Sec	25 Music Sec	39 Social Studies K-12	53 Reading Sec	67 School Board President	81 Gifted/Talented	270 Character Education	298 Grant Writer/Ptnrships
11 Federal Program	26 Business Education	40 Social Studies Elem	54 Remedial Reading K-12	68 Teacher Personnel	82 Video Services	271 Migrant Education	750 Chief Innovation Officer
12 Title I	27 Career & Tech Ed	41 Social Studies Sec	55 Remedial Reading Elem	69 Academic Assessment	83 Substance Abuse Prev	273 Teacher Mentor	751 Chief of Staff
13 Title V	28 Technology Education	42 Science K-12	56 Remedial Reading Sec	70 Research/Development	84 Erate	274 Before/After Sch	752 Social Emotional Learning
15 Asst Superintendent	29 Family/Consumer Science	43 Science Elem	57 Bilingual/ELL	71 Public Information	85 AIDS Education	275 Response To Intervention	

TX-T40

Texas School Directory

DISTRICT PERSONNEL INDEX

NAME/District	JOB FUNCTIONS	PAGE
Hernandez, Olivia/*San Antonio Ind School Dist*	15,57,271	39
Hernandez, Patricia/*Bridgeport Ind School Dist*	11,57,69,271,288,296,298	402
Hernandez, Patrick/*Tuloso-Midway Ind School Dist*	3,5	305
Hernandez, Renee/*Allen Ind School Dist*	16	76
Hernandez, Richard/*Harlandale Ind School Dist*	2,15	32
Hernandez, Roland, Dr/*Corpus Christi Ind Sch Dist*	1	303
Hernandez, Rolando/*La Joya Ind School Dist*	4	219
Hernandez, Rosemary/*Edgewood Ind School Dist*	34	31
Hernandez, Samara/*Como Pickton Cons Ind SD*	4	231
Hernandez, Sandra/*Cuero Ind School Dist*	4	117
Hernandez, Shannon/*Ft Worth Ind School Dist*	45	349
Hernandez, Sylvia/*Bloomington Ind School Dist*	8	381
Hernandez, Tony/*Avalon Ind School Dist*	3	140
Hernandez, Victor/*Clint Ind School Dist*	57	132
Hernandez, Victor/*Gregory-Portland Ind Sch Dist*	67	331
Hernandez, Victor/*Plainview Ind School Dist*	2	175
Herndon, Sommer/*Center Ind School Dist*	38,69	334
Herrera, Hector/*Dayton Ind School Dist*	91	265
Herrera, Karen, Dr/*Killeen Ind School Dist*	20,23	27
Herrera, Marcie/*Sheldon Ind School Dist*	76	200
Herrera, Maria/*Whitney Ind School Dist*	57	228
Herrera, Marianna/*Flatonia Ind School Dist*	271	147
Herrera, Rolando/*Mercedes Ind School Dist*	3	221
Herrin, Debby/*Leveretts Chapel Ind Sch Dist*	2,11,298	328
Herrin, Rick/*Aledo Ind School Dist*	71	312
Herring, Cheryl/*Junction Ind School Dist*	2,84	256
Herring, Cliff/*Southside Ind School Dist*	73	43
Herring, Gloria/*Atlanta Ind School Dist*	16	69
Herring, Jason/*Refugio Ind School Dist*	6	323
Herring, Kathy/*Comanche Ind School Dist*	2	89
Herring, Lisa/*Refugio Ind School Dist*	2,11,57,69,74,270,294,298	323
Herrington, Tina/*Wharton Ind School Dist*	1	390
Herrod, Kristi/*Santa Anna Ind School Dist*	36,57,69,83,271,285	76
Herron, Kevin/*Central Heights Ind Sch Dist*	6	297
Hershey, Paige/*Spring Branch Ind School Dist*	6	200
Hertz, Taffi/*East Central Ind School Dist*	8,15	31
Hervieux, Glenn/*Van Ind School Dist*	84	381
Heryford, Mary/*Seagraves Ind School Dist*	38	157
Herzog, Mitch/*Wylie Ind School Dist*	67	85
Heskett, Christopher, Dr/*Covington ISD School Dist*	1	227
Heskett, Keri/*Covington ISD School Dist*	36,88,270,271	227
Heslip, Eric/*Hemphill Ind School Dist*	73,295	329
Hess, Kristie/*Burton Ind School Dist*	58	386
Hestand, Mary/*Cypress-Fairbanks Ind Sch Dist*	37	184
Hesteande, Blake/*Pilot Point Ind School Dist*	27	125
Hester, Chrissy/*College Station Ind Sch Dist*	16,36,79	55
Hester, Pat/*Carrollton-Farmers Branch ISD*	3,17,274	96
Hettich, Jody/*Winnsboro Ind School Dist*	91	405
Hiatt, Shawn/*Sealy Ind School Dist*	11	22
Hickerson, Corey/*Buffalo Ind School Dist*	83	264
Hickey, Blair/*Prosper Ind School Dist*	58	84
Hickey, Glenda/*Gladewater Ind School Dist*	2,19,73	169
Hickman, Akweta/*Austin Ind School Dist*	58	366
Hickman, Akweta, Dr/*DeSoto Ind School Dist*	58,77	104
Hickman, Jason/*Garland Ind School Dist*	73	105
Hickman, Karen, Dr/*Pasadena Ind School Dist*	8,15,288	198
Hickman, Lauren/*Conroe Ind School Dist*	58	291
Hickman, Seth/*Burleson Ind School Dist*	42,45	246
Hickman, Stormy/*College Station Ind Sch Dist*	68	55
Hicks, David, Dr/*Sherman Ind School Dist*	1	167
Hicks, Della/*Comanche Ind School Dist*	10,36,69,77,83,85	89
Hicks, Gilbert/*Austin ISD Elem School Area 2*	15	367
Hicks, Glen/*Karnack Ind School Dist*	73	208
Hicks, Graydon/*Fort Davis Ind School Dist*	1	241
Hicks, Jason/*Woodville Ind School Dist*	88	375
Hicks, Jeff/*Lone Oak Ind School Dist*	8	236
Hicks, Tim/*Midlothian Ind School Dist*	91	141
Hicks, Todd/*Crosby Ind School Dist*	10,74,273	183
Hicks, Toni, Dr/*Liberty Hill Ind School Dist*	8,15,88,294	398
Hicky, Brooke/*Riviera Ind School Dist*	12,31,69,92	258
Hidalgo, Caleb/*Borger Ind School Dist*	5	237
Hidalgo, Daniel/*Friona Ind School Dist*	3	315
Hidditts, Paula/*Lingleville Ind School Dist*	2	143
Hierholzer, Natalie/*North East Ind School Dist*	36	34
Hieronymus, Bill/*Pampa Ind School Dist*	5	165
Higginbotham, Jd/*Bellville Ind School Dist*	3	21

NAME/District	JOB FUNCTIONS	PAGE
Higgins, Franklin/*Aldine Ind School Dist*	27,31	179
Higgins, Lori/*Baird Ind School Dist*	67	62
Higgins, Marshall/*Marlin Ind School Dist*	5	144
Higgins, Matt/*Jim Ned Cons Ind School Dist*	67	361
Higgins, Misty/*Port Neches-Groves Ind SD*	11,58,88	243
Higgins, William/*Chico Ind School Dist*	1	403
Higgs, Marcus/*Texas City Ind School Dist*	15,68,78	161
Highnote, Therese/*Katy Ind School Dist*	7	151
Hightower, Chris/*Midland Ind School Dist*	39	285
Hightower, Jeffery/*Central Heights Ind Sch Dist*	73	297
Hightower, Maranda/*Brookeland Ind School Dist*	294	240
Hilburn, Kelli/*Denver City Ind School Dist*	37	405
Hildreath, Clint/*North Lamar Ind School Dist*	5	259
Hile, Adam/*Klein Ind School Dist*	8	196
Hile, Adam, Dr/*Bridgeport Ind School Dist*	8,15,72	402
Hill, Ann/*Morton Ind School Dist*	58	75
Hill, Cheryl/*La Poynor Ind School Dist*	4	214
Hill, Colleen/*Garrison Ind School Dist*	11	297
Hill, David/*Goliad Ind School Dist*	3	163
Hill, Daya, Dr/*Nacogdoches Ind School Dist*	8,18	298
Hill, Dedra/*Hartley Ind School Dist*	6	209
Hill, Deena, Dr/*Ft Bend Ind School Dist*	58	149
Hill, Devin/*Van Alstyne Ind School Dist*	16	168
Hill, Eddie/*La Porte Ind School Dist*	16,76,295	198
Hill, Emberly/*Grapevine-Colleyville Ind SD*	36	353
Hill, Glen/*Knox City-O'Brien Cons Ind SD*	10,83,88,275	258
Hill, Guy/*Nocona Ind School Dist*	67	290
Hill, Hutchison/*Pflugerville Ind School Dist*	58	371
Hill, Jan/*Bullard Ind School Dist*	8,11,88,271	336
Hill, Jason/*Keene Ind school Dist*	6	248
Hill, Jim/*Westbrook Ind School Dist*	6	289
Hill, Johnny/*Lake Travis Ind School Dist*	2,15	370
Hill, Jon, Dr/*Dodd City Ind School Dist*	1,83	145
Hill, Julie/*Spring Ind School Dist*	15,751	202
Hill, Justin/*Coppell Ind School Dist*	2	98
Hill, Linda/*Midland Ind School Dist*	47	285
Hill, Lowell/*Bruceville-Eddy Ind Sch Dist*	3	278
Hill, Lynn/*Guthrie Common School Dist*	12,69,88,294	257
Hill, Mariann/*Robert Lee Ind School Dist*	12,57	75
Hill, Matt/*New Deal Ind School Dist*	6	271
Hill, Michael/*Arlington Ind School Dist*	15	343
Hill, Patrice/*Dimmitt Ind School Dist*	34,58	71
Hill, Patterson/*Garrison Ind School Dist*	2	297
Hill, Peggy/*Westbrook Ind School Dist*	12,57	289
Hill, Randy/*Wharton Ind School Dist*	2	390
Hill, Russell/*Morton Ind School Dist*	16	75
Hill, Sara/*McCamey Ind School Dist*	23	377
Hill, Teresa/*Elgin Ind School Dist*	36	24
Hill, Tory, Dr/*Sweeny Ind School Dist*	1	54
Hill, Yvonne/*Seguin Ind School Dist*	91	173
Hillberg, Anthony/*Seguin Ind School Dist*	2,88,298	173
Hillhouse, Leanne, Dr/*Wheeler Ind School Dist*	67	391
Hillhouse, Stacy/*Malakoff Ind School Dist*	91	214
Hilliard, Rory/*Bonham Ind School Dist*	34	145
Hillin, Amy/*Wylie Ind School Dist*	7	84
Hillis, Allison/*Lufkin Ind School Dist*	81	18
Hime, Sheryl/*Conroe Ind School Dist*	42	291
Himes, Darren/*Cross Roads Ind School Dist*	67	214
Himpele, Janice/*Humble Ind School Dist*	2	195
Himphill, Bryan/*Calvert Ind School Dist*	58	324
Hindman, Nathan/*Santa Anna Ind School Dist*	27	76
Hinds, Jennifer/*Stamford Ind School Dist*	8,11,296	250
Hinds, Olga/*Mercedes Ind School Dist*	2,19	221
Hinerman, David/*Hughes Springs Ind Sch Dist*	3,5,91	70
Hinerman, Robert/*Keene Ind School Dist*	16,82	248
Hines, Chris, Dr/*Conroe Ind School Dist*	15	291
Hines, Cory/*Chester Ind School Dist*	1,83	374
Hines, John/*Lometa Ind School Dist*	67	262
Hines, Keeli/*Ira Ind School Dist*	2	333
Hines, Rick/*China Spring Ind School Dist*	67	278
Hinkson, Kirk/*Mt Calm Ind School Dist*	6	228
Hinojosa, Adolfo/*Santa Maria Ind School Dist*	67	67
Hinojosa, Jesse/*Pearsall Ind School Dist*	73,84,295	157
Hinojosa, Lupita, Dr/*Spring Ind School Dist*	79	202
Hinojosa, Maricela/*South Texas Ind School Dist*	83,88	67
Hinojosa, Michael, Dr/*Dallas Ind School Dist*	1	98

School Year 2019-2020   800-333-8802   TX-T41

DISTRICT PERSONNEL INDEX

Market Data Retrieval

NAME/District	JOB FUNCTIONS	PAGE
Hinojosa, Micki/Highland Park Ind Sch Dist	6	108
Hinojosa, Saul/Somerset Ind School Dist	1,11	42
Hinojosa, Sofia/Edinburg Cons Ind School Dist	36,79,83,85,270,275	216
Hinojsa, Susan/Muleshoe Ind School Dist	73,286	22
Hinson, Danielle/Lake Travis Ind School Dist	68	370
Hinton, Barbara/Allen Ind School Dist	81	76
Hipp, Ashley/Plano Ind School Dist	4	82
Hipp, Barry/Cleburne Ind School Dist	3	247
Hipp, Carolsue/Port Aransas Ind School Dist	2,12	305
Hise, Lonnie/Windthorst Ind School Dist	8,31	20
Hise, Lonnie/Windthorst Ind School Dist	1,11	20
Hitchcock, Rebecca/London Ind School Dist	74,88	305
Hittle, Shauna/Tyler Ind School Dist	9,37	337
Hitzelberger, Jim/Highland Park Ind Sch Dist	67	108
Hlavenka, Natalie/Hawkins Ind School Dist	7	404
Hoard, Daniel/Big Spring Ind School Dist	295	233
Hobart, Abigal/Allen Ind School Dist	11,57	76
Hobbs, Jim/Floydada Ind School Dist	34,58	148
Hobbs, Kelly/Pittsburg Ind School Dist	34,58	68
Hobbs, Laura/Diboll Ind School Dist	16	17
Hobbs, Tim/Lufkin Ind School Dist	2	18
Hobden, Bonita/Kaufman Ind School Dist	68	252
Hobson, Bobby/Douglass Ind School Dist	67	297
Hockenberry, James, Dr/Center Ind School Dist	1	334
Hocott, Kim/Pearland Ind School Dist	16,71	53
Hodde, Jason/Burton Ind School Dist	6	386
Hodge, Donna/Keller Ind School Dist	81	354
Hodge, Paul/Lockhart Ind School Dist	295	61
Hodge, Remy/Marlin Ind School Dist	8	144
Hodges, Becky/Patton Springs Ind School Dist	2	126
Hodges, Blake/De Kalb Ind School Dist	67	48
Hodges, Brad/Anderson-Shiro Cons Ind SD	6	171
Hodges, Brenda/Salado Ind School Dist	4	29
Hodges, Cynthia/Killeen Ind School Dist	285	27
Hodges, Lisa/Allen Ind School Dist	68	76
Hodges, Stan/Hull Daisetta Ind School Dist	6	266
Hodgin, Claire/Manor Ind School Dist	43	371
Hodgkins, Mindy/Strawn Ind School Dist	67	311
Hodkinson, Andy/Carlisle Ind School Dist	3,5	327
Hodnett, Brian/Haskell Cons Ind School Dist	6	210
Hodson, Julie/Spring Branch Ind School Dist	11,298	200
Hoedebeck, David/Round Rock Ind School Dist	3	398
Hoehn, Sheila/Oglesby Ind School Dist	76	93
Hoellen, Paige/Georgetown Ind School Dist	42	395
Hoelscher, Russell/Olfen Ind School Dist	73,295	327
Hoelscher, Russell/Paint Rock Ind School Dist	73	90
Hoelscher, Shahala/Highland Ind School Dist	36,69	301
Hoelting, Cory/Nazareth Ind School Dist	73,295	71
Hoff, Elizabeth/Blanco Ind School Dist	16,82	45
Hoffman, Cassie/Lytle Ind School Dist	36,270,273	21
Hoffman, Kevin/Mart Ind School Dist	6	280
Hoffmann, Sean/Seguin Ind School Dist	71	173
Hoffpauir, Gary/East Chambers Ind School Dist	67	72
Hoffpauir, Lynda/Region 5 Ed Service Center	76	244
Hofmann, Shannon/Mason Ind School Dist	58,752	275
Hogan, Cody/Stanton Ind School Dist	6	274
Hogan, Jenifer/Quinlan Ind School Dist	36	237
Hogan, Marion/Cypress-Fairbanks Ind Sch Dist	74	184
Hogg, Jimmy/Cedar Hill Ind School Dist	91	97
Hogue, Aaron/Dawson Ind School Dist	3,5	299
Hogue, Brenda/Shelbyville Ind School Dist	4	335
Hogue, Scott/Electra Ind School Dist	83	391
Hohenberger, Denicia/Cooper Ind School Dist	1,11,57	119
Hohenberger, Steven/Paris Ind School Dist	6	260
Hohlt, Ronnie/Burton Ind School Dist	3	386
Hohmann, Alissa/Coleman Ind School Dist	36	76
Hoke, Janine/Alief Ind School Dist	74	181
Holbert, Cheryl/Henrietta Ind School Dist	31,69,83,85	74
Holbrook, Dianne, Dr/Huntington Ind School Dist	8,11,57,69,88,280,285,298	17
Holcomb, Jennifer/Weatherford Ind School Dist	274	313
Holcomb, Kim/Corsicana Ind School Dist	8,15,34,39	299
Holcomb, Pam/Garland Ind School Dist	73	105
Holcomb, Pamela/Burnet Cons Ind Sch Dist	4	60
Holcombe, Coy, Dr/Eustace Ind School Dist	1,73	214
Holcombe, Laurie/Malakoff Ind School Dist	58	214
Holcombe, Rex/Floydada Ind School Dist	11,57,73,81,84,271,295,296	148
Holden, Natasha/Barbers Hill Ind School Dist	69,294	72
Holden, Russell/Oakwood Ind School Dist	1	264
Holder, Brett/Shallowater Ind School Dist	5	272
Holder, David/Castleberry Ind School Dist	67	347
Holder, Glenda/Clear Creek Ind School Dist	81	158
Holder, Hoby/Gilmer Ind School Dist	3	376
Holder, Jamie/Lindale Ind School Dist	3,15,76	337
Holding, Jeanette/Henrietta Ind School Dist	7	74
Holfpauir, Kenny/West Hardin Co Cons Sch Dist	6	178
Holik, Sandra/Louise Ind School Dist	73,286,295	389
Holland, Amber/Gruver Ind School Dist	9	176
Holland, Ana/Point Isabel Ind Sch Dist	8,16,57,69,72,85,273,274	66
Holland, Bonnie/Katy Ind School Dist	15	151
Holland, Brad/Stanton Ind School Dist	2,19	274
Holland, Carrie/Region 7 Ed Service Center	2,15	171
Holland, David/Birdville Ind School Dist	69,294	346
Holland, Julie/Alvarado Ind School Dist	16,73,295	246
Holland, Kim/Moran Ind School Dist	8,69,288	334
Holland, Michael/Region 6 Ed Service Center	1	384
Holland, Tony/Claude Ind School Dist	58	20
Holle, Geoff/Pflugerville Ind School Dist	4	371
Holleman, Tish/Paris Ind School Dist	2	260
Holley, Aaron/Ector Co Ind School Dist	20,23	129
Holliday, Kris/Alamo Heights Ind School Dist	58,77,78,90	30
Hollie, Gil/Temple Ind School Dist	274	29
Holligan, Alicia/Region 17 Ed Service Center	36,77	272
Hollinger, Beth/Arlington Ind School Dist	15	343
Hollingsworth, Angela/Woodville Ind School Dist	83,85	375
Hollingsworth, Charla/Alief Ind School Dist	16,280	181
Hollingsworth, Jerry/Bandera Ind School Dist	1	23
Hollingsworth, Lacey/Axtell Ind School Dist	58	278
Hollingsworth, Rusty/Crosby Ind School Dist	3	183
Hollingsworth, Tara/Haskell Cons Ind School Dist	58	210
Hollins, Tony/Pine Tree Ind School Dist	3	170
Holloway, Brett/Brookeland Ind School Dist	67	240
Holloway, Charles, Dr/Tioga Ind School Dist	1	167
Holloway, Cindy/Troy Ind School Dist	2	29
Holloway, Deadra/Ft Bend Ind School Dist	11	149
Holloway, Deanne/Flatonia Ind School Dist	16,73	147
Holloway, Jeanne/Chireno ISD School Dist	2,11	297
Holloway, Melody/Elkhart Ind School Dist	38	15
Hollowell, Nancy/Thrall Ind School Dist	4	400
Hollway, Leah/Broaddus Ind School Dist	2,11	329
Hollway, Lucas/Broaddus Ind School Dist	1,83	329
Holly, Mike/Post Ind School Dist	67	162
Holly, Tom/Midland Ind School Dist	73,76,295,297	285
Holman, John/Amarillo Ind School Dist	286	317
Holman, Shane/Giddings Ind School Dist	8,11,57,58,83,88,294,296	263
Holmes, Adrianne/Humble Ind School Dist	298	195
Holmes, Brent/Teague Ind School Dist	73,295	156
Holmes, James/Henderson Ind School Dist	67	327
Holmgreen, Anna/Alice Ind School Dist	8,15,69,275	245
Holmgreen, Ron/Granbury Ind School Dist	15	230
Holt, Brian, Dr/Booker Ind School Dist	1	267
Holt, Dennis/Graford Ind School Dist	1	310
Holt, Kristy/Valley View ISD-Cooke Co	4	91
Holt, Laura, Dr/Birdville Ind School Dist	12,58	346
Holt, Leann/Rocksprings Ind School Dist	58	131

1 Superintendent
2 Bus/Finance/Purchasing
3 Buildings And Grounds
4 Food Service
5 Transportation
6 Athletic
7 Health Services
8 Curric/Instruct K-12
9 Curric/Instruct Elem
10 Curric/Instruct Sec
11 Federal Program
12 Title I
13 Title V
15 Asst Superintendent
16 Instructional Media Svcs
17 Chief Operations Officer
18 Chief Academic Officer
19 Chief Financial Officer
20 Art K-12
21 Art Elem
22 Art Sec
23 Music K-12
24 Music Elem
25 Music Sec
26 Business Education
27 Career & Tech Ed
28 Technology Education
29 Family/Consumer Science
30 Adult Education
31 Career/Sch-to-Work K-12
32 Career/Sch-to-Work Elem
33 Career/Sch-to-Work Sec
34 Early Childhood Ed
35 Health/Phys Education
36 Guidance Services K-12
37 Guidance Services Elem
38 Guidance Services Sec
39 Social Studies K-12
40 Social Studies Elem
41 Social Studies Sec
42 Science K-12
43 Science Elem
44 Science Sec
45 Math K-12
46 Math Elem
47 Math Sec
48 English/Lang Arts K-12
49 English/Lang Arts Elem
50 English/Lang Arts Sec
51 Reading K-12
52 Reading Elem
53 Reading Sec
54 Remedial Reading K-12
55 Remedial Reading Elem
56 Remedial Reading Sec
57 Bilingual/ELL
58 Special Education K-12
59 Special Education Elem
60 Special Education Sec
61 Foreign/World Lang K-12
62 Foreign/World Lang Elem
63 Foreign/World Lang Sec
64 Religious Education K-12
65 Religious Education Elem
66 Religious Education Sec
67 School Board President
68 Teacher Personnel
69 Academic Assessment
70 Research/Development
71 Public Information
72 Summer School
73 Instructional Tech
74 Inservice Training
75 Marketing/Distributive
76 Info Systems
77 Psychological Assess
78 Affirmative Action
79 Student Personnel
80 Driver Ed/Safety
81 Gifted/Talented
82 Video Services
83 Substance Abuse Prev
84 Erate
85 AIDS Education
88 Alternative/At Risk
89 Multi-Cultural Curriculum
90 Social Work
91 Safety/Security
92 Magnet School
93 Parental Involvement
94 Accountability
95 Tech Prep Program
97 Chief Information Officer
98 Chief Technology Officer
270 Character Education
271 Migrant Education
273 Teacher Mentor
274 Before/After Sch
275 Response To Intervention
277 Remedial Math K-12
280 Literacy Coach
285 STEM
286 Digital Learning
288 Common Core Standards
294 Accountability
295 Network System
296 Title II Programs
297 Webmaster
298 Grant Writer/Ptnrships
750 Chief Innovation Officer
751 Chief of Staff
752 Social Emotional Learning

Texas School Directory
DISTRICT PERSONNEL INDEX

NAME/District	JOB FUNCTIONS	PAGE
Holt, Mable/Aldine ISD-Middle Sch Team	15	181
Holt, Susan, Dr/Corpus Christi Ind Sch Dist	8,288	303
Holt, Wesley/Connally Ind School Dist	1	279
Holtkamp, Leslie, Dr/Bryan Ind School Dist	8	54
Holub, Phil/Seymour Ind School Dist	3,5	25
Holubec, Bryan/Thrall Ind School Dist	67	400
Holzapfel, Malinda/Woden Ind School Dist	73,76	298
Holzhaus, Paul/Medina Valley Ind School Dist	2,5,15	284
Homann, Michael/Medina Valley Ind School Dist	2,15	284
Homann, Mike/Pettus Ind School Dist	1,11	25
Homann, Tanya/Lockhart Ind School Dist	2	61
Homer, Bonita/Elgin Ind School Dist	58	24
Homeyer, Lori/Refugio Ind School Dist	58	323
Homeyer, Lori/Woodsboro Ind School Dist	58	324
Hommel, Chad/Clarendon Cons Ind Sch Dist	5	127
Homstead, Gracie/Benjamin Ind School Dist	4	258
Honeycutt, Judy/Silsbee Ind School Dist	27,95	178
Honold, Eduardo/Harris Co Dept of Ed	30	179
Honza, Bill/Ennis Ind School Dist	71	140
Hood, Aaron/Robert Lee Ind School Dist	1,11,288	75
Hood, Greg/Whitehouse Ind School Dist	67	339
Hood, John/Rusk Ind School Dist	4,11,288	73
Hood, Travis/Bridgeport Ind School Dist	58	402
Hook, Mike/Claude Ind School Dist	3,5	20
Hooker, Jason/Chapel Hill Ind School Dist	6	337
Hooker, Tom/Thrall Ind School Dist	1	400
Hooper, Fay/Borger Ind School Dist	2	237
Hooper, Marbella/Angleton Ind School Dist	57,81	51
Hooper, Richard/Ponder Ind School Dist	31,73,297	125
Hooten, Kathleen/Commerce Independent Sch Dist	67	236
Hooten, Kenneth/Linden Kildare Cons Ind SD	2	70
Hooten, Kenton/Lockney Independent Sch Dist	3,5	149
Hooton, Lori/Grand Saline Ind School Dist	82	380
Hoover, Creed/Booker Ind School Dist	67	267
Hoover, Matt/Crowley Ind School Dist	297	347
Hoover, Matthew/Vernon Ind School Dist	6	393
Hope, Michael/Robinson Ind School Dist	1	281
Hopkins, Brandon/Boyd Ind School Dist	6	402
Hopkins, Justin/Mullin Ind School Dist	42	288
Hopkins, Kim/Sam Rayburn Ind School Dist	16	146
Hopkins, Lindsey/Grapevine-Colleyville Ind SD	30,88	353
Hopkins, Norman/Eanes Ind School Dist	3	370
Hopkins, Patty/Gordon Ind School Dist	4	310
Hopkins, Tony/Friendswood Ind Sch Dist	67	160
Hopper, Brandon/Meadow Ind School Dist	6	362
Hopper, Carlton/Austwell Tivoli Ind SD	67	323
Hopper, Craig/De Leon Ind School Dist	58	89
Hopper, Creig/Rising Star Ind Sch Dist	58	129
Hopper, James/Venus Ind School Dist	1	249
Hopson, Donna/Quinlan Ind School Dist	85	237
Hopson, Lily/Livingston Ind School Dist	294	317
Horelica, Missy/Devers Ind School Dist	16,69	265
Hormann, Jody/Leander Ind School Dist	6	396
Horn, Chris/Bloomington Ind School Dist	6	381
Horn, Johnnie/Taylor Ind School Dist	3	399
Horn, Julie/Navasota Ind School Dist	42,45	172
Horn, Kelly/Arlington Ind School Dist	3	343
Hornacky, Libby/Shiner Ind School Dist	7	262
Hornback, Jackie/Sweeny Ind School Dist	2	54
Horne, Kim/Brenham Ind School Dist	2	385
Horner, Glenda, Dr/Cypress-Fairbanks Ind Sch Dist	74,273	184
Horner, Jeff/Midland Ind School Dist	10	285
Hornsby, Ann/Cross Roads Ind School Dist	2	213
Hornsby, Janice/Axtell Ind School Dist	31,73	278
Horrice, Shirley/Bynum Ind School Dist	4	227
Horton, Bill/Wichita Falls Ind School Dist	91	392
Horton, Jeff/Jacksonville Ind School Dist	67	73
Horton, Joanna/Scurry Rosser Ind School Dist	67	253
Horton, Pam/Aquilla Ind School Dist	70	227
Horton, Paula/Jasper Ind School Dist	2,294	240
Horton, Robert, Dr/Conroe Ind School Dist	20,23	291
Horton, Stacie/Wheeler Ind School Dist	2,19,298	391
Horton, Tamela, Dr/Arlington Ind School Dist	8	343
Hosek, Tracy/Keller Ind School Dist	42	354
Hosford, Debbie/Denison Ind School Dist	4	166
Hoskin, Anne/Alief Ind School Dist	47	181
Hoskins, Ken/Lazbuddie Ind School Dist	285	315
Hottman, Sarah/Etoile Ind School Dist	1,11,57,288	297
Hough, Eric/Aubrey Ind School Dist	2,19	120
Houlbec, Cody/Rochelle Ind School Dist	27	278
House, Kelli/Avery Ind School Dist	2	322
Houska, Jennifer/Wheeler Ind School Dist	58	391
Houston, Brandon/Buffalo Ind School Dist	6,35	264
Houston, Cheryl/Seminole Ind School Dist	7,85	158
Houston, Jody/Corpus Christi Ind Sch Dist	4	303
Houy, Dawn/Valentine Ind School Dist	8,36,288	241
Howard-Schwind, Michelle, Dr/DeSoto Ind School Dist	8,15	104
Howard, Aimee/Farmersville Ind School Dist	7	78
Howard, Amy/Grapeland Ind School Dist	57,271	232
Howard, Amy/Grapevine-Colleyville Ind SD	7,35	353
Howard, Chris/Connally Ind School Dist	57,69,294	279
Howard, Dee/Wimberley Ind School Dist	8,11,15,286,288,296,298	212
Howard, Elaine/Boerne Ind School Dist	68,79	253
Howard, Jean/Cooper Ind School Dist	271	120
Howard, Jeff/Brownsboro Ind School Dist	3,5,91	213
Howard, Joy/Borger Ind School Dist	4	237
Howard, Laura/San Angelo Ind School Dist	73	364
Howard, Lisa/China Spring Ind School Dist	11,58	278
Howard, Mason/Brazosport Ind School Dist	67	52
Howard, Mindy/Troy Ind School Dist	27,33,273	29
Howard, Misty/Wimberley Ind School Dist	57	212
Howard, Sandy/Lipan Ind School Dist	271	230
Howard, Sonja/Del Valle Ind School Dist	48	369
Howard, Steve/May Ind School Dist	1,83	59
Howard, Suzie/Ricardo Ind School Dist	7,85	257
Howard, Tana/Sands Consolidated ISD	69,83,270	117
Howard, Teresa/Clyde Consolidated Ind SD	16	62
Howard, Tonia/Lancaster Ind School Dist	18,74	110
Howe, Stephanie/Crawford Ind School Dist	4	279
Howell, Alyssa/Houston Ind School Dist	47	188
Howell, Brandi/Darrouzett Ind School Dist	4	267
Howell, Joe/Grandfalls-Royalty Ind SD	6,8	385
Howell, Sandra/Little Elm Ind School Dist	6	124
Howell, Tracy/Leonard Ind School Dist	271	146
Howes, Rusty/Panhandle Ind School Dist	73,295	69
Howeth, Christie/Knox City-O'Brien Cons Ind SD	34,69,270	258
Howeth, Colin/Knox City-O'Brien Cons Ind SD	1,84	258
Howey, Todd/San Antonio Ind School Dist	6	39
Howse, Greg/Sherman Ind School Dist	58	167
Hoya, Henry/Broaddus Ind School Dist	5	329
Hoyer, Randy, Dr/Orange Grove Ind School Dist	1	245
Hruska, Jed/Reagan Co Ind School Dist	67	321
Hruska, Jessica/Harlingen Cons Ind School Dist	73	64
Hruska, Mike/Dripping Springs Ind Sch Dist	3	210
Hryhorchuk, Sharlene/Deweyville Ind School Dist	4	308
Hubanek, Greg/San Marcos Cons Ind Sch Dist	73,76,295	211
Hubbard, Brandon/Chilton Ind School Dist	1,11	144
Hubbard, Joseph/Jarrell Ind School Dist	295	396
Hubbard, Kim/Peaster Ind School Dist	12,271	313
Hubble, Casey/Breckenridge Ind School Dist	6	341
Huber, Brandon/Goliad Ind School Dist	67	163
Huber, Lori/Valley View ISD-Cooke Co	2	91
Huber, Mollie/Troy Ind School Dist	38	29
Huber, Patricia/Goliad Ind School Dist	9,34	163
Huckabee, Justin/McLeod Ind School Dist	16,73,286,295	70
Huckaby, Chad/Martinsville Ind School Dist	73,76	298
Huddleston, Gena/East Chambers Ind School Dist	2	72
Huddleston, Norman/Hallsburg Ind School Dist	67	279
Huddleston, Shelly/San Angelo Ind School Dist	8,18	364
Huddleston, Sigrid/Sidney Ind School Dist	8,58,88	90
Hudgeons, Jennifer/Cuero Ind School Dist	16	117
Hudgins, Courtney/East Bernard Ind Sch Dist	1	389
Hudson, Buck/Spurger Ind School Dist	27	375
Hudson, Gerald, Dr/Cedar Hill Ind School Dist	1	97
Hudson, Jason/Cumby Ind School Dist	67	231
Hudson, Jason/Wylie Ind School Dist	27	84
Hudson, Kaylinn/Chico Ind School Dist	2	403
Hudson, Kenny/Royse City Ind School Dist	11,15,296	326
Hudson, Larry/Richardson Ind School Dist	5	112
Hudson, Les/Bastrop Ind School Dist	79	23
Hudson, Logan/Miami Ind School Dist	67	324
Hudson, Natalie/Goose Creek Cons Ind Sch Dist	58	187

School Year 2019-2020 800-333-8802

DISTRICT PERSONNEL INDEX

Market Data Retrieval

NAME/District	JOB FUNCTIONS	PAGE
Hudson, Robert/Westphalia Ind School Dist	1,11	145
Hudson, Robert/Westphalia Ind School Dist	6,69,83,270	145
Hudson, Sha-Ree/Neches Ind School Dist	8,12,69,83,88	15
Hudson, Tijuana/Duncanville Ind School Dist	88	104
Hudson, Warren/Venus Ind School Dist	73	249
Huerta, Armando/Odem-Edroy Ind School Dist	6	331
Huerta, Brittany/Sundown Ind School Dist	7	229
Huerta, Rosie/Mathis Ind School Dist	5	331
Hues, Tommy/Shepherd Ind School Dist	73,84	330
Hueske, Debbie/Corrigan-Camden Ind Sch Dist	4	316
Huey, Flint/Hondo Ind School Dist	88	284
Huey, Kathy/White Settlement Ind Sch Dist	4	357
Huff, Audra/Three Rivers Ind School Dist	11,52,58,286,296	268
Huff, Brian/Castleberry Ind School Dist	84,295	347
Huff, Eric/Aubrey Ind School Dist	3,17	120
Huff, Hudson/Keller Ind School Dist	3	354
Huff, Karen/Coleman Ind School Dist	2	76
Huffman, Karen/Crockett Co Cons Common SD	7,85	94
Huffstickler, Robert/Southside Ind School Dist	5	43
Hugg, Randall/Killeen Ind School Dist	6	27
Hughes, Carissa/Coahoma Ind School Dist	35,83,85	234
Hughes, Danielle/Robinson Ind School Dist	57	281
Hughes, Dant/Water Valley Ind School Dist	3,5	365
Hughes, Heather, Dr/Eagle Mtn-Saginaw Ind Sch Dist	58,77	348
Hughes, Holly/Clear Creek Ind School Dist	9,15	158
Hughes, Jessica Lily/Spring Branch Ind School Dist	16	200
Hughes, John/Birdville Ind School Dist	3	346
Hughes, John/Kaufman Ind School Dist	3	252
Hughes, Kayla/Nacogdoches Ind School Dist	58	298
Hughes, Luann/Rockwall Ind School Dist	16,73,76,82,295	325
Hughes, Mary/Shallowater Ind School Dist	7,12,15,69,275,295	272
Hughes, Robyn/Conroe Ind School Dist	4	291
Hughes, Susan/Ft Elliott Cons Ind Sch Dist	58	390
Hughes, Sylvia/Amarillo Ind School Dist	57,271	317
Hughes, Vada/Lufkin Ind School Dist	42	18
Hughes, Windi/Schertz-Cibolo-Univ City ISD	69	173
Huime, Mindy/Midway Ind School Dist	274	280
Hulbert, Jonathan/East Central Ind School Dist	69	31
Hulett, Brian/Springtown Ind School Dist	6	313
Hullender, Deanne/Dallas Co Schools	16,70	95
Hullender, Deanne/Hurst-Euless-Bedford ISD	71	353
Hullihen, Shelly/San Angelo Ind School Dist	15	364
Hullman, David/Eastland Ind School Dist	67	129
Hulme, Jennifer/Mesquite Ind School Dist	12	110
Hulme, Thom/Coppell Ind School Dist	67	98
Humes, Darla/Leander Ind School Dist	35,88,91	396
Humiston, Laurie/Kennedale Ind School Dist	4	355
Hummel, Deborah/Stephenville Ind School Dist	2	144
Humphrey-Sauer, Karen/Fredericksburg Ind School Dist	88	163
Humphrey, Beverly/Lancaster Ind School Dist	6,71	110
Humphrey, Concan/Bonham Ind School Dist	5	145
Humphrey, Deanna/Anahuac Ind School Dist	11,36,57,58,69,83,88	71
Humphrey, Megan/Rockwall Ind School Dist	46	325
Humphrey, Ronnie/Mt Pleasant Ind School Dist	91	363
Humphrey, Troy/Walnut Bend Ind School Dist	1,11,73,83	92
Humphreys, Connie/Rochelle Ind School Dist	58	278
Humphries, Jamie/Seagraves Ind School Dist	6	157
Hungteres, Debbie/Wellington Ind School Dist	4	86
Hunkapillar, Cortney/Denison Ind School Dist	2	166
Hunt, Becky/Allen Ind School Dist	27,31	76
Hunt, Brad/Coppell Ind School Dist	1	98
Hunt, Bud/Miles Ind School Dist	3,5	326
Hunt, Hali/Lake Worth Ind School Dist	68	356
Hunt, Jan/Crane Ind School Dist	1	93
Hunt, John/Kennedale Ind School Dist	67	355
Hunt, Laura/Whitney Ind School Dist	288,298	228
Hunter, Casey/Burkburnett Ind Sch Dist	27,298	391
Hunter, Kandi/Arlington Ind School Dist	45	343
Hunter, Laurie/Santa Anna Ind School Dist	8,12,79,88,274,275	76
Hunter, Mark/Highland Park Ind Sch Dist	295	108
Hunter, Robert/Rockdale Ind School Dist	5	287
Hunter, Sam/Munday Consolidated Ind SD	67	259
Hunter, Tommy, Dr/Sanger Ind School Dist	1	126
Hurd, Clifford/Palmer Ind School Dist	5	141
Hurley, Brian/North East Ind School Dist	68	34
Hurst, Kashonda/Humble Ind School Dist	68	195
Hurst, Luke/McKinney Ind School Dist	81	81
Hurst, Monica/Iola Ind School Dist	73,295	172
Hurst, Terry/Bland Ind School Dist	67	235
Hurst, Thyrun, Dr/Calvert Ind School Dist	1	324
Hurt, Chantele/Blum Ind School Dist	57	227
Hurt, Craig/Henderson Ind School Dist	3,5,91	327
Hurtado, Carolina/Kerrville Ind School Dist	3,91	256
Huschke, Krystal/McMullen Co Ind Sch Dist	2	283
Huseman, Colby/Crosbyton Cons Ind Sch Dist	6	94
Huseman, Mike/Tulia Ind School Dist	2	343
Husen, Natalie/Graham Ind School Dist	11,58	406
Husfeld, Earl/Aledo Ind School Dist	2,19	312
Hutchin, Jill/Brazos Ind School Dist	16	22
Hutchin, Jill/Brazos Ind School Dist	16	22
Hutching, Scott/Castleberry Ind School Dist	45,54,277	347
Hutchins, Climet/Goodrich Ind School Dist	3,5	316
Hutchinson, Kathy/Levelland Ind School Dist	12,58	229
Hutchinson, Leslie/Paducah Ind School Dist	8	93
Hutchison, Christine/Brackett Ind School Dist	77,88	257
Hutchison, David/College Station Ind Sch Dist	73	55
Hutchison, Kenneth/Blooming Grove Ind School Dist	3,5,7	299
Hutsell, Richard/Elysian Fields Ind School Dist	2,11	208
Hutson, Donna/Lake Worth Ind School Dist	67	356
Hutto, Karen/Hudson Ind School Dist	4	17
Hyde, Billie/Texhoma Ind School Dist	4	336
Hyde, Brady/Rocksprings Ind School Dist	67	131
Hyde, David/Navarro Ind School Dist	295	173
Hyde, Duane/Highland Ind School Dist	1,11	301
Hyde, Jk/Mabank Ind School Dist	73,295,297	252
Hyde, Kelly/Navarro Ind School Dist	5	173
Hyde, Shalana/Hudson Ind School Dist	7	17
Hyde, Tonya, Dr/Lackland Ind School Dist	8,11,57,83,88,288	34
Hyden, Steve, Dr/Jasper Ind School Dist	1	240
Hyles, Lisa/Maypearl Ind School Dist	8	141
Hymer, Josh/Bremond Ind School Dist	73,76	324
Hyndran, Justin/Southland Ind School Dist	3,5	162
Hysinger, Monty/Dumas Ind School Dist	1	295
I		
Iacoponelli, Mark/Cuero Ind School Dist	2,15	117
Ibanez, Irma/Corpus Christi Ind Sch Dist	73	303
Ibannez, Clarissa/Rio Grande City Ind Sch Dist	69,294	340
Ibarra-Cantu, Norma, Dr/Brownsville Ind School Dist	10	63
Ibarra, Edgar/Mission Cons Ind Sch Dist	57	222
Ibarra, Hugo/Bryan Ind School Dist	71	54
Ibarra, Laticia/Mission Cons Ind Sch Dist	6	222
Ibarra, Martin/Chapel Hill Ind School Dist	67	337
Ibarra, Sylvia/McAllen Ind School Dist	8,15	221
Ibraheim, Ciara/Yorktown Ind School Dist	54	118
Icenhower, Kim/Texarkana Ind School Dist	73	50
Ideus, John/Sweeny Ind School Dist	91	54
Igo, Tony/Smyer Ind School Dist	9,11,57,271	229
Ikard, Tricia/Maypearl Ind School Dist	58	141
Imnan, Natalie/Bloomburg Ind School Dist	17,69,273	70
Inboden, Cheryl/Deweyville Ind School Dist	16	308
Indelicato, Anthony, Dr/Ft Bend Ind School Dist	15,70,751	149
Infante, Eduardo/Lyford Cons Ind School Dist	1	394
Ingle, Regina/Morton Ind School Dist	271	75

1 Superintendent	16 Instructional Media Svcs	30 Adult Education	44 Science Sec
2 Bus/Finance/Purchasing	17 Chief Operations Officer	31 Career/Sch-to-Work K-12	45 Math K-12
3 Buildings And Grounds	18 Chief Academic Officer	32 Career/Sch-to-Work Elem	46 Math Elem
4 Food Service	19 Chief Financial Officer	33 Career/Sch-to-Work Sec	47 Math Sec
5 Transportation	20 Art K-12	34 Early Childhood Ed	48 English/Lang Arts K-12
6 Athletic	21 Art Elem	35 Health/Phys Education	49 English/Lang Arts Elem
7 Health Services	22 Art Sec	36 Guidance Services K-12	50 English/Lang Arts Sec
8 Curric/Instruct K-12	23 Music K-12	37 Guidance Services Elem	51 Reading K-12
9 Curric/Instruct Elem	24 Music Elem	38 Guidance Services Sec	52 Reading Elem
10 Curric/Instruct Sec	25 Music Sec	39 Social Studies K-12	53 Reading Sec
11 Federal Program	26 Business Education	40 Social Studies Elem	54 Remedial Reading K-12
12 Title I	27 Career & Tech Ed	41 Social Studies Sec	55 Remedial Reading Elem
13 Title V	28 Technology Education	42 Science K-12	56 Remedial Reading Sec
15 Asst Superintendent	29 Family/Consumer Science	43 Science Elem	57 Bilingual/ELL

58 Special Education K-12	72 Summer School	88 Alternative/At Risk	277 Remedial Math K-12
59 Special Education Elem	73 Instructional Tech	89 Multi-Cultural Curriculum	280 Literacy Coach
60 Special Education Sec	74 Inservice Training	90 Social Work	285 STEM
61 Foreign/World Lang K-12	75 Marketing/Distributive	91 Safety/Security	286 Digital Learning
62 Foreign/World Lang Elem	76 Info Systems	92 Magnet School	288 Common Core Standards
63 Foreign/World Lang Sec	77 Psychological Assess	93 Parental Involvement	294 Accountability
64 Religious Education K-12	78 Affirmative Action	95 Tech Prep Program	295 Network System
65 Religious Education Elem	79 Student Personnel	97 Chief Information Officer	296 Title II Programs
66 Religious Education Sec	80 Driver Ed/Safety	98 Chief Technology Officer	297 Webmaster
67 School Board President	81 Gifted/Talented	270 Character Education	298 Grant Writer/Ptnrships
68 Teacher Personnel	82 Video Services	271 Migrant Education	750 Chief Innovation Officer
69 Academic Assessment	83 Substance Abuse Prev	273 Teacher Mentor	751 Chief of Staff
70 Research/Development	84 Erate	274 Before/After Sch	752 Social Emotional Learning
71 Public Information	85 AIDS Education	275 Response To Intervention	

TX-T44

Texas School Directory

DISTRICT PERSONNEL INDEX

NAME/District	JOB FUNCTIONS	PAGE
Ingram, Edward/*Hereford Ind School Dist*	2	119
Ingram, Jennell/*Texarkana Ind School Dist*	273	50
Ingram, Jennifer/*Evant Ind School Dist*	8,13,74,288,294,298	92
Ingram, Jodie/*North Lamar Ind School Dist*	73	259
Ingram, Kelly/*Region 4 Ed Service Center*	8,15	208
Ingram, Rusty/*Hereford Ind School Dist*	2,19	119
Inman, Robert/*Hudson Ind School Dist*	295	17
Inman, Suzie/*Texarkana Ind School Dist*	7	50
Inman, Suzie/*Texarkana Ind School Dist*	7	50
Irby, Melissa/*Abilene Ind School Dist*	2	360
Irvin, Jack/*Pine Tree Ind School Dist*	5	170
Irvin, Jeff/*Quinlan Ind School Dist*	1	237
Irwin, Dale/*Arp Ind School Dist*	6	336
Irwin, Danny/*Nueces Canyon Cons Ind SD*	67	131
Irwin, Lori/*Idalou Ind School Dist*	57,69,270,271	269
Isaacs, Caloby/*Goodrich Ind School Dist*	8,288	316
Isabel, Connie/*Lancaster Ind School Dist*	69	110
Iselt, Sally/*Caldwell Ind School Dist*	5	59
Ishmael, Clint/*Grandview Ind School Dist*	67	248
Iske, Kris/*White Oak Ind School Dist*	6	171
Isnhower, Lynn/*Quanah Ind School Dist*	4	177
Israel, Kimberley/*Eanes Ind School Dist*	76	370
Ivey, Jami/*Athens Ind School Dist*	10,15	213
Ivey, Keitha/*Amarillo Ind School Dist*	76	317
Ivey, Kyle/*Central Ind School Dist*	286	17
Ivey, Martin, Dr/*Brock Ind School Dist*	67	312
Ivey, Robert/*Canton Ind School Dist*	6	380
Ivey, Rusty/*Gilmer Ind School Dist*	73	376
Ivicic, Jackie/*Jarrell Ind School Dist*	5	396
Ivy, Adam/*Thorndale Ind School Dist*	1,11	288
Ivy, Anne/*Ponder Ind School Dist*	38,88	125
Ivy, Cheree/*Wills Point Ind School Dist*	2	381
Ivy, Cindy/*Nacogdoches Ind School Dist*	36,69	298
Ivy, Danita/*Palo Pinto Ind Sch Dist 906*	85	310
Ivy, Keith/*Aubrey Ind School Dist*	6	120
Ivy, Wade/*Kerrville Ind School Dist*	15,68,78,79	256

J

NAME/District	JOB FUNCTIONS	PAGE
Jachade, Jarrett/*Kerrville Ind School Dist*	2,15,16,19,73,76,295	256
Jachade, Katie/*Kerrville Ind School Dist*	7,35,85	256
Jack, Gary/*Callisburg Ind School Dist*	6	90
Jackosn, Wendy/*Overton Ind School Dist*	8,36,69,85	328
Jacks, Joseph/*Tyler Ind School Dist*	84	337
Jacks, Kevin/*Johnson City Ind School Dist*	73	46
Jacks, Patricia/*West Sabine Ind Sch Dist*	69,83	329
Jackson, Amanda/*High Island Ind Sch Dist*	8,11,57,88,273	160
Jackson, Anna/*Lubbock Ind School Dist*	74	270
Jackson, Anthony/*Port Arthur Ind School Dist*	73,76,294,295	243
Jackson, Cara/*Mesquite Ind School Dist*	73,286	110
Jackson, Carla/*Rankin Ind School Dist*	7	377
Jackson, Charlie/*Highland Park Ind Sch Dist*	73,76,98	108
Jackson, Chris, Dr/*Cleburne Ind School Dist*	70	247
Jackson, Christine/*Klein Ind School Dist*	71	196
Jackson, Christine/*Livingston Ind School Dist*	42,45	317
Jackson, Cindy/*Christoval Ind School Dist*	76	364
Jackson, Damon/*Lubbock Ind School Dist*	73,98	270
Jackson, David/*Decatur Ind School Dist*	295	403
Jackson, Don/*Grapeland Ind School Dist*	1,83	232
Jackson, Dora/*Manor Ind School Dist*	47	371
Jackson, Frankie/*Cypress-Fairbanks Ind Sch Dist*	288	184
Jackson, Garrett/*Frisco Ind School Dist*	58	78
Jackson, Gennie/*Kress Ind School Dist*	60	343
Jackson, Herman, Dr/*Ft Worth Ind School Dist*	42	349
Jackson, James/*Benjamin Ind School Dist*	6	258
Jackson, John/*High Island Ind Sch Dist*	6	160
Jackson, Lane/*Ropes Ind School Dist*	6	229
Jackson, Lindy/*Lefors Ind School Dist*	67	165
Jackson, Mark/*Milford Ind School Dist*	13	141
Jackson, Melissa/*Hico Ind School Dist*	57	176
Jackson, Mickie/*Frost Ind School Dist*	1	299
Jackson, Nathan/*Texas City Ind School Dist*	79	161
Jackson, Paula/*Hardin Ind School Dist*	34	265
Jackson, Ray/*Tenaha Ind School Dist*	16,73,295	335
Jackson, Rene/*Granbury Ind School Dist*	88	230
Jackson, Salena/*Pine Tree Ind School Dist*	2	170
Jackson, Tracy/*Willis Ind School Dist*	69	294

NAME/District	JOB FUNCTIONS	PAGE
Jackson, Walter, Dr/*Brenham Ind School Dist*	1	385
Jackwright, Bobby/*Victoria Ind School Dist*	6	382
Jaco, Brent/*Brazosport Ind School Dist*	15,751	52
Jacobs-Worrell, Linda/*Tenaha Ind School Dist*	9	335
Jacobs, Cheryl/*Garland Ind School Dist*	75	105
Jacobs, Doug/*Avinger Ind School Dist*	67	70
Jacobs, Karen, Dr/*Alief Ind School Dist*	44,285	181
Jacobsen, Michael/*Lewisville Ind School Dist*	286	122
Jacobson, David/*Lamar Cons Ind School Dist*	73,76	153
Jacques, Raul/*San Elizario Ind School Dist*	4	135
Jaeger, Clint/*Fayetteville Ind School Dist*	6	147
Jaggard, Tom/*Aransas Co Ind School Dist*	10	19
Jahn, Kathy/*Alief Ind School Dist*	8	181
Jaime, Ashley/*McAllen Ind School Dist*	2	220
Jaime, Michelle/*Farwell Ind School Dist*	7,83	314
Jaksock, Christine/*San Elizario Ind School Dist*	6	135
James, Dana/*Waxahachie Ind School Dist*	40	142
James, Dianne/*Grape Creek Ind School Dist*	67	364
James, George/*Melissa Ind School Dist*	67	81
James, Kelly/*McMullen Co Ind Sch Dist*	69,83,88,270	283
James, Lori/*Dawson Ind School Dist*	4	299
James, Melinda/*Bridge City Ind School Dist*	2	308
James, Molly/*Brazosport Ind School Dist*	7,85	52
James, Rocky/*Rio Hondo Ind School Dist*	6	66
James, Valerie/*Royse City Ind School Dist*	46	326
James, Vicki/*Klein Ind School Dist*	15,79,294	196
Jameson, Garry/*Farmersville Ind School Dist*	8,15,288,294,296,298	78
Jameson, Jay/*Edgewood Ind School Dist*	6	380
Jameson, Patricia/*Krum Ind School Dist*	58,88	122
Jameson, Ronda/*Liberty-Eylau Ind School Dist*	8	48
Jamison, Lynn/*Castleberry Ind School Dist*	58	347
Janacek, Jackie/*College Station Ind Sch Dist*	76	55
Janak, Alice/*Vysehrad Ind School Dist*	67	263
Janda, Catherine/*Comal Ind School Dist*	2	87
Janda, J/*Tomball Ind School Dist*	20,23	203
Janda, Lucas/*Leander Ind School Dist*	2,19	396
Janicek, Chris/*Needville Ind School Dist*	67	154
Jank, Johnny/*Meyersville Ind School Dist*	67	118
Jantzen, Lynn/*Rice Ind School Dist*	1	300
Jaramillo, Andrea/*Seguin Ind School Dist*	48	173
Jaramillo, Annette/*Premont Ind School Dist*	4	246
Jaramillo, Vanessa/*Celina Ind School Dist*	57	78
Jarchow, Theadore, Dr/*Arlington Ind School Dist*	15	343
Jarrell, Travis/*Marathon Ind School Dist*	58	56
Jarrett, Anthony/*Northside Ind School Dist*	10	36
Jarrett, Erin/*Liberty Hill Ind School Dist*	2	398
Jarrott, Cody/*Woodville Ind School Dist*	2,11,15	375
Jarvis, Michael/*Pewitt Cons Ind School Dist*	67	296
Jaso, Ruperto/*Pasadena Ind School Dist*	6	198
Jasper, Shane/*Troup Ind School Dist*	67	337
Jasso, Allison/*Brazosport Ind School Dist*	36	52
Jatzlau, Lamanda/*Bryan Ind School Dist*	16	54
Jefferson, Curtis/*Leggett Ind School Dist*	67	316
Jeffery, Bruce/*New Diana Ind School Dist*	3	376
Jeffery, Nicole/*Crane Ind School Dist*	12,57,88,271	93
Jefferys, Holly/*Bushland Ind School Dist*	67	319
Jeffrey, Emily/*Region 14 Ed Service Center*	2	362
Jeffrey, Kyle/*Highland Ind School Dist*	6	301
Jeffrey, Lisa/*Hudson Ind School Dist*	8	17
Jehlings, Bill/*Howe Ind School Dist*	6	166
Jeitz, Jason/*Centerville Ind School Dist*	1	264
Jemenez, Rudy/*Edinburg Cons Ind School Dist*	90	216
Jenke, Adam/*Coldspring-Oakhurst Cons ISD*	2	330
Jenkins, A/*Irving Ind School Dist*	67	109
Jenkins, Chris/*White Settlement Ind Sch Dist*	8,11,15,16,58,83,271,295	357
Jenkins, Corey/*Trinidad Ind School Dist*	1,11,288	214
Jenkins, Doug/*Spurger Ind School Dist*	3,5	375
Jenkins, Greg/*Tenaha Ind School Dist*	6	335
Jenkins, Jackie/*Turkey-Quitaque Cons Ind SD*	1,11	176
Jenkins, Jeremy/*Mt Enterprise Ind School Dist*	6	328
Jenkins, Lisa/*Frisco Ind School Dist*	4	78
Jenkins, Randy/*Sivells Bend Ind School Dist*	3,5	91
Jenkins, Staci/*Christoval Ind School Dist*	10,69	364
Jenkins, Troy/*New Summerfield Ind Sch Dist*	16,73,297	73
Jennifer, Matteson/*De Kalb Ind School Dist*	2	47
Jennings, Betty/*Burkeville Ind School Dist*	4	300

DISTRICT PERSONNEL INDEX

Market Data Retrieval

NAME/District	JOB FUNCTIONS	PAGE
Jennings, Brian/Carlisle Ind School Dist	73,74,76,295	327
Jennings, Errin/Luling Ind School Dist	10	61
Jennings, Henry/La Vega Ind School Dist	67	279
Jennings, Jessie/Brazosport Ind School Dist	31	52
Jennings, Keith/Hudson Ind School Dist	5	17
Jennings, Melinda, Dr/Marshall Ind School Dist	11,296	209
Jennings, Randall/Rosebud-Lott Ind School Dist	73	145
Jennings, Teresa/Kerens Ind School Dist	67	300
Jennings, Thersa/Hughes Springs Ind Sch Dist	8,11,16,58,88,288,296,298	70
Jennings, Wayne/Plainview Ind School Dist	295	175
Jennings, William/Channelview Ind School Dist	6,7,35,85	183
Jentsch, Clint/Grandview Ind School Dist	37	248
Jerden, Steve/New Deal Ind School Dist	2	271
Jerkins, Courtney/Midway Ind School Dist	40,43	280
Jerkins, Greg/Stafford Municipal Sch Dist	5	155
Jernegen, Farrah/Hallettsville Ind Sch Dist	73,295	262
Jernigan, Laramie/Shamrock Ind School Dist	16,73	390
Jessee, Stanley/Rivercrest Ind School Dist	1	322
Jessen, Terrell/Boling Ind School Dist	73	389
Jessie, Shirrell/Corsicana Ind School Dist	4	299
Jester, Linda/Whitewright Ind School Dist	67	168
Jestis, Heather/Scurry Rosser Ind School Dist	58	253
Jeter, Mendi/Jim Ned Cons Ind School Dist	58	361
Jeter, Neil/Troy Ind School Dist	1	29
Jett, Jeri/Borger Ind School Dist	2	237
Jhonson, Eileen/Henderson Ind School Dist	58	327
Jimenez, Kathleen/Brownsville Ind School Dist	20,23	63
Jimenez, Manuel/Olton Ind School Dist	5	261
Jimenez, Margarito/Progreso Ind School Dist	6	224
Jimenez, Rudy/North East Ind School Dist	30,274	34
Jimenez, Sandra/Lubbock-Cooper Ind Sch Dist	57,271	271
Jimerson, Bret, Dr/Burleson Ind School Dist	1	246
Jimerson, Terence/Jefferson Ind School Dist	88	274
Jimmerson, Antwain/Jefferson Ind School Dist	6	274
Jinkins, Mike/Huntington Ind School Dist	91	17
Jinnette, Preston/Eanes Ind School Dist	295	370
Jobe, Laura/Mesquite Ind School Dist	71,297	110
Joffre, Cassie/Italy Ind School Dist	16	140
Joffre, Lee/Italy Ind School Dist	8	140
Joffre, Lee/Mabank Ind School Dist	1	252
Johns, Angel/Harleton Ind School Dist	8,11,31,69,271,274	208
Johns, Nicole/Galena Park Ind School Dist	275	186
Johnson, Adrian, Dr/Hearne Ind School Dist	1	325
Johnson, Andy/Simms Ind School Dist	8,298	50
Johnson, Angela/Archdiocese Galveston-Houston	15	203
Johnson, Ann, Dr/Humble Ind School Dist	8	195
Johnson, Barbara/Dallas Ind School Dist	35	98
Johnson, Becky/Barbers Hill Ind School Dist	3	72
Johnson, Billy/Crowley Ind School Dist	15,79,83,85	347
Johnson, Billy/Marlin Ind School Dist	67	144
Johnson, Bridget/Aransas Co Ind School Dist	68	19
Johnson, Bridget/Canyon Ind School Dist	58	320
Johnson, Butch/Denver City Ind School Dist	3	405
Johnson, Carol/Richardson Ind School Dist	49	112
Johnson, Casey/Center Point Ind School Dist	8,12,16,73,79,286	255
Johnson, Christine/Aransas Pass Ind School Dist	58	330
Johnson, Connie/Spring Hill Ind School Dist	69	170
Johnson, Debbie/Lexington Ind School Dist	16,82	263
Johnson, Debbie/Maud Ind School Dist	4	49
Johnson, Deborah/Aldine Ind School Dist	41	179
Johnson, Dina/Blanco Ind School Dist	8,11,57,88,271,288,294	45
Johnson, Dixie/Tulia Ind School Dist	58	343
Johnson, Donna/Leon Ind School Dist	4	264
Johnson, Donna/Leveretts Chapel Ind Sch Dist	1	328
Johnson, Eileen/Prosper Ind School Dist	4	84
Johnson, Frank/Holliday Ind School Dist	6	19
Johnson, Gwen/Houston Ind School Dist	7	188

NAME/District	JOB FUNCTIONS	PAGE
Johnson, Jamey, Dr/Brenham Ind School Dist	8,15	385
Johnson, Jason/Daingerfield-Lone Star Ind SD	16,73,295	296
Johnson, Jason/Van Ind School Dist	73	381
Johnson, Jay/Cypress-Fairbanks Ind Sch Dist	28	184
Johnson, Jeanie, Dr/Midway Ind School Dist	79,91	280
Johnson, Jeff/Leonard Ind School Dist	11,84,296	146
Johnson, Jennifer/Comal Ind School Dist	79,275	87
Johnson, Jennifer/Poth Ind School Dist	2	401
Johnson, Jennifer/Rains Ind School Dist	1,11	320
Johnson, Jessica, Dr/Dayton Ind School Dist	1	265
Johnson, Jody/Vega Ind School Dist	1,11	307
Johnson, Joel/Northwest Ind School Dist	6,35	124
Johnson, John/Tyler Ind School Dist	79	337
Johnson, Johnny/Kenedy Co Wide Common Sch Dist	1	254
Johnson, Julea/Bryan Ind School Dist	73	54
Johnson, Julie/Kaufman Ind School Dist	58	252
Johnson, Keith/Caldwell Ind School Dist	73,76	59
Johnson, Kenneth/Judson Ind School Dist	5	33
Johnson, Kim/Kemp Ind School Dist	2	252
Johnson, Kim/Mesquite Ind School Dist	58	110
Johnson, Kimberly/Midway Ind School Dist	46	280
Johnson, Kimberly/Wolfe City Ind School Dist	7	237
Johnson, Kyndra/Richardson Ind School Dist	285	112
Johnson, Lance/Randolph Field Ind School Dist	1	39
Johnson, Lance/S & S Cons Ind School Dist	11,83	167
Johnson, Lauren/Lubbock Ind School Dist	4	269
Johnson, Laurie/Hale Center Ind School Dist	38,83	175
Johnson, Linda/Woodville Ind School Dist	4	375
Johnson, Mandy/Bangs Ind School Dist	5	58
Johnson, Margaret/Joshua Ind School Dist	98	248
Johnson, Mark/Giddings Ind School Dist	67	263
Johnson, Marsha/Kaufman Ind School Dist	294	252
Johnson, Mary/Lumberton Ind School Dist	73,286,297	178
Johnson, Michael/Hallsburg Ind School Dist	73,286	279
Johnson, Michael/Malone Independent School Dist	76	228
Johnson, Michael/Schleicher Co Ind Sch Dist	6	333
Johnson, Michael/Westphalia Ind School Dist	73,76,295	145
Johnson, Michelle/Silsbee Ind School Dist	4	178
Johnson, Mid, Dr/Timpson Ind School Dist	1	335
Johnson, Molly/Breckenridge Ind School Dist	8,11,69,88,273,296	341
Johnson, Mona/Magnolia Ind School Dist	286	292
Johnson, Nancy/Dublin Ind School Dist	7	143
Johnson, Nicholas/DeSoto Ind School Dist	27,285	104
Johnson, Paige/Dublin Ind School Dist	69	143
Johnson, Peggy, Dr/La Vega Ind School Dist	9,11,294,296,298	279
Johnson, Randy/Forsan Ind School Dist	1	234
Johnson, Richard/Bay City Ind School Dist	2,19	275
Johnson, Robin/Blanco Ind School Dist	7	45
Johnson, Sarah/Palestine Ind School Dist	36	15
Johnson, Shane/Cushing Ind School Dist	83,91	297
Johnson, Shane/Cushing Ind School Dist	5,83,91	297
Johnson, Sharise/Idea Public Schools	71	217
Johnson, Sharon/Bruceville-Eddy Ind Sch Dist	9	278
Johnson, Shellie/Keller Ind School Dist	71	354
Johnson, Slade/Wells Ind School Dist	73,295,296	73
Johnson, Stace/Waxahachie Ind School Dist	46	142
Johnson, Stacy/Springtown Ind School Dist	34,58	313
Johnson, Stephanie/Roosevelt Ind School Dist	37	271
Johnson, Steve/Lockhart Ind School Dist	67	61
Johnson, Steve/Miller Grove Ind School Dist	1,11,83	231
Johnson, Sunni, Dr/Northwest Ind School Dist	49,52,55	124
Johnson, Susan/Corsicana Ind School Dist	71,76,93,297	299
Johnson, Susan/Magnolia Ind School Dist	45	292
Johnson, Susan/Victoria Ind School Dist	47	382
Johnson, Teresa/School of Excellence In Ed	11,298	42
Johnson, Terry/Ector Ind School Dist	6	146
Johnson, Terry/Karnes City Ind School Dist	67	250

1 Superintendent	16 Instructional Media Svcs	30 Adult Education	44 Science Sec	58 Special Education K-12	72 Summer School	88 Alternative/At Risk	277 Remedial Math K-12
2 Bus/Finance/Purchasing	17 Chief Operations Officer	31 Career/Sch-to-Work K-12	45 Math K-12	59 Special Education Elem	73 Instructional Tech	89 Multi-Cultural Curriculum	280 Literacy Coach
3 Buildings And Grounds	18 Chief Academic Officer	32 Career/Sch-to-Work Elem	46 Math Elem	60 Special Education Sec	74 Inservice Training	90 Social Work	285 STEM
4 Food Service	19 Chief Financial Officer	33 Career/Sch-to-Work Sec	47 Math Sec	61 Foreign/World Lang K-12	75 Marketing/Distributive	91 Safety/Security	286 Digital Learning
5 Transportation	20 Art K-12	34 Early Childhood Ed	48 English/Lang Arts K-12	62 Foreign/World Lang Elem	76 Info Systems	92 Magnet School	288 Common Core Standards
6 Athletic	21 Art Elem	35 Health/Phys Education	49 English/Lang Arts Elem	63 Foreign/World Lang Sec	77 Psychological Assess	93 Parental Involvement	294 Accountability
7 Health Services	22 Art Sec	36 Guidance Services K-12	50 English/Lang Arts Sec	64 Religious Education K-12	78 Affirmative Action	95 Tech Prep Program	295 Network System
8 Curric/Instruct K-12	23 Music K-12	37 Guidance Services Elem	51 Reading K-12	65 Religious Education Elem	79 Student Personnel	97 Chief Information Officer	296 Title II Programs
9 Curric/Instruct Elem	24 Music Elem	38 Guidance Services Sec	52 Reading Elem	66 Religious Education Sec	80 Driver Ed/Safety	98 Chief Technology Officer	297 Webmaster
10 Curric/Instruct Sec	25 Music Sec	39 Social Studies K-12	53 Reading Sec	67 School Board President	81 Gifted/Talented	270 Character Education	298 Grant Writer/Ptnrships
11 Federal Program	26 Business Education	40 Social Studies Elem	54 Remedial Reading K-12	68 Teacher Personnel	82 Video Services	271 Migrant Education	750 Chief Innovation Officer
12 Title I	27 Career & Tech Ed	41 Social Studies Sec	55 Remedial Reading Elem	69 Academic Assessment	83 Substance Abuse Prev	273 Teacher Mentor	751 Chief of Staff
13 Title V	28 Technology Education	42 Science K-12	56 Remedial Reading Sec	70 Research/Development	84 Erate	274 Before/After Sch	752 Social Emotional Learning
15 Asst Superintendent	29 Family/Consumer Science	43 Science Elem	57 Bilingual/ELL	71 Public Information	85 AIDS Education	275 Response To Intervention	

TX-T46

Texas School Directory

DISTRICT PERSONNEL INDEX

NAME/District	JOB FUNCTIONS	PAGE
Johnson, Terry/McDade Ind School Dist	3,5	24
Johnson, Tommie/Keller Ind School Dist	15,68	354
Johnson, Victrina/Trinidad Ind School Dist	57,58	214
Johnson, Wanda/Tom Bean Ind School Dist	58	168
Johnson, Whitney/Tomball Ind School Dist	4	203
Johnston, Bill, Dr/Red Oak Ind School Dist	2,19	142
Johnston, Camillia/Amarillo Ind School Dist	58	317
Johnston, Chris/Celeste Ind School Dist	73	235
Johnston, Debbie/Newton Ind School Dist	8,69	301
Johnston, Drew/Newton Ind School Dist	6	301
Johnston, Jajean/Grape Creek Ind School Dist	7	364
Johnston, Jason/Leander Ind School Dist	16	396
Johnston, Jessica/Brenham Ind School Dist	71	385
Johnston, Mary, Dr/Rockwall Ind School Dist	8,18	325
Johnston, Ryan/Ed Service Center Region 2	2,76	306
Johnston, Sonya/Whitehouse Ind School Dist	36,69,83	338
Johnston, Susan/Sulphur Springs Ind Sch Dist	58	232
Johnstone, Whitcomb, Dr/Irving Ind School Dist	70	109
Jolivette, Alishia/Houston Ind School Dist	3	188
Jolly, Cynthia/Tahoka Ind School Dist	16	273
Jolly, Darin, Dr/North Hopkins Ind School Dist	1	231
Jolly, Linda/Region 18 Ed Service Center	58	287
Jondron, Dacia/Princeton Ind School Dist	7	84
Jones, Akiko/Mt Enterprise Ind School Dist	58	328
Jones, Becky/Comanche Ind School Dist	58	89
Jones, Beth/San Antonio Ind School Dist	58,77	39
Jones, Bill/Gause Ind School Dist	67	287
Jones, Bobbie/Terlingua Common School Dist	11,83	57
Jones, Brad/Gause Ind School Dist	1,11,83,288	287
Jones, Brad/Rule Ind School Dist	1	210
Jones, Cami/Hardin Ind School Dist	8,11,285,296	265
Jones, Carolyn/Garner Ind School Dist	2,13	312
Jones, Carolyn/Leakey Ind School Dist	5	322
Jones, Cecelia/Little Elm Ind School Dist	71	124
Jones, Chad/Sinton Ind School Dist	1	332
Jones, Charollete/McCamey Ind School Dist	67	377
Jones, Cheryl/Tom Bean Ind School Dist	16,73,82	168
Jones, Chris/Chilton Ind School Dist	6	144
Jones, Chris/Pecos-Barstow-Toyah Ind SD	6,35	323
Jones, Connie/Shamrock Ind School Dist	2	390
Jones, Craig/Kirbyville Cons Ind Sch Dist	6	241
Jones, Dale/Ira Ind School Dist	13	333
Jones, David/Kerrville Ind School Dist	6	256
Jones, Deb/Blanket Ind School Dist	69,83,85,88	58
Jones, Debbie/Columbia Brazoria ISD	5	52
Jones, Debra/Adrian Ind School Dist	7	307
Jones, Dwayne/Crowley Ind School Dist	2	347
Jones, Etola/Shelbyville Ind School Dist	67	335
Jones, George/Garland Ind School Dist	20,23	105
Jones, Glen/Veribest Ind School Dist	10	365
Jones, Greg/Detroit Ind School Dist	2,11	322
Jones, Jason/Blackwell Cons Ind Sch Dist	67	301
Jones, Jason/McMullen Co Ind Sch Dist	1	283
Jones, Jeff/Anna Ind School Dist	91	77
Jones, Jeff/Glasscock Co Ind School Dist	6	163
Jones, Jeff/Harleton Ind School Dist	5	208
Jones, Jeff/Monahans-Wickett-Pyote ISD	3	385
Jones, Jeff/Wortham Ind School Dist	67	156
Jones, Jennifer/Tyler Ind School Dist	36	337
Jones, Jill/Blackwell Cons Ind Sch Dist	2	301
Jones, Joey/Longview Ind School Dist	2,19	169
Jones, Joey/Schleicher Co Ind Sch Dist	5	333
Jones, Joffery, Dr/Klein Ind School Dist	91	196
Jones, Karen/Wink Loving Ind School Dist	57	402
Jones, Keith, Dr/Deweyville Ind School Dist	1,11	308
Jones, Kellie/Greenville Ind School Dist	5	236
Jones, Kevin/Harleton Ind School Dist	73	208
Jones, Kurt/Burnet Cons Ind Sch Dist	6	60
Jones, Kyle, Dr/Lackland Ind School Dist	84	34
Jones, Lanell/Aransas Pass Ind School Dist	4	330
Jones, Laurl/George West Ind School Dist	76	268
Jones, Leann/Palmer Ind School Dist	31	141
Jones, Lisa/Crosby Ind School Dist	2,11,19	183
Jones, Lisa/Era Ind School Dist	12,57	90
Jones, Lisa/Tahoka Ind School Dist	2,4,12,19	273
Jones, Lois/Santa Fe Ind School Dist	90	161
Jones, Lori/Northside Ind School Dist	15,73	36
Jones, Maria/Mineral Wells Ind School Dist	67	310
Jones, Mary/Eastland Ind School Dist	2	129
Jones, Mary/Sunray Ind School Dist	275	296
Jones, Mary, Dr/Eagle Mtn-Saginaw Ind Sch Dist	11,69,88,271,296	348
Jones, Marybeth/Sunray Ind School Dist	35,36,69,83	296
Jones, Matthew/New Braunfels Ind School Dist	16,73,295	88
Jones, Michelle/Hamlin Ind School Dist	58	249
Jones, Mike/Lamar Cons Ind School Dist	5	153
Jones, Mike/Trenton Ind School Dist	6	147
Jones, Mike/Valley Mills Ind School Dist	67	47
Jones, Naiomo/Lockney Independent Sch Dist	11	149
Jones, Niki/Region 8 Ed Service Center	7,271	69
Jones, Patrick/Midland Ind School Dist	8,18	285
Jones, Paul/Boys Ranch Ind School Dist	6,15,275	307
Jones, Paul/Paris Ind School Dist	1	260
Jones, Randy/Athens Ind School Dist	2,19	213
Jones, Robert/Balmorhea Ind School Dist	6	323
Jones, Roberta/Gilmer Ind School Dist	4	376
Jones, Ron/Tyler Ind School Dist	15,68,751	337
Jones, Samantha/De Leon Ind School Dist	4	89
Jones, Shane/Lampasas Ind School Dist	2,19	261
Jones, Shannon/Huffman Ind School Dist	91	195
Jones, Sharon/Edgewood Ind School Dist	2	380
Jones, Shawn/Huntington Ind School Dist	6	17
Jones, Sheila/Quinlan Ind School Dist	58	237
Jones, Shondra/Red Oak Ind School Dist	273	142
Jones, Stacy/Cross Plains Ind Sch Dist	8,69,83,88,275,294	62
Jones, Tamera/Leary Ind School Dist	59	48
Jones, Tammy/Palestine Ind School Dist	15,48,51,54,57,88,271	15
Jones, Tammy/Troup Ind School Dist	1	337
Jones, Taygon/Montague Ind School Dist	67	290
Jones, Terrell/Texline Ind School Dist	1	95
Jones, Thresha/Bloomburg Ind School Dist	67	70
Jones, Tiffanie/Mt Enterprise Ind School Dist	36,69,83,88	328
Jones, Timothy/Dallas Co Schools	3	95
Jones, Todd/Era Ind School Dist	8	90
Jones, Traci/Harleton Ind School Dist	270	208
Jones, Vernora/Tyler Ind School Dist	12	337
Jones, Wes/Granbury Ind School Dist	68	230
Jontra, Stan/Canton Ind School Dist	73,295	380
Jopling, Sandra/Lytle Ind School Dist	83	21
Jordan, Bethany/Pasadena Ind School Dist	2	198
Jordan, Byron/Mt Enterprise Ind School Dist	1,11	328
Jordan, Darelle/Wimberley Ind School Dist	7,83,85	212
Jordan, Elizabeth/Kountze Ind School Dist	4	178
Jordan, Fabiola/Socorro Ind School Dist	45	135
Jordan, Janis/Lake Travis Ind School Dist	74	370
Jordan, Janis, Dr/Northside Ind School Dist	8,15	36
Jordan, Jaretha/Crowley Ind School Dist	74	347
Jordan, Melissa/Devers Ind School Dist	2,295	265
Jordan, Michael/San Antonio Ind School Dist	88	39
Jordan, Sue/Belton Ind School Dist	67	26
Jordan, Vondell/Mason Ind School Dist	280	275
Jordon, Jennifer/Denver City Ind School Dist	4	405
Joseph, Renferd/Manor Ind School Dist	20,23	371
Joseph, Roosevelt/Coldspring-Oakhurst Cons ISD	91	330
Joseph, Stacy/Forney Ind School Dist	16,73	251
Joslien, Elizabeth/Cooper Ind School Dist	38,69,83,288	119
Joslin, Chris/Coahoma Ind School Dist	6	234
Josselet, Kent/Ponder Ind School Dist	2,15,286	125
Jost, Doug/Glasscock Co Ind School Dist	67	163
Joubert, Maggie/Bridge City Ind School Dist	4	308
Joyner, Veronica/Garland Ind School Dist	61	105
Juarez, Mike/Silverton Ind School Dist	3,5	57
Juban, Anda/Hallsville Ind School Dist	81	208
Juergens, Kelly/Celina Ind School Dist	67	78
Juerrero, Rolando/United Ind School Dist	297	387
Junco, Marianne/Santa Fe Ind School Dist	2	161
Jungman, Suzi/Lufkin Ind School Dist	285	18
Junkin, Courtney/Marion Ind School Dist	16,297	172
Jurado, Alicia/Childress Ind School Dist	57	74
Jurado, David/Memphis Ind School Dist	6	175
Jurecek, Lisa/Orange Grove Ind School Dist	16,82	245
Jurek, Dennis/Bellville Ind School Dist	2,19	21
Jurek, Donald/East Central Ind School Dist	5	31

DISTRICT PERSONNEL INDEX

Market Data Retrieval

NAME/District	JOB FUNCTIONS	PAGE
Jurek, Stephen/*Weimar Ind School Dist*	3	87
Justiss, Joseph/*Paris Ind School Dist*	5	260

K

NAME/District	JOB FUNCTIONS	PAGE
Kablaitis, Denise/*Pflugerville Ind School Dist*	7,91	371
Kaffka, Daniel/*Santa Maria Ind School Dist*	91	67
Kahl, Scott/*Arlington Ind School Dist*	15,68,79	343
Kahlden, Ryan/*Waxahachie Ind School Dist*	2,15	142
Kain, Ben/*Leveretts Chapel Ind Sch Dist*	3	328
Kaiser, Bettinae/*South San Antonio Ind Sch Dist*	2,19	42
Kalbas, Edy/*Farwell Ind School Dist*	2,11	314
Kale, Eric/*Hico Ind School Dist*	27	176
Kalina, Cindy/*Schulenburg Ind School Dist*	85	148
Kalina, Kim/*Marshall Ind School Dist*	60	209
Kallus, Sherry/*Holland Ind School Dist*	274	27
Kaluzas, Elizabeth/*Hubbard Ind School Dist*	2	227
Kaminski, David/*Waller Ind School Dist*	67	384
Kammerer, William/*Iredell Ind School Dist*	273	46
Kamradt, Christopher/*Spring Branch Ind School Dist*	4	200
Kane, Diedra/*Wellington Ind School Dist*	8	86
Kanipes, Mark/*Santa Fe Ind School Dist*	6	161
Karch, Shaun/*Thrall Ind School Dist*	2	400
Karchoff, Mark/*Harper Ind School Dist*	6	163
Karl, Carla/*Gold-Burg Ind School Dist*	3	290
Karnes, Jason/*Godley Ind School Dist*	15	247
Karr, Gypsy/*City View Ind School Dist*	67	391
Karr, Lisa/*Hurst-Euless-Bedford ISD*	27,28	353
Karre, Howard/*Sabinal Ind School Dist*	73,286,295	378
Kasch, Bob/*Spring Creek Ind School Dist*	67	238
Kasel, Tim/*Farwell Ind School Dist*	3,5,91	314
Kasper, Brian/*Longview Ind School Dist*	31	169
Kasper, Jennifer/*East Central Ind School Dist*	8	31
Kasper, Melanie/*Jarrell Ind School Dist*	58,275	396
Kassaw, Kim/*Lufkin Ind School Dist*	58	18
Kassen, Alan/*Valley View ISD-Cooke Co*	6	91
Kassman, Lisa/*Katy Ind School Dist*	70	151
Kates, Matt/*La Grange Ind School Dist*	6	147
Kates, Melissa/*Duncanville Ind School Dist*	15,751	104
Katrina, Garrett/*Plainview Ind School Dist*	9	175
Kattner, Vicki/*Godley Ind School Dist*	16	247
Kauffman, Katie/*Lake Travis Ind School Dist*	70	370
Kaufman, John/*Trinity Ind School Dist*	1	374
Kaufmann, Pam/*Rockdale Ind School Dist*	8,11,15,58,288,296,298	287
Kaup, Keith/*Spring Ind School Dist*	5	202
Kautz, Jeff/*Stratford Ind School Dist*	5	336
Kautz, Lynette/*Stratford Ind School Dist*	2,11,84,296	336
Kay, Ashely/*Utopia Ind School Dist*	8,74,271,274	378
Kay, Patricia, Dr/*Crosby Ind School Dist*	15,31,68	183
Kazanas, George, Dr/*Midway Ind School Dist*	1	280
Keach, Kristy/*George West Ind School Dist*	11,69	268
Keahey, Mark/*Region 10 Ed Service Center*	4	116
Kearley, Donna/*Denton Ind School Dist*	16	120
Keasler, Steve/*Carroll Independent Sch Dist*	6	347
Keating, Shannon/*Bells Ind School Dist*	4	165
Kechnie, J P/*Weatherford Ind School Dist*	3	313
Keck, Bradley/*Nocona Ind School Dist*	6	290
Keeler, Stephen/*Benjamin Ind School Dist*	67	258
Keeling, Justin/*Douglass Ind School Dist*	1	297
Keeling, Tammy/*Victoria Ind School Dist*	67	382
Keeling, Whitney/*Waskom Ind School Dist*	6	209
Keen, Susan/*Lancaster Ind School Dist*	58	110
Keene, Kelly/*Liberty Hill Ind School Dist*	7	398
Keene, Teresa/*Newcastle Ind School Dist*	4	406
Keener, Michelle/*Deer Park Ind School Dist*	4	186
Keeney, Chris/*Perrin-Whitt Cons Ind Sch Dist*	67	239
Keeney, Mike/*Aldine Ind School Dist*	71	179
Keeney, Stacey/*Utopia Ind School Dist*	6	378
Keenum, Steve/*Wylie Ind School Dist*	67	361
Keese, Gabe/*Lufkin Ind School Dist*	45	18
Keeton, Wendy/*Sam Rayburn Ind School Dist*	10,60,69,73,286,295	146
Kehoe, Mark/*Azle Ind School Dist*	68	345
Kehrwald, Michelle/*Ysleta Ind School Dist*	42,45	137
Keifler, Megan/*Tatum Ind School Dist*	38	328
Keiser, Chris/*Palestine Ind School Dist*	15	15
Keith, Beth/*Eanes Ind School Dist*	275	370
Keith, Cash/*Uvalde Cons Ind School Dist*	73	378
Keith, Daniel/*Tulia Ind School Dist*	286	343
Keith, Karen/*Lingleville Ind School Dist*	58	143
Keith, Marc, Dr/*Tarkington Ind School Dist*	1	266
Keith, Ray/*Happy Ind School Dist*	1	342
Keith, Tye/*Turkey-Quitaque Cons Ind SD*	6	176
Keithley, David/*Trinity Ind School Dist*	58	374
Kelanic, Jack/*Dallas Ind School Dist*	73,98	98
Kellas, Deb/*Lindale Ind School Dist*	57	337
Keller, Gloria/*Karnes City Ind School Dist*	5	250
Keller, Jason/*Sabinal Ind School Dist*	6	378
Keller, Jon/*Gladewater Ind School Dist*	67	169
Keller, Stephine/*Medina Valley Ind School Dist*	58	284
Keller, Taylor/*Comal Ind School Dist*	42	87
Kellermeier, Mark/*Veribest Ind School Dist*	67	365
Kelley, Brenda/*Alba-Golden Ind School Dist*	2	404
Kelley, Christina/*Atlanta Ind School Dist*	34,58	69
Kelley, Michaelann/*Aldine Ind School Dist*	20	179
Kelley, Mike/*Springtown Ind School Dist*	1	313
Kelley, Rebecca/*Brazosport Ind School Dist*	2,19	52
Kelley, Richard/*River Road Ind School Dist*	1	319
Kelley, Tim/*Eula Ind School Dist*	1	63
Kelley, Tom/*Yoakum Ind School Dist*	1	118
Kelly, Arnie/*Chireno ISD School Dist*	1	297
Kelly, Chad, Dr/*Jacksonville Ind School Dist*	1	72
Kelly, Corey/*Needville Ind School Dist*	73	154
Kelly, Frank/*Madisonville Cons ISD*	3,91	273
Kelly, Jean/*Laneville Ind School Dist*	50	327
Kelly, Jennifer/*Anna Ind School Dist*	33	77
Kelly, Jennifer/*Columbia Brazoria ISD*	58	52
Kelly, John, Dr/*Pearland Ind School Dist*	1	53
Kelly, Mike/*Valley Mills Ind School Dist*	1,11	47
Kelly, Susan/*Carrollton-Farmers Branch ISD*	34,54	96
Kelly, Trudy/*Carrollton-Farmers Branch ISD*	71	96
Kelly, Wayne/*San Saba Ind School Dist*	1,83	332
Kelm, Delbert/*Crawford Ind School Dist*	6	279
Kelmm, Karin/*McKinney Ind School Dist*	35	81
Kelsey, Lena/*Latexo Ind School Dist*	28,286	233
Kelso, John/*Greenville Ind School Dist*	67	236
Kelsoe, Kelli/*Castleberry Ind School Dist*	16	347
Kelton, Shane/*Bronte Ind School Dist*	67	75
Kemmerling, Jeff/*Normangee Ind School Dist*	73,82,286	264
Kemp, Allen/*Perryton Ind School Dist*	3	307
Kemp, Allison/*Palmer Ind School Dist*	29	141
Kemp, Christian/*Hardin Jefferson Ind Sch Dist*	28	177
Kemp, Ken/*Collinsville Ind School Dist*	16,73,295	166
Kemp, Mark/*Aransas Pass Ind School Dist*	11	330
Kemper, James/*Corrigan-Camden Ind Sch Dist*	3,5	316
Kemper, Mary/*Coppell Ind School Dist*	45	98
Kendall, Jim/*Kerens Ind School Dist*	2	300
Kendrick, Kenny/*Humble Ind School Dist*	3	195
Kendrick, Marshall/*Pasadena Ind School Dist*	67	198
Kennedy, Catherine, Dr/*Ysleta Ind School Dist*	15	137
Kennedy, David/*Westhoff Ind School Dist*	1,11,73,83,84	118
Kennedy, Dorothy/*Groveton Ind School Dist*	36,69	374
Kennedy, Edna, Dr/*Burton Ind School Dist*	1,73,83	386
Kennedy, John/*Somerset Ind School Dist*	295	42
Kennedy, Maria/*El Paso Ind School Dist*	6	132
Kennedy, Rhonda/*Covington ISD School Dist*	4	227

---

1 Superintendent	16 Instructional Media Svcs	30 Adult Education	44 Science Sec	58 Special Education K-12	72 Summer School
2 Bus/Finance/Purchasing	17 Chief Operations Officer	31 Career/Sch-to-Work K-12	45 Math K-12	59 Special Education Elem	73 Instructional Tech
3 Buildings And Grounds	18 Chief Academic Officer	32 Career/Sch-to-Work Elem	46 Math Elem	60 Special Education Sec	74 Inservice Training
4 Food Service	19 Chief Financial Officer	33 Career/Sch-to-Work Sec	47 Math Sec	61 Foreign/World Lang K-12	75 Marketing/Distributive
5 Transportation	20 Art K-12	34 Early Childhood Ed	48 English/Lang Arts K-12	62 Foreign/World Lang Elem	76 Info Systems
6 Athletic	21 Art Elem	35 Health/Phys Education	49 English/Lang Arts Elem	63 Foreign/World Lang Sec	77 Psychological Assess
7 Health Services	22 Art Sec	36 Guidance Services K-12	50 English/Lang Arts Sec	64 Religious Education K-12	78 Affirmative Action
8 Curric/Instruct K-12	23 Music K-12	37 Guidance Services Elem	51 Reading K-12	65 Religious Education Elem	79 Student Personnel
9 Curric/Instruct Elem	24 Music Elem	38 Guidance Services Sec	52 Reading Elem	66 Religious Education Sec	80 Driver Ed/Safety
10 Curric/Instruct Sec	25 Music Sec	39 Social Studies K-12	53 Reading Sec	67 School Board President	81 Gifted/Talented
11 Federal Program	26 Business Education	40 Social Studies Elem	54 Remedial Reading K-12	68 Teacher Personnel	82 Video Services
12 Title I	27 Career & Tech Ed	41 Social Studies Sec	55 Remedial Reading Elem	69 Academic Assessment	83 Substance Abuse Prev
13 Title V	28 Technology Education	42 Science K-12	56 Remedial Reading Sec	70 Research/Development	84 Erate
15 Asst Superintendent	29 Family/Consumer Science	43 Science Elem	57 Bilingual/ELL	71 Public Information	85 AIDS Education

88 Alternative/At Risk	277 Remedial Math K-12
89 Multi-Cultural Curriculum	280 Literacy Coach
90 Social Work	285 STEM
91 Safety/Security	286 Digital Learning
92 Magnet School	288 Common Core Standards
93 Parental Involvement	294 Accountability
95 Tech Prep Program	295 Network System
97 Chief Information Officer	296 Title II Programs
98 Chief Technology Officer	297 Webmaster
270 Character Education	298 Grant Writer/Ptnrships
271 Migrant Education	750 Chief Innovation Officer
273 Teacher Mentor	751 Chief of Staff
274 Before/After Sch	752 Social Emotional Learning
275 Response To Intervention	

TX-T48

Texas School Directory

DISTRICT PERSONNEL INDEX

NAME/District	JOB FUNCTIONS	PAGE
Kennedy, Suzanne/*Bonham Ind School Dist*	34	145
Kenney, Kathy/*New Braunfels Ind School Dist*	68	88
Kennon, Paige/*Lamesa Ind School Dist*	37	117
Kent, Katrina/*Iraan-Sheffield Ind Sch Dist*	4	316
Keough, Michael/*Canyon Ind School Dist*	76	320
Kercheville, Kristy/*Liberty Hill Ind School Dist*	31,57	398
Kerin, Pat/*Shallowater Ind School Dist*	4	272
Kern, Catherine/*Ingram Ind School Dist*	7	255
Kern, Larry/*Frost Ind School Dist*	3,5	299
Kerney, Debra/*Canutillo Ind School Dist*	8	131
Kerns, Dane/*Smyer Ind School Dist*	1,83	229
Kerr, Chelsey/*Johnson City Ind School Dist*	4	46
Kerr, Kay/*Channelview Ind School Dist*	68,79	183
Kerr, Sherry/*Kaufman Ind School Dist*	11,57,271	252
Kersh, Becky/*West Ind School Dist*	8	282
Kersh, James/*Lumberton Ind School Dist*	67	178
Kershner, Richard/*Splendora Ind School Dist*	15,273	294
Kersten, Angel/*Angleton Ind School Dist*	5	51
Kersten, Denise/*Bryan Ind School Dist*	16	54
Kessel, Scott/*Aledo Ind School Dist*	88	312
Kessler, Karla/*Alief Ind School Dist*	11,296,298	181
Keuhler, Ronald/*Int'l Leadership of Texas Dist*	2,19	108
Key, Candi/*Throckmorton Ind School Dist*	73,84,295	363
Key, Carl/*New Diana Ind School Dist*	1	376
Key, Dan/*Albany Ind School Dist*	73	334
Key, Jerry/*Harmony Ind School Dist*	67	376
Key, Natalie/*Sanger Ind School Dist*	68	126
Key, Stacy/*Graham Ind School Dist*	7	406
Keys, Mark/*Childress Ind School Dist*	67	74
Keys, Randy/*Van Vleck Ind School Dist*	73,84	276
Khalaf, Elias/*Tioga Ind School Dist*	73	167
Khan, Sandy/*Leander Ind School Dist*	58	396
Khosravi, Anthony/*Harlandale Ind School Dist*	81	32
Kiawatski, Pamela/*Robstown Ind School Dist*	58	305
Kibodeaux, Katie/*Hardin Jefferson Ind Sch Dist*	5	177
Kidd, Karen, Dr/*Prosper Ind School Dist*	8	84
Kidd, Linda/*Big Sandy Ind School Dist*	2	316
Kiehl, Debra/*Greenwood Ind School Dist*	8	285
Kieschnick, Stephanie/*Dime Box Ind School Dist*	2,4	263
Kieschnick, Stuart/*Nederland Ind School Dist*	15,57,88	242
Kieshhnick, Jana/*Odem-Edroy Ind School Dist*	57,58	331
Kile, Doug/*Perryton Ind School Dist*	2,19	307
Kilgore, Richard/*Bruceville-Eddy Ind Sch Dist*	1	278
Kilian, Joy/*Hereford Ind School Dist*	7,58,72	119
Killgo, Jay, Dr/*Vidor Ind School Dist*	1,84	309
Killian, Douglas, Dr/*Pflugerville Ind School Dist*	1	371
Killingsworth, Shelli/*Mexia Ind School Dist*	57,68	267
Killion, Viviana/*Crosby Ind School Dist*	71	183
Killough, Dan/*Winters Ind School Dist*	67	327
Kilman, Lynne/*Teague Ind School Dist*	16	156
Kilmer, Faith/*Broaddus Ind School Dist*	57	329
Kilpatrick, David/*Ennis Ind School Dist*	6	140
Kim, Andrew/*Comal Ind School Dist*	1	87
Kimball, Matt/*Blue Ridge Ind School Dist*	1	77
Kimberly, David/*Klein Ind School Dist*	91	196
Kimble, Glen/*Hudson Ind School Dist*	6	17
Kimbro, Brittany/*Timpson Ind School Dist*	7	335
Kinard, Glen/*Rogers Ind School Dist*	73,295	29
Kincade, Keylon/*Winona Ind School Dist*	6	339
Kincaid, Ronnie/*Region 14 Ed Service Center*	1	362
Kincannon, Susan/*Waco Ind School Dist*	1	281
Kincy, Jesse/*Prairie Valley Ind School Dist*	60	290
Kindrich, Anna/*Jourdanton Ind School Dist*	274	20
Kindsfather, Stacy/*Klein Ind School Dist*	294	196
Kindsfather, Stacy/*Klein Ind School Dist*	69,294	196
Kiner, Dana/*Jim Ned Cons Ind School Dist*	73,286,295	361
King, Annette/*McDade Ind School Dist*	4	24
King, Brandy/*Kennedale Ind School Dist*	68	355
King, Brian/*Chireno ISD School Dist*	8,273	297
King, Carra/*Garland Ind School Dist*	275	105
King, Cathryn/*Region 10 Ed Service Center*	58	116
King, Charlie/*Brock Ind School Dist*	16,73	312
King, Dana/*Lubbock Ind School Dist*	78,90,275	270
King, Daniel, Dr/*Pharr-San Juan-Alamo Ind SD*	1	223
King, Denise/*Barbers Hill Ind School Dist*	285	72
King, Elizabeth/*Humble Ind School Dist*	74	195

NAME/District	JOB FUNCTIONS	PAGE
King, Georgia, Dr/*Beckville Ind School Dist*	8,11,58,83,286,296,298	311
King, James/*Everman Ind School Dist*	79,91	349
King, Jeff/*Irving Ind School Dist*	20,23	109
King, Joey/*Lindale Ind School Dist*	91	337
King, John/*Grandview Ind School Dist*	3	248
King, John/*Longview Ind School Dist*	6,35	169
King, Klint/*Liberty-Eylau Ind School Dist*	6	48
King, Lane/*Mesquite Ind School Dist*	76	110
King, Lester/*Goodrich Ind School Dist*	6	316
King, Monty/*Crane Ind School Dist*	3,5	93
King, Nona/*Connally Ind School Dist*	274	279
King, Paul/*Dallas Co Schools*	2	95
King, Rebecca/*Rockdale Ind School Dist*	16,73,286	287
King, Ronda/*Zephyr Ind School Dist*	4	59
King, Shari/*Region 11 Ed Service Center*	298	360
King, Tacy/*Clear Creek Ind School Dist*	57	158
King, Tamo/*Manor Ind School Dist*	27	371
King, Wendy/*Milano Ind School Dist*	6	287
Kingcade, Tim/*Iowa Park Consolidated Ind SD*	3	392
Kinley, Kevin/*Keller Ind School Dist*	91	354
Kinnaird, Phyllis/*Bonham Ind School Dist*	4	145
Kinnard, Monty/*Perryton Ind School Dist*	67	307
Kinnear, Theresa/*McGregor Ind School Dist*	2	280
Kinsler, Christie/*Jourdanton Ind School Dist*	29	20
Kinslow, Paula/*Clyde Consolidated Ind SD*	8,11,58,69,271,273,298	62
Kinzie, Nancy/*Richardson Ind School Dist*	68	112
Kirby, Denise/*Slaton Ind School Dist*	58	272
Kirby, Jeff/*Poolville Ind School Dist*	1	313
Kirby, Lori/*Blooming Grove Ind School Dist*	37	299
Kirby, Mary/*Rice Ind School Dist*	295	300
Kirby, Synthia/*Wichita Falls Ind School Dist*	27,31,73,95	392
Kirchhoff, Will/*Lovelady Ind School Dist*	6	233
Kirchner, Anthony/*Crowley Ind School Dist*	71	347
Kirk, Sarah/*Peaster Ind School Dist*	2	313
Kirkbride, David, Dr/*Denison Ind School Dist*	13,15,68,78,79,83,294,296	166
Kirkendall, Shelly/*Idalou Ind School Dist*	2,19	269
Kirkland, Amy/*Vega Ind School Dist*	16,73	307
Kirkland, Cathy, Dr/*Athens Ind School Dist*	8,57,69,78,288	213
Kirkpatrick, Coby/*Burleson Ind School Dist*	68,79	246
Kirkpatrick, Lisa, Dr/*Springtown Ind School Dist*	11,31,57,83,88,271,296,298	313
Kirkpatrick, Lynn/*Deer Park Ind School Dist*	67	186
Kirkpatrick, Rick/*Copperas Cove Ind School Dist*	15,91	92
Kirkpatricke, Susan/*Friendswood Ind Sch Dist*	27	160
Kirland, Lesia/*Howe Ind School Dist*	4	166
Kiser, Chris/*Palestine Ind School Dist*	31	15
Kiser, Neil/*Red Lick Ind School Dist*	6	49
Kissko, Marcie/*Lake Travis Ind School Dist*	4	370
Kistner, Rachel/*Red Oak Ind School Dist*	58	142
Kitchens, Susan/*Groveton Ind School Dist*	54	374
Kite, Troy/*Humble Ind School Dist*	6	195
Kitten, Brenda/*Hereford Ind School Dist*	6,35	119
Klabunde, Fritz/*Round Rock Ind School Dist*	5	398
Klammer, Beth/*Navasota Ind School Dist*	39,48	172
Klaska, Dustin/*Perryton Ind School Dist*	6	307
Klatt, Tracy/*Orange Grove Ind School Dist*	73,295	245
Klatt, Will/*Orange Grove Ind School Dist*	67	245
Klaus, Jennifer/*Cypress-Fairbanks Ind Sch Dist*	61	184
Klein, James/*Harlandale Ind School Dist*	79	32
Klein, Kay/*Prairiland Ind School Dist*	2,296	260
Klein, Kelly/*Union Grove Ind School Dist*	298	377
Klein, Millie/*Region 13 Ed Service Center*	15	373
Klein, Stephanie/*Sam Rayburn Ind School Dist*	37	146
Kleinhans, Angela/*Montague Ind School Dist*	16,73	290
Klement, Carol/*Muenster Ind School Dist*	2	91
Klemstein, Jodi/*Comfort Ind School Dist*	16	254
Klepac, Robert/*Bay City Ind School Dist*	67	275
Klimitchek, Missy/*Industrial Ind School Dist*	8,11,74,270,273,294,296	240
Kline, Andrea/*Waxahachie Ind School Dist*	41	142
Kline, Julie/*St Jo Ind School Dist*	73,76,82	290
Kling, Kelsey/*Texas Dept of Education*	20	1
Klink, Renessa/*Wellington Ind School Dist*	69,83,88	86
Kloepper, Eliabeth/*Llano Ind School Dist*	85	268
Klopper, Cathy/*Texarkana Ind School Dist*	285	50
Klopzman, Jeffrey/*Lubbock Ind School Dist*	71	270
Kloth, Debbie/*Pearsall Ind School Dist*	2	157
Kluttz, Les/*Sweeny Ind School Dist*	79	54

DISTRICT PERSONNEL INDEX

Market Data Retrieval

NAME/*District*	JOB FUNCTIONS	PAGE
Knaub, Marla/*South Texas Ind School Dist*	2,15	67
Knaus, Connie/*Holland Ind School Dist*	4	27
Knickerbocker, Tessa/*Ballinger Ind School Dist*	38	326
Knight, Adam/*Alto Ind School Dist*	73	72
Knight, Beverly/*Little Cypress Mauriceville SD*	11,58,68,72,270	308
Knight, Jim/*Lamesa Ind School Dist*	1	117
Knight, Kimber, Dr/*Beaumont Ind School Dist*	73	241
Knight, Lisa/*Midlothian Ind School Dist*	11,57,271,296,298	141
Knight, Mary Ellen/*Winnsboro Ind School Dist*	58	405
Knight, Nate/*Hawley Ind School Dist*	67	250
Knight, Robert/*Ft Stockton Ind School Dist*	83	315
Knight, Robert/*Hondo Ind School Dist*	10,31	284
Knight, Thomas/*Ferris Ind School Dist*	11,54,57,68,69,74,83,294	140
Knighton, Tracy/*Christoval Ind School Dist*	9,11,88	364
Knipp, Jennifer/*Mineola Ind School Dist*	8,57,58,69,74,88,271,286	404
Knobloch, Cd/*Archer City Ind School Dist*	1,11	19
Knolton, Tonya/*Harleton Ind School Dist*	83,88,273	208
Knopp, Tyson/*Linden Kildare Cons Ind SD*	73	70
Knostman, Ryan/*Aransas Pass Ind School Dist*	6	330
Knowlton, John/*Deer Park Ind School Dist*	2	186
Knowlton, Tonya/*Lexington Ind School Dist*	1	263
Knowlton, Virgil/*Ganado Ind School Dist*	11,274	239
Knox, Ashton/*West Orange-Cove Cons ISD*	8	309
Knox, Heather/*West Orange-Cove Cons ISD*	58,90,91	309
Knox, Karl/*School of Excellence In Ed*	2,11	42
Knox, Retta/*Hart Ind School Dist*	13,35,83,85,88	71
Knudsen, Tina/*Lockhart Ind School Dist*	2,19	61
Knudson, Stacey/*San Antonio Ind School Dist*	45	39
Kobosky, David/*Gunter Ind School Dist*	295	166
Koch, Frances/*Victoria Ind School Dist*	2,15	382
Koch, Joe/*Paradise Ind School Dist*	6	403
Kocian, Penny/*Axtell Ind School Dist*	2,10,11,35,57,88	278
Koehl, Kenny/*Columbus Ind School Dist*	3	86
Koelzer, James/*Muenster Ind School Dist*	3	91
Koerth, Stacy, Dr/*Hutto Ind School Dist*	58	396
Koester, Steve/*Goose Creek Cons Ind Sch Dist*	73,286	187
Kohl, Cyndy/*Wichita Falls Ind School Dist*	68	392
Kohler, Theresa, Dr/*Crowley Ind School Dist*	68	347
Kohrman, Jeff/*Spring Ind School Dist*	73,76,295	202
Kolbeck, Bryon/*Lewisville Ind School Dist*	73,76,98,295	122
Kolby, Amberly/*Navasota Ind School Dist*	8,69	172
Kolek, Richard/*Johnson City Ind School Dist*	1	46
Kolenda, Joe/*Spring Branch Ind School Dist*	27,31	200
Kolodziej, Kellie/*Kenedy Ind School Dist*	7	251
Konderla, Joya/*Garrison Ind School Dist*	37	297
Konz, Wendy/*Lake Dallas Ind School Dist*	3,5	122
Koonce, David/*Lewisville Ind School Dist*	76	122
Koons, Jim/*Keller Ind School Dist*	5	354
Koopman, Robert/*Friendswood Ind Sch Dist*	6	160
Kopowski, Sara/*Keller Ind School Dist*	8,275,296	354
Koran, Candace/*Lumberton Ind School Dist*	16,82	178
Korenek, Genelle/*Rockdale Ind School Dist*	2	287
Kornegay, Brent/*George West Ind School Dist*	6	268
Kortan, Maria/*Harlingen Cons Ind School Dist*	74	64
Koskelin, Brad/*Mabank Ind School Dist*	15,68,71	252
Koskelin, Shela/*Mabank Ind School Dist*	31	252
Kostelich, Kristy/*Denver City Ind School Dist*	27	405
Koster, Gena, Dr/*Keller Ind School Dist*	58	354
Kosterman, Chris/*Rockwall Ind School Dist*	20,23	325
Kotar, Edward/*Taylor Ind School Dist*	4	399
Kotsopoulos, Renee/*Garland Ind School Dist*	7,85	105
Kotula, Colette/*Everman Ind School Dist*	11	349
Kouba, Ronda/*Deer Park Ind School Dist*	8,15,296	186
Kovach, Karen/*Del Valle Ind School Dist*	4	369
Kovacs, Kelly/*Schertz-Cibolo-Univ City ISD*	8,69,74	173
Kovar, Becky/*East Bernard Ind Sch Dist*	2,11,294,296	389
Kovar, Jacqueline/*Rice Cons Ind School Dist*	31	87

NAME/*District*	JOB FUNCTIONS	PAGE
Kovar, Shannon/*Grapevine-Colleyville Ind SD*	69	353
Kraft, Jeanne/*Paris Ind School Dist*	71	260
Krajca, Kristi/*Mesquite Ind School Dist*	27,31	110
Kram, Ken/*Weimar Ind School Dist*	67	87
Kramer, Joan/*Fredericksburg Ind School Dist*	30	163
Kramer, Richard/*Nueces Canyon Cons Ind SD*	27	131
Kramer, Toby/*Nueces Canyon Cons Ind SD*	59	131
Kramer, Tracie/*Burton Ind School Dist*	68	386
Kramme, Debbie/*Ft Sam Houston Ind School Dist*	68	32
Kranz, Stephanie/*Lovejoy Ind School Dist*	273	80
Krause, Calvin/*Round Top-Carmine Ind Sch Dist*	67	147
Krause, Curtis/*Giddings Ind School Dist*	5	263
Krchnak, Brenda/*Snook Ind School Dist*	1	59
Kreiter, Erich/*Friendswood Ind School Dist*	91	160
Krenek, Thomas/*El Campo Ind School Dist*	76,84,286	389
Krenger, Lisa/*Alamo Heights Ind School Dist*	67	30
Kretchmar, Ted/*Crowley Ind School Dist*	11,294,296	347
Krichnak, Randall/*Sealy Ind School Dist*	5	22
Kridler, Gene/*Gonzales Ind School Dist*	3,5,17	164
Kriner, Rachel/*Trinity Ind School Dist*	7	374
Krippel, John/*Humble Ind School Dist*	68	195
Kroeger, Brian/*Splendora Ind School Dist*	68	294
Kroeker, Duane/*Ingram Ind School Dist*	6	255
Kroll, Carrie/*Dripping Springs Ind Sch Dist*	67	210
Kroll, Micheal/*Karnes City Ind School Dist*	27,28	250
Krone, Mickey/*Forney Ind School Dist*	5	251
Kronenberger, Kurt/*Bridgeport Ind School Dist*	3,5,15,68	402
Kroontje, Wallie/*Fruitvale Ind School Dist*	3	380
Krsnak, Becki/*Midlothian Ind School Dist*	9	141
Krueger, Jennifer/*Northside Ind School Dist*	7	36
Krueger, Shane/*Hooks Ind School Dist*	1	48
Krueger, Thomas/*Southwest Ind School Dist*	3	43
Krumm, Lisa/*Chapel Hill Ind School Dist*	10	337
Krunnow, Elicia/*Bosqueville Ind School Dist*	57	278
Krusemark, Stony/*Knox City-O'Brien Cons Ind SD*	73,88,286	258
Krusleski, Jerry/*Montgomery Ind School Dist*	73,76,286,295	293
Kubecka, Denise/*Cypress-Fairbanks Ind Sch Dist*	8,15,27	183
Kubena, Nanette/*Brazos Ind School Dist*	31,69,83,85	22
Kucera, David/*Penelope ISD School Dist*	67	228
Kucera, Inez/*Boling Ind School Dist*	9	389
Kucera, Joe, Dr/*Lorena Ind School Dist*	1	280
Kucera, Tony/*Van Vleck Ind School Dist*	67	276
Kuchler, Kathy/*Industrial Ind School Dist*	7	240
Kuddes, Kathy/*Plano Ind School Dist*	20,23	82
Kuecker, Rachelle/*Round Top-Carmine Ind Sch Dist*	6,10,88	147
Kuehler, Ron/*Groom Ind School Dist*	67	69
Kuenstler, Katherine/*Yorktown Ind School Dist*	1	118
Kuhn, John, Dr/*Mineral Wells Ind School Dist*	1	310
Kuhn, Linda/*Grandfalls-Royalty Ind SD*	58	385
Kuhn, Mark/*Grandfalls-Royalty Ind SD*	67	385
Kuhrt, Michael/*Wichita Falls Ind School Dist*	1	392
Kuhrt, Shannon/*Wichita Falls Ind School Dist*	69	392
Kujawa, Rose/*Bremond Ind School Dist*	16	324
Kuklies, Kim/*Lampasas Ind School Dist*	7	261
Kulpa, Dawn/*San Antonio Ind School Dist*	275	39
Kunde, Kevin, Dr/*Marion Ind School Dist*	67	172
Kunkel, Ralph/*Birdville Ind School Dist*	67	346
Kunschik, Veronica/*Crowley Ind School Dist*	750	347
Kuntz, Lindsay/*Medina Ind School Dist*	8,16,57,83,288	23
Kupatt, Leslie/*Rule Ind School Dist*	31,69,270	210
Kurmes, Michele/*Keene Ind School Dist*	58	248
Kusak, Glen/*Yoakum Ind School Dist*	67	118
Kusock, Laura/*Moulton Ind School Dist*	36,69	262
Kutac, Donna/*Louise Ind School Dist*	57	389
Kutsch, Lisa/*Manor Ind School Dist*	47,69,285	371
Kuyatt, Andrea, Dr/*Bishop Cons Ind School Dist*	11,57,296	302
Kuykendall, Christopher/*Oakwood Ind School Dist*	6	264

1 Superintendent	16 Instructional Media Svcs	30 Adult Education	44 Science Sec	58 Special Education K-12	72 Summer School	88 Alternative/At Risk	277 Remedial Math K-12
2 Bus/Finance/Purchasing	17 Chief Operations Officer	31 Career/Sch-to-Work K-12	45 Math K-12	59 Special Education Elem	73 Instructional Tech	89 Multi-Cultural Curriculum	280 Literacy Coach
3 Buildings And Grounds	18 Chief Academic Officer	32 Career/Sch-to-Work Elem	46 Math Elem	60 Special Education Sec	74 Inservice Training	90 Social Work	285 STEM
4 Food Service	19 Chief Financial Officer	33 Career/Sch-to-Work Sec	47 Math Sec	61 Foreign/World Lang K-12	75 Marketing/Distributive	91 Safety/Security	286 Digital Learning
5 Transportation	20 Art K-12	34 Early Childhood Ed	48 English/Lang Arts K-12	62 Foreign/World Lang Elem	76 Info Systems	92 Magnet School	288 Common Core Standards
6 Athletic	21 Art Elem	35 Health/Phys Education	49 English/Lang Arts Elem	63 Foreign/World Lang Sec	77 Psychological Assess	93 Parental Involvement	294 Accountability
7 Health Services	22 Art Sec	36 Guidance Services K-12	50 English/Lang Arts Sec	64 Religious Education K-12	78 Affirmative Action	95 Tech Prep Program	295 Network System
8 Curric/Instruct K-12	23 Music K-12	37 Guidance Services Elem	51 Reading K-12	65 Religious Education Elem	79 Student Personnel	97 Chief Information Officer	296 Title II Programs
9 Curric/Instruct Elem	24 Music Elem	38 Guidance Services Sec	52 Reading Elem	66 Religious Education Sec	80 Driver Ed/Safety	98 Chief Technology Officer	297 Webmaster
10 Curric/Instruct Sec	25 Music Sec	39 Social Studies K-12	53 Reading Sec	67 School Board President	81 Gifted/Talented	270 Character Education	298 Grant Writer/Ptnrships
11 Federal Program	26 Business Education	40 Social Studies Elem	54 Remedial Reading K-12	68 Teacher Personnel	82 Video Services	271 Migrant Education	750 Chief Innovation Officer
12 Title I	27 Career & Tech Ed	41 Social Studies Sec	55 Remedial Reading Elem	69 Academic Assessment	83 Substance Abuse Prev	273 Teacher Mentor	751 Chief of Staff
13 Title V	28 Technology Education	42 Science K-12	56 Remedial Reading Sec	70 Research/Development	84 Erate	274 Before/After Sch	752 Social Emotional Learning
15 Asst Superintendent	29 Family/Consumer Science	43 Science Elem	57 Bilingual/ELL	71 Public Information	85 AIDS Education	275 Response To Intervention	

TX-T50

Texas School Directory

DISTRICT PERSONNEL INDEX

NAME/District	JOB FUNCTIONS	PAGE
Kuykendall, David/*Frisco Ind School Dist*	6	78
Kuykendall, Nancy/*Coolidge Ind School Dist*	2	266
Kvinta, Chris/*Yoakum Ind School Dist*	2,15,71,91,271	118
Kvinta, Kim/*Yoakum Ind School Dist*	37	118
Kwast, Susan/*Sanger Ind School Dist*	2	126
Kyle, Ryan/*Oglesby Ind School Dist*	6	93

L

NAME/District	JOB FUNCTIONS	PAGE
Laaser, Shelley/*Bridgeport Ind School Dist*	4	402
Labbit, Martha/*Central Heights Ind Sch Dist*	11,76,296,298	297
Labbit, Martha/*Central Heights Ind Sch Dist*	84	297
LaBorde, Bobby/*DeSoto Ind School Dist*	2,15	104
Labue, Larry/*Allen Ind School Dist*	8,74	76
Lacefield, Kevin, Dr/*Northwest Ind School Dist*	20,27	124
Lachowicz, Nancy/*Bluff Dale Ind Sch Dist*	69	143
Lackey, Lyle/*Jayton-Girard Ind School Dist*	6,8,11,16,36	255
Lackey, Thomas/*Dodd City Ind School Dist*	67	145
Lacoste-Caputo, Jenny/*Round Rock Ind School Dist*	71	398
Lacy, Gwendolyn/*Beaumont Ind School Dist*	12,34	241
Lacy, Helen/*Brownwood Ind School Dist*	7	58
Ladd, Elaina/*Midland Ind School Dist*	71	285
LaFave, Dan/*Grape Creek Ind School Dist*	297	364
Lafferty, Alice/*Quinlan Ind School Dist*	10	237
Lafferty, Melissa/*Marble Falls Ind School Dist*	2	60
LaGrone, Charlette/*Weatherford Ind School Dist*	93	313
Lahey, Matthew/*Huntsville Ind School Dist*	286	383
Lahrman, Craig/*Ysleta Ind School Dist*	68	137
Lain, Michel/*Union Hill Ind School Dist*	16	377
Laing, Stan/*Northside Ind School Dist*	6	36
Laird, Cindy/*Nederland Ind School Dist*	73,84,95	242
Laird, Mike/*Nederland Ind School Dist*	15,68,91,297	242
Lake, Leann/*Harper Ind School Dist*	8,31,83	163
Lakey, Kandra/*Roby Cons Ind School Dist*	2	148
Laleman, Scott/*South San Antonio Ind Sch Dist*	73,98,295,297	42
Lalor, Elizabeth/*Galena Park Ind School Dist*	8,15	186
Lam, Kevin/*Alamo Heights Ind School Dist*	295	30
Lamb, Chris/*Wylie Ind School Dist*	71,84,97	85
Lamb, Jay/*Groom Ind School Dist*	1,11,84	69
Lamb, Kathleen/*Lexington Ind School Dist*	4	263
Lamb, Michael/*Sulphur Springs Ind Sch Dist*	1	232
Lamb, Pat/*Garland Ind School Dist*	91	105
Lamb, Shawna/*Plemons-Stinnett-Phillips CISD*	34	238
Lamb, Thurston, Dr/*Henderson Ind School Dist*	1	327
Lamb, Trudy/*Follett Ind School Dist*	2	267
Lambden, Dustin/*Edna Ind School Dist*	16,76,295	239
Lamberson, Regan/*Frenship Ind School Dist*	39	269
Lambert, Alan/*Austin Ind School Dist*	20,23	366
Lambert, Cindy/*Hunt Ind School Dist*	11,59,275	255
Lambert, Deborah/*Wellman Union Ind School Dist*	2	362
Lambert, Glenn/*Wylie Ind School Dist*	20	84
Lambert, Holly/*Ingram Ind School Dist*	58	255
Lambeth, Steven/*McLeod Ind School Dist*	6	70
Lambson, Dave/*Birdville Ind School Dist*	73,76,295,297	346
Lament, Scotty/*Union Grove Ind School Dist*	6	377
Lamere, Michael/*Bosqueville Ind School Dist*	5	278
Lamirand, Jerri/*Eanes Ind School Dist*	81,285	370
Lamm, Kristopher/*Lorenzo Ind School Dist*	58	94
Lammers, Christie/*Texarkana Ind School Dist*	4	50
Lampkin, Stacy/*Nacogdoches Ind School Dist*	5	298
Lancaster, Brad, Dr/*Lake Travis Ind School Dist*	1	370
Lancaster, Michelle/*Bushland Ind School Dist*	31	319
Lancaster, Mike/*Evant Ind School Dist*	5	92
Lancaster, Rick/*Early Ind School Dist*	73	58
Lancaster, Rick/*Veribest Ind School Dist*	5	365
Lance, Jennifer/*McLeod Ind School Dist*	8	70
Lance, Randon/*Region 15 Ed Service Center*	295	366
Land, Jennifer/*Belton Ind School Dist*	2,19	26
Land, Liesa/*Brownwood Ind School Dist*	8,83,275,298	58
Landa, Becky/*San Antonio Ind School Dist*	16,74	39
Landeck, Edith, Dr/*United Ind School Dist*	298	387
Landenberger, Lynn/*Driscoll Ind School Dist*	8	304
Landez, Holly/*Killeen Ind School Dist*	286	27
Landin, John/*Coahoma Ind School Dist*	23	234
Landin, Rocio/*Sharyland Ind School Dist*	71	224
Landis, Rick/*North Lamar Ind School Dist*	3	259
Landreth, Shelly/*La Grange Ind School Dist*	8	147
Landrum, Casse/*Poth Ind School Dist*	7,35	401
Landrum, Gina/*Mt Pleasant Ind School Dist*	81	363
Landrum, Jana/*San Benito Cons Ind Sch Dist*	4	66
Landrum, Karla/*Lake Dallas Ind School Dist*	68	122
Landrum, Sharon/*Weatherford Ind School Dist*	2	313
Landry, Barbara/*Brady Ind School Dist*	2	277
Landry, Marie/*Sealy Ind School Dist*	16,82	22
Landry, Tiana/*Waelder Ind School Dist*	2	164
Landua, Susan/*Moody Ind School Dist*	2	281
Lane, Bill/*Azle Ind School Dist*	67	345
Lane, Brad/*Fannindel Ind School Dist*	1,11,73,83	120
Lane, Carol/*Lockney Independent Sch Dist*	8,69,74	149
Lane, Jo/*Latexo Ind School Dist*	2	233
Lane, Lori/*Honey Grove Ind School Dist*	2	146
Lane, Mark/*Kilgore Ind School Dist*	73,82,295,297	169
Lane, Shannon/*Pringle-Morse Cons ISD*	88	177
Lane, Shannon/*Pringle-Morse Cons ISD*	57	177
Lane, Tim/*Saltillo Ind School Dist*	73,286,288	231
Lanford, Barry, Dr/*North East Ind School Dist*	3	34
Lang, Alicia/*Bonham Ind School Dist*	2	145
Langdale, Kenneth/*Aquilla Ind School Dist*	16,73	227
Lange, Natalie/*Brenham Ind School Dist*	67	385
Langford, Amanda/*Gladewater Ind School Dist*	8	169
Langford, Carolyn/*Abbott Ind School Dist*	4	226
Langham, Lynda/*Cushing Ind School Dist*	67	297
Langley, Matt/*Caldwell Ind School Dist*	6	59
Langley, Richele/*Region 8 Ed Service Center*	8,11,15	69
Langlotz, James/*La Vega Ind School Dist*	3,91	279
Langston, Linda/*Abilene Ind School Dist*	7	360
Langston, Shawn/*Kress Ind School Dist*	9	343
Lanham, Lisa/*Advantage Academy Admin Office*	58,88,752	96
Lanham, Sonya/*Covington ISD School Dist*	73,295	227
Lanier, Kathy/*Pleasant Grove Ind School Dist*	76	49
Lanier, Mary Ann/*Winnsboro Ind School Dist*	2	405
Lanier, Matthew/*Orangefield Ind School Dist*	295	309
Lanier, Tammy/*Harris Co Dept of Ed*	71	179
Lankford, Barrett/*Hudson Ind School Dist*	2,19	17
Lankford, Mary/*Sinton Ind School Dist*	285	332
Lanphier, Warren/*Bryan Ind School Dist*	5	54
Lanton, Deanna/*Leakey Ind School Dist*	9,11,58,69,271,294	322
Lantz, Susan/*Comfort Ind School Dist*	73,82,295	254
Lara, Aaron/*La Joya Ind School Dist*	76,295	219
Lara, Alejandra/*Harlingen Cons Ind School Dist*	59	64
Lara, Blanca/*Hidalgo Ind School Dist*	67	217
Lara, Christa/*Hart Ind School Dist*	11,296	71
Lara, Levinia/*Northside Ind School Dist*	15	36
Lara, Peter/*Wink Loving Ind School Dist*	61	402
Lara, Victor/*Flour Bluff Ind School Dist*	23	304
Laredo, Alfredo/*Manor Ind School Dist*	16,73,98,286	371
Larison, Laurie/*Troup Ind School Dist*	7	337
Larkin, Tanya/*Pampa Ind School Dist*	1	165
Larrasquitu, Rosalva/*Brownsville Ind School Dist*	93	63
Larsen, Pier/*Carrollton-Farmers Branch ISD*	39	96
Larson-Hall, Jeri/*Cleburne Ind School Dist*	6	247
Larson, Crystal/*High Island Ind Sch Dist*	2	160
Larson, Todd/*Region 1 Ed Service Center*	58	226
LaRue, Ashley/*Trinity Ind School Dist*	69,83	374
LaRue, Eddie/*Paris Ind School Dist*	295	260
LaRue, Ralph/*Nacogdoches Ind School Dist*	3	298
Lasater, Thad/*College Station Ind Sch Dist*	2	55
Lascsak, Justin/*Mineral Wells Ind School Dist*	286	310
Lashaway, Jay/*Seminole Ind School Dist*	2	158
Lashbrook, Brianna/*Sudan Ind School Dist*	4	261
Lasher, Lenny/*Castleberry Ind School Dist*	6,7,35	347
Lasiter, Cliff/*Slocum ISD School Dist*	1	16
Lass, Mike/*Lockney Independent Sch Dist*	67	149
Lasser, Shelly/*Decatur Ind School Dist*	4	403
Lasseygne, Amber/*Allen Ind School Dist*	2	76
Lassiter, Ross/*Olton Ind School Dist*	6	261
Laster, Nancy/*Marlin Ind School Dist*	16	144
Lathan, Grenita, Dr/*Houston Ind School Dist*	1	188
Latiolais, Pam/*Channelview Ind School Dist*	10	183
Lauer, Cathy/*Nixon-Smiley Cons Ind Sch Dist*	1,11,83	164
Laughinghouse, Stephanie/*Hondo Ind School Dist*	11,54,57,83,271,273,275,296	284
Laughlin, Erin/*Hamshire Fannett Ind Sch Dist*	16	242
Launius, Keri, Dr/*Galveston Ind School Dist*	74	160

DISTRICT PERSONNEL INDEX

Market Data Retrieval

NAME/District	JOB FUNCTIONS	PAGE
Lautzenheifer, Andy/*Medina Ind School Dist*	67	23
Lavake, Ashley/*Stratford Ind School Dist*	12	336
Lavender, Joseph/*Liberty-Eylau Ind School Dist*	295	48
Lavender, Kristin/*Bushland Ind School Dist*	752	319
Laverett, Julie/*Blum Ind School Dist*	58	227
Lawing, Kimberly/*Aransas Co Ind School Dist*	73	19
Lawler, Corbett/*Killeen Ind School Dist*	67	27
Lawless, Erica/*Sunnyvale Ind School Dist*	11,58	113
Lawrence, Amy/*Denton Ind School Dist*	36	120
Lawrence, Christy/*Clear Creek Ind School Dist*	34	158
Lawrence, Cindy/*Richardson Ind School Dist*	58	112
Lawrence, Colton/*Midway Ind School Dist*	4	280
Lawrence, Cynthia/*Lumberton Ind School Dist*	8	178
Lawrence, Howard/*Rising Star Ind Sch Dist*	67	129
Lawrence, Leslie/*Cross Plains Ind Sch Dist*	11	62
Lawrence, Teresa/*Rising Star Ind Sch Dist*	2	129
Lawrence, Yvonne/*Liberty Ind School Dist*	69	266
Lawson, Amanda/*Leggett Ind School Dist*	36,69,88	316
Lawson, Denise/*Holliday Ind School Dist*	76	19
Lawson, Ike/*Happy Ind School Dist*	3,5	342
Lawson, Jill/*Glen Rose Ind School Dist*	4	340
Lawson, Jim/*Royse City Ind School Dist*	3	326
Lawson, Kim, Dr/*Katy Ind School Dist*	9	151
Lawson, Lisa/*Gainesville Ind School Dist*	7,85	91
Lawson, Lisa/*Whitewright Ind School Dist*	16,286	168
Lawson, Mignon/*Abilene Ind School Dist*	30	360
Lawson, Ronnie/*Chilton Ind School Dist*	73	144
Lawson, Sherri/*Spring Branch Ind School Dist*	5	200
Laxson, Felicia/*Menard Ind School Dist*	36,83,88,275	285
Layman, Janna/*Leonard Ind School Dist*	2,298	146
Layman, Lanny/*San Angelo Ind School Dist*	67	364
Layne, Brandon/*Ferris Ind School Dist*	6,35	140
Layne, Garrett/*Rogers Ind School Dist*	12,34,277	28
Layne, Scott/*Dallas Ind School Dist*	3,17	98
Layton, Done/*Malakoff Ind School Dist*	1	214
Lazar, Scott/*Klein Ind School Dist*	3	196
Lazarine, Barbara/*Lufkin Ind School Dist*	9,15,74	18
Lazcano, Elsa/*Ector Co Ind School Dist*	69	130
Lazrine, Diane/*Gause Ind School Dist*	2	287
Le Jeune, Jamie/*Beaumont Ind School Dist*	295	241
Leach, Derek/*Henrietta Ind School Dist*	73,76	74
Leach, Derek/*Midway Ind School Dist*	67	74
Leach, Michele/*Region 8 Ed Service Center*	2,3,19	69
Leach, Randy/*Granbury Ind School Dist*	3,91	230
Leaf, Buster/*Terrell Ind School Dist*	6	253
Leafloor, Garry/*Highland Park Ind School Dist*	3	319
Leal, Armando/*Quanah Ind School Dist*	3	177
Leal, Gilbert/*Brownsville Ind School Dist*	6	63
Leal, Jennifer/*Rockwall Ind School Dist*	81	325
Leal, Jose/*Los Fresnos Cons Ind Sch Dist*	3	66
Leal, Maria/*La Joya Ind School Dist*	298	219
Leal, Ricardo/*Mathis Ind School Dist*	27	331
Leal, Robin/*Maypearl Ind School Dist*	4	141
Leal, Romero/*Edinburg Cons Ind School Dist*	46	216
Lear, Pamela/*Dallas Ind School Dist*	751	98
Leath, Christi/*Goose Creek Cons Ind Sch Dist*	74,81,273	187
Leaverton, Cindy/*City View Ind School Dist*	10,31,83	391
Leavitt, Shannon/*Wildorado Ind Sch Dist*	67	308
LeBlanc, Lakeisha/*Channelview Ind School Dist*	71	183
LeBlanc, Matthew/*Bryan Ind School Dist*	71	54
LeBlanc, Nina, Dr/*West Orange-Cove Cons ISD*	8,11,57,58,90,91,273,288	309
LeBlanc, Susan/*Barbers Hill Ind School Dist*	4	72
LeBlanc, Tim/*Barbers Hill Ind School Dist*	295	72
Lebleu, Michelle/*Angleton Ind School Dist*	58,77	51
Leblew, Michele/*Little Cypress Mauriceville SD*	5	308
Ledbetter, Jack/*Groveton Ind School Dist*	73,83,295	374
Ledbetter, Lane, Dr/*Midlothian Ind School Dist*	1	141

NAME/District	JOB FUNCTIONS	PAGE
Ledbetter, Robert/*Dalhart Ind School Dist*	67	95
Ledford, Thomas/*Argyle Ind School Dist*	3	120
Ledwig, Linda/*Region 3 Ed Service Center*	15,34	383
Lee-Winslow, Debbie/*Mercedes Ind School Dist*	286	221
Lee, Andy/*Mt Enterprise Ind School Dist*	84	328
Lee, Andy/*Mt Enterprise Ind School Dist*	2,68,73,76	328
Lee, Beverley/*Somerset Ind School Dist*	69,294	42
Lee, Brant/*Central Ind School Dist*	67	17
Lee, Christopher/*Garrison Ind School Dist*	5	297
Lee, Cody/*Weatherford Ind School Dist*	76,286	313
Lee, Dan/*Lake Travis Ind School Dist*	5	370
Lee, Danzel/*Corsicana Ind School Dist*	36,79,294	299
Lee, David/*Malta Ind School Dist*	6,9,57,69,74,270	48
Lee, Deann/*Millsap Ind School Dist*	1,11	312
Lee, Debbie/*Garland Ind School Dist*	36	105
Lee, Dewaine/*Strawn Ind School Dist*	6	311
Lee, Donny, Dr/*Buna Ind School Dist*	1	240
Lee, Donny, Dr/*Oakwood Ind School Dist*	288	264
Lee, Emily/*De Kalb Ind School Dist*	11,69	48
Lee, Gerald/*Cleveland Ind School Dist*	3	265
Lee, Ginger/*Timpson Ind School Dist*	4	335
Lee, Heather/*George West Ind School Dist*	31	268
Lee, Honey/*White Settlement Ind Sch Dist*	88	357
Lee, Ingrid/*Region 4 Ed Service Center*	294	208
Lee, Jack/*Blooming Grove Ind School Dist*	1	299
Lee, Jeffrey/*Seguin Ind School Dist*	295	173
Lee, Jessica/*Blooming Grove Ind School Dist*	8,285,288,298	299
Lee, Jose/*Laneville Ind School Dist*	6	327
Lee, Judy/*Dickinson Ind School Dist*	4	159
Lee, Kim/*Texarkana Ind School Dist*	40,49	50
Lee, Kristi, Dr/*Bastrop Ind School Dist*	71,298	23
Lee, Laura/*Eanes Ind School Dist*	68	370
Lee, Margaret/*Texas City Ind School Dist*	2,15	161
Lee, Martha/*Cushing Ind School Dist*	2	297
Lee, Michelle/*Hardin Ind School Dist*	2,19	265
Lee, Michelle/*Mt Enterprise Ind School Dist*	16,270	328
Lee, Robin/*Leggett Ind School Dist*	16	316
Lee, Russell/*Uvalde Cons Ind School Dist*	5	378
Leech, Stan/*Boerne Ind School Dist*	6,35	253
Leeper, Lynly/*Ysleta Ind School Dist*	2,17,19	137
Leer, Rod/*Magnolia Ind School Dist*	27,31,39	292
Lefevers, Toby/*Ector Co Ind School Dist*	73	130
Leflet, Yarda/*Hays Cons Ind School Dist*	79	211
Leftwich, Pam/*Lubbock Ind School Dist*	69,70,294	269
Leger, Rita/*Port Arthur Ind School Dist*	43,285	243
Legg, Carroll/*Sudan Ind School Dist*	5	261
Legg, Kelly/*Dumas Ind School Dist*	8,11,88,296	295
Legore, Kristen/*Seguin Ind School Dist*	79,90	173
LeGrande, Kim/*Mabank Ind School Dist*	4	252
Lehman, Sandra/*Brookesmith Ind School Dist*	8,69	58
Lehne, Brian/*Fredericksburg Ind School Dist*	67	163
Lehnhoff, Scott/*Schertz-Cibolo-Univ City ISD*	6,35	173
Lehr, Ron/*Marshall Ind School Dist*	73,84,295	209
Leib, Mary/*Gatesville Ind School Dist*	67	93
Leirer, Lisa/*Lovejoy Ind School Dist*	274	80
Leivas, Larry/*Dimmitt Ind School Dist*	2,3	71
LeJeune, Adam/*Marlin Ind School Dist*	16,288	144
Leloux, Cathy/*Leggett Ind School Dist*	2,4,11	316
Lemere, Jody/*Pleasanton Ind School Dist*	73,95,297	21
Lemieux, Vick/*Wolfe City Ind School Dist*	295	237
Lemley, J Brett, Dr/*Schertz-Cibolo-Univ City ISD*	10	173
LeMoine, Emily/*Tenaha Ind School Dist*	2,294	335
Lemon, Lisa/*Chapel Hill Ind School Dist*	2	337
Lemon, Molly/*Northside Ind School Dist*	8,11,73	393
Lemond, Stormy/*Forney Ind School Dist*	28	251
Lemonier, Gabrielle, Dr/*DeSoto Ind School Dist*	15	104
Lemons, Jennifer/*Bryan Ind School Dist*	76,79	54

1 Superintendent	16 Instructional Media Svcs	30 Adult Education	44 Science Sec	58 Special Education K-12	72 Summer School	88 Alternative/At Risk	277 Remedial Math K-12
2 Bus/Finance/Purchasing	17 Chief Operations Officer	31 Career/Sch-to-Work K-12	45 Math K-12	59 Special Education Elem	73 Instructional Tech	89 Multi-Cultural Curriculum	280 Literacy Coach
3 Buildings And Grounds	18 Chief Academic Officer	32 Career/Sch-to-Work Elem	46 Math Elem	60 Special Education Sec	74 Inservice Training	90 Social Work	285 STEM
4 Food Service	19 Chief Financial Officer	33 Career/Sch-to-Work Sec	47 Math Sec	61 Foreign/World Lang K-12	75 Marketing/Distributive	91 Safety/Security	286 Digital Learning
5 Transportation	20 Art K-12	34 Early Childhood Ed	48 English/Lang Arts K-12	62 Foreign/World Lang Elem	76 Info Systems	92 Magnet School	288 Common Core Standards
6 Athletic	21 Art Elem	35 Health/Phys Education	49 English/Lang Arts Elem	63 Foreign/World Lang Sec	77 Psychological Assess	93 Parental Involvement	294 Accountability
7 Health Services	22 Art Sec	36 Guidance Services K-12	50 English/Lang Arts Sec	64 Religious Education K-12	78 Affirmative Action	95 Tech Prep Program	295 Network System
8 Curric/Instruct K-12	23 Music K-12	37 Guidance Services Elem	51 Reading K-12	65 Religious Education Elem	79 Student Personnel	97 Chief Infomation Officer	296 Title II Programs
9 Curric/Instruct Elem	24 Music Elem	38 Guidance Services Sec	52 Reading Elem	66 Religious Education Sec	80 Driver Ed/Safety	98 Chief Technology Officer	297 Webmaster
10 Curric/Instruct Sec	25 Music Sec	39 Social Studies K-12	53 Reading Sec	67 School Board President	81 Gifted/Talented	270 Character Education	298 Grant Writer/Ptnrships
11 Federal Program	26 Business Education	40 Social Studies Elem	54 Remedial Reading K-12	68 Teacher Personnel	82 Video Services	271 Migrant Education	750 Chief Innovation Officer
12 Title I	27 Career & Tech Ed	41 Social Studies Sec	55 Remedial Reading Elem	69 Academic Assessment	83 Substance Abuse Prev	273 Teacher Mentor	751 Chief of Staff
13 Title V	28 Technology Education	42 Science K-12	56 Remedial Reading Sec	70 Research/Development	84 Erate	274 Before/After Sch	752 Social Emotional Learning
15 Asst Superintendent	29 Family/Consumer Science	43 Science Elem	57 Bilingual/ELL	71 Public Information	85 AIDS Education	275 Response To Intervention	

TX-T52

Texas School Directory

DISTRICT PERSONNEL INDEX

NAME/District	JOB FUNCTIONS	PAGE
Lemons, Vance/Lockney Independent Sch Dist	27	149
Lenamon, James/McGregor Ind School Dist	1	280
Lenamon, Michelle/McGregor Ind School Dist	16	280
Lenart, Brenda/Abbott Ind School Dist	2	226
Lennon, Jullia/Avery Ind School Dist	7	322
Lentz-Edwards, Lee/Kermit Ind School Dist	67	401
Lentz, Carrie/Waller Ind School Dist	49	384
Lenz, Wade/Hartley Ind School Dist	67	209
Leon, Arcelia/Medina Valley Ind School Dist	8,69	284
Leonard, Charla/Aspermont Ind School Dist	2	342
Leonard, Karen/Childress Ind School Dist	2	74
Leonard, Randy/Klondike Ind School Dist	73,295	117
Leonard, Tom, Dr/Eanes Ind School Dist	1	370
Leopold, Kathy/Dripping Springs Ind Sch Dist	16,73,76,297	210
Leopold, Rob/Windthorst Ind School Dist	73,295	20
Leopold, Scott/Columbus Ind School Dist	2	86
Leos, Jennifer/Cleveland Ind School Dist	4	265
Leplante, Nick/Leveretts Chapel Ind Sch Dist	16,73	328
Leplante, Stephanie/Leveretts Chapel Ind Sch Dist	57	328
Lerma, Carlos/Mission Cons Ind School Dist	5	222
Lerma, Laurie/Alice Ind School Dist	81	245
Lerma, Parisa/Mineral Wells Ind School Dist	58,275	310
Lesak, Manda/Ganado Ind School Dist	31,69,271	239
Lesak, Manda/Ganado Ind School Dist	31,69,271	239
Leschber, Deby/Thorndale Ind School Dist	73,286,295	288
Leshber, Allen/Thorndale Ind School Dist	3	288
Lester, Don/DeSoto Ind School Dist	3	104
Lester, Jay/Abilene Ind School Dist	20,23	360
Lester, Karla, Dr/Ft Worth Ind School Dist	73	349
Lesueur, Larkin/Humble Ind School Dist	27,31	195
Leuba, Ginny/Linden Kildare Cons Ind SD	58	70
Leuschen, Linda/Hitchcock Ind School Dist	68	161
Levandoski, Barbara/Cypress-Fairbanks Ind Sch Dist	9,34	183
Levario, Gloria/Dallas Co Schools	67	96
Levels, Levatta/DeSoto Ind School Dist	15,79	104
Levesque, Marc/Chapel Hill Ind School Dist	1	363
Levien, Luke/Junction Ind School Dist	67	256
Levin, Jason/Victoria Ind School Dist	20,23	382
Levingston, Ceretha/Liberty-Eylau Ind School Dist	11,15,80,298	48
Levrier, Henry/Point Isabel Ind Sch Dist	2,3,11,27,30,83,296	66
Lewandowski, Mark/Tomball Ind School Dist	67	203
Lewis, Bill/Seguin Ind School Dist	16,73,76	173
Lewis, Carol/Hallsburg Ind School Dist	4	279
Lewis, Cindy/Community Ind School Dist	4	78
Lewis, Claude/Bonham Ind School Dist	3	145
Lewis, Dave/Rochelle Ind School Dist	1,11	278
Lewis, David/Arlington Ind School Dist	4	343
Lewis, Dean/Friendswood Ind Sch Dist	5	160
Lewis, Debbie/Fredericksburg Ind School Dist	29	163
Lewis, Debbie/Round Rock Ind School Dist	69,294	398
Lewis, Janie/Callisburg Ind School Dist	2,12	90
Lewis, Jason/Richland Springs Ind Sch Dist	67	332
Lewis, Kelley/Lubbock Ind School Dist	2	269
Lewis, Lee/Moran Ind School Dist	6	334
Lewis, Lezley, Dr/Ft Worth Ind School Dist	74	349
Lewis, Mandi/Sherman Ind School Dist	2	167
Lewis, Maureen, Dr/Longview Ind School Dist	58	169
Lewis, Micha/Grand Saline Ind School Dist	1	380
Lewis, Pat/Marlin Ind School Dist	2,19	144
Lewis, Patricia/Grand Prairie Ind School Dist	11,15	107
Lewis, Randy/Gorman Ind School Dist	3,5	129
Lewis, Rich/Forestburg Ind School Dist	73,286	290
Lewis, Rusty/Splendora Ind School Dist	3	294
Lewis, Sharen/Blooming Grove Ind School Dist	4	299
Lewis, Terry/Savoy Ind School Dist	67	146
Leza, Emma/United Ind School Dist	294	387
Libby, Leanne/Corpus Christi Ind Sch Dist	71	303
Licata, Alexis/Houston Ind School Dist	2,78	188
Licon, Kimberly/Wink Loving Ind School Dist	51,271	402
Licon, Sandra/San Elizario Ind School Dist	67	135
Lide, Mike/Mt Pleasant Ind School Dist	15	363
Lide, Tammi/Wills Point Ind School Dist	7	381
Lieb, James/Pringle-Morse Cons ISD	67	177
Liebman, Amanda/Academy Ind School Dist	69	26
Lieck, Sandra/Carrollton-Farmers Branch ISD	7	96
Liefer, Pene/Bastrop Ind School Dist	68	23
Liepman, Virginia/San Augustine Ind School Dist	1	329
Lieser, Shelli/Chico Ind School Dist	4	403
Liewehr, Jason/Carrollton-Farmers Branch ISD	68	96
Liggett, Keith/Channelview Ind School Dist	67	183
Liggins, Demetrus, Dr/Greenville Ind School Dist	1	236
Light, Joey/Wylie Ind School Dist	1	361
Lightfoot, Delana/Ingleside Ind School Dist	73,286	331
Lightfoot, Jimmy/Gladewater Ind School Dist	15,79	169
Lile, Brent/Booker Ind School Dist	6	267
Lilley, Vickie/Daingerfield-Lone Star Ind SD	34,58,275	296
Lilley, Vickie/Pewitt Cons Ind School Dist	58	296
Lilljedahl, Stacey/Jonesboro Ind School Dist	2	93
Lilly, Earnest/Crandall Ind School Dist	4	251
Limbaugh, Duane/Brady Ind School Dist	1,83	277
Limmer, Josh/Comfort Ind School Dist	3,5,91	254
Limon, Hector/Plains Ind School Dist	73,295	405
Lin, Dawn/Wylie Ind School Dist	4	84
Lincoln, Charles/Crowley Ind School Dist	6	347
Lindeman, Robert/Region 6 Ed Service Center	2,19	384
Lindeman, Todd/Aldine ISD-High Sch Team	15	180
Lindholm, Jon/Marion Ind School Dist	68	172
Lindholm, Kelly/Marion Ind School Dist	1,83	172
Lindley, Alene/Katy Ind School Dist	81	151
Lindsey, Gary/Dallas Co Schools	1	95
Lindsey, Jeanette/Forsan Ind School Dist	11,298	234
Lindsey, Jennifer/Memphis Ind School Dist	295	175
Lindsey, Kenneth/Anna Ind School Dist	3	77
Lindsey, Lara/McKinney Ind School Dist	16,73	80
Lindsey, Lynn/Hemphill Ind School Dist	67	329
Lindsey, Melinda/Kennard Ind Sch Dist	1,11,73	233
Lindsey, Preston/Troup Ind School Dist	5	337
Line, Debbie/Post Ind School Dist	4	162
Linebarger, Les/Nacogdoches Ind School Dist	71	298
Ling, Terry/Warren Ind School Dist	2	375
Link, Stephanie/Elkhart Ind School Dist	7	15
Linley, Tim/Dallas Ind School Dist	20,23	98
Linnstaedter, Jeff/Lorena Ind School Dist	2,19	280
Linscomb, Karen/Cuero Ind School Dist	58,77	117
Linscomb, Steve/Judson Ind School Dist	71	33
Linthicum, Kyle/Spring Hill Ind School Dist	295	170
Linton, Pamela, Dr/Frisco Ind School Dist	68,78	78
Lintzen, Todd/Bridge City Ind School Dist	1	308
Lionberger, Jay/Peaster Ind School Dist	3	313
Lipe, Mike/Schertz-Cibolo-Univ City ISD	20,23	173
Lippa, Adriana/Brownsville Ind School Dist	58	63
Lippard, Stephanie/Sherman Ind School Dist	54,57,74,77,271,273,277	167
Lipscomb, Claudell/Bryan Ind School Dist	5	54
Liptack, Charlotte/Alvin Ind School Dist	39,48	50
Lira, Adam/Splendora Ind School Dist	27,31	294
Lisby, Ronnie/Venus Ind School Dist	3	249
Lischka, Grant/Bellville Ind School Dist	67	22
Lister, Charles/Rio Vista Ind School Dist	73,295	248
Little, Amy/Westwood Ind School Dist	54	16
Little, Cristi/Olney Ind School Dist	58	406
Little, Deborah/Abbott Ind School Dist	298	226
Little, Laura/Castleberry Ind School Dist	294	347
Little, Robert/Taylor Ind School Dist	6	399
Little, Shellie/Gorman Ind School Dist	7	129
Little, Tim, Dr/Perryton Ind School Dist	1	307
Little, Valerie/Prosper Ind School Dist	6	84
Little, Yvonne/Pleasanton Ind School Dist	3,91,295	21
Littlefield, Michael/Harlandale Ind School Dist	73	32
Littlefields, Brad/Millsap Ind School Dist	5	312
Littlejohn, Jim/Clint Ind School Dist	10,15	132
Littrell, Kacie/Leonard Ind School Dist	31,36,58,69,83,88	146
Litvik, Kenny/Nederland Ind School Dist	3,5	242
Litz, Janay/Region 9 Ed Service Center	2	393
Livas, Janie/San Perlita Ind School Dist	11,298	394
Livas, John/Skidmore Tynan Ind SD	6	25
Lively, Debra/Teague Ind School Dist	4	156
Lively, Kenneth/Westwood Ind School Dist	27	16
Lively, Virginia/Alvin Ind School Dist	39	50
Livermore, Ron, Dr/Ysleta Ind School Dist	74	137
Livingston, Mandi/La Vega Ind School Dist	5	279
Llanez, Mesinda/Alpine Ind School Dist	58	56
Lloyd, Donnie/Andrews Ind School Dist	5	16

School Year 2019-2020   800-333-8802

DISTRICT PERSONNEL INDEX

Market Data Retrieval

NAME/District	JOB FUNCTIONS	PAGE
Lloyd, Karen/Mesquite Ind School Dist	72,275	110
Lloyd, Michael/Midland Ind School Dist	73	285
Loan, Tim/Amarillo Ind School Dist	3	317
Lochet, Camille/Austin Ind School Dist	297	366
Lock, Richard/Southside Ind School Dist	6	43
Lock, Tonya/Lefors Ind School Dist	271	165
Locker, Amy/Magnolia Ind School Dist	8,69	292
Lockett, Gwendolyn/Aldine Ind School Dist	40	179
Lockett, Marcella/London Ind School Dist	57	305
Lockhart, Luanne/Mumford Ind School Dist	2	56
Locklin, Jamie/Alamo Heights Ind School Dist	73,295	30
Loeffler, Evelyn/Sierra Blanca Ind School Dist	1,11,73,83	234
Loer, Sarah/Nixon-Smiley Cons Ind Sch Dist	73	164
Loera, Omega/Ector Co Ind School Dist	81	130
Loftin, Dawn/Canton Ind School Dist	5	380
Loftis, Pete/Borger Ind School Dist	3	237
Loftis, Robert/Laneville Ind School Dist	67	327
Lofton, Jeff/Idalou Ind School Dist	6	269
Lofton, Kathy/West Hardin Co Cons Sch Dist	4	178
Lofton, Suzy, Dr/Lago Vista Ind School Dist	8,11,15,296	370
Logan, Ashley/Duncanville Ind School Dist	41	104
Logan, Lisa/Bluff Dale Ind Sch Dist	73,286	143
Logan, Marilyn/Mt Pleasant Ind School Dist	58	363
Logan, Stephen/Burleson Ind School Dist	76,295	246
Lohse, Brenda/Arlington Ind School Dist	298	343
Loman, Theresa/Utopia Ind School Dist	16	378
London, Greg/Bryson Ind School Dist	1,11	238
Londow, Kathy/Port Arthur Ind School Dist	68,79	243
Londrie, Valarie/Los Fresnos Cons Ind Sch Dist	9,16,27,31,57,69,277,298	66
Long Botham, Pamela, Dr/Cuero Ind School Dist	8,11,57,88,285,288,298	117
Long, Asheley/Wellington Ind School Dist	7	86
Long, Bill/Harper Ind School Dist	73,295	163
Long, Clayton/Lipan Ind School Dist	3	230
Long, Cynthia/Campbell Ind School Dist	4	235
Long, Danny/Conroe Ind School Dist	6	291
Long, Gail/Hurst-Euless-Bedford ISD	69	353
Long, Mitchell/East Chambers Ind School Dist	16,73,288	72
Long, Patricia/Pleasant Grove Ind School Dist	26	49
Long, Shelli/Sterling City Ind School Dist	68	342
Long, Sherry/Crosby Ind School Dist	9,37	183
Longley, Cathy/Santo Ind School Dist	12	310
Longoria, David/Raymondville Ind Sch Dist	2,19	394
Longoria, Margie/Taft Ind School Dist	4	332
Longorio, Faith/Goose Creek Cons Ind Sch Dist	39	187
Lons, Paula/Plano Ind School Dist	58	82
Lonsford, Jennifer/Cedar Hill Ind School Dist	58	97
Lookabaugh, Greg/Harris Co Dept of Ed	3	179
Lookingbill, Haylie/Vega Ind School Dist	2	307
Loomis, Chrystal/Roby Cons Ind School Dist	83,85,88,270,273	148
Loomis, Doug/Amarillo Ind School Dist	1	317
Loomis, Robert/Graham Ind School Dist	15,38,68,69,296	406
Looney, Susan/Highland Park Ind School Dist	73	319
Loots, Gage/Leander Ind School Dist	2	396
Loper, Tim/Tyler Ind School Dist	3	337
Lopez, Andy/Covington ISD School Dist	67	227
Lopez, Andy/Sabinal Ind School Dist	3,5	378
Lopez, Brynn/Fayetteville Ind School Dist	8,36,270,273	147
Lopez, Cesar/Brownsville Ind School Dist	3	63
Lopez, Chris/S & S Cons Ind School Dist	67	167
Lopez, Connie/Region 1 Ed Service Center	2,15,19	226
Lopez, Daniel/Diboll Ind School Dist	15	17
Lopez, David/Crystal City Ind School Dist	6	407
Lopez, David/Plainview Ind School Dist	3	175
Lopez, Debbie/Skidmore Tynan Ind SD	16	25
Lopez, Diane/Midland Ind School Dist	9	285
Lopez, Fernando/Pharr-San Juan-Alamo Ind SD	3	223
Lopez, Frank/Andrews Ind School Dist	297	16
Lopez, Frank/Ricardo Ind School Dist	6	257
Lopez, Genaro/Coppell Ind School Dist	3,5,91	98
Lopez, George/Weslaco Ind School Dist	271	225
Lopez, Gerry/Santa Gertrudis Ind Sch Dist	73	258
Lopez, Jesse/Region 13 Ed Service Center	8,15	373
Lopez, Joe/Taft Ind School Dist	1	332
Lopez, Joel/Zapata Co Ind School Dist	6	406
Lopez, Johnnie/Kenedy Ind School Dist	5	251
Lopez, Jose/El Paso Ind School Dist	15,751	132
Lopez, Juan/Point Isabel Ind Sch Dist	58	66
Lopez, Leo/Texas Dept of Education	2,19	1
Lopez, Melissa/Region 1 Ed Service Center	27	226
Lopez, Monica/Iraan-Sheffield Ind Sch Dist	7,83,85	316
Lopez, Nick/Westbrook Ind School Dist	3,5	289
Lopez, Nora/Agua Dulce Ind School Dist	1	302
Lopez, Oscar/Robstown Ind School Dist	67	305
Lopez, Paula/Poteet Ind School Dist	5	21
Lopez, Pete/Lueders-Avoca Ind School Dist	67	250
Lopez, Ricardo, Dr/Garland Ind School Dist	1	105
Lopez, Rosie/Snyder Ind School Dist	57	333
Lopez, Ruben/Taft Ind School Dist	67	332
Lopez, Sandra/Brownsville Ind School Dist	15	63
Lopez, Sebastian/Barbers Hill Ind School Dist	295	72
Lopez, Shannna/Rice Ind School Dist	67	300
Lopez, Sherry/Buckholts Ind School Dist	2,68	287
Lopez, Sonja/Montgomery Ind School Dist	7,15,68,71,273	293
Lopez, Sylvia, Dr/Dallas Ind School Dist	36	98
Lopez, Tricia/Idea Public Schools	58	217
Lopez, Vangie/Taft Ind School Dist	271	332
Loredo, Augustine/Goose Creek Cons Ind Sch Dist	67	187
Lorenz, Emily/Calallen Ind School Dist	15,68,83	302
Losoya, Adam/Buckholts Ind School Dist	67	287
Lotspeich, Catrina/Temple Ind School Dist	20,29	29
Lott, Rebecca/Manor Ind School Dist	83	371
Lott, Richard/Nixon-Smiley Cons Ind Sch Dist	67	164
Lotten, Cindy/Keller Ind School Dist	67	354
Loud, Wonderful/Lubbock Ind School Dist	68	269
Louder, Jermey/Stanton Ind School Dist	67	274
Lough, Betty/Whitehouse Ind School Dist	8,11,57,74,85,273,274,296	338
Loughmiller, Dale/Paris Ind School Dist	73	260
Loupe, Todd/Little Cypress Mauriceville SD	10,30,36,69,85,88	308
Lovaasen, Martha/Elysian Fields Ind School Dist	9	208
Lovato, Krystal/Int'l Leadership of Texas Dist	12	108
Love, Catina/Longview Ind School Dist	69	169
Love, Elisa/Paducah Ind School Dist	4	93
Love, Jim/Evadale Ind School Dist	67	240
Love, Kayleen/Copperas Cove Ind School Dist	68	92
Love, Stephanie/Montague Ind School Dist	4	290
Love, Tamie/Sonora Ind School Dist	85	342
Love, Troy/Hawkins Ind School Dist	5	404
Loveless, Tammy/Royse City Ind School Dist	5	326
Lovell, Alan/Crandall Ind School Dist	3	251
Lovell, Amy/Claude Ind School Dist	67	20
Lovell, Kevin/Lago Vista Ind School Dist	3	370
Lovely, Henryette/Region 7 Ed Service Center	78	171
Loven, Sharyn/Hawkins Ind School Dist	2	404
Lovesmith, Deanna, Dr/Belton Ind School Dist	8,15,88,270,275,286,296,298	26
Lovett, Danny, Dr/Region 5 Ed Service Center	1	244
Lovette, Trent, Dr/La Vernia Ind School Dist	1	401
Lovier, Johnathan/Spring Hill Ind School Dist	6	170
Lovrn, Matt/Stratford Ind School Dist	6	336
Low, Paula/Alto Ind School Dist	271	72
Lowe, Jana/Leggett Ind School Dist	1,11,73	316
Lowe, Matt/Hudson Ind School Dist	67	17
Lowe, Melanie/Newcastle Ind School Dist	54,57	406
Lowe, Pamela/Alief Ind School Dist	286	181

---

1 Superintendent	16 Instructional Media Svcs	30 Adult Education	44 Science Sec	58 Special Education K-12	72 Summer School	88 Alternative/At Risk	277 Remedial Math K-12
2 Bus/Finance/Purchasing	17 Chief Operations Officer	31 Career/Sch-to-Work K-12	45 Math K-12	59 Special Education Elem	73 Instructional Tech	89 Multi-Cultural Curriculum	280 Literacy Coach
3 Buildings And Grounds	18 Chief Academic Officer	32 Career/Sch-to-Work Elem	46 Math Elem	60 Special Education Sec	74 Inservice Training	90 Social Work	285 STEM
4 Food Service	19 Chief Financial Officer	33 Career/Sch-to-Work Sec	47 Math Sec	61 Foreign/World Lang K-12	75 Marketing/Distributive	91 Safety/Security	286 Digital Learning
5 Transportation	20 Art K-12	34 Early Childhood Ed	48 English/Lang Arts K-12	62 Foreign/World Lang Elem	76 Info Systems	92 Magnet School	288 Common Core Standards
6 Athletic	21 Art Elem	35 Health/Phys Education	49 English/Lang Arts Elem	63 Foreign/World Lang Sec	77 Psychological Assess	93 Parental Involvement	294 Accountability
7 Health Services	22 Art Sec	36 Guidance Services K-12	50 English/Lang Arts Sec	64 Religious Education K-12	78 Affirmative Action	95 Tech Prep Program	295 Network System
8 Curric/Instruct K-12	23 Music K-12	37 Guidance Services Elem	51 Reading K-12	65 Religious Education Elem	79 Student Personnel	96 Chief Information Officer	296 Title II Programs
9 Curric/Instruct Elem	24 Music Elem	38 Guidance Services Sec	52 Reading Elem	66 Religious Education Sec	80 Driver Ed/Safety	98 Chief Technology Officer	297 Webmaster
10 Curric/Instruct Sec	25 Music Sec	39 Social Studies K-12	53 Reading Sec	67 School Board President	81 Gifted/Talented	270 Character Education	298 Grant Writer/Ptnrships
11 Federal Program	26 Business Education	40 Social Studies Elem	54 Remedial Reading K-12	68 Teacher Personnel	82 Video Services	271 Migrant Education	750 Chief Innovation Officer
12 Title I	27 Career & Tech Ed	41 Social Studies Sec	55 Remedial Reading Elem	69 Academic Assessment	83 Substance Abuse Prev	273 Teacher Mentor	751 Chief of Staff
13 Title V	28 Technology Education	42 Science K-12	56 Remedial Reading Sec	70 Research/Development	84 Erate	274 Before/After Sch	752 Social Emotional Learning
15 Asst Superintendent	29 Family/Consumer Science	43 Science Elem	57 Bilingual/ELL	71 Public Information	85 AIDS Education	275 Response To Intervention	

Texas School Directory

DISTRICT PERSONNEL INDEX

NAME/District	JOB FUNCTIONS	PAGE
Lowe, Tysha/Cedar Hill Ind School Dist	27,31	97
Lowery, Curtis/Godley Ind School Dist	6	247
Lowery, Donna/Arp Ind School Dist	38	336
Lowery, Jason/Crowley Ind School Dist	5	347
Lowery, Stacey/Evant Ind School Dist	11,57,81,88,271,275,280,296	92
Lowman, Misty/Sunray Ind School Dist	4	296
Lowry, Bret/Franklin Ind School Dist	1	324
Lowry, Clint/Blackwell Cons Ind Sch Dist	6	301
Lowry, Robert, Dr/Coolidge Ind School Dist	1	266
Lowry, Wade/Zephyr Ind School Dist	73	59
Loyless, Leann/Sanger Ind School Dist	8,270	126
Loyola, Andrea/Carlisle Ind School Dist	16	327
Lozano, Angelica/Edgewood Ind School Dist	79	31
Lozano, Arminda/Edinburg Cons Ind School Dist	27,31	216
Lozano, Arturo/Three Rivers Ind School Dist	6,85	268
Lozano, Augustina/Bastrop Ind School Dist	57	23
Lozano, Lisa/Alice Ind School Dist	7	245
Lozano, Roberto/North East Ind School Dist	285	34
Lozano, Steve/Dilley Ind School Dist	11	157
Lucas, Bonnie/Grady Ind School Dist	2,11,296	274
Lucas, Donna/Whitewright Ind School Dist	73,295	168
Lucas, Donnita/Alto Ind School Dist	4	72
Lucas, Lisa/Alamo Heights Ind School Dist	83	30
Lucas, Lyndsay/Levelland Ind School Dist	10	229
Lucas, Matt/Deer Park Ind School Dist	71	186
Lucas, Meredith/Graham Ind School Dist	67	406
Lucas, Russell/Hamlin Ind School Dist	6	249
Lucas, Scott/Whiteface Con Ind School Dist	9,93,274	75
Luce, Tammy/Latexo Ind School Dist	4,84	233
Lucio, David/Tidehaven Ind School Dist	6	276
Luck, Russell/Mt Pleasant Ind School Dist	3	363
Luckie, Lindsay/Ropes Ind School Dist	69,83	229
Luddeke, Matthew/Iraan-Sheffield Ind Sch Dist	6	316
Ludwig, Jill/Lamar Cons Ind School Dist	2,19	153
Ludwig, Tracey/Livingston Ind School Dist	37	317
Luedke, John/Mart Ind School Dist	16,73,82,297	280
Luera, Joseph/O'Donnell Ind School Dist	3,5	273
Luft, Garrett/Lubbock Ind School Dist	81,92,286	270
Lugo, Corina/San Elizario Ind School Dist	93	135
Lugo, Laura/San Marcos Cons Ind Sch Dist	11,69,79,288	211
Lugo, Nora/Harlandale Ind School Dist	45	32
Luhan, Lupe/Socorro Ind School Dist	79	135
Luis, Shannon/Elgin Ind School Dist	8,15,54,61,280	24
Luksovsky, Angela/Weimar Ind School Dist	2	87
Luman, Tina/Pine Tree Ind School Dist	16,82	170
Lumar, Shannon/Killeen Ind School Dist	36	27
Lumpkins, William/Austwell Tivoli Ind SD	36	323
Luna-Taylor, Teresa/Denton Ind School Dist	57,271	120
Luna, Ashley/Crosbyton Cons Ind Sch Dist	7,83	94
Luna, David/Goliad Ind School Dist	73,295	163
Luna, Dianne/Meridian Ind School Dist	58	47
Luna, George/Bishop Cons Ind School Dist	6	302
Luna, Iris/McAllen Ind School Dist	2	220
Luna, Janie/Odem-Edroy Ind School Dist	4	331
Luna, Jeffrey/Poth Ind School Dist	6	401
Luna, Mario/Forney Ind School Dist	20,23	251
Luna, Monica/Valley View Ind School Dist	8,15	225
Luna, Patrick/Randolph Field Ind School Dist	67	39
Luna, Rudy/Lubbock-Cooper Ind Sch Dist	4	271
Lundmark, Jonathan/Brownsboro Ind School Dist	2	213
Lundy, Robert/Hallettsville Ind Sch Dist	67	262
Lunsford, Dan/Frost Ind School Dist	10,74	299
Lunsford, Linda/Martinsville Ind School Dist	68	298
Lunsford, Lindsay/Martinsville Ind School Dist	2	298
Lusk, Kelly/Tom Bean Ind School Dist	1	168
Lusk, Melondy/Clarendon Cons Ind Sch Dist	58	127
Luster, Sandy/Wildorado Ind Sch Dist	2,271	308
Luther, Misty/Texline Ind School Dist	16,57,82	95
Luther, Misty/Texline Ind School Dist	16,82	95
Luton, Carol/Prairie Valley Ind School Dist	69	290
Luttman, Alicia/Aransas Co Ind School Dist	58,270	19
Lux, Brad/Schulenburg Ind School Dist	27	147
Lux, Robyn/Robinson Ind School Dist	4	281
Lykins, Eric/Bangs Ind School Dist	67	58
Lyles, Carl/Medina Valley Ind School Dist	73,295,297	284
Lynch, Billy/Crawford Ind School Dist	2,286	279

NAME/District	JOB FUNCTIONS	PAGE
Lynch, Kevin/Splendora Ind School Dist	2,3,11,15	294
Lynch, Kyle/Canadian Ind School Dist	1,11	213
Lynch, Kyle/Seminole Ind School Dist	1	158
Lynch, Reagan/Gainesville Ind School Dist	11	91
Lynn, Donna/Floresville Ind School Dist	7,85	400
Lynn, Kathryn/Strawn Ind School Dist	2	311
Lynn, Kris/Channelview Ind School Dist	2,15	183
Lynn, Lesa/Gladewater Ind School Dist	2	169
Lynn, Sandra/Stockdale Ind School Dist	10	401
Lyon, Glen/Morton Ind School Dist	67	75
Lyon, Jennifer/Lake Travis Ind School Dist	7	370
Lyon, Lynn/Wylie Ind School Dist	2	84
Lyon, Mark/Texas City Ind School Dist	20,23	161
Lyon, Morris/Hawkins Ind School Dist	1,84	404
Lyons, Andri, Dr/Austin Ind School Dist	79	366
Lyons, Heidi/Denison Ind School Dist	7	166
Lyons, Michael/Channelview Ind School Dist	3	183
Lyons, Suzanne/Ft Bend Ind School Dist	16	149
Lyssy, Braden/Pawnee Ind School Dist	2,3	25
Lyssy, Wayne/Falls City Ind School Dist	67	250
Lytle, Belinda/Haskell Cons Ind School Dist	69,288	210
Lytle, Bobbi/Anson Ind School Dist	11,57,271,296	249

M

NAME/District	JOB FUNCTIONS	PAGE
Maass, David/Oglesby Ind School Dist	1	93
Maass, David/Oglesby Ind School Dist	8,11,16,69,73,286	93
Mabe, Tiffany/Rivercrest Ind School Dist	2,8,11,288,294,296,298	322
Mabry, Lori/Denton Ind School Dist	81	120
Mabry, Ray/Whitney Ind School Dist	67	228
Mac, Tobin/Palestine Ind School Dist	7,83,85	15
Mach, Michael/La Grange Ind School Dist	73	147
Mach, Paul/Waco Ind School Dist	73	281
Machac, Lynne/Schulenburg Ind School Dist	2	147
Machel, Sheri/Kemp Ind School Dist	16	252
Macias, Annette/Ector Co Ind School Dist	69,294	130
Macias, Jessica/Socorro Ind School Dist	8	135
Macias, Linda, Dr/Cypress-Fairbanks Ind Sch Dist	15,294,296	184
Macias, Marco/Canutillo Ind School Dist	4	131
Macias, Marivel/Socorro Ind School Dist	15,68,78	135
Macias, Nancy/Archdiocese Galveston-Houston	4	203
Mack, Lori/Lumberton Ind School Dist	2	178
Mackeben, Mike/Clint Ind School Dist	6	132
Mackeben, Mike/Clint Ind School Dist	6	132
Mackeben, Tammi/Socorro Ind School Dist	36	135
Mackey, Kara/Covington ISD School Dist	69,76	227
Mackey, Theodore/Anna Ind School Dist	285	77
MacLeod, Carol/Brookeland Ind School Dist	58	240
Madden, Amanda/Sabine Ind School Dist	7	170
Maddox, Andrew/Taylor Ind School Dist	88	399
Maddox, Elizabeth/Bartlett Ind School Dist	4	26
Maddox, Kelli/Memphis Ind School Dist	7	175
Maddox, Mike/Lindale Ind School Dist	6,35,83	337
Maddux, Mary/Clifton Ind School Dist	68	46
Madison, Michelle/Peaster Ind School Dist	9,57,88	313
Madkins, Sheilda/School of Excellence In Ed	1	42
Madrid, Gil/Ft Stockton Ind School Dist	15	315
Madrid, Marla/Brackett Ind School Dist	2,11	257
Madrid, Rebecca/Socorro Ind School Dist	7	135
Madrigal, Fidencio/La Gloria Ind School Dist	6	245
Madrigal, Hector/San Benito Cons Ind Sch Dist	8,15	67
Madrigal, Racao/Rio Hondo Ind School Dist	4	66
Maeker, Christy/Katy Ind School Dist	36,77	151
Maeker, Monica/New Home Ind School Dist	2	273
Magallon, Perla/San Elizario Ind School Dist	95	135
MaGee, Elise/Hallsburg Ind School Dist	69	279
MaGee, Patsy/Beaumont Ind School Dist	42	241
MaGee, Sarah/Sealy Ind School Dist	34,58	22
MaGee, Suzanne/Little Cypress Mauriceville SD	4	308
Magers, Lisa/Cleburne Ind School Dist	71,93	247
Maglievaz, Carmen/Natalia Ind School Dist	9	284
Maglisceau, Tom, Dr/Rockwall Ind School Dist	79	325
Maglothin, James/Zavalla Ind School Dist	73	18
Magnum, Laura/Redwater Ind School Dist	7	49
Magura, Lorianne/Lytle Ind School Dist	71	21
Maham, Jill/Avery Ind School Dist	11	322
Mahan, Dana/Dawson Ind School Dist	58	116

School Year 2019-2020   800-333-8802   TX-T55

DISTRICT PERSONNEL INDEX

Market Data Retrieval

NAME/District	JOB FUNCTIONS	PAGE
Mahan, Josh/De Leon Ind School Dist	67	89
Maher, Stephanie/S & S Cons Ind School Dist	2	167
Mahfouz, Monica/Region 5 Ed Service Center	8,27,31	244
Mahlenkamp, Karin/Keller Ind School Dist	34	354
Mahler, Brandon/Ft Elliott Cons Ind Sch Dist	8,88,273	390
Mahler, Charlotte/Olney Ind School Dist	57	406
Mahone, Debra/Elgin Ind School Dist	11	24
Maige, Stan/Garland Ind School Dist	28,295	105
Maika, Sean, Dr/North East Ind School Dist	1	34
Maines, Travis/Vidor Ind School Dist	15,68	309
Maiorano, Tammy/San Marcos Cons Ind Sch Dist	58,77	211
Majors, Ann/Sundown Ind School Dist	69,83,85,88,273	229
Malcik, Carol/Georgetown Ind School Dist	2	395
Malcolm, Kim/Richardson Ind School Dist	61	112
Malcom, Marci, Dr/Lake Dallas Ind School Dist	15	122
Maldonado, Arnold/Odem-Edroy Ind School Dist	3	331
Maldonado, Jay/Webb Cons Ind School Dist	5,12	388
Maldonado, Jennifer/Harlingen Cons Ind School Dist	286	64
Maldonado, Marlene/Cotulla Ind School Dist	38	259
Maldonado, Monica/Diocese Corpus Christi Ed Off	73	306
Maldonado, Phillip/Southland Ind School Dist	271	162
Maldonado, Valarie/Southwest Ind School Dist	7,85	43
Malechuk, Brian, Dr/Katy Ind School Dist	58	151
Maler, Kevin/West Ind School Dist	5	282
Malerba, Cathy, Dr/Round Rock Ind School Dist	69	398
Mallard, Richard/Alamo Heights Ind School Dist	4	30
Mallick, George/Dallas Ind School Dist	76	98
Mallory-Sneed, Wilma/Advantage Academy Admin Office	2,11,19,298	96
Mallory, Jessica/Strawn Ind School Dist	288	311
Malmberg, Kathy/Denton Ind School Dist	7	120
Malone, Chris/Grand Prairie Ind School Dist	73,76,295	107
Malone, Debra/Electra Ind School Dist	4	391
Malone, Debra/Mt Pleasant Ind School Dist	7,15,68	363
Malone, Jennifer/Tatum Ind School Dist	15,69	328
Malone, Joe/Wimberley Ind School Dist	67	212
Malone, Lisa/Paris Ind School Dist	58	260
Malone, Robin/Amarillo Ind School Dist	67	317
Malovets, Tracie/Rogers Ind School Dist	2	28
Manca, Amanda/Texarkana Ind School Dist	76	50
Mancha, Guillermo/Brackett Ind School Dist	1	257
Mancha, Juan/Harlandale Ind School Dist	67	32
Mancias, Renee/Braination Schools	76	30
Mancillas, Yvette/Pharr-San Juan-Alamo Ind SD	34	223
Mandoza, Maribell/Lake Worth Ind School Dist	7	356
Mangallan, Amanda/Terrell Co Ind School Dist	1	362
Mangallan, Sam/Terrell Co Ind School Dist	3	362
Maniatis, Joni/Alief Ind School Dist	275	181
Manley, David/Killeen Ind School Dist	15	27
Manley, Kristie/Burton Ind School Dist	4	386
Manley, Mark/Sweeny Ind School Dist	27	54
Mann, Aimee/La Pryor Ind School Dist	88	407
Mann, Charles/Alvord Ind School Dist	11,73,295	402
Mann, Jeff/College Station Ind Sch Dist	74	55
Mann, Laura/Galena Park Ind School Dist	27,31	186
Mann, Matthew, Dr/Pleasanton Ind School Dist	1	21
Manning, Jan/Calvert Ind School Dist	2	324
Manning, Joan/Copperas Cove Ind School Dist	67	92
Manning, Kristen/Hurst-Euless-Bedford ISD	47	353
Mannino, Gina/Bridge City Ind School Dist	11,15,271,274,294	308
Manous, Aaron/Dimmitt Ind School Dist	6	71
Manriquez, Aurelio/Lyford Cons Ind School Dist	5	394
Manriquez, Ernesto/San Benito Cons Ind Sch Dist	58	67
Mansfield, Brad/Leander Ind School Dist	79	396
Mansfield, Brad/Liberty Hill Ind School Dist	15	398
Mansfield, Tracy/Aldine Ind School Dist	43	179
Mansfield, William/Overton Ind School Dist	73	328
Mansker, Clark/Pettus Ind School Dist	2	25
Manson, Bobby/Celina Ind School Dist	91	78
Manuel, Dianna/Frisco Ind School Dist	27,31	78
Manuel, Elaine/Newcastle Ind School Dist	3,5	406
Manuel, Lacey/Godley Ind School Dist	4	247
Manzo, Maria/Jarrell Ind School Dist	4	396
Maples, Billy/Bushland Ind School Dist	4	319
Maples, Reene/Van Alstyne Ind School Dist	2,11	168
Marable, Dana/De Leon Ind School Dist	1	89
Marable, Michelle/New Caney Ind School Dist	3	293
Marak, Kristin/Hallettsville Ind Sch Dist	2	262
Marak, Lisa/Weimar Ind School Dist	57	87
Marak, Terry/Region 12 Ed Service Center	2,19	283
Marburger, James/Lexington Ind School Dist	5	263
Marbut, Melissa/Whitney Ind School Dist	8,12,273	228
Marcellus, Angela/Int'l Leadership of Texas Dist	79	108
March, Leslie/Hudson Ind School Dist	58	17
Marchbanks, Barbara/McDade Ind School Dist	1,11,288	24
Marcucci, Karen/Mansfield Ind School Dist	67	356
Marcum, Ryan/Manor Ind School Dist	91	371
Marcus, Mere/Brock Ind School Dist	4	312
Marcus, Mike/Waller Ind School Dist	2,19	384
Marcus, Sarah/Waller Ind School Dist	71	384
Marek, Courtney/Brazos Ind School Dist	2	22
Marek, Fran/Joshua Ind School Dist	1	248
Marek, Jan, Dr/Klein Ind School Dist	15	196
Marek, Kimberly/Rogers Ind School Dist	57	29
Marek, Lindsey/Goose Creek Cons Ind Sch Dist	285	187
Mares, Rosemary/Hondo Ind School Dist	15,69,74,91	284
Maresh, Madalyn/Edna Ind School Dist	11,298	239
Margoitta, Vince/Marlin Ind School Dist	3,5	144
Marin, Manuel/Plainview Ind School Dist	3	175
Mariscal, Juanita/Mercedes Ind School Dist	42	221
Markert, Kay/Prairie Lea Ind School Dist	57	61
Markert, Larry/Prairie Lea Ind School Dist	1,11	61
Markgraf, Dondi/Ferris Ind School Dist	3	140
Markham, Bryan/Wheeler Ind School Dist	1,11,83	391
Marks, Ginna/Everman Ind School Dist	58	349
Marks, Sequetta/Dallas Ind School Dist	11	98
Marks, Vance/Johnson City Ind School Dist	3,91	46
Marlar, Corey/La Porte Ind School Dist	3,5,73	198
Marlin, Traci/Midway Ind School Dist	71	280
Marquez, Angelica/Ralls Ind School Dist	271	94
Marquez, Cheryl/Detroit Ind School Dist	57	322
Marquez, Chris/Pearsall Ind School Dist	91	157
Marquez, Fernando/Ysleta Ind School Dist	27,31	137
Marquez, Liza/Socorro Ind School Dist	34	135
Marr, Brian/Klein Ind School Dist	88	196
Marroquin, Lisa/Ector Co Ind School Dist	39	129
Mars, Kayla/Quitman Ind School Dist	2,68	404
Marsh, Amanda/Winona Ind School Dist	8	339
Marsh, Angie/Lake Travis Ind School Dist	2	370
Marsh, Cheryl/Wall Ind School Dist	68	365
Marsh, Joe/Pittsburg Ind School Dist	3,5	68
Marsh, Ronnie/Winona Ind School Dist	3	339
Marsh, Sabreana/Community Ind School Dist	71	78
Marsh, Sherry/Region 20 Ed Service Center	58	45
Marshall, Brenda/Corpus Christi Ind Sch Dist	6	303
Marshall, Brenda/Cushing Ind School Dist	4	297
Marshall, Courtney/Alto Ind School Dist	31,83,88	72
Marshall, Jason/Palestine Ind School Dist	1	15
Marshall, Judd/Mt Pleasant Ind School Dist	1	363
Marshall, Khristopher/Avalon Ind School Dist	1,288	140
Marshall, Laurice/Union Grove Ind School Dist	2,11	377
Marshall, Linda/Huntsville Ind School Dist	11,296	383
Marshall, Rebecca/Hamshire Fannett Ind Sch Dist	69	242
Marshall, Scott/Sundown Ind School Dist	1	229
Marshall, Sydne/Cypress-Fairbanks Ind School Dist	7	183

1 Superintendent	16 Instructional Media Svcs	30 Adult Education	44 Science Sec	58 Special Education K-12	72 Summer School	88 Alternative/At Risk	277 Remedial Math K-12
2 Bus/Finance/Purchasing	17 Chief Operations Officer	31 Career/Sch-to-Work K-12	45 Math K-12	59 Special Education Elem	73 Instructional Tech	89 Multi-Cultural Curriculum	280 Literacy Coach
3 Buildings And Grounds	18 Chief Academic Officer	32 Career/Sch-to-Work Elem	46 Math Elem	60 Special Education Sec	74 Inservice Training	90 Social Work	285 STEM
4 Food Service	19 Chief Financial Officer	33 Career/Sch-to-Work Sec	47 Math Sec	61 Foreign/World Lang K-12	75 Marketing/Distributive	91 Safety/Security	286 Digital Learning
5 Transportation	20 Art K-12	34 Early Childhood Ed	48 English/Lang Arts K-12	62 Foreign/World Lang Elem	76 Info Systems	92 Magnet School	288 Common Core Standards
6 Athletic	21 Art Elem	35 Health/Phys Education	49 English/Lang Arts Elem	63 Foreign/World Lang Sec	77 Psychological Assess	93 Parental Involvement	294 Accountability
7 Health Services	22 Art Sec	36 Guidance Services K-12	50 English/Lang Arts Sec	64 Religious Education K-12	78 Affirmative Action	95 Tech Prep Program	295 Network System
8 Curric/Instruct K-12	23 Music K-12	37 Guidance Services Elem	51 Reading K-12	65 Religious Education Elem	79 Student Personnel	97 Chief Information Officer	296 Title II Programs
9 Curric/Instruct Elem	24 Music Elem	38 Guidance Services Sec	52 Reading Elem	66 Religious Education Sec	80 Driver Ed/Safety	98 Chief Technology Officer	297 Webmaster
10 Curric/Instruct Sec	25 Music Sec	39 Social Studies K-12	53 Reading Sec	67 School Board President	81 Gifted/Talented	270 Character Education	298 Grant Writer/Ptnrships
11 Federal Program	26 Business Education	40 Social Studies Elem	54 Remedial Reading K-12	68 Teacher Personnel	82 Video Services	271 Migrant Education	750 Chief Innovation Officer
12 Title I	27 Career & Tech Ed	41 Social Studies Sec	55 Remedial Reading Elem	69 Academic Assessment	83 Substance Abuse Prev	273 Teacher Mentor	751 Chief of Staff
13 Title V	28 Technology Education	42 Science K-12	56 Remedial Reading Sec	70 Research/Development	84 Erate	274 Before/After Sch	752 Social Emotional Learning
15 Asst Superintendent	29 Family/Consumer Science	43 Science Elem	57 Bilingual/ELL	71 Public Information	85 AIDS Education	275 Response To Intervention	

TX-T56

Texas School Directory

DISTRICT PERSONNEL INDEX

NAME/District	JOB FUNCTIONS	PAGE
Marshall, Toni/Harper Ind School Dist	16	163
Marshall, Tracy/Ft Worth Ind School Dist	70,298	349
Martel, Gary/Moody Ind School Dist	1,11,83	281
Martella, Michele/Comal Ind School Dist	58	87
Martin, Allison/Aspermont Ind School Dist	11	342
Martin, Amanda/Wylie Ind School Dist	36	84
Martin, Angela/Olton Ind School Dist	83	261
Martin, Anna/Hutto Ind School Dist	4	396
Martin, Art/Slaton Ind School Dist	2	272
Martin, Bruce/Rotan Ind School Dist	84	148
Martin, Buck/San Saba Ind School Dist	2	332
Martin, Carol/Bullard Ind School Dist	16	336
Martin, Carrie/Mineral Wells Ind School Dist	4	310
Martin, Chrys/Veribest Ind School Dist	16	365
Martin, Dale/Splendora Ind School Dist	73	294
Martin, Denise/Whitehouse Ind School Dist	50,53	339
Martin, Edi/Millsap Ind School Dist	15,296	312
Martin, Elizabeth/Ft Bend Ind School Dist	15	149
Martin, Erika/Winnsboro Ind School Dist	7	405
Martin, James/Grapeland Ind School Dist	67	232
Martin, Janna Lee/Mineral Wells Ind School Dist	73	310
Martin, Jeff/North Lamar Ind School Dist	67	259
Martin, Jennifer/Randolph Field Ind School Dist	16	39
Martin, John/Hallsville Ind School Dist	15,68,74	208
Martin, Josh/Farmersville Ind School Dist	58,69,77,88	78
Martin, Julie/Grapeland Ind School Dist	2,11	232
Martin, Kim/Whitney Ind School Dist	2	228
Martin, Kyle/Plains Ind School Dist	67	405
Martin, Linda/Runge Ind School Dist	7	251
Martin, Loretta/Longview Ind School Dist	68	169
Martin, Lydia/Hurst-Euless-Bedford ISD	8,15	353
Martin, Mary/Keller Ind School Dist	57	354
Martin, Mary Helen/Denton Ind School Dist	9	120
Martin, Maury/Chico Ind School Dist	5,11,57,58,88,273,285,294	403
Martin, Menell/Luling Ind School Dist	2,19	61
Martin, Michael/Nacogdoches Ind School Dist	68	298
Martin, Mike/May Ind School Dist	73,76,296	59
Martin, Nellie/Hawley Ind School Dist	270,271,273	250
Martin, Paul/Coleman Ind School Dist	73,76,295,297	76
Martin, Paula/Corrigan-Camden Ind Sch Dist	8,11,16,57,286,288,296,298	316
Martin, Philip/Evant Ind School Dist	6	92
Martin, Rachel/Martin's Mill Ind Sch Dist	8,16,73,82	381
Martin, Rose Ann/Richardson Ind School Dist	4	112
Martin, Ruth/Castleberry Ind School Dist	57	347
Martin, Sarah/Katy Ind School Dist	27,51	151
Martin, Sidney/Karnes City Ind School Dist	4	250
Martin, Stacey/Luling Ind School Dist	6	61
Martin, Tana/El Campo Ind School Dist	69	389
Martin, Taylor/Jacksboro Ind Sch Dist	7	239
Martin, Tony/Rio Vista Ind School Dist	1	248
Martindale, Mike/College Station Ind Sch Dist	2,15,19	55
Martindale, Scott/Iola Ind School Dist	1	172
Martinez, Alma Rosa, Dr/East Central Ind School Dist	57	31
Martinez, Angie/McAllen Ind School Dist	57,61	221
Martinez, Anna/Crockett Co Cons Common SD	5	94
Martinez, Anna/Zapata Co Ind School Dist	69	406
Martinez, April/Reagan Co Ind School Dist	4	321
Martinez, Armando/Elgin Ind School Dist	23	24
Martinez, Armando/Socorro Ind School Dist	20,23	135
Martinez, Brenda/San Saba Ind School Dist	8,11,15,57,88,288,296	332
Martinez, Camilo/Valley View Ind School Dist	11,93	225
Martinez, Carlos/Eagle Pass Ind School Dist	23	276
Martinez, Carlos/Weslaco Ind School Dist	73,76,295	225
Martinez, Cesar/Houston ISD-Northwest Area	15	191
Martinez, Christina/Brownfield Ind School Dist	73	362
Martinez, Chuy/Crockett Co Cons Common SD	3	94
Martinez, David/Mathis Ind School Dist	3	331
Martinez, David/Slaton Ind School Dist	57	272
Martinez, Deanna/Edinburg Cons Ind School Dist	7	216
Martinez, Elizabeth/Hughes Springs Ind Sch Dist	4	70
Martinez, Erma/Crystal City Ind School Dist	57	407
Martinez, Esmeralda/Odem-Edroy Ind School Dist	34	331
Martinez, Haley/Seguin Ind School Dist	58	173
Martinez, Hector/Brownwood Ind School Dist	15	58
Martinez, Ilyan/Natalia Ind School Dist	6	284
Martinez, Isaac/Harlandale Ind School Dist	6,35	32
Martinez, Jamie/Van Alstyne Ind School Dist	8,12,57	168
Martinez, Jd/Sherman Ind School Dist	6	167
Martinez, Jennifer/Junction Ind School Dist	16,82	256
Martinez, Jerahiah/Pringle-Morse Cons ISD	3	177
Martinez, Jerry/Dallas Co Schools	68	96
Martinez, Jessica/Harlingen Cons Ind School Dist	297	64
Martinez, Jesus/Rio Grande City Ind Sch Dist	57	340
Martinez, Jesus/San Elizario Ind School Dist	3,5	135
Martinez, Joe/Kingsville Ind School Dist	28,73	257
Martinez, Joe/Spearman Ind School Dist	5	177
Martinez, Jorge/Valley View Ind School Dist	73,84	225
Martinez, Juan, Dr/Clint Ind School Dist	1	132
Martinez, Julio/Valley View Ind School Dist	6	225
Martinez, Lana/Tahoka Ind School Dist	8,83,88,270,280	273
Martinez, Leo/Smyer Ind School Dist	3,5	229
Martinez, Leticia/La Joya Ind School Dist	50	219
Martinez, Luis/Brownsville Ind School Dist	82	63
Martinez, Luis/Diocese of Laredo Ed Office	76,295	388
Martinez, Lydia/Northside Ind School Dist	30,93	36
Martinez, Maggie/Laredo Ind School Dist	79,83	386
Martinez, Manny/Dilley Ind School Dist	6	157
Martinez, Marcena/Cotulla Ind School Dist	4	259
Martinez, Marcus/Calhoun Co Ind School Dist	73,286,295	62
Martinez, Mari/Alief Ind School Dist	34	181
Martinez, Mark/Coleman Ind School Dist	67	76
Martinez, Melissa/El Paso Ind School Dist	71	132
Martinez, Myrna/Edgewood Ind School Dist	2,15,19	31
Martinez, Myrna/Harlandale Ind School Dist	76,295	32
Martinez, Natalie/Alief Ind School Dist	69,294	181
Martinez, Natasha/Winona Ind School Dist	57	339
Martinez, Olivia/Pharr-San Juan-Alamo Ind SD	57,280	223
Martinez, Oscar/Academy Ind School Dist	3	26
Martinez, Oscar/Schleicher Co Ind Sch Dist	3	333
Martinez, Patricia/Rockwall Ind School Dist	57	325
Martinez, Pedro/San Antonio Ind School Dist	1	39
Martinez, Pete/Iola Ind School Dist	6,83,88	172
Martinez, Ricardo/Borden Co Ind School Dist	295	46
Martinez, Rick/Belton Ind School Dist	3	26
Martinez, Robin/Calhoun Co Ind School Dist	2,15	61
Martinez, Rosalinda/Goldthwaite Consolidated ISD	57	288
Martinez, Ruth/Poteet Ind School Dist	7,83,85	21
Martinez, Sandra/Clint Ind School Dist	48	132
Martinez, Sandra/Taylor Ind School Dist	57,271	399
Martinez, Sandra/Taylor Ind School Dist	57	399
Martinez, Sara/Seguin Ind School Dist	88	173
Martinez, Sonya/Pearsall Ind School Dist	8,68,69,79	157
Martinez, Suanne/Mathis Ind School Dist	4	331
Martinez, Susie/Poth Ind School Dist	69	401
Martinez, Tony/Diocese of Victoria Ed Office	2	382
Martinez, Tresa/Haskell Cons Ind School Dist	271	210
Martinez, Veronica/Galena Park Ind School Dist	57	186
Martischnig, Whitney/Seymour Ind School Dist	60	25
Marts, Renee/Lewisville Ind School Dist	43	122
Marwitz, Jill/Holland Ind School Dist	67	27
Marwitz, Stanton/Zephyr Ind School Dist	1,83	59
Marx, David/Texas Dept of Education	11	1
Mascheck, Brant/Columbia Brazoria ISD	6	52
Masek, Andy/Giddings Ind School Dist	3,5	263
Masick, Christina/Spring Branch Ind School Dist	15,71,73,76,97,295	200
Mask, Leanne/Lytle Ind School Dist	67	21
Maskew, Rhudy/Wilson Ind School Dist	6	273
Mason, Bruce/West Rusk Co Cons Ind Sch Dist	5	328
Mason, Chris/Quitman Ind School Dist	8,11,57,69,88,285,296,298	404
Mason, Ralph/Andrews Ind School Dist	6	16
Mason, Shawn/Crosbyton Cons Ind Sch Dist	1	94
Mason, Stacy/Crosbyton Cons Ind Sch Dist	11,69,77	94
Mason, Wayne/Excelsior Ind School Dist	1	334
Massey, Chad/Brock Ind School Dist	6	312
Massey, Danny/Brazosport Ind School Dist	1	52
Massey, Doug/Klein Ind School Dist	4	196
Massey, Kevin/Garland Ind School Dist	47	105
Massingill, Mark/Union Hill Ind School Dist	73	377
Masterson, Amanda/Fruitvale Ind School Dist	69,85,88,270	380
Masterson, Zach/Fruitvale Ind School Dist	93	380
Mata, Enrique/Sharyland Ind School Dist	5	224
Mata, Ernie/Point Isabel Ind Sch Dist	5	66

DISTRICT PERSONNEL INDEX

Market Data Retrieval

NAME/District	JOB FUNCTIONS	PAGE
Mata, Monica/La Villa Ind School Dist	2	220
Mata, Wilfredo/Progreso Ind School Dist	2	224
Matamoros, Kirza/Cleburne Ind School Dist	57	247
Matchett, Amy/Van Vleck Ind School Dist	37	276
Matern, Crystal/Gregory-Portland Ind Sch Dist	16	330
Matheny, Kevin/Central Heights Ind Sch Dist	5	297
Mathes, Cliff/Ennis Ind School Dist	58	140
Mathesen, Jennie/Temple Ind School Dist	58	29
Matheson, Stacey/Danbury Ind School Dist	73,76,295	53
Mathews, David/Dawson Ind School Dist	67	299
Mathews, Dusty/Lexington Ind School Dist	7	263
Mathews, Malisa/Liberty-Eylau Ind School Dist	4	48
Mathews, Michelle/Franklin Ind School Dist	2	324
Mathieu, Troy/Dallas Ind School Dist	6	98
Mathieu, Troy/Grand Prairie Ind School Dist	17	107
Mathiews, Margaret/Woodson Ind School Dist	58,79	363
Mathis, Earl/Sweeny Ind School Dist	67	54
Mathis, John/Galveston Ind School Dist	76,84,295	160
Mathis, Kevin/Hempstead Ind School Dist	2,19	384
Mathis, Olivia/Lake Worth Ind School Dist	297	356
Mathis, Summer/Paradise Ind School Dist	2,19	403
Mathis, Tiffany/Lamar Cons Ind School Dist	58	153
Mathys, Gretchen/Jarrell Ind School Dist	3	396
Matlock, Dale/Everman Ind School Dist	6	349
Matney, Allison, Dr/Katy Ind School Dist	69,70,294	151
Matranga, Mike/Texas City Ind School Dist	91	161
Matson, Craig/Douglass Ind School Dist	58	297
Mattern, Shawn/Elkhart Ind School Dist	5	15
Matterson, Angela/Colmesneil Ind School Dist	1	375
Matthews, David/Grady Ind School Dist	67	274
Matthews, Iyana/Kermit Ind School Dist	4	401
Matthews, James/Wylie Ind School Dist	76	85
Matthews, Jeff/Vidor Ind School Dist	6,35	309
Matthews, John/Celina Ind School Dist	15,68	78
Matthews, Kevin, Dr/Pottsboro Ind School Dist	1	167
Matthews, Patti/Anna Ind School Dist	76	77
Matthews, Phillip/Little Cypress Mauriceville SD	3,91	308
Matthews, Ray/Teague Ind School Dist	15	156
Matthews, Shannon/Central Ind School Dist	37	17
Matthews, Spencer/Kountze Ind School Dist	73,295	178
Matthews, Teresa/Hudson Ind School Dist	90	17
Matthews, Teresa/Kountze Ind School Dist	16	178
Matthews, Vickie/Walcott Ind School Dist	57	119
Matthis, Jepilyn/Conroe Ind School Dist	34,49	291
Matthys, Debbie/Taylor Ind School Dist	69	399
Mattingly, Kim/Cross Roads Ind School Dist	31,69,85	214
Mattson, Denise/Lubbock Ind School Dist	11,57,275,296,298	269
Matula, Georgina/Brazos Ind School Dist	4	22
Matula, Marybeth/Region 3 Ed Service Center	15,76	383
Mault, Brenda/Big Spring Ind School Dist	297	233
Maurizzio, Vanessa/El Paso Ind School Dist	59	132
Maxey, Susan/Luling Ind School Dist	83,85,271	61
Maxfield, Kyle/Bangs Ind School Dist	6	58
Maxwell, Brad/Leonard Ind School Dist	1	146
Maxwell, Connie/Olton Ind School Dist	67	261
Maxwell, Mike/Pleasanton Ind School Dist	295	21
Maxwell, Nathan/Pampa Ind School Dist	68,74,78,273	165
May, Aubrey/Frost Ind School Dist	4	299
May, Cathy/McLeod Ind School Dist	1	70
May, Deanna/Franklin Ind School Dist	57	325
May, Debbie/Winnsboro Ind School Dist	38,85,88	405
May, Eddy/De Kalb Ind School Dist	6	48
May, Gene/Callisburg Ind School Dist	3,5	90
May, Kaci/Tahoka Ind School Dist	57	273
May, Lori/Barbers Hill Ind School Dist	58	72
May, Lori/Denison Ind School Dist	58,77	166
May, Molly/Eanes Ind School Dist	58	370
May, Wendy/Redwater Ind School Dist	31,36,93,270,271,274	49
May, Wendy/Redwater Ind School Dist	31,36,93,270,271,274	49
Maya, Taina/Killeen Ind School Dist	71	27
Mayberry, Sandy/Royal Ind School Dist	2	384
Mayberry, Tammy/Manor Ind School Dist	44	371
Maye, Belinda/Smyer Ind School Dist	73,295	229
Mayeaux, Dolly/Galena Park Ind School Dist	69,294	186
Mayer, Courtney/Northside Ind School Dist	81	36
Mayer, Lisa/Deer Park Ind School Dist	48	186
Mayfield, Carol/Brownsboro Ind School Dist	68	213
Mayfield, Cindy/Holliday Ind School Dist	3	19
Mayfield, Heather/Castleberry Ind School Dist	76	347
Mayfield, Missy/Burkburnett Ind Sch Dist	8,27,57,69,74,88,286,288	391
Mayhan, Jodie/Union Grove Ind School Dist	7	377
Maynard, Russell/Lago Vista Ind School Dist	73	370
Mayo, Carol/Diocese of Dallas Ed Office	73	113
Mayo, Judy/Fredericksburg Ind School Dist	7	163
Mayorquin, Consuelo/Hempstead Ind School Dist	57	384
Mays, Chance, Dr/Mt Enterprise Ind School Dist	10	328
Mays, Kecia/Arlington Ind School Dist	67	343
Mays, Lisa/Troy Ind School Dist	4	29
Mayton, Karen/Midway Ind School Dist	69	280
Maze, Jerry/Region 12 Ed Service Center	1	283
Mazzagate, Roy/Little Cypress Mauriceville SD	16,297	308
McAda, Donna/Mesquite Ind School Dist	69,288	110
McAdams, Brian/Mt Pleasant Ind School Dist	79	363
McAdams, Sunday/Seymour Ind School Dist	16,82	25
McAdoo, Bobbie/Tom Bean Ind School Dist	6	168
McAfee, Mitzi/Region 3 Ed Service Center	15	383
McAlister, Leighanne/Maypearl Ind School Dist	2	141
McAlpin, Shaun/Orangefield Ind School Dist	2,15,298	309
McAlpin, Walter/Colmesneil Ind School Dist	69,88,271,275	375
McAnally, Rosalea/White Deer Ind School Dist	73	69
McAndrew, Wende/Hawley Ind School Dist	4	250
McAnear, Melissa/Cypress-Fairbanks Ind Sch Dist	2	183
McBain, Kelly/Socorro Ind School Dist	70	135
McBee, Morgan/Lefors Ind School Dist	2	165
McBrayer, Cassidy, Dr/Hawley Ind School Dist	1	250
McBrayer, Cassidy, Dr/Whiteface Con Ind School Dist	11	75
McBrayer, Michael/Whiteface Con Ind School Dist	58	75
McBride, Cody/West Sabine Ind Sch Dist	67	329
McBride, Faye/Edgewood Ind School Dist	68	380
McBride, Kristi/Schulenburg Ind School Dist	286	148
McBride, Ticia/Lumberton Ind School Dist	57	178
McBride, Vicki/Garner Ind School Dist	4	312
McBryde, Misti/Stratford Ind School Dist	36,57,58,69,79,85	336
McBurnett, Diana/Region 7 Ed Service Center	11,58	171
McBurnett, Keith/Burnet Cons Ind Sch Dist	1	60
McCabe, Angela/Brazosport Ind School Dist	39	52
McCabe, Ryan/Ennis Ind School Dist	5,285	140
McCafferty, Bryon/Canyon Ind School Dist	2	320
McCain, Leigh/Crane Ind School Dist	2	93
McCaleb, Patti/Utopia Ind School Dist	7	378
McCall, Demetrius/Sheldon Ind School Dist	15	200
McCall, Mark/Bryan Ind School Dist	67	54
McCallester, Ann/Monahans-Wickett-Pyote ISD	7	385
McCallie, Brent/San Angelo Ind School Dist	6,35	364
McCallister, Teresa/Jourdanton Ind School Dist	1,73,83	20
McCampbell, Wallace/North East Ind School Dist	91	34
McCanlies, Holly/Mansfield Ind School Dist	36,83	356
McCann, Erin/Crandall Ind School Dist	71	251
McCann, Steven/Joaquin Ind School Dist	6	335
McCann, Susan/Fruitvale Ind School Dist	2,19,73,298	380
McCarley, Pam/Leonard Ind School Dist	16	146
McCarley, Troy, Dr/Pasadena Ind School Dist	15,70,71	198
McCarter, Sarahbeth/Celina Ind School Dist	2	77
McCarthy, Jeanann/Smithville Ind School Dist	2,19	24

1 Superintendent	16 Instructional Media Svcs	30 Adult Education
2 Bus/Finance/Purchasing	17 Chief Operations Officer	31 Career/Sch-to-Work K-12
3 Buildings And Grounds	18 Chief Academic Officer	32 Career/Sch-to-Work Elem
4 Food Service	19 Chief Financial Officer	33 Career/Sch-to-Work Sec
5 Transportation	20 Art K-12	34 Early Childhood Ed
6 Athletic	21 Art Elem	35 Health/Phys Education
7 Health Services	22 Art Sec	36 Guidance Services K-12
8 Curric/Instruct K-12	23 Music K-12	37 Guidance Services Elem
9 Curric/Instruct Elem	24 Music Elem	38 Guidance Services Sec
10 Curric/Instruct Sec	25 Music Sec	39 Social Studies K-12
11 Federal Program	26 Business Education	40 Social Studies Elem
12 Title I	27 Career & Tech Ed	41 Social Studies Sec
13 Title V	28 Technology Education	42 Science K-12
15 Asst Superintendent	29 Family/Consumer Science	43 Science Elem
44 Science Sec	58 Special Education K-12	72 Summer School
45 Math K-12	59 Special Education Elem	73 Instructional Tech
46 Math Elem	60 Special Education Sec	74 Inservice Training
47 Math Sec	61 Foreign/World Lang K-12	75 Marketing/Distributive
48 English/Lang Arts K-12	62 Foreign/World Lang Elem	76 Info Systems
49 English/Lang Arts Elem	63 Foreign/World Lang Sec	77 Psychological Assess
50 English/Lang Arts Sec	64 Religious Education K-12	78 Affirmative Action
51 Reading K-12	65 Religious Education Elem	79 Student Personnel
52 Reading Elem	66 Religious Education Sec	80 Driver Ed/Safety
53 Reading Sec	67 School Board President	81 Gifted/Talented
54 Remedial Reading K-12	68 Teacher Personnel	82 Video Services
55 Remedial Reading Elem	69 Academic Assessment	83 Substance Abuse Prev
56 Remedial Reading Sec	70 Research/Development	84 Erate
57 Bilingual/ELL	71 Public Information	85 AIDS Education
88 Alternative/At Risk	277 Remedial Math K-12
89 Multi-Cultural Curriculum	280 Literacy Coach
90 Social Work	285 STEM
91 Safety/Security	286 Digital Learning
92 Magnet School	288 Common Core Standards
93 Parental Involvement	294 Accountability
95 Tech Prep Program	295 Network System
97 Chief Information Officer	296 Title II Programs
98 Chief Technology Officer	297 Webmaster
270 Character Education	298 Grant Writer/Ptnrships
271 Migrant Education	750 Chief Innovation Officer
273 Teacher Mentor	751 Chief of Staff
274 Before/After Sch	752 Social Emotional Learning
275 Response To Intervention	

Texas School Directory

DISTRICT PERSONNEL INDEX

NAME/District	JOB FUNCTIONS	PAGE
McCartney, Heather/*Gholson Ind School Dist*	1,83,84,288	279
McCarty, Matt/*Lovejoy Ind School Dist*	4	80
McCarty, Melinda/*Sweetwater ISD School Dist*	11,15,57,61	301
McCarty, Mendy/*Crane Ind School Dist*	4	93
McCarty, Stacey/*Lufkin Ind School Dist*	286	18
McCasland, Brice/*Lovejoy Ind School Dist*	20	80
McCasland, Johnny/*Tulia Ind School Dist*	73,76,295	343
McCasland, Kevin/*Olton Ind School Dist*	1	261
McCasland, Shane/*Overton Ind School Dist*	67	328
McCaughey, James/*Buna Ind School Dist*	295	240
McCauley, David/*Temple Ind School Dist*	68	29
McCawley, Oscar/*Italy Ind School Dist*	73,285	141
McClain, Rachael/*Snyder Ind School Dist*	8	333
McClain, Robert/*Channing Ind School Dist*	1,11,57,288	209
McClanahan, Scott/*Waco Ind School Dist*	81	281
McCland, Deene/*Brookeland Ind School Dist*	294	240
McClean, Pam/*Deer Park Ind School Dist*	13,58,77,83	186
McClean, Robert/*Plains Ind School Dist*	1,11,83	405
McCleery, Joan/*Miles Ind School Dist*	11,45,57,83,270,271,273	326
McClelen, Christy/*Canton Ind School Dist*	4	380
McClellan, Jim/*Sanford-Fritch Ind School Dist*	1,83	238
McClellan, Robb/*Region 14 Ed Service Center*	73	362
McClelland, Natasha/*West Sabine Ind Sch Dist*	2,296	329
McClendon, Alexis/*Duncanville Ind School Dist*	68	104
McClendon, Cole/*Sam Rayburn Ind School Dist*	1	146
McClenny, Cindy/*Lindale Ind School Dist*	4	337
McClimtok, Tom/*Riesel Ind School Dist*	67	281
McCloy, Janice/*Pringle-Morse Cons ISD*	4	177
McClure, Brandon/*Miller Grove Ind School Dist*	27	231
McClure, Doug/*Glen Rose Ind School Dist*	73,76,295	340
McClure, Janis/*Region 8 Ed Service Center*	58	69
McClure, Jeffrey/*Henrietta Ind School Dist*	1	74
McClure, Matt/*Atlanta Ind School Dist*	6,35,85	69
McClure, Tim/*Northwest Ind School Dist*	3,5,15	124
McClure, Vanesa/*Dimmitt Ind School Dist*	16	71
McClurg, Jim/*Pleasant Grove Ind School Dist*	73,297	49
McClurg, Julie/*Pleasant Grove Ind School Dist*	8,11,58,85,285,296	49
McCollister, Adrianna/*Whitharral Ind School Dist*	2	230
McCollister, Nick/*Whitharral Ind School Dist*	8,12,36,69,83,270	230
McComb, Tina/*Gholson Ind School Dist*	4	279
McCone, Michelle/*Ft Worth Ind School Dist*	53,280	349
McCoral, Kim/*Loop Ind School Dist*	58	157
McCord, Brandon/*Snook Ind School Dist*	73,76,286	59
McCord, Henri/*Ezzell Ind School Dist*	67	262
McCord, Kelly, Dr/*Burnet Cons Ind Sch Dist*	10	60
McCord, Michelle, Dr/*Frenship Ind School Dist*	1	269
McCorkle, Hannah/*New Deal Ind School Dist*	16	271
McCormick, Andy/*Richardson Ind School Dist*	297	112
McCormick, Tina/*Venus Ind School Dist*	4	249
McCorquodale, Lisa/*Humble Ind School Dist*	8	195
McCown, Amanda/*Weatherford Ind School Dist*	50	313
McCown, Jan/*Stanton Ind School Dist*	8,15	274
McCown, Milla/*Bangs Ind School Dist*	4	58
McCoy, Pam/*Everman Ind School Dist*	34,57	349
McCoy, Tanis/*Water Valley Ind School Dist*	2,11	365
McCracken, Shanna/*Dayton Ind School Dist*	8	265
McCrary, Angel/*Royse City Ind School Dist*	2	326
McCraw, Brian/*Rocksprings Ind School Dist*	8,12,57,69,88,270	131
McCray, Lisa/*Region 12 Ed Service Center*	73	283
McCreary, Bruce/*Ector Co Ind School Dist*	6	129
McCreary, Mike/*Blue Ridge Ind School Dist*	67	77
McCrory, Micki/*Alvarado Ind School Dist*	42	246
McCroskey, Peaches/*Deer Park Ind School Dist*	15,68	186
McCugh, Kevin/*Brookeland Ind School Dist*	1,83	240
McCuller, Mike/*Comal Ind School Dist*	3	87
McCullough, Jason/*Mt Vernon Ind School Dist*	1	155
McCullough, Jason, Dr/*Region 8 Ed Service Center*	31	69
McCullough, John/*Whitney Ind School Dist*	1	228
McCune, Amanda/*Frisco Ind School Dist*	71,97	78
McCutchan, Sally/*Aransas Pass Ind School Dist*	7	330
McCutchen, Rebecca/*Alpine Ind School Dist*	1	56
McDade, Janet/*Carroll Independent Sch Dist*	79	347
McDaniel, April/*Canyon Ind School Dist*	71	320
McDaniel, Betty/*Center Ind School Dist*	2,19	334
McDaniel, Jeremy/*Hemphill Ind School Dist*	58	329
McDaniel, Norris/*Bryan Ind School Dist*	3	54

NAME/District	JOB FUNCTIONS	PAGE
McDaniel, Rick, Dr/*McKinney Ind School Dist*	1	80
McDaniel, Shellye/*Hubbard Ind School Dist*	271	48
McDaniel, Shirley/*Laneville Ind School Dist*	36,58,69,83	327
McDaniel, Tracy, Dr/*Cypress-Fairbanks Ind Sch Dist*	69	184
McDaris, Debbie/*City View Ind School Dist*	2	391
McDermott, Holly/*Glasscock Co Ind School Dist*	27	163
McDonald, Angela/*Advantage Academy Admin Office*	1	96
McDonald, Brenda/*Anderson-Shiro Cons Ind SD*	73,286	171
McDonald, Cheryl/*Frisco Ind School Dist*	286	78
McDonald, Danny/*Stafford Municipal Sch Dist*	4	155
McDonald, Frank/*Socorro Ind School Dist*	43	135
McDonald, James/*Boyd Ind School Dist*	3	402
McDonald, Kevin/*Advantage Academy Admin Office*	3,5,17	96
McDonald, Sharon/*Glasscock Co Ind School Dist*	58	163
McDonald, Tracy/*Christoval Ind School Dist*	5	364
McDonald, Violita/*Terrell Co Ind School Dist*	13,83	362
McDonnell, Justin/*Collinsville Ind School Dist*	67	166
McDonough, Jimmy/*Los Fresnos Cons Ind Sch Dist*	10,16,27,31,57,58,69,298	66
McDonough, Melissa/*Mumford Ind School Dist*	8,31,36,58,85	56
McDougald, Jamie/*Iola Ind School Dist*	16,85	172
McDowell, Brandon/*Coleman Ind School Dist*	1	76
McDowell, Randy/*Plano Ind School Dist*	2,19	82
McDowell, Stacey/*Deer Park Ind School Dist*	2	186
McDuff, Tammy/*Silsbee Ind School Dist*	57,271	178
McDuffy, Tony/*Linden Kildare Cons Ind SD*	91	70
McDurham, Robin, Dr/*Waco Ind School Dist*	10	281
McEachern, Brad/*Hardin Jefferson Ind Sch Dist*	1	177
McEachern, Mike/*Huffman Ind School Dist*	6	195
McElhany, Talina/*Ore City Ind School Dist*	2	376
McElroy, Samantha/*Huntington Ind School Dist*	4	17
McElyea, Chris/*Winnsboro Ind School Dist*	67	405
McEntyre, Lori/*Paris Ind School Dist*	4	260
McEwen, Kathy/*Port Arthur Ind School Dist*	69	243
McFadden, Duane/*Montgomery Ind School Dist*	10,15	293
McFadden, Leslie/*Garrison Ind School Dist*	58	297
McFall, Dennis/*Austin Ind School Dist*	274	366
McFarland, George, Dr/*Sweetwater ISD School Dist*	1	301
McFarland, Michael, Dr/*Crowley Ind School Dist*	1	347
McGaha, Shad/*Wichita Falls Ind School Dist*	16,73,76,98,295	392
McGahey, Suzanne/*Keller Ind School Dist*	39	354
McGan, Bryan/*Hale Center Ind School Dist*	73	175
McGane, Sherra/*Cedar Hill Ind School Dist*	2	97
McGarvey, Kimberly/*Hallsville Ind School Dist*	7,35,85	208
McGavock, Deborah/*Hico Ind School Dist*	31,36,69	176
McGee, Dustin/*Liberty Ind School Dist*	15	266
McGee, Karla/*Crosby Ind School Dist*	58	183
McGee, Rayanne/*Texline Ind School Dist*	31,58	95
McGeehee, Ben/*Sweetwater ISD School Dist*	6,35	301
McGehee, Harold/*Brooks Co Ind School Dist*	6,35	57
McGehee, Lana/*Paradise Ind School Dist*	16	403
McGhee, Darryl/*Haskell Cons Ind School Dist*	5	210
McGill, Pat/*Harleton Ind School Dist*	67	208
McGilvary, Steven/*Coppell Ind School Dist*	73,98	98
McGinley, James/*Higgins Ind School Dist*	3	268
McGinnis, Jeff/*Snyder Ind School Dist*	73	333
McGinnis, Linda/*Comanche Ind School Dist*	73	89
McGowan, Jenny, Dr/*Klein Ind School Dist*	1,288	196
McGowan, Lucy/*Walcott Ind School Dist*	67	119
McGowen, Charles/*Huntsville Ind School Dist*	5	383
McGowen, Donnie/*Weatherford Ind School Dist*	30	313
McGowen, Robby, Dr/*Region 4 Ed Service Center*	15,79	208
McGraw, Sherry/*Sulphur Springs Ind Sch Dist*	2	232
McGregor, Diana/*North Lamar Ind School Dist*	4	259
McGregor, Heather/*Region 8 Ed Service Center*	74,294	69
McGuire, Julie/*Arlington Ind School Dist*	11	343
McGuire, Maria/*Kenedy Co Wide Common Sch Dist*	81	254
McGuire, Paul/*Clyde Consolidated Ind SD*	73,295	62
McHam, Terry/*Connally Ind School Dist*	5	279
McHazlett, Matthew/*La Pryor Ind School Dist*	1	407
McHenry, Robert/*Springtown Ind School Dist*	73,98,286,295	313
McHenry, Rodney/*Garland Ind School Dist*	68	105
McIlduff, Dan/*Cypress-Fairbanks Ind Sch Dist*	15,57,58,90,280	183
McIlveene, Cindy/*Wolfe City Ind School Dist*	2	237
McInnis, Karen/*Lasara Ind School Dist*	36,83,88,270,275	394
McIntosh, Matt/*Gladewater Ind School Dist*	3	169
McIntyre, Donald/*Princeton Ind School Dist*	10,15,286	84

School Year 2019-2020   800-333-8802   TX-T59

DISTRICT PERSONNEL INDEX

Market Data Retrieval

NAME/District	JOB FUNCTIONS	PAGE
McIntyre, Suzette/Wall Ind School Dist	73,295	365
McKamie, David/Region 12 Ed Service Center	79	283
McKay, Ginger/Goose Creek Cons Ind Sch Dist	11,298	187
McKee, Ashley/Eustace Ind School Dist	67	214
McKee, Jamie/Karnes City Ind School Dist	84	250
McKee, Johnny/Woodville Ind School Dist	3	375
McKee, Norma/Rio Grande City Ind Sch Dist	34	340
McKeithan, Deeone/Spring Ind School Dist	68	202
McKelvain, Travis/Edgewood Ind School Dist	68	31
McKenzie, Michael/Georgetown Ind School Dist	295	395
McKenzie, Tonya/Breckenridge Ind School Dist	7	341
McKethan, Donna/Waco Ind School Dist	27,31	281
McKinley, Michele/Manor Ind School Dist	58	371
McKinney, Carlton/Nixon-Smiley Cons Ind Sch Dist	6	164
McKinney, Lynn/Aledo Ind School Dist	11,15,296	312
McKinney, Mark/Santa Fe Ind School Dist	5	161
McKinney, Sharon/Port Aransas Ind School Dist	1,11	305
McKinnon, Jeff/Nederland Ind School Dist	69	242
McKinnon, Reeann/Glasscock Co Ind School Dist	4	163
McKittrick, Matt/Godley Ind School Dist	67	247
McKnight, Ray/Chester Ind School Dist	67	374
McKnight, Schronda/Bryan Ind School Dist	34	54
McKnight, Winnie/Lovelady Ind School Dist	7	233
McKown, Joan/Iola Ind School Dist	54	172
McLain, Clint, Dr/Dilley Ind School Dist	1	157
McLain, Tammy/Dimmitt Ind School Dist	286	71
McLamore, Mitch/Petrolia Cons Ind School Dist	6	74
McLane, Mitzi/Yantis Ind School Dist	4	405
McLaren, Steve/Klondike Ind School Dist	1,11	117
McLarty, Patrick/Ponder Ind School Dist	3,5	125
McLarty, Paul/Clear Creek Ind School Dist	2,3,15	158
McLarty, Sam/Center Point Ind School Dist	4,5	255
McLaughlin, Bill, Dr/Walcott Ind School Dist	1,11,288	119
McLaurin, Jaime/Devine Ind School Dist	4	283
McLean, Denise/Klein Ind School Dist	297	196
McLean, Holly/Gruver Ind School Dist	73	176
McLean, Scott/Abilene Ind School Dist	3,4,5,15	360
McLear, Blare/Calallen Ind School Dist	10,69	302
McLellan, Loy/Friona Ind School Dist	37,83	315
McLemore, Amber/Martin's Mill Ind Sch Dist	85	381
McLemore, Mitch/Junction Ind School Dist	6	256
McLendon, Deeanna/Blanco Ind School Dist	8,31,36,69,83	45
McLeod, Kimberly/Harris Co Dept of Ed	8,15	179
McLeod, Michael/Mason Ind School Dist	6	275
McLerran, Patti/San Augustine Ind School Dist	2	329
McLver, Ryan/Weimar Ind School Dist	6	87
McMahan, Glenda/Sunnyvale Ind School Dist	69,88,270	113
McMains, Julia, Dr/Palacios Ind School Dist	8,11,16,57,58,271,273,274	275
McManners, Mike/Iola Ind School Dist	27	172
McManus, Becky/Barbers Hill Ind School Dist	2,15	72
McManus, Kim/Caldwell Ind School Dist	69	59
McMath, Barbi/Wills Point Ind School Dist	8,15,285,286,288,294,298	381
McMeans, Bart/Borden Co Ind School Dist	8,11,57,69,88,294,296	46
McMichael, Mechelle/Hubbard Ind School Dist	73,76,270	48
McMillan, Sherri/Newcastle Ind School Dist	270	406
McMillian, Bonnie/Carthage Ind School Dist	7	311
McMillian, David/Santa Fe Ind School Dist	5	161
McMillion, Paula/Anna Ind School Dist	11,57	77
McMillon, Lacey/Red Lick Ind School Dist	2	49
McMurry, Ross/Colmesneil Ind School Dist	6	375
McMurtry, Brad/Troy Ind School Dist	3,68,79,288	29
McMurtry, Linda/Malakoff Ind School Dist	16,82	214
McNab, Maggie/Lubbock-Cooper Ind School Dist	88	271
McNabb, Jean/Ropes Ind School Dist	59	229
McNabb, Terry/Aubrey Ind School Dist	15	120
McNaird, Vickie/Tioga Ind School Dist	4	167
McNeely, Clay/Hereford Ind School Dist	67	119
McNeely, Deborah/Aldine Ind School Dist	275	179
McNeely, Debra/Conroe Ind School Dist	50,63	291
McNeely, Janet/Weatherford Ind School Dist	11	313
McNeill, Diane/Sweeny Ind School Dist	5	54
McNelly, Curt/Miles Ind School Dist	9	326
McNutt, Jamie/Winona Ind School Dist	16,82	339
McOllum, Brenda/Lake Dallas Ind School Dist	9,57,274	122
McPhaul, Tracey/Reagan Co Ind School Dist	73,295	321
McPherson, Cindy/North Hopkins Ind School Dist	4	231
McPherson, Diane/Happy Ind School Dist	4	342
McPherson, Liuren/Blum Ind School Dist	31,69,83,88	227
McPherson, Richard/Blum Ind School Dist	67	227
McPherson, Robert/North Hopkins Ind School Dist	67	231
McQuagge, Dina/Freer Ind School Dist	33,38	128
McQuagge, Steve/Freer Ind School Dist	67	128
McQuarters, Alvin/Irving Ind School Dist	73,98,295	109
McQuary, Beverly/Mildred Ind School Dist	2	300
McSpadden, Karie/Leander Ind School Dist	68	396
McSwain, James/Houston ISD-West Area	15	193
McSwain, Mike/Brock Ind School Dist	2,19	312
McTee, Sonya/Trenton Ind School Dist	4	147
McVey, Tom/Crowell Ind School Dist	6	149
McVicars, Shaun/Forsan Ind School Dist	73,286	234
McWhorter, Claudia/Eanes Ind School Dist	71	370
McWilliams, Dana/McCamey Ind School Dist	5,295,297	377
McWilliams, Jay/Big Spring Ind School Dist	1	233
Mead, Misti/Deer Park Ind School Dist	60	186
Mead, Steve/Aldine Ind School Dist	67	179
Meador, Jeff/Granbury Ind School Dist	71	230
Meador, Tim/Matagorda Ind School Dist	73,295,297	275
Meadow, Aaron/Hempstead Ind School Dist	88	384
Meadow, Myghan/Menard Ind School Dist	58	285
Meadows, Kelly/Little Cypress Mauriceville SD	7	308
Meadows, Tonia/Friendswood Ind Sch Dist	286,295	160
Means, Whitney/Three Rivers Ind School Dist	4	268
Mears, Connie/Redwater Ind School Dist	5	49
Meaux, Robert, Dr/Humble Ind School Dist	76	195
Mechler, Patricia/Medina Valley Ind School Dist	7	284
Medcalf, Melissa/Franklin Ind School Dist	58	325
Medders, Stacey/Anahuac Ind School Dist	3	71
Medellin, Raul/Ysleta Ind School Dist	294	137
Medina, Fernando, Dr/Austin Ind School Dist	68	366
Medina, Marie/Mansfield Ind School Dist	39,81	356
Medina, Raymond/China Spring Ind School Dist	73,295	278
Medlin, Candy/Cypress-Fairbanks Ind Sch Dist	79	184
Medlin, Mike/Royse City Ind School Dist	274	326
Medlock, T/Hamilton Ind School Dist	67	176
Meek, Donnie/Newton Ind School Dist	67	301
Meek, John/Bowie Ind School Dist	3	289
Meek, Kevin/Ft Elliott Cons Ind Sch Dist	27	390
Meek, Mike/Iraan-Sheffield Ind Sch Dist	1,11	316
Meek, Sherry/Anson Ind School Dist	38,83	249
Meek, Stacey/Iraan-Sheffield Ind Sch Dist	16	316
Meek, Tricia/Bells Ind School Dist	1,11	165
Meeks, Allen/Magnolia Ind School Dist	3	292
Meeks, Mike/Lubbock Ind School Dist	6	269
Meff, Jeff/Snook Ind School Dist	8	59
Meier, Susan/Amherst Ind School Dist	2	260
Meier, Tracy/Darrouzett Ind School Dist	273	267
Meigh, Tamara/Crosby Ind School Dist	50	183
Meinzer, Tyke/Haskell Cons Ind School Dist	67	210
Meisel, Emily/Hudson Ind School Dist	16	17
Meisenheimer, Fred/Pleasant Grove Ind School Dist	67	49
Mejia, Hector/Laredo Ind School Dist	2	386
Melendez, Patricia/Weatherford Ind School Dist	2,298	313
Melendrez, Irene/Crystal City Ind School Dist	5	407
Melius, Anette/Hartley Ind School Dist	2	209

1 Superintendent	16 Instructional Media Svcs	30 Adult Education	44 Science Sec	58 Special Education K-12	72 Summer School	88 Alternative/At Risk	277 Remedial Math K-12
2 Bus/Finance/Purchasing	17 Chief Operations Officer	31 Career/Sch-to-Work K-12	45 Math K-12	59 Special Education Elem	73 Instructional Tech	89 Multi-Cultural Curriculum	280 Literacy Coach
3 Buildings And Grounds	18 Chief Academic Officer	32 Career/Sch-to-Work Elem	46 Math Elem	60 Special Education Sec	74 Inservice Training	90 Social Work	285 STEM
4 Food Service	19 Chief Financial Officer	33 Career/Sch-to-Work Sec	47 Math Sec	61 Foreign/World Lang K-12	75 Marketing/Distributive	91 Safety/Security	286 Digital Learning
5 Transportation	20 Art K-12	34 Early Childhood Ed	48 English/Lang Arts K-12	62 Foreign/World Lang Elem	76 Info Systems	92 Magnet School	288 Common Core Standards
6 Athletic	21 Art Elem	35 Health/Phys Education	49 English/Lang Arts Elem	63 Foreign/World Lang Sec	77 Psychological Assess	93 Parental Involvement	294 Accountability
7 Health Services	22 Art Sec	36 Guidance Services K-12	50 English/Lang Arts Sec	64 Religious Education K-12	78 Affirmative Action	95 Tech Prep Program	295 Network System
8 Curric/Instruct K-12	23 Music K-12	37 Guidance Services Elem	51 Reading K-12	65 Religious Education Elem	79 Student Personnel	97 Chief Information Officer	296 Title II Programs
9 Curric/Instruct Elem	24 Music Elem	38 Guidance Services Sec	52 Reading Elem	66 Religious Education Sec	80 Driver Ed/Safety	98 Chief Technology Officer	297 Webmaster
10 Curric/Instruct Sec	25 Music Sec	39 Social Studies K-12	53 Reading Sec	67 School Board President	81 Gifted/Talented	270 Character Education	298 Grant Writer/Ptnrships
11 Federal Program	26 Business Education	40 Social Studies Elem	54 Remedial Reading K-12	68 Teacher Personnel	82 Video Services	271 Migrant Education	750 Chief Innovation Officer
12 Title I	27 Career & Tech Ed	41 Social Studies Sec	55 Remedial Reading Elem	69 Academic Assessment	83 Substance Abuse Prev	273 Teacher Mentor	751 Chief of Staff
13 Title V	28 Technology Education	42 Science K-12	56 Remedial Reading Sec	70 Research/Development	84 Erate	274 Before/After Sch	752 Social Emotional Learning
15 Asst Superintendent	29 Family/Consumer Science	43 Science Elem	57 Bilingual/ELL	71 Public Information	85 AIDS Education	275 Response to Intervention	

TX-T60

Texas School Directory
DISTRICT PERSONNEL INDEX

NAME/District	JOB FUNCTIONS	PAGE
Mello, Cynthia, Sr/*Diocese of Brownsville Ed Off*	1,11	226
Mellon, Neal/*Windthorst Ind School Dist*	58	20
Melton, Jennifer/*Rains Ind School Dist*	58	320
Melton, Melissa/*Rockwall Ind School Dist*	58	325
Melton, Paula/*Peaster Ind School Dist*	4	313
Melton, Ronnie/*Royal Ind School Dist*	27,31	384
Melton, Teresa/*Leveretts Chapel Ind Sch Dist*	271	328
Menard, Joe/*Buna Ind School Dist*	3,5	240
Menchaca, Heidi/*Sinton Ind School Dist*	271	332
Menchaca, Tani/*Priddy Ind School Dist*	271	289
Mendelsohn, Allison/*Waxahachie Ind School Dist*	76	142
Mendez, Christopher/*Whiteface Con Ind School Dist*	280	75
Mendez, Daniel/*Comal Ind School Dist*	75	87
Mendez, Elvira/*Wilson Ind School Dist*	271	273
Mendez, Eric/*Cypress-Fairbanks Ind Sch Dist*	91	184
Mendez, Fernando/*Poteet Ind School Dist*	4	21
Mendez, Joe/*Hereford Ind School Dist*	3,16,17,73,84,286,295	119
Mendez, Marco/*Carrizo Spgs Cons Ind SD*	73,76,84,295	127
Mendez, Patricia/*Brooks Co Ind School Dist*	34,57,58,69	57
Mendez, Porfirio/*Kingsville Ind School Dist*	23	257
Mendez, Ralph/*Mercedes Ind School Dist*	2	221
Mendiola, Carolyn/*Mercedes Ind School Dist*	1	221
Mendoza, David/*Brazosport Ind School Dist*	28,73,76,295	52
Mendoza, John/*Donna Ind School Dist*	88	215
Mendoza, Lisa/*Robstown Ind School Dist*	4	305
Menefee, Deborah/*Willis Ind School Dist*	73	294
Menefee, Melonie/*Buffalo Ind School Dist*	82	264
Meng, Debi/*Bridgeport Ind School Dist*	2	402
Menger, Dinah/*Ft Worth Ind School Dist*	24	349
Menjivar, Chelsea/*Whitewright Ind School Dist*	2	168
Menking, Glenn/*Gonzales Ind School Dist*	67	164
Menn, Dina/*Yorktown Ind School Dist*	37	118
Menton, Lisa/*Red Oak Ind School Dist*	27	142
Mercado, Ana/*Gholson Ind School Dist*	73	279
Mercado, Rosanna/*South San Antonio Ind Sch Dist*	34	42
Merchant, Brian/*Hurst-Euless-Bedford ISD*	5	353
Merchant, Laura/*Forney Ind School Dist*	58	251
Mercier, Donald/*Sinton Ind School Dist*	3	332
Merek, Rodney/*Huntsville Ind School Dist*	3	383
Merka, Carla/*Pasadena Ind School Dist*	2,15,19	198
Merkel, Valerie/*Perryton Ind School Dist*	36	307
Merrick, Brandy/*Plainview Ind School Dist*	68	175
Merrit, Ryan/*Texas Dept of Education*	27	1
Merritt, Kelli/*Lamesa Ind School Dist*	67	117
Merts, Erin/*Yorktown Ind School Dist*	68	118
Mertz, Michael/*Fairfield Ind School Dist*	5	156
Mesa, Brenda/*Birdville Ind School Dist*	45	346
Messer, Zann/*Munday Consolidated Ind SD*	81	259
Messiner, Gwen/*Goodrich Ind School Dist*	2	316
Messinger, Steve/*City View Ind School Dist*	295	391
Messner, Lisa/*Highland Park Ind School Dist*	2	319
Metcalf, Jill/*Aldine Ind School Dist*	5	179
Metcalf, Lisa/*Abilene Ind School Dist*	2	360
Mettauer, Matthew/*Center Ind School Dist*	67	334
Mettlen, Carol/*Diboll Ind School Dist*	38	17
Metts, Rochelle/*Central Ind School Dist*	58	17
Metz, Johnny/*Newton Ind School Dist*	15	301
Metzgar, Heather/*Marble Falls Ind School Dist*	10	60
Metzger, Rebecca/*Joshua Ind School Dist*	2,19	248
Metzig, Mike/*Ropes Ind School Dist*	67	229
Metzler, Donald/*Callisburg Ind School Dist*	1,11	90
Metzler, John/*Forestburg Ind School Dist*	1	290
Meyer, Brenda/*Taft Ind School Dist*	8	332
Meyer, Denise/*Magnolia Ind School Dist*	71	292
Meyer, Lynette/*Ft Bend Ind School Dist*	286	149
Meyer, Randall/*Wharton Ind School Dist*	3,15,68	390
Meyer, Rosanne/*Calallen Ind School Dist*	9,57	302
Meyer, Steve/*Bosqueville Ind School Dist*	3	278
Meyerdirk, Scott/*Gunter Ind School Dist*	67	166
Meyers, Honey Bee/*Brackett Ind School Dist*	4	257
Meyers, Matthew, Dr/*Valley View Ind School Dist*	57,271	225
Meyners, Rusty/*Eustace Ind School Dist*	295	214
Meysembourg, Lisa/*Schulenburg Ind School Dist*	1,11	147
Meysembourg, Lisa/*Woodville Ind School Dist*	1,57	375
Meza-Chavez, Jeannie, Dr/*San Elizario Ind School Dist*	1	135
Meza, Rito/*Socorro Ind School Dist*	5	135
Meza, Tina/*Comstock Ind School Dist*	2	379
Meza, Waymond/*San Felipe-Del Rio Cons Ind SD*	67	379
Mica, Brian/*East Bernard Ind Sch Dist*	67	389
Mica, Peggy/*Round Rock Ind School Dist*	27	398
Michael, Amanda/*Skidmore Tynan Ind SD*	7	25
Michaelewicz, Paul/*Florence Ind School Dist*	1	395
Michalec, Rose/*Archdiocese Galveston-Houston*	2	203
Michels, Paul/*Natalia Ind School Dist*	2	284
Micinski, Gary/*Irving Ind School Dist*	2,19	109
Mickelson, Kristi/*Mullin Ind School Dist*	8,11,83,271,294	288
Mickelson, Kristi/*Mullin Ind School Dist*	1,73	288
Mickelson, Steve/*Brookesmith Ind School Dist*	1	58
Miculka, James/*Northside Ind School Dist*	20,23	36
Middleton, Mace/*Happy Ind School Dist*	67	342
Middleton, Maryann/*Crowley Ind School Dist*	8	347
Migel, Galvan/*Tidehaven Ind School Dist*	5	276
Migl, Leann/*Vysehrad Ind School Dist*	59,275	263
Mijares, Ismael/*Eagle Pass Ind School Dist*	2,15	276
Mijares, Samuel/*Eagle Pass Ind School Dist*	8,15,81,288	276
Mika-Mendez, Leann/*Miles Ind School Dist*	16	326
Mika, Cyndy, Dr/*Little Elm Ind School Dist*	11,15,70,294	124
Mikeal, Laura/*Hudson Ind School Dist*	34	17
Mikesh, Holly/*Center Ind School Dist*	68	334
Mikeska, Charles/*West Ind School Dist*	2,3,91	282
Mikolaycik, Ryan/*Lake Travis Ind School Dist*	4	370
Miksch, Brett/*Sweeny Ind School Dist*	6	54
Milacek, Jim/*Aubrey Ind School Dist*	67	120
Milam, Dwain/*Jacksboro Ind Sch Dist*	1	239
Milan, Cynthia/*Ft Stockton Ind School Dist*	7	315
Miles, Stacy/*Tyler Ind School Dist*	11	337
Miles, Tami/*North Lamar Ind School Dist*	2,296	259
Miles, Tina/*Westbrook Ind School Dist*	59	289
Milini, Christophe/*Pleasanton Ind School Dist*	4	21
Milla, Jennifer/*Edgewood Ind School Dist*	7	31
Millender, Roger/*Brownsboro Ind School Dist*	5	213
Miller-Baker, Mary, Dr/*Edgewood Ind School Dist*	34	31
Miller, Alex/*Hempstead Ind School Dist*	73,98,295,297	384
Miller, Amy/*Wortham Ind School Dist*	83,85	156
Miller, Anna/*Lumberton Ind School Dist*	71	178
Miller, Bethany/*Southland Ind School Dist*	11,296	162
Miller, Billie/*Quinlan Ind School Dist*	2	237
Miller, Brian/*Lackland Ind School Dist*	67	34
Miller, Bryan/*Leander Ind School Dist*	79	396
Miller, Chris/*Columbia Brazoria ISD*	15	52
Miller, Christy/*Palacios Ind School Dist*	2	275
Miller, Craig/*Dallas Ind School Dist*	91	98
Miller, Darlene/*Bovina Ind School Dist*	2	314
Miller, Dawn/*Midland Ind School Dist*	58,77	285
Miller, Doug/*Detroit Ind School Dist*	67	322
Miller, Erica/*Italy Ind School Dist*	69,88,271	140
Miller, Jacquelyn/*Floresville Ind School Dist*	15,68,78,79,273	400
Miller, Jaime/*Ector Co Ind School Dist*	280	130
Miller, Jeff/*Rockdale Ind School Dist*	6	287
Miller, Jennifer/*Birdville Ind School Dist*	39,59	346
Miller, Jennifer/*Cypress-Fairbanks Ind Sch Dist*	73	184
Miller, Jimmy/*Roosevelt Ind School Dist*	6	271
Miller, Julie/*Irving Ind School Dist*	8	109
Miller, Karen/*Eagle Mtn-Saginaw Ind Sch Dist*	74,273	348
Miller, Karie/*Holliday Ind School Dist*	73,84,286	19
Miller, Karin/*Texas Dept of Education*	48,51	1
Miller, Kay/*Bandera Ind School Dist*	5	23
Miller, Kelly/*Dawson Ind School Dist*	2	299
Miller, Leah/*Copperas Cove Ind School Dist*	31,38	92
Miller, Les/*Poth Ind School Dist*	67	401
Miller, Lyle/*Floydada Ind School Dist*	67	148
Miller, M-Lynn/*Claude Ind School Dist*	73,76,286	20
Miller, Matt/*Carroll Independent Sch Dist*	15,68	347
Miller, Melonie/*La Gloria Ind School Dist*	16,57,59,273	245
Miller, Mike/*Judson Ind School Dist*	6	33
Miller, Mikeal/*Van Alstyne Ind School Dist*	6	168
Miller, Monica/*Azle Ind School Dist*	2,11	345
Miller, Neal/*La Grange Ind School Dist*	3,4,5	147
Miller, Ned/*Iowa Park Consolidated Ind SD*	5	392
Miller, Pam/*Avinger Ind School Dist*	2	70
Miller, Patty/*Itasca Ind School Dist*	3	228
Miller, Paul/*Clear Creek Ind School Dist*	3	158

DISTRICT PERSONNEL INDEX

Market Data Retrieval

NAME/District	JOB FUNCTIONS	PAGE
Miller, Paul/McGregor Ind School Dist	7,15,91	280
Miller, Randi/Chico Ind School Dist	6	403
Miller, Randy/Darrouzett Ind School Dist	67	267
Miller, Rebecca/Del Valle Ind School Dist	42	369
Miller, Richard/Center Ind School Dist	73,76	334
Miller, Robert/Edgewood Ind School Dist	69,70	31
Miller, Ryne/Marion Ind School Dist	6	172
Miller, Sarah/Sterling City Ind School Dist	57,58	342
Miller, Shawna/Lewisville Ind School Dist	74	122
Miller, Stan/Bovina Ind School Dist	73,84,295	314
Miller, Stefanie/Spurger Ind School Dist	92,271	375
Miller, Stephen/Olton Ind School Dist	295	261
Miller, Toby/Southland Ind School Dist	1	162
Miller, Toni/Kemp Ind School Dist	27	252
Miller, Torri/Winnsboro Ind School Dist	8,11,58,76,286,288,298	405
Miller, Wade/Tuloso-Midway Ind School Dist	6	305
Miller, William/Valentine Ind School Dist	67	241
Millerick, Tim/Sherman Ind School Dist	67	167
Millican, Chris/Aubrey Ind School Dist	73,295	120
Milligan, Mida, Dr/Garland Ind School Dist	71	105
Milling, Mike/New Caney Ind School Dist	15	293
Millner, Jeff/Canyon Ind School Dist	3	320
Mills-Oller, Kim/Post Ind School Dist	8,11,15,69,270,273	162
Mills, Andy/Rice Ind School Dist	6	300
Mills, Brent/Woodson Ind School Dist	8,57,76	363
Mills, Brooke/Pawnee Ind School Dist	7	25
Mills, Charla/Ralls Ind School Dist	59	94
Mills, Cheryl/Poteet Ind School Dist	1,57	21
Mills, Debi/Wichita Falls Ind School Dist	7	392
Mills, Dee Ann/Brock Ind School Dist	12,298	312
Mills, Linda/Randolph Field Ind School Dist	68	39
Mills, Randy/Fruitvale Ind School Dist	98,295	380
Mills, Sarah/Childress Ind School Dist	8,11,58	74
Mills, Sheri/Carroll Independent Sch Dist	67	347
Milton, Kathy/Richardson Ind School Dist	69	112
Milton, Kathy/Royse City Ind School Dist	69,294	326
Milton, Randy/Shepherd Ind School Dist	4	330
Milum, Jessy/Utopia Ind School Dist	1,288	378
Mims, Jason/Forsan Ind School Dist	2	234
Mims, Mysti/Forsan Ind School Dist	8,57,69,88,271	234
Mimyard, Herb/Goose Creek Cons Ind Sch Dist	3	187
Mincher, Diane/Tioga Ind School Dist	11,88	167
Ming, Keith/Liberty Ind School Dist	33	266
Minix, Winston/Grand Prairie Ind School Dist	27,31	107
Minor, Josh/Hurst-Euless-Bedford ISD	3	353
Minor, Rodney/Int'l Leadership of Texas Dist	5	108
Minor, Todd/Montague Ind School Dist	3,5	290
Minshew, Jill/Llano Ind School Dist	2,19	268
Minter, Alvis/Mexia Ind School Dist	3,5	267
Minter, Keith/Hooks Ind School Dist	73,76,295	48
Minter, Larry/Big Sandy Ind School Dist	6	376
Minyard, Rusty/Evadale Ind School Dist	83,288	240
Miori, Kim/La Grange Ind School Dist	57	147
Miramontes, Gerogina/Tornillo Ind School Dist	58	137
Miranda, Mark/Spring Ind School Dist	3,17	202
Miranda, Patricia/Amarillo Ind School Dist	7,85	317
Miranda, Roxanne/Carrizo Spgs Cons Ind SD	38	127
Mircovich, Karen/Ingleside Ind School Dist	11,57,69,83	331
Mircovich, Troy/Ingleside Ind School Dist	1	331
Mireles, James/Texhoma Ind School Dist	1	336
Mires, Kelly/Coppell Ind School Dist	68	98
Mitchel, Sunny/Bellevue Ind School Dist	295	74
Mitchell, Byron/Elgin Ind School Dist	67	24
Mitchell, Cindy/Boles Ind School Dist	3,5	235
Mitchell, Gary/Broaddus Ind School Dist	16,73,295	329
Mitchell, Jimmie/Manor Ind School Dist	6	371
Mitchell, Lakeisha/Richardson Ind School Dist	44	112

NAME/District	JOB FUNCTIONS	PAGE
Mitchell, Laurie/Katy Ind School Dist	75	151
Mitchell, Michelle/Pine Tree Ind School Dist	4	170
Mitchell, Pam/Pampa Ind School Dist	8,11,15,30,72	165
Mitchell, Pamela/Livingston Ind School Dist	58	317
Mitchell, Renee/Sweeny Ind School Dist	36	54
Mitchell, Richard/Strawn Ind School Dist	1,11	311
Mitchell, Shaelee/Weatherford Ind School Dist	7,83	313
Mitchell, Sharon/Lake Dallas Ind School Dist	5	122
Mitchell, Sherry/Lubbock Ind School Dist	73,286	270
Mitchell, Suzane/Hays Cons Ind School Dist	27	211
Mitchum, Mary/Georgetown Ind School Dist	76,79	395
Mixon, Jason/San Augustine Ind School Dist	8,11,69	329
Mize, Brenda/Burleson Ind School Dist	2	246
Mize, Cody/Winona Ind School Dist	1	339
Mizell, Matthew/Trinidad Ind School Dist	8,274	214
Moats, James/Lindsay Ind School Dist	73	91
Moats, Mara/Edinburg Cons Ind School Dist	74,285	216
Mobley, Billy/Ballinger Ind School Dist	73	326
Mobley, Shane/Sealy Ind School Dist	6	22
Moczgemba, Roxanne/Stockdale Ind School Dist	11,296	401
Moczygemba, Charlotte/Stratford Ind School Dist	4	336
Moczygemba, Cynthia/Randolph Field Ind School Dist	4	39
Moczygemba, Erica/Granger Ind School Dist	7	396
Moczygemba, Lisa/Karnes City Ind School Dist	11,57,88,271	250
Moczygemba, Randy/New Braunfels Ind School Dist	1	88
Moczygemba, Roxanne/Stockdale Ind School Dist	8,69	401
Mode, Eileen/Kennedale Ind School Dist	3	355
Modgling, Jack/Dripping Springs Ind Sch Dist	58,275	210
Modisette, Susan/Plano Ind School Dist	15,36,93	82
Moebes, Todd/Lockhart Ind School Dist	6	61
Moehlig, Scott/Alief Ind School Dist	6	181
Moeller, Delia/Flatonia Ind School Dist	16,73	147
Moffatt, Jared/Van Ind School Dist	6	381
Moffett, John/Claude Ind School Dist	6,83,88,273,275,294	20
Moffett, Lance/Fredericksburg Ind School Dist	6	163
Mogg, Bette/Mesquite Ind School Dist	4	110
Mohan, Cody/Cayuga Ind School Dist	6	14
Moharam, Hossiny/Randolph Field Ind School Dist	3	39
Moiser, Ginny/Dublin Ind School Dist	2	143
Mojica, Alejandro/Victoria Ind School Dist	57,89,271	382
Moke, Martha/New Braunfels Ind School Dist	58	88
Molano, Velma/Hidalgo Ind School Dist	7	217
Molder, Gail/McCamey Ind School Dist	2,11,26	377
Molina, Alexandra/McAllen Ind School Dist	4	220
Molina, James/Poth Ind School Dist	3	401
Molina, Nancy/Moody Ind School Dist	16,69,73,286	281
Molina, Robert/Runge Ind School Dist	67	251
Molinar, Frank/White Settlement Ind Sch Dist	1	357
Molinar, Karen/Ft Worth Ind School Dist	751	349
Molinar, Monica/Aubrey Ind School Dist	57,271	120
Molinar, Savannah/Brackett Ind School Dist	7	257
Molsey, Micah/Nederland Ind School Dist	67	242
Money, Tracy/Forney Ind School Dist	4	251
Moneyhon, Jennifer/Mason Ind School Dist	7,35	275
Monita, Venicia/Stockdale Ind School Dist	57	401
Monjaras, Bonney/Region 6 Ed Service Center	68	384
Monjaras, Mario/Pettus Ind School Dist	4	25
Monk, Bruce/Lovelady Ind School Dist	67	233
Monk, Kristin/Sulphur Springs Ind Sch Dist	9,15	232
Monreal, Julian/Southside Ind School Dist	3	43
Monroe, Judy/Tenaha Ind School Dist	58	335
Monroe, Scott/Carrollton-Farmers Branch ISD	16,73,76,295	96
Monroe, Tanya, Dr/Comfort Ind School Dist	1	254
Monschke, Debbie/Denton Ind School Dist	2	120
Monsivais, Cindy/United Ind School Dist	47	387
Monsizias, Sam/Tahoka Ind School Dist	5,91	273
Montalbo, Nancy/Splendora Ind School Dist	4	294

1 Superintendent	16 Instructional Media Svcs	30 Adult Education	44 Science Sec	58 Special Education K-12	72 Summer School	88 Alternative/At Risk	277 Remedial Math K-12
2 Bus/Finance/Purchasing	17 Chief Operations Officer	31 Career/Sch-to-Work K-12	45 Math K-12	59 Special Education Elem	73 Instructional Tech	89 Multi-Cultural Curriculum	280 Literacy Coach
3 Buildings And Grounds	18 Chief Academic Officer	32 Career/Sch-to-Work Elem	46 Math Elem	60 Special Education Sec	74 Inservice Training	90 Social Work	285 STEM
4 Food Service	19 Chief Financial Officer	33 Career/Sch-to-Work Sec	47 Math Sec	61 Foreign/World Lang K-12	75 Marketing/Distributive	91 Safety/Security	286 Digital Learning
5 Transportation	20 Art K-12	34 Early Childhood Ed	48 English/Lang Arts K-12	62 Foreign/World Lang Elem	76 Info Systems	92 Magnet School	288 Common Core Standards
6 Athletic	21 Art Elem	35 Health/Phys Education	49 English/Lang Arts Elem	63 Foreign/World Lang Sec	77 Psychological Assess	93 Parental Involvement	294 Accountability
7 Health Services	22 Art Sec	36 Guidance Services K-12	50 English/Lang Arts Sec	64 Religious Education K-12	78 Affirmative Action	95 Tech Prep Program	295 Network System
8 Curric/Instruct K-12	23 Music K-12	37 Guidance Services Elem	51 Reading K-12	65 Religious Education Elem	79 Student Personnel	97 Chief Infomation Officer	296 Title II Programs
9 Curric/Instruct Elem	24 Music Elem	38 Guidance Services Sec	52 Reading Elem	66 Religious Education Sec	80 Driver Ed/Safety	98 Chief Technology Officer	297 Webmaster
10 Curric/Instruct Sec	25 Music Sec	39 Social Studies K-12	53 Reading Sec	67 School Board President	81 Gifted/Talented	270 Character Education	298 Grant Writer/Ptnrships
11 Federal Program	26 Business Education	40 Social Studies Elem	54 Remedial Reading K-12	68 Teacher Personnel	82 Video Services	271 Migrant Education	750 Chief Innovation Officer
12 Title I	27 Career & Tech Ed	41 Social Studies Sec	55 Remedial Reading Elem	69 Academic Assessment	83 Substance Abuse Prev	273 Teacher Mentor	751 Chief of Staff
13 Title V	28 Technology Education	42 Science K-12	56 Remedial Reading Sec	70 Research/Development	84 Erate	274 Before/After Sch	752 Social Emotional Learning
15 Asst Superintendent	29 Family/Consumer Science	43 Science Elem	57 Bilingual/ELL	71 Public Information	85 AIDS Education	275 Response To Intervention	

TX-T62

Texas School Directory

DISTRICT PERSONNEL INDEX

NAME/District	JOB FUNCTIONS	PAGE
Montalvo, Connie/*Harlandale Ind School Dist*	16	32
Montalvo, Pamela/*Sharyland Ind School Dist*	8,15	224
Montalvo, Roldan/*Jim Hogg Co Ind School Dist*	6	244
Montelongo, Anthony/*Bushland Ind School Dist*	295,297	319
Montemayor, Adrian/*San Perlita Ind School Dist*	8,58	394
Montemayor, Teresa/*Brownfield Ind Sch Dist*	2,19,68	362
Montenegro, Efren/*Idea Public Schools*	73	217
Montero, Rosalinda/*Alamo Heights Ind School Dist*	297	30
Montes, Alex/*Clifton Ind School Dist*	67	46
Montes, Wayne/*Wells Ind School Dist*	67	73
Montez, Garla/*Aquilla Ind School Dist*	36,57,69	227
Montez, Garla/*Aquilla Ind School Dist*	36,69	227
Montgomery, Ava/*Alief Ind School Dist*	8,15	181
Montgomery, Christopher/*Tomball Ind School Dist*	295	203
Montgomery, Clay/*Spearman Ind School Dist*	1	177
Montgomery, Gina/*River Road Ind School Dist*	84,295	319
Montgomery, Gina/*River Road Ind School Dist*	73,295	319
Montgomery, John/*Allen Ind School Dist*	67	76
Montgomery, Kelli/*Birdville Ind School Dist*	16,286	346
Montgomery, Nancy/*Strawn Ind School Dist*	4	311
Montgomery, Rhiannon/*Weatherford Ind School Dist*	73	313
Montgomery, Rhiannon/*Weatherford Ind School Dist*	73	313
Montgomery, Robert/*Albany Ind School Dist*	67	334
Montgomery, Robert/*McKinney Ind School Dist*	5,91	80
Montgomery, Tracy/*Weatherford Ind School Dist*	295	313
Monto, Roseo/*Bovina Ind School Dist*	88	314
Monzingo, Denise, Dr/*Rockdale Ind School Dist*	1	287
Moody, Darcas/*Splendora Ind School Dist*	5	294
Moody, David, Dr/*Pearland Ind School Dist*	15,68,79	53
Moody, Leslie/*Westbrook Ind School Dist*	2	289
Moody, Sam/*Valley Mills Ind School Dist*	6	47
Moody, Steve/*Iowa Park Consolidated Ind SD*	1	392
Moody, Tania/*Levelland Ind School Dist*	67	229
Moon, Dawn/*Brookeland Ind School Dist*	7	240
Moon, Lisa/*Bruceville-Eddy Ind Sch Dist*	7,85	278
Mooney, Charles/*Plainview Ind School Dist*	3	175
Mooney, Daiann/*Grapevine-Colleyville Ind SD*	2,19	353
Mooneyham, Joe/*Waller Ind School Dist*	5,91	384
Moore-Ellis, Pam/*Clear Creek Ind School Dist*	77	158
Moore, Brian/*Lamar Cons Ind School Dist*	36,69,70,294	153
Moore, Brooks/*Aledo Ind School Dist*	73,98,295	312
Moore, Bryan/*Community Ind School Dist*	2,19,288	78
Moore, Bryan/*Krum Ind School Dist*	2	122
Moore, Candice/*Aldine Ind School Dist*	76,79	179
Moore, Carmen/*Gholson Ind School Dist*	2,13,296	279
Moore, Carson/*Gholson Ind School Dist*	3	279
Moore, Chalet/*Early Ind School Dist*	58	58
Moore, Chenda/*Pearland Ind School Dist*	36,83,88,275	53
Moore, Cheri/*George West Ind School Dist*	67	268
Moore, Chris/*Richardson Ind School Dist*	71	112
Moore, Cindy/*Canadian Ind School Dist*	2	213
Moore, Courtney/*Cuero Ind School Dist*	67	117
Moore, David/*Ft Bend Ind School Dist*	3	149
Moore, Deanna/*Schulenburg Ind School Dist*	58	148
Moore, Derik/*Sheldon Ind School Dist*	71	200
Moore, Douglas/*Balmorhea Ind School Dist*	1,11	323
Moore, George/*Texarkana Ind School Dist*	15,88	50
Moore, Hollis/*Venus Ind School Dist*	11,15,83	249
Moore, James/*Wells Ind School Dist*	1	73
Moore, Jamie/*Panhandle Ind School Dist*	2	69
Moore, Jamye/*Cotton Center Ind School Dist*	27	174
Moore, Janan/*Livingston Ind School Dist*	8,18,69,74	317
Moore, Janette/*Alto Ind School Dist*	57	72
Moore, Jerry/*Celina Ind School Dist*	5	77
Moore, Jonathan/*Galena Park Ind School Dist*	15	186
Moore, Kala/*Jacksonville Ind School Dist*	68	73
Moore, Karen/*Campbell Ind School Dist*	16,286	235
Moore, Kathy/*Elgin Ind School Dist*	298	24
Moore, Kelly/*Union Grove Ind School Dist*	1	377
Moore, Kimberley/*Big Sandy Ind School Dist*	4	316
Moore, Kimberly/*West Oso Ind School Dist*	285	306
Moore, Leland, Dr/*Coldspring-Oakhurst Cons ISD*	1	330
Moore, Lorenzo/*Houston Ind School Dist*	77	188
Moore, Mary-Jane/*Tarkington Ind School Dist*	8,11,57,76,85,88,296,298	266
Moore, Megan/*Texline Ind School Dist*	31,90	95
Moore, Nicole/*Houston ISD-South Area*	15	192
Moore, Paula/*Gainesville Ind School Dist*	11,57,68,83,88,271,298	91
Moore, Ricky/*Rivercrest Ind School Dist*	5	322
Moore, Rob/*Lometa Ind School Dist*	8,16,31,73,273	262
Moore, Robin/*Skidmore Tynan Ind SD*	2	25
Moore, Rocio/*United Ind School Dist*	71	387
Moore, Sandra/*Richardson Ind School Dist*	68,273	112
Moore, Shalee/*Bangs Ind School Dist*	58	58
Moore, Shane/*New Home Ind School Dist*	73	273
Moore, Shawna/*Nueces Canyon Cons Ind SD*	8,11,36,59,69,88,296	131
Moore, Sherry/*Academy Ind School Dist*	2	26
Moore, Sheryl/*Sealy Ind School Dist*	1	22
Moore, Stacie/*Avery Ind School Dist*	67	322
Moore, Tammy/*Willis Ind School Dist*	2,15	294
Moore, Teresa/*Midland Ind School Dist*	11	285
Moore, Terri/*Galena Park Ind School Dist*	15,71,74	186
Moore, Terry/*Jefferson Ind School Dist*	4	274
Moore, Valorie/*Navasota Ind School Dist*	2	172
Moos, Beth/*Pleasanton Ind School Dist*	16,82	21
Moos, Houston/*Sanford-Fritch Ind School Dist*	6	238
Mora, Ben/*Harlandale Ind School Dist*	2	32
Mora, Bernice/*Dell City Ind School Dist*	57	234
Mora, Sylvia/*Keene Ind School Dist*	7,35,85	248
Morales, Edward/*Albany Ind School Dist*	10	334
Morales, Gilbert/*Carrizo Spgs Cons Ind SD*	58	127
Morales, Luke/*Navarro Ind School Dist*	91	173
Morales, Marc/*Bishop Cons Ind School Dist*	67	302
Morales, Marissa/*La Joya Ind School Dist*	7	219
Morales, Melba/*Alvin Ind School Dist*	68	51
Morales, Pedro/*Zapata Co Ind School Dist*	3,5	406
Morales, Rebecca/*United Ind School Dist*	11,95,296	387
Morales, Sylvia/*Edgewood Ind School Dist*	294	31
Morales, Sylvia/*Medina Valley Ind School Dist*	2	284
Moran, Bobbie/*Tom Bean Ind School Dist*	76	168
Moran, Chris/*Whitehouse Ind School Dist*	1	338
Moran, Kevin/*Waller Ind School Dist*	1	384
Morath, Mike/*Texas Dept of Education*	1	1
Morath, Mike/*Winters Ind School Dist*	7	327
Moree, Cody/*Apple Springs Ind School Dist*	2,6,19,31,273	374
Moree, Cody/*Apple Springs Ind School Dist*	1	374
Moreland, Byron/*Greenwood Ind School Dist*	11,15	285
Moreland, Gregg/*Lamesa Ind School Dist*	6	117
Moreland, Mikayle/*Boles Ind School Dist*	2,11,74,296	235
Moreno Hewitt, Andrea, Dr/*Natalia Ind School Dist*	10	284
Moreno-Hewitt, Andrea/*Medina Valley Ind School Dist*	8,57,69	284
Moreno-Recio, Pilar/*Goose Creek Cons Ind Sch Dist*	57	187
Moreno, Angela/*Lorenzo Ind School Dist*	31,54,69,83	94
Moreno, David/*Donna Ind School Dist*	27,33	215
Moreno, Edwardo/*Edinburg Cons Ind School Dist*	15,28,73,84,297	216
Moreno, Eleazar/*Weimar Ind School Dist*	16,76,295	87
Moreno, Emilia/*Region 14 Ed Service Center*	11,57	362
Moreno, Jose, Dr/*Robstown Ind School Dist*	1	305
Moreno, Lupe/*Comanche Ind School Dist*	5	89
Moreno, Raul/*Austin ISD Middle School Area*	15	369
Moreno, Raul/*Roma Ind School Dist*	67	341
Moreno, Rolando/*Valley View Ind School Dist*	2	225
Moreno, Rosi/*Robstown Ind School Dist*	7	305
Moreno, Ruben/*Judson Ind School Dist*	3	33
Morgan, Aaron/*Lamar Cons Ind School Dist*	3	153
Morgan, Amy/*Lumberton Ind School Dist*	7,85	178
Morgan, Bradley/*Buna Ind School Dist*	6	240
Morgan, Cammie/*Utopia Ind School Dist*	36,69,79,83,88,270	378
Morgan, Christi/*Sunnyvale Ind School Dist*	8,15,298	113
Morgan, Dana/*Clear Creek Ind School Dist*	27,31	158
Morgan, Dana/*Slocum ISD School Dist*	2,12	16
Morgan, Denise, Dr/*Campbell Ind School Dist*	1,288	235
Morgan, Joe/*Willis Ind School Dist*	3	294
Morgan, Karen/*Rogers Ind School Dist*	67	29
Morgan, Karen, Dr/*Temple Ind School Dist*	11,294,296	29
Morgan, Lindsay/*Tolar Ind School Dist*	11,58	230
Morgan, Lisa/*Amarillo Ind School Dist*	8,18,83,88	317
Morgan, Matt/*East Central Ind School Dist*	2	31
Morgan, Maxie/*Calvert Ind School Dist*	11,84	324
Morgan, Mike/*Belton Ind School Dist*	15,79	26
Morgan, Mike/*Waxahachie Ind School Dist*	79	142
Morgan, Randall/*Van Alstyne Ind School Dist*	67	168
Morgan, Tammy/*Pilot Point Ind School Dist*	8,69,74,273,275	125

DISTRICT PERSONNEL INDEX

Market Data Retrieval

NAME/District	JOB FUNCTIONS	PAGE
Morgan, Tiffany/*Mildred Ind School Dist*	36,69,83,85,270	300
Morgenroth, Connie/*Cypress-Fairbanks Ind Sch Dist*	2	183
Morin, Monica/*Driscoll Ind School Dist*	9,37,57,69,88,93,270	304
Morisak, Kim/*Forney Ind School Dist*	71,73,97,98	251
Morman, Leslie/*Buffalo Ind School Dist*	274	264
Morman, Tracey/*Amarillo Ind School Dist*	36,270	317
Morril, Rick/*Santa Fe Ind School Dist*	28,73	161
Morris-Kuentz, Holly/*Lake Travis Ind School Dist*	15	370
Morris-Surles, Cassandra, Dr/*Ft Worth Ind School Dist*	34	349
Morris, Adrienne/*McKinney Ind School Dist*	58,69,77	81
Morris, Adrienne/*Melissa Ind School Dist*	58,77	81
Morris, Bobby/*Montgomery Ind School Dist*	3,17	293
Morris, Brian, Dr/*Columbus Ind School Dist*	1	86
Morris, Candy/*Calallen Ind School Dist*	69	302
Morris, Carol/*Rogers Ind School Dist*	7	28
Morris, Charity/*Bland Ind School Dist*	69	235
Morris, Christine/*Balmorhea Ind School Dist*	58,286	323
Morris, Daphne/*Boerne Ind School Dist*	49,52	253
Morris, Doug/*Lamesa Ind School Dist*	8,11,57,83,286,288,296,298	117
Morris, Erich/*Magnolia Ind School Dist*	2,15	292
Morris, Helyn/*Chapel Hill Ind School Dist*	9	337
Morris, Jennie/*Weatherford Ind School Dist*	30	313
Morris, Jill, Dr/*Bryan Ind School Dist*	69,70,76	54
Morris, Katherine/*Sherman Ind School Dist*	27	167
Morris, Kelly/*Venus Ind School Dist*	68	249
Morris, Linda/*Richland Springs Ind Sch Dist*	2	332
Morris, Mary/*Hurst-Euless-Bedford ISD*	11,298	353
Morris, Nancy/*Wills Point Ind School Dist*	73	381
Morris, Roger/*Ector Ind School Dist*	5,275	146
Morris, Tabatha/*Harmony Ind School Dist*	57	376
Morris, Terry/*Klondike Ind School Dist*	5	117
Morris, Zack/*Aspermont Ind School Dist*	1	342
Morrison, Amber/*Holliday Ind School Dist*	7	19
Morrison, Blake/*Diboll Ind School Dist*	6	17
Morrison, Ginger/*Athens Ind School Dist*	11,68,83,296,298	213
Morrison, Michaelene/*Dayton Ind School Dist*	58	265
Morrison, Nancy/*Humble Ind School Dist*	67	195
Morrison, Neil/*Pittsburg Ind School Dist*	16,73,76,295,297	68
Morrison, Rebecca, Dr/*Edinburg Cons Ind School Dist*	2,15,72,274,296,298	216
Morrison, Todd/*Honey Grove Ind School Dist*	1,11	146
Morrison, Tommy/*Cherokee Ind School Dist*	67	332
Morrisson, Kayla/*Lorenzo Ind School Dist*	1,11	94
Morrow, Dan/*Martin's Mill Ind Sch Dist*	67	381
Morrow, Danny/*Van Ind School Dist*	2,3,19,76	381
Morrow, Kathy/*Newton Ind School Dist*	4	301
Morrow, Lenny/*Sands Consolidated ISD*	8,12	117
Morse, Debby/*Grand Saline Ind School Dist*	8,11,57,73,286,288,296,298	380
Morse, Tina/*Martin's Mill Ind Sch Dist*	4	381
Morton, Betsi/*Wichita Falls Ind School Dist*	88	392
Morton, Bonnie/*Spearman Ind School Dist*	16,82	177
Morton, James/*Eastland Ind School Dist*	6	129
Morton, Susan/*Winnsboro Ind School Dist*	1	405
Morton, Wade/*Eustace Ind School Dist*	91	214
Mosby, D'Anne/*Wylie Ind School Dist*	16	84
Moseley, Davy/*Miller Grove Ind School Dist*	73	231
Moseley, Larry/*Elgin Ind School Dist*	5	24
Moser, Kendra/*Caddo Mills Ind Sch Dist*	9	235
Moses, Cindy/*Region 9 Ed Service Center*	8,58,77,275	393
Moses, Joel/*Little Elm Ind School Dist*	3	124
Moses, Troy/*Cotton Center Ind School Dist*	58	174
Mosley, Alisha/*Lovelady Ind School Dist*	4	233
Mosley, Dana/*Lancaster Ind School Dist*	2	110
Mosley, J D/*Schertz-Cibolo-Univ City ISD*	3	173
Mosley, Jean/*Coppell Ind School Dist*	4	98
Moss, Darla/*Midland Ind School Dist*	2,19	285
Moss, Jennifer/*Connally Ind School Dist*	2	279
Moss, Ron/*Midland Ind School Dist*	36	285
Moss, Terri/*Bushland Ind School Dist*	58	319
Mossige, Teresa/*Lamar Cons Ind School Dist*	8,18,288	153
Mostella, Paul/*Tuloso-Midway Ind School Dist*	67	305
Motes, Melissa/*De Kalb Ind School Dist*	73	48
Motley, Kim/*Victoria Ind School Dist*	36	382
Mott, Lisa/*Waxahachie Ind School Dist*	8	142
Mott, Vernagene/*Pflugerville Ind School Dist*	67	371
Moucoulis, Olga/*Edgewood Ind School Dist*	15,751	31
Moulton, Jeannie/*Brackett Ind School Dist*	37,69	257
Moulton, Kelli, Dr/*Galveston Ind School Dist*	1	160
Mount, Jamie/*Humble Ind School Dist*	71	195
Mouser, Greg/*Prairiland Ind School Dist*	6	260
Moy, Betty/*Poth Ind School Dist*	4	401
Moy, Brian/*North East Ind School Dist*	2	34
Moya, Elizabeth/*Ysleta Ind School Dist*	30	137
Moya, Lisa/*Bay City Ind School Dist*	8,18,57,69,88,285,288,294	275
Moya, Raymond/*Zapata Co Ind School Dist*	91	406
Moye, Vicky/*Barbers Hill Ind School Dist*	48	72
Moynihan, David/*Friendswood Ind Sch Dist*	4	160
Muckensturm, Scott/*Royse City Ind School Dist*	67	326
Muckleroy, Jana/*Central Heights Ind Sch Dist*	8,16,57,271,274	297
Mueck, Martin/*Navarro Ind School Dist*	3	173
Muehlberger, Linda, Dr/*Wichita Falls Ind School Dist*	79,93	392
Mueller, Leann/*Stamford Ind School Dist*	31	250
Mueller, Mariana/*Galveston Ind School Dist*	16,73	160
Muery, Jana/*McDade Ind School Dist*	2	24
Muhl, Kirk/*Lexington Ind School Dist*	6	263
Muizers, Dennis/*Lovejoy Ind School Dist*	8,15,69	80
Mulanax, Eddie/*Marshall Ind School Dist*	76	209
Mulkey, Jennifer/*Sanger Ind School Dist*	11,57,296	126
Mullen, Mary/*Lovejoy Ind School Dist*	8	80
Mullenix, Kristi/*Mesquite Ind School Dist*	77	110
Mullens, Eric/*Hempstead Ind School Dist*	11,69,88,271,274,296,298	384
Muller, Robert, Dr/*Belton Ind School Dist*	15	26
Mullin, Melanie/*Wills Point Ind School Dist*	16,73	381
Mullins, Dathan/*Lubbock Ind School Dist*	76,295	270
Mullins, Jada/*Montgomery Ind School Dist*	79	293
Mullins, Jeremy/*Tolar Ind School Dist*	6	230
Mullins, Keith/*Buna Ind School Dist*	67	240
Mullins, Leatha/*Dallas Co Schools*	15,71	95
Mullins, Lisa, Dr/*Pine Tree Ind School Dist*	39,48	170
Mullins, Rene/*Princeton Ind School Dist*	9	84
Mulroney, Malcolm/*Carrollton-Farmers Branch ISD*	3,17	96
Mulvaney, Bernard/*Goose Creek Cons Ind Sch Dist*	6	187
Mundy, Homer/*Paradise Ind School Dist*	67	403
Mundy, Nefertari/*Tomball Ind School Dist*	74	203
Mungia, Andrea/*Raymondville Ind Sch Dist*	8,69	394
Munguia, Yesica/*Paris Ind School Dist*	57	260
Muniz, Jesse/*Carrizo Spgs Cons Ind SD*	2	127
Muniz, Noe/*Roma Ind School Dist*	27,31,83,88	341
Muniz, Norma/*Ft Hancock Ind School Dist*	4	234
Muniz, Oscar/*McLean Ind School Dist*	1	165
Munoz, April/*Chapel Hill Ind School Dist*	57	337
Munoz, Arminda/*Weslaco Ind School Dist*	71	225
Munoz, Chuck/*Chapel Hill Ind School Dist*	73,84,95	337
Munoz, Claudia/*La Joya Ind School Dist*	49	219
Munoz, Esmeralda, Dr/*Sharyland Ind School Dist*	10	224
Munoz, Gabril/*Del Valle Ind School Dist*	79	369
Munoz, Irma/*Idea Public Schools*	3,4,5,295	217
Munoz, Jose/*Eagle Pass Ind School Dist*	73,82,98,295	276
Munoz, Leticia/*Beeville Ind School Dist*	67	25
Munoz, Lucy/*La Joya Ind School Dist*	46	219
Munoz, Michael/*Brackett Ind School Dist*	73	257
Munoz, Stephanie/*San Marcos Cons Ind Sch Dist*	68	211
Munoz, Terry/*New Waverly Ind School Dist*	67	383
Munoz, Tiffany/*Blooming Grove Ind School Dist*	11,69	299
Munro, Loree/*New Caney Ind School Dist*	81	293

#		#		#		#		#		#	
1	Superintendent	16	Instructional Media Svcs	30	Adult Education	44	Science Sec	58	Special Education K-12	72	Summer School
2	Bus/Finance/Purchasing	17	Chief Operations Officer	31	Career/Sch-to-Work K-12	45	Math K-12	59	Special Education Elem	73	Instructional Tech
3	Buildings And Grounds	18	Chief Academic Officer	32	Career/Sch-to-Work Elem	46	Math Elem	60	Special Education Sec	74	Inservice Training
4	Food Service	19	Chief Financial Officer	33	Career/Sch-to-Work Sec	47	Math Sec	61	Foreign/World Lang K-12	75	Marketing/Distributive
5	Transportation	20	Art K-12	34	Early Childhood Ed	48	English/Lang Arts K-12	62	Foreign/World Lang Elem	76	Info Systems
6	Athletic	21	Art Elem	35	Health/Phys Education	49	English/Lang Arts Elem	63	Foreign/World Lang Sec	77	Psychological Assess
7	Health Services	22	Art Sec	36	Guidance Services K-12	50	English/Lang Arts Sec	64	Religious Education K-12	78	Affirmative Action
8	Curric/Instruct K-12	23	Music K-12	37	Guidance Services Elem	51	Reading K-12	65	Religious Education Elem	79	Student Personnel
9	Curric/Instruct Elem	24	Music Elem	38	Guidance Services Sec	52	Reading Elem	66	Religious Education Sec	80	Driver Ed/Safety
10	Curric/Instruct Sec	25	Music Sec	39	Social Studies K-12	53	Reading Sec	67	School Board President	81	Gifted/Talented
11	Federal Program	26	Business Education	40	Social Studies Elem	54	Remedial Reading K-12	68	Teacher Personnel	82	Video Services
12	Title I	27	Career & Tech Ed	41	Social Studies Sec	55	Remedial Reading Elem	69	Academic Assessment	83	Substance Abuse Prev
13	Title V	28	Technology Education	42	Science K-12	56	Remedial Reading Sec	70	Research/Development	84	Erate
15	Asst Superintendent	29	Family/Consumer Science	43	Science Elem	57	Bilingual/ELL	71	Public Information	85	AIDS Education

#		#	
88	Alternative/At Risk	277	Remedial Math K-12
89	Multi-Cultural Curriculum	280	Literacy Coach
90	Social Work	285	STEM
91	Safety/Security	286	Digital Learning
92	Magnet School	288	Common Core Standards
93	Parental Involvement	294	Accountability
95	Tech Prep Program	295	Network System
97	Chief Information Officer	296	Title II Programs
98	Chief Technology Officer	297	Webmaster
270	Character Education	298	Grant Writer/Ptnrships
271	Migrant Education	750	Chief Innovation Officer
273	Teacher Mentor	751	Chief of Staff
274	Before/After Sch	752	Social Emotional Learning
275	Response To Intervention		

TX-T64

Texas School Directory

DISTRICT PERSONNEL INDEX

NAME/District	JOB FUNCTIONS	PAGE
Muntean, Tommy/*Iola Ind School Dist*	3	172
Murdock, Kirk/*Eagle Mtn-Saginaw Ind Sch Dist*	73,295	348
Murff, Janet/*Medina Ind School Dist*	11,58	23
Muri, Scott, Dr/*Ector Co Ind School Dist*	1	129
Murillo, Danica/*Seguin Ind School Dist*	74	173
Murphey, Debra/*Danbury Ind School Dist*	37	53
Murphree, Amanda/*Yoakum Ind School Dist*	7,85	118
Murphy, Aaron/*Columbia Brazoria ISD*	295	52
Murphy, Alysha/*Cotton Center Ind School Dist*	2	174
Murphy, Brenda/*Braination Schools*	8,18	30
Murphy, Christine/*Bluff Dale Ind Sch Dist*	2	143
Murphy, Ethel/*George West Ind School Dist*	58	268
Murphy, Evalene/*Lake Travis Ind School Dist*	15,68	370
Murphy, Kari/*Deer Park Ind School Dist*	73,286,295	186
Murphy, Keith/*Melissa Ind School Dist*	1	81
Murphy, Patrick/*Iredell Ind School Dist*	1,11,73,83,288	46
Murphy, Renae/*Rockwall Ind School Dist*	71	325
Murphy, Valerie/*Cleveland Ind School Dist*	7	265
Murphy, Vanessa/*Hughes Springs Ind Sch Dist*	37	70
Murr, Marty/*Anahuac Ind School Dist*	6	71
Murr, Marty/*San Augustine Ind School Dist*	6	329
Murr, Suzanne/*Azle Ind School Dist*	27	345
Murray, Amy/*Burnet Cons Ind Sch Dist*	7	60
Murray, Ana/*Smithville Ind School Dist*	71,97	24
Murray, Chuck/*Crosby Ind School Dist*	3,91	183
Murray, Emily/*Trinity Ind School Dist*	27	374
Murray, Frank/*Wichita Falls Ind School Dist*	73	392
Murray, Jeffery/*Rule Ind School Dist*	67	210
Murray, Kathleen/*Luling Ind School Dist*	37	61
Murray, Lisa/*Dawson Ind School Dist*	58	299
Murray, Lou Ann/*Cooper Ind School Dist*	7,85	119
Murray, Mark/*Arlington Ind School Dist*	76	343
Murray, Mark/*Pampa Ind School Dist*	27,31	165
Murray, Robin/*Tuloso-Midway Ind School Dist*	298	305
Murray, Tina/*Farmersville Ind School Dist*	76	78
Murray, Vonn, Dr/*La Porte Ind School Dist*	11,69,288,294,296,298	198
Murry, Anjanette, Dr/*Crandall Ind School Dist*	8,11,15,288	251
Murtell, John/*Brazosport Ind School Dist*	9	52
Musgrove, Tracy/*Rains Ind School Dist*	16	320
Mushlian, Druann/*Hardin Jefferson Ind Sch Dist*	11,15,57	177
Musich, Sharon/*Woodsboro Ind School Dist*	275	324
Musick, Patricia/*Willis Ind School Dist*	9	294
Musick, Stu, Dr/*Navasota Ind School Dist*	1	172
Musquiz, Rodolfo/*Eagle Pass Ind School Dist*	48,51,54,61,280,298	276
Myatt, Darla/*Muleshoe Ind School Dist*	34,58	22
Myers, Brenda/*Brownsboro Ind School Dist*	4	213
Myers, Diane/*Friendswood Ind Sch Dist*	15	160
Myers, Kathy/*Commerce Independent Sch Dist*	85	236
Myers, Kim/*Mineola Ind School Dist*	4	404
Myers, Melissa/*Little Elm Ind School Dist*	67	124
Myers, Patricia/*Driscoll Ind School Dist*	73	304
Myers, Rachel/*Commerce Independent Sch Dist*	58	236
Myers, Robert/*Red Oak Ind School Dist*	20,23	142
Myers, Rufus/*Lake Travis Ind School Dist*	2	370
Myers, Susan/*Texas City Ind School Dist*	8,15,16,36,274	161
Myers, Teddye/*Aspermont Ind School Dist*	36,69,83,88,270,271,275	342
Myers, Terry/*Crockett Ind School Dist*	1	232
Mynar, Mary/*Bosqueville Ind School Dist*	4	278
Mynarcik, Larry/*Bynum Ind School Dist*	1,11,83	227
Mynarcik, Lori/*La Vega Ind School Dist*	71	279
Myres, Bryan/*Godley Ind School Dist*	2,11,296	247

N

NAME/District	JOB FUNCTIONS	PAGE
Nace, Michael/*Amherst Ind School Dist*	84,295	260
Nacianceno, Arlando/*La Joya Ind School Dist*	3	219
Nail, Rusty/*Madisonville Cons ISD*	6	273
Najera, Cynthia/*Socorro Ind School Dist*	67	135
Nance, Darin/*Alpine Ind School Dist*	73,295	56
Nanny, Dwin/*Panther Creek Cons Ind SD*	1,11,83	76
Napper, Lisa/*Georgetown Ind School Dist*	15,68	395
Nardozza, Chelsea/*UT Tyler University Acad Dist*	58	338
Nash, Charles/*Centerville Ind School Dist*	67	264
Nash, Kim/*Springtown Ind School Dist*	4	313
Nash, Richard/*Kilgore Ind School Dist*	11,15	169
Nasky, Holley/*Irving Ind School Dist*	81	109
Natividad, Fernando/*Irving Ind School Dist*	11	109

NAME/District	JOB FUNCTIONS	PAGE
Natividad, Lorraine/*Grandfalls-Royalty Ind SD*	2	385
Naugher, Mariella/*Hurst-Euless-Bedford ISD*	4	353
Nauling, Autumn/*North Zulch Ind School Dist*	16	274
Nauman, Patti/*Anahuac Ind School Dist*	8	71
Naumann, Kevin/*Marble Falls Ind School Dist*	67	60
Nava, Ramiro, Dr/*Somerset Ind School Dist*	58	42
Nava, Yoelia/*Sharyland Ind School Dist*	27	224
Navarette, Ed/*Florence Ind School Dist*	67	395
Navariz, Danielle/*Socorro Ind School Dist*	43	135
Navarre, Becky, Dr/*Ft Worth Ind School Dist*	15,95	349
Navarro, Christian/*Edcouch Elsa Ind School Dist*	6,35	215
Navarro, Eva/*Duncanville Ind School Dist*	7,85	104
Navarro, Tommy/*Pearsall Ind School Dist*	67	157
Nazworth, Steven/*Venus Ind School Dist*	8,271	249
Ncelhaney, Roxanne/*Palmer Ind School Dist*	79	141
Neal, Angela/*Region 10 Ed Service Center*	34	116
Neal, Brian/*Savoy Ind School Dist*	1	146
Neal, Carolyn/*North Hopkins Ind School Dist*	7	231
Neal, G W/*Nacogdoches Ind School Dist*	67	298
Neal, Mike/*Clyde Consolidated Ind SD*	286	62
Neal, Rhonda/*Winters Ind School Dist*	2,11	327
Neal, Tracy/*Huntington Ind School Dist*	67	17
Neary, Summer/*Liberty Hill Ind School Dist*	11,296	398
Neatherlin, Jenifer/*Llano Ind School Dist*	31,83,88	268
Neblett, Jeff/*Navasota Ind School Dist*	3	172
Neblett, Pam, Dr/*Garland Ind School Dist*	69,70,294	105
Necessary, Keith/*Jonesboro Ind School Dist*	3	93
Ned, Charles, Dr/*Humble Ind School Dist*	81	195
Nedbalek, Phil/*Westwood Ind School Dist*	5	16
Neddham, Jack/*Hale Center Ind School Dist*	67	175
Needham, Debbie/*New Caney Ind School Dist*	4	293
Needham, Debbie/*Waxahachie Ind School Dist*	73	142
Needham, Jennifer/*Gonzales Ind School Dist*	16,28,73,76,82,297	164
Neel, Diana/*Oakwood Ind School Dist*	2,11,296	264
Neely, Mitzi/*White Oak Ind School Dist*	8,11,57,83,88,273,294,296	171
Neely, Shelli/*Gunter Ind School Dist*	73	166
Neff, Sally/*Colorado Ind School Dist*	67	289
Negri, Thomas/*Ft Bend Ind School Dist*	69	149
Neidert, Amy/*Denison Ind School Dist*	9	166
Neighbors, Lisa/*Midland Ind School Dist*	9	285
Neill, Brenda/*Veribest Ind School Dist*	4	365
Neill, Lindy/*Fairfield Ind School Dist*	83	156
Neira, Claudia/*Int'l Leadership of Texas Dist*	68	108
Nejtek, Kimberly/*Westphalia Ind School Dist*	57,59	145
Nelda Flores, Rosa/*Roma Ind School Dist*	7	341
Nelms, Hilda/*Union Hill Ind School Dist*	4	377
Nelson, Becky/*Andrews Ind School Dist*	7	16
Nelson, Becky/*Mullin Ind School Dist*	57	288
Nelson, Carol/*Alvin Ind School Dist*	1	50
Nelson, Davin/*Daingerfield-Lone Star Ind SD*	6	296
Nelson, Dawn/*East Chambers Ind School Dist*	4	72
Nelson, Garrett/*Shallowater Ind School Dist*	67	272
Nelson, Gregory, Dr/*Ector Co Ind School Dist*	68,78	130
Nelson, Guy/*Rotan Ind School Dist*	67	148
Nelson, Jay/*Hallsville Ind School Dist*	67	208
Nelson, Jennifer/*Ennis Ind School Dist*	11,34,58	140
Nelson, Jenny/*Ganado Ind School Dist*	16,73,286,295,296	239
Nelson, Keith/*Llano Ind School Dist*	3	268
Nelson, Kelisa/*Region 16 Ed Service Center*	58,77	321
Nelson, Mark/*Breckenridge Ind School Dist*	4	341
Nelson, Nicole/*Lamar Cons Ind School Dist*	6,35	153
Nelson, Rebecca/*Weatherford Ind School Dist*	74	313
Nelson, Sharon/*Boyd Ind School Dist*	5	402
Nelson, Sherri/*Skidmore Tynan Ind SD*	58	25
Nelson, Toni/*Little Elm Ind School Dist*	7	124
Nelson, Tyisha/*Carroll Independent Sch Dist*	11,27,57,58,88	347
Nelson, Vicki/*Rice Cons Ind School Dist*	57	87
Nemons, Cynthia/*Houston Ind School Dist*	36	188
Nesbit, Michael/*Medina Valley Ind School Dist*	8,15,69	284
Neshyba, Rose/*Lake Worth Ind School Dist*	1	356
Netera, Eddie/*Alpine Ind School Dist*	67	56
Netro, Tahnee/*Mission Cons Ind School Dist*	58	222
Netterville, Colleen/*Greenville Ind School Dist*	58,68	236
Neudorf, Ramona/*Hart Ind School Dist*	73	71
Neugebauer, Lena/*Montgomery Ind School Dist*	4	293
Neuhoff, Paul/*Region 20 Ed Service Center*	2	45

DISTRICT PERSONNEL INDEX

Market Data Retrieval

NAME/District	JOB FUNCTIONS	PAGE
Neuman, Kami/*Hondo Ind School Dist*	16,82	284
Neuman, Michael/*Sabinal Ind School Dist*	15	378
Neuman, Michael/*Sabinal Ind School Dist*	2,8,11,36,69,77,91	378
New, Donald/*Era Ind School Dist*	6	90
Newby, Randy/*Evant Ind School Dist*	16,73,76,285,295	92
Newcom, Steven/*Eagle Mtn-Saginaw Ind Sch Dist*	67	348
Newcomb, Beverly/*Center Point Ind School Dist*	31	255
Newcomb, Cody/*Center Point Ind School Dist*	1,83	255
Newcomer, Tammie/*Vernon Ind School Dist*	4	393
Newell, Suzanne, Dr/*Grapevine-Colleyville Ind SD*	8,11,16,20,27,36	353
Newhouse, Rhonda/*Spring Ind School Dist*	67	202
Newkirk, Tiffany/*Comal Ind School Dist*	83,90	87
Newman, Belinda/*Eagle Mtn-Saginaw Ind Sch Dist*	76	348
Newman, Bobby/*Nixon-Smiley Cons Ind Sch Dist*	3	164
Newman, Casey/*Woodsboro Ind School Dist*	73,91	324
Newman, Donna, Dr/*North East Ind School Dist*	15	34
Newman, Ed/*Region 12 Ed Service Center*	76	283
Newman, Jarrod/*Academy Ind School Dist*	73,295	26
Newman, Joshua/*Ferris Ind School Dist*	91	140
Newman, Karen/*Dimmitt Ind School Dist*	73,295	71
Newman, Teara/*Rusk Ind School Dist*	7	73
Newsom, Kevin/*Medina Ind School Dist*	1,73	23
Newton, Becky/*Navarro Ind School Dist*	58	173
Newton, Betty/*Huffman Ind School Dist*	5	195
Newton, Garon/*Highland Park Ind School Dist*	4	319
Newton, Sandra/*Tyler Ind School Dist*	20,23	337
Neyman, Jessica/*Georgetown Ind School Dist*	68	395
Nguyen, Nicole/*Calhoun Co Ind School Dist*	4	61
Nichol, Tony/*Olney Ind School Dist*	16,73	406
Nicholas, Beth/*Mesquite Ind School Dist*	15,57,58,69,72,275	110
Nicholas, Kimberlee/*Fairfield Ind School Dist*	7	156
Nicholas, Mike/*Royal Ind School Dist*	73,295	384
Nicholason, Amy/*Blooming Grove Ind School Dist*	2	299
Nichols, Blake/*O'Donnell Ind School Dist*	6	273
Nichols, Brian, Dr/*New Summerfield Ind Sch Dist*	1	73
Nichols, Heather/*Tomball Ind School Dist*	58,270	203
Nichols, Larry/*Calhoun Co Ind School Dist*	1	61
Nichols, Mike/*Academy Ind School Dist*	6	26
Nichols, Sarah/*Hunt Ind School Dist*	16,297	255
Nicholson, Bobby/*Goliad Ind School Dist*	6	163
Nicholson, Justin/*Campbell Ind School Dist*	3	235
Nick, Angela/*Winona Ind School Dist*	4	339
Nick, Kara/*Abernathy Ind School Dist*	36	174
Nickerson, Erik/*Dallas Ind School Dist*	79	98
Nickle, Jeanie/*Navasota Ind School Dist*	8,16	172
Nicks, Joe/*Kaufman Ind School Dist*	8,15,286,288	252
Nicol, Kelly/*Latexo Ind School Dist*	67	233
Niedziela, Joseph/*Ft Worth Ind School Dist*	39	349
Niehues, Kimberly/*Miles Ind School Dist*	58,69	326
Nielsen, David/*Hurst-Euless-Bedford ISD*	297	353
Niemeyer, Mike/*Channelview Ind School Dist*	15	183
Niemyer, Diane/*Liberty-Eylau Ind School Dist*	88	48
Nienstedt, Christy/*Anderson-Shiro Cons Ind SD*	38	171
Nies, Andy/*River Road Ind School Dist*	2,8,11,74,88,270,294,296	319
Nieto, Isidoro/*Weslaco Ind School Dist*	67	225
Nieto, Melissa/*Harlingen Cons Ind School Dist*	68	64
Nine, Mary/*Perryton Ind School Dist*	58	307
Nine, Mary/*Spearman Ind School Dist*	58	177
Nino, Gabby/*Georgetown Ind School Dist*	69	395
Nitsch, Karen/*McAllen Ind School Dist*	81	221
Niven, Scott/*Allen Ind School Dist*	1	76
Nivins, Roosevelt/*Community Ind School Dist*	1	78
Nix, Amy/*Texarkana Ind School Dist*	68	50
Nix, Becky/*Borden Co Ind School Dist*	58,275	46
Nix, Dalton/*Tolar Ind School Dist*	67	230
Nix, Danny/*Burkburnett Ind Sch Dist*	6	391
Nix, Lydia/*Canadian Ind School Dist*	4	213
Nix, Nikki/*Midlothian Ind School Dist*	10	141
Nix, Samuel, Dr/*Duncanville Ind School Dist*	8,69,270,286,288	104
Nix, Toby, Dr/*Pearland Ind School Dist*	27,31,95	53
Nixon, Gerald/*Sweeny Ind School Dist*	68	54
Nixon, Lisa/*Pearland Ind School Dist*	58	53
Nixon, Wendy/*Ganado Ind School Dist*	2	239
Nixson, Gerald/*Hardin Ind School Dist*	1	265
Noack, Dwayne/*Cuero Ind School Dist*	3,91	117
Noack, Kevin/*Palmer Ind School Dist*	1	141
Noahrip, Rocky/*San Vicente Ind School Dist*	2,73	57
Nobis, Sharon/*Lewisville Ind School Dist*	81	122
Noble, Butch/*Clarendon Cons Ind Sch Dist*	71,73,97,98,295	127
Noble, Terre/*Excelsior Ind School Dist*	2	334
Nobles, Tammy/*Victoria Ind School Dist*	13,79	382
Nolan, Elizabeth/*Burkburnett Ind Sch Dist*	81	391
Nolan, Katie/*Fort Davis Ind School Dist*	37	241
Nolen, Christy/*Gunter Ind School Dist*	58	166
Noll, Angie/*Bushland Ind School Dist*	57,271,294	319
Nolte, Joel, Dr/*Huffman Ind School Dist*	8,15	195
Nonaz, Lilian, Dr/*Ector Co Ind School Dist*	8,15	129
Noon, Rebecca/*Everman Ind School Dist*	4,34	349
Nored, Carla/*White Settlement Ind School Dist*	73	357
Norfleet, Kurt/*Frankston Ind School Dist*	3,5	15
Norgaard, Kelli/*Bryan Ind School Dist*	74	54
Noriega, Elvia/*Richardson Ind School Dist*	294	112
Norman, John/*Grapeland Ind School Dist*	76,295	232
Norman, Michael/*Spur Ind School Dist*	6,12	127
Norman, Rusty/*Santa Fe Ind School Dist*	67	161
Norman, Summer/*Chireno ISD School Dist*	69,83,93	297
Norman, Summer/*Hubbard Ind School Dist*	12,31,69,83	227
Norman, Tim/*Hubbard Ind School Dist*	1,11	227
Norrell, Mike/*Clarendon Cons Ind Sch Dist*	1	127
Norriega, Olga/*Donna Ind School Dist*	2	215
Norris, Amber/*Cooper Ind School Dist*	286	120
Norris, Jim/*Midlothian Ind School Dist*	2,15	141
Norris, Stephanie/*Wimberley Ind School Dist*	58	212
Norris, Sybil/*Malakoff Ind School Dist*	11,31,57,58,83,271,296,298	214
Norris, Zach/*Edna Ind School Dist*	4	239
Nors, Raymond/*Hillsboro Ind School Dist*	3,5	227
North, April/*Chisum Ind School Dist*	71,76	259
North, Janice/*Mansfield Ind School Dist*	16,73	356
North, Wayne/*Pecos-Barstow-Toyah Ind SD*	3	323
Northcutt, Amy/*Sulphur Bluff Ind School Dist*	8,58,69,83,274,275	232
Northcutt, Sondra/*Wolfe City Ind School Dist*	57,58	237
Northcutt, Tammy/*Walcott Ind School Dist*	59	119
Northcutt, Virginia/*Longview Ind School Dist*	67	169
Northern, Jeff/*Levelland Ind School Dist*	1	229
Norton, Barry/*Texarkana Ind School Dist*	6	50
Norton, Chris/*Canyon Ind School Dist*	73,285,286	320
Norton, Paul/*Texarkana Ind School Dist*	1	50
Norvil, Tony/*May Ind School Dist*	5	59
Norville, Taylor/*Panhandle Ind School Dist*	9,74	69
Norwood, Pam/*Crowell Ind School Dist*	1	149
Norwood, Ricky/*Crowell Ind School Dist*	3	149
Novak, Jill/*Christoval Ind School Dist*	59	364
Novak, Julie/*Ft Sam Houston Ind School Dist*	2,11	32
Novak, Roy/*Childress Ind School Dist*	27	74
Novander, Francie/*New Braunfels Ind School Dist*	76	88
Novian, Patricia/*Bruceville-Eddy Ind Sch Dist*	4	278
Novotny, Michael/*Salado Ind School Dist*	1	29
Nowak, Shan/*Strawn Ind School Dist*	73	311
Nowlin, Liesa/*De Leon Ind School Dist*	10	89
Noyola, Alicia, Dr/*Harlingen Cons Ind School Dist*	8,18	64
Noyola, Dora/*Waelder Ind School Dist*	67	164
Noyola, Orlando/*Pharr-San Juan-Alamo Ind SD*	79	223
Nuckolls, Dean/*La Poynor Ind School Dist*	6	214
Nugent, Shaun/*Aquilla Ind School Dist*	4	227

---

1 Superintendent	16 Instructional Media Svcs	30 Adult Education	44 Science Sec	58 Special Education K-12	72 Summer School	88 Alternative/At Risk	277 Remedial Math K-12
2 Bus/Finance/Purchasing	17 Chief Operations Officer	31 Career/Sch-to-Work K-12	45 Math K-12	59 Special Education Elem	73 Instructional Tech	89 Multi-Cultural Curriculum	280 Literacy Coach
3 Buildings And Grounds	18 Chief Academic Officer	32 Career/Sch-to-Work Elem	46 Math Elem	60 Special Education Sec	74 Inservice Training	90 Social Work	285 STEM
4 Food Service	19 Chief Financial Officer	33 Career/Sch-to-Work Sec	47 Math Sec	61 Foreign/World Lang K-12	75 Marketing/Distributive	91 Safety/Security	286 Digital Learning
5 Transportation	20 Art K-12	34 Early Childhood Ed	48 English/Lang Arts K-12	62 Foreign/World Lang Elem	76 Info Systems	92 Magnet School	288 Common Core Standards
6 Athletic	21 Art Elem	35 Health/Phys Education	49 English/Lang Arts Elem	63 Foreign/World Lang Sec	77 Psychological Assess	93 Parental Involvement	294 Accountability
7 Health Services	22 Art Sec	36 Guidance Services K-12	50 English/Lang Arts Sec	64 Religious Education K-12	78 Affirmative Action	95 Tech Prep Program	295 Network System
8 Curric/Instruct K-12	23 Music K-12	37 Guidance Services Elem	51 Reading K-12	65 Religious Education Elem	79 Student Personnel	97 Chief Information Officer	296 Title II Programs
9 Curric/Instruct Elem	24 Music Elem	38 Guidance Services Sec	52 Reading Elem	66 Religious Education Sec	80 Driver Ed/Safety	98 Chief Technology Officer	297 Webmaster
10 Curric/Instruct Sec	25 Music Sec	39 Social Studies K-12	53 Reading Sec	67 School Board President	81 Gifted/Talented	270 Character Education	298 Grant Writer/Ptnrships
11 Federal Program	26 Business Education	40 Social Studies Elem	54 Remedial Reading K-12	68 Teacher Personnel	82 Video Services	271 Migrant Education	750 Chief Innovation Officer
12 Title I	27 Career & Tech Ed	41 Social Studies Sec	55 Remedial Reading Elem	69 Academic Assessment	83 Substance Abuse Prev	273 Teacher Mentor	751 Chief of Staff
13 Title V	28 Technology Education	42 Science K-12	56 Remedial Reading Sec	70 Research/Development	84 Erate	274 Before/After Sch	752 Social Emotional Learning
15 Asst Superintendent	29 Family/Consumer Science	43 Science Elem	57 Bilingual/ELL	71 Public Information	85 AIDS Education	275 Response To Intervention	

TX-T66

Texas School Directory
DISTRICT PERSONNEL INDEX

NAME/District	JOB FUNCTIONS	PAGE
Null, Curtis, Dr/*Conroe Ind School Dist*	1	291
Nunez, Christina/*New Caney Ind School Dist*	7	293
Nunez, Debbie/*Corpus Christi Ind Sch Dist*	68	303
Nunez, Lori, Dr/*Alvarado Ind School Dist*	7,11,31,34,83,271,296,298	246
Nunez, Renee/*Archdiocese Galveston-Houston*	8,15,69	203
Nunley, Bob/*Sabinal Ind School Dist*	67	378
Nunn, Judy/*Bosqueville Ind School Dist*	36,69,83,88,275,285,288,294	278
Nunnelly, Melissa/*Port Neches-Groves Ind SD*	4	243
Nutt, Sonya/*Excelsior Ind School Dist*	6,83	334
Nutter, Sarah/*Dalhart Ind School Dist*	8	95
Nye, Debbie/*Allen Ind School Dist*	2	76
Nye, Gary/*Frisco Ind School Dist*	11,69,273,294	78

O

NAME/District	JOB FUNCTIONS	PAGE
O'Brien, John/*Van Vleck Ind School Dist*	1	276
O'Brien, Randal/*Goose Creek Cons Ind Sch Dist*	1	187
O'Cana, Armando, Dr/*La Joya Ind School Dist*	91	219
O'Connor, Dawn/*Cleveland Ind School Dist*	69,294	265
O'Connor, Robert/*Nazareth Ind School Dist*	8,57	71
O'Kelley, Kathleen/*McLeod Ind School Dist*	36	70
O'Neal, Jill/*Sherman Ind School Dist*	68,79	167
O'Neal, Jim/*North Zulch Ind School Dist*	6,60	274
O'Neal, Phillip/*Mansfield Ind School Dist*	6	356
O'Neal, Ronnie/*Bryan Ind School Dist*	2,275	54
O'Neill, Laurie/*Coppell Ind School Dist*	11,298	98
O'Pry, Casey, Dr/*Clear Creek Ind School Dist*	15,68,273	158
O'Quinn, Kayla/*Glen Rose Ind School Dist*	2	340
Oakeley, Cecilia, Dr/*Dallas Ind School Dist*	15,69,70,294	98
Oakes, Bryan/*Quitman Ind School Dist*	6	404
Oates, Brenda/*La Vernia Ind School Dist*	58	401
Oatess, Jan/*Waller Ind School Dist*	58	384
Oats, Margo/*Honey Grove Ind School Dist*	4	146
Obannion, Randy/*Hardin Jefferson Ind Sch Dist*	3,91	177
Obanon, Julie/*Rice Ind School Dist*	2,11,58,68,88	300
Obryant, Verl/*Alpine Ind School Dist*	34	56
Ochoa, Charlie/*Aransas Pass Ind School Dist*	3,5	330
Ochoa, Claudia/*La Joya Ind School Dist*	67	219
Ochoa, Cruz/*Ysleta Ind School Dist*	67	137
Ochoa, Gina/*Orange Grove Ind School Dist*	4	245
Ochoa, Raquel/*Channelview Ind School Dist*	76	183
Ochoa, Velma/*La Joya Ind School Dist*	93	219
Oconner, Robert/*Edna Ind School Dist*	1	239
Oden, Peggy/*Big Sandy Ind School Dist*	58,93	376
Oden, Peggy, Dr/*Gilmer Ind School Dist*	58	376
Oden, Peggy, Dr/*Gladewater Ind School Dist*	58	169
Oden, Peggy, Dr/*Harmony Ind School Dist*	58	376
Odenburg, Sandra/*Clint Ind School Dist*	3	132
Odenthal, Tamara/*Lake Travis Ind School Dist*	2	370
Odenwald, Cliff/*Garland Ind School Dist*	6	105
Odom, Amanda/*South Texas Ind School Dist*	71	67
Odom, Charlotte/*Brookeland Ind School Dist*	8,11,27,57,296,298	240
Odom, Greg/*Dimmitt Ind School Dist*	67	71
Odom, Kenneth/*Mabank Ind School Dist*	67	252
Odom, Pam/*Mabank Ind School Dist*	7,35,85	252
Odonnell, Pat/*Grand Saline Ind School Dist*	3,5,91	380
Ogas, Sylvia/*Ft Stockton Ind School Dist*	57	315
Ogburn, Rusty/*Texarkana Ind School Dist*	27,76,92,295	50
Oglesby, Lori/*Eula Ind School Dist*	31	63
Ogletree, Ben/*Livingston Ind School Dist*	67	317
Ogletree, John, Dr/*Cypress-Fairbanks Ind Sch Dist*	67	184
Ogwumike, Ify/*Cypress-Fairbanks Ind Sch Dist*	15,79	184
Ohlendorf, Kimberly/*Magnolia Ind School Dist*	4	292
Ojeda, Linda/*Marfa Ind School Dist*	6	320
Ojeda, Rosa/*Waller Ind School Dist*	76,97,286	384
Olaslaugua, Roque/*La Pryor Ind School Dist*	73	407
Oldag, Donald/*El Campo Ind School Dist*	295	389
Oles, Reagan/*Canadian Ind School Dist*	9	213
Oliphant, Holly/*Shepherd Ind School Dist*	7	330
Oliphant, Holly/*Shepherd Ind School Dist*	7	330
Oliphant, Roland/*New Waverly Ind School Dist*	5	383
Oliva, Efrain, Dr/*Spring Ind School Dist*	15	202
Oliva, Melissa/*Brownfield Ind Sch Dist*	8,15	362
Olivares, Ismael/*Taft Ind School Dist*	3	332
Olivares, Victor/*Tyler Ind School Dist*	4	337
Olivarez, Alfredo/*Ricardo Ind School Dist*	3,16,83	257
Olivarez, Christie/*Brenham Ind School Dist*	68	385
Olivarez, Isabel/*West Oso Ind School Dist*	69,294	306
Olivarez, Leonel/*San Isidro Ind School Dist*	2,4	341
Olivarez, Rogerio/*Rio Grande City Ind Sch Dist*	23	340
Olivas, Cassie/*Blackwell Cons Ind Sch Dist*	16	301
Olive, Lori/*Oakwood Ind School Dist*	8,69	264
Oliveira, Ana, Dr/*La Joya Ind School Dist*	10	219
Oliver, Debbie/*Midland Ind School Dist*	61	285
Oliver, Garth, Dr/*Louise Ind School Dist*	1	389
Oliver, Heather/*Lometa Ind School Dist*	57,271	262
Oliver, James/*Martin's Mill Ind Sch Dist*	1	381
Oliver, Karla/*Plano Ind School Dist*	15,71,298	82
Oliver, Kathy/*Santa Fe Ind School Dist*	58	161
Oliver, Kaye/*Texarkana Ind School Dist*	5	50
Oliver, Marty/*Godley Ind School Dist*	28,73,295	247
Oliver, Ricky/*Zavalla Ind School Dist*	1	18
Oliver, Robert/*Colorado Ind School Dist*	5	289
Oliver, Shirley/*Lorena Ind School Dist*	4	280
Oliveras-Ortiz, Yanira, Dr/*UT Tyler University Acad Dist*	67	338
Olivier, Jay/*Liberty Hill Ind School Dist*	16	398
Olivo, Diane/*South San Antonio Ind Sch Dist*	7	42
Ollis, Greg/*Channelview Ind School Dist*	1	183
Olmos, Leticia/*Farwell Ind School Dist*	4	314
Olmos, Lorena/*Ysleta Ind School Dist*	297	137
Olson, Cindy/*Coupland Ind School Dist*	2,71,274,294,298	395
Olvera, Carlos/*Brownsville Ind School Dist*	57	63
Oneal, Marva, Dr/*Lamar Cons Ind School Dist*	11	153
Oneal, Thomas, Dr/*Anna Ind School Dist*	2,15,19	77
Oneil, Carl/*Fredericksburg Ind School Dist*	73	163
Oneil, Lyndi/*Schleicher Co Ind Sch Dist*	69,85,88,270,288	333
Oneill, David/*Hico Ind School Dist*	286	176
Oney, Robert/*Slidell Ind School Dist*	3,5,73,76,295	403
Ongoco, Jennifer/*Cypress-Fairbanks Ind Sch Dist*	297	184
Oniel, Ted/*Keene Ind School Dist*	11,88,271	248
Oppelt, Julie/*Medina Valley Ind School Dist*	81	284
Oppermann, Cindy/*Killeen Ind School Dist*	76	27
Oquinn, Jana/*Wells Ind School Dist*	2	73
Ormiston, Chris/*Boerne Ind School Dist*	42	253
Orndorff, Vernon/*Milford Ind School Dist*	1	141
Ornelas, Eliud/*Brownsville Ind School Dist*	5	63
Ornelas, Herman/*Columbia Brazoria ISD*	5	52
Orosco, Alejandro/*Carrizo Spgs Cons Ind SD*	3,5	127
Orosco, Denise/*South San Antonio Ind Sch Dist*	70,76	42
Orosco, Esperanza/*Hays Cons Ind School Dist*	67	211
Orosco, Jeffri/*Hutto Ind School Dist*	2	396
Orozco, Christine/*Medina Valley Ind School Dist*	93	284
Orozco, James/*San Antonio Ind School Dist*	20	39
Orozco, Jesse/*Lyford Cons Ind School Dist*	91	394
Orozco, John/*Tom Bean Ind School Dist*	8,11,74,79,91,296	168
Orozco, John/*Tom Bean Ind School Dist*	10,34	168
Orozco, Juan/*Del Valle Ind School Dist*	16	369
Orozco, Matilda, Dr/*Int'l Leadership of Texas Dist*	15	108
Orozlo, Jon/*Waelder Ind School Dist*	1,11,73,83	164
Orr, Bill/*Ingram Ind School Dist*	2,19	255
Orr, Bill/*Marion Ind School Dist*	2,8	172
Orr, Corri/*Quanah Ind School Dist*	83	177
Orr, John/*Plano Ind School Dist*	2	82
Orr, Terry/*Roby Cons Ind School Dist*	58	148
Orren, Christin/*Terlingua Common School Dist*	57	57
Orsak, Tim/*Olney Ind School Dist*	2	406
Orsak, Vincent/*Fayetteville Ind School Dist*	67	147
Orta, Nelson/*Garland Ind School Dist*	74	105
Ortega Ruiz, Elizabeth/*Corpus Christi Ind Sch Dist*	20	303
Ortega, Alejo/*Texhoma Ind School Dist*	3	336
Ortega, Alma/*La Joya Ind School Dist*	9	219
Ortega, Jamie/*Sharyland Ind School Dist*	2	224
Ortega, Mary/*Seminole Ind School Dist*	30	158
Ortega, Mary Alice/*Woodsboro Ind School Dist*	4	324
Ortega, Richard/*Socorro Ind School Dist*	58,275	135
Ortega, Yvonne/*Farwell Ind School Dist*	93	314
Ortiz, Bertha, Dr/*Edgewood Ind School Dist*	81	31
Ortiz, Carlos/*Three Way Ind School Dist*	73	144
Ortiz, Ernesto/*El Paso Ind School Dist*	3	132
Ortiz, Gina/*San Benito Cons Ind Sch Dist*	69,70,294	67
Ortiz, Marco/*Taylor Ind School Dist*	67	399
Ortiz, Mary/*Poteet Ind School Dist*	90,93	21
Ortiz, Milo/*Aldine Ind School Dist*	3	179

DISTRICT PERSONNEL INDEX

Market Data Retrieval

NAME/District	JOB FUNCTIONS	PAGE
Ortiz, Rebecca/North East Ind School Dist	46	34
Ortolon, Malinda/Newton Ind School Dist	2	301
Osborn, Donnie/Teague Ind School Dist	6	156
Osborne, Charles/Burleson Ind School Dist	11,69	246
Osburn, Clay/Idalou Ind School Dist	16,73	269
Osburn, Clay/Troy Ind School Dist	73,295	29
Oshman, Melissa/Northside Ind School Dist	76	36
Osten, Sharee/Greenville Ind School Dist	4	236
Oswald, Beth Anne/Archer City Ind School Dist	84	19
Oswald, Bethann/Archer City Ind School Dist	73,286,298	19
Otero, Diana, Dr/Ysleta Ind School Dist	58	137
Ott, Bobby, Dr/Temple Ind School Dist	1	29
Ott, Monica/El Campo Ind School Dist	7	389
Ott, Teddy/Ore City Ind School Dist	58,270	377
Ottmers, Deborah/Fredericksburg Ind School Dist	2,15	162
Ouellette, Michael/Katy Ind School Dist	20,23	151
Ouren, Lora/Bryan Ind School Dist	58	54
Ousley, Brian/Orangefield Ind School Dist	4	309
Ovalle Lopez, Maria/Klein Ind School Dist	93	196
Ovalle, Rey/Los Fresnos Cons Ind Sch Dist	4	66
Overbo, Trig/Jayton-Girard Ind School Dist	1	255
Overman, Megan/Eagle Mtn-Saginaw Ind Sch Dist	71	348
Overstreet, Gary/Quinlan Ind School Dist	5	237
Overstreet, Stephen/Tahoka Ind School Dist	6	273
Overton, Jodi/Lipan Ind School Dist	1	230
Owen, Brad/Burkburnett Ind Sch Dist	16,73,82,295	391
Owen, Dana/Friendswood Ind School Dist	71,76	160
Owen, John/Aransas Co Ind School Dist	31	19
Owen, Kathy/Jayton-Girard Ind School Dist	67	255
Owen, Keith/Linden Kildare Cons Ind SD	11,88,288,298	70
Owen, Lonnie/Anderson-Shiro Cons Ind SD	67	171
Owen, Shana/Kerens Ind School Dist	9	300
Owen, Tandi/Forney Ind School Dist	11,294	251
Owen, Tina/Frankston Ind School Dist	4	15
Owens, Auttum/Leary Ind School Dist	2,288	48
Owens, Auttumn/Hubbard Ind School Dist	2	48
Owens, Cary/Abilene Ind School Dist	76,295	360
Owens, Cindy/Corrigan-Camden Ind Sch Dist	2	316
Owens, Frank/Campbell Ind School Dist	67	235
Owens, Greg/Sulphur Springs Ind School Dist	6	232
Owens, Jackie/Tarkington Ind School Dist	37	266
Owens, Janette/White Settlement Ind Sch Dist	2	357
Owens, Jennie/Hedley Ind School Dist	73,295	127
Owens, Les/Venus Ind School Dist	67	249
Owens, Melanie/Tarkington Ind School Dist	5	266
Owens, Mike/Nacogdoches Ind School Dist	16,73,76,297	298
Owens, Ola/Wolfe City Ind School Dist	67	237
Owens, Rissie/Huntsville Ind School Dist	67	383
Owens, Scott/Mesquite Ind School Dist	3	110
Owens, Susie/Laneville Ind School Dist	294	327
Owens, Tatiana, Dr/Port Arthur Ind School Dist	57,271	243
Owings, Kathy/Deer Park Ind School Dist	69,294	186
Ownby, Lorene/Birdville Ind School Dist	9	346
Oyler, Stephanie/Elgin Ind School Dist	31	24
Ozment, Patrece/Boles Ind School Dist	36,83	235
Ozuna, Jessica/Tomball Ind School Dist	27	203
Ozuna, Macy/Alvarado Ind School Dist	295	246
Ozuna, Romeo/Brooks Co Ind School Dist	3,5	57

P

NAME/District	JOB FUNCTIONS	PAGE
Pace, Debbie/Olney Ind School Dist	2	406
Pace, Johnny/Abernathy Ind School Dist	5	174
Pace, Susan/Wills Point Ind School Dist	4	381
Pacheco, Carmen/Hidalgo Ind School Dist	57,61,271	217
Pachiano, Kelly/Floydada Ind School Dist	71	148
Pack, Jeff, Dr/Dickinson Ind School Dist	69,294	159
Pack, Mike/Whitesboro Ind School Dist	5	168

NAME/District	JOB FUNCTIONS	PAGE
Paddie, Mike/Warren Ind School Dist	8,11,74,83	375
Padgett, Gema/Grapevine-Colleyville Ind SD	68	353
Padgett, Lacey, Dr/Ennis Ind School Dist	8	140
Padgett, Renee/Tarkington Ind School Dist	69	266
Padilla, Sylvia/Mathis Ind School Dist	68	331
Padilla, Terry/San Benito Cons Ind Sch Dist	274	67
Paez, Mely/Laredo Ind School Dist	16	386
Pafchall, Rene/Judson Ind School Dist	67	33
Page, Brian/Elgin Ind School Dist	28,73,84,98	24
Page, Cherry/Boling Ind School Dist	2	389
Page, Deanne/Castleberry Ind School Dist	2	347
Page, Jam/Region 15 Ed Service Center	58	366
Page, Mark/Hallsville Ind School Dist	16,28,76,82,295,297	208
Paine, James/Llano Ind School Dist	8,11,280,285,286,288,294,298	268
Painter, Allen/Dayton Ind School Dist	8,12,13,36,79,88,288	265
Painter, Judy/Zephyr Ind School Dist	2	59
Paiva, Brian/Brownfield Ind Sch Dist	3	362
Pajack, Peter/Midlothian Ind School Dist	4	141
Palacios, Aurora/Pharr-San Juan-Alamo Ind SD	4	223
Palacios, David/West Oso Ind School Dist	2	306
Palacios, Jose/Pharr-San Juan-Alamo Ind SD	91	223
Palagonia, Anthony/Int'l Leadership of Texas Dist	15	108
Palazzi, Brian/Clear Creek Ind School Dist	91	158
Palmer, Amber/Hermleigh Ind School Dist	8	333
Palmer, Asisela/Alvord Ind School Dist	7,85	402
Palmer, Becka/Hays Cons Ind School Dist	2	211
Palmer, Cathy, Dr/O'Donnell Ind School Dist	1,11	273
Palmer, Hans/Ft Sam Houston Ind School Dist	34,58	32
Palmer, Joe/Temple Ind School Dist	15,68	29
Pampolina, Ricci/Lumberton Ind School Dist	3	178
Panales, Odette/Benavides Ind School Dist	4	128
Panek, Pat/Crowley Ind School Dist	91	347
Pansmith, Susan/Sheldon Ind School Dist	54,58	200
Pantoja, Angel/Roby Cons Ind School Dist	6	148
Pantoja, Rubina/Harlandale Ind School Dist	39	32
Pape, Pete/Deer Park Ind School Dist	2,15	186
Parada, Arlene/Clint Ind School Dist	67	132
Parady, Gary/Hallsburg Ind School Dist	752	279
Parcell, Earl, Dr/Copperas Cove Ind School Dist	73,286	92
Parchman, Mike/Iowa Park Consolidated Ind SD	76	392
Parchman, Monti/Cranfills Gap ISD School Dist	1,11,73,83	46
Parcus, Natalie/Rosebud-Lott Ind School Dist	11,288	145
Pardo, Ben/Pearland Ind School Dist	6	53
Pardo, Lisa/Grapevine-Colleyville Ind SD	67	353
Parenica, Gayle/Wharton Ind School Dist	8	390
Parham, Clyde/Silverton Ind School Dist	6	57
Parhan, Bart/Haskell Cons Ind School Dist	3	210
Paris-Toulon, Alefia/Wichita Falls Ind School Dist	58	392
Paris, Jane/Goose Creek Cons Ind Sch Dist	271	187
Paris, Patrick/New Caney Ind School Dist	20,23	293
Parish, Deidre/Darrouzett Ind School Dist	1,11	267
Park, Ann/City View Ind School Dist	68	391
Park, Chase/Highland Park Ind Sch Dist	2	108
Park, Debbie/Big Spring Ind School Dist	70	233
Parker-Felder, Lanita/New Summerfield Ind Sch Dist	2	73
Parker, Alice/Cleburne Ind School Dist	6	247
Parker, Angie/Queen City Ind School Dist	68	70
Parker, Bradley/Crowley Ind School Dist	286	347
Parker, Brandi/Hartley Ind School Dist	16,73	209
Parker, Brandie/McLeod Ind School Dist	2	70
Parker, Cheryl/Goose Creek Cons Ind Sch Dist	274	187
Parker, David/Hamshire Fannett Ind Sch Dist	76,286,295	242
Parker, James/Union Hill Ind School Dist	67	377
Parker, Jamie/Silsbee Ind School Dist	69	178
Parker, Jeanne/Spring Ind School Dist	7	202
Parker, Jennifer/Clint Ind School Dist	9	132
Parker, Jennifer/Spring Branch Ind School Dist	15	200

1 Superintendent	16 Instructional Media Svcs	30 Adult Education	44 Science Sec	58 Special Education K-12	72 Summer School	88 Alternative/At Risk	277 Remedial Math K-12
2 Bus/Finance/Purchasing	17 Chief Operations Officer	31 Career/Sch-to-Work K-12	45 Math K-12	59 Special Education Elem	73 Instructional Tech	89 Multi-Cultural Curriculum	280 Literacy Coach
3 Buildings And Grounds	18 Chief Academic Officer	32 Career/Sch-to-Work Elem	46 Math Elem	60 Special Education Sec	74 Inservice Training	90 Social Work	285 STEM
4 Food Service	19 Chief Financial Officer	33 Career/Sch-to-Work Sec	47 Math Sec	61 Foreign/World Lang K-12	75 Marketing/Distributive	91 Safety/Security	286 Digital Learning
5 Transportation	20 Art K-12	34 Early Childhood Ed	48 English/Lang Arts K-12	62 Foreign/World Lang Elem	76 Info Systems	92 Magnet School	288 Common Core Standards
6 Athletic	21 Art Elem	35 Health/Phys Education	49 English/Lang Arts Elem	63 Foreign/World Lang Sec	77 Psychological Assess	93 Parental Involvement	294 Accountability
7 Health Services	22 Art Sec	36 Guidance Services K-12	50 English/Lang Arts Sec	64 Religious Education K-12	79 Affirmative Action	95 Tech Prep Program	295 Network System
8 Curric/Instruct K-12	23 Music K-12	37 Guidance Services Elem	51 Reading K-12	65 Religious Education Elem	80 Student Personnel	97 Chief Information Officer	296 Title II Programs
9 Curric/Instruct Elem	24 Music Elem	38 Guidance Services Sec	52 Reading Elem	66 Religious Education Sec	81 Driver Ed/Safety	98 Chief Technology Officer	297 Webmaster
10 Curric/Instruct Sec	25 Music Sec	39 Social Studies K-12	53 Reading Sec	67 School Board President	82 Gifted/Talented	270 Character Education	298 Grant Writer/Ptnrships
11 Federal Program	26 Business Education	40 Social Studies Elem	54 Remedial Reading K-12	68 Teacher Personnel	83 Video Services	271 Migrant Education	750 Chief Innovation Officer
12 Title I	27 Career & Tech Ed	41 Social Studies Sec	55 Remedial Reading Elem	69 Academic Assessment	83 Substance Abuse Prev	273 Teacher Mentor	751 Chief of Staff
13 Title V	28 Technology Education	42 Science K-12	56 Remedial Reading Sec	70 Research/Development	84 Erate	274 Before/After Sch	752 Social Emotional Learning
15 Asst Superintendent	29 Family/Consumer Science	43 Science Elem	57 Bilingual/ELL	71 Public Information	85 AIDS Education	275 Response To Intervention	

TX-T68

Texas School Directory

DISTRICT PERSONNEL INDEX

NAME/District	JOB FUNCTIONS	PAGE
Parker, Jessica/*Irion Co Ind School Dist*	9	238
Parker, Joel/*Slocum ISD School Dist*	16,73,298	16
Parker, Jonathan/*Harris Co Dept of Ed*	15	179
Parker, Julie/*Mason Ind School Dist*	4	275
Parker, Kathy/*UT Tyler University Acad Dist*	8,18	338
Parker, Kim/*Jasper Ind School Dist*	58,77,88	240
Parker, Lara/*Arp Ind School Dist*	38,57,81	336
Parker, Laura/*Comstock Ind School Dist*	6,8,69,74,273,274	379
Parker, Linda, Dr/*Eagle Mtn-Saginaw Ind Sch Dist*	8,15,34,74,294	348
Parker, Montie/*Allen Ind School Dist*	58	76
Parker, Myliss/*Harlingen Cons Ind School Dist*	81	64
Parker, Nikki/*Iraan-Sheffield Ind Sch Dist*	31,69,79,88,270	316
Parker, Penny/*Harts Bluff Ind School Dist*	59	363
Parker, Rebecca/*Kennard Ind Sch Dist*	67	233
Parker, Ricky/*Elkhart Ind School Dist*	3	15
Parker, Sherry/*Wichita Falls Ind School Dist*	39	392
Parker, Shirley/*Humble Ind School Dist*	4	195
Parker, Sonya/*Shelbyville Ind School Dist*	39	335
Parker, Stacey/*Canutillo Ind School Dist*	39	132
Parker, Tiffany/*Glasscock Co Ind School Dist*	8,31,69,270	163
Parker, Troy/*Jacksonville Ind School Dist*	2	72
Parkerson, Mark/*Mineola Ind School Dist*	11,27,73,77,295	404
Parkhill, Michael/*Era Ind School Dist*	16,73,295	90
Parkhill, Monica/*Valley View ISD-Cooke Co*	8,11,296	91
Parkhurst, Jennifer/*Deweyville Ind School Dist*	12	308
Parkman, Pam/*Marble Falls Ind School Dist*	298	60
Parks, Christine/*Temple Ind School Dist*	71,97	29
Parks, Craig/*Dublin Ind School Dist*	73,84	143
Parks, Diane/*Lamar Cons Ind School Dist*	9,79	153
Parks, Joseph/*Plano Ind School Dist*	91	82
Parks, Pat/*Tatum Ind School Dist*	2	328
Parmer, Rhonda/*Pasadena Ind School Dist*	15	198
Parmley, Pamela, Dr/*McKinney Ind School Dist*	34,274	80
Parnell, Kourtni/*Lorena Ind School Dist*	58	280
Parnum, Jennifer/*Thorndale Ind School Dist*	69	288
Parra, Mary/*Plains Ind School Dist*	4	405
Parris, Corrissa/*Wylie Ind School Dist*	7	361
Parrish, Cari/*Kennard Ind Sch Dist*	2	233
Parrish, Cody/*Hardin Ind School Dist*	67	265
Parrish, Jennifer/*Tom Bean Ind School Dist*	2	168
Parrish, Lisa/*Hamilton Ind School Dist*	69	176
Parrish, Mark/*Springlake-Earth Ind Sch Dist*	67	261
Parrish, Megan/*Coahoma Ind School Dist*	73,76,286,295	234
Parrish, Melody/*Texas Dept of Education*	76	1
Parrish, Stacey/*Evant Ind School Dist*	58,77	92
Parrish, Tammy/*Rochelle Ind School Dist*	11,36,69	278
Parsons, Cindy/*Keller Ind School Dist*	7,83,85	354
Parsons, Glenda/*North Lamar Ind School Dist*	73,95,295	259
Parsons, Mark/*Itasca Ind School Dist*	1	228
Partin, Cary/*Pearland Ind School Dist*	15	53
Parton, Troy/*Munday Consolidated Ind SD*	1,11	258
Pascarella, Debbie/*Harper Ind School Dist*	4	163
Paschall, Theresa/*Crowley Ind School Dist*	36	347
Pasichnyk, Rob/*Belton Ind School Dist*	4	26
Paskell, Angela/*San Antonio Ind School Dist*	42	39
Passmore, Susan/*Goose Creek Cons Ind Sch Dist*	71	187
Patchke, Carla/*Roosevelt Ind School Dist*	7	271
Pate, David/*Richardson Ind School Dist*	2,19	112
Pate, James/*Mabank Ind School Dist*	16	252
Pate, Jason/*Comanche Ind School Dist*	67	89
Pate, Johnny/*Hubbard Ind School Dist*	57	48
Pate, Lynette/*Yoakum Ind School Dist*	68,79	118
Pate, Margie/*De Kalb Ind School Dist*	298	48
Pate, Marnie/*Port Aransas Ind School Dist*	67	305
Pate, Mary/*McMullen Co Ind Sch Dist*	73,76	283
Pate, Rose/*Etoile Ind School Dist*	2,28	297
Patek, Joseph/*Aransas Co Ind School Dist*	1	19
Patek, Trina/*Hallettsville Ind Sch Dist*	34	262
Paterson, Karen/*Anthony Ind School Dist*	16	131
Patillo, Paul/*Region 20 Ed Service Center*	73,76,98	45
Patin, Mary/*Lake Travis Ind School Dist*	11,15,286	370
Patin, Mitzi/*Ft Bend Ind School Dist*	73	149
Patino, Maria/*Lubbock Ind School Dist*	271	270
Patino, Mary/*Silverton Ind School Dist*	4	57
Patrick, Gay/*Dallas Ind School Dist*	16	98
Patrick, Jay/*Jefferson Ind School Dist*	73,295	274

NAME/District	JOB FUNCTIONS	PAGE
Patrick, Jonathan/*Dawson Ind School Dist*	6	116
Patrick, Kati/*Ira Ind School Dist*	7	333
Patrick, Mark/*Kermit Ind School Dist*	16,73,295	401
Patrick, Mary/*Galveston Ind School Dist*	34,58	160
Patschke, Curtis/*Lexington Ind School Dist*	73,295,297	263
Patschke, Jennifer/*Taylor Ind School Dist*	11,296,298	399
Patterson, Brian/*Ira Ind School Dist*	1	333
Patterson, Brian/*Ira Ind School Dist*	6	333
Patterson, Britt/*Rusk Ind School Dist*	67	73
Patterson, Candi/*Orangefield Ind School Dist*	31,36,69,83,93	309
Patterson, Garrett/*Collinsville Ind School Dist*	6	166
Patterson, Janice/*Del Valle Ind School Dist*	2	369
Patterson, Julie/*Cisco Independent Sch Dist*	58,74,92	128
Patterson, Kate/*Bryan Ind School Dist*	58	54
Patterson, Krystal/*Latexo Ind School Dist*	7	233
Patterson, Michelle/*Alief Ind School Dist*	49	181
Patterson, Paula/*Sheldon Ind School Dist*	8,15,18	200
Patterson, Stephen, Dr/*Orangefield Ind School Dist*	1	309
Patterson, Susan/*Arlington Ind School Dist*	27	343
Patton, Cody/*Tioga Ind School Dist*	6	167
Patty, Rae Ann/*Waskom Ind School Dist*	8,69	209
Paul, Eric/*Galveston Ind School Dist*	27	160
Paul, Sue/*Douglass Ind School Dist*	36,69,83,88,270	297
Paulson, Dana/*Leander Ind School Dist*	2	396
Paulson, Stephanie/*Pharr-San Juan-Alamo Ind SD*	39	223
Pavlovsky, Charles/*Archdiocese Galveston-Houston*	68	203
Pawelek, Cynthia/*Elgin Ind School Dist*	294	24
Pawelek, Todd/*Falls City Ind School Dist*	1,11,83	250
Pawelek, Vanessa/*Kenedy Ind School Dist*	2	251
Pawelk, Lindsy/*Pleasanton Ind School Dist*	11,58	21
Paxon, Michael/*Brackett Ind School Dist*	67	257
Payne, Brenda/*Richardson Ind School Dist*	9,15	112
Payne, David/*Lorena Ind School Dist*	295	280
Payne, Larry/*Dumas Ind School Dist*	71,83	295
Payne, Laureen/*Greenville Ind School Dist*	81	236
Payne, Michael/*Carlisle Ind School Dist*	1,11,83	327
Payne, Shalontae/*Duncanville Ind School Dist*	27,31	104
Payne, Stephanie/*Lake Dallas Ind School Dist*	69	122
Payne, Thomas/*Dayton Ind School Dist*	67	265
Payton, Kenneth/*Groom Ind School Dist*	3	69
Paz, Temoc/*Sharyland Ind School Dist*	9	224
Peace, Angie/*Bartlett Ind School Dist*	8,36,69,88	26
Peach, Ken/*Boerne Ind School Dist*	20	253
Peacock, Rory/*Region 11 Ed Service Center*	15,295	360
Peacock, Ryder/*Albany Ind School Dist*	6	334
Peacock, Shannon/*Bloomburg Ind School Dist*	83	70
Pearce, Ricky/*Hempstead Ind School Dist*	67	384
Pearson, Greg/*Brownsboro Ind School Dist*	6,35	213
Pearson, Lisa/*Livingston Ind School Dist*	2	316
Pease, Ben/*Lackland Ind School Dist*	76	34
Peavey, Brandon/*Bridgeport Ind School Dist*	1	402
Peck, Kelley/*Buna Ind School Dist*	8,11,76,271	240
Peck, Nita/*George West Ind School Dist*	2	268
Peddy, Gina/*Carroll Independent Sch Dist*	8,61,81	347
Peddy, Walter/*Woden Ind School Dist*	2	298
Pedersen, Jaclyn/*UT Tyler University Acad Dist*	8,298	338
Pederson, Lyndsey/*Bynum Ind School Dist*	8,11,58,76,286,288	227
Pedroza, Blanca/*Olton Ind School Dist*	271	261
Peebles, Justin/*La Vega Ind School Dist*	73,84,295	279
Peeks, Judy/*Avery Ind School Dist*	4	322
Peel, Rebecca/*Thorndale Ind School Dist*	2	288
Peeler, Barbra/*Jourdanton Ind School Dist*	67	20
Peeples, Cesily/*Marion Ind School Dist*	8	172
Peeples, Scott/*Sunray Ind School Dist*	67	296
Peery, Susan/*Alamo Heights Ind School Dist*	34,72	30
Peese, Evelyn/*Fredericksburg Ind School Dist*	5	162
Peets, Courtney/*Burleson Ind School Dist*	7	246
Pehl, Kit/*Coppell Ind School Dist*	6	98
Peinly, Kim/*Waller Ind School Dist*	2	384
Pelichet, Kyle/*Corpus Christi Ind Sch Dist*	5	303
Pelletier, Jennifer/*Diocese of Fort Worth Ed Off*	1	358
Peltier, Daryl/*Danbury Ind School Dist*	67	53
Peltier, Diane/*Alvin Ind School Dist*	45	50
Pelton, Robin/*Brazosport Ind School Dist*	79,83,270,275	52
Pena-Rodriguez, Audrey/*Point Isabel Ind Sch Dist*	4	66
Pena, Aaron, Dr/*Midway Ind School Dist*	8,15,288	280

School Year 2019-2020   800-333-8802   TX-T69

DISTRICT PERSONNEL INDEX

Market Data Retrieval

NAME/District	JOB FUNCTIONS	PAGE
Pena, Adolfo/Rio Grande City Ind Sch Dist	15	340
Pena, Adrian/Banquete Ind School Dist	2	302
Pena, Albert/San Perlita Ind School Dist	1	394
Pena, Annette/La Feria Ind School Dist	57	65
Pena, Dora/Weslaco Ind School Dist	4	225
Pena, Janie/Weslaco Ind School Dist	8	225
Pena, Jennifer/San Vicente Ind School Dist	83,85,270	57
Pena, Jennifer/Terlingua Common School Dist	36	57
Pena, Leonila/San Benito Cons Ind Sch Dist	16,76,286	67
Pena, Maricela/Robstown Ind School Dist	30	305
Pena, Melissa/Webb Cons Ind School Dist	67	388
Pena, Minerva/Brownsville Ind School Dist	67	63
Pena, Pam/Carrollton-Farmers Branch ISD	71	96
Pena, Rob/Midland Ind School Dist	42	285
Pena, Robert/Cumby Ind School Dist	16,73,295	231
Pena, Rodrigo, Dr/San Diego Ind School Dist	1	128
Pena, Sergio/Mission Cons Ind School Dist	27,31	222
Pena, Virginia/Riviera Ind School Dist	2	258
Pendegraft, Dana/Paint Creek Ind School Dist	67	210
Pendergrass, Susan/Whitharral Ind School Dist	57	230
Penez, Cindy/Corpus Christi Ind Sch Dist	46	303
Penn, Amber/Jacksonville Ind School Dist	57,89,271	73
Penn, Kyle/Westwood Ind School Dist	2,288	16
Penn, Terry/Rockwall Ind School Dist	5	325
Pennell, Amber/Farmersville Ind School Dist	2,19,271	78
Pennell, Elsa/San Antonio Ind School Dist	93	39
Penney, Jennifer/Whitney Ind School Dist	10,31,36,69,83,85,88	228
Penney, Pam/La Poynor Ind School Dist	7,85	214
Pennington, Cathy/Poolville Ind School Dist	8,11,57,58,69,271,296,298	313
Pennington, Stacy/Barbers Hill Ind School Dist	73	72
Penny, Eary/Bosqueville Ind School Dist	7	278
Peno, Maris/Region 5 Ed Service Center	7,298	244
Penrod, Eric, Dr/Killeen Ind School Dist	15	27
Penrod, Florence/Tom Bean Ind School Dist	4	168
Penton, Jennifer/Rockwall Ind School Dist	40,280	325
Pepper, Nancy/Devine Ind School Dist	67	283
Perales, Aaron/Arlington Ind School Dist	93	343
Percival, James/Community Ind School Dist	3,5	78
Peredia, Lori/Ralls Ind School Dist	7,35,85	94
Perez, Aleida/San Antonio Ind School Dist	34	39
Perez, Alfonso/Roma Ind School Dist	2	341
Perez, Barry/Northside Ind School Dist	71	36
Perez, Bertha/La Joya Ind School Dist	88	219
Perez, Carol, Dr/Mission Cons Ind School Dist	1	222
Perez, Cassandra/Arlington Ind School Dist	57,61	343
Perez, Christina/Benavides Ind School Dist	2,5	128
Perez, Daniel/La Villa Ind School Dist	6,69	220
Perez, Deborah/Humble Ind School Dist	50	195
Perez, Doris/Edgewood Ind School Dist	57,61	31
Perez, Frances, Dr/Freer Ind School Dist	8,15,752	128
Perez, Francisco/Navasota Ind School Dist	27,73	172
Perez, Francisco/Schertz-Cibolo-Univ City ISD	5	173
Perez, Gilbert/Benavides Ind School Dist	6	128
Perez, Greg/Benavides Ind School Dist	73,84,285,286	128
Perez, Guadalupe/Diocese of Laredo Ed Office	1	388
Perez, Hector/United Ind School Dist	73,76,286	387
Perez, Jaime/Edinburg Cons Ind School Dist	4	216
Perez, Jessica/Tomball Ind School Dist	34	203
Perez, Liliaana/Somerset Ind School Dist	28,95	42
Perez, Lisa/Odem-Edroy Ind School Dist	83,85	331
Perez, Lyn/Orange Grove Ind School Dist	9	245
Perez, Maria/North East Ind School Dist	7,35	34
Perez, Maryann/La Pryor Ind School Dist	57	407
Perez, Marybelle/Ft Bend Ind School Dist	34	149
Perez, Miguel, Dr/Spring Ind School Dist	15	202
Perez, Mike/Cross Plains Ind Sch Dist	5	62
Perez, Nalsy/Houston Ind School Dist	46	188

NAME/District	JOB FUNCTIONS	PAGE
Perez, Nolan, Dr/Harlingen Cons Ind School Dist	67	64
Perez, Olivia/Carrollton-Farmers Branch ISD	57,61,89,271	96
Perez, Oscar/Ft Bend Ind School Dist	3,17	149
Perez, Peter, Dr/Elgin Ind School Dist	11,15,57,83	24
Perez, Raquel/Jim Hogg Co Ind School Dist	73	244
Perez, Robert/La Villa Ind School Dist	73	220
Perez, Robin, Dr/Nederland Ind School Dist	1	242
Perez, Rosa/Westwood Ind School Dist	34	16
Perez, Rosie/Brooks Co Ind School Dist	4	57
Perez, Santos/Palacios Ind School Dist	3,5	275
Perez, Stephanie/Spring Hill Ind School Dist	69	170
Perez, Steve/Stafford Municipal Sch Dist	16	155
Perez, Victor/Ysleta Ind School Dist	36,57	137
Perkins, Anika/Marshall Ind School Dist	8,27,34,57,81	209
Perkins, Clint/Petrolia Cons Ind School Dist	69,83,88	74
Perkins, Mikaela/Manor Ind School Dist	8,69,280,294,298	371
Perkins, Shane/Farwell Ind School Dist	6	314
Perkins, Wesley/Lake Travis Ind School Dist	3	370
Permann, Becky/Franklin Ind School Dist	295	325
Permentor, Sarah/Comal Ind School Dist	271	87
Peroni, Wendy/Yorktown Ind School Dist	2,11,30,271	118
Peronto, Janice, Dr/Killeen Ind School Dist	58	27
Perrin, Joe/Grandview Ind School Dist	1	248
Perrington, Rhonda/Palestine Ind School Dist	22	15
Perry, David/River Road Ind School Dist	3	319
Perry, Debbie/Midway Ind School Dist	273	280
Perry, Gerald/Mineral Wells Ind School Dist	6	310
Perry, Greg/Little Cypress Mauriceville SD	2,15	308
Perry, Jacob/Waxahachie Ind School Dist	3	142
Perry, Mandi/Knox City-O'Brien Cons Ind SD	7	258
Perry, Mandi/Munday Consolidated Ind SD	7	259
Perry, Mikki/Clarksville Ind School Dist	11,58	322
Perry, Molley/College Station Ind Sch Dist	15,77,751	55
Perry, Robin/Diocese of Tyler Ed Office	1,11	339
Perry, Stephanie/Humble Ind School Dist	8,275	195
Perry, Vicki/Silverton Ind School Dist	271	57
Perryman, Bryan/River Road Ind School Dist	5	319
Perschbacher, Roff/Texline Ind School Dist	8,12,69,288	95
Persyn, Eric/Keller Ind School Dist	6	354
Pesak, Bretina/Rockdale Ind School Dist	27	287
Pesato, Scott/Devine Ind School Dist	73	283
Peschel, Dovie/Needville Ind School Dist	2	154
Pesqueda, Natasha/Charlotte Ind School Dist	16,82	20
Peterka, Joe/Duncanville Ind School Dist	3	104
Peterman, Todd/White Settlement Ind Sch Dist	6	357
Peterman, Todd/White Settlement Ind Sch Dist	6	357
Peters, Andrew/Caldwell Ind School Dist	1,11	59
Peters, Jennifer/Marshall Ind School Dist	7	209
Peters, Joy/Pecos-Barstow-Toyah Ind SD	4	323
Peters, Mary/Hondo Ind School Dist	73,286,295	284
Peters, Mike/Ft Stockton Ind School Dist	6	315
Peters, Scott/Dallas Co Schools	74,77,91	96
Peterson, April/Bonham Ind School Dist	16	145
Peterson, Courtney/Humble Ind School Dist	47	195
Peterson, Dominik/Grand Prairie Ind School Dist	4	107
Peterson, Donna/Texas City Ind School Dist	58	161
Peterson, Donna/Texas City Ind School Dist	58	161
Peterson, Elise/Ore City Ind School Dist	37	377
Peterson, Kathryn/Louise Ind School Dist	8	389
Peterson, Michael/Region 20 Ed Service Center	3	45
Peterson, Michael/Whitesboro Ind School Dist	73,295	168
Peterson, Paula/Nocona Ind School Dist	2	290
Peterson, Shirley/Mt Pleasant Ind School Dist	11	363
Peterson, Steve/Bryan Ind School Dist	3	54
Peterson, Susan/Weslaco Ind School Dist	8,15	225
Petofi-Casal, Christina/Randolph Field Ind School Dist	58	39
Petree, Amber/Friendswood Ind Sch Dist	2	160

1 Superintendent	16 Instructional Media Svcs	30 Adult Education	44 Science Sec	58 Special Education K-12	72 Summer School	88 Alternative/At Risk	277 Remedial Math K-12
2 Bus/Finance/Purchasing	17 Chief Operations Officer	31 Career/Sch-to-Work K-12	45 Math K-12	59 Special Education Elem	73 Instructional Tech	89 Multi-Cultural Curriculum	280 Literacy Coach
3 Buildings And Grounds	18 Chief Academic Officer	32 Career/Sch-to-Work Elem	46 Math Elem	60 Special Education Sec	74 Inservice Training	90 Social Work	285 STEM
4 Food Service	19 Chief Financial Officer	33 Career/Sch-to-Work Sec	47 Math Sec	61 Foreign/World Lang K-12	75 Marketing/Distributive	91 Safety/Security	286 Digital Learning
5 Transportation	20 Art K-12	34 Early Childhood Ed	48 English/Lang Arts K-12	62 Foreign/World Lang Elem	76 Info Systems	92 Magnet School	288 Common Core Standards
6 Athletic	21 Art Elem	35 Health/Phys Education	49 English/Lang Arts Elem	63 Foreign/World Lang Sec	77 Psychological Assess	93 Parental Involvement	294 Accountability
7 Health Services	22 Art Sec	36 Guidance Services K-12	50 English/Lang Arts Sec	64 Religious Education K-12	78 Affirmative Action	95 Tech Prep Program	295 Network System
8 Curric/Instruct K-12	23 Music K-12	37 Guidance Services Elem	51 Reading K-12	65 Religious Education Elem	79 Student Personnel	97 Chief Information Officer	296 Title II Programs
9 Curric/Instruct Elem	24 Music Elem	38 Guidance Services Sec	52 Reading Elem	66 Religious Education Sec	80 Driver Ed/Safety	98 Chief Technology Officer	297 Webmaster
10 Curric/Instruct Sec	25 Music Sec	39 Social Studies K-12	53 Reading Sec	67 School Board President	81 Gifted/Talented	270 Character Education	298 Grant Writer/Ptnrships
11 Federal Program	26 Business Education	40 Social Studies Elem	54 Remedial Reading K-12	68 Teacher Personnel	82 Video Services	271 Migrant Education	750 Chief Innovation Officer
12 Title I	27 Career & Tech Ed	41 Social Studies Sec	55 Remedial Reading Elem	69 Academic Assessment	83 Substance Abuse Prev	273 Teacher Mentor	751 Chief of Staff
13 Title V	28 Technology Education	42 Science K-12	56 Remedial Reading Sec	70 Research/Development	84 Erate	274 Before/After Sch	752 Social Emotional Learning
15 Asst Superintendent	29 Family/Consumer Science	43 Science Elem	57 Bilingual/ELL	71 Public Information	85 AIDS Education	275 Response To Intervention	

Texas School Directory — DISTRICT PERSONNEL INDEX

NAME/District	JOB FUNCTIONS	PAGE
Petree, John/*Region 11 Ed Service Center*	15,58,69,73,74	360
Petrek, Thomas/*Klein Ind School Dist*	2,15	196
Petri, Tony/*Blanco Ind School Dist*	3	45
Petrich, Toni/*Riesel Ind School Dist*	2	281
Petroff, David/*Royse City Ind School Dist*	6	326
Petrzelka, Valerie/*Tomball Ind School Dist*	9	203
Pettit, E/*Bells Ind School Dist*	67	165
Pettit, Pamela/*Bells Ind School Dist*	16,82	165
Petty, Cathy/*Hermleigh Ind School Dist*	1	333
Petty, Lane/*Merkel Ind School Dist*	2	361
Petty, Leigh/*Highland Ind School Dist*	57	301
Petty, Megan/*Cumby Ind School Dist*	8,36,69,270	231
Petty, Mike/*Wells Ind School Dist*	3,5	73
Petty, Mindy/*Lockney Independent Sch Dist*	83,85	149
Pevey, Darren/*Chisum Ind School Dist*	6	259
Peyrot, Tricia/*Waxahachie Ind School Dist*	49,52,55	142
Peyton, Debbie/*Chico Ind School Dist*	295,297	403
Pfeffer, Revard/*Kilgore Ind School Dist*	2,19,298	169
Pfeiffer, Milissa/*Richardson Ind School Dist*	39	112
Pfiel, Becky/*Caddo Mills Ind Sch Dist*	2	235
Pfleging, Sue/*Waco Ind School Dist*	68	281
Phaestka, Cynthia/*Holland Ind School Dist*	7	27
Phalen, Cheryl/*Eagle Mtn-Saginaw Ind Sch Dist*	7	348
Pham, Long/*Ft Bend Ind School Dist*	71,76,97	149
Pharr, Sharah/*Hays Cons Ind School Dist*	11	211
Pharries, Nadine/*Huntsville Ind School Dist*	73	383
Pharris, Greg/*Forney Ind School Dist*	67	251
Phears, Lynn/*Mansfield Ind School Dist*	295	356
Phelps, Ernie/*Farmersville Ind School Dist*	3,5	78
Phelps, Lauren/*Brownfield Ind Sch Dist*	752	362
Phelps, Marie/*Southwest Ind School Dist*	79	43
Phenix, Jaci/*Stafford Municipal Sch Dist*	3	155
Philips, Kana/*Vidor Ind School Dist*	23	309
Phillips, Alethia/*Brainaition Schools*	58	30
Phillips, Anna/*Region 17 Ed Service Center*	58	272
Phillips, Cara/*Normangee Ind School Dist*	10,31	264
Phillips, Christy/*Como Pickton Cons Ind SD*	38	231
Phillips, Connie/*Cuero Ind School Dist*	294	117
Phillips, Craten/*Lago Vista Ind School Dist*	6	370
Phillips, Dedra/*Sweeny Ind School Dist*	76	54
Phillips, Gena/*Newcastle Ind School Dist*	7	406
Phillips, Jason/*Forsan Ind School Dist*	6	234
Phillips, Jeff/*May Ind School Dist*	67	59
Phillips, Jim/*Waller Ind School Dist*	9	384
Phillips, John/*Bronte Ind School Dist*	9,11,52,55	75
Phillips, Kentrell/*Everman Ind School Dist*	8,15,73	349
Phillips, Kim/*Sanger Ind School Dist*	58,84	126
Phillips, Leeton/*St Jo Ind School Dist*	67	290
Phillips, Mike/*Marble Falls Ind School Dist*	3	60
Phillips, Moriah/*Big Sandy Ind School Dist*	73,76,84,286,295	376
Phillips, Renae/*Hallettsville Ind Sch Dist*	16	262
Phillips, Sherry/*Danbury Ind School Dist*	273	53
Phillips, Sherry/*Danbury Ind School Dist*	11,15,57	53
Phillips, Stacy/*Sherman Ind School Dist*	7,36,69,83,275	167
Phillips, Susan/*Matagorda Ind School Dist*	1,11,57,83,288	275
Phillips, Tera/*Normangee Ind School Dist*	9,57,83,270,271,296	264
Phillips, Terry/*Clyde Consolidated Ind SD*	2	62
Phillips, Tony/*Lipan Ind School Dist*	6,8	230
Phillips, Wayne/*Harts Bluff Ind School Dist*	5,73	363
Philpott, Joy/*Hays Cons Ind School Dist*	294	211
Phipps, Robbie/*Dawson Ind School Dist*	7	116
Phipps, Sandy/*Nocona Ind School Dist*	16,82	290
Phipps, Scott/*Crandall Ind School Dist*	73,76,98,286	251
Pichardo, Brandi/*Leakey Ind School Dist*	67	322
Pick, Paul/*Grapeland Ind School Dist*	5	232
Pickens, Andy/*Burleson Ind School Dist*	67	246
Pickens, Dwan/*Region 12 Ed Service Center*	57	283
Pickens, J/*Trent Ind School Dist*	67	361
Pickett, Hubert/*Everman Ind School Dist*	79	349
Pickett, Tammy/*Red Oak Ind School Dist*	5	142
Pickhardt, Irene/*Texas Dept of Education*	42	1
Picon, Raul/*Port Arthur Ind School Dist*	297	243
Picou, Kelsey/*Robstown Ind School Dist*	71	305
Piekarski, Martha/*Canutillo Ind School Dist*	2,19	131
Pieratt, Annaliza/*D'Hanis Ind School Dist*	57	283
Pierce, Casey/*Slidell Ind School Dist*	6	403
Pierce, Daniel/*Cross Roads Ind School Dist*	6	214
Pierce, Georgia/*Leveretts Chapel Ind Sch Dist*	12	328
Pierce, Glen/*Longview Ind School Dist*	76	169
Pierce, Jim/*Texhoma Ind School Dist*	295	336
Pierce, Karyn/*Amarillo Ind School Dist*	27,31	317
Pierce, Kathy/*Poolville Ind School Dist*	9,59	313
Pierce, Melford/*Maud Ind School Dist*	67	49
Pierce, Robbie/*Lytle Ind School Dist*	58	21
Pierce, Tami/*Dayton Ind School Dist*	2,15,19	265
Pierce, Tracy/*Nocona Ind School Dist*	57,271,275	290
Pierce, Wayland/*Glasscock Co Ind School Dist*	8,12,88,274	163
Pierce, Wes/*Region 9 Ed Service Center*	1	393
Piersall, Randy/*Abilene Ind School Dist*	67	360
Pietsch, Shelly/*Bastrop Ind School Dist*	59	23
Pigg, Donna/*Turkey-Quitaque Cons Ind SD*	2	176
Pike, Melissa/*Llano Ind School Dist*	5	268
Pike, Sue/*Deer Park Ind School Dist*	76	186
Piles, Harry/*Lytle Ind School Dist*	8,15,275,286,288	21
Pilip, Christal/*Prairiland Ind School Dist*	7	260
Pilkey, Jacqueline, Dr/*Killeen Ind School Dist*	58	27
Pilkington, Debbie/*Kennard Ind Sch Dist*	16,82	233
Pimentel, Melissa/*Lyford Cons Ind School Dist*	8	394
Pimepel, Milissa/*Lyford Cons Ind School Dist*	69	394
Pina, Patricia/*Goose Creek Cons Ind Sch Dist*	7	187
Pineda, Hector/*Region 15 Ed Service Center*	34	366
Pinedo, Monica/*Marathon Ind School Dist*	57,83,271	56
Pinegar, Lorrine/*Clear Creek Ind School Dist*	71	158
Pinell, David/*Winnsboro Ind School Dist*	285	405
Pinkard, Ritchie/*Mt Pleasant Ind School Dist*	6	363
Pinkerton, Jennifer/*Point Isabel Ind Sch Dist*	67	66
Pinkston, Camille/*Wells Ind School Dist*	4	73
Pinkston, Cassie/*Lone Oak Ind School Dist*	73,76,297	236
Pinnell, David/*Morgan Ind School Dist*	67	47
Pinnell, Janie/*Morgan Ind School Dist*	2	47
Pinnell, Steve/*Winnsboro Ind School Dist*	6	405
Pinner, Sandy/*Chireno ISD School Dist*	36,57,88,271	297
Pinson, Barbara/*Maypearl Ind School Dist*	16	141
Pinyan, Chris/*Rio Vista Ind School Dist*	67	248
Pipak, Molly/*Plano Ind School Dist*	35	82
Piper, Kristen/*Brazosport Ind School Dist*	48,51,54	52
Piper, Pam/*Tom Bean Ind School Dist*	3	168
Pipes, Lynne/*Maypearl Ind School Dist*	59	141
Pipkin, Linda/*Hunt Ind School Dist*	67	255
Pippin, Mable/*Riviera Ind School Dist*	16	258
Pippin, Vicki/*Carrollton-Farmers Branch ISD*	2	96
Pirtele, Chad/*Pleasant Grove Ind School Dist*	1	49
Pitcock, Daniel/*Allen Ind School Dist*	3,5,15,91,295	76
Pittenger, Donna/*Katy Ind School Dist*	4	151
Pittman, Brandi/*Hughes Springs Ind Sch Dist*	7	70
Pittman, Calvin/*Lampasas Ind School Dist*	4	261
Pittman, Curtis/*Colmesneil Ind School Dist*	67	375
Pittman, Curtis/*Fort Davis Ind School Dist*	73	241
Pittman, Michael/*Post Ind School Dist*	6	162
Pitts, Brian/*Longview Ind School Dist*	73,295	169
Pitts, Kevin/*China Spring Ind School Dist*	15	278
Pitts, Kevin/*Richardson Ind School Dist*	6	112
Pitts, Linda/*Boles Ind School Dist*	67	235
Pitts, Peter/*Kingsville Ind School Dist*	2,68	257
Piwetz, Tisha/*Port Aransas Ind School Dist*	298	305
Pizana, James/*Seguin Ind School Dist*	3,5,79,91	173
Pizzini, Gracie/*San Diego Ind School Dist*	8,11,15,79	128
Plant, Curtis/*Kenedy Ind School Dist*	73,84	251
Plany, Doug/*Richardson Ind School Dist*	47	112
Plauche, Lane/*Sabine Pass Ind School Dist*	67	244
Pleasant, Carl/*Temple Ind School Dist*	88	29
Pleasant, Toby/*Spring Hill Ind School Dist*	3	170
Pledger, Colette/*Robinson Ind School Dist*	8,18	281
Plott, Kathleen/*Klein Ind School Dist*	81	196
Plott, Kevin/*Apple Springs Ind School Dist*	8	374
Pluao, Lynn/*Kerrville Ind School Dist*	11,58,83,88,275,298	256
Plyler, Mignon/*Sherman Ind School Dist*	73,295	167
Plymale, Dave/*Goliad Ind School Dist*	1	163
Poage, Liz/*Lamesa Ind School Dist*	2,294	117
Poage, Liz/*Miami Ind School Dist*	2	324
Poage, Ron/*Lampasas Ind School Dist*	73,295	261
Pocius, Clayton/*Flour Bluff Ind School Dist*	3,5	304

School Year 2019-2020 — 800-333-8802

DISTRICT PERSONNEL INDEX

Market Data Retrieval

NAME/District	JOB FUNCTIONS	PAGE
Poe, Matt/Pottsboro Ind School Dist	6	167
Poe, Misty/Diocese of Austin Ed Office	1,11	372
Poenitzsch, Nicole/Dripping Springs Ind Sch Dist	15	210
Poer, Mandy/Spring Creek Ind School Dist	1,11,73,83	238
Pogue, Michael/White Settlement Ind Sch Dist	58	357
Poindexter, Tonya/Crockett Co Cons Common SD	8,69	94
Pokorny, Jolena/Thrall Ind School Dist	11,285	400
Poland, Denise/Aransas Co Ind School Dist	9	19
Polasek, Billy/Pawnee Ind School Dist	73	25
Polasek, Billy/Stockdale Ind School Dist	73	401
Polasek, Holly/Karnes City Ind School Dist	16	250
Polk, Brittanie/Gainesville Ind School Dist	58	91
Polk, Charles/Nederland Ind School Dist	5	242
Polk, Crystel/Crowley Ind School Dist	298	347
Polk, Elizabeth/Austin Ind School Dist	16	366
Polk, James/Gainesville Ind School Dist	6	91
Polk, Larry/Terrell Ind School Dist	15,298	253
Polk, Ray/Karnack Ind School Dist	67	208
Polk, Renee/Pilot Point Ind School Dist	67	125
Pollard, Barrett, Dr/Gatesville Ind School Dist	1	92
Pollard, Jon/Yantis Ind School Dist	73,84	405
Polomo, Ernesto/Gregory-Portland Ind Sch Dist	3	330
Polsen, Elaina/Clear Creek Ind School Dist	71	158
Polster, Misti/Hamilton Ind School Dist	57	176
Polzin, Dyann/Galveston Ind School Dist	68,71	160
Pommerening, Susan/Cameron Ind School Dist	8,11,15	287
Ponce, Geovanny/Houston ISD-East Area	15	189
Poncik, Callie/Academy Ind School Dist	10,74,273	26
Pond, Laurie/Hamlin Ind School Dist	8	249
Pondant, Melanie/Longview Ind School Dist	10	169
Ponder, Barbara/Barbers Hill Ind School Dist	15,68	72
Ponder, Scott/Bells Ind School Dist	6	165
Ponder, Scott/Center Ind School Dist	6	334
Pones, Rosa/Brownsville Ind School Dist	7	63
Pool, Cathy/Tomball Ind School Dist	7,35,85	203
Pool, Lynn/Weatherford Ind School Dist	78,79	313
Poole, Becky/Buffalo Ind School Dist	68,71	264
Poole, Dennis/Borden Co Ind School Dist	67	46
Poole, Greg, Dr/Barbers Hill Ind School Dist	1	72
Poole, Lee/Hunt Ind School Dist	6	255
Pope, Amy/Sweeny Ind School Dist	11,15,69,83,88,275,294,296	54
Pope, Bonnie/Carthage Ind School Dist	16	311
Pope, Faith/Lockhart Ind School Dist	9	61
Pope, Gary/Lamesa Ind School Dist	4	117
Popham, Jacob/Loraine Ind School Dist	6	289
Porras, Amy/Ft Stockton Ind School Dist	274	315
Porras, Ofelia/Texhoma Ind School Dist	271	336
Porter, Amy/Frankston Ind School Dist	7	15
Porter, Brandon/Fredericksburg Ind School Dist	3	162
Porter, Bruce/Patton Springs Ind School Dist	3	127
Porter, Donna/Carthage Ind School Dist	8,11,57,88,285,288,296,298	311
Porter, Jacquie/Texas Dept of Education	34	1
Porter, Kelley/Lefors Ind School Dist	1,11	165
Porter, Luane/Fort Davis Ind School Dist	11	241
Porter, Lynne/Ingleside Ind School Dist	8,15	331
Porter, Ronnie/Troy Ind School Dist	6	29
Porter, Stacey/Cuero Ind School Dist	27	117
Porter, Tracy/Mexia Ind School Dist	286	267
Porter, Veronica/San Augustine Ind School Dist	294	329
Porterfield, Peggy, Dr/Arlington Ind School Dist	69	343
Porterfield, Ty/Douglass Ind School Dist	73,76,286	297
Porterie, Mark, Dr/Port Arthur Ind School Dist	1	243
Portillo, Juvencio/Wilson Ind School Dist	31,36,69	273
Portillo, Luis/Bastrop Ind School Dist	20,23	23
Portillo, Rodrigo/Tornillo Ind School Dist	9	137
Porton, Jason/Vega Ind School Dist	6	307
Portwood, Lance/Columbus Ind School Dist	73,295	86

NAME/District	JOB FUNCTIONS	PAGE
Posey, Dan/Temple Ind School Dist	67	29
Posey, Jeff/Roby Cons Ind School Dist	67	148
Post, Julie/Poteet Ind School Dist	69	21
Postillo, Laura, Dr/Presidio Ind School Dist	8,11,57,58,271,298	320
Pote, Jeffrey/Richards Ind School Dist	6	172
Poteet, Brenda/China Spring Ind School Dist	2	278
Poteet, Brenda/Corsicana Ind School Dist	2,8,15,296	299
Potts, Heather/Ector Co Ind School Dist	76	130
Potts, Kathy/Hitchcock Ind School Dist	7	161
Potts, Ronnie/Keene Ind School Dist	91	248
Pouget, Sylvie/Eanes Ind School Dist	2	370
Poundes, Amanda/Chester Ind School Dist	4	374
Pounds, Sue/Eula Ind School Dist	4	63
Powell, Andy/Axtell Ind School Dist	3	278
Powell, Ashley/Evadale Ind School Dist	8	240
Powell, Brad/Dalhart Ind School Dist	73,76,84,295	95
Powell, Cindy/Arlington Ind School Dist	2,19	343
Powell, Deeann, Dr/Pasadena Ind School Dist	1	198
Powell, Deidre/Nederland Ind School Dist	34,36,54,58,77,79	242
Powell, Donita/Premont Ind School Dist	73	246
Powell, Jackie/Wylie Ind School Dist	76	361
Powell, Jeff/Southwest Ind School Dist	73,84,295	43
Powell, Jonathan/Clint Ind School Dist	5	132
Powell, Kelli/Corpus Christi Ind Sch Dist	10	303
Powell, Mike/Harmony Ind School Dist	3	376
Powell, Rachel/Clear Creek Ind School Dist	46,277	158
Powelson, Stephanie/Donna Ind School Dist	39	215
Powers, Dave/Birdville Ind School Dist	5	346
Powers, Donnie/Sulphur Bluff Ind School Dist	67	232
Powers, Kristi/Nueces Canyon Cons Ind SD	1	131
Powers, Scott, Dr/New Caney Ind School Dist	71	293
Powers, Shana/Diboll Ind School Dist	58	17
Poynor, Greg/Pampa Ind School Dist	6	165
Prachyl, Karen/Red Oak Ind School Dist	76	142
Prado, Connie/South San Antonio Ind Sch Dist	67	42
Prado, Gilberto/Cedar Hill Ind School Dist	19	97
Prater, Ed/Frankston Ind School Dist	73,286,295,298	15
Prater, Kristin/Edgewood Ind School Dist	11,83,288	380
Prater, Kristin/Edgewood Ind School Dist	8,69,88	380
Prather, Brenda/Ralls Ind School Dist	10	94
Pratt, Chris/Splendora Ind School Dist	23	294
Pratt, Kathryn/Whitehouse Ind School Dist	39	338
Pratt, Shawn/McKinney Ind School Dist	6	80
Prentice, Ray/Del Valle Ind School Dist	11	369
Prescher, Karen/Walnut Springs Ind Sch Dist	2	47
Prescher, Lisa/Clifton Ind School Dist	2	46
Presley, Daniel, Dr/Round Rock Ind School Dist	70	398
Presley, Roy/Hallsville Ind School Dist	5	208
Presnall, Jeffrey/Muenster Ind School Dist	73	91
Presto, Darin/Sweeny Ind School Dist	8,294	54
Preston, Curtis/Muleshoe Ind School Dist	67	22
Preston, Gary/Paris Ind School Dist	15,68,273	260
Preston, Morgan/Snyder Ind School Dist	2	333
Preston, Shane/Bridge City Ind School Dist	295	308
Price, Anthony/Goose Creek Cons Ind Sch Dist	15	187
Price, Bud/Palo Pinto Ind Sch Dist 906	67	310
Price, David/Red Lick Ind School Dist	67	49
Price, Erica/Alvin Ind School Dist	42	50
Price, Jennifer/Keller Ind School Dist	69,294	354
Price, John, Dr/Lancaster Ind School Dist	3,17	110
Price, Justin/McKinney Ind School Dist	3	80
Price, Kirk/Milford Ind School Dist	73,286,295	141
Price, Leah/Bruceville-Eddy Ind Sch Dist	73,76,84,286,295	278
Price, Leslie/San Antonio Ind School Dist	71	39
Price, Mia/Denton Ind School Dist	67	120
Price, Mike/Melissa Ind School Dist	4	81
Price, Ronnie/Connally Ind School Dist	83,91	279

1 Superintendent
2 Bus/Finance/Purchasing
3 Buildings And Grounds
4 Food Service
5 Transportation
6 Athletic
7 Health Services
8 Curric/Instruct K-12
9 Curric/Instruct Elem
10 Curric/Instruct Sec
11 Federal Program
12 Title I
13 Title V
15 Asst Superintendent
16 Instructional Media Svcs
17 Chief Operations Officer
18 Chief Academic Officer
19 Chief Financial Officer
20 Art K-12
21 Art Elem
22 Art Sec
23 Music K-12
24 Music Elem
25 Music Sec
26 Business Education
27 Career & Tech Ed
28 Technology Education
29 Family/Consumer Science
30 Adult Education
31 Career/Sch-to-Work K-12
32 Career/Sch-to-Work Elem
33 Career/Sch-to-Work Sec
34 Early Childhood Ed
35 Health/Phys Education
36 Guidance Services K-12
37 Guidance Services Elem
38 Guidance Services Sec
39 Social Studies K-12
40 Social Studies Elem
41 Social Studies Sec
42 Science K-12
43 Science Elem
44 Science Sec
45 Math K-12
46 Math Elem
47 Math Sec
49 English/Lang Arts K-12
49 English/Lang Arts Elem
50 English/Lang Arts Sec
51 Reading K-12
52 Reading Elem
53 Reading Sec
54 Remedial Reading K-12
55 Remedial Reading Elem
56 Remedial Reading Sec
57 Bilingual/ELL
58 Special Education K-12
59 Special Education Elem
60 Special Education Sec
61 Foreign/World Lang K-12
62 Foreign/World Lang Elem
63 Foreign/World Lang Sec
64 Religious Education K-12
65 Religious Education Elem
66 Religious Education Sec
67 School Board President
68 Teacher Personnel
69 Academic Assessment
70 Research/Development
71 Public Information
72 Summer School
73 Instructional Tech
74 Inservice Training
75 Marketing/Distributive
76 Info Systems
77 Psychological Assess
78 Affirmative Action
79 Student Personnel
80 Driver Ed/Safety
81 Gifted/Talented
82 Video Services
83 Substance Abuse Prev
84 Erate
85 AIDS Education
88 Alternative/At Risk
89 Multi-Cultural Curriculum
90 Social Work
91 Safety/Security
92 Magnet School
93 Parental Involvement
94 Accountability
95 Tech Prep Program
96 Chief Information Officer
97 Chief Technology Officer
270 Character Education
271 Migrant Education
273 Teacher Mentor
274 Before/After Sch
275 Response To Intervention
277 Remedial Math K-12
280 Literacy Coach
285 STEM
286 Digital Learning
288 Common Core Standards
294 Accountability
295 Network System
296 Title II Programs
297 Webmaster
298 Grant Writer/Ptnrships
750 Chief Innovation Officer
751 Chief of Staff
752 Social Emotional Learning

TX-T72

Texas School Directory

DISTRICT PERSONNEL INDEX

NAME/District	JOB FUNCTIONS	PAGE
Price, Teri/*Mason Ind School Dist*	2	275
Price, Thomas/*Boerne Ind School Dist*	1	253
Prichard, Jennifer/*Paint Creek Ind School Dist*	73,295	210
Prichard, Lynn/*Highland Park Ind Sch Dist*	4	108
Priddy, Pamela/*San Vicente Ind School Dist*	57	57
Pride, Richard/*Van Ind School Dist*	11,58	381
Pridemore, Kerri/*Belton Ind School Dist*	2	26
Priess, Grant/*Weatherford Ind School Dist*	88	313
Priest, Barbie/*Shallowater Ind School Dist*	58	272
Priest, Greg/*Tyler Ind School Dist*	6,85	337
Prieto, Jerry/*Crosby Ind School Dist*	6	183
Prigge, Regina/*Denison Ind School Dist*	36,69,271,294	166
Prince, Brandon/*Atlanta Ind School Dist*	73,286,297	69
Prince, Donna/*Chillicothe ISD School Dist*	36,69,83,85,88	177
Prince, Kory/*Bullard Ind School Dist*	73	336
Prince, Larry/*Garrison Ind School Dist*	6	297
Priour, Stephen/*East Central Ind School Dist*	3	31
Pritchard, Chris/*Lockney Independent Sch Dist*	73,295	149
Pritchard, Susan/*Brenham Ind School Dist*	274	385
Pritchett, Daniel/*Daingerfield-Lone Star Ind SD*	11	296
Prnka, Rodny/*Joaquin Ind School Dist*	5	335
Probst, Gabby/*Walnut Bend Ind School Dist*	273	92
Probst, Michael/*Brady Ind School Dist*	67	277
Proctor, J R, Dr/*Axtell Ind School Dist*	1	278
Proctor, Stacey/*Robinson Ind School Dist*	2,19	281
Proffitt, Greg/*Wellington Ind School Dist*	6	86
Proffitt, Patrick/*Iredell Ind School Dist*	67	46
Propps, Stacia/*Benjamin Ind School Dist*	2	258
Prosser, Matthew/*Longview Ind School Dist*	71	169
Prouse, Brandon/*Deweyville Ind School Dist*	6	308
Provencio, Art/*Beeville Ind School Dist*	4	25
Province, Michelle/*Birdville Ind School Dist*	7	346
Prudhomme, Donna, Dr/*Beaumont Ind School Dist*	27,31	241
Pruett, Clint/*Dripping Springs Ind Sch Dist*	3	210
Pruett, Craig/*Pflugerville Ind School Dist*	2	371
Pruett, Lynn/*Bremond Ind School Dist*	7	324
Pruitt, Donna/*Pine Tree Ind School Dist*	93	170
Pruitt, John/*Galveston Ind School Dist*	5	160
Pruitt, Kenith/*Canton Ind School Dist*	67	380
Pruitt, Rod/*Region 14 Ed Service Center*	83,85	362
Pruneda, Victor/*Valley View Ind School Dist*	295	225
Pruski, Wayne/*Schertz-Cibolo-Univ City ISD*	19	173
Pruvino, Marina/*Crystal City Ind School Dist*	7,85	407
Pry, Casey, Dr/*Clear Creek Ind School Dist*	15	158
Pryor, Ed/*Coleman Ind School Dist*	11	76
Psencik, Thomas/*Hallettsville Ind Sch Dist*	6	262
Ptasnik, Misty/*Hondo Ind School Dist*	9	284
Puckett, Jim Bob/*Lovejoy Ind School Dist*	6	80
Puente, Alex/*Flour Bluff Ind School Dist*	73,76,84,295	304
Puente, Veronica/*Rio Hondo Ind School Dist*	11,57,58,69	66
Puga, Danee/*Tulia Ind School Dist*	34,58,275	343
Puga, Soor-El/*Marble Falls Ind School Dist*	57	60
Pugh, Denise/*Savoy Ind School Dist*	2	146
Pugh, Donna/*Levelland Ind School Dist*	11,31,57,88,271,274,296,298	229
Pugh, Kyle/*Winona Ind School Dist*	73,84	339
Pugsley, Kim/*Rockwall Ind School Dist*	4	325
Puig, Marc, Dr/*Beeville Ind School Dist*	1	25
Pulate, Cenny/*Johnson City Ind School Dist*	58,69	46
Pullen, Cindy/*Angleton Ind School Dist*	68	51
Pullen, Cyndy/*Columbia Brazoria ISD*	273	52
Pulliam, Lawana/*Canadian Ind School Dist*	8,73	213
Pullin, Clint/*Walnut Springs Ind Sch Dist*	67	47
Pumphrey, Shonna/*Lancaster Ind School Dist*	2,19	110
Purdy, Randy/*Ed Service Center Region 2*	8,16,73	306
Purgahn, Carmen/*Deweyville Ind School Dist*	58	308
Pursch, Kimberly/*Archdiocese Galveston-Houston*	15	203
Pursch, Victoria/*New Braunfels Ind School Dist*	8,15,34,69,294	88
Purser, Rusty/*Greenwood Ind School Dist*	6	285
Pursifull, Kyle/*Allen Ind School Dist*	5	76
Purvis, Daniel/*Cross Plains Ind Sch Dist*	6	62
Pustejovsky, Ben/*Abbott Ind School Dist*	5	226
Pustejovsky, Bob/*Abbott Ind School Dist*	67	226
Pustejovsky, Channa/*Abbott Ind School Dist*	8,11,58,88,285,288,294	226
Pustejovsky, Ed/*Abbott Ind School Dist*	3	226
Pustejovsky, Eric/*Abbott Ind School Dist*	1,57	226
Pustejovsky, Traci/*Penelope ISD School Dist*	73	228

NAME/District	JOB FUNCTIONS	PAGE
Puth, Nina/*East Central Ind School Dist*	58	31
Putnal, Mike/*Alvin Ind School Dist*	91	51
Putnam, Jennifer/*Abilene Ind School Dist*	34	360
Putter, Renee/*Carrollton-Farmers Branch ISD*	6,35	96
Puz, Melony/*Port Arthur Ind School Dist*	44,53	243
Pyburn, Steven/*Hale Center Ind School Dist*	1	175
Pyle, Patrick/*San Antonio Ind School Dist*	39	39
Pyle, Tammy/*Farmersville Ind School Dist*	4	78

Q

NAME/District	JOB FUNCTIONS	PAGE
Quade, Marsha/*Knox City-O'Brien Cons Ind SD*	9,57,271	258
Qualls, Michael/*Bellevue Ind School Dist*	1,11	74
Qualls, Richard/*Pampa Ind School Dist*	67	165
Quarles, Breck/*Palestine Ind School Dist*	5	15
Quarles, Sandra/*Daingerfield-Lone Star Ind SD*	1	296
Quary, John, Dr/*Diocese of Victoria Ed Office*	1	382
Queen, Danielle/*Bronte Ind School Dist*	4	75
Quesada, Patricia, Dr/*San Benito Cons Ind Sch Dist*	57	67
Quesada, Roland, Dr/*George West Ind School Dist*	8,12,57,74,288	268
Quick, Todd/*Lufkin Ind School Dist*	6	18
Quinn, Elizabeth/*Archdiocese Galveston-Houston*	64	203
Quinn, Janice/*Kerens Ind School Dist*	16	300
Quinn, Kaye/*De Leon Ind School Dist*	12,31,36,69,85,88,270,296	89
Quintana, Johnny/*El Paso Ind School Dist*	295	132
Quintna, Larry/*Presidio Ind School Dist*	73	320
Quiorov, Sophia/*Castleberry Ind School Dist*	2	347
Quiraz, Fernando/*Brackett Ind School Dist*	3	257
Quiroga, Jesse/*Edgewood Ind School Dist*	91	31
Quiroz, Gloria/*Stephenville Ind School Dist*	5	144
Quisenberry, Chad/*Devine Ind School Dist*	6	283
Quisenberry, Melissa/*Aledo Ind School Dist*	73	312
Quisenberry, Stephen/*Region 10 Ed Service Center*	68	116

R

NAME/District	JOB FUNCTIONS	PAGE
Rabalais, Carla/*Barbers Hill Ind School Dist*	71	72
Rabalais, Don/*Alvin Ind School Dist*	16,73,76,98	50
Race, Judy/*Lockney Independent Sch Dist*	57	149
Radle, Patti/*San Antonio Ind School Dist*	67	39
Raga, Victor/*Northside Ind School Dist*	57	36
Ragland, Joan/*Hudson Ind School Dist*	73	17
Ragle, Scott/*Sands Consolidated ISD*	73	117
Ragsdale, Lisa/*Florence Ind School Dist*	5	395
Raines, David/*Leon Ind School Dist*	1	264
Raines, Janie/*Timpson Ind School Dist*	2	335
Rainey, Karla/*Van Ind School Dist*	27	381
Rainey, Lance/*Melissa Ind School Dist*	2	81
Rainey, Lisa/*McGregor Ind School Dist*	294	280
Rains, Greg/*Trent Ind School Dist*	3	361
Rains, Lachrisa/*Denver City Ind School Dist*	2,19	405
Rains, Renae/*Iola Ind School Dist*	59	172
Rakestraw, Wally/*Alief Ind School Dist*	73,295	181
Rakin, Sharron/*Kemp Ind School Dist*	67	252
Raley, Craig/*Richardson Ind School Dist*	79	112
Raley, Tim/*Chico Ind School Dist*	67	403
Rally, Joe/*Lefors Ind School Dist*	6	165
Ralson, D'Ann/*Boles Ind School Dist*	7	235
Ralston, Becky/*Rogers Ind School Dist*	8,69,294	28
Ralston, Terry/*Clarendon Cons Ind Sch Dist*	3	127
Ramaker, Tonia/*Aransas Co Ind School Dist*	7	19
Rambin, Ashley/*Joaquin Ind School Dist*	36,57,271	335
Ramer, Ginger/*Liberty Ind School Dist*	2,19	266
Ramerez, Randel/*Sundown Ind School Dist*	16,82,295	229
Rameriz, Ben/*Daingerfield-Lone Star Ind SD*	270	296
Rameriz, Ben/*Daingerfield-Lone Star Ind SD*	270	296
Rameriz, Eddie/*Pecos-Barstow-Toyah Ind SD*	2,15	323
Rameriz, Maryjane/*Hearne Ind School Dist*	67	325
Rameriz, Stephanie/*Coahoma Ind School Dist*	4	234
Ramey, Jamie/*Ganado Ind School Dist*	58	239
Ramirez, Alejandra/*Floydada Ind School Dist*	27,75	148
Ramirez, Alex/*Anthony Ind School Dist*	295	131
Ramirez, Amanda/*Santa Gertrudis Ind Sch Dist*	2	258
Ramirez, Angie/*Corpus Christi Ind Sch Dist*	273	303
Ramirez, Arminda/*Mission Cons Ind School Dist*	271	222
Ramirez, Arsenio/*Seminole Ind School Dist*	5	158
Ramirez, Christopher/*Harlandale Ind School Dist*	5	32
Ramirez, Cynthia/*United Ind School Dist*	58	387

School Year 2019-2020   800-333-8802   TX-T73

DISTRICT PERSONNEL INDEX

Market Data Retrieval

NAME/District	JOB FUNCTIONS	PAGE
Ramirez, Deonicio/Cotulla Ind School Dist	67	259
Ramirez, Diane/Lake Dallas Ind School Dist	7	122
Ramirez, Etna/Jim Hogg Co Ind School Dist	67	244
Ramirez, George/Stanton Ind School Dist	5	274
Ramirez, Guillermo/Hidalgo Ind School Dist	2,3,91	217
Ramirez, Heather/Cotulla Ind School Dist	11	259
Ramirez, Ismael/Sierra Blanca Ind School Dist	6	234
Ramirez, Jennifer/Belton Ind School Dist	58	26
Ramirez, Jennifer/Navasota Ind School Dist	67	172
Ramirez, Jorge/North East Ind School Dist	80	34
Ramirez, Jose/Clint Ind School Dist	39	132
Ramirez, Juana/Southside Ind School Dist	4	43
Ramirez, Kirstie/Point Isabel Ind Sch Dist	11,270,271	66
Ramirez, Liz/Fabens Ind School Dist	7	135
Ramirez, Luz/Judson Ind School Dist	57,271	33
Ramirez, Marla/College Station Ind Sch Dist	57	55
Ramirez, Michael/Carrollton-Farmers Branch ISD	35	96
Ramirez, Mike/Harlandale Ind School Dist	91	32
Ramirez, Myrtala/Laredo Ind School Dist	9	386
Ramirez, Nicole/La Grange Ind School Dist	11	147
Ramirez, Patsy/Rio Grande City Ind Sch Dist	4	340
Ramirez, Randy/Runge Ind School Dist	2	251
Ramirez, Raul/Dilley Ind School Dist	5	157
Ramirez, Raul/United Ind School Dist	4	387
Ramirez, Ricardo/Zapata Co Ind School Dist	67	406
Ramirez, Roberta/Laredo Ind School Dist	15,68	386
Ramirez, Rolando/Valley View Ind School Dist	1	225
Ramirez, Ruben/Devine Ind School Dist	3	283
Ramirez, Shannon/Devine Ind School Dist	2	283
Ramirez, Silvia/Tornillo Ind School Dist	4	137
Ramirez, Stephanie/San Benito Cons Ind Sch Dist	74	67
Ramirez, Susan/United Ind School Dist	52	387
Ramirez, Susanna/Grand Prairie Ind School Dist	15,34,93	107
Ramirez, Suzanne/Los Fresnos Cons Ind Sch Dist	5	66
Ramm, Justin/Lone Oak Ind School Dist	67	236
Ramon, Ralph/Snyder Ind School Dist	67	333
Ramon, Veronica/Driscoll Ind School Dist	67	304
Ramos, Aida/Natalia Ind School Dist	2	284
Ramos, Alice/San Elizario Ind School Dist	73,76,297	135
Ramos, Alicia/El Paso Ind School Dist	71,76,97,295	132
Ramos, Allisan/San Antonio Ind School Dist	4	39
Ramos, Becky/Charlotte Ind School Dist	67	20
Ramos, Cynthia/Lasara Ind School Dist	8,11,69,74,271,273,285	394
Ramos, Eduardo/Pflugerville Ind School Dist	2,3,17	371
Ramos, Freddy/Taft Ind School Dist	73	332
Ramos, Hezila/Presidio Ind School Dist	6	320
Ramos, Jacinto/Ft Worth Ind School Dist	67	349
Ramos, John/Castleberry Ind School Dist	1	347
Ramos, Juan/Plano Ind School Dist	3	82
Ramos, Kelsey/Calallen Ind School Dist	2	302
Ramos, Laura/Amarillo Ind School Dist	54	317
Ramos, Lilian/La Feria Ind School Dist	58	65
Ramos, Manuel/Rocksprings Ind School Dist	6	131
Ramos, Marisela/Canutillo Ind School Dist	271	132
Ramos, Rina/Morton Ind School Dist	9	75
Ramos, Shelly/Texas Dept of Education	8	1
Ramos, Victor/Beeville Ind School Dist	3,27	25
Rampy, Grant/Region 10 Ed Service Center	71	116
Ramsay, Diane/Mt Vernon Ind School Dist	13,16,286	155
Ramsdell, Greta/Sonora Ind School Dist	2	342
Ramsey, Brian/Electra Ind School Dist	6	391
Ramsey, Brian/Merkel Ind School Dist	6	361
Ramsey, Daphne/City View Ind School Dist	4	391
Ramsey, David/Lindale Ind School Dist	36,69	337
Ramsey, James/Pilot Point Ind School Dist	6	125
Ramsey, Tracey/Wimberley Ind School Dist	68	212
Rana, Rashad/Donna Ind School Dist	45	215
Randall, Mary/Mesquite Ind School Dist	15,68,74	110
Randell, Michelle/Alba-Golden Ind School Dist	58	404
Randle, Thomas, Dr/Lamar Cons Ind School Dist	1	153
Randolf, Tracy/Water Valley Ind School Dist	7	365
Randolph, Lyneldon/Lazbuddie Ind School Dist	3,5	315
Randolph, Vicki/Crosby Ind School Dist	49,52,54	183
Raney, Candi/Forestburg Ind School Dist	11	290
Raney, Jessica/Red Lick Ind School Dist	83,85	49
Raney, Jimmy/Forestburg Ind School Dist	67	290
Rangel, Cloris/Dallas Ind School Dist	57	98
Rangel, Enrique/United Ind School Dist	3,15	387
Rangel, Esteban/Laredo Ind School Dist	5	386
Rangel, Xavier/Ralls Ind School Dist	6	94
Raniey, David/Georgetown Ind School Dist	7,36	395
Rankin, Darlene/Katy Ind School Dist	73	151
Rankin, Licey/Motley Co Ind School Dist	57	296
Rankin, Sherry/Jourdanton Ind School Dist	271	20
Ransdell, Dean/Texarkana Ind School Dist	30	50
Ranucci, Jill/Manor Ind School Dist	27	371
Rapp, Lori, Dr/Lewisville Ind School Dist	8,15	122
Rasberry, Marva/Stafford Municipal Sch Dist	16,57,69,74,88,270,288,294	155
Rascoe, Chane, Dr/Lampasas Ind School Dist	1	261
Rascon, Jimmy/Ropes Ind School Dist	3	229
Rasile, Chris/Graham Ind School Dist	295	406
Rasmussen, Myrna/San Antonio Ind School Dist	57	39
Rasnick, D'Wanna/West Hardin Co Cons Sch Dist	8,11,69	178
Raspberry, Lee/Lockhart Ind School Dist	3	61
Rastellini, David/Northside Ind School Dist	2,15	36
Ratcliff, Jay/Big Sandy Ind School Dist	1,11	376
Ratcliff, Kim/Bloomburg Ind School Dist	2	70
Ratcliff, Mark/Alvarado Ind School Dist	3,15,91	246
Rateike, Angie/Whitney Ind School Dist	9,36	228
Ratliff, Haley/Gonzales Ind School Dist	68	164
Ratliff, Laura/Region 3 Ed Service Center	2,3,15	383
Ratliff, Linda/Bangs Ind School Dist	12,57	58
Ratliff, Linda/Boyd Ind School Dist	2	402
Rau, Randall/Hays Cons Ind School Dist	2,19	211
Rauch, Bob/Sterling City Ind School Dist	1	342
Rawlings, Jackie/Matagorda Ind School Dist	4	275
Rawlings, John/Loraine Ind School Dist	73,295	289
Rawlings, Linda/Eanes Ind School Dist	79,752	370
Rawlins, Doug/Stratford Ind School Dist	8,15	336
Rawlins, Mary/Stratford Ind School Dist	13	336
Rawlinson, Gayla/Harris Co Dept of Ed	298	179
Rawls, Rocky/Bronte Ind School Dist	6	75
Ray, Amanda/Blue Ridge Ind School Dist	2	77
Ray, Beth/Celeste Ind School Dist	9,34,271	235
Ray, Bill/Ft Worth Ind School Dist	5	349
Ray, Celia/Belton Ind School Dist	11	26
Ray, Clint/Whitehouse Ind School Dist	2,19	338
Ray, Corey/Gainesville Ind School Dist	4	91
Ray, Jennifer/Paris Ind School Dist	9,81	260
Ray, John/Prairie Lea Ind School Dist	73	61
Ray, Kendra/Lefors Ind School Dist	4	165
Ray, Marsha/Coleman Ind School Dist	4	76
Ray, Natasha/Bridge City Ind School Dist	73	308
Ray, Saugato/Mineral Wells Ind School Dist	295	310
Rayburg, Cheryl/Boerne Ind School Dist	4	253
Rayburn, Liz/Alpine Ind School Dist	4	56
Rayburne, Junior/Alvarado Ind School Dist	45,277	246
Raymond, Todd/Pflugerville Ind School Dist	6	371
Raymond, Tony/Sabine Ind School Dist	67	170
Raz, Ricky/Sweet Home Ind School Dist	67	262
Razo, Norma/La Villa Ind School Dist	5	220
Reach, Jacob/Austin Ind School Dist	15,751	366
Read, Jayson/Childress Ind School Dist	5	74
Read, Joey/Dalhart Ind School Dist	6	95

---

1 Superintendent
2 Bus/Finance/Purchasing
3 Buildings And Grounds
4 Food Service
5 Transportation
6 Athletic
7 Health Services
8 Curric/Instruct K-12
9 Curric/Instruct Elem
10 Curric/Instruct Sec
11 Federal Program
12 Title I
13 Title V
15 Asst Superintendent
16 Instructional Media Svcs
17 Chief Operations Officer
18 Chief Academic Officer
19 Chief Financial Officer
20 Art K-12
21 Art Elem
22 Art Sec
23 Music K-12
24 Music Elem
25 Music Sec
26 Business Education
27 Career & Tech Ed
28 Technology Education
29 Family/Consumer Science
30 Adult Education
31 Career/Sch-to-Work K-12
32 Career/Sch-to-Work Elem
33 Career/Sch-to-Work Sec
34 Early Childhood Ed
35 Health/Phys Education
36 Guidance Services K-12
37 Guidance Services Elem
38 Guidance Services Sec
39 Social Studies K-12
40 Social Studies Elem
41 Social Studies Sec
42 Science K-12
43 Science Elem
44 Science Sec
45 Math K-12
46 Math Elem
47 Math Sec
48 English/Lang Arts K-12
49 English/Lang Arts Elem
50 English/Lang Arts Sec
51 Reading K-12
52 Reading Elem
53 Reading Sec
54 Remedial Reading K-12
55 Remedial Reading Elem
56 Remedial Reading Sec
57 Bilingual/ELL
58 Special Education K-12
59 Special Education Elem
60 Special Education Sec
61 Foreign/World Lang K-12
62 Foreign/World Lang Elem
63 Foreign/World Lang Sec
64 Religious Education K-12
65 Religious Education Elem
66 Religious Education Sec
67 School Board President
68 Teacher Personnel
69 Academic Assessment
70 Research/Development
71 Public Information
72 Summer School
73 Instructional Tech
74 Inservice Training
75 Marketing/Distributive
76 Info Systems
77 Psychological Assess
79 Affirmative Action
80 Driver Ed/Safety
81 Gifted/Talented
82 Video Services
83 Substance Abuse Prev
84 Erate
85 AIDS Education
88 Alternative/At Risk
89 Multi-Cultural Curriculum
90 Social Work
91 Safety/Security
92 Magnet School
93 Parental Involvement
95 Tech Prep Program
97 Chief Infomation Officer
98 Chief Technology Officer
270 Character Education
271 Migrant Education
273 Teacher Mentor
274 Before/After Sch
275 Response To Intervention
277 Remedial Math K-12
280 Literacy Coach
285 STEM
286 Digital Learning
288 Common Core Standards
294 Accountability
295 Network System
296 Title II Programs
297 Webmaster
298 Grant Writer/Ptnrships
750 Chief Innovation Officer
751 Chief of Staff
752 Social Emotional Learning

TX-T74

Texas School Directory
DISTRICT PERSONNEL INDEX

NAME/District	JOB FUNCTIONS	PAGE
Reading, Wilma/*Nueces Canyon Cons Ind SD*	4	131
Ready, Debra/*Austin Ind School Dist*	294	366
Reagan, Yvonne/*Banquete Ind School Dist*	2	302
Reagor, Luke/*Stephenville Ind School Dist*	73	144
Ream, Chuck/*Motley Co Ind School Dist*	5	296
Reasor, Vicki/*Callisburg Ind School Dist*	58	90
Reasor, Vikki/*Muenster Ind School Dist*	58	91
Reasor, Vikki/*Valley View ISD-Cooke Co*	58	91
Reaugh, Graham/*Breckenridge Ind School Dist*	67	341
Reaves, Al/*Alief Ind School Dist*	76	181
Reaves, Randy/*Crowley Ind School Dist*	3	347
Reaves, Steve/*Port Aransas Ind School Dist*	6	305
Reavis, Beth/*Uvalde Cons Ind School Dist*	11,15,296	378
Recek, Brad/*College Station Ind Sch Dist*	295	55
Recer, Josh/*Pottsboro Ind School Dist*	15	167
Reckaway, Sharon/*Gregory-Portland Ind Sch Dist*	10,69,88,270,271,273	330
Redden, Ron/*Brazosport Ind School Dist*	69,294	52
Redden, Tim/*Sundown Ind School Dist*	3,5	229
Redden, Virginia/*Groveton Ind School Dist*	7,35,85	374
Reddock, Andy, Dr/*Flatonia Ind School Dist*	1	147
Redic, Kella/*Teague Ind School Dist*	7	156
Redman, Matthew, Dr/*Rockwall Ind School Dist*	41	325
Redwine, Carolyn/*Westbrook Ind School Dist*	16,82	289
Redwine, Jenni/*Munday Consolidated Ind SD*	34	259
Redwine, Shelia/*Colorado Ind School Dist*	2,11	289
Reece, Cade/*New Waverly Ind School Dist*	83,88	383
Reece, Cliff/*Waco Ind School Dist*	4	281
Reece, Stephanie/*La Villa Ind School Dist*	16,82	220
Reece, Teri/*Abilene Ind School Dist*	58	360
Reed, Ben/*Floresville Ind School Dist*	90	400
Reed, Benji/*Mexia Ind School Dist*	67	267
Reed, Brian/*Anton ISD School Dist*	67	229
Reed, Brian/*Dallas Ind School Dist*	297	98
Reed, Colleen/*Silverton Ind School Dist*	27,73,286,295	57
Reed, Greg/*Waxahachie Ind School Dist*	6	142
Reed, Jeanie/*New Caney Ind School Dist*	286	293
Reed, Julie/*Pasadena Ind School Dist*	58,294	198
Reed, Karen/*Lake Worth Ind School Dist*	69	356
Reed, Laura/*Gholson Ind School Dist*	59	279
Reed, Matt/*New Deal Ind School Dist*	1,11	271
Reed, Michael/*Hamilton Ind School Dist*	6	176
Reed, Mike/*Gordon Ind School Dist*	6	310
Reed, Reagan/*Terlingua Common School Dist*	1	57
Reed, Reagan/*Terlingua Common School Dist*	6	57
Reed, Renneth/*Electra Ind School Dist*	73,295	391
Reed, Roger/*S & S Cons Ind School Dist*	1	167
Reed, Sharon/*Palestine Ind School Dist*	8,69	15
Reed, Sheleah/*Aldine Ind School Dist*	71	179
Reed, Tiffany/*Kress Ind School Dist*	67	343
Reeder, Jeremy/*Northside Ind School Dist*	6	393
Reel, Jodie/*Guthrie Common School Dist*	8,31	257
Rees, Beau, Dr/*Montgomery Ind School Dist*	1	293
Rees, Laurie/*Kerrville Ind School Dist*	273	256
Reese-Taylor, Pamela/*Cedar Hill Ind School Dist*	7	97
Reese, Chris/*Birdville Ind School Dist*	91	346
Reese, Corina/*Fabens Ind School Dist*	15	135
Reese, Joseph/*Silsbee Ind School Dist*	5	178
Reese, Lytia/*Archdiocese Galveston-Houston*	15	203
Reese, Stephanie/*Lake Dallas Ind School Dist*	4	122
Reese, Stephen/*Rivercrest Ind School Dist*	73,295	322
Reeve, Travis/*Cuero Ind School Dist*	6	117
Reeves, Catrina/*Red Oak Ind School Dist*	68	142
Reeves, Deidra/*Greenville Ind School Dist*	2,15,19	236
Reeves, Farley/*Frenship Ind School Dist*	2,15	269
Reeves, Lanna/*Shamrock Ind School Dist*	34,58	390
Reeves, Leshell/*Elgin Ind School Dist*	9	24
Reeves, Marilin/*Krum Ind School Dist*	274	122
Reeves, Phoebe/*Northside Ind School Dist*	67	393
Reeves, Rick/*Conroe Ind School Dist*	2	291
Reeves, Russ/*Rockwall Ind School Dist*	6	325
Regalado, Samantha/*San Antonio Ind School Dist*	4	39
Register, Tina/*Bryson Ind School Dist*	2	238
Rehkopf, Kristie/*Floydada Ind School Dist*	38,69	148
Reichardt, Ryan/*Sealy Ind School Dist*	67	22
Reichelt, Chris/*Conroe Ind School Dist*	81	291
Reid, Brian/*Bellville Ind School Dist*	73,286,295	22
Reid, Christina/*Chapel Hill Ind School Dist*	58	363
Reid, Christina/*Chapel Hill Ind School Dist*	58	363
Reid, Dana/*Frisco Ind School Dist*	81	78
Reid, Linda/*Rockwall Ind School Dist*	69,77,294	325
Reid, Nikki/*Aldine Ind School Dist*	91	179
Reid, Randy/*Denison Ind School Dist*	2,15,91	166
Reidland, Lannise/*Liberty Ind School Dist*	68	266
Reidlinger, Christopher, Dr/*Amarillo Ind School Dist*	23	317
Reimonenq, Precious, Dr/*Goose Creek Cons Ind Sch Dist*	31,36	187
Reina-Garza, Jessica/*Mission Cons Ind School Dist*	49	222
Reinart, Sara/*Happy Ind School Dist*	27,30,31	342
Reisner, Keely/*Rockdale Ind School Dist*	69,77	287
Reitmeier, George/*Klein Ind School Dist*	67	196
Remchel, Alex/*Academy Ind School Dist*	3,11,15,83,88,271,274	26
Remick, Lorrie/*Randolph Field Ind School Dist*	2,19,71	39
Remissong, Patricia, Dr/*Copperas Cove Ind School Dist*	8,15,288	92
Remmers, Pamela/*Nordheim Ind School Dist*	67	118
Remschel, Alex/*Shiner Ind School Dist*	1	262
Rendon, Gloria/*United Ind School Dist*	15	387
Rendon, Hilda/*San Benito Cons Ind Sch Dist*	2,15	66
Rendon, Itzamara/*Laredo Ind School Dist*	34	386
Reneau, Bart/*Garrison Ind School Dist*	67	298
Reneau, Kacie/*Bloomburg Ind School Dist*	58	70
Renegar, Lisa/*San Elizario Ind School Dist*	39,48,69,81,88,275,294	135
Renken, Paula/*Poth Ind School Dist*	1,11	401
Reno-Rollo, Kathryn/*Lubbock Ind School Dist*	1	269
Reno, Elaine/*Olney Ind School Dist*	8,12,288,298	406
Rentz, Crystal/*Dallas Ind School Dist*	72	98
Rergel, Ren/*Santa Rosa Ind School Dist*	3,5	67
Rerich, Theresa/*Weimar Ind School Dist*	4	87
Ressler, Richard/*Texas City Ind School Dist*	5	161
Ressler, Teresa/*Brazos Ind School Dist*	8,11,57,74,271,294	22
Restivo, Rick/*Columbus Ind School Dist*	67	86
Rettig, Eric/*Brenham Ind School Dist*	23	385
Retzlaff, Allen/*Lexington Ind School Dist*	3	263
Revell, Elaine/*Region 7 Ed Service Center*	4	171
Revels, Jeanette/*Flour Bluff Ind School Dist*	68	304
Reville, Sherry/*Quinlan Ind School Dist*	68	237
Rex, Carlinda/*Academy Ind School Dist*	9	26
Rex, Jack/*Wortham Ind School Dist*	16,73	156
Rex, Twilla/*Ennis Ind School Dist*	8,57,69,288	140
Reyas, Erika/*Duncanville Ind School Dist*	34,296	104
Reyenga, Shane/*Kountze Ind School Dist*	8,11,15,69	178
Reyes, Brandon/*Ector Co Ind School Dist*	4	129
Reyes, Cecilia/*Sabinal Ind School Dist*	7	378
Reyes, Corina/*Petersburg Ind School Dist*	36	175
Reyes, Galina/*La Joya Ind School Dist*	4	219
Reyes, Jaime/*Anthony Ind School Dist*	5	131
Reyes, Jissel/*Anthony Ind School Dist*	2	131
Reyes, Laura/*Kress Ind School Dist*	4	343
Reyes, Monica, Dr/*Canutillo Ind School Dist*	7,30,34,36,85,88,93	131
Reyes, Sam/*School of Excellence In Ed*	4	42
Reyes, Velinda/*San Isidro Ind School Dist*	67	341
Reyes, Veronica/*Socorro Ind School Dist*	57	135
Reyes, Vicente/*Dallas Ind School Dist*	8,15	98
Reyna, Amy/*Itasca Ind School Dist*	57,58,88	228
Reyna, Dolores/*Mission Cons Ind School Dist*	298	222
Reyna, Hector/*Socorro Ind School Dist*	73,76,98,295,297	135
Reyna, Jacob/*Jourdanton Ind School Dist*	3	20
Reyna, Jessica/*Deer Park Ind School Dist*	48	186
Reyna, Maricella/*Lackland Ind School Dist*	4	34
Reyna, Mario/*McAllen Ind School Dist*	35	221
Reyna, Rose/*Skidmore Tynan Ind SD*	5	25
Reyna, Yolanda/*Robstown Ind School Dist*	11,57,83	305
Reynolds, Bobby/*Godley Ind School Dist*	3	247
Reynolds, Candice/*New Waverly Ind School Dist*	37	383
Reynolds, David/*Bryan Ind School Dist*	27,31	54
Reynolds, Freda/*Port Arthur Ind School Dist*	34	243
Reynolds, Kathleen/*Kelton Ind School Dist*	16	390
Reynolds, Kent, Dr/*Hallsburg Ind School Dist*	1,11,83,288	279
Reynolds, Michelle/*Lamar Cons Ind School Dist*	2	153
Reynolds, Millie/*North East Ind School Dist*	41	34
Reynolds, Monica/*Beaumont Ind School Dist*	39,81	241
Reynolds, Penny/*Godley Ind School Dist*	4	247
Reynolds, Sandy/*Little Cypress Mauriceville SD*	16	308
Reynolds, Steve/*Adrian Ind School Dist*	1,11	307

DISTRICT PERSONNEL INDEX

Market Data Retrieval

NAME/District	JOB FUNCTIONS	PAGE
Reynolds, Thelma/Harlingen Cons Ind School Dist	11	64
Reynolds, Tracy/Krum Ind School Dist	37	122
Reysinger, Renee/Carthage Ind School Dist	5	311
Reza, Tony/Socorro Ind School Dist	2,19	135
Rhinehart, Ed/Lindale Ind School Dist	3	337
Rhoades, Brandy/Iowa Park Consolidated Ind SD	36	392
Rhoades, Cindy/Dumas Ind School Dist	79,294	295
Rhoades, Jeff/Iowa Park Consolidated Ind SD	67	392
Rhoades, Robin/Moulton Ind School Dist	2	262
Rhoades, Ryan/Plainview Ind School Dist	6	175
Rhoades, Stephen/Lufkin Ind School Dist	27,31,75	18
Rhoades, Wendee/Ropes Ind School Dist	7	229
Rhodes, Angela/Burton Ind School Dist	31,79,88,270	386
Rhodes, Curtis/Needville Ind School Dist	1	154
Rhodes, Melissa/Needville Ind School Dist	16	154
Rhodes, Rick/Gregory-Portland Ind Sch Dist	6	330
Rhodes, Shirley/Newcastle Ind School Dist	2,84	406
Rhone, Kristi/Grandview Ind School Dist	8,11,76,88,285,288,296,298	248
Rhyne, Sean/Pewitt Cons Ind School Dist	76	296
Riberou, Richard, Dr/Edcouch Elsa Ind School Dist	1	215
Rice-Wiltz, Christina/Alvin Ind School Dist	27,31,95	50
Rice, Ben/New Caney Ind School Dist	73	293
Rice, Bobby, Dr/Harts Bluff Ind School Dist	1,11,83	363
Rice, Darrin/Conroe Ind School Dist	2,19	291
Rice, Dawn/Lancaster Ind School Dist	5	110
Rice, Don, Dr/Westwood Ind School Dist	67	16
Rice, Dwight/Anton ISD School Dist	1	229
Rice, Joann/Texarkana Ind School Dist	15,79,93	50
Rice, John/Klein Ind School Dist	5	196
Rice, Joshua/New Caney Ind School Dist	5	293
Rice, Melissa/Harts Bluff Ind School Dist	271	363
Rice, Olivia/Terrell Ind School Dist	71	253
Rice, William/Gainesville Ind School Dist	5	91
Rich, Daniel/Sabine Ind School Dist	73	170
Rich, Jason/Laneville Ind School Dist	73,295	327
Rich, Kimberly/Dickinson Ind School Dist	68,79	159
Rich, Robert, Dr/Melissa Ind School Dist	11,68,271,296	81
Rich, Tim/Sudan Ind School Dist	67	261
Richarb, Michael/Deweyville Ind School Dist	5	308
Richard, Frank/Pine Tree Ind School Dist	67	170
Richard, Jeremy/Connally Ind School Dist	3	279
Richard, Teresa/Center Ind School Dist	275	334
Richard, Tiara/Duncanville Ind School Dist	71	104
Richards, Allen/Italy Ind School Dist	67	140
Richards, Christi/Muleshoe Ind School Dist	11	22
Richards, Cynthia/McAllen Ind School Dist	2,15,19	220
Richards, Debbie/Bryan Ind School Dist	10,42	54
Richards, Doug/Iola Ind School Dist	58,69	172
Richards, Jan/Littlefield Ind School Dist	12,34,57	260
Richards, Laura/Burkburnett Ind Sch Dist	2	391
Richards, R, Dr/Muleshoe Ind School Dist	1,57,83,288	22
Richards, Rick/Littlefield Ind School Dist	2,5,8,11,79,88,92,298	260
Richards, Tammy/Plano Ind School Dist	67	82
Richardson, Angie/Bonham Ind School Dist	13,58	145
Richardson, Angie/Honey Grove Ind School Dist	58	146
Richardson, Christina/Bryan Ind School Dist	8,81	54
Richardson, Connie/Newton Ind School Dist	84	301
Richardson, Dane/White Deer Ind School Dist	1,11,83	69
Richardson, Denise/Van Alstyne Ind School Dist	4	168
Richardson, Dianna/Valley Mills Ind School Dist	16,73,295	47
Richardson, J, Dr/Tatum Ind School Dist	1	328
Richardson, Scott/Christoval Ind School Dist	6	364
Richardson, Terri/Vega Ind School Dist	286	307
Richburg, Brent, Dr/Plainview Ind School Dist	73,76	175
Riche, Sally/McKinney Ind School Dist	58	81
Richey, Roy/Cross Plains Ind Sch Dist	67	62
Richter, Kari/Frost Ind School Dist	58	299
Ricker, Michele/Rankin Ind School Dist	73,295	377
Rickerhauser, Geoffrey/Gregory-Portland Ind Sch Dist	42,45	330
Rickert, Richard/Dimmitt Ind School Dist	5	71
Ricks, Shawn/Huntington Ind School Dist	3	17
Ricks, Todd/Huntington Ind School Dist	5	17
Rictor, Demetrius/Celeste Ind School Dist	6	235
Riddick, Orlando/Midland Ind School Dist	1	285
Riddle, Philip/Natalia Ind School Dist	3	284
Rider, David/Ft Bend Ind School Dist	91	149
Ridge, Michael/Grand Saline Ind School Dist	6	380
Ridge, Pete/Lindale Ind School Dist	5	337
Ridgley, Kimberly, Dr/Northside Ind School Dist	36	36
Rieber, Misty/Lubbock Ind School Dist	8,15,288	269
Rieger, Jennifer/East Bernard Ind Sch Dist	69	389
Riek, Rene/Hurst-Euless-Bedford ISD	58	353
Rielly, Nancy/Salado Ind School Dist	58	29
Riemenschneide, Tammy/Joshua Ind School Dist	69	248
Riester-Wood, Toni/La Vernia Ind School Dist	8	401
Rife, Carrie/La Porte Ind School Dist	7	198
Rife, Racheal/Weatherford Ind School Dist	9,69,74,81,752	313
Rife, Rachel/Weatherford Ind School Dist	8,74,273,285,288	313
Riggen, James/Midland Ind School Dist	3,17,70,91	285
Riggins, Chris/Lamesa Ind School Dist	68	117
Riggs, Jennifer/Bosqueville Ind School Dist	58	278
Riggs, Tommy/Forney Ind School Dist	68	251
Rigney, Phia/Seguin Ind School Dist	5	173
Riley, Gayle/Etoile Ind School Dist	67	297
Riley, Jean/Bland Ind School Dist	3	235
Riley, Kellye/Monahans-Wickett-Pyote ISD	1	385
Riley, Nancy/Academy Ind School Dist	58	26
Riley, Nancy/Holland Ind School Dist	58	27
Riley, Nichole, Dr/Temple Ind School Dist	36,83,275	29
Riley, Rhonda/Throckmorton Ind School Dist	8,11,74,275,294	363
Rimarez, Michael/Devers Ind School Dist	67	265
Rinehart, Amy/Borden Co Ind School Dist	2	46
Riney, Claudia/Diocese of Lubbock Ed Office	8	272
Ringman, Melanie/Carroll Independent Sch Dist	35,41,50	347
Ringo, Brent/Garland Ind School Dist	2,19	105
Ringo, James/Willis Ind School Dist	5	294
Ringo, Johnny/Highland Park Ind Sch Dist	6	108
Ringo, Paula/Glasscock Co Ind School Dist	58	163
Ringo, Tamerah/Coppell Ind School Dist	71	98
Riojas, Omar/Rio Grande City Ind Sch Dist	71	340
Riojas, Oscar/Mercedes Ind School Dist	67	221
Riojas, Oscar/Weslaco Ind School Dist	6	225
Rios, Carlos/San Felipe-Del Rio Cons Ind SD	1	379
Rios, Juan/Trent Ind School Dist	6	361
Rios, Norma/Rule Ind School Dist	4	210
Rios, Roland/Ft Sam Houston Ind School Dist	16,73,295	32
Rios, Ronnie/Harlingen Cons Ind School Dist	23	64
Rios, Silvia, Dr/Laredo Ind School Dist	1	386
Rios, Tracie/McMullen Co Ind School Dist	4	283
Rios, Yolanda/New Caney Ind School Dist	57,271	293
Rippee, Curtis/McKinney Ind School Dist	67	81
Risica, Kim/Mission Cons Ind School Dist	11	222
Risinger, Dena/Terrell Ind School Dist	67	253
Risinger, Ronald, Dr/Orangefield Ind School Dist	67	309
Risner, Justin/Central Ind School Dist	8,11,31,57,69,296,298	17
Risner, Walter/Goodrich Ind School Dist	295	316
Ritchey, Mike/Big Spring Ind School Dist	6,51	233
Ritchie, Bryan/Seminole Ind School Dist	3	158
Ritchie, David/Lamesa Ind School Dist	88	117
Ritchie, Debbie/Pottsboro Ind School Dist	8,11	167
Ritchie, Pat/Clarendon Cons Ind Sch Dist	4	127
Ritter, Rhonda/Hull Daisetta Ind School Dist	286	266
Rivas, Isauro/Brackett Ind School Dist	5	257
Rivas, Norberto/San Elizario Ind School Dist	2,19	135

Code	Function	Code	Function	Code	Function	Code	Function	Code	Function	Code	Function
1	Superintendent	16	Instructional Media Svcs	30	Adult Education	44	Science Sec	58	Special Education K-12	72	Summer School
2	Bus/Finance/Purchasing	17	Chief Operations Officer	31	Career/Sch-to-Work K-12	45	Math K-12	59	Special Education Elem	73	Instructional Tech
3	Buildings And Grounds	18	Chief Academic Officer	32	Career/Sch-to-Work Elem	46	Math Elem	60	Special Education Sec	74	Inservice Training
4	Food Service	19	Chief Financial Officer	33	Career/Sch-to-Work Sec	47	Math Sec	61	Foreign/World Lang K-12	75	Marketing/Distributive
5	Transportation	20	Art K-12	34	Early Childhood Ed	48	English/Lang Arts K-12	62	Foreign/World Lang Elem	76	Info Systems
6	Athletic	21	Art Elem	35	Health/Phys Education	49	English/Lang Arts Elem	63	Foreign/World Lang Sec	77	Psychological Assess
7	Health Services	22	Art Sec	36	Guidance Services K-12	50	English/Lang Arts Sec	64	Religious Education K-12	78	Affirmative Action
8	Curric/Instruct K-12	23	Music K-12	37	Guidance Services Elem	51	Reading K-12	65	Religious Education Elem	79	Student Personnel
9	Curric/Instruct Elem	24	Music Elem	38	Guidance Services Sec	52	Reading Elem	66	Religious Education Sec	80	Driver Ed/Safety
10	Curric/Instruct Sec	25	Music Sec	39	Social Studies K-12	53	Reading Sec	67	School Board President	81	Gifted/Talented
11	Federal Program	26	Business Education	40	Social Studies Elem	54	Remedial Reading K-12	68	Teacher Personnel	82	Video Services
12	Title I	27	Career & Tech Ed	41	Social Studies Sec	55	Remedial Reading Elem	69	Academic Assessment	83	Substance Abuse Prev
13	Title V	28	Technology Education	42	Science K-12	56	Remedial Reading Sec	70	Research/Development	84	Erate
15	Asst Superintendent	29	Family/Consumer Science	43	Science Elem	57	Bilingual/ELL	71	Public Information	85	AIDS Education

Code	Function	Code	Function
88	Alternative/At Risk	277	Remedial Math K-12
89	Multi-Cultural Curriculum	280	Literacy Coach
90	Social Work	285	STEM
91	Safety/Security	286	Digital Learning
92	Magnet School	288	Common Core Standards
93	Parental Involvement	294	Accountability
95	Tech Prep Program	295	Network System
97	Chief Information Officer	296	Title II Programs
98	Chief Technology Officer	297	Webmaster
270	Character Education	298	Grant Writer/Ptnrships
271	Migrant Education	750	Chief Innovation Officer
273	Teacher Mentor	751	Chief of Staff
274	Before/After Sch	752	Social Emotional Learning
275	Response To Intervention		

Texas School Directory
DISTRICT PERSONNEL INDEX

NAME/District	JOB FUNCTIONS	PAGE
Rivas, Paige/Tahoka Ind School Dist	58,275	273
Rivas, Shana/Malta Ind School Dist	59	48
Rivera, Almarie/Azle Ind School Dist	4	345
Rivera, Darrell/Wimberley Ind School Dist	3	212
Rivera, David/Dalhart Ind School Dist	58,275	95
Rivera, Edward/La Villa Ind School Dist	57	220
Rivera, Frank, Dr/La Joya Ind School Dist	8,69	219
Rivera, Jill/Midland Ind School Dist	74	285
Rivera, Matt/Schertz-Cibolo-Univ City ISD	2	173
Rivera, Patricia/Fredericksburg Ind School Dist	11,57,81,271,298	163
Rivera, Rachael/Dalhart Ind School Dist	271	95
Rivera, Ricardo/Mission Cons Ind School Dist	3,15	222
Rivera, Rosela/Balmorhea Ind School Dist	2	323
Rivera, Tiffany/Waxahachie Ind School Dist	5	142
Rivers, Eli/Petrolia Cons Ind School Dist	5	74
Rivers, Jamal/Reagan Co Ind School Dist	3,5	321
Roach, Crystal/Red Lick Ind School Dist	12	49
Roach, Gloria/Channelview Ind School Dist	58	183
Roach, Greg, Dr/Olney Ind School Dist	1	406
Roach, Jaycy/Garner Ind School Dist	11,16,69	312
Roach, Lisa/Rivercrest Ind School Dist	4	322
Roach, Sarah/Hitchcock Ind School Dist	12	161
Roan, Richard/Cooper Ind School Dist	12	119
Roane, Stetson/Raymondville Ind Sch Dist	1	394
Roane, Warren, Dr/Humble Ind School Dist	294	195
Robbins, Jessica/Aransas Co Ind School Dist	57,69	19
Robbins, Patricia/Little Elm Ind School Dist	71	124
Robbins, Sheryl/Bruceville-Eddy Ind Sch Dist	2,68	278
Robeledo, Alison/Wharton Ind School Dist	4	390
Robert, Lori/Edgewood Ind School Dist	73	380
Roberts, Allen/Alvin Ind School Dist	15	50
Roberts, Anthony/Onalaska Ind School Dist	1	317
Roberts, Celeste/New Waverly Ind School Dist	7	383
Roberts, Chance/Bonham Ind School Dist	67	145
Roberts, Cherise/Stafford Municipal Sch Dist	298	155
Roberts, Danny/Prosper Ind School Dist	3	84
Roberts, Georgiann/Ft Worth Ind School Dist	35	349
Roberts, Jamey/Idea Public Schools	68	217
Roberts, Jennett/Natalia Ind School Dist	73,286,295,297	284
Roberts, Jennifer/Lamar Cons Ind School Dist	7,77,83	153
Roberts, Joi/Paris Ind School Dist	58	260
Roberts, Katherine/Venus Ind School Dist	16	249
Roberts, Keri/Goldthwaite Consolidated ISD	67	288
Roberts, Michael/Quinlan Ind School Dist	16,73,295	237
Roberts, Nicole/Alief Ind School Dist	58	181
Roberts, Ross/Little Elm Ind School Dist	15,79	124
Roberts, Scott/Laredo Ind School Dist	298	386
Roberts, Sharon/Mission Cons Ind School Dist	15,81	222
Roberts, Teresa/Bangs Ind School Dist	2	58
Roberts, Troy/Huckabay Ind School Dist	1,83,84	143
Roberts, Ward/Wichita Falls Ind School Dist	81	392
Robertson, Collin/Leon Ind School Dist	67	264
Robertson, Darlenea/Petersburg Ind School Dist	2	175
Robertson, Donna/Smyer Ind School Dist	2	229
Robertson, Jonathan/Sudan Ind School Dist	73,286,298	261
Robertson, Kelly/Alto Ind School Dist	2	72
Robertson, Megan/Follett Ind School Dist	271	267
Robertson, Robert/Klein Ind School Dist	3,15	196
Robertson, Staci/Stamford Ind School Dist	2	250
Robertson, Steve, Dr/Katy Ind School Dist	15	151
Robertson, Thomas/Van Ind School Dist	80	381
Robertson, Thomas/Van Ind School Dist	91	381
Robinett, David/Santa Anna Ind School Dist	1	76
Robins, Becky/Goose Creek Cons Ind Sch Dist	8	187
Robins, Rodney/Ingram Ind School Dist	91	255
Robinson, Arlene/Spurger Ind School Dist	9,69,83	375
Robinson, Barbara/Hillsboro Ind School Dist	68,273	227
Robinson, Becky/Judson Ind School Dist	15	33
Robinson, Bo/Yoakum Ind School Dist	6	118
Robinson, Cody/Lovelady Ind School Dist	3,5,91	233
Robinson, Danielle/West Orange-Cove Cons ISD	4	309
Robinson, Dawn/Troy Ind School Dist	34,37	29
Robinson, Gary/Joshua Ind School Dist	6	248
Robinson, Geneva/La Poynor Ind School Dist	31	214
Robinson, Ginger/Waxahachie Ind School Dist	36,69,294	142
Robinson, Jeff/Waxahachie Ind School Dist	76	142

NAME/District	JOB FUNCTIONS	PAGE
Robinson, Julia/Royse City Ind School Dist	8	326
Robinson, Karen/Meridian Ind School Dist	69,83,85,88,273,274	47
Robinson, Ken/Canyon Ind School Dist	4	320
Robinson, Lacy/Chapel Hill Ind School Dist	8,11,57,271,273,298	363
Robinson, Lafreceia/Cooper Ind School Dist	4	119
Robinson, Larry/Region 12 Ed Service Center	68	283
Robinson, Lisa/Sulphur Springs Ind Sch Dist	8	232
Robinson, Lori/Natalia Ind School Dist	8,271,285	284
Robinson, Melvina/Ft Worth Ind School Dist	46	349
Robinson, Robert/Southwest Ind School Dist	58	43
Robinson, Tina/Lake Worth Ind School Dist	4	356
Robinson, Zachery/Stephenville Ind School Dist	3	144
Robison, Miles/Shepherd Ind School Dist	6	330
Robison, Teresa/Follett Ind School Dist	752	267
Robison, Teresa/Follett Ind School Dist	8,88,752	267
Robison, Todd/Hutto Ind School Dist	71	396
Roble, Gelyn/Alief Ind School Dist	43	181
Robledo, David/Santa Rosa Ind School Dist	2,4,19	67
Robledo, Sandra/Schleicher Co Ind Sch Dist	68	333
Robles Mendez, Deanna/Rio Grande City Ind Sch Dist	2,19	340
Robles, Janet/Pharr-San Juan-Alamo Ind SD	19	223
Robles, Maryhelen/Westhoff Ind School Dist	2	118
Robles, Ronald/Ingleside Ind School Dist	3,5,92	331
Robles, Ronaldo/Monte Alto Ind School Dist	2,19	222
Roby, Deborah/Lewisville Ind School Dist	81	122
Rocha, Andy/Refugio Ind School Dist	67	323
Rocha, Antonio/Friona Ind School Dist	67	315
Rocha, Audrey/Progreso Ind School Dist	4	224
Rocha, Frances/Edcouch Elsa Ind School Dist	15	215
Rocha, Marnie/Canutillo Ind School Dist	15	131
Rocha, Ruben/Corpus Christi Ind Sch Dist	41	303
Rocha, Zelda/Progreso Ind School Dist	57,93	224
Rockefeller, John/Zephyr Ind School Dist	67	59
Rockstead, Maria/Eanes Ind School Dist	2	370
Rockstroh, Bruce/Braination Schools	1	30
Rockwood, Mike/Lamar Cons Ind School Dist	15,71,751	153
Rodarmer, Paul/Tioga Ind School Dist	67	167
Roddy, Clint/Irving Ind School Dist	6	109
Roddy, Meredith/Manor Ind School Dist	57	371
Rodela, Joni/Lubbock Ind School Dist	39	269
Rodell, Angela/Centerville Ind School Dist	16,73	264
Rodell, Courtney/Buffalo Ind School Dist	2,11	264
Roden, Amanda/Apple Springs Ind School Dist	67	374
Roden, Gay/Venus Ind School Dist	57	249
Roden, Kasie/Grand Prairie Ind School Dist	285	107
Roderiguez, Isaac, Dr/La Feria Ind School Dist	8	65
Rodgers, Brannon/Jacksboro Ind Sch Dist	6,35	239
Rodgers, Dean/Chapel Hill Ind School Dist	3,4,5,91	337
Rodgers, Jackie/Bastrop Ind School Dist	58	23
Rodgers, Joel/Amherst Ind School Dist	1,11,83,288	260
Rodgers, Randy/Seguin Ind School Dist	286	173
Rodgers, Scott/Red Oak Ind School Dist	10	142
Rodguiez, Jorge/Stafford Municipal Sch Dist	73,295	155
Rodregez, Martin/Edcouch Elsa Ind School Dist	5	215
Rodrick, Scott/Carrollton-Farmers Branch ISD	2,19	96
Rodriguez, Al/Elgin Ind School Dist	15,68,71,78	24
Rodriguez, Alfonso/La Joya Ind School Dist	47	219
Rodriguez, Alva/Crosbyton Cons Ind Sch Dist	57,271	94
Rodriguez, Ann/Hurst-Euless-Bedford ISD	74	353
Rodriguez, Barbara/San Antonio Ind School Dist	11	39
Rodriguez, Caleb/Grape Creek Ind School Dist	73	364
Rodriguez, Carmelita/Brownsville Ind School Dist	15,68	63
Rodriguez, Christine/Southside Ind School Dist	297	43
Rodriguez, Connie, Dr/Dallas Ind School Dist	77,90	98
Rodriguez, Crystal/San Perlita Ind School Dist	69,83	394
Rodriguez, Cynthia/United Ind School Dist	9,288	387
Rodriguez, David/Castleberry Ind School Dist	68,273	347
Rodriguez, Dawn/Aldine Ind School Dist	69,70,294	179
Rodriguez, Debra/San Perlita Ind School Dist	2	394
Rodriguez, Edgar/Frankston Ind School Dist	69,88,285	15
Rodriguez, Edward/Lackland Ind School Dist	4	34
Rodriguez, Erasmo/Beeville Ind School Dist	15,91	25
Rodriguez, Ernie/Allen Ind School Dist	91	76
Rodriguez, Francisco/Roma Ind School Dist	286	341
Rodriguez, Geronimo/Austin Ind School Dist	67	366
Rodriguez, Gustavo/Ft Bend Ind School Dist	5	149

DISTRICT PERSONNEL INDEX

Market Data Retrieval

NAME/District	JOB FUNCTIONS	PAGE
Rodriguez, Haydee/*La Feria Ind School Dist*	36	65
Rodriguez, Homero/*Southwest Ind School Dist*	15	43
Rodriguez, Inelda/*Dilley Ind School Dist*	271	157
Rodriguez, Jaime/*Pettus Ind School Dist*	67	25
Rodriguez, Janette/*San Benito Cons Ind Sch Dist*	7	66
Rodriguez, Janie/*Zapata Co Ind School Dist*	31,36,81,85,88	406
Rodriguez, Joe/*Ft Bend Ind School Dist*	15	149
Rodriguez, Joe/*Ft Hancock Ind School Dist*	67	234
Rodriguez, Juan/*Abilene Ind School Dist*	3	360
Rodriguez, Juanita/*Donna Ind School Dist*	15,68,79,273	215
Rodriguez, Judi/*Big Spring Ind School Dist*	4	233
Rodriguez, Karla/*Valley View Ind School Dist*	4	225
Rodriguez, Laurie/*Dickinson Ind School Dist*	58,77	159
Rodriguez, Linda/*Sinton Ind School Dist*	67	332
Rodriguez, Liza/*Canutillo Ind School Dist*	71	132
Rodriguez, Manuel/*Valley View Ind School Dist*	20,23	225
Rodriguez, Marcos/*Harlandale Ind School Dist*	4	32
Rodriguez, Maribel/*Progreso Ind School Dist*	8,58	224
Rodriguez, Mario/*Ysleta Ind School Dist*	5	137
Rodriguez, Marisela/*Southwest Ind School Dist*	16	43
Rodriguez, Melanie/*Victoria Ind School Dist*	297	382
Rodriguez, Melissa/*Edinburg Cons Ind School Dist*	13	216
Rodriguez, Michael/*San Elizario Ind School Dist*	27,36,69	135
Rodriguez, Michael/*Uvalde Cons Ind School Dist*	8,15,285	378
Rodriguez, Nancy/*Magnolia Ind School Dist*	57	292
Rodriguez, Nayda/*Carrizo Spgs Cons Ind SD*	38	127
Rodriguez, Norbert, Dr/*Pearsall Ind School Dist*	1	157
Rodriguez, Oscar/*Lingleville Ind School Dist*	3	143
Rodriguez, Refugio/*Aldine Ind School Dist*	23	179
Rodriguez, Reyna/*Rankin Ind School Dist*	4	377
Rodriguez, Ricardo/*Lubbock Ind School Dist*	15,68,78,751	269
Rodriguez, Rick/*La Pryor Ind School Dist*	58	407
Rodriguez, Ruby/*Cuero Ind School Dist*	93	117
Rodriguez, Sandra/*Edinburg Cons Ind School Dist*	93	216
Rodriguez, Saul/*Rio Hondo Ind School Dist*	16,73,295,297	66
Rodriguez, Sayna/*Cotulla Ind School Dist*	2,294	259
Rodriguez, Silvia/*Tornillo Ind School Dist*	4	137
Rodriguez, Steven/*Lackland Ind School Dist*	3	34
Rodriguez, Tonya/*Natalia Ind School Dist*	4	284
Rodriguez, Vicente/*San Elizario Ind School Dist*	295	135
Rodriguez, Xochitl, Dr/*Ft Bend Ind School Dist*	15,79	149
Rodriguez, Yolanda/*Houston ISD-North Area*	15	190
Rodriquez, Belen/*Grady Ind School Dist*	4	274
Rodriquez, Jesse/*San Isidro Ind School Dist*	8,11,16,57,273,280,285	341
Rodriquez, Terri/*Blue Ridge Ind School Dist*	4	77
Roe, Brandie/*Edna Ind School Dist*	8,57,73,83,285,286,288,296	239
Roehling, Charles/*Needville Ind School Dist*	68	154
Roeminguez, Ofelia/*United Ind School Dist*	88	387
Roepke, Diane/*La Vega Ind School Dist*	2	279
Rogers, Brittany/*Nixon-Smiley Cons Ind Sch Dist*	274	164
Rogers, Chad/*Denison Ind School Dist*	6	166
Rogers, Debi/*Terrell Ind School Dist*	58	253
Rogers, Don/*Mt Enterprise Ind School Dist*	67	328
Rogers, Edward/*Marlin Ind School Dist*	36	144
Rogers, Greg/*Wink Loving Ind School Dist*	3,5	402
Rogers, Greg/*Wink Loving Ind School Dist*	298	402
Rogers, Julie/*Frenship Ind School Dist*	48	269
Rogers, Kevin, Dr/*Lewisville Ind School Dist*	1	122
Rogers, Montra, Dr/*Houston Ind School Dist*	10	188
Rogers, Norma/*Central Heights Ind Sch Dist*	2	297
Rogers, Phyllis/*Normangee Ind School Dist*	58	264
Rogers, Renota/*Temple Ind School Dist*	8	29
Rogers, Roxanne/*Industrial Ind School Dist*	2	240
Rogers, Shawn/*Richland Springs Ind Sch Dist*	58	332
Rogers, Tammy/*West Sabine Ind Sch Dist*	4	329
Rogers, Todd/*Argyle Ind School Dist*	6	120
Rogers, Travis/*Graford Ind School Dist*	67	310
Rogers, Trevor/*Lindsay Ind School Dist*	1,11	91
Rogers, Troy/*Lampasas Ind School Dist*	6	261
Rogger, Michael/*Dallas Co Schools*	73	96
Roher, Thad/*Friendswood Ind Sch Dist*	1	160
Rohmfeld, Tom/*Whiteface Con Ind School Dist*	3,5	75
Rohrbach, Kennith, Dr/*Medina Valley Ind School Dist*	1	284
Rohrf, Andrew/*Floresville Ind School Dist*	6	400
Rojas, Elda/*Ft Worth Ind School Dist*	61	349
Rojero, Cecilia/*El Paso Ind School Dist*	12	132
Rokas, Meredith/*East Central Ind School Dist*	11,31,296	31
Roland, Aaron/*Tenaha Ind School Dist*	67	335
Roland, Sara/*Wylie Ind School Dist*	34,58,77	84
Rolen, Clay/*Bells Ind School Dist*	31,58,77,88,93	165
Roll, Nancy/*Alpine Ind School Dist*	11,286,296,298	56
Roller, Jeff/*Amarillo Ind School Dist*	28,73,76,84,98	317
Roller, Jimmie/*Moran Ind School Dist*	67	334
Rollins, Concetta/*Region 5 Ed Service Center*	4	244
Rollins, Yolanda/*Region 12 Ed Service Center*	271	283
Rollwitz, Kim/*Wall Ind School Dist*	7	365
Rolo, Laura/*Archdiocese Galveston-Houston*	8	203
Romans, Mary/*Yorktown Ind School Dist*	7,85	118
Romero-Mueller, Crystal/*Tomball Ind School Dist*	57,81	203
Romero, Angelica/*San Antonio Ind School Dist*	15	39
Romero, Isabel/*San Antonio Ind School Dist*	23	39
Romero, Jacob/*Odem-Edroy Ind School Dist*	67	331
Romero, Laura/*Friona Ind School Dist*	4	315
Romero, Loranda/*Harlingen Cons Ind School Dist*	9,15	64
Romero, Lori/*Harlingen Cons Ind School Dist*	9	64
Romero, Tonya/*Odem-Edroy Ind School Dist*	2	331
Romina, Jan/*Panther Creek Cons Ind SD*	2,19	76
Romine, Mark/*Panther Creek Cons Ind SD*	73	76
Romney, Angela/*Frisco Ind School Dist*	10,81	78
Romo, Rosey/*La Joya Ind School Dist*	58	219
Romos, Marcie/*Shallowater Ind School Dist*	2,19	272
Roney, Neil/*Daingerfield-Lone Star Ind SD*	67	296
Rooney, Nick/*Lewisville Ind School Dist*	297	122
Roper, Bernie, Dr/*Lackland Ind School Dist*	1	34
Roper, Linda/*Region 12 Ed Service Center*	12	283
Ropp, Marilyn/*Barbers Hill Ind School Dist*	58	72
Rosa, Jerry/*Kenedy Co Wide Common Sch Dist*	6	254
Rosales, Albert/*Harlandale Ind School Dist*	71	32
Rosales, Andre/*Nederland Ind School Dist*	295	242
Rosales, Irene/*United Ind School Dist*	7,85	387
Rosas, Elisa/*Lyford Cons Ind School Dist*	2	394
Rosas, Elsa/*Edgewood Ind School Dist*	3	31
Rosatelli, Elizabeth/*Joshua Ind School Dist*	296	248
Rosatelli, Elizabeth/*Joshua Ind School Dist*	58	248
Rose, Janice/*Comal Ind School Dist*	58,79	87
Rose, Joseph/*Rivercrest Ind School Dist*	67	322
Rose, Kristin/*Canton Ind School Dist*	16,82	380
Rose, Nicole/*Cedar Hill Ind School Dist*	47	97
Rose, Randall/*Spurger Ind School Dist*	57	375
Rose, Tracie/*Harts Bluff Ind School Dist*	9	363
Rosebrock, James, Dr/*Corpus Christi Ind Sch Dist*	8,18	303
Rosebrock, James, Dr/*George West Ind School Dist*	1	268
Rosenbaum, Clay/*Blanco Ind School Dist*	1	45
Rosenberger, Michael/*Dallas Ind School Dist*	4	98
Rosenberger, Olga/*Irving Ind School Dist*	4	109
Rosenthal, Liza/*San Antonio Ind School Dist*	69,294	39
Rosillo, Jose/*Valley View Ind School Dist*	67	225
Ross, Charles/*Kermit Ind School Dist*	6	401
Ross, Cody/*Beckville Ind School Dist*	6	311
Ross, James/*Tomball Ind School Dist*	2,19	203
Ross, Johnnie/*Lufkin Ind School Dist*	3,91	18
Ross, Kevin/*Bryan Ind School Dist*	27	54
Ross, Paula/*Cypress-Fairbanks Ind Sch Dist*	15,98	184
Ross, Teri/*Conroe Ind School Dist*	76,295	291

1 Superintendent	16 Instructional Media Svcs	30 Adult Education	44 Science Sec
2 Bus/Finance/Purchasing	17 Chief Operations Officer	31 Career/Sch-to-Work K-12	45 Math K-12
3 Buildings And Grounds	18 Chief Academic Officer	32 Career/Sch-to-Work Elem	46 Math Elem
4 Food Service	19 Chief Financial Officer	33 Career/Sch-to-Work Sec	47 Math Sec
5 Transportation	20 Art K-12	34 Early Childhood Ed	48 English/Lang Arts K-12
6 Athletic	21 Art Elem	35 Health/Phys Education	49 English/Lang Arts Elem
7 Health Services	22 Art Sec	36 Guidance Services K-12	50 English/Lang Arts Sec
8 Curric/Instruct K-12	23 Music K-12	37 Guidance Services Elem	51 Reading K-12
9 Curric/Instruct Elem	24 Music Elem	38 Guidance Services Sec	52 Reading Elem
10 Curric/Instruct Sec	25 Music Sec	39 Social Studies K-12	53 Reading Sec
11 Federal Program	26 Business Education	40 Social Studies Elem	54 Remedial Reading K-12
12 Title I	27 Career & Tech Ed	41 Social Studies Sec	55 Remedial Reading Elem
13 Title V	28 Technology Education	42 Science K-12	56 Remedial Reading Sec
15 Asst Superintendent	29 Family/Consumer Science	43 Science Elem	57 Bilingual/ELL

58 Special Education K-12	72 Summer School	88 Alternative/At Risk	277 Remedial Math K-12
59 Special Education Elem	73 Instructional Tech	89 Multi-Cultural Curriculum	280 Literacy Coach
60 Special Education Sec	74 Inservice Training	90 Social Work	285 STEM
61 Foreign/World Lang K-12	75 Marketing/Distributive	91 Safety/Security	286 Digital Learning
62 Foreign/World Lang Elem	76 Info Systems	92 Magnet School	288 Common Core Standards
63 Foreign/World Lang Sec	77 Psychological Assess	93 Parental Involvement	294 Accountability
64 Religious Education K-12	78 Affirmative Action	95 Tech Prep Program	295 Network System
65 Religious Education Elem	79 Student Personnel	97 Chief Information Officer	296 Title II Programs
66 Religious Education Sec	80 Driver Ed/Safety	98 Chief Technology Officer	297 Webmaster
67 School Board President	81 Gifted/Talented	270 Character Education	298 Grant Writer/Ptnrships
68 Teacher Personnel	82 Video Services	271 Migrant Education	750 Chief Innovation Officer
69 Academic Assessment	83 Substance Abuse Prev	273 Teacher Mentor	751 Chief of Staff
70 Research/Development	84 Erate	274 Before/After Sch	752 Social Emotional Learning
71 Public Information	85 AIDS Education	275 Response To Intervention	

TX-T78

Texas School Directory

DISTRICT PERSONNEL INDEX

NAME/District	JOB FUNCTIONS	PAGE
Rosser, Cameron/Canyon Ind School Dist	8,273	320
Rotan, Wayne/Glen Rose Ind School Dist	1	340
Roten, Charles/Rogers Ind School Dist	6	28
Rothbauer, Chad/Yoakum Ind School Dist	8,11,57,58,69,77,83,88	118
Rother, Deborah/Moulton Ind School Dist	7	262
Roudebush, Leah/Alamo Heights Ind School Dist	5	30
Rouk, Joanie/Aubrey Ind School Dist	8	120
Rouse, Jamie/Miles Ind School Dist	10,88	326
Rouse, Janna/Miles Ind School Dist	73	326
Rouse, Michael/Gordon Ind School Dist	67	310
Rousseau, Joy, Dr/Arp Ind School Dist	16,73,270,286,295	336
Rowan, Harold/Franklin Ind School Dist	3,5	324
Rowan, Stephanie/Carlisle Ind School Dist	57,274	327
Rowden, Mark/Highland Park Ind Sch Dist	91	108
Rowden, Sherry/Westbrook Ind School Dist	8	289
Rowe, Beth/Marshall Ind School Dist	15	209
Rowe, Christi/Central Ind School Dist	37	17
Rowe, Ginger/Midway Ind School Dist	81	280
Rowe, Grady/Bellville Ind School Dist	6	21
Rowe, Pete/Caddo Mills Ind Sch Dist	73	235
Rowe, Pete/Mart Ind School Dist	67	280
Rowe, Rebecca/Scurry Rosser Ind School Dist	7,85	253
Rowe, Tina/Bremond Ind School Dist	27	324
Rowell, Tim/Flatonia Ind School Dist	67	147
Rower, Jennifer/Braination Schools	3,5,17,68	30
Rowland, Dereck/Rains Ind School Dist	3	320
Rowland, Jeff/Marble Falls Ind School Dist	3	60
Royal, Tara/Miami Ind School Dist	16,73,295	324
Royar, Greg/Argyle Ind School Dist	16,295	120
Roybal, Debbie/Denton Ind School Dist	58	120
Roybal, Joanette/Palmer Ind School Dist	7	141
Royce, Shannon/Carthage Ind School Dist	38,270	311
Rozas, Michiel/Houston Ind School Dist	34	188
Rozelle, Carolyn/Northside Ind School Dist	12	36
Rozneck, Paulett/Lubbock Ind School Dist	7,83,85	269
Rubio, Luciano/Harlingen Cons Ind School Dist	5	64
Rubio, Manny/Grapevine-Colleyville Ind SD	5	353
Rubio, Nancy/Dallas Ind School Dist	92	98
Rubio, Sandra/Honey Grove Ind School Dist	57	146
Rucker, Cindy/Santo Ind School Dist	2,84	310
Rucker, James/Sidney Ind School Dist	1,11,73,83	90
Rucker, Margo/Eden Cons Ind School Dist	2	90
Rucker, Mindy/Henderson Ind School Dist	45	327
Rudd, Charla, Dr/La Vega Ind School Dist	8,15	279
Ruddick, Daniel/Alvord Ind School Dist	67	402
Rudock, Michael/Peaster Ind School Dist	5,8,11,68,69,78,83,298	313
Rudolph, Nick/Peaster Ind School Dist	288	313
Rudy, Chad/Frisco Ind School Dist	67	78
Ruedas, Brandy/Gustine Ind School Dist	57	90
Ruedas, Steve/Gustine Ind School Dist	67	90
Ruel Schafer, Deborah/Northside Ind School Dist	31,34	36
Rueter, Jana, Dr/San Angelo Ind School Dist	8,15	364
Ruffin, Greggory/Wylie Ind School Dist	35	361
Ruffin, Mark/Normangee Ind School Dist	1	264
Ruge, Carla/Denton Ind School Dist	27,31,75,95	120
Ruggeri, Mary/Lovejoy Ind School Dist	37	80
Ruggerio, Christopher/Klein Ind School Dist	11	196
Ruggles, Mark, Dr/Lake Dallas Ind School Dist	58	122
Ruiz Mills, Monica/San Marcos Cons Ind Sch Dist	15,68,69	211
Ruiz, Esmarelda/Leakey Ind School Dist	57	322
Ruiz, Manuel/Advantage Academy Admin Office	3	96
Ruiz, Marie/Brenham Ind School Dist	11,57,83	385
Ruiz, Oscar/San Diego Ind School Dist	73,76	128
Ruiz, Rene, Dr/Region 4 Ed Service Center	74	208
Ruiz, Rick/Brooks Co Ind School Dist	8	57
Ruiz, Rita/Irving Ind School Dist	48	109
Ruiz, Rosanna/North East Ind School Dist	47	34
Ruiz, Roxanne/Edgewood Ind School Dist	4	31
Ruiz, Roxanne/Ft Sam Houston Ind School Dist	4	32
Ruiz, Rumalda/Mission Cons Ind School Dist	2,15	222
Ruiz, Sandra/Los Fresnos Cons Ind Sch Dist	36,69,83,88	66
Ruiz, Steve/Lamesa Ind School Dist	7	117
Ruiz, Willie/Alice Ind School Dist	3,5,17,91	245
Rumfield, Alecia/Cotulla Ind School Dist	58	259
Rumsey, Jennifer/Bridge City Ind School Dist	38	308
Runnels, Daniel/Mercedes Ind School Dist	69	221

NAME/District	JOB FUNCTIONS	PAGE
Runnels, Marlon/Montgomery Ind School Dist	91	293
Running, Mary/Cypress-Fairbanks Ind Sch Dist	20,23	184
Rurup, Amanda/Eden Cons Ind School Dist	58	90
Rusek, Pete/Midway Ind School Dist	67	280
Rushing, Elvis/West Orange-Cove Cons ISD	16,73,82	309
Rushing, Lonnie/Clarksville Ind School Dist	5	322
Rusnak, Michele/Austin Ind School Dist	35	366
Russek, Charles/Moran Ind School Dist	3,5	334
Russell-Garcia, Bobbi/Ysleta Ind School Dist	68	137
Russell, Anita/Pampa Ind School Dist	2	165
Russell, Benny/Excelsior Ind School Dist	67	334
Russell, Betsy/Marble Falls Ind School Dist	68	60
Russell, Billy/Hudson Ind School Dist	3	17
Russell, Bonnie/Irving Ind School Dist	76	109
Russell, David/Central Heights Ind Sch Dist	1	297
Russell, Doug/Malta Ind School Dist	67	48
Russell, James/El Campo Ind School Dist	67	389
Russell, Jeff/Wills Point Ind School Dist	15	381
Russell, Jeremy/Alvord Ind School Dist	5	402
Russell, Jim, Dr/Burkburnett Ind Sch Dist	11,15	391
Russell, Josh/Honey Grove Ind School Dist	67	146
Russell, Kayla/Bastrop Ind School Dist	274	23
Russell, Nikita, Dr/Everman Ind School Dist	71	349
Russell, Rick/San Augustine Ind School Dist	5	329
Russell, Samantha/Gause Ind School Dist	59,275	287
Russell, Shawn/Early Ind School Dist	67	58
Russell, Stewart/Livingston Ind School Dist	3,91	316
Russell, Stewart/Pasadena Ind School Dist	91	198
Russell, Tim/Harmony Ind School Dist	6	376
Russell, Wendi/Pecos-Barstow-Toyah Ind SD	271	323
Russo, Joe/Huffman Ind School Dist	4	195
Rust, Amanda/Comfort Ind School Dist	68	254
Rust, Rachel/Wharton Ind School Dist	67	390
Ruthart, Brad/Paris Ind School Dist	91	260
Rutherford, Jerrell/Springtown Ind School Dist	3	313
Rutherford, Jimmy/Uvalde Cons Ind School Dist	3	378
Rutherford, Kathryn/Blanco Ind School Dist	58	45
Rutherford, Leann/Irion Co Ind School Dist	83,88,270	238
Rutherford, Nick/Sweetwater ISD School Dist	76,84,95,286	301
Rutherford, Russ/Gainesville Ind School Dist	20,23	91
Rutherford, Susan/Santa Gertrudis Ind Sch Dist	16,69,82,294	258
Ruthven, Michelle/Elgin Ind School Dist	10	24
Rutkowski, John/Haskell Cons Ind School Dist	73,84,286,295	210
Rutland, Marcy/Dayton Ind School Dist	4	265
Rutledge, Albert/Argyle Ind School Dist	5	120
Rutledge, Becky/UT Tyler University Acad Dist	12	338
Rutledge, Charles/Cooper Ind School Dist	73,76,295	120
Rutledge, Charles/Cooper Ind School Dist	76	120
Rutledge, Tracey/Rising Star Ind Sch Dist	4	129
Ryan, Cheryl/Alvin Ind School Dist	2	50
Ryan, Corey/Leander Ind School Dist	71,97	396
Ryan, Jennifer/Stephenville Ind School Dist	8,57,288	144
Ryan, Paul/Three Way Ind School Dist	1,11,84	144
Ryan, Robin, Dr/Grapevine-Colleyville Ind SD	1	353
Ryan, Sara/Santa Fe Ind School Dist	294	161
Ryan, Wonda/Colmesneil Ind School Dist	2	375
Rychel, Ron/New Braunfels Ind School Dist	11	88
Rye, Terry/Bridgeport Ind School Dist	5	402
Ryman, Louis/Van Vleck Ind School Dist	3	276

S

NAME/District	JOB FUNCTIONS	PAGE
Saavedra, Norma/Elgin Ind School Dist	57	24
Sabatino, Melissa/Austin Ind School Dist	71	366
Sablatura, David/Spring Branch Ind School Dist	27	200
Sack, Frank/Arlington Ind School Dist	297	343
Sadler, Melody/Groesbeck Ind School Dist	11,58	267
Saenz, Eddie/Rio Grande City Ind Sch Dist	8,16,73,76,82,84	340
Saenz, Eli/Waxahachie Ind School Dist	295	142
Saenz, Gisela, Dr/La Joya Ind School Dist	1	219
Saenz, Jorge/Fabens Ind School Dist	58	135
Saenz, Lory/Bovina Ind School Dist	271	314
Saenz, Roberto/Edinburg Cons Ind School Dist	3	216
Saenz, Zelda/Ben Bolt-Palito Blanco ISD	67	245
Saffel, Lisa/Rule Ind School Dist	4	210
Sailer, Andja/Centerville Ind School Dist	8,13,27,36,85,88,271	374
Saint Clair, Darrell/Snook Ind School Dist	2,13,296,298	59

School Year 2019-2020   800-333-8802   TX-T79

DISTRICT PERSONNEL INDEX

Market Data Retrieval

NAME/District	JOB FUNCTIONS	PAGE
Salais, Mark/*Boling Ind School Dist*	4	389
Salazar-Zamora, Martha, Dr/*Tomball Ind School Dist*	1	203
Salazar, Alejos/*La Villa Ind School Dist*	1	220
Salazar, Alex, Dr/*Caldwell Ind School Dist*	8,15,18,57,88	59
Salazar, Amanda/*Ft Bend Ind School Dist*	298	149
Salazar, Gonzalo/*Los Fresnos Cons Ind Sch Dist*	1	66
Salazar, Holly/*London Ind School Dist*	58	305
Salazar, Marco/*Advantage Academy Admin Office*	73,76,286,295	96
Salazar, Marta/*Alice Ind School Dist*	48,93	245
Salazar, Martha/*La Gloria Ind School Dist*	67	245
Salazar, Michelle/*Venus Ind School Dist*	2,19,84,288	249
Salazar, Orlando/*Corpus Christi Ind Sch Dist*	27,36,79,90,285	303
Salazar, Rafael/*Northside Ind School Dist*	5	36
Salazar, Raul/*San Antonio Ind School Dist*	35	39
Salazar, Xochitl/*Tomball Ind School Dist*	11	203
Salcido, Betsabe/*Ector Co Ind School Dist*	57	130
Salcido, Rosie/*Pecos-Barstow-Toyah Ind SD*	37	323
Salcines, Jake/*Sharyland Ind School Dist*	8	224
Saldana, Joan/*Utopia Ind School Dist*	73,76	378
Saldana, Lysandra/*Devine Ind School Dist*	9	283
Saldana, Ray/*San Benito Cons Ind Sch Dist*	79	67
Saldane, Frank/*Ft Hancock Ind School Dist*	6	234
Saldivar, Gil/*Lyford Cons Ind School Dist*	295,297	394
Saldivar, Zaida/*Garland Ind School Dist*	57	105
Sale-Davis, Clara/*Brazosport Ind School Dist*	8,18,288	52
Salee, Will/*Rockwall Ind School Dist*	3	325
Salera, Malesa/*Santa Rosa Ind School Dist*	8,58	67
Salgado, Lilliana/*La Joya Ind School Dist*	71	219
Salgado, Priscilla/*Wink Loving Ind School Dist*	8,11,36,69,83,88,93	402
Salina, Norbert/*Crystal City Ind School Dist*	4	407
Salinas, Amanda/*Klein Ind School Dist*	70	196
Salinas, Angela/*Pharr-San Juan-Alamo Ind SD*	273	223
Salinas, Ben/*Alice Ind School Dist*	67	245
Salinas, Brenda/*Cumby Ind School Dist*	2	231
Salinas, Debbie/*Pharr-San Juan-Alamo Ind SD*	58,77	223
Salinas, Delma/*Robstown Ind School Dist*	81	305
Salinas, Gladice/*Lorenzo Ind School Dist*	57	94
Salinas, Isabel/*Christoval Ind School Dist*	4	364
Salinas, Jose/*Brooks Co Ind School Dist*	27,73,84,295	57
Salinas, Juan/*Lyford Cons Ind School Dist*	4	394
Salinas, Julio/*Ingleside Ind School Dist*	67	331
Salinas, Lenore/*Hidalgo Ind School Dist*	58	217
Salinas, Mario, Dr/*Edinburg Cons Ind School Dist*	15	216
Salinas, Melinda, Dr/*Harlandale Ind School Dist*	68	32
Salinas, Oscar/*La Feria Ind School Dist*	6,35	65
Salinas, Rolando/*Eagle Pass Ind School Dist*	15,78,275	276
Salinas, Rosie/*Sinton Ind School Dist*	73,84	332
Salinas, Rosiosos/*Tornillo Ind School Dist*	4	137
Salinas, Shere, Dr/*Corpus Christi Ind Sch Dist*	47	303
Salinas, Theresa/*Edgewood Ind School Dist*	8	31
Salinas, Xavier/*Edinburg Cons Ind School Dist*	67	216
Salinas, Xavier/*Hidalgo Ind School Dist*	1	217
Salines, Patrick/*Eagle Pass Ind School Dist*	73,95	276
Salizar, Miguel/*Ralls Ind School Dist*	10	94
Salmon, Lisa/*Wylie Ind School Dist*	34,57,69,83,273	361
Salter, John/*New Deal Ind School Dist*	4	271
Salzar, Eugene/*Houston Ind School Dist*	2	188
Salzmann, Patti/*San Antonio Ind School Dist*	15	39
Samaniego, Yvonne/*Ft Hancock Ind School Dist*	11,57,298	234
Sampson, Erika/*Port Arthur Ind School Dist*	4	243
Sampson, Franklin/*Cypress-Fairbanks Ind Sch Dist*	36	184
Sampson, Mark/*Scurry Rosser Ind School Dist*	73	253
Sams, Linda/*Cypress-Fairbanks Ind Sch Dist*	45	184
Samuel, Jennifer/*Everman Ind School Dist*	9,69,288	349
Samuelson, Kandice/*Coupland Ind School Dist*	67	395
San Miguel, Leroy/*Northside Ind School Dist*	3,15	36
Sanches, Veronica/*Lyford Cons Ind School Dist*	68	394
Sanchez, Alissa/*Brooks Co Ind School Dist*	2	57
Sanchez, Amanda/*San Elizario Ind School Dist*	58	135
Sanchez, Andres/*Weslaco Ind School Dist*	2,15	225
Sanchez, Angelica/*United Ind School Dist*	27,31	387
Sanchez, Cynthia/*Sharyland Ind School Dist*	4	224
Sanchez, Daisy/*Bronte Ind School Dist*	36,69,83,85,88,270,273	75
Sanchez, Debbie/*Meridian Ind School Dist*	4	47
Sanchez, Debra/*Gorman Ind School Dist*	57,271	129
Sanchez, Gilbert/*Eagle Pass Ind School Dist*	20,57	276
Sanchez, H T, Dr/*Plainview Ind School Dist*	1	175
Sanchez, Jaime/*Presidio Ind School Dist*	295	320
Sanchez, Joel/*Sierra Blanca Ind School Dist*	67	234
Sanchez, Mari/*Crockett Co Cons Common SD*	76	94
Sanchez, Michael/*San Antonio Ind School Dist*	3	39
Sanchez, Mike/*Vidor Ind School Dist*	91	309
Sanchez, Nancy/*Hidalgo Ind School Dist*	2,11,19	217
Sanchez, Nick/*Schulenburg Ind School Dist*	73,295	148
Sanchez, Omar/*Ft Stockton Ind School Dist*	73	315
Sanchez, Pam/*Georgetown Ind School Dist*	2,19	395
Sanchez, Patti/*Northside Ind School Dist*	9	36
Sanchez, Rawly/*Tyler Ind School Dist*	15	337
Sanchez, Rebecca/*Pharr-San Juan-Alamo Ind SD*	12	223
Sanchez, Reymundo/*Ysleta Ind School Dist*	58	137
Sanchez, Rita/*Comstock Ind School Dist*	4,58,69,73	379
Sanchez, Sammy/*Lamesa Ind School Dist*	3,5,91	117
Sanchez, Sharon/*Northside Ind School Dist*	298	36
Sanchez, Stej/*Dallas Ind School Dist*	45	98
Sanchez, Steve/*Diocese of El Paso Ed Office*	1,11,73	139
Sanchez, Tammy/*Monahans-Wickett-Pyote ISD*	4	385
Sanchez, Valarie/*Comstock Ind School Dist*	12	379
Sanchez, Victoria/*Marathon Ind School Dist*	2	56
Sanderlin, Ted/*Knippa Ind School Dist*	67	378
Sanders, Aaron/*Mt Vernon Ind School Dist*	67	156
Sanders, Allen/*Rockdale Ind School Dist*	83	287
Sanders, Amanda/*Maud Ind School Dist*	8,11,57,271,288,296,298	49
Sanders, Anna/*Wharton Ind School Dist*	82	390
Sanders, Ara/*New Home Ind School Dist*	7	273
Sanders, Daniella/*Arp Ind School Dist*	2	336
Sanders, Donna/*Goldthwaite Consolidated ISD*	58	288
Sanders, Greg/*Jacksboro Ind Sch Dist*	5	239
Sanders, James/*Ennis Ind School Dist*	15,68	140
Sanders, James/*New Waverly Ind School Dist*	3	383
Sanders, James/*Scurry Rosser Ind School Dist*	1,11,83	253
Sanders, Jeff/*Blum Ind School Dist*	1,11	227
Sanders, Jill/*China Spring Ind School Dist*	4	278
Sanders, Kathie/*Cypress-Fairbanks Ind Sch Dist*	11,298	183
Sanders, Leslie/*Savoy Ind School Dist*	85	146
Sanders, Matt/*Midlothian Ind School Dist*	67	141
Sanders, Misti/*Oglesby Ind School Dist*	12	93
Sanders, Nancy/*Wolfe City Ind School Dist*	76	237
Sanders, Russell, Dr/*Mansfield Ind School Dist*	20,23	356
Sanders, Sarah/*Randolph Field Ind School Dist*	81	39
Sanders, Scott/*Lexington Ind School Dist*	67	263
Sanders, Steve/*Brownsboro Ind School Dist*	67	213
Sanders, Wendy/*Morgan Mill Ind School Dist*	1	144
Sanders, Yvette/*East Central Ind School Dist*	68	31
Sanderson, Geoff/*McKinney Ind School Dist*	294	81
Sanderson, Gina/*Everman Ind School Dist*	68	349
Sandford, Blake/*Early Ind School Dist*	6	58
Sandifer, Brenda/*Wylie Ind School Dist*	36,85,88,271	361
Sandifer, Hugh/*Wylie Ind School Dist*	6	361
Sandlin, Nancy/*Buckholts Ind School Dist*	1,11	287
Sandlin, Whilliam/*Buckholts Ind School Dist*	73	287
Sandoval, Frank/*Mexia Ind School Dist*	6	267
Sandoval, Jesse/*Ft Sam Houston Ind School Dist*	5	32
Sandoval, Rosey/*Duncanville Ind School Dist*	57	104
Sandoval, Terri/*Olton Ind School Dist*	11,69,294	261

1 Superintendent
2 Bus/Finance/Purchasing
3 Buildings And Grounds
4 Food Service
5 Transportation
6 Athletic
7 Health Services
8 Curric/Instruct K-12
9 Curric/Instruct Elem
10 Curric/Instruct Sec
11 Federal Program
12 Title I
13 Title V
15 Asst Superintendent
16 Instructional Media Svcs
17 Chief Operations Officer
18 Chief Academic Officer
19 Chief Financial Officer
20 Art K-12
21 Art Elem
22 Art Sec
23 Music K-12
24 Music Elem
25 Music Sec
26 Business Education
27 Career & Tech Ed
28 Technology Education
29 Family/Consumer Science
30 Adult Education
31 Career/Sch-to-Work K-12
32 Career/Sch-to-Work Elem
33 Career/Sch-to-Work Sec
34 Early Childhood Ed
35 Health/Phys Education
36 Guidance Services K-12
37 Guidance Services Elem
38 Guidance Services Sec
39 Social Studies K-12
40 Social Studies Elem
41 Social Studies Sec
42 Science K-12
43 Science Elem
44 Science Sec
45 Math K-12
46 Math Elem
47 Math Sec
48 English/Lang Arts K-12
49 English/Lang Arts Elem
50 English/Lang Arts Sec
51 Reading K-12
52 Reading Elem
53 Reading Sec
54 Remedial Reading K-12
55 Remedial Reading Elem
56 Remedial Reading Sec
57 Bilingual/ELL
58 Special Education K-12
59 Special Education Elem
60 Special Education Sec
61 Foreign/World Lang K-12
62 Foreign/World Lang Elem
63 Foreign/World Lang Sec
64 Religious Education K-12
65 Religious Education Elem
66 Religious Education Sec
67 School Board President
68 Teacher Personnel
69 Academic Assessment
70 Research/Development
71 Public Information
72 Summer School
73 Instructional Tech
74 Inservice Training
75 Marketing/Distributive
76 Info Systems
77 Psychological Assess
78 Affirmative Action
79 Student Personnel
80 Driver Ed/Safety
81 Gifted/Talented
82 Video Services
83 Substance Abuse Prev
84 Erate
85 AIDS Education
88 Alternative/At Risk
89 Multi-Cultural Curriculum
90 Social Work
91 Safety/Security
92 Magnet School
93 Parental Involvement
95 Tech Prep Program
97 Chief Information Officer
98 Chief Technology Officer
270 Character Education
271 Migrant Education
273 Teacher Mentor
274 Before/After Sch
275 Response To Intervention
277 Remedial Math K-12
280 Literacy Coach
285 STEM
286 Digital Learning
288 Common Core Standards
294 Accountability
295 Network System
296 Title II Programs
297 Webmaster
298 Grant Writer/Ptnrships
750 Chief Innovation Officer
751 Chief of Staff
752 Social Emotional Learning

Texas School Directory

DISTRICT PERSONNEL INDEX

NAME/District	JOB FUNCTIONS	PAGE
Sandusky, Julie/*Forestburg Ind School Dist*	58	290
Sanford, Becky/*Colorado Ind School Dist*	4	289
Sanford, Brandon/*Diboll Ind School Dist*	5	17
Sanford, Brenda/*Canton Ind School Dist*	8,11,69	380
Sanford, Brooke/*Highland Ind School Dist*	73	301
Sanford, Kerri/*Diboll Ind School Dist*	4	17
Sanford, Michael/*Chireno ISD School Dist*	67	297
Sanguinetti, Courtney/*Lindale Ind School Dist*	71	337
Santiago, Moises/*Wimberley Ind School Dist*	2,19	212
Santos, Chris/*Cedar Hill Ind School Dist*	91	97
Santos, Juan/*Tomball Ind School Dist*	68	203
Santos, Roberto/*United Ind School Dist*	1	387
Sapp, Lorri/*Midway Ind School Dist*	47	280
Sappington, Jennifer/*Region 3 Ed Service Center*	2,19	383
Sappington, Nathan/*Industrial Ind School Dist*	73,84,295	240
Sappinting, Ray/*Valley View ISD-Cooke Co*	67	91
Sargent, Judy/*Birdville Ind School Dist*	4	346
Sargent, Kristi/*Itasca Ind School Dist*	69	228
Sargent, Ricky/*Hearne Ind School Dist*	6	325
Sartain, J'Ann/*UT Tyler University Acad Dist*	4	338
Satterwhite, Cassie/*Grapeland Ind School Dist*	9,11,34,296	232
Satterwhite, Macy/*Lubbock-Cooper Ind Sch Dist*	15	271
Sattler, Shawn/*Doss Consolidated Common SD*	67	162
Sauceda-Upshaw, Hedith, Dr/*Conroe Ind School Dist*	8,74,273	291
Sauceda, Dora, Dr/*Brownsville Ind School Dist*	8,15	63
Sauceda, Emily/*Edgewood Ind School Dist*	58	31
Sauceda, Emily/*Edgewood Ind School Dist*	58	380
Sauceda, Evelyn/*Nacogdoches Ind School Dist*	57,271	298
Sauceda, Lisa/*Nursery ISD School Dist*	4	382
Saucedo, Arnold/*Menard Ind School Dist*	67	285
Saucedo, Diana/*Eagle Pass Ind School Dist*	16	276
Saucedo, Flavio/*Mumford Ind School Dist*	73	56
Saucke, Mike/*Hubbard Ind School Dist*	3	227
Sauder, Reggie/*Wellington Ind School Dist*	5	86
Saul, Michael/*Sweeny Ind School Dist*	79	54
Saunders, Karen/*Morton Ind School Dist*	1	75
Saunders, Kimberly/*Nordheim Ind School Dist*	2,84	118
Savaell, Bill/*Ponder Ind School Dist*	6	125
Savage, Lisa/*Alvin Ind School Dist*	20,23	50
Savala, Janina/*Crockett Co Cons Common SD*	11,57,288,296,298	94
Savanah, Ken/*Stafford Municipal Sch Dist*	6	155
Saveat, Cindy/*Beaumont Ind School Dist*	79	241
Saveat, Rodney/*Beaumont Ind School Dist*	35	241
Saverline, Charles/*Ricardo Ind School Dist*	67	257
Savoy, Tim/*Hays Cons Ind School Dist*	16,71	211
Sawyer, Sandy/*Robert Lee Ind School Dist*	16,73,76,286	75
Sayavedra, Diana/*Ft Bend Ind School Dist*	8,18,31,69,79	149
Sayers, Georgia/*Kirbyville Cons Ind Sch Dist*	1,11	241
Sayers, Nan/*Diocese of Dallas Ed Office*	2	113
Saylack, Diana/*Lovejoy Ind School Dist*	46	80
Saylor, Shannon, Dr/*Aubrey Ind School Dist*	15,68,79	120
Sazedj, Teresa, Dr/*Stafford Municipal Sch Dist*	13,78,296	155
Scamardo, Anthony/*Mumford Ind School Dist*	67	56
Scarborough, Kendra/*La Poynor Ind School Dist*	2	214
Scarborough, Michael/*Mumford Ind School Dist*	6	56
Scarbourgh, Megan/*Grapevine-Colleyville Ind SD*	274	353
Scarbrough, Carl, Dr/*Alice Ind School Dist*	1	245
Scates, Barbara/*Excelsior Ind School Dist*	16,73,295,297	334
Schaap, Mike/*Smyer Ind School Dist*	6	229
Schacherl, Andrew/*Shiner Ind School Dist*	67	262
Schad, Lenny/*Houston Ind School Dist*	73,76,98,295	188
Schaefer, Carla/*Victoria Ind School Dist*	69,294	382
Schaefer, Dan/*Klein Ind School Dist*	2,19	196
Schaeffer, Kathryn/*Carrollton-Farmers Branch ISD*	69,81	96
Schafer, Brian/*Eastland Ind School Dist*	5	129
Schasteen, Karen/*Clifton Ind School Dist*	58	46
Schaub, Dean/*New Waverly Ind School Dist*	6	383
Schaum, Allison/*Flour Bluff Ind School Dist*	8,12,13,15	304
Scheffler, Dena/*Sanger Ind School Dist*	3	126
Scherr, Donna/*Region 14 Ed Service Center*	275	362
Scherz, Deidre/*Christoval Ind School Dist*	60	364
Schiele, Jim/*Eagle Mtn-Saginaw Ind Sch Dist*	2,19	348
Schiller, Dawn/*Belton Ind School Dist*	69,70	26
Schilling, Karen/*Farwell Ind School Dist*	69	314
Schindewolf, Amy, Dr/*Tomball Ind School Dist*	8,18	203
Schiro, Elsie/*Ft Worth Ind School Dist*	19	349
Schlaud, Jodie/*Iowa Park Consolidated Ind SD*	8,73,285,286,288	392
Schlegel, Angela/*Electra Ind School Dist*	58	391
Schlegel, Anjela/*Iowa Park Consolidated Ind SD*	58	392
Schluter, Traci/*Cypress-Fairbanks Ind Sch Dist*	77	184
Schmidt, Andrew/*Garrison Ind School Dist*	3	297
Schmidt, Cathy/*Teague Ind School Dist*	288,296	156
Schmidt, Don/*Northside Ind School Dist*	15,79	36
Schmidt, Jason/*Seguin Ind School Dist*	9,15	173
Schmidt, Monica/*Pringle-Morse Cons ISD*	16	177
Schmitz, Vivian/*Irving Ind School Dist*	271	109
Schnautz, Brad, Dr/*Grapevine-Colleyville Ind SD*	15	353
Schneider, Bubba/*Damon Ind School Dist*	67	53
Schneider, Dawn/*Devine Ind School Dist*	79	283
Schneider, Julia/*North East Ind School Dist*	34	34
Schneider, Kristi/*Muenster Ind School Dist*	36,69,83,88,270	91
Schneider, Shelly/*Damon Ind School Dist*	286	53
Schneider, Todd/*Bullard Ind School Dist*	1	336
Schnider, Rodney/*Dublin Ind School Dist*	1	143
Schnitta, Mina, Dr/*Huntsville Ind School Dist*	10	383
Schnucker, Kim/*Dumas Ind School Dist*	274	295
Schobajsa, Cheryl/*Water Valley Ind School Dist*	4	365
Schobel, Matt/*Columbus Ind School Dist*	6	86
Schoen, Kathryn/*Round Top-Carmine Ind Sch Dist*	9	147
Schoen, Sheila/*Vidor Ind School Dist*	2	309
Schoenhals, Nieda/*Darrouzett Ind School Dist*	73,286,295	267
Schofield, Brenda/*Region 5 Ed Service Center*	11,30	244
Scholz, Tracy, Dr/*Alief Ind School Dist*	81	181
Schonhoeft, Ross/*Aransas Co Ind School Dist*	4	19
Schonhoeft, Ross/*Ingleside Ind School Dist*	4	331
Schoon, Steve/*Quitman Ind School Dist*	3,5,91	404
Schoppe, Theresa/*Snook Ind School Dist*	68	59
Schoppe, Todd/*La Porte Ind School Dist*	6	198
Schorch, Holly/*McMullen Co Ind Sch Dist*	58,83,88,270	283
Schovajsa, Brandon/*Round Top-Carmine Ind Sch Dist*	1,11,83	147
Schovajsa, Chanda/*Sudan Ind School Dist*	16,82	261
Schrader, Mark/*Palestine Ind School Dist*	73,76,286	15
Schram, Sheila/*Springtown Ind School Dist*	76	313
Schramm, Hannah/*Comal Ind School Dist*	74	87
Schreiber, Shirley/*Northside Ind School Dist*	7	36
Schreitmueller, Joyce/*Diocese of Dallas Ed Office*	11,30	113
Schroader, Barbie/*Borger Ind School Dist*	69,271,285	237
Schroeder, Dena/*New Braunfels Ind School Dist*	69	88
Schroeder, Marshall/*Conroe Ind School Dist*	3	291
Schroeder, Ronnie/*Amherst Ind School Dist*	67	260
Schroedter, Jodi/*Orange Grove Ind School Dist*	2	245
Schronk, Odell/*Grandview Ind School Dist*	5	248
Schuessler, Edwin/*Westwood Ind School Dist*	73,286,295	16
Schuessler, Shelly/*Llano Ind School Dist*	58	268
Schuler, Megan/*Plano Ind School Dist*	7	82
Schulte, Glenn/*Honey Grove Ind School Dist*	6	146
Schulte, Samantha/*Victoria Ind School Dist*	73,76,295	382
Schultz, Craig/*Schulenburg Ind School Dist*	67	148
Schultz, Ida/*Humble Ind School Dist*	2	195
Schultz, Rebbeca/*Oglesby Ind School Dist*	67	93
Schulz, Billy/*Abbott Ind School Dist*	16,73,76,286,295	226
Schulz, Chantel/*Woodsboro Ind School Dist*	8,27,31,36,69,83,88,288	324
Schulz, Marcus/*Splendora Ind School Dist*	6	294
Schulze, Disa/*Danbury Ind School Dist*	3,4,5,91	53
Schulze, Lori/*Odem-Edroy Ind School Dist*	10,11,285	331
Schulze, Renee/*Junction Ind School Dist*	11	256
Schumacher, Kelly/*Klein Ind School Dist*	15,68	196
Schumacker, John/*Gonzales Ind School Dist*	1	164
Schumann, Carla/*Comal Ind School Dist*	20,23	87
Schumann, James/*Agua Dulce Ind School Dist*	2	302
Schumer, Nicole/*Tyler Ind School Dist*	81	337
Schumpert, Melissa/*San Angelo Ind School Dist*	7	364
Schuppert, Phillip/*Forsan Ind School Dist*	3	234
Schuss, Brian/*Katy Ind School Dist*	15,68	151
Schutte, Marian/*Texas Dept of Education*	76	1
Schwab, Maria/*North East Ind School Dist*	49	34
Schwake, Richard/*McGregor Ind School Dist*	3,5	280
Schwartz, Cara/*Pflugerville Ind School Dist*	58	371
Schwartz, Kevin/*Austin Ind School Dist*	73,76,295	366
Schwarz, Kim/*Bosqueville Ind School Dist*	16	278
Schweitzer, Dawna/*Birdville Ind School Dist*	42	346
Schwertner, Paula/*Bushland Ind School Dist*	16	319

School Year 2019-2020 800-333-8802 TX-T81

DISTRICT PERSONNEL INDEX

Market Data Retrieval

NAME/District	JOB FUNCTIONS	PAGE
Schwierjohn, Darryl/*Wink Loving Ind School Dist*	23	402
Schwind, Karen/*New Braunfels Ind School Dist*	7	88
Schwind, Michelle, Dr/*Italy Ind School Dist*	1	140
Schwobell, Ladonna/*Hurst-Euless-Bedford ISD*	49	353
Sciba, Donald/*Boling Ind School Dist*	67	389
Scifres, Jody/*Lubbock Ind School Dist*	91	270
Scisson, Mark/*Sudan Ind School Dist*	3	261
Scisson, Tonjua/*Sudan Ind School Dist*	2	261
Scitern, Stephen/*Anson Ind School Dist*	27,31	249
Scobee, Dustin/*Holliday Ind School Dist*	2	19
Scoggin, Richard/*Weatherford Ind School Dist*	6	313
Scoggins, Gretchen/*Lumberton Ind School Dist*	298	178
Scogin, Debbie/*Harlingen Cons Ind School Dist*	15,68	64
Scogin, Laci/*Jayton-Girard Ind School Dist*	2	255
Scott, Annette, Dr/*Galveston Ind School Dist*	8,11,15	160
Scott, Ben/*Sulphur Springs Ind Sch Dist*	295	232
Scott, Carolyn/*Hallsburg Ind School Dist*	6	279
Scott, Carolyn/*Lazbuddie Ind School Dist*	2	315
Scott, Charla/*Loop Ind School Dist*	16,27	157
Scott, Chris/*Eanes Ind School Dist*	2	370
Scott, Chris/*Tomball Ind School Dist*	42,45	203
Scott, Dana/*Skidmore Tynan Ind SD*	12,296	25
Scott, David/*DeSoto Ind School Dist*	2	104
Scott, David/*Lago Vista Ind School Dist*	67	370
Scott, Donna/*Mexia Ind School Dist*	37	267
Scott, Erik/*Scurry Rosser Ind School Dist*	91	253
Scott, Henry, Dr/*Denison Ind School Dist*	1	166
Scott, Jamie/*Big Spring Ind School Dist*	73,286,295	233
Scott, Jenny/*Albany Ind School Dist*	16,38	334
Scott, John/*Wellington Ind School Dist*	73,295	86
Scott, Jonathan/*Albany Ind School Dist*	1	334
Scott, Kathy/*Snyder Ind School Dist*	11,79	333
Scott, Linda/*Jefferson Ind School Dist*	37	274
Scott, Lyn/*Honey Grove Ind School Dist*	36,69,77,752	146
Scott, Marshall/*Bay City Ind School Dist*	1	275
Scott, Michael/*Alba-Golden Ind School Dist*	73,98	404
Scott, Natosha/*Community Ind School Dist*	11,58	78
Scott, Robert/*Ferris Ind School Dist*	67	140
Scott, Roberta, Dr/*Houston Ind School Dist*	752	188
Scott, Sean, Dr/*Mansfield Ind School Dist*	8,15,288,294	356
Scott, Sheryl/*Clarksville Ind School Dist*	4	322
Scott, Wesley/*Northside Ind School Dist*	2,15	36
Scribner, Ken/*Sanger Ind School Dist*	67	126
Scribner, Kent, Dr/*Ft Worth Ind School Dist*	1	349
Scrivner, Jim/*Irving Ind School Dist*	3	109
Scruggs, Jeremy/*Ennis Ind School Dist*	83,91	140
Scruggs, Sherri/*Joaquin Ind School Dist*	8	335
Seabolt, Michael, Dr/*Marlin Ind School Dist*	11	144
Seago, Mary/*Coldspring-Oakhurst Cons ISD*	16	330
Seale, Becky/*Early Ind School Dist*	2	58
Seale, Robert/*Humble Ind School Dist*	2,19	195
Seale, Sherri/*Pittsburg Ind School Dist*	68	68
Sealey, Darla/*Bovina Ind School Dist*	8,11	314
Seals, Jack, Dr/*Cotulla Ind School Dist*	1	259
Seals, Jared/*Roscoe Collegiate Ind Sch Dist*	16,73	301
Seals, Katherine/*Aldine Ind School Dist*	58	179
Seaman, Sheri/*South San Antonio Ind Sch Dist*	68	42
Searcy, Kevin/*Trinity Ind School Dist*	67	374
Sebesta, Laura/*Snook Ind School Dist*	5,288	59
Sebo, Vince/*Tomball Ind School Dist*	3,6	203
Seckman, Patti/*Paradise Ind School Dist*	8,11,15,74,271,296	403
Sedberry, Jay/*Ropes Ind School Dist*	16,73	229
Sedillo, Marivel/*Hays Cons Ind School Dist*	68	211
Segers, David/*Ganado Ind School Dist*	285	239
Segers, Laura/*Round Rock Ind School Dist*	11	398
Segovia, Rogelio/*San Elizario Ind School Dist*	8,11,15,70,72,274	135
Segura, Kyle/*Port Neches-Groves Ind SD*	5	243
Segura, Matias/*Austin Ind School Dist*	3	366
Segura, Melva/*Weslaco Ind School Dist*	68	225
Seibert, Jay/*Aransas Co Ind School Dist*	6	19
Seigrist, Andrew, Dr/*Tidehaven Ind School Dist*	1	276
Seiler, Russell/*Midway Ind School Dist*	76,295	280
Seimonds, Mildred, Dr/*Wall Ind School Dist*	57	365
Seippe, Pam/*Doss Consolidated Common SD*	11,84,288,296,298,752	162
Seiter, Annie/*Boerne Ind School Dist*	58	253
Self, David/*Denison Ind School Dist*	3	166
Self, Faith/*Childress Ind School Dist*	16	74
Self, Fran/*Perrin-Whitt Cons Ind Sch Dist*	2	239
Self, Ginger/*Coolidge Ind School Dist*	58	266
Self, Kirk/*Canyon Ind School Dist*	5,91	320
Self, Steven/*Muenster Ind School Dist*	1	91
Selig, Emma/*Richardson Ind School Dist*	57	112
Sell, Loren/*Perrin-Whitt Cons Ind Sch Dist*	10	239
Sellers, Aunie/*Ralls Ind School Dist*	67	94
Sellers, Casey/*Rice Ind School Dist*	31	300
Sellers, Daylan/*Seagraves Ind School Dist*	10	157
Sellers, Kellie/*Richardson Ind School Dist*	35	112
Sellers, Leo/*Ira Ind School Dist*	27	333
Sellgren, John/*Hurst-Euless-Bedford ISD*	76	353
Sells, Jennifer/*Texarkana Ind School Dist*	44,47	50
Sells, Katherine/*Lewisville Ind School Dist*	67	122
Seltzer, Mary, Dr/*Northwest Ind School Dist*	9	124
Selznick, Victoria/*Allen Ind School Dist*	16	76
Semdejo, Alma/*Crystal City Ind School Dist*	58	407
Senato, Amy/*Mansfield Ind School Dist*	43	356
Sendejo, Delores/*South San Antonio Ind Sch Dist*	8,18	42
Sendejo, Delores/*Southside Ind School Dist*	67	43
Senter, Nikki/*Overton Ind School Dist*	12	328
Senter, Toyia/*Ropes Ind School Dist*	16	229
Sepeda, Eli/*Roby Cons Ind School Dist*	5	148
Sepkowipz, Brian/*Wellman Union Ind School Dist*	6	362
Sepulveda, Brenda/*Laredo Ind School Dist*	34,73,76	386
Sepulveda, Melinda/*Diocese of Laredo Ed Office*	68	388
Sermas, Pat/*Pasadena Ind School Dist*	36,69	198
Serna, Felix/*Kenedy Co Schools*	67	254
Serna, Felix/*Kenedy Co Wide Common Sch Dist*	67	254
Serna, Norma/*Eagle Pass Ind School Dist*	11,72,271,296,298	276
Serrano, Fabian/*Big Spring Ind School Dist*	67	233
Serrano, Lee/*Pecos-Barstow-Toyah Ind SD*	5	323
Serrano, Sonia/*Pearland Ind School Dist*	10,15	53
Sertuche, Nelda/*Yorktown Ind School Dist*	67	118
Sescota, Rebecca/*Loop Ind School Dist*	4	157
Sessions, Leslie/*Austwell Tivoli Ind SD*	73,295	323
Sessom, Bryan/*Lubbock Ind School Dist*	34	269
Sessom, Charlotte/*Lubbock Ind School Dist*	36	269
Sessums, Michael/*Prairiland Ind School Dist*	67	260
Sestak, Tammy/*Victoria Ind School Dist*	9,93	382
Setser, Jaylyn/*Hughes Springs Ind Sch Dist*	2,11	70
Settle, John/*Sunnyvale Ind School Dist*	6	113
Settle, Kathy/*Irion Co Ind School Dist*	60	238
Settles, Rhiannon/*Waco Ind School Dist*	7	281
Setwalker, Dana/*Colmesneil Ind School Dist*	4	375
Seward, Melissa/*McGregor Ind School Dist*	73,76,286,295	280
Sewell, Cathy/*Duncanville Ind School Dist*	8,18	104
Sewell, Patrish/*Leakey Ind School Dist*	8,36,83,88,275	322
Sewell, Tony/*Coldspring-Oakhurst Cons ISD*	67	330
Sexton, Andy/*Bastrop Ind School Dist*	6,13	23
Sexton, Sandra/*D'Hanis Ind School Dist*	16,73	283
Sexton, Syd/*Region 17 Ed Service Center*	8	272
Seymore, Tim/*Breckenridge Ind School Dist*	1	341
Seymour, Rick/*Neches Ind School Dist*	73,286	15
Shackelford, Catherine/*Collinsville Ind School Dist*	58	166
Shade, Chris/*Denton Ind School Dist*	11,296,298	120
Shafer, Brooklyn/*Joshua Ind School Dist*	30	248

#		#		#		#		#	
1	Superintendent	16	Instructional Media Svcs	30	Adult Education	44	Science Sec	58	Special Education K-12
2	Bus/Finance/Purchasing	17	Chief Operations Officer	31	Career/Sch-to-Work K-12	45	Math K-12	59	Special Education Elem
3	Buildings And Grounds	18	Chief Academic Officer	32	Career/Sch-to-Work Elem	46	Math Elem	60	Special Education Sec
4	Food Service	19	Chief Financial Officer	33	Career/Sch-to-Work Sec	47	Math Sec	61	Foreign/World Lang K-12
5	Transportation	20	Art K-12	34	Early Childhood Ed	48	English/Lang Arts K-12	62	Foreign/World Lang Elem
6	Athletic	21	Art Elem	35	Health/Phys Education	49	English/Lang Arts Elem	63	Foreign/World Lang Sec
7	Health Services	22	Art Sec	36	Guidance Services K-12	50	English/Lang Arts Sec	64	Religious Education K-12
8	Curric/Instruct K-12	23	Music K-12	37	Guidance Services Elem	51	Reading K-12	65	Religious Education Elem
9	Curric/Instruct Elem	24	Music Elem	38	Guidance Services Sec	52	Reading Elem	66	Religious Education Sec
10	Curric/Instruct Sec	25	Music Sec	39	Social Studies K-12	53	Reading Sec	67	School Board President
11	Federal Program	26	Business Education	40	Social Studies Elem	54	Remedial Reading K-12	68	Teacher Personnel
12	Title I	27	Career & Tech Ed	41	Social Studies Sec	55	Remedial Reading Elem	69	Academic Assessment
13	Title V	28	Technology Education	42	Science K-12	56	Remedial Reading Sec	70	Research/Development
15	Asst Superintendent	29	Family/Consumer Science	43	Science Elem	57	Bilingual/ELL	71	Public Information

#		#		#		#	
72	Summer School	88	Alternative/At Risk	277	Remedial Math K-12		
73	Instructional Tech	89	Multi-Cultural Curriculum	280	Literacy Coach		
74	Inservice Training	90	Social Work	285	STEM		
75	Marketing/Distributive	91	Safety/Security	286	Digital Learning		
76	Info Systems	92	Magnet School	288	Common Core Standards		
77	Psychological Assess	93	Parental Involvement	294	Accountability		
78	Affirmative Action	95	Tech Prep Program	295	Network System		
79	Student Personnel	97	Chief Infomation Officer	296	Title II Programs		
80	Driver Ed/Safety	98	Chief Technology Officer	297	Webmaster		
81	Gifted/Talented	270	Character Education	298	Grant Writer/Ptnrships		
82	Video Services	271	Migrant Education	750	Chief Innovation Officer		
83	Substance Abuse Prev	273	Teacher Mentor	751	Chief of Staff		
84	Erate	274	Before/After Sch	752	Social Emotional Learning		
85	AIDS Education	275	Response To Intervention				

TX-T82

Texas School Directory

DISTRICT PERSONNEL INDEX

NAME/District	JOB FUNCTIONS	PAGE
Shafer, Scott/*Mansfield Ind School Dist*	3	356
Shaffer, Carmella/*College Station Ind Sch Dist*	2	55
Shaffer, Pam/*Stanton Ind School Dist*	2	274
Shah, Karen/*Pflugerville Ind School Dist*	294	371
Shahan, Christel/*Munday Consolidated Ind SD*	27,36,69,77,88,294	259
Shahan, Kevin/*San Saba Ind School Dist*	67	332
Shamsid-Deen, Masud/*Richardson Ind School Dist*	31,73	112
Shanna, Shad/*Archer City Ind School Dist*	6	19
Shannon, Beverly/*Hooks Ind School Dist*	88	48
Shannon, Bobbie/*South San Antonio Ind Sch Dist*	27	42
Shannon, Lorraine/*West Orange-Cove Cons ISD*	71	309
Shannon, Tammy/*Belton Ind School Dist*	2	26
Shapiro, Craig/*Austin ISD High School Area*	15	368
Shari, John/*Poolville Ind School Dist*	6	313
Sharp, Ed/*Whitharral Ind School Dist*	1,11,73	230
Sharp, Henry/*Clarksville Ind School Dist*	11	322
Sharp, Leslie/*Borger Ind School Dist*	67	237
Sharp, Randy/*Bangs Ind School Dist*	3	58
Sharp, Randy/*Bastrop Ind School Dist*	73,84	23
Sharp, Rex/*Sabine Ind School Dist*	6	170
Sharp, Vince/*Anna Ind School Dist*	77,83	77
Sharp, Vivian/*West Rusk Co Cons Ind Sch Dist*	73	328
Sharpe, Kristy/*San Antonio Ind School Dist*	4	39
Sharples, Kathy, Dr/*Conroe Ind School Dist*	68	291
Shatto, Steve/*Pleasant Grove Ind School Dist*	3	49
Shaver, Kris/*Buckholts Ind School Dist*	752	287
Shaver, Melissa/*Region 16 Ed Service Center*	34	321
Shaw, Amy/*Trenton Ind School Dist*	31,83,85,88,273	147
Shaw, Brent/*Alvin Ind School Dist*	69,294	51
Shaw, Cameron/*Dawson Ind School Dist*	73,76,295	299
Shaw, Debbie/*Midland Ind School Dist*	20,23	285
Shaw, Diane/*Garner Ind School Dist*	12,34	312
Shaw, Erin/*Wheeler Ind School Dist*	69	391
Shaw, Gary/*Springtown Ind School Dist*	2,19	313
Shaw, Jim/*Sam Rayburn Ind School Dist*	8,11,58,271,273,275	146
Shaw, Kayla/*Klein Ind School Dist*	36,85	196
Shaw, Pamela/*Ft Bend Ind School Dist*	93	149
Shaw, Pamela/*Plemons-Stinnett-Phillips CISD*	4	238
Shaw, Tami/*North East Ind School Dist*	31	34
Shaw, Teresa/*Calallen Ind School Dist*	7,85	302
Shawi, Diane/*Garner Ind School Dist*	7,91	312
Shea, Tracy/*Cleburne Ind School Dist*	286	247
Shear, Pat/*Region 4 Ed Service Center*	73,76	208
Sheedy, Marsha/*Utopia Ind School Dist*	4	378
Sheeley, Brandon/*Palestine Ind School Dist*	67	15
Sheets, Shawn/*Pearsall Ind School Dist*	4	157
Sheffield, Chad/*Bloomburg Ind School Dist*	6	70
Sheffield, Dani/*Aldine Ind School Dist*	4	179
Sheffield, Maria, Dr/*Ft Worth Ind School Dist*	15,58	349
Sheffield, Mary/*Liberty Hill Ind School Dist*	4	398
Sheffield, Melissa/*La Poynor Ind School Dist*	36,83,88	214
Sheffield, Scott/*Whitney Ind School Dist*	5	228
Sheffield, Vincent/*El Paso Ind School Dist*	15,68,78	132
Sheilds, Mike/*McGregor Ind School Dist*	6	280
Shelby, Debra/*Texarkana Ind School Dist*	74	50
Shelhamer, Gene, Dr/*Region 14 Ed Service Center*	67	362
Shelton, Brad/*Midway Ind School Dist*	6	280
Shelton, Gail/*Gatesville Ind School Dist*	4	92
Shelton, Heath/*Leary Ind School Dist*	73,286	48
Shelton, Holly/*Amarillo Ind School Dist*	71	317
Shelton, James/*Buckholts Ind School Dist*	6	287
Shelton, Kenneth/*Pittsburg Ind School Dist*	5	68
Shelton, Mary/*Garland Ind School Dist*	50	105
Shelton, Theresa/*Laneville Ind School Dist*	1,11	327
Shelton, Wendy/*Waskom Ind School Dist*	57	209
Sheneman, Laura/*Region 1 Ed Service Center*	16	226
Shepard, Linda/*Katy Ind School Dist*	57	151
Shepard, Michael/*Community Ind School Dist*	67	78
Shepard, Nicole/*Klein Ind School Dist*	16	196
Shepherd, Karen/*Plano Ind School Dist*	44	82
Shepherd, Leslee/*Keller Ind School Dist*	27	354
Shepherd, Quintin, Dr/*Victoria Ind School Dist*	1	382
Shepherd, Tyler/*Big Spring Ind School Dist*	11,34,57,58,88,271,296,298	233
Shepherd, Wayne/*Lone Oak Ind School Dist*	3	236
Shepler, Gail/*Mathis Ind School Dist*	2,84	331
Sheppard, Scott, Dr/*Huntsville Ind School Dist*	1	383

NAME/District	JOB FUNCTIONS	PAGE
Sheppard, Shelli/*Madisonville Cons ISD*	27,38,69,75	273
Sheppard, Sondra/*Gause Ind School Dist*	4	287
Sherman, Angie/*Victoria Ind School Dist*	5	382
Sherman, Carl/*DeSoto Ind School Dist*	67	104
Sherman, Julie, Dr/*Port Arthur Ind School Dist*	77	243
Sherman, Robin/*Lockney Independent Sch Dist*	280	149
Shermer, Joei/*Wylie Ind School Dist*	9,54	84
Sherrill, Kevin/*Sonora Ind School Dist*	6	342
Sherrin, Rachelle/*Carrollton-Farmers Branch ISD*	4	96
Sherrod, Tim/*Wichita Falls Ind School Dist*	2,19	392
Sherry, Remona/*Kermit Ind School Dist*	7	401
Sherwood, Cathrine/*Honey Grove Ind School Dist*	8,12	146
Sherwood, Peg/*Spring Ind School Dist*	58	202
Shetter, Denise, Dr/*Kermit Ind School Dist*	1	401
Shew, Dennis/*Tarkington Ind School Dist*	2,15	266
Shields, Kenneth/*Shamrock Ind School Dist*	12,57	390
Shields, Kenneth/*Shamrock Ind School Dist*	1	390
Shields, Sharon, Dr/*La Vega Ind School Dist*	1	279
Shields, Tammy/*Celeste Ind School Dist*	2	235
Shiels, Steven/*Ft Bend Ind School Dist*	36,79,90,270,271	149
Shiller, Todd/*Belton Ind School Dist*	15,68,78,273	26
Shimer, Ellen/*Humble Ind School Dist*	34	195
Shimomura, Leslie/*Duncanville Ind School Dist*	16	104
Shipley, Nancy/*Krum Ind School Dist*	11,15	122
Shipman, Bryan/*Blackwell Cons Ind Sch Dist*	8,11,31,36,58,69,83	301
Shipman, Lu Ann/*Schleicher Co Ind School Dist*	16	333
Shipman, Tammy/*Huckabay Ind School Dist*	2	143
Shipp, Greg/*Conroe Ind School Dist*	27,31	291
Shipp, Susan/*Carrollton-Farmers Branch ISD*	42,280,285	96
Shirey, Kandy/*Scurry Rosser Ind School Dist*	9,34	253
Shirley, Crystal/*Terrell Ind School Dist*	2	253
Shirley, Todd/*Prosper Ind School Dist*	79	84
Shivers, Sherry/*Wortham Ind School Dist*	2	156
Shock, Carly/*Region 3 Ed Service Center*	4	383
Shocklee, Lesa/*Mansfield Ind School Dist*	58	356
Shoemake, James/*McKinney Ind School Dist*	4	80
Shoemaker, Don/*Central Heights Ind Sch Dist*	67	297
Shofner, Cindy/*Bloomburg Ind School Dist*	79	70
Shofner, Kristi/*New Caney Ind School Dist*	8	293
Sholmire, Fred/*Spring Ind School Dist*	3	202
Shoppach, Kyle/*Bruceville-Eddy Ind Sch Dist*	6	278
Shore, Julie/*North East Ind School Dist*	20,23	34
Short, Anna/*San Augustine Ind School Dist*	58	329
Short, Cynthia, Dr/*Clear Creek Ind School Dist*	58,83,90,275	158
Short, Scott/*Ennis Ind School Dist*	16,28,73,76,82,286	140
Shoulders, Kim/*New Waverly Ind School Dist*	58	383
Showell, Joseph/*Birdville Ind School Dist*	79,93	346
Shubert, Clyde/*Dublin Ind School Dist*	3,5	143
Shudde, Doug/*Northside Ind School Dist*	16,73	36
Shull, Pat/*Grand Prairie Ind School Dist*	7,85	107
Shulman, Jackie, Dr/*Santa Fe Ind School Dist*	8,12,34,288	161
Shults, Jamie/*Mission Cons Ind School Dist*	42	222
Shultz, Angela/*Sudan Ind School Dist*	57	261
Shultz, Gary/*Campbell Ind School Dist*	6	235
Shultz, Josh/*Westwood Ind School Dist*	3,91	16
Shuman, Jacqueline, Dr/*Santa Fe Ind School Dist*	15	161
Shumate, Darla/*Pewitt Cons Ind School Dist*	73,98,295	296
Shute, Christian/*Slaton Ind School Dist*	81	272
Sibberson, Michael/*Lometa Ind School Dist*	5	262
Sibley, Derick/*Pleasant Grove Ind School Dist*	2,11	49
Sibley, Upenda/*Lancaster Ind School Dist*	4	110
Sieboldt, John/*Jasper Ind School Dist*	91	240
Sifford, Evelin/*Bellville Ind School Dist*	34,37,58	22
Sifford, Nicole/*Dew Ind School Dist*	7	156
Sifre, Pascuala/*Garland Ind School Dist*	57	105
Sigee, Alicia/*West Orange-Cove Cons ISD*	79	309
Sigler, Melissa/*Everman Ind School Dist*	47	349
Signaigo, Stacy/*Manor Ind School Dist*	34	371
Siler, Jill, Dr/*Gunter Ind School Dist*	1	166
Siler, Rebecca/*Bronte Ind School Dist*	11	75
Siler, Tim/*Bronte Ind School Dist*	1,11	75
Silguero, Alberto/*Gregory-Portland Ind Sch Dist*	2	330
Silguero, Robbie/*Webb Cons Ind School Dist*	6	388
Siller, Regina/*Hawley Ind School Dist*	27	250
Silva, Allison/*Bay City Ind School Dist*	71	275
Silva, Hector/*College Station Ind Sch Dist*	5	55

School Year 2019-2020 800-333-8802 TX-T83

DISTRICT PERSONNEL INDEX

Market Data Retrieval

NAME/District	JOB FUNCTIONS	PAGE
Silva, Julie/South San Antonio Ind Sch Dist	58	42
Silva, Lili/McAllen Ind School Dist	27,31	221
Silva, Maria/Canutillo Ind School Dist	57,271	132
Silva, Maria/Cleveland Ind School Dist	8,11,16,57,69,285,294,296	265
Silva, Melana/Calallen Ind School Dist	10	302
Silva, Ralph, Dr/Corpus Christi Ind Sch Dist	273	303
Silva, Rosina/Laredo Ind School Dist	36,88	386
Silva, Toby/Wellington Ind School Dist	3	86
Silvas, Diana/Robstown Ind School Dist	8,15,36,68,285,288	305
Silver, Barbara/Vidor Ind School Dist	76	309
Silvey, Jane/Lindale Ind School Dist	8,74,273	337
Silvius, Pete/Seguin Ind School Dist	35	173
Simmons, Clarence/Birdville Ind School Dist	9	346
Simmons, David, Dr/Martinsville Ind School Dist	1	298
Simmons, Derek/Linden Kildare Cons Ind SD	6	70
Simmons, Jennifer/Paris Ind School Dist	73	260
Simmons, Joann, Dr/UT Tyler University Acad Dist	1	338
Simmons, Lou/Breckenridge Ind School Dist	2	341
Simmons, Mark/Sabine Pass Ind School Dist	16,73	244
Simmons, Monica/Elysian Fields Ind School Dist	8,69	208
Simmons, Scott/Burkburnett Ind Sch Dist	3,91	391
Simmons, Sherri/Texas City Ind School Dist	10	161
Simon, Chris/Jonesboro Ind School Dist	60	93
Simon, Darryl/Spring Ind School Dist	91	202
Simon, Lainey/Junction Ind School Dist	58	256
Simon, Sharon/Lake Dallas Ind School Dist	16,82	122
Simonds, Matthew/Harlandale Ind School Dist	42	32
Simonds, Monica/Richardson Ind School Dist	81	112
Simonds, Monica/Richardson Ind School Dist	81	112
Simons, Denise/Aldine Ind School Dist	69	179
Simons, Tara/Matagorda Ind School Dist	2,84,271	275
Simpson, Amanda/Coppell Ind School Dist	71,97	98
Simpson, Austin/Santa Anna Ind School Dist	6	76
Simpson, Billy/Los Fresnos Cons Ind Sch Dist	73,84,295	66
Simpson, Charlie/Prairie Lea Ind School Dist	3	61
Simpson, Dennis/Stanton Ind School Dist	3	274
Simpson, Dorothy/Pearland Ind School Dist	4	53
Simpson, Eric/Lewisville Ind School Dist	50	122
Simpson, Jennifer/Burnet Cons Ind Sch Dist	58	60
Simpson, Joe/Lorenzo Ind School Dist	2	94
Simpson, Julie/Denton Ind School Dist	2	120
Simpson, Kimberly/Sherman Ind School Dist	16,71	167
Simpson, Michell/De Leon Ind School Dist	16	89
Simpson, Paula/Corsicana Ind School Dist	69	299
Simpson, Sharon/Richardson Ind School Dist	7	112
Simpson, Steve/Arlington Ind School Dist	286	343
Sims, Alison/Abilene Ind School Dist	9	360
Sims, Aubrey/Iowa Park Consolidated Ind SD	6	392
Sims, Brooke/Coppell Ind School Dist	74	98
Sims, Janie, Dr/Athens Ind School Dist	15	213
Sims, Jarvis/Lackland Ind School Dist	5	34
Sims, Jason/Childress Ind School Dist	6	74
Sims, Judy/Whitewright Ind School Dist	91	168
Sims, June/Quitman Ind School Dist	37	404
Sims, Liz/Lake Travis Ind School Dist	9,57	370
Sims, Natalie/Walcott Ind School Dist	16,73	119
Sims, Robby/Rosebud-Lott Ind School Dist	3	145
Sine, David/Johnson City Ind School Dist	6	46
Singh, Guadalupe/Marathon Ind School Dist	1,11	56
Singletary, Joyce/Madisonville Cons ISD	16	273
Singletary, Scott/Madisonville Cons ISD	2	273
Singleton, Penny/Vidor Ind School Dist	27,31,75	309
Sinquefield, Don/Union Hill Ind School Dist	3,5	377
Sipe, Brent/New Caney Ind School Dist	6	293
Sipes, Stephany/Plano Ind School Dist	61	82
Sircar, Diana/Coppell Ind School Dist	2,19	98
Sisco, Trey/Sterling City Ind School Dist	6	342

NAME/District	JOB FUNCTIONS	PAGE
Sisk, Laurie/Tenaha Ind School Dist	57,271	335
Sisneros, Consuelo/Temple Ind School Dist	57	29
Sisneros, Consuelo/Temple Ind School Dist	57	29
Sisneros, Stella/Advantage Academy Admin Office	4	96
Sissom, Todd/Coppell Ind School Dist	76	98
Sitzes, Lori/Celina Ind School Dist	8,11,15	77
Sivak, Marc/Temple Ind School Dist	73,84	29
Sizemore, David/Petrolia Cons Ind School Dist	3	74
Sizemore, Michael/Lubbock Ind School Dist	42,285	269
Sizemore, Sandy/Liberty Ind School Dist	4	266
Skaggs, Mike/Onalaska Ind School Dist	5	317
Skains, Josh/Cedar Hill Ind School Dist	3	97
Skeeler, James/Bosqueville Ind School Dist	1	278
Skelton, Scott/Lufkin Ind School Dist	67	18
Skidmore, Sanvel/Belton Ind School Dist	6	26
Skillern-Jones, Rhonda/Houston Ind School Dist	67	188
Skinner, Chris/Teague Ind School Dist	1	156
Skinner, Christopher/El Campo Ind School Dist	16,73,82	389
Skinner, Karen/Northside Ind School Dist	2,84	393
Skinner, Mark/Gilmer Ind School Dist	67	376
Skinner, Mark/Plano Ind School Dist	5	82
Skinner, Mary/Whitehouse Ind School Dist	47	338
Skinner, Marylynn/Plano Ind School Dist	16	82
Skinner, Melissa/Hempstead Ind School Dist	8	384
Skipper, Barbara, Dr/Bandera Ind School Dist	67	23
Sklenarik, Mark/Miles Ind School Dist	67	326
Skoruppa, Bert/Ganado Ind School Dist	3	239
Skrla, Steve/Brenham Ind School Dist	36	385
Slack, James/Texas Dept of Education	45	1
Slack, Jan/Big Sandy Ind School Dist	58	316
Slate, Angie/Pottsboro Ind School Dist	16,82	167
Slater, James/Connally Ind School Dist	2,15	279
Slater, JR/Follett Ind School Dist	58	267
Slaton, Sam/Argyle Ind School Dist	67	120
Slaughter, Jody/Beaumont Ind School Dist	750	241
Slaughter, Keith/College Station Ind Sch Dist	295	55
Slaughter, Lisa/Sivells Bend Ind School Dist	1,11,83,288	91
Slaughter, Lora/Evant Ind School Dist	36,69,79,83,270,286	92
Slaughter, Shelly/Cumby Ind School Dist	1,11	231
Slaughter, Veronica/United Ind School Dist	48,52,57	387
Slavin, Mavonteine/Higgins Ind School Dist	85	268
Slawson, Belinda/Santa Fe Ind School Dist	274	161
Slayton, Cassandra/Frenship Ind School Dist	8	269
Sledd, Wendy/Copperas Cove Ind School Dist	71,298	92
Sleeper, Lee/Bullard Ind School Dist	3,73	336
Sleeper, Shanna/Ingram Ind School Dist	294	255
Slicker, Lauri/Prosper Ind School Dist	12	84
Sloan, Jared/Rice Cons Ind School Dist	6	87
Sloane, James/Hamilton Ind School Dist	12	176
Sloane, Lacey/Slocum ISD School Dist	37	16
Slover, Gina/Big Spring Ind School Dist	79	233
Smalley, Josh/Orangefield Ind School Dist	6	309
Smalley, Kim/Orangefield Ind School Dist	8,273,286,288	309
Smalskas, Tamy, Dr/Sherman Ind School Dist	15,31	167
Smart, Jamie/Lometa Ind School Dist	51	262
Smedley, Olga/Rio Grande City Ind Sch Dist	9	340
Smelley, Shane/Cushing Ind School Dist	6	297
Smetak, Roger/Jayton-Girard Ind School Dist	11,73,295	255
Smetana, Angie/Grape Creek Ind School Dist	1	364
Smiley, Christina/Coolidge Ind School Dist	12	266
Smiley, Jeff/Lindsay Ind School Dist	6	91
Smilie, Gina/Wylie Ind School Dist	2	84
Smith-Faulkner, Renee/Castleberry Ind School Dist	71,73,95,286	347
Smith-Wick, Angelina/San Diego Ind School Dist	2	128
Smith, Alan/Grapevine-Colleyville Ind SD	91	353
Smith, Amanda/Gonzales Ind School Dist	2,19,81	164
Smith, Andrew/Ricardo Ind School Dist	2,11,296	257

#	Role	#	Role	#	Role	#	Role	#	Role	#	Role
1	Superintendent	16	Instructional Media Svcs	30	Adult Education	44	Science Sec	58	Special Education K-12	72	Summer School
2	Bus/Finance/Purchasing	17	Chief Operations Officer	31	Career/Sch-to-Work K-12	45	Math K-12	59	Special Education Elem	73	Instructional Tech
3	Buildings And Grounds	18	Chief Academic Officer	32	Career/Sch-to-Work Elem	46	Math Elem	60	Special Education Sec	74	Inservice Training
4	Food Service	19	Chief Financial Officer	33	Career/Sch-to-Work Sec	47	Math Sec	61	Foreign/World Lang K-12	75	Marketing/Distributive
5	Transportation	20	Art K-12	34	Early Childhood Ed	48	English/Lang Arts K-12	62	Foreign/World Lang Elem	76	Info Systems
6	Athletic	21	Art Elem	35	Health/Phys Education	49	English/Lang Arts Elem	63	Foreign/World Lang Sec	77	Psychological Assess
7	Health Services	22	Art Sec	36	Guidance Services K-12	50	English/Lang Arts Sec	64	Religious Education K-12	78	Affirmative Action
8	Curric/Instruct K-12	23	Music K-12	37	Guidance Services Elem	51	Reading K-12	65	Religious Education Elem	79	Student Personnel
9	Curric/Instruct Elem	24	Music Elem	38	Guidance Services Sec	52	Reading Elem	66	Religious Education Sec	80	Driver Ed/Safety
10	Curric/Instruct Sec	25	Music Sec	39	Social Studies K-12	53	Reading Sec	67	School Board President	81	Gifted/Talented
11	Federal Program	26	Business Education	40	Social Studies Elem	54	Remedial Reading K-12	68	Teacher Personnel	82	Video Services
12	Title I	27	Career & Tech Ed	41	Social Studies Sec	55	Remedial Reading Elem	69	Academic Assessment	83	Substance Abuse Prev
13	Title V	28	Technology Education	42	Science K-12	56	Remedial Reading Sec	70	Research/Development	84	Erate
15	Asst Superintendent	29	Family/Consumer Science	43	Science Elem	57	Bilingual/ELL	71	Public Information	85	AIDS Education

#	Role	#	Role
88	Alternative/At Risk	277	Remedial Math K-12
89	Multi-Cultural Curriculum	280	Literacy Coach
90	Social Work	285	STEM
91	Safety/Security	286	Digital Learning
92	Magnet School	288	Common Core Standards
93	Parental Involvement	294	Accountability
95	Tech Prep Program	295	Network System
97	Chief Information Officer	296	Title II Programs
98	Chief Technology Officer	297	Webmaster
270	Character Education	298	Grant Writer/Ptnrships
271	Migrant Education	750	Chief Innovation Officer
273	Teacher Mentor	751	Chief of Staff
274	Before/After Sch	752	Social Emotional Learning
275	Response To Intervention		

Texas School Directory

DISTRICT PERSONNEL INDEX

NAME/District	JOB FUNCTIONS	PAGE
Smith, Anne/*Clear Creek Ind School Dist*	43	158
Smith, Ashley/*Friona Ind School Dist*	8	315
Smith, Barbara/*Walnut Bend Ind School Dist*	16	92
Smith, Billye/*Nueces Canyon Cons Ind SD*	2	131
Smith, Blanca/*McCamey Ind School Dist*	10,57	377
Smith, Brenda/*Leveretts Chapel Ind Sch Dist*	83	328
Smith, Brian/*Friendswood Ind Sch Dist*	295	160
Smith, Brie/*Lovejoy Ind School Dist*	81	80
Smith, Bubba/*Panhandle Ind School Dist*	67	69
Smith, Burt/*Salado Ind School Dist*	8,15,36,68,69,91,298	29
Smith, C Keith/*Madisonville Cons ISD*	11,15,31,36,57,58,88,271	273
Smith, Cade, Dr/*Brock Ind School Dist*	1	312
Smith, Calvin/*Timpson Ind School Dist*	285	335
Smith, Carol/*Wylie Ind School Dist*	2,11,296,298	361
Smith, Chad/*Spur Ind School Dist*	27	127
Smith, Chantay/*Aldine Ind School Dist*	46	179
Smith, Charlotte/*Belton Ind School Dist*	7	26
Smith, Chris/*Brownfield Ind Sch Dist*	1	362
Smith, Chris/*Katy Ind School Dist*	2,19	151
Smith, Cindy/*Overton Ind School Dist*	58	328
Smith, Cindy/*Silsbee Ind School Dist*	34,58	178
Smith, Cindy/*Tatum Ind School Dist*	58	328
Smith, Cliff/*Refugio Ind School Dist*	73,295	323
Smith, Craig/*Hitchcock Ind School Dist*	6	161
Smith, Craig/*Poteet Ind School Dist*	297	21
Smith, Dalton/*Bullard Ind School Dist*	5	336
Smith, Dalton/*Bullard Ind School Dist*	5	336
Smith, Darren/*East Chambers Ind School Dist*	3,5,91	72
Smith, David/*Keller Ind School Dist*	4	354
Smith, David/*Troup Ind School Dist*	8,11,57,69,83,88,273	337
Smith, Dawn/*Coldspring-Oakhurst Cons ISD*	4	330
Smith, Dayna, Dr/*Orangefield Ind School Dist*	11,34,57,58,88,271,275,296	309
Smith, Deborah/*Lubbock-Cooper Ind Sch Dist*	27	271
Smith, Derek/*Alba-Golden Ind School Dist*	6	404
Smith, DeWitt/*Region 18 Ed Service Center*	1	287
Smith, Donna, Dr/*Ector Co Ind School Dist*	67	130
Smith, Doug/*Frenship Ind School Dist*	58	269
Smith, Ella/*Keene Ind School Dist*	4	248
Smith, Eric/*Natalia Ind School Dist*	67	284
Smith, Gail, Dr/*Lubbock Ind School Dist*	81	270
Smith, Gayle, Dr/*Sherman Ind School Dist*	9	167
Smith, Glen/*Eula Ind School Dist*	3,91	63
Smith, Greg, Dr/*Clear Creek Ind School Dist*	1	158
Smith, Gwinn/*Comanche Ind School Dist*	37	89
Smith, Heather/*La Grange Ind School Dist*	81	147
Smith, Jack/*Jefferson Ind School Dist*	5	274
Smith, Jacquelyn/*Avinger Ind School Dist*	1,11	70
Smith, James/*Birdville Ind School Dist*	9,34	346
Smith, Jana/*Tioga Ind School Dist*	57,271	167
Smith, Jason/*Joshua Ind School Dist*	295	248
Smith, Jay/*Dime Box Ind School Dist*	8	263
Smith, Jeff/*Hale Center Ind School Dist*	6	175
Smith, Jennifer/*Longview Ind School Dist*	16,73	169
Smith, Jeremy, Dr/*Quitman Ind School Dist*	67	404
Smith, Joe/*Roscoe Collegiate Ind Sch Dist*	3,5	301
Smith, John/*Priddy Ind School Dist*	286	289
Smith, Johnna/*Bridge City Ind School Dist*	37	308
Smith, Josh/*Hudson Ind School Dist*	76,295	17
Smith, Julie/*Diboll Ind School Dist*	16	17
Smith, Kamber/*Shallowater Ind School Dist*	38	272
Smith, Kayne/*Cypress-Fairbanks Ind Sch Dist*	5	183
Smith, Keith/*Madisonville Cons ISD*	1	273
Smith, Kelli/*Olton Ind School Dist*	16,82	261
Smith, Kimberly/*Alief Ind School Dist*	71	181
Smith, Kimberly/*Frisco Ind School Dist*	2,19	78
Smith, Kirsten/*Silsbee Ind School Dist*	2,15	178
Smith, Kisha/*Winnsboro Ind School Dist*	4	405
Smith, Kristy/*Whitney Ind School Dist*	16,73,297	228
Smith, Lamont, Dr/*Elkhart Ind School Dist*	1	15
Smith, Lamont, Dr/*Lancaster Ind School Dist*	294	110
Smith, Lana/*Livingston Ind School Dist*	9,11,57,68,79,83,88,751	317
Smith, Laney/*Madisonville Cons ISD*	73	273
Smith, Larry/*Blanket Ind School Dist*	16,73	58
Smith, Larry/*Canadian Ind School Dist*	67	213
Smith, Larry/*Cleveland Ind School Dist*	5	265
Smith, Larry/*Mason Ind School Dist*	5,88	275
Smith, Laura/*Pittsburg Ind School Dist*	7	68
Smith, Libby/*Devers Ind School Dist*	6	265
Smith, Lisha/*Carlisle Ind School Dist*	31,36	327
Smith, Lloyd/*Murchison Ind Sch Dist*	67	214
Smith, Louanne/*Pleasant Grove Ind School Dist*	38	49
Smith, Luke/*Deweyville Ind School Dist*	67	308
Smith, Marc, Dr/*Duncanville Ind School Dist*	1	104
Smith, Margaret/*Bremond Ind School Dist*	4	324
Smith, Marie/*West Sabine Ind Sch Dist*	57	329
Smith, Marty/*Paducah Ind School Dist*	3	93
Smith, Mary/*Aledo Ind School Dist*	27	312
Smith, Matt/*Humble Ind School Dist*	37	195
Smith, Matt/*Leander Ind School Dist*	8,15,288,751	396
Smith, Melissa/*Buffalo Ind School Dist*	88	264
Smith, Michael/*Comal Ind School Dist*	7,35	87
Smith, Michael/*Savoy Ind School Dist*	10	146
Smith, Michelle/*Lytle Ind School Dist*	1	21
Smith, Monica/*Floydada Ind School Dist*	8	148
Smith, Penny/*Floresville Ind School Dist*	67	400
Smith, Rachel/*Humble Ind School Dist*	46	195
Smith, Randy/*Silsbee Ind School Dist*	6	178
Smith, Ric/*San Felipe-Del Rio Cons Ind SD*	6	379
Smith, Ron/*Lefors Ind School Dist*	3	165
Smith, Roy/*Brady Ind School Dist*	3	277
Smith, Sandra/*Greenwood Ind School Dist*	4	285
Smith, Sandra/*West Rusk Co Cons Ind Sch Dist*	67	328
Smith, Sheila/*Centerville Ind School Dist*	58	374
Smith, Shelia/*Allen Ind School Dist*	15,68	76
Smith, Sherie/*Blackwell Cons Ind Sch Dist*	57	301
Smith, Sherri/*Duncanville Ind School Dist*	74	104
Smith, Stephanie/*Priddy Ind School Dist*	58	289
Smith, Steve/*Leander Ind School Dist*	4	396
Smith, Steven/*Eustace Ind School Dist*	6	214
Smith, Steven/*Nueces Canyon Cons Ind SD*	5	131
Smith, Stuart/*Pampa Ind School Dist*	5	165
Smith, Susan/*Hemphill Ind School Dist*	9,273	329
Smith, Susan/*Saltillo Ind School Dist*	4	231
Smith, Tammy/*Cushing Ind School Dist*	79	297
Smith, Tammy/*Midway Ind School Dist*	79	280
Smith, Terri/*Hurst-Euless-Bedford ISD*	50	353
Smith, Todd/*Azle Ind School Dist*	15	345
Smith, Tony/*Garner Ind School Dist*	6	312
Smith, Tony/*Irion Co Ind School Dist*	4	238
Smith, Tracy/*Bishop Cons Ind School Dist*	39,48	302
Smith, Tracy/*Carrollton-Farmers Branch ISD*	9,15,275	96
Smith, Tracy/*Groesbeck Ind School Dist*	37	267
Smith, Travis/*New Home Ind School Dist*	67	273
Smithers, Ludonna/*Commerce Independent Sch Dist*	68,71,297	236
Smithey, Theresa/*Waxahachie Ind School Dist*	44	142
Smithson, Karen/*New Caney Ind School Dist*	9	293
Snapp, Julie/*Howe Ind School Dist*	2	166
Sneed, Kimberly/*Flour Bluff Ind School Dist*	71	304
Snell, Michelle/*Joshua Ind School Dist*	10	248
Snell, Steven/*Liberty Hill Ind School Dist*	1	398
Snellgrove, Julie/*Stanton Ind School Dist*	11,271	274
Snelson, John/*Dickinson Ind School Dist*	6	159
Snider, Dianne/*Gorman Ind School Dist*	68	129
Snider, Kimberlyn/*Neches Ind School Dist*	11	15
Snider, Randy/*Neches Ind School Dist*	1	15
Snipes, David/*Aquilla Ind School Dist*	67	227
Snodgrass, Christie/*Lohn Ind School Dist*	11,73	277
Snodgrass, Kelley/*Glen Rose Ind School Dist*	67	340
Snook, Joshua/*Winona Ind School Dist*	91	339
Snow, Billy/*Dallas Ind School Dist*	70,750	98
Snow, Zach/*Royse City Ind School Dist*	27,73,285,286	326
Snyder, Dale/*Hillsboro Ind School Dist*	2	227
Snyder, Earl/*Alief Ind School Dist*	46	181
Snyder, Steven/*Ingleside Ind School Dist*	71	331
Snyder, Vanessa/*Alice Ind School Dist*	45	245
Snyder, Wayne/*Region 8 Ed Service Center*	76	69
Soileau, Benny, Dr/*Huffman Ind School Dist*	1	195
Soles, Nancy/*Sweetwater ISD School Dist*	7,85	301
Solice, Davette/*Tornillo Ind School Dist*	2	137
Solis, Cynthia/*La Joya Ind School Dist*	74	219
Solis, Emily/*Frenship Ind School Dist*	71	269
Solis, John/*Raymondville Ind Sch Dist*	67	394

School Year 2019-2020   800-333-8802

DISTRICT PERSONNEL INDEX

Market Data Retrieval

NAME/District	JOB FUNCTIONS	PAGE
Solis, Joshua/Bay City Ind School Dist	73,76,98,295	275
Solis, Judith, Dr/San Antonio Ind School Dist	15	39
Solis, Margarita/Community Ind School Dist	57	78
Solis, Pedro/Ysleta Ind School Dist	4	137
Solis, Ricardo/Rio Grande City Ind Sch Dist	5	340
Solis, Rosie/San Diego Ind School Dist	58	128
Solis, Sulema/Pharr-San Juan-Alamo Ind SD	7,35,85	223
Solis, Yolanda/Karnes City Ind School Dist	36	250
Soliz-Garcia, Velma/Gregory-Portland Ind Sch Dist	8,15,68	330
Soliz, Lori/Sinton Ind School Dist	7	332
Solley, Donna/Birdville Ind School Dist	8	346
Sollock, Laniece/Vidor Ind School Dist	93	309
Solorio, Luis/Harlingen Cons Ind School Dist	35	64
Solorzano, Gina/Marble Falls Ind School Dist	5	60
Somer, Kim/Brazos Ind School Dist	58	22
Somer, Kim/Brazos Ind School Dist	58	22
Somer, Kimberly/Wharton Ind School Dist	58,90	390
Sommerfeld, Tiffany/Waco Ind School Dist	36	281
Sonia, Sonya/Bay City Ind School Dist	34,58	275
Sonnenburg, Jay/Katy Ind School Dist	16	151
Sonntag, Shelley/Valley Mills Ind School Dist	5	47
Sons, Dana/Lewisville Ind School Dist	73	122
Sons, David/Region 11 Ed Service Center	76	360
Sopher, Veronica/Ft Bend Ind School Dist	71	149
Sophie, Weinheimer/Smithville Ind School Dist	7	24
Sormani, Robert/Hutto Ind School Dist	8,15,68,79,88,288	396
Sorola, Anthony, Dr/Lufkin Ind School Dist	13,15,78	18
Sorrell, Tom/Agua Dulce Ind School Dist	73,84	302
Sorrells, Gary/Lone Oak Ind School Dist	2	236
Sorters, Erica/Normangee Ind School Dist	7	264
Sosa, Juan/San Benito Cons Ind Sch Dist	91	67
Sosa, Luci/Corpus Christi Ind Sch Dist	43	303
Sostarich, Scott/Devine Ind School Dist	1	283
Sotelo, Mario/Charlotte Ind School Dist	1,83	20
Soto, Donna/Livingston Ind School Dist	5	317
Soto, Gerry/Harlandale Ind School Dist	3	32
Soto, Mark/San Marcos Cons Ind Sch Dist	6	211
Soto, Roy/Edgewood Ind School Dist	67	380
Soto, Roy/Edgewood Ind School Dist	67	31
Soto, Suzanne/Splendora Ind School Dist	67	294
Souder, Diane/Wellington Ind School Dist	2	86
Southard, Brett/Littlefield Ind School Dist	58	260
Southard, Jon/Blooming Grove Ind School Dist	67	299
Southard, Krystal/Holliday Ind School Dist	59	19
Southern, Jennifer/Nursery ISD School Dist	12	382
Southern, Rodney/Huntsville Ind School Dist	6	383
Sowell, Amanda/Broaddus Ind School Dist	7,85	329
Sowers, Stan/Eustace Ind School Dist	5,15	214
Soza, Chris/Beeville Ind School Dist	6	25
Soza, Chris/Medina Valley Ind School Dist	6	284
Spain, Bobby/Hempstead Ind School Dist	6	384
Spakes, Roger/Winnsboro Ind School Dist	3,5	405
Spalloni, Natalie/Canutillo Ind School Dist	48	132
Spann, David/McKinney Ind School Dist	71,73,84,97	81
Sparkman, Keith/Winona Ind School Dist	88	339
Sparkman, Steven/Quanah Ind School Dist	67	177
Sparks, John/Big Spring Ind School Dist	3,5	233
Sparks, Karla/Somerville Ind School Dist	1,11,83	60
Sparks, Katie/East Chambers Ind School Dist	7	72
Sparks, Larry/West Ind School Dist	67	282
Sparks, Marcy/Socorro Ind School Dist	16	135
Sparks, Troy/Three Way Ind School Dist	5	144
Sparks, Viki/Region 7 Ed Service Center	11	171
Sparling, Rhonda/McLean Ind School Dist	4	165
Spaulding, Karen/Carrollton-Farmers Branch ISD	46,277	96
Spear, Misti/Wichita Falls Ind School Dist	9	392
Spear, Rick/Gordon Ind School Dist	73,295	310
Spearman, Jill/Carlisle Ind School Dist	2	327
Spears, Britt/Lubbock-Cooper Ind Sch Dist	68	271
Spears, Edward/Ft Worth Ind School Dist	30	349
Spears, Kermit/Ft Bend Ind School Dist	68	149
Spears, Leann/Era Ind School Dist	81	90
Spears, Norman/Aransas Co Ind School Dist	3,16,73	19
Speck, Mark/Rockwall Ind School Dist	68,74,79	325
Speck, Paige/Pringle-Morse Cons ISD	2,12,84,298	177
Speed, Jo Ann/Navarro Ind School Dist	2	173
Speegle, Gary/Comanche Ind School Dist	1	89
Speight, Jacob/Waskom Ind School Dist	67	209
Spence, Keari/Rockdale Ind School Dist	7	287
Spencer, Beverley/Lampasas Ind School Dist	5	261
Spencer, Bill/Elysian Fields Ind School Dist	73,84	208
Spencer, Helen/Harris Co Dept of Ed	295	179
Spencer, Kellie/Cedar Hill Ind School Dist	15	97
Spencer, Kim/Malakoff Ind School Dist	2	214
Spencer, Lori/Poth Ind School Dist	58	401
Spencer, Paul/Boerne Ind School Dist	5	253
Spencer, Reggy/Colorado Ind School Dist	1	289
Spencer, Sandra/Harleton Ind School Dist	1	208
Spencer, Tamara/Pflugerville Ind School Dist	71	371
Spenrath, Brad/Comfort Ind School Dist	67	254
Spicer, Kim, Dr/Wylie Ind School Dist	15	84
Spicer, Tiffany, Dr/Leander Ind School Dist	81	396
Spieckerman, Sutton/Zephyr Ind School Dist	58	59
Spikes, Bob/Lueders-Avoca Ind School Dist	1	250
Spikes, Tricia/Trent Ind School Dist	73,295	361
Spindler, Carol/Sterling City Ind School Dist	4	342
Spinhirne, David/Channing Ind School Dist	67	209
Spinks, Sharon/Schleicher Co Ind Sch Dist	285,298	333
Spinn, Craig/Region 13 Ed Service Center	15	373
Spinner, Tracy/Austin Ind School Dist	7	366
Spivey, Chris/Sands Consolidated ISD	3	117
Spivey, Jana/Sands Consolidated ISD	4	117
Spivey, Kyle/Runge Ind School Dist	1	251
Spivey, Reid/Garrison Ind School Dist	1	297
Spivey, Terry/Pleasant Grove Ind School Dist	5,91	49
Spoor, Jodi/Boerne Ind School Dist	8,15,36,74,81,88,273	253
Spradlin, Tony/Wylie Ind School Dist	73,84	361
Sprague, Mark/Krum Ind School Dist	73	122
Sprague, Roy/Cypress-Fairbanks Ind Sch Dist	3,15,17	183
Srambler, Micheele/Castleberry Ind School Dist	9	347
Spreen, Mimi/Palestine Ind School Dist	4	15
Springfield, Kelly/Marathon Ind School Dist	69,93,271	56
Sprinkle, Laura/Region 3 Ed Service Center	286	383
Sprinkles, Kevin/Cameron Ind School Dist	1	287
Sprouse, David, Dr/Kerrville Ind School Dist	67	256
Spurlin, Cliff/McDade Ind School Dist	16,73,295,297	24
Spurlock, Becky/Azle Ind School Dist	6	345
Squiers, Joe/Franklin Ind School Dist	16,28,73,297	324
Squires, Ron/Nordheim Ind School Dist	73	118
Sriritarat, Rapee/Savoy Ind School Dist	73,295	146
St Andre, Jeff/City View Ind School Dist	73,84	391
Stack, Becky/Deer Park Ind School Dist	45	186
Stacy, Lance/Lake Dallas Ind School Dist	67	122
Stafford, Amanda/Archer City Ind School Dist	8,33,85,288,296	19
Stafford, Stephanie/Sterling City Ind School Dist	36,69,83,85	342
Stafford, Tammi/Sweetwater ISD School Dist	69	301
Staggs, Ben/Perrin-Whitt Cons Ind Sch Dist	6,73	239
Stagner, Scott/White Oak Ind School Dist	5	171
Stags, Tommy/Sands Consolidated ISD	67	117
Stahl, Mark/Boerne Ind School Dist	3	253
Stahnke, Curtis/Comanche Ind School Dist	54	89
Staley, Jim/Princeton Ind School Dist	3	84
Stallard, Robert/Ft Stockton Ind School Dist	3	315
Stambaugh, Holly/Joshua Ind School Dist	68	248

1 Superintendent	16 Instructional Media Svcs	30 Adult Education	44 Science Sec	58 Special Education K-12	72 Summer School
2 Bus/Finance/Purchasing	17 Chief Operations Officer	31 Career/Sch-to-Work K-12	45 Math K-12	59 Special Education Elem	73 Instructional Tech
3 Buildings And Grounds	18 Chief Academic Officer	32 Career/Sch-to-Work Elem	46 Math Elem	60 Special Education Sec	74 Inservice Training
4 Food Service	19 Chief Financial Officer	33 Career/Sch-to-Work Sec	47 Math Sec	61 Foreign/World Lang K-12	75 Marketing/Distributive
5 Transportation	20 Art K-12	34 Early Childhood Ed	48 English/Lang Arts K-12	62 Foreign/World Lang Elem	76 Info Systems
6 Athletic	21 Art Elem	35 Health/Phys Education	49 English/Lang Arts Elem	63 Foreign/World Lang Sec	77 Psychological Assess
7 Health Services	22 Art Sec	36 Guidance Services K-12	50 English/Lang Arts Sec	64 Religious Education K-12	78 Affirmative Action
8 Curric/Instruct K-12	23 Music K-12	37 Guidance Services Elem	51 Reading K-12	65 Religious Education Elem	79 Student Personnel
9 Curric/Instruct Elem	24 Music Elem	38 Guidance Services Sec	52 Reading Elem	66 Religious Education Sec	80 Driver Ed/Safety
10 Curric/Instruct Sec	25 Music Sec	39 Social Studies K-12	53 Reading Sec	67 School Board President	81 Gifted/Talented
11 Federal Program	26 Business Education	40 Social Studies Elem	54 Remedial Reading K-12	68 Teacher Personnel	82 Video Services
12 Title I	27 Career & Tech Ed	41 Social Studies Sec	55 Remedial Reading Elem	69 Academic Assessment	83 Substance Abuse Prev
13 Title V	28 Technology Education	42 Science K-12	56 Remedial Reading Sec	70 Research/Development	84 Erate
15 Asst Superintendent	29 Family/Consumer Science	43 Science Elem	57 Bilingual/ELL	71 Public Information	85 AIDS Education

88 Alternative/At Risk	277 Remedial Math K-12
89 Multi-Cultural Curriculum	280 Literacy Coach
90 Social Work	285 STEM
91 Safety/Security	286 Digital Learning
92 Magnet School	288 Common Core Standards
93 Parental Involvement	294 Accountability
95 Tech Prep Program	295 Network System
97 Chief Information Officer	296 Title II Programs
98 Chief Technology Officer	297 Webmaster
270 Character Education	298 Grant Writer/Ptnrships
271 Migrant Education	750 Chief Innovation Officer
273 Teacher Mentor	751 Chief of Staff
274 Before/After Sch	752 Social Emotional Learning
275 Response To Intervention	

TX-T86

Texas School Directory

DISTRICT PERSONNEL INDEX

NAME/District	JOB FUNCTIONS	PAGE
Stancill, Randy/*Van Ind School Dist*	295	381
Standford, Carolyn/*Mineola Ind School Dist*	16	404
Standifer, Brenda/*Lone Oak Ind School Dist*	4	236
Standlee, Becky/*Dimmitt Ind School Dist*	2	71
Standley, Carrie/*Warren Ind School Dist*	16	375
Stanfield, Carolyn/*Freer Ind School Dist*	4	128
Stanfield, Dana/*Nazareth Ind School Dist*	26	71
Stanford, Brandy/*Salado Ind School Dist*	2,11	29
Stanford, Brent/*Red Oak Ind School Dist*	3,5	142
Stanford, Carla/*Corsicana Ind School Dist*	288	299
Stanford, Kevin/*Huntsville Ind School Dist*	2,15,76	383
Stanford, Steve/*Comal Ind School Dist*	71	87
Stanford, Travis/*Spring Branch Ind School Dist*	3,15	200
Stanford, Wade/*Westwood Ind School Dist*	1	16
Stange, Frank/*Alamo Heights Ind School Dist*	68,71	30
Stanghellini, Annett/*Claude Ind School Dist*	4	20
Stanley, Betty/*Sidney Ind School Dist*	4	90
Stanley, Cheri/*Warren Ind School Dist*	73,295	375
Stanley, Danny/*Kilgore Ind School Dist*	57,69,81	169
Stanley, Ken/*Coldspring-Oakhurst Cons ISD*	6,35	330
Stanley, Mark/*Brownwood Ind School Dist*	73,286,295	58
Stanley, Robert/*North Hopkins Ind School Dist*	11	231
Stanley, Ronnie/*Miller Grove Ind School Dist*	58	231
Stanley, Wendy, Dr/*Anna Ind School Dist*	58	77
Stanmore, Jonathan/*Queen City Ind School Dist*	67	70
Stanner, Charlotte/*Atlanta Ind School Dist*	67	69
Stansberry, Amber/*Edna Ind School Dist*	34,58,77	239
Stansberry, Cheryle/*Aransas Pass Ind School Dist*	2	330
Stansbury, Scott/*Round Rock Ind School Dist*	76,84,295,297	398
Stapper, Judy/*Florence Ind School Dist*	76	395
Stark, Brittany/*Pampa Ind School Dist*	38,83,90	165
Starke, Adam/*Socorro Ind School Dist*	11	135
Starkey, Scott/*Whitehouse Ind School Dist*	73	339
Starkweather, Brett/*Grandfalls-Royalty Ind SD*	73	385
Starnes, Curtis/*Granbury Ind School Dist*	295	230
Starnes, Keith/*Stephenville Ind School Dist*	3,91	144
Starnes, Rachel/*Belton Ind School Dist*	76	26
Starr, Michelle/*Spring Ind School Dist*	15	202
Starr, Pamela/*Richland Springs Ind Sch Dist*	73	332
Starr, Shelly/*Hemphill Ind School Dist*	16	329
Starrett, Christy/*Crandall Ind School Dist*	15,68	251
Starrett, Stacy/*Malta Ind School Dist*	1,11	48
Startz, Patricia/*Falls City Ind School Dist*	73,295,298	250
Stary, Alicia/*El Campo Ind School Dist*	11,294,296	389
Statler, Shelly/*Glen Rose Ind School Dist*	16	340
Staugh, Frederek/*Monahans-Wickett-Pyote ISD*	6	385
Staump, Dana/*Medina Ind School Dist*	36	23
Stauty, Gary/*Pleasant Grove Ind School Dist*	4	49
Stearns, Adam/*Magnolia Ind School Dist*	2	292
Steeber, Deana/*Argyle Ind School Dist*	8,11,15,298	120
Steel, Ryan, Dr/*Cisco Independent Sch Dist*	1,11	128
Steele, April/*Ingram Ind School Dist*	4	255
Steele, Cazilda, Dr/*Katy Ind School Dist*	10	151
Steele, Charles/*Covington ISD School Dist*	6	227
Steele, Gwen/*Lake Worth Ind School Dist*	10,280	356
Steele, John/*Ennis Ind School Dist*	295	140
Steele, Natalie/*May Ind School Dist*	11	59
Steelman, Clyde, Dr/*Region 11 Ed Service Center*	1,11	360
Steelman, Trisha/*Friona Ind School Dist*	73,76,286,295	315
Steets, Layne/*Dawson Ind School Dist*	1,11,73	116
Stegall, Shane/*Huckabay Ind School Dist*	67	143
Stegall, Shelly/*Hico Ind School Dist*	10,88	176
Steger, Marilyn/*Bells Ind School Dist*	2	165
Steger, Melissa/*Grand Prairie Ind School Dist*	69	107
Steger, Will/*Bells Ind School Dist*	3,5	165
Stehling, Charli/*Kerrville Ind School Dist*	68	256
Steinbecker, Catrina/*Milano Ind School Dist*	36,69,83,85,88	287
Steinberger, Chad/*Windthorst Ind School Dist*	67	20
Steinbruck, Christopher/*Flour Bluff Ind School Dist*	6	304
Steinert, Michael/*Ft Worth Ind School Dist*	15,79,83	349
Steinkamp, Ricky/*Crawford Ind School Dist*	67	279
Steinley, Kelley/*Garland Ind School Dist*	49	105
Stelter, Cody/*Brenham Ind School Dist*	27,28	385
Step, Krissy/*La Poynor Ind School Dist*	73,295	214
Stephen, Cathy/*Archdiocese Galveston-Houston*	15	203
Stephen, Scott/*Pleasanton Ind School Dist*	2,19	21
Stephens, Beverly/*Belton Ind School Dist*	36	26
Stephens, Erin/*Hull Daisetta Ind School Dist*	2	266
Stephens, James/*Patton Springs Ind School Dist*	73	127
Stephens, Julie/*Carroll Independent Sch Dist*	16,43,46	347
Stephens, Kay/*Linden Kildare Cons Ind SD*	67	70
Stephens, Kurt/*Lufkin Ind School Dist*	88,294	18
Stephens, Lacey/*Mt Vernon Ind School Dist*	36,83,85,88,285	155
Stephens, Mandy/*Sherman Ind School Dist*	4	167
Stephens, Melissa/*Yantis Ind School Dist*	67	405
Stephens, Mike/*Whitewright Ind School Dist*	91	168
Stephens, Pauli/*Howe Ind School Dist*	38	166
Stephens, Phylis/*Burkeville Ind School Dist*	8,31,57,83,88,275,294	300
Stephens, Rebecca/*Mabank Ind School Dist*	8,11,57,69,83,88,294	252
Stephens, Ricky/*Keene Ind School Dist*	1	248
Stephens, Scott/*South San Antonio Ind Sch Dist*	4	42
Stephens, Tamika, Dr/*Aldine Ind School Dist*	2,19	179
Stephens, Todd, Dr/*Magnolia Ind School Dist*	1	292
Stephenson, Angelita/*Coleman Ind School Dist*	58	76
Stephenson, Ann/*Avery Ind School Dist*	59	322
Stephenson, Jane/*West Sabine Ind Sch Dist*	1	329
Sterchy, Sharon, Dr/*Conroe Ind School Dist*	35	291
Steubing, Richard/*Groveton Ind School Dist*	6	374
Stevens, Bettye/*Plemons-Stinnett-Phillips CISD*	2	238
Stevens, Carla/*Manor Ind School Dist*	2	371
Stevens, David/*Arlington Ind School Dist*	91	343
Stevens, Jeffrey/*Era Ind School Dist*	67	90
Stevens, Marcia/*Diocese of Beaumont Sch Office*	1	244
Stevens, Rayann/*Electra Ind School Dist*	275	391
Stevens, Robert/*Taylor Ind School Dist*	58	399
Stevens, Tina/*Millsap Ind School Dist*	4	312
Stevens, Ty/*Sterling City Ind School Dist*	285	342
Stevenson, Alex/*Dodd City Ind School Dist*	6	145
Stevenson, Chris/*Harper Ind School Dist*	1	163
Stevenson, Neal/*Nursery ISD School Dist*	67	382
Stewart, Ashley/*Boerne Ind School Dist*	15	253
Stewart, Becky/*Goldthwaite Consolidated ISD*	4	288
Stewart, Becky/*Goldthwaite Consolidated ISD*	4	288
Stewart, Becky/*Stockdale Ind School Dist*	2	401
Stewart, Bonnie/*Harper Ind School Dist*	8,11,69,74,294,296	163
Stewart, Brad/*Jacksonville Ind School Dist*	68	73
Stewart, Brad/*Lufkin Ind School Dist*	73,295,297	18
Stewart, Carol/*White Oak Ind School Dist*	16	171
Stewart, Deborah, Dr/*Cypress-Fairbanks Ind Sch Dist*	15,68	184
Stewart, Denisa/*Anna Ind School Dist*	68	77
Stewart, Desmontes, Dr/*Gainesville Ind School Dist*	1	91
Stewart, Doug/*Hughes Springs Ind Sch Dist*	73,76,286	70
Stewart, Elizabeth/*Argyle Ind School Dist*	2,19	120
Stewart, Gloria/*Lamar Cons Ind School Dist*	30,57	153
Stewart, Jennifer/*Splendora Ind School Dist*	58	294
Stewart, Katherine/*Grandview Ind School Dist*	16	248
Stewart, Kelli/*North Lamar Ind School Dist*	1	259
Stewart, Kim/*Northside Ind School Dist*	81	36
Stewart, Laura/*Mt Pleasant Ind School Dist*	4	363
Stewart, Leigh/*Broaddus Ind School Dist*	76	329
Stewart, Rob/*Magnolia Ind School Dist*	79,91	292
Stewart, Robert/*Denton Ind School Dist*	15,68,74	120
Stewart, Rusty/*Follett Ind School Dist*	67	267
Stewart, Scott/*Crandall Ind School Dist*	5	251
Stewart, Scott/*Temple Ind School Dist*	6	29
Stewart, Sheryl/*Allen Ind School Dist*	69,294	76
Stewart, Stacy/*Lamesa Ind School Dist*	34,58,77	117
Stewart, Thomas/*Canton Ind School Dist*	3	380
Stickels, David/*Saltillo Ind School Dist*	1,11	231
Stidevent, Wade/*Boling Ind School Dist*	1,83	389
Stidham, Mandy/*O'Donnell Ind School Dist*	67	273
Stieney, Melissaa/*Blue Ridge Ind School Dist*	73	77
Stiles, Blake/*Athens Ind School Dist*	1	213
Stille, Lacrsasha/*Gainesville Ind School Dist*	8,15	91
Stilwell, Travis/*Tolar Ind School Dist*	1	230
Stinson, Gayle, Dr/*Lake Dallas Ind School Dist*	1	122
Stobaugh, Nancy/*Lexington Ind School Dist*	58	263
Stobnicki, Sabrina/*Harts Bluff Ind School Dist*	79,90	363
Stock, Robert/*Pasadena Ind School Dist*	5	198
Stockhorst, Rosanne/*New Braunfels Ind School Dist*	2	88
Stockman, Linda/*Whiteface Con Ind School Dist*	4	75
Stockstill, Greg/*Region 16 Ed Service Center*	73	321

School Year 2019-2020   800-333-8802   TX-T87

DISTRICT PERSONNEL INDEX

Market Data Retrieval

NAME/District	JOB FUNCTIONS	PAGE
Stockton, Dana/Keene Ind School Dist	12,31,36,69,83,270	248
Stockton, Nick/Needville Ind School Dist	295	154
Stockton, Rick/Klein Ind School Dist	83,88	196
Stoddard, Eric/San Vicente Ind School Dist	1,11	57
Stoddard, Jeani/San Vicente Ind School Dist	285	57
Stoecker, Jennifer/Mansfield Ind School Dist	68	356
Stoker, Daryl/New Braunfels Ind School Dist	3	88
Stoker, Kevin/Hawley Ind School Dist	16,73,286	250
Stokes, Brian/Wills Point Ind School Dist	5	381
Stokes, Mark/Hereford Ind School Dist	8,18,45,69	119
Stokes, Willaim/Valley View ISD-Cooke Co	1	91
Stone, Brenda/Quinlan Ind School Dist	4	237
Stone, Christy/Rogers Ind School Dist	4	28
Stone, David/Greenville Ind School Dist	295	236
Stone, Denise/Canton Ind School Dist	2,84	380
Stone, Erin/Buffalo Ind School Dist	7	264
Stone, Jeannie, Dr/Richardson Ind School Dist	1	112
Stone, Jeff/Region 20 Ed Service Center	2,15,73,76	45
Stone, Kenny/Quinlan Ind School Dist	67	237
Stone, Rhonda/Lovelady Ind School Dist	2	233
Stone, Steffanie/Rosebud-Lott Ind School Dist	4	145
Stone, Stephanie/Seminole Ind School Dist	73,286,297	158
Stone, Todd/Lovelady Ind School Dist	8,11,57,58,270,298	233
Stone, Tony/Rosebud-Lott Ind School Dist	5	145
Stoner, Jason/Lago Vista Ind School Dist	2,19	370
Stork, Gwen/Round Top-Carmine Ind Sch Dist	2	147
Story, Mandy/Henrietta Ind School Dist	16	74
Stosberg, Bibiana/Boerne Ind School Dist	57	253
Stotler, Gail/Ft Bend Ind School Dist	4	149
Stout, Jeff/Angleton Ind School Dist	73	51
Stout, Laura, Dr/Corpus Christi Ind Sch Dist	10,273	303
Stout, Linda/Crawford Ind School Dist	9,57,83,85	279
Stout, Robin/Lewisville Ind School Dist	16	122
Stout, Shawn/Seymour Ind School Dist	29	25
Stout, Tally Jo/Region 6 Ed Service Center	27,31	384
Stovall, Jason/Alba-Golden Ind School Dist	67	404
Stover, Bart/Ponder Ind School Dist	27	125
Stover, Shane/Huntington Ind School Dist	10	17
Stovola, Denise/Pilot Point Ind School Dist	57	125
Stowe, Melody/Terrell Ind School Dist	7	253
Strack, Jenny/Florence Ind School Dist	16,82	395
Stracke, Steve/Eanes Ind School Dist	4	370
Strahan, Gina/West Hardin Co Cons Sch Dist	52,55	178
Strain, Becky/Granbury Ind School Dist	39,42,45	230
Strakos, Dan/Pearsall Ind School Dist	3	157
Straley, Robin/Plainview Ind School Dist	8	175
Strange, Kendra/Royal Ind School Dist	8	384
Stratmann, Kay/Dayton Ind School Dist	7	265
Stratton, Diane/Pittsburg Ind School Dist	88,91	68
Strauss, Kim/Brenham Ind School Dist	16,73,76,295	385
Strauss, Mark/Brenham Ind School Dist	8,294	385
Straw, Eldin/Gorman Ind School Dist	67	129
Straw, Sharla/Cotton Center Ind School Dist	57	174
Strayhorn, Jessie/Wolfe City Ind School Dist	3,5	237
Streams, Doris/Tidehaven Ind School Dist	2	276
Street, Jaclyn/Tulia Ind School Dist	7,85	343
Streeter, Kristen/Coppell Ind School Dist	15,68,79	98
Streety, Jim/New Braunfels Ind School Dist	6	88
Streger, Mathew/Blanco Ind School Dist	2,4	45
Strelchun, John/San Antonio Ind School Dist	298	39
Strelec, Sonny/Edna Ind School Dist	3,5,80,91	239
Strenski, Kelly/Wichita Falls Ind School Dist	20,23	392
Stribling, Scott/Georgetown Ind School Dist	67	395
Strick, Rebecca/Ferris Ind School Dist	16,82	140
Strickland, Shane/Springtown Ind School Dist	15,68,273	313
Stricklen, Matt/Sunray Ind School Dist	6,35	296
Stringer, Kobey/Lewisville Ind School Dist	49	122
Stringer, Molly/Huntington Ind School Dist	58	17
Stringer, Myron/Texarkana Ind School Dist	3	50
Stringer, Suzette/Martin's Mill Ind Sch Dist	8,16,73,286	381
Stringer, Tina/Martin's Mill Ind Sch Dist	9,11,88,296,298	381
Striplin, Ronnie/Dawson Ind School Dist	6	299
Stripling, Ernie/Denton Ind School Dist	73,76,98	120
Stripling, Warren/New Caney Ind School Dist	27	293
Stritz, Susan/Sealy Ind School Dist	37	22
Stroebel, Stan/Dumas Ind School Dist	6,35	295
Stroeher, Mark/Doss Consolidated Common SD	1	162
Stroman, Brian/Bloomburg Ind School Dist	1,11	70
Stroman, Kirk/Sweetwater ISD School Dist	58	301
Strong, Judy/Joaquin Ind School Dist	4	335
Strother, John/Panhandle Ind School Dist	69,83,88,270	69
Stroud, Joy/Honey Grove Ind School Dist	7	146
Stroupe, Ernest/Arp Ind School Dist	67	336
Stroy, Kelvin, Dr/Mansfield Ind School Dist	79	356
Stroy, Mia/DeSoto Ind School Dist	15,68	104
Strube, Laura/Region 15 Ed Service Center	15	366
Strubhart, Shane/Harlingen Cons Ind School Dist	71	64
Strunk, Jason/Point Isabel Ind Sch Dist	6	66
Stryk, Rodney/Flatonia Ind School Dist	2	147
Stryk, Rodney/Flatonia Ind School Dist	2,3,5	147
Stuard, Daryl/Bremond Ind School Dist	1	324
Stuart, Jerry/Kilgore Ind School Dist	27	169
Stuart, Lisa/Roby Cons Ind School Dist	52	148
Stuart, Murphey/Victoria Ind School Dist	7	382
Stuart, Randy/Carroll Independent Sch Dist	73	347
Stubblefield, Amanda/Groveton Ind School Dist	9,74,91	374
Stubblefield, Mabisha/Hempstead Ind School Dist	68,74	384
Stubblefiled, Kim/Llano Ind School Dist	9,11,34,51,54,271	268
Stuckly, Cecilia/Coupland Ind School Dist	16,82	395
Stuessel, Eric/Brazos Ind School Dist	73,295	22
Stuhrenberg, Steven/Palacios Ind School Dist	67	275
Stumbaugh, Monte/Hidalgo Ind School Dist	6	217
Sturdivant, Don/Irving Ind School Dist	5,91	109
Sturgeon, Jason/Int'l Leadership of Texas Dist	69	108
Sturm, Jennifer/Westwood Ind School Dist	58	16
Styles, Delisa, Dr/Fredericksburg Ind School Dist	3,8,16,69,74,277,285,294	162
Suarez, Alida/Edinburg Cons Ind School Dist	58,77	216
Suarez, Jesenia/Plains Ind School Dist	2	405
Suarez, Marco/McAllen Ind School Dist	67	221
Suarez, Rebecca/Houston Ind School Dist	71,77,97	188
Suarez, Sylvia, Dr/Seminole Ind School Dist	8,11,15,57,280,288,296	158
Subeldoa, Frank/Dalhart Ind School Dist	5	95
Subia, Reba/Ft Stockton Ind School Dist	297	315
Sudds, Ray/Waskom Ind School Dist	3,5,91	209
Sugerek, Steve/Pettus Ind School Dist	16,73	25
Suggitt, Donna/Waller Ind School Dist	69	384
Suitt, Latrisha/Granbury Ind School Dist	7,27,35,70,75,83,88	230
Sulak, Kimberly/East Bernard Ind Sch Dist	8,31,83,88,270,271	389
Sulak, Melissa/Midway Ind School Dist	9	280
Sullivan, Dotty/Centerville Ind School Dist	57	264
Sullivan, Kaycie/Junction Ind School Dist	73,295	256
Sullivan, Natasha/Bronte Ind School Dist	5	75
Sullivan, Richard/Carthage Ind School Dist	73,76,95,295	311
Sullivan, Vicky, Dr/Northside Ind School Dist	79	36
Sullivan, Wiley/Farmersville Ind School Dist	27,73,295,297	78
Summerhill, Candace/Aledo Ind School Dist	57,74,273,294	312
Summerhill, Candace/White Settlement Ind Sch Dist	8	357
Summerhill, Stacy/Eagle Mtn-Saginaw Ind Sch Dist	8	348
Summers, Christopher/Sealy Ind School Dist	15,294	22
Summers, Christopher/West Oso Ind School Dist	11	306
Summers, Deborah/Royse City Ind School Dist	7	326
Summers, Donna/Pasadena Ind School Dist	70	198
Summers, Mellissa/Dublin Ind School Dist	8,11,31,57,273,286,288,296	143
Summers, Priscilla/Denver City Ind School Dist	16,82	405

1 Superintendent	16 Instructional Media Svcs	30 Adult Education	44 Science Sec	58 Special Education K-12	72 Summer School	88 Alternative/At Risk	277 Remedial Math K-12
2 Bus/Finance/Purchasing	17 Chief Operations Officer	31 Career/Sch-to-Work K-12	45 Math K-12	59 Special Education Elem	73 Instructional Tech	89 Multi-Cultural Curriculum	280 Literacy Coach
3 Buildings And Grounds	18 Chief Academic Officer	32 Career/Sch-to-Work Elem	46 Math Elem	60 Special Education Sec	74 Inservice Training	90 Social Work	285 STEM
4 Food Service	19 Chief Financial Officer	33 Career/Sch-to-Work Sec	47 Math Sec	61 Foreign/World Lang K-12	75 Marketing/Distributive	91 Safety/Security	286 Digital Learning
5 Transportation	20 Art K-12	34 Early Childhood Ed	48 English/Lang Arts K-12	62 Foreign/World Lang Elem	76 Info Systems	92 Magnet School	288 Common Core Standards
6 Athletic	21 Art Elem	35 Health/Phys Education	49 English/Lang Arts Elem	63 Foreign/World Lang Sec	77 Psychological Assess	93 Parental Involvement	294 Accountability
7 Health Services	22 Art Sec	36 Guidance Services K-12	50 English/Lang Arts Sec	64 Religious Education K-12	78 Affirmative Action	95 Tech Prep Program	295 Network System
8 Curric/Instruct K-12	23 Music K-12	37 Guidance Services Elem	51 Reading K-12	65 Religious Education Elem	79 Student Personnel	97 Chief Information Officer	296 Title II Programs
9 Curric/Instruct Elem	24 Music Elem	38 Guidance Services Sec	52 Reading Elem	66 Religious Education Sec	80 Driver Ed/Safety	98 Chief Technology Officer	297 Webmaster
10 Curric/Instruct Sec	25 Music Sec	39 Social Studies K-12	53 Reading Sec	67 School Board President	81 Gifted/Talented	270 Character Education	298 Grant Writer/Ptnrships
11 Federal Program	26 Business Education	40 Social Studies Elem	54 Remedial Reading K-12	68 Teacher Personnel	82 Video Services	271 Migrant Education	750 Chief Innovation Officer
12 Title I	27 Career & Tech Ed	41 Social Studies Sec	55 Remedial Reading Elem	69 Academic Assessment	83 Substance Abuse Prev	273 Teacher Mentor	751 Chief of Staff
13 Title V	28 Technology Education	42 Science K-12	56 Remedial Reading Sec	70 Research/Development	84 Erate	274 Before/After Sch	752 Social Emotional Learning
15 Asst Superintendent	29 Family/Consumer Science	43 Science Elem	57 Bilingual/ELL	71 Public Information	85 AIDS Education	275 Response To Intervention	

TX-T88

Texas School Directory

DISTRICT PERSONNEL INDEX

NAME/District	JOB FUNCTIONS	PAGE
Summers, Regan/*Pleasant Grove Ind School Dist*	37	49
Summers, Sue/*Dimmitt Ind School Dist*	69	71
Sumner, Drew/*Jarrell Ind School Dist*	6	396
Sumner, Rodney/*Tuloso-Midway Ind School Dist*	1	305
Sumrall, Tennie/*Coolidge Ind School Dist*	73,95	266
Sumrow, Steve/*Caddo Mills Ind Sch Dist*	6	235
Sunga-Collier, Jennifer/*South San Antonio Ind Sch Dist*	71	42
Sunosky, Laura/*New Caney Ind School Dist*	79	293
Surdovel, David/*Tomball Ind School Dist*	45	203
Surface, Ally/*Eagle Mtn-Saginaw Ind Sch Dist*	298	348
Surratt, Scott/*Carthage Ind School Dist*	6,35	311
Surratt, Stan/*Lindale Ind School Dist*	1	337
Susen, Kristi/*Brazosport Ind School Dist*	71,97	52
Susser, Catherine/*Corpus Christi Ind Sch Dist*	67	303
Sustaire, Mark/*Saltillo Ind School Dist*	67	231
Sustaita, Calixta/*Lockney Independent Sch Dist*	4	149
Sustaita, Marlena/*Granger Ind School Dist*	4	396
Sutherland, Gary/*Lorena Ind School Dist*	3	280
Sutherland, Russ/*East Chambers Ind School Dist*	6	72
Sutherland, Shannon/*Richland Springs Ind Sch Dist*	4	332
Sutlive, Dawn/*New Summerfield Ind Sch Dist*	4	73
Suttle, Bonnie/*Allen Ind School Dist*	76	76
Suttle, Greg/*McKinney Ind School Dist*	3	80
Sutton, Patricia/*Ft Worth Ind School Dist*	275	349
Sutton, Tom/*Groesbeck Ind School Dist*	67	267
Svoboda, Lisa/*Sealy Ind School Dist*	2,11,19	22
Swaim, Elizabeth/*Aubrey Ind School Dist*	7	120
Swain, Casey/*Martin's Mill Ind Sch Dist*	77	381
Swain, Casey/*Martin's Mill Ind Sch Dist*	58	381
Swain, Michelle/*Round Rock Ind School Dist*	81,92	398
Swan, Jennifer/*Charlotte Ind School Dist*	76,84	20
Swan, Sally/*Spearman Ind School Dist*	7,35,83,85	177
Swan, Tom/*Pasadena Ind School Dist*	30	198
Swaner, Ann/*Mumford Ind School Dist*	16	56
Swank, Jennifer/*Waskom Ind School Dist*	7,85	209
Swanks, Pam/*Dripping Springs Ind Sch Dist*	5	210
Swanlund, Gail/*Iola Ind School Dist*	57	172
Swann, Stan/*Crowley Ind School Dist*	79	347
Swanson, Deborah/*Idalou Ind School Dist*	58	269
Swanson, Eric/*White Oak Ind School Dist*	67	171
Swanson, Jaime/*Beckville Ind School Dist*	4	311
Swanson, William/*Clint Ind School Dist*	44	132
Swarb, Wendy/*Sudan Ind School Dist*	7,85	261
Swart, Marja/*Jim Ned Cons Ind School Dist*	16,82	361
Swartz, David/*Dickinson Ind School Dist*	67	159
Swearengen, Thomas/*Shelbyville Ind School Dist*	5,8,83,85,88	335
Sweeney, Graham, Dr/*Boles Ind School Dist*	1,83	235
Sweeny, Christy/*Campbell Ind School Dist*	7,35	235
Sweet, Cane/*Anna Ind School Dist*	88	77
Sweet, Stephanie/*Savoy Ind School Dist*	58	146
Sweich, Ken/*Rockdale Ind School Dist*	73,76,295	287
Swenson, Jessica/*Galveston Ind School Dist*	58	160
Swenson, Robert/*Lohn Ind School Dist*	67	277
Swick, Bev/*Bremond Ind School Dist*	286	324
Swick, Susan/*Groesbeck Ind School Dist*	38	267
Swift, Joyce/*Princeton Ind School Dist*	69	84
Swinford, Alan/*Crane Ind School Dist*	67	93
Swinney, John/*Crosby Ind School Dist*	67	183
Swinton, Mary/*Plano Ind School Dist*	42	82
Swofford, Malissa/*Nocona Ind School Dist*	73,76	290
Sykora, Carla/*West Ind School Dist*	58	282
Sykora, Janice/*Woodsboro Ind School Dist*	1,11	324
Sylvester, Christie/*Evadale Ind School Dist*	16	240
Sylvester, Tyrone/*Goose Creek Cons Ind Sch Dist*	68	187

T

NAME/District	JOB FUNCTIONS	PAGE
Taber, Chris/*La Vernia Ind School Dist*	6	401
Taber, Karen/*Itasca Ind School Dist*	4	228
Taboada, Celia/*United Ind School Dist*	74	387
Tabor, Ty/*Graford Ind School Dist*	6	310
Tabor, Tyler/*Blanket Ind School Dist*	6	58
Tackett, Chris/*Windthorst Ind School Dist*	6	20
Tackett, Cindy/*Alvord Ind School Dist*	2	402
Tackett, Darla/*Windthorst Ind School Dist*	69,270,271	20
Taff, Norris/*Cleveland Ind School Dist*	6,35	265
Taft, Stephen/*Pine Tree Ind School Dist*	286,295	170

NAME/District	JOB FUNCTIONS	PAGE
Talbert, Brad/*Holland Ind School Dist*	6	27
Talbert, Clarissa/*San Marcos Cons Ind Sch Dist*	58	211
Talbert, David/*Lake Dallas Ind School Dist*	3	122
Talbert, George/*Buna Ind School Dist*	2,3,17	240
Talbert, Kathy, Dr/*Lewisville Ind School Dist*	58	122
Talley, Barry/*Deer Park Ind School Dist*	20,23	186
Talley, Tom/*Bridgeport Ind School Dist*	67	402
Taly, Carol/*Braination Schools*	68	30
Tamez, Fred/*Brownsville Ind School Dist*	35	63
Tamez, Manuel/*Bishop Cons Ind School Dist*	2	302
Tamyo, Emanuel/*Southwest Ind School Dist*	5	43
Tanem, Ginger/*Cleburne Ind School Dist*	45	247
Tanner, Allen/*Frenship Ind School Dist*	3	269
Tanner, Anneliese/*Austin Ind School Dist*	4	366
Tanner, Patrick/*Allen Ind School Dist*	76,295	76
Tanner, Stacy/*Perryton Ind School Dist*	29	307
Tanton, Debbie/*Mesquite Ind School Dist*	273	110
Tapia, Henery/*Huntsville Ind School Dist*	4	383
Tapia, Oscar/*Harlingen Cons Ind School Dist*	3,4,5,15	64
Tarleton, Willie/*Midland Ind School Dist*	5	285
Tarlton, Elyse/*Liberty Hill Ind School Dist*	58,69	398
Tarmon, Donna/*Meridian Ind School Dist*	32,37	47
Tarpley, Clay/*Hamilton Ind School Dist*	1	176
Tarr, Nic/*Higgins Ind School Dist*	6,80	268
Tarrant, John/*Weatherford Ind School Dist*	16,82	313
Tarver, Carolyn/*Little Elm Ind School Dist*	4	124
Tarver, David/*Mineral Wells Ind School Dist*	15,68	310
Tarver, Jodi/*Guthrie Common School Dist*	7	257
Taska, Debra/*Tidehaven Ind School Dist*	5,9,11,69,285,296,298	276
Tatar, Richard/*Port Arthur Ind School Dist*	295	243
Tate, Alyese/*Victoria Ind School Dist*	81	382
Tate, Devin/*Beckville Ind School Dist*	1	311
Tate, Donna/*Pearland Ind School Dist*	298	53
Tate, Karla/*Lockhart Ind School Dist*	274	61
Tate, Lisa/*Fairfield Ind School Dist*	68	156
Tate, Michelle/*Lindale Ind School Dist*	2	337
Tatum, Chris/*Amarillo Ind School Dist*	68	317
Tatum, Cindy/*Decatur Ind School Dist*	2,15	403
Taulton, Bryan/*Goodrich Ind School Dist*	1,11,83	316
Tavenner, Jayne/*Region 6 Ed Service Center*	69	384
Tawater, Chris/*Manor Ind School Dist*	76	371
Taylor, Amy/*Claude Ind School Dist*	752	20
Taylor, Amy/*Claude Ind School Dist*	57,77,81,280,296,752	20
Taylor, Angela/*Claude Ind School Dist*	2,11	20
Taylor, Annette/*Liberty Ind School Dist*	2	266
Taylor, Betsy Adams/*Lubbock-Cooper Ind Sch Dist*	13,296	271
Taylor, Brady/*Woden Ind School Dist*	1	298
Taylor, Brenda/*Kerrville Ind School Dist*	2	256
Taylor, Britney/*Leon Ind School Dist*	3,5	264
Taylor, Carl/*Kelton Ind School Dist*	1,57,288	390
Taylor, Chad/*Liberty Ind School Dist*	6	266
Taylor, Clay/*Tahoka Ind School Dist*	67	273
Taylor, David/*Graford Ind School Dist*	3	310
Taylor, Della/*Harlandale Ind School Dist*	58	32
Taylor, Dori/*Jacksboro Ind Sch Dist*	36,69,83,85	239
Taylor, Doug/*Belton Ind School Dist*	91	26
Taylor, Douglas/*Jim Ned Cons Ind School Dist*	4	361
Taylor, Gordon/*Region 10 Ed Service Center*	1,11	116
Taylor, Howard/*Clarksville Ind School Dist*	73	322
Taylor, Jeane/*Shelbyville Ind School Dist*	7	335
Taylor, Jeanne/*Vidor Ind School Dist*	5	309
Taylor, Jerita/*Bronte Ind School Dist*	42	75
Taylor, Joe/*Hearne Ind School Dist*	3	325
Taylor, John/*Bluff Dale Ind Sch Dist*	1,11,83,288	143
Taylor, Johnny/*Idalou Ind School Dist*	67	269
Taylor, Jon/*Pharr-San Juan-Alamo Ind SD*	20	223
Taylor, Keith/*Jonesboro Ind School Dist*	67	93
Taylor, Kelly/*Calhoun Co Ind School Dist*	13,57,69,74,83,271	61
Taylor, Kerry/*Eanes Ind School Dist*	20,23	370
Taylor, Lahoma/*Chilton Ind School Dist*	2	144
Taylor, Laurie/*Plano Ind School Dist*	9	82
Taylor, Linda/*Boling Ind School Dist*	57	389
Taylor, Linda/*Royse City Ind School Dist*	38	326
Taylor, Logan/*Latexo Ind School Dist*	5	233
Taylor, Lynnette/*Gause Ind School Dist*	16,73,295	287
Taylor, Maggie/*Boys Ranch Ind School Dist*	11,15,298	307

School Year 2019-2020   800-333-8802   TX-T89

DISTRICT PERSONNEL INDEX

Market Data Retrieval

NAME/District	JOB FUNCTIONS	PAGE
Taylor, Mike/Plains Ind School Dist	5	405
Taylor, Netobia/Galveston Ind School Dist	76	160
Taylor, Pam/Cross Roads Ind School Dist	36	214
Taylor, Pam/Mt Calm Ind School Dist	5,8,57,275,288	228
Taylor, Randy/Denison Ind School Dist	5	166
Taylor, Regina/Allen Ind School Dist	298	76
Taylor, Sage/Corrigan-Camden Ind Sch Dist	38	316
Taylor, Sarah/Cleburne Ind School Dist	19	247
Taylor, Shannon/McMullen Co Ind Sch Dist	6	283
Taylor, Sharon/San Augustine Ind School Dist	4	329
Taylor, Sherry/Aledo Ind School Dist	68	312
Taylor, Stephanie/Gholson Ind School Dist	8,286,752	279
Taylor, Stephanie/Sonora Ind School Dist	8,11,27,58,88	342
Taylor, Steve/Denver City Ind School Dist	6	405
Taylor, Susan/Lipan Ind School Dist	73	230
Taylor, Tamika, Dr/Conroe Ind School Dist	69,294	291
Taylor, Tina/Nueces Canyon Cons Ind SD	286	131
Teague, Chad/McKinney Ind School Dist	68	81
Teague, Christopher, Dr/Hillsboro Ind School Dist	67	227
Teal, Glen, Dr/Jim Ned Cons Ind School Dist	1	361
Teal, Suzanne/Carroll Independent Sch Dist	3	347
Tedder, Joel/Normangee Ind School Dist	3,5,91	264
Tedder, Richard/Cross Roads Ind School Dist	1,11	213
Teel, Ken/Boys Ranch Ind School Dist	67	307
Teems, Kelley/Gunter Ind School Dist	3,296	166
Teer, Janet/Miller Grove Ind School Dist	2	231
Teer, Janice/Saltillo Ind School Dist	2	231
Tefertiller, Leif/Monahans-Wickett-Pyote ISD	5	385
Tefertiller, Mary/Wimberley Ind School Dist	4	212
Teichman, Cindy/Iowa Park Consolidated Ind SD	79	392
Tekell, Angela/Waco Ind School Dist	67	281
Tekell, Teressa/Reagan Co Ind School Dist	69	321
Telesca, Julie/Grapevine-Colleyville Ind SD	4	353
Telles, Reyne/Austin Ind School Dist	71	366
Tellez, Myriam/La Joya Ind School Dist	36	219
Tellez, Rita/Ysleta Ind School Dist	45	137
Tellis, Don/Pearland Ind School Dist	3,91	53
Templeton, Carrie/Rankin Ind School Dist	60	377
Templeton, Craig/Harrold Ind School Dist	8,57,69,83,88,273	393
Templeton, Nathan/Laneville Ind School Dist	8,34,74,83,88,271,273	327
Templeton, Robert, Dr/Ingram Ind School Dist	1	255
Templin, Steve/Mabank Ind School Dist	3,91	252
Tencate, Jeannie/Moran Ind School Dist	271	334
Tennery, Jody/Avalon Ind School Dist	9,34	140
Tennison, Clarence/Cross Plains Ind Sch Dist	3	62
Tennison, Travis/Olfen Ind School Dist	6	327
Teran, Rick/Childress Ind School Dist	1,83	74
Terrazas, Daniel/Marion Ind School Dist	11,58	172
Terrazas, Velia/Southwest Ind School Dist	9	43
Terrell, Jennifer/Decatur Ind School Dist	69	403
Terrell, Lance/Levelland Ind School Dist	2,19	229
Terrell, Leah/Booker Ind School Dist	73	267
Terrell, Stain/Paint Creek Ind School Dist	3	210
Terrier, Byron, Dr/Region 5 Ed Service Center	15,16,73	244
Terrill, Josh/Christoval Ind School Dist	295	364
Terry, Becky/Hamlin Ind School Dist	2	249
Terry, Chris/Ft Stockton Ind School Dist	295	315
Terry, Debbie/Pine Tree Ind School Dist	69,288,294	170
Terry, Glenda/Midway Ind School Dist	16	74
Terry, Justin, Dr/Forney Ind School Dist	1	251
Terry, Kelley/Madisonville Cons ISD	4	273
Terry, Kevin/Milano Ind School Dist	73,295	287
Terry, Kim/River Road Ind School Dist	4	319
Terry, Rebecca/Pasadena Ind School Dist	34	198
Terry, Rockney/Marlin Ind School Dist	73	144
Terry, Rueben/Caddo Mills Ind Sch Dist	67	235
Tesch, Kim/Normangee Ind School Dist	36,69,88	264
Tesch, William/Blanco Ind School Dist	6	45
Thacker, Michelle/Hondo Ind School Dist	4	284
Thacker, Robin/Nacogdoches Ind School Dist	4	298
Thane, Michelle/Haskell Cons Ind School Dist	8,11,57,88,273,296,298	210
Thannum, Julie/Carroll Independent Sch Dist	15,71,297	347
Tharpe, Kelly/McGregor Ind School Dist	10	280
Thayer, Tracy/Bandera Ind School Dist	11,31,91,296,298	23
Thedford, Barbara/Industrial Ind School Dist	4	240
Thedford, Lisa/Rice Ind School Dist	4	300
Therwanger, Danielle/Klondike Ind School Dist	8,83,288	117
Therwhanger, Cindy/Seminole Ind School Dist	4	158
Therwhanger, Kerry/Timpson Ind School Dist	6	335
Thias, Irma/Groom Ind School Dist	4	69
Thibodeaux, Adam/Beaumont Ind School Dist	297	241
Thibodeaux, Jason/Sabine Pass Ind School Dist	6	244
Thibodeaux, Jennifer/Nursery ISD School Dist	6	382
Thibodeaux, Michael/Hays Cons Ind School Dist	4	211
Thibodeaux, Stormy/Barbers Hill Ind School Dist	45	72
Thiel, David/La Vega Ind School Dist	4	279
Thies, Heather/Academy Ind School Dist	4	26
Thiessen, Brad/Amarillo Ind School Dist	6	317
Thill, Arland/Fairfield Ind School Dist	73,295	156
Thill, Crystal/Fairfield Ind School Dist	4	156
Thiry, Eric/Yoakum Ind School Dist	3	118
Thixton, Clay/Klondike Ind School Dist	67	117
Thomas-Jimenez, Cinde/Seguin Ind School Dist	67	173
Thomas, Angie/Tarkington Ind School Dist	34	266
Thomas, Ashley/Wichita Falls Ind School Dist	71	392
Thomas, Audrey/Waxahachie Ind School Dist	58	142
Thomas, Autumn/Texarkana Ind School Dist	15	50
Thomas, Cecil/Wheeler Ind School Dist	16,73	391
Thomas, Celina, Dr/Hutto Ind School Dist	1	396
Thomas, Cheyenne/Hermleigh Ind School Dist	57,59	333
Thomas, Christy/Jacksboro Ind Sch Dist	2,84	239
Thomas, Danny/Lorenzo Ind School Dist	73	94
Thomas, Darlene/Motley Co Ind School Dist	2	296
Thomas, Donna/Duncanville Ind School Dist	4	104
Thomas, Edward/Killeen Ind School Dist	5	27
Thomas, George/Socorro Ind School Dist	27,31	135
Thomas, Guy/Waller Ind School Dist	3	384
Thomas, James/Lancaster Ind School Dist	3	110
Thomas, Janie/Gary Ind School Dist	7	311
Thomas, Jean/Carthage Ind School Dist	71	311
Thomas, Jimmie/New Boston Ind School Dist	5	49
Thomas, Jimmy/Bushland Ind School Dist	6	319
Thomas, Kathryn/Brookeland Ind School Dist	4	240
Thomas, Kaylia/Boys Ranch Ind School Dist	8,16	307
Thomas, Kevin/Jacksboro Ind Sch Dist	27	239
Thomas, Kimberley/Monahans-Wickett-Pyote ISD	30,38	385
Thomas, Mark/Birdville Ind School Dist	71	346
Thomas, Mary, Dr/Austin Ind School Dist	11,296,298,752	366
Thomas, Melinda/Kress Ind School Dist	69,83,270	343
Thomas, Mike/Spring Branch Ind School Dist	70	200
Thomas, Robert/Woodsboro Ind School Dist	67	324
Thomas, Robin/Skidmore Tynan Ind SD	8,11,69,83,88,288	25
Thomas, Ross/Abilene Ind School Dist	39	360
Thomas, Roxie/Forsan Ind School Dist	4	234
Thomas, Sam/Chireno ISD School Dist	27	297
Thomas, Scott/Manor Ind School Dist	71	371
Thomas, Scott/Van Ind School Dist	67	381
Thomas, Vicky/Diboll Ind School Dist	1	17
Thomas, Wanda/Houston Ind School Dist	11	188
Thomas, Wesley/Springtown Ind School Dist	69	313
Thomas, Willie/Robinson Ind School Dist	16	281
Thomas, Zack/Ore City Ind School Dist	73	377
Thomason, Jeff/Boles Ind School Dist	6	235
Thomasson, Michael/Harts Bluff Ind School Dist	8,275	363

1 Superintendent	16 Instructional Media Svcs	30 Adult Education	44 Science Sec	58 Special Education K-12	72 Summer School	88 Alternative/At Risk	277 Remedial Math K-12
2 Bus/Finance/Purchasing	17 Chief Operations Officer	31 Career/Sch-to-Work K-12	45 Math K-12	59 Special Education Elem	73 Instructional Tech	89 Multi-Cultural Curriculum	280 Literacy Coach
3 Buildings And Grounds	18 Chief Academic Officer	32 Career/Sch-to-Work Elem	46 Math Elem	60 Special Education Sec	74 Inservice Training	90 Social Work	285 STEM
4 Food Service	19 Chief Financial Officer	33 Career/Sch-to-Work Sec	47 Math Sec	61 Foreign/World Lang K-12	75 Marketing/Distributive	91 Safety/Security	286 Digital Learning
5 Transportation	20 Art K-12	34 Early Childhood Ed	48 English/Lang Arts K-12	62 Foreign/World Lang Elem	76 Info Systems	92 Magnet School	288 Common Core Standards
6 Athletic	21 Art Elem	35 Health/Phys Education	49 English/Lang Arts Elem	63 Foreign/World Lang Sec	77 Psychological Assess	93 Parental Involvement	294 Accountability
7 Health Services	22 Art Sec	36 Guidance Services K-12	50 English/Lang Arts Sec	64 Religious Education K-12	78 Affirmative Action	95 Tech Prep Program	295 Network System
8 Curric/Instruct K-12	23 Music K-12	37 Guidance Services Elem	51 Reading K-12	65 Religious Education Elem	79 Student Personnel	97 Chief Information Officer	296 Title II Programs
9 Curric/Instruct Elem	24 Music Elem	38 Guidance Services Sec	52 Reading Elem	66 Religious Education Sec	80 Driver Ed/Safety	98 Chief Technology Officer	297 Webmaster
10 Curric/Instruct Sec	25 Music Sec	39 Social Studies K-12	53 Reading Sec	67 School Board President	81 Gifted/Talented	270 Character Education	298 Grant Writer/Ptnrships
11 Federal Program	26 Business Education	40 Social Studies Elem	54 Remedial Reading K-12	68 Teacher Personnel	82 Video Services	271 Migrant Education	750 Chief Innovation Officer
12 Title I	27 Career & Tech Ed	41 Social Studies Sec	55 Remedial Reading Elem	69 Academic Assessment	83 Substance Abuse Prev	273 Teacher Mentor	751 Chief of Staff
13 Title V	28 Technology Education	42 Science K-12	56 Remedial Reading Sec	70 Research/Development	84 Erate	274 Before/After Sch	752 Social Emotional Learning
15 Asst Superintendent	29 Family/Consumer Science	43 Science Elem	57 Bilingual/ELL	71 Public Information	85 AIDS Education	275 Response To Intervention	

TX-T90

Texas School Directory — DISTRICT PERSONNEL INDEX

NAME/District	JOB FUNCTIONS	PAGE
Thompson, Bobby/Mt Vernon Ind School Dist	5	155
Thompson, Brandon/Little Elm Ind School Dist	76	124
Thompson, Brian/Brazos Ind School Dist	1	22
Thompson, Charles/Alvarado Ind School Dist	5	246
Thompson, Chris/Graford Ind School Dist	73,295	310
Thompson, Chuck/City View Ind School Dist	16	391
Thompson, Cornel/West Orange-Cove Cons ISD	6	309
Thompson, Daphne/Canton Ind School Dist	58	380
Thompson, Dre/Aldine Ind School Dist	6	179
Thompson, Dwayne/Dallas Ind School Dist	19	98
Thompson, Heather/Graford Ind School Dist	57	310
Thompson, Helen/Blue Ridge Ind School Dist	7	77
Thompson, Jeanne/Whitney Ind School Dist	7	228
Thompson, Jeremy/Era Ind School Dist	1	90
Thompson, Joy/Coleman Ind School Dist	8,12,34,57,296	76
Thompson, Karrie/Hawley Ind School Dist	16,82	250
Thompson, Kathy/Detroit Ind School Dist	1	322
Thompson, Kenneth, Dr/San Antonio Ind School Dist	73,76,97,98	39
Thompson, Kerry/Banquete Ind School Dist	8	302
Thompson, Marjorie/Breckenridge Ind School Dist	57	341
Thompson, Marty/Chester Ind School Dist	3	374
Thompson, Max, Dr/Banquete Ind School Dist	1,11,84	302
Thompson, Michelle/Klein Ind School Dist	42	196
Thompson, Mike/Ranger Ind School Dist	1,73	129
Thompson, Paul/West Rusk Co Cons Ind Sch Dist	91	328
Thompson, Raemi/Big Spring Ind School Dist	8,12,15,52	233
Thompson, Richard/Sharyland Ind School Dist	6	224
Thompson, Robbie/Central Ind School Dist	73	17
Thompson, Ronda/Matagorda Ind School Dist	59	275
Thompson, Ronnie/Liberty-Eylau Ind School Dist	1	48
Thompson, Sandra/Garland Ind School Dist	29	105
Thompson, Stacie/Mt Pleasant Ind School Dist	2,19	363
Thompson, T/Montague Ind School Dist	2	290
Thompson, Terry/Hawley Ind School Dist	3,5,91	250
Thompson, Toni/San Antonio Ind School Dist	15,68,79	39
Thompson, Weldon/Coleman Ind School Dist	3	76
Thoms, Kris/Sundown Ind School Dist	2,11,298	229
Thoreson, Scott/Ysleta Ind School Dist	20,23	137
Thorman, Mike/Cumby Ind School Dist	3,5	231
Thorn, Allison/Central Heights Ind Sch Dist	27,31	297
Thornell, Carey/Georgetown Ind School Dist	274	395
Thornell, Rob, Dr/Northwest Ind School Dist	15	124
Thornhill, Cooper/Blum Ind School Dist	6	227
Thornhill, Sherrie/Silsbee Ind School Dist	8,11,288,296	178
Thornton, Billie/Rio Vista Ind School Dist	2	248
Thornton, Jerry/Overton Ind School Dist	3,5	328
Thornton, Louise/Granger Ind School Dist	2,19	396
Thornton, Robyn/Onalaska Ind School Dist	8,11,16,57,58,69,88	317
Thornton, Rodney/Hico Ind School Dist	6	176
Thornton, Shelley/Westphalia Ind School Dist	2	145
Thornton, Shirley/Flour Bluff Ind School Dist	67	304
Thornton, Vicki/Sabine Ind School Dist	58,77	170
Thornton, Vicki/Spring Hill Ind School Dist	58	170
Thornton, Will/Edgewood Ind School Dist	5	31
Thornton, William/Edgewood Ind School Dist	3,5	380
Thorp, Kathy/Throckmorton Ind School Dist	67	363
Thorsen, Amber/Granger Ind School Dist	12,13,36,69,83,296	396
Thorson, Aaron/Int'l Leadership of Texas Dist	751	108
Thorton, Vicki/White Oak Ind School Dist	34,58	171
Threlkelb, Discha/Fannindel Ind School Dist	2	120
Throgmorton, Rodney/Perryton Ind School Dist	73,295	307
Thuman, Bob/Hamshire Fannett Ind Sch Dist	67	242
Thurman, Denise/St Jo Ind School Dist	83	290
Thurmond, Cynthia/Laneville Ind School Dist	16	327
Thweatt, David/Harrold Ind School Dist	1,11,73	393
Tibo, Roxanna/De Leon Ind School Dist	54	89
Tice, Becky/Barbers Hill Ind School Dist	67	72
Tidwell, Christy/Texarkana Ind School Dist	8,74	50
Tidwell, Coty/Post Ind School Dist	73	162
Tidwell, Diana/Terrell Ind School Dist	4	253
Tidwell, Leanne/Munday Consolidated Ind SD	271	259
Tidwell, Melanie/Whitehouse Ind School Dist	46	338
Tidwell, Rachel/Rice Ind School Dist	7	300
Tidwell, Rick/Bland Ind School Dist	1,83	235
Tieterse, Kelley/Huntsville Ind School Dist	58	383
Tietjan, Kelly/Rivercrest Ind School Dist	16,82	322
Tietjen, Deb/Garland Ind School Dist	57	105
Tieu, Quyen/Sheldon Ind School Dist	58	200
Tijerina, Amaro/Edinburg Cons Ind School Dist	2	216
Tijerina, Candy/Liberty Hill Ind School Dist	57,271	398
Tijerina, Diamond/Mission Cons Ind School Dist	50	222
Tilley, Danette/La Porte Ind School Dist	10	198
Tillman, Tonya/Carrollton-Farmers Branch ISD	11,15	96
Timberlake, Terry/Academy Ind School Dist	295	26
Timmons, David/Penelope ISD School Dist	1	228
Timmons, Mary/Lorena Ind School Dist	67	280
Timms, Joe/McMullen Co Ind Sch Dist	8,31,57,85,273	283
Timms, Stephanie/Three Rivers Ind School Dist	2	268
Tindel, Caleb/Paris Ind School Dist	10,27	260
Tindel, Zeb/Honey Grove Ind School Dist	31	146
Tindol, Charles/Italy Ind School Dist	6	140
Tineda, J'Rae/Shallowater Ind School Dist	16	272
Tingle, Eric/Lake Worth Ind School Dist	8,294	356
Tinker, Chrystal/Leggett Ind School Dist	83	316
Tinney, Alton/San Saba Ind School Dist	5	332
Tinnin, Tierney/Cedar Hill Ind School Dist	97	97
Tinsley, Kristen/Kenedy Co Schools	1	254
Tinsley, Kristen/Kenedy Co Wide Common Sch Dist	11,57,88,271,273,286,288	254
Tinsley, Randy/Bushland Ind School Dist	91	319
Tippett, Joyce/Spurger Ind School Dist	16	375
Tipps, Rod/Sivells Bend Ind School Dist	6,16,59,73	91
Tipton, Beau/Menard Ind School Dist	3,5	285
Tipton, Josh/Midland Ind School Dist	297	285
Tipton, Scott/Bandera Ind School Dist	2	23
Tipton, Tony, Dr/Little Elm Ind School Dist	27,31	124
Tisdale, Jamie/Humble Ind School Dist	68	195
Tisdale, Rick/Llano Ind School Dist	67	268
Todd, Courtney/Milano Ind School Dist	12,57,296	287
Todd, Heidi/Cleburne Ind School Dist	2	247
Todd, Leslie/Anahuac Ind School Dist	38	71
Todd, Lisa/Thorndale Ind School Dist	68	288
Todd, Matthew/Blue Ridge Ind School Dist	8,11,69,74,88,294,298	77
Toelr, Bridgette/Warren Ind School Dist	58,69	375
Tolbert, Kathy/Frisco Ind School Dist	7	78
Toliver, Caroline/Ballinger Ind School Dist	8,11,286,288,296,298	326
Toliver, Lisa/Sulphur Springs Ind Sch Dist	67	232
Tollett, Richard/Lytle Ind School Dist	16,73,76,82,84	21
Tolliver, Duane/Tulia Ind School Dist	6	343
Tolman, Mary/Brownsville Ind School Dist	12	63
Tomalin, Jamie/Rockwall Ind School Dist	2	325
Tomas, Michael/Silsbee Ind School Dist	3	178
Tomas, Monica/Sheldon Ind School Dist	4	200
Tomes, George/Bronte Ind School Dist	23	75
Tomson, Tina/Lovejoy Ind School Dist	2	80
Toney, Nancy/Red Oak Ind School Dist	11,296,298	142
Tonne, Allison/Paint Rock Ind School Dist	16	90
Tooley, Lavern/Hico Ind School Dist	7,85	176
Toon, Rodney/Alvarado Ind School Dist	2	246
Torkelson, Tom/Idea Public Schools	67	217
Torres, Armando/San Perlita Ind School Dist	73,295	394
Torres, Cynthia/La Feria Ind School Dist	8,15	65
Torres, D T/Lometa Ind School Dist	6	262
Torres, Dawn/Eden Cons Ind School Dist	4	90
Torres, Elda/Hutto Ind School Dist	57,294,296	396
Torres, Elizabeth/Eagle Pass Ind School Dist	58	276
Torres, Elizabeth, Dr/Shepherd Ind School Dist	11,57,88,271,288,298	330
Torres, Javier/Dilley Ind School Dist	3	157
Torres, Joe/Edcouch Elsa Ind School Dist	31,73,286	215
Torres, Josie/Sonora Ind School Dist	4	342
Torres, Judith/Edgewood Ind School Dist	74	31
Torres, Ken/Ft Worth Ind School Dist	69	349
Torres, Lelia/Sharyland Ind School Dist	58	224
Torres, Lora/Nixon-Smiley Cons Ind Sch Dist	4	164
Torres, Lynn/Lufkin Ind School Dist	1	18
Torres, Omian/Brenham Ind School Dist	5	385
Torres, Patrick/Red Oak Ind School Dist	8,15,54,277	142
Torres, Randon/Post Ind School Dist	295	162
Torres, Richard/Alief Ind School Dist	5	181
Torres, Roberto/DeSoto Ind School Dist	16,73,76,286,295	104
Torres, Rosa/Harlandale Ind School Dist	57	32
Torres, Rosa Maria/Harris Co Dept of Ed	2	179
Torres, Salanon/Lockhart Ind School Dist	5	61

DISTRICT PERSONNEL INDEX

Market Data Retrieval

NAME/District	JOB FUNCTIONS	PAGE
Torres, Shayla/Olton Ind School Dist	35	261
Torres, Veronica/La Feria Ind School Dist	28,73,295	65
Torrez, Rchard/Burnet Cons Ind Sch Dist	295	60
Torrez, Susan/Corrigan-Camden Ind Sch Dist	73	316
Tortorici, Melissa/Texas City Ind School Dist	71	161
Toscano, Roland/East Central Ind School Dist	1	31
Touchet, Gwyn/Ft Bend Ind School Dist	68	149
Touchet, Nicole/East Chambers Ind School Dist	68	72
Tovar, Elias/Pharr-San Juan-Alamo Ind SD	30	223
Tovar, Eugene/South San Antonio Ind Sch Dist	91	42
Tovar, Sandra/Harlingen Cons Ind School Dist	36	64
Towley, Darrell/Floresville Ind School Dist	3	400
Townsend, George/Manor Ind School Dist	4	371
Townsend, Lee/Santa Fe Ind School Dist	2,19	161
Tracy, Alicia/Whitesboro Ind School Dist	4	168
Tracy, Alicia/Whitesboro Ind School Dist	4	168
Tracy, Jason/Columbia Brazoria ISD	2	52
Tracy, Jennifer/Pleasanton Ind School Dist	7	21
Trailor, Mandy/Sunray Ind School Dist	88,285	296
Tramel, Penny, Dr/College Station Ind School Dist	8,18	55
Tramell, Jacki/Nixon-Smiley Cons Ind Sch Dist	58	164
Trammell, Gina/Cross Roads Ind School Dist	68	214
Tran, Angela/Ft Bend Ind School Dist	57	149
Tran, Rose/Aransas Co Ind School Dist	8,11,30,68,74,78,79	19
Tran, Tuyen/Port Arthur Ind School Dist	16	243
Travis, Casey/Beckville Ind School Dist	67	311
Travis, Joanne/Post Ind School Dist	7	162
Travis, Steven, Dr/Deer Park Ind School Dist	70	186
Traylor, Grace/Jacksonville Ind School Dist	71	73
Traylor, Michelle/Frenship Ind School Dist	73	269
Traynham, Laurie/Leander Ind School Dist	12	396
Traynham, Ralph/Ft Stockton Ind School Dist	1	315
Treadaway, Stanley/Water Valley Ind School Dist	67	365
Treadwell, Lloyd/Ennis Ind School Dist	1	140
Trejo, Araceli/Schertz-Cibolo-Univ City ISD	294	173
Trejo, Charlotte, Dr/Belton Ind School Dist	74,273	26
Trejo, Maria/Cypress-Fairbanks Ind Sch Dist	57,271	184
Tremmel, Patricia/Commerce Independent Sch Dist	15	236
Tresl, Laurie/Connally Ind School Dist	34,58	279
Trevathan, Cliff/Central Ind School Dist	83,91	17
Trevino, Alberto/Santa Rosa Ind School Dist	274	67
Trevino, Ansilee/San Antonio Ind School Dist	4	39
Trevino, Anysia, Dr/La Joya Ind School Dist	15,68	219
Trevino, Diana/Yorktown Ind School Dist	4	118
Trevino, Doloris/El Campo Ind School Dist	8,15,18,57,271,274	389
Trevino, Effron/Jourdanton Ind School Dist	4	20
Trevino, Elias/Weslaco Ind School Dist	57	225
Trevino, Genoveva/Diocese of Brownsville Ed Off	68	226
Trevino, Gilbert, Dr/Floydada Ind School Dist	1	148
Trevino, Jessie/Mission Cons Ind School Dist	7,79	222
Trevino, Joel/La Joya Ind School Dist	2,15	219
Trevino, Joel/North East Ind School Dist	68	34
Trevino, Joyce/Frenship Ind School Dist	4	269
Trevino, Juan/Roma Ind School Dist	4	341
Trevino, Juan/Tomball Ind School Dist	3	203
Trevino, Leticia, Dr/Rio Grande City Ind Sch Dist	10,15,36,69	340
Trevino, Mary/Hughes Springs Ind School Dist	68	70
Trevino, Pilar/Lyford Cons Ind School Dist	16,82,93	394
Trevino, Reuben/McAllen Ind School Dist	3	220
Trevino, Ricardo/Taft Ind School Dist	12	332
Trevino, Sabina/Clear Creek Ind School Dist	76	158
Trevino, Stephen/School of Excellence In Ed	73	42
Trevino, Yvette/Somerset Ind School Dist	7	42
Triamrose, Holly/Atlanta Ind School Dist	68	69
Trigg, Tom, Dr/Highland Park Ind Sch Dist	1	108
Trimble, Jeremy/Eanes Ind School Dist	3,17	370
Trinh, Silvia/Houston Ind School Dist	15,751	188
Tripplett, Brian/Hubbard Ind School Dist	67	48
Troboy, Mary/Big Sandy Ind School Dist	2	376
Trojcak, Robin/Gonzales Ind School Dist	11	164
Trompler, Kelly/Bonham Ind School Dist	15,68,74,79,273	145
Troncoso, Oscar/Anthony Ind School Dist	1	131
Trongaard, Michele/Wylie Ind School Dist	2,15	84
Troqville, Jennifer/Waskom Ind School Dist	11,271,296	209
Trotter, Chris/Cleveland Ind School Dist	1	265
Trotter, Christina/Humble Ind School Dist	69	195
Trotter, Fran/Olton Ind School Dist	2	261
Trotter, Rebecca/Azle Ind School Dist	11	345
Trotter, Tim/Walnut Springs Ind Sch Dist	6	47
Trotts, Sherry/Waco Ind School Dist	15	281
Troup, Eileen/Sinton Ind School Dist	71	332
Trout, Mavis/Diboll Ind School Dist	294	17
Troutman, Shay/Lubbock-Cooper Ind Sch Dist	280	271
Truby, Barbara/Maypearl Ind School Dist	58	141
Trudeau, Bradford/Garland Ind School Dist	4	105
Trudeau, Joel/McMullen Co Ind School Dist	11	283
Truelock, Alann, Dr/Hondo Ind School Dist	1	284
Truelove, Tony/Bangs Ind School Dist	1	58
Truette, Tiarra/Archer City Ind School Dist	12,34	19
Truitt, David/West Ind School Dist	1,11,73,83	282
Truitt, Natasha/Harris Co Dept of Ed	68	179
Trujillo, Gabriel/Grand Prairie Ind School Dist	15	107
Trujillo, Luis/Plainview Ind School Dist	2	175
Trujillo, Michelle/Socorro Ind School Dist	40	135
Trujillo, Mima/Goose Creek Cons Ind Sch Dist	297	187
Trull, Angie/Rains Ind School Dist	34	320
Trull, Clifford/Crosbyton Cons Ind School Dist	67	94
Truman, Dave/Cuero Ind School Dist	84,295	117
Truscheit, Wyatt/Idea Public Schools	2,19	217
Truskowski, Gloria/Katy Ind School Dist	2	151
Tschirhart, Todd/Medina Valley Ind School Dist	5	284
Tubb, Cindy/Cisco Independent Sch Dist	68	128
Tubbs, Shelly/Idalou Ind School Dist	2,11,71	269
Tucker, Bryan/Luling Ind School Dist	3	61
Tucker, Holly/Pewitt Cons Ind School Dist	11,288	296
Tucker, Holly/Texarkana Ind School Dist	8,18	50
Tucker, Jarret/Trenton Ind School Dist	57,271	147
Tucker, Jimmy/Woodville Ind School Dist	67	375
Tucker, Jodie/Whitesboro Ind School Dist	8	168
Tucker, Misti/Schulenburg Ind School Dist	31,36	148
Tucker, Patti/Spurger Ind School Dist	58	375
Tucker, Sky/Levelland Ind School Dist	34	229
Tucker, Stephanie/Hillsboro Ind School Dist	11,31,57,58,271	227
Tucker, Tammy/Rogers Ind School Dist	11,296,298	28
Tucker, Toby/Canyon Ind School Dist	6	320
Tudon, Sara/Los Fresnos Cons Ind Sch Dist	8	66
Tudor, Lori/Keller Ind School Dist	2	354
Tudyk, Frank/Pleasanton Ind School Dist	67	21
Tuggle, Margaret/Crockett Ind School Dist	36	232
Tugwell, Donna/Rusk Ind School Dist	58,77	73
Tuinstra, Missy/Celina Ind School Dist	7,83,85	77
Tullos, Lorene/Pleasanton Ind School Dist	27,35,36,83	21
Tullos, Wendy/Lovelady Ind School Dist	1	233
Tumlinson, Barbie/Gregory-Portland Ind Sch Dist	34,58	330
Tunink, Jennifer/Channelview Ind School Dist	20,23	183
Tunnel, Lynn/Friendswood Ind Sch Dist	68	160
Tunnell, Kim, Dr/Mineola Ind School Dist	1,83,84	404
Tunnell, Olin/Braination Schools	67	30
Turcios, Victor/Broaddus Ind School Dist	3	329
Turlington, Amanda/Weimar Ind School Dist	58	87
Turner Jackson, Alice/Ft Worth Ind School Dist	7	349
Turner, Angela/La Vernia Ind School Dist	73,98,295,297	401
Turner, Brenda/Haskell Cons Ind School Dist	2	210
Turner, Chad/Liberty-Eylau Ind School Dist	67	48

Code	Function	Code	Function	Code	Function	Code	Function	Code	Function	Code	Function
1	Superintendent	16	Instructional Media Svcs	30	Adult Education	44	Science Sec	58	Special Education K-12	72	Summer School
2	Bus/Finance/Purchasing	17	Chief Operations Officer	31	Career/Sch-to-Work K-12	45	Math K-12	59	Special Education Elem	73	Instructional Tech
3	Buildings And Grounds	18	Chief Academic Officer	32	Career/Sch-to-Work Elem	46	Math Elem	60	Special Education Sec	74	Inservice Training
4	Food Service	19	Chief Financial Officer	33	Career/Sch-to-Work Sec	47	Math Sec	61	Foreign/World Lang K-12	75	Marketing/Distributive
5	Transportation	20	Art K-12	34	Early Childhood Ed	48	English/Lang Arts K-12	62	Foreign/World Lang Elem	76	Info Systems
6	Athletic	21	Art Elem	35	Health/Phys Education	49	English/Lang Arts Elem	63	Foreign/World Lang Sec	77	Psychological Assess
7	Health Services	22	Art Sec	36	Guidance Services K-12	50	English/Lang Arts Sec	64	Religious Education K-12	78	Affirmative Action
8	Curric/Instruct K-12	23	Music K-12	37	Guidance Services Elem	51	Reading K-12	65	Religious Education Elem	79	Student Personnel
9	Curric/Instruct Elem	24	Music Elem	38	Guidance Services Sec	52	Reading Elem	66	Religious Education Sec	80	Driver Ed/Safety
10	Curric/Instruct Sec	25	Music Sec	39	Social Studies K-12	53	Reading Sec	67	School Board President	81	Gifted/Talented
11	Federal Program	26	Business Education	40	Social Studies Elem	54	Remedial Reading K-12	68	Teacher Personnel	82	Video Services
12	Title I	27	Career & Tech Ed	41	Social Studies Sec	55	Remedial Reading Elem	69	Academic Assessment	83	Substance Abuse Prev
13	Title V	28	Technology Education	42	Science K-12	56	Remedial Reading Sec	70	Research/Development	84	Erate
15	Asst Superintendent	29	Family/Consumer Science	43	Science Elem	57	Bilingual/ELL	71	Public Information	85	AIDS Education

Code	Function	Code	Function
88	Alternative/At Risk	277	Remedial Math K-12
89	Multi-Cultural Curriculum	280	Literacy Coach
90	Social Work	285	STEM
91	Safety/Security	286	Digital Learning
92	Magnet School	288	Common Core Standards
93	Parental Involvement	294	Accountability
95	Tech Prep Program	295	Network System
97	Chief Information Officer	296	Title II Programs
98	Chief Technology Officer	297	Webmaster
270	Character Education	298	Grant Writer/Ptnrships
271	Migrant Education	750	Chief Innovation Officer
273	Teacher Mentor	751	Chief of Staff
274	Before/After Sch	752	Social Emotional Learning
275	Response To Intervention		

Texas School Directory
DISTRICT PERSONNEL INDEX

NAME/District	JOB FUNCTIONS	PAGE
Turner, Chad/New Caney Ind School Dist	67	293
Turner, Dan/Alief Ind School Dist	91	181
Turner, David/Eula Ind School Dist	8,16,73,82,83,286	63
Turner, Jeff/Allen Ind School Dist	20,23	76
Turner, Jeremy/Community Ind School Dist	6	78
Turner, Jessica/Leon Ind School Dist	6	264
Turner, Josh/Maud Ind School Dist	6	49
Turner, Karen/Lampasas Ind School Dist	58	261
Turner, Kirk/Chireno ISD School Dist	3	297
Turner, Louann/Crockett Ind School Dist	4	232
Turner, Lucas/Hardin Jefferson Ind Sch Dist	76,295,297	177
Turner, Matt/Gilmer Ind School Dist	6	376
Turner, Melinda/Duncanville Ind School Dist	76	104
Turner, Melissa/Northside Ind School Dist	11	36
Turner, Nicole/Hays Cons Ind School Dist	2	211
Turner, Paula/New Boston Ind School Dist	67	49
Turner, Renee/Apple Springs Ind School Dist	4	374
Turner, Renee/Apple Springs Ind School Dist	4	374
Turner, Rhonda/Quitman Ind School Dist	1	404
Turner, Roy/Roosevelt Ind School Dist	3	271
Turner, Ryan/Llano Ind School Dist	270	268
Turner, Scott/Quitman Ind School Dist	73,84,295	404
Turner, Terrance/Hallsville Ind School Dist	91	208
Turner, Tracy/Angleton Ind School Dist	4	51
Turney, Mark/Jacksonville Ind School Dist	5	72
Tusa, Johnny/Waco Ind School Dist	6	281
Tutle, Amy/Sunnyvale Ind School Dist	294	113
Tutt, Kim/Slocum ISD School Dist	38,83,85,88,270,275	16
Tuttle, Cicely/Hurst-Euless-Bedford ISD	15,68	353
Tye, Kevin/Connally Ind School Dist	73	279
Tyerman, Nicholas/Onalaska Ind School Dist	6	317
Tyler, Katelyn/Burleson Ind School Dist	71	246
Tyler, Lauren/Central Heights Ind Sch Dist	38,69,83,85,88	297
Tyndell, Nikki/Edgewood Ind School Dist	57	380
Tyner, Scott/China Spring Ind School Dist	295	278
Tyner, Scott/Tenaha Ind School Dist	1	335
Tyson, Lela/Calhoun Co Ind School Dist	69	62
Tyus, Darcy/Mexia Ind School Dist	58	267

U

NAME/District	JOB FUNCTIONS	PAGE
Ude, Audra/Ft Bend Ind School Dist	294	149
Uecker, David/Hutto Ind School Dist	5	396
Ugarte, Debbie/Rice Cons Ind School Dist	7	87
Ugarte, Diana/Kenedy Ind School Dist	1,11	251
Ukpaka, Cherron/Ft Worth Ind School Dist	52,280	349
Ulcak, Chris/Goliad Ind School Dist	8,15	163
Ulcak, Chris/Nursery ISD School Dist	1,11,73,288	382
Ulibarri, Deborah/Nocona Ind School Dist	69,88	290
Uloth, Sandra/Walnut Springs Ind Sch Dist	16	47
Ulrich, Debbie/Royal Ind School Dist	68	384
Umhoefer, Darrell/Midway Ind School Dist	20,23	280
Umholtz, Alan/Midway Ind School Dist	11	74
Umholtz, Allan/Tahoka Ind School Dist	11	273
Underwood, Dian/San Angelo Ind School Dist	58	364
Underwood, Jay/Anna Ind School Dist	15,68,79	77
Underwood, Matt/Stephenville Ind School Dist	1	144
Underwood, Mickey/Wink Loving Ind School Dist	4	402
Underwood, Rala/Highland Park Ind School Dist	38	319
Underwood, Tommy/Quinlan Ind School Dist	3,5,7,91	237
Underwood, Wesley/San Angelo Ind School Dist	8,18	364
Ungerwood, Sandra/Aubrey Ind School Dist	83,85	120
Unterbrink, Karen/Riviera Ind School Dist	1	258
Upchurch, Carole/Maypearl Ind School Dist	73,295	141
Upchurch, Pam/Queen City Ind School Dist	3,5	70
Upchurch, Sally/Clint Ind School Dist	91	132
Upchurch, Tiffony/Quinlan Ind School Dist	71	237
Upshaw, Sandra/Laneville Ind School Dist	2	327
Uptmore, Patrick/Waco Ind School Dist	74,273	281
Uranga, Natalie/Clear Creek Ind School Dist	36	158
Urban, Paul/Liberty Hill Ind School Dist	76	398
Urbanczyk, James/Floresville Ind School Dist	73,295,297	400
Urbanek, Kevin/Boling Ind School Dist	6	389
Urbano, John/Victoria Ind School Dist	3,91	382
Urbanovsky, Eugene/Milano Ind School Dist	5	287
Urias, Amanda/Kermit Ind School Dist	31,36,270	401
Uribe-Center, Laura/Lytle Ind School Dist	11,68,296,298	21
Uribe, Eugenia/Garrison Ind School Dist	36,57,85	297
Uriegas, Michael/Carrizo Spgs Cons Ind SD	33,68,78,79,91	127
Uriegas, Sandra/Carrizo Spgs Cons Ind SD	11,57	127
Urquizo, Nora/Crowell Ind School Dist	4	149
Urrabazo, Salvadore/Stockdale Ind School Dist	67	401
Urrabazo, Theresa/San Antonio Ind School Dist	69,70,294	39
Uselman, Jeffrey/Round Rock Ind School Dist	16,73,82,286	398
Usery, Jacob/Venus Ind School Dist	295	249
Utech, Travis/Willis Ind School Dist	27,31	294
Uttley, Paul, Dr/Paradise Ind School Dist	1	403

V

NAME/District	JOB FUNCTIONS	PAGE
Vacha, Emily/Snook Ind School Dist	7,35	59
Vaden, Barbara/Lingleville Ind School Dist	16,82	143
Vaden, Kallen/Temple Ind School Dist	2,19	29
Vader, Erin/Diocese of Fort Worth Ed Off	8,70	358
Vahalik, Johnny/San Antonio Ind School Dist	27,31	39
Valacios, Francis/Pharr-San Juan-Alamo Ind SD	69	223
Valderrama, Monica/San Antonio Ind School Dist	57	39
Valdespino, Luis/Arlington Ind School Dist	752	343
Valdez, Criselda/Garland Ind School Dist	9	105
Valdez, Gina/Flour Bluff Ind School Dist	4	304
Valdez, Jane/Eagle Mtn-Saginaw Ind Sch Dist	2	348
Valdez, Jennifer/Alvin Ind School Dist	8,15,37,270	50
Valdez, Marcel/La Pryor Ind School Dist	67	407
Valdez, Rick/Somerset Ind School Dist	91	42
Valdez, Victor/Pflugerville Ind School Dist	16,73,76,295	371
Valdonado, Mary/Brownfield Ind Sch Dist	271	362
Valencia, Albert/Ector Co Ind School Dist	2	129
Valencia, Michael/McCamey Ind School Dist	10	377
Valenta, Rich, Dr/Denton Ind School Dist	15,751	120
Valentine, Jason/Wimberley Ind School Dist	285	212
Valenzuela, Beatriz/Sabinal Ind School Dist	38	378
Valenzuela, Luis/McCamey Ind School Dist	3	377
Valenzuela, Thomas/Crane Ind School Dist	73,295	93
Valeriano, Laura/Sonora Ind School Dist	54	342
Valeriano, Rene/Reagan Co Ind School Dist	83,88	321
Vallejo, Adan/Mercedes Ind School Dist	5	221
Vallejo, Pete/Edcouch Elsa Ind School Dist	16	215
Valles, Ruben/Seagraves Ind School Dist	3,5	157
Valverde, Yirah/Canutillo Ind School Dist	45	132
Van Deaver, Tommy/Maud Ind School Dist	2	49
Van Dyke, Pamela/Eanes Ind School Dist	297	370
Van Fussen, Darren/Devine Ind School Dist	3	283
Van Geem, Edgar/Flour Bluff Ind School Dist	58,77	304
Van Hoose, Dick/Tahoka Ind School Dist	1	273
Van Meter, Trent/Guthrie Common School Dist	73,295	257
Van Ness, Albert/Refugio Ind School Dist	3	323
Van Pelt, Deena/Hardin Jefferson Ind Sch Dist	58	177
Van Pelt, Jennifer/Midway Ind School Dist	2	74
Van Ravensway, Pam/Brownsville Ind School Dist	69,70	63
Van Remmen, Monica/Santo Ind School Dist	57	310
Van Winkle, Chad/Cleburne Ind School Dist	5	247
VanAuken, Jeff/Nixon-Smiley Cons Ind Sch Dist	2,3,5	164
Vance, Cynthia/Union Grove Ind School Dist	4	377
VanCleave, Mason/Hamlin Ind School Dist	67	249
VanCleave, Tim/Robinson Ind School Dist	11,15	281
Vandagriff, Mindi/Aledo Ind School Dist	73,286	77
Vandaveer, Sandra/Sweeny Ind School Dist	58	54
Vandeaver, Pamela/Clarksville Ind School Dist	2,3	322
Vandeaver, Pamela/Mt Vernon Ind School Dist	2	155
Vanderbrook, Catherine/New Braunfels Ind School Dist	4	88
Vanderpool, Stephen/Groom Ind School Dist	8,57,69,275	69
Vandersthaas, Stacy/Quitman Ind School Dist	7	404
Vanderveer, Sean/Sherman Ind School Dist	297	167
Vandervoort, Jessica/Clear Creek Ind School Dist	297	158
Vandeventer, Melissa/Dayton Ind School Dist	2	265
Vandever, John/Texas City Ind School Dist	4	161
Vanley, Nancy/Ector Co Ind School Dist	36	129
Vanmatre, Stephen/Premont Ind School Dist	1,11,288	246
VanMeter, Kalli/Pine Tree Ind School Dist	58	170
Vann, Leslie/Boyd Ind School Dist	1	402
Vannatta, Kelley/Whitehouse Ind School Dist	68	339
Vanover, Finis/Livingston Ind School Dist	6	317
Vanpelt, Beena/Orangefield Ind School Dist	8	309
Vanya, Gary/Hemphill Ind School Dist	6,35	329

DISTRICT PERSONNEL INDEX

Market Data Retrieval

NAME/District	JOB FUNCTIONS	PAGE
Vanzant, Michelle/Krum Ind School Dist	38	122
Vardeman, Rachel/Agua Dulce Ind School Dist	8,11,57,58,69,270	302
Vardeman, Weldonna/Hubbard Ind School Dist	8	227
Vargas-Lew, Linda/Edgewood Ind School Dist	36,78,90	31
Vargas, Carlos/London Ind School Dist	3,5	305
Vargas, Christina/Lasara Ind School Dist	58	394
Vargas, Emilio/Wharton Ind School Dist	3,15	390
Vargas, Irene/Ft Stockton Ind School Dist	271	315
Vargas, Michael/San Benito Cons Ind Sch Dist	67	67
Vargus, Ludy/Crockett Co Cons Common SD	4	94
Varnum, Pam/Pilot Point Ind School Dist	5	125
Varvel, Dennis/Franklin Ind School Dist	67	325
Vaso, Maria/Leander Ind School Dist	61	396
Vasquez, Amador/Lubbock Ind School Dist	45	269
Vasquez, Annette/Driscoll Ind School Dist	2,11	304
Vasquez, Bruno/Canutillo Ind School Dist	3,5	131
Vasquez, Charity/Region 15 Ed Service Center	2	366
Vasquez, Danny/Driscoll Ind School Dist	6	304
Vasquez, Erika/Alice Ind School Dist	42	245
Vasquez, Jill/Wylie Ind School Dist	11,57,271	84
Vasquez, Joe/Los Fresnos Cons Ind Sch Dist	91	66
Vasquez, Laura/Somerset Ind School Dist	5	42
Vasquez, Martha/San Antonio Ind School Dist	61	39
Vasquez, Maury/Somerset Ind School Dist	71	42
Vasquez, Ray/Presidio Ind School Dist	1	320
Vasquez, Roberto/Elgin Ind School Dist	7,91	24
Vasquez, Rosa/Grandfalls-Royalty Ind SD	4	385
Vasquez, Teresa/Kennedale Ind School Dist	7	355
Vaszauskas, Jim, Dr/Mansfield Ind School Dist	1	356
Vaugh, Denice/Cooper Ind School Dist	3	119
Vaughan, Kevin/Andrews Ind School Dist	8,30,58,88,273	16
Vaughan, Lisa/Goose Creek Cons Ind Sch Dist	90	187
Vaughn, Blake/Frisco Ind School Dist	3	78
Vaughn, Jan/North Hopkins Ind School Dist	2	231
Vaughn, Juhree/Windthorst Ind School Dist	2	20
Vaughn, Patricia/Grand Saline Ind School Dist	4	380
Vaughn, Shauni/Wylie Ind School Dist	58,271	361
Vazques, Christina/Lockhart Ind School Dist	57,271	61
Vazquez-Cruz, Juan/Edgewood Ind School Dist	73	31
Vazquez, Gilbert/San Felipe-Del Rio Cons Ind SD	295	379
Vazquez, Lawanda/Apple Springs Ind School Dist	73,76,98	374
Veal-Gooch, Tina/Texarkana Ind School Dist	71	50
Veal, Heidi/Lewisville Ind School Dist	34	122
Vega-Barrio, Rosy/Tornillo Ind School Dist	1	137
Vega, Albert/Canutillo Ind School Dist	286	132
Vega, Erica/Carrizo Spgs Cons Ind SD	4	127
Vega, Jennyann/McAllen Ind School Dist	16,73,82	221
Vega, Judy/McKinney Ind School Dist	49	81
Vega, Nelly/Madisonville Cons ISD	4	273
Vega, Roy/Lasara Ind School Dist	6	394
Vegara, Kathy/Klein Ind School Dist	57,89	196
Vela, Alfredo/Cotulla Ind School Dist	2,5	259
Vela, Alfredo/La Joya Ind School Dist	2,15	219
Vela, Dolores/Austwell Tivoli Ind SD	1	323
Vela, Gilbert/Lyford Cons Ind School Dist	3,5	394
Vela, Librada/San Diego Ind School Dist	67	128
Vela, Queta/Comstock Ind School Dist	4	379
Velazquez, Rolando/Lasara Ind School Dist	67	394
Velazquez, Samaris/Stockdale Ind School Dist	4	401
Velez, Luis/Eagle Pass Ind School Dist	2	276
Veliz, Ramiro/United Ind School Dist	67	387
Vella, Nilda/Seguin Ind School Dist	42	173
Veloz-Powell, Elizabeth, Dr/Alief Ind School Dist	15,68	181
Veno, Tiffany/Garland Ind School Dist	71	105
Ventura, Juan/Pearsall Ind School Dist	5	157
Vera, Daniel/Manor Ind School Dist	68	371
Vera, Javier/United Ind School Dist	20,23	387
Vera, Manuel/West Orange-Cove Cons ISD	5	309
Verduzco, Manuel/Clint Ind School Dist	73,98	132
Vereecke, Matthew, Dr/Diocese of Dallas Ed Office	1	113
Verell, Martina/Beeville Ind School Dist	11	25
Vergo, Donna/Joaquin Ind School Dist	68	335
Verley, Craig/Mission Cons Ind School Dist	71	222
Vernon, Kelly/Perryton Ind School Dist	11	307
Verrett, Lachlin, Dr/Houston Ind School Dist	15,58	188
Verstuyft, Lloyd, Dr/Southwest Ind School Dist	1	43
Verver, Mary/Tulia Ind School Dist	271	343
Vervin, Antonia/Mathis Ind School Dist	16,73	331
Vesely, Todd/Ft Worth Ind School Dist	6	349
Vessels, Ruth/Hereford Ind School Dist	57	119
Vessling, David/Pflugerville Ind School Dist	3	371
Vestal, Ajck/Lovejoy Ind School Dist	98	80
Vestal, Ian/Temple Ind School Dist	4	29
Vestal, Tiffany/Temple Ind School Dist	69,294	29
Vezurk, Blake/Anderson-Shiro Cons Ind SD	2	171
Vick, Christen/Palmer Ind School Dist	67	141
Vickers, Melissa/Woodson Ind School Dist	2,298	363
Vickery, Traci/Garland Ind School Dist	46	105
Vickman, Ann/South Texas Ind School Dist	16	67
Victory, Travis/Clarendon Cons Ind Sch Dist	8	127
Vidaurri, Maria, Dr/Sharyland Ind School Dist	1	224
Vieregge, Rick/Malakoff Ind School Dist	67	214
Vierra, Annette/Round Rock Ind School Dist	68	398
Viertel, Jay/Beeville Ind School Dist	27,36	25
Vies, Marcella, Dr/San Marcos Cons Ind Sch Dist	15,68	211
Vigil, Kelly/Pampa Ind School Dist	16	165
Vigtema, Jackie/Whitehouse Ind School Dist	11,58,271	338
Vijil, Veronica, Dr/Fabens Ind School Dist	1	135
Vilema, Francis/Eagle Pass Ind School Dist	39,42	276
Villa, Diana/Andrews Ind School Dist	68	16
Villafranca, Robert/Somerset Ind School Dist	3,15,79	42
Villagomez, Roxann/United Ind School Dist	274	387
Villalba, Joseph/Goose Creek Cons Ind Sch Dist	2	187
Villalobos, Claudia/Rio Hondo Ind School Dist	67	66
Villaneda, Selena/Ingleside Ind School Dist	16	331
Villanueva, Cheryl/Godley Ind School Dist	31,57,69	247
Villanueva, Connie/Monte Alto Ind School Dist	67	222
Villanueva, Diane/Donna Ind School Dist	58,77,275	215
Villanueva, Gustavo/Abilene Ind School Dist	10,15,27,31	360
Villanueva, Joe/Olton Ind School Dist	3	261
Villareal, Irma/Edinburg Cons Ind School Dist	12	216
Villareal, Joseph/Harlingen Cons Ind School Dist	10	64
Villareal, Ricardo/La Joya Ind School Dist	15,79	219
Villarreal, Adelina/Rio Grande City Ind Sch Dist	27	340
Villarreal, Alicia, Dr/Somerset Ind School ISD	48,51	42
Villarreal, Dan/North East Ind School Dist	2,15,19	34
Villarreal, Ernie/Valentine Ind School Dist	2	241
Villarreal, George/Bovina Ind School Dist	67	314
Villarreal, Heriberto/Santa Rosa Ind School Dist	11,73	67
Villarreal, Hildeliza/Zapata Co Ind School Dist	8	406
Villarreal, Jennifer/Hidalgo Ind School Dist	16	217
Villarreal, John, Dr/Rockwall Ind School Dist	1	325
Villarreal, Juan/South Texas Ind School Dist	3,5,91	67
Villarreal, Laura Zelda/Brownsville Ind School Dist	4	63
Villarreal, Melissa/Sinton Ind School Dist	2,15	332
Villarreal, Nelida/Edinburg Cons Ind School Dist	20,23	216
Villarreal, Rebecca/New Braunfels Ind School Dist	71	88
Villarreal, Richard/Bovina Ind School Dist	3,5	314
Villarreal, Viki/Clifton Ind School Dist	57	46
Villegas, Omar/Lorenzo Ind School Dist	3	94
Villerot, Annette/Del Valle Ind School Dist	1	369
Villiarreal, Sandra Ann/La Joya Ind School Dist	81	219
Vincek, Jamie/Lamar Cons Ind School Dist	74,273	153
Vincelette, Melanie/Lewisville Ind School Dist	7	122

1 Superintendent	16 Instructional Media Svcs	30 Adult Education	44 Science Sec	58 Special Education K-12	72 Summer School
2 Bus/Finance/Purchasing	17 Chief Operations Officer	31 Career/Sch-to-Work K-12	45 Math K-12	59 Special Education Elem	73 Instructional Tech
3 Buildings And Grounds	18 Chief Academic Officer	32 Career/Sch-to-Work Elem	46 Math Elem	60 Special Education Sec	74 Inservice Training
4 Food Service	19 Chief Financial Officer	33 Career/Sch-to-Work Sec	47 Math Sec	61 Foreign/World Lang K-12	75 Marketing/Distributive
5 Transportation	20 Art K-12	34 Early Childhood Ed	48 English/Lang Arts K-12	62 Foreign/World Lang Elem	76 Info Systems
6 Athletic	21 Art Elem	35 Health/Phys Education	49 English/Lang Arts Elem	63 Foreign/World Lang Sec	77 Psychological Assess
7 Health Services	22 Art Sec	36 Guidance Services K-12	50 English/Lang Arts Sec	64 Religious Education K-12	78 Affirmative Action
8 Curric/Instruct K-12	23 Music K-12	37 Guidance Services Elem	51 Reading K-12	65 Religious Education Elem	79 Student Personnel
9 Curric/Instruct Elem	24 Music Elem	38 Guidance Services Sec	52 Reading Elem	66 Religious Education Sec	80 Driver Ed/Safety
10 Curric/Instruct Sec	25 Music Sec	39 Social Studies K-12	53 Reading Sec	67 School Board President	81 Gifted/Talented
11 Federal Program	26 Business Education	40 Social Studies Elem	54 Remedial Reading K-12	68 Teacher Personnel	82 Video Services
12 Title I	27 Career & Tech Ed	41 Social Studies Sec	55 Remedial Reading Elem	69 Academic Assessment	83 Substance Abuse Prev
13 Title V	28 Technology Education	42 Science K-12	56 Remedial Reading Sec	70 Research/Development	84 Erate
15 Asst Superintendent	29 Family/Consumer Science	43 Science Elem	57 Bilingual/ELL	71 Public Information	85 AIDS Education
88 Alternative/At Risk	277 Remedial Math K-12
89 Multi-Cultural Curriculum	280 Literacy Coach
90 Social Work	285 STEM
91 Safety/Security	286 Digital Learning
92 Magnet School	288 Common Core Standards
95 Parental Involvement	294 Accountability
95 Tech Prep Program	295 Network System
97 Chief Information Officer	296 Title II Programs
98 Chief Technology Officer	297 Webmaster
270 Character Education	298 Grant Writer/Ptnrships
271 Migrant Education	750 Chief Innovation Officer
273 Teacher Mentor	751 Chief of Staff
274 Before/After Sch	752 Social Emotional Learning
275 Response To Intervention	

Texas School Directory

DISTRICT PERSONNEL INDEX

NAME/District	JOB FUNCTIONS	PAGE
Vincent, David/*Princeton Ind School Dist*	73	84
Vincent, Debra/*Northside Ind School Dist*	4	393
Vincent, Scott/*Hartley Ind School Dist*	1	209
Vincik, Sherri/*Shiner Ind School Dist*	2,11	262
Vine, Kim, Dr/*Port Arthur Ind School Dist*	8	243
Vineyard, Shelley/*Humble Ind School Dist*	2	195
Vinson, Allison/*Birdville Ind School Dist*	27,30,31,73	346
Vinson, David, Dr/*Wylie Ind School Dist*	1	84
Vinson, Logan/*Anson Ind School Dist*	3,5	249
Vinton, Kim/*Region 20 Ed Service Center*	30	45
Virdell, Keith/*Goldthwaite Consolidated ISD*	6	288
Vivreet, Mary Ellen/*Vidor Ind School Dist*	4	309
Voan, Jennifer/*Sam Rayburn Ind School Dist*	38	146
Voelcker, Wanda/*Mineral Wells Ind School Dist*	7,35,85	310
Voelkel, Carla/*Dickinson Ind School Dist*	1	159
Vogelpohl, Margo/*Round Rock Ind School Dist*	12	398
Voights-Pettit, Tiffany/*Baird Ind School Dist*	4	62
Volger, Doyle/*Lubbock Ind School Dist*	9,15	269
Volkmer, Lisa/*Bay City Ind School Dist*	11,57,271,273,296	275
Volmer, Christie/*Hereford Ind School Dist*	68	119
Volz, Darlene/*San Antonio Ind School Dist*	30	39
Von Borstel, Lisa/*Itasca Ind School Dist*	8,11	228
Vondersaar, Laurie/*Leander Ind School Dist*	15,73,76,295	396
Voradakis, Susan/*Ft Bend Ind School Dist*	10	149
Voss, Serena/*Post Ind School Dist*	38,83,88	162
Voth, Michael/*Lovejoy Ind School Dist*	73	80
Vrooman, Sabrina/*Diocese of Beaumont Sch Office*	2,19	244
Vroonland, David, Dr/*Mesquite Ind School Dist*	1	110
Vu, Arthur/*Harris Co Dept of Ed*	73	179
Vu, Julie, Dr/*Kennedale Ind School Dist*	15	355
Vuittonet, Dianna/*Kress Ind School Dist*	2	343
Vurner, Brett/*Nueces Canyon Cons Ind SD*	16,73,298	131

W

NAME/District	JOB FUNCTIONS	PAGE
Wacker, Susie/*Randolph Field Ind School Dist*	7	39
Waclawczyk, Janlen/*Judson Ind School Dist*	76	33
Waddle, Dawn/*Palmer Ind School Dist*	6	141
Wade, Chris/*Ralls Ind School Dist*	1	94
Wade, Cindi/*Dripping Springs Ind Sch Dist*	84	210
Wade, Cynthia/*May Ind School Dist*	16	59
Wade, Joyce/*Liberty-Eylau Ind School Dist*	5	48
Wade, Melissa/*Frenship Ind School Dist*	11,85	269
Wade, Rhonda, Dr/*Floresville Ind School Dist*	8,36	400
Wade, Tommy/*Jacksonville Ind School Dist*	3,91	72
Wadleigh, Linda, Dr/*La Porte Ind School Dist*	8,15	198
Wager, Sharon/*New Diana Ind School Dist*	73,295	376
Waggoner, Jacob/*Gunter Ind School Dist*	38,83	166
Waggoner, Peggy/*Hico Ind School Dist*	4	176
Wagner, Bill/*La Grange Ind School Dist*	1	147
Wagner, Dennis/*Anahuac Ind School Dist*	1	71
Wagner, Donald/*Diocese of Fort Worth Ed Off*	2,19	358
Wagner, Helen/*Humble Ind School Dist*	35	195
Wagner, Jeremy/*Lubbock-Cooper Ind Sch Dist*	285	271
Wagner, Mark/*Hamshire Fannett Ind Sch Dist*	6,35	242
Wagner, Pam/*Louise Ind School Dist*	2	389
Wagner, Peter/*Southwest Ind School Dist*	6	43
Wagner, Rena/*Winnsboro Ind School Dist*	57	405
Wagner, Shane/*Sweet Home Ind School Dist*	1,11,73,83,84	262
Waide, Paige/*Perryton Ind School Dist*	38	307
Wainscott, Sharon/*Knox City-O'Brien Cons Ind SD*	68	258
Waites, Kanesha, Dr/*Lancaster Ind School Dist*	93	110
Wakefield, Bill/*Bonham Ind School Dist*	3,91	145
Wakeland, Sherri/*Frisco Ind School Dist*	74	78
Walden, Daniel/*Donna Ind School Dist*	91	215
Walden, Lydia/*Highland Park Ind Sch Dist*	36,77,83,88	108
Walden, Steve/*Quinlan Ind School Dist*	91	237
Waldie, Michael/*Gonzales Ind School Dist*	6,35	164
Waldo, Glen/*Nazareth Ind School Dist*	1,11,84,288	71
Waldo, Toni/*Vernon Ind School Dist*	58,275,286	393
Waldrep, Jackie/*Westbrook Ind School Dist*	4	289
Waldrep, Terry/*Pittsburg Ind School Dist*	1	68
Waldrip, Aaron/*Abernathy Ind School Dist*	1	174
Waldrip, Mike, Dr/*Frisco Ind School Dist*	1	78
Waldron, Joseph/*Abilene Ind School Dist*	15,68	360
Waldrop, Colby/*Farwell Ind School Dist*	1	314
Waligura, Leann/*Leakey Ind School Dist*	4	322

NAME/District	JOB FUNCTIONS	PAGE
Walinder, Kari/*Andrews Ind School Dist*	67	16
Walker, Adrienne/*Birdville Ind School Dist*	11,296,298	346
Walker, Amy/*Springtown Ind School Dist*	67	313
Walker, Andre/*Houston Ind School Dist*	6	188
Walker, Angela/*Liberty Ind School Dist*	79	266
Walker, Becky/*Comal Ind School Dist*	27,31,95	87
Walker, Belinda/*West Rusk Co Cons Ind Sch Dist*	2	328
Walker, Christie/*Bowie Ind School Dist*	8,11,57,58,77,88,288,294	289
Walker, Clay/*Little Elm Ind School Dist*	295	124
Walker, Cody/*West Rusk Co Cons Ind Sch Dist*	73,295	328
Walker, Darlene/*Canadian Ind School Dist*	38	213
Walker, David/*Gholson Ind School Dist*	67	279
Walker, David, Dr/*Christoval Ind School Dist*	1	364
Walker, Debbie/*Willis Ind School Dist*	58	294
Walker, Diane/*Everman Ind School Dist*	58	349
Walker, Doretta/*North East Ind School Dist*	295	34
Walker, Fred/*Clear Creek Ind School Dist*	4	158
Walker, Gina/*Hunt Ind School Dist*	2,4	255
Walker, Jeff/*Liberty Hill Ind School Dist*	6,35,85	398
Walker, Jenny/*Olney Ind School Dist*	68	406
Walker, Jimmie, Dr/*Alamo Heights Ind School Dist*	8,81	30
Walker, Joe/*Godley Ind School Dist*	20,23	247
Walker, John/*Commerce Independent Sch Dist*	2	236
Walker, Karrie/*Hays Cons Ind School Dist*	7,85	211
Walker, Kerri/*Bastrop Ind School Dist*	39	23
Walker, Laura/*Tolar Ind School Dist*	73,295	230
Walker, Laurie/*Ennis Ind School Dist*	2,11	140
Walker, Lee/*Muleshoe Ind School Dist*	6	22
Walker, Marcie/*Joshua Ind School Dist*	7	248
Walker, Marcus/*Huntsville Ind School Dist*	27	383
Walker, Maria/*Panhandle Ind School Dist*	57	69
Walker, Mark/*Cleburne Ind School Dist*	6	247
Walker, Marybel/*Hunt Ind School Dist*	3	255
Walker, Michele/*Pine Tree Ind School Dist*	11,57	170
Walker, Rhonda/*Lindale Ind School Dist*	16	337
Walker, Sam/*Lampasas Ind School Dist*	67	261
Walker, Shelli/*Perryton Ind School Dist*	4	307
Walker, Stacy/*Prairiland Ind School Dist*	16,82	260
Walker, Terri/*Katy Ind School Dist*	275	151
Walker, Tiffany/*Georgetown Ind School Dist*	11,57,58,271,285,296	395
Walker, Tyra/*Alief Ind School Dist*	36	181
Walker, Valerie/*School of Excellence In Ed*	285	42
Walker, Whitney/*Lampasas Ind School Dist*	79	261
Wall, Delinda/*Gilmer Ind School Dist*	8,57,83,271	376
Wall, Leigh, Dr/*Santa Fe Ind School Dist*	1	161
Wall, Mike/*Willis Ind School Dist*	6	294
Wall, Missy/*Rockwall Ind School Dist*	90	325
Wall, Murray/*Broaddus Ind School Dist*	5	329
Wall, Valerie/*Pilot Point Ind School Dist*	73,295	125
Walla, Melisa/*Anderson-Shiro Cons Ind SD*	83	171
Wallace, Amanda/*Henderson Ind School Dist*	68,71	327
Wallace, Andrew/*Edna Ind School Dist*	16	239
Wallace, Connie/*Arlington Ind School Dist*	8	343
Wallace, Denise/*Region 5 Ed Service Center*	2	244
Wallace, Donna, Dr/*Van Ind School Dist*	8,54,69,288,294,296	381
Wallace, Jeanne/*Iredell Ind School Dist*	58	46
Wallace, Jeremy/*Center Ind School Dist*	88	334
Wallace, Jerred/*West Sabine Ind Sch Dist*	6	329
Wallace, Ken/*Paint Creek Ind School Dist*	8	210
Wallace, Mike/*Cleburne Ind School Dist*	73	247
Wallace, Mike/*Livingston Ind School Dist*	295	317
Wallace, Payton/*Meridian Ind School Dist*	67	47
Wallace, Shannon/*Shepherd Ind School Dist*	58	330
Wallace, Steven/*Electra Ind School Dist*	9,54	391
Wallace, Todd/*Quinlan Ind School Dist*	6	237
Wallace, Verlene/*Hunt Ind School Dist*	36,69,88,271	255
Wallen, Jason/*Maypearl Ind School Dist*	6,83,270	141
Waller, Don/*Groesbeck Ind School Dist*	295	267
Waller, Jim/*Idalou Ind School Dist*	1,84	269
Waller, Jimmie/*Leveretts Chapel Ind Sch Dist*	67	328
Waller, Mong/*Martinsville Ind School Dist*	11,36,83,85	298
Waller, Nina/*Lubbock Ind School Dist*	2	269
Waller, Rebecca/*Red Oak Ind School Dist*	8	142
Walling, Judy/*Midlothian Ind School Dist*	15	141
Walls, Elizabeth/*Moran Ind School Dist*	58,83	334
Walls, Kayla/*Huckabay Ind School Dist*	6	143

School Year 2019-2020   800-333-8802   TX-T95

DISTRICT PERSONNEL INDEX

Market Data Retrieval

NAME/District	JOB FUNCTIONS	PAGE
Walsh, Tim, Dr/Willis Ind School Dist	79	294
Walsh, Todd/Giddings Ind School Dist	73,295	263
Walter, Brian/Dalhart Ind School Dist	2,19	95
Walter, Dianna/Hubbard Ind School Dist	4	227
Walters, Bart/Rockwall Ind School Dist	27,31	325
Walters, Guy/Center Point Ind School Dist	6	255
Walters, Hayden/Westbrook Ind School Dist	58	289
Walters, Kelly/Rice Ind School Dist	9	300
Walters, LaVelle/Santa Anna Ind School Dist	4	76
Walterscheid, Rick/Goose Creek Cons Ind Sch Dist	5	187
Waltman, Gary/Paducah Ind School Dist	1	93
Walton, Terry/Shelbyville Ind School Dist	3	335
Waltz, Justin/New Boston Ind School Dist	6	49
Wamble, Lori/Brenham Ind School Dist	81	385
Wampler, Lana/City View Ind School Dist	76	391
Wanjura, Christina/Diocese of Amarillo Ed Office	1	319
Wanjura, Christine/Diocese of Lubbock Ed Office	1	272
Wanjura, Sarah/Columbus Ind School Dist	58	86
Ward, Angela/La Vega Ind School Dist	58	279
Ward, Brenda, Dr/Northside Ind School Dist	69,294	36
Ward, Bryan/Cedar Hill Ind School Dist	69	97
Ward, Johnita/Tyler Ind School Dist	69,294	337
Ward, Kermit/Clarksville Ind School Dist	1	322
Ward, Misty/Collinsville Ind School Dist	8,11,296,298	166
Ward, Randel/Alvarado Ind School Dist	3	246
Ward, Rhonda/Katy Ind School Dist	15,74,77,79,83	151
Ward, Robert/Liberty Ind School Dist	5	266
Ward, Stacey/Prairie Valley Ind School Dist	73	290
Ward, Stacy/Lockney Independent Sch Dist	6	149
Ward, Terry/Grapeland Ind School Dist	6	232
Ward, Terry/Harleton Ind School Dist	6	208
Ward, Terry/Harmony Ind School Dist	4	376
Ward, Terry/Northwest Ind School Dist	44	124
Ward, Zach/City View Ind School Dist	27	391
Wardlaw, Mona/Seymour Ind School Dist	58	25
Ware, Angie/Wheeler Ind School Dist	27	391
Ware, Dee/Lorenzo Ind School Dist	5	94
Wargo, Kyle/Region 17 Ed Service Center	1,11	272
Warnasch, Justin/Tomball Ind School Dist	71	203
Warner, Greta/Poteet Ind School Dist	11	21
Warner, Jessica/Marshall Ind School Dist	2	209
Warnke, Kirby/Corpus Christi Ind Sch Dist	91	303
Warnock, Georgeann/Carrollton-Farmers Branch ISD	8,15,74,286	96
Warnock, Jim/Roosevelt Ind School Dist	67	271
Warren, Audrey/Stephenville Ind School Dist	80	144
Warren, Carol/Eustace Ind School Dist	2	214
Warren, Dallis/Lamar Cons Ind School Dist	91	153
Warren, Doug/Wimberley Ind School Dist	6	212
Warren, Erin/Luling Ind School Dist	1,11	61
Warren, Jana/Academy Ind School Dist	37	26
Warren, Joe/Gainesville Ind School Dist	3	91
Warren, Joni/Spring Branch Ind School Dist	58	200
Warren, Rachelle, Dr/Belton Ind School Dist	752	26
Warren, Ryder, Dr/Northwest Ind School Dist	1	124
Warren, Sheri/Kress Ind School Dist	58	343
Warren, Trip/Caldwell Ind School Dist	67	59
Warshaw, Peter/Leander Ind School Dist	20,23	396
Warsing, Mark/Littlefield Ind School Dist	3	260
Warstler, Scott/Frisco Ind School Dist	2	78
Warwick, Helen/Marshall Ind School Dist	67	209
Warzon, Molly/Waller Ind School Dist	4	384
Washam, Wes/Robert Lee Ind School Dist	67	75
Washburn, Todd/Eanes Ind School Dist	8,15,36,275	370
Washington, Cherie, Dr/Ft Worth Ind School Dist	15	349
Washington, Lachele/Lancaster Ind School Dist	275	110
Washington, Yvette/Spring Ind School Dist	2	202
Watassek, Meredith/Ft Bend Ind School Dist	27	149
Waterhouse, Richard/Premont Ind School Dist	67	246
Waters, Brenda, Dr/Pearland Ind School Dist	9,15	53
Waters, David/Nocona Ind School Dist	1	290
Waters, Kelly/El Campo Ind School Dist	1	389
Waters, Kristi/Highland Park Ind School Dist	58	319
Waters, Philo, Dr/Eagle Mtn-Saginaw Ind Sch Dist	68	348
Waters, Walter/Nocona Ind School Dist	4	290
Watkins, Cliff/Glen Rose Ind School Dist	6	340
Watkins, Drew, Dr/Prosper Ind School Dist	1	84
Watkins, Jennifer/Llano Ind School Dist	37	268
Watkins, Scott/Terlingua Common School Dist	67	57
Watley, Delia/Irving Ind School Dist	30	109
Watsmen, Wade/Tyler Ind School Dist	67	337
Watson, Angie/Bushland Ind School Dist	8,11,15,74,296	319
Watson, Annette/Goldthwaite Consolidated ISD	286	288
Watson, Bill/Lewisville Ind School Dist	20,23	122
Watson, Billy/Leonard Ind School Dist	67	146
Watson, Brandi/Henrietta Ind School Dist	88,270	74
Watson, Buddy/DeSoto Ind School Dist	295,297	104
Watson, Casey/Douglass Ind School Dist	2	297
Watson, Craig/Mt Vernon Ind School Dist	58	155
Watson, Danielle/Borger Ind School Dist	38	237
Watson, Diana/McLean Ind School Dist	57	165
Watson, Donna/Evant Ind School Dist	7	92
Watson, Dwight/Yoakum Ind School Dist	5	118
Watson, Elise/Leon Ind School Dist	31,36,69	264
Watson, Heather/Vidor Ind School Dist	39,48	309
Watson, James/Tomball Ind School Dist	28,95	203
Watson, Jamie/Leon Ind School Dist	2,298	264
Watson, Jim/Denton Ind School Dist	5	120
Watson, Josh/Spur Ind School Dist	16,73	127
Watson, Josh/Spur Ind School Dist	16,73	127
Watson, June/Winters Ind School Dist	4	327
Watson, Karleen/Lancaster Ind School Dist	7	110
Watson, Kelli/Lancaster Ind School Dist	73	110
Watson, Kimberly/Latexo Ind School Dist	69	233
Watson, Leslie/Goldthwaite Consolidated ISD	7,85	288
Watson, Natasha, Dr/Spring Ind School Dist	15	202
Watson, Nyla, Dr/Pearland Ind School Dist	8,15,77,273	53
Watson, Rodney, Dr/Spring Ind School Dist	1,288	202
Watson, Teela/Region 11 Ed Service Center	70	360
Watson, Willie/Pflugerville Ind School Dist	68	371
Watts, Eva/Donna Ind School Dist	67	215
Watts, Mike/Leggett Ind School Dist	3,5	316
Wayman, Ric/Princeton Ind School Dist	5	84
Wayt, Chris/Union Grove Ind School Dist	3,5	377
Weatherall, Marcene/Keller Ind School Dist	83	354
Weatherbee, Johnna/Lubbock Ind School Dist	12,93	269
Weatherby, Kim/Brenham Ind School Dist	2	385
Weatherford, Brandon/Broaddus Ind School Dist	3	329
Weatherford, Gary/Ector Co Ind School Dist	3	129
Weatherford, Heather/Spring Creek Ind School Dist	57,58	238
Weatherly, Mark, Dr/New Caney Ind School Dist	10	293
Weaver, Brian/UT Tyler University Acad Dist	69	338
Weaver, Candice/Lazbuddie Ind School Dist	67	315
Weaver, Dandre/DeSoto Ind School Dist	1	104
Weaver, David/Marshall Ind School Dist	71	209
Weaver, Dawn/Collinsville Ind School Dist	7,85	166
Weaver, Dusty/Callisburg Ind School Dist	67	90
Weaver, Dwight/Duncanville Ind School Dist	6,35	104
Weaver, Jeff/Dublin Ind School Dist	67	143
Weaver, Mark/Aspermont Ind School Dist	6	342
Weaver, Michelle/Westphalia Ind School Dist	67	145
Weaver, Neal/Forney Ind School Dist	6	251
Weaver, Teresa/Martinsville Ind School Dist	67	298
Webb, Alexis/Prosper Ind School Dist	288	84
Webb, Beverly/Brownfield Ind Sch Dist	4	362

1 Superintendent	16 Instructional Media Svcs	30 Adult Education
2 Bus/Finance/Purchasing	17 Chief Operations Officer	31 Career/Sch-to-Work K-12
3 Buildings And Grounds	18 Chief Academic Officer	32 Career/Sch-to-Work Elem
4 Food Service	19 Chief Financial Officer	33 Career/Sch-to-Work Sec
5 Transportation	20 Art K-12	34 Early Childhood Ed
6 Athletic	21 Art Elem	35 Health/Phys Education
7 Health Services	22 Art Sec	36 Guidance Services K-12
8 Curric/Instruct K-12	23 Music K-12	37 Guidance Services Elem
9 Curric/Instruct Elem	24 Music Elem	38 Guidance Services Sec
10 Curric/Instruct Sec	25 Music Sec	39 Social Studies K-12
11 Federal Program	26 Business Education	40 Social Studies Elem
12 Title I	27 Career & Tech Ed	41 Social Studies Sec
13 Title V	28 Technology Education	42 Science K-12
15 Asst Superintendent	29 Family/Consumer Science	43 Science Elem
44 Science Sec	58 Special Education K-12	72 Summer School
45 Math K-12	59 Special Education Elem	73 Instructional Tech
46 Math Elem	60 Special Education Sec	74 Inservice Training
47 Math Sec	61 Foreign/World Lang K-12	75 Marketing/Distributive
48 English/Lang Arts K-12	62 Foreign/World Lang Elem	76 Info Systems
49 English/Lang Arts Elem	63 Foreign/World Lang Sec	77 Psychological Assess
50 English/Lang Arts Sec	64 Religious Education K-12	78 Affirmative Action
51 Reading K-12	65 Religious Education Elem	79 Student Personnel
52 Reading Elem	66 Religious Education Sec	80 Driver Ed/Safety
53 Reading Sec	67 School Board President	81 Gifted/Talented
54 Remedial Reading K-12	68 Teacher Personnel	82 Video Services
55 Remedial Reading Elem	69 Academic Assessment	83 Substance Abuse Prev
56 Remedial Reading Sec	70 Research/Development	84 Erate
57 Bilingual/ELL	71 Public Information	85 AIDS Education
88 Alternative/At Risk	277 Remedial Math K-12
89 Multi-Cultural Curriculum	280 Literacy Coach
90 Social Work	285 STEM
91 Safety/Security	286 Digital Learning
92 Magnet School	288 Common Core Standards
93 Parental Involvement	294 Accountability
95 Tech Prep Program	295 Network System
97 Chief Infomation Officer	296 Title II Programs
98 Chief Technology Officer	297 Webmaster
270 Character Education	298 Grant Writer/Ptnrships
271 Migrant Education	750 Chief Innovation Officer
273 Teacher Mentor	751 Chief of Staff
274 Before/After Sch	752 Social Emotional Learning
275 Response To Intervention	

Texas School Directory

DISTRICT PERSONNEL INDEX

NAME/District	JOB FUNCTIONS	PAGE
Webb, Daniel/Andrews Ind School Dist	3,15,91	16
Webb, Darren/Lago Vista Ind School Dist	1	370
Webb, Donny/Hudson Ind School Dist	1,11,57,83	17
Webb, Jeff/Royse City Ind School Dist	15,68,273	326
Webb, Kenny/Comfort Ind School Dist	5	254
Webb, Laurie/Bartlett Ind School Dist	8,11,36,88	26
Webb, Laurinda/Luling Ind School Dist	57,58	61
Webb, Mary/Frisco Ind School Dist	9	78
Webb, Matthew/Humble Ind School Dist	39	195
Webb, Michael, Dr/Tomball Ind School Dist	15	203
Webb, Patty/Joshua Ind School Dist	73	248
Webb, Randy/Malakoff Ind School Dist	73,95,295	214
Webb, Rick, Dr/Cayuga Ind School Dist	1,11,288	14
Webb, Shane/Gatesville Ind School Dist	10	92
Webb, Tracy/Union Grove Ind School Dist	58	377
Webber, Judy/Forney Ind School Dist	8,18,27,30,34,69	251
Webber, Shelly/Lockhart Ind School Dist	7	61
Weber, Joy/Wells Ind School Dist	58	73
Weber, Matthew, Dr/San Antonio Ind School Dist	15	39
Webster, Courtney/Manor Ind School Dist	39	371
Webster, James/Sheldon Ind School Dist	79,83	200
Webster, Kari/Canton Ind School Dist	76,79	380
Webster, Ron/Klein Ind School Dist	91	196
Weddell, Alan/Brazosport Ind School Dist	35	52
Weeks, Russell/Mesquite Ind School Dist	81	110
Weeks, William/Garrison Ind School Dist	16,73,84	297
Weems, Adriana/Winnsboro Ind School Dist	76	405
Weerasinghe, Dash, Dr/Plano Ind School Dist	69,70,294	82
Weger, Josh/Bells Ind School Dist	12	165
Weichel, Kristen/Royse City Ind School Dist	49	326
Weidler, Lance/Rockdale Ind School Dist	3	287
Weikert, Donna, Dr/Luling Ind School Dist	9	61
Weimer, Nanette/Pearland Ind School Dist	15	53
Weinkauf, Gene/Brownsboro Ind School Dist	4	213
Weir, Laura/Region 11 Ed Service Center	2	360
Weirich, Dwayne/Round Rock Ind School Dist	6	398
Weiser, Charlotte/Cisco Independent Sch Dist	16,73	128
Weiser, Charlotte/Cisco Independent Sch Dist	84	128
Weishuhn, Charlotte/Wall Ind School Dist	2	365
Weiss, Gregg, Dr/Silsbee Ind School Dist	1	178
Welch, Bruce/Cotton Center Ind School Dist	3	174
Welch, Chance/Borger Ind School Dist	1	237
Welch, Christie/Detroit Ind School Dist	36	322
Welch, Clete/Eagle Mtn-Saginaw Ind Sch Dist	3,5,17	348
Welch, Danny/Port Aransas Ind School Dist	69,83,85,93	305
Welch, Debbie/Burkburnett Ind Sch Dist	4	391
Welch, Deborah/Rusk Ind School Dist	9	73
Welch, Greg/Clyde Consolidated Ind SD	67	62
Welch, Janae/Deweyville Ind School Dist	2	308
Welch, Janet/Somerset Ind School Dist	4	42
Welch, Mary/Richardson Ind School Dist	68	112
Welch, Philip/Kountze Ind School Dist	2,19	178
Welch, Randy/Mabank Ind School Dist	5	252
Welch, Robb/Grand Prairie Ind School Dist	2,15	107
Welch, Robin/Wildorado Ind Sch Dist	57	308
Welch, Ron/Plains Ind School Dist	6	405
Welch, Tracy/Lake Worth Ind School Dist	6	356
Welker, Sandra/Centerville Ind School Dist	58	264
Wellborn, Harold/Kopperl Ind School Dist	67	47
Wells, Danyell/Cedar Hill Ind School Dist	93	97
Wells, Gina/Big Spring Ind School Dist	68	233
Wells, Jovan, Dr/Garland Ind School Dist	18,298	105
Wells, Pam, Dr/Region 4 Ed Service Center	1	208
Wells, Randi/Carrollton-Farmers Branch ISD	58	96
Wells, Scott/Lingleville Ind School Dist	8,57,88,274,286,288	143
Wells, Starlynn/Celina Ind School Dist	9,88,294	78
Welps, Bryan/River Road Ind School Dist	6	319
Wendel, Daryl/Devine Ind School Dist	8,15,68	283
Wendell, Cynthia/Danbury Ind School Dist	2	53
Wendland, Shelli/Bland Ind School Dist	8	235
Wenmohs, Shelly/Johnson City Ind School Dist	67	46
Wentz, Deanna/Alief Ind School Dist	2,15	181
Wenzel, Jana/Bryan Ind School Dist	73	54
Wermuth, Sharon/San Angelo Ind School Dist	76	364
Wesley, Cheryl/Cedar Hill Ind School Dist	67	97
Wesley, Wade/Jacksboro Ind Sch Dist	8,11,57,271,275,288,296,298	239

NAME/District	JOB FUNCTIONS	PAGE
Wesp, Pete/Randolph Field Ind School Dist	6	39
Wesson, Jay/San Marcos Cons Ind Sch Dist	3	211
West, Anthony/Burkburnett Ind Sch Dist	5	391
West, Brenda/Highland Park Ind Sch Dist	68	108
West, Brent/Cisco Independent Sch Dist	6	128
West, Byron/Henrietta Ind School Dist	6	74
West, Dale/Bells Ind School Dist	6	165
West, Dalton/Florence Ind School Dist	3	395
West, Dana, Dr/Region 10 Ed Service Center	8	116
West, Daniel/Dumas Ind School Dist	2,19	295
West, Filke/Sinton Ind School Dist	4	332
West, Gloria/Bullard Ind School Dist	2	336
West, Jim/Ore City Ind School Dist	3,5	376
West, Keith, Dr/Madisonville Cons ISD	15	273
West, Kelly/Alto Ind School Dist	1	72
West, Lila/Florence Ind School Dist	8	395
West, Marti/Archdiocese San Antonio Ed Off	1	44
West, Nicholas/Dime Box Ind School Dist	1,11,84	263
West, Patricia/Trent Ind School Dist	16	361
West, Ray, Dr/Shelbyville Ind School Dist	1	335
West, Sally/Hunt Ind School Dist	16	255
West, Ted/Electra Ind School Dist	1	391
West, Tempie/Roby Cons Ind School Dist	16	148
West, Tim/Cayuga Ind School Dist	67	14
West, Tim/Prairie Valley Ind School Dist	1,84	290
Westbrook, Ashley/Garland Ind School Dist	12	105
Westbrook, Gary/Anson Ind School Dist	73,98,295	249
Westbrook, Jaime/Azle Ind School Dist	90	345
Westbrook, Jennifer/Centerville Ind School Dist	73	374
Westbrook, Kalinda/Oglesby Ind School Dist	2	93
Westbrook, Randi/Frankston Ind School Dist	2,19	15
Westbrook, Robert/Milano Ind School Dist	1	287
Westbrook, Robert/Schertz-Cibolo-Univ City ISD	67	173
Westbrooks, Ann/Spring Ind School Dist	2,19	202
Westen, Shandra/Anthony Ind School Dist	11,57,58,271	131
Westerberg, Tom/Barbers Hill Ind School Dist	6,35	72
Westerman, Mona/Godley Ind School Dist	3	247
Westfall, Rick, Dr/Keller Ind School Dist	1	354
Westfall, Trumon/Bangs Ind School Dist	11,84	58
Westmoreland, Deborah/Penelope ISD School Dist	4	228
Weston, Blake/Reagan Co Ind School Dist	6	321
Wethington, Nikki/Nazareth Ind School Dist	12	71
Wetzel, Elsie/Gunter Ind School Dist	57,271	166
Wetzel, Julie/Pittsburg Ind School Dist	2	68
Wexler, Sara/San Isidro Ind School Dist	58	341
Whalen, Weldon/Bynum Ind School Dist	27	227
Whaley, David/Buena Vista Ind School Dist	73	315
Whaley, Deanna/Wortham Ind School Dist	37,69	156
Whaley, Norma/Iraan-Sheffield Ind Sch Dist	58	316
Whalin, Lisa/Muleshoe Ind School Dist	2	22
Whalin, Sam/Muleshoe Ind School Dist	3	22
Whalley, Norma/McCamey Ind School Dist	58	377
Wharton, Carol/Poteet Ind School Dist	37	21
Wharton, Kevin/Silsbee Ind School Dist	88	178
Whatley, Diane/Atlanta Ind School Dist	9	69
Wheat, Anita/Moran Ind School Dist	73,295	334
Wheat, Charistie/Haskell Cons Ind School Dist	7,35,83,85	210
Wheat, Jackie/Wichita Falls Ind School Dist	11	392
Wheat, Melinda/Medina Ind School Dist	16	23
Wheatherread, Laura/Holliday Ind School Dist	4	19
Wheatley, Jacklyn/Haskell Cons Ind School Dist	16,82	210
Wheeler, Jacob/Palestine Ind School Dist	3,5	15
Wheeler, Joyce/Int'l Leadership of Texas Dist	73,98	108
Wheeler, Julie/Santa Gertrudis Ind Sch Dist	91	258
Wheeler, Kim/Leonard Ind School Dist	73,295	146
Wheeler, Lela/Crockett Ind School Dist	67	232
Wheeler, Nate/Plains Ind School Dist	76	405
Wheeler, Nate/Whiteface Con Ind School Dist	1	75
Wheeler, Sandi/Spearman Ind School Dist	10,88,270	177
Wheeler, Sheri/Rockdale Ind School Dist	4	287
Wheeler, Sherry/Christoval Ind School Dist	2	364
Wherley, Clifford/Lancaster Ind School Dist	91	110
Wherman, Christy/Murchison Ind Sch Dist	2	214
Wherry, Thomas/Northside Ind School Dist	4	36
Whetstone, Anika/Commerce Independent Sch Dist	4	236
Whintjen, Zeke/Brazosport Ind School Dist	3	52

School Year 2019-2020   800-333-8802   TX-T97

DISTRICT PERSONNEL INDEX

Market Data Retrieval

NAME/District	JOB FUNCTIONS	PAGE
Whisenant, April/Decatur Ind School Dist	58	403
Whisenant, Judy/Levelland Ind School Dist	7	229
Whisenhunt, David/Blanket Ind School Dist	1,11	58
Whitaker, Dale/Dripping Springs Ind Sch Dist	71	210
Whitaker, James/Calvert Ind School Dist	67	324
Whitaker, Lynn/Union Grove Ind School Dist	11,296	377
Whitaker, Norbert, Dr/Duncanville Ind School Dist	79,93,271	104
Whitaker, Richard/Calhoun Co Ind School Dist	6	61
Whitaker, Teresa/Chapel Hill Ind School Dist	68	337
Whitbeck, Christie, Dr/Bryan Ind School Dist	1	54
White, Andrea/Round Top-Carmine Ind Sch Dist	57,271	147
White, Anna/Houston Ind School Dist	15,57	188
White, Anne/Redwater Ind School Dist	58	49
White, Brad/Wink Loving Ind School Dist	67	402
White, Bryan/Patton Springs Ind School Dist	12,288	127
White, Bryan/Patton Springs Ind School Dist	1,11,57	126
White, Chandra/Mt Vernon Ind School Dist	8,11,15,288	155
White, Cody/O'Donnell Ind School Dist	83,88,298	273
White, Connie/Iredell Ind School Dist	69,275	46
White, Cortney/De Kalb Ind School Dist	3,5	48
White, Dan/McKinney Ind School Dist	20,23	80
White, David/De Leon Ind School Dist	73,84	89
White, Dee Dee/Lovejoy Ind School Dist	2	80
White, Deloris/Bloomington Ind School Dist	67	381
White, Derrick/Cisco Independent Sch Dist	3,5	128
White, Eric/Arlington Ind School Dist	6	343
White, Hailey/Klondike Ind School Dist	58	117
White, Heather/Channing Ind School Dist	73,295	209
White, Jackie/Westbrook Ind School Dist	73	289
White, James/Hondo Ind School Dist	79	284
White, Jennifer/Jasper Ind School Dist	295	240
White, Jennifer/Stamford Ind School Dist	69,83,88,270	250
White, John/Quanah Ind School Dist	16,73,295,297	177
White, Judy/Wink Loving Ind School Dist	60	402
White, Karen/Pasadena Ind School Dist	69	198
White, Kelley/Darrouzett Ind School Dist	58	267
White, Kevin/Brady Ind School Dist	11	277
White, Kristy/Higgins Ind School Dist	1,11,83	268
White, Larry/Bryan Ind School Dist	27	54
White, Lisa/Region 14 Ed Service Center	36,58,77	362
White, Lisa/Troup Ind School Dist	2,68	337
White, Margaret/Hemphill Ind School Dist	4	329
White, Marianne/Hurst-Euless-Bedford ISD	274	353
White, Mark/Spring Hill Ind School Dist	67	170
White, Mark/Tomball Ind School Dist	70,294	203
White, Michael/De Kalb Ind School Dist	23	48
White, Mike/Highland Park Ind Sch Dist	2,5,11,15,70	108
White, Pam/Connally Ind School Dist	7	279
White, Penny/West Hardin Co Cons Sch Dist	2	178
White, Robbie/Hawkins Ind School Dist	67	404
White, Robin/Pine Tree Ind School Dist	44,47,285	170
White, Rodney/Sulphur Springs Ind Sch Dist	16,73,295	232
White, Steve/Decatur Ind School Dist	5	403
White, Terell, Dr/Henrietta Ind School Dist	58	74
White, Timmy/Saltillo Ind School Dist	3	231
White, Todd/Perryton Ind School Dist	8,11,57,88,271,298	307
White, Tony/Spring Hill Ind School Dist	5	170
White, Tray/Texas City Ind School Dist	73,76,295,297	161
White, Victor/Deer Park Ind School Dist	1	186
Whitecotton, Melissa/Red Lick Ind School Dist	59	49
Whitefield, Jay/Lubbock-Cooper Ind Sch Dist	79	271
Whitehead, Catherine/Port Arthur Ind School Dist	46	243
Whitehead, Isaiah/Lone Oak Ind School Dist	295	236
Whitehead, Jay/Brazosport Ind School Dist	15,68,74,79,273	52
Whitehead, Larry/Klein Ind School Dist	15,76	196
Whitehead, Mark/Etoile Ind School Dist	59,69	297
Whitehead, Raquel/Gruver Ind School Dist	69,88,270	176
Whitehead, Robert/Merkel Ind School Dist	5	361
Whitehurst, Bob/Frankston Ind School Dist	67	15
Whiteley, Jonie/Eden Cons Ind School Dist	16	90
Whiteley, Shane/Spearman Ind School Dist	16	177
Whitely, Rachel/Bryan Ind School Dist	16	54
Whitenack, Susan/Sherman Ind School Dist	8,11,88,286,288,296,298	167
Whitesell, David/Fort Davis Ind School Dist	67	241
Whitfield, Evan/Coppell Ind School Dist	42	98
Whitfield, Jewel/La Porte Ind School Dist	9	198
Whitis, Judi, Dr/Decatur Ind School Dist	1	403
Whitley, Carol/Rogers Ind School Dist	68,91	29
Whitley, Morgan/Albany Ind School Dist	15	334
Whitley, Sandra/Forney Ind School Dist	286	251
Whitlock, Elaine/Mesquite Ind School Dist	67	110
Whitlow, Sandy/Amarillo Ind School Dist	8,18	317
Whitman, Kevin/Whitehouse Ind School Dist	5	338
Whitman, Rhonda/Dripping Springs Ind Sch Dist	57,69,74,79,271	210
Whitman, Robert/Willis Ind School Dist	15,68	294
Whitmann, Dot/Seguin Ind School Dist	15,68	173
Whitson, Johnny/Menard Ind School Dist	16,73,295	285
Whitson, Phil/Diocese of Amarillo Ed Office	2	319
Whitt, Carla/Corsicana Ind School Dist	7,85	299
Whitt, Sandra/Whitewright Ind School Dist	4	168
Whittemore, Shana/McLeod Ind School Dist	11,57,271,296	70
Whitten, Tammy/Quanah Ind School Dist	10,38	177
Whitten, Trey/Ingram Ind School Dist	3,5	255
Whittington, Holly/Spring Hill Ind School Dist	27,75	170
Whittle, Amy/Hallsville Ind School Dist	7,11,57,77,83,88,275	208
Whittle, Holly/Mabank Ind School Dist	11,57,271,298	275
Whittlesey, Terry/Centerville Ind School Dist	2	374
Whitton, Chyla/North East Ind School Dist	68	34
Whitton, Mary/Pine Tree Ind School Dist	71	170
Whitworth, Betty/Chester Ind School Dist	16	374
Whitworth, Nancy/Tioga Ind School Dist	2	167
Whitworth, Robert/Diocese of Austin Ed Office	8,15	372
Whorton, Vickie/D'Hanis Ind School Dist	2,4	283
Wiatrek, Lyndall/Karnes City Ind School Dist	34	250
Wicker, Eric/North East Ind School Dist	11	34
Wickett, Paul/Pottsboro Ind School Dist	3	167
Widdecombe, Stacey/Lago Vista Ind School Dist	4	370
Widder, Catherine/Alamo Heights Ind School Dist	7	30
Wideman, Justine/North Lamar Ind School Dist	7,35,85	259
Wiebersch, Julie/Caddo Mills Ind Sch Dist	8	235
Wiechmann, Joann, Dr/Grapevine-Colleyville Ind SD	58	353
Wied, Kim/Van Vleck Ind School Dist	7	276
Wiedemann, Cindy/Scurry Rosser Ind School Dist	2	253
Wiederstein, Jody/Higgins Ind School Dist	58	268
Wieding, Alicia/Karnes City Ind School Dist	298	250
Wieding, Ronnie/Poth Ind School Dist	27	401
Wieghat, Rodney/Needville Ind School Dist	3,5	154
Wieland, Shuck/Terrell Ind School Dist	79	253
Wiese, Kenney/Cranfills Gap ISD School Dist	67	46
Wiesman, Karen/Mansfield Ind School Dist	2,15	356
Wiesman, Nicolette/Rogers Ind School Dist	36,85,88,275,288	28
Wiggins, Betti/Houston Ind School Dist	4	188
Wiggins, Bill/Plemons-Stinnett-Phillips CISD	1	238
Wiggins, Kendra/Magnolia Ind School Dist	58	292
Wiggins, Ted/Onalaska Ind School Dist	67	317
Wigington, Chris/Bushland Ind School Dist	1	319
Wigington, Jennifer/Alba-Golden Ind School Dist	11	404
Wilbanks, Edward/Athens Ind School Dist	27	213
Wilbanks, Elizabeth/Ponder Ind School Dist	11,34,57,59,274	125
Wilbanks, Lori/Taylor Ind School Dist	3	399
Wilburn, Justin/Joaquin Ind School Dist	16,73,76,295	335
Wilcox, Craig, Dr/New Summerfield Ind Sch Dist	8,11,57	73
Wilcox, Dave/Atlanta Ind School Dist	12	69
Wilcox, Dave/Atlanta Ind School Dist	3,4,5,10,11,15	69

#		#		#		#		#	
1	Superintendent	16	Instructional Media Svcs	30	Adult Education	44	Science Sec	58	Special Education K-12
2	Bus/Finance/Purchasing	17	Chief Operations Officer	31	Career/Sch-to-Work K-12	45	Math K-12	59	Special Education Elem
3	Buildings And Grounds	18	Chief Academic Officer	32	Career/Sch-to-Work Elem	46	Math Elem	60	Special Education Sec
4	Food Service	19	Chief Financial Officer	33	Career/Sch-to-Work Sec	47	Math Sec	61	Foreign/World Lang K-12
5	Transportation	20	Art K-12	34	Early Childhood Ed	48	English/Lang Arts K-12	62	Foreign/World Lang Elem
6	Athletic	21	Art Elem	35	Health/Phys Education	49	English/Lang Arts Elem	63	Foreign/World Lang Sec
7	Health Services	22	Art Sec	36	Guidance Services K-12	50	English/Lang Arts Sec	64	Religious Education K-12
8	Curric/Instruct K-12	23	Music K-12	37	Guidance Services Elem	51	Reading K-12	65	Religious Education Elem
9	Curric/Instruct Elem	24	Music Elem	38	Guidance Services Sec	52	Reading Elem	66	Religious Education Sec
10	Curric/Instruct Sec	25	Music Sec	39	Social Studies K-12	53	Reading Sec	67	School Board President
11	Federal Program	26	Business Education	40	Social Studies Elem	54	Remedial Reading K-12	68	Teacher Personnel
12	Title I	27	Career & Tech Ed	41	Social Studies Sec	55	Remedial Reading Elem	69	Academic Assessment
13	Title V	28	Technology Education	42	Science K-12	56	Remedial Reading Sec	70	Research/Development
15	Asst Superintendent	29	Family/Consumer Science	43	Science Elem	57	Bilingual/ELL	71	Public Information

#		#		#	
72	Summer School	88	Alternative/At Risk	277	Remedial Math K-12
73	Instructional Tech	89	Multi-Cultural Curriculum	280	Literacy Coach
74	Inservice Training	90	Social Work	285	STEM
75	Marketing/Distributive	91	Safety/Security	286	Digital Learning
76	Info Systems	92	Magnet School	288	Common Core Standards
77	Psychological Assess	93	Parental Involvement	294	Accountability
78	Affirmative Action	95	Tech Prep Program	295	Network System
79	Student Personnel	97	Chief Information Officer	296	Title II Programs
80	Driver Ed/Safety	98	Chief Technology Officer	297	Webmaster
81	Gifted/Talented	270	Character Education	298	Grant Writer/Ptnrships
82	Video Services	271	Migrant Education	750	Chief Innovation Officer
83	Substance Abuse Prev	273	Teacher Mentor	751	Chief of Staff
84	Erate	274	Before/After Sch	752	Social Emotional Learning
85	AIDS Education	275	Response To Intervention		

TX-T98

Texas School Directory
DISTRICT PERSONNEL INDEX

NAME/District	JOB FUNCTIONS	PAGE
Wilcox, Fred/*Timpson Ind School Dist*	5	335
Wilcox, James, Dr/*Longview Ind School Dist*	1	169
Wilcoxson, George/*Wills Point Ind School Dist*	67	381
Wild, Juliana/*Dodd City Ind School Dist*	57	145
Wilde, Christine/*Wall Ind School Dist*	67	365
Wilde, John/*McAllen Ind School Dist*	79	221
Wilds, John/*Alvin Ind School Dist*	84,295	51
Wiley, Karen/*Forestburg Ind School Dist*	51,54,270	290
Wiley, Nan/*Merkel Ind School Dist*	57,271	361
Wilganowski, Rosemary/*Bremond Ind School Dist*	69	324
Wilhelm, Jennifer/*Allen Ind School Dist*	8,15,294	76
Wilkerson, Nicky/*De Leon Ind School Dist*	3,5	89
Wilkerson, Veronica/*Beckville Ind School Dist*	16	311
Wilkes, Tealer/*Miami Ind School Dist*	58	324
Wilkins, Christine/*Crawford Ind School Dist*	16	279
Wilkins, David/*Hico Ind School Dist*	5	176
Wilkins, Dewanye/*Gordon Ind School Dist*	1,83	310
Wilkins, Donna/*Atlanta Ind School Dist*	4	69
Wilkins, Jessica/*Wichita Falls Ind School Dist*	297	392
Wilkins, Marcus/*Elkhart Ind School Dist*	4	15
Wilkins, Sarah/*Boling Ind School Dist*	36	389
Wilkinson, Dawn/*Northside Ind School Dist*	58,88	393
Wilkinson, Debbie/*Newcastle Ind School Dist*	58,73,288	406
Wilkinson, Shelly/*Chester Ind School Dist*	58	374
Wilkinson, Shelly/*Chester Ind School Dist*	58	374
Wilks, Debra/*Fredericksburg Ind School Dist*	34,58,275	163
Wilks, Kellie/*Ector Co Ind School Dist*	16,73,82,98,295	129
Wille, Scott/*Del Valle Ind School Dist*	34	369
Willery, Akilah/*Aldine Ind School Dist*	74	179
Willett Weekly, Julia/*Ector Co Ind School Dist*	11	129
Willett, Donna/*Bryan Ind School Dist*	36,77	54
Willey, Christi/*Hedley Ind School Dist*	58	127
Willey, George, Dr/*Taylor Ind School Dist*	8,18,275	399
Willhite, Patty/*Aledo Ind School Dist*	4	312
Williams-Scott, Melissa/*Dickinson Ind School Dist*	76	159
Williams, Allison/*May Ind School Dist*	57,280,285	59
Williams, Angi, Dr/*Galena Park Ind School Dist*	1	186
Williams, Ann/*Alief Ind School Dist*	67	181
Williams, Beverly/*Blackwell Cons Ind Sch Dist*	4	301
Williams, Brian, Dr/*Palacios Ind School Dist*	68,69,83,294,296,298	275
Williams, Bryan/*Spring Branch Ind School Dist*	15	200
Williams, Carlton/*Nordheim Ind School Dist*	6	118
Williams, Cassandra/*Prosper Ind School Dist*	4	84
Williams, Charlotte/*Queen City Ind School Dist*	1	70
Williams, Cicely/*Houston Ind School Dist*	8	188
Williams, Cliff/*Willis Ind School Dist*	67	294
Williams, Courtney/*Hempstead Ind School Dist*	58	384
Williams, Cynthia/*Spring Ind School Dist*	27,31	202
Williams, Darla/*Howe Ind School Dist*	8,11,15,58,69	166
Williams, Datren/*Conroe Ind School Dist*	67	291
Williams, David/*Detroit Ind School Dist*	73	322
Williams, David/*Godley Ind School Dist*	68,79,91	247
Williams, David/*Seminole Ind School Dist*	6	158
Williams, David/*Waco Ind School Dist*	91	281
Williams, Deborah/*Bells Ind School Dist*	7,35,85	165
Williams, Deborah/*Ector Ind School Dist*	2	146
Williams, Dennis/*Blooming Grove Ind School Dist*	73,76,295	299
Williams, Dennis/*Longview Ind School Dist*	7,15,79,83,88,91,275	169
Williams, Dionne/*Hawkins Ind School Dist*	8,11,58,83,88,296,298	404
Williams, Dobie/*Granbury Ind School Dist*	2	230
Williams, Donald/*Mansfield Ind School Dist*	15,71	356
Williams, Donelle/*Houston Ind School Dist*	43	188
Williams, Doug/*Sunnyvale Ind School Dist*	1	113
Williams, Eva/*Paris Ind School Dist*	34	260
Williams, Frances/*McDade Ind School Dist*	8	24
Williams, Garry/*Lancaster Ind School Dist*	20	110
Williams, Horace/*Longview Ind School Dist*	9,15,36,69,77,286,294	169
Williams, Jackson/*East Bernard Ind Sch Dist*	73,84,295	389
Williams, James/*Int'l Leadership of Texas Dist*	67	108
Williams, Jeremy/*Eastland Ind School Dist*	15	129
Williams, Jeremy/*Wall Ind School Dist*	5,6,8,85,92	365
Williams, Joann/*Alief Ind School Dist*	50	181
Williams, Josh/*Lufkin Ind School Dist*	295	18
Williams, Josh/*Sulphur Springs Ind Sch Dist*	11,15,36,79,88,296	232
Williams, Justen/*Columbia Brazoria ISD*	3	52
Williams, Karl/*Sunnyvale Ind School Dist*	5	113

NAME/District	JOB FUNCTIONS	PAGE
Williams, Kim/*Chisum Ind School Dist*	2,11	259
Williams, Kim/*Schertz-Cibolo-Univ City ISD*	58	173
Williams, Kristin/*Keller Ind School Dist*	2	354
Williams, Laurah/*Eastland Ind School Dist*	27	129
Williams, Leonard/*Mart Ind School Dist*	1	280
Williams, Linda/*Granbury Ind School Dist*	4	230
Williams, Lisa/*Bullard Ind School Dist*	58	336
Williams, Llyod/*Carthage Ind School Dist*	4	311
Williams, Lori/*Plemons-Stinnett-Phillips CISD*	7,35,83,85	238
Williams, Lynn/*Chisum Ind School Dist*	3,5	259
Williams, Mark/*Chillicothe ISD School Dist*	67	177
Williams, Mark/*Evadale Ind School Dist*	6	240
Williams, Marty/*Gatesville Ind School Dist*	5	92
Williams, Melissa/*Clint Ind School Dist*	11	132
Williams, Mike/*Wills Point Ind School Dist*	3	381
Williams, Mike/*Ysleta Ind School Dist*	6,35	137
Williams, Paige/*Crowley Ind School Dist*	7	347
Williams, Pam/*Tarkington Ind School Dist*	73	266
Williams, Patsy/*Trent Ind School Dist*	4	361
Williams, Phillip/*Blum Ind School Dist*	73	227
Williams, Ray/*West Oso Ind School Dist*	4	306
Williams, Rhonda/*Mt Calm Ind School Dist*	4	228
Williams, Robert/*Huntington Ind School Dist*	27	17
Williams, Robin/*Kerens Ind School Dist*	38,69	300
Williams, Sara/*Van Alstyne Ind School Dist*	37	168
Williams, Scott/*Columbia Brazoria ISD*	3	52
Williams, Sharon/*Granbury Ind School Dist*	8,11,36,57,273,296,298	230
Williams, Sheila/*Broaddus Ind School Dist*	4	329
Williams, Sheila/*Evant Ind School Dist*	67	92
Williams, Shemeka/*Lancaster Ind School Dist*	8,15	110
Williams, Sherlene/*Crowell Ind School Dist*	2,12,73,76,295,298	149
Williams, Stephanie/*Chester Ind School Dist*	2,84	374
Williams, Stephanie/*Ft Bend Ind School Dist*	280,285,296	149
Williams, Steve/*Allen Ind School Dist*	6	76
Williams, Susan/*Big Sandy Ind School Dist*	7	376
Williams, Taylor/*Slidell Ind School Dist*	1	403
Williams, Theresa, Dr/*Plano Ind School Dist*	3,17	82
Williams, Tim/*Frenship Ind School Dist*	2,15	269
Williams, Tim/*Lometa Ind School Dist*	3	262
Williams, Tim/*New Boston Ind School Dist*	84	49
Williams, Toby/*Gatesville Ind School Dist*	3	92
Williams, Tracy/*Kennedale Ind School Dist*	71	355
Williams, Tricia/*New Deal Ind School Dist*	38,83,88,270	271
Williams, Wes/*Roscoe Collegiate Ind Sch Dist*	67	301
Williams, Willie/*La Vega Ind School Dist*	6,35	279
Williams, Yolanda/*Waco Ind School Dist*	15	281
Williamson, Emily/*Livingston Ind School Dist*	73	317
Williamson, Jana/*Pampa Ind School Dist*	93	165
Williamson, Janice/*Bryan Ind School Dist*	35	54
Williamson, Laura/*Hull Daisetta Ind School Dist*	7,83,85	266
Williamson, Lena/*Harmony Ind School Dist*	2	376
Williamson, Raelyn/*Madisonville Cons ISD*	7,85	273
Willingham, Jackie/*Cayuga Ind School Dist*	73,295	14
Willis, Cala/*Eastland Ind School Dist*	4	129
Willis, Greg/*West Orange-Cove Cons ISD*	3	309
Willis, Kent/*New Summerfield Ind Sch Dist*	6	73
Willis, Patty/*Dumas Ind School Dist*	67	295
Willis, Randy/*Granger Ind School Dist*	1	396
Willis, Susan/*White Oak Ind School Dist*	7	171
Willis, Tammy, Dr/*Cross Roads Ind School Dist*	286	214
Willmon, Joel/*Ropes Ind School Dist*	1,11	229
Willrich, Kari/*La Grange Ind School Dist*	7	147
Wills, Lisa/*Ector Co Ind School Dist*	8	129
Wills, Sherri/*Beaumont Ind School Dist*	45	241
Willyard, Tracey/*Cedar Hill Ind School Dist*	28,73,95	97
Wilmes, Joan/*Diocese of San Angelo Ed Off*	1	286
Wilroy, Ben/*Livingston Ind School Dist*	68	317
Wilson, Andrea/*Spurger Ind School Dist*	73,295	375
Wilson, Andrew/*Roscoe Collegiate Ind Sch Dist*	285	301
Wilson, Clay/*Savoy Ind School Dist*	6	146
Wilson, Craig/*Temple Ind School Dist*	286	29
Wilson, Crystal/*Ft Bend Ind School Dist*	81	149
Wilson, Cynthia/*Mission Cons Ind School Dist*	10	222
Wilson, Cynthia, Dr/*Dallas Ind School Dist*	71,97	98
Wilson, Debbie/*Groveton Ind School Dist*	4	374
Wilson, Dedee/*Brazosport Ind School Dist*	81,92	52

School Year 2019-2020   800-333-8802

DISTRICT PERSONNEL INDEX

Market Data Retrieval

NAME/District	JOB FUNCTIONS	PAGE
Wilson, Dustin/S & S Cons Ind School Dist	73	167
Wilson, Emily/Brownwood Ind School Dist	16	58
Wilson, Eric/Borger Ind School Dist	6	237
Wilson, Heather/Canyon Ind School Dist	2,15	320
Wilson, Irene/Slidell Ind School Dist	2,12	403
Wilson, Jamie, Dr/Denton Ind School Dist	1	120
Wilson, Janet/Pottsboro Ind School Dist	2	167
Wilson, Jarret/Sulphur Bluff Ind School Dist	73	232
Wilson, John Kevin/Nordheim Ind School Dist	1	118
Wilson, Karen/Spring Branch Ind School Dist	2,15	200
Wilson, Ken/Sabine Ind School Dist	3	170
Wilson, Kevin/Howe Ind School Dist	1	166
Wilson, Lakimberly/Cedar Hill Ind School Dist	46	97
Wilson, Latitia/Longview Ind School Dist	294	169
Wilson, Laurie/Lytle Ind School Dist	6	21
Wilson, Lisa/Highland Park Ind Sch Dist	8,15,34,45,57,81,90	108
Wilson, Lou/Kingsville Ind School Dist	7,85	257
Wilson, Margaret/Carlisle Ind School Dist	4	327
Wilson, Michelle/Region 16 Ed Service Center	68	321
Wilson, Mike/Valley View ISD-Cooke Co	73	91
Wilson, Pam/O'Donnell Ind School Dist	73	273
Wilson, Randal/Arp Ind School Dist	3,5	336
Wilson, Richard/Itasca Ind School Dist	73,295	228
Wilson, Robin, Dr/Waco Ind School Dist	11	281
Wilson, Shannon/Bridgeport Ind School Dist	6	402
Wilson, Shannon/Dalhart Ind School Dist	16,82	95
Wilson, Sheri/Coldspring-Oakhurst Cons ISD	58	330
Wilson, Susan/Carroll Independent Sch Dist	4	347
Wilson, Theresa/Whitehouse Ind School Dist	4	338
Wilson, Tia/Red Oak Ind School Dist	274	142
Wilson, Todd/Chillicothe ISD School Dist	1,11	177
Wilson, Wade/Highland Park Ind School Dist	6	319
Wiltshire, David/Tuloso-Midway Ind School Dist	295	305
Wimberley, December/Union Grove Ind School Dist	57,271	377
Wimberly, David/Connally Ind School Dist	11	279
Wimberly, Ken/Evant Ind School Dist	1	92
Wimmer, Shane/Seminole Ind School Dist	67	158
Wimpee, Amanda/Azle Ind School Dist	8	345
Winans, Kendra/Leander Ind School Dist	11	396
Winchester, Martin/Texas Dept of Education	15,68	1
Windell, Kathy/Venus Ind School Dist	5	249
Windham, Cassie/Palmer Ind School Dist	35	141
Windham, John/Lubbock-Cooper Ind Sch Dist	3	271
Windham, Kelly/Rockdale Ind School Dist	38	287
Windham, Matt/Red Lick Ind School Dist	16,73	49
Windsor, Kathy/Alvin Ind School Dist	11	50
Windsor, Kathy, Dr/Alvin Ind School Dist	8,68,79	50
Wineinger, Lance/Wink Loving Ind School Dist	9	402
Wingate, Angel/Hamshire Fannett Ind Sch Dist	4	242
Winingham, David/Gold-Burg Ind School Dist	41	290
Wink, John/Carthage Ind School Dist	1	311
Wink, John/Tatum Ind School Dist	8,11,57,73,83,271,288,296	328
Winkel, Katt/Lubbock-Cooper Ind School Dist	6	271
Winkelman, Eric/El Paso Ind School Dist	27,31	132
Winkelmann, Audrau/Bellville Ind School Dist	16	22
Winkelmann, Charlotte/Hays Cons Ind School Dist	36	211
Winkenwerder, Dawn/Shiner Ind School Dist	2,68	262
Winkler, Charles/Braination Schools	36,76,84,295	30
Winkler, Charlotte/Dew Ind School Dist	4	156
Winn, Jeanette/Karnes City Ind School Dist	1	250
Winn, Scott/Wylie Ind School Dist	15,79	84
Winovitch, Robert/Lake Travis Ind School Dist	3	370
Winter, Jenny/Lingleville Ind School Dist	36,83	143
Winter, Mike/Gorman Ind School Dist	1,11	129
Winters, Keri/Linden Kildare Cons Ind SD	1,83	70
Wise, Regina/Post Ind School Dist	58	162
Wiseman, Jeff/Little Elm Ind School Dist	16,73,286	124
Wisener, Atticus/Garland Ind School Dist	68	105
Wiswell, Christina, Dr/Round Rock Ind School Dist	36	398
Witcher, Mary/Highland Park Ind Sch Dist	2	108
Witherell, Courtney/Comal Ind School Dist	69,294	87
Witney, Elliott/Spring Branch Ind School Dist	15,70	200
Witt, Dennis/Big Spring Ind School Dist	5	233
Witt, Lisa/McKinney Ind School Dist	41	81
Witte, Kathleen/Quinlan Ind School Dist	11,57,74,271,285,294,298	237
Witte, Laura/North East Ind School Dist	69	34
Witte, Melanie/Kenedy Ind School Dist	69	251
Witten, Aaron/Spearman Ind School Dist	6	177
Woehl, Chris/Lake Travis Ind School Dist	73,76,295	370
Wolf, Adianna/Hereford Ind School Dist	11,296	119
Wolf, Darrell/Mart Ind School Dist	3	280
Wolf, Janet/Center Point Ind School Dist	7,85	255
Wolf, Kenneth/Temple Ind School Dist	3	29
Wolf, Mike/Rochelle Ind School Dist	67	278
Wolf, Steve/Lazbuddie Ind School Dist	1,73	315
Wolf, Tracy/Holland Ind School Dist	2,84	27
Wolfe, Anna/Rochelle Ind School Dist	4	278
Wolfe, Matt/Waco Ind School Dist	295	281
Wolfe, Melissa/Midlothian Ind School Dist	58	141
Wolfe, Nadine/Harlandale Ind School Dist	11,30,85,271,296,298	32
Wolfenbarger, Orlie/Comstock Ind School Dist	1,11,83	379
Wolford, Kathy/Sweeny Ind School Dist	4	54
Wolsch, Edward/Seymour Ind School Dist	31,36,69,77	25
Womack, Brittany/Prairie Valley Ind School Dist	27	290
Womack, Dennis, Dr/Lovejoy Ind School Dist	3,5,15,91	80
Womack, Jimmy/Mansfield Ind School Dist	91	356
Womack, Jody/Colorado Ind School Dist	37	289
Womack, Rosie/Anahuac Ind School Dist	2,5,84	71
Womack, Shelby/Stephenville Ind School Dist	27,73	144
Womble, Ashley/Whitewright Ind School Dist	9,93	168
Wong, Melissa/Nederland Ind School Dist	2	242
Wood, Amy/Granbury Ind School Dist	16,28,73,76	230
Wood, Bill, Dr/Katy Ind School Dist	5	151
Wood, Chris/Cleveland Ind School Dist	67	265
Wood, David/Glasscock Co Ind School Dist	73,286	163
Wood, Dianna/San Saba Ind School Dist	4	332
Wood, James/Karnes City Ind School Dist	6	250
Wood, Jayma/Karnes City Ind School Dist	58	250
Wood, John/Kopperl Ind School Dist	6	47
Wood, Kim/Arp Ind School Dist	4	336
Wood, Maryann/Alvarado Ind School Dist	68,78	246
Wood, Michelle/Wichita Falls Ind School Dist	27,31	392
Wood, Mike/Jefferson Ind School Dist	2	274
Wood, Mike/Kilgore Ind School Dist	6	169
Wood, Robin/River Road Ind School Dist	34,57,58,69,271	319
Wood, Steve/Aledo Ind School Dist	6	312
Wood, Trista/Burkeville Ind School Dist	73	300
Wood, Wes/Snyder Ind School Dist	6	333
Wood, Yuvonne/Kopperl Ind School Dist	2	47
Woodall, Chuck/Ponder Ind School Dist	295	125
Woodall, Trecia/Beckville Ind School Dist	73	311
Woodard, Alicia/Wichita Falls Ind School Dist	2	392
Woodard, David/West Ind School Dist	6	282
Woodard, Joe/Bruceville-Eddy Ind Sch Dist	8,288	278
Woodard, Johnny/Lefors Ind School Dist	5	165
Woodard, La'Evening/Richardson Ind School Dist	91	112
Woodard, Mary/Mesquite Ind School Dist	16	110
Woodard, Mary Claire/Howe Ind School Dist	31	166
Woodard, Michael/Latexo Ind School Dist	1	233
Woodard, Michael/McCamey Ind School Dist	6	377
Woodard, Suzanne/McKinney Ind School Dist	9,15	80
Woodcock, Jodee/Woden Ind School Dist	8,11,294,296,298	298
Woodfin, Jason/Gary Ind School Dist	2,3,5,11,88	311
Woodfin, Terri/Union Grove Ind School Dist	68	377

---

1 Superintendent
2 Bus/Finance/Purchasing
3 Buildings And Grounds
4 Food Service
5 Transportation
6 Athletic
7 Health Services
8 Curric/Instruct K-12
9 Curric/Instruct Elem
10 Curric/Instruct Sec
11 Federal Program
12 Title I
13 Title V
15 Asst Superintendent
16 Instructional Media Svcs
17 Chief Operations Officer
18 Chief Academic Officer
19 Chief Financial Officer
20 Art K-12
21 Art Elem
22 Art Sec
23 Music K-12
24 Music Elem
25 Music Sec
26 Business Education
27 Career & Tech Ed
28 Technology Education
29 Family/Consumer Science
30 Adult Education
31 Career/Sch-to-Work K-12
32 Career/Sch-to-Work Elem
33 Career/Sch-to-Work Sec
34 Early Childhood Ed
35 Health/Phys Education
36 Guidance Services K-12
37 Guidance Services Elem
38 Guidance Services Sec
39 Social Studies K-12
40 Social Studies Elem
41 Social Studies Sec
42 Science K-12
43 Science Elem
44 Science Sec
45 Math K-12
46 Math Elem
47 Math Sec
48 English/Lang Arts K-12
49 English/Lang Arts Elem
50 English/Lang Arts Sec
51 Reading K-12
52 Reading Elem
53 Reading Sec
54 Remedial Reading K-12
55 Remedial Reading Elem
56 Remedial Reading Sec
57 Bilingual/ELL
58 Special Education K-12
59 Special Education Elem
60 Special Education Sec
61 Foreign/World Lang K-12
62 Foreign/World Lang Elem
63 Foreign/World Lang Sec
64 Religious Education K-12
65 Religious Education Elem
66 Religious Education Sec
67 School Board President
68 Teacher Personnel
69 Academic Assessment
70 Research/Development
71 Public Information
72 Summer School
73 Instructional Tech
74 Inservice Training
75 Marketing/Distributive
76 Info Systems
77 Psychological Assess
78 Affirmative Action
79 Student Personnel
80 Driver Ed/Safety
81 Gifted/Talented
82 Video Services
83 Substance Abuse Prev
84 Erate
85 AIDS Education
88 Alternative/At Risk
89 Multi-Cultural Curriculum
90 Social Work
91 Safety/Security
92 Magnet School
93 Parental Involvement
95 Tech Prep Program
97 Chief Information Officer
98 Chief Technology Officer
270 Character Education
271 Migrant Education
273 Teacher Mentor
274 Before/After Sch
275 Response To Intervention
277 Remedial Math K-12
280 Literacy Coach
285 STEM
286 Digital Learning
288 Common Core Standards
294 Accountability
295 Network System
296 Title II Programs
297 Webmaster
298 Grant Writer/Ptnrships
750 Chief Innovation Officer
751 Chief of Staff
752 Social Emotional Learning

TX-T100

Texas School Directory

DISTRICT PERSONNEL INDEX

NAME/District	JOB FUNCTIONS	PAGE
Woodley, Katie/*Elysian Fields Ind School Dist*	36,83	208
Woodruff, Richard/*Conroe Ind School Dist*	39	291
Woodrum, Maria/*Mission Cons Ind School Dist*	4	222
Woods Gage, Tonya/*Royal Ind School Dist*	58	384
Woods-Meals, Jan/*Tom Bean Ind School Dist*	73	168
Woods, Amy/*Higgins Ind School Dist*	2	268
Woods, Brad/*Memphis Ind School Dist*	37	175
Woods, Brian, Dr/*Northside Ind School Dist*	1	36
Woods, Brittney/*Throckmorton Ind School Dist*	2	363
Woods, Charity/*Kennedale Ind School Dist*	8,58	355
Woods, Charles/*Alief Ind School Dist*	2,15	181
Woods, David/*Stephenville Ind School Dist*	5	144
Woods, Krysta/*Prairie Valley Ind School Dist*	29	290
Woods, Lori/*Northside Ind School Dist*	57	393
Woods, Patty/*Dumas Ind School Dist*	4	295
Woodson, Patrice/*Cedar Hill Ind School Dist*	49	97
Woodward, Courtney/*Seymour Ind School Dist*	73,76	25
Woody, Courtney/*Wink Loving Ind School Dist*	7,85	402
Woody, John/*Italy Ind School Dist*	31	140
Woody, Tom/*Meridian Ind School Dist*	73,76,295	47
Woolems, Stacey/*Jasper Ind School Dist*	10,11,69,296	240
Woolen, Sharona/*Marshall Ind School Dist*	58	209
Wooley, Lisa/*Clear Creek Ind School Dist*	44	158
Woolsey, Barbara/*Sweetwater ISD School Dist*	4	301
Woolsey, Denise/*Cherokee Ind School Dist*	2	332
Woosley, Brad/*Denver City Ind School Dist*	67	405
Wooten, Cheryl/*Aledo Ind School Dist*	58	312
Wooten, Troy/*New Caney Ind School Dist*	91	293
Wooten, William/*DeSoto Ind School Dist*	2	104
Wooten, William/*Ferris Ind School Dist*	2	140
Worcester, Terry/*Round Rock Ind School Dist*	3,17	398
Word, Janet/*Childress Ind School Dist*	9	74
Word, Mike/*Clarendon Cons Ind Sch Dist*	11,93	127
Workman, Jim/*Balmorhea Ind School Dist*	13,296	323
Workman, Jim/*Balmorhea Ind School Dist*	8,74,271	323
Workman, Michelle/*Balmorhea Ind School Dist*	69	323
Worrell, Daron/*Rocksprings Ind School Dist*	1,11	131
Worsham, Linda/*Freer Ind School Dist*	5	128
Wortham, Marcus/*Calvert Ind School Dist*	6	324
Wortham, Wanda/*Pleasant Grove Ind School Dist*	294	49
Worthington, Marsha/*Gatesville Ind School Dist*	11,31,36,69,273,275,288	92
Worthington, Mary/*Richardson Ind School Dist*	71	112
Worthy, Bobby/*Whitewright Ind School Dist*	5,8,11,57,74,273,288,294	168
Worthy, Kevin/*Royse City Ind School Dist*	1	326
Woytek, Cheryl/*Columbus Ind School Dist*	4	86
Wozniak, Doug/*San Marcos Cons Ind Sch Dist*	5	211
Wrehe, Scott/*Carroll Independent Sch Dist*	2,15	347
Wren, Joel/*Klein Ind School Dist*	20,23	196
Wren, Nora/*Iola Ind School Dist*	4	172
Wriggle, Megan/*West Rusk Co Cons Ind Sch Dist*	7	328
Wright, Allison/*Three Way Ind School Dist*	59	144
Wright, Anita/*Sidney Ind School Dist*	2	90
Wright, Cheryl/*Goldthwaite Consolidated ISD*	36,69,88,270,271	288
Wright, Cody/*North Hopkins Ind School Dist*	275	231
Wright, David/*Mansfield Ind School Dist*	79	356
Wright, Dianna/*Friona Ind School Dist*	2	315
Wright, Eric/*Eanes Ind School Dist*	76	370
Wright, Eric, Dr/*Hays Cons Ind School Dist*	1	211
Wright, Erica/*McKinney Ind School Dist*	3	80
Wright, Jack/*Aransas Co Ind School Dist*	67	19
Wright, James/*Mt Calm Ind School Dist*	1,11	228
Wright, Jeff/*Liberty-Eylau Ind School Dist*	3,15	48
Wright, Kent/*Prairiland Ind School Dist*	8,16,73	260
Wright, Kerry/*Region 17 Ed Service Center*	2	272
Wright, Lesa/*Ore City Ind School Dist*	38,285	377
Wright, Melanie/*Austwell Tivoli Ind SD*	16	323
Wright, Morgan/*Spurger Ind School Dist*	1	375
Wright, Robert, Dr/*Keller Ind School Dist*	27,31,286	354
Wright, Ronda/*White Settlement Ind Sch Dist*	11	357
Wright, Ronny/*Goldthwaite Consolidated ISD*	1,11,83	288
Wright, Susan/*Glen Rose Ind School Dist*	8,11,58,275,296,298	340
Wright, Telena, Dr/*Argyle Ind School Dist*	1	120
Wright, Tracilynn/*Austin Ind School Dist*	36,88	366
Wright, Tracy/*Banquete Ind School Dist*	67	302
Wrighthood, Debbie/*Bosqueville Ind School Dist*	67	278
Wrinkle, Tammi/*Vernon Ind School Dist*	2	393

NAME/District	JOB FUNCTIONS	PAGE
Wrobleski, Kevin/*Goose Creek Cons Ind Sch Dist*	42	187
Wrzesinski, David/*Robinson Ind School Dist*	12,58	281
Wuest, Kendra/*Pawnee Ind School Dist*	8,12,83,88,294	25
Wunderlich, Jonathan/*Weimar Ind School Dist*	1	87
Wurtz, Steven, Dr/*Arlington Ind School Dist*	8,18	343
Wyatt, Dawn/*Rankin Ind School Dist*	2	377
Wyatt, Jay/*Diboll Ind School Dist*	67	17
Wyatt, Rhonda/*Richland Springs Ind Sch Dist*	8	332
Wyatt, Rhonda/*Richland Springs Ind Sch Dist*	8	332
Wyatt, Ron/*Goose Creek Cons Ind Sch Dist*	68	187
Wyatt, Samuel/*Rankin Ind School Dist*	1	377
Wyatt, Staci/*Happy Ind School Dist*	36	342
Wylie, Aaron/*Eagle Mtn-Saginaw Ind Sch Dist*	4	348
Wylie, Bridget/*Archer City Ind School Dist*	2	19
Wyman, Kathryn/*La Grange Ind School Dist*	58	147
Wynkoop, Gloria/*Somerset Ind School Dist*	68	42
Wynn, Susie/*Booker Ind School Dist*	10,16,69	267
Wynn, Susy/*Booker Ind School Dist*	69	267
Wynne, Latoya/*Aldine ISD-Elem Sch Team 3*	15	180

Y

Y'Herrera, Ymelda/*Braination Schools*	2,19	30
Yager, Candy/*Coldspring-Oakhurst Cons ISD*	68	330
Yakesch, John/*Milano Ind School Dist*	67	287
Yakesch, Pat/*Milano Ind School Dist*	3	287
Yaklin, Terry/*Judson Ind School Dist*	3	33
Yaklin, Toby/*Riviera Ind School Dist*	3	258
Yale, Tiffany/*Tom Bean Ind School Dist*	7	168
Yamaguchi, Yuki/*Hempstead Ind School Dist*	57	384
Yancey, Ronnie/*Tarkington Ind School Dist*	3	266
Yandell, Kevin/*Sabine Ind School Dist*	2	170
Yanke, Mike/*Gruver Ind School Dist*	67	176
Yannotta, David/*Goose Creek Cons Ind Sch Dist*	69,294	187
Yanowski, Randy/*Bremond Ind School Dist*	67	324
Yarborough, Margaret/*George West Ind School Dist*	5	268
Yargo, Julie/*Anderson-Shiro Cons Ind SD*	4	171
Yates, Dana, Dr/*Mercedes Ind School Dist*	15	221
Yates, Heath/*Fruitvale Ind School Dist*	67	380
Yates, Kayla/*Texhoma Ind School Dist*	11,73,83,275,286,288,296	336
Yates, Michelle/*Victoria Ind School Dist*	11	382
Yates, Shelley/*Sabine Ind School Dist*	8,11,83,285,286,288,294,298	170
Ybarra, Barbara/*Bryan Ind School Dist*	8,15,294	54
Ybarra, George/*Killeen Ind School Dist*	2	27
Ybarra, Pete/*Runge Ind School Dist*	3	251
Ybarra, Victoria/*Red Oak Ind School Dist*	4	142
Yeager, Bruce/*Ponder Ind School Dist*	1	125
Yeager, Elizabeth/*Wichita Falls Ind School Dist*	67	392
Yearwood, Brian, Dr/*Manor Ind School Dist*	8,11,15,69,81,294,298	371
Yentzen, Michelle/*Hardin Jefferson Ind Sch Dist*	67	177
Yeschke, Chris/*Leakey Ind School Dist*	1	322
Ying, Shun/*McKinney Ind School Dist*	295	81
Yoakem, Timbra/*Mabank Ind School Dist*	58	252
Yoakum, Dennis/*Commerce Independent Sch Dist*	3,5	236
Yocham, Pam/*Andrews Ind School Dist*	4	16
Yohn, Todd/*Pine Tree Ind School Dist*	295	170
York, Brandy/*Wall Ind School Dist*	58	365
York, Dwain/*Wimberley Ind School Dist*	1	212
York, Jason/*Comal Ind School Dist*	67	87
York, John/*Paducah Ind School Dist*	6	93
Yost, Donna/*Deer Park Ind School Dist*	11	186
Yougblood, Clay/*Garner Ind School Dist*	67	312
Young, Danny/*Silsbee Ind School Dist*	295	178
Young, Darby/*Klein Ind School Dist*	6,35	196
Young, David/*Los Fresnos Cons Ind Sch Dist*	2	66
Young, David, Dr/*Abilene Ind School Dist*	1	360
Young, Gray/*Henderson Ind School Dist*	295	327
Young, James/*La Poynor Ind School Dist*	1	214
Young, Joe/*Brownwood Ind School Dist*	1	58
Young, Kathleen/*Yantis Ind School Dist*	2	405
Young, Kendall/*Kerrville Ind School Dist*	36	256
Young, Lissa/*Gorman Ind School Dist*	4	129
Young, Mark/*Livingston Ind School Dist*	4	317
Young, Mia/*Channelview Ind School Dist*	27,31	183
Young, Michelle/*Galena Park Ind School Dist*	73	186
Young, Misty/*McKinney Ind School Dist*	46	81
Young, Renee/*Lometa Ind School Dist*	58	262

DISTRICT PERSONNEL INDEX

Market Data Retrieval

NAME/District	JOB FUNCTIONS	PAGE
Young, Rhea/Splendora Ind School Dist	16	294
Young, Stacie/Rusk Ind School Dist	2,15,294	73
Young, Tamika/Fabens Ind School Dist	31	135
Young, Todd/McKinney Ind School Dist	31	80
Young, Travis/Dayton Ind School Dist	71,83	265
Youngblood, Emily/Flour Bluff Ind School Dist	2	304
Youngblood, Loydette/Splendora Ind School Dist	36	294
Youngs, Mark/Keller Ind School Dist	2,19	354
Yourman, Thomas/Midway Ind School Dist	3	280
Yznaga, Jerri/Eanes Ind School Dist	3	370

Z

NAME/District	JOB FUNCTIONS	PAGE
Zachary, Louis/Austin Ind School Dist	3	366
Zachary, Nancy/Leonard Ind School Dist	7	146
Zahn, Tony/Grapevine-Colleyville Ind SD	285	353
Zalefnik, Becky/Sheldon Ind School Dist	73,76,285,286	200
Zambiasi, Doug/Frisco Ind School Dist	3,17	78
Zambrano, Jesus/Pharr-San Juan-Alamo Ind SD	67	223
Zambrano, Rosario/Beeville Ind School Dist	57,58	25
Zambrano, Ruth/Harlandale Ind School Dist	93	32
Zamora-Guerra, Norma/McAllen Ind School Dist	71	221
Zamora, Gabe/Olfen Ind School Dist	1,11,57	327
Zamora, Robert/South San Antonio Ind Sch Dist	6	42
Zander, Clint/Bosqueville Ind School Dist	6	278
Zapalac, Charlie/Bryan Ind School Dist	295	54
Zapaliac, Mike/Sealy Ind School Dist	3	22
Zapata-Farmer, Alisa/Socorro Ind School Dist	9,15	135
Zapata, Margarito/Prairie Lea Ind School Dist	67	61
Zapata, Minerva/Driscoll Ind School Dist	4	304
Zapata, Rebecca/Hartley Ind School Dist	4	209
Zapata, Sammy/Aransas Co Ind School Dist	91	19
Zapata, Sylvia/La Joya Ind School Dist	2	219
Zaragoza, David/Southside Ind School Dist	91	43
Zastoupil, Kristin/Forney Ind School Dist	71	251
Zavala, Alberto/Diocese of Brownsville Ed Off	73	226
Zavala, Carmen/Zapata Co Ind School Dist	58	406
Zavala, Santiago/Pharr-San Juan-Alamo Ind SD	297	223
Zeal, Bart/Liberty-Eylau Ind School Dist	91	48
Zeigler, Leah/Kress Ind School Dist	1,11,73,84	343
Zemlicka, Brian, Dr/Region 6 Ed Service Center	15,71	384
Zemlicka, Leslee/Willis Ind School Dist	91	294
Zemo, Matthew/Eanes Ind School Dist	88	370
Zepeda, Ana/Monte Alto Ind School Dist	8	222
Zepeda, Marisela/Pharr-San Juan-Alamo Ind SD	285	223
Zepeda, Raymond/Cypress-Fairbanks Ind Sch Dist	6,35	183
Zepeda, Rocky/Del Valle Ind School Dist	88	369
Zernial, Abby/Lumberton Ind School Dist	2	178
Zertuche, David/Pleasanton Ind School Dist	5	21
Zeske, Karen, Dr/Arlington Ind School Dist	81	343
Zettle, Terry/Irving Ind School Dist	91	109
Zgabay, Zach/Dime Box Ind School Dist	35	263
Ziemer, Jordan, Dr/La Vernia Ind School Dist	71	401
Ziener, Brian, Dr/Mexia Ind School Dist	2,12	267
Zienko, Crystal/Chireno ISD School Dist	58	297
Zigmond, Meghan/Port Aransas Ind School Dist	16	305
Zigtema, Jaculyn/Whitehouse Ind School Dist	58	339
Zimmer, Cherilyn/Mexia Ind School Dist	73	267
Zimmer, Lana/Clear Creek Ind School Dist	47	158
Zimmerer, Diane/Lindsay Ind School Dist	2	91
Zimmerman, Galen/Dripping Springs Ind Sch Dist	6	210
Zimmerman, Lindsey/Point Isabel Ind Sch Dist	38	66
Zimmerman, Marlena/Canutillo Ind School Dist	42	132
Zimmerman, Denise/Spring Ind School Dist	36	202
Zimora, Maria/Duncanville Ind School Dist	11	104
Zinda, Mary/Pleasanton Ind School Dist	81	21
Zingelmann, Robert/Region 4 Ed Service Center	2,3,19	208
Zink, Karen/Redwater Ind School Dist	73	49
Zinke, Courtney/Yoakum Ind School Dist	38	118
Zinn, Troy/Rockdale Ind School Dist	67	287
Zoch, Lus/San Antonio Ind School Dist	74	39
Zoda, Pamela, Dr/Conroe Ind School Dist	11,298	291
Zoeller, Maroba, Dr/Allen Ind School Dist	11	76
Zolman, Phil/Kress Ind School Dist	11,73,286,294,295,298	343
Zorn, Christine/Klein Ind School Dist	45	196
Zorola, Marcos/North East Ind School Dist	76	34
Zuberbueler, Bill/Comstock Ind School Dist	67	379
Zuniga, Ana/Mission Cons Ind School Dist	2	222
Zuniga, Eduardo/United Ind School Dist	15,79,275	387
Zuniga, Irma/La Joya Ind School Dist	57	219
Zuniga, Sandra, Dr/Uvalde Cons Ind School Dist	10	378
Zuniga, Santos/Raymondville Ind Sch Dist	5	394
Zuniga, Tony/Memphis Ind School Dist	5	175
Zunker, Laura/San Marcos Cons Ind Sch Dist	58	211
Zurline, Steve/Carthage Ind School Dist	3,15	311
Zwahr, Charlene/West Hardin Co Cons Sch Dist	16,82	178
Zwattr, Julie/Denton Ind School Dist	71,97	120
Zyla, Sonia/Ed Service Center Region 2	58	306

---

1 Superintendent
2 Bus/Finance/Purchasing
3 Buildings And Grounds
4 Food Service
5 Transportation
6 Athletic
7 Health Services
8 Curric/Instruct K-12
9 Curric/Instruct Elem
10 Curric/Instruct Sec
11 Federal Program
12 Title I
13 Title V
15 Asst Superintendent
16 Instructional Media Svcs
17 Chief Operations Officer
18 Chief Academic Officer
19 Chief Financial Officer
20 Art K-12
21 Art Elem
22 Art Sec
23 Music K-12
24 Music Elem
25 Music Sec
26 Business Education
27 Career & Tech Ed
28 Technology Education
29 Family/Consumer Science
30 Adult Education
31 Career/Sch-to-Work K-12
32 Career/Sch-to-Work Elem
33 Career/Sch-to-Work Sec
34 Early Childhood Ed
35 Health/Phys Education
36 Guidance Services K-12
37 Guidance Services Elem
38 Guidance Services Sec
39 Social Studies K-12
40 Social Studies Elem
41 Social Studies Sec
42 Science K-12
43 Science Elem
44 Science Sec
45 Math K-12
46 Math Elem
47 Math Sec
48 English/Lang Arts K-12
49 English/Lang Arts Elem
50 English/Lang Arts Sec
51 Reading K-12
52 Reading Elem
53 Reading Sec
54 Remedial Reading K-12
55 Remedial Reading Elem
56 Remedial Reading Sec
57 Bilingual/ELL
58 Special Education K-12
59 Special Education Elem
60 Special Education Sec
61 Foreign/World Lang K-12
62 Foreign/World Lang Elem
63 Foreign/World Lang Sec
64 Religious Education K-12
65 Religious Education Elem
66 Religious Education Sec
67 School Board President
68 Teacher Personnel
69 Academic Assessment
70 Research/Development
71 Public Information
72 Summer School
73 Instructional Tech
74 Inservice Training
75 Marketing/Distributive
76 Info Systems
77 Psychological Assess
78 Affirmative Action
79 Student Personnel
80 Driver Ed/Safety
81 Gifted/Talented
82 Video Services
83 Substance Abuse Prev
84 Erate
85 AIDS Education
88 Alternative/At Risk
89 Multi-Cultural Curriculum
90 Social Work
91 Safety/Security
92 Magnet School
93 Parental Involvement
95 Tech Prep Program
97 Chief Information Officer
98 Chief Technology Officer
270 Character Education
271 Migrant Education
273 Teacher Mentor
274 Before/After Sch
275 Response To Intervention
277 Remedial Math K-12
280 Literacy Coach
285 STEM
286 Digital Learning
288 Common Core Standards
294 Accountability
295 Network System
296 Title II Programs
297 Webmaster
298 Grant Writer/Ptnrships
750 Chief Innovation Officer
751 Chief of Staff
752 Social Emotional Learning

TX-T102

Texas School Directory — PRINCIPAL INDEX

NAME/School	PAGE
A	
Aamodt, Mary/*Incarnate Word Academy*	204
Aaron, Lesley/*Wunderlich Intermediate Sch*	198
Abbot, Patti/*O'Connell High Sch*	162
Abbott, Mike/*Granger Sch*	396
Abbs, Mecheal/*Crockett Aec-Pineywoods*	232
Abdi, Diana/*Austin Peace Academy*	373
Abdulrahman, Ibrahim Abu/*Vanguard International Academy*	359
Abel, Angela/*Woodcrest Elem Sch*	244
Abke, Ashley/*It Holleman Elem Sch*	384
Abney, Koby/*New Home Sch*	273
Abohosh, Kelli/*Percy Neblitt Elem Sch*	167
Aboud, Christine/*St Michael's Learning Academy*	207
Abrams, Carrie/*Howard Norman Elem Sch*	396
Abrams, Carrie/*Popham Elem Sch*	369
Abrams, Kari/*Brockett Elem Sch*	120
Abundez, Paul/*La Villa Middle Sch*	220
Acevedo, David/*Highland Sch*	301
Acevedo, Laura/*Anderson Elem Sch*	291
Acevedo, Sophia/*Calder Road Elem Sch*	159
Achimon, Patti/*J W Hayes Primary Sch*	168
Achtermann, Kathryn/*Barton Hills Elem Sch*	366
Acosta, Amy/*Timber Creek Elem Sch*	124
Acosta, Christine/*Taft Junior High Sch*	332
Acosta, Dolores/*Cedar Grove Elem Sch*	137
Acosta, Elena/*Horizon High Sch*	132
Acosta, Mario/*Westwood High Sch*	399
Acosta, Patty/*Monahans High Sch*	385
Acosta, Shannon/*Gerald Sonntag Elem Sch*	79
Acton, Anne/*Oak Hill Academy*	115
Acton, Christopher/*Heritage Sch*	163
Acuna, Antonio/*Del Valle High Sch*	137
Acuna, Sylvia/*Sky Harbor Elem Sch*	43
Adamek, Gabe/*Yoakum Intermediate Sch*	118
Adami, Randolph/*Northbrook High Sch*	201
Adams Pegues, Nakeisha/*Marshall Junior High Sch*	209
Adams, Aisley/*Nimitz 9th Grade Sch*	180
Adams, Amy/*White Rock North Sch*	116
Adams, Crystal/*Teague Elem Sch*	156
Adams, Damon/*Marble Falls High Sch*	60
Adams, James/*Malcolm Rector Technical HS*	298
Adams, Justin/*Crossroads Sch*	205
Adams, Lynn/*Aggieland Country Mont Sch*	56
Adams, Oscar/*Paul Laurence Dunbar High Sch*	351
Adams, Roy/*Disciplinary Alt Ed Program*	186
Adams, Rufina/*Irene C Cardwell Elem Sch*	379
Adams, Scott/*Gateway Academy*	206
Adams, Shalonda/*Pace Alternative Campus*	170
Adams, Steve/*Robert R Shaw Ctr for Steam*	153
Adamson, Steve/*Needville High Sch*	154
Aday, Debbie/*First Christian Day Sch*	143
Adcocok, Carol/*Bisd Ctr Tech & Advanced Lrng*	346
Addison, Lajuan/*Deweyville Elem Sch*	308
Addison, Tammy/*Millsap High Sch*	313
Addison, Tara/*Inspired Vision Secondary Sch [272]*	5
Adhami, Saboohi/*Darul Arqam School-North*	205
Adibi, Masi/*Lake Cities Montessori Sch*	115
Adkins, Erica/*Jefferson Elem Sch*	392
Adkins, Florence, Dr/*La Marque Middle Sch*	161
Adkins, Leon/*Berean Christian Academy*	114
Agan, Rocky/*Pioneer Heritage Middle Sch*	80
Agnew, Doug/*Live Oak Academy*	211
Agnew, Kimberly/*Shadydale Elem Sch*	191
Agrella, Yolanda/*True Cross Catholic Sch*	162
Aguero, Chris/*Austin Jewish Academy*	373
Aguero, Mark/*Tony Gonzalez Elem Sch*	67
Aguilar, Alfredo/*Carlos Truan Jr High Sch*	216
Aguilar, Ana/*Judson Robinson Elem Sch*	190
Aguilar, Dahlia/*Lopez Early College High Sch*	64
Aguilar, Diana/*Progreso High Sch*	224
Aguilar, Kaitlyn/*St Mary of Carmel Sch*	114
Aguilar, Magdalena, Dr/*Keys Academy*	136
Aguilar, Magdalena, Dr/*Options High Sch*	136
Aguilar, Maria/*Hacienda Heights Elem Sch*	138
Aguilar, Sonia/*Idea Academy-Pharr*	218
Aguilar, Susana/*Carmen Avila Elem Sch*	216
Aguilar, Yanira/*Idea Academy-Rio Vista*	218
Aguilar, Zandra/*Eliot Elem Sch*	190
Aguilera, Ignacio/*St Elizabeth Seton Cath Sch*	204
Aguilera, Lilia/*Hughey Elem Sch*	133
Aguirre, Belinda/*R A Hall Elem Sch*	25
Aguirre, Christina/*Wainwright Elem Sch*	192
Aguirre, David/*Taylor Elem Sch*	222
Aguirre, Jesse/*Escontrias Early Childhood Ctr*	136
Aguirre, Jesse/*Escontrias Elem Sch*	136
Aguirre, Jesse/*Keys Elem Academy*	136
Aguirre, Nicole/*Manor Elem Early Learning Ctr*	371
Aguirre, Patricia/*Western Hills Academy*	139
Ahmad, Shahnaj/*R E Good Elem Sch*	97
Ahmed, Huda/*Global Innovation Sch*	155
Ahumada, Irene/*Ramona Elem Sch*	138
Aiken, Brian/*Baytown Junior High Sch*	187
Aikman, Karen/*Hallsville Intermediate Sch*	208
Ainsworth, Lillian/*Northeast Christian Academy*	139
Aitken, Pam/*Prestonwood Elem Sch*	113
Ajibola, Lacey/*Pathfinder Achievement Center*	106
Akala, Beatrice/*Sutton Elem Sch*	194
Akan, Deateria/*Two Dimensions Prep Academy [308]*	13
Akers, Meredith/*Rennell Elem Sch*	185
Akin, Jeff/*Memorial Middle Sch*	405
Akyurek, Atila/*Harmony Sch Fine Arts & Tech [284]*	4
Alamo, Kim/*University Preparatory HS*	305
Alaniz, Adam/*Sudderth Elem Sch*	385
Alaniz, Belinda/*Salazar Crossroads Academy*	305
Alaniz, Eduardo/*Roosevelt Alt Sch*	222
Alaniz, Elizabeth/*Edinburg Classical Academy [297]*	3
Alaniz, Laura/*Harvard Elem Sch*	191
Alarcon, Maricela, Dr/*Lloyd M Knowlton Elem Sch*	38
Alba, Debra/*Santa Rita Elem Sch*	286
Albright, Nancy/*Meadow Oaks Academy*	115
Albritton, Jodie/*Bullard Intermediate Sch*	336
Albury, Tamara/*Young Women's Leadership Acad*	353
Albus, Doug/*Hirschi High Sch*	392
Alcala, Adelina/*Buena Vista Sch*	315
Alcala, Melissa/*Cast Tech High Sch*	40
Alderete, Jodi/*East Side Elem Sch*	73
Aldrin, Renee/*Early College High Sch-Midland*	285
Alejandro, Naomi/*Milam Elem Sch*	392
Alejandro, Susana/*Early Childhood Campus*	256
Aleman, Alberto/*United High Sch*	388
Aleman, Mary, Dr/*Mission Options Academy*	222
Alex, Kristen/*Cypress Elem Sch*	397
Alexander, Ashanta/*Barbara Bush Primary Sch*	232
Alexander, Cheryl/*Handley Elem Sch*	106
Alexander, Clement/*Daniel Webster Elem Sch*	99
Alexander, Joseph/*Indian Spring Middle Sch*	282
Alexander, Lance/*Klein Forest High Sch*	197
Alexander, Lisa/*Walnut Glen Academy Excellence*	107
Alexander, Lori/*Kelley Elem Sch*	405
Alexander, Mandi/*Trenton Elem Sch*	147
Alexander, Melinda/*Colorado Elem Sch*	289
Alexander, Sharon/*Edna Rowe Elem Sch*	99
Alexander, Tammy/*Community Learning Center*	195
Alfaro, Victor/*Riverside Middle Sch*	352
Alford, Patricia/*Gateway Daep Sch*	23
Algier, Kristin/*Uplift Heights Prep Prim Sch [309]*	13
Alireza Abedi, Seyed, Br/*Al-Hadi Sch of Accel Lrng*	205
Allain, Susan/*Zachry Middle Sch*	39
Allen, Carlotta/*Quest Academy*	155
Allen, Charles/*Pearland Jr High School East*	53
Allen, Dee/*Wortham Elem Sch*	156
Allen, Edie/*Sanford Fritch Elem Sch*	238
Allen, Erica/*Heights Elem Sch*	161
Allen, Jamey/*Huffman Elem Sch*	82
Allen, Kathy/*J W Monday Elem Sch*	252
Allen, Kelly/*Ferdinand Herff Academy*	40
Allen, Kerstin/*Club Hill Elem Sch*	105
Allen, Lauri/*Irene Clinkscale Elem Sch*	247

PRINCIPAL INDEX

Market Data Retrieval

NAME/School	PAGE
Allen, Lee/*David Elem Sch*	291
Allen, Manuela/*Premier HS-San Antonio West [297]*	10
Allen, R Scott/*Kinder HS Perform & Visual Art*	192
Allen, Robert/*Rice High Sch*	300
Allen, Salina/*Shugart Elem Sch*	106
Allen, Sandra/*Faith Christian Academy*	390
Allen, Tenisha/*Frederick Douglass Elem Sch*	100
Allen, Teyan/*Spicewood Elem Sch*	399
Allen, Thia/*Dean Highland Elem Sch*	282
Allen, Zachary/*Bishop T K Gorman Cath Sch*	339
Allison, Jennifer/*Lorena Middle Sch*	280
Allman, Chad/*Tomball Junior High Sch*	203
Allred, Jane/*Jefferson Achievement Ctr*	360
Almanza-Pena, Olivia/*Irving Dual Language Academy*	40
Almanza, Anabela/*Southmost Elem Sch*	64
Almanza, Olivia/*Irving Middle Sch*	40
Almaraz, Christina/*Means Young Womens Ldrshp Acad*	369
Almaraz, Elma/*Zapata North Elem Sch*	407
Almendarez, Jose/*Gloria B Sammons Elem Sch*	179
Almond, Jamie/*San Jacinto Elem Sch*	292
Almquist, Lindsie/*Jarrell High Sch*	396
Almquist, Lindsie/*Nadine Johnson Elem Sch*	396
Alongi, Michelle/*Clarence Galm Elem Sch*	36
Alonzo, Brenda/*N L Trevino Elem Sch*	217
Alonzo, Frances/*South Elem Sch*	271
Alonzo, Gloria/*John F Kennedy Elem Sch*	216
Alpern, Laura, Dr/*El Paso Country Day Sch*	139
Alphin, Michael/*Harmony High Sch*	376
Alsup, Ronny/*Rivercrest High Sch*	323
Althage, Philip/*Great Hearts Irving [282]*	4
Althof, Crystal/*Roscoe Collegiate Mont ECC*	301
Althof, Crystal/*Roscoe Elem Sch*	301
Althof, Gregory/*Roscoe Collegiate High Sch*	301
Altindag, Mustafa/*Harmony Sch Innov-Brownsville [284]*	4
Altman, Chris/*Margaret Wills Elem Sch*	318
Altman, Heidi/*St Mary's Sch*	400
Alvarado, Adriana/*Idea Clg Prep-Riverview*	219
Alvarado, Gabe/*Gregory-Portland Mid Sch*	331
Alvarado, Lupita/*Guadalupe Regional Middle Sch*	68
Alvarado, Maria/*Premier HS-Brownsville [297]*	9
Alvarado, Roy/*Ft Stockton High Sch*	315
Alvarado, Roy/*Ft Stockton Middle Sch*	315
Alvarado, Sal/*Flour Bluff Interm Sch*	304
Alvarado, Steve/*Sabinal High Sch*	378
Alvarez, Enrique/*Cantu Elem Sch*	222
Alvarez, Griselda/*C Stainke Elem Sch*	215
Alvarez, Joan/*Idea Clg Prep-McAllen*	219
Alvarez, Joseph/*Luling High Sch*	61
Alvarez, Josie/*Kolda Elem Sch*	303
Alvarez, Marcus/*Wood Middle Sch*	36
Alvarez, Martha/*Raul Perales Middle Sch*	388
Alvarez, Nancy/*Celina Primary Sch*	78
Alvarez, Natalie/*Marian Manor Elem Sch*	138
Alvarez, Pedro/*Memorial High Sch*	221
Alverez, Alison/*Coahoma Elem Sch*	234
Alvidrez, Veronica/*Mission Valley Elem Sch*	138
Alzamora, Roger/*Vista Alt Learning Center*	353
Amason, Nicole/*Calhoun High Sch*	62
Amaya, Efrain/*William B Travis Middle Sch*	221
Amaya, Stephanie/*John Ireland Elem Sch*	101
Ambeau, Lauren/*Brookside Intermediate Sch*	158
Ambrose, Gail/*Christ the King Cathedral Sch*	272
Amerson, De'Monica/*Deloras E Thompson Elem Sch*	202
Amerson, Jeffrey/*Poe Elem Sch*	194
Amerson, Latonia/*Eisenhower 9th Grade Sch*	180
Amley, Hollis/*St John's Sch*	207
Ammerman, Matt/*Borger High Sch*	237
Ammons, Gregg/*Olton High Sch*	261
Amonett, Aaron/*Wylie West Junior High Sch*	361
Amsler, Eric/*Mission Valley Elem Sch*	382
Anagnostis, Anthe/*Creekview Middle Sch*	348
Anaya, Wendy/*Whispering Pines Elem Sch*	196
Ancira, Laura/*Alamo Heights Jr High Sch*	30
Anders, Dustin/*Loraine Sch*	289
Andersen, Kathrina/*Rosemont 6th Grade Center*	352

NAME/School	PAGE
Anderson, Allen/*Uplift Grand Preparatory [309]*	13
Anderson, Andrea/*Uplift Hampton Prep Chtr Sch [309]*	13
Anderson, Anna/*Roark Elem Sch*	345
Anderson, Briana/*KIPP Austin Obras [286]*	6
Anderson, Carolyn/*STEM Academy-Lewisville*	11
Anderson, Cornelius/*Ginnings Elem Sch*	121
Anderson, Cynthia/*Hillside Elem Sch*	133
Anderson, Denise/*Travis Middle Sch*	110
Anderson, Holly/*Bess Race Elem Sch*	347
Anderson, James/*Vistas High Sch*	198
Anderson, Jessie/*Mary McAshan Gibbs PK Center*	383
Anderson, Lucy/*Lakeland Elem Sch*	196
Anderson, Michael/*Cove Charter Academy [295]*	2
Anderson, Rod/*Kirbyville Junior High Sch*	241
Anderson, Shelley/*Anna High Sch*	77
Anderson, Tonya/*John Neely Bryan Elem Sch*	101
Andjelic, Jennifer/*New Caney Elem Sch*	294
Andress, Teresa/*Sam Houston Elem Sch*	121
Andrews, Alissa/*Boyer Elem Sch*	84
Andrews, Blake/*Iraan High Sch*	316
Andrews, Brad/*Coleman Junior High Sch*	142
Andrews, Daniel/*Epic Daep Alt Sch*	72
Andrews, Wilbert, Dr/*Forest Park Middle Sch*	170
Angel, Aura/*D McRae Elem Sch*	350
Angonia, Deanne/*Michael G Killian Middle Sch*	123
Anguiano, Joanne/*Jane A Hambric Sch*	136
Anguiano, Lidia/*Barron Elem Sch*	133
Anguiano, Sonia/*Oaklawn Elem Sch*	351
Annis, Anthony/*Karnes City High Sch*	250
Anthony-Swain, Dayna/*Decker Middle Sch*	371
Anthony, Fred/*Harlandale High Sch*	32
Anthony, Lakisha/*Walter Moses Burton Elem Sch*	151
Antill, Brandy/*Aim Center High Sch*	309
Antoine, Genia/*Pflugerville Elem Sch*	372
Anwar, Zaheer/*Darul Arqam Sch*	205
Apodaca, Jane/*Skipcha Elem Sch*	28
Aponte, Oscar/*Maple Lawn Elem Sch*	101
Appel, Haidi/*Lincoln Middle Sch*	135
Appelt, Jason/*Vysehrad Elem Sch*	263
Apple, Lori/*Haynes Northwest Academy*	392
Appling, Erin/*Parkview Elem Sch*	355
Aquil, Myah/*The Bridge Sch*	207
Aquilar, Leticia/*Progreso Early Clg Academy*	224
Araiza, Dan/*Secondary Alternative Center*	65
Araiza, Marleen/*Dr C M Cash Elem Sch*	67
Arambula-Ruiz, Maria/*Kazen Elem Sch*	387
Arambula, Gerardo/*Gwa Sierra Vista Charter HS [303]*	4
Aranda, Linda/*St Maryis Cathedral Sch*	319
Aranda, Maribel/*Crockett Middle Sch*	130
Arbabi, Alan/*McKinney High Sch*	81
Archer, Amanda/*Westbury Christian Sch*	207
Archer, Ann/*Overton Elem Sch*	270
Archer, Brian/*Joshua Christian Academy*	249
Archer, Dianna/*Splendora High Sch*	294
Archuletta, Lissa/*T S Hancock Elem Sch*	185
Ardoin, Lindsay/*Clark Intermediate Sch*	291
Arellano, Adriana/*Rodriguez Elem Sch*	65
Arenas-Goossen, Megan/*Idea Clg Prep-Tres Lagos*	219
Arenas, Jesus/*New Deal Middle Sch*	271
Arenaz, Georgie/*Copperfield Elem Sch*	371
Arencibia, David/*Colleyville Middle Sch*	353
Arend, Matthew/*Sigler Elem Sch*	83
Arevalo, William/*Texans Can Academy Austin [305]*	12
Arguelles, Sagrario/*Magellan Int'l Sch-Anderson Ln*	373
Arguijo, Serapio/*Lamesa Middle Sch*	117
Arizaga, Rosy/*North Dallas Adventist Academy*	115
Arizmendi, Chester/*Lucio Middle Sch*	64
Arizola, Rosana/*United Middle Sch*	388
Armelin, Todd/*John Winship Elem Sch*	202
Armendarez, Ann/*Windthorst Elem Sch*	20
Armendariz, Alejandro/*Loma Terrace Elem Sch*	138
Armstead, Chastity/*A W Brown Leadership Academy*	1
Armstrong, Amy/*High Point Elem Sch*	27
Armstrong, Danny/*Marathon Sch*	57
Armstrong, Lajuana/*R L Isaacs Elem Sch*	191

Texas School Directory — PRINCIPAL INDEX

NAME/School	PAGE
Armstrong, Penny/East Cliff Elem Sch	331
Armstrong, Tina/Living Word Christian Academy	206
Armstrong, Virginia/Houston Elem Sch	65
Arnett, James/Groves Middle Sch	243
Arnold, Audrey/Lake Pointe Elem Sch	349
Arnold, Chavala/Aw Brown-Fla Early Childhood	1
Arnold, Christine/Dimmitt High Sch	71
Arnold, Natalie/Truett Wilson Middle Sch	125
Arnold, S/Seton Home Charter Education	11
Arnold, Sally/Pathways 3H Campus	9
Arnold, Sally/UT Univ CS-Laurel Ridge	13
Arocha, Michelle/UT Univ CS-Methodist Children	13
Aron, Angela/Burnet Elem Sch	285
Arredondo, Adam/Seymour High Sch	25
Arredondo, Adrianna/Travis Early College High Sch	41
Arredondo, Danitra/Petersen Elem Sch	193
Arredondo, Elizabeth/Kirby Middle Sch	33
Arredondo, Geraldine/Dr Dennis Cantu Health Sci Sch	386
Arredondo, Pamela/Clark Middle Sch	387
Arredondo, Roberto/Dawson Elem Sch	303
Arreola, Mayra/Int'l Ldrshp TX-Windmill Lakes	109
Arreola, Michael/Newman Smith High Sch	97
Arrington, Dara/Gunter Elem Sch	166
Arriola, Roberto/Oralia R Rodriguez Elem Sch	174
Arsenault, Tracy/Vista Ridge Middle Sch	355
Arteaga, Veronica/J B Passmore Elem Sch	37
Arterbery, Cynthia/Valley Ranch Elem Sch	98
Arthur, Jill/Yarbrough Elem Sch	286
Asbun, Vanesa/Lakeland Elem Sch	123
Ash, Claudia/Idea Clg Prep-Pharr	219
Asheim, Betsy/Castle Hills Elem	34
Ashley, Eddie/Champion High Sch	254
Ashley, Mara/Brentwood Christian Sch	373
Ashmore, Julie/Austin Academic Center	232
Askew, Julia/Evolution Academy-Houston [279]	3
Aslan, Sevde/Harmony Sci Acad-Euless [284]	5
Asmerom, Temesghen/Emmett J Conrad High Sch	100
Atchison, Robert/June R Thompson Elem Sch	97
Atchley, Bobby/Brock High Sch	312
Atkins, Jennifer/Charles Rice Learning Center	99
Atkins, Lundy/Nixon-Smiley Elem Sch	164
Atkins, Teresa/Anita Scott Elem Sch	326
Atkinson, Alma/Lamar Elem Sch	65
Atkinson, Diana/Sullivan Elem Sch	67
Atkinson, Nancy/Wheeler Transitional Dev Ctr	110
Atmar, Sandra/Bonham Middle Sch	29
Atteberry, Robert/Kingwood Middle Sch	196
Augustain, George/Lorenzo G Loya Primary Sch	135
Augustus, Lorena/Owens Intermediate Sch	182
Aurich, George/Memorial Hall High Sch	206
Ausbury, Sharon/Trinity Christian Academy	45
Austin, Alesia/West Mesquite High Sch	111
Austin, Ericka/High School Ahead Acad MS	188
Austin, Lynn/Spring Branch Elem Sch	201
Austin, Mareka/Irma Marsh Middle Sch	347
Austin, Michele/North Creek Elem Sch	82
Authier, Kate/Wilemon Steam Academy	143
Autrey, Stephen/Mike Moses Middle Sch	298
Autry, Pat/Lindsay Elem Sch	91
Avci, Orhan/Harmony Sch Innov-Waco [284]	4
Avedician, Rosa/James P Butler Elem Sch	136
Avery, Anthony/Hazel Harvey Peace Elem Sch	351
Avery, Russell/Westview Sch	207
Avery, Terry/West Oso High Sch	306
Avey, Yvonne/Parsons Elem Sch	270
Avie, Erica/R P Harris Elem Sch	190
Avila, Jennifer/Campestre Elem Sch	136
Avila, Leonel/Daniel Ramirez Elem Sch	223
Axelson, Greg/Coppell Middle School North	98
Ayala, Irma/Richard J Wilson Elem Sch	351
Ayala, Rachel/Hudson Elem Sch	64
Ayala, Yvonne/Palmview High Sch	220
Ayci, Mugire/Harmony Sch Exc-Houston [284]	4
Aycock, Beth/Salado High Sch	29
Ayen Metoyer, Nicole/Fleming Middle Sch	190
Ayers, Steve/Newell E Woolls Interm Sch	284
Ayik, Mustafa/Harmony Sch Exc-Laredo [284]	4
Aykanat, Mert/Harmony Sch Innov-San Antonio [284]	4

B

NAME/School	PAGE
Baacke, Debbie/Lutheran South Academy	206
Babine, Krista/The Kinkaid Sch	207
Babineaux, Jamie/Fannindel High Sch	120
Baca, Betty/Harlem Elem Sch	188
Baca, Brooks/Bowman Middle Sch	82
Baca, Genie/Eastridge Elem Sch	318
Baccus, Charlane/Barbara Gordon Montessori Sch	358
Backus, Scott/McDowell Middle Sch	284
Bacom, Barry/Lockhart Pride High Sch	61
Bacon, William/Divide Elem Sch	255
Bacque, Rita/Morningside Elem Sch	123
Badger, Anne/Trinity Christian Academy	116
Badillo, Patricia/L F Blanton Elem Sch	97
Bados, Cecilia/Bradfield Elem Sch	105
Baez, Paul/Rees Elem Sch	182
Baggerly, Julie/Shadow Oaks Elem Sch	201
Baggs, Erin/Kings Academy Chrn Sch	339
Bagley, Charles/Savannah Lakes Elem Sch	51
Bahena, Jo'Anna/Highland Meadows Elem Sch	100
Bailey, Bryan/Lazbuddie Sch	315
Bailey, Christy/Marvin Elem Sch	142
Bailey, Cicely/Earl & Hazel Harris Academy	179
Bailey, Craig/Mt Pleasant High Sch	364
Bailey, Edra/W M Green Elem Sch	352
Bailey, Jennifer, Dr/Johnston McQueen Elem Sch	170
Bailey, Jon/Manor High Sch	371
Bailey, Kasey/Lawson Middle Sch	189
Bailey, Katrina/Kathy Caraway Elem Sch	399
Bailey, Maresa/Lakeview Centennial High Sch	106
Bailey, Mike/Wheeler Sch	391
Bailey, Rod/Nocona Elem Sch	290
Bailey, Tara/Tuscany Heights Elem Sch	36
Bain, Kim/Rowlett Elem Sch	106
Baines, Garrett/Hedley Sch	127
Baird, Kelly/Como Pickton Sch	231
Bairrington, Donna/Greens Prairie Elem Sch	55
Baisy-Dyer, Alieshia/Uplift Luna Prep Primary [309]	13
Baker, Abby/Barbara Walker Elem Sch	251
Baker, Amy/Izetta Sparks Elem Sch	79
Baker, Dana/Wilson Elem Sch	179
Baker, Diana/Bill Hasse Elem Sch	51
Baker, Dianna/Bakers Preparatory Sch	155
Baker, Donna/Nacogdoches Christian Academy	298
Baker, Grae/Austin Montessori Sch	373
Baker, Holly/Imagine Intl Academy-N Texas [029]	5
Baker, Jim/Delay Middle Sch	123
Baker, John/Pearl M Hirsch Elem Sch	202
Baker, Latanya/James Masters Elem Sch	33
Baker, Latanya/Judson Learning Academy	33
Baker, Lisa/Communications Arts High Sch	36
Baker, Megan/Magnolia Parkway Elem Sch	293
Baker, Norma/Maude Moore Wood Elem Sch	28
Baker, Ross/Three Rivers Jr Sr High Sch	268
Baker, Sarah/Carlisle Sch	327
Bakir, Selcuk/Harmony Sci Acad-Lubbock [284]	5
Balboa, Becky/White Oak Middle Sch	171
Balch, Jennifer/Stults Road Elem Sch	113
Balderas, Dianna/Scroggins Elem Sch	191
Balderas, Edward/Larkspur Elem Sch	35
Balderas, Sharon/Park Village Elem Sch	33
Balderrama, Maritza/Lebarron Park Elem Sch	138
Baldwin, Denisse/Annie Purl Elem Sch	395
Balentine, Robert/Academy of Arts at Branson	246
Bales, Amanda/Emerson Elem Sch	318
Ball, Andy/Clifton Middle Sch	46
Ballagh, Sheila/Burleson Early Chldhd Center	31
Ballard, Chrystal/Quitman Junior High Sch	404
Ballard, Nathan/Paso Del Norte Sch	136
Ballard, Sarah/Park Lakes Elem Sch	196

PRINCIPAL INDEX

Market Data Retrieval

NAME/School	PAGE
Ballesteros, Antonio/Longoria Middle Sch	217
Ballesteros, Myrandi/Covenant Christian Academy	358
Ballesteros, Olivia, Dr/David Crockett Elem Sch	303
Balleza, Geraldine/Frank M Tejeda Academy	32
Ballouli, Mahassen/Arabic Immersion Magnet Sch	191
Baloglou, Shelley/Sunrise Elem Sch	318
Balser, Shelby/Tivy High Sch	256
Balzer, Jill/Haltom Middle Sch	346
Balzer, Joanna/Hill Country Montessori Sch	254
Banegas, Wendy/Presa Elem Sch	138
Banfield, Sue/Belton Early Childhood Sch	26
Bankhead, Glenell/Academy Middle Sch	26
Banks, Kevin/Spring Leadership Acad Mid Sch	203
Banks, Victoria/Texas Military Institute	45
Bankston, Penelope/Parkland High Sch	138
Banner, Jeffrey/Shepton High Sch	83
Bannister, Jim/Lawrence D Bell High Sch	354
Bannowsky, Amy/Menard Elem Middle Sch	285
Baptiste, Lasonya/Abraham Lincoln Middle Sch	243
Barba, Jesus/Jose Damian Elem Sch	132
Barbarow, Amber/Arredondo Elem Sch	153
Barber, Douglas/North Mesquite High Sch	111
Barber, Nathan/Emery Weiner Sch	205
Barber, Stacy/Beverly Hills Intermediate Sch	198
Barcelona, Tony/Berry Miller Junior High Sch	53
Barcena, Rosalinda/Liberty Elem Sch	277
Bardo, Brent/Harmony Sch Enrichment-Houston [284]	4
Bare, Stacy/Ischool High University Park [297]	6
Barefield, Elijah/J H Hines Elem Sch	282
Bargas, Jacob/Cameron Dual Lang Magnet Sch	130
Baringer, Todd/Prince of Peace Christian Sch	126
Barker, Cindy/Woodland Hills Elem Sch	196
Barker, Debbie/Hazel S Pattison Elem Sch	152
Barker, Marco/Rosemont Elem & Prep Lang MS	102
Barker, Marco/Rosemont Primary Sch	102
Barker, Tony/Hcal	119
Barksdale, Christopher, Dr/Young Mens Ldrshp Acad-Flornce	104
Barlow, Mary/Coastal Oaks Christian Sch	19
Barmore, Amanda/London Sch	305
Barnes, Aimee/Advantage Academy-Waxahachie	96
Barnes, Anita/Harrell Budd Elem Sch	100
Barnes, Chandra/San Jacinto Christian Academy	319
Barnes, Clinton/Harmony Sch Innov-Carrolltn [284]	4
Barnes, Dana, Dr/Hollenstein Career & Tech Ctr	349
Barnes, Eric/Bray Elem Sch	97
Barnes, Erin/Cedar Grove Elem Sch	317
Barnes, Glenn/Cleveland High Sch	265
Barnes, Joette/Oak Crest Elem Sch	31
Barnes, Katherine/Sacred Heart Sch	19
Barnes, Mark/Bovina Middle Sch	314
Barnes, Peter/Cornerstone Christian Sch	44
Barnes, Raymorris/Spring Forest Middle Sch	201
Barnes, Sonja/Jimmie Tyler Brashear Elem Sch	101
Barnett, Clark/Garrison Senior High Sch	298
Barnett, Joycelyn/William James Middle Sch	352
Barnett, Matt/Woodrow Wilson Jr High Sch	265
Barnett, Mellany/Shelton Sch	116
Barnett, Stacy/Happy Middle High Sch	343
Barnett, Vanette/Highland Park Elem Sch	319
Barochin, Arlene/Uplift Infinity Prep Sch [309]	13
Barr, Randy/Redland Oaks Elem Sch	35
Barr, Roger/Marble Falls Middle Sch	60
Barragan, Amy/Oak Dale Elem Sch	318
Barrayam, Norma/Celestino Mauricio Soto ES	99
Barraza, Alejandra, Dr/Carroll Early Chldhd Center	40
Barraza, Alonzo/Crosby Elem Sch	133
Barraza, Benny/Bivins Elem Sch	317
Barrentine, Daniel/Frisco High Sch	79
Barrera, Aurelia/Berlanga Elem Sch	303
Barrera, Christina/Moses Menger Elem Sch	304
Barrera, Destiny/Spring Meadows Elem Sch	34
Barrera, Gus/Ben Bolt-Palito Blanco HS	245
Barrera, K/St Joseph Sch	246
Barrera, Laura/Roque Guerra Jr Elem Sch	340
Barrera, Lisa/St Paul Catholic Sch	44
Barrera, Roy/Montclair Elem Sch	304
Barreto-Romero, Natascha/Galindo Elem Sch	366
Barreto, Guadalupe/World Languages Institute	352
Barrett, Audra/Woodland Elem Sch	406
Barrett, Bonnie/Daugherty Elem Sch	105
Barrett, Channa, Dr/Austin Middle Sch	109
Barrett, Ellen/Second Baptist Sch	207
Barrett, Jay/Amarillo Area Ctr Advance Lrng	317
Barrett, Justin/Trinity Springs Middle Sch	355
Barrett, Katie/Springridge Elem Sch	113
Barrett, Laura/Yeager Elem Sch	186
Barrientes, Amanda/Olney Junior High Sch	406
Barrientes, Ashlan/New Tech San Antonio High Sch	41
Barrington, Melissa/Barbers Hill Elem Sch South	72
Barrios, Claudia/Cardenas Center	31
Barrios, Sandra/Jack Lowe Sr Elem Sch	100
Barron-Flores, Rebecca/Leon Valley Elem Sch	38
Barron, Amy/Bloomburg Sch	70
Barron, Amy/Pewitt Elem Sch	296
Barron, Jeanette/Cross Plains Elem Sch	62
Barron, Jerrell/Wharton High Sch	390
Barry, Lynne/Meadow Wood Elem Sch	201
Bartlett, Brian/Mexia Junior High Sch	267
Bartlett, Catherine, Dr/Lone Star Elem Sch	293
Bartlett, Donnie/South Grand Prairie 9th GR Ctr	108
Bartley, Damico/Ross Sterling Middle Sch	196
Barto, Suzanne/St Laurence Catholic Sch	155
Bartolotta, Jeffrey/Kirkpatrick Middle Sch	351
Barton, Abigayle/Harvey Elem Sch	257
Barton, Daniel/Shepherd High Sch	330
Barton, Jerrod/Rosebud-Lott High Sch	145
Barton, Lori/Ft Concho Elem Sch	365
Barton, Michelle, Dr/Irvin M Shlenker Sch	206
Bartosh, Ann/Tuloso-Midway High Sch	305
Bartush, Beth/Sacred Heart Sch	92
Basaaran, Adhirai/West Plano Montessori Sch	86
Basham, Cretia/Judy Hajek Elem Sch	247
Basham, Kirby/Grandview High Sch	248
Basham, Mark/Independence Elem Sch	355
Bashinski, Beth/Eternity Christian Sch	205
Bashir, Elora/Qalam Collegiate Academy	116
Basoglu, Mehmet/Harmony Sch Innov-Ft Worth [284]	4
Bass, Lakesha/Stafford Elem Sch	141
Bass, Teri/Sabine Elem Sch	170
Bassano, Brad/Prairiland Junior High Sch	260
Bassett, Gail/Good Shepherd Catholic Sch	114
Bassett, Jana/Bendwood Sch	200
Bassinger, Debra/T H McDonald Middle Sch	111
Batch, Brent/Rio Vista Middle Sch	249
Bateman, Angel/James Williams Elem Sch	152
Batenhorst, Shay/St Anthony's Elem Sch	95
Bates, Allen/Victory Christian Academy	403
Bates, Andrew/Sabine Pass Sch	244
Bates, Jennie/Westwood JHS Math Sci Ldrshp	113
Bates, John/Assumption Catholic Sch	203
Bates, Khristi/Saint Mary's Hall	45
Bathke, John/High Point Elem Sch	172
Bathke, John/Round Top Carmine High Sch	147
Batik, Steffany/New Tech High Sch-Coppell	98
Batiste, Angela/Katherine Johnson Tech Mag Sch	104
Batsell, Deborah/First Baptist Sch	68
Batts, Penny/Trimmier Elem Sch	28
Batts, Sara/Union Hill Sch	377
Bauer, Jennifer/John C French Elem Sch	117
Bauer, Molly/Challenger School-Avery Rnch	400
Bauer, Vivian/Dr Abraham P Cano Fresh Acad	65
Bauer, Vivian/Harlingen High Sch	65
Baughman, Lisa/Industrial Elem Sch East	240
Baughman, Michael/Burkburnett Middle Sch	391
Baum, Kelly/New Home Sch	273
Baumgartner, Richard/Rise Academy	10

Texas School Directory — PRINCIPAL INDEX

NAME/School	PAGE
Baumman, Michelle/*Reuben Johnson Elem Sch*	81
Baxter, Kurt/*Dumas Junior High Sch*	295
Baxter, Stacey/*Denton Calvary Academy*	126
Baxter, Tim/*The Colony High Sch*	124
Bay, Amy/*Sul Ross Elem Sch*	55
Bayarena, Monica/*Coles High Sch & Ed Center*	303
Bayer, Robin/*J O Schulze Elem Sch*	109
Baysinger, Mike/*Pace Academy*	311
Bazan, Lorene/*Sharyland North Jr High Sch*	224
Bazan, Myrna/*Janowski Elem Sch*	191
Bazan, Nelda/*Most Precious Catholic Sch*	306
Bazan, Rodrigo/*Ramiro Barrera Middle Sch*	341
Bazar, Jim, Dr/*Christian School-Castle Hills*	44
Beachum, Deanna/*Eden Elem Sch*	90
Beachum, Lalla/*Mills Elem Sch*	367
Beadles, Staci/*Celeste Junior High Sch*	236
Beafneaux, Rachelle/*R D McAdams Junior High Sch*	160
Beagle, Steven/*Nederland High Sch*	243
Beaird, Miller/*Red Oak High Sch*	142
Beal, Krista/*Gainesville Jr High Sch*	91
Beal, Patricia/*Infinity Early College HS*	293
Beam, Larry/*Butterfield Elem Sch*	126
Bean, John/*Brazos Sch Inquiry-Tidwell [276]*	2
Bean, Lydia/*Newton High Sch*	301
Bean, Talana/*Stonegate Elem Sch*	354
Beane, Wanda/*Commerce Elem Sch*	236
Beasley, Billy/*Brownsboro Intermediate Sch*	213
Beaty, Jason/*Eagle Mountain Elem Sch*	348
Becan, Kimberly/*Wayne A Cox Elem Sch*	125
Becerra, Claudia/*Carver Learning Center*	365
Bechtel, Michelle/*Merryhill Sch*	359
Beck, Edward/*Wellington Junior High Sch*	86
Beck, Marcie/*Leon Heights Elem Sch*	27
Beckerley, Catherine/*Florence Middle Sch*	395
Beckham, Teresa/*Robert F Hunt Elem Sch*	376
Beckley, Pauline/*Holub Middle Sch*	182
Beckman, Anne/*Life School Oak Cliff [290]*	8
Bedair, Cathy/*Gladewater High Sch*	169
Beeler, Barbara/*Seashore Middle Academy*	11
Beene, Amber/*Saginaw Elem Sch*	349
Beesley, Brett/*Dumas Senior High Sch*	295
Beeson, Michael/*Pantego Christian Academy*	359
Beguerie, Elizabeth/*Fusion Acad-Houston Galleria*	206
Behee, Laura/*St Maria Goretti Sch*	358
Behling, Shana/*Oak Run Middle Sch*	89
Behr, Peter/*The Kinkaid Sch*	207
Behrendsen, Kathy/*Barbara Cockrell Elem Sch*	53
Behrman, Shannon/*Grace Covenant Academy*	237
Beistegui, Patricia/*Draw Academy*	2
Belcher, Kristen/*Lamar Elem Sch*	292
Belcher, Randy/*Central Junior High Sch*	354
Belko, Laneil/*Dean H Krueger Elem Sch*	37
Bell, Breyanna/*Kirk Elem Sch*	185
Bell, Cassandra/*Vernon & Kathy Lewis Mid Sch*	181
Bell, Cory/*Boerne Academy*	254
Bell, Dan/*Harmony Sch Innov-Garland [284]*	4
Bell, Demetria/*Ronald E McNair Elem Sch*	102
Bell, Doyle/*Blooming Grove Junior High Sch*	299
Bell, Elisha/*Creekside Elem Sch*	317
Bell, Gloria/*St Louis Early Childhood Ctr*	338
Bell, Myra/*Peck Elem Sch*	193
Bell, Rhea/*Manor Middle Sch*	28
Bell, Ron/*Fort Bend Christian Academy MS*	155
Bell, Roslyn/*Parkway Elem Sch*	348
Bell, Sanee, Dr/*Morton Ranch Jr High Sch*	152
Bell, Terry/*Joan Postma Elem Sch*	185
Bell, Tracey/*Vega Jr Sr High Sch*	308
Bellamy, Catherine/*Labay Middle Sch*	185
Bellard, Linda/*Garcia Elem Sch*	190
Bellomy, Tracy/*Blum Sch*	227
Belote, Tara/*Barrow Elem Sch*	52
Beltran, Karla/*Hickman Elem Sch*	106
Belyeu, Joe/*Liberty Christian Sch*	126
Bemis, Roger/*Msgr Kelly Catholic HS*	244
Benavides, Ben/*Weatherford Elem Sch*	83
Benavides, Claudia/*Senator Judith Zaffirini ES*	388
Benavides, Cristina/*Western Hills Elem Sch*	134
Benavides, Jennifer/*Fox Technical High Sch*	40
Benavides, Kimberly/*George Clarke Elem Sch*	350
Benavides, Mayna/*Walker Junior High Sch*	385
Benavides, Misty/*Premont Early College Academy*	246
Benavides, Perla/*Jose Borrego Middle Sch*	222
Benavides, Tiffany/*Bailey Junior High Sch*	344
Benavidez, Dorene/*KIPP Esperanza Dual Lang Acad [289]*	7
Benavidez, Judith/*Palo Alto Elem Sch*	42
Benavidez, Lilly/*Stafford Early Childhd Ctr*	32
Benavidez, Melissa/*John C Holmgreen Center*	37
Benavidez, Romeo, Dr/*Rosendo Benavides Elem Sch*	220
Bendele, Benicia/*Liberty High Sch*	266
Benford, Melvin/*Dr R D Cathey Middle Sch*	221
Beninga, Melanie/*West Cypress Hills Elem Sch*	371
Benitez, Andrew/*El Paso Leadership Academy*	3
Benitez, Geri/*Monroe S May Jr Elem Sch*	38
Bennet, Cason/*Bellevue Sch*	74
Bennett, Brendia/*Hill Country Adventist Sch*	256
Bennett, Erica/*Early College HS at Timberview*	356
Bennett, Gerald/*Clinton P Russell Elem Sch*	99
Bennett, Jimmy/*East Ridge Elem Sch*	301
Bennett, Kendra/*Henrietta Elem Sch*	74
Bennett, Michelle/*KIPP Sharp Prep [288]*	7
Bennett, Sasha/*West Elem Sch*	271
Bennett, Tiffany/*Genoa Elem Sch*	199
Bennett, Tracey/*Horne Elem Sch*	185
Bennett, Vivian/*David Anthony Middle Sch*	184
Bennett, Wayne/*Aransas Pass High Sch*	330
Bennette, Marla/*Acad of Leadershp & Tech-Mound*	246
Benningfield, Robbye/*Cornerstone Christian Sch*	361
Benscoter, Brian/*Grace Community Jr Sr High Sch*	339
Benskin, Al, Dr/*Waxahachie Challenge Academy*	142
Benson, Terri/*Academy-Science & Health Prof*	291
Bentley, Bernadette/*Petrosky Elem Sch*	182
Bentley, Kim/*Tradewind Elem Sch*	318
Benzor, Irene/*Normandy Crossing Elem Sch*	187
Beran, Christina/*Mary M Boals Elem Sch*	79
Berckenhoff, Lisa/*Ezzell Elem Sch*	262
Berduo, Melina/*Meridian World Charter Sch*	8
Berger, Dennis/*Meadow Sch*	362
Berger, Geri, Dr/*Brandeis High Sch*	36
Bergman, Heather/*Dean Middle Sch*	184
Berkenhoff, Terry/*Nyos Charter School-M M Campus*	8
Bermea, Ana/*Our Lady of Refuge Sch*	277
Bermea, Iliana/*Milam Elem Sch*	286
Bermea, Lynda/*Seadrift Sch*	62
Bermea, Sandy/*Potranco Elem Sch*	284
Bernal-Tamaren, Jennifer/*Jewel C Wietzel Center*	32
Bernal, Erica/*Pleasanton Elem Sch*	21
Bernal, Lorraine/*KIPP UN Mundo Dual Lang Acad [289]*	7
Bernal, Rocio/*L L Hotchkiss Elem Sch*	101
Bernardino, Nancy/*Solar Prep Sch for Girls-Bonhm*	103
Berner, Peter, Dr/*Willow Bend Academy-Plano*	86
Berngen, Frank/*Shamrock Junior High Sch*	391
Bero, Jennifer/*Dennis Miller Elem Sch*	82
Berridge, Elizabeth/*Wheelock Elem Sch*	271
Berringer, Walter/*Chisholm Trail High Sch*	348
Berry, Alan/*Carr Middle Sch*	175
Berryman, Lori/*Western Plateau Elem Sch*	318
Berthel, Scott/*Trinity Christian Academy*	116
Bertrand, Lisa/*Magnolia Intermediate Sch*	293
Beseda, Sunny/*Axtell High Sch*	278
Besgrove, Tracey/*Norwood Elem Sch*	247
Bess, Michelene/*Rapoport Acad-N Campus ES [277]*	10
Bessent, Cynthia/*Baird Elem Sch*	62
Bessent, Cynthia/*Baird Middle Sch*	62
Bessent, Lisa/*Wylie West Elem Sch*	361
Bessire, Chera/*Bennett Elem Sch*	269
Bessire, Cindy/*Muleshoe High Sch*	22
Betak, Tandy/*Flatonia High Sch*	147
Betancourt, Brenda/*Kenneth White Jr High Sch*	222
Betancourt, Vanessa/*El Dorado High Sch*	136
Betencourt, Deeanne/*Anton Sch*	229

School Year 2019-2020 — 800-333-8802

PRINCIPAL INDEX

NAME/School	PAGE
Bethely-Day, Ricci/Judson Secondary Alt Sch	33
Bethencourt, Nancy/Idea Academy-Ingram Hills	218
Bethley, Troy/West Orange-Stark Elem Sch	309
Bettis, Joni/Hoover Elem Sch	345
Betts, Angie/Franklin Elem Sch	392
Betts, Kelly/Tyler Street Christian Academy	116
Betts, Tim/Jose Antonio Navarro Elem Sch	299
Beuscher, Tom/Awty International Sch	205
Bever, Jonathan/Liberty Hill High Sch	398
Beverly, Amy/H C Carleston Elem Sch	53
Bevill-Nelson, Misty/Thomas O Hicks Elem Sch	124
Bewely, Nancy/Parish Sch	206
Bezner, Joy/Cypress Crnty Christian Sch	205
Bholan, Ben, Dr/Arlington College & Career HS	343
Bibler, Amy/Quanah High Sch	177
Bice, Brenda/Stanton Learning Center	119
Bice, Brenda/Tierra Blanca Early Child Cent	119
Bickham, Darrin/Hallettsville High Sch	262
Bickley, Ryan/Grady Burnett Jr Senior HS	85
Bicknell, Greg/W A Porter Elem Sch	346
Bicknell, Joel/St Andrew's Episcopal Day Sch	319
Biddle, Paula/Tyler Classical Academy [297]	13
Biddy, Darla/W F George Middle Sch	392
Bierman, Angela/Brady Elem Sch	277
Bieser, Emily/Advanced Learning Academy	39
Bieser, Kathy/Advanced Learning Academy	39
Bietz, Tiffany/James L Wright Elem Sch	307
Bigenho, Christopher, Dr/Virtual Learning Academy	124
Bigley, Terrance/Burton Hill Elem Sch	350
Biles, Lisa/Selwyn College Prep Sch	126
Billescas, Nelda/Olle Middle Sch	182
Billieter, Amy/Daniels Elem Sch	256
Billings, Belynda/Bowie Elem Sch	153
Billingslea, Amy/Daingerfield Jr High Sch	296
Billingsley, Gary/Miller Grove Sch	231
Bills, Larry/Merkel Middle Sch	361
Billups, Kourtnei/K B Polk Elem Sch	101
Bilton, Bertran/Killough Middle Sch	182
Bilyeu, Denver/Grape Creek Elem Sch	364
Binford, Andy/Central Heights Middle Sch	297
Bingham, Dennis/Premier HS-Irving South [297]	9
Bingham, Gregory/Fairview Junior High Sch	51
Bircher, Kay/Club Estates Elem Sch	303
Bird, Bryan/Bethany Elem Sch	82
Bird, Coby/Southwest Christian Sch-Prep	359
Bird, Thaddeus, Dr/All Saints Episcopal Sch	358
Birdwell, Bethany/Frisco ISD Early Childhood Sch	79
Birdwell, Elizabeth/Pantego Christian Academy	359
Birdwell, Elizabeth/Pantego Christian Academy	359
Birdwell, Matthew, Dr/Ponder High Sch	126
Birkes, Dean/River Road High Sch	319
Birkmire, Suzelle/Meadowbrook Elem Sch	351
Bishop, Kristin/Shepard Elem Sch	83
Bishop, Wade/Ennis High Sch	140
Bissell, Kimberly, Dr/Windsor Park Elem Sch	304
Bitters, Connie/North Elem Sch	357
Bittings, Nikki/Jim Barnes Middle Sch	174
Bixby, Nicole/Arturo Salazar Elem Sch	99
Black, Alfred/West Brazos Junior High Sch	52
Black, Anna/Gateway Alternative Ed Center	391
Black, Bill/Smyer Jr Sr High Sch	229
Black, Philip/Wm B Travis Elem Sch	140
Black, Rikke/Lee Middle Sch	365
Black, Russell/Bowie Intermediate Sch	290
Blackburn, Kim/Seven Hills Elem Sch	125
Blackburn, Sherri/San Leon Elem Sch	160
Blackmon, Heath/Loop Sch	157
Blackshire, Michael/Arrow-Harvest Preparatory Acad [273]	1
Blackstone, Caroline/James A Arthur Interm Sch	355
Blackwell, Brian/Walnut Grove Middle Sch	141
Blackwell, Janet/Rockenbaugh Elem Sch	347
Blackwell, Karena/Longbranch Elem Sch	141
Blackwell, Melanie/Frankston Elem Sch	15

NAME/School	PAGE
Blain, Chad/Pleasant Grove Elem Sch	49
Blain, Laurie/Gus Winston Cain Elem Sch	339
Blain, Mr/Bullard High Sch	336
Blain, Regina/Leonard Elem Sch	146
Blair, Bruce/Ranch Academy	10
Blair, Cindy/Chandler Elem Sch	76
Blair, Cody, Dr/Rider High Sch	392
Blair, Kelly/Rockdale Junior High Sch	288
Blair, Kelsa/Zephyr Sch	59
Blair, Loretta/Beckville Jr Sr High Sch	311
Blair, Rachael/Sageland Elem Sch	138
Blair, Trey/Ft Worth Country Day Sch	359
Blake, Christopher/Three Lakes Middle Sch	338
Blake, David/J W Williams Middle Sch	325
Blake, Matthew, Dr/Texas Military Institute	45
Blake, Yvette, Dr/Mission Glen Elem Sch	150
Blakey, Carmen/Rowlett High Sch	106
Blalock, Joel/Covington Sch	227
Blanchard, Denise/Banquete High Sch	302
Blanchard, Myrna/North Hi Mount Elem Sch	351
Blancher, Lou/Treetops International Sch	12
Blanco, April/Terrace Elem Sch	201
Bland, Cassandra/Como Pickton Sch	231
Bland, Christopher/Gus Garcia Middle Sch	32
Bland, Michael/Lyles Middle Sch	106
Blank, Melissa/Armstrong Middle Sch	82
Blankenship, Michael/V R Eaton High Sch	125
Blanks, Laura Lea/Crisman Sch	171
Blanton, Deeanna/Water Valley Elem Sch	365
Blassingame, Brock/Crockett Intermediate Sch	260
Bledsoe, Justin/William J Thornton Elem Sch	39
Bleggi, Deni/Gulledge Elem Sch	82
Blessing, Andy/Lee Elem Sch	360
Blessum, Anayansi/Winn Elem Sch	368
Blevins, Stacy/Eagle Ridge Elem Sch	355
Bley, Gretchen/John Jay Sci & Engineer Acad	37
Blizzard, Tona/Cannon Elem Sch	353
Block, Melissa/Godley Intermediate Sch	247
Block, Robin/Bridlewood Elem Sch	122
Blocker, Christy/Falls City Elem Sch	250
Blocker, Christy/Falls City High Sch	250
Blodgett, Kris/O L Slaton Middle Sch	270
Bloom, Taleen/Oak Grove Elem Sch	35
Bloomer, Todd/Winston Churchill High Sch	36
Bloomfield, Maria/Otis Brown Elem Sch	110
Blount, Margie/Zelma Hutsell Elem Sch	153
Bluemel, Kelly/Enhanced Horizons	3
Bluemel, Kelly/Hill Country Yth Rch-Najim Sch	5
Bluitt, Jacqueline/Dallas Co Jj Aae-SAU	96
Blythe, Tuck/Masters Sch	212
Boarman, Stacy/Adolphus Elem Sch	153
Boatman, Amy/Salem Lutheran Sch	207
Boatright, Carmen, Dr/Big Springs-Brune Charter Sch	1
Boatright, James/Eastwood High Sch	137
Bobbitt, Dylis/Early Childhood Center	232
Bock, Adam/Thomas Hatchett Elem Sch	38
Bock, Jennifer/Colby Glass Elem Sch	36
Bock, Kara/New Braunfels High Sch	89
Bock, Martha/Bridgeport Elem Sch	402
Bodey, Teresa/Gateway Elem Sch	237
Bodine, Kenneth/New Horizons High Sch	248
Bodine, Kenny/Joshua 9th Grade Campus	248
Boedeker, Mary/Marti Elem Sch	247
Boettger, Cavin, Dr/Denison High Sch	166
Bogard, Rebecca/St John Paul II Catholic Sch	204
Boggan, Alison/Kemp-Carver Elem Sch	55
Bogle, Latecha/Commonwealth Elem Sch	150
Bohacek, John/Family Christian Academy	205
Bohannan, Brandon/Alba-Golden Jr Sr High Sch	404
Bohannon, Jennifer/Butler Elem Sch	344
Bohannon, Katy/Iduma Elem Sch	28
Bohanon, Aundra/Metro Opportunity Sch	351
Bohanon, Aundra/Middle Level Learning Center	351

Texas School Directory — PRINCIPAL INDEX

NAME/School	PAGE
Bohlken, Ada/*Oliver Wendell Holmes High Sch*	38
Boiles, Lea/*Elizabeth Smith Elem Sch*	356
Bojescul, John/*Garner Middle Sch*	35
Bolack, Lauren/*Richland Elem Sch*	113
Bolden, Felicia, Dr/*Lula Belle Goodman Elem Sch*	150
Bolding, Melissa/*Colony Meadows Elem Sch*	150
Boling, Terrence/*Aristoi Classical Academy*	1
Bolton, Beverly/*Meador Elem Sch*	199
Bolton, Roxana/*West Columbia Elem Sch*	52
Bolz, Patricia/*Blanche Dodd Elem Sch*	122
Bomar, Amanda/*Pecan Creek Elem Sch*	121
Bomar, Bonnie, Dr/*Groesbeck High Sch*	267
Bond, Kandy/*Barbara Jordan Elem Sch*	149
Bonner, Rachel/*Criswell Elem Sch*	251
Bonsal, Sheri/*Porter Elem Sch*	294
Bontrager, Lisa/*Legacy Preparatory Chrn Acad*	295
Booe, Kevin/*Jayne Ann Miller Elem Sch*	270
Booker, Mark/*Clardy Elem Sch*	133
Booles, John/*Sendera Ranch Elem Sch*	125
Boone, Diane/*Alt Edu Program Phoenix Campus*	345
Boone, Dianne/*Azle Hornet Academy*	345
Boone, Lindsey/*Hattie Dyer Elem Sch*	122
Boone, Phil/*Wylie Intermediate Sch*	361
Boone, Tanisha/*Dan Powell Intermediate Sch*	349
Booth, Gaila/*Olmos Elem Sch*	35
Booth, Paul/*Meridian Alternative Sch*	47
Booth, Paul/*Meridian Middle High Sch*	47
Booth, Paul/*Whitney Middle Sch*	228
Borchers, Valerie/*Becker Elem Sch*	366
Bordeau, Ginger/*Carpenter Hill Elem Sch*	211
Bordelon, Bryan/*Sharpstown International Acad*	194
Borden, Ray/*Juan Seguin High Sch*	344
Bordner, Jennifer/*Cherokee Sch*	332
Borel, Kyle/*Harmony Sci Acad-Austin [284]*	4
Borel, Kyle/*Vic Robertson Elem Sch*	399
Boren, Jennifer/*Canyon High Sch*	321
Bores, Dinorah/*Walnut Creek Elem Sch*	368
Borg, Bill/*Vanguard College Prepatory Sch*	283
Borgarello, Angela/*Claude Curtsinger Elem Sch*	79
Boring, Richard/*Southard Middle Sch*	84
Borowicz, Sarah/*Giddings Intermediate Sch*	263
Borowicz, Sarah/*Neidig Elem Sch*	24
Borrego, Rosalina/*Raul Longoria Elem Sch*	224
Bosco, Lisa/*Christ the King Sch*	113
Bosley, Mrs/*Huntington Middle Sch*	17
Bosley, Shelly/*Rice Elem Sch*	338
Boswell, Blaise/*Vernon Middle Sch*	394
Boswell, Lea/*Fairmont Elem Sch*	186
Boswell, Scott/*City View Jr Sr High Sch*	391
Bothe, Sheila/*Harvest Christian Academy*	359
Bott, Ryan/*Bryan Adams High Sch*	99
Bottlinger, Nancy/*Carver Elem Sch*	395
Bottoms, Debra/*Liberty Grove Elem Sch*	106
Bouchard, Kai/*Robert Turner Colege-Career HS*	53
Boulware, Shade/*Corsicana High Sch*	299
Bourgeois, Daniel/*Boyd Intermediate Sch*	402
Bourgeois, Daniel/*Boyd Middle Sch*	402
Bourland, Marcus/*LaGrone Advanced Tech Complex*	121
Bowens, Kyalla/*Acton Elem Sch*	104
Bowers, Calvin/*Odem High Sch*	331
Bowers, Lisa/*Luther Jones Elem Sch*	303
Bowers, Melanie/*Helen Edwards Early Chldhd Ctr*	252
Bowie, Kia/*Kohrville Elem Sch*	197
Bowles, Kelsey/*Walter E Floyd Elem Sch*	111
Bowles, Penny/*Sonny & Allegra Nance ES*	125
Bowman, Derek/*Navasota High Sch*	172
Bowman, John/*Gilmer High Sch*	376
Bowman, Melanie/*Rancho Sienna Elem Sch*	398
Bowser, Jimmy/*Jack Faubion Middle Sch*	81
Boyce, Colby/*Atlanta Middle Sch*	69
Boyce, Pamela/*Daep Center*	69
Boyd, Allison/*North Riverside Elem Sch*	355
Boyd, Brandon/*Lufkin High Sch*	18
Boyd, Cecilia/*Lloyd & Dolly Bentsen Elem Sch*	224
Boyd, Dana/*East Point Elem Sch*	137
Boyd, Felicia/*Stephen F Austin Primary*	272
Boyd, Gerald/*Idea Clg Prep-Mays*	219
Boyd, Keith/*Ellis Elem Sch*	344
Boyd, Kristin/*Tom R Ellisor Elem Sch*	293
Boyer, Lesley/*Houston Learning Academy*	206
Boyle, Gretchen/*St Joseph High Sch*	383
Boyle, Laigha/*Grand Prairie Early Clg HS*	107
Boyle, Laigha/*Grand Prairie High Sch*	107
Boysen, Eric/*Kindred Elem Sch*	42
Bozas, Sebastian/*L P Waters Early Childhood Ctr*	236
Bozeman, Linda/*Blanton Elem Sch*	121
Bracamontes, Mario/*Buell Central High Sch*	223
Bracey, Anke/*Boyd Elem Sch*	402
Bradford, Kay, Dr/*Florence Elem Sch*	395
Bradford, Linda/*Holy Rosary Sch*	155
Bradford, Pam/*Pleasant Grove Interm Sch*	49
Bradford, Todd/*Rockwall-Heath High Sch*	325
Brading, Aungelique, Dr/*Viridian Elem Sch*	354
Bradley, Alicia/*T G Terry Elem Sch*	103
Bradley, Elizabeth/*Pope Elem Sch*	185
Bradley, Jeffrey/*Joe Tison Middle Sch*	314
Bradley, Leroy/*Michael R Null Middle Sch*	200
Bradley, Sharon/*Sam Jamison Middle Sch*	53
Bradley, Sheila/*Washington Early Childhood Ctr*	15
Bradshaw, Bill/*Bruce Junior High Sch*	376
Bradshaw, Cathy/*Millsap Elem Sch*	313
Bradshaw, Shawnell/*Hartman Elem Sch*	85
Brady, Beth/*Rodriguez Elem Sch*	41
Brady, Donna/*Winkley Elem Sch*	397
Brakel, Debra/*A G Elder Elem Sch*	248
Braley, Rocio/*M Robinson Elem Sch*	185
Brame, Erica/*Ruby Thompson Elem Sch*	193
Bramlett, Adam/*Eastland High Sch*	129
Bramwell, Ernest/*Clack Middle Sch*	360
Branam, James/*Celeste High Sch*	236
Branch, Greg/*Oakwood Elem Sch*	265
Branch, Laurie/*Henderson Elem Sch*	252
Brandenburg, Sonya/*STEM2 Preparatory Academy*	65
Brandenburger, Corey/*Cross Lutheran Sch*	89
Brandon, Diana/*A L Benavides Elem Sch*	406
Brandstatt, Erin/*Rolling Hills Elem Sch*	319
Brandt, Julie/*Cedar Creek Sch*	44
Brandt, Tom/*W B Travis Vanguard & Academy*	103
Branecky, Robin/*Whispering Hills Achieve Ctr*	147
Brannen, Joe/*New Summerfield Sch*	73
Brannigan, Jim/*St John Paul II High Sch*	306
Branson, Carlon/*Hale Center High Sch*	175
Brantley, Amanda/*Patton Elem Sch*	367
Brashear, Duana/*Peach Creek Elem Sch*	294
Braswell, David/*La Gloria Elem Sch*	245
Braswell, Marci, Dr/*Ricardo Elem Middle Sch*	258
Bratcher, Lorie/*Curtis Elem Sch*	314
Bratton, Billy/*Maya Angelou High Sch*	101
Bratton, Billy/*Village Fair-Elem Daep*	103
Brauer, Gregory/*Veterans Memorial High Sch*	34
Braun, Robin/*Westside Elem Sch*	52
Braun, Tami/*Wellington Elem Sch*	124
Braveboy, Peter/*Barwise Middle Sch*	392
Brawner, Abbey/*Glenwood Private Sch*	295
Brawner, Randy/*Chico High Sch*	403
Bray, Kelly/*Bosqueville Elem Sch*	278
Bray, Kristen/*Mosaic Academy*	319
Bray, Margaret/*Marshall Law & Med Svc Mag HS*	38
Bray, Robert/*Dawson Sch*	299
Breaux, Mark/*Lubbock Christian Sch*	272
Breaux, Paul/*Marshall Middle Sch*	242
Bredt, Lucette/*Richard Milburn Acad-Killeen [298]*	10
Breedlove, Carrie/*Lake Highlands Jr High Sch*	112
Brenz, Susan/*Sadie Woodard Elem Sch*	185
Brewer, James/*Longview High Sch*	170
Brewer, Katherine/*Village Sch*	207
Brewer, Paige/*JW & Ruth Christie Elem Sch*	79
Brewer, Pat/*Yoakum Primary Annex Sch*	118
Brewster, Grace/*Mathews Elem Sch*	368
Brewster, Mike/*Buna High Sch*	240

PRINCIPAL INDEX

Market Data Retrieval

NAME/*School*	PAGE	NAME/*School*	PAGE
Breyer, Roxanne/*Hill School of Fort Worth*	359	Brown, Deion/*Idea Clg Prep-Eastside*	218
Briceno, Felipa/*Townewest Elem Sch*	151	Brown, Derrick/*Young Men's Leadership Academy*	41
Bridges, Aaron/*Chisum Middle Sch*	259	Brown, Frank/*Lincoln Junior High Sch*	330
Bridges, Catherine/*Florence Hill Elem Sch*	107	Brown, Hartwell/*Washington Junior High Sch*	292
Bridges, Jason/*Beckville Sunset Elem Sch*	311	Brown, Heath/*Madisonville High Sch*	273
Bridges, Jeanne/*Orange Grove Elem & Inter Sch*	245	Brown, Jeffrey/*Flower Mound 9th Grade Center*	123
Bridwell, Maria/*Covenant Christian Academy*	226	Brown, Joe/*North Belton Middle Sch*	27
Brinkley-Lopez, Barbara/*Transmountain Early College HS*	134	Brown, Joe/*Springtown Intermediate Sch*	313
Brinkley, Monica/*Rusk Elem Sch*	134	Brown, Joshua/*Int'l Ldrshp TX-Orem*	109
Brinkman, Brenda/*Stephen F Austin Elem Sch*	331	Brown, Karen/*McLean Sixth Grade Sch*	351
Brinkman, Tammy/*Coupland Elem Sch*	395	Brown, Kathy/*Lemm Elem Sch*	197
Brinson, John/*Odyssey Sch*	373	Brown, Katina/*Marshall High Sch*	209
Brisendine, Susan/*Colonial Heights Elem Sch*	362	Brown, Kristi/*Northgate Crossing Elem Sch*	202
Briseno, Anissa/*Roy Roberts Elem Sch*	270	**Brown, Latricia**/*Liberty Hill Middle Sch*	28
Briseno, Juan/*Alvin High Sch*	51	Brown, Lee/*Cloverleaf Elem Sch*	187
Briseno, Norma/*Dublin High Sch*	143	Brown, Leigh/*Godley Middle Sch*	247
Briseno, Tasha/*Shady Grove Elem Sch*	60	Brown, Lisa/*Chandler Intermediate Sch*	213
Brison, Susan/*Dr Joey Pirrung Elem Sch*	111	Brown, Marlena/*Godwin Elem Sch*	84
Bristow, Clarie/*John A Sippel Elem Sch*	173	Brown, Matthew/*Donna Shepard Intermediate Sch*	356
Brittain, Katie/*Rose Haggar Elem Sch*	83	**Brown, Mekasha**/*Summit Education Center*	105
Britton, Alifia/*Double File Trail Elem Sch*	398	Brown, Miranda/*Daep*	279
Britton, Wendy/*West Elem Sch*	345	Brown, Monty, Dr/*Denton Creek Sch*	125
Broadway, Kim/*Hodges Elem Sch*	111	Brown, Omarian/*Crowley Middle Sch*	348
Brock, Brianne/*Charlotte High Sch*	20	Brown, Patrick/*Hardin-Jefferson High Sch*	178
Brock, Brianne/*Charlotte Middle Sch*	20	Brown, Sarah/*Hassler Elem Sch*	197
Brockhoff, Alma/*Zavala Elem Sch*	134	**Brown, Shanah**/*Farmers Branch Elem Sch*	97
Brodt, Elisabeth/*Joe M Adams Junior High Sch*	152	Brown, Shanna/*Harry H Herndon Interm Sch*	326
Brogan, Leonard/*Ridge Point High Sch*	151	Brown, Sharon/*St Paul's Episcopal Sch*	375
Brokovich, Jeffrey/*Johnston Elem Sch*	360	Brown, Shelia/*R M Sorrells Sch-Ed & Soc Srvs*	102
Bromley, Dustin/*Crosby High Sch*	183	Brown, Sonya/*Westwood Junior High Sch*	16
Bromley, Dustin/*Crosby Middle Sch*	183	Brown, Stacie/*The Steam Academy at Mambrino*	230
Bronstad, Mandi/*Speegleville Elem Sch*	281	Brown, Tammy/*Hunt Sch*	255
Brooks, Amber/*Townsell Elem Sch*	110	**Brown, Temeka**/*Dunbar Middle Sch*	159
Brooks, Brian/*Stephen F Austin STEM Academy*	52	Brown, Terri/*Pittsburg Elem Sch*	68
Brooks, Daniel/*Woodlake Hills Middle Sch*	34	Brown, Thurman/*Connally Junior High Sch*	279
Brooks, Dawn/*Adrian Sch*	307	Brown, Tisha/*Gullett Elem Sch*	367
Brooks, Earnest/*La Porte Junior High Sch*	198	Brown, Tressi/*Anna Middle Sch*	77
Brooks, Heather/*Floresville North Elem Sch*	400	Brownell, Robin/*Mildred M Hawk Elem Sch*	121
Brooks, Keith, Dr/*C E King High Sch*	200	Brownfield, Kelly/*Smylie Wilson Middle Sch*	270
Brooks, Marlon/*John L Patton Academic Center*	101	Browning, Scott/*St Paul Lutheran Sch*	359
Brooks, Marlon/*L G Pinkston High Sch*	101	Bruce, Deanna/*Idea Clg Prep-Bluff Sprgs*	218
Brooks, Marlon/*School Cmty Guidance Center*	102	Bruce, Jolene/*Gateway Tech High Sch [292]*	3
Brooks, Marlon/*Village Fair-Lacey Middle Sch*	103	Bruce, Kama/*St Andrew's Episcopal Sch*	373
Brooks, Melodye/*Alvarado Junior High Sch*	246	Bruce, Robert/*Panola Early College High Sch [293]*	9
Brooks, Paula/*Jackie Carden Elem Sch*	348	Bruce, Terri/*Elva C Lobit Middle Sch*	159
Brooks, Rhodena/*Madisonville Elem Sch*	273	Bruha, Patty/*Woodlands Christian Academy*	295
Brooks, Tammie/*Maria Moreno Elem Sch*	101	Bruhn, Kari/*James Patterson Elem Sch*	150
Brooks, Torrance/*Clark Intermediate Sch*	202	**Bruman, Coleman**/*Gilbreath-Reed Career Tech Ctr*	106
Broom, Beverly/*Kitty Hawk Middle Sch*	33	Brumbelow, Rosemary/*Esprit International Sch*	295
Brotemarkle, Jamie/*Spillane Middle Sch*	185	Brumm, Jeremy/*Lutheran South Academy*	206
Brotherton, Brandi/*Alief Early College High Sch*	182	Brungardt, Dianne/*St Philip & St Augustine Acad*	114
Brott, Chris/*R S Kimbrough Middle Sch*	111	Brunk, Glen/*Farrell Elem Sch*	344
Broughton, Debra/*Gloria Marshall Elem Sch*	202	**Brunner, Travis**/*Cowan Elem Sch*	366
Brouillard, Kimberly/*Clear Creek Intermediate Sch*	158	Brusewitz, Paul/*R K Driggers Elem Sch*	38
Brouillard, Kimberly/*League City Intermediate Sch*	159	**Brutonr, Jennifer**/*Kathryn Griffis Elem Sch*	235
Broussard, Carie/*Mauriceville Elem Sch*	308	Bryan, Jeff/*Sunshine Cottage Sch-Deaf Chld*	45
Broussard, Kent/*Splendora Junior High Sch*	294	Bryan, Kin/*Tatum Middle Sch*	328
Brown-Griffin, Kristi/*James R Brooks Middle Sch*	285	Bryan, Melissa/*South Hi Mount Elem Sch*	352
Brown, Andrea/*Bluebonnet Elem Sch*	119	Bryant, Bob/*San Marcos Baptist Academy*	212
Brown, Baldwin/*I M Terrell Elem Sch*	351	Bryant, Bruce/*Canadian Middle Sch*	213
Brown, Bridget/*Wellman-Union Sch*	362	Bryant, Bryan/*Brenham Junior High Sch*	385
Brown, Brittany/*Hillside Elem Sch*	321	Bryant, Darla/*Walcott Elem Sch*	119
Brown, Carlotta/*Madison High Sch*	189	Bryant, James/*Gruver High Sch*	176
Brown, Carrie/*Trinity School of Midland*	286	Bryant, Jennifer/*Shady Shores Elem Sch*	122
Brown, Cheryl/*St James Day Sch*	50	Bryant, Kenneth/*North Shore 10th Grade Ctr*	187
Brown, Cindy/*Fitzgerald Elem Sch*	344	Bryant, Leigh/*Key Sch*	359
Brown, Clifton/*Reagan Co Middle Sch*	321	**Brysch, Karla**/*Poth Elem Sch*	401
Brown, Daniel/*Bastrop Intermediate Sch*	23	**Bryson, Carol**/*Kennedale Alternative Ed Prog*	356
Brown, Darrell/*Major Cheney ES-S Birdville*	346	Buban, Lane/*Travis Bryan High Sch*	55
Brown, David/*Earnest O Woods Interm Sch*	381	Buchanan, Joann/*Frank Madla Elem Sch*	42
Brown, Dawnyell/*Harbach-Ripley Charter Sch*	4	Buck, Angelina/*Midland Alternative Program*	286
Brown, Deb/*Sacred Heart Sch*	295	Buck, Kenneth/*Timberwood Middle Sch*	196
Brown, Deeadra/*MacArthur High Sch*	110	Buck, Kim/*Venus Middle Sch*	249

Texas School Directory — PRINCIPAL INDEX

NAME/School	PAGE
Buckhalton, Kimberly/H F Stevens Middle Sch	348
Buckley, Alice/Applied Learning Academy	350
Buckley, Natalie/Birnham Woods Elem Sch	291
Buckner, Sandra/Kruse Elem Sch	199
Budimir, Daniel/North Bridge Elem Sch	225
Bueno, Erin/San Jacinto Elem Sch	130
Bueno, Madeline/Paul W Ott Elem Sch	38
Buente, Thomas/Shirley J Howsman Elem Sch	38
Bufkin, Kristi/Munday Elem Sch	259
Buhl, Antreshawn/Aldridge Elem Sch	82
Bujanda, Martha/Thomas C Marsh Prep Academy	103
Bujnoch, Melanie/Oak Ridge HS 9th Grade Campus	292
Bull, Jessica/Alvord Middle Sch	402
Bullion, John/Bosque Co Educational Center	47
Bumgarner, Shara/Joy Sch	206
Bundrick, Cindy/Overton Secondary Sch	328
Bunker, Tiffany/St John Early Childhood Center	207
Bunsen, Aracelie/Southwest High Sch	43
Burak, Douglas/Leonides G Cigarroa Elem Sch	101
Buras, Janet/SS Peter & Paul Sch	89
Burbridge, Oliver/Harris Co Juvenile Justice CS	5
Burchett, Becky/Calvary Baptist Sch	295
Burden, Jacquelyn/Foster Elem Sch	344
Burdett, John/Prosper High Sch	84
Burdsal, Sha/Bunche Elem Sch	285
Burgess, Tonya/McGregor Elem Sch	280
Burgin, Cody/De Kalb Middle Sch	48
Burgoon, Andrew/City View Elem Sch	321
Burgy, Matthew/St Mark's Episcopal Sch	207
Burk, Linda/Health Careers High Sch	37
Burke, Kathleen/Early College High Sch	27
Burke, Ryane/Idea Academy-Walzem	218
Burkhalter, Jon/Rusk Junior High Sch	73
Burkhart, Casey/Burnet High Sch	60
Burks, Davida/Centennial Elem Sch	270
Burleson, Brad/Henderson Junior High Sch	144
Burleson, Johnny/TLC Academy	12
Burley, Frances/Parks Elem Sch	199
Burnett, Betsy/Mart High Sch	280
Burnett, Jacqueline, Dr/East Texas Mont Prep Academy	169
Burnett, John/Bremond Middle Sch	324
Burnett, John/KIPP Northeast College Prep [288]	7
Burnett, Mary Helen/Dunn Elem Sch	344
Burnett, Windy/Emile Elem Sch	23
Burnham, Megan/Sally K Ride Elem Sch	292
Burns, Eric/C C Hardy Elem Sch	294
Burns, Francis/Our Lady-Perpetual Help Sch	174
Burns, Janna/Young Womens Leadership Acad	108
Burns, Jennifer/Northside Elem Sch	142
Burns, Kade/Mason High Sch	275
Burns, Mary/St Rita Catholic Sch	358
Burns, Stephanie/KIPP Austin Brave HS [286]	6
Burns, Tommy/Bear Branch Intermediate Sch	292
Burrell, Robert/Wedgwood Middle Sch	352
Burrow, Scott/Pringle-Morse Sch	177
Burrow, Tracie/Parker Elem Sch	286
Burruel, Amanda/Keller Middle Sch	355
Burrus, Jennifer/Mary DeShazo Elem Sch	22
Burt, Beth/Huntsville Intermediate Sch	383
Burt, David/Jasper Junior High Sch	241
Burt, Debbie/Robert S Hyer Elem Sch	108
Burt, Susan/Merriman Park Elem Sch	112
Burton, Christy/Bose Ikard Elem Sch	314
Burton, Evelyn/St Patrick Sch	306
Bush, Reginald/Kashmere High Sch	189
Bustillo, Becca/Otis Spears Elem Sch	79
Butcher, Regina/Susie T Fuentes Elem Sch	211
Butler, Amy/Weatherford Christian Sch	314
Butler, Charlie/Int'l Ldrshp TX-Westpark	109
Butler, Christine, Dr/Bradley Elem Sch	291
Butler, Christy/Kaufman Christian Sch	253
Butler, Dirrick/Sagamore Hill Middle Sch	352
Butler, Gordon/Lake Travis High Sch	370
Butler, John, Dr/Marine Military Academy	68
Butler, Linda/Pershing Park Elem Sch	28

NAME/School	PAGE
Butler, Ralph/Legacy Sch of Sport Sciences	7
Butler, Robert/Krum Middle Sch	122
Butler, Roxana/The Woodlands Classical Acad [297]	12
Butler, Sharla/Permian Basin Classical Acad [297]	9
Butler, Sharla/Scharbauer Elem Sch	286
Butler, Shelly, Dr/Mansfield Legacy High Sch	357
Butler, Stacia/Flossie Floyd Green Elem Sch	77
Butler, Travis/San Juan Diego Cath High Sch	372
Buxton, Becky/Highland Elem Sch	175
Bye, Mario/James E Rudder High Sch	55
Bynum, Clark/Garrison Middle Sch	298
Bynum, Summer/McNiel Middle Sch	392
Byrd, Bryan/Reed Middle Sch	105
Byrd, Derrick/Devine High Sch	283
Byrd, Jeanette/Cummings Elem Sch	182
Byrd, Lindsey/Academy at Nola Dunn	246
Byrne, Troy/Fusion Academy-Plano	85
Byther, Wanda/Reach High Sch	347
Byther, Wanda/Truce Learning Center	347

C

NAME/School	PAGE
Caballero, Cynthia/Nye Elem Sch	388
Caballero, Victor/Garden Park Elem Sch	63
Cabaniss, Angie/Deepwater Elem Sch	186
Cabrera, Lizbeth/Maran-Ata Christian Academy	139
Cabrera, Ronny/College & Career Center	219
Caceres, Bernadett/Donna North High Sch	215
Cadena, Ruben/Alicia R Chacon Int'l Lang Sch	137
Cady, Deana, Dr/Block House Creek Elem Sch	397
Caffery, Susan, Dr/Academy of Science & Tech	291
Caffey, Matt/Olney High Sch	406
Cage, Kristy/Berkner High Sch	112
Cager, Shenikwa/A W Brown Leadership Academy	1
Cagle, Michael/Kennedale High Sch	356
Cahill, Kari/Cross Roads Elem Sch	214
Cain, Andrea/Plummer Middle Sch	181
Cain, Jean/Tegeler Career Center	200
Cain, Jim/Sanger Middle Sch	126
Calcaneo, Eva Alicia/J B Alexander 9th Grade HS	387
Calderon, Jaime/Church Hill Middle Sch	88
Calderon, Laura/Vista Hills Elem Sch	138
Calderon, Nelda/Maria Alicia P Munoz Sch	215
Caldwell, Jason/Winona Elem Sch	339
Caldwell, Jason/Winona Intermediate Sch	339
Caldwell, Randall/Corinth Elem Sch	122
Caldwell, Randall/Lake Dallas Middle Sch	122
Caldwell, Sara/Kennedy Elem Sch	182
Calhoun, Christal/Tool Elem Sch	214
Calk, David/Tuloso-Midway Intermediate Sch	305
Calkins, Matthew/Deer Creek Elem Sch	397
Callahan, Deanna/Seele Elem Sch	89
Callaway, Tim/Christ Academy	393
Callaway, Virginia/Idea Clg Prep-Frontier	218
Callaway, Wayne/Farmersville High Sch	78
Callihan, Kristi/Paris Junior High Sch	260
Callis, Lorana/Jane Wessendorff Middle Sch	154
Callison, Kimberly/Hardwick Elem Sch	270
Calvert, Bryan/Bear Creek Elem Sch	353
Calvert, Darren/Irene L Chavez Excel Academy	37
Calvery, Kimberly/Wills Point Middle Sch	381
Calzada, Sandra/Rio Bravo Middle Sch	138
Camacho, Edgar/Natalia Junior High Sch	284
Camacho, Juanita/El Paso Adventist Jr Academy	139
Camarena, Elizabeth/Premier HS-S Austin [297]	9
Camarena, Emily/Dunaway Elem Sch	142
Camargo, Griselda/Josephine Castaneda Elem Sch	64
Camarillo, Gregorio/Elma Barrera Elem Sch	67
Camarrillo, Michael/Incarnate Word Academy	68
Camden, Paul/Ki Charter Academy	6
Cameron, Amanda/Evans Elem Sch	303
Camp, Alison/Austin Elem Sch	360
Camp, Harry/Memorial Private High Sch	206
Camp, Tracie/Crenshaw Elem & Mid Sch	160
Campa, Rogelio/Santa Maria Middle Sch	67

School Year 2019-2020   800-333-8802   TX-U9

PRINCIPAL INDEX

Market Data Retrieval

NAME/School	PAGE	NAME/School	PAGE
Campbell-Rhone, Khalilah, Dr/Worthing High Sch	189	Carey, Kristen/Tolar Elem Sch	230
Campbell, Alexis/Ray Elem Sch	396	Carielo, Cynthia/Edison High Sch	40
Campbell, Barb/YES Prep Fifth Ward [312]	14	Carlisle, Gordon/Marshall Leadership Academy	107
Campbell, Chelsey/Heritage Middle Sch	269	Carlisle, Kelly/Abernathy Middle Sch	174
Campbell, Gary/Gary W Campbell High Sch	252	Carlisle, Scott/Comanche Early Childhood Ctr	89
Campbell, Holly/Gordon Sch	310	**Carlisle, Scott**/Peaster Middle Sch	313
Campbell, Jasen/Wilmer-Hutchins High Sch	103	Carlisle, Whitney/Dickinson Elem Sch	107
Campbell, Jason/Great Lakes Academy	85	Carlovsky, Ben/Abiding Word Lutheran Sch	205
Campbell, Jonathan, Dr/Forney High Sch	252	Carlton, Yvette/Colmesneil Elem Sch	375
Campbell, Joshua/Mance Park Middle Sch	383	Carmona, Kathleen/Strickland Middle Sch	121
Campbell, Lindsey/Idea Clg Prep-San Juan	219	Carmona, Miguel/Achieve Early College High Sch	221
Campbell, Lisa/Northampton Elem Sch	197	Carnes, Christopher/Herrera Elem Sch	191
Campbell, Lori/Silvercrest Elem Sch	53	Carnett, Stephanie/Carver Center	285
Campbell, Nancy/Odessa Christian Sch	131	Carnigney, Donna/Petersburg Sch	175
Campbell, Robyn/Bernice Chatman Freeman ES	96	Carnley, Jan/DayStar Academy	284
Campbell, Shana/Cranfills Gap Sch	46	Caros, Jason/Founders Classical Acad Lwsvll [297]	3
Campbell, Tracie/Cayuga Sch	14	Carpenter, Antoinette/Whitaker Elem Sch	134
Campos, Evangeline/Browning Elem Sch	191	Carpenter, Barbra/Memorial Christian Academy	30
Campos, Lisa/Oak Meadow Elem Sch	35	Carpenter, Katie/KIPP Austin College Prep [286]	6
Campos, Rosalva/Freer Junior High Sch	128	Carpenter, Sharon/Salyers Elem Sch	202
Canales, Albert/McAllen High Sch	221	Carr, Doug/Christian Heritage Sch	171
Canales, Amanda/Idea Clg Prep-Donna	218	Carr, Edris/Grace Fellowship Christian Sch	115
Canales, Anna/Hebbronville Jr High Sch	244	Carr, Kelley/Lakeside Middle Sch	124
Canales, Judith/Garza-Pena Elem Sch	223	Carr, Lindsay/Belaire Elem Sch	364
Canales, Lydia/Eisenhauer Rd Baptist DC PS	44	**Carranco, John**/Andrews High Sch	16
Canales, Norma/Simon Rivera Early Clg HS	64	Carranco, Lawrence/William Hobby Middle Sch	39
Canales, Renee/Best Elem Sch	182	Carranza, Amy/Roberts Road Elem Sch	384
Canchola, Denise/Patti Welder Middle Sch	382	Carranza, Ericka/B L Gray Junior High Sch	224
Candelaria, Veronica/Horizon Middle Sch	132	Carrasco, Berta/Bradford Elem Sch	364
Canino, Nadia/Holy Family Catholic Sch	161	Carrasco, Lorena/Royalwood Elem Sch	200
Cannon, Mandi/Great Hearts Monte Vista-South [282]	4	Carreathers, Darnisha/Grand Prairie Collegiate Inst	107
Cano, Antonio/La Joya Senior High Sch	220	**Carrejo, Tanya**/Waller Junior High Sch	385
Cano, Ernestina/Vision Academy	217	Carrell, Kelly/Spearman High Sch	177
Cano, Homero/Austin Elem Sch	216	Carreon, Elizabeth/St Patrick Cathedral Sch	139
Cano, Lianna/Madison Elem Sch	41	Carrero, Rebeca/Risd Academy	113
Cano, Mauricio/Robbin E L Washington Elem Sch	138	**Carriaga, Benito**/Sgt Leonel Trevino Elem Sch	224
Cano, Michael/Borger Middle Sch	237	Carridine, Ronnita/Como Montessori Sch	350
Cano, Rodrigo/Whitley Road Elem Sch	355	Carrillo, Alfredo/Liberty Middle Sch	223
Canonico, Marcus/Crossroads High Sch	247	Carrillo, Pamela/Incarnate Word Elem Sch	306
Cantrell, Paige/Medlin Middle Sch	125	Carrington, DeWayne/Timpson Elem Sch	335
Cantu, Adriana/Desert Hills Elem Sch	132	Carrion, Delma/Dilley Elem Sch	157
Cantu, Ana/Burnet Elem Sch	189	Carroll, Karen/Idalou High Sch	269
Cantu, Bertha/Carmen Anaya Elem Sch	223	Carroll, Kimberly/Pro-Vision Academy	10
Cantu, Beth/Timothy Baranoff Elem Sch	367	Carroll, Ryan/Foster Middle Sch	170
Cantu, Cidonio, Dr/Alice High Sch	245	**Carroll, Steven**/Dudley Magnet Sch	382
Cantu, Enrique/Veterans Middle Sch	340	Carruth, Kathy/Holy Family Catholic Academy	114
Cantu, Eric/Connally Elem Sch	279	Carruyo, Alirio/Golden Rule CS-Illinois [281]	3
Cantu, Gilbert/Pearsall Intermediate Sch	157	**Carter, Andrea**/La Vernia Junior High Sch	401
Cantu, Jermaine/Wellington High Sch	86	Carter, Bobbie/Cooper Elem Sch	105
Cantu, Jesus/M D Betts Elem Sch	217	Carter, Carla/Arlon Seay Elem Sch	87
Cantu, Laurie/St Matthew's Episcopal Sch	226	Carter, Charlotte/Bebensee Elem Sch	344
Cantu, Maryjane/Washington Heights Elem Sch	352	Carter, Daniel/Founders Classical Acad Mesq [297]	3
Cantu, Michelle/Alicia Ruiz Elem Sch	387	Carter, Dianne/West Ridge Middle Sch	370
Cantu, Olga/United South High 9th Grade HS	388	Carter, Elisa/Hillcrest Elem Sch	245
Cantu, Oscar/Russell Elem Sch	64	Carter, Erika/Key Middle Sch	191
Cantu, Robert/Claude Sch	20	Carter, Hanna/Forsan Elbow Elem Sch	234
Cantu, Yolanda/Jubilee Leadership Academy [285]	6	**Carter, Hanna**/Forsan Jr Sr High Sch	234
Cantu, Yvette/Noemi Dominguez Elem Sch	65	**Carter, Ida**/J Ruth Smith Academy	179
Capehart, Chelsea/Central Elem Sch	252	Carter, Innetta/Cypresswood Elem Sch	180
Caperton, Desiree, Dr/Fannin Elem Sch	55	Carter, Jana/Royal Ridge Elem Sch	35
Caperton, Elizabeth/Wylie Preparatory Academy	86	Carter, Janee/Lone Oak High Sch	236
Capetillo, Blanca/Highlands Elem Sch	188	Carter, Jason/Roby High Sch	148
Caplinger, Jennifer/Barksdale Elem Sch	82	Carter, Kathryn/L O Donald Elem Sch	101
Carballo, Janie/John F Peeler Elem Sch	101	**Carter, Kimberly**/H O Whitehurst Elem Sch	267
Carcano, Benigna/Idea Academy-Tres Lagos	218	Carter, Kimberly/Port Neches Elem Sch	243
Cardenas, Gerardo/Centro Chrn Alpha Omega Acad	205	**Carter, Tangela**/Zan Wesley Holmes Jr Mid Sch	104
Cardenas, Sonya/Carvajal Early Chldhd Center	40	Carter, Tara/Faith Family Academy-Oak Cliff [280]	3
Cardenas, Trina/Jubilee Highland Hills [285]	6	**Caruso, Carrie**/T H McDonald Junior High Sch	153
Cardenas, Yvette/Pillow Elem Sch	368	Carver, Kelly/Holliday Middle Sch	19
Cardin, Ramona/Edna Mae Fielder Elem Sch	152	Cary, Deborah/Voss Farms Elem Sch	89
Cardin, Richard/Kenedy Middle Sch	251	Cary, Lillie/Reagan Elem Sch	177
Cardoza, Michelle/Berta Palacios Elem Sch	223	**Casal, Kristy**/Lamar Middle Sch	123
Carew, Stacia/Bleyl Middle Sch	184	Casamayor-Ryan, Carmen/Forman Elem Sch	82

Texas School Directory — PRINCIPAL INDEX

NAME/School	PAGE
Casares, Olivia/Lyons Elem Sch	191
Casas, Rebecca/Shaw Spec Emphasis Sch	304
Casas, Sonia/Thigpen-Zavala Elem Sch	221
Casas, Yvette/Chet Burchett Elem Sch	202
Casco, Jairo/James S Hogg Elem Sch	100
Caseltine, Tiffany/Maplebrook Elem Sch	196
Casey, Kayla/Little Cypress Elem Sch	308
Casillas, Michelle/Tom Lea Elem Sch	134
Casler, Andrew/Oak Forest Elem Sch	192
Casper-Teague, Laura/Spring Creek Elem Sch	56
Casquete, Klinger/Bonner Elem Sch	189
Cassidy, Brittaney/Trinity Middle Sch	374
Cassillas, Norma/Borrego Elem Sch	135
Castellanos, Armando/Einstein School Plano	85
Castelline, Lizette/Viola Cobb Elem Sch	183
Castilleja, Georgina/Ruby Sue Clifton Middle Sch	192
Castilleja, Kristy/Canyon Lake High Sch	88
Castillo, Alma/Anita T Dovalina Elem Sch	386
Castillo, Cain/Montana Vista Elem Sch	132
Castillo, Dan/Bovina High Sch	314
Castillo, Diana/Pilgrim Academy	194
Castillo, Elizabeth/Mitchell Elem Sch	193
Castillo, Florinda/Price Elem Sch	42
Castillo, Irma/Science Acad of South Texas	68
Castillo, Jaime/Longview Christian Academy	171
Castillo, Josie/Bruni Middle Sch	388
Castillo, Josie/Oilton Elem Sch	388
Castillo, Martha/Metz Elem Sch	367
Castillo, Miguel/Antonio Bruni Elem Sch	386
Castillo, Miguel/Delco Primary Sch	371
Castillo, Miguel/Horizon Montessori Academy I [301]	5
Castillo, Nancy/Donna High Sch	215
Caston, Paulette/E White Elem Sch	193
Castro, Adriana/Joe E Moreno Elem Sch	191
Castro, Ana/South Texas Prep Academy	68
Castro, Cindy/Oliveira Middle Sch	64
Castro, Deidra/S H Crowley Intermediate Sch	348
Castro, Jackie/Little Flower Sch	44
Castro, Jackie/St Margaret Mary Sch	44
Castro, Leroy/Alvin Junior High Sch	51
Castro, Luciano/Lockhart High Sch	61
Castro, Monica/Ssg Manuel R Puentes Mid Sch	137
Castro, Paul/A Plus Unlimited Potential Sch	205
Cates, Gary/Panhandle Junior High Sch	69
Cates, Kelli/Bob L Kirksey Elem Sch	267
Cates, Read/Edwin F Williams Interm Sch	307
Catuto, Patti/Victory Baptist Academy	314
Caudle, Virginia/Barron Elem Sch	371
Caughlin, Bryan/Wells Elem Sch	73
Cauthen, Jaylynn/Rio Vista Elem Sch	248
Cauthen, Ty/Central Junior High Sch	17
Cavazos-Tucker, Linda/Evers Park Elem Sch	121
Cavazos, Claudia/St Christopher Catholic Sch	204
Cavazos, Darlene/Idea Academy-McAllen	218
Cavazos, Haydee/Kennedy Elem Sch	191
Cavazos, Marla/Anne L MaGee Elem Sch	216
Cavazos, Michelle/Sam Houston Elem Sch	187
Cavazos, Ryan/Robbie E Howard Jr High Sch	142
Cavazos, Ryan/Waxahachie HS of Choice	142
Cawthon, Marsha/Trivium Academy	12
Cawthron, Kathy/Claude Berkman Elem Sch	398
Cayce, Jennifer/Ptaa-Greenville Mid High Sch	10
Cayce, Jennifer/Ptaa-Mesquite Mid High Sch	10
Cazares, Hector/Sam Houston Elem Sch	65
Ceballos, Roger/Benjamin Franklin Middle Sch	99
Ceci, Stacy/O'Dell Elem Sch	78
Cedano, Raquel/Robert M Beren Academy	207
Cegielski, Joe/Van Buren Elem Sch	244
Celorio-Reyes, Yvette/Frank & Sue McBee Elem Sch	367
Centeno, Ivelisse/La Academia De Estrellas CS	7
Center, Kendall/Castroville Elem Sch	284
Cerda, Alma/Monte Alto Elem Sch	223
Cerda, Jesus/Valley View Elem Sch	225
Cerda, Jose/Dr Joaquin Cigarroa Middle Sch	386
Cerda, Sandra/Juan N Seguin Elem Sch	220
Cerna, Jorge/Crystal City High Sch	407
Cerna, Joseph, Dr/Ft Sam Houston Elem Sch	32
Cerny, Bridgette/Hunt Elem Sch	117
Cerroni, Brenda/Bradley Middle Sch	34
Certain, Jason/Dripping Springs Middle Sch	210
Cervantes, Jana/Byron P Steele II High Sch	173
Cervantes, Olga/Truman Price Elem Sch	215
Cervantes, Padgett/Coyote Ridge Elem Sch	122
Cervantes, Thomas/Tornillo Elem Sch	137
Cevallos, Tara/St Austin Catholic Sch	372
Chacon, Miguel/Travis Elem Sch	222
Chacon, Patricia/Palm Grove Elem Sch	64
Chacon, Veronica/Ray Darr Elem Sch	277
Chaddick, Nathan/Ross S Sterling High Sch	188
Chadwick, Freda/Bethesda Christian Sch	358
Chairez, Cynthia/La Feria High Sch	65
Chalberg, Amie/Stonewall Elem Sch	163
Chamberlain, Yolanda/Mva Brownsville CHS [303]	8
Chambers, Ezra/Abernathy High Sch	174
Chambers, Jenci/Abernathy Elem Sch	174
Chambers, Kyle/Oliver Elem Sch	250
Chambers, Lisa, Dr/Tyrrell Elem Sch	243
Chambers, Michele/Ekklesia Christian Sch	358
Chambers, Sarah/Uplift Grand Preparatory [309]	13
Champagne, Mandie/Groves Elem Sch	243
Chandler, Ashley/Yorktown High Sch	118
Chandler, Ashley/Yorktown Junior High Sch	118
Chandler, Christy/Dearing Elem Sch	371
Chandler, Elizabeth/Ella Schorlemmer Elem Sch	382
Chandler, Joseph/Brenham High Sch	385
Chandler, Whitney/Living Rock Academy	89
Chaney, Andrea/Academy Elem Sch	26
Chaney, Cheryl/Weber Elem Sch	159
Chaney, Dexter/KIPP Pleasant Grove Primary [287]	7
Chang, Chaolin/Joslin Elem Sch	366
Chapa, Cassandra/Peete Elem Sch	338
Chapa, Cassandra/Ramey Elem Sch	338
Chapa, Kristina/Finley Elem Sch	387
Chapa, Richard/Industrial Trade Center	161
Chapa, Rosa/Idea Academy-Quest	218
Chaparro, Javier/Legacy Prep Chtr Acad-Mesquite	7
Chapman, Angela/Boone Elem Sch	182
Chapman, Angela/Montgomery Junior High Sch	293
Chapman, Kelly/Henry Bauerschlag Elem Sch	159
Chapman, Shannon/Irion County High Sch	238
Chappell, Jennifer/Trinity Charter Sch-Amarillo [307]	12
Chappell, Ragen/Nolan Richardson Middle Sch	135
Chappell, Reed/Seminole High Sch	158
Chappotin, Chris/Steam Middle Sch	247
Charles, Shanee/Imogene Gideon Elem Sch	357
Chavarria, Anita/Southwest Legacy High Sch	43
Chavera, Linda/Ted Flores Elem Sch	157
Chavez-Gibson, Sarah, Dr/Stanton Elem Sch	134
Chavez-Pinto, Claudia/Energized for Excellence ES	193
Chavez, Erin/Rainard School for the Gifted	206
Chavez, Jennie/Noel Elem Sch	130
Chavez, Leslie/Loma Verde Elem Sch	136
Chavez, Leticia/Eloy Salazar Elem Sch	215
Chavez, Luis/O G Wiederstein Elem Sch	173
Chavez, Mary/Rancho Verde Elem Sch	66
Chavez, Patricia/Indian Creek Elem Sch	43
Chavez, Stephanie/Garrett Elem Sch	200
Chavira, Cristina/Dr Sue Shook Elem Sch	136
Chavis, James/Meadowland CS Stepping Stones	8
Cheatham, Jenny/Shelton Sch	116
Cheek, Roxanne/Aikin Elem Sch	112
Chermak, William/Idea Clg Prep-Ewing Halsell	218
Cherry, Bonita/Waskom Middle Sch	209
Cherry, Brooke/James & Margie Marion ES	77
Cheryl, Fennell/Atascocita Springs Elem Sch	195
Chesser, Brandon/Siebert Elem Sch	129
Chesser, Chuck/Aspermont Elem Sch	342
Chester, Carol/Providence Christian Sch	116
Chesworth, Jennifer/Kentwood Early Childhood Ctr	233
Chevalier, Diane/Harmony Irons-Smith Interm Sch	376

PRINCIPAL INDEX

Market Data Retrieval

NAME/School	PAGE
Cheverier, Mike/*Willow Vista Intermediate Sch*	319
Cheverzer, Mike/*Wildorado Elem Sch*	308
Chew, Stephanie/*Wolflin Elem Sch*	318
Chide, Wendy/*Dickinson Alt Lrng Center*	159
Chilcoat, Jan/*Northside Baptist Sch*	383
Childress, Amy/*Charles Tosch Elem Sch*	111
Chilek, Jeremy/*Lindale High Sch*	337
Chilek, Jeremy/*Lindale Junior High Sch*	337
Chipres, Jorge/*Idea Clg Prep-Kyle*	219
Chirinos, Rebecca/*Peters Colony Elem Sch*	124
Chism, Lauren/*Dr J C Cannaday Elem Sch*	111
Chisum, Jean/*St Philip's Episcopal Sch*	379
Choat, Christopher/*Richardson High Sch*	113
Choate, John/*Christoval Jr Sr High Sch*	364
Choate, Julie/*McCall Elem Sch*	312
Choice, Jameile/*New Tech HS at BF Darrell*	102
Choice, Tai/*Covington Middle Sch*	369
Choice, Vanessa/*Plyler Alternative Educ Sch*	338
Chow-Jackson, Kimberly/*Country Place Elem Sch*	96
Chretien, Princess/*Tekoa Academy-Orange [304]*	11
Christenberry, Laura/*Laura Steele Montessori Acad*	41
Christensen, Dave/*W A Martin Elem Sch*	251
Christensen, Melissa/*Jack M Fields Sr Elem Sch*	196
Christenson, Gina, Dr/*Carroll Bell Elem Sch*	32
Christian, Roy/*Hutto High Sch*	396
Christopher, Bonetha/*Newton Elem Sch*	301
Chritian, Amy/*W C Stripling Middle Sch*	352
Chudej, Shelly/*Robinson Elem Sch*	281
Cintron, Jose/*Energized for Excellence ECC*	193
Cisneros, Kristi/*Pleasant Hill Elem Sch*	367
Cisneros, Sandra/*Southmayd Elem Sch*	190
Claiborne, Catherine/*Nichols Junior High Sch*	344
Clanton, Brad/*Levelland Middle Sch*	229
Clapsaddle, Teresa/*Canutillo High Sch*	132
Clark, Amy/*Lamar Elem Sch*	286
Clark, Becky/*North Dallas Adventist Academy*	115
Clark, Bianca/*Southwest Sch-Empowerment HS [278]*	11
Clark, Chris/*Lamar & Norma Hunt Middle Sch*	79
Clark, Darla/*Shady Oaks Elem Sch*	354
Clark, James/*Lady Bird Johnson Middle Sch*	109
Clark, Jamie/*Story Intermediate Sch*	15
Clark, Jeffrey/*Millsap Middle Sch*	313
Clark, Jerry/*School of Choice*	89
Clark, Kecia/*Uplift Hampton Prep Chtr Sch [309]*	13
Clark, Ollie/*J W Bishop Elem Sch*	349
Clark, Pamela/*Clark High Sch*	82
Clark, Preston/*Pine Forest Elem Sch*	309
Clark, Scootie/*All Saints Episcopal Sch*	244
Clark, Shavon/*Energized for STEM Academy HS*	193
Clark, Tammy/*Granbury Middle Sch*	230
Clark, William/*Step Charter School II*	11
Clarke, Jim/*Grace Academy of Dallas*	115
Clarke, Rachel/*A Plus Up-University Campus*	1
Clason, Brian/*Wayside Sci-Tech Preparatory*	14
Claudia, Sr/*Our Lady of the Rosary Sch*	306
Clausey, Nancy/*Ascension Episcopal Sch*	205
Clay, Jill/*Jackson Elem Sch*	337
Clay, Kellie/*Palmer Elem Sch*	151
Clayman, Dean/*St Mark's School of Texas*	116
Clayton, Alice/*Angleton Junior High Sch*	51
Clayton, Isabell/*Robert G Cole Jr/Sr High Sch*	32
Clayton, Philip/*Provan Opportunity Center*	372
Cleland, Laura/*Crown of Life Lutheran Sch*	358
Clement, Sandra, Dr/*Foy H Moody High Sch*	303
Clements, Carl/*North Plains Opportunity Ctr*	295
Clements, John/*Diboll High Sch*	17
Clements, Kristen/*Pegasus Sch Liberal Arts & Sci*	9
Cleveland, Susan/*John Marshall High Sch*	37
Clifford, Barry/*C W Cline Elem Sch*	160
Clifton, Sherry/*Irving Reg Day Sch Pgrm-Deaf*	109
Clifton, Yaneth/*Slack Elem Sch*	18
Clint, Nicole/*Ben L Brite Elem Sch*	63
Clubb, Shawn/*Hamshire Fannett Middle Sch*	242
Clyne, Brian/*Episcopal Day Sch*	68
Cobb-Eaglin, Lachandra/*Odom Academy*	242
Cobb, Charla/*Mesa Verde Elem Sch*	318
Cobb, Gina/*West Memorial Jr High Sch*	153
Cobb, Marcelina/*Main Street Imtermediate Sch*	399
Cobb, Randy/*Azle High Sch*	345
Cobb, Shelia/*Martinsville Sch*	298
Cobian, Rebecca/*Idea Academy-Edgemere*	217
Coble, Faith/*Kingdom Academy*	206
Cobos, Billy/*Gonzalez Elem Sch*	63
Coburn, Jeff/*Lowe Elem Sch*	84
Coburn, Kenisha/*Kealing Middle Sch*	369
Cochran, Casey/*Wills Point Junior High Sch*	381
Cockrell, Andrea/*Jackson Elem Sch*	83
Cockrell, Stephanie/*Folsom Elem Sch*	84
Cody, Andrew/*Alexander Sch*	114
Cody, Donnie/*Oak Woods Sch*	230
Cody, Kim/*Redwater Junior High Sch*	49
Coe, Annette/*Liberty Hill Middle Sch*	398
Coe, Betsy/*School of the Woods*	207
Coe, Kim/*China Spring Elem Sch*	278
Coffey, Keith/*Aquilla Sch*	227
Coffin, Linda/*Mary Immaculate Sch*	114
Coffman, Judith/*Alton Boyd Elem Sch*	76
Coffman, Lana/*Young Elem Sch*	403
Coggin, Kasey/*Redwater Elem Sch*	49
Cohea, Heather/*Gilbert Mircovich Elem Sch*	331
Cohns, Aishley/*Vernal Lister Elem Sch*	107
Coker, David/*Highland Middle Sch*	348
Coker, Jon/*Abbott Sch*	226
Coker, Michelle/*Mildred Sch*	300
Coker, Shanna/*Mineral Wells Jr High Sch*	310
Cole-Leffel, Ginger/*Sandy McNutt Elem Sch*	345
Cole-White, Kimberly/*Wills Point Primary Sch*	381
Cole, Elisa/*Hoyland Elem Sch*	202
Cole, Latres/*Sunrise-McMillian Elem Sch*	352
Coleman, Amy/*Mata Intermediate Sch*	182
Coleman, Anella/*Young Scholars Acad Excellence*	189
Coleman, Barbara/*Canyon Point Elem Sch*	203
Coleman, Dana/*Academy Intermediate Sch*	26
Coleman, Dollie/*Bay City Junior High Sch*	275
Coleman, Drue/*Alderson Elem Sch*	270
Coleman, Gregory/*Harmony Sci Acad-Plano [284]*	5
Coleman, Joe, Dr/*North Shore Senior High Sch*	187
Coleman, Keishla/*Amber Terrace Discovery ECC*	104
Coleman, Nanette/*Int'l Ldrshp TX-Saginaw*	109
Coleman, Phyliss/*St Helen Sch*	54
Coleman, Rhoda/*Palm Elem Sch*	367
Coleman, Tonya/*Meadowcreek Elem Sch*	348
Collet, Becky/*Bryan Adult Learning Center*	55
Colley, Kent/*Haskell Junior High Sch*	210
Collida, Joanna/*Dodd City Sch*	145
Collier, Jennifer/*Spring Woods High Sch*	201
Collier, Paige/*Reed Elem Sch*	397
Collins, Audrey/*Pietzsch-MacArthur Elem Sch*	242
Collins, Chelsea/*The Kinkaid Sch*	207
Collins, Clarinda/*Baker Koonce Intermediate Sch*	311
Collins, Cory, Dr/*Macario Garcia Middle Sch*	150
Collins, Debbra/*Tsu Charter Lab Sch*	193
Collins, Juanita/*Neal Elem Sch*	55
Collins, Katrina/*Skyview Elem Sch*	113
Collins, Leslie/*Covenant Academy*	205
Collins, Marques/*Kashmere Gardens Elem Sch*	191
Collins, Pamela/*Step by Step Christian Sch*	207
Collins, Quanda/*TCC South-Fwisd Collegiate HS*	352
Collins, Stephen/*High Point Prep Academy*	359
Collins, Tremeka/*King Early Childhood Center*	193
Collinsworth, Barbara/*East Elem Sch*	341
Collison, Heather/*Liberty Hill Elem Sch*	398
Colombero, Kayleigh/*Etoile Acad Charter Sch*	3
Colon, Vanessa/*Johns Elem Sch*	344
Colson, Jo/*Decker Prairie Elem Sch*	203
Colvin, Allan/*Pride Academy*	385

Texas School Directory — PRINCIPAL INDEX

NAME/School	PAGE
Colvin, Charles/*Pathways Alt Learning Center*	242
Colvin, Courtney/*Overton Elem Sch*	368
Colvin, Michael/*Comfort Middle Sch*	254
Colwell, Thomas/*Davis Senior High Sch*	180
Comalander, Gary/*Johnson High Sch*	35
Combs, Lakita/*Metzler Elem Sch*	197
Combs, Terry/*Joseph Hopkins Elem Sch*	33
Compton, Angela/*Geneva Bailey Intermediate Sch*	259
Compton, Beverly/*Advantage Acad-Grand Prairie W*	96
Conaway, Kimberley, Dr/*George Gervin Academy*	3
Condarco, Cesar/*Keefer Crossing Middle Sch*	293
Condren, Christine/*Bssp & Nets*	34
Condren, Christine/*NE Transition Sch*	35
Conely, Teri/*Larson Elem Sch*	344
Conklin, Sandy/*Samuel Beck Elem Sch*	125
Conkwright, Robin/*Dupre Elem Sch*	270
Conley, Alvin/*Nell Burks Elem Sch*	81
Conley, Derrick/*Birch Elem Sch*	170
Conley, Shannon/*Sue Park Broadway Elem Sch*	292
Conn, Teresa/*Silverline Montessori Sch*	54
Connelly, Kimberly/*Union Hill Elem Sch*	399
Connelly, Tom/*San Jacinto Elem Sch*	266
Conner, Jennifer/*Charter Oak Elem Sch*	26
Conner, Jennifer/*Miller Heights Elem Sch*	27
Conness, Monica/*Martin Middle Sch*	369
Conover, Wendy/*Lytle Elem Sch*	21
Conrad, Barbie/*Mabank Junior High Sch*	253
Conrad, Matt/*Murphy Middle Sch*	83
Conrardy, Martin/*Colorado River Collegiate Acad*	23
Conrardy, Martin/*Geneisis High Sch*	23
Constantine, Charmaine/*Ser-Ninos Charter Middle Sch*	11
Constantinescu, Rachel/*Naomi Press Elem Sch*	81
Contreras, Abraham/*Dalton Early Childhood Center*	378
Contreras, Carlos/*Dell City Sch*	234
Contreras, Cindy/*Rivera Elem Sch*	134
Contreras, Elba/*Honore Ligarde Elem Sch*	386
Contreras, Marena/*Tabasco Elem Sch*	220
Conway, Lillan/*Young Learners Elem Sch [278]*	195
Coody, Nina/*Robert E Lee Intermediate Sch*	91
Cook-Costley, Kelly/*Nelda Sullivan Middle Sch*	199
Cook, Brad/*Redwater High Sch*	49
Cook, Connor/*River Oaks Baptist Sch*	207
Cook, Eric/*Covenant Classical Sch*	358
Cook, Jamie/*Mt Pleasant Child Dev Center*	364
Cook, Monica/*Montessori School at Starcreek*	86
Cook, Susan/*Covenant Christian Academy*	358
Cook, Trent/*Neches High Sch*	15
Cook, Tricia/*Canyon Intermediate Sch*	321
Cook, William/*Valentine Sch*	241
Cooke, Cynite/*KIPP Destiny Middle Sch [287]*	7
Cooksey, Marion/*Highpoint School East*	179
Cooksey, Stephen/*Palestine High Sch*	15
Cooksey, Stephen/*Troup Middle Sch*	337
Cooley, Teresa/*Early Primary Sch*	59
Cooley, Thomas/*Kountze Elem Sch*	178
Cooper, Andrea/*Taylor Christian Sch*	226
Cooper, Ashley/*Richardson Classical Academy [297]*	10
Cooper, Brady/*Uplift Hampton Prep Chtr Sch [309]*	13
Cooper, Brent/*Brownsboro High Sch*	213
Cooper, Bridget/*Alton O Bowen Elem Sch*	55
Cooper, Bryan/*Alpha Academy*	292
Cooper, Debbie/*Red Lick Sch*	49
Cooper, Gionet/*Brownfield High Sch*	362
Cooper, Jennifer/*Nimitz Middle Sch*	35
Cooper, Judy/*Paul Belton Early Chldhd Ctr*	237
Cooper, Kerry/*Fine Arts Academy*	357
Cooper, Kerry/*Walsh Elem Sch*	312
Cooper, Lysette/*Cook Jr Elem Sch*	190
Cooper, Marnie/*Fulton Sch*	326
Cooper, Monica/*Lockhart Elem Sch*	193
Cooper, Rebecca/*New Deal Elem Sch*	271
Cooper, Riza/*Elgin Middle Sch*	24
Cooper, Stephanie/*Westbrook Intermediate Sch*	159
Cope, Steven/*Lindsay High Sch*	91
Copeland, Ana/*St Anthony's Elem Sch*	119
Copeland, Brandy/*Goddard Junior High Sch*	286
Copeland, Danielle/*Leo Orr Sr Education Center*	214
Copeland, Danny/*Brookesmith High Sch*	58
Copeland, Jamie/*Harold C Kaffie Middle Sch*	303
Copes, Amy/*Longs Creek Elem Sch*	35
Copley, Jamie/*Baker Elem Sch*	213
Coppedge, Christine/*Williams Elem Sch*	200
Corbett, Sharon/*Annunciation Orthodox Sch*	205
Cordoba, Juan/*Thomas J Rusk Middle Sch*	103
Cordova, Maria/*Brackenridge High Sch*	40
Core, Tina/*Grand Saline Intermediate Sch*	380
Cork, Jenni/*T H Johnson Elem Sch*	399
Cormack, Melanie/*Strawn Sch*	311
Cormier, Eric/*Brazos High Sch*	22
Cormier, Phyllis, Dr/*Victory Early College HS*	180
Cornejo, Nicki/*Trinity Charter Sch-Big Sandy [307]*	12
Cornelius, Bridgette/*Cedar Creek High Sch*	23
Corns, Megan/*Red Oak Elem Sch*	142
Corona, Julie/*Caldwood Elem Sch*	242
Coronado, Paul/*Bright Beginnings Academic Ctr*	362
Correa, Carol/*Peebles Elem Sch*	28
Correa, Maria/*Ruben Chavira Elem Sch*	379
Correa, Yvonne/*Pat Neff Middle Sch*	38
Correll, Melissa/*Career & Technology Institute*	382
Corrington, Molly/*Sam Houston Elem Sch*	299
Corry, Steve/*Deer Park High Sch-S Campus*	186
Cortes-Rangel, Amelia/*Alice Contreras Elem Sch*	350
Cortes, Ami/*Lucy Read Pre-K Sch*	368
Cortez, Angela/*Carney Elem Sch*	122
Cortez, Christina/*George West Primary Sch*	268
Cortez, Eric/*Austwell Tivoli Elem Sch*	323
Cortez, Guadalupe/*Oakhurst Elem Sch*	351
Cortez, Guillermo/*Anson Jones Elem Sch*	99
Cortez, John/*Austwell Tivoli Jr Sr High Sch*	323
Cortez, Maricela/*Alfred Sorensen Elem Sch*	223
Cortez, Rachel/*Hodges Bend Middle Sch*	150
Cortez, Sandra/*Mary & Frank Yturria Elem Sch*	64
Cortina, Julia/*Westcreek Elem Sch*	352
Corzine, Wes/*Huckabay Sch*	143
Coscia, Carla/*Dolores Huerta Elem Sch*	350
Coss, Veronica/*Early Clg High Sch*	398
Cotman, Cassandra/*KIPP Zenith Academy [288]*	7
Cotman, Catherine/*Huntington-Surrey Sch*	373
Cotter, Thomas/*Mabel B Wesley Elem Sch*	189
Cotton, Crenesha/*Ridglea Hills Elem Sch*	351
Cotton, Joshlyn/*Joan Y Ervin Elem Sch*	270
Cotton, Mrs/*Scarborough Elem Sch*	38
Couey, Mauri/*Myatt Elem Sch*	389
Coulson, Deborah/*North Ridge Elem Sch*	346
Coulter, Todd/*Keene Adventist Elem Sch*	249
Counts, Kelly/*Round Rock Christian Academy*	400
Counts, Patrice/*Tom Bean Elem Sch*	168
Courtade, Jodie/*Harlean Beal Elem Sch*	350
Courtney, Dan/*Christ the Redeemer Cath Sch*	204
Courtney, John/*Hudson High Sch*	17
Covan, Christy/*Newport Elem Sch*	183
Covarrubia, Erika/*Dr Americo Paredes Elem Sch*	219
Cover, Mary/*St Luke Catholic Sch*	44
Covey, Paul/*Valle Verde Early College HS*	138
Covin, Steven/*Navarro Early College High Sch*	368
Covington, Stephanie/*Vandagriff Elem Sch*	312
Coward, Jennifer/*Crandall Compass Academy*	251
Cowden, Randiann/*Elkins Elem Sch*	348
Cox, Andrea/*Green Acres Elem Sch*	295
Cox, April/*Kilgore Middle Sch*	169
Cox, Christina/*Coahoma High Sch*	234
Cox, Colter/*Central Elem Sch*	271
Cox, David/*Anton Sch*	229
Cox, Eric/*Moody Middle Sch*	281
Cox, Heather/*Riddle Elem Sch*	80
Cox, Herb, Dr/*Midway Middle Sch*	281
Cox, John/*Eagle Pass High Sch*	276
Cox, Justin/*Coolidge Jr Sr High Sch*	266
Cox, Kathleen/*St Michael Catholic Sch*	204
Cox, Kim/*Mauriceville Middle Sch*	308

PRINCIPAL INDEX

Market Data Retrieval

NAME/School	PAGE	NAME/School	PAGE
Cox, Megan/Mohawk Elem Sch	112	Crowling, Carol/George H W Bush Elem Sch	100
Cox, Stacy/Southwest Elem Sch	27	Crowson, Chad/Stratford High Sch	201
Cox, Stephanie/Liberty Elem Sch	266	Crowther, Melody/Negley Elem Sch	211
Cox, Susan/Spicewood Elem Sch	60	Crumley, Alisha/Garner Fine Arts Academy	107
Cox, Toby/H D Staples Elem Sch	248	Crump, Curtis/Pleasant Valley Elem Sch	318
Coy, Chris, Dr/Hyde Park High Sch	373	Crutcher, Don/Parkside Baptist Academy	116
Crabb, Jessica/Lorenzo Elem Sch	94	Cruz, Debra/Texans Can Acad San Antonio [305]	12
Crabb, Jessica/Lorenzo Jr Sr High Sch	94	Cruz, Emeterio/Sanchez Elem Sch	190
Crabtree, David/Schanen Estates Elem Sch	304	Cruz, Erica/Ozona Elem Sch	94
Crabtree, Kristi/Claybon Elem Sch	251	Cruz, James/McCormick Middle Sch	211
Craft, Adam/Etoile Elem Sch	297	Cruz, Joe/Harvest Christian Academy	226
Craft, Wendy/Lovejoy Elem Sch	80	**Cruz, Jorge**/Francis R Scobee Middle Sch	43
Craig, Emily/Memorial Parkway Jr High Sch	152	Cruz, Katherine/Ashbel Smith Elem Sch	187
Craig, Ian/Trinity Valley Sch	359	Cruz, Linda/Crestview Elem Sch	33
Craig, Lori/Scanlan Oaks Elem Sch	151	Cuadra, Ida/Airport Drive Elem Sch	225
Craighead, Beth/Dr AL Draper Intermediate Sch	85	**Cuarenta, Vanessa**/Morningside Elem Sch	351
Craighead, Jere/Browning Learning Center	326	Cuby, Sabrina/Sterling Aviation High Sch	193
Crain, Michael, Br/Trinity Baptist Temple Academy	359	**Cue, Natalie**/Montague Village Elem Sch	28
Crain, Natasha/Jones Elem Sch	338	Cuellar, Asa/Jhw Inspire Acad-Afton Oaks	31
Crain, Vicki/Cactus Ranch Elem Sch	398	Cuellar, Darcia/College Career & Tech Academy	223
Cramp, Donald, Dr/Duchesne Acad of Sacred Heart	204	**Cuellar, Darcia**/Psja Elvis J Ballew Echs	223
Crane, Carmen/Texas Leadership CS-Abilene	12	Cuenca-Wilson, Veronica/Sun Valley Elem Sch	43
Crane, Regenia/The Phoenix Academy	357	Cueva, Laura/San Pedro Elem Sch	305
Crane, T Leanne/Janice Stanley Scott Elem Sch	79	Cuevas, Patricia/Americas High Sch	135
Crane, Tim/Roosevelt Junior High Sch	271	Cuevas, Roxanne/W B Ray High Sch	304
Crawford, Andrea/North Elem Sch	271	Culberson, Lela/Donna Wernecke Elem Sch	224
Crawford, April/Canyon Creek Elem Sch	398	Culbertson, Lisa/Hockaday Sch	115
Crawford, Daniel/Robert E Lee High Sch	338	**Culley, Kimberly**/Springwoods Village Mid Sch	203
Crawford, Kori/Crockett High Sch	368	Cullum, Norma/Dorothy Adkins Middle Sch	303
Crawford, Steve/Four Points Middle Sch	397	Culpepper, Kristi/Bushland High Sch	319
Crawford, Tamela/Peterson Middle Sch	256	Culwell, Nathan/James W Fannin Middle Sch	318
Crawford, Zach/Martinsville Sch	298	Cumby, Ebony/Jewel Askew Elem Sch	194
Crawley, Amanda/Copperas Cove Jr High Sch	92	Cumings, Rosemarie/Roberts Elem Sch	275
Craytor, Samantha/Crestview Elem Sch	282	Cumming, Sarah/Promise Academy	339
Creamer, Michelle/Leadership Prep Sch	7	Cummings, Courtney/Wichita Christian Sch	393
Creasy, Adam, Dr/Hyde Park Elem Middle Sch	373	Cummings, Michelle, Dr/Sherrod Elem Sch	345
Creeggan, Kristen/Sneed Elem Sch	182	Cummings, Renee/Taylor Creek Elem Sch	261
Creel, Shae/Sachse High Sch	106	**Cummings, Robert**/Lueders-Avoca High Sch	250
Crenshaw, James/Flour Bluff High Sch	304	Cummings, Tommy/Vernon High Sch	394
Crenshaw, Janet/Idea Clg Prep-San Benito	219	Cummins, Betsy/John S Armstrong Elem Sch	108
Crenshaw, Richard/Hudson Middle Sch	17	Cummins, Sara/Covenant Christian Sch	295
Crescenzi, Stacia/Liberal Arts & Science Academy	368	**Cunningham, Bethany**/Huggins Elem Sch	154
Crespo, Romulo/Nacogdoches High Sch	298	Cunningham, C/Georgetown Behavioral Hlth CS	3
Creswell, Shawn/Coulson Tough Elem Sch	291	Cunningham, Karma/Davis Elem Sch	82
Crick, Debbie/Victoria West High Sch	382	Cunningham, Keith/Crockett Elem Sch	212
Crippen, Amy/Mary Martin Elem Sch	314	Cunningham, Liza/Lorena Elem Sch	280
Crisp, Anitra/Ronald E McNair Middle Sch	43	Cunningham, Shannon/Kirby Middle Sch	392
Crisp, Evelyn/Plain Elem Sch	397	Cunningtubby, Alma/Guadalupe Elem Sch	270
Crissey, David/Kiker Elem Sch	366	Cunningtubby, Alma/Jackson Elem Sch	270
Criswell, Kimberly/Jowell Elem Sch	185	Cuny, Erin/Leafspring School-Sonterra	45
Crittenden, Justin/Ingram Tom Moore High Sch	255	Cupit, Larry/Corrigan-Camden Elem Sch	316
Crockett, Tara/Fannin Elem Sch	286	Curl, Michael/Cedar Bayou Junior High Sch	187
Crofford, Shelly/Freiheit Elem Sch	88	Curran, Chaney/Remington Point Elem Sch	349
Croft, Kevin/Polly Ryon Middle Sch	154	Curry, Danielle/Pottsboro Elem Sch	167
Cronkhite, Julie/Danville Middle Sch	88	Curry, Leigh/Elrod Elem Sch	193
Crook, Dameion/Mickey Leland College Prep	191	Curry, Mitchell/Scott Johnson Middle Sch	81
Crosby, Melissa/Fields Store Elem Sch	384	Curry, Rebecca/Cornerstone Christian Academy	56
Cross, Candice/East Elem Sch	271	Curtis, Charmaine/Thurgood Marshall Elem Sch	113
Cross, Chris/Premier Academy	359	Curtis, Josh/Liberty Hill Intermediate Sch	398
Cross, Christy/Huntsville Elem Sch	383	Curtis, Larry/G L Wiley Opportunity Center	282
Cross, James/Cinco Ranch High Sch	152	Curtis, Tina/Barbara C Jordan Interm Sch	173
Cross, Jennifer/Highland Park Elem Sch	50	Curtis, Tonya, Dr/David Crockett Middle Sch	150
Cross, Nancy/Waco Charter Sch	14	Cypert, Karla/Pettus Elem Sch	25
Cross, Patricia/Zavalla High Sch	18	**Cypert, Lauren**/Boon Elem Sch	76
Cross, Stephen/Crane High Sch	93		
Crossland, Kelli/Amanda Rochell Elem Sch	325	**D**	
Crossley, Jill/Rosa Guerrero Elem Sch	134	D'Argo, Carrie/Hughston Elem Sch	82
Crosslin, Lisa/Clara Love Elem Sch	125	D'Lorm, Raul, Dr/Johnny Economedes High Sch	217
Crow, Deborah/Holy Ghost Catholic Sch	204	Daggs, Tammy/River Trails Elem Sch	354
Crow, Jason/Campbell Sch	235	Dagnino, Candice/Uplift Luna Prep Secondary [309]	13
Crow, Shelly/Post High Sch	162	Dahlquist, Michele/Walnut Bend Elem Sch	195
Crowe, David/Legacy of Educl Excellence HS	35	Daily, Ricky/Chandler Elem Sch	213
Crowell, Rebecca/Northside Elem Sch	389	Daily, William/St Mary Magdalen Sch	44

Texas School Directory — PRINCIPAL INDEX

NAME/School	PAGE
Dale, Becky/*East Chambers Elem Sch*	72
Dale, David/*Wheeler Sch*	391
Dalton, Amanda/*Comstock Elem Sch*	79
Dalton, Kelly/*Danish Elem Sch*	184
Dameron, Kim/*Walker Elem Sch*	186
Damron, Josh/*Idalou Middle Sch*	269
Damron, Wayland/*Eula High Sch*	63
Damron, Wayland/*Eula Middle Sch*	63
Dang, Maeli/*Dallas Christian Academy*	115
Daniel, Amy/*Sulphur Bluff Sch*	232
Daniel, Cindy/*Woodland Springs Elem Sch*	355
Daniel, Mahogany/*H M King High Sch*	257
Daniel, Traci/*L H Rather Junior High Sch*	145
Danielle, Taylor/*County Line Elem Sch*	88
Daniels, Bill/*Atascocita High Sch*	195
Daniels, Carra/*Rodger & Ellen Beck Jr HS*	153
Daniels, Christopher, Dr/*Agua Dulce Secondary Sch*	302
Daniels, Isaac/*W P Hobby Elem Sch*	193
Daniels, Jennifer/*Davis Elem Sch*	367
Daniels, Leo-Francis/*Oratory Academy & Athenaeum*	226
Danna, Cathy/*L F Smith Elem Sch*	199
Danner, Dave/*Fannin Elem Sch*	365
Dansby, Wendy/*Newman Int'l Acad-Arlington*	8
Darden, Dana/*Benbrook Elem Sch*	191
Darden, Kimberly/*Pace Center*	53
Darden, Leon/*Chilton Sch*	144
Darden, Tyrone/*George Gervin Academy*	3
Darmstadter, Sally/*Stubblefield Learning Center*	17
Darnall, Stacey/*Zundy Elem Sch*	393
Darnell, Kandi/*Devine Middle Sch*	283
Darrough, Cimberli/*Nci CS Without Walls*	8
Dart, Laura/*Clarke Elem Sch*	27
Darver, Sherri/*St Mark's School of Texas*	116
Daugherty, Melinda/*Smith Elem Sch*	192
Daughtrey, Laurie/*Jourdanton Elem Sch*	20
Daughtry, Keana/*Wilson Elem Sch*	165
Dauphin, Joy/*Millsap Elem Sch*	185
Dauphinais, Sarah/*Laura Ingalls Wilder Inter Sch*	173
Davalos, Lauro/*Pickle Elem Sch*	368
Davalos, Maria/*Spring Oaks Middle Sch*	201
Davenport, Jeff/*Nichols Elem Sch*	38
Davenport, Robin/*Cornerstone Christian Sch*	44
Davenport, Sherri/*Schultz Elem Sch*	197
David, Andrea/*Jarrell Elem Sch*	396
Davidheizar, Paul/*Alpha Omega Academy*	384
Davidson, Shelby/*Van Middle Sch*	381
Davies, MacAire/*Deerwood Elem Sch*	195
Davies, Michael/*St Bernard of Clairvaux Sch*	114
Davies, Michael/*St Paul the Apostle Sch*	114
Davila, Gisela/*George Buddy West Elem Sch*	130
Davila, Jason/*Patrick Henry Middle Sch*	189
Davila, Noemi/*Mission Academy*	41
Davila, Sulema/*Pittman Elem Sch*	394
Davila, Tricia/*William Paschall Elem Sch*	34
Davis-Martin, Kendria/*Byrd Middle Sch*	104
Davis-Troutman, Kristina/*Mistral Early Childhood Center*	194
Davis, Adreana/*Frank Guzick Elem Sch*	100
Davis, Andrea/*Kujawa EC-PK-K Sch*	181
Davis, Ashley/*Cunningham Elem Sch*	392
Davis, Blayne/*Mumford Sch*	56
Davis, Brittney/*Gary Sch*	311
Davis, Cheryl/*Clifford Dunn Elem Sch*	180
Davis, Christine/*Shelton Sch*	116
Davis, Cindy/*Vivian Fowler Elem Sch*	364
Davis, Colvin/*American Preparatory Institute*	30
Davis, Cynthia/*Converse Elem Sch*	33
Davis, Dana/*Junction High Sch*	256
Davis, Derek/*James Bowie 6th Grade Campus*	318
Davis, Eric/*Heritage Academy San Antonio*	5
Davis, Irma/*Dishman Elem Sch*	65
Davis, Jennifer/*E Merle Smith Middle Sch*	332
Davis, Jodi/*Ruth Borchardt Elem Sch*	80
Davis, John/*North Ridge Middle Sch*	346
Davis, Kathryn/*E Kolitz Hebrew Language Acad*	2
Davis, Kaylene/*Bovina Elem Sch*	314
Davis, Keith/*Charles M Blalack Middle Sch*	96
Davis, Kriste/*Crosby Kindergarten Center*	183
Davis, Lisa/*Golden Acres Elem Sch*	199
Davis, Lori/*Lockhart Junior High Sch*	61
Davis, Mandy/*J P Dabbs Elem Sch*	186
Davis, Marcella/*Kennedy Elem Sch*	306
Davis, Margaret/*Alcuin Montessori Sch*	114
Davis, Marian/*Holy Trinity Catholic Sch*	114
Davis, Mark/*Booker T Washington ES*	392
Davis, Melissa/*Comanche Springs Elem Sch*	348
Davis, Melissa/*Pearson Elem Sch*	222
Davis, Nika/*W E Boswell High Sch*	349
Davis, Paul/*Park Meadows Academy*	300
Davis, Renee/*Center for Hearing & Speech*	205
Davis, Ronda/*City View Elem Sch*	391
Davis, Samora/*Tomball Intermediate Sch*	203
Davis, Scott/*Deer Park High Sch-N Campus*	186
Davis, Staci/*Libby Elem Sch*	311
Davis, Stacie/*Lago Vista Intermediate Sch*	370
Davis, Stacy/*Crestview Elem Sch*	269
Davis, Stephanie/*Garland Christian Academy*	115
Davis, Stephanie/*Ridge Creek Elem Sch*	196
Davis, Stephen/*Seminole Success Center*	158
Davis, Steve/*Angleton Christian Sch*	54
Davis, Tabitha, Dr/*Billy Reagan K-8 Educ Ctr*	192
Davis, Vicki/*Travis Elem Sch*	176
Davis, William/*Parnell Elem Sch*	241
Davis, William/*Rhodes School-Lee*	10
Davis, William/*Rspa Northeast-Humble*	10
Davis, William/*Rspa-NE Humble*	10
Davisson, Dustin/*Mountain Valley Middle Sch*	88
Daw, Donny/*Knox Junior High Sch*	292
Daw, Jennifer/*Wilkerson Intermediate Sch*	292
Dawkins, C'Ne/*Meyer Elem Sch*	202
Dawson, Jimmy/*Acton Middle Sch*	230
Day, Debra/*West Hurst Elem Sch*	354
Day, Jennifer/*Wharton Dual Language Academy*	195
Day, Sarah/*Leonard Intermediate Sch*	146
Day, Terry/*Bell County Alternative Sch*	26
Day, Thomas/*Travis Elem Sch*	192
Day, Tim/*Ischolars Magnet Academy*	142
De Hoyos, Brenda/*Hidalgo Academy*	217
De Hoyos, Stacey/*Hafley Development Center*	348
De La Cerda, Antonio/*Valley View Junior High Sch*	225
De La Cruz, Christine/*Sierra Vista Elem Sch*	136
De La Cruz, Enrique/*Lyndon B Johnson Elem Sch*	217
De La Cruz, Veronica/*St Matthews Catholic Sch*	139
De La Fuente, Esequiel/*La Pryor Elem Sch*	407
De La Garza, Brooke/*Schulenburg Elem Sch*	148
De La Huerta, Jesse/*Dobie Middle Sch*	369
De La Pena, Phillip/*Neil Armstrong Elem Sch*	42
De La Rosa, Belinda/*San Carlos Elem Sch*	217
De La Rosa, Marvelia/*Burnet Middle Sch*	369
De La Rosa, Nadia/*Tornillo Intermediate Sch*	137
De La Rosa, Omar/*George West Elem Sch*	268
De La Rosa, Oscar/*Lopez-Riggins Elem Sch*	66
De La Sierra, Blanca/*Paul Keyes Elem Sch*	110
De Leon, Daniel/*Sharpstown High Sch*	189
De Leon, Jose/*Idea Clg Prep-Quest*	219
De Leon, Jose/*Santa Maria Elem Sch*	387
De Los Santos, Celia/*Pullam Elem Sch*	64
De Los Santos, Laura/*Freedom Elem Sch*	387
De Luna, Janis/*Horizon Montessori II [301]*	5
De Santiago, Pablo/*Thomas A Edison Elem Sch*	91
De Saro, Teresita/*Brownsville Lrng Acad High Sch*	63
De Valk, Tina/*KIPP University Prep High Sch [289]*	7
De Wolfe, Robert/*The Summit Sch*	200
De'LaCruz, Maria, Dr/*Big Springs-Cailloux CS*	1
Dean, Julie-Anne/*Vines High Sch*	83
Dean, Michelle/*Cumberland Academy*	2
Dean, Mike/*Calvin Nelms Charter Sch [275]*	2
Dean, Tamara/*Kilgore Primary Sch*	169
Deanda, Javier/*Sgt William Harrell Middle Sch*	222
Deanda, Jennifer/*Mary Allen Elem Sch*	336
Deanda, Luz/*Sylvan Rodriguez Elem Sch*	194

PRINCIPAL INDEX

Market Data Retrieval

NAME/School	PAGE	NAME/School	PAGE
Deanda, Yvette/*Lucy Rede Franco Middle Sch*	320	Dent, Theresa/*Our Lady of the Gulf Cath Sch*	62
Deason, Erin/*Jackson Middle Sch*	35	Denton, Becky/*Cypress Falls High Sch*	184
Deaton, Angie/*Lewisville Learning Center*	123	DeOliveira, Glenisson/*Texas Academy Math & Science*	12
Deaver, Chet, Dr/*Kountze High Sch*	178	DeRosa, Debra/*Mabank Intermediate Sch*	253
Deaver, Terry/*Laura Reeves Primary Sch*	178	DeRouen, Dana/*Bel Air Middle Sch*	137
Deaver, Terry/*Silsbee Elem Sch*	178	DeRouen, Peggy/*Epiphany Montessori Sch*	258
Deaver, Todd/*Poth High Sch*	401	Derrick, Carmen/*Nancy Moseley Elem Sch*	102
Debeaumont, Amber/*Bozman Intermediate Sch*	291	Derrick, Mary/*Mae Stevens Early Learng Acad*	92
Debenport, Brandy/*Morriss Elem Sch*	50	DeSantis, Ann/*Lucas Christian Academy*	86
Debord, Douglas/*Llano Elem Sch*	268	Deslatte, Kaela/*Early Childhood Center*	337
Deboskie, Selena/*Tom W Field Elem Sch*	103	**Devantier, Vicki**/*Beaver Tech Ctr-Math & Science*	105
Deckard, Denise/*San Saba Elem Sch*	332	Devera, Theresa/*Montessori School Downtown*	206
Decker, Karen/*Chico Elem Sch*	403	Devers, Lea/*Central Elem Sch*	122
Deckert, Sarah/*Lake Country Christian Sch*	359	DeVine, Valerie/*North Loop Christian Academy*	139
Deegear, Kelli/*Pecan Trail Interm Sch*	56	Devires, Heather/*Simon Youth Academy*	153
Deer, Errin/*Slocum Sch*	16	Devlin, Rob/*St George Episcopal Sch*	45
Dees, Tamika/*Townley Elem Sch*	349	Devost, Grace/*Green Valley Elem Sch*	187
DeFelice, Nick/*Earl Slaughter Elem Sch*	81	DeWitt, Michelle/*Lyford High Sch*	394
Deflora, Lucretia/*Schiff Elem Sch*	151	Dhalla, Shahveer/*Arlington High Sch*	343
DeHoyos, Martin/*Hommel Elem Sch*	349	**Diaz-Camarillo, Elia**/*Houston Elem Sch*	366
Deister, Beri/*Lakeview Middle Sch*	123	Diaz-Wever, Jesus/*C C Winn High Sch*	276
Deitz, Lynn/*Pine Drive Christian Sch*	162	Diaz, Ana/*Holmsley Elem Sch*	185
Del Bosque, Deborah/*Kenedy High Sch*	251	Diaz, Breanne/*KIPP Austin Vista Middle Sch [286]*	6
Del Bosque, Justin/*Charles Forbes Middle Sch*	395	Diaz, Carmel/*Benito Juarez Middle Sch*	407
Del Hierro, Laura/*Anderson Elem Sch*	78	Diaz, Cesar/*Reed Elem Sch*	185
Del Toro, Mary/*Schenck Elem Sch*	41	Diaz, Flor/*C L Milton Elem Sch*	386
Del Toro, Miguel/*Rosemont Middle Sch*	352	**Diaz, Framy**/*Ridgemont Elem Sch*	151
Delacruz, Audrey/*Sam Tasby Middle Sch*	102	Diaz, Guadalupe/*Idea Academy-Carver*	217
Delacuadra, Richard/*Xavier Educational Academy*	207	**Diaz, Johnny**/*Inez Foster Academy*	40
Delafuente, Cyndi/*Idea Academy-Owassa*	218	Diaz, Judy/*Jensen Elem Sch*	199
Delagarza, Cynthia/*Collins Garden Elem Sch*	40	Diaz, Liza/*Pharr San Juan Alamo North HS*	223
Delagarza, Emmy/*Guzman Elem Sch*	215	**Diaz, Rolando**/*Frank Roberts Elem Sch*	67
Delaguardia, Irma/*Stephen C Foster Elem Sch*	103	Dibley, Glenn/*Legacy Christian Academy*	86
Delamar, Shawna, Dr/*Zack Motley Elem Sch*	111	Dickerson, Joann/*Riverside Applied Lrng Center*	351
Delariva, Cristian/*Spring Woods Middle Sch*	201	Dickerson, Jon/*Scenic Hills Christian Academy*	45
DeLaRosa, Brenda/*Runge Sch*	251	Dickerson, Mindy/*Patricia Paetow High Sch*	152
DeLaRosa, Catherine/*Tenney Sch*	207	Dickey, Courtney/*Meadows Elem Sch*	150
DeLeon, Cathy/*C M MacDonell Elem Sch*	386	Dickey, Elizabeth/*Rosedale Sch*	368
DeLeon, Julie/*Frances Norton Elem Sch*	77	Dickinson, Julie/*Kolter Elem Sch*	194
DeLeon, Lynda/*Paul R Haas Middle Sch*	304	**Dickinson, Michael**/*Liberty Elem Sch*	357
DeLeon, Marco/*Int'l Ldrshp TX-Lanc-DeSoto HS*	109	Dickson, Amy/*George Washington Carver ES*	209
DeLeon, Norma/*J A Garcia Elem Sch*	303	Dickson, Christopher/*Sheldon Early Childhood Acad*	200
DeLeon, Paige/*Prestonwood Christian Academy*	86	Dickson, Gabrelle/*Young Women Steam Acad-Blch Sp*	104
DeLeon, Ricardo/*Pettus Secondary Sch*	25	Dickson, Jennifer/*Pierce Early Childhood Sch*	110
Delestre, Niccole/*Shadowglen Elem Sch*	371	Diehl, Daniel/*Sycamore Springs Middle Sch*	211
DelGado, D'Ann/*MacArthur 9th Grade Sch*	180	Diener, David, Dr/*Grace Academy*	400
DelGado, Freddy/*Amigos Por Vida Charter Sch*	1	Diers, Kelli/*First Baptist Academy*	205
DelGado, Lina/*Veritas Christian Academy*	207	Dietrich, Wendy/*Fredericksburg Primary Sch*	163
DelGado, Mandy/*Breeden Elem Sch*	63	**Dietzman, Kati**/*Robinson High Sch*	281
DelGado, Rachel/*Lieck Elem Sch*	38	Difelice, Kathleen/*Alexander Elem Sch*	182
DelGado, Veronica/*Dallas Park Elem Sch*	348	Diggs, Jairia/*Providence Elem Sch*	121
Delich, Joshua/*Lake Highlands High Sch*	112	Dignan, Nick/*Val Verde Christian Academy*	244
DeLoach, Matthew/*Canyon Middle Sch*	88	Dillard, David/*Wood Elem Sch*	345
Delorge, Renee/*Metroplex Chapel Academy*	359	Dillard, Shamethia/*Helen Major Elm Sch*	202
Delorge, Renee/*New Life Academy*	359	Dilli, Haci/*Sch of Sci & Tech Advancement [299]*	10
Delosontas, Kate/*St James Episcopal Sch*	379	Dimas, Judith/*Hidalgo Early College High Sch*	217
Delpilar, Diana/*Rose M Avalos P-Tech Sch*	180	Diop, Mateen/*Sam Houston High Sch*	41
DeLuna, Alison/*Southwood Valley Elem Sch*	56	DiPalma, Alisa/*Tobias Elem Sch*	211
DeLuna, Angel/*Bluebonnet Trail Elem Sch*	371	Dirksen, Joe/*Grace Community Jr Sr High Sch*	339
Demarest, Susie/*Headwaters Sch*	373	**Disch, Scott**/*West University Elem Sch*	195
Demas, Dawn/*Green Valley Elem Sch*	346	**Dishner, Tony**/*Clifton Career Dev Sch*	368
Dembicki, Robin/*Lucas Christian Academy*	86	Dixon, Cheri/*L E Monahan Elem Sch*	200
Deming-Garcia, Stacy/*Wilshire Elem Sch*	36	Dixon, Richard/*Goodson Middle Sch*	184
Demir, Cetin/*Harmony Sci Acad-Odessa [284]*	5	Dixon, Sharene/*Davis Middle Sch*	40
Demirci, Ekrem/*Sch of Sci & Tech-Corpus Crsti [299]*	11	Dlabaj, Brittany/*Sunnyvale Elem Sch*	113
Demny, Pamela/*Jefferson Elem Sch*	29	DO, Vuong, Sr/*Mary Help of Christians Sch*	389
Denison, Christine/*Uplift Triumph Preparatory [309]*	13	Dobbins, Diana/*Coleman High Sch*	76
Denkeler, Tawnya/*St Paul Lutheran Sch*	306	Dobbins, John/*Marvin P Baker Middle Sch*	304
Denman, Amy/*Green Valley Elem Sch*	173	Dobson, Tarrah/*Nanny Elem Sch*	258
Denning, David/*Grapevine High Sch*	353	Dockery, Charde/*Dan F Long Middle Sch*	96
Dennis, Aimee/*UT Tyler Univ Acad-Tyler*	338	Dockery, Tanya/*Timber Ridge Elem Sch*	28
Dennis, Craig/*Van Alstyne High Sch*	168	Dodd, Chris/*Gunter High Sch*	166
Denson, John, Dr/*Union Hill Sch*	377	Dodd, Ingrid/*Mooneyham Elem Sch*	79

Texas School Directory — Principal Index

NAME/School	PAGE
Dodd, Merideth/Cherry Elem Sch	275
Dodson, Danny/Central Baptist Christian Sch	335
Dodson, Serita/Ida Lee Bright Elem Sch	79
Doering, Mike/Concordia High Sch	400
Doerksen, Craig/Waterloo Sch	373
Dogan, Engin/Harmony Sci Acad-Pflugerville [284]	5
Dolin, Jesse/Mathis Elem Sch	331
Dominguez, Aaron/St Thomas High Sch	204
Dominguez, Andrew/Harlandale Alternative Center	32
Dominguez, Claudia/Willie E Williams Elem Sch	293
Dominguez, David/Ellison High Sch	27
Dominguez, Hector/Crosbyton High Sch	94
Dominguez, Hector/North Avenue Interm Sch	164
Dominguez, Juan/South Elem Sch	286
Dominguez, Laura/Premier HS-El Paso West [297]	9
Dominguez, Tony/Poteet High Sch	21
Donaghey, Kady/Global Prep Academy	348
Donaho, Misty/Hurst Hills Elem Sch	354
Donatti, Fernando/Draw Acad Early Learning Ctr	2
Donehoo, Barbi/Rhea Elem Sch	252
Donlon, Jim/Adventist Christian Academy	295
Donnan, Kimberly/A M Aikin Elem Sch	260
Donnell, Randal/Alternative Learning Center	153
Donnell, Randall/1621 Place Sch	153
Donnell, Randall/Fort Bend Alternative Sch	153
Donnowitz, Matt/Hill Country Christian Sch	373
Donovan, Angela/Haynes Elem Sch	28
Doolan, Tiffany/T F Birmingham Elem Sch	85
Dophied, Glenda/Cockrell Elem Sch	84
Doran, John/Radford Sch	139
Doran, Margaret/Rick Ogden Elem Sch	180
Doria, Sandra/Bill Worsham Elem Sch	181
Doria, Sandra/Evelyn S Thompson Elem Sch	180
Doring, Scott/Collins Intermediate Sch	299
Dorman, Jeffrey/Houston Middle Sch	109
Dornak, Jamie/Moulton High Sch	262
Dorris, Amy/Palo Duro High Sch	318
Doss, Amy/Options Academic High Sch	50
Dotson, Gloria, Dr/Wilson Early College High Sch	243
Dotson, Hardy/Henderson Middle Sch	327
Dotson, Stephanie/Ingleside Primary Sch	331
Doty, Clarissa/Summit Hill Elem Sch	166
Doty, Cristi/Buffalo Gap Elem Sch	361
Doucet, Dawn, Dr/Fallbrook Academy [297]	3
Dougherty, Mera/Idea Academy-Pflugerville	218
Dougherty, Mera/Idea Clg Prep-Pflugerville	219
Doughty, Jason/Great Hearts Forest Heights [282]	4
Douglas, Derrell/Mansfield Timberview High Sch	357
Douglas, Erika/Hempstead Middle Sch	384
Dover, Kenley/Bullard Middle Sch	337
Dow, Angela/Highlands Elem Sch	150
Dowd, Trent/Linda Jobe Middle Sch	357
Dowd, Trent/Mansfield High Sch	357
Dowdy, Chris/Valley Mills Elem Sch	47
Dowell, Deloris/Fred Douglass Early Chldhd Ctr	167
Dowler, Linea/Founders Classical Acad Mesq [297]	3
Downey, Anna/Incarnate Word High Sch	44
Downs, Karen/Avery Elem Sch	322
Doyle, Gerard/Int'l Ldrshp TX-N Richlnd Hill	109
Doyle, Kelly/KIPP Austin Comunidad [286]	6
Dozier, Jennifer/Grace Community Sch	339
Drabek, Bernadette/St Rose of Lima Sch	204
Drabing, Lisa/Kingwood Park High Sch	196
Dracos, Jennifer/Cumby High Sch	231
Dragoo, Scott/Northside Christian Academy	311
Drake, David/Clear Lake High Sch	158
Drake, Jason/Spurger Elem Sch	375
Drake, Paul/Livingston High Sch	317
Drake, Traci/Hubbard Elem Sch	48
Drane, Kristopher/New Waverly High Sch	383
Draper, Tooter/Cisco Junior High Sch	129
Drayton, Martin/Cook Middle Sch	184
Drew, Dana/Friendswood Junior High Sch	160
Driscoll, Susie/Southcrest Christian Sch	272
Driska, Alushka/Rosebud-Lott Elem Sch	145
Driskell, Mark/Miami Sch	324
Driver, Derek/Sulphur Springs High Sch	232
Driver, Jennifer/Mt Vernon Elem Sch	156
Droddy, Leah/Veramendi Elem Sch	89
Druffner, Shana/All Saints Catholic Sch	85
Drummond, Jack/Hill Elem Sch	368
Drummond, Lisa/Wayside Eden Park Academy	14
Drummond, Steve/Commerce High Sch	236
Drury, Brent/Munday High Sch	259
Drysdale, Tim/West Birdville Elementary	346
Duarte, Gabriel/St Peter Prince of Apostles	44
Duarte, Leticia/Truman Elem Sch	217
Dubberke, Scott/Thomas B Gray Elem Sch	179
Dube, Travis/Thrall High Sch	400
Dubose, Clint/San Antonio Academy-Texas	45
Dubose, Ryan/Little Cypress-Mauriceville HS	308
Duce, Jacob/Lebanon Trail High Sch	79
Duck, Patricia/Ware Elem Sch	170
Duckworth, Renee/Naomi Pasemann Elem Sch	399
Dudley, Amanda/Uplift Summit Int'l Prep CS [309]	13
Dudley, Jamie/Ballinger Elem Sch	326
Dudley, Porsha/Arizona Fleming Elem Sch	149
Dudley, Tabitha/Fondren Elem Sch	188
Dudney, Jocelyn/F R Scobee Elem Sch	37
Duffey, Lanina/Adelle R Clark Middle Sch	78
Duffey, Sheraton/Universal Academy-Irving	13
Duffy, Mary Kathryn/St Alban's Episcopal Day Sch	68
Dugan, Tamera/John T White Elem Sch	351
Dugar, Tori/Generation One Academy	206
Dugger, Carolyn/Harker Heights Elem Sch	28
Duhart-Toppen, Mary/Karen Wagner High Sch	33
Duhon, Lindsay/Hanna Springs Elem Sch	261
Duhon, Michelle/Stephen F Austin Elem Sch	188
Duhon, Shawn/Carroll Senior High Sch	347
Duhon, Tammy/Anahuac Middle Sch	71
Duke, Cindy/Crockett Middle Sch	323
Duke, Donna/Harvey Turner Elem Sch	199
Duke, Rusty/Hughes Springs Jr High Sch	70
Dumaine, Jennifer/Ruby Shaw Elem Sch	111
Dumar, Regina/John S Bradfield Elem Sch	108
Dumesnil, Jack/Learning Center	294
Dunaway, Jack/Boulevard Baptist Chrstn Sch	249
Dunbar, Pam/Montessori Academy-Arlington	359
Duncan, Brandon/Refugio High Sch	323
Duncan, Dale/Newman Int'l Acad-Ft Worth	8
Duncan, Dayne/Groesbeck Middle Sch	267
Duncan, Edna/Mabank Daep	252
Duncan, Ray/Academy	252
Duncan, Scott/Willow Creek Elem Sch	196
Duncum, Jared/Clyde Junior High Sch	62
Dunham, Debbie/Dalhart Christian Academy	95
Dunkle, Chris/Saigling Elem Sch	83
Dunlap, Alvis/B McDaniel Intemediate Sch	166
Dunlap, Brenda/Chillicothe Elem Sch	177
Dunlevy, Mary/Eugenia P Rayzor Elem Sch	121
Dunn, Karla/Thunderbird Elem Sch	175
Dunn, Kelly/Meyersville Elem Sch	118
Dunn, Matthew/Chapel Hill Junior High Sch	363
Dunn, Sharon/Stockdale Junior High Sch	401
Dunnam, Jamie/Poolville Junior High Sch	313
Dunphy, David/Jackson Tech Ctr Math Science	106
Dunseth, Vickie/O'Connor Elem Sch	382
Dunworth, Buddy, Dr/McMath Middle Sch	121
Duoto, Tom/East Chambers High Sch	72
Duplantier, Sharon/Uplift Gradus Preparatory [309]	13
DuPont, Yvonne/Dr Mae Jones-Clark Elem Sch	242
DuPree, Carla/Texas High Sch	50
DuPree, John/Leon Valley Christian Academy	45
Duran, Diego/Burbank Elem Sch	190
Duran, Shirley/Boles Elem Sch	235
Durand, Jeff/Rock Prairie Elem Sch	56
Durbin, Andrea/Troy Elem Sch	30
Durbin, Rodrigo/South Hills High Sch	352
Durden, Veronica, Dr/Evolution Academy-Beaumont [279]	3
Duren, Shanta/Ruby Young Elem Sch	104

PRINCIPAL INDEX

Market Data Retrieval

NAME/School	PAGE
Durham-Hunt, Ameka/Pflugerville High Sch	372
Durham, Kristi/Madden Elem Sch	150
Durham, Sherry, Dr/St Cyprian's Episcopal Sch	18
Durling, Debbie/Trinity Christian Sch	116
Durling, Debra/Golden Rule CS-Illinois [281]	3
Durst, Leslie/Hoffmann Lane Elem Sch	88
Dusek, Jennifer/Valley View Elem Sch	370
Dutschmann, Kristen/China Spring Middle Sch	279
Dutton, Barbara/Northside Primary Sch	15
DuVall, Diane/First Christian Academy	54
DuVall, Nicole/Kinder Ranch Elem Sch	88
DuVall, Richard/Doris Miller Middle Sch	212
Dwiggins, Ana Maria/Harris Elem Sch	367
Dwyer, Carmen/Park Elem Sch	134
Dwyer, Polly/Coram Deo Academy	126
Dyal, Lauren/Rosehill Christian Sch	207
Dye, Heidi/Hutchinson Middle Sch	270
Dyer, Brandi/Southside Elem Sch	253
Dyer, Courtney/Lincoln Elem Sch	293
Dyer, Louise/Leadership Academy	7
Dyer, Roby/Chip Richarte High Sch	395
Dyess, Bobby/Troup High Sch	337
Dyke, Peggy/Cypress Bendadventist ES	274
Dykes, Kenneth/Orange Grove Jr High Sch	245
Dykman, Jeannia/Crandall High Sch	251
Dzurilla, Rachel/St Elizabeth of Hungary Sch	114

E

NAME/School	PAGE
Eackles, Michelle/Fairview Elem Sch	167
Earnhart, Leigh/Rasor Elem Sch	83
Eason, Joshua/Richardson North Jr High Sch	113
Eason, Shimona/Smith Elem Sch	202
East, Brian/Deweyville Jr Sr High Sch	308
East, Rusty/Shackelford Elem Sch	142
Easter, Lashon/Northrich Elem Sch	112
Easter, Latoya/Eastview High Sch	395
Easterby, Rebecca/KIPP Sharpstown College Prep [288]	7
Eastlick, Kyna/Willie E Brown Elem Sch	357
Easton, Giselle/George I Sanchez Charter HS	3
Eaton, Jessica/John Hanby Elem Sch	111
Eaton, Phil/Lake Creek High Sch	293
Eaton, Tina/Moody Elem Sch	281
Eberly, Jennifer/Hillcrest Elem Sch	369
Eble, Daniel/Keller Middle Sch	199
Echegaray, Erika/Fanny Finch Elem Sch	81
Eckerman, Kristen/Evelyn Turlington Elem Sch	384
Eckert, Kathleen/Hillwood Middle Sch	355
Eckert, Marcus/Melissa Middle Sch	81
Eckert, Rachel/St Theresa's Catholic Sch	372
Eckford, Christopher, Dr/North Shore Middle Sch	187
Eclarinal, Cathleen/Girls' School of Austin	373
Eddleman, Kyde/Gregory-Portland High Sch	331
Edens, Leslie/Covington Sch	227
Edge, Donna/Justin Wakeland High Sch	79
Edge, Phillip/Construction Careers Academy	36
Edgerton, Travis/Lumberton Middle Sch	178
Edinburgh, Willetta/Einstein School Plano	85
Edison, Richard/University High Sch	282
Edmondson, Kim/Daniel Intermediate Sch	104
Edmunds, Lisa/West Elem Sch	357
Edmundson, Kellie/Crosby Middle Sch	161
Edwards-Flores, Pamela/Yorktown Elem Sch	118
Edwards, Angela/Douglass ECLC	232
Edwards, David/Tiger Academy	24
Edwards, Demedia/Marcella Elem Sch	180
Edwards, Gwen/St Philip Catholic Sch	390
Edwards, Jane/North Park Christian Academy	359
Edwards, Jeanette/Redeemer Episcopal Sch	277
Edwards, Justin/Morningside Middle Sch	351
Edwards, Katherine/Brady High Sch	277
Edwards, Kathleen/Novus Academy	359
Edwards, Meagan/Grissom Elem Sch	192
Edwards, Raymond/Gateway Charter Academy	3
Edwards, Raymond/Gateway Charter Elem Academy	3
Edwards, Robby/Holland High Sch	27
Edwards, Ronnie/Mayde Creek High Sch	152
Edwards, Shannon/Denton Creek Elem Sch	98
Edwards, Sharla/O'Donnell Elem Sch	273
Edwards, Tanya/Baylor Clg of Medicine Acad	192
Edwards, Tiranus/Winfree Academy-N Rchlnd Hills [311]	14
Effa, Marvin, Dr/Bethany Christian Sch	85
Ehrhardt, Debi/Crockett Elem Sch	55
Eilers, Stacy/Hermes Elem Sch	147
Ekmen, Sefik/Harmony Sch Exc-Sugar Land [284]	4
Eksaengsri, Jina/Lujan-Chavez Elem Sch	136
Elachkar, Toufic/McNamara Elem Sch	194
Elarms, Brooke/Pond Springs Elem Sch	399
Elder, Gwendolyn/A & M Consolidated High Sch	55
Elder, Steve/Florence High Sch	395
Elders, Shannon/Fort Worth Academy	358
Eldridge, Tami/Oak Ridge Elem Sch	292
Elias, Alejandro/Pharr San Juan Alamo High Sch	223
Elizondo, Hirma/St Mary's Academy Charter Sch	11
Elizondo, Miguel/Burbank High Sch	40
Elizondo, Monica/Utpb STEM Academy	13
Elizondo, Selina/Speer Elem Sch	345
Ellerbe, Jessie/Ranger Sch	129
Ellington, Brian/Bowie Middle Sch	130
Elliott, Gabriela/Bill Sybert Sch	136
Elliott, Peggy/Southeast Elem Sch	302
Elliott, Robert/Corrigan-Camden Jr High Sch	316
Ellis, David, Dr/Henry Middle Sch	397
Ellis, Galsmine/Bethel SDA Sch	50
Ellis, Keith, Dr/Naaman Forest High Sch	106
Ellis, Kristin/J B Wilmeth Elem Sch	81
Ellis, Robin/James Steele Accelerated HS	125
Ellis, Stephen/North Richland Middle Sch	346
Ellis, Tyler/Meyer High Sch [277]	8
Ellis, Tyler/Quinn Middle Sch [277]	10
Ellis, Virginia/La Vega Junior High Sch	280
Ellison, Chelsey/Taylor Middle Sch	400
Elmore, Renee/Thomas Justiss Elem Sch	260
Elms, Brenda/Oaks Adventist Christian Sch	206
Elrod, Alisha/Greenwood Forest Elem Sch	197
Else, Aaron/Pete & Gracie Hosp Elem Sch	80
Elzy, Tina/Elsik High Sch	182
Emerson, Jennifer/Briscoe Academy	40
Emery, Danny/Settlers Way Elem Sch	151
Emmert, Michelle/Ashleys Private Sch	114
Encarnacion, Oscar/Kennard Sch	233
Endsley, Matthew/Jasper High Sch	83
Endsley, Matthew/Williams High Sch	83
Engel, John/Southwest High Sch	352
Engelbrecht, Rose/Highland Park Elem Sch	40
Engelking, Jill/Renner Middle Sch	83
England, Kristi/Dallas Christian Sch	115
Engleman, Holly/Helping Hand Charter Sch	5
Engleman, Holly/University High Sch	13
Engleman, Holly/UT Univ CS-Settlement Home	13
English, Julie/Jean E Stewart Elem Sch	292
Ennis, Madge/Winfree Academy-Richardson [311]	14
Enos, Brandon/Goliad High Sch	164
Enright, Eric/South Texas Christian Academy	226
Enrique, Ruiz/Falfurrias Elem Sch	57
Ensey, Sheila/Givens Early Childhood Center	260
Eoff, Alesha/Rockdale Elem Sch	287
Ephlin, Patricia, Dr/Pfc Robert Hernandez Mid Sch	399
Epperson, Amber, Dr/Jack Cockrill Middle Sch	81
Epperson, Carolynn/Excel Center-Fort Worth	3
Epperson, Susan/Lee Elem Sch	185
Epps, Beth/Dozier Elem Sch	348
Epps, Trealla/Roberts Elem Sch	194
Erb, Amy/CapRock Elem Sch	354
Erb, Christy/Fall Creek Elem Sch	195
Erbaugh, Matt/San Antonio Christian Mid Sch	45
Erbaugh, Matt/San Antonio Christian Sch	45

Texas School Directory — PRINCIPAL INDEX

NAME/School	PAGE
Erbert, Dani/*Uplift Lee Prep Sch [309]*	108
Erhart, Jesse/*Lakeland Christian Academy*	126
Erickson, Sharon/*Spring Creek Elem Sch*	113
Erie, Linda/*Pleasant Grove Middle Sch*	49
Eriksen, Kristen/*Sunset Valley Elem Sch*	355
Ermoian, Lindy/*Harmony Sci Acad-Waco [284]*	5
Ernest, Brian/*Cele Middle Sch*	371
Ervin, Charles/*South San Antonio Career Ctr*	42
Ervin, Gina/*McMullan Elem Sch*	183
Erwin, Charles/*Timberview Middle Sch*	355
Escalante, Manuel/*Joseph C Martin Elem Sch*	387
Escalante, Manuel/*Woodland Acres Middle Sch*	187
Escalante, Martha/*Willie B Ermel Elem Sch*	179
Escalona, Araceli/*Alton Elem Sch*	222
Escamilla, Christina/*Idea Academy-Mission*	218
Escamilla, Isidro/*Morales Junior High Sch*	378
Escamilla, Jennifer/*Meadow Village Elem Sch*	38
Escamilla, Mikie/*Vincent W Miller Interm Sch*	200
Escanilla, Dinnah/*Ochoa/Milam Steam Academy*	108
Escareno, Marc/*Coronado High Sch*	134
Escobar, Mario/*Eagle Pass Junior High Sch*	276
Escobedo, Ida/*Margaret B Henderson Elem Sch*	101
Escobedo, Rene, Dr/*Holy Cross of San Antonio Sch*	44
Ese, Kathleen/*Bradley Elem Sch*	133
Esparza, Cristina/*Alamo Middle Sch*	223
Esparza, Deborah/*Highland Hills Elem Sch*	40
Esparza, Sylvia/*Montwood Middle Sch*	136
Espino, Manuel/*Barton Elem Sch*	109
Espinosa-Garza, Bertha/*Golfcrest Elem Sch*	192
Espinoza, Catarina/*Aida Escobar Elem Sch*	223
Espinoza, Eric/*YES Prep Southwest [312]*	14
Espinoza, Gracie/*Leon Springs Elem Sch*	38
Espinoza, Maria/*Freeport Elem Sch*	52
Espinoza, Nedia/*Fred Booth Elem Sch*	67
Espitia, N Omar/*A & M Consolidated Middle Sch*	55
Esquivel, Fred/*Ft Worth Adventist Jr Academy*	358
Esquivel, Hector/*Seguin High Sch*	174
Esquivel, Jade/*Int'l Ldrshp TX-Garland*	108
Esquivel, Jose/*Dr Alejo Salinas Sch*	217
Esquivel, Julissa/*Alarcon Elem Sch*	135
Estes, David/*J K Hileman Elem Sch*	70
Estes, Derrick/*Law Elem Sch*	193
Estes, Emily/*Blue Haze Elem Sch*	357
Estorga, Ignacio/*Sun Ridge Middle Sch*	137
Estrada, Janice/*Sacred Heart Sch*	378
Estrada, Joe/*Farine Elem Sch*	109
Estrada, Lisa/*Col John O Ensor Middle Sch*	136
Estrada, Ricardo/*Juarez-Lincoln High Sch*	220
Etheredge, David/*McKinney Christian Academy*	86
Etheridge, Kimberly/*Eagle Lake Primary Sch*	87
Etienne, Nino/*Anne Frank Inspire Academy*	30
Eubank, Laura/*Veribest Sch*	365
Eubank, Teri/*Barton Middle Sch*	211
Eubanks, Ben/*Hico Elem Sch*	176
Eudy, Kenny/*Gustine Sch*	90
Eugenio, Victorius/*Daggett Montessori Elem Sch*	350
Eugenio, Victorius/*De Zavala Elem Sch*	350
Eugenis, Shelbi/*South Elem Sch*	229
Evans, Blake/*Holy Trinity Catholic High Sch*	30
Evans, Bobbie/*Maxdale Elem Sch*	28
Evans, Bradford/*Ector Sch*	146
Evans, Brandon/*Wiley Middle Sch*	397
Evans, Brent/*Sundown High Sch*	229
Evans, Charles/*Covenant Sch*	114
Evans, Darrell/*Dew Elem Sch*	156
Evans, Dustin/*Bland High Sch*	235
Evans, Jan/*Rusk Intermediate Sch*	73
Evans, Julie/*Bess Brannen Elem Sch*	52
Evans, Marc, Dr/*Grace Prep Academy*	359
Evans, Margaret/*West Oso Junior High Sch*	306
Evans, Mike/*Pearce High Sch*	113
Evans, Rebbie/*Winston Sch*	116
Evans, Robin/*San Jacinto Elem Sch*	186
Evans, Terre/*George W Truett Elem Sch*	100
Even, Rosella/*Language Development Center*	277
Everett, Christi/*Snook Sch*	59
Everett, Deshonta, Dr/*Anderson Elem Sch*	193
Everett, Jana/*Caddo Mills High Sch*	235
Everett, Matt/*Leveretts Chapel Sch*	328
Everitt, Terry/*Henderson High Sch*	327
Evers, Rachel/*Union Grove Jr Sr High Sch*	377
Everson, Stacie/*Birkes Elem Sch*	184
Ewald, Deborah/*Leonard Shanklin Elem Sch*	61
Ewerz, Brenda/*Richard Milburn Acad-Lubbock [298]*	10
Ewing, Ann/*A C Jones High Sch*	25
Ewing, Leticia/*Collins Elem Sch*	133
Ewing, Leticia/*Terrace Hills Middle Sch*	135
Ewing, Steven/*South Garland High Sch*	106
Ezell, Tracie/*Teague High Sch*	156

F

NAME/School	PAGE
Fadely, Jody/*Richland Middle Sch*	346
Fahey, Raymond/*Wayside Middle Sch*	349
Failey, Lanica/*Presidential Meadows Elem Sch*	371
Fain, Amy/*Anderson Elem Sch*	18
Fain, Miles/*Texas Sch Blind & Visually Imp*	12
Fairchild, Renee, Dr/*Gonzales Primary Academy*	164
Falcon, Kristin/*Anderson Elem Sch*	202
Falcon, Lisa/*Urban Park Elem Sch*	103
Faldyn, Russell/*Miller Career & Tech Center*	152
Falletich, Maru/*Savannah Heights Interm Sch*	42
Fambrough, Melissa/*Arlington Classics Academy*	1
Fambrough, Susan/*Cedar Creek Elem Sch*	370
Farah, Analisa/*James W Fannin Elem Sch*	303
Farias, Holli/*Kirbyville High Sch*	241
Farias, Maria/*Vanguard Academy-Rembrandt*	13
Farias, Orlando/*Mission Collegiate High Sch*	222
Farish, Andrea/*Dawson Sch*	299
Farley, Matthew/*Center for Career & Tech Ed*	134
Farmer, Carrie/*Bernshausen Elem Sch*	197
Farmer, James/*Founders Classical Acad Schrtz [297]*	3
Farmer, Verna/*John W Carpenter Elem Sch*	101
Farmer, Vonda/*Lee Elem Sch*	235
Farnsworth, Joseph/*Robert E Lee High Sch*	188
Farrell, Norma/*Colonies North Elem Sch*	36
Farrell, Prudence/*Carl O Hamlin Middle Sch*	303
Farris, Bob/*Schell Elem Sch*	83
Farris, Lee/*Crockett Elem Sch*	392
Fasci-Marquez, Dora/*Bruce Aiken Elem Sch*	63
Fatheree, Nancy/*Wilma Fisher Elem Sch*	80
Faucett, Joshua/*New Summerfield Sch*	73
Faulks, Kathryn/*Elm Grove Elem Sch*	211
Favela, Corina/*Brown Middle Sch*	134
Favela, Victor/*Hamlet Elem Sch*	318
Faz, Aracely/*Sacred Heart Sch*	379
Faz, Roel/*Cesar Chavez Elem Sch*	223
Faz, S/*Eisenhower Elem Sch*	216
Feaster, Amy/*Ralls Elem Sch*	94
Fedun, Peggy/*Fredonia Hill Baptist Academy*	298
Fehler, Christina/*L A Gililland Elem Sch*	349
Feimster, Garet/*Judge Barefoot Sanders Law Mag*	101
Feinsteen, Judy/*Towne Creek Sch*	155
Feist, Chayden/*Mullin Middle High Sch*	288
Felder, Iris/*Brookhaven Elem Sch*	27
Felder, Tamera/*Wilson Elem Sch*	186
Feldman, Karen/*Julien C Gallardo Elem Sch*	43
Felix, Dent/*Perryton Kindergarten*	307
Felton, Amy/*St John the Apostle Cath Sch*	358
Felts, Dana/*Grape Creek Elem Sch*	364
Femat, Selma/*Premier HS-Palmview [297]*	9
Fenter, Nichole/*Overton Elem Sch*	328
Fenton, Amanda/*Bowie Primary Sch*	232
Ferguson, Donavan/*Darrouzett Sch*	267
Ferguson, Joseph, Dr/*Hubbard High Sch*	228
Feria, Myrla/*Idea Academy-Eastside*	217
Fernandez, Alesander/*Tijerina Elem Sch*	190
Fernandez, Ana/*Nathaniel Hawthorne Elem Sch*	102
Fernandez, Graciela/*St Raphael Catholic Sch*	139
Fernandez, Irene/*Eligio Kika De La Garza Sch*	220

PRINCIPAL INDEX

Market Data Retrieval

NAME/School	PAGE	NAME/School	PAGE
Fernandez, Jo/Miller Jordan Middle Sch	67	Flores, Dora/Rusk Elem Sch	286
Fernandez, Martha/William Howard Taft High Sch	39	Flores, Edilberto/Mission High Sch	222
Fernandez, Sandra/Adelfa Botello Callejo ES	98	Flores, Eliana/Travis Elem Sch	217
Ferrales, Lorena/Seminary Hills Park Elem Sch	352	Flores, Elsa/M S Ryan Elem Sch	387
Ferrer, Mark/New Diana High Sch	376	**Flores, George**/Oakcrest Intermediate Sch	203
Ferret, Bertrand/Dallas International Sch	85	Flores, George, Dr/Ricky C Bailey Middle Sch	202
Ferreyra, Ely/La Paz Language Academy	139	Flores, Jeff/Frank L Madla Early College HS [291]	3
Ferris, Laila/Mesita Elem Sch	133	Flores, Keri/Western Hills High Sch	352
Fesler, Joe/Gloria Deo Academy	89	Flores, Laura/Dr Leo Cigarroa High Sch	386
Fewell, Jammie/Lytle Primary Sch	21	Flores, Maria/El Jardin Elem Sch	63
Fickel, Keith/Sugar Land Middle Sch	151	Flores, Maria/Guillermo Flores Elem Sch	220
Fidan, Ilker/Harmony Sch Nature & Athletics [284]	4	**Flores, Marittsa**/Richardson Elem Sch	71
Fiedler, Julie/Harper Middle Sch	163	Flores, Maryvel/Lamar Elem Sch	379
Fields, Matthew/Rochelle Sch	278	**Flores, Mrs**/Jimmy Elrod Elem Sch	37
Fields, Robin/Nellie M Reddix Center	38	Flores, Mucia/Charles Borchers Elem Sch	387
Fierro, Michael/Blessed Sacrament Catholic Sch	44	Flores, Nancy/Central Elem Sch	275
Fife, Donna/Elm Grove Elem Sch	195	Flores, Nelly/Raquel Cavazos Elem Sch	222
Fife, Jim/Wonderland Sch	212	Flores, Niranda/Jessie Jensen Elem Sch	224
Figirova, Gary/El Campo Middle Sch	389	**Flores, Olivia**/Judge Oscar De La Fuente ES	67
Figueroa, Autumn/KIPP Climb Academy [288]	6	Flores, Pamela, Dr/Early College High Sch	65
Fike, Jon/Old Union Elem Sch	347	**Flores, Rick**/Rhodes Middle Sch	41
Finch, Bryan/Groveton Jr Sr High Sch	374	Flores, Ricky/Somerset High Sch	42
Finch, Danny/Perryton High Sch	307	Flores, Sandra/Trinity Charter School-Krause [307]	12
Finch, Donna/De Zavala Elem Sch	40	Flores, Sandra/Trinity Charter School-Spring [307]	12
Finch, Melissa/Idea Academy-San Juan	218	Flores, Santos/Columbia Heights Elem Sch	32
Finch, Scot/Hebron High Sch	123	Flores, Umberto/David Sanchez Elem Sch	65
Fine, Michelle/John Glenn Elem Sch	37	Flores, Vanessa/Horn Elem Sch	194
Fingers, Alex/Cross Timbers Middle Sch	353	Flowers, Aeniqua/Rodeo Palms Junior High Sch	51
Finka, Rebecca/Texas Online Preparatory Sch	383	Flowers, Amber/Buna Junior High Sch	240
Finley-Reed, Sheila/John B Connally High Sch	372	**Flowers, Aneiqua**/Manvel High Sch	51
Finnesand, Kerri/Seven Lakes High Sch	153	Flowers, Eddwina/Pioneer Crossing Elem Sch	371
Finster, Dwana/Hope High Sch	62	**Flowers, John**/Highland Heights Elem Sch	188
Fischer, Elizabeth/Coker Elem Sch	34	Flowers, Kelly/Gibson Caldwell Elem Sch	81
Fischer, Jay/Spring Valley Elem Sch	281	Flowers, Sandy/Huntington Intermediate Sch	17
Fisher, Cheryl/Wells Elem Sch	186	Flowers, Shannon/Redeemer Montessori Sch	116
Fisher, Lana/Bluebonnet Elem Sch	122	Floyd, Dexter/Rise Academy	338
Fisher, Toni/The Varnett School-SW [310]	12	**Floyd, Gerald**/Iago Junior High Sch	389
Fisher, Toni/Varnett School-NE [310]	13	**Floyd, Kristal**/Austin Elem Sch	165
Fisher, Vivian/Willow Bend Elem Sch	269	Floyd, Terri/Windermere Primary Sch	372
Fishpaw, John/Austin Academy for Excellence	105	Flynn, Erin, Dr/Katherine Anne Porter Sch	6
Fislar, Kristen/Beaty Early Childhood Sch	82	Flynn, Laura/Mockingbird Elem Sch	98
Fite, Tamara/Tatum Primary Sch	328	Flynn, Sean/Christie Elem Sch	82
Fitzgerald, Natalie/Milam Magnet Elem Sch	130	Foley-Davis, Phyllis/Washington Elem Sch	41
Fitzgerald, Sylvie/Lumin E Dallas Community Sch	8	Foley, Johnie/Leon Junior High Sch	264
Fitzpatrick, Angela/David Crockett Elem Sch	209	Folkes, Lola/Hardy Oak Elem Sch	35
Fitzpatrick, Carrie/Montgomery Elem Sch	293	Folmar, Holly/Sulphur Springs Elem Sch	232
Flaa, Jennifer/Sanger High Sch	126	Fong, Aaron/Bush Elem Sch	285
Flack, Laura/Ball Early Childhood Center	174	Fontana, Anthony/Lewisville HS-B Harmon Campus	123
Flack, Laura/George Vogel Elem Sch	174	Fontenot, Cheryl/Jones Elem Sch	180
Flagler, Duvaughn/S S Dillow Elem Sch	352	Forbis, John/Arden Road Elem Sch	321
Flanagan, Susan/Santa Cruz Elem Sch	212	Ford-Prout, Kelly/Hackney Primary Sch	18
Flanagan, Susan/St Martin De Porres Cath Sch	85	Ford, Alice/Chisholm Trail Elem Sch	126
Flanigan, Rosie/Texoma Alternative Center	392	**Ford, Beverly**/Anne Frank Elem Sch	98
Fleener, Kim/Cuero Junior High Sch	117	Ford, Chris/Full Armor Christian Academy	329
Fleener, Paul/Cuero High Sch	117	**Ford, Cynthia**/Heights High Sch	191
Fleenor, Jeffrey/Dawson Sch	117	Ford, Robert/Manvel Junior High Sch	51
Fleming, Gena/Camacho Elem Sch	397	Ford, Stephanie/Alice W Douse Elem Sch	27
Fleming, Jeneanne/Bowie Junior High Sch	290	Forde, Glenn/El Dorado Elem Sch	35
Fleming, Steve/Dr Kirk Lewis Career & Tech HS	198	Fordyce, Victor, Dr/River City Believers Academy	174
Flemons, Will/Paducah Sch	93	Foreman, Michelle/Texas Serenity Academy	12
Fletcher, Greg/Paradise Junior High Sch	403	Foreman, Michelle/Texas Serenity Academy-Gano	12
Fletcher, Jamie/Tibbals Elem Sch	85	Foreman, Shinnitta/Westwood Elem Sch	16
Fletcher, Stephanie/Waller High Sch	385	Forman, Mark/Uplift Infinity Prep Sch [309]	13
Flinchum, Thomas/Gold-Burg Sch	290	Formby, Marcia/Park Glen Elem Sch	355
Flinn, Christie/Crowell Elem Sch	149	Forney, Darla/White Deer Jr Sr High Sch	69
Flint, Paula, Dr/Flint Academy	358	Forsyth, Alicia/Lefors Sch	165
Flood, Kurtis/Godley High Sch	247	Forsyth, Mike/Vega Elem Sch	81
Florence, Laurie/Hawley Elem Sch	250	Fortenberry, Seth/McGregor High Sch	280
Flores-Guerra, Maria/Evangelina Garza Elem Sch	220	Fortner, Kelli/R Q Sims Intermediate Sch	267
Flores, Ana/Rafael Cantu Jr High Sch	222	Foss, Ivy/Linda Tutt High Sch	126
Flores, Carrie/Durham Elem Sch	191	**Foss, Stacy**/Pease Elem Sch	368
Flores, Clarissa/Lamar Bruni Vergara Middle Sch	388	Foster, Janice/Nova Academy Cedar Hill	8
Flores, Dora/Brewster Sch	216	Foster, Jennifer/Karnes City Primary Sch	250

TX-U20   800-333-8802   School Year 2019-2020

Texas School Directory — PRINCIPAL INDEX

NAME/School	PAGE
Foster, Jennifer/*Roger E Sides Elem Sch*	250
Foster, Judy/*Southwest Elem Sch*	43
Foster, Julie/*Wichita Christian Sch*	393
Foster, Katherine/*Meadows Elem Sch*	83
Foster, Stefani/*Turner Prekindergarten Academy*	142
Foster, Stephanie/*Brown Primary Sch*	24
Foster, Susan/*Boyd High Sch*	402
Foster, Thelma/*Carol Holt Elem Sch*	356
Foster, Tiffany/*T L Pink Elem Sch*	154
Fouche, Erica/*Maud Sch*	49
Fovargue, Keri/*River Oaks Elem Sch*	194
Fowler, Darian/*Merit Academy*	115
Fowler, Jef/*Veritas Academy*	373
Fowler, Jennifer/*Southgate Elem Sch*	106
Fowler, Karli/*I W Evans Intermediate Sch*	145
Fowler, Kendra/*Lamar Elem Sch*	310
Fowler, Letycia/*Harry S Truman Middle Sch*	107
Fox-Norton, Vanessa/*Smith Elem Sch*	41
Fox, Jaime/*Miller Grove Sch*	231
Fox, Mary Lou/*Finley-Oates Elem Sch*	145
Fox, Melody/*Carver Academy Elem Sch*	317
Fox, Merrie/*Randolph Middle Sch*	39
Fox, Monica/*Jean Massieu Acad for the Deaf*	6
Fox, Sean/*Blanco Vista Elem Sch*	211
Fraire, Thomas/*Marine Creek Collegiate HS*	351
Fraker, Jon/*Epiphany Lutheran Sch*	205
Francis, Deborah/*St Joseph Sch*	204
Francis, Theresa/*Notre Dame Sch*	114
Franckowiak, Loren/*Por Vida Academy Charter HS [294]*	9
Franco, Jorge/*Westview Middle Sch*	372
Franco, Sanjuanito/*Capt D Salinas II Elem Sch*	215
Frank, Amy/*Owens Elem Sch*	185
Frank, Gamila/*Living Water Christian Sch*	155
Frank, Patrick/*Yoakum Junior High Sch*	118
Frankhouser, Angela/*Lake Travis Elem Sch*	370
Franklin, Darla/*Florence Black Elem Sch*	111
Franklin, Louisa/*Encinal Elem Sch*	259
Frankson, Kimberly/*Lucile Rogers Ashley Elem Sch*	79
Frauenberger, Kevin/*Hull Daisetta Elem Sch*	266
Frauenberger, Rick/*Grapeland Junior High Sch*	233
Frauenberger, Rick/*Grapeland Secondary Sch*	233
Frauenberger, Rick/*Snook Sch*	59
Frazer, Heath/*Great Oaks Elem Sch*	399
Frazier, Amy/*Iraan Elem Sch*	316
Frazier, Amy/*Iraan Junior High Sch*	316
Frazier, Delsena/*Tyler Early College High Sch*	338
Frazier, Kenneth/*Rule Sch*	210
Frazier, Todd/*Sue E Rattan Elem Sch*	77
Fredo, Ashley/*Morningside Elem Sch*	88
Freed, Kelly/*Lake Pointe Elem Sch*	370
Freelon, Shawki/*Charles A Gill Elem Sch*	99
Freeman, Amber/*Dr Winn Murnin Elem Sch*	37
Freeman, Cheryl/*Clara Oliver Elem Sch*	99
Freeman, Clay/*Montgomery Achievement Center*	327
Freeman, Danny/*Moran Sch*	334
Freeman, Erma/*Lizzie Burgess Alt Sch*	174
Freeman, Prairie/*North Elem Sch*	341
Freeman, Roxie/*Christa McAuliffe Middle Sch*	43
Freeto, Charles/*Waco Center for Youth-Spec Ed*	14
Frei, Danielle/*Locke Hill Elem Sch*	38
Frei, Scott/*Thorndale Middle Sch*	288
Frerking, Jason/*Pearland Jr High School South*	53
Frias, Veronica/*Lancaster Elem Sch*	138
Friede, Kelly/*Summitt Elem Sch*	368
Fries, Jody/*Bobbye Behlau Elem Sch*	36
Frisch, Carl/*Bloomington Elem Sch*	381
Frisch, Kelli/*Edna Bigham Mays Elem Sch*	30
Fritsche, Ron/*Trinity Lutheran Sch*	366
Fritz, Ashleigh/*YES Prep Southside [312]*	14
Froese, Emily/*Coppell Middle School West*	98
Froning, Tammi/*Fred McWhorter Elem Sch*	111
Frost, Lee/*Honey Grove Middle Sch*	146
Frost, Robert/*Willow Wood Junior High Sch*	203
Frye, Erin/*Alexander Elem Sch*	104
Fuchs, Melinda/*Burton Elem Sch*	386
Fuchs, Stephanie/*Firewheel Christian Academy*	115
Fuentes, Anna/*South Park Middle Sch*	304
Fuentes, Debora/*Van Zandt-Guinn Elem Sch*	352
Fugit, Faith/*Elmore Elem Sch*	190
Fuller, Debbie/*Guajardo Elem Sch*	161
Fuller, Jeff/*Irons Junior High Sch*	292
Fuller, Ryan/*West Sabine Jr Sr High Sch*	329
Fulton, Tara/*Gladys Polk Elem Sch*	52
Funderburg, Renee/*Argyle Intermediate Sch*	120
Funderburg, Renee/*Argyle West Elem Sch*	120
Funderburg, Thomas/*Cactus Elem Sch*	295
Funk, Doug, Dr/*Mineral Wells High Sch*	310
Funk, Julia/*Kuehnle Elem Sch*	197
Funkhouser, Jack/*Braun Station Elem Sch*	36
Fuqua, Melissa/*Bay Area Christian Sch*	162
Furlow, Mike/*S W Carter Elem Sch*	335
Furman, Anthony/*Blocker Middle Sch*	161
Furr, Cindy/*Springlake-Earth High Sch*	261
Fusssell, Lila/*Cross of Christ Lutheran Sch*	115

G

NAME/School	PAGE
Gabehart, Cindy/*Pine Tree Senior High Sch*	170
Gabel, Traci/*Woodlands Elem Sch*	319
Gabriel, Krystal/*Bastrop Middle Sch*	23
Gabriel, Michele/*Lion Lane Sch*	201
Gabrysch, Kelly/*Shields Elem Sch*	382
Gaffey, Lesa/*P H Greene Elem Sch*	159
Gage, Kristin/*Paradise Intermediate Sch*	403
Gaines, Joel/*Losoya Intermediate Sch*	43
Gaines, Roger/*Gateway Christian Sch*	45
Gaither, Yolanda/*Apollo Junior High Sch*	112
Gajewski, Mary/*Maggie B Selman Elem Sch*	22
Gajewski, Mary/*Sealy Elem Sch*	22
Galan, Jaymie/*Bowie Elem Sch*	65
Galaviz, Cynthia/*Cimarron Elem Sch*	186
Galdean, Jesse/*Friona Junior High Sch*	315
Galicia, Linda/*Ehrhardt Elem Sch*	197
Galindo-Vargas, Griselda/*Brooke Elem Sch*	366
Galindo, Judy/*Heritage Academy Del Rio*	5
Galindo, Maria/*Desantia Go EC-PK-K Sch*	181
Galindo, Mrs/*Charles E Nash Elem Sch*	350
Galindo, Noe/*Liestman Elem Sch*	182
Galindo, Tanya/*Zavala Magnet Elem Sch*	131
Galinzoga, Sandra/*Antonio Margil Academy*	39
Galinzoga, Sandra/*Wheatley Middle Sch*	41
Gallagher, John/*Nancy Smith Elem Sch*	334
Gallardo, Adrian/*Rankin High Sch*	377
Gallardo, Brenda/*Kay Franklin Elem Sch*	37
Gallardo, Fernando/*Vista Del Futuro Charter Sch*	14
Gallegos, Alecia/*Veritas Christian Academy*	207
Gallegos, Armando, Dr/*Jefferson High Sch*	134
Gallegos, Armando, Dr/*Silva Health Magnet High Sch*	134
Gallegos, Lori/*Kuentz Elem Sch*	38
Gallegos, Norma/*Veterans Memorial Early Clg HS*	64
Gallia, Roseanne/*St Rose of Lima Sch*	148
Galligan, Eileen/*YES Prep Southeast [312]*	14
Gallo, Bill/*Memorial Park Academy*	112
Galoway, Melissa/*Petersburg Sch*	175
Galt, Bria/*Coronado Elem Sch*	318
Galvan, Anna/*Ben Milam Elem Sch*	99
Galvan, Cecilia/*Liberty Junior High Sch*	112
Galvan, David/*New Life Christian Academy*	115
Galvan, Gilbert/*Veterans Memorial Academy*	67
Galvan, Jennifer/*Promise Community Sch Ripley [274]*	10
Galvan, Santana/*Irene Garcia Middle Sch*	220
Gamble, Larea/*Fairview-Miss Jewel Elem Sch*	92
Gamble, Paula/*Weiss High Sch*	372
Gamble, Sherri/*Foster Village Elem Sch*	346
Gamboa, David/*Weslaco East High Sch*	225
Gamboa, Joshua, Dr/*Fasken Elem Sch*	286
Gambrel, Pam/*Winnsboro Elem Sch*	405
Gambrell, Treva/*Jim Ned High Sch*	361
Gamez, Angela/*Dripping Springs High Sch*	210
Gamez, Belinda/*Gillett Intermediate Sch*	257

PRINCIPAL INDEX

Market Data Retrieval

NAME/School	PAGE	NAME/School	PAGE
Gamez, Clotilde/Antonio Gonzalez Middle Sch	387	Garcia, Rosa/Justice Raul A Gonzalez ES	225
Gamotin, Fe, Sr/St Anthony Sch	306	Garcia, Sandra/Graciela Garcia Elem Sch	223
Gandar, Joe/Lincoln Middle Sch	365	Garcia, Sandra/L J Christen Middle Sch	387
Gandy, Meredith/James Mitchell Elem Sch	395	Garcia, Sarah/Sterling H Fly Jr High Sch	407
Gandy, Misty/Eden High Sch	90	Garcia, Selena/Blessing Elem Sch	276
Gann, Charlie/Texas Leadership CS-Midland	12	Garcia, Sheila/Liberty Campus	382
Garcia-Olivo, Mayte/Juan N Seguin Elem Sch	193	Garcia, Silvia/Alton Memorial Junior High Sch	222
Garcia, Adalberto/John Drugan Elem Sch	136	Garcia, Silvia/William Anderson Elem Sch	103
Garcia, Alicia/Providence Catholic Sch	44	**Garcia, Stacy**/High School for Law & Justice	189
Garcia, Amanda/Lamar Elem Sch	392	Garcia, Stephanie/Palacios High Sch	275
Garcia, Angela/Floresville Alternative Ctr	400	Garcia, Tammie/Valley View Early College Sch	225
Garcia, Angelina/Ollie Ogrady Elem Sch	222	**Garcia, Teresa**/General Ricardo Sanchez ES	340
Garcia, Anmarie/Oakwood Terrace Elem Sch	354	Garcia, Tim/Premier HS-Brownwood Early [297]	9
Garcia, Anna/David Crockett Academy	40	Garcia, Valarie/Baskin Elem Sch	39
Garcia, Anna/San Isidro Sch	341	Garcia, Victor/Port Houston Elem Sch	190
Garcia, Azucena/Sanchez Elem Sch	367	Garcia, Vincent/Preston Hollow Elem Sch	102
Garcia, Bob/Texas Early College High Sch [293]	12	Garcia, Yuridia/Houston Gateway Acad-Evergreen	5
Garcia, Bobby/Manor New Tech High Sch	371	**Garcia, Yvette**/Truitt Middle Sch	185
Garcia, Briana/Guerrero Thompson Elem Sch	367	Garcie, Kelye/Olsen Elem Sch	305
Garcia, Charles/Bel Air High Sch	137	Gardea, Becky/Jacinto City Elem Sch	187
Garcia, Chris/Harris Co Detention Center	179	Gardea, Rocio/Seagoville North Elem Sch	102
Garcia, Claudette/Premont Collegiate High Sch	246	Gardner-Valdes, Brenda/Shiloh Sch	54
Garcia, Claudette/San Diego High Sch	128	**Gardner, Aja, Dr**/Cast STEM High Sch	43
Garcia, Corina/Skidmore Tynan Elem Sch	25	Gardner, Brenda/John J Ciavarra Elem Sch	283
Garcia, Dahlia/Zapata South Elem Sch	407	Gardner, Crystal/Hunters Glen Elem Sch	150
Garcia, Daisy/Hueco Elem Sch	136	Gardner, Lazonda/Gardner Preparatory Sch	115
Garcia, Daniel/Hendrickson High Sch	372	Gardner, Lazonda/Xavier Preparatory Sch	116
Garcia, David/Twain MS & Dual Language Acad	41	**Gardner, Melinda**/Walnut Springs Elem Sch	211
Garcia, Diana/Salinas STEM Early College Sch	220	**Gardner, Rose**/Wolfe City High Sch	237
Garcia, Dimitri/Perryton Junior High Sch	307	Garduno, Lourdes/Winnetka Elem Sch	103
Garcia, Edward/Winters Elem Sch	327	Garibaldi, Inge/Louie Welch Middle Sch	194
Garcia, Enrique/St Dominic Savio Catholic HS	400	Garibay, Thania/Casa View Elem Sch	99
Garcia, Eutimio/Premier HS-Comanche [297]	9	**Garinger, Debbie**/Alamo Heights High Sch	30
Garcia, Frank/Raymondville High Sch	394	Garinger, Lynda/Hopewell Middle Sch	399
Garcia, Frank/Raymondville Options Academy	394	Garland, Stephanie/Coram Deo Academy-Collin Cnty	85
Garcia, Gabriela/Gregorio Esparza Elem Sch	37	Garlic, Johnny/B Garza Middle Sch	225
Garcia, Guadalupe/Vida N Clover Elem Sch	224	Garner, Mitzi/Nelson Middle Sch	79
Garcia, Helen/Hornsby-Dunlap Elem Sch	369	Garner, Rick/Blackshear Elem Sch	367
Garcia, Jacob/McCollum High Sch	33	Garnes, Trina/Shekinah Radiance Acad-Garland	11
Garcia, Jaime/Early College High Sch	216	Garnica, Fernando/Anthony High Sch	131
Garcia, Jaime/Santa Rosa High Sch	67	Garnica, Fernando/Anthony Middle Sch	131
Garcia, James/Diamond Hill-Jarvis High Sch	350	Garrabrant, Steve/Lutheran South Academy	206
Garcia, Javier/Southwest Prep Sch SE [302]	11	Garred, Josh/Whitehouse High Sch	339
Garcia, Jennifer/Pleasanton Junior High Sch	21	Garrett-Jones, Alpher/Paul L Dunbar Learning Center	102
Garcia, Jerry/Zapata High Sch	407	Garrett, Danny/Hooks High Sch	48
Garcia, Jose/Domingo Trevino Middle Sch	219	Garrett, Felica/Levi Fry Intermediate Sch	161
Garcia, Joshua/Warren Middle Sch	252	Garrett, James/Brundreet Middle Sch	305
Garcia, Juan Manuel/Crockett Elem Sch	65	Garrett, Jessica/Bushland Middle Sch	319
Garcia, Juanita/Henry B Gonzalez Elem Sch	277	**Garrett, Latoya, Dr**/Briargate Elem Sch	150
Garcia, Judith/J R Harris Elem Sch	190	Garrett, Monica/E M Daggett Middle Sch	350
Garcia, Julio/Highlands High Sch	40	Garrett, Rachel/Valley Ridge Elem Sch	124
Garcia, Kelly/Freeman Elem Sch	105	Garrett, Tara/MacGregor Elem Sch	194
Garcia, Leticia/Newman Elem Sch	388	Garrido, Yolanda/Barrick Elem Sch	190
Garcia, Louella/Lasater Elem Sch	57	**Garrison, Heather**/Griffin Middle Sch	123
Garcia, Magdalena/Crockett Early Education Sch	107	Garrison, Jason/Sanford Fritch High Sch	238
Garcia, Maria/Memorial Elem Sch	194	Garrison, Lisa/Colin Powell Elem Sch	291
Garcia, Marivel/Progreso Elem Sch	224	**Garrison, Matthew**/Maypearl Middle Sch	141
Garcia, Mark/Carlos Coon Elem Sch	36	Garrison, Sarah/Lexington High Sch	263
Garcia, Martina/Salinas Elem Sch	222	Garrison, Tom/Jesuit College Prep Sch	114
Garcia, Mayra/Milton Cooper Elem Sch	202	Gartman, Randy/Winters High Sch	327
Garcia, Michael/Abilene High Sch	360	Garton, Deborah/Life School Lancaster [290]	7
Garcia, Michael/Gonzales High Sch	164	Garver, Carolyn/Autism Treatment Center	114
Garcia, Michelle/Ridgecrest Elem Sch	201	Gary, Staci/Taft Elem Sch	244
Garcia, Miguel/Eastside Memorial High Sch	368	Gary, Sue/Shepherd of the Hills Luth Sch	45
Garcia, Monica/Noonan Elem Sch	245	Garza-Ibarra, Mary/Enrique Camarena Elem Sch	220
Garcia, Nora/St John Berchman's Sch	44	Garza, Adolfo/Incarnate Word Middle Sch	306
Garcia, Norma/La Joya West Academy	220	Garza, Aimee/Brownsville Early Clg HS	63
Garcia, Odette/Roel & Celia Saenz Elem Sch	341	**Garza, Alicia**/Hicks Elem Sch	303
Garcia, Olivia/Benavides Heights Elem Sch	276	**Garza, Amy**/Medio Creek Elem Sch	43
Garcia, Patricia/Collier Elem Sch	32	Garza, Ann Marie/H C Schochler Elem Sch	183
Garcia, Patricia/St Elizabeth Sch	246	Garza, Anna/Idea Academy-Alamo	217
Garcia, Ramon/Alice Landergin Elem Sch	317	**Garza, Annice**/Liberty Middle Sch	66
Garcia, Roberto/Moorhead Junior High Sch	292	**Garza, Anthony**/Wilson & Young Middle Sch	130

Texas School Directory — PRINCIPAL INDEX

NAME/School	PAGE
Garza, Antonio/Idea Clg Prep-Elsa	218
Garza, Barbara/Aesa Preparatory Academy	212
Garza, Christy/Portia Ross Taylor Elem Sch	80
Garza, Crystal/Patricia S Garza Elem Sch	215
Garza, Dan/Rice Challenge Academy	87
Garza, Edgar/Delia Gonzalez Garcia ES	341
Garza, Efrain/S Texas Bus Ed & Tech Acad	68
Garza, Fidel/Veterans Memorial High Sch	222
Garza, Gabriella/Heritage Rose Elem Sch	150
Garza, H/Bruni High Sch	388
Garza, Javier/Keller Elem Sch	64
Garza, Jesus/Valley View High Sch	225
Garza, Jose/Lorenzo De Zavala Elem Sch	217
Garza, Kristine/Woodrow Wilson Elem Sch	221
Garza, Leila/Maverick Elem Sch	41
Garza, Leslie/Woodsboro Elem Sch	324
Garza, Lori/Sharyland High Sch	224
Garza, Marina/Saenz Elem Sch	245
Garza, Marisa/Betty Harwell Middle Sch	216
Garza, Marisa/Narciso Cavazos Elem Sch	220
Garza, Mary/Edinburg South Middle Sch	216
Garza, Melissa/Knippa Sch	378
Garza, Melissa/Lorenzo Dezavala Middle Sch	199
Garza, Myra/Castro Elem Sch	222
Garza, Patricia/Ortiz Elem Sch	64
Garza, Pedro/Legacy Christian Academy	45
Garza, Ramon/Norman Thomas Elem Sch	128
Garza, Ray/Lillion E Luehrs Jr High Sch	302
Garza, Ricardo/East Austin Clg Prep-SW Key	2
Garza, Rosie/C E Vail Elem Sch	65
Garza, San Juana/Francisco Farias Elem Sch	386
Garza, Tammy/Rowland Elem Sch	382
Garza, Tanya/Zavala Elem Sch	65
Garza, Tesilia/Virginia Myers Elem Sch	39
Garza, Tina/Harlingen Sch of Health	65
Garza, Veronica/Ridgeview Elem Sch	35
Garza, Vidal/Tiger Trail Sch	201
Gaskamp, Michelle/James E Randolph Elem Sch	152
Gaskill, Jae/McKinney North High Sch	81
Gassaway, Jim/Bear Branch Elem Sch	292
Gaston, Brian/North Houston Early College HS	192
Gaston, Jill/Center Roughrider Academy	334
Gaston, Jill/Wells High Sch	73
Gates, Gary/Midlothian High Sch	141
Gates, Hannah/Schultz Junior High Sch	385
Gatewood, Howard/Red Oak Middle Sch	142
Gatewood, Steve/Jefferson Co Youth Academy	241
Gathright, Tammy/C P Yeager Elem Sch	303
Gatlin, Donna/Pioneer Elem Sch	406
Gaudette, Philip/East Bernard Elem Sch	389
Gauer, Russell/Whitney Intermediate Sch	228
Gauntt, Shannon/Shady Brook Elem Sch	354
Gavito, Luis/Jjaep Sch	194
Gawryszewski, Alan/Rancier Middle Sch	28
Gawryszewski, Bryan/Fairfield Junior High Sch	156
Gayle, Ginny/Stafford Middle Sch	155
Gayles, Michael, Dr/Ignite Middle Sch	100
Gaytan, Nelda/Cano Gonzalez Elem Sch	216
Gearhart, Ellie/L B Johnson Elem Sch	32
Geary-Smith, Nkosi/Atwood McDonald Elem Sch	350
Gee, Cindy/St Louis Catholic Sch	372
Geeslin, April/Azle Christian Sch	358
Geis, Jaimie/Sugar Mill Elem Sch	151
Gennings, Mindy/Wake Village Elem Sch	50
Gentry, Mr/Meadowbrook Middle Sch	351
Gentry, Olga/St Augustine High Sch	389
Gentry, Tannisha/Forest Brook Middle Sch	188
George, Belinda/Homer Drive Elem Sch	242
George, Jake/Normangee Middle Sch	264
George, Jennifer/Center Point Elem Sch	255
George, King/Plano East Senior High Sch	83
Gerard, Dana/Lutheran High School North	206
Gerard, Lance/Our Savior Lutheran Sch	206
Gerault, Jeanette/Fiest Elem Sch	184
Gerber, Judy/Westlake Lutheran Academy	155
Gerhardt, Rebecca/Richard Milburn Acad-Amarillo [298]	10
Gerik, Misty/Connally Early Childhood Ctr	279
Gerlach, Rebekah/John H Shary Elem Sch	224
Gerletti, Kelly/A Robison Elem Sch	184
German, Jane/Loretto Acad Elem Sch	139
Germany, Stacy/Dolores W McClatchey Elem Sch	141
Gersback, Phil/Douglass Sch	297
Gettys, Joshua/Fort Bend Christian Academy-HS	155
Gex, Robert/Permian High Sch	130
Geyer, Jeanette/Our Lady of Grace Academy	21
Giacchino, Maureen/Mount Carmel Academy	190
Giacumakis, Amie/Ischool High-Hickory Creek [297]	6
Giamanco, PJ/Carroll High Sch	347
Giardino, Lisa/St Peter School the Apostle	358
Giba, Mary Anna/Irvin High Sch	134
Gibbs, David/Cathedral of Life Chrn Sch	114
Gibson, Brian/William Velasquez Elem Sch	154
Gibson, Christine/Prestwick STEM Academy	124
Gibson, Gary/Shadow Ridge Middle Sch	124
Gibson, Holly/Middle College at HCC Gulfton	190
Gibson, Katrina/Seagoville Elem Sch	102
Gibson, Kendra/Levelland Christian Sch	230
Gibson, Kittie/Wink High Sch	402
Gibson, Paula/Park Row Chrn Academy	359
Gibson, Robyn/Paradise Elem Sch	403
Gibson, Sandra/La Vega High Sch	280
Gibson, Scott/Argyle Middle Sch	120
Giddens, Kelly/Stipes Elem Sch	110
Giddens, Terry/Avinger Sch	70
Gielow, Lisa/Nebbie Williams Elem Sch	325
Gifford, Sharon/Magnolia Elem Sch	53
Gijon, Jose/Coldwell Elem Sch	133
Gilbert-Perry, Dana/Vale Middle Sch	38
Gilbert, Andru/Ferris High Sch	140
Gilbert, Caitlin/Saint Constantine Sch	207
Gilbert, Cori/Metro Elem School of Design	304
Gilbert, Jeremy/Highland Park Middle Sch	108
Gilbert, John/Yorktown Christian Academy	306
Gilbert, Rachael/James R Newman Elem Sch	79
Gilbreath, Justin/Dale Jackson Career Center	123
Gilbreath, Kenda/Seymour Elem Sch	25
Gilcrease, Laurie/Hitchcock High Sch	161
Gilder, Charlotte/Jean & Betty Schmalz Elem Sch	152
Giles, Mary/Frederick A Douglass Lrng Acad	265
Giles, Tom/Pewitt Junior High Sch	296
Gilger, Andrea/McMasters Elem Sch	199
Gill, Rob/KIPP Prime College Prep [288]	7
Gillard, Jennifer/Bryson Elem Sch	348
Gillaspie, Sara/Westcliff Elem Sch	352
Gillen, John/Blooming Grove High Sch	299
Gillespie, Catherine/Wolffarth Elem Sch	271
Gillespie, Christina/Poteet Intermediate Campus	21
Gillespie, Gabe/Dunbar College Prep Academy	270
Gilliam, Rhonda/Albert & Iola Davis Malvern ES	81
Gilliam, Tanya/Austin Elem Science Acad	107
Gilmore, Allison/Starrett Elem Sch	345
Gilmore, Earl/O'Banion Middle Sch	106
Gilmore, Leon/Texans Can Acad Houston North [305]	12
Gilmore, Letha/Inspired for Excellence Acad W	194
Gilmore, Marla/Hamshire Fannett Interm Sch	242
Gimble, Missy/Vincent Middle Sch	242
Gipprich, Jessie/Terrell Wells Middle Sch	33
Gipson, Michael/Wilmer-Hutchins Elem Sch	103
Gipson, Winston/James L Coble Middle Sch	357
Girardi, David/Edge Middle Sch	78
Giron, Jasmine/McReynolds Middle Sch	191
Gist, Megan/Linda Lyon Elem Sch	325
Gittens, Stephen/Woodson PK-5 Sch	189
Giuffre, Monica/Falcon Pass Elem Sch	159
Givan, Taryn/Westlawn Elem Sch	50
Givens, Toby, Dr/Harwood Junior High Sch	354
Glass, Andy/Shamrock Elem Sch	391
Glass, Lexy/Gruver Junior High Sch	176
Glass, Raymond/Harper Daep Sch	190
Glass, Raymond/McLean Sch	165

PRINCIPAL INDEX

NAME/School	PAGE
Glasscock, Christopher/*C M Rice Middle Sch*	82
Glasser, Cheryl/*Roberta Rylander Elem Sch*	153
Glen, Smith/*Morton Junior High Sch*	75
Glenewinkel, Niesa/*Creekview Elem Sch*	203
Glenn, Lori/*College Hill Elem Sch*	175
Gloff, Mona/*Hamilton Junior High Sch*	176
Gloria, Olivia/*Benjamin Sch*	258
Glosson, Robyn/*Warren Elem Sch*	375
Gloston, Jerry/*Dequeen Elem Sch*	243
Glover, Gene/*Eagle Lake Intermediate Sch*	87
Glover, Janelle/*Academy of Accelerated Lrng*	1
Glover, Jason/*Mt Vernon High Sch*	156
Glover, Michael/*Prairie Harbor Alternative Sch*	22
Glover, Steve/*Coppell Middle School East*	98
Goad, Lacye/*Kenneth Davis Elem Sch*	357
Goana, Irma/*Highland Forest Elem Sch*	31
Godbolt, Rashad/*Alternative Lrng Ctr-East*	184
Godinez, Delores, Dr/*Cedar Creek Elem Sch*	23
Godoy, Ricardo/*Dr M L Garza-Gonzalez Chtr Sch [283]*	2
Godwin, Quinn/*Hull Daisetta High Sch*	266
Godwin, Quinn/*Hull Daisetta Junior High Sch*	266
Goebel, Vicki/*Glen Rose Junior High Sch*	340
Goebel, Vicki/*Leakey Sch*	322
Goedecke, Keith/*Trinity Lutheran Sch*	207
Goette, Harry/*South Texas Acad Med Professns*	68
Goetzke, Paul/*Norma Krueger Elem Sch-Karrer*	172
Goff, Guamma/*Ischool High the Woodlands [297]*	6
Goff, Jakeb/*Liberty-Eylau Middle Sch*	48
Goforth, Christy/*Hofius Intermediate Sch*	197
Goldsmith, Justin/*Reynolds Middle Sch*	84
Gollihar, Will/*Thomas Buzbee Vocational Sch*	12
Gombert, Jessica/*Geneva School of Boerne*	254
Gomez, Ahna/*Irving High Sch*	109
Gomez, Ana/*St Mary's Sch*	68
Gomez, Carlos/*Canyon Hills Middle Sch*	134
Gomez, Claudia/*Jimmy Carter Early Clg HS*	220
Gomez, Cynthia/*B F Clark Primary Sch*	202
Gomez, Eliza/*Riverside Middle Sch*	67
Gomez, Hector/*Jubilee San Antonio [285]*	6
Gomez, Irma/*John McKeever Elem Sch*	223
Gomez, Jeri/*College Career & Tech Acad*	66
Gomez, Juan/*Crockett Junior High Sch*	232
Gomez, Laura/*Pasadena High Sch*	199
Gomez, Mary/*East Central Heritage Mid Sch*	31
Gomez, Natalie/*Central Middle Sch*	243
Gomez, Nicole/*E T Wrenn Middle Sch*	31
Gomez, Ramiro/*Idea Clg Prep-Edinburg*	218
Gomez, Rosemarie, Dr/*Wilbur E Lucas Elem Sch*	225
Gomez, Ruben/*Southwest Sch-Mangum [278]*	11
Gomez, Zaira/*Cornelius Elem Sch*	192
Gonzales, Amber/*A J Briesemeister Mid Sch*	174
Gonzales, Amy/*Clayton Elem Sch*	366
Gonzales, Blanca/*Lighthouse Charter Sch*	8
Gonzales, Brenda/*William Pearce Elem Sch*	43
Gonzales, Cecilia/*Northside High Sch*	192
Gonzales, Cristabel/*Goliad Elem Sch*	130
Gonzales, Elida/*W J Turner Elem Sch*	352
Gonzales, Graciela/*Augusto Guerra Elem Sch*	223
Gonzales, Guadalupe/*Byron Craig Middle Sch*	360
Gonzales, Henry/*Excel Academy Charter Sch*	3
Gonzales, Jennifer/*Fossil Hill Middle Sch*	355
Gonzales, Jose/*Amherst Sch*	260
Gonzales, Justin/*Alpine High Sch*	56
Gonzales, Justin/*Alpine Middle Sch*	56
Gonzales, Lindsay/*Joseph Gilbert Elem Sch*	369
Gonzales, Magda/*Austin Elem Sch*	64
Gonzales, Marcia/*Floresville Middle Sch*	400
Gonzales, Melissa/*Refugio Junior High Sch*	323
Gonzales, Moises/*Agape Christian Sch*	226
Gonzales, Roger/*Loma Park Elem Sch*	32
Gonzales, Sara/*Somerset Early Chldhd Ctr*	42
Gonzales, Sonia/*Kermit Elem Sch*	402
Gonzales, Tony/*Moises Vela Middle Sch*	65

NAME/School	PAGE
Gonzalez Vela, Rosa/*Emiliano Zapata Elem Sch*	220
Gonzalez, Adriana/*Solar Preparatory for Boys*	103
Gonzalez, Alejandro, Dr/*Gallegos Elem Sch*	189
Gonzalez, Amabilia/*Rodolfo Centeno Elem Sch*	388
Gonzalez, Arturo/*San Jacinto Adult Learning Ctr*	133
Gonzalez, Blanca/*Lighthouse Chtr Sch-B Campus*	8
Gonzalez, Brisa/*Geraldine Palmer Elem Sch*	223
Gonzalez, Carolyn/*Holy Cross Catholic HS*	131
Gonzalez, Charles/*Van Horn Schools*	95
Gonzalez, Claudia/*Marcia R Garza Elem Sch*	223
Gonzalez, Danelo/*Roma Middle Sch*	341
Gonzalez, David/*Ysleta Middle Sch*	138
Gonzalez, Deana/*Jackson Elem Sch*	154
Gonzalez, Ema/*La Paloma Elem Sch*	67
Gonzalez, Epigmenio/*Grulla Elem Sch*	340
Gonzalez, Erica/*East Austin College Prep-MLK*	2
Gonzalez, Federico/*Vanguard Academy-Mozart*	13
Gonzalez, Fernando/*West Oso Elem Sch*	306
Gonzalez, Fernin/*Memorial Middle Sch*	217
Gonzalez, Gerardo/*Theodore Roosevelt Elem Sch*	221
Gonzalez, Ixchell/*Ira C Ogden Academy*	40
Gonzalez, Jennifer/*Bonham Pre-Kindergarten Sch*	211
Gonzalez, Jennifer/*Grady B Rasco Middle Sch*	52
Gonzalez, Joe/*Fredericksburg High Sch*	163
Gonzalez, Joe/*Thompson Learning Center*	34
Gonzalez, Juan/*Patterson Elem Sch*	190
Gonzalez, Laura/*Baty Elem Sch*	369
Gonzalez, Laurie/*Northside Elem Sch*	52
Gonzalez, Linda/*Hereford Preparatory Academy*	119
Gonzalez, Luis, Dr/*Premier HS-San Antonio East [297]*	9
Gonzalez, Melissa/*Lorenzo De Zavala Elem Sch*	101
Gonzalez, Michelle/*Carrizo Springs High Sch*	127
Gonzalez, Nancy/*Port Isabel Junior High Sch*	66
Gonzalez, Olga/*Rafaela T Barrera Elem Sch*	341
Gonzalez, Raul/*Lyford Middle Sch*	394
Gonzalez, Rene/*Bishop Garriga Middle Sch*	306
Gonzalez, Roberto/*Stevens Park Elem Sch*	103
Gonzalez, Samantha/*Bonnie Brae Elem Sch*	350
Gonzalez, Sonia/*Rudy Silva Elem Sch*	225
Gonzalez, Veronica/*Graves Elem Sch*	277
Gonzalez, Yliana/*Ramirez Elem Sch*	128
Good, Sarah/*Highland PK Presbyterian Sch*	115
Good, Tamara/*Edward B Cannan Elem Sch*	294
Goode, Amanda/*Bullard Early Childhood Center*	336
Goodenough, Rob/*Wylie East Junior High Sch*	361
Goodman, Anna/*Wilchester Elem Sch*	201
Goodman, Dorothy/*Depelchin-Richmond Charter Sch*	2
Goodman, Dorothy/*UT Univ CS-Memorial Hermann*	13
Goodman, Dottie/*Texas Neurorehab Center*	373
Goodman, Jennifer/*Odyssey Academy*	8
Goodrich, Sandra/*Knowledge Seeker Christian Sch*	126
Goodrum, Leslie/*Greenwood Elem Sch*	285
Gordon, Britt/*Borden County Sch*	46
Gordon, Christine/*Cavazos Elem Sch*	216
Gordon, Eliza/*Wells Branch Elem Sch*	399
Gordon, Steve/*Valor South Austin*	13
Gordy, Joe/*Graham High Sch*	406
Gore, Cody/*Normangee Elem Sch*	264
Gore, Heather/*Shepherd Primary Sch*	330
Gore, Kristi/*Kirbyville Elem Sch*	241
Gore, Matthew/*Aubrey High Sch*	120
Gorena, Anibal/*Edinburg Alternative Academy*	216
Gorena, Tina/*Prep for Early College HS*	340
Gorka, Dennis/*Conroe 9th Grade High Sch*	291
Gorman, Katherine/*Ella Barnes Elem Sch*	303
Gorman, Paola/*Ford Elem Sch*	291
Gosby, Karen/*Fellowship Christian Academy*	115
Goss, Carita/*Northwood Montessori Sch*	206
Goss, Charelene/*B J Smith Elem Sch*	110
Gosselink, John/*Bastrop High Sch*	23
Goswick, Brandon/*Elysian Fields Middle Sch*	208
Gottwald, Sue/*Shiner Elem Sch*	262
Gouard, Jimmy, Dr/*Sabinal Elem Sch*	378

Texas School Directory — PRINCIPAL INDEX

NAME/School	PAGE
Gouard, Jimmy, Dr/*St Louis Sch*	284
Gouard, Toshia/*Tice Elem Sch*	187
Goudeau, Lois/*St Mary Purification Mont Sch*	204
Gouger, Kathryn/*Brookwood Elem Sch*	158
Gould, Kendall/*Mineola Middle Sch*	404
Gould, Natasha/*Eloise Japhet Academy*	40
Gould, Teri/*Glenmore Elem Sch*	365
Goulden, Melissa/*East Elem Sch*	208
Gounder, Stephanie/*YES Prep Brays Oaks [312]*	14
Gourrier, Steve/*South Early College High Sch*	193
Grable, Victoria/*New Heights Christian Academy*	206
Graf, Ted/*Headwaters Sch*	373
Gragg, Troy/*Sabine Pass Sch*	244
Graham, Betsy/*Prince of Peace Christian Sch*	126
Graham, Kim/*Robert L Stevenson Primary Sch*	51
Graham, Kristi/*Hedgcoxe Elem Sch*	82
Graham, Melanie/*Hidden Lakes Elem Sch*	355
Graham, Susie/*Vaughn Elem Sch*	80
Graham, Wes/*Kline Whitis Elem Sch*	261
Grammer, Carlin/*La Porte High Sch*	198
Gramtages, Charles/*Presbyterian Sch*	206
Granados, Javier/*Martin Middle Sch*	303
Granados, Monica/*Nathan Howell Elem Sch*	351
Grande, Blaire/*Pebble Creek Elem Sch*	56
Grant, Donna/*South Grand Prairie High Sch*	108
Grant, Kim/*Alvarado Intermediate Sch*	246
Grant, Stacy/*Montgomery Christian Academy*	295
Granzin, Kelly/*Wall Elem Sch*	365
Gratt, Francine/*Earl & Lottie Wolford Elem Sch*	81
Graves, Gladys/*Chilton Sch*	144
Graves, Michelle/*Smith Elem Sch*	382
Graves, Perry/*Eldorado High Sch*	333
Graves, Rita/*Lamar High Sch*	194
Gravitt, Van/*Abilene Christian Sch*	361
Gray, Adam/*Vickery Elem Sch*	124
Gray, Brandy/*Chireno Sch*	297
Gray, Carrie/*Rivercrest Elem Sch*	323
Gray, Dameon/*Thelma Jones Elem Sch*	357
Gray, Eric/*Christ the King Cathedral Sch*	272
Gray, Jeremy/*KIPP Somos Collegiate High Sch [289]*	7
Gray, Julie/*Eustace Primary Sch*	214
Gray, Katey, Dr/*Heritage High Sch*	79
Gray, Octavia/*Edward J Briscoe Elem Sch*	350
Gray, Terri/*Joaquin Junior High Sch*	335
Greaff, Gina/*Wheat Elem Sch*	375
Green, Aronda/*Royal Early Childhood Center*	384
Green, Aronda/*Royal Elem Sch*	384
Green, Bianca/*Lee Elem Sch*	107
Green, Elizabeth/*Fort Worth Christian Sch*	358
Green, Jane/*Memorial Middle Sch*	201
Green, Jim/*Industrial High Sch*	240
Green, Juanette/*Jean Hines-Caldwell Elem Sch*	192
Green, Krystle/*Chisholm Ridge Elem Sch*	348
Green, Robert/*Ralph Eickenroht Elem Sch*	202
Green, Shelly/*Plum Creek Elem Sch*	248
Green, Tag/*Providence Christian Sch*	116
Greenberg, Daniel/*Condit Elem Sch*	193
Greene, Jennifer/*YES Prep White Oak [312]*	14
Greenhouse, Lisa/*Paramount Terrace Elem Sch*	318
Greenwell, Timothy/*Liberty Elem Sch*	123
Greenwood, Valencia/*Lucas Pre-K Center*	242
Greer, Carrie/*Yale Elem Sch*	113
Greer, Emily/*Rise School of Austin*	373
Gregory, Geoff/*Huntington Elem Sch*	17
Gregory, Harold/*Greenville Alt Center*	236
Gregory, Harold/*New Horizons Learning Center*	236
Gregory, Kristi/*Achziger Elem Sch*	110
Gregory, Matthew/*Center High Sch*	334
Gregory, Mendy/*Della Icenhower Interm Sch*	356
Gresham, Andy/*Cushing Jr Sr High Sch*	297
Gresham, Katie/*Liberty Christian Academy*	169
Griebel, Janey/*Plum Creek Elem Sch*	61
Griffen, Cody/*Utpb STEM Academy*	13
Griffin, Angie/*Brewer Academy*	40
Griffin, Angie/*Waggoner Creek Elem Sch*	50
Griffin, Kade/*Lomax Junior High Sch*	198
Griffin, Kyella/*Dulles Elem Sch*	150
Griffin, Marc/*Hemphill Senior High Sch*	329
Griffin, Michael/*Amarillo Collegiate Academy*	1
Griffin, Michael/*Amarillo Collegiate Academy [297]*	1
Griffin, Roshanda/*M C Williams Middle Sch*	189
Griffin, Roxxy/*Carolyn G Bukhair Elem Sch*	112
Griffin, Tanis/*George A Thompson Interm Sch*	199
Griffin, Wynette/*Glenhope Elem Sch*	353
Griffith, Deana/*Wylie Primary Sch*	327
Griffith, Erin/*Brock Elem Sch*	312
Griffith, Jeremy/*Sundown Middle Sch*	230
Griffith, Linnea/*Bonnie Holland Elem Sch*	151
Griffith, Victoria/*Hazel Ingram Elem Sch*	140
Griffon, Mark/*Friendswood High Sch*	160
Grimaldo, Veronica/*Dora Romero Elem Sch*	66
Grimaldo, Veronica/*Los Fresnos Elem Sch*	66
Grimes, Danielle/*O A Peterson Elem Sch*	125
Grimes, Justin/*College View High Sch*	55
Grimet, Beth/*Katy Elem Sch*	152
Grimsley, Keri/*Godley Elem Sch*	247
Grisdale, Mark/*Obra D Tompkins High Sch*	152
Grisham, Nikki/*Hawley High Sch*	250
Grissom, Marsha/*Premier HS-Granbury [297]*	9
Groff, Matthew/*Round Rock High Sch*	399
Grogan, Eric/*Rice High Sch*	87
Groholski, Kenneth/*Bremond High Sch*	324
Groppel, Lance/*Colleyville Heritage High Sch*	353
Gross, John/*New Diana Middle Sch*	376
Grossman, Cayla/*Summer Creek Middle Sch*	348
Grossweiler, Philip/*Alonzo De Leon Middle Sch*	221
Grote, Melanie/*Massey Ranch Elem Sch*	53
Groth, Joshua/*Premier HS-Tyler [297]*	10
Groves, Rob/*White Deer Elem Sch*	69
Growdon, James/*Atonement Academy*	44
Grubbs, Holly/*Sam Rutherford Elem Sch*	111
Grubbs, Travis/*High Island Sch*	160
Gruber, Erica/*Oakley Elem Sch*	294
Grubert-Dotson, Shelly/*Brazos Elem Sch*	22
Gruninger, Emily/*Lake Highlands Elem Sch*	112
Gryder, Dee-Dee/*David S Crockett ECC*	140
Guajardo, Lesli/*Braswell High Sch*	121
Guajardo, Michelle/*Ruben Hinojosa Elem Sch*	222
Guajardo, Radha/*Idea Academy-Riverview*	218
Guajardo, Reymundo/*Henry Gonzales Elem Sch*	100
Guajardo, Twila/*Pleasanton High Sch*	21
Guardado, Rafael/*Roberts Elem Sch*	134
Guedea, Cynthia/*Rosita Valley Elem Sch*	277
Guernsey, Marsha, Dr/*Newfound Academy*	115
Guerra, Antonio/*L C Smith Elem Sch*	394
Guerra, Araceli/*W A Todd Middle Sch*	215
Guerra, Carlos/*Montwood High Sch*	136
Guerra, Elida/*Somerset Junior High Sch*	42
Guerra, Juanita/*East Montana Middle Sch*	132
Guerra, Maria/*Beall Elem Sch*	133
Guerra, Maria/*Douglass Elem Sch*	133
Guerra, Maria/*J Henderson Elem Sch*	189
Guerra, Marlen/*Villarreal Elem Sch*	406
Guerra, Mrs/*J F Kennedy Elem Sch*	220
Guerra, Nelda/*Windsong Intermediate Sch*	160
Guerrero, Andi/*Dr Tomas Rivera Elem Sch*	407
Guerrero, Claudia/*Veterans Middle Sch*	215
Guerrero, Joaquin/*South Ward Elem Sch*	170
Guerrero, Liza/*Coronado Village Elem Sch*	33
Guerrero, Liza/*Judson Middle Sch*	33
Guerrero, Maria/*John Doedyns Elem Sch*	223
Guerrero, Mauro/*Socorro Middle Sch*	136
Guerrero, Sarah/*Northbrook Middle Sch*	201
Guerrero, Steve/*Austin High Sch*	189
Guerrero, Yvonne/*Emma Vera Elem Sch*	341
Guidry, Jennifer/*Raye McCoy Elem Sch*	395
Guillary, Daniel/*Dallas Co Jj CS-Drc Campus*	96
Guillen, Maribel/*San Elizario High Sch*	135
Guillen, Mario/*Steubing Ranch Elem Sch*	35
Guillory, Gloria/*Fletcher Elem Sch*	242

PRINCIPAL INDEX

NAME/School	PAGE
Guillory, Julien/Accelerated Center for Ed	186
Guillory, Monica/Prairie Lea Sch	61
Guillory, Tiffany/Yates High Sch	189
Gullekson, Joe/Richard E Cavazos Elem Sch	28
Gulley, Ladonna/J H Florence Elem Sch	111
Gumbs, Jill/Mission Bend Elem Sch	150
Gump, Carolyn/Goodwin Frazier Elem Sch	88
Gunasekera, Vinodh/Providence Classical Sch	206
Gunnels, Casey/Clark Middle Sch	84
Gunnin, Christopher/St Stephen's Episcopal Sch	373
Gunset, Tamara/Lubbock-Cooper Middle Sch	271
Gunter, Steve/Idalou Elem Sch	269
Gurany, Daniel/Riverside High Sch	138
Gurlek, Riza/Harmony Sch Innov-El Paso [284]	4
Gustafson, Peggy/Fannin Elem Sch	133
Gustafson, Peggy/Johnson Elem Sch	133
Gustafson, Peggy/Morehead Middle Sch	135
Gustin, Kendra/Jonesboro Sch	93
Gutgsell, Rachel/Notre Dame Catholic Sch	393
Guthrie, Stuart/Bush Middle Sch	34
Guthrie, Terry/Transition Center	352
Guthrie, Terry, Dr/Boulevard Heights Sch	350
Gutierrez, Alfredo/Dorothea Brown Middle Sch	221
Gutierrez, Alicia/Dr Palmira Mendiola Elem Sch	219
Gutierrez, Elodia/T G Allen Elem Sch	304
Gutierrez, Ericka/Brookwood Forest Elem Sch	293
Gutierrez, Fernando/Instruction & Guidance Center	221
Gutierrez, Jessica/London Sch	305
Gutierrez, Kimberly/St Thomas More Catholic Sch	44
Gutierrez, Laura/Rosemeade Elem Sch	97
Gutierrez, Melba/Barbara Fasken Elem Sch	387
Gutierrez, Melissa/Villa Nueva Elem Sch	64
Gutierrez, Rick/Petronila Elem Sch	302
Gutierrez, Roberto/Waverly Park Elem Sch	352
Gutierrez, Roxanne/Villarreal Elem Sch	39
Gutierrez, Selma/Sam Houston Elem Sch	225
Guy, Gary/Highlands Junior High Sch	188
Guy, Patrick/Rockbrook Elem Sch	124
Guzman, Jorge/Diaz Junior High Sch	217
Guzman, Juan/Scotsdale Elem Sch	138
Guzman, Linda/Vincent Patlan Elem Sch	174
Guzman, Virginia/Immanuel Lutheran Sch	226
Guzzetta, Steve/Garland McMeans Junior HS	152

H

NAME/School	PAGE
Haas, Heather/Annunciation Orthodox Sch	205
Haas, Kevin/Sacred Heart Catholic Sch	263
Haass, Gary/Navarro High Sch	173
Haberer, Manuela/Murray E Boone Elem Sch	38
Haberman, Evette/Second Baptist Sch	207
Habluetzel, Lauren/Bowie Elem Sch	236
Habluetzel, Lauren/Greenville Sixth Grade Center	236
Haddox, Jessica/Klein High Sch	197
Haddox, Tonya/W S Permenter Middle Sch	97
Hadley, Dave/Fossil Ridge High Sch	355
Hadnot, Oliver/College Station Middle Sch	55
Hadziselimovic, Paige/Noel Grisham Middle Sch	399
Haecker, Nicole/Memorial Elem Sch	88
Hafley, Lee/Thorndale High Sch	288
Hafner, Maria/Lizzie Nell C McClure Elem Sch	81
Hagan, Becky/Woodview Elem Sch	201
Hagan, Lysa/Stephen F Austin Univ CS	11
Hager, Hilda/Jack C Binion Elem Sch	346
Hagerty, Nicole/Canyon Vista Middle Sch	398
Hagin, Marsha/Chaparral Star Academy	2
Hagler, David/Anson Middle Sch	249
Hagman, Andy/M B Lamar High Sch	344
Hagood, Tania/Austin Montessori Elem Sch	130
Haider, Wendy/Nolanville Elem Sch	28
Hailey, Jumon/Midland Christian Sch	286
Hailey, Lacey/McNair Elem Sch	121
Hailey, Pamela/Crane Elem Sch	93
Hairston, Valerie/Spc Rafael Hernando Middle Sch	137

NAME/School	PAGE
Hakemack, Amparo, Dr/Texans Can Acad Carrltn-Farmrs [305]	11
Halbardier, Mrs/St Mary Catholic Sch	162
Halbert, Christy/Walnut Springs Sch	47
Halderman, Ralf/Thomas Jefferson High Sch	41
Hale, Nancy/Grapevine Elem Sch	353
Hale, Pam/Mary Evans Elem Sch	77
Haley, Amanda/Lyndon B Johnson Elem Sch	46
Haley, Michael/Marble Falls Elem Sch	60
Hall, Alison/Bluebonnet Elem Sch	23
Hall, Andrea/Dr David C Walker Elem Sch	42
Hall, Carveth/Southside Alternative Sch	43
Hall, Carveth/Waelder Sch	164
Hall, Cherree/Garrett Primary Sch	18
Hall, Dawn/Lincoln Park Sch	64
Hall, Gema/Lakeside Elem Sch	98
Hall, Jennifer/R L Turner High Sch	97
Hall, Keith/Faith Christian Sch	358
Hall, Monica, Dr/Manara Acad-Irving Elem Sch	8
Hall, Theresa/Idea Clg Prep-Harvey Najim	218
Hall, Tra/Bill W Wright Elem Sch	314
Hallam, Cynthia/Abundant Life Christian Sch	1
Hallamek, Jim/Cedar Creek Middle Sch	23
Halliburton, Jamie/Bransford Elem Sch	353
Halliburton, Kelli/Woodstone Elem Sch	36
Hallinan, Mary/Carrillo Elem Sch	189
Hallmark, Todd/Lockney High Sch	149
Halpayne, Christopher/Gateway High Sch	27
Halpayne, Christopher/Gateway Middle Sch	27
Ham, Joshua/San Saba Middle Sch	333
Hamblen, Lisa/James B Havard Elem Sch	187
Hamill, Gloria/Ben Bolt-Palito Blanco ES	245
Hamilton, David/Haltom High Sch	346
Hamilton, Kerry/Dogwood Elem Sch	293
Hamilton, Melanie/Ned E Williams Elem Sch	170
Hamilton, Sam/Saint Mary's Hall	45
Hamilton, Tasha/Missouri City Middle Sch	150
Hamilton, Trent/Trenton Middle Sch	147
Hammack, Carrie/Trinity Episcopal Sch	209
Hammack, Gloria, Dr/Spring Baptist Academy	207
Hammack, Jason/Bland Elem Sch	235
Hammack, Jason/Bland Middle Sch	235
Hammer, Kimberly/Bear Boulevard Pre-School	200
Hammerle, Marlene/John Paul II High Sch	85
Hammond, P Jennifer/Fields Elem Sch	37
Hammond, Scott/Pieper Ranch Middle Sch	88
Hammoudeh, Rawan/Agnes Cotton Academy	39
Hampton, Kendra/Beta Academy	1
Hamric, Barbara/Hedrick Middle Sch	123
Hamrick, Dana/Quitman High Sch	404
Hancock, Jerry/Sam Houston Elem Sch	209
Hancock, Tammy/Rusk Primary Sch	73
Hancock, Tony/West End Elem Sch	22
Hand, Leland/Grand Saline Middle Sch	380
Handcock, Shelley, Dr/Eisenhower Elem Sch	107
Handford, Thamesia/Pershing Elem Sch	41
Handy, Narichica/Bliss Elem Sch	133
Hanes, Scott/Hughes Springs Elem Sch	70
Hang, Qi/Kenley Sch	361
Hanna, Elizabeth/Richard Milburn Acad-CC [298]	10
Hanna, Jennifer/Tom Green Elem Sch	211
Hanna, Phillip/Stratford High Sch	336
Hannah, Aaron/Jacksboro Elem Sch	239
Hannah, Keith/Hillsboro High Sch	227
Hannible, Deidre/East Middle Sch	104
Hannible, Deidre/Woodridge Elem Sch	104
Hannum, Michael/Rockport-Fulton Middle Sch	19
Hansen, Jenifer/Horizon Heights Sch	136
Hanson, Christina, Dr/Maudrie M Walton Elem Sch	351
Hanson, Jessica/Walnut Creek Elem Sch	345
Hanson, Nancy/Logan Elem Sch	133
Hanson, Sandy/Cornerstone Christian Academy	85
Hao, Holly/New Star Sch	86
Haq, Sadia/Islamic School of Irving	115

Texas School Directory

PRINCIPAL INDEX

NAME/School	PAGE
Haq, Sadia/Olive Tree Montessori Academy	8
Harbison, Beth/Desertaire Elem Sch	137
Harbison, Cynthia/Duff Elem Sch	344
Hardesty, Dennis/Goals Learning Center	399
Hardie, Becki/Community Montessori Sch	400
Hardie, Rebekah/Lumin Lindsley Park Cmty Sch	8
Hardin, Candace/Oticel Parker Elem Sch	180
Hardin, Janelle/Clear Spring Elem Sch	88
Hardin, Kennith/Memphis Middle Sch	176
Hardin, Mary/Memorial Elem Sch	83
Harding, Rod/Westlake Academy	14
Harding, Stephen/Pomeroy Elem Sch	199
Hardy, Delisse/Wimbish World Language Academy	345
Hare, Andrea/Hodge Elem Sch	121
Hare, Everett/Bastian Elem Sch	192
Hare, Krystal/Lakeview Elem Sch	321
Harford, Charles/Fruitvale Junior High Sch	380
Harford, Charles/Fruitvale Senior High Sch	380
Harkey, Karen/Choices Leadership Academy	85
Harlan, Tammey/Cambridge Sch	195
Harmon, Kathy/Lucyle Collins Middle Sch	356
Harn, Nancy/Rummel Creek Elem Sch	201
Harper, Andrea/T A Sims Elem Sch	352
Harper, Billy/Harper Elem Sch	163
Harper, Catherine/Northwood Elem Sch	35
Harper, Kristin/Seven Lakes Junior High Sch	153
Harper, Leetha/Uplift Peak Prep Sch [309]	13
Harper, Prentiss/Krimmel Intermediate Sch	197
Harper, Renee/Crain Elem Sch	382
Harrell, Jennifer/Plainview Christian Academy	175
Harrell, Kathleen/Harrison Lane Elem Sch	354
Harrell, Venee/New Pathways Center	65
Harrington, Christina/Travis Early College High Sch	369
Harrington, Elias/Wilderness Oak Elem Sch	36
Harris-Price, Gloria/Bush Elem Sch	182
Harris, Alicia/Bertram Elem Sch	60
Harris, Aliyah/Iman Academy Southeast	206
Harris, Brandon/Borger Intermediate Sch	237
Harris, Debbie/Lawn Elem Sch	361
Harris, Donna/South Lawn Elem Sch	318
Harris, Elizabeth/Devers Elem Sch	265
Harris, Janis/Alice Carlson Applied Lrng Ctr	350
Harris, Jason/Carthage High Sch	311
Harris, Jeremy/Porter High Sch	294
Harris, Karen/Cunningham Elem Sch	193
Harris, Kim/Wharton Alternative Sch	390
Harris, Latracy/Beneke Elem Sch	202
Harris, Lindsay/George Wagner Middle Sch	395
Harris, Lisa/Brookhollow Elem Sch	371
Harris, Mike/Trinity High Sch	354
Harris, Natasha/Hale Elem Sch	344
Harris, Patsy/William's Community Sch	373
Harris, Rachel/Santa Fe High Sch	161
Harris, Robert/Harlan High Sch	37
Harris, Shirley/Two Dimensions Prep-Vickery [308]	13
Harris, Shirley/Two Dimensions-Corsicana [308]	13
Harris, Susan/Sacred Heart Sch	204
Harris, Tonya/Ecia-Sunnyvale	2
Harris, Tonya/Waxahachie High Sch	142
Harris, Tracie/Lamar-Delta Alternative Ctr	260
Harris, Viviana/Houston Elem Sch	292
Harrison, Carol, Dr/Westview Sch	207
Harrison, Carrie/Marine Creek Elem Sch	356
Harrison, Opal/Deady Middle Sch	188
Harrison, Sammi/Anderson High Sch	368
Harshbarger, Paula/Thomas J Rusk Elem Sch	298
Harstrom, Jenny/Lewis Elem Sch	252
Hart-Jackson, Tracie/Gross Elem Sch	193
Hart, Carolyn/Explorations Preparatory Sch	126
Hart, Donna, Dr/Newman Int'l Acad-Arlington	8
Hart, Kristyn/Dobie Primary Sch	112
Hartcraft, Kippie/Dawson-Hillmon Alt Ed Center	70
Hartle, Reece/Austin Achieve Public Sch	1
Hartley, Peter/Meadows Elem Sch	28
Hartsfield, Janeen/Faith Christian Academy	157

NAME/School	PAGE
Harty, Sarah/Cypress Lakes High Sch	184
Harvell, Patrick/Hillsboro Junior High Sch	227
Harvey, Janice/Roberts Middle Sch	154
Harvey, Mike/Pace Sch	372
Haskell, Sterling/Stanton-Smith Elem Sch	339
Haskins, Nicole/Mading Elem Sch	189
Hastings, Brian/Glasscock Co Sch	163
Hatch, Greg/Benito Martinez Elem Sch	136
Hatch, James/Sunnybrook Christian Academy	45
Hatcher, Lindsay/KIPP Nexus Primary-Houston [288]	7
Hatfield, Josh/College Hills Elem Sch	55
Hatfield, Randal/Crockett Elem Sch	237
Hathaway, Vicki/Oak Grove Elem Sch	362
Hatley, Erin/Vine Sch	383
Haug, Eric/Ronald Reagan Elem Sch	397
Haugh, Brett/Mabank High Sch	253
Haugh, Jennifer/Pearson Early Childhood Sch	83
Haugvoll, Laura/Beasley Elem Sch	153
Haulotte, Shannon/Meridian World Charter Sch	8
Hauschild, Kaye/Lakehill Preparatory Sch	115
Hausler, Scott/Positive Redirection Center	67
Havard, Sharon/C T Eddins Elem Sch	81
Hawkes, Dudley/New Waverly Junior High Sch	384
Hawkins, Christopher/Lucy Mae McDonald Elem Sch	140
Hawkins, Malaki/Lagos Elem Sch	371
Hawkins, Mike/Bruceville-Eddy Jr High Sch	278
Hawkins, Rachel/UT Tyler Univ Acad-Longview	338
Hawks, Krystal/Shirley Dill Brothers Elem Sch	51
Haws, Lisa/Felix Morales Elem Sch	198
Hawthorn, Sheri, Dr/Int'l Ldrshp TX-Katy	108
Hawthorne, Leighann/Austin Elem Sch	176
Hawthorne, Shana/Meadows Elem Sch	104
Hawthorne, Shana/West Middle Sch	104
Hawthorne, Stephanie/Barnett Junior High Sch	344
Hawthrone, Wendy/Beltline Elem Sch	110
Hay, Cindy/Thomas Elem Sch	360
Hayden, Terence/Willowridge High Sch	151
Hayes, Brad/Alexander Middle Sch	53
Hayes, David/Wortham High Sch	156
Hayes, David/Wortham Middle Sch	156
Hayes, Michael/Silverton Sch	57
Hayes, Nathan/Crowell High Sch	149
Hayhurst, Bradley/Rotan High Sch	148
Haymark, Christa/Dolly F Vogel Intermediate Sch	291
Haynes, Dimitrise/Amelia Elem Sch	241
Haynes, Holly/Puster Elem Sch	80
Haynes, Sylvia/Aoy Elem Sch	133
Haynes, Terra/Wildcat Learning Alt Center	331
Hays, Joel/Denton High Sch	121
Haytiyev, Serdar/Harmony Sci Acad-Houston [284]	5
Hayunga, Kelly/Old Settlers Elem Sch	123
Hayward, David/Damon Sch	53
Hayward, David/Moulton Elem Sch	262
Head, Sherry/Southwest Prep-Seguin [302]	11
Heard, Margot/St Nicholas Sch	207
Heard, Trialica/Southwest Cmty Christian Acad	207
Hearn, Dennis/McAnally Intermediate Sch	312
Hearn, Donny/Seymour Middle Sch	25
Hearne, Jessika/Varnett School Southeast [310]	13
Heater, Barbara/South Texas HS for Health Prof	68
Heath-Agnew, Brenda/James Garland Walsh Middle Sch	399
Heath, Cliff/Bosqueville Middle Sch	278
Heath, Cliff/Bosqueville Secondary Sch	278
Heath, James/Sharyland Pioneer High Sch	224
Hebert, Forrest/Channing Public Sch	209
Hebert, Jason/Western Academy	207
Hebert, Karen/Buna Elem Sch	240
Hebert, Tommie Jean/Bay Area Montessori House	205
Hecker, Chris/Cypress Park High Sch	184
Heddins, Jennifer/Daep	357
Heers, Lou/Muenster Elem Sch	91
Heffernan, Richard/Ascher Silberstein Elem Sch	99
Heflin, Nathan/Ore City High Sch	377
Heflin, Traci/Plains Elem Sch	405
Heger, Stacy/Weimar High Sch	87

School Year 2019-2020

PRINCIPAL INDEX

Market Data Retrieval

NAME/School	PAGE	NAME/School	PAGE
Heger, Stacy/Weimar Junior High Sch	87	Hernandez, Cesar/Golden Rule CS-Grand Prairie [281]	3
Heil, Henry/Episcopal Sch Dallas-Mid Upper	115	Hernandez, Cesar/Golden Rule CS-Wilmer [281]	4
Heimer, Teresa/Gonzalo & Sofia Garcia ES	132	Hernandez, Christina/Leonelo H Gonzalez Elem Sch	221
Heinchon, Stephanie/Hearne Elem Sch	325	Hernandez, Cristina/Roberta Tipps Elem Sch	357
Heine, Bridgett/Woodridge Forest Middle Sch	294	Hernandez, Daniel/Briscoe Elem Sch	189
Heinroth, Michael/Sweeny Elem Sch	54	Hernandez, David/St Joseph Elem Sch	321
Heintzman, Susan/Mill St Elem Sch	123	Hernandez, Donald/Sam Houston Middle Sch	106
Heinze, Peter/Briarmeadow Charter Sch	193	Hernandez, Gerardo/Edwin J Kiest Elem Sch	100
Heiple, Jeffrey/Holy Trinity Catholic Sch	358	**Hernandez, Gregory**/Frenship High Sch	269
Heiskell, Misty/Dalhart Intermediate Sch	95	Hernandez, Hector/Brownsville Academic Center	63
Heisman, Samuel/Great Hearts Northern Oaks [282]	4	Hernandez, Jessica/Emmott Elem Sch	184
Hejducek, Michael/Fort Settlement Middle Sch	150	Hernandez, Jesus/Judson High Sch	33
Helfferich, Tracey/Imagene Glenn Elem Sch	405	Hernandez, Joaquin/Idea Clg Prep-Judson	219
Helfferich, Tracey/Yantis Sch	405	Hernandez, Jose/Memorial Junior High Sch	277
Helland, Autumn/St Joseph Catholic Sch	143	Hernandez, Jose/Stuchbery Elem Sch	200
Hellman, Angela/Windle Sch for Young Children	121	**Hernandez, L**/Cromack Elem Sch	63
Helm, Maricella, Dr/George W Bush Elem Sch	85	Hernandez, Laura/Judge Andy Mireles Elem Sch	37
Helms, Jody/Rotan Elem Sch	148	Hernandez, Lee/South San Antonio High Sch	43
Hemann, Blanca/Bob Beard Elem Sch	36	**Hernandez, Lee, Dr**/West Campus High Sch	43
Hemenway, Allana/Randolph Elem Sch	39	Hernandez, Leonor/Hebbronville Elem Sch	244
Hemme, Jill/Heritage Elem Sch	353	**Hernandez, Linda**/Pfc Mario Ybarra Elem Sch	225
Hemphill, Darrin/Gisd Alternative Ed Center	106	Hernandez, Lisa/Mark White Elem Sch	194
Hemphill, Mark/Int'l Ldrshp TX-Katy Westpark	108	Hernandez, Lisa/St Cecilia Sch	114
Henderson, Amy/Montessori Children's House	359	Hernandez, Lorena/Henry W Longfellow Academy	100
Henderson, Danny/Savoy Elem Sch	146	Hernandez, Macario/Trinidad Garza Early College	103
Henderson, Ed/Hanes Elem Sch	109	Hernandez, Marcella/St Joseph Sch	139
Henderson, Lindsay/Alice Moore Elementary	121	Hernandez, Margarita/John J Pershing Elem Sch	101
Henderson, Pamela/Clifford Davis Elem Sch	350	Hernandez, Mary/F C Weinert Elem Sch	174
Henderson, Pamela/Riverchase Elem Sch	97	Hernandez, Noemi/Clint Junior High Sch	132
Henderson, Philip/Moss Haven Elem Sch	112	Hernandez, Norma/Jorge R Gutierrez ECC	216
Henderson, Rhonda/Tom Wilson Elem Sch	153	Hernandez, Robert/Sheldon Early Clg High Sch	200
Henderson, Roger/Grape Creek High Sch	364	**Hernandez, Rodrigo**/Santos Livas Elem Sch	224
Hendrickson, John/Field Elem Sch	191	Hernandez, Salud/Dr S Perez Elem Sch	387
Hendrix, Brandi/Montgomery High Sch	293	Hernandez, Talia/Christian Evers Elem Sch	36
Hendrix, Stephanie/Big Sandy Sch	316	Hernandez, Teresa/Mary McLeod Bethune Elem Sch	101
Hendry, Julie/St Patrick Sch	114	**Hernandez, Tony**/Avalon Sch	140
Henke, Charles/Schulenburg High Sch	148	**Hernandez, Veronica**/Humble Elem Sch	196
Henley, Gina/Whitesboro Intermediate Sch	168	Hernandez, Yvonne/Dwight Middle Sch	42
Henley, Glenetta/Curtis Elem Sch	242	**Hernandez, Yvonne**/James Russell Lowell Mid Sch	40
Hennessee, Joe/Visd Alternative Ed Sch	394	**Herndon, Lauri**/Alta Loma Elem Sch	364
Henninger, Elisa/Hawkins High Sch	404	Herndon, Mark/Lawrence A Eckert Elem Sch	180
Heno, Christy/Presbyterian Sch	206	Herrador, Katiuska/Jones Aca of Fine Arts & Dual	344
Henrickson, Jim/Calvary Lutheran Sch	114	**Herrell, Sally**/Clear Creek Intermediate Sch	126
Henry, Cheryl, Dr/Cypress Springs High Sch	184	Herrera, Alberto/Sam Rosen Elem Sch	352
Henry, Darla/Santo Jr Sr High Sch	310	Herrera, Claudia/Carter Junior High Sch	344
Henry, Dea/Northside Interm Sch	327	Herrera, Connie/Kleberg Elem Sch	257
Henry, Delshon/KIPP Pleasant Grove Mid Sch [287]	7	Herrera, Enrique/J M Hanks High Sch	138
Henry, H Phillip/Excel Adventist Academy	155	**Herrera, Jennifer, Dr**/Roy Cisneros Elem Sch	32
Henry, Jamaal/KIPP Polaris Academy for Boys [288]	7	Herrera, Jesus/Baylor Clg Biotech Acad-Rusk	192
Henry, Jason/Eastland Middle Sch	129	Herrera, Leann/Academy Health Sci Prof-STEM	219
Henry, Lonnie/Harmony Junior High Sch	376	Herrera, Miguel/Andrew Jackson Elem Sch	221
Henry, Margaret/St John's Sch	207	Herrera, Patricia/Lomax Elem Sch	198
Henry, Marsha/Parkdale Elem Sch	282	Herrera, Rebecca/Col Menchaca ECC	43
Henry, Shannon/Regents Academy	298	Herrera, Robert/Nettie Baccus Elem Sch	230
Henry, Valerie/Neal Elem Sch	41	Herring, Blaze/Shamrock High Sch	391
Henry, Zachary/Christian Life Preparatory Sch	358	Herring, Greg/Elkhart Intermediate Sch	15
Hensley, Thomas/Klein Oak High Sch	197	**Herring, Lisa**/Callisburg Elem Sch	90
Hensley, Ty/Annapolis Christian Academy	306	Herring, Tana/Elkhart Elem Sch	15
Henson, Belinda/Legacy Classical Chrn Academy	359	Herrington, Aaron/Vidor Junior High Sch	309
Henson, Jack/Texas Academy of Biomed Sci	352	Herron, Marshal/Recovery Education Campus	94
Henson, Jake/Center Middle Sch	334	Herron, Sherry/School of the Woods	207
Henson, Karan/Pays Sch	365	Hertzenberg, Cassie/Glen Loch Elem Sch	291
Hentges, Cynthia/Wyatt Elem Sch	83	Herzberg, Matthew/Mary Lillard Intermediate Sch	357
Hepworth, Ivan/Hill Elem Sch	180	**Hess, Cheri**/Puckett Elem Sch	318
Heras-Salas, Mrs/Howard Burnham Elem Sch	5	Hestand, Kelly/Shadow Creek High Sch	51
Herbin, Michael/Bedichek Middle Sch	369	Hester, Cheryl/Xenia Voigt Elem Sch	399
Herd, Jerry/Clear Path Alt High Sch	158	**Heupel, Nicholas**/May High Sch	59
Heredia, Arick/Crane Middle Sch	93	Heupel, Nick/May Elem Sch	59
Hernanadez, Shea/Flour Bluff Primary Sch	305	Hewitt, Tammie/Smithville Elem Sch	24
Hernandez, Adrian/Idea Clg Prep-Rio Vista	219	Hewlett, John/Lee Elem Sch	368
Hernandez, Beatriz/Perkins Middle Sch	64	Heyward, Kayla/Jhw Inspire Academy-Hays Co	31
Hernandez, Belinda/Arnold Elem Sch	39	Hickerson, Corey/Buffalo High Sch	264
Hernandez, Bryan/Utopia Sch	378	Hickl, Kimberly/Holmes Elem Sch	275

Texas School Directory — PRINCIPAL INDEX

NAME/School	PAGE
Hickman, Darby/*Bobby Shaw Middle Sch*	198
Hickman, Todd/*Temple Christian Academy*	126
Hicks, Bobbye/*St Mark's Episcopal Sch*	207
Hicks, Jessica/*Herfurth Elem Sch*	106
Hicks, Katy/*Fred Elem Sch*	375
Hicks, Kory/*Faith Christian Sch*	358
Hicks, Lisa/*Glenn York Elem Sch*	51
Hicks, Nakimia/*Innovation Design Entrep Acad*	100
Hicks, Natalie/*Mayes Elem Sch*	166
Hicks, Randy/*Seminole Junior High Sch*	158
Hicks, Randy/*Troy High Sch*	30
Hicks, Sam/*Lakeway Elem Sch*	371
Hicks, Sonya/*Mattie A Teague Middle Sch*	181
Hidalgo, Paul/*Alamo Junior High Sch*	285
Hidalgo, Rosie/*Kriewald Road Elem Sch*	43
Higginbotham, Mitzi/*Anahuac Elem Sch*	71
Hilbun, Christine/*Bagdad Elem Sch*	396
Hilcher, Liz/*Timberline Elem Sch*	353
Hildebrand, Sue/*Blackland Prairie Elem Sch*	398
Hildebrandt, Gina/*Rains Junior High Sch*	320
Hill, Alicia/*Zilker Elem Sch*	367
Hill, Colleen/*Garrison Elem Sch*	298
Hill, Donica/*North Texas Collegiate Acad-S [300]*	8
Hill, Glen/*Knox City High Sch*	258
Hill, Jeff/*Burgess Elem Sch*	392
Hill, John/*Driscoll Middle Sch*	34
Hill, Jonathan/*Pittsburg High Sch*	68
Hill, Kernisha/*Palo Alto Middle Sch*	28
Hill, Laura/*Mary Louise Phillips Elem Sch*	351
Hill, Leandra/*Hopkins Elem Sch*	382
Hill, Lynn/*Guthrie Sch*	257
Hill, Mary/*Pine Ridge Elem Sch*	317
Hill, Sally/*Giddens Elem Sch*	397
Hill, Susan/*Westpark Elem Sch*	352
Hill, Tommy/*Bennett & Alma Griffin Mid Sch*	78
Hill, Trenae, Dr/*Pecan Grove Elem Sch*	151
Hillard, Rory/*Bailey Inglish Erly Chldhd Ctr*	145
Hilton, Cooper/*W H Wilson Elem Sch*	98
Hinds, John/*Walzem Elem Sch*	36
Hinds, Troy/*Anson High Sch*	249
Hines, Holly/*Garland High Sch*	105
Hinkle, Craig/*Richland Collegiate High Sch*	10
Hinkle, Rebekah/*Steam Academy at Stribling*	247
Hinojosa, Anna/*Maurice Wolfe Elem Sch*	152
Hinojosa, Heberto/*Fabra Elem Sch*	254
Hinojosa, Judith/*Lorenzo De Zavala Spec Emp Sch*	303
Hinojosa, Linda/*Freer High Sch*	128
Hinojosa, Raul/*Miguel Carrillo Jr Elem Sch*	42
Hinrichsen, Nick/*Fort Worth Christian Sch*	358
Hinson, David/*Central High Sch*	354
Hinson, Jennifer, Dr/*Stuber Elem Sch*	84
Hinson, Julie/*Morton Ranch High Sch*	152
Hinson, Samantha/*Wildwood Elem Sch*	203
Hinton, Tammie/*Red Bluff Elem Sch*	199
Hinton, Tara/*Boulter Middle Sch*	338
Hirt, Kelley/*Chandler Oaks Elem Sch*	398
Hitchcock, Rebecca/*London Sch*	305
Hitt, Dawn/*Adams Elem Sch*	247
Ho, Lyne/*Jefferson Christian Academy*	274
Hobbs, Alleia/*East Handley Elem Sch*	350
Hobbs, Jade/*Giddens Steadham Elem Sch*	106
Hobbs, Kimberly/*Rice Sch*	192
Hobin, Charmaine/*Roosevelt Alexander Elem Sch*	153
Hobson, Kris/*Lake Belton Middle Sch*	27
Hobson, Sarah/*Uplift Infinity Prep Sch [309]*	13
Hodge, Lashawn/*R C Conley Elem Sch*	180
Hodge, Lauren/*Estella Stewart Elem Sch*	383
Hodges, Angela/*Steiner Ranch Elem Sch*	397
Hodges, Mari Jo/*El Paso NE Children's Ed Ctr*	139
Hodges, Sarah/*Wallace Middle Sch*	211
Hodgins, Stephanie/*Willis High Sch*	294
Hodgkinson, Kenneth, Dr/*West Lake Middle Sch*	196
Hodgson, Melinda/*De Kalb Elem Sch*	48
Hodnett, Becky/*Vanguard Preparatory Sch*	116
Hoeffken, Lori/*James Neill Elem Sch*	150

NAME/School	PAGE
Hoffman, Amanda/*Bridge City Middle Sch*	308
Hoffman, Carlos/*Clear Spring Elem Sch*	34
Hoffman, Charles/*Hawley Middle Sch*	250
Hoffman, Veronica/*Lorenzo De Zavala Elem Sch*	407
Hoffstadt, Galen/*St James Episcopal Sch*	306
Hogan, Laura/*Mirus Academy*	206
Hogue, Sam, Dr/*Cotton Vly Early College HS*	135
Holbrook, Ryan/*Mason Elem Sch*	275
Holbrook, Ryan/*Mason Junior High Sch*	275
Holcomb, Dana/*Lampasas Middle Sch*	261
Holcomb, Suzanne/*W A Carpenter Elem Sch*	186
Holden, Russell/*Cayuga Sch*	14
Holden, Shurandia/*Henry Dye Boggess Elem Sch*	82
Holder, Holly/*Glenwood Elem Sch*	318
Holder, Ikie/*Centennial High Sch*	247
Holder, Joni/*Ume Prep Acad-Dallas*	13
Holderman, Amy/*Bennett Elem Sch*	81
Holding, Katie/*Live Oak Elem Sch*	399
Holguin, Alisha/*Lyndon B Johnson Elem Sch*	130
Holguin, Melissa/*Early College Leadership Acad*	42
Holiday, Stacie/*Lively Middle Sch*	369
Holifield, Rolanda/*West Orange-Stark High Sch*	309
Holland, Alfred/*Rosa Parks Elem Sch*	151
Holland, Amber/*Gruver Elem Sch*	176
Holland, Ana/*Bowie Fine Arts Academy*	107
Holland, Brandy/*Austin Elem Sch*	338
Holland, Heather/*L V Stockard Middle Sch*	101
Holland, Kathryn/*George H Gentry Jr High Sch*	187
Holland, Nichole/*Sallye Moore Clg&Career Prep*	108
Holley, Jamie/*KIPP Austin Acad Arts Letters [286]*	6
Holley, Kara/*Phillips Elem Sch*	252
Hollinger, Christal/*Willow Creek Elem Sch*	349
Hollingsworth, Debra/*Jackson Elem Sch*	360
Hollingsworth, Elton/*Woodville Middle Sch*	375
Hollingsworth, Rusty/*Goldthwaite High Sch*	288
Hollis, Rob/*Shallowater High Sch*	272
Hollomon, Casey/*Bellville High Sch*	22
Holloway, Alana/*N Q Henderson Elem Sch*	191
Holloway, Benjamin/*Broaddus Elem Sch*	329
Holman, Courtney/*Klentzman Intermediate Sch*	182
Holmes, Analeasa/*Alma Brewer Strawn Elem Sch*	61
Holmes, Carla/*Emmanuel Christian Sch*	164
Holmes, Jill/*Mora Elem Sch*	38
Holmes, Steve/*Morris Upchurch Middle Sch*	71
Holmes, Steve/*Queen City High Sch*	71
Holmes, Vanessa/*Tyler Career & Technology Ctr*	338
Holmgreen, Judy, Dr/*William Adams Middle Sch*	245
Holt, Cecilia/*Newton Rayzor Elem Sch*	121
Holt, Eric/*Lago Vista Middle Sch*	370
Holt, Gary/*Durham Middle Sch*	123
Holt, Genger/*Seashore Learning Center*	11
Holt, Kelly/*Glenda Dawson High Sch*	53
Holton, Eric/*New Caney High Sch*	294
Honore, Rhonda/*Black Middle Sch*	191
Hood, Brandon/*O H Herman Middle Sch*	276
Hood, Paula/*Paul A Brown Alternative Ctr*	242
Hood, Shannon/*Frost Elem Sch*	154
Hooks, Carlotta/*C F Carr Elem Sch*	99
Hooper Barnett, Chandra/*J L Long Middle Sch*	100
Hooper, Aubrey/*Dallas Co Jj CS-Medlock*	96
Hooper, Aubrey/*Dallas Co Jj CS-Youth Village*	96
Hooper, Jason/*Callisburg Middle High Sch*	90
Hooper, Kyle/*Port Neches Middle Sch*	243
Hooten, Michael/*Trinity Environment Academy*	12
Hooton, Lori/*Grand Saline Elem Sch*	380
Hoover, Dane/*Water Valley Jr Sr High Sch*	365
Hope, Amber/*Hudson Middle Sch*	106
Hopkins, Christina/*Lexington Creek Elem Sch*	150
Hopkins, Crysten/*Greenwood Interm Sch*	285
Hopkins, Emily/*Austin International Sch*	373
Hopkins, Lindsey/*Bridges Accel Lrng Ctr*	353
Hopkins, Lucy/*Barbara Jordan Elem Sch*	99
Hopson, Holly/*Agape Christian Academy*	301
Horan, Ann/*Poetry Community Christian Sch*	253
Horan, Jim/*Most Holy Trinity Sch*	139

PRINCIPAL INDEX

Market Data Retrieval

NAME/School	PAGE
Horan, Shayne/*Fusion Academy-Sugarland*	155
Horgan, Anika/*Lorenzo De Zavala Middle Sch*	110
Hornbuckle, Carinia/*Newman Int'l Acad-Cedar Hill*	8
Horne, Dallas/*Fannin Elem Sch*	299
Horne, Tracy/*Hailey Elem Sch*	291
Horner, Melissa/*Bowie Fine Arts Academy*	285
Horras, Jackie/*Sandra Day O'Connor High Sch*	38
Horton, Adrienne/*Alamo Elem Sch*	315
Horton, Rochelle/*A M Pate Elem Sch*	350
Horton, Shannon/*Ume Prep Acad-Duncanville*	13
Hosack, Brandi/*A N McCallum High Sch*	368
Hoskins, Lashawn/*Accel Inter Academy-Lancaster*	1
Hoskins, Lashawn/*Accelerated Intermediate Acad*	1
Hostas, Jarret/*Premier HS-Midland [297]*	9
Hostetler, Jason/*Prairiland High Sch*	260
Houff, William/*Chapel Hill High Sch*	337
Hough, Kari/*Tipps Elem Sch*	185
Houghtaling, Socorro/*Vermillion Elem Sch*	64
House, Angela/*D C Cannon Elem Sch*	237
House, Calesta/*Tarkington Intermediate Sch*	266
House, James/*St Paul Lutheran Sch*	264
House, Paul/*Clear Falls High Sch*	158
House, Stephanie/*Jhw Inspire Academy-Bell Co*	31
House, Willisa/*Elsie Robertson Middle Sch*	110
Houser, Jill/*The Woodlands HS-9th GR Campus*	292
Houston, Diane/*Big Sandy Sch*	316
Houston, Michael/*Clear Springs High Sch*	158
Houston, Scott/*Barbara Jordan Elem Sch*	130
Houston, Shannon/*Watauga Middle Sch*	346
Hovan, Molly/*Glen Oaks Elem Sch*	81
Howard-Veazy, Chanel/*John Tyler High Sch*	338
Howard, Candy/*South Belt Elem Sch*	199
Howard, Evelyn/*J P Starks Mst Vanguard*	100
Howard, Greg/*Danforth Junior High Sch*	212
Howard, Janet/*Yorkshire Academy*	208
Howard, Kierstin/*Wayside Real Learning Academy*	14
Howard, Pauletta/*Newman Elem Sch*	133
Howell, Amy/*Carl E Schluter Elem Sch*	124
Howell, Amy/*Lance Thompson Elem Sch*	125
Howell, Lisa/*Bel Air Elem Sch*	213
Howell, Ted/*Humble Christian Sch*	206
Howen, M'Lissa/*St Paul's Episcopal Sch*	283
Howle, Jeffrey/*Atems High Sch*	360
Hoyt, Mark/*Good Shepherd Sch*	339
Hranicky, Brad/*Broaddus High Sch*	329
Hranitzky, Jennifer/*Cedar Creek Intermediate Sch*	23
Hubbard, Clayton/*Crockett Elem Sch*	365
Hubbard, Shelby/*The King's Academy*	212
Hubbell, Diane/*Harris Co Youth Village*	179
Hubble, Deborah/*Morton Ranch Elem Sch*	152
Huber, Chris/*Atkins Middle Sch*	270
Huber, Patricia/*Goliad Elem Sch*	164
Hubert, Helen/*La Vernia Intermediate Sch*	401
Hubley, Kelly/*Red Rock Elem Sch*	24
Hudgeons, Lisa/*James Bowie High Sch*	50
Hudgins, Catharine/*Ben Barber Innovation Academy*	356
Hudgins, Catherine/*Frontier High Sch*	356
Hudgins, Clay/*Brazos Middle Sch*	22
Hudgins, Vanessa/*R V Groves Elem Sch*	85
Hudson, Andy/*Brock Junior High Sch*	312
Hudson, Brona/*Dover Elem Sch*	112
Hudson, Cheryl/*Willis Lane Elem Sch*	355
Hudson, Jeff/*Grandview Junior High Sch*	248
Hudson, Nikki/*William B Miller Elem Sch*	103
Hudson, Robert/*Westphalia Sch*	145
Hudson, Tijuana/*Mary E Smithey Pace High Sch*	105
Hudspeth, Melody/*Navasota Junior High Sch*	172
Hudspeth, Scott/*Caddo Mills Aep*	235
Huff, Rebecca/*Elkhart Middle Sch*	15
Huggins, Clay/*Kleb Intermediate Sch*	197
Huggins, Laura/*Canyon Ridge Elem Sch*	34
Hughes-Bestov, Tangela/*Youens Elem Sch*	182
Hughes, David/*Langham Creek High Sch*	185

NAME/School	PAGE
Hughes, Greg/*New Braunfels Middle Sch*	89
Hughes, Howard/*Alamo Education Center*	140
Hughes, Inez/*F L Moffett Primary Sch*	334
Hughes, Jacqueline/*Florence Elem Sch*	355
Hughes, Kristin/*Aaron Parker Elem Sch*	259
Hughes, Mercathia/*Genesis Academy*	58
Hughes, Stephanie/*Lily B Clayton Elem Sch*	351
Hull, Richard/*Katy High Sch*	152
Human, Robin/*Heflin Elem Sch*	182
Humbles, Stacie/*Young Junior High Sch*	345
Hummel, Karlin/*Texas School for the Deaf*	12
Hummel, Nancy/*Oakland Elem Sch*	150
Humphrey, Eric/*Anahuac High Sch*	71
Humphrey, Troy/*Walnut Bend Elem Sch*	92
Humphries, Jame/*Seagraves Junior High Sch*	157
Hungate, Thomas/*Boerne Middle School North*	254
Hunt-French, Joyce/*Country Day Sch of Arlington*	358
Hunt, Brian/*Olton Junior High Sch*	261
Hunt, Kevin/*June W Davis Elem Sch*	348
Hunt, Kristin/*Gateway College Prep Sch [292]*	3
Hunt, Rebekah/*Sycamore Elem Sch*	348
Hunt, Youshawna/*Cimarron Elem Sch*	151
Hunter, Chad/*Vivian Field Middle Sch*	97
Hunter, Gwendolyn/*Pleasantville Elem Sch*	190
Hunter, Kacy/*Central Elem Sch*	393
Hurley, Kristina/*Aloe Elem Sch*	382
Hurst, Bryan/*Arp High Sch*	336
Hurst, Bryan/*Arp Junior High Sch*	336
Hurst, Stacy/*Wright Elem Sch*	271
Hurst, Steve/*Lone Star Elem Sch*	355
Hurtado, Adrian/*Cobb Sixth Grade Campus*	187
Huseman, Amy/*Archer City Elem Sch*	19
Huseman, Chad/*CapRock High Sch*	317
Huseman, Terri/*Will Rogers Elem Sch*	318
Hushen, Bobbie/*Jane Long Elem Sch*	65
Husk, Edward/*Northside Elem Sch*	265
Hussain, Salem/*Raul Quintanilla Middle Sch*	102
Hussey, Barbara/*Texas School for the Deaf*	12
Hutcherson, Dick/*Memphis High Sch*	176
Hutcheson, Jeff/*Smith Elem Sch*	252
Hutcheson, Thayer/*Briargrove Elem Sch*	193
Hutchings, Kyle/*Kemp Junior High Sch*	252
Hutchings, Tammy/*Leonard Junior High Sch*	146
Hutchins, Inez/*Trafton Academy*	207
Hutchins, Jeffery/*Van High Sch*	381
Hutchins, Maryjane/*Lamar Early Education Center*	130
Hutchinson, Donna/*Yavneh Academy-Dallas*	116
Hutchinson, Jeff/*Galena Park Cte Early Clg HS*	187
Hutchinson, Melissa/*Huffman Elem Sch*	195
Hutchinson, Paige/*Lloyd R Ferguson Elem Sch*	159
Hutchison, Barrett/*Morgan Mill Elem Sch*	144
Hutchison, Melissa/*Gainesville High Sch*	91
Hutton, Jeff/*Akin Elem Sch*	175
Huyck, Randalyn/*Avondale Elem Sch*	317
Huynh, Tuyet/*Mike Moseley Elem Sch*	108
Hybner, Karen/*St Joseph Sch*	272
Hyder, H, Dr/*Bammel Middle Sch*	202
Hydock, Chris/*McKinney Christian Academy*	86
Hye, Nuzhat/*Radiant STEM Academy*	116
Hynes, Twyla/*Stafford Elem Sch*	155
Hynes, Twyla/*Stafford Primary Sch*	155
Hypolite, Fabian/*Chapel Hill Preparatory Sch*	99

I

NAME/School	PAGE
Ibarra, Benjamin/*Blanson Cte High Sch*	180
Ibarra, Javier/*AMI Kids Rio Grande Valley*	66
Ibarra, Saul/*Berta Cabaza Middle Sch*	67
Igo, Tony/*Smyer Elem Sch*	229
Igoe, Colin/*St Mark's School of Texas*	116
Iliff, Andrew/*St John Paul II High Sch*	89
Ilski, Melissa/*St Theresa Sch*	204
Infante, Leticia/*James Bonham Elem Sch*	221
Ingalls, Becky/*Avondale House Sch*	205

Texas School Directory — PRINCIPAL INDEX

NAME/School	PAGE
Inge, Joel/*Kingdom Life Academy*	339
Ingle, Regina/*Morton High Sch*	75
Ingram, Jamie/*Keene Junior High Sch*	248
Ingram, Jennifer/*Evant Sch*	92
Ingram, Roland/*Treasure Hills Elem Sch*	65
Ingram, Tai/*KIPP Liberation College Prep [288]*	7
Inklebarger, Angie/*Lubbock-Cooper High Sch*	271
Inman, Jason/*Compass Academy Charter Sch*	2
Insorio, Marygrace/*Uplift Williams Prep Chtr Sch [309]*	13
Ipina, Concepcion/*Dr William Long Elem Sch*	223
Irick, James/*Crossroads High Sch*	92
Irlas, Albert/*Dr Pablo Perez Elem Sch*	221
Isaacs, Calobe/*Goodrich Middle High Sch*	316
Isaly, Timothy/*Early College High Sch*	96
Isom, Leanne/*Arlington Heights Chrn Sch*	306
Israel, Maureen/*YES Prep Northside [312]*	14
Issa, Stephen/*Serenity High Sch*	81
Ivers, Yalonda/*Bells Elem Sch*	165
Ives, Jason/*Elkhart High Sch*	15
Iwasko, Alicia/*Annie Webb Blanton Elem Sch*	99
Iznaola, Jose/*Hector Garcia Early Clg HS*	386

J

NAME/School	PAGE
Jackson, Anson/*Uplift Mighty Preparatory Acad [309]*	13
Jackson, Anthony/*New Life Christian Academy*	45
Jackson, Ashley/*Russell Schupmann Elem Sch*	142
Jackson, Carrie/*Northwest High Sch*	125
Jackson, Chip/*Alkek Elem Sch*	23
Jackson, Darla/*Evans Middle Sch*	81
Jackson, David/*Gregg Elem Sch*	192
Jackson, Deanna/*Maxine & Lutrell Watts ES*	173
Jackson, Gena/*Lamar Elem Sch*	166
Jackson, Hallema/*Key Elem Sch*	344
Jackson, Jake/*West Rusk High Sch*	328
Jackson, Jennifer/*Ft Worth Academy of Fine Arts [306]*	3
Jackson, Jennifer, Dr/*Victor H Hexter Elem Sch*	103
Jackson, Jimmy/*Clifton High Sch*	46
Jackson, Kelly/*Hughes Road Elem Sch*	159
Jackson, Macey/*Community Christian Sch*	309
Jackson, Marion/*Martha Turner Reilly Elem Sch*	101
Jackson, Michael/*Sudie Williams Elem Sch*	103
Jackson, Michelle/*Lago Vista Elem Sch*	370
Jackson, Patricia/*St Jerome Sch*	204
Jackson, Paula/*Hardin Elem Sch*	266
Jackson, Regina/*A C New Middle Sch*	110
Jackson, Ron/*Beaumont United High Sch*	242
Jackson, Serena/*Harmony Sci Acad-Ft Worth [284]*	5
Jackson, Sharron/*Oliver W Holmes Academy*	102
Jackson, Sherqueena/*Irving Elem Sch*	247
Jackson, Stefani/*Cushing Elem Sch*	297
Jackson, Stevanie/*Bonham Elem Sch*	360
Jackson, Susan/*Goose Creek Memorial High Sch*	188
Jacob, Joya/*Oak Hill Academy*	115
Jacobs-Worrell, Linda/*Tenaha Sch*	335
Jacobs, Amy/*Forest North Elem Sch*	398
Jacobs, Annemarie/*Killeen Adventist Jr Academy*	30
Jacobs, Cathy/*Matzke Elem Sch*	185
Jacobs, Gary/*Aim Center*	339
Jacobs, Lisa/*Christian School-Castle Hills*	44
Jacobs, Melissa/*Houston Academy Int'l Studies*	192
Jacobs, Scott/*Central Christian Academy*	205
Jacobson, Vickie/*Maplewood Elem Sch*	368
Jacoby, June, Dr/*Alternative Education Program*	353
Jaen, Jaime/*KIPP Aspire Academy [289]*	6
Jahns, Nancy/*First Baptist Church Sch*	386
Jain, Disha/*Idea Academy-Montopolis*	218
Jaksch, Tiffany/*Round Rock Christian Academy*	400
Jalomo, Jesse/*Parkview School-Levelland*	288
Jalomo, Jesse, Dr/*Parkview School-Lubbock*	288
Jamar, Jacye/*Harrington Elem Sch*	82
James, Cassandria/*Everhart Mgnt Acad/Cltrl Study*	169
James, Christian/*Delta Academy*	133
James, Desiree/*Stafford Intermediate Sch*	155
James, Dj/*Bible Baptist Christian Sch*	393
James, Elizabeth/*Sch of Sci & Tech-Alamo [299]*	10
James, Felicia/*George Bush High Sch*	150
James, Kelly/*Orange Grove Elem Sch*	180
James, Kimberly/*Veterans Memorial High Sch*	304
James, Liesl/*Midway Park Elem Sch*	354
James, Michelle/*David Crockett Elem Sch*	187
Jammer, Dina/*Bush Global Ldrshp Acad*	107
Janczak, Jay/*East Bernard Jr High Sch*	389
Janczak, Jeremy/*East Bernard High Sch*	389
Janecka, Kristy/*Weimar Elem Sch*	87
Jansen, Mary/*Richard Milburn Acad-Odessa [298]*	10
Jansing, Shirley/*Waco Montessori Sch*	283
Janszen, Eric/*Maypearl High Sch*	141
January, Paula/*Roscoe Wilson Elem Sch*	270
Jaquess, Jill/*Terra Vista Middle Sch*	269
Jaramillo, Edgar/*Julian T Saldivar Elem Sch*	101
Jaramillo, Kyla/*Trinity Basin Prep-Ewing*	12
Jaramillo, Will/*Nyos Charter Sch-Lamar Campus*	8
Jarvis, Heath/*Greenville High Sch*	236
Jasenof, Tonya/*Max Vaughan Elem Sch*	77
Jasper, Lashun/*Nova Academy Prichard*	8
Jasper, Lashun/*Nova Academy-Prichard*	8
Jasso, Lorena/*Gillette Elem Sch*	32
Jaster, Creighton/*Lamar Junior High Sch*	154
Jawaid, Constance/*Cedar Crest Elem Sch*	99
Jawanda, Baljeet/*Guidepost Montessori-Stonebria*	86
Jayroe, Brandon/*Douglas Benold Middle Sch*	395
Jazinski, Maria/*Leo J Leo Elem Sch*	220
Jedele, Tania/*Dawson Elem Sch*	366
Jedlicka, Keith/*Boling High Sch*	389
Jedlicka, Shannon/*E Rudd Intermediate Sch*	276
Jeffers, Larry/*Clarendon High Sch*	127
Jefferson, William/*Community Christian Sch*	311
Jeffrey, Kaitlin/*Washington Elem Sch*	234
Jenerson, Andre/*Gainesville State Sch*	3
Jenkins, Amanda/*Orangefield Elem Sch*	309
Jenkins, Carlotta/*Stafford Alt Ed Campus*	155
Jenkins, Heather/*China Spring Intermediate Sch*	279
Jenkins, Kimberly/*Kujawa Elem Sch*	179
Jennings, Cash/*Ozona Middle Sch*	94
Jennings, Donna/*White Oak High Sch*	171
Jenschke, Donna/*Ingram Elem Sch*	255
Jerabek, Jerry/*Lamesa High Sch*	117
Jeremiassen, Kathleen/*Memorial Drive Elem Sch*	201
Jernberg, Jannae/*Chambers Elem Sch*	182
Jessup, Hildegard/*Oak Crest Private Sch*	115
Jeter, M'Kell/*Friona Elem Sch*	315
Jetton, Jason/*Rogers Middle Sch*	84
Jetton, Timothy/*Grape Creek Middle Sch*	364
Jewell, April/*Lorena Primary Sch*	280
Jewell, Mary, Dr/*Earl Rudder Middle Sch*	37
Jimenez, Dora/*Hodges Elem Sch*	270
Jimenez, Elaine/*Fenley PK Center*	32
Jimenez, Iris/*Salvador H Sanchez Middle Sch*	136
Jimenez, Sergio/*Del Rio Middle Sch*	379
Jirasek, Brenda, Dr/*Frank Newman Middle Sch*	259
Job, Dana, Dr/*Universal Academy-Coppell*	13
Johanson, Brandy/*Assets Academy*	51
Johanson, Phil/*Rosebud-Lott Middle Sch*	145
Johnson, Amanda/*Castleman Creek Elem Sch*	280
Johnson, Amanda/*McNeil High Sch*	399
Johnson, Andre/*Lexington Middle Sch*	263
Johnson, Andrea/*Candlewood Elem Sch*	33
Johnson, Bert/*Fairview Accelerated Sch*	365
Johnson, Bianca/*Crockett Middle Sch*	109
Johnson, Brandon/*Mansfield Lake Ridge High Sch*	357
Johnson, Bryan/*Woodway Elem Sch*	352
Johnson, Buffie/*Wedgewood Elem Sch*	159
Johnson, Candace/*Life School Cedar Hill [290]*	7
Johnson, Carlton/*Andrews Alternative Sch*	16
Johnson, Carol/*Brentwood Christian Sch*	373
Johnson, Carol/*Wesley Prep Sch*	116
Johnson, Chastity/*William & Abbie Allen Elem Sch*	80
Johnson, Cheryl, Dr/*J Martin Jacquet Middle Sch*	351
Johnson, Christy/*Early Learning Ctr South*	355

PRINCIPAL INDEX

Market Data Retrieval

NAME/School	PAGE	NAME/School	PAGE
Johnson, Cindy/Abilene Christian Sch	361	Jones, Gary/Grady Sch	274
Johnson, Corrine/Winfree Academy-Grand Prairie [311]	14	Jones, Georgeanna/Woods Elem Sch	338
Johnson, Dana/Bunker Hill Elem Sch	201	Jones, Glen/Veribest Sch	365
Johnson, Daniel/Texans Can Acad Garland [305]	12	Jones, Jeff/Geneva School of Boerne	254
Johnson, Darwert/Data at Adams MS	107	Jones, Jo/Howell Middle Sch	382
Johnson, David/Collinsville High Sch	166	Jones, Joe/Founders Christian Sch	206
Johnson, David/Priority Intervention Academy	270	Jones, Joe/Junction Middle Sch	256
Johnson, Deborah/James F Bay Elem Sch	159	Jones, Justin/Joan Link Elm Sch	202
Johnson, Gerrol/Hartman Middle Sch	192	Jones, Kara/El Paso Jewish Academy	139
Johnson, Gregg/Southland Sch	162	Jones, Karen/Grangerland Interm Sch	291
Johnson, James/Clarksville Middle High Sch	322	**Jones, Kelly**/Goshen Creek Elem Sch	313
Johnson, Janice/Corsciana Middle Sch	299	Jones, Kerri/Forest Meadow Jr High Sch	112
Johnson, Jayme/St John's Episcopal Sch	116	Jones, Khourie/R F Patterson Elem Sch	356
Johnson, Jeanette/Saint Peters Classical Sch	359	Jones, Kim/Clyde Elem Sch	62
Johnson, Jessica/J T Stevens Elem Sch	351	Jones, Kristi/Edgewood Elem Sch	380
Johnson, Jimmi/Springlake-Earth Elem Mid Sch	261	Jones, Kristie/W B Bizzell Academy	172
Johnson, Julie/Nimitz Elem Sch	256	Jones, Larry/Dubiski Career High Sch	107
Johnson, Karyn/Bailey Elem Sch	198	Jones, Lillian/Ringgold Middle Sch	340
Johnson, Kay/Tom C Gooch Elem Sch	103	Jones, Lisa/Progressive High Sch	151
Johnson, Kevin/Lorena High Sch	280	Jones, Logan/Souder Elem Sch	349
Johnson, Kittiya/Edmund Cody Elem Sch	37	Jones, Marion/ACES Alternative	213
Johnson, Lajoyce/Rufus C Burleson Elem Sch	102	Jones, Meghan/Prince of Peace Catholic Sch	85
Johnson, Lakeshia/Malone Elem Sch	228	Jones, Mike/Santa Gertrudis Elem MS	258
Johnson, Latricia, Dr/Meadowbrook Elem Sch	304	Jones, Natalie/O'Bryant Intermediate Sch	22
Johnson, Linda/Immanuel Christian Sch	139	Jones, Natalie/O'Bryant Primary Sch	22
Johnson, Melba/Love Elem Sch	192	**Jones, Nicholas**/Hays Middle Sch	84
Johnson, Mythesia/Eleanor Tinsley Elem Sch	193	Jones, Niki/Harry Stone Montessori Academy	100
Johnson, Noralva/Alma A Pierce Elem Sch	386	Jones, Norman/Besse Coleman Middle Sch	97
Johnson, Pamela/Beulah E Johnson Elem Sch	179	Jones, Randy/Rising Star High Sch	129
Johnson, Paul/Vista Ridge High Sch	397	Jones, Renae/Phoenix Center	253
Johnson, Rhonda/Helotes Elem Sch	37	Jones, Renee/Terrell Alternative Ed Center	253
Johnson, Robert/Hamilton Middle Sch	191	**Jones, Robyn**/River Bend Elem Sch	56
Johnson, Rowena/Lamar Primary Sch	232	Jones, Santrice/Neff Early Learning Center	194
Johnson, Rufus/Texans Can Acad Dallas Ross AV [305]	11	Jones, Shanna/Alex W Spence Middle Sch & Tag	98
Johnson, Rufus/TX Can Acad Dallas Ross Ave	13	Jones, Shannon/Legacy Preparatory Chrn Acad	295
Johnson, Ruth/Howard Dobbs Elem Sch	325	Jones, Shondra/Donald T Shields Elem Sch	142
Johnson, Samantha/Cathelene Thomas Elem Sch	272	Jones, Stacy/Greenwood High Sch	285
Johnson, Sarahdia/Humble Middle Sch	196	Jones, Susan/G W Carver Early Childhood Ctr	140
Johnson, Shandra/Idea Academy-Achieve	217	Jones, Suzanne/Darwin L Gilmore Elem Sch	158
Johnson, Sharon/Bruceville-Eddy Elem Sch	278	Jones, Terri/Angleton Christian Sch	54
Johnson, Sharon/Bruceville-Eddy Interm Sch	278	Jones, Tim/Trinity School of Midland	286
Johnson, Sherrhonda/Center for Success	186	Jones, Tina/Bowie Elem Sch	360
Johnson, Tamekia/William B Travis Elem Sch	209	Jones, Todd/Era Sch	91
Johnson, Tomika/Vernon Price Elem Sch	111	Jones, Traci/Harleton Elem Sch	208
Johnson, Tony/Basswood Elem Sch	354	**Jones, Wendy**/Hillsboro Intermediate Sch	227
Johnson, Tracy/J L Boren Elem Sch	357	**Jones, Wesley**/Cross Plains High Sch	62
Johnson, Travis/Hartsfield Elem Sch	192	Jones, Yolanda/G W Robinson Elem Sch	159
Johnson, Wanda/Milam Elem Sch	133	Jordan, Amanda/North Texas Collegiate Acad-N [300]	8
Johnson, Willie, Dr/South Oak Cliff High Sch	103	Jordan, Christina/Fonwood Early Childhood Center	190
Johnston, April/Blanchette Elem Sch	242	Jordan, Gordon/Boles Middle Sch	235
Johnston, Cherry/Midway Sch	74	Jordan, Jearine/Travis Elem Sch	154
Johnston, Jason, Dr/Allen High Sch	76	Jordan, Pam/St John's Episcopal Sch	116
Johnston, Judy/Lone Star Language Academy	8	Jordan, Shelley/Summit Christian Academy	400
Johnston, Kendy/Overton Ray Elem Sch	391	**Jordan, Tracey**/Ben Milam Elem Sch	287
Johnston, Nicole/Reeves Hinger Elem Sch	321	**Joseph, Abram**/Mesquite Academy Aec of Choice	111
Johnston, Stacey/Sinclair Elem Sch	31	Joseph, Jan/Keys Learning Center	354
Johnston, Steven/Ovilla Christian Sch	143	Joseph, Shon/DeSoto High Sch	104
Jolliff, Michelle/Raymond Mays Middle Sch	30	Joseph, Tanassa/Shsu CS-Little Geniuses Acad	11
Jones, Ahveance/Las Colinas Elem Sch	97	Jost, Brian/Hettie Halstead Elem Sch	92
Jones, Amanda/Frances Corprew Elem Sch	364	Jost, Kathy/Coston Elem Sch	18
Jones, Andra/Gen Tommy Franks Elem Sch	286	Joubert, Connie/Kountze Intermediate Sch	178
Jones, Brad/Gause Elem Sch	287	Juarez-Farias, Sarah/Elgin Elem School North	24
Jones, C/Hamlin Elem Sch	249	Juarez, Deanna/Navarro Elem Sch	61
Jones, Cheryl/Aledo Learning Center	312	Juarez, Josephine/Judson Early College Academy	33
Jones, Cheryl/Evadale Elem Jr High Sch	240	Juarez, Monica/Victoria Walker Elem Sch	188
Jones, Chris/Alternative Learning Center	368	Jubert, Katie/KIPP Truth Elem Sch [287]	7
Jones, Christopher/Gene Pike Middle Sch	125	Judd, Candace/University Park Elem Sch	108
Jones, Cynthia/Premier HS-American Youthworks [297]	9	Judd, Dana/Inspire Academy	359
Jones, Dale/Ira Sch	333	Judice, Stephen/George Junior High Sch	154
Jones, Denise/North Loop Elem Sch	138	Judy, Greg/Stephenville Christian Sch	144
Jones, Dixie/E C Mason Elem Sch	51	**Jung, Nancy**/Jefferson Elem Sch	167
Jones, Donald/Woodrow Wilson Daep Sch	161	Jungmichel, Rhonda/Cibolo Valley Elem Sch	173
Jones, Donna/Academic Behavior Center-East	179	Junot, Charlotte/Helena Park Elem Sch	243

Texas School Directory — PRINCIPAL INDEX

NAME/School	PAGE
Jurica, Jillian/*Bill Brown Elem Sch*	88
Justice, Terry/*Underwood Elem Sch*	16

K

NAME/School	PAGE
Kaai, Kerry/*Hyde Park Elem Sch*	166
Kahil, Kristina/*Faye Webb Elem Sch*	303
Kaiser, Forrest/*Higgins Elem Sch*	339
Kajs, Jeffrey/*Lewisville High Sch*	123
Kalnbach, Brooke/*Austin Elem Sch*	364
Kalnbach, Michael/*Glenn Middle Sch*	365
Kammlah, Mark/*Williams Elem Sch*	345
Kana, Rick/*Barbers Hill High Sch*	72
Kana, Scott/*Edna High Sch*	239
Kane, Deidre/*Wellington Elem Sch*	86
Kangas, Julie/*Concordia Lutheran High Sch*	205
Karanci, Ednan/*Harmony Sch DSC-Houston [284]*	4
Kargbo, Kate/*Walker Station Elem Sch*	151
Karnei, Lisa/*Nordheim Sch*	118
Karns, Heather/*Ysleta Pre-K Center*	138
Karpinski, Angelina/*St Joseph Catholic Sch*	226
Karr, Adrian/*Edith & Ethel Carman Elem Sch*	223
Karr, Ivan/*Sharyland Adv Academic Academy*	224
Karr, Lisa/*Gene A Buinger Cte Academy*	354
Karrer, Ann/*Stone Oak Elem Sch*	35
Kaspar, Karen/*Mary Branch Elem Sch*	55
Kaspar, Karen/*Mary Catherine Harris Sch*	55
Kasper-Hoffman, Gretchen/*Tanglewood Middle Sch*	194
Kassim, Laura/*Palm Tree Academy*	139
Kassir, Patricia/*Spring Branch Acad Institute*	201
Kasson, Jenny/*Bullard Elem Sch*	336
Kastiel, Elizabeth/*Uplift Heights Prep Sch Sec [309]*	13
Kastorunis, Chantel/*Richard J Lee Elem Sch*	98
Kasturi, Tina/*Mona Montessori McKinney*	86
Katial, Monijit/*Paul Revere Middle Sch*	194
Katt, Teresa/*Forest Ridge Elem Sch*	55
Kattner, Diana/*G H Whitcomb Elem Sch*	159
Kattner, Diana/*North Pointe Elem Sch*	159
Kauffman, Theresa, Dr/*Kauffman Leadership Academy*	6
Kaufmann, Monica/*James Nikki Rowe High Sch*	221
Kazda, Caroline/*Margaret L Felty Elem Sch*	142
Kazda, Carrie/*West Elem Sch*	282
Keafer, Katherine/*Longfellow Elem Sch*	194
Kear, Kirk/*Canyon Junior High Sch*	321
Kearns, Kevin/*Wallace Jefferson Middle Sch*	39
Keating, Lance/*Ferris Intermediate Sch*	140
Keck, Shelley/*La Vernia Primary Sch*	401
Keel, Theresa/*Lorenzo De Zavala Elem Sch*	188
Keele, Jami/*Sterling Elem Sch*	342
Keele, Todd/*Llano Junior High Sch*	268
Keenan, Joann/*Theiss Elem Sch*	197
Keene, Don/*Whitesboro Middle Sch*	168
Keesee, Suzanne/*Wheat Middle Sch*	247
Keffer, Trinette/*Great Hearts Northern Oaks [282]*	4
Kegler, Jonathan/*Brook Hill Sch*	339
Kegler, Jonathan/*Brook Hills Lower Sch*	339
Keimig, Brenda/*C J Harris Elem Sch*	53
Keith, Amy/*Kaufman High Sch*	252
Keith, Brian/*West Rusk Junior High Sch*	328
Keith, Mark/*Brandon Elem Sch*	18
Keithan, Jackie/*Michael L Griffin Elem Sch*	152
Keithley, Richard/*Waller Christian Academy*	207
Kellagher, Mary/*Northlake Elem Sch*	112
Kelley, Buddy/*Palacios Junior High Sch*	275
Kelley, Eric/*Trinity High Sch*	374
Kelley, Kim/*Kranz Junior High Sch*	159
Kelley, Kristie/*Dr E R Richter Elem Sch*	265
Kelley, Lesley/*Barbara Cardwell Career Prep*	109
Kelley, Markena/*Brookhollow Christian Academy*	205
Kelley, Michael/*Tarkington Middle Sch*	266
Kelling, Jane/*Ralph Parr Elem Sch*	159
Kellner, Kim/*Bee Cave Elem Sch*	370
Kellogg, Mark/*Edgewood High Sch*	380
Kelly, Alyson/*Humble Classical Academy [297]*	5
Kelly, Beth/*Navo Middle Sch*	121
Kelly, Catherine/*Mark Twain Elem Sch*	112
Kelly, Sonya/*Western Hills Primary Sch*	352
Kelly, Spiller/*Georgetown Alt Program*	395
Kelly, Walter/*Highland Park High Sch*	108
Kemp, Kim/*Gilmer Elem Sch*	376
Kemp, Troy/*Maydell Jenks Elem Sch*	152
Kempf, Kandi/*Gene Howe Elem Sch*	321
Kempson, Phil/*Howe High Sch*	166
Kendirci, Hasan/*Sch of Sci & Tech Excellence [299]*	10
Kendrick, Valarie/*Birdie Alexander Elem Sch*	99
Kendricks, Deborah/*San Jacinto Junior High Sch*	286
Kendziora, Kennith/*Technical Education Center*	151
Kennard, Kay/*Westwood Elem Sch*	201
Kennedy, Brian/*NE Alternative Center*	35
Kennedy, David/*Westhoff Elem Sch*	118
Kennedy, Gloria/*Bayles Elem Sch*	99
Kennedy, Greg/*Buffalo Upper Junior High Sch*	264
Kennedy, James/*Kidwell Elem Sch*	392
Kennell, Abby/*Mason Elem Sch*	397
Kent, Craig/*Cisco High Sch*	128
Keoun, Melanie/*Parkway Elem Sch*	170
Keown, Holly/*Texas City High Sch*	161
Keranen, Michael/*Smithson Valley Middle Sch*	88
Kerby, Sheila/*Bracken Christian Sch*	89
Kern, Jewel/*S M Seabourn Elem Sch*	111
Kerney, Debra, Dr/*Silvestre & Reyes Elem Sch*	132
Kerr, Jenny/*St Pius X Catholic Sch*	44
Kerr, Justice/*Covenant Christian Academy*	358
Kesler, Mary/*Hicks Elem Sch*	182
Ketcher, Ginger/*Tatum Elem Sch*	78
Ketchersid, Dana/*Ropes Sch*	229
Ketchum, Ana/*Jack Taylor Elem Sch*	247
Kettering, Mark/*Diboll Junior High Sch*	17
Key, Catherine/*Victoria Christian Sch*	383
Key, Jeremy/*Eastern Hills Middle Sch*	27
Keys, Irma/*Bridges Sch*	139
Keys, Victor, Dr/*Academic Behavior Sch-West*	179
Khadam-Hir, Steven/*KIPP Acad West MS [288]*	6
Khan, Uzma/*Good Tree Academy*	85
Khan, Veronica/*Premier HS-Laredo [297]*	9
Khandtur, Reena/*Montessori Sch of North Dallas*	86
Khepera, Mene/*Texans Can Acad Dallas Pl Grv [305]*	11
Kho, Arlene/*Energized for Excellence MS*	193
Kibodeaux, Melanie/*Jack E Singley Academy*	109
Kidd, Brannon/*Weatherford High Sch*	314
Kidd, Carole/*Legacy Elem Sch*	269
Kidd, Schonda/*Warner Elem Sch*	186
Kiefer, Michelle/*Shadycrest Elem Sch*	53
Kieser, Stephen/*Faith Lutheran Sch*	85
Kiesling, Pam/*Sunray Middle Sch*	296
Kieth, Kelly/*Tahoka Middle Sch*	273
Kiker, Alison/*St Anne Catholic Sch*	244
Kilborn, Laurie/*San Perlita Sch*	394
Kilgore, Celina/*Pope Elem Sch*	345
Kilkenny, Barbara/*Christian Heritage Sch*	339
Killian, Sara/*Wylie Preparatory Academy*	86
Killo, Sandi/*Notre Dame Sch*	256
Kilpatrick, Vicki/*Frances M Rhodes Elem Sch*	37
Kim-Batra, Jiae/*Cedar Ridge High Sch*	398
Kim, Jaeil/*Idea Clg Prep-Achieve*	218
Kimberling, Kim/*Brock Elem Sch*	246
Kimberly, Diana/*Spring Early College Academy*	202
Kimble, Erika/*A G Hilliard Elem Sch*	188
Kimble, Jepsey/*Clear Lake City Elem Sch*	158
Kimbley, Amelia/*Wester Elem Sch*	271
Kimbriel, Stacy/*David McCall Elem Sch*	82
Kinard, Lori/*Holland Elem Sch*	27
Kincaid, Kimber/*Celina 6th Grade Center*	78
Kindred, Kimberly/*Richardson West Arts & Tech*	113
King-Corbett, Kiashan/*S S Conner Elem Sch*	102
King-Knowles, Melissa/*Dulles High Sch*	150
King, Anna, Dr/*Prairie Vista Middle Sch*	349
King, Ben/*Magnolia West High Sch*	293
King, Carolyn, Dr/*Greenleaf Elem Sch*	294
King, Dale/*St Thomas' Episcopal Sch*	207

PRINCIPAL INDEX

Market Data Retrieval

NAME/School	PAGE	NAME/School	PAGE
King, David/Basis San Antonio Shavano [011]	1	Koenig, Sandra/Perfecto Mancha Elem Sch	277
King, Derick/A C Blunt Middle Sch	330	Koepke, Kurtis/Hartley Sch	210
King, J D/Town East Christian Sch	45	Koepp, Julie/Cross Roads Junior High Sch	214
King, John/Argyle High Sch	120	Koerth, Michelle/Campbell Elem Sch	153
King, Kristi/Roanoke Elem Sch	125	Kohli, Jasmeen/Harmony Sch Ingenuity-Houston [284]	4
King, Lora/Wayne D Boshears Center	338	Kohli, Pinky/Pebblecreek Montessori Sch	86
King, Marissa/Burnet Elem Sch	130	Kolb, Jennifer/Harmony Sci Acad-Garland [284]	5
King, Reba/Mina Elem Sch	24	Kolenda, Joe/Guthrie Center	201
King, Rhett, Dr/John M Tidwell Middle Sch	125	Koller, Mark/Leander Middle Sch	397
King, Stephanie/Walter Hall Elem Sch	159	Komassa, Lori/Oak Hill Elem Sch	367
King, Thomas/Coleman Junior High Sch	76	**Kompelien, Leslie**/Krahn Elem Sch	197
King, Toby/Greenways Intermediate Sch	321	Konesheck, Sara/Sandra Mossman Elem Sch	159
Kinney, Ashley/Herman Jones Elem Sch	384	Konzelman, Jon/Second Baptist Sch	207
Kinney, Brad/Blanco Middle Sch	46	Koonce, Claire/White Oak Primary Sch	171
Kinninger, Garold/Cypress Woods High Sch	184	Koonce, Keith/Panola Charter HS [293]	9
Kinsworthy, Brian/C B Thompson Middle Sch	237	Koontz, Cody/Coppell HS 9th Grade	98
Kipping, Gerard/Randolph Foster High Sch	154	Koontz, Renee/Rodriguez Middle Sch	121
Kirby, Gary/Bryson Sch	238	Koop, Rebecca/Smith Middle Sch	185
Kirby, Jeff/Cotton Center Sch	174	**Kopeck, Karen**/Tradition Elem Sch	31
Kirby, Mallory/Keenan Elem Sch	293	Kopp, Ryan/Santa Fe Junior High Sch	161
Kirby, Synthia/Career Education Center	392	Korenek, Evelyn/Nazareth Academy	383
Kirchner, Dalen/Gillespie County High Sch	163	Korrodi, Diana/Matias De Llano Jr Elem Sch	388
Kirk, Ash/Kenneth D Black Elem Sch	180	Kosednar, Mary/Selwyn College Prep Sch	126
Kirk, Justin/Southwest Christian Sch	359	Kosowsky, Avraham/Mesorah High School for Girls	115
Kirk, Randy/Klein Collins High Sch	197	**Kotara, Daniel**/Merkel Elem Sch	361
Kirkland, Brent/Panhandle High Sch	69	Kottwitz, Sherri/Brewer Middle Sch	357
Kirkland, Tara/Holliday Elem Sch	19	Kraft, Karen/Lone Star High Sch	79
Kirkpatrick, Kellye/William Monnig Middle Sch	352	Kramer, Linda/Hockaday Sch	115
Kirsch, Cynthia/Beth Yeshurun Sch	205	Kramer, Monica/Faith Family Acad-Waxahachie [280]	3
Kiser, Andy/Cisneros Pre-K Sch	105	Krametbauer, Jan/Queen of Peace Catholic Sch	204
Kissire, Michael/Sonora Elemementary Sch	342	Kratky, Dana/Crosby Elem Sch	183
Kitchens, Todd/Margaret Galubenski Achiev Ctr	91	Krause, Bradley/Lutheran High Sch	115
Kitto, Sharyn/Wertheimer Middle Sch	154	Krieger, Amy/Sleepy Hollow Elem Sch	318
Kiture, Andrea/Katy Adventist Christian Sch	206	Krieger, Jeff/Arlington Collegiate High Sch	343
Klaerner, Jennifer, Dr/North Oaks Middle Sch	346	Krol, Tina/Hebron Valley Elem Sch	123
Klander, Charles/West Middle Sch	282	**Kroll, Laura**/Poth Junior High Sch	401
Klapesky, Paula/Mitchell Intermediate Sch	292	Kroll, Ronda/Clifton Elem School PK-5	46
Kleckner, Andrea/Park Crest Elem Sch	106	**Kruse, Cheryl**/Menard High Sch	285
Klein, Darynda/Hairgrove Elem Sch	184	Kubin, Christi/Oliver E Clift Elem Sch	142
Klein, Laura/Hill Country Elem Sch	23	**Kucera, Inez**/Newgulf Elem Sch	389
Kleinhans, Angela/Montague Elem Sch	290	Kucera, Katie/Edna Elem Sch	239
Kleypas, Zachary/Park Crest Middle Sch	372	Kucukbasol, Celil/Harmony Sch Tech-Houston [284]	4
Kline, Kristine/Laura Welch Bush Elem Sch	397	Kuehler, Kellye/Morton Elem Sch	75
Klingenberg, Sherry/Calvin Bledsoe Elem Sch	79	Kuempel, Christopher/Peet Junior High Sch	292
Kluttz, Stacey/Crockett Elem Sch	236	Kuenning, Tod/Bennie Cole Elem Sch	36
Kluttz, Stacey/Katherine G Johnson STEM Acad	236	Kuhlman, Robby/Great Hearts Western Hills [282]	4
Klyng, Karla/Alvin Primary Sch	51	**Kunkel, Kelly**/Gorman High Sch	129
Knapp, Angela/Harmony Sci Acad-Grand Prairie [284]	5	**Kunkel, Kelly**/Gorman Middle Sch	129
Knapp, Misty/W Z Burke Elem Sch	39	Kunschik, Veronica/Travis World Language Academy	108
Knapp, Tom/Westwood Terrace Elem Sch	39	Kuntz, Linda/Our Lady of Victory Sch	358
Knickerbocker, Ryan/Ballinger High Sch	326	Kupcho, Angela/Holy Cross Catholic Sch	276
Knight, Kelly/McKamy Middle Sch	123	**Kuster, Karie**/Brent Elem Sch	124
Knight, Melissa/Harmony Sch Achievement-Houstn [284]	4	Kuster, Karie/Ditto Elem Sch	344
Knight, Robert/Hondo High Sch	284	Kutac, Adam/KIPP Connect Houston Primary [288]	6
Knight, Yolanda/W W Bushman Elem Sch	103	Kutac, Donna/Louise High Sch	390
Knighton, Tracy/Christoval Elem Sch	364	Kutac, Laura/Flatonia Elem Sch	147
Knittle, David/Burbank Middle Sch	190	Kuyatt, Andrea, Dr/Bishop High Sch	302
Knosel, Maria/Raul Yzaguirre Sch for Success	10	**Kwan, Victoria**/Pomona Elem Sch	51
Knowles, Daniel/Ed Willkie Middle Sch	348	**Kwiatkowski, Perla**/Knox Early Chldhd Center	40
Knowles, Danny/Marine Creek Middle Sch	349	Kyle, Matthew/Idea Clg Prep-Mission	219
Knox, Dee/Dulles Middle Sch	150		
Knox, Lois/Jhw Inspire Acad-Williams Hse	31	**L**	
Knutz, Bobbe/Collegiate Acad Tarrant Clg	353	La Rue, Michelle/Rolling Meadows Elem Sch	33
Kocurek, Christopher/Rancho Isabella Elem Sch	52	Labbe-Maginel, Lara/Knowles Elem Sch	397
Koder, Chris/George Anderson Elem Sch	77	**LaBerge, Sarah**/William B Travis High Sch	151
Koehl, Michael/Columbus Alternative Sch	86	Labrado, Claudia/Wee Wisdom Kindergarten	139
Koehler, Karl/Atascocita Middle Sch	195	Lacamu, Jill/Richard Moore Elem Sch	199
Koehler, Laura/Grapevine Middle Sch	353	Lackey, Jon/Jayton-Girard Sch	255
Koehler, Lisa/Liberty Elem Sch	345	Lackey, Kimberly/Pinnacle Intermediate Sch	321
Koehne, Shauna/Haggard Middle Sch	82	Lackey, Lisa/Shadow Forest Elem Sch	196
Koen, Monica/Carrollton Elem Sch	96	Lacoke, Jeff/Ault Elem Sch	184
Koenig, Heath/Collegiate Academy Middle Sch	97	Ladd, Bryan/Lexington Elem Sch	263
Koenig, Neil/New Boston High Sch	49	LaFleur, Cheryl/O V Calvert Elem Sch	180

Texas School Directory — PRINCIPAL INDEX

NAME/School	PAGE
Laflure, Michelle/YES Prep North Centrl [312]	14
Lagle, Nisa/St Louis Catholic Sch	282
Lahrman, Stephanie/North Star Elem Sch	138
Lain, Rosie/Goliad Elem Sch	233
Laird, Emily/Barrett-Lee Early Chldhd Ctr	183
Laird, Robert/Channelview High Sch	183
Lake, Misty/Chapel Hill Elem Sch	363
Lakey, Jamie/Robert Cobb Middle Sch	80
Lalime, Ann/Loraine T Golbow Elem Sch	152
Lalmansingh, Shannon/Summerwood Elem Sch	196
Lam, Edith/Blossom Valley Academy	126
Lam, Mimi/Whidby Elem Sch	193
Lamar, Kelly/Canton Elem Sch	380
Lamb, Jim/Kemp High Sch	252
Lamb, Shawna/Spring Creek Sch	238
Lamb, Shawna/West Texas Elem Sch	238
Lambarri, Blanca/Homer Hanna Early Clg HS	64
Lambert, Elsa/Dr Raul Garza Jr Elem Sch	67
Lambert, Jarod, Dr/Bush Elem Sch	291
Lambert, Kellie/Emma Roberson Elem Sch	230
Lambert, Rachel/La Pryor High Sch	407
Lambert, Tanya/Bill Burden Elem Sch	398
Lambert, Tim/Texas Middle Sch	50
Lambeth, Erin/McLeod Sch	70
Lambropulos, Lori/Energy Institute High Sch	192
Lamers, Patrick/Davis 9th Grade Center	349
Lanas, Patricia/Bonnie Garcia Elem Sch	387
Lancaster, Brittany/Miss May Vernon Elem Sch	326
Lancaster, Tricia/Barron Elem Sch	82
Lance, Jennifer/McLeod Sch	70
Lance, Shawn/Gateway College Prep Sch [292]	3
Land, A'Lesia, Dr/Lighthouse Learning Center	52
Land, Katherine/Doerre Intermediate Sch	197
Land, Nicole/Valley Ranch Elem Sch	294
Landa, Luis/Chavez High Sch	189
Landenberger, Lynn/Driscoll Sch	304
Landeros, Sabina/Santa Fe Elem Sch	247
Landers, Amy/Parkview Christian Academy	283
Landers, Mike/Walnut Grove Elem Sch	347
Landers, Todd/Brazosport Christian Sch	54
Landis, Brad/Winfree Academy-Dallas [311]	14
Landrum, Heather/Dove Elem Sch	353
Landry, Ted/The Woodlands High Sch	292
Lane, Audry/Crenshaw Elem Sch	183
Lane, Claude/Moore Mst Magnet Sch	338
Lane, Deborah/West Sabine Elem Sch	329
Lane, Sharon/Lamar Elem Sch	365
Lane, Tim/Saltillo Sch	231
Lanford, Jacqueline/Barkley-Ruiz Academy	39
Lange, Andrea/Worth Heights Elem Sch	352
Lange, Barbara/Brinker Elem Sch	82
Lange, Tanner/Medina Valley High Sch	284
Langen, Shane/Oak Ridge Elem Sch	269
Langford, Amanda/Gladewater Primary Sch	169
Langford, Chris/Gladewater Middle Sch	169
Langley, Burt/West Rusk Intermediate Sch	328
Langston, Emmalee/E S McKenzie Elem Sch	111
Langston, Robert/Kress Elem Sch	343
Langston, Troy/R L Paschal High Sch	351
Lanier, Jenny/Richardson Heights Elem Sch	113
Laning, Bengie/Brazos River Charter Sch	2
Lapic, Terry/East TX Charter Sch-Chadwick	2
LaPlante, Jennifer/W O Gray Elem Sch	111
LaPrade, Ricky/Grand Saline High Sch	380
Lapuma, Joe/Creekview High Sch	96
Lara, Alejandra/Jefferson Elem Sch	65
Lara, Angel, Dr/Keller Learning Center	355
Lara, Diana/Golden Rule CS-DeSoto [281]	3
Lara, Johnny/W V Swinburn Elem Sch	343
Lara, Krista/Hart Elem Sch	71
Lara, Lucina/E B Reyna Elem Sch	220
Lara, Maria/Garza Elem Sch	63
Larke, Patricia, Dr/Johnson Ferguson Academy	386
LaRoche, Amber/Brentwood Elem Sch	367
LaRocque, Shawnda/Purnell Support Center	124
Larrasquitu, Claudia/Laureles Elem Sch	66
Larsen, Diane/St Pius X High Sch	204
Larson, Kenneth/DeSoto Pvt Sch & Day Care Ctr	115
Lassin, Arlene/Torah Day School of Houston	207
Laster, Kelly/Holy Family Catholic Sch	400
Latchison, Daphanie/Brazos Credit Recovery HS	282
Lathan, Constance/Halpin Early Chldhd Lrng Ctr	193
Lathan, Eric/Anthony Aguirre Junior HS	183
Latimer, Patsy/Smith Elem Sch	270
Latiolais, Toby/Langham Elem Sch	243
Latta, Bruce/All Saints Episcopal Sch	272
Lau, Jill/Harold Cade Middle Sch	382
Lauer, Joyce/Fowler Elem Sch	27
Laufersky, Connie/White Rock Montessori Sch	116
Laugen, Peter/Woodlands Christian Academy	295
Laughlin, Sara/Robinson Intermediate Sch	281
Law, Jay/Mercer-Blumberg Learning Ctr	174
Lawlor, Liz/Levine Academy	86
Lawrason, Paula/Union Grove Middle Sch	28
Lawrence, Jerry/Lubbock Christian Sch	272
Lawson, Deidra/Yellowstone Academy	208
Lawson, Elizabeth/G W Harby Junior High Sch	51
Lawson, Jason/Italy Jr Sr High Sch	141
Lawson, Mignon/Adult Education	360
Lay, Brandi/Whiteside Elem Sch	271
Layne, Garrett/Rogers Elem Sch	29
Layne, Mario/O D Wyatt High Sch	351
Layne, Valerie/Int'l Ldrshp TX-Grand Prairie	108
Layne, Valerie/Int'l Ldrshp TX-Keller Saginaw	109
Layton, Antonio/La Villa Early Clg High Sch	220
Layton, Rachel/Stephen F Austin Middle Sch	55
Lazono-Landry, Patricia/Brooks Int'l Studies Academy	2
Leach, Catherine/Wetmore Elem Sch	36
Leach, Mark/North Heights Alt Sch	318
Leal, Gerardo/Park Place Elem Sch	190
Leal, Grace/Donna Lewis Elem Sch	202
Leal, Lonnie/Clear Lake Intermediate Sch	158
Leal, Marina/Valley View North Elem Sch	225
Leal, Obed/Stell Middle Sch	64
Leal, Pablo/Villareal Elem Sch	66
Leal, Rafael/Mercedes Academic Academy	221
Leamon, Sean/Sonora High Sch	342
Leamon, Sean/Sonora Middle Sch	342
Leath, Caleb/Woodrow Wilson Elem Sch	121
LeBlanc, Jacob, Dr/Katy Junior High Sch	152
LeBlanc, Roxanne/St John Bosco Sch	44
LeBlanc, Shelli/Collins Intermediate Sch	291
Lechler, Pamela/Louise Elem Sch	390
Leclear, Lisa/Jones Elem Sch	286
Lecocq, Karen/Rick Reedy High Sch	80
Leday, Adrian/Watson Tech Center Math & Sci	107
Ledbetter, James/Roosevelt High Sch	271
Ledesma, Sylvia/Robert Vela High Sch	217
Ledford, Amy/Troup Elem Sch	337
LeDoux, Melissa/Black Elem Sch	184
Lee, Brian/York Junior High Sch	292
Lee, Cindy/Bowie Elem Sch	364
Lee, Cleveland/Queens Intermediate Sch	199
Lee, David/Hector P Garcia Middle Sch	100
Lee, David/Malta Elem Sch	48
Lee, Gina/Azle Elem Sch	345
Lee, Jae/Burnett Elem Sch	198
Lee, Jessica/Maypearl Intermediate Sch	141
Lee, Karen/Skaggs Elem Sch	83
Lee, Karen/St Mary's Catholic Sch	92
Lee, Norman/A Plus Academy Secondary [272]	1
Lee, Regina/Gale Pond Alamo Elem Sch	130
Lee, Roneka/Elmer Bondy Intermediate Sch	198
Lee, Sharon/River Pines Elem Sch	196
Lee, Stephanie, Dr/Eddy & Debbie Peach Elem Sch	344
Lee, Tori/KIPP Destiny Elem Sch [287]	7
Lee, Twana/South Waco Elem Sch	282
Leech, Amy/Whitney High Sch	228
Leek, Wayne/Burleson High Sch	246
Leflet, Yarda/Falls Career High Sch	60

PRINCIPAL INDEX

Market Data Retrieval

NAME/School	PAGE
Leger, Jeff/*Vidor Elem Sch*	309
Legg, Danielle/*Henderson Elem Sch*	55
Leggett, Vanikin/*Brule Elem Sch*	172
Legros, Robert/*Cathedral School of St Mary*	372
Lehman, Misti/*Greenwood Hills Elem Sch*	112
Lehman, Sandra/*Brookesmith Elem Sch*	58
Lehmberg, Lori/*Comal Academy*	88
Lehmberg, Lori/*Comal Discipline Center*	88
Leija, Teresa/*Lackland Elem Sch*	34
Leinenkugel, Katie/*Uplift Pinnacle Prep Primary [309]*	13
Leinhauser, Jaime/*Meridian Elem Sch*	47
Leist, Brian/*Rice Junior High Sch*	87
Leite, Renee/*Triangle Adventist Chrn Sch*	244
Leiva, Carlo/*E A Jones Elem Sch*	150
LeJeune, Darrell/*Mary Jo Sheppard Elem Sch*	357
LeJeune, Jeremy/*Burnet Middle Sch*	60
Lemaitre, Barry/*Brooks Lonestar Academy*	2
Lemon, Molly/*Northside Sch*	393
Lemon, Trevor/*Ferndell Henry Center for Lrng*	150
Lemons, Albert/*Atherton Elem Sch*	190
Lennon, Charli/*Red Simon Middle Sch*	211
Lentz, Phillip/*Blue Ridge Middle Sch*	77
Leonard, Allison/*Corinth Classical Academy [297]*	2
Leonard, Joshua/*Blanton Elem Sch*	344
Leonard, Rebecca/*Clear Fork Elem Sch*	61
Leopold, Gary/*Columbus Junior High Sch*	87
Lepley, Kathy/*New Waverly Intermediate Sch*	383
Lerma, George/*Driscoll Middle Sch*	303
Lerma, Jeanette/*Vanguard Academy-Picasso*	13
Lerma, Veronica/*Lyford Elem Sch*	394
Leslie, Robyn/*Pilot Point Middle Sch*	125
Lesniewski, Lindsey/*Gardens Elem Sch*	199
Lester, Abbe/*Jarrell Middle Sch*	396
Letterer, Mark/*Wilson Middle Sch*	83
Leuschner, Mark/*Slocum Sch*	16
Levertov, Rochel/*Hebrew Prep School of Austin*	373
Levy, Catherine/*Dallas International Sch*	115
Lewallen, Allison/*Morris Middle Sch*	199
Lewis, Alicia/*Blackshear Elem Sch*	188
Lewis, Brandi/*Elsie Shands Elem Sch*	111
Lewis, Brandy/*Bella Cameron Elem Sch*	40
Lewis, David/*Walnut Springs Elem Sch*	89
Lewis, Johnny/*Excelsior Sch*	334
Lewis, Ku-Masi/*Texans Can Acad Fw Westcreek [305]*	11
Lewis, Lesia/*West Elem Sch*	296
Lewis, Melanie/*Hardin Intermediate Sch*	105
Lewis, Monica/*Northland Christian Sch*	206
Lewis, Monique/*Central Media Arts Academy*	160
Lewis, Nicole/*Legacy Middle Sch*	31
Lewis, Reginald/*Wings*	104
Lewis, Ricky/*Lillian Elem Sch*	246
Lewis, Steven/*Comanche High Sch*	89
Lewis, Vinson/*Kerr High Sch*	182
Lewis, Wendy/*Mission Bend Christian Academy*	206
Leyva, Alicia/*Horn Elem Sch*	182
Liano, Luis/*Pdn Academy-Vista Del Sol*	9
Liddell, Tamara/*Janet Brockett Elem Sch*	357
Liendo, Jaime/*John B Connally Middle Sch*	37
Liesberger, Lauren/*Kreinhop Elem Sch*	197
Lightfoot, Traci/*Foster Elem Sch*	192
Lightsey, Jeffrey/*New Braunfels HS 9th GR Ctr*	89
Lilie, Ron, Dr/*Waelder Sch*	164
Lillard, Amanda/*Westside Elem Sch*	397
Lilly, Erica/*South Shaver Elem Sch*	200
Lim, Nirmol/*Jones Futures Academy*	192
Limas, Aminta/*Lyndon Baines Johnson Elem Sch*	216
Limon, Angela/*W T Francisco Elem Sch*	346
Limon, Anthony/*Harry Shimotsu Elem Sch*	224
Limon, Marissa/*Dan D Rogers Elem Sch*	99
Linares, Diego/*Opportunity Awareness Center*	152
Linares, Diego, Dr/*Martha Raines High Sch*	152
Lindeman, Todd/*Dwight D Eisenhower High Sch*	180
Lindgren, Ronald/*Timpson High Sch*	335

NAME/School	PAGE
Lindley, Cynthia/*Chandler Elem Sch*	169
Lindsey, Brita/*Texas Connections Academy [181]*	189
Lindsey, Sabrina, Dr/*Academy at Carrie F Thomas*	346
Line, Donette/*Stewart Elem Sch*	161
Liner, Lariza/*Forest Ln Acad of Arts & Comm*	112
Liner, Lariza/*Mitchell Elem Sch*	83
Ling, Stephanie/*Fehl-Price Elem Sch*	242
Linson, Eartha/*Wakefield Elem Sch*	167
Linton, Lisa/*Premier HS-Waco [297]*	10
Lipschitz, Christine/*Uplift White Rock Hills Prep [309]*	13
Lira, Brandi/*Eastwood Academy*	189
Lisle, James/*Haskell Elem Sch*	210
Little, Carolyn/*Bingham Head Start Ctr*	242
Little, Charles/*Vandegrift High Sch*	397
Little, Clayton/*De Kalb High Sch*	48
Little, Vickey/*Teague Intermediate Sch*	156
Littlefield, Michael/*STEM Early College High Sch*	33
Litton, Debbie, Dr/*Wood River Elem Sch*	303
Livas, Shelene/*Ketelsen Elem Sch*	192
Livingston, Steven/*Booker High Sch*	267
Lizardo, Reny/*James Bowie High Sch*	344
Llanos, Armando/*Travis Elem Sch*	134
Lloyd, Jonathan/*Detroit High Sch*	322
Loafman, Casey/*Frenship Middle Sch*	269
Loan, Lisa/*David Crockett Middle Sch*	318
Locke, Connie/*Willow Springs Elem Sch*	28
Locke, Diana/*Corrigan-Camden High Sch*	316
Locke, Kelly/*I N Range Elem Sch*	111
Lockwood, Jonica/*D A Hulcy Steam Middle Sch*	99
Lockyer, Travis/*Annapolis Christian Academy*	306
Loftin, Chris/*Clute Intermediate Sch*	52
Lofton, Darcele/*Bellfort Acad Early Chldhd Ctr*	192
Lofton, Kelle/*Ed Franz Elem Sch*	33
Lofton, Seretha/*Forest Oak Middle Sch*	350
Logan, Bethany/*Smithville Junior High Sch*	24
Logan, Karmen/*Alta Vista Elem Sch*	281
Logan, Robert/*Grace Christian Sch*	226
Logan, Stephanie/*Beverly Cheatham Elem Sch*	76
Lohmiller, Denise, Dr/*Plano Head Start Center*	83
Lohse, Matthew/*Taft High Sch*	332
Lojo, Ken/*Strake Jesuit College Prep Sch*	204
Lomas, Jennifer/*Serna Elem Sch*	35
Lomeli-Bazen, Susana/*Spence Elem Sch*	180
Lomeli, Arturo/*Glenn High Sch*	397
Loney, Lavonda/*Bellaire Elem Sch*	27
Long, Angela/*J O Davis Elem Sch*	109
Long, Barbara/*Rising Star Elem Sch*	129
Long, Corina/*Ehrhart Sch*	3
Long, Karla/*All Saints Episcopal Sch*	339
Long, Kelly/*Frank B Agnew Middle Sch*	111
Long, Larry/*Faith Academy*	383
Long, Lisa/*Hendrick Middle Sch*	82
Long, Rachel/*Coronado Middle Sch*	175
Long, Rebecca, Dr/*Spring Virtual Sch*	203
Long, Robert, Dr/*Edwin M Wells Middle Sch*	202
Long, Stephen/*Travis High School of Choice*	260
Long, Tamara/*Martin Elem Sch*	242
Long, Tim/*Awty International Sch*	205
Longcrier, Roy/*Windthorst High Sch*	20
Longcrier, Roy/*Windthorst Junior High Sch*	20
Longley, Cathy/*Santo Elem Sch*	310
Longonia, Kasie/*Hill Elem Sch*	344
Longoria, Alfonso/*James Tippit Middle Sch*	395
Longoria, Alisia/*Northeast Early Clg High Sch*	368
Longoria, Camille/*Spring Hill Elem Sch*	372
Longoria, Dulia/*Jackson Early Childhood Center*	123
Longoria, Herlinda/*E H Gilbert Elem Sch*	32
Longoria, Lizette/*Audie Murphy Middle Sch*	223
Longoria, Mary/*St George Sch*	358
Longoria, Rose/*James Pace Early Clg HS*	64
Longoria, Sharon/*Mt Sacred Heart Sch*	44
Longoria, Stephanie/*Somerville Elem Sch*	60
Looney, Paul/*Schallert Elem Sch*	245

Texas School Directory — PRINCIPAL INDEX

NAME/School	PAGE
Lopez-Brouse, Melissa/*Michael Elem Sch*	38
Lopez-Rogina, Maria/*Laurenzo ECC*	190
Lopez, Adrian/*Cater Elem Sch*	29
Lopez, Aine/*Seminole Elem Sch*	158
Lopez, Alejandro/*Clemente Martinez Elem Sch*	191
Lopez, Andrea/*Idea Clg Prep-Walzem*	219
Lopez, Angelita/*Lotspeich Elem Sch*	305
Lopez, Annette/*Dr Martha Mead Elem Sch*	37
Lopez, Blanca/*Escobar-Rios Elem Sch*	222
Lopez, Bobby/*Bob Hope Middle High Sch*	1
Lopez, Brynn/*Fayetteville Sch*	147
Lopez, Cristina/*Memorial Intermediate Sch*	245
Lopez, Eduardo/*M B Lamar Middle Sch*	387
Lopez, Elena/*Webb Elem Sch*	345
Lopez, Eli/*Saegert Elem Sch*	28
Lopez, Erica/*Muriel Vance Forbes Academy*	41
Lopez, Gabriel/*West Briar Middle Sch*	195
Lopez, Hector/*Batesville Elem Sch*	378
Lopez, Helena/*Math Science & Tech Magnet Sch*	112
Lopez, Jennifer/*Our Lady of Fatima Sch*	162
Lopez, Jeremy/*Southern Hills Elem Sch*	393
Lopez, Jose/*B H Hamblen Elem Sch*	183
Lopez, Julianna/*Premier HS-Career Tech Ed Ctr [297]*	9
Lopez, Karina/*Edison Middle Sch*	189
Lopez, Linda/*Elodia R Chapa Elem Sch*	220
Lopez, Manuela/*Ed Downs Elem Sch*	67
Lopez, Marco/*Idea Clg Prep-Brownsville*	218
Lopez, Marcos/*Edward K Downing Elem Sch*	130
Lopez, Marisela/*Klein Road Elem Sch*	88
Lopez, Nora/*Agua Dulce Elem Sch*	302
Lopez, Richard/*Fabens Elem Sch*	135
Lopez, Rita/*Parkland Pre-K Center*	138
Lopez, Roberto/*Fannin Middle Sch*	107
Lopez, Sandra/*Armando Cerna Elem Sch*	276
Lopez, Santa/*Hillcrest Elem Sch*	40
Lopez, Sergio/*Alief Middle Sch*	182
Lopez, Sharon/*Seabrook Intermediate Sch*	159
Lopez, Stephanie/*Tom Landry Elem Sch*	97
Lopez, Yolanda/*Webb Primary Sch*	368
Lopez, Zonia/*Sam Houston Elem Sch*	304
Lorge, Bethany/*Edward H White Middle Sch*	35
Loskot, Sonia/*David G Burnet Elem Sch*	99
Lott, Brian/*Cassata High Sch*	358
Lott, Michele/*Liscano Elem Sch*	79
Lott, Stacie/*Fredda Nottingham Alt Educ Ctr*	265
Loughner, Katie/*Chester Elem Sch*	374
Louis, Rodney/*Stelle Claughton Middle Sch*	203
Louis, Shantelle/*Windsor Village Elem Sch*	193
Lourcey, Heather/*The Westwood School-Upper*	116
Lourcey, Heather/*Westwood Montessori/IB Sch*	116
Lovaasen, Martha/*Elysian Fields Elem Sch*	208
Lovato, Lisa/*Dr Linda Henrie Elem Sch*	111
Love, Donald/*Comfort Elem Sch*	254
Love, Ed/*Waco High Sch*	282
Love, Kristy/*Codwell Elem Sch*	190
Lovejoy, Stephen/*St Francis Episcopal Sch*	207
Lovelady, James/*Princeton High Sch*	84
Loveland, Robert/*Cooper Academy at Navarro*	40
Loveland, Robert/*James F Cooper Acad-Navarro*	40
Lovell, Joy/*Thomas Wesley Andrews Elem Sch*	83
Loving, Kellye/*Early Childhood Dev Center*	303
Loving, Kellye/*Oak Park Special Emphasis Sch*	304
Low, Staci/*Bowie Elem Sch*	112
Lowder, David/*Andrews Middle Sch*	16
Lowe, Ashley/*George West Junior High Sch*	268
Lowe, Brian/*North Hopkins Sch*	231
Lowe, Cindy/*Crossroads Academy*	115
Lowe, Jana/*Leggett Sch*	316
Lowe, Jeromy, Dr/*Prince of Peace Christian Sch*	126
Lowe, Sheri/*Tavola Elem Sch*	294
Lowery, C/*Ferris Junior High Sch*	140
Lowery, Carrie/*Catherine Bethke Elem Sch*	151
Lowery, Rhonda/*Lovelady Elem Middle Sch*	233
Lowry, Kasey/*Diane Winborn Elem Sch*	152
Lowry, Laci/*Coolidge Elem Sch*	266

NAME/School	PAGE
Lowry, Nate/*Idea Clg Prep-Weslaco Pike*	219
Loy, Courtney/*Thelma E Page-Richardson ES*	103
Loya-Thomas, Debra/*Sam Houston Elem Sch*	221
Loyola, Eliza/*Menchaca Elem Sch*	367
Lozano-Lerma, Lucy/*Tejas School of Choice*	138
Lozano, Abelardo/*Holbrook Elem Sch*	185
Lozano, Angela/*Houser Elem Sch*	291
Lozano, Elizabeth/*Bellaire Elem Sch*	32
Lozano, Gilberto/*Milam Elem Sch*	292
Lozano, Isabel/*Kendrick Elem Sch*	282
Lucas, Brigit/*Stockdale Elem Sch*	401
Lucas, Euberta/*Sue Creech Elem Sch*	153
Lucas, Heath/*Piney Woods Elem Sch*	294
Lucas, Jennifer/*Gattis Elem Sch*	399
Lucas, Scott/*Whiteface Elem Sch*	75
Lucita, Karen/*Kyle Elem Sch*	211
Luedecke, Jospeh/*Richard Lagow Elem Sch*	102
Lueptow, Lori/*Whittier Elem Sch*	190
Luera, Stevie/*Idea Clg Prep-Owassa*	219
Lugo, Lourdes/*Lundy Elem Sch*	133
Luhn, Elizabeth/*Lone Oak Elem Sch*	236
Lujan-Garcia, Laura/*O'Shea Keleher Elem Sch*	136
Lullo, Vicki/*Thornwood Elem Sch*	201
Lumpkin, Lindsey/*Falcon Early College High Sch*	130
Lumpkins, Janet/*Sheridan Elem Sch*	87
Luna-Bates, Elena/*W T White High Sch*	103
Luna, Adrian/*Nathan Adams Elem Sch*	102
Luna, Alicia, Dr/*Garland Classical Academy [297]*	3
Luna, Ana/*Cogin Memorial Elem Sch*	306
Luna, Caroline/*Alpine Christian Sch*	57
Luna, Raul/*Corina Pena Elem Sch*	219
Luna, Rebecca/*Raul Yzaguirre Middle Sch*	224
Lundquist, Jennifer/*Hillcrest Prof Dev Sch*	282
Lunkin, Tarsha/*Frank D Moates Elem Sch*	104
Lunoff, Manuel/*Robert Driscoll Jr Elem Sch*	305
Lunsford, Dan/*Frost High Sch*	299
Lunz, Joe/*Hill Country Christian Sch*	212
Lusk, Beverly/*Rangel Women's Leadership Sch*	102
Lusk, Dalls/*St Mark Lutheran Sch*	207
Luther, Ginger/*Holiman Elem Sch*	365
Luther, Nikki/*Education Connection*	30
Luther, Timothy/*Wiggs Middle Sch*	135
Luthi, Kyle/*J W Webb Elem Sch*	81
Luton, Kim/*Thrall Middle Sch*	400
Luttrull, Pamelia, Dr/*Brown Middle Sch*	251
Luyster, Kimberly/*Jesse McGowen Elem Sch*	81
Lyday, Tricia/*Frazier Elem Sch*	247
Lyman, Kelsey/*KIPP 3D Academy [288]*	6
Lynch, Colleen/*St Gabriel's Catholic Sch*	372
Lynch, David/*Spring Hill Junior High Sch*	171
Lynch, Ken/*Waxahachie Global High Sch*	142
Lynn, Sandra/*Stockdale High Sch*	401
Lyons-Lewis, Deidra/*Elkins High Sch*	150
Lyons, Brian/*McMillen High Sch*	83
Lyons, Monica/*Guillen Middle Sch*	134
Lyssy, Katherine/*E M Pease Middle Sch*	37
Lyssy, Kim/*Timberwood Park Elem Sch*	88
Lyth, Zena/*Faith Academy*	22
Lytle, Heather/*Liberty Christian Sch*	126

M

NAME/School	PAGE
Maarouf, Mohamad/*KIPP Houston High Sch [288]*	7
Mabry, Candis/*Alto Elem Sch*	72
MacDonald, Sarah/*St Ambrose Sch*	204
MacDougall, Jamie/*Crow Leadership Academy*	344
MacEdo, Maria/*Central Elem Sch*	51
Machicek, Joshua/*Trinity Charter Sch-New Life [307]*	12
Macias, Maria/*St Andrew Catholic Sch*	358
Macias, Ray/*Del Valle Opportunity Center*	369
Macias, Raymond/*Patricia J Blattman Elem Sch*	38
Mackey, Benjamin/*Townview Mag HS-Talent & Gift*	103
Mackey, Scott/*W H Bonner Elem Sch*	17
Mackey, Susan/*Trinity Meadows Interm Sch*	355
Mackey, Thomas/*Dr Pat Henderson Elem Sch*	37

PRINCIPAL INDEX

Market Data Retrieval

NAME/School	PAGE	NAME/School	PAGE
Macklin, Audrey/Austin Parkway Elem Sch	149	**Mansfield, Jason**/Faulk Early Childhood Center	330
Macklin, Chaundra/Joseph J Rhoads Learning Ctr	101	Mansfield, Jason/Kieberger Elem Sch	330
Madden, Billy/Lamar Middle Sch	29	Mantle, Kelly/Forester Elem Sch	37
Madden, Kelly/Kennedy-Powell Elem Sch	29	Mantz, Gary/Freedom Elem Sch	355
Maddin, Tanya/Stubblefield Alternative Acad	294	Manuel, Monica/Career & Tech Education Center	79
Maddoux, Stacey/Ashworth Elem Sch	343	Manuel, Richard/Cal & Walt Wester Middle Sch	79
Maddox, Andrew/Taylor High Sch	399	Mapes, Lauri/Glen Rose Intermediate Sch	340
Maddox, Andrew/Taylor Opportunity Center	400	Maphies, Alicia/Centennial High Sch	79
Maddox, Tannessa/Grace Raymond Academy	180	Maples, Matt/Stonegate Christian Academy	116
Maddox, Virgil/Kahla Middle Sch	185	Maples, Melody/Stiles Middle Sch	397
Mader, William/Sweeny High Sch	54	Marais, Ryno/St Thomas' Episcopal Sch	207
Madison, Michelle/Peaster Elem Sch	313	Marchante, Meredith/Harmony Sci Acad-Katy [284]	5
Madrid-Lacy, Dianna/Strickland Elem Sch	97	Marchiony, Mary/Bishop Dunne Catholic Sch	113
Maedgen, Russell/Lyndon B Johnson High Sch	46	Marcos, Edison/Bexar County Academy [187]	1
Magadance, Steven/International Sch of Americas	35	Mariani, Tammy/Honey Grove High Sch	146
Magallan, Amanda/Sanderson Public Sch	362	Marioni, April/Ann M Garcia-Enriquez Mid Sch	135
MaGee, Christopher/Alvarado High Sch	246	**Mark, Ruffin**/Normangee Senior High Sch	264
Maglievaz, Carmen/Early Childhood Center	284	Markle, Bobby/Caldwell Arts Academy	338
Maglievaz, Carmen/Natalia Elem Sch	284	Marks, Ginna/Behavior Transition Center	230
Mahagan, Vikki, Dr/Sellers Middle Sch	106	Marks, Scott/Waxahachie Preparatory Academy	143
Mahan, Jill/Avery Secondary Sch	322	Maroney, Dawn/Stroman Middle Sch	382
Mahan, Wendy/Cameron Elem Sch	287	**Marquez-Neth, Yvonne**/Calallen Charter High Sch	302
Mahan, Wendy/Cameron Junior High Sch	287	Marquez-Neth, Yvonne/Calallen High Sch	302
Mahar, Craig/Hooks Junior High Sch	48	Marquez, Ashley/Nolan Ryan Junior High Sch	51
Maher, Michael/John Cooper Sch	295	Marquez, Crystal/Sam Houston Elem Sch	130
Mahler, Brandon/Ft Elliott Sch	390	**Marquez, Marizza**/Sunset Valley Elem Sch	367
Mahler, James/W R Hatfield Elem Sch	125	Marquez, Mauricio/Odessa High Sch	130
Mai, Jenae/Colonial Hills Elem Sch	34	Marquez, Michael, Dr/Margaret S McWhirter Elem Sch	159
Maias, Susan/Crestmont Christian Prep Sch	254	Marquez, Monica/Louise Wolff Kahn Elem Sch	101
Mailhiot, Lauren/James Deanda Elem Sch	192	Marquez, Ranulfo/Psja Southwest Echs	224
Maines, Jay/Del Valle Elem Sch	369	**Marr, Brian**/Klein Alternative Ed Center	197
Maisonet, G/St Patrick Catholic Sch	18	Marr, Mallory/Bridgeport Intermediate Sch	402
Majewski, James/Clear Creek High Sch	158	**Marron, Rebecca**/West Memorial Elem Sch	153
Majors, Angela/Montessori Academy-North Texas	169	Marroquin, Christine/Blanche Moore Elem Sch	303
Makel, Erin/St Edward Catholic Sch	204	Marroquin, Ricardo/Harlandale Middle Sch	32
Makuta, Marti/Cavazos Middle Sch	270	Marsh, Kara/Heritage Christian Academy	54
Malcolm, Mitzi/Carver Early Childhood Academy	317	Marsh, Kimberly/Sewell Elem Sch	106
Malcom, Neila/Highland Park Middle Sch	319	Marsh, Robert/Chapin High Sch	134
Maldonado, April/Eagle Springs Elem Sch	195	Marshall, Andrenetta/Keeble EC-PK-K Sch	181
Maldonado, Francisca/Smith Elem Sch	369	Marshall, Cathy/Newton Middle Sch	301
Maldonado, Harold/John Paul Stevens High Sch	37	Marshall, Courtney/Collins Elem Sch	182
Maldonado, Ismael/H M K Care Academy	257	Marshall, Julie/Hays Magnet Academy	130
Maldonado, Sandra/Aikman Elem Sch	119	Marshall, Leanne/Floresville South Elem Sch	400
Maldonado, Virna/Psja T Jefferson Echs	224	**Marshall, Renesiaha**/James R Reynolds Elem Sch	192
Malo, Mark/Magrill EC-PK-K Sch	181	Marshall, Shannon/Dalhart Junior High Sch	95
Malone, Amy/Rahe Bulverde Elem Sch	88	**Marshall, Todd**/Pleasant Grove High Sch	49
Malone, Dwight/Tisd Child & Adolescent Ctr	253	Marshall, Toni/St Peter the Apostle Elem Sch	204
Malone, Eleanore/Griffin Elem Sch	338	Martell, Miguel/Julius L Matthey Middle Sch	43
Malone, Jennifer/Tatum Elem Sch	328	Marti, Lauren/Hildebrandt Intermediate Sch	197
Malone, Lori/W L Higgins Elem Sch	260	Martin, Alexandra/Fowler Elem Sch	392
Malone, Mandy/Barbers Hill Primary Sch	72	Martin, Allie/Klenk Elem Sch	197
Malone, Mark/Randolph High Sch	39	Martin, Amanda/J C Rugel Elem Sch	111
Malone, Sheterric/Dallas Co Jj CS-Main Camp	96	Martin, Ana/Cy-Fair High Sch	184
Malott, Marlo/O Henry Middle Sch	369	Martin, Blain/Devine Intermediate Sch	283
Mamaux, Maria/Jan Aragon Middle Sch	185	Martin, Casey/Good Shepherd Episcopal Sch	115
Mamedov, Ahmed/Sch of Sci & Tech Main [299]	10	Martin, Christine/Victoria Juv Justice Center	382
Manago, Joseph/Andress High Sch	134	**Martin, Curt**/Downing Middle Sch	123
Manchee, Mike/Lorenzo De Zavala Middle Sch	318	Martin, Destini/Dan J Kubacak Elem Sch	161
Mancilla, Grace/Southside Elem Sch	15	Martin, Gordon/Sudan High Sch	261
Mancillas, Yvette/Arnoldo Cantu Elem Sch	223	Martin, Janell/Snyder High Sch	333
Mancini, Angela/George W Carver Elem Sch	187	Martin, Jennifer/David E Smith Elem Sch	346
Mancini, Angela/Hitchcock Primary Sch	161	Martin, Jennifer/Town Center Elem Sch	98
Maness, Michael/Cypress Ranch High Sch	184	Martin, Kimberley/La Vernia High Sch	401
Mangels, Stephanie/Carroll Middle Sch	347	Martin, Kimberly/Galena Park High Sch	187
Mank-Allen, Christina/Data Design & Technology Acad	34	Martin, Kimberly/Stovall EC-PK-K Sch	181
Manley, Julee/Sparta Elem Sch	27	Martin, Leslie/Blossom Elem Sch	260
Manley, William/Santo J Forte Jr High Sch	345	Martin, Ludi/Top of TX Accelerated Ed Ctr	307
Manlove, Kelly/Mary Carroll High Sch	304	Martin, Maya/Idea Academy-Rundberg	218
Mann, Casey/The Jane Justin Sch	359	**Martin, Melissa**/Francone Elem Sch	184
Mann, Karla/McWhorter Elem Sch	270	Martin, Melissa/Providence Classical Sch	206
Mann, Shelley/South Elem Sch	117	Martin, Patti/La Marque Primary Sch	161
Mann, Valerie/P M Akin Elem Sch	85	Martin, Shekita/Linden Kildare High Sch	70
Mans, Melanie/Mockingbird Elem Sch	102	Martin, Starla/Celina Elem Sch	78

Texas School Directory — PRINCIPAL INDEX

NAME/School	PAGE
Martin, Stephanie/*Barbers Hill Elem Sch North*	72
Martinak, Michael/*Bedford Junior High Sch*	353
Martinez-Munoz, Dyanne/*Health Science Academy*	42
Martinez, Amparo/*Hubbard Heights Elem Sch*	351
Martinez, Angelica/*Vanguard Academy-Beethoven*	13
Martinez, Anna/*Dr Malakoff Elem Sch*	387
Martinez, Antonio/*North Side High Sch*	351
Martinez, Beatris/*Classical Center at Vial Sch*	105
Martinez, Belen/*Memorial Middle Sch*	220
Martinez, Bertha/*About Face Alternative ES*	133
Martinez, Bertha/*Lamar Elem Sch*	133
Martinez, Candee/*Trinity Basin Prep-10th Street*	12
Martinez, Carolyn/*Southwest Prep New Directions [302]*	11
Martinez, Carolyn/*Southwest Prep Sch NE [302]*	11
Martinez, Celia/*Juan W Caceres Elem Sch*	215
Martinez, Criselda/*John F Kennedy Elem Sch*	216
Martinez, Daniel/*St Gregory the Great Cath Sch*	44
Martinez, Dawn/*St Anne Sch*	204
Martinez, Diana/*H B Zachry Elem Sch*	386
Martinez, Dora/*Resurrection Catholic Sch*	204
Martinez, Doreen/*Memorial Parkway Elem Sch*	152
Martinez, Edmond/*Clint Early College Academy*	132
Martinez, Eduardo/*Stillman Middle Sch*	64
Martinez, Elisa/*Carrizo Springs Elem Sch*	127
Martinez, Elizabeth/*Hutchins Elem Sch*	42
Martinez, Elsa/*Zapata Middle Sch*	407
Martinez, Esmeralda/*Odem Elem Sch*	331
Martinez, Gilbert/*Eastlake High Sch*	136
Martinez, Gloria/*Sarah King Elem Sch*	41
Martinez, Gracie/*La Encantada Elem Sch*	67
Martinez, Graciela/*John F Kennedy High Sch*	32
Martinez, Greg/*Five Palms Elem Sch*	42
Martinez, Hector/*Alex Sanger Elem Sch*	98
Martinez, Herlinda/*Our Lady of Guadalupe Sch*	388
Martinez, Imelda/*Don Jose Gallego Elem Sch*	386
Martinez, Israel/*Our Lady of Sorrows Sch*	226
Martinez, Jesus/*Seagoville Middle Sch*	102
Martinez, Jo/*Lovelady Jr Sr High Sch*	233
Martinez, Joanna/*Mimi Farley Elem Sch*	307
Martinez, John/*MacKenzie Middle Sch*	270
Martinez, Jose/*Morningside Elem Sch*	64
Martinez, Jose, Dr/*Watkins Middle Sch*	186
Martinez, Junior/*Seagraves Elem Sch*	157
Martinez, Katina/*Short Elem Sch*	345
Martinez, Lillian/*Arrow-Las Americas Lrng Ctr*	1
Martinez, Lorraine/*Dolphin Terrace Elem Sch*	137
Martinez, Louis/*Ysleta Community Learning Ctr*	138
Martinez, Lynn/*Las Yescas Elem Sch*	66
Martinez, Marci/*Cornerstone Christian Academy*	231
Martinez, Maribel/*Seco Mines Elem Sch*	277
Martinez, Marlen/*Ortiz Middle Sch*	190
Martinez, Martha/*Clendenin Elem Sch*	133
Martinez, Maryln/*Diamond Hill Elem Sch*	350
Martinez, Mayra/*Idea Clg Prep-Alamo*	218
Martinez, Nora/*Rangerville Elem Sch*	67
Martinez, Odilia/*Crossroads Alternative Center*	43
Martinez, Odilia/*Resnik Middle Sch*	43
Martinez, Oscar/*W A Meacham Middle Sch*	352
Martinez, Paul/*Calhoun Middle Sch*	121
Martinez, Peter/*MacArthur High Sch*	35
Martinez, Rachel/*Spring Shadows Elem Sch*	201
Martinez, Rick/*Excalibur Sch*	405
Martinez, Ricky/*Denver City High Sch*	405
Martinez, Robert/*Eastwood Knolls Elem Sch*	137
Martinez, Rosalba/*Sanchez-Ochoa Elem Sch*	387
Martinez, Rose/*MacArthur Elem-Interm Sch*	133
Martinez, Rose Ann/*Franklin HS 9th Grade Center*	134
Martinez, Rubelina/*Dr R E Margo Elem Sch*	225
Martinez, Sammy/*Murry Fly Elem Sch*	130
Martinez, Silvia/*Idea Academy-Weslaco Pike*	218
Martinez, Thelma/*Kennedy-Zapata Elem Sch*	388
Martinez, Tony/*Chillicothe High Sch*	177
Martinez, Tudon/*Coop Elem Sch*	190
Martinez, Victoria/*De Zavala Elem Sch*	189
Martinez, Victoria/*Flores-Zapata Elem Sch*	216
Maruska, Sherri/*Thrall Elem Sch*	400
Marvel, Doriane/*Laurel Mountain Elem Sch*	399
Marvin, Douglas/*Quest High Sch*	60
Marx, Karen/*Int'l Ldrshp TX-Garland HS*	108
Marx, Stacey/*Dartmouth Elem Sch*	112
Marz, Carrie/*Bane Elem Sch*	184
Mashburn, Lee/*Sinclair Elem Sch*	192
Masias, Abdullah/*Iman Academy-Southwest*	206
Masini, Scott/*Travis Elem Sch*	212
Mason, Carole/*French Elem Sch*	197
Mason, Courtney/*Krause Elem Sch*	385
Mason, Dale/*Greenville Middle Sch*	236
Mason, David/*Westfield High Sch*	203
Mason, Holly/*Mahaffey Elem Sch*	197
Mason, Joseph/*Palestine Jr High Sch*	15
Mason, MacKee/*Austin Achieve Public Sch*	1
Mason, Nicole/*South Athens Elem Sch*	213
Mason, Rhonda/*Mission West Elem Sch*	150
Massey, Harold/*Las Lomas Elem Sch*	35
Massey, Karla/*Montclair Elem Sch*	106
Massey, Sandi/*Thomas Jefferson High Sch*	103
Masten, Jennifer/*Trinity Basin Prep-Jefferson*	12
Masterson, Lee/*Center Intermediate Sch*	334
Masterson, Zach/*Hallie Randall Elem Sch*	380
Mata-Tausch, Adriana/*Henry Brauchle Elem Sch*	37
Mata, Saron/*Idea Academy-Elsa*	218
Mata, Suzanne/*Clearfork Elem Sch*	16
Matamoros, Erica/*Idea Academy-Brownsville*	217
Matejka, Karen/*Holy Cross Christian Academy*	249
Mathews, Antoinette/*J D Hall Learning Center*	110
Mathews, Lanny/*Deport Elem Sch*	260
Mathis, Lori/*Northside Elem Sch*	104
Mathis, Mark/*Paradise High Sch*	403
Mathis, Sara/*Jacksboro Middle Sch*	239
Mathis, Shabranda/*Whitney M Young Jr Elem Sch*	103
Mathis, Teresa/*Perrin-Whitt Elem Sch*	239
Mathis, Wendy/*Ronald Reagan Middle Sch*	108
Matias, Justin/*Our Lady of Victory Sch*	383
Matous, Stephanie/*Santa Clara Catholic Academy*	114
Matsumoto, Cheryl/*St Luke Sch*	169
Matt, Karen/*Madge Griffith Elem Sch*	52
Matthew, Jadie/*Dilley Early Clg High Sch*	157
Matthews, Jeff/*St Cecilia Catholic Sch*	204
Matthews, John/*Manor Senior High Sch*	371
Matthews, Terri/*Travis Elem Sch*	286
Mattic, Steven/*David K Sellars Elem Sch*	350
Mattingly, Chris/*Briarhill Middle Sch*	122
Mattingly, Jennifer/*McAuliffe Elem Sch*	123
Mattingly, Laura/*Harmony Sci Acad-Bryan [284]*	5
Mattson, Laurie/*Gateway College Prep Sch [292]*	3
Mauldin, Daniel/*Zamora Middle Sch*	43
Maumus, Amy/*St Paul's Preparatory Academy*	359
Maupin, Bruce/*Dodd City Sch*	145
Maw, Erica/*St Thomas' Episcopal Sch*	207
Maxson, Toby/*Heritage Elem Sch*	123
Maxwell, Eleanor/*Cibolo Creek Elem Sch*	254
May, Byron/*Travis Elem Sch*	165
May, Denise/*Big Springs Elem Sch*	112
May, Jimmy/*Perrin Alt Learning Center*	167
May, Julie/*Rogers Middle Sch*	41
May, Nicole/*Legacy Prep Charter Acad-Plano*	7
Mayer, Shelly/*Benbrook Elem Sch*	350
Mayer, Shonda/*Southcrest Christian Sch*	272
Mayes, Beatrice/*Beatrice Mayes Institute CS*	1
Mayes, Crystal/*Robert L Crippen Elem Sch*	294
Mayes, Kymberly/*Southwest Adventist Jr Academy*	116
Mayfield, Chris/*Lovejoy High Sch*	80
Mayfield, Dreama/*La Villita Elem Sch*	97
Mayfield, Gina/*Northbrook Elem Sch*	349
Maynard-Walter, Marva/*Daniels Academy of Science and*	107
Maynard, Patrick/*Lutheran High Sch*	45
Mayo, Jason, Dr/*Temple High Sch*	29
Mays, Chance, Dr/*Mt Enterprise Sch*	328
Mays, Chuck/*Crossroads Christian Academy*	358
Mays, Kassi/*Edgewood Middle Sch*	380

PRINCIPAL INDEX

Market Data Retrieval

NAME/School	PAGE	NAME/School	PAGE
Mays, Schretta/Village Technical Sch	14	McDaniel, Jeremy/Hemphill Middle Sch	329
Mays, Tara/Everette Lee Degolyer Elem Sch	100	McDaniel, Lucinda/Hearne Junior High Sch	325
Mc Mahon, Clint/Milano Junior High Sch	287	McDaniel, Russell/Celina Junior High Sch	78
McAdam, Rachel/San Jacinto Elem Sch	188	McDermand, Lawren/Mt Enterprise Sch	328
McAdams, Kia/Erma Nash Elem Sch	356	McDole, Daphne/Texas Preparatory Sch-Austin	12
McAdams, Michelle/Kay Granger Elem Sch	125	McDonald, Brent/Summer Creek High Sch	196
McAdoo, Alonzo/Cesar Chavez Middle Sch	282	McDonald, Cindy/First Baptist Christian Acad	205
McAfee, Amy/Crandall Middle Sch	251	McDonald, Jessica/J Lyndal Hughes Elem Sch	125
McAfee, Carolanne/St Michael Sch	87	McDonald, Kisha, Dr/T A Howard Middle Sch	357
McAlpin, Walter/Colmesneil High Sch	375	McDonald, Mark/Winona Middle Sch	339
McAlpine, Ross/Barbara Jordan Career Center	191	**McDonald, Michael**/Duncanville High Sch	104
McAnalley, Crystal/Harmony Sch Innov-Euless [284]	4	**McDonald, Natasha**/Sam & Ann Roach Middle Sch	80
McAuliffe, Jason/Hutto Middle Sch	396	McDonald, Shanieka/H I Holland ES-Lisbon	100
McAvoy, Julie/Donna Park Elem Sch	354	McDonald, Tashalon/Morton Elem Sch	344
McBee, Sally/Concordia Lutheran Sch	44	McDoniel, Emily/St John's Episcopal Sch	131
McBride, Tonya/Rspa Northshore	10	McDonough, Michael/Bellaire High Sch	193
McBrinn, Sheila/School for Young Children	207	McDowell, Cody/Sunray Elem Sch	296
McBroom, Casey/Tulia Junior High Sch	343	McDowell, James/Vidor High Sch	309
McCain, Caleb/Shiner High Sch	262	McDowell, Kim/Kemp Intermediate Sch	252
McCalister, Cassandra/Glencrest 6th Grade Middle Sch	350	McDowell, Sara/Pecan Ridge High Sch	289
McCallister, Betty/Apache Elem Sch	315	McElroy, Nancy/Johnson Elem Sch	252
McCanless, Steve/L W Kolarik 9th Grade Center	183	McElroy, Stephanie/Navarro Middle Sch	154
McCanlies, Mark/Richland High Sch	346	McEnerney, Sean/Spicer Alternative Ed Center	22
McCardell, Elisha/Idea Academy-Brackenridge	217	McEwen, Disa/Parsons Pre-K Sch	106
McCarter, Robbi/Brownsboro Elem Sch	213	McFarland, Danny/Sour Lake Elem Sch	178
McCarthy, Hailey/Idea Academy-South Flores	218	McGann, Mary/Rush Elem Sch	270
McCarthy, Mary/Wild Peach Elem Sch	52	McGee, Rhonda/Bluebonnet Elem Sch	354
McCarty, Keri/Bell Manor Elem Sch	354	McGee, Wendy/Purple Sage Elem Sch	187
McCarty, Sara/Tom Bean High Sch	168	McGehee, Shannon/Arthur L Davila Middle Sch	55
McCarty, Sara/Tom Bean Middle Sch	168	McGill, Casandra/Jourdanton Junior High Sch	20
McClain, Brent/Marilyn J Miller Elem Sch	356	McGilvray, Mike/Walden Sch	155
McClanahan, Alena/Lakeview Elem Sch	150	McGinnis, Rodney/Creekside Elem Sch	123
McClarren, Melodie/Academic Career Center	305	McGiothlin, Jody/Grace Christian Academy-Main	239
McClellen, Amy/Adella Young Elem Sch	198	McGlothlin, Jody/Grace Christian Academy-Brock	314
McClendon, Jacquelyn/Workman Junior High Sch	345	McGlothlin, Ross/East Terrell Hills Elem Sch	35
McClendon, Paula/Coldspring Intermediate Sch	330	McGowan, Jenny/I S Rogers Elem Sch	79
McClendon, Paula/James Street Elem Sch	330	McGowan, Karen/Mendez Elem Sch	212
McClendon, Troy/Lamar Elem Sch	165	McGrath, David/Paragon Prep Middle Sch	373
McClenny, Brian/Homer J Morris Middle Sch	221	**McGraw, Leeann**/Austin Elem Sch	323
McClinton, Lisa/KIPP Nexus MS [288]	7	McGraw, Leeann/Pecos Kindergarten	323
McClish, Sean/School at St George Place	194	McGrew, Brodrick/West Orange-Stark Middle Sch	309
McCloskey, Christyn/W I Stevenson Middle Sch	190	McGrew, Shayla/Silverlake Elem Sch	54
McCloud, Stephanie/Umphrey Lee Elem Sch	103	McGruder, Brittany/YES Prep Northline [312]	14
McClung, Cassie/Riverside Park Academy	41	McGruder, Sterlin/Garcia Young Men's Leadership	369
McClure, Charla/Kissam Elem Sch	337	**McGuinness, Catherine**/Martha Reid Elem Sch	357
McClure, Christopher/James Bowie Middle Sch	50	McGuire, Gail/Roth Elem Sch	197
McClure, Krista/Shorehaven Elem Sch	106	McGurk, Linda/St John's Episcopal Day Sch	226
McCollister, Alex/Whitharral Sch	230	McIlvoy, Tammy/Logos Preparatory Academy	155
McCollom, Kelly/C W Beasley Elem Sch	111	McInnis, Sherrie/Cayuga Sch	14
McCollum, Tiffany/Legacy Christian Academy	86	McIntire, Amy/Anson Elem Sch	249
McConnell, Stephanie/Hawkins Elem Sch	404	McIntyre, James/Constance Hulbert Elem Sch	137
McCord, Dena/Atlanta Elem Sch	69	**McIntyre, Rene**/Sheridan Elem Sch	185
McCord, Mark/Stockdick Jr High Sch	153	McKay, Shane/East Central High Sch	31
McCord, Robert/McCullough Junior High Sch	292	McKee, Jennifer/Kinkeade Early Childhood Sch	109
McCorkle, Tina/Don Jeter Elem Sch	51	McKeel, Trish/Chisholm Trail Interm Sch	355
McCormack, Ben/St Elmo Elem Sch	367	McKenna, Daniel/St Gabriel's Catholic Sch	372
McCormick, Debra/Christ the Redeemer Sch	73	McKenzie, Scott, Dr/Sam Rayburn Middle Sch	38
McCormick, Erica/River City Christian Sch	45	McKenzie, Shawn/Folks Middle Sch	37
McCormick, Paul/Cistercian Preparatory Sch	113	McKernan, Dawn, Dr/Robert M Beren Academy	207
McCoy, Cynthia/Robinson Junior High Sch	281	McKey, Lisa/Meyer Elem Sch	154
McCoy, Lesley/Ridgecrest Elem Sch	318	McKinney, Brandi/Bayless Elem Sch	270
McCoy, Mazie/Corpus Christi Catholic Sch	204	McKinney, Brenda/Ben Milam Elem Sch	64
McCoy, Michelle/Bulverde Creek Elem Sch	34	McKinney, Kimberle/Tomball Star Academy	203
McCracken, Geoff/Dayton High Sch	265	McKinney, Lynette/Sweeny Christian Sch	54
McCrae, Sarah/Medina Secondary Sch	23	McKneely, Curt/Miles Sch	326
McCraw, Brian/Rocksprings Sch	131	McKnight, Kimberly/Marlin Elem Sch	145
McCraw, Jolynne/Legacy Christian Academy	244	McLarty, Emily/Borman Elem Sch	121
McCrea, Cynthia/Bible Way Christian Academy	379	McLaughlin, Lisa/Deer Park Elem Sch	186
McCready, Erica/Houston Heights High Sch	5	McLaughlin, Thomas/St John's Sch	207
McCreight, Jeff/New Life Academy	272	McLaughlin, Tom/St Luke's Episcopal Sch	45
McCullum, Marquita/Lake Ridge Elem Sch	97	McLelland, Jennifer/Mva McAllen CHS [303]	8
McCutchen, Terry/Henrietta Junior High Sch	74	McLelland, Jennifer/South Plains CHS [303]	11
McCutcheon, Teresa/Spring Creek Elem Sch	106	McLeod, Angela/Canton Intermediate Sch	380

TX-U40   800-333-8802   School Year 2019-2020

Texas School Directory — PRINCIPAL INDEX

NAME/School	PAGE
McLerran, Delia/*Young Women's Leadership Acad*	41
McLerran, Delia/*Ywla Primary*	41
McMahan, Heather, Dr/*Int'l Ldrshp TX-College Sta*	108
McMains, Julia/*Rogene Worley Middle Sch*	357
McManus, Lisa/*Roosevelt Elem Sch*	192
McMaster, Jess/*Brazos Christian Sch*	56
McMillan, Kim/*Wylie East Elem Sch*	361
McMillion, Rebecca/*St John's Episcopal Sch*	362
McMullan, Kathi/*Agape Christian Academy*	300
McMullen, Jessica/*Jo Ann Ford Elem Sch*	395
McMullen, Kalee/*Kerr Middle Sch*	247
McMurtry, Elizabeth/*Chisholm Trail Elem Sch*	26
McNabb, Danny, Dr/*Ropes Sch*	229
McNally, Patty/*Preston Hollow Presby Sch*	116
McNatt, Tony/*Mt Pleasant Christian Sch*	364
McNeese, Leigh Ann/*Clifton Early Childhood Sch*	109
McNeese, Mitch/*Littlefield Junior High Sch*	261
McNeil, Faye, Dr/*Montgomery Elem Sch*	189
McNeill, Heather/*Premier HS-Texarkana [297]*	10
McNeill, Jerri/*Southside Elem Sch*	52
McNeill, Rodney/*Jack Lummus Interm Sch*	140
McNew, Stephanie/*Blaschke-Sheldon Elem Sch*	331
McNutt, Shelli/*Bremond Elem Sch*	324
McPherson, Scott, Dr/*Springtown High Sch*	313
McQueen, Joey/*Lampasas High Sch*	261
McReynolds, Darrell/*Northpointe Intermediate Sch*	203
McRorey, Joe/*Ingram Middle Sch*	255
McThompson, Robin/*Dragonfly International Sch*	212
McUllough, David/*Brownwood Accelerated High Sch*	58
McWashington, Kelli/*McCowan Middle Sch*	104
McWhorter, Thomas/*A Plus Up-Museum Campus*	1
McWilliams, Marron/*Jean McClung Middle Sch*	351
McWilliams, Michael/*Savannah Elem Sch*	121
McWilliams, Misty/*Roby Elem Sch*	148
McWilliams, Sondra/*Odom Elem Sch*	367
McWilliams, Tamara/*Ozona High Sch*	94
Meacham, Marsha/*Childress Junior High Sch*	74
Meacham, Marsha/*Gateway Academy*	74
Mead, Natalie/*Paloma Creek Elem Sch*	121
Meador, Jerry, Dr/*Woden Junior High Sch*	298
Meador, Tracy/*Arthur McNeil Elem Sch*	81
Meadore, Buffy/*Hillander Sch*	286
Meadows, Margaret/*Velasco Elem Sch*	52
Meadows, Melissa/*North Euless Elem Sch*	354
Means, Kristi/*Longview Early Graduation HS*	170
Means, Sherri/*Sparks Elem Sch*	200
Mease, Eva/*Life School Mountain Creek [290]*	8
Meave, George/*Del Valle Dist Alt Ed Program*	369
Meave, Yolanda/*Diaz-Villarreal Elem Sch*	219
Mebane, Rebecca/*Snyder Junior High Sch*	333
Mechell, Rebekah/*Bell's Hill Elem Sch*	282
Mechura, Marianne/*Our Lady Queen of Peace Sch*	54
Meckel, John/*Burleson Co Alt Sch*	59
Medaris, Joseph/*Lee A McShan Jr Elem Sch*	101
Medford, Bethany/*Cryar Intermediate Sch*	291
Medina, Daniel/*Canutillo Middle Sch*	132
Medina, Danny/*Ft Hancock Middle Sch*	234
Medina, David/*Pasodale Elem Sch*	138
Medina, Gerardo/*Almeda Elem Sch*	192
Medina, Jessie/*Moye Elem Sch*	133
Medina, Lou/*Stinson Middle Sch*	38
Medina, Miriam/*Scarborough Elem Sch*	191
Medlow, Henva/*Don Carter Elem Sch*	153
Medrano, Gabriel/*Anna Education Center*	77
Meek, Amy/*Crestview Elem Sch*	321
Meek, Heather/*Bridge Point Elem Sch*	370
Meek, Julie/*Nesmith Elem Sch*	78
Meeks, Chad/*Key Sch*	359
Meeks, Greg/*Newcomer Center*	344
Meeks, Greg/*Venture High Sch*	345
Meeks, Lauren/*Parkside Elem Sch*	397
Mehaffey, Christina/*Faustina Academy*	115
Mein, John/*St Mary Elem Sch*	163
Meister, Denise/*Hinojosa EC-PK-K Sch*	181
Mejia, Jose/*Zavala Elem Sch*	367
Mejia, Sylvia/*Idea Academy-Weslaco*	218
Melancon, Ann/*Copeland Elem Sch*	184
Melancon, Christine/*Gleason Elem Sch*	184
Melchor, Melissa/*Oates Elem Sch*	190
Meldahl, Sonya/*Christ Community Sch*	295
Melendez, Diaka/*Spring High Sch*	202
Melendez, Julie/*Canutillo Elem Sch*	132
Melendez, Mark/*Hutchinson Elem Sch*	154
Melendez, Michelle/*Harmony Sch Exc-El Paso [284]*	4
Melms, Joseph/*Young Mens Leadership Academy*	108
Melton, Jeremy/*O P Norman Junior High Sch*	252
Mena, Shawn/*Franklin High Sch*	134
Menchaca, Leticia/*Trautmann Middle Sch*	388
Menchaca, Sergio/*Bandera High Sch*	23
Menchaca, Sergio/*Bowie High Sch*	290
Mendez, Christopher/*Whiteface High Sch*	75
Mendez, Jesus/*Mission Ridge Elem Sch*	136
Mendez, Jorge/*Plains High Sch*	406
Mendez, Marisa/*Nelson Early Chldhd Ed Ctr*	41
Mendez, Michelle/*St Jose Sanchez Del Rio Sch*	44
Mendez, Ofelia/*Maedgen Elem Sch*	270
Mendez, Ortencia/*Tierra Blanca Elem Sch*	119
Mendez, Ortencia/*West Central Elem Sch*	119
Mendoza, Ana/*Excellence In Leadership Acad*	3
Mendoza, Cassandra/*J W Nixon High Sch*	386
Mendoza, Hilda/*Lloyd M Bentsen Elem Sch*	220
Mendoza, John/*Disciplinary Alt Ed Program*	215
Mendoza, Margarita/*Glen Cove Elem Sch*	138
Mendoza, Maribel/*Our Lady of Mt Carmel Elem Sch*	204
Mendoza, Michael/*Bassett Middle Sch*	134
Mendoza, Rachel/*Bonham Early Ed Sch*	107
Mendoza, Raul/*Eastwood Heights Elem Sch*	137
Menendez, David/*Eiland Elem Sch*	197
Meneses, Julie/*Bonnie Ellison Elem Sch*	36
Mengwasser, Brad/*Bedford Heights Elem Sch*	353
Mengwasser, Doreen/*Meadow Creek Elem Sch*	354
Mercan, Serit/*Harmony Sch Bus-Dallas [284]*	4
Merchant, Afreen/*Harmony Sci Acad-Sugar Land [284]*	5
Merchant, Diane/*Mainland Prep Classical Acad [297]*	8
Mercury-Owens, Jacqueline/*Clay Classical Academy [297]*	2
Merfa, Roxanne/*Parkland Elem Sch*	138
Merilatt, Courtney/*Garfield Elem Sch*	199
Merkel, Holli/*Itasca Elem Sch*	228
Merrell, Kendra/*Bob Lewis Elem Sch*	36
Merrell, Stefanie/*Shive Elem Sch*	394
Merrett, Luella/*Luella Merrett Elem Sch*	351
Merricks, Michelle/*Emery Elem Sch*	184
Merrill, John/*Montgomery Elem Sch*	35
Merritt, Lakisha/*Martin Weiss Elem Sch*	101
Merriweather, Tiffany/*West Hardin Elem Sch*	178
Meshell, Kelly/*Gilbert Gerdes Jr High Sch*	61
Meshell, Stephanie/*Cypress Ridge High Sch*	184
Messenger, Melissa/*Marshall Kendricks Middle Sch*	199
Messer, Jason/*Central Baptist Academy*	295
Messer, Kent/*Willow Springs Middle Sch*	80
Metcalf, James/*Davis 9th Grade Sch*	180
Metcalfe, Monnie/*Rice Intermediate Middle Sch*	300
Metz, Mike/*Tomball Memorial High Sch*	203
Metzinger, Kathryn, Dr/*Northlake Elem Sch*	106
Meyer, Margie/*Fort Bend Baptist Academy ES*	155
Meyer, Renee/*Dr Antonio Banuelos Elem Sch*	187
Meyer, Sara/*Wells Elem Sch*	83
Meyer, Suzy, Dr/*Crosswinds Accelerated HS*	107
Meyers, Ena/*Diane Patrick Elem Sch*	344
Meza, Maria/*Glenoaks Elem Sch*	37
Micallef, Mark/*Edinburg North High Sch*	216
Michaels, Kristi/*KIPP Austin Beacon Prep [286]*	6
Michaleson, Micheal/*Lockney Elem Sch*	149
Michaud, Troy/*Harvey S Brown Elem Sch*	183
Middlebrooks, Kristin/*Palmer Middle Sch*	142
Middleton, Allison/*Itasca High Sch*	228
Middleton, Bob/*La Vernia Christian Agape Acad*	401
Middleton, Gail/*Leon Elem Sch*	264
Mieth, Rhonda/*Rockport-Fulton High Sch*	19
Mihleder, Stephanie/*Page Middle Sch*	41

PRINCIPAL INDEX

NAME/School	PAGE
Mijares, Betsy/Burley Primary Sch	18
Mike Reyes, Gutierrez/Gutierriez Middle Sch	65
Mike, Tiffany/T H Rogers Sch	194
Mikeal, Laura/W F Peavy Primary Sch	17
Mikkelsen, Kristi/W W Pinkerton Elem Sch	98
Mikolajczyk, Laura/Charlotte Elem Sch	20
Miksch, Brett/Johnson High Sch	211
Miles, Christine/Dr Nixon Elem Sch	133
Miles, Cynthia/Texans Can Acad Dallas Oak Clf [305]	11
Miles, Dana/Pearland Jr High School West	53
Miller, Aaron, Dr/Christian Life Center Academy	205
Miller, Allison/Norma J Paschal Elem Sch	173
Miller, Amy/Sheffield Primary Elem Sch	97
Miller, Andrew/Moody High Sch	281
Miller, Ashley/Miller Elem Sch	79
Miller, Ashley/Rspa-Channelview	10
Miller, Barry/Parmer Lane Elem Sch	372
Miller, Beth/Summit Christian Academy	254
Miller, Byron/Hamshire Fannett Elem Sch	242
Miller, Chad/Ore City Elem Sch	377
Miller, Chris/Blue Ridge High Sch	77
Miller, Cindy/Three Rivers Elem Sch	268
Miller, Clint/Chisum High Sch	259
Miller, Cody/Hidden Forest Elem Sch	35
Miller, Damenion/Winona High Sch	339
Miller, Donisha/Poteet Elem Sch	21
Miller, Elizabeth/Cesar Chavez Elem Sch	124
Miller, Elizabeth/Colin Powell 6th Grade Center	124
Miller, Elizabeth/Swenke Elem Sch	185
Miller, Grant/Scurry Rosser Middle Sch	253
Miller, James/Encino Park Elem Sch	35
Miller, Jason/Cedar Hill High Sch	97
Miller, Jason/Everman Joe C Bean High Sch	349
Miller, Jennifer/Alternative Learning Center	402
Miller, Jessie/Keiko Davidson Elem Sch	152
Miller, John/Cross Roads High Sch	214
Miller, Julie/Patterson Elem Sch	292
Miller, Kardel/Windsong Ranch Elem Sch	84
Miller, Karl/Odessa Career Tch Early Clg HS	130
Miller, Kendall/E M Daggett Elem Sch	350
Miller, Laura/Kermit Junior High Sch	402
Miller, Leah/Clements-Parsons Elem Sch	92
Miller, Lynette/Hastings High Sch	182
Miller, Mindy/Parkview Elem Sch	349
Miller, Natalie/Edris Childres Elliot Elem Sch	79
Miller, Nikki/H G Temple Elem Sch	17
Miller, Nikki/H G Temple Intermediate Sch	17
Miller, Queinnise/Marshall Middle Sch	192
Miller, Rheatha/Foundation School for Autism [297]	3
Miller, Shawn/Raymond Cooper Junior High Sch	85
Miller, Shenequa/Commerce Middle Sch	236
Miller, Stefanie/Spurger High Sch	375
Miller, Stephanie/Laura Bush Elem Sch	199
Miller, Susan/Murchison Elem Sch	214
Miller, Susanne/Olson Elem Sch	77
Miller, Tom/Brooks-Quinn Jones Elem Sch	298
Miller, Tonya/Challenge Early Clg High Sch	191
Miller, Wendy/Harry C Withers Elem Sch	100
Milliner, Rodney/Texans Can Academy-Grant East [305]	12
Mills, Brent/Woodson Sch	363
Mills, Carlette/West Rusk Elem Sch	328
Mills, Keith/Center Point High Sch	255
Mills, Keith/Center Point Middle Sch	255
Mills, Marsha/La Poynor Sch	214
Mills, Monica/Rodriguez Elem Sch	367
Mills, Scott/McCord Elem Sch	394
Mills, Wendy/Norman Elem Sch	368
Mills, Wendy/Sims Elem Sch	368
Mims, Aleia/Uplift Summit Int'l Prep CS [309]	13
Mims, Charles/Rio Vista High Sch	248
Mims, Deedee/New Hope Christian Academy	86
Miner, Pam/Highland Elem Sch	343
Minix, Melissa/Smithfield Elem Sch	346
Minn, Jeff/Victory Place at Coppell	98
Minter, Leslie/Heritage Christian Academy	326
Minton, Ashley/Canyon Ranch Elem Sch	98
Minyard, Rusty/Evadale High Sch	240
Minyen, Valerie/Compass Academy Charter Sch	2
Mira, Jose/Isabel Pierce Sem Elem Sch	79
Miranda, Alicia/Myrtle Cooper Elem Sch	136
Miranda, Fernando/H D Hilley Elem Sch	136
Miranda, Francisco/Nimitz High Sch	110
Miranda, Vanessa/Escuela Montessori-Del Valle	139
Mireles, Carol/Premier HS-Del Rio [297]	9
Mireles, Sherry/Ed Rawlinson Middle Sch	37
Mireles, Tina/Morrill Elem Sch	33
Mishler, Julia/Wellborn Middle Sch	56
Missildine, Justin/Career & Tech Education Center	34
Mitchell, Allison/Panhandle Elem Sch	69
Mitchell, Bridget/Jay Thompson Elem Sch	111
Mitchell, Cathryn/Gorzycki Middle Sch	369
Mitchell, Chavis/Parker Elem Sch	194
Mitchell, Glenn, Dr/Memorial High Sch	243
Mitchell, Judy/Phoenix Learning Center	212
Mitchell, Kalley/Dublin Elem Sch	143
Mitchell, Leah/Stanton Elem Sch	274
Mitchell, Leslye/Highland Village Elem Sch	123
Mitchell, Rachel/Faith Christian Academy	205
Mitchell, Reginal/Thornton Middle Sch	185
Mitchell, Richard/Family Christian Academy	115
Mitchell, Shanica/Young Elem Sch	193
Mitchell, Susan/Beckham Elem Sch	344
Mitchell, Tena/Lakeland Christian Academy	126
Mitzner, Kris, Dr/Tays Junior High Sch	153
Mixer, Blanca/Community of Faith Chrn Sch	139
Mixon, Carol/Canyon Creek Elem Sch	112
Mize, Carol Jo/McLennan Co State Juvenile Sch	8
Mize, Michael/Alba-Golden Jr Sr High Sch	404
Mizell, Matthew/Trinidad Sch	215
Moad, Angie/Gonzales Elem Sch	130
Moeller, Arron/Martha Hunt Elem Sch	83
Moes, Mathew/Iant Quranic Academy	115
Moffatt, Alison/Live Oak Classical Sch	282
Moffett, Daryle/Crowley High Sch	347
Moffitt, Kristin/Westwood-Bales Elem Sch	160
Mogan, Christopher/Decatur High Sch	403
Mohler, Elizabeth/Rutledge Elem Sch	397
Mohler, Holly/School for the Highly Gifted	108
Molina, Amanda/Anderson Mill Elem Sch	398
Molina, Armando/Francisco S Lara Academy	386
Molina, Dora/Blanton Elem Sch	367
Molina, Jose/Spur Sch	127
Molina, Lupe/Allison Elem Sch	366
Molina, Theresa/Karnes City Junior High Sch	250
Molina, Tiffany/Harmony Sch Innov-Austin [284]	4
Molina, Yesena/Edinburg High Sch	216
Molina, Yulia/Dorothy Thompson Middle Sch	224
Molinar, Lorena/Ft Hancock High Sch	234
Molinares, Mary/Arlington Park ECC	99
Molyneaux, Stacey/Blanton Elem Sch	130
Monaghan, Susan/Westbury High Sch	193
Mondik, Mayra/Lamar Middle Sch	369
Mondragon, Mario/Esperanza Medrano Elementary	100
Monrreal, Raymundo/Jaime Escalante Middle Schl	223
Montalbano, Ginger/Duchesne Acad of Sacred Heart	204
Montalvo, Michelle/Caldwell Heights Elem Sch	398
Montalvo, Nicole/Greenbriar Elem Sch	350
Montana, Erika/Friona High Sch	315
Montana, Thomasina/Freedom Elem Sch	43
Montanio, Tracie/Larkspur Elem Sch	397
Montano, James/Jubilee Highland Park [285]	6
Monte, Ernesto/Presidio Elem Sch	320
Montelongo, Alvaro/Looscan Elem Sch	189
Montelongo, Amanda/Lauro Cavazos Elem Sch	130
Montelongo, Bardo/Wayside Sci-Tech Preparatory	14
Montelongo, John/Hightower High Sch	150

Texas School Directory — PRINCIPAL INDEX

NAME/School	PAGE
Montelongo, Jose/*Drs Reed & Mock Elem Sch*	223
Montemayor, Adrian/*San Perlita Sch*	394
Montemayor, David, Dr/*Crawford Elem Sch*	216
Montemayor, Evelia/*Roy P Benavidez Elem Sch*	42
Montemayor, Sara/*Katherine Tarver Elem Sch*	387
Montes, Alexandra/*Western Hills Elem Sch*	352
Montes, Juan/*Francisca Alvarez Elem Sch*	221
Montes, Terry/*Lee Elem Sch*	133
Montez, Jeremiah/*Hfa-Alameda Sch-Art & Design*	5
Montgomery, Phoebe/*Reinhardt Elem Sch*	102
Montgomery, Virdie/*Wylie High Sch*	85
Montoya, Claudia/*Dalhart Elem Sch*	95
Montoya, Linda/*Jones Elem Sch*	55
Moody, Bethany/*Birdwell Elem Sch*	338
Moody, Charles/*The Goodwill Excel Center*	12
Moody, Denise/*Mae Smythe Elem Sch*	199
Moody, John/*Southmore Intermediate Sch*	200
Mooney, Karen/*Weatherford Christian Sch*	314
Mooney, Sean/*St Joseph Catholic Sch*	263
Moore, Billy/*William G Gravitt Jr High Sch*	405
Moore, David/*Viola M Coleman High Sch*	286
Moore, Diana/*Diboll Primary Sch*	17
Moore, Eric/*Effie Morris Elem Sch*	356
Moore, Frances/*Washington Early Childhood Ctr*	209
Moore, Hollis/*Brady Alternative Sch*	277
Moore, Karla/*Alvarado Elem South Sch*	246
Moore, Kathy/*Seminole Primary Sch*	158
Moore, Keith/*Campbell Elem Sch*	367
Moore, Kelley/*Mel Parmley Elem Sch*	294
Moore, Kelly/*Van Alstyne Middle Sch*	168
Moore, Kristane/*Pittsburg Junior High Sch*	68
Moore, Lina/*Bloomington Senior High Sch*	381
Moore, Lola/*Carpenter Elem Sch*	298
Moore, Marilisa/*Crockett Elem Sch*	314
Moore, Marlo/*Connally Primary Sch*	279
Moore, Marty/*Van Intermediate Sch*	381
Moore, Michelle/*Thornton Elem Sch*	29
Moore, Mitchell/*Brownwood High Sch*	58
Moore, Monica/*Velma Penny Elem Sch*	337
Moore, Roy/*Nottingham Elem Sch*	201
Moore, Shauna/*Newman Int'l Acad-Grace*	8
Moore, Shawna/*Nueces Canyon Elem Sch*	131
Moore, Shawna/*Nueces Canyon Jr Sr High Sch*	131
Moore, Shona/*Brady Middle Sch*	277
Moore, Steven/*Maude I Logan Elem Sch*	351
Moore, Susan/*Northwest Special Program Ctr*	125
Moore, Travis/*Danny Jones Middle Sch*	356
Moore, Wendy/*Rebecca Creek Elem Sch*	88
Mora, Carlos/*Jose De Escandon Elem Sch*	221
Mora, Sonya/*Gates Elem Sch*	40
Morales, Ana/*H V Helbing Elem Sch*	350
Morales, Angelee/*Royse City Middle Sch*	326
Morales, Delisa/*KIPP Camino Academy [289]*	6
Morales, Edward/*Albany Jr Sr High Sch*	334
Morales, Ernesto/*Lydia Patterson Institute*	139
Morales, Luke/*Navarro Junior High Sch*	173
Morales, Maeloisa/*Blake Manor Elem Sch*	371
Morales, Marco/*J T Brackenridge Elem Sch*	40
Morales, Nelllie/*La Fe Preparatory Sch*	7
Morales, Nora/*Harmony Sch Exploration-Houstn [284]*	4
Morales, Osvaldo/*Premier HS-El Paso East [297]*	9
Morales, Yvett/*Weslaco High Sch*	225
Moran, Clifton/*Arch H McCulloch Interm Sch*	108
Moran, Katie/*Grace E Hardeman Elem Sch*	346
Moran, Michael/*Woodrow Wilson High Sch*	104
Moran, Tammie/*Franklin Elem Sch*	189
Moran, Tania/*H B Gonzalez Elem Sch*	32
Mordecai, Claudia/*Centerville Jr Sr High Sch*	264
Moreno-Hewitt, Andrea, Dr/*Natalia High Sch*	284
Moreno, Adrian/*Career Center East*	122
Moreno, Carlos/*Jubilee Brownsville [285]*	6
Moreno, Cynthia/*Robert F Koennecke Elem Sch*	174
Moreno, Leann/*Springdale Elem Sch*	352
Moreno, Maria/*Las Americas Newcomer Mid Sch*	194
Moreno, Michael/*Perez Elem Sch*	64
Moreno, Ramiro/*Rio Hondo Middle Sch*	66
Moreno, TJ/*Creedmoor Elem Sch*	369
Morgan, Arthurlyn/*Sue Crouch Intermediate Sch*	348
Morgan, Bill/*Malakoff High Sch*	214
Morgan, Brad/*Tolar Junior High Sch*	231
Morgan, Christopher/*James E Taylor High Sch*	152
Morgan, Jennifer/*Trinity Episcopal Sch*	373
Morgan, Keith/*Naumann Elem Sch*	397
Morgan, Ladonna/*Walnut Creek Private Sch*	359
Morgan, Larry/*Lubbock Adult Learning Center*	8
Morgan, Lindsay/*Tolar High Sch*	231
Morgan, Rhonda/*Madisonville Jr High Sch*	274
Morgan, Scott/*Jollyville Elem Sch*	399
Morman, Katie/*St Jo High Sch*	290
Mormon, Janet/*Jack Frost Elem Sch*	395
Morphis, Jill/*Clyde Intermediate Sch*	62
Morren, Wayne/*Floydada High Sch*	148
Morrill, Kyle/*Trinity Christian Academy*	116
Morris, Andrew/*Valley Hi Elem Sch*	39
Morris, Bailey/*Swift Elem Sch*	345
Morris, Becky/*Challenger Elem Sch*	53
Morris, Christina/*North Belt Elem Sch*	196
Morris, Connie/*Cedar Valley Elem Sch*	27
Morris, Debbie/*Glen Rose Elem Sch*	340
Morris, Jennifer/*Ector Sch*	146
Morris, Jenny/*St Michaels Episcopal Sch*	56
Morris, Kelsie/*Kostoryz Elem Sch*	303
Morris, Laura/*A P Beutel Elem Sch*	52
Morris, Lora/*Larry G Smith Elem Sch*	101
Morris, Marley, Dr/*Career & Technical Ed Center*	195
Morris, Shaunte/*W C Cunningham Middle Sch*	187
Morris, Stacy/*Mineola Elem Sch*	404
Morris, Tammy/*Krum Early Education Center*	122
Morris, Taylor/*Dr Ralph H Poteet High Sch*	111
Morris, Valorie/*Teague Elem Sch*	200
Morris, Vance/*Burkburnett High Sch*	391
Morris, Wendy/*Prestonwood Christian Academy*	86
Morrison-Adams, Jeana/*Floyd Hoffman Middle Sch*	181
Morrison-Adams, Jeana/*Ruby M Reed Academy*	180
Morrison, Brooke/*Texas Leadership CS-Arlington*	12
Morrison, Kevin/*Hillcrest Elem Sch*	243
Morrison, Shannon/*North Ridge Elem Sch*	269
Morrison, Vicky/*James L Collins Catholic Sch*	300
Morrissey, Paul/*Compass Rose Academy*	2
Morrow, Chris/*Blanket Sch*	58
Morrow, Joe/*Texas School of the Arts [306]*	12
Morrow, Lenny/*Sands Sch*	117
Morrow, Ray/*La Grange Intermediate Sch*	147
Morrow, Steve/*Whitewright High Sch*	168
Morton, Cynthia/*McKinney Daep Learning Center*	81
Morton, Kellye/*Rita Smith Elem Sch*	85
Moseley, Doyle/*Liberty Baptist Sch*	126
Moseley, Oralia/*Anthony Elem Sch*	131
Moser, Lacey/*Hart Elem Sch*	80
Moses, Britani, Dr/*Lavace Stewart Elem Sch*	159
Moses, Franklin/*J Frank Dobie High Sch*	199
Moses, Lee/*Rogers High Sch*	29
Moses, Rene/*Jack D Johnson Elem Sch*	347
Mosher, Ronnie/*Woodcreek Elem Sch*	153
Mosley, James/*YES Prep North Forest [312]*	14
Mosley, Kevin/*Legacy Christian Academy*	86
Mosley, Lori/*Rankin Elem Sch*	345
Moss, Corey/*Our Redeemer Lutheran Sch*	116
Moss, Leigh/*Austin Discovery Academy*	1
Moss, Ramon/*Carnegie-Vanguard High Sch*	191
Mosty, Elise/*Classical Center-Brandenburg*	105
Motley, Clark/*Victoria East High Sch*	382
Motomura, Julie/*Bridge City Intermediate Sch*	308
Moton, Gladys/*Griggs EC-PK-K Sch*	181
Moton, Gladys/*Jones EC-PK-K Sch*	181
Mott, Caroline/*Hearne High Sch*	325
Mott, Stephanie/*Int'l Ldrshp TX-Wml-Orem HS*	109
Motzny, Heather/*Sampson Elem Sch*	185
Moussavi, Paul/*Beckendorff Junior High Sch*	151
Mowles, Robert/*Columbia High Sch*	52

School Year 2019-2020

PRINCIPAL INDEX

Market Data Retrieval

NAME/*School*	PAGE	NAME/*School*	PAGE
Moya, Gabriel/*Pease Communication/Tech Acad*	286	Myers, Ron/*Byron Nelson High Sch*	124
Moye, Alan/*Woodcreek Middle Sch*	196	Myers, Tad/*Farmersville Intermediate Sch*	78
Moynihan, Julie/*West Handley Elem Sch*	352	Myers, Tracy/*Hidden Cove Elem Sch*	43
Muceus, Courtney/*First Colony Middle Sch*	150	Myles, Sherqueena/*Inspired Vision Elem Sch [272]*	5
Muckleroy, Jana/*Central Heights Elem Sch*	297	**Mynyk, Ted**/*N A Howry Intermediate Sch*	356
Mudgett, Linda/*Bay Area Christian Sch*	162	**N**	
Muehling, Kristina/*Bryker Woods Elem Sch*	367		
Muele, Pauline/*Indian Ridge Middle Sch*	138	Nabi, Gretchen/*Clarkston Elem Sch*	338
Mueller, Carol/*Redeemer Lutheran Sch*	373	**Nabors, Jennifer**/*O M Roberts Elem Sch*	52
Mueller, David/*St Paul Lutheran Sch*	288	Nagir, Rick/*Brookline Elem Sch*	192
Muhammad, Rashad/*Crowley Learning Center*	348	Nagpal, Divya/*L A Morgan Elem Sch*	160
Mulcahy, Heather/*Jeanette Hayes Elem Sch*	152	Nail, Krista/*Spicewood Park Elem Sch*	43
Muldrew, Jeanne/*Turning Point Secondary Sch*	345	Nail, Tawnya/*Madisonville Intermediate Sch*	273
Mulkey, Jacquelyn/*Focus Academy*	155	Najera, Desi/*Faith Christian Academy*	68
Mull, Sheri/*Wooldridge Elem Sch*	368	Nall, Susan/*Snow Heights Elem Sch*	346
Mullens, Eric/*Hempstead High Sch*	384	Nandayapa, Oscar/*F P Caillet Elem Sch*	100
Mullican, Tim/*McMichael Middle Sch*	298	Nandlal, Carmilla/*Mahanay Elem Sch*	182
Mullin, Beverly/*Coram Deo Academy-Dallas*	114	Nanny, Dwin/*Panther Creek Sch*	76
Mullins, Julie/*Thomas Arnold Elem Sch*	29	Narcisse, Deanna/*Leo A Rizzuto Elem Sch*	198
Mullins, Nancy/*Mid-Valley Christian Sch*	226	**Narcisse, Tiffany**/*Fondren Middle Sch*	193
Mumphord, Karen/*Susannah Dickinson Elem Sch*	154	Narvaez, Jennifer/*Colbert Elem Sch*	265
Mumphrey, Nikita/*Bramlette Elem Sch*	169	Narvaez, Rose, Dr/*Toltech T-STEM Academy*	32
Muniz, Valerie/*Westchester Acad Int'l Studies*	201	Nash, Charles/*Whitewright Middle Sch*	168
Munne, Robert/*Faith Christian Academy*	226	Nash, Christy/*Wichita Falls High Sch*	393
Munoz, Carlos/*A B Duncan Elem Sch*	148	Nash, Patrick/*Discipline Alt Education Pgrm*	97
Munoz, Liz/*Townley Elem Sch*	110	Nasra, Michael, Dr/*Kingwood High Sch*	196
Munoz, Lorenzo/*Raymond Telles/Lafarelle MS*	133	Nasser, Nahla/*St Stephen's Episcopal Sch*	207
Munoz, Maria/*MacArthur Elem Sch*	187	**Nathan, Frymark**/*O H Stowe Elem Sch*	346
Munoz, Martin/*William J Clinton Elem Sch*	220	Nation, Brian/*Hughes Springs High Sch*	70
Munoz, Mindy, Dr/*Creekside Park Jr High Sch*	203	Natividad, Lakshmi/*Lewisville Elem Sch*	123
Munoz, Monica/*Las Palmas Elem Sch*	32	**Nava, Juan**/*Terry High Sch*	154
Munoz, Patricia/*Central Middle Sch*	225	**Nava, Lionel**/*Cesar Chavez Academy*	137
Munoz, Tiffany/*Blooming Grove Elem Sch*	299	**Navaja, Brenda**/*Gilbert Willie Sr Elem Sch*	253
Munoz, Yadira/*Benito Martinez Elem Sch*	234	**Navaja, Brenda**/*Herman Furlough Jr Middle Sch*	253
Munoz, Yvonne/*Wortham Oaks Elem Sch*	34	Navar, Jacquelyn/*Ollie Perry Storm Elem Sch*	41
Munro, Neil/*Fairmont Junior High Sch*	186	**Navarro, Alonda**/*Robert E Lee Elem Sch*	217
Munscher, Jessica/*St Martha Catholic Sch*	204	Navarro, Michelle/*Travis Heights Elem Sch*	367
Munson, Glenda/*Dr Joe Bernal Middle Sch*	37	Navarro, Rosalinda/*Magin Rivas Elem Sch*	215
Murati, Klediol/*Harmony Sci Acad-Beaumont [284]*	5	Navin, Billy/*Kallison Elem Sch*	37
Murati, Klediol/*Harmony Sci Acad-San Antonio [284]*	5	Nazworth, Steven/*Venus Elem Sch*	249
Murdock, Cheryl/*Carroll Elem Sch*	299	Nazworth, Steven/*Venus Primary Sch*	249
Murff, Janel/*Medina Elem Sch*	23	Neal, Celeste/*Joshua High Sch*	248
Murillo, Josefina/*Eladio Martinez Learning Ctr*	100	Neal, Clarice/*Lifestyle Christian Sch*	295
Murphey, Amy/*Nocona Middle Sch*	290	Neal, Francesca/*Raba Elem Sch*	38
Murphy, Angel/*Memorial 9th Grade Academy*	243	Neal, Jen/*Basis San Antonio Prim-Med Ctr [011]*	1
Murphy, David/*Onalaska Elem Sch*	317	Neal, Tyler/*Trinity Christian Jr Sr HS*	272
Murphy, Elizabeth/*Parker Elem Sch*	160	Neatherlin, Jenifer/*Llano High Sch*	268
Murphy, Kim/*Bullard Primary Sch*	337	Necessary, Casey/*Friendship Elem Sch*	355
Murphy, Lance/*Barbers Hill Middle Sch North*	72	Nederveld, Julie/*Serene Hills Elem Sch*	371
Murphy, Mandi/*Hilltop Elem Sch*	120	Neeb, Denise/*Williams Elem Sch*	271
Murphy, Margaret/*Cornerstone Elem Sch*	150	Neeb, Phillip/*Honey Elem Sch*	270
Murphy, Nikki/*Meridith-Dunbar EC Academy*	29	Needham, Jana/*Cambridge Elem Sch*	30
Murphy, Patrick/*Iredell Sch*	47	Neeley, Shawn/*Midway Alternative High Sch*	321
Murphy, Shaye/*Slaton High Sch*	272	Neely, Sharon/*Faith Christian Sch*	358
Murphy, Sheri/*Timber Creek Elem Sch*	317	Negrete, Angelica/*Hart Elem Sch*	133
Murray, Jennifer/*Ross Baldwin Elem Sch*	367	**Nehls, Jill**/*Bentley Elem Sch*	153
Murray, Tonya/*Annie Sims Elem Sch*	363	Nehls, Jill/*Jane Long Elem Sch*	154
Murrell, Kellee/*St Philip's Episcopal Sch*	116	**Neidert, Amy**/*Terrell Elem Sch*	166
Murrell, Mark, Dr/*The Woodlands-College Park HS*	292	Neighbors, Matthew/*Austin Middle Sch*	160
Murry, Stacie/*Markham Elem Sch*	276	Neinast, Terry/*Faith Academy*	383
Murski, Elizabeth/*Dallas Academy*	115	Neisner, Shana/*Columbus Elem Sch*	87
Musgrove, Ronald/*Central High Sch*	17	Nelms-Harris, Valerie/*James Bilhartz Jr Elem Sch*	105
Musselwhite, Mandy/*Aledo Middle Sch*	312	Nelson, Blake/*Heartlight Boarding Sch*	209
Mussey, Reba/*Deep Wood Elem Sch*	398	Nelson, Elizabeth/*Texas Online Preparatory Sch*	383
Mustin, Denise/*Cravens Early Childhood Acad*	200	Nelson, Heidi/*Silver Creek Elem Sch*	345
Mutscher, Travis/*Ridgeview Middle Sch*	399	Nelson, Inetra/*Minshew Elem Sch*	81
Muzquiz, Blanca/*Robert E Lee Elem Sch*	277	Nelson, Julie/*Linda Herrington Elem Sch*	399
Myatt, Jason/*Brentfield Elem Sch*	112	Nelson, Kendra, Dr/*Crosstimbers Academy*	2
Myers, Byron/*Midland Christian Sch*	286	Nelson, Kristy/*Trinity Episcopal Sch*	383
Myers, Chrystal/*Trinity School of Midland*	286	Nelson, Laryn/*Beacon Hill Academy*	39
Myers, Matt/*Curington Elem Sch*	254	**Nelson, Matthew**/*Small Middle Sch*	369
Myers, Norma/*South Loop Elem Sch*	138	Nelson, Sara/*Purple Sage Elem Sch*	399
Myers, Patricia/*Moore Elem Sch*	185	Nelson, Sunday/*Dr Joe Ward Elem Sch*	37

Texas School Directory — PRINCIPAL INDEX

NAME/School	PAGE
Nelson, Susan/*Franklin Middle Sch*	325
Nerren, Cindy/*Trout Primary Sch*	18
Nettles, Jared/*Livingston Junior High Sch*	317
Nettles, Steven/*Westwood High Sch*	16
Neudorf, Ramona/*Hart Junior Senior High Sch*	71
Neuenfeldt, Randolph/*Business Careers High Sch*	36
Neusch, Nancy/*Northwest Elem Sch*	119
Nevarez, Juan/*Juan Seguin Elem Sch*	221
Nevenglosky, Erica/*Covenant Preparatory Sch*	205
Nevermann, Annette/*Lakeshore Elem Sch*	196
Newberry, Todd/*Westwind Elem Sch*	269
Newby, Steve, Dr/*Trinity Christian Academy*	314
Newcomb-Jordan, Amy/*Dowling Elem Sch*	243
Newcomb, Mark, Dr/*St Theresa Sch*	155
Newcomer, Eric/*YES Prep Northbrook MS [312]*	14
Newell, Brooke/*Kenneth E Little Elem Sch*	159
Newman, Allison/*St Thomas Episcopal Sch*	45
Newman, Casey/*William B Travis 6th GR Campus*	318
Newman, Crystal/*Harleton High Sch*	208
Newman, Heather/*South Georgia Elem Sch*	318
Newman, Justin/*Evans Middle Sch*	270
Newman, Kimberly/*Hughes Elem Sch*	84
Newman, Lisa/*A L Steele Enhanced Lrng Ctr*	173
Newman, Max/*Dimmitt Alternative Center*	71
Newman, Natasha/*Pep High Sch*	75
Newman, Sharon/*Buckner Fanning Christian Sch*	44
Newman, Sharon/*Jess Harben Elem Sch*	112
Newman, Shelby/*Texas Virtual Acad Hallsville*	12
Newsome, Lizzy/*Jose A Valdez High Sch*	386
Newton, Ann/*Washington STEM Academy*	286
Newton, Beth/*Murchison Middle Sch*	369
Newton, Jesse/*Valley View Sch*	91
Newton, Joshua/*Madison Middle Sch*	360
Newton, Lucretia/*Lamar Elem Sch*	236
Newton, Michael/*Dyess Elem Sch*	360
Newton, Stan/*West Dallas Community Sch*	116
Nguyen, Tien/*Faith Family Academy-Oak Cliff [280]*	3
Nguyen, Victor/*St Ignatius College Prep Sch*	359
Nichols, Dawn, Dr/*St Michael's Catholic Academy*	372
Nichols, Emily/*John C Webb Elem Sch*	172
Nichols, Felicia, Dr/*St Pius V Sch*	204
Nichols, Kevin/*Premier HS-Huntsville [297]*	9
Nichols, Kevin/*Premier HS-North Houston [297]*	9
Nichols, Linda/*Denver Alternative Center*	392
Nichols, Mary/*Quitman Elem Sch*	404
Nichols, Melissa/*J W Long Elem Sch*	253
Nichols, Melissa/*W H Burnett Early Chldhd Ctr*	253
Nichols, Pike/*Idea Clg Prep-Rundberg*	219
Nicholson, Ricky/*La Marque High Sch*	161
Nickel, Brian/*Rockwall Quest Academy*	325
Nickel, Brian/*Sunnyvale High Sch*	113
Nickell, Page/*Redeemer Lutheran Sch*	359
Nickerson, Shawn/*Blanche K Bruce Elem Sch*	188
Nicklas, Elizabeth/*Cinco Ranch Junior High Sch*	152
Nicks, Rachel/*Smith Elem Sch*	84
Nickson, Michael/*Adelle Turner Elem Sch*	98
Nicolai, Anna/*Jackson-Keller Elem Sch*	35
Nicolas, Lorene/*Sycamore Academy*	249
Niehoff, Jeremi/*Dr Bernard Harris Middle Sch*	34
Niemeyer, Alisa/*Giddings Elem Sch*	263
Nieto, Isidoro/*Keys Academy*	65
Nieto, Karen/*Le Noir Elem Sch*	215
Nieto, Roman/*Mary Burks Marek Elem Sch*	51
Niggli, Michael/*Waltrip High Sch*	192
Nikki, Ms/*Iman Academy Southeast*	206
Nino, Jeanette/*Lamar Academy*	221
Nitahara, Kristina/*Uplift Luna Prep Secondary [309]*	13
Nitz, Todd/*Lutheran High Sch*	115
Nix, Greg/*Richard Milburn Acad-Houston [298]*	10
Nix, Sandra/*Richard Milburn Acad-Pasadena [298]*	10
Nixon, Karen/*George W Carver Early Ed Ctr*	61
Noack, Kathy/*Ralph Pflueger Elem Sch*	211
Nobles, Ken/*Trinity Christian Academy*	314
Nobles, Sandy/*Momentous Sch*	115
Noe, Artha/*Sue Ann Mackey Elem Sch*	111

NAME/School	PAGE
Noeldner, Juli/*Jo Ella Exley Elem Sch*	152
Nolan, Jason/*John Tower Elem Sch*	391
Noonan, Joesph/*St John XXIII Preparatory HS*	204
Noonan, Joseph/*St Anne Catholic Elem Sch*	204
Noorani, Samina/*Uplift Peak Prep Sch [309]*	13
Noriega, Patricia/*Mary Hull Elem Sch*	38
Norman, Coby/*Farwell High Sch*	314
Norman, Michael/*Spur Sch*	127
Norris, Leslie/*Ereckson Middle Sch*	77
Norris, Scott/*Cotulla High Sch*	259
Nors, Angela/*Mt Calm High Sch*	228
Norton, Michael/*Lyndon B Johnson Middle Sch*	46
Norton, Sara/*Sherwood Forest Mont Sch*	207
Norvell, Shelly/*Center Elem Sch*	334
Norwood-Miller, Jamie/*Tarver-Rendon Elem Sch*	357
Norwood, Amy/*Liberty-Eylau Early Chldhd Ctr*	48
Norwood, Bryan/*NE Alternative Center*	35
Norwood, Bryan/*Roosevelt High Sch*	35
Nott, Janis/*Lake Olympia Middle Sch*	150
Novacinski, Laura/*Andre Elem Sch*	184
Novickas, Steve/*Rooster Springs Elem Sch*	210
Nowlin, David/*Texas Empowerment Academy*	12
Nowlin, Lisea/*De Leon High Sch*	89
Nunez, Diana/*W H Adamson High Sch*	103
Nunez, Gina/*Tippin Elem Sch*	134
Nunez, Krystal/*Summit Christian Academy*	384
Nunez, Teresa/*Besteiro Middle Sch*	63
Nunez, Wendy/*Rita Drabek Elem Sch*	151
Nungaray, David/*Bonham Academy*	40
Nungesser, Kelli/*Dellview Elem Sch*	34
Nunn, Neisha/*Texas Empowerment Academy*	12
Nunn, Roby/*Rann Elem Sch*	403
Nusser, Melvin/*Watson Junior High Sch*	23
Nyeman, Shannon/*Faith Christian Academy*	139

O

NAME/School	PAGE
O'Bannon, Patti/*Nash Elem Sch*	50
O'Connor, Ben/*Rowe Lane Elem Sch*	372
O'Connor, Erika/*Colt Elem Sch*	60
O'Donnell, Tiffany/*Harrison-Jefferson-Madison ES*	62
O'Leary, John/*St Anthony Sch*	87
O'Neal, Anita/*Artemisia Bowden Academy*	39
O'Neal, C/*St Thomas Apostle Episc Sch*	207
O'Neal, Kendra/*Shsu CS-Cypress Trails*	11
O'Neal, Renee/*Shsu CS-Brighton Academy*	11
O'Neil, Ted/*Alternative Learning Center*	248
O'Neill, Tonya/*Farwell Elem Sch*	314
O'Sullivan, Kelly/*Ted Polk Middle Sch*	97
O'Toole, Kathleen, Dr/*Founders Classical Acad Leandr [297]*	3
Oakley, Vanessa/*Trent Sch*	361
Oaks, Toby/*Coram Deo Academy-Collin Cnty*	85
Oates, Penny/*Neysa Callison Elem Sch*	399
Obenhaus, Amy/*Arbor Creek Middle Sch*	122
Obersat, Thomas/*Grace Lutheran Sch*	386
Ocana, Michael/*Ann Richards Middle Sch*	219
Oceguera, Vickie/*North Early Learning Center*	309
Ochoa, Berzayda/*Davila Elem Sch*	189
Ochoa, Katy/*Ireland Elem Sch*	130
Ochoa, Nereida/*Ralph G Goodman Elem Sch*	181
Ochs, Vicki/*Caldwell High Sch*	59
Odell, David/*Robert Lee Sch*	75
Odom, Charlotte/*Brookeland Sch*	240
Odom, Kristina/*John & Nelda Partin Elem Sch*	168
Odom, Lisa/*Northstar Sch*	359
Odom, Tracy/*Uplift Summit Int'l Prep CS [309]*	13
Oduwole, Olatunji/*Wharton Junior High Sch*	390
Oestreich, Jane/*Isaacs Early Childhood Sch*	83
Offill, Paul/*River Valley Intermediate Sch*	281
Ogden, Margarita/*Robert E Lee Elem Sch*	318
Ogden, Peggy/*Merrywood Sch*	115
Oge, Debra/*Guess Elem Sch*	242
Ogg, Michael/*Alton Elem Sch*	385
Ogle, Eric/*Lamar Middle Sch*	109
Oglesby, Amy/*Simonton Christian Academy*	155

PRINCIPAL INDEX

Market Data Retrieval

NAME/School	PAGE
Oglesby, Cholly/*Sartartia Middle Sch*	151
Ohara-Sanchez, Kelly/*Arcadia Park Elem Sch*	99
Ojeda, Lynn/*Plano ISD Academy High Sch*	83
Olano, Catherine/*Bens Branch Elem Sch*	293
Oldham, Zac/*Cedar Valley Middle Sch*	398
Olga, Liz/*Frank Macias Elem Sch*	132
Oliphant, Jeremiah/*Bussey Middle Sch*	105
Oliphant, Sheronda/*Ser-Ninos Charter School II*	11
Oliva, Melissa, Dr/*Thomas Jefferson Middle Sch*	243
Olivarez, Linda/*Ignacio Zaragoza Elem Sch*	100
Olivarez, Maria/*Immaculate Conception Sch*	341
Olivarez, Maricela/*Ruben Rodriguez Elem Sch*	216
Olivas, Sarah/*Seguin Christian Academy*	174
Oliver, Carolyn/*Linden Elem Sch*	70
Oliver, Catherine/*Christ Episcopal Sch*	298
Oliver, Jennifer/*Sam Rayburn Steam Acad*	108
Oliver, Joe/*C H Yoe High Sch*	287
Oliver, Lori/*I H Kempner High Sch*	150
Oliver, Megan/*Sealy High Sch*	22
Oliver, Patricia/*Jasper Classical Academy [297]*	6
Oliver, Sherry/*Shallowater Elem Sch*	272
Oliver, Tina/*C O Wilson Middle Sch*	243
Oliver, Tina/*Kaufman Elem Sch*	292
Olmos, Lizet/*Gus Birdwell Elem Sch*	177
Olmstead, Brandi/*Village Technical Sch*	14
Olson, Beth/*Woodway Elem Sch*	281
Olson, Deanna/*Oyster Creek Elem Sch*	151
Olson, Tammany/*Ischool Virtual Academy HS [297]*	6
Olvera, Alejandro/*Ernesto Serna Elem Sch*	136
Olvera, Tracy/*Alvin Elem Sch*	51
Oner, Fatih/*Harmony Sch Adv-Houston [284]*	4
Ontiveros, Artemio/*Brownfield Middle Sch*	362
Ontiveros, Celia/*Palmer-Laakso Elem Sch*	66
Ontiveros, Cynthia/*YW Steam Research & Prep Acad*	133
Ontiveros, Cynthia, Dr/*Armendariz Middle Sch*	134
Ontiveros, Cynthia, Dr/*Young Women's Steam Prep Acad*	134
Ontiveros, Yeni/*Dowell Elem Sch*	133
Opon, Patricia/*St Mark Catholic Sch*	85
Oquin, David/*Highpoint School North*	179
Ordaz, Francisco/*Bowie High Sch*	134
Ordaz, Latonya/*Bill J Elliott Elem Sch*	350
Ordaz, Monica/*Cesar Chavez Elem Sch*	350
Orellana, Marybel/*Lubbock Junior Academy*	272
Orihuela, Kimberly/*Fox Run Elem Sch*	35
Orndorff, Vernon/*Milford Sch*	141
Orsak, Stephanie/*Harmony Elem Sch*	31
Orsborn, Shannon/*Edgewood Intermediate Sch*	380
Orta, Lorie/*Dubose Intermediate Sch*	245
Ortega, Armida/*Kiest Park Christian Academy*	115
Ortega, Benjamin/*Mission Early College High Sch*	136
Ortega, Faustino/*Sul Ross Middle Sch*	38
Ortega, Marty/*Dolores Linton Elem Sch*	37
Ortega, Reyna/*San Martin De Porres Sch*	226
Ortega, Sonja/*First Christian Academy*	226
Ortegon, Vanessa/*J A Kawas Elem Sch*	386
Ortiz Espinell, Sheila/*Gabe P Allen Charter Sch*	100
Ortiz, Irazema/*Our Lady of Guadalupe Sch*	204
Ortiz, Jorge/*L L Pugh Elem Sch*	189
Ortiz, Kathryn/*Woodlawn Elem Sch*	304
Ortiz, Lena/*Atkinson Elem Sch*	198
Ortiz, Moises/*Sidney Lanier High Sch*	41
Ortiz, Nidia/*Juan D Salinas Middle Sch*	220
Ortiz, Patricia, Dr/*Roosevelt Elem Sch*	32
Ortiz, Ricardo/*Rio Hondo Elem Sch*	66
Ortiz, Roberto/*Juarez-Lincoln Elem Sch*	387
Osborn, Deirdre/*Friona Primary Sch*	315
Osburn, Jason/*Temple Charter Academy [295]*	11
Osburn, Thomas/*Lacy Elem Sch*	84
Osby, Mario/*Shelbyville High Sch*	335
Osgood, Chris/*Brazos Sch Inquiry-Bryan [276]*	2
Osten, Shelly/*Miller Elem Sch*	344
Osth, Johan/*North Zulch Sch*	274
Osuna, Norma/*Ysleta Elem Sch*	138
Ott, Jessica/*Kimmie M Brown Elem Sch*	265
Otto, Rebecca/*Big Spring Junior High Sch*	233
Otto, Sarah/*La Grange Middle Sch*	147
Ovalle, Jason/*Strack Intermediate Sch*	197
Oviedo, Maria/*J Z Leyendecker Elem Sch*	386
Owen, Cinda/*Joe K Bryant Elem Sch*	77
Owen, Michelle/*Eastridge Elem Sch*	142
Owen, Rebecca/*Mae Luster Stephen Jr High Sch*	70
Owen, Shana/*Kerens Elem Sch*	300
Owens, Amber/*Hernandez Elem Sch*	212
Owens, Debra/*Collegiate Academy*	160
Owens, Kevin/*Graduation Prep Acad-Navarro*	368
Owolabi, Berky, Dr/*Bammel Elem Sch*	202
Ozier, Renee/*Mt Saint Michael Catholic Sch*	114
Ozuna, Barbara/*W P McLean Middle Sch*	352
Ozuna, Judy/*Early High Sch*	59
Ozuna, Selina/*Remynse Elem Sch*	345
Ozuna, Tambrey, Dr/*Marin B Fenwick Academy*	41

P

NAME/School	PAGE
Paben, Caty/*Premier HS-Brenham Miracle Frm [297]*	9
Pabst, Nadine/*Jubilee Lake View Univ Prep [285]*	6
Pace, Cherie/*Everman Academy High Sch*	349
Pace, Jennifer/*Widen Elem Sch*	367
Pace, Patti/*Monarch Sch*	206
Paceley, Lizette/*Olfen Sch*	327
Pacheco, Eric/*Dillard Spec Achievement Ctr*	77
Pachicano, Linda/*Cottonwood Creek Elem Sch*	396
Padilla, Adriana/*Heights Elem Sch*	386
Padilla, Antonio/*Los Cuates Middle Sch*	66
Padilla, Jacqueline/*A N Rico Elem Sch*	225
Padilla, Jimmy/*Monte Alto Ealry Clg High Sch*	222
Padilla, Tracy/*Somerset Elem Sch*	42
Pagach, Kimberly/*Caldwell Intermediate Sch*	59
Pagano, Michael/*Frazier Elem Sch*	184
Page, Shari/*Aquilla Sch*	227
Paine, Stacey/*Kings Manor Elem Sch*	293
Palacios, Andrew/*Townview Mag HS-Sci & Eng*	103
Palacios, Mario/*Dailey Middle Sch*	369
Palapa, Quetzalcoatl/*Salvador Garcia Middle Sch*	388
Palazzetti, Lisa/*A C Williams Elem Sch*	236
Palividas, Karen/*Holy Spirit Episcopal Sch*	206
Palizo, Agapito/*Killam Elem Sch*	388
Palmer, Amber/*Hermleigh Sch*	333
Palmer, America/*Basis San Antonio Primary N [011]*	1
Palmer, Kakie/*Bear Branch Elem Sch*	195
Palmer, Sherry/*Carver Early Education Center*	130
Palmer, Sonya/*Hillside Acad for Excellence*	106
Palmer, Susan/*Greenhill Sch*	115
Palombo, John/*Pearland High Sch*	53
Pamplin, Gary/*Discipline Ed Alternative Sch*	237
Panachakunnil, Varghese/*Pearsall High Sch*	157
Pancoast, Robert/*Paul Moreno Elem Sch*	134
Pandant, Melanie/*Judson Steam Academy*	170
Pang-Villa, Aida/*Rosita Valley Literacy Academy*	277
Pannell, Dana/*Marcy Elem Sch*	233
Papadimitriou, Michael, Dr/*Academy Careers Engr Science*	291
Papadimitriou, Michael, Dr/*Oak Ridge High Sch*	292
Papaioannou, Sage/*Hamilton Elem Sch*	185
Pappas, Kristen/*KIPP Voyage Academy for Girls [288]*	7
Pappas, Meredith/*Memorial Early Clg HS*	88
Paquin, Patricia/*Univ of Houston Charter Sch*	13
Parcell, Earl/*Martin Walker Elem Sch*	92
Pardo, Judith/*Alpine Elem Sch*	56
Pardo, Yesenia/*Hillcrest Elem Sch*	175
Parduce, Melissa/*Ranch Academy-Tyler*	10
Paredes, Ercilia/*Graham Elem Sch*	367
Parham, Charlene/*Ronnie Crownover Middle Sch*	121
Parham, Melissa/*Pebble Hill High Sch*	136
Paris, Drake/*Teague Junior High Sch*	156
Park, Christopher/*Daniel Singleterry Sr Elem Sch*	215
Parker, Carolyn/*Dessau Elem Sch*	371
Parker, Courtney/*Blackburn Elem Sch*	251

Texas School Directory — PRINCIPAL INDEX

NAME/School	PAGE
Parker, Danieli/North Elem Sch	208
Parker, Gale/Lamkin Elem Sch	185
Parker, Jackson/Elysian Fields High Sch	208
Parker, Jessica/Irion Elem Sch	238
Parker, John/Henry Scott Middle Sch	166
Parker, Laura/Comstock Sch	379
Parker, Lori/Furneaux Elem Sch	97
Parker, Norman/Liberty Christian Sch	126
Parkerson, Tiffany/College Station High Sch	55
Parks, Diane/Joe Hubenak Elem Sch	154
Parks, Precious/KIPP Peace Elem Sch [288]	7
Parmelee, Heather/Kocurek Elem Sch	366
Parnell, Jacqueline/Osborne Elem Sch	191
Parr, Edna/Laura Bush Middle Sch	271
Parr, Vicky/Elisabeth Ney Elem Sch	52
Parra-Malek, Dorcas/Benavidez Elem Sch	193
Parsons, Cristi/Pine Tree Primary Sch	170
Parsons, Valerie/Parkway Elem Sch	124
Parsons, Virginia/Jourdanton High Sch	20
Partida, Clarissa/Sam Rayburn Elem Sch	221
Partida, Maria/J S Adame Elem Sch	215
Pasak, Christina/River Place Elem Sch	397
Pasteur, Jennifer/North Texas Leadership Academy	359
Pasto, James/KIPP Austin Collegiate [286]	6
Pastorino, Louise/Winston School San Antonio	45
Pate, Kevin/Lakeview Elem Sch	252
Patek, Trina/Hallettsville Elem Sch	262
Patenotte, Lisa, Dr/Cage Charter Elem Sch	189
Patin, Melissa/Mark Twain Elem Sch	194
Patin, Nicole/Klein Cain High Sch	197
Patranella, Frank/Wallace Elem Sch	113
Patrick-Sims, Regina/James Bowie Elem Sch	188
Patrick, Linda/Carlisle Elem Sch	82
Patrick, Scott/Bangs High Sch	58
Patterson, Aletha/Santa Anna Elem Sch	76
Patterson, Bruce/Holliday High Sch	19
Patterson, Cathy/Franklin Elem Sch	227
Patterson, Damon/R C Loflin Middle Sch	248
Patterson, Heather/George Ranch High Sch	154
Patterson, Julie/Cisco Learning Center	129
Patterson, Kimberly/Gunter Middle Sch	166
Patterson, Wendy/Roosevelt-Wilson Elem Sch	161
Patton, Carla/Quail Valley Elem Sch	151
Patton, Damian/Highlands Elem Sch	97
Patton, J T/Zue S Bales Intermediate Sch	160
Patton, Tameka/Nancy Neal Elem Sch	357
Patton, Tammy/Christian Heritage Academy	16
Patton, Tim/The Woodlands Methodist Sch	295
Patureau, Misty/Veterans Hill Elem Sch	396
Paul, John/Frassati Catholic High Sch	204
Paul, Marie/Montessori Sch International	45
Paul, Priscilla/Powell Elem Sch	38
Paul, William/Breckenridge High Sch	341
Paulson, Matthew/Ed White E-STEM Magnet Sch	159
Pavlock, Marcy/Anderson-Shiro Elem Sch	171
Pavone, Ryan/Jessup Elem Sch	199
Pawlowski, Elizabeth/John F Ward Elem Sch	159
Payne, Amanda/Virginia Reinhardt Elem Sch	326
Payne, Anne/Caddo Mills Middle Sch	235
Payne, James/Mt Vernon Middle Sch	156
Payne, Terry/Winters Junior High Sch	327
Payne, Thomas/Hudson Bend Middle Sch	370
Payne, Wilma/Camelot Elem Sch	34
Payton, Bob/First Baptist Acad-Univ City	44
Payton, Monique/KIPP Legacy Prep Sch [288]	7
Paz, David, Dr/Mayde Creek Junior High Sch	152
Paz, Mark/El Paso High Sch	134
Peace, Angie/Bartlett Elem Sch	26
Peace, Angie/Bartlett High Sch	26
Peace, Angie/Bartlett Middle Sch	26
Peacock, Ben/Jacksonville High Sch	73
Pearson, Rose/Owen Goodnight Middle Sch	212
Peck, Courtney/North Forney High Sch	252
Peck, Kathy/The Academy	314
Peden, Jamie/Talley Elem Sch	80

NAME/School	PAGE
Peden, Trey/Bettye Myers Middle Sch	121
Pederson, Lyndsey/Bynum Sch	227
Peery, Susan/Howard Early Childhood Center	30
Pegram, Sonja/Larry D Guinn Spec Pgrms Ctr	83
Pegues, Nakeisha/Price T Young Elem Sch	209
Peirson, Jennifer/McKinney Boyd High Sch	81
Pekurney, Kyle/Smithfield Middle Sch	346
Pelking, Priscilla/St Clement's Parish Sch	139
Pelzel, Kathy/Rockdale Intermediate Sch	288
Pemelton, Miscellene/Mva Mercedes CHS [303]	8
Pena-Wilk, Leti/Blazier Elem Sch	366
Pena, Aaron/Woodgate Intermediate Sch	281
Pena, Adolfo/Grulla High Sch	340
Pena, Gilda Jo/R L Martin Elem Sch	64
Pena, Jorge/Rio Grande City High Sch	340
Pena, Katie/Highland Park Elem Sch	368
Pena, Ramiro/Banquete Junior High Sch	302
Pena, Rene/Grulla Middle Sch	340
Pena, Roxanna/Sam Fordyce Elem Sch	220
Pena, Trinidad/Leal Elem Sch	222
Pena, Veronica/Royal Point Academy	45
Pena, Yvette/Alto Bonito Elem Sch	340
Penland, Richard/Benbrook Middle High Sch	350
Penn, Charlotte/Giddings Middle Sch	263
Pennartz, Brian/Bob Hope Elem Sch	43
Pennell, Michael/Highlands Sch	114
Pennington, Amie/Centerville Elem Sch	105
Pennington, Chris/Peaster High Sch	313
Pennington, Pamela/Frostwood Elem Sch	201
Pennix, Tiera/Southminster Sch	155
Penny, Andra, Dr/Cottonwood Creek Elem Sch	98
Penny, Norma/Lomax Middle Sch	199
Pense, Cynthia/Davis Elem Sch	326
Pense, Richard/Ruth Cherry Interm Sch	326
Pentecost, Renee/Little Elm High Sch	124
Pepper, Monty/Sabine High Sch	170
Peragine, Angela/Anderson Elem Sch	343
Peragine, Sheila/Elliott Elem Sch	109
Perales, Ida/Camino Real Middle Sch	137
Perales, Ida/Del Valle Middle Sch	137
Perales, Ida/Memorial Pathway Academy	106
Peraza, Alyssa/Sidney Lanier Expressive Arts	102
Percle, Bridgette/R O'Hara Lanier Middle Sch	52
Pereira, Heather/Uplift North Hills Prep Sch [309]	13
Pereira, Herman/Connally Early Clg Career Tech	279
Perejon, Lola/Helms Elem Sch	191
Perez, Alejandra/Cedar Brook Elem Sch	201
Perez, Alfredo/Gateway to Graduation Academy	67
Perez, Alfredo/Sabas Perez Eng & Tech Sch	387
Perez, Angeles, Dr/Pat Reynolds Elem Sch	202
Perez, Ben/Taylor Ray Elem Sch	154
Perez, Bryan/Anthon Elem Sch	378
Perez, Christine/Poe Middle Sch	41
Perez, Cynthia, Dr/Falfurrias Junior High Sch	57
Perez, Danny/Premier HS-Fort Worth [297]	9
Perez, Dawn/New Frontiers Christian Acad	381
Perez, Elizabeth/Richard King High Sch	304
Perez, Ellie/Presbyterian Pan American Sch	258
Perez, Esmeralda/North Shore Elem Sch	187
Perez, Gabriela/Clark Elem Sch	387
Perez, Iliana/Paige Elem Sch	191
Perez, Jeff/Sweetwater High Sch	302
Perez, Jose/Del Rio High Sch	379
Perez, Jose/Disciplinary Alt Ed Program	225
Perez, Jose/Edgemere Elem Sch	138
Perez, Jose/Santo Nino Elem Sch	387
Perez, Juan/Jim G Martin Elem Sch	37
Perez, Lyn/Orange Grove Primary Sch	245
Perez, Monica/Collins-Parr Elem Sch	128
Perez, Nayeli/Romulo Martinez Elem Sch	224
Perez, Nichole/St Paul Lutheran Sch	226
Perez, Nora/Idea Academy-Edinburg	218
Perez, Perla/Tulia High Sch	343
Perez, Ranier/Energized for STEM Academy MS	193
Perez, Raynaldo/Benavides Secondary Sch	128

School Year 2019-2020 800-333-8802 TX-U47

PRINCIPAL INDEX

Market Data Retrieval

NAME/School	PAGE	NAME/School	PAGE
Perez, Ricardo/*Canterbury Elem Sch*	216	Phillips, Sherry/*Jackson-Roosevelt Elem Sch*	62
Perez, Rosa/*Westwood Primary Sch*	16	**Phillips, Susan**/*Matagorda Sch*	275
Perez, Sandra/*Benavides Elem Sch*	128	Phipps, Brett/*McCarroll Middle Sch*	403
Perez, Sandra/*Del Valle Elem Sch*	137	**Phy, Tim**/*Jefferson Junior High Sch*	274
Perez, Tanya/*Jubilee Destiny [285]*	6	Piatt, Hugh/*Pampa High Sch*	165
Perkins, Clint/*Petrolia Jr Sr High Sch*	74	Pichon, Jules/*Alice Johnson Jr High Sch*	183
Perkins, Cynthia/*Ramirez-Burks Elem Sch*	259	Pidone, Maribel/*Chester Jordan Elem Sch*	136
Perkins, Hugh/*San Augustine Mid High Sch*	329	Pieniazek, Michelle/*Krum High Sch*	122
Perkins, Josiah/*Georgetown Charter Academy [295]*	3	Pierce, Alison/*Timbers Elem Sch*	196
Perkins, Mary/*Breckenridge Jr High Sch*	341	Pierce, Carol/*Huebner Elem Sch*	35
Perkins, Patrick/*Dr John D Horn High Sch*	111	**Pierce, Carrie**/*Lizzie Curtis Elem Sch*	125
Perkins, Tami/*Great Hearts Irving [282]*	4	Pierce, David/*Jack C Hays High Sch*	211
Perry, Agnes/*Debakey High Sch-Health Prof*	191	Pierce, Greg/*S & S Cons Middle Sch*	167
Perry, Brandon/*Willie J Hargrave High Sch*	195	Pierce, Kathy/*Poolville Elem Sch*	313
Perry, Brant, Dr/*Schimelpfenig Middle Sch*	83	Pierce, Kerri/*Vidor Middle Sch*	309
Perry, Chad/*Adaptive Behavior Center*	184	Pierce, Wayland/*Glasscock Co Sch*	163
Perry, Jason/*PCA Dr Terry Robbins Mid Sch*	9	Pierotti, Michael/*Mary Moss Elem Sch*	111
Perry, Jason/*Pineywoods Community Academy*	9	Pierson, David/*North Shore Ninth Grade Center*	187
Perry, Jaunee/*Grace England ECC*	197	Pierson, Serena, Dr/*Austin Elem Sch*	291
Perry, Jennifer/*Lake Dallas Elem Sch*	122	Pileski, Cody/*Fusion Academy-Austin*	373
Perry, Kimberly/*Slaton Junior High Sch*	272	Pillar, Joseph/*Ball High Sch*	160
Perry, Laura, Dr/*Campbell Middle Sch*	184	**Pina, Daniel**/*Edgewood Fine Arts Academy*	31
Perry, Marsha/*Walker Creek Elem Sch*	346	Pina, Daniel/*Emma Frey Discip Alt Ed Pgrm*	31
Perry, Phillip/*Carver Middle Sch*	282	Pine, Courtney/*Dallas Christian Sch*	115
Perry, Phillip/*Fred W Edwards Academy*	29	Pineda, John/*La Grange High Sch*	147
Perry, Robin/*St Gregory Cathedral Sch*	339	**Pineda, Stacy**/*Hollaway Sixth Grade Sch*	339
Perry, Sean/*Homestead Elem Sch*	123	Pinell, David/*Winnsboro High Sch*	405
Perry, Shaun, Dr/*John H Guyer High Sch*	121	**Pingelton, Erin**/*Morningside Elem Sch*	295
Perry, Shawn/*Trent Middle Sch*	80	**Pinkerton, Joshua**/*Somerville Intermediate Sch*	60
Perschbacher, Ross/*Texline Sch*	95	Pinnix, Natasha/*Martin Luther King Academy*	41
Persyn, Anthony/*Northside Alt Middle Sch South*	38	**Pinon, Debra**/*Cable Elem Sch*	36
Persyn, Anthony/*Northside Alt Middle Sch-North*	38	Pinson, Rebekah/*Premier HS-Amarillo [297]*	9
Pesek, Steven/*Sharon Shannon Elem Sch*	326	Pintavalle, Rita/*Brazoswood High Sch*	52
Pesina, Amy/*Washington Elem Sch*	167	Pipkins, Cherish/*Rolling Hills Elem Sch*	110
Pesina, Mr/*Esparza Elem Sch*	216	Pitcher, Mike/*Billie Stevenson Elem Sch*	325
Peters, Brian, Dr/*Groves Elem Sch*	195	Pitchford, Sandra/*Christa McAuliffe Elem Sch*	221
Peters, Jon/*McMillan Junior High Sch*	85	Pitcock, Sonya/*Walter & Lois Curtis Mid Sch*	77
Peters, Mark/*Lifegate Christian Sch*	174	**Pitt, Barbara**/*Monaco Elem Sch*	120
Peters, Renia/*Balch Springs Chrn Academy*	114	**Piwetz, Tisha**/*Woodsboro Jr Sr High Sch*	324
Petersen, Tim/*Antonian College Prep High Sch*	44	**Plake, Cody**/*Leonard High Sch*	146
Peterson, Brady/*Louise Junior High Sch*	390	Plata, Marta/*Manuel Jara Elem Sch*	351
Peterson, Dan/*Aledo High Sch*	312	Playle, Erika/*De La Vina Elem Sch*	216
Peterson, Dan, Dr/*Regents School of Austin*	373	Pleasant, Carl/*Wheatley Alt Ed Center*	29
Peterson, Heather/*Douglas MacArthur High Sch*	180	Plotts, Kevin/*Apple Springs Elem Sch*	374
Peterson, Jeremy/*Van Junior High Sch*	381	Plotts, Kevin/*Apple Springs High Sch*	374
Peterson, John/*James Bowie Elem Sch*	140	Poblano, Claudia/*Del Norte Heights Elem Sch*	137
Peterson, Tiffany/*Dr Harmon W Kelley Elem Sch*	42	Pocquette, Jayne/*Idea Academy-Bluff Springs*	217
Petruccio, Dathan/*Covenant Christian Sch*	295	Podhaski, Randy/*Mountain View Elem Sch*	28
Petruzzini, Heather/*Cunningham Elem Sch*	366	Poe, Gina/*Hamilton High Sch*	176
Petters, Danielle/*H Grady Spruce High Sch*	100	Poehls, Donna/*Bronte Elem Sch*	75
Petty, Ben/*Bear Branch Junior High Sch*	293	**Pohl, Candace**/*DeWalt Alternative Sch*	198
Petty, Cassandra/*Post Elem Sch*	162	Polanco, Ester/*Idea Academy-Kyle*	218
Petty, Mildred/*Martinez Elem Sch*	360	Polites, Constantine/*Idea Clg Prep-South Flores*	219
Petty, Sheira/*Charlotte Anderson Elem Sch*	356	Politi, Jennifer/*Sherman High Sch*	167
Peyton, Angela/*Zavalla Elem Sch*	18	Polk, Brittenie/*W E Chalmers Elem Sch*	91
Pfeifer, Andrea/*James Bonham Middle Sch*	318	Polk, Raymond/*Memorial High School-Cate*	243
Pham, Khanh/*Our Lady of Fatima Sch*	204	Pollack, Scott/*Milstead Middle Sch*	199
Phan, Alycen/*Anna May Daulton Elem Sch*	356	Pollard, Stephen/*Johnston Elem Sch*	109
Pharis, Melanie/*Beaumont Early Clg High Sch*	242	Pollard, Terese/*A A Milne Elem Sch*	193
Phelan, Jennifer/*San Jacinto Intermediate Sch*	199	Pollock, Gary/*Estrada Achievement Center*	40
Phelps, Lisa/*Polser Elem Sch*	124	Pollock, Lindsey/*Garden Oaks Montessori*	191
Phelps, Sandra, Dr/*First Baptist Christian Sch*	60	Polster, Ginger/*Agriculture Science Center*	343
Phelps, Tiffany/*Barton Creek Elem Sch*	370	Polster, Ginger/*Dan Dipert Career & Tech Ctr*	344
Phillips, Amanda/*Booker T Washington Elem Sch*	24	Ponce, Cynthia/*Austin High Sch*	134
Phillips, Bill/*Waterford Oaks Elem Sch*	97	Ponce, Marshall/*Clear Horizons Early Clg HS*	158
Phillips, Carlos/*B T Washington High Sch*	188	Poncho, Crystal/*Snyder Elem Sch*	292
Phillips, Dennis/*Regis Sch of the Sacred Heart*	204	Pond, Cheryl/*Dr Lonnie Green Elem Sch*	379
Phillips, Elizabeth/*Shoreline Academy*	11	Pond, Matt/*Hamlin High Sch*	249
Phillips, Jennifer/*Lipan Sch*	230	Pond, Sue/*Premier HS-Abilene [297]*	9
Phillips, John/*Bronte High Sch*	75	**Pool, Lynn**/*Weatherford 9th Grade Center*	314
Phillips, Kentrel/*Baxter Junior High Sch*	349	Poole, Nicole/*Wayne Stuart Ryan Elem Sch*	121
Phillips, Rebecca/*Ross Elem Sch*	130	Pope, Andrea/*Jacobs Well Elem Sch*	212
Phillips, Robert/*Levelland High Sch*	229	Pope, Geri/*Schertz Elem Sch*	173

Texas School Directory — PRINCIPAL INDEX

NAME/School	PAGE
Pope, Janie/North Zulch Sch	274
Pope, Lillian/Pasadena Classical Academy [297]	9
Pope, Phyllis/Dr JM Ogle Elem Sch	79
Pope, Tammy/Birdville Elem Sch of Fine Art	346
Pope, William/Alliene Mullendore Elem Sch	346
Popillion, Charisma/Charlton-Pollard Elem Sch	242
Porter, Amy/Piner Middle Sch	167
Porter, Barbara/St Francis Sch	373
Porter, Daryl/North Crowley High Sch	348
Porter, Deanna/Lakewood Elem Sch	203
Porter, Dorothy/George Washington Middle Sch	387
Porter, Luane/Fort Davis Jr Sr High Sch	241
Porter, Magan/Dodd Elem Sch	85
Porterfield, Russell/Killeen ISD Career Center	28
Portillo, Adam/Ector Co Youth Alt Center	130
Portillo, Francisco/New World Montessori Sch	139
Portillo, Jp/Wilson Sch	273
Portillo, Ray/Henderson Elem Sch	286
Portillo, Yvonne/Magoffin Middle Sch	135
Portley, Letrice/Piedmont Global Academy	102
Portwood, John/Richards Independent Sch	172
Posey, Rene/Round Rock Opportunity Center	399
Post, Jeffrey/Quail Valley Middle Sch	151
Poth, Dounna/Langford Elem Sch	367
Poth, Julie/Poteet Junior High Sch	21
Potter, Phillip/Walnut Hill Elem Sch	103
Potts, Ami/Hobbs Williams Elem Sch	107
Potts, Jim/Port Aransas High Sch	305
Pounds, Crystal/Danbury High Sch	53
Pounds, Crystal/Danbury Middle Sch	53
Pourchot, Michelle/Roy J Wollam Elem Sch	161
Povich, Christopher, Dr/Grand Oaks High Sch	291
Powell, Brandon/Decker Elem Sch	371
Powell, Chakosha/Libby Cash Maus Middle Sch	79
Powell, Jason/Sundown Elem Sch	229
Powell, Michael/Gary Sch	311
Powell, Nichole/Harper Elem Sch	84
Power, Nanette/Eschool Prep Virtual Sch	50
Powers, Jason/Blackwell Sch	301
Powers, Jennifer/Brooks Wester Middle Sch	356
Prado, Alma/Premier HS-San Juan [297]	10
Prado, Anthony/Fabens High Sch	135
Prado, Arica/All Saints Catholic Sch	358
Prados, Tiffany/KIPP Spirit College Prep [288]	7
Prange, Nathan/Mary Moore Elem Sch	344
Prangner, Elizabeth/Cooley Elem Sch	133
Prater, Wendy/W R Fort Elem Sch	326
Prather, Brenda/Ralls Middle Sch	94
Pratt, Rosalinda/Jill Stone-Vickery Meadow ES	100
Prehn, Amanda/Bee Cave Middle Sch	370
Prejo, Sister Yamila/Father Yermo High Sch	139
Presillas, Delia/Alief Montessori Cmty Sch	1
Presley, Charles/Kilgore High Sch	169
Presley, Denisha/San Marcos High Sch	212
Pressley, Karen/Saginaw High Sch	349
Preston, Mary/Ray Johnson 6th Grade Ctr	349
Preston, Matthew/Cross Oaks Elem Sch	121
Prets, Alice/Greta Oppe Elem Sch	160
Prewitt, Kelley/Dr James P Terry Middle Sch	111
Prezas, John/Fred R Sanders Elem Sch	303
Price, Anji/Cunae International Sch	205
Price, Christy/Brackett High Sch	257
Price, Darren, Dr/Houston Christian High Sch	206
Price, Diane/St Joseph Catholic Sch	358
Price, Jeffrey/Tafolla Middle Sch	41
Price, Jennifer/Inez Carroll Academy	180
Price, Jill/Buckalew Elem Sch	291
Price, Lauren/Marshall Elem Sch	191
Price, Rashunda/Bonnie Gentry Elem Sch	111
Price, Torrey/Baird High Sch	62
Prickett, Erin/Humphrey's Highland Elem Sch	318
Priddy, Elizabeth/Castleberry High Sch	347
Priddy, Greg/Kerens High Sch	300
Priddy, Greg/Kerens Middle Sch	300
Pride, Kari/James F DeLaney Elem Sch	356

NAME/School	PAGE
Priest, Judith/St Gerard Catholic High Sch	44
Priest, Marshall/Rosehill Christian Sch	207
Prince, Jana/Mendenhall Elem Sch	83
Prindle, Niki/Whitestone Elem Sch	397
Pringle, Michelle/Olga Kohlberg Elem Sch	134
Prioleau, Dale/Ellen B Lane Sch	180
Pritchard, Melissa/Mountainview Elem Sch	282
Pritchett, Monte/Crawford High Sch	279
Pritchit, Tracy/Dr Bruce Wood Elem Sch	253
Prnka, Rodny/Joaquin High Sch	335
Pro, Guillermo/Raymond & Tirza Martin HS	387
Proctor, Dawn/Benignus Elem Sch	196
Proper, Sonya/Edna Alternative Sch	239
Provencio, Diana/Herrera Elem Sch	133
Prowell, Ben/Wellman-Union Sch	362
Prueitt, Ellen/KIPP Truth Academy [287]	7
Pruett, Zack/Thomas Elem Sch	83
Pruitt, Marcus/Jones Middle Sch	181
Pruitt, Matthew/Charlie C McKamy Elem Sch	96
Pruitt, Sharonda, Dr/Wilmer Early Chldhd Center	103
Pruneda, Erika/Los Reyes Elem Sch	38
Prusak, Kyla/Robertson Elem Sch	80
Ptasnik, Misty/Meyer Elem Sch	284
Ptomey, Tish/Pat Cooper Elem Sch	395
Puente-Sanchez, Alicia/Durkee Elem Sch	190
Puente, Eileen/Rucker Elem Sch	190
Puente, Elise/Heritage Elem Sch	43
Puentemejia, Maria/Felix Botello Elem Sch	100
Puga, Christopher/Capistrano Elem Sch	137
Puga, Nicolas/Magellan Int'l Sch-Anderson Ln	373
Pugh, Mary, Dr/Doris Cullins-Lake Pointe ES	325
Puishes, Meloni/Kingsland Sch [292]	6
Pulaski, Jonathan/Christian Academy of America	126
Pulido, Martha/Sundown Elem Sch	153
Pulliam, Lynn/Canadian High Sch	213
Punch, Shawna/HCC Life Skills	194
Purdom, Rachael/Ripley House Middle Sch	10
Purdy, Angel/Academy of Choice	200
Purdy, Angel/Cornerstone Academy	201
Purke, Jason/Douglass Sch	297
Purkeypile, Les/Monterey Senior High Sch	270
Purl, Molly/Walter Wilkinson Middle Sch	111
Pursifull, Melissa/Lois Lindsey Elem Sch	77
Pursley, Shannon/Central Athens Elem Sch	213
Putman, Jennifer/Janie Stark Elem Sch	97
Putnam, Jennifer/Long Early Childhood Center	360

Q

Quade, Marsha/Knox City Elem Sch	258
Quadri, Rizvan, Dr/Stephen F Austin High Sch	151
Quick, Matthew/Tatum High Sch	328
Quillin, Wendy/Big Country Elem Sch	43
Quinn, Carrie/Nichols-Saw Mill Elem Sch	293
Quinn, Greg/Magnolia High Sch	293
Quinn, Mike/Audie Murphy Middle Sch	27
Quinn, Zach/Orangefield High Sch	309
Quinones, Aileen/Leadership Acad Mitchell Blvd	351
Quinones, Eileen/Cristo Rey Jesuit Clg Prep HS	205
Quinonez, Eva/E Ray Elem Sch	349
Quintana, Charlotte/Green Elem Sch	133
Quintanilla, Alejandra/Tuloso-Midway Primary Sch	305
Quintanilla, Christian/Ben Milam Elem Sch	221
Quintanilla, Israel/Lasara Elem Sch	394
Quintanilla, Israel/Lasara High Sch	394
Quintela, Charles/Ector Clg Prep Success Acad	130
Quintero, Doris/Honor Roll Sch	155
Quintero, Rhapsody/Mary Lou Fisher Elem Sch	38
Quiroz-Colunga, Laura/William B Travis Elem Sch	304

R

Raab, Joshua/St Mary Magdalene Sch	204
Rachal, Kathy/McDougle Elem Sch	197
Rader, Leslie/Crosby Elem Sch	251
Raesz, Rebecca/Weldon Smith Elem Sch	304

PRINCIPAL INDEX

Market Data Retrieval

NAME/School	PAGE	NAME/School	PAGE
Ragland, Sharon, Dr/*Oakwood Jr Sr High Sch*	265	Rather, Christina/*Dolph Briscoe Middle Sch*	37
Rainey, Dimitrie/*Alcott Elem Sch*	192	Ratliff, Stephanie, Dr/*Frederick Douglass Academy*	40
Rainey, Kenna/*South Elem Sch*	341	Rauls, Heather/*Cedars International Academy*	2
Rainey, Les/*Bay Area Christian Sch*	162	Ravelli, Mark/*Trinity Episcopal Sch*	162
Rainey, Lou Ann/*East Chambers Jr High Sch*	72	Raven, Matrice/*Chisholm Trail Middle Sch*	124
Rainwater, Ashley/*Liberty High Sch*	79	Ravin, Rose/*Veda Knox Elem Sch*	345
Rakay, Rosa/*Psja Sonia Sotomayer HS*	224	Ray-Mullens, Samantha/*Hempstead Elem Sch*	384
Raleeh, Melanie/*Roy Lee Walker Elem Sch*	81	Ray, Beth/*Celeste Elem Sch*	236
Raley, Griselda/*Wright Elem Sch*	33	**Ray, Holly**/*New Caney Middle Sch*	294
Ralston, Melissa/*Giesinger Elem Sch*	291	Ray, Jole/*Mineola Primary Sch*	404
Ralston, Robin/*Hillsboro Elem Sch*	227	Ray, Kristen/*Sycamore Springs Elem Sch*	210
Ramage, James/*Bonham Middle Sch*	130	Ray, Mr/*St Anthony Sch*	11
Ramback, Natalie/*Dell Pickett Elem Sch*	395	Ray, Pam/*Idea Academy-Ewing Halsell*	218
Rambo, Matt/*Tennyson Middle Sch*	282	Ray, Rashad/*Ray D Corbett Junior High Sch*	173
Rameau, Pam/*Alexander Smith Academy*	205	**Ray, Richard**/*Robert Brabham Middle Sch*	294
Ramirez, Adan/*Mission Junior High Sch*	222	Rayborn, Tina/*Buffalo Elem Sch*	264
Ramirez, Adriana/*United South High Sch*	388	Raymer, Chuck/*Montessori Sch of San Antonio*	45
Ramirez, Cameron/*Lakewood Elem Sch*	354	Raymond, Kellie/*Dripping Springs Elem Sch*	210
Ramirez, Clarisa/*Alfonso R Ramirez Elem Sch*	216	Razzack, Zuhaira/*Ilm Academy*	206
Ramirez, Daniel/*Dr Mario Ramirez Elem Sch*	340	**Read, Mike**/*Littlefield High Sch*	261
Ramirez, Gerardo/*George W Bush New Tech Odessa*	130	Read, Shawn/*Boys Ranch High Sch*	307
Ramirez, Herminia/*Bonham Elem Sch*	64	Reagan, Brandt/*Plainview High Sch*	175
Ramirez, Ivan/*Capt Walter E Clarke Mid Sch*	136	Reagan, Carol/*St Philip's Episcopal Sch*	26
Ramirez, Joann/*James Bowie Middle Sch*	318	**Reagan, Cyndy**/*Wise Elem Fine Arts Magnet Sch*	337
Ramirez, Juan/*Morgan Sch*	47	Reaves, Stanton/*Sabine Middle Sch*	170
Ramirez, Lee/*Galena Park Middle Sch*	187	Rebarchek, Jodi/*Trinity Basin Prep-Ft Worth*	12
Ramirez, Maria/*Roma Instructional Sch*	341	Rebecek, Tammy/*Vernagene Mott Elem Sch*	372
Ramirez, Mayra/*J B Jones Muller Elem Sch*	387	Record, Danielle/*Dr Erwin & Elizabeth Pink ES*	79
Ramirez, Myrna/*Beaumont Classical Academy [297]*	1	Redd-Dorsey, Shanequa/*Alto High Sch*	72
Ramirez, Nancy/*Triumph Public CHS [303]*	12	Reddell, Karen/*Harlow Elem Sch*	77
Ramirez, Patricia/*St Anthony Catholic Elem Sch*	44	Redden, Jennifer/*Memorial High Sch*	79
Ramirez, Richard/*Premier HS-New Braunfels [297]*	9	Redning, Lori/*Sam Houston Elem Sch*	140
Ramirez, Rudy/*Angela Leal Elem Sch*	67	Reece, Pamela/*Memorial High Sch*	32
Ramirez, Sandra/*Patton Springs Sch*	127	Reed, Christian/*Scurry Rosser High Sch*	253
Ramirez, Stephanie/*Frontier Elem Sch*	51	Reed, Eddie/*Kathryn S McWhorter Elem Sch*	97
Ramirez, Zachary/*Goliad Elem Sch*	365	Reed, Jill/*Highlander Sch*	115
Ramon, Mayra/*Crespo Elem Sch*	189	Reed, Kevin/*TLC Academy*	12
Ramon, Raul/*Our Lady of Perpetual Help Sch*	306	Reed, Linda/*Vines EC-PK-K Sch*	181
Ramos-Coto, Claudia/*Kelly Elem Sch*	40	Reed, Matt/*New Deal High Sch*	271
Ramos, Amanda/*Back Elem Sch*	105	Reed, Reagan/*Big Bend High Sch*	57
Ramos, Dale/*B L Garza Middle Sch*	216	Reed, Reagan/*Terlingua Elem Sch*	57
Ramos, E Omar/*Green B Trimble Tech High Sch*	350	Reed, Rosemary/*Melba Passmore Elem Sch*	51
Ramos, Elco/*Crockett Elem Sch*	133	Reed, Shad/*Nazareth Sch*	71
Ramos, Iric/*Science Hall Elem Sch*	211	Reeder, Angie/*South Elem Sch*	296
Ramos, Jesus/*Santiago Garcia Elem Sch*	216	Reeders, Bobbie, Dr/*Pathways Academic Campus*	28
Ramos, Jodie/*Wilshire Elem Sch*	354	Reese, Steven/*Wallace Accelerated High Sch*	289
Ramos, Jose/*Dave Blair Elem Sch*	96	Reeve, Robert/*Eustace Intermediate Sch*	214
Ramos, Jose/*Mary Grimes Education Center*	97	Reeves, Alicia/*Deretchin Elem Sch*	291
Ramos, Maryann/*Clear Creek Elem Sch*	27	**Reeves, Christin**/*Emerson Elem Sch*	285
Ramos, Myra/*Patricio Perez Elem Sch*	220	Reeves, Sara/*Ouida Springer Elem Sch*	325
Ramos, Rosa/*Deepwater Junior High Sch*	186	Reeves, Vernon/*Billy Ryan High Sch*	121
Ramos, Stefanie/*Daffron Elem Sch*	82	**Regalado, Kristabel**/*Dowling Elem Sch*	130
Ramos, Stephanie/*Sam Houston Elem Sch*	286	Regan, Tiffany, Dr/*Deer Park Junior High Sch*	186
Ramsey, Kelly/*Greenfield Elem Sch*	348	**Register, Bridget**/*Gatesville Intermediate Sch*	93
Ramsey, Steven/*Westlake High Sch*	370	Register, Bridget/*Gatesville Primary Sch*	93
Randall, Melanie/*David L Walker Interm Sch*	348	Rehan, Susan/*Vera Escamilla Elem Sch*	180
Randle-Filer, Shyulanda/*Smith Magnet Middle Sch*	242	Reid, Melissa/*Crestview Elem Sch*	49
Randle, Derrice/*Maurine Cain Middle Sch*	325	**Reid, Melissa**/*Oakview Primary Sch*	49
Randolph, Kim/*Episcopal High Sch*	205	Reid, Tim/*Central Freshman Campus*	365
Raney, Marthea/*Walipp Tsu Prep Academy*	14	Reidling, Rebecca/*Grace Hartman Elem Sch*	325
Raney, Marthea, Dr/*Lawson Academy*	7	Reile, Hilary/*Sacred Heart Catholic Sch*	401
Raney, Marthea, Dr/*The Lawson Academy*	12	Reilly, Patricia/*Farney Elem Sch*	184
Rangel, Beulah/*Travis Elem Sch*	65	Reinhardt, Becky/*Robb Elem Sch*	378
Rangel, Chris/*Stephens Elem Sch*	121	Reinhart, Tracey/*Montessori Episcopal Sch*	126
Rangel, Linda/*Whittier Elem Sch*	318	Reininger, Charles/*David Tex Hill Middle Sch*	34
Rankin, Brandi/*Bushland Elem Sch*	319	Reisner, Mark/*Greenville Christian Sch*	237
Rankin, Christopher/*McLennan Co Challenge Academy*	282	Reiter, Elizabeth/*KIPP Austin Connections ES [286]*	6
Rankin, Linda/*Como Pickton Sch*	231	**Relf, Amanda**/*Ben Tisinger Elem Sch*	110
Ransleben, Lisa, Dr/*Justin Elem Sch*	125	Remmers, Galen/*Misd Developmental Center*	267
Ransom, Sheila/*Fairfield Elem Sch*	156	**Remschel, Alex**/*Academy High Sch*	26
Rapier, Kerry/*Johnson Daep*	107	Rendon, Armando/*Int'l Ldrshp TX-Keller*	109
Rapp, Kellie/*Polly Tadlock Elem Sch*	80	Rendon, Cara/*James E Poole Elem Sch*	376
Rasco, Becky/*G R Porter Elem Sch*	111	Rendon, Netassha/*Brandenburg Elem Sch*	109

Texas School Directory — PRINCIPAL INDEX

NAME/School	PAGE
Rendon, Silvia/*Ysleta High Sch*	138
Renfro, Anna/*Shady Grove Elem Sch*	355
Renner, Ben/*Cleburne High Sch*	247
Renner, Ben/*Hughes Middle Sch*	247
Reno, Debra/*C D Landolt Elem Sch*	158
Renteria, Christine/*Milton L Kirkpatrick Elem Sch*	351
Renteria, Noe/*Sundown Lane Elem Sch*	321
Resendiz, Pablo/*Holland Middle Sch*	189
Resio, Stella/*Skidmore Tynan Jr High Sch*	26
Revels, Deborah/*Crockett Elem Sch*	232
Reyes, Elizabeth/*Valley View South Elem Sch*	225
Reyes, Fernando/*Harlingen High School South*	65
Reyes, Justin/*Texans Can Acad Houston SW [305]*	12
Reyes, Laura/*Impact Early College High Sch*	188
Reyes, Maria/*Bay City High Sch*	275
Reyes, Martha/*Frank Tejeda Middle Sch*	35
Reyes, Paula/*Govalle Elem Sch*	366
Reyes, Rick/*Elgin High Sch*	24
Reyes, Sandra/*Hector P Garcia Elem Sch*	29
Reyes, Vanessa/*Sam Rayburn High Sch*	199
Reyez, Leida/*Veterans Memorial Elem Sch*	341
Reyna, Angela/*Parkland Middle Sch*	138
Reyna, Eliseo/*Graduation Prep Academy-Travis*	368
Reyna, Eva/*Brentwood Middle Sch*	31
Reyna, Orlando/*Sugar Grove Academy*	189
Reyna, Selina/*DeLeon Elem Sch*	382
Reynolds, Alonzo/*Andy Dekaney High Sch*	202
Reynolds, Donna/*Hood-Case Elem Sch*	51
Reynolds, Fredia/*Wheatley Sch Early Childhood*	243
Reynolds, Keely/*Trinity Charter School-Pegasus [307]*	12
Reynolds, Kent/*Hallsburg Elem Sch*	279
Reynolds, Kimberly/*Valley Oaks Elem Sch*	201
Reynolds, Shanna/*S & S Elem Sch*	167
Reynolds, Tramaine/*Golden Rule CS-Pleasant Grove [281]*	3
Rhea, Iva Nell/*Cypress Cmty Christian Sch*	205
Rhine, Daresa/*Hook Elem Sch*	144
Rhines, Reggie/*Kennedale Junior High Sch*	356
Rhines, Valencia/*Leadership Acad Como ES*	351
Rhodes, Canita/*Snyder Primary Sch*	333
Rhodes, Gloria/*Bonham Elem Sch*	55
Rhodes, Katina/*Bellaire Elem Sch*	354
Rhodes, Lesley/*Adams Elem Sch*	343
Rhodes, Philip/*Dumas Intermediate Sch*	295
Rhodes, William, Dr/*Robert & Felice Bryant ES*	152
Rhodus, Randal/*Hockaday Sch*	115
Rhoten, Wes/*Canton Junior High Sch*	380
Rhymes, Jacqueline/*Golden Meadows Elem Sch*	106
Rice, Calvin/*South Park Middle Sch*	242
Rice, Crystal/*Torres Elem Sch*	382
Rice, Darrell, Dr/*Northside Alternative High Sch*	38
Rice, Donna/*Atlanta Primary Sch*	69
Rice, Michelle/*Hoover Elem Sch*	185
Rice, Robin/*Live Oak Learning Center*	19
Richard, Lisa/*Gregory Luna Middle Sch*	37
Richards, James/*Motley Co Sch*	296
Richards, Jan/*Littlefield Primary Sch*	261
Richards, Joey, Dr/*Southwest Christian Sch-Prep*	359
Richards, Megan/*Valley Creek Elem Sch*	81
Richardson, Dara/*Scudder Primary Sch*	212
Richardson, Darren/*Weldon Elem Sch*	169
Richardson, Jeremy/*Pasadena Memorial High Sch*	199
Richardson, Kimberly/*Thomas L Marsalis Elem Sch*	103
Richardson, Marsha/*Community Christian Sch*	165
Richardson, Melinda/*Navarro Co Alt Educ Ctr*	300
Richardson, Mike/*Cumberland Academy*	2
Richardson, Paula/*Tekoa Academy-Port Arthur [304]*	11
Richardson, Stephen/*Hackberry Elem Sch*	124
Richburg, Leslie/*Edgemere Elem Sch*	175
Richey, Susan/*Richard Milburn Acad-Ft Worth [298]*	10
Richie, Clarisa/*Fain Elem Sch*	392
Richmond, Michael/*Sch of Environmental Education*	172
Richmond, Sarah/*Pittsburg Intermediate Sch*	68
Richter, Gena/*Kor Education Sch*	56
Richter, Laura/*South Knoll Elem Sch*	56
Rickman, Jessica/*Dr Lee Buice Elem Sch*	130
Ricks, Kelly/*Ray & Jamie Wolman Elem Sch*	152
Rico, Adriana/*Britain Elem Sch*	109
Rico, Angel/*Lee Elem Sch*	109
Rico, Oscar, Dr/*Jose Alderete Middle Sch*	132
Riddell, Leslie/*Jo Kelly Sch*	351
Rider, Aris/*Dallas Environmental Sci Acad*	99
Rider, Nathan/*P E Wallace Middle Sch*	364
Ridout, Michael/*Little Cypress Interm Sch*	308
Riebkes, Brenda/*Bear Creek Intermediate Sch*	354
Riek, Rene/*Transition Center*	354
Riepe, Kim/*Life High School-Waxahachie [290]*	7
Rietfors, Gina/*Cross Timbers Intermediate Sch*	356
Riewe, Philip/*Irons Middle Sch*	270
Riggs, Jill/*Herty Primary Sch*	18
Riha, Ruth/*Barrington Place Elem Sch*	149
Rike, Jim/*St Joseph Catholic Sch*	56
Riker, Brad/*James D Gossett Elem Sch*	377
Riley, Chad/*Bishop Lynch High Sch*	113
Riley, Frank/*Bracken Christian Sch*	89
Riley, Phillip/*St Monica Catholic Sch*	114
Riley, Rhonda/*Throckmorton Sch*	363
Rimer, Terri/*Long Elem Sch*	286
Rincon, Lilly/*Jefferson Elem Sch*	192
Rinearson, Robyn/*Glenn Harmon Elem Sch*	357
Rinehart, Nancy/*Atlanta High Sch*	69
Rink, Dawn/*McCoy Elem Sch*	97
Riojas, Amalia/*Sam Houston Elem Sch*	277
Riojas, Jesse, Dr/*Mathis High Sch*	331
Rios-Garcia, Linda/*Huppertz Elem Sch*	40
Rios, Denise/*St Augustine Catholic Sch*	204
Rios, Leah/*Nolan Catholic High Sch*	358
Rios, Manuel/*William D Slider Middle Sch*	137
Rios, Rolando/*Cesar Chavez Middle Sch*	219
Rios, Rosanna/*Kirchner Elem Sch*	277
Ripley, William/*Whitehouse Junior High Sch*	339
Ripple, Dawn/*Ward Elem Sch*	360
Rische, David/*Early Learning Ctr North*	355
Risdal, Kristen/*Abercrombie Academy*	205
Risinger, Jennifer/*Athens Middle Sch*	213
Risley, Reagan/*Canadian Elem Sch*	213
Rispoli, Joe/*Faith Academy of Marble Falls*	60
Rister, Bobby/*T M Clark Elem Sch*	331
Ritchey, David/*Lamesa Success Academy*	117
Ritchey, Garrett/*Clint High Sch*	132
Ritchey, Michael/*Big Spring High Sch*	233
Ritchie, Walter/*Spring Creek Academy*	86
Rivas, Marta/*Ridgegate Elem Sch*	151
Rivas, Monico/*Liberty High Sch*	189
Rivas, Priscilla/*Crockett Charter Elem Sch*	191
Riven, Jay/*Parish Episcopal Sch*	116
Rivera, Conrad/*Pyburn Elem Sch*	187
Rivera, David/*Francisco Barrientes Mid Sch*	216
Rivera, Dion/*Cedric C Smith Elem Sch*	293
Rivera, Edward/*J B Munoz Elem Sch*	220
Rivera, Elizabeth/*Valley Christian High Sch*	68
Rivera, Elva/*John F Kennedy Sch*	221
Rivera, Israel/*Townview Mag HS-Bus & Mngmnt*	103
Rivera, Isreal/*Jose May Elem Sch*	101
Rivera, Jessica/*United Day Sch*	389
Rivera, Ms/*Blackshear Magnet Elem Sch*	130
Rivera, Nora/*North Grammar Elem Sch*	340
Rivera, Vivian/*Legacy Prep Chtr Acad-Mesquite*	7
Rivers, Gregory/*Charles Clyde Ball Academy*	40
Rivers, Jacqueline/*Boude Storey Middle Sch*	99
Rivers, Matt/*Wall Middle Sch*	365
Rivers, Mr/*Connell Middle Sch*	40
Rizo, Kristy/*La Vega IS-H P Miles Campus*	280
Roa, Laura/*Tornillo High Sch*	137
Roach, Christy/*Douglas Elem Sch*	338
Roach, William/*Port Isabel High Sch*	66
Roan, Jared/*San Antonio Christian Mid Sch*	45
Roan, Jared/*San Antonio Christian Sch*	45
Roan, Richard/*Cooper Jr Sr High Sch*	120
Robbins, Ginger/*Graham Junior High Sch*	406
Robbins, Heather/*Pleasant Hill Elem Sch*	397

School Year 2019-2020 800-333-8802 TX-U51

PRINCIPAL INDEX

Market Data Retrieval

NAME/School	PAGE
Roberson, Andre/McAuliffe Middle Sch	150
Roberson, Connie/Willbern Elem Sch	186
Roberson, Jenny/Judy K Miller Elem Sch	357
Roberston, Kennitra/Robinson Middle Sch	83
Robert, Emilie, Dr/Our Lady of Lourdes Cath Sch	162
Robert, Fowler/Alternative Education Ctr	292
Roberts, Ashley/Coahoma Junior High Sch	234
Roberts, Brian/Azle Junior High Sch	345
Roberts, Dana/Achieve Academy	85
Roberts, Franci/Rubicon Academy	295
Roberts, Helen/Kirby Hall Sch	373
Roberts, Jennifer/Billy Baines Middle Sch	149
Roberts, Jill/Trinity Christian Elem Sch	272
Roberts, Joshua/J R Irvin Elem Sch	141
Roberts, Lauren/St Thomas Aquinas Sch	114
Roberts, Leslye/Reagan Elem Sch	360
Roberts, Nikki/Edgar Glover Elem Sch	150
Roberts, Shelley/River Ridge Elem Sch	397
Roberts, Tommy/Bryan Collegiate High Sch	55
Roberts, Virginia/Bob Hope Elem Sch	1
Roberts, William/Huntsville High Sch	383
Robertson, Brad/Brownsboro Junior High Sch	213
Robertson, Dana/Spring Hill Intermediate Sch	171
Robertson, Gena/Fred H Tally Elem Sch	256
Robertson, Kena/George & Deborah Purefoy ES	79
Robertson, Lindy/Housman Elem Sch	201
Robertson, Megan/Follett Sch	268
Robertson, Mindy/Alief Learning Center	182
Robertson, Rachel/Norma Krueger Elem Sch	173
Robinett, Rusty/Spring Hill High Sch	170
Robinson, Amelia, Dr/Academy at World Champions Ctr	295
Robinson, Angela/Cockrell Hill Elem Sch	104
Robinson, Angela/Oak Hills Terrace Elem Sch	38
Robinson, Anita/Benton A Staley Middle Sch	78
Robinson, Annette/Adams Hill Elem Sch	36
Robinson, Britt/The Oakridge Sch	359
Robinson, Cynthia/Cornerstone Christian Sch	366
Robinson, Howard/Carter Park Elem Sch	350
Robinson, Jamie/Van Raub Elem Sch	254
Robinson, Kelli/Lansberry Elem Sch	374
Robinson, Kimberly/Harold Lang Middle Sch	100
Robinson, Mark/James Bowie High Sch	368
Robinson, Marlene/Whitesboro High Sch	168
Robinson, Raymond/Karnes City Early Clg HS	250
Robinson, Timothy/Buda Elem Sch	211
Robinson, Vanessa/Pine Tree Junior High Sch	170
Rocha, Jaime/Galena Park Elem Sch	187
Rocha, John/Bailey Middle Sch	369
Rocha, Mary Ellen/Seguin Early Child Hood Ctr	154
Rochkus, Alan/Harmony Hills Elem Sch	35
Rock, Jennifer/White Oak Intermediate Sch	171
Rockwell, Gayla/St Paul's Preparatory Academy	359
Roddy, Marlene/James Martin High Sch	344
Roddy, Troy/Holy Trinity Episcopal Sch	206
Roden, Kelly/Garden Ridge Elem Sch	123
Roder, Cap, Dr/John M Stuart Career Tech HS	188
Rodgers, Amanda/Braeburn Elem Sch	193
Rodgers, Stacy/Dueitt Middle Sch	202
Rodgers, Teri/Arlington Classics Acad-Bowen	1
Rodriguez-Bohn, Leticia/Burns Elem Sch	63
Rodriguez, Abraham/Salinas Elem Sch	388
Rodriguez, Adriana/Austin Eco Bilingual Sch-South	372
Rodriguez, Alexander/Emerson Elem Sch	193
Rodriguez, Alicia/Thornton Elem Sch	345
Rodriguez, Amanda/Juan Seguin Elem Sch	107
Rodriguez, Beatriz/Burnet Early Childhood Univ ES	160
Rodriguez, Bertha/Cielo Vista Elem Sch	133
Rodriguez, Bertha/Palm Heights Baptist Sch	45
Rodriguez, Charlie/Cox Elem Sch	397
Rodriguez, Cynthia/Blanca E Sanchez Elem Sch	221
Rodriguez, D/Dr Armando Cuellar Middle Sch	225
Rodriguez, Dalia/Solomon P Ortiz Interm Sch	305
Rodriguez, David/Buffalo Creek Elem Sch	200
Rodriguez, Denise/Greentree Elem Sch	195
Rodriguez, Eddie, Dr/Cast Med	40
Rodriguez, Edgar/Frankston High Sch	15
Rodriguez, Edgar/Frankston Middle Sch	15
Rodriguez, Enrique/C A Tatum Elem Sch	99
Rodriguez, Fernando/Lida Hooe Elem Sch	101
Rodriguez, Gerardo/United Step Academy	388
Rodriguez, Guadalupe/Hawthorne Academy	40
Rodriguez, Gunter/Olney Elem Sch	406
Rodriguez, Jaime/Joe Barnhart Magnet Academy	25
Rodriguez, Jaime/Moreno Middle Sch Sch	25
Rodriguez, Jessica/Dr Carlos Castaneda Elem Sch	221
Rodriguez, Jorge/Lewis Elem Sch	190
Rodriguez, Joseph/Nettie Marshall Elem Sch	298
Rodriguez, Kimberly/East Elem Sch	303
Rodriguez, Leticia/Verda Mae Adams Elem Sch	33
Rodriguez, Linda/Olmito Elem Sch	66
Rodriguez, Lisa, Dr/Project Chrysalis Middle Sch	190
Rodriguez, Luci/Welder Elem Sch	332
Rodriguez, Malynn/Odessa Kilpatrick Elem Sch	152
Rodriguez, Mary/Hirsch Elem Sch	40
Rodriguez, Mary/Skinner Elem Sch	64
Rodriguez, Mary Lou/A P Solis Middle Sch	215
Rodriguez, Melissa/Linder Elem Sch	367
Rodriguez, Michelle/Flores Elem Sch	378
Rodriguez, Monica/Mary Hartman Elem Sch	33
Rodriguez, Nancy/Longfellow Middle Sch	41
Rodriguez, Orlando/Mercedes High Sch	222
Rodriguez, Orlando/Sgt Manuel Chacon Middle Sch	222
Rodriguez, Patricia/Del Rio Freshman Sch	379
Rodriguez, Ruben/De Zavala Elem Sch	183
Rodriguez, Rubicela/Carl Waitz Elem Sch	222
Rodriguez, Sandra/Woodland Acres Elem Sch	187
Rodriguez, Terry-Ann/Moises E Molina High Sch	102
Rodriguez, Tracie/Collegiate High Sch	303
Rodriguez, Tracie, Dr/Harold Branch Acad Career/Tech	303
Rodriguez, Veronica/Olivero Garza Elem Sch	224
Rodriquez, Margaret/Stars Accelerated High Sch	230
Roe, Anna/Deer Creek Elem Sch	348
Roe, Brandie/Edna Junior High Sch	239
Roede, Todd/Garcia Middle Sch	181
Roelke, Leda/Crutchfield Elem Sch	167
Rogers-Hall, Sherri/George Peabody Elem Sch	100
Rogers, Holly/Ruth Dowell Middle Sch	81
Rogers, Klinetta/Iuniversity Prep Virtual Acad	353
Rogers, Natalie/Palo Pinto Elem Sch	310
Rogers, Sharla/Reece EC-PK-K Sch	181
Rogers, Tammy/Berry Elem Sch	344
Rohleder, Julie/Caddo Grove Elem Sch	248
Rojas, Fred/College Career Technology Acad	134
Rojas, J Luis/Elm Creek Elem Sch	43
Rojas, Yvonne/W E Greiner Explor Arts Acad	103
Rojo, Blanca/Obadiah Knight Elem Sch	102
Rolen, Clay/Bells High Sch	165
Rolke, Lori/Good Shepherd Episcopal Sch	115
Rollins, Gwyn/Jhw Inspire Acad-Meridell	31
Rollman, Amy/Eagle Heights Elem Sch	345
Roman, Arturo/Devonian Elem Sch	16
Roman, Christine/Cristo Rey Dallas College Prep	114
Roman, Letitia/Magnolia Elem Sch	293
Roman, Ruth/John H Reagan Elem Sch	101
Romano, Oscar/YES Prep Gulfton [312]	14
Rombs, Joshua/Woodroe Petty Elem Sch	332
Romer, Leigh/J C Thompson Elem Sch	125
Romero, Anabel/Jack C Jordan Middle Sch	37
Romero, Jessica/Sch of Sci & Tech-Discovery [299]	11
Romero, Jonatan/Herbert Marcus Elem Sch	100
Romero, Mayra/Shearn Elem Sch	191
Romero, Michelle/Hurshel Antwine Elem Sch	136
Romero, Michelle/Tierra Del Sol Elem Sch	138
Romero, Olga/Lenore Kirk Hall Elem Sch	101
Romero, Sylvia/Robstown High Sch	305
Romine, Larry/River City Christian Sch	45

Texas School Directory — PRINCIPAL INDEX

NAME/School	PAGE
Rood, Chad/*Giddings High Sch*	263
Root, Raymond/*Stafford High Sch*	155
Roper, Sarah/*Van Vleck Elem Sch*	276
Roque, Tiffany/*Hogg Middle Sch*	191
Roraback, Annette/*Creek View Elem Sch*	55
Rosalez, Joey/*Ganado Junior High Sch*	240
Rosas Gonzalez, Maria/*Miraibeau B Lamar Elem Sch*	188
Rosas, Kassidy/*Vega Jr Sr High Sch*	308
Rosas, Maria/*Bonnie P Hopper Primary Sch*	187
Rosatelli, Brian/*Tom & Nita Nichols Middle Sch*	248
Rosberg, Alett/*Lohn Sch*	277
Rose, Bethany/*Forest Hill Elem Sch*	318
Rose, Jim/*Running Brushy Middle Sch*	397
Rose, Karen/*Woodlawn Academy*	41
Rose, Natalie/*Frost Elem Sch*	299
Rose, Theresa/*Barbara Bush Elem Sch*	193
Rose, Tracie/*Harts Bluff Elem Sch*	363
Rosen, Jody/*Frisco Montessori Academy*	237
Rosenbalm, Racquel/*Sherman Elem Sch*	191
Rosenbauer, Kaleena/*KIPP Unity Primary [288]*	7
Rosenbaum, Delia/*St Pius X Sch*	306
Roser, Matthew/*Riverwood Middle Sch*	196
Rosier, Rachel/*Sienna Crossing Elem Sch*	151
Ross-Newby, Sharonda/*Outley Elem Sch*	182
Ross, Angelia/*International Newcomer Academy*	351
Ross, Derrick/*C J & Anne Hyman Elem Sch*	104
Ross, Dwayne/*Iola Junior Senior High Sch*	172
Ross, Jeremy/*Granbury High Sch*	230
Ross, Jill/*Belton High Sch*	26
Ross, Jincy/*Brawner Intermediate Sch*	230
Ross, Kay/*Aledo Christian Sch*	314
Ross, Yvette/*Elaine S Schlather Interm Sch*	173
Rosser, Gaye/*Hutto Elem Sch*	396
Rosson, Penny/*River Road Middle Sch*	319
Rostyne, Greg/*Grayson Christian Sch*	169
Roth, Marla/*Coleman Elem Sch*	247
Roth, Ron/*Legacy Early College High Sch*	399
Rothenberg, Danielle/*Akiba Academy of Dallas*	114
Rothschild, Jeffrey/*Idea Clg Prep-Ingram Hills*	218
Rounds, Bryan/*Cardiff Junior High Sch*	151
Rouse, Jamie/*Miles Sch*	326
Roush, Nicki/*Belmar Elem Sch*	317
Rowan, Stephanie/*Carlisle Sch*	327
Rowden, Sherry/*Westbrook Sch*	289
Rowe, Dina/*Loreta Hickey Elem Sch*	83
Rowland, Michael/*Eustace Middle Sch*	214
Rowley, Joanna/*Mendez Middle Sch*	369
Roy, Geoffrey/*KIPP Connect Houston High Sch [288]*	6
Royal, Renee/*Samuel Houston Elem Sch*	383
Royle, Jonathan/*J C Austin Elem Sch*	111
Rozell, Michelle/*Brook Hill Sch*	339
Rozier, Lezlie/*Ovilla Christian Sch*	143
Rubin, Andrew/*KIPP Academy MS [288]*	6
Rubio, Cristopher/*Idea Clg Prep-Montopolis*	219
Rubio, Cynthia/*Krueger Middle Sch*	35
Rubio, Denise/*Garfield Elem Sch*	379
Rucker, James/*Sidney Sch*	90
Rucker, Timothy/*Compass Center*	73
Ruderman, Chana/*Torah Day School of Dallas*	86
Rudes, Scott/*B T Washington Perform Arts HS*	99
Rudewick, Michael/*Eldorado Elem Sch*	333
Rueda, Sara/*Navarro Elem Sch*	55
Rueter, John, Dr/*McGill Elem Sch*	365
Ruffin-Brown, Patrice/*Kennedy-Curry Middle Sch*	101
Ruiz-Ufland, Aydee/*Ralph Langley Elem Sch*	38
Ruiz, Adriana/*Hawkins Elem Sch*	133
Ruiz, Amanda/*Panda Path Sch*	201
Ruiz, Anabel/*Pleasant Grove Elem Sch*	102
Ruiz, Candice/*Robert T Hill Middle Sch*	102
Ruiz, Claudia/*Franklin Monroe Gilbert ES*	109
Ruiz, Corina/*O'Donnell Intermediate Sch*	135
Ruiz, Jennifer/*Stanton Middle Sch*	274
Ruiz, Justin/*San Jacinto Elem Sch*	318
Ruiz, Lisa/*Kennedy Elem Sch*	277
Ruiz, Lizbeth/*Highland Park Elem Sch*	372
Ruiz, Mario/*Carrizo Springs Interm Sch*	127
Ruiz, Michael/*Geneva Heights Elem Sch*	100
Ruiz, Ruth/*Charles H Milby High Sch*	189
Ruiz, Sylvia/*Roosevelt Elem Sch*	388
Ruiz, Vanessa/*Da Vinci School Science & Arts*	2
Rule, Beth/*Bending Oaks High Sch*	114
Runkles, Joanna/*Capitol Elem Sch*	229
Runnels, Felicia/*St Anthony Cathedral Sch*	244
Runnels, Tony/*Royal High Sch*	384
Rupard, Estella/*Huffines Middle Sch*	123
Rush, Matt/*Allen Academy*	56
Russel, Brenda/*Central Texas Christian Sch*	30
Russell, Chad/*Flower Mound High Sch*	123
Russell, Charles/*Rspa Northwest-Living Word*	10
Russell, Christopher/*Lamar Elem Sch*	88
Russell, David/*Central Heights High Sch*	297
Russell, Jeffrey/*Wills Point High Sch*	381
Russell, Jerry/*Snyder Intermediate Sch*	333
Russell, Jim/*Electra Jr Senior High Sch*	391
Russell, Leah/*Iowa Park High Sch*	392
Russell, Leslie/*Norma Dorsey Elem Sch*	106
Russell, Lonnie/*Gilbert Cuellar Jr Elem Sch*	100
Russell, Matthew/*Pete Ford Middle Sch*	77
Russell, Melissa/*South Hills Elem Sch*	352
Russell, Pearl/*Springtown Elem Sch*	313
Russell, Rebecca/*Colorado High Sch*	289
Russell, Robby/*Colorado Middle Sch*	289
Russell, Robert/*Columbus High Sch*	87
Russell, Trenn/*Heritage Elem Sch*	202
Ruthart, Greg/*Amon Carter-Riverside High Sch*	350
Ruthart, Wendy/*Chisum Elem Sch*	259
Rutherford, Max/*China Spring High Sch*	279
Rutherford, William/*Great Hearts Monte Vista-North [282]*	4
Rutlage, Becky, Dr/*UT Tyler Univ Acad-Palestine*	338
Rutledge, Cheryl/*Aim College & Career Prep Acad*	160
Rutledge, Cheryl/*Collegiate Academy at Weis*	160
Rutzen, George/*Uplift North Hills Prep Sch [309]*	13
Ruvalcaba, Asael/*Rio Hondo High Sch*	66
Ryan, Lesley/*Eanes Elem Sch*	370
Ryan, Randall/*Threeway High Sch*	144
Ryan, Rick/*Trinity Lutheran Sch*	319
Ryan, Scott/*Alternative Education Center*	243
Ryan, Scott/*Port Neches-Groves High Sch*	244
Ryder, Charles/*Meridian World Charter Sch*	8
Rydl, Mary/*Valley Christian Heritage Sch*	226

S

NAME/School	PAGE
Saarie, Lisa/*Chancellor Elem Sch*	182
Sadler, Amy/*Coder Elem Sch*	312
Sadler, Cindy, Dr/*Jubilee Harlingen [285]*	6
Sadler, Latanya/*Pecos High Sch*	323
Sadler, Lisa/*Prairie Valley Sch*	290
Saeed, Raffat/*C E King Middle Sch*	200
Saegert, Jeremy/*Charlie Marshall Elem Sch*	330
Saenz, Corrine/*Reilly Elem Sch*	368
Saenz, Jennifer/*St Michael Sch*	118
Saenz, Larissa/*Austin Middle Sch*	223
Saenz, Marielena/*Cullender Kindergarten*	385
Saenz, Marissa/*Roger Q Mills Elem Sch*	102
Saenz, Rey/*Calallen Middle Sch*	302
Saenz, Sonia, Dr/*Kenmont Montessori Sch*	68
Saettel, Scott/*Heritage Middle Sch*	353
Saffel, Phillip/*New Hope Academy*	271
Safford, Darbie, Dr/*St Mary's Catholic Sch*	171
Sailer, Andja/*Centerville Elem Sch*	374
Sailer, Andja/*Centerville High Sch*	374
Sailors, Pamela/*Southwest Sch-Bissonnet [278]*	11
Sajewski, Kristin/*Iola Elem Sch*	172
Salas, Bonnie/*Brooks Acad-Science Engineerng [130]*	2
Salas, Bonnie/*Brooks Estrella Academy*	2
Salas, Geraldine/*Harmony Sch Innov-Laredo [284]*	4
Salas, Heather/*Lone Star Early Childhood Ctr*	88
Salas, Jacqueline/*Robert R Rojas Elem Sch*	136
Salas, Lorena/*Union Park Elem Sch*	121

PRINCIPAL INDEX

NAME/School	PAGE
Salas, Monica/Hemphill Elem Sch	211
Salas, Naomi/Edward H Cary Middle Sch	99
Salas, Sarah/Sherwood Elem Sch	201
Salazar, Amy/Houston Elem Sch	310
Salazar, Annette/Horizon Montessori III [301]	5
Salazar, Armando/Lyndon B Johnson High Sch	388
Salazar, Emily/Bishop Primary Sch	302
Salazar, Gildardo/Orange Grove High Sch	245
Salazar, Holly/Thousand Oaks Elem Sch	36
Salazar, Jessica/Los Obispos Middle Sch	388
Salazar, Kristina/Akins High Sch	368
Salazar, Wendy/Stafford Elem Sch	32
Salcedo, Reyna/Bill Childress Elem Sch	132
Saldana, Rodrick/Premier HS-Lubbock [297]	9
Saldana, Vanessa/Paciano Prada Elem Sch	388
Saldana, Victor/West Avenue Elem Sch	36
Saldivar, Ildefonso/Roma High Sch	341
Saldivar, Marissa/John & Olive Hinojosa Elem Sch	340
Saldivar, Noemi/Graebner Elem Sch	40
Saldivar, Roel/Baker-Ripley Promise Cmty CS	1
Saldivar, Roel/Promise Cmty Sch-New Nghbr [274]	10
Salerno, Karen/Uplift Wisdom Prep Primary Sch [309]	13
Salgado, Javier/Desert View Middle Sch	137
Salgado, Omar/Bessie Haynes Elem Sch	323
Salinas-DeLeon, Irosema/Claude Cunningham Middle Sch	303
Salinas, Ana/Jefferson Elem Sch	216
Salinas, Blanca/Vanguard Academy-Beethoven	13
Salinas, Carlota/Dr Javier Saenz Middle Sch	219
Salinas, Cuca/Hereford Junior High Sch	119
Salinas, Diana/Florence J Scott Elem Sch	341
Salinas, Fernando/Idea Academy-Rio Grande City	218
Salinas, Geneva/Barrera Veterans Elem Sch	42
Salinas, Geneva/St Matthew Catholic Sch	44
Salinas, Gilberto/Carylene McClendon Elem Sch	78
Salinas, Idani/Ringgold Elem Sch	340
Salinas, Lucia/Leila P Cowart Elem Sch	101
Salinas, Pricilla/Henry Ford Elem Sch	223
Salinas, Reina/Garriga Elem Sch	66
Salinas, Sandra/Lucile M Hendricks Elem Sch	221
Salizar, Miguel/Ralls High Sch	94
Salley, Matthew/Kohfeldt Elem Sch	161
Salmon, Lisa/Wylie West Early Childhood Ctr	361
Salmon, Ricardo/Armando Leal Jr Middle Sch	32
Salmond, Lori/Whitewright Elem Sch	168
Salta, Verna/Alcuin Montessori Sch	114
Salter, Michele/Stewart Creek Elem Sch	293
Salvador, Shameika/Wilson Montessori Elem Sch	195
Salyards, Jennifer/Chamberlin Elem Sch	144
Salyer, Melissa/Fred and Patti Shafer ES	152
Samaniego, Lilly/SS Cyril & Methodius Sch	306
Sammon, Ericka/St Mary Catholic Sch	282
Samples, Kevin/Rockwall High Sch	325
Sampson, Reuben/Lee Elem Sch	243
Samuel, Mark/Shadowbriar Elem Sch	194
San Miguel, Jacqueline/Fred Moore High Sch	121
San Millan, Lance/Pathways High Sch	166
San Segundo, Angelo/Wooten Elem Sch	368
Sanchez, Adolfo/Cathedral High Sch	139
Sanchez, Andrea/Dr Henry Cuellar Elem Sch	387
Sanchez, Annette/Hampton-Moreno-Dugat ECC	25
Sanchez, Celia/San Jacinto Elem Sch	102
Sanchez, Claudia/Carl Wanke Elem Sch	36
Sanchez, Claudia/Winston Elem Sch	32
Sanchez, Cynthia/Putnam Elem Sch	134
Sanchez, Gilma/Barrington Elem Sch	367
Sanchez, Jaime/Pdna Vista Del Sol Mesa CHS [303]	9
Sanchez, Jennifer/Rufino Mendoza Elem Sch	352
Sanchez, Johanna/Hearne Elem Sch	182
Sanchez, Jorge/Harwell Elem Sch	270
Sanchez, Leticia/The Discovery Sch	226
Sanchez, Linda/Bryan Elem Sch	222
Sanchez, Marianela/Vestal Elem Sch	33
Sanchez, Miguel/St Francis of Assisi Cath Sch	204
Sanchez, Mindy/Lee H Means Elem Sch	65
Sanchez, Nancy/Armstrong Elem Sch	149
Sanchez, Patsy/Big Spring Interm Sch	233
Sanchez, Pedro/Coakley Middle Sch	65
Sanchez, Priscilla/Cook Elem Sch	367
Sanchez, Raul/Webb Middle Sch	369
Sanchez, Rubinna/Julius Dorsey Elem Sch	101
Sanchez, Sandra/Bonham Elem Sch	133
Sanchez, Tonya/Greathouse Elem Sch	286
Sanchezvillanu, Elena/De Zavala Elem Sch	212
Sandall, Jana/Dr Allan & Carolyn Bird Ed Ctr	82
Sandate, Irma/Fonville Middle Sch	190
Sandefer, Laura/Acton Academy	372
Sander, Chase/YES Prep Hoffman [312]	14
Sanders-Woods, Tonya/Archway Academy	205
Sanders, Anita/Life School Oak Cliff [290]	8
Sanders, Audrey/Arrow-Liberation Academy [273]	1
Sanders, Brandon/Blakemore Middle Sch	307
Sanders, Elizabeth/High Country Elem Sch	348
Sanders, Jessica/Living Stones Christian Sch	54
Sanders, Katie/St Mary Catholic Sch	309
Sanders, Lasandra/Sch Health Prof-Townview Ctr	102
Sanders, Leatrice/Victory Lakes Intermediate Sch	159
Sanders, Lindsey/John Haley Elem Sch	109
Sanders, Lora/Cecil Everett Elem Sch	259
Sanders, Misti/Oglesby Sch	93
Sanders, Starla/Jacksboro High Sch	239
Sanderson, Michael/Goldthwaite Middle Sch	288
Sanderson, Yancey/Gatesville High Sch	93
Sandles, Gwendolyn/Youngblood Intermediate Sch	183
Sandolph, April/Uplift Mighty Preparatory Acad [309]	13
Sandoval, Elizabeth/Uvalde High Sch	378
Sandoval, Ernesto/J B Alexander High Sch	387
Sandoval, Eva/Lincoln Elem Sch	217
Sandoval, Fernando/Maxfield Elem Sch	129
Sandoval, Juan/Academy High Sch	258
Sandoval, Kathleen/Douglas B Bussey Elem Sch	179
Sandoval, Letty/Early Childhood Center	276
Sandoval, Mario/Northline Elem Sch	191
Sandoval, Mario/Raul Yzaguirre Sch for Success [296]	10
Sandoval, Michael/William Lipscomb Elem Sch	103
Sandoval, Veronica/Thomas Hancock Elem Sch	200
Sandoval, Yesy/Victory Life Academy	59
Sands, Kerri/Richland Elem Sch	346
Sands, Linda/Spurling Christian Academy	359
Sanford, Laureen/Mary Austin Holley Elem Sch	150
Sanford, Rebecca/Mattie B Hambrick Middle Sch	181
Sanjacinto, Kalyn/Carroll Peak Elem Sch	350
Sansom, Jason/Valley Millsjr Sr High Sch	47
Santamaria, Claudia/Uphaus Early Childhood Center	367
Santibanez, Kara/Perez Elem Sch	367
Santos, Jose/Middle College at HCC Fraga	190
Santos, Juanita/Rayburn Elem Sch	33
Santos, Linda/Immaculate Conception Sch	114
Santos, Miranda/D'Hanis Sch	283
Santos, Selma/Blessed Sacrament Sch	388
Sanzo, Sonya, Dr/Reading Junior High Sch	154
Sapaugh, Julie/Brook Ave Elem Sch	282
Sarabia, Auden/Meyerland Perf-Visual Arts MS	194
Sarachene, Lou/Hinojosa Elem Sch	224
Sargent, Kristi/Itasca Middle Sch	228
Sari, Huseyin/Harmony Sci Acad-Carrollton [284]	5
Sarinana, Leanna/Idea Clg Prep-Weslaco	219
Sarminto, Alicia/Runn Elem Sch	215
Sarna, Ezra/Torah Girls Academy	207
Sarpy, April/Galloway Elem Sch	111
Sarpy, Gerald/Mesquite High Sch	111
Satterfield, Cody/Long Intermediate Sch	55
Satterwhite, Cassie/Grapeland Elem Sch	233
Sauceda, Carrie/Rising Scholars Acad of S TX	68
Sauceda, Jacinto/Jo Nelson Middle Sch	67
Sauceda, Richard/Hereford High Sch	119
Sauceda, Victor/Gilbert Intermediate Sch	144

Texas School Directory — PRINCIPAL INDEX

NAME/School	PAGE
Saucedo, Hugo/*Franklin Elem Sch*	40
Saucedo, Sylvia/*San Luis Elem Sch*	277
Sauder, Dorothy/*Tyler Adventist Sch*	339
Sauer, David/*Mineola High Sch*	404
Saul, Joanne/*Dixie Elem Sch*	338
Saunders, Kristin/*Woodlake Elem Sch*	34
Saunders, Suzanne/*I W & Eleanor Hyde Elem Sch*	159
Savage, Shaunna/*Caldwell Middle Sch*	59
Savala, Stephanie/*Goodman Elem Sch*	344
Savant, Cindy/*William Beverly Elem Sch*	83
Sawchak-Mooney, Kelly/*James H Ross Elem Sch*	159
Saxton, Ingia/*Brock Intermediate Sch*	312
Saxton, Janie/*Hastings 9th Grade Center*	182
Saxton, Nikki/*Leveretts Chapel Sch*	328
Sayavedra, Robert/*Guidance Center*	199
Sayler, Melissa/*Selwyn College Prep Sch*	126
Scarborough, Clayton/*North Lamar High Sch*	260
Scarbrough, Maribel/*Epps Island Elem Sch*	197
Schad, Elaine/*Immaculate Conception Catholic*	126
Schaefer, Dina/*Kelly Lane Middle Sch*	372
Schaefer, Kim/*Industrial Junior High Sch*	240
Schaeffer, Pamela/*Shawnee Trail Elem Sch*	80
Schattle, Gerald/*Aldine Education Center*	181
Schecter, Sarah, Dr/*The Oakridge Sch*	359
Scheibmeir, Phillip/*St Marys Catholic Sch*	168
Scheidt, Kemberly/*Dr Johnny T Clark Jr Elem Sch*	187
Schell, Maria/*Grand Prairie Fine Arts Acad*	107
Schellhamer, Kris/*Olsen Park Elem Sch*	318
Schepmann, Darrell/*Memorial Lutheran Sch*	206
Schepmann, Darrell/*Trinity Lutheran Chldrn's Ctr*	207
Schexnaider, Kevin/*Ridgewood Elem Sch*	244
Schiavolin, Jarin/*Regina Mater*	373
Schiller, Judy/*Lakewood Elem Sch*	27
Schilling, Stephanie/*Hillcrest Elem Sch*	295
Schmakel, Madison/*Magnolia Montessori for All*	8
Schmidt, Bob/*Juan Diego Academy*	226
Schmidt, Cathy/*Teague Lion Academy*	156
Schmidt, Chad/*Tomball Elem Sch*	203
Schmidt, Eric/*KIPP Courage College Prep [288]*	6
Schmidt, Linda/*Oak Forest Elem Sch*	196
Schmidt, Tobi/*Schrade Middle Sch*	106
Schminkey, Stephanie/*Arp Elem Sch*	336
Schmitt, Tammi/*Celia Hays Elem Sch*	325
Schneider, Brandy/*John W Armstrong Elem Sch*	106
Schneider, Carol/*Joshua SDA Multi Grade Sch*	249
Schneider, Chesta/*Dublin High Sch*	143
Schneider, Chesta/*Dublin Intermediate Sch*	143
Schneider, Jeff/*Post Oak Montessori Sch*	206
Schock, Jessica/*Old Town Elem Sch*	399
Schodowski, Tim/*Cumberland Academy*	2
Schoen, Kathryn/*Round Top Carmine Elem Sch*	147
Schoonover, Ben/*Bridge Academy*	314
Schott, Patrick, Dr/*Forest Vista Elem Sch*	123
Schratwieser, Melanie/*S C Lee Junior High Sch*	92
Schreiner, Michelle/*McCamey Primary Sch*	377
Schroller, Michael/*Floresville High Sch*	400
Schuenemann, Dawn/*Kaufer High Sch*	258
Schuler, Tami/*Greenspoint Elem Sch*	180
Schulte, Melanie/*Frankford Middle Sch*	82
Schultz, Jennifer/*Garden Ridge Elem Sch*	88
Schultz, Kara/*Ridgetop Elem Sch*	368
Schumacher, Kiley/*Carthage Primary Sch*	311
Schumaker, Kurt/*D'Hanis Sch*	283
Schur, Andria/*Carl Wunsche Sr High Sch*	202
Schutz, Lisa/*Brooks Collegiate Academy*	2
Schwab, Adam/*Cibolo Green Elem Sch*	34
Schwartz, Lisa/*Mozelle Brown Elem Sch*	339
Schwartz, Michael/*Ursula Stephens Elem Sch*	153
Schwartz, Scott/*Silsbee High Sch*	178
Schwartz, Stephen/*Fusion Academy-Southlake*	359
Schwarz, Janice/*Mildred Sch*	300
Schwarz, Steve/*Hill Country High Sch*	256
Schwarz, Steve/*Kerrville Discipline Alt Sch*	256
Schwarz, Therese/*Our Lady of the Hills Cath HS*	256
Schweers, Julie/*Stevenson Middle Sch*	38
Schweitzer, Shelena/*Temple Christian Sch*	359
Schwinger, Joy/*Donald Leonetti Elem Sch*	150
Scires, Shetonia/*Fairfield Intermediate Sch*	156
Scoggins, Kimberly/*Oakmont Elem Sch*	348
Scogin, Machelle/*Spradley Elem Sch*	84
Scott, Allison/*Dirks-Anderson Sch*	241
Scott, Brad/*Idea Clg Prep-Toros*	219
Scott, Chris/*Tomball High Sch*	203
Scott, Dana/*Skidmore Tynan High Sch*	25
Scott, Donald/*Tahoka Elem Sch*	273
Scott, Holly/*Cypress Grove Intermediate Sch*	55
Scott, Jessica/*Mead Middle Sch*	181
Scott, Jessica/*Thomas S Grantham Academy*	181
Scott, Jocelyn/*Zach White Elem Sch*	134
Scott, Kay/*Santa Rita Elem Sch*	365
Scott, Laura/*Scotland Park Elem Sch*	392
Scott, Mandy/*Creekside Intermediate Sch*	158
Scott, Marc/*Joe Lee Johnson Elem Sch*	399
Scott, Nachelle/*Quest Early College High Sch*	196
Scott, Robin/*Sue Wilson Stafford Middle Sch*	80
Scott, Stephanie/*Carrollton Classical Academy [297]*	2
Scott, Tana/*St Pius X Sch*	114
Scott, Toni/*McNeill Elem Sch*	154
Scott, Whitney/*Eastern Hills Elem Sch*	350
Scown, Panchi/*Bonham High Sch*	145
Screen, Kimberly/*Regina-Howell Elem Sch*	242
Scroggin, Raelyn/*Caldwell Elem Sch*	105
Scruggs, Sherry/*Joaquin Elem Sch*	335
Scrutchin, Dorothy/*Chinquapin Prep Sch*	205
Seabolt, Suzanne/*Johnson Ranch Elem Sch*	88
Seagroves, Ronnie/*Shepherd Intermediate Sch*	330
Seamster, Quentyn/*Int'l Ldrshp TX-Arlngtn GR PR*	108
Searcy, Holly/*Nichols Intermediate Sch*	73
Searle, Maria/*Our Lady of Perpetual Help Sch*	114
Sears, Carolyn/*St Vincent De Paul Sch*	204
Seastrunt, Erica/*Washington Elem Sch*	243
Seaton, Tiffany/*Dimmitt Middle Sch*	71
Seawright, Lisa/*La Vega Primary Center*	280
Sebesta, April/*Brookhollow Elem Sch*	18
Sebesta, Marla/*Needville Middle Sch*	154
Seeds, Amy/*Early Childhood Center*	304
Seelke, Chase/*Stamford High Sch*	250
Seely, Amber/*Whitney Elem Sch*	228
Seeton, Jeff/*Brewer High Sch*	357
Segers, David/*Ganado High Sch*	239
Segovia, Julissa/*Weldon Gibson Elem Sch*	304
Segundo, Modesta/*Hargill Elem Sch*	216
Segura, Irma/*Sharp Elem Sch*	64
Segura, Luis/*Julia Garcia Middle Sch*	64
Seidenberger, Angela/*Holy Cross Catholic Academy*	321
Seith, Nan/*Meador Elem Sch*	294
Self, Brandy/*Stephen F Austin Middle Sch*	318
Self, Colby/*Caldwell Elem Sch*	371
Selke, Adrielle/*Eagle Christian Academy*	282
Sell, Loren/*Perrin-Whitt High Sch*	239
Sellers, Daylan/*Seagraves High Sch*	157
Sellman, Rhonda/*Memorial Elem Sch*	225
Seltman, Nicole/*KIPP Austin Leadership ES [286]*	6
Seltzer, Mary/*Lakeview Elem Sch*	125
Semaan, Reem/*YES Prep West [312]*	14
Semmler, Michael/*Dean Learnan Junior High Sch*	153
Sempe, Kim/*Hamilton Middle Sch*	185
Sendejo, Victoria/*Chapel Hill Academy CS*	2
Senne, Tonya/*Jones Elem Sch*	257
Sepeda, Joshua/*Perkins Middle Sch*	89
Septimo, Cecilia/*Jubilee Livingway [285]*	6
Sepulveda, Jesse/*Sgt Jose Carrasco Elem Sch*	136
Sepulveda, Maria/*Idea Academy-Mays*	218
Sepulveda, Mary/*Jose De Escandon Elem Sch*	220
Serenil, Melissa/*Ramirez Charter Sch*	270
Serna Ramirez, Luz/*Veterans Memorial Elem Sch*	388
Serna, Christina/*Park View Intermediate Sch*	199
Serna, Stacy/*Daep*	173
Serrato, Anne Marie/*St Luke Catholic Sch*	68
Sessom, Charlotte/*Byron Martin Advanced Tech Ctr*	270

PRINCIPAL INDEX

NAME/School	PAGE
Setliff, Monte/Lockney Junior High Sch	149
Seward, Clint/Stratford Junior High Sch	336
Sewell, Monte/Chico Junior High Sch	403
Seybert, Jennifer/Abell Junior High Sch	285
Seybert, Jennifer/Young Women's Leadership Acad	286
Seymore, Kimberly/Oran M Roberts Elem Sch	102
Sha, Ting-Ling, Dr/A J Martin Elem Sch	182
Shackelford, Catherine/Collinsville Elem Sch	166
Shackelford, Kelly/Glen Rose High Sch	340
Shafer, Russell/Willis Classical Academy [297]	14
Shah, Vijay/The Humanist Academy	116
Shaikh-Jilani, Iram, Dr/Brighter Horizons Academy	114
Shank, Will/Calvary Chapel Christian Acad	44
Shapiro, Lauren/Catherine Bell Elem Sch	121
Sharber, Donna/Glen Oaks Sch	115
Sharifov, Agil/Harmony Sch Exc-Austin [284]	4
Sharma, Cody/Chinquapin Prep Sch	205
Sharp, Daniel/Kermit High Sch	402
Sharp, Denise/Forest Creek Elem Sch	398
Sharp, Henry/Detroit Elem Sch	322
Sharp, Marcia/Sam Houston Elem Sch	243
Sharp, Sylvia/Cedar Park Charter Academy [295]	2
Sharp, Veronica/Brown Elem Sch	367
Sharpless, Melanie/Founders Classical Acad Frisco [297]	3
Shaum, Kate/Windermere Elem Sch	372
Shaver, Kris/Buckholts Sch	287
Shaw, Diane/Garner Elem Sch	312
Shaw, Fulvia/Dr James Red Duke Elem Sch	51
Shaw, Jennifer/Pineywoods Community Academy	9
Shaw, Jennifer, Dr/PCA Dr Sarah Strinden Elem Sch	9
Shaw, Lori/James Carson Elem Sch	37
Shaw, Natasha/Ann Richards Steam Academy	98
Shaw, Tina/Evolution Academy-Richardson [279]	3
Shealy, Kathryn/Mueller Elem Sch	197
Sheats, Catherine/San Antonio Christian Mid Sch	45
Sheats, Catherine/San Antonio Christian Sch	45
Sheedy, Felicia/Mayde Creek Elem Sch	152
Sheffield, Stacy/Georgia Kimball Elem Sch	111
Shelby, Brett/Dr Bryan C Jack Elem Sch	338
Shelby, Hunter/Stacey Jr Sr High Sch	34
Shelby, Jill/Fort Worth Christian Sch	358
Shelby, Rhonda/Jewel S Houston Academy	181
Shelton, Brenda/Ronald Reagan High Sch	35
Shelton, Michael/Taylor Career & Tech Ctr	242
Shelton, Rob/Geneva School of Boerne	254
Shelton, Ron/Stuard Elem Sch	312
Shelton, Susan/Buffalo Lower Junior High Sch	264
Shepherd, Joy/Life School Red Oak [290]	8
Shepherd, Leslee/Keller Ctr Advanced Learning	355
Sheppard, Sherry/Hunstville Classical Academy [297]	5
Sherfield, Kimberly/J A Hargrave Elem Sch	348
Sherman, Geoffrey/Hubbard Middle Sch	338
Sherman, Melissa/The Fay Sch	207
Sherman, Rachel/Fred Douglass Elem Sch	73
Sherman, Rachel/Owens Elem Sch	338
Sherrill, John/Marfa Jr Sr High Sch	320
Sherrill, Kendra/Claude Sch	20
Sherwood, Bree/Premier HS-San Angelo [297]	9
Sherwood, Mitzi/Honey Grove Elem Sch	146
Shettel, Dixie/Highland Park High Sch	319
Shetzer, Steven/Pershing Middle Sch	194
Shields, Amber/N W Harllee Early Chldhd Ctr	102
Shifflett, Jennifer/Poolville High Sch	313
Shifrine, Deborah/KIPP Shine Prep [288]	7
Shillingburg, Brian/James Bowie Middle Sch	150
Shimmick, Sheila/Colleyville Elem Sch	353
Shinn, Melinda/Startzville Elem Sch	88
Shinn, Melissa/Trautmann Elem Sch	388
Shipley, Jaime/Amy Campbell Elem Sch	151
Shipman, Bryan/Blackwell Sch	301
Shipman, Paul/Hamshire Fannett High Sch	242
Shirey, Kandy/Scurry Rosser Elem Sch	253
Shivers, Vernitra/Thomas Middle Sch	193

NAME/School	PAGE
Shoemake, Julia/First Baptist Academy	115
Shomaker, Harry/Unity Christian Sch	169
Shonamon, Nancy/Nazarene Christian Academy	359
Shook, Betty/San Angelo Christian Academy	366
Short, Jason/Asa Low Jr Intermediate Sch	356
Short, Martha/Idea Academy-Monterrey Park	218
Shoulders, Michelle/Pin Oak Middle Sch	194
Showers, Jenna/Reno Elem Sch	313
Showers, Shauna/Mary Walke Stephens Elem Sch	180
Shreckengast, Craig/High Point Academy	5
Shuck, Jimmy, Dr/Copperas Cove High Sch	92
Shugart, Jessica/Juan Seguin Elem Sch	314
Shull, Keith/Newman Int'l Acad-Mansfield	8
Shumake, Julie/Bonner Elem Sch	338
Shumake, Julie/Mittelstadt Elem Sch	197
Shuman, Larry/Sanger 6th Grade Sch	126
Shuman, Toni/First Baptist Christian Acad	205
Shumate, Audrey/Redwater Middle Sch	49
Shumate, Leigh Anne/Grace Sch	206
Shurley, Andrea/Ursuline Academy	114
Shustella, Kris/Brook Hill Sch	339
Siano, Priscilla/Northwest Crossing Elem Sch	38
Sias, Tomas/Ira Cross Jr Elem Sch	28
Sibberson, Michael/Lometa Sch	262
Sides, Barbara/Industrial Elem Sch West	240
Siegel, Christi/Riojas Elem Sch	372
Sierra, Christine/Los Encinos Ses Elem Sch	303
Sierra, Norma/Mesa Vista Elem Sch	138
Sigurdson, Theresa/Francisco Medrano Middle Sch	100
Sikes, Ginger/Nola Kathryn Wilson Elem Sch	251
Silber, Deborah/Southwest Sch-Discovery MS [278]	11
Silberschlag, Ursula/Aue Elem Sch	36
Silerio, Enedith/De Chaumes Elem Sch	190
Siller, Ms/Herbert Boldt Elem Sch	37
Silliman, Renee, Dr/Hemmenway Elem Sch	185
Silman, Julie/Cooper Elem Sch	120
Silva, Ana/St Pius X Sch	139
Silva, Homero/Loretto Acad-Middle High Sch	139
Silva, Jennifer/Smith Elem Sch	182
Silva, Mark/Webb Elem Sch	261
Silva, Martha/Woodlawn Hills Elem Sch	41
Silva, Teresa/Alonso S Perales Elem Sch	31
Silva, Tizoc/Sharyland Alternative Ed Ctr	224
Silva, Vivian/Democracy Prep Stewart [227]	40
Silver, Jonathan/Austin Waldorf Sch	212
Silverman, Martin/Ricardo Salinas Elem Sch	33
Silvers, Jurahee/Junction Elem Sch	256
Simeon, Joesette/Rspa-E Northshore	10
Simmons, Aaron/YES Prep East End [312]	14
Simmons, Curtis/Schindewolf Intermediate Sch	197
Simmons, Dwain/Skyline High Sch	102
Simmons, Joseph/H R Jefferies Junior High Sch	89
Simmons, Lisa/Keller High Sch	355
Simmons, Shawn/Ponder Junior High Sch	126
Simmons, Sloane/Pine Forest Elem Sch	196
Simmons, Vernon/J Frank Dobie Jr High Sch	173
Simmons, Violet/Sugar Loaf Elem Sch	28
Simons, Everett/White Oak Middle Sch	294
Simons, Tommy/Chisholm Trail Academy	249
Simonton, Haley/KIPP Dream Prep [288]	7
Simpson, Chris/Leander High Sch	397
Simpson, Christine/Rouse High Sch	397
Simpson, E, Dr/A B Anderson Academy	179
Simpson, Michael/Greenhill Sch	115
Simpson, Sandy/Latexo Elem Sch	233
Simpson, Wendy/Hastings Elem Sch	105
Sims, Anthony/Joe Dale Sparks Campus	121
Sims, Debbie/Provident Heights Elem Sch	282
Sims, Julie/Dezavala Elem Sch	285
Sims, Mark/Endeavor HS-J F Campbell Ctr	183
Sims, Mary/St Helen Catholic Sch	400
Simsek, Hakan/Harmony Sch Innov-Sugar Land [284]	4
Singh, Kranti/McSpedden Elem Sch	79

Texas School Directory — PRINCIPAL INDEX

NAME/School	PAGE
Singleton, Julie/*Central Elem Sch*	99
Singleton, Melanie/*Wheeler Ave Christian Academy*	207
Singleton, Steven/*Randall High Sch*	321
Siscer, Latasha/*Mountaintop Learning Center*	206
Sisco-Martinez, Jenny/*Early Childhood Center*	186
Sisk, Christopher/*Coppell Classical Academy [297]*	2
Sisk, Valerie/*Warren High Sch*	39
Sitton, Karli/*Olympia Elem Sch*	33
Sizemore, Patrick/*Bandera Middle Sch*	23
Skarke, Clyde/*Deerpark HS Wolters Campus*	186
Skelton, Jason/*Lake View High Sch*	365
Skelton, Will/*Marcus High Sch*	123
Skinner, Adam/*Huffman Middle Sch*	195
Skinner, Lindsay/*New Boston Middle Sch*	49
Skruch, Sherie/*Ranchview High Sch*	97
Slade, Anne/*Spring Lake Park Elem Sch*	50
Slaten, Lindsay/*Hallsville High Sch*	208
Slater, David/*Magnolia Junior High Sch*	293
Slaton, Joanna, Dr/*South Grand Prairie Echs*	108
Slaughter, Lisa/*Sivells Bend Sch*	91
Slayter, Kim/*Kilgore Intermediate Sch*	169
Sloan, Autumn/*Pease Elem Sch*	130
Sloan, John/*Cedar Park High Sch*	397
Sloan, Laura/*Village Elem Sch*	395
Slone, James/*Ann Whitney Elem Sch*	176
Slovacek, Cindy/*Joe Wright Elem Sch*	73
Smart, Brit/*Oak Hill Academy*	115
Smart, Karen/*Needville Junior High Sch*	154
Smedley, Anthony/*Angleton High Sch*	51
Smejkal, Barbara/*Miller's Point Elem Sch*	33
Smetana, Frances/*Raye-Allen Elem Sch*	29
Smiley, Michael/*Henrietta High Sch*	74
Smith, Alice, Dr/*Llano Christian Academy*	269
Smith, Alison/*Messiah Luth Classical Academy*	359
Smith, Alison/*Midway High Sch*	281
Smith, Amy/*Bay Colony Elem Sch*	159
Smith, Andrea/*East Chambers Primary Sch*	72
Smith, Andrea/*Stewart's Creek Elem Sch*	124
Smith, Angela, Dr/*Boles Junior High Sch*	344
Smith, Armenia/*Glen Couch Elem Sch*	106
Smith, Ashley/*College Street Elem Sch*	337
Smith, Benjamin/*New Tech High Sch at Waskow*	27
Smith, Billye, Dr/*Dickinson High Sch*	159
Smith, Blanca/*McCamey Middle Sch*	377
Smith, Brandon/*Valley Sch*	176
Smith, Brian/*Holy Spirit Episcopal Sch*	206
Smith, Briton/*Founders Classical Acad Flower [297]*	3
Smith, Calvin/*Timpson Middle Sch*	335
Smith, Chad/*Monahans Education Center HS*	385
Smith, Charita/*Travis Intermediate Sch*	292
Smith, Chris/*Spring Branch Middle Sch*	88
Smith, Christopher/*Burges High Sch*	134
Smith, Christopher/*Manor New Tech Middle Sch*	371
Smith, Connie/*North Forest High Sch*	189
Smith, Connie/*Tanglewood Elem Sch*	352
Smith, Daniel/*Sinton High Sch*	332
Smith, Darrell, Dr/*Grace Christian Academy*	206
Smith, Dennis/*Giddings State Sch*	3
Smith, Diana/*Monte Cristo Elem Sch*	217
Smith, Elizabeth/*Cedar Ridge Elem Sch*	282
Smith, Emily/*Branch Sch*	205
Smith, Errol/*Stateline Christian Sch*	95
Smith, Gayle/*Kathlyn Joy Gilliam Academy*	101
Smith, Ginny/*Lamar Elem Sch*	318
Smith, Jana/*Tioga Sch*	167
Smith, Jared/*Lone Oak College St Campus*	236
Smith, Jay/*Dime Box Sch*	263
Smith, Jayne/*Bettye Haun Elem Sch*	82
Smith, Jeff/*Harpool Middle Sch*	121
Smith, Jeffery/*Mineral Wells Academy*	310
Smith, Jennifer/*Mountain Valley Elem Sch*	88
Smith, Jennifer/*North Central Texas Academy*	231
Smith, John/*Eisenhower Middle Sch*	35
Smith, John/*Houston Gateway Academy-Coral*	5
Smith, John/*Tascosa High Sch*	318
Smith, Jonathan/*David W Carter High Sch*	99
Smith, Jonathan/*Deerpark Middle Sch*	398
Smith, Jonnie/*J E Rhodes Elem Sch*	381
Smith, Justin/*Rayburn Intermediate Sch*	55
Smith, Katrina/*Eastern Hills High Sch*	350
Smith, Kelsey/*Austin Elem Sch*	314
Smith, Kendrick/*Liberty-Eylau High Sch*	48
Smith, Kerri/*Oaks Elem Sch*	196
Smith, Kim/*West Foundation Elem Sch*	393
Smith, Lakeisha/*Thomas Tolbert Elem Sch*	103
Smith, Lana/*Livingston High Sch Academy*	317
Smith, Laura/*McKinney Christian Academy*	86
Smith, Leah/*Brentwood Christian Sch*	373
Smith, Leah/*Holland Middle Sch*	27
Smith, Linda/*St Mark's Sch*	139
Smith, Llewellyn/*Justin F Kimball High Sch*	101
Smith, Loyd/*Phoenix Alt Campus 817*	247
Smith, Lucinda/*Rogers Middle Sch*	29
Smith, Lynn/*City Lab High Sch*	99
Smith, Lynn/*Multiple Careers Magnet Center*	102
Smith, Malcolm/*Calvary Episcopal Sch*	155
Smith, Mark/*Art & Pat Goforth Elem Sch*	158
Smith, Mary/*Dezavala Envir Sci Acad*	107
Smith, Megan/*Amy Parks-Heath Elem Sch*	325
Smith, Melissa/*Antonio M Ochoa Elem Sch*	215
Smith, Melissa/*Ed Vanston Middle Sch*	111
Smith, Melissa/*Hollis T Dietz Elem Sch*	251
Smith, Michael/*Bridgeland High Sch*	184
Smith, Michael/*Hurst Junior High Sch*	354
Smith, Michael/*Savoy High Sch*	146
Smith, Michael/*West Hardin High Sch*	179
Smith, Monica/*G W Kennemer Middle Sch*	105
Smith, Nikia/*Int'l Ldrshp TX-East Ft Worth*	108
Smith, Patricia/*Jhw Inspire Acad-Legacy Ranch*	31
Smith, Paul/*Smithville High Sch*	24
Smith, Rahsan/*Polly Ann McRoberts Elem Sch*	152
Smith, Randi/*Bryant Elem Sch*	344
Smith, Rebecca/*Eastside Elem Sch*	265
Smith, Rhonda/*Liberty Middle Sch*	266
Smith, Rotasha/*Conroe High Sch*	291
Smith, Shelby/*Madeley Ranch Elem Sch*	293
Smith, Sherri/*Central Elem Sch*	104
Smith, Susan/*Hemphill Elem Sch*	329
Smith, Susan/*Valley View Sch*	91
Smith, Ted/*Aep Center*	26
Smith, Ted/*Salado Junior High Sch*	29
Smith, Theresa/*Berne Acad Private Sch*	114
Smith, Tim/*Wylie High Sch*	361
Smith, Traci, Dr/*Stonewall Flanders Elem Sch*	33
Smitherman, Christie/*Roland Reynolds Elem Sch*	325
Smock, Farrah/*Parkhill Junior High Sch*	113
Smolka, David/*Bessie Gunstream Elem Sch*	78
Smoot, Cody/*Covenant Preparatory Sch*	205
Smothers, David/*Sweeny Junior High Sch*	54
Smyder, Christa/*A B Harrison Intermediate Sch*	85
Smyder, Greg/*Blue Ridge Elem Sch*	77
Snavely, William/*Memorial Middle Sch*	65
Snavely, William/*Stuart Place Elem Sch*	65
Sneed, Cynthia/*Jubilee Wells Branch [285]*	6
Sneed, Cynthia/*Jubilee-Wells Academies*	6
Sneed, Romikianta/*Martin Luther King Jr Lrng Ctr*	101
Snider, Kimberlyn/*Neches Elem Jr High Sch*	15
Sniffin, Jeanna/*Ronald Thornton Middle Sch*	151
Snokhous, Vicki/*Cypress Creek High Sch*	184
Snook, Don/*West High Sch*	282
Snow, Ronnie/*Malakoff Elem Sch*	214
Snow, Ronny/*Rusk High Sch*	73
Snowden, Ryan/*Wall High Sch*	365
Snyder, Catherine/*Clifton Park Elem Sch*	27
Snyder, Janie/*Southside Elem Sch*	265
Snyder, Robalyn/*Hunters Creek Elem Sch*	201
Snyder, Scott, Dr/*San Saba High Sch*	332
Snyder, Stacia/*Marion High Sch*	172
Sobelman, Patty/*Pines Montessori Sch*	206
Solano, Beatriz/*Kelly Elem Sch*	217

PRINCIPAL INDEX

Market Data Retrieval

NAME/*School*	PAGE	NAME/*School*	PAGE
Solano, Gregorio/*Hidalgo Park Elem Sch*	217	**Spruell, Sandra**/*Coggin Intermediate Sch*	58
Soldevila, Jorge/*Harker Heights High Sch*	28	Spurgeon, Alison/*Palmer Elem Sch*	142
Solis, Lesli/*Medina Valley Middle Sch*	284	Spurgers, Kimberly/*San Jacinto Elem Sch*	365
Solis, Lynda/*Wedgeworth Elem Sch*	143	**Spurlock, Oscar**/*Jerry Junkins Elem Sch*	100
Solis, Maria/*Farias Early Childhood Center*	190	Squalls, Lorie/*Barbara S Austin Elem Sch*	98
Solis, Maria/*Gladys Porter Early Clg HS*	63	Square, Stephanie/*East Early College High Sch*	189
Solis, Maria/*San Benito High Sch*	67	Squiers, Wayne/*Reagan Magnet Elem Sch*	130
Solis, Roger/*Dilley High Sch*	157	Squires, Jared/*Kingdom Preparatory Academy*	272
Soliz, Becky/*Texas Christian Sch*	207	Squyres, Carrie/*Hoffmann Elem Sch*	37
Soliz, Elva/*Camino Real Elem Sch*	211	Sralla, Scott/*Student Reassignment Ctr*	110
Soliz, Maytte/*North Heights Elem Sch*	379	St Clair, Keitha/*Blanco High Sch*	46
Solomon, Dana/*Phillips Elem Sch*	80	St Ama, Michael/*Dr Wright Lassiter Erly Clg HS*	99
Somerhalder, Michelle/*Timber Creek High Sch*	355	St John, Keri/*Bynum Sch*	286
Soriano, Rafael/*Padron Elem Sch*	368	St Julian, Delilah/*Weaver Odom Elem Sch*	180
Sosa, Andi/*Carnahan Elem Sch*	36	Stabile, Amy/*KIPP Explore Academy [288]*	7
Sosa, Melissa/*Samuel Clemens High Sch*	173	Stackhouse, Stephen/*Ft Worth Country Day Sch*	359
Sotelo, Joseph/*Hillcrest High Sch*	100	Stadler, Meredith/*McQueeney Elem Sch*	174
Soto-Dimas, Luz/*Central Elem Sch*	96	**Stafford, Amanda**/*Archer City High Sch*	19
Soto, Ana/*Helen Ball Elem Sch*	136	Stafford, Jill/*Lowery Freshman Center*	77
Soto, Linda/*Lyndon B Johnson Middle Sch*	223	Stafford, Nadia/*Gus A Oleson Elem Sch*	180
Soto, Lisa/*Leon Daiches Elem Sch*	387	Staggs, Becky/*Sojourn Academy*	295
Soto, Patricia/*Academy Academic Enhancemnt-ES*	340	Stahl, Lana/*Eagle Heights Christian Acad*	54
Soto, Samuel/*Bluebonnet Elem Sch*	398	Stahnke, Curtis/*Comanche Elem Sch*	89
Soukup, Theresa/*Brookhaven Sch*	282	Stainbrook, Jacob/*Uplift Wisdom Prep Sec Sch [309]*	13
Soulas, Alexis/*E E & Jovita Mireles Elem Sch*	303	Staley, Michele/*Clear Brook High Sch*	158
Southard, Michelle/*Shallowater Intermediate Sch*	272	Stamos, Caroline/*Fairhill Sch*	115
Southard, Todd/*Pilot Point High Sch*	125	Stanfield, Tanis/*Comquest Academy*	2
Southworth, Chaisleigh/*Raul B Fernandez Elem Sch*	38	Stanley, Debra, Dr/*Mary Grett Sch*	304
Sozar, Abigal/*St Monica Sch*	44	Stanley, Ingrid/*Applegate Adventist Jr Academy*	400
Sparacello, Leslie/*Midland Senior High Sch*	286	Stanmore, Fred/*Life Middle School Waxahachie [290]*	7
Sparks, Brian/*Lamar Elem Sch*	41	Stansberry, Darrin/*Yoakum Primary Sch*	118
Sparks, Kathy/*Victory Christian Academy*	307	Stanton, Sonya/*Euless Junior High Sch*	354
Sparks, Kayla/*Three Way Elem Sch*	144	Stapinski, Camcea/*North Crowley 9th Grade Campus*	348
Sparks, Leticia/*M G Ellis Primary Sch*	351	Stapleton, Kathy/*St Anthony Sch*	68
Sparksgoecke, Kathy/*Grandview Hills Elem Sch*	397	Stapleton, Steven/*Furr High Sch*	189
Spaugh, Donna/*Bayshore Elem Sch*	198	Stapp, Michelle/*Castleberry Elem Sch*	347
Spawn, Amy/*Warren Center*	113	**Starkweather, Brett**/*Grandfalls Royalty Sch*	385
Speaker, Tracy/*Northwest Early College HS*	132	Starnes, Betty/*Hillcrest Sch*	286
Speaks, Monica/*Clear View High Sch*	158	Staten, Charla/*Christene Moss Elem Sch*	350
Spear, Stephanie/*Reese Education Center*	269	Staten, Natasha/*Del Valle Middle Sch*	369
Spearman, Cassandra/*Hay Branch Elem Sch*	28	Statlander, Katie/*Shsu CS-Greengate Academy*	11
Spears, Jennifer/*Wharton Elem Sch*	390	Statos, Jerry/*Manor Excel Academy*	371
Spears, Shelly/*Judy Rucker Elem Sch*	84	Staufert, Martha/*Audelia Creek Elem Sch*	112
Specia, Christopher/*Roan Forest Elem Sch*	35	Stavinoha, Leroy/*Garwood Elem Sch*	87
Specter, Tristan/*Burleson Elem Sch*	130	Stavinoha, Stacey/*Needville Elem Sch*	154
Spedding, Bill/*Keystone Sch*	45	Steed, Melanie/*Chandler Elem Sch*	382
Speer, Sandra/*Brill Elem Sch*	197	Steed, Paige/*Childress High Sch*	74
Speights, Christie/*Horace Mann Junior High Sch*	188	Steele, Ryan/*Mathews Elem Sch*	83
Spellmann, Gerrie/*Woodridge Elem Sch*	30	Steen, Jamila/*Nancy J Cochran Elem Sch*	102
Spelman, Barbara/*New Hope High Sch*	397	Steen, Jill/*Tatom Elem Sch*	385
Spence, Connie, Dr/*Kooken Educational Center*	344	**Steenport, Nathan**/*Doss Elem Sch*	367
Spencer, Antoine/*Otto Middle Sch*	83	Steffens, Dirk/*St Joseph Catholic Sch*	30
Spencer, Dusty/*Canton High Sch*	380	Stegall, Shelly/*Hico Secondary Sch*	176
Spencer, Gloria/*Plato Academy*	138	Steger, Will/*Pritchard Junior High Sch*	165
Spencer, Stefanie/*Spring Branch Middle Sch*	201	Stein, Jean Carol/*Child Montessori Sch*	44
Speyrer, Steven/*Landrum Middle Sch*	201	Stein, Jennifer/*Hardin Junior High Sch*	266
Spicer, Brent/*Saint Mary's Hall*	45	Steinbach, Laura/*Rawson Saunders Sch*	373
Spikes, Bob/*Lueders-Avoca Elem Jr High Sch*	250	**Steinbecker, Catrina**/*Milano High Sch*	287
Spillman, Freda/*Memorial Chrn Academy*	206	Steinberger, Dane/*Herman E Utley Middle Sch*	325
Spitzer, Jennifer/*Owen Elem Sch*	123	Steiner, Bobbie/*Faubion Elem Sch*	397
Spivey, Frances/*Crockett Classical Academy [297]*	2	**Steiner, Bobbie**/*R J Richey Elem Sch*	60
Spivey, Sandra/*Polk Elem Sch*	134	Steinhilber, Halley/*Tate Springs Christian Sch*	359
Spoon, Deborah/*Tom Cox Intermediate Sch*	292	Stell, Robert/*Pflugerville Middle Sch*	372
Spraberry, Cody/*Forest Trail Elem Sch*	370	Stelly, Dana/*Thomas B Francis Elem Sch*	180
Sprang, Gina/*Elsik 9th Grade Center*	182	Stelly, Haley/*Light Farms Elem Sch*	84
Sprayberry, Felicia/*Gonzalez Pre-K Center*	121	Stengler, Waylon/*Harmony Sch Endeavor-Austin [284]*	4
Sprayberry, Kim/*Lynn Lucas Middle Sch*	294	Stepan, Robin/*Laguna Madre Christian Academy*	68
Springer, Gerald/*Pottsboro Middle Sch*	167	**Stephen, Julia**/*Coronado High Sch*	270
Springer, Laura/*Coppell High Sch*	98	**Stephens, Celee**/*Smith Elem Sch*	105
Springs, Marilyn, Sr/*Holy Family Catholic Sch*	306	Stephens, Christofor/*Robert L Thornton Elem Sch*	102
Sprott, Mariea/*Hightower Elem Sch*	82	**Stephens, Jaime**/*Crouch Elem Sch*	344
Sproul, Ross/*Boerne High Sch*	254	Stephens, Jen/*Ortega Elem Sch*	367
Spruell, Carl/*Priddy Sch*	289	Stephens, John/*Ft Worth Country Day Sch*	359

Texas School Directory

PRINCIPAL INDEX

NAME/School	PAGE
Stephens, Kemlyn/*La Academia De Estrellas CS*	7
Stephens, Lisa/*Tarkington High Sch*	266
Stephens, Shelia/*Cleveland Middle Sch*	265
Stephens, Sunee/*Edwards-Johnson Memorial MS*	178
Stephenson, Jennifer/*Ganado Elem Sch*	239
Stephenson, Melody/*Sam Houston Middle Sch*	318
Sterling, Marchelle/*Colin Powell Elem Sch*	107
Sterling, Maureen/*South Euless Elem Sch*	354
Stern, Misty/*Canterbury Episcopal Sch*	114
Sternenberg, Amy/*San Jacinto Christian Academy*	319
Steuernagel, Philip/*Berry Elem Sch*	190
Stevens, Alan/*Boone Elem Sch*	366
Stevens, Courtney/*Era Sch*	91
Stevens, Deidrea/*Cedar Hill Collegiate High Sch*	97
Stevens, James/*Merkel High Sch*	361
Stevens, Louanne/*Alvarado Elem North Sch*	246
Stevens, Theresa/*Slidell Elem Sch*	403
Stevens, Theresa/*Slidell Secondary Sch*	403
Stevens, Ty/*Sterling Middle High Sch*	342
Stevenson, James/*Kountze Middle Sch*	178
Stevenson, Jared/*Wieland Elem Sch*	372
Stevenson, Tatanisha/*Houston Elem Sch*	110
Stevenson, Vicki/*Thomas Elem Sch*	154
Steward, Carmen/*Christa McAuliffe Learning Ctr*	112
Steward, John/*Metcalf Elem Sch*	185
Stewart, Angie/*Legacy Christian Academy*	45
Stewart, Bonnie/*Harper High Sch*	163
Stewart, Cheryl/*Jubilee Academic Center*	6
Stewart, Debra/*Ortiz Elem Sch*	360
Stewart, Denise/*Upland Heights Elem Sch*	269
Stewart, Elizabeth/*Lytle Junior High Sch*	21
Stewart, Harper/*B T Wilson 6th Grade Sch*	256
Stewart, Jennifer/*North Elem Sch*	117
Stewart, Katherine/*Grandview Elem Sch*	248
Stewart, Kelli/*Frank Stone Middle Sch*	259
Stewart, Malinda/*Rice Elem Sch*	292
Stewart, Marguerite/*Westside High Sch*	195
Stewart, Natasha/*Bowie Middle Sch*	109
Stewart, Rockell/*Billy Earl Dade Middle Sch*	99
Stewart, Sandra/*Cedar Park Middle Sch*	397
Stewart, Sara/*Centennial Elem Sch*	82
Stewart, Seymour/*Miller Intermediate Sch*	182
Stewart, Shaunte/*La Vega Elem Sch*	280
Stewart, Thomasine/*Success High Sch*	399
Stewart, Tommy/*Daingerfield High Sch*	296
Stewart, Walter/*Aldine Senior HS*	180
Stichler, Jeffrey/*Caney Creek High Sch*	291
Stickels, David/*Saltillo Sch*	231
Stidom, Wanda/*Live Oak Ridge Middle Sch*	28
Still, Kristin/*Rick Schneider Middle Sch*	199
Still, Peggy/*Brenham Middle Sch*	385
Stillman, Sherry/*Bob & Lola Sandford Elem Sch*	168
Sting, Zachary/*Idea Clg Prep-Brackenridge*	218
Stinnett, Lanette/*Spring Valley Elem Sch*	113
Stitt, Melanie/*Elmer C Watson High Sch*	348
Stockton, Karen/*Post Elem Sch*	185
Stockton, Karen, Dr/*Lieder Elem Sch*	185
Stockton, Mary/*Cleburn Eubanks Interm Sch*	347
Stoddard, Eric/*San Vicente Elem Sch*	57
Stogsdill, Monica/*William R Carmichael Elem Sch*	179
Stoker, Shannon/*Fellowship Academy*	358
Stone, Amy/*Mart Elem Sch*	280
Stone, David/*St James Catholic Sch*	174
Stone, Melinda/*Woodcreek Junior High Sch*	153
Stoner, Heather/*Lago Vista High Sch*	370
Storie, Tyra/*Frank Elem Sch*	197
Storm, Georgann/*Team Sch*	247
Stout, Linda/*Crawford Elem Sch*	279
Stout, Sherry/*Benavides Elem Sch*	63
Stovall, Damien/*Edward Titche Elem Sch*	100
Stover, Shane/*Huntington High Sch*	17
Stowe, Jana/*England Elem Sch*	398
Stowe, Robin/*Crockett Elem Sch*	232
Stoyanoff, Stacy/*Westlake Academy*	14
Stradley, Kim/*Big Sandy High Sch*	376

NAME/School	PAGE
Stradley, Kimberly/*Big Sandy Junior High Sch*	376
Strahan, Marcie/*W T Hall Education Center*	180
Strait, Brandy/*Texas Prep School-San Marcos*	12
Strambler, Meredith/*A V Cato Elem Sch*	347
Stranacher, Danette/*Axtell Elem Sch*	278
Streitmatter, Ardath/*Gene M Reed Elem Sch*	77
Streitmatter, Ardath/*James D Kerr Elem Sch*	77
Stresow, Sandra/*Thomas Manor Elem Sch*	138
Stribling, Johnett/*Vega Elem Sch*	308
Strickland, Aron/*Shallowater Middle Sch*	272
Strickland, Caynon/*Sunset Elem Sch*	295
Strickland, Jeremy/*Trenton High Sch*	147
Strickland, Kerresha/*Toler Elem Sch*	107
Strickland, Kristi, Dr/*Lake Dallas High Sch*	122
Strickland, Kristin/*Arapaho Classical Magnet Sch*	112
Strickland, Magdalena/*Lantrip Elem Sch*	190
Strickland, Mary/*Faith West Academy*	205
Stringer, Suzette/*Martin's Mill Sch*	381
Strittmatter, Rae/*Pilot Point Elem Sch*	125
Strobach, Marta/*Deanna Davenport Elem Sch*	132
Strode, Matt/*Chapel Hill Middle Sch*	337
Stroeher, Mark/*Doss Elem Sch*	162
Strole, Shannon/*Benfer Elem Sch*	196
Stroman, Silvia/*Bloomburg Sch*	70
Strong, Jennifer/*Brushy Creek Elem Sch*	398
Strong, Michael/*Academy of Thought & Industry*	372
Strother, Martha/*Windfern High School of Choice*	186
Stroud, Jesse/*Woden Elem Sch*	298
Stroud, Jesse/*Woden High Sch*	298
Stroud, Tracy/*Nottingham Country Elem Sch*	152
Stuard, Kyle/*Prairie Creek Elem Sch*	113
Stuart, Michael/*Dorothy Smith Pullen Elem Sch*	325
Stuart, Vanessa/*Degan Elem Sch*	123
Stubblefield, Amanda/*Groveton Elem Sch*	374
Stubblefield, David/*Winfree Academy-Lewisville [311]*	14
Stults, Bobby/*Lake Worth High Sch*	356
Stults, Bobby/*Robert E Lee Freshman High Sch*	286
Stults, Mary/*Indian Springs Elem Sch*	88
Stumbaugh, Jennifer/*Los Fresnos 9th & 10th GR Sch*	66
Stumbaugh, Justin/*Los Fresnos High Sch*	66
Sturdivant, Jaime/*Bridgeport High Sch*	402
Sturgeon, James/*Santa Anna High Sch*	76
Suarez, Aracely/*River Oaks Elem Sch*	372
Suarez, Lindsey/*Barber Middle Sch*	159
Subas, Mehmet/*Harmony Sch Sci-Austin [284]*	4
Sublette, Tara/*D P Morris Elem Sch*	356
Suchsland, Sheryl/*Louise Cabaniss Elem Sch*	357
Suders, Shelia/*Citadel Christian Sch*	386
Suess, Carrie/*San Marcos Adventist Jr Acad*	212
Suhr, Kimmarie/*Hyde Park Elem Middle Sch*	373
Sullivan, Dottie/*Centerville Elem Sch*	264
Sullivan, Kathleen/*Hill Country Middle Sch*	370
Sullivan, Marla/*J L Williams-Lovett Ledger ES*	92
Sullivan, Tammy/*Kimberlin Acad for Excellence*	106
Sullivan, Teresa/*Willow Creek Elem Sch*	203
Sullivant, Catherine/*Texas Connections Academy [181]*	189
Summerhill, Randy/*Tannahill Intermediate Sch*	357
Summerhill, William/*Ascension Academy*	321
Summers, Alan/*Sam Houston Math Sci Tech HS*	192
Summers, Brittni/*Dr James D Foster Elem Sch*	281
Summers, Cody/*Bill F Davis Intermediate Sch*	85
Sumners, Staci/*Brown Elem Sch*	270
Sumpter, Jay/*John Jay High Sch*	37
Sundt, Jackie/*M H Specht Elem Sch*	88
Supak, Bobbi/*Navarro Intermediate Sch*	173
Supak, Erin/*Caldwell Elem Sch*	59
Suthers, Becky/*Higgins Sch*	268
Sutton, Angela/*Dodson Primary Sch*	405
Sutton, Brishaun/*Bell Elem Sch*	193
Sutton, Deidra/*Wylie Elem Sch*	327
Sutton, Jennifer/*Buena Vista Elem Sch*	379
Sutton, Jonathan, Dr/*Dr Shirley J Williamson ES*	187
Sveum, Michelle/*Links Academy*	247
Swaby, Bobbie/*Piney Point Elem Sch*	194
Swain, Steven/*Chisholm Trail Middle Sch*	398

PRINCIPAL INDEX

NAME/School	PAGE
Swan, Tom/Community Sch	198
Swaner, Elizabeth/Berkner STEM Academy	112
Swann, Cathy/Joe Lawrence Elem Sch	111
Swann, Leslie/E B Comstock Middle Sch	99
Swanson, Brittany/Mt Auburn Elem Sch	102
Swantner, Elizabeth/Resaca Middle Sch	66
Swanzy, Jenny/Woodland Heights Elem Sch	58
Sweaney, Richard/Brownwood Middle Sch	58
Swearengen, Thomas/Shelbyville Middle Sch	335
Swearingin, James/Trinity Christian Sch	116
Swearingin, Shanna/Ponderosa Elem Sch	202
Swenson, Brandi/Bradford Elem Sch	392
Swenson, Jessica/South Houston Intermediate Sch	200
Swinney, James/Warren High Sch	375
Swize, Georgie/Cora Spencer Elem Sch	356
Sword, Paula/Jackson Intermediate Sch	199
Sylvan, Yvette/Franz Elem Sch	152
Symanik, Julie/Sam Rayburn Sch	146
Symank, Josh/Oakwood Intermediate Sch	55
Symm, Daniel/Bellville Junior High Sch	22

T

NAME/School	PAGE
Tabb, Shello/East Ft Worth Montessori Acad	2
Tabor, Amanda/Alvis C Story Elem Sch	76
Tagle, Adriana/Banquete Elem Sch	302
Talamantes, Irene/Whittier Middle Sch	41
Talamantes, Leslie/Highland Lakes Elem Sch	60
Talamantez, Jill/Connally High Sch	279
Talbert, Patrick/Tidehaven High Sch	276
Talbert, Patrick/Tidehaven Intermediate Sch	276
Taluyo, Arlene/KIPP Intrepid Prep Sch [288]	7
Tamez, Allison/Pearl Hall Elem Sch	199
Tamez, Arely/Vernon Middle Sch	65
Tanguma, Mariselda/Seas Alternative Ed Center	340
Tankersley, Stephanie/Lake Air Mont Magnet Sch	282
Tapia, Erica/Odem Intermediate Sch	331
Tapia, Morella/Wildcat Way Sch	201
Taraba, Susan/North Texas Collegiate Acad-E [300]	8
Tatir, Abdullah/Harmony Sci Acad-Laredo [284]	5
Tatmon, Mellow/Dishman Elem Sch	242
Tatum, Dalea/Allen 6th Grade Campus	317
Tatum, Patricia/Davis Elem Sch	105
Taulton, Bryan, Dr/Hardin High Sch	266
Tavarez, Ishii/Northwood Hills Elem Sch	113
Taylor, Amy/Austin High Sch	368
Taylor, Anabel/Hollibrook Elem Sch	201
Taylor, Anita/Fadden-McKeown-Chambliss ES	25
Taylor, Benjamin/Plains Middle Sch	406
Taylor, Brad/Parkwood Hill Intermediate Sch	355
Taylor, Carol/Huston Academy	5
Taylor, Christopher/Keene Wanda R Smith High Sch	248
Taylor, Donna/Castle Hills Elem Sch	122
Taylor, Everette/Voyde Caraway Elem Sch	179
Taylor, Henry/Thomas Haley Elem Sch	110
Taylor, Israel/Travis Elem Sch	243
Taylor, Jason/Salem Sayers Baptist Academy	45
Taylor, John/Bluff Dale Elem Sch	143
Taylor, Kevin/South Belton Middle Sch	27
Taylor, Lakesha/Dunbar Early Education Center	50
Taylor, Michele/Stinson Elem Sch	83
Taylor, Mindy/Reicher Catholic High Sch	282
Taylor, Pam/Mt Calm Elem Sch	228
Taylor, Pegah/KIPP Connect Houston MS [288]	6
Taylor, Sheri/Bell Elem Sch	338
Taylor, Sheri/James S Hogg Middle Sch	338
Taylor, Sheri/Keeley Elem Sch	106
Taylor, Stephanie/Billy Vandeventer Middle Sch	79
Taylor, Stephanie/Gholson Sch	279
Taylor, Todd/Mansfield Summit High Sch	357
Teaff, Bambi/Harmony Sch Exc-San Antonio [284]	4
Teamann, Amber/Don Whitt Elem Sch	85
Tecklenburg, Jennifer/W W Samuell High Sch	103
Teddy, Amy/Indian Creek Elem Sch	123
Tefertiller, Aaron/Alvord High Sch	402
Tejada, Jessica/Edgewood Elem Sch	201
Telles, Laura/Glass Elem Sch	277
Teltschik, Sophie/Hallettsville Jr High Sch	262
Templeton, Craig/Harrold Sch	393
Tennery, Jody/Avalon Sch	140
Tennison, Alicia/West Side Elem Sch	73
Teran, Tricia/Bonham Elem Sch	285
Terrazas, Leticia/Desert Wind Elem Sch	136
Terrell, David/Frost Elem Sch	192
Terrell, Reginald/Handley Middle Sch	350
Terrell, Trisha/C G Sivells Elem Sch	390
Tessar, Adrienne/William B Travis Elem Sch	188
Tewell, Leslie/Keller-Harvel Elem Sch	355
Thacker, Patricia/Armstrong Elem Sch	291
Tharpe, Kelly/H G Isbill Junior High Sch	280
Thatcher, Laura/Premier HS-Mission [297]	9
Thayer, David/Alice Ponder Elem Sch	356
Theesfield, Debra/Richard Milburn Acad-Midland [298]	10
Theodore, Kecia/Student Opportunity Center	80
Therwhanger, Danielle/Klondike Sch	117
Thetford, Susan/Marion Middle Sch	172
Thibodeaux, Traci/Reve Preparatory Charter Sch	10
Thirston, Brandon, Dr/Liberty-Eylau Elem Sch	48
Thomas-Boone, Sheila/Ennis Junior High Sch	140
Thomas, Angie/Tarkington Primary Sch	266
Thomas, Carla/Culver Elem Sch	153
Thomas, Carla/Smith Elem Sch	154
Thomas, Charlotte/Annie Rainwater Elem Sch	96
Thomas, Chrystal/Scott Elem Sch	29
Thomas, Derrick, Dr/St Philip's Early Clg HS	41
Thomas, Drew/Fannindel Elem Sch	120
Thomas, Ed/San Jacinto Christian Academy	319
Thomas, James/Bayside Intermediate Sch	158
Thomas, Jamila/Uplift Peak Prep Sch [309]	13
Thomas, Jamilla/GW Carver 6th GR STEM Lrng Ctr	110
Thomas, Jenny/Armand Bayou Elem Sch	158
Thomas, Jorly/Fred Roberts Middle Sch	199
Thomas, Keith/George Gervin Academy	3
Thomas, Keith/Ruth Jones McClendon Mid Sch	10
Thomas, Lakisha/T W Browne Middle Sch	103
Thomas, Leslie/Cactus Trails Elem Sch	136
Thomas, Michael/Hamilton Park Pacesetter Magnt	112
Thomas, Pam/Bowie Elem Sch	212
Thomas, Pamela/Duncanville HS Collegiate Acad	104
Thomas, Pamela/Marlin High Sch	145
Thomas, Sheila/Calk-Wilson Elem Sch	303
Thomas, Stephanie/B F Adam Elem Sch	184
Thomas, Susan/Denton Classical Academy [297]	2
Thomas, Suzanne/Premier HS-Dayton [297]	9
Thomas, Tom/Bean Elem Sch	270
Thomas, Tremanya/Wedgwood 6th Grade Middle Sch	352
Thomas, Twyla/Refugio Elem Sch	323
Thomason, Jennifer/Weaver Elem Sch	107
Thomason, Jill/Boles High Sch	235
Thome, Kristen/St Thomas More Sch	204
Thomman, Amy/Johnson Elem Sch	55
Thompson-Conwr, Carolyn/Matthews Alt HS/New Directions	270
Thompson, Bob/Tomball Connections Acadamy	203
Thompson, Dawn/Lovett Elem Sch	194
Thompson, Donna/Coldspring-Oakhurst High Sch	330
Thompson, Fran/St Joseph Catholic Sch	114
Thompson, Jacqueline/Cullen Middle Sch	188
Thompson, James/Anderson-Shiro Jr Sr High Sch	171
Thompson, Jay/Terrell High Sch	253
Thompson, Joseph/Fusion Academy-the Woodlands	295
Thompson, Joy/Coleman Elem Sch	76
Thompson, Kimberly/Garden Villas Elem Sch	192
Thompson, Lauren/Timber Creek Elem Sch	203
Thompson, Luther/Port Arthur Alternative Center	243
Thompson, Roque/Gonzales Junior High Sch	164
Thompson, Shannon/Mountain Peak Elem Sch	141
Thompson, Shay/Waskom Elem Sch	209

Texas School Directory — PRINCIPAL INDEX

NAME/School	PAGE
Thompson, Tamra/*Brandenburg Intermediate Sch*	104
Thompson, Tasia/*Ethridge Elem Sch*	123
Thorman, Jeff/*Zion Lutheran Sch*	116
Thornburg, Keri/*Bassetti Elem Sch*	360
Thornburg, Keri/*Taylor Elem Sch*	360
Thornhill, Anthony/*Lancaster STEM Early Clg HS*	110
Thornhill, Tammy/*West Ward Elem Sch*	28
Thornton, Ann/*Space Center Intermediate Sch*	159
Thornton, Jeff/*Larry Brown Sch*	20
Thornton, Karen/*Waters Elem Sch*	271
Thornton, Robyn/*Onalaska Jr Sr High Sch*	317
Thornton, Yvonne/*Rosa Parks-Millbrook Sch*	110
Thorton, Ritchie/*Estacado Middle Sch*	175
Thrash, Michelle/*A Plus Academy Elementary [272]*	1
Thurman, Denise/*St Jo Elem Sch*	290
Thurmon, Kyle/*Matagorda Sch*	275
Thurmond, Paula/*Southwest Christian Academy*	207
Thurston, Alicia/*Lucille Nash Elem Sch*	252
Thurston, Duane/*Mary Orr Intermediate Sch*	357
Tibayan, Dr/*Presidio High Sch*	320
Tibayan, Edgar, Dr/*Presidio Elem Sch*	320
Tickner, David/*Forestwood Middle Sch*	123
Tidwell, Aaron/*Mildred Sch*	300
Tidwell, Amanda/*Detroit Middle Sch*	322
Tidwell, Sue/*Calvary Christian Academy*	358
Tidwell, Tere/*Northwest Elem Sch*	372
Tiemann, Randy/*Mathis Middle Sch*	331
Tiemann, Wendy/*Timberwilde Elem Sch*	38
Tiet, Cindy/*Ray Daily Elem Sch*	194
Tijerina, Janie/*Edcouch Elsa High Sch*	216
Tiller, Jennifer/*Holy Name Catholic Sch*	44
Tillery, Shelby/*Big Sandy Sch*	316
Timberlake, Dianne/*China Elem Sch*	178
Times, Tricia/*Point Alternative Center*	188
Timm, Ryan/*Baxter Elem Sch*	141
Timmons, David/*Penelope Sch*	228
Timmons, Erika/*L A Nelson Elem Sch*	121
Timms, Joe/*McMullen Co Sch*	283
Tims, Angela/*Don R Daniel 9th Grade Campus*	312
Tindall, Jaime/*Woodson Center for Excellence*	360
Tiner, Brandi/*Alto Middle Sch*	72
Tinnon, Samuel/*Casis Elem Sch*	367
Tinoco, Rafael/*Hidalgo Elem Sch*	217
Tinsley, Kristen/*Sarita Elem Sch*	254
Tippin, Mary/*Goliad Middle Sch*	164
Tipton, Christina/*Fusion Academy-Dallas*	115
Tipton, Krista/*Midlothian Heritage High Sch*	141
Tipton, Verna/*Leon Sablatura Middle Sch*	53
Tisdom, Christy/*Charles R Drew Elem Sch*	183
Tish, Michelle/*Tarver Elem Sch*	27
Tite, Erin/*Florence Campbell Sch*	159
Tobey, Loryn/*Norris Elem Sch*	79
Todd, Courtney/*Milano Elem Sch*	287
Todd, Michele/*Wilson Elem Sch*	65
Todd, Orfelinda/*Vardeman EC-PK-K Sch*	181
Tolbert, Marilyn/*Starpoint Sch*	359
Tolin, K Renee/*St Catherine of Siena Sch*	244
Toliver, Jana/*Lawndale Elem Sch*	318
Tomhave, Kindy/*Sorters Mill Elem Sch*	294
Toney, Kimberly/*Holmquist Elem Sch*	182
Toney, Steven/*E C Brice Elem Sch*	363
Tonne, Allison/*Paint Rock Sch*	90
Toperzer, Grayson/*Emma Ousley Jr HS*	344
Topp, David/*Pilgrim Lutheran Sch*	206
Torbert, Kent/*West Texas High Sch*	238
Torres-Solis, Valerie/*Dessau Middle Sch*	372
Torres-Solis, Valerie/*Paredes Middle Sch*	369
Torres, Dalia/*MaGee Elem Sch*	303
Torres, Jennifer/*Mary Harper Middle Sch*	157
Torres, Jose/*Incarnate Word Academy*	306
Torres, Lou/*Bloomington Middle Sch*	381
Torres, Lou/*Placedo Elem Sch*	382
Torres, Michael/*Travis Middle Sch*	62
Torres, Michael/*W B Green Junior High Sch*	65
Torres, Naida/*Freddy Gonzalez Elem Sch*	216
Torres, Nancy/*Fabens Middle Sch*	135
Torres, Petra/*Del Castillo Elem Sch*	63
Torres, Ricardo/*Champion Elem Sch*	63
Torres, Ruby/*Positive Solutions Charter Sch*	9
Torres, Ruth/*Escandon Elem Sch*	216
Torres, Shannon/*Midland Freshman High Sch*	286
Torrez, Alex/*Ojeda Middle Sch*	369
Torrez, Nick/*Polytechnic High Sch*	351
Torun, Oguzkaan/*Harmony Sch Sci-Houston [284]*	4
Tosh, Sonia/*Hart Elem Sch*	367
Totsuka, Maria/*John Q Adams Elem Sch*	101
Toups, Melanie/*Bridge City Elem Sch*	308
Tovar, Efrain/*Leslie A Stemmons Elem Sch*	101
Tovar, Federico/*Socorro High Sch*	136
Tovar, Letti/*Neal Dillman Elem Sch*	22
Tovar, Margarita/*Dogan Elem Sch*	188
Tovar, Sylvia/*Kingsborough Middle Sch*	33
Towber, Susie/*Herman Lawson Early Chldhd Ctr*	81
Towels, Tanji/*Merrifield Elem Sch*	105
Townley, Amanda/*Crestview Elem Sch*	406
Townsend, Chris/*Van Vleck High Sch*	276
Townsend, Donna/*Ecia-Rowlett*	2
Toy, Adam/*DeWitt Perry Middle Sch*	96
Toycu, Omer/*Harmony Science Acad-Dallas [284]*	5
Tracy-Burke, Leslie/*Jake Silbernagel Elem Sch*	159
Tracy, Henry/*Athens High Sch*	213
Tracy, Jessica/*Hill Country Christian Sch*	373
Tracy, Susan/*St Catherine's Montessori Sch*	204
Trainer, Damon/*East Central Development Ctr*	31
Trammell, Sherri/*Creekside Forest Elem Sch*	203
Tran, Erica/*James Butler Bonham Elem Sch*	189
Tran, Rose/*Fulton 4-5 Learning Center*	19
Tran, Tramy/*Dooley Elem Sch*	82
Travis, Barnes/*Petrolia Elem Sch*	74
Travis, Janet/*Liberty Elem Sch*	355
Traw, Steven/*Sory Elem Sch*	167
Traweek, Stephanie/*Stephenville High Sch*	144
Traylor, Kristine/*T W Ogg Elem Sch*	52
Traylor, Mandy/*Reagan Co Elem Sch*	321
Traylor, Mandy/*Sunray High Sch*	296
Traylor, Pertricee/*Mark Twain Elem Sch*	101
Traylor, Shaketa/*Sidney Poynter Elem Sch*	348
Trdla, Teresa/*Victor Fields Elem Sch*	221
Treadway, Gina/*Gilmer Intermediate Sch*	376
Trejo, Roberto/*Mountain View High Sch*	132
Trejo, Yamila, Sr/*Father Yermo Elem Sch*	139
Trekell, Lawton/*Pride Sch*	17
Tremont, Joshua/*Laneville Sch*	328
Trent, Erin/*Stevens Elem Sch*	189
Trevinio, Belinda/*McDermott Elem Sch*	38
Trevino, Arlene/*United High 9th Grade HS*	388
Trevino, Ashley/*Corpus Christi College Prep HS [294]*	2
Trevino, Criselda/*Farias Elem Sch*	223
Trevino, John/*N M Harrel Elem Sch*	257
Trevino, John, Dr/*Tom Browne Middle Sch*	304
Trevino, Kara/*Killeen High Sch*	28
Trevino, Layla/*Harmony Sci Acad-Brownsville [284]*	5
Trevino, Lorena/*La Union Elem Sch*	340
Trevino, Lori/*Sinton Elem Sch*	332
Trevino, Lydia/*Kelly-Pharr Elem Sch*	223
Trevino, Maribel/*Seale Junior High Sch*	305
Trevino, Marisol/*Manzano Middle Sch*	64
Trevino, Octaviano/*S C Red Elem Sch*	194
Trevino, Olga/*Gwa Townlake CHS [303]*	4
Trevino, Pedro/*Allen & William Arnold ES*	223
Trevino, Roderick/*Scarborough High Sch*	192
Trevino, Rosie/*Bishop Elem Sch*	302
Trevino, Victoria/*H W Schulze Elem Sch*	32
Triana, Teresa/*Salado Intermediate Sch*	31
Tribble, Colleen/*Cats Academy-Student Alt Ctr*	51
Tribble, Dale/*Walt Disney Elem Sch*	51
Trichell, Aurora/*Routh Roach Elem Sch*	106
Trichell, Brian/*Bullock Elem Sch*	105
Trimble, David, Dr/*J P Elder Middle Sch*	351
Trimble, John/*William J Brennan High Sch*	39

PRINCIPAL INDEX

NAME/School	PAGE
Tripplett, Cheryl/*Lucian Adams Elem Sch*	243
Tristan, Marco/*Tornillo Junior High Sch*	137
Tritten, Vanessa/*Bruce Shulkey Elem Sch*	350
Trojcak, Becky/*Angelo Catholic Sch*	366
Trollo, Miriam/*Austin Classical Academy [297]*	1
Troncoso, Adela/*Dora M Sauceda Middle Sch*	215
Trost, Stacy/*Lost Pines Elem Sch*	24
Trotter, Ronnell/*Calvert Sch*	324
Troudt, Sandy/*Indian Springs Middle Sch*	355
Trout, John/*Lakehill Preparatory Sch*	115
Troxell, Daphne/*Texas Virtual Acad Hallsville*	12
True, Melissa/*Heather Glen Elem Sch*	106
Trujillo, Duane/*Carl Schurz Elem Sch*	88
Trull, Angie/*Rains Elem Sch*	320
Tryon, Dawn/*Keith Elem Sch*	185
Tucker, Angela/*New Summerfield Sch*	73
Tucker, Becky/*Arrow-Save Our Streets Ctr [273]*	1
Tucker, Esther/*Central Elem Sch*	144
Tucker, Mark/*O'Brien Middle Sch*	258
Tucker, Matthew/*West Texas Middle Sch*	238
Tucker, Philip/*Texans Can Acad Fw Lancaster [305]*	11
Tucker, Sky/*Levelland ABC*	229
Tucker, Stacy/*Ballinger Junior High Sch*	326
Tucker, Traci, Dr/*Scofield Christian Sch*	116
Tucker, Veronica/*St Anthony of Padua Sch*	295
Tudon, Sandra/*Sanborn Elem Sch*	318
Tufts, Carin/*Amos Elem Sch*	343
Tunnell, Brandon/*Sunnyvale Middle Sch*	113
Tupa, Elizabeth/*Hutchins Elem Sch*	389
Turbeville, Yolanda/*Pena Elem Sch*	64
Turek, Michelle/*Herod Elem Sch*	194
Turel, Mucahit/*Harmony Sci Acad-El Paso [284]*	5
Turnage, Kelly/*Keene Elem Sch*	248
Turner, Amy/*Falcon Ridge Elem Sch*	195
Turner, Annette/*Westbury Christian Sch*	207
Turner, Barberina/*Golden Rule CS-Illinois [281]*	3
Turner, Bric/*Meadow Sch*	362
Turner, Deanna/*Spring Hill Primary Sch*	171
Turner, Debra/*Open Doors Christian Academy*	215
Turner, Devon/*Premier HS-Arlington [297]*	9
Turner, Heather/*Budewig Intermediate Sch*	182
Turner, Jeff/*Mt Pleasant Junior High Sch*	364
Turner, John/*Cleburne Christian Academy*	249
Turner, John/*Village Parkway Chrn Sch*	45
Turner, Kenny/*Hooks Elem Sch*	48
Turner, Leighann/*Joy James Elem Sch*	347
Turner, Ryan/*Packsaddle Elem Sch*	268
Turner, Umoja/*W A Blair Elem Sch*	103
Turner, Virginia/*Travis Middle Sch*	177
Turney, Matt/*Stanton High Sch*	274
Turns, Rhonda/*Dorothy Carlton Center*	184
Twardowski, James/*Baytown Christian Academy*	205
Twedell, Teresa/*Dorris Jones Elem Sch*	325
Tweedy, James/*Ume Prep Acad-Dallas*	13
Tyler, Kyndra/*Lewisville HS-Killough*	123
Tyndell, Justin/*James Bowie Elem Sch*	50
Tyner, Brandy/*Reagan Elem Sch*	365
Tyrrell, Jonathan/*Idea Clg Prep-Monterrey Park*	219
Tyson, Mary/*Escondido Elem Sch*	33
Tyson, Troy/*Franklin D Roosevelt High Sch*	100
Tyson, Troy/*Sarah Zumwalt Middle Sch*	102
Tyus, Joe/*A B McBay Elem Sch*	267

U

NAME/School	PAGE
Uber, Kyle/*Houston Elem Sch*	166
Ude, Edward/*Canales Elem Sch*	63
Uher, Victor/*Wilkinson Elem Sch*	292
Ukegbu, Chinyere/*Stonehill Christian Academy*	373
Ulcak, Chris/*Nursery Elem Sch*	382
Ullmann, Vanessa/*Kessler Sch*	115
Ullrich, Donna/*Humble High Sch*	196
Ulman, Wyvona/*Southridge Elem Sch*	124
Underwood, Jaci/*Stewart Elem Sch*	270
Underwood, Jay/*Kopperl Sch*	47
Upchurch, Alicia/*Baker 6th Grade Campus*	198
Uppchurch, Sara/*Watauga Elem Sch*	346
Upright, De'Ann/*McAndrew Elem Sch*	38
Upshaw, Chantell/*Marcus 9th Grade Center*	123
Upshaw, Kelli/*Landis Elem Sch*	182
Upton, Elisha/*Imagine Intl Academy-N Texas [029]*	5
Ureno Olivaz, Claudia/*Ascarate Elem Sch*	137
Uresti, Antonio/*Lorenzo De Zavala Middle Sch*	220
Urias, Amanda/*Ft Stockton Intermediate Sch*	315
Uribe, Patricia, Dr/*Staggs Acad Intl STEM Studies*	11
Urie, Kimberly/*Burkeville Elem Sch*	300
Urie, Kimberly/*Burkeville Jr Sr High Sch*	300
Usery, Hollye/*Bowie Elem Sch*	299
Usrey, Mary, Dr/*Henry Steubing Elem Sch*	37
Utecht, Lara/*D L Rountree Elem Sch*	77
Uwaga-Sanders, Ogechi, Dr/*Thurgood Marshall High Sch*	151
Uzgoren, Alpaslan/*Sch of Sci & Tech-Houston [299]*	11

V

NAME/School	PAGE
Vaden, Sherrye/*Iboc Christian Academy*	115
Vadillo, Fernando/*Lively Elem Sch*	109
Vaglienty, Stacey/*Zwink Elem Sch*	198
Valadez, Melissa/*St Joseph Academy*	68
Valderas, Joann/*Hebbronville High Sch*	244
Valdez, Carlos/*United South Middle Sch*	388
Valdez, Diana/*West Brook High Sch*	242
Valdez, Lisa/*E B Guerra Elem Sch*	216
Valdez, Louie, Dr/*River Oaks Academy*	206
Valdez, Luis/*Manara Acad-Arlington STEM*	8
Valdez, Maribel/*Derry Elem Sch*	66
Valdez, Melissa/*Memorial Middle Sch*	387
Valdez, Patrick/*Academy of Creative Education*	34
Valdez, Raul/*Myra Green Middle Sch*	394
Valdez, Rodolfo/*Rosemont Elem Sch*	352
Valencia, Michael/*McCamey High Sch*	377
Valencia, Sandra/*Cesar E Chavez Academy [294]*	2
Valentine, Jason/*Wimberley High Sch*	212
Valenzuela, Nancy/*Reynaldo G Garza Elem Sch*	221
Valenzuela, Norma/*Fisher Elem Sch*	198
Valeriano, Rene/*Reagan Co High Sch*	321
Valkenaar, Steven/*Bowie Elem Sch*	289
Valkenaar, Steven/*Bridgeport Middle Sch*	403
Valle, Fred/*St Ignatius Martyr Cath Sch*	372
Vallejo, Diana/*Andrews Elem Sch*	367
Vallejo, Pablo/*Mary Hoge Middle Sch*	225
Valree, Tracey/*Henry Metzger Middle Sch*	33
Valtierra, Jacob/*Riverside Middle Sch*	138
Van Auken, Anita/*Nixon-Smiley Middle Sch*	164
Van Duzee, Codi/*Pearcy STEM Academy*	345
Van Horn, Michelle/*A Habitat for Learning Daycare*	361
Van Loenen, Michael/*Freeman Elem Sch*	199
Van Meter, Trent/*Aspermont High Sch*	342
Van Ness, Cathy/*Rosenberg Elem Sch*	160
Van Nest, Steve/*Evins Regional Juvenile Ctr*	3
Van Ryn, Rebekah/*C D Fulkes Middle Sch*	398
Van Scoyoc, Christy/*Flower Mound Elem Sch*	123
Van Weele, Andy/*Lord of Life Lutheran Sch*	162
Vance, Erin/*J L Lyons Elem Sch*	293
Vance, J/*Rains Intermediate Sch*	320
Vance, Tamra/*Jhw Inspire Acad-Rockdale*	31
Vandermark, Tara, Dr/*Suchma Elementary*	292
Vanderplas, Sam/*St Elizabeth Ann Seton Sch*	358
Vanderpool, Stephen/*Groom Sch*	69
Vanderveer, Monica/*Cleckler-Heald Elem Sch*	225
Vanhoozer, Stan/*Robert E Lee Sr High Sch*	286
Vanicek, Wes/*Georgetown High Sch*	395
Vanloenen, Stacie/*Laura Ingalls Wilder Elem Sch*	51
VanNest, Brian/*Valley West Elem Sch*	194
Vanwassenhove, Christi/*Aldine Middle Sch*	181
Vardeman, Donna/*Hubbard Elem Sch*	228
Varela, Micaela/*Dr Hornedo Middle Sch*	134
Vargas, Becky/*Walter Matthys Elem Sch*	200

Texas School Directory — PRINCIPAL INDEX

NAME/School	PAGE
Vargas, Orlando/Royal Junior High Sch	384
Varisco, Al/St Clare of Assisi Sch	204
Varljen, Nancy/Patsy Sommer Elem Sch	399
Varnado, Dion/M L King Middle Sch	242
Varnado, Donna/Big Sandy Elem Sch	376
Varnell, Matt, Dr/Gunn Junior High Sch	344
Varughese, Reena/Luther & Anna Bolin Elem Sch	77
Vasquez, Aidee/Putegnat Elem Sch	64
Vasquez, Alma/Carroll T Welch Elem Sch	132
Vasquez, Belinda/Bluebonnet Elem Sch	61
Vasquez, Cynthia/Uhland Elem Sch	211
Vasquez, Gloria/Rosehill Elem Sch	203
Vasquez, Jeanette/Robert B Green Academy	41
Vasquez, Laura/Amparo Gutierrez Elem Sch	387
Vasquez, Leslie/Key Sch	359
Vaughan, Stephanie/Olga Leonard Elem Sch	152
Vaughn, Chris/Paris High Sch	260
Vaughn, Kelly/Navarro Mid Sch	190
Vaughn, Lakesha/Rogers Middle Sch	53
Vaughn, Rebecca/Joe M Pirtle Elem Sch	27
Vaughn, Wendi/Prairie Trail Elem Sch	124
Vega, Claudia/Sunset High Sch	103
Vega, Hilda/Trinity Charter Sch-Bokenkamp [307]	12
Vega, Hilga/Trinity Charter Sch-New Hope [307]	12
Vega, Leticia/International High Sch	368
Vega, Lisa/Montessori Acad Hernandez ES	102
Vega, Priscilla/Tuloso-Midway Middle Sch	305
Vega, Rebecca/H A Wooden Elem Sch	142
Vega, Salvador/Oak Meadows Elem Sch	371
Veilleux, Wilfred/General Colin Powell Elem Sch	133
Vela, Adriana/Col Santos Benavides Elem Sch	387
Vela, Enrique/Student Support Center	304
Vela, Joe/Odem Junior High Sch	331
Vela, Jose/Santa Maria High Sch	67
Vela, Jose/Santa Maria Junior High Sch	67
Vela, Nita/Bernarda Jaime Jr High Sch	128
Vela, Rowdy, Dr/Psja Memorial HS	224
Velasquez, Amador/O'Donnell Middle Sch	182
Velasquez, Cynthia/Vista Del Sol Sch	137
Velazquez, Carol/Harris Academy	40
Velazquez, Gregorio/Tynan Early Childhood Ctr	41
Velez, Erika/Woodlands Preparatory Sch	207
Venable, Cindy/Gatesville Junior High Sch	93
Venable, Raymie/Personalized Lrng Prep Houston	102
Venecia, Jeanne/Mercedes Early College HS	221
Venegas, Sarah/Eastwood Middle Sch	138
Vennell, Erin/Adkins Elem Sch	121
Vera, Elizabeth/Medina Valley Lacoste ES	284
Verdooran, Sylvia/Idea Academy-Donna	217
Verdun, Michelle/Peter E Hyland Center	188
Verduzco, Antonio/B H Macon Elem Sch	99
Verduzco, Carlos/La Feria Academy	65
Vermillion, Lance/Regents Academy	298
Vernon, Kristopher/Frank Seale Middle Sch	141
Verreault, Ellen/Glen Park Elem Sch	350
Verstuyft, Julie/W C Andrews Elem Sch	331
Vest, Jennifer/Brenham Elem Sch	385
Vestal, Tiffany/Western Hills Elem Sch	29
Viado, Stephanie/Brazos Bend Elem Sch	150
Vickers, Kari/Pleasanton Primary Sch	21
Vickers, Ron/Jean C Few Primary Sch	241
Vickery, Betty/Calvary Temple Christian Acad	114
Victor, Shannon/Nazarene Christian Academy	119
Victory, Travis/Clarendon Junior High Sch	127
Vidal, Pedro/Egly Elem Sch	63
Vidales, Lorraine/Ricardo Estrada Middle Sch	132
Vidales, Lynnette/Sgt Roberto Ituarte Elem Sch	136
Vidaurri, Kristina, Dr/St Anthony Catholic High Sch	44
Vidaurri, Maria/Salazar Elem Sch	245
Viernes, Chucky/Williams Elem Sch	107
Vilagi, Jeanette/Keystone Sch	45
Vilches, Gina/Ricardo Elem Middle Sch	258
Villafuerte, Theresa/Gallegos Elem Sch	63
Villagomez, Tomas/Valley View 5th Grade Campus	225
Villalobos, Carlos/Red Sands Elem Sch	132
Villalobos, Dora/Hurla M Midkiff Elem Sch	222
Villalobos, Jose/Pete Gallego Elem Sch	277
Villalobos, Malinda/Young Women's Leadership Acad	138
Villalobos, Rachel/Mitzi Bond Elem Sch	133
Villanueva, Jose/3D Academy	215
Villanueva, Natalie/Williams Elem Sch	367
Villareal, Myrtha, Dr/San Isidro Elem Sch	388
Villarreal, Adrianna/Idea Academy-North Mission	218
Villarreal, Albert/Perez Elem Sch	257
Villarreal, Benita/Faulk Middle Sch	63
Villarreal, Benjamin/St Mary's Central Catholic Sch	131
Villarreal, Carla/Elliot Grant Middle Sch	303
Villarreal, Christina/Idea Academy-San Benito	218
Villarreal, Cynthia/D D Hachar Elem Sch	386
Villarreal, Dianabel/Henry B Gonzalez Elem Sch	220
Villarreal, Domingo/La Joya Early College HS	220
Villarreal, Jane/Dr Fermin Calderon Elem Sch	379
Villarreal, Juan/Sam Houston High Sch	345
Villarreal, Lina/Casey Elem Sch	366
Villarreal, Luis/Kennedy Middle Sch	223
Villarreal, Maria/Carrizo Springs Jr High Sch	127
Villarreal, Martha, Dr/Trevino Comm & Fine Art Sch	387
Villarreal, Monica/Frank L Madla Accel Coll Acad [291]	3
Villarreal, Monique/Academy Academic Enhancemnt-MS	340
Villarreal, Odilia/A Villarreal Elem Sch	216
Villarreal, Sugey/Fairmeadows Elem Sch	105
Villarreal, Tammie/Horace Mann Middle Sch	318
Villegas, Dora/Idea Academy-Frontier	218
Villejo, Sylvia/Impact Center	211
Villela, Esther/Ser-Ninos Charter Sch	11
Vincent, Beau/Ore City Middle Sch	377
Vincent, Brenda/Mark Twain Elem Sch	51
Vincent, David/Amarillo High Sch	317
Vincent, Dawes/Travis Elem Sch	236
Vincent, Lucy/Ethridge Elem Sch	105
Vinson, Karen/Kurth Primary Sch	18
Voelkel, Ladonna/Sacred Heart Catholic Sch	148
Voelker, Tracy/Runyan Elem Sch	292
Voges, Todd/Windcrest Elem Sch	36
Voigt, Sarah/Rosanky Christian Academy	24
Voigt, Stacey/South Bosque Elem Sch	281
Voltz, Gail/Varnett School-East [310]	13
Voran, Doug/Westover Park Jr High Sch	321
Voss, Linda/Travis Magnet Elem Sch	130
Voss, Pamela/Dillingham Intermediate Sch	167
Votaw, Cristin/Lorene S Kirkpatrick Elem Sch	141

W

NAME/School	PAGE
Wabrek, Chelle/Episcopal Sch Dallas-Mid Upper	115
Wabrek, Chelle/Episcopal Sch of Dallas-Lower	115
Waddell, Cheryl, Dr/John D Spicer Elem Sch	346
Waddell, Cindy/Sheppard AFB Elem Sch	392
Wade, Dorinda/Dunbar Primary Sch	18
Wade, Von/Fairfield High Sch	156
Wadley, Cleotis/Excel High Sch	170
Wagner, Dave/Idea Clg Prep-N Mission	219
Wagner, Dennis/Barbers Hill Middle Sch South	72
Wagner, Heidi/Anderson Accelerated High Sch	233
Wagner, Michelle/Margaret Long Wisdom High Sch	194
Wagner, Nathan/Westbury Christian Sch	207
Wagner, Shane/Sweet Home Elem Sch	262
Wagnon, Stacy/Carroll Elem Sch	347
Wahl, Michael/Smithson Valley High Sch	88
Waites, Marlon/Pleasant Run Elem Sch	110
Wakefield, Michael/Teravista Elem Sch	399
Walch, Lauren/Fair Oaks Ranch Elem Sch	254
Waldo, Toni/Happy Elem Sch	342
Waldrip, John/Reba Cobb Carroll Elem Sch	80
Waldrop, Katherine/Lumberton Primary Sch	178
Waligura, Alan/Independence High Sch	79
Walker-Daniels, Tracey/Dr Edward Roberson Middle Sch	202
Walker, Christopher/Ashford Elem Sch	193
Walker, Debbie, Sr/St James the Apostle Sch	44
Walker, Hollye/J A Vitovsky Elem Sch	141

PRINCIPAL INDEX

Market Data Retrieval

NAME/*School*	PAGE	NAME/*School*	PAGE
Walker, Hope/*Idea Academy-Harvey Najim*	218	Washington, Courtney/*Carpenter Middle Sch*	82
Walker, Jacob/*Cooke Elem Sch*	247	Washington, Earnest/*Charles R Drew Academy*	181
Walker, Jared/*Netherland Alt Ed Sch*	243	Washington, Kathryn, Dr/*Goodrich Elem Sch*	316
Walker, Jennifer/*E A Lawhon Elem Sch*	53	**Washington, Kenneth**/*Coyle Middle Sch*	105
Walker, Johnna/*Preston Elem Sch*	77	Wasser, Deborah/*Banff Sch*	205
Walker, Jowie/*Blanco Elem Sch*	45	Wasson, Vickie/*Venable Village Elem Sch*	28
Walker, Kate/*Arthur Kramer Elem Sch*	99	Waterhouse, Richard/*George West High Sch*	268
Walker, Kathryn/*Mann Middle Sch*	360	Waters, Bill/*Central High Sch*	365
Walker, Lee/*White Rock Elem Sch*	113	Waters, Dionel/*Int'l Ldrshp TX-Arlington ES*	108
Walker, Lindsay/*Butler Intermediate Sch*	237	Watkins, Anthony/*Carver High Sch*	180
Walker, Lisa/*Holiday Heights Elem Sch*	346	Watkins, Lisa/*Barbers Hill Kindergarten Ctr*	72
Walker, Michael/*Jefferson High Sch*	274	Watkins, Quintin/*Malakoff Middle Sch*	214
Walker, Nicole/*Reaves Elem Sch*	292	Watkins, Ronnie/*Lester Davis Sch*	121
Walker, Sean/*Royse City High Sch*	326	Watkins, Sarah/*Plano Senior High Sch*	83
Walker, Shanda/*Kelso Elem Sch*	193	Watley, Christy/*Hewitt Elem Sch*	280
Walker, Valarie/*Dr Paul Saenz Junior High Sch*	42	**Watson, Angela, Dr**/*Boerne Middle School South*	254
Walker, Valarie/*Milton B Lee Acad of Sci & Eng*	42	Watson, Anthony/*Stony Point High Sch*	399
Wall, Chuck/*Robindell Private Sch*	207	Watson, Chandra/*East Texas Christian Sch*	171
Wall, Debra/*South Davis Elem Sch*	345	Watson, Crystal, Dr/*Chester W Nimitz High Sch*	180
Wall, Rachel/*Haude Elem Sch*	197	Watson, Dixie/*Sanford Fritch Jr High Sch*	238
Wallace, Brodie/*Flour Bluff Junior High Sch*	304	Watson, Emily/*Chester High Sch*	375
Wallace, Christina/*Corinth Classical Academy [297]*	2	Watson, Jennifer/*Creighton Elem Sch*	291
Wallace, Danielle/*John A Baker Elem Sch*	84	Watson, Kassie/*Waskom High Sch*	209
Wallace, Donna/*Mitchell Elem Sch*	55	Watson, Kim/*Kardia Christian Academy*	206
Wallace, Estelia/*Regency Place Elem Sch*	35	Watson, Matthew/*Aristoi Classical Academy*	1
Wallace, Grisel/*Heritage Elem Sch*	198	Watson, Michael, Dr/*Dahlstrom Middle Sch*	211
Wallace, Holly/*E D Walker Middle Sch*	99	**Watson, Sara**/*Reeces Creek Elem Sch*	28
Wallace, James/*J N Ervin Elem Sch*	100	Watson, Sara/*Timmerman Elem Sch*	372
Wallace, Janet/*Midland Academy Charter Sch*	8	Watson, Sharon/*Early Elem Sch*	59
Wallace, Ken/*Paint Creek Sch*	210	Watson, Wade/*Carthage Junior High Sch*	311
Wallace, Michelle/*Travis Primary Sch*	232	Watt, Blanda/*Texas Online Preparatory Sch*	383
Wallace, Robert/*Jackson Middle Sch*	107	Watts, Jennifer/*St Thomas Aquinas Sch*	114
Wallace, Rodney/*Ash High Sch*	175	Watts, Michael/*Disciplinary Alt Ed Program*	55
Wallace, Sheryl/*Fredericksburg Middle Sch*	163	Watts, Roy/*Advantage Acad-Grand Prairie E*	96
Wallace, Steven/*Electra Elem Sch*	391	Watts, Tammy/*North Joshua Elem Sch*	248
Wallace, Suzi/*Newton Collins Elem Sch*	369	Waugh-Freeze, Heather/*Leon Taylor Junior High Sch*	331
Wallace, Yolanda/*Prairie View Elem Sch*	125	Waugh, Kristina/*Richards Young Women Leaders*	369
Wallen, Jason/*Ford High Sch*	237	Waugh, Sam/*Awty International Sch*	205
Waller, Erica/*Tioga Sch*	167	Weatherford, Ashley/*Woodville Intermediate Sch*	375
Waller, Jeffrey/*Stephens Elem Sch*	106	Weatherford, Denise/*Shepherd Middle Sch*	330
Wallin, Nicole/*Uplift North Hills Prep Sch [309]*	13	Weaver, Amanda/*Rhoads Elem Sch*	152
Wallin, Sheryl/*Childrens Sch*	373	**Weaver, Jim**/*Nixon-Smiley High Sch*	164
Walling, Ezra/*Eldorado Middle Sch*	333	Weaver, Johnna/*Lincoln Humanities/Comm HS*	101
Walls, Kalen/*Midland Classical Academy*	286	Weaver, Luci/*Virtual Sch*	200
Walls, Lisa/*Chapa Middle Sch*	211	Webb, Eleanor/*Lancaster High Sch*	110
Wallum, Judy/*Midland Christian Sch*	286	Webb, Homer/*DeSoto Alt Sch*	104
Walsh, Carol/*St Rita Catholic Sch*	114	Webb, Jennifer/*Dallas Christian Sch*	115
Walswick, Stephen/*Central Catholic High Sch*	44	**Webb, Keegan**/*Gatesville Elem Sch*	93
Walters, Ann/*Holy Family Catholic Sch*	358	Webb, Linda, Dr/*Garza Independence High Sch*	368
Walters, Kelly/*Rice Elem Sch*	300	Webb, Margaret/*Holy Spirit Catholic Sch*	44
Walters, Scott/*Ace Alternative Sch*	18	Webb, Sonia/*East Grand Preparatory Academy*	2
Walthall, Karen/*Barrett Elem Sch*	183	Webb, Steffanie/*Creek Valley Middle Sch*	122
Waltmon, Kimberly/*Canyon Ridge Middle Sch*	397	Webb, Zandra/*Cedar Hill 9th Grade Center*	97
Wamble, Matthew/*Burton High Sch*	386	Webber, Melissa/*Haslet Elem Sch*	125
Wanserski-Eska, Katherine/*North Dallas High Sch*	102	Webber, Will/*St Stephen's Episcopal Sch*	212
Ward, Amy/*Ebby Halliday Elem Sch*	99	Webster, Beckie/*Monta Jane Akin Elem Sch*	397
Ward, Cindy/*Rose Garden Elem Sch*	173	Wedgeworth, Carolyn/*Oak Forest Elem Sch*	309
Ward, Daniel/*Fulshear High Sch*	154	Wedgeworth, Tiffany/*New Waverly Elem Sch*	383
Ward, Frank/*Nitsch Elem Sch*	197	Weeden, Diane/*Jennie Reid Elem Sch*	198
Ward, Keri/*Raul C Martinez Elem Sch*	191	Weedman, Leigh/*Green Oaks Sch*	359
Ward, Monica/*Fredericksburg Elem Sch*	163	Weeks, Cerise/*Corpus Christi Montessori Sch*	2
Ward, Nichole/*Nova Academy Scyene*	8	Weeks, John/*West Ave Elem Sch*	282
Ward, Patti/*Marlin Middle Sch*	145	Weeks, Sarah/*Arlington Heights High Sch*	350
Warfield, Markeba/*Bill R Johnson Cte Center*	347	Wegener, Chris/*Yoakum High Sch*	118
Warford, Melissa/*Ginger McNabb Elm Sch*	202	Wegman, John/*J P Bonnette Jr High Sch*	186
Warner, Barbara/*Scoggins Middle Sch*	80	Wehmeyer, Kelly/*Port Oconnor Elem Sch*	62
Warner, Brian/*Palmer High Sch*	142	Weikert, Hank/*Luling Primary Sch*	61
Warner, Susan, Dr/*First Baptist Church Sch*	26	Weiland, Christine/*Miller Elem Sch*	41
Warnock, Matt/*Barbara Bush Middle Sch*	96	Weir, Lisa/*Memorial High Sch*	201
Warren, Dave/*Farmersville Jr High Sch*	78	Weirich, Reese/*Murchison Elem Sch*	372
Warren, Jennifer/*Oveta Culp Hobby Elem Sch*	28	Weiss, Gregg/*Hawkins Middle Sch*	404
Warren, Kaoenya/*Harris Cty Leadership Academy*	5	Weiss, Julie/*Meridiana Elem Sch*	51
Warren, Sherry/*Young Elem Sch*	158	Weiss, Shanna/*Trinity Episcopal Sch*	373

Texas School Directory — PRINCIPAL INDEX

NAME/School	PAGE
Weiss, Tiffany/Travis Science Academy	29
Welborn, Becky/Dripping Springs Christ Acad	212
Welch, David/Barack Obama Male Ldrshp Acad	99
Welch, Deborah/Rusk Elem Sch	73
Welch, Jennifer/Kemp Primary Sch	252
Welch, Joseph/Del Valle High Sch	369
Welch, Mandy/Sweetwater Intermediate Sch	302
Wellman, Randell/Rains High Sch	320
Wells, David/Travis Elem Sch	310
Wells, Demetric/El Campo High Sch	389
Wells, Fidel/Juan Seguin Elem Sch	150
Wells, Jason/Birdville High Sch	346
Wells, Julia/Raguet Elem Sch	298
Wells, Mandy/Sam Houston Elem Sch	55
Wells, Marissa/Uplift Meridian Preparatory [309]	13
Wells, Micah/Robert M Shoemaker High Sch	28
Wells, Sallie/Clariden Sch	358
Wells, Scott/Lingleville Sch	143
Wells, Tina/South Palm Gardens High Sch	225
Wendl, Bill/Prestonwood Christian Academy	86
Wenke, Andrea/South Houston High Sch	199
Wentrcek, Jenna/Starkey Elem Sch	256
Werbiski, Melissa/Paredes Elem Sch	64
Werneke, Amanda/Hebron 9th Grade Campus	123
Wernli, Eric/Jose M Lopez Middle Sch	35
Wernli, Tracy/Hector Garcia Middle Sch	37
Werth, Kori/Oak Point Elem Sch	124
Werts, Bronwyn/Callisburg Middle High Sch	90
Wesley, Melissa/Bea Salazar Sch	96
Wesson, Ricky/Plummer Elem Sch	97
West-Dukes, Edwina/Heritage Elem Sch	355
West, Angela/Seagoville High Sch	102
West, Beth/Rustic Oak Elem Sch	53
West, Darren/New Braunfels Chrn Aca-Lower	89
West, Shannon/LaRue Miller Elem Sch	141
West, Sharon/Crosbyton Elem Sch	94
West, Treasure/Ross Elem Sch	191
Westbrook, Cynthia/Mathis Intermediate Sch	331
Westfall, Darrell/Henderson Middle Sch	178
Westfall, Michael/Community High Sch	78
Westhoff, Beth/Enge-Washington Interm Sch	267
Weston, Craig/Carson Elem Sch	403
Weston, Tiffany/Mildred Jenkins Elem Sch	202
Weyand, Julie/First Baptist Academy	115
Weyman, Robert/Early Middle Sch	59
Whalen, Deborah/St Agnes Academy	204
Wharton, Kevin, Dr/Legacy Christian Academy	244
Wheat, Dave/Lanier Middle Sch	194
Wheat, Michella/Anson Jones Middle Sch	36
Wheeler, Brad, Dr/Heritage Christian Academy	326
Wheeler, DeLynn/Roosevelt Elem Sch	271
Wheeler, Diane/Melillo Middle Sch	199
Whetstone, N/Munday Charter Sch	8
Whetstone, Nicole, Dr/University of Texas Elem CS	13
Whidden, Dawn/Ingleside High Sch	331
Whiffen, Steve/Forney Academic Center	252
Whileyman, Bud/Austin Elem Sch	153
Whisenant, Danny/Lufkin Middle Sch	18
Whisenant, Kris/Latexo High Sch	233
Whisonant, Donna/Anne Sullivan Elem Sch	149
Whistler, Tom/Littlefield Elem Sch	260
Whitaker, Jeffrey/McGowen Elem Sch	191
Whitaker, Lindsey/Jefferson Elem Sch	274
Whitaker, Lindsey/Jefferson Primary Sch	274
Whitaker, Lynn/Union Grove Elem Sch	377
Whitaker, Patsy/Jacksonville Middle Sch	73
White, Amber/Smith Middle Sch	247
White, Amy/Marfa Elem Sch	320
White, Bobby/Stephen F Austin Elem Sch	140
White, Cathy/Leo Center	397
White, Christopher/Crowley HS 9th Grade Campus	348
White, Cody/O'Donnell Jr Sr High Sch	273
White, Darlene/Burton Adventist Academy	358
White, Deana/Purple Heart Elem Sch	136
White, Donita/Advantage Acad-N Duncanville	96
White, Ginger/Wolfe City Elem Sch	237
White, Ian/Freeport Intermediate Sch	52
White, Jodi/Arnold Middle Sch	184
White, John/Lumberton High Sch	178
White, Kendall/Emery Weiner Sch	205
White, Kevin/Stamford Middle Sch	250
White, Kristy/Farwell Junior High Sch	314
White, Marvyn/Tomas Rivera Elem Sch	121
White, Mary, Dr/First Baptist Academy	205
White, Meagan/Blackshear Elem Sch	197
White, Melodie/Jones Early Literacy Center	50
White, Merry/Jefferson Avenue Elem Sch	174
White, Mickey/Drane Learning Center	299
White, Mickey/Pine Tree Middle Sch	170
White, Patricia/Bexar Co Learning Center	31
White, Robert/Mexia High Sch	267
White, Rodney/Young Men's Leadership Academy	353
White, Russell/Franklin High Sch	325
White, Terri/Levelland Intermediate Sch	229
White, Tracy/Gerard Elem Sch	247
White, Troy/Vickers Elem Sch	382
Whitehouse, Marianne/Cheatham Elem Sch	322
Whiteley, Starla/Spearman Junior High Sch	177
Whitely, Janie/Healy-Murphy Center	45
Whiteside, Nicole/Silver Lake Elem Sch	353
Whitfield, Sharon/McFee Elem Sch	185
Whitfield, Shondula/W H Atwell Middle Sch	103
Whitlark, Jennifer/Rapoport Acad-E Campus ES [277]	10
Whitlock, Camilla/College Park Elem Sch	198
Whitmore, Janeen/W H Gaston Middle Sch	103
Whitney, Paige/Alcuin Montessori Sch	114
Whitsel, Tiffany/Rockdale High Sch	288
Whittaker, Shay/Collegiate Prep Academy	97
Whittaker, Shay/High Pointe Elem Sch	97
Whittemore, Shana/McLeod Sch	70
Whittle, Amy/Hallsville Junior High Sch	208
Whittle, Casey/Canyon High Sch	88
Whitton, Rebecca/San Augustine Elem Sch	329
Whitwell, Gary/Trinity School of Texas	171
Whorton, Christopher/Eustace High Sch	214
Wicke, Stacie/Alternative Lrng Ctr-West	184
Wickliffe, Tremayne/Crossroads Alt Tech Sch	182
Wicks, Douglas/Cumby Elem Sch	231
Wiebold, Melinda/Fredonia Elem Sch	298
Wiederhold, Janice/Hidden Hollow Elem Sch	196
Wiedman, Kristina/Warren Junior High Sch	375
Wieland, Amanda/Burleson Collegiate High Sch	246
Wierzowiecki, Heidi/Bonham Elem Sch	364
Wiese, Michelle/I C Evans Elem Sch	391
Wietstruck, Eric/Northland Christian Sch	206
Wiggins, Angela/Judge Frank Berry Middle Sch	111
Wilbanks, Angelica/Estacado High Sch	270
Wilbanks, Janell/Ponder Elem Sch	125
Wilcox, Alba/Jesus Chapel Sch	139
Wilcoxen, Sharon/Cisco Elem Sch	128
Wilder, Becky/Ridgeview Elem Sch	355
Wilder, Kameron/A R Turner Elem Sch	294
Wiley, Kanisha, Dr/Aldine 9th Grade Sch	180
Wiley, Karen/Forestburg Sch	290
Wiley, Maggie/Jersey Village High Sch	185
Wiley, Zachary/Nichols Elem Sch	79
Wilhelm, Tammi/Robert E King Elem Sch	152
Wilhelmi, Gary/Ischool High Lewisville [297]	6
Wilhelmi, Gary/Premier HS-Lewisville [297]	9
Wilhite, Shannon/Lone Oak Middle Sch	236
Wilke, Kate/Lakewood Elem Sch	101
Wilker, Denae/Galatas Elem Sch	291
Wilkerson, Deborah/Luna Elem Sch	106
Wilkerson, Jennifer/William B Travis Middle Sch	318
Wilkerson, Karen/Stehlik Elem Sch	179
Wilkie, Stacy/Oak Creek Elem Sch	88
Wilkins, Claire/Satori Elem Sch	162
Wilkinson, Debbie/Newcastle Sch	406
Wilks, Christi/Burgin Elem Sch	344
Wilks, Teresa/Josefa L Sambrano Elem Sch	135

PRINCIPAL INDEX

Market Data Retrieval

NAME/School	PAGE
Willard, Marian/*James Madison High Sch*	100
Williams, Adrienne/*Jordan Elem Sch*	368
Williams, Alys, Dr/*Memorial Middle Sch*	257
Williams, Andrea/*Pecan Springs Elem Sch*	368
Williams, April/*Young Womens College Prep Acad*	192
Williams, Brent/*Athens Christian Academy*	215
Williams, Brian/*East Side Intermediate Sch*	275
Williams, Bridget/*Alvord Elem Sch*	402
Williams, Carol/*La Porte Elem Sch*	198
Williams, Carrie/*Pampa Learning Center*	165
Williams, Cathy/*Leonard Middle Sch*	351
Williams, Cheryl/*Phoenix High Sch*	24
Williams, Cicely/*Community Services Sch*	191
Williams, Clarence/*Mary Harris Intermediate Sch*	348
Williams, Cody/*Eula Elem Sch*	63
Williams, Curtis/*East Texas Christian Academy*	339
Williams, Darren/*Comfort High Sch*	254
Williams, David/*Shannon High Sch*	346
Williams, Debbie/*E L Kent Elem Sch*	96
Williams, Diadra/*Vineyard Ranch Elem Sch*	36
Williams, Elizabeth/*Colony Bend Elem Sch*	150
Williams, Emily/*Rivertree Academy*	359
Williams, Eva/*Lamar Co Head Start Center*	260
Williams, Frances/*McDade Sch*	24
Williams, Glenda/*North Garland High Sch*	106
Williams, Heather/*Lindsey Elem Sch*	154
Williams, Heather/*Wesley Academy*	207
Williams, Hope/*Idea Academy-Judson*	218
Williams, Ingrid/*Success High Sch*	352
Williams, Janis/*Plano West Senior High Sch*	83
Williams, Jena/*Sulphur Springs Middle Sch*	232
Williams, Jennifer/*Danbury Elem Sch*	53
Williams, Jerona/*Treasure Forest Elem Sch*	201
Williams, John/*Hauke Academic Alt High Sch*	291
Williams, Joseph/*Wheatley High Sch*	189
Williams, Josh/*Lake Country Christian Sch*	359
Williams, Karen/*Longview Christian Sch*	171
Williams, Kaye/*Lamar Consolidated High Sch*	154
Williams, Kelly/*Abbett Elem Sch*	105
Williams, Kenisha/*Twin Creeks Middle Sch*	203
Williams, Latisha/*Patterson Middle Sch*	28
Williams, Laura/*Michael E Fossum Middle Sch*	221
Williams, Lavanta/*Lantern Lane Elem Sch*	150
Williams, Lesley/*Water Oak Sch*	232
Williams, Lisa/*Dale B Davis Elem Sch*	96
Williams, Mary/*Alief Taylor High Sch*	182
Williams, Melanie/*Wolfe City Middle Sch*	237
Williams, Melissa/*William D Surratt Elem Sch*	132
Williams, Mike/*Wylie East High Sch*	85
Williams, Pat, Dr/*Ambassadors Preparatory Acad*	1
Williams, Ridwan/*Winfree Academy-Irving [311]*	14
Williams, Robin/*Galloway Sch*	162
Williams, Ross/*Academy of Dallas-Oak Park [187]*	1
Williams, Sarah/*Spring Garden Elem Sch*	354
Williams, Shannon/*Scott Johnson Elem Sch*	383
Williams, Sharon/*La Marque Elem Sch*	161
Williams, Shelley/*New Horizons Ranch Sch*	8
Williams, Sherry/*John W Runyon Elem Sch*	101
Williams, Sonja/*Arrow-Champions Academy [273]*	1
Williams, Stephanie/*Louis G Lobit Elem Sch*	160
Williams, Tim/*Oak Hills Junior High Sch*	293
Williams, Todd/*House Creek Elementray Sch*	92
Williams, Tomeka/*Eduardo Mata Elem Sch*	99
Williams, Tomicka/*Duryea Elem Sch*	184
Williams, Victor/*Jasper High Sch*	241
Williams, Wayne/*Premier HS-N Austin [297]*	9
Williams, Wendy/*George Washington Carver ES*	105
Williams, Yardley/*Texans Can Acad Houston Hobby [305]*	12
Williamson, Debra/*Lowery Road Elem Sch*	351
Williamson, Lyndsey/*Cooper High Sch*	360
Williamson, Lyndsey/*Holland Medical High Sch*	360
Williford, Robert/*Grace Sch*	206
Willis, Diane/*MacAria Gorena Elem Sch*	217
Willis, Letitia/*Brook Village Eec*	392
Willis, Letitia/*Farris Early Childhood Center*	392
Willis, Letitia/*North West Head Start Center*	392
Willis, Letitia/*Rosewood Head Start Center*	392
Willis, Patricia/*Garcia-Leza EC-PK-K Sch*	181
Willison, Teresa/*Nimitz Middle Sch*	130
Willmann, Kristin/*Gardendale Elem Sch*	32
Willmeth, Karla/*Acton Elem Sch*	230
Willoughby, Mark/*Farley Middle Sch*	396
Wills-Pacheco, Cheryl/*Southwest Preparatory-NW ES*	11
Wills-Pacheco, Sheryl/*Southwest Prep Sch NW [302]*	11
Wills, Carole/*Briarwood Sch*	205
Wills, Jennifer/*O Henry Elem Sch*	113
Wilmes, Joan/*St Ann's Sch*	286
Wilson, Adam/*Griffin Sch*	373
Wilson, Angel/*Gregory-Lincoln Education Ctr*	188
Wilson, Anitra/*Williams Elem Sch*	154
Wilson, Bruce/*Miller HS-Metro Sch of Design*	304
Wilson, Candace/*J B Stephens Elem Sch*	58
Wilson, Caroline/*James Bowie Elem Sch*	100
Wilson, Cherelle/*Nita Pearson Elem Sch*	106
Wilson, Clayton/*Howe Middle Sch*	166
Wilson, Curtis/*Nyos Charter School-M M Campus*	8
Wilson, Damon/*Bangs Middle Sch*	58
Wilson, David/*Celina High Sch*	78
Wilson, Deann/*Sudan Elem Sch*	261
Wilson, Elizabeth, Dr/*Fern Bluff Elem Sch*	398
Wilson, Erwann/*Ramona Bang Elem Sch*	185
Wilson, Gregg/*Clyde High Sch*	62
Wilson, Jack/*I Go Elem Sch*	396
Wilson, Jack/*Jarrell Intermediate Sch*	396
Wilson, John/*Grandview-Hopkins Elem Sch*	164
Wilson, Krista/*Cheri L Cox Elem Sch*	85
Wilson, Krystal/*Riesel High Sch*	281
Wilson, Laurel/*Navarro Elem Sch*	173
Wilson, Lee/*Rivercrest Junior High Sch*	323
Wilson, Mark/*British Int'l Sch of Houston*	205
Wilson, Mark/*Springtown Middle Sch*	313
Wilson, Misty/*Forestridge Elem Sch*	112
Wilson, Nikketta, Dr/*Webb Middle Sch*	107
Wilson, Robby/*Will Rogers Academy*	41
Wilson, Robert/*Post Middle Sch*	162
Wilson, Ryan/*George Dawson Middle Sch*	347
Wilson, Scott/*Elolf Elem Sch*	33
Wilson, Senta/*Int'l Ldrship TX-Lancaster*	108
Wilson, Sheryl/*Cesar Chavez Learning Center*	99
Wilson, Stacie/*Carver Elem Sch*	236
Wilson, Sue/*Hudson Pep Elem Sch*	170
Wilson, Susan/*Calvin Vincent ECC*	161
Wilson, Talisa/*Brooks Oaks Academy*	2
Wimberley, Alan/*STEM Academy-Lewisville [297]*	11
Wimbrey, Willie/*Annette Perry Elem Sch*	356
Winborne, Jamie/*Pampa Junior High Sch*	165
Winchester, Denise/*Ray L Shotwell Middle Sch*	181
Windham, Joel/*Maud Sch*	49
Windsor, Kathy, Dr/*Alvin ISD Career & Tech Ed Ctr*	51
Wineinger, Lance/*Wink Elem Sch*	402
Wing, Beth/*George B Dealey Mont Intl Acad*	100
Wing, John/*Early Childhood Sch*	178
Wing, Paige/*Lumberton Intermediate Sch*	178
Wingard, Amanda/*Neff Elem Sch*	194
Wingfield, Rebecca/*Stan C Stanley Elem Sch*	153
Winicki, Walter/*Creekwood Middle Sch*	195
Winkler, Ray/*Sloan Creek Intermediate Sch*	80
Winn, Jay/*Leon High Sch*	264
Winsett, Nicole/*KIPP Poder Academy [289]*	7
Winslow, Theodora/*Independence Elem Sch*	123
Winstead, Buddy/*Yantis Sch*	405
Winstead, Christina/*Pine Shadows Elem Sch*	201
Winters, Kim/*Pearson Ranch Middle Sch*	399
Wise, Don/*Manor Middle Sch*	371
Wise, Jay/*Jim Ned Middle Sch*	361
Wiseburn, Wendy/*Frazier Elem Sch*	199

Texas School Directory — PRINCIPAL INDEX

NAME/School	PAGE
Wiseman, Donnie/Pat & Katherine Fowler Mid Sch	79
Wiseman, Jennifer/Wally Watkins Elem Sch	85
Wiseman, Ken/Nolan Creek Sch [292]	8
Wisneski, Jamie/Pearson Middle Sch	80
Withrow, Jeff/Sweetwater Middle Sch	302
Witte, Melanie/Kenedy Elem Sch	251
Witten, Tammy/Howe Intermediate Sch	166
Witthaus, Wendi/Hopper Middle Sch	185
Wittich, Rachel/Wedgewood Academy	360
Wittpenn, Keri/Long Academy	194
Wofford, John/Lakeview Elem Sch	124
Wold, Lee/Lola Mae Carter Academy	179
Wolf, Barry/Sealy Junior High Sch	22
Wolf, Chad/Roy J Smith Middle Sch	28
Wolf, Chad/STEM Academy-Killeen	28
Wolfe, B Paul/Cambridge School of Dallas	114
Wolfe, Melonie/North Dallas Adventist Academy	115
Wolff, Lester/Lake Travis Middle Sch	370
Wolff, Shanda/Kendall Elem Sch	254
Wolfgram, Dale/Immanuel Lutheran Sch	263
Womack, Amy/River Oaks Baptist Sch	207
Womack, Clifton/Graford Elem Sch	310
Womack, Clifton/Graford Jr Sr High Sch	310
Womack, Damaris/East Avenue Primary Sch	164
Womack, Keisha/Carolee Booker Elem Sch	202
Womack, Krissy/Harry McKillop Elem Sch	81
Womack, Lori/De Leon Elem Sch	89
Wommack, Carman/Moss Elem Sch	233
Wong, Rodrigo/Idea Clg Prep-Edgemere	218
Wood, Jennifer/Somerville High Sch	60
Wood, Jody/Riesel High Sch	281
Wood, Joel/Filemon B Vela Middle Sch	63
Wood, Jyl/Pittsburg Primary Sch	68
Wood, Lindsey/Dorie Miller Interm Sch	140
Wood, Liz/Salyards Middle Sch	185
Wood, Susan/Lake Jackson Intermediate Sch	52
Wood, Xan/League City Elem Sch	159
Woodard, Crystal/La Poynor Sch	214
Woodard, Joe/Bruceville-Eddy High Sch	278
Woodard, Latreia/Foerster Elem Sch	188
Woodington, Allison/Windsor Elem Sch	318
Woods, Charles/Klein Intermediate Sch	197
Woods, Jerry, Dr/Tom C Clark High Sch	38
Woods, Jessie/Burrus Elem Sch	190
Woods, Monica/Oak Springs Elem Sch	368
Woods, Tonya/Southwest Schools-Phoenix [278]	11
Woodson, Beverly/St Philip's Academy-Frisco	86
Woodward, Beth/Little Elem Sch	344
Woodward, Denise/Manara Acad Leadership Acad	8
Woodworth, Karen/Venus High Sch	249
Wooldridge, Toron, Dr/Blue Ridge Elem Sch	149
Woolley, Tim/Bridge City High Sch	308
Woolley, Trevor/Ulrich Intermediate Sch	197
Wooten, Darla/Pilot Point Intermediate Sch	125
Wooten, Diane/St Francis DeSales Sch	204
Wooten, Kandra/Isbell Elem Sch	79
Wooten, Kenneth/Melissa High Sch	81
Wooten, Michelle/Lisd STEM Academy at Donaldson	123
Worcester, Trevor/Greenhill Sch	115
Word, Janet/Childress Elem Sch	74
Word, Janet/Gateway Academy	74
Word, Mike/Clarendon Elem Sch	127
Workman, Jim/Balmorhea Sch	323
Workman, Jim/Gonzales Elem Sch	164
Works, Phillip/Beckville Jr Sr High Sch	311
Worley, Dawn/Jstem Academy	33
Worrell, Daron/Brackett Junior High Sch	257
Worth, Donald/Tahoka High Sch	273
Wortham, Atiya/Stephen F Austin Elem Sch	265
Wrather, Sherri/Copperfield Elem Sch	33
Wrege, Thomas/Zion Lutheran Sch	400
Wright, Amanda/Central Elem Sch	17
Wright, Angela/Versia L Williams Elem Sch	352
Wright, April/Lowery Elem Sch	185
Wright, Arla/Goldthwaite Elem Sch	288
Wright, Bryndan/Mullin Elem Sch	288
Wright, Bryndan/Mullin Oaks Sch	288
Wright, Dee/East Elem Sch	58
Wright, Elsa/Thomas J Stovall Middle Sch	181
Wright, Gail/West Main Elem Sch	110
Wright, Greg/Pottsboro High Sch	167
Wright, Jimmy/Golden Rule CS-Sunnyside [281]	3
Wright, Julia/Meyerpark Charter Sch	8
Wright, Karen/Aubrey Middle Sch	120
Wright, Kevin/Alba-Golden Elem Sch	404
Wright, Kodi/North Hopkins Sch	231
Wright, Kyle/E J Moss Intermediate Sch	337
Wright, Randall/Harleton Junior High Sch	208
Wright, Rian, Dr/KIPP Sunnyside High Sch [288]	7
Wright, Richard/Falfurrias High Sch	57
Wright, Scot/Dalhart High Sch	95
Wright, Stephanie/Nocona High Sch	290
Wright, Tiffany/Elite College Prep Acad-Bowie	3
Wright, Tiffany/Houston Gateway Elite Clg Prep	5
Wright, Traci Lynn/Lyndon B Johnson High Sch	368
Wrinkle, Rea/Orangefield Junior High Sch	309
Wrobleske, Kathleen/Connection School of Houston	205
Wuest, Kendra/Pawnee Sch	25
Wulfsberg, Marisa/Northern Hills Elem Sch	35
Wurzbach, Kristin/Pecan Valley Elem Sch	31
Wyatt, April/Whitt Fine Arts Academy	108
Wyatt, Julie/Talkington Sch Young Women	270
Wyatt, Lori/Albright Middle Sch	182
Wyatt, Rhonda/Richland Springs Sch	332
Wyles, Theresa/St Mary's Catholic Sch	30
Wylie, Jay/Pewitt High Sch	296
Wyllie, Shani/Attucks Middle Sch	188
Wynne, Stephanie/Shirley Hall Middle Sch	314
Wynns, Shelly/Cross Timbers Elem Sch	345
Wyrick, Mike/Don Durham Intermediate Sch	347

Y

NAME/School	PAGE
Yackel, Neely/Shiner Catholic School-St Paul	263
Yaffie, David/Clements High Sch	150
Yampey, Debbie/Parkwood Elem Sch	186
Yates, Emma/Stahl Elem Sch	35
Yates, Kayla/Texhoma Elem Sch	336
Yates, Rosemary/Elfida P Chavez Elem Sch	136
Ybarra, Diana/Rafael Galvan Elem Sch	304
Ybarsabal, Amanda/KIPP Generations Collegiate HS [288]	7
Yeaman, Charlee/Highland Park Elem Sch	243
Yeaman, Jason/Little Cypress Jr High Sch	308
Yeilding, Linda/Texoma Christian Sch	169
Yilmaz, Ali/Harmony Sch Innov-Houston [284]	4
Yilmaz, Ilker/Harmony Sci Acad-Cedar Park [284]	5
Yilmaz, Kamil/Harmony Sch Endeavor-Houston [284]	4
Ying, Chung/Mandarin Immersion Magnet Sch	194
Yocham, Steven/Winston School San Antonio	45
Yoder, Elizabeth/M H Moore Elem Sch	351
Yoes, Richard/Brazosport High Sch	52
Yoest, Beth, Sr/St Peter's Memorial Sch	389
York, Ashley/Nolan Middle Sch	28
York, Jeff/Haskell High Sch	210
York, John/Muenster High Sch	91
York, Russ/Ambleside School of Fredericks	163
Young, Atina/Carroll Elem Sch	200
Young, Catherine/Noel A Smith Elem Sch	79
Young, Christine/Northwest Elem Sch	58
Young, Douglas/Lubbock Senior High Sch	270
Young, Jeannette/Capitol School-Austin	373
Young, Lisa/Bette Perot Elem Sch	354
Young, Lisa/O C Taylor Elem Sch	353
Young, Michael/Thorndale Elem Sch	288
Young, Steve/Orr Elem Sch	338
Young, Terry/Woodville High Sch	375
Young, Vickie/La Mesa Elem Sch	175
Youngberg, Nikol, Dr/Flour Bluff Elem Sch	304
Youngblood, Brenda/Weldon Corbell Elem Sch	80
Youngs, Irene/Pebble Hills Elem Sch	138

PRINCIPAL INDEX

Market Data Retrieval

NAME/*School*	PAGE
Youree, Mark/*S & S Cons High Sch*	167
Ysasi, Marcus/*Chapel Hill High Sch*	363
Ysquierdo, Rachelle/*Sheldon Elem Sch*	200
Yttredahl, Bob/*Lakehill Preparatory Sch*	115
Yturralde, Jason/*Henderson Middle Sch*	135
Yturralde, Jason/*Ross Middle Sch*	135
Yu, Byong Chang/*Idea Clg Prep-Carver*	218
Yzaguirre, Henry/*Southside High Sch*	43

Z

NAME/*School*	PAGE
Zacharias, Cheri/*McGregor Primary Sch*	280
Zacharias, Melissa/*Robinson Primary Sch*	281
Zachary, Sharri/*Elisha M Pease Elem Sch*	100
Zagala, Erika/*Allen Elem Sch*	36
Zahn, Jerod/*Shackelford Junior High Sch*	345
Zamarripa, Martin/*Garcia Elem Sch*	107
Zamarripa, Sofia/*Adult Education Center*	350
Zambiasi, Travis/*Lawler Middle Sch*	79
Zamora, David/*H E Charles Middle Sch*	134
Zamora, Efrain/*Marcell Elem Sch*	222
Zamora, Lindolfo/*Hope Academy*	220
Zamora, Marco/*Cte Early College High Sch*	225
Zamora, Rosario/*Premier HS-Pharr [297]*	9
Zamora, Yvonne/*Mims Elem Sch*	222
Zamzow, Devon/*Pearsall Junior High Sch*	157
Zandt, Derek/*Eddie Finley Jr High Sch*	142
Zapalac, Callene/*Schulenburg High Sch*	148
Zapata, Andrea/*Richey Elem Sch*	199
Zapata, Jerry/*Meadowland CS-Oaks Acad*	8
Zaqat, Baha/*Iman Academy-Southwest*	206
Zaravar, Nidia/*Atherton Elem Sch*	343
Zaravar, Nidia/*Corey Acad Fine Arts*	344
Zarzosa, Edna/*South Houston Elem Sch*	199
Zavala, Alberto/*John R Good Elem Sch*	109
Zavala, Beatriz/*El Paso Academy West*	3
Zavala, Beatriz/*Sierra Blanca Sch*	235
Zavala, Betty/*Kaiser Elem Sch*	197
Zavala, Frank/*Alan B Shepard Middle Sch*	42
Zavala, Jennifer/*Wilson Elem Sch*	41
Zavala, Loretta/*Lytle High Sch*	21
Zbylut, Amy/*Kleberg Elem Sch*	101
Zebold, Jennifer/*Briscoe Junior High Sch*	153
Zeissel, Karen/*Calvary Christian Sch*	68
Zelezinski, Diana/*Foster Elem Sch*	195
Zepeda, Andrea/*Alamo Elem Sch*	187
Zepeda, Juanita/*J W Arndt Elem Sch*	387
Zerbe, Kari/*Rise School of Dallas*	116
Zertuche, Alma/*Bear Creek Elem Sch*	151
Zimmerman, Casey/*Friendship Pre-Sch & Chrn Acad*	244
Zimmerman, Steven/*Madison High Sch*	35
Zipkes, Steven/*Cedars Intl Next Generation HS*	2
Zolman, Phil/*Kress Jr Sr High Sch*	343
Zukowski, Cindy/*Furr Elem Sch*	84
Zuniga-Barrera, Celia/*San Felipe Memorial Middle Sch*	379
Zuniga, Edith/*Progreso Early Childhood Sch*	224
Zuniga, Karen/*Lehman High Sch*	211
Zuniga, Paulita/*Premier HS-Pflugerville [297]*	9
Zupa, Michele/*Richardson Terrace Elem Sch*	113
Zuppardo, Marilena/*Dallas Co Jj Aae-Letot Ctr*	96
Zurita, Barbra/*St Augustine Elem Middle Sch*	388

Texas School Directory

DISTRICT & SCHOOL TELEPHONE INDEX

School/City/County DISTRICT/CITY/COUNTY	PID	TELEPHONE NUMBER	PAGE
3D Academy/*Donna*/Hidalgo	11454070	956/464-1254	215
1621 Place Sch/*Rosenberg*/Fort Bend	04282755	832/223-0950	153

A

School/City/County	PID	TELEPHONE	PAGE
A & M Consolidated High Sch/*College Sta*/Brazos	01001966	979/764-5500	55
A & M Consolidated Middle Sch/*College Sta*/Brazos	04918978	979/764-5575	55
A A Milne Elem Sch/*Houston*/Harris	03336688	713/778-3420	193
A B Anderson Academy/*Houston*/Harris	01022702	281/878-0370	179
A B Duncan Elem Sch/*Floydada*/Floyd	01017989	806/983-5332	148
A B Harrison Intermediate Sch/*Wylie*/Collin	04451750	972/429-3300	85
A B McBay Elem Sch/*Mexia*/Limestone	01824330	254/562-4030	267
A C Blunt Middle Sch/*Aransas Pass*/San Patricio	03050470	361/758-2711	330
A C Jones High Sch/*Beeville*/Bee	00996071	361/362-6000	25
A C New Middle Sch/*Mesquite*/Dallas	03011797	972/882-5600	110
A C Williams Elem Sch/*Commerce*/Hunt	02127434	903/886-3758	236
A G Elder Elem Sch/*Joshua*/Johnson	04755178	817/202-2500	248
A G Hilliard Elem Sch/*Houston*/Harris	01026473	713/635-3085	188
A Habitat for Learning Daycare/*Abilene*/Taylor	11011032	325/692-2481	361
A J Briesemeister Mid Sch/*Seguin*/Guadalupe	01021643	830/401-8711	174
A J Martin Elem Sch/*Houston*/Harris	01022984	281/983-8363	182
A L Benavides Elem Sch/*San Ygnacio*/Zapata	01062257	956/765-5611	406
A L Steele Enhanced Lrng Ctr/*Schertz*/Guadalupe	04448870	210/945-6401	173
A M Aikin Elem Sch/*Paris*/Lamar	02110481	903/737-7443	260
A M Pate Elem Sch/*Fort Worth*/Tarrant	01053220	817/815-3800	350
A N McCallum High Sch/*Austin*/Travis	01056404	512/414-2519	368
A N Rico Elem Sch/*Weslaco*/Hidalgo	04288448	956/969-6815	225
A P Beutel Elem Sch/*Lake Jackson*/Brazoria	01001552	979/730-7165	52
A P Solis Middle Sch/*Donna*/Hidalgo	01029607	956/464-1650	215
A Plus Academy Elem/*Dallas*/Dallas	04932168	972/557-5578	1
A Plus Academy Secondary/*Dallas*/Dallas	12238831	469/677-1000	1
A Plus Unlimited Potential Sch/*Houston*/Harris	12043143	713/658-1881	205
A Plus Up-Museum Campus/*Houston*/Harris	12261436	713/955-7543	1
A Plus Up-University Campus/*Houston*/Harris	12261448	713/955-7583	1
A R Turner Elem Sch/*Willis*/Montgomery	01042776	936/856-1289	294
A Robison Elem Sch/*Cypress*/Harris	05272105	281/213-1700	184
A V Cato Elem Sch/*Fort Worth*/Tarrant	01052305	817/252-2400	347
A Villarreal Elem Sch/*Edinburg*/Hidalgo	04873287	956/289-2377	216
A W Brown Leadership Academy/*Dallas*/Dallas	04881557	972/709-4700	1
Aaron Parker Elem Sch/*Powderly*/Lamar	01036674	903/732-3066	259
Abbett Elem Sch/*Garland*/Dallas	03266320	972/675-3000	105
ABBOTT IND SCH DIST/***ABBOTT***/***HILL***	01030709	254/582-3011	226
Abbott Sch/*Abbott*/Hill	01030711	254/582-3011	226
Abell Junior High Sch/*Midland*/Midland	04036996	432/689-6200	285
Abercrombie Academy/*Spring*/Harris	02750158	281/374-1730	205
Abernathy Elem Sch/*Abernathy*/Hale	01021758	806/298-4930	174
Abernathy High Sch/*Abernathy*/Hale	01021760	806/298-2563	174
ABERNATHY IND SCH DIST/***ABERNATHY***/***HALE***	01021746	806/298-2563	174
Abernathy Middle Sch/*Abernathy*/Hale	01021772	806/298-4921	174
Abiding Word Lutheran Sch/*Houston*/Harris	04993368	281/895-7048	205
Abilene Christian Sch/*Abilene*/Taylor	01481158	325/672-6200	361
Abilene High Sch/*Abilene*/Taylor	01172632	325/677-1731	360
ABILENE IND SCH DIST/***ABILENE***/***TAYLOR***	01054523	325/677-1444	360
About Face Alternative ES/*El Paso*/El Paso	11982285	915/236-3150	133
Abraham Lincoln Middle Sch/*Port Arthur*/Jefferson	01033787	409/984-8700	243
Abundant Life Christian Sch/*La Marque*/Galveston	11715276	409/935-8773	1
Acad of Leadershp & Tech-Mound/*Burleson*/Johnson	01034858	817/245-3100	246
Academic Behavior Center-East/*Houston*/Harris	04144256	713/242-8036	179
Academic Behavior Sch-West/*Houston*/Harris	11134464	713/339-9411	179
Academic Career Center/*Corp Christi*/Nueces	03396432	361/903-6450	305
Academy/*Mabank*/Kaufman	11457060	903/880-1600	252
Academy Academic Enhancemnt-ES/*Rio Grande Cy*/Starr	12038564	956/716-6941	340
Academy Academic Enhancemnt-MS/*Rio Grande Cy*/Starr	12038576	956/352-6324	340
Academy at Carrie F Thomas/*N Richlnd Hls*/Tarrant	01881144	817/547-3000	346
Academy at Nola Dunn/*Burleson*/Johnson	04919726	817/245-3300	246
Academy at World Champions Ctr/*Spring*/Montgomery	12322690	281/292-6284	295
Academy Careers Engr Science/*Conroe*/Montgomery	12311079	832/482-6700	291
Academy Elem Sch/*LTL RVR Acad*/Bell	00996277	254/982-4621	26
Academy Health Sci Prof-STEM/*La Joya*/Hidalgo	12233544	956/323-2250	219
Academy High Sch/*Kingsville*/Kleberg	04362991	361/384-5041	258
Academy High Sch/*LTL RVR Acad*/Bell	03397632	254/982-4201	26
ACADEMY IND SCH DIST/***LTL RVR ACAD***/***BELL***	00996253	254/982-4304	26
Academy Intermediate Sch/*LTL RVR Acad*/Bell	12104450	254/982-0150	26
Academy Middle Sch/*LTL RVR Acad*/Bell	03397620	254/982-4620	26
Academy of Accelerated Lrng/*Houston*/Harris	05242760	713/773-4766	1
Academy of Arts at Branson/*Burleson*/Johnson	05091169	817/245-3600	246
Academy of Choice/*Houston*/Harris	01027312	713/251-1500	200
Academy of Creative Education/*San Antonio*/Bexar	03471953	210/407-0740	34
Academy of Dallas-Oak Park/*Dallas*/Dallas	04881583	214/371-9600	1
Academy of Science & Tech/*The Woodlands*/Montgomery	05358436	936/709-3250	291
Academy of Thought & Industry/*Austin*/Travis	12362420	512/910-8980	372
Academy-Science & Health Prof/*Conroe*/Montgomery	05358448	936/709-5731	291
Accel Inter Academy-Lancaster/*Lancaster*/Dallas	11824968	972/227-2105	1
Accelerated Center for Ed/*Houston*/Harris	04284399	832/386-3672	186
Accelerated Intermediate Acad/*Houston*/Harris	05010919	713/728-9330	1
Ace Alternative Sch/*Lufkin*/Angelina	02126674	936/630-4152	18
ACES Alternative/*Brownsboro*/Henderson	11450361	903/852-8046	213
Achieve Academy/*Wylie*/Collin	10968951	972/429-2390	85
Achieve Early College High Sch/*McAllen*/Hidalgo	11557402	956/872-1653	221
Achziger Elem Sch/*Mesquite*/Dallas	11447132	972/290-4180	110
Acton Academy/*Austin*/Travis	11914692	512/320-0596	372
Acton Elem Sch/*Dallas*/Dallas	01539169	972/708-2400	104
Acton Elem Sch/*Granbury*/Hood	01826326	817/408-4200	230
Acton Middle Sch/*Granbury*/Hood	04033918	817/408-4800	230
Adams Elem Sch/*Arlington*/Tarrant	11919549	682/867-2130	343
Adams Elem Sch/*Cleburne*/Johnson	01034884	817/202-2000	247
Adams Hill Elem Sch/*San Antonio*/Bexar	00998029	210/397-1400	36
Adaptive Behavior Center/*Houston*/Harris	02045367	281/897-4174	184
Adelfa Botello Callejo ES/*Dallas*/Dallas	11827960	972/892-5700	98
Adella Young Elem Sch/*Pasadena*/Harris	01881900	713/740-0784	198
Adelle R Clark Middle Sch/*Frisco*/Collin	04916877	469/633-4600	78
Adelle Turner Elem Sch/*Dallas*/Dallas	01008378	972/794-6300	98
Adkins Elem Sch/*Lantana*/Denton	12033344	940/369-1300	121
Adolphus Elem Sch/*Richmond*/Fort Bend	11923631	832/223-4700	153
ADRIAN IND SCH DIST/***ADRIAN***/***OLDHAM***	01045522	806/538-6203	307
Adrian Sch/*Adrian*/Oldham	01045534	806/538-6203	307
Adult Education/*Abilene*/Taylor	01538244	325/671-4419	360
Adult Education Center/*Fort Worth*/Tarrant	01538232	817/492-7960	350
Advanced Learning Academy/*San Antonio*/Bexar	12169955	210/738-9760	39
Advanced Learning Academy/*San Antonio*/Bexar	12177469	210/738-9763	39
Advantage Acad-Grand Prairie E/*Grand Prairie*/Dallas	12234859	214/276-5800	96
Advantage Acad-Grand Prairie W/*Grand Prairie*/Dallas	11134414	214/276-5800	96
Advantage Acad-N Duncanville/*Dallas*/Dallas	04819774	214/276-5800	96
ADVANTAGE ACADEMY ADMIN OFFICE/***DUNCANVILLE***/***DALLAS***	11824891	214/276-5800	96
Advantage Academy-Waxahachie/*Waxahachie*/Dallas	02743064	972/937-9851	96
Adventist Christian Academy/*Conroe*/Montgomery	11239258	936/756-5078	295
Aep Center/*Belton*/Bell	03394563	254/215-2571	26
Aesa Preparatory Academy/*Austin*/Hays	11825601	512/560-5584	212
Agape Christian Academy/*Corsicana*/Navarro	12042266	903/641-0900	300
Agape Christian Academy/*Newton*/Newton	11727700	409/379-4611	301
Agape Christian Sch/*Mission*/Hidalgo	02123581	956/585-9773	226
Aggieland Country Mont Sch/*College Sta*/Brazos	02853449	979/696-1674	56
Agnes Cotton Academy/*San Antonio*/Bexar	00998380	210/738-9780	39
Agriculture Science Center/*Arlington*/Tarrant	12231132	682/867-9500	343
Agua Dulce Elem Sch/*Agua Dulce*/Nueces	01043990	361/998-2335	302
AGUA DULCE IND SCH DIST/***AGUA DULCE***/***NUECES***	01043988	361/998-2542	302

School Year 2019-2020   800-333-8802   TX-V1

DISTRICT & SCHOOL TELEPHONE INDEX

Market Data Retrieval

School/City/County DISTRICT/CITY/COUNTY	PID	TELEPHONE NUMBER	PAGE
Agua Dulce Secondary Sch/*Agua Dulce*/Nueces	03394173	361/998-2214	302
Aida Escobar Elem Sch/*Pharr*/Hidalgo	01030498	956/354-2920	223
Aikin Elem Sch/*Dallas*/Dallas	01881869	469/593-1820	112
Aikman Elem Sch/*Hereford*/Deaf Smith	01012991	806/363-7640	119
Aim Center/*Whitehouse*/Smith	04748022	903/839-5556	339
Aim Center High Sch/*Vidor*/Orange	04288125	409/951-8780	309
Aim College & Career Prep Acad/*Galveston*/Galveston	11557127	409/761-6302	160
Airport Drive Elem Sch/*Weslaco*/Hidalgo	03251959	956/969-6770	225
Akiba Academy of Dallas/*Dallas*/Dallas	01012135	214/295-3400	114
Akin Elem Sch/*Hale Center*/Hale	01021825	806/839-2121	175
Akins High Sch/*Austin*/Travis	04917687	512/841-9900	368
Al-Hadi Sch of Accel Lrng/*Houston*/Harris	11233888	713/787-5000	205
Alamo Education Center/*Ennis*/Ellis	12037302	972/872-7332	140
Alamo Elem Sch/*Baytown*/Harris	01023574	281/420-4595	187
Alamo Elem Sch/*Fort Stockton*/Pecos	01046849	432/336-4016	315
Alamo Heights High Sch/*San Antonio*/Bexar	00996930	210/820-8850	30
ALAMO HEIGHTS IND SCH DIST/SAN ANTONIO/BEXAR	00996928	210/824-2483	30
Alamo Heights Jr High Sch/*San Antonio*/Bexar	00996942	210/824-3231	30
Alamo Junior High Sch/*Midland*/Midland	01041435	432/689-1700	285
Alamo Middle Sch/*Alamo*/Hidalgo	03055494	956/354-2550	223
Alan B Shepard Middle Sch/*San Antonio*/Bexar	00999396	210/623-1875	42
Alarcon Elem Sch/*San Elizario*/El Paso	01016181	915/872-3930	135
Alba-Golden Elem Sch/*Alba*/Wood	01061796	903/768-2472	404
ALBA-GOLDEN IND SCH DIST/ALBA/WOOD	01061784	903/768-2472	404
Alba-Golden Jr Sr High Sch/*Alba*/Wood	01061801	903/768-2472	404
ALBANY IND SCH DIST/ALBANY/SHACKELFORD	01050216	325/762-2823	334
Albany Jr Sr High Sch/*Albany*/Shackelford	01050228	325/762-3974	334
Albert & Iola Davis Malvern ES/*McKinney*/Collin	04948507	469/302-5300	81
Albright Middle Sch/*Houston*/Harris	02201468	281/983-8411	182
Alcott Elem Sch/*Houston*/Harris	01025091	713/732-3540	192
Alcuin Montessori Sch/*Dallas*/Dallas	01754266	972/239-1745	114
Alderson Elem Sch/*Lubbock*/Lubbock	01038555	806/219-8000	270
Aldine 9th Grade Sch/*Houston*/Harris	04805022	281/878-6800	180
Aldine Education Center/*Houston*/Harris	04949824	281/985-6685	181
ALDINE IND SCH DIST/HOUSTON/HARRIS	01022697	281/449-1011	179
ALDINE ISD-ELEM SCH TEAM 1/HOUSTON/HARRIS	12107347	281/985-6467	179
ALDINE ISD-ELEM SCH TEAM 2/HOUSTON/HARRIS	12107359	281/985-6159	179
ALDINE ISD-ELEM SCH TEAM 3/HOUSTON/HARRIS	12107361	281/985-6956	180
ALDINE ISD-HIGH SCH TEAM/HOUSTON/HARRIS	12107397	281/985-6427	180
ALDINE ISD-MIDDLE SCH TEAM/HOUSTON/HARRIS	12107385	281/985-6689	181
ALDINE ISD-PRIMARY TEAM/HOUSTON/HARRIS	12368280	281/449-1011	181
Aldine Middle Sch/*Houston*/Harris	01022714	281/985-6580	181
Aldine Senior HS/*Houston*/Harris	01022726	281/448-5231	180
Aldridge Elem Sch/*Richardson*/Collin	01006473	469/752-0000	82
Aledo Christian Sch/*Aledo*/Parker	04924630	817/441-7357	314
Aledo High Sch/*Aledo*/Parker	01046320	817/441-8711	312
ALEDO IND SCH DIST/ALEDO/PARKER	01046306	817/441-8327	312
Aledo Learning Center/*Aledo*/Parker	04920646	817/441-5176	312
Aledo Middle Sch/*Aledo*/Parker	01046332	817/441-5198	312
Alex Sanger Elem Sch/*Dallas*/Dallas	01008392	972/749-7600	98
Alex W Spence Middle Sch & Tag/*Dallas*/Dallas	01008407	972/925-2300	98
Alexander Elem Sch/*Duncanville*/Dallas	01010307	972/708-2500	104
Alexander Elem Sch/*Houston*/Harris	02227280	281/983-8300	182
Alexander Middle Sch/*Pearland*/Brazoria	10909242	832/736-6700	53
Alexander Sch/*Richardson*/Dallas	02192702	972/690-9210	114
Alexander Smith Academy/*Houston*/Harris	02083917	713/266-0920	205
Alfonso R Ramirez Elem Sch/*Edinburg*/Hidalgo	11558236	956/289-2425	216
Alfred Sorensen Elem Sch/*San Juan*/Hidalgo	01030486	956/354-2910	223
Alice Carlson Applied Lrng Ctr/*Fort Worth*/Tarrant	04024462	817/815-5700	350
Alice Christian Sch/*Alice*/Jim Wells	04993837	361/668-6636	246
Alice Contreras Elem Sch/*Fort Worth*/Tarrant	04924757	817/814-7800	350
Alice High Sch/*Alice*/Jim Wells	01034535	361/664-0126	245
ALICE IND SCH DIST/ALICE/JIM WELLS	01034511	361/664-0981	245
Alice Johnson Jr High Sch/*Channelview*/Harris	01023093	281/452-8030	183
Alice Landergin Elem Sch/*Amarillo*/Potter	01047130	806/326-4650	317
Alice Moore Elementary/*Denton*/Denton	01013294	940/369-3500	121
Alice Ponder Elem Sch/*Mansfield*/Tarrant	01054121	817/299-7700	356
Alice W Douse Elem Sch/*Killeen*/Bell	12231338	254/336-7480	27
Alicia R Chacon Int'l Lang Sch/*El Paso*/El Paso	04364793	915/434-9200	137
Alicia Ruiz Elem Sch/*Laredo*/Webb	04013243	956/473-3300	387
Alief Early College High Sch/*Houston*/Harris	11557074	281/988-3010	182
ALIEF IND SCH DIST/HOUSTON/HARRIS	01022972	281/498-8110	181
Alief Learning Center/*Houston*/Harris	03052155	281/983-8000	182
Alief Middle Sch/*Houston*/Harris	01023017	281/983-8422	182
Alief Montessori Cmty Sch/*Houston*/Harris	04813902	281/530-9406	1
Alief Taylor High Sch/*Houston*/Harris	04943179	281/988-3500	182
Alkek Elem Sch/*Bandera*/Bandera	00995780	830/796-6223	23
All Saints Catholic Sch/*Dallas*/Collin	04841923	214/217-3300	85
All Saints Catholic Sch/*Fort Worth*/Tarrant	01054341	817/624-2670	358
All Saints Episcopal Sch/*Beaumont*/Jefferson	01034303	409/892-1755	244
All Saints Episcopal Sch/*Fort Worth*/Tarrant	01054248	817/560-5700	358
All Saints Episcopal Sch/*Lubbock*/Lubbock	01039262	806/745-7701	272
All Saints Episcopal Sch/*Tyler*/Smith	02084052	903/579-6000	339
Allen & William Arnold ES/*Pharr*/Hidalgo	01030383	956/354-2710	223
Allen 6th Grade Campus/*Amarillo*/Potter	10008355	806/326-3770	317
Allen Academy/*Bryan*/Brazos	01002180	979/776-0731	56
Allen Elem Sch/*San Antonio*/Bexar	00998172	210/397-0800	36
Allen High Sch/*Allen*/Collin	01006007	972/727-0400	76
ALLEN IND SCH DIST/ALLEN/COLLIN	01005986	972/727-0511	76
Alliene Mullendore Elem Sch/*N Richlnd Hls*/Tarrant	01052111	817/547-1900	346
Allison Elem Sch/*Austin*/Travis	01056026	512/414-2004	366
Alma A Pierce Elem Sch/*Laredo*/Webb	01059195	956/273-4300	386
Alma Brewer Strawn Elem Sch/*Dale*/Caldwell	12168858	512/398-0630	61
Almeda Elem Sch/*Houston*/Harris	01025106	713/434-5620	192
Aloe Elem Sch/*Victoria*/Victoria	01058452	361/788-9509	382
Alonso S Perales Elem Sch/*San Antonio*/Bexar	00997166	210/444-8350	31
Alonzo De Leon Middle Sch/*McAllen*/Hidalgo	03392606	956/632-8800	221
Alpha Academy/*Magnolia*/Montgomery	05264976	281/252-2265	292
Alpha Omega Academy/*Huntsville*/Walker	04993435	936/438-8833	384
Alpine Christian Sch/*Alpine*/Brewster	11076226	432/837-5757	57
Alpine Elem Sch/*Alpine*/Brewster	01002207	432/837-7730	56
Alpine High Sch/*Alpine*/Brewster	01002219	432/837-7710	56
ALPINE IND SCH DIST/ALPINE/BREWSTER	01002192	432/837-7700	56
Alpine Middle Sch/*Alpine*/Brewster	01002221	432/837-7720	56
Alt Edu Program Phoenix Campus/*Azle*/Tarrant	04452168	817/444-4564	345
Alta Loma Elem Sch/*San Angelo*/Tom Green	01055541	325/947-3914	364
Alta Vista Elem Sch/*Waco*/McLennan	01040144	254/662-3050	281
Alternative Education Center/*Port Neches*/Jefferson	04747717	409/722-5924	243
Alternative Education Ctr/*Magnolia*/Montgomery	11924855	281/252-2275	292
Alternative Education Program/*Euless*/Tarrant	04748230	817/354-3398	353
Alternative Learning Center/*Austin*/Travis	03008673	512/414-2554	368
Alternative Learning Center/*Bridgeport*/Wise	05270080	940/683-1830	402
Alternative Learning Center/*Keene*/Johnson	04247482	817/774-5370	248
Alternative Learning Center/*Rosenberg*/Fort Bend	03250826	832/223-0900	153
Alternative Lrng Ctr-East/*Houston*/Harris	04036661	281/897-4171	184
Alternative Lrng Ctr-West/*Katy*/Harris	11457503	281/855-4310	184
Alto Bonito Elem Sch/*Rio Grande Cy*/Starr	04867965	956/487-6295	340
Alto Elem Sch/*Alto*/Cherokee	01005211	936/587-7174	72
Alto High Sch/*Alto*/Cherokee	01005223	936/858-7110	72
ALTO IND SCH DIST/ALTO/CHEROKEE	01005209	936/858-7101	72
Alto Middle Sch/*Alto*/Cherokee	04745056	936/858-7140	72
Alton Boyd Elem Sch/*Allen*/Collin	01824093	972/727-0560	76
Alton Elem Sch/*Alton*/Hidalgo	01388128	956/323-7600	222
Alton Elem Sch/*Brenham*/Washington	01059054	979/277-3870	385
Alton Memorial Junior High Sch/*Alton*/Hidalgo	05275418	956/323-5000	222
Alton O Bowen Elem Sch/*Bryan*/Brazos	04278455	979/209-1300	55
Alvarado Elem North Sch/*Alvarado*/Johnson	02896960	817/783-6863	246
Alvarado Elem South Sch/*Alvarado*/Johnson	01034808	817/783-6880	246
Alvarado High Sch/*Alvarado*/Johnson	01034779	817/783-6940	246

Texas School Directory

DISTRICT & SCHOOL TELEPHONE INDEX

School/City/County DISTRICT/CITY/COUNTY	PID	TELEPHONE NUMBER	PAGE
ALVARADO IND SCH DIST/*Alvarado*/ **JOHNSON**	01034767	817/783-6800	246
Alvarado Intermediate Sch/*Alvarado*/Johnson	04453849	817/783-6825	246
Alvarado Junior High Sch/*Alvarado*/Johnson	01034793	817/783-6840	246
Alvin Elem Sch/*Alvin*/Brazoria	01001394	281/585-2511	51
Alvin High Sch/*Alvin*/Brazoria	01001409	281/245-3000	51
ALVIN IND SCH DIST/*Alvin*/ **BRAZORIA**	01001382	281/388-1130	50
Alvin ISD Career & Tech Ed Ctr/*Manvel*/ Brazoria	12177550	281/245-2160	51
Alvin Junior High Sch/*Alvin*/Brazoria	01001411	281/245-2770	51
Alvin Primary Sch/*Alvin*/Brazoria	01001423	281/585-2531	51
Alvis C Story Elem Sch/*Allen*/Collin	03004055	972/727-0570	76
Alvord Elem Sch/*Alvord*/Wise	01061538	940/427-2881	402
Alvord High Sch/*Alvord*/Wise	01061540	940/427-9643	402
ALVORD IND SCH DIST/*Alvord*/**WISE**	01061526	940/427-5975	402
Alvord Middle Sch/*Alvord*/Wise	03008219	940/427-5511	402
Amanda Rochell Elem Sch/*Rockwall*/Rockwall	02104092	972/771-2112	325
Amarillo Area Ctr Advance Lrng/*Amarillo*/ Potter	04922773	806/326-2800	317
Amarillo Collegiate Academy/*Amarillo*/ Randall	12260626	806/352-0171	1
Amarillo Collegiate Academy/*Amarillo*/ Randall	11014577	806/352-0171	1
Amarillo High Sch/*Amarillo*/Potter	01047142	806/326-2000	317
AMARILLO IND SCH DIST/*Amarillo*/ **POTTER**	01047128	806/326-1000	317
Ambassadors Preparatory Acad/*Galveston*/ Galveston	11013858	409/762-1115	1
Amber Terrace Discovery ECC/*Desoto*/Dallas	01525948	972/223-8757	104
Ambleside School of Fredericks/*Fredericksbrg*/ Gillespie	11223522	830/990-9059	163
Amelia Elem Sch/*Beaumont*/Jefferson	01034107	409/617-6000	241
American Preparatory Institute/*Killeen*/ Bell	11239375	254/526-1321	30
Americas High Sch/*El Paso*/El Paso	04455952	915/937-2800	135
AMHERST IND SCH DIST/*Amherst*/ **LAMB**	01036882	806/246-7729	260
Amherst Sch/*Amherst*/Lamb	01036894	806/246-3221	260
AMI Kids Rio Grande Valley/*Los Fresnos*/ Cameron	04809858	956/233-5795	66
Amigos Por Vida Charter Sch/*Houston*/Harris	04881600	713/349-9945	1
Amon Carter-Riverside High Sch/*Fort Worth*/ Tarrant	01052537	817/814-9000	350
Amos Elem Sch/*Arlington*/Tarrant	01051636	682/867-4700	343
Amparo Gutierrez Elem Sch/*Laredo*/Webb	04013231	956/473-4400	387
Amy Campbell Elem Sch/*Fulshear*/Harris	12308307	281/234-4500	151
Amy Parks-Heath Elem Sch/*Heath*/Rockwall	04364078	972/772-4300	325
Anahuac Elem Sch/*Anahuac*/Chambers	01005089	409/267-3600	71
Anahuac High Sch/*Anahuac*/Chambers	01005091	409/267-3600	71
ANAHUAC IND SCH DIST/*Anahuac*/ **CHAMBERS**	01005077	409/267-3600	71
Anahuac Middle Sch/*Anahuac*/Chambers	01005106	409/267-2042	71
Anderson Accelerated High Sch/*Big Spring*/ Howard	05092357	432/264-4115	233
Anderson Elem Sch/*Arlington*/Tarrant	05347853	682/867-7750	343
Anderson Elem Sch/*Conroe*/Montgomery	01042477	936/709-5300	291
Anderson Elem Sch/*Houston*/Harris	01024700	713/726-3600	193
Anderson Elem Sch/*Lufkin*/Angelina	02201793	936/632-5527	18
Anderson Elem Sch/*Plano*/Collin	04868555	469/633-2300	78
Anderson Elem Sch/*Spring*/Harris	02110613	281/891-8360	202
Anderson High Sch/*Austin*/Travis	01056442	512/414-2538	368
Anderson Mill Elem Sch/*Austin*/Williamson	01541411	512/428-3700	398
ANDERSON-SHIRO CONS IND SD/ **ANDERSON/GRIMES**	01021344	936/873-4500	171
Anderson-Shiro Elem Sch/*Anderson*/Grimes	01021356	936/873-4525	171
Anderson-Shiro Jr Sr High Sch/*Anderson*/ Grimes	03049299	936/873-4550	171
Andre Elem Sch/*Cypress*/Harris	10030322	281/463-5500	184
Andress High Sch/*El Paso*/El Paso	01015735	915/236-4000	134
Andrew Jackson Elem Sch/*McAllen*/Hidalgo	01030008	956/971-4277	221
Andrews Alternative Sch/*Andrews*/Andrews	04801909	432/524-1946	16
Andrews Elem Sch/*Austin*/Travis	01056038	512/414-1770	367
Andrews High Sch/*Andrews*/Andrews	00994724	432/524-1910	16
ANDREWS IND SCH DIST/*Andrews*/ **ANDREWS**	00994700	432/523-3640	16
Andrews Middle Sch/*Andrews*/Andrews	00994712	432/524-1940	16
Andy Dekaney High Sch/*Houston*/Harris	10910007	281/891-7260	202
Angela Leal Elem Sch/*San Benito*/Cameron	11713436	956/276-5055	67
Angelo Catholic Sch/*San Angelo*/Tom Green	01055931	325/949-1747	366
Angleton Christian Sch/*Angleton*/Brazoria	10016039	979/864-3842	54
Angleton High Sch/*Angleton*/Brazoria	01001497	979/864-8001	51

School/City/County DISTRICT/CITY/COUNTY	PID	TELEPHONE NUMBER	PAGE
ANGLETON IND SCH DIST/*Angleton*/ **BRAZORIA**	01001473	979/864-8000	51
Angleton Junior High Sch/*Angleton*/Brazoria	01001485	979/864-8002	51
Anita Scott Elem Sch/*Royse City*/Rockwall	05096779	972/636-3300	326
Anita T Dovalina Elem Sch/*Laredo*/Webb	02201200	956/273-3320	386
Ann M Garcia-Enriquez Mid Sch/*San Elizario*/ El Paso	03004184	915/872-3960	135
Ann Richards Middle Sch/*Mission*/Hidalgo	04868610	956/323-2860	219
Ann Richards Steam Academy/*Dallas*/Dallas	11919903	972/892-5400	98
Ann Whitney Elem Sch/*Hamilton*/Hamilton	01022178	254/386-8166	176
Anna Education Center/*Anna*/Collin	12363278	972/924-1340	77
Anna High Sch/*Anna*/Collin	03051010	972/924-1100	77
ANNA IND SCH DIST/**ANNA**/**COLLIN**	01006021	972/924-1000	77
Anna May Daulton Elem Sch/*Grand Prairie*/ Tarrant	10028226	817/299-6640	356
Anna Middle Sch/*Anna*/Collin	01006045	972/924-1200	77
Annapolis Christian Academy/*Corp Christi*/ Nueces	04144218	361/991-6004	306
Anne Frank Elem Sch/*Dallas*/Dallas	04757035	972/502-5900	98
Anne Frank Inspire Academy/*San Antonio*/ Bexar	12035108	210/638-5900	30
Anne L MaGee Elem Sch/*Edinburg*/Hidalgo	05275183	956/289-2306	216
Anne Sullivan Elem Sch/*Sugar Land*/ Fort Bend	12169553	281/327-2860	149
Annette Perry Elem Sch/*Mansfield*/Tarrant	11464960	817/804-2800	356
Annie Purl Elem Sch/*Georgetown*/Williamson	01060895	512/943-5080	395
Annie Rainwater Elem Sch/*Carrollton*/Dallas	04282860	972/968-2800	96
Annie Sims Elem Sch/*Mt Pleasant*/Titus	01055371	903/575-2062	363
Annie Webb Blanton Elem Sch/*Dallas*/Dallas	01008433	972/794-1700	99
Annunciation Orthodox Sch/*Houston*/Harris	01601815	713/470-5630	205
Anson Elem Sch/*Anson*/Jones	01035204	325/823-3361	249
Anson High Sch/*Anson*/Jones	01035216	325/823-2404	249
ANSON IND SCH DIST/*Anson*/**JONES**	01035199	325/823-3671	249
Anson Jones Elem Sch/*Dallas*/Dallas	01009217	972/794-4700	99
Anson Jones Middle Sch/*San Antonio*/Bexar	00998031	210/397-2100	36
Anson Middle Sch/*Anson*/Jones	01834153	325/823-2771	249
Anthon Elem Sch/*Uvalde*/Uvalde	01057800	830/591-2988	378
Anthony Aguirre Junior HS/*Houston*/Harris	11927730	281/860-3300	183
Anthony Elem Sch/*Anthony*/El Paso	00705561	915/886-6510	131
Anthony High Sch/*Anthony*/El Paso	01015371	915/886-6550	131
ANTHONY IND SCH DIST/*Anthony*/ **EL PASO**	01015357	915/886-6500	131
Anthony Middle Sch/*Anthony*/El Paso	04935392	915/886-6530	131
ANTON ISD SCH DIST/**ANTON**/**HOCKLEY**	01031090	806/997-2301	229
Anton Sch/*Anton*/Hockley	01031117	806/997-5211	229
Antonian College Prep High Sch/*San Antonio*/ Bexar	00999736	210/344-9265	44
Antonio Bruni Elem Sch/*Laredo*/Webb	01059200	956/273-3000	386
Antonio Gonzalez Middle Sch/*Laredo*/Webb	05027326	956/473-7000	387
Antonio M Ochoa Elem Sch/*Donna*/Hidalgo	01029566	956/464-1900	215
Antonio Margil Academy/*San Antonio*/Bexar	00998512	210/738-9805	39
Aoy Elem Sch/*El Paso*/El Paso	01015929	915/236-0175	133
Apache Elem Sch/*Fort Stockton*/Pecos	01046851	432/336-4161	315
Apollo Junior High Sch/*Richardson*/Dallas	01826168	469/593-7900	112
Apple Springs Elem Sch/*Apple Springs*/ Trinity	01057056	936/831-2241	374
Apple Springs High Sch/*Apple Springs*/ Trinity	04033475	936/831-2241	374
APPLE SPRINGS IND SCH DIST/ **APPLE SPRINGS/TRINITY**	01057044	936/831-3344	374
Applegate Adventist Jr Academy/*Round Rock*/ Williamson	11816870	512/388-7870	400
Applied Learning Academy/*Fort Worth*/ Tarrant	04035837	817/815-5500	350
AQUILLA IND SCH DIST/*Aquilla*/ **HILL**	01030735	254/694-3770	227
Aquilla Sch/*Aquilla*/Hill	01030747	254/694-3770	227
Arabic Immersion Magnet Sch/*Houston*/Harris	12105026	713/556-8940	191
ARANSAS CO IND SCH DIST/ **ROCKPORT/ARANSAS**	00995120	361/790-2212	19
Aransas Pass High Sch/*Aransas Pass*/ San Patricio	01049504	361/758-3248	330
ARANSAS PASS IND SCH DIST/ **ARANSAS PASS/SAN PATRICIO**	01049487	361/758-3466	330
Arapaho Classical Magnet Sch/*Richardson*/ Dallas	01011636	469/593-6400	112
Arbor Creek Middle Sch/*Carrollton*/Denton	04288747	469/713-5971	122
Arcadia Park Elem Sch/*Dallas*/Dallas	01008445	972/502-5300	99
Arch H McCulloch Interm Sch/*Dallas*/Dallas	01011040	214/780-3500	108
ARCHDIOCESE GALVESTON-HOUSTON/ **HOUSTON/HARRIS**	01027855	713/741-8704	203

DISTRICT & SCHOOL TELEPHONE INDEX

Market Data Retrieval

School/City/County DISTRICT/CITY/COUNTY	PID	TELEPHONE NUMBER	PAGE
ARCHDIOCESE SAN ANTONIO ED OFF/			
SAN ANTONIO/BEXAR	00999724	210/734-2620	44
Archer City Elem Sch/*Archer City*/Archer	00995209	940/574-4506	19
Archer City High Sch/*Archer City*/Archer	04915782	940/574-4713	19
ARCHER CITY IND SCH DIST/			
ARCHER CITY/ARCHER	00995182	940/574-4536	19
Archway Academy/*Houston*/Harris	10019031	713/328-0780	205
Arden Road Elem Sch/*Amarillo*/Randall	03008075	806/677-2360	321
Argyle High Sch/*Argyle*/Denton	04879102	940/262-7777	120
ARGYLE IND SCH DIST/ARGYLE/			
DENTON	01013177	940/464-7241	120
Argyle Intermediate Sch/*Argyle*/Denton	11746196	940/464-5100	120
Argyle Middle Sch/*Argyle*/Denton	05026736	940/246-2126	120
Argyle West Elem Sch/*Argyle*/Denton	12364557	940/464-7241	120
Aristoi Classical Academy/*Katy*/Harris	04459489	281/391-5003	1
Arizona Fleming Elem Sch/*Houston*/Fort Bend	04287937	281/634-4600	149
Arlington Classics Acad-Bowen/*Arlington*/Tarrant	11737145	817/303-1553	1
Arlington Classics Academy/*Arlington*/Tarrant	04890871	817/274-2008	1
Arlington College & Career HS/*Arlington*/Tarrant	12365630	682/867-9600	343
Arlington Collegiate High Sch/*Arlington*/Tarrant	12034893	817/515-3550	343
Arlington Heights Chrn Sch/*Corp Christi*/Nueces	02770378	361/241-0090	306
Arlington Heights High Sch/*Fort Worth*/Tarrant	01052551	817/815-1000	350
Arlington High Sch/*Arlington*/Tarrant	01051648	682/867-8100	343
ARLINGTON IND SCH DIST/ARLINGTON/			
TARRANT	01051624	682/867-4611	343
Arlington Park ECC/*Dallas*/Dallas	12318596	972/749-5500	99
Arlon Seay Elem Sch/*Spring Branch*/Comal	04478863	830/885-8700	87
Armand Bayou Elem Sch/*Houston*/Galveston	01523689	281/284-5100	158
Armando Cerna Elem Sch/*Eagle Pass*/Maverick	01041148	830/758-7004	276
Armando Leal Jr Middle Sch/*San Antonio*/Bexar	00997532	210/989-2400	32
Armendariz Middle Sch/*El Paso*/El Paso	04806650	915/236-4800	134
Armstrong Elem Sch/*Conroe*/Montgomery	01042491	936/709-3400	291
Armstrong Elem Sch/*Missouri City*/Fort Bend	11079591	281/634-9410	149
Armstrong Middle Sch/*Plano*/Collin	01525900	469/752-4600	82
Arnold Elem Sch/*San Antonio*/Bexar	00998419	210/438-6530	39
Arnold Middle Sch/*Cypress*/Harris	01023201	281/897-4700	184
Arnoldo Cantu Elem Sch/*San Juan*/Hidalgo	04032794	956/354-2850	223
Arp Elem Sch/*Arp*/Smith	01050553	903/859-4650	336
Arp High Sch/*Arp*/Smith	01050565	903/859-4917	336
ARP IND SCH DIST/ARP/SMITH	01050541	903/859-8482	336
Arp Junior High Sch/*Arp*/Smith	03047370	903/859-4936	336
Arredondo Elem Sch/*Richmond*/Fort Bend	12107816	832/223-4800	153
Arrow-Champions Academy/*Houston*/Harris	12039099	832/446-6762	1
Arrow-Harvest Preparatory Acad/*Houston*/Harris	11729459	281/872-5201	1
Arrow-Las Americas Lrng Ctr/*Houston*/Harris	11848615	832/582-7327	1
Arrow-Liberation Academy/*Missouri City*/Fort Bend	11729485	281/969-7766	1
Arrow-Save Our Streets Ctr/*Bryan*/Brazos	12113956	979/703-1810	1
Art & Pat Goforth Elem Sch/*League City*/Galveston	05009570	281/284-6000	158
Artemisia Bowden Academy/*San Antonio*/Bexar	00998744	210/738-9770	39
Arthur Kramer Elem Sch/*Dallas*/Dallas	03247764	972/794-8300	99
Arthur L Davila Middle Sch/*Bryan*/Brazos	11079292	979/209-7150	55
Arthur McNeil Elem Sch/*McKinney*/Collin	04948492	469/302-5200	81
Arturo Salazar Elem Sch/*Dallas*/Dallas	10023109	972/502-1800	99
Asa Low Jr Intermediate Sch/*Mansfield*/Tarrant	11452187	817/299-3640	356
Ascarate Elem Sch/*El Paso*/El Paso	01016301	915/434-7400	137
Ascension Academy/*Amarillo*/Randall	11236749	806/342-0515	321
Ascension Episcopal Sch/*Houston*/Harris	01410850	713/783-0260	205
Ascher Silberstein Elem Sch/*Dallas*/Dallas	01008471	972/794-1900	99
Ash High Sch/*Plainview*/Hale	04019467	806/293-6010	175
Ashbel Smith Elem Sch/*Baytown*/Harris	01023586	281/420-4615	187
Ashford Elem Sch/*Houston*/Harris	01418424	281/368-2120	193
Ashleys Private Sch/*Cedar Hill*/Dallas	12105052	972/291-1313	114
Ashworth Elem Sch/*Arlington*/Tarrant	04456774	682/867-4800	343
Aspermont Elem Sch/*Aspermont*/Stonewall	01051428	940/989-3323	342
Aspermont High Sch/*Aspermont*/Stonewall	01051430	940/989-2707	342
ASPERMONT IND SCH DIST/ASPERMONT/			
STONEWALL	01051416	940/989-3355	342
Assets Academy/*Alvin*/Brazoria	04282494	281/331-1690	51
Assumption Catholic Sch/*Houston*/Harris	01028017	281/447-2132	203
Atascocita High Sch/*Humble*/Harris	10028628	281/641-7500	195
Atascocita Middle Sch/*Humble*/Harris	02202371	281/641-4600	195

School/City/County DISTRICT/CITY/COUNTY	PID	TELEPHONE NUMBER	PAGE
Atascocita Springs Elem Sch/*Humble*/Harris	11552672	281/641-3600	195
Atems High Sch/*Abilene*/Taylor	11452955	325/794-4140	360
Athens Christian Academy/*Athens*/Henderson	11231763	903/675-5135	215
Athens High Sch/*Athens*/Henderson	01029255	903/677-6920	213
ATHENS IND SCH DIST/ATHENS/			
HENDERSON	01029231	903/677-6900	213
Athens Middle Sch/*Athens*/Henderson	01029243	903/677-3030	213
Atherton Elem Sch/*Arlington*/Tarrant	01548471	682/867-4900	343
Atherton Elem Sch/*Houston*/Harris	01025405	713/671-4100	190
Atkins Middle Sch/*Lubbock*/Lubbock	01038529	806/219-3000	270
Atkinson Elem Sch/*Houston*/Harris	01026643	713/740-0520	198
Atlanta Elem Sch/*Atlanta*/Cass	01004683	903/796-7164	69
Atlanta High Sch/*Atlanta*/Cass	01004695	903/796-4411	69
ATLANTA IND SCH DIST/ATLANTA/			
CASS	01004671	903/796-4194	69
Atlanta Middle Sch/*Atlanta*/Cass	01004700	903/796-7928	69
Atlanta Primary Sch/*Atlanta*/Cass	01004712	903/796-8115	69
Atonement Academy/*San Antonio*/Bexar	04308543	210/695-2240	44
Attucks Middle Sch/*Houston*/Harris	01025156	713/732-3670	188
Atwood McDonald Elem Sch/*Fort Worth*/Tarrant	01053086	817/815-4800	350
Aubrey High Sch/*Aubrey*/Denton	01013218	940/668-3900	120
AUBREY IND SCH DIST/AUBREY/			
DENTON	01013191	940/668-0060	120
Aubrey Middle Sch/*Aubrey*/Denton	04747389	940/668-0200	120
Audelia Creek Elem Sch/*Dallas*/Dallas	05272650	469/593-2900	112
Audie Murphy Middle Sch/*Alamo*/Hidalgo	11552854	956/354-2530	223
Audie Murphy Middle Sch/*Fort Hood*/Bell	05347827	254/336-6530	27
Aue Elem Sch/*San Antonio*/Bexar	10913217	210/397-6750	36
Augusto Guerra Elem Sch/*Alamo*/Hidalgo	05098789	956/354-2810	223
Ault Elem Sch/*Cypress*/Harris	04285331	281/373-2800	184
Austin Academic Center/*Sulphur Spgs*/Hopkins	10020937	903/885-4942	232
Austin Academy for Excellence/*Garland*/Dallas	01010735	972/926-2620	105
Austin Achieve Public Sch/*Austin*/Travis	11816935	512/522-4190	1
Austin Classical Academy/*Austin*/Travis	11925146	512/371-8933	1
Austin Discovery Academy/*Austin*/Travis	11009297	512/674-0700	1
Austin Eco Bilingual Sch-South/*Austin*/Travis	12107232	512/299-5731	372
Austin Elem Sch/*Abilene*/Taylor	01172840	325/690-3920	360
Austin Elem Sch/*Conroe*/Montgomery	01042532	936/709-8400	291
Austin Elem Sch/*Edinburg*/Hidalgo	01029786	956/289-2331	216
Austin Elem Sch/*Harlingen*/Cameron	01003768	956/427-3060	64
Austin Elem Sch/*Memphis*/Hall	01022099	806/259-5930	176
Austin Elem Sch/*Pampa*/Gray	01020144	806/669-4760	165
Austin Elem Sch/*Pecos*/Reeves	01048407	432/447-7541	323
Austin Elem Sch/*Richmond*/Fort Bend	03323552	832/223-1000	153
Austin Elem Sch/*San Angelo*/Tom Green	01055797	325/659-3636	364
Austin Elem Sch/*Tyler*/Smith	01050967	903/262-1765	338
Austin Elem Sch/*Weatherford*/Parker	03051917	817/598-2848	314
Austin Elem Science Acad/*Grand Prairie*/Dallas	01011002	972/343-4600	107
Austin High Sch/*Austin*/Travis	01056650	512/414-2505	368
Austin High Sch/*El Paso*/El Paso	01015515	915/236-4200	134
Austin High Sch/*Houston*/Harris	01024712	713/924-1600	189
AUSTIN IND SCH DIST/AUSTIN/			
TRAVIS	01055993	512/414-1700	366
Austin International Sch/*Austin*/Travis	04944094	512/331-7806	373
AUSTIN ISD ELEM SCH AREA 1/			
AUSTIN/TRAVIS	04032316	512/414-1708	366
AUSTIN ISD ELEM SCH AREA 2/			
AUSTIN/TRAVIS	04032304	512/414-0038	367
AUSTIN ISD HIGH SCH AREA/			
AUSTIN/TRAVIS	04032328	512/414-4471	368
AUSTIN ISD MIDDLE SCH AREA/			
AUSTIN/TRAVIS	12033332	512/414-4481	369
Austin Jewish Academy/*Austin*/Travis	04879580	512/735-8350	373
Austin Middle Sch/*Galveston*/Galveston	01019236	409/761-3500	160
Austin Middle Sch/*Irving*/Dallas	01532006	972/600-3100	109
Austin Middle Sch/*San Juan*/Hidalgo	01030345	956/354-2570	223
Austin Montessori Elem Sch/*Odessa*/Ector	01014561	432/456-1029	130
Austin Montessori Sch/*Austin*/Travis	02861812	512/892-0253	373
Austin Parkway Elem Sch/*Sugar Land*/Fort Bend	03247049	281/634-4001	149
Austin Peace Academy/*Austin*/Travis	04994001	512/926-1737	373
Austin Waldorf Sch/*Austin*/Hays	02779594	512/288-5942	212
Austwell Tivoli Elem Sch/*Tivoli*/Refugio	01048445	361/286-3222	323
AUSTWELL TIVOLI IND SD/TIVOLI/			
REFUGIO	01048419	361/286-3212	
Austwell Tivoli Jr Sr High Sch/*Tivoli*/Refugio	01048433	361/286-3212	323

TX-V4 800-333-8802 School Year 2019-2020

Texas School Directory

DISTRICT & SCHOOL TELEPHONE INDEX

School/City/County DISTRICT/CITY/COUNTY	PID	TELEPHONE NUMBER	PAGE
Autism Treatment Center/*Dallas*/Dallas	11221304	972/644-2076	114
AVALON IND SCH DIST/*AVALON*/ELLIS	01014937	972/627-3251	140
Avalon Sch/*Avalon*/Ellis	01014949	972/627-3251	140
Avery Elem Sch/*Avery*/Red River	01048093	903/684-3116	322
AVERY IND SCH DIST/*AVERY*/ **RED RIVER**	01048081	903/684-3460	322
Avery Secondary Sch/*Avery*/Red River	01048108	903/684-3431	322
AVINGER IND SCH DIST/*AVINGER*/ **CASS**	01004724	903/562-1355	70
Avinger Sch/*Avinger*/Cass	01004736	903/562-1355	70
Avondale Elem Sch/*Amarillo*/Potter	01047166	806/326-4000	317
Avondale House Sch/*Houston*/Harris	11228156	713/993-9544	205
Aw Brown-Fla Early Childhood/*Dallas*/Dallas	12161721	214/330-8686	1
Awty International Sch/*Houston*/Harris	01875391	713/686-4850	205
Axtell Elem Sch/*Axtell*/McLennan	03321425	254/863-5419	278
Axtell High Sch/*Axtell*/McLennan	01039547	254/863-5301	278
AXTELL IND SCH DIST/*AXTELL*/ **MCLENNAN**	01039535	254/863-5301	278
Azle Christian Sch/*Azle*/Tarrant	12168444	817/444-9964	358
Azle Elem Sch/*Azle*/Tarrant	01051985	817/444-1312	345
Azle High Sch/*Azle*/Tarrant	01051997	817/444-5555	345
Azle Hornet Academy/*Azle*/Tarrant	11848782	817/444-4564	345
AZLE IND SCH DIST/*AZLE*/TARRANT	01051973	817/444-3235	345
Azle Junior High Sch/*Azle*/Tarrant	01052006	817/444-2564	345

B

School/City/County	PID	TELEPHONE	PAGE
B F Adam Elem Sch/*Houston*/Harris	01023196	281/897-4485	184
B F Clark Primary Sch/*Houston*/Harris	03393806	281/891-8600	202
B Garza Middle Sch/*Weslaco*/Hidalgo	04748890	956/969-6774	225
B H Hamblen Elem Sch/*Channelview*/Harris	04457027	281/457-8720	183
B H Macon Elem Sch/*Dallas*/Dallas	01008500	972/794-1500	99
B J Smith Elem Sch/*Mesquite*/Dallas	04807226	972/882-7080	110
B L Garza Middle Sch/*Edinburg*/Hidalgo	04873249	956/289-2480	216
B L Gray Junior High Sch/*Mission*/Hidalgo	01030541	956/580-5333	224
B McDaniel Intemediate Sch/*Denison*/Grayson	01020352	903/462-7200	166
B T Washington High Sch/*Houston*/Harris	01023885	713/696-6600	188
B T Washington Perform Arts HS/*Dallas*/ Dallas	01010163	972/925-1200	99
B T Wilson 6th Grade Sch/*Kerrville*/Kerr	03050509	830/257-2207	256
Back Elem Sch/*Rowlett*/Dallas	02226547	972/475-1884	105
Bagdad Elem Sch/*Leander*/Williamson	04866777	512/570-5900	396
Bailey Elem Sch/*Pasadena*/Harris	01026655	713/740-0528	198
Bailey Inglish Erly Chldhd Ctr/*Bonham*/ Fannin	01017410	903/583-8141	145
Bailey Junior High Sch/*Arlington*/Tarrant	01051650	682/867-0700	344
Bailey Middle Sch/*Austin*/Travis	04034259	512/414-4990	369
Baird Elem Sch/*Baird*/Callahan	01003299	325/854-1400	62
Baird High Sch/*Baird*/Callahan	01003304	325/854-1400	62
BAIRD IND SCH DIST/*BAIRD*/ **CALLAHAN**	01003287	325/854-1400	62
Baird Middle Sch/*Baird*/Callahan	10016704	325/854-1400	62
Baker 6th Grade Campus/*La Porte*/Harris	01026394	281/604-6884	198
Baker Elem Sch/*Canadian*/Hemphill	01029217	806/323-5386	213
Baker Koonce Intermediate Sch/*Carthage*/ Panola	01046227	903/693-8611	311
Baker-Ripley Promise Cmty CS/*Houston*/ Harris	11457515	713/273-3731	1
Bakers Preparatory Sch/*Stafford*/Fort Bend	11236050	281/403-2100	155
Balch Springs Chrn Academy/*Balch Springs*/ Dallas	02152295	972/286-8511	114
Ball Early Childhood Center/*Seguin*/ Guadalupe	01021693	830/401-1281	174
Ball High Sch/*Galveston*/Galveston	01019092	409/766-5700	160
Ballinger Elem Sch/*Ballinger*/Runnels	01048811	325/365-3527	326
Ballinger High Sch/*Ballinger*/Runnels	01048835	325/365-3547	326
BALLINGER IND SCH DIST/*BALLINGER*/ **RUNNELS**	01048809	325/365-3588	326
Ballinger Junior High Sch/*Ballinger*/ Runnels	01048823	325/365-3537	326
BALMORHEA IND SCH DIST/*BALMORHEA*/ **REEVES**	01048251	432/375-2223	323
Balmorhea Sch/*Balmorhea*/Reeves	01048263	432/375-2224	323
Bammel Elem Sch/*Houston*/Harris	01027477	281/891-8150	202
Bammel Middle Sch/*Houston*/Harris	01027489	281/891-7900	202
Bandera High Sch/*Bandera*/Bandera	01558103	830/796-6254	23
BANDERA IND SCH DIST/*BANDERA*/ **BANDERA**	00995778	830/796-3313	23
Bandera Middle Sch/*Bandera*/Bandera	00995792	830/460-3899	23
Bane Elem Sch/*Houston*/Harris	01023213	713/460-6140	184
Banff Sch/*Houston*/Harris	03414436	281/444-9326	205
Bangs High Sch/*Bangs*/Brown	01002415	325/752-6822	58
BANGS IND SCH DIST/*BANGS*/BROWN	01002398	325/752-6612	58

School/City/County DISTRICT/CITY/COUNTY	PID	TELEPHONE NUMBER	PAGE
Bangs Middle Sch/*Bangs*/Brown	02056160	325/752-6088	58
Banquete Elem Sch/*Banquete*/Nueces	01044023	361/387-4329	302
Banquete High Sch/*Banquete*/Nueces	01044035	361/387-8588	302
BANQUETE IND SCH DIST/*BANQUETE*/ **NUECES**	01044011	361/387-2551	302
Banquete Junior High Sch/*Banquete*/Nueces	01044047	361/387-2551	302
Barack Obama Male Ldrshp Acad/*Dallas*/ Dallas	11732755	972/749-2100	99
Barbara Bush Elem Sch/*Houston*/Harris	04016063	281/368-2150	193
Barbara Bush Middle Sch/*Irving*/Dallas	04756299	972/968-3700	96
Barbara Bush Primary Sch/*Sulphur Spgs*/ Hopkins	04746000	903/439-6170	232
Barbara C Jordan Interm Sch/*Cibolo*/ Guadalupe	04808804	210/619-4250	173
Barbara Cardwell Career Prep/*Irving*/Dallas	03053252	972/600-6140	109
Barbara Cockrell Elem Sch/*Pearland*/ Brazoria	10909266	832/736-6600	53
Barbara Fasken Elem Sch/*Laredo*/Webb	10007399	956/473-4700	387
Barbara Gordon Montessori Sch/*Colleyville*/ Tarrant	01754321	817/354-6670	358
Barbara Jordan Career Center/*Houston*/ Harris	01023809	713/636-6900	191
Barbara Jordan Elem Sch/*Dallas*/Dallas	01009126	972/925-8100	99
Barbara Jordan Elem Sch/*Odessa*/Ector	03248744	432/456-1299	130
Barbara Jordan Elem Sch/*Richmond*/Fort Bend	05098430	281/634-2800	149
Barbara S Austin Elem Sch/*Coppell*/Dallas	03005956	214/496-7300	98
Barbara Walker Elem Sch/*Heartland*/Kaufman	11540514	972/427-6030	251
Barber Middle Sch/*Dickinson*/Galveston	05345958	281/229-6900	159
Barbers Hill Elem Sch North/*Mont Belvieu*/ Chambers	12109204	281/567-2221	72
Barbers Hill Elem Sch South/*Mont Belvieu*/ Chambers	04939647	281/576-3421	72
Barbers Hill High Sch/*Mont Belvieu*/ Chambers	01005132	281/576-3400	72
BARBERS HILL IND SCH DIST/ **MONT BELVIEU/CHAMBERS**	01005118	281/576-2221	72
Barbers Hill Kindergarten Ctr/*Mont Belvieu*/ Chambers	11080485	281/576-3407	72
Barbers Hill Middle Sch North/*Mont Belvieu*/ Chambers	02055726	281/576-2221	72
Barbers Hill Middle Sch South/*Mont Belvieu*/ Chambers	01005144	281/576-2221	72
Barbers Hill Primary Sch/*Mont Belvieu*/ Chambers	01005120	281/576-2221	72
Barkley-Ruiz Academy/*San Antonio*/Bexar	00999308	210/978-7940	39
Barksdale Elem Sch/*Plano*/Collin	04454893	469/752-0100	82
Barnett Junior High Sch/*Arlington*/Tarrant	04035772	682/867-5000	344
Barrera Veterans Elem Sch/*Von Ormy*/Bexar	05027259	866/465-8808	42
Barrett Elem Sch/*Crosby*/Harris	03321683	281/328-9317	183
Barrett-Lee Early Chldhd Ctr/*Channelview*/ Harris	11563047	281/860-3827	183
Barrick Elem Sch/*Houston*/Harris	01025778	281/405-2500	190
Barrington Elem Sch/*Austin*/Travis	01056052	512/414-2008	367
Barrington Place Elem Sch/*Sugar Land*/ Fort Bend	03328590	281/634-4040	149
Barron Elem Sch/*El Paso*/El Paso	05101831	915/236-5075	133
Barron Elem Sch/*Pflugerville*/Travis	11818531	512/594-4300	371
Barron Elem Sch/*Plano*/Collin	01006370	469/752-0200	82
Barrow Elem Sch/*Brazoria*/Brazoria	01001722	979/991-1740	52
Bartlett Elem Sch/*Bartlett*/Bell	00996291	254/527-3353	26
Bartlett High Sch/*Bartlett*/Bell	00996306	254/527-3351	26
BARTLETT IND SCH DIST/*BARTLETT*/ **BELL**	00996289	254/527-4247	26
Bartlett Middle Sch/*Bartlett*/Bell	12037297	254/527-4247	26
Barton Creek Elem Sch/*Austin*/Travis	03397096	512/732-9180	370
Barton Elem Sch/*Irving*/Dallas	01011222	972/600-4100	109
Barton Hills Elem Sch/*Austin*/Travis	01056064	512/414-2013	366
Barton Middle Sch/*Buda*/Hays	04037524	512/268-1472	211
Barwise Middle Sch/*Wichita Falls*/Wichita	01172955	940/235-1108	392
Basis San Antonio Prim-Med Ctr/*San Antonio*/ Bexar	11931717	210/319-5525	1
Basis San Antonio Primary N/*San Antonio*/ Bexar	12101123	210/775-4125	1
Basis San Antonio Shavano/*San Antonio*/ Bexar	12239756	210/874-9250	1
Baskin Elem Sch/*San Antonio*/Bexar	00998562	210/438-6535	39
Bassett Middle Sch/*El Paso*/El Paso	01015527	915/236-6350	134
Bassetti Elem Sch/*Abilene*/Taylor	04015318	325/690-3720	360
Basswood Elem Sch/*Fort Worth*/Tarrant	11448540	817/744-6500	354
Bastian Elem Sch/*Houston*/Harris	01024724	713/732-5830	192
Bastrop High Sch/*Bastrop*/Bastrop	00995857	512/772-7200	23

School Year 2019-2020   800-333-8802   TX-V5

DISTRICT & SCHOOL TELEPHONE INDEX

Market Data Retrieval

School/City/County DISTRICT/CITY/COUNTY	PID	TELEPHONE NUMBER	PAGE
BASTROP IND SCH DIST/*BASTROP*/			
BASTROP	00995833	512/321-2292	23
Bastrop Intermediate Sch/*Bastrop*/Bastrop	04278651	512/772-7450	23
Bastrop Middle Sch/*Bastrop*/Bastrop	02855681	512/772-7400	23
Batesville Elem Sch/*Batesville*/Uvalde	01057812	830/376-4221	378
Baty Elem Sch/*Austin*/Travis	02848834	512/386-3450	369
Baxter Elem Sch/*Midlothian*/Ellis	03050896	469/856-6100	141
Baxter Junior High Sch/*Fort Worth*/Tarrant	01052484	817/568-3530	349
Bay Area Christian Sch/*League City*/Galveston	01410719	281/332-4814	162
Bay Area Montessori House/*Houston*/Harris	04993291	281/480-7022	205
Bay City High Sch/*Bay City*/Matagorda	01040821	979/401-1100	275
BAY CITY IND SCH DIST/*BAY CITY*/			
MATAGORDA	01040819	979/401-1000	275
Bay City Junior High Sch/*Bay City*/Matagorda	01040833	979/401-1600	275
Bay Colony Elem Sch/*Dickinson*/Galveston	01018995	281/229-6200	159
Bayles Elem Sch/*Dallas*/Dallas	01008512	972/749-8900	99
Bayless Elem Sch/*Lubbock*/Lubbock	01038543	806/219-5000	270
Baylor Clg Biotech Acad-Rusk/*Houston*/Harris	01024580	713/226-4543	192
Baylor Clg of Medicine Acad/*Houston*/Harris	11920330	713/942-1932	192
Bayshore Elem Sch/*La Porte*/Harris	01026409	281/604-4600	198
Bayside Intermediate Sch/*League City*/Galveston	11554826	281/284-3000	158
Baytown Christian Academy/*Baytown*/Harris	02123749	281/421-4150	205
Baytown Junior High Sch/*Baytown*/Harris	01023598	281/420-4560	187
Bea Salazar Sch/*Carrollton*/Dallas	04449147	972/968-5900	96
Beacon Hill Academy/*San Antonio*/Bexar	00998392	210/738-9765	39
Beall Elem Sch/*El Paso*/El Paso	01015539	915/236-8075	133
Bean Elem Sch/*Lubbock*/Lubbock	01038660	806/219-5100	270
Bear Boulevard Pre-School/*Houston*/Harris	04949874	713/251-7900	200
Bear Branch Elem Sch/*Kingwood*/Harris	01809354	281/641-1600	195
Bear Branch Elem Sch/*Magnolia*/Montgomery	02202450	281/356-4771	292
Bear Branch Intermediate Sch/*Magnolia*/Montgomery	05097656	281/252-2031	292
Bear Branch Junior High Sch/*Magnolia*/Montgomery	04450524	281/356-6088	293
Bear Creek Elem Sch/*Euless*/Tarrant	03047411	817/305-4860	353
Bear Creek Elem Sch/*Houston*/Harris	01832090	281/237-5600	151
Bear Creek Intermediate Sch/*Keller*/Tarrant	01054028	817/744-3650	354
Beasley Elem Sch/*Beasley*/Fort Bend	01018256	832/223-1100	153
Beatrice Mayes Institute CS/*Houston*/Harris	05010880	713/747-5629	1
Beaty Early Childhood Sch/*Plano*/Collin	05096834	469/752-4200	82
Beaumont Classical Academy/*Beaumont*/Jefferson	11713113	409/434-4549	1
Beaumont Early Clg High Sch/*Beaumont*/Jefferson	12305551	409/617-6600	242
BEAUMONT IND SCH DIST/*BEAUMONT*/			
JEFFERSON	01034092	409/617-5000	241
Beaumont United High Sch/*Beaumont*/Jefferson	01033402	409/617-5400	242
Beaver Tech Ctr-Math & Science/*Garland*/Dallas	01010515	972/494-8301	105
Bebensee Elem Sch/*Arlington*/Tarrant	03051266	682/867-5100	344
Beckendorff Junior High Sch/*Katy*/Harris	05337042	281/237-8800	151
Becker Elem Sch/*Austin*/Travis	01056076	512/414-2019	366
Beckham Elem Sch/*Arlington*/Tarrant	04949317	682/867-6600	344
BECKVILLE IND SCH DIST/*BECKVILLE*/			
PANOLA	01046186	903/678-3311	311
Beckville Jr Sr High Sch/*Beckville*/Panola	01046203	903/678-3851	311
Beckville Sunset Elem Sch/*Beckville*/Panola	01046198	903/678-3601	311
Bedford Heights Elem Sch/*Bedford*/Tarrant	01391644	817/788-3150	353
Bedford Junior High Sch/*Bedford*/Tarrant	01053749	817/788-3101	353
Bedichek Middle Sch/*Austin*/Travis	01056088	512/414-3265	369
Bee Cave Elem Sch/*Austin*/Travis	04868414	512/533-6250	370
Bee Cave Middle Sch/*Austin*/Travis	12366490	737/931-2400	370
BEEVILLE IND SCH DIST/*BEEVILLE*/			
BEE	00996069	361/358-7111	25
Behavior Transition Center/*Granbury*/Hood	04749399	817/408-4400	230
Bel Air Elem Sch/*Athens*/Henderson	01029267	903/677-6980	213
Bel Air High Sch/*El Paso*/El Paso	01016313	915/434-2000	137
Bel Air Middle Sch/*El Paso*/El Paso	01016442	915/434-2200	137
Belaire Elem Sch/*San Angelo*/Tom Green	01055553	325/659-3639	364
Bell County Alternative Sch/*LTL RVR Acad*/Bell	04800462	254/982-3505	26
Bell Elem Sch/*Houston*/Harris	01826285	281/983-2800	193
Bell Elem Sch/*Tyler*/Smith	01050761	903/262-1820	338
Bell Manor Elem Sch/*Bedford*/Tarrant	01053763	817/354-3370	354
Bell's Hill Elem Sch/*Waco*/McLennan	01040156	254/754-4171	282
Bella Cameron Elem Sch/*San Antonio*/Bexar	00998732	210/978-7960	40
Bellaire Elem Sch/*Hurst*/Tarrant	01053751	817/285-3230	354
Bellaire Elem Sch/*Killeen*/Bell	00996447	254/336-1410	27
Bellaire Elem Sch/*San Antonio*/Bexar	01545209	210/989-2850	32
Bellaire High Sch/*Bellaire*/Harris	01024736	713/295-3704	193
BELLEVUE IND SCH DIST/*BELLEVUE*/			
CLAY	01005481	940/928-2104	74
Bellevue Sch/*Bellevue*/Clay	01005493	940/928-2104	74
Bellfort Acad Early Chldhd Ctr/*Houston*/Harris	11456195	713/640-0950	192
Bells Elem Sch/*Bells*/Grayson	01020247	903/965-3601	165
Bells High Sch/*Bells*/Grayson	03006780	903/965-3603	165
BELLS IND SCH DIST/*BELLS*/**GRAYSON**	01020235	903/965-7721	165
Bellville High Sch/*Bellville*/Austin	00995546	979/865-3681	22
BELLVILLE IND SCH DIST/*BELLVILLE*/			
AUSTIN	00995534	979/865-3133	21
Bellville Junior High Sch/*Bellville*/Austin	02224317	979/865-5966	22
Belmar Elem Sch/*Amarillo*/Potter	01047178	806/326-4050	317
Beltline Elem Sch/*Lancaster*/Dallas	02225373	972/218-1608	110
Belton Early Childhood Sch/*Belton*/Bell	12032429	254/215-3700	26
Belton High Sch/*Belton*/Bell	00996320	254/215-2200	26
BELTON IND SCH DIST/*BELTON*/**BELL**	00996318	254/215-2000	26
Ben Barber Innovation Academy/*Mansfield*/Tarrant	05347413	682/314-1600	356
Ben Bolt-Palito Blanco ES/*Ben Bolt*/Jim Wells	02110869	361/664-9568	245
Ben Bolt-Palito Blanco HS/*Ben Bolt*/Jim Wells	01034640	361/664-9822	245
BEN BOLT-PALITO BLANCO ISD/			
BEN BOLT/**JIM WELLS**	01034638	361/664-9904	245
Ben L Brite Elem Sch/*Brownsville*/Cameron	10754889	956/698-3000	63
Ben Milam Elem Sch/*Cameron*/Milam	01041772	254/697-3641	287
Ben Milam Elem Sch/*Dallas*/Dallas	02109810	972/749-5600	99
Ben Milam Elem Sch/*Harlingen*/Cameron	01003770	956/427-3150	64
Ben Milam Elem Sch/*McAllen*/Hidalgo	01029920	956/971-4333	221
Ben Tisinger Elem Sch/*Mesquite*/Dallas	01011416	972/882-5120	110
Benavides Elem Sch/*Benavides*/Duval	01014195	361/256-3030	128
Benavides Elem Sch/*Brownsville*/Cameron	04873445	956/350-3250	63
Benavides Heights Elem Sch/*Eagle Pass*/Maverick	01041069	830/758-7006	276
BENAVIDES IND SCH DIST/*BENAVIDES*/			
DUVAL	01014171	361/256-3000	128
Benavides Secondary Sch/*Benavides*/Duval	01014183	361/256-3040	128
Benavidez Elem Sch/*Houston*/Harris	04016099	713/778-3350	193
Benbrook Elem Sch/*Fort Worth*/Tarrant	01052587	817/815-6400	350
Benbrook Elem Sch/*Houston*/Harris	01023897	713/613-2502	191
Benbrook Middle High Sch/*Fort Worth*/Tarrant	11711878	817/815-7100	350
Bending Oaks High Sch/*Dallas*/Dallas	03122580	972/669-0000	114
Bendwood Sch/*Houston*/Harris	01027099	713/251-5200	200
Beneke Elem Sch/*Houston*/Harris	02892158	281/891-8450	202
Benfer Elem Sch/*Klein*/Harris	01539171	832/484-6000	196
Benignus Elem Sch/*Klein*/Harris	10028094	832/484-7750	196
Benito Juarez Middle Sch/*Crystal City*/Zavala	01062324	830/374-8105	407
Benito Martinez Elem Sch/*El Paso*/El Paso	03399343	915/937-8001	136
Benito Martinez Elem Sch/*Fort Hancock*/Hudspeth	01032185	915/769-1602	234
Benjamin Franklin Middle Sch/*Dallas*/Dallas	02896324	972/502-7100	99
BENJAMIN IND SCH DIST/*BENJAMIN*/**KNOX**	01036442	940/459-2231	258
Benjamin Sch/*Benjamin*/Knox	01036454	940/459-2231	258
Bennett & Alma Griffin Mid Sch/*Frisco*/Collin	05343431	469/633-4900	78
Bennett Elem Sch/*McKinney*/Collin	05243324	469/302-5400	81
Bennett Elem Sch/*Wolfforth*/Lubbock	01038438	806/866-4443	269
Bennie Cole Elem Sch/*San Antonio*/Bexar	12170124	210/398-2100	36
Bens Branch Elem Sch/*Porter*/Montgomery	05356127	281/577-8700	293
Bentley Elem Sch/*Richmond*/Fort Bend	12169474	832/223-4900	153
Benton A Staley Middle Sch/*Frisco*/Collin	01006215	469/633-4500	78
Berean Christian Academy/*Irving*/Dallas	01479868	972/438-1440	114
Berkner High Sch/*Richardson*/Dallas	01011648	469/593-7000	112
Berkner STEM Academy/*Richardson*/Dallas	12033746	469/593-7021	112
Berlanga Elem Sch/*Corp Christi*/Nueces	11717365	361/878-2160	303
Bernarda Jaime Jr High Sch/*San Diego*/Duval	01014303	361/279-3382	128
Berne Acad Private Sch/*Lancaster*/Dallas	02734958	972/218-7373	114
Bernice Chatman Freeman ES/*Irving*/Dallas	05350018	972/968-1700	96
Bernshausen Elem Sch/*Tomball*/Harris	11926994	832/375-8000	197
Berry Elem Sch/*Arlington*/Tarrant	01051662	682/867-0850	344
Berry Elem Sch/*Houston*/Harris	01025780	713/696-2700	190
Berry Miller Junior High Sch/*Pearland*/Brazoria	11079553	281/997-3900	53
Berta Cabaza Middle Sch/*San Benito*/Cameron	01004279	956/361-6600	67
Berta Palacios Elem Sch/*Pharr*/Hidalgo	01030369	956/354-2690	223

Texas School Directory
DISTRICT & SCHOOL TELEPHONE INDEX

School/City/County DISTRICT/CITY/COUNTY	PID	TELEPHONE NUMBER	PAGE
Bertram Elem Sch/*Bertram*/Burnet	01002764	512/355-2111	60
Bess Brannen Elem Sch/*Lake Jackson*/Brazoria	01001564	979/730-7170	52
Bess Race Elem Sch/*Crowley*/Tarrant	01052367	817/297-5080	347
Besse Coleman Middle Sch/*Cedar Hill*/Dallas	10006369	972/293-4505	97
Bessie Gunstream Elem Sch/*Frisco*/Collin	05092618	469/633-3100	78
Bessie Haynes Elem Sch/*Pecos*/Reeves	01048328	432/447-7497	323
Best Elem Sch/*Houston*/Harris	03397797	713/988-6445	182
Besteiro Middle Sch/*Brownsville*/Cameron	04034302	956/544-3900	63
Beta Academy/*Houston*/Harris	12105038	832/331-2460	1
Beth Yeshurun Elem Sch/*Houston*/Harris	01480324	713/666-1884	205
Bethany Christian Sch/*Plano*/Collin	02733710	972/596-5811	85
Bethany Elem Sch/*Plano*/Collin	04032988	469/752-0300	82
Bethel SDA Sch/*Texarkana*/Bowie	02850409	903/838-4215	50
Bethesda Christian Sch/*Fort Worth*/Tarrant	03141861	817/281-6446	358
Bette Perot Elem Sch/*Keller*/Tarrant	05350757	817/744-4600	354
Betty Harwell Middle Sch/*Edinburg*/Hidalgo	01029712	956/289-2440	216
Bettye Haun Elem Sch/*Plano*/Collin	04751122	469/752-1600	82
Bettye Myers Middle Sch/*Shady Shores*/Denton	11919472	940/369-1500	121
Beulah E Johnson Elem Sch/*Houston*/Harris	01022867	281/985-6510	179
Beverly Cheatham Elem Sch/*Allen*/Collin	11552270	972/396-3016	76
Beverly Hills Intermediate Sch/*Houston*/Harris	01026667	713/740-0420	198
Bexar Co Learning Center/*San Antonio*/Bexar	04915627	210/335-1745	31
Bexar County Academy/*San Antonio*/Bexar	04890857	210/432-8600	1
Bible Baptist Christian Sch/*Wichita Falls*/Wichita	02153964	940/723-2446	393
Bible Way Christian Academy/*Del Rio*/Val Verde	04994087	830/775-9921	379
Big Bend High Sch/*Terlingua*/Brewster	10915655	432/371-2281	57
Big Country Elem Sch/*San Antonio*/Bexar	03011632	210/645-7560	43
Big Sandy Elem Sch/*Big Sandy*/Upshur	01057381	903/636-5287	376
Big Sandy High Sch/*Big Sandy*/Upshur	04033487	903/636-5287	376
BIG SANDY IND SCH DIST/**BIG SANDY**/**UPSHUR**	01057379	903/636-5287	376
BIG SANDY IND SCH DIST/**LIVINGSTON**/**POLK**	01046954	936/563-1000	316
Big Sandy Junior High Sch/*Big Sandy*/Upshur	04801272	903/636-5287	376
Big Sandy Sch/*Dallardsville*/Polk	01046966	936/563-1000	316
Big Spring High Sch/*Big Spring*/Howard	01031909	432/264-3641	233
BIG SPRING IND SCH DIST/**BIG SPRING**/**HOWARD**	01031870	432/264-3600	233
Big Spring Interm Sch/*Big Spring*/Howard	12102658	432/264-4121	233
Big Spring Junior High Sch/*Big Spring*/Howard	01032032	432/264-4135	233
Big Springs Elem Sch/*Garland*/Dallas	01826170	469/593-8100	112
Big Springs-Brune Charter Sch/*Leakey*/Real	05011016	830/232-7101	1
Big Springs-Cailloux CS/*Ingram*/Kerr	11014149	830/367-6100	1
Bill Brown Elem Sch/*Spring Branch*/Comal	03391121	830/885-1400	88
Bill Burden Elem Sch/*Liberty Hill*/Williamson	10905179	512/260-4400	398
Bill Childress Elem Sch/*Vinton*/El Paso	04451918	915/877-7700	132
Bill F Davis Intermediate Sch/*Wylie*/Collin	05350185	972/429-3325	85
Bill Hasse Elem Sch/*Alvin*/Brazoria	01001435	281/585-3397	51
Bill J Elliott Elem Sch/*Fort Worth*/Tarrant	03053020	817/815-4600	350
Bill R Johnson Cte Center/*Crowley*/Tarrant	11561996	817/297-3018	347
Bill Sybert Sch/*El Paso*/El Paso	05153420	915/937-4400	136
Bill W Wright Elem Sch/*Weatherford*/Parker	01878434	817/598-2828	314
Bill Worsham Elem Sch/*Houston*/Harris	01022910	281/985-6520	181
Billie Stevenson Elem Sch/*Rockwall*/Rockwall	11918492	469/698-7474	325
Billy Baines Middle Sch/*Missouri City*/Fort Bend	10027894	281/634-6870	149
Billy Earl Dade Middle Sch/*Dallas*/Dallas	01009152	972/749-3800	99
Billy Reagan K-8 Educ Ctr/*Houston*/Harris	11820558	713/556-9575	192
Billy Ryan High Sch/*Denton*/Denton	01013256	940/369-3000	121
Billy Vandeventer Middle Sch/*Frisco*/Collin	11820065	469/633-4350	79
Bingham Head Start Ctr/*Beaumont*/Jefferson	01034262	409/617-6200	242
Birch Elem Sch/*Longview*/Gregg	01021150	903/295-5120	170
Birdie Alexander Elem Sch/*Dallas*/Dallas	01008419	972/749-3100	99
Birdville Elem Sch of Fine Art/*Haltom City*/Tarrant	01052044	817/547-1500	346
Birdville High Sch/*N RichInd Hls*/Tarrant	04872245	817/547-8000	346
BIRDVILLE IND SCH DIST/**HALTOM CITY**/**TARRANT**	01052032	817/547-5700	346
Birdwell Elem Sch/*Tyler*/Smith	01050773	903/262-1870	338
Birkes Elem Sch/*Houston*/Harris	05272090	281/345-3300	184
Birnham Woods Elem Sch/*Spring*/Montgomery	11449726	832/663-4200	291
Bisd Ctr Tech & Advanced Lrng/*N RichInd Hls*/Tarrant	11559175	817/547-3800	346
BISHOP CONS IND SCH DIST/**BISHOP**/**NUECES**	01044059	361/584-3591	302
Bishop Dunne Catholic Sch/*Dallas*/Dallas	01012379	214/339-6561	113
Bishop Elem Sch/*Bishop*/Nueces	01044085	361/584-3571	302
Bishop Garriga Middle Sch/*Corp Christi*/Nueces	03015975	361/851-0853	306
Bishop High Sch/*Bishop*/Nueces	01044061	361/584-2547	302
Bishop Lynch High Sch/*Dallas*/Dallas	01012381	214/324-3607	113
Bishop Primary Sch/*Bishop*/Nueces	04446987	361/584-2434	302
Bishop T K Gorman Cath Sch/*Tyler*/Smith	01012745	903/561-2424	339
Bivins Elem Sch/*Amarillo*/Potter	01047348	806/326-4100	317
Black Elem Sch/*Cypress*/Harris	10025987	281/320-7145	184
Black Middle Sch/*Houston*/Harris	01023990	713/613-2505	191
Blackburn Elem Sch/*Forney*/Kaufman	05341433	972/564-7008	251
Blackland Prairie Elem Sch/*Round Rock*/Williamson	04945880	512/424-8600	398
Blackshear Elem Sch/*Austin*/Travis	01056090	512/414-2021	367
Blackshear Elem Sch/*Houston*/Harris	01024334	713/942-1481	188
Blackshear Elem Sch/*Tomball*/Harris	11713931	832/375-7600	197
Blackshear Magnet Elem Sch/*Odessa*/Ector	01014573	432/456-1279	130
BLACKWELL CONS IND SCH DIST/**BLACKWELL**/**NOLAN**	01043794	325/282-2311	301
Blackwell Sch/*Blackwell*/Nolan	01809691	325/282-2311	301
Blake Manor Elem Sch/*Manor*/Travis	10915033	512/278-4200	371
Blakemore Middle Sch/*Boys Ranch*/Oldham	04145377	806/534-2361	307
Blanca E Sanchez Elem Sch/*McAllen*/Hidalgo	10910887	956/971-1100	221
Blanche Dodd Elem Sch/*Krum*/Denton	03252692	940/482-2603	122
Blanche K Bruce Elem Sch/*Houston*/Harris	01024360	713/226-4560	188
Blanche Moore Elem Sch/*Corp Christi*/Nueces	01044580	361/878-2660	303
Blanchette Elem Sch/*Beaumont*/Jefferson	01034121	409/617-6300	242
Blanco Elem Sch/*Blanco*/Blanco	01000493	830/833-4338	45
Blanco High Sch/*Blanco*/Blanco	01000508	830/833-4337	46
BLANCO IND SCH DIST/**BLANCO**/**BLANCO**	01000481	830/833-4414	45
Blanco Middle Sch/*Blanco*/Blanco	04012342	830/833-5570	46
Blanco Vista Elem Sch/*San Marcos*/Hays	11079424	512/268-8506	211
Bland Elem Sch/*Celeste*/Hunt	01032240	903/527-5480	235
Bland High Sch/*Farmersville*/Hunt	01032252	903/776-2161	235
BLAND IND SCH DIST/**MERIT**/**HUNT**	01032238	903/776-2239	235
Bland Middle Sch/*Celeste*/Hunt	04746189	903/527-5490	235
BLANKET IND SCH DIST/**BLANKET**/**BROWN**	01002427	325/748-5311	58
Blanket Sch/*Blanket*/Brown	01002441	325/748-3341	58
Blanson Cte High Sch/*Houston*/Harris	12309648	281/591-4950	180
Blanton Elem Sch/*Argyle*/Denton	11128570	940/369-0700	121
Blanton Elem Sch/*Arlington*/Tarrant	01051674	682/867-1000	344
Blanton Elem Sch/*Austin*/Travis	01056105	512/414-2026	367
Blanton Elem Sch/*Odessa*/Ector	02126416	432/456-1259	130
Blaschke-Sheldon Elem Sch/*Ingleside*/San Patricio	01172606	361/776-3050	331
Blazier Elem Sch/*Austin*/Travis	10907256	512/841-8800	366
Blessed Sacrament Catholic Sch/*San Antonio*/Bexar	00999762	210/824-3381	44
Blessed Sacrament Sch/*Laredo*/Webb	01045182	956/722-1222	388
Blessing Elem Sch/*Blessing*/Matagorda	01040974	979/843-4330	276
Bleyl Middle Sch/*Houston*/Harris	01023237	281/897-4340	184
Bliss Elem Sch/*El Paso*/El Paso	01015747	915/236-5150	133
Block House Creek Elem Sch/*Leander*/Williamson	03003130	512/570-7600	397
Blocker Middle Sch/*Texas City*/Galveston	01019482	409/916-0700	161
BLOOMBURG IND SCH DIST/**BLOOMBURG**/**CASS**	01004750	903/728-5216	70
Bloomburg Sch/*Bloomburg*/Cass	01004762	903/728-5216	70
Blooming Grove Elem Sch/*Blooming GRV*/Navarro	03393179	903/695-2541	299
Blooming Grove High Sch/*Blooming GRV*/Navarro	01043407	903/695-2541	299
BLOOMING GROVE IND SCH DIST/**BLOOMING GRV**/**NAVARRO**	01043392	903/695-2541	299
Blooming Grove Junior High Sch/*Blooming GRV*/Navarro	04364690	903/695-2541	299
Bloomington Elem Sch/*Bloomington*/Victoria	01058323	361/333-8003	381
BLOOMINGTON IND SCH DIST/**BLOOMINGTON**/**VICTORIA**	01058311	361/333-8016	381
Bloomington Middle Sch/*Bloomington*/Victoria	04745159	361/333-8008	381
Bloomington Senior High Sch/*Bloomington*/Victoria	01058347	361/333-8011	381
Blossom Elem Sch/*Blossom*/Lamar	01487293	903/982-5230	260
Blossom Valley Academy/*Lewisville*/Denton	04023133	972/436-3613	126
Blue Haze Elem Sch/*Fort Worth*/Tarrant	03049067	817/367-2583	357
Blue Ridge Elem Sch/*Blue Ridge*/Collin	01006069	972/752-5554	77

DISTRICT & SCHOOL TELEPHONE INDEX

Market Data Retrieval

School/City/County DISTRICT/CITY/COUNTY	PID	TELEPHONE NUMBER	PAGE
Blue Ridge Elem Sch/*Houston*/Fort Bend	01018127	281/634-4520	149
Blue Ridge High Sch/*Blue Ridge*/Collin	01006071	972/752-5554	77
BLUE RIDGE IND SCH DIST/			
BLUE RIDGE/COLLIN	01006057	972/752-5554	77
Blue Ridge Middle Sch/*Blue Ridge*/Collin	04009553	972/752-4243	77
Bluebonnet Elem Sch/*Bastrop*/Bastrop	05350159	512/772-7680	23
Bluebonnet Elem Sch/*Flower Mound*/Denton	04920464	469/713-5195	122
Bluebonnet Elem Sch/*Fort Worth*/Tarrant	05090799	817/744-4500	354
Bluebonnet Elem Sch/*Hereford*/Deaf Smith	01013000	806/363-7650	119
Bluebonnet Elem Sch/*Lockhart*/Caldwell	10002662	512/398-0900	61
Bluebonnet Elem Sch/*Round Rock*/Williamson	02893982	512/428-7700	398
Bluebonnet Trail Elem Sch/*Austin*/Travis	01056909	512/278-4125	371
Bluff Dale Elem Sch/*Bluff Dale*/Erath	01017006	254/728-3277	143
BLUFF DALE IND SCH DIST/			
BLUFF DALE/ERATH	01016997	254/728-3277	143
BLUM IND SCH DIST/BLUM/HILL	01030761	254/874-5231	227
Blum Sch/*Blum*/Hill	01030773	254/874-5231	227
Bob & Lola Sandford Elem Sch/*Van Alstyne*/ Grayson	12306804	903/712-1900	168
Bob Beard Elem Sch/*Helotes*/Bexar	05274000	210/397-6600	36
Bob Hope Elem Sch/*Port Arthur*/Jefferson	12260638	409/983-3244	1
Bob Hope Elem Sch/*San Antonio*/Bexar	00999580	210/927-8180	43
Bob Hope Middle High Sch/*Port Arthur*/ Jefferson	11663609	409/983-3244	1
Bob L Kirksey Elem Sch/*Booker*/Lipscomb	01038141	806/658-4559	267
Bob Lewis Elem Sch/*San Antonio*/Bexar	04942022	210/397-2650	36
Bobby Shaw Middle Sch/*Pasadena*/Harris	11129433	713/740-5268	198
Bobbye Behlau Elem Sch/*San Antonio*/Bexar	11552048	210/398-1000	36
Boerne Academy/*Boerne*/Kendall	04432106	830/572-2600	254
Boerne High Sch/*Boerne*/Kendall	01035826	830/357-2200	254
BOERNE IND SCH DIST/BOERNE/			
KENDALL	01035814	830/357-2000	253
Boerne Middle School North/*Boerne*/Kendall	01035840	830/357-3100	254
Boerne Middle School South/*Boerne*/Kendall	04916815	830/357-3300	254
Boles Elem Sch/*Quinlan*/Hunt	01032276	903/883-2161	235
Boles High Sch/*Quinlan*/Hunt	04800632	903/883-2918	235
BOLES IND SCH DIST/QUINLAN/HUNT	01032264	903/883-4464	235
Boles Junior High Sch/*Arlington*/Tarrant	03011694	682/867-8000	344
Boles Middle Sch/*Quinlan*/Hunt	05101192	903/883-4464	235
Boling High Sch/*Boling*/Wharton	01059547	979/657-2816	389
BOLING IND SCH DIST/BOLING/			
WHARTON	01059535	979/657-2770	389
Bonham Academy/*San Antonio*/Bexar	00999059	210/228-3300	40
Bonham Early Ed Sch/*Grand Prairie*/Dallas	01010917	972/262-4255	107
Bonham Elem Sch/*Abilene*/Taylor	01172747	325/690-3745	360
Bonham Elem Sch/*Bryan*/Brazos	01002025	979/209-1200	55
Bonham Elem Sch/*El Paso*/El Paso	01015541	915/236-8150	133
Bonham Elem Sch/*Harlingen*/Cameron	01003782	956/427-3070	64
Bonham Elem Sch/*Midland*/Midland	01041538	432/240-6000	285
Bonham Elem Sch/*San Angelo*/Tom Green	02896843	325/947-3917	364
Bonham High Sch/*Bonham*/Fannin	01017381	903/583-5567	145
BONHAM IND SCH DIST/BONHAM/			
FANNIN	01017367	903/583-5526	145
Bonham Middle Sch/*Odessa*/Ector	01014585	432/456-0429	130
Bonham Middle Sch/*Temple*/Bell	00996722	254/215-6600	29
Bonham Pre-Kindergarten Sch/*San Marcos*/ Hays	12109436	512/393-6031	211
Bonner Elem Sch/*Houston*/Harris	01025417	713/943-5740	189
Bonner Elem Sch/*Tyler*/Smith	01050785	903/262-1920	338
Bonnie Brae Elem Sch/*Fort Worth*/Tarrant	05275872	817/814-3700	350
Bonnie Ellison Elem Sch/*San Antonio*/Bexar	12033631	210/398-1850	36
Bonnie Garcia Elem Sch/*Laredo*/Webb	05350707	956/473-8900	387
Bonnie Gentry Elem Sch/*Mesquite*/Dallas	05273680	972/290-4140	111
Bonnie Holland Elem Sch/*Katy*/Harris	11128609	281/234-0500	151
Bonnie P Hopper Primary Sch/*Highlands*/ Harris	02110651	281/420-4685	187
Booker High Sch/*Booker*/Lipscomb	01038153	806/658-4521	267
BOOKER IND SCH DIST/BOOKER/			
LIPSCOMB	01038139	806/658-4501	267
Booker T Washington Elem Sch/*Elgin*/Bastrop	00995895	512/281-3411	24
Booker T Washington ES/*Wichita Falls*/ Wichita	01173222	940/235-1196	392
Boon Elem Sch/*Allen*/Collin	10006242	972/747-3331	76
Boone Elem Sch/*Austin*/Travis	02890540	512/414-2537	366
Boone Elem Sch/*Houston*/Harris	01023067	281/983-8308	182
BORDEN CO IND SCH DIST/GAIL/			
BORDEN	01000546	806/756-4313	46
Borden County Sch/*Gail*/Borden	01000558	806/756-4313	46
Borger High Sch/*Borger*/Hutchinson	01032654	806/273-1029	237
BORGER IND SCH DIST/BORGER/			
HUTCHINSON	01032642	806/273-6481	237
Borger Intermediate Sch/*Borger*/Hutchinson	10026955	806/273-4342	237

School/City/County DISTRICT/CITY/COUNTY	PID	TELEPHONE NUMBER	PAGE
Borger Middle Sch/*Borger*/Hutchinson	01032680	806/273-1037	237
Borman Elem Sch/*Denton*/Denton	01013232	940/369-2500	121
Borrego Elem Sch/*San Elizario*/El Paso	04939403	915/872-3910	135
Bose Ikard Elem Sch/*Weatherford*/Parker	01046605	817/598-2818	314
Bosque Co Educational Center/*Meridian*/ Bosque	04826533	254/435-6098	47
Bosqueville Elem Sch/*Waco*/McLennan	01039573	254/752-6006	278
BOSQUEVILLE IND SCH DIST/			
WACO/MCLENNAN	01039561	254/757-3113	278
Bosqueville Middle Sch/*Waco*/McLennan	12036188	254/759-7077	278
Bosqueville Secondary Sch/*Waco*/McLennan	11456781	254/752-8513	278
Boude Storey Middle Sch/*Dallas*/Dallas	01008548	972/925-8700	99
Boulevard Baptist Chrstn Sch/*Burleson*/ Johnson	11663582	817/295-4342	249
Boulevard Heights Sch/*Fort Worth*/Tarrant	01052599	817/814-6400	350
Boulter Middle Sch/*Tyler*/Smith	01050797	903/262-1390	338
Bovina Elem Sch/*Bovina*/Parmer	01046667	806/251-1336	314
Bovina High Sch/*Bovina*/Parmer	11565124	806/251-1336	314
BOVINA IND SCH DIST/BOVINA/			
PARMER	01046655	806/251-1336	314
Bovina Middle Sch/*Bovina*/Parmer	11565112	806/251-1336	314
Bowie Elem Sch/*Abilene*/Taylor	01172759	325/671-4770	360
Bowie Elem Sch/*Bowie*/Montague	01042221	940/689-2950	289
Bowie Elem Sch/*Corsicana*/Navarro	01043433	903/872-6541	299
Bowie Elem Sch/*Dallas*/Dallas	01011741	469/593-6000	112
Bowie Elem Sch/*Greenville*/Hunt	01032460	903/457-2676	236
Bowie Elem Sch/*Harlingen*/Cameron	01003794	956/427-3080	65
Bowie Elem Sch/*Rosenberg*/Fort Bend	01018268	832/223-1200	153
Bowie Elem Sch/*San Angelo*/Tom Green	01055670	325/947-3921	364
Bowie Elem Sch/*San Marcos*/Hays	01029152	512/393-6200	212
Bowie Fine Arts Academy/*Grand Prairie*/ Dallas	01010929	972/262-7348	107
Bowie Fine Arts Academy/*Midland*/Midland	01041540	432/240-6100	285
Bowie High Sch/*Bowie*/Montague	01042207	940/689-2840	290
Bowie High Sch/*El Paso*/El Paso	01015931	915/236-7000	134
BOWIE IND SCH DIST/BOWIE/			
MONTAGUE	01042180	940/872-1151	289
Bowie Intermediate Sch/*Bowie*/Montague	01042192	940/689-2895	290
Bowie Junior High Sch/*Bowie*/Montague	01042219	940/689-2975	290
Bowie Middle Sch/*Irving*/Dallas	01011131	972/600-3000	109
Bowie Middle Sch/*Odessa*/Ector	01014597	432/456-0439	130
Bowie Primary Sch/*Sulphur Spgs*/Hopkins	01031648	903/885-3772	232
Bowman Middle Sch/*Plano*/Collin	01006423	469/752-4800	82
Boyd Elem Sch/*Boyd*/Wise	01061564	940/433-9520	402
Boyd High Sch/*Boyd*/Wise	01061576	940/433-9580	402
BOYD IND SCH DIST/BOYD/WISE	01061552	940/433-2327	402
Boyd Intermediate Sch/*Boyd*/Wise	03046924	940/433-9540	402
Boyd Middle Sch/*Boyd*/Wise	02056196	940/433-9560	402
Boyer Elem Sch/*Prosper*/Collin	12307042	469/219-2240	84
Boys Ranch High Sch/*Boys Ranch*/Oldham	01484485	806/534-0032	307
BOYS RANCH IND SCH DIST/			
BOYS RANCH/OLDHAM	01484461	806/534-2221	307
Bozman Intermediate Sch/*Conroe*/Montgomery	11449738	936/709-1800	291
Bracken Christian Sch/*Bulverde*/Comal	02192427	830/438-3211	89
Brackenridge High Sch/*San Antonio*/Bexar	00999140	210/228-1200	40
Brackett High Sch/*Brackettville*/Kinney	01036234	830/563-2480	257
BRACKETT IND SCH DIST/BRACKETTVILLE/			
KINNEY	01036222	830/563-2491	257
Brackett Junior High Sch/*Brackettville*/ Kinney	03410650	830/563-2480	257
Bradfield Elem Sch/*Garland*/Dallas	01010773	972/494-8303	105
Bradford Elem Sch/*Iowa Park*/Wichita	01060077	940/592-5841	392
Bradford Elem Sch/*San Angelo*/Tom Green	01055577	325/659-3645	364
Bradley Elem Sch/*El Paso*/El Paso	02129860	915/236-5225	133
Bradley Elem Sch/*Spring*/Montgomery	12231883	832/482-6800	291
Bradley Middle Sch/*San Antonio*/Bexar	02178328	210/356-2600	34
Brady Alternative Sch/*Brady*/McCulloch	04447383	325/597-2170	277
Brady Elem Sch/*Brady*/McCulloch	01039456	325/597-2590	277
Brady High Sch/*Brady*/McCulloch	01039432	325/597-2491	277
BRADY IND SCH DIST/BRADY/			
MCCULLOCH	01039420	325/597-2301	277
Brady Middle Sch/*Brady*/McCulloch	01039444	325/597-8110	277
Braeburn Elem Sch/*Houston*/Harris	01024748	713/295-5210	193
BRAINATION SCHOOLS/SAN ANTONIO/			
BEXAR	11701354	210/638-5000	30
Bramlette Elem Sch/*Longview*/Gregg	01021007	903/803-5600	169
Branch Sch/*Houston*/Harris	02757144	713/465-0288	205
Brandeis High Sch/*San Antonio*/Bexar	11104146	210/397-8200	36
Brandenburg Elem Sch/*Irving*/Dallas	01011208	972/600-7100	109
Brandenburg Intermediate Sch/*Duncanville*/ Dallas	04011788	972/708-3100	104
Brandon Elem Sch/*Lufkin*/Angelina	02201808	936/632-5513	18

Texas School Directory

DISTRICT & SCHOOL TELEPHONE INDEX

School/City/County DISTRICT/CITY/COUNTY	PID	TELEPHONE NUMBER	PAGE
Bransford Elem Sch/*Colleyville*/Tarrant	04030497	817/305-4920	353
Braswell High Sch/*Aubrey*/Denton	12165375	972/347-7700	121
Braun Station Elem Sch/*San Antonio*/Bexar	02178330	210/397-1550	36
Brawner Intermediate Sch/*Granbury*/Hood	04947747	817/408-4950	230
Bray Elem Sch/*Cedar Hill*/Dallas	01008287	972/291-4231	97
Brazos Bend Elem Sch/*Sugar Land*/Fort Bend	04749777	281/634-5180	150
Brazos Christian Sch/*Bryan*/Brazos	02164690	979/823-1000	56
Brazos Credit Recovery HS/*Waco*/McLennan	05275884	254/754-9422	282
Brazos Elem Sch/*Orchard*/Austin	00995649	979/478-6610	22
Brazos High Sch/*Wallis*/Austin	00995637	979/478-6832	22
BRAZOS IND SCH DIST/**WALLIS/ AUSTIN**	00995625	979/478-6551	22
Brazos Middle Sch/*Wallis*/Austin	00995663	979/478-6814	22
Brazos River Charter Sch/*Nemo*/Somervell	05011030	254/898-9226	2
Brazos Sch Inquiry-Bryan/*Bryan*/Brazos	04890900	979/774-5032	2
Brazos Sch Inquiry-Tidwell/*Houston*/Harris	11136503	713/681-1960	2
Brazosport Christian Sch/*Lake Jackson*/ Brazoria	02164951	979/297-0722	54
Brazosport High Sch/*Freeport*/Brazoria	01001576	979/730-7260	52
BRAZOSPORT IND SCH DIST/ **CLUTE/BRAZORIA**	01001540	979/730-7000	52
Brazoswood High Sch/*Clute*/Brazoria	01001588	979/730-7300	52
Breckenridge High Sch/*Breckenridge*/ Stephens	01051349	254/559-2231	341
BRECKENRIDGE IND SCH DIST/ **BRECKENRIDGE/STEPHENS**	01051325	254/559-2278	341
Breckenridge Jr High Sch/*Breckenridge*/ Stephens	01051337	254/559-6581	341
Breeden Elem Sch/*Brownsville*/Cameron	11819107	956/554-4730	63
Bremond Elem Sch/*Bremond*/Robertson	04033669	254/746-7145	324
Bremond High Sch/*Bremond*/Robertson	01048562	254/746-7061	324
BREMOND IND SCH DIST/**BREMOND/ ROBERTSON**	01048550	254/746-7145	324
Bremond Middle Sch/*Bremond*/Robertson	04033449	254/746-5022	324
Brenham Elem Sch/*Brenham*/Washington	01059066	979/277-3880	385
Brenham High Sch/*Brenham*/Washington	01059078	979/277-3800	385
BRENHAM IND SCH DIST/**BRENHAM/ WASHINGTON**	01059042	979/277-3700	385
Brenham Junior High Sch/*Brenham*/Washington	04755087	979/277-3830	385
Brenham Middle Sch/*Brenham*/Washington	01059080	979/277-3845	385
Brent Elem Sch/*Little Elm*/Denton	04920127	972/947-9451	124
Brentfield Elem Sch/*Dallas*/Dallas	01399658	469/593-5740	112
Brentwood Christian Sch/*Austin*/Travis	01481201	512/835-5983	373
Brentwood Elem Sch/*Austin*/Travis	01056611	512/414-2039	367
Brentwood Middle Sch/*San Antonio*/Bexar	00997099	210/444-7675	31
Brewer Academy/*San Antonio*/Bexar	04874944	210/438-6825	40
Brewer High Sch/*Fort Worth*/Tarrant	01054212	817/367-1200	357
Brewer Middle Sch/*Fort Worth*/Tarrant	01054195	817/367-1267	357
Brewster Sch/*Edinburg*/Hidalgo	01029683	956/289-2334	216
Briargate Elem Sch/*Missouri City*/Fort Bend	01541320	281/634-4560	150
Briargrove Elem Sch/*Houston*/Harris	01024358	713/917-3600	193
Briarhill Middle Sch/*Lewisville*/Denton	04364652	469/713-5975	122
Briarmeadow Charter Sch/*Houston*/Harris	04755544	713/458-5500	193
Briarwood Sch/*Houston*/Harris	01480518	281/493-1070	205
Bridge Academy/*Weatherford*/Parker	11551903	817/598-2847	314
Bridge City Elem Sch/*Bridge City*/Orange	01045649	409/735-0900	308
Bridge City High Sch/*Bridge City*/Orange	01045613	409/735-1600	308
BRIDGE CITY IND SCH DIST/ **BRIDGE CITY/ORANGE**	01045601	409/735-1501	308
Bridge City Intermediate Sch/*Bridge City*/ Orange	04450079	409/792-8800	308
Bridge City Middle Sch/*Bridge City*/Orange	01045625	409/735-1700	308
Bridge Point Elem Sch/*Austin*/Travis	04748010	512/732-9200	370
Bridgeland High Sch/*Cypress*/Harris	12233166	832/349-7600	184
Bridgeport Elem Sch/*Bridgeport*/Wise	01061590	940/683-5955	402
Bridgeport High Sch/*Bridgeport*/Wise	01061605	940/683-4064	402
BRIDGEPORT IND SCH DIST/ **BRIDGEPORT/WISE**	01061588	940/683-5124	402
Bridgeport Intermediate Sch/*Bridgeport*/ Wise	04028169	940/683-5784	402
Bridgeport Middle Sch/*Bridgeport*/Wise	01061617	940/683-2273	403
Bridges Accel Lrng Ctr/*Colleyville*/Tarrant	04750520	817/251-5474	353
Bridges Sch/*El Paso*/El Paso	02233320	915/532-6647	139
Bridlewood Elem Sch/*Flower Mound*/Denton	04812635	469/713-5193	122
Bright Beginnings Academic Ctr/*Brownfield*/ Terry	11710135	806/637-0757	362
Brighter Horizons Academy/*Garland*/Dallas	03556591	972/675-2062	114
Brill Elem Sch/*Klein*/Harris	01832131	832/484-6150	197
Brinker Elem Sch/*Plano*/Collin	03047423	469/752-0500	82
Briscoe Academy/*San Antonio*/Bexar	00999085	210/228-3305	40
Briscoe Elem Sch/*Houston*/Harris	01025429	713/924-1740	189
Briscoe Junior High Sch/*Richmond*/Fort Bend	04946016	832/223-4000	153

School/City/County DISTRICT/CITY/COUNTY	PID	TELEPHONE NUMBER	PAGE
Britain Elem Sch/*Irving*/Dallas	01011246	972/600-3800	109
British Int'l Sch of Houston/*Katy*/Harris	05135806	713/290-9025	205
Broaddus Elem Sch/*Broaddus*/San Augustine	03473638	936/872-3315	329
Broaddus High Sch/*Broaddus*/San Augustine	01049358	936/872-3610	329
BROADDUS IND SCH DIST/**BROADDUS/ SAN AUGUSTINE**	01049334	936/872-3041	329
Brock Elem Sch/*Brock*/Parker	01046356	817/592-6555	312
Brock Elem Sch/*Burleson*/Johnson	11396997	817/245-3800	246
Brock High Sch/*Weatherford*/Parker	04034443	817/596-7425	312
BROCK IND SCH DIST/**BROCK/PARKER**	01046344	817/594-7642	312
Brock Intermediate Sch/*Brock*/Parker	12306957	817/594-8017	312
Brock Junior High Sch/*Brock*/Parker	05342164	817/594-3195	312
Brockett Elem Sch/*Aubrey*/Denton	01013206	940/668-0036	120
Bronte Elem Sch/*Bronte*/Coke	01005766	325/473-2251	75
Bronte High Sch/*Bronte*/Coke	03397163	325/473-2521	75
BRONTE IND SCH DIST/**BRONTE/COKE**	01005754	325/473-2511	75
Brook Ave Elem Sch/*Waco*/McLennan	04869949	254/750-3562	282
Brook Hill Sch/*Bullard*/Smith	04881765	903/894-5000	339
Brook Hills Lower Sch/*Bullard*/Smith	11226263	903/894-4164	339
Brook Village Eec/*Wichita Falls*/Wichita	04875261	940/235-1132	392
Brooke Elem Sch/*Austin*/Travis	01056129	512/414-2043	366
BROOKELAND IND SCH DIST/ **BROOKELAND/JASPER**	01033141	409/698-2677	240
Brookeland Elem Sch/*Brookeland*/Jasper	01033153	409/698-2677	240
Brookesmith Elem Sch/*Brookesmith*/Brown	04247755	325/643-3023	58
Brookesmith High Sch/*Brookesmith*/Brown	01002477	325/643-3023	58
BROOKESMITH IND SCH DIST/ **BROOKESMITH/BROWN**	01002453	325/643-3023	58
Brookhaven Elem Sch/*Killeen*/Bell	04027646	254/336-1440	27
Brookhaven Sch/*West*/McLennan	12109369	254/981-2240	282
Brookhollow Christian Academy/*Houston*/ Harris	11976793	281/649-6813	205
Brookhollow Elem Sch/*Lufkin*/Angelina	00994944	936/639-3100	18
Brookhollow Elem Sch/*Pflugerville*/Travis	04363555	512/594-5200	371
Brookline Elem Sch/*Houston*/Harris	01025431	713/845-7400	192
Brooks Acad-Science Engineerng/*San Antonio*/ Bexar	11014113	210/388-0288	2
BROOKS CO IND SCH DIST/**FALFURRIAS/ BROOKS**	01002336	361/325-5681	57
Brooks Collegiate Academy/*San Antonio*/ Bexar	12235841		2
Brooks Estrella Academy/*San Antonio*/Bexar	12162165	210/257-5175	2
Brooks Int'l Studies Academy/*San Antonio*/ Bexar	12161953	210/998-4452	2
Brooks Lonestar Academy/*San Antonio*/Bexar	12260640	210/998-4452	2
Brooks Oaks Academy/*San Antonio*/Bexar	12260652	210/627-6013	2
Brooks Wester Middle Sch/*Mansfield*/Tarrant	05091638	682/314-1800	356
Brooks-Quinn Jones Elem Sch/*Nacogdoches*/ Nacogdoches	01420532	936/569-5040	298
Brookside Intermediate Sch/*Friendswood*/ Galveston	04365321	281/284-3600	158
Brookwood Elem Sch/*Houston*/Galveston	02043278	281/284-5600	158
Brookwood Forest Elem Sch/*Porter*/ Montgomery	12313974	281/577-8820	293
Brown Elem Sch/*Austin*/Travis	01056686	512/414-2047	367
Brown Elem Sch/*Lubbock*/Lubbock	01038567	806/219-5300	270
Brown Middle Sch/*El Paso*/El Paso	10907127	915/774-4080	134
Brown Middle Sch/*Forney*/Kaufman	01035589	972/564-3967	251
Brown Primary Sch/*Smithville*/Bastrop	00995986	512/237-2519	24
Brownfield High Sch/*Brownfield*/Terry	01055096	806/637-4523	362
BROWNFIELD IND SCH DIST/ **BROWNFIELD/TERRY**	01055084	806/637-2591	362
Brownfield Middle Sch/*Brownfield*/Terry	01055113	806/637-7521	362
Browning Elem Sch/*Houston*/Harris	01023914	713/867-5140	191
Browning Learning Center/*Royse City*/ Rockwall	04940036	972/635-5077	326
Brownsboro Elem Sch/*Brownsboro*/Henderson	01029334	903/852-6461	213
Brownsboro High Sch/*Brownsboro*/Henderson	01029346	903/852-2321	213
BROWNSBORO IND SCH DIST/ **BROWNSBORO/HENDERSON**	01029322	903/852-3701	213
Brownsboro Intermediate Sch/*Brownsboro*/ Henderson	02131710	903/852-7325	213
Brownsboro Junior High Sch/*Brownsboro*/ Henderson	03050080	903/852-6931	213
Brownsville Academic Center/*Brownsville*/ Cameron	04015758	956/504-6305	63
Brownsville Early Clg HS/*Brownsville*/ Cameron	11103831	956/698-1476	63
BROWNSVILLE IND SCH DIST/ **BROWNSVILLE/CAMERON**	01003445	956/548-8000	63
Brownsville Lrng Acad High Sch/*Brownsville*/ Cameron	12315154	956/548-8630	63

School Year 2019-2020   800-333-8802   TX-V9

DISTRICT & SCHOOL TELEPHONE INDEX

Market Data Retrieval

School/City/County DISTRICT/CITY/COUNTY	PID	TELEPHONE NUMBER	PAGE
Brownwood Accelerated High Sch/Brownwood/Brown	04011283	325/646-1652	58
Brownwood High Sch/Brownwood/Brown	01002491	325/646-9549	58
BROWNWOOD IND SCH DIST/BROWNWOOD/BROWN	01002489	325/643-5644	58
Brownwood Middle Sch/Brownwood/Brown	01002506	325/646-9545	58
Bruce Aiken Elem Sch/Brownsville/Cameron	04456748	956/986-5200	63
Bruce Junior High Sch/Gilmer/Upshur	01057446	903/841-7600	376
Bruce Shulkey Elem Sch/Fort Worth/Tarrant	01052628	817/814-8400	350
Bruceville-Eddy Elem Sch/Eddy/McLennan	01039597	254/859-5525	278
Bruceville-Eddy High Sch/Eddy/McLennan	01039602	254/859-5525	278
BRUCEVILLE-EDDY IND SCH DIST/EDDY/MCLENNAN	01039585	254/859-5525	278
Bruceville-Eddy Interm Sch/Eddy/McLennan	04946872	254/859-5525	278
Bruceville-Eddy Jr High Sch/Eddy/McLennan	04448428	254/859-5525	278
Brule Elem Sch/Navasota/Grimes	04145418	936/825-4275	172
Brundreet Middle Sch/Port Aransas/Nueces	02224575	361/749-1209	305
Bruni High Sch/Bruni/Webb	01059169	361/747-5415	388
Bruni Middle Sch/Bruni/Webb	01059157	361/747-5415	388
Brushy Creek Elem Sch/Round Rock/Williamson	02126894	512/428-3000	398
Bryan Adams High Sch/Dallas/Dallas	01008550	972/502-4900	99
Bryan Adult Learning Center/Bryan/Brazos	04810962	979/703-7740	55
Bryan Collegiate High Sch/Bryan/Brazos	10911154	979/209-2790	55
Bryan Elem Sch/Mission/Hidalgo	01030230	956/323-4800	222
BRYAN IND SCH DIST/BRYAN/BRAZOS	01002013	979/209-1000	54
Bryant Elem Sch/Arlington/Tarrant	04035760	682/867-5200	344
Bryker Woods Elem Sch/Austin/Travis	01056131	512/414-2054	367
Bryson Elem Sch/Fort Worth/Tarrant	02846472	817/237-8306	348
BRYSON IND SCH DIST/BRYSON/JACK	01032898	940/392-3281	238
Bryson Sch/Bryson/Jack	01032903	940/392-2601	238
Bssp & Nets/San Antonio/Bexar	00997697	210/356-7520	34
Buckalew Elem Sch/The Woodlands/Montgomery	04806765	281/465-3400	291
BUCKHOLTS IND SCH DIST/BUCKHOLTS/MILAM	01041722	254/593-3011	287
Buckholts Sch/Buckholts/Milam	01041734	254/593-2744	287
Buckner Fanning Christian Sch/San Antonio/Bexar	04844212	210/402-6905	44
Buda Elem Sch/Buda/Hays	02855813	512/268-8439	211
Budewig Intermediate Sch/Houston/Harris	05272193	281/988-3200	182
Buell Central High Sch/Pharr/Hidalgo	04365955	956/354-2500	223
Buena Vista Elem Sch/Del Rio/Val Verde	02128294	830/778-4600	379
BUENA VISTA IND SCH DIST/IMPERIAL/PECOS	01046801	432/536-2225	315
Buena Vista Sch/Imperial/Pecos	01046813	432/536-2336	315
Buffalo Creek Elem Sch/Houston/Harris	04751029	713/251-5300	200
Buffalo Elem Sch/Buffalo/Leon	01037563	903/322-2473	264
Buffalo Gap Elem Sch/Buffalo Gap/Taylor	02112300	325/572-3533	361
Buffalo High Sch/Buffalo/Leon	01037575	903/322-2473	264
BUFFALO IND SCH DIST/BUFFALO/LEON	01037551	903/322-3765	264
Buffalo Lower Junior High Sch/Buffalo/Leon	04281804	903/322-2473	264
Buffalo Upper Junior High Sch/Buffalo/Leon	12311445	903/322-2473	264
Bullard Early Childhood Center/Bullard/Smith	12225224	903/894-6389	336
Bullard Elem Sch/Bullard/Smith	01050589	903/894-2930	336
Bullard High Sch/Bullard/Smith	01050591	903/894-3272	336
BULLARD IND SCH DIST/BULLARD/SMITH	01050577	903/894-6639	336
Bullard Intermediate Sch/Bullard/Smith	04939415	903/894-6793	336
Bullard Middle Sch/Bullard/Smith	02178782	903/894-6533	337
Bullard Primary Sch/Bullard/Smith	11131371	903/894-2890	337
Bullock Elem Sch/Garland/Dallas	01010553	972/494-8308	105
Bulverde Creek Elem Sch/San Antonio/Bexar	10003343	210/407-1000	34
Buna Elem Sch/Buna/Jasper	01033189	409/994-4840	240
Buna High Sch/Buna/Jasper	01033191	409/994-4811	240
BUNA IND SCH DIST/BUNA/JASPER	01033177	409/994-5101	240
Buna Junior High Sch/Buna/Jasper	01033206	409/994-4860	240
Bunche Elem Sch/Midland/Midland	12104371	432/240-8600	285
Bunker Hill Elem Sch/Houston/Harris	01027104	713/251-5400	201
Burbank Elem Sch/Houston/Harris	01025819	713/696-2690	190
Burbank High Sch/San Antonio/Bexar	00999231	210/228-1210	40
Burbank Middle Sch/Houston/Harris	01025821	713/696-2720	190
Burges High Sch/El Paso/El Paso	01015553	915/236-7200	134
Burgess Elem Sch/Wichita Falls/Wichita	01172993	940/235-1136	392
Burgin Elem Sch/Arlington/Tarrant	04918930	682/867-1300	344
Burkburnett High Sch/Burkburnett/Wichita	01059937	940/569-1411	391
BURKBURNETT IND SCH DIST/BURKBURNETT/WICHITA	01059925	940/569-3326	391
Burkburnett Middle Sch/Burkburnett/Wichita	01059949	940/569-3381	391
Burkeville Elem Sch/Burkeville/Newton	01043689	409/565-4284	300
BURKEVILLE IND SCH DIST/BURKEVILLE/NEWTON	01043677	409/565-2201	300
Burkeville Jr Sr High Sch/Burkeville/Newton	01043691	409/565-4284	300
Burleson Co Alt Sch/Caldwell/Burleson	04802135	979/567-2670	59
Burleson Collegiate High Sch/Burleson/Johnson	12168107	817/245-1600	246
Burleson Early Chldhd Center/San Antonio/Bexar	11713515	210/444-7725	31
Burleson Elem Sch/Odessa/Ector	01014602	432/456-1039	130
Burleson High Sch/Burleson/Johnson	01034834	817/245-0000	246
BURLESON IND SCH DIST/BURLESON/JOHNSON	01034810	817/245-1000	246
BURLESON MILAM SPEC SERV CO-OP/MILANO/MILAM	11551771	512/455-7801	288
Burley Primary Sch/Lufkin/Angelina	11446023	936/639-3100	18
BURNET CONS IND SCH DIST/BURNET/BURNET	01002752	512/756-2124	60
Burnet Early Childhood Univ ES/Galveston/Galveston	11563372	409/761-6470	160
Burnet Elem Sch/Houston/Harris	01025443	713/924-1780	189
Burnet Elem Sch/Midland/Midland	01041461	432/240-6200	285
Burnet Elem Sch/Odessa/Ector	01014614	432/456-1049	130
Burnet High Sch/Burnet/Burnet	01002788	512/756-6193	60
Burnet Middle Sch/Austin/Travis	01056179	512/414-3225	369
Burnet Middle Sch/Burnet/Burnet	01002790	512/756-6182	60
Burnett Elem Sch/Houston/Harris	01548433	713/740-0536	198
Burns Elem Sch/Brownsville/Cameron	02202682	956/548-8490	63
Burrus Elem Sch/Houston/Harris	01023926	713/867-5180	190
Burton Adventist Academy/Arlington/Tarrant	02233708	817/572-0081	358
Burton Elem Sch/Burton/Washington	01059119	979/289-2175	386
Burton High Sch/Burton/Washington	01059121	979/289-3830	386
Burton Hill Elem Sch/Fort Worth/Tarrant	01052630	817/815-1400	350
BURTON IND SCH DIST/BURTON/WASHINGTON	01059107	979/289-3131	386
Bush Elem Sch/Houston/Harris	04750128	713/272-3220	182
Bush Elem Sch/Midland/Midland	03250242	432/240-6300	285
Bush Elem Sch/The Woodlands/Montgomery	04454881	936/709-1600	291
Bush Global Ldrshp Acad/Grand Prairie/Dallas	04751524	972/237-1628	107
Bush Middle Sch/San Antonio/Bexar	04807886	210/356-2900	34
Bushland Elem Sch/Amarillo/Potter	01047570	806/359-5410	319
Bushland High Sch/Amarillo/Potter	10008070	806/359-6683	319
BUSHLAND IND SCH DIST/AMARILLO/POTTER	01047568	806/359-6683	319
Bushland Middle Sch/Bushland/Potter	05345960	806/359-5418	319
Business Careers High Sch/San Antonio/Bexar	03403530	210/397-7070	36
Bussey Middle Sch/Garland/Dallas	01010436	972/494-8391	105
Butler Elem Sch/Arlington/Tarrant	01399775	682/867-1010	344
Butler Intermediate Sch/Quinlan/Hunt	01032587	903/356-1400	237
Butterfield Elem Sch/Sanger/Denton	11148269	940/458-4377	126
BYNUM IND SCH DIST/BYNUM/HILL	01030797	254/531-2341	227
Bynum Sch/Bynum/Hill	01030802	254/623-4251	227
Bynum Sch/Midland/Midland	04268682	432/520-0075	286
Byrd Middle Sch/Duncanville/Dallas	01010319	972/708-3400	104
Byron Craig Middle Sch/Abilene/Taylor	10913243	325/794-4100	360
Byron Martin Advanced Tech Ctr/Lubbock/Lubbock	12037857	806/219-2800	270
Byron Nelson High Sch/Trophy Club/Denton	11452321	817/698-5600	124
Byron P Steele II High Sch/Cibolo/Guadalupe	10004347	210/619-4000	173

C

School/City/County	PID	TELEPHONE NUMBER	PAGE
C A Tatum Elem Sch/Dallas/Dallas	10023185	972/502-2000	99
C B Thompson Middle Sch/Quinlan/Hunt	01032604	903/356-1500	237
C C Hardy Elem Sch/Willis/Montgomery	01042788	936/856-1241	294
C C Winn High Sch/Eagle Pass/Maverick	04806894	830/757-0828	276
C D Fulkes Middle Sch/Round Rock/Williamson	01061136	512/428-3100	398
C D Landolt Elem Sch/Friendswood/Galveston	02043254	281/284-5200	158
C E King High Sch/Houston/Harris	01027025	281/727-3500	200
C E King Middle Sch/Houston/Harris	01027037	281/727-4300	200
C E Vail Elem Sch/La Feria/Cameron	04871069	956/797-8460	65
C F Carr Elem Sch/Dallas/Dallas	01008586	972/794-4300	99
C G Sivells Elem Sch/Wharton/Wharton	01059717	979/532-6866	390
C H Yoe High Sch/Cameron/Milam	01041796	254/697-3902	287
C J & Anne Hyman Elem Sch/Dallas/Dallas	05275107	972/708-6700	104
C J Harris Elem Sch/Pearland/Brazoria	01001863	281/485-4024	53
C L Milton Elem Sch/Laredo/Webb	01059224	956/273-4200	386
C M MacDonell Elem Sch/Laredo/Webb	01059377	956/273-4000	386

TX-V10   800-333-8802   School Year 2019-2020

Texas School Directory

DISTRICT & SCHOOL TELEPHONE INDEX

School/City/County DISTRICT/CITY/COUNTY	PID	TELEPHONE NUMBER	PAGE
C M Rice Middle Sch/*Plano*/Collin	04867288	469/752-6000	82
C O Wilson Middle Sch/*Nederland*/Jefferson	01033672	409/727-6224	243
C P Yeager Elem Sch/*Corp Christi*/Nueces	01044774	361/878-2920	303
C Stainke Elem Sch/*Donna*/Hidalgo	01809366	956/464-1940	215
C T Eddins Elem Sch/*McKinney*/Collin	04808426	469/302-6600	81
C W Beasley Elem Sch/*Mesquite*/Dallas	02128555	972/882-5160	111
C W Cline Elem Sch/*Friendswood*/Galveston	01019054	281/482-1201	160
Cable Elem Sch/*San Antonio*/Bexar	00998043	210/397-2850	36
Cactus Elem Sch/*Cactus*/Moore	01042829	806/966-5102	295
Cactus Ranch Elem Sch/*Round Rock*/Williamson	04945892	512/424-8000	398
Cactus Trails Elem Sch/*El Paso*/El Paso	12364416	915/938-2600	136
Caddo Grove Elem Sch/*Joshua*/Johnson	10002650	817/202-2500	248
Caddo Mills Aep/*Caddo Mills*/Hunt	04503884	903/527-2075	235
Caddo Mills High Sch/*Caddo Mills*/Hunt	01032317	903/527-3164	235
CADDO MILLS IND SCH DIST/ CADDO MILLS/HUNT	01032290	903/527-6056	235
Caddo Mills Middle Sch/*Caddo Mills*/Hunt	02180046	903/527-3161	235
Cage Charter Elem Sch/*Houston*/Harris	01024750	713/924-1700	189
Cal & Walt Wester Middle Sch/*Frisco*/Collin	05092644	469/633-4800	79
Calallen Charter High Sch/*Corp Christi*/Nueces	12163054	361/242-6800	302
Calallen High Sch/*Corp Christi*/Nueces	01044140	361/242-5626	302
CALALLEN IND SCH DIST/CORP CHRISTI/ NUECES	01044114	361/242-5600	302
Calallen Middle Sch/*Corp Christi*/Nueces	01044152	361/242-5672	302
Calder Road Elem Sch/*Dickinson*/Galveston	11553951	281/229-7500	159
Caldwell Arts Academy/*Tyler*/Smith	01050840	903/262-2250	338
Caldwell Elem Sch/*Caldwell*/Burleson	01002659	979/567-2404	59
Caldwell Elem Sch/*Garland*/Dallas	01010450	972/926-2500	105
Caldwell Elem Sch/*Round Rock*/Travis	05098466	512/594-6400	371
Caldwell Heights Elem Sch/*Round Rock*/Williamson	04867329	512/428-7300	398
Caldwell High Sch/*Caldwell*/Burleson	01002661	979/567-2401	59
CALDWELL IND SCH DIST/CALDWELL/ BURLESON	01002647	979/567-2400	59
Caldwell Intermediate Sch/*Caldwell*/Burleson	02178457	979/567-2403	59
Caldwell Middle Sch/*Caldwell*/Burleson	01002673	979/567-2402	59
Caldwood Elem Sch/*Beaumont*/Jefferson	01034133	409/617-6025	242
CALHOUN CO IND SCH DIST/ PORT LAVACA/CALHOUN	01003158	361/552-9728	61
Calhoun High Sch/*Port Lavaca*/Calhoun	01003160	361/552-3775	62
Calhoun Middle Sch/*Denton*/Denton	01013244	940/369-2400	121
Calk-Wilson Elem Sch/*Corp Christi*/Nueces	01044255	361/878-2860	303
Callisburg Elem Sch/*Gainesville*/Cooke	01007300	940/612-4196	90
CALLISBURG IND SCH DIST/ GAINESVILLE/COOKE	01007271	940/665-0540	90
Callisburg Middle High Sch/*Gainesville*/Cooke	04801959	940/665-0961	90
Calvary Baptist Sch/*Conroe*/Montgomery	02193031	936/756-0743	295
Calvary Chapel Christian Acad/*Universal Cty*/Bexar	11231684	210/658-8337	44
Calvary Christian Academy/*Fort Worth*/Tarrant	02192520	817/332-3351	358
Calvary Christian Sch/*Harlingen*/Cameron	02233265	956/425-1882	68
Calvary Episcopal Sch/*Richmond*/Fort Bend	01410707	281/342-3161	155
Calvary Lutheran Sch/*Dallas*/Dallas	01410575	214/343-7457	114
Calvary Temple Christian Acad/*Mesquite*/Dallas	04992807	972/286-4935	114
CALVERT IND SCH DIST/CALVERT/ ROBERTSON	01048586	979/364-2824	324
Calvert Sch/*Calvert*/Robertson	01048603	979/364-2845	324
Calvin Bledsoe Elem Sch/*Frisco*/Collin	10016699	469/633-3600	79
Calvin Nelms Charter Sch/*Katy*/Harris	04890950	281/398-8031	2
Calvin Vincent ECC/*Texas City*/Galveston	12035653	409/916-0512	161
Camacho Elem Sch/*Leander*/Williamson	12106082	512/570-7800	397
Cambridge Elem Sch/*San Antonio*/Bexar	00996954	210/822-3611	30
Cambridge Sch/*Humble*/Harris	12109101	281/641-7445	195
Cambridge School of Dallas/*Dallas*/Dallas	10000195	214/357-2995	114
Camelot Elem Sch/*San Antonio*/Bexar	00997673	210/407-1400	34
Cameron Dual Lang Magnet Sch/*Odessa*/Ector	01014626	432/456-1059	130
Cameron Elem Sch/*Cameron*/Milam	01041760	254/697-2381	287
CAMERON IND SCH DIST/CAMERON/ MILAM	01041758	254/697-3512	287
Cameron Junior High Sch/*Cameron*/Milam	01041784	254/697-2131	287
Camey Elem Sch/*The Colony*/Denton	01541306	469/713-5951	122
Camino Real Elem Sch/*Niederwald*/Hays	11079412	512/268-8505	211
Camino Real Middle Sch/*El Paso*/El Paso	03250876	915/434-8300	137
Campbell Elem Sch/*Austin*/Travis	01056313	512/414-2056	367
Campbell Elem Sch/*Sugar Land*/Fort Bend	04923313	832/223-1300	153
CAMPBELL IND SCH DIST/CAMPBELL/ HUNT	01032329	903/862-3259	235
Campbell Middle Sch/*Houston*/Harris	01829433	281/897-4300	184
Campbell Sch/*Campbell*/Hunt	01032331	903/862-3253	235
Campestre Elem Sch/*El Paso*/El Paso	02177037	915/937-7300	136
Canadian Elem Sch/*Canadian*/Hemphill	02224903	806/323-9331	213
Canadian High Sch/*Canadian*/Hemphill	01029229	806/323-5373	213
CANADIAN IND SCH DIST/CANADIAN/ HEMPHILL	01029205	806/323-5393	213
Canadian Middle Sch/*Canadian*/Hemphill	01532068	806/323-5351	213
Canales Elem Sch/*Brownsville*/Cameron	01003603	956/548-8900	63
Candlewood Elem Sch/*San Antonio*/Bexar	03236181	210/662-1060	33
Caney Creek High Sch/*Conroe*/Montgomery	04486688	936/709-2000	291
Cannon Elem Sch/*Grapevine*/Tarrant	01053684	817/251-5680	353
Cano Gonzalez Elem Sch/*Edinburg*/Hidalgo	04452792	956/289-2380	216
Canterbury Elem Sch/*Edinburg*/Hidalgo	03010626	956/289-2374	216
Canterbury Episcopal Sch/*Desoto*/Dallas	04903882	972/572-7200	114
Canton Elem Sch/*Canton*/Van Zandt	01526162	903/567-6521	380
Canton High Sch/*Canton*/Van Zandt	01058103	903/567-6561	380
CANTON IND SCH DIST/CANTON/ VAN ZANDT	01058086	903/567-4179	380
Canton Intermediate Sch/*Canton*/Van Zandt	03318399	903/567-6418	380
Canton Junior High Sch/*Canton*/Van Zandt	01058098	903/567-4329	380
Cantu Elem Sch/*Alton*/Hidalgo	02201391	956/323-7400	222
Canutillo Elem Sch/*Canutillo*/El Paso	01015395	915/877-7600	132
Canutillo High Sch/*El Paso*/El Paso	01015412	915/877-7800	132
CANUTILLO IND SCH DIST/EL PASO/ EL PASO	01015383	915/877-7400	131
Canutillo Middle Sch/*Canutillo*/El Paso	01548392	915/877-7900	132
Canyon Creek Elem Sch/*Austin*/Williamson	04806478	512/428-2800	398
Canyon Creek Elem Sch/*Richardson*/Dallas	01011650	469/593-6500	112
Canyon High Sch/*Canyon*/Randall	01047946	806/677-2740	321
Canyon High Sch/*New Braunfels*/Comal	01006916	830/221-2400	88
Canyon Hills Middle Sch/*El Paso*/El Paso	01015761	915/236-6450	134
CANYON IND SCH DIST/CANYON/ RANDALL	01047934	806/677-2600	320
Canyon Intermediate Sch/*Canyon*/Randall	05341445	806/677-2800	321
Canyon Junior High Sch/*Canyon*/Randall	01047958	806/677-2700	321
Canyon Lake High Sch/*Fischer*/Comal	10913281	830/885-1700	88
Canyon Middle Sch/*New Braunfels*/Comal	01006928	830/221-2300	88
Canyon Point Elem Sch/*Tomball*/Harris	11127784	281/357-3122	203
Canyon Ranch Elem Sch/*Irving*/Dallas	12366074	214/496-7200	98
Canyon Ridge Elem Sch/*San Antonio*/Bexar	10003331	210/407-1600	34
Canyon Ridge Middle Sch/*Austin*/Williamson	05345582	512/570-3500	397
Canyon Vista Middle Sch/*Austin*/Williamson	02223935	512/464-8100	398
Capistrano Elem Sch/*El Paso*/El Paso	01545247	915/434-8600	137
Capitol Elem Sch/*Levelland*/Hockley	01031131	806/894-4715	229
Capitol School-Austin/*Austin*/Travis	11237262	512/467-7006	373
CapRock Elem Sch/*Keller*/Tarrant	11436262	817/744-6400	354
CapRock High Sch/*Amarillo*/Potter	01047207	806/326-2200	317
Capt D Salinas II Elem Sch/*Alamo*/Hidalgo	04363012	956/783-1332	215
Capt Walter E Clarke Mid Sch/*El Paso*/El Paso	04035265	915/937-5600	136
Cardenas Center/*San Antonio*/Bexar	11447247	210/444-7826	31
Cardiff Junior High Sch/*Katy*/Harris	11128594	281/234-0600	151
Career & Tech Education Center/*Frisco*/Collin	11103855	469/633-6780	79
Career & Tech Education Center/*San Antonio*/Bexar	12315130	210/407-0743	34
Career & Technical Ed Center/*Humble*/Harris	05093143	281/641-7950	195
Career & Technology Institute/*Victoria*/Victoria	01540120	361/788-9288	382
Career Center East/*Lewisville*/Denton	11553705	469/713-5211	122
Career Education Center/*Wichita Falls*/Wichita	12230891	940/235-4316	392
Carl E Schluter Elem Sch/*Haslet*/Denton	11710238	817/698-3900	124
Carl O Hamlin Middle Sch/*Corp Christi*/Nueces	01044449	361/878-4210	303
Carl Schurz Elem Sch/*New Braunfels*/Comal	01006978	830/627-6680	88
Carl Waitz Elem Sch/*Alton*/Hidalgo	04012550	956/323-6600	222
Carl Wanke Elem Sch/*San Antonio*/Bexar	10020690	210/397-6700	36
Carl Wunsche Sr High Sch/*Spring*/Harris	01027544	281/891-7650	202
Carlisle Elem Sch/*Plano*/Collin	02225610	469/752-0600	82
CARLISLE IND SCH DIST/HENDERSON/ RUSK	01048940	903/861-3801	327
Carlisle Sch/*Henderson*/Rusk	01048952	903/861-3801	327
Carlos Coon Elem Sch/*San Antonio*/Bexar	01824079	210/397-7250	36
Carlos Truan Jr High Sch/*Edcouch*/Hidalgo	01029633	956/262-5820	216
Carmen Anaya Elem Sch/*Pharr*/Hidalgo	10914285	956/784-8500	223
Carmen Avila Elem Sch/*Edinburg*/Hidalgo	05275171	956/289-2307	216
Carnahan Elem Sch/*San Antonio*/Bexar	11104093	210/397-5850	36
Carnegie-Vanguard High Sch/*Houston*/Harris	05099290	713/732-3690	191

DISTRICT & SCHOOL TELEPHONE INDEX

Market Data Retrieval

School/City/County DISTRICT/CITY/COUNTY	PID	TELEPHONE NUMBER	PAGE
Carol Holt Elem Sch/*Arlington*/Tarrant	10908834	817/299-6460	356
Carolee Booker Elem Sch/*Houston*/Harris	11077232	281/891-8750	202
Carolyn G Bukhair Elem Sch/*Dallas*/Dallas	05350769	469/593-4900	112
Carpenter Elem Sch/*Nacogdoches*/Nacogdoches	01043299	936/569-5070	298
Carpenter Hill Elem Sch/*Buda*/Hays	11555545	512/268-8509	211
Carpenter Middle Sch/*Plano*/Collin	01824108	469/752-5000	82
Carr Middle Sch/*Hale Center*/Hale	03391470	806/839-2141	175
Carrillo Elem Sch/*Houston*/Harris	04021721	713/924-1870	189
CARRIZO SPGS CONS IND SD/ **CARRIZO SPGS/DIMMIT**	01014030	830/876-3503	127
Carrizo Springs Elem Sch/*Carrizo Spgs*/ Dimmit	01014066	830/876-3513	127
Carrizo Springs High Sch/*Carrizo Spgs*/ Dimmit	01014054	830/876-9393	127
Carrizo Springs Interm Sch/*Carrizo Spgs*/ Dimmit	01014080	830/876-3561	127
Carrizo Springs Jr High Sch/*Carrizo Spgs*/ Dimmit	01014078	830/876-2496	127
Carroll Bell Elem Sch/*San Antonio*/Bexar	00997398	210/989-2900	32
Carroll Early Chldhd Center/*San Antonio*/ Bexar	11539981	210/978-7965	40
Carroll Elem Sch/*Corsicana*/Navarro	01043495	903/872-3074	299
Carroll Elem Sch/*Houston*/Harris	11080382	281/727-4100	200
Carroll Elem Sch/*Southlake*/Tarrant	03006766	817/949-4300	347
Carroll High Sch/*Southlake*/Tarrant	01052288	817/949-5600	347
CARROLL INDEPENDENT SCH DIST/ **SOUTHLAKE/TARRANT**	01052252	817/949-8222	347
Carroll Middle Sch/*Southlake*/Tarrant	04918552	817/949-5400	347
Carroll Peak Elem Sch/*Fort Worth*/Tarrant	01053244	817/814-0700	350
Carroll Senior High Sch/*Southlake*/Tarrant	01052276	817/949-5800	347
Carroll T Welch Elem Sch/*El Paso*/El Paso	04452003	915/926-4400	132
Carrollton Classical Academy/*Carrollton*/ Dallas	11014589	972/245-2900	2
Carrollton Elem Sch/*Carrollton*/Dallas	01008158	972/968-1200	96
CARROLLTON-FARMERS BRANCH ISD/ **CARROLLTON/DALLAS**	01008134	972/968-6100	96
Carson Elem Sch/*Decatur*/Wise	04914233	940/393-7500	403
Carter Junior High Sch/*Arlington*/Tarrant	01051698	682/867-1700	344
Carter Park Elem Sch/*Fort Worth*/Tarrant	01052654	817/815-8600	350
Carthage High Sch/*Carthage*/Panola	01046239	903/693-2552	311
CARTHAGE IND SCH DIST/CARTHAGE/ **PANOLA**	01046215	903/693-3806	311
Carthage Junior High Sch/*Carthage*/Panola	01046265	903/693-2751	311
Carthage Primary Sch/*Carthage*/Panola	02104468	903/693-2254	311
Carvajal Early Chldhd Center/*San Antonio*/ Bexar	00999097	210/978-7970	40
Carver Academy Elem Sch/*Amarillo*/Potter	03248031	806/326-4150	317
Carver Center/*Midland*/Midland	10005236	432/240-6400	285
Carver Early Childhood Academy/*Amarillo*/ Potter	04866167	806/326-4200	317
Carver Early Education Center/*Odessa*/Ector	02856257	432/456-1069	130
Carver Elem Sch/*Georgetown*/Williamson	01060900	512/943-5070	395
Carver Elem Sch/*Greenville*/Hunt	01032472	903/457-0777	236
Carver High Sch/*Houston*/Harris	01022805	281/878-0310	180
Carver Learning Center/*San Angelo*/ Tom Green	01055589	325/659-3648	365
Carver Middle Sch/*Waco*/McLennan	01040273	254/757-0787	282
Carylene McClendon Elem Sch/*Nevada*/Collin	03046895	972/843-6800	78
Casa View Elem Sch/*Dallas*/Dallas	01008598	972/749-7700	99
Casey Elem Sch/*Austin*/Travis	04869846	512/841-6900	366
Casis Elem Sch/*Austin*/Travis	01056143	512/414-2062	367
Cassata High Sch/*Fort Worth*/Tarrant	02115106	817/926-1745	358
Cast Med/*San Antonio*/Bexar	12309911	210/228-3380	40
Cast STEM High Sch/*Von Ormy*/Bexar	12364519	210/622-4810	43
Cast Tech High Sch/*San Antonio*/Bexar	12238972	210/554-2700	40
Castle Hills Elem Sch/*Lewisville*/Denton	05091729	469/713-5952	122
Castle Hills Elem Sch/*San Antonio*/Bexar	00997685	210/407-1800	34
Castleberry Elem Sch/*Fort Worth*/Tarrant	01052317	817/252-2300	347
Castleberry Elem Sch/*Fort Worth*/Tarrant	01052329	817/252-2100	347
CASTLEBERRY IND SCH DIST/ **FORT WORTH/TARRANT**	01052290	817/252-2000	347
Castleman Creek Elem Sch/*Hewitt*/McLennan	11449568	254/761-5755	280
Castro Elem Sch/*Mission*/Hidalgo	01030242	956/323-6800	222
Castroville Elem Sch/*Castroville*/Medina	01041318	830/931-2117	284
Cater Elem Sch/*Temple*/Bell	00996734	254/215-7444	29
Cathedral High Sch/*El Paso*/El Paso	01016727	915/532-3238	139
Cathedral of Life Chrn Sch/*Balch Springs*/ Dallas	05078296	972/286-4845	114
Cathedral School of St Mary/*Austin*/Travis	01003005	512/476-1480	372
Cathelene Thomas Elem Sch/*Slaton*/Lubbock	01039236	806/828-5805	272
Catherine Bell Elem Sch/*Little Elm*/Denton	12168676	972/347-7200	121
Catherine Bethke Elem Sch/*Katy*/Harris	12169943	281/234-4200	151

School/City/County DISTRICT/CITY/COUNTY	PID	TELEPHONE NUMBER	PAGE
Cats Academy-Student Alt Ctr/*Angleton*/ Brazoria	04013578	979/864-8003	51
Cavazos Elem Sch/*McAllen*/Hidalgo	01029736	956/289-2535	216
Cavazos Middle Sch/*Lubbock*/Lubbock	04032639	806/219-3200	270
CAYUGA IND SCH DIST/TENN COLONY/ **ANDERSON**	00994401	903/928-2102	14
Cayuga Sch/*Tenn Colony*/Anderson	00994425	903/928-2102	14
Cecil Everett Elem Sch/*Paris*/Lamar	01418503	903/737-2061	259
Cedar Bayou Junior High Sch/*Baytown*/Harris	01023603	281/420-4570	187
Cedar Brook Elem Sch/*Houston*/Harris	04032225	713/251-5500	201
Cedar Creek Elem Sch/*Austin*/Travis	01829548	512/732-9120	370
Cedar Creek Elem Sch/*Cedar Creek*/Bastrop	04030734	512/772-7600	23
Cedar Creek High Sch/*Cedar Creek*/Bastrop	11555739	512/772-7300	23
Cedar Creek Intermediate Sch/*Cedar Creek*/ Bastrop	05350161	512/772-7475	23
Cedar Creek Middle Sch/*Cedar Creek*/Bastrop	04917883	512/772-7425	23
Cedar Creek Sch/*San Antonio*/Bexar	12231510	210/822-3792	44
Cedar Crest Elem Sch/*Dallas*/Dallas	01008380	972/925-7400	99
Cedar Grove Elem Sch/*El Paso*/El Paso	01016349	915/434-7600	137
Cedar Grove Elem Sch/*Livingston*/Polk	12034984	936/328-2240	317
Cedar Hill 9th Grade Center/*Cedar Hill*/ Dallas	10006371	469/272-2050	97
Cedar Hill Collegiate High Sch/*Cedar Hill*/ Dallas	11718747	469/272-2021	97
Cedar Hill High Sch/*Cedar Hill*/Dallas	01008299	469/272-2000	97
CEDAR HILL IND SCH DIST/ **CEDAR HILL/DALLAS**	01008275	972/291-1581	97
Cedar Park Charter Academy/*Cedar Park*/ Williamson	12113891	512/331-2980	2
Cedar Park High Sch/*Cedar Park*/Williamson	04808490	512/570-1200	397
Cedar Park Middle Sch/*Cedar Park*/ Williamson	01061045	512/570-3100	397
Cedar Ridge Elem Sch/*Waco*/McLennan	01040182	254/756-1241	282
Cedar Ridge High Sch/*Round Rock*/Williamson	11557414	512/704-0100	398
Cedar Valley Elem Sch/*Killeen*/Bell	04027634	254/336-1480	27
Cedar Valley Middle Sch/*Austin*/Williamson	04030306	512/428-2300	398
Cedars International Academy/*Austin*/Travis	05011066	512/419-1551	2
Cedars Intl Next Generation HS/*Austin*/ Travis	12260664	512/956-4406	2
Cedric C Smith Elem Sch/*Magnolia*/ Montgomery	04922890	281/252-2300	293
Cele Middle Sch/*Pflugerville*/Travis	11923447	512/594-3000	371
Celeste Elem Sch/*Celeste*/Hunt	01032367	903/568-4721	236
Celeste High Sch/*Celeste*/Hunt	04034417	903/568-4721	236
CELESTE IND SCH DIST/CELESTE/ **HUNT**	01032355	903/568-4825	235
Celeste Junior High Sch/*Celeste*/Hunt	04034405	903/568-4721	236
Celestino Mauricio Soto ES/*Dallas*/Dallas	10023111	972/502-5100	99
Celia Hays Elem Sch/*Rockwall*/Rockwall	10911013	469/698-2800	325
Celina 6th Grade Center/*Celina*/Collin	12035641	469/742-9105	78
Celina Elem Sch/*Celina*/Collin	03046596	469/742-9103	78
Celina High Sch/*Celina*/Collin	01006100	469/742-9102	78
CELINA IND SCH DIST/CELINA/ **COLLIN**	01006083	469/742-9100	77
Celina Junior High Sch/*Celina*/Collin	01006095	469/742-9101	78
Celina Primary Sch/*Celina*/Collin	12230877	469/742-9104	78
Centennial Elem Sch/*Lubbock*/Lubbock	10911037	806/219-7800	270
Centennial Elem Sch/*Plano*/Collin	04867276	469/752-0700	82
Centennial High Sch/*Burleson*/Johnson	11547794	817/245-0250	247
Centennial High Sch/*Frisco*/Collin	05272595	469/633-5600	79
Center Elem Sch/*Center*/Shelby	01050280	936/598-3625	334
Center for Career & Tech Ed/*El Paso*/ El Paso	01015462	915/236-7900	134
Center for Hearing & Speech/*Houston*/Harris	01875353	713/523-3633	205
Center for Success/*Houston*/Harris	04922888	832/386-3637	186
Center High Sch/*Center*/Shelby	01050292	936/598-6173	334
CENTER IND SCH DIST/CENTER/ **SHELBY**	01050278	936/598-5642	334
Center Intermediate Sch/*Center*/Shelby	01050307	936/598-6148	334
Center Middle Sch/*Center*/Shelby	01050319	936/598-5619	334
Center Point Elem Sch/*Center Point*/Kerr	01035981	830/634-2257	255
Center Point High Sch/*Center Point*/Kerr	01035993	830/634-2244	255
CENTER POINT IND SCH DIST/ **CENTER POINT/KERR**	01035979	830/634-2171	255
Center Point Middle Sch/*Center Point*/Kerr	04452883	830/634-2244	255
Center Roughrider Academy/*Center*/Shelby	12305721	936/598-1540	334
Centerville Elem Sch/*Centerville*/Leon	01037599	903/536-2235	264
Centerville Elem Sch/*Garland*/Dallas	01010462	972/926-2510	105
Centerville Elem Sch/*Groveton*/Trinity	01057082	936/642-1597	374
Centerville High Sch/*Groveton*/Trinity	04033451	936/642-1597	374
CENTERVILLE IND SCH DIST/ **CENTERVILLE/LEON**	01037587	903/536-7812	264

Texas School Directory

DISTRICT & SCHOOL TELEPHONE INDEX

School/City/County DISTRICT/CITY/COUNTY	PID	TELEPHONE NUMBER	PAGE
CENTERVILLE IND SCH DIST/ **GROVETON/TRINITY**	01057070	936/642-1597	374
Centerville Jr Sr High Sch/Centerville/ Leon	01037604	903/536-2625	264
Central Athens Elem Sch/Athens/Henderson	01029279	903/677-6960	213
Central Baptist Academy/Magnolia/ Montgomery	02153782	281/356-2861	295
Central Baptist Christian Sch/Center/ Shelby	02153550	936/598-3642	335
Central Catholic High Sch/San Antonio/ Bexar	00999774	210/225-6794	44
Central Christian Academy/Houston/Harris	04836708	713/468-3248	205
Central Elem Sch/Angleton/Brazoria	02895174	979/864-8004	51
Central Elem Sch/Carrollton/Dallas	04364494	972/968-1300	96
Central Elem Sch/Duncanville/Dallas	01010321	972/708-2600	104
Central Elem Sch/Lewisville/Denton	01013414	469/713-5976	122
Central Elem Sch/Lubbock/Lubbock	11715329	806/776-2150	271
Central Elem Sch/Mabank/Kaufman	01035694	903/880-1380	252
Central Elem Sch/Palacios/Matagorda	01040924	361/972-2911	275
Central Elem Sch/Pollok/Angelina	04028286	936/853-9390	17
Central Elem Sch/Seagoville/Dallas	01008603	972/749-6800	99
Central Elem Sch/Stephenville/Erath	01017147	254/965-3716	144
Central Elem Sch/Vernon/Wilbarger	01060572	940/553-1859	393
Central Freshman Campus/San Angelo/ Tom Green	01055620	325/659-3576	365
Central Heights Elem Sch/Nacogdoches/ Nacogdoches	01043081	936/552-3424	297
Central Heights High Sch/Nacogdoches/ Nacogdoches	04364963	936/552-3408	297
CENTRAL HEIGHTS IND SCH DIST/ **NACOGDOCHES/NACOGDOCHES**	01043079	936/564-2681	297
Central Heights Middle Sch/Nacogdoches/ Nacogdoches	11710032	936/552-3441	297
Central High Sch/Fort Worth/Tarrant	05273460	817/744-2000	354
Central High Sch/Pollok/Angelina	00994798	936/853-2167	17
Central High Sch/San Angelo/Tom Green	01055591	325/659-3434	365
CENTRAL IND SCH DIST/POLLOK/ **ANGELINA**	00994774	936/853-2216	16
Central Junior High Sch/Euless/Tarrant	01053775	817/354-3350	354
Central Junior High Sch/Pollok/Angelina	00994803	936/853-2115	17
Central Media Arts Academy/Galveston/ Galveston	01019119	409/761-6200	160
Central Middle Sch/Nederland/Jefferson	01033684	409/727-5765	243
Central Middle Sch/Weslaco/Hidalgo	04014209	956/969-6710	225
Central Texas Christian Sch/Temple/Bell	04993112	254/939-5700	30
Centro Chrn Alpha Omega Acad/Houston/ Harris	11229136	713/697-6726	205
Cesar Chavez Academy/El Paso/El Paso	04035631	915/434-9600	137
Cesar Chavez Elem Sch/Fort Worth/Tarrant	05096509	817/815-0300	350
Cesar Chavez Elem Sch/Little Elm/Denton	05070490	972/947-9452	124
Cesar Chavez Elem Sch/Pharr/Hidalgo	04870326	956/354-2720	223
Cesar Chavez Learning Center/Dallas/Dallas	04757176	972/925-1000	99
Cesar Chavez Middle Sch/Mission/Hidalgo	03266356	956/323-2800	219
Cesar Chavez Middle Sch/Waco/McLennan	05221194	254/750-3736	282
Cesar E Chavez Academy/Corp Christi/Nueces	11015557	361/561-5651	2
Challenge Early Clg High Sch/Houston/ Harris	05280396	713/664-9712	191
Challenger Elem Sch/Pearland/Brazoria	04033906	281/485-7912	53
Challenger School-Avery Rnch/Austin/ Williamson	11702592	512/341-8000	400
Chamberlin Elem Sch/Stephenville/Erath	01017159	254/968-2311	144
Chambers Elem Sch/Houston/Harris	01023029	281/983-8313	182
Champion Elem Sch/Brownsville/Cameron	04945103	956/832-6200	63
Champion High Sch/Boerne/Kendall	11080502	830/357-2600	254
Chancellor Elem Sch/Houston/Harris	01541344	281/983-8318	182
Chandler Elem Sch/Allen/Collin	10028472	469/467-1400	76
Chandler Elem Sch/Chandler/Henderson	01029358	903/849-3400	213
Chandler Elem Sch/Kilgore/Gregg	01020912	903/988-3904	169
Chandler Elem Sch/Victoria/Victoria	01058593	361/788-9587	382
Chandler Intermediate Sch/Chandler/ Henderson	05097709	903/849-6436	213
Chandler Oaks Elem Sch/Round Rock/ Williamson	11553315	512/704-0400	398
Channelview High Sch/Channelview/Harris	01023081	281/452-1450	183
CHANNELVIEW IND SCH DIST/ **CHANNELVIEW/HARRIS**	01023079	281/452-8002	183
CHANNING IND SCH DIST/CHANNING/ **HARTLEY**	01028794	806/235-3432	209
Channing Public Sch/Channing/Hartley	01028809	806/235-3719	209
Chapa Middle Sch/Kyle/Hays	10022753	512/268-8500	211
Chaparral Star Academy/Austin/Travis	04846595	512/989-2672	2
Chapel Hill Academy CS/Fort Worth/Tarrant	11453296	817/289-0242	2
Chapel Hill Elem Sch/Mt Pleasant/Titus	05099953	903/572-4586	363
Chapel Hill High Sch/Mt Pleasant/Titus	11078028	903/572-3925	363
Chapel Hill High Sch/Tyler/Smith	01050620	903/566-2311	337
CHAPEL HILL IND SCH DIST/ **MT PLEASANT/TITUS**	01055307	903/572-8096	363
CHAPEL HILL IND SCH DIST/ **TYLER/SMITH**	01050606	903/566-2441	337
Chapel Hill Junior High Sch/Mt Pleasant/ Titus	01055319	903/572-3925	363
Chapel Hill Middle Sch/Tyler/Smith	02856659	903/566-1491	337
Chapel Hill Preparatory Sch/Dallas/Dallas	01010187	972/794-2400	99
Chapin High Sch/El Paso/El Paso	04918655	915/236-4400	134
Charles A Gill Elem Sch/Dallas/Dallas	01008615	972/749-8400	99
Charles Borchers Elem Sch/Laredo/Webb	05102940	956/473-7200	387
Charles Clyde Ball Academy/San Antonio/ Bexar	00998756	210/438-6845	40
Charles E Nash Elem Sch/Fort Worth/Tarrant	01053153	817/814-9400	350
Charles Forbes Middle Sch/Georgetown/ Williamson	04946640	512/943-5150	395
Charles H Milby High Sch/Houston/Harris	01025455	713/928-7401	189
Charles M Blalack Middle Sch/Carrollton/ Dallas	02894132	972/968-3500	96
Charles R Drew Academy/Houston/Harris	01022740	281/878-0360	181
Charles R Drew Elem Sch/Crosby/Harris	01418383	281/328-9306	183
Charles Rice Learning Center/Dallas/Dallas	01008627	972/749-1100	99
Charles Tosch Elem Sch/Mesquite/Dallas	01011428	972/882-5000	111
Charlie C McKamy Elem Sch/Dallas/Dallas	04020545	972/968-2400	96
Charlie Marshall Elem Sch/Aransas Pass/ San Patricio	01049499	361/758-3455	330
Charlotte Anderson Elem Sch/Arlington/ Tarrant	02897471	817/299-7760	356
Charlotte Elem Sch/Charlotte/Atascosa	00995340	830/277-1710	20
Charlotte High Sch/Charlotte/Atascosa	00995352	830/277-1432	20
CHARLOTTE IND SCH DIST/CHARLOTTE/ **ATASCOSA**	00995338	830/277-1431	20
Charlotte Middle Sch/Charlotte/Atascosa	00995364	830/277-1646	20
Charlton-Pollard Elem Sch/Beaumont/ Jefferson	01033476	409/617-6075	242
Charter Oak Elem Sch/Temple/Bell	12367638	254/215-4000	26
Chavez High Sch/Houston/Harris	04922101	713/495-6950	189
Cheatham Elem Sch/Clarksville/Red River	01048134	903/427-3891	322
Cheri L Cox Elem Sch/Sachse/Collin	05356206	972/429-2500	85
CHEROKEE IND SCH DIST/CHEROKEE/ **SAN SABA**	01049889	325/622-4298	332
Cherokee Sch/Cherokee/San Saba	01049891	325/622-4298	332
Cherry Elem Sch/Bay City/Matagorda	01040857	979/401-1300	275
Chester Elem Sch/Chester/Tyler	01057202	936/969-2211	374
Chester High Sch/Chester/Tyler	04362666	936/969-2211	375
CHESTER IND SCH DIST/CHESTER/ **TYLER**	01057197	936/969-2211	374
Chester Jordan Elem Sch/El Paso/El Paso	10911673	915/937-8801	136
Chester W Nimitz High Sch/Houston/Harris	01824213	281/443-7480	180
Chet Burchett Elem Sch/Spring/Harris	10006943	281/891-8630	202
Chico Elem Sch/Chico/Wise	01061631	940/644-2220	403
Chico High Sch/Chico/Wise	03317773	940/644-5783	403
CHICO IND SCH DIST/CHICO/WISE	01061629	940/644-2228	403
Chico Junior High Sch/Chico/Wise	03317785	940/644-5550	403
Child Montessori Sch/San Antonio/Bexar	04993801	210/493-6550	44
Childrens Sch/Austin/Travis	02780464	512/453-1126	373
Childress Elem Sch/Childress/Childress	01005467	940/937-6313	74
Childress High Sch/Childress/Childress	01005443	940/937-6131	74
CHILDRESS IND SCH DIST/CHILDRESS/ **CHILDRESS**	01005431	940/937-2501	74
Childress Junior High Sch/Childress/ Childress	01005455	940/937-3641	74
Chillicothe Elem Sch/Chillicothe/Hardeman	01022362	940/852-5521	177
Chillicothe High Sch/Chillicothe/Hardeman	01022374	940/852-5391	177
CHILLICOTHE ISD SCH DIST/ **CHILLICOTHE/HARDEMAN**	01022350	940/852-5391	177
CHILTON IND SCH DIST/CHILTON/ **FALLS**	01017202	254/546-1200	144
Chilton Sch/Chilton/Falls	01017214	254/546-1200	144
China Elem Sch/China/Hardin	01022441	409/981-6410	178
China Spring Elem Sch/China Spring/ McLennan	01039626	254/836-4635	278
China Spring High Sch/China Spring/ McLennan	01039638	254/836-1771	279
CHINA SPRING IND SCH DIST/ **CHINA SPRING/MCLENNAN**	01039614	254/836-1115	278
China Spring Intermediate Sch/Waco/ McLennan	04914805	254/759-1200	279

DISTRICT & SCHOOL TELEPHONE INDEX

Market Data Retrieval

School/City/County DISTRICT/CITY/COUNTY	PID	TELEPHONE NUMBER	PAGE
China Spring Middle Sch/*China Spring*/McLennan	03413054	254/836-4611	279
Chinquapin Prep Sch/*Highlands*/Harris	01802722	281/426-5551	205
Chip Richarte High Sch/*Georgetown*/Williamson	03400801	512/943-5120	395
CHIRENO ISD SCH DIST/CHIRENO/NACOGDOCHES	01043108	936/362-2132	297
Chireno Sch/*Chireno*/Nacogdoches	01043110	936/362-2132	297
Chisholm Ridge Elem Sch/*Fort Worth*/Tarrant	10003692	817/232-0715	348
Chisholm Trail Academy/*Keene*/Johnson	01480697	817/641-6626	249
Chisholm Trail Elem Sch/*Belton*/Bell	10003721	254/316-5100	26
Chisholm Trail Elem Sch/*Sanger*/Denton	03011228	940/458-5297	126
Chisholm Trail High Sch/*Fort Worth*/Tarrant	11818062	817/232-7112	348
Chisholm Trail Interm Sch/*Fort Worth*/Tarrant	04288113	817/744-3800	355
Chisholm Trail Middle Sch/*Rhome*/Denton	04804626	817/215-0600	124
Chisholm Trail Middle Sch/*Round Rock*/Williamson	01824419	512/428-2500	398
Chisum Elem Sch/*Paris*/Lamar	01036612	903/737-2820	259
Chisum High Sch/*Paris*/Lamar	12315049	903/737-2800	259
CHISUM IND SCH DIST/PARIS/LAMAR	01036600	903/737-2830	259
Chisum Middle Sch/*Paris*/Lamar	12315037	903/737-2806	259
Choices Leadership Academy/*Dallas*/Collin	11227530	972/662-0665	85
Christ Academy/*Wichita Falls*/Wichita	01060481	940/692-2853	393
Christ Community Sch/*Shenandoah*/Montgomery	04993485	936/321-6300	295
Christ Episcopal Sch/*Nacogdoches*/Nacogdoches	01043380	936/564-0621	298
Christ the King Cathedral Sch/*Lubbock*/Lubbock	01047673	806/795-8283	272
Christ the King Sch/*Dallas*/Dallas	01012393	214/365-1234	113
Christ the Redeemer Cath Sch/*Houston*/Harris	12164979	281/469-8440	204
Christ the Redeemer Sch/*Rusk*/Cherokee	11222566	903/683-1404	73
Christa McAuliffe Elem Sch/*McAllen*/Hidalgo	02897237	956/971-4400	221
Christa McAuliffe Learning Ctr/*Richardson*/Dallas	04030667	469/593-5800	112
Christa McAuliffe Middle Sch/*San Antonio*/Bexar	03323394	210/623-6260	43
Christene Moss Elem Sch/*Fort Worth*/Tarrant	01052862	817/815-3600	350
Christian Academy of America/*Double Oak*/Denton	12313780	972/539-1458	126
Christian Evers Elem Sch/*San Antonio*/Bexar	04015461	210/397-2550	36
Christian Heritage Academy/*Palestine*/Anderson	11465134	903/723-4685	16
Christian Heritage Sch/*Longview*/Gregg	04927864	903/663-4151	171
Christian Heritage Sch/*Tyler*/Smith	02165060	903/593-2702	339
Christian Life Center Academy/*Kingwood*/Harris	11237834	281/319-4673	205
Christian Life Preparatory Sch/*Fort Worth*/Tarrant	11549015	817/293-1500	358
Christian School-Castle Hills/*San Antonio*/Bexar	02165046	210/878-1000	44
Christie Elem Sch/*Plano*/Collin	01006382	469/752-0800	82
Christoval Elem Sch/*Christoval*/Tom Green	01055498	325/896-2446	364
CHRISTOVAL IND SCH DIST/CHRISTOVAL/TOM GREEN	01055486	325/896-2520	364
Christoval Jr Sr High Sch/*Christoval*/Tom Green	03055937	325/896-2355	364
Church Hill Middle Sch/*New Braunfels*/Comal	04479764	830/221-2800	88
Cibolo Creek Elem Sch/*Boerne*/Kendall	10031039	830/357-4400	254
Cibolo Green Elem Sch/*San Antonio*/Bexar	11558705	210/407-1200	34
Cibolo Valley Elem Sch/*Cibolo*/Guadalupe	12108638	210/619-4700	173
Cielo Vista Elem Sch/*El Paso*/El Paso	01015577	915/236-8375	133
Cimarron Elem Sch/*Houston*/Harris	01023421	832/386-3240	186
Cimarron Elem Sch/*Katy*/Harris	02110273	281/237-6900	151
Cinco Ranch High Sch/*Katy*/Harris	04866040	281/237-7000	152
Cinco Ranch Junior High Sch/*Katy*/Harris	04939350	281/237-7300	152
Cisco Elem Sch/*Cisco*/Eastland	01014377	254/442-1219	128
Cisco High Sch/*Cisco*/Eastland	01014365	254/442-3051	128
CISCO INDEPENDENT SCH DIST/CISCO/EASTLAND	01014353	254/442-3056	128
Cisco Junior High Sch/*Cisco*/Eastland	03246459	254/442-3004	129
Cisco Learning Center/*Cisco*/Eastland	04448040	254/442-4852	129
Cisneros Pre-K Sch/*Garland*/Dallas	10008123	972/271-7160	105
Cistercian Preparatory Sch/*Irving*/Dallas	01012408	469/499-5400	113
Citadel Christian Sch/*Brenham*/Washington	04937077	979/830-8480	386
City Lab High Sch/*Dallas*/Dallas	12305604	972/749-2700	99
City View Elem Sch/*Amarillo*/Randall	11450397	806/677-2500	321
City View Elem Sch/*Wichita Falls*/Wichita	01060003	940/855-2351	391
CITY VIEW IND SCH DIST/WICHITA FALLS/WICHITA	01059999	940/855-4042	391
City View Jr Sr High Sch/*Wichita Falls*/Wichita	04868385	940/855-7511	391
Clack Middle Sch/*Abilene*/Taylor	04015306	325/692-1961	360
Clara Love Elem Sch/*Justin*/Denton	11452333	817/698-6600	125
Clara Oliver Elem Sch/*Dallas*/Dallas	01008641	972/749-3400	99
Clardy Elem Sch/*El Paso*/El Paso	01015589	915/236-8450	133
Clarence Galm Elem Sch/*San Antonio*/Bexar	03010690	210/397-1150	36
CLARENDON CONS IND SCH DIST/CLARENDON/DONLEY	01014119	806/874-2062	127
Clarendon Elem Sch/*Clarendon*/Donley	01014121	806/874-3855	127
Clarendon High Sch/*Clarendon*/Donley	01014133	806/874-2181	127
Clarendon Junior High Sch/*Clarendon*/Donley	04278467	806/874-3232	127
Clariden Sch/*Southlake*/Tarrant	03268031	682/237-0400	358
Clark Elem Sch/*Laredo*/Webb	01059482	956/473-4600	387
Clark High Sch/*Plano*/Collin	01877387	469/752-7200	82
Clark Intermediate Sch/*Houston*/Harris	05273264	281/891-8540	202
Clark Intermediate Sch/*Spring*/Montgomery	12311067	281/939-0600	291
Clark Middle Sch/*Laredo*/Webb	01826352	956/473-7500	387
Clark Middle Sch/*Princeton*/Collin	01006538	469/952-5404	84
Clarke Elem Sch/*Fort Hood*/Bell	01525869	254/336-1510	27
Clarkston Elem Sch/*Tyler*/Smith	01050802	903/262-1980	338
CLARKSVILLE IND SCH DIST/CLARKSVILLE/RED RIVER	01048110	903/427-3891	322
Clarksville Middle High Sch/*Clarksville*/Red River	01048158	903/427-3891	322
Classical Center at Vial Sch/*Garland*/Dallas	01010589	972/240-3710	105
Classical Center-Brandenburg/*Garland*/Dallas	01010424	972/926-2630	105
Claude Berkman Elem Sch/*Round Rock*/Williamson	01061095	512/464-8250	398
Claude Cunningham Middle Sch/*Corp Christi*/Nueces	01044346	361/878-4720	303
Claude Curtsinger Elem Sch/*Frisco*/Collin	04360292	469/633-2100	79
CLAUDE IND SCH DIST/CLAUDE/ARMSTRONG	00995302	806/226-7331	20
Claude Sch/*Claude*/Armstrong	00995314	806/226-7331	20
Clay Classical Academy/*Dallas*/Dallas	11663049	214/467-4143	2
Claybon Elem Sch/*Forney*/Kaufman	04947113	972/564-7023	251
Clayton Elem Sch/*Austin*/Travis	10023678	512/841-9200	366
Clear Brook High Sch/*Friendswood*/Galveston	03052416	281/284-2100	158
Clear Creek Elem Sch/*Fort Hood*/Bell	03334551	254/336-1550	27
Clear Creek High Sch/*League City*/Galveston	01018828	281/284-1700	158
CLEAR CREEK IND SCH DIST/LEAGUE CITY/GALVESTON	01018816	281/284-0000	158
Clear Creek Intermediate Sch/*League City*/Galveston	11449116	281/284-2300	158
Clear Creek Intermediate Sch/*Sanger*/Denton	01013658	940/458-7476	126
Clear Falls High Sch/*League City*/Galveston	11554838	281/284-1100	158
Clear Fork Elem Sch/*Lockhart*/Caldwell	01003055	512/398-0450	61
Clear Horizons Early Clg HS/*Houston*/Galveston	10908872	281/929-4657	158
Clear Lake City Elem Sch/*Houston*/Galveston	01018830	281/284-4200	158
Clear Lake High Sch/*Houston*/Galveston	01018854	281/284-1900	158
Clear Lake Intermediate Sch/*Houston*/Galveston	01018842	281/284-3200	158
Clear Path Alt High Sch/*Webster*/Galveston	05096901	281/284-1600	158
Clear Spring Elem Sch/*New Braunfels*/Comal	11559840	830/837-7300	88
Clear Spring Elem Sch/*San Antonio*/Bexar	00997702	210/407-2000	34
Clear Springs High Sch/*League City*/Galveston	10908884	281/284-1300	158
Clear View High Sch/*Webster*/Galveston	03052404	281/284-1500	158
Clearfork Elem Sch/*Andrews*/Andrews	02202723	432/524-1930	16
Cleburn Eubanks Interm Sch/*Southlake*/Tarrant	04946157	817/949-5200	347
Cleburne Christian Academy/*Cleburne*/Johnson	04993007	817/641-2857	249
Cleburne High Sch/*Cleburne*/Johnson	01526095	817/202-1200	247
CLEBURNE IND SCH DIST/CLEBURNE/JOHNSON	01034872	817/202-1100	247
Cleckler-Heald Elem Sch/*Weslaco*/Hidalgo	04288450	956/969-6888	225
Clemente Martinez Elem Sch/*Houston*/Harris	04289935	713/224-1424	191
Clements High Sch/*Sugar Land*/Fort Bend	02201444	281/634-2150	150
Clements-Parsons Elem Sch/*Copperas Cove*/Coryell	01007568	254/547-2235	92
Clendenin Elem Sch/*El Paso*/El Paso	02205402	915/236-5300	133
Cleveland Elem Sch/*Cleveland*/Liberty	01037721	281/592-8752	265
CLEVELAND IND SCH DIST/CLEVELAND/LIBERTY	01037719	281/592-8717	265
Cleveland Middle Sch/*Cleveland*/Liberty	01037733	281/593-1148	265
Clifford Davis Elem Sch/*Fort Worth*/Tarrant	05096511	817/815-8700	350
Clifford Dunn Elem Sch/*Houston*/Harris	02894376	281/233-4320	180

Texas School Directory

DISTRICT & SCHOOL TELEPHONE INDEX

School/City/County DISTRICT/CITY/COUNTY	PID	TELEPHONE NUMBER	PAGE
Clifton Career Dev Sch/*Austin*/Travis	02127836	512/414-3614	368
Clifton Early Childhood Sch/*Irving*/Dallas	04872960	972/600-4200	109
Clifton Elem School PK-5/*Clifton*/Bosque	01808910	254/675-1875	46
Clifton High Sch/*Clifton*/Bosque	01808908	254/675-1845	46
CLIFTON IND SCH DIST/CLIFTON/ BOSQUE	01808893	254/675-2827	46
Clifton Middle Sch/*Clifton*/Bosque	03248665	254/675-1855	46
Clifton Park Elem Sch/*Killeen*/Bell	00996459	254/336-1580	27
Clint Early College Academy/*Clint*/El Paso	12031607	915/926-8100	132
Clint High Sch/*Clint*/El Paso	01015448	915/926-8300	132
CLINT IND SCH DIST/EL PASO/ EL PASO	01015424	915/926-4000	132
Clint Junior High Sch/*Clint*/El Paso	01826209	915/926-8000	132
Clinton P Russell Elem Sch/*Dallas*/Dallas	01009748	972/925-8300	99
Cloverleaf Elem Sch/*Houston*/Harris	01023433	832/386-3200	187
Club Estates Elem Sch/*Corp Christi*/Nueces	02109066	361/878-3780	303
Club Hill Elem Sch/*Garland*/Dallas	01010486	972/926-2520	105
Clute Intermediate Sch/*Clute*/Brazoria	01001605	979/730-7230	52
CLYDE CONSOLIDATED IND SD/ CLYDE/CALLAHAN	01003316	325/893-4222	62
Clyde Elem Sch/*Clyde*/Callahan	01003328	325/893-4788	62
Clyde High Sch/*Clyde*/Callahan	01003330	325/893-2161	62
Clyde Intermediate Sch/*Clyde*/Callahan	04245305	325/893-2815	62
Clyde Junior High Sch/*Clyde*/Callahan	01003342	325/893-5788	62
Coahoma Elem Sch/*Coahoma*/Howard	01032068	432/394-5000	234
Coahoma High Sch/*Coahoma*/Howard	01032070	432/394-5000	234
COAHOMA IND SCH DIST/COAHOMA/ HOWARD	01032056	432/394-5000	234
Coahoma Junior High Sch/*Coahoma*/Howard	01032082	432/394-5000	234
Coakley Middle Sch/*Harlingen*/Cameron	01003809	956/427-3000	65
Coastal Oaks Christian Sch/*Rockport*/ Aransas	04993851	361/790-9597	19
Cobb Sixth Grade Campus/*Houston*/Harris	04884092	832/386-2100	187
Cockrell Elem Sch/*Prosper*/Collin	11831868	469/219-2130	84
Cockrell Hill Elem Sch/*Desoto*/Dallas	03005994	972/230-1692	104
Coder Elem Sch/*Aledo*/Parker	01046318	817/441-6095	312
Codwell Elem Sch/*Houston*/Harris	01826297	713/732-3580	190
Coggin Intermediate Sch/*Brownwood*/Brown	02199918	325/646-0462	58
Cogin Memorial Elem Sch/*Corp Christi*/ Nueces	03017507	361/991-6968	306
Coker Elem Sch/*San Antonio*/Bexar	00997714	210/407-2200	34
Col John O Ensor Middle Sch/*El Paso*/ El Paso	04916102	915/937-6000	136
Col Menchaca ECC/*San Antonio*/Bexar	12307951	210/882-1600	43
Col Santos Benavides Elem Sch/*Laredo*/Webb	01059509	956/473-4900	387
Colbert Elem Sch/*Dayton*/Liberty	05342516	936/258-2727	265
Colby Glass Elem Sch/*San Antonio*/Bexar	00998316	210/397-1950	36
Coldspring Intermediate Sch/*Coldspring*/ San Jacinto	02896465	936/653-1152	330
COLDSPRING-OAKHURST CONS ISD/ COLDSPRING/SAN JACINTO	01049401	936/653-1115	330
Coldspring-Oakhurst High Sch/*Coldspring*/ San Jacinto	01049413	936/653-1140	330
Coldwell Elem Sch/*El Paso*/El Paso	01015591	915/236-8525	133
Coleman Elem Sch/*Cleburne*/Johnson	01034901	817/202-2030	247
Coleman Elem Sch/*Coleman*/Coleman	03047942	325/625-3546	76
Coleman Elem Sch/*Coleman*/Coleman	01005833	325/625-2156	76
COLEMAN IND SCH DIST/COLEMAN/ COLEMAN	01005819	325/625-3575	76
Coleman Junior High Sch/*Coleman*/Coleman	03391339	325/625-3593	76
Coleman Junior High Sch/*Waxahachie*/Ellis	12311366	972/923-4790	142
Coles High Sch & Ed Center/*Corp Christi*/ Nueces	03051008	361/878-7380	303
Colin Powell 6th Grade Center/*Little Elm*/ Denton	12168274	972/947-9446	124
Colin Powell Elem Sch/*Grand Prairie*/Dallas	04751536	972/642-3961	107
Colin Powell Elem Sch/*The Woodlands*/ Montgomery	04284545	936/709-1700	291
College & Career Center/*La Joya*/Hidalgo	11449477	956/323-2230	219
College Career & Tech Acad/*Los Fresnos*/ Cameron	12368357	956/254-5296	66
College Career & Tech Academy/*Pharr*/ Hidalgo	11128532	956/784-8515	223
College Career Technology Acad/*El Paso*/ El Paso	04288278	915/236-7700	134
College Hill Elem Sch/*Plainview*/Hale	01021930	806/293-6035	175
College Hills Elem Sch/*College Sta*/Brazos	01001978	979/764-5565	55
College Park Elem Sch/*Deer Park*/Harris	01026411	281/604-4400	198
College Station High Sch/*College Sta*/ Brazos	11823641	979/694-5800	55
COLLEGE STATION IND SCH DIST/ COLLEGE STA/BRAZOS	01001954	979/764-5400	55

School/City/County DISTRICT/CITY/COUNTY	PID	TELEPHONE NUMBER	PAGE
College Station Middle Sch/*College Sta*/ Brazos	01001980	979/764-5545	55
College Street Elem Sch/*Lindale*/Smith	01050694	903/881-4350	337
College View High Sch/*College Sta*/Brazos	04451205	979/764-5540	55
Collegiate Acad Tarrant Clg/*Hurst*/Tarrant	12035897	817/515-6775	353
Collegiate Academy/*Galveston*/Galveston	11557103	409/761-6100	160
Collegiate Academy at Weis/*Galveston*/ Galveston	01019200	409/761-6200	160
Collegiate Academy Middle Sch/*Cedar Hill*/ Dallas	03237795	469/272-2021	97
Collegiate High Sch/*Corp Christi*/Nueces	10912586	361/698-2425	303
Collegiate Prep Academy/*Cedar Hill*/Dallas	12108626	972/293-4502	97
Colleyville Elem Sch/*Colleyville*/Tarrant	01053696	817/305-4940	353
Colleyville Heritage High Sch/*Colleyville*/ Tarrant	04447890	817/305-4700	353
Colleyville Middle Sch/*Colleyville*/Tarrant	01539262	817/305-4900	353
Collier Elem Sch/*San Antonio*/Bexar	00997403	210/989-2950	32
Collins Elem Sch/*El Paso*/El Paso	02043216	915/236-5375	133
Collins Elem Sch/*Houston*/Harris	04868127	713/272-3250	182
Collins Garden Elem Sch/*San Antonio*/Bexar	00999102	210/228-3310	40
Collins Intermediate Sch/*Corsicana*/Navarro	01043469	903/872-3979	299
Collins Intermediate Sch/*The Woodlands*/ Montgomery	03325342	281/298-3800	291
Collins-Parr Elem Sch/*San Diego*/Duval	01014286	361/279-3382	128
Collinsville Elem Sch/*Collinsville*/Grayson	10902036	903/429-3077	166
Collinsville High Sch/*Collinsville*/Grayson	01020285	903/429-6164	166
COLLINSVILLE IND SCH DIST/ COLLINSVILLE/GRAYSON	01020261	903/429-6272	166
Colmesneil Elem Sch/*Colmesneil*/Tyler	01057238	409/837-5757	375
Colmesneil High Sch/*Colmesneil*/Tyler	01057240	409/837-2225	375
COLMESNEIL IND SCH DIST/ COLMESNEIL/TYLER	01057226	409/837-5757	375
Colonial Heights Elem Sch/*Brownfield*/Terry	01055125	806/637-4282	362
Colonial Hills Elem Sch/*San Antonio*/Bexar	00997726	210/407-2400	34
Colonies North Elem Sch/*San Antonio*/Bexar	00998067	210/397-1700	36
Colony Bend Elem Sch/*Sugar Land*/Fort Bend	02126387	281/634-4080	150
Colony Meadows Elem Sch/*Sugar Land*/ Fort Bend	03393181	281/634-4120	150
Colorado Elem Sch/*Colorado City*/Mitchell	01042104	325/728-3471	289
Colorado High Sch/*Colorado City*/Mitchell	01042075	325/728-3424	289
COLORADO IND SCH DIST/COLORADO CITY/ MITCHELL	01042063	325/728-5312	289
Colorado Middle Sch/*Colorado City*/Mitchell	01042087	325/728-2673	289
Colorado River Collegiate Acad/*Bastrop*/ Bastrop	12037144	512/772-7230	23
Colt Elem Sch/*Marble Falls*/Burnet	02845612	830/693-3474	60
COLUMBIA BRAZORIA ISD/WEST COLUMBIA/ BRAZORIA	01001710	979/345-5147	52
Columbia Heights Elem Sch/*San Antonio*/ Bexar	00997415	210/989-3000	32
Columbia High Sch/*West Columbia*/Brazoria	01001746	979/799-1720	52
Columbus Alternative Sch/*Columbus*/Colorado	12313194	979/732-2963	86
Columbus Elem Sch/*Columbus*/Colorado	01006758	979/732-2078	87
Columbus High Sch/*Columbus*/Colorado	01006760	979/732-5746	87
COLUMBUS IND SCH DIST/COLUMBUS/ COLORADO	01006746	979/732-5704	86
Columbus Junior High Sch/*Columbus*/Colorado	01006772	979/732-2891	87
Comal Academy/*New Braunfels*/Comal	12178267	830/221-2950	88
Comal Discipline Center/*New Braunfels*/ Comal	11450921	830/221-2950	88
COMAL IND SCH DIST/NEW BRAUNFELS/ COMAL	01006887	830/221-2000	87
Comanche Early Childhood Ctr/*Comanche*/ Comanche	12173669	325/356-2440	89
Comanche Elem Sch/*Comanche*/Comanche	03004677	325/356-2727	89
Comanche High Sch/*Comanche*/Comanche	01531985	325/356-2581	89
COMANCHE IND SCH DIST/COMANCHE/ COMANCHE	01007051	325/356-2727	89
Comanche Springs Elem Sch/*Fort Worth*/ Tarrant	10902995	817/847-8700	348
Comfort Elem Sch/*Comfort*/Kendall	01035876	830/995-6410	254
Comfort High Sch/*Comfort*/Kendall	01035888	830/995-6430	254
COMFORT IND SCH DIST/COMFORT/ KENDALL	01035864	830/995-6400	254
Comfort Middle Sch/*Comfort*/Kendall	04035174	830/995-6420	254
Commerce Elem Sch/*Commerce*/Hunt	01032393	903/886-3757	236
Commerce High Sch/*Commerce*/Hunt	01032408	903/886-3756	236
COMMERCE INDEPENDENT SCH DIST/ COMMERCE/HUNT	01032381	903/886-3755	236
Commerce Middle Sch/*Commerce*/Hunt	01032410	903/886-3795	236
Commonwealth Elem Sch/*Sugar Land*/Fort Bend	04749789	281/634-5120	150

DISTRICT & SCHOOL TELEPHONE INDEX

Market Data Retrieval

School/City/County DISTRICT/CITY/COUNTY	PID	TELEPHONE NUMBER	PAGE
Communications Arts High Sch/*San Antonio*/Bexar	04368713	210/397-6043	36
Community Christian Sch/*Mineral Wells*/Palo Pinto	02208222	940/328-1333	311
Community Christian Sch/*Orange*/Orange	02208234	409/883-4531	309
Community Christian Sch/*Pampa*/Gray	04835687	806/665-3393	165
Community High Sch/*Nevada*/Collin	03003128	972/843-6500	78
COMMUNITY IND SCH DIST/*NEVADA*/ **COLLIN**	01006124	972/843-8400	78
Community Learning Center/*Humble*/Harris	04370259	281/641-7400	195
Community Montessori Sch/*Georgetown*/Williamson	02785098	512/863-7920	400
Community of Faith Chrn Sch/*El Paso*/El Paso	02744094	915/584-2561	139
Community Sch/*Pasadena*/Harris	12037077	713/740-4048	198
Community Services Sch/*Houston*/Harris	11717509	713/967-5285	191
Como Montessori Sch/*Fort Worth*/Tarrant	01052707	817/815-7200	350
COMO PICKTON CONS IND SD/ **COMO/HOPKINS**	01031466	903/488-3671	231
Como Pickton Sch/*Como*/Hopkins	01031478	903/488-3671	231
Compass Academy Charter Sch/*Odessa*/Ector	11733955	432/272-1836	2
Compass Center/*Jacksonville*/Cherokee	04448997	903/589-3926	73
Compass Rose Academy/*San Antonio*/Bexar	12260676	210/540-9265	2
Comquest Academy/*Tomball*/Harris	04881662	281/516-0611	2
Comstock Elem Sch/*McKinney*/Collin	11820091	469/633-3900	79
COMSTOCK IND SCH DIST/*COMSTOCK*/ **VAL VERDE**	01057898	432/292-4444	379
Comstock Sch/*Comstock*/Val Verde	01057903	432/292-4444	379
Concordia High Sch/*Round Rock*/Williamson	10015372	512/248-2547	400
Concordia Lutheran High Sch/*Tomball*/Harris	02233344	281/351-2547	205
Concordia Lutheran Sch/*San Antonio*/Bexar	00999657	210/479-1477	44
Condit Elem Sch/*Bellaire*/Harris	01024762	713/295-5255	193
Connally Early Childhood Ctr/*Waco*/McLennan	12179895	254/750-7160	279
Connally Early Clg Career Tech/*Waco*/McLennan	12311201	254/296-6700	279
Connally Elem Sch/*Waco*/McLennan	01039690	254/750-7100	279
Connally High Sch/*Waco*/McLennan	01039652	254/296-6700	279
CONNALLY IND SCH DIST/*WACO*/ **MCLENNAN**	01039640	254/296-6460	279
Connally Junior High Sch/*Elm Mott*/McLennan	01039664	254/296-7700	279
Connally Primary Sch/*Elm Mott*/McLennan	05048758	254/296-7600	279
Connection School of Houston/*Cypress*/Harris	12177859	832/544-6031	205
Connell Middle Sch/*San Antonio*/Bexar	00999009	210/438-6835	40
Conroe 9th Grade High Sch/*Conroe*/Montgomery	11920433	936/709-4000	291
Conroe High Sch/*Conroe*/Montgomery	01042453	936/709-5700	291
CONROE IND SCH DIST/*CONROE*/ **MONTGOMERY**	01042439	936/709-7752	291
Constance Hulbert Elem Sch/*El Paso*/El Paso	05231151	915/434-6900	137
Construction Careers Academy/*San Antonio*/Bexar	11448978	210/397-4294	36
Converse Elem Sch/*Converse*/Bexar	00997594	210/945-1210	33
Cook Elem Sch/*Austin*/Travis	01391917	512/414-2510	367
Cook Jr Elem Sch/*Houston*/Harris	01025833	713/636-6040	190
Cook Middle Sch/*Houston*/Harris	02896673	281/897-4400	184
Cooke Elem Sch/*Cleburne*/Johnson	01034949	817/202-2060	247
Cooley Elem Sch/*El Paso*/El Paso	01015606	915/236-8600	133
Coolidge Elem Sch/*Coolidge*/Limestone	01038024	254/786-2206	266
COOLIDGE IND SCH DIST/*COOLIDGE*/ **LIMESTONE**	01038012	254/786-2206	266
Coolidge Jr Sr High Sch/*Coolidge*/Limestone	04914453	254/786-4612	266
Coop Elem Sch/*Houston*/Harris	01025857	713/696-2630	190
Cooper Academy at Navarro/*San Antonio*/Bexar	04455500	210/438-6810	40
Cooper Elem Sch/*Cooper*/Delta	01013115	903/395-2111	120
Cooper Elem Sch/*Garland*/Dallas	01010747	972/675-3010	105
Cooper High Sch/*Abilene*/Taylor	01172709	325/691-1000	360
COOPER IND SCH DIST/*COOPER*/**DELTA**	01013103	903/395-2111	119
Cooper Jr Sr High Sch/*Cooper*/Delta	01013127	903/395-2111	120
Copeland Elem Sch/*Houston*/Harris	04016635	281/856-1400	184
Coppell Classical Academy/*Coppell*/Dallas	11459680	972/393-3077	2
Coppell High Sch/*Coppell*/Dallas	01008342	214/496-6100	98
Coppell HS 9th Grade/*Coppell*/Dallas	12310867	214/496-3800	98
COPPELL IND SCH DIST/*COPPELL*/ **DALLAS**	01008328	214/496-6000	98
Coppell Middle School East/*Coppell*/Dallas	03247099	214/496-6600	98
Coppell Middle School North/*Coppell*/Dallas	04808799	214/496-7100	98
Coppell Middle School West/*Coppell*/Dallas	02109353	214/496-8600	98
Copperas Cove High Sch/*Copperas Cove*/Coryell	01007570	254/547-2534	92
COPPERAS COVE IND SCH DIST/ **COPPERAS COVE/CORYELL**	01007556	254/547-1227	92
Copperas Cove Jr High Sch/*Copperas Cove*/Coryell	01007582	254/547-6959	92
Copperfield Elem Sch/*Austin*/Travis	04803050	512/594-5800	371
Copperfield Elem Sch/*Converse*/Bexar	12034178	210/619-0460	33
Cora Spencer Elem Sch/*Grand Prairie*/Tarrant	10028214	817/299-6680	356
Coram Deo Academy/*Flower Mound*/Denton	10000183	682/237-0232	126
Coram Deo Academy-Collin Cnty/*Plano*/Collin	11825883	469/854-1300	85
Coram Deo Academy-Dallas/*Dallas*/Dallas	11825871	972/385-6410	114
Corey Acad Fine Arts/*Arlington*/Tarrant	02897172	682/867-3900	344
Corina Pena Elem Sch/*Penitas*/Hidalgo	10914405	956/323-2750	219
Corinth Classical Academy/*Corinth*/Denton	12161733	940/497-0059	2
Corinth Elem Sch/*Corinth*/Denton	03391432	940/497-4010	122
Cornelius Elem Sch/*Houston*/Harris	01025144	713/845-7405	192
Cornerstone Academy/*Houston*/Harris	04808921	713/251-1600	201
Cornerstone Christian Academy/*Bryan*/Brazos	11712236	979/694-8200	56
Cornerstone Christian Academy/*Granbury*/Hood	04937625	817/910-8076	231
Cornerstone Christian Academy/*McKinney*/Collin	11227968	972/562-8200	85
Cornerstone Christian Sch/*Abilene*/Taylor	03023398	325/676-8232	361
Cornerstone Christian Sch/*San Angelo*/Tom Green	03025580	325/655-3439	366
Cornerstone Christian Sch/*San Antonio*/Bexar	04953655	210/979-6161	44
Cornerstone Elem Sch/*Sugar Land*/Fort Bend	10912873	281/634-6400	150
Coronado Elem Sch/*Amarillo*/Potter	01047219	806/326-4250	318
Coronado High Sch/*El Paso*/El Paso	01015943	915/236-2000	134
Coronado High Sch/*Lubbock*/Lubbock	01038581	806/219-1100	270
Coronado Middle Sch/*Plainview*/Hale	01021942	806/293-6020	175
Coronado Village Elem Sch/*Universal Cty*/Bexar	00997609	210/945-5110	33
Corpus Christi Catholic Sch/*Houston*/Harris	01027908	713/664-3351	204
Corpus Christi College Prep HS/*Corp Christi*/Nueces	11016109	361/225-4240	2
CORPUS CHRISTI IND SCH DIST/ **CORP CHRISTI/NUECES**	01044176	361/695-7200	303
Corpus Christi Montessori Sch/*Corp Christi*/Nueces	10016766	361/852-0707	2
Corrigan-Camden Elem Sch/*Corrigan*/Polk	01047013	936/398-2501	316
Corrigan-Camden High Sch/*Corrigan*/Polk	01047001	936/398-2543	316
CORRIGAN-CAMDEN IND SCH DIST/ **CORRIGAN/POLK**	01046980	936/398-4040	316
Corrigan-Camden Jr High Sch/*Corrigan*/Polk	03004316	936/398-2962	316
Corsicana Middle Sch/*Corsicana*/Navarro	01043445	430/775-6200	299
Corsicana High Sch/*Corsicana*/Navarro	01043457	903/874-8211	299
CORSICANA IND SCH DIST/*CORSICANA*/ **NAVARRO**	01043421	903/874-7441	299
Coston Elem Sch/*Lufkin*/Angelina	00994956	936/639-3118	18
COTTON CENTER IND SCH DIST/ **COTTON CENTER/HALE**	01021784	806/879-2160	174
Cotton Center Sch/*Cotton Center*/Hale	01021796	806/879-2176	174
Cotton Vly Early College HS/*Fabens*/El Paso	11716505	915/765-2609	135
Cottonwood Creek Elem Sch/*Coppell*/Dallas	04454166	214/496-8300	98
Cottonwood Creek Sch/*Hutto*/Williamson	10020808	512/759-5430	396
Cotulla High Sch/*Cotulla*/La Salle	01037214	830/879-2374	259
COTULLA IND SCH DIST/*COTULLA*/ **LA SALLE**	01037197	830/879-3073	259
Coulson Tough Elem Sch/*Spring*/Montgomery	05093014	281/465-5900	291
Country Day Sch of Arlington/*Arlington*/Tarrant	03016864	817/275-0851	358
Country Place Elem Sch/*Carrollton*/Dallas	01418242	972/968-1400	96
County Line Elem Sch/*New Braunfels*/Comal	02896908	830/627-6610	88
Coupland Elem Sch/*Coupland*/Williamson	01060821	512/856-2422	395
COUPLAND IND SCH DIST/*COUPLAND*/ **WILLIAMSON**	01060819	512/856-2422	395
Cove Charter Academy/*Copperas Cove*/Coryell	11932060	254/238-8231	2
Covenant Academy/*Cypress*/Harris	05347190	281/373-2233	205
Covenant Christian Academy/*Colleyville*/Tarrant	02164705	817/281-4333	358
Covenant Christian Academy/*McAllen*/Hidalgo	04993916	956/686-7886	226
Covenant Christian Sch/*Conroe*/Montgomery	02192439	936/890-8080	295
Covenant Classical Sch/*Fort Worth*/Tarrant	11234985	817/820-0884	358
Covenant Preparatory Sch/*Humble*/Harris	04247016	281/359-1090	205
Covenant Sch/*Dallas*/Dallas	10000573	214/358-5818	114
COVINGTON ISD SCH DIST/*COVINGTON*/ **HILL**	01030826	254/854-2215	227
Covington Middle Sch/*Austin*/Travis	02891130	512/414-3276	369
Covington Sch/*Covington*/Hill	01030838	254/854-2215	227
Cowan Elem Sch/*Austin*/Travis	04917699	512/841-2700	366

Texas School Directory
DISTRICT & SCHOOL TELEPHONE INDEX

School/City/County DISTRICT/CITY/COUNTY	PID	TELEPHONE NUMBER	PAGE
Cox Elem Sch/*Cedar Park*/Williamson	04939960	512/570-6000	397
Coyle Middle Sch/*Rowlett*/Dallas	01010498	972/475-3711	105
Coyote Ridge Elem Sch/*Carrollton*/Denton	10014574	469/713-5994	122
Crain Elem Sch/*Victoria*/Victoria	01058531	361/573-7453	382
Crandall Compass Academy/*Crandall*/Kaufman	04744650	972/427-6100	251
Crandall High Sch/*Crandall*/Kaufman	01035553	972/427-6150	251
CRANDALL IND SCH DIST/**CRANDALL/ KAUFMAN**	01035539	972/427-6000	251
Crandall Middle Sch/*Crandall*/Kaufman	01553165	972/427-6080	251
Crane Elem Sch/*Crane*/Crane	01007829	432/558-1050	93
Crane High Sch/*Crane*/Crane	01007843	432/558-1030	93
CRANE IND SCH DIST/**CRANE/CRANE**	01007817	432/558-1022	93
Crane Middle Sch/*Crane*/Crane	01007831	432/558-1040	93
CRANFILLS GAP ISD SCH DIST/ CRANFILLS GAP/BOSQUE	01000601	254/597-2505	46
Cranfills Gap Sch/*Cranfills Gap*/Bosque	01000625	254/597-2505	46
Cravens Early Childhood Acad/*Houston*/Harris	05090593	281/727-2100	200
Crawford Elem Sch/*Crawford*/McLennan	01039717	254/486-9083	279
Crawford Elem Sch/*Edinburg*/Hidalgo	11558250	956/289-2410	216
Crawford High Sch/*Crawford*/McLennan	01039729	254/486-2381	279
CRAWFORD IND SCH DIST/**CRAWFORD/ MCLENNAN**	01039705	254/486-2381	279
Creedmoor Elem Sch/*Creedmoor*/Travis	10020949	512/386-3950	369
Creek Valley Middle Sch/*Carrollton*/Denton	05010464	469/713-5184	122
Creek View Elem Sch/*College Sta*/Brazos	11446047	979/694-5890	55
Creekside Elem Sch/*Lewisville*/Denton	03325550	469/713-5953	123
Creekside Elem Sch/*Livingston*/Polk	04286103	936/328-2150	317
Creekside Forest Elem Sch/*Spring*/Harris	11449556	281/357-4526	203
Creekside Intermediate Sch/*League City*/Galveston	04015253	281/284-3500	158
Creekside Park Jr High Sch/*The Woodlands*/Harris	12169333	281/357-3282	203
Creekview Elem Sch/*The Woodlands*/Harris	12107854	281/357-3070	203
Creekview High Sch/*Carrollton*/Dallas	04810182	972/968-4800	96
Creekview Middle Sch/*Fort Worth*/Tarrant	05341897	817/237-4261	348
Creekwood Middle Sch/*Kingwood*/Harris	02125503	281/641-4400	195
Creighton Elem Sch/*Conroe*/Montgomery	04948399	936/709-2900	291
Crenshaw Elem & Mid Sch/*Crystal Beach*/Galveston	11563396	409/761-6350	160
Crenshaw Elem Sch/*Channelview*/Harris	02846408	281/457-3080	183
Crespo Elem Sch/*Houston*/Harris	04016104	713/845-7492	189
Crestmont Christian Prep Sch/*Boerne*/Kendall	12363072	210/254-4534	254
Crestview Elem Sch/*Canyon*/Randall	04365503	806/677-2780	321
Crestview Elem Sch/*Graham*/Young	01062116	940/549-6023	406
Crestview Elem Sch/*Live Oak*/Bexar	01379490	210/945-5111	33
Crestview Elem Sch/*Lubbock*/Lubbock	03240675	806/794-3661	269
Crestview Elem Sch/*New Boston*/Bowie	01001071	903/628-6521	49
Crestview Elem Sch/*Waco*/McLennan	01040194	254/776-1704	282
Crisman Sch/*Longview*/Gregg	02233332	903/758-9741	171
Cristo Rey Dallas College Prep/*Dallas*/Dallas	12238881	469/844-7956	114
Cristo Rey Jesuit Clg Prep HS/*Houston*/Harris	11450464	281/501-1298	205
Criswell Elem Sch/*Forney*/Kaufman	02894259	972/564-1609	251
Crockett Aec-Pineywoods/*Crockett*/Houston	04800993	936/546-5972	232
Crockett Charter Elem Sch/*Houston*/Harris	01023902	713/802-4780	191
Crockett Classical Academy/*Crockett*/Houston	11848914	936/546-0487	2
CROCKETT CO CONS COMMON SD/ OZONA/CROCKETT	01007855	325/392-5501	94
Crockett Early Education Sch/*Grand Prairie*/Dallas	12225169	972/262-5353	107
Crockett Elem Sch/*Borger*/Hutchinson	01032666	806/273-1054	237
Crockett Elem Sch/*Bryan*/Brazos	01002051	979/209-2960	55
Crockett Elem Sch/*Crockett*/Houston	01031741	936/544-3758	232
Crockett Elem Sch/*El Paso*/El Paso	01015618	915/236-8675	133
Crockett Elem Sch/*Greenville*/Hunt	01032484	903/457-2684	236
Crockett Elem Sch/*Harlingen*/Cameron	01003811	956/427-3090	65
Crockett Elem Sch/*San Angelo*/Tom Green	01055606	325/947-3925	365
Crockett Elem Sch/*San Marcos*/Hays	01029138	512/393-6400	212
Crockett Elem Sch/*Weatherford*/Parker	01046576	817/598-2811	314
Crockett Elem Sch/*Wichita Falls*/Wichita	01173002	940/235-1140	392
Crockett High Sch/*Austin*/Travis	01056167	512/414-2532	368
Crockett High Sch/*Crockett*/Houston	01553139	936/544-2193	232
CROCKETT IND SCH DIST/**CROCKETT/ HOUSTON**	01031715	936/544-2125	232
Crockett Intermediate Sch/*Paris*/Lamar	01036703	903/737-7450	260
Crockett Junior High Sch/*Crockett*/Houston	01031727	936/544-2125	232
Crockett Middle Sch/*Irving*/Dallas	01011143	972/600-4700	109
Crockett Middle Sch/*Odessa*/Ector	01014640	432/456-0449	130
Crockett Middle Sch/*Pecos*/Reeves	01048392	432/447-7461	323
Cromack Elem Sch/*Brownsville*/Cameron	01003512	956/548-8820	63
Crosby Elem Sch/*Crosby*/Harris	11697698	281/328-9360	183
Crosby Elem Sch/*El Paso*/El Paso	01015773	915/236-5450	133
Crosby Elem Sch/*Forney*/Kaufman	10002648	972/564-7002	251
Crosby High Sch/*Crosby*/Harris	01023158	281/328-9237	183
CROSBY IND SCH DIST/**CROSBY/ HARRIS**	01023134	281/328-9200	183
Crosby Kindergarten Center/*Crosby*/Harris	03321695	281/328-9370	183
Crosby Middle Sch/*Crosby*/Harris	01023160	281/328-9264	183
Crosby Middle Sch/*Hitchcock*/Galveston	01019286	409/316-6542	161
CROSBYTON CONS IND SCH DIST/ CROSBYTON/CROSBY	01007908	806/675-7331	94
Crosbyton Elem Sch/*Crosbyton*/Crosby	01007946	806/675-7331	94
Crosbyton High Sch/*Crosbyton*/Crosby	01007922	806/675-7331	94
Cross Lutheran Sch/*New Braunfels*/Comal	02733863	830/625-3969	89
Cross Oaks Elem Sch/*Crossroads*/Denton	11559151	972/347-7100	121
Cross of Christ Lutheran Sch/*Desoto*/Dallas	03142815	972/223-9586	115
Cross Plains Elem Sch/*Cross Plains*/Callahan	01003366	254/725-6123	62
Cross Plains High Sch/*Cross Plains*/Callahan	01003378	254/725-6121	62
CROSS PLAINS IND SCH DIST/ CROSS PLAINS/CALLAHAN	01003354	254/725-6121	62
Cross Roads Elem Sch/*Malakoff*/Henderson	03390397	903/489-1774	214
Cross Roads High Sch/*Malakoff*/Henderson	01029372	903/489-1275	214
CROSS ROADS IND SCH DIST/ MALAKOFF/HENDERSON	01029360	903/489-2001	213
Cross Roads Junior High Sch/*Malakoff*/Henderson	03390385	903/489-2667	214
Cross Timbers Elem Sch/*Azle*/Tarrant	04813158	817/444-3802	345
Cross Timbers Intermediate Sch/*Arlington*/Tarrant	04149268	817/299-3560	356
Cross Timbers Middle Sch/*Grapevine*/Tarrant	04447905	817/251-5320	353
Crossroads Academy/*Cedar Hill*/Dallas	11231830	972/293-9093	115
Crossroads Alt Tech Sch/*Houston*/Harris	10028252	281/988-3266	182
Crossroads Alternative Center/*San Antonio*/Bexar	12169618	210/622-4670	43
Crossroads Christian Academy/*Fort Worth*/Tarrant	11226768	817/378-0100	358
Crossroads High Sch/*Burleson*/Johnson	04808177	817/245-0500	247
Crossroads High Sch/*Copperas Cove*/Coryell	04452053	254/547-9164	92
Crossroads Sch/*Houston*/Harris	04023353	713/977-1221	205
Crosstimbers Academy/*Weatherford*/Parker	10795027	817/594-6220	2
Crosswinds Accelerated HS/*Grand Prairie*/Dallas	03393387	972/522-2950	107
Crouch Elem Sch/*Grand Prairie*/Tarrant	04456786	682/867-0200	344
Crow Leadership Academy/*Arlington*/Tarrant	01051703	682/867-1850	344
Crowell Elem Sch/*Crowell*/Foard	01018098	940/684-1878	149
Crowell High Sch/*Crowell*/Foard	01018103	940/684-1331	149
CROWELL IND SCH DIST/**CROWELL/ FOARD**	01018086	940/684-1403	149
Crowley High Sch/*Crowley*/Tarrant	01052379	817/297-5810	347
Crowley HS 9th Grade Campus/*Crowley*/Tarrant	04364315	817/297-5845	348
CROWLEY IND SCH DIST/**CROWLEY/ TARRANT**	01052355	817/297-5800	347
Crowley Learning Center/*Crowley*/Tarrant	04755128	817/297-6992	348
Crowley Middle Sch/*Fort Worth*/Tarrant	04035459	817/370-5650	348
Crown of Life Lutheran Sch/*Colleyville*/Tarrant	04836916	817/251-1881	358
Crutchfield Elem Sch/*Sherman*/Grayson	01020649	903/891-6565	167
Cryar Intermediate Sch/*Conroe*/Montgomery	05344667	936/709-7300	291
Crystal City High Sch/*Crystal City*/Zavala	01062336	830/374-2341	407
CRYSTAL CITY IND SCH DIST/ CRYSTAL CITY/ZAVALA	01062295	830/374-2367	407
Cte Early College High Sch/*Weslaco*/Hidalgo	12032649	956/969-6742	225
Cuero High Sch/*Cuero*/De Witt	01013696	361/275-1900	117
CUERO IND SCH DIST/**CUERO/DE WITT**	01013684	361/275-1900	117
Cuero Junior High Sch/*Cuero*/De Witt	01013701	361/275-1900	117
CULBERSON CO ALLAMOORE IND SD/ VAN HORN/CULBERSON	01008029	432/283-2245	95
Cullen Middle Sch/*Houston*/Harris	01024798	713/746-8180	188
Cullender Kindergarten/*Monahans*/Ward	01832234	432/943-5252	385
Culver Elem Sch/*Rosenberg*/Fort Bend	12364131	832/223-5600	153
Cumberland Academy/*Tyler*/Smith	04813445	903/581-2890	2
Cumby Elem Sch/*Cumby*/Hopkins	01857301	903/994-2260	231
Cumby High Sch/*Cumby*/Hopkins	05342736	903/994-2260	231
CUMBY IND SCH DIST/**CUMBY/HOPKINS**	01031492	903/994-2260	231
Cummings Elem Sch/*Houston*/Harris	02201470	281/983-8328	182
Cunae International Sch/*Spring*/Harris	11720776	281/516-3770	205
Cunningham Elem Sch/*Austin*/Travis	01056155	512/414-2067	366

DISTRICT & SCHOOL TELEPHONE INDEX

School/City/County DISTRICT/CITY/COUNTY	PID	TELEPHONE NUMBER	PAGE
Cunningham Elem Sch/*Houston*/Harris	01024774	713/295-5223	193
Cunningham Elem Sch/*Wichita Falls*/Wichita	01173014	940/235-1144	392
Curington Elem Sch/*Boerne*/Kendall	01035852	830/357-4000	254
Curtis Elem Sch/*Beaumont*/Jefferson	01034248	409/617-6050	242
Curtis Elem Sch/*Weatherford*/Parker	03006065	817/598-2838	314
Cushing Elem Sch/*Cushing*/Nacogdoches	01043146	936/326-4234	297
CUSHING IND SCH DIST/**CUSHING**/ **NACOGDOCHES**	01043134	936/326-4890	297
Cushing Jr Sr High Sch/*Cushing*/Nacogdoches	01043158	936/326-4890	297
Cy-Fair High Sch/*Cypress*/Harris	01023249	281/897-4600	184
Cypress Bendadventist ES/*Jefferson*/Marion	02234386	903/665-7402	274
Cypress Cmty Christian Sch/*Houston*/Harris	02164731	281/469-8829	205
Cypress Creek High Sch/*Houston*/Harris	01548407	281/897-4200	184
Cypress Elem Sch/*Cedar Park*/Williamson	03049378	512/570-5400	397
Cypress Falls High Sch/*Houston*/Harris	04016582	281/856-1000	184
Cypress Grove Intermediate Sch/*College Sta*/ Brazos	04282470	979/694-5600	55
Cypress Lakes High Sch/*Katy*/Harris	11077385	281/856-3800	184
Cypress Park High Sch/*Cypress*/Harris	12165296	346/227-6000	184
Cypress Ranch High Sch/*Cypress*/Harris	11077373	281/373-2300	184
Cypress Ridge High Sch/*Houston*/Harris	05026322	281/807-8000	184
Cypress Springs High Sch/*Cypress*/Harris	04751598	281/345-3000	184
Cypress Woods High Sch/*Cypress*/Harris	10025999	281/213-1800	184
CYPRESS-FAIRBANKS IND SCH DIST/ **HOUSTON/HARRIS**	01023184	281/897-4000	183
Cypresswood Elem Sch/*Humble*/Harris	12104395	281/227-3370	180

D

School/City/County	PID	TELEPHONE	PAGE
D A Hulcy Steam Middle Sch/*Dallas*/Dallas	12109462	214/932-7400	99
D C Cannon Elem Sch/*Quinlan*/Hunt	02199607	903/356-1300	237
D D Hachar Elem Sch/*Laredo*/Webb	01059248	956/273-3500	386
D L Rountree Elem Sch/*Allen*/Collin	01005998	972/727-0550	77
D McRae Elem Sch/*Fort Worth*/Tarrant	01052733	817/814-0500	350
D P Morris Elem Sch/*Arlington*/Tarrant	04804377	817/299-7860	356
D'HANIS IND SCH DIST/**D HANIS**/ **MEDINA**	01041162	830/363-7216	283
D'Hanis Sch/*D Hanis*/Medina	01041174	830/363-7216	283
Da Vinci School Science & Arts/*El Paso*/ El Paso	11014125	915/584-4024	2
Daep/*China Spring*/McLennan	12035158	254/836-0676	279
Daep/*Schertz*/Guadalupe	05342920	210/945-6413	173
Daep/*WHT Settlemt*/Tarrant	11935426	817/367-1364	357
Daep Center/*Atlanta*/Cass	04447060	903/799-1044	69
Daffron Elem Sch/*Plano*/Collin	03333791	469/752-0900	82
Daggett Montessori Elem Sch/*Fort Worth*/ Tarrant	04946054	817/814-6300	350
Dahlstrom Middle Sch/*Buda*/Hays	02855796	512/268-8441	211
Dailey Middle Sch/*Austin*/Travis	11556226	512/386-3600	369
Daingerfield High Sch/*Daingerfield*/Morris	01042958	903/645-3968	296
Daingerfield Jr High Sch/*Daingerfield*/ Morris	01042960	903/645-2261	296
DAINGERFIELD-LONE STAR IND SD/ **DAINGERFIELD/MORRIS**	01042946	903/645-2239	296
Dale B Davis Elem Sch/*Carrollton*/Dallas	01418254	972/968-1500	96
Dale Jackson Career Center/*Lewisville*/ Denton	03254145	469/713-5186	123
Dalhart Christian Academy/*Dalhart*/Dallam	04994099	806/244-6482	95
Dalhart Elem Sch/*Dalhart*/Dallam	01008081	806/244-7350	95
Dalhart High Sch/*Dalhart*/Dallam	01008093	806/244-7300	95
DALHART IND SCH DIST/**DALHART**/ **DALLAM**	01008067	806/244-7810	95
Dalhart Intermediate Sch/*Dalhart*/Dallam	02882402	806/244-7380	95
Dalhart Junior High Sch/*Dalhart*/Dallam	01008079	806/244-7825	95
Dallas Academy/*Dallas*/Dallas	01012771	214/324-1481	115
Dallas Christian Academy/*Dallas*/Dallas	03017399	214/528-6327	115
Dallas Christian Sch/*Mesquite*/Dallas	01479820	972/270-5495	115
Dallas Co Jj Aae-Letot Ctr/*Dallas*/Dallas	11571214	214/956-2036	96
Dallas Co Jj Aae-SAU/*Dallas*/Dallas	11571202	214/860-4370	96
Dallas Co Jj CS-Drc Campus/*Dallas*/Dallas	11571197	214/637-6136	96
Dallas Co Jj CS-Main Camp/*Dallas*/Dallas	04893603	214/637-6136	96
Dallas Co Jj CS-Medlock/*Dallas*/Dallas	11571173	972/225-9735	96
Dallas Co Jj CS-Youth Village/*Dallas*/ Dallas	11571185	972/225-9735	96
DALLAS CO SCHOOLS/**DALLAS**/**DALLAS**	02090673	214/944-4545	95
Dallas Environmental Sci Acad/*Dallas*/ Dallas	01009853	972/794-3950	99
DALLAS IND SCH DIST/**DALLAS**/ **DALLAS**	01008354	972/925-3700	98
Dallas International Sch/*Dallas*/Collin	11748015	469/250-0001	85
Dallas International Sch/*Dallas*/Dallas	05162275	972/991-6379	115
Dallas Park Elem Sch/*Fort Worth*/Tarrant	05092565	817/370-5620	348

School/City/County DISTRICT/CITY/COUNTY	PID	TELEPHONE NUMBER	PAGE
Dalton Early Childhood Center/*Uvalde*/ Uvalde	01057836	830/591-4933	378
DAMON IND SCH DIST/**DAMON**/ **BRAZORIA**	01001796	979/742-3457	53
Damon Sch/*Damon*/Brazoria	01001801	979/742-3457	53
Dan D Rogers Elem Sch/*Dallas*/Dallas	01008718	972/794-8800	99
Dan Dipert Career & Tech Ctr/*Arlington*/ Tarrant	12231144	682/867-9500	344
Dan F Long Middle Sch/*Dallas*/Dallas	02128713	972/968-4100	96
Dan J Kubacak Elem Sch/*Santa Fe*/Galveston	04920414	409/925-9600	161
Dan Powell Intermediate Sch/*Fort Worth*/ Tarrant	10012411	817/568-3523	349
Danbury Elem Sch/*Danbury*/Brazoria	01001825	979/922-8787	53
Danbury High Sch/*Danbury*/Brazoria	01001837	979/922-1226	53
DANBURY IND SCH DIST/**DANBURY**/ **BRAZORIA**	01001813	979/922-1218	53
Danbury Middle Sch/*Danbury*/Brazoria	05027015	979/922-1226	53
Danforth Junior High Sch/*Wimberley*/Hays	04744832	512/847-2181	212
Daniel Intermediate Sch/*Duncanville*/Dallas	03048166	972/708-3200	104
Daniel Ramirez Elem Sch/*Pharr*/Hidalgo	02178378	956/354-2880	223
Daniel Singleterry Sr Elem Sch/*Donna*/ Hidalgo	05330317	956/464-1845	215
Daniel Webster Elem Sch/*Dallas*/Dallas	01008720	972/794-6100	99
Daniels Academy of Science and/*Grand Prairie*/ Dallas	01010840	972/264-7803	107
Daniels Elem Sch/*Kerrville*/Kerr	01036131	830/257-2208	256
Danish Elem Sch/*Houston*/Harris	10002143	281/955-4981	184
Danny Jones Middle Sch/*Mansfield*/Tarrant	05347425	682/314-4600	356
Danville Middle Sch/*New Braunfels*/Comal	12307298	830/837-7400	88
DARROUZETT IND SCH DIST/ **DARROUZETT**/**LIPSCOMB**	01038165	806/624-2221	267
Darrouzett Sch/*Darrouzett*/Lipscomb	01038177	806/624-3001	267
Dartmouth Elem Sch/*Richardson*/Dallas	01011662	469/593-8400	112
Darul Arqam Sch/*Houston*/Harris	04993239	713/948-0094	205
Darul Arqam School-North/*Houston*/Harris	11551185	281/583-1984	205
Darwin L Gilmore Elem Sch/*League City*/ Galveston	10004191	281/284-6400	158
Data at Adams MS/*Grand Prairie*/Dallas	01010943	972/262-1934	107
Data Design & Technology Acad/*San Antonio*/ Bexar	11452230	210/356-2237	34
Daugherty Elem Sch/*Garland*/Dallas	01010759	972/926-2530	105
Dave Blair Elem Sch/*Farmers BRNCH*/Dallas	05098363	972/968-1000	96
David Anthony Middle Sch/*Cypress*/Harris	12032314	281/373-5660	184
David Crockett Academy/*San Antonio*/Bexar	00998421	210/738-9785	40
David Crockett Elem Sch/*Baytown*/Harris	02128567	281/420-4645	187
David Crockett Elem Sch/*Corp Christi*/ Nueces	01044310	361/878-2220	303
David Crockett Elem Sch/*Marshall*/Harrison	01028639	903/927-8880	209
David Crockett Middle Sch/*Amarillo*/Potter	01047221	806/326-3300	318
David Crockett Middle Sch/*Richmond*/ Fort Bend	10912859	281/634-6380	150
David E Smith Elem Sch/*Haltom City*/Tarrant	01052056	817/547-1600	346
David Elem Sch/*The Woodlands*/Montgomery	03325354	281/298-4700	291
David G Burnet Elem Sch/*Dallas*/Dallas	01008744	972/794-3000	99
David K Sellars Elem Sch/*Fort Worth*/ Tarrant	01052757	817/815-9200	350
David L Walker Interm Sch/*Fort Worth*/ Tarrant	11562005	817/568-2745	348
David McCall Elem Sch/*Plano*/Collin	10008331	469/752-4500	82
David S Crockett ECC/*Ennis*/Ellis	05035012	972/872-7131	140
David Sanchez Elem Sch/*La Feria*/Cameron	10915265	956/797-8550	65
David Tex Hill Middle Sch/*San Antonio*/ Bexar	12033540	210/356-8000	34
David W Carter High Sch/*Dallas*/Dallas	01008691	214/932-5700	99
Davila Elem Sch/*Houston*/Harris	03336690	713/924-1851	189
Davis 9th Grade Center/*Everman*/Tarrant	11006336	817/568-5280	349
Davis 9th Grade Sch/*Houston*/Harris	11919707	281/873-1800	180
Davis Elem Sch/*Austin*/Travis	04015150	512/414-2580	367
Davis Elem Sch/*Garland*/Dallas	01010503	972/494-8205	105
Davis Elem Sch/*Plano*/Collin	01006394	469/752-1000	82
Davis Elem Sch/*Royse City*/Rockwall	03004586	972/636-9549	326
Davis Middle Sch/*San Antonio*/Bexar	00998768	210/978-7920	40
Davis Senior High Sch/*Houston*/Harris	11821277	281/539-4070	180
Dawson Elem Sch/*Austin*/Travis	01056430	512/414-2070	366
Dawson Elem Sch/*Corp Christi*/Nueces	04754916	361/878-0140	303
DAWSON IND SCH DIST/**DAWSON**/ **NAVARRO**	01043524	254/578-1031	299
DAWSON IND SCH DIST/**WELCH**/**DAWSON**	01012795	806/489-7461	116
Dawson Sch/*Dawson*/Navarro	01043536	254/578-1031	299
Dawson Sch/*Welch*/Dawson	01012812	806/489-7461	117
Dawson-Hillmon Alt Ed Center/*Queen City*/ Cass	04744234	903/796-0774	70

Texas School Directory

DISTRICT & SCHOOL TELEPHONE INDEX

School/City/County DISTRICT/CITY/COUNTY	PID	TELEPHONE NUMBER	PAGE
DayStar Academy/*Castroville*/Medina	11815400	830/931-0808	284
Dayton High Sch/*Dayton*/Liberty	01037795	936/258-2510	265
DAYTON IND SCH DIST/**DAYTON**/ **LIBERTY**	01037771	936/258-2667	265
De Chaumes Elem Sch/*Houston*/Harris	01025869	713/696-2676	190
De Kalb Elem Sch/*De Kalb*/Bowie	01000821	903/667-2328	48
De Kalb High Sch/*De Kalb*/Bowie	01000833	903/667-2422	48
DE KALB IND SCH DIST/**DE KALB**/ **BOWIE**	01000819	903/667-2566	47
De Kalb Middle Sch/*De Kalb*/Bowie	01000845	903/667-2834	48
De La Vina Elem Sch/*Edinburg*/Hidalgo	02856025	956/289-2366	216
De Leon Elem Sch/*De Leon*/Comanche	01007104	254/893-8220	89
De Leon High Sch/*De Leon*/Comanche	01007116	254/938-8240	89
DE LEON IND SCH DIST/**DE LEON**/ **COMANCHE**	01007099	254/893-8210	89
De Zavala Elem Sch/*Channelview*/Harris	01023108	281/452-6008	183
De Zavala Elem Sch/*Fort Worth*/Tarrant	01052771	817/814-5600	350
De Zavala Elem Sch/*Houston*/Harris	01025479	713/924-1888	189
De Zavala Elem Sch/*San Antonio*/Bexar	00999138	210/978-7975	40
De Zavala Elem Sch/*San Marcos*/Hays	02896087	512/393-6250	212
Deady Middle Sch/*Houston*/Harris	01025560	713/845-7411	188
Dean H Krueger Elem Sch/*San Antonio*/Bexar	10009488	210/397-3850	37
Dean Highland Elem Sch/*Waco*/McLennan	01040209	254/752-3751	282
Dean Leaman Junior High Sch/*Fulshear*/ Fort Bend	12165301	832/223-5200	153
Dean Middle Sch/*Houston*/Harris	01023225	713/460-6153	184
Deanna Davenport Elem Sch/*Canutillo*/ El Paso	03325469	915/886-6400	132
Dearing Elem Sch/*Round Rock*/Travis	12033045	512/594-4500	371
Debakey High Sch-Health Prof/*Houston*/ Harris	01385437	713/741-2410	191
Decatur High Sch/*Decatur*/Wise	01061679	940/393-7200	403
DECATUR IND SCH DIST/**DECATUR**/ **WISE**	01061655	940/393-7100	403
Decker Elem Sch/*Austin*/Travis	04866090	512/278-4141	371
Decker Middle Sch/*Austin*/Travis	11397056	512/278-4630	371
Decker Prairie Elem Sch/*Magnolia*/Harris	02202606	281/357-3134	203
Deep Wood Elem Sch/*Round Rock*/Williamson	01541423	512/464-4400	398
Deepwater Elem Sch/*Pasadena*/Harris	01023330	832/668-8300	186
Deepwater Junior High Sch/*Pasadena*/Harris	01023442	832/668-7600	186
Deer Creek Elem Sch/*Cedar Park*/Williamson	05345570	512/570-6300	397
Deer Creek Elem Sch/*Crowley*/Tarrant	01401433	817/297-5880	348
Deer Park Elem Sch/*Deer Park*/Harris	01023354	832/668-8000	186
Deer Park High Sch-N Campus/*Deer Park*/ Harris	01023366	832/668-7300	186
Deer Park High Sch-S Campus/*Deer Park*/ Harris	02203014	832/668-7200	186
DEER PARK IND SCH DIST/**DEER PARK**/ **HARRIS**	01023316	832/668-7000	186
Deer Park Junior High Sch/*Deer Park*/Harris	01023378	832/668-7500	186
Deerpark HS Wolters Campus/*Deer Park*/ Harris	03391224	832/668-7400	186
Deerpark Middle Sch/*Austin*/Williamson	03067784	512/464-6600	398
Deerwood Elem Sch/*Kingwood*/Harris	02848688	281/641-2200	195
Degan Elem Sch/*Lewisville*/Denton	01013438	469/713-5967	123
Del Castillo Elem Sch/*Brownsville*/Cameron	01003536	956/982-2600	63
Del Norte Heights Elem Sch/*El Paso*/El Paso	01016351	915/434-2400	137
Del Rio Freshman Sch/*Del Rio*/Val Verde	02202333	830/778-4400	379
Del Rio High Sch/*Del Rio*/Val Verde	01057965	830/778-4300	379
Del Rio Middle Sch/*Del Rio*/Val Verde	01057977	830/778-4500	379
Del Valle Dist Alt Ed Program/*Austin*/ Travis	12035067	512/386-3180	369
Del Valle Elem Sch/*Del Valle*/Travis	05102914	512/386-3350	369
Del Valle Elem Sch/*El Paso*/El Paso	11713022	915/434-9300	137
Del Valle High Sch/*Del Valle*/Travis	01056791	512/386-3200	369
Del Valle High Sch/*El Paso*/El Paso	03010975	915/434-3000	137
DEL VALLE IND SCH DIST/**DEL VALLE**/ **TRAVIS**	01056789	512/386-3010	369
Del Valle Middle Sch/*Del Valle*/Travis	01056806	512/386-3400	369
Del Valle Middle Sch/*El Paso*/El Paso	01545259	915/434-3300	137
Del Valle Opportunity Center/*Del Valle*/ Travis	03473547	512/386-3300	369
Delay Middle Sch/*Lewisville*/Denton	01013440	469/713-5191	123
Delco Primary Sch/*Austin*/Travis	05098454	512/594-6200	371
DeLeon Elem Sch/*Victoria*/Victoria	02112257	361/788-9553	382
Delia Gonzalez Garcia ES/*Rio Grande Cy*/ Starr	04452352	956/849-8450	341
DELL CITY IND SCH DIST/**DELL CITY**/ **HUDSPETH**	01032147	915/964-2663	234
Dell City Sch/*Dell City*/Hudspeth	01032159	915/964-2663	234
Dell Pickett Elem Sch/*Georgetown*/ Williamson	04034962	512/943-5050	395
Della Icenhower Interm Sch/*Arlington*/ Tarrant	05350068	817/299-2700	356
Dellview Elem Sch/*San Antonio*/Bexar	00997738	210/407-2600	34
Deloras E Thompson Elem Sch/*Houston*/Harris	04452871	281/891-8480	202
Delta Academy/*El Paso*/El Paso	04828543	915/774-0447	133
Democracy Prep Stewart/*San Antonio*/Bexar	00998988	210/438-6875	40
Denison High Sch/*Denison*/Grayson	01020326	903/462-7125	166
DENISON IND SCH DIST/**DENISON**/ **GRAYSON**	01020297	903/462-7000	166
Dennis Miller Elem Sch/*Richardson*/Collin	04366791	469/752-2700	82
Denton Calvary Academy/*Denton*/Denton	05302023	940/320-1944	126
Denton Classical Academy/*Denton*/Denton	12162957	940/565-8333	2
Denton Creek Elem Sch/*Coppell*/Dallas	04808787	214/496-8100	98
Denton Creek Sch/*Roanoke*/Denton	04917845	817/215-0920	125
Denton High Sch/*Denton*/Denton	04011817	940/369-2000	121
DENTON IND SCH DIST/**DENTON**/ **DENTON**	01013220	940/369-0000	120
Denver Alternative Center/*Wichita Falls*/ Wichita	04286921	940/235-1101	392
Denver City High Sch/*Denver City*/Yoakum	01062037	806/592-5950	405
DENVER CITY IND SCH DIST/ **DENVER CITY/YOAKUM**	01062013	806/592-5900	405
Depelchin-Richmond Charter Sch/*Richmond*/ Fort Bend	12100428	713/558-3980	2
Deport Elem Sch/*Deport*/Lamar	01036806	903/652-3325	260
Dequeen Elem Sch/*Port Arthur*/Jefferson	01033763	409/984-8900	243
Deretchin Elem Sch/*The Woodlands*/ Montgomery	10007569	832/592-8700	291
Derry Elem Sch/*Port Isabel*/Cameron	01004073	956/943-0070	66
Desantia Go EC-PK-K Sch/*Houston*/Harris	04805010	281/985-7500	181
Desert Hills Elem Sch/*El Paso*/El Paso	03051345	915/926-4500	132
Desert View Middle Sch/*El Paso*/El Paso	02131071	915/434-5300	137
Desert Wind Elem Sch/*El Paso*/El Paso	05272313	915/937-7800	136
Desertaire Elem Sch/*El Paso*/El Paso	03325495	915/434-6400	137
DeSoto Alt Sch/*Desoto*/Dallas	04749296	972/223-2242	104
DeSoto High Sch/*Desoto*/Dallas	01010266	972/230-0726	104
DESOTO IND SCH DIST/**DESOTO**/ **DALLAS**	01010242	972/223-6666	104
DeSoto Pvt Sch & Day Care Ctr/*Desoto*/ Dallas	02734829	972/223-6450	115
Dessau Elem Sch/*Austin*/Travis	03011656	512/594-4600	371
Dessau Middle Sch/*Austin*/Travis	04920206	512/594-2600	372
Detroit Elem Sch/*Detroit*/Red River	01048184	903/674-3137	322
Detroit High Sch/*Detroit*/Red River	05256864	903/674-2646	322
DETROIT IND SCH DIST/**DETROIT**/ **RED RIVER**	01048172	903/674-6131	322
Detroit Middle Sch/*Detroit*/Red River	01048196	903/674-2646	322
Devers Elem Sch/*Devers*/Liberty	01037836	936/549-7591	265
DEVERS IND SCH DIST/**DEVERS**/ **LIBERTY**	01037824	936/549-7591	265
Devine High Sch/*Devine*/Medina	01041215	830/851-0895	283
DEVINE IND SCH DIST/**DEVINE**/ **MEDINA**	01041198	830/851-0795	283
Devine Intermediate Sch/*Devine*/Medina	03318844	830/851-0495	283
Devine Middle Sch/*Devine*/Medina	01041227	830/851-0695	283
Devonian Elem Sch/*Andrews*/Andrews	00994736	432/524-1950	16
Dew Elem Sch/*Teague*/Freestone	01018440	903/389-2828	156
DEW IND SCH DIST/**TEAGUE**/ **FREESTONE**	01018438	903/389-2828	156
DeWalt Alternative Sch/*La Porte*/Harris	02223870	281/604-6900	198
Deweyville Elem Sch/*Orange*/Newton	01043720	409/746-2731	308
DEWEYVILLE IND SCH DIST/ **ORANGE/NEWTON**	01043718	409/746-2731	308
Deweyville Jr Sr High Sch/*Orange*/Newton	01043732	409/746-2685	308
DeWitt Perry Middle Sch/*Carrollton*/Dallas	01008225	972/968-4400	96
Dezavala Elem Sch/*Midland*/Midland	01041485	432/240-6600	285
Dezavala Envir Sci Acad/*Grand Prairie*/ Dallas	01540015	972/642-0448	107
Diamond Hill Elem Sch/*Fort Worth*/Tarrant	01052783	817/815-0400	350
Diamond Hill-Jarvis High Sch/*Fort Worth*/ Tarrant	01052795	817/815-0000	350
Diane Patrick Elem Sch/*Grand Prairie*/ Tarrant	12105985	682/867-0600	344
Diane Winborn Elem Sch/*Katy*/Harris	02131679	281/237-6650	152
Diaz Junior High Sch/*Hidalgo*/Hidalgo	02202436	956/843-4350	217
Diaz-Villarreal Elem Sch/*Mission*/Hidalgo	04457833	956/323-2470	219
Diboll High Sch/*Diboll*/Angelina	00994839	936/829-5626	17
DIBOLL IND SCH DIST/**DIBOLL**/ **ANGELINA**	00994815	936/829-4718	17
Diboll Junior High Sch/*Diboll*/Angelina	00994841	936/829-5225	17
Diboll Primary Sch/*Diboll*/Angelina	03240314	936/829-4671	17

School Year 2019-2020   800-333-8802   TX-V19

DISTRICT & SCHOOL TELEPHONE INDEX

Market Data Retrieval

School/City/County DISTRICT/CITY/COUNTY	PID	TELEPHONE NUMBER	PAGE
Dickinson Alt Lrng Center/*Dickinson*/Galveston	04747810	281/229-6300	159
Dickinson Elem Sch/*Grand Prairie*/Dallas	02126727	972/641-1664	107
Dickinson High Sch/*Dickinson*/Galveston	01018983	281/229-6400	159
DICKINSON IND SCH DIST/DICKINSON/GALVESTON	01018969	281/229-6000	159
Dillard Spec Achievement Ctr/*Allen*/Collin	04913148	972/727-7163	77
Dilley Early Clg High Sch/*Dilley*/Frio	12171752	830/965-1814	157
Dilley Elem Sch/*Dilley*/Frio	01018581	830/965-1313	157
Dilley High Sch/*Dilley*/Frio	01018593	830/965-1814	157
DILLEY IND SCH DIST/DILLEY/FRIO	01018579	830/965-1912	157
Dillingham Intermediate Sch/*Sherman*/Grayson	01020601	903/891-6495	167
DIME BOX IND SCH DIST/DIME BOX/LEE	01037422	979/884-2324	263
Dime Box Sch/*Dime Box*/Lee	01037446	979/884-3366	263
Dimmitt Alternative Center/*Dimmitt*/Castro	04448636	806/647-5186	71
Dimmitt High Sch/*Dimmitt*/Castro	01004970	806/647-3105	71
DIMMITT IND SCH DIST/DIMMITT/CASTRO	01004968	806/647-3101	71
Dimmitt Middle Sch/*Dimmitt*/Castro	01004994	806/647-3108	71
DIOCESE CORPUS CHRISTI ED OFF/CORP CHRISTI/NUECES	01045170	361/882-6191	306
DIOCESE OF AMARILLO ED OFFICE/AMARILLO/POTTER	01047659	806/383-2243	319
DIOCESE OF AUSTIN ED OFFICE/AUSTIN/TRAVIS	01420568	512/949-2497	372
DIOCESE OF BEAUMONT SCH OFFICE/BEAUMONT/JEFFERSON	01034339	409/924-4322	244
DIOCESE OF BROWNSVILLE ED OFF/SAN JUAN/HIDALGO	01004372	956/784-5051	226
DIOCESE OF DALLAS ED OFFICE/DALLAS/DALLAS	01012367	214/528-2360	113
DIOCESE OF EL PASO ED OFFICE/EL PASO/EL PASO	01016703	915/872-8426	139
DIOCESE OF FORT WORTH ED OFF/FORT WORTH/TARRANT	01054339	817/560-3300	358
DIOCESE OF LAREDO ED OFFICE/LAREDO/WEBB	04938095	956/753-5208	388
DIOCESE OF LUBBOCK ED OFFICE/LUBBOCK/LUBBOCK	02204290	806/795-8283	272
DIOCESE OF SAN ANGELO ED OFF/MIDLAND/TOM GREEN	01055929	432/684-4563	286
DIOCESE OF TYLER ED OFFICE/TYLER/SMITH	03014660	903/534-1077	339
DIOCESE OF VICTORIA ED OFFICE/VICTORIA/VICTORIA	02181727	361/573-0828	382
Dirks-Anderson Sch/*Fort Davis*/Jeff Davis	01033335	432/426-4454	241
Disciplinary Alt Ed Program/*Bryan*/Brazos	04034211	979/209-2752	55
Disciplinary Alt Ed Program/*Deer Park*/Harris	10011792	832/668-7407	186
Disciplinary Alt Ed Program/*Donna*/Hidalgo	04750051	956/464-1954	215
Disciplinary Alt Ed Program/*Weslaco*/Hidalgo	05273472	956/969-6916	225
Discipline Alt Education Pgrm/*Cedar Hill*/Dallas	04918289	972/293-4504	97
Discipline Ed Alternative Sch/*Quinlan*/Hunt	04871203	903/356-1575	237
Dishman Elem Sch/*Beaumont*/Jefferson	04806923	409/617-6250	242
Dishman Elem Sch/*Combes*/Cameron	01003823	956/427-3100	65
Ditto Elem Sch/*Arlington*/Tarrant	01548483	682/867-3100	344
Divide Elem Sch/*Mountain Home*/Kerr	01036026	830/640-3322	255
DIVIDE IND SCH DIST/MOUNTAIN HOME/KERR	01036014	830/640-3322	255
Dixie Elem Sch/*Tyler*/Smith	01050814	903/262-2040	338
Dobie Middle Sch/*Austin*/Travis	01056181	512/414-3270	369
Dobie Primary Sch/*Dallas*/Dallas	01011727	469/593-4100	112
DODD CITY IND SCH DIST/DODD CITY/FANNIN	01017422	903/583-7585	145
Dodd City Sch/*Dodd City*/Fannin	01017434	903/583-7585	145
Dodd Elem Sch/*Wylie*/Collin	04876899	972/429-3440	85
Dodson Primary Sch/*Denver City*/Yoakum	12036009	806/592-5931	405
Doerre Intermediate Sch/*Klein*/Harris	02227187	832/249-5700	197
Dogan Elem Sch/*Houston*/Harris	01025481	713/671-4110	188
Dogwood Elem Sch/*New Caney*/Montgomery	12305707	281/577-2960	293
Dolly F Vogel Intermediate Sch/*Spring*/Montgomery	04948387	832/663-4300	291
Dolores Huerta Elem Sch/*Fort Worth*/Tarrant	05344526	817/814-4400	350
Dolores Linton Elem Sch/*San Antonio*/Bexar	02110120	210/397-0750	37
Dolores W McClatchey Elem Sch/*Midlothian*/Ellis	12172665	469/856-6600	141
Dolph Briscoe Middle Sch/*San Antonio*/Bexar	11552153	210/398-1100	37
Dolphin Terrace Elem Sch/*El Paso*/El Paso	01016363	915/434-6500	137
Domingo Trevino Middle Sch/*Alton*/Hidalgo	11557050	956/323-2810	219
Don Carter Elem Sch/*Richmond*/Fort Bend	12308371	832/223-5500	153
Don Durham Intermediate Sch/*Southlake*/Tarrant	04449458	817/949-5300	347
Don Jeter Elem Sch/*Manvel*/Brazoria	05011729	281/245-3055	51
Don Jose Gallego Elem Sch/*Laredo*/Webb	01059212	956/273-3100	386
Don R Daniel 9th Grade Campus/*Aledo*/Parker	11712042	817/441-4504	312
Don Whitt Elem Sch/*Sachse*/Collin	11434795	972/429-2560	85
Donald Leonetti Elem Sch/*Missouri City*/Fort Bend	12232124	281/327-3190	150
Donald T Shields Elem Sch/*Glenn Heights*/Ellis	02132049	972/617-4799	142
Donna High Sch/*Donna*/Hidalgo	01029578	956/464-1700	215
DONNA IND SCH DIST/DONNA/HIDALGO	01029554	956/464-1600	215
Donna Lewis Elem Sch/*Houston*/Harris	10022478	281/891-8720	202
Donna North High Sch/*Donna*/Hidalgo	11920093	956/464-4190	215
Donna Park Elem Sch/*Hurst*/Tarrant	01053799	817/285-3285	354
Donna Shepard Intermediate Sch/*Mansfield*/Tarrant	04949135	817/299-5940	356
Donna Wernecke Elem Sch/*McAllen*/Hidalgo	10915344	956/928-1063	224
Dooley Elem Sch/*Plano*/Collin	02130895	469/752-1100	82
Dora M Sauceda Middle Sch/*Donna*/Hidalgo	05343522	956/464-1360	215
Dora Romero Elem Sch/*Brownsville*/Cameron	11711581	956/254-5210	66
Dorie Miller Interm Sch/*Ennis*/Ellis	05035000	972/872-3775	140
Doris Cullins-Lake Pointe ES/*Rowlett*/Rockwall	03049304	972/412-3070	325
Doris Miller Middle Sch/*San Marcos*/Hays	04365060	512/393-6660	212
Dorothea Brown Middle Sch/*McAllen*/Hidalgo	01523706	956/632-8700	221
Dorothy Adkins Middle Sch/*Corp Christi*/Nueces	12106551	361/878-3800	303
Dorothy Carlton Center/*Cypress*/Harris	02045379	281/213-1950	184
Dorothy Smith Pullen Elem Sch/*Rockwall*/Rockwall	04846739	972/772-1177	325
Dorothy Thompson Middle Sch/*Progreso*/Hidalgo	02178213	956/565-6539	224
Dorris Jones Elem Sch/*Rockwall*/Rockwall	05100186	972/772-1070	325
DOSS CONSOLIDATED COMMON SD/DOSS/GILLESPIE	01019664	830/669-2411	162
Doss Elem Sch/*Austin*/Travis	01056193	512/414-2365	367
Doss Elem Sch/*Doss*/Gillespie	01019676	830/669-2411	162
Double File Trail Elem Sch/*Round Rock*/Williamson	02893994	512/428-7400	398
Douglas B Bussey Elem Sch/*Houston*/Harris	05274115	281/878-1501	179
Douglas Benold Middle Sch/*Georgetown*/Williamson	04455421	512/943-5090	395
Douglas Elem Sch/*Tyler*/Smith	01050838	903/262-2100	338
Douglas MacArthur High Sch/*Houston*/Harris	01022764	281/985-6330	180
Douglass ECLC/*Sulphur Spgs*/Hopkins	01031650	903/885-4516	232
Douglass Elem Sch/*El Paso*/El Paso	01015955	915/236-8750	133
DOUGLASS IND SCH DIST/DOUGLASS/NACOGDOCHES	01043160	936/569-9804	297
Douglass Sch/*Douglass*/Nacogdoches	01043172	936/569-9804	297
Dove Elem Sch/*Grapevine*/Tarrant	01053701	817/251-5700	353
Dover Elem Sch/*Richardson*/Dallas	01011674	469/593-4200	112
Dowell Elem Sch/*El Paso*/El Paso	01015785	915/236-5525	133
Dowling Elem Sch/*Odessa*/Ector	01014652	432/456-1079	130
Dowling Elem Sch/*Port Arthur*/Jefferson	01033775	409/984-4960	243
Downing Middle Sch/*Flower Mound*/Denton	05091705	469/713-5962	123
Dozier Elem Sch/*Fort Worth*/Tarrant	12166367	817/847-6340	348
Dr Abraham P Cano Fresh Acad/*Harlingen*/Cameron	11920172	956/430-4900	65
Dr AL Draper Intermediate Sch/*Wylie*/Collin	10915708	972/429-3350	85
Dr Alejo Salinas Sch/*Hidalgo*/Hidalgo	04867757	956/843-4250	217
Dr Allan & Carolyn Bird Ed Ctr/*Plano*/Collin	11717987	469/752-2200	82
Dr Americo Paredes Elem Sch/*Mission*/Hidalgo	10028202	956/323-2730	219
Dr Antonio Banuelos Elem Sch/*Baytown*/Harris	12035809	281/420-1230	187
Dr Armando Cuellar Middle Sch/*Weslaco*/Hidalgo	01030632	956/969-6720	225
Dr Bernard Harris Middle Sch/*San Antonio*/Bexar	10023393	210/356-4100	34
Dr Bruce Wood Elem Sch/*Terrell*/Kaufman	04149177	972/563-3750	253
Dr Bryan C Jack Elem Sch/*Tyler*/Smith	10911520	903/262-3260	338
Dr C M Cash Elem Sch/*San Benito*/Cameron	01004188	956/361-6700	67
Dr Carlos Castaneda Elem Sch/*McAllen*/Hidalgo	04948064	956/632-8882	221
Dr David C Walker Elem Sch/*San Antonio*/Bexar	11015480	210/654-4411	42
Dr Dennis Cantu Health Sci Sch/*Laredo*/Webb	11924685	956/795-3874	386
Dr E R Richter Elem Sch/*Dayton*/Liberty	02129937	936/258-7126	265

Texas School Directory

DISTRICT & SCHOOL TELEPHONE INDEX

School/City/County DISTRICT/CITY/COUNTY	PID	TELEPHONE NUMBER	PAGE
Dr Edward Roberson Middle Sch/*Houston*/Harris	11452010	281/891-7700	202
Dr Erwin & Elizabeth Pink ES/*Frisco*/Collin	10004672	469/633-3500	79
Dr Fermin Calderon Elem Sch/*Del Rio*/Val Verde	04145389	830/778-4620	379
Dr Harmon W Kelley Elem Sch/*San Antonio*/Bexar	04813457	210/431-9881	42
Dr Henry Cuellar Elem Sch/*Laredo*/Webb	04875211	956/473-2700	387
Dr Hornedo Middle Sch/*El Paso*/El Paso	04288280	915/236-3300	134
Dr J C Cannaday Elem Sch/*Mesquite*/Dallas	03050963	972/882-5060	111
Dr James D Foster Elem Sch/*Riesel*/McLennan	04914647	254/896-2297	281
Dr James P Terry Middle Sch/*Mesquite*/Dallas	10027337	972/882-5650	111
Dr James Red Duke Elem Sch/*Manvel*/Brazoria	12035926	281/245-3400	51
Dr Javier Saenz Middle Sch/*Penitas*/Hidalgo	05346794	956/323-2830	219
Dr JM Ogle Elem Sch/*McKinney*/Collin	10022387	469/633-3525	79
Dr Joaquin Cigarroa Middle Sch/*Laredo*/Webb	02201183	956/273-6100	386
Dr Joe Bernal Middle Sch/*San Antonio*/Bexar	12033629	210/398-1900	37
Dr Joe Ward Elem Sch/*San Antonio*/Bexar	05273434	210/397-6800	37
Dr Joey Pirrung Elem Sch/*Mesquite*/Dallas	03011929	972/882-7170	111
Dr John D Horn High Sch/*Mesquite*/Dallas	04914817	972/882-5200	111
Dr Johnny T Clark Jr Elem Sch/*Baytown*/Harris	12035794	281/420-7450	187
Dr Kirk Lewis Career & Tech HS/*Houston*/Harris	11927247	713/740-5320	198
Dr Lee Buice Elem Sch/*Odessa*/Ector	12105741	432/456-1339	130
Dr Leo Cigarroa High Sch/*Laredo*/Webb	02201195	956/273-6800	386
Dr Linda Henrie Elem Sch/*Dallas*/Dallas	12108872	972/290-4200	111
Dr Lonnie Green Elem Sch/*Del Rio*/Val Verde	04878263	830/778-4750	379
Dr M L Garza-Gonzalez Chtr Sch/*Corp Christi*/Nueces	04467515	361/881-9988	2
Dr Mae Jones-Clark Elem Sch/*Beaumont*/Jefferson	01033517	409/617-6350	242
Dr Malakoff Elem Sch/*Laredo*/Webb	10007387	956/473-4800	387
Dr Mario Ramirez Elem Sch/*Rio Grande Cy*/Starr	10005925	956/487-4457	340
Dr Martha Mead Elem Sch/*San Antonio*/Bexar	10020676	210/397-1750	37
Dr Nixon Elem Sch/*El Paso*/El Paso	03399862	915/236-5900	133
Dr Pablo Perez Elem Sch/*McAllen*/Hidalgo	10910899	956/971-1125	221
Dr Palmira Mendiola Elem Sch/*Mission*/Hidalgo	11719258	956/323-2420	219
Dr Pat Henderson Elem Sch/*San Antonio*/Bexar	11552139	210/398-1050	37
Dr Paul Saenz Junior High Sch/*San Antonio*/Bexar	11015507	210/431-9881	42
Dr R D Cathey Middle Sch/*McAllen*/Hidalgo	01030010	956/971-4300	221
Dr R E Margo Elem Sch/*Weslaco*/Hidalgo	01030656	956/969-6800	225
Dr Ralph H Poteet High Sch/*Mesquite*/Dallas	02894388	972/882-5300	111
Dr Raul Garza Jr Elem Sch/*San Benito*/Cameron	04768448	956/361-6900	67
Dr S Perez Elem Sch/*Laredo*/Webb	02895083	956/473-3600	387
Dr Shirley J Williamson ES/*Houston*/Harris	10003367	832/386-4000	187
Dr Sue Shook Elem Sch/*El Paso*/El Paso	10911697	915/937-7100	136
Dr Tomas Rivera Elem Sch/*Crystal City*/Zavala	12363785	830/374-8078	407
Dr William Long Elem Sch/*Pharr*/Hidalgo	01030371	956/354-2750	223
Dr Winn Murnin Elem Sch/*San Antonio*/Bexar	10020688	210/397-4550	37
Dr Wright Lassiter Erly Clg HS/*Dallas*/Dallas	04019821	214/860-2356	99
Dragonfly International Sch/*Dripping Spgs*/Hays	11221940	512/858-9780	212
Drane Learning Center/*Corsicana*/Navarro	12306165	903/874-8281	299
Draw Acad Early Learning Ctr/*Houston*/Harris	12163913	713/706-3729	2
Draw Academy/*Houston*/Harris	05099252	713/706-3729	2
Dripping Springs Christ Acad/*Dripping Spgs*/Hays	11829671	512/858-9738	212
Dripping Springs Elem Sch/*Dripping Spgs*/Hays	02845545	512/858-3700	210
Dripping Springs High Sch/*Dripping Spgs*/Hays	01029035	512/858-3100	210
DRIPPING SPRINGS IND SCH DIST/DRIPPING SPGS/HAYS	01029011	512/858-3000	210
Dripping Springs Middle Sch/*Dripping Spgs*/Hays	02845557	512/858-3400	210
DRISCOLL IND SCH DIST/DRISCOLL/NUECES	01044798	361/387-7349	304
Driscoll Middle Sch/*Corp Christi*/Nueces	01044358	361/878-4600	303
Driscoll Middle Sch/*San Antonio*/Bexar	04017768	210/356-3200	34
Driscoll Sch/*Driscoll*/Nueces	01044803	361/387-7349	304
Drs Reed & Mock Elem Sch/*San Juan*/Hidalgo	04840278	956/354-2890	223

School/City/County DISTRICT/CITY/COUNTY	PID	TELEPHONE NUMBER	PAGE
Dubiski Career High Sch/*Grand Prairie*/Dallas	11452668	972/343-7800	107
Dublin Elem Sch/*Dublin*/Erath	01017020	254/445-2577	143
Dublin High Sch/*Dublin*/Erath	01017032	254/445-0362	143
DUBLIN IND SCH DIST/DUBLIN/ERATH	01017018	254/445-3341	143
Dublin Intermediate Sch/*Dublin*/Erath	04865527	254/445-2618	143
Dubose Intermediate Sch/*Alice*/Jim Wells	01034547	361/664-7512	245
Duchesne Acad of Sacred Heart/*Houston*/Harris	01027910	713/468-8211	204
Dudley Magnet Sch/*Victoria*/Victoria	01058476	361/788-9517	382
Dueitt Middle Sch/*Spring*/Harris	02110625	281/891-7800	202
Duff Elem Sch/*Arlington*/Tarrant	01051727	682/867-2000	344
Dulles Elem Sch/*Sugar Land*/Fort Bend	01525998	281/634-5830	150
Dulles High Sch/*Sugar Land*/Fort Bend	01018153	281/634-5600	150
Dulles Middle Sch/*Sugar Land*/Fort Bend	02201456	281/634-5750	150
DUMAS IND SCH DIST/DUMAS/MOORE	01042817	806/935-6461	295
Dumas Intermediate Sch/*Dumas*/Moore	11562988	806/935-6474	295
Dumas Junior High Sch/*Dumas*/Moore	01042831	806/935-4155	295
Dumas Senior High Sch/*Dumas*/Moore	01042843	806/935-4151	295
Dunaway Elem Sch/*Waxahachie*/Ellis	03008788	972/923-4646	142
Dunbar College Prep Academy/*Lubbock*/Lubbock	01038593	806/219-3400	270
Dunbar Early Education Center/*Texarkana*/Bowie	01001241	903/794-8112	50
Dunbar Middle Sch/*Dickinson*/Galveston	01019004	281/229-6600	159
Dunbar Primary Sch/*Lufkin*/Angelina	00995027	936/630-4500	18
Duncanville High Sch/*Duncanville*/Dallas	01010333	972/708-3700	104
Duncanville HS Collegiate Acad/*Duncanville*/Dallas	12368888	972/708-3885	104
DUNCANVILLE IND SCH DIST/DUNCANVILLE/DALLAS	01010292	972/708-2000	104
Dunn Elem Sch/*Arlington*/Tarrant	01051739	682/867-3200	344
Dupre Elem Sch/*Lubbock*/Lubbock	01038608	806/219-5400	270
Durham Elem Sch/*Houston*/Harris	01023976	713/613-2527	191
Durham Middle Sch/*Lewisville*/Denton	05091717	469/713-5963	123
Durkee Elem Sch/*Houston*/Harris	01025871	713/696-2835	190
Duryea Elem Sch/*Katy*/Harris	05346627	281/856-5174	184
Dwight D Eisenhower High Sch/*Houston*/Harris	01022776	281/878-0900	180
Dwight Middle Sch/*San Antonio*/Bexar	00999425	210/977-7300	42
Dyess Elem Sch/*Abilene*/Taylor	01172905	325/690-3795	360

E

School/City/County DISTRICT/CITY/COUNTY	PID	TELEPHONE NUMBER	PAGE
E A Jones Elem Sch/*Missouri City*/Fort Bend	01018141	281/634-4960	150
E A Lawhon Elem Sch/*Pearland*/Brazoria	01001851	281/412-1445	53
E B Comstock Middle Sch/*Dallas*/Dallas	01008689	972/794-1300	99
E B Guerra Elem Sch/*Edinburg*/Hidalgo	04873263	956/289-2530	216
E B Reyna Elem Sch/*Palmview*/Hidalgo	03323423	956/323-2390	220
E C Brice Elem Sch/*Mt Pleasant*/Titus	01055383	903/575-2057	363
E C Mason Elem Sch/*Manvel*/Brazoria	01001447	281/245-2832	51
E D Walker Middle Sch/*Dallas*/Dallas	10023159	972/502-6100	99
E E & Jovita Mireles Elem Sch/*Corp Christi*/Nueces	04913980	361/878-0120	303
E H Gilbert Elem Sch/*San Antonio*/Bexar	00997489	210/989-3050	32
E J Moss Intermediate Sch/*Lindale*/Smith	01050670	903/881-4200	337
E Kolitz Hebrew Language Acad/*San Antonio*/Bexar	11931767	210/302-6900	2
E L Kent Elem Sch/*Carrollton*/Dallas	03248988	972/968-2000	96
E M Daggett Elem Sch/*Fort Worth*/Tarrant	01052745	817/814-5500	350
E M Daggett Middle Sch/*Fort Worth*/Tarrant	01052848	817/814-5200	350
E M Pease Middle Sch/*San Antonio*/Bexar	00998081	210/397-2950	37
E Merle Smith Middle Sch/*Sinton*/San Patricio	01049786	361/364-6840	332
E Ray Elem Sch/*Fort Worth*/Tarrant	01052472	817/568-3545	349
E Rudd Intermediate Sch/*Van Vleck*/Matagorda	02889773	979/245-6561	276
E S McKenzie Elem Sch/*Mesquite*/Dallas	02110065	972/882-5140	111
E T Wrenn Middle Sch/*San Antonio*/Bexar	00997154	210/444-8475	31
E White Elem Sch/*Houston*/Harris	01024657	713/778-3490	193
Eagle Christian Academy/*Waco*/McLennan	02951194	254/772-2122	282
Eagle Heights Christian Acad/*Pearland*/Brazoria	02730237	281/485-6330	54
Eagle Heights Elem Sch/*Fort Worth*/Tarrant	01052018	817/237-4161	345
Eagle Lake Intermediate Sch/*Eagle Lake*/Colorado	01006796	979/234-3531	87
Eagle Lake Primary Sch/*Eagle Lake*/Colorado	01006801	979/234-3531	87
Eagle Mountain Elem Sch/*Fort Worth*/Tarrant	01052410	817/236-7191	348
EAGLE MTN-SAGINAW IND SCH DIST/SAGINAW/TARRANT	01052408	817/232-0880	348
Eagle Pass High Sch/*Eagle Pass*/Maverick	01041083	830/773-2381	276
EAGLE PASS IND SCH DIST/EAGLE PASS/MAVERICK	01041057	830/773-5181	276

DISTRICT & SCHOOL TELEPHONE INDEX

Market Data Retrieval

School/City/County DISTRICT/CITY/COUNTY	PID	TELEPHONE NUMBER	PAGE
Eagle Pass Junior High Sch/*Eagle Pass*/Maverick	01041095	830/758-7037	276
Eagle Ridge Elem Sch/*Keller*/Tarrant	10970942	817/744-6300	355
Eagle Springs Elem Sch/*Humble*/Harris	10028604	281/641-3100	195
Eanes Elem Sch/*Austin*/Travis	01056856	512/732-9100	370
EANES IND SCH DIST/AUSTIN/TRAVIS	01056844	512/732-9000	370
Earl & Hazel Harris Academy/*Houston*/Harris	04867202	281/878-7900	179
Earl & Lottie Wolford Elem Sch/*McKinney*/Collin	04920713	469/302-4700	81
Earl Rudder Middle Sch/*San Antonio*/Bexar	02178366	210/397-5000	37
Earl Slaughter Elem Sch/*McKinney*/Collin	04358122	469/302-6100	81
Early Childhood Campus/*Kerrville*/Kerr	04866569	830/257-1335	256
Early Childhood Center/*Corp Christi*/Nueces	04450469	361/694-9036	304
Early Childhood Center/*Crockett*/Houston	02762010	936/544-2125	232
Early Childhood Center/*Eagle Pass*/Maverick	01877416	830/758-7027	276
Early Childhood Center/*Lindale*/Smith	04945634	903/881-4400	337
Early Childhood Center/*Natalia*/Medina	04273405	830/663-9739	284
Early Childhood Center/*Pasadena*/Harris	11133147	832/668-8390	186
Early Childhood Dev Center/*Corp Christi*/Nueces	04498186	361/825-3366	303
Early Childhood Sch/*Lumberton*/Hardin	04288888	409/923-7695	178
Early Clg High Sch/*Round Rock*/Williamson	12230839	512/704-1650	398
Early College High Sch/*Dallas*/Dallas	10030815	972/968-6200	96
Early College High Sch/*Edcouch*/Hidalgo	12035550	956/262-4731	216
Early College High Sch/*Fort Hood*/Bell	12107050	254/336-0260	27
Early College High Sch/*Harlingen*/Cameron	10910928	956/430-9690	65
Early College High Sch-Midland/*Midland*/Midland	11565681	432/685-4641	285
Early College HS at Timberview/*Arlington*/Tarrant	12305599	682/314-1391	356
Early College Leadership Acad/*Somerset*/Bexar	12109503	855/999-4634	42
Early Elem Sch/*Early*/Brown	01002568	325/646-5511	59
Early High Sch/*Early*/Brown	01002570	325/643-4593	59
EARLY IND SCH DIST/EARLY/BROWN	01002556	325/646-7934	58
Early Learning Ctr North/*Fort Worth*/Tarrant	11558743	817/744-6700	355
Early Learning Ctr South/*Fort Worth*/Tarrant	12232813	817/743-8300	355
Early Middle Sch/*Early*/Brown	02131916	325/643-5665	59
Early Primary Sch/*Early*/Brown	04036659	325/643-9622	59
Earnest O Woods Interm Sch/*Wills Point*/Van Zandt	03049873	903/873-5100	381
East Austin Clg Prep-SW Key/*Austin*/Travis	11540643	512/287-5000	2
East Austin College Prep-MLK/*Austin*/Travis	11849023	512/287-5050	2
East Avenue Primary Sch/*Gonzales*/Gonzales	01019872	830/672-2826	164
East Bernard Elem Sch/*East Bernard*/Wharton	01059585	979/335-7519	389
East Bernard High Sch/*East Bernard*/Wharton	01059597	979/335-7519	389
EAST BERNARD IND SCH DIST/EAST BERNARD/WHARTON	01059573	979/335-7519	389
East Bernard Jr High Sch/*East Bernard*/Wharton	02056184	979/335-7519	389
East Central Development Ctr/*San Antonio*/Bexar	02896910	210/633-3020	31
East Central Heritage Mid Sch/*San Antonio*/Bexar	04748632	210/648-4546	31
East Central High Sch/*San Antonio*/Bexar	00997001	210/649-2951	31
EAST CENTRAL IND SCH DIST/SAN ANTONIO/BEXAR	00996992	210/648-7861	31
East Chambers Elem Sch/*Winnie*/Chambers	04943117	409/296-6100	72
East Chambers High Sch/*Winnie*/Chambers	01005182	409/296-4184	72
EAST CHAMBERS IND SCH DIST/WINNIE/CHAMBERS	01005156	409/296-6100	72
East Chambers Jr High Sch/*Winnie*/Chambers	01005168	409/296-4183	72
East Chambers Primary Sch/*Winnie*/Chambers	01005170	409/296-2980	72
East Cliff Elem Sch/*Portland*/San Patricio	01049554	361/777-4255	331
East Early College High Sch/*Houston*/Harris	10021618	713/847-4809	189
East Elem Sch/*Breckenridge*/Stephens	01051351	254/559-6531	341
East Elem Sch/*Brownwood*/Brown	02199932	325/646-2937	58
East Elem Sch/*Corp Christi*/Nueces	01044138	361/242-5938	303
East Elem Sch/*Hallsville*/Harrison	03322209	903/668-5984	208
East Elem Sch/*Lubbock*/Lubbock	12309208	806/776-2109	271
East Ft Worth Montessori Acad/*Fort Worth*/Tarrant	02774764	817/496-3003	2
East Grand Preparatory Academy/*Dallas*/Dallas	11014876	214/824-4747	2
East Handley Elem Sch/*Fort Worth*/Tarrant	01052836	817/815-4400	350
East Middle Sch/*Desoto*/Dallas	01010254	972/223-0690	104
East Montana Middle Sch/*El Paso*/El Paso	04032110	915/926-5200	132
East Point Elem Sch/*El Paso*/El Paso	01016375	915/434-4500	137
East Ridge Elem Sch/*Sweetwater*/Nolan	01043926	325/235-5282	301
East Side Elem Sch/*Jacksonville*/Cherokee	01005259	903/586-5146	73
East Side Intermediate Sch/*Palacios*/Matagorda	01040936	361/972-2544	275
East Terrell Hills Elem Sch/*San Antonio*/Bexar	00997764	210/407-2800	35
East Texas Christian Academy/*Tyler*/Smith	02233435	903/561-8642	339
East Texas Christian Sch/*Longview*/Gregg	04931657	903/757-7891	171
East Texas Mont Prep Academy/*Longview*/Gregg	12226450	903/803-5000	169
East TX Charter Sch-Chadwick/*Longview*/Gregg	04891576	903/753-9400	2
Eastern Hills Elem Sch/*Fort Worth*/Tarrant	01052898	817/815-4500	350
Eastern Hills High Sch/*Fort Worth*/Tarrant	01052903	817/815-4000	350
Eastern Hills Middle Sch/*Harker HTS*/Bell	03007320	254/336-1100	27
Eastlake High Sch/*El Paso*/El Paso	11552945	915/937-3600	136
Eastland High Sch/*Eastland*/Eastland	01014420	254/631-5000	129
EASTLAND IND SCH DIST/EASTLAND/EASTLAND	01014406	254/631-5120	129
Eastland Middle Sch/*Eastland*/Eastland	01014432	254/631-5040	129
Eastridge Elem Sch/*Amarillo*/Potter	01047233	806/326-4300	318
Eastridge Elem Sch/*Red Oak*/Ellis	04030760	972/617-2266	142
Eastside Elem Sch/*Cleveland*/Liberty	04756005	281/592-0125	265
Eastside Memorial High Sch/*Austin*/Travis	01056002	512/414-5810	368
Eastview High Sch/*Georgetown*/Williamson	04807903	512/943-1800	395
Eastwood Academy/*Houston*/Harris	04943430	713/924-1697	189
Eastwood Heights Elem Sch/*El Paso*/El Paso	01016387	915/434-4600	137
Eastwood High Sch/*El Paso*/El Paso	01016399	915/434-4000	137
Eastwood Knolls Elem Sch/*El Paso*/El Paso	01016416	915/434-4400	137
Eastwood Middle Sch/*El Paso*/El Paso	01016404	915/434-4300	138
Ebby Halliday Elem Sch/*Dallas*/Dallas	11732743	972/925-1800	99
Ecia-Rowlett/*Rowlett*/Dallas	11014424	972/412-8080	2
Ecia-Royse City/*Royse City*/Rockwall	12260688	972/636-2600	2
Ecia-Sunnyvale/*Sunnyvale*/Dallas	11014412	214/628-9152	2
Ector Clg Prep Success Acad/*Odessa*/Ector	01014664	432/456-0479	130
ECTOR CO IND SCH DIST/ODESSA/ECTOR	01014547	432/456-0000	129
Ector Co Youth Alt Center/*Odessa*/Ector	01826194	432/456-0049	130
ECTOR IND SCH DIST/ECTOR/FANNIN	01017458	903/961-2355	146
Ector Sch/*Ector*/Fannin	01857193	903/961-2355	146
Ed Downs Elem Sch/*San Benito*/Cameron	01004190	956/361-6720	67
Ed Franz Elem Sch/*Live Oak*/Bexar	00997647	210/655-6241	33
Ed Rawlinson Middle Sch/*San Antonio*/Bexar	05273410	210/397-4900	37
ED SERVICE CENTER REGION 2/CORP CHRISTI/NUECES	01045003	361/561-8400	306
Ed Vanston Middle Sch/*Mesquite*/Dallas	01011442	972/882-5801	111
Ed White E-STEM Magnet Sch/*El Lago*/Galveston	01018866	281/284-4300	159
Ed Willkie Middle Sch/*Fort Worth*/Tarrant	11449415	817/237-9631	348
Edcouch Elsa High Sch/*Edcouch*/Hidalgo	01029657	956/262-6074	216
EDCOUCH ELSA IND SCH DIST/EDCOUCH/HIDALGO	01029621	956/262-6000	215
Eddie Finley Jr High Sch/*Waxahachie*/Ellis	01015333	972/923-4680	142
Eddy & Debbie Peach Elem Sch/*Arlington*/Tarrant	12170095	682/867-6100	344
EDEN CONS IND SCH DIST/EDEN/CONCHO	01007180	325/869-4121	90
Eden Elem Sch/*Eden*/Concho	01007192	325/869-4121	90
Eden High Sch/*Eden*/Concho	01007207	325/869-4121	90
Edgar Glover Elem Sch/*Missouri City*/Fort Bend	04287949	281/634-4920	150
Edge Middle Sch/*Nevada*/Collin	01006136	972/843-6670	78
Edgemere Elem Sch/*El Paso*/El Paso	01016428	915/434-4700	138
Edgemere Elem Sch/*Plainview*/Hale	01021954	806/293-6040	175
Edgewood Elem Sch/*Edgewood*/Van Zandt	01058127	903/896-4332	380
Edgewood Elem Sch/*Houston*/Harris	01027116	713/251-5600	201
Edgewood Fine Arts Academy/*San Antonio*/Bexar	04954465	210/444-7925	31
Edgewood High Sch/*Edgewood*/Van Zandt	01058139	903/896-4856	380
EDGEWOOD IND SCH DIST/EDGEWOOD/VAN ZANDT	01058115	903/896-4332	380
EDGEWOOD IND SCH DIST/SAN ANTONIO/BEXAR	00997075	210/444-4500	31
Edgewood Intermediate Sch/*Edgewood*/Van Zandt	04913368	903/896-2134	380
Edgewood Middle Sch/*Edgewood*/Van Zandt	02948599	903/896-1530	380
Edinburg Alternative Academy/*Edinburg*/Hidalgo	04429068	956/289-2598	216
Edinburg Classical Academy/*Edinburg*/Hidalgo	11848938	956/720-4361	3
EDINBURG CONS IND SCH DIST/EDINBURG/HIDALGO	01029671	956/289-2300	216
Edinburg High Sch/*Edinburg*/Hidalgo	01029695	956/289-2400	216
Edinburg North High Sch/*Edinburg*/Hidalgo	03392644	956/289-2500	216

Texas School Directory

DISTRICT & SCHOOL TELEPHONE INDEX

School/City/County DISTRICT/CITY/COUNTY	PID	TELEPHONE NUMBER	PAGE
Edinburg South Middle Sch/*Edinburg*/Hidalgo	02110285	956/289-2415	216
Edison High Sch/*San Antonio*/Bexar	00998627	210/738-9720	40
Edison Middle Sch/*Houston*/Harris	01025493	713/924-1800	189
Edith & Ethel Carman Elem Sch/*San Juan*/Hidalgo	03055482	956/354-2700	223
Edmund Cody Elem Sch/*San Antonio*/Bexar	02178342	210/397-1650	37
Edna Alternative Ed/*Edna*/Jackson	12032613	361/782-9051	239
Edna Bigham Mays Elem Sch/*Troy*/Bell	04939037	254/938-0304	30
Edna Elem Sch/*Edna*/Jackson	01033000	361/782-2953	239
Edna High Sch/*Edna*/Jackson	01033024	361/782-5255	239
EDNA IND SCH DIST/**EDNA**/**JACKSON**	01032991	361/782-3573	239
Edna Junior High Sch/*Edna*/Jackson	01033036	361/782-2351	239
Edna Mae Fielder Elem Sch/*Katy*/Harris	04032823	281/237-6450	152
Edna Rowe Elem Sch/*Dallas*/Dallas	01009724	972/749-8800	99
Edris Childres Elliot Elem Sch/*McKinney*/Collin	11103881	469/633-3750	79
Eduardo Mata Elem Sch/*Dallas*/Dallas	04755439	972/749-7500	99
Education Connection/*Killeen*/Bell	11229124	254/526-9299	30
Edward B Cannan Elem Sch/*Willis*/Montgomery	04872180	936/890-8660	294
Edward H Cary Middle Sch/*Dallas*/Dallas	01008756	972/502-7600	99
Edward H White Middle Sch/*San Antonio*/Bexar	00997972	210/356-5900	35
Edward J Briscoe Elem Sch/*Fort Worth*/Tarrant	03253385	817/814-0300	350
Edward K Downing Elem Sch/*Odessa*/Ector	12105727	432/456-1319	130
Edward Titche Elem Sch/*Dallas*/Dallas	01008770	972/794-2100	100
Edwards-Johnson Memorial MS/*Silsbee*/Hardin	01022647	409/980-7870	178
Edwin F Williams Interm Sch/*Perryton*/Ochiltree	01045467	806/435-3436	307
Edwin J Kiest Elem Sch/*Dallas*/Dallas	01008782	972/502-5600	100
Edwin M Wells Middle Sch/*Houston*/Harris	01541368	281/891-7750	202
Effie Morris Elem Sch/*Lake Worth*/Tarrant	01054080	817/306-4260	356
Egly Elem Sch/*Brownsville*/Cameron	01539987	956/548-8850	63
Ehrhardt Elem Sch/*Klein*/Harris	02057554	832/484-6200	197
Ehrhart Sch/*Beaumont*/Jefferson	05010983	409/839-8200	3
Eiland Elem Sch/*Houston*/Harris	04033047	832/484-6900	197
Einstein School Plano/*Plano*/Collin	12362107	972/564-8040	85
Eisenhauer Rd Baptist DC PS/*San Antonio*/Bexar	02869096	210/655-6831	44
Eisenhower 9th Grade Sch/*Houston*/Harris	04805034	281/878-7700	180
Eisenhower Elem Sch/*Edinburg*/Hidalgo	01029815	956/289-2540	216
Eisenhower Elem Sch/*Grand Prairie*/Dallas	01010864	972/262-3717	107
Eisenhower Middle Sch/*San Antonio*/Bexar	00997752	210/356-3500	35
Ekklesia Christian Sch/*Fort Worth*/Tarrant	04993045	817/332-1202	358
El Campo Elem Sch/*Wharton*/Wharton	01059614	979/543-6341	389
EL CAMPO IND SCH DIST/**EL CAMPO**/**WHARTON**	01059602	979/543-6771	389
El Campo Middle Sch/*El Campo*/Wharton	01059626	979/543-6362	389
El Dorado Elem Sch/*San Antonio*/Bexar	00997776	210/407-3000	35
El Dorado High Sch/*El Paso*/El Paso	05272296	915/937-3200	136
El Jardin Elem Sch/*Brownsville*/Cameron	01003550	956/831-6000	63
El Paso Academy East/*El Paso*/El Paso	10015164	915/590-8589	3
El Paso Academy West/*El Paso*/El Paso	04932209	915/845-7997	3
El Paso Adventist Jr Academy/*El Paso*/El Paso	01480104	915/855-7312	139
El Paso Country Day Sch/*El Paso*/El Paso	02950310	915/533-4492	139
El Paso High Sch/*El Paso*/El Paso	01015967	915/236-2500	134
EL PASO IND SCH DIST/**EL PASO**/**EL PASO**	01015450	915/230-2000	132
EL PASO ISD-ELEMENTARY/**EL PASO**/**EL PASO**	11982247	915/230-2485	133
EL PASO ISD-HIGH SCHOOLS/**EL PASO**/**EL PASO**	11982259	915/236-2500	134
EL PASO ISD-MIDDLE SCHOOLS/**EL PASO**/**EL PASO**	11982261	915/230-2213	134
El Paso Jewish Academy/*El Paso*/El Paso	01875303	915/833-0808	139
El Paso Leadership Academy/*El Paso*/El Paso	12113970	915/298-3900	3
El Paso NE Children's Ed Ctr/*El Paso*/El Paso	02869371	915/751-9487	139
Eladio Martinez Learning Ctr/*Dallas*/Dallas	03336925	972/794-6900	100
Elaine S Schlather Interm Sch/*Cibolo*/Guadalupe	11457333	210/619-4300	173
Eldorado Elem Sch/*Eldorado*/Schleicher	01050008	325/853-2514	333
Eldorado High Sch/*Eldorado*/Schleicher	01049994	325/853-2514	333
Eldorado Middle Sch/*Eldorado*/Schleicher	03005889	325/853-2514	333
Eleanor Tinsley Elem Sch/*Houston*/Harris	04951645	713/778-8400	193
Electra Elem Sch/*Electra*/Wichita	01060027	940/432-3815	391
ELECTRA IND SCH DIST/**ELECTRA**/**WICHITA**	01060015	940/495-3683	391
Electra Jr Senior High Sch/*Electra*/Wichita	01060039	940/432-3812	391
Elfida P Chavez Elem Sch/*El Paso*/El Paso	04757310	915/937-8300	136
Elgin Elem School North/*Elgin*/Bastrop	11559034	512/281-3457	24
Elgin High Sch/*Elgin*/Bastrop	00995900	512/281-3438	24
ELGIN IND SCH DIST/**ELGIN**/**BASTROP**	00995883	512/281-3434	24
Elgin Middle Sch/*Elgin*/Bastrop	00995912	512/281-3382	24
Eligio Kika De La Garza Sch/*Mission*/Hidalgo	02949050	956/323-2380	220
Eliot Elem Sch/*Houston*/Harris	01025895	713/671-3670	190
Elisabeth Ney Elem Sch/*Lake Jackson*/Brazoria	01001617	979/730-7190	52
Elisha M Pease Elem Sch/*Dallas*/Dallas	01008794	214/932-3800	100
Elite College Prep Acad-Bowie/*Houston*/Harris	12114003	832/649-2700	3
Elizabeth Smith Elem Sch/*Mansfield*/Tarrant	05347384	817/299-6980	356
Elkhart Elem Sch/*Elkhart*/Anderson	00994449	903/764-2979	15
Elkhart High Sch/*Elkhart*/Anderson	00994451	903/764-5161	15
ELKHART IND SCH DIST/**ELKHART**/**ANDERSON**	00994437	903/764-2952	15
Elkhart Intermediate Sch/*Elkhart*/Anderson	11711842	903/764-8535	15
Elkhart Middle Sch/*Elkhart*/Anderson	04446688	903/764-2459	15
Elkins Elem Sch/*Fort Worth*/Tarrant	03049055	817/237-0805	348
Elkins High Sch/*Missouri City*/Fort Bend	04016350	281/634-2600	150
Ella Barnes Elem Sch/*Corp Christi*/Nueces	04019443	361/878-7330	303
Ella Schorlemmer Elem Sch/*Victoria*/Victoria	11450115	361/788-2860	382
Ellen B Lane Sch/*Houston*/Harris	01022788	281/985-6350	180
Elliot Grant Middle Sch/*Corp Christi*/Nueces	04286488	361/878-3740	303
Elliott Elem Sch/*Irving*/Dallas	01011155	972/600-4300	109
Ellis Elem Sch/*Arlington*/Tarrant	03250709	682/867-7900	344
Ellison High Sch/*Killeen*/Bell	01829366	254/336-0600	27
Elm Creek Elem Sch/*Atascosa*/Bexar	04750738	210/622-4430	43
Elm Grove Elem Sch/*Buda*/Hays	04920244	512/268-8440	211
Elm Grove Elem Sch/*Kingwood*/Harris	01829457	281/641-1700	195
Elma Barrera Elem Sch/*Santa Rosa*/Cameron	03345823	956/636-9870	67
Elmer Bondy Intermediate Sch/*Pasadena*/Harris	04036972	713/740-0430	198
Elmer C Watson High Sch/*Fort Worth*/Tarrant	04747999	817/238-7925	348
Elmore Elem Sch/*Houston*/Harris	11932539	713/672-7466	190
Elodia R Chapa Elem Sch/*Mission*/Hidalgo	04031714	956/323-2400	220
Eloise Japhet Academy/*San Antonio*/Bexar	00998782	210/228-3345	40
Elolf Elem Sch/*Converse*/Bexar	04288101	210/661-1130	33
Eloy Salazar Elem Sch/*Donna*/Hidalgo	05343534	956/464-1977	215
Elrod Elem Sch/*Houston*/Harris	01024786	713/778-3330	193
Elsie Robertson Middle Sch/*Lancaster*/Dallas	01011363	972/218-1660	110
Elsie Shands Elem Sch/*Mesquite*/Dallas	01011454	972/290-4020	111
Elsik 9th Grade Center/*Houston*/Harris	04809107	281/988-3239	182
Elsik High Sch/*Houston*/Harris	01418369	281/988-3150	182
Elva C Lobit Middle Sch/*Dickinson*/Galveston	12167347	281/229-7700	159
Elysian Fields Elem Sch/*Elysian Flds*/Harrison	01028445	903/633-2465	208
Elysian Fields High Sch/*Elysian Flds*/Harrison	01028469	903/633-2455	208
ELYSIAN FIELDS IND SCH DIST/**ELYSIAN FLDS**/**HARRISON**	01028433	903/633-2420	208
Elysian Fields Middle Sch/*Elysian Flds*/Harrison	04363359	903/633-2306	208
Emerson Elem Sch/*Amarillo*/Potter	01047245	806/326-4350	318
Emerson Elem Sch/*Houston*/Harris	01024425	713/917-3630	193
Emerson Elem Sch/*Midland*/Midland	01041502	432/240-6700	285
Emery Elem Sch/*Katy*/Harris	11560497	281/855-9080	184
Emery Weiner Sch/*Houston*/Harris	02848262	832/204-5900	205
Emile Elem Sch/*Bastrop*/Bastrop	00995845	512/772-7620	23
Emiliano Zapata Elem Sch/*Mission*/Hidalgo	05278977	956/323-2700	220
Emma Frey Discip Alt Ed Pgrm/*San Antonio*/Bexar	04788826	210/444-8230	31
Emma Ousley Jr HS/*Arlington*/Tarrant	04757023	682/867-5700	344
Emma Roberson Elem Sch/*Granbury*/Hood	02848482	817/408-4500	230
Emma Vera Elem Sch/*Roma*/Starr	04282200	956/849-4552	341
Emmanuel Christian Sch/*Gonzales*/Gonzales	02191631	830/519-4086	164
Emmett J Conrad High Sch/*Dallas*/Dallas	10023147	972/502-2300	100
Emmott Elem Sch/*Houston*/Harris	02848729	281/897-4500	184
Encinal Elem Sch/*Encinal*/La Salle	01037240	956/948-5324	259
Encino Park Elem Sch/*San Antonio*/Bexar	03250319	210/407-3200	35
Endeavor HS-J F Campbell Ctr/*Channelview*/Harris	04034015	281/457-0086	183
Energized for Excellence ECC/*Houston*/Harris	11077000	281/779-4411	193
Energized for Excellence ES/*Houston*/Harris	04815091	713/773-3600	193
Energized for Excellence MS/*Houston*/Harris	11076991	713/773-3600	193
Energized for STEM Academy HS/*Houston*/Harris	11555428	713/641-1630	193

DISTRICT & SCHOOL TELEPHONE INDEX

Market Data Retrieval

School/City/County DISTRICT/CITY/COUNTY	PID	TELEPHONE NUMBER	PAGE
Energized for STEM Academy MS/*Houston*/Harris	11555416	713/773-3600	193
Energy Institute High Sch/*Houston*/Harris	11920328	713/802-4620	192
Enge-Washington Interm Sch/*Groesbeck*/Limestone	03318155	254/729-4103	267
England Elem Sch/*Austin*/Williamson	11821320	512/704-1200	398
Enhanced Horizons/*Ingram*/Kerr	12163066	830/367-4330	3
Ennis High Sch/*Ennis*/Ellis	01014975	972/872-3500	140
ENNIS IND SCH DIST/ENNIS/ELLIS	01014963	972/872-7000	140
Ennis Junior High Sch/*Ennis*/Ellis	02131538	972/872-3850	140
Enrique Camarena Elem Sch/*Mission*/Hidalgo	10028197	956/323-2720	220
Epic Daep Alt Sch/*Mont Belvieu*/Chambers	10915277	281/576-2221	72
Epiphany Lutheran Sch/*Houston*/Harris	03018630	713/896-1316	205
Epiphany Montessori Sch/*Kingsville*/Kleberg	01036428	361/592-2871	258
Episcopal Day Sch/*Brownsville*/Cameron	01004360	956/542-5231	68
Episcopal High Sch/*Bellaire*/Harris	02950346	713/512-3400	205
Episcopal Sch Dallas-Mid Upper/*Dallas*/Dallas	01875195	214/358-4368	115
Episcopal Sch of Dallas-Lower/*Dallas*/Dallas	10015803	214/353-5818	115
Epps Island Elem Sch/*Houston*/Harris	01026291	832/484-5800	197
ERA IND SCH DIST/ERA/COOKE	01007312	940/665-5961	90
Era Sch/*Era*/Cooke	01007324	940/665-5961	91
Ereckson Middle Sch/*Allen*/Collin	05343144	972/747-3308	77
Erma Nash Elem Sch/*Mansfield*/Tarrant	01054133	817/299-6900	356
Ernesto Serna Elem Sch/*El Paso*/El Paso	04916114	915/937-4800	136
Escandon Elem Sch/*Edinburg*/Hidalgo	01029798	956/289-2545	216
Eschool Prep Virtual Sch/*Texarkana*/Bowie	12362470	903/794-3651	50
Escobar-Rios Elem Sch/*Mission*/Hidalgo	11079333	956/323-8400	222
Escondido Elem Sch/*Converse*/Bexar	12308010	210/662-2250	33
Escontrias Early Childhood Ctr/*El Paso*/El Paso	04487761	915/937-4200	136
Escontrias Elem Sch/*El Paso*/El Paso	01016222	915/937-4100	136
Escuela Montessori-Del Valle/*El Paso*/El Paso	02869424	915/584-9215	139
Esparza Elem Sch/*Edinburg*/Hidalgo	05275195	956/289-2308	216
Esperanza Medrano Elementary/*Dallas*/Dallas	01010058	972/794-3300	100
Esprit International Sch/*The Woodlands*/Montgomery	11903772	281/298-9200	295
Estacado High Sch/*Lubbock*/Lubbock	01038622	806/766-1400	270
Estacado Middle Sch/*Plainview*/Hale	01021966	806/293-6015	175
Estella Stewart Elem Sch/*Huntsville*/Walker	01058725	936/435-6700	383
Estrada Achievement Center/*San Antonio*/Bexar	03056175	210/438-6820	40
Eternity Christian Sch/*Houston*/Harris	04993241	281/999-5107	205
Ethridge Elem Sch/*Garland*/Dallas	01010785	972/675-3020	105
Ethridge Elem Sch/*The Colony*/Denton	03325548	469/713-5954	123
Etoile Acad Charter Sch/*Houston*/Harris	12310673	713/201-5714	3
Etoile Elem Sch/*Etoile*/Nacogdoches	01043201	936/465-9404	297
ETOILE IND SCH DIST/ETOILE/NACOGDOCHES	01043196	936/465-9404	297
Eugenia P Rayzor Elem Sch/*Argyle*/Denton	05096444	940/369-4100	121
Eula Elem Sch/*Clyde*/Callahan	01003392	325/529-3212	63
Eula High Sch/*Clyde*/Callahan	04914685	325/529-3605	63
EULA IND SCH DIST/CLYDE/CALLAHAN	01003380	325/529-3186	63
Eula Middle Sch/*Clyde*/Callahan	04914673	325/529-3605	63
Euless Junior High Sch/*Euless*/Tarrant	01053804	817/354-3340	354
Eustace High Sch/*Eustace*/Henderson	01029401	903/425-5161	214
EUSTACE IND SCH DIST/EUSTACE/HENDERSON	01029384	903/425-5151	214
Eustace Intermediate Sch/*Eustace*/Henderson	04447266	903/425-5181	214
Eustace Middle Sch/*Eustace*/Henderson	01029396	903/425-5171	214
Eustace Primary Sch/*Eustace*/Henderson	03008685	903/425-5191	214
Evadale Elem Jr High Sch/*Evadale*/Jasper	01033220	409/276-1337	240
Evadale High Sch/*Evadale*/Jasper	04032653	409/276-1337	240
EVADALE IND SCH DIST/EVADALE/JASPER	01033218	409/276-1337	240
Evangelina Garza Elem Sch/*Mission*/Hidalgo	11449489	956/323-2350	220
Evans Elem Sch/*Corp Christi*/Nueces	01044360	361/878-2240	303
Evans Middle Sch/*Lubbock*/Lubbock	01038634	806/219-3600	270
Evans Middle Sch/*McKinney*/Collin	05343168	469/302-7100	81
EVANT IND SCH DIST/EVANT/CORYELL	01007635	254/471-3160	92
Evant Sch/*Evant*/Coryell	01007647	254/471-5536	92
Evelyn S Thompson Elem Sch/*Houston*/Harris	01022790	281/878-0333	180
Evelyn Turlington Elem Sch/*Hockley*/Waller	11456975	936/372-0100	384
Everette Lee Degolyer Elem Sch/*Dallas*/Dallas	04282781	972/794-2800	100
Everhart Mgnt Acad/Cltrl Study/*Longview*/Gregg	01857234	903/803-5400	169
Everman Academy High Sch/*Everman*/Tarrant	11929623	817/568-3520	349
EVERMAN IND SCH DIST/FORT WORTH/TARRANT	01052460	817/568-3500	349
Everman Joe C Bean High Sch/*Everman*/Tarrant	01052496	817/568-5200	349
Evers Park Elem Sch/*Denton*/Denton	02845923	940/369-2600	121
Evins Regional Juvenile Ctr/*Edinburg*/Hidalgo	04220525	956/289-5500	3
Evolution Academy-Beaumont/*Beaumont*/Jefferson	11931779	409/239-5553	3
Evolution Academy-Houston/*Spring*/Harris	11932503	281/907-6440	3
Evolution Academy-Richardson/*Richardson*/Dallas	05220982	972/907-3755	3
Excalibur Sch/*Denver City*/Yoakum	04746232	806/592-5950	405
Excel Academy Charter Sch/*Houston*/Harris	12161977	713/222-4577	3
Excel Adventist Academy/*Missouri City*/Fort Bend	11222932	281/835-0770	155
Excel Center-Fort Worth/*Fort Worth*/Tarrant	11704447	817/335-6429	3
Excel High Sch/*Longview*/Gregg	11718759	903/295-6753	170
Excellence In Leadership Acad/*Mission*/Hidalgo	11816387	956/424-9504	3
Excelsior Elem Sch/*Center*/Shelby	01050333	936/598-5866	334
EXCELSIOR IND SCH DIST/CENTER/SHELBY	01050321	936/598-5866	334
Explorations Preparatory Sch/*Flower Mound*/Denton	12314069	972/539-0601	126
Ezzell Elem Sch/*Hallettsville*/Lavaca	01037276	361/798-4448	262
EZZELL IND SCH DIST/HALLETTSVILLE/LAVACA	01037264	361/798-4448	262

F

School/City/County DISTRICT/CITY/COUNTY	PID	TELEPHONE NUMBER	PAGE
F C Weinert Elem Sch/*Seguin*/Guadalupe	01021667	830/401-1241	174
F L Moffett Primary Sch/*Center*/Shelby	03161380	936/598-6266	334
F P Caillet Elem Sch/*Dallas*/Dallas	01008847	972/794-3200	100
F R Scobee Elem Sch/*San Antonio*/Bexar	03010705	210/397-0700	37
Fabens Elem Sch/*Fabens*/El Paso	01016155	915/765-2650	135
Fabens High Sch/*Fabens*/El Paso	01016131	915/765-2620	135
FABENS IND SCH DIST/FABENS/EL PASO	01016129	915/765-2600	135
Fabens Middle Sch/*Fabens*/El Paso	01016143	915/765-2630	135
Fabra Elem Sch/*Boerne*/Kendall	03005841	830/357-4200	254
Fadden-McKeown-Chambliss ES/*Beeville*/Bee	00996083	361/362-6050	25
Fain Elem Sch/*Wichita Falls*/Wichita	01173026	940/235-1148	392
Fair Oaks Ranch Elem Sch/*Fair Oaks*/Kendall	04369729	830/357-4800	254
Fairfield Elem Sch/*Fairfield*/Freestone	01018464	903/389-2148	156
Fairfield High Sch/*Fairfield*/Freestone	01018476	903/389-4177	156
FAIRFIELD IND SCH DIST/FAIRFIELD/FREESTONE	01018452	903/389-2532	156
Fairfield Intermediate Sch/*Fairfield*/Freestone	11719284	903/389-7095	156
Fairfield Junior High Sch/*Fairfield*/Freestone	01018490	903/389-4210	156
Fairhill Sch/*Dallas*/Dallas	02083761	972/233-1026	115
Fairmeadows Elem Sch/*Duncanville*/Dallas	01010345	972/708-2700	105
Fairmont Elem Sch/*Pasadena*/Harris	03323318	832/668-8500	186
Fairmont Junior High Sch/*Pasadena*/Harris	04281567	832/668-7800	186
Fairview Accelerated Sch/*San Angelo*/Tom Green	04247444	325/651-7656	365
Fairview Elem Sch/*Sherman*/Grayson	01020613	903/891-6580	167
Fairview Junior High Sch/*Alvin*/Brazoria	11070973	281/245-3100	51
Fairview-Miss Jewel Elem Sch/*Copperas Cove*/Coryell	01007594	254/547-4212	92
Faith Academy/*Bellville*/Austin	04935146	979/865-1811	22
Faith Academy/*Victoria*/Victoria	02156693	361/573-2484	383
Faith Academy of Marble Falls/*Marble Falls*/Burnet	04933318	830/798-1333	60
Faith Christian Academy/*Brownsville*/Cameron	11222944	956/546-7726	68
Faith Christian Academy/*Dilley*/Frio	04993655	830/965-1324	157
Faith Christian Academy/*El Paso*/El Paso	04994180	915/594-3305	139
Faith Christian Academy/*Palmhurst*/Hidalgo	11934989	956/581-1465	226
Faith Christian Academy/*Pasadena*/Harris	04856679	713/943-9978	205
Faith Christian Academy/*Wharton*/Wharton	10985662	979/531-1000	390
Faith Christian Sch/*Grapevine*/Tarrant	04872403	817/442-9144	358
Faith Family Acad-Waxahachie/*Waxahachie*/Ellis	02161739	972/937-3704	3
Faith Family Academy-Oak Cliff/*Dallas*/Dallas	04850326	214/375-7682	3
Faith Lutheran Sch/*Plano*/Collin	02083735	972/423-7448	85
Faith West Academy/*Katy*/Harris	03417373	281/391-5683	205
Falcon Early College High Sch/*Odessa*/Ector	12105765	432/456-6429	130
Falcon Pass Elem Sch/*Houston*/Galveston	05096884	281/284-6200	159
Falcon Ridge Elem Sch/*Huffman*/Harris	12310594	281/324-7100	195
Falfurrias Elem Sch/*Falfurrias*/Brooks	01002350	361/325-8040	57

Texas School Directory

DISTRICT & SCHOOL TELEPHONE INDEX

School/City/County DISTRICT/CITY/COUNTY	PID	TELEPHONE NUMBER	PAGE
Falfurrias High Sch/*Falfurrias*/Brooks	01002362	361/325-8091	57
Falfurrias Junior High Sch/*Falfurrias*/Brooks	01002374	361/325-8071	57
Fall Creek Elem Sch/*Humble*/Harris	11079618	281/641-3400	195
Fallbrook Academy/*Houston*/Harris	12315362	281/880-1360	3
Falls Career High Sch/*Marble Falls*/Burnet	10020822	830/798-3621	60
Falls City Elem Sch/*Falls City*/Karnes	01035371	830/254-3551	250
Falls City High Sch/*Falls City*/Karnes	01035383	830/254-3551	250
FALLS CITY IND SCH DIST/FALLS CITY/KARNES	01035369	830/254-3551	250
Family Christian Academy/*Dallas*/Dallas	11231799	214/324-4399	115
Family Christian Academy/*Houston*/Harris	05422582	713/455-4483	205
Fannin Elem Sch/*Bryan*/Brazos	01002063	979/209-3800	55
Fannin Elem Sch/*Corsicana*/Navarro	01043471	903/874-3728	299
Fannin Elem Sch/*El Paso*/El Paso	01015797	915/236-5600	133
Fannin Elem Sch/*Midland*/Midland	01041552	432/240-6800	286
Fannin Elem Sch/*San Angelo*/Tom Green	01055682	325/947-3930	365
Fannin Middle Sch/*Grand Prairie*/Dallas	01010931	972/262-8668	107
Fannindel Elem Sch/*Pecan Gap*/Delta	01013153	903/359-6314	120
Fannindel High Sch/*Ladonia*/Delta	01013165	903/367-7251	120
FANNINDEL IND SCH DIST/LADONIA/DELTA	01013141	903/367-7251	120
Fanny Finch Elem Sch/*McKinney*/Collin	01006253	469/302-5600	81
Farias Early Childhood Center/*Houston*/Harris	10003898	713/691-8730	190
Farias Elem Sch/*Alamo*/Hidalgo	01030448	956/354-2760	223
Farine Elem Sch/*Irving*/Dallas	01011129	972/600-7900	109
Farley Middle Sch/*Hutto*/Williamson	11080526	512/759-2050	396
Farmers Branch Elem Sch/*Farmers BRNCH*/Dallas	01008172	972/968-1600	97
Farmersville High Sch/*Farmersville*/Collin	01006150	972/782-7757	78
FARMERSVILLE IND SCH DIST/FARMERSVILLE/COLLIN	01006148	972/782-6601	78
Farmersville Intermediate Sch/*Farmersville*/Collin	04918851	972/782-8108	78
Farmersville Jr High Sch/*Farmersville*/Collin	01006162	972/782-6202	78
Farney Elem Sch/*Cypress*/Harris	04916334	281/373-2850	184
Farrell Elem Sch/*Grand Prairie*/Tarrant	03250711	682/867-0300	344
Farris Early Childhood Center/*Wichita Falls*/Wichita	11444661	940/235-4302	392
Farwell Elem Sch/*Farwell*/Parmer	01046708	806/481-9131	314
Farwell High Sch/*Farwell*/Parmer	01046710	806/481-3351	314
FARWELL IND SCH DIST/FARWELL/PARMER	01046693	806/481-3371	314
Farwell Junior High Sch/*Farwell*/Parmer	01046722	806/481-9260	314
Fasken Elem Sch/*Midland*/Midland	12104369	432/240-8400	286
Father Yermo Elem Sch/*El Paso*/El Paso	01016739	915/533-4693	139
Father Yermo High Sch/*El Paso*/El Paso	01016741	915/533-3185	139
Faubion Elem Sch/*Cedar Park*/Williamson	01061019	512/570-7500	397
Faulk Early Childhood Center/*Aransas Pass*/San Patricio	01049516	361/758-3141	330
Faulk Middle Sch/*Brownsville*/Cameron	01003562	956/548-8500	63
Faustina Academy/*Irving*/Dallas	05331220	972/254-6726	115
Faye Webb Elem Sch/*Corp Christi*/Nueces	10025846	361/878-2740	303
FAYETTEVILLE IND SCH DIST/FAYETTEVILLE/FAYETTE	01017666	979/378-4242	147
Fayetteville Sch/*Fayetteville*/Fayette	01017678	979/378-4242	147
Fehl-Price Elem Sch/*Beaumont*/Jefferson	01034195	409/617-6400	242
Felix Botello Elem Sch/*Dallas*/Dallas	10023094	972/502-4600	100
Felix Morales Elem Sch/*Pasadena*/Harris	04015629	713/740-0664	198
Fellowship Academy/*Kennedale*/Tarrant	11231907	817/483-2400	358
Fellowship Christian Academy/*Dallas*/Dallas	11824994	214/672-9200	115
Fenley PK Center/*San Antonio*/Bexar	12173774	210/921-7000	32
Ferdinand Herff Academy/*San Antonio*/Bexar	00998823	210/228-3330	40
Fern Bluff Elem Sch/*Round Rock*/Williamson	04017794	512/428-2100	398
Ferndell Henry Center for Lrng/*Rosharon*/Fort Bend	11561910	281/327-6000	150
Ferris High Sch/*Ferris*/Ellis	01015060	972/544-3737	140
FERRIS IND SCH DIST/FERRIS/ELLIS	01015034	972/544-3858	140
Ferris Intermediate Sch/*Ferris*/Ellis	03241681	972/544-8662	140
Ferris Junior High Sch/*Ferris*/Ellis	01015058	972/544-2279	140
Field Elem Sch/*Houston*/Harris	01024009	713/867-5190	191
Fields Elem Sch/*San Antonio*/Bexar	12170112	210/398-2150	37
Fields Store Elem Sch/*Waller*/Waller	05035062	936/931-4050	384
Fiest Elem Sch/*Houston*/Harris	03251961	281/463-5838	184
Filemon B Vela Middle Sch/*Brownsville*/Cameron	03325586	956/548-7770	63
Fine Arts Academy/*Fort Worth*/Tarrant	10904852	817/367-5396	357
Finley Elem Sch/*Laredo*/Webb	03007514	956/473-4500	387
Finley-Oates Elem Sch/*Bonham*/Fannin	01017379	903/640-4090	145
Firewheel Christian Academy/*Garland*/Dallas	02207228	972/495-0851	115
First Baptist Acad-Univ City/*Universal Cty*/Bexar	02165084	210/658-5331	44
First Baptist Academy/*Dallas*/Dallas	01480972	972/453-1321	115
First Baptist Academy/*Houston*/Harris	04798924	713/290-2500	205
First Baptist Christian Acad/*Pasadena*/Harris	03371705	281/991-9191	205
First Baptist Christian Sch/*Marble Falls*/Burnet	02731140	830/693-3930	60
First Baptist Church Sch/*Beeville*/Bee	04993693	361/358-4161	26
First Baptist Church Sch/*Brenham*/Washington	02783583	979/836-6411	386
First Baptist Sch/*Brownsville*/Cameron	01479686	956/542-4854	68
First Christian Academy/*Pearland*/Brazoria	11236048	281/760-4201	54
First Christian Academy/*Weslaco*/Hidalgo	11226122	956/968-9030	226
First Christian Day Sch/*Waxahachie*/Ellis	02743088	972/937-1952	143
First Colony Middle Sch/*Sugar Land*/Fort Bend	02857380	281/634-3240	150
Fisher Elem Sch/*Pasadena*/Harris	01026679	713/740-0552	198
Fitzgerald Elem Sch/*Arlington*/Tarrant	02226418	682/867-5300	344
Five Palms Elem Sch/*San Antonio*/Bexar	00999437	210/645-3850	42
Flatonia Elem Sch/*Flatonia*/Fayette	01017707	361/865-2941	147
Flatonia High Sch/*Flatonia*/Fayette	01017719	361/865-2941	147
FLATONIA IND SCH DIST/FLATONIA/FAYETTE	01017692	361/865-2941	147
Fleming Middle Sch/*Houston*/Harris	01025584	713/671-4170	190
Fletcher Elem Sch/*Beaumont*/Jefferson	01033505	409/617-6100	242
Flint Academy/*Arlington*/Tarrant	11225843	817/277-0620	358
Florence Black Elem Sch/*Mesquite*/Dallas	01011478	972/882-7240	111
Florence Campbell Sch/*League City*/Galveston	12365642	281/284-6600	159
Florence Elem Sch/*Florence*/Williamson	01060845	254/793-2497	395
Florence Elem Sch/*Southlake*/Tarrant	01538684	817/744-4700	355
Florence High Sch/*Florence*/Williamson	01060857	254/793-2495	395
Florence Hill Elem Sch/*Grand Prairie*/Dallas	01010876	972/264-0802	107
FLORENCE IND SCH DIST/FLORENCE/WILLIAMSON	01060833	254/793-2850	395
Florence J Scott Elem Sch/*Roma*/Starr	01051246	956/849-1175	341
Florence Middle Sch/*Florence*/Williamson	03472414	254/793-2504	395
Flores Elem Sch/*Uvalde*/Uvalde	01057824	830/591-2976	378
Flores-Zapata Elem Sch/*Edinburg*/Hidalgo	11558248	956/289-2445	216
Floresville Alternative Ctr/*Floresville*/Wilson	04363244	830/393-5368	400
Floresville High Sch/*Floresville*/Wilson	01061277	830/393-5370	400
FLORESVILLE IND SCH DIST/FLORESVILLE/WILSON	01061265	830/393-5300	400
Floresville Middle Sch/*Floresville*/Wilson	01061291	830/393-5350	400
Floresville North Elem Sch/*Floresville*/Wilson	01061306	830/393-5310	400
Floresville South Elem Sch/*Floresville*/Wilson	03050705	830/393-5325	400
Flossie Floyd Green Elem Sch/*Allen*/Collin	04356411	972/727-0370	77
Flour Bluff Elem Sch/*Corp Christi*/Nueces	01044827	361/694-9500	304
Flour Bluff High Sch/*Corp Christi*/Nueces	01044839	361/694-9100	304
FLOUR BLUFF IND SCH DIST/CORP CHRISTI/NUECES	01044815	361/694-9000	304
Flour Bluff Interm Sch/*Corp Christi*/Nueces	01044841	361/694-9400	304
Flour Bluff Junior High Sch/*Corp Christi*/Nueces	01044853	361/694-9300	304
Flour Bluff Primary Sch/*Corp Christi*/Nueces	01420544	361/694-9400	305
Flower Mound 9th Grade Center/*Flower Mound*/Denton	12033942	469/713-5999	123
Flower Mound Elem Sch/*Flower Mound*/Denton	02857433	469/713-5955	123
Flower Mound High Sch/*Flower Mound*/Denton	04850936	469/713-5192	123
Floyd Hoffman Middle Sch/*Houston*/Harris	01399749	713/613-7670	181
Floydada High Sch/*Floydada*/Floyd	01017991	806/983-2340	148
FLOYDADA IND SCH DIST/FLOYDADA/FLOYD	01017977	806/983-3498	148
Focus Academy/*Sugar Land*/Fort Bend	12230671	281/240-0663	155
Foerster Elem Sch/*Houston*/Harris	01024803	713/726-3604	188
Folks Middle Sch/*San Antonio*/Bexar	11918193	210/398-1600	37
FOLLETT IND SCH DIST/FOLLETT/LIPSCOMB	01038191	806/653-2301	267
Follett Sch/*Follett*/Lipscomb	01038206	806/653-2301	268
Folsom Elem Sch/*Prosper*/Collin	01006564	469/219-2110	84
Fondren Elem Sch/*Houston*/Harris	01025194	713/726-3611	188
Fondren Middle Sch/*Houston*/Harris	01024815	713/778-3360	193
Fonville Middle Sch/*Houston*/Harris	01025912	713/696-2825	190
Fonwood Early Childhood Center/*Houston*/Harris	11931066	713/633-0781	190
Ford Elem Sch/*Spring*/Montgomery	01829495	832/592-5700	291

School Year 2019-2020   800-333-8802   TX-V25

DISTRICT & SCHOOL TELEPHONE INDEX

Market Data Retrieval

School/City/County DISTRICT/CITY/COUNTY	PID	TELEPHONE NUMBER	PAGE
Ford High Sch/*Quinlan*/Hunt	01032599	903/356-1600	237
Forest Brook Middle Sch/*Houston*/Harris	11563140	713/631-7720	188
Forest Creek Elem Sch/*Round Rock*/ Williamson	04452338	512/464-5350	398
Forest Hill Elem Sch/*Amarillo*/Potter	01047269	806/326-4400	318
Forest Ln Acad of Arts & Comm/*Dallas*/ Dallas	04850900	469/593-1850	112
Forest Meadow Jr High Sch/*Dallas*/Dallas	01011686	469/593-1500	112
Forest North Elem Sch/*Austin*/Williamson	01541435	512/464-6750	398
Forest Oak Middle Sch/*Fort Worth*/Tarrant	01052927	817/815-8200	350
Forest Park Middle Sch/*Longview*/Gregg	01021019	903/446-2510	170
Forest Ridge Elem Sch/*College Sta*/Brazos	10012318	979/694-5801	55
Forest Trail Elem Sch/*Austin*/Travis	02222400	512/732-9160	370
Forest Vista Elem Sch/*Flower Mound*/Denton	04757229	469/713-5194	123
FORESTBURG IND SCH DIST/ **FORESTBURG/MONTAGUE**	01042257	940/964-2323	290
Forestburg Sch/*Forestburg*/Montague	01042269	940/964-2323	290
Forester Elem Sch/*San Antonio*/Bexar	11104108	210/397-0200	37
Forestridge Elem Sch/*Dallas*/Dallas	01011698	469/593-8500	112
Forestwood Middle Sch/*Flower Mound*/Denton	04036063	469/713-5972	123
Forman Elem Sch/*Plano*/Collin	01006411	469/752-1200	82
Forney Academic Center/*Forney*/Kaufman	04750063	469/762-4350	252
Forney High Sch/*Forney*/Kaufman	01035591	469/762-4200	252
FORNEY IND SCH DIST/FORNEY/ **KAUFMAN**	01035565	972/564-4055	251
Forsan Elbow Elem Sch/*Forsan*/Howard	01032109	432/457-0091	234
FORSAN IND SCH DIST/FORSAN/ **HOWARD**	01032094	432/457-2223	234
Forsan Jr Sr High Sch/*Forsan*/Howard	01032111	432/457-2223	234
Fort Bend Alternative Sch/*Rosenberg*/ Fort Bend	04478306	281/239-3431	153
Fort Bend Baptist Academy ES/*Sugar Land*/ Fort Bend	04993538	281/263-9100	155
Fort Bend Christian Academy MS/*Sugar Land*/ Fort Bend	05291955	281/263-9191	155
Fort Bend Christian Academy-HS/*Sugar Land*/ Fort Bend	05291967	281/263-9175	155
FORT DAVIS IND SCH DIST/ **FORT DAVIS/JEFF DAVIS**	01033323	432/426-4440	241
Fort Davis Jr Sr High Sch/*Fort Davis*/ Jeff Davis	01033347	432/426-4444	241
Fort Settlement Middle Sch/*Sugar Land*/ Fort Bend	04947149	281/634-6440	150
Fort Worth Academy/*Fort Worth*/Tarrant	02233459	817/370-1191	358
Fort Worth Christian Sch/*N Richlnd Hls*/ Tarrant	01481005	817/281-6504	358
Fossil Hill Middle Sch/*Fort Worth*/Tarrant	03047071	817/744-3050	355
Fossil Ridge High Sch/*Fort Worth*/Tarrant	04366662	817/744-1700	355
Foster Elem Sch/*Arlington*/Tarrant	01051753	682/867-5350	344
Foster Elem Sch/*Houston*/Harris	01024827	713/746-8260	192
Foster Elem Sch/*Kingwood*/Harris	01026162	281/641-1400	195
Foster Middle Sch/*Longview*/Gregg	01021033	903/446-2710	170
Foster Village Elem Sch/*N Richlnd Hls*/ Tarrant	02110900	817/547-3100	346
Foundation School for Autism/*San Antonio*/ Bexar	11832563	210/402-0253	3
Founders Christian Sch/*Spring*/Harris	12368228	281/602-8006	206
Founders Classical Acad Flower/*Flower Mound*/ Denton	12161745	972/899-2521	3
Founders Classical Acad Frisco/*Frisco*/Hunt	12363735	972/532-0952	3
Founders Classical Acad Leandr/*Leander*/ Williamson	12042216	512/259-0103	3
Founders Classical Acad Lwsvll/*Lewisville*/ Denton	11662980	469/464-3415	3
Founders Classical Acad Mesq/*Mesquite*/ Dallas	12161757	469/453-0977	3
Founders Classical Acad Schrtz/*Schertz*/ Guadalupe	12173554	210/510-2618	3
Four Points Middle Sch/*Austin*/Williamson	11557036	512/570-3700	397
Fowler Elem Sch/*Killeen*/Bell	00996485	254/336-1760	27
Fowler Elem Sch/*Wichita Falls*/Wichita	01173040	940/235-1152	392
Fox Run Elem Sch/*San Antonio*/Bexar	03329025	210/407-3400	35
Fox Technical High Sch/*San Antonio*/Bexar	00998483	210/738-9730	40
Foy H Moody High Sch/*Corp Christi*/Nueces	01044396	361/878-7340	303
Frances Corprew Elem Sch/*Mt Pleasant*/Titus	01055395	903/575-2050	364
Frances M Rhodes Elem Sch/*San Antonio*/ Bexar	05097747	210/397-4000	37
Frances Norton Elem Sch/*Allen*/Collin	04749014	972/396-6918	77
Francis R Scobee Middle Sch/*San Antonio*/ Bexar	04868218	210/645-7500	43
Francisca Alvarez Elem Sch/*McAllen*/Hidalgo	01029994	956/971-4471	221
Francisco Barrientes Mid Sch/*Edinburg*/ Hidalgo	10909981	956/289-2430	216
Francisco Farias Elem Sch/*Laredo*/Webb	01059262	956/273-3400	386
Francisco Medrano Middle Sch/*Dallas*/Dallas	11130315	972/925-1300	100
Francisco S Lara Academy/*Laredo*/Webb	04752619	956/273-7900	386
Francone Elem Sch/*Houston*/Harris	02045393	281/897-4512	184
Frank & Sue McBee Elem Sch/*Austin*/Travis	04917675	512/841-2500	367
Frank B Agnew Middle Sch/*Mesquite*/Dallas	01011492	972/882-5750	111
Frank D Moates Elem Sch/*Glenn Heights*/ Dallas	03047100	972/230-2881	104
Frank Elem Sch/*Klein*/Harris	10910198	832/375-7000	197
Frank Guzick Elem Sch/*Dallas*/Dallas	10023173	972/502-3900	100
Frank L Madla Accel Coll Acad/*San Antonio*/ Bexar	04802630	210/533-3655	3
Frank L Madla Early College HS/*San Antonio*/ Bexar	12163016	210/486-3686	3
Frank M Tejeda Academy/*San Antonio*/Bexar	04035112	210/989-4900	32
Frank Macias Elem Sch/*Horizon City*/El Paso	04931906	915/926-4600	132
Frank Madla Elem Sch/*San Antonio*/Bexar	00999499	210/645-3800	42
Frank Newman Middle Sch/*Cotulla*/La Salle	01037226	830/879-4376	259
Frank Roberts Elem Sch/*San Benito*/Cameron	01004205	956/361-6740	67
Frank Seale Middle Sch/*Midlothian*/Ellis	02896398	972/775-6145	141
Frank Stone Middle Sch/*Paris*/Lamar	01036650	903/737-2041	259
Frank Tejeda Middle Sch/*San Antonio*/Bexar	04946341	210/356-5600	35
Frankford Middle Sch/*Dallas*/Collin	04811497	469/752-5200	82
Franklin D Roosevelt High Sch/*Dallas*/ Dallas	01008861	972/925-6800	100
Franklin Elem Sch/*Hillsboro*/Hill	01172474	254/582-4130	227
Franklin Elem Sch/*Houston*/Harris	01025508	713/924-1820	189
Franklin Elem Sch/*San Antonio*/Bexar	00998407	210/738-9790	40
Franklin Elem Sch/*Wichita Falls*/Wichita	01172967	940/235-1156	392
Franklin High Sch/*El Paso*/El Paso	04035681	915/236-2200	134
Franklin High Sch/*Franklin*/Robertson	01048627	979/828-7100	325
Franklin HS 9th Grade Center/*El Paso*/ El Paso	11982273	915/236-2400	134
FRANKLIN IND SCH DIST/FRANKLIN/ **ROBERTSON**	01048615	979/828-7000	324
Franklin Middle Sch/*Franklin*/Robertson	03391262	979/828-7200	325
Franklin Monroe Gilbert ES/*Irving*/Dallas	04451176	972/600-0400	109
Frankston Elem Sch/*Frankston*/Anderson	04272528	903/876-2214	15
Frankston High Sch/*Frankston*/Anderson	00994487	903/876-3219	15
FRANKSTON IND SCH DIST/FRANKSTON/ **ANDERSON**	00994463	903/876-2556	15
Frankston Middle Sch/*Frankston*/Anderson	04272530	903/876-2215	15
Franz Elem Sch/*Katy*/Harris	05344318	281/237-8600	152
Frassati Catholic High Sch/*Spring*/Harris	12115693	832/616-3217	204
Frazier Elem Sch/*Burleson*/Johnson	01034822	817/245-3000	247
Frazier Elem Sch/*Houston*/Harris	01387318	713/740-0560	199
Frazier Elem Sch/*Houston*/Harris	02177946	713/896-3475	184
Fred and Patti Shafer ES/*Katy*/Harris	11822049	281/234-1900	152
Fred Booth Elem Sch/*San Benito*/Cameron	01004217	956/361-6860	67
Fred Douglass Early Chldhd Ctr/*Sherman*/ Grayson	01418345	903/891-6545	167
Fred Douglass Elem Sch/*Jacksonville*/ Cherokee	02226860	903/586-6519	73
Fred Elem Sch/*Fred*/Tyler	01057290	409/429-3240	375
Fred H Tally Elem Sch/*Kerrville*/Kerr	05100368	830/257-2222	256
Fred McWhorter Elem Sch/*Mesquite*/Dallas	01011466	972/882-7020	111
Fred Moore High Sch/*Denton*/Denton	03473535	940/369-4000	121
Fred R Sanders Elem Sch/*Corp Christi*/ Nueces	01044645	361/878-2820	303
Fred Roberts Middle Sch/*Houston*/Harris	12160739	713/740-5390	199
Fred W Edwards Academy/*Temple*/Bell	12035770	254/215-6944	29
Fredda Nottingham Alt Educ Ctr/*Dayton*/ Liberty	12168509	936/257-4100	265
Freddy Gonzalez Elem Sch/*Edinburg*/Hidalgo	01418498	956/289-2520	216
Frederick A Douglass Lrng Acad/*Cleveland*/ Liberty	11078602	281/592-7595	265
Frederick Douglass Academy/*San Antonio*/ Bexar	00998770	210/228-3315	40
Frederick Douglass Elem Sch/*Dallas*/Dallas	03247805	972/794-1400	100
Fredericksburg Elem Sch/*Fredericksbrg*/ Gillespie	01019717	830/997-9595	163
Fredericksburg High Sch/*Fredericksbrg*/ Gillespie	01019705	830/997-7551	163
FREDERICKSBURG IND SCH DIST/ **FREDERICKSBRG/GILLESPIE**	01019688	830/997-9551	162
Fredericksburg Middle Sch/*Fredericksbrg*/ Gillespie	01857222	830/997-7657	163
Fredericksburg Primary Sch/*Fredericksbrg*/ Gillespie	01401419	830/997-7421	163
Fredonia Elem Sch/*Nacogdoches*/Nacogdoches	01043304	936/569-5080	298

Texas School Directory

DISTRICT & SCHOOL TELEPHONE INDEX

School/City/County DISTRICT/CITY/COUNTY	PID	TELEPHONE NUMBER	PAGE
Fredonia Hill Baptist Academy/*Nacogdoches*/ Nacogdoches	01875511	936/564-4472	298
Freedom Elem Sch/*Keller*/Tarrant	05090804	817/744-4800	355
Freedom Elem Sch/*Laredo*/Webb	12231455	956/473-1600	387
Freedom Elem Sch/*San Antonio*/Bexar	10012095	210/882-1603	43
Freeman Elem Sch/*Garland*/Dallas	01010400	972/494-8371	105
Freeman Elem Sch/*Houston*/Harris	01026681	713/740-0568	199
Freeport Elem Sch/*Freeport*/Brazoria	01001655	979/730-7175	52
Freeport Intermediate Sch/*Freeport*/ Brazoria	01001629	979/730-7240	52
Freer High Sch/*Freer*/Duval	01809201	361/394-6717	128
FREER IND SCH DIST/*FREER*/*DUVAL*	01809196	361/394-6025	128
Freer Junior High Sch/*Freer*/Duval	01809213	361/394-7102	128
Freiheit Elem Sch/*New Braunfels*/Comal	01006954	830/221-2700	88
French Elem Sch/*Spring*/Harris	12110681	832/375-8100	197
Frenship High Sch/*Wolfforth*/Lubbock	01038426	806/866-4440	269
FRENSHIP IND SCH DIST/*WOLFFORTH*/ *LUBBOCK*	01038402	806/866-9541	269
Frenship Middle Sch/*Wolfforth*/Lubbock	02177075	806/866-4464	269
Friendship Elem Sch/*Keller*/Tarrant	10028551	817/744-6200	355
Friendship Pre-Sch & Chrn Acad/*Beaumont*/ Jefferson	11243613	409/898-0489	244
Friendswood High Sch/*Friendswood*/Galveston	01019030	281/482-3413	160
FRIENDSWOOD IND SCH DIST/ *FRIENDSWOOD*/*GALVESTON*	01019028	281/482-1267	160
Friendswood Junior High Sch/*Friendswood*/ Galveston	01019042	281/996-6200	160
Friona Elem Sch/*Friona*/Parmer	01046746	806/250-2240	315
Friona High Sch/*Friona*/Parmer	01046758	806/250-3951	315
FRIONA IND SCH DIST/*FRIONA*/ *PARMER*	01046734	806/250-2747	315
Friona Junior High Sch/*Friona*/Parmer	01046760	806/250-2788	315
Friona Primary Sch/*Friona*/Parmer	03241514	806/250-3935	315
Frisco High Sch/*Frisco*/Collin	01006203	469/633-5500	79
FRISCO IND SCH DIST/*FRISCO*/ *COLLIN*	01006186	469/633-6000	78
Frisco ISD Early Childhood Sch/*Frisco*/ Collin	11448485	469/633-3825	79
Frisco Montessori Academy/*Frisco*/Hunt	04929537	972/712-7400	237
Frontier Elem Sch/*Angleton*/Brazoria	03393026	979/864-8005	51
Frontier High Sch/*Mansfield*/Tarrant	11715393	682/314-1600	356
Frost Elem Sch/*Frost*/Navarro	11833866	903/682-2541	299
Frost Elem Sch/*Houston*/Harris	01025209	713/732-3490	192
Frost Elem Sch/*Richmond*/Fort Bend	04923325	832/223-1500	154
Frost High Sch/*Frost*/Navarro	01043562	903/682-2541	299
FROST IND SCH DIST/*FROST*/*NAVARRO*	01043550	903/682-2711	299
Frostwood Elem Sch/*Houston*/Harris	01027128	713/251-5700	201
FRUITVALE IND SCH DIST/*FRUITVALE*/ *VAN ZANDT*	01058141	903/896-1191	380
Fruitvale Junior High Sch/*Fruitvale*/ Van Zandt	03397101	903/896-4363	380
Fruitvale Senior High Sch/*Fruitvale*/ Van Zandt	04810936	903/896-4363	380
FT BEND IND SCH DIST/*SUGAR LAND*/ *FORT BEND*	01018115	281/634-1000	149
Ft Concho Elem Sch/*San Angelo*/Tom Green	01055632	325/659-3654	365
FT ELLIOTT CONS IND SCH DIST/ *BRISCOE*/*WHEELER*	01059779	806/375-2454	390
Ft Elliott Sch/*Briscoe*/Wheeler	01059781	806/375-2454	390
Ft Hancock High Sch/*Fort Hancock*/Hudspeth	01032197	915/769-1604	234
FT HANCOCK IND SCH DIST/ *FORT HANCOCK*/*HUDSPETH*	01032173	915/769-3811	234
Ft Hancock Middle Sch/*Fort Hancock*/ Hudspeth	05099111	915/769-1603	234
Ft Sam Houston Elem Sch/*San Antonio*/Bexar	01534951	210/368-8800	32
FT SAM HOUSTON IND SCH DIST/ *SAN ANTONIO*/*BEXAR*	01534949	210/368-8701	32
Ft Stockton High Sch/*Fort Stockton*/Pecos	01046887	432/336-4101	315
FT STOCKTON IND SCH DIST/ *FORT STOCKTON*/*PECOS*	01046837	432/336-4000	315
Ft Stockton Intermediate Sch/*Fort Stockton*/ Pecos	01539224	432/336-4141	315
Ft Stockton Middle Sch/*Fort Stockton*/Pecos	01046899	432/336-4131	315
Ft Worth Academy of Fine Arts/*Fort Worth*/ Tarrant	04146113	817/924-1482	3
Ft Worth Adventist Jr Academy/*Fort Worth*/ Tarrant	04993069	817/370-7177	358
Ft Worth Country Day Sch/*Fort Worth*/ Tarrant	01054250	817/732-7718	359
FT WORTH IND SCH DIST/*FORT WORTH*/ *TARRANT*	01052525	817/871-2000	349
Full Armor Christian Academy/*Henderson*/ Rusk	04467046	903/655-8489	329
Fulshear High Sch/*Fulshear*/Fort Bend	12165313	832/223-5000	154
Fulton 4-5 Learning Center/*Fulton*/Aransas	00995132	361/790-2240	19
Fulton Sch/*Heath*/Rockwall	10756473	972/772-4445	326
Furneaux Elem Sch/*Carrollton*/Dallas	02178081	972/968-1800	97
Furr Elem Sch/*McKinney*/Collin	12363826	469/219-2280	84
Furr High Sch/*Houston*/Harris	01025510	713/675-1118	189
Fusion Acad-Houston Galleria/*Houston*/ Harris	12312217	713/963-9096	206
Fusion Academy-Austin/*Austin*/Travis	12312190	512/330-0188	373
Fusion Academy-Dallas/*Dallas*/Dallas	12312205	214/363-4615	115
Fusion Academy-Plano/*Plano*/Collin	12312229	972/403-9018	85
Fusion Academy-Southlake/*Southlake*/Tarrant	12312231	817/416-0306	359
Fusion Academy-Sugarland/*Sugar Land*/ Fort Bend	12312243	281/207-9506	155
Fusion Academy-the Woodlands/*The Woodlands*/ Montgomery	12312255	281/419-1436	295

G

School/City/County DISTRICT/CITY/COUNTY	PID	TELEPHONE NUMBER	PAGE
G H Whitcomb Elem Sch/*Houston*/Galveston	01018878	281/284-4900	159
G L Wiley Opportunity Center/*Waco*/McLennan	04036714	254/757-3829	282
G R Porter Elem Sch/*Mesquite*/Dallas	02043204	972/290-4000	111
G W Carver Early Childhood Ctr/*Ennis*/Ellis	11456743	972/872-3730	140
G W Harby Junior High Sch/*Alvin*/Brazoria	02109420	281/585-6626	51
G W Kennemer Middle Sch/*Dallas*/Dallas	03244592	972/708-3600	105
G W Robinson Elem Sch/*Seabrook*/Galveston	10025949	281/284-6500	159
Gabe P Allen Charter Sch/*Dallas*/Dallas	01008885	972/794-5100	100
Gainesville High Sch/*Gainesville*/Cooke	01007362	940/665-5528	91
GAINESVILLE IND SCH DIST/ *GAINESVILLE*/*COOKE*	01007348	940/665-4362	91
Gainesville Jr High Sch/*Gainesville*/Cooke	01007374	940/665-4062	91
Gainesville State Sch/*Gainesville*/Cooke	04459697	940/665-0701	3
Galatas Elem Sch/*The Woodlands*/Montgomery	04014625	936/709-5000	291
Gale Pond Alamo Elem Sch/*Odessa*/Ector	01014559	432/456-1019	130
Galena Park Cte Early Clg HS/*Houston*/ Harris	12235047	281/459-7198	187
Galena Park Elem Sch/*Galena Park*/Harris	01023457	832/386-1670	187
Galena Park High Sch/*Galena Park*/Harris	01023471	832/386-2800	187
GALENA PARK IND SCH DIST/ *HOUSTON*/*HARRIS*	01023419	832/386-1000	186
Galena Park Middle Sch/*Galena Park*/Harris	01023469	832/386-1700	187
Galindo Elem Sch/*Austin*/Travis	03249279	512/414-1756	366
Gallegos Elem Sch/*Brownsville*/Cameron	04945127	956/547-4230	63
Gallegos Elem Sch/*Houston*/Harris	04016116	713/924-1830	189
Galloway Elem Sch/*Mesquite*/Dallas	01011404	972/882-5101	111
Galloway Sch/*Friendswood*/Galveston	04934738	281/338-9510	162
GALVESTON IND SCH DIST/*GALVESTON*/ *GALVESTON*	01019078	409/766-5100	160
Ganado Elem Sch/*Ganado*/Jackson	01033062	361/771-4250	239
Ganado High Sch/*Ganado*/Jackson	01033074	361/771-4300	239
GANADO IND SCH DIST/*GANADO*/ *JACKSON*	01033050	361/771-4200	239
Ganado Junior High Sch/*Ganado*/Jackson	11690729	361/771-4309	240
Garcia Elem Sch/*Grand Prairie*/Dallas	01010967	972/237-0001	107
Garcia Elem Sch/*Houston*/Harris	04016130	713/696-2900	190
Garcia Middle Sch/*Houston*/Harris	12309674	281/878-3730	181
Garcia Young Men's Leadership/*Austin*/ Travis	10907220	512/841-9400	369
Garcia-Leza EC-PK-K Sch/*Houston*/Harris	11448875	281/985-6037	181
Garden Oaks Montessori/*Houston*/Harris	01024023	713/696-2930	191
Garden Park Elem Sch/*Brownsville*/Cameron	01003574	956/982-2630	63
Garden Ridge Elem Sch/*Flower Mound*/Denton	04016025	469/713-5956	123
Garden Ridge Elem Sch/*Garden Ridge*/Comal	01006930	830/885-1794	88
Garden Villas Elem Sch/*Houston*/Harris	01025211	713/845-7484	192
Gardendale Elem Sch/*San Antonio*/Bexar	00997221	210/444-8150	32
Gardens Elem Sch/*Pasadena*/Harris	01026693	713/740-0576	199
Gardner Preparatory Sch/*Lancaster*/Dallas	12033320	972/275-1539	115
Garfield Elem Sch/*Del Rio*/Val Verde	01057991	830/778-4700	379
Garfield Elem Sch/*Houston*/Harris	01026708	713/740-0584	199
Garland Christian Academy/*Garland*/Dallas	01012226	972/487-0043	115
Garland Classical Academy/*Garland*/Dallas	11459678	972/840-1100	3
Garland High Sch/*Garland*/Dallas	01010539	972/494-8492	105
GARLAND IND SCH DIST/*GARLAND*/ *DALLAS*	01010395	972/494-8201	105
Garland McMeans Junior HS/*Katy*/Harris	04908454	281/237-8000	152
Garner Elem Sch/*Weatherford*/Parker	01046382	940/682-4251	312
Garner Fine Arts Academy/*Grand Prairie*/ Dallas	03007265	972/262-5000	107
GARNER IND SCH DIST/*WEATHERFORD*/ *PARKER*	01046370	940/682-4251	312
Garner Middle Sch/*San Antonio*/Bexar	00997788	210/356-3800	35

School Year 2019-2020   800-333-8802   TX-V27

DISTRICT & SCHOOL TELEPHONE INDEX

School/City/County DISTRICT/CITY/COUNTY	PID	TELEPHONE NUMBER	PAGE
Garrett Elem Sch/*Houston*/Harris	11717432	281/727-4200	200
Garrett Primary Sch/*Lufkin*/Angelina	00994968	936/634-8418	18
Garriga Elem Sch/*Port Isabel*/Cameron	01004085	956/943-0080	66
Garrison Elem Sch/*Garrison*/Nacogdoches	01043225	936/347-7010	298
GARRISON IND SCH DIST/GARRISON/ NACOGDOCHES	01043213	936/347-7000	297
Garrison Middle Sch/*Garrison*/Nacogdoches	04762779	936/347-7020	298
Garrison Senior High Sch/*Garrison*/Nacogdoches	01043237	936/347-7030	298
Garwood Elem Sch/*Garwood*/Colorado	01006813	979/758-3531	87
GARY IND SCH DIST/GARY/PANOLA	01046277	903/685-2291	311
Gary Sch/*Gary*/Panola	01046289	903/685-2291	311
Gary W Campbell High Sch/*Kaufman*/Kaufman	04451982	972/932-8789	252
Garza Elem Sch/*Brownsville*/Cameron	01539975	956/982-2660	63
Garza Independence Acad/*Austin*/Travis	04806686	512/414-8600	368
Garza-Pena Elem Sch/*San Juan*/Hidalgo	03009263	956/354-2800	223
Gates Elem Sch/*San Antonio*/Bexar	00998964	210/978-7980	40
Gatesville Elem Sch/*Gatesville*/Coryell	01007673	254/865-7262	93
Gatesville High Sch/*Gatesville*/Coryell	01007685	254/865-8281	93
GATESVILLE IND SCH DIST/ GATESVILLE/CORYELL	01007661	254/865-7251	92
Gatesville Intermediate Sch/*Gatesville*/Coryell	04447292	254/865-2526	93
Gatesville Junior High Sch/*Gatesville*/Coryell	01007697	254/865-8271	93
Gatesville Primary Sch/*Gatesville*/Coryell	01007702	254/865-7264	93
Gateway Academy/*Childress*/Childress	04446420	940/937-3099	74
Gateway Academy/*Houston*/Harris	11225398	713/659-7900	206
Gateway Alternative Ed Center/*Burkburnett*/Wichita	04745991	940/569-0850	391
Gateway Charter Academy/*Dallas*/Dallas	11848823	214/375-1921	3
Gateway Charter Elem Academy/*Dallas*/Dallas	05010775	214/375-2039	3
Gateway Christian Sch/*San Antonio*/Bexar	01410525	210/674-5703	45
Gateway College Prep Sch/*Georgetown*/Williamson	11704485	512/868-4947	3
Gateway Daep Sch/*Bastrop*/Bastrop	03399240	512/772-7820	23
Gateway Elem Sch/*Borger*/Hutchinson	02126753	806/273-1044	237
Gateway High Sch/*Killeen*/Bell	03107724	254/336-1700	27
Gateway Middle Sch/*Killeen*/Bell	04368763	254/336-1690	27
Gateway Tech High Sch/*Georgetown*/Williamson	11539840	512/868-5299	3
Gateway to Graduation Academy/*San Benito*/Cameron	11558755	956/361-6446	67
Gattis Elem Sch/*Round Rock*/Williamson	04017809	512/428-2000	399
Gause Elem Sch/*Gause*/Milam	01041813	979/279-5891	287
GAUSE IND SCH DIST/GAUSE/MILAM	01041801	979/279-5891	287
Gen Tommy Franks Elem Sch/*Midland*/Midland	01041473	432/240-6500	286
Gene A Buinger Cte Academy/*Bedford*/Tarrant	01053957	817/354-3542	354
Gene Howe Elem Sch/*Amarillo*/Randall	01047960	806/677-2380	321
Gene M Reed Elem Sch/*Allen*/Collin	02200385	972/727-0580	77
Gene Pike Middle Sch/*Justin*/Denton	01013555	817/215-0400	125
Geneisis High Sch/*Bastrop*/Bastrop	11450452	512/772-7230	23
General Colin Powell Elem Sch/*El Paso*/El Paso	11449207	915/774-7775	133
General Ricardo Sanchez ES/*Rio Grande Cy*/Starr	04949173	956/487-7043	340
Generation One Academy/*Houston*/Harris	11817305	713/654-8008	206
Genesis Academy/*Brookesmith*/Brown	12366804	713/955-4414	58
Geneva Bailey Intermediate Sch/*Paris*/Lamar	04749583	903/737-7971	259
Geneva Heights Elem Sch/*Dallas*/Dallas	01009645	972/749-7400	100
Geneva School of Boerne/*Boerne*/Kendall	10013659	830/755-6101	254
Genoa Elem Sch/*Houston*/Harris	01026710	713/740-0592	199
George & Deborah Purefoy ES/*Frisco*/Collin	11558365	469/633-3875	79
George A Thompson Interm Sch/*Houston*/Harris	01026980	713/740-0510	199
George Anderson Elem Sch/*Allen*/Collin	04749002	972/396-6924	77
George B Dealey Mont Intl Acad/*Dallas*/Dallas	04282779	972/794-8400	100
George Buddy West Elem Sch/*Odessa*/Ector	12105739	432/456-1329	130
George Bush High Sch/*Richmond*/Fort Bend	04947125	281/634-6060	150
George Clarke Elem Sch/*Fort Worth*/Tarrant	01052939	817/814-6100	350
George Dawson Middle Sch/*Southlake*/Tarrant	05070660	817/949-5500	347
George Gervin Academy/*San Antonio*/Bexar	04467125	210/568-8800	3
George H Gentry Jr High Sch/*Baytown*/Harris	02179712	281/420-4590	187
George H W Bush Elem Sch/*Addison*/Dallas	11713307	972/925-1700	100
George I Sanchez Charter HS/*Houston*/Harris	02083905	713/926-1112	3
George Junior High Sch/*Rosenberg*/Fort Bend	02110091	832/223-3600	154
George Peabody Elem Sch/*Dallas*/Dallas	01008902	972/794-5200	100
George Ranch High Sch/*Richmond*/Fort Bend	11553494	832/223-4200	154
George Vogel Elem Sch/*Seguin*/Guadalupe	03391119	830/401-8745	174
George W Bush Elem Sch/*Wylie*/Collin	12109785	972/429-2600	85
George W Bush New Tech Odessa/*Odessa*/Ector	04420854	432/456-6989	130
George W Carver Early Ed Ctr/*Lockhart*/Caldwell	01003043	512/398-0060	61
George W Carver Elem Sch/*Baytown*/Harris	01023627	281/420-4600	187
George W Truett Elem Sch/*Dallas*/Dallas	01008926	972/749-8000	100
George Wagner Middle Sch/*Georgetown*/Williamson	12232306	512/943-1830	395
George Washington Carver ES/*Garland*/Dallas	10907385	972/487-4415	105
George Washington Carver ES/*Karnack*/Harrison	01028586	903/679-3111	209
George Washington Middle Sch/*Laredo*/Webb	04364030	956/473-7600	387
George West Elem Sch/*George West*/Live Oak	01038268	361/449-1914	268
George West High Sch/*George West*/Live Oak	01038270	361/449-1914	268
GEORGE WEST IND SCH DIST/ GEORGE WEST/LIVE OAK	01038256	361/449-1914	268
George West Junior High Sch/*George West*/Live Oak	01038282	361/449-1914	268
George West Primary Sch/*George West*/Live Oak	01038294	361/449-1914	268
Georgetown Alt Program/*Georgetown*/Williamson	04946652	512/943-5196	395
Georgetown Behavioral Hlth CS/*Georgetown*/Williamson	12362690	254/644-9111	3
Georgetown Charter Academy/*Georgetown*/Williamson	12100375	512/863-9236	3
Georgetown High Sch/*Georgetown*/Williamson	01060871	512/943-5100	395
GEORGETOWN IND SCH DIST/ GEORGETOWN/WILLIAMSON	01060869	512/943-5000	395
Georgia Kimball Elem Sch/*Mesquite*/Dallas	02856051	972/290-4120	111
Gerald Sonntag Elem Sch/*McKinney*/Collin	11558353	469/633-3850	79
Geraldine Palmer Elem Sch/*Pharr*/Hidalgo	01030412	956/354-2860	223
Gerard Elem Sch/*Cleburne*/Johnson	02855825	817/202-2130	247
GHOLSON IND SCH DIST/WACO/ MCLENNAN	01039731	254/829-1528	279
Gholson Sch/*Waco*/McLennan	01039743	254/829-1528	279
Gibson Caldwell Elem Sch/*McKinney*/Collin	01006291	469/302-5500	81
Giddens Elem Sch/*Cedar Park*/Williamson	04455809	512/570-5600	397
Giddens Steadham Elem Sch/*Rowlett*/Dallas	04866650	972/463-5887	106
Giddings Elem Sch/*Giddings*/Lee	01037460	979/542-2886	263
Giddings High Sch/*Giddings*/Lee	01037472	979/542-3351	263
GIDDINGS IND SCH DIST/GIDDINGS/ LEE	01037458	979/542-2854	263
Giddings Intermediate Sch/*Giddings*/Lee	04745458	979/542-4403	263
Giddings Middle Sch/*Giddings*/Lee	01037484	979/542-2057	263
Giddings State Sch/*Giddings*/Lee	01809562	979/542-4500	3
Giesinger Elem Sch/*Conroe*/Montgomery	03325366	936/709-2600	291
Gilbert Cuellar Jr Elem Sch/*Dallas*/Dallas	04457754	972/749-6400	100
Gilbert Gerdes Jr High Sch/*Luling*/Caldwell	01003110	830/875-2121	61
Gilbert Intermediate Sch/*Stephenville*/Erath	02222149	254/968-4664	144
Gilbert Mircovich Elem Sch/*Ingleside*/San Patricio	04800888	361/776-1683	331
Gilbert Willie Sr Elem Sch/*Terrell*/Kaufman	01035761	972/563-1443	253
Gilbreath-Reed Career Tech Ctr/*Garland*/Dallas	12231340	972/487-4588	106
Gillespie County High Sch/*Fredericksbrg*/Gillespie	05351634	830/990-4598	163
Gillett Intermediate Sch/*Kingsville*/Kleberg	01036313	361/595-8200	257
Gillette Elem Sch/*San Antonio*/Bexar	00997441	210/989-3100	32
Gilmer Elem Sch/*Gilmer*/Upshur	01057410	903/841-7700	376
Gilmer High Sch/*Gilmer*/Upshur	01057422	903/841-7500	376
GILMER IND SCH DIST/GILMER/ UPSHUR	01057408	903/841-7400	376
Gilmer Intermediate Sch/*Gilmer*/Upshur	01057434	903/841-7800	376
Ginger McNabb Elm Sch/*Spring*/Harris	10022466	281/891-8690	202
Ginnings Elem Sch/*Denton*/Denton	01013268	940/369-2700	121
Girls' School of Austin/*Austin*/Travis	10914936	512/478-7827	373
Gisd Alternative Ed Center/*Garland*/Dallas	04806387	972/926-2691	106
Givens Early Childhood Center/*Paris*/Lamar	01036741	903/737-7466	260
Gladewater High Sch/*Gladewater*/Gregg	01020883	903/845-5591	169
GLADEWATER IND SCH DIST/ GLADEWATER/GREGG	01020857	903/845-6991	169
Gladewater Middle Sch/*Gladewater*/Gregg	01020895	903/845-2243	169
Gladewater Primary Sch/*Gladewater*/Gregg	01020871	903/845-2254	169
Gladys Polk Elem Sch/*Richwood*/Brazoria	01001590	979/730-7200	52
Gladys Porter Early Clg HS/*Brownsville*/Cameron	01003653	956/548-7800	63
Glass Elem Sch/*Eagle Pass*/Maverick	01041100	830/758-7042	277
GLASSCOCK CO IND SCH DIST/ GARDEN CITY/GLASSCOCK	1019781	432/354-2230	163
Glasscock Co Sch/*Garden City*/Glasscock	01019808	432/354-2244	163
Gleason Elem Sch/*Houston*/Harris	04916358	281/517-6800	184

Texas School Directory
DISTRICT & SCHOOL TELEPHONE INDEX

School/City/County DISTRICT/CITY/COUNTY	PID	TELEPHONE NUMBER	PAGE
Glen Couch Elem Sch/Garland/Dallas	10008111	972/240-1801	106
Glen Cove Elem Sch/El Paso/El Paso	01824196	915/434-5500	138
Glen Loch Elem Sch/The Woodlands/Montgomery	02110388	281/298-4900	291
Glen Oaks Elem Sch/McKinney/Collin	01006265	469/302-6400	81
Glen Oaks Sch/Dallas/Dallas	02740000	972/231-3135	115
Glen Park Elem Sch/Fort Worth/Tarrant	01052941	817/815-8800	350
Glen Rose Elem Sch/Glen Rose/Somervell	01051090	254/898-3500	340
Glen Rose High Sch/Glen Rose/Somervell	01051105	254/898-3800	340
GLEN ROSE IND SCH DIST/GLEN ROSE/SOMERVELL	01051088	254/898-3900	340
Glen Rose Intermediate Sch/Glen Rose/Somervell	04010760	254/898-3600	340
Glen Rose Junior High Sch/Glen Rose/Somervell	02056172	254/898-3700	340
Glencrest 6th Grade Middle Sch/Fort Worth/Tarrant	01809885	817/815-8400	350
Glenda Dawson High Sch/Pearland/Brazoria	05231486	281/412-8800	53
Glenhope Elem Sch/Colleyville/Tarrant	04363660	817/251-5720	353
Glenmore Elem Sch/San Angelo/Tom Green	01055644	325/659-3657	365
Glenn Harmon Elem Sch/Arlington/Tarrant	03047083	817/299-7780	357
Glenn High Sch/Leander/Williamson	12165387	512/570-1400	397
Glenn Middle Sch/San Angelo/Tom Green	01055694	325/947-3841	365
Glenn York Elem Sch/Pearland/Brazoria	11711139	281/245-2100	51
Glenoaks Elem Sch/San Antonio/Bexar	00998110	210/397-2300	37
Glenwood Elem Sch/Amarillo/Potter	01047271	806/326-4450	318
Glenwood Private Sch/Conroe/Montgomery	02768844	936/756-1223	295
Global Innovation Sch/Sugar Land/Fort Bend	04265159	281/980-5800	155
Global Prep Academy/Crowley/Tarrant	11926968	817/297-3018	348
Gloria B Sammons Elem Sch/Houston/Harris	01022946	281/878-0955	179
Gloria Deo Academy/Bulverde/Comal	11818725	830/708-5463	89
Gloria Marshall Elem Sch/Spring/Harris	11719038	281/491-4900	202
Goals Learning Center/Round Rock/Williamson	12167488	512/464-5153	399
Goddard Junior High Sch/Midland/Midland	01041514	432/689-1300	286
Godley Elem Sch/Godley/Johnson	01034975	817/389-3838	247
Godley High Sch/Godley/Johnson	03392539	817/592-4320	247
GODLEY IND SCH DIST/GODLEY/JOHNSON	01034963	817/389-2536	247
Godley Intermediate Sch/Godley/Johnson	04914752	817/389-2382	247
Godley Middle Sch/Godley/Johnson	03392527	817/389-2121	247
Godwin Elem Sch/Princeton/Collin	04868000	469/952-5402	84
GOLD-BURG IND SCH DIST/BOWIE/MONTAGUE	01042283	940/872-3562	290
Gold-Burg Elem Sch/Bowie/Montague	01042295	940/872-3562	290
Golden Acres Elem Sch/Pasadena/Harris	01026722	713/740-0600	199
Golden Meadows Elem Sch/Garland/Dallas	01010541	972/494-8373	106
Golden Rule CS-DeSoto/Desoto/Dallas	11663673	469/248-4463	3
Golden Rule CS-Grand Prairie/Grand Prairie/Dallas	11832202	214/988-3257	3
Golden Rule CS-Illinois/Dallas/Dallas	05220994	214/333-9330	3
Golden Rule CS-Pleasant Grove/Dallas/Dallas	11663661	469/341-5780	3
Golden Rule CS-Sunnyside/Dallas/Dallas	11663659	214/393-6911	3
Golden Rule CS-Wilmer/Wilmer/Dallas	12260729	972/525-6204	4
GOLDTHWAITE CONSOLIDATED ISD/GOLDTHWAITE/MILLS	01041942	325/648-3531	288
Goldthwaite Elem Sch/Goldthwaite/Mills	01041954	325/648-3055	288
Goldthwaite High Sch/Goldthwaite/Mills	01041966	325/648-3081	288
Goldthwaite Middle Sch/Goldthwaite/Mills	04871851	325/648-3630	288
Golfcrest Elem Sch/Houston/Harris	01025522	713/845-7425	192
Goliad Elem Sch/Big Spring/Howard	01031959	432/264-4111	233
Goliad Elem Sch/Goliad/Goliad	01019846	361/645-3206	164
Goliad Elem Sch/Odessa/Ector	01014690	432/456-1109	130
Goliad Elem Sch/San Angelo/Tom Green	01055656	325/659-3660	365
Goliad High Sch/Goliad/Goliad	01019834	361/645-3257	164
GOLIAD IND SCH DIST/GOLIAD/GOLIAD	01019810	361/645-3259	163
Goliad Middle Sch/Goliad/Goliad	01019822	361/645-3146	164
Gonzales Elem Sch/Gonzales/Gonzales	04885747	830/672-1467	164
Gonzales Elem Sch/Odessa/Ector	01014705	432/456-1119	130
Gonzales High Sch/Gonzales/Gonzales	01019896	830/672-7535	164
GONZALES IND SCH DIST/GONZALES/GONZALES	01019860	830/672-9551	164
Gonzales Junior High Sch/Gonzales/Gonzales	01019901	830/672-8641	164
Gonzales Primary Academy/Gonzales/Gonzales	12103303	830/519-4110	164
Gonzalez Elem Sch/Brownsville/Cameron	02892134	956/831-6030	63
Gonzalez Pre-K Center/Denton/Denton	11559163	940/369-4360	121
Gonzalo & Sofia Garcia ES/El Paso/El Paso	10915318	915/877-1200	132
Good Shepherd Catholic Sch/Garland/Dallas	01012410	972/272-6533	114
Good Shepherd Episcopal Sch/Dallas/Dallas	01012329	214/357-1610	115
Good Shepherd Sch/Tyler/Smith	11236452	903/592-4045	339
Good Tree Academy/Plano/Collin	11975268	972/836-6322	85
Goodman Elem Sch/Arlington/Tarrant	01051777	682/867-2200	344
Goodrich Elem Sch/Goodrich/Polk	01047037	936/365-1100	316
GOODRICH IND SCH DIST/GOODRICH/POLK	01047025	936/365-1100	316
Goodrich Middle High Sch/Goodrich/Polk	05341885	936/365-1100	316
Goodson Middle Sch/Cypress/Harris	04943765	281/373-2350	184
Goodwater Mont Charter Sch/Georgetown/Williamson	12260731	512/966-5484	4
Goodwin Frazier Elem Sch/New Braunfels/Comal	01006942	830/221-2200	88
GOOSE CREEK CONS IND SCH DIST/BAYTOWN/HARRIS	01023562	281/420-4800	187
Goose Creek Memorial High Sch/Baytown/Harris	11079620	281/421-4400	188
GORDON IND SCH DIST/GORDON/PALO PINTO	01045950	254/693-5582	310
Gordon Sch/Gordon/Palo Pinto	01045962	254/693-5342	310
Gorman High Sch/Gorman/Eastland	01014468	254/734-3171	129
GORMAN IND SCH DIST/GORMAN/EASTLAND	01014444	254/734-3171	129
Gorman Middle Sch/Gorman/Eastland	11718917	254/734-3171	129
Gorzycki Middle Sch/Austin/Travis	11540667	512/841-8600	369
Goshen Creek Elem Sch/Springtown/Parker	01046540	817/220-0272	313
Govalle Elem Sch/Austin/Travis	01056222	512/414-2078	366
Grace Academy/Georgetown/Williamson	05270004	512/864-9500	400
Grace Academy of Dallas/Dallas/Dallas	02858293	214/696-5648	115
Grace Christian Academy/Houston/Harris	11234624	281/488-4883	206
Grace Christian Academy-Brock/Brock/Parker	12365147	682/262-9288	314
Grace Christian Academy-Main/Perrin/Jack	12365135	682/262-9288	239
Grace Christian Sch/Pharr/Hidalgo	04953485	956/787-0701	226
Grace Community Jr Sr High Sch/Tyler/Smith	04304028	903/566-5661	339
Grace Community Sch/Tyler/Smith	02123593	903/593-1977	339
Grace Covenant Academy/Frisco/Hunt	12107787	972/836-9422	237
Grace E Hardeman Elem Sch/Watauga/Tarrant	01052070	817/547-2800	346
Grace England ECC/Houston/Harris	11822714	832/375-7900	197
Grace Fellowship Christian Sch/Sunnyvale/Dallas	05287071	972/226-4499	115
Grace Hartman Elem Sch/Rockwall/Rockwall	05100198	972/772-2080	325
Grace Lutheran Sch/Brenham/Washington	01059133	979/836-2030	386
Grace Prep Academy/Arlington/Tarrant	04867563	817/557-3399	359
Grace Raymond Academy/Houston/Harris	01022817	281/985-6550	180
Grace Sch/Houston/Harris	02992461	713/782-4421	206
Graciela Garcia Elem Sch/Pharr/Hidalgo	05098791	956/354-2790	223
Graduation Prep Acad-Navarro/Austin/Travis	12179613	512/414-2896	368
Graduation Prep Academy-Travis/Austin/Travis	12179601	512/414-6635	368
Grady B Rasco Middle Sch/Lake Jackson/Brazoria	04363749	979/730-7225	52
Grady Burnett Jr Senior HS/Wylie/Collin	05350197	972/429-3200	85
GRADY IND SCH DIST/LENORAH/MARTIN	01040730	432/459-2444	274
Grady Sch/Lenorah/Martin	01040742	432/459-2445	274
Graebner Elem Sch/San Antonio/Bexar	00999164	210/228-3320	40
Graford Elem Sch/Graford/Palo Pinto	01045998	940/664-3101	310
GRAFORD IND SCH DIST/GRAFORD/PALO PINTO	01045986	940/664-3101	310
Graford Jr Sr High Sch/Graford/Palo Pinto	04750087	940/664-3101	310
Graham Elem Sch/Austin/Travis	01056234	512/414-2395	367
Graham High Sch/Graham/Young	01062130	940/549-1504	406
GRAHAM IND SCH DIST/GRAHAM/YOUNG	01062104	940/549-0595	406
Graham Junior High Sch/Graham/Young	01062128	940/549-2002	406
Granbury High Sch/Granbury/Hood	01031399	817/408-4600	230
GRANBURY IND SCH DIST/GRANBURY/HOOD	01031375	817/408-4000	230
Granbury Middle Sch/Granbury/Hood	01031404	817/408-4850	230
Grand Oaks High Sch/Spring/Montgomery	12312360	281/939-0000	291
Grand Prairie Collegiate Inst/Grand Prairie/Dallas	11925689	972/343-3120	107
Grand Prairie Early Clg HS/Grand Prairie/Dallas	12168614	972/809-5711	107
Grand Prairie Fine Arts Acad/Grand Prairie/Dallas	11925677	972/237-5603	107
Grand Prairie High Sch/Grand Prairie/Dallas	01010888	972/809-5711	107
GRAND PRAIRIE IND SCH DIST/GRAND PRAIRIE/DALLAS	01010814	972/264-6141	107
Grand Saline Elem Sch/Grand Saline/Van Zandt	01058177	903/962-7526	380
Grand Saline High Sch/Grand Saline/Van Zandt	01058189	903/962-7533	380

DISTRICT & SCHOOL TELEPHONE INDEX

Market Data Retrieval

School/City/County DISTRICT/CITY/COUNTY	PID	TELEPHONE NUMBER	PAGE
GRAND SALINE IND SCH DIST/			
GRAND SALINE/VAN ZANDT	01058165	903/962-7546	380
Grand Saline Intermediate Sch/*Grand Saline*/Van Zandt	04447216	903/962-5515	380
Grand Saline Middle Sch/*Grand Saline*/Van Zandt	02108646	903/962-7537	380
Grandfalls Royalty Sch/*Grandfalls*/Ward	01058945	432/547-2266	385
GRANDFALLS-ROYALTY IND SD/			
GRANDFALLS/WARD	01058919	432/547-2266	385
Grandview Elem Sch/*Grandview*/Johnson	01035008	817/866-4600	248
Grandview High Sch/*Grandview*/Johnson	01035010	817/866-4520	248
Grandview Hills Elem Sch/*Austin*/Williamson	10914340	512/570-6800	397
GRANDVIEW IND SCH DIST/GRANDVIEW/			
JOHNSON	01034999	817/866-4500	248
Grandview Junior High Sch/*Grandview*/Johnson	02200555	817/866-4660	248
Grandview-Hopkins Elem Sch/*Groom*/Gray	01020065	806/669-3831	164
GRANDVIEW-HOPKINS IND SCH DIST/			
GROOM/GRAY	01020053	806/669-3831	164
GRANGER IND SCH DIST/GRANGER/			
WILLIAMSON	01060912	512/859-2613	396
Granger Sch/*Granger*/Williamson	01060924	512/859-2173	396
Grangerland Interm Sch/*Conroe*/Montgomery	02126856	936/709-3500	291
Grape Creek Elem Sch/*San Angelo*/Tom Green	01055527	325/655-1735	364
Grape Creek High Sch/*San Angelo*/Tom Green	04447151	325/653-1852	364
GRAPE CREEK IND SCH DIST/			
SAN ANGELO/TOM GREEN	01055515	325/658-7823	364
Grape Creek Middle Sch/*San Angelo*/Tom Green	04748060	325/655-1735	364
Grapeland Elem Sch/*Grapeland*/Houston	01031765	936/687-2317	233
GRAPELAND IND SCH DIST/GRAPELAND/			
HOUSTON	01031753	936/687-4619	232
Grapeland Junior High Sch/*Grapeland*/Houston	05342152	936/687-2351	233
Grapeland Secondary Sch/*Grapeland*/Houston	01031777	936/687-4661	233
Grapevine Elem Sch/*Grapevine*/Tarrant	04281232	817/251-5735	353
Grapevine High Sch/*Grapevine*/Tarrant	01053713	817/251-5210	353
Grapevine Middle Sch/*Grapevine*/Tarrant	01053725	817/251-5660	353
GRAPEVINE-COLLEYVILLE IND SD/			
GRAPEVINE/TARRANT	01053672	817/251-5200	353
Graves Elem Sch/*Eagle Pass*/Maverick	01041071	830/758-7043	277
Grayson Christian Sch/*Sherman*/Grayson	02153897	903/892-3304	169
Great Hearts Forest Heights/*San Antonio*/Bexar	12362731	210/892-3665	4
Great Hearts Irving/*Irving*/Dallas	12163004	469/759-3030	4
Great Hearts Monte Vista-North/*San Antonio*/Bexar	12177225	210/888-9485	4
Great Hearts Monte Vista-South/*San Antonio*/Bexar	12160961	210/888-9485	4
Great Hearts Northern Oaks/*San Antonio*/Bexar	12160662	210/888-9483	4
Great Hearts Western Hills/*San Antonio*/Bexar	12362729	210/888-9488	4
Great Lakes Academy/*Plano*/Collin	10000391	972/517-7498	85
Great Oaks Elem Sch/*Round Rock*/Williamson	04754447	512/464-6850	399
Greathouse Elem Sch/*Midland*/Midland	04037005	432/240-6900	286
Green Acres Elem Sch/*Dumas*/Moore	01042855	806/935-4157	295
Green B Trimble Tech High Sch/*Fort Worth*/Tarrant	01052953	817/815-2500	350
Green Elem Sch/*El Paso*/El Paso	04035667	915/236-3000	133
Green Oaks Sch/*Arlington*/Tarrant	11231359	817/496-5100	359
Green Valley Elem Sch/*Houston*/Harris	01023483	832/386-4390	187
Green Valley Elem Sch/*N RichInd Hls*/Tarrant	04015605	817/547-3400	346
Green Valley Elem Sch/*Schertz*/Guadalupe	05275793	210/619-4450	173
Greenbriar Elem Sch/*Fort Worth*/Tarrant	01052965	817/814-7400	350
Greenfield Elem Sch/*Fort Worth*/Tarrant	10022868	817/237-0357	348
Greenhill Sch/*Addison*/Dallas	01012783	972/628-5400	115
Greenleaf Elem Sch/*Splendora*/Montgomery	05352262	281/689-8020	294
Greens Prairie Elem Sch/*College Sta*/Brazos	11709435	979/694-5870	55
Greenspoint Elem Sch/*Houston*/Harris	12165765	281/985-7800	180
Greentree Elem Sch/*Kingwood*/Harris	02125527	281/641-1900	195
Greenville Alt Center/*Greenville*/Hunt	04750517	903/457-2688	236
Greenville Christian Sch/*Greenville*/Hunt	02164884	903/454-1111	237
Greenville High Sch/*Greenville*/Hunt	02177063	903/457-2550	236
GREENVILLE IND SCH DIST/			
GREENVILLE/HUNT	01032446	903/457-2500	236
Greenville Middle Sch/*Greenville*/Hunt	01032501	903/457-2620	236
Greenville Sixth Grade Center/*Greenville*/Hunt	01032496	903/457-2660	236
Greenways Intermediate Sch/*Amarillo*/Randall	05264885	806/677-2460	321
Greenwood Elem Sch/*Midland*/Midland	01041409	432/685-7821	285
Greenwood Forest Elem Sch/*Houston*/Harris	01026306	832/484-5700	197
Greenwood High Sch/*Midland*/Midland	01041411	432/685-7806	285
Greenwood Hills Elem Sch/*Richardson*/Dallas	01011703	469/593-6100	112
GREENWOOD IND SCH DIST/MIDLAND/			
MIDLAND	01041394	432/683-6461	285
Greenwood Interm Sch/*Midland*/Midland	12365070	432/685-7819	285
Gregg Elem Sch/*Houston*/Harris	01025223	713/845-7432	192
Gregorio Esparza Elem Sch/*San Antonio*/Bexar	00998093	210/397-1850	37
Gregory Luna Middle Sch/*San Antonio*/Bexar	05347580	210/397-5300	37
Gregory-Lincoln Education Ctr/*Houston*/Harris	01024035	713/942-1400	188
Gregory-Portland High Sch/*Portland*/San Patricio	01049566	361/777-4251	331
GREGORY-PORTLAND IND SCH DIST/			
PORTLAND/SAN PATRICIO	01049530	361/777-1091	330
Gregory-Portland Mid Sch/*Portland*/San Patricio	01049578	361/777-4042	331
Greta Oppe Elem Sch/*Galveston*/Galveston	03012210	409/761-6500	160
Griffin Elem Sch/*Tyler*/Smith	01050888	903/262-2310	338
Griffin Middle Sch/*The Colony*/Denton	02179554	469/713-5973	123
Griffin Sch/*Austin*/Travis	11233606	512/454-5797	373
Griggs EC-PK-K Sch/*Houston*/Harris	12309698	281/985-3760	181
Grissom Elem Sch/*Houston*/Harris	01025247	713/434-5660	192
Groesbeck High Sch/*Groesbeck*/Limestone	01038062	254/729-4101	267
GROESBECK IND SCH DIST/GROESBECK/			
LIMESTONE	01038048	254/729-4100	267
Groesbeck Middle Sch/*Groesbeck*/Limestone	01038074	254/729-4102	267
GROOM IND SCH DIST/GROOM/CARSON	01004554	806/248-7474	69
Groom Sch/*Groom*/Carson	01004566	806/248-7474	69
Gross Elem Sch/*Houston*/Harris	04951633	713/778-8450	193
Groves Elem Sch/*Groves*/Jefferson	01033969	409/962-1531	243
Groves Elem Sch/*Humble*/Harris	12235944	281/641-5000	195
Groves Middle Sch/*Groves*/Jefferson	01034054	409/962-0225	243
Groveton Elem Sch/*Groveton*/Trinity	01057111	936/642-1182	374
GROVETON IND SCH DIST/GROVETON/			
TRINITY	01057109	936/642-1473	374
Groveton Jr Sr High Sch/*Groveton*/Trinity	01057123	936/642-1128	374
Grulla Elem Sch/*Rio Grande Cy*/Starr	01051131	956/487-3306	340
Grulla High Sch/*Rio Grande Cy*/Starr	11559515	956/487-7278	340
Grulla Middle Sch/*Grulla*/Starr	01051129	956/487-5558	340
Gruver Elem Sch/*Gruver*/Hansford	01022269	806/733-2031	176
Gruver High Sch/*Gruver*/Hansford	01022271	806/733-2477	176
GRUVER IND SCH DIST/GRUVER/			
HANSFORD	01022257	806/733-2001	176
Gruver Junior High Sch/*Gruver*/Hansford	01022283	806/733-2081	176
Guadalupe Elem Sch/*Lubbock*/Lubbock	01038672	806/219-5500	270
Guadalupe Regional Middle Sch/*Brownsville*/Cameron	05153559	956/504-5568	68
Guajardo Elem Sch/*Texas City*/Galveston	01019547	409/916-0300	161
Guerrero Thompson Elem Sch/*Austin*/Travis	11923215	512/414-8400	367
Guess Elem Sch/*Beaumont*/Jefferson	01033531	409/617-6125	242
Guidance Center/*Pasadena*/Harris	04896318	713/740-0792	199
Guidepost Montessori-Brush Crk/*Cedar Park*/Williamson	11902194	512/259-3333	400
Guidepost Montessori-Stonebria/*Frisco*/Collin	05423146	214/387-8202	86
Guillen Middle Sch/*El Paso*/El Paso	01015979	915/236-4900	134
Guillermo Flores Elem Sch/*Mission*/Hidalgo	02104535	956/323-2760	220
Gulledge Elem Sch/*Plano*/Collin	04366777	469/752-1300	82
Gullett Elem Sch/*Austin*/Travis	01056246	512/414-2082	367
Gunn Junior High Sch/*Arlington*/Tarrant	01051789	682/867-5400	344
Gunter Elem Sch/*Gunter*/Grayson	01020455	903/433-5315	166
Gunter High Sch/*Gunter*/Grayson	03055925	903/433-1542	166
GUNTER IND SCH DIST/GUNTER/			
GRAYSON	01020443	903/433-4750	166
Gunter Middle Sch/*Gunter*/Grayson	04447981	903/433-1545	166
Gus A Oleson Elem Sch/*Houston*/Harris	01022922	281/985-6530	180
Gus Birdwell Elem Sch/*Spearman*/Hansford	01022324	806/659-2565	177
Gus Garcia Middle Sch/*San Antonio*/Bexar	00997245	210/444-8075	32
Gus Winston Cain Elem Sch/*Whitehouse*/Smith	01051002	903/839-5600	339
GUSTINE IND SCH DIST/GUSTINE/			
COMANCHE	01007128	325/667-7981	90
Gustine Sch/*Gustine*/Comanche	01007130	325/667-7303	90
Guthrie Center/*Houston*/Harris	01545273	713/251-1300	201
GUTHRIE COMMON SCH DIST/			
GUTHRIE/KING	01036193	806/596-4466	257
Guthrie Sch/*Guthrie*/King	01036210	806/596-4466	257
Gutierriez Middle Sch/*Harlingen*/Cameron	04748711	956/430-4400	65
Guzman Elem Sch/*Donna*/Hidalgo	03321475	956/464-1920	215

Texas School Directory

DISTRICT & SCHOOL TELEPHONE INDEX

School/City/County DISTRICT/CITY/COUNTY	PID	TELEPHONE NUMBER	PAGE
GW Carver 6th GR STEM Lrng Ctr/*Lancaster*/Dallas	11711995	972/218-1577	110
Gwa Sierra Vista Charter HS/*Laredo*/Webb	11663647	956/723-0345	4
Gwa Townlake CHS/*Laredo*/Webb	04891631	956/722-0747	4

H

School/City/County	PID	TELEPHONE	PAGE
H A Wooden Elem Sch/*Red Oak*/Ellis	01015254	972/617-2977	142
H B Gonzalez Elem Sch/*San Antonio*/Bexar	00997233	210/444-7800	32
H B Zachry Elem Sch/*Laredo*/Webb	01540132	956/273-4900	386
H C Carleston Elem Sch/*Pearland*/Brazoria	02112245	281/412-1412	53
H C Schochler Elem Sch/*Channelview*/Harris	01023110	281/452-2880	183
H D Hilley Elem Sch/*El Paso*/El Paso	02109509	915/937-8400	136
H D Staples Elem Sch/*Joshua*/Johnson	01035034	817/202-2500	248
H E Charles Middle Sch/*El Paso*/El Paso	01418280	915/236-6550	134
H F Stevens Middle Sch/*Crowley*/Tarrant	01052381	817/297-5840	348
H G Isbill Junior High Sch/*Mc Gregor*/McLennan	01039901	254/840-3251	280
H G Temple Elem Sch/*Diboll*/Angelina	00994827	936/829-6950	17
H G Temple Intermediate Sch/*Diboll*/Angelina	11917058	936/829-6900	17
H Grady Spruce High Sch/*Dallas*/Dallas	01008940	972/892-5500	100
H I Holland ES-Lisbon/*Dallas*/Dallas	01009384	972/749-1900	100
H M K Care Academy/*Kingsville*/Kleberg	11934599	361/595-8600	257
H M King High Sch/*Kingsville*/Kleberg	01036296	361/595-8600	257
H O Whitehurst Elem Sch/*Groesbeck*/Limestone	02845595	254/729-4104	267
H R Jefferies Junior High Sch/*Comanche*/Comanche	01007087	325/356-5220	89
H V Helbing Elem Sch/*Fort Worth*/Tarrant	01052991	817/815-0500	350
H W Schulze Elem Sch/*San Antonio*/Bexar	00997518	210/989-3250	32
Hacienda Heights Elem Sch/*El Paso*/El Paso	01016430	915/434-2500	138
Hackberry Elem Sch/*Frisco*/Denton	05277088	972/947-9453	124
Hackney Primary Sch/*Lufkin*/Angelina	00994970	936/634-3324	18
Hafley Development Center/*Fort Worth*/Tarrant	10003719	817/232-2071	348
Haggard Middle Sch/*Plano*/Collin	01006435	469/752-5400	82
Hailey Elem Sch/*The Woodlands*/Montgomery	01829483	832/663-4100	291
Hairgrove Elem Sch/*Houston*/Harris	03398246	713/896-5015	184
Hale Center High Sch/*Hale Center*/Hale	01021837	806/839-2452	175
HALE CENTER IND SCH DIST/HALE CENTER/HALE	01021813	806/839-2451	175
Hale Elem Sch/*Arlington*/Tarrant	04808701	682/867-1530	344
Hallettsville Elem Sch/*Hallettsville*/Lavaca	01037290	361/798-2242	262
Hallettsville High Sch/*Hallettsville*/Lavaca	01037305	361/798-2242	262
HALLETTSVILLE IND SCH DIST/HALLETTSVILLE/LAVACA	01037288	361/798-2242	262
Hallettsville Jr High Sch/*Hallettsville*/Lavaca	01037317	361/798-2242	262
Hallie Randall Elem Sch/*Fruitvale*/Van Zandt	01058153	903/896-4466	380
Hallsburg Elem Sch/*Waco*/McLennan	01039767	254/875-2331	279
HALLSBURG IND SCH DIST/WACO/MCLENNAN	01039755	254/875-2331	279
Hallsville High Sch/*Hallsville*/Harrison	01028500	903/668-5990	208
HALLSVILLE IND SCH DIST/HALLSVILLE/HARRISON	01028483	903/668-5990	208
Hallsville Intermediate Sch/*Hallsville*/Harrison	01558139	903/668-5989	208
Hallsville Junior High Sch/*Hallsville*/Harrison	01028524	903/668-5986	208
Halpin Early Chldhd Lrng Ctr/*Houston*/Harris	04454946	713/778-6720	193
Haltom High Sch/*Haltom City*/Tarrant	01052082	817/547-6000	346
Haltom Middle Sch/*Haltom City*/Tarrant	01052094	817/547-4000	346
Hamilton Elem Sch/*Cypress*/Harris	03327182	281/370-0990	185
Hamilton High Sch/*Hamilton*/Hamilton	01022180	254/386-8167	176
HAMILTON IND SCH DIST/HAMILTON/HAMILTON	01022166	254/386-3149	176
Hamilton Junior High Sch/*Hamilton*/Hamilton	02200804	254/386-8168	176
Hamilton Middle Sch/*Cypress*/Harris	04016594	281/320-7000	185
Hamilton Middle Sch/*Houston*/Harris	01024047	713/802-4725	191
Hamilton Park Pacesetter Magnt/*Dallas*/Dallas	01011715	469/593-3900	112
Hamlet Elem Sch/*Amarillo*/Potter	01047283	806/326-4500	318
Hamlin Elem Sch/*Hamlin*/Jones	01035230	325/576-3191	249
Hamlin High Sch/*Hamlin*/Jones	01035242	325/576-3624	249
HAMLIN IND SCH DIST/HAMLIN/JONES	01035228	325/576-2722	249
Hampton-Moreno-Dugat ECC/*Beeville*/Bee	00996095	361/362-6040	25
Hamshire Fannett Elem Sch/*Beaumont*/Jefferson	01033622	409/794-1412	242
Hamshire Fannett High Sch/*Hamshire*/Jefferson	01033634	409/243-2131	242
HAMSHIRE FANNETT IND SCH DIST/HAMSHIRE/JEFFERSON	01033610	409/243-2133	242
Hamshire Fannett Interm Sch/*Beaumont*/Jefferson	03394238	409/794-1558	242
Hamshire Fannett Middle Sch/*Beaumont*/Jefferson	01033646	409/794-1502	242
Handley Elem Sch/*Garland*/Dallas	01010606	972/926-2540	106
Handley Middle Sch/*Fort Worth*/Tarrant	01052989	817/815-4200	350
Hanes Elem Sch/*Irving*/Dallas	01011167	972/600-3600	109
Hanna Springs Elem Sch/*Lampasas*/Lampasas	01037123	512/556-2152	261
Happy Elem Sch/*Happy*/Swisher	01051521	806/558-2561	342
HAPPY IND SCH DIST/HAPPY/SWISHER	01051519	806/558-5331	342
Happy Middle High Sch/*Happy*/Swisher	01051533	806/558-5311	343
Harbach-Ripley Charter Sch/*Houston*/Harris	11834456	713/669-5202	4
Hardin Elem Sch/*Hardin*/Liberty	01037850	936/298-2114	266
Hardin High Sch/*Liberty*/Liberty	01037862	936/298-2118	266
HARDIN IND SCH DIST/HARDIN/LIBERTY	01037848	936/298-2112	265
Hardin Intermediate Sch/*Duncanville*/Dallas	03048178	972/708-3300	105
HARDIN JEFFERSON IND SCH DIST/SOUR LAKE/HARDIN	01022439	409/981-6400	177
Hardin Junior High Sch/*Hardin*/Liberty	11014838	936/298-2054	266
Hardin-Jefferson High Sch/*Sour Lake*/Hardin	01022453	409/981-6430	178
Hardwick Elem Sch/*Lubbock*/Lubbock	01038684	806/219-5600	270
Hardy Oak Elem Sch/*San Antonio*/Bexar	04924549	210/407-3600	35
Hargill Elem Sch/*Hargill*/Hidalgo	01029724	956/289-2338	216
Harker Heights Elem Sch/*Harker HTS*/Bell	00996497	254/336-2050	28
Harker Heights High Sch/*Harker HTS*/Bell	04368787	254/336-0800	28
Harlan High Sch/*San Antonio*/Bexar	12230310	210/398-2200	37
Harlandale Alternative Center/*San Antonio*/Bexar	00997544	210/989-5200	32
Harlandale High Sch/*San Antonio*/Bexar	00997465	210/989-1000	32
HARLANDALE IND SCH DIST/SAN ANTONIO/BEXAR	00997350	210/989-4300	32
Harlandale Middle Sch/*San Antonio*/Bexar	00997453	210/989-2000	32
Harlean Beal Elem Sch/*Fort Worth*/Tarrant	01052915	817/815-8500	350
Harlem Elem Sch/*Baytown*/Harris	01023639	281/420-4910	188
Harleton Elem Sch/*Harleton*/Harrison	01028548	903/777-4092	208
Harleton High Sch/*Harleton*/Harrison	01028550	903/777-2711	208
HARLETON IND SCH DIST/HARLETON/HARRISON	01028536	903/777-8601	208
Harleton Junior High Sch/*Harleton*/Harrison	01028562	903/777-3010	208
HARLINGEN CONS IND SCH DIST/HARLINGEN/CAMERON	01003756	956/430-9500	64
Harlingen High Sch/*Harlingen*/Cameron	01003847	956/427-3600	65
Harlingen High School South/*Harlingen*/Cameron	02893932	956/427-3800	65
Harlingen Sch of Health/*Harlingen*/Cameron	12032285	956/430-4078	65
Harlow Elem Sch/*Anna*/Collin	12226230	972/924-1320	77
Harmony Elem Sch/*San Antonio*/Bexar	00997013	210/633-0231	31
Harmony High Sch/*Big Sandy*/Upshur	01057472	903/725-7270	376
Harmony Hills Elem Sch/*San Antonio*/Bexar	00997790	210/407-3800	35
HARMONY IND SCH DIST/BIG SANDY/UPSHUR	01057458	903/725-5492	376
Harmony Irons-Smith Interm Sch/*Big Sandy*/Upshur	04946303	903/725-7270	376
Harmony Junior High Sch/*Big Sandy*/Upshur	02845870	903/725-5485	376
Harmony Sch Achievement-Houstn/*Houston*/Harris	12260743	281/855-2500	4
Harmony Sch Adv-Houston/*Houston*/Harris	11734947	281/741-8899	4
Harmony Sch Bus-Dallas/*Dallas*/Collin	11818189	214/321-0100	4
Harmony Sch DSC-Houston/*Houston*/Harris	11557062	281/861-5105	4
Harmony Sch Endeavor-Austin/*Austin*/Williamson	11734923	512/284-9880	4
Harmony Sch Endeavor-Houston/*Houston*/Harris	11548449	281/999-8400	4
Harmony Sch Enrichment-Houston/*Houston*/Harris	12260755	281/999-0606	4
Harmony Sch Exc-Austin/*Austin*/Travis	11512608	512/693-0000	4
Harmony Sch Exc-El Paso/*El Paso*/El Paso	12179235	915/307-4772	4
Harmony Sch Exc-Houston/*Houston*/Harris	11013652	713/983-8668	4
Harmony Sch Exc-Laredo/*Laredo*/Webb	12260767	956/791-0007	4
Harmony Sch Exc-San Antonio/*San Antonio*/Bexar	12162658	210/645-7166	4
Harmony Sch Exc-Sugar Land/*Sugar Land*/Fort Bend	12309363	832/532-0728	4
Harmony Sch Exploration-Houstn/*Houston*/Harris	11932541	832/831-7406	4
Harmony Sch Fine Arts & Tech/*Houston*/Harris	11559046	832/433-7001	4

School Year 2019-2020   800-333-8802   TX-V31

DISTRICT & SCHOOL TELEPHONE INDEX

Market Data Retrieval

School/City/County DISTRICT/CITY/COUNTY	PID	TELEPHONE NUMBER	PAGE
Harmony Sch Ingenuity-Houston/*Houston*/Harris	11448306	713/664-1020	4
Harmony Sch Innov-Austin/*Austin*/Travis	12163705	512/300-0895	4
Harmony Sch Innov-Brownsville/*Brownsville*/Cameron	12260779	956/544-1348	4
Harmony Sch Innov-Carrolltn/*Carrollton*/Denton	11548451	469/892-5556	4
Harmony Sch Innov-El Paso/*El Paso*/El Paso	11446918	915/757-2929	4
Harmony Sch Innov-Euless/*Euless*/Tarrant	12039051	817/554-2800	4
Harmony Sch Innov-Ft Worth/*Fort Worth*/Tarrant	11818359	817/386-5505	4
Harmony Sch Innov-Garland/*Garland*/Dallas	12179223	469/814-0059	4
Harmony Sch Innov-Houston/*Houston*/Harris	11013664	713/541-3030	4
Harmony Sch Innov-Laredo/*Laredo*/Webb	12163042	956/568-9495	4
Harmony Sch Innov-San Antonio/*San Antonio*/Bexar	11559096	210/265-1715	4
Harmony Sch Innov-Sugar Land/*Sugar Land*/Fort Bend	11719789	281/302-6445	4
Harmony Sch Innov-Waco/*Waco*/McLennan	12260781	254/235-0321	4
Harmony Sch Nature & Athletics/*Dallas*/Dallas	11559084	972/296-1000	4
Harmony Sch Sci-Austin/*Austin*/Travis	11013688	512/821-1700	4
Harmony Sch Sci-Houston/*Houston*/Harris	05010878	713/729-4400	4
Harmony Sch Tech-Houston/*Houston*/Harris	11734935	281/444-1555	4
Harmony Sci Acad-Austin/*Austin*/Travis	05301706	512/835-7900	4
Harmony Sci Acad-Beaumont/*Beaumont*/Jefferson	11013690	409/838-4000	5
Harmony Sci Acad-Brownsville/*Brownsville*/Cameron	11132143	956/574-9555	5
Harmony Sci Acad-Bryan/*Bryan*/Brazos	11013705	979/779-2100	5
Harmony Sci Acad-Carrollton/*Carrollton*/Denton	12163729	972/394-9560	5
Harmony Sci Acad-Cedar Park/*Austin*/Travis	12235231	512/494-5151	5
Harmony Sci Acad-El Paso/*El Paso*/El Paso	10915825	915/859-4620	5
Harmony Sci Acad-Euless/*Euless*/Tarrant	11548463	817/354-3000	5
Harmony Sci Acad-Ft Worth/*Fort Worth*/Tarrant	11013640	817/263-0700	5
Harmony Sci Acad-Garland/*Garland*/Dallas	11559060	972/212-4777	5
Harmony Sci Acad-Grand Prairie/*Grand Prairie*/Dallas	11132131	972/642-9911	5
Harmony Sci Acad-Houston/*Houston*/Harris	11565021	713/492-0214	5
Harmony Sci Acad-Katy/*Katy*/Fort Bend	11735630	832/437-3926	5
Harmony Sci Acad-Laredo/*Laredo*/Webb	11132076	956/712-1177	5
Harmony Sci Acad-Lubbock/*Lubbock*/Lubbock	11013717	806/747-1000	5
Harmony Sci Acad-Odessa/*Odessa*/Ector	11559058	432/363-6000	5
Harmony Sci Acad-Pflugerville/*Pflugerville*/Travis	11132090	512/251-5000	5
Harmony Sci Acad-Plano/*Plano*/Collin	12260793	972/596-0041	5
Harmony Sci Acad-San Antonio/*San Antonio*/Bexar	11013729	210/674-7788	5
Harmony Sci Acad-Sugar Land/*Sugar Land*/Fort Bend	11132088	281/265-2525	5
Harmony Sci Acad-Waco/*Waco*/McLennan	11013731	254/751-7878	5
Harmony Science Acad-Cypress/*Cypress*/Harris	12362717	281/444-1555	5
Harmony Science Acad-Dallas/*Dallas*/Dallas	05368041	469/730-2477	5
Harold Branch Acad Career/Tech/*Corp Christi*/Nueces	11925017	361/878-4780	303
Harold C Kaffie Middle Sch/*Corp Christi*/Nueces	03050999	361/878-3700	303
Harold Cade Middle Sch/*Victoria*/Victoria	11557115	361/788-2840	382
Harold Lang Middle Sch/*Dallas*/Dallas	10908353	972/925-2400	100
Harper Daep Sch/*Houston*/Harris	02129858	713/802-4760	190
Harper Elem Sch/*Harper*/Gillespie	01019743	830/864-4044	163
Harper Elem Sch/*Princeton*/Collin	11076666	469/952-5400	84
Harper High Sch/*Harper*/Gillespie	10005119	830/864-4044	163
HARPER IND SCH DIST/HARPER/ GILLESPIE	01019731	830/864-4044	163
Harper Middle Sch/*Harper*/Gillespie	11445768	830/864-4044	163
Harpool Middle Sch/*Argyle*/Denton	11128556	940/369-1700	121
Harrell Budd Elem Sch/*Dallas*/Dallas	01008964	972/502-8400	100
Harrington Elem Sch/*Plano*/Collin	01824134	469/752-1500	82
Harris Academy/*San Antonio*/Bexar	00999190	210/228-1220	40
HARRIS CO DEPT OF ED/HOUSTON/ HARRIS	02091055	713/694-6300	179
Harris Co Detention Center/*Houston*/Harris	03475428	713/222-4100	179
Harris Co Juvenile Justice CS/*Houston*/Harris	04813536	713/222-4100	5
Harris Co Youth Village/*Seabrook*/Harris	01809328	281/326-2521	179
Harris Cty Leadership Academy/*Katy*/Harris	05010830	713/222-4629	5
Harris Elem Sch/*Austin*/Travis	01056258	512/414-2085	367
Harrison Lane Elem Sch/*Hurst*/Tarrant	01053816	817/285-3270	354

School/City/County DISTRICT/CITY/COUNTY	PID	TELEPHONE NUMBER	PAGE
Harrison-Jefferson-Madison ES/*Port Lavaca*/Calhoun	01003196	361/552-5253	62
HARROLD IND SCH DIST/HARROLD/ WILBARGER	01060508	940/886-2213	393
Harrold Sch/*Harrold*/Wilbarger	01060510	940/886-2213	393
Harry C Withers Elem Sch/*Dallas*/Dallas	03336937	972/794-5000	100
Harry H Herndon Interm Sch/*Fate*/Rockwall	11462431	469/721-8101	326
Harry McKillop Elem Sch/*Melissa*/Collin	01006332	972/837-2632	81
Harry S Truman Middle Sch/*Grand Prairie*/Dallas	02110340	972/641-7676	107
Harry Shimotsu Elem Sch/*Mission*/Hidalgo	10915332	956/583-5643	224
Harry Stone Montessori Academy/*Dallas*/Dallas	04020765	972/794-3400	100
Hart Elem Sch/*Austin*/Travis	04806703	512/841-2100	367
Hart Elem Sch/*El Paso*/El Paso	01015981	915/236-8825	133
Hart Elem Sch/*Hart*/Castro	01005027	806/938-2142	71
Hart Elem Sch/*Lucas*/Collin	04914568	469/742-8200	80
HART IND SCH DIST/HART/CASTRO	01005015	806/938-2143	71
Hart Junior Senior High Sch/*Hart*/Castro	01005039	806/938-2141	71
HARTLEY IND SCH DIST/HARTLEY/ HARTLEY	01028823	806/365-4458	209
Hartley Sch/*Hartley*/Hartley	01028835	806/365-4458	210
Hartman Elem Sch/*Wylie*/Collin	01006617	972/429-3480	85
Hartman Middle Sch/*Houston*/Harris	01025118	713/845-7435	192
Harts Bluff Elem Sch/*Mt Pleasant*/Titus	01055357	903/577-1146	363
HARTS BLUFF IND SCH DIST/ MT PLEASANT/TITUS	01055345	903/577-1146	363
Hartsfield Elem Sch/*Houston*/Harris	01024841	713/746-8280	192
Harvard Elem Sch/*Houston*/Harris	01024061	713/867-5210	191
Harvest Christian Academy/*Edinburg*/Hidalgo	11135951	956/383-8967	226
Harvest Christian Academy/*Watauga*/Tarrant	04888139	817/485-1660	359
Harvey Elem Sch/*Kingsville*/Kleberg	01036260	361/592-4327	257
Harvey S Brown Elem Sch/*Houston*/Harris	10012394	281/860-1400	183
Harvey Turner Elem Sch/*Pasadena*/Harris	04015631	713/740-0768	199
Harwell Elem Sch/*Lubbock*/Lubbock	01038579	806/219-5700	270
Harwood Junior High Sch/*Bedford*/Tarrant	01053828	817/354-3360	354
HASKELL CONS IND SCH DIST/ HASKELL/HASKELL	01028873	940/864-2602	210
Haskell Elem Sch/*Haskell*/Haskell	01028885	940/864-2654	210
Haskell High Sch/*Haskell*/Haskell	01172448	940/864-8535	210
Haskell Junior High Sch/*Rochester*/Haskell	01028940	940/864-5981	210
Haslet Elem Sch/*Haslet*/Denton	01013529	817/215-0850	125
Hassler Elem Sch/*Klein*/Harris	04853586	832/484-7100	197
Hastings 9th Grade Center/*Houston*/Harris	04809119	281/988-3139	182
Hastings Elem Sch/*Duncanville*/Dallas	01010357	972/708-2800	105
Hastings High Sch/*Houston*/Harris	01023005	281/988-3110	182
Hattie Dyer Elem Sch/*Krum*/Denton	01013359	940/482-2604	122
Haude Elem Sch/*Spring*/Harris	01026318	832/484-5600	197
Hauke Academic Alt High Sch/*Conroe*/Montgomery	01541409	936/709-3420	291
Hawkins Elem Sch/*El Paso*/El Paso	01015620	915/236-8900	133
Hawkins Elem Sch/*Hawkins*/Wood	01061625	903/769-0536	404
Hawkins High Sch/*Hawkins*/Wood	01061837	903/769-0571	404
HAWKINS IND SCH DIST/HAWKINS/ WOOD	01061813	903/769-2181	404
Hawkins Middle Sch/*Hawkins*/Wood	01553270	903/769-0552	404
Hawley Elem Sch/*Hawley*/Jones	01035278	325/537-2721	250
Hawley High Sch/*Hawley*/Jones	04801674	325/537-2722	250
HAWLEY IND SCH DIST/HAWLEY/JONES	01035266	325/537-2214	249
Hawley Middle Sch/*Hawley*/Jones	01035280	325/537-2070	250
Hawthorne Academy/*San Antonio*/Bexar	00998457	210/738-9795	40
Hay Branch Elem Sch/*Killeen*/Bell	02897213	254/336-2080	28
Haynes Elem Sch/*Killeen*/Bell	11718474	254/336-6750	28
Haynes Northwest Academy/*Wichita Falls*/Wichita	01173064	940/235-1160	392
HAYS CONS IND SCH DIST/KYLE/HAYS	01029059	512/268-2141	211
Hays Magnet Academy/*Odessa*/Ector	01014717	432/456-1129	130
Hays Middle Sch/*Frisco*/Collin	12363838	469/219-2260	84
Hazel Harvey Peace Elem Sch/*Fort Worth*/Tarrant	11554553	817/814-8800	351
Hazel Ingram Elem Sch/*Ferris*/Ellis	01015046	972/544-3212	140
Hazel S Pattison Elem Sch/*Katy*/Harris	03249126	281/237-5450	152
Hcal/*Hereford*/Deaf Smith	12172081	806/363-7720	119
HCC Life Skills/*Houston*/Harris	11555492	713/718-6882	194
Headwaters Sch/*Austin*/Travis	11228364	512/443-8843	373
Headwaters Sch/*Austin*/Travis	11551197	512/480-8142	373
Health Careers High Sch/*San Antonio*/Bexar	02226559	210/397-5400	37
Health Science Academy/*San Antonio*/Bexar	11712602	210/977-7278	42
Healy-Murphy Center/*San Antonio*/Bexar	01479533	210/223-2944	45
Hearne Elem Sch/*Hearne*/Robertson	01048653	979/279-3341	325
Hearne Elem Sch/*Houston*/Harris	03007837	281/983-8333	182
Hearne High Sch/*Hearne*/Robertson	01048665	979/279-2332	325

Texas School Directory

DISTRICT & SCHOOL TELEPHONE INDEX

School/City/County DISTRICT/CITY/COUNTY	PID	TELEPHONE NUMBER	PAGE
HEARNE IND SCH DIST/*Hearne*/			
ROBERTSON	01048641	979/279-3200	325
Hearne Junior High Sch/*Hearne*/Robertson	01048689	979/279-2449	325
Heartlight Boarding Sch/*Hallsville*/			
Harrison	12313986	903/668-2173	209
Heather Glen Elem Sch/*Garland*/Dallas	01010577	972/270-2881	106
Hebbronville Elem Sch/*Hebbronville*/			
Jim Hogg	01034482	361/527-3203	244
Hebbronville High Sch/*Hebbronville*/			
Jim Hogg	01034494	361/527-3203	244
Hebbronville Jr High Sch/*Hebbronville*/			
Jim Hogg	01034509	361/527-3203	244
Hebrew Prep School of Austin/*Austin*/Travis	04994025	512/977-0770	373
Hebron 9th Grade Campus/*Carrollton*/Denton	11553717	469/713-5996	123
Hebron High Sch/*Carrollton*/Denton	04850948	469/713-5183	123
Hebron Valley Elem Sch/*Carrollton*/Denton	03249607	469/713-5182	123
Hector Garcia Early Clg HS/*Laredo*/Webb	11073676	956/273-7700	386
Hector Garcia Middle Sch/*San Antonio*/Bexar	11448966	210/397-8400	37
Hector P Garcia Elem Sch/*Temple*/Bell	00996746	254/215-6100	29
Hector P Garcia Middle Sch/*Dallas*/Dallas	10908339	972/502-5500	100
Hedgcoxe Elem Sch/*Plano*/Collin	03333806	469/752-1700	82
HEDLEY IND SCH DIST/*Hedley*/			
DONLEY	01014145	806/856-5323	127
Hedley Sch/*Hedley*/Donley	01014157	806/856-5323	127
Hedrick Middle Sch/*Lewisville*/Denton	01013464	469/713-5188	123
Heflin Elem Sch/*Houston*/Harris	02177972	281/531-1144	182
Heights Elem Sch/*Laredo*/Webb	01059274	956/273-3600	386
Heights Elem Sch/*Texas City*/Galveston	01019511	409/916-0500	161
Heights High Sch/*Houston*/Harris	01024229	713/865-4400	191
Helen Ball Elem Sch/*El Paso*/El Paso	04365979	915/937-8201	136
Helen Edwards Early Chldhd Ctr/*Kaufman*/			
Kaufman	05278238	972/932-0800	252
Helen Major Elm Sch/*Houston*/Harris	11452008	281/891-8870	202
Helena Park Elem Sch/*Nederland*/Jefferson	01033696	409/722-0462	243
Helms Elem Sch/*Houston*/Harris	01024073	713/867-5130	191
Helotes Elem Sch/*Helotes*/Bexar	00998122	210/397-3800	37
Helping Hand Charter Sch/*Austin*/Travis	12362705	512/751-4534	5
Hemmenway Elem Sch/*Katy*/Harris	11077361	281/856-9870	185
Hemphill Elem Sch/*Hemphill*/Sabine	01049279	409/787-3371	329
Hemphill Elem Sch/*Kyle*/Hays	04920256	512/268-4688	211
HEMPHILL IND SCH DIST/*Hemphill*/			
SABINE	01049267	409/787-3371	329
Hemphill Middle Sch/*Hemphill*/Sabine	04448301	409/787-3371	329
Hemphill Senior High Sch/*Hemphill*/Sabine	01049281	409/787-3371	329
Hempstead Elem Sch/*Hempstead*/Waller	01058787	979/826-2452	384
Hempstead High Sch/*Hempstead*/Waller	01058799	979/826-3331	384
HEMPSTEAD IND SCH DIST/*Hempstead*/			
WALLER	01058775	979/826-3304	384
Hempstead Middle Sch/*Hempstead*/Waller	01058804	979/826-2530	384
Henderson Elem Sch/*Bryan*/Brazos	01002087	979/209-1560	55
Henderson Elem Sch/*Forney*/Kaufman	05277064	972/564-7100	252
Henderson Elem Sch/*Midland*/Midland	01041526	432/240-7000	286
Henderson High Sch/*Henderson*/Rusk	01049009	903/655-5000	327
HENDERSON IND SCH DIST/*Henderson*/			
RUSK	01048976	903/655-5000	327
Henderson Junior High Sch/*Stephenville*/			
Erath	01017173	254/968-6967	144
Henderson Middle Sch/*El Paso*/El Paso	01015632	915/236-0700	135
Henderson Middle Sch/*Henderson*/Rusk	01878458	903/655-5400	327
Henderson Middle Sch/*Sour Lake*/Hardin	01022465	409/981-6420	178
Hendrick Middle Sch/*Plano*/Collin	03008221	469/752-5600	82
Hendrickson High Sch/*Pflugerville*/Travis	05276010	512/594-1100	372
Henrietta Elem Sch/*Henrietta*/Clay	01005558	940/720-7910	74
Henrietta High Sch/*Henrietta*/Clay	01005560	940/720-7930	74
HENRIETTA IND SCH DIST/*Henrietta*/			
CLAY	01005546	940/720-7900	74
Henrietta Junior High Sch/*Henrietta*/Clay	01005572	940/720-7920	74
Henry B Gonzalez Elem Sch/*Eagle Pass*/			
Maverick	04871071	830/758-7099	277
Henry B Gonzalez Elem Sch/*Mission*/Hidalgo	04868622	956/323-2460	220
Henry Bauerschlag Elem Sch/*League City*/			
Galveston	05009582	281/284-6100	159
Henry Brauchle Elem Sch/*San Antonio*/Bexar	03324958	210/397-1500	37
Henry Dye Boggess Elem Sch/*Murphy*/Collin	05096858	469/752-4000	82
Henry Ford Elem Sch/*Pharr*/Hidalgo	01030424	956/354-2770	223
Henry Gonzales Elem Sch/*Dallas*/Dallas	10023161	972/502-3300	100
Henry Metzger Middle Sch/*San Antonio*/Bexar	05347712	210/662-2210	33
Henry Middle Sch/*Cedar Park*/Williamson	05093052	512/570-3400	397
Henry Scott Middle Sch/*Denison*/Grayson	12037869	903/462-7180	166
Henry Steubing Elem Sch/*San Antonio*/Bexar	04754760	210/397-4390	37
Henry W Longfellow Academy/*Dallas*/Dallas	01008988	972/749-5400	100
Herbert Boldt Elem Sch/*San Antonio*/Bexar	12106989	210/398-2000	37
Herbert Marcus Elem Sch/*Dallas*/Dallas	01008990	972/794-2900	100
Hereford High Sch/*Hereford*/Deaf Smith	01013024	806/363-7620	119
HEREFORD IND SCH DIST/*Hereford*/			
DEAF SMITH	01012989	806/363-7600	119
Hereford Junior High Sch/*Hereford*/			
Deaf Smith	01013036	806/363-7630	119
Hereford Preparatory Academy/*Hereford*/			
Deaf Smith	11823639	806/363-7740	119
Herfurth Elem Sch/*Rowlett*/Dallas	03055511	972/475-7994	106
Heritage Academy Del Rio/*Del Rio*/Val Verde	12260808	830/774-6230	5
Heritage Academy San Antonio/*Windcrest*/			
Bexar	12178566	210/354-7753	5
Heritage Christian Academy/*Pearland*/			
Brazoria	11230240	713/436-8422	54
Heritage Christian Academy/*Rockwall*/			
Rockwall	04763230	972/772-3003	326
Heritage Elem Sch/*Deer Park*/Harris	10901434	281/604-2600	198
Heritage Elem Sch/*Grapevine*/Tarrant	03389659	817/305-4820	353
Heritage Elem Sch/*Houston*/Harris	04912754	281/891-8510	202
Heritage Elem Sch/*Keller*/Tarrant	03009859	817/744-4900	355
Heritage Elem Sch/*Lewisville*/Denton	04036518	469/713-5985	123
Heritage Elem Sch/*San Antonio*/Bexar	04876435	210/882-1607	43
Heritage High Sch/*Frisco*/Collin	11448473	469/633-5900	79
Heritage Middle Sch/*Colleyville*/Tarrant	04012598	817/305-4790	353
Heritage Middle Sch/*Lubbock*/Lubbock	11717781	806/794-9400	269
Heritage Rose Elem Sch/*Rosharon*/Fort Bend	11551599	281/327-5400	150
Heritage Sch/*Fredericksbrg*/Gillespie	04761359	830/997-6597	163
Herman E Utley Middle Sch/*Rockwall*/			
Rockwall	11453741	972/771-5281	325
Herman Furlough Jr Middle Sch/*Terrell*/			
Kaufman	01035797	972/563-7501	253
Herman Jones Elem Sch/*Prairie View*/Waller	04012354	936/372-4200	384
Herman Lawson Early Chldhd Ctr/*McKinney*/			
Collin	11447144	469/302-2400	81
Hermes Elem Sch/*La Grange*/Fayette	01017745	979/968-4100	147
HERMLEIGH IND SCH DIST/*Hermleigh*/			
SCURRY	01050046	325/863-2451	333
Hermleigh Sch/*Hermleigh*/Scurry	01050058	325/863-2451	333
Hernandez Elem Sch/*San Marcos*/Hays	01029164	512/393-6100	212
Herod Elem Sch/*Houston*/Harris	01024653	713/778-3315	194
Herrera Elem Sch/*El Paso*/El Paso	11449192	915/774-7700	133
Herrera Elem Sch/*Houston*/Harris	04016697	713/696-2800	191
Herty Primary Sch/*Lufkin*/Angelina	00994982	936/639-2241	18
Hettie Halstead Elem Sch/*Copperas Cove*/			
Coryell	01007609	254/547-3440	92
Hewitt Elem Sch/*Hewitt*/McLennan	02045422	254/761-5750	280
Hfa-Alameda Sch-Art & Design/*San Antonio*/			
Bexar	11832379	210/226-4031	5
Hickman Elem Sch/*Garland*/Dallas	01382825	972/675-3150	106
Hicks Elem Sch/*Corp Christi*/Nueces	01044504	361/878-2200	303
Hicks Elem Sch/*Houston*/Harris	04453239	281/983-8040	182
Hico Elem Sch/*Hico*/Hamilton	01022207	254/796-2183	176
HICO IND SCH DIST/*Hico*/**HAMILTON**	01022192	254/796-2182	176
Hico Secondary Sch/*Hico*/Hamilton	04867874	254/796-2184	176
Hidalgo Academy/*Hidalgo*/Hidalgo	04921432	956/843-4390	217
Hidalgo Early College High Sch/*Hidalgo*/			
Hidalgo	01553127	956/843-4300	217
Hidalgo Elem Sch/*Hidalgo*/Hidalgo	01029839	956/843-4225	217
HIDALGO IND SCH DIST/*Hidalgo*/			
HIDALGO	01029827	956/843-4404	217
Hidalgo Park Elem Sch/*Pharr*/Hidalgo	05341421	956/843-4275	217
Hidden Cove Elem Sch/*San Antonio*/Bexar	02894326	210/623-6220	43
Hidden Forest Elem Sch/*San Antonio*/Bexar	01824031	210/407-4000	35
Hidden Hollow Elem Sch/*Kingwood*/Harris	03333521	281/641-2400	196
Hidden Lakes Elem Sch/*Keller*/Tarrant	04921614	817/744-5000	355
Higgins Elem Sch/*Whitehouse*/Smith	03049902	903/839-5580	339
HIGGINS IND SCH DIST/*Higgins*/			
LIPSCOMB	01038220	806/852-2171	268
Higgins Sch/*Higgins*/Lipscomb	01038232	806/852-2631	268
High Country Elem Sch/*Fort Worth*/Tarrant	04946597	817/306-8007	348
HIGH ISLAND IND SCH DIST/			
HIGH ISLAND/GALVESTON	01019250	409/286-5317	160
High Island Sch/*High Island*/Galveston	01019262	409/286-5313	160
High Point Academy/*Fort Worth*/Tarrant	12163353	817/600-6401	5
High Point Elem Sch/*Navasota*/Grimes	10025822	936/825-1130	172
High Point Elem Sch/*Temple*/Bell	11926047	254/316-5000	27
High Point Prep Academy/*Arlington*/Tarrant	11231749	817/394-3100	359
High Pointe Elem Sch/*Cedar Hill*/Dallas	02893114	972/291-7874	97
High School Ahead Acad MS/*Houston*/Harris	11555507	713/696-2643	188
High School for Law & Justice/*Houston*/			
Harris	02227527	713/867-5100	189
Highland Elem Sch/*Plainview*/Hale	01021978	806/293-6045	175

School Year 2019-2020   800-333-8802   **TX-V33**

DISTRICT & SCHOOL TELEPHONE INDEX

Market Data Retrieval

School/City/County DISTRICT/CITY/COUNTY	PID	TELEPHONE NUMBER	PAGE
Highland Elem Sch/*Tulia*/Swisher	01051583	806/995-4141	343
Highland Forest Elem Sch/*San Antonio*/Bexar	05070141	210/333-7385	31
Highland Heights Elem Sch/*Houston*/Harris	01024085	713/696-2920	188
Highland Hills Elem Sch/*San Antonio*/Bexar	00998835	210/438-6860	40
HIGHLAND IND SCH DIST/*ROSCOE*/ NOLAN	01043859	325/766-3652	301
Highland Lakes Elem Sch/*Granite SHLS*/ Burnet	04801777	830/798-3650	60
Highland Meadows Elem Sch/*Dallas*/Dallas	05345764	972/502-5200	100
Highland Middle Sch/*Fort Worth*/Tarrant	04808828	817/847-5143	348
Highland Park Elem Sch/*Amarillo*/Potter	03315878	806/335-1334	319
Highland Park Elem Sch/*Austin*/Travis	01056260	512/414-2090	368
Highland Park Elem Sch/*Nederland*/Jefferson	01033701	409/722-0236	243
Highland Park Elem Sch/*Pflugerville*/Travis	10022416	512/594-6800	372
Highland Park Elem Sch/*San Antonio*/Bexar	00998847	210/228-3335	40
Highland Park Elem Sch/*Texarkana*/Bowie	01001253	903/794-8001	50
Highland Park High Sch/*Amarillo*/Potter	04914441	806/335-2821	319
Highland Park High Sch/*Dallas*/Dallas	01011052	214/780-3700	108
HIGHLAND PARK IND SCH DIST/ DALLAS/DALLAS	01011038	214/780-3000	108
HIGHLAND PARK IND SCH DIST/ AMARILLO/POTTER	01047582	806/335-2823	319
Highland Park Middle Sch/*Amarillo*/Potter	01047594	806/335-2821	319
Highland Park Middle Sch/*Dallas*/Dallas	04360125	214/780-3600	108
Highland PK Presbyterian Sch/*Dallas*/Dallas	01479741	214/525-6500	115
Highland Sch/*Roscoe*/Nolan	01043861	325/766-3651	301
Highland Village Elem Sch/*Lewisville*/ Denton	02131019	469/713-5957	123
Highlander Sch/*Dallas*/Dallas	01479935	214/348-3220	115
Highlands Elem Sch/*Cedar Hill*/Dallas	03006493	972/291-0496	97
Highlands Elem Sch/*Highlands*/Harris	01023641	281/420-4900	188
Highlands Elem Sch/*Sugar Land*/Fort Bend	02892926	281/634-4160	150
Highlands High Sch/*San Antonio*/Bexar	00998859	210/438-6800	40
Highlands Junior High Sch/*Highlands*/Harris	01023653	281/420-4695	188
Highlands Sch/*Irving*/Dallas	04146175	972/554-1980	114
Highpoint School East/*Houston*/Harris	04747133	713/696-2160	179
Highpoint School North/*Houston*/Harris	04942228	713/696-2195	179
Hightower Elem Sch/*Plano*/Collin	04811473	469/752-1800	82
Hightower High Sch/*Missouri City*/Fort Bend	04808610	281/634-5240	150
Hildebrandt Intermediate Sch/*Spring*/Harris	01026320	832/249-5100	197
Hill Country Adventist Sch/*Kerrville*/Kerr	03017349	830/257-3903	256
Hill Country Christian Sch/*Austin*/Travis	04880797	512/331-7036	373
Hill Country Christian Sch/*San Marcos*/Hays	04993980	512/353-8976	212
Hill Country Elem Sch/*Pipe Creek*/Bandera	04362599	830/535-6151	23
Hill Country High Sch/*Kerrville*/Kerr	03473511	830/257-2232	256
Hill Country Middle Sch/*Austin*/Travis	01401445	512/732-9220	370
Hill Country Montessori Sch/*Boerne*/Kendall	11849683	830/229-5377	254
Hill Country Yth Rch-Najim Sch/*Ingram*/Kerr	12100387	830/367-6100	5
Hill Elem Sch/*Arlington*/Tarrant	01051791	682/867-2300	344
Hill Elem Sch/*Austin*/Travis	01056272	512/414-2369	368
Hill Elem Sch/*Houston*/Harris	05097228	281/878-7775	180
Hill School of Fort Worth/*Fort Worth*/ Tarrant	01875597	817/923-9482	359
Hillander Sch/*Midland*/Midland	01480829	432/684-8681	286
Hillcrest Elem Sch/*Alice*/Jim Wells	01034561	361/660-2095	245
Hillcrest Elem Sch/*Austin*/Travis	02130429	512/386-3550	369
Hillcrest Elem Sch/*Dumas*/Moore	01042867	806/935-5629	295
Hillcrest Elem Sch/*Nederland*/Jefferson	01033713	409/722-3484	243
Hillcrest Elem Sch/*Plainview*/Hale	01021980	806/293-6050	175
Hillcrest Elem Sch/*San Antonio*/Bexar	00999176	210/228-3340	40
Hillcrest High Sch/*Dallas*/Dallas	01009009	972/502-6800	100
Hillcrest Prof Dev Sch/*Waco*/McLennan	04288668	254/772-4286	282
Hillcrest Sch/*Midland*/Midland	04994154	432/570-7444	286
Hillsboro Elem Sch/*Hillsboro*/Hill	03008269	254/582-4140	227
Hillsboro High Sch/*Hillsboro*/Hill	01172498	254/582-4100	227
HILLSBORO IND SCH DIST/*HILLSBORO*/ HILL	01030852	254/582-8585	227
Hillsboro Intermediate Sch/*Hillsboro*/Hill	05026750	254/582-4170	227
Hillsboro Junior High Sch/*Hillsboro*/Hill	01172503	254/582-4120	227
Hillside Acad for Excellence/*Garland*/ Dallas	01010591	972/926-2550	106
Hillside Elem Sch/*Amarillo*/Randall	11450402	806/677-2520	321
Hillside Elem Sch/*El Paso*/El Paso	01015644	915/236-0100	133
Hilltop Elem Sch/*Argyle*/Denton	01013189	940/464-0564	120
Hillwood Middle Sch/*Fort Worth*/Tarrant	04921638	817/744-3350	355
Hinojosa EC-PK-K Sch/*Houston*/Harris	04754485	281/985-4750	181
Hinojosa Elem Sch/*Mission*/Hidalgo	05278381	956/584-4990	224
Hirsch Elem Sch/*San Antonio*/Bexar	00998809	210/978-7985	40
Hirschi High Sch/*Wichita Falls*/Wichita	01173076	940/235-1070	392
Hitchcock High Sch/*Hitchcock*/Galveston	01019298	409/316-6544	161
HITCHCOCK IND SCH DIST/*HITCHCOCK*/ GALVESTON	01019274	409/316-6545	160

School/City/County DISTRICT/CITY/COUNTY	PID	TELEPHONE NUMBER	PAGE
Hitchcock Primary Sch/*Hitchcock*/Galveston	11719272	409/316-6467	161
Hobbs Williams Elem Sch/*Grand Prairie*/ Dallas	11157155	972/522-2700	107
Hockaday Sch/*Dallas*/Dallas	01012123	214/363-6311	115
Hodge Elem Sch/*Denton*/Denton	03009732	940/369-2800	121
Hodges Bend Middle Sch/*Houston*/Fort Bend	03011395	281/634-3000	150
Hodges Elem Sch/*Balch Springs*/Dallas	01011430	972/290-4040	111
Hodges Elem Sch/*Lubbock*/Lubbock	01038701	806/219-5800	270
Hoffmann Elem Sch/*San Antonio*/Bexar	11448954	210/397-8350	37
Hoffmann Lane Elem Sch/*New Braunfels*/Comal	05090684	830/221-2500	88
Hofius Intermediate Sch/*Spring*/Harris	12315764	832/375-8800	197
Hogg Middle Sch/*Houston*/Harris	01024097	713/802-4700	191
Holbrook Elem Sch/*Houston*/Harris	01857260	713/460-6165	185
Holiday Heights Elem Sch/*N Richlnd Hls*/ Tarrant	01052109	817/547-2600	346
Holiman Elem Sch/*San Angelo*/Tom Green	01055668	325/659-3663	365
Holland Elem Sch/*Holland*/Bell	00996409	254/657-2525	27
Holland High Sch/*Holland*/Bell	00996411	254/657-2523	27
HOLLAND IND SCH DIST/*HOLLAND*/ BELL	00996394	254/657-0175	27
Holland Medical High Sch/*Abilene*/Taylor	11452943	325/794-4120	360
Holland Middle Sch/*Holland*/Bell	04245161	254/657-2224	27
Holland Middle Sch/*Houston*/Harris	02043319	713/671-3860	189
Hollaway Sixth Grade Sch/*Whitehouse*/Smith	01051026	903/839-5656	339
Hollenstein Career & Tech Ctr/*Fort Worth*/ Tarrant	11713527	817/306-1925	349
Hollibrook Elem Sch/*Houston*/Harris	01023263	713/251-5800	201
Holliday Elem Sch/*Holliday*/Archer	00995223	940/586-1986	19
Holliday High Sch/*Holliday*/Archer	00995235	940/586-1624	19
HOLLIDAY IND SCH DIST/*HOLLIDAY*/ ARCHER	00995211	940/586-1281	19
Holliday Middle Sch/*Holliday*/Archer	02844802	940/586-1314	19
Hollis T Dietz Elem Sch/*Heartland*/Kaufman	12231118	972/427-6050	251
Holmes Elem Sch/*Bay City*/Matagorda	01040883	979/401-1400	275
Holmquist Elem Sch/*Houston*/Harris	10910174	281/988-3024	182
Holmsley Elem Sch/*Houston*/Harris	02848731	281/463-5885	185
Holub Middle Sch/*Houston*/Harris	02126428	281/983-8433	182
Holy Cross Catholic Academy/*Amarillo*/ Randall	01047661	806/355-9637	321
Holy Cross Catholic HS/*Odessa*/Ector	12368852	432/713-0143	131
Holy Cross Catholic Sch/*Bay City*/Matagorda	01027922	979/245-5632	276
Holy Cross Christian Academy/*Burleson*/ Johnson	11228405	817/295-7232	249
Holy Cross of San Antonio Sch/*San Antonio*/ Bexar	00999803	210/433-9395	44
Holy Family Catholic Academy/*Irving*/Dallas	01012422	972/255-0205	114
Holy Family Catholic Sch/*Austin*/Williamson	04911827	512/246-4455	400
Holy Family Catholic Sch/*Corp Christi*/ Nueces	01045211	361/884-9142	306
Holy Family Catholic Sch/*Fort Worth*/ Tarrant	01054353	817/737-4201	358
Holy Family Catholic Sch/*Galveston*/ Galveston	01028029	409/765-6607	161
Holy Ghost Catholic Sch/*Houston*/Harris	01027934	713/668-5327	204
Holy Name Catholic Sch/*San Antonio*/Bexar	00999815	210/333-7356	44
Holy Rosary Sch/*Rosenberg*/Fort Bend	01857272	281/342-5813	155
Holy Spirit Catholic Sch/*San Antonio*/Bexar	00999839	210/349-1169	44
Holy Spirit Episcopal Sch/*Houston*/Harris	01875389	713/468-5138	206
Holy Trinity Catholic High Sch/*Temple*/Bell	04885072	254/771-0787	30
Holy Trinity Catholic Sch/*Dallas*/Dallas	01012434	214/526-5113	114
Holy Trinity Catholic Sch/*Grapevine*/ Tarrant	04307159	817/421-8000	358
Holy Trinity Episcopal Sch/*Houston*/Harris	05256826	281/459-4323	206
Homer Drive Elem Sch/*Beaumont*/Jefferson	03326839	409/617-6225	242
Homer Hanna Early Clg HS/*Brownsville*/ Cameron	01003586	956/548-7600	64
Homer J Morris Middle Sch/*McAllen*/Hidalgo	02856726	956/618-7300	221
Homestead Elem Sch/*Carrollton*/Denton	04850950	469/713-5181	123
Hommel Elem Sch/*Everman*/Tarrant	01526148	817/568-3540	349
Hondo High Sch/*Hondo*/Medina	01041241	830/426-3341	284
HONDO IND SCH DIST/*HONDO*/MEDINA	01041239	830/426-3027	284
Honey Elem Sch/*Lubbock*/Lubbock	02202101	806/219-5900	270
Honey Grove Elem Sch/*Honey Grove*/Fannin	01017484	903/378-2264	146
Honey Grove High Sch/*Honey Grove*/Fannin	01017496	903/378-2264	146
HONEY GROVE IND SCH DIST/ HONEY GROVE/FANNIN	01017472	903/378-2264	146
Honey Grove Middle Sch/*Honey Grove*/Fannin	03240302	903/378-2264	146
Honor Roll Sch/*Sugar Land*/Fort Bend	04028066	281/265-7888	155
Honore Ligarde Elem Sch/*Laredo*/Webb	03052959	956/273-3900	386
Hood-Case Elem Sch/*Alvin*/Brazoria	04750829	281/585-5786	51
Hook Elem Sch/*Stephenville*/Erath	04945567	254/968-3213	144
Hooks Elem Sch/*Hooks*/Bowie	01000869	903/547-2291	48

Texas School Directory

DISTRICT & SCHOOL TELEPHONE INDEX

School/City/County DISTRICT/CITY/COUNTY	PID	TELEPHONE NUMBER	PAGE
Hooks High Sch/*Hooks*/Bowie	01000871	903/547-2215	48
HOOKS IND SCH DIST/**HOOKS**/**BOWIE**	01000857	903/547-6077	48
Hooks Junior High Sch/*Hooks*/Bowie	01000883	903/547-2568	48
Hoover Elem Sch/*Azle*/Tarrant	04035916	817/444-7766	345
Hoover Elem Sch/*Katy*/Harris	12233154	832/667-7301	185
Hope Academy/*La Joya*/Hidalgo	10912469	956/323-2900	220
Hope High Sch/*Port Lavaca*/Calhoun	03397084	361/552-7084	62
Hopewell Middle Sch/*Round Rock*/Williamson	04452340	512/464-5200	399
Hopkins Elem Sch/*Victoria*/Victoria	01058517	361/788-9527	382
Hopper Middle Sch/*Cypress*/Harris	10966680	281/463-5353	185
Horace Mann Junior High Sch/*Baytown*/Harris	01023665	281/420-4585	188
Horace Mann Middle Sch/*Amarillo*/Potter	01047295	806/326-3700	318
Horizon Heights Sch/*El Paso*/El Paso	02199516	915/937-7400	136
Horizon High Sch/*El Paso*/El Paso	05100344	915/926-4200	132
Horizon Middle Sch/*El Paso*/El Paso	10004359	915/926-4700	132
Horizon Montessori Academy I/*McAllen*/Hidalgo	11014905	956/631-0234	5
Horizon Montessori II/*Weslaco*/Hidalgo	11014917	956/969-0044	5
Horizon Montessori III/*Harlingen*/Cameron	11564699	956/423-8200	5
Horn Elem Sch/*Bellaire*/Harris	01024865	713/295-5264	194
Horn Elem Sch/*Houston*/Harris	10002894	281/988-3223	182
Horne Elem Sch/*Houston*/Harris	02045381	281/463-5954	185
Hornsby-Dunlap Elem Sch/*Austin*/Travis	02907117	512/386-3650	369
House Creek Elementray Sch/*Copperas Cove*/Coryell	11715173	254/518-3000	92
Houser Elem Sch/*Conroe*/Montgomery	02126868	832/663-4000	291
Housman Elem Sch/*Houston*/Harris	01027154	713/251-5900	201
Houston Academy Int'l Studies/*Houston*/Harris	10021620	713/942-1430	192
Houston Christian High Sch/*Houston*/Harris	01480441	713/580-6000	206
Houston Elem Sch/*Austin*/Travis	01532094	512/414-2517	366
Houston Elem Sch/*Conroe*/Montgomery	01042544	936/709-5100	292
Houston Elem Sch/*Denison*/Grayson	01020340	903/462-7300	166
Houston Elem Sch/*Harlingen*/Cameron	01003859	956/427-3110	65
Houston Elem Sch/*Lancaster*/Dallas	01011349	972/218-1512	110
Houston Elem Sch/*Mineral Wells*/Palo Pinto	01046083	940/325-3427	310
Houston Gateway Acad-Evergreen/*Houston*/Harris	04926781	713/649-2706	5
Houston Gateway Academy-Coral/*Houston*/Harris	05221314	713/923-5060	5
Houston Gateway Elite Clg Prep/*Houston*/Harris	12260822	832/649-2700	5
Houston Heights High Sch/*Houston*/Harris	04891825	713/868-9797	5
HOUSTON IND SCH DIST/**HOUSTON**/**HARRIS**	01023770	713/556-6000	188
HOUSTON ISD-ACHIEVE 180/**HOUSTON**/**HARRIS**	12310958	713/556-7102	188
HOUSTON ISD-EAST AREA/**HOUSTON**/**HARRIS**	12170253	713/556-8998	189
HOUSTON ISD-NORTH AREA/**HOUSTON**/**HARRIS**	12170239	713/556-8998	190
HOUSTON ISD-NORTHWEST AREA/**HOUSTON**/**HARRIS**	12179974	713/556-8999	191
HOUSTON ISD-SOUTH AREA/**HOUSTON**/**HARRIS**	12170241	713/556-4447	192
HOUSTON ISD-WEST AREA/**HOUSTON**/**HARRIS**	12170265	713/556-9123	193
Houston Learning Academy/*Houston*/Harris	11238412	281/449-1532	206
Houston Middle Sch/*Irving*/Dallas	01532018	972/600-7500	109
Howard Burnham Elem Sch/*El Paso*/El Paso	04813952	915/584-9499	5
Howard Dobbs Elem Sch/*Rockwall*/Rockwall	01048720	972/771-5232	325
Howard Early Childhood Center/*San Antonio*/Bexar	00996966	210/832-5900	30
Howard Norman Elem Sch/*Hutto*/Williamson	12167701	512/759-5480	396
Howe High Sch/*Howe*/Grayson	01020493	903/532-3236	166
HOWE IND SCH DIST/**HOWE**/**GRAYSON**	01020479	903/532-3228	166
Howe Intermediate Sch/*Howe*/Grayson	01020481	903/532-3320	166
Howe Middle Sch/*Howe*/Grayson	01020508	903/532-3286	166
Howell Middle Sch/*Victoria*/Victoria	01058529	361/578-1561	382
Hoyland Elem Sch/*Houston*/Harris	11451987	281/891-8810	202
Hubbard Elem Sch/*De Kalb*/Bowie	01000912	903/667-2645	48
Hubbard Elem Sch/*Hubbard*/Hill	01030929	254/576-2359	228
Hubbard Heights Elem Sch/*Fort Worth*/Tarrant	01053000	817/814-7500	351
Hubbard High Sch/*Hubbard*/Hill	01030931	254/576-2549	228
HUBBARD IND SCH DIST/**DE KALB**/**BOWIE**	01000900	903/667-2645	48
HUBBARD IND SCH DIST/**HUBBARD**/**HILL**	01030917	254/576-2564	227
Hubbard Middle Sch/*Tyler*/Smith	01050864	903/262-1560	338
HUCKABAY IND SCH DIST/**STEPHENVILLE**/**ERATH**	01017056	254/968-5274	143
Huckabay Sch/*Stephenville*/Erath	01017068	254/968-8476	143
Hudson Bend Middle Sch/*Austin*/Travis	04920189	512/533-6400	370
Hudson Elem Sch/*Brownsville*/Cameron	04808517	956/574-6400	64
Hudson High Sch/*Lufkin*/Angelina	00994877	936/875-9232	17
HUDSON IND SCH DIST/**LUFKIN**/**ANGELINA**	00994853	936/875-3351	17
Hudson Middle Sch/*Lufkin*/Angelina	00994889	936/875-9295	17
Hudson Middle Sch/*Sachse*/Dallas	04035473	972/675-3070	106
Hudson Pep Elem Sch/*Longview*/Gregg	01021045	903/803-5100	170
Huebner Elem Sch/*San Antonio*/Bexar	04755867	210/407-4200	35
Hueco Elem Sch/*El Paso*/El Paso	02199528	915/937-7600	136
Huffines Middle Sch/*Lewisville*/Denton	01541318	469/713-5990	123
Huffman Elem Sch/*Huffman*/Harris	03004768	281/324-1399	195
Huffman Elem Sch/*Plano*/Collin	02225593	469/752-1900	82
HUFFMAN IND SCH DIST/**HUFFMAN**/**HARRIS**	01026112	281/324-1871	195
Huffman Middle Sch/*Huffman*/Harris	01026136	281/324-2598	195
Huggins Elem Sch/*Fulshear*/Fort Bend	02045355	832/223-1600	154
Hughes Elem Sch/*McKinney*/Collin	12172897	469/219-2230	84
Hughes Middle Sch/*Burleson*/Johnson	01034846	817/245-0600	247
Hughes Road Elem Sch/*Dickinson*/Galveston	02846496	281/229-6700	159
Hughes Springs Elem Sch/*Hughes Spgs*/Cass	01004798	903/639-3881	70
Hughes Springs High Sch/*Hughes Spgs*/Cass	01004803	903/639-3841	70
HUGHES SPRINGS IND SCH DIST/**HUGHES SPGS**/**CASS**	01004786	903/639-3800	70
Hughes Springs Jr High Sch/*Hughes Spgs*/Cass	01004815	903/639-3812	70
Hughey Elem Sch/*El Paso*/El Paso	01015656	915/236-0250	133
Hughston Elem Sch/*Plano*/Collin	01401366	469/752-2000	82
Hull Daisetta Elem Sch/*Hull*/Liberty	01037898	936/536-6321	266
Hull Daisetta High Sch/*Daisetta*/Liberty	01037903	936/536-6321	266
HULL DAISETTA IND SCH DIST/**DAISETTA**/**LIBERTY**	01037886	936/536-6321	266
Hull Daisetta Junior High Sch/*Daisetta*/Liberty	01037915	936/536-6321	266
Humble Christian Sch/*Humble*/Harris	11225128	281/441-1313	206
Humble Classical Academy/*Humble*/Harris	11925184	281/913-5107	5
Humble Elem Sch/*Humble*/Harris	01026174	281/641-1100	196
Humble High Sch/*Humble*/Harris	01026186	281/641-6300	196
HUMBLE IND SCH DIST/**HUMBLE**/**HARRIS**	01026150	281/641-1000	195
Humble Middle Sch/*Humble*/Harris	01026198	281/641-4000	196
Humphrey's Highland Elem Sch/*Amarillo*/Potter	01047312	806/326-4550	318
Hunstville Classical Academy/*Huntsville*/Walker	11014591	936/291-0203	5
Hunt Elem Sch/*Cuero*/De Witt	01013713	361/275-1900	117
HUNT IND SCH DIST/**HUNT**/**KERR**	01036038	830/238-4893	255
Hunt Sch/*Hunt*/Kerr	01036040	830/238-4893	255
Hunters Creek Elem Sch/*Houston*/Harris	01027166	713/251-6000	201
Hunters Glen Elem Sch/*Missouri City*/Fort Bend	02857366	281/634-4640	150
Huntington Elem Sch/*Huntington*/Angelina	00994906	936/876-5194	17
Huntington High Sch/*Huntington*/Angelina	00994910	936/876-4150	17
HUNTINGTON IND SCH DIST/**HUNTINGTON**/**ANGELINA**	00994891	936/876-4287	17
Huntington Intermediate Sch/*Huntington*/Angelina	03319513	936/876-3432	17
Huntington Middle Sch/*Huntington*/Angelina	00994920	936/876-4722	17
Huntington-Surrey Sch/*Austin*/Travis	03141897	512/502-5400	373
Huntsville Elem Sch/*Huntsville*/Walker	03318985	936/293-2888	383
Huntsville High Sch/*Huntsville*/Walker	01058696	936/435-6100	383
HUNTSVILLE IND SCH DIST/**HUNTSVILLE**/**WALKER**	01058672	936/435-6300	383
Huntsville Intermediate Sch/*Huntsville*/Walker	01058701	936/293-2717	383
Huppertz Elem Sch/*San Antonio*/Bexar	00998548	210/438-6580	40
Hurla M Midkiff Elem Sch/*Palmhurst*/Hidalgo	05274969	956/323-7000	222
Hurshel Antwine Elem Sch/*El Paso*/El Paso	10005559	915/937-6400	136
Hurst Hills Elem Sch/*Hurst*/Tarrant	01053830	817/285-3295	354
Hurst Junior High Sch/*Hurst*/Tarrant	01053842	817/285-3220	354
HURST-EULESS-BEDFORD ISD/**BEDFORD**/**TARRANT**	01053737	817/283-4461	353
Huston Academy/*Stephenville*/Erath	04891605	254/965-8883	5
Hutchins Elem Sch/*El Campo*/Wharton	01059638	979/543-5481	389
Hutchins Elem Sch/*San Antonio*/Bexar	00999449	210/977-7200	42
Hutchinson Elem Sch/*Richmond*/Fort Bend	10004086	832/223-1700	154
Hutchinson Middle Sch/*Lubbock*/Lubbock	01038713	806/219-3800	270
Hutto Elem Sch/*Hutto*/Williamson	01060962	512/759-2094	396
Hutto High Sch/*Hutto*/Williamson	01060950	512/759-4700	396
HUTTO IND SCH DIST/**HUTTO**/**WILLIAMSON**	01060948	512/759-3771	396

School Year 2019-2020   800-333-8802   **TX-V35**

DISTRICT & SCHOOL TELEPHONE INDEX

Market Data Retrieval

School/City/County DISTRICT/CITY/COUNTY	PID	TELEPHONE NUMBER	PAGE
Hutto Middle Sch/*Hutto*/Williamson	04866430	512/759-4541	396
Hyde Park Elem Middle Sch/*Austin*/Travis	02084131	512/465-8338	373
Hyde Park Elem Sch/*Denison*/Grayson	01020364	903/462-7350	166
Hyde Park High Sch/*Austin*/Travis	12361218	512/465-8333	373

I

School/City/County	PID	TELEPHONE	PAGE
I C Evans Elem Sch/*Burkburnett*/Wichita	01059987	940/569-3311	391
I Go Elem Sch/*Jarrell*/Williamson	12363412	512/746-4805	396
I H Kempner High Sch/*Sugar Land*/Fort Bend	03048946	281/634-2300	150
I M Terrell Elem Sch/*Fort Worth*/Tarrant	04812398	817/815-1900	351
I N Range Elem Sch/*Mesquite*/Dallas	01011507	972/882-5180	111
I S Rogers Elem Sch/*Frisco*/Collin	03003116	469/633-2000	79
I W & Eleanor Hyde Elem Sch/*League City*/Galveston	04365307	281/284-5800	159
I W Evans Intermediate Sch/*Bonham*/Fannin	01017393	903/583-2914	145
Iago Junior High Sch/*Boling*/Wharton	01059559	979/657-2826	389
Iant Quranic Academy/*Richardson*/Dallas	11234856	972/231-5698	115
Iboc Christian Academy/*Dallas*/Dallas	05013026	972/572-4262	115
Ida Lee Bright Elem Sch/*Frisco*/Collin	04942357	469/633-2700	79
Idalou Elem Sch/*Idalou*/Lubbock	01038464	806/892-2524	269
Idalou High Sch/*Idalou*/Lubbock	01038476	806/892-2123	269
IDALOU IND SCH DIST/IDALOU/LUBBOCK	01038452	806/892-1900	269
Idalou Middle Sch/*Idalou*/Lubbock	01038488	806/892-2133	269
Idea Academy-Achieve/*Haltom City*/Hidalgo	12368254	817/885-4700	217
Idea Academy-Alamo/*Alamo*/Hidalgo	11557098	956/588-4005	217
Idea Academy-Bluff Springs/*Austin*/Hidalgo	12173877	512/822-4200	217
Idea Academy-Brackenridge/*San Antonio*/Hidalgo	12232033	210/239-4300	217
Idea Academy-Brownsville/*Brownsville*/Hidalgo	11824061	956/832-5150	217
Idea Academy-Carver/*San Antonio*/Hidalgo	11824073	210/223-8885	217
Idea Academy-Donna/*Donna*/Hidalgo	04931827	956/464-0203	217
Idea Academy-Eastside/*San Antonio*/Hidalgo	12106836	210/239-4800	217
Idea Academy-Edgemere/*El Paso*/Hidalgo	12311639	915/444-0200	217
Idea Academy-Edinburg/*Edinburg*/Hidalgo	11728807	956/287-6100	218
Idea Academy-Elsa/*Elsa*/Hidalgo	12311653	956/567-4700	218
Idea Academy-Ewing Halsell/*San Antonio*/Hidalgo	12232045	210/239-4850	218
Idea Academy-Frontier/*Brownsville*/Hidalgo	10751801	956/541-2002	218
Idea Academy-Harvey Najim/*San Antonio*/Hidalgo	12232069	210/239-4900	218
Idea Academy-Ingram Hills/*San Antonio*/Hidalgo	12311732	210/529-3700	218
Idea Academy-Judson/*San Antonio*/Hidalgo	12173827	210/529-3600	218
Idea Academy-Kyle/*Kyle*/Hidalgo	12309789	512/822-4300	218
Idea Academy-Mays/*San Antonio*/Hidalgo	12173841	210/529-3200	218
Idea Academy-McAllen/*McAllen*/Hidalgo	11824085	956/429-4100	218
Idea Academy-Mission/*Mission*/Hidalgo	10751837	956/583-8315	218
Idea Academy-Monterrey Park/*San Antonio*/Hidalgo	12106874	210/239-4200	218
Idea Academy-Montopolis/*Austin*/Hidalgo	11819121	512/646-2800	218
Idea Academy-North Mission/*Mission*/Hidalgo	12106769	956/424-4300	218
Idea Academy-Owassa/*Pharr*/Hidalgo	12311677	956/588-4300	218
Idea Academy-Pflugerville/*Pflugerville*/Hidalgo	12311689	512/822-4700	218
Idea Academy-Pharr/*Pharr*/Hidalgo	11557086	956/283-1515	218
Idea Academy-Quest/*Edinburg*/Hidalgo	10751825	956/287-1003	218
Idea Academy-Rio Grande City/*Rio Grande Cy*/Hidalgo	12230047	956/263-4900	218
Idea Academy-Rio Vista/*Socorro*/Hidalgo	12311706	915/444-0188	218
Idea Academy-Riverview/*Brownsville*/Hidalgo	12106783	956/832-5900	218
Idea Academy-Rundberg/*Austin*/Hidalgo	12106800	512/822-4800	218
Idea Academy-San Benito/*San Benito*/Hidalgo	10751813	956/399-5252	218
Idea Academy-San Juan/*San Juan*/Hidalgo	11455098	956/702-5150	218
Idea Academy-South Flores/*San Antonio*/Hidalgo	11926786	210/239-4150	218
Idea Academy-Tres Lagos/*McAllen*/Hidalgo	12232007	956/375-8550	218
Idea Academy-Walzem/*San Antonio*/Hidalgo	12106898	210/239-4600	218
Idea Academy-Weslaco/*Weslaco*/Hidalgo	11728819	956/351-4100	218
Idea Academy-Weslaco Pike/*Weslaco*/Hidalgo	12042163	956/351-4850	218
Idea Clg Prep-Achieve/*Haltom City*/Hidalgo	12368266	817/885-4700	218
Idea Clg Prep-Alamo/*Alamo*/Hidalgo	11751933	956/588-4005	218
Idea Clg Prep-Bluff Sprgs/*Austin*/Hidalgo	12173865	512/822-4200	218
Idea Clg Prep-Brackenridge/*San Antonio*/Hidalgo	12232021	210/239-4300	218
Idea Clg Prep-Brownsville/*Brownsville*/Hidalgo	11926798	956/832-5150	218
Idea Clg Prep-Carver/*San Antonio*/Hidalgo	12106824	210/223-8885	218
Idea Clg Prep-Donna/*Donna*/Hidalgo	11751945	956/464-0203	218
Idea Clg Prep-Eastside/*San Antonio*/Hidalgo	12106848	210/239-4800	218
Idea Clg Prep-Edgemere/*El Paso*/Hidalgo	12311627	915/444-0200	218
Idea Clg Prep-Edinburg/*Edinburg*/Hidalgo	11751907	956/287-6100	218
Idea Clg Prep-Elsa/*Elsa*/Hidalgo	12311641	956/567-4700	218
Idea Clg Prep-Ewing Halsell/*San Antonio*/Hidalgo	12232423	210/239-4850	218
Idea Clg Prep-Frontier/*Brownsville*/Hidalgo	11751969	956/541-2002	218
Idea Clg Prep-Harvey Najim/*San Antonio*/Hidalgo	12232057	210/239-4900	218
Idea Clg Prep-Ingram Hills/*San Antonio*/Hidalgo	12311720	210/529-3700	218
Idea Clg Prep-Judson/*San Antonio*/Hidalgo	12173839	210/529-3600	218
Idea Clg Prep-Kyle/*Kyle*/Hidalgo	12309791	512/822-4300	219
Idea Clg Prep-Mays/*San Antonio*/Hidalgo	12173853	210/529-3200	219
Idea Clg Prep-McAllen/*McAllen*/Hidalgo	11926815	956/429-4100	219
Idea Clg Prep-Mission/*Mission*/Hidalgo	11751919	956/583-8315	219
Idea Clg Prep-Monterrey Park/*San Antonio*/Hidalgo	12106886	210/239-4200	219
Idea Clg Prep-Montopolis/*Austin*/Hidalgo	11926827	512/646-2800	219
Idea Clg Prep-N Mission/*McAllen*/Hidalgo	12106771	956/424-4300	219
Idea Clg Prep-Owassa/*Pharr*/Hidalgo	12311665	956/588-4300	219
Idea Clg Prep-Pflugerville/*Pflugerville*/Hidalgo	12311691	512/822-4700	219
Idea Clg Prep-Pharr/*Pharr*/Hidalgo	11751957	956/283-1515	219
Idea Clg Prep-Quest/*Edinburg*/Hidalgo	11751971	956/287-1003	219
Idea Clg Prep-Rio Vista/*Socorro*/Hidalgo	12311718	915/444-0188	219
Idea Clg Prep-Riverview/*Brownsville*/Hidalgo	12106795	956/832-5900	219
Idea Clg Prep-Rundberg/*Austin*/Hidalgo	12106812	512/822-4800	219
Idea Clg Prep-San Benito/*San Benito*/Hidalgo	11732690	956/399-5252	219
Idea Clg Prep-San Juan/*San Juan*/Hidalgo	11748039	956/588-4021	219
Idea Clg Prep-South Flores/*San Antonio*/Hidalgo	12106862	210/239-4150	219
Idea Clg Prep-Toros/*Pharr*/Hidalgo	12173889	956/266-3772	219
Idea Clg Prep-Tres Lagos/*McAllen*/Hidalgo	12232019	956/252-9227	219
Idea Clg Prep-Walzem/*San Antonio*/Hidalgo	12106903	210/239-4600	219
Idea Clg Prep-Weslaco/*Weslaco*/Hidalgo	11751921	956/351-4100	219
Idea Clg Prep-Weslaco Pike/*Weslaco*/Hidalgo	12042199	956/351-4850	219
IDEA PUBLIC SCHOOLS/WESLACO/HIDALGO	11131307	956/377-8000	217
Iduma Elem Sch/*Killeen*/Bell	05271864	254/336-2590	28
Ignacio Zaragoza Elem Sch/*Dallas*/Dallas	01008732	972/749-8600	100
Ignite Middle Sch/*Dallas*/Dallas	12318601	972/794-7770	100
Ilm Academy/*Houston*/Harris	10986874	713/464-4720	206
Imagene Glenn Elem Sch/*Yantis*/Wood	05342645	903/383-2462	405
Imagine Intl Academy-N Texas/*McKinney*/Collin	11827738	214/491-1500	5
Iman Academy Southeast/*Houston*/Harris	04927670	713/910-3626	206
Iman Academy-Southwest/*Houston*/Harris	04927668	281/498-1345	206
Immaculate Conception Catholic/*Denton*/Denton	04420696	940/381-1155	126
Immaculate Conception Sch/*Grand Prairie*/Dallas	01012446	972/264-8777	114
Immaculate Conception Sch/*Rio Grande Cy*/Starr	01004384	956/487-2558	341
Immanuel Christian Sch/*El Paso*/El Paso	11231593	915/778-6160	139
Immanuel Lutheran Sch/*Giddings*/Lee	01037525	979/542-3319	263
Immanuel Lutheran Sch/*Mercedes*/Hidalgo	05324930	956/565-3208	226
Imogene Gideon Elem Sch/*Arlington*/Tarrant	04949123	817/299-7800	357
Impact Center/*Buda*/Hays	04359932	512/268-8473	211
Impact Early College High Sch/*Baytown*/Harris	11552593	281/420-4802	188
Incarnate Word Academy/*Brownsville*/Cameron	01004401	956/546-4486	68
Incarnate Word Academy/*Corp Christi*/Nueces	01045209	361/883-0857	306
Incarnate Word Academy/*Houston*/Harris	01027984	713/227-3637	204
Incarnate Word Elem Sch/*Corp Christi*/Nueces	01045235	361/883-0857	306
Incarnate Word High Sch/*San Antonio*/Bexar	00999841	210/829-3100	44
Incarnate Word Middle Sch/*Corp Christi*/Nueces	01045247	361/883-0857	306
Independence Elem Sch/*Fort Worth*/Tarrant	10028549	817/744-6100	355
Independence Elem Sch/*Lewisville*/Denton	11079577	469/713-5212	123
Independence High Sch/*Frisco*/Collin	12032895	469/633-5400	79
Indian Creek Elem Sch/*Carrollton*/Denton	02857445	469/713-5180	123
Indian Creek Elem Sch/*San Antonio*/Bexar	00999621	210/623-6520	43
Indian Ridge Middle Sch/*El Paso*/El Paso	03250864	915/434-5400	138
Indian Spring Middle Sch/*Waco*/McLennan	11819339	254/757-6200	282
Indian Springs Elem Sch/*San Antonio*/Comal	11825106	830/609-6298	88
Indian Springs Middle Sch/*Keller*/Tarrant	04945945	817/744-3200	355
Industrial Elem Sch East/*Vanderbilt*/Jackson	01033139	361/284-3317	240
Industrial Elem Sch West/*Inez*/Jackson	01033115	361/782-3325	240

Texas School Directory

DISTRICT & SCHOOL TELEPHONE INDEX

School/City/County DISTRICT/CITY/COUNTY	PID	TELEPHONE NUMBER	PAGE
Industrial High Sch/*Vanderbilt*/Jackson	01033098	361/284-3216	240
INDUSTRIAL IND SCH DIST/ VANDERBILT/JACKSON	01033086	361/284-3226	240
Industrial Junior High Sch/*Vanderbilt*/Jackson	01033103	361/284-3226	240
Industrial Trade Center/*Texas City*/Galveston	12232409	409/916-0710	161
Inez Carroll Academy/*Houston*/Harris	01022843	281/878-0340	180
Inez Foster Academy/*San Antonio*/Bexar	00998873	210/438-6855	40
Infinity Early College HS/*Porter*/Montgomery	11927900	281/577-2890	293
Ingleside High Sch/*Ingleside*/San Patricio	01172589	361/776-2712	331
INGLESIDE IND SCH DIST/INGLESIDE/ SAN PATRICIO	01049592	361/776-7631	331
Ingleside Primary Sch/*Ingleside*/San Patricio	01172577	361/776-3060	331
Ingram Elem Sch/*Ingram*/Kerr	01036064	830/367-5751	255
INGRAM IND SCH DIST/INGRAM/KERR	01036052	830/367-5517	255
Ingram Middle Sch/*Ingram*/Kerr	12160313	830/367-4111	255
Ingram Tom Moore High Sch/*Ingram*/Kerr	02110857	830/367-4111	255
Innovation Design Entrep Acad/*Dallas*/Dallas	12109474	972/794-6800	100
Inspire Academy/*Colleyville*/Tarrant	12322884	817/966-4821	359
Inspired for Excellence Acad W/*Houston*/Harris	11555404	832/834-5295	194
Inspired Vision Elem Sch/*Dallas*/Dallas	04931762	214/391-7964	5
Inspired Vision Secondary Sch/*Dallas*/Dallas	05000304	972/285-5758	5
Instruction & Guidance Center/*McAllen*/Hidalgo	04014699	956/971-4393	221
Int'l Ldrship TX-Lancaster/*Lancaster*/Dallas	12233726	469/862-4237	108
Int'l Ldrshp TX-Arlington ES/*Arlington*/Dallas	11917955	817/496-0400	108
Int'l Ldrshp TX-Arlngtn GR PR/*Grand Prairie*/Dallas	12163779	682/808-5960	108
Int'l Ldrshp TX-College Sta/*College Sta*/Dallas	12313637	979/704-6027	108
Int'l Ldrshp TX-East Ft Worth/*Fort Worth*/Dallas	12233752	817/395-1766	108
Int'l Ldrshp TX-Garland/*Garland*/Dallas	11928502	972/414-8000	108
Int'l Ldrshp TX-Garland HS/*Garland*/Dallas	11931937	972/414-3414	108
Int'l Ldrshp TX-Grand Prairie/*Grand Prairie*/Dallas	12233738	469/348-7960	108
Int'l Ldrshp TX-Katy/*Katy*/Dallas	12233788	281/394-9417	108
Int'l Ldrshp TX-Katy Westpark/*Richmond*/Dallas	12233805	832/222-9470	108
Int'l Ldrshp TX-Keller/*Fort Worth*/Dallas	12043155	817/665-0646	109
Int'l Ldrshp TX-Keller Saginaw/*Fort Worth*/Dallas	12233776	682/250-3701	109
Int'l Ldrshp TX-Lanc-DeSoto HS/*Desoto*/Dallas	12313601	469/786-2850	109
Int'l Ldrshp TX-N Richlnd Hill/*N Richlnd Hls*/Dallas	12233764	817/576-9031	109
Int'l Ldrshp TX-Orem/*Houston*/Dallas	12313625	713/987-9435	109
Int'l Ldrshp TX-Saginaw/*Fort Worth*/Dallas	12233697	682/250-3600	109
Int'l Ldrshp TX-Westpark/*Houston*/Dallas	12233790	346/203-4126	109
Int'l Ldrshp TX-Windmill Lakes/*Houston*/Dallas	12233817	832/667-0453	109
Int'l Ldrshp TX-Wml-Orem HS/*Houston*/Dallas	12313613	832/649-6817	109
INT'L LEADERSHIP OF TEXAS DIST/ RICHARDSON/DALLAS	12261400	972/479-9078	108
International High Sch/*Austin*/Travis	10007258	512/414-6817	368
International Newcomer Academy/*Fort Worth*/Tarrant	04143214	817/815-5600	351
International Sch of Americas/*San Antonio*/Bexar	04284260	210/356-0900	35
Iola Elem Sch/*Iola*/Grimes	03410624	936/394-2361	172
IOLA IND SCH DIST/IOLA/GRIMES	01021370	936/394-2361	172
Iola Junior Senior High Sch/*Iola*/Grimes	01021382	936/394-2361	172
IOWA PARK CONSOLIDATED IND SD/ IOWA PARK/WICHITA	01060065	940/592-4193	392
Iowa Park High Sch/*Iowa Park*/Wichita	01060091	940/592-2144	392
Ira C Ogden Academy/*San Antonio*/Bexar	00998586	210/738-9815	40
Ira Cross Jr Elem Sch/*Killeen*/Bell	05271876	254/336-2550	28
IRA IND SCH DIST/IRA/SCURRY	01050072	325/573-2628	333
Ira Sch/*Ira*/Scurry	01050096	325/573-2628	333
Iraan Elem Sch/*Iraan*/Pecos	01046916	432/639-2524	316
Iraan High Sch/*Iraan*/Pecos	01046928	432/639-2512	316
Iraan Junior High Sch/*Iraan*/Pecos	01046930	432/639-2512	316
IRAAN-SHEFFIELD IND SCH DIST/ IRAAN/PECOS	01046904	432/639-2512	316

School/City/County DISTRICT/CITY/COUNTY	PID	TELEPHONE NUMBER	PAGE
IREDELL IND SCH DIST/IREDELL/ BOSQUE	01000637	254/364-2411	46
Iredell Sch/*Iredell*/Bosque	01000649	254/364-2411	47
Ireland Elem Sch/*Odessa*/Ector	01014731	432/456-1149	130
Irene C Cardwell Elem Sch/*Del Rio*/Val Verde	01058062	830/778-4650	379
Irene Clinkscale Elem Sch/*Burleson*/Johnson	11540497	817/245-3900	247
Irene Garcia Middle Sch/*Mission*/Hidalgo	05278989	956/323-2840	220
Irene L Chavez Excel Academy/*San Antonio*/Bexar	03403542	210/397-8120	37
IRION CO IND SCH DIST/MERTZON/ IRION	01032862	325/835-6111	238
Irion County High Sch/*Mertzon*/Irion	04914659	325/835-2881	238
Irion Elem Sch/*Mertzon*/Irion	01032874	325/835-3991	238
Irma Marsh Middle Sch/*Fort Worth*/Tarrant	01052331	817/252-2200	347
Irons Junior High Sch/*Conroe*/Montgomery	11818024	936/709-8500	292
Irons Middle Sch/*Lubbock*/Lubbock	03251143	806/219-4000	270
Irvin High Sch/*El Paso*/El Paso	01015802	915/236-4600	134
Irvin M Shlenker Sch/*Houston*/Harris	03276284	713/270-6127	206
Irving Dual Language Academy/*San Antonio*/Bexar	12317724	210/738-9740	40
Irving Elem Sch/*Cleburne*/Johnson	01034937	817/202-2100	247
Irving High Sch/*Irving*/Dallas	01011179	972/600-6300	109
IRVING IND SCH DIST/IRVING/ DALLAS	01011105	972/600-5000	109
Irving Middle Sch/*San Antonio*/Bexar	00998641	210/738-9740	40
Irving Reg Day Sch Pgrm-Deaf/*Irving*/Dallas	11923473	972/600-3800	109
Isaacs Early Childhood Sch/*Plano*/Collin	11475608	469/752-3480	83
Isabel Pierce Sem Elem Sch/*Frisco*/Collin	10022399	469/633-3575	79
Isbell Elem Sch/*Frisco*/Collin	05343443	469/633-3400	79
Ischolars Magnet Academy/*Red Oak*/Ellis	11934276	972/617-4747	142
Ischool High Lewisville/*Lewisville*/Denton	11663013	972/317-2470	6
Ischool High the Woodlands/*The Woodlands*/Montgomery	11932266	936/231-8594	6
Ischool High University Park/*Houston*/Harris	11925201	281/251-5770	6
Ischool High-Hickory Creek/*Hickory Creek*/Denton	12161769	940/321-1144	6
Ischool Virtual Academy HS/*Lewisville*/Denton	12362652	888/729-0622	6
Islamic School of Irving/*Irving*/Dallas	10013673	972/812-2220	115
It Holleman Elem Sch/*Waller*/Waller	01824407	936/372-9196	384
ITALY IND SCH DIST/ITALY/ELLIS	01015072	972/483-1815	140
Italy Jr Sr High Sch/*Italy*/Ellis	01015096	972/483-7411	141
Itasca Elem Sch/*Itasca*/Hill	01030967	254/687-2922	228
Itasca High Sch/*Itasca*/Hill	01030979	254/687-2922	228
ITASCA IND SCH DIST/ITASCA/HILL	01030955	254/687-2922	228
Itasca Middle Sch/*Itasca*/Hill	03395048	254/687-2922	228
Iuniversity Prep Virtual Acad/*Grapevine*/Tarrant	12035885	855/779-7357	353
Izetta Sparks Elem Sch/*Frisco*/Collin	05092620	469/633-3000	79

J

School/City/County DISTRICT/CITY/COUNTY	PID	TELEPHONE NUMBER	PAGE
J A Garcia Elem Sch/*Corp Christi*/Nueces	01044425	361/878-2280	303
J A Hargrave Elem Sch/*Fort Worth*/Tarrant	05343649	817/370-5630	348
J A Kawas Elem Sch/*Laredo*/Webb	02178005	956/273-3700	386
J A Vitovsky Elem Sch/*Midlothian*/Ellis	04944680	469/856-6400	141
J B Alexander 9th Grade HS/*Laredo*/Webb	12308204	956/473-1300	387
J B Alexander High Sch/*Laredo*/Webb	04287846	956/473-5800	387
J B Jones Muller Elem Sch/*Laredo*/Webb	04875194	956/473-3900	387
J B Munoz Elem Sch/*La Villa*/Hidalgo	01029906	956/262-9357	220
J B Passmore Elem Sch/*San Antonio*/Bexar	00998134	210/397-0500	37
J B Stephens Elem Sch/*Bangs*/Brown	01002403	325/752-7236	58
J B Wilmeth Elem Sch/*McKinney*/Collin	10006656	469/302-7400	81
J C Austin Elem Sch/*Mesquite*/Dallas	03249164	972/882-7220	111
J C Rugel Elem Sch/*Mesquite*/Dallas	01011519	972/882-7260	111
J C Thompson Elem Sch/*Haslet*/Denton	11715599	817/698-3800	125
J D Hall Learning Center/*Lancaster*/Dallas	03397606	972/218-1441	110
J E Rhodes Elem Sch/*Van*/Van Zandt	01058244	903/963-8386	381
J F Kennedy Elem Sch/*Penitas*/Hidalgo	01029853	956/323-2330	220
J Frank Dobie High Sch/*Houston*/Harris	01026734	713/740-0370	199
J Frank Dobie Jr High Sch/*Cibolo*/Guadalupe	01021564	210/619-4100	173
J H Florence Elem Sch/*Mesquite*/Dallas	01011521	972/290-4080	111
J H Hines Elem Sch/*Waco*/McLennan	01040247	254/753-1362	282
J Henderson Elem Sch/*Houston*/Harris	01025546	713/924-1730	189
J K Hileman Elem Sch/*Queen City*/Cass	01809029	903/796-6304	70
J L Boren Elem Sch/*Mansfield*/Tarrant	01881950	817/299-7740	357
J L Long Middle Sch/*Dallas*/Dallas	01009047	972/502-4700	100
J L Lyons Elem Sch/*Magnolia*/Montgomery	04033877	281/356-8115	293
J L Williams-Lovett Ledger ES/*Copperas Cove*/Coryell	03319032	254/542-1001	92
J Lyndal Hughes Elem Sch/*Roanoke*/Denton	10012332	817/698-1900	125

School Year 2019-2020   800-333-8802   TX-V37

DISTRICT & SCHOOL TELEPHONE INDEX

Market Data Retrieval

School/City/County DISTRICT/CITY/COUNTY	PID	TELEPHONE NUMBER	PAGE
J M Hanks High Sch/*El Paso*/El Paso	01824184	915/434-5000	138
J Martin Jacquet Middle Sch/*Fort Worth*/Tarrant	02180448	817/815-3500	351
J N Ervin Elem Sch/*Dallas*/Dallas	01009059	972/749-3700	100
J O Davis Elem Sch/*Irving*/Dallas	03329219	972/600-4900	109
J O Schulze Elem Sch/*Irving*/Dallas	01011181	972/600-3500	109
J P Bonnette Jr High Sch/*Deer Park*/Harris	01824225	832/668-7700	186
J P Dabbs Elem Sch/*Deer Park*/Harris	01548421	832/668-8100	186
J P Elder Middle Sch/*Fort Worth*/Tarrant	01053012	817/814-4100	351
J P Starks Mst Vanguard/*Dallas*/Dallas	03006663	972/502-8800	100
J R Harris Elem Sch/*Houston*/Harris	01025534	713/924-1860	190
J R Irvin Elem Sch/*Midlothian*/Ellis	01015175	469/856-6000	141
J Ruth Smith Academy/*Houston*/Harris	01022855	713/613-7650	179
J S Adame Elem Sch/*Donna*/Hidalgo	10908858	956/461-4010	215
J T Brackenridge Elem Sch/*San Antonio*/Bexar	00999061	210/978-7950	40
J T Stevens Elem Sch/*Fort Worth*/Tarrant	01053438	817/814-8500	351
J W Arndt Elem Sch/*Laredo*/Webb	04875209	956/473-2800	387
J W Bishop Elem Sch/*Everman*/Tarrant	01052501	817/568-3575	349
J W Hayes Primary Sch/*Whitesboro*/Grayson	05274086	903/564-4281	168
J W Long Elem Sch/*Terrell*/Kaufman	01035785	972/563-1448	253
J W Monday Elem Sch/*Kaufman*/Kaufman	01035618	972/932-3513	252
J W Nixon High Sch/*Laredo*/Webb	01059298	956/273-7400	386
J W Webb Elem Sch/*McKinney*/Collin	01006277	469/302-6000	81
J W Williams Middle Sch/*Rockwall*/Rockwall	01048744	972/771-8313	325
J Z Leyendecker Elem Sch/*Laredo*/Webb	01059341	956/273-3800	386
Jacinto City Elem Sch/*Houston*/Harris	01023495	832/386-4600	187
Jack C Binion Elem Sch/*Richland Hls*/Tarrant	01052068	817/547-1800	346
Jack C Hays High Sch/*Buda*/Hays	01029085	512/268-2911	211
Jack C Jordan Middle Sch/*San Antonio*/Bexar	04035203	210/397-6150	37
Jack Cockrill Middle Sch/*McKinney*/Collin	11130810	469/302-7900	81
Jack D Johnson Elem Sch/*Southlake*/Tarrant	01052264	817/949-4500	347
Jack E Singley Academy/*Irving*/Dallas	04942096	972/600-5300	109
Jack Faubion Middle Sch/*McKinney*/Collin	02895992	469/302-6900	81
Jack Frost Elem Sch/*Georgetown*/Williamson	02896752	512/943-5020	395
Jack Lowe Sr Elem Sch/*Dallas*/Dallas	10023197	972/502-1700	100
Jack Lummus Interm Sch/*Ennis*/Ellis	11563358	972/872-7060	140
Jack M Fields Sr Elem Sch/*Humble*/Harris	04457948	281/641-2700	196
Jack Taylor Elem Sch/*Burleson*/Johnson	02895265	817/245-3200	247
Jackie Carden Elem Sch/*Fort Worth*/Tarrant	03236375	817/370-5600	348
Jacksboro Elem Sch/*Jacksboro*/Jack	01032939	940/567-7206	239
Jacksboro High Sch/*Jacksboro*/Jack	01032941	940/567-7204	239
JACKSBORO IND SCH DIST/*JACKSBORO*/JACK	01032927	940/567-7203	239
Jacksboro Middle Sch/*Jacksboro*/Jack	01032953	940/567-7205	239
Jackson Early Childhood Center/*Lewisville*/Denton	10004098	469/713-5986	123
Jackson Elem Sch/*Abilene*/Taylor	01172852	325/690-3602	360
Jackson Elem Sch/*Lubbock*/Lubbock	01038737	806/219-6000	270
Jackson Elem Sch/*Plano*/Collin	01401378	469/752-2100	83
Jackson Elem Sch/*Rosenberg*/Fort Bend	01018244	832/223-1800	154
Jackson Elem Sch/*Tyler*/Smith	01050632	903/566-3411	337
Jackson Intermediate Sch/*Pasadena*/Harris	01026746	713/740-0440	199
Jackson Middle Sch/*Grand Prairie*/Dallas	01010826	972/264-2704	107
Jackson Middle Sch/*San Antonio*/Bexar	00997805	210/356-4400	35
Jackson Tech Ctr Math Science/*Garland*/Dallas	01010412	972/494-8362	106
Jackson-Keller Elem Sch/*San Antonio*/Bexar	03250307	210/407-4400	35
Jackson-Roosevelt Elem Sch/*Port Lavaca*/Calhoun	01003201	361/552-3317	62
Jacksonville High Sch/*Jacksonville*/Cherokee	01005285	903/586-3661	73
JACKSONVILLE IND SCH DIST/*JACKSONVILLE/CHEROKEE*	01005235	903/586-6511	72
Jacksonville Middle Sch/*Jacksonville*/Cherokee	01005273	903/586-3686	73
Jacobs Well Elem Sch/*Wimberley*/Hays	03047007	512/847-5558	212
Jaime Escalante Middle Schl/*Pharr*/Hidalgo	11552866	956/354-2670	223
Jake Silbernagel Elem Sch/*Dickinson*/Galveston	01881871	281/229-6800	159
James & Margie Marion ES/*Allen*/Collin	05276163	214/495-6784	77
James A Arthur Interm Sch/*Kennedale*/Tarrant	01054042	817/563-8300	355
James B Havard Elem Sch/*Houston*/Harris	04808866	832/386-3710	187
James Bilhartz Jr Elem Sch/*Dallas*/Dallas	05275092	972/708-6600	105
James Bonham Elem Sch/*McAllen*/Hidalgo	01029932	956/971-4440	221
James Bonham Middle Sch/*Amarillo*/Potter	01047180	806/326-3100	318
James Bowie 6th Grade Campus/*Amarillo*/Potter	12033722	806/326-3270	318
James Bowie Elem Sch/*Baytown*/Harris	01023677	281/420-4605	188
James Bowie Elem Sch/*Dallas*/Dallas	01009085	972/925-6600	100

School/City/County DISTRICT/CITY/COUNTY	PID	TELEPHONE NUMBER	PAGE
James Bowie Elem Sch/*Ennis*/Ellis	03007942	972/872-7234	140
James Bowie Elem Sch/*Simms*/Bowie	01001198	903/543-2245	50
James Bowie High Sch/*Arlington*/Tarrant	03397876	682/867-4400	344
James Bowie High Sch/*Austin*/Travis	03249267	512/414-5247	368
James Bowie High Sch/*Simms*/Bowie	01001203	903/543-2275	50
James Bowie Middle Sch/*Amarillo*/Potter	01047192	806/326-3200	318
James Bowie Middle Sch/*Richmond*/Fort Bend	11715410	281/327-6200	150
James Bowie Middle Sch/*Simms*/Bowie	11128908	903/543-2275	50
James Butler Bonham Elem Sch/*Houston*/Harris	01024346	713/778-3480	189
James Carson Elem Sch/*San Antonio*/Bexar	04809042	210/397-1100	37
James D Gossett Elem Sch/*Rankin*/Upton	01057666	432/693-2455	377
James D Kerr Elem Sch/*Allen*/Collin	04913136	214/495-6765	77
James Deanda Elem Sch/*Houston*/Harris	11735135	713/556-9550	192
James E Poole Elem Sch/*Big Sandy*/Upshur	01057460	903/725-7270	376
James E Randolph Elem Sch/*Fulshear*/Harris	12033801	281/234-3800	152
James E Rudder High Sch/*Bryan*/Brazos	11079280	979/209-7900	55
James E Taylor High Sch/*Katy*/Harris	02045408	281/237-3100	152
James F Bay Elem Sch/*Seabrook*/Galveston	01018880	281/284-4600	159
James F Cooper Acad-Navarro/*San Antonio*/Bexar	11451858	210/438-6810	40
James F DeLaney Elem Sch/*Kennedale*/Tarrant	03004354	817/563-8400	356
James Garland Walsh Middle Sch/*Round Rock*/Williamson	11130834	512/704-0800	399
James H Ross Elem Sch/*League City*/Galveston	01018921	281/284-4500	159
James L Coble Middle Sch/*Arlington*/Tarrant	10028240	682/314-4900	357
James L Collins Catholic Sch/*Corsicana*/Navarro	01012458	903/872-1751	300
James L Wright Elem Sch/*Perryton*/Ochiltree	01045493	806/435-2371	307
James Madison High Sch/*Dallas*/Dallas	01009114	972/925-2800	100
James Martin High Sch/*Arlington*/Tarrant	02177415	682/867-8600	344
James Masters Elem Sch/*Converse*/Bexar	11452280	210/945-1150	33
James Mitchell Elem Sch/*Georgetown*/Williamson	11079644	512/943-1820	395
James Neill Elem Sch/*Richmond*/Fort Bend	12232136	281/327-3760	150
James Nikki Rowe High Sch/*McAllen*/Hidalgo	03323564	956/632-5100	221
James P Butler Elem Sch/*El Paso*/El Paso	11920536	915/937-8901	136
James Pace Early Clg HS/*Brownsville*/Cameron	01418228	956/548-7700	64
James Patterson Elem Sch/*Richmond*/Fort Bend	12232112	281/327-4260	150
James R Brooks Middle Sch/*Midland*/Midland	04477651	432/685-7837	285
James R Newman Elem Sch/*Frisco*/Collin	12032883	469/633-3975	79
James R Reynolds Elem Sch/*Houston*/Harris	01025352	713/731-5590	192
James Russell Lowell Mid Sch/*San Antonio*/Bexar	00999205	210/228-1225	40
James S Hogg Elem Sch/*Dallas*/Dallas	01009097	972/502-8600	100
James S Hogg Middle Sch/*Tyler*/Smith	01050852	903/262-1500	338
James Steele Accelerated HS/*Roanoke*/Denton	11554462	817/698-5800	125
James Street Elem Sch/*Coldspring*/San Jacinto	01049437	936/653-1187	330
James Tippit Middle Sch/*Georgetown*/Williamson	01060883	512/943-5040	395
James W Fannin Elem Sch/*Corp Christi*/Nueces	01044372	361/878-2260	303
James W Fannin Middle Sch/*Amarillo*/Potter	01047257	806/326-3500	318
James Williams Elem Sch/*Katy*/Harris	04917493	281/237-7200	152
Jan Aragon Middle Sch/*Houston*/Harris	04943753	281/856-5100	185
Jane A Hambric Sch/*El Paso*/El Paso	04916126	915/937-4600	136
Jane Long Elem Sch/*Harlingen*/Cameron	02856037	956/427-3140	65
Jane Long Elem Sch/*Richmond*/Fort Bend	01018282	832/223-1900	154
Jane Wessendorff Middle Sch/*Rosenberg*/Fort Bend	01018270	832/223-3300	154
Janet Brockett Elem Sch/*Arlington*/Tarrant	10006888	817/299-6620	357
Janice Stanley Scott Elem Sch/*McKinney*/Collin	12027993	469/633-4000	79
Janie Stark Elem Sch/*Farmers BRNCH*/Dallas	01008201	972/968-3300	97
Janowski Elem Sch/*Houston*/Harris	01025962	713/696-2844	191
Jarrell Elem Sch/*Jarrell*/Williamson	12036944	512/746-2170	396
Jarrell High Sch/*Jarrell*/Williamson	12036920	512/746-2188	396
JARRELL IND SCH DIST/*JARRELL*/WILLIAMSON	01060974	512/746-2124	396
Jarrell Intermediate Sch/*Jarrell*/Williamson	12036956	512/746-4805	396
Jarrell Middle Sch/*Jarrell*/Williamson	12036932	512/746-4180	396
Jasper Classical Academy/*Jasper*/Jasper	11456212	409/489-9222	6
Jasper High Sch/*Jasper*/Jasper	01523720	409/384-3242	241
Jasper High Sch/*Plano*/Collin	04453887	469/752-7400	83
JASPER IND SCH DIST/*JASPER/JASPER*	01033244	409/384-2401	240
Jasper Junior High Sch/*Jasper*/Jasper	01033268	409/384-3585	241

TX-V38   800-333-8802   School Year 2019-2020

Texas School Directory

DISTRICT & SCHOOL TELEPHONE INDEX

School/City/County DISTRICT/CITY/COUNTY	PID	TELEPHONE NUMBER	PAGE
Jay Thompson Elem Sch/*Mesquite*/Dallas	04364810	972/882-7190	111
Jayne Ann Miller Elem Sch/*Lubbock*/Lubbock	01038696	806/219-8100	270
JAYTON-GIRARD IND SCH DIST/ JAYTON/KENT	01035931	806/237-2991	255
Jayton-Girard Sch/*Jayton*/Kent	01035943	806/237-2991	255
Jean & Betty Schmalz Elem Sch/*Houston*/ Harris	04948741	281/237-4500	152
Jean C Few Primary Sch/*Jasper*/Jasper	04867989	409/489-9808	241
Jean E Stewart Elem Sch/*Montgomery*/ Montgomery	12028600	936/709-4200	292
Jean Hines-Caldwell Elem Sch/*Houston*/ Harris	10003903	713/726-3700	192
Jean Massieu Acad for the Deaf/*Arlington*/ Tarrant	04892441	817/460-0396	6
Jean McClung Middle Sch/*Fort Worth*/Tarrant	11711919	817/815-5300	351
Jeanette Hayes Elem Sch/*Katy*/Harris	04452247	281/237-3200	152
Jefferson Achievement Ctr/*Abilene*/Taylor	01172735	325/794-4150	360
Jefferson Avenue Elem Sch/*Seguin*/Guadalupe	01021679	830/401-8727	174
Jefferson Christian Academy/*Jefferson*/ Marion	01480805	903/665-3973	274
Jefferson Co Youth Academy/*Beaumont*/ Jefferson	04913382	409/720-4078	241
Jefferson Elem Sch/*Edinburg*/Hidalgo	01029803	956/289-2385	216
Jefferson Elem Sch/*Harlingen*/Cameron	01003861	956/427-3120	65
Jefferson Elem Sch/*Houston*/Harris	01025986	713/696-2778	192
Jefferson Elem Sch/*Jefferson*/Marion	01040699	903/665-2461	274
Jefferson Elem Sch/*Sherman*/Grayson	01020625	903/891-6610	167
Jefferson Elem Sch/*Temple*/Bell	00996772	254/215-5500	29
Jefferson Elem Sch/*Wichita Falls*/Wichita	01173117	940/235-1168	392
Jefferson High Sch/*El Paso*/El Paso	01015694	915/236-7400	134
Jefferson High Sch/*Jefferson*/Marion	01040704	903/665-2461	274
JEFFERSON IND SCH DIST/JEFFERSON/ MARION	01040687	903/665-2461	274
Jefferson Junior High Sch/*Jefferson*/Marion	01040728	903/665-2461	274
Jefferson Primary Sch/*Jefferson*/Marion	10015023	903/665-2461	274
Jennie Reid Elem Sch/*La Porte*/Harris	01026382	281/604-4500	198
Jensen Elem Sch/*Pasadena*/Harris	01026758	713/740-0608	199
Jerry Junkins Elem Sch/*Carrollton*/Dallas	10019885	972/502-2400	100
Jersey Village High Sch/*Jersey Vlg*/Harris	01023275	713/896-3400	185
Jess Harben Elem Sch/*Richardson*/Dallas	01399660	469/593-8800	112
Jesse McGowen Elem Sch/*McKinney*/Collin	10909187	469/302-7500	81
Jessie Jensen Elem Sch/*Mission*/Hidalgo	01030539	956/580-5252	224
Jessup Elem Sch/*Houston*/Harris	01026760	713/740-0616	199
Jesuit College Prep Sch/*Dallas*/Dallas	01012460	972/387-8700	114
Jesus Chapel Sch/*El Paso*/El Paso	04020985	915/593-1153	139
Jewel Askew Elem Sch/*Houston*/Harris	01826273	281/368-2100	194
Jewel C Wietzel Center/*San Antonio*/Bexar	01541289	210/989-3280	32
Jewel S Houston Academy/*Houston*/Harris	05274127	281/878-7745	181
Jhw Inspire Acad-Afton Oaks/*San Antonio*/ Bexar	04814011	210/638-5500	31
Jhw Inspire Acad-Legacy Ranch/*Gonzales*/ Bexar	12174120	210/638-5300	31
Jhw Inspire Acad-Meridell/*Liberty Hill*/ Bexar	12035110	512/528-2100	31
Jhw Inspire Acad-Rockdale/*Rockdale*/Bexar	11701378	210/638-5700	31
Jhw Inspire Acad-Williams Hse/*Lometa*/Bexar	11832331	210/638-5800	31
Jhw Inspire Academy-Bell Co/*Killeen*/Bell	12233219	254/618-4280	31
Jhw Inspire Academy-Hays Co/*San Marcos*/ Bexar	05243312	210/638-5400	31
Jill Stone-Vickery Meadow ES/*Dallas*/Dallas	04810405	972/502-7900	100
Jim Barnes Middle Sch/*Seguin*/Guadalupe	05342023	830/401-8756	174
Jim G Martin Elem Sch/*San Antonio*/Bexar	11552141	210/398-1400	37
JIM HOGG CO IND SCH DIST/ HEBBRONVILLE/JIM HOGG	01034470	361/527-3203	244
JIM NED CONS IND SCH DIST/ TUSCOLA/TAYLOR	01054896	325/554-7500	361
Jim Ned High Sch/*Tuscola*/Taylor	01054913	325/554-7755	361
Jim Ned Middle Sch/*Tuscola*/Taylor	04745032	325/554-7870	361
Jimmie Tyler Brashear Elem Sch/*Dallas*/ Dallas	10023123	972/502-2600	101
Jimmy Carter Early Clg HS/*La Joya*/Hidalgo	11719260	956/323-2200	220
Jimmy Elrod Elem Sch/*San Antonio*/Bexar	03050511	210/397-1800	37
Jjaep Sch/*Houston*/Harris	11555480	713/556-7140	194
Jo Ann Ford Elem Sch/*Georgetown*/Williamson	05343742	512/943-5180	395
Jo Ella Exley Elem Sch/*Katy*/Harris	05344306	281/237-8400	152
Jo Kelly Sch/*Fort Worth*/Tarrant	01809897	817/815-5900	351
Jo Nelson Middle Sch/*Santa Rosa*/Cameron	03345835	956/636-9850	67
Joan Link Elm Sch/*Houston*/Harris	02178299	281/891-8390	202
Joan Postma Elem Sch/*Cypress*/Harris	10747989	281/345-3660	185
Joan Y Ervin Elem Sch/*Lubbock*/Lubbock	01038725	806/219-8200	270
Joaquin Elem Sch/*Joaquin*/Shelby	01050369	936/269-3128	335
Joaquin High Sch/*Joaquin*/Shelby	01050383	936/269-3128	335
JOAQUIN IND SCH DIST/JOAQUIN/ SHELBY	01050357	936/269-3128	335
Joaquin Junior High Sch/*Joaquin*/Shelby	05035086	936/269-3128	335
Joe Barnhart Magnet Academy/*Beeville*/Bee	12225626	361/358-6262	25
Joe Dale Sparks Campus/*Denton*/Denton	11452929	940/349-2468	121
Joe E Moreno Elem Sch/*Houston*/Harris	10003886	281/405-2150	191
Joe Hubenak Elem Sch/*Richmond*/Fort Bend	11447223	832/223-2900	154
Joe K Bryant Elem Sch/*Anna*/Collin	01006033	972/924-1300	77
Joe Lawrence Elem Sch/*Mesquite*/Dallas	01011533	972/882-7000	111
Joe Lee Johnson Elem Sch/*Austin*/Williamson	12167476	512/704-1400	399
Joe M Adams Junior High Sch/*Fulshear*/ Harris	12367406	281/234-3400	152
Joe M Pirtle Elem Sch/*Temple*/Bell	01876931	254/215-3400	27
Joe Tison Middle Sch/*Weatherford*/Parker	04748761	817/598-2960	314
Joe Wright Elem Sch/*Jacksonville*/Cherokee	01005297	903/586-5286	73
John & Nelda Partin Elem Sch/*Van Alstyne*/ Grayson	01020754	903/482-8805	168
John & Olive Hinojosa Elem Sch/*Rio Grande Cy*/ Starr	03323320	956/487-3710	340
John A Baker Elem Sch/*McKinney*/Collin	10915198	469/219-2120	84
John A Sippel Elem Sch/*Schertz*/Guadalupe	11130511	210/619-4600	173
John B Connally High Sch/*Austin*/Travis	04454221	512/594-0800	372
John B Connally Middle Sch/*San Antonio*/ Bexar	04809054	210/397-1000	37
John C French Elem Sch/*Cuero*/De Witt	01013725	361/275-1900	117
John C Holmgreen Center/*San Antonio*/Bexar	01539963	210/397-6100	37
John C Webb Elem Sch/*Navasota*/Grimes	02227852	936/825-1120	172
John Cooper Sch/*The Woodlands*/Montgomery	03161354	281/367-0900	295
John D Spicer Elem Sch/*Haltom City*/Tarrant	03393014	817/547-3300	346
John Doedyns Elem Sch/*San Juan*/Hidalgo	01030400	956/354-2740	223
John Drugan Elem Sch/*El Paso*/El Paso	10005547	915/937-6800	136
John F Kennedy Elem Sch/*Edinburg*/Hidalgo	04452807	956/289-2390	216
John F Kennedy Elem Sch/*Elsa*/Hidalgo	01029669	956/262-6027	216
John F Kennedy High Sch/*San Antonio*/Bexar	00997269	210/444-8040	32
John F Kennedy Sch/*Mercedes*/Hidalgo	01030163	956/514-2300	221
John F Peeler Elem Sch/*Dallas*/Dallas	01009140	972/502-8300	101
John F Ward Elem Sch/*Houston*/Galveston	03325524	281/284-5400	159
John Glenn Elem Sch/*San Antonio*/Bexar	00998146	210/397-2250	37
John H Guyer High Sch/*Denton*/Denton	10001826	940/369-1000	121
John H Reagan Elem Sch/*Dallas*/Dallas	01009190	972/502-8200	101
John H Shary Elem Sch/*Mission*/Hidalgo	04359918	956/580-5282	224
John Haley Elem Sch/*Irving*/Dallas	01011193	972/600-6600	109
John Hanby Elem Sch/*Mesquite*/Dallas	01011545	972/882-5040	111
John Ireland Elem Sch/*Dallas*/Dallas	01009164	972/749-4900	101
John J Ciavarra Elem Sch/*Devine*/Medina	01041203	830/851-0395	283
John J Pershing Elem Sch/*Dallas*/Dallas	01009176	972/794-8600	101
John Jay High Sch/*San Antonio*/Bexar	00998158	210/397-2700	37
John Jay Sci & Engineer Acad/*San Antonio*/ Bexar	04809016	210/397-2773	37
John L Patton Academic Center/*Dallas*/ Dallas	11551393	214/932-5160	101
John M Stuart Career Tech HS/*Baytown*/ Harris	01023691	281/420-4550	188
John M Tidwell Middle Sch/*Roanoke*/Denton	11554474	817/698-5900	125
John Marshall High Sch/*San Antonio*/Bexar	00998160	210/397-7100	37
John McKeever Elem Sch/*Alamo*/Hidalgo	01030357	956/354-2680	223
John Neely Bryan Elem Sch/*Dallas*/Dallas	01008562	972/502-8500	101
John Paul II High Sch/*Plano*/Collin	10015360	972/867-0005	85
John Paul Stevens High Sch/*San Antonio*/ Bexar	10009490	210/397-6450	37
John Q Adams Elem Sch/*Dallas*/Dallas	01008366	972/794-1200	101
John R Good Elem Sch/*Irving*/Dallas	01011210	972/600-3300	109
John S Armstrong Elem Sch/*Dallas*/Dallas	01011064	214/780-3100	108
John S Bradfield Elem Sch/*Dallas*/Dallas	01011076	214/780-3200	108
John T White Elem Sch/*Fort Worth*/Tarrant	11711907	817/814-7900	351
John Tower Elem Sch/*Wichita Falls*/Wichita	01059975	940/855-3221	391
John Tyler High Sch/*Tyler*/Smith	01050876	903/262-2850	338
John W Armstrong Elem Sch/*Sachse*/Dallas	05096808	972/414-7480	106
John W Carpenter Elem Sch/*Dallas*/Dallas	01009205	972/794-6000	101
John W Runyon Elem Sch/*Dallas*/Dallas	01009736	972/749-6100	101
John Winship Elem Sch/*Spring*/Harris	01027491	281/891-8210	202
Johnny Economedes High Sch/*Edinburg*/ Hidalgo	04922905	956/289-2450	217
Johns Elem Sch/*Arlington*/Tarrant	01051765	682/867-2500	344
JOHNSON CITY IND SCH DIST/ JOHNSON CITY/BLANCO	01000510	830/868-7410	46
Johnson Daep/*Grand Prairie*/Dallas	03007253	972/262-7244	107
Johnson Elem Sch/*Bryan*/Brazos	01002099	979/209-1460	55
Johnson Elem Sch/*El Paso*/El Paso	01016002	915/236-3925	133
Johnson Elem Sch/*Forney*/Kaufman	01035577	972/564-3397	252
Johnson Ferguson Academy/*Brenham*/ Washington	10016027	979/836-4156	386

School Year 2019-2020 800-333-8802 TX-V39

DISTRICT & SCHOOL TELEPHONE INDEX

Market Data Retrieval

School/City/County DISTRICT/CITY/COUNTY	PID	TELEPHONE NUMBER	PAGE
Johnson High Sch/*Buda*/Hays	12362133	512/268-2141	211
Johnson High Sch/*San Antonio*/Bexar	11128518	210/356-0400	35
Johnson Ranch Elem Sch/*Bulverde*/Comal	11450945	830/885-8600	88
Johnston Elem Sch/*Abilene*/Taylor	01172797	325/671-4845	360
Johnston Elem Sch/*Irving*/Dallas	01011117	972/600-7700	109
Johnston McQueen Elem Sch/*Longview*/Gregg	01021095	903/803-5300	170
Jollyville Elem Sch/*Austin*/Williamson	04017811	512/428-2200	399
Jones Aca of Fine Arts & Dual/*Arlington*/Tarrant	01051894	682/867-3580	344
Jones Early Literacy Center/*Texarkana*/Bowie	01001239	903/793-4871	50
Jones EC-PK-K Sch/*Humble*/Harris	11074694	281/446-1576	181
Jones Elem Sch/*Brackettville*/Kinney	01036246	830/563-2492	257
Jones Elem Sch/*Bryan*/Brazos	03400605	979/209-3900	55
Jones Elem Sch/*Humble*/Harris	11074682	281/446-6168	180
Jones Elem Sch/*Midland*/Midland	01041576	432/240-7200	286
Jones Elem Sch/*Tyler*/Smith	01050890	903/262-2360	338
Jones Futures Academy/*Houston*/Harris	12037089	713/733-1111	192
Jones Middle Sch/*Humble*/Harris	12309662	281/985-3720	181
JONESBORO IND SCH DIST/**JONESBORO**/**CORYELL**	01007714	254/463-2111	93
Jonesboro Sch/*Jonesboro*/Coryell	01007726	254/463-2111	93
Jordan Elem Sch/*Austin*/Travis	04014936	512/414-2578	368
Jorge R Gutierrez ECC/*Edcouch*/Hidalgo	04931956	956/262-0040	216
Jose A Valdez High Sch/*Laredo*/Webb	11713072	956/273-8000	386
Jose Alderete Middle Sch/*Canutillo*/El Paso	10022258	915/877-6600	132
Jose Antonio Navarro Elem Sch/*Corsicana*/Navarro	01043483	903/874-1011	299
Jose Borrego Middle Sch/*Monte Alto*/Hidalgo	10901379	956/262-1374	222
Jose Damian Elem Sch/*El Paso*/El Paso	04011128	915/877-6800	132
Jose De Escandon Elem Sch/*McAllen*/Hidalgo	02043333	956/971-4511	221
Jose De Escandon Elem Sch/*Mission*/Hidalgo	04039156	956/323-2410	220
Jose M Lopez Middle Sch/*San Antonio*/Bexar	10911051	210/356-5000	35
Jose May Elem Sch/*Dallas*/Dallas	12169125	972/749-4800	101
Josefa L Sambrano Elem Sch/*San Elizario*/El Paso	04278584	915/872-3950	135
Joseph C Martin Elem Sch/*Laredo*/Webb	01059236	956/273-4100	387
Joseph Gilbert Elem Sch/*Austin*/Travis	11732729	512/386-3800	369
Joseph Hopkins Elem Sch/*San Antonio*/Bexar	00997623	210/661-1120	33
Joseph J Rhoads Learning Ctr/*Dallas*/Dallas	01009231	972/749-1000	101
Josephine Castaneda Elem Sch/*Brownsville*/Cameron	01003483	956/548-8800	64
Joshua 9th Grade Campus/*Joshua*/Johnson	11718565	817/202-2500	248
Joshua Christian Academy/*Joshua*/Johnson	11225984	817/295-7377	249
Joshua High Sch/*Joshua*/Johnson	01035046	817/202-2500	248
JOSHUA IND SCH DIST/**JOSHUA**/**JOHNSON**	01035022	817/426-7500	248
Joshua SDA Multi Grade Sch/*Joshua*/Johnson	03405758	817/556-2109	249
Joslin Elem Sch/*Austin*/Travis	01056301	512/414-2094	366
Jourdanton Elem Sch/*Jourdanton*/Atascosa	00995388	830/769-2121	20
Jourdanton High Sch/*Jourdanton*/Atascosa	00995390	830/769-2350	20
JOURDANTON IND SCH DIST/**JOURDANTON**/**ATASCOSA**	00995376	830/769-3548	20
Jourdanton Junior High Sch/*Jourdanton*/Atascosa	02111899	830/769-2234	20
Jowell Elem Sch/*Katy*/Harris	02896661	281/463-5966	185
Joy James Elem Sch/*Fort Worth*/Tarrant	01052343	817/252-2500	347
Joy Sch/*Houston*/Harris	05026578	713/523-0660	206
Jstem Academy/*Converse*/Bexar	12177574	210/945-1159	33
Juan D Salinas Middle Sch/*Mission*/Hidalgo	11449465	956/323-2850	220
Juan Diego Academy/*Mission*/Hidalgo	11715240	956/583-2752	226
Juan N Seguin Elem Sch/*Houston*/Harris	05099305	713/845-5600	193
Juan N Seguin Elem Sch/*Mission*/Hidalgo	05346809	956/323-2710	220
Juan Seguin Elem Sch/*Grand Prairie*/Dallas	05342619	972/522-7100	107
Juan Seguin Elem Sch/*McAllen*/Hidalgo	01172462	956/971-4565	221
Juan Seguin Elem Sch/*Richmond*/Fort Bend	11448409	281/634-9850	150
Juan Seguin Elem Sch/*Weatherford*/Parker	01046588	817/598-2814	314
Juan Seguin High Sch/*Arlington*/Tarrant	05096561	682/867-6700	344
Juan W Caceres Elem Sch/*Donna*/Hidalgo	03410222	956/464-1995	215
Juarez-Lincoln Elem Sch/*Laredo*/Webb	04038449	956/473-3000	387
Juarez-Lincoln High Sch/*Mission*/Hidalgo	04031726	956/323-2890	220
Jubilee Academic Center/*San Antonio*/Bexar	05010672	210/333-6227	6
Jubilee Brownsville/*Brownsville*/Cameron	12044616	956/509-2690	6
Jubilee Destiny/*Harlingen*/Cameron	12044628	956/708-2040	6
Jubilee Harlingen/*Harlingen*/Cameron	12044630	956/708-2030	6
Jubilee Highland Hills/*San Antonio*/Bexar	12044599	210/634-7590	6
Jubilee Highland Park/*San Antonio*/Bexar	11834523	210/801-8030	6
Jubilee Kingsville/*Kingsville*/Kleberg	11929221	361/516-0840	6
Jubilee Lake View Univ Prep/*San Antonio*/Bexar	12238532	210/963-3900	6
Jubilee Leadership Academy/*Brownsville*/Cameron	12260834	956/641-4250	6
Jubilee Livingway/*Brownsville*/Cameron	12044642	956/708-2020	6
Jubilee San Antonio/*San Antonio*/Bexar	12044604	210/278-3880	6
Jubilee Wells Branch/*Austin*/Travis	11932046	512/872-8440	6
Jubilee-Wells Academies/*Austin*/Travis	12108834	512/872-8440	6
Judge Andy Mireles Elem Sch/*San Antonio*/Bexar	11713905	210/398-1500	37
Judge Barefoot Sanders Law Mag/*Dallas*/Dallas	01553048	972/925-5950	101
Judge Frank Berry Middle Sch/*Mesquite*/Dallas	04750116	972/882-5850	111
Judge Oscar De La Fuente ES/*San Benito*/Cameron	10026656	956/361-6820	67
Judson Early College Academy/*Universal Cty*/Bexar	11452278	210/619-0200	33
Judson High Sch/*Converse*/Bexar	04813213	210/945-1100	33
JUDSON IND SCH DIST/**LIVE OAK**/**BEXAR**	00997582	210/945-5100	33
Judson Learning Academy/*San Antonio*/Bexar	04362381	210/651-4080	33
Judson Middle Sch/*Converse*/Bexar	11561582	210/357-0801	33
Judson Robinson Elem Sch/*Houston*/Harris	05099288	713/450-7107	190
Judson Secondary Alt Sch/*Converse*/Bexar	04448648	210/619-0330	33
Judson Steam Academy/*Longview*/Gregg	01021071	903/446-2610	170
Judy Hajek Elem Sch/*Burleson*/Johnson	11220609	817/245-3700	247
Judy K Miller Elem Sch/*Mansfield*/Tarrant	12104993	817/299-7550	357
Judy Rucker Elem Sch/*Prosper*/Collin	10011510	469/219-2100	84
Julia Garcia Middle Sch/*Brownsville*/Cameron	05095737	956/832-6300	64
Julian T Saldivar Elem Sch/*Dallas*/Dallas	04456499	972/794-2000	101
Julien C Gallardo Elem Sch/*San Antonio*/Bexar	10012071	210/882-1609	43
Julius Dorsey Elem Sch/*Dallas*/Dallas	01009255	972/749-6300	101
Julius L Matthey Middle Sch/*San Antonio*/Bexar	00999542	210/882-1601	43
Junction Elem Sch/*Junction*/Kimble	01036167	325/446-2055	256
Junction High Sch/*Junction*/Kimble	01036179	325/446-3326	256
JUNCTION IND SCH DIST/**JUNCTION**/**KIMBLE**	01036155	325/446-3510	256
Junction Middle Sch/*Junction*/Kimble	01036181	325/446-2464	256
June R Thompson Elem Sch/*Carrollton*/Dallas	01008263	972/968-3400	97
June W Davis Elem Sch/*Fort Worth*/Tarrant	12367121	817/885-5700	348
Justice Raul A Gonzalez ES/*Weslaco*/Hidalgo	01030606	956/969-6760	225
Justin Elem Sch/*Justin*/Denton	01013531	817/215-0800	125
Justin F Kimball High Sch/*Dallas*/Dallas	01009035	972/502-2100	101
Justin Wakeland High Sch/*Frisco*/Collin	10031936	469/633-5700	79
JW & Ruth Christie Elem Sch/*Frisco*/Collin	04868543	469/633-2400	79

K

School/City/County	PID	TELEPHONE NUMBER	PAGE
K B Polk Elem Sch/*Dallas*/Dallas	01009267	972/794-8900	101
Kahla Middle Sch/*Houston*/Harris	10000559	281/345-3260	185
Kaiser Elem Sch/*Houston*/Harris	01832129	832/484-6100	197
Kallison Elem Sch/*San Antonio*/Bexar	12230712	210/398-2350	37
Kardia Christian Academy/*Houston*/Harris	11224605	281/378-4040	206
Karen Wagner High Sch/*San Antonio*/Bexar	10003446	210/662-5000	33
KARNACK IND SCH DIST/**KARNACK**/**HARRISON**	01028574	903/679-3117	208
Karnes City Early Clg HS/*Karnes City*/Karnes	12169905	830/780-2321	250
Karnes City High Sch/*Karnes City*/Karnes	01035436	830/780-2321	250
KARNES CITY IND SCH DIST/**KARNES CITY**/**KARNES**	01035395	830/780-2321	250
Karnes City Junior High Sch/*Karnes City*/Karnes	01809495	830/780-2321	250
Karnes City Primary Sch/*Karnes City*/Karnes	12169917	830/780-2321	250
Kashmere Gardens Elem Sch/*Houston*/Harris	01025998	713/671-4160	191
Kashmere High Sch/*Houston*/Harris	01026007	713/636-6400	189
Katherine Anne Porter Sch/*Wimberley*/Hays	04892453	512/847-6867	6
Katherine G Johnson STEM Acad/*Greenville*/Hunt	12305680	903/454-5050	236
Katherine Johnson Tech Mag Sch/*Desoto*/Dallas	12309442	972/274-8026	104
Katherine Tarver Elem Sch/*Laredo*/Webb	01059315	956/273-4800	387
Kathlyn Joy Gilliam Academy/*Dallas*/Dallas	11552842	972/925-1400	101
Kathryn Griffis Elem Sch/*Caddo Mills*/Hunt	11075648	903/527-3525	235
Kathryn S McWhorter Elem Sch/*Dallas*/Dallas	04945086	972/968-2600	97
Kathy Caraway Elem Sch/*Austin*/Williamson	01824421	512/464-5500	399
Katy Adventist Christian Sch/*Katy*/Harris	12314007	281/392-5603	206
Katy Elem Sch/*Katy*/Harris	01026241	281/237-6550	152
Katy High Sch/*Katy*/Harris	01026253	281/237-9700	152
KATY IND SCH DIST/**KATY**/**HARRIS**	01026227	281/396-6000	151
Katy Junior High Sch/*Katy*/Harris	01026265	281/237-6800	152
Kaufer High Sch/*Riviera*/Kleberg	01036416	361/296-3607	258

Texas School Directory
DISTRICT & SCHOOL TELEPHONE INDEX

School/City/County DISTRICT/CITY/COUNTY	PID	TELEPHONE NUMBER	PAGE
Kauffman Leadership Academy/Cleburne/Johnson	12260846	682/459-2800	6
Kaufman Christian Sch/Kaufman/Kaufman	04762822	972/932-4672	253
Kaufman Elem Sch/Spring/Montgomery	10027832	832/592-5600	292
Kaufman High Sch/Kaufman/Kaufman	01035632	972/932-2811	252
KAUFMAN IND SCH DIST/KAUFMAN/ KAUFMAN	01035606	972/932-2622	252
Kay Franklin Elem Sch/San Antonio/Bexar	11918181	210/398-1700	37
Kay Granger Elem Sch/Keller/Denton	10913114	817/698-1100	125
Kazen Elem Sch/Laredo/Webb	04038425	956/473-4200	387
Kealing Middle Sch/Austin/Travis	02891142	512/414-3214	369
Keeble EC-PK-K Sch/Houston/Harris	04805008	281/878-6860	181
Keefer Crossing Middle Sch/New Caney/Montgomery	02179009	281/577-8841	293
Keeley Elem Sch/Rowlett/Dallas	03397462	972/412-2140	106
Keenan Elem Sch/Montgomery/Montgomery	01042659	936/276-5500	293
Keene Adventist Elem Sch/Keene/Johnson	01480685	817/645-9125	249
Keene Elem Sch/Keene/Johnson	01035072	817/774-5320	248
KEENE IND SCH DIST/KEENE/JOHNSON	01035060	817/774-5200	248
Keene Junior High Sch/Keene/Johnson	04354578	817/774-5311	248
Keene Wanda R Smith High Sch/Keene/Johnson	04354580	817/774-5220	248
Keiko Davidson Elem Sch/Katy/Harris	12033813	281/234-2500	152
Keith Elem Sch/Cypress/Harris	05346615	281/213-1744	185
Keller Ctr Advanced Learning/Keller/Tarrant	12170186	817/743-8000	355
Keller Elem Sch/Brownsville/Cameron	11449269	956/547-4400	64
Keller High Sch/Keller/Tarrant	02222424	817/744-1400	355
KELLER IND SCH DIST/KELLER/ TARRANT	01053983	817/744-1000	354
Keller Learning Center/Keller/Tarrant	03392735	817/744-4465	355
Keller Middle Sch/Keller/Tarrant	01054004	817/744-2900	355
Keller Middle Sch/Pasadena/Harris	11129419	713/740-5284	199
Keller-Harvel Elem Sch/Keller/Tarrant	01053995	817/744-5100	355
Kelley Elem Sch/Denver City/Yoakum	01062025	806/592-5920	405
Kelly Elem Sch/Pharr/Hidalgo	02202424	956/843-4200	217
Kelly Elem Sch/San Antonio/Bexar	00999152	210/228-3350	40
Kelly Lane Middle Sch/Pflugerville/Travis	10022428	512/594-2800	372
Kelly-Pharr Elem Sch/Pharr/Hidalgo	03055470	956/354-2870	223
Kelso Elem Sch/Houston/Harris	01024889	713/845-7451	193
KELTON IND SCH DIST/WHEELER/ WHEELER	01059808	806/826-5795	390
Kelton Sch/Wheeler/Wheeler	01059810	806/826-5795	390
Kemp High Sch/Kemp/Kaufman	01035670	903/498-9222	252
KEMP IND SCH DIST/KEMP/KAUFMAN	01035656	903/498-1314	252
Kemp Intermediate Sch/Kemp/Kaufman	03018719	903/498-1362	252
Kemp Junior High Sch/Kemp/Kaufman	02055350	903/498-1343	252
Kemp Primary Sch/Kemp/Kaufman	01035668	903/498-1404	252
Kemp-Carver Elem Sch/Bryan/Brazos	01002075	979/209-3700	55
Kendall Elem Sch/Boerne/Kendall	04916803	830/357-4600	254
Kendrick Elem Sch/Waco/McLennan	01040261	254/752-3316	282
KENEDY CO SCHOOLS/SARITA/KENEDY	02091342	361/294-5381	254
KENEDY CO WIDE COMMON SCH DIST/ SARITA/KENEDY	01035905	361/294-5381	254
Kenedy Elem Sch/Kenedy/Karnes	01035474	830/583-4100	251
Kenedy High Sch/Kenedy/Karnes	01035462	830/583-4100	251
KENEDY IND SCH DIST/KENEDY/ KARNES	01035450	830/583-4100	251
Kenedy Middle Sch/Kenedy/Karnes	01035486	830/583-4100	251
Kenley Sch/Abilene/Taylor	11231658	325/698-3220	361
Kenmont Montessori Sch/Brownsville/Cameron	02825997	956/542-0500	68
KENNARD IND SCH DIST/KENNARD/ HOUSTON	01031791	936/655-2161	233
Kennard Sch/Kennard/Houston	01031806	936/655-2161	233
Kennedale Alternative Ed Prog/Kennedale/Tarrant	04918253	817/563-8060	356
Kennedale High Sch/Kennedale/Tarrant	01054066	817/563-8100	356
KENNEDALE IND SCH DIST/KENNEDALE/ TARRANT	01054030	817/563-8000	355
Kennedale Junior High Sch/Kennedale/Tarrant	01054054	817/563-8200	356
Kennedy Elem Sch/Corp Christi/Nueces	01045089	361/806-5920	306
Kennedy Elem Sch/Eagle Pass/Maverick	05000940	830/758-7189	277
Kennedy Elem Sch/Houston/Harris	01024126	713/696-2686	191
Kennedy Elem Sch/Houston/Harris	01418371	281/983-8338	182
Kennedy Middle Sch/Pharr/Hidalgo	11552878	956/354-2650	223
Kennedy-Curry Middle Sch/Dallas/Dallas	01009401	972/925-1600	101
Kennedy-Powell Elem Sch/Temple/Bell	00996760	254/215-6000	29
Kennedy-Zapata Elem Sch/El Cenizo/Webb	04364042	956/473-4100	388
Kenneth D Black Elem Sch/Houston/Harris	03246772	281/878-0350	180
Kenneth Davis Elem Sch/Arlington/Tarrant	04949111	817/299-7840	357
Kenneth E Little Elem Sch/Bacliff/Galveston	01018971	281/229-7000	159
Kenneth White Jr High Sch/Mission/Hidalgo	03052090	956/323-3600	222
Kentwood Early Childhood Ctr/Big Spring/Howard	11816399	432/264-4130	233
Kerens Elem Sch/Kerens/Navarro	01043598	903/396-7941	300
Kerens High Sch/Kerens/Navarro	01043603	903/396-2931	300
KERENS IND SCH DIST/KERENS/ NAVARRO	01043586	903/396-2924	299
Kerens Middle Sch/Kerens/Navarro	02846642	903/396-2570	300
Kermit Elem Sch/Kermit/Winkler	01061473	432/586-1020	402
Kermit High Sch/Kermit/Winkler	01061447	432/586-1050	402
KERMIT IND SCH DIST/KERMIT/ WINKLER	01061423	432/586-1000	401
Kermit Junior High Sch/Kermit/Winkler	01061461	432/586-1040	402
Kerr High Sch/Houston/Harris	04285094	281/983-8484	182
Kerr Middle Sch/Burleson/Johnson	04748955	817/245-0750	247
Kerrville Discipline Alt Sch/Kerrville/Kerr	04037536	830/257-1332	256
KERRVILLE IND SCH DIST/KERRVILLE/ KERR	01036076	830/257-2200	256
Kessler Sch/Dallas/Dallas	03371468	214/942-2220	115
Ketelsen Elem Sch/Houston/Harris	01024138	713/220-5050	192
Key Elem Sch/Arlington/Tarrant	01399787	682/867-5500	344
Key Middle Sch/Houston/Harris	01025900	713/636-6000	191
Key Sch/Fort Worth/Tarrant	03141835	817/446-3738	359
Keys Academy/El Paso/El Paso	04284337	915/937-4000	136
Keys Academy/Harlingen/Cameron	03401518	956/427-3220	65
Keys Elem Academy/El Paso/El Paso	12032132	915/937-4104	136
Keys Learning Center/Euless/Tarrant	03052260	817/354-3580	354
Keystone Sch/San Antonio/Bexar	01000467	210/735-4022	45
Ki Charter Academy/San Marcos/Hays	12108066	512/618-0787	6
Kidwell Elem Sch/Iowa Park/Wichita	01060089	940/592-4322	392
Kieberger Elem Sch/Aransas Pass/San Patricio	01049528	361/758-3113	330
Kiest Park Christian Academy/Dallas/Dallas	02207101	214/331-1536	115
Kiker Elem Sch/Austin/Travis	04014948	512/414-2584	366
Kilgore High Sch/Kilgore/Gregg	01020974	903/988-3901	169
KILGORE IND SCH DIST/KILGORE/ GREGG	01020900	903/988-3900	169
Kilgore Intermediate Sch/Kilgore/Gregg	01020936	903/988-3903	169
Kilgore Middle Sch/Kilgore/Gregg	01020962	903/988-3902	169
Kilgore Primary Sch/Kilgore/Gregg	01020950	903/988-3905	169
Killam Elem Sch/Laredo/Webb	11077452	956/473-2600	388
Killeen Adventist Jr Academy/Killeen/Bell	02233760	254/699-9466	30
Killeen High Sch/Killeen/Bell	00996514	254/336-7208	28
KILLEEN IND SCH DIST/KILLEEN/ BELL	00996423	254/336-0000	27
Killeen ISD Career Center/Killeen/Bell	01601774	254/336-3800	28
Killough Middle Sch/Houston/Harris	01526021	281/983-8444	182
Kimberlin Acad for Excellence/Garland/Dallas	01010565	972/926-2560	106
Kimmie M Brown Elem Sch/Dayton/Liberty	01037783	936/257-2796	265
Kinder HS Perform & Visual Art/Houston/Harris	01023811	713/942-1960	192
Kinder Ranch Elem Sch/San Antonio/Comal	11719428	830/609-6702	88
Kindred Elem Sch/San Antonio/Bexar	00999451	210/977-7575	42
King Early Childhood Center/Houston/Harris	05349928	713/797-7900	193
Kingdom Academy/Houston/Harris	11230329	713/450-0021	206
Kingdom Life Academy/Tyler/Smith	12169527	903/283-3444	339
Kingdom Preparatory Academy/Lubbock/Lubbock	11227059	806/767-9334	272
Kings Academy Chrn Sch/Tyler/Smith	11222425	903/534-9992	339
Kings Manor Elem Sch/Kingwood/Montgomery	04946030	281/577-2940	293
Kingsborough Middle Sch/San Antonio/Bexar	00997477	210/989-2200	33
Kingsland Sch/Kingsland/Llano	12260858	325/388-0020	6
KINGSVILLE IND SCH DIST/ KINGSVILLE/KLEBERG	01036258	361/592-3387	257
Kingwood High Sch/Kingwood/Harris	02067860	281/641-6900	196
Kingwood Middle Sch/Kingwood/Harris	01540039	281/641-4200	196
Kingwood Park High Sch/Kingwood/Harris	04286189	281/641-6600	196
Kinkeade Early Childhood Sch/Irving/Dallas	04872984	972/600-6500	109
KIPP 3D Academy/Houston/Harris	11704356	832/230-0566	6
KIPP Acad West MS/Houston/Harris	12163810	832/230-0573	6
KIPP Academy MS/Houston/Harris	04454489	832/328-1051	6
KIPP Aspire Academy/San Antonio/Bexar	05282588	210/735-7300	6
KIPP Austin Acad Arts Letters/Austin/Travis	11702499	512/501-3640	6
KIPP Austin Beacon Prep/Austin/Travis	11823457	512/651-1918	6
KIPP Austin Brave HS/Austin/Travis	12260860	512/651-2225	6
KIPP Austin College Prep/Austin/Travis	05243348	512/501-4969	6
KIPP Austin Collegiate/Austin/Travis	11702487	512/501-3586	6
KIPP Austin Comunidad/Austin/Travis	11702504	512/501-3911	6
KIPP Austin Connections ES/Austin/Travis	11834389	512/651-5537	6

School Year 2019-2020   800-333-8802   TX-V41

DISTRICT & SCHOOL TELEPHONE INDEX

Market Data Retrieval

School/City/County DISTRICT/CITY/COUNTY	PID	TELEPHONE NUMBER	PAGE
KIPP Austin Leadership ES/*Austin*/Travis	11932498	512/651-2168	6
KIPP Austin Obras/*Austin*/Travis	11932486	512/651-2069	6
KIPP Austin Vista Middle Sch/*Austin*/Travis	11823469	512/651-1921	6
KIPP Camino Academy/*San Antonio*/Bexar	11702516	210/829-4200	6
KIPP Climb Academy/*Houston*/Harris	12260872	832/230-0578	6
KIPP Connect Houston High Sch/*Houston*/Harris	12320252	281/879-3023	6
KIPP Connect Houston MS/*Houston*/Harris	12163860	281/879-3023	6
KIPP Connect Houston Primary/*Houston*/Harris	12260884	281/879-3023	6
KIPP Courage College Prep/*Houston*/Harris	11823483	713/251-3800	6
KIPP Destiny Elem Sch/*Dallas*/Dallas	11931949	972/323-4220	7
KIPP Destiny Middle Sch/*Dallas*/Dallas	12161135	972/323-4225	7
KIPP Dream Prep/*Houston*/Harris	10805268	832/230-0566	7
KIPP Esperanza Dual Lang Acad/*San Antonio*/Bexar	12032326	210/888-6601	7
KIPP Explore Academy/*Houston*/Harris	11704409	832/230-0547	7
KIPP Generations Collegiate HS/*Houston*/Harris	11834432	832/230-0566	7
KIPP Houston High Sch/*Houston*/Harris	11704332	832/328-1082	7
KIPP Intrepid Prep Sch/*Houston*/Harris	11396117	281/879-3100	7
KIPP Legacy Prep Sch/*Houston*/Harris	11704423	832/230-0567	7
KIPP Liberation College Prep/*Houston*/Harris	11014620	832/230-0564	7
KIPP Nexus MS/*Houston*/Harris	12305654	832/230-0553	7
KIPP Nexus Primary-Houston/*Houston*/Harris	12260896	832/230-0553	7
KIPP Northeast College Prep/*Houston*/Harris	11931951	832/230-0567	7
KIPP Peace Elem Sch/*Houston*/Harris	11818658	832/230-0564	7
KIPP Pleasant Grove Mid Sch/*Dallas*/Dallas	12260913	972/323-4235	7
KIPP Pleasant Grove Primary/*Dallas*/Dallas	12260901	972/323-4230	7
KIPP Poder Academy/*San Antonio*/Bexar	12112586	210/888-6513	7
KIPP Polaris Academy for Boys/*Houston*/Harris	11014618	832/230-0567	7
KIPP Prime College Prep/*Houston*/Harris	12174285	832/230-0578	7
KIPP Sharp Prep/*Houston*/Harris	11409714	281/879-3000	7
KIPP Sharpstown College Prep/*Houston*/Harris	11449817	281/879-3005	7
KIPP Shine Prep/*Houston*/Harris	11220245	832/328-1051	7
KIPP Somos Collegiate High Sch/*San Antonio*/Bexar	12367937		7
KIPP Spirit College Prep/*Houston*/Harris	10817168	832/230-0562	7
KIPP Sunnyside High Sch/*Houston*/Harris	11704320	832/230-0562	7
KIPP Truth Academy/*Dallas*/Dallas	10031895	972/323-4215	7
KIPP Truth Elem Sch/*Dallas*/Dallas	12161123	972/323-4240	7
KIPP UN Mundo Dual Lang Acad/*San Antonio*/Bexar	11823495	210/824-1905	7
KIPP Unity Primary/*Houston*/Harris	12112598	832/230-0572	7
KIPP University Prep High Sch/*San Antonio*/Bexar	11445407	210/290-8720	7
KIPP Voyage Academy for Girls/*Houston*/Harris	11704368	832/230-0567	7
KIPP Zenith Academy/*Houston*/Harris	11916121	832/230-0562	7
Kirby Hall Sch/*Austin*/Travis	02084143	512/474-1770	373
Kirby Middle Sch/*San Antonio*/Bexar	00997635	210/661-1140	33
Kirby Middle Sch/*Wichita Falls*/Wichita	01173155	940/235-1113	392
KIRBYVILLE CONS IND SCH DIST/ KIRBYVILLE/JASPER	01033282	409/423-2284	241
Kirbyville Elem Sch/*Kirbyville*/Jasper	01033309	409/423-8526	241
Kirbyville High Sch/*Kirbyville*/Jasper	01033311	409/423-7500	241
Kirbyville Junior High Sch/*Kirbyville*/Jasper	01033294	409/420-0692	241
Kirchner Elem Sch/*Quemado*/Maverick	01041112	830/758-7045	277
Kirk Elem Sch/*Houston*/Harris	04916346	713/849-8250	185
Kirkpatrick Middle Sch/*Fort Worth*/Tarrant	01053115	817/814-4200	351
Kissam Elem Sch/*Tyler*/Smith	04278649	903/566-8334	337
Kitty Hawk Middle Sch/*Universal Cty*/Bexar	01523665	210/945-1220	33
Kleb Intermediate Sch/*Klein*/Harris	02178275	832/249-5500	197
Kleberg Elem Sch/*Dallas*/Dallas	01009279	972/749-6500	101
Kleberg Elem Sch/*Kingsville*/Kleberg	01036272	361/592-2615	257
Klein Alternative Ed Center/*Klein*/Harris	05273769	832/249-4801	197
Klein Cain High Sch/*Houston*/Harris	12223247	832/375-8400	197
Klein Collins High Sch/*Spring*/Harris	04941626	832/484-5500	197
Klein Forest High Sch/*Houston*/Harris	02043321	832/484-4500	197
Klein High Sch/*Klein*/Harris	01026332	832/484-4000	197
KLEIN IND SCH DIST/KLEIN/HARRIS	01026289	832/249-4000	196
Klein Intermediate Sch/*Houston*/Harris	02227204	832/249-4900	197
Klein Oak High Sch/*Spring*/Harris	02178263	832/484-5000	197
Klein Road Elem Sch/*New Braunfels*/Comal	11436248	830/221-1700	88
Klenk Elem Sch/*Houston*/Harris	04017938	832/484-6800	197
Klentzman Intermediate Sch/*Houston*/Harris	04364444	281/983-8477	182
Kline Whitis Elem Sch/*Lampasas*/Lampasas	01037159	512/556-8291	261
KLONDIKE IND SCH DIST/LAMESA/ DAWSON	01012824	806/462-7334	117
Klondike Sch/*Lamesa*/Dawson	01012850	806/462-7332	117
KNIPPA IND SCH DIST/KNIPPA/ UVALDE	01057692	830/934-2176	378
Knippa Sch/*Knippa*/Uvalde	01057721	830/934-2176	378
Knowledge Seeker Christian Sch/*Lewisville*/Denton	04992728	972/353-3981	126
Knowles Elem Sch/*Cedar Park*/Williamson	05272442	512/570-6200	397
Knox City Elem Sch/*Knox City*/Knox	01036519	940/657-3147	258
Knox City High Sch/*Knox City*/Knox	01036521	940/657-3565	258
KNOX CITY-O'BRIEN CONS IND SD/ KNOX CITY/KNOX	01036507	940/657-3521	258
Knox Early Chldhd Center/*San Antonio*/Bexar	00999334	210/228-3365	40
Knox Junior High Sch/*The Woodlands*/Montgomery	01829471	832/592-8400	292
Kocurek Elem Sch/*Austin*/Travis	02890538	512/414-2547	366
Kohfeldt Elem Sch/*Texas City*/Galveston	01019523	409/916-0400	161
Kohrville Elem Sch/*Tomball*/Harris	05096092	832/484-7200	197
Kolda Elem Sch/*Corp Christi*/Nueces	11821100	361/878-2980	303
Kolter Elem Sch/*Houston*/Harris	01024891	713/726-3630	194
Kooken Educational Center/*Arlington*/Tarrant	03250694	682/867-7152	344
KOPPERL IND SCH DIST/KOPPERL/ BOSQUE	01000663	254/889-3502	47
Kopperl Sch/*Kopperl*/Bosque	01000675	254/889-3502	47
Kor Education Sch/*College Sta*/Brazos	12173906	979/777-1213	56
Kostoryz Elem Sch/*Corp Christi*/Nueces	01044487	361/878-2540	303
Kountze Elem Sch/*Kountze*/Hardin	01022532	409/246-3877	178
Kountze High Sch/*Kountze*/Hardin	01022518	409/246-3474	178
KOUNTZE IND SCH DIST/KOUNTZE/ HARDIN	01022491	409/246-3352	178
Kountze Intermediate Sch/*Kountze*/Hardin	11073028	409/246-8230	178
Kountze Middle Sch/*Kountze*/Hardin	01022520	409/246-3551	178
Krahn Elem Sch/*Klein*/Harris	02178287	832/484-6500	197
Kranz Junior High Sch/*Dickinson*/Galveston	12307107	281/309-3600	159
Krause Elem Sch/*Brenham*/Washington	01059092	979/277-3860	385
Kreinhop Elem Sch/*Spring*/Harris	05347592	832/484-7400	197
Kress Elem Sch/*Kress*/Swisher	01051557	806/684-2326	343
KRESS IND SCH DIST/KRESS/SWISHER	01051545	806/684-2652	343
Kress Jr Sr High Sch/*Kress*/Swisher	01051569	806/684-2651	343
Kriewald Road Elem Sch/*San Antonio*/Bexar	04808983	210/645-7550	43
Krimmel Intermediate Sch/*Klein*/Harris	10804836	832/375-7200	197
Krueger Middle Sch/*San Antonio*/Bexar	00997829	210/356-4700	35
Krum Early Education Center/*Krum*/Denton	11126912	940/482-2605	122
Krum High Sch/*Krum*/Denton	01013361	940/482-2601	122
KRUM IND SCH DIST/KRUM/DENTON	01013347	940/482-6000	122
Krum Middle Sch/*Krum*/Denton	02131112	940/482-2602	122
Kruse Elem Sch/*Pasadena*/Harris	01026772	713/740-0624	199
Kuehnle Elem Sch/*Klein*/Harris	03245510	832/484-6650	197
Kuentz Elem Sch/*Helotes*/Bexar	11448992	210/397-8050	38
Kujawa EC-PK-K Sch/*Houston*/Harris	11074709	281/878-1514	181
Kujawa Elem Sch/*Houston*/Harris	05274103	281/878-1530	179
Kurth Primary Sch/*Lufkin*/Angelina	00994994	936/639-3279	18
Kyle Elem Sch/*Kyle*/Hays	01029097	512/268-3311	211

L

School/City/County DISTRICT/CITY/COUNTY	PID	TELEPHONE NUMBER	PAGE
L A Gililland Elem Sch/*Fort Worth*/Tarrant	01052422	817/232-0331	349
L A Morgan Elem Sch/*Galveston*/Galveston	01019169	409/761-6700	160
L A Nelson Elem Sch/*Denton*/Denton	10909125	940/369-1400	121
L B Johnson Elem Sch/*San Antonio*/Bexar	00997300	210/444-8175	32
L C Smith Elem Sch/*Raymondville*/Willacy	01060730	956/689-8172	394
L E Monahan Elem Sch/*Houston*/Harris	02176095	281/454-2900	200
L F Blanton Elem Sch/*Carrollton*/Dallas	01008146	972/968-1100	97
L F Smith Elem Sch/*Pasadena*/Harris	01026942	713/740-0720	199
L G Pinkston High Sch/*Dallas*/Dallas	01009281	972/502-2700	101
L H Rather Junior High Sch/*Bonham*/Fannin	01017408	903/583-7474	145
L J Christen Middle Sch/*Laredo*/Webb	01059327	956/273-6400	387
L L Hotchkiss Elem Sch/*Dallas*/Dallas	01009293	972/749-7000	101
L L Pugh Elem Sch/*Houston*/Harris	01025716	713/671-3820	189
L O Donald Elem Sch/*Dallas*/Dallas	01009308	972/794-5300	101
L P Waters Early Childhood Ctr/*Greenville*/Hunt	04948583	903/457-2680	236
L V Stockard Middle Sch/*Dallas*/Dallas	01009310	972/794-5700	101
L W Kolarik 9th Grade Center/*Channelview*/Harris	11158020	713/378-3400	183
La Academia De Estrellas CS/*Dallas*/Dallas	11014632	214/946-8908	7
La Encantada Elem Sch/*San Benito*/Cameron	01004229	956/361-6760	67
La Fe Preparatory Sch/*El Paso*/El Paso	11015478	915/533-4690	7
La Feria Academy/*La Feria*/Cameron	11540019	956/797-8360	65
La Feria High Sch/*La Feria*/Cameron	01003952	956/797-8370	65

Texas School Directory
DISTRICT & SCHOOL TELEPHONE INDEX

School/City/County DISTRICT/CITY/COUNTY	PID	TELEPHONE NUMBER	PAGE
LA FERIA IND SCH DIST/*LA FERIA*/**CAMERON**	01003940	956/797-8300	65
La Gloria Elem Sch/*Falfurrias*/Jim Wells	02129353	361/325-2330	245
LA GLORIA IND SCH DIST/*FALFURRIAS*/**JIM WELLS**	01034664	361/325-2330	245
La Grange High Sch/*La Grange*/Fayette	01017757	979/968-4800	147
LA GRANGE IND SCH DIST/*LA GRANGE*/**FAYETTE**	01017721	979/968-7000	147
La Grange Intermediate Sch/*La Grange*/Fayette	04235996	979/968-4700	147
La Grange Middle Sch/*La Grange*/Fayette	01017769	979/968-4747	147
La Joya Early College HS/*La Joya*/Hidalgo	11930593	956/323-2930	220
LA JOYA IND SCH DIST/*LA JOYA*/**HIDALGO**	01029841	956/323-2000	219
La Joya Senior High Sch/*La Joya*/Hidalgo	01029865	956/323-2870	220
La Joya West Academy/*La Joya*/Hidalgo	04287901	956/323-2260	220
La Marque Elem Sch/*La Marque*/Galveston	01019339	409/908-5056	161
La Marque High Sch/*La Marque*/Galveston	01019353	409/938-4261	161
La Marque Middle Sch/*La Marque*/Galveston	01019377	409/938-4286	161
La Marque Primary Sch/*La Marque*/Galveston	04808268	409/935-3020	161
La Mesa Elem Sch/*Plainview*/Hale	03236428	806/293-6055	175
La Paloma Elem Sch/*San Benito*/Cameron	02845935	956/361-6780	67
La Paz Language Academy/*El Paso*/El Paso	11224320	915/584-5100	139
La Porte Elem Sch/*La Porte*/Harris	01026435	281/604-4700	198
La Porte High Sch/*La Porte*/Harris	01026447	281/604-7500	198
LA PORTE IND SCH DIST/*LA PORTE*/**HARRIS**	01026370	281/604-7000	198
La Porte Junior High Sch/*La Porte*/Harris	01026459	281/604-6600	198
LA POYNOR IND SCH DIST/*LARUE*/**HENDERSON**	01029413	903/876-4057	214
La Poynor Sch/*Larue*/Henderson	01029425	903/876-4057	214
La Pryor Elem Sch/*La Pryor*/Zavala	04033437	830/365-4009	407
La Pryor High Sch/*La Pryor*/Zavala	01062386	830/365-4007	407
LA PRYOR IND SCH DIST/*LA PRYOR*/**ZAVALA**	01062374	830/365-4000	407
La Union Elem Sch/*Rio Grande Cy*/Starr	01051143	956/487-3404	340
La Vega Elem Sch/*Waco*/McLennan	01039793	254/299-6755	280
La Vega High Sch/*Waco*/McLennan	01039810	254/299-6820	280
LA VEGA IND SCH DIST/*WACO*/**MCLENNAN**	01039779	254/299-6700	279
La Vega IS-H P Miles Campus/*Bellmead*/McLennan	01039781	254/299-6770	280
La Vega Junior High Sch/*Waco*/McLennan	01039808	254/299-6790	280
La Vega Primary Center/*Waco*/McLennan	02223557	254/299-6730	280
La Vernia Christian Agape Acad/*La Vernia*/Wilson	12165545	830/779-6361	401
La Vernia High Sch/*La Vernia*/Wilson	01061332	830/779-6630	401
LA VERNIA IND SCH DIST/*LA VERNIA*/**WILSON**	01061318	830/779-6600	401
La Vernia Intermediate Sch/*La Vernia*/Wilson	01061320	830/779-6640	401
La Vernia Junior High Sch/*La Vernia*/Wilson	03004445	830/779-6650	401
La Vernia Primary Sch/*La Vernia*/Wilson	04931891	830/779-6660	401
La Villa Early Clg High Sch/*La Villa*/Hidalgo	03245560	956/262-4715	220
LA VILLA IND SCH DIST/*LA VILLA*/**HIDALGO**	01029891	956/262-4755	220
La Villa Middle Sch/*La Villa*/Hidalgo	04247511	956/262-4760	220
La Villita Elem Sch/*Irving*/Dallas	11157442	972/968-6900	97
Labay Middle Sch/*Houston*/Harris	02226121	281/463-5800	185
Lackland Elem Sch/*San Antonio*/Bexar	01808843	210/357-5053	34
LACKLAND IND SCH DIST/*SAN ANTONIO*/**BEXAR**	01808829	210/357-5000	34
Lacy Elem Sch/*Princeton*/Collin	01006514	469/952-5401	84
Lady Bird Johnson Middle Sch/*Irving*/Dallas	11717092	972/600-0500	109
Lago Vista Elem Sch/*Lago Vista*/Travis	01056882	512/267-8340	370
Lago Vista High Sch/*Lago Vista*/Travis	01526150	512/267-8300	370
LAGO VISTA IND SCH DIST/*LAGO VISTA*/**TRAVIS**	01056870	512/267-8300	370
Lago Vista Intermediate Sch/*Lago Vista*/Travis	12169606	512/267-8300	370
Lago Vista Middle Sch/*Lago Vista*/Travis	04745044	512/267-8300	370
Lagos Elem Sch/*Manor*/Travis	12230267	512/278-4000	371
LaGrone Advanced Tech Complex/*Denton*/Denton	10021852	940/369-4850	121
Laguna Madre Christian Academy/*Laguna Vista*/Cameron	11230123	956/943-4446	68
Lake Air Mont Magnet Sch/*Waco*/McLennan	01040297	254/772-1910	282
Lake Belton Middle Sch/*Temple*/Bell	04916310	254/215-2900	27
Lake Cities Montessori Sch/*Garland*/Dallas	11902182	214/440-4930	115
Lake Country Christian Sch/*Fort Worth*/Tarrant	02164834	817/236-8703	359
Lake Creek High Sch/*Montgomery*/Montgomery	12363058	936/276-4000	293
Lake Dallas Elem Sch/*Lake Dallas*/Denton	02130728	940/497-2222	122
Lake Dallas High Sch/*Corinth*/Denton	01013397	940/497-4031	122
LAKE DALLAS IND SCH DIST/**LAKE DALLAS**/**DENTON**	01013373	940/497-4039	122
Lake Dallas Middle Sch/*Lake Dallas*/Denton	01809172	940/497-4037	122
Lake Highlands Elem Sch/*Dallas*/Dallas	01011753	469/593-2100	112
Lake Highlands High Sch/*Dallas*/Dallas	01011765	469/593-1000	112
Lake Highlands Jr High Sch/*Dallas*/Dallas	01011777	469/593-1600	112
Lake Jackson Intermediate Sch/*Lake Jackson*/Brazoria	01001643	979/730-7250	52
Lake Olympia Middle Sch/*Missouri City*/Fort Bend	04016348	281/634-3520	150
Lake Pointe Elem Sch/*Austin*/Travis	05070218	512/533-6500	370
Lake Pointe Elem Sch/*Fort Worth*/Tarrant	11072787	817/236-8801	349
Lake Ridge Elem Sch/*Cedar Hill*/Dallas	05097826	972/293-4501	97
Lake Travis Elem Sch/*Austin*/Travis	10011871	512/533-6300	370
Lake Travis High Sch/*Austin*/Travis	02223571	512/533-6100	370
LAKE TRAVIS IND SCH DIST/**AUSTIN**/**TRAVIS**	02178653	512/533-6000	370
Lake Travis Middle Sch/*Spicewood*/Travis	02223595	512/533-6200	370
Lake View High Sch/*San Angelo*/Tom Green	01055711	325/659-3500	365
Lake Worth High Sch/*Lake Worth*/Tarrant	01054092	817/306-4200	356
LAKE WORTH IND SCH DIST/**LAKE WORTH**/**TARRANT**	01054078	817/306-4200	356
Lakehill Preparatory Sch/*Dallas*/Dallas	01479923	214/826-2931	115
Lakeland Christian Academy/*Lewisville*/Denton	11230800	972/219-3939	126
Lakeland Elem Sch/*Humble*/Harris	01026203	281/641-1200	196
Lakeland Elem Sch/*Lewisville*/Denton	01013476	469/713-5992	123
Lakeshore Elem Sch/*Houston*/Harris	11450347	281/641-3500	196
Lakeside Elem Sch/*Coppell*/Dallas	04030277	214/496-7600	98
Lakeside Middle Sch/*Little Elm*/Denton	03007693	972/947-9445	124
Lakeview Centennial High Sch/*Garland*/Dallas	01525950	972/240-3740	106
Lakeview Elem Sch/*Amarillo*/Randall	03007825	806/677-2830	321
Lakeview Elem Sch/*Little Elm*/Denton	10012605	972/947-9454	124
Lakeview Elem Sch/*Mabank*/Kaufman	04454087	903/880-1360	252
Lakeview Elem Sch/*Sugar Land*/Fort Bend	01018165	281/634-4200	150
Lakeview Elem Sch/*Trophy Club*/Denton	02200775	817/215-0750	125
Lakeview Middle Sch/*The Colony*/Denton	03249360	469/713-5974	123
Lakeway Elem Sch/*Austin*/Travis	01029047	512/533-6350	371
Lakewood Elem Sch/*Belton*/Bell	02895071	254/215-3100	27
Lakewood Elem Sch/*Dallas*/Dallas	01009322	972/749-7300	101
Lakewood Elem Sch/*Euless*/Tarrant	01053854	817/354-3375	354
Lakewood Elem Sch/*Tomball*/Harris	02202618	281/357-3260	203
Lamar & Norma Hunt Middle Sch/*Frisco*/Collin	11558341	469/633-5200	79
Lamar Academy/*McAllen*/Hidalgo	03052612	956/632-3222	221
Lamar Bruni Vergara Middle Sch/*Laredo*/Webb	10021577	956/473-6600	388
Lamar Co Head Start Center/*Paris*/Lamar	12170863	903/737-7469	260
LAMAR CONS IND SCH DIST/**ROSENBERG**/**FORT BEND**	01018232	832/223-0000	153
Lamar Consolidated High Sch/*Rosenberg*/Fort Bend	01018294	832/223-3000	154
Lamar Early Education Center/*Odessa*/Ector	01014743	432/456-1159	130
Lamar Elem Sch/*Amarillo*/Potter	01047324	806/326-4600	318
Lamar Elem Sch/*Del Rio*/Val Verde	01058000	830/778-4730	379
Lamar Elem Sch/*Denison*/Grayson	01020376	903/462-7400	166
Lamar Elem Sch/*El Paso*/El Paso	01016014	915/236-3150	133
Lamar Elem Sch/*Greenville*/Hunt	01032525	903/457-0765	236
Lamar Elem Sch/*Harlingen*/Cameron	01003873	956/427-3130	65
Lamar Elem Sch/*Midland*/Midland	01041588	432/240-7300	286
Lamar Elem Sch/*Mineral Wells*/Palo Pinto	01046045	940/325-5303	310
Lamar Elem Sch/*New Braunfels*/Comal	01857143	830/627-6890	88
Lamar Elem Sch/*Pampa*/Gray	01020170	806/669-4880	165
Lamar Elem Sch/*San Angelo*/Tom Green	01055565	325/947-3900	365
Lamar Elem Sch/*San Antonio*/Bexar	00998574	210/738-9800	41
Lamar Elem Sch/*The Woodlands*/Montgomery	01042489	832/592-5800	292
Lamar Elem Sch/*Wichita Falls*/Wichita	01173129	940/235-1172	392
Lamar High Sch/*Houston*/Harris	01024487	713/522-5960	194
Lamar Junior High Sch/*Rosenberg*/Fort Bend	01018309	832/223-3200	154
Lamar Middle Sch/*Austin*/Travis	01056325	512/414-3217	369
Lamar Middle Sch/*Flower Mound*/Denton	03010456	469/713-5966	123
Lamar Middle Sch/*Irving*/Dallas	01011234	972/600-4400	109
Lamar Middle Sch/*Temple*/Bell	00996784	254/215-6444	29
Lamar Primary Sch/*Sulphur Spgs*/Hopkins	01031674	903/885-4550	232
Lamar-Delta Alternative Ctr/*Paris*/Lamar	04750178	903/669-0188	260
Lamesa High Sch/*Lamesa*/Dawson	01012898	806/872-8385	117
LAMESA IND SCH DIST/*LAMESA*/**DAWSON**	01012862	806/872-5461	117
Lamesa Middle Sch/*Lamesa*/Dawson	01012903	806/872-8301	117

School Year 2019-2020 800-333-8802 TX-V43

DISTRICT & SCHOOL TELEPHONE INDEX

Market Data Retrieval

School/City/County DISTRICT/CITY/COUNTY	PID	TELEPHONE NUMBER	PAGE
Lamesa Success Academy/*Lamesa*/Dawson	11917199	806/872-5410	117
Lamkin Elem Sch/*Cypress*/Harris	01023287	281/897-4775	185
Lampasas High Sch/*Lampasas*/Lampasas	01037135	512/564-2310	261
LAMPASAS IND SCH DIST/**LAMPASAS**/**LAMPASAS**	01037111	512/556-6224	261
Lampasas Middle Sch/*Lampasas*/Lampasas	01037147	512/556-3101	261
Lancaster Elem Sch/*El Paso*/El Paso	02200074	915/434-3400	138
Lancaster High Sch/*Lancaster*/Dallas	01011351	972/218-1800	110
LANCASTER IND SCH DIST/**LANCASTER**/**DALLAS**	01011337	972/218-1400	110
Lancaster STEM Early Clg HS/*Lancaster*/Dallas	12308450	972/218-1800	110
Lance Thompson Elem Sch/*Argyle*/Denton	12363151	817/698-1800	125
Landis Elem Sch/*Houston*/Harris	03252862	281/983-8343	182
Landrum Middle Sch/*Houston*/Harris	01027130	713/251-3700	201
LANEVILLE IND SCH DIST/**LANEVILLE**/**RUSK**	01049061	903/863-5353	327
Laneville Sch/*Laneville*/Rusk	01049085	903/863-5353	328
Langford Elem Sch/*Austin*/Travis	02110118	512/414-1765	367
Langham Creek High Sch/*Houston*/Harris	02848717	281/463-5400	185
Langham Elem Sch/*Nederland*/Jefferson	01033725	409/722-4324	243
Language Development Center/*Eagle Pass*/Maverick	04021707	830/758-7047	277
Lanier Middle Sch/*Houston*/Harris	01024504	713/942-1900	194
Lansberry Elem Sch/*Trinity*/Trinity	01057159	936/594-3567	374
Lantern Lane Elem Sch/*Missouri City*/Fort Bend	01826235	281/634-4680	150
Lantrip Elem Sch/*Houston*/Harris	01025596	713/924-1670	190
LAREDO IND SCH DIST/**LAREDO**/**WEBB**	01059183	956/273-1000	386
Larkspur Elem Sch/*Leander*/Williamson	12365513	512/570-8100	397
Larkspur Elem Sch/*San Antonio*/Bexar	00997831	210/407-4600	35
Larry Brown Sch/*Jourdanton*/Atascosa	04450251	830/769-2925	20
Larry D Guinn Spec Pgrms Ctr/*Plano*/Collin	11718943	469/752-6900	83
Larry G Smith Elem Sch/*Mesquite*/Dallas	10908327	972/502-4800	101
Larson Elem Sch/*Grand Prairie*/Tarrant	04754461	682/867-0000	344
LaRue Miller Elem Sch/*Midlothian*/Ellis	11122306	469/856-6500	141
Las Americas Newcomer Mid Sch/*Houston*/Harris	05099329	713/773-5300	194
Las Colinas Elem Sch/*Irving*/Dallas	02894120	972/968-2200	97
Las Lomas Elem Sch/*San Antonio*/Bexar	11820455	210/356-7000	35
Las Palmas Elem Sch/*San Antonio*/Bexar	10007179	210/444-8050	32
Las Yescas Elem Sch/*San Benito*/Cameron	01004011	956/233-6955	66
Lasara Elem Sch/*Lasara*/Willacy	01060649	956/642-3271	394
Lasara High Sch/*Lasara*/Willacy	11564974	956/642-3271	394
LASARA IND SCH DIST/**LASARA**/**WILLACY**	01060637	956/642-3271	394
Lasater Elem Sch/*Falfurrias*/Brooks	01002386	361/325-8060	57
Latexo Elem Sch/*Latexo*/Houston	01031832	936/546-5630	233
Latexo High Sch/*Latexo*/Houston	04748876	936/544-5638	233
LATEXO IND SCH DIST/**LATEXO**/**HOUSTON**	01031820	936/544-5664	233
Laura Bush Elem Sch/*Houston*/Harris	10029000	713/740-0928	199
Laura Bush Middle Sch/*Lubbock*/Lubbock	11716490	806/776-0750	271
Laura Ingalls Wilder Elem Sch/*Pearland*/Brazoria	10908169	281/245-3090	51
Laura Ingalls Wilder Inter Sch/*Schertz*/Guadalupe	04746270	210/619-4200	173
Laura Reeves Primary Sch/*Silsbee*/Hardin	01022594	409/980-7850	178
Laura Steele Montessori Acad/*San Antonio*/Bexar	12305537	210/438-6870	41
Laura Welch Bush Elem Sch/*Austin*/Williamson	05102952	512/570-6100	397
Laurel Mountain Elem Sch/*Austin*/Williamson	02893970	512/464-4300	399
Laureles Elem Sch/*Los Fresnos*/Cameron	04918758	956/254-5141	66
Laurenzo ECC/*Houston*/Harris	05349916	713/924-0350	190
Lauro Cavazos Elem Sch/*Odessa*/Ector	03248732	432/456-1309	130
Lavace Stewart Elem Sch/*Kemah*/Galveston	01019315	281/284-4700	159
Law Elem Sch/*Houston*/Harris	01025285	713/732-3630	193
Lawler Middle Sch/*Frisco*/Collin	12308345	469/633-4150	79
Lawn Elem Sch/*Lawn*/Taylor	01054901	325/583-2256	361
Lawndale Elem Sch/*Amarillo*/Potter	01047336	806/326-4700	318
Lawrence A Eckert Elem Sch/*Houston*/Harris	04032586	281/985-6380	180
Lawrence D Bell High Sch/*Hurst*/Tarrant	01053787	817/282-2551	354
Lawson Academy/*Houston*/Harris	12160595	713/225-1551	7
Lawson Middle Sch/*Houston*/Harris	01025168	713/434-5600	189
LAZBUDDIE IND SCH DIST/**LAZBUDDIE**/**PARMER**	01046772	806/965-2156	315
Lazbuddie Sch/*Lazbuddie*/Parmer	01046796	806/965-2153	315
Le Noir Elem Sch/*Donna*/Hidalgo	03252991	956/464-1685	215
Leadership Acad Como ES/*Fort Worth*/Tarrant	01052692	817/815-6500	351
Leadership Acad Mitchell Blvd/*Fort Worth*/Tarrant	01053127	817/815-9000	351

School/City/County DISTRICT/CITY/COUNTY	PID	TELEPHONE NUMBER	PAGE
Leadership Academy/*Tyler*/Smith	12261199	903/561-1002	7
Leadership Prep Sch/*Frisco*/Collin	11712808	972/294-6921	7
Leafspring School-Sonterra/*San Antonio*/Bexar	05312896	210/495-5222	45
League City Elem Sch/*League City*/Galveston	01018907	281/284-4400	159
League City Intermediate Sch/*League City*/Galveston	02178029	281/284-3400	159
LEAKEY IND SCH DIST/**LEAKEY**/**REAL**	01048055	830/232-5595	322
Leakey Sch/*Leakey*/Real	01048067	830/232-5595	322
Leal Elem Sch/*Mission*/Hidalgo	02227943	956/323-4600	222
Leander High Sch/*Leander*/Williamson	01061021	512/570-1000	397
LEANDER IND SCH DIST/**LEANDER**/**WILLIAMSON**	01061007	512/570-0000	396
Leander Middle Sch/*Leander*/Williamson	04455811	512/570-3200	397
Learning Center/*New Caney*/Montgomery	04754227	281/577-2850	294
Leary Elem Sch/*Texarkana*/Bowie	01000936	903/838-8960	48
LEARY IND SCH DIST/**TEXARKANA**/**BOWIE**	01000924	903/838-8960	48
Lebanon Trail High Sch/*Frisco*/Collin	12165399	469/633-6600	79
Lebarron Park Elem Sch/*El Paso*/El Paso	01824172	915/434-3500	138
Lee A McShan Jr Elem Sch/*Dallas*/Dallas	10006802	972/502-3800	101
Lee Elem Sch/*Abilene*/Taylor	01172838	325/671-4895	360
Lee Elem Sch/*Austin*/Travis	01056600	512/414-2098	368
Lee Elem Sch/*Caddo Mills*/Hunt	01032305	903/527-3162	235
Lee Elem Sch/*El Paso*/El Paso	01826211	915/236-5675	133
Lee Elem Sch/*Grand Prairie*/Dallas	01010979	972/262-6785	107
Lee Elem Sch/*Houston*/Harris	10002155	713/849-8281	185
Lee Elem Sch/*Irving*/Dallas	01011301	972/600-7800	109
Lee Elem Sch/*Port Arthur*/Jefferson	01033866	409/984-8300	243
Lee H Means Elem Sch/*Harlingen*/Cameron	11434783	956/427-3377	65
Lee Middle Sch/*San Angelo*/Tom Green	01055759	325/947-3871	365
LEFORS IND SCH DIST/**LEFORS**/**GRAY**	01020077	806/835-2533	165
Lefors Sch/*Lefors*/Gray	01020089	806/835-2533	165
Legacy Christian Academy/*Beaumont*/Jefferson	10915423	409/924-0500	244
Legacy Christian Academy/*Frisco*/Collin	05256802	469/633-1330	86
Legacy Christian Academy/*San Antonio*/Bexar	02192647	210/674-0490	45
Legacy Classical Chrn Academy/*Haslet*/Tarrant	12313998	817/382-2322	359
Legacy Early College High Sch/*Taylor*/Williamson	12036839	512/352-9596	399
Legacy Elem Sch/*Lubbock*/Lubbock	12035172	806/792-3800	269
Legacy Middle Sch/*San Antonio*/Bexar	10029787	210/648-3118	31
Legacy of Educl Excellence HS/*San Antonio*/Bexar	00997910	210/356-0800	35
Legacy Prep Charter Acad-Plano/*Plano*/Collin	11916884	469/998-0213	7
Legacy Prep Chtr Acad-Mesquite/*Mesquite*/Dallas	11917503	469/287-8610	7
Legacy Preparatory Chrn Acad/*Magnolia*/Montgomery	11224514	936/337-2000	295
Legacy Sch of Sport Sciences/*Spring*/Harris	12362664	713/396-0837	7
LEGGETT IND SCH DIST/**LEGGETT**/**POLK**	01047051	936/398-2804	316
Leggett Sch/*Leggett*/Polk	01047063	936/398-2412	316
Lehman High Sch/*Kyle*/Hays	05352365	512/268-8454	211
Leila P Cowart Elem Sch/*Dallas*/Dallas	01009334	972/794-5500	101
Lemm Elem Sch/*Spring*/Harris	02110675	832/484-6300	197
Lenore Kirk Hall Elem Sch/*Dallas*/Dallas	01009346	972/794-5400	101
Leo A Rizzuto Elem Sch/*La Porte*/Harris	02223856	281/604-6500	198
Leo Center/*Leander*/Williamson	03390816	512/570-2230	397
Leo J Leo Elem Sch/*Mission*/Hidalgo	02848456	956/323-2370	220
Leo Orr Sr Education Center/*Malakoff*/Henderson	04866349	903/489-4132	214
Leon Daiches Elem Sch/*Laredo*/Webb	01059339	956/273-3200	387
Leon Elem Sch/*Jewett*/Leon	01037630	903/626-1425	264
Leon Heights Elem Sch/*Belton*/Bell	00996356	254/215-3200	27
Leon High Sch/*Jewett*/Leon	01037642	903/626-1475	264
LEON IND SCH DIST/**JEWETT**/**LEON**	01037628	903/626-1400	264
Leon Junior High Sch/*Jewett*/Leon	03004495	903/626-1450	264
Leon Sablatura Middle Sch/*Pearland*/Brazoria	04752451	281/412-1500	53
Leon Springs Elem Sch/*San Antonio*/Bexar	03397656	210/397-4400	38
Leon Taylor Junior High Sch/*Ingleside*/San Patricio	01172591	361/776-2232	331
Leon Valley Christian Academy/*San Antonio*/Bexar	11225192	210/684-5662	45
Leon Valley Elem Sch/*San Antonio*/Bexar	00998184	210/397-4650	38
Leonard Elem Sch/*Leonard*/Fannin	01017513	903/587-2316	146
Leonard High Sch/*Leonard*/Fannin	01017525	903/587-3556	146
LEONARD IND SCH DIST/**LEONARD**/**FANNIN**	01017501	903/587-2318	146

Texas School Directory

DISTRICT & SCHOOL TELEPHONE INDEX

School/City/County DISTRICT/CITY/COUNTY	PID	TELEPHONE NUMBER	PAGE
Leonard Intermediate Sch/*Leonard*/Fannin	04920622	903/587-8303	146
Leonard Junior High Sch/*Leonard*/Fannin	03242219	903/587-2315	146
Leonard Middle Sch/*Fort Worth*/Tarrant	01053048	817/815-6200	351
Leonard Shanklin Elem Sch/*Luling*/Caldwell	01003108	830/875-2515	61
Leonelo H Gonzalez Elem Sch/*McAllen*/Hidalgo	03392618	956/971-4577	221
Leonides G Cigarroa Elem Sch/*Dallas*/Dallas	10023202	972/502-2900	101
Leslie A Stemmons Elem Sch/*Dallas*/Dallas	01009358	972/794-4900	101
Lester Davis Sch/*Denton*/Denton	04748242	940/369-4050	121
Levelland ABC/*Levelland*/Hockley	01857296	806/894-6959	229
Levelland Christian Sch/*Levelland*/Hockley	04994116	806/894-6019	230
Levelland High Sch/*Levelland*/Hockley	01031167	806/894-8515	229
LEVELLAND IND SCH DIST/LEVELLAND/HOCKLEY	01031129	806/894-9628	229
Levelland Intermediate Sch/*Levelland*/Hockley	01031143	806/894-3060	229
Levelland Middle Sch/*Levelland*/Hockley	01031179	806/894-6355	229
LEVERETTS CHAPEL IND SCH DIST/OVERTON/RUSK	01049097	903/834-6675	328
Leveretts Chapel Sch/*Overton*/Rusk	01049102	903/834-3181	328
Levi Fry Intermediate Sch/*Texas City*/Galveston	01019535	409/916-0600	161
Levine Academy/*Dallas*/Collin	02848286	972/248-3032	86
Lewis Elem Sch/*Forney*/Kaufman	10027973	972/564-7102	252
Lewis Elem Sch/*Houston*/Harris	01025601	713/845-7453	190
Lewisville Elem Sch/*Lewisville*/Denton	11553729	469/713-5995	123
Lewisville High Sch/*Lewisville*/Denton	01013488	469/713-5190	123
Lewisville HS-B Harmon Campus/*Lewisville*/Denton	11718369	469/713-5201	123
Lewisville HS-Killough/*Lewisville*/Denton	04754710	469/713-5987	123
LEWISVILLE IND SCH DIST/LEWISVILLE/DENTON	01013402	469/713-5200	122
Lewisville Learning Center/*Lewisville*/Denton	03249621	469/713-5185	123
Lexington Creek Elem Sch/*Missouri City*/Fort Bend	04287951	281/634-5000	150
Lexington Elem Sch/*Lexington*/Lee	04354140	979/773-2525	263
Lexington High Sch/*Lexington*/Lee	02112312	979/773-2255	263
LEXINGTON IND SCH DIST/LEXINGTON/LEE	01037496	979/773-2254	263
Lexington Middle Sch/*Lexington*/Lee	01037513	979/773-2254	263
Libby Cash Maus Middle Sch/*Frisco*/Collin	11558327	469/633-5250	79
Libby Elem Sch/*Carthage*/Panola	01046253	903/693-8862	311
Liberal Arts & Science Academy/*Austin*/Travis	10907244	512/414-5272	368
Liberty Baptist Sch/*Lewisville*/Denton	11231646	972/436-3493	126
Liberty Campus/*Victoria*/Victoria	03250747	361/788-9650	382
Liberty Christian Academy/*Sherman*/Grayson	12042369	903/328-6037	169
Liberty Christian Sch/*Argyle*/Denton	02207175	940/294-2000	126
Liberty Elem Sch/*Azle*/Tarrant	02043371	817/444-1317	345
Liberty Elem Sch/*Colleyville*/Tarrant	10003276	817/744-6000	355
Liberty Elem Sch/*Eagle Pass*/Maverick	05095816	830/758-7156	277
Liberty Elem Sch/*Flower Mound*/Denton	05091690	469/713-5958	123
Liberty Elem Sch/*Fort Worth*/Tarrant	01054200	817/367-1357	357
Liberty Elem Sch/*Liberty*/Liberty	01037953	936/336-3603	266
Liberty Grove Elem Sch/*Rowlett*/Dallas	10907397	972/487-4416	106
Liberty High Sch/*Frisco*/Collin	10750675	469/633-5800	79
Liberty High Sch/*Houston*/Harris	10003939	713/458-5555	189
Liberty High Sch/*Liberty*/Liberty	01037939	936/336-6483	266
Liberty Hill Elem Sch/*Liberty Hill*/Williamson	01061071	512/379-3260	398
Liberty Hill High Sch/*Liberty Hill*/Williamson	01418620	512/260-5500	398
LIBERTY HILL IND SCH DIST/LIBERTY HILL/WILLIAMSON	01061069	512/260-5580	398
Liberty Hill Intermediate Sch/*Liberty Hill*/Williamson	04918112	512/379-3200	398
Liberty Hill Middle Sch/*Killeen*/Bell	04811409	254/336-1370	28
Liberty Hill Middle Sch/*Liberty Hill*/Williamson	02109432	512/379-3300	398
LIBERTY IND SCH DIST/LIBERTY/LIBERTY	01037927	936/336-7213	266
Liberty Junior High Sch/*Dallas*/Dallas	01399672	469/593-7888	112
Liberty Middle Sch/*Liberty*/Liberty	01037941	936/336-3582	266
Liberty Middle Sch/*Pharr*/Hidalgo	01030450	956/354-2610	223
Liberty Middle Sch/*San Benito*/Cameron	05356139	956/233-3900	66
Liberty-Eylau Early Chldhd Ctr/*Texarkana*/Bowie	01000962	903/831-5352	48
Liberty-Eylau Elem Sch/*Texarkana*/Bowie	01000986	903/831-5390	48
Liberty-Eylau High Sch/*Texarkana*/Bowie	01000974	903/832-1530	48
LIBERTY-EYLAU IND SCH DIST/TEXARKANA/BOWIE	01000948	903/832-1535	48
Liberty-Eylau Middle Sch/*Texarkana*/Bowie	01000998	903/838-5555	48
Lida Hooe Elem Sch/*Dallas*/Dallas	01009360	972/794-6700	101
Lieck Elem Sch/*San Antonio*/Bexar	11713917	210/398-1450	38
Lieder Elem Sch/*Houston*/Harris	01829445	281/463-5928	185
Liestman Elem Sch/*Houston*/Harris	01826261	281/983-8348	182
Life High School-Waxahachie/*Waxahachie*/Ellis	12103913	469/708-4444	7
Life Middle School Waxahachie/*Waxahachie*/Ellis	11595442	972/937-0715	7
Life School Cedar Hill/*Cedar Hill*/Dallas	11595428	972/293-2825	7
Life School Lancaster/*Lancaster*/Dallas	11014515	972/274-7950	7
Life School Mountain Creek/*Dallas*/Dallas	11935359	214/623-0012	8
Life School Oak Cliff/*Dallas*/Dallas	04814401	214/376-8200	8
Life School Red Oak/*Red Oak*/Ellis	11014503	469/552-9200	8
Lifegate Christian Sch/*Seguin*/Guadalupe	04924381	830/372-0850	174
Lifestyle Christian Sch/*Conroe*/Montgomery	04937479	936/756-9383	295
Light Farms Elem Sch/*Celina*/Collin	12109010	469/219-2140	84
Lighthouse Charter Sch/*San Antonio*/Bexar	05282667	210/674-4100	8
Lighthouse Chtr Sch-B Campus/*San Antonio*/Bexar	12163171	210/257-6746	8
Lighthouse Learning Center/*Clute*/Brazoria	04033700	979/730-7340	52
Lillian Elem Sch/*Alvarado*/Johnson	01035125	817/783-6815	246
Lillion E Luehrs Jr High Sch/*Bishop*/Nueces	01044073	361/584-3576	302
Lily B Clayton Elem Sch/*Fort Worth*/Tarrant	01053050	817/814-5400	351
Lincoln Elem Sch/*Edinburg*/Hidalgo	04806507	956/289-2525	217
Lincoln Elem Sch/*Montgomery*/Montgomery	12363060	936/276-4700	293
Lincoln Humanities/Comm HS/*Dallas*/Dallas	01009372	972/925-7600	101
Lincoln Junior High Sch/*Coldspring*/San Jacinto	01049425	936/653-1166	330
Lincoln Middle Sch/*El Paso*/El Paso	01016026	915/236-3400	135
Lincoln Middle Sch/*San Angelo*/Tom Green	01055723	325/659-3550	365
Lincoln Park/*Brownsville*/Cameron	02127733	956/548-7880	64
Linda Herrington Elem Sch/*Round Rock*/Williamson	11714416	512/704-1900	399
Linda Jobe Middle Sch/*Mansfield*/Tarrant	11452199	682/314-4400	357
Linda Lyon Elem Sch/*Heath*/Rockwall	12232370	214/771-4910	325
Linda Tutt High Sch/*Sanger*/Denton	04865618	940/458-5701	126
Lindale High Sch/*Lindale*/Smith	01050668	903/881-4050	337
LINDALE IND SCH DIST/LINDALE/SMITH	01050656	903/881-4000	337
Lindale Junior High Sch/*Lindale*/Smith	01050682	903/881-4150	337
Linden Elem Sch/*Linden*/Cass	01826144	903/756-5471	70
LINDEN KILDARE CONS IND SD/LINDEN/CASS	01004827	903/756-7071	70
Linden Kildare High Sch/*Linden*/Cass	01004865	903/756-5314	70
Linder Elem Sch/*Austin*/Travis	01056349	512/414-2398	367
Lindsay Elem Sch/*Lindsay*/Cooke	01007439	940/668-8923	91
Lindsay High Sch/*Lindsay*/Cooke	05341419	940/668-8474	91
LINDSAY IND SCH DIST/LINDSAY/COOKE	01007427	940/668-8923	91
Lindsey Elem Sch/*Katy*/Fort Bend	12230815	832/223-5400	154
LINGLEVILLE IND SCH DIST/LINGLEVILLE/ERATH	01017082	254/968-2596	143
Lingleville Sch/*Lingleville*/Erath	01017094	254/968-2596	143
Links Academy/*Godley*/Johnson	12368931	817/592-4212	247
Lion Lane Sch/*Houston*/Harris	04949862	713/251-6100	201
LIPAN IND SCH DIST/LIPAN/HOOD	01031416	254/646-2266	230
Lipan Sch/*Lipan*/Hood	01031428	254/646-2266	230
Liscano Elem Sch/*Frisco*/Collin	12308357	469/633-2275	79
Lisd STEM Academy at Donaldson/*Flower Mound*/Denton	03249372	469/713-5198	123
Little Cypress Elem Sch/*Orange*/Orange	01045663	409/886-2838	308
Little Cypress Interm Sch/*Orange*/Orange	01529994	409/886-4245	308
Little Cypress Jr High Sch/*Orange*/Orange	01045687	409/883-2317	308
LITTLE CYPRESS MAURICEVILLE SD/ORANGE/ORANGE	01045651	409/883-2232	308
Little Cypress-Mauriceville HS/*Orange*/Orange	01045675	409/886-5821	308
Little Elem Sch/*Arlington*/Tarrant	01051844	682/867-3300	344
Little Elm High Sch/*Little Elm*/Denton	01401392	972/947-9443	124
LITTLE ELM IND SCH DIST/LITTLE ELM/DENTON	01013490	972/947-9340	124
Little Flower Sch/*San Antonio*/Bexar	00999865	210/732-9207	44
Littlefield Elem Sch/*Littlefield*/Lamb	01036923	806/385-6217	260
Littlefield High Sch/*Littlefield*/Lamb	01036947	806/385-5683	261
LITTLEFIELD IND SCH DIST/LITTLEFIELD/LAMB	01036911	806/385-3844	260
Littlefield Junior High Sch/*Littlefield*/Lamb	01036959	806/385-3922	261
Littlefield Primary Sch/*Littlefield*/Lamb	01036961	806/385-3922	261
Live Oak Academy/*Buda*/Hays	04923882	512/268-8462	211
Live Oak Classical Sch/*Waco*/McLennan	10900870	254/714-1007	282

School Year 2019-2020   800-333-8802   TX-V45

DISTRICT & SCHOOL TELEPHONE INDEX

Market Data Retrieval

School/City/County DISTRICT/CITY/COUNTY	PID	TELEPHONE NUMBER	PAGE
Live Oak Elem Sch/*Austin*/Williamson	03007356	512/428-3800	399
Live Oak Learning Center/*Rockport*/Aransas	00995144	361/790-2260	19
Live Oak Ridge Middle Sch/*Killeen*/Bell	05097058	254/336-2490	28
Lively Elem Sch/*Irving*/Dallas	01011258	972/600-6700	109
Lively Middle Sch/*Austin*/Travis	01056210	512/414-3207	369
Living Rock Academy/*Bulverde*/Comal	12314198	830/387-2929	89
Living Stones Christian Sch/*Alvin*/Brazoria	02192398	281/331-0086	54
Living Water Christian Sch/*Rosenberg*/Fort Bend	04856667	281/342-6336	155
Living Word Christian Academy/*Houston*/Harris	02153641	713/686-5538	206
Livingston High Sch/*Livingston*/Polk	01047099	936/967-1600	317
Livingston High Sch Academy/*Livingston*/Polk	12305719	936/328-8600	317
LIVINGSTON IND SCH DIST/LIVINGSTON/POLK	01047075	936/328-2100	316
Livingston Junior High Sch/*Livingston*/Polk	01047104	936/328-2120	317
Lizzie Burgess Alt Sch/*Seguin*/Guadalupe	03049706	830/379-1108	174
Lizzie Curtis Elem Sch/*Fort Worth*/Denton	12363333	817/541-8901	125
Lizzie Nell C McClure Elem Sch/*McKinney*/Collin	11555600	469/302-9400	81
Llano Christian Academy/*Llano*/Llano	12314186	325/247-4942	269
Llano Elem Sch/*Llano*/Llano	01038359	325/247-5718	268
Llano High Sch/*Llano*/Llano	01038361	325/248-2200	268
LLANO IND SCH DIST/LLANO/LLANO	01038347	325/247-4747	268
Llano Junior High Sch/*Llano*/Llano	01038373	325/247-4659	268
Lloyd & Dolly Bentsen Elem Sch/*McAllen*/Hidalgo	10011417	956/686-0426	224
Lloyd M Bentsen Elem Sch/*Mission*/Hidalgo	04946822	956/323-2480	220
Lloyd M Knowlton Elem Sch/*San Antonio*/Bexar	02848509	210/397-2600	38
Lloyd R Ferguson Elem Sch/*League City*/Galveston	03325536	281/284-5500	159
Locke Hill Elem Sch/*San Antonio*/Bexar	00998196	210/397-1600	38
Lockhart Elem Sch/*Houston*/Harris	01024906	713/942-1950	193
Lockhart High Sch/*Lockhart*/Caldwell	01003067	512/398-0300	61
LOCKHART IND SCH DIST/LOCKHART/CALDWELL	01003031	512/398-0000	61
Lockhart Junior High Sch/*Lockhart*/Caldwell	01003079	512/398-0770	61
Lockhart Pride High Sch/*Lockhart*/Caldwell	03399549	512/398-0130	61
Lockney Elem Sch/*Lockney*/Floyd	01018036	806/652-3321	149
Lockney High Sch/*Lockney*/Floyd	01018048	806/652-3325	149
LOCKNEY INDEPENDENT SCH DIST/LOCKNEY/FLOYD	01018024	806/652-2104	149
Lockney Junior High Sch/*Lockney*/Floyd	01018050	806/652-2236	149
Logan Elem Sch/*El Paso*/El Paso	01015814	915/236-5750	133
Logos Preparatory Academy/*Sugar Land*/Fort Bend	11223950	281/565-6467	155
LOHN IND SCH DIST/LOHN/MCCULLOCH	01039482	325/344-5749	277
Lohn Sch/*Lohn*/McCulloch	01039494	325/344-5749	277
Lois Lindsey Elem Sch/*McKinney*/Collin	11916925	972/908-4000	77
Lola Mae Carter Academy/*Houston*/Harris	04805046	281/878-7760	179
Loma Park Elem Sch/*San Antonio*/Bexar	00997295	210/444-8250	32
Loma Terrace Elem Sch/*El Paso*/El Paso	01016454	915/434-2600	138
Loma Verde Elem Sch/*El Paso*/El Paso	05153418	915/937-8600	136
Lomax Elem Sch/*La Porte*/Harris	01824251	281/604-4300	198
Lomax Junior High Sch/*La Porte*/Harris	02894168	281/604-6700	198
Lomax Middle Sch/*Pasadena*/Harris	10913279	713/740-5230	199
LOMETA IND SCH DIST/LOMETA/LAMPASAS	01037161	512/752-3384	262
Lometa Sch/*Lometa*/Lampasas	01037173	512/752-3384	262
LONDON IND SCH DIST/CORP CHRISTI/NUECES	01044865	361/855-0183	305
London Sch/*Corp Christi*/Nueces	01044877	361/855-0092	305
Lone Oak College St Campus/*Lone Oak*/Hunt	12233934	903/634-2071	236
Lone Oak Elem Sch/*Lone Oak*/Hunt	01032551	903/662-5151	236
Lone Oak High Sch/*Lone Oak*/Hunt	01032563	903/662-0980	236
LONE OAK IND SCH DIST/LONE OAK/HUNT	01032549	903/662-5427	236
Lone Oak Middle Sch/*Lone Oak*/Hunt	03020255	903/662-5121	236
Lone Star Early Childhood Ctr/*New Braunfels*/Comal	12312578	830/627-6820	88
Lone Star Elem Sch/*Fort Worth*/Tarrant	04921626	817/744-5200	355
Lone Star Elem Sch/*Montgomery*/Montgomery	10031443	936/276-4500	293
Lone Star High Sch/*Frisco*/Collin	11558315	469/633-5300	79
Lone Star Language Academy/*Plano*/Collin	12260925	972/244-7220	8
Long Academy/*Houston*/Harris	01024449	713/778-3380	194
Long Early Childhood Center/*Abilene*/Taylor	01172802	325/671-4594	360
Long Elem Sch/*Midland*/Midland	01041564	432/240-7400	286
Long Intermediate Sch/*Bryan*/Brazos	03244683	979/209-6500	55
Longbranch Elem Sch/*Midlothian*/Ellis	01015151	469/856-6200	141
Longfellow Elem Sch/*Houston*/Harris	01025297	713/295-5268	194
Longfellow Middle Sch/*San Antonio*/Bexar	00998495	210/438-6520	41
Longoria Middle Sch/*Edinburg*/Hidalgo	11719416	956/289-2486	217
Longs Creek Elem Sch/*San Antonio*/Bexar	04757061	210/407-4800	35
Longview Christian Academy/*Longview*/Gregg	02153665	903/759-0626	171
Longview Christian Sch/*Longview*/Gregg	02207292	903/297-3501	171
Longview Early Graduation HS/*Longview*/Gregg	01809304	903/381-3921	170
Longview High Sch/*Longview*/Gregg	01021083	903/663-1301	170
LONGVIEW IND SCH DIST/LONGVIEW/GREGG	01020986	903/381-2200	169
LOOP IND SCH DIST/LOOP/GAINES	01018684	806/487-6412	157
Loop Sch/*Loop*/Gaines	01018696	806/487-6412	157
Looscan Elem Sch/*Houston*/Harris	01026021	713/696-2760	189
Lopez Early College High Sch/*Brownsville*/Cameron	04034314	956/982-7400	64
Lopez-Riggins Elem Sch/*Los Fresnos*/Cameron	02894314	956/233-6916	66
LORAINE IND SCH DIST/LORAINE/MITCHELL	01042128	325/737-2225	289
Loraine Sch/*Loraine*/Mitchell	01042130	325/737-2225	289
Loraine T Golbow Elem Sch/*Katy*/Harris	03249114	281/237-5350	152
Lord of Life Lutheran Sch/*Friendswood*/Galveston	04993564	281/482-0481	162
Lorena Elem Sch/*Lorena*/McLennan	01039834	254/857-4613	280
Lorena High Sch/*Lorena*/McLennan	01039846	254/857-4604	280
LORENA IND SCH DIST/LORENA/MCLENNAN	01039822	254/857-3616	280
Lorena Middle Sch/*Lorena*/McLennan	02890033	254/857-4621	280
Lorena Primary Sch/*Lorena*/McLennan	05352054	254/857-8909	280
Lorene S Kirkpatrick Elem Sch/*Maypearl*/Ellis	01015113	972/435-1010	141
Lorenzo De Zavala Elem Sch/*Baytown*/Harris	04019479	281/420-4920	188
Lorenzo De Zavala Elem Sch/*Crystal City*/Zavala	01062300	830/374-8080	407
Lorenzo De Zavala Elem Sch/*Dallas*/Dallas	02109822	972/892-6400	101
Lorenzo De Zavala Elem Sch/*Edinburg*/Hidalgo	03267063	956/289-2350	217
Lorenzo De Zavala Middle Sch/*Amarillo*/Potter	10008367	806/326-3400	318
Lorenzo De Zavala Middle Sch/*Irving*/Dallas	05090555	972/600-6000	110
Lorenzo De Zavala Middle Sch/*La Joya*/Hidalgo	01029889	956/323-2770	220
Lorenzo De Zavala Spec Emp Sch/*Corp Christi*/Nueces	01044786	361/878-2720	303
Lorenzo Dezavala Middle Sch/*Pasadena*/Harris	05102885	713/740-0544	199
Lorenzo Elem Sch/*Lorenzo*/Crosby	01007960	806/634-5593	94
Lorenzo G Loya Primary Sch/*San Elizario*/El Paso	03394161	915/872-3940	135
LORENZO IND SCH DIST/LORENZO/CROSBY	01007958	806/634-5591	94
Lorenzo Jr Sr High Sch/*Lorenzo*/Crosby	01007972	806/634-5592	94
Loreta Hickey Elem Sch/*Plano*/Collin	05096860	469/752-4100	83
Loretto Acad Elem Sch/*El Paso*/El Paso	01016806	915/566-8400	139
Loretto Acad-Middle High Sch/*El Paso*/El Paso	01016791	915/566-8400	139
Los Cuates Middle Sch/*Los Fresnos*/Cameron	01004047	956/254-5182	66
Los Encinos Ses Elem Sch/*Corp Christi*/Nueces	01044516	361/878-2600	303
Los Fresnos 9th & 10th GR Sch/*San Benito*/Cameron	11456901	956/254-5250	66
LOS FRESNOS CONS IND SCH DIST/LOS FRESNOS/CAMERON	01004009	956/254-5000	65
Los Fresnos Elem Sch/*Los Fresnos*/Cameron	01004023	956/233-6900	66
Los Fresnos High Sch/*Los Fresnos*/Cameron	01004035	956/254-5300	66
Los Obispos Middle Sch/*Laredo*/Webb	04455926	956/473-7800	388
Los Reyes Elem Sch/*Helotes*/Bexar	11822843	210/398-1200	38
Losoya Intermediate Sch/*San Antonio*/Bexar	03008245	210/882-1602	43
Lost Pines Elem Sch/*Bastrop*/Bastrop	05350173	512/772-7700	24
Lotspeich Elem Sch/*Robstown*/Nueces	01044920	361/767-6655	305
Louie Welch Middle Sch/*Houston*/Harris	02043307	713/778-3300	194
Louis G Lobit Elem Sch/*Dickinson*/Galveston	12167335	281/229-7600	160
Louise Cabaniss Elem Sch/*Grand Prairie*/Tarrant	11073690	817/299-6480	357
Louise Elem Sch/*Louise*/Wharton	01059676	979/648-2262	390
Louise High Sch/*Louise*/Wharton	01059688	979/648-2202	390
LOUISE IND SCH DIST/LOUISE/WHARTON	01059664	979/648-2982	389
Louise Junior High Sch/*Louise*/Wharton	11071812	979/648-2262	390
Louise Wolff Kahn Elem Sch/*Dallas*/Dallas	04757102	972/502-1400	101
Love Elem Sch/*Houston*/Harris	01024140	713/867-0840	192
Lovejoy Elem Sch/*Allen*/Collin	01006239	469/742-8100	80
Lovejoy High Sch/*Lucas*/Collin	10025858	469/742-8700	80

Texas School Directory
DISTRICT & SCHOOL TELEPHONE INDEX

School/City/County DISTRICT/CITY/COUNTY	PID	TELEPHONE NUMBER	PAGE
LOVEJOY IND SCH DIST/ALLEN/			
COLLIN	01006227	469/742-8000	80
Lovelady Elem Middle Sch/*Lovelady*/Houston	01031856	936/636-7832	233
LOVELADY IND SCH DIST/LOVELADY/			
HOUSTON	01031844	936/636-7616	233
Lovelady Jr Sr High Sch/*Lovelady*/Houston	01031868	936/636-7636	233
Lovett Elem Sch/*Houston*/Harris	01024918	713/295-5258	194
Lowe Elem Sch/*Princeton*/Collin	12363606	469/952-5400	84
Lowery Elem Sch/*Houston*/Harris	02126430	281/463-5900	185
Lowery Freshman Center/*Allen*/Collin	04866741	972/396-6975	77
Lowery Road Elem Sch/*Fort Worth*/Tarrant	04919439	817/815-4700	351
Lubbock Adult Learning Center/*Lubbock*/Lubbock	04018516	806/281-5750	8
Lubbock Christian Sch/*Lubbock*/Lubbock	01480714	806/796-8700	272
LUBBOCK IND SCH DIST/LUBBOCK/			
LUBBOCK	01038490	806/766-1000	269
Lubbock Junior Academy/*Lubbock*/Lubbock	11816545	806/793-8614	272
Lubbock Senior High Sch/*Lubbock*/Lubbock	01038751	806/219-1600	270
Lubbock-Cooper High Sch/*Lubbock*/Lubbock	01039042	806/863-7105	271
LUBBOCK-COOPER IND SCH DIST/LUBBOCK/LUBBOCK	01039030	806/863-7100	271
Lubbock-Cooper Middle Sch/*Lubbock*/Lubbock	01039066	806/863-7104	271
Lucas Christian Academy/*Lucas*/Collin	04954415	972/429-4362	86
Lucas Pre-K Center/*Beaumont*/Jefferson	01033567	409/617-6450	242
Lucian Adams Elem Sch/*Port Arthur*/Jefferson	11826356	409/984-4100	243
Lucile M Hendricks Elem Sch/*McAllen*/Hidalgo	11104017	956/971-1145	221
Lucile Rogers Ashley Elem Sch/*Frisco*/Collin	10016687	469/633-3700	79
Lucille Nash Elem Sch/*Kaufman*/Kaufman	01035644	972/932-6415	252
Lucio Middle Sch/*Brownsville*/Cameron	04751184	956/831-4550	64
Lucy Mae McDonald Elem Sch/*Ferris*/Ellis	05230717	972/544-3405	140
Lucy Read Pre-K Sch/*Austin*/Travis	10025468	512/419-9400	368
Lucy Rede Franco Middle Sch/*Presidio*/Presidio	01047881	432/229-3113	320
Lucyle Collins Middle Sch/*Fort Worth*/Tarrant	10030970	817/306-4250	356
Lueders-Avoca Elem Jr High Sch/*Lueders*/Jones	01035307	325/228-4211	250
Lueders-Avoca High Sch/*Avoca*/Jones	01035319	325/773-2785	250
LUEDERS-AVOCA IND SCH DIST/LUEDERS/JONES	01035292	325/228-4211	250
Luella Merrett Elem Sch/*Fort Worth*/Tarrant	01053309	817/815-6600	351
Lufkin High Sch/*Lufkin*/Angelina	00995015	936/632-7721	18
LUFKIN IND SCH DIST/LUFKIN/ANGELINA	00994932	936/634-6696	18
Lufkin Middle Sch/*Lufkin*/Angelina	00995003	936/630-4444	18
Lujan-Chavez Elem Sch/*El Paso*/El Paso	04941793	915/937-8700	136
Lula Belle Goodman Elem Sch/*Fresno*/Fort Bend	04921547	281/634-5985	150
Luling High Sch/*Luling*/Caldwell	02884137	830/875-2458	61
LULING IND SCH DIST/LULING/CALDWELL	01003093	830/875-3191	61
Luling Primary Sch/*Luling*/Caldwell	02200969	830/875-2223	61
Lumberton High Sch/*Lumberton*/Hardin	01022568	409/923-7890	178
LUMBERTON IND SCH DIST/LUMBERTON/HARDIN	01022544	409/923-7580	178
Lumberton Intermediate Sch/*Lumberton*/Hardin	02046505	409/923-7790	178
Lumberton Middle Sch/*Lumberton*/Hardin	01022556	409/923-7581	178
Lumberton Primary Sch/*Lumberton*/Hardin	01022570	409/923-7490	178
Lumin E Dallas Community Sch/*Dallas*/Dallas	04814358	214/824-8950	8
Lumin Lindsley Park Cmty Sch/*Dallas*/Dallas	05013143	214/321-9155	8
Luna Elem Sch/*Garland*/Dallas	02226107	972/675-3040	106
Lundy Elem Sch/*El Paso*/El Paso	11449180	915/230-5075	133
Luther & Anna Bolin Elem Sch/*Parker*/Collin	04913124	214/495-6750	77
Luther Jones Elem Sch/*Corp Christi*/Nueces	03333090	361/878-0100	303
Lutheran High Sch/*Dallas*/Dallas	02152257	214/349-8912	115
Lutheran High Sch/*San Antonio*/Bexar	04951152	210/694-4962	45
Lutheran High School North/*Houston*/Harris	02157324	713/880-3131	206
Lutheran South Academy/*Houston*/Harris	01410771	281/464-8299	206
Lydia Patterson Institute/*El Paso*/El Paso	01480075	915/533-8286	139
LYFORD CONS IND SCH DIST/LYFORD/WILLACY	01060651	956/347-3900	394
Lyford Elem Sch/*Lyford*/Willacy	03050743	956/347-3911	394
Lyford High Sch/*Lyford*/Willacy	01060675	956/347-3909	394
Lyford Middle Sch/*Lyford*/Willacy	01060687	956/347-3910	394
Lyles Middle Sch/*Garland*/Dallas	03009378	972/240-3720	106
Lyndon B Johnson Elem Sch/*Edinburg*/Hidalgo	01878410	956/289-2358	217
Lyndon B Johnson Elem Sch/*Johnson City*/Blanco	01000522	830/868-4028	46
Lyndon B Johnson Elem Sch/*Odessa*/Ector	03248756	432/456-1289	130
Lyndon B Johnson High Sch/*Austin*/Travis	01056454	512/414-2543	368
Lyndon B Johnson High Sch/*Johnson City*/Blanco	01000534	830/868-4025	46
Lyndon B Johnson High Sch/*Laredo*/Webb	04946377	956/473-5100	388
Lyndon B Johnson Middle Sch/*Johnson City*/Blanco	04245240	830/868-9025	46
Lyndon B Johnson Middle Sch/*Pharr*/Hidalgo	01826314	956/354-2590	223
Lyndon Baines Johnson Elem Sch/*Elsa*/Hidalgo	03237393	956/262-2161	216
Lynn Lucas Middle Sch/*Willis*/Montgomery	02177996	936/856-1274	294
Lyons Elem Sch/*Houston*/Harris	04036312	713/696-2870	191
Lytle Elem Sch/*Lytle*/Atascosa	00995417	830/709-5130	21
Lytle High Sch/*Lytle*/Atascosa	00995429	830/709-5105	21
LYTLE IND SCH DIST/LYTLE/ATASCOSA	00995405	830/709-5100	21
Lytle Junior High Sch/*Lytle*/Atascosa	04940361	830/709-5115	21
Lytle Primary Sch/*Lytle*/Atascosa	04972534	830/709-5140	21

M

School/City/County DISTRICT/CITY/COUNTY	PID	TELEPHONE NUMBER	PAGE
M B Lamar High Sch/*Arlington*/Tarrant	01051832	682/867-8300	344
M B Lamar Middle Sch/*Laredo*/Webb	01059353	956/273-6200	387
M C Williams Middle Sch/*Houston*/Harris	01024152	713/696-2600	189
M D Betts Elem Sch/*Edinburg*/Hidalgo	04873251	956/289-2560	217
M G Ellis Primary Sch/*Fort Worth*/Tarrant	05096523	817/814-3800	351
M H Moore Elem Sch/*Fort Worth*/Tarrant	01053062	817/815-0600	351
M H Specht Elem Sch/*San Antonio*/Comal	05090701	830/885-1500	88
M L King Middle Sch/*Beaumont*/Jefferson	01033452	409/617-5850	242
M Robinson Elem Sch/*Katy*/Harris	11077359	281/855-1240	185
M S Ryan Elem Sch/*Laredo*/Webb	01059365	956/273-4400	387
Mabank Daep/*Mabank*/Kaufman	05090983	903/880-1320	252
Mabank High Sch/*Mabank*/Kaufman	01035709	903/880-1600	253
MABANK IND SCH DIST/MABANK/KAUFMAN	01035682	903/880-1300	252
Mabank Intermediate Sch/*Mabank*/Kaufman	01035711	903/880-1640	253
Mabank Junior High Sch/*Mabank*/Kaufman	11157167	903/880-1670	253
Mabel B Wesley Elem Sch/*Houston*/Harris	01024164	713/696-2860	189
MacAria Gorena Elem Sch/*Edinburg*/Hidalgo	11719404	956/289-2460	217
Macario Garcia Middle Sch/*Sugar Land*/Fort Bend	04365876	281/634-3160	150
MacArthur 9th Grade Sch/*Houston*/Harris	04867214	281/985-7400	180
MacArthur Elem Sch/*Galena Park*/Harris	01023445	832/386-4630	187
MacArthur Elem-Interm Sch/*El Paso*/El Paso	01015668	915/236-0625	133
MacArthur High Sch/*Irving*/Dallas	01011260	972/600-7200	110
MacArthur High Sch/*San Antonio*/Bexar	00997740	210/356-7600	35
MacGregor Elem Sch/*Houston*/Harris	01024932	713/942-1990	194
MacKenzie Middle Sch/*Lubbock*/Lubbock	01038763	806/219-4200	270
Madden Elem Sch/*Richmond*/Fort Bend	12105313	281/327-2740	150
Madeley Ranch Elem Sch/*Montgomery*/Montgomery	11456987	936/276-4600	293
Madge Griffith Elem Sch/*Clute*/Brazoria	03316729	979/730-7180	52
Mading Elem Sch/*Houston*/Harris	01025302	713/732-3560	189
Madison Elem Sch/*San Antonio*/Bexar	00998471	210/438-6545	41
Madison High Sch/*Houston*/Harris	01025273	713/433-9801	189
Madison High Sch/*San Antonio*/Bexar	01523677	210/356-1400	35
Madison Middle Sch/*Abilene*/Taylor	01172814	325/692-5661	360
MADISONVILLE CONS ISD/MADISONVILLE/MADISON	01040596	936/348-2797	273
Madisonville Elem Sch/*Madisonville*/Madison	01040601	936/348-2261	273
Madisonville High Sch/*Madisonville*/Madison	01040613	936/348-2721	273
Madisonville Intermediate Sch/*Madisonville*/Madison	02131772	936/348-2921	273
Madisonville Jr High Sch/*Madisonville*/Madison	01040625	936/348-3587	274
Mae Luster Stephen Jr High Sch/*Linden*/Cass	01004841	903/756-5381	70
Mae Smythe Elem Sch/*Pasadena*/Harris	01026954	713/740-0728	199
Mae Stevens Early Learng Acad/*Copperas Cove*/Coryell	01007623	254/547-8289	92
Maedgen Elem Sch/*Lubbock*/Lubbock	01038775	806/219-6200	270
MaGee Elem Sch/*Corp Christi*/Nueces	01044164	361/242-5900	303
Magellan Int'l Sch-Anderson Ln/*Austin*/Travis	11927118	512/782-2327	373
Maggie B Selman Elem Sch/*Sealy*/Austin	00995596	979/885-6659	22
Magin Rivas Elem Sch/*Donna*/Hidalgo	02895124	956/464-1990	215
Magnolia Elem Sch/*Magnolia*/Montgomery	01042594	281/356-6434	293
Magnolia Elem Sch/*Pearland*/Brazoria	10909254	281/727-1750	53
Magnolia High Sch/*Magnolia*/Montgomery	01042609	281/356-3572	293
MAGNOLIA IND SCH DIST/MAGNOLIA/MONTGOMERY	01042582	281/356-3571	292
Magnolia Intermediate Sch/*Magnolia*/Montgomery	05097644	281/252-2033	293

School Year 2019-2020 800-333-8802 TX-V47

DISTRICT & SCHOOL TELEPHONE INDEX

School/City/County DISTRICT/CITY/COUNTY	PID	TELEPHONE NUMBER	PAGE
Magnolia Junior High Sch/*Magnolia*/Montgomery	01042611	281/356-1327	293
Magnolia Montessori for All/*Austin*/Travis	12114041	512/522-2429	8
Magnolia Parkway Elem Sch/*Magnolia*/Montgomery	11127095	281/252-7440	293
Magnolia West High Sch/*Magnolia*/Montgomery	10028642	281/252-2550	293
Magoffin Middle Sch/*El Paso*/El Paso	01015826	915/774-4040	135
Magrill EC-PK-K Sch/*Humble*/Harris	01399751	281/233-4300	181
Mahaffey Elem Sch/*Tomball*/Harris	12166783	832/375-8300	197
Mahanay Elem Sch/*Houston*/Harris	01023043	281/983-8355	182
Main Street Imtermediate Sch/*Taylor*/Williamson	02199750	512/352-3634	399
Mainland Prep Classical Acad/*La Marque*/Galveston	04814425	409/934-9100	8
Major Cheney ES-S Birdville/*Haltom City*/Tarrant	01052185	817/547-2300	346
Malakoff Elem Sch/*Malakoff*/Henderson	01029451	903/489-0313	214
Malakoff High Sch/*Malakoff*/Henderson	01029463	903/489-1527	214
MALAKOFF IND SCH DIST/MALAKOFF/HENDERSON	01029449	903/489-1152	214
Malakoff Middle Sch/*Malakoff*/Henderson	01029475	903/489-0264	214
Malcolm Rector Technical HS/*Nacogdoches*/Nacogdoches	04363402	936/205-1000	298
Malone Elem Sch/*Malone*/Hill	01030993	254/533-2321	228
MALONE INDEPENDENT SCH DIST/MALONE/HILL	01030981	254/533-2321	228
Malta Elem Sch/*New Boston*/Bowie	01001021	903/667-2950	48
MALTA IND SCH DIST/NEW BOSTON/BOWIE	01001019	903/667-2950	48
Manara Acad Leadership Acad/*Irving*/Dallas	12260949	972/304-1155	8
Manara Acad-Arlington STEM/*Arlington*/Tarrant	12260937	972/304-1155	8
Manara Acad-Irving Elem Sch/*Irving*/Dallas	11453595	972/304-1155	8
Mance Park Middle Sch/*Huntsville*/Walker	01881986	936/435-6400	383
Mandarin Immersion Magnet Sch/*Houston*/Harris	11820546	713/295-5276	194
Mann Middle Sch/*Abilene*/Taylor	01172826	325/672-8493	360
Manor Elem Early Learning Ctr/*Manor*/Travis	04174081	512/278-4100	371
Manor Excel Academy/*Manor*/Travis	04447747	512/278-4075	371
Manor High Sch/*Manor*/Travis	12363163	512/278-4800	371
MANOR IND SCH DIST/MANOR/TRAVIS	01056894	512/278-4000	371
Manor Middle Sch/*Killeen*/Bell	00996526	254/336-1310	28
Manor Middle Sch/*Manor*/Travis	01056923	512/278-4600	371
Manor New Tech High Sch/*Manor*/Travis	10915057	512/278-4875	371
Manor New Tech Middle Sch/*Manor*/Travis	12230255	512/278-4663	371
Manor Senior High Sch/*Manor*/Travis	01056911	512/278-4665	371
Mansfield High Sch/*Mansfield*/Tarrant	01054145	682/314-0100	357
MANSFIELD IND SCH DIST/TARRANT	01054119	817/299-6300	356
Mansfield Lake Ridge High Sch/*Mansfield*/Tarrant	11818622	682/314-0400	357
Mansfield Legacy High Sch/*Mansfield*/Tarrant	10908822	682/314-0600	357
Mansfield Summit High Sch/*Arlington*/Tarrant	04363438	682/314-0800	357
Mansfield Timberview High Sch/*Arlington*/Tarrant	05347401	682/314-1300	357
Manuel Jara Elem Sch/*Fort Worth*/Tarrant	01052680	817/814-4500	351
Manvel High Sch/*Manvel*/Brazoria	10021199	281/245-2232	51
Manvel Junior High Sch/*Manvel*/Brazoria	12104541	281/245-3700	51
Manzano Middle Sch/*Brownsville*/Cameron	11554890	956/548-9800	64
Maple Lawn Elem Sch/*Dallas*/Dallas	01009413	972/925-2500	101
Maplebrook Elem Sch/*Humble*/Harris	04948753	281/641-2900	196
Maplewood Elem Sch/*Austin*/Travis	01056375	512/414-4402	368
Maran-Ata Christian Academy/*El Paso*/El Paso	11234832	915/592-1909	139
MARATHON IND SCH DIST/MARATHON/BREWSTER	01002233	432/386-4431	56
Marathon Sch/*Marathon*/Brewster	01002245	432/386-4431	57
Marble Falls Elem Sch/*Marble Falls*/Burnet	01002831	830/693-2385	60
Marble Falls High Sch/*Marble Falls*/Burnet	01002843	830/693-4375	60
MARBLE FALLS IND SCH DIST/MARBLE FALLS/BURNET	01002817	830/693-4357	60
Marble Falls Middle Sch/*Marble Falls*/Burnet	01002855	830/693-4439	60
Marcell Elem Sch/*Mission*/Hidalgo	01030254	956/323-6400	222
Marcella Elem Sch/*Houston*/Harris	10907103	281/878-0860	180
Marcia R Garza Elem Sch/*Alamo*/Hidalgo	01030436	956/354-2780	223
Marcus 9th Grade Center/*Flower Mound*/Denton	12033930	469/713-5998	123
Marcus High Sch/*Flower Mound*/Denton	02132104	469/713-5196	123
Marcy Elem Sch/*Big Spring*/Howard	01031997	432/264-4144	233
Marfa Elem Sch/*Marfa*/Presidio	01047831	432/729-4252	320
MARFA IND SCH DIST/MARFA/PRESIDIO	01047829	432/729-4252	320
Marfa Jr Sr High Sch/*Marfa*/Presidio	01047843	432/729-4252	320
Margaret B Henderson Elem Sch/*Dallas*/Dallas	01009396	972/749-2900	101
Margaret Galubenski Achiev Ctr/*Gainesville*/Cooke	04801868	940/665-0277	91
Margaret L Felty Elem Sch/*Waxahachie*/Ellis	11131981	972/923-4616	142
Margaret Long Wisdom High Sch/*Houston*/Harris	01024566	713/787-1700	194
Margaret S McWhirter Elem Sch/*Webster*/Galveston	01018919	281/284-4800	159
Margaret Wills Elem Sch/*Amarillo*/Potter	01047350	806/326-5650	318
Maria Alicia P Munoz Sch/*Donna*/Hidalgo	04750049	956/464-1310	215
Maria Moreno Elem Sch/*Dallas*/Dallas	04456475	972/502-3100	101
Marian Manor Elem Sch/*El Paso*/El Paso	01016466	915/434-3600	138
Marilyn J Miller Elem Sch/*Fort Worth*/Tarrant	10030968	817/306-4280	356
Marin B Fenwick Academy/*San Antonio*/Bexar	00998524	210/438-6540	41
Marine Creek Collegiate HS/*Fort Worth*/Tarrant	12101135	817/515-7784	351
Marine Creek Elem Sch/*Lake Worth*/Tarrant	03241277	817/306-4200	356
Marine Creek Middle Sch/*Fort Worth*/Tarrant	12365771	817/847-2945	349
Marine Military Academy/*Harlingen*/Cameron	01004499	956/423-6006	68
Marion High Sch/*Marion*/Guadalupe	01021502	830/914-1075	172
MARION IND SCH DIST/MARION/GUADALUPE	01021485	830/914-2803	172
Marion Middle Sch/*Marion*/Guadalupe	01021514	830/914-1070	172
Mark Twain Elem Sch/*Alvin*/Brazoria	01001461	281/585-5318	51
Mark Twain Elem Sch/*Dallas*/Dallas	01009425	972/749-3000	101
Mark Twain Elem Sch/*Houston*/Harris	01025039	713/295-5230	194
Mark Twain Elem Sch/*Richardson*/Dallas	01011789	469/593-4800	112
Mark White Elem Sch/*Houston*/Harris	12170291	713/556-6571	194
Markham Elem Sch/*Markham*/Matagorda	01040986	979/843-4340	276
Marlin Elem Sch/*Marlin*/Falls	01017240	254/883-3232	145
Marlin High Sch/*Marlin*/Falls	01017252	254/883-2394	145
MARLIN IND SCH DIST/MARLIN/FALLS	01017238	254/883-3585	144
Marlin Middle Sch/*Marlin*/Falls	02128282	254/883-9241	145
Marshall Elem Sch/*Houston*/Harris	01026564	281/636-4606	191
Marshall High Sch/*Marshall*/Harrison	01028677	903/927-8800	209
MARSHALL IND SCH DIST/MARSHALL/HARRISON	01028603	903/927-8700	209
Marshall Junior High Sch/*Marshall*/Harrison	01028665	903/927-8784	209
Marshall Kendricks Middle Sch/*Pasadena*/Harris	12160727	713/740-5380	199
Marshall Law & Med Svc Mag HS/*San Antonio*/Bexar	12365678	210/397-7199	38
Marshall Leadership Academy/*Grand Prairie*/Dallas	05342621	972/522-7200	107
Marshall Middle Sch/*Beaumont*/Jefferson	01034157	409/617-5900	242
Marshall Middle Sch/*Houston*/Harris	01025950	713/226-2600	192
Mart Elem Sch/*Mart*/McLennan	01039860	254/876-2762	280
Mart High Sch/*Mart*/McLennan	01039884	254/876-2574	280
MART IND SCH DIST/MART/MCLENNAN	01039858	254/876-2523	280
Martha Hunt Elem Sch/*Murphy*/Collin	10008343	469/752-4400	83
Martha Raines High Sch/*Katy*/Harris	11565095	281/237-1500	152
Martha Reid Elem Sch/*Arlington*/Tarrant	05347396	817/299-6960	357
Martha Turner Reilly Elem Sch/*Dallas*/Dallas	01009683	972/749-7800	101
Marti Elem Sch/*Cleburne*/Johnson	01034913	817/202-1650	247
Martin Elem Sch/*Beaumont*/Jefferson	01033579	409/617-6425	242
Martin Luther King Academy/*San Antonio*/Bexar	00998885	210/978-7935	41
Martin Luther King Jr Lrng Ctr/*Dallas*/Dallas	01008677	972/502-8100	101
Martin Middle Sch/*Austin*/Travis	01056387	512/414-3243	369
Martin Middle Sch/*Corp Christi*/Nueces	01044530	361/878-4690	303
Martin Walker Elem Sch/*Copperas Cove*/Coryell	01545211	254/547-2283	92
Martin Weiss Elem Sch/*Dallas*/Dallas	01009437	972/749-4000	101
MARTIN'S MILL IND DIST/BEN WHEELER/VAN ZANDT	01058191	903/479-3872	381
Martin's Mill Sch/*Ben Wheeler*/Van Zandt	01058206	903/479-3234	381
Martinez Elem Sch/*Abilene*/Taylor	01172694	325/794-4160	360
MARTINSVILLE IND SCH DIST/NACOGDOCHES/NACOGDOCHES	01043249	936/564-3455	298
Martinsville Sch/*Nacogdoches*/Nacogdoches	01043251	936/564-3455	298
Marvin Elem Sch/*Waxahachie*/Ellis	01015307	972/923-4670	142
Marvin P Baker Middle Sch/*Corp Christi*/Nueces	01044217	361/878-4600	304

School/City/County DISTRICT/CITY/COUNTY	PID	TELEPHONE NUMBER	PAGE
Mary & Frank Yturria Elem Sch/*Brownsville*/Cameron	04015746	956/350-3200	64
Mary Allen Elem Sch/*Stratford*/Sherman	01050498	806/366-3340	336
Mary Austin Holley Elem Sch/*Houston*/Fort Bend	10912861	281/634-3850	150
Mary Branch Elem Sch/*Bryan*/Brazos	03325598	979/209-2900	55
Mary Burks Marek Elem Sch/*Pearland*/Brazoria	05346304	281/245-3232	51
Mary Carroll High Sch/*Corp Christi*/Nueces	01044542	361/878-5140	304
Mary Catherine Harris Sch/*Bryan*/Brazos	11452319	979/209-2812	55
Mary DeShazo Elem Sch/*Muleshoe*/Bailey	00995704	806/272-7364	22
Mary E Smithey Pace High Sch/*Duncanville*/Dallas	04037689	972/708-2470	105
Mary Evans Elem Sch/*Allen*/Collin	11079840	972/747-3373	77
Mary Grett Sch/*Corp Christi*/Nueces	01532070	361/878-1738	304
Mary Grimes Education Center/*Carrollton*/Dallas	01525936	972/968-5600	97
Mary Harper Middle Sch/*Dilley*/Frio	01018608	830/965-2195	157
Mary Harris Intermediate Sch/*Fort Worth*/Tarrant	11562017	817/370-7571	348
Mary Hartman Elem Sch/*San Antonio*/Bexar	05272234	210/564-1520	33
Mary Help of Christians Sch/*Laredo*/Webb	01045259	956/722-3966	389
Mary Hoge Middle Sch/*Weslaco*/Hidalgo	04034871	956/969-6730	225
Mary Hull Elem Sch/*San Antonio*/Bexar	00998213	210/397-0950	38
Mary Immaculate Sch/*Farmers BRNCH*/Dallas	01012484	972/243-7105	114
Mary Jo Sheppard Elem Sch/*Mansfield*/Tarrant	10006876	817/299-6600	357
Mary Lillard Intermediate Sch/*Mansfield*/Tarrant	10028238	817/276-6260	357
Mary Lou Fisher Elem Sch/*San Antonio*/Bexar	10020705	210/397-4450	38
Mary Louise Phillips Elem Sch/*Fort Worth*/Tarrant	01053256	817/815-1600	351
Mary M Boals Elem Sch/*Frisco*/Collin	05272600	469/633-3300	79
Mary Martin Elem Sch/*Weatherford*/Parker	04452675	817/598-2910	314
Mary McAshan Gibbs PK Center/*Huntsville*/Walker	01058684	936/435-6550	383
Mary McLeod Bethune Elem Sch/*Dallas*/Dallas	04456516	972/502-1300	101
Mary Moore Elem Sch/*Arlington*/Tarrant	03325457	682/867-8900	344
Mary Moss Elem Sch/*Mesquite*/Dallas	04033023	972/882-7130	111
Mary Orr Intermediate Sch/*Mansfield*/Tarrant	01172618	817/299-2600	357
Mary Walke Stephens Elem Sch/*Houston*/Harris	01022893	281/985-6560	180
Mason Elem Sch/*Cedar Park*/Williamson	04282365	512/570-5500	397
Mason Elem Sch/*Mason*/Mason	01040792	325/347-1122	275
Mason High Sch/*Mason*/Mason	01040807	325/347-1122	275
MASON IND SCH DIST/**MASON**/**MASON**	01040780	325/347-1144	275
Mason Junior High Sch/*Mason*/Mason	11447003	325/347-1122	275
Massey Ranch Elem Sch/*Pearland*/Brazoria	10028082	281/727-1700	53
Masters Sch/*San Marcos*/Hays	04824925	512/392-4322	212
Mata Intermediate Sch/*Houston*/Harris	04868696	281/983-7800	182
MATAGORDA IND SCH DIST/**MATAGORDA**/**MATAGORDA**	01040895	979/863-7693	275
Matagorda Sch/*Matagorda*/Matagorda	01040900	979/863-7693	275
Math Science & Tech Magnet Sch/*Richardson*/Dallas	04366818	469/593-7300	112
Mathews Elem Sch/*Austin*/Travis	01056399	512/414-4406	368
Mathews Elem Sch/*Plano*/Collin	03014672	469/752-2300	83
Mathis Elem Sch/*Mathis*/San Patricio	01049657	361/547-4106	331
Mathis High Sch/*Mathis*/San Patricio	01049669	361/547-3322	331
MATHIS IND SCH DIST/**MATHIS**/**SAN PATRICIO**	01049645	361/547-3378	331
Mathis Intermediate Sch/*Mathis*/San Patricio	01049671	361/547-2472	331
Mathis Middle Sch/*Mathis*/San Patricio	01049683	361/547-2381	331
Matias De Llano Jr Elem Sch/*Laredo*/Webb	04038437	956/473-4000	388
Matthews Alt HS/New Directions/*Lubbock*/Lubbock	04285006	806/219-2600	270
Mattie A Teague Middle Sch/*Humble*/Harris	01022881	281/233-4310	181
Mattie B Hambrick Middle Sch/*Houston*/Harris	01022829	281/985-6570	181
Matzke Elem Sch/*Houston*/Harris	01023299	281/897-4450	185
MAUD IND SCH DIST/**MAUD**/**BOWIE**	01001033	903/585-2219	49
Maud Sch/*Maud*/Bowie	01001045	903/585-2219	49
Maude I Logan Elem Sch/*Fort Worth*/Tarrant	01052812	817/815-3700	351
Maude Moore Wood Elem Sch/*Killeen*/Bell	00996461	254/336-1650	28
Maudrie M Walton Elem Sch/*Fort Worth*/Tarrant	01053335	817/815-3300	351
Maurice Wolfe Elem Sch/*Houston*/Harris	01026239	281/237-2250	152
Mauriceville Elem Sch/*Orange*/Orange	02179023	409/745-1615	308
Mauriceville Middle Sch/*Orange*/Orange	01045699	409/745-3970	308
Maurine Cain Middle Sch/*Rockwall*/Rockwall	04846727	972/772-1170	325
Maverick Elem Sch/*San Antonio*/Bexar	00998603	210/438-6550	41
Max Vaughan Elem Sch/*Allen*/Collin	03235333	972/727-0470	77
Maxdale Elem Sch/*Killeen*/Bell	04941896	254/336-2460	28
Maxfield Elem Sch/*Gorman*/Eastland	01014456	254/734-3171	129
Maxine & Lutrell Watts ES/*Cibolo*/Guadalupe	04871980	210/619-4400	173
May Elem Sch/*May*/Brown	01002594	254/259-3711	59
May High Sch/*May*/Brown	01002609	254/259-2131	59
MAY IND SCH DIST/**MAY**/**BROWN**	01002582	254/259-2091	59
Maya Angelou High Sch/*Dallas*/Dallas	01809134	972/925-7000	101
Mayde Creek Elem Sch/*Houston*/Harris	02201626	281/237-3950	152
Mayde Creek High Sch/*Houston*/Harris	02227266	281/237-3000	152
Mayde Creek Junior High Sch/*Houston*/Harris	02110261	281/237-3900	152
Maydell Jenks Elem Sch/*Katy*/Harris	12169931	281/234-4100	152
Mayes Elem Sch/*Denison*/Grayson	01020390	903/462-7500	166
Maypearl High Sch/*Maypearl*/Ellis	03007033	972/435-1020	141
MAYPEARL IND SCH DIST/**MAYPEARL**/**ELLIS**	01015101	972/435-2116	141
Maypearl Intermediate Sch/*Maypearl*/Ellis	12102581	972/435-1099	141
Maypearl Middle Sch/*Maypearl*/Ellis	05092187	972/435-1015	141
McAllen High Sch/*McAllen*/Hidalgo	01030034	956/632-3100	221
MCALLEN IND SCH DIST/**MCALLEN**/**HIDALGO**	01029918	956/618-6000	220
McAnally Intermediate Sch/*Aledo*/Parker	05276395	817/441-8347	312
McAndrew Elem Sch/*Boerne*/Bexar	11918179	830/398-1750	38
McAuliffe Elem Sch/*Lewisville*/Denton	03010470	469/713-5959	123
McAuliffe Middle Sch/*Houston*/Fort Bend	02892914	281/634-3360	150
McCall Elem Sch/*Willow Park*/Parker	11102356	817/441-4500	312
McCamey High Sch/*Mc Camey*/Upton	01057642	432/652-3666	377
MCCAMEY IND SCH DIST/**MC CAMEY**/**UPTON**	01057616	432/652-3666	377
McCamey Middle Sch/*Mc Camey*/Upton	01057628	432/652-3666	377
McCamey Primary Sch/*Mc Camey*/Upton	01057630	432/652-3666	377
McCarroll Middle Sch/*Decatur*/Wise	01061681	940/393-7300	403
McCollum High Sch/*San Antonio*/Bexar	00997427	210/989-1500	33
McCord Elem Sch/*Vernon*/Wilbarger	02178469	940/553-4381	394
McCormick Middle Sch/*Buda*/Hays	12170722	512/268-8508	211
McCowan Middle Sch/*Glenn Heights*/Dallas	10904773	972/274-8090	104
McCoy Elem Sch/*Carrollton*/Dallas	01826156	972/968-2300	97
McCullough Junior High Sch/*Spring*/Montgomery	01526136	832/592-5100	292
MCDADE IND SCH DIST/**MC DADE**/**BASTROP**	00995936	512/273-2522	24
McDade Sch/*Mc Dade*/Bastrop	00995948	512/273-2522	24
McDermott Elem Sch/*San Antonio*/Bexar	04015473	210/397-5100	38
McDougle Elem Sch/*Houston*/Harris	05347607	832/484-7550	197
McDowell Middle Sch/*Hondo*/Medina	01041253	830/426-2261	284
McFee Elem Sch/*Katy*/Harris	10966678	281/463-5380	185
McGill Elem Sch/*San Angelo*/Tom Green	01055735	325/947-3934	365
McGowen Elem Sch/*Houston*/Harris	01025924	713/636-6979	191
McGregor Elem Sch/*Mc Gregor*/McLennan	01039925	254/840-3204	280
McGregor High Sch/*Mc Gregor*/McLennan	01039913	254/840-2853	280
MCGREGOR IND SCH DIST/**MC GREGOR**/**MCLENNAN**	01039896	254/840-2828	280
McGregor Primary Sch/*Mc Gregor*/McLennan	12035146	254/840-2973	280
McKamy Middle Sch/*Flower Mound*/Denton	04754722	469/713-5991	123
McKinney Boyd High Sch/*McKinney*/Collin	10028496	469/302-3400	81
McKinney Christian Academy/*McKinney*/Collin	04931152	214/544-2658	86
McKinney Daep Learning Center/*McKinney*/Collin	03396808	469/302-7800	81
McKinney High Sch/*McKinney*/Collin	01006289	469/302-5700	81
MCKINNEY IND SCH DIST/**MCKINNEY**/**COLLIN**	01006241	469/302-4000	80
McKinney North High Sch/*McKinney*/Collin	04920684	469/302-4300	81
MCLEAN IND SCH DIST/**MCLEAN**/**GRAY**	01020106	806/779-2301	165
McLean Sch/*McLean*/Gray	01020118	806/779-2301	165
McLean Sixth Grade Sch/*Fort Worth*/Tarrant	04919441	817/814-5700	351
McLennan Co Challenge Academy/*Waco*/McLennan	04873471	254/754-0803	282
McLennan Co State Juvenile Sch/*Mart*/McLennan	04885175	254/297-8200	8
MCLEOD IND SCH DIST/**MC LEOD**/**CASS**	01004891	903/796-7181	70
McLeod Sch/*Bivins*/Cass	01004906	903/796-7181	70
McMasters Elem Sch/*Pasadena*/Harris	01026784	713/740-0640	199
McMath Middle Sch/*Denton*/Denton	04810895	940/369-3300	121
McMichael Middle Sch/*Nacogdoches*/Nacogdoches	01043342	936/552-0519	298
McMillan Junior High Sch/*Wylie*/Collin	01172436	972/492-3225	85
McMillen High Sch/*Plano*/Collin	11717999	469/752-8600	83
McMullan Elem Sch/*Channelview*/Harris	01878408	281/452-1154	183
MCMULLEN CO IND SCH DIST/**TILDEN**/**MCMULLEN**	01040560	361/274-2000	283
McMullen Co Sch/*Tilden*/McMullen	01040572	361/274-2000	283

DISTRICT & SCHOOL TELEPHONE INDEX

School/City/County DISTRICT/CITY/COUNTY	PID	TELEPHONE NUMBER	PAGE
McNair Elem Sch/*Denton*/Denton	03009744	940/369-3600	121
McNamara Elem Sch/*Houston*/Harris	01024982	713/778-3460	194
McNeil High Sch/*Austin*/Williamson	03007306	512/464-6300	399
McNeill Elem Sch/*Richmond*/Fort Bend	11397070	832/223-2800	154
McNiel Middle Sch/*Wichita Falls*/Wichita	01173143	940/235-1118	392
McQueeney Elem Sch/*Mc Queeney*/Guadalupe	01021722	830/401-8738	174
McReynolds Middle Sch/*Houston*/Harris	01025613	713/671-3650	191
McSpedden Elem Sch/*Frisco*/Collin	12032871	469/633-4025	79
McWhorter Elem Sch/*Lubbock*/Lubbock	01038799	806/219-6100	270
Mead Middle Sch/*Houston*/Harris	12309650	281/985-3700	181
Meador Elem Sch/*Houston*/Harris	01026796	713/740-0648	199
Meador Elem Sch/*Willis*/Montgomery	11130523	936/890-7550	294
Meadow Creek Elem Sch/*Bedford*/Tarrant	03249009	817/354-3500	354
MEADOW IND SCH DIST/MEADOW/TERRY	01055149	806/539-2246	362
Meadow Oaks Academy/*Mesquite*/Dallas	03143091	972/285-6895	115
Meadow Sch/*Meadow*/Terry	01055163	806/539-2246	362
Meadow Village Elem Sch/*San Antonio*/Bexar	00998225	210/397-0650	38
Meadow Wood Elem Sch/*Houston*/Harris	01027178	713/251-6200	201
Meadowbrook Elem Sch/*Corp Christi*/Nueces	01044554	361/878-2620	304
Meadowbrook Elem Sch/*Fort Worth*/Tarrant	01053098	817/815-4900	351
Meadowbrook Middle Sch/*Fort Worth*/Tarrant	01053103	817/815-4300	351
Meadowcreek Elem Sch/*Fort Worth*/Tarrant	02897196	817/370-5690	348
Meadowland CS Stepping Stones/*San Antonio*/Bexar	12362779	830/331-4094	8
Meadowland CS-Oaks Acad/*Boerne*/Kendall	11704435	830/331-4094	8
Meadows Elem Sch/*Desoto*/Dallas	02895253	972/224-0960	104
Meadows Elem Sch/*Fort Hood*/Bell	00996540	254/336-1870	28
Meadows Elem Sch/*Meadows Place*/Fort Bend	01018189	281/634-4720	150
Meadows Elem Sch/*Plano*/Collin	01006356	469/752-2400	83
Means Young Womens Ldrshp Acad/*Austin*/Travis	01056284	512/414-3234	369
Medina Elem Sch/*Medina*/Bandera	01172412	830/589-2731	23
MEDINA IND SCH DIST/MEDINA/BANDERA	00995807	830/589-2855	23
Medina Secondary Sch/*Medina*/Bandera	04450172	830/589-2851	23
Medina Valley High Sch/*Castroville*/Medina	01041289	830/931-2243	284
MEDINA VALLEY IND SCH DIST/CASTROVILLE/MEDINA	01041277	830/931-2243	284
Medina Valley Lacoste ES/*La Coste*/Medina	01041291	830/985-3421	284
Medina Valley Middle Sch/*Castroville*/Medina	01041306	830/931-2243	284
Medio Creek Elem Sch/*San Antonio*/Bexar	11711232	210/622-4950	43
Medlin Middle Sch/*Trophy Club*/Denton	04804614	817/215-0500	125
Mel Parmley Elem Sch/*Willis*/Montgomery	03053044	936/856-1231	294
Melba Passmore Elem Sch/*Alvin*/Brazoria	04033346	281/585-6696	51
Melillo Middle Sch/*Houston*/Harris	11129421	713/740-5260	199
Melissa High Sch/*Melissa*/Collin	02848901	972/837-4216	81
MELISSA IND SCH DIST/MELISSA/COLLIN	01006320	972/837-2411	81
Melissa Middle Sch/*Melissa*/Collin	11445811	972/837-4355	81
Memorial 9th Grade Academy/*Port Arthur*/Jefferson	01033880	409/984-4900	243
Memorial Christian Academy/*Killeen*/Bell	02725103	254/526-5403	30
Memorial Chrn Academy/*Houston*/Harris	11231490	281/493-3700	206
Memorial Drive Elem Sch/*Houston*/Harris	01027180	713/251-6300	201
Memorial Early Clg HS/*New Braunfels*/Comal	04429056	830/885-1798	88
Memorial Elem Sch/*Houston*/Harris	01024176	713/867-5150	194
Memorial Elem Sch/*New Braunfels*/Comal	04808971	830/627-6470	88
Memorial Elem Sch/*Plano*/Collin	01006447	469/752-2500	83
Memorial Elem Sch/*Weslaco*/Hidalgo	03251973	956/969-6780	225
Memorial Hall High Sch/*Houston*/Harris	01480269	713/688-5566	206
Memorial High Sch/*Frisco*/Collin	12308333	469/633-7300	79
Memorial High Sch/*Houston*/Harris	01027207	713/251-2515	201
Memorial High Sch/*McAllen*/Hidalgo	02110364	956/632-5201	221
Memorial High Sch/*Port Arthur*/Jefferson	01033919	409/984-4000	243
Memorial High Sch/*San Antonio*/Bexar	00997312	210/444-8300	32
Memorial High School-Cate/*Port Arthur*/Jefferson	01033892	409/984-4750	243
Memorial Intermediate Sch/*Alice*/Jim Wells	01034597	361/660-2080	245
Memorial Junior High Sch/*Eagle Pass*/Maverick	02896128	830/758-7053	277
Memorial Lutheran Sch/*Houston*/Harris	02235706	713/782-4022	206
Memorial Middle Sch/*Edinburg*/Hidalgo	01029700	956/289-2470	217
Memorial Middle Sch/*Harlingen*/Cameron	01003835	956/427-3020	65
Memorial Middle Sch/*Houston*/Harris	01027192	713/251-3900	201
Memorial Middle Sch/*Kingsville*/Kleberg	01036337	361/595-8675	257
Memorial Middle Sch/*Laredo*/Webb	01059303	956/273-6600	387
Memorial Middle Sch/*Mission*/Hidalgo	04287896	956/323-2820	220
Memorial Middle Sch/*Winnsboro*/Wood	01061954	903/342-5711	405
Memorial Park Academy/*Richardson*/Dallas	12309040	469/593-0450	112
Memorial Parkway Elem Sch/*Katy*/Harris	01832117	281/237-5850	152
Memorial Parkway Jr High Sch/*Katy*/Harris	02177049	281/237-5800	152
Memorial Pathway Academy/*Garland*/Dallas	01010618	972/926-2650	106
Memorial Private High Sch/*Houston*/Harris	10989888	281/759-2288	206
Memphis High Sch/*Memphis*/Hall	01022104	806/259-5910	176
MEMPHIS IND SCH DIST/MEMPHIS/HALL	01022087	806/259-5900	175
Memphis Middle Sch/*Memphis*/Hall	01022116	806/259-5920	176
Menard Elem Middle Sch/*Menard*/Menard	01041370	325/396-2348	285
Menard High Sch/*Menard*/Menard	01041382	325/396-2513	285
MENARD IND SCH DIST/MENARD/MENARD	01041368	325/396-2404	285
Menchaca Elem Sch/*Austin*/Travis	01056363	512/414-2333	367
Mendenhall Elem Sch/*Plano*/Collin	01006368	469/752-2600	83
Mendez Elem Sch/*San Marcos*/Hays	11540461	512/393-6060	212
Mendez Middle Sch/*Austin*/Travis	03011682	512/414-3284	369
Mercedes Academic Academy/*Mercedes*/Hidalgo	12032962	956/825-5076	221
Mercedes Early College HS/*Mercedes*/Hidalgo	11074515	956/825-5180	221
Mercedes High Sch/*Mercedes*/Hidalgo	01030175	956/514-2100	222
MERCEDES IND SCH DIST/MERCEDES/HIDALGO	01030149	956/514-2000	221
Mercer-Blumberg Learning Ctr/*Seguin*/Guadalupe	04453980	830/401-8690	174
Meridian Alternative Sch/*Meridian*/Bosque	04804391	254/435-6047	47
Meridian Elem Sch/*Meridian*/Bosque	01000704	254/435-2731	47
MERIDIAN IND SCH DIST/MERIDIAN/BOSQUE	01000699	254/435-2081	47
Meridian Middle High Sch/*Meridian*/Bosque	04357740	254/435-2723	47
Meridian World Charter Sch/*Round Rock*/Williamson	11729502	512/660-5230	8
Meridiana Elem Sch/*Iowa Colony*/Brazoria	12169113	281/245-3636	51
Meridith-Dunbar EC Academy/*Temple*/Bell	00996710	254/215-6700	29
Merit Academy/*Dallas*/Dallas	11929128	214/736-8375	115
Merkel Elem Sch/*Merkel*/Taylor	01054951	325/928-4795	361
Merkel High Sch/*Merkel*/Taylor	01054949	325/928-4667	361
MERKEL IND SCH DIST/MERKEL/TAYLOR	01054925	325/928-5813	361
Merkel Middle Sch/*Merkel*/Taylor	01054937	325/928-5511	361
Merrifield Elem Sch/*Duncanville*/Dallas	01010369	972/708-2900	105
Merriman Park Elem Sch/*Dallas*/Dallas	01881132	469/593-2800	112
Merryhill Sch/*Arlington*/Tarrant	11551733	817/472-9494	359
Merrywood Sch/*Duncanville*/Dallas	02734910	972/298-0130	115
Mesa Verde Elem Sch/*Amarillo*/Potter	01047362	806/326-4800	318
Mesa Vista Elem Sch/*El Paso*/El Paso	01016478	915/434-2700	138
Mesita Elem Sch/*El Paso*/El Paso	01016038	915/236-6850	133
Mesorah High School for Girls/*Dallas*/Dallas	05343041	214/420-1990	115
Mesquite Academy Aec of Choice/*Mesquite*/Dallas	04366404	972/882-7570	111
Mesquite High Sch/*Mesquite*/Dallas	01011569	972/882-7800	111
MESQUITE IND SCH DIST/MESQUITE/DALLAS	01011399	972/288-6411	110
Messiah Luth Classical Academy/*Keller*/Tarrant	11235070	817/431-5486	359
Metcalf Elem Sch/*Houston*/Harris	03398234	281/856-1152	185
Metro Elem School of Design/*Corp Christi*/Nueces	01044671	361/878-2780	304
Metro Opportunity Sch/*Fort Worth*/Tarrant	01881948	817/814-6700	351
Metroplex Chapel Academy/*Euless*/Tarrant	04423686	817/267-1000	359
Metz Elem Sch/*Austin*/Travis	01056416	512/414-4408	367
Metzler Elem Sch/*Spring*/Harris	10001943	832/484-7900	197
Mexia High Sch/*Mexia*/Limestone	01038103	254/562-4010	267
MEXIA IND SCH DIST/MEXIA/LIMESTONE	01038086	254/562-4000	267
Mexia Junior High Sch/*Mexia*/Limestone	01038115	254/562-4020	267
Meyer Elem Sch/*Hondo*/Medina	01041265	830/426-3161	284
Meyer Elem Sch/*Houston*/Harris	01526033	281/891-8270	202
Meyer Elem Sch/*Richmond*/Fort Bend	02856972	832/223-2000	154
Meyer High Sch/*Waco*/McLennan	11478832	254/754-2288	8
Meyerland Perf-Visual Arts MS/*Houston*/Harris	01024695	713/726-3616	194
Meyerpark Charter Sch/*Houston*/Harris	11014797	713/729-9712	8
Meyersville Elem Sch/*Meyersville*/De Witt	01013749	361/275-3639	118
MEYERSVILLE IND SCH DIST/MEYERSVILLE/DE WITT	01013737	361/277-5817	118
MIAMI IND SCH DIST/MIAMI/ROBERTS	01048536	806/868-3971	324
Miami Sch/*Miami*/Roberts	01048548	806/868-3971	324
Michael E Fossum Middle Sch/*McAllen*/Hidalgo	11104029	956/971-1105	221
Michael Elem Sch/*San Antonio*/Bexar	04865943	210/397-3900	38
Michael G Killian Middle Sch/*Lewisville*/Denton	10910617	469/713-5977	123
Michael L Griffin Elem Sch/*Katy*/Harris	10027870	281/237-8700	152
Michael R Null Middle Sch/*Houston*/Harris	01027075	281/436-2800	200

Texas School Directory
DISTRICT & SCHOOL TELEPHONE INDEX

School/City/County DISTRICT/CITY/COUNTY	PID	TELEPHONE NUMBER	PAGE
Mickey Leland College Prep/Houston/Harris	11717523	713/226-2668	191
Mid-Valley Christian Sch/Weslaco/Hidalgo	02153952	956/968-6232	226
Middle College at HCC Fraga/Houston/Harris	12107725	713/228-3408	190
Middle College at HCC Gulfton/Houston/Harris	12107737	713/662-2551	190
Middle Level Learning Center/Fort Worth/Tarrant	02110314	817/814-6800	351
Midland Academy Charter Sch/Midland/Midland	04903076	432/686-0003	8
Midland Alternative Program/Midland/Midland	11924829	432/240-4700	286
Midland Christian Sch/Midland/Midland	01480843	432/694-1661	286
Midland Classical Academy/Midland/Midland	12169747	432/694-0995	286
Midland Freshman High Sch/Midland/Midland	01041497	432/689-1200	286
MIDLAND IND SCH DIST/MIDLAND/MIDLAND	01041423	432/689-1000	285
Midland Senior High Sch/Midland/Midland	01041590	432/689-1100	286
Midlothian Heritage High Sch/Midlothian/Ellis	12109058	469/856-5400	141
Midlothian High Sch/Midlothian/Ellis	01015163	469/856-5100	141
MIDLOTHIAN IND SCH DIST/MIDLOTHIAN/ELLIS	01015137	469/856-5000	141
Midway Alternative High Sch/Canyon/Randall	11450385	806/677-2455	321
Midway High Sch/Waco/McLennan	01039951	254/761-5650	281
MIDWAY IND SCH DIST/HENRIETTA/CLAY	01005584	940/476-2215	74
MIDWAY IND SCH DIST/WOODWAY/MCLENNAN	01039937	254/761-5600	280
Midway Middle Sch/Hewitt/McLennan	01557642	254/761-5680	281
Midway Park Elem Sch/Euless/Tarrant	01053866	817/354-3380	354
Midway Sch/Henrietta/Clay	01005596	940/476-2215	74
Miguel Carrillo Jr Elem Sch/San Antonio/Bexar	04364107	210/977-7550	42
Mike Moseley Elem Sch/Grand Prairie/Dallas	10910631	972/522-2800	108
Mike Moses Middle Sch/Nacogdoches/Nacogdoches	03317591	936/569-5001	298
Milam Elem Sch/Conroe/Montgomery	01042441	936/709-5200	292
Milam Elem Sch/El Paso/El Paso	01015838	915/236-0325	133
Milam Elem Sch/Midland/Midland	01041459	432/240-7500	286
Milam Elem Sch/Wichita Falls/Wichita	01172979	940/235-1176	392
Milam Magnet Elem Sch/Odessa/Ector	01014755	432/456-1169	130
Milano Elem Sch/Milano/Milam	02110106	512/455-2062	287
Milano High Sch/Milano/Milam	05242631	512/455-9333	287
MILANO IND SCH DIST/MILANO/MILAM	01041825	512/455-2533	287
Milano Junior High Sch/Milano/Milam	01041849	512/455-6701	287
MILDRED IND SCH DIST/CORSICANA/NAVARRO	01043615	903/872-6505	300
Mildred Jenkins Elem Sch/Spring/Harris	01526045	281/891-8300	202
Mildred M Hawk Elem Sch/Corinth/Denton	10001838	940/369-1800	121
Mildred Sch/Corsicana/Navarro	01043627	903/872-6505	300
MILES IND SCH DIST/MILES/RUNNELS	01048847	325/468-2861	326
Miles Sch/Miles/Runnels	01048859	325/468-2861	326
MILFORD IND SCH DIST/MILFORD/ELLIS	01015187	972/493-2911	141
Milford Sch/Milford/Ellis	01015199	972/493-2921	141
Mill St Elem Sch/Lewisville/Denton	01013426	469/713-5965	123
Miller Career & Tech Center/Katy/Harris	03053264	281/237-6300	152
Miller Elem Sch/Arlington/Tarrant	02132180	682/867-8400	344
Miller Elem Sch/Little Elm/Collin	12167282	469/633-2075	79
Miller Elem Sch/San Antonio/Bexar	00998926	210/978-7995	41
MILLER GROVE IND SCH DIST/CUMBY/HOPKINS	01031521	903/459-3288	231
Miller Grove Sch/Cumby/Hopkins	01031533	903/459-3288	231
Miller Heights Elem Sch/Belton/Bell	00996368	254/215-3300	27
Miller HS-Metro Sch of Design/Corp Christi/Nueces	01044621	361/878-5100	304
Miller Intermediate Sch/Houston/Harris	04914594	281/531-3430	182
Miller Jordan Middle Sch/San Benito/Cameron	02112520	956/361-6650	67
Miller's Point Elem Sch/Converse/Bexar	03007875	210/945-5114	33
Mills Elem Sch/Austin/Travis	04806698	512/841-2400	367
Millsap Elem Sch/Cypress/Harris	01548419	281/897-4470	185
Millsap Elem Sch/Millsap/Parker	03321516	940/682-4489	313
Millsap High Sch/Millsap/Parker	01046409	940/682-4994	313
MILLSAP IND SCH DIST/MILLSAP/PARKER	01046394	940/682-4994	312
Millsap Middle Sch/Millsap/Parker	04941389	940/682-4489	313
Milstead Middle Sch/Houston/Harris	10913267	713/740-5238	199
Milton B Lee Acad of Sci & Eng/San Antonio/Bexar	11589998	210/431-9881	42
Milton Cooper Elem Sch/Houston/Harris	10006931	281/891-8660	202
Milton L Kirkpatrick Elem Sch/Fort Worth/Tarrant	01053036	817/814-4600	351
Mimi Farley Elem Sch/Boys Ranch/Oldham	01484473	806/534-2248	307
Mims Elem Sch/Mission/Hidalgo	02856714	956/323-4400	222
Mina Elem Sch/Bastrop/Bastrop	00995869	512/772-7640	24
Mineola Elem Sch/Mineola/Wood	01061875	903/569-2466	404
Mineola High Sch/Mineola/Wood	01061887	903/569-3000	404
MINEOLA IND SCH DIST/MINEOLA/WOOD	01061851	903/569-2448	404
Mineola Middle Sch/Mineola/Wood	01061899	903/569-5338	404
Mineola Primary Sch/Mineola/Wood	01061863	903/569-5488	404
Mineral Wells Academy/Mineral Wells/Palo Pinto	04921341	940/325-3033	310
Mineral Wells High Sch/Mineral Wells/Palo Pinto	01046069	940/325-4408	310
MINERAL WELLS IND SCH DIST/MINERAL WELLS/PALO PINTO	01046019	940/325-6404	310
Mineral Wells Jr High Sch/Mineral Wells/Palo Pinto	01046071	940/325-0711	310
Minshew Elem Sch/McKinney/Collin	05343156	469/302-7300	81
Miraibeau B Lamar Elem Sch/Baytown/Harris	01023706	281/420-4625	188
Mirus Academy/Katy/Harris	11662942	281/392-4477	206
Misd Developmental Center/Mexia/Limestone	11444879	254/562-4023	267
Miss May Vernon Elem Sch/Fate/Rockwall	10907086	972/635-5006	326
Mission Academy/San Antonio/Bexar	11128049	210/438-6880	41
Mission Bend Christian Academy/Houston/Harris	11235288	281/497-4057	206
Mission Bend Elem Sch/Houston/Fort Bend	02126375	281/634-4240	150
Mission Collegiate High Sch/Alton/Hidalgo	11848811	956/323-6120	222
MISSION CONS IND SCH DIST/MISSION/HIDALGO	01030228	956/323-5500	222
Mission Early College High Sch/El Paso/El Paso	10751124	915/937-1200	136
Mission Glen Elem Sch/Houston/Fort Bend	02892938	281/634-4280	150
Mission High Sch/Mission/Hidalgo	01030266	956/323-5700	222
Mission Junior High Sch/Mission/Hidalgo	01030278	956/323-3300	222
Mission Options Academy/Mission/Hidalgo	11818103	956/323-3960	222
Mission Ridge Elem Sch/El Paso/El Paso	12030782	915/938-2000	136
Mission Valley Elem Sch/El Paso/El Paso	03250888	915/434-3700	138
Mission Valley Elem Sch/Victoria/Victoria	01540118	361/788-9514	382
Mission West Elem Sch/Houston/Fort Bend	03393193	281/634-4320	150
Missouri City Middle Sch/Missouri City/Fort Bend	01526007	281/634-3440	150
Mistral Early Childhood Center/Houston/Harris	10003927	713/773-6253	194
Mitchell Elem Sch/Bryan/Brazos	04884949	979/209-1400	55
Mitchell Elem Sch/Dallas/Collin	04016324	469/752-2800	83
Mitchell Elem Sch/Houston/Harris	01025625	713/991-8190	193
Mitchell Intermediate Sch/The Woodlands/Montgomery	04454037	832/592-8500	292
Mittelstadt Elem Sch/Klein/Harris	03397216	832/484-6700	197
Mitzi Bond Elem Sch/El Paso/El Paso	02129884	915/236-2925	133
Mockingbird Elem Sch/Coppell/Dallas	03393466	214/496-8200	98
Mockingbird Elem Sch/Dallas/Dallas	01009891	972/749-7200	102
Mohawk Elem Sch/Richardson/Dallas	01011791	469/593-6600	112
Moises E Molina High Sch/Dallas/Dallas	04755477	972/502-1000	102
Moises Vela Middle Sch/Harlingen/Cameron	10007698	956/427-3479	65
Momentous Sch/Dallas/Dallas	03414371	214/915-1890	115
Mona Montessori McKinney/McKinney/Collin	03137975	972/542-5825	86
Monaco Elem Sch/Aubrey/Denton	05342918	940/668-0000	120
Monahans Education Center HS/Monahans/Ward	05277052	432/943-2019	385
Monahans High Sch/Monahans/Ward	01058995	432/943-2519	385
MONAHANS-WICKETT-PYOTE ISD/MONAHANS/WARD	01058957	432/943-6711	385
Monarch Sch/Houston/Harris	04937950	713/479-0800	206
Monroe S May Jr Elem Sch/San Antonio/Bexar	04754758	210/397-2000	38
Monta Jane Akin Elem Sch/Leander/Williamson	12230803	512/570-8000	397
Montague Elem Sch/Montague/Montague	01042324	940/894-2811	290
MONTAGUE IND SCH DIST/MONTAGUE/MONTAGUE	01042312	940/894-2811	290
Montague Village Elem Sch/Fort Hood/Bell	04806569	254/336-2230	28
Montana Vista Elem Sch/El Paso/El Paso	02845636	915/926-5307	132
Montclair Elem Sch/Corp Christi/Nueces	01044578	361/878-0160	304
Montclair Elem Sch/Garland/Dallas	01010620	972/279-4041	106
Monte Alto Ealry Clg High Sch/Edcouch/Hidalgo	11540485	956/262-6152	222
Monte Alto Elem Sch/Monte Alto/Hidalgo	01030321	956/262-6101	223
MONTE ALTO IND SCH DIST/MONTE ALTO/HIDALGO	01030319	956/262-1381	222
Monte Cristo Elem Sch/Edinburg/Hidalgo	03344415	956/289-2362	217
Monterey Senior High Sch/Lubbock/Lubbock	01038804	806/219-1900	270

DISTRICT & SCHOOL TELEPHONE INDEX

Market Data Retrieval

School/City/County DISTRICT/CITY/COUNTY	PID	TELEPHONE NUMBER	PAGE
Montessori Acad Hernandez ES/*Dallas*/Dallas	04456463	972/925-2700	102
Montessori Academy-Arlington/*Arlington*/Tarrant	03016931	817/274-1548	359
Montessori Academy-North Texas/*Sherman*/Grayson	11973222	903/893-3500	169
Montessori Children's House/*Fort Worth*/Tarrant	01481055	817/732-0252	359
Montessori Episcopal Sch/*Lewisville*/Denton	01410680	972/221-3533	126
Montessori Sch International/*San Antonio*/Bexar	02982832	210/614-1665	45
Montessori Sch of North Dallas/*Dallas*/Collin	03404493	972/985-8844	86
Montessori Sch of San Antonio/*San Antonio*/Bexar	01754242	210/492-3553	45
Montessori School at Starcreek/*Allen*/Collin	11589651	972/727-2800	86
Montessori School Downtown/*Houston*/Harris	04885591	713/520-6801	206
Montgomery Achievement Center/*Henderson*/Rusk	12312956	903/655-5552	327
Montgomery Christian Academy/*Montgomery*/Montgomery	12361311	936/622-4598	295
Montgomery Elem Sch/*Houston*/Harris	01025314	713/434-5640	189
Montgomery Elem Sch/*Montgomery*/Montgomery	01042635	936/597-6333	293
Montgomery Elem Sch/*San Antonio*/Bexar	00997843	210/407-5000	35
Montgomery High Sch/*Montgomery*/Montgomery	02177984	936/276-3000	293
MONTGOMERY IND SCH DIST/MONTGOMERY/MONTGOMERY	01042623	936/276-2000	293
Montgomery Junior High Sch/*Montgomery*/Montgomery	01042647	936/276-3300	293
Montwood High Sch/*El Paso*/El Paso	03323473	915/937-2400	136
Montwood Middle Sch/*El Paso*/El Paso	04753182	915/937-5800	136
Moody Elem Sch/*Moody*/McLennan	01039987	254/853-2155	281
Moody High Sch/*Moody*/McLennan	01039999	254/853-3622	281
MOODY IND SCH DIST/MOODY/MCLENNAN	01039975	254/853-2172	281
Moody Middle Sch/*Moody*/McLennan	03392876	254/853-2181	281
Mooneyham Elem Sch/*McKinney*/Collin	10912720	469/633-3650	79
Moore Elem Sch/*Houston*/Harris	02110352	281/370-4040	185
Moore Mst Magnet Sch/*Tyler*/Smith	01050905	903/262-1640	338
Moorhead Junior High Sch/*Conroe*/Montgomery	01042568	936/709-2400	292
Mora Elem Sch/*San Antonio*/Bexar	12309064	210/398-2400	38
Morales Junior High Sch/*Uvalde*/Uvalde	02222448	830/591-2980	378
MORAN IND SCH DIST/MORAN/SHACKELFORD	01050242	325/945-3101	334
Moran Sch/*Moran*/Shackelford	01050254	325/945-3101	334
Morehead Middle Sch/*El Paso*/El Paso	01016040	915/236-3500	135
Moreno Middle Sch/*Beeville*/Bee	00996124	361/358-6262	25
MORGAN IND SCH DIST/MORGAN/BOSQUE	01000728	254/635-2311	47
Morgan Mill Elem Sch/*Morgan Mill*/Erath	01017123	254/968-4921	144
MORGAN MILL IND SCH DIST/MORGAN MILL/ERATH	01017111	254/968-4921	144
Morgan Sch/*Morgan*/Bosque	02112192	254/635-2311	47
Morningside Elem Sch/*Brownsville*/Cameron	02892122	956/982-2760	64
Morningside Elem Sch/*Dumas*/Moore	01042879	806/935-4153	295
Morningside Elem Sch/*Fort Worth*/Tarrant	01053139	817/814-0600	351
Morningside Elem Sch/*New Braunfels*/Comal	11079436	830/837-7100	88
Morningside Elem Sch/*The Colony*/Denton	04036075	469/713-5970	123
Morningside Middle Sch/*Fort Worth*/Tarrant	01053141	817/815-8300	351
Morrill Elem Sch/*San Antonio*/Bexar	00997491	210/989-3150	33
Morris Middle Sch/*Houston*/Harris	05347877	713/740-0672	199
Morris Upchurch Middle Sch/*Queen City*/Cass	01809017	903/796-6412	71
Morriss Elem Sch/*Texarkana*/Bowie	10907438	903/791-2262	50
Morton Elem Sch/*Arlington*/Tarrant	01558880	682/867-5600	344
Morton Elem Sch/*Morton*/Cochran	01005687	806/266-5505	75
Morton High Sch/*Morton*/Cochran	01005699	806/266-5505	75
MORTON IND SCH DIST/MORTON/COCHRAN	01005675	806/266-5505	75
Morton Junior High Sch/*Morton*/Cochran	01005704	806/266-5505	75
Morton Ranch Elem Sch/*Katy*/Harris	11128611	281/234-0300	152
Morton Ranch High Sch/*Katy*/Harris	05344320	281/237-7800	152
Morton Ranch Jr High Sch/*Katy*/Harris	05264718	281/237-7400	152
Mosaic Academy/*Amarillo*/Potter	11223649	817/204-0300	319
Moses Menger Elem Sch/*Corp Christi*/Nueces	01044566	361/878-2640	304
Moss Elem Sch/*Big Spring*/Howard	01032006	432/264-4148	233
Moss Haven Elem Sch/*Dallas*/Dallas	01525974	469/593-2200	112
Most Holy Trinity Sch/*El Paso*/El Paso	01483948	915/751-2566	139
Most Precious Catholic Sch/*Corp Christi*/Nueces	01600471	361/852-4800	306
MOTLEY CO IND SCH DIST/MATADOR/MOTLEY	01043043	806/347-2676	296
Motley Co Sch/*Matador*/Motley	01043055	806/347-2676	296
Moulton Elem Sch/*Moulton*/Lavaca	01037331	361/596-4605	262
Moulton High Sch/*Moulton*/Lavaca	01037343	361/596-4691	262
MOULTON IND SCH DIST/MOULTON/LAVACA	01037329	361/596-4609	262
Mount Carmel Academy/*Houston*/Harris	05099238	713/643-2008	190
Mountain Peak Elem Sch/*Midlothian*/Ellis	04745800	469/856-6300	141
Mountain Valley Elem Sch/*Canyon Lake*/Comal	11926877	830/885-9500	88
Mountain Valley Middle Sch/*Canyon Lake*/Comal	11079450	830/885-1300	88
Mountain View Elem Sch/*Harker HTS*/Bell	03051503	254/336-1900	28
Mountain View High Sch/*El Paso*/El Paso	03237408	915/926-5000	132
Mountaintop Learning Center/*Houston*/Harris	04993332	713/808-9284	206
Mountainview Elem Sch/*Waco*/McLennan	01040314	254/772-2520	282
Moye Elem Sch/*El Paso*/El Paso	01015890	915/774-4000	133
Mozelle Brown Elem Sch/*Whitehouse*/Smith	01539250	903/839-5610	339
Msgr Kelly Catholic HS/*Beaumont*/Jefferson	01034365	409/866-2351	244
Mt Auburn Elem Sch/*Dallas*/Dallas	01009487	972/749-8500	102
Mt Calm Elem Sch/*Mount Calm*/Hill	01031014	254/993-2611	228
Mt Calm High Sch/*Mount Calm*/Hill	11710484	254/993-2611	228
MT CALM IND SCH DIST/MOUNT CALM/HILL	01031002	254/993-2611	228
MT ENTERPRISE IND SCH DIST/MT ENTERPRISE/RUSK	01049126	903/822-3575	328
Mt Enterprise Sch/*Mt Enterprise*/Rusk	01049140	903/822-3545	328
Mt Pleasant Child Dev Center/*Mt Pleasant*/Titus	04870091	903/575-2092	364
Mt Pleasant Christian Sch/*Mt Pleasant*/Titus	04992883	903/577-1550	364
Mt Pleasant High Sch/*Mt Pleasant*/Titus	01055400	903/575-2020	364
MT PLEASANT IND SCH DIST/MT PLEASANT/TITUS	01055369	903/575-2000	363
Mt Pleasant Junior High Sch/*Mt Pleasant*/Titus	04747494	903/575-2110	364
Mt Sacred Heart Sch/*San Antonio*/Bexar	00999877	210/342-6711	44
Mt Saint Michael Catholic Sch/*Dallas*/Dallas	04430299	214/337-0244	114
Mt Vernon Elem Sch/*Mount Vernon*/Franklin	01018397	903/537-2266	156
Mt Vernon High Sch/*Mount Vernon*/Franklin	01018402	903/537-3700	156
MT VERNON IND SCH DIST/MOUNT VERNON/FRANKLIN	01018385	903/537-2546	155
Mt Vernon Middle Sch/*Mount Vernon*/Franklin	01018414	903/537-2267	156
Mueller Elem Sch/*Klein*/Harris	11452113	832/375-7300	197
Muenster Elem Sch/*Muenster*/Cooke	04281610	940/759-2282	91
Muenster High Sch/*Muenster*/Cooke	01007477	940/759-2281	91
MUENSTER IND SCH DIST/MUENSTER/COOKE	01007453	940/759-2281	91
Muleshoe High Sch/*Muleshoe*/Bailey	00995728	806/272-7302	22
MULESHOE IND SCH DIST/MULESHOE/BAILEY	00995699	806/272-7400	22
Mullin Elem Sch/*Mullin*/Mills	12166240	325/985-3374	288
MULLIN IND SCH DIST/MULLIN/MILLS	01041978	325/985-3374	288
Mullin Middle High Sch/*Mullin*/Mills	01041980	325/985-3374	288
Mullin Oaks Sch/*Brownwood*/Mills	12166214	325/203-5315	288
Multiple Careers Magnet Center/*Dallas*/Dallas	01010046	972/925-2200	102
MUMFORD IND SCH DIST/MUMFORD/BRAZOS	01048691	979/279-3678	56
Mumford Sch/*Mumford*/Brazos	01048706	979/279-3678	56
Munday Charter Sch/*Austin*/Travis	12362676	512/791-2270	8
MUNDAY CONSOLIDATED IND SD/MUNDAY/KNOX	01036533	940/422-4241	258
Munday Elem Sch/*Munday*/Knox	01036545	940/422-4321	259
Munday High Sch/*Munday*/Knox	01036557	940/422-4321	259
Murchison Elem Sch/*Murchison*/Henderson	01029499	903/469-3636	214
Murchison Elem Sch/*Pflugerville*/Travis	04920191	512/594-6000	372
MURCHISON IND SCH DIST/MURCHISON/HENDERSON	01029487	903/469-3636	214
Murchison Middle Sch/*Austin*/Travis	01392129	512/414-3254	369
Muriel Vance Forbes Academy/*San Antonio*/Bexar	00998938	210/438-6850	41
Murphy Middle Sch/*Murphy*/Collin	05274397	469/752-7000	83
Murray E Boone Elem Sch/*San Antonio*/Bexar	00998237	210/397-1450	38
Murry Fly Elem Sch/*Odessa*/Ector	02178251	432/456-1269	130
Mva Brownsville CHS/*Brownsville*/Cameron	12320159	956/372-1433	8
Mva McAllen CHS/*McAllen*/Hidalgo	04892465	956/618-2303	8
Mva Mercedes CHS/*Mercedes*/Hidalgo	11014802	956/565-5417	8
Myatt Elem Sch/*El Campo*/Wharton	03007019	979/543-7514	389
Myra Green Middle Sch/*Raymondville*/Willacy	01060742	956/689-8171	394
Myrtle Cooper Elem Sch/*El Paso*/El Paso	03009847	915/937-7700	136

Texas School Directory
DISTRICT & SCHOOL TELEPHONE INDEX

School/City/County DISTRICT/CITY/COUNTY	PID	TELEPHONE NUMBER	PAGE
N			
N A Howry Intermediate Sch/*Lake Worth*/Tarrant	01054107	817/306-4200	356
N L Trevino Elem Sch/*Edinburg*/Hidalgo	04873275	956/289-2550	217
N M Harrel Elem Sch/*Kingsville*/Kleberg	01036351	361/592-9305	257
N Q Henderson Elem Sch/*Houston*/Harris	01025637	713/671-4195	191
N W Harllee Early Chldhd Ctr/*Dallas*/Dallas	12169711	972/925-6500	102
Naaman Forest High Sch/*Garland*/Dallas	03055523	972/675-3091	106
Nacogdoches Christian Academy/*Nacogdoches*/Nacogdoches	11829657	936/462-1021	298
Nacogdoches High Sch/*Nacogdoches*/Nacogdoches	01043316	936/564-2466	298
NACOGDOCHES IND SCH DIST/NACOGDOCHES/NACOGDOCHES	01043275	936/569-5000	298
Nadine Johnson Elem Sch/*Hutto*/Williamson	05221338	512/759-5400	396
Nancy J Cochran Elem Sch/*Dallas*/Dallas	01008665	972/794-4600	102
Nancy Moseley Elem Sch/*Dallas*/Dallas	01009516	972/749-6700	102
Nancy Neal Elem Sch/*Mansfield*/Tarrant	11715408	817/299-1270	357
Nancy Smith Elem Sch/*Albany*/Shackelford	01050230	325/762-3384	334
Nanny Elem Sch/*Riviera*/Kleberg	01036404	361/296-2446	258
Naomi Pasemann Elem Sch/*Taylor*/Williamson	04803438	512/352-1016	399
Naomi Press Elem Sch/*McKinney*/Collin	10909175	469/302-7600	81
Narciso Cavazos Elem Sch/*Mission*/Hidalgo	04805979	956/323-2430	220
Nash Elem Sch/*Nash*/Bowie	01001289	903/838-4321	50
Natalia Elem Sch/*Natalia*/Medina	01041332	830/663-2837	284
Natalia High Sch/*Natalia*/Medina	01041344	830/663-4417	284
NATALIA IND SCH DIST/NATALIA/MEDINA	01041320	830/663-4416	284
Natalia Junior High Sch/*Natalia*/Medina	01041356	830/663-4027	284
Nathan Adams Elem Sch/*Dallas*/Dallas	01009530	972/794-2600	102
Nathan Howell Elem Sch/*Haltom City*/Tarrant	01053191	817/814-9300	351
Nathaniel Hawthorne Elem Sch/*Dallas*/Dallas	01009504	972/749-4700	102
Naumann Elem Sch/*Cedar Park*/Williamson	04808488	512/570-5800	397
Navarro Co Alt Educ Ctr/*Corsicana*/Navarro	12307640	903/872-4502	300
Navarro Early College High Sch/*Austin*/Travis	01056337	512/414-2514	368
Navarro Elem Sch/*Bryan*/Brazos	03047837	979/209-1260	55
Navarro Elem Sch/*Lockhart*/Caldwell	01003081	512/398-0690	61
Navarro Elem Sch/*Seguin*/Guadalupe	01021538	830/372-1933	173
Navarro High Sch/*Seguin*/Guadalupe	01021540	830/372-1931	173
NAVARRO IND SCH DIST/SEGUIN/GUADALUPE	01021526	830/372-1930	173
Navarro Intermediate Sch/*Seguin*/Guadalupe	04745018	830/372-1943	173
Navarro Junior High Sch/*Seguin*/Guadalupe	10774188	830/401-5550	173
Navarro Mid Sch/*Houston*/Harris	01025003	713/924-1760	190
Navarro Middle Sch/*Rosenberg*/Fort Bend	03009861	832/223-3700	154
Navasota High Sch/*Navasota*/Grimes	01021423	936/825-4250	172
NAVASOTA IND SCH DIST/NAVASOTA/GRIMES	01021409	936/825-4200	172
Navasota Junior High Sch/*Navasota*/Grimes	01021435	936/825-4225	172
Navo Middle Sch/*Aubrey*/Denton	10021876	972/347-7500	121
Nazarene Christian Academy/*Crowley*/Tarrant	10754384	817/297-7003	359
Nazarene Christian Academy/*Hereford*/Deaf Smith	11230525	806/364-1697	119
Nazareth Academy/*Victoria*/Victoria	00999906	361/573-6651	383
NAZARETH IND SCH DIST/NAZARETH/CASTRO	01005041	806/945-2231	71
Nazareth Sch/*Nazareth*/Castro	01005053	806/945-2231	71
Nci CS Without Walls/*Houston*/Harris	11016111	713/779-4856	8
NE Alternative Center/*San Antonio*/Bexar	04017782	210/356-7400	35
NE Transition Sch/*San Antonio*/Bexar	11452216	210/356-7520	35
Neal Dillman Elem Sch/*Muleshoe*/Bailey	00995730	806/272-7383	22
Neal Elem Sch/*Bryan*/Brazos	04753481	979/209-3860	55
Neal Elem Sch/*San Antonio*/Bexar	00998445	210/738-9810	41
Nebbie Williams Elem Sch/*Rockwall*/Rockwall	04454130	972/772-0502	325
Neches Elem Jr High Sch/*Neches*/Anderson	00994504	903/584-3401	15
Neches High Sch/*Neches*/Anderson	00994516	903/584-3311	15
NECHES IND SCH DIST/NECHES/ANDERSON	00994499	903/584-3311	15
Ned E Williams Elem Sch/*Longview*/Gregg	11818074	903/803-5500	170
Nederland High Sch/*Nederland*/Jefferson	01033737	409/727-2741	243
NEDERLAND IND SCH DIST/NEDERLAND/JEFFERSON	01033660	409/724-2391	242
Needville Elem Sch/*Needville*/Fort Bend	01018361	979/793-4241	154
Needville High Sch/*Needville*/Fort Bend	01018373	979/793-4158	154
NEEDVILLE IND SCH DIST/NEEDVILLE/FORT BEND	01018347	979/793-4158	154
Needville Junior High Sch/*Needville*/Fort Bend	04912857	979/793-4250	154
Needville Middle Sch/*Needville*/Fort Bend	02128749	979/793-3027	154
Neff Early Learning Center/*Houston*/Harris	12170200	713/778-3470	194
Neff Elem Sch/*Houston*/Harris	01024528	713/556-9566	194
Negley Elem Sch/*Kyle*/Hays	10022739	512/268-8501	211
Neidig Elem Sch/*Elgin*/Bastrop	10001163	512/281-9702	24
Neil Armstrong Elem Sch/*San Antonio*/Bexar	00999463	210/623-8787	42
Nelda Sullivan Middle Sch/*Pasadena*/Harris	12170162	713/740-5420	199
Nell Burks Elem Sch/*McKinney*/Collin	01006306	469/302-6200	81
Nellie M Reddix Center/*San Antonio*/Bexar	00998201	210/397-2401	38
Nelson Early Chldhd Ed Ctr/*San Antonio*/Bexar	12305630	210/438-6555	41
Nelson Middle Sch/*Frisco*/Collin	12167268	469/633-4100	79
Nesmith Elem Sch/*Lavon*/Collin	11148374	972/843-6100	78
Netherland Alt Ed Sch/*Nederland*/Jefferson	04748993	409/727-5241	243
Nettie Baccus Elem Sch/*Granbury*/Hood	03007681	817/408-4300	230
Nettie Marshall Elem Sch/*Nacogdoches*/Nacogdoches	01043328	936/569-5062	298
New Boston High Sch/*New Boston*/Bowie	01001083	903/628-6551	49
NEW BOSTON IND SCH DIST/NEW BOSTON/BOWIE	01001069	903/628-2521	49
New Boston Middle Sch/*New Boston*/Bowie	01001095	903/628-6588	49
New Braunfels Chrn Aca-Lower/*New Braunfels*/Comal	02733954	830/629-6222	89
New Braunfels High Sch/*New Braunfels*/Comal	01007001	830/627-6000	89
New Braunfels HS 9th GR Ctr/*New Braunfels*/Comal	11822324	830/629-8600	89
NEW BRAUNFELS IND SCH DIST/NEW BRAUNFELS/COMAL	01006966	830/643-5700	88
New Braunfels Middle Sch/*New Braunfels*/Comal	01007013	830/627-6270	89
New Caney Elem Sch/*New Caney*/Montgomery	01042673	281/577-8720	294
New Caney High Sch/*New Caney*/Montgomery	01042685	281/577-2800	294
NEW CANEY IND SCH DIST/NEW CANEY/MONTGOMERY	01042661	281/577-8600	293
New Caney Middle Sch/*Porter*/Montgomery	10915576	281/577-8860	294
New Deal Elem Sch/*New Deal*/Lubbock	01039092	806/746-5849	271
New Deal High Sch/*New Deal*/Lubbock	01039107	806/746-5933	271
NEW DEAL IND SCH DIST/NEW DEAL/LUBBOCK	01039080	806/746-5833	271
New Deal Middle Sch/*New Deal*/Lubbock	03047265	806/746-6633	271
New Diana High Sch/*Diana*/Upshur	01057513	903/663-8001	376
NEW DIANA IND SCH DIST/DIANA/UPSHUR	01057484	903/663-8000	376
New Diana Middle Sch/*Diana*/Upshur	04034388	903/663-8002	376
New Frontiers Christian Acad/*Wills Point*/Van Zandt	11224148	903/873-2440	381
New Heights Christian Academy/*Houston*/Harris	04993198	713/861-9101	206
NEW HOME IND SCH DIST/NEW HOME/LYNN	01039274	806/924-7543	273
New Home Sch/*New Home*/Lynn	01039286	806/924-7543	273
New Hope Academy/*Lubbock*/Lubbock	12230229	806/863-7109	271
New Hope Christian Academy/*Plano*/Collin	12239861	972/656-9951	86
New Hope High Sch/*Leander*/Williamson	05102976	512/570-2200	397
New Horizons High Sch/*Joshua*/Johnson	04278675	817/202-2500	248
New Horizons Learning Center/*Greenville*/Hunt	03396200	903/457-2688	236
New Horizons Ranch Sch/*Goldthwaite*/Mills	02897586	325/938-5513	8
New Life Academy/*Euless*/Tarrant	12306397	817/267-1000	359
New Life Academy/*Lubbock*/Lubbock	02191667	806/763-0117	272
New Life Christian Academy/*Dallas*/Dallas	12166771	214/327-6522	115
New Life Christian Academy/*San Antonio*/Bexar	04993758	210/679-6001	45
New Pathways Center/*Harlingen*/Cameron	05096705	956/427-3250	65
New Star Sch/*Plano*/Collin	11222607	972/897-9217	86
NEW SUMMERFIELD IND SCH DIST/NEW SUMMERFLD/CHEROKEE	01005340	903/726-3306	73
New Summerfield Sch/*New Summerfld*/Cherokee	01005352	903/726-3306	73
New Tech High Sch at Waskow/*Belton*/Bell	04871461	254/215-2500	27
New Tech High Sch-Coppell/*Coppell*/Dallas	11132636	214/496-5900	98
New Tech HS at BF Darrell/*Dallas*/Dallas	02109834	214/932-7600	102
New Tech San Antonio High Sch/*San Antonio*/Bexar	11926023	210/978-7900	41
New Waverly Elem Sch/*New Waverly*/Walker	01058751	936/344-2900	383
New Waverly High Sch/*New Waverly*/Walker	01058749	936/344-6451	383
NEW WAVERLY IND SCH DIST/NEW WAVERLY/WALKER	01058737	936/344-6751	383
New Waverly Intermediate Sch/*New Waverly*/Walker	05342176	936/344-6601	383
New Waverly Junior High Sch/*New Waverly*/Walker	03047174	936/344-2246	384
New World Montessori Sch/*El Paso*/El Paso	05342542	915/593-8091	139
NEWCASTLE IND SCH DIST/NEWCASTLE/YOUNG	01062166	940/846-3531	406
Newcastle Sch/*Newcastle*/Young	01062178	940/846-3531	406

School Year 2019-2020 800-333-8802 TX-V53

DISTRICT & SCHOOL TELEPHONE INDEX

Market Data Retrieval

School/City/County DISTRICT/CITY/COUNTY	PID	TELEPHONE NUMBER	PAGE
Newcomer Center/*Arlington*/Tarrant	04808713	682/867-7100	344
Newell E Woolls Interm Sch/*Hondo*/Medina	04911932	830/426-7666	284
Newfound Academy/*Carrollton*/Dallas	11227097	214/390-1749	115
Newgulf Elem Sch/*Boling*/Wharton	01059561	979/657-2837	389
Newman Elem Sch/*El Paso*/El Paso	01015840	915/236-5825	133
Newman Elem Sch/*Laredo*/Webb	02109975	956/473-3800	388
Newman Int'l Acad-Arlington/*Arlington*/Tarrant	11704473	682/207-5175	8
Newman Int'l Acad-Cedar Hill/*Cedar Hill*/Dallas	12161991	972/293-5460	8
Newman Int'l Acad-Ft Worth/*Fort Worth*/Tarrant	12260987	817/655-2255	8
Newman Int'l Acad-Grace/*Arlington*/Tarrant	12260975	682/220-9210	8
Newman Int'l Acad-Mansfield/*Mansfield*/Tarrant	12260963	682/400-4010	8
Newman Smith High Sch/*Carrollton*/Dallas	01418266	972/968-5200	97
Newport Elem Sch/*Crosby*/Harris	02181595	281/328-9330	183
Newton Collins Elem Sch/*Austin*/Travis	12307925	512/386-3900	369
Newton Elem Sch/*Newton*/Newton	01043768	409/420-6600	301
Newton High Sch/*Newton*/Newton	01043782	409/420-6600	301
NEWTON IND SCH DIST/**NEWTON**/**NEWTON**	01043744	409/420-6600	301
Newton Middle Sch/*Newton*/Newton	01043770	409/420-6600	301
Newton Rayzor Elem Sch/*Denton*/Denton	01013282	940/369-3700	121
Neysa Callison Elem Sch/*Round Rock*/Williamson	11130860	512/704-0700	399
Nichols Elem Sch/*Frisco*/Collin	11820089	469/633-3950	79
Nichols Elem Sch/*San Antonio*/Bexar	05097759	210/397-4050	38
Nichols Intermediate Sch/*Jacksonville*/Cherokee	04932429	903/541-0213	73
Nichols Junior High Sch/*Arlington*/Tarrant	01051856	682/867-2600	344
Nichols-Saw Mill Elem Sch/*Magnolia*/Montgomery	05097632	281/252-2133	293
Nimitz 9th Grade Sch/*Houston*/Harris	04867226	281/209-8200	180
Nimitz Elem Sch/*Kerrville*/Kerr	01036117	830/257-2209	256
Nimitz High Sch/*Irving*/Dallas	01011272	972/600-5700	110
Nimitz Middle Sch/*Odessa*/Ector	01014767	432/456-0469	130
Nimitz Middle Sch/*San Antonio*/Bexar	00997855	210/356-5300	35
Nita Pearson Elem Sch/*Rowlett*/Dallas	05345439	972/463-7568	106
Nitsch Elem Sch/*Houston*/Harris	02110687	832/484-6400	197
NIXON-SMILEY CONS IND SCH DIST/**NIXON**/**GONZALES**	01019937	830/582-1536	164
Nixon-Smiley Elem Sch/*Smiley*/Gonzales	01019949	830/582-1536	164
Nixon-Smiley High Sch/*Nixon*/Gonzales	01019951	830/582-1536	164
Nixon-Smiley Middle Sch/*Nixon*/Gonzales	01019963	830/582-1536	164
Nocona Elem Sch/*Nocona*/Montague	01042362	940/825-3151	290
Nocona High Sch/*Nocona*/Montague	01042348	940/825-3264	290
NOCONA IND SCH DIST/**NOCONA**/**MONTAGUE**	01042336	940/825-3267	290
Nocona Middle Sch/*Nocona*/Montague	01042350	940/825-3121	290
Noel A Smith Elem Sch/*Frisco*/Collin	04744612	469/633-2200	79
Noel Elem Sch/*Odessa*/Ector	02126404	432/456-1249	130
Noel Grisham Middle Sch/*Austin*/Williamson	01530034	512/428-2650	399
Noemi Dominguez Elem Sch/*La Feria*/Cameron	01003988	956/797-8430	65
Nola Kathryn Wilson Elem Sch/*Crandall*/Kaufman	04454312	972/427-6040	251
Nolan Catholic High Sch/*Fort Worth*/Tarrant	01054377	817/457-2920	358
Nolan Creek Sch/*Belton*/Bell	12260999	254/939-4491	8
Nolan Middle Sch/*Killeen*/Bell	00996552	254/336-1150	28
Nolan Richardson Middle Sch/*El Paso*/El Paso	04806648	915/236-6650	135
Nolan Ryan Junior High Sch/*Pearland*/Brazoria	11070985	281/245-3210	51
Nolanville Elem Sch/*Nolanville*/Bell	00996564	254/336-2180	28
Noonan Elem Sch/*Alice*/Jim Wells	01034602	361/664-7591	245
NORDHEIM IND SCH DIST/**NORDHEIM**/**DE WITT**	01013751	361/938-5211	118
Nordheim Sch/*Nordheim*/De Witt	01013763	361/938-5211	118
Norma Dorsey Elem Sch/*Rowlett*/Dallas	04450976	972/463-5595	106
Norma J Paschal Elem Sch/*Schertz*/Guadalupe	05275781	210/619-4500	173
Norma Krueger Elem Sch/*Marion*/Guadalupe	01021497	830/914-1060	173
Norma Krueger Elem Sch-Karrer/*Marion*/Guadalupe	05343326	830/914-1065	172
Norman Elem Sch/*Austin*/Travis	01056466	512/414-2347	368
Norman Thomas Elem Sch/*Freer*/Duval	01809225	361/394-6800	128
Normandy Crossing Elem Sch/*Houston*/Harris	05274440	832/386-1600	187
Normangee Elem Sch/*Normangee*/Leon	01037666	936/396-9999	264
NORMANGEE IND SCH DIST/**NORMANGEE**/**LEON**	01037654	936/396-3111	264
Normangee Middle Sch/*Normangee*/Leon	11459642	936/396-3111	264
Normangee Senior High Sch/*Normangee*/Leon	11459654	936/396-6111	264
Norris Elem Sch/*Frisco*/Collin	12107000	469/633-4075	79
North Avenue Interm Sch/*Gonzales*/Gonzales	01019913	830/672-9557	164
North Belt Elem Sch/*Humble*/Harris	01026215	281/641-1300	196
North Belton Middle Sch/*Temple*/Bell	04035887	254/316-5200	27
North Bridge Elem Sch/*Weslaco*/Hidalgo	03393076	956/969-6810	225
North Central Texas Academy/*Granbury*/Hood	02153562	254/897-4822	231
North Creek Elem Sch/*Melissa*/Collin	10901135	972/837-4530	82
North Crowley 9th Grade Campus/*Fort Worth*/Tarrant	05271553	817/297-5896	348
North Crowley High Sch/*Fort Worth*/Tarrant	04807680	817/263-1250	348
North Dallas Adventist Academy/*Richardson*/Dallas	02850552	972/234-6322	115
North Dallas High Sch/*Dallas*/Dallas	01009499	972/925-1500	102
North Early Learning Center/*Orange*/Orange	01045845	409/882-5434	309
NORTH EAST IND SCH DIST/**SAN ANTONIO**/**BEXAR**	00997661	210/407-0000	34
North Elem Sch/*Breckenridge*/Stephens	01051363	254/559-6511	341
North Elem Sch/*Fort Worth*/Tarrant	01054224	817/367-1323	357
North Elem Sch/*Hallsville*/Harrison	01028495	903/668-5981	208
North Elem Sch/*Lamesa*/Dawson	01012915	806/872-5428	117
North Elem Sch/*Lubbock*/Lubbock	05027065	806/776-2700	271
North Euless Elem Sch/*Euless*/Tarrant	01053878	817/354-3505	354
North Forest High Sch/*Houston*/Harris	01026526	713/636-4300	189
North Forney High Sch/*Forney*/Kaufman	11465029	469/762-4210	252
North Garland High Sch/*Garland*/Dallas	01010632	972/675-3120	106
North Grammar Elem Sch/*Rio Grande Cy*/Starr	01051155	956/716-6618	340
North Heights Alt Sch/*Amarillo*/Potter	01047489	806/326-2850	318
North Heights Elem Sch/*Del Rio*/Val Verde	01058024	830/778-4777	379
North Hi Mount Elem Sch/*Fort Worth*/Tarrant	01053165	817/815-1500	351
NORTH HOPKINS IND SCH DIST/**SULPHUR SPGS**/**HOPKINS**	01031545	903/945-2192	231
North Hopkins Sch/*Sulphur Spgs*/Hopkins	01031557	903/945-2192	231
North Houston Early College HS/*Houston*/Harris	11152284	713/696-6168	192
North Joshua Elem Sch/*Burleson*/Johnson	04452364	817/426-7500	248
North Lamar High Sch/*Paris*/Lamar	01036662	903/737-2011	260
NORTH LAMAR IND SCH DIST/**PARIS**/**LAMAR**	01036636	903/737-2000	259
North Loop Christian Academy/*El Paso*/El Paso	04994192	915/859-8090	139
North Loop Elem Sch/*El Paso*/El Paso	01016480	915/434-2800	138
North Mesquite High Sch/*Mesquite*/Dallas	01011571	972/882-7900	111
North Oaks Middle Sch/*Haltom City*/Tarrant	01052135	817/547-4600	346
North Park Christian Academy/*N Richlnd Hls*/Tarrant	03380196	817/498-8456	359
North Plains Opportunity Ctr/*Dumas*/Moore	12033978	806/935-8774	295
North Pointe Elem Sch/*Houston*/Galveston	04365319	281/284-5900	159
North Richland Middle Sch/*N Richlnd Hls*/Tarrant	01052123	817/547-4200	346
North Ridge Elem Sch/*Lubbock*/Lubbock	02895198	806/793-6686	269
North Ridge Elem Sch/*N Richlnd Hls*/Tarrant	03052492	817/547-3200	346
North Ridge Middle Sch/*N Richlnd Hls*/Tarrant	03251894	817/547-5200	346
North Riverside Elem Sch/*Fort Worth*/Tarrant	04806789	817/744-5300	355
North Shore 10th Grade Ctr/*Houston*/Harris	12307999	832/386-4880	187
North Shore Elem Sch/*Houston*/Harris	01023500	832/386-4660	187
North Shore Middle Sch/*Houston*/Harris	01023524	832/386-2600	187
North Shore Ninth Grade Center/*Houston*/Harris	01023512	832/386-3400	187
North Shore Senior High Sch/*Houston*/Harris	04837788	832/386-4100	187
North Side High Sch/*Fort Worth*/Tarrant	01053177	817/814-4000	351
North Star Elem Sch/*El Paso*/El Paso	05097620	915/434-6700	138
North Texas Collegiate Acad-E/*Little Elm*/Denton	05010787	972/292-3562	8
North Texas Collegiate Acad-N/*Denton*/Denton	11014400	940/383-1972	8
North Texas Collegiate Acad-S/*Lewisville*/Denton	11014395	972/221-3564	8
North Texas Leadership Academy/*Keller*/Tarrant	12105480	817/562-2931	359
North West Head Start Center/*Wichita Falls*/Wichita	11551915	940/322-1905	392
NORTH ZULCH IND SCH DIST/**NORTH ZULCH**/**MADISON**	01040637	936/241-7100	274
North Zulch Sch/*North Zulch*/Madison	01040649	936/241-7100	274
Northampton Elem Sch/*Spring*/Harris	01026356	832/484-5550	197
Northbrook Elem Sch/*Fort Worth*/Tarrant	11072775	817/232-0086	349
Northbrook High Sch/*Houston*/Harris	01027221	713/251-2800	201
Northbrook Middle Sch/*Houston*/Harris	03397905	713/251-4100	201
Northeast Christian Academy/*El Paso*/El Paso	02152348	915/755-1155	139
Northeast Early Clg High Sch/*Austin*/Travis	01056296	512/414-2523	368

Texas School Directory
DISTRICT & SCHOOL TELEPHONE INDEX

School/City/County DISTRICT/CITY/COUNTY	PID	TELEPHONE NUMBER	PAGE
Northern Hills Elem Sch/*San Antonio*/Bexar	02126167	210/407-5200	35
Northgate Crossing Elem Sch/*Spring*/Harris	11077244	281/891-8780	202
Northlake Elem Sch/*Dallas*/Dallas	01011806	469/593-2300	112
Northlake Elem Sch/*Garland*/Dallas	01382928	972/494-8359	106
Northland Christian Sch/*Houston*/Harris	02153445	281/440-1060	206
Northline Elem Sch/*Houston*/Harris	01026045	713/696-2890	191
Northpointe Intermediate Sch/*Tomball*/Harris	05279385	281/357-3020	203
Northrich Elem Sch/*Richardson*/Dallas	01011818	469/593-6200	112
Northside Alt Middle Sch South/*San Antonio*/Bexar	04503949	210/397-2070	38
Northside Alt Middle Sch-North/*San Antonio*/Bexar	04774710	210/397-2070	38
Northside Alternative High Sch/*San Antonio*/Bexar	02226432	210/397-7080	38
Northside Baptist Sch/*Victoria*/Victoria	01481287	361/578-1568	383
Northside Christian Academy/*Carthage*/Panola	04992924	903/693-7700	311
Northside Elem Sch/*Angleton*/Brazoria	01001514	979/864-8006	52
Northside Elem Sch/*Cleveland*/Liberty	01037757	281/592-4628	265
Northside Elem Sch/*Desoto*/Dallas	01010278	972/224-6709	104
Northside Elem Sch/*El Campo*/Wharton	01059640	979/543-5812	389
Northside Elem Sch/*Waxahachie*/Ellis	01015319	972/923-4610	142
Northside High Sch/*Houston*/Harris	01025974	713/226-4900	192
NORTHSIDE IND SCH DIST/**SAN ANTONIO**/**BEXAR**	00998017	210/397-8500	36
NORTHSIDE IND SCH DIST/**VERNON**/**WILBARGER**	01060534	940/552-2551	393
Northside Interm Sch/*Henderson*/Rusk	01878446	903/655-5300	327
Northside Primary Sch/*Palestine*/Anderson	00994542	903/731-8020	15
Northside Sch/*Vernon*/Wilbarger	01060546	940/552-2551	393
Northstar Sch/*Arlington*/Tarrant	11157002	817/478-5852	359
Northwest Crossing Elem Sch/*San Antonio*/Bexar	02178354	210/397-0600	38
Northwest Early College HS/*El Paso*/El Paso	11080497	915/877-1700	132
Northwest Elem Sch/*Austin*/Travis	02896075	512/594-4400	372
Northwest Elem Sch/*Brownwood*/Brown	01002520	325/646-0707	58
Northwest Elem Sch/*Hereford*/Deaf Smith	01013048	806/363-7660	119
Northwest High Sch/*Justin*/Denton	01013543	817/215-0200	125
NORTHWEST IND SCH DIST/**JUSTIN**/**DENTON**	01013517	817/215-0000	124
Northwest Special Program Ctr/*Justin*/Denton	03473145	817/215-0900	125
Northwood Elem Sch/*San Antonio*/Bexar	00997840	210/407-5400	35
Northwood Hills Elem Sch/*Dallas*/Dallas	01011820	469/593-4300	113
Northwood Montessori Sch/*Houston*/Harris	01601827	281/444-9433	206
Norwood Elem Sch/*Burleson*/Johnson	01522623	817/245-3400	247
Notre Dame Catholic Sch/*Wichita Falls*/Wichita	01054389	940/692-6041	393
Notre Dame Sch/*Dallas*/Dallas	01012496	214/720-3911	114
Notre Dame Sch/*Kerrville*/Kerr	00999918	830/257-6707	256
Nottingham Country Elem Sch/*Katy*/Harris	02130223	281/237-5500	152
Nottingham Elem Sch/*Houston*/Harris	01027233	713/251-6400	201
Nova Academy Cedar Hill/*Cedar Hill*/Dallas	12261008	972/291-1900	8
Nova Academy Prichard/*Dallas*/Dallas	11935361	972/808-7470	8
Nova Academy Scyene/*Dallas*/Dallas	05368065	214/381-3088	8
Nova Academy-Prichard/*Dallas*/Dallas	04931786	972/808-7470	8
Novus Academy/*Grapevine*/Tarrant	11224473	817/488-4555	359
NUECES CANYON CONS IND SD/**BARKSDALE**/**EDWARDS**	01014872	830/234-3514	131
Nueces Canyon Elem Sch/*Camp Wood*/Edwards	01014884	830/597-3218	131
Nueces Canyon Jr Sr High Sch/*Barksdale*/Edwards	01014896	830/234-3524	131
Nursery Elem Sch/*Victoria*/Victoria	01058426	361/575-6882	382
NURSERY ISD SCH DIST/**VICTORIA**/**VICTORIA**	01058414	361/575-6882	382
Nye Elem Sch/*Laredo*/Webb	01059494	956/473-3700	388
Nyos Charter Sch-Lamar Campus/*Austin*/Travis	05286508	512/583-6967	8
Nyos Charter School-M M Campus/*Austin*/Travis	04814451	512/275-1593	8

O

School/City/County DISTRICT/CITY/COUNTY	PID	TELEPHONE NUMBER	PAGE
O A Peterson Elem Sch/*Fort Worth*/Denton	11104081	817/698-5000	125
O C Taylor Elem Sch/*Colleyville*/Tarrant	02895095	817/305-4870	353
O D Wyatt High Sch/*Fort Worth*/Tarrant	01053189	817/815-8000	351
O G Wiederstein Elem Sch/*Cibolo*/Guadalupe	01021629	210/619-4550	173
O H Herman Middle Sch/*Van Vleck*/Matagorda	01041045	979/245-6401	276
O H Stowe Elem Sch/*Haltom City*/Tarrant	01052147	817/547-2400	346
O Henry Elem Sch/*Garland*/Dallas	01011844	469/593-8200	113
O Henry Middle Sch/*Austin*/Travis	01056478	512/414-3229	369
O L Slaton Middle Sch/*Lubbock*/Lubbock	01038907	806/219-4400	270
O M Roberts Elem Sch/*Lake Jackson*/Brazoria	01001667	979/730-7205	52
O P Norman Junior High Sch/*Kaufman*/Kaufman	01035620	972/932-2410	252
O V Calvert Elem Sch/*Houston*/Harris	03399812	281/985-6360	180
O'Banion Middle Sch/*Garland*/Dallas	01010644	972/279-6103	106
O'Brien Middle Sch/*O Brien*/Knox	01534016	940/657-3731	258
O'Bryant Intermediate Sch/*Bellville*/Austin	04354243	979/865-3671	22
O'Bryant Primary Sch/*Bellville*/Austin	00995560	979/865-5907	22
O'Connell High Sch/*Galveston*/Galveston	01028031	409/765-5534	162
O'Connor Elem Sch/*Victoria*/Victoria	01058555	361/788-9572	382
O'Dell Elem Sch/*Celina*/Collin	12230865	469/742-9106	78
O'Donnell Elem Sch/*Odonnell*/Lynn	01039327	806/428-3244	273
O'DONNELL IND SCH DIST/**ODONNELL**/**LYNN**	01039315	806/428-3241	273
O'Donnell Intermediate Sch/*Fabens*/El Paso	01016167	915/765-2640	135
O'Donnell Jr Sr High Sch/*Odonnell*/Lynn	01039339	806/428-3247	273
O'Donnell Middle Sch/*Houston*/Harris	04015459	281/495-6000	182
O'Shea Keleher Elem Sch/*El Paso*/El Paso	03009823	915/937-7200	136
Oak Creek Elem Sch/*New Braunfels*/Comal	11450933	830/837-7200	88
Oak Crest Elem Sch/*San Antonio*/Bexar	00997037	210/648-9484	31
Oak Crest Private Sch/*Carrollton*/Dallas	10968597	214/483-5400	115
Oak Dale Elem Sch/*Amarillo*/Potter	01047374	806/326-4850	318
Oak Forest Elem Sch/*Houston*/Harris	01024205	713/613-2536	192
Oak Forest Elem Sch/*Humble*/Harris	04367599	281/641-2800	196
Oak Forest Elem Sch/*Vidor*/Orange	01045766	409/951-8860	309
Oak Grove Elem Sch/*Brownfield*/Terry	01055137	806/637-6455	362
Oak Grove Elem Sch/*San Antonio*/Bexar	00997879	210/407-5600	35
Oak Hill Academy/*Dallas*/Dallas	04992819	214/353-8804	115
Oak Hill Elem Sch/*Austin*/Travis	01056480	512/414-2336	367
Oak Hills Junior High Sch/*Montgomery*/Montgomery	04801935	936/276-4300	293
Oak Hills Terrace Elem Sch/*San Antonio*/Bexar	00998251	210/397-0550	38
Oak Meadow Elem Sch/*San Antonio*/Bexar	03396315	210/407-5800	35
Oak Meadows Elem Sch/*Austin*/Travis	11434769	512/278-4175	371
Oak Park Special Emphasis Sch/*Corp Christi*/Nueces	01044592	361/878-2120	304
Oak Point Elem Sch/*Oak Point*/Denton	11074503	972/947-9455	124
Oak Ridge Elem Sch/*Conroe*/Montgomery	01042518	832/592-5900	292
Oak Ridge Elem Sch/*Lubbock*/Lubbock	11445847	806/794-5200	269
Oak Ridge High Sch/*Conroe*/Montgomery	02126870	832/592-5300	292
Oak Ridge HS 9th Grade Campus/*Conroe*/Montgomery	11552464	281/465-5000	292
Oak Run Middle Sch/*New Braunfels*/Comal	03391092	830/627-6400	89
Oak Springs Elem Sch/*Austin*/Travis	01056492	512/414-4413	368
Oak Woods Sch/*Granbury*/Hood	03325691	817/408-4750	230
Oakcrest Intermediate Sch/*Cypress*/Harris	12107830	281/357-3033	203
Oakhurst Elem Sch/*Fort Worth*/Tarrant	01053206	817/814-9500	351
Oakland Elem Sch/*Richmond*/Fort Bend	10027909	281/634-3730	150
Oaklawn Elem Sch/*Fort Worth*/Tarrant	01053218	817/815-9100	351
Oakley Elem Sch/*New Caney*/Montgomery	11719246	281/577-5970	294
Oakmont Elem Sch/*Fort Worth*/Tarrant	04454207	817/370-5610	348
Oaks Adventist Christian Sch/*Cypress*/Harris	11229629	713/896-0071	206
Oaks Elem Sch/*Humble*/Harris	02108634	281/641-1890	196
Oakview Primary Sch/*New Boston*/Bowie	11527574	903/628-8900	49
Oakwood Elem Sch/*Oakwood*/Leon	01037692	903/545-2106	265
OAKWOOD IND SCH DIST/**OAKWOOD**/**LEON**	01037680	903/545-2666	264
Oakwood Intermediate Sch/*College Sta*/Brazos	02111241	979/764-5530	55
Oakwood Jr Sr High Sch/*Oakwood*/Leon	01037707	903/545-2140	265
Oakwood Terrace Elem Sch/*Euless*/Tarrant	01053880	817/354-3386	354
Oates Elem Sch/*Houston*/Harris	01025649	713/671-3800	190
Obadiah Knight Elem Sch/*Dallas*/Dallas	01009542	972/749-5300	102
Obra D Tompkins High Sch/*Katy*/Harris	11925897	281/234-1000	152
Ochoa/Milam Steam Academy/*Grand Prairie*/Dallas	01010838	972/262-7131	108
Odem Elem Sch/*Odem*/San Patricio	01049712	361/368-8121	331
Odem High Sch/*Odem*/San Patricio	01049724	361/368-8121	331
Odem Intermediate Sch/*Odem*/San Patricio	12310491	361/368-8121	331
Odem Junior High Sch/*Odem*/San Patricio	01049736	361/368-8121	331
ODEM-EDROY IND SCH DIST/**ODEM**/**SAN PATRICIO**	01049700	361/368-8121	331
Odessa Career Tch Early Clg HS/*Odessa*/Ector	12105753	432/456-6409	130
Odessa Christian Sch/*Odessa*/Ector	01480063	432/362-6311	131
Odessa High Sch/*Odessa*/Ector	01014779	432/456-0029	130
Odessa Kilpatrick Elem Sch/*Katy*/Harris	05273628	281/237-7600	152
Odom Academy/*Beaumont*/Jefferson	01034183	409/617-5925	242
Odom Elem Sch/*Austin*/Travis	01056507	512/414-2388	367
Odyssey Academy/*Galveston*/Galveston	04892740	409/750-9289	8
Odyssey Sch/*Austin*/Travis	04891289	512/472-2262	373

DISTRICT & SCHOOL TELEPHONE INDEX

Market Data Retrieval

School/City/County DISTRICT/CITY/COUNTY	PID	TELEPHONE NUMBER	PAGE
OGLESBY IND SCH DIST/OGLESBY/ CORYELL	01007740	254/456-2271	93
Oglesby Sch/Oglesby/Coryell	01007752	254/456-2271	93
Oilton Elem Sch/Bruni/Webb	01059171	361/586-5415	388
Ojeda Middle Sch/Austin/Travis	05301744	512/386-3500	369
Old Settlers Elem Sch/Flower Mound/Denton	04288759	469/713-5993	123
Old Town Elem Sch/Round Rock/Williamson	03052337	512/428-7600	399
Old Union Elem Sch/Southlake/Tarrant	04946145	817/949-4600	347
OLFEN IND SCH DIST/ROWENA/ RUNNELS	01048873	325/442-4301	327
Olfen Sch/Rowena/Runnels	01048885	325/442-4301	327
Olga Kohlberg Elem Sch/El Paso/El Paso	04757401	915/236-2850	134
Olga Leonard Elem Sch/Katy/Harris	12367418	281/234-4600	152
Olive Tree Montessori Academy/Fort Worth/ Tarrant	12043533	817/460-5000	8
Oliveira Middle Sch/Brownsville/Cameron	01877351	956/548-8530	64
Oliver E Clift Elem Sch/Waxahachie/Ellis	11718709	972/923-4720	142
Oliver Elem Sch/Stamford/Jones	01035333	325/307-3765	250
Oliver W Holmes Academy/Dallas/Dallas	01009566	972/925-8500	102
Oliver Wendell Holmes High Sch/San Antonio/ Bexar	00998263	210/397-7000	38
Olivero Garza Elem Sch/Mission/Hidalgo	02884125	956/580-5353	224
Olle Middle Sch/Houston/Harris	01023055	281/983-8455	182
Ollie Ogrady Elem Sch/Mission/Hidalgo	03009926	956/323-4200	222
Ollie Perry Storm Elem Sch/San Antonio/ Bexar	00999255	210/978-8005	41
Olmito Elem Sch/Brownsville/Cameron	05356141	956/233-3950	66
Olmos Elem Sch/San Antonio/Bexar	00997881	210/407-6000	35
Olney Elem Sch/Olney/Young	01062207	940/564-5608	406
Olney High Sch/Olney/Young	01062219	940/564-5637	406
OLNEY IND SCH DIST/OLNEY/YOUNG	01062192	940/564-3519	406
Olney Junior High Sch/Olney/Young	01062221	940/564-3517	406
Olsen Elem Sch/Port Aransas/Nueces	01809756	361/749-1212	305
Olsen Park Elem Sch/Amarillo/Potter	01047386	806/326-4900	318
Olson Elem Sch/Allen/Collin	11451963	972/562-1800	77
Olton High Sch/Olton/Lamb	01036997	806/285-2691	261
OLTON IND SCH DIST/OLTON/LAMB	01036973	806/285-2641	261
Olton Junior High Sch/Olton/Lamb	01037006	806/285-2681	261
Olympia Elem Sch/Universal Cty/Bexar	02109949	210/945-5113	33
Onalaska Elem Sch/Onalaska/Polk	01809811	936/646-1010	317
ONALASKA IND SCH DIST/ONALASKA/ POLK	01809809	936/646-1000	317
Onalaska Jr Sr High Sch/Onalaska/Polk	03391406	936/646-1020	317
Open Doors Christian Academy/Gun Barrel Cy/ Henderson	04025129	903/887-3621	215
Opportunity Awareness Center/Katy/Harris	02045410	281/237-6350	152
Options Academic High Sch/Texarkana/Bowie	04920490	903/793-5632	50
Options High Sch/El Paso/El Paso	10911685	915/937-1300	136
Oralia R Rodriguez Elem Sch/Seguin/ Guadalupe	11589807	830/401-8774	174
Oran M Roberts Elem Sch/Dallas/Dallas	01009554	972/749-8700	102
Orange Grove Elem & Inter Sch/Orange Grove/ Jim Wells	03008776	361/384-9358	245
Orange Grove Elem Sch/Houston/Harris	01022934	281/985-6540	180
Orange Grove High Sch/Orange Grove/ Jim Wells	01034705	361/384-2330	245
ORANGE GROVE IND SCH DIST/ ORANGE GROVE/JIM WELLS	01034688	361/384-2495	245
Orange Grove Jr High Sch/Orange Grove/ Jim Wells	01523732	361/384-2323	245
Orange Grove Primary Sch/Orange Grove/ Jim Wells	01034690	361/384-2316	245
Orangefield Elem Sch/Orange/Orange	01045728	409/735-5346	309
Orangefield High Sch/Orange/Orange	01045742	409/735-3851	309
ORANGEFIELD IND SCH DIST/ ORANGE/ORANGE	01045704	409/735-5337	309
Orangefield Junior High Sch/Orange/Orange	01045730	409/735-6737	309
Oratory Academy & Athenaeum/Pharr/Hidalgo	02760646	956/781-3056	226
Ore City Elem Sch/Ore City/Upshur	01057537	903/968-3300	377
Ore City High Sch/Ore City/Upshur	01057549	903/968-3300	377
ORE CITY IND SCH DIST/ORE CITY/ UPSHUR	01057525	903/968-3300	376
Ore City Middle Sch/Ore City/Upshur	03047289	903/968-3300	377
Orr Elem Sch/Tyler/Smith	01050917	903/262-2400	338
Ortega Elem Sch/Austin/Travis	01056519	512/414-4417	367
Ortiz Elem Sch/Abilene/Taylor	04015320	325/671-4945	360
Ortiz Elem Sch/Brownsville/Cameron	01003500	956/698-1100	64
Ortiz Middle Sch/Houston/Harris	05099317	713/845-5650	190
Osborne Elem Sch/Houston/Harris	01024217	281/405-2525	191
Oticel Parker Elem Sch/Houston/Harris	04367563	281/233-8930	180
Otis Brown Elem Sch/Irving/Dallas	01011284	972/600-4000	110
Otis Spears Elem Sch/Frisco/Collin	05092632	469/633-2900	79

School/City/County DISTRICT/CITY/COUNTY	PID	TELEPHONE NUMBER	PAGE
Otto Middle Sch/Plano/Collin	11554802	469/752-8500	83
Ouida Springer Elem Sch/Rockwall/Rockwall	05351622	972/772-7160	325
Our Lady of Fatima Sch/Galena Park/Harris	01028043	713/674-5832	204
Our Lady of Fatima Sch/Texas City/ Galveston	01028055	409/945-3326	162
Our Lady of Grace Academy/Pleasanton/ Atascosa	11818787	830/569-8073	21
Our Lady of Guadalupe Sch/Houston/Harris	01028067	713/224-6904	204
Our Lady of Guadalupe Sch/Laredo/Webb	01045261	956/722-3915	388
Our Lady of Lourdes Cath Sch/Hitchcock/ Galveston	01028081	409/925-3224	162
Our Lady of Mt Carmel Elem Sch/Houston/ Harris	01028093	713/643-0676	204
Our Lady of Perpetual Help Sch/Corp Christi/ Nueces	01045273	361/991-3305	306
Our Lady of Perpetual Help Sch/Dallas/ Dallas	01012513	214/351-3396	114
Our Lady of Refuge Sch/Eagle Pass/Maverick	00999944	830/773-3531	277
Our Lady of Sorrows Sch/McAllen/Hidalgo	01004425	956/686-3651	226
Our Lady of the Gulf Cath Sch/Port Lavaca/ Calhoun	04467826	361/552-6140	62
Our Lady of the Hills Cath HS/Kerrville/ Kerr	05286390	830/895-0501	256
Our Lady of the Rosary Sch/Corp Christi/ Nueces	11532658	361/939-9847	306
Our Lady of Victory Sch/Fort Worth/Tarrant	01054391	817/924-5123	358
Our Lady of Victory Sch/Victoria/Victoria	00999968	361/575-5391	383
Our Lady Queen of Peace Sch/Richwood/ Brazoria	02903551	979/265-3909	54
Our Lady-Perpetual Help Sch/Selma/ Guadalupe	00999932	210/651-6811	174
Our Redeemer Lutheran Sch/Dallas/Dallas	01012288	214/368-1371	116
Our Savior Lutheran Sch/Houston/Harris	01027702	713/290-8277	206
Outley Elem Sch/Houston/Harris	04033009	281/584-0655	182
Overton Elem Sch/Austin/Travis	10901745	512/841-9300	368
Overton Elem Sch/Lubbock/Lubbock	01038830	806/219-6300	270
Overton Elem Sch/Overton/Rusk	01049164	903/834-6144	328
OVERTON IND SCH DIST/OVERTON/ RUSK	01049152	903/834-6145	328
Overton Ray Elem Sch/Burkburnett/Wichita	01059951	940/569-5253	391
Overton Secondary Sch/Overton/Rusk	01049176	903/834-6143	328
Oveta Culp Hobby Elem Sch/Fort Hood/Bell	05347815	254/336-6500	28
Ovilla Christian Sch/Red Oak/Ellis	04881844	972/617-1177	143
Owen Elem Sch/The Colony/Denton	03010482	469/713-5950	123
Owen Goodnight Middle Sch/San Marcos/Hays	01029140	512/393-6550	212
Owens Elem Sch/Houston/Harris	02201547	281/463-5915	185
Owens Elem Sch/Tyler/Smith	02846264	903/262-2175	338
Owens Intermediate Sch/Houston/Harris	04285109	281/983-8466	182
Oyster Creek Elem Sch/Sugar Land/Fort Bend	04851033	281/634-5910	151
Ozona Elem Sch/Ozona/Crockett	01007879	325/392-5501	94
Ozona High Sch/Ozona/Crockett	01007867	325/392-5501	94
Ozona Middle Sch/Ozona/Crockett	01007881	325/392-5501	94

P

School/City/County DISTRICT/CITY/COUNTY	PID	TELEPHONE NUMBER	PAGE
P E Wallace Middle Sch/Mt Pleasant/Titus	01055424	903/575-2040	364
P H Greene Elem Sch/Webster/Galveston	01523691	281/284-5000	159
P M Akin Elem Sch/Wylie/Collin	03052911	972/429-3400	85
Pace Academy/Carthage/Panola	12312774	903/694-7554	311
Pace Alternative Campus/Longview/Gregg	11718761	903/295-5130	170
Pace Center/Pearland/Brazoria	05070268	281/412-1599	53
Pace Sch/Pflugerville/Travis	11544405	512/594-1900	372
Paciano Prada Elem Sch/Laredo/Webb	04287822	956/473-3500	388
Packsaddle Elem Sch/Kingsland/Llano	04913423	325/388-8129	268
Padron Elem Sch/Austin/Travis	12035213	512/841-9600	368
PADUCAH IND SCH DIST/PADUCAH/ COTTLE	01007776	806/492-3524	93
Paducah Sch/Paducah/Cottle	01007805	806/492-2009	93
Page Middle Sch/San Antonio/Bexar	00999267	210/228-1230	41
Paige Elem Sch/Houston/Harris	01025807	713/696-2855	191
PAINT CREEK IND SCH DIST/ HASKELL/HASKELL	01028914	940/864-2471	210
Paint Creek Sch/Haskell/Haskell	01028926	940/864-2471	210
PAINT ROCK IND SCH DIST/ PAINT ROCK/CONCHO	01007245	325/732-4314	90
Paint Rock Sch/Paint Rock/Concho	01007257	325/732-4314	90
Palacios High Sch/Palacios/Matagorda	01040948	361/972-2571	275
PALACIOS IND SCH DIST/PALACIOS/ MATAGORDA	01040912	361/972-5491	275
Palacios Junior High Sch/Palacios/ Matagorda	01040950	361/972-2417	275
Palestine High Sch/Palestine/Anderson	00994578	903/731-8005	15

TX-V56　　　800-333-8802　　　School Year 2019-2020

Texas School Directory
DISTRICT & SCHOOL TELEPHONE INDEX

School/City/County DISTRICT/CITY/COUNTY	PID	TELEPHONE NUMBER	PAGE
PALESTINE IND SCH DIST/PALESTINE/ ANDERSON	00994528	903/731-8000	15
Palestine Jr High Sch/*Palestine*/Anderson	02200373	903/731-8008	15
Palm Elem Sch/*Austin*/Travis	03008659	512/414-2545	367
Palm Grove Elem Sch/*Brownsville*/Cameron	01418230	956/982-3850	64
Palm Heights Baptist Sch/*San Antonio*/Bexar	02727814	210/923-8600	45
Palm Tree Academy/*El Paso*/El Paso	12314162	915/229-2190	139
Palmer Elem Sch/*Missouri City*/Fort Bend	02857378	281/634-4760	151
Palmer Elem Sch/*Palmer*/Ellis	01015228	972/449-3132	142
Palmer High Sch/*Palmer*/Ellis	01015230	972/449-3487	142
PALMER IND SCH DIST/PALMER/ELLIS	01015216	972/449-3389	141
Palmer Middle Sch/*Palmer*/Ellis	03047241	972/449-3319	142
Palmer-Laakso Elem Sch/*San Benito*/Cameron	04452663	956/254-5121	66
Palmview High Sch/*Mission*/Hidalgo	05100954	956/323-2880	220
Palo Alto Elem Sch/*San Antonio*/Bexar	00999475	210/977-7125	42
Palo Alto Middle Sch/*Killeen*/Bell	04368775	254/336-1200	28
Palo Duro High Sch/*Amarillo*/Potter	01047398	806/326-2400	318
Palo Pinto Elem Sch/*Palo Pinto*/Palo Pinto	01046112	940/659-2745	310
PALO PINTO IND SCH DIST 906/ PALO PINTO/PALO PINTO	01046100	940/659-2745	310
Paloma Creek Elem Sch/*Aubrey*/Denton	10909137	972/347-7300	121
Pampa High Sch/*Pampa*/Gray	01020194	806/669-4800	165
PAMPA IND SCH DIST/PAMPA/GRAY	01020132	806/669-4700	165
Pampa Junior High Sch/*Pampa*/Gray	01020182	806/669-4900	165
Pampa Learning Center/*Pampa*/Gray	03394056	806/669-4750	165
Panda Path Sch/*Houston*/Harris	04949850	713/251-8000	201
Panhandle Elem Sch/*Panhandle*/Carson	01004607	806/537-3579	69
Panhandle High Sch/*Panhandle*/Carson	01004619	806/537-3851	69
PANHANDLE IND SCH DIST/PANHANDLE/ CARSON	01004592	806/537-3568	69
Panhandle Junior High Sch/*Panhandle*/Carson	01004621	806/537-3541	69
Panola Charter HS/*Carthage*/Panola	04930366	903/693-6355	9
Panola Early College High Sch/*Carthage*/ Panola	11834391	903/693-6355	9
Pantego Christian Academy/*Arlington*/ Tarrant	02123531	817/460-3315	359
Pantego Christian Academy/*Mansfield*/ Tarrant	11224667	817/522-5900	359
PANTHER CREEK CONS IND SD/ VOSS/COLEMAN	01005950	325/357-4449	76
Panther Creek Sch/*Voss*/Coleman	01005962	325/357-4449	76
Paradise Elem Sch/*Paradise*/Wise	01061734	940/969-5046	403
Paradise High Sch/*Paradise*/Wise	04020791	940/969-5010	403
PARADISE IND SCH DIST/PARADISE/ WISE	01061722	940/969-2501	403
Paradise Intermediate Sch/*Paradise*/Wise	04866428	940/969-5032	403
Paradise Junior High Sch/*Paradise*/Wise	04431073	940/969-5034	403
Paragon Prep Middle Sch/*Austin*/Travis	04846624	512/459-5040	373
Paramount Terrace Elem Sch/*Amarillo*/Potter	01047403	806/326-4950	318
Paredes Elem Sch/*Brownsville*/Cameron	04945115	956/574-5582	64
Paredes Middle Sch/*Austin*/Travis	04904264	512/841-6800	369
Paris High Sch/*Paris*/Lamar	01036753	903/737-7400	260
PARIS IND SCH DIST/PARIS/LAMAR	01036698	903/737-7473	260
Paris Junior High Sch/*Paris*/Lamar	01036777	903/737-7434	260
Parish Episcopal Sch/*Dallas*/Dallas	01012290	972/239-8011	116
Parish Sch/*Houston*/Harris	02757156	713/467-4696	206
Park Crest Elem Sch/*Garland*/Dallas	01010656	972/926-2571	106
Park Crest Middle Sch/*Pflugerville*/Travis	04363543	512/594-2400	372
Park Elem Sch/*El Paso*/El Paso	03399874	915/236-5975	134
Park Glen Elem Sch/*Fort Worth*/Tarrant	03319006	817/744-5400	355
Park Lakes Elem Sch/*Humble*/Harris	10028616	281/641-3200	196
Park Meadows Academy/*Corsicana*/Navarro	12174144	903/872-2391	300
Park Place Elem Sch/*Houston*/Harris	01025663	713/845-7458	190
Park Row Chrn Academy/*Arlington*/Tarrant	02775316	817/277-1021	359
Park View Intermediate Sch/*Pasadena*/Harris	01026801	713/740-0460	199
Park Village Elem Sch/*San Antonio*/Bexar	00997659	210/637-4890	33
Parkdale Elem Sch/*Waco*/McLennan	01040352	254/772-2170	282
Parker Elem Sch/*Galveston*/Galveston	01019183	409/761-6600	160
Parker Elem Sch/*Houston*/Harris	01024956	713/726-3634	194
Parker Elem Sch/*Midland*/Midland	02199968	432/240-7600	286
Parkhill Junior High Sch/*Dallas*/Dallas	01881857	469/593-5600	113
Parkland Elem Sch/*El Paso*/El Paso	01016492	915/434-6600	138
Parkland High Sch/*El Paso*/El Paso	01016519	915/434-6000	138
Parkland Middle Sch/*El Paso*/El Paso	01016507	915/434-6300	138
Parkland Pre-K Center/*El Paso*/El Paso	11919381	915/435-7800	138
Parks Elem Sch/*Pasadena*/Harris	01026813	713/740-0680	199
Parkside Baptist Academy/*Mesquite*/Dallas	11235367	972/613-7833	116
Parkside Elem Sch/*Georgetown*/Williamson	11130779	512/570-7100	397
Parkview Christian Academy/*Waco*/McLennan	02153938	254/753-0159	283
Parkview Elem Sch/*Fort Worth*/Tarrant	02105412	817/744-5500	355
Parkview Elem Sch/*Fort Worth*/Tarrant	11072763	817/237-5121	349
Parkview School-Levelland/*Levelland*/Mills	12166238	806/568-1420	288
Parkview School-Lubbock/*Lubbock*/Mills	12166226	806/568-1420	288
Parkway Elem Sch/*Fort Worth*/Tarrant	04282341	817/568-5710	348
Parkway Elem Sch/*Lewisville*/Denton	04364420	469/713-5979	124
Parkway Elem Sch/*Longview*/Gregg	01021174	903/295-5151	170
Parkwood Elem Sch/*Pasadena*/Harris	01023392	832/668-8200	186
Parkwood Hill Intermediate Sch/*Fort Worth*/ Tarrant	04921602	817/744-4000	355
Parmer Lane Elem Sch/*Austin*/Travis	02178304	512/594-4000	372
Parnell Elem Sch/*Jasper*/Jasper	01033256	409/384-2212	241
Parsons Elem Sch/*Lubbock*/Lubbock	01038610	806/219-6400	270
Parsons Pre-K Sch/*Garland*/Dallas	10008109	972/675-8065	106
Pasadena Classical Academy/*Pasadena*/Harris	11925196	281/372-8999	9
Pasadena High Sch/*Pasadena*/Harris	01026825	713/740-0310	199
PASADENA IND SCH DIST/PASADENA/ HARRIS	01026631	713/740-0000	198
Pasadena Memorial High Sch/*Pasadena*/Harris	05273408	713/740-0390	199
Paso Del Norte Sch/*El Paso*/El Paso	05272301	915/937-6200	136
Pasodale Elem Sch/*El Paso*/El Paso	01016521	915/434-8500	138
Pat & Katherine Fowler Mid Sch/*Plano*/ Collin	10912691	469/633-5050	79
Pat Cooper Elem Sch/*Georgetown*/Williamson	02223026	512/943-5060	395
Pat Neff Middle Sch/*San Antonio*/Bexar	00998275	210/397-4100	38
Pat Reynolds Elem Sch/*Houston*/Harris	01027506	281/891-8240	202
Pathfinder Achievement Center/*Garland*/ Dallas	01545223	972/494-8520	106
Pathways 3H Campus/*Mountain Home*/Kerr	12362640	512/560-8132	9
Pathways Academic Campus/*Killeen*/Bell	03474618	254/336-7250	28
Pathways Alt Learning Center/*Beaumont*/ Jefferson	03394525	409/617-5206	242
Pathways High Sch/*Denison*/Grayson	04453186	903/462-7150	166
Patricia J Blattman Elem Sch/*San Antonio*/ Bexar	05273422	210/397-4600	38
Patricia Paetow High Sch/*Katy*/Harris	12231259	281/234-4900	152
Patricia S Garza Elem Sch/*Donna*/Hidalgo	04868012	956/464-1886	215
Patricio Perez Elem Sch/*Mission*/Hidalgo	04868634	956/323-2450	220
Patrick Henry Middle Sch/*Houston*/Harris	01026057	713/696-2650	189
Patsy Sommer Elem Sch/*Austin*/Williamson	11130858	512/704-0600	399
Patterson Elem Sch/*Conroe*/Montgomery	12033033	936/709-4300	292
Patterson Elem Sch/*Houston*/Harris	01025675	713/943-5750	190
Patterson Middle Sch/*Killeen*/Bell	00996473	254/336-7100	28
Patti Welder Middle Sch/*Victoria*/Victoria	01058634	361/575-4553	382
Patton Elem Sch/*Austin*/Travis	02857328	512/414-1780	367
PATTON SPRINGS IND SCH DIST/ AFTON/DICKENS	01013933	806/689-2220	126
Patton Springs Sch/*Afton*/Dickens	01013945	806/689-2220	127
Paul A Brown Alternative Ctr/*Beaumont*/ Jefferson	04948466	409/617-5720	242
Paul Belton Early Chldhd Ctr/*Borger*/ Hutchinson	01032678	806/273-1059	237
Paul Keyes Elem Sch/*Irving*/Dallas	01011296	972/600-3400	110
Paul L Dunbar Learning Center/*Dallas*/ Dallas	01009578	972/794-6600	102
Paul Laurence Dunbar High Sch/*Fort Worth*/ Tarrant	01053232	817/815-3000	351
Paul Moreno Elem Sch/*El Paso*/El Paso	04918667	915/236-0400	134
Paul R Haas Middle Sch/*Corp Christi*/Nueces	01044451	361/878-4240	304
Paul Revere Middle Sch/*Houston*/Harris	02111942	713/917-3500	194
Paul W Ott Elem Sch/*San Antonio*/Bexar	05347578	210/397-5550	38
PAWNEE IND SCH DIST/PAWNEE/BEE	00996148	361/456-7256	25
Pawnee Sch/*Pawnee*/Bee	00996162	361/456-7256	25
Pays Sch/*San Angelo*/Tom Green	11925122	325/947-3912	365
PCA Dr Sarah Strinden Elem Sch/*Lufkin*/ Angelina	12263111	936/634-5515	9
PCA Dr Terry Robbins Mid Sch/*Lufkin*/ Angelina	12263123	936/634-5515	9
Pdn Academy-Vista Del Sol/*El Paso*/El Paso	11834420	915/298-3637	9
Pdna Vista Del Sol Mesa CHS/*El Paso*/ El Paso	04892738	915/532-7216	9
Peach Creek Elem Sch/*Splendora*/Montgomery	01042738	281/689-3114	294
Pearce High Sch/*Richardson*/Dallas	01011739	469/593-5000	113
Pearcy STEM Academy/*Arlington*/Tarrant	04918928	682/867-5555	345
Pearl Hall Elem Sch/*South Houston*/Harris	01026837	713/740-0688	199
Pearl M Hirsch Elem Sch/*Spring*/Harris	01824263	281/891-8330	202
Pearland High Sch/*Pearland*/Brazoria	01001887	281/997-7445	53
PEARLAND IND SCH DIST/PEARLAND/ BRAZORIA	01001849	281/485-3203	53
Pearland Jr High School East/*Pearland*/ Brazoria	01001875	281/485-2481	53
Pearland Jr High School South/*Pearland*/ Brazoria	05070256	281/727-1500	53
Pearland Jr High School West/*Pearland*/ Brazoria	04033889	281/412-1222	53

School Year 2019-2020   800-333-8802   TX-V57

DISTRICT & SCHOOL TELEPHONE INDEX

Market Data Retrieval

School/City/County DISTRICT/CITY/COUNTY	PID	TELEPHONE NUMBER	PAGE
Pearsall High Sch/*Pearsall*/Frio	01018646	830/334-8011	157
PEARSALL IND SCH DIST/*PEARSALL*/ FRIO	01018610	830/334-8001	157
Pearsall Intermediate Sch/*Pearsall*/Frio	01018658	830/334-3316	157
Pearsall Junior High Sch/*Pearsall*/Frio	01018660	830/334-8021	157
Pearson Early Childhood Sch/*Plano*/Collin	05096872	469/752-4300	83
Pearson Elem Sch/*Mission*/Hidalgo	01030280	956/323-4000	222
Pearson Middle Sch/*Frisco*/Collin	12110057	469/633-4450	80
Pearson Ranch Middle Sch/*Austin*/Williamson	12226541	512/704-1500	399
Pease Communication/Tech Acad/*Midland*/Midland	01041605	432/240-7700	286
Pease Elem Sch/*Austin*/Travis	01056533	512/414-4428	368
Pease Elem Sch/*Odessa*/Ector	01014781	432/456-1179	130
Peaster Elem Sch/*Weatherford*/Parker	01046435	817/341-5000	313
Peaster High Sch/*Weatherford*/Parker	04750544	817/341-5000	313
PEASTER IND SCH DIST/*WEATHERFORD*/ PARKER	01046423	817/341-5000	313
Peaster Middle Sch/*Weatherford*/Parker	04750532	817/341-5000	313
Pebble Creek Elem Sch/*College Sta*/Brazos	04451190	979/764-5595	56
Pebble Hill High Sch/*El Paso*/El Paso	11552933	915/937-9400	136
Pebble Hills Elem Sch/*El Paso*/El Paso	02110596	915/434-5600	138
Pebblecreek Montessori Sch/*Plano*/Collin	05312535	972/908-3797	86
Pecan Creek Elem Sch/*Denton*/Denton	05273692	940/369-4400	121
Pecan Grove Elem Sch/*Richmond*/Fort Bend	03048934	281/634-4800	151
Pecan Ridge High Sch/*Mullin*/Mills	12166252	325/372-4091	289
Pecan Springs Elem Sch/*Austin*/Travis	01056545	512/414-4445	368
Pecan Trail Interm Sch/*College Sta*/Brazos	12233178	979/694-5874	56
Pecan Valley Elem Sch/*San Antonio*/Bexar	00997063	210/333-1230	31
Peck Elem Sch/*Houston*/Harris	01024920	713/845-7463	193
Pecos High Sch/*Pecos*/Reeves	01048380	432/447-7400	323
Pecos Kindergarten/*Pecos*/Reeves	01857387	432/447-7596	323
PECOS-BARSTOW-TOYAH IND SD/ PECOS/REEVES	01048304	432/447-7201	323
Peebles Elem Sch/*Killeen*/Bell	00996576	254/336-2120	28
Peet Junior High Sch/*Conroe*/Montgomery	01042570	936/709-3700	292
Peete Elem Sch/*Tyler*/Smith	01050979	903/262-2460	338
Pegasus Sch Liberal Arts & Sci/*Dallas*/Dallas	04757970	214/740-9991	9
Pena Elem Sch/*Brownsville*/Cameron	11449257	956/547-7100	64
PENELOPE ISD SCH DIST/*PENELOPE*/ HILL	01031026	254/533-2215	228
Penelope Sch/*Penelope*/Hill	01031038	254/533-2215	228
Pep High Sch/*Pep*/Cochran	04011518	806/933-4499	75
Percy Neblitt Elem Sch/*Sherman*/Grayson	10900820	903/891-6670	167
Perez Elem Sch/*Austin*/Travis	10030463	512/841-9100	367
Perez Elem Sch/*Brownsville*/Cameron	01003641	956/982-2800	64
Perez Elem Sch/*Kingsville*/Kleberg	01036301	361/592-8511	257
Perfecto Mancha Elem Sch/*Eagle Pass*/Maverick	11559802	830/758-7216	277
Perkins Middle Sch/*Brownsville*/Cameron	03011230	956/831-8770	64
Perkins Middle Sch/*De Leon*/Comanche	03047277	254/893-8230	89
Permian Basin Classical Acad/*Midland*/Midland	12363723	432/217-6122	9
Permian High Sch/*Odessa*/Ector	01014793	432/456-0039	130
Perrin Alt Learning Center/*Denison*/Grayson	11075600	903/891-6680	167
PERRIN-WHITT CONS IND SCH DIST/ PERRIN/JACK	01032965	940/798-3718	239
Perrin-Whitt Elem Sch/*Perrin*/Jack	01032989	940/798-2395	239
Perrin-Whitt High Sch/*Perrin*/Jack	04032665	940/798-3718	239
Perryton High Sch/*Perryton*/Ochiltree	01045479	806/435-3633	307
PERRYTON IND SCH DIST/*PERRYTON*/ OCHILTREE	01045455	806/435-5478	307
Perryton Junior High Sch/*Perryton*/Ochiltree	01553191	806/435-3601	307
Perryton Kindergarten/*Perryton*/Ochiltree	04865008	806/435-2463	307
Pershing Elem Sch/*San Antonio*/Bexar	00998897	210/738-9820	41
Pershing Middle Sch/*Houston*/Harris	01024877	713/295-5240	194
Pershing Park Elem Sch/*Killeen*/Bell	00996588	254/336-1790	28
Personalized Lrng Prep Houston/*Dallas*/Dallas	01009803	972/749-5800	102
Pete & Gracie Hosp Elem Sch/*Frisco*/Collin	12032869	469/633-4050	80
Pete Ford Middle Sch/*Allen*/Collin	01006019	972/727-0590	77
Pete Gallego Elem Sch/*Eagle Pass*/Maverick	04871083	830/758-7130	277
Peter E Hyland Center/*Baytown*/Harris	01023615	281/420-4555	188
Peters Colony Elem Sch/*The Colony*/Denton	02112142	469/713-5179	124
PETERSBURG IND SCH DIST/ PETERSBURG/HALE	01021863	806/667-3585	175
Petersburg Sch/*Petersburg*/Hale	01021875	806/667-3585	175
Petersen Elem Sch/*Houston*/Harris	01025326	713/434-5630	193
Peterson Middle Sch/*Kerrville*/Kerr	01036090	830/257-2204	256
PETROLIA CONS IND SCH DIST/ PETROLIA/CLAY	01005601	940/524-3555	74
Petrolia Elem Sch/*Petrolia*/Clay	11071707	940/524-3433	74
Petrolia Jr Sr High Sch/*Petrolia*/Clay	01005625	940/524-3264	74
Petronila Elem Sch/*Robstown*/Nueces	01044097	361/387-2834	302
Petrosky Elem Sch/*Houston*/Harris	02043280	281/983-8366	182
Pettus Elem Sch/*Pettus*/Bee	00996186	361/375-2296	25
PETTUS IND SCH DIST/*PETTUS*/BEE	00996174	361/375-2296	25
Pettus Secondary Sch/*Pettus*/Bee	00996198	361/375-2296	25
PEWITT CONS IND SCH DIST/ OMAHA/MORRIS	01043005	903/884-2136	296
Pewitt Elem Sch/*Omaha*/Morris	01043017	903/884-2404	296
Pewitt High Sch/*Omaha*/Morris	01043029	903/884-2293	296
Pewitt Junior High Sch/*Omaha*/Morris	01043031	903/884-2505	296
Pfc Mario Ybarra Elem Sch/*Weslaco*/Hidalgo	01030644	956/969-6587	225
Pfc Robert Hernandez Mid Sch/*Round Rock*/Williamson	11557438	512/424-8800	399
Pflugerville Elem Sch/*Pflugerville*/Travis	01056947	512/594-3800	372
Pflugerville High Sch/*Pflugerville*/Travis	01056959	512/594-0500	372
PFLUGERVILLE IND SCH DIST/ PFLUGERVILLE/TRAVIS	01056935	512/594-0000	371
Pflugerville Middle Sch/*Pflugerville*/Travis	01056961	512/594-2000	372
Pharr San Juan Alamo High Sch/*San Juan*/Hidalgo	01030474	956/354-2300	223
Pharr San Juan Alamo North HS/*Pharr*/Hidalgo	03325732	956/354-2360	223
PHARR-SAN JUAN-ALAMO IND SD/ PHARR/HIDALGO	01030333	956/354-2000	223
Phillips Elem Sch/*Frisco*/Collin	11820077	469/633-3925	80
Phillips Elem Sch/*Kaufman*/Kaufman	02178770	972/932-4500	252
Phoenix Alt Campus 817/*Cleburne*/Johnson	04807719	817/202-2090	247
Phoenix Center/*Terrell*/Kaufman	04450122	972/563-6319	253
Phoenix High Sch/*Elgin*/Bastrop	04028327	512/281-9774	24
Phoenix Learning Center/*San Marcos*/Hays	03381061	512/393-6864	212
Pickle Elem Sch/*Austin*/Travis	04943820	512/841-8400	368
Piedmont Global Academy/*Dallas*/Dallas	01009138	972/749-4100	102
Pieper Ranch Middle Sch/*San Antonio*/Comal	12307286	830/885-9600	88
Pierce Early Childhood Sch/*Irving*/Dallas	04872972	972/600-3700	110
Pietzsch-MacArthur Elem Sch/*Beaumont*/Jefferson	01034212	409/617-6475	242
Pilgrim Academy/*Houston*/Harris	01024530	713/458-4672	194
Pilgrim Lutheran Sch/*Houston*/Harris	01027714	713/432-7082	206
Pillow Elem Sch/*Austin*/Travis	01056557	512/414-2350	368
Pilot Point Elem Sch/*Pilot Point*/Denton	02844814	940/686-8710	125
Pilot Point High Sch/*Pilot Point*/Denton	01013593	940/686-8740	125
PILOT POINT IND SCH DIST/ PILOT POINT/DENTON	01013581	940/686-8700	125
Pilot Point Intermediate Sch/*Pilot Point*/Denton	04865058	940/686-8720	125
Pilot Point Middle Sch/*Pilot Point*/Denton	02055336	940/686-8730	125
Pin Oak Middle Sch/*Bellaire*/Harris	05099331	713/295-6500	194
Pine Drive Christian Sch/*Hitchcock*/Galveston	02828262	281/534-4881	162
Pine Forest Elem Sch/*Humble*/Harris	02848690	281/641-2100	196
Pine Forest Elem Sch/*Vidor*/Orange	01045778	409/951-8800	309
Pine Ridge Elem Sch/*Livingston*/Polk	01047087	936/328-2160	317
Pine Shadows Elem Sch/*Houston*/Harris	01027245	713/251-6500	201
PINE TREE IND SCH DIST/*LONGVIEW*/ GREGG	01021148	903/295-5000	170
Pine Tree Junior High Sch/*Longview*/Gregg	02222797	903/295-5081	170
Pine Tree Middle Sch/*Longview*/Gregg	01021198	903/295-5160	170
Pine Tree Primary Sch/*Longview*/Gregg	01021203	903/295-5095	170
Pine Tree Senior High Sch/*Longview*/Gregg	01021162	903/295-5031	170
Piner Middle Sch/*Sherman*/Grayson	01020651	903/891-6470	167
Pines Montessori Sch/*Kingwood*/Harris	02233368	281/358-8933	206
Piney Point Elem Sch/*Houston*/Harris	01024542	713/917-3610	194
Piney Woods Elem Sch/*Splendora*/Montgomery	11465524	281/689-3073	294
Pineywoods Community Academy/*Lufkin*/Angelina	04892752	936/634-5515	9
Pinnacle Intermediate Sch/*Amarillo*/Randall	12306969	806/677-2570	321
Pioneer Crossing Elem Sch/*Austin*/Travis	11456535	512/278-4250	371
Pioneer Elem Sch/*Graham*/Young	01062142	940/549-2442	406
Pioneer Heritage Middle Sch/*Frisco*/Collin	05092656	469/633-4700	80
Pittman Elem Sch/*Raymondville*/Willacy	01060766	956/689-8173	394
Pittsburg Elem Sch/*Pittsburg*/Camp	01004528	903/856-6472	68
Pittsburg High Sch/*Pittsburg*/Camp	01004542	903/856-3646	68
PITTSBURG IND SCH DIST/*PITTSBURG*/ CAMP	01004504	903/856-3628	68
Pittsburg Intermediate Sch/*Pittsburg*/Camp	05026748	903/855-3395	68
Pittsburg Junior High Sch/*Pittsburg*/Camp	01004530	903/856-6432	68
Pittsburg Primary Sch/*Pittsburg*/Camp	01004516	903/856-6482	68
Placedo Elem Sch/*Placedo*/Victoria	01058359	361/333-8000	382
Plain Elem Sch/*Leander*/Williamson	10023288	512/570-6600	397

Texas School Directory
DISTRICT & SCHOOL TELEPHONE INDEX

School/City/County DISTRICT/CITY/COUNTY	PID	TELEPHONE NUMBER	PAGE
Plains Elem Sch/*Plains*/Yoakum	01062099	806/456-7401	405
Plains High Sch/*Plains*/Yoakum	01062075	806/456-7401	406
PLAINS IND SCH DIST/PLAINS/ YOAKUM	01062063	806/456-7401	405
Plains Middle Sch/*Plains*/Yoakum	01062087	806/456-7401	406
Plainview Christian Academy/*Plainview*/Hale	04950861	806/296-6034	175
Plainview Elem Sch/*Plainview*/Hale	01022001	806/293-6005	175
PLAINVIEW IND SCH DIST/PLAINVIEW/ HALE	01021904	806/296-6392	175
Plano East Senior High Sch/*Plano*/Collin	02130900	469/752-9000	83
Plano Head Start Center/*Plano*/Collin	11423992	469/752-7160	83
PLANO IND SCH DIST/PLANO/COLLIN	01006344	469/752-8100	82
Plano ISD Academy High Sch/*Plano*/Collin	11925378	972/905-8100	83
Plano Senior High Sch/*Plano*/Collin	01401380	469/752-9300	83
Plano West Senior High Sch/*Plano*/Collin	04867290	469/752-9600	83
Plato Academy/*El Paso*/El Paso	04918277	915/434-9000	138
Pleasant Grove Elem Sch/*Dallas*/Dallas	04456504	972/892-5000	102
Pleasant Grove Elem Sch/*Texarkana*/Bowie	01001124	903/838-0528	49
Pleasant Grove Elem Sch/*Texarkana*/Bowie	02893059	903/832-8005	49
PLEASANT GROVE IND SCH DIST/ TEXARKANA/BOWIE	01001112	903/831-4086	49
Pleasant Grove Interm Sch/*Texarkana*/Bowie	11555076	903/832-0001	49
Pleasant Grove Middle Sch/*Texarkana*/Bowie	01558115	903/831-4295	49
Pleasant Hill Elem Sch/*Austin*/Travis	01056569	512/414-4453	367
Pleasant Hill Elem Sch/*Leander*/Williamson	05345568	512/570-6400	397
Pleasant Run Elem Sch/*Lancaster*/Dallas	01011375	972/218-1538	110
Pleasant Valley Elem Sch/*Amarillo*/Potter	01047415	806/326-5000	318
Pleasanton Elem Sch/*Pleasanton*/Atascosa	00995467	830/569-1340	21
Pleasanton High Sch/*Pleasanton*/Atascosa	00995479	830/569-1250	21
PLEASANTON IND SCH DIST/ PLEASANTON/ATASCOSA	00995431	830/569-1200	21
Pleasanton Junior High Sch/*Pleasanton*/ Atascosa	00995481	830/569-1280	21
Pleasanton Primary Sch/*Pleasanton*/Atascosa	04750958	830/569-1325	21
Pleasantville Elem Sch/*Houston*/Harris	01025699	713/671-3840	190
PLEMONS-STINNETT-PHILLIPS CISD/ STINNETT/HUTCHINSON	01032836	806/878-2858	238
Plum Creek Elem Sch/*Joshua*/Johnson	02893085	817/202-2500	248
Plum Creek Elem Sch/*Lockhart*/Caldwell	02896116	512/398-0570	61
Plummer Elem Sch/*Cedar Hill*/Dallas	01008316	972/291-4058	97
Plummer Middle Sch/*Houston*/Harris	10000456	281/539-4000	181
Plyler Alternative Educ Sch/*Tyler*/Smith	02223272	903/262-3070	338
Poe Elem Sch/*Houston*/Harris	01024970	713/535-3780	194
Poe Middle Sch/*San Antonio*/Bexar	00998794	210/228-1235	41
Poetry Community Christian Sch/*Terrell*/ Kaufman	11227152	972/563-7227	253
Point Alternative Center/*Highlands*/Harris	11721641	281/420-4630	188
POINT ISABEL IND SCH DIST/ PORT ISABEL/CAMERON	01004061	956/943-0000	66
Polk Elem Sch/*El Paso*/El Paso	02129872	915/236-2775	134
Polly Ann McRoberts Elem Sch/*Katy*/Harris	04757073	281/237-2000	152
Polly Ryon Middle Sch/*Richmond*/Fort Bend	11923643	832/223-4500	154
Polly Tadlock Elem Sch/*Frisco*/Collin	11103879	469/633-3775	80
Polser Elem Sch/*Carrollton*/Denton	04364664	469/713-5978	124
Polytechnic High Sch/*Fort Worth*/Tarrant	01053270	817/814-0000	351
Pomeroy Elem Sch/*Pasadena*/Harris	01026849	713/740-0696	199
Pomona Elem Sch/*Manvel*/Brazoria	12231015	281/245-3670	51
Pond Springs Elem Sch/*Austin*/Williamson	01061112	512/464-4200	399
Ponder Elem Sch/*Ponder*/Denton	04272542	940/479-8230	125
Ponder High Sch/*Ponder*/Denton	01013622	940/479-8210	126
PONDER IND SCH DIST/PONDER/ DENTON	01013610	940/479-8200	125
Ponder Junior High Sch/*Ponder*/Denton	10012667	940/479-8220	126
Ponderosa Elem Sch/*Houston*/Harris	01027518	281/891-8180	202
Poolville Elem Sch/*Poolville*/Parker	01046461	817/599-3308	313
Poolville High Sch/*Poolville*/Parker	05101037	817/599-5134	313
POOLVILLE IND SCH DIST/POOLVILLE/ PARKER	01046459	817/594-4452	313
Poolville Junior High Sch/*Poolville*/Parker	05101025	817/594-4539	313
Pope Elem Sch/*Arlington*/Tarrant	01051868	682/867-2750	345
Pope Elem Sch/*Cypress*/Harris	11919379	281/373-2340	185
Popham Elem Sch/*Del Valle*/Travis	01056820	512/386-3750	369
Por Vida Academy Charter HS/*San Antonio*/ Bexar	00999750	210/775-1132	9
Port Aransas High Sch/*Port Aransas*/Nueces	01044891	361/749-1206	305
PORT ARANSAS IND SCH DIST/ PORT ARANSAS/NUECES	01044889	361/749-1200	305
Port Arthur Alternative Center/*Port Arthur*/ Jefferson	01526083	409/984-8650	243
PORT ARTHUR IND SCH DIST/ PORT ARTHUR/JEFFERSON	01033749	409/989-6222	243
Port Houston Elem Sch/*Houston*/Harris	01025704	713/671-3890	190
Port Isabel High Sch/*Port Isabel*/Cameron	01004097	956/943-0030	66
Port Isabel Junior High Sch/*Port Isabel*/ Cameron	01808958	956/943-0060	66
Port Neches Elem Sch/*Port Neches*/Jefferson	01033983	409/722-2262	243
Port Neches Middle Sch/*Port Neches*/ Jefferson	01033995	409/722-8115	243
Port Neches-Groves High Sch/*Port Neches*/ Jefferson	01034004	409/729-7644	244
PORT NECHES-GROVES IND SD/ PORT NECHES/JEFFERSON	01033957	409/722-4244	243
Port Oconnor Elem Sch/*Port O Connor*/ Calhoun	01003249	361/983-2341	62
Porter Elem Sch/*Porter*/Montgomery	01042714	281/577-2920	294
Porter High Sch/*Porter*/Montgomery	11713462	281/577-5900	294
Portia Ross Taylor Elem Sch/*Plano*/Collin	10023941	469/633-3625	80
Positive Redirection Center/*San Benito*/ Cameron	03390543	956/361-6275	67
Positive Solutions Charter Sch/*San Antonio*/ Bexar	04848074	210/299-1025	9
Post Elem Sch/*Houston*/Harris	01023304	713/896-3488	185
Post Elem Sch/*Post*/Garza	01019602	806/495-3414	162
Post High Sch/*Post*/Garza	01019614	806/495-2770	162
POST IND SCH DIST/POST/GARZA	01019597	806/495-3343	162
Post Middle Sch/*Post*/Garza	01019626	806/495-2874	162
Post Oak Montessori Sch/*Bellaire*/Harris	01875406	713/661-6688	206
Poteet Elem Sch/*Poteet*/Atascosa	00995508	830/742-3503	21
Poteet High Sch/*Poteet*/Atascosa	00995510	830/742-3521	21
POTEET IND SCH DIST/POTEET/ ATASCOSA	00995493	830/742-3567	21
Poteet Intermediate Campus/*Poteet*/Atascosa	05278812	830/742-3697	21
Poteet Junior High Sch/*Poteet*/Atascosa	00995522	830/742-3571	21
Poth Elem Sch/*Poth*/Wilson	01061356	830/484-3321	401
Poth High Sch/*Poth*/Wilson	01061368	830/484-3322	401
POTH IND SCH DIST/POTH/WILSON	01061344	830/484-3330	401
Poth Junior High Sch/*Poth*/Wilson	01061370	830/484-3323	401
Potranco Elem Sch/*San Antonio*/Medina	10012552	830/931-2243	284
Pottsboro Elem Sch/*Pottsboro*/Grayson	01020534	903/771-2981	167
Pottsboro High Sch/*Pottsboro*/Grayson	01020546	903/771-0085	167
POTTSBORO IND SCH DIST/POTTSBORO/ GRAYSON	01020510	903/771-0083	167
Pottsboro Middle Sch/*Pottsboro*/Grayson	01418333	903/771-2982	167
Powell Elem Sch/*San Antonio*/Bexar	00998328	210/397-0450	38
Prairie Creek Elem Sch/*Richardson*/Dallas	01011856	469/593-6300	113
Prairie Harbor Alternative Sch/*Wallis*/ Austin	11931834	979/478-6020	22
PRAIRIE LEA IND SCH DIST/ PRAIRIE LEA/CALDWELL	01003122	512/488-2328	61
Prairie Lea Sch/*Prairie Lea*/Caldwell	01003134	512/488-2328	61
Prairie Trail Elem Sch/*Flower Mound*/Denton	04364432	469/713-5980	124
PRAIRIE VALLEY IND SCH DIST/ NOCONA/MONTAGUE	01042374	940/825-4425	290
Prairie Valley Sch/*Nocona*/Montague	01042386	940/825-4425	290
Prairie View Elem Sch/*Rhome*/Denton	04804597	817/215-0550	125
Prairie Vista Middle Sch/*Fort Worth*/ Tarrant	10902983	817/847-9210	349
Prairiland High Sch/*Pattonville*/Lamar	01036818	903/652-5681	260
PRAIRILAND IND SCH DIST/ PATTONVILLE/LAMAR	01036789	903/652-6476	260
Prairiland Junior High Sch/*Pattonville*/ Lamar	10001412	903/652-5681	260
Premier Academy/*Keller*/Tarrant	11228144	817/745-0034	359
Premier HS-Abilene/*Abilene*/Taylor	04932182	325/698-8111	9
Premier HS-Amarillo/*Amarillo*/Randall	12100416	806/367-5447	9
Premier HS-American Youthworks/*Austin*/ Travis	04459453	512/744-1954	9
Premier HS-Arlington/*Arlington*/Tarrant	12261058	682/350-8865	9
Premier HS-Brenham Miracle Frm/*Brenham*/ Washington	11925237	979/836-0901	9
Premier HS-Brownsville/*Brownsville*/Cameron	04881674	956/550-0084	9
Premier HS-Brownwood Early/*Early*/Brown	11925249	325/643-3735	9
Premier HS-Career Tech Ed Ctr/*Edinburg*/ Hidalgo	12160856	956/386-1793	9
Premier HS-Comanche/*Comanche*/Comanche	11815474	325/356-9673	9
Premier HS-Dayton/*Dayton*/Liberty	11848835	936/257-8017	9
Premier HS-Del Rio/*Del Rio*/Val Verde	04881703	830/703-1631	9
Premier HS-El Paso East/*El Paso*/El Paso	12161939	915/633-1598	9
Premier HS-El Paso West/*El Paso*/El Paso	11565617	915/581-4300	9
Premier HS-Fort Worth/*Fort Worth*/Tarrant	04881715	817/731-2028	9
Premier HS-Granbury/*Granbury*/Hood	11565629	817/573-0435	9
Premier HS-Huntsville/*Huntsville*/Walker	11565631	936/439-5204	9
Premier HS-Irving South/*Irving*/Dallas	11848847	972/254-1016	9
Premier HS-Laredo/*Laredo*/Webb	04881727	956/723-7788	9

School Year 2019-2020   800-333-8802   TX-V59

DISTRICT & SCHOOL TELEPHONE INDEX

Market Data Retrieval

School/City/County DISTRICT/CITY/COUNTY	PID	TELEPHONE NUMBER	PAGE
Premier HS-Lewisville/*Lewisville*/Denton	11925275	972/521-1592	9
Premier HS-Lubbock/*Lubbock*/Lubbock	04881739	806/763-1518	9
Premier HS-Midland/*Midland*/Midland	04891588	432/682-0384	9
Premier HS-Mission/*Mission*/Hidalgo	11014486	956/424-9290	9
Premier HS-N Austin/*Austin*/Travis	11565655	512/614-4537	9
Premier HS-New Braunfels/*New Braunfels*/Comal	11565643	830/609-6606	9
Premier HS-North Houston/*Houston*/Harris	12173542	281/537-7272	9
Premier HS-Palmview/*Palmview*/Hidalgo	11014498	956/584-8458	9
Premier HS-Pflugerville/*Pflugerville*/Travis	12160844	512/969-5100	9
Premier HS-Pharr/*Pharr*/Hidalgo	04891590	956/781-8800	9
Premier HS-S Austin/*Austin*/Travis	05010713	512/444-8442	9
Premier HS-San Angelo/*San Angelo*/Tom Green	12363747	325/823-7758	9
Premier HS-San Antonio East/*San Antonio*/Bexar	12261046	210/650-0944	9
Premier HS-San Antonio West/*San Antonio*/Bexar	12261034	830/587-4730	10
Premier HS-San Juan/*San Juan*/Hidalgo	11565679	956/961-4721	10
Premier HS-Texarkana/*Texarkana*/Bowie	12173578	430/200-4385	10
Premier HS-Tyler/*Tyler*/Smith	04881741	903/592-5222	10
Premier HS-Waco/*Waco*/McLennan	04881753	254/752-0441	10
Premont Collegiate High Sch/*Premont*/Jim Wells	01034755	361/348-3915	246
Premont Early College Academy/*Premont*/Jim Wells	01034729	361/348-3915	246
PREMONT IND SCH DIST/**PREMONT**/**JIM WELLS**	01034717	361/348-3915	246
Prep for Early College HS/*Rio Grande Cy*/Starr	12235401	956/352-6349	340
Presa Elem Sch/*El Paso*/El Paso	01016533	915/434-8700	138
Presbyterian Pan American Sch/*Kingsville*/Kleberg	01036430	361/592-4307	258
Presbyterian Sch/*Houston*/Harris	03560229	713/520-0284	206
Presidential Meadows Elem Sch/*Manor*/Travis	10915045	512/278-4225	371
Presidio Elem Sch/*Presidio*/Presidio	01047879	432/229-3200	320
Presidio High Sch/*Presidio*/Presidio	02887866	432/229-3365	320
PRESIDIO IND SCH DIST/**PRESIDIO**/**PRESIDIO**	01047867	432/229-3275	320
Preston Elem Sch/*Allen*/Collin	12230487	972/908-8780	77
Preston Hollow Elem Sch/*Dallas*/Dallas	01009619	972/794-8500	102
Preston Hollow Presby Sch/*Dallas*/Dallas	01479791	214/368-3886	116
Prestonwood Christian Academy/*Plano*/Collin	04924628	972/820-5300	86
Prestonwood Elem Sch/*Dallas*/Dallas	01011868	469/593-6700	113
Prestwick STEM Academy/*The Colony*/Denton	12036918	972/947-9450	124
Price Elem Sch/*San Antonio*/Bexar	00999487	210/977-7225	42
Price T Young Elem Sch/*Marshall*/Harrison	01028689	903/927-8850	209
PRIDDY IND SCH DIST/**PRIDDY**/**MILLS**	01042001	325/966-3323	289
Priddy Sch/*Priddy*/Mills	01042013	325/966-3323	289
Pride Academy/*Brenham*/Washington	04449886	979/277-3890	385
Pride Sch/*Huntington*/Angelina	04282949	936/876-4287	17
Prince of Peace Catholic Sch/*Plano*/Collin	03410363	972/380-5505	85
Prince of Peace Christian Sch/*Carrollton*/Denton	02858281	972/447-0532	126
Princeton High Sch/*Princeton*/Collin	01006526	469/952-5405	84
PRINCETON IND SCH DIST/**PRINCETON**/**COLLIN**	01006502	469/952-5400	84
PRINGLE-MORSE CONS ISD/**MORSE**/**HANSFORD**	01022295	806/733-2507	177
Pringle-Morse Sch/*Morse*/Hansford	01022300	806/733-2507	177
Priority Intervention Academy/*Lubbock*/Lubbock	02110302	806/219-2400	270
Pritchard Junior High Sch/*Bells*/Grayson	01020259	903/965-4835	165
Pro-Vision Academy/*Houston*/Harris	04922034	713/748-0030	10
Progreso Early Childhood Sch/*Progreso*/Hidalgo	05349801	956/565-1168	224
Progreso Early Clg Academy/*Progreso*/Hidalgo	11928019	956/565-4142	224
Progreso Elem Sch/*Progreso*/Hidalgo	11540473	956/514-9502	224
Progreso High Sch/*Progreso*/Hidalgo	02203923	956/565-4142	224
PROGRESO IND SCH DIST/**PROGRESO**/**HIDALGO**	01030503	956/565-3002	224
Progressive High Sch/*Missouri City*/Fort Bend	04365890	281/634-2900	151
Project Chrysalis Middle Sch/*Houston*/Harris	04454453	713/924-1700	190
Promise Academy/*Tyler*/Smith	12166757	903/630-7369	339
Promise Cmty Sch-New Nghbr/*Houston*/Harris	12162012	713/273-3731	10
Promise Community Sch Ripley/*Houston*/Harris	05195052	713/315-6429	10
Prosper High Sch/*Prosper*/Collin	04169012	469/219-2180	84
PROSPER IND SCH DIST/**PROSPER**/**COLLIN**	01006552	469/219-2000	84
Provan Opportunity Center/*Pflugerville*/Travis	04299198	512/594-3600	372
Providence Catholic Sch/*San Antonio*/Bexar	00999970	210/224-6651	44
Providence Christian Sch/*Dallas*/Dallas	04992845	214/302-2800	116
Providence Classical Sch/*Spring*/Harris	11824877	281/320-0500	206
Providence Elem Sch/*Aubrey*/Denton	05343455	940/369-1900	121
Provident Heights Elem Sch/*Waco*/McLennan	01040364	254/750-3930	282
Psja Elvis J Ballew Echs/*Pharr*/Hidalgo	11454408	956/354-2520	223
Psja Memorial HS/*Alamo*/Hidalgo	04754033	956/354-2420	224
Psja Sonia Sotomayer HS/*Pharr*/Hidalgo	03346566	956/354-2510	224
Psja Southwest Echs/*Pharr*/Hidalgo	11552880	956/354-2480	224
Psja T Jefferson Echs/*Pharr*/Hidalgo	11128520	956/784-8525	224
Ptaa-Greenville Mid High Sch/*Greenville*/Hunt	12261010	903/454-7153	10
Ptaa-Mesquite Mid High Sch/*Mesquite*/Dallas	12261022	972/375-9672	10
Puckett Elem Sch/*Amarillo*/Potter	01548469	806/326-5050	318
Pullam Elem Sch/*Brownsville*/Cameron	11449245	956/547-3700	64
Purnell Support Center/*Lewisville*/Denton	12170136	469/713-5199	124
Purple Heart Elem Sch/*El Paso*/El Paso	12105064	915/938-2200	136
Purple Sage Elem Sch/*Austin*/Williamson	02126909	512/428-3500	399
Purple Sage Elem Sch/*Houston*/Harris	03397981	832/386-3100	187
Puster Elem Sch/*Fairview*/Collin	11127760	469/742-8300	80
Putegnat Elem Sch/*Brownsville*/Cameron	01003457	956/548-8930	64
Putnam Elem Sch/*El Paso*/El Paso	01016052	915/236-3225	134
Pyburn Elem Sch/*Houston*/Harris	01023536	832/386-3150	187

Q

School/City/County	PID	TELEPHONE NUMBER	PAGE
Qalam Collegiate Academy/*Richardson*/Dallas	12043234	972/437-2526	116
Quail Valley Elem Sch/*Missouri City*/Fort Bend	01418319	281/634-5040	151
Quail Valley Middle Sch/*Missouri City*/Fort Bend	01541332	281/634-3600	151
Quanah High Sch/*Quanah*/Hardeman	01022403	940/663-2791	177
QUANAH IND SCH DIST/**QUANAH**/**HARDEMAN**	01022398	940/663-2281	177
Queen City High Sch/*Queen City*/Cass	01004932	903/796-8259	71
QUEEN CITY IND SCH DIST/**QUEEN CITY**/**CASS**	01004920	903/796-8256	70
Queen of Peace Catholic Sch/*Houston*/Harris	01028122	713/921-1558	204
Queens Intermediate Sch/*Houston*/Harris	01026851	713/740-0470	199
Quest Academy/*Stafford*/Fort Bend	12367779	281/261-9200	155
Quest Early College High Sch/*Humble*/Harris	04303971	281/641-7300	196
Quest High Sch/*Burnet*/Burnet	04238546	512/756-6747	60
QUINLAN IND SCH DIST/**QUINLAN**/**HUNT**	01032575	903/356-1200	237
Quinn Middle Sch/*Waco*/McLennan	11478820	254/754-8000	10
Quitman Elem Sch/*Quitman*/Wood	01061916	903/763-5000	404
Quitman High Sch/*Quitman*/Wood	01061928	903/763-5000	404
QUITMAN IND SCH DIST/**QUITMAN**/**WOOD**	01061904	903/763-5000	404
Quitman Junior High Sch/*Quitman*/Wood	01061930	903/763-5000	404

R

School/City/County	PID	TELEPHONE NUMBER	PAGE
R A Hall Elem Sch/*Beeville*/Bee	00996112	361/362-6060	25
R C Conley Elem Sch/*Houston*/Harris	02201389	281/537-5418	180
R C Loflin Middle Sch/*Joshua*/Johnson	01035058	817/202-2500	248
R D McAdams Junior High Sch/*Dickinson*/Galveston	01019016	281/229-7100	160
R E Good Elem Sch/*Carrollton*/Dallas	01008196	972/968-1900	97
R F Patterson Elem Sch/*Arlington*/Tarrant	04456736	817/563-8600	356
R J Richey Elem Sch/*Burnet*/Burnet	10758794	512/756-2609	60
R K Driggers Elem Sch/*San Antonio*/Bexar	10913205	210/397-5900	38
R L Isaacs Elem Sch/*Houston*/Harris	01025558	713/671-4120	191
R L Martin Elem Sch/*Brownsville*/Cameron	01003548	956/982-2730	64
R L Paschal High Sch/*Fort Worth*/Tarrant	01053282	817/814-5000	351
R L Turner High Sch/*Carrollton*/Dallas	01008237	972/968-5400	97
R M Sorrells Sch-Ed & Soc Srvs/*Dallas*/Dallas	01553036	972/925-5940	102
R O'Hara Lanier Middle Sch/*Freeport*/Brazoria	04363737	979/730-7220	52
R P Harris Elem Sch/*Houston*/Harris	01025728	713/450-7100	190
R Q Sims Intermediate Sch/*Mexia*/Limestone	02890966	254/562-4025	267
R S Kimbrough Middle Sch/*Mesquite*/Dallas	04033035	972/882-5900	111
R V Groves Elem Sch/*Wylie*/Collin	05035294	972/429-3460	85
Raba Elem Sch/*San Antonio*/Bexar	04921406	210/397-1350	38
Radford Sch/*El Paso*/El Paso	01016686	915/565-2700	139
Radiant STEM Academy/*Irving*/Dallas	12225690	214/245-5125	116
Rafael Cantu Jr High Sch/*Palmhurst*/Hidalgo	11079321	956/323-7800	222
Rafael Galvan Elem Sch/*Corp Christi*/Nueces	03333105	361/878-2800	304

Texas School Directory

DISTRICT & SCHOOL TELEPHONE INDEX

School/City/County DISTRICT/CITY/COUNTY	PID	TELEPHONE NUMBER	PAGE
Rafaela T Barrera Elem Sch/*Roma*/Starr	04282212	956/486-2475	341
Raguet Elem Sch/*Nacogdoches*/Nacogdoches	01043330	936/569-5052	298
Rahe Bulverde Elem Sch/*Bulverde*/Comal	01006899	830/885-1600	88
Rainard School for the Gifted/*Houston*/Harris	02998518	713/647-7246	206
Rains Elem Sch/*Mumford*/Rains	01047908	903/473-2222	320
Rains High Sch/*Emory*/Rains	01047910	903/473-2222	320
RAINS IND SCH DIST/**EMORY**/**RAINS**	01047893	903/473-2222	320
Rains Intermediate Sch/*Emory*/Rains	05276888	903/473-2222	320
Rains Junior High Sch/*Emory*/Rains	01047922	903/473-2222	320
Ralls Elem Sch/*Ralls*/Crosby	01007996	806/253-2546	94
Ralls High Sch/*Ralls*/Crosby	01008005	806/253-2571	94
RALLS IND SCH DIST/**RALLS**/**CROSBY**	01007984	806/253-2509	94
Ralls Middle Sch/*Ralls*/Crosby	04245410	806/253-2549	94
Ralph Eickenroht Elem Sch/*Houston*/Harris	11451999	281/891-8840	202
Ralph G Goodman Elem Sch/*Houston*/Harris	01022831	281/878-0355	181
Ralph Langley Elem Sch/*San Antonio*/Bexar	11448980	210/397-0150	38
Ralph Parr Elem Sch/*League City*/Galveston	11449099	281/284-4100	159
Ralph Pfluger Elem Sch/*Buda*/Hays	11555533	512/268-8510	211
Ramey Elem Sch/*Tyler*/Smith	01050929	903/262-2505	338
Ramirez Charter Sch/*Lubbock*/Lubbock	02907064	806/219-6500	270
RAMIREZ COMMON SCH DIST/**REALITOS**/**DUVAL**	01014250	361/539-4343	128
Ramirez Elem Sch/*Realitos*/Duval	01014262	361/539-4343	128
Ramirez-Burks Elem Sch/*Cotulla*/La Salle	01037202	830/879-2511	259
Ramiro Barrera Middle Sch/*Roma*/Starr	11072220	956/486-2670	341
Ramona Bang Elem Sch/*Houston*/Harris	03327209	281/897-4760	185
Ramona Elem Sch/*El Paso*/El Paso	01016545	915/434-7700	138
Ranch Academy/*Canton*/Van Zandt	04892776	903/479-3601	10
Ranch Academy-Tyler/*Canton*/Van Zandt	11704722	903/479-3601	10
Rancho Isabella Elem Sch/*Angleton*/Brazoria	02845947	979/864-8007	52
Rancho Sienna Elem Sch/*Georgetown*/Williamson	12305733	512/260-4450	398
Rancho Verde Elem Sch/*Brownsville*/Cameron	11129861	956/254-5230	66
Ranchview High Sch/*Irving*/Dallas	05098375	972/968-5000	97
Rancier Middle Sch/*Killeen*/Bell	00996590	254/336-1250	28
Randall High Sch/*Amarillo*/Randall	03048928	806/677-2333	321
Randolph Elem Sch/*Universal Cty*/Bexar	01601798	210/357-2345	39
RANDOLPH FIELD IND SCH DIST/**UNIVERSAL CTY**/**BEXAR**	01601786	210/357-2300	39
Randolph Foster High Sch/*Richmond*/Fort Bend	04946028	832/223-3800	154
Randolph High Sch/*Universal Cty*/Bexar	01601803	210/357-2400	39
Randolph Middle Sch/*Universal Cty*/Bexar	03237745	210/357-2430	39
Rangel Women's Leadership Sch/*Dallas*/Dallas	05345752	972/749-5200	102
RANGER IND SCH DIST/**RANGER**/**EASTLAND**	01014470	254/647-1187	129
Ranger Sch/*Ranger*/Eastland	02046048	254/647-3216	129
Rangerville Elem Sch/*San Benito*/Cameron	01004255	956/361-6840	67
Rankin Elem Sch/*Arlington*/Tarrant	01051870	682/867-2800	345
Rankin High Sch/*Rankin*/Upton	01057678	432/693-2451	377
RANKIN IND SCH DIST/**RANKIN**/**UPTON**	01057654	432/693-2461	377
Rann Elem Sch/*Decatur*/Wise	01061667	940/393-7600	403
Rapoport Acad-E Campus ES/*Waco*/McLennan	04814009	254/799-4191	10
Rapoport Acad-N Campus ES/*Waco*/McLennan	11848897	254/313-1313	10
Raquel Cavazos Elem Sch/*Mission*/Hidalgo	05275420	956/323-7200	222
Rasor Elem Sch/*Plano*/Collin	03456666	469/752-2900	83
Raul B Fernandez Elem Sch/*San Antonio*/Bexar	03324960	210/397-1900	38
Raul C Martinez Elem Sch/*Houston*/Harris	04016128	713/671-3680	191
Raul Longoria Elem Sch/*Pharr*/Hidalgo	01540077	956/354-2820	224
Raul Perales Middle Sch/*Laredo*/Webb	12308230	956/473-6800	388
Raul Quintanilla Middle Sch/*Dallas*/Dallas	04755465	972/502-3200	102
Raul Yzaguirre Middle Sch/*San Juan*/Hidalgo	04919568	956/354-2630	224
Raul Yzaguirre Sch for Success/*Brownsville*/Cameron	12168901	956/574-7100	10
Raul Yzaguirre Sch for Success/*Houston*/Harris	04467565	713/640-3700	10
Rawson Saunders Sch/*Austin*/Travis	11231672	512/476-8382	373
Ray & Jamie Wolman Elem Sch/*Katy*/Harris	11822025	281/234-1700	152
Ray D Corbett Junior High Sch/*Schertz*/Guadalupe	01021588	210/619-4150	173
Ray Daily Elem Sch/*Houston*/Harris	10910514	281/368-2111	194
Ray Darr Elem Sch/*Eagle Pass*/Maverick	02855904	830/758-7060	277
Ray Elem Sch/*Hutto*/Williamson	10904797	512/759-5450	396
Ray Johnson 6th Grade Ctr/*Fort Worth*/Tarrant	12115617	817/615-3670	349
Ray L Shotwell Middle Sch/*Houston*/Harris	01857246	281/878-0960	181
Rayburn Elem Sch/*San Antonio*/Bexar	00997506	210/989-3200	33
Rayburn Intermediate Sch/*Bryan*/Brazos	03244695	979/209-6600	55
Raye McCoy Elem Sch/*Georgetown*/Williamson	01420570	512/943-5030	395
Raye-Allen Elem Sch/*Temple*/Bell	00996796	254/215-5800	29
Raymond & Tirza Martin HS/*Laredo*/Webb	01059391	956/273-7100	387
Raymond Cooper Junior High Sch/*Wylie*/Collin	10748361	972/429-3250	85
Raymond Mays Middle Sch/*Troy*/Bell	02887828	254/938-2543	30
Raymond Telles/Lafarelle MS/*El Paso*/El Paso	04288292	915/236-7800	133
Raymondville High Sch/*Raymondville*/Willacy	01060778	956/689-8170	394
RAYMONDVILLE IND SCH DIST/**RAYMONDVILLE**/**WILLACY**	01060716	956/689-2471	394
Raymondville Options Academy/*Raymondville*/Willacy	12312401	956/689-8185	394
Reach High Sch/*Fort Worth*/Tarrant	04359994	817/252-2390	347
Reading Junior High Sch/*Richmond*/Fort Bend	11553482	832/223-4400	154
Reagan Co Elem Sch/*Big Lake*/Reagan	01048029	325/884-3741	321
Reagan Co High Sch/*Big Lake*/Reagan	01048031	325/884-3714	321
REAGAN CO IND SCH DIST/**BIG LAKE**/**REAGAN**	01048017	325/884-3705	321
Reagan Co Middle Sch/*Big Lake*/Reagan	01048043	325/884-3728	321
Reagan Elem Sch/*Abilene*/Taylor	01172785	325/690-3627	360
Reagan Elem Sch/*Quanah*/Hardeman	01022415	940/663-2171	177
Reagan Elem Sch/*San Angelo*/Tom Green	01055709	325/659-3666	365
Reagan Magnet Elem Sch/*Odessa*/Ector	01014808	432/456-1189	130
Reaves Elem Sch/*Conroe*/Montgomery	01042506	936/709-5400	292
Reba Cobb Carroll Elem Sch/*Frisco*/Collin	10912718	469/633-3725	80
Rebecca Creek Elem Sch/*Spring Branch*/Comal	05090696	830/885-1800	88
Recovery Education Campus/*Ralls*/Crosby	12103195	806/253-2549	94
Red Bluff Elem Sch/*Pasadena*/Harris	01026863	713/740-0704	199
RED LICK IND SCH DIST/**TEXARKANA**/**BOWIE**	01001136	903/838-8230	49
Red Lick Sch/*Texarkana*/Bowie	01001148	903/838-8230	49
Red Oak Elem Sch/*Red Oak*/Ellis	01015266	972/617-3523	142
Red Oak High Sch/*Red Oak*/Ellis	01015280	972/617-3535	142
RED OAK IND SCH DIST/**RED OAK**/**ELLIS**	01015242	972/617-2941	142
Red Oak Middle Sch/*Red Oak*/Ellis	01015278	972/617-0066	142
Red Rock Elem Sch/*Red Rock*/Bastrop	04453253	512/772-7660	24
Red Sands Elem Sch/*El Paso*/El Paso	04880400	915/926-5400	132
Red Simon Middle Sch/*Kyle*/Hays	11454393	512/268-8507	211
Redeemer Episcopal Sch/*Eagle Pass*/Maverick	01410939	830/773-5122	277
Redeemer Lutheran Sch/*Austin*/Travis	01056997	512/451-6478	373
Redeemer Lutheran Sch/*Fort Worth*/Tarrant	01411012	817/560-0032	359
Redeemer Montessori Sch/*Irving*/Dallas	02851063	972/257-3517	116
Redland Oaks Elem Sch/*San Antonio*/Bexar	03250321	210/407-6200	35
Redwater Elem Sch/*Redwater*/Bowie	01001162	903/671-3425	49
Redwater High Sch/*Redwater*/Bowie	01001174	903/671-3421	49
REDWATER IND SCH DIST/**REDWATER**/**BOWIE**	01001150	903/671-3481	49
Redwater Junior High Sch/*Redwater*/Bowie	04840228	903/671-3227	49
Redwater Middle Sch/*Redwater*/Bowie	02130182	903/671-3412	49
Reece EC-PK-K Sch/*Houston*/Harris	04453875	281/878-0800	181
Reeces Creek Elem Sch/*Killeen*/Bell	03244700	254/336-2150	28
Reed Elem Sch/*Cedar Park*/Williamson	12035720	512/570-7700	397
Reed Elem Sch/*Houston*/Harris	03397931	713/896-5035	185
Reed Middle Sch/*Duncanville*/Dallas	01010371	972/708-3500	105
Rees Elem Sch/*Houston*/Harris	02227307	281/531-1444	182
Reese Education Center/*Lubbock*/Lubbock	04748981	806/885-4910	269
Reeves Hinger Elem Sch/*Canyon*/Randall	01047972	806/677-2870	321
Refugio Elem Sch/*Refugio*/Refugio	01048483	361/526-4844	323
Refugio High Sch/*Refugio*/Refugio	01048469	361/526-2344	323
REFUGIO IND SCH DIST/**REFUGIO**/**REFUGIO**	01048457	361/526-2325	323
Refugio Junior High Sch/*Refugio*/Refugio	11848902	361/526-2434	323
Regency Place Elem Sch/*San Antonio*/Bexar	00997893	210/407-6400	35
Regents Academy/*Nacogdoches*/Nacogdoches	11225788	936/559-7343	298
Regents School of Austin/*Austin*/Travis	04295910	512/899-8095	373
Regina Mater/*Austin*/Travis	12361488	512/524-1799	373
Regina-Howell Elem Sch/*Beaumont*/Jefferson	01034236	409/617-6190	242
REGION 1 ED SERVICE CENTER/**EDINBURG**/**HIDALGO**	01030553	956/984-6000	226
REGION 3 ED SERVICE CENTER/**VICTORIA**/**VICTORIA**	01058438	361/573-0731	383
REGION 4 ED SERVICE CENTER/**HOUSTON**/**HARRIS**	01027556	713/462-7708	208
REGION 5 ED SERVICE CENTER/**BEAUMONT**/**JEFFERSON**	01034298	409/951-1700	244
REGION 6 ED SERVICE CENTER/**HUNTSVILLE**/**WALKER**	01058763	936/435-8400	384
REGION 7 ED SERVICE CENTER/**KILGORE**/**GREGG**	01021291	903/988-6700	171
REGION 8 ED SERVICE CENTER/**PITTSBURG**/**TITUS**	01055450	903/575-2600	69

DISTRICT & SCHOOL TELEPHONE INDEX

Market Data Retrieval

School/City/County DISTRICT/CITY/COUNTY	PID	TELEPHONE NUMBER	PAGE
REGION 9 ED SERVICE CENTER/			
WICHITA FALLS/WICHITA	01060120	940/322-6928	393
REGION 10 ED SERVICE CENTER/			
RICHARDSON/DALLAS	01012032	972/348-1700	116
REGION 11 ED SERVICE CENTER/			
WHT SETTLEMT/TARRANT	01054171	817/740-3600	360
REGION 12 ED SERVICE CENTER/			
WACO/MCLENNAN	01040120	254/297-1212	283
REGION 13 ED SERVICE CENTER/			
AUSTIN/TRAVIS	02101545	512/919-5313	373
REGION 14 ED SERVICE CENTER/			
ABILENE/TAYLOR	01054975	325/675-8600	362
REGION 15 ED SERVICE CENTER/			
SAN ANGELO/TOM GREEN	01055814	325/658-6571	366
REGION 16 ED SERVICE CENTER/			
AMARILLO/RANDALL	01047984	806/677-5000	321
REGION 17 ED SERVICE CENTER/			
LUBBOCK/LUBBOCK	01039248	806/792-4000	272
REGION 18 ED SERVICE CENTER/			
MIDLAND/MIDLAND	01041693	432/563-2380	287
REGION 19 ED SERVICE CENTER/			
EL PASO/EL PASO	01016246	915/780-5052	139
REGION 20 ED SERVICE CENTER/			
SAN ANTONIO/BEXAR	00999645	210/370-5200	45
Regis Sch of the Sacred Heart/*Houston*/Harris	04022050	713/682-8383	204
Reicher Catholic High Sch/*Waco*/McLennan	01002879	254/752-8349	282
Reilly Elem Sch/*Austin*/Travis	01056583	512/414-4464	368
Reinhardt Elem Sch/*Dallas*/Dallas	01009695	972/749-7900	102
Remington Point Elem Sch/*Fort Worth*/Tarrant	05276890	817/232-1342	349
Remynse Elem Sch/*Grand Prairie*/Tarrant	04949290	682/867-0500	345
Rennell Elem Sch/*Cypress*/Harris	11560485	281/213-1550	185
Renner Middle Sch/*Plano*/Collin	03333818	469/752-5800	83
Reno Elem Sch/*Azle*/Parker	04884937	817/221-5001	313
Resaca Middle Sch/*Los Fresnos*/Cameron	04019481	956/254-5159	66
Resnik Middle Sch/*Von Ormy*/Bexar	12165789	210/623-6589	43
Resurrection Catholic Sch/*Houston*/Harris	01028134	713/674-5545	204
Reuben Johnson Elem Sch/*McKinney*/Collin	04750647	469/302-6500	81
Reve Preparatory Charter Sch/*Houston*/Harris	12362638	832/982-2083	10
Reynaldo G Garza Elem Sch/*McAllen*/Hidalgo	02199475	956/971-4554	221
Reynolds Middle Sch/*Prosper*/Collin	11555026	469/219-2165	84
Rhea Elem Sch/*Forney*/Kaufman	11130652	469/762-4157	252
Rhoads Elem Sch/*Katy*/Harris	05344332	281/237-8500	152
Rhodes Middle Sch/*San Antonio*/Bexar	00999279	210/978-7925	41
Rhodes School-Lee/*Houston*/Harris	11013872	281/458-4334	10
Ricardo Elem Middle Sch/*Kingsville*/Kleberg	01036387	361/592-6465	258
Ricardo Estrada Middle Sch/*El Paso*/El Paso	11561556	915/926-4800	132
RICARDO IND SCH DIST/KINGSVILLE/ KLEBERG	01036375	361/593-0703	257
Ricardo Salinas Elem Sch/*Universal Cty*/Bexar	10754970	210/659-5045	33
Rice Challenge Academy/*Eagle Lake*/Colorado	12305642	979/234-3531	87
RICE CONS IND SCH DIST/ALTAIR/ COLORADO	01006784	979/234-3531	87
Rice Elem Sch/*Conroe*/Montgomery	01829469	936/709-2700	292
Rice Elem Sch/*Rice*/Navarro	01043653	903/326-4151	300
Rice Elem Sch/*Tyler*/Smith	01050931	903/262-2555	338
Rice High Sch/*Altair*/Colorado	01006825	979/234-3531	87
Rice High Sch/*Rice*/Navarro	04867769	903/326-4502	300
RICE IND SCH DIST/RICE/NAVARRO	01043641	903/326-4287	300
Rice Intermediate Middle Sch/*Rice*/Navarro	11552971	903/326-4190	300
Rice Junior High Sch/*Altair*/Colorado	11540057	979/234-3531	87
Rice/*Houston*/Harris	04289923	713/349-1800	192
Richard E Cavazos Elem Sch/*Nolanville*/Bell	11449336	254/336-7000	28
Richard J Lee Elem Sch/*Irving*/Dallas	12035330	214/496-7900	98
Richard J Wilson Elem Sch/*Fort Worth*/Tarrant	01053385	817/814-7700	351
Richard King High Sch/*Corp Christi*/Nueces	01044475	361/906-3400	304
Richard Lagow Elem Sch/*Dallas*/Dallas	01009669	972/749-6600	102
Richard Milburn Acad-Amarillo/*Amarillo*/Randall	05011004	806/463-2284	10
Richard Milburn Acad-CC/*Corp Christi*/Nueces	04892788	361/225-4424	10
Richard Milburn Acad-Ft Worth/*Fort Worth*/Tarrant	05286584	817/731-7627	10
Richard Milburn Acad-Houston/*Houston*/Harris	05286572	281/209-3505	10
Richard Milburn Acad-Killeen/*Killeen*/Bell	04893160	254/634-4444	10
Richard Milburn Acad-Lubbock/*Lubbock*/Lubbock	04892790	806/740-0811	10
Richard Milburn Acad-Midland/*Midland*/Midland	04892805	432/203-9829	10
Richard Milburn Acad-Odessa/*Odessa*/Ector	05286596	432/614-1859	10
Richard Milburn Acad-Pasadena/*Pasadena*/Harris	12261072	832/730-4570	10
Richard Moore Elem Sch/*Houston*/Harris	01881895	713/740-0656	199
RICHARDS IND SCH DIST/RICHARDS/ GRIMES	01021459	936/851-2364	172
Richards Independent Sch/*Richards*/Grimes	01021461	936/851-2364	172
Richards Young Women Leaders/*Austin*/Travis	10907232	512/414-3236	369
Richardson Classical Academy/*Richardson*/Dallas	12162969	972/479-9584	10
Richardson Elem Sch/*Dimmitt*/Castro	01005003	806/647-4131	71
Richardson Heights Elem Sch/*Richardson*/Dallas	01011870	469/593-4400	113
Richardson High Sch/*Richardson*/Dallas	01011882	469/593-3000	113
RICHARDSON IND SCH DIST/ RICHARDSON/DALLAS	01011624	469/593-0000	112
Richardson North Jr High Sch/*Richardson*/Dallas	01011909	469/593-5300	113
Richardson Terrace Elem Sch/*Richardson*/Dallas	01011911	469/593-8700	113
Richardson West Arts & Tech/*Richardson*/Dallas	01011923	469/593-3700	113
Richey Elem Sch/*Pasadena*/Harris	01026875	713/740-0712	199
Richland Collegiate High Sch/*Dallas*/Dallas	11014864	972/761-6888	10
Richland Elem Sch/*Richardson*/Dallas	01399684	469/593-4650	113
Richland Elem Sch/*Richland Hls*/Tarrant	01052159	817/547-2000	346
Richland High Sch/*N Richlnd Hls*/Tarrant	01052161	817/547-7000	346
Richland Middle Sch/*Richland Hls*/Tarrant	01052173	817/547-4400	346
RICHLAND SPRINGS IND SCH DIST/ RICHLAND SPGS/SAN SABA	01049918	325/452-3524	332
Richland Springs Sch/*Richland Spgs*/San Saba	01049920	325/452-3427	332
Rick Ogden Elem Sch/*Humble*/Harris	11555351	281/233-8901	180
Rick Reedy High Sch/*Frisco*/Collin	12106991	469/633-6400	80
Rick Schneider Middle Sch/*Houston*/Harris	10028991	713/740-0920	199
Ricky C Bailey Middle Sch/*Spring*/Harris	10022480	281/891-8000	202
Riddle Elem Sch/*Plano*/Collin	05272612	469/633-3200	80
Rider High Sch/*Wichita Falls*/Wichita	01173179	940/235-1077	392
Ridge Creek Elem Sch/*Humble*/Harris	11925081	281/641-3700	196
Ridge Point High Sch/*Missouri City*/Fort Bend	11561908	281/327-5200	151
Ridgecrest Elem Sch/*Amarillo*/Potter	01047427	806/326-5100	318
Ridgecrest Elem Sch/*Houston*/Harris	01027257	713/251-6600	201
Ridgegate Elem Sch/*Houston*/Fort Bend	02126399	281/634-4840	151
Ridgemont Elem Sch/*Houston*/Fort Bend	01018191	281/634-4880	151
Ridgetop Elem Sch/*Austin*/Travis	01056595	512/414-4469	368
Ridgeview Elem Sch/*Keller*/Tarrant	11710329	817/744-6600	355
Ridgeview Elem Sch/*San Antonio*/Bexar	00997908	210/407-6600	35
Ridgeview Middle Sch/*Round Rock*/Williamson	04938875	512/424-8400	399
Ridgewood Elem Sch/*Port Neches*/Jefferson	01034016	409/722-7641	244
Ridglea Hills Elem Sch/*Fort Worth*/Tarrant	01053294	817/815-1700	351
Riesel High Sch/*Riesel*/McLennan	01040027	254/896-3171	281
RIESEL IND SCH DIST/RIESEL/ MCLENNAN	01040003	254/896-6411	281
Ringgold Elem Sch/*Rio Grande Cy*/Starr	01051181	956/716-6929	340
Ringgold Middle Sch/*Rio Grande Cy*/Starr	01051167	956/716-6851	340
Rio Bravo Middle Sch/*El Paso*/El Paso	04754435	915/434-8400	138
Rio Grande City High Sch/*Rio Grande Cy*/Starr	01051193	956/488-6000	340
RIO GRANDE CITY IND SCH DIST/ RIO GRANDE CY/STARR	01051117	956/716-6702	340
Rio Hondo Elem Sch/*Rio Hondo*/Cameron	01004114	956/748-1050	66
Rio Hondo High Sch/*Rio Hondo*/Cameron	01004126	956/748-1200	66
RIO HONDO IND SCH DIST/RIO HONDO/ CAMERON	01004102	956/748-1000	66
Rio Hondo Middle Sch/*Rio Hondo*/Cameron	01004138	956/748-1150	66
Rio Vista Elem Sch/*Rio Vista*/Johnson	03047198	817/373-2151	248
Rio Vista High Sch/*Rio Vista*/Johnson	01035149	817/373-2009	248
RIO VISTA IND SCH DIST/RIO VISTA/ JOHNSON	01035137	817/373-2241	248
Rio Vista Middle Sch/*Rio Vista*/Johnson	03246520	817/373-2241	249
Riojas Elem Sch/*Pflugerville*/Travis	11548542	512/594-4100	372
Ripley House Middle Sch/*Houston*/Harris	11827790	713/315-6429	10
Risd Academy/*Dallas*/Dallas	03010755	469/593-3300	113
Rise Academy/*Lubbock*/Lubbock	04892817	806/744-0438	10
Rise Academy/*Tyler*/Smith	04808579	903/262-3040	338
Rise School of Austin/*Austin*/Travis	05313785	512/891-1682	373
Rise School of Dallas/*Dallas*/Dallas	05378163	214/373-7473	116
Rising Scholars Acad of S TX/*San Benito*/Cameron	12104589	956/399-4358	68

TX-V62   800-333-8802   School Year 2019-2020

Texas School Directory

DISTRICT & SCHOOL TELEPHONE INDEX

School/City/County DISTRICT/CITY/COUNTY	PID	TELEPHONE NUMBER	PAGE
Rising Star Elem Sch/*Rising Star*/Eastland	01014523	254/643-2431	129
Rising Star High Sch/*Rising Star*/Eastland	01014535	254/643-3521	129
RISING STAR IND SCH DIST/			
RISING STAR/EASTLAND	01014511	254/643-1981	129
Rita Drabek Elem Sch/*Sugar Land*/Fort Bend	04947929	281/634-6570	151
Rita Smith Elem Sch/*Wylie*/Collin	10915693	972/429-2540	85
River Bend Elem Sch/*College Sta*/Brazos	12363591	979/694-5841	56
River City Believers Academy/*Selma*/Guadalupe	12052039	210/656-2999	174
River City Christian Sch/*San Antonio*/Bexar	11225570	210/384-0297	45
River Oaks Academy/*Houston*/Harris	11238424	713/783-7200	206
River Oaks Baptist Sch/*Houston*/Harris	01480350	713/623-6938	207
River Oaks Elem Sch/*Austin*/Travis	04035825	512/594-5000	372
River Oaks Elem Sch/*Houston*/Harris	01418436	713/942-1460	194
River Pines Elem Sch/*Humble*/Harris	10911544	281/641-3300	196
River Place Elem Sch/*Austin*/Williamson	10914338	512/570-6900	397
River Ridge Elem Sch/*Austin*/Williamson	11450995	512/570-7300	397
River Road High Sch/*Amarillo*/Potter	01047611	806/383-8867	319
RIVER ROAD IND SCH DIST/			
AMARILLO/POTTER	01047609	806/381-7800	319
River Road Middle Sch/*Amarillo*/Potter	01047635	806/383-8721	319
River Trails Elem Sch/*Fort Worth*/Tarrant	05097046	817/285-3235	354
River Valley Intermediate Sch/*Mc Gregor*/McLennan	11567299	254/761-5699	281
Rivera Elem Sch/*El Paso*/El Paso	01418292	915/236-3700	134
Riverchase Elem Sch/*Coppell*/Dallas	04920311	972/968-2900	97
Rivercrest Elem Sch/*Bogata*/Red River	01048225	903/632-5214	323
Rivercrest High Sch/*Bogata*/Red River	01048237	903/632-5204	323
RIVERCREST IND SCH DIST/			
BOGATA/RED RIVER	01048213	903/632-5203	322
Rivercrest Junior High Sch/*Bogata*/Red River	01048249	903/632-0878	323
Riverside Applied Lrng Center/*Fort Worth*/Tarrant	01052604	817/815-5800	351
Riverside High Sch/*El Paso*/El Paso	01016571	915/434-7000	138
Riverside Middle Sch/*El Paso*/El Paso	01016583	915/434-7300	138
Riverside Middle Sch/*Fort Worth*/Tarrant	01053323	817/814-9200	352
Riverside Middle Sch/*San Benito*/Cameron	10031924	956/361-6940	67
Riverside Park Academy/*San Antonio*/Bexar	00999281	210/228-3355	41
Rivertree Academy/*Fort Worth*/Tarrant	12363395	817/420-9310	359
Riverwood Middle Sch/*Kingwood*/Harris	03394719	281/641-4800	196
RIVIERA IND SCH DIST/RIVIERA/			
KLEBERG	01036399	361/296-3101	258
Roan Forest Elem Sch/*San Antonio*/Bexar	05101544	210/407-6800	35
Roanoke Elem Sch/*Roanoke*/Denton	01013579	817/215-0650	125
Roark Elem Sch/*Arlington*/Tarrant	01051882	682/867-2900	345
Robb Elem Sch/*Uvalde*/Uvalde	01057848	830/591-4947	378
Robbie E Howard Jr High Sch/*Waxahachie*/Ellis	11131979	972/923-4771	142
Robbin E L Washington Elem Sch/*El Paso*/El Paso	04948313	915/434-5900	138
Robert & Felice Bryant ES/*Katy*/Harris	12231285	281/234-4300	152
Robert B Green Academy/*San Antonio*/Bexar	00999293	210/228-3325	41
Robert Brabham Middle Sch/*Willis*/Montgomery	05351684	936/890-2312	294
Robert Cobb Middle Sch/*Frisco*/Collin	11558339	469/633-4300	80
Robert Driscoll Jr Elem Sch/*Robstown*/Nueces	01044932	361/767-6641	305
Robert E King Elem Sch/*Katy*/Harris	04948739	281/237-6850	152
Robert E Lee Elem Sch/*Amarillo*/Potter	01047439	806/326-4750	318
Robert E Lee Elem Sch/*Eagle Pass*/Maverick	01041124	830/758-7062	277
Robert E Lee Elem Sch/*Edinburg*/Hidalgo	01029762	956/289-2342	217
Robert E Lee Freshman High Sch/*Midland*/Midland	01041447	432/689-1250	286
Robert E Lee High Sch/*Baytown*/Harris	01023718	281/420-4535	188
Robert E Lee High Sch/*Tyler*/Smith	01050943	903/262-2625	338
Robert E Lee Intermediate Sch/*Gainesville*/Cooke	04752671	940/668-6662	91
Robert E Lee Sr High Sch/*Midland*/Midland	01041617	432/689-1600	286
Robert F Hunt Elem Sch/*Diana*/Upshur	04034376	903/663-8004	376
Robert F Koennecke Elem Sch/*Seguin*/Guadalupe	03009914	830/401-8741	174
Robert G Cole Jr/Sr High Sch/*San Antonio*/Bexar	11074890	210/368-8730	32
Robert L Crippen Elem Sch/*Porter*/Montgomery	04450653	281/577-8740	294
Robert L Stevenson Primary Sch/*Alvin*/Brazoria	01534121	281/585-3349	51
Robert L Thornton Elem Sch/*Dallas*/Dallas	01009657	972/794-8000	102
ROBERT LEE IND SCH DIST/			
ROBERT LEE/COKE	01005780	325/453-4555	75
Robert Lee Sch/*Robert Lee*/Coke	01005792	325/453-4555	75
Robert M Beren Academy/*Houston*/Harris	01027790	713/723-7170	207
Robert M Shoemaker High Sch/*Killeen*/Bell	04368804	254/336-0900	28
Robert R Rojas Elem Sch/*El Paso*/El Paso	03009835	915/937-8500	136
Robert R Shaw Ctr for Steam/*Katy*/Harris	12239457	281/396-7670	153
Robert S Hyer Elem Sch/*Dallas*/Dallas	01011088	214/780-3300	108
Robert T Hill Middle Sch/*Dallas*/Dallas	01009700	972/502-5700	102
Robert Turner Colege-Career HS/*Pearland*/Brazoria	11917266	281/727-1600	53
Robert Vela High Sch/*Edinburg*/Hidalgo	11822910	956/289-2650	217
Roberta Rylander Elem Sch/*Katy*/Harris	05344344	281/237-8300	153
Roberta Tipps Elem Sch/*Mansfield*/Tarrant	05273642	817/299-6920	357
Roberts Elem Sch/*Bay City*/Matagorda	01040869	979/401-1500	275
Roberts Elem Sch/*El Paso*/El Paso	01016064	915/236-3775	134
Roberts Elem Sch/*Houston*/Harris	01024944	713/295-5272	194
Roberts Middle Sch/*Fulshear*/Fort Bend	12364129	832/223-5300	154
Roberts Road Elem Sch/*Hockley*/Waller	02896178	936/931-0300	384
Robertson Elem Sch/*Little Elm*/Collin	10912706	469/633-3675	80
Robindell Private Sch/*Houston*/Harris	01480300	713/667-9895	207
Robinson Elem Sch/*Robinson*/McLennan	03319501	254/662-5000	281
Robinson Elem Sch/*Robinson*/McLennan	01040053	254/662-3840	281
ROBINSON IND SCH DIST/ROBINSON/			
MCLENNAN	01040039	254/662-0194	281
Robinson Intermediate Sch/*Robinson*/McLennan	04939374	254/662-6113	281
Robinson Junior High Sch/*Robinson*/McLennan	01040065	254/662-3843	281
Robinson Middle Sch/*Plano*/Collin	04145391	469/752-6200	83
Robinson Primary Sch/*Robinson*/McLennan	01040041	254/662-0251	281
Robstown High Sch/*Robstown*/Nueces	01044944	361/387-5999	305
ROBSTOWN IND SCH DIST/ROBSTOWN/			
NUECES	01044906	361/767-6600	305
ROBY CONS IND SCH DIST/ROBY/			
FISHER	01017886	325/776-2222	148
Roby Elem Sch/*Roby*/Fisher	01017903	325/776-2222	148
Roby High Sch/*Roby*/Fisher	04914544	325/776-2223	148
ROCHELLE IND SCH DIST/ROCHELLE/			
MCCULLOCH	01039509	325/243-5224	278
Rochelle Sch/*Rochelle*/McCulloch	01039511	325/243-5224	278
Rock Prairie Elem Sch/*College Sta*/Brazos	03236399	979/764-5570	56
Rockbrook Elem Sch/*Lewisville*/Denton	05271852	469/713-5968	124
Rockdale Elem Sch/*Rockdale*/Milam	01041863	512/430-6030	287
Rockdale Elem Sch/*Rockdale*/Milam	01041875	512/430-6140	288
ROCKDALE IND SCH DIST/ROCKDALE/			
MILAM	01041851	512/430-6000	287
Rockdale Intermediate Sch/*Rockdale*/Milam	11540631	512/430-6200	288
Rockdale Junior High Sch/*Rockdale*/Milam	01041887	512/430-6100	288
Rockenbaugh Elem Sch/*Southlake*/Tarrant	04747315	817/949-4700	347
Rockport-Fulton High Sch/*Rockport*/Aransas	00995168	361/790-2220	19
Rockport-Fulton Middle Sch/*Rockport*/Aransas	00995170	361/790-2230	19
ROCKSPRINGS IND SCH DIST/			
ROCKSPRINGS/EDWARDS	01014901	830/683-4137	131
Rocksprings Sch/*Rocksprings*/Edwards	01014913	830/683-2140	131
Rockwall High Sch/*Rockwall*/Rockwall	01048732	972/771-7339	325
ROCKWALL IND SCH DIST/ROCKWALL/			
ROCKWALL	01048718	972/771-0605	325
Rockwall Quest Academy/*Rockwall*/Rockwall	04364080	972/772-2077	325
Rockwall-Heath High Sch/*Heath*/Rockwall	10012693	972/772-2474	325
Rodeo Palms Junior High Sch/*Manvel*/Brazoria	01001459	281/245-2078	51
Rodger & Ellen Beck Jr HS/*Katy*/Harris	04452259	281/237-3300	153
Rodolfo Centeno Elem Sch/*Laredo*/Webb	05350692	956/473-8800	388
Rodriguez Elem Sch/*Austin*/Travis	04869858	512/841-7200	367
Rodriguez Elem Sch/*Harlingen*/Cameron	05343338	956/430-4060	65
Rodriguez Elem Sch/*San Antonio*/Bexar	00999188	210/978-8000	41
Rodriguez Middle Sch/*Aubrey*/Denton	12305616	972/347-7050	121
Roel & Celia Saenz Elem Sch/*Roma*/Starr	11072232	956/849-7230	341
Rogene Worley Middle Sch/*Mansfield*/Tarrant	01172620	682/314-5100	357
Roger E Sides Elem Sch/*Karnes City*/Karnes	01035424	830/780-2321	250
Roger Q Mills Elem Sch/*Dallas*/Dallas	01009671	972/925-7500	102
Rogers Elem Sch/*Rogers*/Bell	00996655	254/642-3250	29
Rogers High Sch/*Rogers*/Bell	00996667	254/642-3224	29
ROGERS IND SCH DIST/ROGERS/BELL	00996643	254/642-3802	28
Rogers Middle Sch/*Pearland*/Brazoria	05271723	832/736-6400	53
Rogers Middle Sch/*Prosper*/Collin	04920672	469/219-2150	84
Rogers Middle Sch/*Rogers*/Bell	04365125	254/642-3011	29
Rogers Middle Sch/*San Antonio*/Bexar	00998811	210/438-6840	41
Roland Reynolds Elem Sch/*Franklin*/Robertson	01048639	979/828-7300	325
Rolling Hills Elem Sch/*Amarillo*/Potter	01047623	806/383-8621	319
Rolling Hills Elem Sch/*Lancaster*/Dallas	03240417	972/218-1525	110
Rolling Meadows Elem Sch/*San Antonio*/Bexar	11561570	210/945-5700	33
Roma High Sch/*Roma*/Starr	01051272	956/849-1333	341

DISTRICT & SCHOOL TELEPHONE INDEX

Market Data Retrieval

School/City/County DISTRICT/CITY/COUNTY	PID	TELEPHONE NUMBER	PAGE
ROMA IND SCH DIST/ROMA/STARR	01051222	956/849-1377	341
Roma Instructional Sch/Roma/Starr	04365333	956/849-2803	341
Roma Middle Sch/Roma/Starr	01051284	956/849-1434	341
Romulo Martinez Elem Sch/Mission/Hidalgo	04918722	956/584-4900	224
Ronald E McNair Elem Sch/Dallas/Dallas	03018692	972/794-6200	102
Ronald E McNair Middle Sch/Atascosa/Bexar	00999633	210/622-4480	43
Ronald Reagan Elem Sch/Cedar Park/Williamson	11450971	512/570-7200	397
Ronald Reagan High Sch/San Antonio/Bexar	04865876	210/356-1800	35
Ronald Reagan Middle Sch/Grand Prairie/Dallas	05342633	972/522-7300	108
Ronald Thornton Middle Sch/Missouri City/Fort Bend	12312011	281/327-3870	151
Ronnie Crownover Middle Sch/Corinth/Denton	05096432	940/369-4700	121
Roosevelt Alexander Elem Sch/Katy/Harris	04803646	281/237-7100	153
Roosevelt Alt Sch/Mission/Hidalgo	03393521	956/323-3900	222
Roosevelt Elem Sch/Houston/Harris	01026069	713/696-2820	192
Roosevelt Elem Sch/Laredo/Webb	04455938	956/473-3400	388
Roosevelt Elem Sch/Lubbock/Lubbock	01039121	806/842-3284	271
Roosevelt Elem Sch/San Antonio/Bexar	10007167	210/444-8375	32
Roosevelt High Sch/Lubbock/Lubbock	01039145	806/842-3283	271
Roosevelt High Sch/Windcrest/Bexar	00997934	210/356-2200	35
ROOSEVELT IND SCH DIST/LUBBOCK/LUBBOCK	01039119	806/842-3282	271
Roosevelt Junior High Sch/Lubbock/Lubbock	04917869	806/842-3218	271
Roosevelt-Wilson Elem Sch/Texas City/Galveston	01019559	409/916-0200	161
Rooster Springs Elem Sch/Austin/Hays	10904981	512/465-6200	210
ROPES IND SCH DIST/ROPESVILLE/HOCKLEY	01031234	806/562-4031	229
Ropes Sch/Ropesville/Hockley	01031246	806/562-4031	229
Roque Guerra Jr Elem Sch/Rio Grande Cy/Starr	01051210	956/716-6982	340
Rosa Guerrero Elem Sch/El Paso/El Paso	04035679	915/236-3075	134
Rosa Parks Elem Sch/Fresno/Fort Bend	10912885	281/634-6390	151
Rosa Parks-Millbrook Sch/Lancaster/Dallas	02896788	972/218-1564	110
Rosanky Christian Academy/Rosanky/Bastrop	11229617	512/360-3109	24
Roscoe Collegiate High Sch/Roscoe/Nolan	01043902	325/766-3327	301
ROSCOE COLLEGIATE IND SCH DIST/ROSCOE/NOLAN	01043885	325/766-3629	301
Roscoe Collegiate Mont ECC/Roscoe/Nolan	12232605	325/766-3323	301
Roscoe Elem Sch/Roscoe/Nolan	01043897	325/766-3323	301
Roscoe Wilson Elem Sch/Lubbock/Lubbock	01038866	806/219-7500	270
Rose Garden Elem Sch/Schertz/Guadalupe	01021590	210/619-4350	173
Rose Haggar Elem Sch/Dallas/Collin	04366789	469/752-1400	83
Rose M Avalos P-Tech Sch/Houston/Harris	12365616	281/985-2100	180
Rosebud-Lott Elem Sch/Lott/Falls	01017290	254/583-7965	145
Rosebud-Lott Elem Sch/Lott/Falls	11565461	254/583-7967	145
ROSEBUD-LOTT IND SCH DIST/LOTT/FALLS	01017276	254/583-4510	145
Rosebud-Lott Middle Sch/Lott/Falls	01017317	254/583-7962	145
Rosedale Sch/Austin/Travis	02127848	512/414-3617	368
Rosehill Christian Sch/Tomball/Harris	04466535	281/351-8114	207
Rosehill Elem Sch/Tomball/Harris	05279373	281/357-3075	203
Rosemeade Elem Sch/Carrollton/Dallas	02227905	972/968-3000	97
Rosemont 6th Grade Center/Fort Worth/Tarrant	04866222	817/814-7300	352
Rosemont Elem & Prep Lang MS/Dallas/Dallas	01009712	972/749-5000	102
Rosemont Elem Sch/Fort Worth/Tarrant	11711880	817/815-5200	352
Rosemont Middle Sch/Fort Worth/Tarrant	01053347	817/814-7200	352
Rosemont Primary Sch/Dallas/Dallas	10006797	972/502-3850	102
Rosenberg Elem Sch/Galveston/Galveston	11451078	409/761-6800	160
Rosendo Benavides Elem Sch/Sullivan City/Hidalgo	02202876	956/323-2360	220
Rosewood Head Start Center/Wichita Falls/Wichita	05364552	940/235-4309	392
Rosita Valley Elem Sch/Eagle Pass/Maverick	04021692	830/758-7065	277
Rosita Valley Literacy Academy/Eagle Pass/Maverick	04806911	830/758-7067	277
Ross Baldwin Elem Sch/Austin/Travis	11552555	512/841-8900	367
Ross Elem Sch/Houston/Harris	01025792	713/226-4550	191
Ross Elem Sch/Odessa/Ector	01014810	432/456-1199	130
Ross Middle Sch/El Paso/El Paso	01015670	915/236-0800	135
Ross S Sterling High Sch/Baytown/Harris	01023728	281/420-4500	188
Ross Sterling Middle Sch/Humble/Harris	10911532	281/641-6000	196
Rotan Elem Sch/Rotan/Fisher	01017927	325/735-3182	148
Rotan High Sch/Rotan/Fisher	01017939	325/735-3041	148
ROTAN IND SCH DIST/ROTAN/FISHER	01017915	325/735-2332	148
Roth Elem Sch/Spring/Harris	02227163	832/484-6600	197
Round Rock Christian Academy/Round Rock/Williamson	02785165	512/255-4491	400
Round Rock High Sch/Round Rock/Williamson	01061124	512/464-6000	399

School/City/County DISTRICT/CITY/COUNTY	PID	TELEPHONE NUMBER	PAGE
ROUND ROCK IND SCH DIST/ROUND ROCK/WILLIAMSON	01061083	512/464-5000	398
Round Rock Opportunity Center/Round Rock/Williamson	02949476	512/428-2900	399
Round Top Carmine Elem Sch/Round Top/Fayette	01017783	979/249-3200	147
Round Top Carmine High Sch/Carmine/Fayette	01017795	979/278-3252	147
ROUND TOP-CARMINE IND SCH DIST/CARMINE/FAYETTE	01017771	979/278-3252	147
Rouse High Sch/Leander/Williamson	11130781	512/570-2000	397
Routh Roach Elem Sch/Garland/Dallas	01010668	972/926-2580	106
Rowe Lane Elem Sch/Pflugerville/Travis	10006852	512/594-6600	372
Rowland Elem Sch/Victoria/Victoria	01058567	361/788-9549	382
Rowlett Elem Sch/Rowlett/Dallas	01010670	972/475-3380	106
Rowlett High Sch/Rowlett/Dallas	04450988	972/463-1712	106
Roy Cisneros Elem Sch/San Antonio/Bexar	00997130	210/444-7850	32
Roy J Smith Middle Sch/Killeen/Bell	12225949	254/336-1050	28
Roy J Wollam Elem Sch/Santa Fe/Galveston	02897134	409/925-2770	161
Roy Lee Walker Elem Sch/McKinney/Collin	04920701	469/302-4600	81
Roy P Benavidez Elem Sch/San Antonio/Bexar	00999401	210/677-7175	42
Roy Roberts Elem Sch/Lubbock/Lubbock	10911025	806/219-7900	270
Royal Early Childhood Center/Brookshire/Waller	03393686	281/934-3147	384
Royal Elem Sch/Brookshire/Waller	01058828	281/934-3166	384
Royal High Sch/Brookshire/Waller	01058842	281/934-2215	384
ROYAL IND SCH DIST/PATTISON/WALLER	01058816	281/934-2248	384
Royal Junior High Sch/Brookshire/Waller	01058830	281/934-2241	384
Royal Point Academy/San Antonio/Bexar	04993825	210/674-5310	45
Royal Ridge Elem Sch/San Antonio/Bexar	05118975	210/407-7000	35
Royalwood Elem Sch/Houston/Harris	01027051	281/454-2700	200
Royse City High Sch/Royse City/Rockwall	01048794	972/636-9991	326
ROYSE CITY IND SCH DIST/ROYSE CITY/ROCKWALL	01048770	972/636-2413	326
Royse City Middle Sch/Royse City/Rockwall	01048782	972/636-9544	326
Rspa Northeast-Humble/Humble/Harris	12361505	281/319-9300	10
Rspa Northshore/Houston/Harris	12361517	281/459-9797	10
Rspa Northwest-Living Word/Houston/Harris	12261216	832/562-2822	10
Rspa-Channelview/Channelview/Harris	12261228	281/864-7015	10
Rspa-E Northshore/Houston/Harris	11933832	281/459-9797	10
Rspa-NE Humble/Humble/Harris	12261204	281/319-9300	10
Ruben Chavira Elem Sch/Del Rio/Val Verde	03009598	830/778-4660	379
Ruben Hinojosa Elem Sch/Mercedes/Hidalgo	01030151	956/514-2277	222
Ruben Rodriguez Elem Sch/Edcouch/Hidalgo	02857005	956/262-4712	216
Rubicon Academy/The Woodlands/Montgomery	04932431	936/273-9111	295
Ruby M Reed Academy/Houston/Harris	04285276	281/985-6670	180
Ruby Shaw Elem Sch/Mesquite/Dallas	02201884	972/882-7060	111
Ruby Sue Clifton Middle Sch/Houston/Harris	02043292	713/613-2516	192
Ruby Thompson Elem Sch/Houston/Harris	01024994	713/746-8250	193
Ruby Young Elem Sch/Desoto/Dallas	01010280	972/223-6505	104
Rucker Elem Sch/Houston/Harris	01025687	713/845-7467	190
Rudy Silva Elem Sch/Weslaco/Hidalgo	01030618	956/969-6790	225
Rufino Mendoza Elem Sch/Fort Worth/Tarrant	01052769	817/814-4700	352
Rufus C Burleson Elem Sch/Dallas/Dallas	01008574	972/749-4500	102
RULE IND SCH DIST/RULE/HASKELL	01028964	940/997-2521	210
Rule Sch/Rule/Haskell	01028976	940/997-2521	210
Rummel Creek Elem Sch/Houston/Harris	01027269	713/251-6700	201
RUNGE IND SCH DIST/RUNGE/KARNES	01035503	830/239-4315	251
Runge Sch/Runge/Karnes	01035515	830/239-4315	251
Runn Elem Sch/Donna/Hidalgo	01029619	956/464-1864	215
Running Brushy Middle Sch/Cedar Park/Williamson	04915809	512/570-3300	397
Runyan Elem Sch/Conroe/Montgomery	01042520	936/709-2800	292
Rush Elem Sch/Lubbock/Lubbock	01038880	806/219-6700	270
Rusk Elem Sch/El Paso/El Paso	01015682	915/236-0475	134
Rusk Elem Sch/Midland/Midland	01041629	432/240-7800	286
Rusk Elem Sch/Rusk/Cherokee	01005376	903/683-6106	73
Rusk High Sch/Rusk/Cherokee	01005388	903/683-5401	73
RUSK IND SCH DIST/RUSK/CHEROKEE	01005364	903/683-5592	73
Rusk Intermediate Sch/Rusk/Cherokee	05341859	903/683-1726	73
Rusk Junior High Sch/Rusk/Cherokee	01005390	903/683-2502	73
Rusk Primary Sch/Rusk/Cherokee	02130194	903/683-6106	73
Russell Elem Sch/Brownsville/Cameron	01003689	956/548-8960	64
Russell Schupmann Elem Sch/Glenn Heights/Ellis	02894003	972/617-2685	142
Rustic Oak Elem Sch/Pearland/Brazoria	04033891	281/482-5400	53
Ruth Borchardt Elem Sch/Plano/Collin	04942826	469/633-2800	80
Ruth Cherry Interm Sch/Royse City/Rockwall	11462443	972/636-3301	326
Ruth Dowell Middle Sch/McKinney/Collin	01006318	469/302-6700	81
Ruth Jones McClendon Mid Sch/San Antonio/Bexar	12261412	210/568-8800	10
Rutledge Elem Sch/Austin/Williamson	10006890	512/570-6500	397

Texas School Directory
DISTRICT & SCHOOL TELEPHONE INDEX

School/City/County DISTRICT/CITY/COUNTY	PID	TELEPHONE NUMBER	PAGE
S			
S & S Cons High Sch/*Sadler*/Grayson	01020584	903/564-3768	167
S & S CONS IND SCH DIST/ SADLER/GRAYSON	01020560	903/564-6051	167
S & S Cons Middle Sch/*Sadler*/Grayson	02857184	903/564-7626	167
S & S Elem Sch/*Southmayd*/Grayson	01020572	903/893-0767	167
S C Lee Junior High Sch/*Copperas Cove*/Coryell	04452041	254/542-7877	92
S C Red Elem Sch/*Houston*/Harris	01025340	713/726-3638	194
S H Crowley Intermediate Sch/*Crowley*/Tarrant	11079711	817/297-5960	348
S M Seabourn Elem Sch/*Mesquite*/Dallas	01011583	972/882-7040	111
S S Conner Elem Sch/*Dallas*/Dallas	01009798	972/749-8200	102
S S Dillow Elem Sch/*Fort Worth*/Tarrant	01052800	817/814-0400	352
S Texas Bus Ed & Tech Acad/*Edinburg*/Cameron	01809005	956/383-1684	68
S W Carter Elem Sch/*Shelbyville*/Shelby	01050400	936/598-7363	335
Sabas Perez Eng & Tech Sch/*Laredo*/Webb	05347968	956/795-3800	387
Sabinal Elem Sch/*Sabinal*/Uvalde	01057745	830/988-2436	378
Sabinal High Sch/*Sabinal*/Uvalde	01057757	830/988-2475	378
SABINAL IND SCH DIST/SABINAL/ UVALDE	01057733	830/988-2472	378
Sabine Elem Sch/*Kilgore*/Gregg	01021227	903/984-5320	170
Sabine High Sch/*Gladewater*/Gregg	01021239	903/984-8587	170
SABINE IND SCH DIST/GLADEWATER/ GREGG	01021215	903/984-8564	170
Sabine Middle Sch/*Gladewater*/Gregg	01021241	903/984-4767	170
SABINE PASS IND SCH DIST/ SABINE PASS/JEFFERSON	01034066	409/971-2321	244
Sabine Pass Sch/*Sabine Pass*/Jefferson	01034078	409/971-2321	244
Sachse High Sch/*Sachse*/Dallas	05096793	972/414-7450	106
Sacred Heart Catholic Sch/*Floresville*/Wilson	01000027	830/393-2117	401
Sacred Heart Catholic Sch/*Hallettsville*/Lavaca	00999994	361/798-4251	263
Sacred Heart Catholic Sch/*La Grange*/Fayette	01002893	979/968-3223	148
Sacred Heart Sch/*Conroe*/Montgomery	01028146	936/756-3848	295
Sacred Heart Sch/*Crosby*/Harris	01028158	281/328-6561	204
Sacred Heart Sch/*Del Rio*/Val Verde	00999982	830/775-3274	379
Sacred Heart Sch/*Muenster*/Cooke	01054432	940/759-2511	92
Sacred Heart Sch/*Rockport*/Aransas	02136942	361/463-8963	19
Sacred Heart Sch/*Uvalde*/Uvalde	01000015	830/278-2661	378
Sadie Woodard Elem Sch/*Cypress*/Harris	12105167	281/373-2303	185
Saegert Elem Sch/*Killeen*/Bell	10030724	254/336-6660	28
Saenz Elem Sch/*Alice*/Jim Wells	01034573	361/664-4981	245
Sagamore Hill Elem Sch/*Fort Worth*/Tarrant	01053361	817/815-5000	352
Sageland Elem Sch/*El Paso*/El Paso	01016595	915/434-2900	138
Saginaw Elem Sch/*Fort Worth*/Tarrant	01052434	817/232-0631	349
Saginaw High Sch/*Fort Worth*/Tarrant	10003707	817/306-0914	349
Saigling Elem Sch/*Plano*/Collin	01540003	469/752-3000	83
Saint Constantine Sch/*Houston*/Harris	12320630	832/975-7075	207
Saint Mary's Hall/*San Antonio*/Bexar	00999669	210/483-9100	45
Saint Peters Classical Sch/*Fort Worth*/Tarrant	11226859	817/294-0124	359
Salado High Sch/*Salado*/Bell	00996681	254/947-6985	29
SALADO IND SCH DIST/SALADO/BELL	00996679	254/947-6900	29
Salado Intermediate Sch/*San Antonio*/Bexar	00997051	210/648-3310	31
Salado Junior High Sch/*Salado*/Bell	11075765	254/947-6935	29
Salazar Crossroads Academy/*Robstown*/Nueces	02127343	361/767-6600	305
Salazar Elem Sch/*Alice*/Jim Wells	01034626	361/664-6263	245
Salem Lutheran Sch/*Tomball*/Harris	01027817	281/351-8223	207
Salem Sayers Baptist Academy/*Adkins*/Bexar	02984658	210/649-1178	45
Salinas Elem Sch/*Alton*/Hidalgo	04809755	956/323-6200	222
Salinas Elem Sch/*Laredo*/Webb	01548500	956/473-3200	388
Salinas STEM Early College Sch/*La Joya*/Hidalgo	11823615	956/323-2240	220
Sally K Ride Elem Sch/*The Woodlands*/Montgomery	02200012	281/465-2800	292
Sallye Moore Clg&Career Prep/*Grand Prairie*/Dallas	04945177	972/660-2261	108
SALTILLO IND SCH DIST/SALTILLO/ HOPKINS	01031571	903/537-2386	231
Saltillo Sch/*Saltillo*/Hopkins	01031583	903/537-2386	231
Salvador Garcia Middle Sch/*Laredo*/Webb	04364054	956/473-5000	388
Salvador H Sanchez Middle Sch/*El Paso*/El Paso	03323485	915/937-5200	136
Salyards Middle Sch/*Cypress*/Harris	11713137	281/373-2400	185
Salyers Elem Sch/*Spring*/Harris	01027520	281/891-8570	202
Sam & Ann Roach Middle Sch/*Frisco*/Collin	10004684	469/633-5000	80
Sam Fordyce Elem Sch/*Sullivan City*/Hidalgo	05100942	956/323-2490	220
Sam Houston Elem Sch/*Bryan*/Brazos	03007784	979/209-1360	55
Sam Houston Elem Sch/*Corp Christi*/Nueces	01044463	361/878-2520	304
Sam Houston Elem Sch/*Corsicana*/Navarro	10902048	903/874-6971	299
Sam Houston Elem Sch/*Denton*/Denton	02177025	940/369-2900	121
Sam Houston Elem Sch/*Eagle Pass*/Maverick	04806909	830/758-7069	277
Sam Houston Elem Sch/*Ennis*/Ellis	01015008	972/872-7285	140
Sam Houston Elem Sch/*Houston*/Harris	10910655	832/386-4430	187
Sam Houston Elem Sch/*La Feria*/Cameron	01003990	956/797-8490	65
Sam Houston Elem Sch/*Marshall*/Harrison	01028718	903/927-8860	209
Sam Houston Elem Sch/*McAllen*/Hidalgo	01030072	956/971-4484	221
Sam Houston Elem Sch/*Midland*/Midland	01041631	432/240-7100	286
Sam Houston Elem Sch/*Odessa*/Ector	01014834	432/456-1139	130
Sam Houston Elem Sch/*Port Arthur*/Jefferson	01033878	409/984-4800	243
Sam Houston Elem Sch/*Weslaco*/Hidalgo	11713357	956/969-6740	225
Sam Houston High Sch/*Arlington*/Tarrant	01051909	682/867-8200	345
Sam Houston High Sch/*San Antonio*/Bexar	00998861	210/978-7900	41
Sam Houston Math Sci Tech HS/*Houston*/Harris	01025936	713/696-0200	192
Sam Houston Middle Sch/*Amarillo*/Potter	01047300	806/326-3600	318
Sam Houston Middle Sch/*Garland*/Dallas	01010694	972/926-2640	106
Sam Jamison Middle Sch/*Pearland*/Brazoria	02179841	281/412-1440	53
Sam Rayburn Elem Sch/*McAllen*/Hidalgo	02043357	956/971-4363	221
Sam Rayburn High Sch/*Pasadena*/Harris	01026928	713/740-0330	199
SAM RAYBURN IND SCH DIST/ IVANHOE/FANNIN	01017549	903/664-2255	146
Sam Rayburn Middle Sch/*San Antonio*/Bexar	00998287	210/397-2150	38
Sam Rayburn Sch/*Ivanhoe*/Fannin	01017563	903/664-2165	146
Sam Rayburn Steam Acad/*Grand Prairie*/Dallas	01010993	972/264-8900	108
Sam Rosen Elem Sch/*Fort Worth*/Tarrant	01053373	817/814-4800	352
Sam Rutherford Elem Sch/*Mesquite*/Dallas	01011595	972/290-4060	111
Sam Tasby Middle Sch/*Dallas*/Dallas	10023135	972/502-1900	102
Sampson Elem Sch/*Cypress*/Harris	05096743	281/213-1600	185
Samuel Beck Elem Sch/*Trophy Club*/Denton	04804573	817/215-0450	125
Samuel Clemens High Sch/*Schertz*/Guadalupe	01021605	210/945-6501	173
Samuel Houston Elem Sch/*Huntsville*/Walker	01058713	936/435-6750	383
San Angelo Christian Academy/*San Angelo*/Tom Green	02120993	325/651-8363	366
SAN ANGELO IND SCH DIST/ SAN ANGELO/TOM GREEN	01055539	325/947-3700	364
San Antonio Academy-Texas/*San Antonio*/Bexar	01479466	210/733-7331	45
San Antonio Christian Mid Sch/*San Antonio*/Bexar	04993734	210/248-1635	45
San Antonio Christian Sch/*San Antonio*/Bexar	01479519	210/340-1864	45
SAN ANTONIO IND SCH DIST/ SAN ANTONIO/BEXAR	00998366	210/554-2200	39
San Augustine Elem Sch/*San Augustine*/San Augustine	01049372	936/275-3424	329
SAN AUGUSTINE IND SCH DIST/ SAN AUGUSTINE/SAN AUGUSTINE	01049360	936/275-2306	329
San Augustine Mid High Sch/*San Augustine*/San Augustine	01049384	936/275-9603	329
SAN BENITO CONS IND SCH DIST/ SAN BENITO/CAMERON	01004140	956/361-6100	66
San Benito High Sch/*San Benito*/Cameron	01004267	956/361-6500	67
San Carlos Elem Sch/*Edinburg*/Hidalgo	03012193	956/289-2370	217
San Diego High Sch/*San Diego*/Duval	01014315	361/279-1840	128
SAN DIEGO IND SCH DIST/SAN DIEGO/ DUVAL	01014274	361/279-3382	128
San Elizario High Sch/*San Elizario*/El Paso	01016193	915/872-3970	135
SAN ELIZARIO IND SCH DIST/ SAN ELIZARIO/EL PASO	01016179	915/872-3900	135
San Felipe Memorial Middle Sch/*Del Rio*/Val Verde	01058012	830/778-4560	379
SAN FELIPE-DEL RIO CONS IND SD/ DEL RIO/VAL VERDE	01057941	830/778-4000	379
San Isidro Elem Sch/*Laredo*/Webb	12308242	956/473-6700	388
SAN ISIDRO IND SCH DIST/ SAN ISIDRO/STARR	01051296	956/481-3100	341
San Isidro Sch/*San Isidro*/Starr	01051301	956/481-3100	341
San Jacinto Adult Learning Ctr/*El Paso*/El Paso	04806662	915/230-3200	133
San Jacinto Christian Academy/*Amarillo*/Potter	02207034	806/372-2285	319
San Jacinto Elem Sch/*Amarillo*/Potter	01047465	806/326-5200	318
San Jacinto Elem Sch/*Baytown*/Harris	01023744	281/420-4670	188
San Jacinto Elem Sch/*Conroe*/Montgomery	02110390	281/465-7700	292
San Jacinto Elem Sch/*Dallas*/Dallas	01009815	972/749-4200	102
San Jacinto Elem Sch/*Deer Park*/Harris	01023407	832/668-7900	186
San Jacinto Elem Sch/*Liberty*/Liberty	01037965	936/336-3161	266
San Jacinto Elem Sch/*Odessa*/Ector	01014846	432/456-1219	130

DISTRICT & SCHOOL TELEPHONE INDEX

Market Data Retrieval

School/City/County DISTRICT/CITY/COUNTY	PID	TELEPHONE NUMBER	PAGE
San Jacinto Elem Sch/*San Angelo*/Tom Green	01055773	325/659-3675	365
San Jacinto Intermediate Sch/*Pasadena*/Harris	01026930	713/740-0480	199
San Jacinto Junior High Sch/*Midland*/Midland	01041643	432/689-1350	286
San Juan Diego Cath High Sch/*Austin*/Travis	05153523	512/804-1935	372
San Leon Elem Sch/*Dickinson*/Galveston	10905131	281/229-7400	160
San Luis Elem Sch/*Eagle Pass*/Maverick	01041136	830/758-7071	277
San Marcos Adventist Jr Acad/*San Marcos*/Hays	02233851	512/392-9475	212
San Marcos Baptist Academy/*San Marcos*/Hays	01029190	512/353-2400	212
SAN MARCOS CONS IND SCH DIST/SAN MARCOS/HAYS	01029114	512/393-6700	211
San Marcos High Sch/*San Marcos*/Hays	01029176	512/393-6800	212
San Martin De Porres Sch/*Weslaco*/Hidalgo	04880149	956/973-8642	226
San Pedro Elem Sch/*Robstown*/Nueces	01044918	361/767-6648	305
SAN PERLITA IND SCH DIST/SAN PERLITA/WILLACY	01060780	956/248-5563	394
San Perlita Sch/*San Perlita*/Willacy	01857430	956/248-5250	394
San Saba Elem Sch/*San Saba*/San Saba	01049956	325/372-3019	332
San Saba High Sch/*San Saba*/San Saba	01049968	325/372-3786	332
SAN SABA IND SCH DIST/SAN SABA/SAN SABA	01049944	325/372-3771	332
San Saba Middle Sch/*San Saba*/San Saba	01418577	325/372-3200	333
San Vicente Elem Sch/*Bg BND NTL Pk*/Brewster	01002271	432/477-2220	57
SAN VICENTE IND SCH DIST/BG BND NTL PK/BREWSTER	01002269	432/477-2220	57
Sanborn Elem Sch/*Amarillo*/Potter	01047477	806/326-5250	318
Sanchez Elem Sch/*Austin*/Travis	01056521	512/414-4423	367
Sanchez Elem Sch/*Houston*/Harris	02857964	713/845-7472	190
Sanchez-Ochoa Elem Sch/*Laredo*/Webb	01059250	956/273-4500	387
Sanderson Public Sch/*Sanderson*/Terrell	01055060	432/345-2515	362
Sandra Day O'Connor High Sch/*Helotes*/Bexar	04809030	210/397-4800	38
Sandra Mossman Elem Sch/*League City*/Galveston	11449104	281/284-4000	159
SANDS CONSOLIDATED ISD/ACKERLY/DAWSON	01012941	432/353-4888	117
Sands Sch/*Ackerly*/Dawson	01012953	432/353-4744	117
Sandy McNutt Elem Sch/*Arlington*/Tarrant	12170100	682/867-9100	345
Sanford Fritch Elem Sch/*Fritch*/Hutchinson	01032783	806/397-0159	238
Sanford Fritch High Sch/*Fritch*/Hutchinson	01032800	806/359-0159	238
Sanford Fritch Jr High Sch/*Fritch*/Hutchinson	02178225	806/397-0159	238
SANFORD-FRITCH IND SCH DIST/FRITCH/HUTCHINSON	01032771	806/397-0159	238
Sanger 6th Grade Sch/*Sanger*/Denton	11148257	940/458-3699	126
Sanger High Sch/*Sanger*/Denton	01528122	940/458-7497	126
SANGER IND SCH DIST/SANGER/DENTON	01013646	940/458-7438	126
Sanger Middle Sch/*Sanger*/Denton	01013660	940/458-7916	126
Santa Anna Elem Sch/*Santa Anna*/Coleman	01005936	325/348-3138	76
Santa Anna High Sch/*Santa Anna*/Coleman	01005948	325/348-3137	76
SANTA ANNA IND SCH DIST/SANTA ANNA/COLEMAN	01005924	325/348-3136	76
Santa Clara Catholic Academy/*Dallas*/Dallas	04309341	214/333-9423	114
Santa Cruz Elem Sch/*Buda*/Hays	11396428	512/312-2137	212
Santa Fe Elem Sch/*Cleburne*/Johnson	10905143	817/202-2300	247
Santa Fe High Sch/*Santa Fe*/Galveston	01019444	409/927-3100	161
SANTA FE IND SCH DIST/SANTA FE/GALVESTON	01019432	409/925-3526	161
Santa Fe Junior High Sch/*Santa Fe*/Galveston	01019456	409/925-9300	161
Santa Gertrudis Elem MS/*Kingsville*/Kleberg	01809548	361/384-5046	258
SANTA GERTRUDIS IND SCH DIST/KINGSVILLE/KLEBERG	01809536	361/384-5087	258
Santa Maria Elem Sch/*Laredo*/Webb	01059406	956/273-4600	387
Santa Maria High Sch/*Santa Maria*/Cameron	04036453	956/565-9144	67
SANTA MARIA IND SCH DIST/SANTA MARIA/CAMERON	01004308	956/565-6308	67
Santa Maria Junior High Sch/*Santa Maria*/Cameron	12319966	956/565-5348	67
Santa Maria Middle Sch/*Santa Maria*/Cameron	04036441	956/565-5039	67
Santa Rita Elem Sch/*Midland*/Midland	02199956	432/240-7900	286
Santa Rita Elem Sch/*San Angelo*/Tom Green	01055785	325/659-3672	365
Santa Rosa High Sch/*Santa Rosa*/Cameron	01004334	956/636-9830	67
SANTA ROSA IND SCH DIST/SANTA ROSA/CAMERON	01004322	956/636-9800	67
Santiago Garcia Elem Sch/*Edcouch*/Hidalgo	01029645	956/262-4741	216
Santo Elem Sch/*Santo*/Palo Pinto	02110417	940/769-3215	310
SANTO IND SCH DIST/SANTO/PALO PINTO	01046124	940/769-2835	310
Santo J Forte Jr High Sch/*Azle*/Tarrant	04866973	817/270-1133	345
Santo Jr Sr High Sch/*Santo*/Palo Pinto	04749167	940/769-3847	310
Santo Nino Elem Sch/*Laredo*/Webb	01059418	956/273-4700	387
Santos Livas Elem Sch/*Alamo*/Hidalgo	04288527	956/354-2860	224
Sarah King Elem Sch/*San Antonio*/Bexar	00999229	210/978-7990	41
Sarah Zumwalt Middle Sch/*Dallas*/Dallas	01009827	972/749-3600	102
Sarita Elem Sch/*Sarita*/Kenedy	01035929	361/294-5381	254
Sartartia Middle Sch/*Sugar Land*/Fort Bend	04947137	281/634-6310	151
Satori Elem Sch/*Galveston*/Galveston	10009660	409/763-7022	162
Savannah Elem Sch/*Aubrey*/Denton	10021864	972/347-7400	121
Savannah Heights Interm Sch/*Von Ormy*/Bexar	10915253	866/852-9863	42
Savannah Lakes Elem Sch/*Rosharon*/Brazoria	11070961	281/245-3214	51
Savoy Elem Sch/*Savoy*/Fannin	01017587	903/965-7738	146
Savoy High Sch/*Savoy*/Fannin	04942151	903/965-4024	146
SAVOY IND SCH DIST/SAVOY/FANNIN	01017575	903/965-5262	146
Scanlan Oaks Elem Sch/*Missouri City*/Fort Bend	05345520	281/634-3950	151
Scarborough Elem Sch/*Houston*/Harris	01026100	713/696-2710	191
Scarborough Elem Sch/*San Antonio*/Bexar	11104110	210/397-8000	38
Scarborough High Sch/*Houston*/Harris	01024231	713/613-2200	192
Scenic Hills Christian Academy/*San Antonio*/Bexar	02234441	210/523-2312	45
Sch Health Prof-Townview Ctr/*Dallas*/Dallas	02896295	972/925-5930	102
Sch of Environmental Education/*Plantersville*/Grimes	04775116	936/894-2141	172
Sch of Sci & Tech Advancement/*Houston*/Harris	12261113	713/266-2522	10
Sch of Sci & Tech Excellence/*Houston*/Harris	12261149	832/672-6671	10
Sch of Sci & Tech Main/*San Antonio*/Bexar	10916001	210/804-0222	10
Sch of Sci & Tech Northwest/*San Antonio*/Bexar	12362755	210/530-8366	10
Sch of Sci & Tech-Alamo/*San Antonio*/Bexar	11527615	210/657-6400	10
Sch of Sci & Tech-Corpus Crsti/*Corp Christi*/Nueces	11457876	361/851-2450	11
Sch of Sci & Tech-Discovery/*Leon Valley*/Bexar	11155274	210/543-1111	11
Sch of Sci & Tech-Houston/*Houston*/Harris	12261137	346/270-2101	11
Sch of Sci & Tech-Sugarland/*Richmond*/Fort Bend	12362743	210/530-8366	11
Schallert Elem Sch/*Alice*/Jim Wells	01034614	361/664-6361	245
Schanen Estates Elem Sch/*Corp Christi*/Nueces	01044669	361/878-2940	304
Scharbauer Elem Sch/*Midland*/Midland	02848420	432/240-8000	286
Schell Elem Sch/*Richardson*/Collin	10911738	469/752-6600	83
Schenck Elem Sch/*San Antonio*/Bexar	00998902	210/438-6865	41
Schertz Elem Sch/*Schertz*/Guadalupe	01021617	210/619-4650	173
SCHERTZ-CIBOLO-UNIV CITY ISD/SCHERTZ/GUADALUPE	01021552	210/945-6200	173
Schiff Elem Sch/*Missouri City*/Fort Bend	11079589	281/634-9450	151
Schimelpfenig Middle Sch/*Plano*/Collin	02108000	469/752-6400	83
Schindewolf Intermediate Sch/*Spring*/Harris	05096080	832/249-5900	197
SCHLEICHER CO IND SCH DIST/ELDORADO/SCHLEICHER	01049982	325/853-2514	333
School at St George Place/*Houston*/Harris	05099343	713/625-1499	194
School Cmty Guidance Center/*Dallas*/Dallas	04020753	972/925-7000	102
School for the Highly Gifted/*Grand Prairie*/Dallas	12113968	972/343-7864	108
School for Young Children/*Houston*/Harris	02754207	713/520-8310	207
School of Choice/*New Braunfels*/Comal	04452091	830/629-8650	89
SCHOOL OF EXCELLENCE IN ED/SAN ANTONIO/BEXAR	11828823	210/431-9881	42
School of the Woods/*Houston*/Harris	01410898	713/686-8811	207
Schrade Middle Sch/*Rowlett*/Dallas	04806375	972/463-8790	106
Schulenburg Elem Sch/*Schulenburg*/Fayette	01553074	979/743-4221	148
Schulenburg High Sch/*Schulenburg*/Fayette	01017824	979/743-3605	148
SCHULENBURG IND SCH DIST/SCHULENBURG/FAYETTE	01017800	979/743-3448	147
Schultz Elem Sch/*Tomball*/Harris	04286969	832/484-7000	197
Schultz Junior High Sch/*Waller*/Waller	01018177	936/931-9103	385
Science Acad of South Texas/*Mercedes*/Cameron	04017380	956/565-4620	68
Science Hall Elem Sch/*Kyle*/Hays	10022741	512/268-8502	211
Scofield Christian Sch/*Dallas*/Dallas	02123543	214/349-6843	116
Scoggins Middle Sch/*McKinney*/Collin	11103867	469/633-5150	80
Scotland Park Elem Sch/*Wichita Falls*/Wichita	01173038	940/235-1180	392
Scotsdale Elem Sch/*El Paso*/El Paso	01016600	915/434-4800	138
Scott Elem Sch/*Temple*/Bell	00996825	254/215-6222	29
Scott Johnson Elem Sch/*Huntsville*/Walker	01881974	936/293-2866	383
Scott Johnson Middle Sch/*McKinney*/Collin	04922266	469/302-4900	81
Scroggins Elem Sch/*Houston*/Harris	01026095	713/671-4130	191

Texas School Directory
DISTRICT & SCHOOL TELEPHONE INDEX

School/City/County DISTRICT/CITY/COUNTY	PID	TELEPHONE NUMBER	PAGE
Scudder Primary Sch/*Wimberley*/Hays	01029102	512/847-3407	212
Scurry Rosser Elem Sch/*Scurry*/Kaufman	01035735	972/452-8823	253
Scurry Rosser High Sch/*Scurry*/Kaufman	01035747	972/452-8823	253
SCURRY ROSSER IND SCH DIST/ SCURRY/KAUFMAN	01035723	972/452-8823	253
Scurry Rosser Middle Sch/*Scurry*/Kaufman	02857249	972/452-8823	253
Seabrook Intermediate Sch/*Seabrook*/ Galveston	01018933	281/284-3100	159
Seadrift Sch/*Seadrift*/Calhoun	01003184	361/785-3511	62
Seagoville Elem Sch/*Seagoville*/Dallas	01009839	972/892-7900	102
Seagoville High Sch/*Dallas*/Dallas	01009841	972/892-5900	102
Seagoville Middle Sch/*Dallas*/Dallas	02109846	972/892-7100	102
Seagoville North Elem Sch/*Seagoville*/ Dallas	11824530	972/892-5300	102
Seagraves Elem Sch/*Seagraves*/Gaines	01018725	806/387-2015	157
Seagraves High Sch/*Seagraves*/Gaines	01018737	806/387-2520	157
SEAGRAVES IND SCH DIST/SEAGRAVES/ GAINES	01018713	806/387-2035	157
Seagraves Junior High Sch/*Seagraves*/Gaines	01018749	806/387-2646	157
Seale Junior High Sch/*Robstown*/Nueces	01539200	361/767-6631	305
Sealy Elem Sch/*Sealy*/Austin	04238493	979/885-3852	22
Sealy High Sch/*Sealy*/Austin	00995613	979/885-3515	22
SEALY IND SCH DIST/SEALY/AUSTIN	00995584	979/885-3516	22
Sealy Junior High Sch/*Sealy*/Austin	03245376	979/885-3292	22
Seas Alternative Ed Center/*Garciasville*/ Starr	03390531	956/488-0014	340
Seashore Learning Center/*Corp Christi*/ Nueces	04467553	361/949-1222	11
Seashore Middle Academy/*Corp Christi*/ Nueces	10971128	361/654-1134	11
Seco Mines Elem Sch/*Eagle Pass*/Maverick	02127018	830/758-7073	277
Second Baptist Sch/*Houston*/Harris	01480348	713/365-2310	207
Secondary Alternative Center/*Harlingen*/ Cameron	04931530	956/427-3210	65
Seele Elem Sch/*New Braunfels*/Comal	01007037	830/627-6750	89
Seguin Christian Academy/*Seguin*/Guadalupe	11238175	830/433-4131	174
Seguin Early Child Hood Ctr/*Richmond*/ Fort Bend	04803775	832/223-2200	154
Seguin High Sch/*Seguin*/Guadalupe	01021734	830/401-8000	174
SEGUIN IND SCH DIST/SEGUIN/ GUADALUPE	01021631	830/401-8600	173
Sellers Middle Sch/*Garland*/Dallas	01010709	972/494-8337	106
Selwyn College Prep Sch/*Argyle*/Denton	01013672	940/382-6771	126
Seminary Hills Park Elem Sch/*Fort Worth*/ Tarrant	05344538	817/814-7600	352
Seminole Elem Sch/*Seminole*/Gaines	01018775	432/758-3615	158
Seminole High Sch/*Seminole*/Gaines	01018787	432/758-5873	158
SEMINOLE IND SCH DIST/SEMINOLE/ GAINES	01018751	432/758-3662	158
Seminole Junior High Sch/*Seminole*/Gaines	01018799	432/758-9431	158
Seminole Primary Sch/*Seminole*/Gaines	01018804	432/758-5841	158
Seminole Success Center/*Seminole*/Gaines	04447242	432/758-2772	158
Senator Judith Zaffirini ES/*Laredo*/Webb	04875223	956/473-2900	388
Sendera Ranch Elem Sch/*Haslet*/Denton	11104079	817/698-3500	125
Ser-Ninos Charter Middle Sch/*Houston*/ Harris	12320238	713/592-6055	11
Ser-Ninos Charter Sch/*Houston*/Harris	04459465	713/667-6145	11
Ser-Ninos Charter School II/*Houston*/Harris	11832317	713/432-9400	11
Serene Hills Elem Sch/*Austin*/Travis	11074254	512/533-7400	371
Serenity High Sch/*McKinney*/Collin	04920696	469/302-7830	81
Serna Elem Sch/*San Antonio*/Bexar	04017770	210/407-7200	35
Seton Home Charter Education/*San Antonio*/ Bexar	12362767	512/560-8132	11
Settlers Way Elem Sch/*Sugar Land*/Fort Bend	02226688	281/634-4360	151
Seven Hills Elem Sch/*Newark*/Denton	03055509	817/215-0700	125
Seven Lakes High Sch/*Katy*/Harris	10002870	281/237-2800	153
Seven Lakes Junior High Sch/*Katy*/Harris	11822051	281/234-2100	153
Sewell Elem Sch/*Sachse*/Dallas	04035461	972/675-3050	106
Seymour Elem Sch/*Seymour*/Baylor	00996033	940/889-2533	25
Seymour High Sch/*Seymour*/Baylor	00996045	940/889-2947	25
SEYMOUR IND SCH DIST/SEYMOUR/ BAYLOR	00996021	940/889-3525	24
Seymour Middle Sch/*Seymour*/Baylor	05035153	940/889-4548	25
Sgt Jose Carrasco Elem Sch/*El Paso*/El Paso	12307494	915/938-2400	136
Sgt Leonel Trevino Elem Sch/*San Juan*/ Hidalgo	01540065	956/354-2900	224
Sgt Manuel Chacon Middle Sch/*Mercedes*/ Hidalgo	01030187	956/514-2200	222
Sgt Roberto Ituarte Elem Sch/*El Paso*/ El Paso	10021888	915/937-7000	136
Sgt William Harrell Middle Sch/*Mercedes*/ Hidalgo	12225315	956/825-5140	222

School/City/County DISTRICT/CITY/COUNTY	PID	TELEPHONE NUMBER	PAGE
Shackelford Elem Sch/*Waxahachie*/Ellis	03049029	972/923-4666	142
Shackelford Junior High Sch/*Arlington*/ Tarrant	01399799	682/867-3600	345
Shadow Creek High Sch/*Pearland*/Brazoria	12165442	281/245-3800	51
Shadow Forest Elem Sch/*Kingwood*/Harris	04038176	281/641-2600	196
Shadow Oaks Elem Sch/*Houston*/Harris	01027271	713/251-6800	201
Shadow Ridge Middle Sch/*Flower Mound*/ Denton	10004103	469/713-5984	124
Shadowbriar Elem Sch/*Houston*/Harris	04016087	281/368-2160	194
Shadowglen Elem Sch/*Manor*/Travis	12108327	512/278-4700	371
Shady Brook Elem Sch/*Bedford*/Tarrant	01053919	817/354-3513	354
Shady Grove Elem Sch/*Burnet*/Burnet	01002776	512/756-2126	60
Shady Grove Elem Sch/*Keller*/Tarrant	03392747	817/744-5600	355
Shady Oaks Elem Sch/*Hurst*/Tarrant	01053921	817/285-3240	354
Shady Shores Elem Sch/*Shady Shores*/Denton	10753706	940/497-4035	122
Shadycrest Elem Sch/*Pearland*/Brazoria	01001899	281/412-1404	53
Shadydale Elem Sch/*Houston*/Harris	01026605	713/633-5150	191
Shallowater Elem Sch/*Shallowater*/Lubbock	01039169	806/832-4531	272
Shallowater High Sch/*Shallowater*/Lubbock	01039183	806/832-4531	272
SHALLOWATER IND SCH DIST/ SHALLOWATER/LUBBOCK	01039157	806/832-4531	272
Shallowater Intermediate Sch/*Shallowater*/ Lubbock	01039171	806/832-4531	272
Shallowater Middle Sch/*Shallowater*/Lubbock	03241667	806/832-4531	272
Shamrock Elem Sch/*Shamrock*/Wheeler	01059860	806/256-3227	391
Shamrock High Sch/*Shamrock*/Wheeler	04801715	806/256-2241	391
SHAMROCK IND SCH DIST/SHAMROCK/ WHEELER	01059858	806/256-3492	390
Shamrock Junior High Sch/*Shamrock*/Wheeler	04801703	806/256-3227	391
Shannon High Sch/*Haltom City*/Tarrant	03329348	817/547-5400	346
Sharon Shannon Elem Sch/*Rockwall*/Rockwall	10911001	469/698-2900	326
Sharp Elem Sch/*Brownsville*/Cameron	01003691	956/982-2930	64
Sharpstown High Sch/*Houston*/Harris	01024607	713/771-7215	189
Sharpstown International Acad/*Houston*/ Harris	01024619	713/778-3440	194
Sharyland Adv Academic Academy/*Mission*/ Hidalgo	12035342	956/584-6467	224
Sharyland Alternative Ed Ctr/*Mission*/ Hidalgo	12035366	956/584-6407	224
Sharyland High Sch/*Mission*/Hidalgo	01526069	956/580-5300	224
SHARYLAND IND SCH DIST/MISSION/ HIDALGO	01030527	956/580-5200	224
Sharyland North Jr High Sch/*McAllen*/ Hidalgo	10011429	956/686-1415	224
Sharyland Pioneer High Sch/*Mission*/Hidalgo	12035354	956/271-1600	224
Shaw Spec Emphasis Sch/*Corp Christi*/Nueces	01044528	361/878-2100	304
Shawnee Trail Elem Sch/*Frisco*/Collin	04917247	469/633-2500	80
Shearn Elem Sch/*Houston*/Harris	01025376	713/295-5236	191
Sheffield Primary Elem Sch/*Dallas*/Dallas	02845715	972/968-3100	97
Shekinah Radiance Acad-Garland/*Dallas*/ Dallas	12163365	214/320-2500	11
Shelbyville High Sch/*Shelbyville*/Shelby	01050412	936/598-7323	335
SHELBYVILLE IND SCH DIST/ SHELBYVILLE/SHELBY	01050395	936/598-2641	335
Shelbyville Middle Sch/*Shelbyville*/Shelby	01553244	936/598-5146	335
Sheldon Early Childhood Acad/*Houston*/ Harris	11452034	281/456-6800	200
Sheldon Early Clg High Sch/*Houston*/Harris	12033772	281/727-3500	200
Sheldon Elem Sch/*Houston*/Harris	01027063	281/456-6700	200
SHELDON IND SCH DIST/HOUSTON/ HARRIS	01027013	281/727-2000	200
Shelton Sch/*Dallas*/Dallas	11829970	972/774-1772	116
Shepard Elem Sch/*Plano*/Collin	01006461	469/752-3100	83
Shepherd High Sch/*Shepherd*/San Jacinto	01049463	936/628-3371	330
SHEPHERD IND SCH DIST/SHEPHERD/ SAN JACINTO	01049449	936/628-3396	330
Shepherd Intermediate Sch/*Shepherd*/ San Jacinto	01553232	936/628-6764	330
Shepherd Middle Sch/*Shepherd*/San Jacinto	04801870	936/628-3377	330
Shepherd of the Hills Luth Sch/*San Antonio*/ Bexar	02235378	210/614-3741	45
Shepherd Primary Sch/*Shepherd*/San Jacinto	01049451	936/628-3302	330
Sheppard AFB Elem Sch/*Sheppard Afb*/Wichita	01173181	940/235-1184	392
Shepton High Sch/*Plano*/Collin	02225634	469/752-7600	83
Sheridan Elem Sch/*Katy*/Harris	04016609	281/856-1420	185
Sheridan Elem Sch/*Sheridan*/Colorado	01006837	979/234-3531	87
Sherman Elem Sch/*Houston*/Harris	01024372	713/226-2627	191
Sherman High Sch/*Sherman*/Grayson	01020663	903/891-6440	167
SHERMAN IND SCH DIST/SHERMAN/ GRAYSON	01020596	903/891-6400	167
Sherrod Elem Sch/*Arlington*/Tarrant	02109262	682/867-3700	345
Sherwood Elem Sch/*Houston*/Harris	01027283	713/251-6900	201

DISTRICT & SCHOOL TELEPHONE INDEX

Market Data Retrieval

School/City/County DISTRICT/CITY/COUNTY	PID	TELEPHONE NUMBER	PAGE
Sherwood Forest Mont Sch/*Houston*/Harris	02757120	713/464-5791	207
Shields Elem Sch/*Victoria*/Victoria	01058579	361/788-9593	382
Shiloh Sch/*Manvel*/Brazoria	11230630	281/489-1290	54
Shiner Catholic School-St Paul/*Shiner*/Lavaca	04972522	361/594-2313	263
Shiner Elem Sch/*Shiner*/Lavaca	01037367	361/594-8106	262
Shiner High Sch/*Shiner*/Lavaca	01037379	361/594-3131	262
SHINER IND SCH DIST/SHINER/LAVACA	01037355	361/594-3121	262
Shirley Dill Brothers Elem Sch/*Pearland*/Brazoria	12231027	281/388-1130	51
Shirley Hall Middle Sch/*Weatherford*/Parker	01046629	817/598-2822	314
Shirley J Howsman Elem Sch/*San Antonio*/Bexar	00998299	210/397-2350	38
Shive Elem Sch/*Vernon*/Wilbarger	01060596	940/553-4309	394
Shorehaven Elem Sch/*Garland*/Dallas	01010711	972/494-8346	106
Shoreline Academy/*Taft*/San Patricio	04447278	361/528-3356	11
Short Elem Sch/*Arlington*/Tarrant	01051911	682/867-5850	345
Shsu CS-Brighton Academy/*The Woodlands*/Montgomery	10986484	281/465-4111	11
Shsu CS-Cypress Trails/*Spring*/Harris	12261242	936/294-3229	11
Shsu CS-Greengate Academy/*Spring*/Harris	04792205	281/288-0880	11
Shsu CS-Little Geniuses Acad/*Humble*/Harris	12136491	832/995-5916	11
Shugart Elem Sch/*Garland*/Dallas	03009380	972/240-3700	106
SIDNEY IND SCH DIST/SIDNEY/COMANCHE	01007154	254/842-5500	90
Sidney Lanier Expressive Arts/*Dallas*/Dallas	01009774	972/794-4400	102
Sidney Lanier High Sch/*San Antonio*/Bexar	00999310	210/978-7910	41
Sidney Poynter Elem Sch/*Fort Worth*/Tarrant	10004622	817/568-5730	348
Sidney Sch/*Sidney*/Comanche	01007178	254/842-5500	90
Siebert Elem Sch/*Eastland*/Eastland	01014418	254/631-5080	129
Sienna Crossing Elem Sch/*Missouri City*/Fort Bend	04808608	281/634-3680	151
SIERRA BLANCA IND SCH DIST/SIERRA BLANCA/HUDSPETH	01032202	915/369-3741	234
Sierra Blanca Sch/*Sierra Blanca*/Hudspeth	01032214	915/369-2781	235
Sierra Vista Elem Sch/*El Paso*/El Paso	04035277	915/937-8100	136
Sigler Elem Sch/*Plano*/Collin	01006409	469/752-3200	83
Silsbee Elem Sch/*Silsbee*/Hardin	03047916	409/980-7856	178
Silsbee High Sch/*Silsbee*/Hardin	01022635	409/980-7877	178
SILSBEE IND SCH DIST/SILSBEE/HARDIN	01022582	409/980-7800	178
Silva Health Magnet High Sch/*El Paso*/El Paso	04035693	915/236-7600	134
Silver Creek Elem Sch/*Azle*/Tarrant	03004067	817/444-0257	345
Silver Lake Elem Sch/*Grapevine*/Tarrant	04363658	817/251-5750	353
Silvercrest Elem Sch/*Pearland*/Brazoria	05070244	832/736-6000	53
Silverlake Elem Sch/*Pearland*/Brazoria	04807678	713/436-8000	54
Silverline Montessori Sch/*Pearland*/Brazoria	11818804	713/436-5070	54
SILVERTON IND SCH DIST/SILVERTON/BRISCOE	01002300	806/823-2476	57
Silverton Sch/*Silverton*/Briscoe	01002312	806/823-2476	57
Silvestre & Reyes Elem Sch/*El Paso*/El Paso	12167646	915/877-1300	132
SIMMS IND SCH DIST/SIMMS/BOWIE	01001186	903/543-2219	50
Simon Rivera Early Clg HS/*Brownsville*/Cameron	03095767	956/831-8700	64
Simon Youth Academy/*Katy*/Harris	12231261	281/396-6050	153
Simonton Christian Academy/*Simonton*/Fort Bend	04496059	281/346-2303	155
Sims Elem Sch/*Austin*/Travis	01056636	512/414-4488	368
Sinclair Elem Sch/*Houston*/Harris	01024243	713/867-5161	192
Sinclair Elem Sch/*San Antonio*/Bexar	02129743	210/648-4620	31
Sinton Elem Sch/*Sinton*/San Patricio	01049798	361/364-6900	332
Sinton High Sch/*Sinton*/San Patricio	01049803	361/364-6650	332
SINTON IND SCH DIST/SINTON/SAN PATRICIO	01049762	361/364-6800	332
SIVELLS BEND IND SCH DIST/GAINESVILLE/COOKE	01007489	940/665-6411	91
Sivells Bend Sch/*Gainesville*/Cooke	01007491	940/665-6411	91
Skaggs Elem Sch/*Plano*/Collin	04453899	469/752-3300	83
Skidmore Tynan Elem Sch/*Skidmore*/Bee	00996227	361/287-3425	25
Skidmore Tynan High Sch/*Skidmore*/Bee	00996239	361/287-3426	25
SKIDMORE TYNAN IND SD/SKIDMORE/BEE	00996215	361/287-3426	25
Skidmore Tynan Jr High Sch/*Skidmore*/Bee	00996241	361/287-3426	26
Skinner Elem Sch/*Brownsville*/Cameron	01003639	956/982-2830	64
Skipcha Elem Sch/*Harker HTS*/Bell	10030736	254/336-6690	28
Sky Harbor Elem Sch/*San Antonio*/Bexar	02110429	210/623-6580	43
Skyline High Sch/*Dallas*/Dallas	01009865	972/502-3400	102
Skyview Elem Sch/*Dallas*/Dallas	01011935	469/593-2400	113
Slack Elem Sch/*Lufkin*/Angelina	00995065	936/639-2279	18
Slaton High Sch/*Slaton*/Lubbock	01039212	806/828-5833	272
SLATON IND SCH DIST/SLATON/LUBBOCK	01039195	806/828-6591	272
Slaton Junior High Sch/*Slaton*/Lubbock	01039224	806/828-6583	272
Sleepy Hollow Elem Sch/*Amarillo*/Potter	02127757	806/326-5300	318
Slidell Elem Sch/*Decatur*/Wise	01061760	940/466-3118	403
SLIDELL IND SCH DIST/SLIDELL/WISE	01061758	940/535-5260	403
Slidell Secondary Sch/*Slidell*/Wise	04804755	940/535-5260	403
Sloan Creek Intermediate Sch/*Fairview*/Collin	11127772	469/742-8400	80
SLOCUM ISD SCH DIST/ELKHART/ANDERSON	00994633	903/478-3624	16
Slocum Sch/*Elkhart*/Anderson	00994657	903/478-3624	16
Small Middle Sch/*Austin*/Travis	04869872	512/841-6700	369
Smith Elem Sch/*Austin*/Travis	01056832	512/386-3850	369
Smith Elem Sch/*Duncanville*/Dallas	01010383	972/708-3000	105
Smith Elem Sch/*Forney*/Kaufman	11130640	469/762-4158	252
Smith Elem Sch/*Houston*/Harris	01023031	281/983-8380	182
Smith Elem Sch/*Houston*/Harris	01024255	713/613-2542	192
Smith Elem Sch/*Lubbock*/Lubbock	03008714	806/219-6800	270
Smith Elem Sch/*Princeton*/Collin	12105076	469/952-5411	84
Smith Elem Sch/*Richmond*/Fort Bend	01018323	832/223-2300	154
Smith Elem Sch/*San Antonio*/Bexar	00998976	210/228-3360	41
Smith Elem Sch/*Spring*/Harris	02892146	281/891-8420	202
Smith Elem Sch/*Victoria*/Victoria	01058581	361/788-9605	382
Smith Magnet Middle Sch/*Beaumont*/Jefferson	01033426	409/617-5825	242
Smith Middle Sch/*Cleburne*/Johnson	01034896	817/202-1500	247
Smith Middle Sch/*Cypress*/Harris	11451482	281/213-1010	185
Smithfield Elem Sch/*N Richlnd Hls*/Tarrant	01052197	817/547-2100	346
Smithfield Middle Sch/*N Richlnd Hls*/Tarrant	01418589	817/547-5000	346
Smithson Valley High Sch/*Spring Branch*/Comal	01525924	830/885-1000	88
Smithson Valley Middle Sch/*Spring Branch*/Comal	01006904	830/885-1200	88
Smithville Elem Sch/*Smithville*/Bastrop	00995998	512/237-2406	24
Smithville High Sch/*Smithville*/Bastrop	00996007	512/237-2451	24
SMITHVILLE IND SCH DIST/SMITHVILLE/BASTROP	00995974	512/237-2487	24
Smithville Junior High Sch/*Smithville*/Bastrop	00996019	512/237-2407	24
Smyer Elem Sch/*Smyer*/Hockley	01031284	806/234-2935	229
SMYER IND SCH DIST/SMYER/HOCKLEY	01031272	806/234-2935	229
Smyer Jr Sr High Sch/*Smyer*/Hockley	03399070	806/234-2935	229
Smylie Wilson Middle Sch/*Lubbock*/Lubbock	01039004	806/219-4600	270
Sneed Elem Sch/*Houston*/Harris	03328655	713/789-6979	182
SNOOK IND SCH DIST/SNOOK/BURLESON	01002685	979/272-8307	59
Snook Sch/*Snook*/Burleson	01002697	979/272-8307	59
Snow Heights Elem Sch/*N Richlnd Hls*/Tarrant	01052202	817/547-2200	346
Snyder Elem Sch/*Spring*/Montgomery	11920445	832/663-4400	292
Snyder High Sch/*Snyder*/Scurry	01050163	325/574-8800	333
SNYDER IND SCH DIST/SNYDER/SCURRY	01050101	325/574-8900	333
Snyder Intermediate Sch/*Snyder*/Scurry	12033851	325/574-8650	333
Snyder Junior High Sch/*Snyder*/Scurry	01050137	325/574-8700	333
Snyder Primary Sch/*Snyder*/Scurry	01050125	325/574-8600	333
Socorro High Sch/*El Paso*/El Paso	01016234	915/937-2000	136
SOCORRO IND SCH DIST/EL PASO/EL PASO	01016208	915/937-0000	135
Socorro Middle Sch/*El Paso*/El Paso	03323629	915/937-5001	136
Sojourn Academy/*Conroe*/Montgomery	04993497	281/298-5800	295
Solar Prep Sch for Girls-Bonhm/*Dallas*/Dallas	12169735	972/749-4300	103
Solar Preparatory for Boys/*Dallas*/Dallas	12318613	972/794-7100	103
Solomon P Ortiz Interm Sch/*Robstown*/Nueces	03051929	361/767-6662	305
Somerset Early Chldhd Ctr/*Somerset*/Bexar	04912027	866/852-9865	42
Somerset Elem Sch/*Somerset*/Bexar	00999358	866/852-9864	42
Somerset High Sch/*Somerset*/Bexar	00999372	866/852-9861	42
SOMERSET IND SCH DIST/SOMERSET/BEXAR	00999346	866/852-9858	42
Somerset Junior High Sch/*Von Ormy*/Bexar	00999360	866/852-9862	42
Somerville Elem Sch/*Somerville*/Burleson	01002726	979/596-1502	60
Somerville High Sch/*Somerville*/Burleson	01002738	979/596-1534	60
SOMERVILLE IND SCH DIST/SOMERVILLE/BURLESON	01002714	979/596-2153	60
Somerville Intermediate Sch/*Somerville*/Burleson	12363369	979/596-7502	60
Sonny & Allegra Nance ES/*Fort Worth*/Denton	10012320	817/698-1950	125

Texas School Directory
DISTRICT & SCHOOL TELEPHONE INDEX

School/City/County DISTRICT/CITY/COUNTY	PID	TELEPHONE NUMBER	PAGE
Sonora Elemementary Sch/*Sonora*/Sutton	01051480	325/387-6940	342
Sonora High Sch/*Sonora*/Sutton	01051492	325/387-6940	342
SONORA IND SCH DIST/*SONORA*/ SUTTON	01051478	325/387-6940	342
Sonora Middle Sch/*Sonora*/Sutton	01051507	325/387-6940	342
Sorters Mill Elem Sch/*Porter*/Montgomery	10903339	281/577-8780	294
Sory Elem Sch/*Sherman*/Grayson	11070650	903/891-6650	167
Souder Elem Sch/*Everman*/Tarrant	01052513	817/568-3580	349
Sour Lake Elem Sch/*Sour Lake*/Hardin	01022489	409/981-6440	178
South Athens Elem Sch/*Athens*/Henderson	01029281	903/677-6970	213
South Belt Elem Sch/*Houston*/Harris	11450000	713/740-5276	199
South Belton Middle Sch/*Belton*/Bell	11712341	254/215-3000	27
South Bosque Elem Sch/*Waco*/McLennan	03322443	254/761-5720	281
South Davis Elem Sch/*Arlington*/Tarrant	01051715	682/867-3800	345
South Early College High Sch/*Houston*/Harris	10003915	713/732-3623	193
South Elem Sch/*Breckenridge*/Stephens	01051375	254/559-6554	341
South Elem Sch/*Daingerfield*/Morris	01172539	903/645-3501	296
South Elem Sch/*Lamesa*/Dawson	01012927	806/872-5401	117
South Elem Sch/*Levelland*/Hockley	01031181	806/894-6255	229
South Elem Sch/*Lubbock*/Lubbock	01039078	806/863-7102	271
South Elem Sch/*Midland*/Midland	01041655	432/240-8100	286
South Euless Elem Sch/*Euless*/Tarrant	01053892	817/354-3521	354
South Garland High Sch/*Garland*/Dallas	01010682	972/926-2700	106
South Georgia Elem Sch/*Amarillo*/Potter	01047441	806/326-5350	318
South Grand Prairie 9th GR Ctr/*Grand Prairie*/Dallas	05092034	972/264-1769	108
South Grand Prairie Echs/*Grand Prairie*/Dallas	12168602	972/343-7640	108
South Grand Prairie High Sch/*Grand Prairie*/Dallas	01010981	972/343-1500	108
South Hi Mount Elem Sch/*Fort Worth*/Tarrant	01053397	817/815-1800	352
South Hills Elem Sch/*Fort Worth*/Tarrant	01053402	817/814-5800	352
South Hills High Sch/*Fort Worth*/Tarrant	04815261	817/814-7000	352
South Houston Elem Sch/*South Houston*/Harris	01026887	713/740-0736	199
South Houston High Sch/*South Houston*/Harris	01026899	713/740-0350	199
South Houston Intermediate Sch/*South Houston*/Harris	01026904	713/740-0490	200
South Knoll Elem Sch/*College Sta*/Brazos	01001992	979/764-5580	56
South Lawn Elem Sch/*Amarillo*/Potter	01047453	806/326-5400	318
South Loop Elem Sch/*El Paso*/El Paso	01016612	915/434-8800	138
South Oak Cliff High Sch/*Dallas*/Dallas	01009786	214/932-7000	103
South Palm Gardens High Sch/*Weslaco*/Hidalgo	04034869	956/969-6621	225
South Park Middle Sch/*Beaumont*/Jefferson	01034200	409/617-5875	242
South Park Middle Sch/*Corp Christi*/Nueces	01044633	361/878-4720	304
South Plains CHS/*Lubbock*/Lubbock	04893598	806/744-0330	11
South San Antonio Career Ctr/*San Antonio*/Bexar	01877349	210/977-7350	42
South San Antonio High Sch/*San Antonio*/Bexar	00999504	210/977-7400	43
SOUTH SAN ANTONIO IND SCH DIST/ SAN ANTONIO/BEXAR	00999384	210/977-7000	42
South Shaver Elem Sch/*Pasadena*/Harris	01026916	713/740-0842	200
South Texas Acad Med Professns/*Olmito*/Cameron	01808996	956/214-6100	68
South Texas Christian Academy/*McAllen*/Hidalgo	03017375	956/682-1117	226
South Texas HS for Health Prof/*Mercedes*/Cameron	02231815	956/565-2237	68
SOUTH TEXAS IND SCH DIST/ MERCEDES/CAMERON	01808984	956/565-2454	67
South Texas Prep Academy/*Edinburg*/Cameron	11123908	956/381-5522	68
South Waco Elem Sch/*Waco*/McLennan	01040405	254/753-6802	282
South Ward Elem Sch/*Longview*/Gregg	01021112	903/803-5200	170
Southard Middle Sch/*Princeton*/Collin	05342724	469/952-5403	84
Southcrest Christian Sch/*Lubbock*/Lubbock	04994130	806/797-7400	272
Southeast Elem Sch/*Sweetwater*/Nolan	01172553	325/235-9222	302
Southern Hills Elem Sch/*Wichita Falls*/Wichita	01172981	940/235-1188	393
Southgate Elem Sch/*Garland*/Dallas	01010723	972/926-2590	106
SOUTHLAND IND SCH DIST/*SOUTHLAND*/ GARZA	01019638	806/996-5339	162
Southland Sch/*Southland*/Garza	01019640	806/996-5339	162
Southmayd Elem Sch/*Houston*/Harris	01025742	713/924-1720	190
Southminster Elem Sch/*Missouri City*/Fort Bend	03371547	281/261-8872	155
Southmore Intermediate Sch/*Pasadena*/Harris	01026966	713/740-0500	200
Southmost Elem Sch/*Brownsville*/Cameron	03051620	956/548-8870	64
Southridge Elem Sch/*Lewisville*/Denton	04850912	469/713-5187	124
Southside Alternative Sch/*San Antonio*/Bexar	04745094	210/882-1604	43
Southside Elem Sch/*Angleton*/Brazoria	01001526	979/864-8008	52
Southside Elem Sch/*Cleveland*/Liberty	01037769	281/592-0594	265
Southside Elem Sch/*Mabank*/Kaufman	02199542	903/880-1340	253
Southside Elem Sch/*Palestine*/Anderson	00994592	903/731-8023	15
Southside High Sch/*San Antonio*/Bexar	00999530	210/882-1606	43
SOUTHSIDE IND SCH DIST/*SAN ANTONIO*/ BEXAR	00999516	210/882-1600	43
Southwest Adventist Jr Academy/*Dallas*/Dallas	02233667	214/948-1666	116
Southwest Christian Academy/*Houston*/Harris	02995516	281/561-7400	207
Southwest Christian Sch/*Fort Worth*/Tarrant	02233447	817/294-0350	359
Southwest Christian Sch-Prep/*Fort Worth*/Tarrant	11566087	817/294-9596	359
Southwest Cmty Christian Acad/*Houston*/Harris	04797516	281/575-9400	207
Southwest Elem Sch/*Belton*/Bell	00996370	254/215-3500	27
Southwest Elem Sch/*San Antonio*/Bexar	00999592	210/622-4420	43
Southwest High Sch/*Fort Worth*/Tarrant	01053414	817/814-8000	352
Southwest High Sch/*San Antonio*/Bexar	00999619	210/622-4500	43
SOUTHWEST IND SCH DIST/*SAN ANTONIO*/ BEXAR	00999578	210/622-4300	43
Southwest Legacy High Sch/*Von Ormy*/Bexar	12230906	210/623-6539	43
Southwest Prep New Directions/*San Antonio*/Bexar	12164888	210/829-8017	11
Southwest Prep Sch NE/*San Antonio*/Bexar	04813469	210/829-8017	11
Southwest Prep Sch NW/*San Antonio*/Bexar	10019055	210/432-2634	11
Southwest Prep Sch SE/*San Antonio*/Bexar	10019043	210/333-1403	11
Southwest Prep-Seguin/*Seguin*/Guadalupe	12261151	830/549-5930	11
Southwest Preparatory-NW ES/*San Antonio*/Bexar	12261163	210/819-7860	11
Southwest Sch-Bissonnet/*Houston*/Harris	12027931	713/988-5839	11
Southwest Sch-Discovery MS/*Houston*/Harris	05010854	713/954-9528	11
Southwest Sch-Empowerment HS/*Houston*/Harris	12260690	713/954-9528	11
Southwest Sch-Mangum/*Houston*/Harris	11704784	713/688-0505	11
Southwest Schools-Phoenix/*Houston*/Harris	12100181	346/571-6060	11
Southwood Valley Elem Sch/*College Sta*/Brazos	02202761	979/764-5590	56
Space Center Intermediate Sch/*Houston*/Galveston	04015265	281/284-3300	159
Sparks Elem Sch/*Pasadena*/Harris	02225115	713/740-0744	200
Sparta Elem Sch/*Belton*/Bell	03049598	254/215-3600	27
Spc Rafael Hernando Middle Sch/*El Paso*/El Paso	11449398	915/937-9800	137
Spearman High Sch/*Spearman*/Hansford	01022336	806/659-2584	177
SPEARMAN IND SCH DIST/*SPEARMAN*/ HANSFORD	01022312	806/659-3233	177
Spearman Junior High Sch/*Spearman*/Hansford	01022348	806/659-2563	177
Speegleville Elem Sch/*Waco*/McLennan	01040118	254/761-5730	281
Speer Elem Sch/*Arlington*/Tarrant	01051923	682/867-4000	345
Spence Elem Sch/*Houston*/Harris	10000468	281/539-4050	180
Spicer Alternative Ed Center/*Bellville*/Austin	04754318	979/865-7095	22
Spicewood Elem Sch/*Austin*/Williamson	01061150	512/428-3600	399
Spicewood Elem Sch/*Spicewood*/Burnet	05341407	830/798-3675	60
Spicewood Park Elem Sch/*San Antonio*/Bexar	11712389	210/622-4999	43
Spillane Middle Sch/*Cypress*/Harris	10000547	281/213-1645	185
Splendora High Sch/*Splendora*/Montgomery	01042740	281/689-8008	294
SPLENDORA IND SCH DIST/*SPLENDORA*/ MONTGOMERY	01042726	281/689-3128	294
Splendora Junior High Sch/*Splendora*/Montgomery	01042752	281/689-6343	294
Spradley Elem Sch/*Frisco*/Collin	12307030	469/219-2250	84
Spring Baptist Academy/*Spring*/Harris	12235633	281/353-5448	207
Spring Branch Acad Institute/*Houston*/Harris	12308826	713/251-1901	201
Spring Branch Elem Sch/*Houston*/Harris	01027295	713/251-7000	201
SPRING BRANCH IND SCH DIST/ HOUSTON/HARRIS	01027087	713/464-1511	200
Spring Branch Middle Sch/*Houston*/Harris	01027300	713/251-4400	201
Spring Branch Middle Sch/*Spring Branch*/Comal	04808189	830/885-8800	88
Spring Creek Academy/*Plano*/Collin	12314150	972/517-6730	86
Spring Creek Elem Sch/*College Sta*/Brazos	12104242	979/694-5838	56
Spring Creek Elem Sch/*Dallas*/Dallas	01011947	469/593-4500	113
Spring Creek Elem Sch/*Garland*/Dallas	02127769	972/675-3060	106
SPRING CREEK IND SCH DIST/ SKELLYTOWN/HUTCHINSON	01032812	806/273-6791	238
Spring Creek Sch/*Skellytown*/Hutchinson	01032824	806/273-6791	238

DISTRICT & SCHOOL TELEPHONE INDEX

School/City/County DISTRICT/CITY/COUNTY	PID	TELEPHONE NUMBER	PAGE
Spring Early College Academy/Houston/Harris	11719040	281/891-6880	202
Spring Forest Middle Sch/Houston/Harris	01027324	713/251-4600	201
Spring Garden Elem Sch/Bedford/Tarrant	02201614	817/354-3395	354
Spring High Sch/Spring/Harris	01027532	281/891-7000	202
Spring Hill Elem Sch/Pflugerville/Travis	04454233	512/594-5400	372
Spring Hill High Sch/Longview/Gregg	01021277	903/446-3300	170
SPRING HILL IND SCH DIST/ LONGVIEW/GREGG	01021253	903/759-4404	170
Spring Hill Intermediate Sch/Longview/Gregg	01021265	903/323-7701	171
Spring Hill Junior High Sch/Longview/Gregg	01021289	903/323-7718	171
Spring Hill Primary Sch/Longview/Gregg	04906509	903/323-7848	171
SPRING IND SCH DIST/HOUSTON/ HARRIS	01027465	281/891-6000	202
Spring Lake Park Elem Sch/Texarkana/Bowie	03007045	903/794-7525	50
Spring Leadership Acad Mid Sch/Houston/Harris	12365941	281/891-8050	203
Spring Meadows Elem Sch/San Antonio/Bexar	02896855	210/662-1050	34
Spring Oaks Middle Sch/Houston/Harris	01027336	713/251-4800	201
Spring Shadows Elem Sch/Houston/Harris	01027348	713/251-7100	201
Spring Valley Elem Sch/Dallas/Dallas	01011961	469/593-4600	113
Spring Valley Elem Sch/Hewitt/McLennan	02906967	254/761-5710	281
Spring Virtual Sch/Houston/Harris	11927728	281/891-6223	203
Spring Woods High Sch/Houston/Harris	01027362	713/251-3100	201
Spring Woods Middle Sch/Houston/Harris	01027350	713/251-5000	201
Springdale Elem Sch/Fort Worth/Tarrant	01053426	817/814-9600	352
Springlake-Earth Elem Mid Sch/Earth/Lamb	01037056	806/257-3310	261
Springlake-Earth High Sch/Earth/Lamb	01037068	806/257-3819	261
SPRINGLAKE-EARTH IND SCH DIST/ EARTH/LAMB	01037044	806/257-3310	261
Springridge Elem Sch/Richardson/Dallas	01011959	469/593-8600	113
Springtown Elem Sch/Springtown/Parker	01046538	817/220-2498	313
Springtown High Sch/Springtown/Parker	01046526	817/220-3888	313
SPRINGTOWN IND SCH DIST/ SPRINGTOWN/PARKER	01046514	817/220-7243	313
Springtown Intermediate Sch/Springtown/Parker	04918459	817/220-1219	313
Springtown Middle Sch/Springtown/Parker	02894962	817/220-7455	313
Springwoods Village Mid Sch/Spring/Harris	12365953	281/891-8100	203
SPUR IND SCH DIST/SPUR/DICKENS	01013969	806/271-3272	127
Spur Sch/Spur/Dickens	01013983	806/271-3385	127
Spurger Elem Sch/Spurger/Tyler	01057264	409/429-3464	375
Spurger High Sch/Spurger/Tyler	01057276	409/429-3464	375
SPURGER IND SCH DIST/SPURGER/ TYLER	01057252	409/429-3464	375
Spurling Christian Academy/Arlington/Tarrant	11915191	817/465-1122	359
SS Cyril & Methodius Sch/Corp Christi/Nueces	01045314	361/853-9392	306
SS Peter & Paul Sch/New Braunfels/Comal	01000065	830/625-4531	89
Ssg Manuel R Puentes Mid Sch/El Paso/El Paso	11920524	915/937-9200	137
St Agnes Academy/Houston/Harris	01028237	713/219-5400	204
St Alban's Episcopal Day Sch/Harlingen/Cameron	01479662	956/428-2326	68
St Ambrose Sch/Houston/Harris	01028172	713/686-6990	204
St Andrew Catholic Sch/Fort Worth/Tarrant	01054456	817/924-8917	358
St Andrew's Episcopal Day Sch/Amarillo/Potter	01047647	806/376-9501	319
St Andrew's Episcopal Sch/Austin/Travis	01057018	512/452-5779	373
St Ann's Sch/Midland/Midland	01055967	432/684-4563	286
St Anne Catholic Elem Sch/Tomball/Harris	02229707	281/351-0093	204
St Anne Catholic Sch/Beaumont/Jefferson	01034391	409/832-5939	244
St Anne Sch/Houston/Harris	01028249	713/526-3279	204
St Anthony Cathedral Sch/Beaumont/Jefferson	01034406	409/832-3486	244
St Anthony Catholic Elem Sch/San Antonio/Bexar	01000106	210/732-8801	44
St Anthony Catholic High Sch/San Antonio/Bexar	01000118	210/832-5600	44
St Anthony of Padua Sch/The Woodlands/Montgomery	04942785	281/296-0300	295
St Anthony Sch/Columbus/Colorado	01000091	979/732-5505	87
St Anthony Sch/Dallas/Dallas	01012549	214/421-3645	11
St Anthony Sch/Harlingen/Cameron	01004437	956/423-2486	68
St Anthony Sch/Robstown/Nueces	01045326	361/387-3814	306
St Anthony's Elem Sch/Dalhart/Dallam	01047702	806/244-4811	95
St Anthony's Elem Sch/Hereford/Deaf Smith	01047714	806/364-1952	119
St Augustine Catholic Sch/Houston/Harris	01028213	713/946-9050	204
St Augustine Elem Middle Sch/Laredo/Webb	01045443	956/724-1176	388
St Augustine High Sch/Laredo/Webb	01045338	956/724-8131	389

School/City/County DISTRICT/CITY/COUNTY	PID	TELEPHONE NUMBER	PAGE
St Austin Catholic Sch/Austin/Travis	01002922	512/477-3751	372
St Bernard of Clairvaux Sch/Dallas/Dallas	01012563	214/321-2897	114
St Catherine of Siena Sch/Port Arthur/Jefferson	01034418	409/962-3011	244
St Catherine's Montessori Sch/Houston/Harris	01600469	713/665-2195	204
St Cecilia Catholic Sch/Houston/Harris	01028251	713/468-9515	204
St Cecilia Sch/Dallas/Dallas	01012525	214/948-8628	114
St Christopher Catholic Sch/Houston/Harris	01028275	713/649-0009	204
St Clare of Assisi Sch/Houston/Harris	04423703	281/286-3395	204
St Clement's Parish Sch/El Paso/El Paso	01016698	915/533-4248	139
St Cyprian's Episcopal Sch/Lufkin/Angelina	00995118	936/632-1720	18
St Dominic Savio Catholic HS/Austin/Williamson	11564704	512/388-8846	400
St Edward Catholic Sch/Spring/Harris	01534303	281/353-4570	204
St Elizabeth Ann Seton Sch/Keller/Tarrant	04928583	817/431-4845	358
St Elizabeth of Hungary Sch/Dallas/Dallas	01012575	214/331-5139	114
St Elizabeth Sch/Alice/Jim Wells	01045340	361/664-6271	246
St Elizabeth Seton Cath Sch/Houston/Harris	04484109	281/463-1444	204
St Elmo Elem Sch/Austin/Travis	01056648	512/414-4477	367
St Francis DeSales Sch/Houston/Harris	01028287	713/774-4447	204
St Francis Episcopal Sch/Houston/Harris	01027726	713/458-6100	207
St Francis of Assisi Cath Sch/Houston/Harris	01028299	713/674-1966	204
St Francis Sch/Austin/Travis	12314019	512/454-0848	373
St Gabriel's Catholic Sch/Austin/Travis	04879073	512/327-7755	372
St George Episcopal Sch/San Antonio/Bexar	01479569	210/342-4263	45
St George Sch/Fort Worth/Tarrant	01054468	817/222-1221	358
St Gerard Catholic High Sch/San Antonio/Bexar	01000156	210/533-8061	44
St Gregory Cathedral Sch/Tyler/Smith	01012587	903/595-4109	339
St Gregory the Great Cath Sch/San Antonio/Bexar	01000041	210/342-0281	44
St Helen Catholic Sch/Georgetown/Williamson	05153535	512/868-0744	400
St Helen Sch/Pearland/Brazoria	04794227	281/485-2845	54
St Ignatius College Prep Sch/Fort Worth/Tarrant	11571446	817/801-4801	359
St Ignatius Martyr Cath Sch/Austin/Travis	01002934	512/442-8547	372
St James Catholic Sch/Seguin/Guadalupe	01000168	830/379-2878	174
St James Day Sch/Texarkana/Bowie	01479595	903/793-5554	50
St James Episcopal Sch/Corp Christi/Nueces	01045132	361/883-0835	306
St James Episcopal Sch/Del Rio/Val Verde	01058074	830/775-9911	379
St James the Apostle Sch/San Antonio/Bexar	01000170	210/924-1201	44
St Jerome Sch/Houston/Harris	01028184	713/468-7946	204
St Jo Elem Sch/Saint Jo/Montague	01042415	940/995-2541	290
St Jo High Sch/Saint Jo/Montague	01042427	940/995-2532	290
ST JO IND SCH DIST/SAINT JO/ MONTAGUE	01042403	940/995-2668	290
St John Berchman's Sch/San Antonio/Bexar	02203703	210/433-0411	44
St John Bosco Sch/San Antonio/Bexar	01000182	210/432-8011	44
St John Early Childhood Center/Cypress/Harris	12314057	281/304-5546	207
St John Paul II Catholic Sch/Houston/Harris	03077765	281/496-1500	204
St John Paul II High Sch/Corp Christi/Nueces	11401516	361/855-5744	306
St John Paul II High Sch/New Braunfels/Comal	11705142	830/643-0802	89
St John the Apostle Cath Sch/N Richlnd Hls/Tarrant	01054470	817/284-2228	358
St John XXIII Preparatory HS/Katy/Harris	10756215	281/693-1000	204
St John's Episcopal Day Sch/McAllen/Hidalgo	01410874	956/686-0231	226
St John's Episcopal Sch/Abilene/Taylor	01055034	325/695-8870	362
St John's Episcopal Sch/Dallas/Dallas	01012305	214/328-9131	116
St John's Episcopal Sch/Odessa/Ector	01410692	432/337-6431	131
St John's Sch/Houston/Harris	01028421	713/850-0222	207
St Jose Sanchez Del Rio Sch/San Antonio/Bexar	05286340	210/497-0323	44
St Joseph Academy/Brownsville/Cameron	01004449	956/542-3581	68
St Joseph Catholic Sch/Arlington/Tarrant	04420701	817/419-6800	358
St Joseph Catholic Sch/Bryan/Brazos	01002946	979/822-6641	56
St Joseph Catholic Sch/Edinburg/Hidalgo	01004451	956/383-3957	226
St Joseph Catholic Sch/Killeen/Bell	01002958	254/634-7272	30
St Joseph Catholic Sch/Richardson/Dallas	05153547	972/234-4679	114
St Joseph Catholic Sch/Waxahachie/Ellis	04021874	972/937-0956	143
St Joseph Catholic Sch/Yoakum/Lavaca	01000223	361/293-9000	263
St Joseph Elem Sch/Amarillo/Randall	01047740	806/359-1604	321
St Joseph High Sch/Victoria/Victoria	01000209	361/573-2446	383
St Joseph Sch/Alice/Jim Wells	01045388	361/664-4642	246
St Joseph Sch/Baytown/Harris	01028304	281/422-9749	204

Texas School Directory
DISTRICT & SCHOOL TELEPHONE INDEX

School/City/County DISTRICT/CITY/COUNTY	PID	TELEPHONE NUMBER	PAGE
St Joseph Sch/*El Paso*/El Paso	01016882	915/566-1661	139
St Joseph Sch/*Slaton*/Lubbock	01047752	806/828-6761	272
St Laurence Catholic Sch/*Sugar Land*/Fort Bend	04022048	281/980-0500	155
St Louis Catholic Sch/*Austin*/Travis	01002972	512/454-0384	372
St Louis Catholic Sch/*Waco*/McLennan	01002960	254/754-2041	282
St Louis Early Childhood Ctr/*Tyler*/Smith	01050955	903/262-1180	338
St Louis Sch/*Castroville*/Medina	03266318	830/931-3544	284
St Luke Catholic Sch/*Brownsville*/Cameron	04307317	956/544-7982	68
St Luke Catholic Sch/*San Antonio*/Bexar	01000053	210/434-2011	44
St Luke Sch/*Denison*/Grayson	02083840	903/465-2653	169
St Luke's Episcopal Sch/*San Antonio*/Bexar	00999695	210/826-0664	45
St Margaret Mary Sch/*San Antonio*/Bexar	01000259	210/534-6137	44
St Maria Goretti Sch/*Arlington*/Tarrant	01054482	817/275-5081	358
St Mark Catholic Sch/*Plano*/Collin	02181155	972/578-0610	85
St Mark Lutheran Sch/*Houston*/Harris	01027740	713/468-2623	207
St Mark's Episcopal Sch/*Houston*/Harris	01027752	713/667-7030	207
St Mark's Sch/*El Paso*/El Paso	02743387	915/581-2032	139
St Mark's School of Texas/*Dallas*/Dallas	01012147	214/346-8000	116
St Martha Catholic Sch/*Kingwood*/Harris	04420543	281/358-5523	204
St Martin De Porres Cath Sch/*Prosper*/Collin	11815292	469/362-2400	85
St Mary Catholic Sch/*League City*/Galveston	02138017	281/332-4014	162
St Mary Catholic Sch/*Orange*/Orange	01034444	409/883-8913	309
St Mary Catholic Sch/*West*/McLennan	01002996	254/826-5991	282
St Mary Elem Sch/*Fredericksbrg*/Gillespie	01000273	830/997-3914	163
St Mary Magdalen Sch/*San Antonio*/Bexar	01000285	210/735-1381	44
St Mary Magdalene Sch/*Humble*/Harris	04942797	281/446-8535	204
St Mary of Carmel Sch/*Dallas*/Dallas	01012630	214/748-2934	114
St Mary Purification Mont Sch/*Houston*/Harris	02114011	713/522-9276	204
St Mary's Academy Charter Sch/*Beeville*/Bee	01045390	361/358-5601	11
St Mary's Catholic Sch/*Gainesville*/Cooke	01054494	940/665-5395	92
St Mary's Catholic Sch/*Longview*/Gregg	01012642	903/753-1657	171
St Mary's Catholic Sch/*Temple*/Bell	01003017	254/778-8141	30
St Mary's Central Catholic Sch/*Odessa*/Ector	01055981	432/337-6052	131
St Mary's Sch/*Brownsville*/Cameron	01004463	956/546-1805	68
St Mary's Sch/*Taylor*/Williamson	01002908	512/352-2313	400
St Maryis Cathedral Sch/*Amarillo*/Potter	01047776	806/376-9112	319
St Marys Cathedral Sch/*Sherman*/Grayson	01012654	903/893-2127	168
St Matthew Catholic Sch/*San Antonio*/Bexar	04145793	210/696-7433	44
St Matthew's Episcopal Sch/*Edinburg*/Hidalgo	01560651	956/383-4202	226
St Matthews Catholic Sch/*El Paso*/El Paso	11532828	915/581-8801	139
St Michael Catholic Sch/*Houston*/Harris	01028196	713/621-6847	204
St Michael Sch/*Cuero*/De Witt	01000326	361/274-3554	118
St Michael Sch/*Weimar*/Colorado	01000338	979/725-8461	87
St Michael's Catholic Academy/*Austin*/Travis	02229537	512/328-2323	372
St Michael's Learning Academy/*Houston*/Harris	12314021	713/977-0566	207
St Michaels Episcopal Sch/*Bryan*/Brazos	01002178	979/822-2715	56
St Monica Catholic Sch/*Dallas*/Dallas	01012537	214/351-5688	114
St Monica Sch/*Converse*/Bexar	01000340	210/658-6701	44
St Nicholas Sch/*Houston*/Harris	04993227	713/791-9977	207
St Patrick Cathedral Sch/*El Paso*/El Paso	01016959	915/532-4142	139
St Patrick Catholic Sch/*Lufkin*/Angelina	01034450	936/634-6719	18
St Patrick Sch/*Corp Christi*/Nueces	01045302	361/852-1211	306
St Patrick Sch/*Dallas*/Dallas	01012678	214/348-8070	114
St Paul Catholic Sch/*San Antonio*/Bexar	01000376	210/732-2741	44
St Paul Lutheran Sch/*Bishop*/Nueces	01045156	361/584-2778	306
St Paul Lutheran Sch/*Fort Worth*/Tarrant	01054298	817/332-4563	359
St Paul Lutheran Sch/*Giddings*/Lee	01037549	979/366-2218	264
St Paul Lutheran Sch/*McAllen*/Hidalgo	01030694	956/682-2345	226
St Paul Lutheran Sch/*Thorndale*/Milam	01041930	512/898-2711	288
St Paul the Apostle Sch/*Richardson*/Dallas	01012680	972/235-3263	114
St Paul's Episcopal Sch/*Waco*/McLennan	01040546	254/753-0246	283
St Paul's Episcopal Sch/*Woodville*/Tyler	03017789	409/283-7555	375
St Paul's Preparatory Academy/*Arlington*/Tarrant	04886014	817/561-3500	359
St Peter Prince of Apostles/*San Antonio*/Bexar	01000388	210/824-3171	44
St Peter School the Apostle/*WHT Settlemt*/Tarrant	01054511	817/246-2032	358
St Peter the Apostle Elem Sch/*Houston*/Harris	01028330	713/747-9484	204
St Peter's Memorial Sch/*Laredo*/Webb	01045417	956/723-6302	389
St Philip & St Augustine Acad/*Dallas*/Dallas	01012707	214/381-4973	114
St Philip Catholic Sch/*El Campo*/Wharton	01000405	979/543-2901	390
St Philip's Academy-Frisco/*Frisco*/Collin	11735226	214/929-7787	86
St Philip's Early Clg HS/*San Antonio*/Bexar	12034403	210/486-2406	41
St Philip's Episcopal Sch/*Beeville*/Bee	01410496	361/358-6242	26
St Philip's Episcopal Sch/*Dallas*/Dallas	02083797	214/421-5221	116
St Philip's Episcopal Sch/*Uvalde*/Uvalde	01057886	830/278-1350	379
St Pius V Sch/*Pasadena*/Harris	01028354	713/472-5172	204
St Pius X Catholic Sch/*San Antonio*/Bexar	01000417	210/824-6431	44
St Pius X High Sch/*Houston*/Harris	01028366	713/692-3581	204
St Pius X Sch/*Corp Christi*/Nueces	01045429	361/992-1343	306
St Pius X Sch/*Dallas*/Dallas	01012719	972/279-2339	114
St Pius X Sch/*El Paso*/El Paso	01016961	915/772-6598	139
St Raphael Catholic Sch/*El Paso*/El Paso	01857181	915/598-2241	139
St Rita Catholic Sch/*Dallas*/Dallas	01012721	972/239-3203	114
St Rita Catholic Sch/*Fort Worth*/Tarrant	01054444	817/451-9383	358
St Rose of Lima Sch/*Houston*/Harris	01028378	713/691-0104	204
St Rose of Lima Sch/*Schulenburg*/Fayette	01000429	979/743-3080	148
St Stephen's Episcopal Sch/*Austin*/Travis	01057032	512/327-1213	373
St Stephen's Episcopal Sch/*Houston*/Harris	01410886	713/821-9100	207
St Stephen's Episcopal Sch/*Wimberley*/Hays	04012811	512/847-9857	212
St Theresa Sch/*Houston*/Harris	01028380	713/864-4536	204
St Theresa Sch/*Sugar Land*/Fort Bend	11532830	281/494-1156	155
St Theresa's Catholic Sch/*Austin*/Travis	02903484	512/451-7105	372
St Thomas Apostle Episc Sch/*Houston*/Harris	01410800	281/333-1340	207
St Thomas Aquinas Sch/*Dallas*/Dallas	01012733	214/826-0566	114
St Thomas Episcopal Sch/*San Antonio*/Bexar	01875080	210/494-3509	45
St Thomas High Sch/*Houston*/Harris	01028392	713/864-6348	204
St Thomas More Catholic Sch/*San Antonio*/Bexar	01000443	210/655-2882	44
St Thomas More Sch/*Houston*/Harris	01028407	713/729-3434	204
St Thomas' Episcopal Sch/*Houston*/Harris	01027788	713/666-3111	207
St Vincent De Paul Sch/*Houston*/Harris	01028201	713/666-2345	204
Stacey Jr Sr High Sch/*San Antonio*/Bexar	01808831	210/357-5100	34
Stafford Alt Ed Campus/*Stafford*/Fort Bend	04503858	281/261-9270	155
Stafford Early Childhd Ctr/*San Antonio*/Bexar	11713503	210/444-7900	32
Stafford Elem Sch/*Italy*/Ellis	01015084	972/483-6342	141
Stafford Elem Sch/*San Antonio*/Bexar	00997324	210/444-8400	32
Stafford Elem Sch/*Stafford*/Fort Bend	04942008	281/261-9229	155
Stafford High Sch/*Stafford*/Fort Bend	03316793	281/261-9239	155
Stafford Intermediate Sch/*Stafford*/Fort Bend	04010289	281/208-6100	155
Stafford Middle Sch/*Stafford*/Fort Bend	03316781	281/261-9215	155
STAFFORD MUNICIPAL SCH DIST/STAFFORD/FORT BEND	02228624	281/261-9200	154
Stafford Primary Sch/*Stafford*/Fort Bend	02228636	281/261-9203	155
Staggs Acad Intl STEM Studies/*Laredo*/Webb	12361206	956/326-2861	11
Stahl Elem Sch/*San Antonio*/Bexar	01881821	210/407-7400	35
Stamford High Sch/*Stamford*/Jones	01035357	325/307-3614	250
STAMFORD IND SCH DIST/STAMFORD/JONES	01035321	325/773-2705	250
Stamford Middle Sch/*Stamford*/Jones	01035345	325/455-0978	250
Stan C Stanley Elem Sch/*Katy*/Harris	11448564	281/234-1400	153
Stanton Elem Sch/*El Paso*/El Paso	01015876	915/236-6125	134
Stanton Elem Sch/*Stanton*/Martin	01040766	432/756-2285	274
Stanton High Sch/*Stanton*/Martin	01040778	432/756-3326	274
STANTON IND SCH DIST/STANTON/MARTIN	01040754	432/607-3700	274
Stanton Learning Center/*Hereford*/Deaf Smith	02224654	806/363-7610	119
Stanton Middle Sch/*Stanton*/Martin	01418539	432/756-2544	274
Stanton-Smith Elem Sch/*Whitehouse*/Smith	11072373	903/839-5730	339
Starkey Elem Sch/*Kerrville*/Kerr	01036105	830/257-2210	256
Starpoint Sch/*Fort Worth*/Tarrant	02238186	817/257-7141	359
Starrett Elem Sch/*Grand Prairie*/Tarrant	03011709	682/867-0400	345
Stars Accelerated High Sch/*Granbury*/Hood	04282236	817/408-4450	230
Startzville Elem Sch/*Canyon Lake*/Comal	01397026	830/885-8000	88
Stateline Christian Sch/*Texline*/Dallam	11231660	806/362-4320	95
Steam Academy at Stribling/*Burleson*/Johnson	01034860	817/245-3500	247
Steam Middle Sch/*Burleson*/Johnson	12107206	817/245-1500	247
Stehlik Elem Sch/*Houston*/Harris	04032603	281/878-0300	179
Steiner Ranch Elem Sch/*Austin*/Williamson	04455823	512/570-5700	397
Stell Middle Sch/*Brownsville*/Cameron	01003706	956/698-0363	64
Stelle Claughton Middle Sch/*Houston*/Harris	05273252	281/891-7950	203
STEM Academy/*Killeen*/Bell	12366244	254/336-7836	28
STEM Academy-Lewisville/*Lewisville*/Denton	12261175	972/829-4492	11
STEM Academy-Lewisville/*Lewisville*/Denton	11663037	972/316-6700	11
STEM Early College High Sch/*San Antonio*/Bexar	12032986	210/989-3500	33
STEM2 Preparatory Academy/*Harlingen*/Cameron	12364650	956/368-6100	65
Step by Step Christian Sch/*Tomball*/Harris	02751786	281/351-2888	207
Step Charter School II/*Houston*/Harris	11014890	281/988-7797	11

School Year 2019-2020 800-333-8802 TX-V71

DISTRICT & SCHOOL TELEPHONE INDEX

Market Data Retrieval

School/City/County DISTRICT/CITY/COUNTY	PID	TELEPHONE NUMBER	PAGE
Stephen C Foster Elem Sch/*Dallas*/Dallas	01009762	972/794-8100	103
Stephen F Austin Elem Sch/*Baytown*/Harris	01023756	281/420-4620	188
Stephen F Austin Elem Sch/*Dayton*/Liberty	01037800	936/258-2535	265
Stephen F Austin Elem Sch/*Ennis*/Ellis	01015010	972/872-7190	140
Stephen F Austin Elem Sch/*Gregory*/San Patricio	01049542	361/777-4252	331
Stephen F Austin High Sch/*Sugar Land*/Fort Bend	04365888	281/634-2000	151
Stephen F Austin Middle Sch/*Amarillo*/Potter	01047154	806/326-3000	318
Stephen F Austin Middle Sch/*Bryan*/Brazos	03400590	979/209-6700	55
Stephen F Austin Primary/*Slaton*/Lubbock	01039200	806/828-5813	272
Stephen F Austin STEM Academy/*Freeport*/Brazoria	01001679	979/730-7160	52
Stephen F Austin Univ CS/*Nacogdoches*/Nacogdoches	05097979	936/468-5899	11
Stephens Elem Sch/*Rowlett*/Dallas	04284301	972/463-5790	106
Stephens Elem Sch/*Shady Shores*/Denton	11128568	940/369-0800	121
Stephenville Christian Sch/*Stephenville*/Erath	11231737	254/965-4821	144
Stephenville High Sch/*Stephenville*/Erath	01017161	254/968-4141	144
STEPHENVILLE IND SCH DIST/STEPHENVILLE/ERATH	01017135	254/968-7990	144
Sterling Aviation High Sch/*Houston*/Harris	01025338	713/991-0510	193
STERLING CITY IND SCH DIST/STERLING CITY/STERLING	01051387	325/378-4781	342
Sterling Elem Sch/*Sterling City*/Sterling	01051399	325/378-5821	342
Sterling H Fly Jr High Sch/*Crystal City*/Zavala	01062350	830/374-2371	407
Sterling Middle High Sch/*Sterling City*/Sterling	04503834	325/378-5821	342
Steubing Ranch Elem Sch/*San Antonio*/Bexar	10003329	210/407-7600	35
Stevens Elem Sch/*Houston*/Harris	01024267	713/613-2546	189
Stevens Park Elem Sch/*Dallas*/Dallas	01009889	972/794-4200	103
Stevenson Middle Sch/*San Antonio*/Bexar	01379921	210/397-7300	38
Stewart Creek Elem Sch/*Montgomery*/Montgomery	05231216	936/276-3500	293
Stewart Elem Sch/*Hitchcock*/Galveston	01018892	409/316-6543	161
Stewart Elem Sch/*Lubbock*/Lubbock	01038921	806/219-6900	270
Stewart's Creek Elem Sch/*The Colony*/Denton	02179566	469/713-5960	124
Stiles Middle Sch/*Leander*/Williamson	11823330	512/570-3800	397
Stillman Middle Sch/*Brownsville*/Cameron	01003495	956/698-1000	64
Stinson Elem Sch/*Richardson*/Collin	04916281	469/752-3400	83
Stinson Middle Sch/*San Antonio*/Bexar	03398131	210/397-3600	38
Stipes Elem Sch/*Irving*/Dallas	10023240	972/600-4500	110
Stockdale Elem Sch/*Stockdale*/Wilson	01061394	830/996-1612	401
Stockdale High Sch/*Stockdale*/Wilson	01061409	830/996-3103	401
STOCKDALE IND SCH DIST/STOCKDALE/WILSON	01061382	830/996-3551	401
Stockdale Junior High Sch/*Stockdale*/Wilson	01061411	830/996-3153	401
Stockdick Jr High Sch/*Katy*/Harris	12231273	281/234-2700	153
Stone Oak Elem Sch/*San Antonio*/Bexar	04455407	210/407-7800	35
Stonegate Christian Academy/*Irving*/Dallas	02164872	972/790-0070	116
Stonegate Elem Sch/*Bedford*/Tarrant	01053933	817/285-3250	354
Stonehill Christian Academy/*Pflugerville*/Travis	02233734	512/763-2776	373
Stonewall Elem Sch/*Stonewall*/Gillespie	01019729	830/990-4599	163
Stonewall Flanders Elem Sch/*San Antonio*/Bexar	00997439	210/989-3300	33
Stony Point High Sch/*Round Rock*/Williamson	04867317	512/428-7000	399
Story Intermediate Sch/*Palestine*/Anderson	01808788	903/731-8015	15
Stovall EC-PK-K/*Houston*/Harris	03336016	281/591-8500	181
Strack Intermediate Sch/*Klein*/Harris	01539183	832/249-5400	197
Strake Jesuit College Prep Sch/*Houston*/Harris	01028419	713/774-7651	204
Stratford High Sch/*Houston*/Harris	01027374	713/251-3400	201
Stratford High Sch/*Stratford*/Sherman	01050515	806/366-3330	336
STRATFORD IND SCH DIST/STRATFORD/SHERMAN	01050486	806/366-3300	336
Stratford Junior High Sch/*Stratford*/Sherman	01050503	806/366-3320	336
STRAWN IND SCH DIST/STRAWN/PALO PINTO	01046150	254/672-5313	311
Strawn Sch/*Strawn*/Palo Pinto	02111318	254/672-5313	311
Strickland Elem Sch/*Farmers BRNCH*/Dallas	01008213	972/968-2500	97
Strickland Middle Sch/*Denton*/Denton	01013323	940/369-4200	121
Stroman Middle Sch/*Victoria*/Victoria	01058464	361/578-2711	382
Stuard Elem Sch/*Aledo*/Parker	04920634	817/441-5103	312
Stuart Place Elem Sch/*Harlingen*/Cameron	01003897	956/427-3160	65
Stubblefield Alternative Acad/*Willis*/Montgomery	04282262	936/856-1302	294
Stubblefield Learning Center/*Lufkin*/Angelina	04447034	936/634-1100	17
Stuber Elem Sch/*Prosper*/Collin	12363840	469/219-2290	84
Stuchbery Elem Sch/*Houston*/Harris	01026978	713/740-0752	200
Student Opportunity Center/*Frisco*/Collin	04916889	469/633-6700	80
Student Reassignment Ctr/*Irving*/Dallas	04451059	972/600-3900	110
Student Support Center/*Corp Christi*/Nueces	02203040	361/878-2840	304
Stults Road Elem Sch/*Dallas*/Dallas	01011973	469/593-2500	113
Success High Sch/*Fort Worth*/Tarrant	04420725	817/815-2700	352
Success High Sch/*Round Rock*/Williamson	11561946	512/704-1300	399
Suchma Elementary/*Conroe*/Montgomery	12368785	936/709-4400	292
Sudan Elem Sch/*Sudan*/Lamb	01037094	806/227-2431	261
Sudan High Sch/*Sudan*/Lamb	01037109	806/227-2431	261
SUDAN IND SCH DIST/SUDAN/LAMB	01037082	806/227-2431	261
Sudderth Elem Sch/*Monahans*/Ward	01059028	432/943-5101	385
Sudie Williams Elem Sch/*Dallas*/Dallas	01010204	972/794-8700	103
Sue Ann Mackey Elem Sch/*Balch Springs*/Dallas	05345623	972/290-4160	111
Sue Creech Elem Sch/*Katy*/Harris	04917481	281/237-8850	153
Sue Crouch Intermediate Sch/*Fort Worth*/Tarrant	10019718	817/370-5670	348
Sue E Rattan Elem Sch/*Anna*/Collin	10901123	972/924-1400	77
Sue Park Broadway Elem Sch/*Spring*/Montgomery	10910992	281/465-2900	292
Sue Wilson Stafford Middle Sch/*Frisco*/Collin	11103843	469/633-5100	80
Sugar Grove Academy/*Houston*/Harris	04454477	713/271-0214	189
Sugar Land Middle Sch/*Sugar Land*/Fort Bend	01418321	281/634-3080	151
Sugar Loaf Elem Sch/*Killeen*/Bell	00996605	254/336-1940	28
Sugar Mill Elem Sch/*Sugar Land*/Fort Bend	02226664	281/634-4440	151
Sul Ross Elem Sch/*Bryan*/Brazos	01002154	979/209-1500	55
Sul Ross Middle Sch/*San Antonio*/Bexar	00998304	210/397-6350	38
Sullivan Elem Sch/*San Benito*/Cameron	01004293	956/361-6880	67
SULPHUR BLUFF IND SCH DIST/SULPHUR BLUFF/HOPKINS	01031595	903/945-2460	232
Sulphur Bluff Sch/*Sulphur Bluff*/Hopkins	01809407	903/945-2460	232
Sulphur Springs Elem Sch/*Sulphur Spgs*/Hopkins	01031636	903/855-8466	232
Sulphur Springs High Sch/*Sulphur Spgs*/Hopkins	01031698	903/885-2158	232
SULPHUR SPRINGS IND SCH DIST/SULPHUR SPGS/HOPKINS	01031624	903/885-2153	232
Sulphur Springs Middle Sch/*Sulphur Spgs*/Hopkins	01031686	903/885-7741	232
Summer Creek High Sch/*Houston*/Harris	11450335	281/641-5400	196
Summer Creek Middle Sch/*Crowley*/Tarrant	11079723	817/297-5090	348
Summerwood Elem Sch/*Houston*/Harris	05344198	281/641-3000	196
Summit Christian Academy/*Boerne*/Kendall	12313948	210/254-4534	254
Summit Christian Academy/*Cedar Park*/Williamson	02153598	512/250-1369	400
Summit Christian Academy/*Huntsville*/Walker	04993447	936/295-9601	384
Summit Education Center/*Duncanville*/Dallas	04450419	972/708-2570	105
Summit Hill Elem Sch/*Howe*/Grayson	12365989	903/745-4100	166
Summitt Elem Sch/*Austin*/Travis	01056662	512/414-4484	368
Sun Ridge Middle Sch/*El Paso*/El Paso	04941808	915/937-6600	137
Sun Valley Elem Sch/*San Antonio*/Bexar	00999607	210/645-7570	43
Sundown Elem Sch/*Katy*/Harris	02177051	281/237-5400	153
Sundown Elem Sch/*Sundown*/Hockley	01031313	806/229-5021	229
Sundown High Sch/*Sundown*/Hockley	01031325	806/229-2511	229
SUNDOWN IND SCH DIST/SUNDOWN/HOCKLEY	01031301	806/229-3021	229
Sundown Lane Elem Sch/*Amarillo*/Randall	01539248	806/677-2400	321
Sundown Middle Sch/*Sundown*/Hockley	01031337	806/229-4691	230
Sunnybrook Christian Academy/*San Antonio*/Bexar	04938239	210/674-8000	45
Sunnyvale Elem Sch/*Sunnyvale*/Dallas	10022090	972/226-7601	113
Sunnyvale High Sch/*Sunnyvale*/Dallas	11076680	972/203-4600	113
SUNNYVALE IND SCH DIST/SUNNYVALE/DALLAS	01012018	972/226-5974	113
Sunnyvale Middle Sch/*Sunnyvale*/Dallas	01012020	972/226-2922	113
Sunray Elem Sch/*Sunray*/Moore	01042922	806/948-4222	296
Sunray High Sch/*Sunray*/Moore	01042934	806/948-5515	296
SUNRAY IND SCH DIST/SUNRAY/MOORE	01042910	806/948-4411	296
Sunray Middle Sch/*Sunray*/Moore	04929329	806/948-4444	296
Sunrise Elem Sch/*Amarillo*/Potter	01047491	806/326-5450	318
Sunrise-McMillian Elem Sch/*Fort Worth*/Tarrant	01053440	817/815-3900	352
Sunset Elem Sch/*Dumas*/Moore	01042881	806/935-2127	295
Sunset High Sch/*Dallas*/Dallas	01009906	972/502-1500	103
Sunset Valley Elem Sch/*Austin*/Travis	01056674	512/414-2392	367
Sunset Valley Elem Sch/*Fort Worth*/Tarrant	12170198	817/743-8200	355

Texas School Directory

DISTRICT & SCHOOL TELEPHONE INDEX

School/City/County DISTRICT/CITY/COUNTY	PID	TELEPHONE	PAGE NUMBER
Sunshine Cottage Sch-Deaf Chld/*San Antonio*/Bexar	01479430	210/824-0579	45
Susannah Dickinson Elem Sch/*Sugar Land*/Fort Bend	04033621	832/223-1400	154
Susie T Fuentes Elem Sch/*Kyle*/Hays	04920268	512/268-7827	211
Sutton Elem Sch/*Houston*/Harris	01024633	713/778-3400	194
Sweeny Christian Sch/*Sweeny*/Brazoria	02729575	979/548-6001	54
Sweeny Elem Sch/*Sweeny*/Brazoria	01001930	979/491-8300	54
Sweeny High Sch/*Sweeny*/Brazoria	01001928	979/491-8100	54
SWEENY IND SCH DIST/SWEENY/BRAZORIA	01001904	979/491-8000	54
Sweeny Junior High Sch/*Sweeny*/Brazoria	01001942	979/491-8200	54
Sweet Home Elem Sch/*Sweet Home*/Lavaca	01037393	361/293-3221	262
SWEET HOME IND SCH DIST/SWEET HOME/LAVACA	01037381	361/293-3221	262
Sweetwater High Sch/*Sweetwater*/Nolan	01043976	325/235-4371	302
Sweetwater Intermediate Sch/*Sweetwater*/Nolan	01043940	325/235-3491	302
SWEETWATER ISD SCH DIST/SWEETWATER/NOLAN	01043914	325/235-8601	301
Sweetwater Middle Sch/*Sweetwater*/Nolan	01043952	325/236-6303	302
Swenke Elem Sch/*Cypress*/Harris	11451494	281/213-1200	185
Swift Elem Sch/*Arlington*/Tarrant	01051935	682/867-4100	345
Sycamore Academy/*Keene*/Johnson	12313833	817/645-0895	249
Sycamore Elem Sch/*Fort Worth*/Tarrant	01052393	817/568-5700	348
Sycamore Springs Elem Sch/*Austin*/Hays	12305666	512/858-3900	210
Sycamore Springs Middle Sch/*Austin*/Hays	12305678	512/858-3600	211
Sylvan Rodriguez Elem Sch/*Houston*/Harris	05009532	713/295-3870	194

T

School/City/County	PID	TELEPHONE	PAGE
T A Howard Middle Sch/*Arlington*/Tarrant	04170619	682/314-1050	357
T A Sims Elem Sch/*Fort Worth*/Tarrant	03253361	817/814-0800	352
T F Birmingham Elem Sch/*Wylie*/Collin	02845650	972/429-3420	85
T G Allen Elem Sch/*Corp Christi*/Nueces	01044188	361/878-2140	304
T G Terry Elem Sch/*Dallas*/Dallas	01009944	972/749-3200	103
T H Johnson Elem Sch/*Taylor*/Williamson	11712004	512/365-7114	399
T H McDonald Junior High Sch/*Katy*/Harris	03397618	281/237-5300	153
T H McDonald Middle Sch/*Mercedes*/Hidalgo	01011557	972/882-5700	111
T H Rogers Sch/*Houston*/Harris	01024578	713/917-3565	194
T L Pink Elem Sch/*Richmond*/Fort Bend	04746309	832/223-2100	154
T M Clark Elem Sch/*Portland*/San Patricio	01049580	361/777-4045	331
T S Hancock Elem Sch/*Houston*/Harris	01023251	281/897-4523	185
T W Browne Middle Sch/*Dallas*/Dallas	01009970	972/502-2500	103
T W Ogg Elem Sch/*Clute*/Brazoria	01001681	979/730-7195	52
Tabasco Elem Sch/*La Joya*/Hidalgo	04805981	956/323-2440	220
Tafolla Middle Sch/*San Antonio*/Bexar	00999322	210/978-7930	41
Taft Elem Sch/*Port Arthur*/Jefferson	01034028	409/962-2262	244
Taft High Sch/*Taft*/San Patricio	01049865	361/528-2636	332
TAFT IND SCH DIST/TAFT/SAN PATRICIO	01049827	361/528-2636	332
Taft Junior High Sch/*Taft*/San Patricio	01049877	361/528-2636	332
Tahoka Elem Sch/*Tahoka*/Lynn	01039365	806/561-4350	273
Tahoka High Sch/*Tahoka*/Lynn	01039377	806/561-4538	273
TAHOKA IND SCH DIST/TAHOKA/LYNN	01039341	806/561-4105	273
Tahoka Middle Sch/*Tahoka*/Lynn	04038413	806/561-4539	273
Talkington Sch Young Women/*Lubbock*/Lubbock	11434771	806/219-2200	270
Talley Elem Sch/*Frisco*/Collin	12308151	469/633-2175	80
Tanglewood Elem Sch/*Fort Worth*/Tarrant	01053464	817/814-5900	352
Tanglewood Middle Sch/*Houston*/Harris	04016075	713/625-1411	194
Tannahill Intermediate Sch/*Fort Worth*/Tarrant	04803452	817/367-1370	357
Tarkington High Sch/*Cleveland*/Liberty	01038000	281/592-7739	266
TARKINGTON IND SCH DIST/CLEVELAND/LIBERTY	01037977	281/592-8781	266
Tarkington Intermediate Sch/*Cleveland*/Liberty	03319642	281/592-6134	266
Tarkington Middle Sch/*Cleveland*/Liberty	01037991	281/592-7737	266
Tarkington Primary Sch/*Cleveland*/Liberty	01037989	281/592-7736	266
Tarver Elem Sch/*Temple*/Bell	10900868	254/215-3800	27
Tarver-Rendon Elem Sch/*Burleson*/Tarrant	01054169	817/299-7880	357
Tascosa High Sch/*Amarillo*/Potter	01047506	806/326-2600	318
Tate Springs Christian Sch/*Arlington*/Tarrant	11746275	817/478-7091	359
Tatom Elem Sch/*Monahans*/Ward	01059030	432/943-2769	385
Tatum Elem Sch/*Farmersville*/Collin	01006174	972/782-7251	78
Tatum Elem Sch/*Tatum*/Rusk	01049190	903/947-0352	328
Tatum High Sch/*Tatum*/Rusk	01049205	903/947-6482	328
TATUM IND SCH DIST/TATUM/RUSK	01049188	903/947-6482	328
Tatum Middle Sch/*Tatum*/Rusk	01418565	903/947-6482	328
Tatum Primary Sch/*Tatum*/Rusk	02230108	903/947-6485	328
Tavola Elem Sch/*New Caney*/Montgomery	01878422	281/577-2900	294

School/City/County DISTRICT/CITY/COUNTY	PID	TELEPHONE	PAGE NUMBER
Taylor Career & Tech Ctr/*Beaumont*/Jefferson	03054763	409/617-5740	242
Taylor Christian Sch/*McAllen*/Hidalgo	01875456	956/686-7574	226
Taylor Creek Elem Sch/*Copperas Cove*/Lampasas	11445263	512/564-2585	261
Taylor Elem Sch/*Abilene*/Taylor	01172864	325/671-4970	360
Taylor Elem Sch/*Mercedes*/Hidalgo	01030216	956/514-2388	222
Taylor High Sch/*Taylor*/Williamson	01061186	512/365-6326	399
TAYLOR IND SCH DIST/TAYLOR/WILLIAMSON	01061162	512/365-1391	399
Taylor Middle Sch/*Taylor*/Williamson	01061198	512/352-2815	400
Taylor Opportunity Center/*Taylor*/Williamson	12036827	512/365-8089	400
Taylor Ray Elem Sch/*Rosenberg*/Fort Bend	02045343	832/223-2400	154
Tays Junior High Sch/*Katy*/Harris	12168896	281/234-2400	153
TCC South-Fwisd Collegiate HS/*Fort Worth*/Tarrant	12172483	817/515-4402	352
Teague Elem Sch/*Pasadena*/Harris	01548457	713/740-0760	200
Teague Elem Sch/*Teague*/Freestone	01018517	254/739-2611	156
Teague High Sch/*Teague*/Freestone	01018529	254/739-2532	156
TEAGUE IND SCH DIST/TEAGUE/FREESTONE	01018505	254/739-1300	156
Teague Intermediate Sch/*Teague*/Freestone	02055037	254/739-3303	156
Teague Junior High Sch/*Teague*/Freestone	04447993	254/739-3011	156
Teague Lion Academy/*Teague*/Freestone	12166991	254/739-1444	156
Team Sch/*Cleburne*/Johnson	04014560	817/202-2160	247
Technical Education Center/*Sugar Land*/Fort Bend	03393789	281/634-5671	151
Ted Flores Elem Sch/*Pearsall*/Frio	01018672	830/334-4108	157
Ted Polk Middle Sch/*Carrollton*/Dallas	04756287	972/968-4600	97
Tegeler Career Center/*Pasadena*/Harris	04036984	713/740-0410	200
Tejas School of Choice/*El Paso*/El Paso	03010987	915/434-9900	138
Tekoa Academy-Orange/*Orange*/Orange	11704796	409/886-9864	11
Tekoa Academy-Port Arthur/*Port Arthur*/Jefferson	04903105	409/982-5400	11
Temple Charter Academy/*Temple*/Bell	04886131	254/778-8682	11
Temple Christian Academy/*Flower Mound*/Denton	10017318	972/874-8700	126
Temple Christian Sch/*Fort Worth*/Tarrant	01410991	817/457-0770	359
Temple High Sch/*Temple*/Bell	00996837	254/215-7000	29
TEMPLE IND SCH DIST/TEMPLE/BELL	00996708	254/215-8473	29
TENAHA IND SCH DIST/TENAHA/SHELBY	01050424	936/248-5000	335
Tenaha Sch/*Tenaha*/Shelby	01050448	936/248-5000	335
Tenney Sch/*Houston*/Harris	01480415	713/783-6990	207
Tennyson Middle Sch/*Waco*/McLennan	01040429	254/772-1440	282
Teravista Elem Sch/*Round Rock*/Williamson	11130846	512/704-0500	399
TERLINGUA COMMON SCH DIST/TERLINGUA/BREWSTER	01002283	432/371-2281	57
Terlingua Elem Sch/*Terlingua*/Brewster	01002295	432/371-2281	57
Terra Vista Middle Sch/*Lubbock*/Lubbock	10030372	806/796-0076	269
Terrace Elem Sch/*Houston*/Harris	01027386	713/251-7200	201
Terrace Hills Middle Sch/*El Paso*/El Paso	01015888	915/236-6750	135
Terrell Alternative Ed Center/*Terrell*/Kaufman	04875687	972/563-6319	253
TERRELL CO IND SCH DIST/SANDERSON/TERRELL	01055046	432/345-2515	362
Terrell Elem Sch/*Denison*/Grayson	01020314	903/462-7550	166
Terrell High Sch/*Terrell*/Kaufman	01035802	972/563-7525	253
TERRELL IND SCH DIST/TERRELL/KAUFMAN	01035759	972/563-7504	253
Terrell Wells Middle Sch/*San Antonio*/Bexar	00997568	210/989-2600	33
Terry High Sch/*Rosenberg*/Fort Bend	02110089	832/223-3400	154
Texans Can Acad Carrltn-Farmrs/*Dallas*/Dallas	11014163	972/243-2178	11
Texans Can Acad Dallas Oak Clf/*Dallas*/Dallas	04924769	214/943-2244	11
Texans Can Acad Dallas Pl Grv/*Dallas*/Dallas	11014151	972/225-1194	11
Texans Can Acad Dallas Ross AV/*Dallas*/Dallas	04467113	214/824-4226	11
Texans Can Acad Fw Lancaster/*Fort Worth*/Tarrant	05011042	817/735-1515	11
Texans Can Acad Fw Westcreek/*Fort Worth*/Tarrant	04925787	817/531-3223	11
Texans Can Acad Garland/*Garland*/Dallas	12260705	972/441-7202	12
Texans Can Acad Houston Hobby/*Houston*/Harris	11567304	832/379-4226	12
Texans Can Acad Houston North/*Houston*/Harris	04813407	713/659-4226	12
Texans Can Acad Houston SW/*Houston*/Harris	12260810	281/918-4316	12

DISTRICT & SCHOOL TELEPHONE INDEX

Market Data Retrieval

School/City/County DISTRICT/CITY/COUNTY	PID	TELEPHONE NUMBER	PAGE
Texans Can Acad San Antonio/San Antonio/Bexar	05010634	210/923-1226	12
Texans Can Academy Austin/Austin/Travis	05220944	512/477-4226	12
Texans Can Academy-Grant East/Dallas/Dallas	12163717	972/228-4226	12
TEXARKANA IND SCH DIST/TEXARKANA/BOWIE	01001215	903/794-3651	50
Texas Academy Math & Science/Denton/Denton	04022153	940/565-3606	12
Texas Academy of Biomed Sci/Fort Worth/Tarrant	11711892	817/515-1660	352
Texas Christian Sch/Houston/Harris	04481066	281/550-6060	207
Texas City High Sch/Texas City/Galveston	01019561	409/916-0800	161
TEXAS CITY IND SCH DIST/TEXAS CITY/GALVESTON	01019470	409/916-0100	161
Texas Connections Academy/Houston/Harris	11555399	281/661-8293	189
TEXAS DEPT OF EDUCATION/AUSTIN/TRAVIS	00994396	512/463-9734	1
Texas Early College High Sch/Marshall/Harrison	11704655	903/935-4109	12
Texas Empowerment Academy/Austin/Travis	04813483	512/494-1076	12
Texas Empowerment Academy/Austin/Travis	12161824	512/928-0118	12
Texas High Sch/Texarkana/Bowie	01001344	903/794-3891	50
Texas Leadership CS-Abilene/Abilene/Taylor	12115758	325/480-3500	12
Texas Leadership CS-Arlington/Arlington/Tarrant	12115710	817/385-9338	12
Texas Leadership CS-Midland/Midland/Midland	11930804	432/242-7117	12
Texas Middle Sch/Texarkana/Bowie	01001306	903/793-5631	50
Texas Military Institute/San Antonio/Bexar	01000479	210/698-7171	45
Texas Neurorehab Center/Austin/Travis	02204654	512/444-4835	373
Texas Online Preparatory Sch/Lewisville/Walker	11931896	888/263-6497	383
Texas Prep School-San Marcos/San Marcos/Hays	04949678	512/805-3000	12
Texas Preparatory Sch-Austin/Austin/Travis	11932242	512/928-3000	12
Texas Sch Blind & Visually Imp/Austin/Travis	01810078	512/454-8631	12
Texas School for the Deaf/Austin/Travis	01810107	512/462-5353	12
Texas School of the Arts/Edgecliff Vlg/Tarrant	11013860	817/732-8372	12
Texas Serenity Academy/Houston/Harris	04893184	281/820-9540	12
Texas Serenity Academy-Gano/Houston/Harris	12261187	713/699-3443	12
Texas Virtual Acad Hallsville/Lewisville/Denton	11014888	866/360-0161	12
Texhoma Elem Sch/Texhoma/Sherman	00863137	806/827-7400	336
TEXHOMA IND SCH DIST/TEXHOMA/SHERMAN	01050527	806/827-7400	336
TEXLINE IND SCH DIST/TEXLINE/DALLAM	01008108	806/362-4667	95
Texline Sch/Texline/Dallam	01008110	806/362-4284	95
Texoma Alternative Center/Iowa Park/Wichita	04911451	940/592-1410	392
Texoma Christian Sch/Sherman/Grayson	02747773	903/893-7076	169
The Academy/Weatherford/Parker	11237547	817/598-0722	314
The Bridge Sch/Houston/Harris	12313845	713/974-2066	207
The Colony High Sch/The Colony/Denton	02896623	469/713-5178	124
The Discovery Sch/Edinburg/Hidalgo	02761183	956/381-1117	226
The Fay Sch/Houston/Harris	03560358	713/681-8300	207
The Goodwill Excel Center/Austin/Travis	12163030	512/531-5500	12
The Humanist Academy/Irving/Dallas	12180325	972/646-1085	116
The Jane Justin Sch/Fort Worth/Tarrant	12314033	817/390-2831	359
The King's Academy/Dripping Spgs/Hays	12032211	512/858-4700	212
The Kinkaid Sch/Houston/Harris	01027647	713/782-1640	207
The Lawson Academy/Houston/Harris	05273965	713/225-1551	12
The Oakridge Sch/Arlington/Tarrant	02205385	817/451-4994	359
The Phoenix Academy/Mansfield/Tarrant	04452699	682/314-1700	357
The Steam Academy at Mambrino/Granbury/Hood	04749387	817/408-4900	230
The Summit Sch/Pasadena/Harris	05347889	713/740-0290	200
The Varnett School-SW/Houston/Harris	02950372	713/723-4699	12
The Westwood School-Upper/Dallas/Dallas	12313857	972/239-8598	116
The Woodlands Classical Acad/The Woodlands/Montgomery	11848964	936/242-1541	12
The Woodlands High Sch/The Woodlands/Montgomery	04454025	936/709-1200	292
The Woodlands HS-9th GR Campus/The Woodlands/Montgomery	04923777	832/592-8200	292
The Woodlands Methodist Sch/Spring/Montgomery	12313936	281/882-8220	295
The Woodlands-College Park HS/The Woodlands/Montgomery	10007571	936/709-3000	292
Theiss Elem Sch/Klein/Harris	01026368	832/484-5900	197
Thelma E Page-Richardson ES/Dallas/Dallas	11925964	972/892-8100	103
Thelma Jones Elem Sch/Arlington/Tarrant	05273630	817/299-6940	357
Theodore Roosevelt Elem Sch/McAllen/Hidalgo	01030060	956/971-4424	221
Thigpen-Zavala Elem Sch/McAllen/Hidalgo	01030101	956/971-4377	221
Thomas A Edison Elem Sch/Gainesville/Cooke	01007415	940/665-6091	91
Thomas Arnold Elem Sch/Salado/Bell	00996693	254/947-6925	29
Thomas B Francis Elem Sch/Houston/Harris	01022960	281/985-6500	180
Thomas B Gray Elem Sch/Houston/Harris	03246760	281/878-0660	179
Thomas Buzbee Vocational Sch/New Waverly/Walker	03395660	936/344-7238	12
Thomas C Marsh Prep Academy/Dallas/Dallas	01009994	972/502-6600	103
Thomas Elem Sch/Abilene/Taylor	04015344	325/671-4995	360
Thomas Elem Sch/Plano/Collin	01824110	469/752-3500	83
Thomas Elem Sch/Richmond/Fort Bend	11447211	832/223-4600	154
Thomas Haley Elem Sch/Irving/Dallas	01011313	972/600-7000	110
Thomas Hancock Elem Sch/Houston/Harris	12169486	713/740-5430	200
Thomas Hatchett Elem Sch/San Antonio/Bexar	05347566	210/397-6850	38
Thomas J Rusk Elem Sch/Nacogdoches/Nacogdoches	05343118	936/569-3100	298
Thomas J Rusk Middle Sch/Dallas/Dallas	01010008	972/925-2000	103
Thomas J Stovall Middle Sch/Houston/Harris	01022958	281/878-0670	181
Thomas Jefferson High Sch/Dallas/Dallas	01009956	972/502-7300	103
Thomas Jefferson High Sch/San Antonio/Bexar	00998639	210/438-6570	41
Thomas Jefferson Middle Sch/Port Arthur/Jefferson	01033907	409/984-4860	243
Thomas Justiss Elem Sch/Paris/Lamar	01036765	903/737-7458	260
Thomas L Marsalis Elem Sch/Dallas/Dallas	01009968	972/749-3500	103
Thomas Manor Elem Sch/El Paso/El Paso	01016624	915/434-7500	138
Thomas Middle Sch/Houston/Harris	01025089	713/732-3500	193
Thomas O Hicks Elem Sch/Frisco/Denton	05347372	469/713-5981	124
Thomas S Grantham Academy/Houston/Harris	02225696	281/985-6590	181
Thomas Tolbert Elem Sch/Dallas/Dallas	04456487	972/794-5900	103
Thomas Wesley Andrews Elem Sch/Plano/Collin	05096846	469/752-3900	83
Thompson Learning Center/Converse/Bexar	11452266	210/945-5053	34
Thorndale Elem Sch/Thorndale/Milam	01041916	512/898-2912	288
Thorndale High Sch/Thorndale/Milam	01041928	512/898-2321	288
THORNDALE IND SCH DIST/THORNDALE/MILAM	01041904	512/898-2538	288
Thorndale Middle Sch/Thorndale/Milam	04800694	512/898-2670	288
Thornton Elem Sch/Arlington/Tarrant	01051947	682/867-4200	345
Thornton Elem Sch/Temple/Bell	00996849	254/215-5700	29
Thornton Middle Sch/Katy/Harris	04036142	281/856-1500	185
Thornwood Elem Sch/Houston/Harris	01027398	713/251-7300	201
Thousand Oaks Elem Sch/San Antonio/Bexar	01881833	210/407-8000	36
Thrall Elem Sch/Thrall/Williamson	01061239	512/898-5293	400
Thrall High Sch/Thrall/Williamson	04944331	512/898-5193	400
THRALL IND SCH DIST/THRALL/WILLIAMSON	01061227	512/898-0062	400
Thrall Middle Sch/Thrall/Williamson	01061241	512/898-5328	400
Three Lakes Middle Sch/Tyler/Smith	01050759	903/952-4400	338
Three Rivers Elem Sch/Three Rivers/Live Oak	01038311	361/786-3592	268
THREE RIVERS IND SCH DIST/THREE RIVERS/LIVE OAK	01038309	361/786-3626	268
Three Rivers Jr Sr High Sch/Three Rivers/Live Oak	01038323	361/786-3531	268
Three Way Elem Sch/Stephenville/Erath	01017197	254/965-6496	144
THREE WAY IND SCH DIST/STEPHENVILLE/ERATH	01017185	254/965-6496	144
Threeway High Sch/Stephenville/Erath	12309894	254/965-9496	144
THROCKMORTON IND SCH DIST/THROCKMORTON/THROCKMORTON	01055228	940/849-2411	363
Throckmorton Sch/Throckmorton/Throckmorton	01055230	940/849-9981	363
Thunderbird Elem Sch/Plainview/Hale	01022013	806/293-6060	175
Thurgood Marshall Elem Sch/Dallas/Dallas	10007430	469/593-6800	113
Thurgood Marshall High Sch/Missouri City/Fort Bend	05098442	281/634-6630	151
Tibbals Elem Sch/Murphy/Collin	10011936	972/429-2520	85
Tice Elem Sch/Houston/Harris	01881883	832/386-4050	187
Tidehaven High Sch/Elmaton/Matagorda	01040998	979/843-4310	276
TIDEHAVEN IND SCH DIST/ELMATON/MATAGORDA	01040962	979/843-4300	276
Tidehaven Intermediate Sch/Elmaton/Matagorda	01041007	361/843-4320	276
Tierra Blanca Early Child Cent/Hereford/Deaf Smith	12364870	806/363-7680	119
Tierra Blanca Elem Sch/Hereford/Deaf Smith	01013074	806/363-7680	119
Tierra Del Sol Elem Sch/El Paso/El Paso	02110601	915/434-5800	138
Tiger Academy/Smithville/Bastrop	12173451	512/237-5142	24

TX-V74   800-333-8802   School Year 2019-2020

Texas School Directory
DISTRICT & SCHOOL TELEPHONE INDEX

School/City/County DISTRICT/CITY/COUNTY	PID	TELEPHONE NUMBER	PAGE
Tiger Trail Sch/*Houston*/Harris	04949886	713/251-8100	201
Tijerina Elem Sch/*Houston*/Harris	02111954	713/924-1790	190
Timber Creek Elem Sch/*Flower Mound*/Denton	01824146	469/713-5961	124
Timber Creek Elem Sch/*Livingston*/Polk	02223894	936/328-2180	317
Timber Creek Elem Sch/*The Woodlands*/Harris	11815943	281/357-3060	203
Timber Creek High Sch/*Fort Worth*/Tarrant	11448552	817/744-2300	355
Timber Ridge Elem Sch/*Killeen*/Bell	10002052	254/336-6630	28
Timberline Elem Sch/*Grapevine*/Tarrant	02043383	817/251-5770	353
Timbers Elem Sch/*Humble*/Harris	02125515	281/641-2000	196
Timberview Middle Sch/*Fort Worth*/Tarrant	11551458	817/744-2600	355
Timberwilde Elem Sch/*San Antonio*/Bexar	02110132	210/397-0400	38
Timberwood Middle Sch/*Humble*/Harris	04808672	281/641-3800	196
Timberwood Park Elem Sch/*San Antonio*/Comal	11079448	830/609-6705	88
Timmerman Elem Sch/*Pflugerville*/Travis	02848822	512/594-4200	372
Timothy Baranoff Elem Sch/*Austin*/Travis	04869834	512/841-7100	367
Timpson Elem Sch/*Timpson*/Shelby	04748333	936/254-2462	335
Timpson High Sch/*Timpson*/Shelby	01050462	936/254-3125	335
TIMPSON IND SCH DIST/*TIMPSON*/ SHELBY	01050450	936/254-2463	335
Timpson Middle Sch/*Timpson*/Shelby	04801727	936/254-2078	335
TIOGA IND SCH DIST/*TIOGA*/GRAYSON	01020699	940/437-2366	167
Tioga Sch/*Tioga*/Grayson	01020704	940/437-2366	167
Tippin Elem Sch/*El Paso*/El Paso	05344409	915/230-5150	134
Tipps Elem Sch/*Houston*/Harris	05272117	281/345-3350	185
Tisd Child & Adolescent Ctr/*Terrell*/Kaufman	03004639	972/551-8960	253
Tivy High Sch/*Kerrville*/Kerr	01036129	830/257-2212	256
TLC Academy/*San Angelo*/Tom Green	11231713	325/653-3200	12
Tobias Elem Sch/*Kyle*/Hays	05273226	512/268-8437	211
Tolar Elem Sch/*Tolar*/Hood	01031442	254/835-4028	230
Tolar High Sch/*Tolar*/Hood	04869999	254/835-4316	231
TOLAR IND SCH DIST/*TOLAR*/HOOD	01031430	254/835-4718	230
Tolar Junior High Sch/*Tolar*/Hood	11074632	254/835-5207	231
Toler Elem Sch/*Garland*/Dallas	01545235	972/226-3922	107
Toltech T-STEM Academy/*San Antonio*/Bexar	11819951	210/444-8425	32
Tom & Nita Nichols Middle Sch/*Burleson*/Johnson	12305692	817/202-2500	248
Tom Bean Elem Sch/*Tom Bean*/Grayson	01020728	903/546-6333	168
Tom Bean High Sch/*Tom Bean*/Grayson	01020730	903/546-6319	168
TOM BEAN IND SCH DIST/*TOM BEAN*/GRAYSON	01020716	903/546-6076	168
Tom Bean Middle Sch/*Tom Bean*/Grayson	03047746	903/546-6161	168
Tom Browne Middle Sch/*Corp Christi*/Nueces	01044243	361/878-4270	304
Tom C Clark High Sch/*San Antonio*/Bexar	01824067	210/397-5150	38
Tom C Gooch Elem Sch/*Dallas*/Dallas	01009918	972/794-2500	103
Tom Cox Intermediate Sch/*Spring*/Montgomery	11157117	281/465-3200	292
Tom Green Elem Sch/*Buda*/Hays	02896740	512/268-8438	211
Tom Landry Elem Sch/*Irving*/Dallas	04449123	972/968-2100	97
Tom Lea Elem Sch/*El Paso*/El Paso	11449178	915/230-5450	134
Tom R Ellisor Elem Sch/*Magnolia*/Montgomery	10012148	281/252-7400	293
Tom W Field Elem Sch/*Dallas*/Dallas	01010010	972/794-2700	103
Tom Wilson Elem Sch/*Katy*/Harris	11822037	281/234-1600	153
Tomas Rivera Elem Sch/*Denton*/Denton	04281579	940/369-3800	121
Tomball Connections Academy/*Tomball*/Harris	03396494	281/357-3281	203
Tomball Elem Sch/*Tomball*/Harris	01027582	281/357-3280	203
Tomball High Sch/*Tomball*/Harris	01027594	281/357-3220	203
TOMBALL IND SCH DIST/*TOMBALL*/HARRIS	01027568	281/357-3100	203
Tomball Intermediate Sch/*Tomball*/Harris	01027611	281/357-3150	203
Tomball Junior High Sch/*Tomball*/Harris	01027609	281/357-3000	203
Tomball Memorial High Sch/*Tomball*/Harris	11709411	281/357-3230	203
Tomball Star Academy/*Tomball*/Harris	12305549	281/357-3222	203
Tony Gonzalez Elem Sch/*Santa Maria*/Cameron	01004310	956/565-5348	67
Tool Elem Sch/*Kemp*/Henderson	10901070	903/432-2637	214
Top of TX Accelerated Ed Ctr/*Perryton*/Ochiltree	04913576	806/434-0389	307
Torah Day School of Dallas/*Dallas*/Collin	11180683	972/964-0090	86
Torah Day School of Houston/*Houston*/Harris	02824565	713/777-2000	207
Torah Girls Academy/*Houston*/Harris	11919018	713/936-0644	207
Tornillo Elem Sch/*Tornillo*/El Paso	03442718	915/765-3100	137
Tornillo High Sch/*Tornillo*/El Paso	01016284	915/765-3550	137
TORNILLO IND SCH DIST/*TORNILLO*/EL PASO	01016260	915/765-3000	137
Tornillo Intermediate Sch/*Tornillo*/El Paso	11078274	915/765-3350	137
Tornillo Junior High Sch/*Tornillo*/El Paso	04745111	915/765-3400	137
Torres Elem Sch/*Victoria*/Victoria	11450103	361/788-2850	382
Town Center Elem Sch/*Coppell*/Dallas	04278687	214/496-7800	98
Town East Christian Sch/*San Antonio*/Bexar	02191679	210/648-2601	45
Towne Creek Sch/*Missouri City*/Fort Bend	02995554	281/499-8030	155
Townewest Elem Sch/*Sugar Land*/Fort Bend	01826247	281/634-4480	151
Townley Elem Sch/*Fort Worth*/Tarrant	11457462	817/568-3560	349
Townley Elem Sch/*Irving*/Dallas	01829407	972/600-6800	110
Townsell Elem Sch/*Irving*/Dallas	05273094	972/600-5500	110
Townview Mag HS-Bus & Mngmnt/*Dallas*/Dallas	01009449	972/925-5920	103
Townview Mag HS-Sci & Eng/*Dallas*/Dallas	02228090	972/925-5960	103
Townview Mag HS-Talent & Gift/*Dallas*/Dallas	02200490	972/925-5970	103
Tradewind Elem Sch/*Amarillo*/Potter	10912237	806/326-5500	318
Tradition Elem Sch/*Saint Hedwig*/Bexar	00997025	210/649-2021	31
Trafton Academy/*Houston*/Harris	11239234	713/723-3732	207
Transition Center/*Bedford*/Tarrant	01809938	817/354-3537	354
Transition Center/*Fort Worth*/Tarrant	05344514	817/814-6418	352
Transmountain Early College HS/*El Paso*/El Paso	11076848	915/236-5000	134
Trautmann Elem Sch/*Laredo*/Webb	02176576	956/473-3100	388
Trautmann Middle Sch/*Laredo*/Webb	04455940	956/473-7400	388
Travis Bryan High Sch/*Bryan*/Brazos	01002049	979/209-2400	55
Travis Early College High Sch/*Austin*/Travis	01056727	512/414-2527	369
Travis Early College High Sch/*San Antonio*/Bexar	11128063	210/738-9830	41
Travis Elem Sch/*Edinburg*/Hidalgo	04487747	956/289-2354	217
Travis Elem Sch/*El Paso*/El Paso	01015709	915/236-6200	134
Travis Elem Sch/*Greenville*/Hunt	01032537	903/457-2696	236
Travis Elem Sch/*Harlingen*/Cameron	01003902	956/427-3170	65
Travis Elem Sch/*Houston*/Harris	01024281	713/802-4790	192
Travis Elem Sch/*Memphis*/Hall	01022128	806/259-5940	176
Travis Elem Sch/*Mercedes*/Hidalgo	01030199	956/514-2366	222
Travis Elem Sch/*Midland*/Midland	01041667	432/240-8200	286
Travis Elem Sch/*Mineral Wells*/Palo Pinto	01046095	940/325-7801	310
Travis Elem Sch/*Pampa*/Gray	01020211	806/669-4950	165
Travis Elem Sch/*Port Arthur*/Jefferson	01033933	409/984-4700	243
Travis Elem Sch/*Rosenberg*/Fort Bend	01018335	832/223-2500	154
Travis Elem Sch/*San Marcos*/Hays	01029188	512/393-6450	212
Travis Heights Elem Sch/*Austin*/Travis	01056698	512/414-4495	367
Travis High School of Choice/*Paris*/Lamar	04751081	903/737-7560	260
Travis Intermediate Sch/*Conroe*/Montgomery	01042465	936/709-7000	292
Travis Magnet Elem Sch/*Odessa*/Ector	01014858	432/456-1229	130
Travis Middle Sch/*Irving*/Dallas	01011325	972/600-0100	110
Travis Middle Sch/*Port Lavaca*/Calhoun	01003275	361/552-3784	62
Travis Middle Sch/*Quanah*/Hardeman	01022427	940/663-2226	177
Travis Primary Sch/*Sulphur Spgs*/Hopkins	01031703	903/885-5246	232
Travis Science Academy/*Temple*/Bell	00996851	254/215-6300	29
Travis World Language Academy/*Grand Prairie*/Dallas	01011014	972/262-2990	108
Treasure Forest Elem Sch/*Houston*/Harris	04477675	713/251-7400	201
Treasure Hills Elem Sch/*Harlingen*/Cameron	02045331	956/427-3180	65
Treetops International Sch/*Euless*/Tarrant	02084090	817/283-1771	12
TRENT IND SCH DIST/*TRENT*/TAYLOR	01054987	325/862-6125	361
Trent Middle Sch/*Frisco*/Collin	12107012	469/633-4400	80
Trent Sch/*Trent*/Taylor	01054999	325/862-6125	361
Trenton Elem Sch/*Trenton*/Fannin	01017616	903/989-2244	147
Trenton High Sch/*Trenton*/Fannin	01017628	903/989-2242	147
TRENTON IND SCH DIST/*TRENTON*/FANNIN	01017604	903/989-2245	146
Trenton Middle Sch/*Trenton*/Fannin	05341861	903/989-2243	147
Trevino Comm & Fine Art Sch/*Laredo*/Webb	04289753	956/273-7800	387
Triangle Adventist Chrn Sch/*Groves*/Jefferson	03405772	409/963-3806	244
Trimmier Elem Sch/*Killeen*/Bell	04806571	254/336-2270	28
Trinidad Garza Early College/*Dallas*/Dallas	10023965	214/860-3680	103
TRINIDAD IND SCH DIST/*TRINIDAD*/HENDERSON	01029504	903/778-2673	214
Trinidad Sch/*Trinidad*/Henderson	01029516	903/778-2415	215
Trinity Baptist Temple Academy/*Fort Worth*/Tarrant	04993071	817/237-4255	359
Trinity Basin Prep-10th Street/*Dallas*/Dallas	11849059	214/296-9302	12
Trinity Basin Prep-Ewing/*Dallas*/Dallas	04890998	214/942-8846	12
Trinity Basin Prep-Ft Worth/*Fort Worth*/Tarrant	11849073	817/840-7501	12
Trinity Basin Prep-Jefferson/*Dallas*/Dallas	11849061	214/941-4881	12
Trinity Charter Sch-Amarillo/*Amarillo*/Randall	12322705	512/706-7566	12
Trinity Charter Sch-Big Sandy/*Big Sandy*/Upshur	11930634	903/565-6801	12
Trinity Charter Sch-Bokenkamp/*Corp Christi*/Nueces	12100492	361/994-1214	12
Trinity Charter Sch-New Hope/*McAllen*/Hidalgo	12260951	361/563-7979	12
Trinity Charter Sch-New Life/*Canyon Lake*/Comal	10014706	830/964-4390	12
Trinity Charter School-Krause/*Katy*/Fort Bend	11014943	281/392-7505	12

School Year 2019-2020   800-333-8802

DISTRICT & SCHOOL TELEPHONE INDEX

Market Data Retrieval

School/City/County DISTRICT/CITY/COUNTY	PID	TELEPHONE NUMBER	PAGE
Trinity Charter School-Pegasus/*Lockhart*/Caldwell	11935505	512/432-1655	12
Trinity Charter School-Spring/*Spring*/Harris	12322717	512/706-7566	12
Trinity Christian Academy/*Addison*/Dallas	01802667	972/931-8325	116
Trinity Christian Academy/*San Antonio*/Bexar	02192659	210/653-2800	45
Trinity Christian Academy/*Willow Park*/Parker	04880814	817/441-7901	314
Trinity Christian Elem Sch/*Lubbock*/Lubbock	04145913	806/791-6581	272
Trinity Christian Jr Sr HS/*Lubbock*/Lubbock	02164987	806/791-6583	272
Trinity Christian Sch/*Cedar Hill*/Dallas	02159360	972/291-2505	116
Trinity Environment Academy/*Dallas*/Dallas	12109450	972/920-6558	12
Trinity Episcopal Sch/*Austin*/Travis	04885319	512/472-9525	373
Trinity Episcopal Sch/*Galveston*/Galveston	01019535	409/765-9391	162
Trinity Episcopal Sch/*Marshall*/Harrison	01028782	903/938-3513	209
Trinity Episcopal Sch/*Victoria*/Victoria	01058660	361/573-3220	383
Trinity High Sch/*Euless*/Tarrant	01053945	817/571-0271	354
Trinity High Sch/*Trinity*/Trinity	03006778	936/594-3560	374
TRINITY IND SCH DIST/**TRINITY**/**TRINITY**	01057147	936/594-3569	374
Trinity Lutheran Chldrn's Ctr/*Houston*/Harris	01027831	713/224-3207	207
Trinity Lutheran Sch/*Amarillo*/Potter	01048005	806/352-5620	319
Trinity Lutheran Sch/*San Angelo*/Tom Green	01055917	325/947-1275	366
Trinity Lutheran Sch/*Spring*/Harris	01027829	281/376-5810	207
Trinity Meadows Interm Sch/*Keller*/Tarrant	10031613	817/744-4300	355
Trinity Middle Sch/*Trinity*/Trinity	01057161	936/594-2321	374
Trinity School of Midland/*Midland*/Midland	01041708	432/697-3281	286
Trinity School of Texas/*Longview*/Gregg	01021332	903/753-0612	171
Trinity Springs Middle Sch/*Fort Worth*/Tarrant	10748270	817/744-3500	355
Trinity Valley Sch/*Fort Worth*/Tarrant	01054274	817/321-0100	359
Triumph Public CHS/*San Benito*/Cameron	11704461	956/276-9930	12
Trivium Academy/*Carrollton*/Denton	12173425	469/855-5531	12
Troup Elem Sch/*Troup*/Smith	01050711	903/842-3071	337
Troup High Sch/*Troup*/Smith	01050723	903/842-3065	337
TROUP IND SCH DIST/**TROUP**/**SMITH**	01050709	903/842-3067	337
Troup Middle Sch/*Troup*/Smith	01050735	903/842-3081	337
Trout Primary Sch/*Lufkin*/Angelina	00995077	936/639-3274	18
Troy Elem Sch/*Troy*/Bell	00996904	254/938-2503	30
Troy High Sch/*Troy*/Bell	00996916	254/938-2561	30
TROY IND SCH DIST/**TROY**/**BELL**	00996899	254/938-2595	29
Truce Learning Center/*Fort Worth*/Tarrant	04451554	817/252-2490	347
True Cross Catholic Sch/*Dickinson*/Galveston	01028225	281/337-5212	162
Truett Wilson Middle Sch/*Haslet*/Denton	11818543	817/698-7900	125
Truitt Middle Sch/*Houston*/Harris	03327194	281/856-1100	185
Truman Elem Sch/*Edinburg*/Hidalgo	01029748	956/289-2555	217
Truman Price Elem Sch/*Donna*/Hidalgo	01418486	956/464-1303	215
Tsu Charter Lab Sch/*Houston*/Harris	10910502	713/313-6754	193
Tulia High Sch/*Tulia*/Swisher	01051595	806/995-2759	343
TULIA IND SCH DIST/**TULIA**/**SWISHER**	01051571	806/995-4591	343
Tulia Junior High Sch/*Tulia*/Swisher	01051600	806/995-4842	343
Tuloso-Midway High Sch/*Corp Christi*/Nueces	02226315	361/903-6700	305
TULOSO-MIDWAY IND SCH DIST/**CORP CHRISTI**/**NUECES**	01045015	361/903-6400	305
Tuloso-Midway Intermediate Sch/*Corp Christi*/Nueces	01045053	361/903-6550	305
Tuloso-Midway Middle Sch/*Corp Christi*/Nueces	01045041	361/903-6600	305
Tuloso-Midway Primary Sch/*Corp Christi*/Nueces	02129004	361/903-6500	305
TURKEY-QUITAQUE CONS IND SD/**TURKEY**/**HALL**	01022130	806/455-1411	176
Turner Prekindergarten Academy/*Waxahachie*/Ellis	12225913	972/923-4690	142
Turning Point Secondary Sch/*Arlington*/Tarrant	04039053	682/867-3050	345
Tuscany Heights Elem Sch/*San Antonio*/Bexar	11558717	210/407-8200	36
Twain MS & Dual Language Acad/*San Antonio*/Bexar	00998536	210/738-9745	41
Twin Creeks Middle Sch/*Spring*/Harris	02227620	281/891-7850	203
Two Dimensions Prep Academy/*Houston*/Harris	04886143	281/227-4700	13
Two Dimensions Prep-Vickery/*Houston*/Harris	11704813	281/227-4700	13
Two Dimensions-Corsicana/*Corsicana*/Navarro	11704801	281/227-4700	13
TX Can Acad Dallas Ross Ave/*Dallas*/Dallas	12362688	214/824-4226	13
Tyler Adventist Sch/*Tyler*/Smith	02234398	903/595-6706	339
Tyler Career & Technology Ctr/*Tyler*/Smith	12311108	903/262-1024	338
Tyler Classical Academy/*Tyler*/Smith	11848976	903/504-5690	13
Tyler Early College High Sch/*Tyler*/Smith	12305563	903/262-3040	338
TYLER IND SCH DIST/**TYLER**/**SMITH**	01050747	903/262-1000	337

School/City/County DISTRICT/CITY/COUNTY	PID	TELEPHONE NUMBER	PAGE
Tyler Street Christian Academy/*Dallas*/Dallas	01012343	214/941-9717	116
Tynan Early Childhood Ctr/*San Antonio*/Bexar	00998990	210/738-9835	41
Tyrrell Elem Sch/*Port Arthur*/Jefferson	01033921	409/984-4660	243

U

Uhland Elem Sch/*Uhland*/Hays	12308395	512/268-8503	211
Ulrich Intermediate Sch/*Houston*/Harris	11551939	832/375-7500	197
Ume Prep Acad-Dallas/*Dallas*/Dallas	11849102	214/445-6243	13
Ume Prep Acad-Duncanville/*Duncanville*/Dallas	12261254	972/296-0084	13
Umphrey Lee Elem Sch/*Dallas*/Dallas	01009023	972/749-3900	103
Underwood Elem Sch/*Andrews*/Andrews	00994762	432/524-1960	16
Union Grove Elem Sch/*Gladewater*/Upshur	01057563	903/845-3481	377
UNION GROVE IND SCH DIST/**GLADEWATER**/**UPSHUR**	01057551	903/845-5509	377
Union Grove Jr Sr High Sch/*Gladewater*/Upshur	01057575	903/845-5506	377
Union Grove Middle Sch/*Harker HTS*/Bell	05347839	254/336-6580	28
Union Hill Elem Sch/*Round Rock*/Williamson	05096030	512/424-8700	399
UNION HILL IND SCH DIST/**GILMER**/**UPSHUR**	01057587	903/762-2140	377
Union Hill Sch/*Gilmer*/Upshur	01057599	903/762-2138	377
Union Park Elem Sch/*Aubrey*/Denton	12368759	940/369-0900	121
United Day Sch/*Laredo*/Webb	01481304	956/723-7261	389
United High 9th Grade HS/*Laredo*/Webb	12308228	956/473-2400	388
United High Sch/*Laredo*/Webb	01059511	956/473-5600	388
UNITED IND SCH DIST/**LAREDO**/**WEBB**	01059470	956/473-6201	387
United Middle Sch/*Laredo*/Webb	02949177	956/473-7300	388
United South High 9th Grade HS/*Laredo*/Webb	12308199	956/473-1400	388
United South High Sch/*Laredo*/Webb	03336171	956/473-5400	388
United South Middle Sch/*Laredo*/Webb	03336169	956/473-7700	388
United Step Academy/*Laredo*/Webb	04875182	956/473-6500	388
Unity Christian Sch/*Denison*/Grayson	11816375	903/465-1909	169
Univ of Houston Charter Sch/*Houston*/Harris	04757982	713/743-9111	13
Universal Academy-Coppell/*Coppell*/Dallas	05010696	972/393-5834	13
Universal Academy-Irving/*Irving*/Dallas	04813500	972/255-1800	13
University High Sch/*Austin*/Travis	12161915	512/382-0072	13
University High Sch/*Waco*/McLennan	01040431	254/756-1843	282
University of Texas Elem CS/*Austin*/Travis	05286613	512/495-3300	13
University Park Elem Sch/*Dallas*/Dallas	01011090	214/780-3400	108
University Preparatory HS/*Corp Christi*/Nueces	10022117	361/694-9780	305
Uphaus Early Childhood Center/*Austin*/Travis	11848744	512/414-5520	367
Upland Heights Elem Sch/*Lubbock*/Lubbock	12234768	806/698-6611	269
Uplift Gradus Preparatory/*Desoto*/Dallas	12160870	214/451-5551	13
Uplift Grand Preparatory/*Grand Prairie*/Dallas	12038928	972/854-0600	13
Uplift Hampton Prep Chtr Sch/*Dallas*/Dallas	11150365	972/421-1982	13
Uplift Heights Prep Prim Sch/*Dallas*/Dallas	12240339	214/873-9700	13
Uplift Heights Prep Sch Sec/*Dallas*/Dallas	11589417	214/442-7094	13
Uplift Infinity Prep Sch/*Irving*/Dallas	11728900	469/621-9200	13
Uplift Lee Prep Sch/*Grand Prairie*/Dallas	12106927	972/262-6785	108
Uplift Luna Prep Primary/*Dallas*/Dallas	11574498	214/442-7882	13
Uplift Luna Prep Secondary/*Dallas*/Dallas	11826069	214/445-3300	13
Uplift Meridian Preparatory/*Fort Worth*/Tarrant	11818593	817/288-1700	13
Uplift Mighty Preparatory Acad/*Fort Worth*/Tarrant	11828287	817/288-3800	13
Uplift North Hills Prep Sch/*Irving*/Dallas	04758039	972/501-0645	13
Uplift Peak Prep Sch/*Dallas*/Dallas	10804630	214/276-0879	13
Uplift Pinnacle Prep Primary/*Dallas*/Dallas	11728912	214/442-6100	13
Uplift Summit Int'l Prep CS/*Arlington*/Tarrant	10969852	817/287-5121	13
Uplift Triumph Preparatory/*Dallas*/Dallas	11927912	972/590-5100	13
Uplift White Rock Hills Prep/*Dallas*/Dallas	12238477	469/914-7500	13
Uplift Williams Prep Chtr Sch/*Dallas*/Dallas	11150377	214/276-0352	13
Uplift Wisdom Prep Primary Sch/*Dallas*/Dallas	12240353	972/330-7291	13
Uplift Wisdom Prep Sec Sch/*Dallas*/Dallas	12240341	972/330-7291	13
Urban Park Elem Sch/*Dallas*/Dallas	01010022	972/794-1100	103
Ursula Stephens Elem Sch/*Katy*/Harris	10913293	281/234-0200	153
Ursuline Academy/*Dallas*/Dallas	01012757	469/232-1800	114
UT Tyler Univ Acad-Longview/*Longview*/Smith	12317035	903/663-8219	338
UT Tyler Univ Acad-Palestine/*Palestine*/Smith	12100143	903/705-4330	338
UT Tyler Univ Acad-Tyler/*Tyler*/Smith	11917888	903/705-4330	338

Texas School Directory

DISTRICT & SCHOOL TELEPHONE INDEX

School/City/County DISTRICT/CITY/COUNTY	PID	TELEPHONE NUMBER	PAGE
UT TYLER UNIVERSITY ACAD DIST/			
TYLER/SMITH	12317047	903/730-3988	338
UT Univ CS-Laurel Ridge/*San Antonio*/Bexar	12100454	210/491-9400	13
UT Univ CS-Memorial Hermann/*Houston*/Harris	12100430	713/939-7272	13
UT Univ CS-Methodist Children/*Waco*/McLennan	12100442	512/471-4864	13
UT Univ CS-Settlement Home/*Austin*/Travis	12100466	512/836-2150	13
UTOPIA IND SCH DIST/UTOPIA/			
UVALDE	01057769	830/966-1928	378
Utopia Sch/*Utopia*/Uvalde	01057783	830/966-3339	378
Utpb STEM Academy/*Odessa*/Ector	12105492	432/552-2580	13
UVALDE CONS IND SCH DIST/			
UVALDE/UVALDE	01057795	830/278-6655	378
Uvalde High Sch/*Uvalde*/Uvalde	01057850	830/591-2950	378
V			
V R Eaton High Sch/*Fort Worth*/Denton	12106745	817/698-7300	125
Val Verde Christian Academy/*Groves*/Jefferson	11748821	409/962-8822	244
Vale Middle Sch/*San Antonio*/Bexar	11104122	210/397-5700	38
VALENTINE IND SCH DIST/VALENTINE/			
JEFF DAVIS	01033359	432/467-2671	241
Valentine Sch/*Valentine*/Jeff Davis	01033361	432/467-2671	241
Valle Verde Early College HS/*El Paso*/El Paso	10908638	915/434-1500	138
Valley Christian Heritage Sch/*Alamo*/Hidalgo	02873645	956/787-9743	226
Valley Christian High Sch/*Brownsville*/Cameron	01754254	956/542-5222	68
Valley Creek Elem Sch/*McKinney*/Collin	03396793	469/302-4800	81
Valley Hi Elem Sch/*San Antonio*/Bexar	00998330	210/397-0350	39
Valley Mills Elem Sch/*Valley Mills*/Bosque	01000766	254/932-5526	47
VALLEY MILLS IND SCH DIST/			
VALLEY MILLS/BOSQUE	01000754	254/932-5210	47
Valley Millsjr Sr High Sch/*Valley Mills*/Bosque	01000778	254/932-5251	47
Valley Oaks Elem Sch/*Houston*/Harris	01027403	713/251-7500	201
Valley Ranch Elem Sch/*Irving*/Dallas	04454178	214/496-8500	98
Valley Ranch Elem Sch/*Porter*/Montgomery	10760084	281/577-8760	294
Valley Ridge Elem Sch/*Lewisville*/Denton	04452235	469/713-5982	124
Valley Sch/*Turkey*/Hall	01022154	806/455-1411	176
Valley View 5th Grade Campus/*Pharr*/Hidalgo	11136967	956/340-1400	225
Valley View Early College Sch/*Hidalgo*/Hidalgo	12035055	956/340-1200	225
Valley View Elem Sch/*Austin*/Travis	02127599	512/732-9140	370
Valley View Elem Sch/*Hidalgo*/Hidalgo	01030577	956/340-1450	225
Valley View High Sch/*Pharr*/Hidalgo	03049653	956/340-1500	225
VALLEY VIEW IND SCH DIST/			
PHARR/HIDALGO	01030565	956/340-1000	225
VALLEY VIEW ISD-COOKE CO/			
VALLEY VIEW/COOKE	01007506	940/726-3659	91
Valley View Junior High Sch/*Pharr*/Hidalgo	03322948	956/340-1300	225
Valley View North Elem Sch/*Pharr*/Hidalgo	04801208	956/340-1600	225
Valley View Sch/*Valley View*/Cooke	01007518	940/726-3659	91
Valley View South Elem Sch/*Hidalgo*/Hidalgo	10915538	956/340-1650	225
Valley West Elem Sch/*Houston*/Harris	04454465	713/773-6151	194
Valor South Austin/*Austin*/Travis	12366787	512/646-4170	13
Van Alstyne High Sch/*Van Alstyne*/Grayson	01020766	903/482-8803	168
VAN ALSTYNE IND SCH DIST/			
VAN ALSTYNE/GRAYSON	01020742	903/482-8802	168
Van Alstyne Middle Sch/*Van Alstyne*/Grayson	01020778	903/482-8804	168
Van Buren Elem Sch/*Groves*/Jefferson	01034030	409/962-6511	244
Van High Sch/*Van*/Van Zandt	01058256	903/963-8623	381
Van Horn Schools/*Van Horn*/Culberson	01008043	432/283-2245	95
VAN IND SCH DIST/VAN/VAN ZANDT	01058232	903/963-8713	381
Van Intermediate Sch/*Van*/Van Zandt	11917723	903/963-8331	381
Van Junior High Sch/*Van*/Van Zandt	01058268	903/963-8321	381
Van Middle Sch/*Van*/Van Zandt	11070076	903/963-1461	381
Van Raub Elem Sch/*Boerne*/Kendall	12313481	830/357-4100	254
Van Vleck Elem Sch/*Van Vleck*/Matagorda	01041021	979/245-8681	276
Van Vleck High Sch/*Van Vleck*/Matagorda	01041033	979/245-4664	276
VAN VLECK IND SCH DIST/VAN VLECK/			
MATAGORDA	01041019	979/323-5000	276
Van Zandt-Guinn Elem Sch/*Fort Worth*/Tarrant	01052977	817/815-2000	352
Vandagriff Elem Sch/*Aledo*/Parker	03250474	817/441-8771	312
Vandegrift High Sch/*Austin*/Williamson	11450983	512/570-2300	397
Vanguard Academy-Beethoven/*Edinburg*/Hidalgo	12261266	956/318-0211	13
Vanguard Academy-Mozart/*Alamo*/Hidalgo	11932632	956/702-2548	13
Vanguard Academy-Picasso/*Pharr*/Hidalgo	11833995	956/702-0134	13
Vanguard Academy-Rembrandt/*Pharr*/Hidalgo	05010957	956/781-1701	13
Vanguard College Prepatory Sch/*Waco*/McLennan	01480790	254/772-8111	283
Vanguard International Academy/*Arlington*/Tarrant	11813816	817/274-6444	359
Vanguard Preparatory Sch/*Dallas*/Dallas	12313819	972/404-1616	116
Vardeman EC-PK-K Sch/*Houston*/Harris	12309686	281/985-3740	181
Varnett School Southeast/*Houston*/Harris	12261230	713/726-7654	13
Varnett School-East/*Houston*/Harris	11015533	713/637-6574	13
Varnett School-NE/*Houston*/Harris	11015545	713/631-4396	13
Vaughn Elem Sch/*Frisco*/Collin	12167270	469/633-2575	80
Veda Knox Elem Sch/*Arlington*/Tarrant	04949329	682/867-2051	345
Vega Elem Sch/*McKinney*/Collin	05243300	469/302-5100	81
Vega Elem Sch/*Vega*/Oldham	01045560	806/267-2126	308
VEGA IND SCH DIST/VEGA/OLDHAM	01045558	806/267-2123	307
Vega Jr Sr High Sch/*Vega*/Oldham	01045572	806/267-2126	308
Velasco Elem Sch/*Freeport*/Brazoria	01001708	979/730-7210	52
Velma Penny Elem Sch/*Lindale*/Smith	04366167	903/881-4250	337
Venable Village Elem Sch/*Fort Hood*/Bell	04368799	254/336-1980	28
Venture High Sch/*Arlington*/Tarrant	01051741	682/867-6400	345
Venus Elem Sch/*Venus*/Johnson	04884054	972/366-3748	249
Venus High Sch/*Venus*/Johnson	01035187	972/366-8815	249
VENUS IND SCH DIST/VENUS/JOHNSON	01035163	972/366-3448	249
Venus Middle Sch/*Venus*/Johnson	04287731	972/366-3358	249
Venus Primary Sch/*Venus*/Johnson	01035175	972/366-3268	249
Vera Escamilla Elem Sch/*Houston*/Harris	04032598	281/985-6390	180
Veramendi Elem Sch/*New Braunfels*/Comal	12235932	830/608-5900	89
Verda Mae Adams Elem Sch/*San Antonio*/Bexar	00997362	210/989-2800	33
VERIBEST IND SCH DIST/VERIBEST/			
TOM GREEN	01055826	325/655-2851	365
Veribest Sch/*Veribest*/Tom Green	01055838	325/655-2851	365
Veritas Academy/*Austin*/Travis	11228273	512/891-1673	373
Veritas Christian Academy/*Bellaire*/Harris	11234595	713/773-9605	207
Vermillion Elem Sch/*Brownsville*/Cameron	02110584	956/831-6060	64
Vernagene Mott Elem Sch/*Pflugerville*/Travis	12235360	512/594-4700	372
Vernal Lister Elem Sch/*Garland*/Dallas	04367678	972/675-3030	107
Vernon & Kathy Lewis Mid Sch/*Houston*/Harris	11555363	281/209-8257	181
Vernon High Sch/*Vernon*/Wilbarger	01060601	940/553-3377	394
VERNON IND SCH DIST/VERNON/			
WILBARGER	01060560	940/553-1900	393
Vernon Middle Sch/*Harlingen*/Cameron	01003914	956/427-3040	65
Vernon Middle Sch/*Vernon*/Wilbarger	01060613	940/552-6231	394
Vernon Price Elem Sch/*Garland*/Dallas	02128543	972/290-4100	111
Versia L Williams Elem Sch/*Fort Worth*/Tarrant	01053490	817/814-9700	352
Vestal Elem Sch/*San Antonio*/Bexar	00997570	210/989-3350	33
Veterans Hill Elem Sch/*Round Rock*/Williamson	12033459	512/759-3030	396
Veterans Memorial Academy/*San Benito*/Cameron	04941884	956/276-6000	67
Veterans Memorial Early Clg HS/*Brownsville*/Cameron	11554905	956/574-5600	64
Veterans Memorial Elem Sch/*Laredo*/Webb	12105208	956/473-1200	388
Veterans Memorial Elem Sch/*Roma*/Starr	12034776	956/849-1717	341
Veterans Memorial High Sch/*Corp Christi*/Nueces	12106563	361/878-7900	304
Veterans Memorial High Sch/*Mission*/Hidalgo	04288802	956/323-3000	222
Veterans Memorial High Sch/*San Antonio*/Bexar	12165428	210/619-0222	34
Veterans Middle Sch/*Donna*/Hidalgo	04892130	956/464-1350	215
Veterans Middle Sch/*Rio Grande Cy*/Starr	10903509	956/488-0252	340
Vic Robertson Elem Sch/*Round Rock*/Williamson	02043395	512/428-3300	399
Vickers Elem Sch/*Victoria*/Victoria	01058610	361/788-9579	382
Vickery Elem Sch/*Flower Mound*/Denton	05271840	469/713-5969	124
Victor Fields Elem Sch/*McAllen*/Hidalgo	01029982	956/971-4344	221
Victor H Hexter Elem Sch/*Dallas*/Dallas	01010034	972/502-5800	103
Victoria Christian Sch/*Victoria*/Victoria	11238357	361/573-5345	383
Victoria East High Sch/*Victoria*/Victoria	01058622	361/788-2820	382
VICTORIA IND SCH DIST/VICTORIA/			
VICTORIA	01058440	361/576-3131	382
Victoria Juv Justice Center/*Victoria*/Victoria	11819327	361/575-0399	382
Victoria Walker Elem Sch/*Baytown*/Harris	10907505	281/421-1800	188
Victoria West High Sch/*Victoria*/Victoria	01058608	361/788-2830	382
Victory Baptist Academy/*Weatherford*/Parker	12317164	817/596-2711	314
Victory Christian Academy/*Decatur*/Wise	12364818	940/626-4730	403
Victory Christian Academy/*Perryton*/Ochiltree	04994104	806/435-3476	307
Victory Early College HS/*Houston*/Harris	10907098	281/810-5675	180

School Year 2019-2020   800-333-8802   TX-V77

DISTRICT & SCHOOL TELEPHONE INDEX

Market Data Retrieval

School/City/County DISTRICT/CITY/COUNTY	PID	TELEPHONE NUMBER	PAGE
Victory Lakes Intermediate Sch/*League City*/Galveston	05096896	281/284-3700	159
Victory Life Academy/*Brownwood*/Brown	04993150	325/641-2223	59
Victory Place at Coppell/*Coppell*/Dallas	04940323	214/496-8032	98
Vida N Clover Elem Sch/*San Juan*/Hidalgo	01030395	956/354-2730	224
Vidor Elem Sch/*Vidor*/Orange	01045780	409/951-8830	309
Vidor High Sch/*Vidor*/Orange	01045792	409/951-8900	309
VIDOR IND SCH DIST/VIDOR/ORANGE	01045754	409/951-8700	309
Vidor Junior High Sch/*Vidor*/Orange	01045807	409/951-8970	309
Vidor Middle Sch/*Vidor*/Orange	02201901	409/951-8880	309
Villa Nueva Elem Sch/*Brownsville*/Cameron	01003720	956/542-3957	64
Village Elem Sch/*Georgetown*/Williamson	04807915	512/943-5140	395
Village Fair-Elem Daep/*Dallas*/Dallas	04503872	972/925-7000	103
Village Fair-Lacey Middle Sch/*Dallas*/Dallas	04282767	972/925-7000	103
Village Parkway Chrn Sch/*San Antonio*/Bexar	03569158	210/680-8187	45
Village Sch/*Houston*/Harris	01875377	281/496-7900	207
Village Technical Sch/*Duncanville*/Dallas	11934264	469/454-4441	14
Villareal Elem Sch/*Olmito*/Cameron	01004059	956/233-3975	66
Villarreal Elem Sch/*San Antonio*/Bexar	00998108	210/397-5800	39
Villarreal Elem Sch/*Zapata*/Zapata	01062283	956/765-4321	406
Vincent Middle Sch/*Beaumont*/Jefferson	01034286	409/617-5950	242
Vincent Patlan Elem Sch/*Seguin*/Guadalupe	03009902	830/401-1221	174
Vincent W Miller Interm Sch/*Pasadena*/Harris	01026992	713/740-0450	200
Vine Sch/*Victoria*/Victoria	12113059	361/212-8463	383
Vines EC-PK-K Sch/*Houston*/Harris	04867197	281/878-7950	181
Vines High Sch/*Plano*/Collin	01525912	469/752-7800	83
Vineyard Ranch Elem Sch/*San Antonio*/Bexar	11820443	210/356-7200	36
Viola Cobb Elem Sch/*Channelview*/Harris	01023122	281/452-7788	183
Viola M Coleman High Sch/*Midland*/Midland	03052143	432/689-5000	286
Virginia Myers Elem Sch/*San Antonio*/Bexar	04754772	210/397-6650	39
Virginia Reinhardt Elem Sch/*Rockwall*/Rockwall	02856908	972/771-5247	326
Viridian Elem Sch/*Arlington*/Tarrant	12033447	817/864-0550	354
Virtual Learning Academy/*Flower Mound*/Denton	12170148	972/350-1870	124
Virtual Sch/*Pasadena*/Harris	12169371	713/740-0124	200
Visd Alternative Ed Sch/*Vernon*/Wilbarger	04941224	940/552-2252	394
Vision Academy/*Edinburg*/Hidalgo	11558262	956/289-2584	217
Vista Alt Learning Center/*Colleyville*/Tarrant	04447917	817/251-5466	353
Vista Del Futuro Charter Sch/*El Paso*/El Paso	11728974	915/855-8143	14
Vista Del Sol Sch/*El Paso*/El Paso	02199530	915/937-7500	137
Vista Hills Elem Sch/*El Paso*/El Paso	01545261	915/434-5700	138
Vista Ridge High Sch/*Cedar Park*/Williamson	05272430	512/570-1800	397
Vista Ridge Middle Sch/*Fort Worth*/Tarrant	12232825	817/743-8400	355
Vistas High Sch/*Houston*/Harris	10797594	832/484-7650	198
Vivian Field Middle Sch/*Farmers BRNCH*/Dallas	01008184	972/968-3900	97
Vivian Fowler Elem Sch/*Mt Pleasant*/Titus	01055412	903/575-2070	364
Voss Farms Elem Sch/*New Braunfels*/Comal	12235920	830/608-5800	89
Voyde Caraway Elem Sch/*Houston*/Harris	04019039	281/878-0320	179
Vysehrad Elem Sch/*Hallettsville*/Lavaca	01037410	361/798-4118	263
VYSEHRAD IND SCH DIST/HALLETTSVILLE/LAVACA	01037408	361/798-4118	263

W

School/City/County DISTRICT/CITY/COUNTY	PID	TELEPHONE NUMBER	PAGE
W A Blair Elem Sch/*Dallas*/Dallas	01010113	972/794-1600	103
W A Carpenter Elem Sch/*Deer Park*/Harris	01023328	832/668-8400	186
W A Martin Elem Sch/*Crandall*/Kaufman	01035541	972/427-6020	251
W A Meacham Middle Sch/*Fort Worth*/Tarrant	01053517	817/815-0200	352
W A Porter Elem Sch/*Hurst*/Tarrant	01418591	817/547-2900	346
W A Todd Middle Sch/*Donna*/Hidalgo	11920108	956/464-1800	215
W B Bizzell Academy/*Navasota*/Grimes	11927950	936/825-4296	172
W B Green Junior High Sch/*La Feria*/Cameron	01003976	956/797-8400	65
W B Ray High Sch/*Corp Christi*/Nueces	01044736	361/878-7300	304
W B Travis Vanguard & Academy/*Dallas*/Dallas	04921951	972/794-7500	103
W C Andrews Elem Sch/*Portland*/San Patricio	02046517	361/777-4048	331
W C Cunningham Middle Sch/*Houston*/Harris	02177726	832/386-4470	187
W C Stripling Middle Sch/*Fort Worth*/Tarrant	01053529	817/815-1300	352
W E Boswell High Sch/*Fort Worth*/Tarrant	01052446	817/237-3314	349
W E Chalmers Elem Sch/*Gainesville*/Cooke	01007386	940/665-4147	91
W E Greiner Explor Arts Acad/*Dallas*/Dallas	01010072	972/925-7100	103
W F George Middle Sch/*Iowa Park*/Wichita	01060106	940/592-2196	392
W F Peavy Primary Sch/*Lufkin*/Angelina	04933980	936/875-9344	17
W H Adamson High Sch/*Dallas*/Dallas	01010084	972/749-1400	103
W H Atwell Middle Sch/*Dallas*/Dallas	01010175	972/794-6400	103
W H Bonner Elem Sch/*Lufkin*/Angelina	00994865	936/875-9212	17
W H Burnett Early Chldhd Ctr/*Terrell*/Kaufman	01035773	972/563-1452	253
W H Gaston Middle Sch/*Dallas*/Dallas	01010096	972/502-5400	103
W H Wilson Elem Sch/*Coppell*/Dallas	04010411	214/496-7500	98
W I Stevenson Middle Sch/*Houston*/Harris	04149074	713/943-5700	190
W J Turner Elem Sch/*Fort Worth*/Tarrant	01053488	817/814-4900	352
W L Higgins Elem Sch/*Paris*/Lamar	03161392	903/737-2081	260
W M Green Elem Sch/*Fort Worth*/Tarrant	01053543	817/815-8900	352
W O Gray Elem Sch/*Balch Springs*/Dallas	04850388	972/882-7280	111
W P Hobby Elem Sch/*Houston*/Harris	01025259	713/434-5650	193
W P McLean Middle Sch/*Fort Worth*/Tarrant	01053555	817/814-5300	352
W R Fort Elem Sch/*Royse City*/Rockwall	05356165	972/636-3304	326
W R Hatfield Elem Sch/*Justin*/Denton	04804585	817/215-0350	125
W S Permenter Middle Sch/*Cedar Hill*/Dallas	01008304	972/291-5270	97
W T Francisco Elem Sch/*Haltom City*/Tarrant	01052226	817/547-1700	346
W T Hall Education Center/*Houston*/Harris	04922785	281/985-7446	180
W T White High Sch/*Dallas*/Dallas	01010125	972/502-6200	103
W V Swinburn Elem Sch/*Tulia*/Swisher	01051612	806/995-4309	343
W W Bushman Elem Sch/*Dallas*/Dallas	01010137	972/749-1800	103
W W Pinkerton Elem Sch/*Coppell*/Dallas	01008330	214/496-6800	98
W W Samuell High Sch/*Dallas*/Dallas	01010149	972/892-5100	103
W Z Burke Elem Sch/*San Antonio*/Bexar	04921391	210/397-1300	39
Waco Center for Youth-Spec Ed/*Waco*/McLennan	03217276	254/756-2171	14
Waco Charter Sch/*Waco*/McLennan	04467527	254/754-8169	14
Waco High Sch/*Waco*/McLennan	01040376	254/776-1150	282
WACO IND SCH DIST/WACO/MCLENNAN	01040132	254/755-9473	281
Waco Montessori Sch/*Waco*/McLennan	03404182	254/754-3966	283
WAELDER IND SCH DIST/WAELDER/GONZALES	01020003	830/788-7161	164
Waelder Sch/*Waelder*/Gonzales	01020015	830/788-7221	164
Waggoner Creek Elem Sch/*Texarkana*/Bowie	12232289	903/255-3301	50
Wainwright Elem Sch/*Houston*/Harris	01024293	713/613-2550	192
Wake Village Elem Sch/*Wake Village*/Bowie	01001356	903/838-4261	50
Wakefield Elem Sch/*Sherman*/Grayson	01020675	903/891-6595	167
Walcott Elem Sch/*Hereford*/Deaf Smith	01013098	806/289-5222	119
WALCOTT IND SCH DIST/HEREFORD/DEAF SMITH	01013086	806/289-5222	119
Walden Sch/*Sugar Land*/Fort Bend	01875339	281/980-0022	155
Walipp Tsu Prep Academy/*Houston*/Harris	11733967	713/741-3600	14
Walker Creek Elem Sch/*N Richlnd Hls*/Tarrant	10004701	817/547-3500	346
Walker Elem Sch/*Katy*/Harris	04916322	281/345-3200	186
Walker Junior High Sch/*Monahans*/Ward	01059004	432/943-4622	385
Walker Station Elem Sch/*Sugar Land*/Fort Bend	04016336	281/634-4400	151
Wall Elem Sch/*Wall*/Tom Green	01055864	325/651-7790	365
Wall High Sch/*Wall*/Tom Green	03238775	325/651-7521	365
WALL IND SCH DIST/WALL/TOM GREEN	01055840	325/651-7790	365
Wall Middle Sch/*Wall*/Tom Green	01055876	325/651-7648	365
Wallace Accelerated High Sch/*Colorado City*/Mitchell	10016742	325/728-2392	289
Wallace Elem Sch/*Dallas*/Dallas	01011985	469/593-2600	113
Wallace Jefferson Middle Sch/*San Antonio*/Bexar	11104134	210/397-3700	39
Wallace Middle Sch/*Kyle*/Hays	01029073	512/268-2891	211
Waller Christian Academy/*Waller*/Harris	11934393	936/372-0901	207
Waller High Sch/*Waller*/Waller	01058892	936/372-3654	385
WALLER IND SCH DIST/WALLER/WALLER	01058866	936/931-3685	384
Waller Junior High Sch/*Waller*/Waller	04803268	936/931-1353	385
Wally Watkins Elem Sch/*Wylie*/Collin	11551850	972/429-2580	85
Walnut Bend Elem Sch/*Gainesville*/Cooke	01007544	940/665-5990	92
Walnut Bend Elem Sch/*Houston*/Harris	01024645	713/917-3540	195
WALNUT BEND IND SCH DIST/GAINESVILLE/COOKE	01007532	940/665-5990	92
Walnut Creek Elem Sch/*Austin*/Travis	01056703	512/414-4499	368
Walnut Creek Elem Sch/*Azle*/Tarrant	01052020	817/444-4045	345
Walnut Creek Private Sch/*Mansfield*/Tarrant	03565530	817/473-4406	359
Walnut Glen Academy Excellence/*Garland*/Dallas	01010797	972/494-8330	107
Walnut Grove Elem Sch/*Southlake*/Tarrant	04356710	817/949-4400	347
Walnut Grove Middle Sch/*Midlothian*/Ellis	10016792	469/856-5700	141
Walnut Hill Elem Sch/*Dallas*/Dallas	01010151	972/502-7800	103
Walnut Springs Elem Sch/*Dripping Spgs*/Hays	04447371	512/858-3800	211
Walnut Springs Elem Sch/*New Braunfels*/Comal	03240699	830/627-6540	89
WALNUT SPRINGS IND SCH DIST/WALNUT SPGS/BOSQUE	01000780	254/797-2133	47
Walnut Springs Sch/*Walnut Spgs*/Bosque	01000792	254/797-2133	47
Walsh Elem Sch/*Aledo*/Parker	12226448	817/207-3355	312

Texas School Directory
DISTRICT & SCHOOL TELEPHONE INDEX

School/City/County DISTRICT/CITY/COUNTY	PID	TELEPHONE NUMBER	PAGE
Walt Disney Elem Sch/*Alvin*/Brazoria	01881065	281/585-6234	51
Walter & Lois Curtis Mid Sch/*Allen*/Collin	04288072	972/727-0340	77
Walter E Floyd Elem Sch/*Balch Springs*/Dallas	01011480	972/882-7100	111
Walter Hall Elem Sch/*League City*/Galveston	02043266	281/284-5300	159
Walter Matthys Elem Sch/*South Houston*/Harris	04015617	713/740-0632	200
Walter Moses Burton Elem Sch/*Fresno*/Fort Bend	04452273	281/634-5080	151
Walter Wilkinson Middle Sch/*Mesquite*/Dallas	01011600	972/882-5950	111
Waltrip High Sch/*Houston*/Harris	01024308	713/688-1361	192
Walzem Elem Sch/*San Antonio*/Bexar	00997958	210/407-8400	36
Ward Elem Sch/*Abilene*/Taylor	04015332	325/690-3666	360
Ware Elem Sch/*Longview*/Gregg	01021136	903/803-5700	170
Warner Elem Sch/*Cypress*/Harris	10915473	281/213-1650	186
Warren Center/*Garland*/Dallas	11923679	972/926-2671	113
Warren Elem Sch/*Warren*/Tyler	01057305	409/547-2247	375
Warren High Sch/*San Antonio*/Bexar	05097761	210/397-4200	39
Warren High Sch/*Warren*/Tyler	01057317	409/547-2243	375
WARREN IND SCH DIST/**WARREN**/**TYLER**	01057288	409/547-2241	375
Warren Junior High Sch/*Warren*/Tyler	01057329	409/547-2246	375
Warren Middle Sch/*Forney*/Kaufman	11130638	469/762-4156	252
Washington Early Childhood Ctr/*Marshall*/Harrison	02110637	903/927-8790	209
Washington Early Childhood Ctr/*Palestine*/Anderson	11556367	903/731-8030	15
Washington Elem Sch/*Big Spring*/Howard	01032044	432/264-4126	234
Washington Elem Sch/*Port Arthur*/Jefferson	01033751	409/984-8600	243
Washington Elem Sch/*San Antonio*/Bexar	00999023	210/738-9840	41
Washington Elem Sch/*Sherman*/Grayson	01020687	903/891-6700	167
Washington Heights Elem Sch/*Fort Worth*/Tarrant	01053567	817/815-0700	352
Washington Junior High Sch/*Conroe*/Montgomery	04923399	936/709-7400	292
Washington STEM Academy/*Midland*/Midland	01041679	432/240-8300	286
Waskom Elem Sch/*Waskom*/Harrison	01028726	903/687-3361	209
Waskom High Sch/*Waskom*/Harrison	01028768	903/687-3361	209
WASKOM IND SCH DIST/**WASKOM**/**HARRISON**	01028744	903/687-3361	209
Waskom Middle Sch/*Waskom*/Harrison	01028770	903/687-3361	209
Watauga Elem Sch/*Watauga*/Tarrant	01052238	817/547-2700	346
Watauga Middle Sch/*Watauga*/Tarrant	01052240	817/547-4800	346
Water Oak Sch/*Sulphur Spgs*/Hopkins	11231634	903/439-3044	232
Water Valley Elem Sch/*Water Valley*/Tom Green	01055890	325/484-2478	365
WATER VALLEY IND SCH DIST/**WATER VALLEY**/**TOM GREEN**	01055888	325/484-2478	365
Water Valley Jr Sr High Sch/*Water Valley*/Tom Green	01055905	325/484-2478	365
Waterford Oaks Elem Sch/*Cedar Hill*/Dallas	03396535	972/291-5290	97
Waterloo Sch/*Austin*/Travis	12263709	512/447-7781	373
Waters Elem Sch/*Lubbock*/Lubbock	02226705	806/219-7000	271
Watkins Middle Sch/*Houston*/Harris	02179803	281/463-5850	186
Watson Junior High Sch/*Muleshoe*/Bailey	00995716	806/272-7349	23
Watson Tech Center Math & Sci/*Garland*/Dallas	01010527	972/926-2600	107
Waverly Park Elem Sch/*Fort Worth*/Tarrant	01053579	817/815-6700	352
Waxahachie Challenge Academy/*Waxahachie*/Ellis	12313089	972/923-4695	142
Waxahachie Global High Sch/*Waxahachie*/Ellis	04282298	972/923-4761	142
Waxahachie High Sch/*Waxahachie*/Ellis	01015321	972/923-4600	142
Waxahachie HS of Choice/*Waxahachie*/Ellis	11134141	972/923-4758	142
WAXAHACHIE IND SCH DIST/**WAXAHACHIE**/**ELLIS**	01015292	972/923-4631	142
Waxahachie Preparatory Academy/*Waxahachie*/Ellis	12165650	972/937-0440	143
Wayne A Cox Elem Sch/*Roanoke*/Denton	11924910	817/698-7200	125
Wayne D Boshears Center/*Tyler*/Smith	11925108	903/262-1350	338
Wayne Stuart Ryan Elem Sch/*Denton*/Denton	04948765	940/369-4600	121
Wayside Altamira Academy/*Austin*/Travis	12161771	512/220-9105	14
Wayside Eden Park Academy/*Austin*/Travis	04813419	512/358-1800	14
Wayside Middle Sch/*Fort Worth*/Tarrant	01052458	817/232-0541	349
Wayside Real Learning Academy/*Austin*/Travis	12107244	512/438-7325	14
Wayside Sci-Tech Preparatory/*Austin*/Travis	11934082	512/220-9120	14
Weatherford 9th Grade Center/*Weatherford*/Parker	05264938	817/598-2847	314
Weatherford Christian Sch/*Weatherford*/Parker	11133549	817/596-7807	314
Weatherford Elem Sch/*Plano*/Collin	01006485	469/752-3600	83
Weatherford High Sch/*Weatherford*/Parker	01046617	817/598-2858	314
WEATHERFORD IND SCH DIST/**WEATHERFORD**/**PARKER**	01046564	817/598-2800	313
Weaver Elem Sch/*Garland*/Dallas	01010448	972/494-8311	107
Weaver Odom Elem Sch/*Houston*/Harris	01022752	281/878-0390	180
WEBB CONS IND SCH DIST/**BRUNI**/**WEBB**	01059145	361/747-5415	388
Webb Elem Sch/*Arlington*/Tarrant	04035758	682/867-4300	345
Webb Elem Sch/*Olton*/Lamb	01036985	806/285-2657	261
Webb Middle Sch/*Austin*/Travis	04014950	512/414-3258	369
Webb Middle Sch/*Garland*/Dallas	01383049	972/675-3080	107
Webb Primary Sch/*Austin*/Travis	11848732	512/414-8830	368
Weber Elem Sch/*Houston*/Galveston	05243063	281/284-6300	159
Wedgewood Academy/*Fort Worth*/Tarrant	11225685	817/924-9095	360
Wedgewood Elem Sch/*Friendswood*/Galveston	04032017	281/284-5700	159
Wedgeworth Elem Sch/*Waxahachie*/Ellis	02845820	972/923-4640	143
Wedgwood 6th Grade Middle Sch/*Fort Worth*/Tarrant	04143226	817/814-8300	352
Wedgwood Middle Sch/*Fort Worth*/Tarrant	01053581	817/814-8200	352
Wee Wisdom Kindergarten/*El Paso*/El Paso	02869436	915/592-6036	139
Weimar Elem Sch/*Weimar*/Colorado	01006851	979/725-6009	87
Weimar High Sch/*Weimar*/Colorado	01006863	979/725-9504	87
WEIMAR IND SCH DIST/**WEIMAR**/**COLORADO**	01006849	979/725-9504	87
Weimar Junior High Sch/*Weimar*/Colorado	01006875	979/725-9515	87
Weiss High Sch/*Pflugerville*/Travis	12235786	512/594-1400	372
Welder Elem Sch/*Sinton*/San Patricio	01049815	361/364-6600	332
Weldon Corbell Elem Sch/*Frisco*/Collin	10022404	469/633-3550	80
Weldon Elem Sch/*Gladewater*/Gregg	02223492	903/845-6921	169
Weldon Gibson Elem Sch/*Corp Christi*/Nueces	01044437	361/878-2500	304
Weldon Smith Elem Sch/*Corp Christi*/Nueces	01044700	361/878-2760	304
Wellborn Middle Sch/*College Sta*/Brazos	12307511	979/694-5880	56
Wellington Elem Sch/*Flower Mound*/Denton	04812776	469/713-5989	124
Wellington Elem Sch/*Wellington*/Collingsworth	01006710	806/447-3112	86
Wellington High Sch/*Wellington*/Collingsworth	01006722	806/447-3172	86
WELLINGTON IND SCH DIST/**WELLINGTON**/**COLLINGSWORTH**	01006708	806/447-3102	86
Wellington Junior High Sch/*Wellington*/Collingsworth	01006734	806/447-3152	86
WELLMAN UNION IND SCH DIST/**WELLMAN**/**TERRY**	01055199	806/637-4910	362
Wellman-Union Sch/*Wellman*/Terry	01055204	806/637-4619	362
Wells Branch Elem Sch/*Austin*/Williamson	02856740	512/428-3400	399
Wells Elem Sch/*Cypress*/Harris	12233142	832/349-7400	186
Wells Elem Sch/*Plano*/Collin	01824122	469/752-3700	83
Wells Elem Sch/*Wells*/Cherokee	01005417	936/867-4400	73
Wells High Sch/*Wells*/Cherokee	01005429	936/867-4400	73
WELLS IND SCH DIST/**WELLS**/**CHEROKEE**	01005405	936/867-4466	73
Wellspring Christian Acad/*Denton*/Denton	04023145	940/591-9900	126
Wertheimer Middle Sch/*Rosenberg*/Fort Bend	11151656	832/223-4100	154
Weslaco East High Sch/*Weslaco*/Hidalgo	04920323	956/969-6950	225
Weslaco High Sch/*Weslaco*/Hidalgo	01420491	956/969-6700	225
WESLACO IND SCH DIST/**WESLACO**/**HIDALGO**	01030589	956/969-6500	225
Wesley Academy/*Houston*/Harris	04907230	713/266-3341	207
Wesley Prep Sch/*Dallas*/Dallas	11020813	214/706-9568	116
West Ave Elem Sch/*Waco*/McLennan	04944666	254/750-3900	282
West Avenue Elem Sch/*San Antonio*/Bexar	00997960	210/407-8600	36
West Birdville Elementary/*Haltom City*/Tarrant	01052214	817/547-2500	346
West Brazos Junior High Sch/*Brazoria*/Brazoria	01001784	979/991-1730	52
West Briar Middle Sch/*Houston*/Harris	05099355	281/368-2140	195
West Brook High Sch/*Beaumont*/Jefferson	01034145	409/617-5500	242
West Campus High Sch/*San Antonio*/Bexar	12364868		43
West Central Elem Sch/*Hereford*/Deaf Smith	11558016	806/363-7690	119
West Columbia Elem Sch/*West Columbia*/Brazoria	01001760	979/799-1760	52
West Cypress Hills Elem Sch/*Spicewood*/Travis	12036803	512/533-7500	371
West Dallas Community Sch/*Dallas*/Dallas	04929056	214/634-1927	116
West Elem Sch/*Daingerfield*/Morris	01172541	903/645-2901	296
West Elem Sch/*Fort Worth*/Tarrant	01054236	817/367-1334	357
West Elem Sch/*Grand Prairie*/Tarrant	04757047	682/867-0100	345
West Elem Sch/*Lubbock*/Lubbock	11078016	806/776-0700	271
West Elem Sch/*West*/McLennan	01040508	254/981-2000	282
West End Elem Sch/*Industry*/Austin	00995572	979/357-2595	22
West Foundation Elem Sch/*Wichita Falls*/Wichita	04456695	940/235-1192	393

School Year 2019-2020   800-333-8802   TX-V79

DISTRICT & SCHOOL TELEPHONE INDEX

Market Data Retrieval

School/City/County DISTRICT/CITY/COUNTY	PID	TELEPHONE NUMBER	PAGE
West Handley Elem Sch/*Fort Worth*/Tarrant	04285898	817/815-5100	352
WEST HARDIN CO CONS SCH DIST/			
SARATOGA/HARDIN	01022659	936/274-5061	178
West Hardin Elem Sch/*Saratoga*/Hardin	01022661	936/274-5061	178
West Hardin High Sch/*Saratoga*/Hardin	01022673	936/274-5061	179
West High Sch/*West*/McLennan	01040510	254/981-2050	282
West Hurst Elem Sch/*Hurst*/Tarrant	01053969	817/285-3290	354
WEST IND SCH DIST/WEST/MCLENNAN	01040481	254/981-2050	282
West Lake Middle Sch/*Humble*/Harris	12320161	281/641-5800	196
West Main Elem Sch/*Lancaster*/Dallas	01011387	972/218-1551	110
West Memorial Elem Sch/*Katy*/Harris	01026277	281/237-6600	153
West Memorial Jr High Sch/*Katy*/Harris	01529982	281/237-6400	153
West Mesquite High Sch/*Mesquite*/Dallas	01525962	972/882-7600	111
West Middle Sch/*Desoto*/Dallas	03005982	972/230-1820	104
West Middle Sch/*West*/McLennan	01040091	254/981-2120	282
WEST ORANGE-COVE CONS ISD/			
ORANGE/ORANGE	01045819	409/882-5437	309
West Orange-Stark Elem Sch/*Orange*/Orange	01045821	409/882-5630	309
West Orange-Stark High Sch/*Orange*/Orange	01045936	409/882-5570	309
West Orange-Stark Middle Sch/*Orange*/Orange	01045948	409/882-5520	309
West Oso Elem Sch/*Corp Christi*/Nueces	01045106	361/806-5930	306
West Oso High Sch/*Corp Christi*/Nueces	01045118	361/806-5960	306
WEST OSO IND SCH DIST/CORP CHRISTI/			
NUECES	01045065	361/806-5900	306
West Oso Junior High Sch/*Corp Christi*/			
Nueces	01045091	361/806-5950	306
West Plano Montessori Sch/*Plano*/Collin	02733526	972/618-8844	86
West Ridge Middle Sch/*Austin*/Travis	03008738	512/732-9240	370
WEST RUSK CO CONS IND SCH DIST/			
NEW LONDON/RUSK	01049217	903/392-7850	328
West Rusk Elem Sch/*New London*/Rusk	01049229	903/895-0179	328
West Rusk High Sch/*New London*/Rusk	01049243	903/392-7857	328
West Rusk Intermediate Sch/*New London*/Rusk	11818232	903/895-4685	328
West Rusk Junior High Sch/*New London*/Rusk	01049255	903/392-7855	328
West Sabine Elem Sch/*Pineland*/Sabine	01049308	409/584-2205	329
WEST SABINE IND SCH DIST/			
PINELAND/SABINE	01049293	409/584-2655	329
West Sabine Jr Sr High Sch/*Pineland*/Sabine	01049310	409/584-2525	329
West Side Elem Sch/*Jacksonville*/Cherokee	01005302	903/586-5165	73
West Texas Elem Sch/*Stinnett*/Hutchinson	03006558	806/878-2103	238
West Texas High Sch/*Stinnett*/Hutchinson	03006534	806/878-2456	238
West Texas Middle Sch/*Stinnett*/Hutchinson	03006546	806/878-2247	238
West University Elem Sch/*Houston*/Harris	01025041	713/295-5215	195
West Ward Elem Sch/*Killeen*/Bell	00996617	254/336-1830	28
WESTBROOK IND SCH DIST/WESTBROOK/			
MITCHELL	01042154	325/644-2311	289
Westbrook Intermediate Sch/*Friendswood*/			
Galveston	10007777	281/284-3800	159
Westbrook Sch/*Westbrook*/Mitchell	01042178	325/644-2311	289
Westbury Christian Sch/*Houston*/Harris	02083890	713/551-8100	207
Westbury High Sch/*Houston*/Harris	01025053	713/723-6015	193
Westchester Acad Int'l Studies/*Houston*/			
Harris	04920555	713/251-1800	201
Westcliff Elem Sch/*Fort Worth*/Tarrant	01053593	817/814-6000	352
Westcreek Elem Sch/*Fort Worth*/Tarrant	01053608	817/814-8600	352
Wester Elem Sch/*Lubbock*/Lubbock	01038971	806/219-7100	271
Western Academy/*Houston*/Harris	11744045	713/461-7000	207
Western Hills Academy/*El Paso*/El Paso	02869486	915/584-6642	139
Western Hills Elem Sch/*El Paso*/El Paso	01016117	915/774-4060	134
Western Hills Elem Sch/*Fort Worth*/Tarrant	01053610	817/815-6800	352
Western Hills Elem Sch/*Temple*/Bell	00996887	254/215-5600	29
Western Hills High Sch/*Benbrook*/Tarrant	01053658	817/815-6000	352
Western Hills Primary Sch/*Fort Worth*/			
Tarrant	04919453	817/815-6900	352
Western Plateau Elem Sch/*Amarillo*/Potter	01047520	806/326-5550	318
Westfield High Sch/*Houston*/Harris	01526057	281/891-7130	203
Westhoff Elem Sch/*Westhoff*/De Witt	01013799	830/236-5519	118
WESTHOFF IND SCH DIST/WESTHOFF/			
DE WITT	01013787	830/236-5519	118
Westlake Academy/*Westlake*/Denton	05286601	817/490-5757	14
Westlake High Sch/*Austin*/Travis	01056868	512/732-9280	370
Westlake Lutheran Academy/*Richmond*/			
Fort Bend	11455426	281/341-9910	155
Westlawn Elem Sch/*Texarkana*/Bowie	01001265	903/223-4252	50
Westover Park Jr High Sch/*Amarillo*/Randall	04365022	806/677-2420	321
Westpark Elem Sch/*Fort Worth*/Tarrant	03053018	817/815-7000	352
WESTPHALIA IND SCH DIST/			
LOTT/FALLS	01017329	254/584-4988	145
Westphalia Sch/*Lott*/Falls	01017343	254/584-4988	145
Westside Elem Sch/*Angleton*/Brazoria	01001538	979/848-8990	52
Westside Elem Sch/*Cedar Park*/Williamson	11130767	512/570-7000	397
Westside High Sch/*Houston*/Harris	04815065	281/920-8000	195
Westview Middle Sch/*Austin*/Travis	03049952	512/594-2200	372
Westview Sch/*Houston*/Harris	02749604	713/973-1900	207
Westwind Elem Sch/*Lubbock*/Lubbock	04356617	806/799-3731	269
Westwood Elem Sch/*Houston*/Harris	01027439	713/251-2100	201
Westwood Elem Sch/*Palestine*/Anderson	00994671	903/729-1771	16
Westwood High Sch/*Austin*/Williamson	02126911	512/464-4000	399
Westwood High Sch/*Palestine*/Anderson	00994683	903/729-1773	16
WESTWOOD IND SCH DIST/PALESTINE/			
ANDERSON	00994669	903/729-1776	16
Westwood JHS Math Sci Ldrshp/*Dallas*/Dallas	01011997	469/593-3600	113
Westwood Junior High Sch/*Palestine*/			
Anderson	00994695	903/723-0423	16
Westwood Montessori/IB Sch/*Dallas*/Dallas	03144174	972/239-8598	116
Westwood Primary Sch/*Palestine*/Anderson	02111760	903/729-1774	16
Westwood Terrace Elem Sch/*San Antonio*/			
Bexar	00998342	210/397-0300	39
Westwood-Bales Elem Sch/*Friendswood*/			
Galveston	01019066	281/482-3341	160
Wetmore Elem Sch/*San Antonio*/Bexar	04946339	210/407-8800	36
Wharton Alternative Sch/*Wharton*/Wharton	04033645	979/532-6262	390
Wharton Dual Language Academy/*Houston*/			
Harris	01024310	713/535-3771	195
Wharton Elem Sch/*Wharton*/Wharton	01059729	979/532-6882	390
Wharton High Sch/*Wharton*/Wharton	01059731	979/532-6800	390
WHARTON IND SCH DIST/WHARTON/			
WHARTON	01059690	979/532-3612	390
Wharton Junior High Sch/*Wharton*/Wharton	01059743	979/532-6840	390
Wheat Elem Sch/*Woodville*/Tyler	01057367	409/283-2452	375
Wheat Middle Sch/*Cleburne*/Johnson	01034925	817/202-1300	247
Wheatley Alt Ed Center/*Temple*/Bell	04753106	254/215-5655	29
Wheatley High Sch/*Houston*/Harris	01025651	713/671-3900	189
Wheatley Middle Sch/*San Antonio*/Bexar	00998952	210/738-9750	41
Wheatley Sch Early Childhood/*Port Arthur*/			
Jefferson	01033854	409/984-8750	243
Wheeler Ave Christian Academy/*Houston*/			
Harris	11458272	713/579-2792	207
WHEELER IND SCH DIST/WHEELER/			
WHEELER	01059896	806/826-5241	391
Wheeler Sch/*Wheeler*/Wheeler	01059901	806/826-5241	391
Wheeler Transitional Dev Ctr/*Irving*/Dallas	04015710	972/600-3750	110
Wheelock Elem Sch/*Lubbock*/Lubbock	01038995	806/219-7200	271
Whidby Elem Sch/*Houston*/Harris	01025065	713/746-8170	193
Whispering Hills Achieve Ctr/*Flatonia*/			
Fayette	12035093	361/865-3083	147
Whispering Pines Elem Sch/*Humble*/Harris	03394159	281/641-2500	196
Whitaker Elem Sch/*El Paso*/El Paso	03006895	915/236-6275	134
White Deer Elem Sch/*White Deer*/Carson	01004657	806/883-2311	69
WHITE DEER IND SCH DIST/			
WHITE DEER/CARSON	01004633	806/883-2311	69
White Deer Jr Sr High Sch/*White Deer*/			
Carson	01004669	806/883-2311	69
White Oak High Sch/*White Oak*/Gregg	01021320	903/291-2004	171
WHITE OAK IND SCH DIST/WHITE OAK/			
GREGG	01021306	903/291-2200	171
White Oak Intermediate Sch/*White Oak*/Gregg	03380988	903/291-2101	171
White Oak Middle Sch/*Porter*/Montgomery	01042697	281/577-8800	294
White Oak Middle Sch/*White Oak*/Gregg	01399737	903/291-2055	171
White Oak Primary Sch/*White Oak*/Gregg	01021318	903/291-2160	171
White Rock Elem Sch/*Dallas*/Dallas	01012006	469/593-2700	113
White Rock Montessori Sch/*Dallas*/Dallas	02735706	214/324-5580	116
White Rock North Sch/*Dallas*/Dallas	02180709	214/348-7410	116
WHITE SETTLEMENT IND SCH DIST/			
FORT WORTH/TARRANT	01054183	817/367-1300	357
WHITEFACE CON IND SCH DIST/			
WHITEFACE/COCHRAN	01005728	806/287-1154	75
Whiteface Elem Sch/*Whiteface*/Cochran	01005730	806/287-1285	75
Whiteface High Sch/*Whiteface*/Cochran	01005742	806/287-1104	75
Whitehouse High Sch/*Whitehouse*/Smith	01051014	903/839-5551	339
WHITEHOUSE IND SCH DIST/			
WHITEHOUSE/SMITH	01050993	903/839-5500	338
Whitehouse Junior High Sch/*Whitehouse*/			
Smith	04946298	903/839-5590	339
Whitesboro High Sch/*Whitesboro*/Grayson	01020807	903/564-4114	168
WHITESBORO IND SCH DIST/			
WHITESBORO/GRAYSON	01020780	903/564-4200	168
Whitesboro Intermediate Sch/*Whitesboro*/			
Grayson	01020792	903/564-4180	168
Whitesboro Middle Sch/*Whitesboro*/Grayson	01020819	903/564-4236	168
Whiteside Elem Sch/*Lubbock*/Lubbock	02202096	806/219-7300	271
Whitestone Elem Sch/*Leander*/Williamson	01061033	512/570-7400	397
Whitewright Elem Sch/*Whitewright*/Grayson	01020833	903/364-2155	168
Whitewright High Sch/*Whitewright*/Grayson	01020845	903/364-2155	168

Texas School Directory
DISTRICT & SCHOOL TELEPHONE INDEX

School/City/County DISTRICT/CITY/COUNTY	PID	TELEPHONE	PAGE NUMBER
WHITEWRIGHT IND SCH DIST/			
WHITEWRIGHT/GRAYSON	01020821	903/364-2155	168
Whitewright Middle Sch/Whitewright/Grayson	01397038	903/364-2155	168
WHITHARRAL IND SCH DIST/			
WHITHARRAL/HOCKLEY	01031349	806/299-1184	230
Whitharral Sch/Whitharral/Hockley	01031351	806/299-1135	230
Whitley Road Elem Sch/Watauga/Tarrant	02854388	817/744-5800	355
Whitney Elem Sch/Whitney/Hill	01031064	254/694-3456	228
Whitney High Sch/Whitney/Hill	01031076	254/694-3457	228
WHITNEY IND SCH DIST/WHITNEY/ HILL	01031052	254/694-2254	228
Whitney Intermediate Sch/Whitney/Hill	04762949	254/694-7303	228
Whitney M Young Jr Elem Sch/Dallas/Dallas	01010230	972/749-2000	103
Whitney Middle Sch/Whitney/Hill	01031088	254/946-6568	228
Whitt Fine Arts Academy/Grand Prairie/ Dallas	04945189	972/264-5024	108
Whittier Elem Sch/Amarillo/Potter	01047532	806/326-5600	318
Whittier Elem Sch/Houston/Harris	01025754	713/671-3810	190
Whittier Middle Sch/San Antonio/Bexar	00998653	210/738-9755	41
Wichita Christian Sch/Wichita Falls/ Wichita	11829499	940/763-1347	393
Wichita Falls High Sch/Wichita Falls/ Wichita	01173234	940/235-1084	393
WICHITA FALLS IND SCH DIST/			
WICHITA FALLS/WICHITA	01060132	940/235-1000	392
Widen Elem Sch/Austin/Travis	03008661	512/414-2556	367
Wieland Elem Sch/Pflugerville/Travis	10911269	512/594-3900	372
Wiggs Middle Sch/El Paso/El Paso	02907038	915/236-3600	135
Wilbur E Lucas Elem Sch/Hidalgo/Hidalgo	05090543	956/340-1700	225
Wilchester Elem Sch/Houston/Harris	01027441	713/251-7700	201
Wild Peach Elem Sch/Brazoria/Brazoria	02109494	979/991-1750	52
Wildcat Learning Alt Center/Portland/ San Patricio	12368802	361/777-4051	331
Wildcat Way Sch/Houston/Harris	05092864	713/251-8200	201
Wilderness Oak Elem Sch/San Antonio/Bexar	10003317	210/407-9200	36
Wildorado Elem Sch/Wildorado/Oldham	01045596	806/426-3317	308
WILDORADO IND SCH DIST/WILDORADO/ OLDHAM	01045584	806/426-3317	308
Wildwood Elem Sch/Tomball/Harris	12107842	281/357-3040	203
Wilemon Steam Academy/Waxahachie/Ellis	12313118	972/923-4780	143
Wiley Middle Sch/Leander/Williamson	10023290	512/570-3600	397
Wilkerson Intermediate Sch/The Woodlands/ Montgomery	01042556	832/592-8900	292
Wilkinson Elem Sch/Conroe/Montgomery	11449714	936/709-1500	292
Will Rogers Academy/San Antonio/Bexar	00998665	210/738-9825	41
Will Rogers Elem Sch/Amarillo/Potter	01047544	806/326-5150	318
Willbern Elem Sch/Houston/Harris	04019194	281/897-3820	186
William & Abbie Allen Elem Sch/Frisco/ Collin	11448497	469/633-3800	80
William Adams Middle Sch/Alice/Jim Wells	01034523	361/660-2055	245
William Anderson Elem Sch/Dallas/Dallas	01010199	972/749-6200	103
William B Miller Elem Sch/Dallas/Dallas	01010060	972/502-8700	103
William B Travis 6th GR Campus/Amarillo/ Potter	12033710	806/326-3870	318
William B Travis Elem Sch/Baytown/Harris	01023768	281/420-4660	188
William B Travis Elem Sch/Corp Christi/ Nueces	01044724	361/878-2700	304
William B Travis Elem Sch/Marshall/ Harrison	01028732	903/927-8780	209
William B Travis High Sch/Richmond/ Fort Bend	10027882	281/634-7000	151
William B Travis Middle Sch/Amarillo/ Potter	01047518	806/326-3800	318
William B Travis Middle Sch/McAllen/ Hidalgo	01030113	956/971-4242	221
William Beverly Elem Sch/Allen/Collin	04810120	469/752-0400	83
William D Slider Middle Sch/El Paso/ El Paso	03399355	915/857-5804	137
William D Surratt Elem Sch/Clint/El Paso	01015436	915/926-8200	132
William G Gravitt Jr High Sch/Denver City/ Yoakum	01062051	806/592-5940	405
William Hobby Middle Sch/San Antonio/Bexar	00998354	210/397-6300	39
William Howard Taft High Sch/San Antonio/ Bexar	02848511	210/397-6000	39
William J Brennan High Sch/San Antonio/ Bexar	11552165	210/398-1250	39
William J Clinton Elem Sch/Penitas/Hidalgo	10914417	956/323-2740	220
William J Thornton Elem Sch/San Antonio/ Bexar	03252111	210/397-3950	39
William James Middle Sch/Fort Worth/ Tarrant	01053622	817/814-0200	352
William Lipscomb Elem Sch/Dallas/Dallas	01010101	972/794-7300	103
William Monnig Middle Sch/Fort Worth/ Tarrant	01053634	817/815-1200	352
William Paschall Elem Sch/San Antonio/ Bexar	04945921	210/662-2240	34
William Pearce Elem Sch/San Antonio/Bexar	00999566	210/882-1605	43
William R Carmichael Elem Sch/Houston/ Harris	01857258	281/878-0345	179
William Velasquez Elem Sch/Richmond/ Fort Bend	10030748	832/223-2600	154
William's Community Sch/Austin/Travis	12240183	512/250-5700	373
Williams Elem Sch/Arlington/Tarrant	04019871	682/867-5900	345
Williams Elem Sch/Austin/Travis	01532109	512/414-2525	367
Williams Elem Sch/Garland/Dallas	01010802	972/926-2610	107
Williams Elem Sch/Lubbock/Lubbock	01418515	806/219-7400	271
Williams Elem Sch/Pasadena/Harris	01027001	713/740-0776	200
Williams Elem Sch/Richmond/Fort Bend	02856984	832/223-2700	154
Williams High Sch/Plano/Collin	01006459	469/752-8300	83
Willie B Ermel Elem Sch/Houston/Harris	01532020	713/466-5220	179
Willie E Brown Elem Sch/Mansfield/Tarrant	04804365	817/299-5860	357
Willie E Williams Elem Sch/Magnolia/ Montgomery	04363103	281/356-6866	293
Willie J Hargrave High Sch/Huffman/Harris	01026124	281/324-1845	195
Willis Classical Academy/Willis/Montgomery	11459692	936/890-0100	14
Willis High Sch/Willis/Montgomery	01042805	936/856-1250	294
WILLIS IND SCH DIST/WILLIS/ MONTGOMERY	01042764	936/856-1200	294
Willis Lane Elem Sch/Keller/Tarrant	04749313	817/744-5700	355
Willow Bend Academy-Plano/Plano/Collin	11564405	972/599-7882	86
Willow Bend Elem Sch/Lubbock/Lubbock	10030360	806/796-0090	269
Willow Creek Elem Sch/Kingwood/Harris	03051474	281/641-2300	196
Willow Creek Elem Sch/Saginaw/Tarrant	11555557	817/232-2845	349
Willow Creek Elem Sch/Tomball/Harris	04806717	281/357-3080	203
Willow Springs Elem Sch/Killeen/Bell	02897225	254/336-2020	28
Willow Springs Middle Sch/Allen/Collin	11924908	469/742-8500	80
Willow Vista Intermediate Sch/Amarillo/ Potter	11445586	806/383-8820	319
Willow Wood Junior High Sch/Tomball/Harris	05279397	281/357-3030	203
Willowridge High Sch/Houston/Fort Bend	02043230	281/634-2450	151
Wills Point High Sch/Wills Point/Van Zandt	01058294	903/873-5100	381
WILLS POINT IND SCH DIST/ WILLS POINT/VAN ZANDT	01058270	903/873-3161	381
Wills Point Junior High Sch/Wills Point/ Van Zandt	04803488	903/873-5100	381
Wills Point Middle Sch/Wills Point/ Van Zandt	01058309	903/873-5100	381
Wills Point Primary Sch/Wills Point/ Van Zandt	01058282	903/873-5100	381
Wilma Fisher Elem Sch/Frisco/Collin	04942369	469/633-2600	80
Wilmer Early Chldhd Center/Wilmer/Dallas	12169723	469/660-7296	103
Wilmer-Hutchins Elem Sch/Dallas/Dallas	11732779	972/925-2600	103
Wilmer-Hutchins High Sch/Dallas/Dallas	11732767	972/925-2900	103
Wilshire Elem Sch/Euless/Tarrant	01053971	817/354-3529	354
Wilshire Elem Sch/San Antonio/Bexar	00997984	210/407-9400	36
Wilson & Young Middle Sch/Odessa/Ector	01014729	432/456-0459	130
Wilson Early College High Sch/Port Arthur/ Jefferson	12310233	409/984-8960	243
Wilson Elem Sch/Harlingen/Cameron	01381510	956/427-3190	65
Wilson Elem Sch/Houston/Harris	02201535	281/463-5941	186
Wilson Elem Sch/Houston/Harris	04019041	281/878-0990	179
Wilson Elem Sch/Pampa/Gray	01020223	806/669-4930	165
Wilson Elem Sch/San Antonio/Bexar	00998718	210/738-9845	41
WILSON IND SCH DIST/WILSON/LYNN	01039391	806/628-6261	273
Wilson Middle Sch/Plano/Collin	01006497	469/752-6700	83
Wilson Montessori Elem Sch/Houston/Harris	01024671	713/942-1470	195
Wilson Sch/Wilson/Lynn	01039406	806/628-6261	273
Wimberley High Sch/Wimberley/Hays	02855801	512/847-5729	212
WIMBERLEY IND SCH DIST/WIMBERLEY/ HAYS	02903408	512/847-2414	212
Wimbish World Language Academy/Arlington/ Tarrant	01051961	682/867-6000	345
Windcrest Elem Sch/San Antonio/Bexar	00997996	210/407-9600	36
Windermere Elem Sch/Pflugerville/Travis	03318997	512/594-4800	372
Windermere Primary Sch/Pflugerville/Travis	04803048	512/594-5600	372
Windfern High School of Choice/Houston/ Harris	04455419	281/807-8684	186
Windle Sch for Young Children/Denton/ Denton	01826182	940/369-3900	121
Windsong Intermediate Sch/Friendswood/ Galveston	04851071	281/482-0111	160
Windsong Ranch Elem Sch/Prosper/Collin	12172885	469/219-2220	84
Windsor Elem Sch/Amarillo/Potter	02178031	806/326-5700	318
Windsor Park Elem Sch/Corp Christi/Nueces	01044750	361/878-3770	304

School Year 2019-2020   800-333-8802   TX-V81

DISTRICT & SCHOOL TELEPHONE INDEX

Market Data Retrieval

School/City/County DISTRICT/CITY/COUNTY	PID	TELEPHONE NUMBER	PAGE
Windsor Village Elem Sch/*Houston*/Harris	01025388	713/726-3642	193
Windthorst Elem Sch/*Windthorst*/Archer	00995285	940/423-6679	20
Windthorst High Sch/*Windthorst*/Archer	00995297	940/423-6680	20
WINDTHORST IND SCH DIST/			
WINDTHORST/ARCHER	00995273	940/423-6688	20
Windthorst Junior High Sch/*Windthorst*/Archer	11450737	940/423-6605	20
Winfree Academy-Dallas/*Dallas*/Dallas	12044264	469/930-5199	14
Winfree Academy-Grand Prairie/*Grand Prairie*/Dallas	11013901	214/204-2030	14
Winfree Academy-Irving/*Irving*/Dallas	05010763	972/251-2010	14
Winfree Academy-Lewisville/*Lewisville*/Denton	05009843	214/222-2200	14
Winfree Academy-N Rchlnd Hills/*Richland Hls*/Tarrant	11013913	817/590-2240	14
Winfree Academy-Richardson/*Richardson*/Dallas	05009855	972/234-9855	14
Wings/*Desoto*/Dallas	12108999	972/274-8219	104
Wink Elem Sch/*Wink*/Winkler	01061497	432/527-3880	402
Wink High Sch/*Wink*/Winkler	01061502	432/527-3880	402
WINK LOVING IND SCH DIST/			
WINK/WINKLER	01061485	432/527-3880	402
Winkley Elem Sch/*Leander*/Williamson	10023276	512/570-6700	397
Winn Elem Sch/*Austin*/Travis	01056739	512/414-2390	368
Winnetka Elem Sch/*Dallas*/Dallas	01010216	972/749-5100	103
Winnsboro Elem Sch/*Winnsboro*/Wood	01061966	903/342-3548	405
Winnsboro High Sch/*Winnsboro*/Wood	01061978	903/342-3641	405
WINNSBORO IND SCH DIST/WINNSBORO/			
WOOD	01061942	903/342-3737	405
Winona Elem Sch/*Winona*/Smith	01051040	903/939-4800	339
Winona High Sch/*Winona*/Smith	01051052	903/939-4100	339
WINONA IND SCH DIST/WINONA/SMITH	01051038	903/939-4000	339
Winona Intermediate Sch/*Winona*/Smith	12034673	903/939-4800	339
Winona Middle Sch/*Winona*/Smith	02129377	903/939-4040	339
Winston Churchill High Sch/*San Antonio*/Bexar	00998005	210/356-0000	36
Winston Elem Sch/*San Antonio*/Bexar	00997348	210/444-8450	32
Winston Sch/*Dallas*/Dallas	01875286	214/691-6950	116
Winston School San Antonio/*San Antonio*/Bexar	02083644	210/615-6544	45
Winters Elem Sch/*Winters*/Runnels	01048926	325/754-5577	327
Winters High Sch/*Winters*/Runnels	01048938	325/754-5516	327
WINTERS IND SCH DIST/WINTERS/			
RUNNELS	01048914	325/754-5574	327
Winters Junior High Sch/*Winters*/Runnels	04865369	325/754-5518	327
Wise Elem Fine Arts Magnet Sch/*Tyler*/Smith	01050618	903/566-2271	337
Wm B Travis Elem Sch/*Ennis*/Ellis	01015022	972/872-7455	140
Woden Elem Sch/*Woden*/Nacogdoches	01043366	936/564-2386	298
Woden High Sch/*Woden*/Nacogdoches	04921808	936/564-7903	298
WODEN IND SCH DIST/NACOGDOCHES/			
NACOGDOCHES	01043354	936/564-2073	298
Woden Junior High Sch/*Woden*/Nacogdoches	04921793	936/564-2481	298
Wolfe City Elem Sch/*Wolfe City*/Hunt	01032628	903/496-7333	237
Wolfe City High Sch/*Wolfe City*/Hunt	01032630	903/496-2891	237
WOLFE CITY IND SCH DIST/			
WOLFE CITY/HUNT	01032616	903/496-2283	237
Wolfe City Middle Sch/*Wolfe City*/Hunt	02131320	903/496-7333	237
Wolffarth Elem Sch/*Lubbock*/Lubbock	01039016	806/219-7600	271
Wolflin Elem Sch/*Amarillo*/Potter	01047556	806/326-5750	318
Wonderland Sch/*San Marcos*/Hays	01480609	512/392-9404	212
Wood Elem Sch/*Arlington*/Tarrant	01881936	682/867-1100	345
Wood Middle Sch/*San Antonio*/Bexar	02126143	210/356-6200	36
Wood River Elem Sch/*Corp Christi*/Nueces	02896130	361/242-7560	303
Woodcreek Elem Sch/*Katy*/Harris	10913308	281/234-0100	153
Woodcreek Junior High Sch/*Katy*/Harris	11128582	281/234-0800	153
Woodcreek Middle Sch/*Houston*/Harris	11552684	281/641-5200	196
Woodcrest Elem Sch/*Port Neches*/Jefferson	01034042	409/724-2309	244
Woodgate Intermediate Sch/*Waco*/McLennan	04034912	254/761-5690	281
Woodlake Elem Sch/*San Antonio*/Bexar	01878381	210/662-2220	34
Woodlake Hills Middle Sch/*San Antonio*/Bexar	04446468	210/661-1110	34
Woodland Acres Elem Sch/*Houston*/Harris	01023548	832/386-2220	187
Woodland Acres Middle Sch/*Houston*/Harris	01023550	832/386-4700	187
Woodland Elem Sch/*Graham*/Young	01062154	940/549-4090	406
Woodland Heights Elem Sch/*Brownwood*/Brown	01002544	325/646-8633	58
Woodland Hills Elem Sch/*Kingwood*/Harris	01401421	281/641-1500	196
Woodland Springs Elem Sch/*Keller*/Tarrant	05350745	817/744-5900	355
Woodlands Christian Academy/*The Woodlands*/Montgomery	04930603	936/273-2555	295
Woodlands Elem Sch/*Amarillo*/Potter	04866179	806/326-5800	319
Woodlands Preparatory Sch/*Tomball*/Harris	05275511	281/561-0600	207
Woodlawn Academy/*San Antonio*/Bexar	00998691	210/438-6560	41
Woodlawn Elem Sch/*Corp Christi*/Nueces	01044762	361/878-2900	304
Woodlawn Hills Elem Sch/*San Antonio*/Bexar	00998706	210/438-6565	41
Woodridge Elem Sch/*Desoto*/Dallas	01881845	972/223-3800	104
Woodridge Elem Sch/*San Antonio*/Bexar	00996980	210/826-8021	30
Woodridge Forest Middle Sch/*Porter*/Montgomery	12033875	281/577-8880	294
Woodroe Petty Elem Sch/*Taft*/San Patricio	01049853	361/528-2636	332
Woodrow Wilson Daep Sch/*Texas City*/Galveston	05278379	409/916-0280	161
Woodrow Wilson Elem Sch/*Denton*/Denton	01013335	940/369-4500	121
Woodrow Wilson Elem Sch/*McAllen*/Hidalgo	01030125	956/971-4525	221
Woodrow Wilson High Sch/*Dallas*/Dallas	01010228	972/502-4400	104
Woodrow Wilson Jr High Sch/*Dayton*/Liberty	01037812	936/258-2309	265
Woods Elem Sch/*Tyler*/Smith	01050981	903/262-1280	338
Woodsboro Elem Sch/*Woodsboro*/Refugio	01048500	361/543-4518	324
WOODSBORO IND SCH DIST/WOODSBORO/			
REFUGIO	01048495	361/543-4518	324
Woodsboro Jr Sr High Sch/*Woodsboro*/Refugio	01048512	361/543-4622	324
Woodson Center for Excellence/*Abilene*/Taylor	04304133	325/671-4736	360
WOODSON IND SCH DIST/WOODSON/			
THROCKMORTON	01055254	940/345-6521	363
Woodson PK-5 Sch/*Houston*/Harris	01025120	713/732-3600	189
Woodson Sch/*Woodson*/Throckmorton	01055266	940/345-6521	363
Woodstone Elem Sch/*San Antonio*/Bexar	01824043	210/407-9800	36
Woodview Elem Sch/*Houston*/Harris	01027453	713/251-7800	201
Woodville High Sch/*Woodville*/Tyler	01057343	409/283-3714	375
WOODVILLE IND SCH DIST/WOODVILLE/			
TYLER	01057331	409/283-3752	375
Woodville Intermediate Sch/*Woodville*/Tyler	02224393	409/283-2549	375
Woodville Middle Sch/*Woodville*/Tyler	01057355	409/283-3714	375
Woodway Elem Sch/*Fort Worth*/Tarrant	03340342	817/814-8700	352
Woodway Elem Sch/*Waco*/McLennan	01039949	254/761-5740	281
Wooldridge Elem Sch/*Austin*/Travis	01056741	512/414-2353	368
Wooten Elem Sch/*Austin*/Travis	01056753	512/414-2315	368
Workman Junior High Sch/*Arlington*/Tarrant	01051686	682/867-1200	345
World Languages Institute/*Fort Worth*/Tarrant	12033796	817/815-2200	352
Worth Heights Elem Sch/*Fort Worth*/Tarrant	01053646	817/814-6200	352
Wortham Elem Sch/*Wortham*/Freestone	01018555	254/765-3523	156
Wortham High Sch/*Wortham*/Freestone	04800292	254/765-3094	156
WORTHAM IND SCH DIST/WORTHAM/			
FREESTONE	01018543	254/765-3095	156
Wortham Middle Sch/*Wortham*/Freestone	04800280	254/765-3523	156
Wortham Oaks Elem Sch/*San Antonio*/Bexar	12308008	210/945-5750	34
Worthing High Sch/*Houston*/Harris	01025170	713/733-3433	189
Wright Elem Sch/*Lubbock*/Lubbock	01039028	806/219-7700	271
Wright Elem Sch/*San Antonio*/Bexar	00997520	210/989-3400	33
Wunderlich Intermediate Sch/*Houston*/Harris	01418450	832/249-5200	198
Wyatt Elem Sch/*Plano*/Collin	04916293	469/752-3800	83
Wylie East Elem Sch/*Abilene*/Taylor	12365305	325/437-2330	361
Wylie East High Sch/*Wylie*/Collin	10915710	972/429-3150	85
Wylie East Junior High Sch/*Abilene*/Taylor	12110124	325/437-2360	361
Wylie Elem Sch/*Henderson*/Rusk	01048988	903/655-5200	327
Wylie High Sch/*Abilene*/Taylor	01055022	325/690-1181	361
Wylie High Sch/*Wylie*/Collin	01172424	972/429-3100	85
WYLIE IND SCH DIST/ABILENE/			
TAYLOR	01055008	325/692-4353	361
WYLIE IND SCH DIST/WYLIE/COLLIN	01006605	972/429-3000	84
Wylie Intermediate Sch/*Abilene*/Taylor	02180137	325/692-7961	361
Wylie Preparatory Academy/*Wylie*/Collin	10013908	972/442-1388	86
Wylie Primary Sch/*Henderson*/Rusk	01049035	903/655-5100	327
Wylie West Early Childhood Ctr/*Abilene*/Taylor	01055010	325/437-2351	361
Wylie West Elem Sch/*Abilene*/Taylor	03241710	325/692-6554	361
Wylie West Junior High Sch/*Abilene*/Taylor	04235960	325/695-1910	361
X			
Xavier Educational Academy/*Houston*/Harris	12361232	832/303-9638	207
Xavier Preparatory Sch/*Dallas*/Dallas	12234615	214/372-4524	116
Xenia Voigt Elem Sch/*Round Rock*/Williamson	01413929	512/428-7500	399
Y			
Yale Elem Sch/*Richardson*/Dallas	01399696	469/593-8300	113
YANTIS IND SCH DIST/YANTIS/WOOD	01061980	903/383-2463	405
Yantis Sch/*Yantis*/Wood	01061992	903/383-2462	405
Yarbrough Elem Sch/*Midland*/Midland	12104357	432/240-8500	286
Yates High Sch/*Houston*/Harris	01024451	713/748-5400	189
Yavneh Academy-Dallas/*Dallas*/Dallas	04149270	214/295-3500	116
Yeager Elem Sch/*Houston*/Harris	01418395	281/440-4914	186
Yellowstone Academy/*Houston*/Harris	05342750	713/741-8000	208

Texas School Directory
DISTRICT & SCHOOL TELEPHONE INDEX

School/City/County DISTRICT/CITY/COUNTY	PID	TELEPHONE NUMBER	PAGE
YES Prep Brays Oaks/*Houston*/Harris	11834470	713/967-8400	14
YES Prep East End/*Houston*/Harris	10758861	713/967-7800	14
YES Prep Fifth Ward/*Houston*/Harris	11935373	713/924-0600	14
YES Prep Gulfton/*Houston*/Harris	11014101	713/967-9805	14
YES Prep Hoffman/*Houston*/Harris	12044551	713/924-5400	14
YES Prep North Centrl/*Houston*/Harris	10758847	281/227-2044	14
YES Prep North Forest/*Houston*/Harris	11563138	713/967-8600	14
YES Prep Northbrook MS/*Houston*/Harris	12044549	713/251-4200	14
YES Prep Northline/*Houston*/Harris	12261278	713/842-5400	14
YES Prep Northside/*Houston*/Harris	11720037	713/924-0400	14
YES Prep Southeast/*Houston*/Harris	04813275	713/910-2510	14
YES Prep Southside/*Houston*/Harris	12163028	713/924-5500	14
YES Prep Southwest/*Houston*/Fort Bend	10758859	713/413-0001	14
YES Prep West/*Houston*/Harris	11540370	713/967-8200	14
YES Prep White Oak/*Houston*/Harris	11934410	713/924-5300	14
Yoakum High Sch/*Yoakum*/De Witt	01013816	361/293-3442	118
YOAKUM IND SCH DIST/YOAKUM/ DE WITT	01013804	361/293-3162	118
Yoakum Intermediate Sch/*Yoakum*/De Witt	01013828	361/293-3001	118
Yoakum Junior High Sch/*Yoakum*/De Witt	01013830	361/293-3111	118
Yoakum Primary Annex Sch/*Yoakum*/De Witt	01013842	361/293-3312	118
Yoakum Primary Sch/*Yoakum*/De Witt	01013854	361/293-2011	118
York Junior High Sch/*Spring*/Montgomery	02856829	832/592-8600	292
Yorkshire Academy/*Houston*/Harris	02753253	281/531-6088	208
Yorktown Christian Academy/*Corp Christi*/Nueces	04993899	361/985-9960	306
Yorktown Elem Sch/*Yorktown*/De Witt	01013880	361/564-2252	118
Yorktown High Sch/*Yorktown*/De Witt	01013878	361/564-2252	118
YORKTOWN IND SCH DIST/YORKTOWN/ DE WITT	01013866	361/564-2252	118
Yorktown Junior High Sch/*Yorktown*/De Witt	02177398	361/564-2252	118
Youens Elem Sch/*Houston*/Harris	01022996	281/983-8383	182
Young Elem Sch/*Decatur*/Wise	11562081	940/393-7400	403
Young Elem Sch/*Houston*/Harris	01025015	713/732-3590	193
Young Elem Sch/*Seminole*/Gaines	01018763	432/758-3636	158
Young Junior High Sch/*Arlington*/Tarrant	01881924	682/867-3400	345
Young Learners Elem Sch/*Houston*/Harris	11834509	713/772-7100	195
Young Men's Leadership Academy/*Fort Worth*/Tarrant	11821318	817/815-3400	353
Young Men's Leadership Academy/*San Antonio*/Bexar	12106458	210/354-9652	41
Young Mens Ldrshp Acad-Flornce/*Dallas*/Dallas	01008835	972/749-6000	104
Young Mens Leadership Academy/*Grand Prairie*/Dallas	11823304	972/264-8651	108
Young Scholars Acad Excellence/*Houston*/Harris	04813251	713/654-1404	189
Young Women Steam Acad-Blch Sp/*Balch Springs*/Dallas	11919886	972/892-5800	104
Young Women's Leadership Acad/*El Paso*/El Paso	12177988	915/434-1300	138
Young Women's Leadership Acad/*Fort Worth*/Tarrant	11554541	817/815-2400	353
Young Women's Leadership Acad/*Midland*/Midland	12364935	432/240-8700	286
Young Women's Leadership Acad/*San Antonio*/Bexar	11128051	210/438-6525	41
Young Women's Steam Prep Acad/*El Paso*/El Paso	12368735	915/236-4830	134
Young Womens College Prep Acad/*Houston*/Harris	11717511	713/942-1441	192
Young Womens Leadership Acad/*Grand Prairie*/Dallas	11823299	972/343-7400	108
Youngblood Intermediate Sch/*Houston*/Harris	04453265	281/983-8020	183
Ysleta Community Learning Ctr/*El Paso*/El Paso	04918265	915/434-9400	138
Ysleta Elem Sch/*El Paso*/El Paso	01016648	915/434-8900	138
Ysleta High Sch/*El Paso*/El Paso	01016650	915/434-8000	138
YSLETA IND SCH DIST/EL PASO/ EL PASO	01016296	915/434-0000	137
Ysleta Middle Sch/*El Paso*/El Paso	01399713	915/434-8200	138
Ysleta Pre-K Center/*El Paso*/El Paso	02857110	915/434-9500	138
YW Steam Research & Prep Acad/*El Paso*/El Paso	12233427	915/236-4830	133
Ywla Primary/*San Antonio*/Bexar	12365472	210/554-2710	41

Z

School/City/County	PID	TELEPHONE NUMBER	PAGE
Zach White Elem Sch/*El Paso*/El Paso	01016105	915/236-2700	134
Zachry Middle Sch/*San Antonio*/Bexar	02848523	210/397-7400	39
Zack Motley Elem Sch/*Mesquite*/Dallas	01011612	972/882-5080	111
Zamora Middle Sch/*San Antonio*/Bexar	10023317	210/977-7278	43
Zan Wesley Holmes Jr Mid Sch/*Dallas*/Dallas	11825364	214/932-7800	104

School/City/County DISTRICT/CITY/COUNTY	PID	TELEPHONE NUMBER	PAGE
ZAPATA CO IND SCH DIST/ZAPATA/ ZAPATA	01062245	956/765-6546	406
Zapata High Sch/*Zapata*/Zapata	01062271	956/765-0280	407
Zapata Middle Sch/*Zapata*/Zapata	02178471	956/765-6542	407
Zapata North Elem Sch/*Zapata*/Zapata	02199970	956/765-6917	407
Zapata South Elem Sch/*Zapata*/Zapata	01062269	956/765-4332	407
Zavala Elem Sch/*Austin*/Travis	01056765	512/414-2318	367
Zavala Elem Sch/*El Paso*/El Paso	01015711	915/236-0550	134
Zavala Elem Sch/*Harlingen*/Cameron	01003938	956/427-3200	65
Zavala Magnet Elem Sch/*Odessa*/Ector	01014860	432/456-1239	131
Zavalla Elem Sch/*Zavalla*/Angelina	00995091	936/897-2611	18
Zavalla High Sch/*Zavalla*/Angelina	00995106	936/897-2301	18
ZAVALLA IND SCH DIST/ZAVALLA/ ANGELINA	00995089	936/897-2271	18
Zelma Hutsell Elem Sch/*Katy*/Harris	01832105	281/237-6500	153
ZEPHYR IND SCH DIST/ZEPHYR/BROWN	01002611	325/739-5331	59
Zephyr Sch/*Zephyr*/Brown	01002623	325/739-5331	59
Zilker Elem Sch/*Austin*/Travis	01056777	512/414-2327	367
Zion Lutheran Sch/*Dallas*/Dallas	01012355	214/363-1630	116
Zion Lutheran Sch/*Georgetown*/Williamson	01061253	512/863-5345	400
Zue S Bales Intermediate Sch/*Friendswood*/Galveston	12367808	281/482-8255	160
Zundy Elem Sch/*Wichita Falls*/Wichita	01060405	940/235-1123	393
Zwink Elem Sch/*Spring*/Harris	11822726	832/375-7800	198

Texas School Directory

DISTRICT URL INDEX

DISTRICT	URL	PAGE
Abbott Ind School Dist	abbottisd.org/	226
Abernathy Ind School Dist	abernathyisd.com/	174
Abilene Ind School Dist	abileneisd.org	360
Academy Ind School Dist	academyisd.net/	26
Adrian Ind School Dist	adrianisd.net/	307
Advantage Academy Admin Office	advantageisd.com/	96
Agua Dulce Ind School Dist	adisd.esc2.net/	302
Alamo Heights Ind School Dist	ahisd.net/	30
Alba-Golden Ind School Dist	agisd.com/	404
Albany Ind School Dist	albanyisd.net/	334
Aldine Ind School Dist	aldineisd.org/	179
Aledo Ind School Dist	aledo.k12.tx.us/	312
Alice Ind School Dist	aliceisd.net/	245
Alief Ind School Dist	aliefisd.net/	181
Allen Ind School Dist	allenisd.org	76
Alpine Ind School Dist	alpine.esc18.net/	56
Alto Ind School Dist	alto.esc7.net/	72
Alvarado Ind School Dist	alvaradoisd.net/	246
Alvin Ind School Dist	alvinisd.net/	50
Alvord Ind School Dist	alvordisd.net/	402
Amarillo Ind School Dist	amaisd.org/	317
Amherst Ind School Dist	amherstisd.schooldesk.net/	260
Anahuac Ind School Dist	sites.google.com/aisdpanthers.com/anahuacisd/home	71
Anderson-Shiro Cons Ind SD	ascisd.net/	171
Andrews Ind School Dist	andrews.esc18.net	16
Angleton Ind School Dist	angletonisd.net/	51
Anna Ind School Dist	annaisd.org/	77
Anson Ind School Dist	ansontigers.com/	249
Anthony Ind School Dist	anthonyisd.net/	131
Anton ISD School Dist	antonisd.org/	229
Apple Springs Ind School Dist	asisd.com/	374
Aquilla Ind School Dist	aquillaisd.net/	227
Aransas Co Ind School Dist	acisd.org/	19
Aransas Pass Ind School Dist	apisd.org/	330
Archer City Ind School Dist	archercityisd.net/	19
Argyle Ind School Dist	argyleisd.com/	120
Arlington Ind School Dist	aisd.net/	343
Arp Ind School Dist	home.arpisd.org/	336
Aspermont Ind School Dist	aspermontisd.com/	342
Athens Ind School Dist	athensisd.net/	213
Atlanta Ind School Dist	atlisd.net/	69
Aubrey Ind School Dist	aubreyisd.net/	120
Austin Ind School Dist	austinisd.org/	366
Austwell Tivoli Ind SD	atisd.net/	323
Avalon Ind School Dist	avalonisd.net/	140
Avery Ind School Dist	averyisd.net/	322
Avinger Ind School Dist	avingerisd.net/	70
Axtell Ind School Dist	axtellisd.net/	278
Azle Ind School Dist	azleisd.net/	345
Baird Ind School Dist	bairdisd.net/	62
Ballinger Ind School Dist	ballingerisd.net/	326
Balmorhea Ind School Dist	bisdbears.esc18.net/	323
Bandera Ind School Dist	banderaisd.net/	23
Bangs Ind School Dist	bangsisd.net	58
Banquete Ind School Dist	banqueteisd.esc2.net	302
Barbers Hill Ind School Dist	bhisd.net	72
Bartlett Ind School Dist	bartlett.txed.net/	26
Bastrop Ind School Dist	bisdtx.org/	23
Bay City Ind School Dist	bcblackcats.net/	275
Beaumont Ind School Dist	bmtisd.com/	241
Beckville Ind School Dist	beckvilleisd.net/home	311
Beeville Ind School Dist	beevilleisd.net/	25
Bellevue Ind School Dist	bellevueisd.org/	74
Bells Ind School Dist	bellsisd.net/	165
Bellville Ind School Dist	bellvilleisd.org/	21
Belton Ind School Dist	bisd.net	26
Ben Bolt-Palito Blanco ISD	bbpbschools.net	245
Benavides Ind School Dist	benavidesisd.net/	128
Benjamin Ind School Dist	benjaminisd.net/	258
Big Sandy Ind School Dist	bigsandyisd.net/	316
Big Sandy Ind School Dist	bigsandyisd.org/	376
Big Spring Ind School Dist	bsisd.esc18.net/	233
Birdville Ind School Dist	birdvilleschools.net/	346

School Year 2019-2020 800-333-8802 TX-W1

DISTRICT URL INDEX

Market Data Retrieval

DISTRICT	URL	PAGE
Bishop Cons Ind School Dist	bishopcisd.esc2.net	302
Blackwell Cons Ind Sch Dist	blackwellhornets.org/	301
Blanco Ind School Dist	blancoisd.com/	45
Bland Ind School Dist	blandisd.net/	235
Blanket Ind School Dist	blanketisd.net/	58
Bloomburg Ind School Dist	bloomburgisd.net/	70
Blooming Grove Ind School Dist	bgisd.org/	299
Bloomington Ind School Dist	bes.bisd-tx.org/	381
Blue Ridge Ind School Dist	brisd.net/	77
Bluff Dale Ind Sch Dist	bdisd.net/	143
Blum Ind School Dist	blumisd.net/	227
Boerne Ind School Dist	boerne-isd.net	253
Boles Ind School Dist	bolesisd.com/	235
Boling Ind School Dist	bolingisd.net/	389
Bonham Ind School Dist	bonhamisd.org	145
Booker Ind School Dist	bookerisd.net/	267
Borden Co Ind School Dist	bcisd.net/	46
Borger Ind School Dist	borgerisd.net	237
Bosqueville Ind School Dist	bosquevilleisd.org/15969_1	278
Bovina Ind School Dist	bovinaisd.org/	314
Bowie Ind School Dist	bowieisd.net/	289
Boyd Ind School Dist	boydisd.net/	402
Boys Ranch Ind School Dist	boysranchisd.org/	307
Brackett Ind School Dist	brackettisd.net/	257
Brady Ind School Dist	bradyisd.org/	277
Braination Schools	braination.net/	30
Brazos Ind School Dist	brazosisd.net/	22
Brazosport Ind School Dist	brazosportisd.net/	52
Breckenridge Ind School Dist	breckenridgeisd.org/	341
Bremond Ind School Dist	bremondisd.net/	324
Brenham Ind School Dist	brenhamisd.net/	385
Bridge City Ind School Dist	bridgecityisd.net/	308
Bridgeport Ind School Dist	high.bridgeportisd.net/	402
Broaddus Ind School Dist	broaddusisd.net/	329
Brock Ind School Dist	brockisd.net/	312
Bronte Ind School Dist	bronteisd.net/	75
Brookeland Ind School Dist	brookelandisd.net/	240
Brookesmith Ind School Dist	brookesmithisd.net	58
Brooks Co Ind School Dist	bcisdistrict.net/	57
Brownfield Ind Sch Dist	brownfieldisd.net/home	362
Brownsboro Ind School Dist	gobearsgo.net/	213
Brownsville Ind School Dist	bisd.us/	63
Brownwood Ind School Dist	brownwoodisd.org/	58
Bruceville-Eddy Ind Sch Dist	beisd.net/Page/1	278
Bryan Ind School Dist	bryanisd.org	54
Bryson Ind School Dist	brysonisd.net/	238
Buckholts Ind School Dist	buckholtsisd.net/	287
Buena Vista Ind School Dist	bvisd.net/	315
Buffalo Ind School Dist	buffaloisd.net/	264
Bullard Ind School Dist	bullardisd.net/	336
Buna Ind School Dist	bunaisd.net/	240
Burkburnett Ind Sch Dist	burkburnettisd.org/	391
Burkeville Ind School Dist	burkevilleisd.org/	300
Burleson Ind School Dist	burlesonisd.net/	246
Burnet Cons Ind Sch Dist	burnetcisd.net/	60
Burton Ind School Dist	burtonisd.net/	386
Bushland Ind School Dist	bushlandisd.net/cms/One.aspx	319
Bynum Ind School Dist	bynumisd.net/	227
Caddo Mills Ind Sch Dist	caddomillsisd.org/caddomillsisd/site/default.asp	235
Calallen Ind School Dist	calallen.k12.tx.us/	302
Caldwell Ind School Dist	caldwellisd.net/	59
Calhoun Co Ind School Dist	calcoisd.org/	61
Callisburg Ind School Dist	cisdtx.net/site/default.aspx?PageID=1	90
Calvert Ind School Dist	calvertisd.com/	324
Cameron Ind School Dist	cameronisd.net/	287
Campbell Ind School Dist	campbellisd.org/	235
Canadian Ind School Dist	canadianisd.net/	213
Canton Ind School Dist	cantonisd.net/	380
Canutillo Ind School Dist	canutillo-isd.org/	131
Canyon Ind School Dist	canyonisd.net	320
Carlisle Ind School Dist	carlisleisd.org/	327
Carrizo Spgs Cons Ind SD	cscisd.net/	127
Carroll Independent Sch Dist	southlakecarroll.edu	347
Carrollton-Farmers Branch ISD	cfbisd.edu/	96

TX-W2   800-333-8802   **School Year 2019-2020**

Texas School Directory

DISTRICT URL INDEX

DISTRICT	URL	PAGE
Carthage Ind School Dist	carthageisd.org/	311
Castleberry Ind School Dist	castleberryisd.net	347
Cayuga Ind School Dist	cayugaisd.com/	14
Cedar Hill Ind School Dist	chisd.com	97
Celeste Ind School Dist	207.235.128.200/Celeste/	235
Celina Ind School Dist	celinaisd.com/	77
Center Ind School Dist	centerisd.org/	334
Center Point Ind School Dist	cpisd.net	255
Centerville Ind School Dist	centerville.k12.tx.us/	264
Centerville Ind School Dist	centervilleisd.net	374
Central Heights Ind Sch Dist	centralhts.org/	297
Central Ind School Dist	centralisd.com	16
Channelview Ind School Dist	cvisd.org/site/default.aspx?PageID=1	183
Channing Ind School Dist	region16.net/channingisd/	209
Chapel Hill Ind School Dist	chapelhillisd.org/	337
Chapel Hill Ind School Dist	chisddevils.com/	363
Charlotte Ind School Dist	charlotteisd.net/	20
Cherokee Ind School Dist	cherokeeisd.net	332
Chester Ind School Dist	chesterisd.com/	374
Chico Ind School Dist	chicoisdtx.net/	403
Childress Ind School Dist	childressisd.net/	74
Chillicothe ISD School Dist	cisd-tx.net/	177
Chilton Ind School Dist	chiltonisd.org/	144
China Spring Ind School Dist	chinaspringisd.net/	278
Chireno ISD School Dist	chirenoisd.org/	297
Chisum Ind School Dist	chisumisd.org/	259
Christoval Ind School Dist	christovalisd.org/	364
Cisco Independent Sch Dist	ciscoisd.net/	128
City View Ind School Dist	cityview-isd.net/	391
Clarendon Cons Ind Sch Dist	clarendonisd.net/	127
Clarksville Ind School Dist	clarksvilleisd.net/home	322
Claude Ind School Dist	claudeisd.net/	20
Clear Creek Ind School Dist	ccisd.net	158
Cleburne Ind School Dist	cleburne.k12.tx.us	247
Cleveland Ind School Dist	clevelandisd.org/	265
Clifton Ind School Dist	cliftonisd.org/	46
Clint Ind School Dist	clintweb.net/	132
Clyde Consolidated Ind SD	clyde.esc14.net	62
Coahoma Ind School Dist	coahomaisd.com/	234
Coldspring-Oakhurst Cons ISD	cocisd.org/	330
Coleman Ind School Dist	colemanisd.com/	76
College Station Ind Sch Dist	csisd.org/	55
Collinsville Ind School Dist	collinsvilleisd.org/	166
Colmesneil Ind School Dist	colmesneilisd.net	375
Colorado Ind School Dist	ccity.esc14.net	289
Columbia Brazoria ISD	cbisd.com/	52
Columbus Ind School Dist	columbusisd.org/	86
Comal Ind School Dist	comalisd.org/	87
Comanche Ind School Dist	comancheisd.net/	89
Comfort Ind School Dist	comfort.txed.net/	254
Commerce Independent Sch Dist	commerceisd.org/	236
Community Ind School Dist	communityisd.org/	78
Como Pickton Cons Ind SD	cpcisd.net/	231
Comstock Ind School Dist	comstockisd.net/	379
Connally Ind School Dist	connally.org/	279
Conroe Ind School Dist	conroeisd.net/	291
Coolidge Ind School Dist	coolidgeisd.org/	266
Cooper Ind School Dist	cooperisd.net/	119
Coppell Ind School Dist	coppellisd.com	98
Copperas Cove Ind School Dist	ccisd.com/	92
Corpus Christi Ind Sch Dist	ccisd.us/	303
Corrigan-Camden Ind Sch Dist	ccisdtx.com/	316
Corsicana Ind School Dist	cisd.org/	299
Cotton Center Ind School Dist	cottoncenterisd.org/	174
Cotulla Ind School Dist	cotullaisd.org	259
Coupland Ind School Dist	couplandisd.org/	395
Covington ISD School Dist	covingtonisd.org/	227
Crandall Ind School Dist	crandall-isd.net/	251
Crane Ind School Dist	craneisd.com/	93
Cranfills Gap ISD School Dist	cranfillsgapisd.net/	46
Crawford Ind School Dist	crawford-isd.net/	279
Crockett Co Cons Common SD	ozonaschools.net/	94
Crockett Ind School Dist	crockettisd.net/	232
Crosby Ind School Dist	crosbyisd.org/	183

DISTRICT URL INDEX

DISTRICT	URL	PAGE
Crosbyton Cons Ind Sch Dist	crosbyton.k12.tx.us/	94
Cross Plains Ind Sch Dist	crossplainsisd.net/	62
Cross Roads Ind School Dist	crossroadsisd.org/	213
Crowell Ind School Dist	crowellisd.net/	149
Crowley Ind School Dist	crowley.k12.tx.us	347
Crystal City Ind School Dist	crystalcityisd.org/	407
Cuero Ind School Dist	cueroisd.org	117
Culberson Co Allamoore Ind SD	ccaisd.net/	95
Cumby Ind School Dist	cumbyisd.net/	231
Cushing Ind School Dist	cushingisd.org/	297
Cypress-Fairbanks Ind Sch Dist	cfisd.net	183
D'Hanis Ind School Dist	dhanisisd.net/	283
Daingerfield-Lone Star Ind SD	dlsisd.org/	296
Dalhart Ind School Dist	dalhartisd.org/	95
Dallas Ind School Dist	dallasisd.org/	98
Damon Ind School Dist	damonisd.net/	53
Danbury Ind School Dist	danburyisd.org	53
Darrouzett Ind School Dist	darrouzettisd.net	267
Dawson Ind School Dist	dawson.esc17.net/	116
Dawson Ind School Dist	dawsonisd.net/	299
Dayton Ind School Dist	daytonisd.net/	265
De Kalb Ind School Dist	dekalbisd.net/	47
De Leon Ind School Dist	deleon.esc14.net/	89
Decatur Ind School Dist	decaturisd.us/decatur/site/default.asp	403
Deer Park Ind School Dist	dpisd.org/	186
Del Valle Ind School Dist	dvisd.net/	369
Dell City Ind School Dist	dellcity.schoolwires.com/dellcity/site/default.asp	234
Denison Ind School Dist	denisonisd.net/	166
Denton Ind School Dist	dentonisd.org/	120
Denver City Ind School Dist	dcisd.org/	405
DeSoto Ind School Dist	desotoisd.org	104
Detroit Ind School Dist	detroiteagles.net/	322
Devers Ind School Dist	deversisd.net/	265
Devine Ind School Dist	devineisd.org/	283
Dew Ind School Dist	dewisd.org/	156
Deweyville Ind School Dist	deweyvilleisd.com/	308
Diboll Ind School Dist	dibollisd.com/	17
Dickinson Ind School Dist	dickinsonisd.org/	159
Dilley Ind School Dist	dilleyisd.net/	157
Dime Box Ind School Dist	dimeboxisd.net/	263
Dimmitt Ind School Dist	dimmittisd.net	71
Dodd City Ind School Dist	doddcityisd.org/	145
Donna Ind School Dist	donnaisd.net/	215
Doss Consolidated Common SD	dossccsd.org/	162
Douglass Ind School Dist	douglassisd.com/pages/Douglass_Schools	297
Dripping Springs Ind Sch Dist	dsisd.txed.net/	210
Driscoll Ind School Dist	driscollisd.us/	304
Dublin Ind School Dist	dublin.k12.tx.us/	143
Dumas Ind School Dist	dumasisd.org/	295
Duncanville Ind School Dist	duncanvilleisd.org/	104
Eagle Mtn-Saginaw Ind Sch Dist	emsisd.com/emsisd	348
Eagle Pass Ind School Dist	eaglepassisd.net/	276
Eanes Ind School Dist	eanesisd.net/	370
Early Ind School Dist	earlyisd.net/	58
East Bernard Ind Sch Dist	ebisd.org/	389
East Central Ind School Dist	ecisd.net/	31
East Chambers Ind School Dist	eastchambers.net/	72
Eastland Ind School Dist	eastland.esc14.net/	129
Ector Co Ind School Dist	ectorcountyisd.org/site/default.aspx?PageID=1	129
Ector Ind School Dist	ectorisd.net/	146
Edcouch Elsa Ind School Dist	eeisd.org/	215
Eden Cons Ind School Dist	edencisd.net/	90
Edgewood Ind School Dist	eisd.net/	31
Edgewood Ind School Dist	edgewood-isd.net/default.aspx?name=dis.homepage	380
Edinburg Cons Ind School Dist	ecisd.us	216
Edna Ind School Dist	ednaisd.org/	239
El Campo Ind School Dist	ecisd.org/	389
El Paso Ind School Dist	episd.org	132
Electra Ind School Dist	electraisd.net/	391
Elgin Ind School Dist	elginisd.net	24
Elkhart Ind School Dist	elkhartisd.org/	15
Elysian Fields Ind School Dist	efisd.net/	208
Ennis Ind School Dist	ennis.k12.tx.us/	140
Era Ind School Dist	eraisd.net/	90

Texas School Directory

DISTRICT URL INDEX

DISTRICT	URL	PAGE
Etoile Ind School Dist	etoile.esc7.net	297
Eula Ind School Dist	eulaisd.us/	63
Eustace Ind School Dist	eustaceisd.net/	214
Evadale Ind School Dist	evadalek12.net/	240
Evant Ind School Dist	evantisd.org/	92
Everman Ind School Dist	eisd.org/	349
Excelsior Ind School Dist	excelsior.esc7.net/	334
Ezzell Ind School Dist	ezzellisd.org/	262
Fabens Ind School Dist	fabensisd.net/	135
Fairfield Ind School Dist	fairfield.k12.tx.us/	156
Falls City Ind School Dist	fcisd.net/	250
Fannindel Ind School Dist	fannindelisd.net/	120
Farmersville Ind School Dist	farmersvilleisd.net/	78
Farwell Ind School Dist	farwellschools.org/	314
Fayetteville Ind School Dist	fayettevilleisd.net/	147
Ferris Ind School Dist	ferrisisd.org	140
Flatonia Ind School Dist	flatoniaisd.net/	147
Florence Ind School Dist	florenceisd.net/	395
Floresville Ind School Dist	fisd.us/	400
Flour Bluff Ind School Dist	flourbluffschools.net	304
Floydada Ind School Dist	floydadaisd.esc17.net/?template=m	148
Follett Ind School Dist	follettisd.net/	267
Forestburg Ind School Dist	forestburgisd.net	290
Forney Ind School Dist	forneyisd.net/#!forney-academic-center/c253r	251
Forsan Ind School Dist	forsan.esc18.net/	234
Fort Davis Ind School Dist	fdisd.com/	241
Franklin Ind School Dist	franklinisd.net/	324
Frankston Ind School Dist	frankstonisd.net/	15
Fredericksburg Ind School Dist	fisd.org/	162
Freer Ind School Dist	freerisd.org/	128
Frenship Ind School Dist	frenship.net/	269
Friendswood Ind Sch Dist	fisdk12.net/	160
Friona Ind School Dist	frionaisd.com	315
Frisco Ind School Dist	friscoisd.org/	78
Frost Ind School Dist	frostisd.org/	299
Fruitvale Ind School Dist	fruitvaleisd.com/	380
Ft Bend Ind School Dist	fortbendisd.com/	149
Ft Elliott Cons Ind Sch Dist	fecisd.net/	390
Ft Hancock Ind School Dist	fhisd.net/	234
Ft Sam Houston Ind School Dist	fshisd.net/	32
Ft Stockton Ind School Dist	fsisd.net	315
Ft Worth Ind School Dist	fwisd.org/	349
Gainesville Ind School Dist	gainesvilleisd.org/	91
Galena Park Ind School Dist	galenaparkisd.com/	186
Galveston Ind School Dist	gisd.org	160
Ganado Ind School Dist	ganadoisd.org/	239
Garland Ind School Dist	garlandisd.net	105
Garner Ind School Dist	garnerisd.net	312
Garrison Ind School Dist	garrisonisd.com/	297
Gary Ind School Dist	garyisd.org/	311
Gatesville Ind School Dist	gatesvilleisd.org/	92
Gause Ind School Dist	gauseisd.net/	287
George West Ind School Dist	gwisd.esc2.net/	268
Georgetown Ind School Dist	georgetownisd.org/	395
Gholson Ind School Dist	gholsonisd.org/	279
Giddings Ind School Dist	giddingsisd.net/	263
Gilmer Ind School Dist	gilmerisd.org/	376
Gladewater Ind School Dist	gladewaterisd.com	169
Glasscock Co Ind School Dist	gckats.net/	163
Glen Rose Ind School Dist	grisd.net	340
Godley Ind School Dist	godleyisd.net/	247
Gold-Burg Ind School Dist	goldburgisd.net/	290
Goldthwaite Consolidated ISD	goldisd.net/	288
Goliad Ind School Dist	goliadisd.org/	163
Gonzales Ind School Dist	gonzalesisd.net/	164
Goodrich Ind School Dist	goodrichisd.net/	316
Goose Creek Cons Ind Sch Dist	gccisd.net/	187
Gordon Ind School Dist	gordonisd.net/	310
Gorman Ind School Dist	gorman.esc14.net/	129
Grady Ind School Dist	gradyisd.org/	274
Graford Ind School Dist	grafordisd.net/	310
Graham Ind School Dist	grahamisd.com/	406
Granbury Ind School Dist	granburyisd.org/	230
Grand Prairie Ind School Dist	gpisd.org/site/default.aspx?PageID=1	107

School Year 2019-2020   800-333-8802   TX-W5

DISTRICT URL INDEX

Market Data Retrieval

DISTRICT	URL	PAGE
Grand Saline Ind School Dist	grandsalineisd.net/	380
Grandfalls-Royalty Ind SD	grisd.com/	385
Grandview Ind School Dist	gvisd.org/	248
Grandview-Hopkins Ind Sch Dist	gvhisd.net/	164
Granger Ind School Dist	grangerisd.net/	396
Grape Creek Ind School Dist	grapecreekisd.net/	364
Grapeland Ind School Dist	grapelandisd.net/	232
Grapevine-Colleyville Ind SD	gcisd-k12.org/	353
Greenville Ind School Dist	greenvilleisd.com/	236
Greenwood Ind School Dist	greenwood.esc18.net	285
Gregory-Portland Ind Sch Dist	g-pisd.org/	330
Groesbeck Ind School Dist	groesbeck.k12.tx.us	267
Groom Ind School Dist	groomisd.net/	69
Groveton Ind School Dist	grovetonisd.net/	374
Gruver Ind School Dist	gruverisd.net/	176
Gunter Ind School Dist	gunterisd.org/	166
Gustine Ind School Dist	gustine.esc14.net/	90
Guthrie Common School Dist	guthriejags.com/	257
Hale Center Ind School Dist	hcisdowls.net/	175
Hallettsville Ind Sch Dist	hisdbrahmas.org/	262
Hallsburg Ind School Dist	hallsburgisd.com/	279
Hallsville Ind School Dist	hisd.com	208
Hamilton Ind School Dist	hamiltonisd.org/	176
Hamlin Ind School Dist	hamlin.esc14.net/	249
Hamshire Fannett Ind Sch Dist	hfisd.net/	242
Happy Ind School Dist	happyisd.net/	342
Hardin Ind School Dist	hardinisd.net/	265
Hardin Jefferson Ind Sch Dist	hjisd.net/	177
Harlandale Ind School Dist	harlandale.net/	32
Harleton Ind School Dist	harletonisd.net/	208
Harlingen Cons Ind School Dist	hcisd.org/	64
Harmony Ind School Dist	harmonyisd.net/	376
Harper Ind School Dist	harper.txed.net/	163
Harrold Ind School Dist	harroldisd.net/	393
Hart Ind School Dist	hartisd.net/	71
Hartley Ind School Dist	hartleyisd.net/	209
Harts Bluff Ind School Dist	hbisd.net/	363
Haskell Cons Ind School Dist	haskell.esc14.net/	210
Hawkins Ind School Dist	hawkinsisd.org/	404
Hawley Ind School Dist	hawley.esc14.net/	249
Hays Cons Ind School Dist	hayscisd.net/	211
Hearne Ind School Dist	hearne.k12.tx.us/	325
Hedley Ind School Dist	hedleyisd.net/	127
Hemphill Ind School Dist	hemphill.esc7.net/	329
Hempstead Ind School Dist	hempsteadisd.org/	384
Henderson Ind School Dist	hendersonisd.org/	327
Henrietta Ind School Dist	henrietta-isd.net/	74
Hereford Ind School Dist	herefordisd.net/	119
Hermleigh Ind School Dist	hermleigh.esc14.net/	333
Hico Ind School Dist	hico-isd.net/	176
Hidalgo Ind School Dist	hidalgo-isd.org/	217
Higgins Ind School Dist	higginsisd.net/	268
High Island Ind Sch Dist	highislandisd.com/	160
Highland Ind School Dist	highland.esc14.net/	301
Highland Park Ind Sch Dist	hpisd.org	108
Highland Park Ind School Dist	hpisd.net	319
Hillsboro Ind School Dist	hillsboroisd.org/	227
Hitchcock Ind School Dist	hitchcockisd.org/	160
Holland Ind School Dist	hollandisd.org/	27
Holliday Ind School Dist	hollidayisd.net/	19
Hondo Ind School Dist	hondoisd.net/	284
Honey Grove Ind School Dist	honeygroveisd.net/	146
Hooks Ind School Dist	hooksisd.net/	48
Houston Ind School Dist	houstonisd.org/	188
Howe Ind School Dist	howeisd.net/site/default.aspx?PageID=1	166
Hubbard Ind School Dist	hubbardisd.net/	48
Hubbard Ind School Dist	hubbardisd.com/	227
Huckabay Ind School Dist	hisd.us/hisd/site/default.asp	143
Hudson Ind School Dist	hudsonisd.org/	17
Huffman Ind School Dist	huffmanisd.net/	195
Hughes Springs Ind Sch Dist	hsisd.net	70
Hull Daisetta Ind School Dist	hdisd.net/	266
Humble Ind School Dist	humble.k12.tx.us	195
Hunt Ind School Dist	huntisd.org/	255

Texas School Directory

DISTRICT URL INDEX

DISTRICT	URL	PAGE
Huntington Ind School Dist	huntingtonisd.com	17
Huntsville Ind School Dist	huntsville-isd.org/	383
Hurst-Euless-Bedford ISD	hebisd.edu	353
Hutto Ind School Dist	hutto.txed.net/	396
Idalou Ind School Dist	idalouisd.net/	269
Idea Public Schools	ideapublicschools.org/	217
Industrial Ind School Dist	industrialisd.org/site/default.aspx?PageID=1	240
Ingleside Ind School Dist	inglesideisd.org/	331
Ingram Ind School Dist	ingramisd.net/	255
Int'l Leadership of Texas Dist	iltexasdistrict.org/	108
Iola Ind School Dist	iolaisd.net/	172
Iowa Park Consolidated Ind SD	ipcisd.net/	392
Ira Ind School Dist	ira.esc14.net	333
Iraan-Sheffield Ind Sch Dist	isisd.esc18.net/	316
Iredell Ind School Dist	iredell-isd.com/	46
Irion Co Ind School Dist	irion-isd.org	238
Irving Ind School Dist	irvingisd.net/	109
Italy Ind School Dist	italyisd.org/	140
Itasca Ind School Dist	itascaisd.org/	228
Jacksboro Ind Sch Dist	jacksboroisd.net/	239
Jacksonville Ind School Dist	jisd.org/	72
Jarrell Ind School Dist	jarrellisd.org/	396
Jasper Ind School Dist	jasperisd.net/	240
Jayton-Girard Ind School Dist	jaytonjaybirds.com/	255
Jefferson Ind School Dist	jeffersonisd.org	274
Jim Hogg Co Ind School Dist	jhcisdpk12.org/	244
Jim Ned Cons Ind School Dist	jimned.esc14.net/	361
Joaquin Ind School Dist	joaquinisd.net/	335
Johnson City Ind School Dist	jc.txed.net/	46
Jonesboro Ind School Dist	jonesboroisd.net/	93
Joshua Ind School Dist	joshuaisd.org/	248
Jourdanton Ind School Dist	jourdantonisd.net/	20
Judson Ind School Dist	judsonisd.org/	33
Junction Ind School Dist	junctionisd.net/	256
Karnack Ind School Dist	karnackisd.org/	208
Karnes City Ind School Dist	kcisd.net	250
Katy Ind School Dist	katyisd.org/	151
Kaufman Ind School Dist	kaufmanisd.net/	252
Keene Ind School Dist	keeneisd.org/keene/site/default.asp	248
Keller Ind School Dist	kellerisd.net	354
Kelton Ind School Dist	keltonisd.com/	390
Kemp Ind School Dist	kempisd.org/	252
Kenedy Co Wide Common Sch Dist	sarita.esc2.net/	254
Kenedy Ind School Dist	kenedyisd.com/	251
Kennard Ind Sch Dist	kennardisd.net/	233
Kennedale Ind School Dist	kennedaleisd.net/Domain/8	355
Kerens Ind School Dist	kerensisd.org/	299
Kermit Ind School Dist	kermitisd.org/	401
Kerrville Ind School Dist	kerrvilleisd.net/	256
Kilgore Ind School Dist	kisd.org/	169
Killeen Ind School Dist	killeenisd.org	27
Kingsville Ind School Dist	kingsvilleisd.com/	257
Kirbyville Cons Ind Sch Dist	kirbyvillecisd.org/	241
Klein Ind School Dist	kleinisd.net/	196
Klondike Ind School Dist	klondike.esc17.net/	117
Knippa Ind School Dist	knippaisd.net/	378
Knox City-O'Brien Cons Ind SD	knoxcityschools.net/	258
Kopperl Ind School Dist	kopperlisd.org/	47
Kountze Ind School Dist	kountzeisd.org/	178
Kress Ind School Dist	kressonline.net	343
Krum Ind School Dist	krumisd.net/	122
La Feria Ind School Dist	laferiaisd.org	65
La Gloria Ind School Dist	lagloriaisd.esc2.net/	245
La Grange Ind School Dist	lgisd.net/	147
La Joya Ind School Dist	lajoyaisd.com/	219
La Porte Ind School Dist	lpisd.org/	198
La Poynor Ind School Dist	lapoynorisd.net/	214
La Pryor Ind School Dist	lapryor.net/	407
La Vega Ind School Dist	lavegaisd.org	279
La Vernia Ind School Dist	lvisd.org/	401
La Villa Ind School Dist	lavillaisd.org/	220
Lackland Ind School Dist	lacklandisd.net/	34
Lago Vista Ind School Dist	lagovistaisd.net/	370
Lake Dallas Ind School Dist	ldisd.net	122

School Year 2019-2020 800-333-8802 TX-W7

DISTRICT URL INDEX

Market Data Retrieval

DISTRICT	URL	PAGE
Lake Travis Ind School Dist	laketravis.txed.net/	370
Lake Worth Ind School Dist	lake-worth.k12.tx.us	356
Lamar Cons Ind School Dist	lcisd.org	153
Lamesa Ind School Dist	lamesa.esc17.net	117
Lampasas Ind School Dist	lisdtx.org/	261
Lancaster Ind School Dist	lancasterisd.org/	110
Laneville Ind School Dist	lanevilleisd.org/	327
Laredo Ind School Dist	laredoisd.org/	386
Lasara Ind School Dist	lasaraisd.net/	394
Latexo Ind School Dist	latexoisd.net	233
Lazbuddie Ind School Dist	lazbuddieisd.org/	315
Leakey Ind School Dist	leakeyisd.org/	322
Leander Ind School Dist	leanderisd.org/	396
Leary Ind School Dist	learyisd.net/	48
Lefors Ind School Dist	leforsisd.net/	165
Leggett Ind School Dist	leggettisd.net/	316
Leon Ind School Dist	leonisd.net	264
Leonard Ind School Dist	leonardisd.net/	146
Levelland Ind School Dist	levellandisd.net/	229
Leveretts Chapel Ind Sch Dist	leverettschapelisd.net/	328
Lewisville Ind School Dist	lisd.net	122
Lexington Ind School Dist	lexingtonisd.net/	263
Liberty Hill Ind School Dist	libertyhill.txed.net/	398
Liberty Ind School Dist	libertyisd.net/	266
Liberty-Eylau Ind School Dist	leisd.net/	48
Lindale Ind School Dist	lindaleeagles.org/	337
Linden Kildare Cons Ind SD	lkcisd.net/	70
Lindsay Ind School Dist	lindsayisd.org	91
Lingleville Ind School Dist	lingleville.k12.tx.us/lingleville/site/default.asp	143
Lipan Ind School Dist	lipanindians.net/	230
Little Cypress Mauriceville SD	lcmcisd.org/	308
Little Elm Ind School Dist	littleelmisd.net/	124
Littlefield Ind School Dist	littlefield.k12.tx.us/	260
Livingston Ind School Dist	livingstonisd.com/	316
Llano Ind School Dist	llanoisd.org/	268
Lockhart Ind School Dist	lockhartisd.org/	61
Lockney Independent Sch Dist	lockneyisd.net/	149
Lohn Ind School Dist	lohnisd.net/	277
Lometa Ind School Dist	lometaisd.org/	262
London Ind School Dist	londonisd.net/	305
Lone Oak Ind School Dist	loisd.net/	236
Longview Ind School Dist	lisd.org	169
Loop Ind School Dist	loopisd.net/	157
Loraine Ind School Dist	loraine.esc14.net/	289
Lorena Ind School Dist	lorenaisd.net/	280
Lorenzo Ind School Dist	lorenzoisd.net/	94
Los Fresnos Cons Ind Sch Dist	lfcisd.net/	65
Louise Ind School Dist	louiseisd.net/	389
Lovejoy Ind School Dist	lovejoyisd.net	80
Lovelady Ind School Dist	loveladyisd.net/	233
Lubbock Ind School Dist	lubbockisd.org/	269
Lubbock-Cooper Ind Sch Dist	lcisd.net	271
Lueders-Avoca Ind School Dist	laisd.esc14.net/	250
Lufkin Ind School Dist	lufkinisd.org	18
Luling Ind School Dist	luling.txed.net/	61
Lumberton Ind School Dist	lumberton.k12.tx.us	178
Lyford Cons Ind School Dist	lyfordcisd.net/	394
Lytle Ind School Dist	lytleisd.org/	21
Mabank Ind School Dist	mabankisd.net/	252
Madisonville Cons ISD	madisonvillecisd.org/	273
Magnolia Ind School Dist	magnoliaisd.org/	292
Malakoff Ind School Dist	malakoffisd.org/	214
Malone Independent School Dist	maloneisd.org	228
Malta Ind School Dist	maltaisd.net/	48
Manor Ind School Dist	manorisd.net	371
Mansfield Ind School Dist	mansfieldisd.org	356
Marathon Ind School Dist	marathonisd.net/	56
Marble Falls Ind School Dist	mfisd.ss3.sharpschool.com/	60
Marfa Ind School Dist	marfaisd.com/	320
Marion Ind School Dist	marionisd.net/	172
Marlin Ind School Dist	marlinisd.org/	144
Marshall Ind School Dist	marshallisd.com/	209
Mart Ind School Dist	martisd.org/	280
Martin's Mill Ind Sch Dist	martinsmillisd.net/	381

Texas School Directory

DISTRICT URL INDEX

DISTRICT	URL	PAGE
Martinsville Ind School Dist	martinsvilleisd.com/	298
Mason Ind School Dist	masonisd.net	275
Matagorda Ind School Dist	matagordaisd.org	275
Mathis Ind School Dist	mathisisd.org/	331
Maud Ind School Dist	maudisd.net/	49
May Ind School Dist	mayisd.com/	59
Maypearl Ind School Dist	maypearlisd.org/	141
McAllen Ind School Dist	mcallenisd.org/	220
McCamey Ind School Dist	mcisd.esc18.net/	377
McDade Ind School Dist	mcdadeisd.org/	24
McGregor Ind School Dist	mcgregor-isd.org/	280
McKinney Ind School Dist	mckinneyisd.net/	80
McLean Ind School Dist	mcleanisd.com/	165
McLeod Ind School Dist	mcleodisd.net/	70
McMullen Co Ind Sch Dist	mcisd.us/	283
Meadow Ind School Dist	meadowisd.net	362
Medina Ind School Dist	medinaisd.org/	23
Medina Valley Ind School Dist	mvisd.com/	284
Melissa Ind School Dist	melissaisd.org/	81
Memphis Ind School Dist	memphisisd.net/	175
Menard Ind School Dist	menardisd.net/	285
Mercedes Ind School Dist	misdtx.net/	221
Meridian Ind School Dist	meridianisd.org/	47
Merkel Ind School Dist	merkel.esc14.net/	361
Mesquite Ind School Dist	mesquiteisd.org	110
Mexia Ind School Dist	mexiaisd.net/	267
Meyersville Ind School Dist	meyersvilleisd.org/	118
Miami Ind School Dist	miamiisd.net/	324
Midland Ind School Dist	midlandisd.net/Domain/1	285
Midlothian Ind School Dist	misd.gs/	141
Midway Ind School Dist	midwayisd.net/	74
Midway Ind School Dist	midwayisd.org/	280
Milano Ind School Dist	milanoisd.net/	287
Mildred Ind School Dist	mildredisd.org/	300
Miles Ind School Dist	miles.netxv.net/	326
Milford Ind School Dist	milfordisd.org/	141
Miller Grove Ind School Dist	mgisd.net/	231
Millsap Ind School Dist	millsapisd.net/	312
Mineola Ind School Dist	mineolaisd.net/	404
Mineral Wells Ind School Dist	mwisd.net	310
Mission Cons Ind School Dist	mcisd.net/	222
Monahans-Wickett-Pyote ISD	mwpisd.esc18.net/	385
Montague Ind School Dist	montagueisd.org	290
Monte Alto Ind School Dist	montealtoisd.org/	222
Montgomery Ind School Dist	misd.org	293
Moody Ind School Dist	moodyisd.org	281
Moran Ind School Dist	moran.esc14.net/	334
Morgan Ind School Dist	morganisd.org/	47
Morgan Mill Ind School Dist	mmisd.us/	144
Morton Ind School Dist	mortonisd.net/	75
Motley Co Ind School Dist	motleyco.org/	296
Moulton Ind School Dist	moultonisd.net/	262
Mt Calm Ind School Dist	mcisd1.org/	228
Mt Enterprise Ind School Dist	meisd.esc7.net/	328
Mt Pleasant Ind School Dist	mpisd.net/	363
Mt Vernon Ind School Dist	mtvernonisd.net/	155
Muenster Ind School Dist	muensterisd.net/	91
Muleshoe Ind School Dist	muleshoeisd.net/	22
Mullin Ind School Dist	mullinisd.net/	288
Mumford Ind School Dist	mumford.k12.tx.us/	56
Munday Consolidated Ind SD	mundaycisd.net/	258
Murchison Ind Sch Dist	murchisonisd.com/	214
Nacogdoches Ind School Dist	nacisd.org/	298
Natalia Ind School Dist	nataliaisd.net/	284
Navarro Ind School Dist	nisd.us/	173
Navasota Ind School Dist	navasotaisd.org	172
Nazareth Ind School Dist	nazarethisd.net/	71
Neches Ind School Dist	nechesisd.com/#!	15
Nederland Ind School Dist	nederland.k12.tx.us/	242
Needville Ind School Dist	needvilleisd.com	154
New Boston Ind School Dist	nbschools.net/	49
New Braunfels Ind School Dist	nbisd.org/default.aspx?name=dis.homepage	88
New Caney Ind School Dist	newcaneyisd.org/	293
New Deal Ind School Dist	ndisd.net/	271

School Year 2019-2020   800-333-8802

DISTRICT URL INDEX

Market Data Retrieval

DISTRICT	URL	PAGE
New Diana Ind School Dist	ndisd.org/	376
New Home Ind School Dist	newhomeisd.org/	273
New Summerfield Ind Sch Dist	nsisd.sprnet.org/	73
New Waverly Ind School Dist	new-waverly.k12.tx.us/	383
Newcastle Ind School Dist	newcastle-isd.net/	406
Newton Ind School Dist	newtonisd.net/	301
Nixon-Smiley Cons Ind Sch Dist	nixonsmiley.net/	164
Nocona Ind School Dist	noconaisd.net/	290
Nordheim Ind School Dist	nordheimisd.org/	118
Normangee Ind School Dist	normangeeisd.org/	264
North East Ind School Dist	neisd.net/	34
North Hopkins Ind School Dist	northhopkins.net/	231
North Lamar Ind School Dist	northlamar.net/	259
North Zulch Ind School Dist	nzisd.org/	274
Northside Ind School Dist	nisd.net	36
Northside Ind School Dist	northsideisd.us/	393
Northwest Ind School Dist	nisdtx.org	124
Nueces Canyon Cons Ind SD	nccisd.net/	131
Nursery ISD School Dist	nurseryisd.org/	382
O'Donnell Ind School Dist	odonnell.esc17.net/	273
Oakwood Ind School Dist	oakwoodisd.net/	264
Odem-Edroy Ind School Dist	oeisd.org/	331
Oglesby Ind School Dist	oglesbyisd.net/	93
Olfen Ind School Dist	olfenisd.net/	327
Olney Ind School Dist	olneyisd.net/	406
Olton Ind School Dist	oltonisd.net/	261
Onalaska Ind School Dist	onalaskaisd.net/vnews/display.v/SEC/JSHS	317
Orange Grove Ind School Dist	ogisd.net/	245
Orangefield Ind School Dist	orangefieldisd.net/	309
Ore City Ind School Dist	ocisd.net/	376
Overton Ind School Dist	overtonisd.net/	328
Paducah Ind School Dist	paducahisd.org/	93
Paint Creek Ind School Dist	pcisd.org/	210
Paint Rock Ind School Dist	paintrock.netxv.net/	90
Palacios Ind School Dist	palaciosisd.org/	275
Palestine Ind School Dist	palestineschools.org/	15
Palmer Ind School Dist	palmer-isd.org/	141
Palo Pinto Ind Sch Dist 906	palopintoisd.net/	310
Pampa Ind School Dist	pampaisd.net	165
Panhandle Ind School Dist	panhandleisd.net/	69
Panther Creek Cons Ind SD	pcreek.net/	76
Paradise Ind School Dist	pisd.net	403
Paris Ind School Dist	parisisd.net	260
Pasadena Ind School Dist	pasadenaisd.org/	198
Patton Springs Ind School Dist	pattonsprings.net/	126
Pawnee Ind School Dist	pawneeisd.net/	25
Pearland Ind School Dist	pearlandisd.org	53
Pearsall Ind School Dist	pearsallisd.org/	157
Peaster Ind School Dist	peaster.net/	313
Pecos-Barstow-Toyah Ind SD	pbtisd.esc18.net/	323
Penelope ISD School Dist	penelopeisd.org/	228
Perrin-Whitt Cons Ind Sch Dist	pwcisd.net	239
Perryton Ind School Dist	perrytonisd.com/	307
Petersburg Ind School Dist	petersburgisd.net/	175
Petrolia Cons Ind School Dist	petroliaisd.org/	74
Pettus Ind School Dist	pettusisd.org/	25
Pewitt Cons Ind School Dist	pewittcisd.net/	296
Pflugerville Ind School Dist	pfisd.net/	371
Pharr-San Juan-Alamo Ind SD	psjaisd.us/	223
Pilot Point Ind School Dist	pilotpointisd.com/	125
Pine Tree Ind School Dist	ptisd.org/	170
Pittsburg Ind School Dist	pittsburgisd.net/	68
Plains Ind School Dist	plainsisd.net/	405
Plainview Ind School Dist	plainview.k12.tx.us	175
Plano Ind School Dist	pisd.edu/	82
Pleasant Grove Ind School Dist	pgisd.net/	49
Pleasanton Ind School Dist	pisd.us/	21
Plemons-Stinnett-Phillips CISD	pspcisd.net/	238
Point Isabel Ind Sch Dist	pi-isd.net/	66
Ponder Ind School Dist	ponderisd.net/	125
Poolville Ind School Dist	poolville.net/	313
Port Aransas Ind School Dist	paisd.net/	305
Port Arthur Ind School Dist	paisd.org	243
Port Neches-Groves Ind SD	pngisd.org/	243

Texas School Directory

DISTRICT URL INDEX

DISTRICT	URL	PAGE
Post Ind School Dist	postisd.net/	162
Poteet Ind School Dist	poteet.k12.tx.us/	21
Poth Ind School Dist	pothisd.us/	401
Pottsboro Ind School Dist	pottsboroisd.org/	167
Prairie Lea Ind School Dist	prairielea.txed.net/	61
Prairie Valley Ind School Dist	prairievalleyisd.net/	290
Prairiland Ind School Dist	prairiland.net/	260
Premont Ind School Dist	premontisd.net/	246
Presidio Ind School Dist	presidio-isd.net/	320
Priddy Ind School Dist	priddyisd.net/	289
Princeton Ind School Dist	princetonisd.net/	84
Pringle-Morse Cons ISD	pringlemorsecisd.net/	177
Progreso Ind School Dist	progreso.schooldesk.net/	224
Prosper Ind School Dist	prosper-isd.net	84
Quanah Ind School Dist	qisd.net/	177
Queen City Ind School Dist	qcisd.net/	70
Quinlan Ind School Dist	quinlanisd.net/	237
Quitman Ind School Dist	quitmanisd.net/	404
Rains Ind School Dist	rainsisd.org/	320
Ralls Ind School Dist	rallsisd.org/	94
Ramirez Common School Dist	ramirezcsd.esc2.net/	128
Randolph Field Ind School Dist	rfisd.net/	39
Ranger Ind School Dist	ranger.esc14.net/	129
Rankin Ind School Dist	rankinisd.net	377
Raymondville Ind Sch Dist	raymondvilleisd.org/	394
Reagan Co Ind School Dist	reagancountyisd.net/	321
Red Lick Ind School Dist	redlickisd.com/	49
Red Oak Ind School Dist	redoakisd.org/	142
Redwater Ind School Dist	redwaterisd.org/	49
Refugio Ind School Dist	refugioisd.net/	323
Ricardo Ind School Dist	ricardoisd.us/	257
Rice Cons Ind School Dist	ricecisd.org	87
Rice Ind School Dist	rice-isd.org/	300
Richards Ind School Dist	richardsisd.net/	172
Richardson Ind School Dist	risd.org/group/schools/schools_main.html	112
Richland Springs Ind Sch Dist	rscoyotes.net/	332
Riesel Ind School Dist	rieselisd.org/	281
Rio Grande City Ind Sch Dist	rgccisd.org/	340
Rio Hondo Ind School Dist	riohondoisd.net/	66
Rio Vista Ind School Dist	rvisd.net/	248
Rising Star Ind Sch Dist	risingstarisd.org/	129
River Road Ind School Dist	rrisd.net/	319
Rivercrest Ind School Dist	rivercrestisd.net/	322
Riviera Ind School Dist	rivieraisd.us/	258
Robert Lee Ind School Dist	rlisd.net	75
Robinson Ind School Dist	risdweb.org/	281
Robstown Ind School Dist	robstownisd.org/	305
Roby Cons Ind School Dist	robycisd.org/	148
Rochelle Ind School Dist	rochelleisd.net/	278
Rockdale Ind School Dist	rockdaleisd.net/	287
Rocksprings Ind School Dist	rockspringsisd.net/	131
Rockwall Ind School Dist	rockwallisd.com	325
Rogers Ind School Dist	rogersisd.org/	28
Roma Ind School Dist	romaisd.com/	341
Roosevelt Ind School Dist	roosevelt.k12.tx.us/	271
Ropes Ind School Dist	ropesisd.us/	229
Roscoe Collegiate Ind Sch Dist	roscoe.esc14.net/default.aspx?name=risd.home	301
Rosebud-Lott Ind School Dist	rlisd.org	145
Rotan Ind School Dist	rotan.org/	148
Round Rock Ind School Dist	roundrockisd.org/	398
Round Top-Carmine Ind Sch Dist	rtcisd.net/	147
Royal Ind School Dist	royal-isd.net/	384
Royse City Ind School Dist	rcisd.org/	326
Rule Ind School Dist	rule.esc14.net/	210
Runge Ind School Dist	rungeisd.org/	251
Rusk Ind School Dist	ruskisd.net/	73
S & S Cons Ind School Dist	sscisd.net/	167
Sabinal Ind School Dist	sabinalisd.net/	378
Sabine Ind School Dist	sabineisd.org/	170
Sabine Pass Ind School Dist	sabinepass.net/	244
Salado Ind School Dist	saladoisd.org/	29
Saltillo Ind School Dist	saltilloisd.net/	231
Sam Rayburn Ind School Dist	srisd.org	146
San Angelo Ind School Dist	saisd.org	364

School Year 2019-2020   800-333-8802   TX-W11

DISTRICT URL INDEX

Market Data Retrieval

DISTRICT	URL	PAGE
San Antonio Ind School Dist	saisd.net/main/	39
San Augustine Ind School Dist	saisd.us/	329
San Benito Cons Ind Sch Dist	sbcisd.net/	66
San Diego Ind School Dist	sdisd.esc2.net/	128
San Elizario Ind School Dist	seisd.net/	135
San Felipe-Del Rio Cons Ind SD	sfdr-cisd.org	379
San Isidro Ind School Dist	sanisidroisd.org/	341
San Marcos Cons Ind Sch Dist	smcisd.net/	211
San Perlita Ind School Dist	spisd.org/	394
San Saba Ind School Dist	san-saba.net/	332
San Vicente Ind School Dist	svisd.com/	57
Sands Consolidated ISD	sands.esc17.net/	117
Sanford-Fritch Ind School Dist	sfisd.net/	238
Sanger Ind School Dist	sangerisd.net/	126
Santa Anna Ind School Dist	santaannaisd.net/	76
Santa Fe Ind School Dist	sfisd.org/	161
Santa Gertrudis Ind Sch Dist	sgisd.net/	258
Santa Maria Ind School Dist	smisd.net/	67
Santa Rosa Ind School Dist	srtx.org/	67
Santo Ind School Dist	santoisd.net	310
Savoy Ind School Dist	savoyisd.org/	146
Schertz-Cibolo-Univ City ISD	scuc.txed.net	173
Schleicher Co Ind Sch Dist	scisd.net/	333
School of Excellence In Ed	excellence-sa.org/	42
Schulenburg Ind School Dist	schulenburgisd.net/	147
Scurry Rosser Ind School Dist	scurry-rosser.com	253
Seagraves Ind School Dist	seagravesisd.net/	157
Sealy Ind School Dist	sealyisd.com/	22
Seguin Ind School Dist	seguin.k12.tx.us/	173
Seminole Ind School Dist	seminoleisd.net	158
Seymour Ind School Dist	seymour-isd.net/	24
Shallowater Ind School Dist	shallowaterisd.net/	272
Shamrock Ind School Dist	shamrockisd.net/	390
Sharyland Ind School Dist	sharylandisd.org	224
Shelbyville Ind School Dist	shelbyville.k12.tx.us/	335
Sheldon Ind School Dist	sheldonisd.com	200
Shepherd Ind School Dist	shepherdisd.net/	330
Sherman Ind School Dist	shermanisd.net	167
Shiner Ind School Dist	shinerisd.net/	262
Sidney Ind School Dist	sidney.esc14.net/	90
Sierra Blanca Ind School Dist	sierrablancaisd.net/	234
Silsbee Ind School Dist	silsbeeisd.org/	178
Silverton Ind School Dist	silvertonisd.net/	57
Simms Ind School Dist	simmsisd.net/	50
Sinton Ind School Dist	sintonisd.net	332
Sivells Bend Ind School Dist	sivellsbendisd.net	91
Skidmore Tynan Ind SD	stbobcats.net/	25
Slaton Ind School Dist	slatonisd.net/	272
Slidell Ind School Dist	slidellisd.net/	403
Slocum ISD School Dist	slocumisd.org/	16
Smithville Ind School Dist	smithvilleisd.org/	24
Smyer Ind School Dist	smyer-isd.org	229
Snook Ind School Dist	snookisd.com/	59
Snyder Ind School Dist	snyderisd.net/	333
Socorro Ind School Dist	sisd.net	135
Somerset Ind School Dist	sisdk12.edlioschool.com/	42
Somerville Ind School Dist	somervilleisd.org/	60
Sonora Ind School Dist	sonoraisd.net/	342
South San Antonio Ind Sch Dist	southsanisd.net/	42
South Texas Ind School Dist	stisd.net	67
Southland Ind School Dist	southlandisd.net/	162
Southside Ind School Dist	southsideisd.org/	43
Southwest Ind School Dist	swisd.net/	43
Spearman Ind School Dist	spearmanisd.net/	177
Splendora Ind School Dist	splendoraisd.org/	294
Spring Branch Ind School Dist	springbranchisd.com/	200
Spring Creek Ind School Dist	springcreekisd.net/	238
Spring Hill Ind School Dist	shisd.net/	170
Spring Ind School Dist	springisd.org/	202
Springlake-Earth Ind Sch Dist	springlake-earth.org	261
Springtown Ind School Dist	springtownisd.net/	313
Spur Ind School Dist	spurbulldogs.com/	127
Spurger Ind School Dist	spurgerisd.org/	375
St Jo Ind School Dist	saintjoisd.net/	290

TX-W12 800-333-8802 School Year 2019-2020

Texas School Directory

DISTRICT URL INDEX

DISTRICT	URL	PAGE
Stafford Municipal Sch Dist	staffordmsd.org/	154
Stamford Ind School Dist	stamford.esc14.net/	250
Stanton Ind School Dist	stanton.esc18.net/	274
Stephenville Ind School Dist	sville.us/	144
Sterling City Ind School Dist	sterlingcityisd.net/	342
Stockdale Ind School Dist	stockdaleisd.org/	401
Stratford Ind School Dist	stratfordisd.net/	336
Strawn Ind School Dist	strawnschool.net/	311
Sudan Ind School Dist	sudanisd.net/	261
Sulphur Bluff Ind School Dist	sulphurbluffisd.net/	232
Sulphur Springs Ind Sch Dist	ssisd.net/	232
Sundown Ind School Dist	sundownisd.com/	229
Sunnyvale Ind School Dist	sunnyvaleisd.com/	113
Sunray Ind School Dist	region16.net/sunrayisd/	296
Sweeny Ind School Dist	sweenyisd.org/	54
Sweet Home Ind School Dist	sweethomeisd.org/	262
Sweetwater ISD School Dist	sweetwaterisd.net	301
Taft Ind School Dist	taftisd.net/	332
Tahoka Ind School Dist	tahokaisd.us/	273
Tarkington Ind School Dist	tarkingtonisd.net/	266
Tatum Ind School Dist	tatumisd.org/	328
Taylor Ind School Dist	taylorisd.org/	399
Teague Ind School Dist	teagueisd.org/	156
Temple Ind School Dist	tisd.org/	29
Tenaha Ind School Dist	tenahaisd.com/	335
Terlingua Common School Dist	terlinguacsd.com/	57
Terrell Co Ind School Dist	terrell.esc18.net/	362
Terrell Ind School Dist	terrellisd.org/	253
Texarkana Ind School Dist	txkisd.net/	50
Texas City Ind School Dist	tcisd.org/	161
Texhoma Ind School Dist	texhomaisd.net/	336
Texline Ind School Dist	texlineisd.net/	95
Thorndale Ind School Dist	thorndale.txed.net	288
Thrall Ind School Dist	thrallisd.com/	400
Three Rivers Ind School Dist	trisd.org/	268
Three Way Ind School Dist	twisd.us/	144
Throckmorton Ind School Dist	throck.org/	363
Tidehaven Ind School Dist	tidehavenisd.com	276
Timpson Ind School Dist	timpsonisd.com/	335
Tioga Ind School Dist	tiogaisd.net/	167
Tolar Ind School Dist	tolarisd.org/tolarisd/site/default.asp	230
Tom Bean Ind School Dist	tombean-isd.org	168
Tomball Ind School Dist	tomballisd.net/	203
Tornillo Ind School Dist	tisd.us/	137
Trent Ind School Dist	trentisd.org/	361
Trenton Ind School Dist	trentonisd.com/	146
Trinidad Ind School Dist	trinidadisd.com/	214
Trinity Ind School Dist	trinityisd.net/	374
Troup Ind School Dist	troupisd.org/	337
Troy Ind School Dist	troyisd.org/	29
Tulia Ind School Dist	tuliaisd.net/	343
Tuloso-Midway Ind School Dist	tmisd.us/	305
Turkey-Quitaque Cons Ind SD	valleypatriots.com/	176
Tyler Ind School Dist	tylerisd.org/	337
Union Grove Ind School Dist	uniongroveisd.org/	377
Union Hill Ind School Dist	uhisd.com/	377
United Ind School Dist	uisd.net/	387
UT Tyler University Acad Dist	uttia.org/	338
Utopia Ind School Dist	utopiaisd.net/	378
Uvalde Cons Ind School Dist	ucisd.net/	378
Valentine Ind School Dist	valentineisd.com/	241
Valley Mills Ind School Dist	vmisd.net/	47
Valley View Ind School Dist	vviewisd.net/	225
Valley View ISD-Cooke Co	vvisd.net/	91
Van Alstyne Ind School Dist	vanalstyneisd.org/	168
Van Ind School Dist	vanschools.org/	381
Van Vleck Ind School Dist	vvisd.org/	276
Vega Ind School Dist	vegalonghorn.com/	307
Venus Ind School Dist	venusisd.net/	249
Veribest Ind School Dist	veribestisd.net/	365
Vernon Ind School Dist	vernonisd.org/	393
Victoria Ind School Dist	visd.com	382
Vidor Ind School Dist	vidorisd.org/	309
Vysehrad Ind School Dist	vysehrad.k12.tx.us/	263

School Year 2019-2020 800-333-8802

DISTRICT URL INDEX

Market Data Retrieval

DISTRICT	URL	PAGE
Waco Ind School Dist	wacoisd.org	281
Waelder Ind School Dist	waelderisd.org/	164
Walcott Ind School Dist	walcottisd.com/	119
Wall Ind School Dist	wallisd.net/	365
Waller Ind School Dist	wallerisd.net/	384
Walnut Bend Ind School Dist	walnutbendisd.net/site/default.aspx?PageID=1	92
Walnut Springs Ind Sch Dist	walnutspringsisd.net/	47
Warren Ind School Dist	warrenisd.net/	375
Waskom Ind School Dist	waskomisd.net/	209
Water Valley Ind School Dist	wvisd.net/Page/1	365
Waxahachie Ind School Dist	wisd.org/	142
Weatherford Ind School Dist	weatherfordisd.com/	313
Webb Cons Ind School Dist	webbcisd.org/	388
Weimar Ind School Dist	weimarisd.org	87
Wellington Ind School Dist	wellingtonisd.net/	86
Wellman Union Ind School Dist	wellman.esc17.net/	362
Wells Ind School Dist	wells.esc7.net	73
Weslaco Ind School Dist	wisd.us/	225
West Hardin Co Cons Sch Dist	westhardin.org/	178
West Ind School Dist	westisd.net/	282
West Orange-Cove Cons ISD	woccisd.net/	309
West Oso Ind School Dist	westosoisd.net/	306
West Rusk Co Cons Ind Sch Dist	westrusk.esc7.net	328
West Sabine Ind Sch Dist	westsabineisd.net/	329
Westbrook Ind School Dist	westbrookisd.com/	289
Westhoff Ind School Dist	westhoffisd.org/	118
Westphalia Ind School Dist	westphaliaisd.org/	145
Westwood Ind School Dist	westwoodisd.net/	16
Wharton Ind School Dist	whartonisd.net/	390
Wheeler Ind School Dist	wheelerschools.net/	391
White Deer Ind School Dist	whitedeerisd.net/	69
White Oak Ind School Dist	woisd.net/isd/	171
White Settlement Ind Sch Dist	wsisd.com/	357
Whiteface Con Ind School Dist	whitefaceschool.net/	75
Whitehouse Ind School Dist	whitehouseisd.org/	338
Whitesboro Ind School Dist	whitesboroisd.org/	168
Whitewright Ind School Dist	whitewrightisd.com/	168
Whitharral Ind School Dist	whitharralisd.org/	230
Whitney Ind School Dist	whitney.k12.tx.us/	228
Wichita Falls Ind School Dist	wfisd.net/	392
Wildorado Ind Sch Dist	wildoradoisd.org/	308
Willis Ind School Dist	willisisd.org/	294
Wills Point Ind School Dist	wpisd.com/	381
Wilson Ind School Dist	wilson.esc17.net/	273
Wimberley Ind School Dist	wimberleyisd.net/	212
Windthorst Ind School Dist	windthorstisd.net/	20
Wink Loving Ind School Dist	wlisd.net/	402
Winnsboro Ind School Dist	winnsboroisd.org/	405
Winona Ind School Dist	winonaisd.org/home/	339
Winters Ind School Dist	wintersisd.org/	327
Woden Ind School Dist	wodenisd.org/	298
Wolfe City Ind School Dist	wcisd.net/	237
Woodsboro Ind School Dist	wisd.net	324
Woodson Ind School Dist	woodsonisd.net/	363
Woodville Ind School Dist	woodvilleeagles.org/	375
Wortham Ind School Dist	worthamisd.org/	156
Wylie Ind School Dist	wylieisd.net	84
Wylie Ind School Dist	wyliebulldogs.org/	361
Yantis Ind School Dist	yantisisd.net/	405
Yoakum Ind School Dist	yoakumisd.net	118
Yorktown Ind School Dist	yisd.org/	118
Ysleta Ind School Dist	yisd.net/	137
Zapata Co Ind School Dist	zcisd.org/	406
Zavalla Ind School Dist	zavallaisd.org/	18
Zephyr Ind School Dist	zephyrisd.net/	59

MDR School Directory
CHARTER MANAGEMENT ORGANIZATION (CMO) INDEX

CMO No.	PID	CMO Name	Address	Phone
001	11912383	Estem Public Charter Schools	200 River Market Ave Ste 225, Little Rock AR 72201	(501) 324-9200
002	11916092	KIPP Delta Public Schools	415 Ohio, Helena AR 72342	(870) 753-9035
003	12319502	Lisa Academy Foundation	10825 Financial Centre Pkwy, Little Rock AR 72211	(501) 916-9450
004	11912826	Academy of Tucson Inc	10720 E 22nd St, Tucson AZ 85748	(520) 733-0096
005	11914305	Accelerated Learning Ctr	4105 E Shea Blvd, Phoenix AZ 85028	(602) 485-0309
006	11914288	Allen-Cochran Enterprises	1700 E Elliot Rd Ste 9, Tempe AZ 85284	(480) 632-1940
007	11914264	American Basic Schools LLC	131 E Southern Ave, Mesa AZ 85210	(480) 655-7868
008	11928033	American Leadership Acad Inc	2250 E Germann Rd Ste 14, Chandler AZ 85286	(480) 420-2101
009	11912761	Arizona Agribus&Equine Ctr Org	315 E Mulberry Dr, Phoenix AZ 85012	(602) 297-8500
010	11912759	Arizona Charter Schools	5704 E Grant Rd, Tucson AZ 85712	(520) 545-0575
011	11912723	Basis School Inc	7975 N Hayden Rd Ste B202, Scottsdale AZ 85258	(480) 289-2088
012	11914525	Benjamin Franklin Chtr Schools	690 E Warner Rd, Gilbert AZ 85296	(480) 264-3710
013	11912668	Blueprint Education	5651 W Talavi Blvd Ste 170, Glendale AZ 85306	(602) 674-5555
014	11914226	Bright Beginnings School Inc	400 N Andersen Blvd, Chandler AZ 85224	(480) 821-1404
015	11912620	CAFA Inc	4055 E Warner Rd, Gilbert AZ 85296	(480) 635-1900
016	11913387	Career Success Schools	3816 N 27th Ave, Phoenix AZ 85017	(602) 285-5525
017	11913351	Center for Academic Success	1843 Paseo San Luis, Sierra Vista AZ 85635	(520) 458-9309
018	11914173	Compass High School Inc	PO Box 17810, Tucson AZ 85731	(520) 296-4070
019	11914159	Cornerstone Charter School Inc	7107 N Black Canyon Hwy, Phoenix AZ 85021	(602) 595-2198
020	11914147	Country Gardens Educl Svcs	6313 W Southern Ave, Laveen AZ 85339	(602) 237-3741
021	11914111	Eastpointe High School Inc	8495 E Broadway Blvd, Tucson AZ 85710	(520) 731-8180
022	11914068	Educational Impact Inc	1950 E Placita Sin Nombre, Tucson AZ 85718	(520) 407-1200
023	11914044	Eduprize Schools Inc	4567 W Roberts Rd, Queen Creek AZ 85142	(480) 888-1610
024	11912395	Espiritu Community Development	4848 S 2nd St, Phoenix AZ 85040	(602) 243-7788
025	11914032	GAR LLC	8253 W Thunderbird Rd Ste 105, Peoria AZ 85381	(602) 334-4104
026	11913234	Great Hearts Academies	4801 E Washington St Ste 250, Phoenix AZ 85034	(602) 438-7045
027	11913985	Heritage Academy Inc	32 S Center St, Mesa AZ 85210	(480) 969-5641
028	11914434	Humanities & Sciences Acad US	5201 N 7th St, Phoenix AZ 85014	(602) 650-1333
029	11911781	Imagine Southwest Regional	1843 W 16th Ave, Apache Jct AZ 85120	(480) 355-0502
030	11913179	Kingman Academy of Learning	3410 N Burbank St, Kingman AZ 86409	(928) 681-2400
031	11913167	Leading Edge Charter Solutions	633 E Ray Rd Ste 132, Gilbert AZ 85296	(480) 633-0414
032	11913143	Learning Matters Educl Group	4744 W Grovers Ave, Glendale AZ 85308	(602) 439-5026
033	11913959	Legacy Traditional Schools	3125 S Gilbert Rd, Chandler AZ 85286	(480) 270-5438
034	11914599	Leona Group LLC-AZ	7878 N 16th St Ste 150, Phoenix AZ 85020	(602) 953-2933
035	11914381	Mgrm Pinnacle Education Inc	2224 W Southern Ave Ste 1, Tempe AZ 85282	(480) 755-8222
036	11913911	Montessori Schoolhouse Tucson	1301 E Fort Lowell Rd, Tucson AZ 85719	(520) 319-8668
037	11913923	Montessori Schools Flagstaff	2212 E Cedar Ave, Flagstaff AZ 86004	(928) 774-1600
038	12305874	Pima Prevention Partnership	924 N Alvernon Way, Tucson AZ 85711	(520) 791-2711
039	12306309	Plc Charter Schools	2504 S 91st Ave, Tolleson AZ 85353	(623) 474-2120
040	11912101	Pointe Educational Services	10215 N 43rd Ave, Phoenix AZ 85051	(602) 843-2014
041	11913519	PPEP and Affiliates	802 E 46th St, Tucson AZ 85713	(520) 622-3553
042	11913856	Rose Management Group	3686 W Orange Grove Rd Ste 192, Tucson AZ 85741	(520) 797-4884
043	11913832	Self Development Chtr Sch Org	1709 N Greenfield Rd, Mesa AZ 85205	(480) 641-2640
044	11913337	Sequoia Schools-Edkey Inc	1460 S Horne Bldg 6, Mesa AZ 85204	(480) 461-3200
045	11912979	Skyline Education	7450 S 40th St 7500, Phoenix AZ 85042	(877) 225-2118
046	11913349	Sonoran Schools Inc	1489 W Elliot Rd Ste 103, Gilbert AZ 85233	(480) 940-5440
047	11913806	Southern Arizona Cmty Acad Inc	2470 N Tucson Blvd, Tucson AZ 85716	(520) 319-6113
048	11912929	The Charter Foundation Inc	1150 N Country Club Rd Ste 100, Tucson AZ 85716	(520) 296-1100
049	11911901	The Edge School Inc	2555 E 1st St, Tucson AZ 85716	(520) 881-1389
050	11912890	Tucson International Academy	2700 W Broadway Blvd, Tucson AZ 85745	(520) 792-3255
051	11912802	Albert Einstein Academies	3035 Ash St, San Diego CA 92102	(619) 795-1190
052	11913686	Alliance College-Ready Pub Sch	601 S Figueroa St Fl 4, Los Angeles CA 90017	(213) 943-4930
053	12305812	Alpha Public Schools	PO Box 21366, San Jose CA 95151	(408) 455-6355
054	12262961	Alta Public Schools	2410 Broadway, Huntington Pk CA 90255	(323) 923-0383
055	11912785	American Indian Model Schools	171 12th St, Oakland CA 94607	(510) 893-8701
056	12262911	Amethod Public Schools	2101 Livingston St, Oakland CA 94606	(510) 436-0172
057	11913648	Aspire Public Schools	1001 22nd Ave Ste 100, Oakland CA 94606	(510) 434-5000
058	11912656	Bright Star Education Group	600 S La Fayette Park Pl, Los Angeles CA 90057	(323) 954-9957
059	11913404	California Montessori Projects	5330A Gibbons Dr Ste 700, Carmichael CA 95608	(916) 971-2432
060	11913399	Camino Nuevo Charter Academy	3435 W Temple St, Los Angeles CA 90026	(213) 417-3400

CHARTER MANAGEMENT ORGANIZATION (CMO) INDEX

Market Data Retrieval

CMO No.	PID	CMO Name	Address	Phone
061	11912709	Ceiba Public Schools	260 W Riverside Dr, Watsonville CA 95076	(831) 740-8800
062	12260028	Citizens of the World Chtr Sch	5371 Wilshire Blvd Ste 210, Los Angeles CA 90036	(323) 634-7109
063	11912565	Civicorps Schools	101 Myrtle St, Oakland CA 94607	(510) 992-7800
064	11912539	Community Learning Center Schs	1900 3rd St, Alameda CA 94501	(510) 263-9266
065	11912527	Core-Cmty Options Resources Ed	321 16th St, Marysville CA 95901	(530) 742-2786
066	12110435	Downtown College Prep	1400 Parkmoor Ave Ste 206, San Jose CA 95126	(408) 271-8120
067	12261486	Ednovate Inc	3939 S Vermont Ave, Los Angeles CA 90037	(213) 454-0599
068	11912436	Education for Change	333 Hegenberger Rd Ste 600, Oakland CA 94621	(510) 568-7936
069	11912412	Environmental Charter Schools	2625 Manhattn Bch Blvd Ste 100, Redondo Beach CA 90278	(310) 214-3408
070	11913301	Envision Education	111 Myrtle St Ste 203, Oakland CA 94607	(510) 451-2415
071	12179015	Equitas Academy Chtr Sch Inc	1700 W Pico Blvd, Los Angeles CA 90015	(213) 201-0440
072	12305824	Fenton Charter Public Schools	8928 Sunland Blvd, Sun Valley CA 91352	(818) 962-3630
073	11912357	Five Keys Charter Schools Inc	70 Oak Grove St, San Francisco CA 94107	(415) 734-3310
074	12262935	Fortune School of Education	2890 Gateway Oaks Dr Ste 100, Sacramento CA 95833	(916) 924-8633
075	11913258	Gateway Community Charters	5112 Arnold Ave Ste A, McClellan CA 95652	(916) 286-5129
076	11912319	Golden Valley Charter Schools	3585 Maple St Ste 101, Ventura CA 93003	(805) 642-3435
077	11913595	Green Dot Public Schools	1149 S Hill St Ste 600, Los Angeles CA 90015	(323) 565-1600
078	12239598	Grimmway Schools	5080 California Ave Ste 100, Bakersfield CA 93309	(661) 432-7880
079	11912280	High Desert Partnsp Acad Excel	17500 Mana Rd, Apple Valley CA 92307	(760) 946-5414
080	11913222	High Tech High	2861 Womble Rd, San Diego CA 92106	(619) 243-5000
081	11913583	ICEF Public Schools	3855 W Slauson Ave, Los Angeles CA 90043	(323) 290-6900
082	11912266	Innovative Education Managemnt	4535 Missouri Flat Rd Ste 1A, Placerville CA 95667	(800) 979-4436
083	11913375	Isana Academies	3580 Wilshire Blvd Ste 1130, Los Angeles CA 90010	(323) 291-1211
084	11913181	King-Chavez Neighborhood Schs	415 31st St, San Diego CA 92102	(619) 525-7320
085	11916054	KIPP Bay Area Public Schools	1000 Broadway Ste 460, Oakland CA 94607	(510) 465-5477
086	11913571	KIPP Foundation	135 Main St Ste 1700, San Francisco CA 94105	(415) 399-1556
087	11916169	KIPP LA Public Schools	3601 E 1st St, Los Angeles CA 90063	(213) 489-4461
088	12115045	KIPP San Diego Clg Prep Public	1475 6th Ave, San Diego CA 92101	(619) 233-3242
089	11913155	Leadership Public Schools	99 Linden St, Oakland CA 94607	(510) 830-3780
090	12260030	Los Angeles Education Corps	3635 Atlantic Ave, Long Beach CA 90807	(562) 216-1790
091	11913557	Magnolia Ed & Research Fdn	250 E 1st St Ste 1500, Los Angeles CA 90012	(213) 628-3634
092	11912187	National Univ Academy System	2030 University Dr, Vista CA 92083	(760) 630-4080
093	12262777	Navigator Schools	650 San Benito St Ste 230, Hollister CA 95023	(831) 217-4880
094	12361373	Olive Grove Charter Schools	2353 S Broadway, Santa Maria CA 93454	(805) 623-1111
095	11935907	Opportunities for Learning	320 N Halstead St Ste 220, Pasadena CA 91107	(888) 207-1119
096	11913052	Options for Youth Inc	320 N Halstead St Ste 280, Pasadena CA 91107	(888) 389-9992
097	12262923	Pacific Charter Institute	1401 El Camino Ave Ste 510, Sacramento CA 95815	(866) 992-9033
098	11912125	Para Los Ninos PCS	5000 Hollywood Blvd, Los Angeles CA 90027	(213) 250-4800
099	11913521	Partnerships to Uplift Cmty	1405 N San Fernando Blvd 303, Burbank CA 91504	(818) 559-7699
100	11912060	Real Journey Academies	1425 W Foothill Blvd Ste 100, Upland CA 91786	(909) 888-8458
101	11912046	Roads Education Organization	2999 Cleveland Ave Ste D, Santa Rosa CA 95403	(707) 843-4676
102	11912034	Rocketship Education	350 Twin Dolphin Dr Ste 109, Redwood City CA 94065	(877) 806-0920
103	11911872	Rocklin Academy Charter Schs	2204 Plaza Dr Ste 200, Rocklin CA 95765	(916) 778-4544
104	11912008	Semillas Sociedad Civil	4736 Huntington Dr S, Los Angeles CA 90032	(323) 352-3148
105	11911987	St Hope Public Schools	PO Box 5038, Sacramento CA 95817	(916) 649-7900
106	12101381	Summit Public Schools	780 Broadway St, Redwood City CA 94063	(650) 257-9880
107	11911925	The Accelerated School	116 E Mlk Jr Blvd, Los Angeles CA 90011	(323) 235-6343
108	11911884	The Learner-Centered School	3325 Hacienda Way, Antioch CA 94509	(925) 755-7311
109	11911846	Tracy Learning Center	51 E Beverly Pl, Tracy CA 95376	(209) 290-0511
110	11911822	Value Schools	680 Wilshire Pl Ste 315, Los Angeles CA 90005	(213) 388-8676
111	12306244	Western Sierra Charter Schools	41267 Highway 41, Oakhurst CA 93644	(559) 642-1422
112	12262791	Ypi Charter Schools	10660 White Oak Ave B101, Granada Hills CA 91344	(818) 834-5805
113	12321684	Colorado Early College Network	4405 N Chestnut St Ste E, Colorado Spgs CO 80907	(719) 955-4685
114	12322432	Global Village Charter Collab	10701 Melody Dr Ste 610, Denver CO 80234	(720) 353-4113
115	11916078	KIPP Colorado	1390 Lawrence St Ste 200, Denver CO 80204	(303) 934-3245
116	12305886	Rocky Mountain Prep Schools	7808 Cherry Creek Dr S, Denver CO 80231	(720) 863-8920
117	12110356	Strive Preparatory Schools	2480 W 26th Ave Ste 360B, Denver CO 80211	(720) 772-4300
118	12322626	Tatonka Education Services	10375 Park Meadows Dr Ste 230, Lone Tree CO 80124	(303) 296-6500
119	11913090	The New America Schools Netwk	925 S Niagara St Ste 140/400, Denver CO 80224	(303) 800-0058
120	11913698	Achievement First Network	370 James St Ste 404, New Haven CT 06513	(203) 773-3223

MDR School Directory
CHARTER MANAGEMENT ORGANIZATION (CMO) INDEX

CMO No.	PID	CMO Name	Address	Phone
121	11915414	Jumoke Academy Inc	999 Asylum Ave Ste 200, Hartford CT 06105	(860) 216-9636
122	11913650	Aspira Educl Management Org	1220 L St NW Ste 701, Washington DC 20005	(202) 835-3600
123	11913363	Center City Public Charter Sch	900 2nd St NE Ste 221, Washington DC 20002	(202) 589-0202
124	11912591	Cesar Chavez Public Chtr Schs	709 12th St SE, Washington DC 20003	(202) 547-3975
125	11912503	DC Prep	707 Edgewood St NE, Washington DC 20017	(202) 635-4590
126	11913260	Friendship Public Charter Sch	111 O St NW, Washington DC 20001	(202) 281-1700
127	11914836	KIPP DC	2600 Virginia Ave NW Ste 900, Washington DC 20037	(202) 223-4505
128	11912010	See Forever Foundation	600 Pnnsylvnia Ave SE Ste 210, Washington DC 20003	(202) 797-8250
129	11911860	The Seed Foundation	1730 Rh Isl Ave NW Ste 1102, Washington DC 20036	(202) 785-4123
130	11914680	Academica	6340 Sunset Dr, Miami FL 33143	(305) 669-2906
131	11914549	Accelerated Learning Solutions	5850 T G Lee Blvd Ste 345, Orlando FL 32822	(888) 437-9353
132	11914496	Charter School Associates Inc	5471 N University Dr, Coral Springs FL 33067	(954) 414-5767
133	11914678	Charter Schools USA	800 Corporate Dr Ste 700, Ft Lauderdale FL 33334	(954) 202-3500
134	11912541	Cmty & Eco Dev Org Gadsden Co	20 E Washington St, Quincy FL 32351	(850) 627-7656
135	11914630	Edisonlearning Inc	1 E Broward Blvd Ste 1111, Ft Lauderdale FL 33301	(877) 890-7088
136	12261709	Forza Education Management LLC	7815 111th Ter E, Parrish FL 34219	(727) 642-9319
137	11916420	Imagine South Florida Regional	13790 NW 4th St Ste 108, Sunrise FL 33325	(954) 870-5023
138	11916406	Imagine Southeast Regional	755 Town Center Blvd, Palm Coast FL 32164	(888) 709-8010
139	11916157	KIPP Jacksonville Schools	1440 McDuff Ave N, Jacksonville FL 32254	(904) 683-6643
140	12179651	Lake Wales Charter Schools	130 E Central Ave, Lake Wales FL 33853	(863) 679-6560
141	11913569	Lighthouse Academies	29140 Chapel Park Dr Bldg 5A, Wesley Chapel FL 33543	(800) 901-6943
142	11913947	LII Licensing Inc	6710 86th Ave N, Pinellas Park FL 33782	(727) 768-0989
143	11914379	Rader Group	101A Business Centre Dr, Miramar Beach FL 32550	(850) 650-3984
144	11913789	Superior Schools	861 N Hercules Ave, Clearwater FL 33765	(727) 799-1200
145	11916224	KIPP Metro Atlanta Schools	504 Fair St SW Ste 300, Atlanta GA 30313	(404) 924-6310
146	12240195	Mountain Ed Chtr High School	1963 Tom Bell Rd, Cleveland GA 30528	(706) 219-4664
147	12259990	Gem Innovation Schools	PO Box 86, Deary ID 83823	(208) 238-1388
148	11913466	Acero Charter Schools Inc	209 W Jackson Blvd Ste 500, Chicago IL 60606	(312) 637-3900
149	11913662	American Quality Schools Corp	1315 Butterfield Rd Ste 224, Chicago IL 60615	(312) 226-3355
150	11912670	Betty Shabazz Intl Chtr Sch	7822 S Dobson Ave, Chicago IL 60619	(773) 651-1221
151	11912606	Catalyst Schools	6727 S California Ave, Chicago IL 60629	(773) 295-7001
152	11912553	Civitas Education Partners	901 W Jackson Blvd Ste 205, Chicago IL 60607	(312) 733-6790
153	11913636	Concept Schools	1336 Basswood Rd, Schaumburg IL 60173	(847) 824-3380
154	11912333	Galapagos Charter	3051 Rotary Rd, Rockford IL 61109	(779) 368-0852
155	11914812	KIPP Chicago	2007 S Halsted St, Chicago IL 60608	(312) 733-8108
156	12110447	Lawndale Educ & Reg Network	3021 W Carroll Ave, Chicago IL 60612	(773) 584-4399
157	11913545	Noble Network of Charter Sch	1 N State St Ste 700, Chicago IL 60602	(312) 521-5287
158	11913038	Perspectives Charter Schools	1530 S State St Ste 200, Chicago IL 60605	(312) 604-2200
159	12260016	Regeneration Schools	1816 W Garfield Blvd, Chicago IL 60609	(773) 778-9455
160	11913246	GEO Foundation	1630 N Meridian St Ste 350, Indianapolis IN 46202	(317) 536-1027
161	12315427	Goodwill Education Initiatives	1635 W Michigan St, Indianapolis IN 46222	(317) 524-4265
162	11916145	KIPP Indy Public Schools	1740 E 30th St, Indianapolis IN 46218	(317) 547-5477
163	12179027	Tindley Accelerated Schools	3960 Meadows Dr, Indianapolis IN 46205	(317) 545-1745
164	11913430	Algiers Charter School Assoc	2401 Westbend Pkwy Ste 2001, New Orleans LA 70114	(504) 302-7001
165	12115203	Collegiate Academies	7301 Dwyer Rd, New Orleans LA 70126	(504) 503-0008
166	11930816	Crescent City Schools	3811 N Galvez St, New Orleans LA 70117	(504) 708-4136
167	11912369	Firstline Schools Inc	300 N Broad St Ste 207, New Orleans LA 70119	(504) 267-9038
168	11930725	Friends of King Schools	1617 Caffin Ave, New Orleans LA 70117	(504) 940-2243
169	12179039	Inspirenola Charter Schools	2401 Westbend Pkwy Ste 4040, New Orleans LA 70114	(504) 227-3057
170	12259213	Jcfa Charter Schools	475 Manhattan Blvd, Harvey LA 70058	(504) 410-3121
171	11916250	KIPP New Orleans Schools	1307 Oretha Castle Haley Blvd, New Orleans LA 70113	(504) 373-6269
172	11912058	Renew Schools Inc	1607 S Carrollton Ave, New Orleans LA 70118	(504) 367-3307
173	11911913	The Choice Foundation	3201 Live Oak St, New Orleans LA 70118	(504) 861-8370
174	12110411	The Einstein Group Inc	5316 Michoud Blvd, New Orleans LA 70129	(504) 324-7450
175	11913296	Excel Academy	58 Moore St, East Boston MA 02128	(617) 874-4080
176	11916171	KIPP Massachusetts Pub CH Schs	90 High Rock St, Lynn MA 01902	(781) 598-1609
177	12306086	The Community Group	190 Hampshire St Ste 2, Lawrence MA 01840	(978) 682-6628
178	12260004	Up Education Network	90 Canal St Ste 600, Boston MA 02114	(617) 307-5980
179	11913428	Baltimore Curriculum Project	2707 E Fayette St, Baltimore MD 21224	(410) 675-7000
180	11912577	City Neighbors Inc	4301 Raspe Ave, Baltimore MD 21206	(410) 325-2627

CHARTER MANAGEMENT ORGANIZATION (CMO) INDEX

Market Data Retrieval

CMO No.	PID	CMO Name	Address	Phone
181	11914666	Connections Academy	10960 Grantchester Way, Columbia MD 21044	(443) 529-1000
182	11916470	Imagine Mid-Atlantic Regional	4415 Nicole Dr Ste C, Lanham MD 20706	(301) 316-1802
183	11915830	KIPP Baltimore	4701 Greenspring Ave Rm 115, Baltimore MD 21209	(410) 367-0807
184	11912228	Living Classrooms Foundation	802 S Caroline St, Baltimore MD 21231	(410) 685-0295
185	11914252	American Institutional Mgmt	5728 Schaefer Rd Ste 200, Dearborn MI 48126	(313) 624-2000
186	11914240	Bardwell Group	19800 Beech Daly Rd, Redford MI 48240	(313) 450-0642
187	11914501	Charter School Admin Services	20820 Greenfield Rd, Oak Park MI 48237	(248) 569-7787
188	11914484	Choice Schools Associates LLC	5251 Clyde Park Ave SW, Wyoming MI 49509	(616) 785-8440
189	11911858	Cornerstone Education Group	306 E 4th St, Royal Oak MI 48067	(248) 439-6228
190	11914642	CS Partners LLC	869 S Old US 23 Ste 500, Brighton MI 48114	(810) 229-5145
191	11914094	EdTec Central LLC	10 S Main St Ste 100, Mount Clemens MI 48043	(248) 582-8100
192	11914343	Education Enrichmnet Services	19236 W 11 Mile Rd, Lathrup Vlg MI 48076	(248) 905-5030
193	11914070	Education Management&Networks	27704 Franklin Rd, Southfield MI 48034	(248) 327-7673
194	11912345	Foundation for Behavioral Res	600 S Lincoln St, Augusta MI 49012	(269) 731-5796
195	11914446	Global Educational Excellence	2455 S Industrial Hwy Ste A, Ann Arbor MI 48104	(734) 369-9500
196	11914018	Hamadeh Educational Services	PO Box 1440, Dearborn MI 48121	(313) 565-0507
197	11914006	Hanley-Harper Group Inc	20542 Harper Ave, Harper Woods MI 48225	(313) 347-0026
198	11913973	Innovative Teaching Solutions	18470 W 10 Mile Rd Ste 100, Southfield MI 48075	(248) 799-2780
199	11913961	Lakeshore Educl Management	12955 Robins Ridge Rd, Charlevoix MI 49720	(231) 547-4264
200	11916597	Leona Group LLC-Midwest	2125 University Park Dr, Okemos MI 48864	(517) 333-9030
201	11912204	Midland Charter Initiative	4653 Bailey Bridge Rd, Midland MI 48640	(989) 496-2404
202	11913935	MJ Management Services Inc	PO Box 1014, Flat Rock MI 48134	(734) 675-5505
203	11914575	National Heritage Academies	3850 Broadmoor Ave SE Ste 201, Grand Rapids MI 49512	(877) 223-6402
204	11913868	PrepNet LLC	3755 36th St SE Ste 250, Grand Rapids MI 49512	(616) 726-8900
205	12038734	Promise Schools	15000 Trojan St, Detroit MI 48235	(313) 964-2339
206	11914367	Romine Group LLC	7877 Stead St Ste 100, Utica MI 48317	(586) 731-5300
207	11913818	Solid Rock Management Company	3031 W Grand Blvd Ste 524, Detroit MI 48202	(313) 873-7625
208	11913753	Technical Academy Group LLC	4801 Oakman Blvd, Dearborn MI 48126	(313) 625-4700
209	11911793	Youth Visions Solutions	1450 25th St, Detroit MI 48216	(313) 558-9022
210	12262284	Harvest Network of Schools	1300 Olson Memorial Hwy, Minneapolis MN 55411	(612) 876-4105
211	12262301	Hiawatha Academies	1611 E 46th St, Minneapolis MN 55407	(612) 455-4004
212	12115033	KIPP Minnesota Public Schools	5034 Oliver Ave N, Minneapolis MN 55430	(612) 287-9700
213	12262387	MN Transitions Charter Schs	2872 26th Ave S, Minneapolis MN 55406	(612) 722-9013
214	11914355	Sabis Educational Systems	6385 Beach Rd, Eden Prairie MN 55344	(952) 918-1850
215	12261462	Confluence Academies	611 N 10th St Ste 525, Saint Louis MO 63101	(314) 588-8554
216	12115021	KIPP Kansas City	2700 E 18th St Ste 155B, Kansas City MO 64127	(816) 241-3994
217	11916303	KIPP St Louis Public Schools	1310 Papin St Ste 203, Saint Louis MO 63103	(314) 349-1388
218	12115019	KIPP Charlotte Public Schools	931 Wilann Dr, Charlotte NC 28215	(704) 537-2044
219	11916119	KIPP Enc College Prep Pub Schs	320 Pleasant Hill Rd, Gaston NC 27832	(252) 308-6932
220	12179431	Teamcfa	9935D Rea Rd Ste 167, Charlotte NC 28277	(704) 774-3038
221	12309351	The Roger Bacon Academy	3610 Thaddeus Lott Ln NE, Leland NC 28451	(910) 655-3600
222	12306593	College Achieve Ctl CS Network	365 Emerson Ave, Plainfield NJ 07062	(908) 625-1879
223	12110332	Ilearn Schools Inc	33-00 Broadway Ste 301, Fair Lawn NJ 07410	(201) 773-9140
224	11916327	KIPP New Jersey	60 Park Pl Ste 802, Newark NJ 07102	(973) 622-0905
225	11912694	Beginning with Children Fndn	217 Havemeyer St Ste 2, Brooklyn NY 11211	(212) 750-9320
226	11912644	Brighter Choice Charter Schs	250 Central Ave, Albany NY 12206	(518) 694-4100
227	11912498	Democracy Prep Public Schools	1767 Park Ave Fl 4, New York NY 10035	(212) 281-1248
228	12262894	Excellence Community Schools	2090 7th Ave Ste 605, New York NY 10027	(212) 222-5071
229	11912371	Explore Schools Inc	20 Jay St Ste 211, Brooklyn NY 11201	(718) 989-6730
230	12161604	Great Oaks Foundation	200 Broadway 3rd Fl, New York NY 10038	(917) 239-3641
231	11912292	Harlem Village Academies	15 Penn Plz Ste 15, New York NY 10001	(646) 812-9501
232	12114986	KIPP Albany Public Schools	321 Northern Blvd, Albany NY 12210	(518) 694-9494
233	11914824	KIPP NYC Public Schools	1501 Broadway Ste 1000, New York NY 10036	(212) 991-2610
234	11912084	Public Prep Network Inc	441 E 148th St, Bronx NY 10455	(212) 346-6000
235	11912943	Success Academy Charter Schls	95 Pine St Fl 6, New York NY 10005	(646) 597-4641
236	11913478	Uncommon Schools	826 Broadway Fl 9, New York NY 10003	(212) 844-3584
237	11914563	Victory Education Partners	135 W 40 St Fl 5, New York NY 10036	(212) 786-7900
238	12179819	Accel Schools	4700 Rockside Rd Ste 345, Independence OH 44131	(216) 583-5230
239	11913416	Breakthrough Charter Schools	3615 Superior Ave E Ste 4403A, Cleveland OH 44114	(216) 456-2086
240	11912632	Buckeye on-Line School Success	119 E 5th St, E Liverpool OH 43920	(330) 385-1987

MDR School Directory
CHARTER MANAGEMENT ORGANIZATION (CMO) INDEX

CMO No.	PID	CMO Name	Address	Phone
241	12106575	Carpe Diem Learning Systems	301 N Breiel Blvd Ste B, Middletown OH 45042	(513) 217-3400
242	11914654	Constellation Schools	5730 Broadview Rd, Parma OH 44134	(216) 712-7600
243	12319069	Educational Solutions	1500 W 3rd Ave Ste 125, Columbus OH 43212	(614) 299-1007
244	11914460	Eschool Consultants	4480 Refugee Rd, Columbus OH 43232	(614) 322-7996
245	11916509	Imagine Ohio Regional	11518 Banning Rd, Mount Vernon OH 43050	(614) 930-1184
246	11916066	KIPP Columbus	2980 Inspire Dr, Columbus OH 43224	(614) 263-6137
247	11914393	Performance Academies LLC	2 Easton Oval Ste 525, Columbus OH 43219	(614) 512-2151
248	11913480	Summit Academy Management	2791 Mogadore Rd, Akron OH 44312	(330) 670-8470
249	12363034	United Schools Network	1469 E Main St, Columbus OH 43205	(614) 299-5284
250	12305745	KIPP Okc Public Schools	PO Box 776, Oklahoma City OK 73101	(405) 425-4622
251	12115069	KIPP Tulsa Public Charter Schs	1661 E Virgin St, Tulsa OK 74106	(918) 794-8652
252	12361452	Santa Fe South Public Schools	4825 S Shields Blvd, Oklahoma City OK 73129	(405) 601-5440
253	11913117	Mastery Lrng Inst-Arthur Acad	13717 SE Division St, Portland OR 97236	(503) 762-6061
254	11914185	Charter School Management Inc	419 Avenue of the States, Chester PA 19013	(610) 447-0200
255	11912448	EdSys Inc	201 Stanwix St Ste 100, Pittsburgh PA 15222	(412) 690-2489
256	11916274	KIPP Philadelphia Public Schs	5070 Parkside Ave Ste 3500D, Philadelphia PA 19131	(215) 294-8596
257	11913129	Mastery Charter Schools	5700 Wayne Ave, Philadelphia PA 19144	(215) 866-9000
258	11914408	Omnivest Properties Management	115 Pheasant Run Ste 210, Newtown PA 18940	(215) 497-8301
259	11913026	Propel Schools	3447 E Carson St Ste 200, Pittsburgh PA 15203	(412) 325-7305
260	11912888	Universal Companies Inc	800 S 15th St, Philadelphia PA 19146	(215) 391-4161
261	12312499	Charter Institute at Erskine	1201 Main St Ste 300, Columbia SC 29201	(803) 849-2464
262	12161719	Capstone Education Group	PO Box 22569, Memphis TN 38122	(901) 416-3640
263	11914628	Chancelight Behavioral Hlth-Ed	1321 Murfreesboro Pike Ste 702, Nashville TN 37217	(615) 361-4000
264	12319629	Freedom Prep Academy Network	778 Parkrose Ave, Memphis TN 38109	(901) 881-1149
265	12038813	Gestalt Community Schools	2650 Thsnd Oaks Blvd Ste 1400, Memphis TN 38118	(901) 213-5161
266	12305850	Green Dot Pub Schs-Tennessee	4950 Fairley Rd, Memphis TN 38109	(901) 730-8160
267	11916200	KIPP Memphis Collegiate Schs	2670 Union Avenue Ext Ste 1100, Memphis TN 38112	(901) 452-2682
268	11916236	KIPP Nashville	123 Douglas Ave, Nashville TN 37207	(615) 226-4484
269	12038825	Lead Public Schools	2835 Brick Church Pike, Nashville TN 37207	(615) 815-1264
270	12110461	Republic Schools	3307 Brick Church Pike, Nashville TN 37207	(615) 921-6620
271	11911896	The Influence 1 Foundation	665 Madison Ave, Memphis TN 38103	(901) 526-1944
272	11912993	A Plus Charter Schools	8225 Bruton Rd, Dallas TX 75217	(214) 381-3226
273	12315738	Arrow Academy	PO Box 12207, College Sta TX 77842	(979) 703-8820
274	11913105	Baker-Ripley	PO Box 271389, Houston TX 77277	(713) 667-9400
275	11912618	Calvin Nelms Charter Schools	20625 Clay Rd, Katy TX 77449	(281) 398-8031
276	11912486	Democratic Schools Research	410 Bethel Ln, Bryan TX 77802	(979) 775-2152
277	11912450	East Waco Innovative Sch Dev	1020 Elm St Ste 100, Waco TX 76704	(254) 754-8000
278	11913325	Educational Leadership Inc	3333 Bering Dr Ste 200, Houston TX 77057	(713) 784-6345
279	12361414	Evolution Academy Charter Schs	1101 S Sherman St, Richardson TX 75081	(972) 907-3755
280	11913284	Faith Family Academy Chtr Schs	1608 Osprey Dr, Desoto TX 75115	(972) 224-4110
281	11912321	Golden Rule Schools Inc	2602 W Illinois Ave, Dallas TX 75233	(214) 333-9330
282	12160947	Great Hearts Texas	824 Broadway St Ste 101, San Antonio TX 78215	(210) 888-9475
283	11912307	Gulf Coast Council of La Raza	4129 Greenwood Dr, Corp Christi TX 78416	(361) 881-9988
284	11913624	Harmony Pub Schs-Cosmos Found	9321 W Sam Houston Pkwy S, Houston TX 77099	(713) 343-3333
285	11913193	Jubilee Academic Center Inc	4434 Roland Rd, San Antonio TX 78222	(210) 333-6227
286	11915828	KIPP Texas Public Schs Austin	8509 FM 969 Ste 513, Austin TX 78724	(512) 501-3643
287	11916080	KIPP Texas Public Schs Dallas	1545 S Ewing Ave, Dallas TX 75216	(972) 323-4200
288	11916133	KIPP Texas Public Schs Houston	10711 Kipp Way Dr, Houston TX 77099	(832) 328-1051
289	11916298	KIPP Texas Public Schs Sa	731 Fredericksburg Rd, San Antonio TX 78201	(210) 787-3197
290	11913131	Life School	132 E Ovilla Rd Ste 1A, Red Oak TX 75154	(469) 850-5433
291	11912163	New Frontiers Public Schools	138 Fair Ave, San Antonio TX 78223	(210) 519-3900
292	11913040	Orenda Education	2951 Williams Dr, Georgetown TX 78628	(512) 869-3020
293	11912137	Panola Charter Schools	PO Box 610, Carthage TX 75633	(903) 693-6355
294	11912096	Por Vida Inc	1135 Mission Rd, San Antonio TX 78210	(210) 532-8816
295	12113918	Priority Charter Schools	275 FM 2483, Morgans Point TX 76513	(254) 206-2013
296	11913014	Raul Yzaguirre Sch-Success Org	2950 Broadway St, Houston TX 77017	(713) 640-3700
297	12233855	Responsive Education Solutions	PO Box 292730, Lewisville TX 75029	(972) 316-3663
298	11913507	Richard Milburn Academy Inc	1263 Terminal Loop Rd, Mc Queeney TX 78123	(830) 557-6181
299	11913002	Riverwalk Education Foundation	5300 Wurzbach Rd, San Antonio TX 78238	(210) 957-1955
300	11912981	Salvaging Teens at Risk Inc	4601 N Interstate 35, Denton TX 76207	(940) 383-6655

CHARTER MANAGEMENT ORGANIZATION (CMO) INDEX

Market Data Retrieval

CMO No.	PID	CMO Name	Address	Phone
301	11911999	South Texas Educ Technologies	2402 E Business 83, Weslaco TX 78596	(956) 969-3092
302	11912967	Southwest Winners Foundation	1258 Austin Hwy, San Antonio TX 78209	(210) 829-8017
303	11912955	Student Alternatives Program	PO Box 15644, San Antonio TX 78212	(210) 227-0295
304	11912931	Tekoa Academy Accel Studies	326 Thomas Blvd, Port Arthur TX 77640	(409) 982-5400
305	11913674	Texans Can Academies	325 W 12th St, Dallas TX 75208	(214) 944-1985
306	11911937	Texas Center for Arts & Acad	3901 S Hulen St, Fort Worth TX 76109	(817) 766-2390
307	11912905	Trinity Charter Schools	8305 Cross Park Dr, Austin TX 78754	(512) 706-7564
308	11911834	Two Dimensions Prep Chtr Acad	12121 Veterans Memorial Dr, Houston TX 77067	(281) 227-4700
309	11913454	Uplift Education	1825 Market Ctr Blvd Ste 500, Dallas TX 75207	(469) 621-8500
310	11911810	Varnett Public School Inc	5025 S Willow Dr, Houston TX 77035	(713) 667-4051
311	11912876	Winfree Academy Charter Schs	1555 Valwood Pkwy Ste 160, Carrollton TX 75006	(972) 869-3250
312	11912864	YES Prep Public Schools	5515 South Loop E Ste B, Houston TX 77033	(713) 967-9000
313	11914616	Imagine Schools Inc	1900 Gallows Rd Ste 250, Vienna VA 22182	(703) 527-2600
314	11914604	K12 Inc	2300 Corporate Park Dr, Herndon VA 20171	(866) 283-0300
315	12305836	Green Dot Pub Schs-Washington	4800 S 188th St Ste 250, Seatac WA 98188	(253) 382-2400
316	12306000	Seeds of Health Inc	1445 S 32nd St, Milwaukee WI 53215	(414) 672-3430